Lockwood-Post
Directory of Pulp & Paper Mills

Table of Contents

Introduction	iii
Headquarters and Pulp and Paper Mills in the United States	1
Headquarters and Pulp and Paper Mills in Canada	105
Headquarters and Pulp and Paper Mills in Europe	137
Headquarters and Pulp and Paper Mills in Asia and Oceania	385
Headquarters and Pulp and Paper Mills in Latin America	781
Headquarters and Pulp and Paper Mills in Africa	875
Pulp and Paper Grades Produced	903
Measurements and Grade List Glossary	1035
Country Index	1036
Index of Offices, Headquarters, and Mills	1037

RAYMOND H. FOGLER
LIBRARY
ORONO, MAINE

The cover image is Montes del Plata - Punta Pereira Mill, Zona Franca, Punta Pereira, Colonia, Uruguay

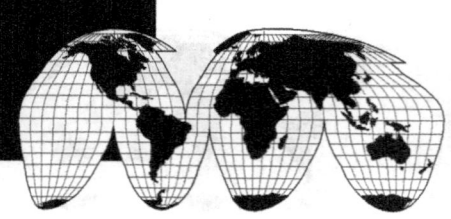

Lockwood-Post
Directory of Pulp & Paper Mills

Global Engineers and Cost Benchmarking Analysts for Mill Intelligence

Atlanta, USA
Jon Rager – Senior Vice President, Analytics
Michael Jones - Director, Cost Benchmarking: Packaging and Tissue
William Studstill - Director, Cost Benchmarking: Graphic Papers
Ryan Burgess - Analyst, Cost Benchmarking
Sheila Rezak - Product Manager, Mill Intelligence

Brussels, Belgium
David Lees - Analyst, Mill Intelligence, Lockwood-Post Directory

Helsinki, Finland
Ville Henttonen - Senior Product Manager, Cost Benchmarking
Sampsa Veiljalanien - Analyst, Mill Intelligence

Shanghai/Beijing, China
Portia Zhao - Senior Product Manager, Cost Benchmarking
Sarah Xu - Analyst, Mill Intelligence
Olivia Qiu - Production Assistant
JJ Meng - Analyst, Cost Benchmarking

Editorial Staff

North America: PPI Pulp & Paper Week
Will Mies - Editorial Director
Greg Rudder - Editor
Chris Cook - Deputy Editor
James McLaren - Sr. News Editor
Bryan Smith - Deputy Editor
Chris Lyddan - Contributing Editor

Europe: PPI Europe
Steven Sachoff - Editor
Daniela Wortmann - Deputy Editor
Irina Van den Neste – Senior News Editor
Eva Nyman - News Editor
Anne Grimbert - News Editor

Latin America: PPI Latin America
Renata Mercante - Editor
Marina Faleiros - News Editor

Asia: PPI Asia
Nick Chang - Editor, Singapore
Jessica Zimbalatti - Senior News Editor, Brisbane
Rita Yao - News Editor, Shanghai
Marlene Otepina - Associate Editor, Shanghai

Executives
Charles Rutstein: Chief Executive Officer
Iain Murray: Chief Operating Officer
Matt Graves: Senior Vice President
Todd Petracek: Vice President, Pulp & Paper, News, Markets & Prices

Publishing Staff
Anne-Chantal Bodart: Graphic Design Manager
Martin Dolega: Snr. Web. Developer
Teresa Wann: Director of Production

Offices

Corporate Headquarters/Publishing Office
4 Alfred Circle • Bedford, MA 01730 USA
Tel: +1.866.271.8525 • Fax: +1.781.271.0337

European Editorial Office
523 Avenue Louise • B-1050 Brussels, Belgium
Tel: +32.2.536.0748 • Fax: +32.2.537.5626

North American Editorial Office
900 Circle 75 Parkway, Suite 1200 • Atlanta, GA 30339
Tel: +1.770.373.3100 • Fax: +1.770.373.3005

Latin American Editorial Office
R. Br. de Capanema, 343 - 7° andar • Jardins - São Paulo - Brazil
CEP 01411-011
Tel: +55.11.3064.3192 • Fax: +55.11.2504.5151

Asian Editorial Offices
6 Shenton Way #15-08 • DBS Building Tower 2 • Singapore 068890
Tel: +65.6395.5868 • Fax: +65.6293.6966

9th Floor, Ciro's Plaza, 388 Nanjing West Road
Shanghai 200003, China
Tel: +86.21.6157.3988 • Fax: +86.21.6157.3999

Other RISI Offices
1441 Sachem Place, Suite 2 • Charlottesville, VA 22901
Tel: +1.434.978.2927 • Fax: +1.434.978.1184

1999 Harrison St., Suite 2010 • Oakland, CA 94612 USA
Tel: +1.510.922.8816 • Fax: +1.510.879.7642

Mannerheimintie 40 D 84 • FI-00100 Helsinki, Finland
Tel: +358.9.348.9344

RISI Consulting (Beijing) Co., Ltd.
Unite 907-908, 9/F • SOHO Nexus Center
A19 North East Third Ring Road • Chaoyang, Beijing, P.R. China
Tel: +86.10.5870.6088 • Fax: +86.10.5870.6099

Lockwood-Post
Directory of Pulp & Paper Mills

VISIT THE LOCKWOOD-POST DIRECTORIES ONLINE:
www.risi.com/directories
VISIT OUR WEBSITE:: www.risi.com
RISI Customer Care
In North America call 866.271.8525
Outside North America call +32.2.536.0748
Online: www.risi.com • Email: info@risi.com
Fax: 781.734.8998 (U.S.) or +32.2.537.5626 (Belgium)
ISBN: 978-1-932426-08-3
Copyright © 2015 by RISI, Inc.

RISI
Boston • Brussels • Atlanta • San Francisco • Shanghai
Beijing • Helsinki • São Paulo • Singapore

Lockwood-Post
Directory of Pulp & Paper Mills

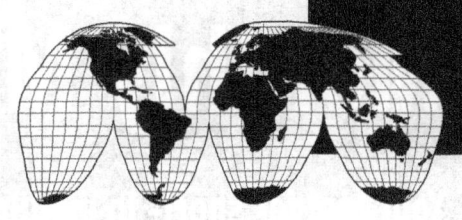

The Lockwood-Post Directory is the indispensable guide to pulp and paper mills, and companies in Africa, the Americas, Asia and Europe.

Now printed bi-annually, this publication provides insights on mill operations and company ownership details for all major pulp and paper mills worldwide.

Originally founded as Lockwood's Directory of the Paper and Allied Trade in August 1873, the Directory was merged with the Post's Pulp and Paper Directory, forming the Lockwood-Post Directory for North America.

In 2003, the International Pulp & Paper Directory was integrated with the Lockwood-Post Directory, and it is now presented as a single global edition. Over the years, this guide has become a fixture on the shelves of professionals throughout the Pulp and Paper industry.

The data for the new 2015-2016 edition comes from RISI's Asset Database*. This information combines the old Lockwood-Post Online Directory of Pulp & Paper Mills and elements from its cost benchmarking service, Analytical Cornerstone 4.0. RISI constantly strives to improve the accuracy of the data in each edition. From its Atlanta, Brussels, Helsinki and Shanghai offices, RISI has updated the data for mills and headquarters thanks to its research analysts speaking various countries' native languages. In addition to this, the Lockwood-Post Directory benefits fully from the breadth of RISI resources in its offices in Beijing, Sao Paulo, Singapore and all over North America. The contents are reviewed for accuracy by the world's largest editorial staff devoted to the pulp and paper industry, as well as analysts, engineers and economists from RISI's Mill Intelligence Services. Feedback from readers has also been a great help to improving the overall accuracy of this comprehensive Directory.

Just before the Country Index, towards the end of the publication, is an explanation of the grades and units of measurements used. RISI's sincere hope is that the quality of this information is higher than it has ever been.

About the information RISI collects: The information supplied in the Lockwood-Post Directory is obtained through the generous cooperation of many of the mills and companies listed, as well as that of RISI's network of international contributors around the world. RISI also receives references from the various Pulp and Paper Associations throughout the world. The publishers extend their thanks to all the individuals who contribute to this annual effort.

The information published herein is, in general, as received from the respondents and, in some instances, may have been augmented by data from other reliable and public sources. Every effort is made to provide dependable data; however, the publishers cannot accept any responsibility for inaccuracies or omissions resulting from incorrect or incomplete information supplied. Additionally, reference in any listing to an item of equipment by its trade name should not be considered as endorsement of that item.

RISI welcomes your comments on the 2015-2016 edition of the Lockwood-Post Directory, please e-mail: directories@risi.com with any suggestions or comments.

Jon Rager
Senior Vice President, Analytics

*RISI's Asset Database was built in partnership with our clients to deliver comprehensive mill and market equipment, consumption and investment information to pulp and paper industry professionals around the world. The Asset Database offers the information you need to develop a more competitive sales and marketing strategy.

RISI offers a full range of mill intelligence products, including mill and company production information, key personnel details, equipment data, mill projects, and comprehensive cost and profit data.
http://www.risiinfo.com/pages/product/pulp-paper/mill-intelligence.jsp

Monthly Monitor Service

Your tool for short- to medium term planning in global pulp and paper markets

RISI's monitor, or commentary, service provides monthly economic analysis and a two-year forecast of global pulp and paper markets by region and grade.

Each of our monitors analyzes current market trends, forecasts near-term developments, and provides historical and forecasted price summaries using RISI's proprietary benchmark prices.

With a subscription to any of RISI's monthly monitors, you receive access to:

- **Commentaries**- written market summaries and insights from RISI's globally-based, grade-focused economists; including relevant figures and appendix tables

- **Descriptive tables and data charts**- summaries and forecasts for major market indicators such as supply, demand, imports, and pricing by grade and region

RISI's monthly monitors include:

Asian Pulp and Paper Monitor
For more information, please visit
www.risi.com/appm

Paper Packaging Monitor
For more information, please visit
www.risi.com/ppm

Paper Packaging Monitor Europe
For more information, please visit
www.risi.com/ppme

Paper Trader
For more information, please visit
www.risi.com/papertrader

Paper Trader Europe
For more information, please visit
www.risi.com/pte

World Dissolving Pulp Monitor
For more information, please visit
www.risi.com/wdpm

World Pulp Monthly
For more information, please visit
www.risi.com/wpm

World Recovered Paper Monitor
For more information, please visit
www.risi.com/wrpm

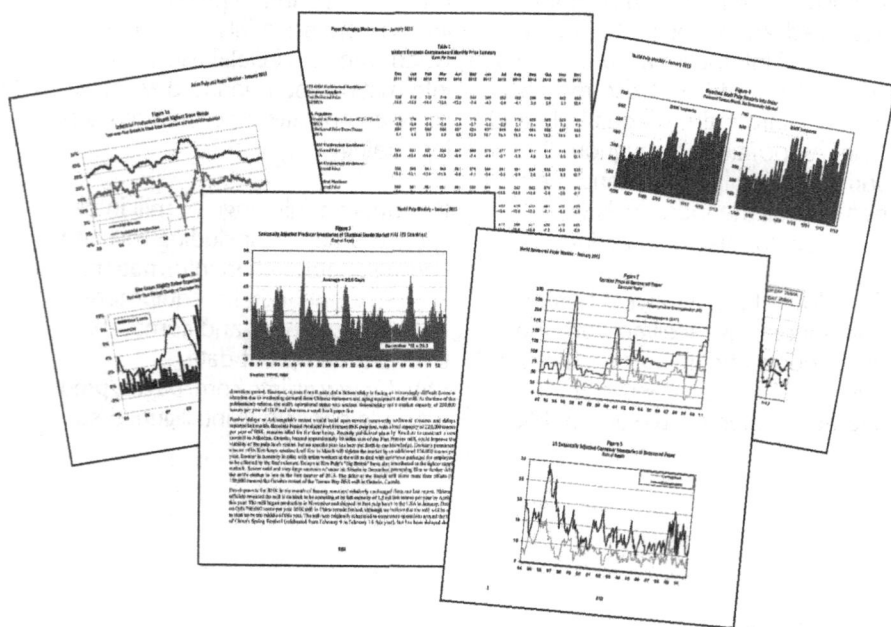

 Learn more at www.risi.com/monitors

PULP and PAPER MILLS in the United States

This section contains data about Headquarters and Pulp and paper mills. Information available in this section includes company, email and internet addresses, ownership, personnel, type of operation, Grades and capacities, production data, paper machines and equipment used.

Ⓗ preceding company denotes company's headquarters location.
Ⓜ preceding company denotes a mill location.
Imperial units of measurement are used in the U.S. mill entries in this directory. Metric units of measurement are used in mill entries of all other regions and countries.

Companies that may have closed in the year preceding publication are included in this current edition. However certain data, such as total capacities, may not show in that entry. Some companies are indicated as being "closed", "idle", "for sale", "bankrupt," etc. and will be removed from the directory in the next edition unless their status changes.

Companies that have closed down in previous years are not included.

Data correct as of early November 2014.

N.B.: Not all listings have data for all categories.

ALABAMA

ⓂAlabama Paper Products, LLC
Tuscaloosa Mill
Ownership: Maryland Paper
1300 Industrial Park Drive
Tuscaloosa, AL 35401
USA
 Phone: (1) 205-339-9660
 Fax: (1) 205-339-9883
 Web Address: www.alabamapaperproducts.com
Personnel:
 Pres. & CEO: Mathew Chakola
 Email: mchakola@marylandpaper.com
 Mill Mgr: Akbar Lotfi
 Phone: (1) 205-339-9660
 Fax: (1) 205-339-9883
 Email: alotfi@alabamapaperproducts.com
 Shipping and Receiving: Frank Cannon
 Phone: (1) 205-339-9660
 Fax: (1) 205-339-9883
 Email: fcannon@alabamapaperproducts.com
 General Forman: Wade Mansfield
 Phone: (1) 205-339-9660
 Fax: (1) 205-339-9883
 Email: wmansfield@alabamapaperproducts.com
 Maint Mgr: Len Hill
 Phone: (1) 205-339-9660
 Fax: (1) 205-339-9883
 Email: lhill@alabamapaperproducts.com
 Office Mgr.: Wanda Tunnell
 Phone: (1) 205-339-9660
 Fax: (1) 205-339-9883
 Email: wtunnell@alabamapaperproducts.com
Type of Operation: Paperboard mill
Paper/Paperboard Grades and Capacities:
 Total paper and paperboard capacity: 14,991 st/y
 Specialty and industrial: 14,991 st/y

ⓂBoise Paper
Jackson Mill
Previously Boise Inc.
Ownership: 100% by Packaging Corp. of America
4585 Industrial Rd
Jackson, AL 36545
USA
 Phone: (1) 251-246-4461
 Fax: (1) 251-246-7643
 Web Address: www.boisepaper.com
Personnel:
 Mill Mgr.: Rusty Burns
 Phone: (1) 251-246-4461
 Fax: (1) 251-246-7643
 Email: rustyburns@boisepaper.com
 Cust. Rel., Commun. & Gorvern. Affairs Mgr.: Marty Parker
 Phone: (1) 251-246-8238
 Fax: (1) 208-385-9048
 Email: martyparker@boisepaper.com
 Eng. & Environ. Mgr. : Trey Wilson
 Phone: (1) 251-246-4461
 Fax: (1) 251-246-7643
 Email: treywilson@boisepaper.com
Total Employees at this Location: 540
Type of Operation: Pulp mill, Paper mill
Pulp Grades and Capacities:
 Total pulp capacity: 309,893 st/y
 Chemical Pulp: 249,843 st/y
 Recycled Pulping: 60,050 st/y
Pulp Mill Data:
 Chemical Pulping Systems:
 Batch digesters: 6
 Bleach Plant Systems: 1
 Chemical Pulping System - Line 1, Type: Hardwood/Softwood, Sequence: DEoDED
 Chemical Recovery Equipment:
 Evaporator lines: 1
 Recovery boilers: 1
 Lime Kiln
 Recycled Fiber Treatment Lines:
 Pulpers: 1
Paper/Paperboard Grades and Capacities:
 Total paper and paperboard capacity: 485,413 st/y
 Uncoated woodfree/freesheet: 485,413 st/y
Paper and Paperboard Mill Data:
 Stock Preparation:
 Pulpers: 2
 Refiners: 2
 Paper Machines: 2
 J-1, fourdrinier, total capacity 92,800 st/y, Trim width 216 in, Uncoated woodfree/freesheet
 J-3, GapFormer, total capacity 392,613 st/y, Trim width 352 in, Uncoated woodfree/freesheet
 Finishing Equipment:
 Rewinders: 1
 Sheeters: 4 at 480,000 st/y
 Energy Data:
 Power boilers: 3
 Steam turbines: 1 at 18 MW
 Electrical demand for mill: 1,351 MWh/D

ⓂGeorgia-Pacific LLC
Brewton Mill
32224 US 31
Brewton, AL 36426
USA
Mailing Address: PO Box 709, Brewton, AL 36427-0709, USA
 Phone: (1) 251-867-3621
 Fax: (1) 251-867-8353
 Web Address: www.gp.com
Personnel:
 VP. & Gen. Mgr.: Jeff Joyce
 Phone: (1) 251-867-3621
 Fax: (1) 251-867-8353
 Email: jtjoyce@gapac.com
 Paper Mill Mgr.: Steven Claytor
 Phone: (1) 251-867-3621 Ext. 454
 Fax: (1) 251-867-8353
 Email: steven.claytor@gapac.com
 Purch. Mgr.: Steve Whitted
 Phone: (1) 251-867-3621
 Fax: (1) 251-867-8353
 Email: steve.whitted@gapac.com
 Power Supt.: Thomas E. Evans
 Phone: (1) 251-867-3621 Ext. 150
 Fax: (1) 251-867-8353
 Email: thomas.evans@gapac.com
 Environ. & Compliance Ldr.: Roberto Flores
 Phone: (1) 251-867-8358
 Fax: (1) 251-867-8353
 Email: roberto.flores@gapac.com
Total Employees at this Location: 453
Type of Operation: Pulp mill, Paperboard mill
Pulp Grades and Capacities:
 Total pulp capacity: 495,094 st/y
 Chemical Pulp: 495,094 st/y
Pulp Mill Data:
 Chemical Pulping Systems:
 Batch digesters: 8
Pulp Lines: 2
 Bleach Plant Systems: 1
 1, Sequence: DEopDED
 Chemical Recovery Equipment:
 Evaporator lines: 1
 Recovery boilers: 3
 Lime Kiln
Paper/Paperboard Grades and Capacities:
 Total paper and paperboard capacity: 499,800 st/y
 Linerboard: 305,235 st/y
 Boxboard/cartonboard: 194,565 st/y
Paper and Paperboard Mill Data:
 Stock Preparation:
 Pulpers:
 Paper Machines: 2

LOCKWOOD-POST DIRECTORY 2015-2016   Pulp and Paper Mills - United States

Alabama

No. 1, fourdrinier, total capacity 194,565 st/y, Trim width 202 in, Boxboard/cartonboard
No. 2, fourdrinier, total capacity 305,235 st/y, Trim width 202 in, Linerboard
Coating Machines: 1
PM 1, total capacity 195,106 st/y., on machine
Finishing Equipment:
Calenders: 1
Sheeters: 1
Energy Data:
Power boilers: 3
Steam turbines: 3 at 15.6, 15.6, 18.3 MW
Electrical demand for mill: 1,323 MWh/D

ⓂGeorgia-Pacific LLC
Naheola Mill
7530 Hwy 114
Pennington, AL 36916
USA
 Phone: (1) 205-459-1900
 Fax: (1) 205-459-1303
 Web Address: www.gp.com
Personnel:
VP & Mill Mgr.: Kelvin J. Hill
 Phone: (1) 205-459-1900
 Fax: (1) 205-459-1303
 Email: kelvin.hill@gapac.com
Facility Contr.: Paul J. Cramer
 Phone: (1) 205-459-1900
 Fax: (1) 205-459-1303
 Email: paul.cramer@gapac.com
Dir, Tech Oper.: John Rogers
 Phone: (1) 205-459-1900
 Fax: (1) 205-459-1303
 Email: john.rogers@gapac.com
Converting Oper. Supt: Michael Cook
 Phone: (1) 205-459-1900
 Fax: (1) 205-459-1303
 Email: michael.cook@gapac.com
Total Employees at this Location: 765
Type of Operation: Pulp mill, Paper mill, Paperboard mill
Pulp Grades and Capacities:
Total pulp capacity: 610,786 st/y
Pulp available for market: 29,514 st/y
Chemical Pulp: 610,786 st/y
Pulp Mill Data:
 Chemical Pulping Systems:
 Batch digesters: 8
 Continuous digesters: 1
 Bleach Plant Systems: 2
 Chemical Pulping System - 1, Type: Hardwood/Softwood, Sequence: DEoDD
 Chemical Pulping System - 2, Type: Hardwood/Softwood, Sequence: DEopDD
 Chemical Recovery Equipment:
 Evaporator lines: 2
 Recovery boilers: 1
 Lime Kiln
 Pulp Dryers:
 Fourdriniers 1, Pulp Dryers 1
Paper/Paperboard Grades and Capacities:
Total paper and paperboard capacity: 579,054 st/y
Tissue: 248,829 st/y
Boxboard/cartonboard: 330,225 st/y
Paper and Paperboard Mill Data:
Paper Machines: 7
No. 1, crescent former, total capacity 27,489 st/y, Trim width 184 in, Tissue
No. 2, fourdrinier, total capacity 107,100 st/y, Trim width 172 in, Boxboard/cartonboard
No. 3, fourdrinier, total capacity 223,125 st/y, Trim width 215 in, Boxboard/cartonboard
No. 4, crescent former, total capacity 46,410 st/y, Trim width 184 in, Tissue
No. 5, crescent former, total capacity 46,410 st/y, Trim width 184 in, Tissue
No. 6, crescent former, Yankee dryer, total capacity 48,195 st/y, Trim width 184 in, Tissue
No. 7, crescent former, total capacity 80,325 st/y, Trim width 258 in, Tissue
Coating Machines: 3
No. 1, on machine
No. 2, on machine
No. 3, on machine
Energy Data:
Power boilers: 5
Steam turbines: 3 at 85 MW
Electrical demand for mill: 1,803 MWh/D

ⓂGP Cellulose, LLC
Alabama River Cellulose Mill
Ownership: Georgia-Pacific LLC
Lena Landegger Highway, County Road 39
Perdue Hill, Claiborne, AL 36470
USA
Mailing Address: PO Box 100, Perdue Hill, AL 36470, USA
 Phone: (1) 251-575-2000
 Fax: (1) 251-743-8432
 Email: info@gpcellulose.com
 Web Address: www.gpcellulose.com
Personnel:
VP. & Gen. Mgr.: Timothy McIlwain
 Phone: (1) 251-575-2000
 Fax: (1) 251-743-8432
 Email: timothy.mcilwain@gapac.com
Contr.: Donna Maxwell
 Phone: (1) 251-575-2000
 Fax: (1) 251-743-8432
 Email: donna.maxwell@gapac.com
Production Unit Mgr.: Shannon McKenzie
 Phone: (1) 251-575-2000
 Fax: (1) 251-743-8432
 Email: shannon.mckenzie@gapac.com
Fiberline & Recaust Mgr.: Robert Diercks
 Phone: (1) 251-575-2000
 Fax: (1) 251-743-8432
 Email: robert.diercks@gapac.com
Total Employees at this Location: 420
Type of Operation: Pulp mill
Pulp Grades and Capacities:
Total pulp capacity: 1,022,735 st/y
Pulp available for market: 992,060 st/y
Chemical Pulp: 1,022,735 st/y
Pulp Mill Data:
 Chemical Pulping Systems:
 Continuous digesters: 3
Pulp Lines: 2
 Bleach Plant Systems: 2
 Andritz (Pulp Dryer #D2), Sequence: O_2 DEpDD, Capacity 606,999.6 admt/y
 Canron (Pulp Dryer #1), Sequence: DEpDEpD, Capacity 535,999.8 admt/y
 Chemical Recovery Equipment:
 Evaporator lines: 2
 Recovery boilers: 2
 Lime Kiln
 Pulp Dryers:
 Flakt dryer 1, Fourdriniers 1, Ross Dryer 1
Energy Data:
Power boilers: 3
Steam turbines: 4 at 48, 69, 110(2) MW
Electrical demand for mill: 2,275 MWh/D

ⓂInternational Paper Co.
Courtland Mill
Mill is closed (Two of the four Courtland PMs were shut in November 2013 and the last two PMs were closed February 1-2, 2014.)
16504 County Rd 150
Courtland, AL 35618
USA
Mailing Address: PO Box 189, Courtland, AL 35618, USA
 Phone: (1) 256-637-2741
 Fax: (1) 256-637-5116
 Email: (firstname.lastname@ipaper.com)
 Web Address: www.internationalpaper.com
Total Employees at this Location: 825
Type of Operation: Pulp mill, Paper mill
Pulp Mill Data:
 Chemical Pulping Systems:
 Continuous digesters: 3
 Bleach Plant Systems: 2
 2, Type: Sunds, Sequence: O_2 DEoD
 Chemical Recovery Equipment:
 Evaporator lines: 1
 Recovery boilers: 2
 Lime Kiln
Paper and Paperboard Mill Data:
Paper Machines: 2
No. 34, fourdrinier, total capacity 214,153 st/y, Trim width 258 in
No. 35, Bel-Baie II, total capacity 312,306 st/y, Trim width 352 in
Coating Machines: 1
No. 1, total capacity 115,741 st/y., off machine
Finishing Equipment:
Supercalenders: 1
Sheeters: 6
Energy Data:
Power boilers: 4
Combustion turbines: 1 at 35 MW
Steam turbines: 2 at 90 MW

ⓂInternational Paper Co.
Pine Hill Mill
Previously Weyerhaeuser
7600 Hwy 10 West
Pine Hill, AL 36769
USA
Mailing Address: PO Box 250, Pine Hill, AL 36769, USA
 Phone: (1) 334-963-4391
 Fax: (1) 334-963-2763
 Web Address: www.internationalpaper.com
Personnel:
Mill Mgr.: Janet Neighbors
 Phone: (1) 334-963-4391
 Fax: (1) 334-963-2763
 Email: janet.neighbors@ipaper.com
Oper. Mgr.: David E. Stringfellow
 Phone: (1) 334-963-4391
 Fax: (1) 334-963-2763
 Email: david.stringfellow@ipaper.com
Total Employees at this Location: 379
Type of Operation: Paperboard mill
Pulp Grades and Capacities:
Total pulp capacity: 913,511 st/y
Chemical Pulp: 699,380 st/y
Recycled Pulping: 214,131 st/y
Pulp Mill Data:
 Chemical Pulping Systems:
 Continuous digesters: 2
 Chemical Recovery Equipment:
 Evaporator lines: 2
 Recovery boilers: 1
 Lime Kiln
 Recycled Fiber Treatment Lines:
 Recycled packaging pulping lines: 1 at 214,000 admt/y
Paper/Paperboard Grades and Capacities:
Total paper and paperboard capacity: 870,009 st/y
Linerboard: 557,634 st/y
Corrugating medium/fluting: 312,375 st/y
Paper and Paperboard Mill Data:
 Stock Preparation:
 Pulpers: 2
Paper Machines: 2
No. 1, fourdrinier, total capacity 557,634 st/y, Trim width 318 in, Linerboard
No. 2, fourdrinier, total capacity 312,375 st/y, Trim width 258 in, Corrugating medium/fluting
Finishing Equipment:
Calenders: 3
Rewinders: 2
Energy Data:

Alabama

Power boilers: 2
Steam turbines: 2 at 73 MW
Electrical demand for mill: 1,743 MWh/D

ⓜInternational Paper Co.
Prattville Mill
100 Jensen Rd
Prattville, AL 36067
USA
  Phone: (1) 334-361-5000
  Fax: (1) 334-361-5845
  Email: (firstname.lastname@ipaper.com)
  Web Address: www.internationalpaper.com
Personnel:
  Gen. Mgr.: Carl Gunter
  Phone: (1) 334-361-5000
  Fax: (1) 334-361-5845
  Email: carl.gunter@ipaper.com
  Process Contr. Mgr.: Stacy L. Starnes
  Phone: (1) 334-361-5000
  Fax: (1) 334-361-5845
  Email: stacy.starnes@ipaper.com
  Pulp Mill Tech. Assist.: Mandy Ledkins
  Phone: (1) 334-361-5000
  Fax: (1) 334-361-5845
  Email: mandy.ledkins@ipaper.com
  Maint. Coordinator: Ryan Nair
  Phone: (1) 334-361-5000
  Fax: (1) 334-361-5845
  Email: ryan.nair@ipaper.com
Total Employees at this Location: 574
Type of Operation: Paper mill, Paperboard mill
Pulp Grades and Capacities:
  Total pulp capacity: 1,186,872 st/y
  Chemical Pulp: 1,026,108 st/y
  Recycled Pulping: 160,764 st/y
Pulp Mill Data:
  Chemical Pulping Systems:
  Continuous digesters: 3
  Chemical Recovery Equipment:
  Evaporator lines: 3
  Recovery boilers: 2
  Lime Kiln
  Recycled Fiber Treatment Lines:
  Recycled packaging pulping lines: 1 at 158,730 admt/y
Paper/Paperboard Grades and Capacities:
  Total paper and paperboard capacity: 1,119,909 st/y
  Linerboard: 1,119,909 st/y
Paper and Paperboard Mill Data:
  Stock Preparation:
  Pulpers: 1
  Refiners: 19
Paper Machines: 2
  No. 1, fourdrinier, total capacity 610,470 st/y, Trim width 308 in, Linerboard
  No. 2, fourdrinier, total capacity 509,439 st/y, Trim width 330 in, Linerboard
Finishing Equipment:
  Winders: 1
Energy Data:
  Power boilers: 2
  Steam turbines: 2 at 80 MW
  Electrical demand for mill: 2,382 MWh/D

ⓜInternational Paper Co.
Riverdale Mill
601 County Rd 78
Selma, AL 36701
USA
Mailing Address: PO Box 1409, Selma, AL 36702, USA
  Phone: (1) 334-418-5349
  Fax: (1) 334-418-5110
  Email: (firstname.lastname@ipaper.com)
  Web Address: www.internationalpaper.com
Personnel:
  Mill Mgr.: James E. Bruce
  Phone: (1) 334-418-5349
  Fax: (1) 334-418-5110
  Email: james.bruce@ipaper.com
  Manuf. Excellence Mgr.: Chris Hayter
  Phone: (1) 334-418-5349
  Fax: (1) 334-418-5110
  Email: chris.hayter@ipaper.com
  Vibration Analyst: Emmett C. Pitts
  Phone: (1) 334-418-5349
  Fax: (1) 334-418-5110
  Email: emmett.pitts@ipaper.com
  Assist. Superintendent PM #16 (From May 2014): Chris Jackson
  Phone: (1) 334-418-5349
  Fax: (1) 334-418-5110
  Email: chris.jackson@ipaper.com
  Purch. Mgr. (From June 2014): Tammy Lyons
  Phone: (1) 334-418-5225
  Fax: (1) 334-418-5113
  Email: tammy.lyons@ipaper.com
Total Employees at this Location: 540
Type of Operation: Paper mill
Pulp Grades and Capacities:
  Total pulp capacity: 550,135 st/y
  Chemical Pulp: 420,986 st/y
  Recycled Pulping: 129,148 st/y
Pulp Mill Data:
  Chemical Pulping Systems:
  Batch digesters: 10
  Bleach Plant Systems: 3
  Chemical Pulping System - 1, Type: Softwood, Sequence: DEopDED, Capacity 200,000 admt/y
  Chemical Pulping System - 2, Type: Hardwood, Sequence: DEopDED, Capacity 250,000 admt/y
  Recycled Deinked Pulping System, Sequence: P
  Chemical Recovery Equipment:
  Evaporator lines: 3
  Recovery boilers: 2
  Lime Kiln
  Recycled Fiber Treatment Lines:
  Flotation deinking lines: 1 at 105,159
Paper/Paperboard Grades and Capacities:
  Total paper and paperboard capacity: 649,597 st/y
  Uncoated woodfree/freesheet: 649,597 st/y
Paper and Paperboard Mill Data:
  Stock Preparation:
  Pulpers:
Paper Machines: 2
  No. 15, twin-wire, total capacity 235,568 st/y, Trim width 322 in, Uncoated woodfree/freesheet
  No. 16, twin-wire, total capacity 414,029 st/y, Trim width 362 in, Uncoated woodfree/freesheet
Finishing Equipment:
  Sheeters: 5
Energy Data:
  Power boilers: 3
  Combustion turbines: 1 at 54 MW
  Steam turbines: 1 at 40 MW
  Electrical demand for mill: 1,941 MWh/D

ⓜKimberly-Clark Corp.
Mobile Mill
200 Bay Bridge Rd
Mobile, AL 36652
USA
  Phone: (1) 251-330-3000
  Fax: (1) 251-452-6329
  Web Address: www.kimberly-clark.com
Personnel:
  Eng. Tech. Ldr.: John Fortner
  Phone: (1) 251-330-3000
  Fax: (1) 251-452-6329
  Email: jfortner@kcc.com
  Maint./Reliability Ldr.: Mark Bosarge
  Phone: (1) 251-330-3000
  Fax: (1) 251-452-6329
  Email: mbosarge@kcc.com
  Snr. HR Associate: George Watson
  Phone: (1) 251-330-3000
  Fax: (1) 251-452-6329
  Email: gwatson@kcc.com
  Buyer: Craig Jones
  Phone: (1) 251-330-3000
  Fax: (1) 251-452-6329
  Email: cjones@kcc.com
Total Employees at this Location: 293
Type of Operation: Paper mill
Pulp Grades and Capacities:
  Total pulp capacity: 123,069 st/y
  Recycled Pulping: 123,069 st/y
Pulp Mill Data:
  Pulp Lines: 1
  Bleach Plant Systems: 1
  Recycled Deinked Pulping System
  Recycled Fiber Treatment Lines:
  Flotation deinking lines: 1
Paper/Paperboard Grades and Capacities:
  Total paper and paperboard capacity: 275,604 st/y
  Tissue: 275,604 st/y
Paper and Paperboard Mill Data:
  Stock Preparation:
  Pulpers:
Paper Machines: 5
  No. 5, TAD, total capacity 49,980 st/y, Trim width 204 in, Tissue
  No. 6, crescent former, total capacity 46,767 st/y, Trim width 204 in, Tissue
  No. 7, crescent former, total capacity 58,905 st/y, Trim width 203 in, Tissue
  No. 8, crescent former, total capacity 55,692 st/y, Trim width 203 in, Tissue
  No. 11, crescent former, total capacity 64,260 st/y, Trim width 203 in, Tissue
Energy Data:
  Power boilers: 5
  Steam turbines: 4 at 125 MW
  Electrical demand for mill: 992 MWh/D

ⓜMeadWestvaco Corporation
Mahrt Mill
Hwy 165 S
Cottonton, AL 36851
USA
Mailing Address: PO Box 940, Phenix City, AL 36868-0940, USA
  Phone: (1) 334-855-4711, 687-4896
  Fax: (1) 334-855-5151
  Web Address: www.mwv.com
Personnel:
  VP. Oper.: Scott Fryer
  Phone: (1) 334-855-5609
  Fax: (1) 334-855-5151
  Email: scott.fryer@mwv.com
  Maint. Mgr.: Larry Casey
  Phone: (1) 334-855-4711
  Fax: (1) 334-855-5151
  Email: larry.casey@mwv.com
  Finan. Dir.: David Eakes
  Phone: (1) 334-855-4711
  Fax: (1) 334-855-5151
  Email: david.eakes@mwv.com
  Wood Procurement Mgr. Mahrt Operations: Ben Smith
  Phone: (1) 334-855-4711
  Fax: (1) 334-855-5151
  Email: ben.smith@mwv.com
  Environ. Mgr.: Pamela Dohney
  Phone: (1) 334-855-4711
  Fax: (1) 334-855-5151
  Email: pamela.dohney@mwv.com
  No. 2 Paper Machine Supt.: Kenneth Jones
  Phone: (1) 334-855-4711
  Fax: (1) 334-855-5151
  Email: ken.jones@mwv.com
Total Employees at this Location: 672
Type of Operation: Pulp mill, Paperboard mill
Pulp Grades and Capacities:
  Total pulp capacity: 996,923 st/y
  Chemical Pulp: 827,704 st/y
  Recycled Pulping: 169,219 st/y
Pulp Mill Data:
  Chemical Pulping Systems:

Alabama

Batch digesters: 6
Continuous digesters: 1
Chemical Recovery Equipment:
Evaporator lines: 1
Recovery boilers: 2
Lime Kiln
Recycled Fiber Treatment Lines:
Pulpers: 1 at 182,099
Paper/Paperboard Grades and Capacities:
Total paper and paperboard capacity: 1,064,574 st/y
Boxboard/cartonboard: 1,064,574 st/y
Paper and Paperboard Mill Data:
Stock Preparation:
Pulpers: 6
Refiners: 18
Paper Machines: 2
No. 1, twin-wire, total capacity 504,084 st/y, Trim width 258 in, Boxboard/cartonboard
No. 2, twin-wire, total capacity 560,490 st/y, Trim width 300 in, Boxboard/cartonboard
Coating Machines: 2
PM 1, total capacity 518,078 st/y., on machine
PM 2, total capacity 553,351 st/y., on machine
Finishing Equipment:
Winders: 2
Energy Data:
Power boilers: 4
Combustion turbines: 1 at 25 MW
Steam turbines: 2 at 88 MW
Electrical demand for mill: 2,532 MWh/D

ⓜ Mobile Paperboard Corp.
Mobile Mill
Ownership: 100% by Newark Recycled Paperboard Solutions
701 Mobile St
Mobile, AL 36617-2019
USA
Phone: (1) 251-478-6391
Fax: (1) 251-478-5125
Web Address: www.newarkpb.com
Personnel:
Gen. Mgr.: Chris Conrad
Phone: (1) 251-478-6391
Fax: (1) 251-478-5125
Email: cconrad@tngus.com
Contr.: Kerri Byrd
Phone: (1) 251-478-6391
Fax: (1) 251-478-5125
Email: kbyrd@tngus.com
Plt. Mgr.: Michael Raymond
Phone: (1) 251-478-6391
Fax: (1) 251-478-5125
Email: mraymond@tngus.com
Gen. Sls. Mgr.: Ed Kneip
Phone: (1) 251-478-6391
Fax: (1) 251-478-5125
Email: ekneip@tngus.com
Total Employees at this Location: 161
Type of Operation: Paperboard mill
Pulp Grades and Capacities:
Total pulp capacity: 149,595 st/y
Recycled Pulping: 149,595 st/y
Pulp Mill Data:
Recycled Fiber Treatment Lines:
Recycled packaging pulping lines: 2
Paper/Paperboard Grades and Capacities:
Total paper and paperboard capacity: 146,013 st/y
Boxboard/cartonboard: 146,013 st/y
Paper and Paperboard Mill Data:
Stock Preparation:
Pulpers: 2
Refiners: 8
Paper Machines: 2
No. 1, fourdrinier, total capacity 62,832 st/y, Trim width 81 in, Boxboard/cartonboard
No. 2, fourdrinier, total capacity 83,181 st/y, Trim width 102 in, Boxboard/cartonboard
Energy Data:
Power boilers: 1
Electrical demand for mill: 185 MWh/D

ⓜ National Gypsum Co.
Anniston Mill
4811 US Hwy 78 W
Oxford, AL 36203
USA
Phone: (1) 256-831-6900
Fax: (1) 256-835-2688
Web Address: www.nationalgypsum.com
Personnel:
Mill Mgr.: Neal E Stephenson
Phone: (1) 256-831-6900
Fax: (1) 256-835-2688
Email: nestephenson@nationalgypsum.com
Office Mgr.: David Phillips
Phone: (1) 256-831-6900
Fax: (1) 256-835-2688
Email: dphillips@nationalgypsum.com
Admin. Mgr.: Alan Goodwin
Phone: (1) 256-831-6900
Fax: (1) 256-835-2688
Purch. Mgr.: Raymond G Syracuse
Phone: (1) 256-831-6900
Fax: (1) 256-835-2688
Email: rgsyracuse@nationalgypsum.com
Total Employees at this Location: 78
Type of Operation: Paperboard mill
Pulp Grades and Capacities:
Total pulp capacity: 80,288 st/y
Recycled Pulping: 80,288 st/y
Pulp Mill Data:
Recycled Fiber Treatment Lines:
Recycled packaging pulping lines: 1
Paper/Paperboard Grades and Capacities:
Total paper and paperboard capacity: 77,112 st/y
Boxboard/cartonboard: 77,112 st/y
Paper and Paperboard Mill Data:
Stock Preparation:
Pulpers: 3
Refiners: 4
Paper Machines: 1
No. 1, cylinder (9), total capacity 77,112 st/y, Trim width 103 in, Boxboard/cartonboard
Finishing Equipment:
Winders: 1
Calenders: 2
Energy Data:
Power boilers: 2
Electrical demand for mill: 98 MWh/D

ⓜ Resolute FP US Inc.
Coosa Pines Mill
Ownership: 100% by Resolute Forest Products Canada Inc.
17589 Plant Rd
Coosa Pines, AL 35044-0555
USA
Phone: (1) 256-378-5541
Fax: (1) 256-378-2165
Email: info@resolutefp.com
Web Address: www.resolutefp.com
Personnel:
VP. & Gen. Mgr.: Scott A. Palmer
Phone: (1) 256-378-2146
Fax: (1) 256-378-2147
Email: scott.palmer@resolutefp.com
Tech. Serv. Mgr.: Sébastien P. Kidd
Phone: (1) 256-378-2628
Fax: (1) 256-378-2165
Email: sebastien.kidd@resolutefp.com
Ross Dryer Oper. Coord.: Gregory Graben
Phone: (1) 256-378-2662
Fax: (1) 256-378-2165
Email: greg.graben@resolutefp.com
Environ. Eng.: Jeremy Daughtry
Phone: (1) 256-378-5541
Fax: (1) 256-378-2165
Email: jeremy.daughtry@resolutefp.com
Total Employees at this Location: 260
Type of Operation: Pulp mill
Pulp Grades and Capacities:
Total pulp capacity: 308,904 st/y
Pulp available for market: 289,884 st/y
Chemical Pulp: 308,904 st/y
Pulp Mill Data:
Chemical Pulping Systems:
Batch digesters: 5
Bleach Plant Systems: 1
No. 1, Sequence: DEoDEpD
Chemical Recovery Equipment:
Recovery boilers: 2
Lime Kiln
Pulp Dryers:
Fourdriniers 1, Ross Dryer 1
Paper and Paperboard Mill Data:
Stock Preparation:
Pulpers: 2
Finishing Equipment:
Winders: 2
Calenders: 2
Energy Data:
Power boilers: 5
Steam turbines: 6 at 30 MW
Electrical demand for mill: 694 MWh/D

ⓜ RockTenn Co.
Demopolis Mill
28270 US Hwy 80 W
Demopolis, AL 36732-5121
USA
Phone: (1) 334-289-1242
Fax: (1) 334-289-6410
Web Address: www.rocktenn.com
Personnel:
Gen. Mgr.: James Grantham
Phone: (1) 334-289-6274
Fax: (1) 334-289-6410
Email: jgrantham@rocktenn.com
Strategic Proj. Mgr.: Marty Duckworth
Phone: (1) 334-289-6273
Fax: (1) 334-289-5257
Email: mduckworth@rocktenn.com
Reliability Mgr.: Michael (Mike) Hill
Phone: (1) 334-289-6274
Fax: (1) 334-289-6410
Email: mhill@rocktenn.com
Bus. Serv. Mgr.: Shone Jones
Phone: (1) 334-289-6274
Fax: (1) 334-289-6410
Email: sjones@rocktenn.com
Board Machine Superint.: Michael Etheridge
Phone: (1) 334-289-6274
Fax: (1) 334-289-6410
Email: metheridge@rocktenn.com
Total Employees at this Location: 465
Type of Operation: Pulp mill, Paperboard mill
Pulp Grades and Capacities:
Total pulp capacity: 425,185 st/y
Pulp available for market: 102,102 st/y
Chemical Pulp: 425,185 st/y
Pulp Mill Data:
Chemical Pulping Systems:
Continuous digesters: 2
Bleach Plant Systems: 2
No. 1, Type: Swd, Sequence: DEopDED
No. 2, Type: Hwd, Sequence: DEopD
Chemical Recovery Equipment:
Evaporator lines: 1
Recovery boilers: 1
Lime Kiln
Pulp Dryers:
Air Float dryers 1
Paper/Paperboard Grades and Capacities:
Total paper and paperboard capacity: 339,864 st/y
Boxboard/cartonboard: 339,864 st/y
Paper and Paperboard Mill Data:
Stock Preparation:
Pulpers: 2

Refiners: 6
Paper Machines: 1
No. 1, top former, total capacity 339,864 st/y, Trim width 218 in, Boxboard/cartonboard
Coating Machines: 1
No. 1, total capacity 329,586 st/y., on machine
Finishing Equipment:
Winders: 1
Calenders: 2
Energy Data:
Power boilers: 3
Steam turbines: 2 at 11.0, 17.75 (shutdown (2012)) MW
Electrical demand for mill: 937 MWh/D

ⓂRockTenn Co.
Stevenson Mill
1611 County Rd 85
Stevenson, AL 35772-0908
USA
Mailing Address: PO Box 508, Stevenson, AL 35772-0908, USA
Phone: (1) 256-437-2161
Fax: (1) 256-437-3301
Web Address: www.rocktenn.com
Personnel:
PM Mgr. (From January 2014): Michael (Mick) Forbes
Phone: (1) 256-437-2161
Fax: (1) 256-437-3301
Email: mforbes@rocktenn.com
Sr. Systems Engineer: Keith Yeager
Phone: (1) 256-437-2161
Fax: (1) 256-437-3301
Email: kyeager@rocktenn.com
HR Mgr.: Duke Cumbelich
Phone: (1) 256-437-2161
Fax: (1) 256-437-3301
Email: dcumbelich@rocktenn.com
Eng. Mgr.: Bruce Roberts
Phone: (1) 256-437-2161
Fax: (1) 256-437-3301
Email: broberts@rocktenn.com
Total Employees at this Location: 382
Type of Operation: Pulp mill, Paperboard mill
Pulp Grades and Capacities:
Total pulp capacity: 917,083 st/y
Chemical Pulp: 467,505 st/y
Recycled Pulping: 449,577 st/y
Pulp Mill Data:
Chemical Pulping Systems:
Continuous digesters: 2
Pulp Lines: 5
Chemical Recovery Equipment:
Evaporator lines: 1
Recovery boilers: 1
Recycled Fiber Treatment Lines:
Pulpers: 3 at 480,000 admt/y
Paper/Paperboard Grades and Capacities:
Total paper and paperboard capacity: 885,003 st/y
Corrugating medium/fluting: 885,003 st/y
Paper and Paperboard Mill Data:
Stock Preparation:
Refiners: 12
Paper Machines: 2
No. 1, fourdrinier, total capacity 451,962 st/y, Trim width 312 in, Corrugating medium/fluting
No. 2, fourdrinier, total capacity 433,041 st/y, Trim width 314 in, Corrugating medium/fluting
Energy Data:
Power boilers: 4

ⓂSCA Tissue North America, L.L.C.
Barton Mill
Ownership: 100% by SCA - Svenska Cellulosa Aktiebolaget
1834 Haley Dr.
Cherokee, AL 35616
USA
Mailing Address: PO Box 348, Barton, AL 35616-0348, USA
Phone: (1) 256-370-8100
Fax: (1) 256-370-8195
Web Address: www.scatissue.com
Personnel:
Site Mgr.: John Crane
Phone: (1) 256-370-8108
Fax: (1) 256-370-8195
Email: john.crane@sca.com
Maint. & Reliability Ldr.: Richard Stutts
Phone: (1) 256-370-8100
Fax: (1) 256-370-8195
Email: richard.stutts@sca.com
Reg. HR Mgr. Southeast: Bryan Dyar
Phone: (1) 256-370-8112
Fax: (1) 256-370-8195
Email: bryan.dyar@sca.com
Safety Mgr.: Alicia Gist
Phone: (1) 256-370-8119
Fax: (1) 256-370-8195
Email: alicia.gist@sca.com
Tech. Serv. Mgr. (From January 2014): Andrew Chorney
Phone: (1) 256-370-8100
Fax: (1) 256-370-8195
Email: andrew.chorney@sca.com
Environ. Mgr.: Robin Wood
Phone: (1) 256-370-8125
Fax: (1) 256-370-8195
Email: robin.wood@sca.com
Reg. Logist. Mgr.: Robert Matthew James
Phone: (1) 256-370-8252
Fax: (1) 256-370-8195
Email: matt.james@sca.com
Procurement Mgr.: Mark Segars
Phone: (1) 256-370-8100
Fax: (1) 256-370-8195
Email: mark.segars@sca.com
Total Employees at this Location: 490
Type of Operation: Paper mill
Pulp Grades and Capacities:
Total pulp capacity: 185,989 st/y
Recycled Pulping: 185,989 st/y
Pulp Mill Data:
Pulp Lines: 2
Bleach Plant Systems: 2
DIP
DIP
Recycled Fiber Treatment Lines:
Flotation deinking lines: 2 at 265,000
Paper/Paperboard Grades and Capacities:
Total paper and paperboard capacity: 175,287 st/y
Tissue: 175,287 st/y
Paper and Paperboard Mill Data:
Paper Machines: 2
No. 12, crescent former, total capacity 101,745 st/y, Trim width 214 in, Tissue
No. 14, crescent former, total capacity 73,542 st/y, Trim width 214 in, Tissue
Energy Data:
Power boilers: 1
Electrical demand for mill: 697 MWh/D

ARIZONA

①Royal Paper
Ownership: Private
31201 W. Thayer Rd
Phoenix, AZ 85337
USA
Phone: (1) 602-258-9007, 800-258-9007
Fax: (1) 800-965-9007
Email: info@royalpaper.us
Web Address: www.royalpaper.us
Personnel:
Pres. & CEO: Nassar Sarrafzadeh
Phone: (1) 602-258-9007, 800-258-9007
Fax: (1) 800-965-9007
COO: Bob Sarrafzadeh
Phone: (1) 602-258-9007, 800-258-9007
Fax: (1) 800-965-9007
Exec. VP Mktg.: Sepehr Dardashtyn
Phone: (1) 602-258-9007, 800-258-9007
Fax: (1) 800-965-9007
Exec. VP Mktg.: Siamak Dardashtyn
Phone: (1) 602-258-9007, 800-258-9007
Fax: (1) 800-965-9007
CFO: Sunil Kanuga
Phone: (1) 602-258-9007, 800-258-9007
Fax: (1) 800-965-9007
VP Oper.: Sal Mannino
Phone: (1) 602-258-9007, 800-258-9007
Fax: (1) 800-965-9007
Total Employees of Company: 50
Mill Locations:
Royal Paper, Gila Bend, 31201 W. Thayer Rd, Phoenix, AZ 85337, USA, Capacity: 32,130 st/y, (Paper mill)
Phone: (1) 602-258-9007, 800-258-9007
Fax: (1) 800-965-9007
Email: info@royalpaper.us

ⓂRoyal Paper
Gila Bend
31201 W. Thayer Rd
Phoenix, AZ 85337
USA
Phone: (1) 602-258-9007, 800-258-9007
Fax: (1) 800-965-9007
Email: info@royalpaper.us
Web Address: www.royalpaper.us
Personnel:
Plt. Mgr.: Erik Sowirka
Phone: (1) 800-258-9007
Fax: (1) 800-965-9007
Contr.: Kim Lubbers
Phone: (1) 800-258-9007
Fax: (1) 800-965-9007
Qlty. Mgr.: Mary Holt
Phone: (1) 800-258-9007
Fax: (1) 800-965-9007
Total Employees at this Location: 50
Type of Operation: Paper mill
Paper/Paperboard Grades and Capacities:
Total paper and paperboard capacity: 32,130 st/y
Tissue: 32,130 st/y
Paper and Paperboard Mill Data:
Stock Preparation:
Pulpers:
Paper Machines: 1
No. 1, crescent former, total capacity 32,130 st/y, Trim width 102 in, Tissue
Energy Data:
Power boilers: 1
Electrical demand for mill: 79 MWh/D

ⓂSCA Tissue North America, L.L.C.
Flagstaff Mill
Ownership: 100% by SCA - Svenska Cellulosa Aktiebolaget
1600 E Butler Av
Flagstaff, AZ 86001
USA
Phone: (1) 928-774-7375
Fax: (1) 928-774-9546
Email: americas@sca.com
Web Address: www.sca.com/us
Personnel:
Oper. Mgr.: Michael Yoder
Phone: (1) 928-774-7375
Fax: (1) 928-774-9546
Email: michael.yoder@sca.com
Process Eng & Oper. Mgr.: Thomas Orgler
Phone: (1) 928-774-7375
Fax: (1) 928-774-9546
Email: thomas.orgler@sca.com

Arkansas

Sr. Account Executive: Perry Ceccarelli
Phone: (1) 928-774-7375
Fax: (1) 928-774-9546
Email: perry.ceccarelli@sca.com
Environ. Asst.: Annikki Chamberlain
Phone: (1) 928-774-7375
Fax: (1) 928-774-9546
Email: annikki.chamberlain@sca.com
Total Employees at this Location: 75
Type of Operation: Paper mill
Pulp Grades and Capacities:
Total pulp capacity: 66,147 st/y
Recycled Pulping: 66,147 st/y
Pulp Mill Data:
Bleach Plant Systems: 1
DIP
Recycled Fiber Treatment Lines:
Pulpers: 1 at 88,845 admt/y
Paper/Paperboard Grades and Capacities:
Total paper and paperboard capacity: 61,761 st/y
Tissue: 61,761 st/y
Paper and Paperboard Mill Data:
Stock Preparation:
Pulpers: 3
Refiners: 2
Paper Machines: 2
No. 5, crescent former, total capacity 32,844 st/y, Trim width 127 in, Tissue
No. 6, crescent former, total capacity 28,917 st/y, Trim width 133 in, Tissue
Energy Data:
Power boilers: 1
Electrical demand for mill: 186 MWh/D

ARKANSAS

ⓂClearwater Paper Corporation
Cypress Bend Mill, McGehee Mill
5082 Arkansas 4
McGehee, Arkansas City, AR 71630
USA
Mailing Address: PO Box 727, McGehee, AR 71654-0727, USA
Phone: (1) 870-877-2662
Fax: (1) 870-877-3380
Web Address: www.clearwaterpaper.com
Personnel:
Mill Mgr.: Bill Horne
Phone: (1) 870-877-2662
Fax: (1) 870-877-3380
Email: bill.horne@clearwaterpaper.com
Environ., Safety & Health and HR Mgr.: Judy A. Holt
Phone: (1) 870-877-2662
Fax: (1) 870-877-3380
Email: judy.holt@clearwaterpaper.com
Pulp & Utilities Mgr.: Malcolm E. Massey
Phone: (1) 870-877-2662
Fax: (1) 870-877-3380
Email: malcolm.massey@clearwaterpaper.com
Fiber Supply Mgr.: Ben Garner
Phone: (1) 870-877-2662
Fax: (1) 870-877-3380
Email: ben.garner@clearwaterpaper.com
Product Mgr.: Lynn Weatherly
Phone: (1) 870-877-2662
Fax: (1) 870-877-3380
Email: lynn.weatherly@clearwaterpaper.com
Total Employees at this Location: 264
Type of Operation: Paperboard mill
Pulp Grades and Capacities:
Total pulp capacity: 57,470 st/y
Chemical Pulp: 57,470 st/y
Pulp Mill Data:
Chemical Pulping Systems:
Batch digesters: 4
Bleach Plant Systems: 1

1, Sequence: DEopDED
Chemical Recovery Equipment:
Evaporator lines: 1
Recovery boilers: 1
Lime Kiln
Paper/Paperboard Grades and Capacities:
Total paper and paperboard capacity: 312,018 st/y
Boxboard/cartonboard: 312,018 st/y
Paper and Paperboard Mill Data:
Stock Preparation:
Pulpers: 1
Refiners: 8
Paper Machines: 1
No. 1, fourdrinier, total capacity 312,018 st/y, Trim width 220 in, Boxboard/cartonboard
Coating Machines: 1
CM 1, total capacity 317,460 st/y., on machine
Finishing Equipment:
Winders: 1
Calenders: 3
Energy Data:
Power boilers: 1
Steam turbines: 1 at 32 MW
Electrical demand for mill: 772 MWh/D

ⓂDomtar Corporation
Ashdown Mill
285 Hwy 71 South
Ashdown, AR 71822
USA
Phone: (1) 870-898-2711
Fax: (1) 870-898-4724
Web Address: www.domtar.com
Personnel:
Gen. Mgr.: Bob Grygotis
Phone: (1) 870-898-2711
Fax: (1) 870-898-4724
Email: bob.grygotis@domtar.com
Commun. & Government. Rel. Mgr.: Tammy Waters
Phone: (1) 870-898-2711 ext. 6635
Fax: (1) 870-898-4724
Email: tammy.waters@domtar.com
Oper. Mgr.: John O'Donnell
Phone: (1) 870-898-2711
Fax: (1) 870-898-4724
Email: john.odonnell@domtar.com
Maint. Mgr.: Doug Minor
Phone: (1) 870-898-2711
Fax: (1) 870-898-4724
Email: doug.minor@domtar.com
Mgr., Eng.: Bernie Kreul
Phone: (1) 870-898-2711
Fax: (1) 870-898-4724
Email: bernard.kreul@domtar.com
Total Employees at this Location: 850
Type of Operation: Pulp mill, Paper mill
Pulp Grades and Capacities:
Total pulp capacity: 912,320 st/y
Pulp available for market: 249,884 st/y
Chemical Pulp: 912,320 st/y
Pulp Mill Data:
Chemical Pulping Systems:
Batch digesters: 10
Continuous digesters: 1
Pulp Lines: 3
Bleach Plant Systems: 3
#2, Type: SWD, Sequence: O₂ DEopDD, Capacity 327,594.8 admt/y
1A, Type: HWD, Sequence: DEopDD, Capacity 282,695.1 admt/y
1B, Type: HWD, Sequence: DEopDD, Capacity 282,695.1 admt/y
Chemical Recovery Equipment:
Evaporator lines: 2
Recovery boilers: 2
Lime Kiln
Pulp Dryers:
Air Float dryers 1
Paper/Paperboard Grades and Capacities:

Total paper and paperboard capacity: 767,381 st/y
Uncoated woodfree/freesheet: 767,381 st/y
Paper and Paperboard Mill Data:
Stock Preparation:
Refiners: 4
Paper Machines: 3
No. 62, fourdrinier, total capacity 196,307 st/y, Trim width 280 in, Uncoated woodfree/freesheet
No. 63, twin-wire, total capacity 207,014 st/y, Trim width 240 in, Uncoated woodfree/freesheet
No. 64, twin-wire, total capacity 364,060 st/y, Trim width 350 in, Uncoated woodfree/freesheet
Finishing Equipment:
Winders: 4
Calenders: 4
Rewinders: 1
Sheeters: 5
Energy Data:
Power boilers: 5
Steam turbines: 4 at 15.6, 42.0, 33.3, 38.8 MW
Electrical demand for mill: 3,068 MWh/D

ⓂEvergreen Packaging Inc.
Pine Bluff Mill
5201 Fairfield Rd
Pine Bluff, AR 71601
USA
Phone: (1) 870-541-5600
Fax: (1) 870-541-5788
Email: evergreen.packaging@everpack.com
Web Address: www.evergreenpackaging.com
Personnel:
Mill Mgr.: Craig Lichty
Phone: (1) 870-541-5600
Fax: (1) 870-541-5788
Email: craig.lichty@everpack.com
Bus. Unit Mgr., Bleached Board & Qlty. Assurance: Bill Wilson
Phone: (1) 870-541-5600
Fax: (1) 870-541-5788
Email: bill.wilson@everpack.com
Procurement Mgr.: Mike Boyd
Phone: (1) 870-541-5600
Fax: (1) 870-541-5788
Email: mike.boyd@everpack.com
Area Mgr.: Steve Ratliff
Phone: (1) 870-541-5600
Fax: (1) 870-541-5788
Email: steve.ratliff@everpack.com
HR. Mgr.: Terry Steen
Phone: (1) 870-541-5600
Fax: (1) 870-541-5788
Email: terry.steen@everpack.com
Total Employees at this Location: 931
Type of Operation: Paper mill, Paperboard mill
Pulp Grades and Capacities:
Total pulp capacity: 571,980 st/y
Chemical Pulp: 515,069 st/y
Mechanical Pulp: 56,911 st/y
Pulp Mill Data:
Chemical Pulping Systems:
Batch digesters: 13
Mechanical Pulping Systems:
Conventional grinders
Bleach Plant Systems: 2
Chemical Pulping System, Type: Softwood, Sequence: DEopDD, Capacity 290,000 admt/y
Chemical Pulping System, Type: Hardwood, Sequence: DEoD, Capacity 244,000.2 admt/y
Chemical Recovery Equipment:
Evaporator lines: 2
Recovery boilers: 3
Lime Kiln
Paper/Paperboard Grades and Capacities:
Total paper and paperboard capacity: 631,394 st/y
Uncoated mechanical/groundwood: 23,914 st/y
Coated mechanical/groundwood: 158,116 st/y
Boxboard/cartonboard: 449,364 st/y
Paper and Paperboard Mill Data:
Paper Machines: 2

No. 1, SymFormer, total capacity 187,741 st/y, Trim width 277 in, Coated mechanical/groundwood, Uncoated mechanical/groundwood
No. 2, (PE Extruder - 4), fourdrinier, total capacity 449,364 st/y, Trim width 275 in, Boxboard/cartonboard

Coating Machines: 5
No. 1, total capacity 189,594 st/y., off machine
No. 2
No. 3
No. 4
No. 5

Finishing Equipment:
Supercalenders: 2

Energy Data:
Power boilers: 3
Steam turbines: 3 at 20, 25, 40 MW
Electrical demand for mill: 1,891 MWh/D

ⓂGeorgia-Pacific LLC
Crossett Mill
100 Mill Supply Rd
Crossett, AR 71635
USA
Mailing Address: PO Box 3333, Crossett, AR 71635, USA
Phone: (1) 870-567-8000, 870-567-5365
Fax: (1) 870-364-5123
Web Address: www.gp.com
Personnel:
VP Manuf.: Gary W. Kaiser
Phone: (1) 870-567-8000
Fax: (1) 870-364-5123
Email: gary.kaiser@gapac.com
Contr.: Barbara A. Welch
Phone: (1) 870-567-8000
Fax: (1) 870-364-5123
Email: barbara.welch@gapac.com
Maint. Reliability Ldr.: Dewayne Ford
Phone: (1) 870-567-8000
Fax: (1) 870-364-5123
Email: dewayne.ford@gapac.com
Total Employees at this Location: 880
Type of Operation: Paper mill, Paperboard mill
Pulp Grades and Capacities:
Total pulp capacity: 608,998 st/y
Chemical Pulp: 608,998 st/y

Pulp Mill Data:
Chemical Pulping Systems:
Batch digesters: 13
Continuous digesters: 1
Bleach Plant Systems: 2
2, Sequence: DEopDD
Chemical Recovery Equipment:
Evaporator lines: 1
Recovery boilers: 1
Lime Kiln

Paper/Paperboard Grades and Capacities:
Total paper and paperboard capacity: 615,111 st/y
Tissue: 268,821 st/y
Boxboard/cartonboard: 346,290 st/y

Paper and Paperboard Mill Data:
Stock Preparation:
Pulpers:

Paper Machines: 7
No. 2, fourdrinier, total capacity 132,090 st/y, Trim width 198 in, Boxboard/cartonboard
No. 3, fourdrinier, total capacity 214,200 st/y, Trim width 198 in, Boxboard/cartonboard
No. 4, crescent former, Yankee dryer, total capacity 44,268 st/y, Trim width 102 in, Tissue
No. 5, crescent former, Yankee dryer, total capacity 32,130 st/y, Trim width 102 in, Tissue
No. 6, crescent former, Yankee dryer, total capacity 62,475 st/y, Trim width 208 in, Tissue
No. 7, crescent former, total capacity 64,260 st/y, Trim width 208 in, Tissue
No. 8, eTAD, total capacity 65,688 st/y, Trim width 206 in, Tissue

Coating Machines: 1

No. 3, total capacity 213,845 st/y., on machine
Energy Data:
Power boilers: 4
Steam turbines: 3 at 92 MW
Electrical demand for mill: 1,956 MWh/D

ⓂGreen Bay Packaging Inc.
Morrilton Mill
338 Highway 113 S, P.O. Box 711
Morrilton, AR 72110
USA
Mailing Address: PO Box 711, Morrilton, AR 72110, USA
Phone: (1) 501-354-4521
Fax: (1) 501-354-9290
Web Address: www.gbp.com
Personnel:
VP. & Gen. Mgr.: Matthew A. Szymanski
Phone: (1) 501-354-4521
Fax: (1) 501-354-9290
Email: mszymans@gbp.com
Oli & Gas Mgr. (From 2014): Scott Meek
Phone: (1) 501-354-4521
Fax: (1) 501-354-9290
Email: smeek@gbp.com
VP. & Gen. Mgr., Fiber Resource & Pinecrest Lumber Div.: Dave Cawein
Phone: (1) 501-354-4521
Fax: (1) 501-354-9290
Email: dcawein@gbp.com
buyer: David Andrew
Phone: (1) 501-354-4521
Fax: (1) 501-354-9290
Email: dandrews@gbp.com
Div. Contr.: Dean Warren
Phone: (1) 501-354-4521
Fax: (1) 501-354-9290
Email: dwarren@gbp.com
Pulp Mill Supt.: Jack Williamson
Phone: (1) 501-354-4521
Fax: (1) 501-354-9290
Email: jwilliamson@gbp.com
Total Employees at this Location: 374
Type of Operation: Pulp mill, Paperboard mill
Pulp Grades and Capacities:
Total pulp capacity: 448,846 st/y
Chemical Pulp: 245,577 st/y
Recycled Pulping: 203,268 st/y

Pulp Mill Data:
Chemical Pulping Systems:
Batch digesters: 5
Pulp Lines: 3
Chemical Recovery Equipment:
Evaporator lines: 2
Recovery boilers: 1
Lime Kiln
Recycled Fiber Treatment Lines:
Recycled packaging pulping lines: 1 at 285,494 admt/y

Paper/Paperboard Grades and Capacities:
Total paper and paperboard capacity: 429,828 st/y
Linerboard: 322,728 st/y
Corrugating medium/fluting: 107,100 st/y

Paper and Paperboard Mill Data:
Paper Machines: 2
No. 1, top former, total capacity 251,328 st/y, Trim width 200 in, Linerboard
No. 2, top former, total capacity 178,500 st/y, Trim width 164 in, Linerboard, Corrugating medium/fluting

Finishing Equipment:
Winders: 2
Calenders: 2

Energy Data:
Power boilers: 3
Electrical demand for mill: 746 MWh/D

ⓂMondi
Pine Bluff Mill
Mill is previously: Graphic Packaging International, Inc.
1701 Jefferson Parkway
Pine Bluff, AR 71601
USA
Mailing Address: PO Box 20700, Pine Bluff, AR 71601, USA
Phone: (1) 870-541-5000
Fax: (1) 870-541-5060
Email: info@mondigroup.com
Web Address: www.mondigroup.com
Personnel:
Mill Mgr. (From 2014): Richard Johnson
Phone: (1) 870-541-5000
Fax: (1) 870-541-5060
Email: richard.johnson@mondigroup.com
HR Mgr.: Melissa Schulze
Phone: (1) 870-541-5207
Fax: (1) 870-541-5095
Email: melissa.schulze@mondigroup.com
Environ. & Qlty. Mgr.: Amber Zajac
Phone: (1) 870-541-5000
Fax: (1) 870-541-5060
Email: amber.zajac@mondigroup.com
Safety & Health Mgr.: Don Murphy
Phone: (1) 870-541-5000
Fax: (1) 870-541-5060
Email: don.murphy@mondigroup.com
Sls. Mgr.: Shane Livingston
Phone: (1) 870-541-5000
Fax: (1) 870-541-5060
Email: shane.livingston@mondigroup.com
Total Employees at this Location: 178
Type of Operation: Paper mill
Pulp Grades and Capacities:
Total pulp capacity: 165,644 st/y
Chemical Pulp: 123,631 st/y
Recycled Pulping: 42,012 st/y

Pulp Mill Data:
Chemical Pulping Systems:
Batch digesters: 3
Chemical Recovery Equipment:
Evaporator lines: 1
Recovery boilers: 1
Lime Kiln
Recycled Fiber Treatment Lines:
Recycled packaging pulping lines: 1 at 38,580

Paper/Paperboard Grades and Capacities:
Total paper and paperboard capacity: 158,508 st/y
Packaging papers: 158,508 st/y

Paper and Paperboard Mill Data:
Stock Preparation:
Pulpers: 1
Refiners: 4
Paper Machines: 1
No. 1, fourdrinier, total capacity 158,508 st/y, Trim width 154 in, Packaging papers

Energy Data:
Power boilers: 2
Electrical demand for mill: 315 MWh/D

CALIFORNIA

ⓂCalifornia Paperboard Corp.
Santa Clara Mill
Ownership: 100% by Newark Recycled Paperboard Solutions
525 Mathew St
Santa Clara, CA 95050
USA
Mailing Address: PO Box 58044, Santa Clara, CA 95052, USA
Phone: (1) 408-727-7377
Fax: (1) 408-988-0585
Web Address: www.newarkpb.com
Personnel:
Gen. Mgr.: Mike Grover

California

Phone: (1) 408-727-7377
Fax: (1) 408-988-0585
Email: mgrover@tngus.com
Tech Mgr.: Keith Wharton
Phone: (1) 408-727-7377
Fax: (1) 408-988-0585
Asst Mill Mgr.: Lee Holmes
Phone: (1) 408-727-7377
Fax: (1) 408-988-0585
Total Employees at this Location: 60
Type of Operation: Paperboard mill
Pulp Grades and Capacities:
 Total pulp capacity: 86,870 st/y
 Recycled Pulping: 86,870 st/y
Pulp Mill Data:
 Recycled Fiber Treatment Lines:
 Recycled packaging pulping lines
Paper/Paperboard Grades and Capacities:
 Total paper and paperboard capacity: 84,252 st/y
 Linerboard: 2,142 st/y
 Corrugating medium/fluting: 82,110 st/y
Paper and Paperboard Mill Data:
Paper Machines: 1
 No. 2, fourdrinier, total capacity 84,252 st/y, Trim width 100 in, Corrugating medium/fluting, Linerboard
Energy Data:
 Power boilers: 2
 Electrical demand for mill: 87 MWh/D

ⓂG-P Gypsum LLC
San Leandro Mill
Ownership: Georgia-Pacific LLC
1988 Marina Blvd
San Leandro, CA 94550
USA
Mailing Address: 1988 Marina Blvd, San Leandro, CA 94577-3207, USA
 Phone: (1) 510-483-7580
 Fax: (1) 510-483-5430
 Web Address: www.gp.com,
 www.buildgp.com/Georgia-Pacific-Gypsum
Personnel:
 Plt. Mgr.: Fred J. Curcio
 Phone: (1) 510-483-7580
 Fax: (1) 510-483-5430
 Email: fjcurcio@gapac.com
 Mfg. Mgr./Assist. Plt. Mgr.: Duane W. Dohse
 Phone: (1) 510-483-7580
 Fax: (1) 510-483-5430
 Email: dwdohse@gapac.com
Total Employees at this Location: 75
Type of Operation: Paper mill
Pulp Grades and Capacities:
 Total pulp capacity: 83,523 st/y
 Recycled Pulping: 83,523 st/y
Paper/Paperboard Grades and Capacities:
 Total paper and paperboard capacity: 80,325 st/y
 Boxboard/cartonboard: 80,325 st/y
Paper and Paperboard Mill Data:
 Stock Preparation:
 Pulpers: 3
 Refiners: 1
Paper Machines: 1
 No. 1, fourdrinier, total capacity 80,325 st/y, Trim width 162 in, Boxboard/cartonboard
Finishing Equipment:
 Winders: 1
 Calenders: 1
 Rewinders: 1
Energy Data:
 Power boilers: 2
 Electrical demand for mill: 128 MWh/D

ⓂGraphic Packaging International Inc.
Santa Clara Mill
2600 De La Cruz Blvd
Santa Clara, CA 95050
USA
 Phone: (1) 408-496-5118
 Fax: (1) 408-496-5027
 Web Address: www.graphicpkg.com
Personnel:
 Resident Mgr.: Dick Johnston
 Phone: (1) 408-496-5084
 Fax: (1) 408-496-5027
 Email: dick.johnston@graphicpkg.com
 Mill Mgr.: Jeff Mih
 Phone: (1) 408-496-5118
 Fax: (1) 408-496-5027
 Email: jeff.mih@graphicpkg.com
 Contr.: Douglas Evans
 Phone: (1) 408-496-5118
 Fax: (1) 408-496-5027
 Email: doug.evans@graphicpkg.com
 HR Mgr. & Enviro. Mgr.: Rick L. Horne
 Phone: (1) 408-496-5118
 Fax: (1) 408-496-5027
 Email: rick.horne@graphicpkg.com
Total Employees at this Location: 128
Type of Operation: Paperboard mill
Pulp Grades and Capacities:
 Total pulp capacity: 126,255 st/y
 Recycled Pulping: 126,255 st/y
Pulp Mill Data:
 Recycled Fiber Treatment Lines:
 Pulpers: 1 at 123,787
Paper/Paperboard Grades and Capacities:
 Total paper and paperboard capacity: 139,230 st/y
 Boxboard/cartonboard: 139,230 st/y
Paper and Paperboard Mill Data:
 Stock Preparation:
 Pulpers:
Paper Machines: 1
 No. 1, multi-wire, total capacity 139,230 st/y, Trim width 136 in, Boxboard/cartonboard
Coating Machines: 2
 No. 1, total capacity 130,071 st/y., on machine No. 2
Finishing Equipment:
 Rewinders: 1
Energy Data:
 Power boilers: 2
 Combustion turbines: 1 at 25 MW
 Steam turbines: 1 at 5 MW
 Electrical demand for mill: 233 MWh/D

ⓂGusmerCellulo
Fresno Mill
Ownership: 100% by Gusmer Enterprises Inc.
81 M St
Fresno, CA 93721
USA
 Phone: (1) 559-485-2692
 Fax: (1) 559-485-4254
 Email: info@gusmercellulo.com
 Web Address: www.gusmerenterprises.com
Personnel:
 Prod. Mgr.: Jim Lunt
 Phone: (1) 559-485-2692
 Fax: (1) 559-485-4254
 Email: jlunt@gusmerenterprises.com
 Tech Sls.: Etienne (Tim) Ossun
 Phone: (1) 559-485-2692
 Fax: (1) 559-485-4254
 Email: eossun@gusmerenterprises.com
 Cust Service Mgr.: Christine Caudell
 Phone: (1) 559-485-2692
 Fax: (1) 559-485-4254
 Email: ccaudell@gusmerenterprises.com
Type of Operation: Paper mill
Paper/Paperboard Grades and Capacities:
 Total paper and paperboard capacity: 2,999 st/y
 Specialty and industrial: 2,999 st/y

ⓂKimberly-Clark Corp.
Fullerton Mill
2001 E Orangethorpe Ave
Fullerton, CA 92831-5326
USA
 Phone: (1) 714-773-7500
 Fax: (1) 714-773-9291
 Web Address: www.kimberly-clark.com
Personnel:
 Sr. Process Eng.: Doug Lamb
 Phone: (1) 714-773-7500
 Fax: (1) 714-773-9291
 Email: dlamb@kcc.com
Total Employees at this Location: 104
Type of Operation: Paper mill
Paper/Paperboard Grades and Capacities:
 Total paper and paperboard capacity: 66,045 st/y
 Tissue: 66,045 st/y
Paper and Paperboard Mill Data:
 Stock Preparation:
 Pulpers: 3
 Refiners: 4
Paper Machines: 2
 No. 1, crescent former, Yankee dryer, total capacity 29,988 st/y, Trim width 172 in, Tissue
 No. 2, crescent former, Yankee dryer, total capacity 36,057 st/y, Trim width 172 in, Tissue
Energy Data:
 Power boilers: 1
 Combustion turbines: 1 at 13.4 MW
 Electrical demand for mill: 168 MWh/D

ⓂNew-Indy Containerboard LLC
Ownership: The Kraft Group, Schwarz Partners, LP
5100 E Jurupa St
Ontario, CA 91761-3618
USA
 Phone: (1) 909-937-7300
 Fax: (1) 909-937-7308
 Web Address: www.new-indy.com
Personnel:
 COO: Richard Hartman
 Phone: (1) 909-937-7300
 Fax: (1) 909-937-7308
 Maint. Mgr.: Dave Winn
 Phone: (1) 909-937-7300
 Fax: (1) 909-937-7308
 Corporate Dir. HR Mgr.: Christine Lacey
 Phone: (1) 909-937-7300
 Fax: (1) 909-937-7308
 Tech Mgr.: Victor Kumpera
 Phone: (1) 909-937-7300
 Fax: (1) 909-937-7308
Mill Locations:
 New-Indy Containerboard LLC, Port Hueneme Mill, 5936 Perkins Rd, Oxnard, CA 93033, USA, Capacity: 215,985 st/y, (Paperboard mill)
 Phone: (1) 805-986-3881
 Fax: (1) 805-488-5186
 New-Indy Containerboard LLC, Ontario Mill, 5100 E Jurupa St, Ontario, CA 91761-3618, USA, Capacity: 333,795 st/y, (Paperboard mill)
 Phone: (1) 909-937-7300
 Fax: (1) 909-937-7308

ⓂNew-Indy Containerboard LLC
Port Hueneme Mill
Previously International Paper Co.
5936 Perkins Rd
Oxnard, CA 93033
USA
Mailing Address: PO Box 519, Port Hueneme, CA 93044, USA
 Phone: (1) 805-986-3881
 Fax: (1) 805-488-5186
 Web Address: new-indy.com
Personnel:
 Maint. Mgr.: Charles Wilson
 Phone: (1) 805-986-3881
 Fax: (1) 805-488-5186
 Buss Unit Mgr.: Jay Loppnow
 Phone: (1) 805-986-3881
 Fax: (1) 805-488-5186
 Paper Machine Supt.: Michael McGinty
 Phone: (1) 805-986-3881

Fax: (1) 805-488-5186
Plant Eng Mgr.: Jeffrey Larson
Phone: (1) 805-986-3881
Fax: (1) 805-488-5186
Mechanical Eng Mgr.: Elise Woolworth
Phone: (1) 805-986-3881
Fax: (1) 805-488-5186
Total Employees at this Location: 87
Type of Operation: Paperboard mill
Pulp Grades and Capacities:
  Total pulp capacity: 221,984 st/y
  Recycled Pulping: 221,984 st/y
Pulp Mill Data:
  Recycled Fiber Treatment Lines:
  Pulpers: 1 at 242,504
Paper/Paperboard Grades and Capacities:
  Total paper and paperboard capacity: 215,985 st/y
  Corrugating medium/fluting: 215,985 st/y
Paper and Paperboard Mill Data:
  Stock Preparation:
  Pulpers: 1
  Refiners: 4
Paper Machines: 1
No. 1, fourdrinier, total capacity 215,985 st/y, Trim width 170 in, Corrugating medium/fluting
Energy Data:
Power boilers: 1
Combustion turbines: 1 at 28 MW
Electrical demand for mill: 247 MWh/D

ⓜNew-Indy Containerboard LLC
Ontario Mill
Previously International Paper Co. mill
5100 E Jurupa St
Ontario, CA 91761-3618
USA
  Phone: (1) 909-937-7300
  Fax: (1) 909-937-7308
  Web Address: new-indy.com
Personnel:
  COO: Richard Hartman
  Phone: (1) 909-937-7300
  Fax: (1) 909-937-7308
  Maint. Mgr.: Dave Winn
  Phone: (1) 909-937-7300
  Fax: (1) 909-937-7308
  HR Mgr.: Christine Lacey
  Phone: (1) 909-937-7300
  Fax: (1) 909-937-7308
  Tech. Mgr.: Victor Kumpera
  Phone: (1) 909-937-7300
  Fax: (1) 909-937-7308
Total Employees at this Location: 150
Type of Operation: Paperboard mill
Pulp Grades and Capacities:
  Total pulp capacity: 348,613 st/y
  Recycled Pulping: 348,613 st/y
Pulp Mill Data:
  Recycled Fiber Treatment Lines:
  Pulpers: 1 at 379,189
Paper/Paperboard Grades and Capacities:
  Total paper and paperboard capacity: 333,795 st/y
  Linerboard: 333,795 st/y
Paper and Paperboard Mill Data:
Paper Machines: 1
No. 1, top-wire former, total capacity 333,795 st/y, Trim width 259 in, Linerboard
Energy Data:
Power boilers
Combustion turbines: 1 at 37 MW
Electrical demand for mill: 394 MWh/D

ⓜNewark Pacific Paperboard Corp.
Los Angeles Mill
Ownership: Newark Recycled Paperboard Solutions
6001 S Eastern Ave
Los Angeles, CA 90040
USA
  Phone: (1) 323-728-7500
  Fax: (1) 323-724-7570
  Web Address: www.newarkpb.com.
Personnel:
  Plt. Mgr.: Andrew Peek
  Phone: (1) 323-724-7500 Ext: 7521
  Fax: (1) 323-724-7570
  Email: apeek@tngus.com
  Sls. Mgr.: Keith A. Standridge
  Phone: (1) 323-728-7500
  Fax: (1) 323-724-7570
  Email: kstandridge@tngus.com
  Sls. Mgr.: Matthew Mullen
  Phone: (1) 323-728-7500
  Fax: (1) 323-724-7570
  Email: mmullen@tngus.com
  Tech. Dir.: Mike Lipp
  Phone: (1) 323-728-7500
  Fax: (1) 323-724-7570
  Email: mlipp@tngus.com
Total Employees at this Location: 74
Type of Operation: Paperboard mill
Pulp Grades and Capacities:
  Total pulp capacity: 61,473 st/y
  Recycled Pulping: 61,473 st/y
Pulp Mill Data:
  Recycled Fiber Treatment Lines:
  Recycled packaging pulping lines
Paper/Paperboard Grades and Capacities:
  Total paper and paperboard capacity: 64,974 st/y
  Boxboard/cartonboard: 64,974 st/y
Paper and Paperboard Mill Data:
  Stock Preparation:
  Pulpers: 3
  Refiners: 6
Paper Machines: 1
No. 1, cylinder (9), total capacity 64,974 st/y, Trim width 96 in, Boxboard/cartonboard
Coating Machines: 1
No. 1, total capacity 66,138 st/y., on machine
Finishing Equipment:
Sheeters: 1 at 17,000 st/y
Energy Data:
Power boilers: 2
Steam turbines: 1 at 1 MW
Electrical demand for mill: 92 MWh/D

ⓜPABCO Paper
Ownership: PABCO Building Products LLC
4460 Pacific Blvd.
Vernon, CA 90058-2206
USA
  Phone: (1) 323-581-6113
  Fax: (1) 323-581-0125
  Web Address: www.pabcopaper.com
Personnel:
  Pres.: Ryan Lucchetti
  Phone: (1) 323-581-6113
  Fax: (1) 323-581-0125
  Email: ryan.lucchetti@paccoast.com
  VP, Product Qlty, Paper: Michael Willoughby
  Phone: (1) 323-581-6113
  Fax: (1) 323-581-0125
  Email: michael.willoughby@paccoast.com
  Plt. Mgr.: William J Fraser
  Phone: (1) 323-581-6113
  Fax: (1) 323-581-0125
  Email: william.fraser@paccoast.com
  Tech. Dir.: Mark Wasson
  Phone: (1) 323-826-6919
  Fax: (1) 323-571-0125
  Email: mark.wasson@paccoast.com
  Asst. Plt. Mgr. Eng. & Maint.: Larry Leonardho
  Phone: (1) 323-581-6113
  Fax: (1) 323-581-0125
  Email: larry.leornadho@paccoast.com
  Sls. Mgr.: Dave Evans
  Phone: (1) 323-826-6907
  Fax: (1) 323-581-9681
  Email: dave.evans@paccoast.com
  Cust. Serv.: Laura Balthazar
  Phone: (1) 323-826-6917
  Fax: (1) 323-581-9681
  Email: laura.balthazar@paccoast.com
Mill Locations:
PABCO Paper, Vernon Mill, 4460 Pacific Blvd., Vernon, CA 90058-2206, USA, Capacity: 67,116 st/y, (Paper mill)
  Phone: (1) 323-581-6113
  Fax: (1) 323-581-0125

ⓜPABCO Paper
Vernon Mill
4460 Pacific Blvd.
Vernon, CA 90058-2206
USA
  Phone: (1) 323-581-6113
  Fax: (1) 323-581-0125
  Web Address: www.pabcopaper.com
Personnel:
  VP, Product Qlty, Paper Manuf.: Michael Willoughby
  Phone: (1) 323-581-6113
  Fax: (1) 323-581-0125
  Email: michael.willoughby@paccoast.com
  Plt. Mgr.: William J Fraser
  Phone: (1) 323-581-6113
  Fax: (1) 323-581-0125
  Email: bill.fraser@paccoast.com
  Tech. Dir.: Mark Wasson
  Phone: (1) 323-826-6919
  Fax: (1) 323-581-0125
  Email: mark.wasson@paccoast.com
  Asst. Plt. Mgr. Eng. & Maint.: Larry Leonardho
  Phone: (1) 323-581-6113
  Fax: (1) 323-581-0125
  Email: larry.leonardho@paccoast.com
  Sls. Mgr.: David Evans
  Phone: (1) 323-826-6907
  Fax: (1) 323-581-0125
  Email: dave.evans@paccoast.com
  Plt. Supt.: Mike E. Zermeno
  Phone: (1) 323-581-6113
  Fax: (1) 323-581-0125
  Email: mike.zermeno@paccoast.com
Total Employees at this Location: 78
Type of Operation: Paper mill
Pulp Grades and Capacities:
  Total pulp capacity: 69,655 st/y
  Recycled Pulping: 69,655 st/y
Pulp Mill Data:
  Recycled Fiber Treatment Lines:
  Recycled packaging pulping lines: 1
Paper/Paperboard Grades and Capacities:
  Total paper and paperboard capacity: 67,116 st/y
  Linerboard: 5,355 st/y
  Boxboard/cartonboard: 61,761 st/y
Paper and Paperboard Mill Data:
  Stock Preparation:
  Pulpers: 2
  Refiners: 2
Paper Machines: 1
No. 1, cylinder (7), total capacity 67,116 st/y, Trim width 104 in, Boxboard/cartonboard, Linerboard
Coating Machines: 1
No. 1, on machine
Energy Data:
Power boilers: 4
Electrical demand for mill: 85 MWh/D

ⓜPaper Pak Industries
1941 White Avenue
La Verne, CA 91750
USA
  Phone: (1) 909-392-1750
  Fax: (1) 909-392-1760
  Email: customerservice@paperpakindustries.com
  Web Address: www.paperpakindustries.com
Personnel:
  Pres. & CEO: Ron Jensen
  Phone: (1) 909-392-1750
  Fax: (1) 909-392-1760

Connecticut

Email: rjensen@paperpakindustries.com
VP, Sls. & Mktg.: John Terrien
Phone: (1) 909-392-1750
Fax: (1) 909-392-1760
Email: jterrien@paperpakindustries.com
Dir., Adv. Technology: Sayandro Versteylen
Phone: (1) 909-392-1750
Fax: (1) 909-392-1760
Email: sversteylen@paperpakindustries.com
VP & Gen. Counsel: Marty Michael
Phone: (1) 909-392-1750
Fax: (1) 909-392-1760
Email: mmichael@paperpakindustries.com
Plt. Mgr.: Robert Schindel
Phone: (1) 909-392-1750
Fax: (1) 909-392-1760
Email: bschindel@paperpakindustries.com
Dir. Oper.: Harvey Nafius
Phone: (1) 909-392-1750
Fax: (1) 909-392-1760
Email: hnafius@paperparkindustries.com
Mill Locations:
Paper Pak Industries, Washington Mill, 1 PaperPak Parkway, Washington, GA 30673, USA, Capacity: 7,899 st/y, (Paper mill)
Phone: (1) 706-678-6600
Fax: (1) 706-678-3810
Paper Pak Industries, La Verne Mill, 1941 White Avenue, La Verne, CA 91750, USA, Capacity: 15,400 st/y, (Paper mill)
Phone: (1) 909-392-1750
Fax: (1) 909-392-1760
Email: customerservice@paperpakindustries.com

ⓂPaper Pak Industries
La Verne Mill
1941 White Avenue
La Verne, CA 91750
USA
Phone: (1) 909-392-1750
Fax: (1) 909-392-1760
Email: customerservice@paperpakindustries.com
Web Address: www.paperpakindustries.com
Personnel:
Pres. & CEO: Ron Jensen
Phone: (1) 909-392-1750
Fax: (1) 909-392-1760
Email: rjensen@paperpakindustries.com
VP, Sls. & Mktg.: John Terrien
Phone: (1) 909-392-1750
Fax: (1) 909-392-1760
Email: jterrien@paperpakindustries.com
Dir., Adv. Technology: Sayandro Versteylen
Phone: (1) 909-392-1750
Fax: (1) 909-392-1760
Email: sversteylen@paperpakindustries.com
VP & Gen. Counsel: Marty Michael
Phone: (1) 909-392-1750
Fax: (1) 909-392-1760
Email: mmichael@paperpakindustries.com
Plt. Mgr.: Robert Schindel
Phone: (1) 909-392-1750
Fax: (1) 909-392-1760
Email: bschindel@paperpakindustries.com
Type of Operation: Paper mill
Paper/Paperboard Grades and Capacities:
Total paper and paperboard capacity: 15,400 st/y
Tissue: 15,400 st/y

ⓂProcter & Gamble Paper Products Co.
Oxnard Mill
800 N Rice Av
Oxnard, CA 93030
USA
Phone: (1) 805-485-8871
Fax: (1) 805-983-8908
Web Address: www.pg.com
Personnel:
Plt. Mgr.: Kara Roeder
Phone: (1) 805-485-8871
Fax: (1) 805-983-8908

Eng. Mgr.: Thorsten Streppel
Phone: (1) 805-485-8871
Fax: (1) 805-983-8908
Email: streppel.t@pg.com
Project Mgr & Tech. Eng.: Michael Grabowski
Phone: (1) 805-485-8871
Fax: (1) 805-983-8908
Email: grabowski.m@pg.com
Total Employees at this Location: 175
Type of Operation: Paper mill
Paper/Paperboard Grades and Capacities:
Total paper and paperboard capacity: 146,370 st/y
Tissue: 146,370 st/y
Paper and Paperboard Mill Data:
Stock Preparation:
Pulpers:
Paper Machines: 2
No. 1, TAD, total capacity 66,045 st/y, Trim width 205 in, Tissue
No. 2, TAD, total capacity 80,325 st/y, Trim width 205 in, Tissue
Energy Data:
Power boilers
Combustion turbines: 2 at 68 MW
Electrical demand for mill: 531 MWh/D

ⓂSmurfit Kappa Orange County
Ownership: 100% by Smurfit Kappa Group
13400 E. Nelson Ave
City of Industry, CA 91746-2331
USA
Phone: (1) 626-271-1350, 800-306-8326
Fax: (1) 678-989-8500
Web Address: www.smurfitkappa.com/vHome/us/Pages/Default.aspx
Personnel:
CEO: Gregory (Greg) V. Hall
Phone: (1) 626-333-6363
Fax: (1) 678-989-8500
Email: greg.hall@smurfitkappa.com
Dir. Of Finan.: Bruce Huffman
Phone: (1) 626-333-6363
Fax: (1) 678-989-8500
Email: bruce.huffman@smurfitkappa.com
Total Employees of Company: 3,000
Mill Locations:
Smurfit Kappa Orange County, Forney Mill, 855 East Hwy 80, Forney, TX 75126, USA, Capacity: 336,294 st/y, (Paperboard mill)
Phone: (1) 214-515-6400, 888-870-4582
Fax: (1) 214-515-6499

ⓂSonoco Products Co.
City of Industry Mill
166 N Baldwin Park Blvd
City of Industry, CA 91746
USA
Phone: (1) 626-369-6927
Fax: (1) 626-369-1688
Web Address: www.sonoco.com
Personnel:
Plt. Mgr.: Salvador Juarez
Phone: (1) 626-369-6927
Fax: (1) 626-369-1688
Email: salvador.juarez@sonoco.com
Account Mgr.: Darlene Zern
Phone: (1) 626-369-6927
Fax: (1) 626-369-1688
Email: darlene.zern@sonoco.com
Process Supervisor.: Fernando Alday
Phone: (1) 626-369-6927
Fax: (1) 626-369-1688
Email: fernando.alday@sonoco.com
Total Employees at this Location: 53
Type of Operation: Paperboard mill
Pulp Grades and Capacities:
Total pulp capacity: 33,956 st/y
Recycled Pulping: 33,956 st/y
Paper/Paperboard Grades and Capacities:
Total paper and paperboard capacity: 32,844 st/y

Boxboard/cartonboard: 32,844 st/y
Paper and Paperboard Mill Data:
Stock Preparation:
Pulpers: 2
Refiners: 2
Paper Machines: 1
No. 1, cylinder (7), total capacity 32,844 st/y, Trim width 80 in, Boxboard/cartonboard
Finishing Equipment:
Winders: 1
Energy Data:
Power boilers: 2
Electrical demand for mill: 43 MWh/D

ⓂSpecialty Paper Mills Inc.
8844 S. Millergrove Dr
Santa Fe Springs, CA 90670
USA
Mailing Address: PO Box 3188, Santa Fe Springs, CA 90670-0188, USA
Phone: (1) 562-699-1051
Fax: (1) 562-699-3284
Web Address: www.gabrielcontainer.com
Personnel:
Pres.: Ronald H. Gabriel
Phone: (1) 562-699-1051
Fax: (1) 562-699-3284
Mill Mgr.: Lorenzo J. Apostol
Phone: (1) 562-699-1051
Fax: (1) 562-699-3284
Email: lorenzo@gabrielcontainer.com
Total Employees of Company: 30
Mill Locations:
Specialty Paper Mills Inc., Santa Fe Springs Mill, 8844 S. Millergrove Dr, Santa Fe Springs, CA 90670, USA, Capacity: 72,000 st/y, (Paperboard mill)
Phone: (1) 562-699-1051
Fax: (1) 562-699-3284

ⓂSpecialty Paper Mills Inc.
Santa Fe Springs Mill
8844 S. Millergrove Dr
Santa Fe Springs, CA 90670
USA
Mailing Address: PO Box 3188, Santa Fe Springs, CA 90670-0188, USA
Phone: (1) 562-699-1051
Fax: (1) 562-699-3284
Web Address: www.gabrielcontainer.com
Personnel:
Pres.: Ronald H. Gabriel
Phone: (1) 562-699-1051
Fax: (1) 562-699-3284
Mill Mgr.: Lorenzo J. Apostol
Phone: (1) 562-699-1051
Fax: (1) 562-699-3284
Email: lorenzo@gabrielcontainer.com
Total Employees at this Location: 30
Type of Operation: Paperboard mill
Paper/Paperboard Grades and Capacities:
Total paper and paperboard capacity: 72,000 st/y
Corrugating medium/fluting: 72,000 st/y
Paper and Paperboard Mill Data:
Stock Preparation:
Pulpers: 2
Refiners: 2
Paper Machines: 1
No. 1, (2nd hand, started up December 2010), four-drinier, total capacity 72,000 st/y, Trim width 140 in, Corrugating medium/fluting

CONNECTICUT

ⓂClearwater Paper Corporation
East Hartford Mill
Two Forbes St
East Hartford, CT 06108
USA

Connecticut

Mailing Address: PO Box 280096, East Hartford, CT 06128-0096, USA
Phone: (1) 860-289-7496
Fax: (1) 860-289-5142
Email: info@clearwaterpaper.com
Web Address: www.clearwaterpaper.com
Personnel:
Mill Mgr.: James Dickerson
Phone: (1) 860-289-7496
Fax: (1) 860-289-5142
Email: james.dickerson@clearwaterpaper.com
Mill Supt.: Kevin Riley
Phone: (1) 860-289-7496
Fax: (1) 860-289-5142
Email: kevin.riley@clearwaterpaper.com
Total Employees at this Location: 72
Type of Operation: Paper mill
Paper/Paperboard Grades and Capacities:
Total paper and paperboard capacity: 33,915 st/y
Tissue: 33,915 st/y
Paper and Paperboard Mill Data:
  Stock Preparation:
  Pulpers: 3
  Refiners: 5
Paper Machines: 2
No. 1, crescent former, total capacity 12,495 st/y, Trim width 126 in, Tissue
No. 2, crescent former, total capacity 21,420 st/y, Trim width 120 in, Tissue
Energy Data:
Power boilers: 2
Combustion turbines: 1 at 3 MW
Electrical demand for mill: 93 MWh/D

ⓜFusion Paperboard

Ownership: 100% by OpenGate Capital (Private)
495 Inland Road
Versailles, CT 06383
USA
Mailing Address: PO Box 238, Versailles, CT 06383-0238, USA
Phone: (1) 860-823-3600, 888-823-2976
Fax: (1) 860-822-8257, 860-823-3693
Email: info@fusionpaperboard.com
Web Address: www.fusionpaperboard.com
Personnel:
COO: Ghislain Levesque
Phone: (1) 860-823-3600
Fax: (1) 860-822-8257
Email: glevesque@fusionpaperboard.com
CFO: Joshua Duhaime
Phone: (1) 860-823-3600
Fax: (1) 860-822-8257
Email: jduhaime@fusionpaperboard.com
Gen. Mgr. (From January 2013): Joel Laroche
Phone: (1) 860-823-3600
Fax: (1) 860-822-8257
Email: jlaroche@fusionpaperboard.com
VP Sls & Mktg. (From January 2013): Hank Somer
Phone: (1) 860-823-3600
Fax: (1) 860-822-8257
Email: hsomer@fusionpaperboard.com
Dir., Sls.: Ronnie Guerrette
Phone: (1) 860-823-3600
Fax: (1) 860-822-8257
Email: rguerrette@fusionpaperboard.com
HR. Mgr.: Shannon Haddad
Phone: (1) 860-823-3600
Fax: (1) 860-822-8257
Email: shaddad@fusionpaperboard.com
Total Employees of Company: 144
Mill Locations:
Fusion Paperboard, Versailles (Sprague) Mill, 495 Inland Road, Versailles, CT 06383, USA, (Paperboard mill)
Phone: (1) 860-823-3600, 888-823-2976
Fax: (1) 860-822-8257, 860-823-3693
Email: info@fusionpaperboard.com

ⓜFusion Paperboard
Versailles (Sprague) Mill

Mill is for sale, closed (mill was idled on August 16, 2014 and site, including Paper Machine and related stock preparation equipment, put up for sale.)
495 Inland Road
Versailles, CT 06383
USA
Mailing Address: PO Box 238, Versailles, CT 06383-0238, USA
Phone: (1) 860-823-3600, 888-823-2976
Fax: (1) 860-822-8257, 860-823-3693
Email: info@fusionpaperboard.com
Web Address: www.fusionpaperboard.com
Personnel:
COO: Ghislain Levesque
Phone: (1) 860-823-3600
Fax: (1) 860-822-8257
Email: glevesque@fusionpaperboard.com
CFO: Joshua Duhaime
Phone: (1) 860-823-3600
Fax: (1) 860-822-8257
Email: jduhaime@fusionpaperboard.com
Gen. Mgr.: Joel Laroche
Phone: (1) 860-823-3600
Fax: (1) 860-822-8257
Email: jlaroche@fusionpaperboard.com
VP Sls & Mktg.: Hank Somer
Phone: (1) 860-823-3600
Fax: (1) 860-822-8257
Email: hsomer@fusionpaperboard.com
Dir., Sls.: Ronnie Guerrette
Phone: (1) 860-823-3600
Fax: (1) 860-822-8257
Email: rguerrette@fusionpaperboard.com
Logistic Dir. & Fiber Procurement Mgr.: Mike D'Auria
Phone: (1) 860-823-3600
Fax: (1) 860-822-8257
Email: mdauria@fusionpaperboard.com
Total Employees at this Location: 140
Type of Operation: Paperboard mill
Pulp Mill Data:
  Recycled Fiber Treatment Lines:
  Pulpers: 1 at 131,173
Paper and Paperboard Mill Data:
  Stock Preparation:
  Pulpers: 5
  Refiners: 5
Paper Machines: 1
No. 1, Inverformer, total capacity 138,516 st/y, Trim width 148 in
Coating Machines: 2
No. 1, total capacity 138,889 st/y., on machine
No. 2, total capacity 138,889 st/y., on machine
Energy Data:
Power boilers: 1
Steam turbines: 1 at 20 MW

ⓜFutureMark Paper Group

Ownership: 100% by The Watermill Group
315 Post Road West
Westport, CT 06880
USA
Phone: (1) 203-202-7777, 866-580-8325
Email: info@futuremarkpaper.com
Web Address: www.futuremarkpaper.com
Personnel:
Pres. & CEO: Stephen Silver
Phone: (1) 203-202-7777
Fax: (1) 708-389-8237
Email: steve.silver@futuremarkpaper.com
Snr. VP, Mktg & Tech. Serv.: Tim Nicholson
Phone: (1) 203-202-7777
Fax: (1) 708-389-8237
VP. Oper.: Steven Smith
Phone: (1) 203-202-7777
Fax: (1) 708-389-8237
Email: steve.smith@futuremarkpaper.com
VP., Sls. & Mktg.: Paul E. Bradshaw
Phone: (1) 203-202-7777
Fax: (1) 708-389-8237
Email: paul.bradshaw@futuremarkpaper.com

Total Employees of Company: 300
Mill Locations:
FutureMark Paper Group, Alsip Mill, 13101 S Pulaski Rd, Alsip, IL 60803, USA, (Pulp mill, Paper mill)
Phone: (1) 708-272-8700, 866-580-8325
Fax: (1) 708-389-8237
FutureMark Paper Group, Manistique Mill, 453 S Mackinac Ave, Manistique, MI 49854, USA, Capacity: 143,241 st/y, (Paper mill)
Phone: (1) 906-341-2175
Fax: (1) 906-341-5635

ⓜKimberly-Clark Corp.
New Milford Mill

58 Pickett District Rd
New Milford, CT 06776-4493
USA
Phone: (1) 860-354-4481
Fax: (1) 860-355-6689
Web Address: www.kimberly-clark.com
Personnel:
Mill Mgr.: Gary Wright
Phone: (1) 860-354-4481
Fax: (1) 860-355-6689
Email: gary.wright@kcc.com
Reliability Strat. Ldr.: Emily Hutter
Phone: (1) 860-354-4481
Fax: (1) 860-355-6689
Email: emily.hutter@kcc.com
Stores Team Ldr.: Marilyn MacLaren
Phone: (1) 860-354-4481
Fax: (1) 860-355-6689
Email: marilyn.maclaren@kcc.com
Total Employees at this Location: 137
Type of Operation: Paper mill
Paper/Paperboard Grades and Capacities:
Total paper and paperboard capacity: 80,325 st/y
Tissue: 80,325 st/y
Paper and Paperboard Mill Data:
  Stock Preparation:
  Pulpers: 2
  Refiners: 7
Paper Machines: 2
No. 1, crescent former, Yankee dryer, total capacity 39,270 st/y, Trim width 168 in, Tissue
No. 2, crescent former, Yankee dryer, total capacity 41,055 st/y, Trim width 168 in, Tissue
Finishing Equipment:
Rewinders: 2
Energy Data:
HRSG boiler: 3
Combustion turbines: 2 at 30 MW
Steam turbines: 1 at 4 MW
Electrical demand for mill: 205 MWh/D

ⓜLydall, Inc.

Ownership: Public
One Colonial Rd
Manchester, CT 06042
USA
Mailing Address: PO Box 151, Manchester, CT 06045-0151, USA
Phone: (1) 860-646-1233
Fax: (1) 860-646-4917
Email: info@lydall.com
Web Address: www.lydall.com
Personnel:
Chmn.: W. Leslie Duffy
Phone: (1) 860-646-1233
Fax: (1) 860-646-4917
Email: wduffy@lydall.com
Pres. & CEO: Dale G. Barnhart
Phone: (1) 860-646-1233
Fax: (1) 860-646-4917
Email: dbarnhart@lydall.com
Exec. VP & CFO: Robert K. Julian
Phone: (1) 860-646-1233
Fax: (1) 860-646-4917
Email: rjulian@lydall.com
VP & Gen. Counsel & Sec.: Chad A. McDaniel

Connecticut

Phone: (1) 860-646-1233
Fax: (1) 860-646-4917
Email: cmcdaniel@lydall.com
VP HR: Mona G. Estey
Phone: (1) 860-646-1233
Fax: (1) 860-646-4917
Email: mestey@lydall.com
VP, Chief Accounting Officer & Treas.: James V. Laughlan
Phone: (1) 860-646-1233
Fax: (1) 860-646-4917
Email: etumer@lydall.com
Total Employees of Company: 1,600
Total Employees at this Location: 50
Mill Locations:
Lydall Filtration Separation SAS, Melrand Mill, Saint-Rivalain, F-56310 Melrand, France, Capacity: 3,307 st/y, (Paper mill)
Phone: (33) 2 97 28 53 00
Fax: (33) 2 97 39 58 90
Lydall, Inc, Green Island Mill, 68 George St, Green Island, NY 12183, USA, Capacity: 7,000 st/y, (Paper mill)
Phone: (1) 518-273-6320
Fax: (1) 518-273-6361
Lydall, Inc., Rochester Mill, 134 Chestnut Hill Rd, Rochester, NH 03867, USA, Capacity: 3,999 st/y, (Paper mill)
Phone: (1) 603-332-4600
Fax: (1) 603-332-9602

⑪Rand Whitney Containerboard
Ownership: 100% by The Kraft Group
Rte 163
Montville, CT 06353
USA
Mailing Address: PO Box 336, Montville, CT 06353, USA
Phone: (1) 860-848-1900
Fax: (1) 860-848-8900
Email: info@randwhitney.com
Web Address: www.randwhitney.com
Personnel:
Tech. Dir.: Kathy Pflugbeil
Phone: (1) 860-425-3711
Fax: (1) 860-848-8900
Email: kathyp@rwcb.com
HR Mgr.: Maureen Sullivan Smith
Phone: (1) 860-425-3704
Fax: (1) 860-848-8900
Email: maureens@rwcb.com
Maint. Mgr.: Ron Chase
Phone: (1) 860-425-3704
Fax: (1) 860-848-8900
Email: ronc@rwcb.com
Total Employees of Company: 110
Mill Locations:
Rand Whitney Containerboard, Montville Mill, Rte 163, Montville, CT 06353, USA, Capacity: 224,910 st/y, (Paper mill, Paperboard mill)
Phone: (1) 860-848-1900
Fax: (1) 860-848-8900
Email: info@randwhitney.com

⑪Rand Whitney Containerboard
Montville Mill
Rte 163
Montville, CT 06353
USA
Mailing Address: PO Box 336, Montville, CT 06353, USA
Phone: (1) 860-848-1900
Fax: (1) 860-848-8900
Email: info@randwhitney.com
Web Address: www.randwhitney.com
Personnel:
Tech. Dir.: Kathy Pflugbeil
Phone: (1) 860-848-1900
Fax: (1) 860-848-8900
Email: kathyp@rwcb.com
HR Mgr.: Maureen Sullivan Smith
Phone: (1) 860-425-3704
Fax: (1) 860-848-8900
Email: maureens@rwcb.com
Supt.: Tom Nunes
Phone: (1) 860-848-1900
Fax: (1) 860-848-8900
Email: tomn@rwcb.com
Purch. Mgr.: Karl Klein
Phone: (1) 860-848-1900
Fax: (1) 860-848-8900
Email: karlk@rwcb.com
Total Employees at this Location: 110
Type of Operation: Paper mill, Paperboard mill
Pulp Grades and Capacities:
Total pulp capacity: 234,857 st/y
Recycled Pulping: 234,857 st/y
Pulp Mill Data:
Recycled Fiber Treatment Lines:
Recycled packaging pulping lines: 1 at 240,000 admt/y
Paper/Paperboard Grades and Capacities:
Total paper and paperboard capacity: 224,910 st/y
Linerboard: 224,910 st/y
Paper and Paperboard Mill Data:
Paper Machines: 1
No. 2, Bel-Bond, total capacity 224,910 st/y, Trim width 185 in, Linerboard
Energy Data:
Power boilers: 1
Combustion turbines: 1 at 15 MW
Electrical demand for mill: 346 MWh/D

⑪RockTenn Co.
Uncasville Mill
125 Depot Rd
Uncasville, CT 06382
USA
Phone: (1) 860-848-1500
Fax: (1) 860-848-1956
Web Address: www.rocktenn.com
Personnel:
Mgr., MRO Inventory Systems: John Terrall
Phone: (1) 860-848-1500
Fax: (1) 860-848-1956
Email: jterrall@rocktenn.com
Safety Mgr.: John Deveau
Phone: (1) 860-848-1500
Fax: (1) 860-848-1956
Email: jdeveau@rocktenn.com
HR Mgr.: Sandra Lamotte
Phone: (1) 860-848-1500
Fax: (1) 860-848-1956
Email: slamotte@rocktenn.com
Eng. & Maint. Mgr.: Nicholas Tamburrino
Phone: (1) 860-639-2325
Fax: (1) 860-848-1956
Total Employees at this Location: 81
Type of Operation: Paperboard mill
Pulp Grades and Capacities:
Total pulp capacity: 340,197 st/y
Recycled Pulping: 169,539 st/y
Pulp Mill Data:
Recycled Fiber Treatment Lines:
Pulpers: 1 at 173,060
Paper/Paperboard Grades and Capacities:
Total paper and paperboard capacity: 329,154 st/y
Corrugating medium/fluting: 329,154 st/y
Paper and Paperboard Mill Data:
Stock Preparation:
Pulpers: 2
Refiners: 4
Paper Machines: 2
No. 1, fourdrinier, total capacity 164,934 st/y, Trim width 196 in, Corrugating medium/fluting
No. 3, fourdrinier, total capacity 164,220 st/y, Trim width 196 in, Corrugating medium/fluting
Finishing Equipment:
Rewinders: 4
Energy Data:
Power boilers: 1
Steam turbines: 1 at 2.8 MW
Electrical demand for mill: 225 MWh/D

⑪Simkins Industries Inc.
Ownership: Simkins Family (Private)
317 Foxon Rd
East Haven, CT 06513
USA
Phone: (1) 203-787-7171
Fax: (1) 203-787-5454
Email: sales@simkinsindustries.com
Web Address: www.simkinsindustries.com
Personnel:
Pres.: Leon J Simkins
Phone: (1) 203-787-7171 Ext. 390
Fax: (1) 203-787-5454
Email: lsimkins@simkinsindustries.com
VP, Sls Southern Region: D. Wayne Clark
Phone: (1) 423-838-8358
Email: wclark@simkinsindustries.com
VP, Sls Northern Region: Bryan Coyne
Phone: (1) 781-479-6721
Email: bcoyne@simkinsindustries.com
Mill Locations:
Deerfield Tissue, LLC, Augusta Mill, 4302 Mike Padgett Hwy, Augusta, GA 30906, USA, Capacity: 21,000 st/y, (Paper mill)
Phone: (1) 706-798-7677
Fax: (1) 706-798-7684
Glassine Canada Inc., Quebec City Mill, 1245 Boulevard Montmorency, Quebec City, QC, Canada G1J 5L6, Capacity: 13,773 st/y, (Paper mill)
Phone: (1) 418-522-8262
Fax: (1) 418-648-2725
Email: sales@glassinecanada.qc.ca, customerservice@glassinecanada.qc.ca

⑪White Birch Paper Company
Ownership: 100% by Black Diamond White Birch Investment (BDWBI)
80 Field Point Rd
Greenwich, CT 06830
USA
Mailing Address: PO Box 3443, Greenwich, CT 06830, USA
Phone: (1) 203-661-3344
Fax: (1) 203-661-3349
Web Address: www.whitebirchpaper.com
Personnel:
Chmn. & CEO: Peter M. Brant
Phone: (1) 203-661-3344
Fax: (1) 203-661-3349
Email: pbrant@whitebirchpaper.com
Pres & COO: Christopher Brant
Phone: (1) 203-661-3344
Fax: (1) 203-661-3349
Email: cbrant@whitebirchpaper.com
Snr. VP, CFO: Edward D. Sherrick
Phone: (1) 203-661-3344
Fax: (1) 203-661-3349
Email: esherrick@whitebirchpaper.com
Snr. VP, Oper.: Jean Blais
Phone: (1) 203-661-3344
Fax: (1) 203-661-3349
Email: jblais@whitebirchpaper.com
VP, Finan. & Treasurer: Russ lowder
Phone: (1) 203-661-3344
Fax: (1) 203-661-3349
Email: rlowder@whitebirchpaper.com
VP, Sls.: Grant Schneider
Phone: (1) 203-661-3344
Fax: (1) 203-661-3349
Email: gschneider@whitebirchpaper.com
Mill Locations:
Bear Island Paper Co., LLC, Ashland Mill, 10026 Old Ridge Rd, Ashland, VA 23005, USA, Capacity: 257,755 st/y, (Pulp mill, Paper mill)
Phone: (1) 804-227-3394
Fax: (1) 804-227-4014
F.F. Soucy SEC, Riviere du Loup Mill, 191 Delage St,

Riviere du Loup, QC, Canada G5R 3Z1, Capacity: 293,171 st/y, (Paper mill)
Phone: (1) 418-862-6941
Fax: (1) 418-867-1134
Papier Masson, Gatineau Mill, 2 Montreal Rd W, Gatineau, QC, Canada J8M 2E1, Capacity: 267,593 st/y, (Paper mill)
Phone: (1) 819-986-4300
Fax: (1) 819-986-7331 (Admin), 819-986-6522 (Maint / Eng / Purch)
Email: resshuma@whitebirchpaper.com
Stadacona Inc, Stadacona Mill, 10 Blvd des Capucins, Quebec City, QC, Canada G1K 7H9, Capacity: 285,301 st/y, (Paper mill)
Phone: (1) 418-525-2500
Fax: (1) 418-525-2987

Windsor-Stevens Inc.
99 Stevens Mill Rd.
Windsor, CT 06095
USA
Mailing Address: PO Box 500, Poquonock, CT 06064-0500, USA
Phone: (1) 860-683-1515
Fax: (1) 860-683-1558
Email: info@windsorstevens.com
Web Address: www.windsor-stevens.com
Personnel:
Pres.: Bill Brennan
Phone: (1) 860-683-1515
Fax: (1) 860-683-1558
COO: Ralph Tropeano
Phone: (1) 860-683-1515
Fax: (1) 860-683-1558
Admin. Asst.: Dori Fairbairn
Phone: (1) 860-683-1515
Fax: (1) 860-683-1558
Mill Locations:
Windsor-Stevens Inc., Poquonock Mill, 99 Stevens Mill Rd., Windsor, CT 06095, USA, Capacity: 4,000 st/y, (Paper mill)
Phone: (1) 860-683-1515
Fax: (1) 860-683-1558
Email: info@windsor-stevens.com

Windsor-Stevens Inc.
Poquonock Mill
99 Stevens Mill Rd.
Windsor, CT 06095
USA
Mailing Address: PO Box 500, Poquonock, CT 06064-0500, USA
Phone: (1) 860-683-1515
Fax: (1) 860-683-1558
Email: info@windsor-stevens.com
Web Address: www.windsor-stevens.com
Personnel:
COO: Ralph Tropeano
Phone: (1) 860-683-1515
Fax: (1) 860-683-1558
Contr.: Jill Criscitelli
Phone: (1) 860-683-1515
Fax: (1) 860-683-1558
Prod. Mgr.: Frank Lupacchino
Phone: (1) 860-683-1515
Fax: (1) 860-683-1558
Admin. Asst.: Dori Fairbairn
Phone: (1) 860-683-1515
Fax: (1) 860-683-1558
Type of Operation: Paper mill
Paper/Paperboard Grades and Capacities:
Total paper and paperboard capacity: 4,000 st/y
Packaging papers
Specialty and industrial
Paper and Paperboard Mill Data:
Stock Preparation:
Pulpers: 1
Refiners: 3
Paper Machines: 1
No. 1, Rotoformer, total capacity 4,000 st/y, Trim width 56 in, Packaging papers, Specialty and industrial, Boxboard/cartonboard
Coating Machines: 1
No. 1, total capacity 4,200 st/y., off machine

FLORIDA

Atlas Paper Mills LLC
Hialeah Mill
Ownership: 100% by Peak Rock Capital
3725 East 10th Court
Hialeah, FL 33013
USA
Phone: (1) 305-636-5740
Fax: (1) 305-685-6714
Email: office@atlaspapermills.com
Web Address: www.atlaspapermills.com
Personnel:
Pres. & CEO: Jim W. Brown
Phone: (1) 305-636-5741
Fax: (1) 305-685-6714
Email: jbrown@atlaspapermills.com
CFO: Robert P. Penvose Jr.
Phone: (1) 305-636-5740
Fax: (1) 305-685-6714
Email: rpenvose@atlaspapermills.com
VP, Supply Chain: John Cioffi
Phone: (1) 305-636-5740
Fax: (1) 305-685-6714
Email: jcioffi@atlaspapermills.com
VP, Oper.: Juan Michelena
Phone: (1) 305-636-5740
Fax: (1) 305-685-6714
Email: jmichelena@atlaspapermills.com
VP, Manuf. (since July 2014): David DeMarzo
Phone: (1) 305-636-5740
Fax: (1) 305-685-6714
Email: ddemarzo@atlaspapermills.com
Dir., Tech.: Sixto Delgado
Phone: (1) 305-636-5740
Fax: (1) 305-685-6714
Email: sdelgado@atlaspapermills.com
Total Employees of Company: 250
Total Employees at this Location: 63
Type of Operation: Paper mill
Pulp Grades and Capacities:
Total pulp capacity: 39,238 st/y
Recycled Pulping: 39,238 st/y
Pulp Mill Data:
Bleach Plant Lines:
Deinked Pulp Line, Sequence: P
Recycled Fiber Treatment Lines:
Flotation deinking lines
Paper/Paperboard Grades and Capacities:
Total paper and paperboard capacity: 36,414 st/y
Tissue: 36,414 st/y
Paper and Paperboard Mill Data:
Paper Machines: 2
No. 1, crescent former, Yankee dryer, total capacity 18,564 st/y, Trim width 122 in, Tissue
No. 2, crescent former, total capacity 17,850 st/y, Trim width 122 in, Tissue
Finishing Equipment:
Rewinders: 3 at 28,000 st/y
Energy Data:
Power boilers: 2
Electrical demand for mill: 120 MWh/D

Georgia-Pacific LLC
Palatka Mill
215 County Road 216
Palatka, FL 32177
USA
Mailing Address: PO Box 919, Palatka, FL 32178-0919, USA
Phone: (1) 386-325-2001
Fax: (1) 386-325-6141
Web Address: www.gp.com
Personnel:
Bus. Ldr. (Acting Mill Mgr.): Kevin J. Curry
Phone: (1) 386-325-2001
Fax: (1) 386-325-6141
Email: kevin.curry@gapac.com
Tech. Capability Ldr.: Joseph Webster
Phone: (1) 386-325-2001
Fax: (1) 386-325-6141
Email: joseph.webster@gapac.com
Mgr., HR: Karin Brown
Phone: (1) 386-325-2001
Fax: (1) 386-325-6141
Email: karin.brown@gapac.com
Dir., Commercialization NACP: Ted Kennedy
Phone: (1) 386-325-2001
Fax: (1) 386-325-6141
Email: ted.kennedy@gapac.com
Product Stream Ldr.: Keith Francis
Phone: (1) 386-325-2001
Fax: (1) 386-325-6141
Email: keith.francis@gapac.com
Total Employees at this Location: 600
Type of Operation: Paper mill, Paperboard mill
Pulp Grades and Capacities:
Total pulp capacity: 467,354 st/y
Chemical Pulp: 467,354 st/y
Pulp Mill Data:
Chemical Pulping Systems:
Batch digesters: 13
Bleach Plant Systems: 1
Chemical Pulping System, Type: Hardwood/Softwood, Sequence: DEpDP
Chemical Recovery Equipment:
Evaporator lines: 1
Recovery boilers: 1
Lime Kiln
Paper/Paperboard Grades and Capacities:
Total paper and paperboard capacity: 533,001 st/y
Tissue: 220,626 st/y
Packaging papers: 287,385 st/y
Specialty and industrial: 7,140 st/y
Linerboard: 17,850 st/y
Paper and Paperboard Mill Data:
Paper Machines: 5
No. 1, fourdrinier, total capacity 166,005 st/y, Trim width 220 in, Packaging papers, Specialty and industrial, Linerboard
No. 2, fourdrinier, total capacity 146,370 st/y, Trim width 218 in, Packaging papers
No. 3, twin-wire, total capacity 64,260 st/y, Trim width 212 in, Tissue
No. 4, twin-wire, total capacity 72,471 st/y, Trim width 215 in, Tissue
No. 5, twin-wire, total capacity 83,895 st/y, Trim width 212 in, Tissue
Energy Data:
Power boilers: 4
Steam turbines: 4 at 94 MW
Electrical demand for mill: 1,647 MWh/D

GP Cellulose, LLC
Foley Cellulose Mill (Perry Mill)
Ownership: Georgia-Pacific LLC
One Buckeye Drive
Perry, FL 32348
USA
Phone: (1) 850-584-1121
Fax: (1) 850-584-1722
Email: info@gpcellulose.com
Web Address: www.gpcellulose.com
Personnel:
Mill Mgr. (From 2014): Lee Davis
Phone: (1) 850-584-1121
Fax: (1) 850-584-1722

Florida

Email: lee.davis2@gapac.com
Oper. Mgr.: Walker Bassett
Phone: (1) 850-584-1448
Fax: (1) 850-584-1722
Email: walker.bassett@gapac.com
Pub. Affairs Mgr.: Scott Mixon
Phone: (1) 850-584-1121 Ext. 1524
Fax: (1) 850-584-1722
Email: scott.mixon@gapac.com
Buyer (Purch. Agent): Hope Lynn
Phone: (1) 850-584-1121
Fax: (1) 850-584-1722
Email: hope.lynn@gapac.com
Product Mgr.: Loren Forbus
Phone: (1) 850-584-1121
Fax: (1) 850-584-1722
Email: loren.forbus@gapac.com
HR Mgr.: David Hager
Phone: (1) 850-584-1121
Fax: (1) 850-584-1722
Email: david.hager@gapac.com
Snr. Mgr. - Environ. Permitting Containerboard & Cellulose Div.: David C. Weeden
Phone: (1) 850-584-1121
Fax: (1) 850-584-1722
Email: david.weeden@gapac.com
Paper Machine Technology Mgr.: Phil Powers
Phone: (1) 850-584-1121
Fax: (1) 850-584-1722
Email: philip.powers@gapac.com
Total Employees at this Location: 573
Type of Operation: Pulp mill
Pulp Grades and Capacities:
Total pulp capacity: 549,157 st/y
Pulp available for market: 512,755 st/y
Chemical Pulp: 549,157 st/y

Pulp Mill Data:
Chemical Pulping Systems:
Batch digesters: 19
Pulp Lines: 2
Bleach Plant Systems: 2
Chemical Pulping System, Type: Softwood, Sequence: O_2 DEDED, Capacity 219,356.3 adst/y
Chemical Pulping System, Type: Softwood, Sequence: O_2 DEDED, Capacity 328,483.2 adst/y
Chemical Recovery Equipment:
Evaporator lines: 1
Recovery boilers: 2
Lime Kiln
Pulp Dryers:
Fourdriniers 1, Fourdriniers 1
Energy Data:
Power boilers
Steam turbines: 4 at 44.4, 25 MW
Electrical demand for mill: 1,362 MWh/D

ⓜInternational Paper Co.
Pensacola Mill
375 Muscogee Rd
Cantonment, FL 32533
USA
Mailing Address: PO Box 87, Cantonment, FL 32533-0087, USA
Phone: (1) 850-968-2121
Fax: (1) 850-968-4297
Email: (firstname.lastname@ipaper.com)
Web Address: www.ipaper.com
Personnel:
Mill Mgr.: Bretton DeJong
Phone: (1) 850-968-2121
Fax: (1) 850-968-4297
Email: bretton.dejong@ipaper.com
Maint. & Eng. Mgr.: Brent Griffin
Phone: (1) 850-968-2121
Fax: (1) 850-968-4297
Email: brent.griffin@ipaper.com
Environ. Mgr.: John Taylor
Phone: (1) 850-968-2121
Fax: (1) 850-968-4297
Email: john.taylor@ipaper.com

E & I Supervisor: Richard Zamzow
Phone: (1) 850-968-2121
Fax: (1) 850-968-4297
Email: richard.zamzow@ipaper.com
Health & Safety Mgr.: Lizz Littler
Phone: (1) 850-968-2121
Fax: (1) 850-968-4297
Email: lizz.littler@ipaper.com
Total Employees at this Location: 426
Type of Operation: Pulp mill, Paperboard mill
Pulp Grades and Capacities:
Total pulp capacity: 623,707 st/y
Pulp available for market: 164,934 st/y
Chemical Pulp: 623,707 st/y

Pulp Mill Data:
Chemical Pulping Systems:
Batch digesters: 12
Continuous digesters: 1
Bleach Plant Systems: 1
Chemical Pulping System, Type: Softwood, Sequence: O_2 DEoD
Chemical Recovery Equipment:
Evaporator lines: 1
Recovery boilers: 2
Lime Kiln
Pulp Dryers:
Fourdriniers 1
Paper/Paperboard Grades and Capacities:
Total paper and paperboard capacity: 535,500 st/y
Linerboard: 535,500 st/y
Paper and Paperboard Mill Data:
Stock Preparation:
Pulpers: 3
Refiners: 10
Paper Machines: 1
No. 5, top-wire, total capacity 535,500 st/y, Trim width 348 in, Linerboard
Energy Data:
Power boilers: 2
Steam turbines: 2 at 82.8 MW
Electrical demand for mill: 1,820 MWh/D

ⓜRayonier Advanced Materials Inc.
Ownership: Public
1301 Riverplace Boulevard Suite 2300
Jacksonville, FL 32207
USA
Phone: (1) 904-357-4600
Fax: (1) 904-357-9101
Web Address: www.rayonieram.com, www.rayonier.com
Personnel:
Chmn., Pres., & CEO: Paul G. Boynton
Phone: (1) 904-357-9100
Fax: (1) 904-357-9101
Email: paul.boynton@rayonier.com
Snr. VP. & CFO: Benson K. Woo
Phone: (1) 904-357-9100
Fax: (1) 904-357-9101
Snr. VP. & Gen. Counsel: Michael R. Herman
Phone: (1) 904-357-9100
Fax: (1) 904-357-9101
Email: michael.herman@rayonier.com
Snr. VP, Public Affairs & Commun.: Charles H. Hood
Phone: (1) 904-357-9100
Fax: (1) 904-357-9101
Email: charles.hood@rayonier.com
Snr. VP, Commercial: Thomas Benner
Phone: (1) 904-357-9100
Fax: (1) 904-357-9101
Snr. VP, Advanced Materials Performance Fibers (plans to retire effective December 31, 2014): Jack M. Kriesel
Phone: (1) 904-357-9100
Fax: (1) 904-357-9101
Email: jack.kriesel@rayonier.com
Snr. VP., HR: James (Jay) L. Posze Jr.
Phone: (1) 904-357-9100
Fax: (1) 904-357-9101
Email: jay.posze@rayonier.com
Snr. VP., Corp. Develop. & Strat. Plan. (Eff. March 31,

2014): Frank Ruperto
Phone: (1) 904-357-9186
Fax: (1) 904-357-9848
Total Employees of Company: 1,600
Mill Locations:
Rayonier Advanced Materials Inc., Fernandina Beach Plant, Gum Street, Fernandina Beach, FL 32034, USA, (Pulp mill)
Phone: (1) 904-261-3611
Fax: (1) 904-261-7226
Rayonier Advanced Materials Inc., Jesup Plant, 4470 Savannah Hwy, Jesup, GA 31545, USA, (Pulp mill)
Phone: (1) 912-427-5000, 912-588-8000
Fax: (1) 912-427-5587

ⓜRayonier Advanced Materials Inc.
Fernandina Beach Plant
Previously Rayonier Inc.
Gum Street
Fernandina Beach, FL 32034
USA
Mailing Address: PO Box 2002, Fernandina Beach, FL 32034, USA
Phone: (1) 904-261-3611
Fax: (1) 904-261-7226
Web Address: www.rayonieram.com, www.rayonier.com
Personnel:
Gen. Mgr.: Clifton A. McDonald
Phone: (1) 904-557-3171
Fax: (1) 904-261-7226
Email: ca.mcdonald@rayonieram.com
Utilities Mgr.: McKinley Ravenell
Phone: (1) 904-261-3611
Fax: (1) 904-261-7226
Email: mckinley.ravenell@rayonieram.com
Value-Added Bus. Dir. (From March 2014): Jeff Lawrence
Phone: (1) 904-321-1009
Fax: (1) 904-261-7226
Email: jeff.lawrence@rayonier.com
Environ. Mgr, Forestry Practices & Compliance: Ben H. Cazzell
Phone: (1) 904-321-5555
Fax: (1) 904-261-7226
Email: ben.cazell@rayonier.com
Total Employees at this Location: 277
Type of Operation: Pulp mill
Pulp Grades and Capacities:
Total pulp capacity: 193,548 st/y
Pulp available for market: 181,806 st/y
Chemical Pulp: 193,548 st/y

Pulp Mill Data:
Chemical Pulping Systems:
Batch digesters: 6
Pulp Lines: 1
Bleach Plant Systems: 1
1, Sequence: CEHD
Chemical Recovery Equipment:
Evaporator lines: 1
Recovery boilers: 1
Pulp Dryers:
Fourdriniers 1
Energy Data:
Power boilers: 1
Steam turbines: 2 at 20, 22.5 MW
Electrical demand for mill: 521 MWh/D

ⓜRockTenn Co.
Fernandina Beach Mill
600 North 8th Street
Fernandina Beach, FL 32034-3321
USA
Mailing Address: P.O. Box 2000, Fernandina Beach, FL 32034, USA
Phone: (1) 904-277-5854, 904-261-5551
Fax: (1) 904-277-5888
Web Address: www.rocktenn.com
Personnel:
Div. Contr.: Art Renfro

Florida

Phone: (1) 904-261-5551
Fax: (1) 904-277-5888
Email: arenfro@rocktenn.com
Eng. Mgr.: Tom Keenan
Phone: (1) 904-261-5551
Fax: (1) 904-277-5888
Email: tkeenan@rocktenn.com
Area Wood Procurement: Donald Murphy
Phone: (1) 904-261-5551
Fax: (1) 904-277-5888
Email: dmurphy@rocktenn.com
Total Employees at this Location: 447
Type of Operation: Pulp mill, Paperboard mill
Pulp Grades and Capacities:
Total pulp capacity: 981,541 st/y
Chemical Pulp: 807,114 st/y
Recycled Pulping: 174,427 st/y
Pulp Mill Data:
Chemical Pulping Systems:
Batch digesters: 7
Continuous digesters: 1
Chemical Recovery Equipment:
Evaporator lines: 1
Recovery boilers: 2
Lime Kiln
Recycled Fiber Treatment Lines:
Recycled packaging pulping lines at 176,000
Paper/Paperboard Grades and Capacities:
Total paper and paperboard capacity: 929,985 st/y
Linerboard: 929,985 st/y
Paper and Paperboard Mill Data:
Stock Preparation:
Pulpers: 2
Refiners: 14
Paper Machines: 2
No. 3, fourdrinier, total capacity 515,865 st/y, Trim width 244 in, Linerboard
No. 4, fourdrinier, total capacity 414,120 st/y, Trim width 244 in, Linerboard
Finishing Equipment:
Winders: 1
Energy Data:
Power boilers: 2
Steam turbines: 2 at 108 MW
Electrical demand for mill: 1,936 MWh/D

ⓜRockTenn Co.
Panama City Mill
One Everitt Avenue
Panama City, FL 32401-6900
USA
Phone: (1) 850-785-4311
Fax: (1) 850-763-6290
Web Address: www.rocktenn.com
Personnel:
Gen. Mgr. (From March 2014): Tommy Martin
Phone: (1) 850-785-4311
Fax: (1) 850-763-6290
Email: tmartin2@rocktenn.com
Snr. HR Representative: Amy Ellis
Phone: (1) 850-785-4311
Fax: (1) 850-763-6290
Email: aellis@rocktenn.com
Snr. Procurement Specialist: Joni Montgomery
Phone: (1) 850-785-4311
Fax: (1) 850-763-6290
Email: jmontgomery@rocktenn.com
Account Supervisor: Lance Cothern
Phone: (1) 850-785-4311
Fax: (1) 850-763-6290
Email: lcothern@rocktenn.com
Total Employees at this Location: 411
Type of Operation: Pulp mill, Paperboard mill
Pulp Grades and Capacities:
Total pulp capacity: 660,740 st/y
Pulp available for market: 292,026 st/y
Chemical Pulp: 660,740 st/y
Pulp Mill Data:
Chemical Pulping Systems:
Batch digesters: 22
Bleach Plant Systems: 1
Chemical Pulping System, Type: Hardwood/Softwood, Sequence: DEopDEopD
Chemical Recovery Equipment:
Evaporator lines: 3
Recovery boilers: 2
Lime Kiln
Recycled Fiber Treatment Lines:
Recycled packaging pulping lines: 1 at 20,000 admt/y
Pulp Dryers:
Fourdriniers 1
Paper/Paperboard Grades and Capacities:
Total paper and paperboard capacity: 335,937 st/y
Linerboard: 335,937 st/y
Paper and Paperboard Mill Data:
Stock Preparation:
Refiners: 5
Paper Machines: 1
No. 1, fourdrinier, total capacity 335,937 st/y, Trim width 221 in, Linerboard
Finishing Equipment:
Calenders: 1
Energy Data:
Power boilers: 3
Steam turbines: 3 at 20, 10, 4 MW
Electrical demand for mill: 1,190 MWh/D

ⓜRockTenn Co.
Seminole Mill
9469 Eastport Rd
Jacksonville, FL 32226-6998
USA
Mailing Address: PO Box 26998, Jacksonville, FL 32218-0998, USA
Phone: (1) 904-751-6400
Fax: (1) 904-714-3276
Web Address: www.rocktenn.com
Personnel:
Gen. Mgr. (From May 2014): Robert F Dansby
Phone: (1) 904-751-6400
Fax: (1) 904-714-3276
Process Contrl Maint. Supervisor: Hank McNally
Phone: (1) 904-751-6400
Fax: (1) 904-714-3276
Email: hmcnally@rocktenn.com
Maint. & Eng. Mgr: Stan Davidson
Phone: (1) 904-751-6400
Fax: (1) 904-714-3276
Procurement Mgr.: Rodolfo Marquez
Phone: (1) 904-751-6400
Fax: (1) 904-714-3276
Email: rmarquez@rocktenn.com
Environ. Mgr.: Michele Rundlett
Phone: (44) 904-751-6400
Fax: (44) 904-714-3276
Email: mrundlet@rocktenn.com
Total Employees at this Location: 161
Type of Operation: Paperboard mill
Pulp Grades and Capacities:
Total pulp capacity: 622,402 st/y
Recycled Pulping: 622,402 st/y
Pulp Mill Data:
Recycled Fiber Treatment Lines:
Pulpers: 1 at 656,966
Paper/Paperboard Grades and Capacities:
Total paper and paperboard capacity: 600,117 st/y
Linerboard: 401,982 st/y
Corrugating medium/fluting: 198,135 st/y
Paper and Paperboard Mill Data:
Stock Preparation:
Pulpers: 3
Refiners: 2
Paper Machines: 2
No. 1, fourdrinier, total capacity 198,135 st/y, Trim width 214 in, Corrugating medium/fluting
No. 2, fourdrinier, total capacity 401,982 st/y, Trim width 255 in, Linerboard
Finishing Equipment:
Winders: 2
Energy Data:
Power boilers: 1
Steam turbines: 1 at 16, 250 MW

ⓜRoses Southeast Papers, LLC
Sanford Mill
3401 St. Johns Parkway
Sanford, FL 32771
USA
Phone: (1) 407-330-9118
Email: info@rosesnm.com
Web Address: www.rosessouthwest.com
Personnel:
Exec. VP. & Gen. Mgr.: Enrique Todd
Phone: (1) 407-330-9118
Fax: (1) 407-330-9641
Email: etodd@atlastissue.com
Gen. Mgr.: Juan Carlos Casillas
Phone: (1) 407-330-9118
Fax: (1) 407-330-9641
Email: jcasillas@rosesnm.com
Total Employees at this Location: 115
Type of Operation: Paper mill
Pulp Mill Data:
Recycled Fiber Treatment Lines:
Pulpers: 1 at 7,165
Paper/Paperboard Grades and Capacities:
Total paper and paperboard capacity: 29,988 st/y
Tissue: 29,988 st/y
Paper and Paperboard Mill Data:
Stock Preparation:
Pulpers:
Paper Machines: 1
No. 1, crescent former, total capacity 29,988 st/y, Trim width 107 in, Tissue
Finishing Equipment:
Rewinders: 2
Energy Data:
Power boilers
Electrical demand for mill: 73 MWh/D

ⓞⓜSofidel America Corporation
Haines City Mill
Company is previously Cellynne Corp.
Ownership: 100% by Sofidel Group
1006 Marley Drive
Haines City, FL 33844
USA
Phone: (1) 800-443-6099
Fax: (1) 863-547-1101
Web Address: www.sofidelamerica.com
Personnel:
CEO: Tony Curtis
Phone: (1) 800-443-6099
Fax: (1) 863-547-1101
Exec. VP: Marc Allegre
Phone: (1) 800-443-6099 Ext. 1092
Fax: (1) 863-547-1101
Email: marc.allegre@sofidelamerica.com
Mill. Mgr.: Jerôme Bareth
Phone: (1) 800-443-6099 Ext. 1124
Fax: (1) 863-547-1101
Email: jerome.bareth@sofidelamerica.com
CTO: Alberto Cinelli
Phone: (1) 863-547-1100
Fax: (1) 863-547-1101
Email: alberto.cinelli@sofidelamerica.com
Paper Mill Mgr.: Jeff Hammonds
Phone: (1) 800-443-6099 Ext. 1109
Fax: (1) 863-547-1101
Email: jeff.hammonds@sofidelamerica.com
HR & Safety Dir.: Jorge Altieri
Phone: (1) 800-443-6099 Ext. 1085
Fax: (1) 863-547-1101
Email: jorge.altieri@sofidelamerica.com
Total Employees of Company: 345
Total Employees at this Location: 58
Type of Operation: Paper mill

Georgia

Paper/Paperboard Grades and Capacities:
Total paper and paperboard capacity: 74,970 st/y
Tissue: 74,970 st/y
Paper and Paperboard Mill Data:
Stock Preparation:
Pulpers: 1
Refiners: 1
Paper Machines: 2
No. 1, crescent former, Yankee dryer, total capacity 39,270 st/y, Trim width 102 in, Tissue
No. 2, crescent former, Yankee dryer, total capacity 35,700 st/y, Trim width 102 in, Tissue
Energy Data:
Power boilers: 2
Electrical demand for mill: 183 MWh/D

GEORGIA

ⓂAugusta Select Tissue, LLC
Ownership: 100% by Select Product Group LP
3452 Cookie Road
Augusta, GA 30906
USA
Phone: (1) 706-796-1999
Fax: (1) 706-796-8496
Personnel:
Pulp Mill Mgr., Tech.Dir.: Don Brown
Phone: (1) 706-796-1999
Fax: (1) 706-796-8496
Email: dbrown@augustaselecttissue.com
Contr.: Lisa Glevenyak
Phone: (1) 706-796-1999
Fax: (1) 706-796-8496
Email: lglevenyak@augustaselecttissue.com
Qlty. Mgr. & Project Eng.: Jeffrey Pettit
Phone: (1) 706-796-1999
Fax: (1) 706-796-8496
Email: jpettit@augustaselecttissue.com
Fiber Procurement Mgr.: Mike Muza
Phone: (1) 706-796-1999
Fax: (1) 706-796-8496
Email: mmuza@augustaselecttissue.com
Total Employees of Company: 65
Mill Locations:
Augusta Select Tissue, LLC, Augusta Mill, 3452 Cookie Road, Augusta, GA 30906, USA, Capacity: 33,915 st/y, (Pulp mill, Paper mill)
Phone: (1) 706-796-1999
Fax: (1) 706-796-8496

ⓂAugusta Select Tissue, LLC
Augusta Mill
3452 Cookie Road
Augusta, GA 30906
USA
Phone: (1) 706-796-1999
Fax: (1) 706-796-8496
Personnel:
Pulp Mill Mgr., Tech Dir.: Don Brown
Phone: (1) 706-796-1999
Fax: (1) 706-796-8496
Email: dbrown@augustaselecttissue.com
Logist. Mgr., Procurement: Linda Rader
Phone: (1) 706-796-1999
Fax: (1) 706-796-8496
Email: lrader@augustaselecttissue.com
Total Employees at this Location: 65
Type of Operation: Pulp mill, Paper mill
Pulp Grades and Capacities:
Total pulp capacity: 36,241 st/y
Recycled Pulping: 36,241 st/y
Pulp Mill Data:
Bleach Plant Lines:
DIP Pulping System, Sequence: HS
Recycled Fiber Treatment Lines:
Flotation deinking lines: 1
Pulpers: 2
Paper/Paperboard Grades and Capacities:
Total paper and paperboard capacity: 33,915 st/y
Tissue: 33,915 st/y
Paper and Paperboard Mill Data:
Stock Preparation:
Refiners: 2
Paper Machines: 1
No. 1, crescent former, Yankee dryer, total capacity 33,915 st/y, Trim width 106 in, Tissue
Energy Data:
Power boilers: 2
Electrical demand for mill: 99 MWh/D

ⓂAustell Boxboard
Austell Boxboard Mill #1
Ownership: 100% by Caraustar Industries, Inc.
3300 Joe Jerkins Boulevard
Austell, GA 30106
USA
Mailing Address: PO Box 157, Austell, GA 30168, USA
Phone: (1) 770-948-3100
Fax: (1) 770-732-3403
Email: millgroup.abb@caraustar.com
Web Address: www.caraustar.com
Personnel:
VP, Gen. Mgr.: James Jordan
Phone: (1) 770-948-3100
Fax: (1) 770-732-3403
Email: james.jordan@caraustar.com
Mill Mgr., Mill No.1: Rob Maino
Phone: (1) 770-948-3100
Fax: (1) 770-745-3713
Email: rob.maino@caraustar.com
Procurement Mgr.: Jon M. Steadman
Phone: (1) 770-745-3778
Fax: (1) 770-732-3403
Email: jon.steadman@caraustar.com
Total Employees at this Location: 70
Type of Operation: Paperboard mill
Pulp Grades and Capacities:
Total pulp capacity: 73,716 st/y
Recycled Pulping: 73,716 st/y
Pulp Mill Data:
Recycled Fiber Treatment Lines:
Pulpers
Paper/Paperboard Grades and Capacities:
Total paper and paperboard capacity: 71,400 st/y
Boxboard/cartonboard: 71,400 st/y
Paper and Paperboard Mill Data:
Stock Preparation:
Pulpers: 4
Refiners: 4
Paper Machines: 1
No. 1, cylinder (10), total capacity 71,400 st/y, Trim width 92 in, Boxboard/cartonboard
Finishing Equipment:
Calenders: 1
Sheeters: 1
Energy Data:
Electrical demand for mill: 98 MWh/D

ⓂAustell Boxboard
Austell Boxboard Mill # 2
Ownership: 100% by Caraustar Industries, Inc.
3300-3400 Joe Jerkins Blvd
Austell, GA 30106
USA
Mailing Address: PO Box 157, Austell, GA 30168, USA
Phone: (1) 770-948-3100
Fax: (1) 770-732-3403, 770-732-3433
Email: millgroup.abb@caraustar.com
Web Address: www.caraustar.com
Personnel:
VP, Gen. Mgr.: James Jordan
Phone: (1) 770-948-3100
Fax: (1) 770-732-3403
Email: james.jordan@caraustar.com
Prod. Supervisor: Mike Jenkins
Phone: (1) 770-948-3100
Fax: (1) 770-732-3403
Email: mike.jenkins@caraustar.com
Procurement Mgr.: Jon M. Steadman
Phone: (1) 770-745-3778
Fax: (1) 770-732-3403
Email: jon.steadman@caraustar.com
Tech. Mgr.: Chris Goryl
Phone: (1) 770-948-3100
Fax: (1) 770-732-3403
Email: chris.goryl@caraustar.com
Total Employees at this Location: 97
Type of Operation: Paperboard mill
Pulp Grades and Capacities:
Total pulp capacity: 100,508 st/y
Recycled Pulping: 100,508 st/y
Pulp Mill Data:
Recycled Fiber Treatment Lines:
Pulpers: 3
Paper/Paperboard Grades and Capacities:
Total paper and paperboard capacity: 99,960 st/y
Boxboard/cartonboard: 99,960 st/y
Paper and Paperboard Mill Data:
Stock Preparation:
Pulpers: 3
Refiners: 4
Paper Machines: 1
No. 1, cylinder (10), total capacity 99,960 st/y, Trim width 108 in, Boxboard/cartonboard
Finishing Equipment:
Winders: 1 at 97,000 st/y
Energy Data:
Power boilers: 1
Electrical demand for mill: 130 MWh/D

ⓂCaraustar Industries, Inc.
Ownership: 100% by H.I.G. Capital, LLC (Private)
5000 Austell-Powder Springs Road, Suite 300
Austell, GA 30106-3227
USA
Mailing Address: PO Box 115, Austell, GA 30168-0115, USA
Phone: (1) 770-948-3101
Email: info@caraustar.com
Web Address: www.caraustar.com
Personnel:
Pres. & CEO: Michael C. Patton
Phone: (1) 770-948-3101
Email: michael.patton@caraustar.com
VP, Sls & Mktg. of Mill Group: Greg A. Bartlett
Phone: (1) 770-948-3101
Email: greg.bartlett@caraustar.com
VP, Recovered Fiber Group: Gregory B. Cottrell
Phone: (1) 770-948-3101
Email: gcottrell@caraustar.com
VP, Finan. & CAO: William A. Nix III
Phone: (1) 770-948-3101
Email: william.nix@caraustar.com
VP, HR: Keith Lolley
Phone: (1) 770-948-3101
Email: keith.lolley@caraustar.com
VP Sls.: Mark I. Maley
Phone: (1) 770-948-3101
Email: mark.maley@caraustar.com
Total Employees of Company: 3,500
Total Employees at this Location: 150
Mill Locations:
Austell Boxboard, Austell Boxboard Mill #1, 3300 Joe Jerkins Boulevard, Austell, GA 30106, USA, Capacity: 71,400 st/y, (Paperboard mill)
Phone: (1) 770-948-3100
Fax: (1) 770-732-3403
Email: millgroup.abb@caraustar.com
Austell Boxboard, Austell Boxboard Mill # 2, 3300-3400 Joe Jerkins Blvd, Austell, GA 30106, USA, Capacity: 99,960 st/y, (Paperboard mill)

Georgia

Phone: (1) 770-948-3100
Fax: (1) 770-732-3403, 770-732-3433
Email: millgroup.abb@caraustar.com
Carotell Paperboard, Taylors Mill, 873 Alexander Dr, Taylors, SC 29687, USA, Capacity: 78,540 st/y, (Paperboard mill)
Phone: (1) 864-244-6221
Fax: (1) 864-292-8856
Cincinnati Paperboard, Cincinnati Mill, 5500 Wooster Rd, Cincinnati, OH 45226, USA, Capacity: 80,325 st/y, (Paperboard mill)
Phone: (1) 513-871-7112
Fax: (1) 513-871-7971
Email: millgroup.austell@caraustar.com
Sweetwater Paperboard, Austell Mill, 3500 Joe Jerkins Blvd, Austell, GA 30106-3227, USA, Capacity: 117,810 st/y, (Paperboard mill)
Phone: (1) 770-944-9350
Fax: (1) 770-732-3402
Email: info@caraustar.com
Tacoma Paperboard, Tacoma Mill, 808 E. 26th St., Tacoma, WA 98421, USA, Capacity: 48,195 st/y, (Paperboard mill)
Phone: (1) 253-627-1197
Fax: (1) 253-627-0380
Email: greg.bartlett@caraustar.com
Tama Paperboard, Tama Mill, 117 Siegel St, Tama, IA 52339-2616, USA, Capacity: 80,682 st/y, (Paperboard mill)
Phone: (1) 641-484-2884
Fax: (1) 641-484-4234

⑩Deerfield Tissue, LLC
Augusta Mill
Ownership: Simkins Industries Inc.
4302 Mike Padgett Hwy
Augusta, GA 30906
USA
Phone: (1) 706-798-7677
Fax: (1) 706-798-7684
Personnel:
Owner: Bob Dinneweth
Phone: (1) 706-798-7677
Fax: (1) 706-798-7684
Machine Supt.: Anthony Dinneweth
Phone: (1) 706-798-7677
Fax: (1) 706-798-7684
Mgr.: Brian Dawson
Phone: (1) 706-798-7677
Fax: (1) 706-798-7684
Type of Operation: Paper mill
Paper/Paperboard Grades and Capacities:
Total paper and paperboard capacity: 21,000 st/y
Tissue: 21,000 st/y
Paper and Paperboard Mill Data:
Stock Preparation:
Pulpers: 4
Paper Machines: 2
No. 1, fourdrinier, Trim width 90 in, Tissue
No. 2, fourdrinier, Trim width 100 in, Tissue
Finishing Equipment:
Supercalenders: 1
Rewinders: 4

⑪Georgia-Pacific LLC
Ownership: 100% by Koch Industries (Private)
133 Peachtree Street North East
Atlanta, GA 30303
USA
Mailing Address: PO Box 105605, Atlanta, GA 30348, USA
Phone: (1) 404-652-4000
Fax: (1) 404-652-4581
Web Address: www.gp.com
Personnel:
CEO & Pres.: James Hannan
Phone: (1) 404-652-4000
Fax: (1) 404-652-4581
Email: james.hannan@gapac.com

CFO & Snr. VP.: Tyler Woolson
Phone: (1) 404-652-4000
Fax: (1) 404-652-4581
Email: tyler.woolson@gapac.com
Exec. VP, Consumer Products Group: Kathleen A. Walters
Phone: (1) 404-652-4000
Fax: (1) 404-652-4581
Email: kathleen.walters@gapac.com
Exec. VP, Packaging: Christian Fischer
Phone: (1) 404-652-4000
Fax: (1) 404-652-4581
Email: christian.fischer@gapac.com
Exec. VP, Building Products: Mark Luetters
Phone: (1) 404-652-4000
Fax: (1) 404-652-4581
Email: mark.luetters@gapac.com
Snr. VP, HR: Julie Brehm
Phone: (1) 404-652-4000
Fax: (1) 404-652-4581
Email: julie.brehm@gapac.com
Snr. VP, Gen. Counsel: Tye Darland
Phone: (1) 404-652-4000
Fax: (1) 404-652-4581
Email: tye.darland@gapac.com
Snr. VP, Commun, Govern., & Public Affairs: Sheila M. Weidman
Phone: (1) 404-652-4000
Fax: (1) 404-652-4581
Email: david.park@gapac.com
Snr. VP, Strat. & Bus. Devlpt.: David Park
Phone: (1) 404-652-4000
Fax: (1) 404-652-4581
VP, Chief Sustainability Officer: william Frerking
Phone: (1) 404-652-4000
Fax: (1) 404-652-4581
Email: william.frerking@gapac.com
Total Employees of Company: 35,000
Mill Locations:
G-P Gypsum LLC, San Leandro Mill, 1988 Marina Blvd, San Leandro, CA 94550, USA, Capacity: 80,325 st/y, (Paper mill)
Phone: (1) 510-483-7580
Fax: (1) 510-483-5430
Georgia-Pacific LLC, Camas Mill, 401 NE Adams St, Camas, WA 98607-2133, USA, Capacity: 285,537 st/y, (Pulp mill, Paper mill)
Phone: (1) 360-834-3021
Fax: (1) 360-834-8176
Georgia-Pacific LLC, Brewton Mill, 32224 US 31, Brewton, AL 36426, USA, Capacity: 499,800 st/y, (Pulp mill, Paperboard mill)
Phone: (1) 251-867-3621
Fax: (1) 251-867-8353
GP Cellulose, LLC, Leaf River Cellulose Mill, 157 Buck Creek Rd, New Augusta, MS 39462, USA, (Pulp mill)
Phone: (1) 601-964-8411
Fax: (1) 601-964-7248
Email: info@gpcellulose.com
Georgia-Pacific LLC, Broadway Street/West Mill, 1919 S Broadway, Green Bay, WI 54304, USA, Capacity: 384,846 st/y, (Paper mill)
Phone: (1) 920-435-8821
Fax: (1) 920-435-3703
Georgia-Pacific LLC, Big Island Mill, 9363 Lee Jackson Hwy, Big Island, VA 24526, USA, Capacity: 597,975 st/y, (Pulp mill, Paperboard mill)
Phone: (1) 434-299-5911
Fax: (1) 434-299-5222
Georgia-Pacific LLC, Cedar Springs Mill, 12551 Georgia 273, Cedar Springs, GA 39832, USA, Capacity: 1,022,805 st/y, (Paperboard mill)
Phone: (1) 229-372-5541
Fax: (1) 229-372-5191
Georgia-Pacific LLC, Wauna Mill, 92326 Taylorsville Rd, Rte 2, Box 2185, Clatskanie, OR 97016-9299, USA, Capacity: 343,791 st/y, (Paper mill)
Phone: (1) 503-455-2221
Fax: (1) 503-455-3562
Georgia-Pacific LLC, Crossett Mill, 100 Mill Supply Rd, Crossett, AR 71635, USA, Capacity: 615,111 st/y, (Paper

mill, Paperboard mill)
Phone: (1) 870-567-8000, 870-567-5365
Fax: (1) 870-364-5123
Georgia-Pacific LLC, Day Street/East Mill, 500 Day St, Green Bay, WI 54302, USA, Capacity: 110,313 st/y, (Paper mill)
Phone: (1) 920-433-6200
Fax: (1) 920-433-6352
Georgia-Pacific LLC, Halsey Mill, 30470 American Dr, Halsey, OR 97348, USA, Capacity: 109,599 st/y, (Pulp mill, Paper mill)
Phone: (1) 541-369-2293
Fax: (1) 541-369-1327
Georgia-Pacific LLC, Monticello Mill, 604 NA Sandifer Rd, Monticello, MS 39654, USA, Capacity: 1,113,840 st/y, (Paperboard mill)
Phone: (1) 601-587-7711, 601-587-3204
Fax: (1) 601-587-4532
Georgia-Pacific LLC, Muskogee Mill, 4901 Chandler Rd, Muskogee, OK 74403, USA, Capacity: 364,140 st/y, (Paper mill)
Phone: (1) 918-683-7671
Fax: (1) 918-683-1609
Georgia-Pacific LLC, Naheola Mill, 7530 Hwy 114, Pennington, AL 36916, USA, Capacity: 579,054 st/y, (Pulp mill, Paper mill, Paperboard mill)
Phone: (1) 205-459-1900
Fax: (1) 205-459-1303
Georgia-Pacific LLC, Plattsburgh Mill, 327 Margaret St, Plattsburgh, NY 12901, USA, Capacity: 45,339 st/y, (Paper mill)
Phone: (1) 518-561-3500
Fax: (1) 518-562-6533
Georgia-Pacific LLC, Port Hudson Mill, 1000 West Mount Pleasant Zachary Road, Zachary, LA 70791, USA, Capacity: 822,528 st/y, (Paper mill)
Phone: (1) 225-654-1700
Fax: (1) 225-654-7722
Georgia-Pacific LLC, Savannah River Mill, 393 Fort Howard Rd, Rincon, GA 31326, USA, Capacity: 466,242 st/y, (Paper mill)
Phone: (1) 912-826-5216
Fax: (1) 912-806-2363
Georgia-Pacific LLC, Thorold Mill, 319 Allanburg Rd, Thorold, ON, Canada L2V 5C3, Capacity: 126,764 st/y, (Paperboard mill)
Phone: (1) 905-227-6651
Fax: (1) 905-227-8120
Georgia-Pacific LLC, Toledo Mill, 1400 S.E. Butler Bridge Road, Toledo, OR 97391, USA, Capacity: 894,285 st/y, (Pulp mill, Paperboard mill)
Phone: (1) 541-336-2211
Fax: (1) 541-336-8214
Georgia-Pacific LLC, Palatka Mill, 215 County Road 216, Palatka, FL 32177, USA, Capacity: 533,001 st/y, (Paper mill, Paperboard mill)
Phone: (1) 386-325-2001
Fax: (1) 386-325-6141
GP Cellulose, LLC, Foley Cellulose Mill (Perry Mill), One Buckeye Drive, Perry, FL 32348, USA, (Pulp mill)
Phone: (1) 850-584-1121
Fax: (1) 850-584-1722
Email: info@gpcellulose.com
GP Cellulose, LLC, Brunswick Cellulose Mill, 1400 West 9th St, Brunswick, GA 31520, USA, (Pulp mill)
Phone: (1) 912-265-5780
Fax: (1) 912-265-8060
Email: info@gpcellulose.com
GP Cellulose, LLC, Alabama River Cellulose Mill, Lena Landegger Highway, County Road 39, Perdue Hill, Claiborne, AL 36470, USA, (Pulp mill)
Phone: (1) 251-575-2000
Fax: (1) 251-743-8432
Email: info@gpcellulose.com
Industria Panameña de Papel SA, Chilibre Mill (50% owned), Milla 15, Carretera Boyd Roosevelt, 0816-02543 San Vicente, Zona Chilibre, Panama, Capacity: 33,056 st/y, (Paper mill, Paperboard mill)
Phone: (507) 216 6555/6031
Fax: (507) 16 6766
Email: vanipel@cw.panama.net

Georgia

① Ⓜ GP Cellulose, LLC
Brunswick Cellulose Mill
Ownership: Georgia-Pacific LLC
W. 9th St
Brunswick, GA 31520
USA
Mailing Address: PO Box 1438, Brunswick, GA 31521, USA
  Phone: (1) 912-265-5780
  Fax: (1) 912-265-8060
  Web Address: www.gpcellulose.com
Personnel:
  VP. & Gen. Mgr.: David Martinez
  Phone: (1) 912-265-5780
  Fax: (1) 912-265-8060
  Email: daamarti@gapac.com
  #5 Pulp Machines Optimizer: John Watson
  Phone: (1) 912-265-5780
  Fax: (1) 912-265-8060
  Email: john.watson@gapac.com
  Labor Rel. Mgr.: Siobhan Foley
  Phone: (1) 912-265-5780
  Fax: (1) 912-265-8060
Total Employees at this Location: 561
Type of Operation: Pulp mill
Pulp Grades and Capacities:
  Total pulp capacity: 1,000,732 st/y
  Pulp available for market: 942,477 st/y
  Chemical Pulp: 1,000,732 st/y
Pulp Mill Data:
  Chemical Pulping Systems:
  Batch digesters: 19
  Pulp Lines: 1
  Bleach Plant Systems: 3
  1, Sequence: O_2 DEopDED
  2, Sequence: O_2 DEopDED
  3, Sequence: O_2 DEopDED
  Chemical Recovery Equipment:
  Evaporator lines: 1
  Recovery boilers: 2
  Lime Kiln
  Pulp Dryers:
  Air Float dryers 1, Flakt dryer 1, Flakt dryer 1, Fourdriniers 1
Energy Data:
  Power boilers: 3
  Steam turbines: 2 at 70.2 MW
  Electrical demand for mill: 2,050 MWh/D

Ⓜ Georgia-Pacific LLC
Cedar Springs Mill
12551 Georgia 273
Cedar Springs, GA 39832
USA
Mailing Address: PO Box 44, Cedar Springs, GA 31732-0044, USA
  Phone: (1) 229-372-5541
  Fax: (1) 229-372-5191
  Web Address: www.gp.com
Personnel:
  VP & Gen. Mgr.: George J. Cifelli
  Phone: (1) 229-372-5541
  Fax: (1) 229-372-5191
  Email: george.cifelli@gapac.com
  Dir., Plan. & Analysis: Rick Douglas
  Phone: (1) 229-372-5541
  Fax: (1) 229-372-5191
  Email: rick.douglas@gapac.com
  IT Mgr.: David Buie
  Phone: (1) 229-372-5320
  Fax: (1) 229-372-5191
  Email: david.buie@gapac.com
Total Employees at this Location: 537
Type of Operation: Paperboard mill
Pulp Grades and Capacities:
  Total pulp capacity: 1,074,359 st/y
  Chemical Pulp: 981,683 st/y
  Recycled Pulping: 92,676 st/y
Pulp Mill Data:
  Chemical Pulping Systems:
  Batch digesters: 11
  Continuous digesters: 1
  Chemical Recovery Equipment:
  Evaporator lines: 2
  Recovery boilers: 3
  Lime Kiln
  Recycled Fiber Treatment Lines:
  Pulpers: 1 at 96,781
Paper/Paperboard Grades and Capacities:
  Total paper and paperboard capacity: 1,022,805 st/y
  Linerboard: 796,110 st/y
  Corrugating medium/fluting: 226,695 st/y
Paper and Paperboard Mill Data:
  Paper Machines: 3
  No. 1, fourdrinier, total capacity 439,110 st/y, Trim width 256 in, Linerboard
  No. 2, fourdrinier, total capacity 357,000 st/y, Trim width 254 in, Linerboard
  No. 3, fourdrinier, total capacity 226,695 st/y, Trim width 258 in, Corrugating medium/fluting
Energy Data:
  Power boilers: 2
  Steam turbines: 2 at 48, 45 MW
  Electrical demand for mill: 2,196 MWh/D

Ⓜ Georgia-Pacific LLC
Savannah River Mill
393 Fort Howard Rd
Rincon, GA 31326
USA
  Phone: (1) 912-826-5216
  Fax: (1) 912-806-2363
  Web Address: www.gp.com
Personnel:
  VP, Manuf.: Monty Brown
  Phone: (1) 912-826-5216
  Fax: (1) 912-806-2363
  Email: montoya.brown@gapac.com
  Environ. Mgr.: Brent G. Howell
  Phone: (1) 912-826-5216
  Fax: (1) 912-806-2363
  Email: brent.howell@gapac.com
Total Employees at this Location: 850
Type of Operation: Paper mill
Pulp Grades and Capacities:
  Total pulp capacity: 455,887 st/y
  Recycled Pulping: 455,887 st/y
Pulp Mill Data:
  Bleach Plant Systems: 1
  Recycled Deinked Pulping System, Sequence: H
  Recycled Fiber Treatment Lines:
  Flotation deinking lines
Paper/Paperboard Grades and Capacities:
  Total paper and paperboard capacity: 466,242 st/y
  Tissue: 466,242 st/y
Paper and Paperboard Mill Data:
  Stock Preparation:
  Pulpers:
  Paper Machines: 5
  No. 16, twin-wire, total capacity 93,177 st/y, Trim width 263 in, Tissue
  No. 17, twin-wire, total capacity 131,376 st/y, Trim width 263 in, Tissue
  No. 18, twin-wire, total capacity 89,250 st/y, Trim width 263 in, Tissue
  No. 19, twin-wire, total capacity 73,899 st/y, Trim width 263 in, Tissue
  No. 20, twin-wire, total capacity 78,540 st/y, Trim width 263 in, Tissue
Energy Data:
  Power boilers: 4
  HRSG boiler
  Combustion turbines: 2 at 25, 25 MW
  Steam turbines: 2 at 45, 45 MW
  Electrical demand for mill: 1,803 MWh/D

① GP Cellulose, LLC
Ownership: Georgia-Pacific LLC
133 Peachtree Street North East
Atlanta, GA 30303
USA
  Phone: (1) 404-652-4000
  Fax: (1) 404-652-4581
  Email: info@gppackaging.com
  Web Address: gpcellulose.com
Personnel:
  Pres.: Patrick J Boushka
  Phone: (1) 404-652-4000
  Fax: (1) 404-652-4581
  Email: pboushka@gapac.com
  VP. Sls. & Mktg. Sls.: Munir Abdallah
  Phone: (1) 404-652-4000
  Fax: (1) 404-652-4581
  Email: mabdallah@gapac.com
  VP., Tech. Serv. Containerboard & Cellulose Division: Jeff Vermilyea
  Phone: (1) 404-652-4000
  Fax: (1) 404-652-4581
  Email: jeff.vermilyea@gapac.com
Mill Locations:
  GP Cellulose, LLC, Leaf River Cellulose Mill, 157 Buck Creek Rd, New Augusta, MS 39462, USA, (Pulp mill)
  Phone: (1) 601-964-8411
  Fax: (1) 601-964-7248
  Email: info@gpcellulose.com
  GP Cellulose, LLC, Foley Cellulose Mill (Perry Mill), One Buckeye Drive, Perry, FL 32348, USA, (Pulp mill)
  Phone: (1) 850-584-1121
  Fax: (1) 850-584-1722
  Email: info@gpcellulose.com
  GP Cellulose, LLC, Brunswick Cellulose Mill, 1400 West 9th St, Brunswick, GA 31520, USA, (Pulp mill)
  Phone: (1) 912-265-5780
  Fax: (1) 912-265-8060
  Email: info@gpcellulose.com
  GP Cellulose, LLC, Alabama River Cellulose Mill, Lena Landegger Highway, County Road 39, Perdue Hill, Claiborne, AL 36470, USA, (Pulp mill)
  Phone: (1) 251-575-2000
  Fax: (1) 251-743-8432
  Email: info@gpcellulose.com

① Graphic Packaging International Inc.
Ownership: 100% by Graphic Packaging Holding Co.
1500 Riveredge Parkway NW
Atlanta, GA 30328
USA
  Phone: (1) 770-644-3000
  Fax: (1) 770-644-2999
  Web Address: www.graphicpkg.com
Personnel:
  Pres. & CEO: David W. Scheible
  Phone: (1) 770-644-3000
  Fax: (1) 770-644-2999
  Email: david.scheible@graphicpkg.com
  COO: Michael P. Doss
  Phone: (1) 770-644-3000
  Fax: (1) 770-644-2999
  Email: michael.doss@graphicpkg.com
  Snr. VP., Finan. (Eff. October 1, 2014 & CFO Eff. January 1, 2015): Stephen R. Scherger
  Phone: (1) 770-644-3000
  Fax: (1) 770-644-2999
  Snr. VP. & CFO (Special Advisor Eff. January 1, 2015 & to retire on March 1, 2015): Daniel J. Blount
  Phone: (1) 770-644-3000
  Fax: (1) 770-644-2999
  Email: daniel.blount@graphicpkg.com
  Snr. VP., Gen. Council & Sec. (From Feb. 2014): Lauren S. Tashma
  Phone: (1) 770-644-3000
  Fax: (1) 770-644-2999
  Snr. VP., Mills Div.: Alan R. Nichols
  Phone: (1) 770-644-3000
  Fax: (1) 770-644-2999
  Snr. VP., HR (From July 15, 2013): Carla J. Chaney
  Phone: (1) 770-644-3000
  Fax: (1) 770-644-2999

Snr. VP., Beverage Packaging Div.: Michael R. Schmal
Phone: (1) 770-644-3000
Fax: (1) 770-644-2999
Email: michael.schmal@graphicpkg.com
Snr. VP., Flexible Div.: R. Allen Ennis Jr.
Phone: (1) 770-644-3000
Fax: (1) 770-644-2999
Snr. Consumer Packaging Division (From October 1, 2014): Michael Ukropina
Phone: (1) 770-644-3000
Fax: (1) 770-644-2999
Total Employees of Company: 12,722
Mill Locations:
Graphic Packaging International Inc., Battle Creek Mill, 79 E Fountain St, Battle Creek, MI 49017-4198, USA, Capacity: 173,145 st/y, (Paperboard mill)
Phone: (1) 269-963-4004
Fax: (1) 269-963-1306
Graphic Packaging International Inc., Middletown Mill, 407 Charles St, Middletown, OH 45042-2192, USA, Capacity: 162,792 st/y, (Paperboard mill)
Phone: (1) 513-424-4200
Fax: (1) 513-424-4325
Graphic Packaging International Inc., Santa Clara Mill, 2600 De La Cruz Blvd, Santa Clara, CA 95050, USA, Capacity: 139,230 st/y, (Paperboard mill)
Phone: (1) 408-496-5118
Fax: (1) 408-496-5027
Graphic Packaging International Inc., Kalamazoo Mill, 1500 N Pitcher St, Kalamazoo, MI 49007-2539, USA, Capacity: 460,530 st/y, (Paperboard mill)
Phone: (1) 269-383-5000
Fax: (1) 269-383-5135
Graphic Packaging International Inc., Macon Mill, 100 Riverwood International Way, Macon, GA 31206-2098, USA, Capacity: 584,409 st/y, (Paperboard mill)
Phone: (1) 478-788-6160
Fax: (1) 478-784-2562
Graphic Packaging International Inc., West Monroe Mill, 1000 Jonesboro Rd, West Monroe, LA 71292, USA, Capacity: 910,707 st/y, (Paperboard mill)
Phone: (1) 318-362-2000
Fax: (1) 318-362-2133

ⓜGraphic Packaging International Inc.
Macon Mill
100 Riverwood International Way
Macon, GA 31206-2098
USA
Phone: (1) 478-788-6160
Fax: (1) 478-784-2562
Web Address: www.graphicpkg.com
Personnel:
Res. Mgr. (From January 2014): Scott Grimes
Phone: (1) 478-788-6160
Fax: (1) 478-784-2562
Email: scott.grimes@graphicpkg.com
Process Cntr. & IT Mgr.: Mike Gillespie
Phone: (1) 478-788-6160
Fax: (1) 478-784-2562
Email: mike.gillespie@graphicpkg.com
Snr. Buyer: Jack Kipe
Phone: (1) 478-788-6160
Fax: (1) 478-784-2562
Email: jack.kipe@graphicpkg.com
Mgr., Safety & Health: Bruce Oberstadt
Phone: (1) 478-788-6160
Fax: (1) 478-784-2562
Email: bruce.oberstadt@graphicpkg.com
Total Employees at this Location: 515
Type of Operation: Paperboard mill
Pulp Grades and Capacities:
Total pulp capacity: 537,930 st/y
Chemical Pulp: 444,664 st/y
Recycled Pulping: 93,265 st/y
Pulp Mill Data:
Chemical Pulping Systems:
Batch digesters: 8
Chemical Recovery Equipment:
Evaporator lines: 1
Recovery boilers: 1
Lime Kiln
Recycled Fiber Treatment Lines:
Recycled packaging pulping lines
Paper/Paperboard Grades and Capacities:
Total paper and paperboard capacity: 584,409 st/y
Boxboard/cartonboard: 584,409 st/y
Paper and Paperboard Mill Data:
Paper Machines: 2
No. 1, fourdrinier, total capacity 314,160 st/y, Trim width 200 in, Boxboard/cartonboard
No. 2, fourdrinier, total capacity 270,249 st/y, Trim width 186 in, Boxboard/cartonboard
Coating Machines: 2
PM 1, total capacity 30,864 st/y., on machine
PM 2, total capacity 270,062 st/y., on machine
Energy Data:
Power boilers: 4
Steam turbines: 4 at 77.5 MW
Electrical demand for mill: 1,264 MWh/D

ⓜHollingsworth & Vose Co.
Hawkinsville Mill
300 Industrial Blvd
Hawkinsville, GA 31036
USA
Phone: (1) 478-783-3200
Fax: (1) 478-783-3292
Email: info@hovo.com
Web Address: www.hollingsworth-vose.com
Personnel:
Mill Mgr.: John Follett
Phone: (1) 478-783-3200 ext. 5220
Fax: (1) 478-783-3292
Email: john.follett@hovo.com
Qlt. Mgr.: Gary Sharpe
Phone: (1) 478-783-3200
Fax: (1) 478-783-3292
Email: gary.sharpe@hovo.com
Manuf. Mgr.: Drew Cravey
Phone: (1) 478-783-3200
Fax: (1) 478-783-3292
Email: drew.cravey@hovo.com
Type of Operation: Paper mill
Paper/Paperboard Grades and Capacities:
Total paper and paperboard capacity: 12,500 st/y
Specialty and industrial
Paper and Paperboard Mill Data:
Paper Machines: 2
No. 1, Rotoformer, Trim width 80 in, Specialty and industrial
No. 2, Rotoformer, Trim width 36 in, Specialty and industrial

ⓜInternational Paper Co.
Augusta Mill
4278 Mike Padgett Hwy
Augusta, GA 30906
USA
Mailing Address: PO Box 1425, Augusta, GA 30903-1425, USA
Phone: (1) 706-798-5711
Fax: (1) 706-796-5599
Email: (firstname.lastname@ipaper.com)
Web Address: www.internationalpaper.com
Personnel:
Mill Mgr.: J. Richard (Dick) Jackson Jr.
Phone: (1) 706-796-5609
Fax: (1) 706-796-5599
Email: dick.jackson@ipaper.com
Qlty. Mgr.: David R. DeLong
Phone: (1) 706-796-5345
Fax: (1) 901-334-3507
Email: david.delong@ipaper.com
HR Mgr.: Jeff Carmack
Phone: (1) 706-798-5711
Fax: (1) 706-796-5599
Email: jeff.carmack@ipaper.com
Contr.: Sean Hassel
Phone: (1) 706-798-5711
Fax: (1) 706-796-5599
Email: sean.hassel@ipaper.com
Mgr., PS&D: Jennifer Schwarz
Phone: (1) 706-798-5711
Fax: (1) 706-796-5599
Email: jennifer.schwarz@ipaper.com
Total Employees at this Location: 658
Type of Operation: Paperboard mill
Pulp Grades and Capacities:
Total pulp capacity: 496,029 st/y
Chemical Pulp: 496,029 st/y
Pulp Mill Data:
Chemical Pulping Systems:
Continuous digesters: 1
Bleach Plant Systems: 3
Hardwood Pulp Line, Sequence: DEopD
Hardwood/Softwood Pulp Line, Sequence: DEopDD
Chemical Recovery Equipment:
Recovery boilers: 1
Lime Kiln
Paper/Paperboard Grades and Capacities:
Total paper and paperboard capacity: 526,575 st/y
Boxboard/cartonboard: 526,575 st/y
Paper and Paperboard Mill Data:
Stock Preparation:
Pulpers: 9
Refiners: 15
Paper Machines: 2
No. 1, Bel-Bond, total capacity 240,975 st/y, Trim width 215 in, Boxboard/cartonboard
No. 3, DuoFormer, total capacity 285,600 st/y, Trim width 216 in, Boxboard/cartonboard
Coating Machines: 3
PM 1, total capacity 260,141 st/y., on machine
PM 2, total capacity 149,912 st/y., on machine
PM 3, total capacity 299,824 st/y., on machine
Energy Data:
Power boilers: 2
Steam turbines: 3 at 84.8 MW
Electrical demand for mill: 1,653 MWh/D

ⓜInternational Paper Co.
IP Augusta
4278 Mike Padgett Hwy
Augusta, GA 30906
USA
Mailing Address: PO Box 1425, Augusta, GA 30903-1425, USA
Phone: (1) 706-798-5711
Fax: (1) 706-796-5599
Email: (firstname.lastname@ipaper.com)
Web Address: www.internationalpaper.com
Total Employees at this Location: 731
Type of Operation: Paperboard mill

ⓜInternational Paper Co.
Savannah Mill
1201 West Lathrop Avenue
Savannah, GA 31415
USA
Mailing Address: PO Box 570, Savannah, GA 31402, USA
Phone: (1) 912-238-6000, 912-238-6789
Email: (firstname.lastname@ipaper.com)
Web Address: www.internationalpaper.com
Personnel:
Mill Mgr.: Ralph Stagner
Phone: (1) 912-238-6000
Fax: (1) 912-238-6040
Email: ralph.stagner@ipaper.com
Product Performance Mgr.: George Katula
Phone: (1) 912-238-6000
Fax: (1) 912-238-6040
Email: george.katula@ipaper.com
Eng. Grp. Ldr.: Wendell Ryle
Phone: (1) 912-238-6000
Fax: (1) 912-238-6040
Email: wendell.ryle@ipaper.com
Purch. Mgr.: Ty Cobb
Phone: (1) 912-238-6000, 912-238-6789

Georgia

Fax: (1) 912-238-6040
Email: ty.cobb@ipaper.com
Environ. Mgr.: Donna Katula
Phone: (1) 912-238-6000
Fax: (1) 912-238-6040
Email: donna.katula@ipaper.com
Total Employees at this Location: 664
Type of Operation: Paper mill, Paperboard mill
Pulp Grades and Capacities:
Total pulp capacity: 1,032,990 st/y
Chemical Pulp: 861,349 st/y
Recycled Pulping: 171,641 st/y
Pulp Mill Data:
Chemical Pulping Systems:
Batch digesters: 18
Continuous digesters: 2
Chemical Recovery Equipment:
Evaporator lines: 5
Recovery boilers: 2
Lime Kiln
Recycled Fiber Treatment Lines:
Recycled packaging pulping lines
Paper/Paperboard Grades and Capacities:
Total paper and paperboard capacity: 979,965 st/y
Packaging papers: 196,350 st/y
Linerboard: 783,615 st/y
Paper and Paperboard Mill Data:
Paper Machines: 3
No. 5, fourdrinier, total capacity 196,350 st/y, Trim width 218 in, Packaging papers
No. 6, fourdrinier, total capacity 248,115 st/y, Trim width 220 in, Linerboard
No. 8, (2 Fourdrinier with 2 ENP Press.), fourdrinier (2), total capacity 535,500 st/y, Trim width 340 in, Linerboard
Energy Data:
Power boilers: 4
Steam turbines: 8 at 191.6 MW
Electrical demand for mill: 2,066 MWh/D

ⓂInternational Paper Co.
Rome Mill
238 MaysBridge Rd.
Rome, GA 30165
USA
Mailing Address: PO Box 1551, Rome, GA 30162-1551, USA
Phone: (1) 706-232-0851
Fax: (1) 706-236-5443
Web Address: www.internationalpaper.com
Personnel:
Mill Mgr. (Eff. June 2014): Brant Oberg
Phone: (1) 706-232-0851
Fax: (1) 706-236-5443
Email: brant.oberg@ipaper.com
Environ. and Safety (EHS) Mgr.: Russ Foulke
Phone: (1) 706-236-8499
Fax: (1) 706-236-5443
Email: russ.foulke@ipaper.com
Eng. & Tech. Mgr.: Tommy Barnes
Phone: (1) 706-236-8487
Fax: (1) 706-236-5443
Email: tommy.barnes@ipaper.com
HR Mgr.: Robert Heath
Phone: (44) 706-236-5341
Fax: (44) 706-236-5443
Email: robert.heath@ipaper.com
Total Employees at this Location: 456
Type of Operation: Paper mill, Paperboard mill
Pulp Grades and Capacities:
Total pulp capacity: 919,104 st/y
Chemical Pulp: 836,435 st/y
Recycled Pulping: 82,669 st/y
Pulp Mill Data:
Chemical Pulping Systems:
Batch digesters: 15
Pulp Lines: 2
Chemical Recovery Equipment:
Evaporator lines: 3
Recovery boilers: 1
Lime Kiln
Recycled Fiber Treatment Lines:
Recycled packaging pulping lines: 1 at 81,570
Paper/Paperboard Grades and Capacities:
Total paper and paperboard capacity: 870,009 st/y
Linerboard: 870,009 st/y
Paper and Paperboard Mill Data:
Stock Preparation:
Refiners: 4
Paper Machines: 2
No. 1, fourdrinier, total capacity 489,090 st/y, Trim width 235 in, Linerboard
No. 2, fourdrinier, total capacity 380,919 st/y, Trim width 237 in, Linerboard
Finishing Equipment:
Winders: 2 at 460,000 st/y, 390,000 st/y
Energy Data:
Power boilers: 2
Steam turbines: 4 at 65 MW
Electrical demand for mill: 1,825 MWh/D

ⓂInterstate Paper L.L.C.
Riceboro Mill
Ownership: Interstate Resources, Inc.
2366 Interstate Paper Rd
Riceboro, GA 31323
USA
Phone: (1) 912-884-3371
Fax: (1) 912-884-3426
Email: info@interstatepaper.com
Web Address: www.interstatepaper.com
Personnel:
VP & Gen. Mgr. Timber/Lumber: Tom Norris
Phone: (1) 912-884-3371
Fax: (1) 912-884-7011
Email: tom.norris@interstatepaper.com
Gen. Mgr.: Al Cantrell
Phone: (1) 912-884-3371
Fax: (1) 912-884-3426
Email: al.cantrell@interstatepaper.com
Oper. Mgr.: Michael Hardy
Phone: (1) 912-884-3371
Fax: (1) 912-884-6513
Email: michael.hardy@interstatepaper.com
Dir. Procurement & Mill Sls.: Nick Shwayri
Phone: (1) 912-884-3371 Ext. 7216
Fax: (1) 912-884-7255
Email: nick.shwayri@interstatepaper.com
Total Employees at this Location: 234
Type of Operation: Pulp mill, Paper mill, Paperboard mill
Pulp Grades and Capacities:
Total pulp capacity: 367,244 st/y
Chemical Pulp: 311,422 st/y
Recycled Pulping: 66,526 st/y
Pulp Mill Data:
Chemical Pulping Systems:
Batch digesters: 5
Bleach Plant Systems: 1
Chemical Recovery Equipment:
Evaporator lines: 2
Recovery boilers: 1
Lime Kiln
Recycled Fiber Treatment Lines:
Pulpers: 1 at 71,350 admt/y
Paper/Paperboard Grades and Capacities:
Total paper and paperboard capacity: 350,217 st/y
Linerboard: 350,217 st/y
Paper and Paperboard Mill Data:
Stock Preparation:
Refiners: 7
Paper Machines: 1
No. 1, top-wire, total capacity 350,217 st/y, Trim width 170 in, Linerboard
Finishing Equipment:
Winders: 1 at 323,100 st/y
Calenders: 1
Energy Data:
Power boilers: 1
Steam turbines: 1 at 14.5 MW
Electrical demand for mill: 768 MWh/D

ⓂNeenah Paper, Inc.
3460 Preston Ridge Road, Suite 600
Alpharetta, GA 30005
USA
Phone: (1) 678-518-3242/678-566-6500
Fax: (1) 678-518-3287
Web Address: www.neenah.com
Personnel:
Chrmn.: Sean T. Erwin
Phone: (1) 678-518-3281
Fax: (1) 678-518-3287
Email: sean.erwin@neenahpaper.com
Pres. & CEO: John P. O'Donnell
Phone: (1) 678-518-3242
Fax: (1) 678-518-3287
Email: john.odonnell@neenahpaper.com
Snr. VP, Gen. Counsel & Sec.: Steven S. Heinrichs
Phone: (1) 678-518-3242
Fax: (1) 678-518-3287
Email: steven.heinrichs@neenahpaper.com
Snr. VP, CFO & Treasurer: Bonnie C. Lind
Phone: (1) 678-518-3242
Fax: (1) 678-518-3287
Email: bonnie.lind@neenahpaper.com
Snr. VP, Sls. & Mktg.: James Caudill
Phone: (1) 678-518-3242
Fax: (1) 678-518-3287
Email: james.caudill@neenahpaper.com
VP, HR: Richard Read
Phone: (1) 678-518-3230
Fax: (1) 678-518-3287
Email: rread@neenahpaper.com
Total Employees of Company: 1,875
Total Employees at this Location: 100
Mill Locations:
Neenah Gessner GmbH, Bruckmühl Mill, Otto-von-Steinbeis-Str. 14b, D-83052 Bruckmühl, Germany, Capacity: 27,557 st/y, (Paper mill)
Phone: (49) 8062 7030
Fax: (49) 8062 703255
Neenah Gessner GmbH, Feldkirchen-Westerham Mill, Weidacher Str. 30, D-83620 Feldkirchen-Westerham, Germany, Capacity: 33,069 st/y, (Paper mill)
Phone: (49) 8062 703 0
Fax: (49) 8062 703 461
Email: c.koegl@neenah.de
Neenah Lahnstein, Lahnstein Mill, Auf Brühl 15-27, D-56112 Lahnstein, Germany, Capacity: 18,739 st/y, (Paper mill)
Phone: (49) 2621 1770
Fax: (49) 2621 177609
Email: lahnstein@neenah.de
Neenah Paper, Inc., Neenah Mill, 135 N Commercial St, Neenah, WI 54956, USA, Capacity: 48,184 st/y, (Paper mill)
Phone: (1) 920-721-1376, 800-558-5061
Fax: (1) 302-655-5049
Neenah Paper, Inc., Appleton Mill, 600 S Vulcan St, Appleton, WI 54915, USA, Capacity: 35,692 st/y, (Paper mill)
Phone: (1) 920-738-8332
Fax: (1) 920-738-8308
Neenah Paper, Inc., Munising Mill, 501 E Munising Ave, Munising, MI 49862-1490, USA, Capacity: 32,123 st/y, (Paper mill)
Phone: (1) 906-387-2700
Fax: (1) 906-387-2935
Neenah Paper, Inc., Whiting Mill, 3243 Whiting Rd, Stevens Point, WI 54481-6300, USA, Capacity: 139,199 st/y, (Paper mill)
Phone: (1) 715-345-5050
Fax: (1) 715-345-5043

ⓂPackaging Corp. of America
Valdosta Mill
5495 Lake Park-Clyattville Rd
Valdosta, GA 31601
USA

Georgia

Mailing Address: PO Box 1048, Valdosta, GA 31603-1048, USA
 Phone: (1) 229-559-7911
 Fax: (1) 229-559-0546
 Web Address: www.packagingcorp.com
Personnel:
 Mill Mgr. (Eff. 2014): W. Kirk Thomas
 Phone: (1) 229-559-7911
 Fax: (1) 229-559-0546
 Email: kirk.thomas@packagingcorp.com
 Snr. Dir., Corp. Eng - Mechanical Reliability (Eff. 2014): David Carmon
 Phone: (1) 229-559-7911
 Fax: (1) 229-559-0546
 Email: dcarmon@packagingcorp.com
 Purch. Mgr.: Clint Yager
 Phone: (1) 229-559-7911
 Fax: (1) 229-559-0546
 Email: cyager@packagingcorp.com
 Sr. Eng.: Britton Powell
 Phone: (1) 229-559-7911
 Fax: (1) 229-559-0546
 Email: bpowell@packagingcorp.com
 Woodlands Mgr. (Gen. Mgr. - Fiber Management): Donald Pope
 Phone: (1) 229-559-2366
 Fax: (1) 229-559-0546
 Email: dpope@packagingcorp.com
 Prod. Mgr.: Kent Thomas
 Phone: (1) 229-559-7911
 Fax: (1) 229-559-0546
 Email: kthomas@packagingcorp.com
Total Employees at this Location: 359
Type of Operation: Pulp mill, Paperboard mill
Pulp Grades and Capacities:
 Total pulp capacity: 589,277 st/y
 Chemical Pulp: 589,277 st/y
Pulp Mill Data:
 Chemical Pulping Systems:
 Batch digesters: 10
 Chemical Recovery Equipment:
 Evaporator lines: 1
 Recovery boilers: 1
 Lime Kiln
Paper/Paperboard Grades and Capacities:
 Total paper and paperboard capacity: 560,133 st/y
 Linerboard: 560,133 st/y
Paper and Paperboard Mill Data:
 Stock Preparation:
 Pulpers: 1
 Refiners: 7
Paper Machines: 1
 No. 1, fourdrinier, total capacity 560,133 st/y, Trim width 224 in, Linerboard
Finishing Equipment:
 Calenders: 2
 Rewinders: 1
Energy Data:
 Power boilers: 3
 Steam turbines: 1 at 52 MW
 Electrical demand for mill: 1,191 MWh/D

ⓂPaper Pak Industries
Washington Mill
1 PaperPak Parkway
Washington, GA 30673
USA
 Phone: (1) 706-678-6600
 Fax: (1) 706-678-3810
 Web Address: www.paperpakindustries.com
Personnel:
 Plt. Mgr.: Stephen Newton
 Phone: (1) 706-678-6600
 Fax: (1) 706-678-3810
 Email: snewton@paperpakindustries.com
Type of Operation: Paper mill
Paper/Paperboard Grades and Capacities:
 Total paper and paperboard capacity: 7,899 st/y
 Tissue: 7,899 st/y
Paper and Paperboard Mill Data:
Paper Machines: 1
 No. 1, total capacity 7,900 st/y, Tissue

ⓗPratt Industries (USA)
Ownership: Visy Pulp & Paper
1800 C Sarasota Business Parkway
Conyers, GA 30013
USA
 Phone: (1) 770-918-5678
 Fax: (1) 770-918-5679
 Email: info@prattindustries.com
 Web Address: www.prattindustries.com
Personnel:
 Chmn. & CEO: Anthony Pratt
 Phone: (1) 770-918-5678
 Fax: (1) 770-918-5679
 Email: apratt@prattindustries.com
 CEO: Brian McPheely
 Phone: (1) 770-918-5678
 Fax: (1) 770-918-5679
 Email: bmcpheely@prattindustries.com
 VP, Sls. & Mktg.: David Dennis
 Phone: (1) 770-918-5678
 Fax: (1) 770-918-5679
 Email: ddennis@prattindustries.com
 Mill Mgr.: Allen Bowdler
 Phone: (1) 770-918-5678
 Fax: (1) 770-918-5679
 Email: abowdler@prattindustries.com
 Prod. Mgr.: Arnie Corell
 Phone: (1) 770-918-5678
 Fax: (1) 770-918-5679
 Email: acorell@prattindustries.com
Total Employees of Company: 4,000
Total Employees at this Location: 115
Mill Locations:
 Pratt Industries (USA), Conyers Mill, 1800 A Sarasota Business Parkway, Conyers, GA 30013, USA, Capacity: 365,925 st/y, (Paper mill, Paperboard mill)
 Phone: (1) 770-922-5400, 770-918-5678
 Fax: (1) 770-922-7572
 Email: info@prattindustries.com
 Pratt Industries (USA), Shreveport Mill, 10429 Richard Pratt Drive, Shreveport, LA 71115, USA, Capacity: 374,850 st/y, (Paperboard mill)
 Phone: (1) 318-797-7375
 Pratt Industries (USA), Staten Island Mill, 4435 Victory Blvd, Staten Island, NY 10314, USA, Capacity: 373,065 st/y, (Paper mill, Paperboard mill)
 Phone: (1) 718-355-6754
 Fax: (1) 718-370-1115

ⓂPratt Industries (USA)
Conyers Mill
Ownership: Visy Pulp & Paper
1800 A Sarasota Business Parkway
Conyers, GA 30013
USA
 Phone: (1) 770-922-5400, 770-918-5678
 Fax: (1) 770-922-7572
 Email: info@prattindustries.com
 Web Address: www.prattindustries.com, www.visy.com.au
Personnel:
 Mill Mgr.: Allen Bowdler
 Phone: (1) 770-922-5400, 770-918-5678
 Fax: (1) 770-922-7572
 Email: abowdler@prattindustries.com
 Procurement Mgr.: Linda Stevens
 Phone: (1) 770-922-5400
 Fax: (1) 770-922-7572
 Email: lstevens@prattindustries.com
 Eng. Mgr.: Mark Mays
 Phone: (1) 770-922-5400, 770-918-5678
 Fax: (1) 770-922-7572
 Email: mmays@prattindustries.com
 Oper. Mgr. (From December 2013): Arnie Correll
 Phone: (1) 770-922-5400, 770-918-5678
 Fax: (1) 770-922-7572
 Email: acorrell@prattindustries.com
Total Employees at this Location: 98
Type of Operation: Paper mill, Paperboard mill
Pulp Grades and Capacities:
 Total pulp capacity: 374,148 st/y
 Recycled Pulping: 374,148 st/y
Pulp Mill Data:
 Recycled Fiber Treatment Lines:
 Recycled packaging pulping lines: 1
Paper/Paperboard Grades and Capacities:
 Total paper and paperboard capacity: 365,925 st/y
 Linerboard: 274,533 st/y
 Corrugating medium/fluting: 91,392 st/y
Paper and Paperboard Mill Data:
 Stock Preparation:
 Pulpers: 1
Paper Machines: 1
 No. 12, twin-wire, total capacity 365,925 st/y, Trim width 200 in, Linerboard, Corrugating medium/fluting
Finishing Equipment:
 Winders: 1
 Calenders: 1
Energy Data:
 Power boilers: 1
 Steam turbines: 1 at 9 MW
 Electrical demand for mill: 482 MWh/D

ⓂProcter & Gamble Paper Products Co.
Albany Mill
512 Liberty Expwy SE
Albany, GA 31705
USA
Mailing Address: PO Box 1747, Albany, GA 31702, USA
 Phone: (1) 229-430-8260
 Web Address: www.pg.com
Personnel:
 Plt. Mgr.: Fidel Torres
 Phone: (1) 229-430-8260
 Towel Oper. Dept. Ldr.: Devin Sanders
 Phone: (1) 229-430-8260
 Papermaking. Oper. Mgr. (From December 2013): Robert Cisneros
 Phone: (1) 229-430-8260
Total Employees at this Location: 450
Type of Operation: Paper mill
Paper/Paperboard Grades and Capacities:
 Total paper and paperboard capacity: 365,211 st/y
 Tissue: 365,211 st/y
Paper and Paperboard Mill Data:
Paper Machines: 6
 No. 1, TAD, total capacity 57,834 st/y, Trim width 205 in, Tissue
 No. 2, TAD, total capacity 57,834 st/y, Trim width 205 in, Tissue
 No. 3, TAD, total capacity 58,548 st/y, Trim width 205 in, Tissue
 No. 4, TAD, total capacity 58,905 st/y, Trim width 205 in, Tissue
 No. 5, TAD, total capacity 67,830 st/y, Trim width 205 in, Tissue
 No. 6, TAD, total capacity 64,260 st/y, Trim width 205 in, Tissue
Energy Data:
 Power boilers: 2
 Electrical demand for mill: 1,324 MWh/D

ⓂRayonier Advanced Materials Inc.
Jesup Plant
Previously Rayonier Inc.
4470 Savannah Hwy
Jesup, GA 31545
USA
Mailing Address: PO Box 2070, Jesup, GA 31598, USA
 Phone: (1) 912-427-5000, 912-588-8000
 Fax: (1) 912-427-5587
 Web Address: www.rayonieram.com, www.rayonier.com

Georgia

Personnel:
VP., Manuf. Oper.: William Manzer
Phone: (1) 912-427-5000
Fax: (1) 912-427-5587
Email: bill.manzer@rayonieram.com
Gen. Mgr.: Jack Perrett
Phone: (1) 912-427-5000
Fax: (1) 912-427-5587
Email: jack.perrett@rayonieram.com
Proj. Mgr., Celullose Specialities: Jay Jukkala
Phone: (1) 912-427-5000
Fax: (1) 912-427-5587
Email: jay.jukkala@rayonieram.com
Pulp Mill Mgr. (From October 2014): Mark Carden
Phone: (1) 912-427-5522
Fax: (1) 912-427-5587
Email: mark.carden@rayonieram.com
Total Employees at this Location: 817
Type of Operation: Pulp mill
Pulp Grades and Capacities:
Total pulp capacity: 619,330 st/y
Pulp available for market: 580,833 st/y
Chemical Pulp: 619,330 st/y
Pulp Mill Data:
Chemical Pulping Systems:
Batch digesters: 26
Pulp Lines: 3
Bleach Plant Systems: 3
Chemical Pulping System - A, Type: Hardwood/Softwood, Sequence: CdEoD(H)DD
Chemical Pulping System - B, Type: Hardwood/Softwood, Sequence: CdEoD(H)DD
Chemical Pulping System - C, Type: ECF- Hardwood/Softwood, Sequence: O_2 DEoDED
Chemical Recovery Equipment:
Evaporator lines: 1
Recovery boilers: 2
Lime Kiln
Pulp Dryers:
Fourdriniers 1, Fourdriniers 1, Fourdriniers 1
Energy Data:
Power boilers: 3
Steam turbines: 6 at 5, 5, 8, 8, 30, 27 MW
Electrical demand for mill: 1,613 MWh/D

ⓜResolute FP Augusta LLC
Augusta Mill
Ownership: 52.50% by Resolute Forest Products Canada Inc., 47.50% by Woodbridge Company
2434 Doug Bernard Pkwy
Augusta, GA 30906
USA
Mailing Address: PO Box 1647, Augusta, GA 30913, USA
Phone: (1) 706-798-3440
Fax: (1) 706-312-6473
Email: info@resolutefp.com
Web Address: www.resolutefp.com
Personnel:
Gen. Mgr. (from 2014): Derrick Lindgren
Phone: (1) 706-798-3440
Fax: (1) 706-312-6473
Email: derrick.lindgren@resolutefp.com
Prod. Mgr. (From July 2014): Wayne Griffin
Phone: (1) 706-798-3440
Fax: (1) 706-312-6473
Email: wayne.griffin@resolutefp.com
Quality Mgr.: Brian Norris
Phone: (1) 706-798-3440 Ext. 300
Fax: (1) 706-312-6473
Email: bnorris@resolutefp.com
Finan. Mgr.: Barbara Cole
Phone: (1) 706-798-3440 Ext. 100
Fax: (1) 706-312-6473
Email: bcole@resolutefp.com
Safety Mgr.: Jim Herrmann
Phone: (1) 706-798-3440 Ext: 266
Fax: (1) 706-312-6473
Email: jim.herrmann@resolutefp.com

Exec. Asist. to Gen. Mgr.: Willa J. Thomas
Phone: (1) 706-798-3440 Ext. 101
Fax: (1) 706-312-6473
Email: willia.thomas@resolutefp.com
Total Employees at this Location: 266
Type of Operation: Pulp mill, Paper mill
Pulp Grades and Capacities:
Total pulp capacity: 448,361 st/y
Mechanical Pulp: 344,636 st/y
Recycled Pulping: 103,726 st/y
Pulp Mill Data:
Mechanical Pulping Systems:
TMP systems: 4
Recycled Fiber Treatment Lines:
Flotation deinking lines: 1 at 200,000 admt/y
Paper/Paperboard Grades and Capacities:
Total paper and paperboard capacity: 438,773 st/y
Newsprint: 438,773 st/y
Paper and Paperboard Mill Data:
Stock Preparation:
Pulpers: 2
Refiners: 2
Paper Machines: 2
No. 1, SymFormer, total capacity 204,630 st/y, Trim width 300 in, Newsprint
No. 2, SymFormer, total capacity 234,144 st/y, Trim width 324 in, Newsprint
Finishing Equipment:
Winders: 2
Energy Data:
Power boilers: 2
TMP Reboiler
Electrical demand for mill: 3,028 MWh/D

ⓜRockTenn Co.
Ownership: Public
504 Thrasher St
Norcross, GA 30071
USA
Mailing Address: PO Box 4098, Norcross, GA 30091-4098, USA
Phone: (1) 770-448-2193
Fax: (1) 770-263-4483
Email: webmaster@rocktenn.com
Web Address: www.rocktenn.com
Personnel:
CEO: Steven C. Voorhees
Phone: (1) 770-448-2193
Fax: (1) 770-263-4483
Email: svoorhess@rocktenn.com
Pres., Paper Solution: James B. Porter III
Phone: (1) 770-448-2193
Fax: (1) 770-263-4483
Email: jporter@rocktenn.com
Pres., Packaging Solutions: Michael E. Kiepura
Phone: (1) 770-448-2193
Fax: (1) 770-263-4483
Email: mkiepura@rocktenn.com
Exec. VP. & CFO: Ward H. Dickson
Phone: (1) 770-448-2193
Fax: (1) 770-263-4483
Exec. VP., Market Develop.: Richard E. Steed
Phone: (1) 770-448-2193
Fax: (1) 770-263-4483
Email: rsteed@rocktenn.com
Exec. VP., HR: Jennifer Graham Johnson
Phone: (1) 770-448-2193
Fax: (1) 770-263-4483
Email: jjohnson@rocktenn.com
Exec. VP., Gen. Counsel & Sec.: Robert B. McIntosh
Phone: (1) 770-448-2193
Fax: (1) 770-263-4483
Email: rmcintosh@rocktenn.com
Exec. VP., Mill Oper.: Thomas M. Stigers
Phone: (1) 770-448-2193
Fax: (1) 770-263-4483
Email: tstigers@rocktenn.com
Exec. VP., Merchandising Displays & Folding Cartons: Craig A. Gunckel
Phone: (1) 770-448-2193

Fax: (1) 770-263-4483
Snr. VP & Gen. Mgr. Recycling: Gregory L. King
Phone: (1) 770-448-2193
Fax: (1) 770-263-4483
Email: gking@rocktenn.com
Snr. VP & Snr. Environ. Counsel: Nina E. Butler
Phone: (1) 770-448-2193
Fax: (1) 770-263-4483
Email: nbutler@rocktenn.com
Total Employees of Company: 25,800
Total Employees at this Location: 350
Mill Locations:
RockTenn Co., Demopolis Mill, 28270 US Hwy 80 W, Demopolis, AL 36732-5121, USA, Capacity: 339,864 st/y, (Pulp mill, Paperboard mill)
Phone: (1) 334-289-1242
Fax: (1) 334-289-6410
RockTenn Co., Battle Creek Mill, 177 Angell St, Battle Creek, MI 49015-1958, USA, Capacity: 159,936 st/y, (Paperboard mill)
Phone: (1) 269-963-5511
Fax: (1) 269-969-7166
RockTenn Co., Chattanooga Mill, 701 Manufacturers Rd, Chattanooga, TN 37405, USA, Capacity: 139,944 st/y, (Paperboard mill)
Phone: (1) 423-266-7381
Fax: (1) 423-265-1496
RockTenn Co., Cincinnati Mill, 3347 Madison Rd, Cincinnati, OH 45209, USA, Capacity: 54,978 st/y, (Paperboard mill)
Phone: (1) 513-871-5000
Fax: (1) 513-533-2154
RockTenn Co., Coshocton Mill, 500 N 4th St, Coshocton, OH 43812-1119, USA, Capacity: 309,876 st/y, (Paperboard mill)
Phone: (1) 740-622-6543
Fax: (1) 740-622-5297
RockTenn Co., Dallas Mill, 1120 E Clarendon Dr, Dallas, TX 75203, USA, Capacity: 127,092 st/y, (Paperboard mill)
Phone: (1) 214-941-3400
Fax: (1) 214-941-8048
RockTenn Co., Stroudsburg Mill, Paper Mill Rd, Delaware Water Gap, PA 18327, USA, Capacity: 79,968 st/y, (Paperboard mill)
Phone: (1) 570-476-0120
Fax: (1) 570-476-9553
RockTenn Co., Eaton Mill, 800A S Romy St, Eaton, IN 47338, USA, Capacity: 63,903 st/y, (Paperboard mill)
Phone: (1) 765-396-3317
Fax: (1) 765-396-9243
RockTenn Co., Fernandina Beach Mill, 600 North 8th Street, Fernandina Beach, FL 32034-3321, USA, Capacity: 929,985 st/y, (Pulp mill, Paperboard mill)
Phone: (1) 904-277-5854, 904-261-5551
Fax: (1) 904-277-5888
RockTenn Co., Florence Mill, 2202 Paper Mill Road, Florence, SC 29506 , USA, Capacity: 682,941 st/y, (Paperboard mill)
Phone: (1) 843-667-6252, 843-662-0313
Fax: (1) 843-673-0310
RockTenn Co., Hodge Mill, Mill Street, C/S 3700, Hodge, LA 71247-3700, USA, Capacity: 825,027 st/y, (Paper mill, Paperboard mill)
Phone: (1) 318-259-4421
Fax: (1) 318-259-5355
Email: webmaster@rocktenn.com
RockTenn Co., Hopewell Mill, 910 Industrial St, Hopewell, VA 23860, USA, Capacity: 550,137 st/y, (Pulp mill, Paperboard mill)
Phone: (1) 804-541-9600
Fax: (1) 804-541-9770
RockTenn Co., La Tuque Mill, 1000 Chemin de L'Usine, La Tuque, QC, Canada G9X 3P8, Capacity: 475,881 st/y, (Paperboard mill)
Phone: (1) 819-676-8100
Fax: (1) 819-676-8145
RockTenn Co., Panama City Mill, One Everitt Avenue, Panama City, FL 32401-6900, USA, Capacity: 335,937 st/y, (Pulp mill, Paperboard mill)
Phone: (1) 850-785-4311
Fax: (1) 850-763-6290

Georgia

RockTenn Co., Saint Paul Mill, 2250 Wabash Ave, Saint Paul, MN 55114-1895, USA, Capacity: 368,067 st/y, (Paperboard mill)
Phone: (1) 651-641-4938
Fax: (1) 651-641-4791
RockTenn Co., Seminole Mill, 9469 Eastport Rd, Jacksonville, FL 32226-6998, USA, Capacity: 600,117 st/y, (Paperboard mill)
Phone: (1) 904-751-6400
Fax: (1) 904-714-3276
RockTenn Co., Missisquoi Mill, Mill St, Sheldon Springs, VT 05485, USA, (Paperboard mill)
Phone: (1) 802-933-7733
Fax: (1) 802-933-5326
RockTenn Co., Stevenson Mill, 1611 County Rd 85, Stevenson, AL 35772-0908, USA, Capacity: 885,003 st/y, (Pulp mill, Paperboard mill)
Phone: (1) 256-437-2161
Fax: (1) 256-437-3301
RockTenn Co., Uncasville Mill, 125 Depot Rd, Uncasville, CT 06382, USA, Capacity: 329,154 st/y, (Paperboard mill)
Phone: (1) 860-848-1500
Fax: (1) 860-848-1956
RockTenn Co., West Point Mill, 19th & Main Sts, West Point, VA 23181, USA, Capacity: 896,070 st/y, (Pulp mill, Paper mill, Paperboard mill)
Phone: (1) 804-843-5000
Fax: (1) 804-843-5439
Email: webmaster@rocktenn.com
RockTenn Co., Tacoma Mill, 801 East Portland Ave, Tacoma, WA 98421, USA, Capacity: 424,830 st/y, (Pulp mill, Paper mill, Paper mill, Paperboard mill)
Phone: (1) 253-572-2150
Fax: (1) 253-596-0159
RockTenn Co., Solvay Mill, 53 Industrial Drive, Syracuse, NY 13204-1035, USA, Capacity: 805,035 st/y, (Paperboard mill)
Phone: (1) 315-484-9050
Fax: (1) 315-484-9434
Email: webmaster@rocktenn.com
Seven Hills Paperboard, LLC, Lynchburg Mill (49% owned), 1801 Concord Turnpike-Lower Basin, Lynchburg, VA 24504-0980, USA, Capacity: 103,173 st/y, (Paperboard mill)
Phone: (1) 434-847-5521
Fax: (1) 434-846-4611
Email: dvandeford@rocktenn.com

ⓘSchweitzer-Mauduit International Inc.
100 North Point Center East, Suite 600
Alpharetta, GA 30022-8246
USA
Phone: (1) 770-569-4200
Fax: (1) 770-569-4212
Email: products@swm-us.com
Web Address: www.swmintl.com
Personnel:
Chmn. & CEO: Frederic Villoutreix
Phone: (1) 770-569-4200
Fax: (1) 770-569-4275
Email: frederic.villoutreix@swm-us.com
Exec. VP, CFO: Jeffrey Cook
Phone: (1) 770-569-4200
Fax: (1) 770-569-4212
Email: jeff.cook@swm-us.com
Exec. VP, Paper Bus.: Otto Herbst
Phone: (1) 770-569-4200
Fax: (1) 770-569-4212
Email: otto.herbst@swm-us.com
Exec. VP, Tobacco Bus.: Michel Fievez
Phone: (1) 770-569-4200
Fax: (1) 770-569-4212
Email: michel.fievez@swm-us.com
COO: Stephen (Steve) Dunmead
Phone: (1) 770-569-4200
Fax: (1) 770-569-4212
Email: steve.dunmead@swm-us.com
Contr. (From November 2013): Bob Cardin
Phone: (1) 770-569-4200
Fax: (1) 770-569-4212
Total Employees of Company: 3,000

Total Employees at this Location: 80
Mill Locations:
China Tobacco Mauduit (Jiangmen) Paper Industry Company Ltd., Jiangmen Mill (50% owned), Aizia Ling, Fengsheng Industrial Base West Zone, Tangxia Township, Jiangmen 529085, China, Capacity: 19,841 st/y, (Paper mill)
Phone: (86) 750 3132 300/ 3626 262
Fax: (86) 750 3385 228
Email: hr@ct-pdm.com, lihuining@ct-pdm.com
Papeteries de Mauduit SA, Mauduit Mill, Kérisole BP 34, F-29393 Quimperlé, France, Capacity: 66,138 st/y, (Pulp mill, Paper mill)
Phone: (33) 2 98 06 20 00
Fax: (33) 2 98 06 20 94
Papeteries de Saint-Girons, Saint-Girons Mill, Faubourg de la Moulasse, PO Box 20071, F-09201 Eycheil, Saint-Girons, France, Capacity: 16,534 st/y, (Pulp mill, Paper mill)
Phone: (33) 5 34 14 35 00
Fax: (33) 5 61 66 77 22
Schweitzer-Mauduit do Brasil, Santanésia do Piraí Mill (99% owned), Av. Darcy Vargas 325 5° Distrito de Piraí, 27195-000 Santanésia do Piraí, RJ, Brazil, Capacity: 40,785 st/y, (Paper mill)
Phone: (55) 24 2447 5000/5200
Fax: (55) 24 2443 5570
Schweitzer-Mauduit International Inc., Medan Mill, Jln. Brigjend. Zein Hamid Km 6.9, Titi Kuning, 20146 Medan, Indonesia, Capacity: 3,527 st/y, (Paper mill)
Phone: (62) 61 7867 648/ 973
Fax: (62) 61 7863 004
Schweitzer-Mauduit International Inc., Ancram Mill, 2424 State Route 82, Ancram, NY 12502-5414, USA, Capacity: 10,000 st/y, (Paper mill)
Phone: (1) 518-329-4222
Fax: (1) 518-329-1161
Schweitzer-Mauduit International Inc., Spotswood Mill, 85 Main St, Spotswood, NJ 08884, USA, Capacity: 47,000 st/y, (Pulp mill, Paper mill)
Phone: (1) 732-723-6100
Fax: (1) 732-251-3814

ⓘSP Fiber Technologies LLC (SPFT)
709 Papermill Road
Dublin, GA 31027
USA
Phone: (1) 478-272-1600
Fax: (1) 478-275-5301
Web Address: spfibertech.com
Personnel:
Pres. & CEO (from end 2013): Allen Byrd
Phone: (1) 478-272-1600
Fax: (1) 478-275-5301
CFO (From Dec. 23, 2013): Dwayne Miller
Phone: (1) 478-272-1600
Fax: (1) 404-979-6615
VP, Manuf.: Edward Bortz
Email: edward.bortz@spfibertech.com
VP, HR.: John Lee
Phone: (1) 478-272-1600
Fax: (1) 478-275-5301
Email: john.lee@spfibertech.com
Corp. Contr.: Tom Ryan
Phone: (1) 478-272-1600
Fax: (1) 404-979-6615
Gen. Mgr.- Dublin Mill: Karl Christiansen
Phone: (1) 478-272-1600
Fax: (1) 404-979-6615
Email: karl.christiansen@spfibertech.com
Power Plt. Maint. Mgr. (Interim): Kellam Orr
Phone: (1) 478-272-1600
Fax: (1) 478-275-5301
Procurement & Recycling Dir.: Beverly Timmins
Phone: (1) 478-272-1600
Fax: (1) 404-979-6615
Mill Locations:
SP Fiber Technologies LLC (SPFT), Dublin Mill, 709 Papermill Rd, Dublin, GA 31027, USA, Capacity: 589,097 st/y, (Pulp mill, Paper mill)
Phone: (1) 478-272-1600

Fax: (1) 478-275-5301
SP Fiber Technologies LLC (SPFT), Newberg Mill, 1301 Wynooski St, Newberg, OR 97132, USA, Capacity: 226,273 st/y, (Pulp mill, Paper mill)
Phone: (1) 503-538-2151
Fax: (1) 503-537-6322

ⓘSP Fiber Technologies LLC (SPFT)
Dublin Mill
Previously SP Newsprint Co.
709 Papermill Rd
Dublin, GA 31027
USA
Mailing Address: 709 Papermill Road, Dublin, GA 31027, USA
Phone: (1) 478-272-1600
Fax: (1) 478-275-5301
Web Address: spfibertech.com
Personnel:
Gen. Mgr.: Karl Christiansen
Phone: (1) 478-272-1600
Fax: (1) 478-275-5301
Email: karl.christianson@spfibertech.com
Power Maint. Mgr. (Interim): Kellam Orr
Phone: (1) 478-272-1600
Fax: (1) 478-275-5301
Email: kellam.orr@spfibertech.com
Total Employees at this Location: 280
Type of Operation: Pulp mill, Paper mill
Pulp Grades and Capacities:
Total pulp capacity: 601,732 st/y
Recycled Pulping: 601,732 st/y
Pulp Mill Data:
Pulp Lines: 2
Bleach Plant Systems: 1
Recycled Pulp Line, Sequence: P, Capacity 660,000 admt/y
Recycled Fiber Treatment Lines:
Pulpers: 4 at 1,200,000 admt/y
Washing deinking lines: 2 at 595,000 admt/y
Paper/Paperboard Grades and Capacities:
Total paper and paperboard capacity: 589,097 st/y
Newsprint: 153,472 st/y
Packaging papers: 107,037 st/y
Linerboard: 49,190 st/y
Corrugating medium/fluting: 279,398 st/y
Paper and Paperboard Mill Data:
Stock Preparation:
Refiners: 4
Paper Machines: 2
No. 1, Bel-Baie II, total capacity 232,176 st/y, Trim width 301 in, Newsprint, Packaging papers
No. 2, SpeedFormer HS, total capacity 356,921 st/y, Trim width 328 in, Packaging papers, Corrugating medium/fluting, Linerboard
Finishing Equipment:
Winders: 3
Calenders: 3
Rewinders: 1
Energy Data:
Power boilers: 2
HRSG boiler: 1
Combustion turbines: 1 at 38.8 MW
Steam turbines: 1 at 42 MW
Electrical demand for mill: 1,209 MWh/D

ⓘSP Fiber Technologies LLC (SPFT)
SP Tech- Dublin
Previously SP Newsprint Co.
709 Papermill Rd
Dublin, GA 31027
USA
Mailing Address: 709 Papermill Road, Dublin, GA 31027, USA
Phone: (1) 478-272-1600
Fax: (1) 478-275-5301
Web Address: spfibertech.com
Total Employees at this Location: 315
Type of Operation: Pulp mill, Paper mill

Idaho

ⓂSweetwater Paperboard
Austell Mill
Ownership: 100% by Caraustar Industries, Inc.
3500 Joe Jerkins Blvd
Austell, GA 30106-3227
USA
Mailing Address: PO Box 665, Austell, GA 30168, USA
 Phone: (1) 770-944-9350
 Fax: (1) 770-732-3402
 Email: info@caraustar.com
 Web Address: www.caraustar.com
Personnel:
 PM Tech. Assist.: Justin Mattingly
 Phone: (1) 770-944-9350
 Fax: (1) 770-732-3402
 Email: justin.mattingly@caraustar.com
 Tech. Serv. Mgr. - Mill Group (Eff May 2014): Tommy Wilson
 Phone: (1) 770-745-3715
 Fax: (1) 770-732-3402
 Email: tommy.wilson@caraustar.com
Total Employees at this Location: 80
Type of Operation: Paperboard mill
Pulp Grades and Capacities:
 Total pulp capacity: 122,662 st/y
 Recycled Pulping: 122,662 st/y
Pulp Mill Data:
 Recycled Fiber Treatment Lines:
 Pulpers: 3 at 112,000 admt/y
Paper/Paperboard Grades and Capacities:
 Total paper and paperboard capacity: 117,810 st/y
 Boxboard/cartonboard: 117,810 st/y
Paper and Paperboard Mill Data:
 Stock Preparation:
 Pulpers: 3
 Refiners: 2
Paper Machines: 1
 No. 1, cylinder (8), total capacity 117,810 st/y, Trim width 159 in, Boxboard/cartonboard
Finishing Equipment:
 Winders: 1
Energy Data:
 Power boilers: 1
 Steam turbines
 Electrical demand for mill: 164 MWh/D

ⓂWeyerhaeuser Co.
Flint River Mill
2449 Stagecoach Road
Oglethorpe, GA 31068
USA
Mailing Address: PO Box 238, Oglethorpe, GA 31068-0238, USA
 Phone: (1) 478-472-2527
 Email: pulpgeneral@weyerhaeuser.com
 Web Address: www.weyerhaeuser.com
Personnel:
 Environ. Mgr.: Jay Sum
 Phone: (1) 478-472-2527
 Email: jay.sum@weyerhaeuser.com
 Raw Mat. Mgr: Randy Starling
 Phone: (1) 478-472-5267
 Email: randy.starling@weyerhaeuser.com
 Utilities Oper. Mgr.: Leroy Porter
 Phone: (1) 478-472-5267
 Email: leroy.porter@weyerhaeuser.com
Total Employees at this Location: 270
Type of Operation: Pulp mill
Pulp Grades and Capacities:
 Total pulp capacity: 426,707 st/y
 Pulp available for market: 402,176 st/y
 Chemical Pulp: 426,707 st/y
Pulp Mill Data:
 Chemical Pulping Systems:
 Continuous digesters: 1
 Bleach Plant Systems: 1
 Chemical Pulping System, Type: Softwood Line, Sequence: O_2 DEoD

Chemical Recovery Equipment:
 Evaporator lines: 1
 Recovery boilers: 1
 Lime Kiln
Pulp Dryers:
 Fourdriniers 1
Energy Data:
 Power boilers: 1
 Steam turbines: 1 at 46 MW
 Electrical demand for mill: 901 MWh/D

ⓂWeyerhaeuser Co.
Port Wentworth Mill
1 Bonnybridge Rd
Port Wentworth, GA 31407
USA
 Phone: (1) 912-964-1271
 Fax: (1) 912-966-4339
 Email: pulpGeneral@weyerhaeuser.com
 Web Address: www.weyerhaeuser.com
Personnel:
 Mill Mgr.: Bob Williams
 Phone: (1) 912-964-1271
 Fax: (1) 912-966-4339
 Email: bob.williams2@weyerhaeuser.com
 Environ. Mgr.: Chris Blocker
 Phone: (1) 912-964-1271
 Fax: (1) 912-966-4339
 Email: chris.blocker@weyerhaeuser.com
 Manuf. Serv. Mgr.: Rick Hamilton
 Phone: (1) 912-964-1271
 Fax: (1) 912-966-4339
 Email: rick.hamilton@weyerhaeuser.com
 Utilites Oper. Mgr.: David Slagel
 Phone: (1) 912-964-1271
 Fax: (1) 912-966-4339
 Email: david.slagel@weyerhaeuser.com
 HR. Mgr.: Amy Bashor
 Phone: (1) 912-964-1271
 Fax: (1) 912-966-4339
 Email: Amy.Bashor@weyerhaeuser.com
Total Employees at this Location: 320
Type of Operation: Pulp mill
Pulp Grades and Capacities:
 Total pulp capacity: 361,475 st/y
 Pulp available for market: 341,574 st/y
 Chemical Pulp: 361,475 st/y
Pulp Mill Data:
 Chemical Pulping Systems:
 Continuous digesters: 1
 Bleach Plant Systems: 1
 Chemical Pulping System, Type: Softwood, Sequence: O_2 DEoDED
 Chemical Recovery Equipment:
 Evaporator lines: 1
 Recovery boilers: 1
 Lime Kiln
 Pulp Dryers:
 Fourdriniers 1
Energy Data:
 Power boilers: 4
 Steam turbines: 4 at 73 MW
 Electrical demand for mill: 853 MWh/D

IDAHO

ⓗBoise Paper
Ownership: 100% by Packaging Corp. of America
1111 W Jefferson St, Ste 200
Boise, ID 83702-5388
USA
Mailing Address: PO Box 990050, Boise, ID 83799-0050, USA
 Phone: (1) 208-384-7000
 Fax: (1) 208-384-7189
 Email: PaperQuestions@BoisePaper.com, marketpulp@boiseinc.com
 Web Address: www.boisepaper.com
Personnel:
 Pres. & CEO: Alexander Toeldte
 Phone: (1) 208-384-6161
 Fax: (1) 208-384-7189
 Email: alexandertoeldte@boiseinc.com
 Exec. VP & COO: Judith M Lassa
 Phone: (1) 208-384-6161
 Fax: (1) 208-384-7189
 Email: judithlassa@boiseinc.com
 Snr. VP. & CFO: Samuel K. Cotterell
 Phone: (1) 208-384-6161
 Fax: (1) 208-384-7189
 Email: samuelcotterell@boiseinc.com
 Snr. VP Technology & Supply Chain: Bob Strenge
 Phone: (1) 208-384-6161
 Fax: (1) 208-384-7189
 Email: bobstrenge@boiseinc.com
 Snr. VP, Gen. Counsel, Sec.: Karen E. Gowland
 Phone: (1) 208-384-7394
 Fax: (1) 208-384-4912
 Email: karengowland@boiseinc.com
 VP, HR & Corp. Commun.: Virgina Aulin
 Phone: (1) 208-384-6161
 Fax: (1) 208-384-7189
 Email: virginiaaulin@boiseinc.com
 VP, Contr.: Bernadette Madarieta
 Phone: (1) 208-384-6161
 Fax: (1) 208-384-7189
 Email: bernadettemadarieta@boiseinc.com
 VP, CIO: Robert Egan
 Phone: (1) 208-384-6161
 Fax: (1) 208-384-7189
 Email: robertegan@boiseinc.com
 VP, Paper Manuf.: Terry Ward
 Phone: (1) 208-384-6161
 Fax: (1) 208-384-7189
 Email: terryward@boiseinc.com
 VP, Corp. Develop.: Bob Tracy
 Phone: (1) 208-384-6161
 Fax: (1) 208-384-7189
 Email: bobtracy@boiseinc.com
Mill Locations:
 Boise Paper, International Falls Mill, 400 Second St, International Falls, MN 56649-2327, USA, Capacity: 424,736 st/y, (Pulp mill, Paper mill)
 Phone: (1) 218-285-5011
 Fax: (1) 218-285-5210
 Boise Paper, Jackson Mill, 4585 Industrial Rd, Jackson, AL 36545, USA, Capacity: 485,413 st/y, (Pulp mill, Paper mill)
 Phone: (1) 251-246-4461
 Fax: (1) 251-246-7643
 Boise Paper, Wallula Mill, 31831 West Hwy 12, Wallula, WA 99363, USA, Capacity: 324,828 st/y, (Pulp mill, Paper mill, Paperboard mill)
 Phone: (1) 509-547-2411
 Fax: (1) 509-545-3298

ⓂClearwater Paper Corporation
Lewiston Mill
803 Mill Rd
Lewiston, ID 83501
USA
Mailing Address: PO Box 1126, Lewiston, ID 83501-1126, USA
 Phone: (1) 208-799-0123/208-799-1644 (Terri Rice)
 Fax: (1) 208-799-1488
 Web Address: www.clearwaterpaper.com
Personnel:
 VP, Mill Oper. (since August 2013): Jay Backus
 Phone: (1) 208-799-0123
 Fax: (1) 208-799-1488
 Email: jay.backus@clearwaterpaper.com
 Plt. Mgr.: Donnie Ely
 Phone: (1) 208-799-0123
 Fax: (1) 208-799-1488
 Email: donnie.ely@clearwaterpaper.com
 Pulp/P&R/Utilities Mgr: Don Holmes
 Phone: (1) 208-799-0123
 Fax: (1) 208-799-1488

Email: don.homes@clearwaterpaper.com
Purch. Mgr.: Traci Greco
Phone: (1) 208-799-1608
Fax: (1) 208-799-1488
Email: traci.greco@clearwaterpaper.com
Fiber Resource Mgr.: Nick Jagelski
Phone: (1) 208-791-6889
Fax: (1) 208-799-1969
Email: nick.jagelski@clearwaterpaper.com
Environ. Mgr.: Sue Somers
Phone: (1) 208-799-4104
Fax: (1) 208-799-1788
Email: sue.somers@clearwaterpaper.com
Mgr., Mill Tech. Serv.: Howard Ray
Phone: (1) 208-799-1030
Fax: (1) 208-799-1488
Email: howard.ray@clearwaterpaper.com
Snr. HR Mgr: Scott M. Corbitt
Phone: (1) 208-799-1226
Fax: (1) 208-799-1524
Email: scott.corbitt@clearwaterpaper.com
Total Employees at this Location: 858
Type of Operation: Pulp mill, Paper mill, Paperboard mill
Pulp Grades and Capacities:
Total pulp capacity: 628,305 st/y
Pulp available for market: 79,968 st/y
Chemical Pulp: 628,305 st/y

Pulp Mill Data:
Chemical Pulping Systems:
Batch digesters: 12
Continuous digesters: 2
Bleach Plant Systems: 2
Chemical Pulping System - 1, Type: Softwood, Sequence: O_2 DEoDD, Capacity 400,000 admt/y
Chemical Pulping System - 2, Type: Sawdust, Sequence: DEopD, Capacity 145,000 admt/y
Chemical Recovery Equipment:
Evaporator lines: 1
Recovery boilers: 2
Lime Kiln
Pulp Dryers:
Fourdriniers 1, Ross Dryer 1
Paper/Paperboard Grades and Capacities:
Total paper and paperboard capacity: 622,965 st/y
Tissue: 189,924 st/y
Boxboard/cartonboard: 433,041 st/y
Paper and Paperboard Mill Data:
Stock Preparation:
Pulpers: 3
Refiners: 7
Paper Machines: 5
No. 1 L, crescent former, total capacity 38,199 st/y, Trim width 156 in, Tissue
No. 2 L, crescent former, total capacity 74,970 st/y, Trim width 206 in, Tissue
No. 3 L, crescent former, total capacity 76,755 st/y, Trim width 204 in, Tissue
B1, Bel-Bond, total capacity 203,133 st/y, Trim width 204 in, Boxboard/cartonboard
B2, (PE Coater), Bel-Bond, total capacity 229,908 st/y, Trim width 204 in, Boxboard/cartonboard
Coating Machines: 2
CM 1, total capacity 203,153 st/y., on machine
CM 2, total capacity 229,938 st/y., on machine
Finishing Equipment:
Rewinders: 2
Energy Data:
Power boilers: 4
Steam turbines: 4 at 114 MW
Electrical demand for mill: 2,342 MWh/D

ILLINOIS

ⓜAhlstrom Engine Filtration, L.L.C.
Taylorville Mill
Ownership: Ahlstrom Corporation Oy
1200 E Elm St
Taylorville, IL 62568
USA
Mailing Address: PO Box 680, Taylorville, IL 62568, USA
Phone: (1) 217-824-9611
Fax: (1) 217-824-9514
Email: investor@ahlstrom.com, corporate.communications@ahlstrom.com
Web Address: www.ahlstrom.com
Personnel:
Plt. Mgr.: Michael Hady
Phone: (1) 217-824-9611
Fax: (1) 217-824-9514
Email: mike.hady@ahlstrom.com
HR Mgr.: Terry Dolenc
Phone: (1) 217-824-9611
Fax: (1) 217-824-9514
Email: terry.dolenc@ahlstrom.com
Total Employees at this Location: 131
Type of Operation: Paper mill
Paper/Paperboard Grades and Capacities:
Total paper and paperboard capacity: 26,000 st/y
Specialty and industrial: 26,000 st/y
Paper and Paperboard Mill Data:
Paper Machines: 1
PM 1, deltaformer, total capacity 26,000 st/y, Trim width 126 in, Specialty and industrial
Finishing Equipment:
Rewinders: 2
Energy Data:
Power boilers: 2

ⓜFutureMark Paper Group
Alsip Mill
Mill is closed (was indefinitely closed by late August 2014)
13101 S Pulaski Rd
Alsip, IL 60803
USA
Phone: (1) 708-272-8700, 866-580-8325
Fax: (1) 708-389-8237
Web Address: www.futuremarkpaper.com
Personnel:
VP Oper. (from Jan 1, 2014): Everett O'Neill
Phone: (1) 708-272-8700
Fax: (1) 708-389-8237
Email: everett.oneill@futuremarkpaper.com
Qlty. System Mgr.: Tanuj Bajaj
Phone: (1) 708-272-8700
Fax: (1) 708-389-8237
Email: tanuj.bajaj@futuremarkpaper.com
Utility Mgr.: Rick Flowers
Phone: (1) 708-272-8700
Fax: (1) 708-389-8237
Email: rick.flowers@futuremarkpaper.com
Total Employees at this Location: 170
Type of Operation: Pulp mill, Paper mill
Pulp Mill Data:
Pulp Lines: 1
Bleach Plant Lines:
Recycled Pulp Line, Sequence: P
Recycled Fiber Treatment Lines:
Pulpers
Paper and Paperboard Mill Data:
Stock Preparation:
Pulpers: 1
Paper Machines: 1
No. 1, SymFormer R, total capacity 164,184 st/y, Trim width 236 in
Coating Machines: 1
PM 5, total capacity 153,219 st/y., on machine
Finishing Equipment:
Supercalenders: 1
Energy Data:
Power boilers: 2

ⓜOx Paperboard LLC
Pekin Mill
1525 S 2nd St
Pekin, IL 61554
USA
Mailing Address: PO Box 520, Pekin, IL 61554-0520, USA
Phone: (1) 309-346-4118
Fax: (1) 309-346-2150
Web Address: www.oxpaperboard.com
Personnel:
Gen. Mgr.: Jeff Lyman
Phone: (1) 309-346-4118 Ext: 270
Fax: (1) 309-346-2150
Email: jlyman@oxpaperboard.com
Process/ Environ. Engineer Mgr.II: Clayton Staley
Phone: (1) 309-346-4118
Fax: (1) 309-346-2150
Email: cstaley@oxpaperboard.com
Total Employees at this Location: 47
Type of Operation: Paperboard mill
Pulp Grades and Capacities:
Total pulp capacity: 43,779 st/y
Recycled Pulping: 43,779 st/y
Pulp Mill Data:
Recycled Fiber Treatment Lines:
Recycled packaging pulping lines
Paper/Paperboard Grades and Capacities:
Total paper and paperboard capacity: 42,840 st/y
Boxboard/cartonboard: 42,840 st/y
Paper and Paperboard Mill Data:
Stock Preparation:
Pulpers: 3
Refiners: 3
Paper Machines: 1
No. 1, cylinder (8), total capacity 42,840 st/y, Trim width 67 in, Boxboard/cartonboard
Finishing Equipment:
Calenders: 1
Rewinders: 1
Sheeters: 1
Energy Data:
Power boilers: 2
Steam turbines: 1 at 1.5 MW
Electrical demand for mill: 57 MWh/D

ⓘIVEX Protective Packaging
Ownership: 100% by Forest Resources LLC
8100 South 77th Ave
Bridgeview, IL 60455
USA
Phone: (1) 708-728-8000
Fax: (1) 708-458-5221
Web Address: www.ivexpackaging.com
Personnel:
Pres.: Paul Gaulin
Phone: (1) 708-728-8000
Fax: (1) 708-458-5221
VP, Sls. & Mktg.: Tom Trauscht
Phone: (1) 708-728-8000
Fax: (1) 708-458-5221
Account Mgr.: Bruce MacLean

ⓘⓜIvex Specialty Paper, LLC
Peoria Mill
Ownership: 100% by Forest Resources LLC
1 Sloan St
Peoria, IL 61603
USA
Mailing Address: PO Box 1820, Peoria, IL 61656, USA
Phone: (1) 309-686-3830
Fax: (1) 309-686-0324
Web Address: www.ivexsp.com
Personnel:
Mill Mgr.: Mark Reardon
Phone: (1) 309-686-3830 Ext: 7112
Fax: (1) 309-686-0324
Prod. Mgr.: Robert Gruse
Phone: (1) 309-686-3830
Fax: (1) 309-686-0324
HR. Mgr.: Angie Spann

Illinois

Phone: (1) 309-686-3830 Ext: 7110
Fax: (1) 309-686-0324
Account. & Purch.: Chuck Erwin
Phone: (1) 309-686-3830 Ext: 7115
Fax: (1) 309-686-0324
Total Employees at this Location: 45
Type of Operation: Paper mill
Paper/Paperboard Grades and Capacities:
Total paper and paperboard capacity: 11,000 st/y
Packaging papers
Paper and Paperboard Mill Data:
Stock Preparation:
Pulpers: 3
Refiners: 3
Paper Machines: 1
PM 1, fourdrinier, total capacity 11,000 st/y, Trim width 76 in, Packaging papers
Coating Machines: 1
No. 1, total capacity 16,000 st/y., off machine
Finishing Equipment:
Calenders: 2
Energy Data:
Power boilers: 2

⊕KapStone Paper and Packaging Corp
Ownership: Public
1101 Skokie Blvd. Suite 300
Northbrook, IL 60062
USA
Phone: (1) 847-239-8800
Fax: (1) 847-205-7551
Email: information@kapstonepaper.com
Web Address: www.kapstonepaper.com
Personnel:
Chmn. & CEO: Roger W. Stone
Phone: (1) 847-239-8800
Fax: (1) 847-205-7551
Email: roger.stone@kapstonepaper.com
Pres., COO & Dir.: Matthew Kaplan
Phone: (1) 847-239-8800
Fax: (1) 847-205-7551
Email: matthew.kaplan@kapstonepaper.com
VP & CFO: Andrea K. Tarbox
Phone: (1) 847-239-8800
Fax: (1) 847-205-7551
Email: andrea.tarbox@kapstonepaper.com
Pres. KapStone Kraft Paper Corp.: Randy J. Nebel
Phone: (1) 847-239-8800
Fax: (1) 847-205-7551
Pres. KapStone Container Corp.: Timothy P. Keneally
Phone: (1) 847-239-8800
Fax: (1) 847-205-7551
Reg. VP: Jeff Corke
Phone: (1) 847-239-8800
Fax: (1) 847-205-7551
Email: jeff.corkel@kapstonepaper.com
VP: Mark Favre
Phone: (1) 847-239-8800
Fax: (1) 847-205-7551
Email: markfavre@kapstonepaper.com
Total Employees of Company: 4,601
Mill Locations:
KapStone Kraft Paper Corporation, Cowpens Mill, 139 Price Farm Rd, Cowpens, SC 29330, USA, Capacity: 239,904 st/y, (Paperboard mill)
Phone: (1) 864-463-9090, 864-463-1722
Fax: (1) 864-463-9585
Email: information@kapstonepaper.com
KapStone Kraft Paper Corporation, Longview Mill, 300 Fibre Way, Longview, WA 98632, USA, Capacity: 1,106,343 st/y, (Pulp mill, Paper mill, Paperboard mill)
Phone: (1) 360-425-1550
Fax: (1) 360-230-5135
KapStone Kraft Paper Corporation, Roanoke Rapids Mill, 100 Gaston Road, Roanoke Rapids, NC 27870-1911, USA, Capacity: 439,824 st/y, (Pulp mill, Paper mill, Paperboard mill)
Phone: (1) 252-533-6000
Fax: (1) 252-533-6401
Email: information@kapstonepaper.com
KapStone Paper Charleston Kraft LLC, North Charleston Mill, 5600 Virginia Ave, North Charleston, SC 29406, USA, Capacity: 878,187 st/y, (Paper mill, Paperboard mill)
Phone: (1) 843-745-3000
Fax: (1) 843-745-3067

⊕Packaging Corp. of America
Ownership: Public
1900 West Field Ct
Lake Forest, IL 60045
USA
Phone: (1) 847-482-3000/800-456-4725
Fax: (1) 847-482-4545
Web Address: www.packagingcorp.com
Personnel:
CEO: Mark W. Kowlzan
Phone: (1) 847-482-3000
Fax: (1) 847-482-4545
Email: mkowlzan@packagingcorp.com
Exec. VP, Corrugated Products: Thomas A. Hassfurther
Phone: (1) 847-482-3000
Fax: (1) 847-482-4545
Email: thassfurther@packagingcorp.com
Snr. VP & CFO: Richard B. West
Phone: (1) 847-482-3000
Fax: (1) 847-482-4545
Email: rwest@packagingcorp.com
Snr. VP. Sls. & Mktg. Corrugated Products: Thomas H. Walton
Phone: (1) 847-482-3000
Fax: (1) 847-482-4545
Email: twalton@packagingcorp.com
Snr. VP. Paper (From October 2013): Judith M. Lassa
Phone: (1) 847-482-2111
Fax: (1) 847-482-4545
Email: scalhoun@packagingcorp.com
VP, Sec. & Gen. Counsel: Kent A. Pflederer
Phone: (1) 847-482-3000
Fax: (1) 847-482-4545
Email: kpflederer@packagingcorp.com
VP., Containerboard Mill Oper. (From July 2013): Charles J. (Jack) Carter
Phone: (1) 847-482-3000
Fax: (1) 847-482-4545
Email: ccarter@packagingcorp.com
Total Employees of Company: 13,600
Total Employees at this Location: 200
Mill Locations:
Packaging Corp. of America, DeRidder Mill, 4200 Hwy 190 W, DeRidder, LA 70634, USA, Capacity: 968,898 st/y, (Pulp mill, Paperboard mill)
Phone: (1) 337-462-4300
Fax: (1) 337-462-4330
Boise Paper, International Falls Mill, 400 Second St, International Falls, MN 56649-2327, USA, Capacity: 424,736 st/y, (Pulp mill, Paper mill)
Phone: (1) 218-285-5011
Fax: (1) 218-285-5210
Boise Paper, Jackson Mill, 4585 Industrial Rd, Jackson, AL 36545, USA, Capacity: 485,413 st/y, (Pulp mill, Paper mill)
Phone: (1) 251-246-4461
Fax: (1) 251-246-7643
Boise Paper, Wallula Mill, 31831 West Hwy 12, Wallula, WA 99363, USA, Capacity: 324,828 st/y, (Pulp mill, Paper mill, Paperboard mill)
Phone: (1) 509-547-2411
Fax: (1) 509-545-3298
Packaging Corp. of America, Counce Mill, 6715 Hwy 57, Counce, TN 38326, USA, Capacity: 1,066,716 st/y, (Paperboard mill)
Phone: (1) 731-689-3111
Fax: (1) 731-689-1471
Packaging Corp. of America, Filer City Mill, 2246 Udell St, Filer City, MI 49634, USA, Capacity: 456,603 st/y, (Pulp mill, Paperboard mill)
Phone: (1) 231-723-9951
Fax: (1) 231-723-1395
Packaging Corp. of America, Tomahawk Mill, N9090 County Rd E, Tomahawk, WI 54487, USA, Capacity: 970,683 st/y, (Paperboard mill)
Phone: (1) 715-453-2131
Fax: (1) 715-453-0470
Packaging Corp. of America, Valdosta Mill, 5495 Lake Park-Clyattville Rd, Valdosta, GA 31601, USA, Capacity: 560,133 st/y, (Pulp mill, Paperboard mill)
Phone: (1) 229-559-7911
Fax: (1) 229-559-0546

⊕UPM North America
Ownership: UPM-Kymmene Corporation
999 Oakmont Plaza Drive, Suite 200
Westmont, IL 60559-5517
USA
Phone: (1) 630-850-3310, 866-300-4175
Fax: (1) 630-850-3325
Email: info@upm-kymmene.com
Web Address: www.upm-kymmene.com
Personnel:
VP, Gen. Mgr.: Angelo LaMantia
Phone: (1) 630-850-3310
Fax: (1) 630-850-3325
Email: angelo.lamantina@upm.com
VP, Converting Papers: John Smedley
Phone: (1) 630-850-3310
Fax: (1) 630-850-3325
Email: john.smedley@upm.com
Tech. Sls. Dir.: Ian Hamilton
Phone: (1) 630-850-3310
Fax: (1) 630-850-3325
Email: ian.hamilton@upm.com
Project Mgr., Inside Sls & Serv. Mgr.: Wade Smith
Phone: (1) 630-850-3310
Fax: (1) 630-850-3325
Email: wade.smith@upm.com
Mill Locations:
UPM North America, Madison Paper Mill, 1 Main Street, Madison, ME 04950, USA, Capacity: 242,014 st/y, (Pulp mill, Paper mill)
Phone: (1) 207-696-3307
Fax: (1) 207-696-1125
UPM North America, Blandin Paper Mill, 115 First St SW, Grand Rapids, MN 55744-3699, USA, Capacity: 396,183 st/y, (Paper mill)
Phone: (1) 218-327-6200
Fax: (1) 218-327-6212
Email: info@upm-kymmene.com

⊕United States Gypsum Co.
125 S Franklin St
Chicago, IL 60606-4678
USA
Mailing Address: PO Box 6721, Chicago, IL 60680-6721, USA
Phone: (1) 312-606-4000
Fax: (1) 312-606-3700
Email: usg4you@usg.com
Web Address: www.usg.com
Personnel:
Chmn., Pres & CEO: James S. Metcalf
Phone: (1) 312-606-4000
Fax: (1) 312-606-3700
Email: jmetcalf@usg.com
ExecVP, Gen. Counsel: Stanley L. Ferguson
Phone: (1) 312-606-4000
Fax: (1) 312-606-3700
Email: sferguson@usg.com
Exec. VP., Oper.: Christopher R. Griffin
Phone: (1) 312-606-4000
Fax: (1) 312-606-3700
Email: cgriffin@usg.com
Exec. VP. & CFO: Matthew F. Hilzinger
Phone: (1) 312-606-4000
Fax: (1) 312-606-3700
Email: mhilzinger@usg.com
Snr. VP. & Pres. & CEO L & W Supply Corp.: Brendan J. Deely
Phone: (1) 312-606-4000
Fax: (1) 312-606-3700
Email: bdeely@usg.com
Snr. VP. & Chief Technology Officer: Dominic A. Dannessa

Phone: (1) 312-606-4000
Fax: (1) 312-606-3700
Email: ddannessa@usg.com
Snr. VP, HR: Brian J. Cook
Phone: (1) 312-606-4000
Fax: (1) 312-606-3700
Email: bcook@usg.com
Snr. VP., Bus. Develop & Operational Serv.: D. Rick Lowes
Phone: (1) 312-606-4000
Fax: (1) 312-606-3700
Email: rlowes@usg.com
Corp. Accounting Mgr.: Mona Carroll
Phone: (1) 312-606-4000
Fax: (1) 312-606-3700
Email: mcarroll@usg.com
Total Employees of Company: 8,900
Mill Locations:
Otsego Paper Inc., Otsego Mill, 320 N Farmer St, Otsego, MI 49078, USA, Capacity: 199,920 st/y, (Pulp mill, Paperboard mill)
Phone: (1) 269-692-6141
Fax: (1) 269-692-2060
United States Gypsum Co., Galena Park Mill, 1201 Mayo Shell Rd, Galena Park, TX 77547, USA, Capacity: 74,970 st/y, (Paperboard mill)
Phone: (1) 713-308-5400
Fax: (1) 713-308-5401
United States Gypsum Co., North Kansas City Mill, 1115 Armour Rd, North Kansas City, MO 64116-3783, USA, Capacity: 76,041 st/y, (Paperboard mill)
Phone: (1) 816-471-4298
Fax: (1) 816-471-1463
United States Gypsum Co., Oakfield Mill, 275 Maple Avenue, Oakfield, NY 14125-0773, USA, Capacity: 79,968 st/y, (Paperboard mill)
Phone: (1) 585-948-5221
Fax: (1) 585-948-5018

INDIANA

ⓜHartford City Paper, LLC
Ownership: 100% by Forest Resources
501 S Spring St
Hartford City, IN 47348
USA
Mailing Address: PO Box 30, Hartford City, IN 47348, USA
Phone: (1) 765-348-5440
Fax: (1) 765-348-7355
Email: hcpmail@hcpaper.com
Web Address: www.atlasholdingsllc.com/business-segments/packaging.aspx?id=7
Personnel:
Gen. Mgr.: Phil Freel
Phone: (1) 765-348-5440
Fax: (1) 765-348-7355
Email: philf@hcpaper.com
VP Sls.: Daisy Hessler
Phone: (1) 765-348-5440
Fax: (1) 765-348-7355
Email: daisyh@hcpaper.com
Total Employees of Company: 83
Mill Locations:
Hartford City Paper, LLC, Hartford City Mill, 501 S Spring St, Hartford City, IN 47348, USA, Capacity: 132,090 st/y, (Paperboard mill)
Phone: (1) 765-348-5440
Fax: (1) 765-348-7355
Email: hcpmail@hcpaper.com

ⓜHartford City Paper, LLC
Hartford City Mill
501 S Spring St
Hartford City, IN 47348
USA
Mailing Address: PO Box 30, Hartford City, IN 47348, USA
Phone: (1) 765-348-5440
Fax: (1) 765-348-7355
Email: hcpmail@hcpaper.com
Web Address: www.atlasholdingsllc.com/business-segments/packaging.aspx?id=7
Personnel:
Gen. Mgr.: Phil Freel
Phone: (1) 765-348-5440
Fax: (1) 765-348-7355
Email: philf@hcpaper.com
VP. Sls. - HCP Recycling: Mike Friskney
Phone: (1) 260-347-4739
Fax: (1) 260-347-4150
Email: mikef@hcpaper.com
Div. Contr.: Brad Roddeffer
Phone: (1) 765-348-5440
Fax: (1) 765-348-7355
Email: bradr@hcpaper.com
Cust. Serv. Mgr.: Christy Manor
Phone: (1) 765-348-7364
Fax: (1) 765-348-7355
Email: christym@hcpaper.com
Total Employees at this Location: 76
Type of Operation: Paperboard mill
Pulp Grades and Capacities:
Total pulp capacity: 137,968 st/y
Recycled Pulping: 137,968 st/y
Pulp Mill Data:
Recycled Fiber Treatment Lines:
Pulpers: 1
Paper/Paperboard Grades and Capacities:
Total paper and paperboard capacity: 132,090 st/y
Packaging papers: 2,142 st/y
Specialty and industrial: 6,783 st/y
Corrugating medium/fluting: 123,165 st/y
Paper and Paperboard Mill Data:
Stock Preparation:
Pulpers: 1
Refiners: 2
Paper Machines: 1
No. 1, (with Valmet Hi-PLI Press Section), fourdrinier, total capacity 132,090 st/y, Trim width 168 in, Corrugating medium/fluting, Packaging papers, Specialty and industrial
Energy Data:
Power boilers: 2
Electrical demand for mill: 192 MWh/D

ⓜInternational Paper Co.
Newport Mill
Mill is a previous Temple-Inland mill
2585 E 200 North
Cayuga, IN 47928-8153
USA
Phone: (1) 765-492-3341
Fax: (1) 765-492-4832
Web Address: www.internationalpaper.com
Personnel:
Mill Mgr.: Derek Depuydt
Phone: (1) 765-492-3341 Ext.: 203
Fax: (1) 765-492-4832
Email: derek.depuydt@ipaper.com
Contr.: Craig Doty
Phone: (1) 765-492-3341 Ext.: 200
Fax: (1) 765-492-4832
Email: craig.doty@ipaper.com
HR Mgr.: Rusty Akers
Phone: (1) 765-492-3341 Ext.: 208
Fax: (1) 765-492-4321
Email: rusty.akers@ipaper.com
Eng. Mgr.: Paul M. Crowell
Phone: (1) 765-492-3341 Ext.: 358
Fax: (1) 765-492-4832
Email: paul.crowell@ipaper.com
Tech. Mgr.: Michael Curts
Phone: (1) 765-492-3341
Fax: (1) 765-492-4832
Email: mike.curts@ipaper.com
Total Employees at this Location: 133
Type of Operation: Paperboard mill
Pulp Grades and Capacities:
Total pulp capacity: 385,310 st/y
Recycled Pulping: 385,310 st/y
Pulp Mill Data:
Recycled Fiber Treatment Lines:
Pulpers: 3 at 400,000 admt/y
Paper/Paperboard Grades and Capacities:
Total paper and paperboard capacity: 369,852 st/y
Linerboard: 89,250 st/y
Corrugating medium/fluting: 78,540 st/y
Boxboard/cartonboard: 202,062 st/y
Paper and Paperboard Mill Data:
Stock Preparation:
Pulpers: 3
Refiners: 6
Paper Machines: 1
No. 1, fourdrinier, total capacity 369,852 st/y, Trim width 245 in, Linerboard, Corrugating medium/fluting, Boxboard/cartonboard
Finishing Equipment:
Calenders: 1
Rewinders: 1 at 400,000 st/y
Energy Data:
Power boilers
Electrical demand for mill: 448 MWh/D

ⓜPaperWorks Industries, Inc.
Wabash Mill
455 W Factory St
Wabash, IN 46992
USA
Mailing Address: PO Box 217, Wabash, IN 46992-0217, USA
Phone: (1) 260-563-3102
Fax: (1) 260-569-3404
Email: info@paperwrks.com
Web Address: www.paperwrks.com
Personnel:
Gen. Mgr.: Richard Townley
Phone: (1) 260-563-3102
Fax: (1) 260-569-3404
Email: richard.townley@paperwrks.com
Purch. Mgr.: Sherri Schnepp
Phone: (1) 260-563-3102
Fax: (1) 260-569-3404
Email: sherri.schnepp@paperwrks.com
HR Mgr.: Lynn Huddleston
Phone: (1) 260-563-3102
Fax: (1) 260-569-3404
Email: lynn.huddleston@paperwrks.com
Total Employees at this Location: 196
Type of Operation: Paperboard mill
Pulp Grades and Capacities:
Total pulp capacity: 141,170 st/y
Recycled Pulping: 141,170 st/y
Pulp Mill Data:
Recycled Fiber Treatment Lines:
Recycled packaging pulping lines: 1 at 143,629
Paper/Paperboard Grades and Capacities:
Total paper and paperboard capacity: 145,656 st/y
Boxboard/cartonboard: 145,656 st/y
Paper and Paperboard Mill Data:
Stock Preparation:
Pulpers: 6
Refiners: 6
Paper Machines: 2
No. 1, Ultraformer (8), total capacity 85,323 st/y, Trim width 108 in, Boxboard/cartonboard
No. 2, cylinder (10), total capacity 60,333 st/y, Trim width 88 in, Boxboard/cartonboard
Coating Machines: 2
PM 1, total capacity 94,246 st/y., on machine
PM 2, total capacity 62,831 st/y., on machine
Finishing Equipment:
Sheeters: 2
Energy Data:
Power boilers: 3

Iowa

ⓜRockTenn Co.
Eaton Mill
800A S Romy St
Eaton, IN 47338
USA
Phone: (1) 765-396-3317
Fax: (1) 765-396-9243
Web Address: www.rocktenn.com
Personnel:
Gen. Mgr.: Mike Mullinix
Phone: (1) 765-396-3317
Fax: (1) 765-396-9243
Email: mmullinix@rocktenn.com
Prod. Mgr.: Andrew Olfier
Phone: (1) 765-396-3317
Fax: (1) 765-396-9243
Email: aolfier@rocktenn.com
Supply Chain Mgr.: Greg Walters
Phone: (1) 765-396-3317
Fax: (1) 765-396-9243
Email: gwalters@rocktenn.com
Total Employees at this Location: 63
Type of Operation: Paperboard mill
Pulp Grades and Capacities:
Total pulp capacity: 64,050 st/y
Recycled Pulping: 64,050 st/y
Pulp Mill Data:
Recycled Fiber Treatment Lines:
Recycled packaging pulping lines
Paper/Paperboard Grades and Capacities:
Total paper and paperboard capacity: 63,903 st/y
Boxboard/cartonboard: 63,903 st/y
Paper and Paperboard Mill Data:
Stock Preparation:
Pulpers: 2
Refiners: 4
Paper Machines: 1
No. 1, cylinder (9), total capacity 63,903 st/y, Trim width 80 in, Boxboard/cartonboard
Energy Data:
Power boilers: 1

IOWA

ⓜInternational Paper Co.
Cedar Rapids Mill
4600 C Street SW
Cedar Rapids, IA 52404
USA
Mailing Address: PO Box 3250, Cedar Rapids, IA 52406-3250, USA
Phone: (1) 319-365-2100
Fax: (1) 319-365-0436
Web Address: www.internationalpaper.com
Personnel:
Mill Mgr. (From 2014): Clifford T. Murphy
Phone: (1) 319-365-2100
Fax: (1) 319-365-0436
Email: clifford.murphy@ipaper.com
Manuf. Mgr.: John Fields
Phone: (1) 319-365-2100
Fax: (1) 319-365-0436
Email: john.fields@ipaper.com
Maint. Mgr.: Patrick Geiger
Phone: (1) 319-365-2100
Fax: (1) 319-365-0436
Email: patrick.geiger@ipaper.com
Total Employees at this Location: 226
Type of Operation: Paperboard mill
Pulp Grades and Capacities:
Total pulp capacity: 1,021,605 st/y
Recycled Pulping: 1,021,605 st/y
Pulp Mill Data:
Recycled Fiber Treatment Lines:
Pulpers: 5 at 1,089,616 admt/y

Paper/Paperboard Grades and Capacities:
Total paper and paperboard capacity: 989,961 st/y
Linerboard: 388,059 st/y
Corrugating medium/fluting: 601,902 st/y
Paper and Paperboard Mill Data:
Stock Preparation:
Refiners: 8
Paper Machines: 2
No. 1, (PM has Concept IV MH Headbox and ENP-C @8500 PLI), fourdrinier, total capacity 451,962 st/y, Trim width 280 in, Corrugating medium/fluting
No. 2, (Bel Liner ENP-C), fourdrinier, total capacity 537,999 st/y, Trim width 274 in, Linerboard, Corrugating medium/fluting
Finishing Equipment:
Winders: 2 at 970,000 st/y
Energy Data:
Electrical demand for mill: 1,302 MWh/D

ⓜTama Paperboard
Tama Mill
Ownership: 100% by Caraustar Industries, Inc.
117 Siegel St
Tama, IA 52339-2616
USA
Phone: (1) 641-484-2884
Fax: (1) 641-484-4234
Web Address: www.caraustar.com
Personnel:
Oper. Mgr.: John A. Richter
Phone: (1) 641-484-2884
Fax: (1) 641-484-4234
Email: john.richter@caraustar.com
Sls. Mgr.: Margaret Wolfe
Phone: (1) 641-484-2884
Fax: (1) 641-484-4234
Email: margaret.wolfe@caraustar.com
Cust. Serv.: Kim McAdoo
Phone: (1) 641-484-2884
Fax: (1) 641-484-4234
Email: kim.mcadoo@caraustar.com
Total Employees at this Location: 92
Type of Operation: Paperboard mill
Pulp Grades and Capacities:
Total pulp capacity: 76,351 st/y
Recycled Pulping: 76,351 st/y
Pulp Mill Data:
Recycled Fiber Treatment Lines:
Pulpers: 1 at 58,422
Paper/Paperboard Grades and Capacities:
Total paper and paperboard capacity: 80,682 st/y
Boxboard/cartonboard: 80,682 st/y
Paper and Paperboard Mill Data:
Stock Preparation:
Pulpers: 3
Refiners: 5
Paper Machines: 1
No. 1, cylinder (8), total capacity 80,682 st/y, Trim width 86 in, Boxboard/cartonboard
Coating Machines: 1
No. 1, total capacity 72,090 st/y., on machine
Finishing Equipment:
Rewinders: 1
Sheeters: 1
Energy Data:
Power boilers: 1
Electrical demand for mill: 123 MWh/D

KANSAS

ⓜSonoco Products Co.
Hutchinson Mill
100 N Halstead
Hutchinson, KS 67501
USA
Mailing Address: PO Box 1267, Hutchinson, KS 67504-1267, USA
Phone: (1) 620-662-2331
Fax: (1) 620-662-4276
Web Address: www.sonoco.com
Personnel:
Qlty. Mgr.: Joe Black
Phone: (1) 620-662-2331
Fax: (1) 620-662-4276
Email: joe.black@sonoco.com
Admin. Mgr.: Dorcee Ayres
Phone: (1) 620-662-2331 ext. 149
Fax: (1) 620-662-4276
Email: dorcee.ayres@sonoco.com
Total Employees at this Location: 116
Type of Operation: Paperboard mill
Pulp Grades and Capacities:
Total pulp capacity: 101,485 st/y
Recycled Pulping: 101,485 st/y
Paper/Paperboard Grades and Capacities:
Total paper and paperboard capacity: 99,960 st/y
Boxboard/cartonboard: 99,960 st/y
Paper and Paperboard Mill Data:
Stock Preparation:
Pulpers: 5
Refiners: 17
Paper Machines: 2
No. 1, cylinder (8), total capacity 41,055 st/y, Trim width 81 in, Boxboard/cartonboard
No. 2, cylinder (8), total capacity 58,905 st/y, Trim width 102 in, Boxboard/cartonboard
Energy Data:
Power boilers: 1
Electrical demand for mill: 146 MWh/D

KENTUCKY

ⓜAhlstrom Filtration LLC
Madisonville Plant
Ownership: 100% by Ahlstrom Corporation Oy
215 Nebo Rd
Madisonville, KY 42431
USA
Mailing Address: PO Box 1708, Madisonville, KY 42431, USA
Phone: (1) 270-821-0140
Fax: (1) 270-824-1577
Email: investor@ahlstrom.com, corporate.communications@ahlstrom.com
Web Address: www.ahlstrom.com
Personnel:
Plt. Mgr.: Dennis L. Molle
Phone: (1) 270-824-1573
Fax: (1) 270-824-1577
Email: dennis.molle@ahlstrom.com
Total Employees at this Location: 130
Type of Operation: Paper mill
Paper/Paperboard Grades and Capacities:
Total paper and paperboard capacity: 22,999 st/y
Specialty and industrial: 22,999 st/y
Paper and Paperboard Mill Data:
Stock Preparation:
Pulpers: 2
Refiners: 2
Paper Machines: 1
PM 1, fourdrinier, total capacity 23,000 st/y, Trim width 120 in, Specialty and industrial
Energy Data:
Power boilers: 1

ⓜDomtar Corporation
Hawesville Mill
Hwy. 1406, 58 Wescor Road
Hawesville, KY 42348
USA

Kentucky

Mailing Address: PO Box 130, Hawesville, KY 42348, USA
Phone: (1) 270-927-6961
Fax: (1) 270-927-9929
Web Address: www.domtar.com
Personnel:
Gen. Mgr.: Steve Henry
Phone: (1) 270-927-6961
Fax: (1) 270-927-9929
Email: steve.henry@domtar.com
Maint. Mgr.: Larry Bryant
Phone: (1) 270-927-6961
Fax: (1) 270-927-9929
Email: larry.bryant@domtar.com
Reliability Eng.: Hanna Fortwendel
Phone: (1) 270-927-6961
Fax: (1) 270-927-9929
Email: hanna.fortwendel@domtar.com
Wood Procurement Mgr.: Dan Allard
Phone: (1) 270-927-7214
Fax: (1) 270-927-7237
Email: daniel.allard@domtar.com
Total Employees at this Location: 430
Type of Operation: Pulp mill, Paper mill
Pulp Grades and Capacities:
Total pulp capacity: 470,525 st/y
Pulp available for market: 108,218 st/y
Chemical Pulp: 470,525 st/y
Pulp Mill Data:
Chemical Pulping Systems:
Continuous digesters: 2
Pulp Lines: 1
Bleach Plant Systems: 2
Chemical Pulping System - No. 2, Type: Hardwood Line, Sequence: DEopD
Chemical Pulping System - No. 3, Type: Hardwood Line, Sequence: DEopD
Chemical Recovery Equipment:
Evaporator lines: 2
Recovery boilers: 2
Lime Kiln
Pulp Dryers:
Pulp Dryers 1
Paper/Paperboard Grades and Capacities:
Total paper and paperboard capacity: 571,074 st/y
Uncoated woodfree/freesheet: 571,074 st/y
Paper and Paperboard Mill Data:
Stock Preparation:
Pulpers: 1
Refiners: 3
Paper Machines: 2
No. 1, fourdrinier, total capacity 187,384 st/y, Trim width 274 in, Uncoated woodfree/freesheet
No. 2, fourdrinier, total capacity 383,690 st/y, Trim width 315 in, Uncoated woodfree/freesheet
Finishing Equipment:
Calenders: 2
Rewinders: 2
Energy Data:
Power boilers: 2
Steam turbines: 1 at 88.4 MW

ⓜInternational Paper Co.
Henderson Mill
1500 Commonwealth Dr
Henderson, KY 42420
USA
Phone: (1) 270-831-6000
Fax: (1) 270-830-9750
Web Address: www.internationalpaper.com
Personnel:
Mill Mgr.: Kally Hodgson
Phone: (1) 270-831-6000
Fax: (1) 270-830-9750
Email: kally.hodgson@ipaper.com
Prod. Mgr.: Michael Olive
Phone: (1) 270-831-6000
Fax: (1) 270-830-9750
Email: michael.olive@ipaper.com
Manuf. Mgr.: Bob Dekarske
Phone: (1) 270-831-6000
Fax: (1) 270-830-9750
Email: bob.dekarske@ipaper.com
Total Employees at this Location: 85
Type of Operation: Paperboard mill
Pulp Grades and Capacities:
Total pulp capacity: 227,409 st/y
Recycled Pulping: 227,409 st/y
Pulp Mill Data:
Recycled Fiber Treatment Lines:
Pulpers: 1 at 249,900 admt/y
Paper/Paperboard Grades and Capacities:
Total paper and paperboard capacity: 219,912 st/y
Linerboard: 82,110 st/y
Corrugating medium/fluting: 137,802 st/y
Paper and Paperboard Mill Data:
Paper Machines: 1
No. 1, (PM has C-Former top wire and Hydra-Nip pre-calender), fourdrinier, total capacity 219,912 st/y, Trim width 188 in, Linerboard, Corrugating medium/fluting
Energy Data:
Power boilers: 1
Steam turbines: 1 at 88 MW
Electrical demand for mill: 291 MWh/D

ⓜInternational Paper Co.
Maysville Mill
Mill is a previous Temple-Inland mill
1241 West 2nd Street
Maysville, KY 41056
USA
Mailing Address: PO Box 688, Maysville, KY 41056, USA
Phone: (1) 606-564-2616 / 606-564-2617 (emergency # only)
Fax: (1) 606-564-2618
Web Address: www.internationalpaper.com
Personnel:
Mill Mgr. (from September 2013): Steven P. Braun
Phone: (1) 606-564-2601
Fax: (1) 606-564-2618
Email: steven.braun@ipaper.com
Tech. & Environ. Mgr.: Melissa Wiegand
Phone: (1) 606-564-2641
Fax: (1) 606-564-2618
Email: melissa.wiegand@ipaper.com
Prod. Mgr. & Manuf. Excellence Mgr.: Neal Tutor
Phone: (1) 606-564-2634
Fax: (1) 606-564-2618
Email: neal.tutor@ipaper.com
HR Mgr.: Becky Moore
Phone: (1) 606-564-2614
Fax: (1) 606-564-2618
Email: becky.moore@ipaper.com
Logist. Mgr.: Robin Stewart
Phone: (1) 606-564-2638
Fax: (1) 606-564-2618
Email: robin.stewart@ipaper.com
Total Employees at this Location: 142
Type of Operation: Pulp mill, Paperboard mill, Paperboard mill
Pulp Grades and Capacities:
Total pulp capacity: 475,591 st/y
Recycled Pulping: 475,591 st/y
Pulp Mill Data:
Recycled Fiber Treatment Lines:
Pulpers: 1 at 559,303
Paper/Paperboard Grades and Capacities:
Total paper and paperboard capacity: 460,530 st/y
Linerboard: 321,300 st/y
Corrugating medium/fluting: 139,230 st/y
Paper and Paperboard Mill Data:
Stock Preparation:
Pulpers: 2
Refiners: 2
Paper Machines: 1
No. 1, fourdrinier, total capacity 460,530 st/y, Trim width 284 in, Linerboard, Corrugating medium/fluting
Finishing Equipment:
Winders: 1 at 425,000 st/y
Calenders: 1
Energy Data:
Power boilers: 1
Steam turbines
Electrical demand for mill: 522 MWh/D

ⓜKimberly-Clark Corp.
Owensboro Mill
601 Innovative Way
Owensboro, KY 42301
USA
Phone: (1) 270-764-4400
Fax: (1) 270-764-4598
Web Address: www.kimberly-clark.com
Personnel:
Mill Mgr.: Grover Hardin
Phone: (1) 270-764-3179
Fax: (1) 270-764-4598
Email: ghardin@kcc.com
Eng. Mgr.: Mike Monroe
Phone: (1) 270-764-4400
Fax: (1) 270-764-4598
Email: mmonroe@kcc.com
Safety Ldr.: Pamela Dickens
Phone: (1) 270-764-4400
Fax: (1) 270-764-4598
Total Employees at this Location: 173
Type of Operation: Paper mill
Pulp Grades and Capacities:
Total pulp capacity: 97,508 st/y
Recycled Pulping: 97,508 st/y
Pulp Mill Data:
Bleach Plant Lines:
Recycled Deinked Pulping System, Sequence: HYP
Recycled Fiber Treatment Lines:
Flotation deinking lines: 1 at 107,584
Paper/Paperboard Grades and Capacities:
Total paper and paperboard capacity: 134,589 st/y
Tissue: 134,589 st/y
Paper and Paperboard Mill Data:
Stock Preparation:
Pulpers:
Paper Machines: 2
No. 1, crescent former, total capacity 56,049 st/y, Trim width 208 in, Tissue
No. 2, TAD, total capacity 78,540 st/y, Trim width 208 in, Tissue
Energy Data:
Power boilers: 1
Electrical demand for mill: 584 MWh/D

ⓜNewPage Corporation
Wickliffe Mill
1724 Fort Jefferson Hill Rd.
Wickliffe, KY 42087
USA
Mailing Address: PO Box 278, Wickliffe, KY 42087, USA
Phone: (1) 270-335-4000
Fax: (1) 270-335-4110
Web Address: www.newpagecorp.com
Personnel:
Mill Mgr.: John Fuller
Phone: (1) 270-335-4201
Fax: (1) 270-335-4110
Email: john.fuller@newpagecorp.com
Pub. Affairs Mgr. & HR Dir.: Michael Mazzone
Phone: (1) 270-335-4306
Fax: (1) 270-335-4110
Email: michael.mazzone@newpagecorp.com
Prod. Mgr.: Steven Weber
Phone: (1) 270-335-4000
Fax: (1) 270-335-4110
Email: steven.weber@newpagecorp.com
Total Employees at this Location: 450
Type of Operation: Pulp mill, Paper mill
Pulp Grades and Capacities:
Total pulp capacity: 290,299 st/y

Louisiana

Pulp available for market: 96,412 st/y
Chemical Pulp: 290,299 st/y
Pulp Mill Data:
Chemical Pulping Systems:
Continuous digesters: 1
Bleach Plant Systems: 1
Chemical Pulping System, Type: Hardwood/Softwood, Sequence: DEDD
Chemical Recovery Equipment:
Evaporator lines: 1
Recovery boilers: 1
Lime Kiln
Pulp Dryers:
Flash dryers 1
Paper/Paperboard Grades and Capacities:
Total paper and paperboard capacity: 285,537 st/y
Uncoated woodfree/freesheet: 33,908 st/y
Coated woodfree/freesheet: 251,630 st/y
Paper and Paperboard Mill Data:
Stock Preparation:
Pulpers: 5
Refiners: 5
Paper Machines: 1
No. 1, fourdrinier, total capacity 285,537 st/y, Trim width 231 in, Coated woodfree/freesheet, Uncoated wood-free/freesheet
Coating Machines: 1
No. 1, total capacity 297,619 st/y., off machine
Finishing Equipment:
Supercalenders: 2
Rewinders: 2
Energy Data:
Power boilers: 3
Electrical demand for mill: 1,003 MWh/D

ⓂⓂ Wausau Paper Towel & Tissue, LLC
Harrodsburg Mill
Ownership: Wausau Paper Corp.
1150 Industry Rd
Harrodsburg, KY 40330
USA
  Phone: (1) 859-734-0538
  Fax: (1) 859-734-8219
  Web Address: www.wausaupaper.com
Personnel:
VP., Oper.: Gary Rudemiller
  Phone: (1) 859-734-0538
  Fax: (1) 859-734-8219
  Email: grudemiller@wausaupaper.com
Dir. Finan.: Norm Fortier
  Phone: (1) 859-734-0538
  Fax: (1) 859-734-8219
  Email: nfortier@wausaupaper.com
Dir. Manf'.: Ed Jadczak
  Phone: (1) 859-734-0538
  Fax: (1) 859-734-8219
  Email: ejadczak@wausaupaper.com
Total Employees at this Location: 470
Type of Operation: Paper mill
Mill Locations:
Wausau Paper Towel & Tissue, LLC, Middletown Mill, 700 Columbia Ave., Middletown, OH 45042, USA, Capacity: 126,735 st/y, (Pulp mill, Paper mill)
  Phone: (1) 513-424-2999
  Fax: (1) 513-420-8570
  Email: contactbaywest@wausaupaper.com
Paper/Paperboard Grades and Capacities:
Total paper and paperboard capacity: 74,967 st/y
Tissue: 74,967 st/y
Paper and Paperboard Mill Data:
Paper Machines: 1
No. 1, ATMOS, total capacity 74,967 st/y, Trim width 220 in, Tissue
Energy Data:
Power boilers
Electrical demand for mill: 160 MWh/D

LOUISIANA

Ⓜ Packaging Corp. of America
DeRidder Mill
4200 Hwy 190 W
DeRidder, LA 70634
USA
Mailing Address: PO Box 1060, DeRidder, LA 70634-1060, USA
  Phone: (1) 337-462-4300
  Fax: (1) 337-462-4330
  Web Address: www.packagingcorp.com
Personnel:
Prod. Mgr.: Billy Goodman
  Phone: (1) 337-462-4300
  Fax: (1) 337-462-4330
  Email: billygoodman@packagingcorp.com
Maint. Superint.: Mike Holt
  Phone: (1) 337-462-4300
  Fax: (1) 337-462-4330
  Email: mikeholt@boisepaper.com
Procurement Mgr.: Dana Hall
  Phone: (1) 337-462-4300
  Fax: (1) 337-462-4330
  Email: danahall@packagingcorp.com
Environ. Mgr.: Blaine Butaud
  Phone: (1) 337-462-4300
  Fax: (1) 337-462-4330
  Email: blainebutaud@boisepaper.com
Purch. Agent: Pat McBride
  Phone: (1) 337-462-4300
  Fax: (1) 337-462-4330
  Email: patmcbride@boisepaper.com
Total Employees at this Location: 436
Type of Operation: Pulp mill, Paperboard mill
Pulp Grades and Capacities:
Total pulp capacity: 1,018,068 st/y
Chemical Pulp: 724,823 st/y
Recycled Pulping: 293,245 st/y
Pulp Mill Data:
Chemical Pulping Systems:
Batch digesters: 8
Bleach Plant Lines:
(Batch digester - Kraft Pulp), Sequence: DEopDD
Chemical Recovery Equipment:
Evaporator lines: 6
Recovery boilers: 1
Lime Kiln
Recycled Fiber Treatment Lines:
Recycled packaging pulping lines: 1 at 297,619
Paper/Paperboard Grades and Capacities:
Total paper and paperboard capacity: 968,898 st/y
Linerboard: 897,498 st/y
Corrugating medium/fluting: 71,400 st/y
Paper and Paperboard Mill Data:
Stock Preparation:
Pulpers: 3
Refiners: 11
Paper Machines: 2
No. 1, fourdrinier, total capacity 614,040 st/y, Trim width 300 in, Linerboard
No. 3, Bel-Baie II, total capacity 354,858 st/y, Trim width 299 in, Linerboard, Corrugating medium/fluting
Finishing Equipment:
Calenders: 4
Rewinders: 3
Energy Data:
Power boilers: 4
Steam turbines: 1 at 61.5 MW
Electrical demand for mill: 1,882 MWh/D

Ⓜ Georgia-Pacific LLC
Port Hudson Mill
1000 West Mount Pleasant Zachary Road
Zachary, LA 70791
USA

Mailing Address: PO Box 430, Zachary, LA 70791, USA
  Phone: (1) 225-654-1700
  Fax: (1) 225-654-7722
  Web Address: www.gp.com
Personnel:
VP, Oper.: Keith Wahoske
  Phone: (1) 225-654-1700
  Fax: (1) 225-654-7722
  Email: keith.wahoske@gapac.com
Prod. Ldr.: Paul Medlin
  Phone: (1) 225-654-1700
  Fax: (1) 225-654-7722
  Email: paul.medlin@gapac.com
Purch. & Stores Mgr.: Stan Marshall
  Phone: (1) 225-654-1700
  Fax: (1) 225-654-7722
Total Employees at this Location: 691
Type of Operation: Paper mill
Pulp Grades and Capacities:
Total pulp capacity: 700,749 st/y
Chemical Pulp: 700,749 st/y
Pulp Mill Data:
Chemical Pulping Systems:
Batch digesters: 4
Continuous digesters: 2
Bleach Plant Systems: 2
Chemical Pulping System, Type: Hardwood/Softwood, Sequence: DEopDD
Chemical Pulping System, Type: Hardwood/Softwood, Sequence: DEopDD
Chemical Recovery Equipment:
Evaporator lines: 1
Recovery boilers: 2
Lime Kiln
Paper/Paperboard Grades and Capacities:
Total paper and paperboard capacity: 822,528 st/y
Uncoated woodfree/freesheet: 631,890 st/y
Tissue: 190,638 st/y
Paper and Paperboard Mill Data:
Paper Machines: 4
No. 3, SymFormer, total capacity 312,375 st/y, Trim width 349 in, Uncoated woodfree/freesheet
No. 4, SymFormer, total capacity 319,515 st/y, Trim width 349 in, Uncoated woodfree/freesheet
No. 5, eTAD, total capacity 110,670 st/y, Trim width 290 in, Tissue
No. 6, eTAD, total capacity 79,968 st/y, Trim width 205 in, Tissue
Finishing Equipment:
Supercalenders: 1
Rewinders: 2
Sheeters: 3
Energy Data:
Power boilers: 3
Steam turbines: 2 at 60, 60 MW
Electrical demand for mill: 2,770 MWh/D

Ⓜ Graphic Packaging International Inc.
West Monroe Mill
1000 Jonesboro Rd
West Monroe, LA 71292
USA
Mailing Address: PO Box 35800, West Monroe, LA 71294-5800, USA
  Phone: (1) 318-362-2000
  Fax: (1) 318-362-2133
  Web Address: www.graphicpkg.com
Personnel:
VP. & Resident Mgr. (From February 2013): Tony Hobson
  Phone: (1) 318-362-2000
  Fax: (1) 318-362-2133
  Email: hobsont@graphicpkg.com
Manuf. Mgr.: Ken Meissner
  Phone: (1) 318-362-2000
  Fax: (1) 318-362-2133
  Email: ken.meissner@graphicpkg.com
Wood Procurement Mgr.: Tony Diaz
  Phone: (1) 318-362-2000

Louisiana

Fax: (1) 318-362-2133
Email: tony.diaz@graphicpkg.com
Tech. Serv. Mgr.: Robby McReynolds
Phone: (1) 318-362-2000
Fax: (1) 318-362-2133
Email: robby.mcreynolds@graphicpkg.com
Prod. Contr. Mgr.: Chris Babin
Phone: (1) 318-362-2000
Fax: (1) 318-362-2133
Email: chris.babin@graphicpkg.com
Total Employees at this Location: 751
Type of Operation: Paperboard mill
Pulp Grades and Capacities:
 Total pulp capacity: 859,862 st/y
 Chemical Pulp: 724,160 st/y
 Recycled Pulping: 135,702 st/y
Pulp Mill Data:
 Chemical Pulping Systems:
 Continuous digesters: 4
 Chemical Recovery Equipment:
 Evaporator lines: 2
 Recovery boilers: 2
 Lime Kiln
 Recycled Fiber Treatment Lines:
 Pulpers: 1 at 21,054
Paper/Paperboard Grades and Capacities:
 Total paper and paperboard capacity: 910,707 st/y
 Packaging papers: 43,554 st/y
 Corrugating medium/fluting: 130,305 st/y
 Boxboard/cartonboard: 736,848 st/y
Paper and Paperboard Mill Data:
Paper Machines: 4
 No. 1, fourdrinier, total capacity 130,305 st/y, Trim width 160 in, Corrugating medium/fluting
 No. 5, fourdrinier, total capacity 43,554 st/y, Trim width 118 in, Packaging papers
 No. 6, fourdrinier (2), total capacity 409,836 st/y, Trim width 230 in, Boxboard/cartonboard
 No. 7, fourdrinier (3), total capacity 327,012 st/y, Trim width 232 in, Boxboard/cartonboard
Coating Machines: 2
 No. 6, total capacity 410,053 st/y., on machine
 No. 7, total capacity 327,381 st/y., on machine
Energy Data:
 Power boilers: 4
 Steam turbines: 5 at 63 MW
 Electrical demand for mill: 1,999 MWh/D

ⓜInternational Paper Co.
Bogalusa Mill
Mill is a previous Temple-Inland mill
401 Ave U
Bogalusa, LA 70429-1060
USA
Mailing Address: PO Box 1060, Bogalusa, LA 70427, USA
Phone: (1) 985-732-8000
Fax: (1) 985-732-8480
Web Address: www.internationalpaper.com
Personnel:
Mill Mgr.: Bernie Chascin
Phone: (1) 985-732-8000
Fax: (1) 985-732-8480
Email: bernie.chascin@ipaper.com
Maint. & Reliability Mgr.: Michael Reed
Phone: (1) 985-732-8000
Fax: (1) 985-732-8480
Email: michael.reed@ipaper.com
Mgr. Manuf. Excellence: Marianne Smith
Phone: (1) 985-732-8000
Fax: (1) 985-732-8480
Email: marianne.smith@ipaper.com
Total Employees at this Location: 425
Type of Operation: Pulp mill, Paperboard mill
Pulp Grades and Capacities:
 Total pulp capacity: 878,602 st/y
 Chemical Pulp: 683,066 st/y
 Recycled Pulping: 195,536 st/y
Pulp Mill Data:
 Chemical Pulping Systems:
 Continuous digesters: 2
Pulp Lines: 2
 Chemical Recovery Equipment:
 Evaporator lines: 1
 Recovery boilers: 2
 Lime Kiln
 Recycled Fiber Treatment Lines:
 Pulpers: 1 at 196,000 admt/y
 Pulpers: 1 at 179,000
Paper/Paperboard Grades and Capacities:
 Total paper and paperboard capacity: 830,025 st/y
 Linerboard: 830,025 st/y
Paper and Paperboard Mill Data:
 Stock Preparation:
 Pulpers: 2
 Refiners: 12
Paper Machines: 2
 No. 7, (ENP Press), total capacity 357,000 st/y, Trim width 196 in, Linerboard
 No. 8, (ENP Press.), total capacity 473,025 st/y, Trim width 278 in, Linerboard
Energy Data:
 Power boilers: 3
 Steam turbines: 3 at 96 MW
 Electrical demand for mill: 1,885 MWh/D

ⓜInternational Paper Co.
Red River Mill
Hwy 480
Campti, LA 71411
USA
Mailing Address: PO Box 377, Campti, LA 71411, USA
Phone: (1) 318-476-3392
Fax: (1) 318-476-2712
Web Address: www.internationalpaper.com
Personnel:
Mill Mgr. (From January, 2014): Hunter Whiteley
Phone: (1) 318-476-3392
Fax: (1) 318-476-2712
Email: hunter.whiteley@ipapaer.com
Oper. & Maint. Coord. (From February 2013): Jose Antezana
Phone: (1) 318-476-3392
Fax: (1) 318-476-2712
Email: jose.antezana@ipaper.com
Ppr Mill Supt: Steve Birdwell
Phone: (1) 318-476-3392
Fax: (1) 318-476-2712
Email: steve.birdwell@ipaper.com
Finished Product Mgr.: Chris J. Loach
Phone: (1) 318-476-3392
Fax: (1) 318-476-2712
Email: chris.loach@ipaper.com
Total Employees at this Location: 356
Type of Operation: Pulp mill, Paperboard mill
Pulp Grades and Capacities:
 Total pulp capacity: 1,035,122 st/y
 Chemical Pulp: 458,991 st/y
 Recycled Pulping: 576,131 st/y
Pulp Mill Data:
 Chemical Pulping Systems:
 Batch digesters: 6
 Chemical Recovery Equipment:
 Recovery boilers: 1
 Lime Kiln
 Recycled Fiber Treatment Lines:
 Pulpers: 4 at 520,000 admt/y
Paper/Paperboard Grades and Capacities:
 Total paper and paperboard capacity: 979,965 st/y
 Linerboard: 979,965 st/y
Paper and Paperboard Mill Data:
 Stock Preparation:
 Pulpers: 4
 Refiners: 11
Paper Machines: 2
 No. 1, Bel-Bond, total capacity 498,015 st/y, Trim width 260 in, Linerboard
 No. 2, fourdrinier, total capacity 481,950 st/y, Trim width 255 in, Linerboard
Finishing Equipment:
 Calenders: 3
 Rewinders: 2
Energy Data:
 Power boilers: 3
 Steam turbines: 3 at 67.5 MW
 Electrical demand for mill: 1,683 MWh/D

ⓜInternational Paper Co.
Mansfield Mill
1202 Hwy 509
Mansfield, LA 71052
USA
Mailing Address: PO Box 999, Mansfield, LA 71052, USA
Phone: (1) 318-872-5100
Fax: (1) 318-872-4779
Email: (firstname.lastname@ipaper.com)
Web Address: www.internationalpaper.com
Personnel:
Mill Mgr.: Kevin Driscoll
Phone: (1) 318-872-5100
Fax: (1) 318-872-4779
Email: kevin.driscoll@ipaper.com
Project Mgr.: Jay Bhima
Phone: (1) 318-872-5100
Fax: (1) 318-872-4779
Email: jay.bhima@ipaper.com
Process Eng.: Candice Watson
Phone: (1) 318-872-5100
Fax: (1) 318-872-4779
Email: candice.watson@ipaper.com
Mgr. HR: Lynne Given
Phone: (1) 318-872-5100
Fax: (1) 318-872-4779
Email: lynne.given@ipaper.com
Total Employees at this Location: 575
Type of Operation: Pulp mill, Paperboard mill
Pulp Grades and Capacities:
 Total pulp capacity: 1,666,274 st/y
 Chemical Pulp: 1,063,056 st/y
 Recycled Pulping: 603,219 st/y
Pulp Mill Data:
 Chemical Pulping Systems:
 Continuous digesters: 3
 Bleach Plant Systems: 1
 Chemical Recovery Equipment:
 Evaporator lines: 2
 Recovery boilers: 2
 Lime Kiln
 Recycled Fiber Treatment Lines:
 Flotation deinking lines: 1
 Pulpers: 2 at 757,275 admt/y
 Recycled packaging pulping lines: 1 at 479,992 admt/y
Paper/Paperboard Grades and Capacities:
 Total paper and paperboard capacity: 1,580,082 st/y
 Linerboard: 1,169,175 st/y
 Corrugating medium/fluting: 410,907 st/y
Paper and Paperboard Mill Data:
Paper Machines: 3
 No. 1, fourdrinier, total capacity 658,665 st/y, Trim width 349 in, Linerboard
 No. 2, fourdrinier, total capacity 410,907 st/y, Trim width 348 in, Corrugating medium/fluting
 No. 3, fourdrinier, total capacity 510,510 st/y, Trim width 348 in, Linerboard
Energy Data:
 Power boilers: 2
 Combustion turbines: 1 at 25 MW
 Steam turbines: 3 at 110 MW
 Electrical demand for mill: 2,961 MWh/D

ⓜKPAQ Industries LLC
Ownership: 100% by Amzak Capital Management
2105 Hwy 964
Saint Francisville, LA 70775
USA

Maine

Phone: (1) 225-336-2530
Web Address: www.kpaq.com
Personnel:
Pres. & CEO: Bob Boschee
Phone: (1) 225-336-2530
Email: bob.boschee@kpaq.com
VP, Admin.: Michele Conrod
Phone: (1) 225-336-2530
Email: michele.conrod@kpaq.com
CFO: Paula Moreau
Phone: (1) 225-336-2530
Email: paula.moreau@kpaq.com
VP, Sls. & Mktg.: Michael Butler
Phone: (1) 225-336-2530
Email: mike.butler@kpaq.com
Total Employees of Company: 295
Mill Locations:
KPAQ Industries LLC, Saint Francisville Mill, 2105 Hwy 964, Saint Francisville, LA 70775, USA, Capacity: 229,908 st/y, (Pulp mill, Paper mill, Paperboard mill)
Phone: (1) 225-336-2530

ⓂKPAQ Industries LLC
Saint Francisville Mill
2105 Hwy 964
Saint Francisville, LA 70775
USA
Phone: (1) 225-336-2530
Web Address: www.kpaq.com
Personnel:
Pres. & CEO: Bob Boschee
Phone: (1) 225-336-2530
Email: bob.boschee@kpaq.com
CFO: Paula Moreau
Phone: (1) 225-336-2530
Email: paula.moreau@kpaq.com
VP, Admin.: Michele Conrod
Phone: (1) 225-336-2551
Email: michele.conrod@kpaq.com
VP, Sls. Mgr. & Mktg.: Michael Butler
Phone: (1) 225-336-2530
Email: mike.butler@kpaq.com
Procurement Mgr.: Eldon Hopf
Phone: (1) 225-336-2530
Email: eldon.hopf@kpaq.com
Total Employees at this Location: 295
Type of Operation: Pulp mill, Paper mill, Paperboard mill
Pulp Grades and Capacities:
Total pulp capacity: 256,747 st/y
Pulp available for market: 14,994 st/y
Chemical Pulp: 256,747 st/y
Pulp Mill Data:
Chemical Pulping Systems:
Continuous digesters: 1
Pulp Lines: 1
Chemical Recovery Equipment:
Evaporator lines: 1
Recovery boilers: 1
Lime Kiln
Pulp Dryers:
Twin Wire 1
Paper/Paperboard Grades and Capacities:
Total paper and paperboard capacity: 229,908 st/y
Packaging papers: 79,968 st/y
Linerboard: 149,940 st/y
Paper and Paperboard Mill Data:
Stock Preparation:
Refiners: 3
Paper Machines: 2
K1, fourdrinier, total capacity 199,920 st/y, Trim width 236 in, Linerboard, Packaging papers
K2, twin-wire, total capacity 44,982 st/y, Trim width 151 in, Packaging papers
Energy Data:
Power boilers: 2
Steam turbines: 1 at 15 MW
Electrical demand for mill: 837 MWh/D

ⓂPratt Industries (USA)
Shreveport Mill
Ownership: Visy Pulp & Paper
10429 Richard Pratt Drive
Shreveport, LA 71115
USA
Phone: (1) 318-797-7375
Web Address: www.prattindustries.com
Personnel:
Gen. Mgr.: Luis Henao
Phone: (1) 318-797-7375
Email: lhenao@prattindustries.com
Mill Mgr.: Ed Kersey
Phone: (1) 318-797-7375
Email: ekersey@prattindustries.com
Prod. Mgr.: Mike Michaud
Phone: (1) 318-797-7375
Email: mmichaud@prattindustries.com
Env. Dir.: Travis Horsch
Phone: (1) 318-797-7375
Email: thorsch@prattindustries.com
Total Employees at this Location: 110
Type of Operation: Paperboard mill
Pulp Grades and Capacities:
Total pulp capacity: 384,284 st/y
Recycled Pulping: 384,284 st/y
Pulp Mill Data:
Recycled Fiber Treatment Lines:
Pulpers: 1 at 399,471
Paper/Paperboard Grades and Capacities:
Total paper and paperboard capacity: 374,850 st/y
Linerboard: 149,940 st/y
Corrugating medium/fluting: 224,910 st/y
Paper and Paperboard Mill Data:
Stock Preparation:
Pulpers: 1
Paper Machines: 1
No. 15, GapFormer, total capacity 374,850 st/y, Trim width 220 in, Linerboard, Corrugating medium/fluting
Finishing Equipment:
Winders: 1
Calenders: 1
Energy Data:
Power boilers: 1
Electrical demand for mill: 450 MWh/D

ⓂRockTenn Co.
Hodge Mill
Mill Street, C/S 3700
Hodge, LA 71247-3700
USA
Phone: (1) 318-259-4421
Fax: (1) 318-259-5355
Email: webmaster@rocktenn.com
Web Address: www.rocktenn.com
Personnel:
Gen. Mgr.: Mike Ballew
Phone: (1) 318-259-4421
Fax: (1) 318-259-5355
Email: mballew@rocktenn.com
Oper. Mgr.: Don Holtzclaw
Phone: (1) 318-259-4421
Fax: (1) 318-259-5355
Email: dholtzclaw@rocktenn.com
Purch. Mgr.: Wade Wright
Phone: (1) 318-259-4421
Fax: (1) 318-259-5355
Email: wwright@rocktenn.com
Pulp, Power & Rec. Mgr. (From April 2013): Todd Pyles
Phone: (1) 318-259-4421
Fax: (1) 318-259-5355
Email: tpyles@rocktenn.com
Total Employees at this Location: 394
Type of Operation: Paper mill, Paperboard mill
Pulp Grades and Capacities:
Total pulp capacity: 864,084 st/y
Chemical Pulp: 734,472 st/y
Recycled Pulping: 129,613 st/y
Pulp Mill Data:
Chemical Pulping Systems:
Continuous digesters: 2
Chemical Recovery Equipment:
Evaporator lines: 3
Recovery boilers: 2
Lime Kiln
Recycled Fiber Treatment Lines:
Pulpers: 1 at 152,337 admt/y
Paper/Paperboard Grades and Capacities:
Total paper and paperboard capacity: 825,027 st/y
Linerboard: 825,027 st/y
Paper and Paperboard Mill Data:
Stock Preparation:
Refiners:
Paper Machines: 2
No. 4, fourdrinier, total capacity 332,367 st/y, Trim width 224 in, Linerboard
No. 5, fourdrinier, total capacity 492,660 st/y, Trim width 355 in, Linerboard
Energy Data:
Power boilers: 2
Turbines at 3, 4, 16, 25, 24 MW
Electrical demand for mill: 1,706 MWh/D

MAINE

ⓂCascades Auburn Fiber, Inc.
Auburn Mill
Ownership: Cascades Inc.
586 Lewiston Junction Rd
Auburn, ME 04210-8847
USA
Phone: (1) 207-753-5300
Fax: (1) 207-753-5333
Web Address: www.cascades.com
Personnel:
Mill Mgr.: Tony Newman
Phone: (1) 207-753-5300
Fax: (1) 207-753-5333
Email: tony_newman@cascades.com
Manuf. Mgr.: Scott Alexander
Phone: (1) 207-753-5300
Fax: (1) 207-753-5333
Email: scott_alexander@cascades.com
Total Employees at this Location: 47
Type of Operation: Pulp mill
Pulp Grades and Capacities:
Total pulp capacity: 84,411 st/y
Pulp available for market: 82,824 st/y
Recycled Pulping: 84,411 st/y
Pulp Mill Data:
Bleach Plant Lines:
Dinking Pulp Line, Sequence: P
Recycled Fiber Treatment Lines:
Flotation deinking lines
Pulp Dryers:
Wet Lap machine 1
Energy Data:
Electrical demand for mill: 109 MWh/D

ⓂGreat Northern Paper Co. LLC.
Ownership: 100% by Cate $treet Capital
50 Main St
East Millinocket, ME 04430
USA
Phone: (1) 207-723-5131, 207-723-2351
Fax: (1) 207-723-2660, 207-723-2200
Email: gnpaperco.com,
tdyer@gnpapercompany.com
Web Address: greatnorthernpaper.com
Personnel:
Pres.: Ned Dwyer
Phone: (1) 207-723-5131
Fax: (1) 207-723-2660
Email: ndwyer@gnpapercompany.com

CEO: Richard Cyr
Phone: (1) 207-723-5131
Fax: (1) 207-723-2660
Email: rcyr@gnpapercompany.com
Dir. Finan.: Robert J. Desrosiers
Phone: (1) 207-723-5131
Fax: (1) 207-723-2660
Email: rdesrosiers@gnpapercompany.com
Director of Sales: Todd Dyer
Phone: (1) 203-209-1392
Fax: (1) 207-723-2492
Email: tdyer@gnpapercompany.com
Total Employees of Company: 252
Mill Locations:
Great Northern Paper Co. LLC., East Millinocket Mill, 50 Main St, East Millinocket, ME 04430, USA, (Paper mill)
Phone: (1) 207-723-5131, 207-723-2351
Fax: (1) 207-723-2660, 207-723-2492

ⓜGreat Northern Paper Co. LLC.
East Millinocket Mill
Mill is for sale, closed, under bankruptcy protection (The mill stopped producing paper in January 2014 and laid off 212 of 256 workers on February 6, 2014. Filed for Chapter 7 bankruptcy)
50 Main St
East Millinocket, ME 04430
USA
Phone: (1) 207-723-5131, 207-723-2351
Fax: (1) 207-723-2660, 207-723-2492
Web Address: greatnorthernpaper.com
Personnel:
Pres.: Ned Dwyer
Phone: (1) 207-723-5131
Fax: (1) 207-723-2660
Email: ndwyer@gnpapercompany.com
Quality Assurance: Rodney Nicholson
Phone: (1) 207-723-5131
Fax: (1) 207-723-2660
Email: rnicholson@gnpapercompany.com
Maint. Planner: Paul Mackin
Phone: (1) 207-723-2273
Fax: (1) 207-723-2522
Email: pmackin@gnpapercompany.com
Tech. Mgr.: Mary Wagner
Phone: (1) 207-723-5131
Fax: (1) 207-723-2660
Email: mwagner@gnpapercompany.com
Total Employees at this Location: 252
Type of Operation: Paper mill
Pulp Mill Data:
Mechanical Pulping Systems:
Conventional grinders
Pulp Lines: 2
Bleach Plant Lines:
SGW Pulp Line, Sequence: PY
Recycled Fiber Treatment Lines:
Flotation deinking lines at 115,741
Energy Data:
Power boilers: 1
Steam turbines at 6 MW

ⓜLincoln Paper and Tissue, LLC
Ownership: First Paper Holding LLC, PCG Capital Partners
50 Katadin Avenue
Lincoln, ME 04457
USA
Mailing Address: P.O. Box 490, Lincoln, ME 04457, USA
Phone: (1) 207-794-0600, 866-744-3200 (toll free)
Fax: (1) 207-794-3964
Email: info@lpt.com
Web Address: www.lpt.com
Personnel:
Pres. & CEO: Keith Van Scotter
Phone: (1) 207-794-0600
Fax: (1) 207-794-3964
Email: kvanscotter@lpt.com
CFO: John Wissmann
Phone: (1) 207-794-0600
Fax: (1) 207-794-3964
Email: jwissmann@lpt.com
VP, Oper.: Marco L'Italien
Phone: (1) 207-794-0600
Fax: (1) 207-794-3964
Email: mlitalien@lpt.com
Total Employees of Company: 200
Mill Locations:
Lincoln Paper and Tissue, LLC, Lincoln Mill, 50 Katadin Avenue, Lincoln, ME 04457, USA, Capacity: 73,185 st/y, (Paper mill)
Phone: (1) 207-794-0600/ 866-744-3200 (toll free)
Fax: (1) 207-794-3964
Email: info@lpt.com

ⓜLincoln Paper and Tissue, LLC
Lincoln Mill
50 Katadin Avenue
Lincoln, ME 04457
USA
Mailing Address: P.O. Box 490, Lincoln, ME 04457, USA
Phone: (1) 207-794-0600/ 866-744-3200 (toll free)
Fax: (1) 207-794-3964
Email: info@lpt.com
Web Address: www.lpt.com
Personnel:
VP, Oper.: Marco L'Italien
Phone: (1) 207-794-0600
Fax: (1) 207-794-3964
Email: mlitalien@lpt.com
Dir., Develop.: Ralph Lichtenberg
Phone: (1) 207-794-0624
Fax: (1) 207-794-3964
Email: rlichtenberg@lpt.com
Environ. & Safety Mgr.: Dennis C. McComb
Phone: (1) 207-249-8229
Fax: (1) 207-794-3964
Email: dmccomb@lpt.com
Safety Mgr.: Neil Brackley
Phone: (1) 207-794-0641
Fax: (1) 207-794-3964
Email: nbrackley@lpt.com
Total Employees at this Location: 150
Type of Operation: Paper mill
Pulp Mill Data:
Chemical Pulping Systems:
Continuous digesters: 2
Bleach Plant Systems: 1
Chemical Pulping System, Type: Softwood/Hardwood/Sawdust, Sequence: DO2DEP
Chemical Recovery Equipment:
Evaporator lines: 6
Recovery boilers: 1
Lime Kiln
Pulp Dryers:
Fourdriniers 1
Paper/Paperboard Grades and Capacities:
Total paper and paperboard capacity: 73,185 st/y
Tissue: 73,185 st/y
Paper and Paperboard Mill Data:
Stock Preparation:
Pulpers:
Paper Machines: 3
No. 6, crescent former, Yankee dryer, total capacity 19,992 st/y, Trim width 96 in, Tissue
No. 7, crescent former, Yankee dryer, total capacity 19,992 st/y, Trim width 110 in, Tissue
No. 8, crescent former, total capacity 33,201 st/y, Trim width 105 in, Tissue
Energy Data:
Power boilers: 4
Steam turbines: 2 at 13.5 MW
Electrical demand for mill: 188 MWh/D

ⓜNewPage Corporation
Rumford Mill
Mill is for sale (on October 30, 2014, Catalyst Paper Corporation entered into an Asset Purchase Agreement with NewPage Corporation to purchase the Rumford pulp and paper mill.)
35 Hartford St
Rumford, ME 04276-1000
USA
Phone: (1) 207-364-4521
Fax: (1) 207-369-2531
Web Address: www.newpagecorp.com
Personnel:
VP, Oper. & Mill Mgr.: Gerald A. LeClaire
Phone: (1) 207-364-4521
Fax: (1) 207-369-2531
Email: gerald.leclaire@newpagecorp.com
Dir., Fiber Supply & Pub. Affairs: Anthony Lyons
Phone: (1) 207-369-2615
Fax: (1) 207-369-2531
Email: anthony.lyons@newpagecorp.com
Dir., HR & Commun.: Janet Hall
Phone: (1) 207-364-4521
Fax: (1) 207-369-2531
Email: janet.hall@newpagecorp.com
Snr. Eng. (From July 2014): Blue Keim
Phone: (1) 207-364-4521
Fax: (1) 207-369-2531
Email: blue.keim@newpagecorp.com
Contr.: Kelly Berry
Phone: (1) 207-364-4521
Fax: (1) 207-369-2531
Email: kelly.berry@newpagecorp.com
IT Mgr.: Jon Federico
Phone: (1) 207-364-4521
Fax: (1) 207-369-2531
Email: jon.federico@newpagecorp.com
Maint., Eng. & Purch. Mgr.: Shannon Dwyer
Phone: (1) 207-364-4521
Fax: (1) 207-369-2531
Email: shannon.dwyer@newpagecorp.com
Total Employees at this Location: 851
Type of Operation: Pulp mill, Paper mill
Pulp Grades and Capacities:
Total pulp capacity: 471,265 st/y
Pulp available for market: 102,708 st/y
Chemical Pulp: 409,300 st/y
Mechanical Pulp: 61,965 st/y
Pulp Mill Data:
Chemical Pulping Systems:
Batch digesters: 10
Continuous digesters: 1
Mechanical Pulping Systems:
Conventional grinders
Pulp Lines: 3
Bleach Plant Systems: 2
Chemical Pulping System - 1, Type: Softwood, Sequence: DEopD, Capacity 196,350.3 admt/y
Chemical Pulping System - 2, Type: Hardwood, Sequence: DEopD, Capacity 284,391.5 admt/y
Chemical Recovery Equipment:
Evaporator lines: 1
Recovery boilers: 1
Lime Kiln
Pulp Dryers:
Fourdriniers 1
Paper/Paperboard Grades and Capacities:
Total paper and paperboard capacity: 522,890 st/y
Uncoated woodfree/freesheet: 7,138 st/y
Coated woodfree/freesheet: 230,214 st/y
Coated mechanical/groundwood: 258,768 st/y
Specialty and industrial: 26,769 st/y
Paper and Paperboard Mill Data:
Stock Preparation:
Pulpers: 3
Refiners: 18
Paper Machines: 3
No. 10, fourdrinier, total capacity 160,615 st/y, Trim width 158 in, Coated woodfree/freesheet, Coated mechanical/groundwood
No. 12, Bel-Form, total capacity 98,153 st/y, Trim width 138 in, Coated woodfree/freesheet, Coated mechanical/groundwood, Specialty and industrial

Maine

No. 15, fourdrinier, total capacity 264,122 st/y, Trim width 282 in, Coated mechanical/groundwood, Coated woodfree/freesheet, Uncoated woodfree/freesheet
Coating Machines: 3
No. 10, total capacity 160,935 st/y, on machine
No. 12, total capacity 97,002 st/y, on machine
No. 15, total capacity 254,630 st/y, on machine
Finishing Equipment:
Supercalenders: 4
Rewinders: 7
Energy Data:
Power boilers: 3
Steam turbines: 2 at 85, 10 MW
Hydro turbines: 6 at 39.4 MW
Electrical demand for mill: 666 MWh/D

(M) Old Town Fuel and Fiber
Ownership: 100% by Patriarch Partners, LLC
24 Portland Street
Old Town, ME 04468
USA
Mailing Address: P.O. Box 564, Old Town, ME 04468, USA
  Phone: (1) 207-827-0600, 207-827-7711
  Fax: (1) 207-827-8888
  Email: dan.bird@oldtownff.com
  Web Address: www.oldtownff.com
Personnel:
  Pres.: Dick Arnold
  Phone: (1) 207-827-0600
  Fax: (1) 207-827-8888
  Email: dick.arnold@oldtownff.com
  Mat. Mgr.: Everett Deschenes
  Phone: (1) 207-827-0600
  Fax: (1) 207-827-8888
  Email: everett.deschenes@oldtownff.com
  Maint. Mgr.: Kevin Paradis
  Phone: (1) 207-827-0600
  Fax: (1) 207-827-8888
  Email: kevin.paradis@oldtownff.com
  IT & HR Dir.: Daniel J. Bird
  Phone: (1) 207-745-5788
  Fax: (1) 207-827-8888
  Email: dan.bird@oldtownff.com
Total Employees of Company: 205
Mill Locations:
Old Town Fuel and Fiber, Maine Mill, 24 Portland Street, Old Town, ME 04468, USA, (Pulp mill)
  Phone: (1) 207-827-7711, 207-827-0600
  Fax: (1) 207-827-8888

(M) Old Town Fuel and Fiber
Maine Mill
Mill is temporarily closed ((Old Town Fuel & Fiber indefinitely suspended operations from August 13, 2014. Expera Specialty Solutions, LLC on Nov. 11, 2014 entered into a definitive agreement to acquire certain assets related to the Old Town Fuel & Fiber pulp mill)
24 Portland Street
Old Town, ME 04468
USA
Mailing Address: P.O. Box 564, Old Town, ME 04468, USA
  Phone: (1) 207-827-7711, 207-827-0600
  Fax: (1) 207-827-8888
  Web Address: www.oldtownff.com
Personnel:
  Pres.: Dick Arnold
  Phone: (1) 207-827-0600
  Fax: (1) 207-827-8888
  Email: dick.arnold@oldtownff.com
  Gen. Mgr.: Michael Footer
  Phone: (1) 207-827-0600
  Fax: (1) 207-827-8888
  Email: michael.footer@oldtownff.com
  IT & HR Dir.: Daniel Bird
  Phone: (1) 207-745-5788
  Fax: (1) 207-827-8888
  Email: dan.bird@oldtownff.com
  Maint. Mgr.: Kevin Paradis
  Phone: (1) 207-827-0600
  Fax: (1) 207-827-8888
  Email: kevin.paradis@oldtownff.com
Total Employees at this Location: 160
Type of Operation: Pulp mill
Pulp Mill Data:
  Chemical Pulping Systems:
  Continuous digesters: 2
  Bleach Plant Systems: 1
  Chemical Pulping System, Type: Softwood, Sequence: DEoDopND, Capacity 215,000 admt/y
  Chemical Recovery Equipment:
  Evaporator lines: 2
  Recovery boilers: 1
  Lime Kiln
  Pulp Dryers:
  Flakt dryer 1
Energy Data:
Power boilers: 1
Combustion turbines: 1 at 9.5 MW
Steam turbines: 3 at 17.1 MW
Hydro turbines

(M) Sappi Fine Paper North America
Somerset Mill
Ownership: Sappi Limited
1329 Waterville Road
Skowhegan, ME 04976
USA
  Phone: (1) 207-238-3000
  Fax: (1) 207-453-4532
  Web Address: www.sappi.com
Personnel:
  Man. Dir. & Mill Mgr.: Michael Haws
  Phone: (1) 207-238-3000
  Fax: (1) 207-453-4532
  Email: mike.haws@sappi.com
  Bus. Unit Ldr.: Edward Glasheen
  Phone: (1) 207-238-3000
  Fax: (1) 207-453-4532
  Email: edward.glasheen@sappi.com
  Eng. Project Mgr.: Mark Durkee
  Phone: (1) 207-238-3000
  Fax: (1) 207-453-4532
  Email: mark.durkee@sappi.com
  Supply Chain Mgr.: Nick Buck
  Phone: (1) 207-238-3000
  Fax: (1) 207-453-4532
  Email: nick.buck@sappi.com
  Utilities Area Oper. Mgr.: Todd Anderson
  Phone: (1) 207-238-3000
  Fax: (1) 207-453-4532
  Email: todd.anderson@sappi.com
Total Employees at this Location: 767
Type of Operation: Pulp mill, Paper mill
Pulp Grades and Capacities:
Total pulp capacity: 561,082 st/y
Pulp available for market: 86,574 st/y
Chemical Pulp: 561,082 st/y
Pulp Mill Data:
  Chemical Pulping Systems:
  Continuous digesters: 1
  Bleach Plant Systems: 1
  Chemical Pulping System, Type: Hardwood/Softwood, Sequence: DEoD
  Chemical Recovery Equipment:
  Evaporator lines: 1
  Recovery boilers: 1
  Lime Kiln
  Pulp Dryers:
  Flakt dryer 1
Paper/Paperboard Grades and Capacities:
Total paper and paperboard capacity: 876,242 st/y
Coated woodfree/freesheet: 856,611 st/y
Specialty and industrial: 19,631 st/y
Paper and Paperboard Mill Data:
  Stock Preparation:
  Pulpers:
Paper Machines: 3
No. 1, Bel-Bond, total capacity 306,952 st/y, Trim width 285 in, Coated woodfree/freesheet
No. 2, Bel-Bond, total capacity 230,214 st/y, Trim width 285 in, Coated woodfree/freesheet, Specialty and industrial
No. 3, Bel-Baie, total capacity 339,075 st/y, Trim width 285 in, Coated woodfree/freesheet
Coating Machines: 3
No. 1, total capacity 292,659 st/y, on machine
No. 2, total capacity 224,868 st/y, on machine
No. 3, total capacity 31,746 st/y, on machine
Energy Data:
Power boilers: 1
Steam turbines: 2 at 108 MW
Electrical demand for mill: 2,401 MWh/D

(M) Sappi Fine Paper North America
Westbrook Mill
Ownership: Sappi Limited
89 Cumberland St
Westbrook, ME 04092
USA
  Phone: (1) 207-856-4000
  Fax: (1) 207-856-1346
  Email: info@sappi.com
  Web Address: www.sappi.com
Personnel:
  Man. Dir.: Donna Cassese
  Phone: (1) 207-856-4925
  Fax: (1) 207-856-1346
  Email: donna.cassese@sappi.com
  Mgr., Basepaper Develop.: James DeWitt
  Phone: (1) 207-856-4000
  Fax: (1) 207-856-1346
  Email: james.dewitt@sappi.com
  Utilities Oper. Mgr.: Gary Couture
  Phone: (1) 207-856-4000
  Fax: (1) 207-856-1346
  Email: gary.couture@sappi.com
  Environ., Health & Safety Specialist: Gordon Lane
  Phone: (1) 207-856-4073
  Fax: (1) 207-856-1346
  Email: gordon.lane@sappi.com
Total Employees at this Location: 135
Type of Operation: Paper mill
Pulp Grades and Capacities:
Total pulp capacity: 4,050 st/y
Recycled Pulping: 4,050 st/y
Pulp Mill Data:
  Chemical Recovery Equipment:
  Recovery boilers: 1
Paper/Paperboard Grades and Capacities:
Total paper and paperboard capacity: 38,548 st/y
Specialty and industrial: 38,548 st/y
Paper and Paperboard Mill Data:
Paper Machines: 1
No. 9, fourdrinier, total capacity 38,548 st/y, Trim width 126 in, Specialty and industrial
Coating Machines: 6
No. 1, off machine
No. 2, off machine
No. 3, off machine
No. 4, off machine
No. 5, off machine
No. 6, off machine
Energy Data:
Power boilers: 3
Steam turbines: 2
Hydro turbines: 6 at 8 MW
Electrical demand for mill: 101 MWh/D

(1) Twin Rivers Paper, LLC
Ownership: 50% by Atlas Holdings, 50% by Blue Wolf Capital Partners
707 Sable Oaks Drive, Suite #010
South Portland, ME 04106
USA
  Phone: (1) 207-523-2350 / 800-920-9988

Maine

Fax: (1) 207-523-2392
Web Address: www.twinriverspaper.com
Personnel:
Pres.: Kenneth Winterhalter
Phone: (1) 207-523-2350
Fax: (1) 207-523-2392
Email: kenneth.winterhalter@twinriverspaper.com
CEO: Tim Lowe
Phone: (1) 207-523-2350
Fax: (1) 207-523-2392
Email: tim.lowe@twinriverspaper.com
CFO: Wayne Gosse
Phone: (1) 207-523-2350
Fax: (1) 207-523-2392
Email: wayne.gosse@twinriverspaper.com
Chief Restructuring Officer: Adam Levy
Phone: (1) 207-523-2350
Fax: (1) 207-523-2392
Email: adam.levy@twinriverspaper.com
VP., Forestry & Sawmill Oper.: Jean-Pierre Grenon
Phone: (1) 207-523-2350
Fax: (1) 207-523-2392
Email: jean-pierre.grenon@twinriverspaper.com
VP., Oper.: Brian Sass
Phone: (1) 207-728-8109
Fax: (1) 207-728-8556
Email: brian.sass@twinriverspaper.com
VP., Sls.: Tony Rigelman
Phone: (1) 207-523-2350
Fax: (1) 207-523-2392
Bus Develop. & Mktg. Mgr.: Dave Deger
Phone: (1) 207-523-2355
Fax: (1) 207-523-2392
Email: dave.deger@twinriverspaper.com
Dir. Pulp & Energy: Dale Paterson
Phone: (1) 207-523-2350
Fax: (1) 207-523-2392
Total Employees of Company: 1,300
Total Employees at this Location: 10
Mill Locations:
Twin Rivers Paper, LLC, Madawaska and Edmundston Mills (East Paper Operations), 82 Bridge Ave., Madawaska, ME 04756, USA, Capacity: 367,629 st/y, (Pulp mill, Paper mill)
Phone: (1) 207-728-3321
Fax: 207-728-8701

ⓜTwin Rivers Paper, LLC
Madawaska and Edmundston Mills (East Paper Operations)
82 Bridge Ave.
Madawaska, ME 04756
USA
Phone: (1) 207-728-3321
Fax: (1) 207-728-8701
Web Address: www.twinriverspaper.com
Personnel:
Gen. Mgr.: Gary Curtis
Phone: (1) 207-728-8617
Fax: (1) 207-728-8556
Email: gary.curtis@twinriverspaper.com
Environ. Mgr.: Eric Carrier
Phone: (1) 207-728-8617
Fax: (1) 207-728-8556
Email: eric.carrier@twinriverspaper.com
Dir. Product Dev.: Bruce Wellman
Phone: (1) 207-728-8419
Fax: (1) 207-728-8738
Email: bruce.wellman@twinriverspaper.com
Total Employees at this Location: 825
Type of Operation: Pulp mill, Paper mill
Pulp Grades and Capacities:
Total pulp capacity: 282,756 st/y
Chemical Pulp: 237,723 st/y
Mechanical Pulp: 42,522 st/y
Recycled Pulping: 2,511 st/y
Pulp Mill Data:
Chemical Pulping Systems:
Batch digesters: 8
Mechanical Pulping Systems:
Conventional grinders: 6
Pulp Lines: 2
Bleach Plant Systems: 4
Sulfite, Sequence: D/CEopDH, Capacity 220,999.8 admt/y
Chemical Recovery Equipment:
Evaporator lines: 1
Recovery boilers: 1
Lime Kiln
Paper/Paperboard Grades and Capacities:
Total paper and paperboard capacity: 367,629 st/y
Uncoated woodfree/freesheet: 94,584 st/y
Uncoated mechanical/groundwood: 82,092 st/y
Coated woodfree/freesheet: 5,354 st/y
Specialty and industrial: 185,599 st/y
Paper and Paperboard Mill Data:
Stock Preparation:
Pulpers: 4
Paper Machines: 5
No. 3, fourdrinier, total capacity 55,323 st/y, Trim width 177 in, Specialty and industrial, Coated woodfree/freesheet
No. 4, fourdrinier, total capacity 48,184 st/y, Trim width 180 in, Uncoated woodfree/freesheet
No. 5, fourdrinier, total capacity 78,523 st/y, Trim width 208 in, Specialty and industrial
No. 7, fourdrinier, total capacity 67,815 st/y, Trim width 215 in, Uncoated woodfree/freesheet, Specialty and industrial
No. 8, fourdrinier, total capacity 117,784 st/y, Trim width 258 in, Uncoated mechanical/groundwood, Specialty and industrial
Coating Machines: 4
No. 1, off machine
No. 2, off machine
PM 3, total capacity 55,115 st/y., on machine
PM 7, on machine
Finishing Equipment:
Winders: 8
Calenders: 1
Supercalenders: 2
Rewinders: 3
Energy Data:
Power boilers: 1
Steam turbines: 2 at 20, 46 (Edmundston) MW
Electrical demand for mill: 900 MWh/D

ⓜUPM North America
Madison Paper Mill
Previously Madison Paper Industries (Myllykoski)
Ownership: UPM-Kymmene Corporation
1 Main Street
Madison, ME 04950
USA
Mailing Address: PO Box 129, Madison, ME 04950-0129, USA
Phone: (1) 207-696-3307
Fax: (1) 207-696-1125
Web Address: www.upm.com
Personnel:
Gen. Mgr.: E. Russell Drechsel
Phone: (1) 207-696-3307
Fax: (1) 207-696-1125
Email: russ.drechsel@upm.com
Mgr., Sustainability: Daniel Mallett
Phone: (1) 207-696-1116
Fax: (1) 207-696-1125
Email: daniel.mallett@upm.com
Mech. Fibre & Tech. Mgr.: Randy D. Charette
Phone: (1) 207-696-3307
Fax: (1) 207-696-1125
Email: randy.charette@upm.com
Dir., Oper.: Michael Doiron
Phone: (1) 207-696-3307
Fax: (1) 207-696-1125
Email: michael.doiron@upm.com
HR Generalist: Kimberly Willette
Phone: (1) 207-696-3307
Fax: (1) 207-696-1125
Email: kim.willette@upm.com
Total Employees at this Location: 215
Type of Operation: Pulp mill, Paper mill
Pulp Grades and Capacities:
Total pulp capacity: 142,768 st/y
Mechanical Pulp: 142,768 st/y
Pulp Mill Data:
Mechanical Pulping Systems:
Pressurized grinders: 6
Bleach Plant Systems: 1
No. 1, Type: Dithionite, Sequence: P/Y, Capacity 120,000 admt/y
Paper/Paperboard Grades and Capacities:
Total paper and paperboard capacity: 242,014 st/y
Uncoated mechanical/groundwood: 242,014 st/y
Paper and Paperboard Mill Data:
Stock Preparation:
Pulpers: 2
Refiners: 4
Paper Machines: 1
No. 3, OptiFormer, total capacity 242,014 st/y, Trim width 283 in, Uncoated mechanical/groundwood
Finishing Equipment:
Supercalenders: 3
Energy Data:
Power boilers: 3
Steam turbines at 3 MW
Hydro turbines: 13 at 25.8 MW
Electrical demand for mill: 1,049 MWh/D

ⓜVerso Paper Corp.
Androscoggin Mill
300 Riley Rd.
Jay, ME 04239
USA
Mailing Address: PO Box 20, Jay, ME 04239, USA
Phone: (1) 207-897-3431
Fax: (1) 207-897-6360
Web Address: www.versopaper.com
Personnel:
Mill Mgr.: Marc Connor
Phone: (1) 207-897-3431
Fax: (1) 207-897-6360
Email: marc.connor@versopaper.com
IT Mgr.: Dave Michaud
Phone: (1) 207-897-3431
Fax: (1) 207-897-6360
Email: dave.michaud@versopaper.com
Mgr., Tech. Serv.: Stephen Provencal
Phone: (1) 207-897-3431
Fax: (1) 207-897-6360
Email: stephen.provencal@versopaper.com
Contr.: Stacey Abbott
Phone: (1) 207-897-3431
Fax: (1) 207-897-6360
Email: stacey.abbott@versopaper.com
Wood Prep. Mgr. (Area Mgr.): Jeff Irish
Phone: (1) 207-897-3431
Fax: (1) 207-897-6360
Email: jeff.irish@versopaper.com
Mgr. Coating & Additive: Tim Borchardt
Phone: (1) 207-897-3431
Fax: (1) 207-897-6360
Email: tim.borchardt@versopaper.com
Total Employees at this Location: 990
Type of Operation: Pulp mill, Paper mill
Pulp Grades and Capacities:
Total pulp capacity: 494,960 st/y
Pulp available for market: 89,230 st/y
Chemical Pulp: 368,778 st/y
Mechanical Pulp: 126,181 st/y
Pulp Mill Data:
Chemical Pulping Systems:
Continuous digesters: 2
Mechanical Pulping Systems:
Conventional grinders: 6
Bleach Plant Systems: 2
Groundwood, Sequence: HS, Capacity 125,661.4 admt/y
Hardwood, Sequence: DEopD, Capacity 152,336.9 admt/y

Maryland

Softwood, Sequence: O_2 DEopD, Capacity 272,927.7 admt/y
Chemical Recovery Equipment:
Evaporator lines: 1
Recovery boilers: 2
Lime Kiln
Pulp Dryers:
Fourdriniers 1
Paper/Paperboard Grades and Capacities:
Total paper and paperboard capacity: 633,178 st/y
Uncoated woodfree/freesheet: 49,969 st/y
Coated woodfree/freesheet: 174,891 st/y
Coated mechanical/groundwood: 354,780 st/y
Specialty and industrial: 53,538 st/y
Paper and Paperboard Mill Data:
Paper Machines: 4
No. 2, fourdrinier, total capacity 154,904 st/y, Trim width 204 in, Coated mechanical/groundwood
No. 3, fourdrinier, total capacity 199,876 st/y, Trim width 276 in, Coated mechanical/groundwood
No. 4, fourdrinier, total capacity 224,860 st/y, Trim width 269 in, Coated woodfree/freesheet, Uncoated woodfree/freesheet
No. 5, (production contracted to Thilmany), fourdrinier, Yankee dryer, total capacity 53,538 st/y, Trim width 228 in, Specialty and industrial
Coating Machines: 3
No. 1, total capacity 154,872 st/y., on machine
No. 2, total capacity 199,846 st/y., on machine
No. 3, total capacity 224,868 st/y., on machine
Finishing Equipment:
Supercalenders: 3 at 170,855 st/y, 220,459 st/y, 248,016 st/y
Energy Data:
Power boilers: 2
Steam turbines: 3 at 25, 25, 30 MW
Hydro turbines: 4 at 11.9 MW
Electrical demand for mill: 1,946 MWh/D

ⓂVerso Paper Corp.
Bucksport Mill
Mill is Verso Paper announced plans to close Bucksport Mill, Maine. The closure of the mill is expected to occur in Q4 2014.
2 River Rd
Bucksport, ME 04416
USA
Mailing Address: PO Box 1200, Bucksport, ME 04416, USA
 Phone: (1) 207-469-1700
 Fax: (1) 207-469-1704
 Web Address: www.versopaper.com
Personnel:
Mill Mgr.: Matthew Archambeau
Phone: (1) 207-469-1700
Fax: (1) 207-469-1704
Email: matthew.archambeau@versopaper.com
Dir., Prod. Develop.: Mike Farrington
Phone: (1) 207-469-1700
Fax: (1) 207-469-1704
Email: mike.farrington@versopaper.com
Mgr., Manuf. Support Pulp & Fiber: Dennis Castonguay
Phone: (1) 207-469-1700
Fax: (1) 207-469-1704
Email: dennis.castonguay1@versopaper.com
Fiber Supply Mgr.: James Contino
Phone: (1) 207-469-1700
Fax: (1) 207-469-1704
Email: james.contino@versopaper.com
Mill Contr.: Christine Urquhart
Phone: (1) 207-469-1700
Fax: (1) 207-469-1704
Email: christine.urquhart@versopaper.com
Total Employees at this Location: 615
Type of Operation: Paper mill
Pulp Grades and Capacities:
Total pulp capacity: 154,087 st/y
Mechanical Pulp: 154,087 st/y
Pulp Mill Data:
 Mechanical Pulping Systems:

Conventional grinders: 12
TMP systems: 1
Bleach Plant Systems: 2
2, Type: Low density Sodium Hydrosulphite, Sequence: H
Paper/Paperboard Grades and Capacities:
Total paper and paperboard capacity: 403,321 st/y
Uncoated woodfree/freesheet: 21,415 st/y
Uncoated mechanical/groundwood: 8,923 st/y
Coated mechanical/groundwood: 342,644 st/y
Specialty and industrial: 30,338 st/y
Paper and Paperboard Mill Data:
 Stock Preparation:
 Pulpers:
Paper Machines: 3
No. 1, fourdrinier, total capacity 60,677 st/y, Trim width 211 in, Specialty and industrial, Uncoated woodfree/freesheet, Uncoated mechanical/groundwood
No. 4, fourdrinier, total capacity 137,415 st/y, Trim width 212 in, Coated mechanical/groundwood
No. 5, fourdrinier, total capacity 205,230 st/y, Trim width 286 in, Coated mechanical/groundwood
Coating Machines: 3
No. 4, total capacity 133,929 st/y., on machine
No. 5, total capacity 201,720 st/y., on machine
PM 1, total capacity 60,626 st/y., off machine
Finishing Equipment:
 Supercalenders: 6
 Rewinders: 2
Energy Data:
Power boilers: 3
HRSG boiler
Steam turbines: 3 at 85, 174 MW
Electrical demand for mill: 1,541 MWh/D

ⒽⓂWoodland Pulp LLC
Baileyville Mill
144 Main Street
Baileyville, ME 04694-9656
USA
 Phone: (1) 207-427-3311
 Fax: (1) 207-427-4102/4183
 Web Address: woodlandpulp.com
Personnel:
CEO: Arvind K. Agarwal
Phone: (1) 207-427-3311
Fax: (1) 207-427-4183
Email: ak.agarwal@woodlandpulp.com
Dir.: Bert Martin
Phone: (1) 207-427-3311
Fax: (1) 207-427-4102/4183
Email: bert.martin@woodlandpulp.com
Contr.: James L Oliver
Phone: (1) 207-427-3311
Fax: (1) 207-427-4102/4183
Email: james.oliver@woodlandpulp.com
Mill Mgr.: Paul Jack
Phone: (1) 207-427-3311
Fax: (1) 207-427-4102/4183
Email: paul.jack@woodlandpulp.com
Quality & Tech. Mgr.: Darrell Salisbury
Phone: (1) 207-427-3311
Fax: (1) 207-427-4102/4183
Email: darrell.salisbury@woodlandpulp.com
Safety & Env. Mgr.: Colin Scott Beal
Phone: (1) 207-427-3311
Fax: (1) 207-427-4183
Email: collin.beal@woodlandpulp.com
HR Mgr.: Candace Robb
Phone: (1) 207-427-3311
Fax: (1) 207-427-4183
Email: candy.robb@woodlandpulp.com
Total Employees at this Location: 300
Type of Operation: Pulp mill
Pulp Grades and Capacities:
Total pulp capacity: 450,287 st/y
Pulp available for market: 440,741 st/y
Chemical Pulp: 450,287 st/y
Pulp Mill Data:
 Chemical Pulping Systems:

Continuous digesters: 1
Pulp Lines: 1
Bleach Plant Systems: 1
No. 1, Type: ECF, Sequence: DEopDED
Chemical Recovery Equipment:
Evaporator lines: 2
Recovery boilers: 1
Lime Kiln
Pulp Dryers:
Fourdriniers 1
Energy Data:
Power boilers: 1
Steam turbines: 2 at 48.3 MW
Hydro turbines: 10 at 18.9 MW
Electrical demand for mill: 970 MWh/D

MARYLAND

ⓂMaryland Paper
16151 Elliott Parkway
Williamsport, MD 21795
USA
 Phone: (1) 301-223-6550
 Fax: (1) 301-223-7730
 Email: info@marylandpaper.com
 Web Address: www.marylandpaper.com
Personnel:
Pres., CEO: Mathew Chakola
Phone: (1) 301-223-6550
Fax: (1) 301-223-7730
Email: mchakola@marylandpaper.com
Oper. Mgr.: George Delaplaine
Phone: (1) 301-223-6550
Fax: (1) 301-223-7730
Email: gdelaplaine@marylandpaper.com
Prod. Mgr.: Ron Baker
Phone: (1) 301-223-6550
Fax: (1) 301-223-7730
Email: rbaker@marylandpaper.com
Contr.: Debi Dennis
Phone: (1) 301-223-6550
Fax: (1) 301-223-7730
Email: ddennis@marylandpaper.com
Spec. Sales & Raw Mat. Purch.: Cherian Thomas
Phone: (1) 301-223-6550
Fax: (1) 301-223-7730
Email: cthomas@marylandpaper.com
Safety Mgr.: Bernard Keefer
Phone: (1) 301-223-6550
Fax: (1) 301-223-7730
Email: bkeefer@marylandpaper.com
Ship & Receiving: Jeff Hooper
Phone: (1) 301-223-6550
Fax: (1) 301-223-7730
Email: jhooper@marylandpaper.com
Total Employees of Company: 70
Mill Locations:
Alabama Paper Products, LLC, Tuscaloosa Mill, 1300 Industrial Park Drive, Tuscaloosa, AL 35401, USA, Capacity: 14,991 st/y, (Paperboard mill)
Phone: (1) 205-339-9660
Fax: (1) 205-339-9883
Maryland Paper, Williamsport Mill, 16151 Elliott Parkway, Williamsport, MD 21795, USA, Capacity: 110,229 st/y, (Paper mill)
Phone: (1) 301-223-6550
Fax: (1) 301-223-7730
Email: info@marylandpaper.com

ⓂMaryland Paper
Williamsport Mill
16151 Elliott Parkway
Williamsport, MD 21795
USA
 Phone: (1) 301-223-6550
 Fax: (1) 301-223-7730

Email: info@marylandpaper.com
Web Address: www.marylandpaper.com
Personnel:
Pres., CEO: Mathew Chakola
Phone: (1) 301-223-6550
Fax: (1) 301-223-7730
Email: mchakola@marylandpaper.com
Oper. Mgr.: George Delaplaine
Phone: (1) 301-223-6550
Fax: (1) 301-223-7730
Email: gdelaplaine@marylandpaper.com
Prod. Mgr.: Ron Baker
Phone: (1) 301-223-6550
Fax: (1) 301-223-7730
Email: rbaker@marylandpaper.com
Contr: Debi Dennis
Phone: (1) 301-223-6550
Fax: (1) 301-223-7730
Email: ddennis@marylandpaper.com
Spec.Sales & Raw Mat. Purch.: Cherian Thomas
Phone: (1) 301-223-6550
Fax: (1) 301-223-7730
Email: cthomas@marylandpaper.com
Safety: Bernard Keefer
Phone: (1) 301-223-6550
Fax: (1) 301-223-7730
Email: bkeefer@marylandpaper.com
Ship & Receiving: Jeff Hooper
Phone: (1) 301-223-6550
Fax: (1) 301-223-7730
Email: jhooper@marylandpaper.com
Total Employees at this Location: 70
Type of Operation: Paper mill
Paper/Paperboard Grades and Capacities:
Total paper and paperboard capacity: 110,229 st/y
Specialty and industrial: 110,229 st/y

Ⓜ**NewPage Corporation**
Luke Mill
300 Pratt St
Luke, MD 21540-1099
USA
Phone: (1) 301-359-3311
Fax: (1) 301-359-2004
Web Address: www.newpagecorp.com
Personnel:
Mill Mgr.: Richard Watro
Phone: (1) 301-359-3311
Fax: (1) 301-359-2004
Email: richard.watro@newpagecorp.com
Pub. Rel. Mgr.: Patsy Koontz
Phone: (1) 301-359-3311
Fax: (1) 301-359-2004
Email: patricia.koontz@newpagecorp.com
Dir., Tech.: Michelle Layman
Phone: (1) 301-359-3311
Fax: (1) 301-359-2004
Email: michelle.layman@newpagecorp.com
Maint. & Eng. Area Mgr.: Victor Proietti
Phone: (1) 301-359-3311
Fax: (1) 301-359-2004
Email: victor.proietti@newpagecorp.com
Prod. Mgr.: Donald Wilkinson
Phone: (1) 301-359-3311
Fax: (1) 301-359-2004
Email: donald.wilkinson@newpagecorp.com
Total Employees at this Location: 849
Type of Operation: Paper mill
Pulp Grades and Capacities:
Total pulp capacity: 339,199 st/y
Chemical Pulp: 339,199 st/y
Pulp Mill Data:
Chemical Pulping Systems:
Batch digesters: 12
Bleach Plant Systems: 2
Chemical Pulping System, Type: Softwood, Sequence: DEPD, Capacity 80,908.3 admt/y
Chemical Pulping System, Type: Hardwood, Sequence: DEoD, Capacity 242,504.4 admt/y
Chemical Recovery Equipment:
Evaporator lines: 1
Recovery boilers: 2
Lime Kiln
Paper/Paperboard Grades and Capacities:
Total paper and paperboard capacity: 509,684 st/y
Coated woodfree/freesheet: 381,192 st/y
Specialty and industrial: 128,492 st/y
Paper and Paperboard Mill Data:
Paper Machines: 2
No. 8, DuoFormer, total capacity 263,051 st/y, Trim width 212 in, Coated woodfree/freesheet
No. 9, fourdrinier, total capacity 246,633 st/y, Trim width 212 in, Coated woodfree/freesheet, Specialty and industrial
Coating Machines: 2
PM 8, total capacity 260,141 st/y, on machine
PM 9, total capacity 243,607 st/y, on machine
Finishing Equipment:
Supercalenders: 4
Sheeters: 3
Energy Data:
Power boilers: 3
Steam turbines: 2 at 65 MW
Electrical demand for mill: 1,254 MWh/D

MASSACHUSETTS

Ⓗ**Crane & Co., Inc.**
30 South St
Dalton, MA 01226-1799
USA
Phone: (1) 413-684-2600 / 413-684-6316
Fax: (1) 413-684-0726
Web Address: www.crane.com
Personnel:
Chmn.: Charles Kittredge
Phone: (1) 413-684-2600 / 413-684-6316
Fax: (1) 413-684-0726
CEO: Stephen P. DeFalco
Phone: (1) 413-684-2600 / 413-684-6316
Fax: (1) 413-684-0726
Email: spdefalco@crane.com
VP, HR: Jay Wickliff
Phone: (1) 413-684-2600 / 413-684-6316
Fax: (1) 413-684-0726
Email: jdwickliff@crane.com
VP, Tech. Materials: Dennis G. Lockyer
Phone: (1) 413-684-2600 / 413-684-6316
Fax: (1) 413-684-0726
Email: dglockyer@crane.com
Prod. Mgr.: Arthur Sanders
Phone: (1) 413-684-2600 / 413-684-6316
Fax: (1) 413-684-0726
Project Leader: Dwight H Reid
Phone: (1) 413-684-2600 / 413-684-6316
Fax: (1) 413-684-0726
Email: dhreid@crane.com
Total Employees of Company: 1,400
Mill Locations:
Crane & Co., Inc., Bay State Mill, 30 Main Street, Dalton, MA 01226, USA, Capacity: 10,500 st/y, (Paper mill)
Phone: (1) 413-684-2600
Fax: (1) 413-684-4278
Crane & Co., Inc., Byron Weston Mill, 800 Main St, Dalton, MA 01226, USA, Capacity: 25,000 st/y, (Paper mill)
Phone: (1) 413-684-1234, 800-233-0748
Fax: (1) 413-684-0726, 800-331-8660
Crane & Co., Inc., Wahconah Mill, 130 Housatonic Street, Dalton, MA 01226, USA, Capacity: 21,000 st/y, (Paper mill)
Phone: (1) 413-684-2600
Fax: (1) 413-684-0875
Crane AB, Tumba Mill, Tumbavägen 5, SE-147 82 Tumba, Sweden, Capacity: 7,716 st/y, (Paper mill)
Phone: (46) 8 57869500
Fax: (46) 8 57869800
Email: info@cranecurrency.com

Ⓜ**Crane & Co., Inc.**
Bay State Mill
30 Main Street
Dalton, MA 01226
USA
Phone: (1) 413-684-2600
Fax: (1) 413-684-4278
Web Address: www.crane.com
Personnel:
Mgr., Workforce Develop.: Donald J. Drosehn
Phone: (1) 413-684-2600
Fax: (1) 413-684-4278
Email: djdrosehn@crane.com
HR Mgr.: Barbara Chaput
Phone: (1) 413-684-2600
Fax: (1) 413-684-4278
Type of Operation: Paper mill
Paper/Paperboard Grades and Capacities:
Total paper and paperboard capacity: 10,500 st/y
Uncoated woodfree/freesheet: 10,500 st/y
Paper and Paperboard Mill Data:
Stock Preparation:
Pulpers: 2
Paper Machines: 1
No. 1, fourdrinier, total capacity 10,500 st/y, Trim width 97 in, Uncoated woodfree/freesheet

Ⓜ**Crane & Co., Inc.**
Byron Weston Mill
800 Main St
Dalton, MA 01226
USA
Phone: (1) 413-684-1234, 800-233-0748
Fax: (1) 413-684-0726, 800-331-8660
Web Address: www.crane.com
Personnel:
Mill Mgr.: Donald J. Dorsehn
Phone: (1) 413-684-1234, 800-233-0748
Fax: (1) 413-684-0726, 800-331-8660
Email: djdorsehn@crane.com
Chief Eng.: Edward A. Goddard
Phone: (1) 413-684-1234, 800-233-0748
Fax: (1) 413-684-0726, 800-331-8660
Email: eagoddard@crane.com
Type of Operation: Paper mill
Paper/Paperboard Grades and Capacities:
Total paper and paperboard capacity: 25,000 st/y
Uncoated woodfree/freesheet
Specialty and industrial
Paper and Paperboard Mill Data:
Stock Preparation:
Pulpers: 4
Refiners: 2
Paper Machines: 2
No. 1, fourdrinier, Trim width 92 in
No. 2, fourdrinier, Trim width 96 in
Finishing Equipment:
Rewinders: 3
Sheeters: 4

Ⓜ**Crane & Co., Inc.**
Wahconah Mill
130 Housatonic Street
Dalton, MA 01226
USA
Phone: (1) 413-684-2600
Fax: (1) 413-684-0875
Web Address: www.crane.com
Personnel:
Mill Mgr: Bill Bartz
Phone: (1) 413-684-2600
Fax: (1) 413-684-4278
Prod Mgr: Joseph McCasland
Phone: (1) 413-684-2600
Fax: (1) 413-684-4278
Coord.: Sandra Racine
Phone: (1) 413-684-2600
Fax: (1) 413-684-4278
Type of Operation: Paper mill

Massachusetts

Paper/Paperboard Grades and Capacities:
Total paper and paperboard capacity: 21,000 st/y
Uncoated woodfree/freesheet: 21,000 st/y
Paper and Paperboard Mill Data:
Paper Machines: 2
No. 1, fourdrinier, Trim width 114 in, Uncoated woodfree/freesheet
No. 2, fourdrinier, Trim width 81 in, Uncoated woodfree/freesheet

ⒽCrocker Technical Papers
Company is for sale (FiberMark has acquired the assets of Crocker Technical Papers, based in Fitchburg, MA. The deal is expected to close in August.)
Ownership: 100% by Family-owned
431 Westminster Street
Fitchburg, MA 01420-4700
USA
  Phone: (1) 978-345-7771
  Fax: (1) 978-342-4052
  Web Address: www.crockertech.com
Personnel:
  Pres.: Larry Gelsomini
  Phone: (1) 978-345-7771
  Fax: (1) 978-342-4052
  Email: lgelsomini@crockertech.com
  VP, Sls.: Ron Imig
  Phone: (1) 978-345-7771
  Fax: (1) 978-342-4052
  Email: rimig@crockertech.com
  VP, Admin.: Bruce Whitney
  Phone: (1) 978-345-7771
  Fax: (1) 978-342-4052
  Email: bwhitney@crockertech.com
  VP, Oper.: Donald Brutvan
  Phone: (1) 978-345-7771
  Fax: (1) 978-342-4052
  Email: dbrutvan@crockertech.com
  Dir., Tech.: Chris Dembrosky
  Phone: (1) 978-345-7771
  Fax: (1) 978-342-4052
  Email: cdembrosky@crockertech.com
  Cust. Serv.: Berni Maguy
  Phone: (1) 978-345-7771
  Fax: (1) 978-342-4052
  Email: bmaguy@crockertech.com
Total Employees of Company: 41
Mill Locations:
Crocker Technical Papers, Fitchburg Mill, 431 Westminster Street, Fitchburg, MA 01420-4700, USA, Capacity: 15,983 st/y, (Paper mill)
  Phone: (1) 978-345-7771
  Fax: (1) 978-342-4052

ⓂCrocker Technical Papers
Fitchburg Mill
431 Westminster Street
Fitchburg, MA 01420-4700
USA
  Phone: (1) 978-345-7771
  Fax: (1) 978-342-4052
  Web Address: www.crockertech.com
Personnel:
  Pres.: Larry Gelsomini
  Phone: (1) 978-345-7771
  Fax: (1) 978-342-4052
  Email: lgelsomini@crockertech.com
  VP, Admin.: Bruce Whitney
  Phone: (1) 978-345-7771
  Fax: (1) 978-342-4052
  Email: bwhitney@crockertech.com
  VP, Oper. (Mill Oper.): Donald Brutvan
  Phone: (1) 978-345-7771
  Fax: (1) 978-342-4052
  Email: dbrutvan@crockertech.com
  Dir., Tech.: Chris Dembrosky
  Phone: (1) 978-345-7771
  Fax: (1) 978-342-4052
  Email: cdembrosky@crockertech.com
  Cust. Serv. & Schedulling: Berni Maguy
  Phone: (1) 978-345-7771
  Fax: (1) 978-342-4052
  Email: bmaguy@crockertech.com
Total Employees at this Location: 41
Type of Operation: Paper mill
Paper/Paperboard Grades and Capacities:
Total paper and paperboard capacity: 15,983 st/y
Uncoated woodfree/freesheet
Coated woodfree/freesheet
Packaging papers
Specialty and industrial
Boxboard/cartonboard
Paper and Paperboard Mill Data:
Stock Preparation:
Pulpers: 2
Refiners: 3
Paper Machines: 1
No. 1, (4-vat cylinder + 1-FC Former.), cylinder (4), total capacity 14,000 st/y, Trim width 94 in, Uncoated woodfree/freesheet, Packaging papers, Specialty and industrial, Boxboard/cartonboard
Finishing Equipment:
Calenders: 2
Sheeters: 2
Energy Data:
Power boilers: 1

ⒽErving Industries Inc.
Company is bankrupt
120 E Main St
Erving, MA 01344
USA
  Phone: (1) 413-422-2700
  Fax: (1) 413-422-2710
  Web Address: www.ervingpaper.com
Personnel:
  Chmn.: Charles B. Housen
  Phone: (1) 413-422-2700
  Fax: (1) 413-422-2710
  Email: chousen@ervingpaper.com
  CEO & Pres.: Morris Housen
  Phone: (1) 413-422-2700 Ext. 299
  Email: mhpaperboy@ervingpapermill.com
  HR Mgr.: Kathy Gibbs
  Phone: (1) 413-422-2700
  Fax: (1) 413-422-2710
  Email: kgibbs@ervingpaper.com
  Assist. Contrl.: Karine A. Nowick
  Phone: (1) 413-422-2700
  Fax: (1) 413-422-2710
  Email: knowick@ervingpaper.com
Total Employees at this Location: 340
Mill Locations:
Erving Paper Mills Inc., Erving Mill, 97 E Main St, Erving, MA 01344, USA, Capacity: 46,410 st/y, (Pulp mill, Paper mill)
  Phone: (1) 413-422-2700
  Fax: (1) 413-422-2710

ⓂErving Paper Mills Inc.
Erving Mill
Mill is bankrupt (filed for Chapter 11 bankruptcy protection on April 20, 2009)
Ownership: Erving Industries Inc.
97 E Main St
Erving, MA 01344
USA
  Phone: (1) 413-422-2700
  Fax: (1) 413-422-2710
  Web Address: www.ervingpaper.com
Personnel:
  Mgr.: Gary Sakowicz
  Phone: (1) 413-422-2700
  Fax: (1) 413-422-2710
  Email: gsakowicz@ervingpapermill.com
  Supt.: Mike Peterson
  Phone: (1) 413-422-2700
  Fax: (1) 413-422-2710
  Email: mpeterson@ervingpapermill.com
  Purch. Mgr.: Jean Woodcock
  Phone: (1) 413-422-2700 Ext. 269
  Fax: (1) 413-422-2710
  Email: jwoodcock@ervingpapermill.com
Total Employees at this Location: 120
Type of Operation: Pulp mill, Paper mill
Pulp Grades and Capacities:
Total pulp capacity: 49,698 st/y
Recycled Pulping: 49,698 st/y
Pulp Mill Data:
Bleach Plant Systems: 1
Deinked Pulp Line
Recycled Fiber Treatment Lines:
Flotation deinking lines: 1
Paper/Paperboard Grades and Capacities:
Total paper and paperboard capacity: 46,410 st/y
Tissue: 46,410 st/y
Paper and Paperboard Mill Data:
Stock Preparation:
Pulpers: 4
Refiners: 4
Paper Machines: 3
No. 3, crescent former, total capacity 16,065 st/y, Trim width 105 in, Tissue
No. 4, crescent former, total capacity 6,069 st/y, Trim width 85 in, Tissue
No. 5, crescent former, total capacity 24,276 st/y, Trim width 104 in, Tissue
Energy Data:
Power boilers: 3
Steam turbines: 1 at 2.5 MW
Electrical demand for mill: 127 MWh/D

ⒽFiberMark North America, Inc.
Ownership: 100% by American Securities Capital Partners LLC
70 Front Street
West Springfield, MA
USA
  Phone: (1) 413 533-0699, 533-0338
  Fax: (1) 413 532-4810, 535-2463
  Web Address: www.fibermark.com
Personnel:
  Pres. & CEO: Anthony MacLaurin
  Phone: (1) 413 533-0699
  Fax: (1) 413 532-4810
  CFO & Snr. VP. Finan.: Craig Thiel
  Phone: (1) 413 533-0699
  Fax: (1) 413 532-4810
  Snr. VP. Oper.: Mike Wright
  Phone: (1) 413 533-0699
  Fax: (1) 413 532-4810
  VP. Cust. Srvcs & Int. Sls.: Jeff Hopkins
  Phone: (1) 413 533-0699
  Fax: (1) 413 532-4810
Total Employees of Company: 1,850
Mill Locations:
FiberMark North America, Inc., Brattleboro Mill, 161 Wellington Rd, Brattleboro, VT 05301, USA, Capacity: 42,999 st/y, (Paper mill)
  Phone: (1) 802-257-0365
  Fax: (1) 802-257-5973
  Email: service@fibermark.com

ⒽHollingsworth & Vose Co.
112 Washington St
East Walpole, MA 02032
USA
  Phone: (1) 508-850-2000
  Fax: (1) 508-668-3557
  Email: info@hovo.com
  Web Address: www.hollingsworth-vose.com
Personnel:
  Chrmn.: Gordon W. Moran
  Phone: (1) 508-850-2000
  Fax: (1) 508-668-3557
  Email: gordon.moran@hovo.com
  Pres. & CEO: Valentine Hollingsworth
  Phone: (1) 508-850-2000

Massachusetts

Fax: (1) 508-668-3557
Email: valentine.hollingsworth@hovo.com
VP, Finan. & CFO: Jeff Sherer
Phone: (1) 508-850-2000
Fax: (1) 508-668-3557
Email: jeff.sherer@hovo.com
VP, Chief Tech. Officer: John Fitzgerald
Phone: (1) 508-850-2000
Fax: (1) 508-668-3557
Email: john.fitzgerald@hovo.com
VP, Gen. Mgr.: David Von Loesecke
Phone: (1) 508-850-2000
Fax: (1) 508-668-3557
Email: david.vonloesecke@hovo.com
VP & Gen Mgr High Efficiency & Specialty BU: Mike Clark
Phone: (1) 508-850-2000
Fax: (1) 508-668-3557
Email: mike.clark@hovo.com
VP & Gen. Mgr., Energy and Industrial BU: John Madej
Phone: (1) 508-850-2000
Fax: (1) 508-668-3557
Email: john.madej@hovo.com
VP, HR: ken Fausnacht
Phone: (1) 508-850-2232
Fax: (1) 508-668-3557
Email: ken.fausnacht@hovo.com
Dir., Eng.: Edward Bregman
Phone: (1) 508-850-2000
Fax: (1) 508-668-3557
Email: edward.bregman@hovo.com
Dir., Bus. Develop.: Angelika Mayman
Phone: (1) 508-850-2205
Fax: (1) 508-668-3557
Email: angelika.mayman@hovo.com
VP, Gen. Mgr.: Josh Ayer
Phone: (1) 508-850-2000
Fax: (1) 508-668-3557
Email: josh.ayer@hovo.com
Mill Locations:
Hollingsworth & Vose GmbH, Hatzfeld Mill, Berleburgerstr. 71, D-35116 Hatzfeld, Germany, Capacity: 17,857 st/y, (Paper mill)
Phone: (49) 6467 801-0/4110
Fax: (49) 6467 801 4202/4126
Email: mail@hovo.de
Hollingsworth & Vose Co., East Walpole Mill, 112 Washington St, East Walpole, MA 02032, USA, Capacity: 15,750 st/y, (Paper mill)
Phone: (1) 508-668-0295, 508-850-2000
Fax: (1) 508-668-3057, 508-668-3557
Email: info@hovo.com
Hollingsworth & Vose Co., Easton Mill, 5035 County Rte 113, Greenwich, NY 12834, USA, Capacity: 22,000 st/y, (Paper mill)
Phone: (1) 518-695-4814, 518-695-3266
Fax: (1) 518-695-4659, 518-695-3771 Main Office
Email: info@hovo.com
Hollingsworth & Vose Co., Greenwich Mill, 3235 County Rte 113, Greenwich, NY 12834, USA, Capacity: 5,000 st/y, (Paper mill)
Phone: (1) 518-695-4814
Fax: (1) 518-695-3771
Email: info@hovo.com
Hollingsworth & Vose Co., Hawkinsville Mill, 300 Industrial Blvd, Hawkinsville, GA 31036, USA, Capacity: 12,500 st/y, (Paper mill)
Phone: (1) 478-783-3200
Fax: (1) 478-783-3292
Email: info@hovo.com
Hollingsworth & Vose Co., West Groton Mill, 219 Townsend Rd; P.O. Box 168, West Groton, MA 01472, USA, Capacity: 17,500 st/y, (Paper mill)
Phone: (1) 978-448-3311
Fax: (1) 978-448-3090
Email: info@hovo.com
Hollingsworth & Vose Co. Ltd., Postlip Mills, Winchcombe, Cheltenham GL54 5BB, United Kingdom, Capacity: 11,023 st/y, (Pulp mill, Paper mill)
Phone: (44) 1242 602 227
Fax: (44) 1242 604 099
Email: hollingsworth@hovo.co.uk

Hovomex S.A. de C.V., Apizaco Mill, Km. 1.2, Camino a Col. Morelos, 90308 Apizaco, Mexico, Capacity: 9,921 st/y, (Paper mill)
Phone: (52) 241 41 72555/70773
Fax: (52) 241 41 70708/80026
Email: info@hovo.com.mx, bortiz@hovo.com.mx

ⓜHollingsworth & Vose Co.
East Walpole Mill
112 Washington St
East Walpole, MA 02032
USA
Phone: (1) 508-668-0295, 508-850-2000
Fax: (1) 508-668-3057, 508-668-3557
Email: info@hovo.com
Web Address: www.hollingsworth-vose.com
Personnel:
Dir., Oper: Mike Baumann
Phone: (1) 508-850-2000
Fax: (1) 508-668-3557
Email: mbaumann@hovo.com
Sls & Mktg Dir.: Per Lindblom
Phone: (1) 508-850-2000
Fax: (1) 508-668-3557
Email: plindblom@hovo.com
Supply Chain Mgr.: Joe Hall
Phone: (1) 508-850-2000
Fax: (1) 508-668-3557
Total Employees at this Location: 35
Type of Operation: Paper mill
Paper/Paperboard Grades and Capacities:
Total paper and paperboard capacity: 15,750 st/y
Coated woodfree/freesheet
Packaging papers
Specialty and industrial
Boxboard/cartonboard
Paper and Paperboard Mill Data:
Stock Preparation:
Pulpers: 3
Refiners: 4
Paper Machines: 2
No. 1, cylinder (4), Trim width 108 in
No. 2, fourdrinier, Trim width 82 in
Energy Data:
Power boilers: 4

ⓜHollingsworth & Vose Co.
West Groton Mill
219 Townsend Rd; P.O. Box 168
West Groton, MA 01472
USA
Mailing Address: PO Box 168, West Groton, MA 01472, USA
Phone: (1) 978-448-3311
Fax: (1) 978-448-3090
Email: info@hovo.com
Web Address: www.hollingsworth-vose.com
Personnel:
Plt. Mgr.: Robert Moore
Phone: (1) 978-448-3311
Fax: (1) 978-448-3090
Email: rob.moore@hovo.com
Lead Operator: Ed Nee
Phone: (1) 978-448-3311
Fax: (1) 978-448-3090
Email: ed.nee@hovo.com
R & D Mgr.: Larry Turner
Phone: (1) 978-448-3311
Fax: (1) 978-448-3090
Email: lturner@hovo.com
Paper Mach. Supt. #5: Dana Page
Phone: (1) 978-448-3311
Fax: (1) 978-448-3090
Email: dana.page@hovo.com
Paper Machine Supt. #7: Bob Corey
Phone: (1) 978-448-3311
Fax: (1) 978-448-3090
Email: bob.corey@hovo.com
Process Mgr. #5 PM: Ken Gargan
Phone: (1) 978-448-3311

Fax: (1) 978-448-3090
Email: ken.gargan@hovo.com
Process Mgr. #7 PM: Bill Krichbaum
Phone: (1) 978-448-3311
Fax: (1) 978-448-3090
Email: bill.krichbaum@hovo.com
Total Employees at this Location: 218
Type of Operation: Paper mill
Paper/Paperboard Grades and Capacities:
Total paper and paperboard capacity: 17,500 st/y
Packaging papers
Specialty and industrial
Paper and Paperboard Mill Data:
Stock Preparation:
Pulpers: 3
Paper Machines: 2
No. 5, fourdrinier, Trim width 72 in
No. 7, Rotoformer, Trim width 110 in
Finishing Equipment:
Rewinders: 2
Sheeters: 2
Energy Data:
Power boilers: 3

ⓜNewark America
Fitchburg Mill
Ownership: Newark Recycled Paperboard Solutions
100 Newark Way
Fitchburg, MA 01420
USA
Phone: (1) 978-665-2600
Fax: (1) 978-665-2750
Web Address: www.newarkpb.com.
Personnel:
Gen. Mgr.: Dana Pelletier
Phone: (1) 978-665-2600
Fax: (1) 978-665-2750
Email: dPelletier@tngus.com
Tech. Mgr.: John Glasier
Phone: (1) 978-665-2600
Fax: (1) 978-665-2750
Email: jglasier@tngus.com
Sls. & Procurement: Brad Cole
Phone: (1) 978-665-2600
Fax: (1) 978-665-2750
Email: bcole@tngus.com
Total Employees at this Location: 105
Type of Operation: Paperboard mill
Pulp Grades and Capacities:
Total pulp capacity: 108,763 st/y
Recycled Pulping: 108,763 st/y
Paper/Paperboard Grades and Capacities:
Total paper and paperboard capacity: 106,029 st/y
Linerboard: 95,319 st/y
Boxboard/cartonboard: 10,710 st/y
Paper and Paperboard Mill Data:
Paper Machines: 1
No. 1, DuoFormer D, total capacity 106,029 st/y, Trim width 124 in, Linerboard, Boxboard/cartonboard
Energy Data:
Power boilers: 2
Steam turbines: 1 at 6.25 MW
Electrical demand for mill: 122 MWh/D

ⒽⓜOnyx Specialty Papers, Inc
South Lee Mill
40 Willow St
South Lee, MA 01260-0188
USA
Phone: (1) 413-243-1231
Fax: (1) 413-243-4602
Email: Info@onyxpapers.com
Web Address: www.onyxpapers.com
Personnel:
Pres & Owner: Patricia C. Begrowicz
Phone: (1) 413-243-1231
Fax: (1) 413-243-4602
Email: pbegrowicz@onyxpapers.com

Massachusetts

Exec. VP, Sls. & Bus. Dev.: Christopher R. Mathews
Phone: (1) 413-243-1231
Fax: (1) 413-243-4602
Email: cmathews@onyxpapers.com
Dir., Oper.: John Healy
Phone: (1) 413-243-1231
Fax: (1) 413-243-4602
Email: jhealy@onyxpapers.com
Contr.: Charlie Stengl
Phone: (1) 413-243-1231
Fax: (1) 413-243-4602
Email: cstengl@onyxpapers.com
Tech & Qlty Mgr.: Steve Maggio
Phone: (1) 413-243-1231
Fax: (1) 413-243-4602
Email: smaggio@onyxpapers.com
Environ. Mgr.: Dan Grant
Phone: (1) 413-243-1231
Fax: (1) 413-243-4602
Email: dgrant@onyxpapers.com
Oper. Support Mgr.: Don Zukowski
Phone: (1) 413-243-1231
Fax: (1) 413-243-4602
Email: dzukowski@onyxpapers.com
Supply Chain Mgr.: Lyn Biasin
Phone: (1) 413-243-1231
Fax: (1) 413-243-4602
Email: lbiasin@onyxpapers.com
Total Employees of Company: 122
Total Employees at this Location: 122
Type of Operation: Paper mill
Paper/Paperboard Grades and Capacities:
 Total paper and paperboard capacity: 10,000 st/y
 Specialty and industrial: 10,000 st/y
Paper and Paperboard Mill Data:
 Stock Preparation:
 Pulpers: 11
 Refiners: 16
Paper Machines: 2
PM 1, fourdrinier, total capacity 5,000 st/y, Trim width 64 in, Specialty and industrial
PM 2, fourdrinier, total capacity 5,000 st/y, Trim width 74 in, Specialty and industrial
Finishing Equipment:
 Rewinders: 3
Energy Data:
 Power boilers: 6

ⓂPaperlogic
Company is previously Southworth Co.
Ownership: Southworth Co.
265 Main Street
Agawam, MA 01001-1822
USA
 Phone: (1) 413-789-1200
 Fax: (1) 413-863-3196
 Email: info.Paperlogic@southworth.com
 Web Address: www.paperlogic.com
Personnel:
 Pres., CEO: David C. Southworth
 Phone: (1) 413-789-1200
 Fax: (1) 413-863-3196
 Email: dsouthworth@southworth.com
 Snr. Mktg. Mgr.: Kyle Biedenbach
 Phone: (1) 413-789-1200
 Fax: (1) 413-863-3196
 Email: kbiedenbach@southworth.com
 Product Mgr. Specialty Paper: Robert J. Binnal Sr.
 Phone: (1) 413-789-1200
 Fax: (1) 413-863-3196
Total Employees of Company: 155
Mill Locations:
Paperlogic, Turners Falls Mill, 36 Canal St, Turners, Falls, MA 01376-1106, USA, Capacity: 9,000 st/y, (Paper mill)
 Phone: (1) 413-863-4326
 Fax: (1) 413-863-3196
 Email: info.Paperlogic@southworth.com

ⓂPaperlogic
Turners Falls Mill
Previously Southworth Co.
36 Canal St
Turners, Falls, MA 01376-1106
USA
Mailing Address: PO Box 717, Turners Falls, MA 01376-0717, USA
 Phone: (1) 413-863-4326
 Fax: (1) 413-863-3196
 Email: info.Paperlogic@southworth.com
 Web Address: www.paperlogic.com
Personnel:
 Tech. Dir., Mill Mgr.: Ken Schelling
 Phone: (1) 413-863-4326 x 265
 Fax: (1) 413-863-3196
 Email: kschelling@southworth.com
 Prod. Mgr.: Rob Binnall
 Phone: (1) 413-863-4326 x 222
 Fax: (1) 413-863-3196
 Email: rbinnall@southworth.com
 Prod. Mgr.: Charlie Blanker
 Phone: (1) 413-863-4326 x240
 Fax: (1) 413-863-3196
 Email: cblanker@southworth.com
 Cust. Serv.: John Helbig
 Phone: (1) 413-863-4326 x 236
 Fax: (1) 413-863-3196
 Email: jhelbig@southworth.com
 Prod. Develop. Mgr.: Paul Bitters
 Phone: (1) 413-863-4326 x 255
 Fax: (1) 413-863-3196
 Email: pbiters@southworth.com
Type of Operation: Paper mill
Pulp Mill Data:
 Chemical Pulping Systems:
 Batch digesters: 2
Paper/Paperboard Grades and Capacities:
 Total paper and paperboard capacity: 9,000 st/y
 Uncoated woodfree/freesheet
Paper and Paperboard Mill Data:
 Stock Preparation:
 Refiners: 3
Paper Machines: 1
No. 1, fourdrinier, total capacity 9,000 st/y, Trim width 112 in, Uncoated woodfree/freesheet
Finishing Equipment:
 Supercalenders: 3
 Rewinders: 2
 Sheeters: 1
Energy Data:
 Power boilers: 4

ⓂSappi Fine Paper North America
Ownership: Sappi Limited
225 Franklin St, 28th floor
Boston, MA 02110
USA
 Phone: (1) 617-423-7300
 Fax: (1) 617-423-5494
 Email: (firstname.lastname@sappi.com)
 Web Address: www.sappi.com/na
Personnel:
 Pres. & CEO: Mark Gardner
 Phone: (1) 617-423-7300
 Fax: (1) 617-423-5494
 Email: mark.gardner@sappi.com
 Exec. VP, Coated Bus. & Chief Sustainability Officer: Jennifer Miller
 Phone: (1) 617-423-7300
 Fax: (1) 617-423-5494
 Email: jennifer.miller@sappi.com
 VP, Finan. & CFO: Annette Luchene
 Phone: (1) 617-423-7300
 Fax: (1) 617-423-5494
 Email: annette.luchene@sappi.com
 VP, Corp. Develop. & CIO: Anne R. Ayer
 Phone: (1) 617-423-7300
 Fax: (1) 617-423-5494
 Email: anne.ayer@sappi.com
 VP, HR & Gen. Counsel: Sarah Manchester
 Phone: (1) 617-423-7300
 Fax: (1) 617-423-5494
 Email: sarah.manchester@sappi.com
 VP, Manuf.: John Donahue
 Phone: (1) 617-423-7300
 Fax: (1) 617-423-5494
 Email: john.donahue@sappi.com
 VP R&D & Innovation: Beth Cormier
 Phone: (1) 617-423-7300
 Fax: (1) 617-423-5494
 Email: beth.cormier@sappi.com
 VP, Procurement & Fiber: Deece Hannigan
 Phone: (1) 617-423-7300
 Fax: (1) 617-423-5494
 Email: deece.hannigan@sappi.com
 VP & Gen. Mgr. Spec. Bus.: Bob E. Weeden
 Phone: (1) 617-423-7300
 Fax: (1) 617-423-5494
 Email: robert.weeden@sappi.com
 VP, Sls. & Bus. Develop.: Bob Forsberg
 Phone: (1) 617-423-7300
 Fax: (1) 617-423-5494
 Email: bob.forsberg@sappi.com
 Mktg. Mgr.: Mark Hittie
 Phone: (1) 617-423-7300
 Fax: (1) 617-423-5494
 Email: mark.hittie@sappi.com
Mill Locations:
Sappi Fine Paper North America, Cloquet Mill, 2201 Avenue B, Cloquet, MN 55720, USA, Capacity: 364,140 st/y, (Pulp mill, Paper mill)
 Phone: (1) 218-879-2300
 Fax: (1) 218-879-0648
Sappi Fine Paper North America, Somerset Mill, 1329 Waterville Road, Skowhegan, ME 04976, USA, Capacity: 876,242 st/y, (Pulp mill, Paper mill)
 Phone: (1) 207-238-3000
 Fax: (1) 207-453-4532
Sappi Fine Paper North America, Westbrook Mill, 89 Cumberland St, Westbrook, ME 04092, USA, Capacity: 38,548 st/y, (Paper mill)
 Phone: (1) 207-856-4000
 Fax: (1) 207-856-1346
 Email: info@sappi.com

ⓂSeaman Paper Company
Otter River Mill
Previously Seaman Paper Co. of Massachusetts, Inc.
51 Main St
Otter River, MA 01436
USA
Mailing Address: PO Box 21, Baldwinville, MA 01436, USA
 Phone: (1) 978-939-1151
 Fax: (1) 978-939-2359
 Email: info@satinwrap.com
 Web Address: www.seamanpaper.com
Personnel:
 VP., Puch.: Sean Whittle
 Phone: (1) 978-939-1151
 Fax: (1) 978-939-2359
 Treas.: Joe Lichwell
 Phone: (1) 978-939-1151
 Fax: (1) 978-939-2359
 Email: joe@seamanpaper.com
 IT Mgr.: Jeff Dickens
 Phone: (1) 978-939-1151
 Fax: (1) 978-939-2359
 Email: jeff@seamanpaper.com
Total Employees at this Location: 49
Type of Operation: Paper mill
Pulp Grades and Capacities:
 Total pulp capacity: 2,274 st/y
 Recycled Pulping: 2,274 st/y
Paper/Paperboard Grades and Capacities:
 Total paper and paperboard capacity: 35,692 st/y
 Tissue: 21,415 st/y
 Specialty and industrial: 14,277 st/y

Paper and Paperboard Mill Data:
Stock Preparation:
Pulpers: 3
Refiners: 5
Paper Machines: 2
No. 1, fourdrinier, total capacity 18,560 st/y, Trim width 83 in, Specialty and industrial, Tissue
No. 2, Yankee dryer, total capacity 17,132 st/y, Trim width 123 in, Specialty and industrial, Tissue
Energy Data:
Power boilers: 2
Steam turbines: 1 at 3 MW

ⓗSeaman Paper Company
Ownership: Private
35 Wilkins Road
Gardner, MA 01440
USA
  Phone: (1) 978-632-1513, 800-784-7783
  Fax: (1) 978-632-6319
  Email: info@satinwrap.com
  Web Address: www.seamanpaper.com
Personnel:
  Pres.: George D. Jones
  Phone: (1) 978-632-1513
  Fax: (1) 978-632-6319
  VP, Sls.: James B. Jones
  Phone: (1) 978-632-1513
  Fax: (1) 978-632-6319
  Email: jbjones@seamanpaper.com
  VP, Purch.: Sean Whittle
  Phone: (1) 978-632-1513
  Fax: (1) 978-632-6319
  VP Manuf.: Gene Reardon
  Phone: (1) 978-632-1513
  Fax: (1) 978-632-6319
  Treas.: Joseph Lichwell
  Phone: (1) 978-632-1513
  Fax: (1) 978-632-6319
  Email: joe@seamanpaper.com
Total Employees of Company: 53
Mill Locations:
Seaman Paper Company, Otter River Mill, 51 Main St, Otter River, MA 01436, USA, Capacity: 35,692 st/y, (Paper mill)
  Phone: (1) 978-939-1151
  Fax: (1) 978-939-2359
  Email: info@satinwrap.com

ⓜSonoco Products Co.
Holyoke Mill
200 S Water St
Holyoke, MA 01040
USA
  Phone: (1) 413-536-4546
  Fax: (1) 413-536-0903
  Web Address: www.sonoco.com
Personnel:
  Mill Mgr.: David Schultz
  Phone: (1) 413-536-4546
  Fax: (1) 413-536-0903
  Email: dave.schultz@sonoco.com
  Logist. & Procurement Supervisor: Donald Ingram
  Phone: (1) 413-536-4546
  Fax: (1) 413-536-0903
Total Employees at this Location: 62
Type of Operation: Paperboard mill
Pulp Grades and Capacities:
Total pulp capacity: 67,420 st/y
Recycled Pulping: 67,420 st/y
Paper/Paperboard Grades and Capacities:
Total paper and paperboard capacity: 66,045 st/y
Boxboard/cartonboard: 66,045 st/y
Paper and Paperboard Mill Data:
Stock Preparation:
Pulpers: 3
Refiners: 2
Paper Machines: 1
No. 1, cylinder (7), total capacity 66,045 st/y, Trim width 116 in, Boxboard/cartonboard

Finishing Equipment:
Rewinders: 1
Energy Data:
Power boilers
Electrical demand for mill: 92 MWh/D

MICHIGAN

ⓜClearwater Paper Corporation
Menominee Mill
144 First St
Menominee, MI 49858
USA
  Phone: (1) 906-863-5595
  Fax: (1) 906-864-3320
  Email: info@clearwaterpaper.com
  Web Address: www.clearwaterpaper.com
Personnel:
  Sr. Mill Mgr. Neenah Mill & Menominee Mill: Kevin French
  Phone: (1) 906-863-5595 Ext. 5318
  Fax: (1) 906-864-3320
  Email: kevin.french@clearwaterpaper.com
  Qlty Cntrl Mgr.: Mike Lovedale
  Phone: (1) 906-863-5595 Ext. 5327
  Fax: (1) 906-864-3320
  Email: mike.lovedale@clearwaterpaper.com
  Maint. & Eng. Mgr.: Adam Nykanen
  Phone: (1) 906-863-5595 Ext. 5328
  Fax: (1) 906-864-3320
  Email: adam.nykanen@clearwaterpaper.com
Total Employees at this Location: 55
Type of Operation: Paper mill
Paper/Paperboard Grades and Capacities:
Total paper and paperboard capacity: 35,692 st/y
Specialty and industrial: 35,692 st/y
Paper and Paperboard Mill Data:
Stock Preparation:
Pulpers: 4
Refiners: 2
Paper Machines: 1
No. 2, fourdrinier, total capacity 35,692 st/y, Trim width 128 in, Specialty and industrial
Finishing Equipment:
Supercalenders: 2
Rewinders: 4
Energy Data:
Power boilers: 1
Electrical demand for mill: 97 MWh/D

ⓜDomtar Corporation
Port Huron Mill
1700 Washington Ave.
Port Huron, MI 48060
USA
Mailing Address: PO Box 5003, Port Huron, MI 48060-5003, USA
  Phone: (1) 810-982-0191
  Fax: (1) 810-982-7124
  Web Address: www.domtar.com
Personnel:
  Mill Mgr.: Rick Vannan
  Phone: (1) 810-982-0191
  Fax: (1) 810-982-7124
  Email: rick.vannan@domtar.com
  Purch. & Logist. Mgr.: Markus Knecht
  Phone: (1) 810-982-0191
  Fax: (1) 810-982-7124
  Email: markus.knecht@domtar.com
  Plt. Eng.: Scott Oberhellman
  Phone: (1) 810-982-0191
  Fax: (1) 810-982-7124
  Email: scott.oberhellman@domtar.com
Total Employees at this Location: 230
Type of Operation: Paper mill
Paper/Paperboard Grades and Capacities:
Total paper and paperboard capacity: 112,430 st/y

Uncoated woodfree/freesheet: 42,831 st/y
Specialty and industrial: 69,600 st/y
Paper and Paperboard Mill Data:
Stock Preparation:
Pulpers: 5
Refiners: 15
Paper Machines: 4
No. 5, fourdrinier, total capacity 14,277 st/y, Trim width 116 in, Uncoated woodfree/freesheet
No. 6, Yankee dryer, total capacity 28,554 st/y, Trim width 127 in, Specialty and industrial
No. 7, fourdrinier, total capacity 28,554 st/y, Trim width 156 in, Uncoated woodfree/freesheet
No. 8, Yankee dryer, total capacity 41,046 st/y, Trim width 186 in, Specialty and industrial
Finishing Equipment:
Rewinders: 1
Energy Data:
Power boilers: 3
Steam turbines: 1 at 7 MW
Electrical demand for mill: 234 MWh/D

ⓞⓜDunn Paper
Port Huron Mill
Ownership: 100% by Wingate Partners
218 Riverview St
Port Huron, MI 48060
USA
  Phone: (1) 810-984-5523
  Fax: (1) 810-984-5830
  Web Address: www.dunnpaper.com
Personnel:
  Pres. & CEO: Brent Earnshaw
  Phone: (1) 810-984-5523 Ext.: 3157
  Fax: (1) 810-984-5830
  Email: earnshawb@dunnpaper.com
  VP, Sls. & Mktg.: Rick Voss
  Phone: (1) 513-553-1134
  Fax: (1) 810-984-5830
  Email: vossr@dunnpaper.com
  Oper. Mgr.: David Barr
  Phone: (1) 810-984-5523
  Fax: (1) 810-984-5830
  Email: barrd@dunnpaper.com
  Sen Acct Exec.: David DeBoer
  Phone: (1) 608-779-9958
  Fax: (1) 810-984-5830
  Email: deboerd@dunnpaper.com
Total Employees of Company: 190
Total Employees at this Location: 190
Type of Operation: Paper mill
Paper/Paperboard Grades and Capacities:
Total paper and paperboard capacity: 86,394 st/y
Specialty and industrial: 86,394 st/y
Paper and Paperboard Mill Data:
Stock Preparation:
Pulpers: 8
Refiners: 14
Paper Machines: 4
No. 1, fourdrinier, Yankee dryer, total capacity 18,921 st/y, Trim width 125 in, Specialty and industrial
No. 2, fourdrinier, Yankee dryer, total capacity 10,353 st/y, Trim width 121 in, Specialty and industrial
No. 3, fourdrinier, Yankee dryer, total capacity 33,915 st/y, Trim width 134 in, Specialty and industrial
No. 4, fourdrinier, Yankee dryer, total capacity 23,205 st/y, Trim width 124 in, Specialty and industrial
Coating Machines: 3
CM 1, on machine
CM 3
CM 4
Finishing Equipment:
Rewinders: 1
Energy Data:
Power boilers: 2
Combustion turbines: 3 at 15 MW
Electrical demand for mill: 188 MWh/D

Michigan

ⓜFrench Paper Co.
Ownership: French Family (Private)
100 French St
Niles, MI 49120
USA
  Phone: (1) 269.683.1100
  Fax: (1) 269-683-3025
  Web Address: www.frenchpaper.com
Personnel:
  Chmn.: Edward French
  Phone: (1) 269-683-1100
  Fax: (1) 269-683-3025
  Email: jerryfrench@frenchpaper.com
  Pres.: Jerry French
  Phone: (1) 269-683-1100
  Fax: (1) 269-683-3025
  Email: jerryfrench@frenchpaper.com
  VP, Oper.: Shane Fenske
  Phone: (1) 269-683-1100
  Fax: (1) 269-683-3025
  Email: shanefenske@frenchpaper.com
  Reg. Acc. Mgr.: Rebecca Canter
  Phone: (1) 269-683-1100
  Fax: (1) 269-683-3025
  Email: rebeccacanter@frenchpaper.com
  PM Supt.: Rod Toll
  Phone: (1) 269-683-1100
  Fax: (1) 269-683-3025
  Email: rodtoll@frenchpaper.com
Total Employees of Company: 75
Mill Locations:
  French Paper Co., Niles Mill, 100 French St, Niles, MI 49120, USA, Capacity: 19,631 st/y, (Paper mill)
  Phone: (1) 269-683-1100
  Fax: (1) 269-683-3025

ⓜFrench Paper Co.
Niles Mill
100 French St
Niles, MI 49120
USA
  Phone: (1) 269-683-1100
  Fax: (1) 269-683-3025
  Web Address: www.frenchpaper.com
Personnel:
  Gen. Mgr.: Brian French
  Phone: (1) 269-683-1100
  Fax: (1) 269-683-3025
  Email: french@frenchpaper.com
  Oper. Mgr.: Jeff Honour
  Phone: (1) 269-683-1100
  Fax: (1) 269-683-3025
  Email: honour@frenchpaper.com
  PM Supt.: Rod Toll
  Phone: (1) 269-683-1100
  Fax: (1) 269-683-3025
  Email: toll@frenchpaper.com
Total Employees at this Location: 50
Type of Operation: Paper mill
Pulp Grades and Capacities:
  Total pulp capacity: 1,715 st/y
  Recycled Pulping: 1,715 st/y
Paper/Paperboard Grades and Capacities:
  Total paper and paperboard capacity: 19,631 st/y
  Uncoated woodfree/freesheet: 19,631 st/y
Paper and Paperboard Mill Data:
  Stock Preparation:
  Pulpers: 3
  Refiners: 6
Paper Machines: 1
  No. 1, fourdrinier, total capacity 19,631 st/y, Trim width 107 in, Uncoated woodfree/freesheet
Finishing Equipment:
  Sheeters: 2
Energy Data:
  Power boilers: 1
  Hydro turbines: 4 at 1.25 MW
  Electrical demand for mill: 35 MWh/D

ⓜFutureMark Paper Group
Manistique Mill
Previously Manistique Papers Inc.
453 S Mackinac Ave
Manistique, MI 49854
USA
  Phone: (1) 906-341-2175
  Fax: (1) 906-341-5635
  Web Address: www.futuremarkpaper.com
Personnel:
  Pres. & CEO: Matthew Nightingale
  Phone: (1) 906-341-2175
  Fax: (1) 906-341-5635
  Email: matthew.nightingale@futuremarkpaper.com
  Executive VP & General Manager: Jon Johnson
  Phone: (1) 906-341-4204
  Fax: (1) 906-341-5635
  Email: jon.johnson@futuremarkpaper.com
  Waste Paper Procurement Mgr.: Eric Bourdo
  Phone: (1) 224-643-7067
  Fax: (1) 906-341-7099
  Email: eric.bourdo@futuremarkpaper.com
  HR Mgr.: David Tennyson
  Phone: (1) 906-341-2175
  Fax: (1) 906-341-5635
  Email: david.tennyson@futuremarkpaper.com
Total Employees at this Location: 140
Type of Operation: Paper mill
Pulp Grades and Capacities:
  Total pulp capacity: 148,698 st/y
  Recycled Pulping: 148,698 st/y
Pulp Mill Data:
  Bleach Plant Systems: 1
  Recycled Pulping System
  Recycled Fiber Treatment Lines:
  Flotation deinking lines: 1 at 180,000 admt/y
  Pulpers: 1 at 180,000 admt/y
Paper/Paperboard Grades and Capacities:
  Total paper and paperboard capacity: 143,241 st/y
  Uncoated mechanical/groundwood: 115,694 st/y
  Packaging papers: 27,546 st/y
Paper and Paperboard Mill Data:
Paper Machines: 1
  No. 1, DuoFormer F, total capacity 143,241 st/y, Trim width 147 in, Packaging papers, Uncoated mechanical/groundwood
Finishing Equipment:
  Calenders: 1
  Rewinders: 1
Energy Data:
  Power boilers: 2
  Electrical demand for mill: 359 MWh/D

ⓜGraphic Packaging International Inc.
Battle Creek Mill
79 E Fountain St
Battle Creek, MI 49017-4198
USA
  Phone: (1) 269-963-4004
  Fax: (1) 269-963-1306
  Web Address: www.graphicpkg.com
Personnel:
  Resident Mgr.: Mark Reed
  Phone: (1) 269-963-4004
  Fax: (1) 269-963-1306
  Email: mark.reed@graphicpkg.com
  Oper. Mgr.: Ronald L. Fox
  Phone: (1) 269-963-4004
  Fax: (1) 269-963-1306
  Email: ron.fox@graphicpkg.com
  Fiber Mgr.: Joel Burkle
  Phone: (1) 269-963-4004
  Fax: (1) 269-963-1306
  Email: joel.burkle@graphicpkg.com
Total Employees at this Location: 207
Type of Operation: Paperboard mill
Pulp Grades and Capacities:
  Total pulp capacity: 155,103 st/y
  Recycled Pulping: 155,103 st/y
Pulp Mill Data:
Pulp Lines: 1
  Recycled Fiber Treatment Lines:
  Pulpers: 1
Paper/Paperboard Grades and Capacities:
  Total paper and paperboard capacity: 173,145 st/y
  Boxboard/cartonboard: 173,145 st/y
Paper and Paperboard Mill Data:
  Stock Preparation:
  Pulpers:
  Refiners: 1
Paper Machines: 2
  No. 1, cylinder (7), total capacity 89,607 st/y, Trim width 95 in, Boxboard/cartonboard
  No. 2, Ultraformer (6), total capacity 83,538 st/y, Trim width 120 in, Boxboard/cartonboard
Coating Machines: 2
  No. 1, total capacity 81,570 st/y., on machine
  No. 2, total capacity 80,467 st/y., on machine
Finishing Equipment:
  Sheeters: 1
Energy Data:
  Power boilers: 1
  Steam turbines: 1 at 6 MW
  Electrical demand for mill: 284 MWh/D

ⓜGraphic Packaging International Inc.
Kalamazoo Mill
1500 N Pitcher St
Kalamazoo, MI 49007-2539
USA
  Phone: (1) 269-383-5000
  Fax: (1) 269-383-5135
  Web Address: www.graphicpkg.com
Personnel:
  VP - Recycled Mill Div.: Michael Farrell
  Phone: (1) 269-383-5000
  Fax: (1) 269-383-5135
  Email: mike.farrell@graphicpkg.com
  Resident Mill Mgr.: Scott LeBeau
  Phone: (1) 269-383-5000
  Fax: (1) 269-383-5135
  Email: scott.lebeau@graphicpkg.com
  Contr.: Julie Richmond
  Phone: (1) 269-383-5000
  Fax: (1) 269-383-5135
  Email: julie.richmond@graphicpkg.com
  Buyer: Cecilia Grauman
  Phone: (1) 269-383-5000
  Fax: (1) 269-383-5135
  Email: graumanc@graphicpkg.com
Total Employees at this Location: 282
Type of Operation: Paperboard mill
Pulp Grades and Capacities:
  Total pulp capacity: 412,415 st/y
  Recycled Pulping: 412,415 st/y
Pulp Mill Data:
  Recycled Fiber Treatment Lines:
  Pulpers: 2 at 422,840
Paper/Paperboard Grades and Capacities:
  Total paper and paperboard capacity: 460,530 st/y
  Boxboard/cartonboard: 460,530 st/y
Paper and Paperboard Mill Data:
  Stock Preparation:
  Pulpers: 10
Paper Machines: 2
  K1, fourdrinier (3), total capacity 349,503 st/y, Trim width 146 in, Boxboard/cartonboard
  K3, cylinder (6), total capacity 111,027 st/y, Trim width 120 in, Boxboard/cartonboard
Coating Machines: 2
  CM 1, total capacity 321,318 st/y., on machine
  CM 3, total capacity 114,638 st/y., on machine
Energy Data:
  Power boilers: 3
  Steam turbines: 2 at 4, 7.5 MW
  Electrical demand for mill: 586 MWh/D

Michigan

ⓘGreat Lakes Tissue Co.
Ownership: Clarence Roznowski
437 S Main St
Cheboygan, MI 49721
USA
 Phone: (1) 231-627-0200
 Fax: (1) 231-627-3906
 Email: info@greatlakestissue.com
 Web Address: www.greatlakestissue.com
Personnel:
 Pres. & CEO: Clarence Rozlowski
 Phone: (1) 231-627-0200
 Fax: (1) 231-627-3906
 Elec. Eng.: Todd Corbin
 Phone: (1) 231-627-0200
 Fax: (1) 231-627-3906
 Mill Mgr.: Jerry Melching
 Phone: (1) 231-627-0200
 Fax: (1) 231-627-3906
 Email: jerry.melching@greatlakestissue.com
 Project Mgr.: Arthur Roznowski
 Phone: (1) 231-627-0200
 Fax: (1) 231-627-3906
 Email: arthur.roznowski@greatlakestissue.com
Total Employees of Company: 80
Mill Locations:
Great Lakes Tissue Co., Cheboygan Mill, 437 S Main St, Cheboygan, MI 49721, USA, Capacity: 22,134 st/y, (Paper mill)
 Phone: (1) 231-627-0200
 Fax: (1) 231-627-0242
 Email: info@greatlakestissue.com

ⓘGreat Lakes Tissue Co.
Cheboygan Mill
437 S Main St
Cheboygan, MI 49721
USA
 Phone: (1) 231-627-0200
 Fax: (1) 231-627-0242
 Email: info@greatlakestissue.com
 Web Address: www.greatlakestissue.com
Personnel:
 Maint. Mgr.: Mike Dodd
 Phone: (1) 231-627-0200
 Fax: (1) 231-627-0242
 Email: mdodd@greatlakestissue.com
 Proj. Mgr.: Arthur Roznowski
 Phone: (1) 231-627-0200
 Fax: (1) 231-627-0242
 Email: arthus.roznowski@greatlakestissue.com
Total Employees at this Location: 80
Type of Operation: Paper mill
Pulp Grades and Capacities:
 Total pulp capacity: 23,691 st/y
 Recycled Pulping: 23,691 st/y
Pulp Mill Data:
Pulp Lines: 1
 Bleach Plant Systems: 1
 DIP
 Recycled Fiber Treatment Lines:
 Pulpers: 1 at 27,557
Paper/Paperboard Grades and Capacities:
 Total paper and paperboard capacity: 22,134 st/y
 Tissue: 22,134 st/y
Paper and Paperboard Mill Data:
Paper Machines: 2
No. 8, crescent former, total capacity 10,353 st/y, Trim width 128 in, Tissue
No. 9, crescent former, total capacity 11,781 st/y, Trim width 130 in, Tissue
Energy Data:
 Power boilers: 2
 Hydro turbines: 1 at 1.5 MW
 Electrical demand for mill: 78 MWh/D

ⓘNeenah Paper, Inc.
Munising Mill
501 E Munising Ave
Munising, MI 49862-1490
USA
 Phone: (1) 906-387-2700
 Fax: (1) 906-387-2935
 Web Address: www.neenah.com
Personnel:
 Dir., Finan.: Mark Arrieri
 Phone: (1) 906-387-2700
 Fax: (1) 906-387-2935
 Email: mark.arrieri@neenahpaper.com
 Qlty. & Continuous Improvement Mgr.: Todd Swenson
 Phone: (1) 906-387-7551
 Fax: (1) 906-387-2935
 Email: todd.swenson@neenahpaper.com
 Supply Chain Mgr.: Chris Gethers
 Phone: (1) 906-387-7551
 Fax: (1) 906-387-2935
 Email: chris.gethers@neenahpaper.com
 Purch. Analyst: Kathy Matson
 Phone: (1) 906-387-7551
 Fax: (1) 906-387-2935
 Email: kathy.matson@neenahpaper.com
Total Employees at this Location: 100
Type of Operation: Paper mill
Paper/Paperboard Grades and Capacities:
 Total paper and paperboard capacity: 32,123 st/y
 Specialty and industrial: 32,123 st/y
Paper and Paperboard Mill Data:
 Stock Preparation:
 Pulpers: 4
 Refiners: 2
Paper Machines: 2
No. 1, fourdrinier, total capacity 16,061 st/y, Trim width 120 in, Specialty and industrial
No. 2, fourdrinier, total capacity 16,061 st/y, Trim width 120 in, Specialty and industrial
Coating Machines: 1
No. 1, off machine
Finishing Equipment:
 Supercalenders: 2
 Rewinders: 5
 Sheeters: 2
Energy Data:
 Power boilers: 2
 Electrical demand for mill: 75 MWh/D

ⓘNewPage Corporation
Escanaba Mill
7100 County Rd 426, M.5 Rd
Escanaba, MI 49829
USA
Mailing Address: PO Box 757, Escanaba, MI 49829-0757, USA
 Phone: (1) 906-786-1660
 Fax: (1) 906-789-3221, 789-3206
 Web Address: www.newpagecorp.com
Personnel:
 Mill Mgr.: Roger Rouleau
 Phone: (1) 906-786-1660
 Fax: (1) 906-789-3221
 Email: roger.rouleau@newpagecorp.com
 Environ. Mgr.: Todd Schmidt
 Phone: (1) 906-233-2929
 Fax: (1) 906-233-2266
 Email: todd.schmidt@newpagecorp.com
 Tech. Dir. (From March 2013): Steven Bennett
 Phone: (1) 906-786-1660
 Fax: (1) 906-789-3221
 Email: steven.bennett@newpagecorp.com
 Commun. Mgr.: Jackie Pride
 Phone: (1) 906-233-2690
 Fax: (1) 906-789-3221
 Email: jackie.pride@newpagecorp.com
 Prod. Mgr.: Jeffrey Boulden
 Phone: (1) 906-233-2357
 Fax: (1) 906-789-3221
 Email: jeffrey.boulden@newpagecorp.com
Total Employees at this Location: 996
Type of Operation: Pulp mill, Paper mill
Pulp Grades and Capacities:
 Total pulp capacity: 538,554 st/y
 Chemical Pulp: 461,793 st/y
 Mechanical Pulp: 76,761 st/y
Pulp Mill Data:
 Chemical Pulping Systems:
 Batch digesters: 8
 Mechanical Pulping Systems:
 RMP systems: 1
 Bleach Plant Lines:
 Chemical Pulping System, Sequence: DEopDED
 Mechanical - RMP Pulping System, Sequence: P
 Chemical Recovery Equipment:
 Evaporator lines: 1
 Recovery boilers: 1
 Lime Kiln
 Pulp Dryers:
 Flash dryers
Paper/Paperboard Grades and Capacities:
 Total paper and paperboard capacity: 779,873 st/y
 Uncoated woodfree/freesheet: 62,461 st/y
 Coated woodfree/freesheet: 378,337 st/y
 Coated mechanical/groundwood: 324,798 st/y
 Specialty and industrial: 14,277 st/y
Paper and Paperboard Mill Data:
 Stock Preparation:
 Pulpers: 5
 Refiners: 18
Paper Machines: 3
No. 1, fourdrinier, total capacity 189,168 st/y, Trim width 143 in, Coated woodfree/freesheet, Uncoated woodfree/freesheet
No. 3, fourdrinier, total capacity 283,752 st/y, Trim width 273 in, Coated woodfree/freesheet, Coated mechanical/groundwood, Uncoated woodfree/freesheet, Specialty and industrial
No. 4, fourdrinier, total capacity 306,952 st/y, Trim width 273 in, Coated mechanical/groundwood, Uncoated woodfree/freesheet
Coating Machines: 3
No. 1, total capacity 197,310 st/y., off machine
No. 3, total capacity 263,448 st/y., off machine
No. 4, total capacity 252,425 st/y., off machine
Finishing Equipment:
 Supercalenders: 6
 Rewinders: 2
Energy Data:
 Power boilers: 4
 Steam turbines: 3 at 103 MW
 Hydro turbines: 3 at 9.2 MW
 Electrical demand for mill: 2,339 MWh/D

ⓘOtsego Paper Inc.
Otsego Mill
Ownership: 100% by United States Gypsum Co.
320 N Farmer St
Otsego, MI 49078
USA
Mailing Address: PO Box 155, Otsego, MI 49078-0155, USA
 Phone: (1) 269-692-6141
 Fax: (1) 269-692-2060
 Web Address: www.usg.com
Personnel:
 Plt. Mgr.: Henry Krell
 Phone: (1) 269-692-6141
 Fax: (1) 269-692-2060
 Email: hkrell@usg.com
 Paper Mill Mgr.: Tom Oldham
 Phone: (1) 269-692-6141
 Fax: (1) 269-692-2060
 Email: toldham@usg.com
 Snr. Environ. Eng.: Dale Turton
 Phone: (1) 269-692-6141
 Fax: (1) 269-692-2060
 Email: dturton@usg.com
 Contr.: Thomas Benchina
 Phone: (1) 269-692-6141
 Fax: (1) 269-692-2060
 Email: tbenchina@usg.com
Total Employees at this Location: 130

Michigan

Type of Operation: Pulp mill, Paperboard mill
Pulp Grades and Capacities:
 Total pulp capacity: 208,687 st/y
 Recycled Pulping: 208,687 st/y
Pulp Mill Data:
 Recycled Fiber Treatment Lines:
 Recycled packaging pulping lines: 3 at 100,000 admt/y
Paper/Paperboard Grades and Capacities:
 Total paper and paperboard capacity: 199,920 st/y
 Boxboard/cartonboard: 199,920 st/y
Paper and Paperboard Mill Data:
 Stock Preparation:
 Pulpers: 7
 Refiners: 3
Paper Machines: 1
 No. 1, fourdrinier, total capacity 199,920 st/y, Trim width 162 in, Boxboard/cartonboard
Finishing Equipment:
 Winders: 1 at 300,000 st/y
Energy Data:
 Power boilers: 1
 Combustion turbines: 2 at 20 MW
 Electrical demand for mill: 334 MWh/D

ⓜOx Paperboard LLC
Constantine Mill
Previously Berry Plastics Holding Corporation. Ox Paperboard purchased this mill in early 2012.
700 Centreville Rd
Constantine, MI 49042
USA
Mailing Address: PO Box 187, Constantine, MI 49042, USA
 Phone: (1) 269-435-2425
 Fax: (1) 269-435-7510
 Web Address: www.oxpaperboard.com
Personnel:
 Gen. Mgr.: Timothy Michaels
 Phone: (1) 269-435-2425 Ext. 411
 Fax: (1) 269-435-7510
 Email: timmichaels@oxpaperboard.com
 Purch. Agent: Chris Malott
 Phone: (1) 269-435-2425 Ext. 427
 Fax: (1) 269-435-7510
 Email: chrismalott@oxpaperboard.com
 Building Products Tech. Dir.: Paul Lautrup
 Phone: (1) 269-435-2425
 Fax: (1) 269-435-7510
 Email: paullautrup@oxpaperboard.com
 Cust. Serv. & Logist. Mgr.: Tera Loker
 Phone: (1) 269-435-2425
 Fax: (1) 269-435-7510
 Email: teraloker@oxpaperboard.com
Total Employees at this Location: 90
Type of Operation: Paperboard mill
Pulp Grades and Capacities:
 Total pulp capacity: 55,878 st/y
 Recycled Pulping: 55,878 st/y
Pulp Mill Data:
 Recycled Fiber Treatment Lines:
 Recycled packaging pulping lines
Paper/Paperboard Grades and Capacities:
 Total paper and paperboard capacity: 53,907 st/y
 Boxboard/cartonboard: 53,907 st/y
Paper and Paperboard Mill Data:
 Stock Preparation:
 Pulpers: 1
 Refiners: 4
Paper Machines: 1
 No. 1, cylinder (9), total capacity 53,907 st/y, Trim width 100 in, Boxboard/cartonboard
Energy Data:
 Power boilers: 2
 Electrical demand for mill: 75 MWh/D

ⓜPackaging Corp. of America
Filer City Mill
2246 Udell St
Filer City, MI 49634
USA
Mailing Address: PO Box 5, Filer City, MI 49634-0005, USA
 Phone: (1) 231-723-9951
 Fax: (1) 231-723-1395
 Web Address: www.packagingcorp.com
Personnel:
 Mill Mgr.: Robert Peretin
 Phone: (1) 231-723-3552
 Fax: (1) 231-723-1396
 Email: rperetin@packagingcorp.com
 Paper Machines & Shipping Mgr.: Michael Thompson
 Phone: (1) 231-723-1391
 Fax: (1) 231-723-1396
 Email: mthompson@packagingcorp.com
 Paper Mill Supt.: Maureen A. Barry
 Phone: (1) 231-723-9951
 Fax: (1) 231-723-1396
 Email: mbarry@packagingcorp.com
 Tech. Mgr.: John D. Rakoski
 Phone: (1) 231-723-9951
 Fax: (1) 231-723-1396
 Email: jrakoski@packagingcorp.com
 Snr Proj. Eng.: Randy Stoykovich
 Phone: (1) 231-723-9951
 Fax: (1) 231-723-1396
 Email: rstoykovich@packagingcorp.com
 Woodlands Mgr.: Todd Siegert
 Phone: (1) 231-723-9951
 Fax: (1) 231-723-1396
 Email: tsiegert@packagingcorp.com
Total Employees at this Location: 344
Type of Operation: Pulp mill, Paperboard mill
Pulp Grades and Capacities:
 Total pulp capacity: 472,485 st/y
 Chemical Pulp: 265,898 st/y
 Recycled Pulping: 206,587 st/y
Pulp Mill Data:
 Chemical Pulping Systems:
 Continuous digesters: 3
 Recycled Fiber Treatment Lines:
 Pulpers: 2 at 178,500 admt/y
Paper/Paperboard Grades and Capacities:
 Total paper and paperboard capacity: 456,603 st/y
 Corrugating medium/fluting: 456,603 st/y
Paper and Paperboard Mill Data:
Paper Machines: 3
 No. 1, fourdrinier, total capacity 77,112 st/y, Trim width 148 in, Corrugating medium/fluting
 No. 2, fourdrinier, total capacity 200,991 st/y, Trim width 158 in, Corrugating medium/fluting
 No. 3, fourdrinier, total capacity 178,500 st/y, Trim width 159 in, Corrugating medium/fluting
Energy Data:
 Power boilers: 3
 Steam turbines: 3 at 17.5 MW
 Electrical demand for mill: 845 MWh/D

ⓜResolute FP US Inc.
Menominee Mill
Previously Fibrek Inc.
Ownership: 100% by Resolute Forest Products Canada Inc.
701 Fourth Ave.
Menominee, MI 49858
USA
Mailing Address: PO Box 277, Menominee, MI 49858-0277, USA
 Phone: (1) 906 863-9936, 906-863-8137
 Fax: (1) 906-864-9108
 Web Address: www.resolutefp.com
Personnel:
 Gen. Mgr.: Todd Clausen
 Phone: (1) 906-864-9159
 Fax: (1) 906-863-7488
 Email: todd.clausen@resolutefp.com
 Tech. Serv. Mgr.: Mary Goyette
 Phone: (1) 906-864-9157
 Fax: (1) 906-864-9108
 Email: mary.goyette@resolutefp.com
 Maint. Mgr.: Jason Zorn
 Phone: (1) 906-864-9144
 Fax: (1) 906-864-9179
 Email: jason.zorn@resolutefp.com
 Project Eng.: Kirk Kontny
 Phone: (1) 906-864-9167
 Fax: (1) 906-864-9108
 Email: kirk.kontny@resolutefp.com
 HR Coord.: Pam Neville
 Phone: (1) 906-863-8137
 Fax: (1) 906-864-9108
 Email: pam.neville@resolutefp.com
 Logistics Coord.: Diane Erickson
 Phone: (1) 906-864-9139
 Fax: (1) 906-864-9147
 Email: diane.erickson@resolutefp.com
 Assist. Prod. Mgr.: Greg Russell
 Phone: (1) 906-863-8137
 Fax: (1) 906-864-9108
 Email: greg.russell@resolutefp.com
 Tech. Mgr.: Michael Maeder
 Phone: (1) 906-863-8137
 Fax: (1) 906-864-9108
 Email: michael.maeder@resolutefp.com
Total Employees at this Location: 105
Type of Operation: Pulp mill
Pulp Grades and Capacities:
 Total pulp capacity: 199,057 st/y
 Pulp available for market: 196,350 st/y
 Recycled Pulping: 199,057 st/y
Pulp Mill Data:
Pulp Lines: 1
 Bleach Plant Systems: 1
 Deinkd Pulp Line, Sequence: PFAS, Capacity 187,389.8 admt/y
 Recycled Fiber Treatment Lines:
 Flotation deinking lines: 1 at 190,697 admt/y
 Pulp Dryers:
 Air Float dryers 1
Energy Data:
 Power boilers
 Electrical demand for mill: 310 MWh/D

ⓜRockTenn Co.
Battle Creek Mill
177 Angell St
Battle Creek, MI 49015-1958
USA
 Phone: (1) 269-963-5511
 Fax: (1) 269-969-7166
 Web Address: www.rocktenn.com
Personnel:
 VP. & Gen. Mgr.: Tom (Thomas) D. Crockett
 Phone: (1) 269-969-7116
 Fax: (1) 269-969-7166
 Email: tdcrockett@rocktenn.com
 Safety Coord.: Megan Foster
 Phone: (1) 269-969-7116
 Fax: (1) 269-969-7166
 Email: mfoster@rocktenn.com
 Sls. Mgr.: Roberto Balaguer
 Phone: (1) 269-969-7116
 Fax: (1) 269-969-7166
 Email: rbalaguer@rocktenn.com
 Prod. Superint.: Stephen Rudy
 Phone: (1) 269-969-7116
 Fax: (1) 269-969-7166
 Email: srudy@rocktenn.com
 Maint. Superint.: Mark Arnett
 Phone: (1) 269-969-7116
 Fax: (1) 269-969-7166
 Email: marnett@rocktenn.com
Total Employees at this Location: 168
Type of Operation: Paperboard mill
Pulp Grades and Capacities:
 Total pulp capacity: 140,278 st/y
 Recycled Pulping: 140,278 st/y
Pulp Mill Data:
 Recycled Fiber Treatment Lines:

Pulpers: 1 at 164,793
Paper/Paperboard Grades and Capacities:
Total paper and paperboard capacity: 159,936 st/y
Boxboard/cartonboard: 159,936 st/y
Paper and Paperboard Mill Data:
  Stock Preparation:
  Pulpers: 4
Paper Machines: 1
No. 1, Bel-Bond, total capacity 159,936 st/y, Trim width 129 in, Boxboard/cartonboard
Coating Machines: 1
No. 1, total capacity 159,832 st/y., on machine
Finishing Equipment:
  Sheeters: 1
Energy Data:
Power boilers: 2
Steam turbines: 2 at 2 MW

Ⓜ **Verso Paper Corp.**
Quinnesec Mill
W6705 US Highwway 2
Quinnesec, MI 49870-0211
USA
Mailing Address: PO Box 211, Norway, MI 49870-0211, USA
  Phone: (1) 906-779-3200
  Fax: (1) 906-779-3307
  Web Address: www.versopaper.com
Personnel:
Mill Mgr.: Adam St. John
  Phone: (1) 906-779-3200
  Fax: (1) 906-779-3307
  Email: adam.stjohn@versopaper.com
Prod. Mgr: John Jessen
  Phone: (1) 906-779-3200
  Fax: (1) 906-779-3307
  Email: john.jessen@versopaper.com
EHS Manager: Jeff Maule
  Phone: (1) 906-779-3370
  Fax: (1) 906-779-3307
  Email: jeff.maule@versopaper.com
Fiberline Mgr.: Brian LaBrash
  Phone: (1) 906-779-3200
  Fax: (1) 906-779-3307
  Email: brian.labrash@versopaper.com
Commun. Mgr.: Mark Pontti
  Phone: (1) 906-779-3200
  Fax: (1) 906-779-3307
  Email: mark.pontti@versopaper.com
Total Employees at this Location: 472
Type of Operation: Pulp mill, Paper mill
Pulp Grades and Capacities:
Total pulp capacity: 484,781 st/y
Pulp available for market: 279,398 st/y
Chemical Pulp: 484,781 st/y
Pulp Mill Data:
  Chemical Pulping Systems:
  Continuous digesters: 1
  Bleach Plant Systems: 1
  Chemical Pulping System - 1, Type: Hardwood, Sequence: O₂ DEopDD, Capacity 475,000 admt/y
  Chemical Recovery Equipment:
  Evaporator lines: 1
  Recovery boilers: 1
  Lime Kiln
  Pulp Dryers:
  Flakt dryer 1
Paper/Paperboard Grades and Capacities:
Total paper and paperboard capacity: 424,736 st/y
Coated woodfree/freesheet: 424,736 st/y
Paper and Paperboard Mill Data:
  Stock Preparation:
  Pulpers:
Paper Machines: 1
No. 41, fourdrinier, total capacity 424,736 st/y, Trim width 287 in, Coated woodfree/freesheet
Coating Machines: 1
No. 1, total capacity 410,053 st/y., on machine
Finishing Equipment:

Supercalenders: 1
Energy Data:
Power boilers: 2
Steam turbines: 2 at 28, 30 MW
Electrical demand for mill: 1,791 MWh/D

Ⓜ **White Pigeon Paper Co.**
Ownership: *Artistic Carton Co.*
15781 River St
White Pigeon, MI 49099
USA
Mailing Address: PO Box 277, White Pigeon, MI 49099, USA
  Phone: (1) 269-483-7601
  Fax: (1) 269-483-9989
  Email: sales@whitepigeonpaper.com
  Web Address: www.whitepigeonpaper.com
Personnel:
VP & Gen. Mgr.: Dave DiBiaggio
  Phone: (1) 269-483-7601 Ext. 4226
  Fax: (1) 269-483-9989
  Email: ddibiaggio@whitepigeonpaper.com
Plt. Contr.: Nick Schiffli
  Phone: (1) 269-483-7601
  Fax: (1) 269-483-9989
  Email: nschiffli@whitepigeonpaper.com
Cust. Service Mgr.: Aucunas Brandy
  Phone: (1) 269-483-7601
  Fax: (1) 269-483-9989
  Email: abrandy@whitepigeonpaper.com
Storeroom Mgr.: Timothy McAllister
  Phone: (1) 269-483-7601
  Fax: (1) 269-483-9989
  Email: tmcallister@whitepigeonpaper.com
Total Employees of Company: 105
Mill Locations:
White Pigeon Paper Co., White Pigeon Mill, 15781 River St, White Pigeon, MI 49099, USA, Capacity: 74,970 st/y, (Paperboard mill)
  Phone: (1) 269-483-7601
  Fax: (1) 269-483-9989
  Email: sales@whitepigeonpaper.com

Ⓜ **White Pigeon Paper Co.**
White Pigeon Mill
15781 River St
White Pigeon, MI 49099
USA
Mailing Address: PO Box 277, White Pigeon, MI 49099, USA
  Phone: (1) 269-483-7601
  Fax: (1) 269-483-9989
  Email: sales@whitepigeonpaper.com
  Web Address: www.whitepigeonpaper.com
Personnel:
VP & Gen. Mgr.: Dave DiBiaggio
  Phone: (1) 269-483-7601 Ext. 4226
  Fax: (1) 269-483-9989
  Email: ddibiaggio@whitepigeonpaper.com
Plt. Contr.: Nick Schiffli
  Phone: (1) 269-483-7601
  Fax: (1) 269-483-9989
  Email: nschiffli@whitepigeonpaper.com
Purch. Mgr.: Patsy Brown
  Phone: (1) 269-483-7601
  Fax: (1) 269-483-9989
  Email: pbrown@whitepigeonpaper.com
Total Employees at this Location: 92
Type of Operation: Paperboard mill
Pulp Grades and Capacities:
Total pulp capacity: 71,239 st/y
Recycled Pulping: 71,239 st/y
Pulp Mill Data:
  Recycled Fiber Treatment Lines:
  Pulpers: 1 at 65,035
Paper/Paperboard Grades and Capacities:
Total paper and paperboard capacity: 74,970 st/y
Boxboard/cartonboard: 74,970 st/y
Paper and Paperboard Mill Data:

Stock Preparation:
Pulpers: 4
Refiners: 5
Paper Machines: 1
No. 3, Ultraformer (7), total capacity 74,970 st/y, Trim width 110 in, Boxboard/cartonboard
Coating Machines: 1
PM 3, total capacity 71,649 st/y., on machine
Finishing Equipment:
  Rewinders: 1
Energy Data:
Power boilers: 2
Electrical demand for mill: 101 MWh/D

MINNESOTA

Ⓜ **Boise Paper**
International Falls Mill
Previously Boise Inc.
Ownership: *100% by Packaging Corp. of America*
400 Second St
International Falls, MN 56649-2327
USA
  Phone: (1) 218-285-5011
  Fax: (1) 218-285-5210
  Web Address: www.boisepaper.com
Personnel:
Mill Mgr.: Bert Brown
  Phone: (1) 218-285-5011
  Fax: (1) 218-285-5210
  Email: bertbrown@boisepaper.com
Purch. Mgr.: Jan Klow
  Phone: (1) 218-285-5011
  Fax: (1) 218-285-5210
  Email: janklow@boisepaper.com
Pub. Affairs Mgr.: Lori Lyman
  Phone: (1) 218-285-5312
  Fax: (1) 218-285-5210
  Email: lorilyman@boisepaper.com
Total Employees at this Location: 580
Type of Operation: Pulp mill, Paper mill
Pulp Grades and Capacities:
Total pulp capacity: 313,235 st/y
Chemical Pulp: 313,235 st/y
Pulp Mill Data:
  Chemical Pulping Systems:
  Batch digesters: 8
  Bleach Plant Systems: 1
  # 1, Type: HW/SW Swing, Sequence: DEopD, Capacity 360,000 admt/y
  Chemical Recovery Equipment:
  Evaporator lines: 1
  Recovery boilers: 1
  Lime Kiln
Paper/Paperboard Grades and Capacities:
Total paper and paperboard capacity: 424,736 st/y
Uncoated woodfree/freesheet: 415,813 st/y
Specialty and industrial: 8,923 st/y
Paper and Paperboard Mill Data:
  Stock Preparation:
  Pulpers: 16
  Refiners: 14
Paper Machines: 2
No. 3, fourdrinier, total capacity 80,307 st/y, Trim width 165 in, Uncoated woodfree/freesheet, Specialty and industrial
I-1, twin-wire, total capacity 344,429 st/y, Trim width 345 in, Uncoated woodfree/freesheet
Coating Machines: 2
No. 2, total capacity 42,000 st/y., off machine
No. 4, total capacity 42,989 st/y., on machine
Finishing Equipment:
  Supercalenders: 1 at 42,840 st/y
  Rewinders: 3
  Sheeters: 5 at 389,991 st/y

Minnesota

Energy Data:
Power boilers: 5
Steam turbines: 3 at 47 MW
Hydro turbines: 7 at 10 MW
Electrical demand for mill: 1,305 MWh/D

ⓗLiberty Diversified Industries
Ownership: Fiterman Family (Private)
5600 N Hwy 169
New Hope, MN 55428-3096
USA
  Phone: (1) 763-536-6600
  Fax: (1) 763-536-6685
  Email: info@libertydiversified.com
  Web Address: www.libertydiversified.com
Personnel:
Pres: Michael B. Fiterman
  Phone: (1) 763-536-6600
  Fax: (1) 763-536-6685
  Email: michaelfiterman@libertydiversified.com
VP, Organization & Talent Development: Robert Meekin
  Phone: (1) 763-536-6600
  Fax: (1) 763-536-6685
  Email: robertmeekin@libertydiversified.com
CIO: Alla Johnson
  Phone: (1) 763-536-6600
  Fax: (1) 763-536-6685
  Email: allajohnson@libertydiversified.com
CFO: Byron Wieberdink
  Phone: (1) 763-536-6600
  Fax: (1) 763-536-6685
  Email: byronwieberdink@libertydiversified.com
Total Employees of Company: 1,400
Mill Locations:
Liberty Paper Inc., Becker Mill, 13500 Liberty Ln, Becker, MN 55308, USA, Capacity: 229,908 st/y, (Paperboard mill)
  Phone: (1) 763-261-6100
  Fax: (1) 763-261-5311
  Email: sales@libertypaper.com

ⓜLiberty Paper Inc.
Becker Mill
Ownership: Liberty Diversified Industries
13500 Liberty Ln
Becker, MN 55308
USA
Mailing Address: PO Box 429, Becker, MN 55308, USA
  Phone: (1) 763-261-6100
  Fax: (1) 763-261-5311
  Email: sales@libertypaper.com
  Web Address: www.libertypaper.com
Personnel:
VP, Paper Manuf. (Eff. September 2014) & Gen. Mgr.: Larry M. Newell
  Phone: (1) 763-261-6112
  Fax: (1) 763-261-5311
  Email: larrynewell@libertypaper.com
Mill Mgr.: Chuck Legatt
  Phone: (1) 763-261-6100
  Fax: (1) 763-261-5311
  Email: chucklegatt@libertypaper.com
key Account. Mgr.: Dean Flicker
  Phone: (1) 763-261-6100
  Fax: (1) 763-261-5311
  Email: deanflicker@libertypaper.com
Bus. Analyst: Glenn M. Stimler
  Phone: (1) 763-261-6100
  Fax: (1) 763-261-5311
  Email: glennstimler@libertypaper.com
Maint. Mgr.: Kip Averill
  Phone: (1) 763-261-6100
  Fax: (1) 763-261-5311
  Email: kipaverill@libertypaper.com
Environ. Eng.: Tim Swanson
  Phone: (1) 763-261-6155
  Fax: (1) 763-261-5311
  Email: timswanson@libertypaper.com
Total Employees at this Location: 100
Type of Operation: Paperboard mill
Pulp Grades and Capacities:
Total pulp capacity: 241,185 st/y
Recycled Pulping: 241,185 st/y
Pulp Mill Data:
Pulp Lines: 1
  Recycled Fiber Treatment Lines:
  Pulpers: 1 at 220,899
Paper/Paperboard Grades and Capacities:
Total paper and paperboard capacity: 229,908 st/y
Linerboard: 229,908 st/y
Paper and Paperboard Mill Data:
  Stock Preparation:
  Refiners: 1
Paper Machines: 1
No. 1, twin-wire, total capacity 229,908 st/y, Trim width 184 in, Linerboard
Coating Machines: 1
No. 1
Finishing Equipment:
Rewinders: 1

ⓜNewPage Corporation
Duluth Paper Mill
100 N Central Ave
Duluth, MN 55807-2400
USA
  Phone: (1) 218-628-5100
  Fax: (1) 218-628-0310
  Web Address: www.newpagecorp.com
Personnel:
Mill Mgr.: John Bastian
  Phone: (1) 218-628-5100
  Fax: (1) 218-628-0310
  Email: john.bastian@newpagecorp.com
Dir., HR: Laura Molter
  Phone: (1) 218-628-5100
  Fax: (1) 218-628-0310
  Email: laura.molter@newpagecorp.com
Maint. & Eng. Mgr: James Bittinger
  Phone: (1) 218-628-5318
  Fax: (1) 218-628-0310
  Email: james.bittinger@newpagecorp.com
Cust. Serv. Mgr.: Dawn Polaski
  Phone: (1) 218-628-5100
  Fax: (1) 218-628-0310
  Email: dawn.polaski@newpagecorp.com
Training & Mill Oper. Support: Kalee Hermanson
  Phone: (1) 218-628-5340
  Fax: (1) 218-628-0310
  Email: kalee.hermanson@newpagecorp.com
Total Employees at this Location: 225
Type of Operation: Pulp mill, Paper mill
Pulp Grades and Capacities:
Total pulp capacity: 121,508 st/y
Mechanical Pulp: 121,508 st/y
Pulp Mill Data:
  Mechanical Pulping Systems:
  Pressurized grinders: 6
Pulp Lines: 6
  Bleach Plant Lines:
  PGW Mechanical Pulp, Sequence: HP
Paper/Paperboard Grades and Capacities:
Total paper and paperboard capacity: 269,560 st/y
Uncoated mechanical/groundwood: 269,560 st/y
Paper and Paperboard Mill Data:
  Stock Preparation:
  Pulpers:
Paper Machines: 1
No. 1, GapFormer, total capacity 269,560 st/y, Trim width 295 in, Uncoated mechanical/groundwood
Finishing Equipment:
Supercalenders: 3
Rewinders: 2
Energy Data:
Power boilers: 4
Steam turbines: 4 at 122 MW
Hydro turbines: 1 at 10.7 MW

ⓜNewPage Corporation
Duluth Pulp Mill
4920 Recycle Way
Duluth, MN 55807
USA
  Phone: (1) 218-628-5100
  Fax: (1) 218-628-0310
  Web Address: www.newpagecorp.com
Personnel:
Mill Mgr.: John Bastian
  Phone: (1) 218-628-5100
  Fax: (1) 218-628-0310
  Email: john.bastian@newpagecorp.com
Maint & Eng Mgr.: James Bittinger
  Phone: (1) 218-628-5318
  Fax: (1) 218-628-0310
  Email: james.bittinger@newpagecorp.com
Mill Field Specialist: Andy Brunette
  Phone: (1) 218-628-5100
  Fax: (1) 218-628-0310
  Email: andy.brunette@newpagecorp.com
Total Employees at this Location: 44
Type of Operation: Pulp mill
Pulp Grades and Capacities:
Total pulp capacity: 103,771 st/y
Pulp available for market: 102,315 st/y
Recycled Pulping: 103,771 st/y
Pulp Mill Data:
  Bleach Plant Systems: 2
  1, Type: two-stage P-R. towers, Sequence: P
  Recycled Fiber Treatment Lines:
  Pulpers: 1 at 132,937
  Pulp Dryers:
  Wet Lap machine 1
Energy Data:
Power boilers: 1
Electrical demand for mill: 128 MWh/D

ⓜRockTenn Co.
Saint Paul Mill
2250 Wabash Ave
Saint Paul, MN 55114-1895
USA
  Phone: (1) 651-641-4938
  Fax: (1) 651-641-4791
  Web Address: www.rocktenn.com
Personnel:
Gen. Mgr.: Bob Carpenter
  Phone: (1) 651-641-4938
  Fax: (1) 651-641-4791
  Email: bcarpent@rocktenn.com
Eng. Mgr. : Gary Myhrman
  Phone: (1) 651-641-4938
  Fax: (1) 651-641-4791
  Email: gmyhrman@rocktenn.com
Div. Mgr., Stock Prep.: Tom Barton
  Phone: (1) 651-641-4938
  Fax: (1) 651-641-4791
  Email: tbarton@rocktenn.com
Total Employees at this Location: 365
Type of Operation: Paperboard mill
Pulp Grades and Capacities:
Total pulp capacity: 369,987 st/y
Recycled Pulping: 369,987 st/y
Pulp Mill Data:
  Recycled Fiber Treatment Lines:
  Pulpers: 2 at 398,258
Paper/Paperboard Grades and Capacities:
Total paper and paperboard capacity: 368,067 st/y
Corrugating medium/fluting: 199,920 st/y
Boxboard/cartonboard: 168,147 st/y
Paper and Paperboard Mill Data:
  Stock Preparation:
  Pulpers: 4
  Refiners: 13
Paper Machines: 4
No. 1, cylinder (7), total capacity 76,041 st/y, Trim width 110 in, Boxboard/cartonboard

No. 2, cylinder (8), total capacity 92,106 st/y, Trim width 130 in, Boxboard/cartonboard
No. 4, fourdrinier, total capacity 94,605 st/y, Trim width 127 in, Corrugating medium/fluting
No. 5, fourdrinier, total capacity 105,315 st/y, Trim width 135 in, Corrugating medium/fluting
Coating Machines: 2
No. 1, total capacity 72,751 st/y., on machine
No. 2, total capacity 87,081 st/y., on machine
Finishing Equipment:
Rewinders: 1
Sheeters: 1
Energy Data:
Power boilers: 4
Steam turbines: 1 at 14 MW

ⓜSappi Fine Paper North America
Cloquet Mill
Ownership: Sappi Limited
2201 Avenue B
Cloquet, MN 55720
USA
Mailing Address: 2201 Avenue B, Post Office Box 511, Cloquet, MN 55720, USA
  Phone: (1) 218-879-2300
  Fax: (1) 218-879-0648
  Web Address: www.na.sappi.com/aboutus
Personnel:
Man. Dir. & Mill Mgr. (Since November 2, 2013): Mike Schultz
  Phone: (1) 218-879-0652
  Fax: (1) 218-879-0648
  Email: mike.schultz@sappi.com
Eng. Mgr.: Richard L. Morgan
  Phone: (1) 218-879-2341
  Fax: (1) 218-879-0686
  Email: rick.morgan@sappi.com
Environ. Mgr.: Robert Shilling
  Phone: (1) 218-879-2300
  Fax: (1) 218-879-0648
  Email: robert.shilling@sappi.com
Prod. Mgr.: Kraig Melin
  Phone: (1) 218-879-2300
  Fax: (1) 218-879-0648
  Email: kraig.melin@sappi.com
Total Employees at this Location: 569
Type of Operation: Pulp mill, Paper mill
Pulp Grades and Capacities:
Total pulp capacity: 386,214 st/y
Pulp available for market: 363,611 st/y
Chemical Pulp: 386,214 st/y
Pulp Mill Data:
  Chemical Pulping Systems:
  Batch digesters: 8
Pulp Lines: 1
Bleach Plant Systems: 1
1, Type: ZD-Eop-D, Sequence: O_2 ZD1 EopD2, Capacity 308,642.0 admt/y
  Chemical Recovery Equipment:
  Evaporator lines: 1
  Recovery boilers: 2
  Lime Kiln
  Pulp Dryers:
  Air Float dryers 1, Twin Wire 1
Paper/Paperboard Grades and Capacities:
Total paper and paperboard capacity: 364,140 st/y
Coated woodfree/freesheet: 364,140 st/y
Paper and Paperboard Mill Data:
  Stock Preparation:
  Pulpers: 4
  Refiners: 9
Paper Machines: 2
No. 4, Bel-Bond, total capacity 174,930 st/y, Trim width 194 in, Coated woodfree/freesheet
No. 12, Bel-Bond, total capacity 189,210 st/y, Trim width 194 in, Coated woodfree/freesheet
Coating Machines: 4
PM 12, total capacity 181,878 st/y., on machine
PM 12, total capacity 181,878 st/y., off machine

PM 4, total capacity 147,707 st/y., on machine
PM 4, total capacity 147,707 st/y., off machine
Finishing Equipment:
Supercalenders: 2
Rewinders: 3
Sheeters: 4
Energy Data:
Power boilers: 3
Steam turbines: 3 at 89 MW
Hydro turbines: 4 at 5.8 MW
Electrical demand for mill: 1,517 MWh/D

ⓜUPM North America
Blandin Paper Mill
Ownership: UPM-Kymmene Corporation
115 First St SW
Grand Rapids, MN 55744-3699
USA
  Phone: (1) 218-327-6200
  Fax: (1) 218-327-6212
  Email: info@upm-kymmene.com
  Web Address: www.upm.com
Personnel:
Gen. Mgr.: Joe Maher
  Phone: (1) 218-327-6200
  Fax: (1) 218-327-6212
  Email: joe.maher@upm-kymmene.com
Bus. Contr.: Jim Kent
  Phone: (1) 218-327-6200
  Fax: (1) 218-327-6212
  Email: jim.kent@upm-kymmene.com
Mgr., Maint.: Greg Chandler
  Phone: (1) 218-327-6200
  Fax: (1) 218-327-6212
  Email: greg.chandler@upm-kymmene.com
Mgr., Forest.: Jim Marshall
  Phone: (1) 218-327-6200
  Fax: (1) 218-327-6212
  Email: jim.marshall@upm-kymmene.com
Environ. Mgr.: Nathan Waech
  Phone: (1) 218-327-6200
  Fax: (1) 218-327-6212
  Email: nathan.waech@upm-kymmene.com
Mgr., Cust. Service: Kevin Gilbert
  Phone: (1) 218-327-6200
  Fax: (1) 218-327-6212
  Email: kevin.gilbert@upm-kymmene.com
Total Employees at this Location: 456
Type of Operation: Paper mill
Pulp Grades and Capacities:
Total pulp capacity: 67,272 st/y
Mechanical Pulp: 67,272 st/y
Pulp Mill Data:
  Mechanical Pulping Systems:
  Pressurized grinders: 2
Pulp Lines: 2
Bleach Plant Systems: 2
No. 1, Type: PGW, Sequence: P
No. 2, Type: PGW, Sequence: HS
Paper/Paperboard Grades and Capacities:
Total paper and paperboard capacity: 396,183 st/y
Coated mechanical/groundwood: 396,183 st/y
Paper and Paperboard Mill Data:
Paper Machines: 2
No. 5, fourdrinier, total capacity 121,353 st/y, Trim width 175 in, Coated mechanical/groundwood
No. 6, twin-wire, total capacity 274,829 st/y, Trim width 306 in, Coated mechanical/groundwood
Coating Machines: 2
CM 3, total capacity 121,252 st/y., off machine
CM 5, total capacity 274,471 st/y., off machine
Finishing Equipment:
Supercalenders: 8
Energy Data:
Power boilers: 4
Steam turbines: 1 at 31.5 MW
Hydro turbines: 1 at 2 MW
Electrical demand for mill: 1,490 MWh/D

MISSISSIPPI

ⓜBurrows Paper
Pickens Mill
196 Burrow Drive
Pickens, MS 39146
USA
Mailing Address: P.O. Box 987, Little Falls, NY 13365-0987, USA
  Phone: (1) 662-468-2183
  Fax: (1) 662-468-2860
  Email: papersales@burrowspaper.com
  Web Address: www.burrowspaper.com
Personnel:
Plt. Mgr.: Joe Roberts
  Phone: (1) 662-468-2183
  Fax: (1) 662-468-2860
  Email: jroberts@burrowspaper.com
Qlty. Mgr.: Shad Morgan
  Phone: (1) 662-468-2183
  Fax: (1) 662-468-2860
  Email: smorgan@burrowspaper.com
Total Employees at this Location: 41
Type of Operation: Paper mill
Paper/Paperboard Grades and Capacities:
Total paper and paperboard capacity: 10,710 st/y
Specialty and industrial: 10,710 st/y
Paper and Paperboard Mill Data:
  Stock Preparation:
  Pulpers: 1
  Refiners: 3
Paper Machines: 1
No. 41, fourdrinier, total capacity 10,710 st/y, Trim width 123 in, Specialty and industrial
Energy Data:
Power boilers: 1
Electrical demand for mill: 14 MWh/D

ⓜClearwater Paper Corporation
Wiggins Mill
1321 S Magnolia Dr
Wiggins, MS 39577-9615
USA
Mailing Address: 1321 S Magnolia Dr, Wiggins, MS 39577, USA
  Phone: (1) 601-928-5205
  Fax: (1) 601-928-3601
  Web Address: www.clearwaterpaper.com
Personnel:
Mill Mgr.: Sherrill Mayton
  Phone: (1) 601-928-5205
  Fax: (1) 601-928-3601
  Email: sherrill.mayton@clearwaterpaper.com
Purch. Mgr.: Paul Martinez
  Phone: (1) 601-928-5205
  Fax: (1) 601-928-3601
  Email: paul.martinez@clearwaterpaper.com
Oper. Mgr.: Gavin Black
  Phone: (1) 601-928-5205
  Fax: (1) 601-928-3601
  Email: gavin.black@clearwaterpaper.com
PM#2 Supt.: Eli Collier
  Phone: (1) 601-928-5205 Ext. 5236
  Fax: (1) 601-928-2910
  Email: eli.collier@clearwaterpaper.com
Safety Mgr.: Bill Rabby
  Phone: (1) 601-928-5205
  Fax: (1) 601-928-3601
  Email: bill.rabby@clearwaterpaper.com
Total Employees at this Location: 80
Type of Operation: Paper mill
Paper/Paperboard Grades and Capacities:
Total paper and paperboard capacity: 58,905 st/y
Tissue: 26,061 st/y
Specialty and industrial: 32,844 st/y
Paper and Paperboard Mill Data:
  Stock Preparation:
  Pulpers: 1
  Refiners: 4

Mississippi

Paper Machines: 2
No. 1, fourdrinier, total capacity 32,844 st/y, Trim width 180 in, Specialty and industrial
No. 2, fourdrinier, total capacity 26,061 st/y, Trim width 130 in, Tissue
Coating Machines: 1
PM1, total capacity 32,844 st/y., on machine
Finishing Equipment:
Calenders: 1
Rewinders: 1
Energy Data:
Power boilers: 1
Electrical demand for mill: 97 MWh/D

ⓜGP Cellulose, LLC
Leaf River Cellulose Mill
Ownership: Georgia-Pacific LLC
157 Buck Creek Rd
New Augusta, MS 39462
USA
Mailing Address: PO Box 329, New Augusta, MS 39462-0329, USA
Phone: (1) 601-964-8411
Fax: (1) 601-964-7248
Email: info@gpcellulose.com
Web Address: www.gpcellulose.com
Personnel:
Gen. Mgr.: Arlis Hicks
Phone: (1) 601-964-8411
Fax: (1) 601-964-7248
Email: arlis.hicks@gapac.com
Mill Mgr.: Richard King
Phone: (1) 601-964-8411
Fax: (1) 601-964-7248
Email: richard.king@gapac.com
Purch. & Stores Mgr.: Zachary Parker
Phone: (1) 601-964-8411
Fax: (1) 601-964-7248
Email: zachary.parker@gapac.com
Total Employees at this Location: 284
Type of Operation: Pulp mill
Pulp Grades and Capacities:
Total pulp capacity: 685,116 st/y
Pulp available for market: 655,602 st/y
Chemical Pulp: 685,116 st/y
Pulp Mill Data:
Chemical Pulping Systems:
Continuous digesters: 1
Pulp Lines: 1
Bleach Plant Systems: 1
Chemical Pulping System, Type: Softwood, Sequence: O_2 DEopDED
Chemical Recovery Equipment:
Evaporator lines: 1
Recovery boilers: 1
Lime Kiln
Pulp Dryers:
Flakt dryer 1
Energy Data:
Power boilers: 1
Steam turbines: 2 at 25, 25 MW
Electrical demand for mill: 1,555 MWh/D

ⓜGeorgia-Pacific LLC
Monticello Mill
604 NA Sandifer Rd
Monticello, MS 39654
USA
Phone: (1) 601-587-7711, 601-587-3204
Fax: (1) 601-587-4532
Web Address: www.gp.com
Personnel:
Mill Mgr.: Brent A. Collins
Phone: (1) 601-587-7711
Fax: (1) 601-587-4532
Email: bacollin@gapac.com
Wood & Fiber Supply Group Mgr.: John V. Rushing
Phone: (1) 601-587-1125
Fax: (1) 601-587-4532
Email: jvrushin@gapac.com

Proj. Eng.: John Zimmerman
Phone: (1) 601-587-7711
Fax: (1) 601-587-4532
Total Employees at this Location: 446
Type of Operation: Paperboard mill
Pulp Grades and Capacities:
Total pulp capacity: 1,177,414 st/y
Chemical Pulp: 897,726 st/y
Recycled Pulping: 279,689 st/y
Pulp Mill Data:
Chemical Pulping Systems:
Continuous digesters: 2
Chemical Recovery Equipment:
Evaporator lines: 2
Recovery boilers: 2
Lime Kiln
Recycled Fiber Treatment Lines:
Recycled packaging pulping lines at 275,573
Paper/Paperboard Grades and Capacities:
Total paper and paperboard capacity: 1,113,840 st/y
Linerboard: 1,113,840 st/y
Paper and Paperboard Mill Data:
Paper Machines: 2
No. 1, fourdrinier, total capacity 399,840 st/y, Trim width 250 in, Linerboard
No. 2, fourdrinier, total capacity 714,000 st/y, Trim width 312 in, Linerboard
Energy Data:
Power boilers: 1
Steam turbines: 2 at 36.5, 31 MW
Electrical demand for mill: 2,288 MWh/D

ⓜInternational Paper Co.
Vicksburg Mill
Hwy 3 North
Vicksburg, MS 39156
USA
Mailing Address: PO Box 950, Vicksburg, MS 39180, USA
Phone: (1) 601-638-3665
Fax: (1) 601-631-8355
Email: (firstname.lastname@ipaper.com)
Web Address: www.internationalpaper.com
Personnel:
Mill Mgr.: Tom Olstad
Phone: (1) 601-638-3665
Fax: (1) 601-631-8355
Email: thomas.olstad@ipaper.com
Area Process Mgr.: Lee Harrell
Phone: (1) 601-638-3665
Fax: (1) 601-631-8355
Email: lee.harrell@ipaper.com
Bus. Unit Mgr. Power & Utilities: Naser S. Jaber
Phone: (1) 601-638-3665
Fax: (1) 601-631-8355
Email: naser.jaber@ipaper.com
Bus. Mgr.: Rodney D. Franklin
Phone: (1) 601-638-3665
Fax: (1) 601-631-8355
Email: rodney.franklin@ipaper.com
Fiber Supply Specialist: Ramey Harrell
Phone: (1) 601-638-3665
Fax: (1) 601-631-8355
Email: ramey.harrell@ipaper.com
Total Employees at this Location: 293
Type of Operation: Pulp mill, Paperboard mill
Pulp Grades and Capacities:
Total pulp capacity: 595,880 st/y
Chemical Pulp: 517,971 st/y
Recycled Pulping: 77,909 st/y
Pulp Mill Data:
Chemical Pulping Systems:
Continuous digesters: 2
Chemical Recovery Equipment:
Evaporator lines: 1
Recovery boilers: 1
Lime Kiln
Recycled Fiber Treatment Lines:
Recycled packaging pulping lines at 71,000 admt/y
Paper/Paperboard Grades and Capacities:
Total paper and paperboard capacity: 565,131 st/y
Linerboard: 493,731 st/y
Corrugating medium/fluting: 71,400 st/y
Paper and Paperboard Mill Data:
Paper Machines: 1
No. 1, fourdrinier, total capacity 565,131 st/y, Trim width 348 in, Linerboard, Corrugating medium/fluting
Energy Data:
Power boilers: 1
Steam turbines: 2 at 50.5 MW
Electrical demand for mill: 1,209 MWh/D

ⓜResolute FP US Inc.
Grenada Mill
Ownership: 100% by Resolute Forest Products Canada Inc.
1000 Papermill Rd
Grenada, MS 38901
USA
Mailing Address: PO Box 849, Grenada, MS 38902-0849, USA
Phone: (1) 662-227-7900
Fax: (1) 662-227-7901
Email: info@resolutefp.com
Web Address: www.resolutefp.com
Personnel:
Gen. Mgr.: Rob Wise
Phone: (1) 662-227-7980
Fax: (1) 662-227-7901
Email: rob.wise@resolutefp.com
Paper Machine Mgr.: Glen Deese
Phone: (1) 662-227-7986
Fax: (1) 662-227-7901
Email: glen.deese@resolutefp.com
Wood Procurement Mgr.: Bryan McCartney
Phone: (1) 662-227-7916
Fax: (1) 662-227-7901
Email: bryan.mccartney@resolutefp.com
Maint. & Eng. Mgr.: Gary W. Fant
Phone: (1) 662-227-7997
Fax: (1) 662-227-7901
Email: gary.fant@resolutefp.com
Total Employees at this Location: 173
Type of Operation: Pulp mill, Paper mill
Pulp Grades and Capacities:
Total pulp capacity: 266,454 st/y
Mechanical Pulp: 266,454 st/y
Pulp Mill Data:
Mechanical Pulping Systems:
TMP systems: 3
Bleach Plant Lines:
Mechanical TMP Pulping System, Type: Softwood Line, Sequence: H
Paper/Paperboard Grades and Capacities:
Total paper and paperboard capacity: 271,134 st/y
Newsprint: 271,134 st/y
Paper and Paperboard Mill Data:
Stock Preparation:
Pulpers:
Paper Machines: 1
No. 1, Bel-Baie III, total capacity 271,134 st/y, Trim width 329 in, Newsprint
Finishing Equipment:
Winders: 1 at 279,000 st/y
Calenders: 1
Energy Data:
Power boilers: 2
TMP Reboiler: 1
Electrical demand for mill: 2,290 MWh/D

ⓜMississippi River Corp.
Ownership: 100% by Von Drehle Corp.
30 Majorca Rd
Natchez, MS 39120
USA
Mailing Address: PO Box 727, Natchez, MS 39121-0727, USA
Phone: (1) 601-445-0100
Fax: (1) 601-442-6599

Email: info@msriver.com
Web Address: www.msriver.com
Personnel:
Pres. & CEO: Robert C. Garland
Phone: (1) 601-445-0100
Fax: (1) 601-442-6599
Email: rgarland@msriver.com
VP, Purch.: Joseph Albrycht
Phone: (1) 601-445-0100
Fax: (1) 601-442-6599
Email: jalbrycht@msriver.com
VP, Finan.: Steven V. Schreiber
Phone: (1) 601-445-0100
Fax: (1) 601-442-6599
Email: sschreiber@msriver.com
VP, Process Eng. & Product Develop.: Tanya Smith Richardson
Phone: (1) 601-445-1856
Fax: (1) 601-442-6599
Email: tanya@msriver.com
VP, Sls.: Karen Ziemba
Phone: (1) 906-792-9051
Fax: (1) 601-442-6599
Email: kziemba@msriver.com
Total Employees of Company: 70

ⓜVon Drehle Corp.
Natchez Mill
30 Majorca Rd
Natchez, MS 39120
USA
Mailing Address: PO Box 727, Natchez, MS 39121-0727, USA
Phone: (1) 601-445-0100
Fax: (1) 601-442-6599
Email: sales@vondrehle.com
Web Address: www.vondrehle.com
Personnel:
Consultant: Lynn Patt
Phone: (1) 601-445-0100
Fax: (1) 601-442-6599
VP, Process Eng. & Product Develop.: Tanya Richardson
Phone: (1) 601-445-0100
Fax: (1) 601-442-6599
Total Employees at this Location: 70
Type of Operation: Pulp mill
Pulp Mill Data:
Bleach Plant Lines:
No. 1, Sequence: P
Recycled Fiber Treatment Lines:
Flotation deinking lines
Pulp Dryers:
Wet Lap machine 1
Energy Data:
Power boilers: 1

ⓜWeyerhaeuser Co.
Columbus Mill
4335 Carson Road, Hwy 792
Columbus, MS 39703
USA
Mailing Address: PO Box 1830, Columbus, MS 39703, USA
Phone: (1) 662-243-4000
Web Address: www.weyerhaeuser.com
Personnel:
VP, Mill Mgr.: Kent L Walker
Phone: (1) 662-243-4000
Email: kent.walker1@weyerhaeuser.com
Tech. Dir.: Dana Shelton
Phone: (1) 662-243-4000
Email: dana.shelton@weyerhaeuser.com
Eng. & Maint. Mgr.: Dwayne Robbins
Phone: (1) 662-243-4000
Email: dwayne.robbins@weyerhaeuser.com
Finan. Analyst: Melissa Aldridge
Phone: (1) 662-243-4000
Email: melissa.aldridge@weyerhaeuser.com
Total Employees at this Location: 350
Type of Operation: Pulp mill
Pulp Grades and Capacities:
Total pulp capacity: 553,761 st/y
Pulp available for market: 523,773 st/y
Chemical Pulp: 553,761 st/y
Pulp Mill Data:
Chemical Pulping Systems:
Continuous digesters: 1
Bleach Plant Systems: 1
Kraft Line, Type: Sunds, Sequence: O₂ DEopDD, Capacity 535,500.4 admt/y
Chemical Recovery Equipment:
Evaporator lines: 1
Recovery boilers: 1
Lime Kiln
Pulp Dryers:
Fourdriniers 1
Energy Data:
Power boilers: 1
Steam turbines: 4 at 120, 4 (stand-by) MW
Electrical demand for mill: 1,222 MWh/D

MISSOURI

ⓜProcter & Gamble Paper Products Co.
Cape Girardeau Mill
14484 State Hwy 177
Cape Girardeau, Jackson, MO 63755
USA
Phone: (1) 573-651-9200, 573 339-9243
Web Address: www.pg.com
Personnel:
Tissue Oper. Ldr.: John Spencer
Phone: (1) 573-651-9200
Bounty Converting Oper. Mgr.: NaKeia Grimes
Phone: (1) 573-651-9200
Bus. Ldr.: Heather Fudge LaMar
Phone: (1) 573-651-9200
Total Employees at this Location: 250
Type of Operation: Paper mill
Paper/Paperboard Grades and Capacities:
Total paper and paperboard capacity: 205,275 st/y
Tissue: 205,275 st/y
Paper and Paperboard Mill Data:
Stock Preparation:
Pulpers:
Paper Machines: 3
No. 1, TAD, total capacity 64,260 st/y, Trim width 205 in, Tissue
No. 2, TAD, total capacity 62,475 st/y, Trim width 205 in, Tissue
No. 3, TAD, total capacity 78,540 st/y, Trim width 205 in, Tissue
Energy Data:
Power boilers: 2
Electrical demand for mill: 773 MWh/D

ⓜUnited States Gypsum Co.
North Kansas City Mill
1115 Armour Rd
North Kansas City, MO 64116-3783
USA
Phone: (1) 816-471-4298
Fax: (1) 816-471-1463
Web Address: www.usg.com
Personnel:
Plt. Mgr.: Jason Kankey
Phone: (1) 816-559-3627
Fax: (1) 816-471-1463
Email: jkankey@usg.com
Serv. & Supply Chain Mgr.: Dale Alden
Phone: (1) 816-471-4298
Fax: (1) 816-471-1463
Email: dalden@usg.com
Type of Operation: Paperboard mill
Pulp Grades and Capacities:
Total pulp capacity: 79,178 st/y
Recycled Pulping: 79,178 st/y
Paper/Paperboard Grades and Capacities:
Total paper and paperboard capacity: 76,041 st/y
Boxboard/cartonboard: 76,041 st/y
Paper and Paperboard Mill Data:
Stock Preparation:
Pulpers: 1
Refiners: 2
Paper Machines: 1
No. 1, cylinder (7), total capacity 76,041 st/y, Trim width 106 in, Boxboard/cartonboard
Finishing Equipment:
Calenders: 1
Rewinders: 1
Energy Data:
Power boilers: 1
Electrical demand for mill: 94 MWh/D

NEVADA

ⓜClearwater Paper Corporation
Las Vegas Mill
3901 North Donna St.
North Las Vegas, NV 89030
USA
Phone: (1) 702-657-2400
Fax: (1) 702-657-1572
Email: firstname.lastname@clearwaterpaper.com
Web Address: www.clearwaterpaper.com
Personnel:
Plt. Mgr.: Gary Blosl
Phone: (1) 702-657-2400
Fax: (1) 702-657-1572
Email: gary.blosl@clearwaterpaper.com
HR Mgr.: Jody Bernal
Phone: (1) 702-657-2454
Fax: (1) 509-444-9756
Email: jody.bernal@clearwaterpaper.com
Process Contr. Supervisor: Ian Drazin
Phone: (1) 702-657-2408
Fax: (1) 509-444-9707
Email: ian.drazin@clearwaterpaper.com
Tech. Mgr.: PJ (Paul) Borowitz
Phone: (1) 702-657-2400
Fax: (1) 702-657-1572
Email: paul.borowitz@clearwaterpaper.com
Total Employees at this Location: 37
Type of Operation: Paper mill
Paper/Paperboard Grades and Capacities:
Total paper and paperboard capacity: 37,842 st/y
Tissue: 37,842 st/y
Paper and Paperboard Mill Data:
Stock Preparation:
Pulpers:
Paper Machines: 1
No. 1V, TAD, total capacity 37,842 st/y, Trim width 102 in, Tissue
Energy Data:
Power boilers
Electrical demand for mill: 139 MWh/D

NEW HAMPSHIRE

ⓘⓜ3M Tilton
Tilton Mill
One Paper Trail
Tilton, NH 03276-0739
USA
Mailing Address: P.O. Box 739, Tilton, NH 03276-0739, USA
Phone: (1) 866-357-2737, 603-286-4891
Fax: (1) 603-286-4859
Email: info@iptllc.net
Web Address: www.iptllc.net

New Hampshire

Personnel:
VP, Oper.: Joseph LaPlante
Phone: (1) 603-545-3013
Fax: (1) 603-286-4859
Global Bus. Develop. Mgr.: John DiCarlo
Phone: (1) 603-545-3040
Fax: (1) 603-286-4859
Email: jmdicarlo@mmm.com
Tech. Dir.: David S. Stankes
Phone: (1) 603-545-3026
Fax: (1) 603-286-4859
Email: dsstankes@mmm.com
HR Mgr.: Susan LaFlamme
Phone: (1) 603-545-3041
Fax: (1) 603-286-4859
Total Employees of Company: 60
Total Employees at this Location: 60
Type of Operation: Paper mill, Paperboard mill
Paper/Paperboard Grades and Capacities:
Total paper and paperboard capacity: 3,000 st/y
Specialty and industrial: 2,000 st/y
Boxboard/cartonboard: 1,000 st/y
Paper and Paperboard Mill Data:
Stock Preparation:
Pulpers: 1
Refiners: 1
Paper Machines: 2
PM 1, cylinder (4), Trim width 38 in
PM 2, cylinder, Trim width 48 in
Coating Machines: 1
No. 1, off machine
Finishing Equipment:
Rewinders: 3
Sheeters: 1
Energy Data:
Power boilers: 1

APC Paper Company, Inc
Claremont Mill
Ownership: 100% by APC Paper Group
130 Sullivan St.
Claremont, NH 03743
USA
Phone: (1) 603-542-6330
Fax: (1) 603-543-1485
Email: tgray@apcpaper.com
Web Address: www.apcpaper.com
Personnel:
Pres.: Frank Tarantino
Phone: (1) 603-542-6330
Fax: (1) 603-543-1485
Email: ftarantino@apcpaper.com
VP Finance.: Tom Moore
Phone: (1) 603-542-6330
Fax: (1) 603-543-1485
Email: tmoore@apcpaper.com
Mill Mgr.: Brian Caisse
Phone: (1) 603-542-6330
Fax: (1) 603-543-1485
Email: bcaisse@apcpaper.com
Sls. Mgr.: Travis Gray
Phone: (1) 603-542-6330 Ext. 12
Fax: (1) 603-543-1485
Email: tgray@apcpaper.com
Oper. Mgr.: Dave Harris
Phone: (1) 603-542-6330
Fax: (1) 603-543-1485
Email: dharris@apcpaper.com
Dir. Purch. Clairmont Mill & Norfolk Mill: Dennis Chaffee
Phone: (1) 603-542-6330
Fax: (1) 603-543-1485
Email: dchaffee@apcpaper.com
Total Employees at this Location: 60
Type of Operation: Paper mill
Mill Locations:
APC Paper Company of New York, Inc., Norfolk Mill, 100 Remington Ave., P.O. Box 756, Norfolk, NY 13667, USA, Capacity: 59,976 st/y, (Paper mill)
Phone: (1) 315-384-4225
Fax: (1) 315-384-4148

Email: tgray@apcpaper.com
Pulp Grades and Capacities:
Total pulp capacity: 37,095 st/y
Recycled Pulping: 37,095 st/y
Pulp Mill Data:
Recycled Fiber Treatment Lines:
Recycled packaging pulping lines: 1 at 41,667
Paper/Paperboard Grades and Capacities:
Total paper and paperboard capacity: 34,986 st/y
Packaging papers: 34,986 st/y
Paper and Paperboard Mill Data:
Stock Preparation:
Pulpers: 2
Refiners: 4
Paper Machines: 1
No. 1, fourdrinier, total capacity 34,986 st/y, Trim width 123 in, Packaging papers
Energy Data:
Power boilers: 2
Electrical demand for mill: 65 MWh/D

Gorham Paper and Tissue, LLC
Ownership: 100% by Patriarch Partners, LLC
72 Cascades Flats
Gorham, NH 03581
USA
Phone: (1) 603-342-2000
Fax: (1) 603-342-2261
Web Address: www.gorhampt.com
Personnel:
Owner: Lynn Tilton
Phone: (1) 603-342-2000
Fax: (1) 603-342-2261
Email: lynn.tilton@gorhampt.com
CEO: Michael Cummings
Phone: (1) 603-342-3644
Fax: (1) 603-342-2261
Email: mike.cummings@gorhampat.com
CFO (From November 2013): Wayne Johnson
Phone: (1) 603-342-3632
Fax: (1) 603-342-2261
Email: wayne.johnson@gorhampt.com
Total Employees of Company: 240
Mill Locations:
Gorham Paper and Tissue, LLC, Gorham Mill, 72 Cascades Flats, Gorham, NH 03581, USA, Capacity: 77,826 st/y, (Paper mill)
Phone: (1) 603-342-2000
Fax: (1) 603-342-2261

Gorham Paper and Tissue, LLC
Gorham Mill
Mill is machines are running on a day-to-day basis as orders allow
72 Cascades Flats
Gorham, NH 03581
USA
Phone: (1) 603-342-2000
Fax: (1) 603-342-2261
Web Address: www.gorhampt.com
Personnel:
Eng. & Maint. Mgr.: Andy Hartford
Phone: (1) 603-342-2000 Ext. 3322
Fax: (1) 603-342-2261
Email: andy.hartford@gorhampt.com
Environ. Dir.: Ryan Carrier
Phone: (1) 603-342-2000 Ext. 3363
Fax: (1) 603-342-2261
Email: ryan.carrier@gorhampt.com
Total Employees at this Location: 100
Type of Operation: Paper mill
Pulp Grades and Capacities:
Total pulp capacity: 40,652 st/y
Recycled Pulping: 40,652 st/y
Pulp Mill Data:
Recycled Fiber Treatment Lines:
Pulpers
Paper/Paperboard Grades and Capacities:
Total paper and paperboard capacity: 77,826 st/y

Tissue: 77,826 st/y
Paper and Paperboard Mill Data:
Stock Preparation:
Pulpers: 6
Refiners: 15
Paper Machines: 2
No. 6, crescent former, total capacity 36,057 st/y, Trim width 105 in, Tissue
No. 9, crescent former, total capacity 41,769 st/y, Trim width 180 in, Tissue
Energy Data:
Power boilers: 3

Lydall, Inc.
Rochester Mill
134 Chestnut Hill Rd
Rochester, NH 03867
USA
Mailing Address: PO Box 1960, Rochester, NH 03866-1960, USA
Phone: (1) 603-332-4600
Fax: (1) 603-332-9602
Web Address: www.lydall.com
Personnel:
Mgr./Dir.: Jeff Miller
Phone: (1) 603-332-4600
Fax: (1) 603-332-9602
Email: jmiller@lydall.com
Manuf. Mgr.: Adam Burnett
Phone: (1) 603-332-4600
Fax: (1) 603-332-9602
Email: aburnett@lydall.com
HR Mgr.: Lucy Bleau
Phone: (1) 603-332-4600
Fax: (1) 603-332-9602
Email: lbleau@lydall.com
Total Employees at this Location: 110
Type of Operation: Paper mill
Paper/Paperboard Grades and Capacities:
Total paper and paperboard capacity: 3,999 st/y
Packaging papers: 3,999 st/y
Specialty and industrial
Paper and Paperboard Mill Data:
Stock Preparation:
Pulpers: 1
Refiners: 1
Paper Machines: 1
No. 1, Rotoformer, total capacity 4,000 st/y, Trim width 68 in, Packaging papers, Specialty and industrial
Finishing Equipment:
Calenders: 1
Rewinders: 1
Sheeters: 1
Energy Data:
Power boilers: 1

Monadnock Paper Mills, Inc.
Ownership: Family owned (Private)
117 Antrim Rd
Bennington, NH 03442-4205
USA
Mailing Address: info@mpm.com
Phone: (1) 603-588-3311
Fax: (1) 603-588-3158
Web Address: www.mpm.com
Personnel:
Chmn., CEO: Richard G. Verney
Phone: (1) 603-588-3311
Fax: (1) 603-588-3158
Email: rverney@mpm.com
CFO & Treas.: Andrew M. Manns
Phone: (1) 603-588-3311
Fax: (1) 603-588-3158
Email: amanns@mpm.com
VP, R&D, Tech. Serv.: Paul M. Ciccone
Phone: (1) 603-588-3311
Fax: (1) 603-588-3158
Email: pciccone@mpm.com
VP, HR: Joseph A. Fletcher
Phone: (1) 603-588-3311

Fax: (1) 603-588-3158
Email: jfletcher@mpm.com
Dir., Supply Chain: Gilbert Malnati
Phone: (1) 603-588-3311
Fax: (1) 603-588-3158
Email: gmalnati@mpm.com
Mgr. Environ. Serv. (From September 2014): Brian Maloy
Phone: (1) 603-588-3311
Fax: (1) 603-588-3158
VP, Sls. & Mktg. (From November 2014): Brendan Lesch
Phone: (1) 603-588-3311
Fax: (1) 603-588-3158
Total Employees of Company: 176
Mill Locations:
Monadnock Paper Mills, Inc., Bennington Mill, 117 Antrim Rd, Bennington, NH 03442-4205, USA, Capacity: 24,000 st/y, (Paper mill)
Phone: (1) 603-588-3311
Fax: (1) 603-588-3158
Email: info@mpm.com

ⓜMonadnock Paper Mills, Inc.
Bennington Mill
117 Antrim Rd
Bennington, NH 03442-4205
USA
Phone: (1) 603-588-3311
Fax: (1) 603-588-3158
Email: info@mpm.com
Web Address: www.mpm.com
Personnel:
Tech. Serv. Mgr.: Steven Jones
Phone: (1) 603-588-3311
Fax: (1) 603-588-3158
Email: sjones@mpm.com
Environ. Mgr. (Eff. September 2014): Brian Maloy
Phone: (1) 603-588-3311
Fax: (1) 603-588-3158
Snr. Proj. Mgr.: Tom Graczyk
Phone: (1) 603-588-3311
Fax: (1) 603-588-3158
Email: tgraczyk@mpm.com
Total Employees at this Location: 176
Type of Operation: Paper mill
Paper/Paperboard Grades and Capacities:
Total paper and paperboard capacity: 24,000 st/y
Uncoated woodfree/freesheet
Coated woodfree/freesheet
Paper and Paperboard Mill Data:
  Stock Preparation:
  Pulpers: 3
  Refiners: 3
Paper Machines: 2
No. 1, fourdrinier, Trim width 88 in, Uncoated woodfree/freesheet
No. 2, fourdrinier, Trim width 101 in, Uncoated woodfree/freesheet
Coating Machines: 1
No. 1
Finishing Equipment:
Calenders: 2
Sheeters: 2
Energy Data:
Power boilers: 2

NEW JERSEY

ⓜNewark Recycled Paperboard Solutions
Company is for sale (Caraustar Industries has entered into an agreement to acquire The Newark Group, Inc. The acquisition is subject to customary closing conditions and required regulatory approvals.)
Ownership: 52% by DDJ Capital Management, 48% by other private

20 Jackson Dr
Cranford, NJ 07016
USA
Phone: (1) 908-276-4000
Fax: (1) 908-276-9126
Web Address: www.newarkpb.com
Personnel:
Pres & CEO: Frank Papa
Phone: (1) 908-276-4000
Fax: (1) 908-276-9126
Email: fpapa@tngus.com
VP & CFO: Gregg M. Kam
Phone: (1) 908-276-4000
Fax: (1) 908-276-9126
Email: gkam@tngus.com
Snr. VP, Converted Products: James Carbine
Phone: (1) 908-276-4000
Fax: (1) 908-276-9126
Email: jcarbine@tngus.com
Snr. VP, Recovery & Recycling: Johnny Gold
Phone: (1) 908-276-4000
Fax: (1) 908-276-9126
Email: jgold@tngus.com
Snr. VP, HR: Manny Silva
Phone: (1) 908-276-4000
Fax: (1) 908-276-9126
Email: msilva@tngus.com
Snr. VP, Paperboard Mills: Dick Poppe
Phone: (1) 908-276-4000
Fax: (1) 908-276-9126
Email: dpoppe@tngus.com
VP, Sls. & Mktg.: Paul Spitale
Phone: (1) 908-276-4000
Fax: (1) 908-276-9126
Email: pspitale@tngus.com
Mktg. Mgr.: Susanne Batchelor
Phone: (1) 908-276-4000 ext. 247
Fax: (1) 908-276-9126
Email: sbatchelor@tngus.com
Total Employees of Company: 1,500
Total Employees at this Location: 60
Mill Locations:
California Paperboard Corp., Santa Clara Mill, 525 Mathew St, Santa Clara, CA 95050, USA, Capacity: 84,252 st/y, (Paperboard mill)
Phone: (1) 408-727-7377
Fax: (1) 408-988-0585
Mobile Paperboard Corp., Mobile Mill, 701 Mobile St, Mobile, AL 36617-2019, USA, Capacity: 146,013 st/y, (Paperboard mill)
Phone: (1) 251-478-6391
Fax: (1) 251-478-5125
Newark America, Fitchburg Mill, 100 Newark Way, Fitchburg, MA 01420, USA, Capacity: 106,029 st/y, (Paperboard mill)
Phone: (1) 978-665-2600
Fax: (1) 978-665-2750
Newark Pacific Paperboard Corp., Los Angeles Mill, 6001 S Eastern Ave, Los Angeles, CA 90040, USA, Capacity: 64,974 st/y, (Paperboard mill)
Phone: (1) 323-728-7500
Fax: (1) 323-724-7570
Ohio Paperboard Corp., Baltimore Board Mill, 310 Water St, Baltimore, OH 43105-1272, USA, Capacity: 117,810 st/y, (Paperboard mill)
Phone: (1) 740-862-4167
Fax: (1) 740-862-8320
Wisconsin Paperboard Corp., Milwaukee Mill, 1514 E Thomas Ave., Milwaukee, WI 53211-4397, USA, Capacity: 164,934 st/y, (Paperboard mill)
Phone: (1) 414-271-9000
Fax: (1) 414-271-9001

ⓜSchweitzer-Mauduit International Inc.
Spotswood Mill
85 Main St
Spotswood, NJ 08884
USA
Phone: (1) 732-723-6100

Fax: (1) 732-251-3814
Web Address: www.swmintl.com
Personnel:
Purch. Agt: John Pastor
Phone: (1) 732-723-6100
Fax: (1) 732-251-3814
Email: john.pastor@swm-us.com
Total Employees at this Location: 298
Type of Operation: Pulp mill, Paper mill
Pulp Grades and Capacities:
Pulp Mill Data:
  Chemical Pulping Systems:
  Batch digesters: 5
Paper/Paperboard Grades and Capacities:
Total paper and paperboard capacity: 47,000 st/y
Specialty and industrial: 47,000 st/y
Paper and Paperboard Mill Data:
  Stock Preparation:
  Refiners: 20
Paper Machines: 7
No. 1, fourdrinier, Trim width 128 in, Specialty and industrial
No. 2, fourdrinier, Trim width 128 in, Specialty and industrial
No. 3, fourdrinier, Trim width 128 in, Specialty and industrial
No. 4, fourdrinier, Trim width 128 in, Specialty and industrial
No. 5, fourdrinier, Trim width 137 in, Specialty and industrial
No. 6, fourdrinier, Trim width 137 in, Specialty and industrial
No. 7, fourdrinier, Trim width 137 in, Specialty and industrial

ⓜSealed Air Corp.
Ownership: Public
200 Riverfront Blvd.
Woodpark, NJ 07407
USA
Phone: (1) 201-791-7600
Fax: (1) 201-703-4205
Web Address: www.sealedair.com
Personnel:
Chmn.: William V. Hickey
Phone: (1) 201-791-7600
Fax: (1) 201-703-4205
Email: william.hickey@sealedair.com
Pres. & CEO: Jerome A Peribere
Phone: (1) 201-791-7600
Fax: (1) 201-703-4205
Email: jerome.peribere@sealedair.com
Snr. VP. & CFO: Carol P. Lowe
Phone: (1) 201-791-7600
Fax: (1) 201-703-4205
Email: carol.lowe@sealedair.com
Contrl. & Chief Accounting Officer: William G. Stiehl
Phone: (1) 201-791-7600
Fax: (1) 201-703-4205
Email: william.stiehl@sealedair.com
VP, Gen. Counsel & Sec.: H. Kathrine White
Phone: (1) 201-791-7600
Fax: (1) 201-703-4205
Email: kathrine.white@sealedair.com
Exec. Dir. Corp. Commun.: Ken Aurichio
Phone: (1) 201-791-7600
Fax: (1) 201-703-4205
Email: Ken.Aurichio@sealedair.com
VP.: Carole M. De Mayo
Phone: (1) 201-791-7600
Fax: (1) 201-703-4205
Email: carole.demayo@sealedair.com
VP.: Ilham Kadri
Phone: (1) 201-791-7600
Fax: (1) 201-703-4205
Email: ilham.kadri@sealedair.com
VP.: Larry Pillote
Phone: (1) 201-791-7600
Fax: (1) 201-703-4205
Email: larry.pillote@sealedair.com
Total Employees of Company: 25,000
Total Employees at this Location: 80
Mill Locations:
Sealed Air Corp., Lenoir Mill, 2075 NW Valway Rd, Lenoir, NC 28645, USA, Capacity: 7,000 st/y, (Paper mill)
Phone: (1) 828-726-2100
Fax: (1) 828-754-0580

New Mexico

Email: specialtymaterials-na@sealedair.com
Sealed Air Corp., Modena Mill, 22 Meredith Ct, Modena, PA 19358, USA, Capacity: 28,999 st/y, (Paper mill)
Phone: (1) 610-384-2650
Fax: (1) 610-384-2605
Sealed Air Corp., Reading Mill, 450 Riverfront Dr, Reading, PA 19602, USA, Capacity: 25,000 st/y, (Paper mill)
Phone: (1) 610-375-4281
Fax: (1) 610-375-6443

ⓘⓜSoundview Paper Co.
Elmwood Park Mill
Ownership: 100% by Atlas Holdings
1 Market St
Elmwood Park, NJ 07407
USA
Phone: (1) 201-796-4000; 855-756-9566
Fax: (1) 201-796-0470
Web Address: www.soundviewpaper.com
Personnel:
Chmn. (Eff. September 2014): George Wurtz
Phone: (1) 201-796-4000
Fax: (1) 201-796-0470
Email: gwurtz@soundviewpaper.com
Pres. & CEO (Eff. September 23, 2014): Karl Meyers
Phone: (1) 201-796-4000
Fax: (1) 201-796-0470
CFO & Snr. VP.: John Sickler
Phone: (1) 201-796-4000
Fax: (1) 201-796-0470
Snr. VP, Oper. & Technology: Tim Crawford
Phone: (1) 201-796-4000
Fax: (1) 201-796-0470
Email: tcrawford@soundviewpaper.com
Snr. VP of Sls. & Mktg.: John McLean
Phone: (1) 201-796-4000
Fax: (1) 201-796-0470
Email: jmclean@soundviewpaper.com
Snr. Chief Counsel & Secretary: Carrie Williamson
Phone: (1) 201-796-4000
Fax: (1) 201-796-0470
Email: cwilliamson@soundviewpaper.com
COO (Away from Home Division): Karl Meyers
Phone: (1) 201-796-4000
Fax: (1) 201-796-0470
VP. Sls.: Jim Rochford
Phone: (1) 201-796-4000
Fax: (1) 201-796-0470
Email: jrochford@soundviewpaper.com
VP, Fiber Div. (As of June 2014): William (Bill) Schlenger
Phone: (1) 201-796-4000
Fax: (1) 201-796-0470
Email: wschlenger@soundviewpaper.com
Dir., Eng.: Mark Vertucci
Phone: (1) 201-796-4000
Fax: (1) 201-796-0470
Email: mvertucci@soundviewpaper.com
Chief Procurement Officer: Eddie Oliveira
Phone: (1) 201-796-4000
Fax: (1) 201-796-0470
Email: eoliveira@soundviewpaper.com
Total Employees of Company: 1,050
Total Employees at this Location: 105
Type of Operation: Paper mill
Mill Locations:
Soundview Paper Co., Putney Mill, 67 Kathan Meadow Road, Putney, VT 05346, USA, Capacity: 26,418 st/y, (Pulp mill, Paper mill)
Phone: (1) 802-387-5571
Fax: (1) 802-387-5297
Pulp Grades and Capacities:
Total pulp capacity: 149,665 st/y
Recycled Pulping: 149,665 st/y
Pulp Mill Data:
Recycled Fiber Treatment Lines:
Flotation deinking lines: 1
Paper/Paperboard Grades and Capacities:
Total paper and paperboard capacity: 139,944 st/y
Tissue: 139,944 st/y
Paper and Paperboard Mill Data:
Stock Preparation:
Pulpers:
Paper Machines: 2
No. 10, DuoFormer, Yankee dryer, total capacity 73,185 st/y, Trim width 217 in, Tissue
No. 11, crescent former, Yankee dryer, total capacity 66,759 st/y, Trim width 205 in, Tissue
Energy Data:
Power boilers: 2
Electrical demand for mill: 438 MWh/D

NEW MEXICO

ⓜBio-PAPPEL International
Prewitt Mill
Ownership: 100% by Bio-PAPPEL, S.A.B. de C.V.
County Rd 19
Prewitt, NM 87045
USA
Mailing Address: PO Box 100, Prewitt, NM 87045-0100, USA
Phone: (1) 505-876-2100
Fax: (1) 505-876-2313
Web Address: www.biopappel.com/en
Personnel:
Mill Mgr.: Isaac Rosas
Phone: (1) 505-876-2100
Fax: (1) 505-876-2313
Email: irosas@biopappel.com
Fiber Procurement Mgr.: Zhariff Valle
Phone: (1) 505-224-2329 Ext. 10129
Fax: (1) 505-876-2313
Email: zvalle@biopappel.com
Tech. Mgr.: John Shaw
Phone: (1) 505-876-2100
Fax: (1) 505-876-2313
Email: jshaw@biopappel.com
Total Employees at this Location: 90
Type of Operation: Paperboard mill
Pulp Grades and Capacities:
Total pulp capacity: 259,606 st/y
Recycled Pulping: 259,606 st/y
Pulp Mill Data:
Recycled Fiber Treatment Lines:
Recycled packaging pulping lines at 232,804
Paper/Paperboard Grades and Capacities:
Total paper and paperboard capacity: 249,900 st/y
Packaging papers: 19,635 st/y
Linerboard: 217,770 st/y
Corrugating medium/fluting: 12,495 st/y
Paper and Paperboard Mill Data:
Stock Preparation:
Pulpers: 1
Refiners: 5
Paper Machines: 1
No. 1, twin-wire, total capacity 249,900 st/y, Trim width 186 in, Linerboard, Corrugating medium/fluting, Packaging papers
Energy Data:
Power boilers
Combustion turbines at 250 MW
Electrical demand for mill: 345 MWh/D

ⓘRoses Southeast Papers, LLC
Ownership: 100% by Atlas Southeast Papers, Inc. an affiliate of Peak Rock Capital
1701 2nd St. SW
Albuquerque, NM 87102
USA
Phone: (1) 505-842-0134
Fax: (1) 505-242-0342
Email: info@rosesnm.com
Web Address: www.rosessouthwest.com
Personnel:
Pres. & CEO: Roberto Espat Sr.
Phone: (1) 505-842-0134
Fax: (1) 505-242-0342
Email: respat@rosesnm.com
Co. Chmn.: Rose Marie Espat
Phone: (1) 505-842-0134
Fax: (1) 505-242-0342
Email: rmespat@rosesnm.com
COO: Arnin Espat
Phone: (1) 505-842-0134
Fax: (1) 505-242-0342
Email: aespat@rosesnm.com
HR: Ken Rearick
Phone: (1) 505-842-0134
Fax: (1) 505-242-0342
Email: krearick@rosesnm.com
Total Employees of Company: 250
Mill Locations:
Roses Southeast Papers, LLC, Sanford Mill, 3401 St. Johns Parkway, Sanford, FL 32771, USA, Capacity: 29,988 st/y, (Paper mill)
Phone: (1) 407-330-9118
Email: info@rosesnm.com

NEW YORK

ⓜAPC Paper Company of New York, Inc.
Norfolk Mill
Ownership: APC Paper Company, Inc
100 Remington Ave., P.O. Box 756
Norfolk, NY 13667
USA
Phone: (1) 315-384-4225
Fax: (1) 315-384-4148
Email: tgray@apcpaper.com
Web Address: www.apcpaper.com
Personnel:
Mill Mgr.: Allen Ames
Phone: (1) 315-384-4225
Fax: (1) 315-384-4148
Email: aames@apcpaper.com
Maint. Supervisor: Richard Tieman
Phone: (1) 315-384-4225
Fax: (1) 315-384-4148
Email: rtieman@apcpaper.com
Total Employees at this Location: 55
Type of Operation: Paper mill
Pulp Grades and Capacities:
Total pulp capacity: 63,317 st/y
Recycled Pulping: 63,317 st/y
Pulp Mill Data:
Recycled Fiber Treatment Lines:
Recycled packaging pulping lines: 1 at 57,319
Paper/Paperboard Grades and Capacities:
Total paper and paperboard capacity: 59,976 st/y
Packaging papers: 47,838 st/y
Corrugating medium/fluting: 12,138 st/y
Paper and Paperboard Mill Data:
Stock Preparation:
Pulpers: 3
Refiners: 3
Paper Machines: 1
No. 1, fourdrinier, total capacity 59,976 st/y, Trim width 152 in, Packaging papers, Corrugating medium/fluting
Energy Data:
Power boilers: 2
Electrical demand for mill: 98 MWh/D

ⓘBurrows Paper
Ownership: 100% by Private
501 W Main St
Little Falls, NY 13365
USA

New York

Mailing Address: PO Box 987, Little Falls, NY 13365-0987, USA
Phone: (1) 315-823-2300
Fax: (1) 315-823-0867
Email: papersales@burrowspaper.com
Web Address: www.burrowspaper.com
Personnel:
Pres. & COO: Rose Mihaly
Phone: (1) 315-823-2300 Ext.: 1712
Fax: (1) 315-823-0867
Email: rmihaly@burrowspaper.com
CFO: Philip Paras
Phone: (1) 315-823-2300 Ext.: 1712
Fax: (1) 315-823-0867
Email: ppahars@burrowspaper.com
Snr. VP, Gen. Mgr., Paper Group: Hai Q Ninh
Phone: (1) 315-823-2300 Ext.:1721
Fax: (1) 315-823-2417
Email: hninh@burrowspaper.com
VP, Manuf. & Eng.: John D. Sterzinar
Phone: (1) 315-823-2300 Ext.: 1706
Fax: (1) 315-823-0867
Email: jsterzinar@burrowspaper.com
VP, Sls., Paper Group: Duane E. Judd
Phone: (1) 315-823-2300 Ext.: 1702
Fax: (1) 315-823-0867
Email: djudd@burrowspaper.com
Sls. Mgr.: Timothy T Wood
Phone: (1) 315-823-2300
Fax: (1) 315-823-0867
Email: twood@burrowspaper.com
HR Generalist: Jennifer Crandall
Phone: (1) 315-266-1704
Fax: (1) 315-83-2584
Email: jcrandall@burrowspaper.com
Dir., Environ., Health & Safety: Maryanne Ray
Phone: (1) 315-823-2300
Fax: (1) 315-823-0867
Email: mray@burrowspaper.com
Total Employees of Company: 724
Total Employees at this Location: 69
Mill Locations:
Burrows Paper, Mill Street Facility, 730 E Mill St, Little Falls, NY 13365, USA, Capacity: 29,988 st/y, (Paper mill)
Phone: (1) 315-823-2300
Fax: (1) 315-823-0867
Email: papersales@burrowspaper.com
Burrows Paper, Mohawk Valley Facility, 489 W Main St, Little Falls, NY 13365, USA, Capacity: 11,065 st/y, (Paper mill)
Phone: (1) 315-823-2300
Fax: (1) 315-823-0867
Email: papersales@burline.com
Burrows Paper, Lyonsdale Mill, 7801 Lyonsdale Rd, Lyons Falls, NY 13368, USA, Capacity: 18,000 st/y, (Paper mill)
Phone: (1) 315-348-8491
Fax: (1) 315-348-6808
Email: papersales@burrowspaper.com
Burrows Paper, Pickens Mill, 196 Burrow Drive, Pickens, MS 39146, USA, Capacity: 10,710 st/y, (Paper mill)
Phone: (1) 662-468-2183
Fax: (1) 662-468-2860
Email: papersales@burrowspaper.com

ⓂBurrows Paper
Mill Street Facility
730 E Mill St
Little Falls, NY 13365
USA
Mailing Address: P.O. Box 987, Little Falls, NY 13365-0987, USA
Phone: (1) 315-823-2300
Fax: (1) 315-823-0867
Email: papersales@burrowspaper.com
Web Address: www.burrowspaper.com
Personnel:
VP Sls,: Duane Judd
Phone: (1) 315-823-2300 Ext. 1702
Fax: (1) 315-823-3892
Email: djudd@burrowspaper.com
Total Employees at this Location: 69
Type of Operation: Paper mill
Paper/Paperboard Grades and Capacities:
Total paper and paperboard capacity: 29,988 st/y
Specialty and industrial: 29,988 st/y
Paper and Paperboard Mill Data:
Stock Preparation:
Pulpers: 2
Refiners: 4
Paper Machines: 2
No. 2, (MG), Yankee dryer, total capacity 7,854 st/y, Trim width 96 in, Specialty and industrial
No. 3, (MG), Yankee dryer, total capacity 22,134 st/y, Trim width 132 in, Specialty and industrial
Energy Data:
Power boilers: 2
Electrical demand for mill: 50 MWh/D

ⓂBurrows Paper
Mohawk Valley Facility
489 W Main St
Little Falls, NY 13365
USA
Mailing Address: PO Box 987, Little Falls, NY 13365-0987, USA
Phone: (1) 315-823-2300
Fax: (1) 315-823-0867
Email: papersales@burline.com
Web Address: www.burrowspaper.com
Personnel:
Qlty. Mgr.: Eric Eisert
Phone: (1) 315-823-2300
Fax: (1) 315-823-0867
Email: eeisert@burrowspaper.com
Total Employees at this Location: 30
Type of Operation: Paper mill
Paper/Paperboard Grades and Capacities:
Total paper and paperboard capacity: 11,065 st/y
Specialty and industrial: 11,065 st/y
Paper and Paperboard Mill Data:
Stock Preparation:
Refiners: 1
Paper Machines: 1
No. 12, fourdrinier, total capacity 11,065 st/y, Trim width 90 in, Specialty and industrial
Energy Data:
Power boilers
Electrical demand for mill: 20 MWh/D

ⓂBurrows Paper
Lyonsdale Mill
7801 Lyonsdale Rd
Lyons Falls, NY 13368
USA
Mailing Address: P.O. Box 987, Little Falls, NY 13365-0987, USA
Phone: (1) 315-348-8491
Fax: (1) 315-348-6808
Email: papersales@burrowspaper.com
Web Address: www.burrowspaper.com
Personnel:
Mgr.: Dennis Gigliotti
Phone: (1) 315-348-8491
Fax: (1) 315-348-6808
Email: dgigliotti@burrowspaper.com
Total Employees at this Location: 41
Type of Operation: Paper mill
Paper/Paperboard Grades and Capacities:
Total paper and paperboard capacity: 18,000 st/y
Specialty and industrial: 18,000 st/y
Paper and Paperboard Mill Data:
Stock Preparation:
Pulpers: 2
Refiners: 2
Paper Machines: 1
No. 32, fourdrinier, total capacity 18,000 st/y, Trim width 162 in, Specialty and industrial

ⓗCarthage Specialty Paperboard
Ownership: Climax Acquisition LLC, DeltaPoint Capital Management
7840 State Rte 26
Lowville, NY 13367-1290
USA
Phone: (1) 315-376-8000
Fax: (1) 315-376-2034
Web Address: www.carthagespbd.com
Personnel:
CEO, Pres., Paperboard Div.: Patrick (Pat) J Purdy
Phone: (1) 315-376-8000
Fax: (1) 315-376-2034
Email: pat.purdy@carthagespbd.com
VP. Admin.: Jill Boliver
Phone: (1) 315-376-8000
Fax: (1) 315-376-2034
Email: jill.boliver@carthagespbd.com
Logist & Conv Service Mgr.: Earl LaLone
Phone: (1) 315-493-5523
Fax: (1) 315-493-0485
Email: earl.lalone@carthagespbd.com
Total Employees of Company: 272
Total Employees at this Location: 205
Mill Locations:
Carthage Specialty Paperboard, Carthage Mill, 30 Champion St, Carthage, NY 13619, USA, Capacity: 59,976 st/y, (Paperboard mill)
Phone: (1) 315-493-2120
Fax: (1) 315-493-0812

ⓂCascades Tissue Group
Mechanicville Mill
Ownership: 100% by Cascades Inc.
510 S Main St
Mechanicville, NY 12118
USA
Mailing Address: PO Box 630, Mechanicville, NY 12118, USA
Phone: (1) 518-664-8400
Fax: (1) 518-664-7306
Web Address: www.afh.cascades.com
Personnel:
Contr.: Francois David Leblanc
Phone: (1) 518-664-8400
Fax: (1) 518-664-7306
Email: francois-david_leblanc@cascades.com
HR Mgr., Personnel Dir.: Keith Nicholas
Phone: (1) 518-664-8400
Fax: (1) 518-664-7306
Email: keith_nicholas@cascades.com
Tech. Support: Sophia Ferraro
Phone: (1) 518-664-8400
Fax: (1) 518-664-7306
Email: sophia_ferraro@cascades.com
Total Employees at this Location: 45
Type of Operation: Paper mill
Pulp Grades and Capacities:
Total pulp capacity: 61,753 st/y
Recycled Pulping: 61,753 st/y
Pulp Mill Data:
Recycled Fiber Treatment Lines:
Recycled packaging pulping lines: 1
Paper/Paperboard Grades and Capacities:
Total paper and paperboard capacity: 57,834 st/y
Tissue: 57,834 st/y
Paper and Paperboard Mill Data:
Stock Preparation:
Pulpers: 2
Refiners: 2
Paper Machines: 1
No. 1, crescent former, Yankee dryer, total capacity 57,834 st/y, Trim width 168 in, Tissue
Finishing Equipment:
Calenders: 1
Rewinders: 1
Energy Data:
Power boilers: 1
Electrical demand for mill: 116 MWh/D

New York

ⓜClearwater Paper Corporation
Natural Dam Mill
4921 State Highway 58
Gouverneur, NY 13642
USA
Mailing Address: PO Box 98, Gouverneur, NY 13642, USA
  Phone: (1) 315-287-1200
  Fax: (1) 315-287-1111
  Web Address: www.clearwaterpaper.com
Personnel:
  Plt. Mgr.: Jeremy Bartholomew
  Phone: (1) 315-287-7192
  Fax: (1) 315-287-1111
  Email: jeremy.bartholomew@clearwaterpaper.com
  Contr.: Diane Lallier
  Phone: (1) 315-287-1200
  Fax: (1) 315-287-1111
  Email: diane.lallier@clearwaterpaper.com
  Oper. Mgr.: Marlon Howson
  Phone: (1) 315-287-1200
  Fax: (1) 315-287-1111
  Email: marlon.howson@clearwaterpaper.com
  Purch. Specialist II: Tracie Prashaw
  Phone: (1) 315-287-7194
  Fax: (1) 315-287-1111
  Email: tracie.prashaw@clearwaterpaper.com
Total Employees at this Location: 120
Type of Operation: Paper mill
Paper/Paperboard Grades and Capacities:
  Total paper and paperboard capacity: 38,913 st/y
  Tissue: 38,913 st/y
Paper and Paperboard Mill Data:
  Stock Preparation:
  Pulpers: 3
  Refiners: 3
Paper Machines: 2
No. 2, crescent former, total capacity 17,136 st/y, Trim width 126 in, Tissue
No. 3, crescent former, total capacity 21,777 st/y, Trim width 120 in, Tissue
Finishing Equipment:
  Rewinders: 1
Energy Data:
Power boilers: 2
Hydro turbines: 3 at 1.2 MW
Electrical demand for mill: 107 MWh/D

ⓜCarthage Specialty Paperboard
Carthage Mill
30 Champion St
Carthage, NY 13619
USA
  Phone: (1) 315-493-2120
  Fax: (1) 315-493-0812
  Web Address: www.carthagespbd.com
Personnel:
  VP, Sls. & Mktg.: Michael Lambert
  Phone: (1) 315-493-5516
  Fax: (1) 315-493-0812
  Email: michael.lambert@carthagespbd.com
  Sls. Serv. Mgr.: Tina Pomerville
  Phone: (1) 315-493-5513
  Fax: (1) 315-493-0812
  Email: tina.pomerville@carthagespbd.com
  Inside Sls. Mgr.: Jon Hirschey
  Phone: (1) 315-493-5515
  Fax: (1) 315-493-0812
  Email: jon.hirschey@carthagespbd.com
  Cust. Srvce. Mgr.: Rebecca Rogers
  Phone: (1) 315-493-5552
  Fax: (1) 315-493-0485
  Email: rebecca.rogers@carthagespbd.com
Total Employees at this Location: 76
Type of Operation: Paperboard mill
Pulp Grades and Capacities:
  Total pulp capacity: 61,648 st/y
  Recycled Pulping: 61,648 st/y
Pulp Mill Data:
  Recycled Fiber Treatment Lines:
  Recycled packaging pulping lines: 2
Paper/Paperboard Grades and Capacities:
  Total paper and paperboard capacity: 59,976 st/y
  Boxboard/cartonboard: 59,976 st/y
Paper and Paperboard Mill Data:
  Stock Preparation:
  Pulpers: 4
  Refiners: 6
Paper Machines: 1
No. 1, cylinder (8), total capacity 59,976 st/y, Trim width 106 in, Boxboard/cartonboard
Energy Data:
Power boilers
Steam turbines: 1

ⓗCottrell Paper Co., Inc.
Ownership: 100% by shareholders
1135 Rock City Rd
Rock City Falls, NY 12863
USA
Mailing Address: PO Box 35, Rock City Falls, NY 12863-0035, USA
  Phone: (1) 518-885-1702, 800-948-3559
  Fax: (1) 518-885-0741
  Email: josh@cottrellpaper.com, cottrell@nycap.rr.com
  Web Address: www.cottrellpaper.com
Personnel:
  Pres, Treas, Purch.: Jack Cottrell
  Phone: (1) 518-885-1702, 800-948-3559
  Fax: (1) 518-885-0741
  Email: jack@cottrellpaper.com
  VP, Prod., Sec., Chief Eng.: Ben Cottrell
  Phone: (1) 518-885-1702, 800-948-3559
  Fax: (1) 518-885-0741
  Email: ben@cottrellpaper.com
  Qlty. Contrl.: Josh Cottrell
  Phone: (1) 518-885-1702, 800-948-3559
  Fax: (1) 518-885-0741
  Email: josh@cottrellpaper.com
Total Employees of Company: 36
Mill Locations:
Cottrell Paper Co., Inc., Rock City Falls Mill, 1135 Rock City Rd, Rock City Falls, NY 12863, USA, Capacity: 2,000 st/y, (Paper mill)
  Phone: (1) 518-885-1702, 800-948-3559
  Fax: (1) 518-885-0741
  Email: josh@cottrellpaper.com, cottrell@nycap.rr.com

ⓜCottrell Paper Co., Inc.
Rock City Falls Mill
1135 Rock City Rd
Rock City Falls, NY 12863
USA
Mailing Address: PO Box 35, Rock City Falls, NY 12863-0035, USA
  Phone: (1) 518-885-1702, 800-948-3559
  Fax: (1) 518-885-0741
  Email: josh@cottrellpaper.com, cottrell@nycap.rr.com
  Web Address: www.cottrellpaper.com
Personnel:
  Pres, Treas, Purch.: Jack Cottrell
  Phone: (1) 518-885-1702
  Fax: (1) 518-885-0741
  Email: jack@cottrellpaper.com
  VP, Prod., Sec., Chief Eng.: Ben Cottrell
  Phone: (1) 518-885-1702
  Fax: (1) 518-885-0741
  Email: ben@cottrellpaper.com
  Pulp & Paper Eng.: Josh Cottrell
  Phone: (1) 518-885-1702
  Fax: (1) 518-885-0741
  Email: josh@cottrellpaper.com
  Maint. Mgr.: Darren Costanzo
  Phone: (1) 518-885-1702
  Fax: (1) 518-885-0741
  Email: darren@cottrellpaper.com
Total Employees at this Location: 36
Type of Operation: Paper mill

Paper/Paperboard Grades and Capacities:
  Total paper and paperboard capacity: 2,000 st/y
  Packaging papers: 400 st/y
  Specialty and industrial: 1,600 st/y
  Boxboard/cartonboard
Paper and Paperboard Mill Data:
  Stock Preparation:
  Pulpers: 1
  Refiners: 2
Paper Machines: 1
PM 1, cylinder (7), total capacity 2,000 st/y, Trim width 72 in, Packaging papers, Specialty and industrial
Finishing Equipment:
  Supercalenders: 1
Energy Data:
Power boilers: 1

ⓗⓜFinch Paper, LLC
Glens Falls Mill
Ownership: Atlas Holdings LLC, Blue Wolf Capital Management LLC
1 Glen St
Glens Falls, NY 12801-2167
USA
  Phone: (1) 518-793-2541
  Fax: (1) 518-793-7364
  Email: webmaster@finchpaper.com
  Web Address: www.finchpaper.com
Personnel:
  Owner: Eric Finch
  Phone: (1) 518-793-2541
  Fax: (1) 518-793-7364
  Email: efinch@finchpaper.com
  Pres. & CEO: Debabrata Mukherjee Ph.D.
  Phone: (1) 518-793-2541
  Fax: (1) 518-793-7364
  Email: dmukherjee@finchpaper.com
  VP Tech. & Develop.: Thomas D. Ruch
  Phone: (1) 518-793-2541 ext. 55
  Fax: (1) 518-793-7364
  Email: truch@finchpaper.com
  Mill Mgr.: Stephanie Picard
  Phone: (1) 518-793-2541
  Fax: (1) 518-793-7364
  Email: stephanie.picard@finchpaper.com
  Environ., Health & Safety Mgr.: Sandra LeBarron
  Phone: (1) 518-793-2541 ext. 53
  Fax: (1) 518-793-7364
  Email: slebarron@finchpaper.com
  Contr.: Steven McDonald
  Phone: (1) 518-792-4925
  Fax: (1) 518-793-7364
  Email: smcdonald@finchpaper.com
  Bus. Dev. Mgr.: Gary Dow
  Phone: (1) 605-484-5866
  Email: gary.dow@finchpaper.com
Total Employees of Company: 768
Total Employees at this Location: 600
Type of Operation: Pulp mill, Paper mill
Pulp Grades and Capacities:
  Total pulp capacity: 149,844 st/y
  Chemical Pulp: 143,501 st/y
  Recycled Pulping: 6,343 st/y
Pulp Mill Data:
  Chemical Pulping Systems:
  Continuous digesters: 1
  Bleach Plant Systems: 1
  Chemcial Pulping System, Type: Softwood/Hardwood Line, Sequence: DED
  Chemical Recovery Equipment:
  Evaporator lines: 1
  Recovery boilers: 4
Paper/Paperboard Grades and Capacities:
  Total paper and paperboard capacity: 249,845 st/y
  Uncoated woodfree/freesheet: 249,845 st/y
Paper and Paperboard Mill Data:
  Stock Preparation:
  Pulpers:
Paper Machines: 4

New York

No. 1, fourdrinier, total capacity 41,046 st/y, Trim width 108 in, Uncoated woodfree/freesheet
No. 2, fourdrinier, total capacity 42,831 st/y, Trim width 106 in, Uncoated woodfree/freesheet
No. 3, fourdrinier, total capacity 53,538 st/y, Trim width 136 in, Uncoated woodfree/freesheet
No. 4, fourdrinier, total capacity 112,430 st/y, Trim width 175 in, Uncoated woodfree/freesheet
Finishing Equipment:
  Sheeters: 4
Energy Data:
Power boilers: 6
Steam turbines: 1 at 28 MW
Hydro turbines at 10 MW

First Quality Tissue LLC
Ownership: 100% by Damaghi Family (Private)
Cuttermill Rd. Suite 500
Great Neck, NY 11021
USA
  Phone: (1) 516-829-3030
  Fax: (1) 516-829-4949
  Email: fqtsales@firstquality.com
  Web Address: www.firstquality.com
Personnel:
  Pres.: Kambiz Damaghi
  Phone: (1) 516-829-3030
  Fax: (1) 516-829-4949
  Email: kdamaghi@firstquality.com
  VP, Sls. & Mktg.: Dan Murphy
  Dir. Finan. & Treasury: Richard Martorella
  Phone: (1) 516-829-3030
  Fax: (1) 516-829-4949
  Email: rmartorella@firstquality.com
  Global Mktg. Ldr.: Richard Usuquen
  Phone: (1) 516-829-3030
  Fax: (1) 516-829-4949
  Email: rusuquen@firstquality.com
  Dir., HR: Shani Loren
  Phone: (1) 516-829-3030
  Fax: (1) 516-829-4949
  Email: sloren@firstquality.com
Total Employees of Company: 3,600
Mill Locations:
First Quality Tissue LLC, Lock Haven Mill, 904 Woods Avenue, Lock Haven, PA 17745, USA, Capacity: 122,094 st/y, (Paper mill)
  Phone: (1) 570-748-1200
  Fax: (1) 570-748-0874
  Email: fqtsales@firstquality.com
First Quality Tissue LLC, Anderson Mill, 441 Masters Blvd, Anderson, SC 29626-6127, USA, Capacity: 119,952 st/y, (Paper mill)
  Phone: (1) 800-726-6910, 516-829-3030 (NY HQ number), 864-437-2085
  Email: se.info@firstquality.com

Florelle Tissue Corporation
Company is from July 4, 2008. Acquired by Florelle Tissue and is due to reopen as a tissue mill in mid 2012
Bridge St
Brownville, NY 13615
USA
  Phone: (1) 315-782-4500
  Fax: (1) 315-782-3964
Personnel:
  CEO: Richard M Kessel
  Phone: (1) 315-782-4500, 315-405-4203
  Fax: (1) 315-782-3964
  Pres.: Harry Minas
  Phone: (1) 315-782-4500, 315-405-4203
  Fax: (1) 315-782-3964
  Exec. Assist.: Brenda O' Connor
  Phone: (1) 315-782-4500, 315-405-4203
  Fax: (1) 315-782-3964

Flower City Tissue Mills Co.
Ownership: Private
700 Driving Park Avenue
Rochester, NY 14613
USA
Mailing Address: PO Box 13497, Rochester, NY 14613-0497, USA
  Phone: (1) 585-458-9200
  Fax: (1) 585-458-3812
  Email: wrapture@flowercitytissue.com
  Web Address: www.flowercitytissue.com
Personnel:
  Pres.: William F. Shafer III
  Phone: (1) 585-458-9200
  Fax: (1) 585-458-3812
  Machine Supt.: Scott Bentley
  Phone: (1) 585-458-9200
  Fax: (1) 585-458-3812
  Email: scott@flowercitytissue.com
  Account. Mgr.: Luke Shafer
  Phone: (1) 585-458-9200
  Fax: (1) 585-458-3812
  Email: luke@flowercitytissue.com
  Sls & Mktg Mgr.: Donald MacDonald
  Phone: (1) 585-458-9200
  Fax: (1) 585-458-3812
  Email: donm@flowercitytissue.com
Total Employees of Company: 60
Mill Locations:
Flower City Tissue Mills Co., Rochester Mill, 700 Driving Park Avenue, Rochester, NY 14613, USA, Capacity: 8,000 st/y, (Paper mill)
  Phone: (1) 585-458-9200
  Fax: (1) 585-458-3812

Flower City Tissue Mills Co.
Rochester Mill
700 Driving Park Avenue
Rochester, NY 14613
USA
Mailing Address: PO Box 13497, Rochester, NY 14613-0497, USA
  Phone: (1) 585-458-9200
  Fax: (1) 585-458-3812
  Web Address: www.flowercitytissue.com
Personnel:
  Pres., Gen. Mgr.: William F. Shafer III
  Phone: (1) 585-458-9200
  Fax: (1) 585-458-3812
  Machine Tender: Scott Bentley
  Phone: (1) 585-458-9200
  Fax: (1) 585-458-3812
  Email: scott@flowercitytissue.com
  Sls. Mktg. Mgr.: Donald MacDonald
  Phone: (1) 585-458-9200
  Fax: (1) 585-458-3812
  Email: donm@flowercitytissue.com
  Account Mgr.: Luke Shafer
  Phone: (1) 585-458-9200
  Fax: (1) 585-458-3812
  Email: luke@flowercitytissue.com
Total Employees at this Location: 50
Type of Operation: Paper mill
Paper/Paperboard Grades and Capacities:
  Total paper and paperboard capacity: 8,000 st/y
  Tissue: 8,000 st/y
Paper and Paperboard Mill Data:
Paper Machines: 1
No. 1, fourdrinier, total capacity 8,000 st/y, Trim width 82 in, Tissue
Finishing Equipment:
  Winders: 1
  Calenders: 1
  Rewinders: 2
  Sheeters: 2

Georgia-Pacific LLC
Plattsburgh Mill
327 Margaret St
Plattsburgh, NY 12901
USA
  Phone: (1) 518-561-3500
  Fax: (1) 518-562-6533
  Web Address: www.gp.com
Personnel:
  Oper. Mgr.: Timothy Boshart
  Phone: (1) 518-561-3500
  Fax: (1) 518-562-6533
  Paper Machine Mgr.: Brenda Lokey
  Phone: (1) 518-561-3500
  Fax: (1) 518-562-6533
  Maint. Ldr.: Michael Bell
  Phone: (1) 518-561-3500
  Fax: (1) 518-562-6533
  Email: michael.bell@gapac.com
Total Employees at this Location: 119
Type of Operation: Paper mill
Paper/Paperboard Grades and Capacities:
  Total paper and paperboard capacity: 45,339 st/y
  Tissue: 45,339 st/y
Paper and Paperboard Mill Data:
  Stock Preparation:
  Pulpers: 2
Paper Machines: 1
No. 7, crescent former, total capacity 45,339 st/y, Trim width 125 in, Tissue
Energy Data:
Power boilers
Electrical demand for mill: 132 MWh/D

Greenpac Mill, LLC
Ownership: 59.70% by Norampac, 20.10% by Jamestown Container and another industry converter, 20.20% by Caisse de dépôt et placement du Québec
4001 Packard Rd
Niagara Falls, NY 14303
USA
  Phone: (1) 716-299-0560
  Email: info@cascades.com
  Web Address: www.greenpacmill.com, www.norampac.com, www.cascades.com
Personnel:
  Gen. Mgr.: Murray Hewitt
  Phone: (1) 716-524-3101
  Email: murray_hewitt@norampac.com
Total Employees of Company: 118
Mill Locations:
Greenpac Mill, LLC, Greenpac Mill, 4001 Packard Rd, Niagara Falls, NY 14303, USA, Capacity: 540,141 st/y, (Paper mill)
  Phone: (1) 716-299-0560

Hollingsworth & Vose Co.
Greenwich Mill
3235 County Rte 113
Greenwich, NY 12834
USA
  Phone: (1) 518-695-4814
  Fax: (1) 518-695-3771
  Email: info@hovo.com
  Web Address: www.hollingsworth-vose.com
Personnel:
  Mill Mgr.: Dino Rosati
  Phone: (1) 518-695-4814
  Fax: (1) 518-695-3771
  Email: drosati@hovo.com
  Snr. Research Tech.: Norris Pike
  Phone: (1) 518-695-4814
  Fax: (1) 518-695-3771
  Email: npike@hovo.com
  Oper. Mgr.: Jason Snyder
  Phone: (1) 518-695-4814
  Fax: (1) 518-695-3771
Type of Operation: Paper mill
Paper/Paperboard Grades and Capacities:
  Total paper and paperboard capacity: 5,000 st/y
  Specialty and industrial
Paper and Paperboard Mill Data:
  Stock Preparation:
  Pulpers: 1
Paper Machines: 1

New York

No. 1, Rotoformer, total capacity 5,000 st/y, Trim width 71 in, Specialty and industrial
Energy Data:
Power boilers: 2

ⓜHollingsworth & Vose Co.
Easton Mill
5035 County Rte 113
Greenwich, NY 12834
USA
Phone: (1) 518-695-4814, 518-695-3266
Fax: (1) 518-695-4659, 518-695-3771 Main Office
Email: info@hovo.com
Web Address: www.hollingsworth-vose.com
Personnel:
Mill Mgr.: Dino Rosati
Phone: (1) 518-695-4814
Fax: (1) 518-695-3771
Email: drosati@hovo.com
Site Mgr.: Michael Rowland
Phone: (1) 518-695-4814
Fax: (1) 518-695-3771
Total Employees at this Location: 181
Type of Operation: Paper mill
Paper/Paperboard Grades and Capacities:
Total paper and paperboard capacity: 22,000 st/y
Packaging papers
Specialty and industrial
Paper and Paperboard Mill Data:
Stock Preparation:
Pulpers: 3
Refiners: 2
Paper Machines: 3
No. 1, fourdrinier, Trim width 100 in
No. 2, Rotoformer, Trim width 90 in
No. 3, Rotoformer, Trim width 81 in
Energy Data:
Power boilers: 1

ⓜInternational Paper Co.
Ticonderoga Mill
568 Shore-Airport Road
Ticonderoga, NY 12883
USA
Phone: (1) 518-585-5300
Fax: (1) 518-585-5358
Email: (firstname.lastname@ipaper.com)
Web Address: www.internationalpaper.com
Personnel:
Mill Mgr.: Chris Mallon
Phone: (1) 518-585-5300
Fax: (1) 518-585-5358
Email: chris.mallon@ipaper.com
Assist. PM Mgr.: Tyler McQueen
Phone: (1) 518-585-5300
Fax: (1) 518-585-5358
Mgr., PS&D: Eugene Fox Jr.
Phone: (1) 518-585-5300
Fax: (1) 518-585-5358
Email: eugene.fox@ipaper.com
Purch. & Stores Mgr.: Ashley Sennett
Phone: (1) 518-585-5300
Fax: (1) 518-585-5358
Email: ashley.sennett@ipaper.com
Process Contr. Mgr.: Edward Dawson
Phone: (1) 518-585-5300
Fax: (1) 518-585-5358
Email: edward.dawson@ipaper.com
Commun. Mgr.: Donna Wadsworth
Phone: (1) 518-585-5300
Fax: (1) 518-585-5358
Email: donna.wadsworth@ipaper.com
Total Employees at this Location: 500
Type of Operation: Paper mill
Pulp Grades and Capacities:
Total pulp capacity: 238,566 st/y
Chemical Pulp: 238,566 st/y
Pulp Mill Data:
Chemical Pulping Systems:
Continuous digesters: 1
Bleach Plant Systems: 1
Chemical Pulping System, Type: Hardwood/Softwood, Sequence: DEOpDEpD, Capacity 220,000 admt/y
Chemical Recovery Equipment:
Evaporator lines: 1
Recovery boilers: 1
Paper/Paperboard Grades and Capacities:
Total paper and paperboard capacity: 299,814 st/y
Uncoated woodfree/freesheet: 299,814 st/y
Paper and Paperboard Mill Data:
Stock Preparation:
Pulpers:
Paper Machines: 2
No. 7, fourdrinier, total capacity 108,861 st/y, Trim width 210 in, Uncoated woodfree/freesheet
No. 8, fourdrinier, total capacity 190,953 st/y, Trim width 280 in, Uncoated woodfree/freesheet
Finishing Equipment:
Sheeters: 3
Energy Data:
Power boilers: 1
Steam turbines at 42 MW
Electrical demand for mill: 906 MWh/D

ⓜIrving Tissue Inc.
Fort Edward Mill
Ownership: J.D. Irving, Ltd.
1 Eddy St
Fort Edward, NY 12828
USA
Phone: (1) 518-747-4151
Fax: (1) 518-747-3397
Web Address: www.irvingconsumerproducts.com, www.irvingtissue.com
Personnel:
Mill Mgr.: Eric Dawson
Phone: (1) 518-747-4151
Fax: (1) 518-747-3397
Email: eric.dawson@irvingpaper.com
Eng., Maint., & Facilities Mgr.: Eric Anderson
Phone: (1) 518-747-4151
Fax: (1) 518-747-3397
Email: eric.anderson@irvingpaper.com
Continuous Improvement Mgr.: Kevin Jones
Phone: (1) 518-747-4151
Fax: (1) 518-747-3397
Email: kevin.jones@irvingpaper.com
Total Employees at this Location: 94
Type of Operation: Paper mill
Paper/Paperboard Grades and Capacities:
Total paper and paperboard capacity: 51,765 st/y
Tissue: 51,765 st/y
Paper and Paperboard Mill Data:
Stock Preparation:
Pulpers:
Paper Machines: 2
No. 3, fourdrinier, total capacity 18,921 st/y, Trim width 97 in, Tissue
No. 4, TAD, total capacity 32,844 st/y, Trim width 98 in, Tissue
Energy Data:
Power boilers: 2
Electrical demand for mill: 161 MWh/D

ⓜLydall, Inc.
Green Island Mill
68 George St
Green Island, NY 12183
USA
Mailing Address: PO Box 328, Troy, NY 12181, USA
Phone: (1) 518-273-6320
Fax: (1) 518-273-6361
Web Address: www.lydall.com
Personnel:
Dir., Oper.: Terrance Dingman
Phone: (1) 518-273-6320 x1087
Fax: (1) 518-273-6361
Email: tdingman@lydall.com
Mgr., P&P Mills & Convert.: Anthony Herrick
Phone: (1) 518-880-1089
Fax: (1) 518-273-6361
Email: aherrick@lydall.com
Contr.: Timothy Riley
Phone: (1) 518-880-1065
Fax: (1) 518-273-6361
Email: treilly@lydall.com
Total Employees at this Location: 106
Type of Operation: Paper mill
Paper/Paperboard Grades and Capacities:
Total paper and paperboard capacity: 7,000 st/y
Specialty and industrial: 7,000 st/y
Paper and Paperboard Mill Data:
Stock Preparation:
Pulpers: 2
Paper Machines: 2
PM 1, fourdrinier, Trim width 100 in, Specialty and industrial
PM 2, cylinder (2), Trim width 100 in, Specialty and industrial
Coating Machines: 1
No. 1, total capacity 4,200 st/y., off machine
Finishing Equipment:
Calenders: 2
Rewinders: 3
Energy Data:
Power boilers: 2

ⓜⓜMohawk Fine Papers Inc.
Cohoes Mill
Ownership: O'Connor Family (Private)
465 Saratoga St
Cohoes, NY 12047
USA
Mailing Address: PO Box 497, Cohoes, NY 12047, USA
Phone: (1) 800-843-6455/518-237-1740
Fax: (1) 518-237-7394
Web Address: www.mohawkconnects.com
Personnel:
Chmn. & CEO: Thomas D. O'Connor Jr.
Phone: (1) 518-237-1740
Fax: (1) 518-237-7394
Email: oconnot1@mohawkpaper.com
Pres. & CFO: Jack F. Haren
Phone: (1) 518-237-1740
Fax: (1) 518-237-7394
Email: harenj@mohawkpaper.com
VP Bus. Develop. & Creative Dir.: Christopher M. Harrold
Phone: (1) 518-237-1740
Fax: (1) 518-237-7394
Email: chris.harrold@mohawkpaper.com
VP. Sls.: Melissa Stevens
Phone: (1) 518-237-1740
Fax: (1) 518-237-7394
Email: melissa.stevens@mohawkpaper.com
VP. Environ. & Energy Stewardship: Michelle A. Carpenter
Phone: (1) 518-237-1740
Fax: (1) 518-237-7394
Email: michelle.carpenter@mohawkpaper.com
VP, New York Oper. (Cahoes & Waterford Mill & Specialty convert. Center) (From 2014): Dolph Beyer
Phone: (1) 518-237-1740
Fax: (1) 518-237-7394
Email: dolph.beyer@mohawkpaper.com
DistricSls. Mgr.: Gary Bucci
Phone: (1) 518-237-1740
Fax: (1) 518-237-7394
Email: gary.bucci@mohawkpaper.com
Mill Mgr. (From 2014): Terry Nagy
Phone: (1) 518-237-1740
Fax: (1) 518-237-7394
Email: terry.nagy@mohawkpaper.com
Sr. Finan. Analyst: Patrick Sheridan
Phone: (1) 518-237-1740
Fax: (1) 518-237-7394
Email: patrick.sheridan@mohawkpaper.com
Environ. Prog. Mgr.: Kathleen Doherty
Phone: (1) 518-237-1740
Fax: (1) 518-237-7394

New York

Email: kathleen.doherty@mohawkpaper.com
Total Employees of Company: 580
Total Employees at this Location: 85
Type of Operation: Paper mill
Mill Locations:
Mohawk Fine Papers Inc., Waterford Mill, One O'Connor Drive, Waterford, NY 12188, USA, Capacity: 53,538 st/y, (Paper mill)
 Phone: (1) 518-237-1740
 Fax: (1) 518-237-7394
 Email: webmaster@mohawkpaper.com
Pulp Grades and Capacities:
 Total pulp capacity: 4,470 st/y
 Recycled Pulping: 4,470 st/y
Paper/Paperboard Grades and Capacities:
 Total paper and paperboard capacity: 51,754 st/y
 Uncoated woodfree/freesheet: 51,754 st/y
Paper and Paperboard Mill Data:
 Stock Preparation:
 Pulpers: 2
 Refiners: 3
Paper Machines: 1
No. 1, fourdrinier, total capacity 51,754 st/y, Trim width 100 in, Uncoated woodfree/freesheet
Energy Data:
Power boilers: 3
Electrical demand for mill: 95 MWh/D

ⓜMohawk Fine Papers Inc.
Waterford Mill
One O'Connor Drive
Waterford, NY 12188
USA
Mailing Address: 465 Saratoga St., Cohoes, NY 12047, USA
 Phone: (1) 518-237-1740
 Fax: (1) 518-237-7394
 Email: webmaster@mohawkpaper.com
 Web Address: www.mohawkconnects.com
Personnel:
 VP, New York Oper (From 2014): Dolph Beyer
 Email: dolph.beyer@mohawkpaper.com
 Proj. Team Ldr.: Gregory Taylor
 Phone: (1) 518-237-1740
 Fax: (1) 518-237-7394
 Email: gregory.taylor@mohawkpaper.com
Total Employees at this Location: 100
Type of Operation: Paper mill
Pulp Grades and Capacities:
 Total pulp capacity: 4,615 st/y
 Recycled Pulping: 4,615 st/y
Paper/Paperboard Grades and Capacities:
 Total paper and paperboard capacity: 53,538 st/y
 Uncoated woodfree/freesheet: 53,538 st/y
Paper and Paperboard Mill Data:
 Stock Preparation:
 Pulpers: 2
 Refiners: 7
Paper Machines: 2
No. 1, fourdrinier, total capacity 35,692 st/y, Trim width 77 in, Uncoated woodfree/freesheet
No. 2, fourdrinier, total capacity 17,846 st/y, Trim width 64 in, Uncoated woodfree/freesheet
Energy Data:
Power boilers: 3
Electrical demand for mill: 95 MWh/D

ⓜNewton Falls Fine Papers Company, LLC
Company is for sale, temporarily closed
Ownership: 100% by Scotia Investments
875 County Route 60
Newton Falls, NY 13666
USA
 Phone: (1) 315-848-2406
 Fax: (1) 315-848-3325
 Email: info@newtonfallsfinepaper.com
 Web Address: newtonfallsfinepaper.com
Personnel:
 VP Oper.: Andy LeRoux
 Phone: (1) 315-848-2406
 Fax: (1) 315-848-3325
 Exec. Assist.: Cynthia VanBrocklin
 Phone: (1) 315-848-3321 Ext 203
 Fax: (1) 315-848-3325
 Email: cvanbrocklin@newtonfallsfp.com
 Mgr.: Chuck Downey
 Phone: (1) 315-848-2406
 Fax: (1) 315-848-3325
 Email: cdowney@newtonfallsfp.com
 Mktg.Mgr.: Jay Rogers
 Phone: (1) 315-848-2406
 Fax: (1) 315-848-3325
 Email: jrogers@newtonfallsfp.com
 Cust.Service Mgr.: Mary Wood
 Phone: (1) 315-848-2406
 Fax: (1) 315-848-3325
 Email: mwood@newtonfallsfp.com

ⓜGreenpac Mill, LLC
Greenpac Mill
Ownership: 59.70% by Norampac
4001 Packard Rd
Niagara Falls, NY 14303
USA
 Phone: (1) 716-299-0560
 Web Address: www.greenpacmill.com
Personnel:
 Gen. Mgr.: Murray Hewitt
 Phone: (1) 716-524-3101
 Email: murray_hewitt@norampac.com
 Contrl.: Sal Sciarrino
 Email: sal_sciarrino@norampac.com
 Mech. Specialist: Kelly Robbins
 Email: kelly_robbins@norampac.com
 Team Ldr.: Forrest Adams
 Email: forrest_adams@norampac.com
Total Employees at this Location: 134
Type of Operation: Paper mill
Pulp Grades and Capacities:
 Total pulp capacity: 554,549 st/y
 Recycled Pulping: 554,549 st/y
Pulp Mill Data:
 Recycled Fiber Treatment Lines:
 Recycled packaging pulping lines
Paper/Paperboard Grades and Capacities:
 Total paper and paperboard capacity: 540,141 st/y
 Linerboard: 540,141 st/y
Paper and Paperboard Mill Data:
Paper Machines: 1
No. 1, fourdrinier, total capacity 540,141 st/y, Trim width 328 in, Linerboard
Energy Data:
Electrical demand for mill: 447 MWh/D

ⓜNorampac Industries Inc.
Niagara Falls Mill
Ownership: 100% by Cascades Inc.
4001 Packard Rd
Niagara Falls, NY 14303
USA
 Phone: (1) 716-285-3681
 Fax: (1) 716-285-3767
 Email: niagarafalls_info@norampac.com
 Web Address: www.norampac.com
Personnel:
 Regional Gen. Mgr. - Containerboard & Boxboard (From 2014): Danick Lavoie
 Phone: (1) 450-461-8602
 Email: danick_lavoie@norampac.com
 Prod. Mgr. (From 2014): Michael hansen
 Phone: (1) 716-285-3681
 Fax: (1) 716-285-3767
 Email: mike_hansen@norampac.com
 Paper Machine #1 Production Supervisor: Troy A. McLean
 Phone: (1) 716-285-3681
 Fax: (1) 716-285-3767
 Email: troy_mclean@norampac.com
 Mech. Mgr.: Clark Willett
 Phone: (1) 716-285-3681
 Fax: (1) 716-285-3767
 Email: clark_willett@norampac.com
Total Employees at this Location: 128
Type of Operation: Paperboard mill
Pulp Grades and Capacities:
 Total pulp capacity: 328,137 st/y
 Recycled Pulping: 328,137 st/y
Pulp Mill Data:
 Recycled Fiber Treatment Lines:
 Recycled packaging pulping lines: 1
Paper/Paperboard Grades and Capacities:
 Total paper and paperboard capacity: 313,803 st/y
 Corrugating medium/fluting: 313,803 st/y
Paper and Paperboard Mill Data:
 Stock Preparation:
 Pulpers: 2
 Refiners: 7
Paper Machines: 2
No. 1, fourdrinier, total capacity 222,768 st/y, Trim width 186 in, Corrugating medium/fluting
No. 2, fourdrinier, total capacity 91,035 st/y, Trim width 186 in, Corrugating medium/fluting
 Finishing Equipment:
 Winders: 2 at 10,000 st/y
Energy Data:
Power boilers: 3
Electrical demand for mill: 406 MWh/D

ⓜⓜOmniafiltra, LLC
Beaver Falls Mill
9547 Main St
Beaver Falls, NY 13305
USA
Mailing Address: PO Box 520, Beaver Falls, NY 13305, USA
 Phone: (1) 315-346-7300
 Fax: (1) 315-346-7301
 Email: info@omniafiltra.com
 Web Address: www.omniafiltra.it
Personnel:
 VP, Sls & Mktg.: Fred Burgess
 Phone: (1) 315-346-7300
 Fax: (1) 315-346-7301
 Email: fredburgess@omniafiltra.com
 Bus. Develop. & Sls. Mgr.: Pete Gendreau
 Phone: (1) 315-346-7300
 Fax: (1) 315-346-7301
 Email: petegendreau@omniafiltra.com
 Mill Mgr.: Scott Sauer
 Phone: (1) 315-346-7300
 Fax: (1) 315-346-7301
 Email: scottsauer@omniafiltra.com
 Tech. Dir.: Francis Pottokaran
 Phone: (1) 315-346-7300
 Fax: (1) 315-346-7301
 Email: francispottokaran@omniafiltra.com
 Cust. Service, Ship. & Receiving: Patti Arndt
 Phone: (1) 315-346-7300
Type of Operation: Pulp mill, Paper mill
Pulp Grades and Capacities:
 Total pulp capacity: 17,500 st/y
 Mechanical Pulp: 17,500 st/y
Pulp Mill Data:
 Mechanical Pulping Systems:
 RMP systems: 1
Paper/Paperboard Grades and Capacities:
 Total paper and paperboard capacity: 17,500 st/y
 Packaging papers
 Specialty and industrial
 Boxboard/cartonboard
Paper and Paperboard Mill Data:
 Stock Preparation:
 Pulpers: 6
 Refiners: 2
Paper Machines: 2
No. 1, cylinder (5), Trim width 64 in

New York

No. 2, fourdrinier, total capacity 17,500 st/y, Trim width 84 in
Finishing Equipment:
Rewinders: 1

ⓜPotsdam Specialty Paper Inc.
Ownership: Private
547A Sissonville Rd
Potsdam, NY 13676
USA
Phone: (1) 315-265-4000
Fax: (1) 315-265-4004
Email: sales@pspi.us.com
Web Address: www.pspi.us.com
Personnel:
CEO: Mike Huth
Phone: (1) 315-265-4000
Fax: (1) 315-265-4004
Email: mike.huth@pspi.us.com
Pres.: Kenny Weiqun Zhang
Phone: (1) 315-265-4000
Fax: (1) 315-265-4004
Email: kenny.zhang@pspi.us.com
Tech. Mgr.: Joel P. Behm
Phone: (1) 315-265-4000
Fax: (1) 315-265-4004
Email: joel.behm@pspi.us.com
Bus. Mgr.: Tracy Champion
Phone: (1) 315-265-4000
Fax: (1) 315-265-4004
Email: tracy.champion@pspi.us.com
Total Employees of Company: 80
Mill Locations:
Potsdam Specialty Paper Inc., Cedar Mill, 547A Sissonville Rd, Potsdam, NY 13676, USA, Capacity: 28,554 st/y, (Paper mill)
Phone: (1) 315-265-4000
Fax: (1) 315-265-4004
Email: sales@pspi.us.com

ⓜPotsdam Specialty Paper Inc.
Cedar Mill
547A Sissonville Rd
Potsdam, NY 13676
USA
Phone: (1) 315-265-4000
Fax: (1) 315-265-4004
Email: sales@pspi.us.com
Web Address: www.pspi.us.com
Personnel:
Oper. Mgr.: Douglass H. Drumm
Phone: (1) 315-265-4000
Fax: (1) 315-265-4004
Email: doug.drumm@pspi.us.com
Bus. Support Mgr.: Tracy Champion
Phone: (1) 315-265-4000
Fax: (1) 315-265-4004
Email: tracy.champion@pspi.us.com
Technology Mgr.: Joel P. Behm
Phone: (1) 315-265-4000
Fax: (1) 315-265-4004
Email: joel.behm@pspi.us.com
Purch. Supervisor: Roxanne Kilgore
Phone: (1) 315-265-4000
Fax: (1) 315-265-4004
Email: roxanne.kilgore@pspi.us.com
Environ. Mgr.: Kristin Basford
Phone: (1) 315-265-4000 Ext: 5673
Fax: (1) 315-265-4004
Email: kristin.basford@pspi.us.com
Total Employees at this Location: 80
Type of Operation: Paper mill
Pulp Grades and Capacities:
Total pulp capacity: 2,985 st/y
Recycled Pulping: 2,985 st/y
Pulp Mill Data:
Paper/Paperboard Grades and Capacities:
Total paper and paperboard capacity: 28,554 st/y
Specialty and industrial: 28,554 st/y

Paper and Paperboard Mill Data:
Paper Machines: 1
No. 3, fourdrinier, total capacity 28,554 st/y, Trim width 124 in, Specialty and industrial
Energy Data:
Power boilers: 3
Electrical demand for mill: 58 MWh/D

ⓜPratt Industries (USA)
Staten Island Mill
Ownership: Visy Pulp & Paper
4435 Victory Blvd
Staten Island, NY 10314
USA
Phone: (1) 718-355-6754
Fax: (1) 718-370-1115
Web Address: www.prattindustries.com, www.visy.com.au
Personnel:
Gen. Mgr. (From May 2014): Muneer Ahmad
Phone: (1) 718-355-6754
Fax: (1) 718-370-1115
Email: mahmad@prattindustries.com
Plt. Mgr.: Dennis Pena
Phone: (1) 718-355-6754
Fax: (1) 718-370-1115
Email: dpena@prattindustries.com
Total Employees at this Location: 111
Type of Operation: Paper mill, Paperboard mill
Pulp Grades and Capacities:
Total pulp capacity: 381,571 st/y
Recycled Pulping: 381,571 st/y
Pulp Mill Data:
Recycled Fiber Treatment Lines:
Recycled packaging pulping lines: 1 at 403,439
Paper/Paperboard Grades and Capacities:
Total paper and paperboard capacity: 373,065 st/y
Linerboard: 242,760 st/y
Corrugating medium/fluting: 130,305 st/y
Paper and Paperboard Mill Data:
Stock Preparation:
Pulpers: 1
Paper Machines: 1
No. 14, GapFormer, total capacity 373,065 st/y, Trim width 200 in, Linerboard, Corrugating medium/fluting
Energy Data:
Power boilers: 1
Electrical demand for mill: 500 MWh/D

ⓜRockTenn Co.
Solvay Mill
53 Industrial Drive
Syracuse, NY 13204-1035
USA
Phone: (1) 315-484-9050
Fax: (1) 315-484-9434
Email: webmaster@rocktenn.com
Web Address: www.rocktenn.com
Personnel:
Gen. Mgr. (From October 2014): Peter Tantalo
Phone: (1) 315-484-9050
Fax: (1) 315-484-9434
Email: ptantalo@rocktenn.com
Fiber Procurement Mgr.: Scott Reed
Phone: (1) 315-484-9050
Fax: (1) 315-484-9434
Email: sreed@rocktenn.com
Dir., Strat. Proj. & Technology Paper Solutions - Mill Operations - Technical Resource Group: Jose Iribarne Ph.D
Phone: (1) 315-703-9363
Fax: (1) 315-703-9463
Email: jiribarne@rocktenn.com
Assist. Contrl.: Pam Hanrahan
Phone: (1) 315-484-9050
Fax: (1) 315-484-9434
Email: phanrahan@rocktenn.com
Total Employees at this Location: 239
Type of Operation: Paperboard mill
Pulp Grades and Capacities:

Total pulp capacity: 830,492 st/y
Recycled Pulping: 830,492 st/y
Pulp Mill Data:
Recycled Fiber Treatment Lines:
Recycled packaging pulping lines: 3 at 871,473
Paper/Paperboard Grades and Capacities:
Total paper and paperboard capacity: 805,035 st/y
Linerboard: 533,001 st/y
Corrugating medium/fluting: 272,034 st/y
Paper and Paperboard Mill Data:
Stock Preparation:
Pulpers: 3
Refiners: 9
Paper Machines: 3
No. 1, fourdrinier, total capacity 227,766 st/y, Trim width 188 in, Linerboard
No. 2, fourdrinier, total capacity 305,235 st/y, Trim width 190 in, Linerboard
No. 3, fourdrinier, total capacity 272,034 st/y, Trim width 190 in, Corrugating medium/fluting

ⓜSCA Tissue North America, L.L.C.
Encore Paper
Ownership: 100% by SCA - Svenska Cellulosa Aktiebolaget
1 River St
South Glens Falls, NY 12803
USA
Phone: (1) 518-793-5684
Fax: (1) 518-793-2650
Email: torkusa@sca.com
Web Address: www.scatissue.com, www.torkusa.com
Personnel:
Plt. Mgr.: Terry Miller
Phone: (1) 518-793-5684
Fax: (1) 518-793-2650
Email: terry.miller@sca.com
Purch. Mgr.: Mindy Kearns
Phone: (1) 518-793-5684
Fax: (1) 518-793-2650
Email: mindy.kearns@sca.com
Proj. Mgr. Americas Product Supply: John Kreul
Phone: (1) 920-720-4794
Email: john.kreul@sca.com
Supt: Bill Cook
Phone: (1) 518-793-5684
Fax: (1) 518-793-2650
Email: bill.cook@sca.com
Total Employees at this Location: 320
Type of Operation: Paper mill
Pulp Grades and Capacities:
Total pulp capacity: 95,039 st/y
Recycled Pulping: 95,039 st/y
Pulp Mill Data:
Bleach Plant Systems: 1
DIP
Recycled Fiber Treatment Lines:
Pulpers: 1 at 108,289 admt/y
Paper/Paperboard Grades and Capacities:
Total paper and paperboard capacity: 88,893 st/y
Tissue: 88,893 st/y
Paper and Paperboard Mill Data:
Stock Preparation:
Pulpers: 4
Refiners: 2
Paper Machines: 3
No. 9, crescent former, total capacity 30,702 st/y, Trim width 140 in, Tissue
No. 10, crescent former, total capacity 19,278 st/y, Trim width 85 in, Tissue
No. 11, crescent former, Yankee dryer, total capacity 38,913 st/y, Trim width 143 in, Tissue
Finishing Equipment:
Rewinders: 4
Energy Data:
Power boilers: 2
Electrical demand for mill: 289 MWh/D

North Carolina

ⓂSchweitzer-Mauduit International Inc.
Ancram Mill
2424 State Route 82
Ancram, NY 12502-5414
USA
Mailing Address: PO Box 10, Ancram, NY 12502-0010, USA
Phone: (1) 518-329-4222
Fax: (1) 518-329-1161
Web Address: www.swmintl.com
Personnel:
Mill Mgr.: Gary Kennedy
Phone: (1) 518-329-5150
Fax: (1) 518-329-1161
Email: gkennedy@swmintl.com
Eng & Maint. Mgr.: Bruce Barnard
Phone: (1) 518-329-5117
Fax: (1) 518-329-1161
Email: bbarnard@swmintl.com
Eng., Maint. & Util. Mgr.: John Tennier
Phone: (1) 518-329-5113
Fax: (1) 518-329-1161
Email: jtennier@swmintl.com
Buyer: Leroy Ferguson
Phone: (1) 518-329-5115
Fax: (1) 518-329-1161
Email: lferguson@swmintl.com
Total Employees at this Location: 121
Type of Operation: Paper mill
Paper/Paperboard Grades and Capacities:
Total paper and paperboard capacity: 10,000 st/y
Specialty and industrial: 9,999 st/y
Paper and Paperboard Mill Data:
Stock Preparation:
Pulpers: 4
Refiners: 7
Paper Machines: 2
No. 1, inclined, total capacity 6,800 st/y, Trim width 87 in, Specialty and industrial
No. 2, fourdrinier, total capacity 3,200 st/y, Trim width 56 in, Specialty and industrial
Finishing Equipment:
Winders: 5 at 7,900 st/y
Energy Data:
Power boilers: 2
Electrical demand for mill: 55 MWh/D

ⓂUnited States Gypsum Co.
Oakfield Mill
275 Maple Avenue
Oakfield, NY 14125-0773
USA
Phone: (1) 585-948-5221
Fax: (1) 585-948-5018
Web Address: www.usg.com
Personnel:
Plt. Mgr.: Jim Perry
Phone: (1) 585-948-5221
Fax: (1) 585-948-5018
Email: jperry@usg.com
Paper Mill Mgr.: Greg E. Gelder
Phone: (1) 585-948-5221
Fax: (1) 585-948-5018
Email: ggelder@usg.com
Eng. Mgr.: Mike F. Pedro
Phone: (1) 585-948-5221
Fax: (1) 585-948-5018
Email: mpedro@usg.com
Total Employees at this Location: 98
Type of Operation: Paperboard mill
Pulp Grades and Capacities:
Total pulp capacity: 83,207 st/y
Recycled Pulping: 83,207 st/y
Paper/Paperboard Grades and Capacities:
Total paper and paperboard capacity: 79,968 st/y
Boxboard/cartonboard: 79,968 st/y
Paper and Paperboard Mill Data:
Stock Preparation:
Pulpers: 2
Refiners: 3
Paper Machines: 1
No. 1, cylinder (7), total capacity 79,968 st/y, Trim width 162 in, Boxboard/cartonboard
Finishing Equipment:
Calenders: 1
Rewinders: 1
Energy Data:
Power boilers: 1
HRSG boiler: 1
Combustion turbines: 1 at 5.8 MW
Electrical demand for mill: 128 MWh/D

NORTH CAROLINA

ⓂCascades Tissue Group
Rockingham Mill
Ownership: 100% by Cascades Inc.
805 Midway Rd
Rockingham, NC 28379
USA
Mailing Address: PO Box 578, Rockingham, NC 28380, USA
Phone: (1) 910-895-4033
Fax: (1) 910-895-9887
Web Address: www.afh.cascades.com
Personnel:
Paper Mill Mgr.: Mickey Lee
Phone: (1) 910-895-4033
Fax: (1) 910-895-9887
Email: mickey_lee@cascades.com
Purch. Mgr.: Alan Raines
Phone: (1) 910-895-4033
Fax: (1) 910-895-9887
Email: alan_raines@cascades.com
Converting Mgr.: Adam Boulware
Phone: (1) 910-895-4033
Fax: (1) 910-895-9887
Email: adam_boulware@cascades.com
Total Employees at this Location: 130
Type of Operation: Pulp mill, Paper mill
Pulp Grades and Capacities:
Total pulp capacity: 67,171 st/y
Recycled Pulping: 67,171 st/y
Pulp Mill Data:
Bleach Plant Systems: 1
Recycled Deinked Pulping System
Recycled Fiber Treatment Lines:
Flotation deinking lines: 1 at 55,000 admt/y
Pulpers: 2 at 75,000 admt/y
Washing deinking lines: 2 at 55,000 admt/y
Paper/Paperboard Grades and Capacities:
Total paper and paperboard capacity: 62,832 st/y
Tissue: 62,832 st/y
Paper and Paperboard Mill Data:
Stock Preparation:
Pulpers: 2
Refiners: 2
Paper Machines: 2
No. 1, fourdrinier, Yankee dryer, total capacity 24,990 st/y, Trim width 121 in, Tissue
No. 2, twin-wire, total capacity 37,842 st/y, Trim width 108 in, Tissue
Finishing Equipment:
Winders: 1
Rewinders: 5 at 27,557 st/y
Energy Data:
Power boilers: 2
Electrical demand for mill: 198 MWh/D

ⓂClearwater Paper Corporation
Shelby Mill
687 Washburn Switch Rd.
Shelby, NC 28150
USA
Phone: (1) 704-476-3801
Fax: (1) 704-481-8955
Web Address: www.clearwaterpaper.com
Personnel:
Mill Mgr.: Vince Reese
Phone: (1) 704-476-3801
Fax: (1) 704-481-8955
Email: vince.reese@clearwaterpaper.com
PM Supervisor: Gareth Beattie
Phone: (1) 704-476-3801
Fax: (1) 704-481-8955
Email: gareth.beattie@clearwaterpaper.com
Maint. Mgr.: Keith McCoy
Phone: (1) 704-476-3801
Fax: (1) 704-481-8955
Email: keith.mccoy@clearwaterpaper.com
Snr. Proj. Mgr.: Gregory Pering
Phone: (1) 704-476-3801
Fax: (1) 704-481-8955
Email: gregory_pering@clearwaterpaper.com
Procces Eng.: Tony Burnette
Phone: (1) 704-476-3801
Fax: (1) 704-481-8955
Email: tony.burnette@clearwaterpaper.com
PM Mgr.: Dwain Eberhard
Phone: (1) 704-476-3801
Fax: (1) 704-481-8955
Email: dwain.eberhard@clearwaterpaper.com
Total Employees at this Location: 57
Type of Operation: Paper mill
Paper/Paperboard Grades and Capacities:
Total paper and paperboard capacity: 69,972 st/y
Tissue: 69,972 st/y
Paper and Paperboard Mill Data:
Paper Machines: 1
No. 5, TAD, total capacity 69,972 st/y, Trim width 200 in, Tissue
Energy Data:
Power boilers: 1

ⓂDomtar Corporation
Plymouth Mill
Highway 149
Plymouth, NC 27962
USA
Mailing Address: PO Box 787, Plymouth, NC 27962, USA
Phone: (1) 252-793-8111
Fax: (1) 252-793-8164
Web Address: www.domtar.com
Personnel:
Mill Mgr. (Eff. September 2014): Allan Bohn
Phone: (1) 252-793-8111
Fax: (1) 252-793-8164
Email: allan.bohn@domtar.com
Environ. Mgr.: Diane Hardison
Phone: (1) 252-793-8111
Fax: (1) 252-793-8164
Email: diane.hardison@domtar.com
Raw Materials Supply/Woodyard Mgr.: Marvin Hare
Phone: (1) 252-793-8073
Fax: (1) 252-793-8164
Email: marvin.hare@domtar.com
Snr. Proj. Eng.: Jimmy Spruill
Phone: (1) 252-793-8111
Fax: (1) 252-793-8164
Email: jimmy.spruill@domtar.com
Exec. Assistant to Mill Mgr.: Carol M. Waters
Phone: (1) 252-793-8890
Fax: (1) 252-793-8164
Email: carol.waters@domtar.com
Maint. & Eng. Mgr. (from October 2014): Bill Ward
Phone: (1) 252-793-8111
Fax: (1) 252-793-8164
Email: bill.ward@domtar.com
Total Employees at this Location: 410
Type of Operation: Pulp mill, Paper mill
Pulp Grades and Capacities:
Total pulp capacity: 541,902 st/y
Pulp available for market: 511,574 st/y
Chemical Pulp: 541,902 st/y
Pulp Mill Data:
Chemical Pulping Systems:

North Carolina

Continuous digesters: 2
Pulp Lines: 2
Bleach Plant Systems: 2
Chemical Pulping System - Line 2, Type: Softwood, Sequence: O_2 DEopDP
Chemical Recovery Equipment:
Evaporator lines: 1
Recovery boilers: 1
Lime Kiln
Pulp Dryers:
Fourdriniers 1
Energy Data:
Power boilers: 3
Steam turbines: 4 at 127.5 MW
Electrical demand for mill: 1,347 MWh/D

ⓂEvergreen Packaging Inc.
Canton Mill
175 Main St
Canton, NC 28716
USA
Mailing Address: PO Box 4000, Canton, NC 28716, USA
Phone: (1) 828-646-2000
Fax: (1) 828-646-6732
Web Address: www.evergreenpackaging.com
Personnel:
Gen. Mgr., Mill Oper.: Dane Griswold
Phone: (1) 828-646-2840
Fax: (1) 828-646-6732
Email: dane.griswold@everpack.com
Mgr. Prod.: Victor Orr
Phone: (1) 828-646-2000
Fax: (1) 828-646-6732
Email: victor.orr@everpack.com
Fiber Procurement Mgr.: Tom Lassiter
Phone: (1) 828-646-2000
Fax: (1) 828-646-6732
Email: tom.lassiter@everpack.com
Total Employees at this Location: 900
Type of Operation: Pulp mill, Paper mill, Paperboard mill
Pulp Grades and Capacities:
Total pulp capacity: 541,839 st/y
Chemical Pulp: 531,930 st/y
Recycled Pulping: 9,909 st/y
Pulp Mill Data:
Chemical Pulping Systems:
Batch digesters: 18
Pulp Lines: 2
Bleach Plant Systems: 2
No. 1, Type: Hardwood, Sequence: O_2 DEoD
No. 2, Type: Softwood, Sequence: O_2 DEopD
Chemical Recovery Equipment:
Evaporator lines: 2
Recovery boilers: 2
Lime Kiln
Paper/Paperboard Grades and Capacities:
Total paper and paperboard capacity: 583,695 st/y
Uncoated woodfree/freesheet: 237,405 st/y
Specialty and industrial: 27,132 st/y
Boxboard/cartonboard: 319,158 st/y
Paper and Paperboard Mill Data:
Stock Preparation:
Pulpers: 16
Refiners: 10
Paper Machines: 4
No. 11, fourdrinier, total capacity 74,256 st/y, Trim width 219 in, Uncoated woodfree/freesheet, Specialty and industrial
No. 12, fourdrinier, total capacity 81,396 st/y, Trim width 219 in, Uncoated woodfree/freesheet, Specialty and industrial, Boxboard/cartonboard
No. 19, fourdrinier, total capacity 314,874 st/y, Trim width 230 in, Boxboard/cartonboard
No. 20, fourdrinier, total capacity 145,656 st/y, Trim width 226 in, Uncoated woodfree/freesheet
Energy Data:
Power boilers: 4
Steam turbines: 6 at 50 MW
Electrical demand for mill: 1,399 MWh/D

ⓂInternational Paper Co.
Riegelwood Mill
865 John L Riegel Rd
Riegelwood, NC 28456-0008
USA
Phone: (1) 910-655-2211
Fax: (1) 910-655-6119
Email: (firstname.lastname@ipaper.com)
Web Address: www.internationalpaper.com
Personnel:
Mill Mgr.: Floyd Whitmire
Phone: (1) 910-655-2211
Fax: (1) 910-655-6119
Email: floyd.whitmire@ipaper.com
Finished Products Mgr.: Edwin J. Senko
Phone: (1) 910-655-2211
Fax: (1) 910-655-6119
Email: ed.senko@ipaper.com
Area Manager-Chemical Recovery: Andy Knoll
Phone: (1) 910-655-2211
Fax: (1) 910-655-6119
Email: andy.knoll@ipaper.com
Total Employees at this Location: 758
Type of Operation: Pulp mill, Paperboard mill
Pulp Grades and Capacities:
Total pulp capacity: 894,171 st/y
Pulp available for market: 475,167 st/y
Chemical Pulp: 894,171 st/y
Pulp Mill Data:
Chemical Pulping Systems:
Batch digesters: 16
Continuous digesters: 1
Bleach Plant Systems: 3
Chemical Pulping System, Type: Hardwood, Sequence: DEopDD
Chemical Pulping System, Type: Softwood, Sequence: O_2 DEopDD
Chemical Recovery Equipment:
Evaporator lines
Recovery boilers: 3
Lime Kiln
Pulp Dryers:
Flakt dryer 1, Fourdriniers 1
Paper/Paperboard Grades and Capacities:
Total paper and paperboard capacity: 424,830 st/y
Boxboard/cartonboard: 424,830 st/y
Paper and Paperboard Mill Data:
Stock Preparation:
Pulpers: 3
Paper Machines: 2
No. 15, fourdrinier, total capacity 224,910 st/y, Trim width 216 in, Boxboard/cartonboard
No. 18, fourdrinier, total capacity 199,920 st/y, Trim width 216 in, Boxboard/cartonboard
Coating Machines: 2
No. 1, total capacity 224,868 st/y., on machine
No. 2, total capacity 196,208 st/y., on machine
Finishing Equipment:
Rewinders: 1
Sheeters: 2
Energy Data:
Power boilers: 5
Steam turbines: 3 at 58 MW
Electrical demand for mill: 2,098 MWh/D

ⓄⓂJackson Paper Manufacturing Co.
Sylva Mill
152 W Main St
Sylva, NC 28779
USA
Mailing Address: PO Box 667, Sylva, NC 28779, USA
Phone: (1) 828-586-5534
Fax: (1) 828-586-6755
Email: jmurphy@jacksonpaper.net
Web Address: www.jacksonpaper-nc.com
Personnel:
Chmn. & CEO: Timothy L. Campbell
Phone: (1) 828-586-5534 Ext. 20
Fax: (1) 828-586-6755
Email: tcampbell@jacksonpaper.net
Pres. & COO: Nicki Slusser
Phone: (1) 828-586-5534
Fax: (1) 828-586-6755
Email: nslusser@jacksonpaper.net
VP & CFO: Jeffrey L. Murphy
Phone: (1) 828-586-5534 Ext. 205
Fax: (1) 828-586-6755
Email: jmurphy@jacksonpaper.net
VP, Finan.: Tammy Francis
Phone: (1) 828-586-5534
Fax: (1) 828-586-6755
Email: tfrancis@jacksonpaper.net
VP, Sls. : Scott Price
Phone: (1) 828-586-5534 Ext. 276
Fax: (1) 828-631-0954
Email: sprice@jacksonpaper.net
Plt. Mgr.: Ken Rogers
Phone: (1) 828-586-5534
Fax: (1) 828-631-0954
Email: krogers@jacksonpaper.net
Total Employees of Company: 121
Total Employees at this Location: 121
Type of Operation: Paperboard mill
Pulp Grades and Capacities:
Total pulp capacity: 119,655 st/y
Recycled Pulping: 119,655 st/y
Pulp Mill Data:
Recycled Fiber Treatment Lines:
Pulpers: 1 at 150,000 admt/y
Paper/Paperboard Grades and Capacities:
Total paper and paperboard capacity: 114,240 st/y
Corrugating medium/fluting: 114,240 st/y
Paper and Paperboard Mill Data:
Stock Preparation:
Pulpers: 1
Refiners: 3
Paper Machines: 1
No. 1, fourdrinier, total capacity 114,240 st/y, Trim width 131 in, Corrugating medium/fluting
Energy Data:
Power boilers: 1
Steam turbines: 1 at 0.6 MW

ⓂKapStone Kraft Paper Corporation
Roanoke Rapids Mill
Ownership: 100% by KapStone Paper and Packaging Corp
100 Gaston Road
Roanoke Rapids, NC 27870-1911
USA
Mailing Address: 100 Gaston Road, Roanoke Rapids, NC 27870-1911, USA
Phone: (1) 252-533-6000
Fax: (1) 252-533-6401
Email: information@kapstonepaper.com
Web Address: www.kapstonepaper.com
Personnel:
VP, Mill Oper.: Bill Kessinger
Phone: (1) 252-533-6000
Fax: (1) 252-533-6401
Email: bill.kessinger@kapstonepaper.com
Environ. Mgr.: Mike Knudson
Phone: (1) 252-533-6000
Fax: (1) 252-533-6401
Email: mike.knudson@kapstonepaper.com
HR & Safety Mgr.: Chris Wilkins
Phone: (1) 252-533-6000
Fax: (1) 252-533-6401
Email: chris.wilkins@kapstonepaper.com
Fiber Supply Mgr.: Bernard Rose
Phone: (1) 252-533-6000
Fax: (1) 252-533-6401
Email: bernard.rose@kapstonepaper.com
Tech. Serv. & Sls. Mgr.: Fred Martin
Phone: (1) 252-533-6000
Fax: (1) 252-533-6401
Email: fred.martin@kapstonepaper.com
Total Employees at this Location: 490
Type of Operation: Pulp mill, Paper mill, Paperboard mill

North Carolina

Pulp Grades and Capacities:
Total pulp capacity: 463,806 st/y
Chemical Pulp: 463,806 st/y
Pulp Mill Data:
Chemical Pulping Systems:
Batch digesters: 12
Pulp Lines: 3
Chemical Recovery Equipment:
Evaporator lines: 1
Recovery boilers: 1
Lime Kiln
Paper/Paperboard Grades and Capacities:
Total paper and paperboard capacity: 439,824 st/y
Packaging papers: 199,920 st/y
Linerboard: 239,904 st/y
Paper and Paperboard Mill Data:
Stock Preparation:
Pulpers: 1
Refiners: 2
Paper Machines: 2
No. 3, Tri Nip press, total capacity 204,204 st/y, Trim width 228 in, Packaging papers, Linerboard
No. 4, total capacity 235,620 st/y, Trim width 228 in, Packaging papers, Linerboard
Finishing Equipment:
Winders: 2 at 400,000 st/y
Calenders: 1
Energy Data:
Power boilers: 1
Steam turbines: 1 at 24 MW
Electrical demand for mill: 1,041 MWh/D

ⓜNational Gypsum Co.
Ownership: Private
2001 Rexford Rd
Charlotte, NC 28211
USA
 Phone: (1) 704-365-7300
 Fax: (1) 704-365-7423
 Email: ng@nationalgypsum.com
 Web Address: www.nationalgypsum.com
Personnel:
Chrmn., Pres. & CEO: Thomas C. Nelson
 Phone: (1) 704-365-7300
 Fax: (1) 704-365-7423
 Email: tcnelson@nationalgypsum.com
VP., Gen Counsel & Sec.: Sam A. Schiffman
 Phone: (1) 704-365-7300
 Fax: (1) 704-365-7423
 Email: saschiffman@nationalgypsum.com
VP., R&D: Craig C. Robertson
 Phone: (1) 704-365-7300
 Fax: (1) 704-365-7423
 Email: ccrobertson@nationalgypsum.com
VP., Manuf. Oper. & Eng.: John M. Corsi
 Phone: (1) 704-365-7300
 Fax: (1) 704-365-7423
 Email: jmcorsi@nationalgypsum.com
Dir. Commun.: Nancy H. Spurlock
 Phone: (1) 704-365-7300
 Fax: (1) 704-365-7423
 Email: nhspurlock@nationalgypsum.com
Mgr, Mktg Comm: Renee A. Cieslikowski
 Phone: (1) 704-365-7300
 Fax: (1) 704-365-7423
 Email: racieslikowski@nationalgypsum.com
Mktg. Mgr.: David B. Drummond
 Phone: (1) 704-365-7293
 Fax: (1) 704-365-7423
 Email: dbdrummond@nationalgypsum.com
Mill Locations:
National Gypsum Co., Milton Plant, 2586 Old Route 15, New Columbia, PA 17856, USA, Capacity: 112,098 st/y, (Paperboard mill)
 Phone: (1) 570-538-2531
 Fax: (1) 570-538-5898
National Gypsum Co., Anniston Mill, 4811 US Hway 78 W, Oxford, AL 36201, USA, Capacity: 77,112 st/y, (Paperboard mill)
 Phone: (1) 256-831-6900
 Fax: (1) 256-835-2688
National Gypsum Co., Pryor Mill, 4189 Hunt Street, Pryor, OK 74361, USA, Capacity: 89,964 st/y, (Paperboard mill)
 Phone: (1) 918-825-0142
 Fax: (1) 918-825-7094

ⓜSealed Air Corp.
Lenoir Mill
2075 NW Valway Rd
Lenoir, NC 28645
USA
Mailing Address: PO Box 1018, Lenoir, NC 28645, USA
 Phone: (1) 828-726-2100
 Fax: (1) 828-754-0580
 Email: specialtymaterials-na@sealedair.com
 Web Address: www.sealedair.com
Personnel:
VP & Gen. Mgr.: Jonathan Baker
 Phone: (1) 828-726-2100
 Fax: (1) 828-754-0580
 Email: jon.baker@sealedair.com
Plt & Prod Mgr.: Ed Frost
 Phone: (1) 828-726-2100
 Fax: (1) 828-754-0580
 Email: ed.frost@sealedair.com
IT Mgr.: Larry Spears
 Phone: (1) 828-726-2100
 Fax: (1) 828-754-0580
 Email: larry.spears@sealedair.com
Type of Operation: Paper mill
Paper/Paperboard Grades and Capacities:
Total paper and paperboard capacity: 7,000 st/y
Specialty and industrial: 7,000 st/y
Paper and Paperboard Mill Data:
Stock Preparation:
Pulpers: 2
Refiners: 2
Paper Machines: 1
PM #1, Yankee dryer, fourdrinier, total capacity 7,000 st/y, Trim width 88 in, Specialty and industrial
Energy Data:
Power boilers: 1

ⓜVon Drehle Corp.
Ownership: 50% by Raymond Von Drehle, 50% by Steve Von Drehle
612 Third Avenue NE
Hickory, NC 28601-5164
USA
 Phone: (1) 828-322-1805
 Fax: (1) 828-322-4145
 Email: sales@vondrehle.com
 Web Address: www.vondrehle.com
Personnel:
Chrmn.: Steve Von Drehle
 Phone: (1) 828-322-1805
 Fax: (1) 828-322-4145
 Email: steve.vondrehle@vondrehle.com
Pres. & CEO: Randy Bergman
 Phone: (1) 828-322-1805
 Fax: (1) 828-322-4145
 Email: randy.bergman@vondrehle.com
VP Oper.: Carey Latimer
 Phone: (1) 828-322-1805
 Fax: (1) 828-322-4145
 Email: carey.latimer@vondrehle.com
CFO: Craig Keenan
 Phone: (1) 828-322-1805
 Fax: (1) 828-322-4145
 Email: craig.keenan@vondrehle.com
V.P. of Manufacturing: Joe Pankratz
 Phone: (1) 828-322-1805
 Fax: (1) 828-322-4145
 Email: joe.pankratz@vondrehle.com
Lean Oper. Mgr.: Travis von Drehle
 Phone: (1) 828-322-1805
 Fax: (1) 828-322-4145
 Email: travis.vondrehle@vondrehle.com
Sls. Dir.: Jim Tant
 Phone: (1) 828-322-1805
 Fax: (1) 828-322-4145
 Email: jim.tant@vondrehle.com
Regional Mgr.: Duke Thomas
 Phone: (1) 828-322-1805
 Fax: (1) 828-322-4145
 Email: duke.thomas@vondrehle.com
Total Employees of Company: 320
Total Employees at this Location: 25
Mill Locations:
Von Drehle Corp., Cordova Mill, 126 1st St, Cordova, NC 28330, USA, Capacity: 57,120 st/y, (Paper mill)
 Phone: (1) 910-410-9131, 828-322-1805
 Fax: (1) 828-322-4145
 Email: sales@vondrehle.com
Von Drehle Corp., Natchez Mill, 30 Majorca Rd, Natchez, MS 39120, USA, (Pulp mill)
 Phone: (1) 601-445-0100
 Fax: (1) 601-442-6599
 Email: sales@vondrehle.com

ⓜVon Drehle Corp.
Cordova Mill
126 1st St
Cordova, NC 28330
USA
Mailing Address: PO Box 159, Cordova, NC 28330, USA
 Phone: (1) 910-410-9131, 828-322-1805
 Fax: (1) 828-322-4145
 Email: sales@vondrehle.com
 Web Address: www.vondrehle.com
Personnel:
Prod. Mgr.: Steve Watkins
 Phone: (1) 910-410-9131
 Fax: (1) 828-322-4145
 Email: steve.watkins@vondrehle.com
Paper Mill Supt.: Vernon Self
 Phone: (1) 910-410-9131
 Fax: (1) 828-322-4145
 Email: vernon.self@vondrehle.com
Eng. Mgr.: Doug Bailey
 Phone: (1) 910-410-9131 Ext. 215
 Fax: (1) 828-322-4145
 Email: doug.bailey@vondrehle.com
Office Mgr./HR Mgr.: Brenda Gainey
 Phone: (1) 910-410-9131
 Fax: (1) 828-322-4145
 Email: brenda.gainey@vondrehle.com
Total Employees at this Location: 90
Type of Operation: Paper mill
Pulp Grades and Capacities:
Total pulp capacity: 61,012 st/y
Recycled Pulping: 61,012 st/y
Pulp Mill Data:
Pulp Lines: 1
Bleach Plant Systems: 1
No. 1, Type: Direct Borol Injection (DBI), Sequence: P/HS
Recycled Fiber Treatment Lines:
Pulpers: 2
Washing deinking lines: 1 at 70,000 admt/y
Paper/Paperboard Grades and Capacities:
Total paper and paperboard capacity: 57,120 st/y
Tissue: 57,120 st/y
Paper and Paperboard Mill Data:
Stock Preparation:
Pulpers:
Paper Machines: 2
No. 1, crescent former, Yankee dryer, total capacity 27,132 st/y, Trim width 102 in, Tissue
No. 2, crescent former, Yankee dryer, total capacity 29,988 st/y, Trim width 102 in, Tissue
Energy Data:
Power boilers: 1
Electrical demand for mill: 159 MWh/D

ⓜWeyerhaeuser Co.
New Bern Mill
1785 Weyerhaeuser Rd,
Vanceboro, NC 28526-7606
USA

Ohio

Phone: (1) 252-633-7100
Fax: (1) 252-633-7529
Email: pulpgeneral@weyerhaeuser.com
Web Address: www.weyerhaeuser.com
Personnel:
Unit Mgr.: Gerald Cooper
Phone: (1) 919-633-7338
VP, Mill Mgr.: John Ashley
Phone: (1) 252-633-7100
Fax: (1) 252-633-7529
Email: john.ashley@weyerhaeuser.com
Prod Line & Utility Mgr.: Denise Martin
Phone: (1) 252-633-7100
Fax: (1) 252-633-7529
Email: denise.martin@weyerhaeuser.com
Capital Proj. Eng.: Greg Golike
Phone: (1) 252-633-7100
Fax: (1) 252-633-7529
Email: greg.golike@weyerhaeuser.com
Prod. Mgr.: Scott Lonadier
Phone: (1) 252-633-7100
Fax: (1) 252-633-7529
Email: scott.lonadier@weyerhaeuser.com
Total Employees at this Location: 281
Type of Operation: Pulp mill
Pulp Grades and Capacities:
Total pulp capacity: 374,754 st/y
Pulp available for market: 352,593 st/y
Chemical Pulp: 374,754 st/y
Pulp Mill Data:
Chemical Pulping Systems:
Continuous digesters: 1
Bleach Plant Systems: 1
Chemical Pulping System, Type: Softwood, Sequence: O_2 DEopD, Capacity 331,999.6 admt/y
Chemical Recovery Equipment:
Evaporator lines: 1
Recovery boilers: 1
Lime Kiln
Pulp Dryers:
Flakt dryer 1
Energy Data:
Power boilers: 1
Steam turbines: 1 at 38.1 MW

OHIO

ⓜCheney Pulp & Paper Co.
1000 Anderson Street
Franklin, OH 45005
USA
Mailing Address: PO Box 215, Franklin, OH 45005, USA
Phone: (1) 937-746-9991
Fax: (1) 937-746-3884
Web Address: www.cheneypulp.com
Personnel:
Pres.: Mark Snyder
Phone: (1) 937-746-9991 Ext.12
Fax: (1) 937-746-3884
Email: marksnyder@cheneypulp.com
Tech. Dir.: Jeff Truax
Phone: (1) 937-746-9991 Ext.16
Fax: (1) 937-746-3884
Email: jefftruax@cheneypulp.com
Maint. Mgr.: Tony Priest
Phone: (1) 937-746-9991
Fax: (1) 937-746-3884
Email: tpriest@cheneypulp.com
Admin. Asst.: Mary Chase
Phone: (1) 937-746-9991
Fax: (1) 937-746-3884
Email: mchase@cheneypulp.com
Mill Locations:
Cheney Pulp & Paper Co., Franklin Mill, 1000 Anderson Street, Franklin, OH 45005, USA, (Pulp mill)

Phone: (1) 937-746-9991
Fax: (1) 937-746-3884

ⓜCheney Pulp & Paper Co.
Franklin Mill
1000 Anderson Street
Franklin, OH 45005
USA
Mailing Address: PO Box 215, Franklin, OH 45005, USA
Phone: (1) 937-746-9991
Fax: (1) 937-746-3884
Web Address: www.cheneypulp.com
Personnel:
Pres.: Mark Snyder
Phone: (1) 937-746-9991 ext. 12
Fax: (1) 937-746-3884
Email: marksnyder@cheneypulp.com
Maint. Mgr.: Tony Priest
Phone: (1) 937-746-9991 Ext 13
Fax: (1) 937-746-3884
Email: tpriest@cheneypulp.com
Admin. Asst.: Mary Chase
Phone: (1) 937-746-9991 ext. 11
Fax: (1) 937-746-3884
Email: mchase@cheneypulp.com
Total Employees at this Location: 35
Type of Operation: Pulp mill
Pulp Grades and Capacities:
Total pulp capacity: 12,000 st/y
Pulp available for market: 12,000 st/y
Pulp Mill Data:
Chemical Pulping Systems:
Batch digesters: 4
Pulp Lines: 1
Bleach Plant Lines:
No. 1, Sequence: H
Recycled Fiber Treatment Lines:
Pulpers: 1 at 10,500 admt/y
Energy Data:
Power boilers: 1

ⓜCincinnati Paperboard
Cincinnati Mill
Ownership: 100% by Caraustar Industries, Inc.
5500 Wooster Rd
Cincinnati, OH 45226
USA
Phone: (1) 513-871-7112
Fax: (1) 513-871-7971
Email: millgroup.austell@caraustar.com
Web Address: www.caraustar.com
Personnel:
Gen. Mgr.: Luke Galloway
Phone: (1) 513-871-7112
Fax: (1) 513-871-7971
Email: luke.galloway@caraustar.com
Ship. & Waste Paper Receiving Mgr.: Donald Macbeth
Phone: (1) 513-871-7112
Fax: (1) 513-871-7971
Email: don.macbeth@caraustar.com
Total Employees at this Location: 77
Type of Operation: Paperboard mill
Pulp Grades and Capacities:
Total pulp capacity: 81,899 st/y
Recycled Pulping: 81,899 st/y
Pulp Mill Data:
Recycled Fiber Treatment Lines:
Pulpers
Paper/Paperboard Grades and Capacities:
Total paper and paperboard capacity: 80,325 st/y
Boxboard/cartonboard: 80,325 st/y
Paper and Paperboard Mill Data:
Stock Preparation:
Pulpers: 2
Refiners: 4
Paper Machines: 1

No. 1, cylinder (8), total capacity 80,325 st/y, Trim width 118 in, Boxboard/cartonboard
Finishing Equipment:
Calenders: 2
Rewinders: 1
Energy Data:
Power boilers: 2
Electrical demand for mill: 104 MWh/D

ⓜFibercorr Inc.
670 17th St NW
Massillon, OH 44647
USA
Mailing Address: PO Box 453, Massillon, OH 44646, USA
Phone: (1) 330-837-5151
Fax: (1) 330-837-9109
Web Address: www.fibercorr.com
Personnel:
Plant. Mgr.: Allan Lynch
Phone: (1) 330.837.5151 Ext.318
Fax: (1) 330-837-9109
Email: lynch@fibercorr.com
Sls.Mgr.: Donnie Peters
Phone: (1) 330.837.5151 Ext.311
Fax: (1) 330-837-9109
Email: peters@fibercorr.com
Controller: Ralph Reisinger
Phone: (1) 330.837.5151 Ext.313
Fax: (1) 330-837-9109
Email: reisinger@fibercorr.com
Admin.Mgr., Office Mgr.: Mark Goodnight
Phone: (1) 330.837.5151 Ext.312
Fax: (1) 330-837-9109
Email: goodnight@fibercorr.com
Mill Locations:
Fibercorr Inc., Massillon Mill, 670 17th St NW, Massillon, OH 44647, USA, Capacity: 89,250 st/y, (Paperboard mill)
Phone: (1) 330-837-5151
Fax: (1) 330-837-9109

ⓜFibercorr Inc.
Massillon Mill
670 17th St NW
Massillon, OH 44647
USA
Mailing Address: PO Box 453, Massillon, OH 44646, USA
Phone: (1) 330-837-5151
Fax: (1) 330-837-9109
Web Address: www.fibercorr.com
Personnel:
Plt. Mgr.: Allan Lynch
Phone: (1) 330-837-5151 Ext 318
Fax: (1) 330-837-9109
Email: lynch@fibercorr.com
Office Mgr./Tech.: Donald J. Peters
Phone: (1) 330-837-5151 Ext.: 311
Fax: (1) 330-837-9109
Email: peters@fibercorr.com
Information System Mgr.: Mark Goodnight
Phone: (1) 330-837-5151 Ext 312
Fax: (1) 330-837-9109
Email: goodnight@fibercorr.com
Contr.: Ralph Reisinger
Phone: (1) 330-837-5151 Ext: 313
Fax: (1) 330-837-9109
Email: reisinger@fibercorr.com
Total Employees at this Location: 90
Type of Operation: Paperboard mill
Pulp Grades and Capacities:
Total pulp capacity: 92,561 st/y
Recycled Pulping: 92,561 st/y
Pulp Mill Data:
Recycled Fiber Treatment Lines:
Pulpers: 2 at 100,309
Paper/Paperboard Grades and Capacities:
Total paper and paperboard capacity: 89,250 st/y
Corrugating medium/fluting: 89,250 st/y
Paper and Paperboard Mill Data:

Stock Preparation:
  Pulpers: 2
  Refiners: 6
Paper Machines: 2
  No. 1, fourdrinier, total capacity 41,055 st/y, Trim width 105 in, Corrugating medium/fluting
  No. 2, fourdrinier, total capacity 48,195 st/y, Trim width 105 in, Corrugating medium/fluting
Energy Data:
  Power boilers: 6
  Electrical demand for mill: 125 MWh/D

ⓂGlatfelter
Chillicothe Mill
401 S Paint St
Chillicothe, OH 45601
USA
Mailing Address: PO Box 2500, Chillicothe, OH 45601, USA
  Phone: (1) 740-772-3111
  Fax: (1) 740-772-0024
  Web Address: www.glatfelter.com
Personnel:
  Mgr, Product Performance: Phil Butchers
  Phone: (1) 740-772-3139
  Fax: (1) 740-772-0024
  Email: philip.butchers@glatfelter.com
  Dir., Environ. Health & Safety: Katherine Wiedeman
  Phone: (1) 740-772-3387
  Fax: (1) 740-772-0024
  Email: kwiedeman@glatfelter.com
  Sr. Process Improv. Eng.: Paul Deschene
  Phone: (1) 740-772-3111
  Fax: (1) 740-772-0024
  Email: paul.deschene@glatfelter.com
Total Employees at this Location: 950
Type of Operation: Pulp mill, Paper mill
Pulp Grades and Capacities:
  Total pulp capacity: 354,782 st/y
  Chemical Pulp: 338,586 st/y
  Recycled Pulping: 16,197 st/y
Pulp Mill Data:
  Chemical Pulping Systems:
  Batch digesters: 8
Pulp Lines: 1
  Bleach Plant Systems: 1
  Chemical Pulping System, Sequence: DEopD
  Chemical Recovery Equipment:
  Evaporator lines: 1
  Recovery boilers: 1
  Lime Kiln
Paper/Paperboard Grades and Capacities:
  Total paper and paperboard capacity: 394,398 st/y
  Uncoated woodfree/freesheet: 394,398 st/y
Paper and Paperboard Mill Data:
  Stock Preparation:
  Pulpers:
Paper Machines: 4
  No. 10, fourdrinier, total capacity 66,030 st/y, Trim width 200 in, Uncoated woodfree/freesheet
  No. 12, twin-wire, total capacity 219,507 st/y, Trim width 300 in, Uncoated woodfree/freesheet
  No. 23, fourdrinier, total capacity 49,969 st/y, Trim width 163 in, Uncoated woodfree/freesheet
  No. 24, fourdrinier, total capacity 58,892 st/y, Trim width 176 in, Uncoated woodfree/freesheet
Coating Machines: 3
  No. 1/2, off machine
  No. 12, total capacity 95,000 st/y, off machine
  No. 32, off machine
Finishing Equipment:
  Winders: 5
  Supercalenders: 2
  Rewinders: 13
  Sheeters: 8
Energy Data:
  Power boilers: 4
  Steam turbines: 4 at 83 MW
  Electrical demand for mill: 1,250 MWh/D

ⓂGraphic Packaging International Inc.
Middletown Mill
407 Charles St
Middletown, OH 45042-2192
USA
  Phone: (1) 513-424-4200
  Fax: (1) 513-424-4325
  Web Address: www.graphicpkg.com
Personnel:
  Resident Mill Mgr. (From August 2014): James (Matt) Sullivan
  Phone: (1) 513-424-4200
  Fax: (1) 513-424-4325
  Email: matt.sullivan@graphicpkg.com
  Contr.: Neil Shockey
  Phone: (1) 513-424-4200
  Fax: (1) 513-424-4325
  Email: neil.shockey@graphicpkg.com
  Continuous Improvement Mgr.: Judy Arvan
  Phone: (1) 513-424-4200
  Fax: (1) 513-424-4325
  Email: judy.arvan@graphicpkg.com
Total Employees at this Location: 142
Type of Operation: Paperboard mill
Pulp Grades and Capacities:
  Total pulp capacity: 157,430 st/y
  Recycled Pulping: 157,430 st/y
Pulp Mill Data:
  Recycled Fiber Treatment Lines:
  Recycled packaging pulping lines: 1
Paper/Paperboard Grades and Capacities:
  Total paper and paperboard capacity: 162,792 st/y
  Boxboard/cartonboard: 162,792 st/y
Paper and Paperboard Mill Data:
  Stock Preparation:
  Pulpers:
Paper Machines: 1
  No. 1, cylinder (6), total capacity 162,792 st/y, Trim width 124 in, Boxboard/cartonboard
Coating Machines: 1
  No. 1, total capacity 158,179 st/y., on machine
Finishing Equipment:
  Sheeters: 1
Energy Data:
  Power boilers: 4
  Electrical demand for mill: 281 MWh/D

ⒽGreif Inc.
425 Winter Rd
Delaware, OH 43015
USA
  Phone: (1) 740-549-6000
  Fax: (1) 740-549-6100
  Web Address: www.greif.com
Personnel:
  Exec. Chmn.: Michael J. Gasser
  Phone: (1) 740-549-6000
  Fax: (1) 740-549-6100
  Email: michael.gasser@greif.com
  Pres., CEO: David B. Fischer
  Phone: (1) 740-549-6000
  Fax: (1) 740-549-6100
  Email: david.fischer@greif.com
  Exec. VP & CFO (From May 2014): Lawrence A. Hilsheimer
  Phone: (1) 740-549-6000
  Fax: (1) 740-549-6100
  Exec. VP & Gen. Counsel: Gary R. Martz
  Phone: (1) 740-549-6000
  Fax: (1) 740-549-6100
  Email: gary.martz@greif.com
  COO, effective Jan. 1, 2014: Peter G. Watson
  Phone: (1) 740-549-6000
  Fax: (1) 740-549-6100
  Div. Pres., Sr. VP, IP&S - Europe: Ivan Signorelli
  Phone: (1) 740-549-6000
  Fax: (1) 740-549-6100
  Email: ivan.signorelli@greif.com
  VP, Corp. Finan. Contr. (Eff. April 2014): David Lloyd
  Phone: (1) 740-549-6000
  Fax: (1) 740-549-6100
  VP, Bus. Managerial Contr. (Eff. April 2014): Chris Luffler
  Phone: (1) 740-549-6000
  Fax: (1) 740-549-6100
Total Employees of Company: 13,085
Mill Locations:
  Greif Inc., Massillon Mill, 9420 Warmington St, Massillon, OH 44646, USA, Capacity: 224,910 st/y, (Pulp mill, Paper mill, Paperboard mill)
  Phone: (1) 330-879-2101
  Fax: (1) 330-879-5974
  Greif Inc., Riverville Mill, 861 Fibre Plant Rd, Amherst, VA 24521, USA, Capacity: 499,800 st/y, (Pulp mill, Paper mill, Paperboard mill)
  Phone: (1) 434-933-4100
  Fax: (1) 434-933-4148

ⓂGreif Inc.
Massillon Mill
9420 Warmington St
Massillon, OH 44646
USA
Mailing Address: PO Box 675, Massillon, OH 44648-0675, USA
  Phone: (1) 330-879-2101
  Fax: (1) 330-879-5974
  Web Address: www.greif.com
Personnel:
  Tech. Dir.: Jordan Brodsky
  Phone: (1) 330-879-2101
  Fax: (1) 330-879-5974
  Email: jordan.brodsky@greif.com
  HR Mgr. & Recovered Fiber Buyer: Jamie Cutcher
  Phone: (1) 330-879-2101
  Fax: (1) 330-879-5974
  Email: jamie.cutcher@greif.com
  Dir., Sls. & Mktg.: Rick Moreland
  Phone: (1) 330-879-2101
  Fax: (1) 330-879-5974
  Email: rick.moreland@greif.com
  Project Eng. Mgr.: Jarvais Wilson
  Phone: (1) 330-879-2101
  Fax: (1) 330-879-5974
  Email: jarvais.wilson@greif.com
  Plt Eng.: Jack Eschliman
  Phone: (1) 330-879-2101
  Fax: (1) 330-879-5703
  Email: jack.eschliman@greif.com
Total Employees at this Location: 101
Type of Operation: Pulp mill, Paper mill, Paperboard mill
Pulp Grades and Capacities:
  Total pulp capacity: 230,760 st/y
  Recycled Pulping: 230,760 st/y
Pulp Mill Data:
Pulp Lines: 1
  Recycled Fiber Treatment Lines:
  Recycled packaging pulping lines: 1 at 230,000 admt/y
Paper/Paperboard Grades and Capacities:
  Total paper and paperboard capacity: 224,910 st/y
  Corrugating medium/fluting: 224,910 st/y
Paper and Paperboard Mill Data:
  Stock Preparation:
  Pulpers: 2
  Refiners: 3
Paper Machines: 2
  No. 1, fourdrinier, total capacity 82,110 st/y, Trim width 110 in, Corrugating medium/fluting
  No. 2, fourdrinier, total capacity 142,800 st/y, Trim width 152 in, Corrugating medium/fluting
Finishing Equipment:
  Rewinders: 2 at 175,000 st/y
Energy Data:
  HRSG boiler: 1
  Combustion turbines: 1 at 5.8 MW
  Electrical demand for mill: 360 MWh/D

Ohio

ⓃNewPage Corporation
Ownership: 80% by Cerberus Capital Management, LP (Private)
8540 Gander Creek Drive
Miamisburg, OH 45342
USA
　Phone: (1) 937-242-9500, 800-895-2248
　Fax: (1) 800-987-5281
　Web Address: www.newpagecorp.com
Personnel:
　Pres. & CEO: George F. Martin
　Phone: (1) 937-242-9168
　Fax: (1) 937-242-9325
　Email: gfm4@newpagecorp.com
　Snr. VP., & CFO: Jay A Epstein
　Phone: (1) 937-242-9500
　Fax: (1) 800-987-5281
　Email: jay.epstein@newpagecorp.com
　Snr. VP. & CAO: Daniel A. Clark
　Phone: (1) 937-242-9051
　Fax: (1) 937-242-9325
　Email: dac1@newpagecorp.com
　Snr. VP., Oper.: L. Mark Lukacs
　Phone: (1) 937-242-9068
　Fax: (1) 937-242-4444
　Email: lm18@newpagecorp.com
　Snr. VP., Gen. Counsel and Sec.: David L. Santez
　Phone: (1) 937-242-9500
　Fax: (1) 800-987-5281
　Email: david.santez@newpagecorp.com
　VP., Mktg.: Steve DeVoe
　Phone: (1) 937-242-9668
　Fax: (1) 937-242-9329
　Email: sjd6@newpagecorp.com
　VP., Environ., Health & Safety: David Bonistall
　Phone: (1) 938-242-9033
　Fax: (1) 800-987-5281
　Email: david.bonistall@newpagecorp.com
　Contr. & Chief Accountant (CAO): Linda Sheffield
　Phone: (1) 937-242-9500
　Fax: (1) 800-987-5281
　Email: linda.sheffield@newpagecorp.com
　Dir., Commun.: Shawn L. Hall
　Phone: (1) 937-242-9373
　Fax: (1) 937-242-9329
　Email: shawn.hall@newpagecorp.com
Total Employees of Company: 5,600
Total Employees at this Location: 350
Mill Locations:
NewPage Corporation, Biron Mill, 621 N Biron Dr, Wisconsin Rapids, WI 54495-8050, USA, Capacity: 399,752 st/y, (Paper mill)
　Phone: (1) 715-422-2236
　Fax: (1) 715-422-2403
NewPage Corporation, Wisconsin Rapids Paper Mill, 310 N. 3rd Ave., Wisconsin Rapids, WI 54495-8050, USA, Capacity: 553,228 st/y, (Pulp mill, Paper mill)
　Phone: (1) 715-422-1616, 715-422-4067
　Fax: (1) 715-422-3982
NewPage Corporation, Duluth Paper Mill, 100 N Central Ave, Duluth, MN 55807-2400, USA, Capacity: 269,560 st/y, (Pulp mill, Paper mill)
　Phone: (1) 218-628-5100
　Fax: (1) 218-628-0310
NewPage Corporation, Duluth Pulp Mill, 4920 Recycle Way, Duluth, MN 55807, USA, (Pulp mill)
　Phone: (1) 218-628-5100
　Fax: (1) 218-628-0310
NewPage Corporation, Escanaba Mill, 7100 County Rd 426, M.5 Rd, Escanaba, MI 49829, USA, Capacity: 779,873 st/y, (Pulp mill, Paper mill)
　Phone: (1) 906-786-1660
　Fax: (1) 906-789-3221, 789-3206
NewPage Corporation, Luke Mill, 300 Pratt St, Luke, MD 21540-1099, USA, Capacity: 509,684 st/y, (Paper mill)
　Phone: (1) 301-359-3311
　Fax: (1) 301-359-2004
NewPage Corporation, Rumford Mill, 35 Hartford St, Rumford, ME 04276-1000, USA, Capacity: 522,890 st/y, (Pulp mill, Paper mill)
　Phone: (1) 207-364-4521
　Fax: (1) 207-369-2531
NewPage Corporation, Stevens Point Mill, 707 Arlington Pl, Stevens Point, WI 54481, USA, Capacity: 169,538 st/y, (Paper mill)
　Phone: (1) 715-345-8060
　Fax: (1) 715-345-8001
NewPage Corporation, Wickliffe Mill, 1724 Fort Jefferson Hill Rd., Wickliffe, KY 42087, USA, Capacity: 285,537 st/y, (Pulp mill, Paper mill)
　Phone: (1) 270-335-4000
　Fax: (1) 270-335-4110

ⓂOhio Paperboard Corp.
Baltimore Board Mill
Ownership: 100% by Newark Recycled Paperboard Solutions
310 Water St
Baltimore, OH 43105-1272
USA
　Phone: (1) 740-862-4167
　Fax: (1) 740-862-8320
　Web Address: www.newarkpb.com
Personnel:
　Mill Mgr.: Nate Ridings
　Phone: (1) 740-862-3572
　Fax: (1) 740-862-8320
　Email: nridings@tngus.com
　Sls. Mgr.: Jeff Gressick
　Phone: (1) 740-862-4167
　Fax: (1) 740-862-8320
　Email: jgressick@tngus.com
　Tech. Mgr.: Kevin McMunn
　Phone: (1) 740-862-3569
　Fax: (1) 740-862-8320
　Email: kmcmunn@tngus.com
　HR Mgr.: Anita Owens
　Phone: (1) 740-862-3584
　Fax: (1) 740-862-8320
　Email: aowens@tngus.com
　Contr.: Kelly Adkins
　Phone: (1) 740-862-3561
　Fax: (1) 740-862-8320
　Email: kadkins@tngus.com
Total Employees at this Location: 139
Type of Operation: Paperboard mill
Pulp Grades and Capacities:
　Total pulp capacity: 121,767 st/y
　Recycled Pulping: 121,767 st/y
Pulp Mill Data:
Pulp Lines: 1
　Recycled Fiber Treatment Lines:
　Pulpers: 1 at 135,692
Paper/Paperboard Grades and Capacities:
　Total paper and paperboard capacity: 117,810 st/y
　Corrugating medium/fluting: 32,130 st/y
　Boxboard/cartonboard: 85,680 st/y
Paper and Paperboard Mill Data:
　Stock Preparation:
　Refiners: 2
Paper Machines: 2
　No. 1, cylinder (5), total capacity 85,680 st/y, Trim width 132 in, Boxboard/cartonboard
　No. 2, cylinder (4), total capacity 32,130 st/y, Trim width 87 in, Corrugating medium/fluting
Energy Data:
　Power boilers: 1
　Electrical demand for mill: 167 MWh/D

ⓄOhio Pulp Mills Inc.
Ownership: Donco Paper Supply Company
2100 Losantiville Rd
Cincinnati, OH 45237
USA
　Phone: (1) 513-631-0208
　Fax: (1) 513-351-2129
　Email: doncol@aol.com
　Web Address: www.doncopaper.com
Personnel:
　Chmn.: Robert Mendelson
　Phone: (1) 312-337-7822
　Fax: (1) 312-337-7891
　Email: robert.mendelson@doncosolutions.com
　Exec. VP: Charles Cyra
　Phone: (1) 312-337-7822
　Fax: (1) 312-337-7891
　Email: chuck.cyra@doncosolutions.com
　Dir., Mktg.: Jeffrey Sunderman
　Phone: (1) 312-337-7822
　Fax: (1) 312-337-7891
　Email: jeff.sunderman@doncosolutions.com
　Sls. Mgr.: Thomas Imming
　Phone: (1) 513-631-0208
　Fax: (1) 513-351-2129
　Email: tom.imming@doncosolutions.com
　Contrl.: Theresa Aili
　Phone: (1) 513-631-0208
　Fax: (1) 513-351-2129
　Email: theresa.aili@doncosolutions.com
Mill Locations:
Ohio Pulp Mills Inc., Cincinnati Mill, 2100 Losantiville Rd, Cincinnati, OH 45237, USA, (Pulp mill)
　Phone: (1) 513-631-0208
　Fax: (1) 513-351-2129
　Email: doncol@aol.com

ⓄOhio Pulp Mills Inc.
Cincinnati Mill
2100 Losantiville Rd
Cincinnati, OH 45237
USA
　Phone: (1) 513-631-0208
　Fax: (1) 513-351-2129
　Email: doncol@aol.com
　Web Address: www.doncopaper.com
Personnel:
　Mill Mgr.: Steve Baker
　Phone: (1) 513-631-7400
　Fax: (1) 513-351-2129
　Email: steve.baker@doncosolutions.com
　Sls. Mgr.: Thomas Imming
　Phone: (1) 513-731-0208
　Fax: (1) 513-351-2129
　Email: tom.imming@doncosolutions.com
　Contr.: Theresa Aili
　Phone: (1) 513-631-7400
　Fax: (1) 513-351-2129
　Email: theresa.ali@doncosolutions.com
Type of Operation: Pulp mill
Pulp Grades and Capacities:
　Total pulp capacity: 17,500 st/y
　Recycled Pulping: 17,500 st/y

ⓅProcter & Gamble Paper Products Co.
Ownership: Public
One Procter & Gamble Plz
Cincinnati, OH 45202
USA
Mailing Address: PO Box 599, Cincinnati, OH 45201-0599, USA
　Phone: (1) 513-983-1100
　Fax: (1) 513-386-1887
　Web Address: www.pg.com
Personnel:
　CEO & Pres.: Alan George "A.G." Lafley
　Phone: (1) 513-983-1100
　Fax: (1) 513-945-6758
　Email: lafley.a@pg.com
　CFO: Jon R. Moeller
　Phone: (1) 513-983-1100
　Fax: (1) 513-945-6758
　Email: moeller.j@pg.com
　Pres., Latin America & Global Club, Cash & Carry Channel: Tarek Farahat
　Phone: (1) 513-983-1100
　Fax: (1) 513-945-6758
　Email: uribe.j@pg.com
　Group Pres., NA & Global Hyper, Super Mass Channel: Melanie L Healey

Ohio

Phone: (1) 513-983-1100
Fax: (1) 513-945-6758
Email: healey.m@pg.com
VP., Corp.: Nancy K. Swanson
Phone: (1) 513-983-1100
Fax: (1) 513-945-6758
Email: swanson.n@pg.com
Chief Legal Officer & Sec.: Deborah P. Majoras
Phone: (1) 513-983-1100
Fax: (1) 513-945-6758
Email: majoras.d@pg.com
Chief HR Officer: Mark Biegger
Phone: (1) 513-983-1100
Fax: (1) 513-945-6758
Officer on Special Assignment: Bruce Brown
Phone: (1) 513-983-1100
Fax: (1) 513-945-6758
Email: brown.b@pg.com
Total Employees of Company: 121,000
Mill Locations:
Procter & Gamble Paper Products Co., Box Elder Mill, 5000 North Iowa Springs Road, Brigham City, UT, USA, Capacity: 79,968 st/y, (Paper mill)
Procter & Gamble Paper Products Co., Albany Mill, 512 Liberty Expwy SE, Albany, GA 31705, USA, Capacity: 365,211 st/y, (Paper mill)
Phone: (1) 229-430-8260
Procter & Gamble Paper Products Co., Cape Girardeau Mill, 14484 State Hwy 177, Cape Girardeau, Jackson, MO 63755, USA, Capacity: 205,275 st/y, (Paper mill)
Phone: (1) 573-651-9200, 573 339-9243
Procter & Gamble Paper Products Co., Fox River Plant, 501 Eastman Ave, Green Bay, WI 54302, USA, Capacity: 334,152 st/y, (Paper mill)
Phone: (1) 920-430-2101
Fax: (1) 920-433-2571
Procter & Gamble Paper Products Co., Mehoopany Mill, Rte 87, Mehoopany, PA 18629, USA, Capacity: 419,118 st/y, (Paper mill)
Phone: (1) 570-833-5141
Fax: (1) 570-833-3281
Procter & Gamble Paper Products Co., Oxnard Mill, 800 N Rice Av, Oxnard, CA 93030, USA, Capacity: 146,370 st/y, (Paper mill)
Phone: (1) 805-485-8871
Fax: (1) 805-983-8908
Procter & Gamble de Mexico S. de R.L. de C.V., Apizaco Mill, Km. 115.5, Carretera Los Reyes Zacatepec, 90300 Apizaco, Mexico, Capacity: 82,639 st/y, (Paper mill)
Phone: (52) 1 241 41 899 70
Email: tinajero@pg.com, reyes.mg.4@pg.com, lira.r.1@pg.com

ⓂRockTenn Co.
Cincinnati Mill
Mill is due to permanently close by the end of 2014.
3347 Madison Rd
Cincinnati, OH 45209
USA
Phone: (1) 513-871-5000
Fax: (1) 513-533-2154
Web Address: www.rocktenn.com
Personnel:
Mill Mgr.: Timothy E. Hagenbuch
Phone: (1) 513-871-5000
Fax: (1) 513-533-2154
Email: thagenbuch@rocktenn.com
Process Contr. Eng.: Brian Elwell
Phone: (1) 513-871-5000
Fax: (1) 513-533-2154
Email: belwell@rocktenn.com
Environ., Health & Safety Mgr.: Rod Mamula
Phone: (1) 513-533-2116
Fax: (1) 513-533-2154
Email: rmamula@rocktenn.com
Total Employees at this Location: 63
Type of Operation: Paperboard mill
Pulp Grades and Capacities:
Total pulp capacity: 55,416 st/y
Recycled Pulping: 55,416 st/y
Paper/Paperboard Grades and Capacities:
Total paper and paperboard capacity: 54,978 st/y
Boxboard/cartonboard: 54,978 st/y
Paper and Paperboard Mill Data:
Stock Preparation:
Pulpers: 2
Refiners: 3
Paper Machines: 1
No. 1, cylinder (8), total capacity 54,978 st/y, Trim width 82 in, Boxboard/cartonboard
Energy Data:
Power boilers: 1

ⓂRockTenn Co.
Coshocton Mill
500 N 4th St
Coshocton, OH 43812-1119
USA
Phone: (1) 740-622-6543
Fax: (1) 740-622-5297
Web Address: www.rocktenn.com
Personnel:
Gen. Mgr. (From May 2013): Steve Devlin
Phone: (1) 740-522-2201
Fax: (1) 740-622-5297
Email: sdevlin@rocktenn.com
Contr.: Mark D. Layton
Phone: (1) 740-622-6543
Fax: (1) 740-622-5297
Email: mlayton@rocktenn.com
Tech. Mgr.: Randall A. Hothem
Phone: (1) 740-522-2274
Fax: (1) 740-622-5297
Email: rhothem@rocktenn.com
Paper Machine Superint.: James (Jim) Hinkel
Phone: (1) 740-622-6543
Fax: (1) 740-622-6543
Email: jhinkel@rocktenn.com
Paper Mill Supt.: Max Crown
Phone: (1) 740-622-6543
Fax: (1) 740-622-5297
Email: mcrown@rocktenn.com
Environ. Mgr.: Joe Bulzan
Phone: (1) 740-622-6543
Fax: (1) 740-622-5297
Email: jbulzan@rocktenn.com
Total Employees at this Location: 203
Type of Operation: Paperboard mill
Pulp Grades and Capacities:
Total pulp capacity: 324,465 st/y
Chemical Pulp: 212,158 st/y
Recycled Pulping: 112,306 st/y
Pulp Mill Data:
Chemical Pulping Systems:
Continuous digesters: 2
Chemical Recovery Equipment:
Evaporator lines: 1
Recovery boilers: 2
Recycled Fiber Treatment Lines:
Pulpers: 1 at 121,803
Paper/Paperboard Grades and Capacities:
Total paper and paperboard capacity: 309,876 st/y
Corrugating medium/fluting: 309,876 st/y
Paper and Paperboard Mill Data:
Stock Preparation:
Pulpers: 1
Refiners: 9
Paper Machines: 2
No. 1, fourdrinier, total capacity 174,930 st/y, Trim width 167 in, Corrugating medium/fluting
No. 2, fourdrinier, total capacity 134,946 st/y, Trim width 158 in, Corrugating medium/fluting
Energy Data:
Power boilers: 1
Steam turbines: 1 at 16.5 MW

ⓗValley Converting Co.
Ownership: Private
405 Daniels St
Toronto, OH 43964
USA
Mailing Address: PO Box 279, Toronto, OH 43964, USA
Phone: (1) 740-537-2152
Fax: (1) 740-537-2977
Email: mike@valleyconverting.com
Web Address: www.valleyconverting.com
Personnel:
Pres.: Michael D. Biasi
Phone: (1) 740-537-2152
Fax: (1) 740-537-2977
Email: mike@valleyconverting.com
Mill Mgr.: Rich Brandt
Phone: (1) 740-537-2152
Fax: (1) 740-537-2977
Email: rich@valleyconverting.com
Sls. Mgr.: Mark Seermiller
Phone: (1) 740-537-2152
Fax: (1) 740-537-2977
Email: mark@valleyconverting.com
Total Employees of Company: 50
Mill Locations:
Valley Converting Co., Toronto Mill, 405 Daniels St, Toronto, OH 43964, USA, Capacity: 21,777 st/y, (Paperboard mill)
Phone: (1) 740-537-2152
Fax: (1) 740-537-2977
Email: mike@valleyconverting.com

ⓂValley Converting Co.
Toronto Mill
405 Daniels St
Toronto, OH 43964
USA
Mailing Address: PO Box 279, Toronto, OH 43964, USA
Phone: (1) 740-537-2152
Fax: (1) 740-537-2977
Email: mike@valleyconverting.com
Web Address: www.valleyconverting.com
Personnel:
Mill Mgr.: Rich Brandt
Phone: (1) 740-537-2152
Fax: (1) 740-537-2977
Email: rich@valleyconverting.com
Mktg. Mgr.: Mark Seermiller
Phone: (1) 740-537-2152
Fax: (1) 740-537-2977
Email: mark@valleyconverting.com
Total Employees at this Location: 38
Type of Operation: Paperboard mill
Pulp Grades and Capacities:
Total pulp capacity: 22,329 st/y
Recycled Pulping: 22,329 st/y
Pulp Mill Data:
Recycled Fiber Treatment Lines:
Recycled packaging pulping lines
Paper/Paperboard Grades and Capacities:
Total paper and paperboard capacity: 21,777 st/y
Boxboard/cartonboard: 21,777 st/y
Paper and Paperboard Mill Data:
Paper Machines: 1
No. 1, cylinder (8), total capacity 21,777 st/y, Trim width 88 in, Boxboard/cartonboard
Finishing Equipment:
Rewinders: 1
Sheeters: 2
Energy Data:
Power boilers
Electrical demand for mill: 29 MWh/D

ⓂWausau Paper Towel & Tissue, LLC
Middletown Mill
Ownership: Wausau Paper Corp.
700 Columbia Ave.
Middletown, OH 45042
USA
Phone: (1) 513-424-2999
Fax: (1) 513-420-8570
Email: contactbaywest@wausaupaper.com
Web Address: www.wausaupaper.com
Personnel:
VP Special Proj.: John E. Wells

Oklahoma

Phone: (1) 513-424-2999
Fax: (1) 513-420-8570
Email: jwells@wausaupaper.com
Purch. Mgr.: Christopher J. Villano
Phone: (1) 513-217-3627
Fax: (1) 513-420-8570
Email: cvillano@wausaupaper.com
Total Employees at this Location: 185
Type of Operation: Pulp mill, Paper mill
Pulp Grades and Capacities:
Total pulp capacity: 116,010 st/y
Recycled Pulping: 116,010 st/y
Pulp Mill Data:
Bleach Plant Lines:
Deinked Pulp Line, Sequence: HS
Recycled Fiber Treatment Lines:
Flotation deinking lines
Paper/Paperboard Grades and Capacities:
Total paper and paperboard capacity: 126,735 st/y
Tissue: 126,735 st/y
Paper and Paperboard Mill Data:
Paper Machines: 2
No. 1, fourdrinier, Yankee dryer, total capacity 91,035 st/y, Trim width 57 in, Tissue
No. 2, twin-wire, total capacity 35,700 st/y, Trim width 47 in, Tissue
Energy Data:
Electrical demand for mill: 489 MWh/D

ⓜWeidmann Electrical Technology Inc.
Howard Mill
Ownership: 100% by Wicor Group
700 W Court St
Urbana, OH 43078
USA
Phone: (1) 937 652 1220
Fax: (1) 937-652-1722
Email: service.weti@wicor.com
Web Address: www.weidmann-electrical.com
Total Employees at this Location: 110
Type of Operation: Paper mill
Paper and Paperboard Mill Data:
Stock Preparation:
Pulpers: 4
Refiners: 2
Finishing Equipment:
Sheeters: 2
Energy Data:
Power boilers: 1

OKLAHOMA

ⓜGeorgia-Pacific LLC
Muskogee Mill
4901 Chandler Rd
Muskogee, OK 74403
USA
Phone: (1) 918-683-7671
Fax: (1) 918-683-1609
Web Address: www.gp.com
Personnel:
VP, Manuf.: Rodney Bond
Phone: (1) 918-683-7671
Fax: (1) 918-683-1609
Email: rodney.bond@gapac.com
Total Employees at this Location: 549
Type of Operation: Paper mill
Pulp Grades and Capacities:
Total pulp capacity: 389,915 st/y
Recycled Pulping: 389,915 st/y
Pulp Mill Data:
Bleach Plant Systems: 1
Recycled Deinked Pulping System, Sequence: HP
Recycled Fiber Treatment Lines:
Flotation deinking lines: 1 at 382,826
Paper/Paperboard Grades and Capacities:
Total paper and paperboard capacity: 364,140 st/y
Tissue: 364,140 st/y
Paper and Paperboard Mill Data:
Paper Machines: 5
No. 11, twin-wire, Yankee dryer, total capacity 49,980 st/y, Trim width 295 in, Tissue
No. 12, twin-wire, Yankee dryer, total capacity 85,680 st/y, Trim width 195 in, Tissue
No. 13, twin-wire, Yankee dryer, total capacity 67,830 st/y, Trim width 195 in, Tissue
No. 14, twin-wire, Yankee dryer, total capacity 78,540 st/y, Trim width 263 in, Tissue
No. 15, twin-wire, Yankee dryer, total capacity 82,110 st/y, Trim width 263 in, Tissue
Energy Data:
Power boilers: 4
Steam turbines: 3 at 115 MW
Electrical demand for mill: 1,572 MWh/D

ⓜInternational Paper Co.
Valliant Mill
890 Weyerhaeuser Lane
Valliant, OK 74764
USA
Mailing Address: PO Box 890, Valliant, OK 74764-0890, USA
Phone: (1) 580-933-7211
Fax: (1) 580-933-1567
Web Address: www.internationalpaper.com
Personnel:
Mill Mgr.: Peter Thompson
Phone: (1) 580-933-7211
Fax: (1) 580-933-1567
Email: pete.thompson@ipaper.com
Area Mgr.: Donald Gross
Phone: (1) 580-933-7211
Fax: (1) 580-933-1567
Email: donald.gross@ipaper.com
Utility Mgr.: Joseph Moore
Phone: (1) 580-933-7211
Fax: (1) 580-933-1567
Email: joseph.moore@ipaper.com
Total Employees at this Location: 462
Type of Operation: Paperboard mill
Pulp Grades and Capacities:
Total pulp capacity: 1,419,624 st/y
Chemical Pulp: 811,435 st/y
Recycled Pulping: 608,189 st/y
Pulp Mill Data:
Chemical Pulping Systems:
Continuous digesters: 3
Chemical Recovery Equipment:
Evaporator lines: 1
Recovery boilers: 1
Lime Kiln
Recycled Fiber Treatment Lines:
Pulpers: 3 at 678,300 admt/y
Paper/Paperboard Grades and Capacities:
Total paper and paperboard capacity: 1,349,817 st/y
Linerboard: 927,486 st/y
Corrugating medium/fluting: 422,331 st/y
Paper and Paperboard Mill Data:
Stock Preparation:
Pulpers: 6
Refiners: 21
Paper Machines: 2
No. 1, Bel-Bond, total capacity 927,486 st/y, Trim width 355 in, Linerboard
No. 2, fourdrinier, total capacity 422,331 st/y, Trim width 261 in, Corrugating medium/fluting
Finishing Equipment:
Calenders: 6
Rewinders: 3
Energy Data:
Power boilers: 2
Steam turbines: 1 at 68 MW
Electrical demand for mill: 2,512 MWh/D

ⓜKimberly-Clark Corp.
Jenks Mill
13252 S Yale Pl
Jenks, OK 74037
USA
Mailing Address: PO Box 3000, Jenks, OK 74037-3000, USA
Phone: (1) 918-366-5000
Fax: (1) 918-366-5050
Web Address: www.kimberly-clark.com
Personnel:
Plt. Mgr.: Eric Draheim
Phone: (1) 918-366-5000
Fax: (1) 918-366-5050
Email: edraheim@kcc.com
Eng. Tech. Ldr. (From September 2013): Greg Ryan
Phone: (1) 918-366-5000
Fax: (1) 918-366-5050
Email: greg.ryan@kcc.com
R&E Tech. Strategist (From January 2014): Mike Baldwin
Phone: (1) 918-366-5000
Fax: (1) 918-366-5050
Email: mbaldwin@kcc.com
Total Employees at this Location: 150
Type of Operation: Paper mill
Paper/Paperboard Grades and Capacities:
Total paper and paperboard capacity: 175,287 st/y
Tissue: 175,287 st/y
Paper and Paperboard Mill Data:
Stock Preparation:
Pulpers:
Paper Machines: 2
No. 1, TAD, total capacity 82,110 st/y, Trim width 200 in, Tissue
No. 2, TAD, total capacity 93,177 st/y, Trim width 172 in, Tissue
Energy Data:
Power boilers: 2
Electrical demand for mill: 608 MWh/D

ⓜNational Gypsum Co.
Pryor Mill
4189 Hunt Street
Pryor, OK 74361
USA
Phone: (1) 918-825-0142
Fax: (1) 918-825-7094
Web Address: www.nationalgypsum.com
Personnel:
Plt. Mgr.: Trey Jackson
Phone: (1) 918-825-0142
Fax: (1) 918-825-7094
Eng. Mgr.: Tim Lawson
Phone: (1) 918-825-0142
Fax: (1) 918-825-7094
Total Employees at this Location: 80
Type of Operation: Paperboard mill
Pulp Grades and Capacities:
Total pulp capacity: 94,197 st/y
Recycled Pulping: 94,197 st/y
Paper/Paperboard Grades and Capacities:
Total paper and paperboard capacity: 89,964 st/y
Boxboard/cartonboard: 89,964 st/y
Paper and Paperboard Mill Data:
Stock Preparation:
Refiners: 5
Paper Machines: 1
No. 1, fourdrinier (2), total capacity 89,964 st/y, Trim width 104 in, Boxboard/cartonboard
Finishing Equipment:
Rewinders: 1
Energy Data:
Electrical demand for mill: 111 MWh/D

ⓞⓜOrchids Paper Products Co.
Pryor Mill
4826 Hunt Street
Pryor, OK 74361
USA

Phone: (1) 918-825-0616, 800-832-4908
Fax: (1) 918-825-7998
Web Address: www.orchidspaper.com
Personnel:
  Chmn. of the Board: Steven R. Berlin
  Phone: (1) 918-825-0616, 800-832-4908
  Fax: (1) 918-825-7998
  CFO: Keith R. Schroeder
  Phone: (1) 918-825-0616 Ext.
  Fax: (1) 918-825-7998
  Email: krschroeder@orchidspaper.com
  VP, Sls & Mktg: Dan Daniels
  Phone: (1) 918-825-0616, 800-832-4908
  Fax: (1) 918-825-7998
  Dir., Eng: Lonnie Harper
  Phone: (1) 918-825-0616, 800-832-4908
  Fax: (1) 918-825-7998
  Maint. Mgr.: Bob Ocker
  Phone: (1) 918-825-0616, 800-832-4908
  Fax: (1) 918-825-7998
Total Employees of Company: 296
Total Employees at this Location: 167
Type of Operation: Paper mill
Pulp Grades and Capacities:
  Total pulp capacity: 60,615 st/y
  Recycled Pulping: 60,615 st/y
Pulp Mill Data:
  Bleach Plant Systems: 1
  Recycled Deinked Pulping System
  Recycled Fiber Treatment Lines:
  Pulpers: 1 at 79,696
Paper/Paperboard Grades and Capacities:
  Total paper and paperboard capacity: 56,763 st/y
  Tissue: 56,763 st/y
Paper and Paperboard Mill Data:
Paper Machines: 4
  No. 1, crescent former, total capacity 5,712 st/y, Trim width 79 in, Tissue
  No. 2, crescent former, total capacity 7,140 st/y, Trim width 93 in, Tissue
  No. 3, crescent former, Yankee dryer, total capacity 8,925 st/y, Trim width 103 in, Tissue
  No. 4, crescent former, Yankee dryer, total capacity 34,986 st/y, Trim width 102 in, Tissue
Energy Data:
  Power boilers: 1
  Electrical demand for mill: 166 MWh/D

ⓂRepublic Paperboard Co. LLC
Ownership: Eagle Materials Inc. (Public)
8801 S.W. Lee Blvd.
Lawton, OK 73505-9764
USA
  Phone: (1) 580-510-2200
  Fax: (1) 580-510-2242
  Email: info@eaglematerials.com
  Web Address: www.eaglematerials.com
Personnel:
  Pres.: Lisa McGregor
  Phone: (1) 580-510-2226
  Fax: (1) 580-510-2242
  Email: lmcgregor@lawtonpaperboard.com
  VP., Technology & Serv.: Dan Frenette
  Phone: (1) 580-510-2263
  Fax: (1) 580-510-2242
  Email: dfrenette@lawtonpaperboard.com
  VP., Finan.: Brian Sibley
  Phone: (1) 580-510-2251
  Fax: (1) 580-510-2242
  Email: bsibley@lawtonpaperboard.com
Total Employees of Company: 135
Mill Locations:
Republic Paperboard Co. LLC, Lawton Mill, 8801 S.W. Lee Blvd., Lawton, OK 73505-9764, USA, Capacity: 319,872 st/y, (Paperboard mill)
  Phone: (1) 580-510-2200
  Fax: (1) 580-510-2242
  Email: info@eaglematerials.com

ⓂRepublic Paperboard Co. LLC
Lawton Mill
8801 S.W. Lee Blvd.
Lawton, OK 73505-9764
USA
  Phone: (1) 580-510-2200
  Fax: (1) 580-510-2242
  Email: info@eaglematerials.com
  Web Address: www.eaglematerials.com
Personnel:
  Pres.: Lisa McGregor
  Phone: (1) 580-510-2226
  Fax: (1) 580-510-2242
  Email: lmcgregor@lawtonpaperboard.com
  VP., Technology & Serv.: Dan Frenette
  Phone: (1) 580-510-2263
  Fax: (1) 580-510-2242
  Email: dfrenette@lawtonpaperboard.com
  VP., Finan.: Brian Sibley
  Phone: (1) 580-510-2251
  Fax: (1) 580-510-2242
  Email: bsibley@lawtonpaperboard.com
  Maint. & Eng. Mgr.: Mike Mazur
  Phone: (1) 580-510-2224
  Fax: (1) 580-510-2242
  Email: mmazur@lawtonpaperboard.com
  QCS Eng.: Brandon Baggett
  Phone: (1) 580-510-2224
  Fax: (1) 580-510-2242
Total Employees at this Location: 135
Type of Operation: Paperboard mill
Pulp Grades and Capacities:
  Total pulp capacity: 330,876 st/y
  Recycled Pulping: 330,876 st/y
Pulp Mill Data:
Pulp Lines: 1
  Recycled Fiber Treatment Lines:
  Pulpers: 1 at 125,000 admt/y
  Pulpers: 1 at 350,000
Paper/Paperboard Grades and Capacities:
  Total paper and paperboard capacity: 319,872 st/y
  Linerboard: 84,966 st/y
  Corrugating medium/fluting: 34,986 st/y
  Boxboard/cartonboard: 199,920 st/y
Paper and Paperboard Mill Data:
  Stock Preparation:
  Pulpers: 2
  Refiners: 5
Paper Machines: 1
  No. 1, DuoFormer, total capacity 319,872 st/y, Trim width 159 in, Boxboard/cartonboard, Linerboard, Corrugating medium/fluting
Energy Data:
  Power boilers: 2
  Electrical demand for mill: 365 MWh/D

OREGON

ⓄCascade Pacific Pulp, LLC
Ownership: 100% by International Grand Investment Corporation
30480 American Dr
Halsey, OR 97348
USA
Mailing Address: PO Box 400, 97348 Halsey
  Phone: (1) 541-369-1128
  Fax: (1) 541-369-1741
  Email: info@cascadepulp.com
  Web Address: www.cascadepulp.com
Personnel:
  Gen. Mgr.: Pat Rank
  Phone: (1) 541-369-1167
  Fax: (1) 541-369-1124
  Email: prank@cascadepulp.com
  Prod. Mgr.: Paul Horton
  Phone: (1) 541-369-1179
  Fax: (1) 541-369-1168
  Email: phorton@cascadepulp.com
  HR Mgr.: Kim Kammerer
  Phone: (1) 541-369-1114
  Fax: (1) 541-369-1741
  Email: kkammerer@cascadepulp.com
  Tech. Mgr.: Lisa Scott
  Phone: (1) 541-369-1752
  Fax: (1) 541-369-1725
  Email: lscott@cascadepulp.com
  Maint. Coord.: Daniel Boydston
  Phone: (1) 541-369-1142
  Fax: (1) 541-369-1103
  Email: dboydston@cascadepulp.com
  Environ. Mgr.: Lori Blau
  Phone: (1) 541-369-1174
  Fax: (1) 541-369-1609
  Email: lblau@cascadepulp.com
Total Employees of Company: 187
Mill Locations:
Cascade Pacific Pulp, LLC, Halsey Mill, 30480 American Dr, Halsey, OR 97348, USA, (Pulp mill)
  Phone: (1) 541-369-1128
  Fax: (1) 541-369-1741
  Email: info@cascadepulp.com

ⓂCascade Pacific Pulp, LLC
Halsey Mill
30480 American Dr
Halsey, OR 97348
USA
Mailing Address: PO Box 400, Halsey, OR 97348, USA
  Phone: (1) 541-369-1128
  Fax: (1) 541-369-1741
  Email: info@cascadepulp.com
  Web Address: www.cascadepulp.com
Personnel:
  Gen. Mgr.: Pat Rank
  Phone: (1) 541-369-1128
  Fax: (1) 541-369-1741
  Email: prank@cascadepulp.com
  Prod. Mgr.: Paul Horton
  Phone: (1) 541-369-1128
  Fax: (1) 541-369-1741
  Email: phorton@cascadepulp.com
  Tech. Mgr.: Lisa Scott
  Phone: (1) 541-369-1128
  Fax: (1) 541-369-1741
  Email: lscott@cascadepulp.com
  Maint. Coord.: Daniel Boydston
  Phone: (1) 541-369-1128
  Fax: (1) 541-369-1741
  Email: dboydston@cascadepulp.com
  Environ. Mgr.: Lori Blau
  Phone: (1) 541-369-1128
  Fax: (1) 541-369-1741
  Email: lblau@cascadepulp.com
Total Employees at this Location: 187
Type of Operation: Pulp mill
Pulp Grades and Capacities:
  Total pulp capacity: 227,091 st/y
  Pulp available for market: 223,912 st/y
  Chemical Pulp: 227,091 st/y
Pulp Mill Data:
  Chemical Pulping Systems:
  Continuous digesters: 3
Pulp Lines: 1
  Bleach Plant Systems: 1
  Chemical Pulping System, Type: Sawdust/Softwood, Sequence: O_2 DEopDED, Capacity 224,867.7 admt/y
  Chemical Recovery Equipment:
  Evaporator lines: 1
  Recovery boilers: 1
  Lime Kiln
  Pulp Dryers:
  Flakt dryer 1, Fourdriniers 1
Energy Data:
  Power boilers: 2
  Electrical demand for mill: 456 MWh/D

Oregon

ⓂCascades Tissue Group
Saint Helens Mill
Ownership: 100% by Cascades Inc.
1300 Kaster Rd
Saint Helens, OR 97051
USA
  Phone: (1) 503-397-9372
  Fax: (1) 503-397-9440 (ofc); 9304 (shpg)
  Web Address: www.afh.cascades.com
Personnel:
  Mill Mgr.: Eric Prochnow
  Phone: (1) 503-397-9405
  Fax: (1) 503-397-9440
  Email: eric_prochnow@cascades.com
  Stock Prep. & Environ. Supervisor: Todd Christianson
  Phone: (1) 503-397-9372
  Fax: (1) 503-397-9440
  Email: todd_christianson@cascades.com
Total Employees at this Location: 88
Type of Operation: Paper mill
Pulp Grades and Capacities:
  Total pulp capacity: 10,943 st/y
  Recycled Pulping: 10,943 st/y
Paper/Paperboard Grades and Capacities:
  Total paper and paperboard capacity: 119,952 st/y
  Tissue: 119,952 st/y
Paper and Paperboard Mill Data:
  Stock Preparation:
  Pulpers: 1
  Refiners: 1
Paper Machines: 2
No. 2, twin-wire, total capacity 54,978 st/y, Trim width 194 in, Tissue
No. 3, crescent former, Yankee dryer, total capacity 64,974 st/y, Trim width 248 in, Tissue
Energy Data:
Power boilers: 2
Electrical demand for mill: 300 MWh/D

ⓂGeorgia-Pacific LLC
Wauna Mill
92326 Taylorsville Rd, Rte 2, Box 2185
Clatskanie, OR 97016-9299
USA
  Phone: (1) 503-455-2221
  Fax: (1) 503-455-3562
  Web Address: www.gp.com
Personnel:
  Mill Mgr.: Steve Francoeur
  Phone: (1) 503-455-2221
  Fax: (1) 503-455-3562
  Email: steve.francoeur@gapac.com
  IT Mgr.: Nick Skimas
  Phone: (1) 503-455-2221
  Fax: (1) 503-455-3562
  Email: nick.skimas@gapac.com
  Pub. Rel. Mgr.: Kristi Ward
  Phone: (1) 503-455-3214
  Fax: (1) 503-455-3562
  Email: kristi.ward@gapac.com
Total Employees at this Location: 710
Type of Operation: Paper mill
Pulp Grades and Capacities:
  Total pulp capacity: 319,067 st/y
  Chemical Pulp: 319,067 st/y
Pulp Mill Data:
  Chemical Pulping Systems:
  Continuous digesters: 2
  Bleach Plant Systems: 2
  Chemical Pulping System, Type: Hardwood/Softwood, Sequence: DEopDD
  Chemical Pulping System, Type: Sawdust, Sequence: DEoD
  Chemical Recovery Equipment:
  Evaporator lines: 1
  Recovery boilers: 1
  Lime Kiln
Paper/Paperboard Grades and Capacities:
  Total paper and paperboard capacity: 343,791 st/y
  Tissue: 343,791 st/y
Paper and Paperboard Mill Data:
  Stock Preparation:
  Pulpers: 4
  Refiners: 6
Paper Machines: 5
No. 1, Yankee dryer, total capacity 46,053 st/y, Trim width 184 in, Tissue
No. 2, Yankee dryer, total capacity 56,763 st/y, Trim width 184 in, Tissue
No. 5, Yankee dryer, total capacity 89,250 st/y, Trim width 276 in, Tissue
No. 6, Yankee dryer, TAD, total capacity 80,325 st/y, Trim width 263 in, Tissue
No. 7, TAD, total capacity 71,400 st/y, Trim width 204 in, Tissue
Finishing Equipment:
  Rewinders: 1
Energy Data:
Power boilers: 1
Combustion turbines: 1 at 24 MW
Steam turbines: 1 at 36 MW
Electrical demand for mill: 1,478 MWh/D

ⓂGeorgia-Pacific LLC
Halsey Mill
30470 American Dr
Halsey, OR 97348
USA
Mailing Address: PO Box 215, Halsey, OR 97348, USA
  Phone: (1) 541-369-2293
  Fax: (1) 541-369-1327
  Web Address: www.gp.com
Personnel:
  VP. & Mill Mgr.: George Munn
  Phone: (1) 541-369-2293
  Fax: (1) 541-369-1327
  Email: george.munn@gapac.com
  Contr.: Reuben Swindoll
  Phone: (1) 541-369-2293
  Fax: (1) 541-369-1327
  Email: reuben.swindoll@gapac.com
  Purch. Mgr.: Ed Sherman
  Phone: (1) 541-369-2293
  Fax: (1) 541-369-1327
  Email: ed.sherman@gapac.com
  Safety Mgr.: Joe Ciullo
  Phone: (1) 541-369-2293
  Fax: (1) 541-369-1327
  Email: joe.ciullo@gapac.com
Total Employees at this Location: 230
Type of Operation: Pulp mill, Paper mill
Pulp Grades and Capacities:
  Total pulp capacity: 90,031 st/y
  Pulp available for market: 35,700 st/y
  Recycled Pulping: 90,031 st/y
Pulp Mill Data:
  Bleach Plant Lines:
  Deinked Pulp Line, Sequence: P
  Recycled Fiber Treatment Lines:
  Washing deinking lines: 1 at 125,000 admt/y
  Pulp Dryers:
  Wet Lap machine 1
Paper/Paperboard Grades and Capacities:
  Total paper and paperboard capacity: 109,599 st/y
  Tissue: 109,599 st/y
Paper and Paperboard Mill Data:
  Stock Preparation:
  Pulpers: 2
  Refiners: 2
Paper Machines: 2
No. 1, twin-wire, Yankee dryer, total capacity 50,694 st/y, Trim width 186 in, Tissue
No. 2, twin-wire, total capacity 58,905 st/y, Trim width 186 in, Tissue
Energy Data:
Electrical demand for mill: 382 MWh/D

ⓂGeorgia-Pacific LLC
Toledo Mill
1400 S.E. Butler Bridge Road
Toledo, OR 97391
USA
Mailing Address: PO Box 580, Toledo, OR 97391, USA
  Phone: (1) 541-336-2211
  Fax: (1) 541-336-8214
  Web Address: www.gp.com
Personnel:
  VP & Gen. Mgr.: Kenneth Li
  Phone: (1) 541-336-2211
  Fax: (1) 541-336-8214
  Email: kenneth.li@gapac.com
  Snr. Div. Contr.: Kari T. Murk
  Phone: (1) 541-336-2211
  Fax: (1) 541-336-8214
  Email: ktmurk@gapac.com
  IT Mgr.: Larry L. Davis
  Phone: (1) 541-336-2211
  Fax: (1) 541-336-8214
  Email: lldavis@gapac.com
Total Employees at this Location: 409
Type of Operation: Pulp mill, Paperboard mill
Pulp Grades and Capacities:
  Total pulp capacity: 929,411 st/y
  Chemical Pulp: 462,000 st/y
  Recycled Pulping: 467,410 st/y
Pulp Mill Data:
  Chemical Pulping Systems:
  Batch digesters: 11
  Continuous digesters: 1
  Chemical Recovery Equipment:
  Evaporator lines: 3
  Recovery boilers: 2
  Lime Kiln
  Recycled Fiber Treatment Lines:
  Recycled packaging pulping lines at 469,687
Paper/Paperboard Grades and Capacities:
  Total paper and paperboard capacity: 894,285 st/y
  Linerboard: 565,845 st/y
  Corrugating medium/fluting: 328,440 st/y
Paper and Paperboard Mill Data:
Paper Machines: 3
No. 1, fourdrinier, total capacity 355,215 st/y, Trim width 245 in, Linerboard
No. 2, fourdrinier, total capacity 217,770 st/y, Trim width 160 in, Corrugating medium/fluting
No. 3, fourdrinier, total capacity 321,300 st/y, Trim width 246 in, Linerboard, Corrugating medium/fluting
Energy Data:
Power boilers: 4
Steam turbines: 1 at 22.5 MW
Electrical demand for mill: 1,519 MWh/D

ⓂInternational Paper Co.
Springfield Mill
801 42nd St
Springfield, OR 97478-5781
USA
  Phone: (1) 541-741-5700
  Fax: (1) 541-741-5662
  Web Address: www.internationalpaper.com
Personnel:
  Mill Mgr.: David Castro
  Phone: (1) 541-741-5700
  Fax: (1) 541-741-5662
  Email: david.castro@ipaper.com
  EHS&S Mgr.: Scott Freeburn
  Phone: (1) 541-741-5700
  Fax: (1) 541-741-5662
  Email: scott.freeburn@ipaper.com
  Process Eng. (From November 2013): Lindsey Speed
  Phone: (1) 541-741-5700
  Fax: (1) 541-741-5662
  Email: lindsey.speed@ipaper.com
Total Employees at this Location: 244
Type of Operation: Paper mill, Paperboard mill
Pulp Grades and Capacities:

Total pulp capacity: 629,663 st/y
Chemical Pulp: 414,508 st/y
Recycled Pulping: 215,154 st/y
Pulp Mill Data:
Chemical Pulping Systems:
Batch digesters: 1
Continuous digesters: 3
Chemical Recovery Equipment:
Evaporator lines: 1
Recovery boilers: 2
Lime Kiln
Recycled Fiber Treatment Lines:
Pulpers: 1 at 229,277
Paper/Paperboard Grades and Capacities:
Total paper and paperboard capacity: 630,105 st/y
Linerboard: 630,105 st/y
Paper and Paperboard Mill Data:
Stock Preparation:
Pulpers: 4
Refiners: 10
Paper Machines: 1
No. 2, Bel-Bond, total capacity 630,105 st/y, Trim width 256 in, Linerboard
Finishing Equipment:
Rewinders
Energy Data:
Power boilers: 3
Steam turbines: 4 at 77 MW
Electrical demand for mill: 1,217 MWh/D

ⓂSP Fiber Technologies LLC (SPFT)
Newberg Mill
Previously SP Newsprint Co.
1301 Wynooski St
Newberg, OR 97132
USA
  Phone: (1) 503-538-2151
  Fax: (1) 503-537-6322
  Web Address: spfibertech.com
Personnel:
  Gen. Mgr.: Scott Wagener
  Phone: (1) 503-538-2151
  Fax: (1) 503-537-6322
  Email: scott.wagener@spfibertech.com
  VP Manuf.: Edward Bortz
  Phone: (1) 503-538-2151
  Fax: (1) 503-537-6322
  Email: edward.bortz@spfibertech.com
  Pulp & Power Mgr.: Dave Walsh
  Phone: (1) 503-538-2151
  Fax: (1) 503-537-6322
  Shift Mill Mgr.: Michael Grace
  Phone: (1) 503-538-2151
  Fax: (1) 503-537-6322
  Improvement Mgr.: Pat Huerta
  Phone: (1) 503-538-2151
  Fax: (1) 503-537-6322
  HR & Safety Mgr.: Jorge Rodriquez
  Phone: (1) 503-538-2151
  Fax: (1) 503-537-6322
  Reg. Contr.: Randy Blank
  Phone: (1) 503-538-2151
  Fax: (1) 503-537-6322
Total Employees at this Location: 215
Type of Operation: Pulp mill, Paper mill
Pulp Grades and Capacities:
Total pulp capacity: 233,216 st/y
Mechanical Pulp: 116,608 st/y
Recycled Pulping: 116,608 st/y
Pulp Mill Data:
Mechanical Pulping Systems:
RMP systems: 1
TMP systems: 3
Pulp Lines: 2
Recycled Fiber Treatment Lines:
Flotation deinking lines: 1 at 300,000 admt/y
Pulpers: 1 at 300,000 admt/y
Paper/Paperboard Grades and Capacities:
Total paper and paperboard capacity: 226,273 st/y
Newsprint: 226,273 st/y
Paper and Paperboard Mill Data:
Paper Machines: 1
No. 6, DuoFormer C, total capacity 226,273 st/y, Trim width 300 in, Newsprint
Finishing Equipment:
Winders: 2
Calenders: 2
Energy Data:
Power boilers: 1
Combustion turbines: 1 at 45 (idle) MW
Steam turbines: 2 at 33 MW
Electrical demand for mill: 1,222 MWh/D

ⓄⓂWest Linn Paper Co.
West Linn Mill
Ownership: 100% by Belgravia Investments
4800 Mill St
West Linn, OR 97068
USA
  Phone: (1) 503-557-6500
  Fax: (1) 503-557-6616
  Web Address: www.wlinpco.com
Personnel:
  Pres.: Tom Gallagher
  Phone: (1) 503-557-6500, 740-286-2148
  Fax: (1) 503-557-6616
  Email: tgallagher@westlinnpaper.com
  COO.: Brian Konen
  Phone: (1) 503-557-6500
  Fax: (1) 503-557-6616
  Email: bkonen@westlinnpaper.com
  Tech. Dir.: Kit Corrigan
  Phone: (1) 503-557-6500
  Fax: (1) 503-557-6616
  Email: kcorrigan@westlinnpaper.com
  Dir., Mktg.: Jill Crossley
  Phone: (1) 503-557-6512
  Fax: (1) 503-557-6616
  Email: jcrossley@westlinnpaper.com
Total Employees of Company: 250
Total Employees at this Location: 250
Type of Operation: Paper mill
Pulp Grades and Capacities:
Total pulp capacity: 8,614 st/y
Recycled Pulping: 8,614 st/y
Paper/Paperboard Grades and Capacities:
Total paper and paperboard capacity: 267,691 st/y
Coated woodfree/freesheet: 267,691 st/y
Paper and Paperboard Mill Data:
Stock Preparation:
Pulpers:
Paper Machines: 3
No. 1, fourdrinier, total capacity 91,015 st/y, Trim width 147 in, Coated woodfree/freesheet
No. 2, fourdrinier, total capacity 80,307 st/y, Trim width 148 in, Coated woodfree/freesheet
No. 3, fourdrinier, total capacity 96,369 st/y, Trim width 147 in, Coated woodfree/freesheet
Coating Machines: 3
PM 1, total capacity 89,286 st/y., on machine
PM 2, total capacity 78,263 st/y., on machine
PM 3, total capacity 94,797 st/y., on machine
Finishing Equipment:
Winders: 3
Supercalenders: 4
Rewinders: 1
Energy Data:
Power boilers: 3
Electrical demand for mill: 526 MWh/D

PENNSYLVANIA

ⓂAhlstrom Filtration LLC
Mount Holly Springs Mill
Ownership: 100% by Ahlstrom Corporation Oy
122 W Butler St
Mount Holly Springs, PA 17065
USA
Mailing Address: 122 West Butler Street, Mount Holly Springs, PA 17065-0238, USA
  Phone: (1) 717-486-3438
  Fax: (1) 717-486-6413
  Email: investor@ahlstrom.com, corporate.communications@ahlstrom.com
  Web Address: www.ahlstrom.com
Personnel:
  Tech. Mgr.: Frank Cousart
  Phone: (1) 717-486-3438
  Fax: (1) 717-486-6413
  Email: frank.cousart@ahlstrom.com
  Key account Mgr.: Rod Komlenic
  Phone: (1) 717-486-3438
  Fax: (1) 717-486-6413
  Email: rod.komlenic@ahlstrom.com
  Product Mgr.: Tonia Showers
  Phone: (1) 717-486-3438
  Fax: (1) 717-486-6413
  Email: tonia.showers@ahlstrom.com
  Process Speciallist: Kim Canter
  Phone: (1) 717-486-3438
  Fax: (1) 717-486-6413
  Email: kim.canter@ahlstrom.com
Type of Operation: Paper mill
Paper/Paperboard Grades and Capacities:
Total paper and paperboard capacity: 5,500 st/y
Specialty and industrial: 5,500 st/y
Paper and Paperboard Mill Data:
Stock Preparation:
Pulpers: 2
Refiners: 5
Paper Machines: 1
No. 1, fourdrinier, total capacity 5,500 st/y, Trim width 80 in, Specialty and industrial
Finishing Equipment:
Calenders: 1
Rewinders: 3
Sheeters: 2
Energy Data:
Power boilers: 1

ⓂAmerican Eagle Paper Mills Inc.
Ownership: 100% by Team Ten LLC
1600 Pennsylvania Avenue
Tyrone, PA 16686
USA
  Phone: (1) 814-684-1610
  Fax: (1) 814-684-6166
  Web Address: www.aepaper.com
Personnel:
  Pres. & CEO: Michael Grimm
  Phone: (1) 814-684-1610
  Fax: (1) 814-684-6166
  Email: mgrimm@aepaper.com
  Exec. VP, Oper.: Scott Igoe
  Phone: (1) 814-684-1610
  Fax: (1) 814-684-6166
  Email: sigoe@aepaper.com
  Sls. Mgr.: Richard Koch
  Phone: (1) 814-684-6130
  Fax: (1) 814-684-6166
  Email: rkoch@aepaper.com
  Cust. Serv. Mgr.: Angie Cleckner
  Phone: (1) 814-684-6146
  Fax: (1) 814-684-6101
  Email: acleckner@aepaper.com
  Dir., HR: Lori McGovern
  Phone: (1) 814-684-1610
  Fax: (1) 814-684-6101
  Email: lmcgovern@aepaper.com
  Sec., Treas.: Clark Adelman
  Phone: (1) 814-684-6134
  Fax: (1) 814-684-6101
  Email: cadelman@aepaper.com
Total Employees of Company: 230
Mill Locations:

Pennsylvania

American Eagle Paper Mills Inc., Tyrone Mill, 1600 Pennsylvania Avenue, Tyrone, PA 16686, USA, Capacity: 85,661 st/y, (Paper mill)
Phone: (1) 814-684-1610
Fax: (1) 814-684-6166

ⓜAmerican Eagle Paper Mills Inc.
Tyrone Mill
1600 Pennsylvania Avenue
Tyrone, PA 16686
USA
Phone: (1) 814-684-1610
Fax: (1) 814-684-6166
Web Address: www.aepaper.com
Personnel:
Pres. & CEO: Mike Grimm
Phone: (1) 814-684-1610
Fax: (1) 814-684-6166
Email: mgrimm@aepaper.com
Exec. VP, Oper.: Scott Igoe
Phone: (1) 814-684-6191
Fax: (1) 814-684-6166
Email: sigoe@aepaper.com
Contr.: Brent McManigal
Phone: (1) 814-684-6143
Fax: (1) 814-684-6166
Email: bmcmanigal@aepaper.com
Sls. Mgr.: Richard Koch
Phone: (1) 908-996-6130
Fax: (1) 814-684-6166
Email: rkoch@aepaper.com
Cust. Serv. Mgr.: Angie Cleckner
Phone: (1) 814-684-6146
Fax: (1) 814-684-6166
Email: acleckner@aepaper.com
Total Employees at this Location: 160
Type of Operation: Paper mill
Pulp Grades and Capacities:
Total pulp capacity: 59,115 st/y
Recycled Pulping: 59,115 st/y
Pulp Mill Data:
Bleach Plant Systems: 1
Recycled Deinked Pulping System, Sequence: CEHH, Capacity 22,610.2 adst/y
Recycled Fiber Treatment Lines:
Flotation deinking lines: 1 at 27,557
Paper/Paperboard Grades and Capacities:
Total paper and paperboard capacity: 85,661 st/y
Uncoated woodfree/freesheet: 85,661 st/y
Paper and Paperboard Mill Data:
Stock Preparation:
Pulpers: 2
Refiners: 6
Paper Machines: 2
No. 3, fourdrinier, total capacity 58,892 st/y, Trim width 152 in, Uncoated woodfree/freesheet
No. 4, fourdrinier, total capacity 26,769 st/y, Trim width 84 in, Uncoated woodfree/freesheet
Finishing Equipment:
Supercalenders: 1
Rewinders: 4
Sheeters: 1
Energy Data:
Power boilers: 1
Steam turbines: 1 at 7.5 MW
Electrical demand for mill: 182 MWh/D

ⓜAppvion, Inc.
Roaring Spring Mill
Previously Appleton Papers Inc.
100 Paper Mill Rd
Roaring Spring, PA 16673-1488
USA
Phone: (1) 814-224-2131
Fax: (1) 814-224-6540
Web Address: www.appvion.com
Personnel:
Mill Mgr.: William Roepke
Phone: (1) 814-224-2131 Ext. 6618
Fax: (1) 814-224-6540
Email: wroepke@appvion.com
Prod. Supervisor: Brodie Brockman
Phone: (1) 814-224-2131
Fax: (1) 814-224-6540
Email: bbrockman@appvion.com
Tech. Mgr.: Andrea Forbes
Phone: (1) 814-224-2131
Fax: (1) 814-224-6540
Email: aforbes@appvion.com
Associate Reliability Engineer: Mark Taylor
Phone: (1) 814-224-6334
Fax: (1) 814-224-6310
Email: mtaylor@appvion.com
Total Employees at this Location: 375
Type of Operation: Pulp mill, Paper mill
Pulp Grades and Capacities:
Total pulp capacity: 90,070 st/y
Chemical Pulp: 90,070 st/y
Pulp Mill Data:
Chemical Pulping Systems:
Batch digesters: 5
Pulp Lines: 1
Bleach Plant Systems: 3
Chemical Pulping System, Type: Hardwood, Sequence: DEopD, Capacity 90,000 admt/y
Chemical Recovery Equipment:
Evaporator lines: 1
Recovery boilers: 1
Lime Kiln
Paper/Paperboard Grades and Capacities:
Total paper and paperboard capacity: 137,415 st/y
Uncoated woodfree/freesheet: 137,415 st/y
Paper and Paperboard Mill Data:
Stock Preparation:
Pulpers: 2
Refiners: 5
Paper Machines: 3
No. 1, fourdrinier, total capacity 67,815 st/y, Trim width 115 in, Uncoated woodfree/freesheet
No. 2, fourdrinier, total capacity 46,400 st/y, Trim width 123 in, Uncoated woodfree/freesheet
No. 3, fourdrinier, total capacity 23,200 st/y, Trim width 72 in, Uncoated woodfree/freesheet
Coating Machines: 3
No. 1, on machine
No. 2, on machine
No. 3, on machine
Energy Data:
Power boilers: 2
Electrical demand for mill: 450 MWh/D

ⓜCascades Tissue Group
Ransom Mill
Ownership: 100% by Cascades Inc.
1 Main St
Ransom, PA 18653-00004
USA
Mailing Address: PO Box 6000, Pittston Township, PA 18640-6000, USA
Phone: (1) 570-388-6161
Fax: (1) 570-883-4125
Web Address: www.afh.cascades.com
Personnel:
Plt. Mgr. - Ransom & Pittston Mills (From Jan 1, 2014): Mike Breen
Phone: (1) 570-388-6161
Fax: (1) 570-883-4125
Email: mike_breen@cascades.com
Purch. Mgr.: John Raban
Phone: (1) 570-388-6161
Fax: (1) 570-883-4125
Email: john_raban@cascades.com
Total Employees at this Location: 75
Type of Operation: Paper mill
Pulp Grades and Capacities:
Total pulp capacity: 67,347 st/y
Recycled Pulping: 67,347 st/y
Pulp Mill Data:
Recycled Fiber Treatment Lines:
Flotation deinking lines: 1
Paper/Paperboard Grades and Capacities:
Total paper and paperboard capacity: 62,832 st/y
Tissue: 62,832 st/y
Paper and Paperboard Mill Data:
Stock Preparation:
Pulpers: 4
Refiners: 3
Paper Machines: 2
No. 3, crescent former, total capacity 33,915 st/y, Trim width 135 in, Tissue
No. 4, crescent former, total capacity 28,917 st/y, Trim width 165 in, Tissue
Energy Data:
Power boilers: 2
Electrical demand for mill: 219 MWh/D

ⓜDomtar Corporation
Johnsonburg Mill
100 Center St
Johnsonburg, PA 15845
USA
Phone: (1) 814-965-2521, 800-458-4640
Fax: (1) 814-965-6231
Web Address: www.domtar.com
Personnel:
Gen. Mgr.: Grant Forrest
Phone: (1) 814-965-2521
Fax: (1) 814-965-6383
Email: grant.forrest@domtar.com
Paper Mill Mgr.: Bob Paladino
Phone: (1) 814-965-2521
Fax: (1) 814-965-6231
Email: bob.paladino@domtar.com
Purch. Mgr.: Sam Rosenhoover
Phone: (1) 814-965-6204
Fax: (1) 814-965-6287
Email: sam.rosenhoover@domtar.com
Wood Proc. Mgr.: Daniel Evans
Phone: (1) 814-965-6399
Fax: (1) 814-965-6235
Email: dan.evans@domtar.com
Maint. Team Ldr.: Darrell Berger
Phone: (1) 814-965-2521
Fax: (1) 814-965-6231
Email: darrell.berger@domtar.com
Logistic Supervisor: Frank Cherry
Phone: (1) 814-965-2521
Fax: (1) 814-965-6231
Email: frank.cherry@domtar.com
Total Employees at this Location: 390
Type of Operation: Pulp mill, Paper mill
Pulp Grades and Capacities:
Total pulp capacity: 216,619 st/y
Chemical Pulp: 216,619 st/y
Pulp Mill Data:
Chemical Pulping Systems:
Continuous digesters: 1
Pulp Lines: 1
Bleach Plant Systems: 1
Chemical Pulping System, Type: Hardwood, Sequence: DEopD
Chemical Recovery Equipment:
Evaporator lines: 1
Recovery boilers: 1
Lime Kiln
Paper/Paperboard Grades and Capacities:
Total paper and paperboard capacity: 355,137 st/y
Uncoated woodfree/freesheet: 355,137 st/y
Paper and Paperboard Mill Data:
Stock Preparation:
Pulpers: 3
Refiners:
Paper Machines: 2
No. 1, fourdrinier, total capacity 73,169 st/y, Trim width 180 in, Uncoated woodfree/freesheet
No. 5, twin-wire, total capacity 281,968 st/y, Trim width 232 in, Uncoated woodfree/freesheet
Finishing Equipment:

Pennsylvania

Calenders: 1
Rewinders: 2
Energy Data:
Power boilers: 4
Steam turbines: 1 at 60 MW
Electrical demand for mill: 899 MWh/D

ⓜFirst Quality Tissue LLC
Lock Haven Mill
904 Woods Avenue
Lock Haven, PA 17745
USA
  Phone: (1) 570-748-1200
  Fax: (1) 570-748-0874
  Email: fqtsales@firstquality.com
  Web Address: www.firstquality.com
Personnel:
  Product Develop. Mgr.: Alex Neeb
  Phone: (1) 570-748-1200
  Fax: (1) 570-748-0874
  Email: aneeb@firstquality.com
  HR Mgr.: Dana Wallis
  Phone: (1) 570-748-1200
  Fax: (1) 570-748-0874
  Email: dwallis@firstquality.com
  Product Mgr.: Kerry Bierly Herbster
  Phone: (1) 570-748-1200
  Fax: (1) 570-748-0874
  Email: kherbster@firstquality.com
  Tech. Serv.: Allyn Shultis
  Phone: (1) 570-748-1200
  Fax: (1) 570-748-0874
  Email: ashultis@firstquality.com
  Dir., Finan.: Patrick Sinner
  Phone: (1) 570-748-1200
  Fax: (1) 570-748-0874
  Email: psinner@firstquality.com
Total Employees at this Location: 140
Type of Operation: Paper mill
Paper/Paperboard Grades and Capacities:
  Total paper and paperboard capacity: 122,094 st/y
  Tissue: 122,094 st/y
Paper and Paperboard Mill Data:
  Stock Preparation:
  Pulpers:
Paper Machines: 2
  No. 1, crescent former, TAD, total capacity 72,114 st/y, Trim width 210 in, Tissue
  No. 2, crescent former, TAD, total capacity 49,980 st/y, Trim width 210 in, Tissue
Energy Data:
Power boilers: 2
Electrical demand for mill: 451 MWh/D

ⓜGlatfelter
Ownership: Public
96 S George St, Suite 500
York, PA 17401
USA
  Phone: (1) 717-225-4711
  Fax: (1) 717-846-7208
  Email: pr@glatfelter.com
  Web Address: www.glatfelter.com
Personnel:
  Chmn., CEO: Dante C. Parrini
  Phone: (1) 717-225-4711
  Fax: (1) 717-846-7208
  Email: dante.parrini@glatfelter.com
  Exec. VP. & CFO (Eff. March 1, 2014): John P. Jacunski
  Phone: (1) 717-225-4711
  Fax: (1) 717-846-7208
  Email: john.jacunski@glatfelter.com
  Snr. VP. & Gen. Mgr., Composite Fibers Business Unit (Eff. March 1, 2014): Martin Rapp
  Phone: (1) 717-225-4711
  Fax: (1) 717-846-7208
  Email: martin.rapp@glatfelter.com
  Snr. VP. HR & Admin. (Eff. March 1, 2014): William T. Yanavitch II
  Phone: (1) 717-225-4711
  Fax: (1) 717-846-7208
  Email: william.yanavitch@glatfelter.com
  Snr. VP. Corp. Strat. (Eff. March 1, 2014): Christopher W Astley
  Phone: (1) 717-225-4711
  Fax: (1) 717-846-7208
  Email: christopher.astley@glatfelter.com
  VP. & Gen. Mgr. Specialty Papers Business Unit (SPBU): Brian E. Janki
  Phone: (1) 717-225-4711
  Fax: (1) 717-846-7208
  Email: brian.janki@glatfelter.com
  VP., Gen. Counsel, and Corporate Secretary: Kent K. Matsumoto
  Phone: (1) 717-225-4711
  Fax: (1) 717-846-7208
  Email: kent.matsumoto@glatfelter.com
  VP., Global Supply Chain & IT: Mark A. Sullivan
  Phone: (1) 717-225-4711
  Fax: (1) 717-846-7208
  Email: mark.sullivan@glatfelter.com
  VP., Finan.: David C. Elder
  Phone: (1) 717-225-4711
  Fax: (1) 717-846-7208
  Email: david.elder@glatfelter.com
Total Employees of Company: 4,403
Mill Locations:
Glatfelter, Chillicothe Mill, 401 S Paint St, Chillicothe, OH 45601, USA, Capacity: 394,398 st/y, (Pulp mill, Paper mill)
  Phone: (1) 740-772-3111
  Fax: (1) 740-772-0024
Dresden Papier GmbH, Dresden Mill, Pirnaer Str. 31-33, D-01809 Heidenau, Germany, Capacity: 66,138 st/y, (Paper mill)
  Phone: (49) 3529 554-0
  Fax: (49) 3529 554-180
  Email: wallpaperbase@glatfelter.com
Glatfelter Gernsbach GmbH & Co. KG, Gernsbach Mill, Hördener Str. 5, D-76593 Gernsbach, Germany, Capacity: 46,296 st/y, (Paper mill)
  Phone: (49) 7224 660
  Fax: (49) 7224 66274
  Email: composite.fibers@glatfelter.com
Glatfelter UK Ltd., Lydney Paper Mill, Church Rd., Lydney GL15 5EJ, United Kingdom, Capacity: 16,534 st/y, (Paper mill)
  Phone: (44) 1594 842 235
  Fax: (44) 1594 844 213
  Email: info@glatfelter.com; uksales@glatfelter.com
Glatfelter, Scaër Mill, BP 2, F-29390 Scaër, France, Capacity: 6,614 st/y, (Paper mill)
  Phone: (33) 2 98 66 42 00
  Fax: (33) 2 98 59 09 98
  Email: service.france@glatfelter.com
Glatfelter, Spring Grove Mill, 228 S Main St, Spring Grove, PA 17362, USA, Capacity: 339,075 st/y, (Pulp mill, Paper mill)
  Phone: (1) 717-225-4711
  Fax: (1) 717-225-6834
  Email: pr@glatfelter.com
Newtech Pulp Inc., Lanao del Norte Mill, Bo. Maria Cristina, Balo-I, 9217 Lanao del Norte, Philippines, (Pulp mill)
  Phone: (63) 2 893 7640
  Fax: (63) 2 893 2819
  Email: info@glatfelter.com
Spezialpapierfabrik Oberschmitten GmbH, Nidda/Ober-Schmitten Mill, Rhönstr. 13, D-63667 Nidda/Ober-Schmitten, Germany, Capacity: 13,773 st/y, (Paper mill)
  Phone: (49) 6043 80801
  Fax: (49) 6043 8081 00
  Email: info@spo-gmbh.de

ⓜGlatfelter
Spring Grove Mill
228 S Main St
Spring Grove, PA 17362
USA
  Phone: (1) 717-225-4711
  Fax: (1) 717-225-6834
  Email: pr@glatfelter.com
  Web Address: www.glatfelter.com
Personnel:
  Mill Mgr.: Robert L. Inners II
  Phone: (1) 717-225-4711
  Fax: (1) 717-225-6834
  Email: rinners@glatfelter.com
  Dir. Supply Chain: Mark Keller
  Phone: (1) 717-225-4711
  Fax: (1) 717-225-6834
  Email: mkeller@glatfelter.com
  HR Mgr., Personnel Dir.: Laurie Donahoue
  Phone: (1) 717-225-4711
  Fax: (1) 717-225-6834
  Email: ldonahoue@glatfelter.com
  Prod. Mgr.: Eric J. Hanson
  Phone: (1) 717-225-4711
  Fax: (1) 717-225-6834
  Email: ehanson@glatfelter.com
  Mktg. Mgr.: Heath Frye
  Phone: (1) 717-225-4711
  Fax: (1) 717-225-6834
  Email: hfrye@glatfelter.com
Total Employees at this Location: 700
Type of Operation: Pulp mill, Paper mill
Pulp Grades and Capacities:
  Total pulp capacity: 268,014 st/y
  Chemical Pulp: 268,014 st/y
Pulp Mill Data:
  Chemical Pulping Systems:
  Batch digesters: 9
  Continuous digesters: 1
  Bleach Plant Systems: 2
  Chemical Pulping System, Type: Hardwood, Sequence: O_2 DEpD
  Chemical Pulping System, Type: Softwood, Sequence: O_2 DEpD
  Chemical Recovery Equipment:
  Evaporator lines: 2
  Recovery boilers: 1
  Lime Kiln
Paper/Paperboard Grades and Capacities:
  Total paper and paperboard capacity: 339,075 st/y
  Uncoated woodfree/freesheet: 289,106 st/y
  Specialty and industrial: 49,969 st/y
Paper and Paperboard Mill Data:
  Stock Preparation:
  Pulpers: 4
  Refiners: 25
Paper Machines: 5
  No. 1, fourdrinier, total capacity 57,107 st/y, Trim width 172 in, Uncoated woodfree/freesheet
  No. 2, fourdrinier, total capacity 39,261 st/y, Trim width 160 in, Uncoated woodfree/freesheet
  No. 5, fourdrinier, total capacity 17,846 st/y, Trim width 92 in, Uncoated woodfree/freesheet
  No. 7, top wire C former, total capacity 114,215 st/y, Trim width 170 in, Uncoated woodfree/freesheet
  No. 8, SymFormer, total capacity 110,646 st/y, Trim width 192 in, Uncoated woodfree/freesheet, Specialty and industrial
Coating Machines: 1
  No. 1, total capacity 53,000 st/y., off machine
Finishing Equipment:
  Supercalenders: 2
  Rewinders: 4
  Sheeters: 5
Energy Data:
Power boilers: 4
Steam turbines: 3 at 101 MW
Electrical demand for mill: 1,075 MWh/D

ⓜKimberly-Clark Corp.
Chester Mill
Front St & Av of the States
Chester, PA 19013
USA
  Phone: (1) 610-874-4331
  Fax: (1) 610-499-6238

Pennsylvania

Web Address: www.kimberly-clark.com
Personnel:
Oper. Ldr.: Jacob Dombroski
Phone: (1) 610-874-4331
Fax: (1) 610-499-6238
Email: jacob.dombroski@kcc.com
Contr.: Tom Brooks
Phone: (1) 610-874-4331
Fax: (1) 610-499-6238
Email: tom.brooks@kcc.com
Eng. Mgr.: Victor M. Gentile
Phone: (1) 610-874-4331
Fax: (1) 610-499-6238
Email: vgentile@kcc.com
Total Employees at this Location: 295
Type of Operation: Paper mill
Paper/Paperboard Grades and Capacities:
Total paper and paperboard capacity: 250,257 st/y
Tissue: 250,257 st/y
Paper and Paperboard Mill Data:
  Stock Preparation:
  Pulpers:
Paper Machines: 5
No. 12, twin-wire, total capacity 44,625 st/y, Trim width 177 in, Tissue
No. 16, crescent former, total capacity 26,775 st/y, Trim width 177 in, Tissue
No. 17, twin-wire, total capacity 44,625 st/y, Trim width 177 in, Tissue
No. 18, crescent former, total capacity 67,830 st/y, Trim width 195 in, Tissue
No. 19, TAD, total capacity 66,402 st/y, Trim width 198 in, Tissue
Energy Data:
Power boilers: 2
Steam turbines: 1 at 67 MW
Electrical demand for mill: 852 MWh/D

ⓜNational Gypsum Co.
Milton Plant
2586 Old Route 15
New Columbia, PA 17856
USA
Mailing Address: PO Box 210, Milton, PA 17886, USA
Phone: (1) 570-538-2531
Fax: (1) 570-538-5898
Web Address: www.nationalgypsum.com
Personnel:
Mill Ldr.: Dave Eltz
Phone: (1) 570-538-2531
Fax: (1) 570-538-5898
Regional Sls. Mgr.: Tim Hessert
Phone: (1) 570-538-2531
Fax: (1) 570-538-5898
Plt/Oper./Maint. Mgr.: Joseph Rosenberger
Phone: (1) 570-538-2531
Fax: (1) 570-538-5898
Total Employees at this Location: 75
Type of Operation: Paperboard mill
Pulp Grades and Capacities:
Total pulp capacity: 116,868 st/y
Recycled Pulping: 116,868 st/y
Paper/Paperboard Grades and Capacities:
Total paper and paperboard capacity: 112,098 st/y
Boxboard/cartonboard: 112,098 st/y
Paper and Paperboard Mill Data:
  Stock Preparation:
  Refiners: 6
Paper Machines: 1
No. 1, cylinder (9), total capacity 112,098 st/y, Trim width 153 in, Boxboard/cartonboard
Finishing Equipment:
Calenders: 2
Rewinders: 1
Energy Data:
Power boilers: 1
Electrical demand for mill: 145 MWh/D

ⓜNewman & Company, Inc.
Ownership: 100% by private company

6101 Tacony St
Philadelphia, PA 19135
USA
Phone: (1) 215-333-8700, 800-523-3256 (Toll Free)
Fax: (1) 215-332-8586
Email: first.lastname@newmanpaperboard.com
Web Address: www.newmanpaperboard.com
Personnel:
Pres., CEO: Bernard Newman
Phone: (1) 215-333-8700 Ext.1200
Fax: (1) 215-332-8586
Email: bud.newman@newmanpaperboard.com
VP Oper.: Michael Ferman
Phone: (1) 215-333-8700
Fax: (1) 215-332-8586
Email: michael.ferman@newmanpaperboard.com
VP: David Newman
Phone: (1) 215-333-8700
Fax: (1) 215-332-8586
Email: david.newman@newmanpaperboard.com
VP, Sls.: Charles Wismer
Phone: (1) 215-333-8700 Ext.1216
Fax: (1) 215-992-5735
Email: charlie.wismer@newmanpaperboard.com
Prod. Mgr., Sls.: Joe Partito
Phone: (1) 215-333-8700 Ext.1250
Fax: (1) 215-992-5739
Email: joe.partito@newmanpaperboard.com
Logist. Mgr.: Nick DelBuono
Phone: (1) 215-333-8700 Ext.1213
Fax: (1) 215-992-5731
Email: nick.delbuono@newmanpaperboard.com
Total Employees of Company: 200
Mill Locations:
Newman & Company, Inc., Philadelphia Mill, 6101 Tacony St, Philadelphia, PA 19135, USA, Capacity: 74,970 st/y, (Paperboard mill)
Phone: (1) 215-333-8700, 800-523-2356 (toll free)
Fax: (1) 215-332-8586, 332-8686 (Sales Dept)
Email: sales@newmanpaperboard.com

ⓜNewman & Company, Inc.
Philadelphia Mill
6101 Tacony St
Philadelphia, PA 19135
USA
Phone: (1) 215-333-8700, 800-523-2356 (toll free)
Fax: (1) 215-332-8586, 332-8686 (Sales Dept)
Email: sales@newmanpaperboard.com
Web Address: www.newmanpaperboard.com
Personnel:
Pres. & CEO: Bernard Newman
Phone: (1) 215-333-8700 Ext.1200
Fax: (1) 215-332-8586, 332-8686 (Sales Dept)
Email: bernard.newman@newmanpaperboard.com
VP, Sls. & Prod.: Charles Wismer
Phone: (1) 215-333-8700 Ext.1216
Fax: (1) 215-332-8586, 332-8686 (Sales Dept)
Email: charlie.wismer@newmanpaperboard.com
Prod. Mgr./Sls.: Joe Partito
Phone: (1) 215-333-8700 Ext.1250
Fax: (1) 215-332-8586, 332-8686 (Sales Dept)
Email: joe.partito@newmanpaperboard.com
Logist. Mgr.: Nick DelBuono
Phone: (1) 215-333-8700
Fax: (1) 215-332-8586, 332-8686 (Sales Dept)
Email: nick.delbuono@newmanpaperboard.com
Total Employees at this Location: 200
Type of Operation: Paperboard mill
Pulp Grades and Capacities:
Total pulp capacity: 77,731 st/y
Recycled Pulping: 77,731 st/y
Pulp Mill Data:
  Recycled Fiber Treatment Lines:
  Pulpers: 2 at 240 admt/y
Paper/Paperboard Grades and Capacities:
Total paper and paperboard capacity: 74,970 st/y
Boxboard/cartonboard: 74,970 st/y
Paper and Paperboard Mill Data:
  Stock Preparation:

Pulpers: 3
Refiners: 1
Paper Machines: 1
No. 1, cylinder (8), total capacity 74,970 st/y, Trim width 116 in, Boxboard/cartonboard
Finishing Equipment:
Calenders: 2
Sheeters: 2
Energy Data:
Power boilers: 1
Steam turbines: 1 at 2 MW
Electrical demand for mill: 102 MWh/D

ⓗⓜPaperWorks Industries, Inc.
Philadelphia Mill
Ownership: Sun Capital Partners, Inc.
5000 Flat Rock Rd
Philadelphia, PA 19127
USA
Phone: (1) 215-984-7000
Fax: (1) 215-984-7181
Web Address: www.paperwrks.com
Personnel:
Pres., CEO (Eff. March 24, 2014): Kevin Kwilinski
Phone: (1) 215-984-7023
Fax: (1) 215-984-7181
CFO: Robert J. Nobile
Phone: (1) 215-984-7023
Fax: (1) 215-984-7181
Email: robert.nobile@paperwrks.com
Exec. VP., Packaging Group: J. Joseph Moynihan
Phone: (1) 215-984-7000
Fax: (1) 215-984-7181
Email: joseph.moynihan@paperwrks.com
Snr. VP., Packaging Sls & Bus. Develop. (Eff. April 2014): Mark P. Roy
Phone: (1) 215-984-7008
Fax: (1) 215-984-7181
Email: mark.roy@paperwrks.com
Snr. VP., Oper. (Eff. April 2014): Clint Rutledge
Phone: (1) 215-984-7000
Fax: (1) 215-984-7181
VP, HR: Dan Sassi
Phone: (1) 215-984-7175
Fax: (1) 215-984-7181
Email: dan.sassi@paperwrks.com
Gen. Mgr.: Frank DelGrego
Phone: (1) 215-984-7057
Fax: (1) 215-984-7181
Email: frank.delgrego@paperwrks.com
Contr.: Glenn Hummel
Phone: (1) 215-984-7000
Fax: (1) 215-984-7181
Email: glenn.hummel@paperwrks.com
Snr. Dir., Sls & Mktg.: Jerry Tassone
Phone: (1) 215-984-7000
Fax: (1) 215-984-7181
Email: jerry.tassone@paperwrks.com
Total Employees of Company: 1,850
Total Employees at this Location: 141
Type of Operation: Paperboard mill
Mill Locations:
PaperWorks Industries, Inc., Wabash Mill, 455 W Factory St, Wabash, IN 46992, USA, Capacity: 145,656 st/y, (Paperboard mill)
Phone: (1) 260-563-3102
Fax: (1) 260-569-3404
Email: info@paperwrks.com
Pulp Grades and Capacities:
Total pulp capacity: 132,071 st/y
Recycled Pulping: 132,071 st/y
Pulp Mill Data:
  Recycled Fiber Treatment Lines:
  Pulpers: 1 at 121,252
Paper/Paperboard Grades and Capacities:
Total paper and paperboard capacity: 134,589 st/y
Boxboard/cartonboard: 134,589 st/y
Paper and Paperboard Mill Data:
  Stock Preparation:
  Pulpers:

Pennsylvania

Paper Machines: 1
No. 6, Ultraformer (8), total capacity 134,589 st/y, Trim width 144 in, Boxboard/cartonboard
Coating Machines: 1
No. 2, total capacity 124,559 st/y., on machine
Energy Data:
Power boilers: 2

ⓂProcter & Gamble Paper Products Co.
Mehoopany Mill
Rte 87
Mehoopany, PA 18629
USA
Mailing Address: PO Box 32, Mehoopany, PA 18629, USA
Phone: (1) 570-833-5141
Fax: (1) 570-833-3281
Web Address: www.pg.com
Personnel:
Oper. Dept. Mgr.: Tomasz Kasperkowicz
Phone: (1) 570-833-5141
Fax: (1) 570-833-3281
Email: kasperkowicz.t@pg.com
Facility Management: Gina Reese
Phone: (1) 570-833-5141
Fax: (1) 570-833-3281
Process Eng.: Michael Klees
Phone: (1) 570-833-5141
Fax: (1) 570-833-3281
Email: klees.m@pg.com
Total Employees at this Location: 348
Type of Operation: Paper mill
Paper/Paperboard Grades and Capacities:
Total paper and paperboard capacity: 419,118 st/y
Tissue: 419,118 st/y
Paper and Paperboard Mill Data:
Stock Preparation:
Pulpers:
Paper Machines: 8
No. 1, TAD, total capacity 44,982 st/y, Trim width 200 in, Tissue
No. 2, TAD, total capacity 44,982 st/y, Trim width 200 in, Tissue
No. 3, TAD, total capacity 48,552 st/y, Trim width 200 in, Tissue
No. 4, TAD, total capacity 44,982 st/y, Trim width 200 in, Tissue
No. 5, TAD, total capacity 43,554 st/y, Trim width 200 in, Tissue
No. 6, TAD, total capacity 43,554 st/y, Trim width 200 in, Tissue
No. 7, TAD, total capacity 69,615 st/y, Trim width 200 in, Tissue
No. 8, TAD, total capacity 78,897 st/y, Trim width 200 in, Tissue
Energy Data:
Power boilers: 3
Combustion turbines: 1 at 48 MW
Electrical demand for mill: 1,624 MWh/D

ⓂRockTenn Co.
Stroudsburg Mill
Paper Mill Rd
Delaware Water Gap, PA 18327
USA
Phone: (1) 570-476-0120
Fax: (1) 570-476-9553
Web Address: www.rocktenn.com
Personnel:
Gen. Mgr.: John McCarthy
Phone: (1) 570-476-0120
Fax: (1) 570-476-9553
Email: jmccarthy@rocktenn.com
Maint & Eng Mgr.: Gerry L. Craig
Phone: (1) 570-476-0120 Ext: 13
Fax: (1) 570-476-9553
Email: gcraig@rocktenn.com
HR & Safety Mgr.: Jane Burkholder
Phone: (1) 570-476-0120

Fax: (1) 570-476-9553
Email: jburkholder@rocktenn.com
Total Employees at this Location: 113
Type of Operation: Paperboard mill
Pulp Grades and Capacities:
Total pulp capacity: 69,736 st/y
Recycled Pulping: 69,736 st/y
Pulp Mill Data:
Recycled Fiber Treatment Lines:
Pulpers: 1 at 71,759
Paper/Paperboard Grades and Capacities:
Total paper and paperboard capacity: 79,968 st/y
Boxboard/cartonboard: 79,968 st/y
Paper and Paperboard Mill Data:
Stock Preparation:
Pulpers: 3
Refiners: 4
Paper Machines: 1
No. 1, cylinder (8), total capacity 79,968 st/y, Trim width 94 in, Boxboard/cartonboard
Coating Machines: 2
No. 1, total capacity 79,916 st/y., on machine
No. 1
Energy Data:
Power boilers: 2

ⓘSCA Tissue North America, L.L.C.
Ownership: 100% by SCA - Svenska Cellulosa Aktiebolaget
Cira Centre 2929 Arch St., Suite 2600
Philadelphia, PA 19104
USA
Phone: (1) 610-499-3700
Fax: (1) 610-499-3391
Web Address: www.torkusa.com, www.tena-usa.com, www.scanorthamerica.com
Personnel:
Pres.: Don Lewis
Phone: (1) 610-499-3700
Fax: (1) 610-499-3391
Email: don.lewis@sca.com
VP, Product Supply: Fred Albrecht
Phone: (1) 610-499-3700
Fax: (1) 610-499-3391
Email: fred.albrecht@sca.com
VP, Commun.: Amy Bellcourt
Phone: (1) 518 369-8880
Fax: (1) 518 742-5706
Email: amy.bellcourt@sca.com
VP, Product & Mktg., SCA Tissue North America: John Drengler
Phone: (1) 610-499-3700
Fax: (1) 610-499-3391
Email: john.drengler@sca.com
VP, Sls. & Mktg.: Joe Russo
Phone: (1) 610-499-3700
Fax: (1) 610-499-3391
Email: joe.russo@sca.com
VP, Product Plan. & Logist.: Mike Jansen
Phone: (1) 610-499-3700
Fax: (1) 610-499-3391
Email: mike.jansen@sca.com
VP, Strategic Accounts: David Rizley
Phone: (1) 610-499-3700
Fax: (1) 610-499-3391
Email: david.rizley@sca.com
Dir. of Engineering for SCA North America: Mark Phiscator
Phone: (1) 610-499-3700
Fax: (1) 610-499-3391
Email: mark.phiscator@sca.com
Mill Locations:
SCA Tissue North America, L.L.C., Encore Paper, 1 River St, South Glens Falls, NY 12803, USA, Capacity: 88,893 st/y, (Paper mill)
Phone: (1) 518-793-5684
Fax: (1) 518-793-2650
Email: torkusa@sca.com
SCA Tissue North America, L.L.C., Barton Mill, 1834 Haley Dr., Cherokee, AL 35616, USA, Capacity: 175,287

st/y, (Paper mill)
Phone: (1) 256-370-8100
Fax: (1) 256-370-8195
SCA Tissue North America, L.L.C., Flagstaff Mill, 1600 E Butler Av, Flagstaff, AZ 86001, USA, Capacity: 61,761 st/y, (Paper mill)
Phone: (1) 928-774-7375
Fax: (1) 928-774-9546
Email: americas@sca.com
SCA Tissue North America, L.L.C., Menasha Mill, 190 Tayco Street, Menasha, WI 54952, USA, Capacity: 209,559 st/y, (Paper mill)
Phone: (1) 920-727-2910
Fax: (1) 920-727-2902
Email: info@sca.com

ⓂSealed Air Corp.
Modena Mill
22 Meredith Ct
Modena, PA 19358
USA
Mailing Address: PO Box 158, Modena, PA 19358-0158, USA
Phone: (1) 610-384-2650
Fax: (1) 610-384-2605
Web Address: www.sealedair.com
Personnel:
Plt. Mgr.: Tom Krall
Phone: (1) 215-384-2650
Fax: (1) 215-384-2605
Email: tom.krall@sealedair.com
Cust. Serv.: Rachel Holmes
Phone: (1) 215-384-2650
Fax: (1) 215-384-2605
Email: rachel.holmes@sealedair.com
Type of Operation: Paper mill
Paper/Paperboard Grades and Capacities:
Total paper and paperboard capacity: 28,999 st/y
Specialty and industrial
Paper and Paperboard Mill Data:
Stock Preparation:
Pulpers: 2
Refiners: 2
Paper Machines: 1
PM 1, fourdrinier, total capacity 29,000 st/y, Trim width 108 in, Packaging papers, Specialty and industrial
Energy Data:
Power boilers: 1

ⓂSealed Air Corp.
Reading Mill
450 Riverfront Dr
Reading, PA 19602
USA
Phone: (1) 610-375-4281
Fax: (1) 610-375-6443
Web Address: www.sealedair.com
Personnel:
VP. & Gen. Mgr. Paper Mills: Mike Feeney
Phone: (1) 610-375-4281
Fax: (1) 610-375-6443
Email: mike.feeney@sealedair.com
Oper. Dir.: Brian Blackford
Phone: (1) 610-375-4281
Fax: (1) 610-375-6443
Email: brian.blackford@sealedair.com
Materials Mgr.: Joseph Squadrito
Phone: (1) 484-786-7144
Fax: (1) 610-375-6443
Email: joseph.squadrito@sealedair.com
Total Employees at this Location: 42
Type of Operation: Paper mill
Paper/Paperboard Grades and Capacities:
Total paper and paperboard capacity: 25,000 st/y
Specialty and industrial: 25,000 st/y
Paper and Paperboard Mill Data:
Stock Preparation:
Pulpers: 5
Refiners: 2
Paper Machines: 1

South Carolina

PM 1, fourdrinier, total capacity 25,000 st/y, Trim width 90 in, Specialty and industrial
Finishing Equipment:
 Winders: 1
Energy Data:
Power boilers: 2
Electrical demand for mill: 48 MWh/D

ⓂUnited Corrstack LLC
Reading Mill
Ownership: Interstate Resources, Inc.
720 Laurel St
Reading, PA 19602
USA
 Phone: (1) 610-374-3000
 Fax: (1) 610-376-8215
 Email: info@InterstateResources.com
 Web Address: www.unitedcorrstack.com
Personnel:
 Gen. Mgr.: Arthur McLaughlin
 Phone: (1) 610-374-3000 Ext. 3202
 Fax: (1) 610-376-8215
 Email: amclaughlin@unitedcorrstack.com
 Eng. & Maint. Mgr.: Ken Day
 Phone: (1) 610-374-3000
 Fax: (1) 610-376-8215
 Email: kday@unitedcorrstack.com
 Purch. Mgr.: Art Murphy
 Phone: (1) 610-374-3000 Ext. 3270
 Fax: (1) 610-376-8215
 Email: art.murphy@unitedcorrstack.com
Total Employees at this Location: 73
Type of Operation: Paperboard mill
Pulp Grades and Capacities:
 Total pulp capacity: 180,786 st/y
 Recycled Pulping: 201,831 st/y
Pulp Mill Data:
 Recycled Fiber Treatment Lines:
 Recycled packaging pulping lines: 1
Paper/Paperboard Grades and Capacities:
 Total paper and paperboard capacity: 172,788 st/y
 Corrugating medium/fluting: 172,788 st/y
Paper and Paperboard Mill Data:
 Stock Preparation:
 Pulpers: 1
 Refiners: 3
Paper Machines: 1
No. 3, fourdrinier, total capacity 172,788 st/y, Trim width 166 in, Corrugating medium/fluting
Finishing Equipment:
 Winders: 1
Energy Data:
Power boilers: 2
Steam turbines at 30 MW
Electrical demand for mill: 195 MWh/D

SOUTH CAROLINA

ⓂCarotell Paperboard
Taylors Mill
Ownership: 100% by Caraustar Industries, Inc.
873 Alexander Dr
Taylors, SC 29687
USA
Mailing Address: PO Box 2329, Greer, SC 29652-2329, USA
 Phone: (1) 864-244-6221
 Fax: (1) 864-292-8856
 Web Address: www.caraustar.com
Personnel:
 Gen. Mgr.: Donnie Mason
 Phone: (1) 864-244-6221
 Fax: (1) 864-292-8856
 Email: dmason@caraustar.com
 Tech. Mgr.: Cecilia Locke

 Phone: (1) 864-244-6221
 Fax: (1) 864-292-8856
 Email: clocke@caraustar.com
Total Employees at this Location: 88
Type of Operation: Paperboard mill
Pulp Grades and Capacities:
 Total pulp capacity: 80,427 st/y
 Recycled Pulping: 80,427 st/y
Pulp Mill Data:
 Recycled Fiber Treatment Lines:
 Pulpers
Paper/Paperboard Grades and Capacities:
 Total paper and paperboard capacity: 78,540 st/y
 Boxboard/cartonboard: 78,540 st/y
Paper and Paperboard Mill Data:
 Stock Preparation:
 Pulpers: 4
 Refiners: 4
Paper Machines: 1
No. 1, cylinder (10), total capacity 78,540 st/y, Trim width 108 in, Boxboard/cartonboard
Finishing Equipment:
 Calenders: 2
 Rewinders: 1 at 100,000 st/y
 Sheeters: 1 at 100,000 st/y
Energy Data:
Power boilers: 1
Electrical demand for mill: 101 MWh/D

ⓂDomtar Corporation
Marlboro Mill
585 Willamette Road
Bennettsville, SC 29512
USA
Mailing Address: PO Box 678, Bennettsville, SC 29512, USA
 Phone: (1) 843-479-0200
 Fax: (1) 843-479-0608
 Web Address: www.domtar.com
Personnel:
 Mill Mgr. (Eff. September 2014): Dennis Askew
 Phone: (1) 843-479-0200
 Fax: (1) 843-479-0608
 Email: dennis.askew@domtar.com
 Pulp & Utility Mgr.: Chris Gore
 Phone: (1) 843-479-8913
 Fax: (1) 843-479-0608
 Email: chris.gore@domtar.com
 Maint. Mgr.: Robbie Ammons
 Phone: (1) 843-479-0200
 Fax: (1) 843-479-0608
 Email: robbie.ammons@domtar.com
Total Employees at this Location: 320
Type of Operation: Pulp mill, Paper mill
Pulp Grades and Capacities:
 Total pulp capacity: 363,023 st/y
 Pulp available for market: 51,157 st/y
 Chemical Pulp: 363,023 st/y
Pulp Mill Data:
 Chemical Pulping Systems:
 Batch digesters: 8
Pulp Lines: 1
 Bleach Plant Systems: 1
 Chemical Pulping System - Line 1, Type: Hardwood/Softwood, Sequence: O_2 DEopD, Capacity 426,807.8 admt/y
 Chemical Recovery Equipment:
 Evaporator lines: 1
 Recovery boilers: 1
 Lime Kiln
 Pulp Dryers:
 Pulp Dryers 1
Paper/Paperboard Grades and Capacities:
 Total paper and paperboard capacity: 350,854 st/y
 Uncoated woodfree/freesheet: 280,183 st/y
 Specialty and industrial: 70,670 st/y
Paper and Paperboard Mill Data:
Paper Machines: 1
No. 1, SymFormer R, total capacity 350,854 st/y, Trim width 329 in, Uncoated woodfree/freesheet, Specialty and industrial
Energy Data:
Power boilers: 2
Steam turbines: 1 at 50 MW
Electrical demand for mill: 1,270 MWh/D

ⓂFirst Quality Tissue LLC
Anderson Mill
441 Masters Blvd
Anderson, SC 29626-6127
USA
 Phone: (1) 800-726-6910, 516-829-3030 (NY HQ number), 864-437-2085
 Email: se.info@firstquality.com
 Web Address: www.firstquality.com
Personnel:
 Dir., Oper.: Doug Zirbel
 Phone: (1) 864-437-2085
 Email: dzirbel@firstquality.com
 Tech. Mgr. Paper/Converting: Nathan Jones
 Phone: (1) 864-437-2085
 Email: njones@firstquality.com
 Product Develop. Chem. Mgr.: Karthik K. Ramaratnam
 Phone: (1) 864-437-2011
 Email: kkramaratnam@firstquality.com
 Process Develop. Mgr.: Justin S. Pence
 Phone: (1) 864-437-2085
 Email: jspence@firstquality.com
 Prod. Mgr.: Louis LeBrun
 Phone: (1) 864-437-2085
 Email: llebrun@firstquality.com
Total Employees at this Location: 109
Type of Operation: Paper mill
Paper/Paperboard Grades and Capacities:
 Total paper and paperboard capacity: 119,952 st/y
 Tissue: 119,952 st/y
Paper and Paperboard Mill Data:
 Stock Preparation:
 Pulpers:
Paper Machines: 2
No. 3, C-wrap, total capacity 69,972 st/y, Trim width 213 in, Tissue
No. 4, C-wrap, total capacity 49,980 st/y, Trim width 213 in, Tissue
Energy Data:
Power boilers: 2
Electrical demand for mill: 459 MWh/D

ⓂInternational Paper Co.
Eastover Mill
4001 McCords Ferry Rd
Eastover, SC 29044
USA
Mailing Address: PO Box B, Eastover, SC 29044, USA
 Phone: (1) 803-353-7700
 Fax: (1) 803-353-7981
 Email: (firstname.lastname@ipaper.com)
 Web Address: www.internationalpaper.com
Personnel:
 Area Mgr.: Steve Frierson
 Phone: (1) 803-353-7700
 Fax: (1) 803-353-7981
 Email: steve.frierson@ipaper.com
 Maint. Mgr.: Andy Brady
 Phone: (1) 803-353-7700
 Fax: (1) 803-353-7981
 Email: andy.brady@ipaper.com
 Commun. Mgr.: Yamur Hossain
 Phone: (1) 803-353-7653
 Fax: (1) 803-353-7981
 Email: yamur.hossain@ipaper.com
Total Employees at this Location: 600
Type of Operation: Pulp mill, Paper mill
Pulp Grades and Capacities:
 Total pulp capacity: 729,549 st/y
 Pulp available for market: 110,185 st/y
 Chemical Pulp: 729,549 st/y
Pulp Mill Data:

South Carolina

Chemical Pulping Systems:
Continuous digesters: 2
Bleach Plant Lines:
Hardwood, Sequence: O_2 DEoD
Softwood, Sequence: O_2 DEopD
Chemical Recovery Equipment:
Recovery boilers: 2
Lime Kiln
Pulp Dryers:
Flakt dryer 1, Foudriniers 1
Paper/Paperboard Grades and Capacities:
Total paper and paperboard capacity: 729,904 st/y
Uncoated woodfree/freesheet: 729,904 st/y
Paper and Paperboard Mill Data:
Paper Machines: 2
No. 1, DuoFormer, total capacity 346,214 st/y, Trim width 346 in, Uncoated woodfree/freesheet
No. 2, Bel-Baie III, total capacity 383,690 st/y, Trim width 346 in, Uncoated woodfree/freesheet
Energy Data:
Power boilers: 2
Steam turbines: 2 at 110 MW
Electrical demand for mill: 2,615 MWh/D

ⓜInternational Paper Co.
Georgetown Mill
700 S Kaminski
Georgetown, SC 29440
USA
Phone: (1) 843-546-6111
Fax: (1) 843-546-6129
Email: (firstname.lastname@ipaper.com)
Web Address: www.internationalpaper.com
Personnel:
Gen. Mgr.: Dru Kraus
Phone: (1) 843-546-6111
Fax: (1) 843-546-6129
Email: dru.kraus@ipaper.com
Manuf. Mgr.: Steve McNelly
Phone: (1) 843-546-6111
Fax: (1) 843-546-6129
Email: steve.mcnelly@ipaper.com
Maint. Mgr.: Andy McKellar
Phone: (1) 843-546-6111
Fax: (1) 843-546-6129
Email: andy.mckellar@ipaper.com
PS&D Area Mgr.: Felicia S. Wilson
Phone: (1) 843-545-2215
Fax: (1) 843-546-6129
Email: felicia.wilson@ipaper.com
Region Mgr., Global sourcing, Fiber Supply: Mike P. Macedo
Phone: (1) 843-546-6111
Fax: (1) 843-546-6129
Email: mike.macedo@ipaper.com
Total Employees at this Location: 650
Type of Operation: Pulp mill, Paper mill
Pulp Grades and Capacities:
Total pulp capacity: 656,817 st/y
Pulp available for market: 360,213 st/y
Chemical Pulp: 644,198 st/y
Recycled Pulping: 12,619 st/y
Pulp Mill Data:
Chemical Pulping Systems:
Continuous digesters: 6
Bleach Plant Systems: 3
Chemical Pulping System, Type: Hardwood, Sequence: DEopD
Chemical Pulping System, Type: Swing, Sequence: DEopDD
Chemical Pulping System, Type: Softwood, Sequence: DEopDED
Chemical Recovery Equipment:
Evaporator lines: 1
Recovery boilers: 2
Lime Kiln
Pulp Dryers:
Flakt dryer 1
Paper/Paperboard Grades and Capacities:
Total paper and paperboard capacity: 319,515 st/y
Uncoated woodfree/freesheet: 319,515 st/y
Paper and Paperboard Mill Data:
Stock Preparation:
Pulpers:
Paper Machines: 2
No. 1, Bel-Bond, total capacity 169,575 st/y, Trim width 188 in, Uncoated woodfree/freesheet
No. 2, fourdrinier, total capacity 149,940 st/y, Trim width 190 in, Uncoated woodfree/freesheet
Energy Data:
Power boilers: 2
Steam turbines: 3 at 95.7 MW

ⓜKapStone Kraft Paper Corporation
Cowpens Mill
Ownership: 100% by KapStone Paper and Packaging Corp
139 Price Farm Rd
Cowpens, SC 29330
USA
Phone: (1) 864-463-9090, 864-463-1722
Fax: (1) 864-463-9585
Email: information@kapstonepaper.com
Web Address: www.kapstonepaper.com
Personnel:
VP. Mill. Oper.: Jeff Volker
Phone: (1) 864-463-9090
Fax: (1) 864-463-9585
Email: jeff.volker@kapstonepaper.com
Tech. Serv. Mgr.: Michael Mclean
Phone: (1) 864-463-9090
Fax: (1) 864-463-9585
Email: michael.mclean@kapstonepaper.com
Prod. Mgr.: Bobby O'Neal
Phone: (1) 864-463-9090
Fax: (1) 864-463-9585
Email: bobby.oneal@kapstonepaper.com
Maint. Mgr.: Scott Bolf
Phone: (1) 864-463-9090
Fax: (1) 864-463-9585
Email: scott.bolf@kapstonepaper.com
Plant Eng.: Tony Foti
Phone: (1) 864-463-9090
Fax: (1) 864-463-9585
Email: tony.foti@kapstonepaper.com
Environ. & Qlty. Mgr.: Matt Gasperetti
Phone: (1) 864-463-9090
Fax: (1) 864-463-9585
Office Mgr.: Angela Neal
Phone: (1) 864-463-9090
Fax: (1) 864-463-9585
Email: angela.neal@kapstonepaper.com
Total Employees at this Location: 108
Type of Operation: Paperboard mill
Pulp Grades and Capacities:
Total pulp capacity: 246,660 st/y
Recycled Pulping: 246,660 st/y
Pulp Mill Data:
Recycled Fiber Treatment Lines:
Pulpers: 1 at 261,243
Paper/Paperboard Grades and Capacities:
Total paper and paperboard capacity: 239,904 st/y
Linerboard: 139,944 st/y
Corrugating medium/fluting: 99,960 st/y
Paper and Paperboard Mill Data:
Stock Preparation:
Pulpers: 2
Refiners: 5
Paper Machines: 1
No. 1, top former, total capacity 239,904 st/y, Trim width 165 in, Linerboard, Corrugating medium/fluting
Energy Data:
Power boilers: 2
Electrical demand for mill: 277 MWh/D

ⓜKapStone Paper Charleston Kraft LLC
North Charleston Mill
Ownership: 100% by KapStone Paper and Packaging Corp
5600 Virginia Ave
North Charleston, SC 29406
USA
Mailing Address: PO Box 118005, Charleston, SC 29423-8005, USA
Phone: (1) 843-745-3000
Fax: (1) 843-745-3067
Web Address: www.kapstonepaper.com
Personnel:
VP. & Gen. Mgr.: Bruce Hoffman
Phone: (1) 843-745-3000
Fax: (1) 843-745-3067
Email: bruce.hoffman@kapstonepaper.com
Contr.: Aubrey M. Mallett
Phone: (1) 843-745-3000
Fax: (1) 843-745-3067
Email: aubrey.mallett@kapstonepaper.com
Dir., HR: Debbie Lightfoot
Phone: (1) 843-745-3000
Fax: (1) 843-745-3067
Email: debbie.lightfoot@kapstonepaper.com
Dir. Mktg.: John Benson
Phone: (1) 843-745-3000
Fax: (1) 843-745-3067
Email: john.benson@kapstonepaper.com
Fiber & Utilities Supt.: Wesley Kosin
Phone: (1) 843-745-3000
Fax: (1) 843-745-3067
Email: wesley.kosin@kapstonepaper.com
Environ., Health & Safety (EHS) Mgr.: Duane Mummert
Phone: (1) 843-745-3000
Fax: (1) 843-745-3067
Email: duane.mummert@kapstonepaper.com
Total Employees at this Location: 780
Type of Operation: Paper mill, Paperboard mill
Pulp Grades and Capacities:
Total pulp capacity: 917,674 st/y
Chemical Pulp: 917,674 st/y
Pulp Mill Data:
Chemical Pulping Systems:
Batch digesters: 15
Continuous digesters: 1
Chemical Recovery Equipment:
Evaporator lines: 4
Recovery boilers: 2
Pulp Dryers:
Fourdriniers 1
Paper/Paperboard Grades and Capacities:
Total paper and paperboard capacity: 878,187 st/y
Packaging papers: 246,330 st/y
Linerboard: 503,337 st/y
Corrugating medium/fluting: 8,925 st/y
Boxboard/cartonboard: 119,595 st/y
Paper and Paperboard Mill Data:
Stock Preparation:
Pulpers: 3
Refiners: 10
Paper Machines: 3
No. 1, total capacity 319,515 st/y, Trim width 225 in, Linerboard, Boxboard/cartonboard
No. 2, fourdrinier, total capacity 255,255 st/y, Trim width 225 in, Packaging papers, Corrugating medium/fluting
No. 3, fourdrinier, total capacity 303,417 st/y, Trim width 246 in, Linerboard
Finishing Equipment:
Rewinders: 1
Energy Data:
Power boilers: 4
Steam turbines: 1 at 99 MW
Electrical demand for mill: 2,165 MWh/D

ⓜKimberly-Clark Corp.
Beech Island Mill
246 Old Jackson Hwy
Beech Island, SC 29842-4542
USA
Phone: (1) 803-827-1100
Fax: (1) 803-827-6022
Web Address: www.kimberly-clark.com

South Carolina

Personnel:
Mill Mgr.: John H. Pownall
Phone: (1) 803-827-1100
Fax: (1) 803-827-6022
Email: john.pownall@kcc.com
Eng. Snr. Mgr.: Kevin Sartain
Phone: (1) 803-827-1100
Fax: (1) 803-827-6022
Email: ksartain@kcc.com
Oper. Mgr.: Cory Vanness
Phone: (1) 803-827-6165
Fax: (1) 803-827-6022
Email: cory.vanness@kcc.com
Environ. Mgr.: Matt Campanaro
Phone: (1) 803-827-1100
Fax: (1) 803-827-6022
Email: matthew.campanaro@kcc.com
Mech. Eng.: Josh Berezansky
Phone: (1) 803-827-1100
Fax: (1) 803-827-6022
Email: joshua.berezansky@kcc.com
Total Employees at this Location: 250
Type of Operation: Paper mill
Paper/Paperboard Grades and Capacities:
Total paper and paperboard capacity: 264,537 st/y
Tissue: 264,537 st/y
Paper and Paperboard Mill Data:
Stock Preparation:
Pulpers: 3
Refiners: 3
Paper Machines: 4
No. 1, crescent former, total capacity 55,335 st/y, Trim width 204 in, Tissue
No. 2, crescent former, total capacity 60,690 st/y, Trim width 204 in, Tissue
No. 3, TAD, total capacity 73,542 st/y, Trim width 204 in, Tissue
No. 4, TAD, total capacity 74,970 st/y, Trim width 204 in, Tissue
Energy Data:
Power boilers: 2
Electrical demand for mill: 873 MWh/D

Ⓜ Resolute FP US Inc.
Catawba Mill
Ownership: 100% by Resolute Forest Products Canada Inc.
5300 Cureton Ferry Rd
Catawba, SC 29704
USA
Mailing Address: PO Box 7, Catawba, SC 29704-0007, USA
Phone: (1) 803-981-8000
Fax: (1) 803-981-8181
Email: info@resolutefp.com
Web Address: www.resolutefp.com
Personnel:
Gen. Mgr.: Patrick Moore
Phone: (1) 803-981-8000
Fax: (1) 803-981-8181
Email: patrick.moore@resolutefp.com
Oper. Mgr. (From 2014): Mark Swenson
Phone: (1) 803-981-8625
Fax: (1) 803-981-8181
Email: mark.swenson@resolutefp.com
Eng. Mgr.: Roger Nussman
Phone: (1) 803-981-8000
Fax: (1) 803-981-8181
Email: roger.nussman@resolutefp.com
Environ. Mgr.: Dale Herendeen
Phone: (1) 803-981-8000
Fax: (1) 803-981-8181
Email: dale.herendeen@resolutefp.com
Maint. Supt. (From May 2014): Mike Allen
Phone: (1) 803-981-8000
Fax: (1) 803-981-8181
Email: mike.allen@resolutefp.com
Assist. Maint. Superint. Power & Woodyard: Bobby Polk
Phone: (1) 803-981-8227
Fax: (1) 803-981-8539
Email: bobby.polk@resolutefp.com
Total Employees at this Location: 675
Type of Operation: Pulp mill, Paper mill
Pulp Grades and Capacities:
Total pulp capacity: 636,036 st/y
Pulp available for market: 236,111 st/y
Chemical Pulp: 437,206 st/y
Mechanical Pulp: 198,830 st/y
Pulp Mill Data:
Chemical Pulping Systems:
Continuous digesters: 1
Mechanical Pulping Systems:
TMP systems: 2
Bleach Plant Lines:
SW, Type: Kraft, Sequence: O_2 DEopDD, Capacity 529,100.5 admt/y
TMP-1, Sequence: P, Capacity 76,609.3 admt/y
TMP-2, Sequence: H, Capacity 130,000 admt/y
Chemical Recovery Equipment:
Evaporator lines: 3
Recovery boilers: 2
Lime Kiln
Pulp Dryers:
Flakt dryer 1
Paper/Paperboard Grades and Capacities:
Total paper and paperboard capacity: 583,194 st/y
Coated mechanical/groundwood: 583,194 st/y
Paper and Paperboard Mill Data:
Paper Machines: 2
No. 2, (Former Type model: Twin-wire - Bel Bond HC), twin-wire, total capacity 226,273 st/y, Trim width 296 in, Coated mechanical/groundwood
No. 3, Bel-Baie III, total capacity 356,921 st/y, Trim width 352 in, Coated mechanical/groundwood
Coating Machines: 3
No. 1, total capacity 149,912 st/y., off machine
No. 2, total capacity 197,751 st/y., off machine
No. 3, total capacity 348,325 st/y., on machine
Finishing Equipment:
Calenders
Supercalenders: 4
Energy Data:
Power boilers: 2
Steam turbines: 2 at 50 MW
Electrical demand for mill: 3,083 MWh/D

Ⓜ RockTenn Co.
Florence Mill
2202 Paper Mill Road
Florence, SC 29506
USA
Mailing Address: PO Box 100544, Florence, SC 29501-0544, USA
Phone: (1) 843-667-6252, 843-662-0313
Fax: (1) 843-673-0310
Web Address: www.rocktenn.com
Personnel:
Oper. Mgr.: Steve Davidson
Phone: (1) 843-667-6252
Fax: (1) 843-673-0310
Email: stdavidson@rocktenn.com
Maint. Mgr.: Tom Hardy
Phone: (1) 843-667-6252
Fax: (1) 843-673-0310
Email: tohardy@rocktenn.com
Supt PM2: Craig Faling
Phone: (1) 843-667-6252
Fax: (1) 843-673-0310
Email: cfaling@rocktenn.com
Region Mgr., Wood Procurement: Dan Cox
Phone: (1) 843-667-6252
Fax: (1) 843-673-0310
Email: dmcox@rocktenn.com
Total Employees at this Location: 333
Type of Operation: Paperboard mill
Pulp Grades and Capacities:
Total pulp capacity: 718,497 st/y
Chemical Pulp: 584,870 st/y
Recycled Pulping: 133,628 st/y
Pulp Mill Data:
Chemical Pulping Systems:
Batch digesters: 9
Chemical Recovery Equipment:
Evaporator lines: 1
Recovery boilers: 1
Lime Kiln
Recycled Fiber Treatment Lines:
Pulpers: 1 at 139,231
Paper/Paperboard Grades and Capacities:
Total paper and paperboard capacity: 682,941 st/y
Linerboard: 682,941 st/y
Paper and Paperboard Mill Data:
Stock Preparation:
Pulpers: 3
Refiners: 4
Paper Machines: 3
No. 1, fourdrinier, total capacity 261,681 st/y, Trim width 166 in, Linerboard
No. 2, fourdrinier, total capacity 228,123 st/y, Trim width 166 in, Linerboard
No. 3, fourdrinier, total capacity 193,137 st/y, Trim width 168 in, Linerboard
Energy Data:
Power boilers: 3
Steam turbines: 3 at 96 MW
Electrical demand for mill: 1,417 MWh/D

Ⓗ Ⓜ Sonoco Products Co.
Hartsville Mill
Ownership: Public
1 N Second St
Hartsville, SC 29550
USA
Mailing Address: PO Box 160, Hartsville, SC 29551-0160, USA
Phone: (1) 843-339-6047/383-7000
Fax: (1) 843-383-3394/7978
Web Address: www.sonoco.com
Personnel:
Exec. Chmn.: Harris E. DeLoach Jr.
Phone: (1) 843-339-6047
Fax: (1) 843-383-3394
Email: harris.deloach@sonoco.com
Pres. & CEO: M. Jack Sanders
Phone: (1) 843-339-6047
Fax: (1) 843-383-3394
Email: jack.sanders@sonoco.com
CFO: Barry L Saunders
Phone: (1) 843-339-6047
Fax: (1) 843-383-3394
Snr. VP., Global Consumer Packaging and Services: Rob C. Tiede
Phone: (1) 843-339-6047
Fax: (1) 843-383-3394
Snr. VP., Global Industrial Products and Protective Solutions: John M. Colyer
Phone: (1) 843-339-6047/383-7000
Fax: (1) 843-383-3394/7978
VP., Protective Solutions: Vicki B. Arthur
Phone: (1) 843-339-6047
Fax: (1) 843-383-3394
Email: vicki.arthur@sonoco.com
VP., HR: Allan H. McLeland
Phone: (1) 843-339-6047
Fax: (1) 843-383-3394
Email: allan.mcleland@sonoco.com
VP., Primary Materials Group NA: Marty F. Pignone
Phone: (1) 843-339-6047
Fax: (1) 843-383-3394
Email: marty.pignone@sonoco.com
VP., Investor Rel. & Corp. Affairs: Roger P. Schrum
Phone: (1) 843-339-6047
Fax: (1) 843-383-3394
Email: roger.schrum@sonoco.com
VP., CIO: Bernard W. Campbell
Phone: (1) 843-339-6047
Fax: (1) 843-383-3394
Email: bernard.campbell@sonoco.com
VP., Rigid Paper & Plastics, Europe: Sean Cairns

Phone: (1) 843-339-6047
Fax: (1) 843-383-3394
Email: sean.cairns@sonoco.com
VP, Mktg. & Innovation: Marcy Thompson
Phone: (1) 843-339-6047
Fax: (1) 843-383-3394
Gen. Mgr. Hartsville Mill: Ronald Byrd
Phone: (1) 843-339-6047
Fax: (1) 843-383-3394
Email: ronald.byrd@sonoco.com
Total Employees of Company: 19,900
Total Employees at this Location: 360
Type of Operation: Paperboard mill
Mill Locations:
PT Papertech Indonesia, Subang Mill, Jln. Raya Cipeundeuy Km 1, Desa Cipeundeuy, 41272 Subang, Indonesia, Capacity: 66,138 st/y, (Paper mill)
Phone: (62) 260 710645
Fax: (62) 260 710644
Email: pti@id.papertech.com
PT Papertech Indonesia, Blabak Mill, Jalan Sanggrahan Gatak No.23, 56511 Blabak, Mungkid, Indonesia, Capacity: 28,660 st/y, (Paperboard mill)
Papertech S.L., Tudela Mill, Aptdo. 18 / Carr. de Pamplona, 2, E-31500 Tudela, Spain, Capacity: 60,626 st/y, (Paperboard mill)
Phone: (34) 948 823400
Fax: (34) 948 827756
Email: comercial@papertech.com
PT Papertech Indonesia, Unit II, Kabupaten Magelang, Jl. Sanggrahan Gatak No. 23, Desa Mungkid, 56511 Kecamatan Mungkid, Kabupaten Magelang, Indonesia, Capacity: 19,290 st/y, (Paperboard mill)
Phone: (62) 293 327231
Fax: (62) 293 327230
Email: pti@id.papertech.com
Sonoco Alcore-Demolli srl, Ciriè Mill, Loc. Olivetti 47, Frazione Devesi, IT-10073 Ciriè, (TO), Italy, Capacity: 71,649 st/y, (Paper mill)
Phone: (39) 011 9225311
Fax: (39) 011 9207772
Email: cvl@demolli.it
Sonoco-Alcore Oy, Karhula Board Mill, Karhulantie 160, FI-48601 Karhula, Finland, Capacity: 88,183 st/y, (Paperboard mill)
Phone: (358) 1023 42300
Fax: (358) 5 266 887
Email: (firstname.lastname@sonoco-alcore.net)
Sonoco Board Mills Ltd., Stainland Mill, Stainland, Holywell Green, Halifax HX4 9PY, United Kingdom, Capacity: 71,649 st/y, (Paperboard mill)
Phone: (44) 1422 374 741
Fax: (44) 1422 311 725 / 1422 371 495
Sonoco de Colombia Ltda, Cali Mill, Carrera 7 No. 34-120, Cali, Colombia, Capacity: 36,991 st/y, (Paperboard mill)
Phone: (57) 2 681 8600
Fax: (57) 2 438 4736
Sonoco do Brasil Ltda., Londrina Mill, Rua Noitibó, 157, Vila Yara, 86027-000 Londrina, PR, Brazil, Capacity: 45,648 st/y, (Paper mill, Paperboard mill)
Phone: (55) 43 3377 7761
Fax: (55) 43 3377 7700
Email: antonio.silva@sonoco.com.br
Sonoco Hellas, Stavrohori Mill, 10.5 km Kilkis Doirani National Road, GR-61100 Stavrohori, Kilkis, Greece, Capacity: 27,557 st/y, (Paper mill, Paperboard mill)
Phone: (30) 23 41051558
Fax: (30) 23 41051267
Sonoco Ltd., Brantford Mill, 33 Park Av E, Brantford, ON, Canada N3T 5T5, Capacity: 57,120 st/y, (Paperboard mill)
Phone: (1) 519-752-6591
Fax: (1) 519-752-8399
Email: info@sonoco.com
Sonoco Ltd., Trent Valley Mill, Hwy 33 North of Hwy 401, Glen Miller, ON, Canada K8V 5P6, Capacity: 124,950 st/y, (Paperboard mill)
Phone: (1) 613-392-1231
Fax: (1) 613-392-2485
Email: info@sonoco.com
Sonoco Products Co., City of Industry Mill, 166 N Baldwin Park Blvd, City of Industry, CA 91746, USA, Capacity: 32,844 st/y, (Paperboard mill)
Phone: (1) 626-369-6927
Fax: (1) 626-369-1688
Sonoco Products Co., Holyoke Mill, 200 S Water St, Holyoke, MA 01040, USA, Capacity: 66,045 st/y, (Paperboard mill)
Phone: (1) 413-536-4546
Fax: (1) 413-536-0903
Sonoco Products Co., Hutchinson Mill, 100 N Halstead, Hutchinson, KS 67501, USA, Capacity: 99,960 st/y, (Paperboard mill)
Phone: (1) 620-662-2331
Fax: (1) 620-662-4276
Sonoco Products Co., Menasha Mill, 69 Washington St, Menasha, WI 54952, USA, Capacity: 169,932 st/y, (Paperboard mill)
Phone: (1) 920-725-7115
Fax: (1) 920-725-4869
Sonoco Products Co., Newport Mill, 766 Industrial Rd, Newport, TN 37821, USA, Capacity: 121,380 st/y, (Paperboard mill)
Phone: (1) 423-623-8611
Fax: (1) 423-613-1291
Sonoco Products Co., Richmond Mill, 1850 Commerce Rd, Richmond, VA 23224, USA, Capacity: 99,960 st/y, (Paperboard mill)
Phone: (1) 804-233-5411
Fax: (1) 804-232-7061
Sonoco Products Co., Sumner Mill, Steele Av, Sumner, WA 98390, USA, Capacity: 37,485 st/y, (Paperboard mill)
Phone: (1) 253-863-6366
Fax: (1) 253-863-0223
Sonoco de México, S.A. de C.V., Santa Clara Mill, Calle Hidalgo No. 175, 55540 Santa Clara Ecatepec, Mexico, Capacity: 66,111 st/y, (Paperboard mill)
Phone: (52) 55 9171 0100/101
Fax: (52) 55 9171 0114/0110/0111
Email: ofi.ventas@sonoco.com
Sonoco Paper France SAS, Schweighouse Mill, 5 rue de la Gare-BP 10318, F-67507 Schweighouse sur Moder, France, Capacity: 94,797 st/y, (Pulp mill, Paper mill, Paperboard mill)
Phone: (33) 3 88 72 64 00/0910
Fax: (33) 3 88 72 64 34
U.S. Paper Mills Corp., De Pere Mill, 800 Fort Howard Ave, De Pere, WI 54115, USA, Capacity: 39,984 st/y, (Paperboard mill)
Phone: (1) 920-336-4229
Fax: (1) 920-336-6104
Pulp Grades and Capacities:
Total pulp capacity: 442,813 st/y
Chemical Pulp: 109,031 st/y
Recycled Pulping: 333,782 st/y
Pulp Mill Data:
Chemical Pulping Systems:
Continuous digesters: 1
Chemical Recovery Equipment:
Evaporator lines: 1
Recovery boilers: 1
Recycled Fiber Treatment Lines:
Pulpers: 1 at 355,379
Paper/Paperboard Grades and Capacities:
Total paper and paperboard capacity: 428,757 st/y
Corrugating medium/fluting: 193,137 st/y
Boxboard/cartonboard: 235,620 st/y
Paper and Paperboard Mill Data:
Stock Preparation:
Pulpers: 12
Refiners: 21
Paper Machines: 7
No. 1, cylinder (6), total capacity 23,205 st/y, Trim width 95 in, Boxboard/cartonboard
No. 3, cylinder (6), total capacity 26,775 st/y, Trim width 95 in, Boxboard/cartonboard
No. 4, cylinder (8), total capacity 85,680 st/y, Trim width 110 in, Boxboard/cartonboard
No. 6, cylinder (7), total capacity 39,270 st/y, Trim width 80 in, Boxboard/cartonboard
No. 7, cylinder (6), total capacity 35,700 st/y, Trim width 79 in, Boxboard/cartonboard
No. 9, cylinder (4), total capacity 24,990 st/y, Trim width 120 in, Boxboard/cartonboard
No. 10, fourdrinier, total capacity 193,137 st/y, Trim width 176 in, Corrugating medium/fluting
Finishing Equipment:
Calenders: 12
Rewinders: 8
Energy Data:
Power boilers: 7
Steam turbines: 2 at 24 MW
Electrical demand for mill: 641 MWh/D

TENNESSEE

ⓜCascades Tissue Group
Memphis Mill
Ownership: 100% by Cascades Inc.
1535 Thomas St
Memphis, TN 38107
USA
Phone: (1) 901-523-9118
Fax: (1) 901-526-1756
Web Address: www.afh.cascades.com
Personnel:
Mill Mgr. (From Jan. 1, 2014): Clyde Smith
Email: clyde_smith@cascades.com
Paper Machine Supervisor: Jason McKay
Phone: (1) 901-523-9118
Fax: (1) 901-526-1756
Email: jason_mckay@cascades.com
Sls. Mgr.: Rookie Murphy
Phone: (1) 901-523-9118
Fax: (1) 901-526-1756
Email: rookie_murphy@cascades.com
Total Employees at this Location: 55
Type of Operation: Paper mill
Pulp Grades and Capacities:
Total pulp capacity: 49,408 st/y
Recycled Pulping: 49,408 st/y
Pulp Mill Data:
Pulp Lines: 1
Bleach Plant Lines:
Recycled Pulping System, Type: Deinked
Recycled Fiber Treatment Lines:
Flotation deinking lines: 1 at 47,950
Paper/Paperboard Grades and Capacities:
Total paper and paperboard capacity: 46,053 st/y
Tissue: 46,053 st/y
Paper and Paperboard Mill Data:
Stock Preparation:
Refiners: 1
Paper Machines: 1
No. 1, crescent former, Yankee dryer, total capacity 46,053 st/y, Trim width 200 in, Tissue
Finishing Equipment:
Rewinders: 2
Energy Data:
Power boilers: 1
Electrical demand for mill: 139 MWh/D

ⓜDomtar Corporation
Kingsport Mill
100 Clinchfield St
Kingsport, TN 37660
USA
Phone: (1) 423-247-7111
Fax: (1) 423-392-2719
Web Address: www.domtar.com
Personnel:
VP, Oper. Performance: Charlie Floyd
Phone: (1) 423-392-2700
Fax: (1) 423-392-2719
Email: charlie.floyd@domtar.com

Tennessee

Mill Mgr.: Bill Macpherson
Phone: (1) 423-392-3742
Fax: (1) 423-247-2649
Email: bill.macpherson@domtar.com
Fiberline Mgr.: Jeff Chamberlin
Phone: (1) 423-392-2729
Fax: (1) 423-392-2790
Email: jeff.chamberlin@domtar.com
Purch. Mgr.: Sidney Hammonds
Phone: (1) 423-392-2784
Fax: (1) 423-392-2719
Email: sidney.hammonds@domtar.com
HR Mgr.: Thomas (Tom) K Segelhorst
Phone: (1) 423-392-2742
Fax: (1) 423-392-2824
Email: tom.segelhorst@domtar.com
Total Employees at this Location: 325
Type of Operation: Pulp mill, Paper mill
Pulp Grades and Capacities:
Total pulp capacity: 295,049 st/y
Chemical Pulp: 295,049 st/y
Pulp Mill Data:
Chemical Pulping Systems:
Batch digesters: 6
Continuous digesters: 1
Pulp Lines: 1
Bleach Plant Systems: 1
Chemical Pulping System, Type: Andritz 3 stage - Hardwood, Sequence: O_2 DEpD
Chemical Recovery Equipment:
Evaporator lines: 1
Recovery boilers: 1
Lime Kiln
Paper/Paperboard Grades and Capacities:
Total paper and paperboard capacity: 414,029 st/y
Uncoated woodfree/freesheet: 414,029 st/y
Paper and Paperboard Mill Data:
Stock Preparation:
Pulpers:
Paper Machines: 1
K1, SpeedFormer MB, total capacity 414,029 st/y, Trim width 346 in, Uncoated woodfree/freesheet
Finishing Equipment:
Rewinders: 1
Energy Data:
Power boilers: 2
Steam turbines: 1 at 50 MW

ⓘEvergreen Packaging Inc.
Ownership: 100% by Rank Group, New Zealand
5350 Poplar Avenue, Suite 600
Memphis, TN 38119
USA
Phone: (1) 319-399-3200
Fax: (1) 319-399-3543
Web Address: www.evergreenpackaging.com
Personnel:
Chmn.: Thomas J. Degnan
Phone: (1) 319-399-3200
Fax: (1) 319-399-3543
Pres. & CEO: Malcolm Bundey
Phone: (1) 319-399-3200
Fax: (1) 319-399-3543
Mill Locations:
Evergreen Packaging Inc., Canton Mill, 175 Main St, Canton, NC 28716, USA, Capacity: 583,695 st/y, (Pulp mill, Paper mill, Paperboard mill)
Phone: (1) 828-646-2000
Fax: (1) 828-646-6732
Evergreen Packaging Inc., Pine Bluff Mill, 5201 Fairfield Rd, Pine Bluff, AR 71601, USA, Capacity: 631,394 st/y, (Paper mill, Paperboard mill)
Phone: (1) 870-541-5600
Fax: (1) 870-541-5788
Email: evergreen.packaging@everpack.com

ⓘHood Container Corporation
Ownership: Private
2877 Septer Road
Waverly, TN 37185
USA
Phone: (1) 931-535-2161
Fax: (1) 931-535-2160
Personnel:
Pres. & COO (Eff. March 13, 2014): Charles E. Hodges
Mill Mgr.: Wayne Morgan
Phone: (1) 931-535-2161
Fax: (1) 931-535-2160
Email: wayne.morgan@hoodcontainer.com
HR. Mgr.: Angie Hedge
Phone: (1) 931-535-2161
Fax: (1) 931-535-2160
Email: angie.hedge@hoodcontainer.com
Sls. & Mktg. Mgr.: Ron Zimbelman
Phone: (1) 931-535-2161
Fax: (1) 931-535-2160
Email: ron.zimbelman@hoodcontainer.com
Contr.: Tracy Smith
Phone: (1) 931-535-2161
Fax: (1) 931-535-2160
Email: tracy.smith@hoodcontainer.com
Mill Locations:
Hood Container Corporation, New Johnsonville Mill, 2877 Septer Road, Waverly, TN 37185, USA, Capacity: 365,925 st/y, (Paperboard mill)
Phone: (1) 931-535-2161
Fax: (1) 931-535-2160

ⓂHood Container Corporation
New Johnsonville Mill
Previously International Paper Co.
2877 Septer Road
Waverly, TN 37185
USA
Mailing Address: PO Box 299, New Johnsonville, TN 37134, USA
Phone: (1) 931-535-2161
Fax: (1) 931-535-2160
Personnel:
Mill Mgr.: Wayne Morgan
Phone: (1) 931-535-2161
Fax: (1) 931-535-2160
Email: wayne.morgan@hoodcontainer.com
HR. Mgr.: Angie Hedge
Phone: (1) 931-535-2161
Fax: (1) 931-535-2160
Email: angie.hedge@hoodcontainer.com
Sls. & Mktg. Mgr.: Ron Zimbelman
Phone: (1) 931-535-2161
Fax: (1) 931-535-2160
Email: ron.zimbelman@hoodcontainer.com
Contr.: Tracy Smith
Phone: (1) 931-535-2161
Fax: (1) 931-535-2160
Email: tracy.smith@hoodcontainer.com
Total Employees at this Location: 190
Type of Operation: Paperboard mill
Pulp Grades and Capacities:
Total pulp capacity: 380,007 st/y
Chemical Pulp: 228,377 st/y
Recycled Pulping: 151,630 st/y
Pulp Mill Data:
Chemical Pulping Systems:
Continuous digesters: 1
Chemical Recovery Equipment:
Evaporator lines: 4
Recycled Fiber Treatment Lines:
Pulpers: 1 at 164,572
Paper/Paperboard Grades and Capacities:
Total paper and paperboard capacity: 365,925 st/y
Corrugating medium/fluting: 365,925 st/y
Paper and Paperboard Mill Data:
Stock Preparation:
Pulpers: 1
Paper Machines: 1
No. 1, fourdrinier, total capacity 365,925 st/y, Trim width 245 in, Corrugating medium/fluting
Energy Data:
Power boilers: 3
Electrical demand for mill: 567 MWh/D

ⓘInternational Paper Co.
Ownership: Public, Norges Bank
6400 Poplar Ave
Memphis, TN 38197
USA
Phone: (1) 901-419-9000
Fax: (1) 901-763-6140
Email: internationalpaper.comm@ipaper.com, (firstname.lastname@ipaper.com)
Web Address: www.internationalpaper.com
Personnel:
Chmn. & CEO (CEO until October 31 and Chmn. until December 31, 2014.): John V. Faraci
Phone: (1) 901-419-9000
Fax: (1) 901-763-6140
Email: john.faraci@ipaper.com
Pres. & COO (CEO effective November 1, 2014 and Chmn. of the board effective January 1, 2015.): Mark S. Sutton
Phone: (1) 901-419-9000
Fax: (1) 901-763-6140
Email: mark.sutton@ipaper.com
Snr. VP, Corp. Devlpt.: C. Cato Ealy
Phone: (1) 901-419-9000
Fax: (1) 901-763-6140
Email: c.ealy@ipaper.com
Snr. VP, & CFO: Carol L. Roberts
Phone: (1) 901-419-9000
Fax: (1) 901-763-6140
Email: carol.roberts@ipaper.com
Snr. VP, industrial packaging (effective November 1, 2014): Timothy S. Nicholls
Phone: (1) 901-419-9000
Fax: (1) 901-763-6140
Email: tim.nicholls@ipaper.com
Snr. VP, : HR, Comm. and global government relations, responsibilities for supply chain and IP India: Thomas G. Kadien
Phone: (1) 901-419-9000
Fax: (1) 901-763-6140
Email: thomas.kadien@ipaper.com
Snr. VP, : Container the Americas: William Hoel
Phone: (1) 901-419-9000
Fax: (1) 901-763-6140
Email: william.hoel@ipaper.com
Snr. VP, N.A. papers, pulp and consumer packaging (effective November 1, 2014): W Michael Amick Jr.
Phone: (1) 901-419-9000
Fax: (1) 901-763-6140
VP Finan. & Contr.: Terri Herrington
Phone: (1) 901-419-9000
Fax: (1) 901-763-6140
Email: terri.herrington@ipaper.com
VP & Gen. Mgr. Containerboard & Recycling: Thomas A. Cleves
Phone: (1) 901-419-9000
Fax: (1) 901-763-6140
Email: thomas.cleves@ipaper.com
Dir. Investment Strategy, Containerboard (from Nov. 1, 2013): Todd Crutcher
Phone: (1) 901-419-9000
Fax: (1) 901-763-6140
Email: todd.crutcher@ipaper.com
Total Employees of Company: 70,000
Total Employees at this Location: 67
Mill Locations:
Copikas Kagit ve Oluklu Mukavva Kutu A.S., Olmuksa Copikas Mill, Ankara Yolu 4 km, Corum, Turkey, Capacity: 33,069 st/y, (Paperboard mill)
Phone: (90) 364 2350050
Fax: (90) 364 2350067
Email: sales.corum@ipaper.com
Groupe CMCP - La Compagnie Marocaine des Cartons et Papiers, Kenitra Mill, Quartier Industriel, Boite Postale 94, MA 14000 Kenitra, Morocco, Capacity: 132,275 st/y, (Paperboard mill)
Phone: (212) 537 399000
Fax: (212) 537 378557/8638
Email: contact@ipaper.com
International Paper & Sun Paper Cartonboard Co., Ltd., Yanzhou Mill (55% owned), 1# Youyi Road, Yanzhou

Tennessee

272100, China, Capacity: 1,488,095 st/y, (Paperboard mill)
Phone: (86) 537 389 8588
Fax: (86) 537 389 8502
International Paper APPM Ltd., Kadiam Mill (96.50% owned), Industrial Dev Area, Kadiyam Mandal, 533 126 Madhavarayudu Palem, East Godavari District, A.P., India, Capacity: 76,058 st/y, (Pulp mill, Paper mill, Paperboard mill)
Phone: (91) 883 2424651/52/53/54/55
Fax: (91) 883 2453538
Email: appmcp@andhapaper.com
International Paper APPM Ltd., Rajahmundry Mill (96.50% owned), Shriramnagar, 533 105 Rajahmundry, East Godavari, A.P., India, Capacity: 216,042 st/y, (Pulp mill, Paper mill)
Phone: (91) 883 2471831 to 37
Fax: (91) 883 2461764/2471383
Email: appmrjy@andhrapaper.com
International Paper Co., Bogalusa Mill, 401 Ave U, Bogalusa, LA 70429-1060, USA, Capacity: 830,025 st/y, (Pulp mill, Paper mill, Paperboard mill)
Phone: (1) 985-732-8000
Fax: (1) 985-732-8480
International Paper Co., Augusta Mill, 4278 Mike Padgett Hwy, Augusta, GA 30906, USA, Capacity: 526,575 st/y, (Paperboard mill)
Phone: (1) 706-798-5711
Fax: (1) 706-796-5599
Email: (firstname.lastname@ipaper.com)
International Paper Co., Red River Mill, Hwy 480, Campti, LA 71411, USA, Capacity: 979,965 st/y, (Pulp mill, Paperboard mill)
Phone: (1) 318-476-3392
Fax: (1) 318-476-2712
International Paper Co., Pensacola Mill, 375 Muscogee Rd, Cantonment, FL 32533, USA, Capacity: 535,500 st/y, (Pulp mill, Paperboard mill)
Phone: (1) 850-968-2121
Fax: (1) 850-968-4297
Email: (firstname.lastname@ipaper.com)
International Paper Co., Cedar Rapids Mill, 4600 C Street SW, Cedar Rapids, IA 52404, USA, Capacity: 989,961 st/y, (Paperboard mill)
Phone: (1) 319-365-2100
Fax: (1) 319-365-0436
International Paper Co., Courtland Mill, 16504 County Rd 150, Courtland, AL 35618, USA, (Pulp mill, Paper mill)
Phone: (1) 256-637-2741
Fax: (1) 256-637-5116
Email: (firstname.lastname@ipaper.com)
International Paper Co., Texarkana Mill, 9978 FM Rd. 3129, Domino, TX 75572, USA, Capacity: 674,730 st/y, (Paperboard mill)
Phone: (1) 903-796-7101
Fax: (1) 903-796-1960
Email: (firstname.lastname@ipaper.com)
International Paper Co., Eastover Mill, 4001 McCords Ferry Rd, Eastover, SC 29044, USA, Capacity: 729,904 st/y, (Pulp mill, Paper mill)
Phone: (1) 803-353-7700
Fax: (1) 803-353-7981
Email: (firstname.lastname@ipaper.com)
International Paper Co., Franklin Mill, 34040 Union Camp Dr, Franklin, VA 23851-0178, USA, (Pulp mill, Paper mill, Paperboard mill)
Phone: (1) 757-569-4641
Fax: (1) 757-569-4545
Email: (firstname.lastname@ipaper.com)
International Paper Co., Georgetown Mill, 700 S Kaminski, Georgetown, SC 29440, USA, Capacity: 319,515 st/y, (Pulp mill, Paper mill)
Phone: (1) 843-546-6111
Fax: (1) 843-546-6129
Email: (firstname.lastname@ipaper.com)
International Paper Co., Henderson Mill, 1500 Commonwealth Dr, Henderson, KY 42420, USA, Capacity: 219,912 st/y, (Paperboard mill)
Phone: (1) 270-831-6000
Fax: (1) 270-830-9750
International Paper Co., Mansfield Mill, 1202 Hwy 509,
Mansfield, LA 71052, USA, Capacity: 1,580,082 st/y, (Pulp mill, Paperboard mill)
Phone: (1) 318-872-5100
Fax: (1) 318-872-4779
Email: (firstname.lastname@ipaper.com)
International Paper Co., Pine Hill Mill, 7600 Hwy 10 West, Pine Hill, AL 36769, USA, Capacity: 870,009 st/y, (Paperboard mill)
Phone: (1) 334-963-4391
Fax: (1) 334-963-2763
International Paper Co., Prattville Mill, 100 Jensen Rd, Prattville, AL 36067, USA, Capacity: 1,119,909 st/y, (Paper mill, Paperboard mill)
Phone: (1) 334-361-5000
Fax: (1) 334-361-5845
Email: (firstname.lastname@ipaper.com)
International Paper Co., Vicksburg Mill, Hwy 3 North, Vicksburg, MS 39156, USA, Capacity: 565,131 st/y, (Pulp mill, Paperboard mill)
Phone: (1) 601-638-3665
Fax: (1) 601-631-8355
Email: (firstname.lastname@ipaper.com)
International Paper Co., Riegelwood Mill, 865 John L Riegel Rd, Riegelwood, NC 28456-0008, USA, Capacity: 424,830 st/y, (Pulp mill, Paperboard mill)
Phone: (1) 910-655-2211
Fax: (1) 910-655-6119
Email: (firstname.lastname@ipaper.com)
International Paper Co., Savannah Mill, 1201 West Lathrop Avenue, Savannah, GA 31415, USA, Capacity: 979,965 st/y, (Paper mill, Paperboard mill)
Phone: (1) 912-238-6000, 912-238-6789
Email: (firstname.lastname@ipaper.com)
International Paper Co., Riverdale Mill, 601 County Rd 78, Selma, AL 36701, USA, Capacity: 649,597 st/y, (Paper mill)
Phone: (1) 334-418-5349
Fax: (1) 334-418-5110
Email: (firstname.lastname@ipaper.com)
International Paper Co., Springfield Mill, 801 42nd St, Springfield, OR 97478-5781, USA, Capacity: 630,105 st/y, (Paper mill, Paperboard mill)
Phone: (1) 541-741-5700
Fax: (1) 541-741-5662
International Paper Co., Ticonderoga Mill, 568 Shore-Airport Road, Ticonderoga, NY 12883, USA, Capacity: 299,814 st/y, (Paper mill)
Phone: (1) 518-585-5300
Fax: (1) 518-585-5358
Email: (firstname.lastname@ipaper.com)
International Paper Co., Valliant Mill, 890 Weyerhaeuser Lane, Valliant, OK 74764, USA, Capacity: 1,349,817 st/y, (Paperboard mill)
Phone: (1) 580-933-7211
Fax: (1) 580-933-1567
International Paper - Kwidzyn Sp. z o.o., Kwidzyn Mill, Lotnicza 1, PL-82500 Kwidzyn, Poland, Capacity: 851,521 st/y, (Pulp mill, Paper mill, Paperboard mill)
Phone: (48) 55 2798000
Fax: (48) 55 2798451
International Paper do Brasil Ltda., Luiz Antônio Mill, Rodovia SP 255, Km. 41, 240, 14210-000 Luiz Antonio, SP, Brazil, Capacity: 407,685 st/y, (Pulp mill, Paper mill)
Phone: (55) 16 3986 9000
Fax: (55) 16 3986 1620
Email: sac@ipaperbr.com
International Paper Co., Maysville Mill, 1241 West 2nd Street, Maysville, KY 41056, USA, Capacity: 460,530 st/y, (Pulp mill, Paperboard mill, Paperboard mill)
Phone: (1) 606-564-2616/606-564-2617 (emergency # only)
Fax: (1) 606-564-2618
International Paper, Empaques Industriales de México S.A. de C.V., Xalapa Mill, Carretera Antigua Jalapa-Coatepec Km. 3.8 Predio La Yerbabuena, 91000 Xalapa, Mexico, Capacity: 26,759 st/y, (Paper mill, Paperboard mill)
Phone: (52) 228 818 6777
Fax: (52) 228 818 3533
International Paper do Brasil Ltda., Mogi Guaçu Mill, Rodovia, SP-340, Km 171, CP 10, 13840-970 Mogi
Guaçu, SP, Brazil, Capacity: 490,324 st/y, (Pulp mill, Paper mill)
Phone: (55) 19 3861 8593 / 8121
Fax: (55) 19 3861 8412 / 1098
Email: sac@ipaperbr.com
International Paper Co., Newport Mill, 2585 E 200 North, Cayuga, IN 47928-8153, USA, Capacity: 369,852 st/y, (Paperboard mill)
Phone: (1) 765-492-3341
Fax: (1) 765-492-4832
International Paper Co., Orange Mill, 1750 Inland Rd, Orange, TX 77632, USA, Capacity: 795,039 st/y, (Paperboard mill)
Phone: (1) 409-746-2441
Fax: (1) 409-746-7210
International Paper Co., Rome Mill, 238 Mays Bridge Rd., Rome, GA 30165, USA, Capacity: 870,009 st/y, (Paper mill, Paperboard mill)
Phone: (1) 706-232-0851
Fax: (1) 706-236-5443
International Paper SA, Saillat Mill, Usine de Saillat, BP 1 Saillat-sur-Vienne, F-87206 Saint-Junien, France, Capacity: 264,550 st/y, (Pulp mill, Paper mill)
Phone: (33) 5 55 43 48 00
Fax: (33) 5 55 43 48 65
Email: firstname.lastname@ipaper.com
ZAO International Paper, Svetogorsk Mill, ul. Zavodskaya 17, 188991 Svetogorsk, Russia, Capacity: 529,101 st/y, (Pulp mill, Paper mill, Paperboard mill)
Phone: (7) 813 7843504/5 688 4100
Fax: (7) 813 7844 061/5 688 4900
Email: skbf@mail.ru
International Paper do Brasil Ltda., Três Lagoas Mill, Rodovia MS 395 KM 21, 79601-970 Três Lagoas, MT, Brazil, Capacity: 225,880 st/y, (Paper mill)
Phone: (55) 67 2105 6161
Fax: (55) 67 2105 6240
Email: sac@ipaperbr.com
Olmuksa International Paper-Sabanci Ambalaj Sanayi ve Ticaret A.S., Olmuksa Edirne Mill (87.50% owned), Sazlidere Mevkii, Pk. 110 Tayakadin Köyü, TR-22160 Edirne, Turkey, Capacity: 77,160 st/y, (Pulp mill, Paper mill)
Phone: (90) 284 268 64 24
Fax: (90) 284 268 62 42
Email: contacttr@ipaper.com
Orsa International Paper Embalagens S.A, Nova Campina Mill, Rodovia Luiz José Sguário, km 31 - Taquari Guassú, 18400-000 Nova Campina, SP, Brazil, Capacity: 201,875 st/y, (Pulp mill, Paperboard mill)
Phone: (55) 15 3521 9600
Fax: (55) 15 3521 9718
Orsa International Paper Embalagens S.A, Franco da Rocha Mill, Av. Pacaembu 495 - Bairro dos Abreus, 07810 000 Franco da Rocha, SP, Brazil, Capacity: 55,093 st/y, (Paperboard mill)
Phone: (55) 11 4811 8000
Email: comercial@orsaip.com.br
Orsa International Paper Embalagens S.A, Paulínia Mill, Rua Henedina R.O. Bresler, 150 - Bela Vista, 13140-000 Paulínia, SP, Brazil, Capacity: 145,602 st/y, (Pulp mill, Paper mill, Paperboard mill)
Phone: (55) 19 3844 2600
Fax: (55) 19 3874 2279

ⓜKimberly-Clark Corp.
Loudon Mill
5600 Kimberly Way
Loudon, TN 37774
USA
Phone: (1) 865-988-7000
Fax: (1) 865-988-7012
Web Address: www.kimberly-clark.com

Personnel:
Oper. Team Ldr.: Kimberly Samry
Phone: (1) 865-988-7000
Fax: (1) 865-988-7012
Email: ksamry@kcc.com
Manuf. Mgr.: Jeff Chelette
Phone: (1) 865-988-7000
Fax: (1) 865-988-7012

Tennessee

Email: jeff.chelette@kcc.com
Total Employees at this Location: 210
Type of Operation: Paper mill
Pulp Grades and Capacities:
  Total pulp capacity: 83,373 st/y
  Recycled Pulping: 83,373 st/y
Pulp Mill Data:
  Bleach Plant Lines:
  Deinked Pulp Line
  Recycled Fiber Treatment Lines:
  Flotation deinking lines
Paper/Paperboard Grades and Capacities:
  Total paper and paperboard capacity: 142,086 st/y
  Tissue: 142,086 st/y
Paper and Paperboard Mill Data:
  Stock Preparation:
  Pulpers:
Paper Machines: 4
No. 1, crescent former, total capacity 26,418 st/y, Trim width 262 in, Tissue
No. 2, crescent former, total capacity 27,489 st/y, Trim width 124 in, Tissue
No. 3, TAD, total capacity 29,274 st/y, Trim width 124 in, Tissue
No. 4, TAD, total capacity 58,905 st/y, Trim width 124 in, Tissue
Energy Data:
Power boilers: 1
Electrical demand for mill: 506 MWh/D

ⓜK.T.G. (USA) L.P.
Memphis Mill
Ownership: Kruger Inc.
400 Mahannah Ave.
Memphis, TN 38107-1021
USA
  Phone: (1) 901-260-3900
  Fax: (1) 901-260-3910
  Web Address: www.ktgusa.com
Personnel:
Gen. Mgr. (From November 2013): Fred Ceruti
Phone: (1) 901-260-3921
Fax: (1) 901-260-3910
Email: fred_ceruti@ktgusa.com
TAD Mill Mgr. (From May 2013): Marc Surprenant
Phone: (1) 901-260-3900 Ext: 9050
Fax: (1) 901-260-3910
Email: marc.surprenant@krugerproducts.ca
Qlty. Mgr.: Jim Szaroletta
Phone: (1) 901-260-3900
Fax: (1) 901-260-3910
Email: jim_szaroletta@ktgusa.com
VP US Bus. Mgr.: Dan Clarahan
Phone: (1) 901-260-3900
Fax: (1) 901-260-3910
Email: dan.clarahan@krugerproducts.com
Purch. Mgr.: Matt McAdams
Phone: (1) 901-260-3900
Fax: (1) 901-260-3910
Email: matt_mcadams@ktgusa.com
Purch. Superintendent: Cindy Davis
Phone: (1) 901-260-3926
Fax: (1) 901-260-3927
Email: cindy_davis@ktgusa.com
Total Employees at this Location: 485
Type of Operation: Paper mill
Paper/Paperboard Grades and Capacities:
Total paper and paperboard capacity: 106,743 st/y
Tissue: 106,743 st/y
Paper and Paperboard Mill Data:
  Stock Preparation:
  Pulpers: 4
  Refiners: 8
Paper Machines: 3
No. 1, crescent former, total capacity 32,844 st/y, Trim width 172 in, Tissue
No. 3, crescent former, total capacity 23,919 st/y, Trim width 172 in, Tissue
No. 5, TAD, total capacity 49,980 st/y, Trim width 208 in, Tissue

Energy Data:
Power boilers: 3

ⓜPackaging Corp. of America
Counce Mill
6715 Hwy 57
Counce, TN 38326
USA
Mailing Address: PO Box 33, Counce, TN 38326, USA
  Phone: (1) 731-689-3111
  Fax: (1) 731-689-1471
  Web Address: www.packagingcorp.com
Personnel:
Pulp Mill Mgr.: Keith DeBerry
Phone: (1) 731-689-3111
Fax: (1) 731-689-1471
Email: kdeberry@packagingcorp.com
Mgr.: Richard Holland
Phone: (1) 731-689-1356
Fax: (1) 731-689-1471
Email: rholland@packagingcorp.com
Pulp/Woodyard Mgr.: Rob Willhelm
Phone: (1) 731-689-3111
Fax: (1) 731-689-1471
Email: rwillhelm@packagingcorp.com
Purch. & Traffic Mgr.: David E. Lawrence
Phone: (1) 731-689-3111
Fax: (1) 731-689-1471
Email: dlawrence@packagingcorp.com
Eng. Mgr.: Jerry Blakely
Phone: (1) 731-689-3111
Fax: (1) 731-689-1471
Email: jblakely@packagingcorp.com
Snr. Proj. Eng.: Jim Meredith
Phone: (1) 731-689-3111
Fax: (1) 731-689-1471
Email: jmeredith@packagingcorp.com
Electrical Eng.: Justin D. Wood
Phone: (1) 731-689-3111
Fax: (1) 731-689-1471
Email: jwood@packagingcorp.com
Total Employees at this Location: 542
Type of Operation: Paperboard mill
Pulp Grades and Capacities:
  Total pulp capacity: 1,122,207 st/y
  Chemical Pulp: 920,210 st/y
  Recycled Pulping: 201,997 st/y
Pulp Mill Data:
  Chemical Pulping Systems:
  Batch digesters: 9
  Chemical Recovery Equipment:
  Evaporator lines: 1
  Recovery boilers: 3
  Lime Kiln
  Recycled Fiber Treatment Lines:
  Recycled packaging pulping lines: 1 at 206,680 admt/y
Paper/Paperboard Grades and Capacities:
  Total paper and paperboard capacity: 1,066,716 st/y
  Linerboard: 1,066,716 st/y
Paper and Paperboard Mill Data:
Paper Machines: 2
No. 1, fourdrinier, total capacity 574,056 st/y, Trim width 240 in, Linerboard
No. 2, fourdrinier, total capacity 492,660 st/y, Trim width 240 in, Linerboard
Energy Data:
Power boilers: 2
Steam turbines: 2 at 46.5, 48 MW
Electrical demand for mill: 1,928 MWh/D

ⓜResolute FP US Inc.
Calhoun Mill
Ownership: 100% by Resolute Forest Products Canada Inc.
5020 Hwy 11 S
Calhoun, TN 37309-5249
USA
  Phone: (1) 423-336-2211

Fax: (1) 423-336-7150/7950
Email: info@resolutefp.com
Web Address: www.resolutefp.com
Personnel:
Mill Mgr.: Rob Martin
Phone: (1) 423-336-7987
Fax: (1) 423-336-7150
Email: rob.martin@resolutefp.com
Dir., HR: James Brigham SPHR
Phone: (1) 423-336-2211
Fax: (1) 423-336-7150
Email: james.brigham@resolutefp.com
Tech. Serv. Mgr.: John E. Griffey
Phone: (1) 423-336-7559
Fax: (1) 423-336-7150
Email: john.griffey@resolutefp.com
Finishing, Shipping, Logistics Mgr.: Nicholas Chance
Phone: (1) 423-336-2211
Fax: (1) 423-336-7150
Email: nick.chance@resolutefp.com
Reliability Eng.: Lance Bennett
Phone: (1) 423-336-7822
Fax: (1) 423-336-7150
Email: lance.bennett@resolutefp.com
Environ., Tech., & Continuous Improvement Mgr. (From October 2014): Lori Chalker
Phone: (1) 423-336-7591
Fax: (1) 423-336-7150
Email: lori.chalker@resolutefp.com
Safety & Health Mgr.: Larry Vest
Phone: (1) 423-336-7217
Fax: (1) 423-336-7150
Email: larry.vest@resolutefp.com
Total Employees at this Location: 517
Type of Operation: Pulp mill, Paper mill
Pulp Grades and Capacities:
  Total pulp capacity: 724,913 st/y
  Pulp available for market: 159,769 st/y
  Chemical Pulp: 355,854 st/y
  Mechanical Pulp: 335,536 st/y
  Recycled Pulping: 33,524 st/y
Pulp Mill Data:
  Chemical Pulping Systems:
  Batch digesters: 1
  Mechanical Pulping Systems:
  TMP systems
  Bleach Plant Systems: 2
  Chemical Pulping System, Sequence: O_2 DEopD
  Mechanical (TMP) Pulping System, Sequence: P
  Chemical Recovery Equipment:
  Evaporator lines
  Recovery boilers: 1
  Lime Kiln
  Recycled Fiber Treatment Lines:
  Pulpers: 1 at 41,887
  Pulp Dryers:
  Flakt dryer 1
Paper/Paperboard Grades and Capacities:
  Total paper and paperboard capacity: 570,602 st/y
  Newsprint: 49,190 st/y
  Uncoated mechanical/groundwood: 521,412 st/y
Paper and Paperboard Mill Data:
  Stock Preparation:
  Pulpers:
Paper Machines: 3
No. 3, twin-wire, total capacity 155,440 st/y, Trim width 256 in, Uncoated mechanical/groundwood
No. 4, twin-wire, total capacity 179,051 st/y, Trim width 252 in, Uncoated mechanical/groundwood
No. 5, Bel-Baie II, total capacity 236,111 st/y, Trim width 298 in, Newsprint, Uncoated mechanical/groundwood
Coating Machines: 1
PM4, on machine
Energy Data:
Power boilers: 5
TMP Reboiler
Steam turbines: 3 at 19, 19, 25 MW
Electrical demand for mill: 3,956 MWh/D

ⓂRockTenn Co.
Chattanooga Mill
701 Manufacturers Rd
Chattanooga, TN 37405
USA
Mailing Address: 701 Manufactures Road, Chattanooga, TN 37405, USA
  Phone: (1) 423-266-7381
  Fax: (1) 423-265-1496
  Web Address: www.rocktenn.com
Personnel:
  Gen. Mgr.: Patrick Cowan
  Phone: (1) 423-266-7381
  Fax: (1) 423-265-1496
  Email: pcowan@rocktenn.com
  Assist. Gen. Mgr.: Mark Murphy
  Phone: (1) 423-266-7381
  Fax: (1) 423-265-1496
  Email: mmurphy@rocktenn.com
  Plt. Supt.: Michael McDougal
  Phone: (1) 423-266-7381 Ext. 116
  Fax: (1) 423-265-1496
  Email: mmcdougal@rocktenn.com
  Sls. Exec.: Alan Templeton
  Phone: (1) 423-266-7381
  Fax: (1) 423-265-1496
  Email: atempleton@rocktenn.com
  Environ. & Safety Mgr.: John Barlew
  Phone: (1) 423-266-7381
  Fax: (1) 423-265-1496
  Email: jbarlew@rocktenn.com
Total Employees at this Location: 138
Type of Operation: Paperboard mill
Pulp Grades and Capacities:
  Total pulp capacity: 142,490 st/y
  Recycled Pulping: 142,490 st/y
Pulp Mill Data:
  Recycled Fiber Treatment Lines:
  Recycled packaging pulping lines
Paper/Paperboard Grades and Capacities:
  Total paper and paperboard capacity: 139,944 st/y
  Boxboard/cartonboard: 139,944 st/y
Paper and Paperboard Mill Data:
  Stock Preparation:
  Pulpers: 4
  Refiners: 3
Paper Machines: 2
No. 1, cylinder (9), total capacity 71,400 st/y, Trim width 118 in, Boxboard/cartonboard
No. 2, cylinder (9), total capacity 68,544 st/y, Trim width 118 in, Boxboard/cartonboard
Finishing Equipment:
  Sheeters: 1
Energy Data:
  Power boilers: 2

ⓂSonoco Products Co.
Newport Mill
766 Industrial Rd
Newport, TN 37821
USA
  Phone: (1) 423-623-8611
  Fax: (1) 423-613-1291
  Web Address: www.sonoco.com
Personnel:
  Plt. Mgr.: Shawn McIntosh
  Phone: (1) 423-623-8611
  Fax: (1) 423-613-1291
Total Employees at this Location: 171
Type of Operation: Paperboard mill
Pulp Grades and Capacities:
  Total pulp capacity: 123,973 st/y
  Recycled Pulping: 123,973 st/y
Paper/Paperboard Grades and Capacities:
  Total paper and paperboard capacity: 121,380 st/y
  Boxboard/cartonboard: 121,380 st/y
Paper and Paperboard Mill Data:
  Stock Preparation:
  Pulpers: 3
  Refiners: 6
Paper Machines: 2
No. 1, cylinder (7), total capacity 64,260 st/y, Trim width 90 in, Boxboard/cartonboard
No. 2, cylinder (9), total capacity 57,120 st/y, Trim width 88 in, Boxboard/cartonboard
Energy Data:
  Power boilers: 2
  Electrical demand for mill: 165 MWh/D

ⓂSouthern Cellulose Products Inc.
Ownership: Archer Daniels Midland Co.
103 W 45th St
Chattanooga, TN 37410
USA
Mailing Address: PO Box 2278, Chattanooga, TN 37409, USA
  Phone: (1) 423-821-1561
  Fax: (1) 423-821-2624
  Web Address: www.adm.com
Personnel:
  Snr. Plt. Mgr.: Kyle Hutton
  Phone: (1) 423-821-1561
  Fax: (1) 423-821-2624
  Email: kyle.hutton@adm.com
  Bus. Mgr.: Mark Wirkus
  Phone: (1) 423-821-1561
  Fax: (1) 423-821-2624
  Email: mark.wirkus@adm.com
  Sls. Mgr.: Ricky Weiger
  Phone: (1) 423-821-1561
  Fax: (1) 423-821-2624
  Manuf. Dir.: Jerry Morton
  Phone: (1) 423-821-1561
  Fax: (1) 423-821-2624
Total Employees of Company: 100
Mill Locations:
Southern Cellulose Products Inc., Chattanooga Mill, 103 W 45th St, Chattanooga, TN 37410, USA, (Pulp mill)
  Phone: (1) 423-821-1561
  Fax: (1) 423-821-2624

ⓂSouthern Cellulose Products Inc.
Chattanooga Mill
103 W 45th St
Chattanooga, TN 37410
USA
Mailing Address: PO Box 2278, Chattanooga, TN 37409, USA
  Phone: (1) 423-821-1561
  Fax: (1) 423-821-2624
  Web Address: www.adm.com
Total Employees at this Location: 100
Type of Operation: Pulp mill
Pulp Grades and Capacities:
  Total pulp capacity: 64,000 st/y
Pulp Mill Data:
  Chemical Pulping Systems:
  Continuous digesters: 1
  Bleach Plant Systems: 1
  Line 1, Type: Linters
Energy Data:
  Power boilers: 1

ⓘVerso Paper Corp.
Ownership: 73% by Apollo Management L.P., 27% by investing public
6775 Lenox Center Court, Suite 400
Memphis, TN 38115
USA
  Phone: (1) 877-837-7606, 901-369-4100
  Fax: (1) 901-369-4174
  Web Address: www.versopaper.com
Personnel:
  Pres. & CEO: David J. Paterson
  Phone: (1) 877-837-7606
  Fax: (1) 901-369-4174
  Email: david.paterson@versopaper.com
  Snr. VP. & CFO: Robert P. Mundy
  Phone: (1) 901-369-4185
  Fax: (1) 901-369-4174
  Email: robert.mundy@versopaper.com
  Snr. VP., Manuf. & Energy: Lyle J. Fellows
  Phone: (1) 877-837-7606
  Fax: (1) 901-369-4174
  Email: lyle.fellows@versopaper.com
  Snr. VP., Sls., Mktg. & Prod. Devlpt.: Michael A. Weinhold
  Phone: (1) 877-837-7606
  Fax: (1) 901-369-4174
  Email: michael.weinhold@versopaper.com
  Snr. VP., Gen. Counsel & Sec.: Peter H. Kesser
  Phone: (1) 877-837-7606
  Fax: (1) 901-369-4174
  Email: peter.kesser@versopaper.com
  VP., HR: Kenneth D. Sawyer
  Phone: (1) 901-369-4233
  Fax: (1) 901-369-4174
  Email: kenny.sawyer@versopaper.com
  VP., Integrated Plan. & Cntrl.: Joseph C. Duffy
  Phone: (1) 877-837-7606
  Fax: (1) 901-369-4174
  Email: joseph.duffy@versopaper.com
  VP. & CIO: Benjamin Hinchman IV
  Phone: (1) 877-837-7606
  Fax: (1) 901-369-4174
  Email: benjamin.hinchman@versopaper.com
Total Employees of Company: 2,100
Mill Locations:
Verso Paper Corp., Androscoggin Mill, 300 Riley Rd., Jay, ME 04239, USA, Capacity: 633,178 st/y, (Pulp mill, Paper mill)
  Phone: (1) 207-897-3431
  Fax: (1) 207-897-6360
Verso Paper Corp., Bucksport Mill, 2 River Rd, Bucksport, ME 04416, USA, Capacity: 403,321 st/y, (Paper mill)
  Phone: (1) 207-469-1700
  Fax: (1) 207-469-1704
Verso Paper Corp., Quinnesec Mill, W6705 US Highwway 2, Quinnesec, MI 49870-0211, USA, Capacity: 424,736 st/y, (Pulp mill, Paper mill)
  Phone: (1) 906-779-3200
  Fax: (1) 906-779-3307

TEXAS

ⓘBio-PAPPEL International
Ownership: 100% by Bio-PAPPEL, S.A.B. de C.V.
1301 S. Bowen Road
Arlington, TX 76013
USA
  Phone: (1) 972-591-4005
  Fax: (1) 972-591-4028
  Web Address: www.biopappel.com/en
Personnel:
  Pres & CEO: Miguel Rincon
  Phone: (1) 972-591-4005
  Fax: (1) 972-591-4028
  Email: mrincon@biopappel.com
  Pres., US Oper.: Herb Baez
  Phone: (1) 972-591-4005
  Fax: (1) 972-591-4028
  Email: hbaez@biopappel.com
  Bus. Develop. Mgr.: Ignacio Parra
  Phone: (1) 972-591-4005
  Fax: (1) 972-591-4028
  Email: iparra@biopappel.com
  Sls. Mgr.: Torryea Calderon
  Phone: (1) 972-591-4005
  Fax: (1) 972-591-4028
  Email: tcalderon@biopappel.com
  Commercial Dir.: Wilfrido Rincon
  Phone: (1) 972-591-4005
  Fax: (1) 972-591-4028
  Email: wrincon@biopappel.com
  Procurement Mgr.: Rogelio Silva
  Phone: (1) 972-591-4005

Texas

Fax: (1) 972-591-4028
Email: rsilva@biopappel.com
Finan. & Admin. Mgr.: Eduardo Arizpe
Phone: (1) 972-591-4005
Fax: (1) 972-591-4028
Email: earizpe@biopappel.com
Total Employees of Company: 179
Total Employees at this Location: 5
Mill Locations:
Bio-PAPPEL International, Prewitt Mill, County Rd 19, Prewitt, NM 87045, USA, Capacity: 249,900 st/y, (Paperboard mill)
Phone: (1) 505-876-2100
Fax: (1) 505-876-2313

ⓂInternational Paper Co.
Texarkana Mill
9978 FM Rd. 3129
Domino, TX 75572
USA
Mailing Address: PO Box 870, Texarkana, TX 75504, USA
Phone: (1) 903-796-7101
Fax: (1) 903-796-1960
Email: (firstname.lastname@ipaper.com)
Web Address: www.internationalpaper.com
Personnel:
Mill Mgr. (since January 2014): Matthew Barbour
Phone: (1) 903-796-7101
Fax: (1) 903-796-1960
Email: matt.barbour@ipaper.com
Prod. Mgr.: Joseph Fierst
Phone: (1) 903-796-7101
Fax: (1) 903-796-1960
Email: joesph.fierst@ipaper.com
Mgr., PS&D (Finishing & Shipping): Troy Ashmore
Phone: (1) 903-796-7101
Fax: (1) 903-796-1960
Email: troy.ashmore@ipaper.com
Bus. Mgr., Power: Jeff Carter
Phone: (1) 903-796-7101
Fax: (1) 903-796-1960
Email: jeff.carter@ipaper.com
Bus. Mgr., Pulp: Mark Bruyns
Phone: (1) 903-796-7101
Fax: (1) 903-796-1960
Email: mark.bruyns@ipaper.com
Bus. Mgr., Paper: Jason Hoffman
Phone: (1) 903-796-7101
Fax: (1) 903-796-1960
Email: jason.hoffman@ipaper.com
Maint. Mgr.: Will Thomas
Phone: (1) 903-796-7101
Fax: (1) 903-796-1960
Email: will.thomas@ipaper.com
Safety Mgr.: Cheri Stuart
Phone: (1) 903-796-7101
Fax: (1) 903-796-1960
Email: cheri.stuart@ipaper.com
Environ. Eng.: Anil Patel
Phone: (1) 903-796-7101
Fax: (1) 903-796-1960
Email: anil.patel@ipaper.com
Total Employees at this Location: 702
Type of Operation: Paperboard mill
Pulp Grades and Capacities:
Total pulp capacity: 670,844 st/y
Chemical Pulp: 670,844 st/y
Pulp Mill Data:
Chemical Pulping Systems:
Batch digesters: 16
Pulp Lines: 2
Bleach Plant Systems: 2
Chemical Pulping System - A line, Type: Hardwood, Sequence: DEoDD, Capacity 364,000.2 admt/y
Chemical Pulping System - B line, Type: Hardwwood/Softwood, Sequence: O₂ DEopDD, Capacity 243,000.4 admt/y
Chemical Recovery Equipment:
Evaporator lines: 1
Recovery boilers: 2
Lime Kiln
Paper/Paperboard Grades and Capacities:
Total paper and paperboard capacity: 674,730 st/y
Boxboard/cartonboard: 674,730 st/y
Paper and Paperboard Mill Data:
Paper Machines: 2
No. 1, fourdrinier, total capacity 310,590 st/y, Trim width 219 in, Boxboard/cartonboard
No. 3, fourdrinier, total capacity 364,140 st/y, Trim width 291 in, Boxboard/cartonboard
Coating Machines: 3
No. 5, off machine
No. 7, off machine
PM 1, total capacity 296,517 st/y., on machine
Energy Data:
Power boilers: 2
Steam turbines: 2 at 65 MW
Electrical demand for mill: 1,898 MWh/D

ⓂInternational Paper Co.
Orange Mill
Mill is a previous Temple-Inland mill.
1750 Inland Rd
Orange, TX 77632
USA
Phone: (1) 409-746-2441
Fax: (1) 409-746-7210
Web Address: www.internationalpaper.com
Personnel:
Mill Mgr.: Anitra Collins
Phone: (1) 409-746-2441
Fax: (1) 409-746-7210
Email: anitra.collins@ipaper.com
Oper. Mgr. (From May 2014): Mike Lyles
Phone: (1) 409-746-2441
Fax: (1) 409-746-7210
Email: mike.lyles@ipaper.com
Cust. Service Mgr.: Doug Myers
Phone: (1) 409-746-2441
Fax: (1) 409-746-7210
Email: doug.myers@ipaper.com
HR Mgr.: Carl Schreier
Phone: (1) 409-746-2441
Fax: (1) 409-746-7210
Email: carl.schreier@ipaper.com
Total Employees at this Location: 355
Type of Operation: Paperboard mill
Pulp Grades and Capacities:
Total pulp capacity: 842,293 st/y
Chemical Pulp: 673,834 st/y
Recycled Pulping: 168,459 st/y
Pulp Mill Data:
Chemical Pulping Systems:
Continuous digesters: 2
Chemical Recovery Equipment:
Evaporator lines: 1
Recovery boilers: 2
Lime Kiln
Recycled Fiber Treatment Lines:
Pulpers: 1 at 172,178
Paper/Paperboard Grades and Capacities:
Total paper and paperboard capacity: 795,039 st/y
Linerboard: 795,039 st/y
Paper and Paperboard Mill Data:
Stock Preparation:
Pulpers: 2
Refiners: 0
Paper Machines: 2
No. 1, Bel-Bond, total capacity 518,007 st/y, Trim width 238 in, Linerboard
No. 2, Bel-Bond, total capacity 277,032 st/y, Trim width 238 in, Linerboard
Energy Data:
Power boilers: 4
Steam turbines: 1 at 48 MW
Electrical demand for mill: 1,638 MWh/D

ⒽKimberly-Clark Corp.
Ownership: Public
351 Phelps Dr
Irving, TX 75038
USA
Mailing Address: PO Box 619100, DFW Arpt Sta, Dallas, TX 75261-9100, USA
Phone: (1) 972-281-1200
Fax: (1) 972-281-1490
Web Address: www.kimberly-clark.com
Personnel:
Chmn. & CEO: Thomas J. Falk
Phone: (1) 972-281-1200
Fax: (1) 972-281-1490
Email: tfalk@kcc.com
Pres., Kimberly-Clark Professional (KCP): Kim Underhill
Phone: (1) 972-281-1200
Fax: (1) 972-281-1490
Pres., Global Health Care: Joanne B. Bauer
Phone: (1) 972-281-1200
Fax: (1) 972-281-1490
Email: jbauer@kcc.com
Pres. global brands and innovation: Anthony (Tony) J. Palmer
Phone: (1) 972-281-1200
Fax: (1) 972-281-1490
Email: apalmer@kcc.com
Group Pres. K-C International (KCI): Elane B. Stock
Phone: (1) 972-281-1200
Fax: (1) 972-281-1490
Email: estock@kcc.com
Pres., K-C North America: Michael Hsu
Phone: (1) 972-281-1200
Fax: (1) 972-281-1490
Email: mhsu@kcc.com
Snr. VP. & CFO: Mark A. Buthman
Phone: (1) 972-281-1200
Fax: (1) 972-281-1490
Email: mbuthman@kcc.com
Snr. VP., HR: Lizanne C. Gottung
Phone: (1) 972-281-1200
Fax: (1) 972-281-1490
Email: lgottung@kcc.com
Snr. VP., Gen. Counsel: Thomas J. Mielke
Phone: (1) 972-281-1200
Fax: (1) 972-281-1490
Email: tmielke@kcc.com
Snr. VP. & Chief Strategy Officer: Nancy Loewe
Phone: (1) 972-281-1200
Fax: (1) 972-281-1490
Email: nloewe@kcc.com
VP & Treasurer: Karen Leets
Phone: (1) 972-281-1200
Fax: (1) 972-281-1490
Email: kleets@kcc.com
VP. & Chief Marketing Officer: Clive Sirkin
Phone: (1) 972-281-1200
Fax: (1) 972-281-1490
Email: csirkin@kcc.com
Snr. Dir., Global Labor Rel.: Bill Bombardier
Phone: (1) 972-281-1200
Fax: (1) 972-281-1490
Email: bbombardier@kcc.com
Total Employees of Company: 56,748
Mill Locations:
Colombiana Kimberly Colpapel S.A., Medellin Mill, Calle 12 #1111 Vereda, Canaan Barbosa, Medellin, Colombia, Capacity: 25,185 st/y, (Pulp mill, Paper mill)
Phone: (57) 4 3789200
Colombiana Kimberly Colpapel S.A., Puerto Tejada Mill, 201 mts después del Pte. El Hormiguero via Cali - Pto Tejada, Puerto Tejada, Cauca, Colombia, Capacity: 71,620 st/y, (Paper mill)
Phone: (57) 2 3187700 ext. 2084
Hogla-Kimberly Ltd., Hadera Mill (50.10% owned), 4 Myzer Street, Industrial Zone Hadera, 38101 Hadera, Israel, Capacity: 34,171 st/y, (Paper mill)
Phone: (972) 4 634 9232
Fax: (972) 4 632 6761
Hogla-Kimberly Ltd., Naharya Mill (50.10% owned), Industrial Zone PO Box 313, 46101 Naharya, Israel,

Capacity: 28,660 st/y, (Paper mill)
Phone: (972) 4 9106100
Fax: (972) 4 9823255
Kimberly Bolivia S.A., Santa Cruz Mill, Parque Industrial M 5, 6937 Santa Cruz de la Sierra, Bolivia, Capacity: 18,739 st/y, (Paper mill)
Phone: (591) 3 3465159
Fax: (591) 3 3470094
Kimberly-Clark Srl, Alanno Scalo Mill, Località S. Emidio, I-65020 Alanno Scalo, (PE), Italy, Capacity: 44,092 st/y, (Paper mill)
Phone: (39) 085 854 0800
Fax: (39) 085 854 2849
Kimberly-Clark de México S.A. de C.V., Bajio Mill, Av. Doctor Rafael Ayala, Echevarri Km. 0.5 Libramiento a Tequisquiapan, 76800 San Juan del Rio, Mexico, Capacity: 297,500 st/y, (Paper mill)
Phone: (52) 427 271 8500, 442 272 8282
Fax: (52) 427 271 8504, 442 272 8030
Kimberly-Clark Ltd., Barrow-in-Furness Mill, PO Box 25, Barrow-in-Furness LA14 4QX, United Kingdom, Capacity: 143,298 st/y, (Pulp mill, Paper mill)
Phone: (44) 1229 495 000
Fax: (44) 1229 495 001
Kimberly-Clark S.A., Bernal Mill, Espora 50, 1876 Bernal, Argentina, Capacity: 38,565 st/y, (Paper mill)
Phone: (54) 11 4365 7209
Fax: (54) 11 4365 7244
Email: gustavo.magnani@kcc.com
Kimberly-Clark de Centroamérica S.A., Sitio Del Nino Mill, Km. 32 Carretera a San Juan Opico, Sitio Del Nino, El Salvador, Capacity: 97,199 st/y, (Paper mill)
Phone: (503) 2319 4500
Kimberly-Clark Taiwan, Chungli Mill, 240, Chung Hsin Rd., Hsin Wu 32750, Taiwan, Capacity: 25,353 st/y, (Paper mill)
Phone: (886) 3 4772772
Fax: (886) 3 4772777
Email: chungming.huang@kcc.com
Kimberly-Clark Ltd., Coleshill Mill, Flint Site, Aber Road, Flint CH6 5EX, United Kingdom, Capacity: 31,966 st/y, (Paper mill)
Phone: (44) 1352 805 000
Fax: (44) 1352 805 001
Kimberly-Clark Brasil Ind. e Com. de Produtos de Higiene Ltda., Correia Pinto Mill, Rodovia BR 116, km 218 s/n°, 88535-000 Correia Pinto, SC, Brazil, Capacity: 63,750 st/y, (Paper mill)
Phone: (55) 49 3243 6000
Fax: (55) 49 3243 6004
Email: sacprofessional@kcc.com
Kimberly-Clark Costa Rica, SA, San José Mill (81% owned), San Antonio de Belen Aptdo. 10271, San José, Costa Rica, Capacity: 22,037 st/y, (Pulp mill, Paper mill)
Phone: (506) 506 298 3100
Fax: (506) 506 239 0805
Kimberly-Clark de México S.A. de C.V., Cepamisa, Domicilio Conocido, Ejido de Cointzio, Municipio de Morelia, 58341 Morelia, Mexico, Capacity: 49,583 st/y, (Pulp mill, Paper mill)
Phone: (52) 443 322 3700
Fax: (52) 443 322 3709
Kimberly-Clark Ltd., Delyn Mill, Flint Site, Aber Road, Flint CH6 5EX, United Kingdom, Capacity: 33,069 st/y, (Paper mill)
Phone: (44) 1352 805 000
Fax: (44) 1352 805 001
Kimberly-Clark de México S.A. de C.V., Ecatepec Mill, Avenida de las Torres No. 87, Col. Jajalpa, San Cristobal, 55090 Ecatepec de Morelos, Mexico, Capacity: 156,620 st/y, (Paper mill)
Phone: (52) 55 5836 2400
Fax: (52) 55 5836 2403 /10
Kimberly-Clark Taiwan, Hsinying Mill, 321, Tai Tze Rd., Hsinying 73044, Taiwan, Capacity: 44,092 st/y, (Paper mill)
Phone: (886) 6 6563446
Fax: (886) 6 6561436
Email: chente.yang@kcc.com
Kimberly-Clark Products (Malaysia) Sdn. Bhd., Kluang Mill, 4-1/2 Mile Jalan Mersing, 86007 Kluang, Malaysia, Capacity: 44,092 st/y, (Paper mill)
Phone: (60) 7 787 9381
Fax: (60) 7 787 9234/170
Kimberly-Clark Venezuela, C.A., Maracay Mill, Aptdo. 173, Zona Ind. La Hamaca 2da. transversal 160-4, Maracay, Venezuela, Capacity: 46,042 st/y, (Paper mill)
Phone: (58) 243 550 1511
Fax: (58) 243 550 1502
Kimberly-Clark Australia Pty Ltd., Millicent Mill, Princes Highway, Millicent, SA 5280, Australia, Capacity: 99,206 st/y, (Paper mill)
Phone: (61) 8 8721 4200
Fax: (61) 8 8723 2253
Kimberly-Clark Brasil Ind. e Com. de Produtos de Higiene Ltda., Mogi das Cruzes Mill, Estrada da Casa Grande, km 59 s/n°- Cocuera, 08710-971 Mogi das Cruzes, SP, Brazil, Capacity: 79,884 st/y, (Paper mill)
Phone: (55) 11 4793 5000
Fax: (55) 11 4793 5000
Email: sacprofessional@kcc.com
Kimberly-Clark GmbH, Niederbipp Mill, Rotboden 1, CH-4704 Niederbipp, Switzerland, Capacity: 51,808 st/y, (Paper mill)
Phone: (41) 32 633 51 11
Fax: (41) 32 633 51 00
Kimberly-Clark Ltd., Northfleet Mill, Thames House, Crete Hall Rd., Northfleet, Gravesend DA11 9AD, United Kingdom, Capacity: 82,672 st/y, (Pulp mill, Paper mill)
Phone: (44) 1474 336 000
Fax: (44) 1474 336 478
Kimberly-Clark de México S.A. de C.V., Orizaba Mill, Avenida San Juan 1, Escamela Iztaczoquitlan, 94452 Orizaba, Mexico, Capacity: 104,676 st/y, (Pulp mill, Paper mill)
Phone: (52) 272 728 2800
Fax: (52) 272 728 2844
Email: salvador.ortegal@kcc.com
Kimberly-Clark Thailand Ltd., Pathumthani Mill, 54 Moo 6 Tambon Bangkayang, Amphur Muang, Pathumthani 12000, Thailand, Capacity: 22,046 st/y, (Paper mill)
Phone: (66) 2 598 2700-14
Fax: (66) 2 975 3099/5982711
Kimberly-Clark Thailand Ltd., Samut Prakan Mill, 58 Moo 2 Poochaosamingprai Road, Tambon Bangyapraek, Amphur Phrapradaeng 10130, Thailand, Capacity: 19,282 st/y, (Paper mill)
Phone: (66) 2 755 9011-13
Fax: (66) 2 384 3594
Kimberly-Clark de México S.A. de C.V., Ramos Arizpe Mill, Carretera Monterey Saltillo, Km. 21.4, 25900 Ramos Arizpe, Mexico, Capacity: 170,787 st/y, (Paper mill)
Phone: (52) 844 411 0100
Fax: (52) 844 411 0137
Kimberly-Clark Srl, Romagnano Sesia Mill, Via S. Martino 16, I-28078 Romagnano Sesia, (NO), Italy, Capacity: 126,764 st/y, (Paper mill)
Phone: (39) 0163 821200
Fax: (39) 0163 821202
Kimberly-Clark S.A., Salamanca Mill, Carr. Florida de Liébana, km. 3,8, E-37120 Doñinos, Spain, Capacity: 55,115 st/y, (Paper mill)
Phone: (34) 92 333 0011
Fax: (34) 92 333 0030/0115
Kimberly-Clark SAS, Sotteville-les-Rouen Mill, 8 rue Antoine Lavoisier, F-76300 Sotteville-les-Rouen, France, Capacity: 27,557 st/y, (Pulp mill, Paper mill)
Phone: (33) 2 35 64 38 00
Fax: (33) 2 35 65 53 74
Kimberly-Clark of SA (Pty) Ltd., Enstra Mill, East Geduld Rd., Enstra, Springs 1560, South Africa, Capacity: 59,524 st/y, (Paper mill)
Phone: (27) 11 360 7000
Fax: (27) 11 360 7001
Kimberly-Clark Taiwan, Tayuan Mill, 262 Chung Shan Rd., Tayuan 33759, Taiwan, Capacity: 44,083 st/y, (Paper mill)
Phone: (886) 3 386 4935
Fax: (886) 3 386 4400
Email: Lance.Yang@kcc.com
Kimberly-Clark de México S.A. de C.V., San Martin Texmelucan Mill, Av. Revolucion No. 1, Santamaria, Moyotzingo, 74129 San Martin Texmelucan, Mexico, Capacity: 29,907 st/y, (Paper mill)
Phone: (52) 248 485 0477/0055
Fax: (52) 248 485 0015
Kimberly-Clark SNC, Toul Mill, Z.A.C. de Villey-St-Etienne, F-54212 Toul, France, Capacity: 88,183 st/y, (Paper mill)
Phone: (33) 3 83 65 34 34
Fax: (33) 3 83 65 34 78
Kimberly-Clark Peru S.A., Puente de Piedra Mill, Av. del Pinar 180, Chacarilla del Estanque, Santiago de Surco, Lima, Peru, Capacity: 73,981 st/y, (Pulp mill, Paper mill)
Phone: (51) 1 618 1800
Fax: (51) 1 436 3189
Email: kcastellanos@kcc.com.pe, j.testino@kc.com
Kimberly-Clark GmbH, Koblenz Mill, Carl-Spaeter-Str. 17, D-56070 Koblenz, Germany, Capacity: 41,887 st/y, (Paper mill)
Phone: (49) 261 9227 0
Fax: (49) 261 9227 494 / 488
Email: afhde@kcc.com
Kimberly-Clark Corp., Beech Island Mill, 246 Old Jackson Hwy, Beech Island, SC 29842-4542, USA, Capacity: 264,537 st/y, (Paper mill)
Phone: (1) 803-827-1100
Fax: (1) 803-827-6022
Kimberly-Clark Corp., Chester Mill, Front St & Av of the States, Chester, PA 19013, USA, Capacity: 250,257 st/y, (Paper mill)
Phone: (1) 610-874-4331
Fax: (1) 610-499-6238
Kimberly-Clark Corp., Fullerton Mill, 2001 E Orangethorpe Ave, Fullerton, CA 92831-5326, USA, Capacity: 66,045 st/y, (Paper mill)
Phone: (1) 714-773-7500
Fax: (1) 714-773-9291
Kimberly-Clark Corp., Jenks Mill, 13252 S Yale Pl, Jenks, OK 74037, USA, Capacity: 175,287 st/y, (Paper mill)
Phone: (1) 918-366-5000
Fax: (1) 918-366-5050
Kimberly-Clark Corp., Marinette Mill, 3120 Riverside Ave., Marinette, WI 54143, USA, Capacity: 44,982 st/y, (Paper mill)
Phone: (1) 715-735-6644
Fax: (1) 715-735-4002
Kimberly-Clark Corp., Mobile Mill, 200 Bay Bridge Rd, Mobile, AL 36652, USA, Capacity: 275,604 st/y, (Paper mill)
Phone: (1) 251-330-3000
Fax: (1) 251-452-6329
Kimberly-Clark Corp., New Milford Mill, 58 Pickett District Rd, New Milford, CT 06776-4493, USA, Capacity: 80,325 st/y, (Paper mill)
Phone: (1) 860-354-4481
Fax: (1) 860-355-6689
Kimberly-Clark Corp., Owensboro Mill, 601 Innovative Way, Owensboro, KY 42301, USA, Capacity: 134,589 st/y, (Paper mill)
Phone: (1) 270-764-4400
Fax: (1) 270-764-4598
Kimberly-Clark Corp., Loudon Mill, 5600 Kimberly Way, Loudon, TN 37774, USA, Capacity: 142,086 st/y, (Paper mill)
Phone: (1) 865-988-7000
Fax: (1) 865-988-7012
Kimberly-Clark of Canada, Huntsville Mill, 570 Ravenscliffe Rd., Huntsville, ON, Canada P1H 2A1, Capacity: 35,343 st/y, (Paper mill)
Phone: (1) 705-788-5200
Fax: (1) 705-788-5272
Olayan Kimberly-Clark (Bahrain) W.L.L., Isa Town Mill, South Alba Industrial Area, Isa Town, Bahrain, Capacity: 51,808 st/y, (Paper mill)
Phone: (973) 17 830-688
Fax: (973) 17 830-449
Email: okb@olayangroup.com, kuginm@kcc.com
Shanghai Kimberly-Clark (China) Paper Co. Ltd., Shanghai Mill (80% owned), 139 Jinshatan, Songjiang District, Shanghai 201600, China, Capacity: 26,455 st/y, (Paper mill)

Texas

Phone: (86) 21 5782 2671
Fax: (86) 21 5782 0386
Email: wesen.zha@kcc.com
Yuhan-Kimberly Ltd., Daejeon Mill (70% owned), 41-1, Munpyeong-dong, Daedeok-gu, 306-220 Daejeon-si, South Korea, Capacity: 19,400 st/y, (Paper mill)
Phone: (82) 42 939-7100
Fax: (82) 42 931-7105/06
Email: webmaster.korea@y-k.co.kr
Yuhan-Kimberly Ltd., Kimcheon Mill (70% owned), 746-1, Daegwang-dong, 740-170 Gimcheon-si, South Korea, Capacity: 117,945 st/y, (Paper mill)
Phone: (82) 54 420-5500
Fax: (82) 54 420-5555
Email: webmaster.korea@y-k.co.kr
Yuhan-Kimberly Ltd., Kunpo Mill (70% owned), 27-4, Dangjeong-dong, 435-831 Gunpo-si, South Korea, Capacity: 25,353 st/y, (Paper mill)
Phone: (82) 31 450-8567
Fax: (82) 31 455-9609
Email: webmaster.korea@y-k.co.kr

ⓂMeadWestvaco Corporation
Evadale Mill
1913 FM 105
Evadale, TX 77615
USA
Mailing Address: PO Box 816, Silsbee, TX 77656, USA
Phone: (1) 409-276-3243
Fax: (1) 409-276-3108
Web Address: www.mwv.com
Personnel:
VP, Evadale Oper.: James H. Gresham Jr.
Phone: (1) 409-276-3243
Fax: (1) 409-276-3108
Email: james.gresham@mwv.com
Qlty. Assur. Mgr.: Todd Quick
Phone: (1) 409-276-3243
Fax: (1) 409-276-3108
Email: todd.quick@mwv.com
Paper Mill Superint. (From September 2013): Darrell Deaton
Phone: (1) 409-276-3243
Fax: (1) 409-276-3108
Email: darrell.deaton@mwv.com
Electrical Reliability Eng.: Thomas Vescovi
Phone: (1) 409-276-3243
Fax: (1) 409-276-3108
Email: thomas.vescovi@mwv.com
Total Employees at this Location: 668
Type of Operation: Pulp mill, Paperboard mill
Pulp Grades and Capacities:
Total pulp capacity: 674,843 st/y
Pulp available for market: 89,250 st/y
Chemical Pulp: 674,843 st/y
Pulp Mill Data:
Chemical Pulping Systems:
Continuous digesters: 2
Bleach Plant Systems: 2
Chemical Pulping System, Type: ECF - Softwood, Sequence: DEopDP, Capacity 428,399.5 admt/y
Chemical Pulping System, Type: ECF - Hardwood, Sequence: DEopDP, Capacity 356,999.6 admt/y
Chemical Recovery Equipment:
Evaporator lines: 3
Recovery boilers: 2
Lime Kiln
Pulp Dryers:
Pulp Dryers 1
Paper/Paperboard Grades and Capacities:
Total paper and paperboard capacity: 583,695 st/y
Boxboard/cartonboard: 583,695 st/y
Paper and Paperboard Mill Data:
Paper Machines: 2
No. 4, fourdrinier, total capacity 235,620 st/y, Trim width 232 in, Boxboard/cartonboard
No. 5, fourdrinier, total capacity 348,075 st/y, Trim width 268 in, Boxboard/cartonboard
Coating Machines: 1
PM 5, total capacity 348,325 st/y., on machine

Energy Data:
Power boilers: 4
Steam turbines: 3 at 62.0 MW
Electrical demand for mill: 2,162 MWh/D

ⓂRockTenn Co.
Dallas Mill
1120 E Clarendon Dr
Dallas, TX 75203
USA
Phone: (1) 214-941-3400
Fax: (1) 214-941-8048
Web Address: www.rocktenn.com
Personnel:
Gen. Mgr.: David R. Pearson
Phone: (1) 214-257-2603
Fax: (1) 214-941-8048
Email: dpearson@rocktenn.com
Maint. Mgr.: Troy White
Phone: (1) 214-941-3400
Fax: (1) 214-941-8048
Email: twhite@rocktenn.com
Cust. Service Mgr.: Alfredo Gallegos
Phone: (1) 214-941-3400
Fax: (1) 214-941-8048
Email: agallegos@rocktenn.com
Buyer: David Hendrickson
Phone: (1) 214-941-3400
Fax: (1) 214-941-8048
Email: dhendrickson@rocktenn.com
Total Employees at this Location: 110
Type of Operation: Paperboard mill
Pulp Grades and Capacities:
Total pulp capacity: 115,358 st/y
Recycled Pulping: 115,358 st/y
Pulp Mill Data:
Recycled Fiber Treatment Lines:
Recycled packaging pulping lines: 1
Paper/Paperboard Grades and Capacities:
Total paper and paperboard capacity: 127,092 st/y
Boxboard/cartonboard: 127,092 st/y
Paper and Paperboard Mill Data:
Stock Preparation:
Pulpers: 2
Refiners: 2
Paper Machines: 1
No. 1, Ultraformer, total capacity 127,092 st/y, Trim width 106 in, Boxboard/cartonboard
Coating Machines: 1
No. 1, total capacity 110,009 st/y., on machine
Energy Data:
Power boilers: 2
Steam turbines: 1 at 4.2 MW

ⓂSmurfit Kappa Orange County
Forney Mill
Previously Orange County Container Group, LLC
Ownership: 100% by Smurfit Kappa Group
855 East Hwy 80
Forney, TX 75126
USA
Mailing Address: PO Box 847, Forney, TX 75126, USA
Phone: (1) 214-515-6400, 888-870-4582
Fax: (1) 214-515-6499
Web Address: www.smurfitkappa.com/vHome/us/Pages/Default.aspx
Personnel:
COO (VP., Oper.): Dave Nelson
Phone: (1) 214-515-6400
Fax: (1) 214-515-6499
Email: david.nelson@smurfitkappa.com
Liner Mill Mgr.: Bryan Norwood
Phone: (1) 214-515-6442
Fax: (1) 214-515-6498
Email: bryan.norwood@smurfitkappa.com
Dir., Sls. & Mktg.: William (Bill) Baker
Phone: (1) 214-515-6408
Fax: (1) 214-515-6499
Email: william.baker@smurfitkappa.com

Gen. Mgr. Div. Coated Products: Chris Blockhus
Phone: (1) 214-515-6421
Fax: (1) 214-515-6499
Email: chris.blockhus@smurfitkappa.com
Gen. Mgr. Div. Converting: Mike Meyer
Phone: (1) 214-515-6407
Fax: (1) 214-515-6486
Email: mike.meyer@smurfitkappa.com
Purch. Mgr.: Andrew Kern
Phone: (1) 214-515-6400
Fax: (1) 214-515-6499
Email: andrew.kern@smurfitkappa.com
Total Employees at this Location: 182
Type of Operation: Paperboard mill
Pulp Grades and Capacities:
Total pulp capacity: 353,665 st/y
Recycled Pulping: 353,665 st/y
Pulp Mill Data:
Recycled Fiber Treatment Lines:
Pulpers: 2 at 342,813
Recycled packaging pulping lines: 2 at 313,503
Paper/Paperboard Grades and Capacities:
Total paper and paperboard capacity: 336,294 st/y
Linerboard: 250,257 st/y
Corrugating medium/fluting: 86,037 st/y
Paper and Paperboard Mill Data:
Stock Preparation:
Pulpers: 4
Paper Machines: 2
No. 1, fourdrinier, total capacity 86,037 st/y, Trim width 98 in, Corrugating medium/fluting
No. 2, fourdrinier, total capacity 250,257 st/y, Trim width 240 in, Linerboard
Finishing Equipment:
Calenders: 2
Rewinders: 2
Energy Data:
Power boilers: 2
Combustion turbines: 1 at 4 MW
Steam turbines: 1 at 3 MW
Electrical demand for mill: 381 MWh/D

ⓂUnited States Gypsum Co.
Galena Park Mill
1201 Mayo Shell Rd
Galena Park, TX 77547
USA
Mailing Address: PO Box 525, Galena Park, TX 77547, USA
Phone: (1) 713-308-5400
Fax: (1) 713-308-5401
Web Address: www.usg.com
Personnel:
Mill Mgr.: Eric Pieper
Phone: (1) 713-308-5400
Fax: (1) 713-308-5401
Email: epieper@usg.com
Corp. Tech. Mgr.: Paula M. McKnight
Phone: (1) 713-308-5400
Fax: (1) 713-308-5401
Plt. Eng.: Michael Harper
Phone: (1) 713-308-5400
Fax: (1) 713-308-5401
Email: mharper@usg.com
Type of Operation: Paperboard mill
Pulp Grades and Capacities:
Total pulp capacity: 78,369 st/y
Recycled Pulping: 78,369 st/y
Paper/Paperboard Grades and Capacities:
Total paper and paperboard capacity: 74,970 st/y
Boxboard/cartonboard: 74,970 st/y
Paper and Paperboard Mill Data:
Stock Preparation:
Pulpers: 2
Refiners: 2
Paper Machines: 1
No. 1, cylinder (8), total capacity 74,970 st/y, Trim width 106 in, Boxboard/cartonboard
Finishing Equipment:
Rewinders: 1

Energy Data:
Power boilers: 1
Electrical demand for mill: 97 MWh/D

UTAH

ⓜProcter & Gamble Paper Products Co.
Box Elder Mill
5000 North Iowa Springs Road
Brigham City, UT
USA
 Web Address: www.pg.com
Personnel:
 Mill Mgr.: Joseph Tomon
 Phone: (1) 513-983-1100
 Fax: (1) 513-386-1887
 Oper. Mgr.: John McKay
 Phone: (1) 513-983-1100
 Fax: (1) 513-386-1887
Total Employees at this Location: 90
Type of Operation: Paper mill
Paper/Paperboard Grades and Capacities:
 Total paper and paperboard capacity: 79,968 st/y
 Tissue: 79,968 st/y
Paper and Paperboard Mill Data:
 Stock Preparation:
 Pulpers:
Paper Machines: 1
 No. 1, TAD, total capacity 79,968 st/y, Trim width 295 in, Tissue
Energy Data:
 Power boilers: 4
 Electrical demand for mill: 270 MWh/D

VERMONT

ⓞⓜFiberMark North America, Inc.
Brattleboro Mill
Ownership: 100% by American Securities Capital Partners LLC
161 Wellington Rd
Brattleboro, VT 05301
USA
 Phone: (1) 802-257-0365
 Fax: (1) 802-257-5973
 Email: service@fibermark.com
 Web Address: www.fibermark.com
Personnel:
 Gen. Mgr.: James Sherman
 Phone: (1) 802-257-0365
 Fax: (1) 802-257-5973
Total Employees of Company: 250
Total Employees at this Location: 250
Type of Operation: Paper mill
Paper/Paperboard Grades and Capacities:
 Total paper and paperboard capacity: 42,999 st/y
 Specialty and industrial: 42,999 st/y
Paper and Paperboard Mill Data:
 Stock Preparation:
 Pulpers: 3
 Refiners: 4
Paper Machines: 1
 PM 1, Ultraformer, total capacity 43,000 st/y, Trim width 86 in, Specialty and industrial
Coating Machines: 2
 CM 1, off machine
 CM 2, off machine
Finishing Equipment:
 Rewinders: 1

ⓜRockTenn Co.
Missisquoi Mill
Mill St
Sheldon Springs, VT 05485
USA
Mailing Address: PO Box 98, Sheldon Springs, VT 05485, USA
 Phone: (1) 802-933-7733
 Fax: (1) 802-933-5326
 Web Address: www.rocktenn.com
Personnel:
 Gen. Mgr.: Wade Taylor
 Phone: (1) 802-933-7733
 Fax: (1) 802-933-5326
 Email: wtaylor@rocktenn.com
 Asst Gen Mgr.: Jim Barden
 Phone: (1) 802-933-7733
 Fax: (1) 802-933-5326
 Email: jbarden@rocktenn.com
 Tech. Dir.: Roger Thieken
 Phone: (1) 802-933-7733
 Fax: (1) 802-933-5326
 Email: rthieken@rocktenn.com
Total Employees at this Location: 119
Type of Operation: Paperboard mill
Pulp Mill Data:
 Recycled Fiber Treatment Lines:
 Recycled packaging pulping lines: 1
Paper and Paperboard Mill Data:
 Stock Preparation:
 Pulpers: 6
 Refiners: 6
Coating Machines: 2
 No. 1, total capacity 49,603 st/y., on machine
 No. 2, on machine
Finishing Equipment:
 Sheeters: 2
Energy Data:
 Power boilers: 4
 Steam turbines: 1 at 1 MW

ⓜSoundview Paper Co.
Putney Mill
Previously Putney Paper Co.
67 Kathan Meadow Road
Putney, VT 05346
USA
Mailing Address: PO Box 226, Putney, VT 05346, USA
 Phone: (1) 802-387-5571
 Fax: (1) 802-387-5297
 Web Address: soundviewpaper.com
Personnel:
 VP, Finan.: Tom Moore
 Phone: (1) 802-387-5571
 Fax: (1) 802-387-5297
 Email: tmoore@soundviewpaper.com
 Cust. Serv. Mgr.: Toni Collins
 Phone: (1) 802-387-5571
 Fax: (1) 802-387-5297
 Email: tcollins@soundviewpaper.com
 Prod. Mgr.: Dave Harris
 Phone: (1) 802-387-5571
 Fax: (1) 802-387-5297
 Email: dharris@soundviewpaper.com
 Maint. Mgr.: Ron Nichols
 Phone: (1) 802-387-5571
 Fax: (1) 802-387-5297
 Email: nichols@soundviewpaper.com
 Environ. Mgr.: Bruce Raymond
 Phone: (1) 802-387-5571
 Fax: (1) 802-387-5297
 Email: braymond@asoundviewpaper.com
Total Employees at this Location: 53
Type of Operation: Pulp mill, Paper mill
Pulp Grades and Capacities:
 Total pulp capacity: 28,316 st/y
 Recycled Pulping: 28,316 st/y
Pulp Mill Data:
 Bleach Plant Systems: 1

 Recycled Deinked Pulping System
 Recycled Fiber Treatment Lines:
 Pulpers: 1 at 36,927
Paper/Paperboard Grades and Capacities:
 Total paper and paperboard capacity: 26,418 st/y
 Tissue: 26,418 st/y
Paper and Paperboard Mill Data:
 Stock Preparation:
 Pulpers: 2
 Refiners: 2
Paper Machines: 2
 No. 3, fourdrinier, total capacity 8,925 st/y, Trim width 90 in, Tissue
 No. 4, fourdrinier, total capacity 17,493 st/y, Trim width 103 in, Tissue
Energy Data:
 Power boilers: 2
 Electrical demand for mill: 48 MWh/D

ⓜWeidmann Electrical Technology Inc.
Saint Johnsbury Mill
Ownership: 100% by Wicor Group
One Gordon Mills Way
Saint Johnsbury, VT 05819
USA
Mailing Address: PO Box 903, St. Johnsbury, VT 05819-0903, USA
 Phone: (1) 802-748-3936
 Fax: (1) 802-748-3897
 Email: service.weti@wicor.com
 Web Address: www.weidmann-electrical.com
Personnel:
 VP & Gen. Mgr.: John M. Goodrich
 Phone: (1) 802-748-3936
 Fax: (1) 802-748-8029
 Email: john.goodrich@wicor.com
 VP, HR: Patti Harvey
 Phone: (1) 802-748-3936
 Fax: (1) 802-748-3897
 Email: patti.harvey@wicor.com
 Eng. Mgr.: William Phelps
 Phone: (1) 802-748-3936
 Fax: (1) 802-748-3897
 Email: william.phelps@wicor.com
 Eng. Mgr.: Justin Crocker
 Phone: (1) 802-748-3936
 Fax: (1) 802-748-3897
 Email: justin.crocker@wicor.com
 HR Business partner: Kilee Willey
 Phone: (1) 802-748-3936
 Fax: (1) 802-748-8029
 Email: kilee.willey@wicor.com
Total Employees at this Location: 217
Type of Operation: Paperboard mill
Paper/Paperboard Grades and Capacities:
 Total paper and paperboard capacity: 15,000 st/y
 Boxboard/cartonboard: 15,000 st/y
Paper and Paperboard Mill Data:
 Stock Preparation:
 Pulpers: 2
 Refiners: 6
Paper Machines: 2
 PM 1, dry vat, Trim width 148 in, Boxboard/cartonboard
 PM 2, cylinder (1), Trim width 126 in, Boxboard/cartonboard
Finishing Equipment:
 Calenders: 2
Energy Data:
 Power boilers: 2
 Electrical demand for mill: 3 MWh/D

VIRGINIA

ⓜBear Island Paper Co., LLC
Ashland Mill
Ownership: 100% by White Birch Paper Company

Virginia

10026 Old Ridge Rd
Ashland, VA 23005
USA
  Phone: (1) 804-227-3394
  Fax: (1) 804-227-4014
  Web Address: www.whitebirchpaper.com
Personnel:
  Gen. Mgr.: Wayne Griffin
  Phone: (1) 804-227-3394
  Fax: (1) 804-227-4014
  Email: wgriffin@bi.whitebirchpaper.com
  Purch. Mgr.: Cheree Stamper
  Phone: (1) 804-227-3394
  Fax: (1) 804-227-4014
  Email: cstamper@bi.whitebirchpaper.com
  Mgr., HR: Patricia Nowell
  Phone: (1) 804-227-3394
  Fax: (1) 804-227-4014
  Email: pnowell@bi.whitebirchpaper.com
  Supt, Paper Mill: Don Anderson
  Phone: (1) 804-227-3394
  Fax: (1) 804-227-4014
  Email: danderson@bi.whitebirchpaper.com
  Mgr., IT: Jimmy Ogle
  Phone: (1) 804-227-3394
  Fax: (1) 804-227-4014
  Email: jogle@bi.whitebirchpaper.com
  Process Eng.: Laura Beauchesne
  Phone: (1) 804-227-3394
  Fax: (1) 804-227-4014
  Email: lbeauchesne@bi.whitebirchpaper.com
  Contr.: Seth Hobart
  Phone: (1) 804-227-3394
  Fax: (1) 804-227-4014
  Email: shobart@bi.whitebirchpaper.com
  Pulping Oper. Supervisor: Melvin Lesane
  Phone: (1) 804-227-4048
  Fax: (1) 804-227-4014
  Email: mlesane@bi.whitebirchpaper.com
Total Employees at this Location: 190
Type of Operation: Pulp mill, Paper mill
Pulp Grades and Capacities:
  Total pulp capacity: 264,634 st/y
  Mechanical Pulp: 205,091 st/y
  Recycled Pulping: 59,543 st/y
Pulp Mill Data:
  Mechanical Pulping Systems:
  TMP systems: 4
  Bleach Plant Systems: 1
  No. 1, Sequence: HS, Capacity 386,750.4 admt/y
  Recycled Fiber Treatment Lines:
  Flotation deinking lines at 83,075
Paper/Paperboard Grades and Capacities:
  Total paper and paperboard capacity: 257,755 st/y
  Newsprint: 257,755 st/y
Paper and Paperboard Mill Data:
  Paper Machines: 1
  No. 1, Bel-Baie II, total capacity 257,755 st/y, Trim width 302 in, Newsprint
Energy Data:
  Power boilers: 3
  Electrical demand for mill: 1,765 MWh/D

ⓜGeorgia-Pacific LLC
Big Island Mill
9363 Lee Jackson Hwy
Big Island, VA 24526
USA
Mailing Address: PO Box 40, Big Island, VA 24526-0040, USA
  Phone: (1) 434-299-5911
  Fax: (1) 434-299-5222
  Web Address: www.gp.com
Personnel:
  VP., Oper.: Eldon Brammer
  Phone: (1) 434-299-5911
  Fax: (1) 434-299-5222
  Email: egbramme@gapac.com
  Fiber Mgr.: Dennis Austin
  Phone: (1) 434-299-5911
  Fax: (1) 434-299-5222
  Email: ddaustin@gapac.com
  Logist. Mgr.: Iris Sharpe
  Phone: (1) 434-299-5911
  Fax: (1) 434-299-5222
  Email: itsharpe@gapac.com
  Dept. Assist.: Kathy Bryant
  Phone: (1) 434-299-5911
  Fax: (1) 434-299-5222
  Email: krbryant@gapac.com
Total Employees at this Location: 341
Type of Operation: Pulp mill, Paperboard mill
Pulp Grades and Capacities:
  Total pulp capacity: 620,312 st/y
  Chemical Pulp: 194,756 st/y
  Recycled Pulping: 425,556 st/y
Pulp Mill Data:
  Chemical Pulping Systems:
  Continuous digesters: 5
  Chemical Recovery Equipment:
  Evaporator lines: 1
  Recovery boilers: 1
Paper/Paperboard Grades and Capacities:
  Total paper and paperboard capacity: 597,975 st/y
  Linerboard: 285,600 st/y
  Corrugating medium/fluting: 312,375 st/y
Paper and Paperboard Mill Data:
  Paper Machines: 3
  No. 1, (with LNP), fourdrinier, total capacity 98,175 st/y, Trim width 100 in, Corrugating medium/fluting
  No. 3, (with ENP.), fourdrinier, total capacity 214,200 st/y, Trim width 168 in, Corrugating medium/fluting
  No. 4, (with LNP), fourdrinier, total capacity 285,600 st/y, Trim width 185 in, Linerboard
Energy Data:
  Power boilers: 3
  Steam turbines: 1 at 7.5 MW
  Hydro turbines: 7 at 2 MW
  Electrical demand for mill: 1,075 MWh/D

ⓜGreif Inc.
Riverville Mill
861 Fibre Plant Rd
Amherst, VA 24521
USA
Mailing Address: PO Box 339, Amherst, VA 24521, USA
  Phone: (1) 434-933-4100
  Fax: (1) 434-933-4148
  Web Address: www.greif.com
Personnel:
  VP Mill Oper. (From 2014): David T. Scott
  Phone: (1) 434-933-4159
  Fax: (1) 434-933-4148
  Email: david.scott@greif.com
  Maint. Mgr.: Michael Zalegowski
  Phone: (1) 434-933-4100
  Fax: (1) 434-933-4148
  Email: michael.zalegowski@greif.com
  Tech. Mgr.: Mitchell V. Heishman
  Phone: (1) 434-933-4100
  Fax: (1) 434-933-4148
  Email: mitch.heishman@greif.com
  OCC Buyer, Shppng: Leonard R. Brown
  Phone: (1) 434-933-4100
  Fax: (1) 434-933-4148
  Email: leonard.brown@greif.com
  Sr Proj. Mgr.: Brad Maines
  Phone: (1) 434-933-4100
  Fax: (1) 434-933-4148
  Email: brad.maines@greif.com
Total Employees at this Location: 243
Type of Operation: Pulp mill, Paper mill, Paperboard mill
Pulp Grades and Capacities:
  Total pulp capacity: 516,229 st/y
  Chemical Pulp: 207,413 st/y
  Recycled Pulping: 308,816 st/y
Pulp Mill Data:
  Chemical Pulping Systems:
  Continuous digesters: 1
  Chemical Recovery Equipment:
  Evaporator lines: 1
  Recovery boilers: 1
  Recycled Fiber Treatment Lines:
  Recycled packaging pulping lines: 1 at 276,124 admt/y
Paper/Paperboard Grades and Capacities:
  Total paper and paperboard capacity: 499,800 st/y
  Linerboard: 199,920 st/y
  Corrugating medium/fluting: 299,880 st/y
Paper and Paperboard Mill Data:
  Stock Preparation:
  Pulpers: 1
  Refiners: 10
  Paper Machines: 2
  No. 1, fourdrinier, total capacity 299,880 st/y, Trim width 260 in, Corrugating medium/fluting
  No. 2, (ENP Press.), fourdrinier, total capacity 199,920 st/y, Trim width 180 in, Linerboard
  Finishing Equipment:
  Rewinders: 2
Energy Data:
  Power boilers: 4
  Electrical demand for mill: 934 MWh/D

ⓜInternational Paper Co.
Franklin Mill
34040 Union Camp Dr
Franklin, VA 23851-0178
USA
  Phone: (1) 757-569-4641
  Fax: (1) 757-569-4545
  Email: (firstname.lastname@ipaper.com)
  Web Address: www.internationalpaper.com
Personnel:
  Pulp Mill Area Mgr.: Steve Cook
  Phone: (1) 757-569-4641
  Fax: (1) 757-569-4545
  Email: steve.cook@ipaper.com
  Prod. Mgr.: Margot Harding
  Phone: (1) 757-569-4641
  Fax: (1) 757-569-4545
  Email: margot.harding@ipaper.com
  HR Generalist: Lindsay Pope
  Phone: (1) 757-569-4641
  Fax: (1) 757-569-4545
  Email: lindsay.pope@ipaper.com
Total Employees at this Location: 200
Type of Operation: Pulp mill, Paper mill, Paperboard mill
Pulp Grades and Capacities:
  Total pulp capacity: 317,934 st/y
  Pulp available for market: 299,880 st/y
  Chemical Pulp: 317,934 st/y
Pulp Mill Data:
  Chemical Pulping Systems:
  Continuous digesters: 2
  Pulp Lines: 1
  Bleach Plant Systems: 3
  Chemical Pulping System, Type: Softwood Line, Sequence: O_2 DEoD
  Chemical Recovery Equipment:
  Evaporator lines: 4
  Recovery boilers: 3
  Lime Kiln
  Pulp Dryers:
  Fourdriniers 1
Energy Data:
  Power boilers: 2
  Steam turbines: 3 at 15.6, 20, 28 MW
  Hydro turbines: 1 at 59 MW
  Electrical demand for mill: 759 MWh/D

ⓞInterstate Resources, Inc.
Ownership: 100% by INDEVCO - Industrial Development Company sal
1800 N Kent St, Suite 1200
Arlington, VA 22209-2145
USA

Virginia

Phone: (1) 703-243-3355
Fax: (1) 703-243-4681
Email: admin@iripaper.com
Web Address: www.iripaper.com
Personnel:
Chmn. & CEO: Antoine N. Frem
Phone: (1) 703-243-3355
Fax: (1) 703-243-4681
Email: antoine.frem@iripaper.com
Pres. & COO: Jim Morgan
Phone: (1) 703-243-3355
Fax: (1) 703-243-4681
Email: jmorgan@iripaper.com
CFO: Pierre Khatter
Phone: (1) 703-243-3355
Fax: (1) 703-243-4681
Email: pierre.khatter@iripaper.com
Exec. Treasure & Corp. Secretary: Ramez Skaff
Phone: (1) 703-243-3355
Fax: (1) 703-243-4681
Email: ramez.skaff@iripaper.com
VP, HR: Susan Newman
Phone: (1) 703-243-3355
Fax: (1) 703-243-4681
Email: susan.newman@iripaper.com
Corp. Contr.: Paul D. Zimmerman
Phone: (1) 703-243-3355
Fax: (1) 703-243-4681
Email: paul.zimmerman@iripaper.com
Total Employees of Company: 1,500
Total Employees at this Location: 14
Mill Locations:
Interstate Paper Industries, Sadat City Mill, 85 km North of Cairo Desert Road, P.O. Box 165, Sadat City, Egypt, Capacity: 82,672 st/y, (Paper mill)
Phone: (20) 4 8261 3080/77
Fax: (20) 4 8261 3076
Email: papermaking@indevcogroup.com , pcd@indevcogroup.com, info@ipitissue.com
Interstate Paper L.L.C., Riceboro Mill, 2366 Interstate Paper Rd, Riceboro, GA 31323, USA, Capacity: 350,217 st/y, (Pulp mill, Paper mill, Paperboard mill)
Phone: (1) 912-884-3371
Fax: (1) 912-884-3426
Email: info@interstatepaper.com
Unipak Tissue Mill, Jbeil Mill, Old Seaside Road, Halat, Jbeil, Lebanon, Capacity: 19,841 st/y, (Paper mill)
Phone: (961) 9 478911/2/3
Fax: (961) 9 478909
Email: exportsales@unipak-tissue-mill.com, customercare@utmlb.com
United Corrstack LLC, Reading Mill, 720 Laurel St, Reading, PA 19602, USA, Capacity: 172,788 st/y, (Paperboard mill)
Phone: (1) 610-374-3000
Fax: (1) 610-376-8215
Email: info@InterstateResources.com

ⓂMeadWestvaco Corporation
Ownership: Public
501 South 5th Street
Richmond, VA 23219-0501
USA
Phone: (1) 804-444-1000
Fax: (1) 804-327-6363
Web Address: www.mwv.com
Personnel:
Chmn., CEO: John A. Luke Jr
Phone: (1) 804-444-1101
Fax: (1) 804-327-6363
Email: john.luke@mwv.com
Exec. VP, & Pres. Packaging: Dr. Robert K Beckler
Phone: (1) 804-444-1000
Fax: (1) 804-327-6363
Exec. VP. & Pres. Global Oper.: Robert A. Feeser
Phone: (1) 804-444-1000
Fax: (1) 804-327-6363
Snr. VP & CFO: E. Mark Rajkowski
Phone: (1) 804-444-1125
Fax: (1) 804-327-6363
Email: mark.rajkowski@mwv.com
Snr. VP, HR, Commun. & Meadwestvaco Foundation: Linda V. Schreiner
Phone: (1) 804-444-1125
Fax: (1) 804-327-6363
Email: linda.schreiner@mwv.com
Snr. VP, Technology: Mark T. Watkins
Phone: (1) 804-444-1107
Fax: (1) 804-327-6363
Email: mark.watkins@mwv.com
Snr. VP., Home, Health & Beauty Packaging: Peter C. Durette
Phone: (1) 804-444-1123
Fax: (1) 804-327-6363
Email: peter.durette@mwv.com
VP. Global Commun.: Donna Ownes Cox
Phone: (1) 804-444-7762
Fax: (1) 804-327-6363
Email: donna.owenscox@mwv.com
VP. Corp. Affairs: Ned S. Massee
Phone: (1) 804-444-5216
Fax: (1) 804-327-6363
Email: ned.massee@mwv.com
VP, Safety, Health & Environ.: Dirk Krouskop
Phone: (1) 804-444-6227
Fax: (1) 804-327-6363
Email: dirk.krouskop@mwv.com
VP. & Contrl.: Brent A. Harwood
Phone: (1) 804-444-1000
Fax: (1) 804-327-6363
Email: brent.harwood@mwv.com
Dir., Bus. Intelligence: William Bloom
Phone: (1) 804-444-1000
Fax: (1) 804-327-6363
Email: william.bloom@mwv.com
Mktg. Mgr.: Mike Mueller
Phone: (1) 804-444-2509
Fax: (1) 804-327-6363
Email: michael.mueller@mwv.com
Total Employees of Company: 16,000
Mill Locations:
MeadWestvaco Corporation, Mahrt Mill, Hwy 165 S, Cottonton, AL 36851, USA, Capacity: 1,064,574 st/y, (Pulp mill, Paperboard mill)
Phone: (1) 334-855-4711, 687-4896
Fax: (1) 334-855-5151
MeadWestvaco Corporation, Covington Mill, 104 E Riverside St, Covington, VA 24426-1238, USA, Capacity: 928,200 st/y, (Paper mill, Paperboard mill)
Phone: (1) 540-969-5000
Fax: (1) 540-969-5778
MeadWestvaco Corporation, Evadale Mill, 1913 FM 105, Evadale, TX 77615, USA, Capacity: 583,695 st/y, (Pulp mill, Paperboard mill)
Phone: (1) 409-276-3243
Fax: (1) 409-276-3108
Rigesa, Celulose, Papel e Embalagens Ltda., Três Barras Mill, Av. Rigesa, 2.400, Bairro João Paulo II, 89490-000 Três Barras, SC, Brazil, Capacity: 479,306 st/y, (Pulp mill, Paperboard mill)
Phone: (55) 47 3621 5400
Fax: (55) 47 3622 5324
Rigesa, Celulose, Papel e Embalagens Ltda., Valinhos Mill, Rua 13 de Maio 755 Centro, 13276 020 Valinhos, SP, Brazil, (Paperboard mill)
Phone: (55) 19 3869 9000/ 38699160
Fax: (55) 19 3869 9270
Email: antonio.puccinelli@mwv.com
Ruby Macons Ltd., Morai Mill, Survey No.56/1, Morai, India, Capacity: 102,315 st/y, (Paperboard mill)
Email: mail@rubymacons.com
Ruby Macons Ltd., Vapi Mill, 789/4, 3rd Phase Road G.I.D.C., 396 195 Vapi, India, Capacity: 70,833 st/y, (Paperboard mill)
Phone: (91) 260 3050000
Fax: (91) 260 2410910
Email: mail@rubymacons.com

ⓂMeadWestvaco Corporation
Covington Mill
104 E Riverside St
Covington, VA 24426-1238
USA
Phone: (1) 540-969-5000
Fax: (1) 540-969-5778
Web Address: www.mwv.com
Personnel:
VP. Oper. (From December 2014): Rod Strong
Phone: (1) 540-969-5000
Fax: (1) 540-969-5778
Email: rod.strong@mwv.com
Prod. Mgr. (From March 2014): Craig Lane
Phone: (1) 540-969-5347
Fax: (1) 540-969-5317
Email: craig.lane@mwv.com
Wood Oper. Superintedent: Michael Grist
Phone: (1) 540-969-5000
Fax: (1) 540-969-5778
Email: michael.grist@mwv.com
Paper Mill Shift Oper. Mgr. (From August 2014): Alex Kessinger
Phone: (1) 540-969-5000
Fax: (1) 540-969-5778
Email: alex.kessinger@mwv.com
Total Employees at this Location: 1,080
Type of Operation: Paper mill, Paperboard mill
Pulp Grades and Capacities:
Total pulp capacity: 881,696 st/y
Chemical Pulp: 881,696 st/y
Pulp Mill Data:
Chemical Pulping Systems:
Batch digesters: 18
Bleach Plant Systems: 3
No. 1, Sequence: O_2 DED
Chemical Recovery Equipment:
Evaporator lines: 1
Recovery boilers: 2
Lime Kiln
Paper/Paperboard Grades and Capacities:
Total paper and paperboard capacity: 928,200 st/y
Boxboard/cartonboard: 928,200 st/y
Paper and Paperboard Mill Data:
Stock Preparation:
Refiners: 22
Paper Machines: 3
No. 1, DuoFormer D, total capacity 357,000 st/y, Trim width 274 in, Boxboard/cartonboard
No. 2, DuoFormer D, total capacity 374,850 st/y, Trim width 276 in, Boxboard/cartonboard
No. 8, Bel-Bond, total capacity 196,350 st/y, Trim width 196 in, Boxboard/cartonboard
Coating Machines: 3
No. 1, total capacity 357,143 st/y., on machine
No. 2, total capacity 374,780 st/y., on machine
No. 8, total capacity 196,208 st/y., on machine
Energy Data:
Power boilers: 6
Steam turbines: 4 at 9.5, 21, 31, 56 MW
Electrical demand for mill: 2,352 MWh/D

ⓂRockTenn Co.
Hopewell Mill
910 Industrial St
Hopewell, VA 23860
USA
Mailing Address: PO Box 201, Hopewell, VA 23860, USA
Phone: (1) 804-541-9600
Fax: (1) 804-541-9770
Web Address: www.rocktenn.com
Personnel:
Mill Mgr.: David Anderson
Phone: (1) 804-541-9600
Fax: (1) 804-541-9770
Email: danderson@rocktenn.com
Maint. & Reliability Mgr.: Tim Paasch
Phone: (1) 804-541-9600
Fax: (1) 804-541-9770
Email: tpaasch@rocktenn.com
Snr. Puch. Specialist: Randy Clevenger
Phone: (1) 804-541-9600

Washington

Fax: (1) 804-541-9770
Quality Assur Mgr.: Charles Brinkley
Phone: (1) 804-541-9605
Fax: (1) 804-541-9770
Email: cbrinkle@rocktenn.com
Account Mgr.: Barbara Houston
Phone: (1) 804-541-9600
Fax: (1) 804-541-9770
Email: bhouston@rocktenn.com
HR Mgr.: Sheila Shannon
Phone: (1) 804-541-9600
Fax: (1) 804-541-9770
Email: sshannon@rocktenn.com
Total Employees at this Location: 283
Type of Operation: Pulp mill, Paperboard mill
Pulp Grades and Capacities:
Total pulp capacity: 579,046 st/y
Chemical Pulp: 436,946 st/y
Recycled Pulping: 142,099 st/y
Pulp Mill Data:
Chemical Pulping Systems:
Batch digesters: 12
Pulp Lines: 1
Chemical Recovery Equipment:
Evaporator lines: 3
Recovery boilers: 1
Lime Kiln
Recycled Fiber Treatment Lines:
Pulpers: 1 at 89,646 admt/y
Paper/Paperboard Grades and Capacities:
Total paper and paperboard capacity: 550,137 st/y
Linerboard: 550,137 st/y
Paper and Paperboard Mill Data:
Stock Preparation:
Pulpers: 1
Refiners: 4
Paper Machines: 1
No. 2, fourdrinier, total capacity 550,137 st/y, Trim width 255 in, Linerboard
Energy Data:
Power boilers: 1
Steam turbines: 1 at 48 MW
Electrical demand for mill: 1,087 MWh/D

ⓜRockTenn Co.
West Point Mill
19th & Main Sts
West Point, VA 23181
USA
Mailing Address: PO Box 100, West Point, VA 23181, USA
Phone: (1) 804-843-5000
Fax: (1) 804-843-5439
Email: webmaster@rocktenn.com
Web Address: www.rocktenn.com
Personnel:
Gen. Mgr.: Chris Broome
Phone: (1) 804-843-5650
Fax: (1) 804-843-5369
Email: cbroome@rocktenn.com
Oper. Mgr.: Daniel Rowland
Phone: (1) 804-843-5000
Fax: (1) 804-843-5369
Email: drowland@rocktenn.com
Environ. Mgr.: Carole Hamner
Phone: (1) 804-843-5270
Fax: (1) 804-843-5369
Email: chamner@rocktenn.com
Total Employees at this Location: 475
Type of Operation: Pulp mill, Paper mill, Paperboard mill
Pulp Grades and Capacities:
Total pulp capacity: 900,661 st/y
Chemical Pulp: 541,408 st/y
Recycled Pulping: 359,253 st/y
Pulp Mill Data:
Chemical Pulping Systems:
Batch digesters: 8
Continuous digesters: 1
Bleach Plant Systems: 1
1 (Continuous Digester), Type: Chemetics - Hardwood/Softwood, Sequence: DEoD
Chemical Recovery Equipment:
Evaporator lines: 1
Recovery boilers: 2
Lime Kiln
Recycled Fiber Treatment Lines:
Recycled packaging pulping lines: 2
Paper/Paperboard Grades and Capacities:
Total paper and paperboard capacity: 896,070 st/y
Linerboard: 712,929 st/y
Corrugating medium/fluting: 183,141 st/y
Paper and Paperboard Mill Data:
Stock Preparation:
Pulpers: 3
Refiners: 16
Paper Machines: 3
No. 1, fourdrinier, total capacity 183,141 st/y, Trim width 228 in, Corrugating medium/fluting
No. 2, fourdrinier, total capacity 314,874 st/y, Trim width 256 in, Linerboard
No. 3, fourdrinier (3), total capacity 398,055 st/y, Trim width 256 in, Linerboard
Finishing Equipment:
Calenders: 3
Rewinders: 2
Energy Data:
Power boilers: 2
Steam turbines: 7 at 4, 10, 25, 15, 44 MW
Electrical demand for mill: 2,182 MWh/D

ⓜSeven Hills Paperboard, LLC
Lynchburg Mill
Ownership: 49% by RockTenn Co., 51% by Lafarge Corporation
1801 Concord Turnpike-Lower Basin
Lynchburg, VA 24504-0980
USA
Phone: (1) 434-847-5521
Fax: (1) 434-846-4611
Email: dvandeford@rocktenn.com
Web Address: www.rocktenn.com
Personnel:
Gen. Mgr.: Edward N. Melton
Phone: (1) 434-847-5521
Fax: (1) 434-846-4611
Email: emelton@rocktenn.com
Prod Mgr Graphics: Jonathan Dunlap
Phone: (1) 434-847-5521
Fax: (1) 434-846-4611
Email: jdunlap@rocktenn.com
Total Employees at this Location: 85
Type of Operation: Paperboard mill
Pulp Grades and Capacities:
Total pulp capacity: 107,531 st/y
Recycled Pulping: 107,531 st/y
Paper/Paperboard Grades and Capacities:
Total paper and paperboard capacity: 103,173 st/y
Boxboard/cartonboard: 103,173 st/y
Paper and Paperboard Mill Data:
Stock Preparation:
Pulpers: 3
Refiners: 4
Paper Machines: 1
No. 1, fourdrinier, total capacity 103,173 st/y, Trim width 110 in, Boxboard/cartonboard
Coating Machines: 1
No. 1, off machine
Energy Data:
Power boilers: 1
Electrical demand for mill: 184 MWh/D

ⓜSonoco Products Co.
Richmond Mill
1850 Commerce Rd
Richmond, VA 23224
USA
Mailing Address: PO Box 1155, Richmond, VA 23218, USA
Phone: (1) 804-233-5411
Fax: (1) 804-232-7061
Web Address: www.sonoco.com
Personnel:
Pres. US Paper Mills: Scott Brown
Phone: (1) 804-233-5411 ext. 252
Fax: (1) 804-232-7061
Email: scott.brown@sonoco.com
Plt. Mgr.: Greg Goode
Phone: (1) 804-233-5411
Fax: (1) 804-232-7061
Email: greg.goode@sonoco.com
Gen. Mgr.: Max Dillon
Phone: (1) 804-233-5411 ext. 241
Fax: (1) 804-232-7061
Email: max.dillon@sonoco.com
Total Employees at this Location: 85
Type of Operation: Paperboard mill
Pulp Grades and Capacities:
Total pulp capacity: 100,918 st/y
Recycled Pulping: 100,918 st/y
Paper/Paperboard Grades and Capacities:
Total paper and paperboard capacity: 99,960 st/y
Boxboard/cartonboard: 99,960 st/y
Paper and Paperboard Mill Data:
Stock Preparation:
Pulpers: 4
Refiners: 5
Paper Machines: 1
No. 1, cylinder (7), total capacity 99,960 st/y, Trim width 140 in, Boxboard/cartonboard
Energy Data:
Power boilers: 1

ⓜST Tissue, LLC
Franklin Mill
Ownership: 100% by ST Paper, LLC
34040 Union Camp Dr
Franklin, VA 23851-0178
USA
Phone: (1) 757-304-5040
Email: info@sttissuellc.com, sales@sttissuellc.com
Web Address: www.sttissuellc.com
Personnel:
Mill Mgr.: James Maness
Phone: (1) 757-304-5040
Total Employees at this Location: 80
Type of Operation: Paper mill
Pulp Grades and Capacities:
Total pulp capacity: 74,510 st/y
Recycled Pulping: 74,510 st/y
Pulp Mill Data:
Bleach Plant Systems: 1
Recycled Pulping System, Type: Deinked, Sequence: P
Recycled Fiber Treatment Lines:
Flotation deinking lines: 1
Paper/Paperboard Grades and Capacities:
Total paper and paperboard capacity: 69,972 st/y
Tissue: 69,972 st/y
Paper and Paperboard Mill Data:
Paper Machines: 1
No. 6, fourdrinier, total capacity 69,972 st/y, Trim width 306 in, Tissue
Energy Data:
Electrical demand for mill: 233 MWh/D

WASHINGTON

ⓜBoise Paper
Boise Wallula
31831 West Hwy 12
Wallula, WA 99363
USA

Washington

Mailing Address: PO Box 500, Wallula, WA 99363-0500, USA
  Phone: (1) 509-547-2411
  Fax: (1) 509-545-3298
  Web Address: www.boiseinc.com
Total Employees at this Location: 449
Type of Operation: Pulp mill, Paper mill, Paperboard mill
Energy Data:
  Electrical demand for mill: 1,002 MWh/D

Boise Paper
Wallula Mill
Previously Boise Inc.
Ownership: 100% by Packaging Corp. of America
31831 West Hwy 12
Wallula, WA 99363
USA
Mailing Address: PO Box 500, Wallula, WA 99363-0500, USA
  Phone: (1) 509-547-2411
  Fax: (1) 509-545-3298
  Web Address: www.boisepaper.com
Personnel:
  Mill Mgr.: Sean M. Krajnik
  Phone: (1) 509-545-3201
  Fax: (1) 509-545-3298
  Email: seankrajnik@boisepaper.com
  Reliability Mgr.: Neil Heeney
  Phone: (1) 509-547-2411
  Fax: (1) 509-545-3298
  Email: neilheeney@boisepaper.com
  Pulp Mill Assis. Supt.: Andrew Anacker
  Phone: (1) 509-547-2411
  Fax: (1) 509-545-3298
  Email: andrewanacker@boisepaper.com
Total Employees at this Location: 449
Type of Operation: Pulp mill, Paper mill, Paperboard mill
Pulp Grades and Capacities:
  Total pulp capacity: 399,029 st/y
  Pulp available for market: 142,060 st/y
  Chemical Pulp: 328,489 st/y
  Recycled Pulping: 70,540 st/y
Pulp Mill Data:
  Chemical Pulping Systems:
  Continuous digesters: 4
  Bleach Plant Systems: 2
  (Cont. Digester Kraft - HW), Type: Hardwood, Sequence: DEoDEpD
  (Cont. Digester Kraft - SW), Type: Softwood, Sequence: DEoDEpD
  (Cont. Digester Sawdust - bleached), Type: DEoDEPoD - Sawdust
  Chemical Recovery Equipment:
  Evaporator lines: 1
  Recovery boilers: 2
  Lime Kiln
  Pulp Dryers:
  Fourdriniers 1
Paper/Paperboard Grades and Capacities:
  Total paper and paperboard capacity: 324,828 st/y
  Uncoated woodfree/freesheet: 74,597 st/y
  Specialty and industrial: 114,215 st/y
  Corrugating medium/fluting: 136,017 st/y
Paper and Paperboard Mill Data:
  Stock Preparation:
  Pulpers: 5
  Refiners: 5
Paper Machines: 2
  No. 2, fourdrinier, total capacity 136,017 st/y, Trim width 155 in, Corrugating medium/fluting
  No. 3, (Former Type model: Bel Baie II), twin-wire, total capacity 188,811 st/y, Trim width 245 in, Uncoated woodfree/freesheet, Specialty and industrial
Coating Machines: 1
  No. 1, on machine
Energy Data:
  Power boilers: 3
  Electrical demand for mill: 1,002 MWh/D

Clearwater Paper Corporation
Ownership: Public
601 W. Riverside Avenue, Suite 1100
Spokane, WA 99201
USA
  Phone: (1) 509-344-5900
  Fax: (1) 509-835-1555
  Web Address: www.clearwaterpaper.com
Personnel:
  Member board of directors: Beth E. Ford
  Phone: (1) 509-344-5900
  Fax: (1) 509-835-1555
  Email: beth.ford@clearwaterpaper.com
  Member board of directors: Kevin J. Hunt
  Phone: (1) 509-344-5900
  Fax: (1) 509-835-1555
  Email: kevin.hunt@clearwaterpaper.com
  Pres. & CEO: Linda K. Massman
  Phone: (1) 509-344-5900
  Fax: (1) 509-835-1555
  Email: linda.massman@clearwaterpaper.com
  Snr. VP & CFO: John D. Hertz
  Phone: (1) 509-344-5900
  Fax: (1) 509-835-1555
  Email: john.hertz@clearwaterpaper.com
  Snr. VP, Pres. of Consumer Products Div.: Thomas A. Colgrove
  Phone: (1) 509-344-5943
  Fax: (1) 509-342-2605
  Email: thomas.colgrove@clearwaterpaper.com
  Snr. VP, Pres. Pulp & Paperboard Div.: Dan G. Johansen
  Phone: (1) 509-344-5939
  Fax: (1) 509-342-2598
  Email: dan.johansen@clearwaterpaper.com
  Snr. VP, Gen. Counsel & Corp. Sec.: Michael S. Gadd
  Phone: (1) 509-344-5900
  Fax: (1) 509-835-1555
  Email: michael.gadd@clearwaterpaper.com
  Snr. VP, HR: Jackson O. Lynch
  Phone: (1) 509-344-5900
  Fax: (1) 509-835-1555
  Email: jackson.lynch@clearwaterpaper.com
Total Employees of Company: 3,860
Mill Locations:
  Clearwater Paper Corporation, East Hartford Mill, Two Forbes St, East Hartford, CT 06108, USA, Capacity: 33,915 st/y, (Paper mill)
  Phone: (1) 860-289-7496
  Fax: (1) 860-289-5142
  Email: info@clearwaterpaper.com
  Clearwater Paper Corporation, Ladysmith Mill, 1215 East Worden Ave., Ladysmith, WI 54848-2079, USA, Capacity: 53,193 st/y, (Pulp mill, Paper mill)
  Phone: (1) 715-532-5541
  Fax: (1) 715-532-5542
  Email: info@clearwaterpaper.com
  Clearwater Paper Corporation, Las Vegas Mill, 3901 North Donna St., North Las Vegas, NV 89030, USA, Capacity: 37,842 st/y, (Paper mill)
  Phone: (1) 702-657-2400
  Fax: (1) 702-657-1572
  Email: firstname.lastname@clearwaterpaper.com
  Clearwater Paper Corporation, Lewiston Mill, 803 Mill Rd, Lewiston, ID 83501, USA, Capacity: 622,965 st/y, (Pulp mill, Paper mill, Paperboard mill)
  Phone: (1) 208-799-0123/208-799-1644 (Terri Rice)
  Fax: (1) 208-799-1488
  Clearwater Paper Corporation, Cypress Bend Mill, McGehee Mill, 5082 Arkansas 4, McGehee, Arkansas City, AR 71630, USA, Capacity: 312,018 st/y, (Paperboard mill)
  Phone: (1) 870-877-2662
  Fax: (1) 870-877-3380
  Clearwater Paper Corporation, Menominee Mill, 144 First St, Menominee, MI 49858, USA, Capacity: 35,692 st/y, (Paper mill)
  Phone: (1) 906-863-5595
  Fax: (1) 906-864-3320
  Email: info@clearwaterpaper.com
  Clearwater Paper Corporation, Natural Dam Mill, 4921 State Highway 58, Gouverneur, NY 13642, USA, Capacity: 38,913 st/y, (Paper mill)
  Phone: (1) 315-287-1200
  Fax: (1) 315-287-1111
  Clearwater Paper Corporation, Lakeview Mill, 249 N Lake St, Neenah, WI 54956, USA, Capacity: 83,895 st/y, (Paper mill)
  Phone: (1) 920-721-9800
  Fax: (1) 920-721-9831
  Email: info@clearwaterpaper.com
  Clearwater Paper Corporation, Saint Catharines Mill, 45 Merritt St, Saint Catharines, ON, Canada L2T 1J4, Capacity: 48,909 st/y, (Paper mill)
  Phone: (1) 905-680-3000
  Fax: (1) 905-227-1899
  Email: info@clearwaterpaper.com
  Clearwater Paper Corporation, Wiggins Mill, 1321 S Magnolia Dr, Wiggins, MS 39577-9615, USA, Capacity: 58,905 st/y, (Paper mill)
  Phone: (1) 601-928-5205
  Fax: (1) 601-928-3601
  Clearwater Paper Corporation, Shelby Mill, 687 Washburn Switch Rd, Shelby, NC 28150, USA, Capacity: 69,972 st/y, (Paper mill)
  Phone: (1) 704-476-3801
  Fax: (1) 704-481-8955

Cosmo Specialty Fibers, Inc.
Ownership: 100% by The Gores Group LLC
1701 1st St
Cosmopolis, WA 98537
USA
Mailing Address: PO Box 539, Cosmopolis, WA 98537, USA
  Phone: (1) 360-500-4600
  Fax: (1) 360-537-8304, 360-500-4601
  Web Address: www.cosmospecialtyfibers.com
Personnel:
  Bd. Mbr.: Scott Marshall
  Phone: (1) 360-500-4600
  Fax: (1) 360-500-4601
  CEO: Michael W. Entz
  Phone: (1) 360-500-4600
  Fax: (1) 360-537-8304
  Email: mentz@cosmospecialtyfibers.com
  CFO: Regina G Wyse
  Phone: (1) 360-500-4600
  Fax: (1) 360-537-8304
  Email: rwyse@cosmospecialtyfibers.com
  Snr. VP., Global Sls. Pulp: Warren Pullen
  Phone: (1) 1-914-696-9025, 1-914-310-4121 Mobile
  Fax: (1) 360-500-4601
  Email: jwpullen@cng-inc.com
  VP. Govern. Rel., Mktg & Commun.: Robert Buchan
  Phone: (1) 360-500-4600
  Fax: (1) 360-537-8304
  Email: rbuchan@cosmospecialtyfibers.com
  HR Dir.: Scott Wilding
  Phone: (1) 360-500-4600
  Fax: (1) 360-537-8304
  Email: swilding@cosmospecialtyfibers.com
  Dir., Fiber Resources: Larry Davis
  Phone: (1) 360-500-4600
  Fax: (1) 360-537-8304
  Email: ldavis@cosmospecialtyfibers.com
  Mill Mgr.: James E. Smith
  Phone: (1) 360-500-4600
  Fax: (1) 360-537-8304
  Email: jsmith@cosmospecialtyfibers.com
  Contracting & Procurement Mgr.: Sandy L. Corrion
  Phone: (1) 360-500-4643
  Fax: (1) 360-537-8304
  Email: scorrion@cosmospecialtyfibers.com
  Safety & Healthy Mgr.: Donna J. Parsons
  Phone: (1) 360-500-4651
  Fax: (1) 360-537-8304
  Email: dparsons@cosmospecialtyfibers.com
Mill Locations:
  Cosmo Specialty Fibers, Inc., Cosmopolis Mill, 1701 1st St, Cosmopolis, WA 98537, USA, (Pulp mill)
  Phone: (1) 360-532-7110, 360-500-4600
  Fax: (1) 360-537-8304, 360-500-4601

Washington

ⓂCosmo Specialty Fibers, Inc.
Cosmopolis Mill
1701 1st St
Cosmopolis, WA 98537
USA
Mailing Address: PO Box 539, Cosmopolis, WA 98537, USA
Phone: (1) 360-532-7110, 360-500-4600
Fax: (1) 360-537-8304, 360-500-4601
Web Address: www.cosmospecialtyfibers.com
Personnel:
Mill Mgr.: James Smith
Phone: (1) 360-532-7110
Fax: (1) 360-537-8304
Email: jsmith@cosmospecialtyfibers.com
Dir. of Fiber Resources: Larry Davis
Phone: (1) 360-500-4628
Fax: (1) 360-500-4601
Email: ldavis@cosmospecialtyfibers.com
HR. Dir.: Scott Wilding
Phone: (1) 360-500?4600
Fax: (1) 360-500-4601
Email: swilding@cosmospecialtyfibers.com
Safety & Health Mgr.: Donna J. Parsons
Phone: (1) 360-500-4651
Fax: (1) 360-500-4601
Email: dparsons@cosmospecialtyfibers.com
Contracting and Procurement Mgr.: Sandy L. Corrion
Phone: (1) 360.500.4643
Fax: (1) 360-500-4601
Email: scorrion@cosmospecialtyfibers.com
Environ. Mgr.: Craig McKinney
Phone: (1) 360-500-4638
Fax: (1) 360-537-8304
Email: cmckinney@cosmospecialtyfibers.com
Total Employees at this Location: 200
Type of Operation: Pulp mill
Pulp Grades and Capacities:
Total pulp capacity: 164,058 st/y
Pulp available for market: 154,259 st/y
Chemical Pulp: 164,058 st/y
Pulp Mill Data:
Chemical Pulping Systems:
Batch digesters: 9
Bleach Plant Systems: 1
No. 1, Sequence: DOEDP
Chemical Recovery Equipment:
Recovery boilers: 3
Pulp Dryers:
Flakt dryer 1, Fourdriniers 1
Energy Data:
Power boilers: 1
Steam turbines: 2 at 7.5, 7.5 MW
Electrical demand for mill: 366 MWh/D

ⓂGeorgia-Pacific LLC
Camas Mill
401 NE Adams St
Camas, WA 98607-2133
USA
Phone: (1) 360-834-3021
Fax: (1) 360-834-8176
Web Address: www.gp.com
Personnel:
VP Manuf., Mill Mgr. (From April 2014): Joe Ertolacci
Phone: (1) 360-834-8482
Fax: (1) 360-834-8186
Email: joseph.ertolacci@gapac.com
Mgr., Qlty. Product Management: Lyle Bays
Phone: (1) 360-834-8482
Fax: (1) 360-834-8186
Email: lyle.bays@gapac.com
Convert. Supt.: Tom Long
Phone: (1) 360-834-8482
Fax: (1) 360-834-8186
Email: tom.long@gapac.com
Total Employees at this Location: 488
Type of Operation: Pulp mill, Paper mill
Pulp Grades and Capacities:
Total pulp capacity: 241,477 st/y
Chemical Pulp: 241,477 st/y
Pulp Mill Data:
Chemical Pulping Systems:
Batch digesters: 13
Continuous digesters: 2
Bleach Plant Systems: 3
No. 1, Type: Sawdust, Sequence: DEoDED, Capacity 45,000 admt/y
No. 2, Type: Softwood, Sequence: O_2 DEpD, Capacity 238,000.4 admt/y
No. 3, Type: Hardwood, Sequence: DEopD, Capacity 115,000 admt/y
Chemical Recovery Equipment:
Evaporator lines: 1
Recovery boilers: 1
Lime Kiln
Pulp Dryers:
Wet Lap machine
Paper/Paperboard Grades and Capacities:
Total paper and paperboard capacity: 285,537 st/y
Uncoated woodfree/freesheet: 237,353 st/y
Tissue: 48,184 st/y
Paper and Paperboard Mill Data:
Stock Preparation:
Pulpers:
Paper Machines: 2
No. 11, TAD, total capacity 48,184 st/y, Trim width 165 in, Tissue
No. 20, Bel-Baie II, total capacity 237,353 st/y, Trim width 295 in, Uncoated woodfree/freesheet
Finishing Equipment:
Sheeters: 2
Energy Data:
Power boilers: 2
Steam turbines: 1 at 52 MW
Electrical demand for mill: 929 MWh/D

ⓂHarbor Paper LLC
Ownership: 100% by Elliott Rust Companies
801 23rd St
Hoquiam, WA 98550
USA
Phone: (1) 360-532-9600 or 877-548-3424 (toll free)
Fax: (1) 360-538-5636
Email: tle@harborpaper.com
Web Address: www.harborpaper.com/
Personnel:
Pres & CEO: John Begley
Phone: (1) 360-532-9600
Fax: (1) 360-538-5636
Email: jbegley@harborpaper.com
Prod. Mgr.: Bill McClelland
Phone: (1) 360-532-9600
Fax: (1) 360-538-5636
Email: bmcclelland@harborpaper.com
Utility Mgr.: John Pellegrini
Phone: (1) 360-532-9600
Fax: (1) 360-538-5636
Email: jpellegrini@harborpaper.com
Account Mgr. & Tech. Serv. Mgr.: Gary Braden
Phone: (1) 360-532-9600
Fax: (1) 360-538-5636
Email: gbarden@harborpaper.com
Total Employees of Company: 175
Mill Locations:
Harbor Paper LLC, Hoquiam Mill, 801 23rd St, Hoquiam, WA 98550, USA, (Paper mill)
Phone: (1) 360-532-9600 or 877-548-3424 (toll free)
Fax: (1) 360-538-5636
Email: tle@harborpaper.com

ⓂHarbor Paper LLC
Hoquiam Mill
Mill is closed (Idled from January, 2013, permanently closed from January 2014, mill will be sold off piece-by-piece and the buildings demolished)
801 23rd St
Hoquiam, WA 98550
USA
Phone: (1) 360-532-9600 or 877-548-3424 (toll free)
Fax: (1) 360-538-5636
Email: tle@harborpaper.com
Web Address: www.harborpaper.com
Personnel:
Pres. & CEO: John Begley
Phone: (1) 360-532-9600
Fax: (1) 360-538-5636
Email: jbegley@harborpaper.com
Prod. Mgr.: Bill McClelland
Phone: (1) 360-532-9600
Fax: (1) 360-538-5636
Email: bmcclelland@harborpaper.com
Utility Mgr.: John Pellegrini
Phone: (1) 360-532-9600
Fax: (1) 360-538-5636
Email: jpellegrini@harborpaper.com
Account Mgr.& Tech. Serv. Mgr.: Gary Braden
Phone: (1) 360-532-9600
Fax: (1) 360-538-5636
Email: gbarden@harborpaper.com
Total Employees at this Location: 175
Type of Operation: Paper mill
Paper and Paperboard Mill Data:
Stock Preparation:
Pulpers: 6
Refiners: 6
Paper Machines: 2
No. 1, fourdrinier, total capacity 80,307 st/y, Trim width 185 in
No. 2, fourdrinier, total capacity 74,953 st/y, Trim width 160 in
Finishing Equipment:
Rewinders: 2
Sheeters: 4
Energy Data:
Power boilers: 2
Steam turbines: 1 at 15.6 MW

ⓂInland Empire Paper Co.
Ownership: 100% by Cowles Company
3320 N Argonne Rd
Millwood, Spokane, WA
USA
Phone: (1) 509-924-1911
Fax: (1) 509-927-8461
Email: iep@iepco.com
Web Address: www.iepco.com
Personnel:
Pres. & Gen. Mgr.: Kevin Rasler
Phone: (1) 509-924-1911
Fax: (1) 509-927-8461
Email: kevinrasler@iepco.com
PM Supt.: Chris Averyt
Phone: (1) 509-924-1911
Fax: (1) 509-927-8461
Email: chrisaveryt@iepco.com
Total Employees of Company: 128
Mill Locations:
Inland Empire Paper Co., Millwood Mill, 3320 N Argonne Rd, Millwood, Spokane, WA 99212-2099, USA, Capacity: 196,759 st/y, (Pulp mill, Paper mill)
Phone: (1) 509-924-1911
Fax: (1) 509-927-8461
Email: iep@iepco.com

ⓂInland Empire Paper Co.
Millwood Mill
3320 N Argonne Rd
Millwood, Spokane, WA 99212-2099
USA
Phone: (1) 509-924-1911
Fax: (1) 509-927-8461
Email: iep@iepco.com
Web Address: www.iepco.com
Personnel:
Pres. & Gen. Mgr.: Kevin Rasler

Washington

Phone: (1) 509-924-1911
Fax: (1) 509-927-8461
Email: kevinrasler@iepco.com
Environ. Mgr.: Doug Krapas
Phone: (1) 509-924-1911
Fax: (1) 509-927-8461
Email: dougkrapas@iepco.com
Bus. Mgr.: Shirene Young
Phone: (1) 508-850-2232
Fax: (1) 509-927-8461
Email: shireneyoung@iepco.com
Mktg. & Sls. Mgr.: Glenn Owens
Phone: (1) 509-924-1911
Fax: (1) 509-927-8461
Email: glennowens@iepco.com
Forest Oper. Mgr.: Paul Buckland
Phone: (1) 509-924-1911
Fax: (1) 509-927-8461
Email: paulbuckland@iepco.com
Pulp Mill Supt.: Luke Huntley
Phone: (1) 509-924-1911
Fax: (1) 509-927-8461
Email: lukehuntley@iepco.com
Paper Machine Supt.: Chris Averyt
Phone: (1) 509-924-1911
Fax: (1) 509-927-8461
Email: chrisaveryt@iepco.com
Total Employees at this Location: 112
Type of Operation: Pulp mill, Paper mill
Pulp Grades and Capacities:
 Total pulp capacity: 195,273 st/y
 Mechanical Pulp: 156,218 st/y
 Recycled Pulping: 39,055 st/y
Pulp Mill Data:
 Mechanical Pulping Systems:
 TMP systems: 1
 Bleach Plant Systems: 2
 Mechanical TMP Pulping System, Type: Softwood
 Recycled Deinked Pulping System, Sequence: P
 Recycled Fiber Treatment Lines:
 Flotation deinking lines: 4 at 74,680 admt/y
 Pulpers: 1 at 91,821 admt/y
 Washing deinking lines: 2 at 30,589 admt/y
Paper/Paperboard Grades and Capacities:
 Total paper and paperboard capacity: 196,759 st/y
 Newsprint: 143,634 st/y
 Uncoated mechanical/groundwood: 53,125 st/y
Paper and Paperboard Mill Data:
 Stock Preparation:
 Pulpers: 2
 Refiners: 1
Paper Machines: 1
 No. 5, DuoFormer TQv, total capacity 196,759 st/y, Trim width 227 in, Newsprint, Uncoated mechanical/groundwood
Finishing Equipment:
 Winders: 1
 Calenders: 2
Energy Data:
 Power boilers: 3
 TMP Reboiler: 1
 Electrical demand for mill: 1,284 MWh/D

ⓘⓜ KapStone Kraft Paper Corporation
Longview Mill
Company is previously Longview Fibre Paper and Packaging Inc.
Ownership: 100% by KapStone Paper and Packaging Corp
300 Fibre Way
Longview, WA 98632
USA
Mailing Address: PO Box 639, Longview, WA 98632, USA
 Phone: (1) 360-425-1550
 Fax: (1) 360-230-5135
 Web Address: www.fibreshield.com, www.kapstonepaper.com
Personnel:
 VP. Mill Oper. (From October 2014): Paul E. Duncan
 Phone: (1) 360-575-5372
 Fax: (1) 360-230-5135
 Email: paul.duncan@kapstonepaper.com
 Dir. Sls. & Mktg.: William P. Lindsay
 Phone: (1) 360-575-5242
 Fax: (1) 360-230-5135
 Email: william.lindsay@kapstonepaper.com
 Snr. Dir. HR: Gary Parafinczuk
 Phone: (1) 360-575-52271
 Fax: (1) 360-230-3265
 Email: gary.parafinczuk@kapstonepaper.com
 Dir. Eng., Env., and Safety: Patrick Ortiz
 Phone: (1) 360-575-5242
 Fax: (1) 360-230-5135
Total Employees at this Location: 875
Type of Operation: Pulp mill, Paper mill, Paperboard mill
Mill Locations:
KapStone Kraft Paper Corporation, Cowpens Mill, 139 Price Farm Rd, Cowpens, SC 29330, USA, Capacity: 239,904 st/y, (Paperboard mill)
 Phone: (1) 864-463-9090, 864-463-1722
 Fax: (1) 864-463-9585
 Email: information@kapstonepaper.com
KapStone Kraft Paper Corporation, Roanoke Rapids Mill, 100 Gaston Road, Roanoke Rapids, NC 27870-1911, USA, Capacity: 439,824 st/y, (Pulp mill, Paper mill, Paperboard mill)
 Phone: (1) 252-533-6000
 Fax: (1) 252-533-6401
 Email: information@kapstonepaper.com
Pulp Grades and Capacities:
 Total pulp capacity: 1,191,430 st/y
 Pulp available for market: 35,700 st/y
 Chemical Pulp: 813,658 st/y
 Recycled Pulping: 377,772 st/y
Pulp Mill Data:
 Chemical Pulping Systems:
 Continuous digesters: 4
 Pulp Lines: 4
 Chemical Recovery Equipment:
 Evaporator lines: 5
 Recovery boilers: 3
 Lime Kiln
 Recycled Fiber Treatment Lines:
 Pulpers: 2 at 400,400 admt/y
 Pulp Dryers:
 Fourdriniers 1
Paper/Paperboard Grades and Capacities:
 Total paper and paperboard capacity: 1,106,343 st/y
 Packaging papers: 413,763 st/y
 Specialty and industrial: 5,712 st/y
 Linerboard: 477,666 st/y
 Corrugating medium/fluting: 209,202 st/y
Paper and Paperboard Mill Data:
 Stock Preparation:
 Pulpers: 15
 Refiners: 46
Paper Machines: 5
No. 5, fourdrinier, total capacity 60,690 st/y, Trim width 185 in, Packaging papers, Specialty and industrial
No. 7, fourdrinier, total capacity 308,448 st/y, Trim width 167 in, Linerboard
No. 10, fourdrinier, total capacity 414,120 st/y, Trim width 242 in, Linerboard, Corrugating medium/fluting
No. 11, fourdrinier, total capacity 192,780 st/y, Trim width 238 in, Packaging papers
No. 12, fourdrinier, total capacity 166,005 st/y, Trim width 240 in, Packaging papers
Finishing Equipment:
 Calenders: 1
Energy Data:
 Power boilers: 4
 HRSG boiler
 Combustion turbines: 1 at 57.8 (idle) MW
 Steam turbines: 6 at 55 MW

ⓘ Nippon Paper Industries USA Co., Ltd.
Ownership: Nippon Paper Industries Co., Ltd.
1815 Marine Dr
Port Angeles, WA 98363
USA
Mailing Address: P.O. Box 271, Port Angeles, WA 98362, USA
 Phone: (1) 360-565-7063, 360-457-4474
 Fax: (1) 360-452-6576
 Email: questions@npiusa.com
 Web Address: www.npiusa.com, www.nipponpapergroup.com/e/index.html
Personnel:
 Pres.: Yoshihiro Sagawa
 Phone: (1) 360-565-7063
 Fax: (1) 360-452-6576
 Email: Yoshihiro.sagawa@npiusa.com
 Treasurer: Yoichiro Nakada
 Phone: (1) 360-565-7063
 Fax: (1) 360-452-6576
 Email: yoichiro.nakada@npiusa.com
 Snr. Advisor: David Tamaki
 Phone: (1) 360-565-7063
 Fax: (1) 360-452-6576
 Email: david.tamaki@npiusa.com
 VP, Sls. & Mktg.: John Howell
 Email: john.howell@npiusa.com
 VP, Sls.: Geoff Shaw
 Phone: (1) 360-565-7063
 Fax: (1) 360-452-6576
 Cust. Serv. Representative: Kathy Konopaski
 Phone: (1) 360-565-7063
 Fax: (1) 360-452-6576
Total Employees of Company: 220
Total Employees at this Location: 220
Mill Locations:
Nippon Paper Industries USA Co., Ltd., Port Angeles Mill, 1902 Marine Dr, Port Angeles, WA 98362, USA, Capacity: 163,310 st/y, (Pulp mill, Paper mill)
 Phone: (1) 360-457-4474
 Fax: (1) 360-452-6576
 Email: questions@npiusa.com

ⓘⓜ Nippon Paper Industries USA Co., Ltd.
Port Angeles Mill
Ownership: Nippon Paper Industries Co., Ltd.
1902 Marine Dr
Port Angeles, WA 98362
USA
Mailing Address: PO Box 271, Port Angeles, WA 98362, USA
 Phone: (1) 360-457-4474
 Fax: (1) 360-452-6576
 Email: questions@npiusa.com
 Web Address: www.npiusa.com, www.nipponpapergroup.com/e/index.html
Personnel:
 VP Mill, Power Mgr. (Eff. March 27, 2014): Steven R. Johnson
 Phone: (1) 360-565-7034
 Fax: (1) 360-452-6576
 Email: steven.johnson@npiusa.com
 Plt. Contr.: Mary Sue French
 Phone: (1) 360-457-4474
 Fax: (1) 360-452-6576
 Email: mary.french@npiusa.com
 Proj. Mgr.: Gary J. Holmquist
 Phone: (1) 360-457-4474
 Fax: (1) 360-452-6576
 Email: gary.holmquist@npiusa.com
 Maint. Mgr.: Ken Sugg
 Phone: (1) 360-457-4474
 Fax: (1) 360-452-6576
 Email: ken.sugg@npiusa.com
 HR Mgr.: Cathy Price
 Phone: (1) 360-457-4474
 Fax: (1) 360-452-6576

Washington

Email: cathy.price@npiusa.com
Pulp Supt.: Jamie Strouf
Phone: (1) 360-457-4474
Fax: (1) 360-452-6576
Email: jamie.strouf@npiusa.com
Environ. Dir.: Paul Perlwitz
Phone: (1) 360-457-4474
Fax: (1) 360-452-6576
Email: paul.perlwitz@npiusa.com
Total Employees at this Location: 200
Type of Operation: Pulp mill, Paper mill
Pulp Grades and Capacities:
Total pulp capacity: 144,795 st/y
Mechanical Pulp: 100,868 st/y
Recycled Pulping: 43,926 st/y
Pulp Mill Data:
Mechanical Pulping Systems:
RMP systems: 3
Bleach Plant Systems: 2
Mechanical RMP Pulping System, Type: Softwood, Sequence: PY
Recycled Deinked Pulping System
Recycled Fiber Treatment Lines:
Flotation deinking lines: 1 at 99,206 admt/y
Pulpers: 1 at 99,206 admt/y
Paper/Paperboard Grades and Capacities:
Total paper and paperboard capacity: 163,310 st/y
Uncoated mechanical/groundwood: 163,310 st/y
Paper and Paperboard Mill Data:
Stock Preparation:
Pulpers:
Paper Machines: 2
No. 2, Top Flyte, total capacity 60,995 st/y, Trim width 154 in, Uncoated mechanical/groundwood
No. 3, Top Flyte, total capacity 102,315 st/y, Trim width 222 in, Uncoated mechanical/groundwood
Finishing Equipment:
Winders: 2 at 165,000 st/y
Energy Data:
Power boilers
Steam turbines: 1 at 20 MW

ⓂNorth Pacific Paper Corp. (Norpac)
Longview Mill
Ownership: 50% by Weyerhaeuser Co., 50% by Nippon Paper Industries Co., Ltd.
3000 Industrial Way
Longview, WA 98632
USA
Mailing Address: PO Box 2069, Longview, WA 98632, USA
Phone: (1) 360-636-6400
Fax: (1) 360-636-6881
Web Address: www.weyerhaeuser.com
Personnel:
VP, Mill Mgr: Craig Anneberg
Phone: (1) 360-636-6400
Fax: (1) 360-636-6881
Email: craig.anneberg@weyerhaeuser.com
Mgr, Cust Serv.: Tom Rozwod
Phone: (1) 360-636-6400
Fax: (1) 360-636-6881
Email: tom.rozwod@weyerhaeuser.com
Training Mgr.: Ross Lovie
Phone: (1) 360-636-7148
Fax: (1) 360-636-6881
Email: ross.lovie@weyerhaeuser.com
Total Employees at this Location: 450
Type of Operation: Paper mill
Pulp Grades and Capacities:
Total pulp capacity: 819,013 st/y
Mechanical Pulp: 695,169 st/y
Recycled Pulping: 123,844 st/y
Pulp Mill Data:
Mechanical Pulping Systems:
TMP systems: 2
Bleach Plant Systems: 1
Mechanical TMP Pulping System - 1, Type: Softwood, Sequence: P

Recycled Fiber Treatment Lines:
Flotation deinking lines: 1 at 236,111 admt/y
Paper/Paperboard Grades and Capacities:
Total paper and paperboard capacity: 836,227 st/y
Newsprint: 310,880 st/y
Uncoated mechanical/groundwood: 525,347 st/y
Paper and Paperboard Mill Data:
Stock Preparation:
Pulpers: 16
Refiners: 3
Paper Machines: 3
No. 1, Bel-Baie II, total capacity 271,528 st/y, Trim width 346 in, Newsprint
No. 2, Bel-Baie II, total capacity 289,236 st/y, Trim width 341 in, Newsprint, Uncoated mechanical/groundwood
No. 3, Bel-Baie III, total capacity 275,463 st/y, Trim width 318 in, Uncoated mechanical/groundwood
Energy Data:
Power boilers
Electrical demand for mill: 5,610 MWh/D

ⓂPonderay Newsprint Co.
Usk Mill
Ownership: 40% by Resolute Forest Products Canada Inc., 13.50% by Copley Press, 13.50% by Gannett, 27% by McClatchy News, 6% by MediaNews
422767 State Hwy 20
Usk, WA 99180-9771
USA
Phone: (1) 509-445-1511
Fax: (1) 509-445-1233
Web Address: www.resolutefp.com
Personnel:
Gen. Mgr.: Myron Johnson
Phone: (1) 509-445-2142
Fax: (1) 509-445-1233
Email: myron.johnson@resolutefp.com
Papermachine Mgr.: Bernie Kessler
Phone: (1) 509-445-1511
Fax: (1) 509-445-1233
Email: bernie.kessler@resolutefp.com
Tech. Mgr.: Brad Bardwell
Phone: (1) 509-445-1511 Ext. 2175
Fax: (1) 509-445-1233
Email: brad.bardwell@resolutefp.com
Utilities Mgr.: Pete Poquette
Phone: (1) 509-445-2302
Fax: (1) 509-445-1233
Email: pete.poquette@resolutefp.com
Oper. Team Mgr.: Greg Matlock
Phone: (1) 509-445-2138
Fax: (1) 509-445-1233
Email: gregory.matlock@resolutefp.com
Pulping Mgr. TMP & Recycle: Robert Grace
Phone: (1) 509-445-2154
Fax: (1) 509-445-1233
Email: bob.grace@resolutefp.com
Mech. Maint. Mgr.: Todd Behrend
Phone: (1) 509-445-2183
Fax: (1) 509-445-1233
Email: todd.behrend@resolutefp.com
Total Employees at this Location: 177
Type of Operation: Pulp mill, Paper mill
Pulp Grades and Capacities:
Total pulp capacity: 274,294 st/y
Mechanical Pulp: 266,331 st/y
Recycled Pulping: 7,962 st/y
Pulp Mill Data:
Mechanical Pulping Systems:
TMP systems: 2
Bleach Plant Lines:
Mechanical TMP Pulping System, Type: Softwood, Sequence: H
Recycled Fiber Treatment Lines:
Flotation deinking lines: 1 at 47,399
Paper/Paperboard Grades and Capacities:
Total paper and paperboard capacity: 268,773 st/y
Newsprint: 268,773 st/y

Paper and Paperboard Mill Data:
Paper Machines: 1
No. 1, SpeedFormer HS, total capacity 268,773 st/y, Trim width 328 in, Newsprint
Energy Data:
Power boilers: 1
TMP Reboiler: 1

ⓄⓂPort Townsend Paper Corp.
Port Townsend Mill
Ownership: Private
100 Paper Mill Hill Rd
Port Townsend, WA 98368
USA
Mailing Address: PO Box 3170, Port Townsend, WA 98368, USA
Phone: (1) 360-385-3170, 360-379-4224 (general mill info)
Fax: (1) 360-385-0355
Email: community_relations@ptpc.com
Web Address: www.ptpc.com
Personnel:
Exec. Chmn.: Dale Stahl
Phone: (1) 360-385-3170
Fax: (1) 360-385-0355
Pres.: Roger P Hagan
Phone: (1) 360-385-3170
Fax: (1) 360-385-0355
Email: rogerh@ptpc.com
Gen. Sls. Mgr.: Kevin Wright
Phone: (1) 360-385-3170
Fax: (1) 360-385-0355
Email: kevinw@ptpc.com
Fiber Supply Mgr.: George Cave
Phone: (1) 360-385-3170
Fax: (1) 360-385-0355
Email: georgec@ptpc.com
Tech. Serv. Mgr.: Kristi Kobetich
Phone: (1) 360-385-3170
Fax: (1) 360-385-0355
Email: kristik@ptpc.com
Total Employees of Company: 600
Total Employees at this Location: 325
Type of Operation: Pulp mill, Paper mill, Paperboard mill
Pulp Grades and Capacities:
Total pulp capacity: 322,902 st/y
Pulp available for market: 92,820 st/y
Chemical Pulp: 213,810 st/y
Recycled Pulping: 109,092 st/y
Pulp Mill Data:
Chemical Pulping Systems:
Batch digesters: 12
Continuous digesters: 1
Chemical Recovery Equipment:
Evaporator lines: 1
Recovery boilers: 1
Lime Kiln
Recycled Fiber Treatment Lines:
Pulpers: 1 at 98,104
Pulp Dryers:
Fourdriniers 1, Other dryers 1
Paper/Paperboard Grades and Capacities:
Total paper and paperboard capacity: 217,770 st/y
Packaging papers: 76,755 st/y
Linerboard: 83,895 st/y
Corrugating medium/fluting: 57,120 st/y
Paper and Paperboard Mill Data:
Stock Preparation:
Refiners: 4
Paper Machines: 1
No. 2, fourdrinier, total capacity 217,770 st/y, Trim width 238 in, Linerboard, Corrugating medium/fluting, Packaging papers
Finishing Equipment:
Winders: 1
Calenders: 1
Rewinders: 2
Sheeters: 2

Washington

Energy Data:
Power boilers: 4
Steam turbines: 3 at 14.5 MW
Hydro turbines: 1 at 0.4 MW
Electrical demand for mill: 540 MWh/D

ⓜRockTenn Co.
Tacoma Mill
Previously Simpson Tacoma Kraft Co.
801 East Portland Ave
Tacoma, WA 98421
USA
  Phone: (1) 253-572-2150
  Fax: (1) 253-596-0159
  Web Address: www.rocktenn.com
Personnel:
  Paper Mill Mgr.: Tom Blake
  Phone: (1) 253-572-2150
  Fax: (1) 253-596-0159
  Email: tblake@rocktenn.com
  Gen. Sls. Mgr.: Paul Hensel
  Phone: (1) 253-572-2150
  Fax: (1) 253-596-0159
  Email: phensel@rocktenn.com
  Sourcing Mgr.: Lori Smith
  Phone: (1) 253-572-2150
  Fax: (1) 253-596-0159
  Email: lsmith@rocktenn.com
  Oper. Mgr.: John Brandt
  Phone: (1) 253-572-2150
  Fax: (1) 253-596-0159
  Email: jbrandt@rocktenn.com
  Paper Mill Shift Supervisor: John Sly
  Phone: (1) 253-572-2150
  Fax: (1) 253-596-0159
  Email: jsly@rocktenn.com
  Environ. Mgr. (From May 2013): Lester Keel
  Phone: (1) 253-572-2150
  Fax: (1) 253-596-0159
  Email: lkeel@rocktenn.com
  Cust. Serv. Mgr.: Tara Sorensen
  Phone: (1) 253-596-0178
  Fax: (1) 253-596-0159
  Email: tsorensen@rocktenn.com
Total Employees at this Location: 385
Type of Operation: Pulp mill, Paper mill, Paper mill, Paperboard mill
Pulp Grades and Capacities:
Total pulp capacity: 495,611 st/y
Pulp available for market: 59,976 st/y
Chemical Pulp: 377,711 st/y
Recycled Pulping: 117,900 st/y
Pulp Mill Data:
Chemical Pulping Systems:
Continuous digesters: 2
Bleach Plant Systems: 1
Chemical Pulping System, Type: Softwood, Sequence: DEopD
Chemical Recovery Equipment:
Evaporator lines: 3
Recovery boilers: 1
Lime Kiln
Recycled Fiber Treatment Lines:
Pulpers: 1 at 84,877
Pulp Dryers:
Flakt dryer 1, Flakt dryer 1, Fourdriniers 1, Fourdriniers 1
Paper/Paperboard Grades and Capacities:
Total paper and paperboard capacity: 424,830 st/y
Linerboard: 424,830 st/y
Paper and Paperboard Mill Data:
Stock Preparation:
Pulpers: 2
Refiners: 8
Paper Machines: 2
No. 13, fourdrinier, total capacity 89,250 st/y, Trim width 164 in, Linerboard
No. 14, fourdrinier (2), total capacity 335,580 st/y, Trim width 240 in, Linerboard
Finishing Equipment:
Calenders: 2

Rewinders: 1
Energy Data:
Power boilers: 2
Steam turbines: 1 at 55 MW
Electrical demand for mill: 1,074 MWh/D

ⓜSimpson Paper Co.
Ownership: Simpson Investment Co.
917 E. 11th Street
Tacoma, WA 98421
USA
  Phone: (1) 253-779-6400
  Web Address: www.simpson.com
Personnel:
  Chmn Bd: Colin F. Moseley
  Phone: (1) 253-779-6400
  Email: cmoseley@simpson.com
  Pres: Ray Tennison
  Phone: (1) 253-779-6400
  Email: rtennis@simpson.com
  Dir. Sls. & Mktg.: Laurie Creech
  Phone: (1) 253-779-6400
  Email: lcreech@simpson.com

ⓜSonoco Products Co.
Sumner Mill
Steele Av
Sumner, WA 98390
USA
Mailing Address: PO Box 489, Sumner, WA 98390, USA
  Phone: (1) 253-863-6366
  Fax: (1) 253-863-0223
  Web Address: www.sonoco.com
Personnel:
  Reg Mfg Mgr: Kishor Jhala
  Phone: (1) 253-863-6366
  Fax: (1) 253-863-0223
  MillWright/Mechanicals: Dan Kini
  Phone: (1) 253-863-6366
  Fax: (1) 253-863-0223
  Email: dan.kini@sonoco.com
Total Employees at this Location: 59
Type of Operation: Paperboard mill
Pulp Grades and Capacities:
Total pulp capacity: 38,501 st/y
Recycled Pulping: 38,501 st/y
Paper/Paperboard Grades and Capacities:
Total paper and paperboard capacity: 37,485 st/y
Boxboard/cartonboard: 37,485 st/y
Paper and Paperboard Mill Data:
Stock Preparation:
Pulpers: 2
Refiners: 4
Paper Machines: 1
No. 1, cylinder (8), total capacity 37,485 st/y, Trim width 88 in, Boxboard/cartonboard
Finishing Equipment:
Sheeters: 1
Energy Data:
Power boilers: 2
Electrical demand for mill: 53 MWh/D

ⓜTacoma Paperboard
Tacoma Mill
Ownership: 100% by Caraustar Industries, Inc.
808 E. 26th St.
Tacoma, WA 98421
USA
  Phone: (1) 253-627-1197
  Fax: (1) 253-627-0380
  Email: greg.bartlett@caraustar.com
  Web Address: www.caraustar.com
Personnel:
  Gen. Mgr.: Mark Lindstrom
  Phone: (1) 253-627-1197
  Fax: (1) 253-627-0380
  Email: mark.lindstrom@caraustar.com
  Process Eng.: Mike Trussell
  Phone: (1) 253-627-1197

  Fax: (1) 253-627-0380
  Email: mike.trussell@caraustar.com
Total Employees at this Location: 49
Type of Operation: Paperboard mill
Pulp Grades and Capacities:
Total pulp capacity: 49,034 st/y
Recycled Pulping: 49,034 st/y
Pulp Mill Data:
Recycled Fiber Treatment Lines:
Pulpers
Paper/Paperboard Grades and Capacities:
Total paper and paperboard capacity: 48,195 st/y
Boxboard/cartonboard: 48,195 st/y
Paper and Paperboard Mill Data:
Stock Preparation:
Pulpers: 3
Refiners: 5
Paper Machines: 1
No. 1, cylinder (10), total capacity 48,195 st/y, Trim width 84 in, Boxboard/cartonboard
Finishing Equipment:
Rewinders: 1
Energy Data:
Power boilers: 2
Electrical demand for mill: 64 MWh/D

ⓜWeyerhaeuser Co.
Company is Weyerhaeuser Company will move its headquarters from Federal Way, Wash., to 200 Occidental Avenue in Seattle, Wash. The move will occur in mid to late 2016 when construction of the new building is complete
Ownership: Public
33663 Weyerhaeuser Way South
Federal Way, WA 98003
USA
  Phone: (1) 253-924-2345
  Fax: (1) 253-924-4652 Procurement Hotline
  Email: PubRelations@weyerhaeuser.com, purchasing.contact@weyerhaeuser.com
  Web Address: www.weyerhaeuser.com
Personnel:
  Pres. & CEO: Doyle R. Simons
  Phone: (1) 253-924-2345
  Fax: (1) 253-924-465
  Email: doyle.simons@weyerhaeuser.com
  Exec. VP & CFO: Patricia (Patty) M. Bedient
  Phone: (1) 253-924-2345
  Fax: (1) 253-924-4652
  Email: patricia.bedient@weyerhaeuser.com
  Snr. VP., Timberlands (From January 2014): Rhonda Hunter
  Phone: (1) 253-924-2345
  Fax: (1) 253-924-4652
  Snr. VP., Cellulose Fibers: Shrinivasan Chandrasekaran
  Phone: (1) 253-924-2345
  Fax: (1) 253-924-4652
  Email: shrinivasan.chandrasekaran@weyerhaeuser.com
  Snr. VP., Gen. Counsel (from July 2014): Devin Stockfish
  Phone: (1) 253-924-2345
  Fax: (1) 253-924-4652
  Snr. VP., Oriented Strand Board, Engineered Lumber Products and Distribution: Cathy Slater
  Phone: (1) 253-924-2345
  Fax: (1) 253-924-4652
  Email: cathy.slater@weyerhaeuser.com
  Snr. VP., Lumber (From August 21, 2013): Adrian Blocker
  Phone: (1) 253-924-2345
  Fax: (1) 253-924-4652 Procurement
  Snr. VP., HR and Invest. Rel. (Eff. August 2014): Denise Merle
  Phone: (1) 253-924-2345
  Fax: (1) 253-924-4652
  VP., Govern Rel., Environ., Health & Safety: Kristen Sawin
  Phone: (1) 253-924-2345
  Fax: (1) 253-924-4652
  VP., & Chief Accounting Officer.: Jeanne M. Hillman
  Phone: (1) 253-924-2345
  Fax: (1) 253-924-4652
  Email: jeanne.hillman@weyerhaeuser.com

Washington

Dir., Invest. Rel. (Eff. April 2014): Beth Baum
Phone: (1) 253-924-2345
Fax: (1) 253-924-4652
Total Employees of Company: 13,000
Mill Locations:
North Pacific Paper Corp. (Norpac), Longview Mill (50% owned), 3000 Industrial Way, Longview, WA 98632, USA, Capacity: 836,227 st/y, (Paper mill)
Phone: (1) 360-636-6400
Fax: (1) 360-636-6881
Weyerhaeuser Co., Columbus Mill, 4335 Carson Road, Hwy 792, Columbus, MS 39703, USA, (Pulp mill)
Phone: (1) 662-243-4000
Weyerhaeuser Co., Longview Mill, 3401 Industrial Way 98632, Longview, WA 98632-9285, USA, Capacity: 303,450 st/y, (Pulp mill, Paperboard mill)
Phone: (1) 360-636-6812 / 360-425-2150
Fax: (1) 360-636-6382
Email: bleachedpaperboard@weyerhaeuser.com
Weyerhaeuser Co., New Bern Mill, 1785 Weyerhaeuser Rd, Vanceboro, NC 28526-7606, USA, (Pulp mill)
Phone: (1) 252-633-7100
Fax: (1) 252-633-7529
Email: pulpgeneral@weyerhaeuser.com
Weyerhaeuser Co., Flint River Mill, 2449 Stagecoach Road, Oglethorpe, GA 31068, USA, (Pulp mill)
Phone: (1) 478-472-2527
Email: pulpgeneral@weyerhaeuser.com
Weyerhaeuser Co., Port Wentworth Mill, 1 Bonnybridge Rd, Port Wentworth, GA 31407, USA, (Pulp mill)
Phone: (1) 912-964-1271
Fax: (1) 912-966-4339
Email: pulpGeneral@weyerhaeuser.com
Weyerhaeuser Company Ltd., Grande Prairie Mill, Mailbag 1020, Grande Prairie, AB, Canada T8V 3A9, (Pulp mill)
Phone: (1) 780-539-8500
Fax: (1) 780-539-8500

ⓂWeyerhaeuser Co.
Longview Mill
3401 Industrial Way 98632
Longview, WA 98632-9285
USA
Mailing Address: PO Box 188, Longview, WA 98632-7117, USA
Phone: (1) 360-636-6812 / 360-425-2150
Fax: (1) 360-636-6382
Email: bleachedpaperboard@weyerhaeuser.com
Web Address: www.weyerhaeuser.com
Personnel:
Environ. Mgr.: Bryan Wood
Phone: (1) 360-636-6812 / 360-425-2150
Fax: (1) 360-636-6382
Email: bryan.wood@weyerhaeuser.com
Safety & EMS Mgr.: Terry Alexander
Phone: (1) 360-891-3376
Fax: (1) 360-636-6382
Email: terry.alexander@weyerhaeuser.com
Portfolio Mgr.: Jim Bunker
Phone: (1) 360-636-6812 / 360-425-2150
Fax: (1) 360-636-6382
Email: jim.bunker@weyerhaeuser.com
Fiberline Mgr.: Graham Bailey
Phone: (1) 360-636-6812 / 360-425-2150
Fax: (1) 360-636-6382
Email: graham.bailey@weyerhaeuser.com
Total Employees at this Location: 465
Type of Operation: Pulp mill, Paperboard mill
Pulp Grades and Capacities:
Total pulp capacity: 442,770 st/y
Pulp available for market: 136,944 st/y
Chemical Pulp: 442,770 st/y
Pulp Mill Data:
Chemical Pulping Systems:
Continuous digesters: 1
Pulp Lines: 1
Bleach Plant Systems: 1
Chemical Pulping System, Type: Softwood/Hardwood, Sequence: O₂ DEopDD

Chemical Recovery Equipment:
Evaporator lines: 2
Recovery boilers: 1
Lime Kiln
Pulp Dryers:
Other dryers 1, Wet Lap machine 1
Paper/Paperboard Grades and Capacities:
Total paper and paperboard capacity: 303,450 st/y
Boxboard/cartonboard: 303,450 st/y
Paper and Paperboard Mill Data:
Stock Preparation:
Refiners: 6
Paper Machines: 1
No. 3, fourdrinier, total capacity 303,450 st/y, Trim width 200 in, Boxboard/cartonboard
Finishing Equipment:
Rewinders: 1
Energy Data:
Power boilers: 4
Steam turbines: 3 at 51.4 MW
Electrical demand for mill: 1,428 MWh/D

WEST VIRGINIA

ⓂOx Paperboard LLC
Ownership: OX Industries
164 Eyster Road
Halltown, WV 25423-0070
USA
Mailing Address: PO Box 70, Halltown, WV 25423-0010, USA
Phone: (1) 304-725-2076
Fax: (1) 304-728-7544
Email: kirkmathews@oxpaperboard.com, jcappellano@oxpaperboard.com
Web Address: www.oxpaperboard.com
Personnel:
Pres. & Owner: Kevin J. Hayward
Phone: (1) 304-725-2076
Fax: (1) 304-728-7544
Email: khayward@oxpaperboard.com
Exec. VP, Owner/Partner: Matthew D. Sullivan
Phone: (1) 304-725-2076
Fax: (1) 304-728-7544
Email: msullivan@oxpaperboard.com
VP., HR: Kathy Ambrose
Phone: (1) 304-725-2076
Fax: (1) 304-728-7544
Email: kambrose@oxpaperboard.com
Purch. Agent: Bryan Roesch
Phone: (1) 304-725-2076
Fax: (1) 304-728-7544
Email: broesch@oxpaperboard.com
Total Employees of Company: 230
Mill Locations:
Ox Paperboard LLC, Pekin Mill, 1525 S 2nd St, Pekin, IL 61554, USA, Capacity: 42,840 st/y, (Paperboard mill)
Phone: (1) 309-346-4118
Fax: (1) 309-346-2150
Ox Paperboard LLC, Constantine Mill, 700 Centreville Rd, Constantine, MI 49042, USA, Capacity: 53,907 st/y, (Paperboard mill)
Phone: (1) 269-435-2425
Fax: (1) 269-435-7510
Ox Paperboard LLC, Halltown Mill, 164 Eyster Rd, Halltown, WV 25423-0070, USA, Capacity: 49,980 st/y, (Paperboard mill)
Phone: (1) 304-725-2076
Fax: (1) 304-728-7544
Email: kirkmathews@oxpaperboard.com

ⓂOx Paperboard LLC
Halltown Mill
164 Eyster Rd
Halltown, WV 25423-0070
USA
Mailing Address: PO Box 70, Halltown, WV 25423-0010, USA
Phone: (1) 304-725-2076
Fax: (1) 304-728-7544
Email: kirkmathews@oxpaperboard.com
Web Address: www.oxpaperboard.com
Personnel:
Pres. & Owner: Kevin J. Hayward
Phone: (1) 304-725-2076
Fax: (1) 304-728-7544
Email: khayward@oxpaperboard.com
Exec. VP, Owner/Partner: Matthew D. Sullivan
Phone: (1) 304-725-2076
Fax: (1) 304-728-7544
Email: msullivan@oxpaperboard.com
Maint. Mechanic: Andrew Austill
Phone: (1) 304-725-2076
Fax: (1) 304-728-7544
Cust. Serv. Mgr.: Jim Lanham
Phone: (1) 800-820-3687
Fax: (1) 304-728-8714
Email: jlanham@oxpaperboard.com
Total Employees at this Location: 80
Type of Operation: Paperboard mill
Pulp Grades and Capacities:
Total pulp capacity: 51,653 st/y
Recycled Pulping: 51,653 st/y
Pulp Mill Data:
Recycled Fiber Treatment Lines:
Pulpers
Paper/Paperboard Grades and Capacities:
Total paper and paperboard capacity: 49,980 st/y
Boxboard/cartonboard: 49,980 st/y
Paper and Paperboard Mill Data:
Stock Preparation:
Pulpers: 8
Refiners: 8
Paper Machines: 1
No. 2, cylinder (9), total capacity 49,980 st/y, Trim width 90 in, Boxboard/cartonboard
Finishing Equipment:
Winders: 1 at 30,000 st/y
Calenders: 1
Rewinders: 1 at 33,069 st/y
Sheeters: 1 at 42,000 st/y
Energy Data:
Power boilers: 1
Steam turbines: 1
Electrical demand for mill: 68 MWh/D

ⓂResolute FP US Inc.
Fairmont Mill
Previously Fibrek Inc.
Ownership: 100% by Resolute Forest Products Canada Inc.
702 AFR Dr
Fairmont, WV 26554
USA
Phone: (1) 304-368-0900
Fax: (1) 304-368-2826
Web Address: www.resolutefp.com
Personnel:
Gen. Mgr.: Brian Wilmoth
Phone: (1) 304-368-0900
Fax: (1) 304-368-2826
Email: brian.wilmoth@resolutefp.com
Contr.: Jill Lake
Phone: (1) 304-368-0900
Fax: (1) 304-368-2826
Email: jill.lake@resolutefp.com
Maint. Planner Mgr.: Chris Oliverio
Phone: (1) 304-333-6166
Fax: (1) 304-368-2823
Email: chris.oliverio@resolutefp.com
Fiber Line Mgr.: Steven Demyon
Phone: (1) 304-333-6188
Fax: (1) 304-368-1997
Email: steven.demyon@resolutefp.com
Maint. I & E Mgr.: Brad Morgan

Wisconsin

Phone: (1) 304-328-0900
Fax: (1) 304-368-2826
Email: brad.morgan@resolutefp.com
Total Employees at this Location: 115
Type of Operation: Pulp mill
Pulp Grades and Capacities:
Total pulp capacity: 239,897 st/y
Pulp available for market: 236,898 st/y
Recycled Pulping: 239,897 st/y

Pulp Mill Data:
Bleach Plant Systems: 1
DIP Pulping Sytem, Sequence: PFAS, Capacity 236,992.9 admt/y
Recycled Fiber Treatment Lines:
Flotation deinking lines: 2 at 240,300 admt/y
Pulpers: 2 at 352,734 admt/y
Washing deinking lines: 3 at 240,300 admt/y
Pulp Dryers:
Air Float dryers 1
Energy Data:
Power boilers
Electrical demand for mill: 436 MWh/D

WISCONSIN

ⓘAppleton Coated LLC
Ownership: 100% by Arjowiggins SAS
540 Prospect St
Combined Locks, WI 54113
USA
Phone: (1) 920-788-3550
Fax: (1) 920-687-3590
Web Address: www.appletoncoated.com
Personnel:
Pres. & CEO: Douglas Osterberg
Phone: (1) 920-788-3550 Ext.: 3473
Fax: (1) 920-687-3590
Email: dosterberg@appletoncoated.com
VP, Mktg & Cust. Svc.: Ann Whalen
Phone: (1) 920-788-3550 Ext.: 3809
Fax: (1) 920-687-3590
Email: awhalen@appletoncoated.com
VP, IT.: Bob Cramer
Phone: (1) 920-788-3550 Ext.: 3430
Fax: (1) 920-687-3590
Email: bcramer@appletoncoated.com
Exec. Dir. - Publishing Papers, Dir. Pricing, Cust. Serv.: Mike Baker
Phone: (1) 920-788-3550
Fax: (1) 920-687-3590
Email: mbaker@appletoncoated.com
Dir., Oper.: Mark Pikturna
Phone: (1) 920-788-3550 Ext.: 3454
Fax: (1) 920-687-3590
Email: mpikturna@appletoncoated.com
Prod. Mgr.: Howard Kirby
Phone: (1) 920-788-3550
Fax: (1) 920-687-3590
Email: hkirby@appletoncoated.com
Total Employees of Company: 800
Total Employees at this Location: 30
Mill Locations:
Appleton Coated LLC, Combined Locks Mill, 540 Prospect St, Combined Locks, WI 54113, USA, Capacity: 399,752 st/y, (Paper mill)
Phone: (1) 920-788-3550
Fax: (1) 920-687-3590

ⓘAppleton Coated LLC
Combined Locks Mill
Mill is for sale (Mill is expected to be sold during the course of 2014)
Ownership: 100% by Arjowiggins SAS
540 Prospect St
Combined Locks, WI 54113
USA

Mailing Address: PO Box 129, Combined Locks, WI 54113-0129, USA
Phone: (1) 920-788-3550
Fax: (1) 920-687-3590
Web Address: www.appletoncoated.com
Personnel:
VP Operations, Mill Mgr.: Mark Pikturna
Phone: (1) 920-788-3550 Ext. 3454
Fax: (1) 920-687-3590
Email: mpikturna@appletoncoated.com
Utilities and Environ. Supt.: Dave Wardecke
Phone: (1) 920-788-3550 Ext. 3495
Fax: (1) 920-687-3590
Email: dwardecke@appletoncoated.com
Tranport. Mgr.: Angie Slinger
Phone: (1) 920-788-3550
Fax: (1) 920-687-3590
Email: aslinger@appletoncoated.com
Total Employees at this Location: 425
Type of Operation: Paper mill
Pulp Grades and Capacities:
Total pulp capacity: 25,999 st/y
Recycled Pulping: 25,999 st/y

Pulp Mill Data:
Chemical Pulping Systems:
Continuous digesters: 2
Bleach Plant Lines:
No. 1, Sequence: P
Paper/Paperboard Grades and Capacities:
Total paper and paperboard capacity: 399,752 st/y
Uncoated woodfree/freesheet: 69,957 st/y
Coated woodfree/freesheet: 308,380 st/y
Coated mechanical/groundwood: 3,569 st/y
Specialty and industrial: 17,846 st/y
Paper and Paperboard Mill Data:
Stock Preparation:
Pulpers: 6
Refiners: 13
Paper Machines: 3
No. 1, twin-wire, total capacity 74,953 st/y, Trim width 123 in, Coated woodfree/freesheet, Coated mechanical/groundwood
No. 6, twin-wire, total capacity 129,919 st/y, Trim width 230 in, Uncoated woodfree/freesheet, Coated woodfree/freesheet
No. 7, twin-wire, total capacity 194,879 st/y, Trim width 226 in, Coated woodfree/freesheet, Uncoated woodfree/freesheet, Specialty and industrial
Coating Machines: 3
PM 1, total capacity 67,791 st/y., off machine
PM 6, total capacity 109,127 st/y., on machine
PM 7, total capacity 114,638 st/y., off machine
Finishing Equipment:
Winders: 2
Calenders: 2
Sheeters: 2
Energy Data:
Power boilers: 3
HRSG boiler
Combustion turbines: 1 at 48 MW
Electrical demand for mill: 800 MWh/D

ⓘAppvion, Inc.
Ownership: 100% by employees (Private)
825 E Wisconsin Avenue
Appleton, WI 54911
USA
Mailing Address: PO Box 359, Appleton, WI 54912-0359, USA
Phone: (1) 920-734-9841
Fax: (1) 920-991-8796
Web Address: www.appvion.com
Personnel:
Chmn., & CEO: Mark R. Richards
Phone: (1) 920-734-9841
Fax: (1) 920-991-8796
Email: mrichards@appvion.com
Pres. Paper Div.: Kevin Gilligan
Phone: (1) 920-734-9841
Fax: (1) 920-991-8796

Email: kgilligan@appvion.com
VP, carbonless and specialty papers business: Ethan Haas
Phone: (1) 920-734-9841
Fax: (1) 920-991-8796
Email: ehaas@appvion.com
Snr. VP Finan. & CFO: Thomas J. Ferree
Phone: (1) 920-734-9841
Fax: (1) 920-991-8796
Email: tferree@appvion.com
Snr. VP., HR: Kerry S. Arent
Phone: (1) 920-734-9841
Fax: (1) 920-991-8796
Email: karent@appvion.com
Snr. VP & Gen. Mgr. carbonless and security papers business (from Dec 5, 2013): Matt Denton
Phone: (1) 920-734-9841
Fax: (1) 920-991-8796
VP, Bus. Develop.: Ted E. Goodwin
Phone: (1) 920-734-9841
Fax: (1) 920-991-8796
Email: tgoodwin@appvion.com
VP Finan. & Contr.: Jeffrey J. Fletcher
Phone: (1) 920-734-9841
Fax: (1) 920-991-8796
Email: jfletcher@appvion.com
VP Company Sec. & Gen. Counsel: Tami L. Van Straten
Phone: (1) 920-734-9841
Fax: (1) 920-991-8796
Email: tvanstraten@appvion.com
VP, continuous improvement: Jason Schulist
Phone: (1) 920-734-9841
Fax: (1) 920-991-8796
Email: jschulist@appvion.com
Total Employees of Company: 1,700
Mill Locations:
Appvion, Inc., Roaring Spring Mill, 100 Paper Mill Rd, Roaring Spring, PA 16673-1488, USA, Capacity: 137,415 st/y, (Pulp mill, Paper mill)
Phone: (1) 814-224-2131
Fax: (1) 814-224-6540

ⓘBeloit Box Board Co
Ownership: Private
801 Second St
Beloit, WI 53511
USA
Mailing Address: PO Box 386, Beloit, WI 53512-0386, USA
Phone: (1) 608-365-6671, 800-852-2447 (Sls)
Fax: (1) 608-365-9696
Email: jnichols@beloitboxboard.com
Web Address: www.beloitboxboard.com
Personnel:
Pres.: Andrew H. Chamberlain
Phone: (1) 608-365-6671, 800-852-2447 (Sls)
Fax: (1) 608-365-9696
Email: achamberlain@beloitboxboard.com
Contr.: Marlon Knittel
Phone: (1) 608-365-6671, 800-852-2447 (Sls)
Fax: (1) 608-365-9696
Email: mknittel@beloitboxboard.com
Mill Mgr.: Richard L. Schneider
Phone: (1) 608-365-6671, 800-852-2447 (Sls)
Fax: (1) 608-365-9696
Email: rschneider@beloitboxboard.com
HR Mgr.: Mike Masterson
Phone: (1) 608-365-6671, 800-852-2447 (Sls)
Fax: (1) 608-365-9696
Email: mmasterson@beloitboxboard.com
Total Employees of Company: 54
Mill Locations:
Beloit Box Board Co, Beloit Mill, 801 Second St, Beloit, WI 53511, USA, Capacity: 19,992 st/y, (Paperboard mill)
Phone: (1) 608-365-6671, 800-852-2447 (Sls)
Fax: (1) 608-365-9696
Email: jnichols@beloitboxboard.com

ⓘBeloit Box Board Co
Beloit Mill
801 Second St

Wisconsin

Beloit, WI 53511
USA
Mailing Address: PO Box 386, Beloit, WI 53512-0386, USA
  Phone: (1) 608-365-6671, 800-852-2447 (Sls)
  Fax: (1) 608-365-9696
  Email: jnichols@beloitboxboard.com
  Web Address: www.beloitboxboard.com
Personnel:
  Mill Mgr.: Ryan Morris
  Phone: (1) 608-365-6671
  Fax: (1) 608-365-9696
  Email: rmorris@beloitboxboard.com
  Contr.: Marlon Knittel
  Phone: (1) 608-365-6671
  Fax: (1) 608-365-9696
  Email: mknittel@beloitboxboard.com
  Cust. Svc., Prod. Mgr.: Jerry Nichols
  Phone: (1) 608-365-6671
  Fax: (1) 608-365-9696
  Email: jnichols@beloitboxboard.com
  Sls. Mgr.: Erik Chamberlain
  Phone: (1) 608-365-6671
  Fax: (1) 608-365-9696
  Email: echamberlain@beloitboxboard.com
  HR Mgr.: Mike Masterson
  Phone: (1) 608-365-6671
  Fax: (1) 608-365-9696
  Email: mmasterson@beloitboxboard.com
Total Employees at this Location: 54
Type of Operation: Paperboard mill
Pulp Grades and Capacities:
  Total pulp capacity: 20,651 st/y
  Recycled Pulping: 20,651 st/y
Pulp Mill Data:
  Recycled Fiber Treatment Lines:
  Recycled packaging pulping lines: 1
Paper/Paperboard Grades and Capacities:
  Total paper and paperboard capacity: 19,992 st/y
  Boxboard/cartonboard: 19,992 st/y
Paper and Paperboard Mill Data:
  Stock Preparation:
  Pulpers: 2
  Refiners: 2
Paper Machines: 1
  No. 1, cylinder (7), total capacity 19,992 st/y, Trim width 77 in, Boxboard/cartonboard
Finishing Equipment:
  Sheeters: 1
Energy Data:
  Power boilers: 1
  Electrical demand for mill: 26 MWh/D

ⓘⓂ BPM, Inc.
Peshtigo Mill
Ownership: 100% by James Azzar
200 W. Front St.
Peshtigo, WI 54157
USA
Mailing Address: PO Box 149, Peshtigo, WI 54157-0149, USA
  Phone: (1) 715-582-4551
  Fax: (1) 715-582-4853
  Email: bpm@bpmpaper.com
  Web Address: www.bpmpaper.com
Personnel:
  Gen. Mgr.: James S. Koronkiewicz
  Phone: (1) 715-582-5223
  Fax: (1) 715-582-4853
  Email: jsk@bpmpaper.com
  Converting Mgr.: Mark S. Bruemmer
  Phone: (1) 715-582-5280
  Fax: (1) 715-582-4853
  Email: msb@bpmpaper.com
  Contr., HR: Ann Britten
  Phone: (1) 715-582-5358
  Fax: (1) 715-582-4853
  Email: amb@bpmpaper.com
  Tech. Mgr.: Ryan Day
  Phone: (1) 715-582-5247
  Fax: (1) 715-582-4853
  Email: rpd@bpmpaper.com
  Plt. Eng.: Steve Peterich
  Phone: (1) 715-582-5290
  Fax: (1) 715-582-4853
  Email: sjp@bpmpaper.com
  Converting Mgr. for Printing & Plexible Packaging - Oconto Falls & Peshtigo Facilities: Rod Wiltzius
  Phone: (1) 715-582-4551
  Fax: (1) 715-582-4853
  Email: rjw@bpmpaper.com
  Traffic, Purch. Mgr.: Vicki Lange
  Phone: (1) 715-582-5229
  Fax: (1) 715-582-4853
  Email: vll@bpmpaper.com
Total Employees of Company: 110
Total Employees at this Location: 85
Type of Operation: Paper mill
Paper/Paperboard Grades and Capacities:
  Total paper and paperboard capacity: 69,600 st/y
  Uncoated woodfree/freesheet: 49,969 st/y
  Specialty and industrial: 19,631 st/y
Paper and Paperboard Mill Data:
  Stock Preparation:
  Pulpers: 2
  Refiners: 8
Paper Machines: 2
  No. 1, (MG (Machine-glazed)), fourdrinier, total capacity 19,631 st/y, Trim width 123 in, Specialty and industrial
  No. 2, fourdrinier, total capacity 49,969 st/y, Trim width 123 in, Uncoated woodfree/freesheet
Coating Machines: 1
  No. 1, on machine
Finishing Equipment:
  Rewinders: 8
  Sheeters: 3
Energy Data:
  Power boilers: 1
  Electrical demand for mill: 89 MWh/D

ⓂCascades Tissue Group
Eau Claire Mill
Ownership: 100% by Cascades Inc.
1200 Forest St
Eau Claire, WI 54703
USA
  Phone: (1) 715-834-3461
  Fax: (1) 715-833-3140
  Web Address: www.afh.cascades.com
Personnel:
  Mill Mgr.: Rick Parr
  Phone: (1) 715-833-3186
  Fax: (1) 715-833-3140
  Email: rick_parr@cascades.com
  Mktg. Dir.: Brian S. Carlson
  Phone: (1) 715-833-3168
  Fax: (1) 715-833-3140
  Email: brian_carlson@cascades.com
  Maint. Mgr.: Darrin Groom
  Phone: (1) 715-834-3461
  Fax: (1) 715-833-3140
  Email: darrin_groom@cascades.com
  Admin. Asst.: Carla Peterson
  Phone: (1) 715-834-3461
  Fax: (1) 715-833-3140
  Email: carla_peterson@cascades.com
Total Employees at this Location: 125
Type of Operation: Pulp mill, Paper mill
Pulp Grades and Capacities:
  Total pulp capacity: 58,779 st/y
  Recycled Pulping: 58,779 st/y
Pulp Mill Data:
  Bleach Plant Systems: 1
  No. 1, Type: deinked Capacity 55,114.6 admt/y
  Recycled Fiber Treatment Lines:
  Flotation deinking lines: 2
  Pulpers: 2
  Washing deinking lines: 2
Paper/Paperboard Grades and Capacities:
  Total paper and paperboard capacity: 62,118 st/y
  Tissue: 62,118 st/y
Paper and Paperboard Mill Data:
  Stock Preparation:
  Pulpers: 2
  Refiners: 2
Paper Machines: 2
  No. 3, fourdrinier, total capacity 27,489 st/y, Trim width 126 in, Tissue
  No. 5, fourdrinier, total capacity 34,629 st/y, Trim width 129 in, Tissue
Finishing Equipment:
  Rewinders: 10
Energy Data:
  Power boilers: 1
  Electrical demand for mill: 237 MWh/D

ⓂClearwater Paper Corporation
Ladysmith Mill
Previously Cellu Tissue
1215 East Worden Ave.
Ladysmith, WI 54848-2079
USA
  Phone: (1) 715-532-5541
  Fax: (1) 715-532-5542
  Email: info@clearwaterpaper.com
  Web Address: www.clearwaterpaper.com
Personnel:
  Mill Mgr.: Keith Schenk
  Phone: (1) 715-532-5541
  Fax: (1) 715-532-5542
  Email: keith.schenk@clearwaterpaper.com
  Environ. Mgr.: Kevin Ovans
  Phone: (1) 715-532-5541
  Fax: (1) 715-532-5542
  Email: kevin.ovans@clearwaterpaper.com
  Mechanical Engineer II: Nick Sovacool
  Phone: (1) 715-532-5541 Ext. 6140
  Fax: (1) 715-532-5542
  Email: nick.sovacool@clearwaterpaper.com
Total Employees at this Location: 85
Type of Operation: Pulp mill, Paper mill
Pulp Grades and Capacities:
  Total pulp capacity: 53,449 st/y
  Recycled Pulping: 53,449 st/y
Pulp Mill Data:
  Bleach Plant Lines:
  DIP Pulping System
  Recycled Fiber Treatment Lines:
  Pulpers: 2 at 63,051 admt/y
Paper/Paperboard Grades and Capacities:
  Total paper and paperboard capacity: 53,193 st/y
  Tissue: 53,193 st/y
Paper and Paperboard Mill Data:
  Stock Preparation:
  Pulpers: 2
  Refiners: 5
Paper Machines: 2
  No. 1, crescent former, Yankee dryer, total capacity 19,278 st/y, Trim width 148 in, Tissue
  No. 4, crescent former, total capacity 33,915 st/y, Trim width 104 in, Tissue
Energy Data:
  Power boilers: 1
  Electrical demand for mill: 184 MWh/D

ⓂClearwater Paper Corporation
Lakeview Mill
249 N Lake St
Neenah, WI 54956
USA
  Phone: (1) 920-721-9800
  Fax: (1) 920-721-9831
  Email: info@clearwaterpaper.com
  Web Address: www.clearwaterpaper.com
Personnel:
  Sr. Mill Mgr.: Kevin French
  Phone: (1) 920-721-9800
  Fax: (1) 920-721-9831

Email: kevin.french@clearwaterpaper.com
Eng. & Utilities Mgr.: Mic Dworak
Phone: (1) 920-721-9800
Fax: (1) 920-721-9831
Email: mic.dworak@clearwaterpaper.com
Converting Superintendent: Tammy Harrer
Phone: (1) 920-721-9800
Fax: (1) 920-721-9831
Email: tammy.harrer@clearwaterpaper.com
Buyer: Angie Moore
Phone: (1) 920-721-9800
Fax: (1) 920-721-9831
Email: angie.moore@clearwaterpaper.com
Qlty. Assurance Mgr.: Daniel Phillips
Phone: (1) 920-721-9800
Fax: (1) 920-721-9831
Email: daniel.phillips@clearwaterpaper.com
Total Employees at this Location: 205
Type of Operation: Paper mill
Paper/Paperboard Grades and Capacities:
Total paper and paperboard capacity: 83,895 st/y
Tissue: 83,895 st/y
Paper and Paperboard Mill Data:
Stock Preparation:
Pulpers:
Paper Machines: 5
No. 1, crescent former, Yankee dryer, total capacity 15,351 st/y, Trim width 120 in, Tissue
No. 2, crescent former, Yankee dryer, total capacity 19,278 st/y, Trim width 160 in, Tissue
No. 3, crescent former, Yankee dryer, total capacity 17,136 st/y, Trim width 120 in, Tissue
No. 4, crescent former, Yankee dryer, total capacity 16,065 st/y, Trim width 120 in, Tissue
No. 5, crescent former, Yankee dryer, total capacity 16,065 st/y, Trim width 120 in, Tissue
Energy Data:
Power boilers: 3
Electrical demand for mill: 242 MWh/D

ⓜCorenso North America
Wisconsin Rapids Mill
Mill is for sale (Powerflute has signed a conditional agreement with Stora Enso to acquire the coreboard and core manufacturer Corenso. The deal is expected to be closed in Q4 2014.)
Ownership: Corenso United Oy Ltd.
800 Fremont Street
Wisconsin Rapids, WI 54495-8050
USA
Mailing Address: PO Box 1057, Wisconsin Rapids, WI 54495, USA
Phone: (1) 715-422-7800
Fax: (1) 715-422-7874
Email: corenso.northamerica@storaenso.com
Web Address: www.corenso.com
Personnel:
Pres.: Tom Janke
Phone: (1) 715-422-7800
Fax: (1) 715-422-7874
Email: tom.janke@storaenso.com
Dir., Sls.: Mark Ellis
Phone: (1) 715-422-7800
Fax: (1) 715-422-7874
Email: mark.ellis@storaenso.com
HR. Mgr.: Tracy Fitzgerald
Phone: (1) 715-422-7800
Fax: (1) 715-422-7874
Email: tracy.fitzgerald@storaenso.com
Prod. Mgr. Board Machine: Allen Paul
Phone: (1) 715-422-7800
Fax: (1) 715-422-7874
Prod. Mgr. Converting Operation: Jeffrey Pfeifer
Phone: (1) 715-422-7800
Fax: (1) 715-422-7874
Email: jeff.pfeifer@storaenso.com
Total Employees at this Location: 47
Type of Operation: Paperboard mill
Pulp Grades and Capacities:
Total pulp capacity: 95,830 st/y
Recycled Pulping: 95,830 st/y
Pulp Mill Data:
Recycled Fiber Treatment Lines:
Pulpers
Paper/Paperboard Grades and Capacities:
Total paper and paperboard capacity: 93,891 st/y
Boxboard/cartonboard: 93,891 st/y
Paper and Paperboard Mill Data:
Paper Machines: 1
No. 12, fourdrinier, total capacity 93,891 st/y, Trim width 127 in, Boxboard/cartonboard
Energy Data:
Electrical demand for mill: 150 MWh/D

ⓜDomtar Corporation
Nekoosa Mill
301 Point Basse Ave
Nekoosa, WI 54457-1422
USA
Phone: (1) 715-886-7076/715-886-7111
Fax: (1) 715-886-7620
Web Address: www.domtar.com
Personnel:
Gen. Mgr. (as of September 15, 2014): Matt Fischer
Phone: (1) 715-886-7076
Fax: (1) 715-886-7620
Email: matt.fischer@domtar.com
Oper. Mgr.: Bryan M. Lewis
Phone: (1) 715-886-7183
Fax: (1) 715-886-7620
Email: bryan.lewis@domtar.com
Fiber & Recovery Mgr.: Christopher J. Bodette
Phone: (1) 715-886-7611
Fax: (1) 715-886-7620
Email: christopher.bodette@domtar.com
Purch. Mgr.: Dean Curtis
Phone: (1) 715-886-7146
Fax: (1) 715-886-7620
Email: dean.curtis@domtar.com
Mgr., Commun. & Government Relations: Craig Timm
Phone: (1) 715-887-5061
Fax: (1) 715-887-5020
Email: craig.timm@domtar.com
Total Employees at this Location: 350
Type of Operation: Paper mill
Pulp Grades and Capacities:
Total pulp capacity: 167,803 st/y
Pulp available for market: 29,514 st/y
Chemical Pulp: 153,982 st/y
Recycled Pulping: 13,822 st/y
Pulp Mill Data:
Chemical Pulping Systems:
Batch digesters: 9
Pulp Lines: 1
Bleach Plant Systems: 1
Chemical Pulping System, Type: Hardwood/Softwood, Sequence: DEopD, Capacity 182,980.6 admt/y
Chemical Recovery Equipment:
Evaporator lines: 1
Recovery boilers: 1
Lime Kiln
Paper/Paperboard Grades and Capacities:
Total paper and paperboard capacity: 149,907 st/y
Uncoated woodfree/freesheet: 149,907 st/y
Paper and Paperboard Mill Data:
Stock Preparation:
Pulpers:
Paper Machines: 3
No. 2, fourdrinier, total capacity 49,969 st/y, Trim width 175 in, Uncoated woodfree/freesheet
No. 4, fourdrinier, total capacity 35,692 st/y, Trim width 106 in, Uncoated woodfree/freesheet
No. 9, fourdrinier, total capacity 64,246 st/y, Trim width 159 in, Uncoated woodfree/freesheet
Energy Data:
Power boilers: 3
Steam turbines: 3 at 31.6 MW
Hydro turbines: 5 at 3.2 MW

ⓜDomtar Corporation
Rothschild Mill
200 N Grand Ave
Rothschild, WI 54474-1197
USA
Phone: (1) 715-359-3101
Fax: (1) 715-355-6347
Web Address: www.domtar.com
Personnel:
Interim Mill Mgr. (From September 2014), Environ., Health & Safety Mgr.: Kathy Collins
Phone: (1) 715-355-6309
Fax: (1) 715-355-6347
Email: kathy.collins3@domtar.com
Unit Ldr.: David Faucett
Phone: (1) 715-359-3101
Fax: (1) 715-355-6347
Email: dave.faucett@domtar.com
Convert. Mgr.: Conrad S. Sternot
Phone: (1) 715-241-6534
Fax: (1) 715-355-6348
Email: conrad.sternot@domtar.com
Snr. Proj. Mgr.: Tim Holcomb
Phone: (1) 715-355-6344
Fax: (1) 715-355-6215
Email: tim.holcomb@domtar.com
Total Employees at this Location: 205
Type of Operation: Pulp mill, Paper mill
Pulp Grades and Capacities:
Total pulp capacity: 71,642 st/y
Chemical Pulp: 71,642 st/y
Pulp Mill Data:
Chemical Pulping Systems:
Batch digesters: 4
Pulp Lines: 1
Bleach Plant Systems: 1
No. 1, Type: TCF, Sequence: EoPP
Chemical Recovery Equipment:
Evaporator lines: 1
Paper/Paperboard Grades and Capacities:
Total paper and paperboard capacity: 135,630 st/y
Uncoated woodfree/freesheet: 135,630 st/y
Paper and Paperboard Mill Data:
Stock Preparation:
Pulpers:
Paper Machines: 1
No. 5, Bel-Bond, total capacity 135,630 st/y, Trim width 215 in, Uncoated woodfree/freesheet
Finishing Equipment:
Sheeters: 5
Energy Data:
Power boilers: 4
Steam turbines: 1 at 4.6 MW
Hydro turbines: 7 at 4.4 MW

ⓓⓜExpera Specialty Solutions
Kaukauna Mill
Company is previously Thilmany Papers
Ownership: 100% by Expera Specialty Solutions
600 Thilmany Rd
Kaukauna, WI 54130
USA
Mailing Address: PO Box 600, Kaukauna, WI 54130, USA
Phone: (1) 800-847-8022, 920-766-4611
Fax: (1) 920-766-8920
Email: info@experaspecialty.com
Web Address: www.experaspecialty.com
Personnel:
Mill. Mgr. Kaukauna: Steve Myers
Phone: (1) 920-766-4611
Fax: (1) 920-766-8920
Email: steve.myers@experaspecialty.com
Dir., Mktg. & Bus. Devlpt.: Dean Dalebroux
Phone: (1) 920-766-8919
Fax: (1) 920-766-8920
Email: dean.dalebroux@experaspecialty.com
Maint. Mgr.: Gary J. Frassetto
Phone: (1) 920-766-4611

Wisconsin

Fax: (1) 920-766-8920
Email: gary.frassetto@experaspecialty.com
Total Employees of Company: 1,800
Total Employees at this Location: 645
Type of Operation: Pulp mill, Paper mill
Mill Locations:
Expera Specialty Solutions, Nicolet Mill, 200 Main Ave, De Pere, WI 54115-2299, USA, Capacity: 80,325 st/y, (Paper mill)
  Phone: (1) 920-336-4211
  Fax: (1) 920-337-1228
  Email: info@experaspecialty.com
Expera Specialty Solutions, Mosinee Mill, 100 Main Street, Mosinee, WI 54455, USA, Capacity: 130,305 st/y, (Paper mill)
  Phone: (1) 715-693-2111
  Fax: (1) 715-693-4723
  Email: info@experaspecialty.com
Expera Specialty Solutions, Rhinelander Mill, 515 W Davenport St, Rhinelander, WI 54501, USA, Capacity: 152,439 st/y, (Paper mill)
  Phone: (1) 715-369-4100
  Fax: (1) 715-369-4450
  Email: info@experaspecialty.com
Pulp Grades and Capacities:
  Total pulp capacity: 115,361 st/y
  Chemical Pulp: 115,361 st/y
Pulp Mill Data:
  Chemical Pulping Systems:
  Batch digesters: 4
Pulp Lines: 1
  Bleach Plant Systems: 1
  Chemical Recovery Equipment:
  Recovery boilers: 2
  Lime Kiln
Paper/Paperboard Grades and Capacities:
  Total paper and paperboard capacity: 195,279 st/y
  Specialty and industrial: 195,279 st/y
Paper and Paperboard Mill Data:
  Stock Preparation:
  Pulpers: 11
  Refiners: 27
Paper Machines: 5
No. 11, Yankee dryer, total capacity 29,988 st/y, Trim width 120 in, Specialty and industrial
No. 12, Yankee dryer, total capacity 34,986 st/y, Trim width 150 in, Specialty and industrial
No. 13, Yankee dryer, total capacity 45,339 st/y, Trim width 162 in, Specialty and industrial
No. 14, Yankee dryer, total capacity 29,988 st/y, Trim width 186 in, Specialty and industrial
No. 15, Yankee dryer, total capacity 54,978 st/y, Trim width 163 in, Specialty and industrial
Coating Machines: 1
No. 13, on machine
Finishing Equipment:
  Winders: 6
  Calenders: 6
  Supercalenders: 1 at 60,000 st/y
  Rewinders: 13
Energy Data:
Power boilers: 3
Steam turbines: 4 at 40.5 MW
Electrical demand for mill: 617 MWh/D

ⓜExpera Specialty Solutions
Nicolet Mill
Previously Thilmany Papers
Ownership: 100% by Expera Specialty Solutions
200 Main Ave
De Pere, WI 54115-2299
USA
  Phone: (1) 920-336-4211
  Fax: (1) 920-337-1228
  Email: info@experaspecialty.com
  Web Address: www.experaspecialty.com
Personnel:
Mill Mgr.: Lee Hammen
  Phone: (1) 920-336-4211
  Fax: (1) 920-337-1228
  Email: lee.hammen@experaspecialty.com
Qlty. & Cust. Tech. Serv. Mgr.: Joel Neuville
  Phone: (1) 920-336-4211
  Fax: (1) 920-337-1228
  Email: joel.neuville@experaspecialty.com
Pwr. Eng. & Team Trainer: Michael Grimmer
  Phone: (1) 920-336-4211
  Fax: (1) 920-337-1228
  Email: michael.grimmer@experaspecialty.com
Total Employees at this Location: 235
Type of Operation: Paper mill
Paper/Paperboard Grades and Capacities:
  Total paper and paperboard capacity: 80,325 st/y
  Specialty and industrial: 80,325 st/y
Paper and Paperboard Mill Data:
  Stock Preparation:
  Pulpers: 8
  Refiners: 6
Paper Machines: 2
No. 3, foudrinier, total capacity 39,270 st/y, Trim width 141 in, Specialty and industrial
No. 4, foudrinier, total capacity 41,055 st/y, Trim width 141 in, Specialty and industrial
Finishing Equipment:
  Winders
  Supercalenders: 4
  Rewinders: 3
Energy Data:
Power boilers: 4
Hydro turbines: 5

ⓜExpera Specialty Solutions
Mosinee Mill
Previously Wasau Paper
Ownership: 100% by Expera Specialty Solutions
100 Main Street
Mosinee, WI 54455
USA
  Phone: (1) 715-693-2111
  Fax: (1) 715-693-4723
  Email: info@experaspecialty.com
  Web Address: www.experaspecialty.com
Personnel:
Mill Mgr.: Gary Garand
  Phone: (1) 715-693-2111
  Fax: (1) 715-693-4723
  Email: gary.garand@experaspecialty.com
Dir., Procurement: Rob Kudick
  Phone: (1) 715-693-2111
  Fax: (1) 715-693-4723
  Email: rob.kudick@experaspecialty.com
Dir., Bus. Analysis: Jeff Baars
  Phone: (1) 715-693-2111
  Fax: (1) 715-693-4723
  Email: jeff.baars@experaspecialty.com
Pwr. & Rec. Supt.: Jeff Osterberg
  Phone: (1) 715-693-2111
  Fax: (1) 715-693-4723
  Email: jeff.osterberg@experaspecialty.com
Tech. Mgr.: Lisa Schultz
  Phone: (1) 715-693-2111
  Fax: (1) 715-693-4723
  Email: lisa.schultz@experaspecialty.com
Total Employees at this Location: 392
Type of Operation: Paper mill
Pulp Grades and Capacities:
  Total pulp capacity: 136,467 st/y
  Chemical Pulp: 136,467 st/y
Pulp Mill Data:
  Chemical Pulping Systems:
  Batch digesters: 6
  Chemical Recovery Equipment:
  Evaporator lines: 1
  Recovery boilers: 1
  Lime Kiln
Paper/Paperboard Grades and Capacities:
  Total paper and paperboard capacity: 130,305 st/y
  Specialty and industrial: 130,305 st/y
Paper and Paperboard Mill Data:
  Stock Preparation:
  Pulpers: 4
  Refiners: 5
Paper Machines: 4
No. 1, foudrinier, total capacity 24,633 st/y, Trim width 96 in, Specialty and industrial
No. 2, foudrinier, total capacity 29,274 st/y, Trim width 120 in, Specialty and industrial
No. 3, foudrinier, total capacity 42,126 st/y, Trim width 144 in, Specialty and industrial
No. 4, foudrinier, total capacity 34,272 st/y, Trim width 100 in, Specialty and industrial
Finishing Equipment:
  Rewinders: 6
Energy Data:
Power boilers: 3
Steam turbines: 2 at 15, 5 MW
Hydro turbines: 3 at 1, 2, 1 MW
Electrical demand for mill: 448 MWh/D

ⓜExpera Specialty Solutions
Rhinelander Mill
Previously Wasau Paper
Ownership: 100% by Expera Specialty Solutions
515 W Davenport St
Rhinelander, WI 54501
USA
  Phone: (1) 715-369-4100
  Fax: (1) 715-369-4450
  Email: info@experaspecialty.com
  Web Address: www.experaspecialty.com
Personnel:
VP., Coated Product: John P. Engel
  Phone: (1) 715-369-4129
  Fax: (1) 715-369-4450
  Email: john.engel@experaspecialty.com
Mill Mgr.: Jeff Verdoorn
  Phone: (1) 715-369-4480
  Fax: (1) 715-369-4293
  Email: jeff.verdoorn@experaspecialty.com
Dir., Procurement: Linda Fox
  Phone: (1) 715-369-4100
  Fax: (1) 715-369-4450
  Email: linda.fox@experaspecialty.com
Snr. Prod. Develop. Engineer: John A. Theisen
  Phone: (1) 715-369-4202
  Fax: (1) 715-369-4293
  Email: john.theisen@experaspecialty.com
Maint. Reliability Specialist: Bill Gray
  Phone: (1) 715-369-4202
  Fax: (1) 715-369-4293
  Email: bill.gray@experaspecialty.com
Total Employees at this Location: 330
Type of Operation: Paper mill
Paper/Paperboard Grades and Capacities:
  Total paper and paperboard capacity: 152,439 st/y
  Packaging papers
  Specialty and industrial: 152,439 st/y
Paper and Paperboard Mill Data:
  Stock Preparation:
  Pulpers:
Paper Machines: 4
No. 6, foudrinier, total capacity 41,769 st/y, Trim width 162 in, Specialty and industrial
No. 7, foudrinier, total capacity 41,769 st/y, Trim width 160 in, Specialty and industrial
No. 8, foudrinier, total capacity 12,852 st/y, Trim width 114 in, Specialty and industrial, Packaging papers
No. 9, foudrinier, total capacity 56,049 st/y, Trim width 162 in, Specialty and industrial, Packaging papers
Coating Machines: 2
No. 1, total capacity 25,000 st/y., off machine
No. 2, off machine
Finishing Equipment:
  Winders: 4
  Supercalenders: 3
  Rewinders: 5
Energy Data:
Power boilers: 6

Wisconsin

Hydro turbines: 1 at 2.12 MW
Electrical demand for mill: 594 MWh/D

ⓂFlambeau River Papers, LLC
Ownership: CellMark Paper, William Butch Johnson
200 First Ave. North
Park Falls, WI 54552
USA
Mailing Address: PO Box 340, Park Falls, WI 54552, USA
  Phone: (1) 715-762-3231
  Fax: (1) 715-762-5299
  Web Address: www.flambeauriverpapers.com
Personnel:
  Pres., CEO: Butch Johnson
  Phone: (1) 715-762-3231
  Fax: (1) 715-762-5299
  Email: bjohnson@flambeauriverpapers.com
  Lignin Product Mgr.: Bill Tomczak
  Phone: (1) 715-762-3231
  Fax: (1) 715-762-5299
  Email: btomczak@flambeauriverpapers.com
  Environ. Oper. Mgr.: Herman Luedtke
  Phone: (1) 715-762-3231
  Fax: (1) 715-762-5299
  Email: hluedtke@flambeauriverpapers.com
  Purch. Mgr.: Kathy Lueloff
  Phone: (1) 715-762-3231
  Fax: (1) 715-762-5299
  Email: klueloff@flambeauriverpapers.com
Total Employees of Company: 310
Mill Locations:
Flambeau River Papers, LLC, Park Falls Mill, 200 First Ave. North, Park Falls, WI 54552, USA, Capacity: 151,692 st/y, (Pulp mill, Paper mill)
  Phone: (1) 715-762-3231
  Fax: (1) 715-762-5299

ⓂFlambeau River Papers, LLC
Park Falls Mill
200 First Ave. North
Park Falls, WI 54552
USA
Mailing Address: PO Box 340, Park Falls, WI 54552, USA
  Phone: (1) 715-762-3231
  Fax: (1) 715-762-5299
  Web Address: www.flambeauriverpapers.com
Personnel:
  Pres. & Gen. Mgr.: Randy Stoeckel
  Phone: (1) 715-762-3231
  Fax: (1) 715-762-5299
  Email: rstoeckel@flambeauriverpapers.com
  Purch. Mgr.: Kathy Lueloff
  Phone: (1) 715-762-3231
  Fax: (1) 715-762-5299
  Email: klueloff@flambeauriverpapers.com
  Lignin Product Mgr.: Bill Tomczak
  Phone: (1) 715-762-5235
  Fax: (1) 715-762-5299
  Email: btomczak@flambeauriverpapers.com
  Environ. Oper. Mgr.: Herman A. Luedtke
  Phone: (1) 715-762-3231
  Fax: (1) 715-762-5299
  Email: hluedtke@flambeauriverpapers.com
Total Employees at this Location: 300
Type of Operation: Pulp mill, Paper mill
Pulp Grades and Capacities:
  Total pulp capacity: 87,618 st/y
  Chemical Pulp: 54,925 st/y
  Recycled Pulping: 32,693 st/y
Pulp Mill Data:
  Chemical Pulping Systems:
  Batch digesters: 3
  Bleach Plant Systems: 2
  Recycled Deinked Pulping System, Sequence: P
  Sulfite Pulping System, Type: (TCF) O Delignification-H Hardwood, Sequence: O₂ H
  Chemical Recovery Equipment:
  Evaporator lines: 1
  Recycled Fiber Treatment Lines:
  Flotation deinking lines
Paper/Paperboard Grades and Capacities:
  Total paper and paperboard capacity: 151,692 st/y
  Uncoated woodfree/freesheet: 151,692 st/y
Paper and Paperboard Mill Data:
  Stock Preparation:
  Pulpers: 3
  Refiners: 7
Paper Machines: 3
No. 1, fourdrinier, total capacity 32,123 st/y, Trim width 95 in, Uncoated woodfree/freesheet
No. 2, fourdrinier, total capacity 35,692 st/y, Trim width 118 in, Uncoated woodfree/freesheet
No. 3, fourdrinier, total capacity 83,877 st/y, Trim width 157 in, Uncoated woodfree/freesheet
Finishing Equipment:
  Calenders: 3
  Rewinders: 1
  Sheeters: 3
Energy Data:
Power boilers: 4
Steam turbines: 1 at 5.7 MW
Electrical demand for mill: 431 MWh/D

ⒽⓂFox River Fiber Co., LLC
De Pere Mill
Ownership: Private
1751 W. Matthew Dr.
De Pere, WI 54115-9131
USA
  Phone: (1) 920-339-9880
  Fax: (1) 920-339-9875
  Email: akositzke@foxriverfiber.com, garchambault@foxriverfiber.com
  Web Address: foxriverfiber.com
Personnel:
  Pres.: Gregory P. Archambault
  Phone: (1) 920-339-9880 ext.32
  Fax: (1) 920-339-9875
  Email: garchambault@foxriverfiber.com
  VP, Eng., Maint., & Utilitiesy: Dave Stevenson
  Phone: (1) 920-339-9880
  Fax: (1) 920-339-9875
  Email: dstevenson@foxriverfiber.com
  VP, Sls: Ted Heimerman
  Phone: (1) 920-347-4430
  Fax: (1) 920-339-9875
  Prod. Mgr.: Mark Hunter
  Phone: (1) 920-339-9880
  Fax: (1) 920-339-9875
  Email: mark@foxriverfiber.com
  Snr. Accountant: Thias Shefchik
  Phone: (1) 920-339-9880
  Fax: (1) 920-339-9875
  Email: tshefchik@foxriverfiber.com
  Inside Sls. & Logistics Mgr.: Tricia Delain
  Phone: (1) 920-339-9880 Ext. 28
  Fax: (1) 920-339-9875
  Email: tdelain@foxriverfiber.com
  Sls. Mgr.: Bill Moe
  Phone: (1) 920-339-9880
  Fax: (1) 920-339-9875
  Email: william@foxriverfiber.com
  Reliability Engineer: Rick Dallmann
  Phone: (1) 920-339-9880
  Fax: (1) 920-339-9875
Total Employees at this Location: 50
Type of Operation: Pulp mill
Pulp Grades and Capacities:
  Total pulp capacity: 152,850 st/y
  Pulp available for market: 149,940 st/y
  Recycled Pulping: 152,850 st/y
Pulp Mill Data:
  Bleach Plant Lines:
  Recycle Pulp Line, Sequence: H
  Recycled Fiber Treatment Lines:
  Pulpers: 2 at 200,000 admt/y
  Pulp Dryers:
  Wet Lap machine 1
Energy Data:
Power boilers
Electrical demand for mill: 205 MWh/D

ⓂGeorgia-Pacific LLC
Broadway Street/West Mill
1919 S Broadway
Green Bay, WI 54304
USA
Mailing Address: PO Box 19130, Green Bay, WI 54307-9130, USA
  Phone: (1) 920-435-8821
  Fax: (1) 920-435-3703
  Web Address: www.gp.com
Personnel:
  Dir, Logist. & Transportation: Paul Snider
  Phone: (1) 920-438-4716
  Fax: (1) 920-435-3703
  Email: paul.snider@gapac.com
  Environ. Mgr.: Kenneth J. Graves
  Phone: (1) 920-438-2587
  Fax: (1) 920-435-3703
  Email: kenneth.graves@gapac.com
  Maint. Mgr.: Kevin Dickey
  Phone: (1) 920-438-2766
  Fax: (1) 920-435-3703
  Email: kevin.dickey@gapac.com
Total Employees at this Location: 800
Type of Operation: Paper mill
Pulp Grades and Capacities:
  Total pulp capacity: 411,758 st/y
  Recycled Pulping: 411,758 st/y
Pulp Mill Data:
  Bleach Plant Systems: 1
  Recycled Fiber Treatment Lines:
  Pulpers: 1 at 539,021
Paper/Paperboard Grades and Capacities:
  Total paper and paperboard capacity: 384,846 st/y
  Tissue: 384,846 st/y
Paper and Paperboard Mill Data:
  Stock Preparation:
  Pulpers: 7
  Refiners: 7
Paper Machines: 7
No. 1, crescent former, total capacity 74,970 st/y, Trim width 262 in, Tissue
No. 5, crescent former, total capacity 45,339 st/y, Trim width 124 in, Tissue
No. 6, crescent former, total capacity 45,696 st/y, Trim width 124 in, Tissue
No. 7, crescent former, total capacity 32,130 st/y, Trim width 124 in, Tissue
No. 8, crescent former, total capacity 26,061 st/y, Trim width 128 in, Tissue
No. 9, crescent former, total capacity 62,475 st/y, Trim width 195 in, Tissue
No. 10, crescent former, total capacity 98,175 st/y, Trim width 263 in, Tissue
Energy Data:
Power boilers: 6
Steam turbines: 5 at 129 MW
Electrical demand for mill: 1,745 MWh/D

ⓂGeorgia-Pacific LLC
Day Street/East Mill
500 Day St
Green Bay, WI 54302
USA
Mailing Address: PO Box 23790, Green Bay, WI 54305-3790, USA
  Phone: (1) 920-433-6200
  Fax: (1) 920-433-6352
  Web Address: www.gp.com
Personnel:
  Mill Mgr.: Mike Stankevitz
  Phone: (1) 920-433-6200
  Fax: (1) 920-433-6352
  Email: michael.stankevitz@gapac.com

Wisconsin

Prod. Planner: Johnna Spry
Phone: (1) 920-433-6200
Fax: (1) 920-433-6352
Email: johnna.spry@gapac.com
NACP Commercialization & Strategic Initiatives Oper. Mgr.: John Mladucky
Phone: (1) 920-433-6200
Fax: (1) 920-433-6352
Email: john.mladucky@gapac.com
Total Employees at this Location: 250
Type of Operation: Paper mill
Paper/Paperboard Grades and Capacities:
Total paper and paperboard capacity: 110,313 st/y
Tissue: 110,313 st/y
Paper and Paperboard Mill Data:
Stock Preparation:
Pulpers:
Paper Machines: 3
No. 1, crescent former, total capacity 26,775 st/y, Trim width 130 in, Tissue
No. 7, crescent former, total capacity 39,984 st/y, Trim width 186 in, Tissue
No. 9, eTAD, total capacity 43,554 st/y, Trim width 186 in, Tissue
Energy Data:
Power boilers: 1
Electrical demand for mill: 321 MWh/D

ⒽGreen Bay Packaging Inc.
Ownership: Kress Family (Private)
1700 N Webster Ct
Green Bay, WI 54302
USA
Mailing Address: PO Box 19017, Green Bay, WI 54307-9017, USA
Phone: (1) 920-433-5111
Fax: (1) 920-433-5471
Web Address: www.gbp.com
Personnel:
Chmn.: James F. Kress
Phone: (1) 920-433-5111
Fax: (1) 920-433-5471
Email: jkress@gbp.com
Pres. & CEO: William F. Kress
Phone: (1) 920-433-5111
Fax: (1) 920-433-5471
Snr. VP, Gen. Counsel: Scott Wochos
Phone: (1) 920-433-5111
Fax: (1) 920-433-5471
Email: swochos@gbp.com
Manuf. Dir. (Coated Product Oper.): Jeff Menzel
Phone: (1) 920-337-1790
Fax: (1) 920-433-5471
Email: jmenzel@gbpcoated.com
Admin. Coord.: Deana Martin
Phone: (1) 920-433-5171
Fax: (1) 920-438-5171
Email: dmartin@gbp.com
Territory Mgr.: Ryan Aulenbacher
Phone: (1) 920-433-5111
Fax: (1) 920-433-5471
Email: raulenbacher@gbp.com
Contr.: Vern Peterson
Phone: (1) 920-433-5111
Fax: (1) 920-433-5471
Email: vpeterson@gbp.com
Total Employees of Company: 3,100
Total Employees at this Location: 90
Mill Locations:
Green Bay Packaging Inc., Green Bay Mill, 1601 N Quincy, Green Bay, WI 54302, USA, Capacity: 239,904 st/y, (Paperboard mill)
Phone: (1) 920-433-5000
Fax: (1) 920-433-5105
Green Bay Packaging Inc., Morrilton Mill, 338 Highway 113 S, P.O. Box 711, Morrilton, AR 72110, USA, Capacity: 429,828 st/y, (Pulp mill, Paperboard mill)
Phone: (1) 501-354-4521
Fax: (1) 501-354-9290

ⓂGreen Bay Packaging Inc.
Green Bay Mill
1601 N Quincy
Green Bay, WI 54302
USA
Mailing Address: PO Box 19017, Green Bay, WI 54307-9017, USA
Phone: (1) 920-433-5000
Fax: (1) 920-433-5105
Web Address: www.gbp.com
Personnel:
Exec. VP: Bryan Hollenbach
Phone: (1) 920-433-5000
Fax: (1) 920-433-5105
Email: bhollenb@gbp.com
VP Containerboard Sls.: Jeff Walch
Phone: (1) 920-433-5016
Fax: (1) 920-433-5105
Email: jwalch@gbp.com
Plant Eng.: Todd DeRoach
Phone: (1) 920-433-5000
Fax: (1) 920-433-5105
Email: tderoach@gbp.com
Dir. of Compliance & Environ Mgr. - Wausau Div.: Jennifer J. Peplinski
Phone: (1) 715-843-8192
Email: jpeplinski@gbp.com
Qlty. Mgr.: Robert D. Mihalski
Phone: (1) 920-433-5000
Fax: (1) 920-433-5105
Email: rmihalsk@gbp.com
Secondary Fiber Supt.: Tony Wester
Phone: (1) 920-433-5000
Fax: (1) 920-433-5105
Email: twester@gbp.com
Div. Accounting, Office Mgr.: Joan Lardinois
Phone: (1) 920-433-5000
Fax: (1) 920-433-5105
Email: jlardinois@gbp.com
Total Employees at this Location: 131
Type of Operation: Paperboard mill
Pulp Grades and Capacities:
Total pulp capacity: 248,330 st/y
Recycled Pulping: 248,330 st/y
Pulp Mill Data:
Recycled Fiber Treatment Lines:
Pulpers: 1 at 264,550
Paper/Paperboard Grades and Capacities:
Total paper and paperboard capacity: 239,904 st/y
Linerboard: 119,952 st/y
Corrugating medium/fluting: 119,952 st/y
Paper and Paperboard Mill Data:
Stock Preparation:
Pulpers: 2
Paper Machines: 1
No. 1, Bel-Bond, total capacity 239,904 st/y, Trim width 162 in, Linerboard, Corrugating medium/fluting
Energy Data:
Power boilers: 2
Electrical demand for mill: 303 MWh/D

ⒽGusmer Enterprises Inc.
1401 Ware Street
Waupaca, Wisconsin, 54981-1365
USA
Phone: (1) 715-258-5525
Fax: (1) 715-258-8488
Web Address: www.gusmerenterprises.com
Personnel:
VP, Gen. Mgr.: Chris Gusmer
Phone: (1) 715-258-4698 Ext 119
Fax: (1) 715-258-8488
Email: cgusmer@gusmerenterprises.com
Dir.: Bob Menzies
Phone: (1) 715-258-5525
Fax: (1) 715-258-8488
Email: bmenzies@gusmerenterprises.com
Prod. Mgr.: Gary Prochnow
Phone: (1) 715-258-5525
Fax: (1) 715-258-8488
Email: gprochnow@gusmerenterprises.com
Technol. Mgr.: Wayne Poole
Phone: (1) 715-258-5525
Fax: (1) 715-258-8488
Email: wpoole@gusmerenterprises.com
Prod & Mktg Mgr.: Deborah Fenske
Phone: (1) 715-258-5525
Fax: (1) 715-258-8488
Email: dfenske@gusmerenterprises.com
Total Employees at this Location: 65
Mill Locations:
Gusmer Enterprises Inc., Waupaca Mill, 1401 Ware Street, Waupaca, WI 54981-1365, USA, Capacity: 4,200 st/y, (Pulp mill, Paper mill, Paperboard mill)
Phone: (1) 715-258-5525
Fax: (1) 715-258-8488
Email: sales@gusmerenterprises.com
GusmerCellulo, Fresno Mill, 81 M St, Fresno, CA 93721, USA, Capacity: 2,999 st/y, (Paper mill)
Phone: (1) 559-485-2692
Fax: (1) 559-485-4254
Email: info@gusmercellulo.com

ⓂGusmer Enterprises Inc.
Waupaca Mill
1401 Ware Street
Waupaca, WI 54981-1365
USA
Mailing Address: 1401 Ware Street, Waupaca, WI 54981-0329, USA
Phone: (1) 715-258-5525
Fax: (1) 715-258-8488
Email: sales@gusmerenterprises.com
Web Address: www.gusmerenterprises.com
Personnel:
Exec. VP, Gen. Mgr.: Chris Gusmer
Phone: (1) 715-258-4698 Ext 119
Fax: (1) 715-258-8488
Email: cgusmer@gusmerenterprises.com
Prod. Mgr.: Gary Prochnow
Phone: (1) 715-258-5525
Fax: (1) 715-258-8488
Email: gprochnow@gusmerenterprises.com
IT Specialist: Wayne Poole
Phone: (1) 715-258-5525
Fax: (1) 715-258-8488
Email: wpoole@gusmerenterprises.com
Total Employees at this Location: 65
Type of Operation: Pulp mill, Paper mill, Paperboard mill
Paper/Paperboard Grades and Capacities:
Total paper and paperboard capacity: 4,200 st/y
Specialty and industrial
Boxboard/cartonboard
Paper and Paperboard Mill Data:
Stock Preparation:
Refiners: 2
Paper Machines: 1
PM 1, fourdrinier, total capacity 4,200 st/y, Trim width 54 in, Specialty and industrial
Energy Data:
Power boilers: 1

ⓂKimberly-Clark Corp.
Marinette Mill
3120 Riverside Ave.
Marinette, WI 54143
USA
Phone: (1) 715-735-6644
Fax: (1) 715-735-4002
Web Address: www.kimberly-clark.com
Personnel:
Mill Mgr.: Dan T. Macke
Phone: (1) 715-735-4500
Fax: (1) 715-735-4002
Email: dtmacke@kcc.com
Total Employees at this Location: 80
Type of Operation: Paper mill
Paper/Paperboard Grades and Capacities:
Total paper and paperboard capacity: 44,982 st/y

Tissue: 44,982 st/y
Paper and Paperboard Mill Data:
Paper Machines: 1
No. 5, crescent former, TAD, total capacity 44,982 st/y, Trim width 124 in, Tissue
Energy Data:
Power boilers: 3
Electrical demand for mill: 173 MWh/D

ⓂLittle Rapids Corp.
2273 Larsen Road
Green Bay, WI 54303
USA
Mailing Address: PO Box 19031, Green Bay, WI 54307-9031, USA
 Phone: (1) 920-496-3040
 Fax: (1) 920-494-5340
 Email: em@littlerapids.com
 Web Address: www.littlerapids.com
Personnel:
 Pres. & CEO: Kirk S. Ryan
 Phone: (1) 920-496-3040
 Fax: (1) 920-494-5340
 Email: kryan@littlerapids.com
 VP., HR: John Wirch
 Phone: (1) 920-490-5209
 Fax: (1) 920-494-5340
 Email: jwirch@littlerapids.com
 VP., Sls.: Brian Segrin
 Phone: (1) 920-490-5209
 Fax: (1) 920-494-5340
 Cust. Serv. Mgr.: Gene Bortolameolli
 Phone: (1) 920-490-5209
 Fax: (1) 920-494-5340
Mill Locations:
 Shawano Specialty Papers, Shawano Mill, W7575 Poplar Road, Shawano, WI 54166, USA, Capacity: 69,288 st/y, (Paper mill)
 Phone: (1) 715-526-2181, 800-543-5554 (toll free)
 Fax: (1) 920-496-4612
 Email: paper@littlerapids.com

ⓂNeenah Paper, Inc.
Neenah Mill
135 N Commercial St
Neenah, WI 54956
USA
Mailing Address: 1376 Kimberly Drive, Neenah, WI 54956, USA
 Phone: (1) 920-721-1376, 800-558-5061
 Fax: (1) 302-655-5049
 Web Address: www.neenah.com
Personnel:
 Mill Mgr. Neenah & Appleton Mills: Howard Piotrowski
 Phone: (1) 920-721-1111
 Fax: (1) 302-655-5049
 Email: howard.piotrowski@neenah.com
 Cust. Mktg. Mgr.: Chris Schneider
 Phone: (1) 920-721-1376
 Fax: (1) 302-655-5049
 Email: chris.schneider@neenahpaper.com
Total Employees at this Location: 80
Type of Operation: Paper mill
Pulp Grades and Capacities:
 Total pulp capacity: 2,157 st/y
 Recycled Pulping: 2,157 st/y
Paper/Paperboard Grades and Capacities:
 Total paper and paperboard capacity: 48,184 st/y
 Uncoated woodfree/freesheet: 48,184 st/y
Paper and Paperboard Mill Data:
 Stock Preparation:
 Pulpers:
Paper Machines: 2
No. 3, fourdrinier, total capacity 19,631 st/y, Trim width 110 in, Uncoated woodfree/freesheet
No. 8, fourdrinier, total capacity 28,554 st/y, Trim width 120 in, Uncoated woodfree/freesheet
Finishing Equipment:
 Supercalenders: 2
 Rewinders: 3
 Sheeters: 6
Energy Data:
 Power boilers: 4
 Steam turbines: 1 at 6.5 MW
 Electrical demand for mill: 91 MWh/D

ⓂNeenah Paper, Inc.
Appleton Mill
600 S Vulcan St
Appleton, WI 54915
USA
 Phone: (1) 920-738-8332
 Fax: (1) 920-738-8308
 Web Address: www.neenah.com
Personnel:
 Mill Mgr. Appleton & Neenah Mills: Howard Piotrowski
 Phone: (1) 920-721-1111
 Email: howard.piotrowski@neenah.com
 Tech. Mgr.: Kenneth Wahl
 Phone: (1) 920-738-8303
 Fax: (1) 920-738-8308
 Email: kenneth.wahl@neenahpaper.com
 Asset Ldr.: Cathy Bennett
 Phone: (1) 920-738-8303
 Fax: (1) 920-738-8308
 Email: catherine.bennett@neenahpaper.com
 Environ. Eng/Utilities Supervisor: David Linden
 Phone: (1) 920-738-8303
 Fax: (1) 920-738-8308
 Email: david.linden@neenahpaper.com
Total Employees at this Location: 125
Type of Operation: Paper mill
Pulp Grades and Capacities:
 Total pulp capacity: 4,805 st/y
 Recycled Pulping: 4,805 st/y
Paper/Paperboard Grades and Capacities:
 Total paper and paperboard capacity: 35,692 st/y
 Uncoated woodfree/freesheet: 35,692 st/y
Paper and Paperboard Mill Data:
 Stock Preparation:
 Pulpers: 5
 Refiners: 8
Paper Machines: 2
No. 4, fourdrinier, total capacity 21,772 st/y, Trim width 100 in, Uncoated woodfree/freesheet
No. 5, fourdrinier, total capacity 13,920 st/y, Trim width 76 in, Uncoated woodfree/freesheet
Finishing Equipment:
 Winders: 2
 Calenders: 2
 Rewinders: 1
 Sheeters: 3
Energy Data:
 Power boilers: 3
 Hydro turbines: 5 at 1 MW
 Electrical demand for mill: 60 MWh/D

ⓂNeenah Paper, Inc.
Whiting Mill
3243 Whiting Rd
Stevens Point, WI 54481-6300
USA
 Phone: (1) 715-345-5050
 Fax: (1) 715-345-5043
 Web Address: www.neenah.com
Personnel:
 Snr. Plt.I Mgr.: Gregg Aiken
 Phone: (1) 715-345-5050
 Fax: (1) 715-345-5043
 Email: gregg.aiken@neenahpaper.com
 Mill Mgr. (From December 2013): David Paulus
 Phone: (1) 715-345-5050
 Fax: (1) 715-345-5043
 Email: dave.paulus@neenahpaper.com
 Asset Ldr II - Retail Product Develop.: Jill Goffin
 Phone: (1) 715-345-5050
 Fax: (1) 715-345-5043
 Email: jill.goffin@neenahpaper.com
 Eng. Mgr.: Brian Bayorgeon
 Phone: (1) 715-345-5050
 Fax: (1) 715-345-5043
 Email: brian.bayorgeon@neenahpaper.com
Total Employees at this Location: 225
Type of Operation: Paper mill
Pulp Grades and Capacities:
 Total pulp capacity: 14,808 st/y
 Recycled Pulping: 14,808 st/y
Paper/Paperboard Grades and Capacities:
 Total paper and paperboard capacity: 139,199 st/y
 Uncoated woodfree/freesheet: 139,199 st/y
Paper and Paperboard Mill Data:
 Stock Preparation:
 Pulpers:
Paper Machines: 4
No. 5, fourdrinier, total capacity 24,984 st/y, Trim width 105 in, Uncoated woodfree/freesheet
No. 6, fourdrinier, total capacity 26,769 st/y, Trim width 129 in, Uncoated woodfree/freesheet
No. 7, fourdrinier, total capacity 43,544 st/y, Trim width 140 in, Uncoated woodfree/freesheet
No. 8, fourdrinier, total capacity 43,901 st/y, Trim width 139 in, Uncoated woodfree/freesheet
Finishing Equipment:
 Sheeters: 3
Energy Data:
 Power boilers: 2
 Steam turbines at 3.1 MW
 Electrical demand for mill: 229 MWh/D

ⓂNewPage Corporation
Biron Mill
Mill is for sale (on October 30, 2014, Catalyst Paper Corporation entered into an Asset Purchase Agreement with NewPage Corporation to purchase the Biron paper mill.)
621 N Biron Dr
Wisconsin Rapids, WI 54495-8050
USA
Mailing Address: PO Box 8050, Wisconsin Rapids, WI 54495-8050, USA
 Phone: (1) 715-422-2236
 Fax: (1) 715-422-2403
 Web Address: www.newpagecorp.com
Personnel:
 Mill Mgr.: Sean Wallace
 Phone: (1) 715-422-2236
 Fax: (1) 715-422-2403
 Email: sean.wallace@newpagecorp.com
 Tech. Mgr.: Brent Nelson
 Phone: (1) 715-422-2236
 Fax: (1) 715-422-2403
 Email: brent.nelson@newpagecorp.com
 Dir., HR: Mary A. Manley
 Phone: (1) 715-422-2184
 Fax: (1) 715-422-2534
 Email: mary.manley@newpagecorp.com
 Environ. Mgr. Biron & Wisconsin Rapids Mills (from August 2013): Steven Lewens
 Phone: (1) 715-422-3553
 Fax: (1) 715-422-2403
 Email: steven.lewens@newpagecorp.com
Total Employees at this Location: 421
Type of Operation: Paper mill
Pulp Grades and Capacities:
 Total pulp capacity: 80,600 st/y
 Mechanical Pulp: 80,600 st/y
Pulp Mill Data:
 Mechanical Pulping Systems:
 Conventional grinders: 6
 TMP systems: 3
 Bleach Plant Lines:
 SGW Pulping System, Sequence: P
 TMP Pulping System, Sequence: P
Paper/Paperboard Grades and Capacities:
 Total paper and paperboard capacity: 399,752 st/y
 Coated mechanical/groundwood: 399,752 st/y
Paper and Paperboard Mill Data:
 Stock Preparation:
 Pulpers:

Wisconsin

Paper Machines: 2
No. 25, twin-wire, total capacity 132,061 st/y, Trim width 185 in, Coated mechanical/groundwood
No. 26, twin-wire, total capacity 267,691 st/y, Trim width 289 in, Coated mechanical/groundwood
Coating Machines: 2
No. 1, total capacity 131,173 st/y., off machine
No. 2, total capacity 243,607 st/y., on machine
Finishing Equipment:
Supercalenders: 11
Rewinders: 6
Sheeters: 9
Energy Data:
Power boilers: 5
Hydro turbines: 2 at 21 MW
Electrical demand for mill: 1,640 MWh/D

ⓜNewPage Corporation
Wisconsin Rapids Paper Mill
310 N. 3rd Ave.
Wisconsin Rapids, WI 54495-8050
USA
Mailing Address: P.O. Box 8050, Wisconsin Rapids, WI 54495-8050, USA
  Phone: (1) 715-422-1616, 715-422-4067
  Fax: (1) 715-422-3982
  Web Address: www.newpagecorp.com
Personnel:
Prod. Mgr. (Interim Mill Mgr. 2014): Tim Budelier
  Phone: (1) 715-422-3161
  Fax: (1) 715-422-3982
  Email: tim.budelier@newpagecorp.com
Prod. Capability Ldr.: Terry Dolan
  Phone: (1) 715-422-4096
  Fax: (1) 715-422-3982
  Email: terry.dolan@newpagecorp.com
Maint Supt.: Ronald J. Herman
  Phone: (1) 715-422-3963
  Fax: (1) 715-422-4149
  Email: ron.herman@newpagecorp.com
Qlty. Contrl. Supervisor: Kyle Warras
  Phone: (1) 715-422-3440
  Fax: (1) 715-422-3982
  Email: kyle.warras@newpagecorp.com
Oper. Team Ldr. Sheeting: Mike Spoon
  Phone: (1) 715-422-1616
  Fax: (1) 715-422-3982
  Email: mike.spoon@newpagecorp.com
Total Employees at this Location: 620
Type of Operation: Pulp mill, Paper mill
Pulp Grades and Capacities:
Total pulp capacity: 501,712 st/y
Pulp available for market: 137,731 st/y
Chemical Pulp: 501,712 st/y
Pulp Mill Data:
Chemical Pulping Systems:
Continuous digesters: 2
Pulp Lines: 2
Bleach Plant Systems: 2
Chemical Pulping System, Type: Hardwood - DEEopDD
Chemical Pulping System, Type: Hardwood/Softwood - DDEopD
Chemical Recovery Equipment:
Evaporator lines
Recovery boilers: 3
Lime Kiln
Pulp Dryers:
Pulp Dryers 1, Wet Lap machine 1, Wet Lap machine 1
Paper/Paperboard Grades and Capacities:
Total paper and paperboard capacity: 553,228 st/y
Coated woodfree/freesheet: 553,228 st/y
Paper and Paperboard Mill Data:
Stock Preparation:
Pulpers:
Paper Machines: 2
No. 14, twin-wire, total capacity 162,399 st/y, Trim width 146 in, Coated woodfree/freesheet
No. 16, twin-wire, total capacity 390,829 st/y, Trim width 236 in, Coated woodfree/freesheet
Coating Machines: 2
PM 14, total capacity 144,951 st/y., off machine
PM 16, total capacity 350,529 st/y., off machine
Finishing Equipment:
Supercalenders: 5
Rewinders: 6
Sheeters: 9
Energy Data:
Power boilers
Steam turbines: 2 at 39, 40 MW
Electrical demand for mill: 1,985 MWh/D

ⓜNewPage Corporation
Stevens Point Mill
707 Arlington Pl
Stevens Point, WI 54481
USA
Mailing Address: PO Box 227, Stevens Point, WI 54481, USA
  Phone: (1) 715-345-8060
  Fax: (1) 715-345-8001
  Web Address: www.newpagecorp.com
Personnel:
Mill Mgr.: John Reichert
  Phone: (1) 715-345-8060
  Fax: (1) 715-345-8001
  Email: john.reichert@newpagecorp.com
Environ. Mgr.: Deanna Webster
  Phone: (1) 715-345-8060
  Fax: (1) 715-345-8001
  Email: deanna.webster@newpagecorp.com
Exec. Dir. of Sales and Bus. Devlpt.: David M Diekelman
  Phone: (1) 715-345-8060
  Fax: (1) 715-345-8001
  Email: david.diekelman@newpagecorp.com
Asset Develop. & Energy Mgr.: Duane Spinler
  Phone: (1) 715-345-8060
  Fax: (1) 715-345-8001
  Email: duane.spinler@newpagecorp.com
Total Employees at this Location: 252
Type of Operation: Paper mill
Paper/Paperboard Grades and Capacities:
Total paper and paperboard capacity: 169,538 st/y
Specialty and industrial: 169,538 st/y
Paper and Paperboard Mill Data:
Stock Preparation:
Pulpers: 3
Refiners: 1
Paper Machines: 2
No. 34, fourdrinier, Yankee dryer, total capacity 83,877 st/y, Trim width 160 in, Specialty and industrial
No. 35, fourdrinier, Yankee dryer, total capacity 85,661 st/y, Trim width 160 in, Specialty and industrial
Coating Machines: 2
No. 4, total capacity 80,688 st/y., on machine
No. 5, total capacity 82,672 st/y., on machine
Finishing Equipment:
Rewinders: 4
Energy Data:
Power boilers: 2
Steam turbines: 1 at 7.6 MW
Electrical demand for mill: 407 MWh/D

ⓜPackaging Corp. of America
Tomahawk Mill
N9090 County Rd E
Tomahawk, WI 54487
USA
  Phone: (1) 715-453-2131
  Fax: (1) 715-453-0470
  Web Address: www.packagingcorp.com
Personnel:
Mill Mgr. (From April 2013): Adam Webster
  Phone: (1) 715-453-2131
  Fax: (1) 715-453-0470
  Email: awebster@packagingcorp.com
Purch. Mgr.: Dave Hawkinson
  Phone: (1) 715-453-0422
  Fax: (1) 715-453-0470
  Email: dhawkinson@packagingcorp.com
HR Mgr.: Ronald D. Zimmerman
  Phone: (1) 715-453-2131
  Fax: (1) 715-453-0470
  Email: rzimmerman@packagingcorp.com
Cust. Serv. Mgr.: Leisa R. Gustafson
  Phone: (1) 715-453-2131
  Fax: (1) 715-453-0470
  Email: lgustafson@packagingcorp.com
Total Employees at this Location: 437
Type of Operation: Paperboard mill
Pulp Grades and Capacities:
Total pulp capacity: 1,005,626 st/y
Chemical Pulp: 366,135 st/y
Recycled Pulping: 201,950 st/y
Pulp Mill Data:
Chemical Pulping Systems:
Continuous digesters: 4
Chemical Recovery Equipment:
Evaporator lines: 2
Recovery boilers: 1
Recycled Fiber Treatment Lines:
Pulpers: 1 at 204,255
Paper/Paperboard Grades and Capacities:
Total paper and paperboard capacity: 970,683 st/y
Corrugating medium/fluting: 970,683 st/y
Paper and Paperboard Mill Data:
Stock Preparation:
Pulpers: 1
Refiners: 8
Paper Machines: 3
No. 1, fourdrinier, total capacity 121,737 st/y, Trim width 140 in, Corrugating medium/fluting
No. 2, twin-wire, total capacity 428,400 st/y, Trim width 254 in, Corrugating medium/fluting
No. 4, twin-wire, total capacity 420,546 st/y, Trim width 254 in, Corrugating medium/fluting
Energy Data:
Power boilers: 4
Steam turbines: 2 at 12.5 MW
Hydro turbines: 3 at 3 MW
Electrical demand for mill: 1,038 MWh/D

ⓜProcter & Gamble Paper Products Co.
Fox River Plant
501 Eastman Ave
Green Bay, WI 54302
USA
Mailing Address: PO Box 8020, Green Bay, WI 54308-8020, USA
  Phone: (1) 920-430-2101
  Fax: (1) 920-433-2571
  Web Address: www.pg.com
Personnel:
Oper. Dept. Ldr.: Michael Rader
  Phone: (1) 920-430-2101
  Fax: (1) 920-433-2571
Maint. Mgr.: Russell Reynolds
  Phone: (1) 920-430-2101
  Fax: (1) 920-433-2571
Total Employees at this Location: 450
Type of Operation: Paper mill
Paper/Paperboard Grades and Capacities:
Total paper and paperboard capacity: 334,152 st/y
Tissue: 334,152 st/y
Paper and Paperboard Mill Data:
Stock Preparation:
Pulpers:
Paper Machines: 6
No. 10, TAD, total capacity 48,552 st/y, Trim width 198 in, Tissue
No. 11, TAD, total capacity 46,767 st/y, Trim width 198 in, Tissue
No. 12, TAD, total capacity 49,980 st/y, Trim width 198 in, Tissue
No. 13, TAD, total capacity 48,195 st/y, Trim width 198 in, Tissue

Wisconsin

No. 14, TAD, total capacity 60,690 st/y, Trim width 198 in, Tissue
No. 15, TAD, total capacity 79,968 st/y, Trim width 198 in, Tissue
Energy Data:
Power boilers: 3
Electrical demand for mill: 1,248 MWh/D

ⓂSCA Tissue North America, L.L.C.
Menasha Mill
Ownership: 100% by SCA - Svenska Cellulosa Aktiebolaget
190 Tayco Street
Menasha, WI 54952
USA
Mailing Address: PO Box 2400, Neenah, WI 54957-2400, USA
  Phone: (1) 920-727-2910
  Fax: (1) 920-727-2902
  Email: info@sca.com
  Web Address: www.scatissue.com
Personnel:
  Plt. Mgr.: Gary Shadick
  Phone: (1) 920-727-2942
  Fax: (1) 920-727-2902
  Email: gary.shadick@sca.com
  Regional Dir.: Tom Mettlach
  Phone: (1) 920-727-2910
  Fax: (1) 920-727-2902
  Email: tom.mettlach@sca.com
  Eng. Service Dir.: Mark K. Phiscator
  Phone: (1) 920-720-4527
  Fax: (1) 920-727-2902
  Email: mark.phiscator@sca.com
  Oper. Specialist: Nancy Taylor
  Phone: (1) 920-727-2910
  Fax: (1) 920-727-2902
  Email: nancy.taylor@sca.com
  Environ. Eng.: Paul Johnson
  Phone: (1) 920-727-2910
  Fax: (1) 920-727-2902
  Email: paul.johnson@sca.com
Total Employees at this Location: 229
Type of Operation: Paper mill
Pulp Grades and Capacities:
  Total pulp capacity: 223,982 st/y
  Recycled Pulping: 223,982 st/y
Pulp Mill Data:
Pulp Lines: 3
  Bleach Plant Lines:
  Recycled Pulping System, Type: Deinked, Sequence: CEP
  Recycled Fiber Treatment Lines:
  Flotation deinking lines: 1
Paper/Paperboard Grades and Capacities:
  Total paper and paperboard capacity: 209,559 st/y
  Tissue: 209,559 st/y
Paper and Paperboard Mill Data:
Paper Machines: 3
No. 2, crescent former, total capacity 31,059 st/y, Trim width 133 in, Tissue
No. 3, crescent former, total capacity 71,400 st/y, Trim width 208 in, Tissue
No. 4, C-wrap, Yankee dryer, total capacity 107,100 st/y, Trim width 214 in, Tissue
Energy Data:
Power boilers: 3
Electrical demand for mill: 848 MWh/D

ⓂShawano Specialty Papers
Shawano Mill
Ownership: Little Rapids Corp.
W7575 Poplar Road
Shawano, WI 54166
USA
  Phone: (1) 715-526-2181, 800-543-5554 (toll free)
  Fax: (1) 920-496-4612
  Email: paper@littlerapids.com
  Web Address: www.littlerapids.com,
www.shawanospecialtypapers.com
Personnel:
  VP Oper.: Ronald Thiry
  Phone: (1) 715-526-2181
  Fax: (1) 920-496-4612
  Email: rthiry@littlerapids.com
  Tech. Dir.: Jerry Bartman
  Phone: (1) 715-526-2181
  Fax: (1) 920-496-4612
  Email: jbartman@littlerapids.com
  Purch. Mgr.: Paul Grassl
  Phone: (1) 715-526-2181
  Fax: (1) 920-496-4612
  Email: pgrassl@littlerapids.com
  Sls. & Mktg. Mgr.: Jeremy Roemer
  Phone: (1) 715-526-2181
  Fax: (1) 920-496-4612
  Email: jroemer@littlerapids.com
  Bus. Develop. Mgr: Brett Buratti
  Phone: (1) 715-526-2181
  Fax: (1) 920-496-4612
  Email: bburatti@littlerapids.com
Total Employees at this Location: 112
Type of Operation: Paper mill
Paper/Paperboard Grades and Capacities:
  Total paper and paperboard capacity: 69,288 st/y
  Tissue: 36,049 st/y
  Specialty and industrial: 33,239 st/y
Paper and Paperboard Mill Data:
Paper Machines: 3
No. 1, fourdrinier, total capacity 19,631 st/y, Trim width 96 in, Specialty and industrial, Tissue
No. 2, fourdrinier, total capacity 19,676 st/y, Trim width 124 in, Specialty and industrial
No. 3, fourdrinier, total capacity 29,981 st/y, Trim width 132 in, Specialty and industrial, Tissue
Energy Data:
Power boilers: 2
Electrical demand for mill: 154 MWh/D

ⓂSonoco Products Co.
Menasha Mill
69 Washington St
Menasha, WI 54952
USA
  Phone: (1) 920-725-7115
  Fax: (1) 920-725-4869
  Web Address: www.sonoco.com
Personnel:
  Plt. Mgr.: Troy Huebner
  Phone: (1) 920-725-7115
  Fax: (1) 920-725-4869
  Email: troy.huebner@sonoco.com
  Purch. Mgr.: Julie Lamers
  Phone: (1) 920-725-7115
  Fax: (1) 920-725-4869
  Email: julie.lamers@sonoco.com
  Sls. Mgr.: Bill Sommer
  Phone: (1) 920-725-7115
  Fax: (1) 920-725-4869
  Email: bill.sommer@sonoco.com
Total Employees at this Location: 100
Type of Operation: Paperboard mill
Pulp Grades and Capacities:
  Total pulp capacity: 140,770 st/y
  Recycled Pulping: 140,770 st/y
Paper/Paperboard Grades and Capacities:
  Total paper and paperboard capacity: 169,932 st/y
  Corrugating medium/fluting: 84,966 st/y
  Boxboard/cartonboard: 84,966 st/y
Paper and Paperboard Mill Data:
  Stock Preparation:
  Pulpers: 3
  Refiners: 6
Paper Machines: 2
No. 1, cylinder (7), total capacity 84,966 st/y, Trim width 72 in, Boxboard/cartonboard
No. 2, fourdrinier, total capacity 49,980 st/y, Trim width 102 in, Corrugating medium/fluting
Finishing Equipment:
Sheeters: 1
Energy Data:
Power boilers: 1
Steam turbines
Electrical demand for mill: 194 MWh/D

ⓂST Paper, LLC
Ownership: 100% by Tak Investments, Inc
106 E Central Ave
Oconto Falls, WI 54154
USA
  Phone: (1) 920-846-3411
  Fax: (1) 920-846-4410
  Email: info@stpaperllc.com
  Web Address: www.stpaperllc.com/index.html
Personnel:
  Pres. & CEO: Sharad Tak
  Phone: (1) 920-846-3411
  Fax: (1) 920-846-4410
  Gen. Mgr.: Maury Keesler
  Phone: (1) 920-846-3411
  Fax: (1) 920-846-4410
  Plt. Mgr.: Steve Lea
  Phone: (1) 920-846-3411
  Fax: (1) 920-846-4410
  Email: stephenfl@stpaperllc.com
  Sls. Mgr.: Lee Luft
  Phone: (1) 920-255-6222
  Fax: (1) 920-846-4410
  Email: leeluft@wildblue.net
  Eng.Mgr.: Ron Splingaire
  Phone: (1) 920-846-3411
  Fax: (1) 920-846-4410
Total Employees of Company: 171
Mill Locations:
STTissue, LLC, Franklin Mill, 34040 Union Camp Dr, Franklin, VA 23851-0178, USA, Capacity: 69,972 st/y, (Paper mill)
  Phone: (1) 757-304-5040
  Email: info@sttissuellc.com, sales@sttissuellc.com
ST Paper, LLC, Oconto Falls Mill, 106 E Central Ave, Oconto Falls, WI 54154, USA, Capacity: 64,260 st/y, (Pulp mill, Paper mill)
  Phone: (1) 920-846-3411
  Fax: (1) 920-846-4410
  Email: info@stpaperllc.com

ⓂST Paper, LLC
Oconto Falls Mill
106 E Central Ave
Oconto Falls, WI 54154
USA
  Phone: (1) 920-846-3411
  Fax: (1) 920-846-4410
  Email: info@stpaperllc.com
  Web Address: www.stpaperllc.com/index.html
Personnel:
  Plt. Mgr.: Steve Lea
  Phone: (1) 920-846-3411
  Fax: (1) 920-846-4410
  Email: stephenfl@stpaperllc.com
  Plt. Eng Mgr.: Ron Splingaire
  Phone: (1) 920-846-3411
  Fax: (1) 920-846-4410
  Email: ron.splingaire@stpaperllc.com
Total Employees at this Location: 91
Type of Operation: Pulp mill, Paper mill
Pulp Grades and Capacities:
  Total pulp capacity: 68,690 st/y
  Recycled Pulping: 68,690 st/y
Pulp Mill Data:
  Bleach Plant Systems: 1
  Recycled Deinked Pulping System, Sequence: H
  Recycled Fiber Treatment Lines:
  Flotation deinking lines at 49,724
Paper/Paperboard Grades and Capacities:
  Total paper and paperboard capacity: 64,260 st/y
  Tissue: 64,260 st/y
Paper and Paperboard Mill Data:

Wisconsin

Stock Preparation:
  Pulpers:
Paper Machines: 2
  No. 1, crescent former, total capacity 32,844 st/y, Trim width 138 in, Tissue
  No. 2, crescent former, total capacity 31,416 st/y, Trim width 108 in, Tissue
Energy Data:
  Power boilers: 2
  Electrical demand for mill: 217 MWh/D

ⓜU.S. Paper Mills Corp.
De Pere Mill
Ownership: Sonoco Products Co.
800 Fort Howard Ave
De Pere, WI 54115
USA
Mailing Address: PO Box 5850, De Pere, WI 54115-5850, USA
  Phone: (1) 920-336-4229
  Fax: (1) 920-336-6104
  Web Address: www.sonoco.com
Personnel:
  Sls. Mgr.: Mark Molina
  Phone: (1) 920-336-4229
  Fax: (1) 920-336-6104
  Email: mark.molina@sonoco.com
  Snr. Process Eng.: Nicholas Krueger
  Phone: (1) 920-336-4229
  Fax: (1) 920-336-6104
  Email: nicholas.krueger@sonoco.com
  Snr. Mill Supply Mgr.: Merilee Blowers
  Phone: (1) 920-336-4229
  Fax: (1) 920-336-6104
  Email: merilee.blowers@sonoco.com
Total Employees at this Location: 62
Type of Operation: Paperboard mill
Pulp Grades and Capacities:
  Total pulp capacity: 41,978 st/y
  Recycled Pulping: 41,978 st/y
Paper/Paperboard Grades and Capacities:
  Total paper and paperboard capacity: 39,984 st/y
  Boxboard/cartonboard: 39,984 st/y
Paper and Paperboard Mill Data:
  Stock Preparation:
    Pulpers: 2
    Refiners: 2
  Paper Machines: 1
    No. 1, fourdrinier, total capacity 39,984 st/y, Trim width 72 in, Boxboard/cartonboard
  Energy Data:
    Power boilers: 2
    Electrical demand for mill: 60 MWh/D

ⓜWausau Paper Corp.
Ownership: Public
100 Paper Place
Mosinee, WI 54455-9099
USA
  Phone: (1) 715-693-4470
  Fax: (1) 715-692-2082
  Web Address: www.wausaupaper.com
Personnel:
  Chmn. of the Board & CEO: Michael C. Burandt
  Phone: (1) 715-693-4470
  Fax: (1) 715-692-2082
  Email: burandt@wausaupaper.com
  Pres. & COO: Matthew L. Urmanski
  Phone: (1) 715-693-4470
  Fax: (1) 715-692-2082
  Email: murmanski@wausaupaper.com
  Chmn.: Gary W. Freels
  Phone: (1) 715-693-4470
  Fax: (1) 715-692-2082
  Email: gfrells@wausaupaper.com
  Snr. VP., Oper.: Patrick J. Medvecz
  Phone: (1) 715-693-4470
  Fax: (1) 715-692-2082
  Email: pmedvecz@wausaupaper.com
  Snr. VP., Paper: Michael W Nelson
  Phone: (1) 715-693-4470
  Fax: (1) 715-692-2082
  Email: mnelson@wausaupaper.com
  Snr. VP. & CFO: Sherri L. Lemmer
  Phone: (1) 715-693-4470
  Fax: (1) 715-692-2082
  Email: slemmer@wausaupaper.com
  Snr. VP., HR: Curtis R. Schmidt
  Phone: (1) 715-693-4470
  Fax: (1) 715-692-2082
  Email: cschmidt@wausaupaper.com
  Dir Sls.: Bob Steif
  Phone: (1) 715-693-4470
  Fax: (1) 715-692-2082
  Email: bsteif@wausaupaper.com
Total Employees of Company: 1,900
Total Employees at this Location: 36
Mill Locations:
Wausau Paper Towel & Tissue, LLC, Harrodsburg Mill, 1150 Industry Rd, Harrodsburg, KY 40330, USA, Capacity: 74,967 st/y, (Paper mill)
  Phone: (1) 859-734-0538
  Fax: (1) 859-734-8219
Wausau Paper Towel & Tissue, LLC, Middletown Mill, 700 Columbia Ave., Middletown, OH 45042, USA, Capacity: 126,735 st/y, (Pulp mill, Paper mill)
  Phone: (1) 513-424-2999
  Fax: (1) 513-420-8570
  Email: contactbaywest@wausaupaper.com

ⓜWhiting Paper Co.
Ownership: 100% by company CEO Tom Danz
100 River St
Menasha, WI 54952
USA
Mailing Address: PO Box 28, Menasha, WI 54952-0028, USA
  Phone: (1) 920-722-3351
  Fax: (1) 920-722-9553
  Web Address: www.whitingpaper.com
Personnel:
  CEO & Owner: Thomas A. Danz
  Phone: (1) 920-722-3351
  Fax: (1) 920-722-9553
  Email: tom.whitingpaper@tds.net
  Chmn.: George A Whiting III
  Phone: (1) 920-722-3351
  Fax: (1) 920-722-9553
  Exec. VP, Sec. & Treas.: Debbie Olander
  Phone: (1) 920-722-3351
  Fax: (1) 920-722-9553
Total Employees of Company: 32
Mill Locations:
Whiting Paper Co., Menasha Mill, 100 River St, Menasha, WI 54952, USA, Capacity: 7,200 st/y, (Paper mill)
  Phone: (1) 920-722-3351
  Fax: (1) 920-722-9553

ⓜWhiting Paper Co.
Menasha Mill
100 River St
Menasha, WI 54952
USA
Mailing Address: PO Box 28, Menasha, WI 54952-0028, USA
  Phone: (1) 920-722-3351
  Fax: (1) 920-722-9553
  Web Address: www.whitingpaper.com
Personnel:
  Exec. VP. Finan.: Debbie Orlander
  Phone: (1) 920-722-3351
  Fax: (1) 920-722-9553
  Sls. Mgr.: Bonnie Hoffman
  Phone: (1) 920-722-3351
  Fax: (1) 920-722-9553
  Prod. Mgr.: Thomas Strebe
  Phone: (1) 920-722-3351
  Fax: (1) 920-722-9553
  VP Sls.: Tripp Whitting
  Phone: (1) 920-722-3351
  Fax: (1) 920-722-9553
Total Employees at this Location: 32
Type of Operation: Paper mill
Paper/Paperboard Grades and Capacities:
  Total paper and paperboard capacity: 7,200 st/y
  Uncoated woodfree/freesheet: 7,200 st/y
Paper and Paperboard Mill Data:
  Stock Preparation:
    Pulpers: 2
    Refiners: 2
  Paper Machines: 1
    No. 1, fourdrinier, total capacity 7,200 st/y, Trim width 75 in, Uncoated woodfree/freesheet
  Finishing Equipment:
    Winders: 1
    Calenders: 1
    Rewinders: 1
    Sheeters: 2
  Energy Data:
    Power boilers: 1
    Electrical demand for mill: 18 MWh/D

ⓜWisconsin Paperboard Corp.
Milwaukee Mill
Ownership: 100% by Newark Recycled Paperboard Solutions
1514 E Thomas Ave.
Milwaukee, WI 53211-4397
USA
  Phone: (1) 414-271-9000
  Fax: (1) 414-271-9001
  Web Address: www.newarkpb.com.
Personnel:
  Gen. Mgr.: Chris Chappell
  Phone: (1) 414-271-9000
  Fax: (1) 414-271-9001
  Email: cchappell@tngus.com
  Tech. Dir.: Dave Jacobs
  Phone: (1) 414-271-9000
  Fax: (1) 414-271-9001
  Email: djacobs@tngus.com
  Contr.: Daniel Gumm
  Phone: (1) 414-319-3964
  Fax: (1) 414-271-9001
  Email: dgumm@tngus.com
Total Employees at this Location: 165
Type of Operation: Paperboard mill
Pulp Grades and Capacities:
  Total pulp capacity: 168,114 st/y
  Recycled Pulping: 168,114 st/y
Pulp Mill Data:
  Recycled Fiber Treatment Lines:
  Recycled packaging pulping lines
Paper/Paperboard Grades and Capacities:
  Total paper and paperboard capacity: 164,934 st/y
  Boxboard/cartonboard: 164,934 st/y
Paper and Paperboard Mill Data:
Paper Machines: 2
  No. 1, cylinder (8), total capacity 73,899 st/y, Trim width 115 in, Boxboard/cartonboard
  No. 2, cylinder (8), total capacity 91,035 st/y, Trim width 126 in, Boxboard/cartonboard
Finishing Equipment:
  Sheeters: 2
Energy Data:
  Power boilers: 2
  Steam turbines: 1 at 4 MW
  Electrical demand for mill: 217 MWh/D

PULP and PAPER MILLS in Canada

ALBERTA

ⓂAlberta Newsprint Co. Ltd.
Whitecourt Mill
Ownership: 50% by West Fraser Timber Co. Ltd., 50% by Whitecourt Newsprint L.P.
10km West, Hwy 43
Whitecourt, AB
Canada, T7S 1P9
Mailing Address: PO Box 9000, Whitecourt, AB, Canada, T7S 1P9
 Phone: (1) 780-778-7000
 Fax: (1) 780-778-7070
 Email: ancmill@albertanewsprint.com
 Web Address: www.albertanewsprint.com
Personnel:
 Pres. & CEO: Ronald N. Stern
 Phone: (1) 780-778-7000
 Fax: (1) 780-778-7070
 Gen. Mgr.: Mike Putzke
 Phone: (1) 780-778-7000
 Fax: (1) 780-778-7070
 Contr.: Lindsay Moyle
 Phone: (1) 780-778-7026
 Fax: (1) 780-778-7070
 Pulping & Utilities Supt.: Surendra Singh
 Phone: (1) 780-778-7027
 Fax: (1) 780-778-7070
 Pres. Sls: Dale A. Band
 Phone: (1) 630-848-9193
 Fax: (1) 630-245-0337
 Email: dband@albertanewsprint.com
 Tech. Dir.: Gary Smith
 Phone: (1) 780-778-7053
 Fax: (1) 780-778-7070
 Material Management Supervisor: Audrey Droesse
 Phone: (1) 780-778-7062
 Fax: (1) 780-778-7070
Total Employees at this Location: 200
Type of Operation: Paper mill
Pulp Grades and Capacities:
 Total pulp capacity: 276,986 mt/y
 Mechanical Pulp: 276,986 mt/y
Pulp Mill Data:
 Mechanical Pulping Systems:
 CTMP systems: 3
Pulp Lines: 3
 Bleach Plant Systems: 1
 Mechanical CTMP Pulping System, Type: Softwood, Sequence: HS
Paper/Paperboard Grades and Capacities:
 Total paper and paperboard capacity: 271,320 mt/y
 Newsprint: 271,320 mt/y
Paper and Paperboard Mill Data:
 Paper Machines: 1
 No. 1, DuoFormer F, total capacity 271,320 mt/y, Trim width 8.37 m, Newsprint
Finishing Equipment:
 Winders: 1
Energy Data:
 Power boilers: 2
 TMP Reboiler: 1

ⓂAlberta-Pacific Forest Industries Inc. (Al-Pac)
Ownership: 30% by Oji Holdings Corportation, 70% by Mitsubishi Corporation
Box 8000
Boyle, AB
Canada, AB T0A 0M0
Mailing Address: P.O. Box 8000, Boyle, AB, Canada, AB T0A 0M0
 Phone: (1) 780-525-8000
 Fax: (1) 780-525-8423
 Email: info@alpac.ca
 Web Address: www.alpac.ca
Personnel:
 Chmn. & CEO: Sam Terao
 Phone: 780-525-8000
 Fax: (1) 780-525-8095
 Email: osamu.terao@mitsubishicorp.com
 Pres. & COO: Allan Ward
 Phone: (1) 780-525-8000
 Fax: (1) 780-525-8095
 Email: al.ward@alpac.ca
 VP., Finan & CFO: Dale Bencharsky
 Phone: (1) 780-525-8000
 Fax: (1) 780-525-8095
 Email: dale.bencharsky@alpac.ca
 VP Pulp   : Daryl Nichol
 Phone: (1) 780-525-8000
 Fax: (1) 780-525-8095
 Email: daryl.nichol@alpac.ca
Total Employees of Company: 259
Mill Locations:
Alberta-Pacific Forest Industries Inc. (Al-Pac), Boyle Mill, Box 8000, Boyle, AB, Canada AB T0A 0M0, (Pulp mill)
 Phone: (1) 780-525-8000, 800-661-5210
 Fax: (1) 780-525-8423
 Email: info@alpac.ca

ⓂAlberta-Pacific Forest Industries Inc. (Al-Pac)
Boyle Mill
Box 8000
Boyle, AB
Canada, AB T0A 0M0
Mailing Address: P.O. Box 8000, Boyle, AB, Canada, AB T0A 0M0
 Phone: (1) 780-525-8000, 800-661-5210
 Fax: (1) 780-525-8423
 Email: info@alpac.ca
 Web Address: www.alpac.ca
Personnel:
 Chmn. & CEO: Sam Terao
 Phone: (1) 780-525-8000
 Fax: (1) 780-525-8095
 Email: osamu.terao@mitsubishicorp.com
 Pres. & COO: Allan Ward
 Phone: (1) 780-525-8150
 Fax: (1) 780-525-8095
 Email: al.ward@alpac.ca
 VP., Finan & CFO: Dale Bencharsky
 Phone: (1) 780-525-8000
 Fax: (1) 780-525-8095
 Email: dale.bencharsky@alpac.ca
 VP Pulp: Daryl Nichol
 Phone: (1) 780-525-8232
 Fax: (1) 780-525-8095
 Email: daryl.nichol@alpac.ca
 Dir., Chip & Biomass Procurement: Randy McNamara
 Phone: (1) 780-525-8059
 Fax: (1) 780-525-8095
 Email: randy.mcnamara@alpac.ca
Total Employees at this Location: 259
Type of Operation: Pulp mill
Pulp Grades and Capacities:
 Total pulp capacity: 659,461 mt/y
 Pulp available for market: 650,097 mt/y
 Chemical Pulp: 659,461 mt/y
Pulp Mill Data:
 Chemical Pulping Systems:
 Continuous digesters: 1
Pulp Lines: 1
 Bleach Plant Systems: 1
 Chemical Pulping system - Metso, Sequence: O_2 DEopD, Capacity 653,000 admt/y
 Chemical Recovery Equipment:
 Evaporator lines: 1
 Recovery boilers: 1
 Lime Kiln
 Pulp Dryers:
 Flakt dryer 1, Fourdriniers 1
Energy Data:
 Power boilers: 1
 Combustion turbines: 1 at 13 MW
 Steam turbines: 3 at 41, 41, 30 MW
 Electrical demand for mill: 1,325 MWh/D

ⓂDaishowa-Marubeni International Ltd.
Peace River Pulp Division
Ownership: 50% by Nippon Paper Industries Co., Ltd.
Peace River, AB
Canada, T8S 1V7
Mailing Address: Postal Bag 4400, Peace River, AB, Canada, T8S 1V7
 Phone: (1) 780-624-7000
 Fax: (1) 780-624-7329
 Email: webmaster@dmi.ca
 Web Address: www.dmi.ca
Personnel:
 Gen. Mgr.: Tim Lanteigne
 Phone: (1) 780-624-7000
 Fax: (1) 780-624-7329
 Email: tlanteigne@dmi.com
 Mill Mgr.: Bill Downing
 Phone: (1) 780-624-7000
 Fax: (1) 780-624-7329
 Email: bdowning@dmi.com
 Environ. Mgr.: Thomas Tarpey
 Phone: (1) 780-624-7000
 Fax: (1) 780-624-7329
 Email: ttarpey@dmi.com
 Contr.: Marvin Baker
 Phone: (1) 780-618-4100
 Fax: (1) 780-624-7079
 Email: mbaker@dmi.com
 Maint. & Eng. Mgr.: Shawn Elliott
 Phone: (1) 780-624-7000
 Fax: (1) 780-624-7329
 Email: selliott@dmi.com
 HR Mgr.: Rob LaFontaine
 Phone: (1) 780-624-7000
 Fax: (1) 780-624-7329
 Email: rlafontaine@dmi.com
 Woodlands Mgr.: Stefan Szabo
 Phone: (1) 780-624-7000
 Fax: (1) 780-624-7329
 Email: sszabo@prpddmi.com
Total Employees at this Location: 301
Type of Operation: Pulp mill
Pulp Grades and Capacities:
 Total pulp capacity: 499,235 mt/y
 Pulp available for market: 491,946 mt/y

Alberta

Chemical Pulp: 499,235 mt/y
Pulp Mill Data:
Chemical Pulping Systems:
Continuous digesters: 1
Pulp Lines: 1
Bleach Plant Systems: 1
Chemical Pulping System, Type: hardwood/Softwood, Sequence: O_2 DEopDD
Chemical Recovery Equipment:
Evaporator lines: 1
Recovery boilers: 1
Lime Kiln
Pulp Dryers:
Flakt dryer 1
Energy Data:
Power boilers: 1
Steam turbines: 2 at 45, 25 MW
Electrical demand for mill: 916 MWh/D

ⓂHinton Pulp
Hinton Pulp
Ownership: 100% by West Fraser Timber Co. Ltd.
760 Switzer Dr
Hinton, AB
Canada, T7V 1V7
  Phone: (1) 780-865-2251
  Fax: (1) 780-865-8538
  Web Address: www.westfraser.com
Personnel:
  Gen. Mgr.: Brian Grantham
  Phone: (1) 780-865-2251
  Fax: (1) 780-865-8538
  Email: brian.grantham@westfraser.com
  Pulp Mill Supt.: Paulo Kapronczai
  Phone: (1) 780-865-2251
  Fax: (1) 780-865-8538
  Email: paulo.kapronczai@westfraser.com
Total Employees at this Location: 342
Type of Operation: Pulp mill
Pulp Grades and Capacities:
  Total pulp capacity: 427,138 mt/y
  Pulp available for market: 419,832 mt/y
  Chemical Pulp: 427,138 mt/y
Pulp Mill Data:
Chemical Pulping Systems:
Continuous digesters: 1
Pulp Lines: 1
Bleach Plant Systems: 1
Chemical Pulping System - 1, Type: 3-stages of washing - Softwood Line, Sequence: O_2 DEopD
Chemical Recovery Equipment:
Evaporator lines: 1
Recovery boilers: 2
Lime Kiln
Pulp Dryers:
Air Float dryers 1, Fourdriniers 1
Energy Data:
Power boilers: 3
Steam turbines: 2 at 23, 28 MW
Electrical demand for mill: 1,003 MWh/D

ⓂMillar Western Forest Products Ltd.
Ownership: 100% by Private, family owned
16640 111th Ave
Edmonton, AB
Canada, T5M 2S5
  Phone: (1) 780-486-8200
  Fax: (1) 780-486-8282
  Email: mwfp@millarwestern.com
  Web Address: www.millarwestern.com
Personnel:
  Co-Chmn.: H. MacKenzie Millar
  Phone: (1) 780-486-8200
  Fax: (1) 780-486-8282
  Email: hmillar@millarwestern.com
  Pres. & CEO: J. Craig Armstrong
  Phone: (1) 780-486-8231
  Fax: (1) 780-486-8282
  Email: jarmstrong@millarwestern.com
  Snr. VP: Carol Cotton
  Phone: (1) 780-486-8290
  Fax: (1) 780-486-8282
  Email: ccotton@millarwestern.com
  Snr. VP, Pulp: Ronald J. Reis
  Phone: (1) 780-486-8200
  Fax: (1) 780-486-8282
  Email: rreis@millarwestern.com
  VP, Finan. & CFO: David Anderson
  Phone: (1) 780-486-8219
  Fax: (1) 780-486-8282
  Email: danderson@millarwestern.com
  VP, HR: Brian McConkey
  Phone: (1) 780-486-8267
  Fax: (1) 780-486-8282
  Email: bmcconkey@millarwestern.com
  Logist. Mgr.: Greg Simpson
  Phone: (1) 780-486-8281
  Fax: (1) 780-486-8282
  Email: gsimpson@millarwestern.com
Total Employees of Company: 562
Total Employees at this Location: 60
Mill Locations:
Millar Western Forest Products Ltd., Whitecourt Pulp Mill, Whitecourt, AB, Canada T7S1A1, (Pulp mill)
  Phone: (1) 780-778-2036
  Fax: (1) 780-778-4384
  Email: mwfp@millarwestern.com

ⓂMillar Western Forest Products Ltd.
Whitecourt Pulp Mill
Whitecourt, AB
Canada, T7S1A1
Mailing Address: PO Box 1072, Whitecourt, AB, Canada, T7S 1N9
  Phone: (1) 780-778-2036
  Fax: (1) 780-778-4384
  Email: mwfp@millarwestern.com
  Web Address: www.millarwestern.com
Personnel:
  Mill Mgr.: Dave Martell
  Phone: (1) 780-778-2036 Ext. 4244
  Fax: (1) 780-778-4384
  Email: dmartell@millarwestern.com
  Maint. & Eng. Mgr.: Mark Wright
  Phone: (1) 780-778-2036
  Fax: (1) 780-778-4384
  Email: mwright@millarwestern.com
  Prod. Supervisor: Shayne Wadlow
  Phone: (1) 780-778-2036
  Fax: (1) 780-778-4384
  Email: swadlow@millarwestern.com
  Contr.: Lindsay Moyle
  Phone: (1) 780-778-2036
  Fax: (1) 780-778-4384
  Email: lmoyle@millarwestern.com
  Environ. Supt.: Jeff Shipton
  Phone: (1) 780-778-2036
  Fax: (1) 780-778-4384
  Email: jshipton@millarwestern.com
Total Employees at this Location: 106
Type of Operation: Pulp mill
Pulp Grades and Capacities:
  Total pulp capacity: 324,809 mt/y
  Pulp available for market: 319,872 mt/y
  Mechanical Pulp: 324,809 mt/y
Pulp Mill Data:
Mechanical Pulping Systems:
BCTMP systems: 1
Pulp Lines: 2
Bleach Plant Systems: 2
Mechanical BCTMP Pulping System, Type: Multi-stage, Sequence: PP, Capacity 155,000 admt/y
Pulp Dryers:
Flash dryers 1, Flash dryers 1
Energy Data:
Power boilers: 1
TMP Reboiler: 1
Electrical demand for mill: 1,456 MWh/D

ⓂSlave Lake Pulp Corp.
Slave Lake Pulp Mill
Ownership: 100% by West Fraser Timber Co. Ltd.
P.O. Box 1790
Slave Lake, AB
Canada, T0G 2A0
Mailing Address: PO Box 1790, Slave Lake, AB, Canada, T0G 2A0
  Phone: (1) 780-849-7777
  Fax: (1) 780-849-7725
  Web Address: www.westfraser.com
Personnel:
  Gen. Mgr.: Tony McWhannel
  Phone: (1) 780-849-7777
  Fax: (1) 780-849-7725
  Email: tony.mcwhannel@westfraser.com
  Eng Technologist: Gary Romelus
  Phone: (1) 780-849-7722
  Fax: (1) 780-849-7785
  Email: gary.romelus@westfraser.com
  Payroll Coordinator.: Lynda Paterson
  Phone: (1) 780-849-7777
  Fax: (1) 780-849-7725
  Email: lynda.paterson@westfraser.com
Total Employees at this Location: 100
Type of Operation: Pulp mill
Pulp Grades and Capacities:
  Total pulp capacity: 243,508 mt/y
  Pulp available for market: 239,904 mt/y
  Mechanical Pulp: 243,508 mt/y
Pulp Mill Data:
Mechanical Pulping Systems:
BCTMP systems: 3
Pulp Lines: 1
Bleach Plant Systems: 1
Mechanical BCTMP Pulping System, Type: 2 stage peroxide, Sequence: PP, Capacity 254,600 admt/y
Pulp Dryers:
Flash dryers 1
Energy Data:
Power boilers: 3
TMP Reboiler: 1
Electrical demand for mill: 1,390 MWh/D

ⓂWeyerhaeuser Company Ltd.
Grande Prairie Mill
Ownership: 100% by Weyerhaeuser Co.
Mailbag 1020
Grande Prairie, AB
Canada, T8V 3A9
Mailing Address: Mailbag 1020, Grande Prairie, AB, Canada, T8V 3A9
  Phone: (1) 780-539-8500
  Fax: (1) 780-539-8500
  Web Address: www.weyerhaeuser.com
Personnel:
  Pulp Mill Mgr.: Aleasa Tasker
  Phone: (1) 780-539-8500
  Fax: (1) 780-539-8500
  Email: aleasa.tasker@weyerhaeuser.com
  Pub. Affairs Ldr. (Alberta): Wayne Roznowsky
  Phone: (1) 780-539-8832
  Fax: (1) 780-539-8500
  Email: wayne.roznowsky@weyerhaeuser.com
  Tech. Mgr.: Brad Farquhar
  Phone: (1) 780-539-8500
  Fax: (1) 780-539-8500
  Email: brad.farquhar@weyerhaeuser.com
  HR Mgr. (Alberta): Norm Carlberg
  Phone: (1) 780-539-8500
  Fax: (1) 780-539-8500
  Email: norm.carlberg@weyerhaeuser.com
  Oper. Mgr.: Darren Lapp
  Phone: (1) 780-539-8500
  Fax: (1) 780-539-8500
  Email: darren.lapp@weyerhaeuser.com
  Cust. Serv. Mgr.: Heidi Yang
  Phone: (1) 780-539-8500
  Fax: (1) 780-539-8500

Email: heidi.yang@weyerhaeuser.com
Maint. Mgr.: Doug Stangier
Phone: (1) 780-539-8500
Fax: (1) 780-539-8500
Email: doug.stangier@weyerhaeuser.com
Environ. Mgr.: Grant Bourree
Phone: (1) 780-539-8500
Fax: (1) 780-539-8500
Email: grant.bourree@weyerhaeuser.com
Total Employees at this Location: 319
Type of Operation: Pulp mill
Pulp Grades and Capacities:
Total pulp capacity: 384,680 mt/y
Pulp available for market: 379,848 mt/y
Chemical Pulp: 384,680 mt/y
Pulp Mill Data:
Chemical Pulping Systems:
Continuous digesters: 1
Pulp Lines: 1
Bleach Plant Systems: 1
Chemical Pulping System, Type: Softwood Line, Sequence: O_2 DEopDED, Capacity 370,000 admt/y
Chemical Recovery Equipment:
Evaporator lines: 1
Recovery boilers: 1
Lime Kiln
Pulp Dryers:
Air Float dryers 1, Fourdriniers 1
Energy Data:
Power boilers: 1
Steam turbines: 4 at 34, 50, 30, 48 MW
Electrical demand for mill: 837 MWh/D

BRITISH COLUMBIA

ⓂCanfor Corp.
Ownership: 100% by the public
100-1700 W. 75th Ave
Vancouver, BC
Canada, V6P 6G2
 Phone: (1) 604-661-5241
 Fax: (1) 604-661-5235
 Email: info@canfor.com
 Web Address: www.canfor.com
Personnel:
Gen. Mgr., Lumber Sls.: Frank Turnbull
Phone: (1) 604-661-5241
Email: frank.turnbull@canfor.com
Chmn.: Ronald Cliff
Phone: (1) 604-661-5241
Fax: (1) 604-661-5235
Email: ronald.cliff@canfor.com
Pres. & CEO: Don Kayne
Phone: (1) 604-661-5241
Fax: (1) 604-661-5235
Email: don.kayne@canfor.com
Snr. VP, Corp. & Legal Affairs & Corp. Sec.: David Calabrigo
Phone: (1) 604-661-5241
Fax: (1) 604-661-5235
Email: david.calibrigo@canfor.com
Snr. VP., Sls. & Mktg.: Wayne Guthrie
Phone: (1) 604-661-5241
Fax: (1) 604-661-5235
Email: wayne.gutherie@canfor.com
Snr. VPn, Finan. & CFO: Alan Nicholl
Phone: (1) 604-661-5241
Fax: (1) 604-661-5235
Email: alan.nicholl@canfor.com
VP. & Treasurer: Patric Elliot
Phone: (1) 604-661-5241
Fax: (1) 604-661-5235
Email: patric.elliot@canfor.com
VP., HR: Onkar Athwal
Phone: (1) 604-661-5241
Fax: (1) 604-661-5235
Email: oncar.athwal@canfor.com

Total Employees of Company: 5,351
Mill Locations:
Canfor Corp., Taylor Mill, 8300 Cherry Avenue East, Taylor, BC, Canada V0C 2K0, (Pulp mill)
 Phone: (1) 250-789-9300
 Fax: (1) 250-789-3089
 Email: CPPM@canfor.ca
Canfor Pulp Ltd., Intercontinental Mill (50.20% owned), 2533 Prince George Pulp Mill Rd, Prince George, BC, Canada V2N 2K3, (Pulp mill)
 Phone: (1) 250-563-0161
 Fax: (1) 250-561-3921
 Email: info@canforpulp.com
Canfor Pulp Ltd., Northwood Mill (50.20% owned), 5353 Northwood Pulp Mill Rd, Prince George, BC, Canada V2L 4W2, (Pulp mill)
 Phone: (1) 250-962-3600
 Fax: (1) 250-962-3638
 Email: info@canforpulp.com
Canfor Pulp Ltd., Prince George (Pulp & Paper) Mill (50.20% owned), 2789 Prince George Pulp Mill Road, Prince George, BC, Canada V2N 2K3, Capacity: 152,082 mt/y, (Pulp mill, Paper mill)
 Phone: (1) 250-563-0161
 Fax: (1) 250-561-3627
 Email: info@canforpulp.com

ⓂCanfor Corp.
Taylor Mill
8300 Cherry Avenue East
Taylor, BC
Canada, V0C 2K0
Mailing Address: PO Box 330, Taylor, BC, Canada, V0C 2K0
 Phone: (1) 250-789-9300
 Fax: (1) 250-789-3089
 Email: CPPM@canfor.ca
 Web Address: www.canfor.com
Personnel:
Gen. Mgr.: Ted St. John
Phone: (1) 250-789-9300
Fax: (1) 250-789-3089
Email: ted.st.john@canfor.com
Prod. Mgr.: Hal Bulmer
Phone: (1) 250-789-9300
Fax: (1) 250-789-3089
Email: hal.bulmer@canfor.com
Energy and Env. Mgr.: Craig Thomson
Phone: (1) 250-789-9300
Fax: (1) 250-789-3089
Email: craig.thomson@canfor.com
Tech. & Cust. Serv. Mgr. & Mktg Mgr.: Darren Guliov
Phone: (1) 250-789-9300
Fax: (1) 250-789-3089
Email: darren.givliov@canfor.com
Purch. Mgr.: Dan Hogg
Phone: (1) 250-789-9300
Fax: (1) 250-789-3089
Email: dan.hogg@canfor.com
Total Employees at this Location: 110
Type of Operation: Pulp mill
Pulp Grades and Capacities:
Total pulp capacity: 217,312 mt/y
Pulp available for market: 214,200 mt/y
Mechanical Pulp: 217,312 mt/y
Pulp Mill Data:
Mechanical Pulping Systems:
BCTMP systems: 2
Pulp Lines: 2
Bleach Plant Systems: 2
Mechanical BCTMP Pulping System, Sequence: PP, Capacity 220,000 admt/y
Pulp Dryers:
Flash dryers 1, Flash dryers 1
Energy Data:
Power boilers: 1
TMP Reboiler: 1
Electrical demand for mill: 1,150 MWh/D

ⓂCanfor Pulp Ltd.
Intercontinental Mill
Ownership: 50.20% by Canfor Corp., 49.80% by the public
2533 Prince George Pulp Mill Rd
Prince George, BC
Canada, V2N 2K3
Mailing Address: PO Box 6000, Prince George, BC, Canada, V2N 2K3
 Phone: (1) 250-563-0161
 Fax: (1) 250-561-3921
 Email: info@canforpulp.com
 Web Address: www.canforpulp.com
Personnel:
Pres. CPLP: Brett Robinson
Phone: (1) 250-563-0161
Fax: (1) 250-561-3921
Email: brett.robinson@canforpulp.com
Maint. Mgr.: Pam Woyciehouski
Phone: (1) 250-563-0161
Fax: (1) 250-561-3921
Email: pam.woyciehouski@canforpulp.com
Cust. Service Mgr.: Jeff Bennett
Phone: (1) 250-563-0161
Fax: (1) 250-561-3921
Email: jeff.bennett@canforpulp.com
Total Employees at this Location: 270
Type of Operation: Pulp mill
Pulp Grades and Capacities:
Total pulp capacity: 324,756 mt/y
Pulp available for market: 319,872 mt/y
Chemical Pulp: 324,756 mt/y
Pulp Mill Data:
Chemical Pulping Systems:
Continuous digesters: 1
Pulp Lines: 1
Bleach Plant Systems: 1
Chemical Pulping System, Type: Softwood Line, Sequence: O_2 DEopDEpD, Capacity 328,100 admt/y
Chemical Recovery Equipment:
Evaporator lines: 1
Recovery boilers: 1
Lime Kiln
Pulp Dryers:
Flakt dryer 1
Energy Data:
Power boilers: 1
Steam turbines: 1 at 25 MW
Electrical demand for mill: 756 MWh/D

ⓂCanfor Pulp Ltd.
Northwood Mill
Ownership: 50.20% by Canfor Corp., 49.80% by the public
5353 Northwood Pulp Mill Rd
Prince George, BC
Canada, V2L 4W2
Mailing Address: PO Box 9000, Prince George, BC, Canada, V2L 4W2
 Phone: (1) 250-962-3600
 Fax: (1) 250-962-3638
 Email: info@canforpulp.com
 Web Address: www.canforpulp.com
Personnel:
Gen. Mgr.: Sotirios Korogonas
Phone: (1) 250-962-3680
Fax: (1) 250-962-3602
Email: Sotirios.Korogonas@canforpulp.com
Snr. Process Contr. Eng.: Dan Laing
Phone: (1) 250-962-3600
Fax: (1) 250-962-3602
Email: dan.laing@canforpulp.com
Proj. Coord.: Joe Rea
Phone: (1) 250-962-3600
Fax: (1) 250-962-3602
Email: joe.rea@canforpulp.com
Reliability Specialist: Troy Belbeck
Phone: (1) 250-962-3600
Fax: (1) 250-962-3602

British Columbia

Email: troy.belbeck@canforpulp.com
Total Employees at this Location: 460
Type of Operation: Pulp mill
Pulp Grades and Capacities:
  Total pulp capacity: 608,785 mt/y
  Pulp available for market: 600,117 mt/y
  Chemical Pulp: 608,785 mt/y
Pulp Mill Data:
  Chemical Pulping Systems:
  Continuous digesters: 2
Pulp Lines: 2
  Bleach Plant Systems: 2
  Chemical Pulping System - No.1, Type: Softwood, Sequence: O_2 DEOpDEpD, Capacity 301,070 admt/y
  Chemical Pulping System - No.2, Type: Softwood, Sequence: O_2 DEopDED, Capacity 327,250 admt/y
  Chemical Recovery Equipment:
  Evaporator lines: 2
  Recovery boilers: 2
  Lime Kiln
  Pulp Dryers:
  Flakt dryer 1, Flakt dryer 1, Fourdriniers 1
Energy Data:
  Power boilers: 2
  Steam turbines: 2 at 56 MW
  Electrical demand for mill: 1,333 MWh/D

ⓂCanfor Pulp Ltd.
Prince George (Pulp & Paper) Mill
Ownership: 50.20% by Canfor Corp., 49.80% by the public
2789 Prince George Pulp Mill Road
Prince George, BC
Canada, V2N 2K3
Mailing Address: PO Box 6000, Prince George, BC, Canada, V2N 2K3
  Phone: (1) 250-563-0161
  Fax: (1) 250 561-3627
  Email: info@canforpulp.com
  Web Address: www.canforpulp.com
Personnel:
  VP Oper.: Martin Pudlas
  Phone: (1) 250-563-0161
  Fax: (1) 250 561-3627
  Email: martin.pudlas@canforpulp.com
  Environ. Supervisor: Adam Lancaster
  Phone: (1) 250-563-0161
  Fax: (1) 250 561-3627
  Email: adam.lancaster@canforpulp.com
Total Employees at this Location: 366
Type of Operation: Pulp mill, Paper mill
Pulp Grades and Capacities:
  Total pulp capacity: 307,462 mt/y
  Pulp available for market: 144,942 mt/y
  Chemical Pulp: 307,462 mt/y
Pulp Mill Data:
  Chemical Pulping Systems:
  Continuous digesters: 2
Pulp Lines: 2
  Bleach Plant Systems: 1
  Chemical Pulping System - 1, Type: Softwood, Sequence: DEopD, Capacity 195,000 admt/y
  Chemical Recovery Equipment:
  Evaporator lines: 2
  Recovery boilers: 1
  Lime Kiln
  Pulp Dryers:
  Flakt dryer 1, Fourdriniers 1
Paper/Paperboard Grades and Capacities:
  Total paper and paperboard capacity: 152,082 mt/y
  Packaging papers: 152,082 mt/y
Paper and Paperboard Mill Data:
  Stock Preparation:
  Refiners: 4
Paper Machines: 1
  No. 1, fourdrinier, total capacity 152,082 mt/y, Trim width 5.68 m, Packaging papers
Finishing Equipment:
  Rewinders: 1 at 144,000 mt/y

Energy Data:
Power boilers: 2
Steam turbines: 1 at 48 MW
Electrical demand for mill: 798 MWh/D

ⓄⓂCariboo Pulp & Paper Co.
Cariboo Mill
Ownership: 50% by West Fraser Timber Co. Ltd., 25% by Nippon Paper Industries Co., Ltd., 25% by Daishowa-Marubeni International Ltd.
50 North Star Rd
Quesnel, BC
Canada, V2J 3J6
Mailing Address: PO Box 7500, Quesnel, BC, Canada, V2J 3J6
  Phone: (1) 250-992-0200
  Fax: (1) 250-991-0747
  Web Address: www.westfraser.com, www.dmi.ca
Personnel:
  Gen. Mgr.: Bruce Eby
  Phone: (1) 250-992-0251
  Fax: (1) 250-991-0747
  Email: bruce.eby@westfraser.com
  Eng. & Maint. Mgr.: Dave Needham
  Phone: (1) 250-992-0200
  Fax: (1) 250-991-0747
  Email: dave.needham@westfraser.com
  Steam and Recov. Mgr.: Dan McRae
  Phone: (1) 250-992-0200
  Fax: (1) 250-991-0747
  Email: dan.mcrae@westfraser.com
  Fibre Line & Tech. Mgr.: Steve Bird
  Phone: (1) 250-992-0232
  Fax: (1) 250-991-0747
  Email: steve.bird@westfraser.com
  HR Mgr.: Bob Norman
  Phone: (1) 250-992-0200
  Fax: (1) 250-991-0747
  Email: bob.norman@westfraser.com
  Contr. & Wood Supply Mgr.: Charlie Ragsdale
  Phone: (1) 250-992-0200
  Fax: (1) 250-991-0747
  Email: charlie.ragsdale@westfraser.com
Total Employees of Company: 320
Total Employees at this Location: 289
Type of Operation: Pulp mill
Pulp Grades and Capacities:
  Total pulp capacity: 353,724 mt/y
  Pulp available for market: 348,432 mt/y
  Chemical Pulp: 353,724 mt/y
Pulp Mill Data:
  Chemical Pulping Systems:
  Continuous digesters: 1
Pulp Lines: 1
  Bleach Plant Systems: 1
  No. 1, Sequence: O_2 DEOpDEpD
  Chemical Recovery Equipment:
  Evaporator lines: 1
  Recovery boilers: 1
  Lime Kiln
  Pulp Dryers:
  Air Float dryers 1, Fourdriniers 1
Energy Data:
Power boilers: 1
Steam turbines: 2 at 34, 30 MW
Electrical demand for mill: 799 MWh/D

ⓄCatalyst Paper Corporation
Ownership: 100% by the public
3600 Lysander Lane, 2nd Floor
Richmond, BC
Canada, V7B 1C3
  Phone: (1) 604-247-4400
  Fax: (1) 604-654-4048/604-247-0512
  Web Address: www.catalystpaper.com
Personnel:
  Pres. & CEO.: Joe Nemeth
  Phone: (1) 604-247-4400
  Fax: (1) 604-654-4048

Email: joe.nemeth@catalystpaper.com
  Snr. VP., HR: Stephen Boniferro
  Phone: (1) 604-247-4400
  Fax: (1) 604-654-4048
  Email: stephen.boniferro@catalystpaper.com
  Snr. VP. Sls. & Mktg. (From April 2014): Jim Bayles
  Phone: (1) 604-247-4400
  Fax: (1) 604-654-4048
  VP Finance, CFO: Brian Baarda
  Phone: (1) 604-247-4710
  Fax: (1) 604-654-4048
  Email: brian.baarda@catalystpaper.com
Total Employees of Company: 1,611
Total Employees at this Location: 70
Mill Locations:
Catalyst Paper Corporation, Crofton Mill, 8541 Hay Road, Crofton, BC, Canada V0R 1R0, Capacity: 340,935 mt/y, (Pulp mill, Paper mill)
  Phone: (1) 250-246-6100
  Fax: (1) 250-246-6300
  Email: contactus@catalystpaper.com
Catalyst Paper Corporation, Port Alberni Mill, 4000 Stamp Ave, Port Alberni, BC, Canada V9Y 5J7, Capacity: 339,864 mt/y, (Paper mill)
  Phone: (1) 250-723-2161
  Fax: (1) 250-724-7498
  Email: contactus@catalystpaper.com
Catalyst Paper Corporation, Powell River Mill, 5775 Ash Avenue, Powell River, BC, Canada V8A 4R3, Capacity: 469,098 mt/y, (Paper mill)
  Phone: (1) 604-483-3722
  Fax: (1) 604-483-2951
  Email: contactus@catalystpaper.com

ⓂCatalyst Paper Corporation
Crofton Mill
8541 Hay Road
Crofton, BC
Canada, V0R 1R0
Mailing Address: PO Box 70, Crofton, BC, Canada, V0R 1R0
  Phone: (1) 250-246-6100
  Fax: (1) 250-246-6300
  Email: contactus@catalystpaper.com
  Web Address: www.catalystpaper.com
Personnel:
  VP. & Gen. Mgr.: Robert Belanger
  Phone: (1) 250-246-6100
  Fax: (1) 250-246-6300
  Email: robert.belanger@catalystpaper.com
  Eng. & Tech. Serv. Mgr.: Berk Borrett
  Phone: (1) 250-246-6100
  Fax: (1) 250-246-6300
  Email: berk.borrett@catalystpaper.com
  Maint. Mgr.: Dennis Maltais
  Phone: (1) 250-246-6100
  Fax: (1) 250-246-6300
  Email: dennis.maltais@catalystpaper.com
  Oper. Specialist (Kraft Mill - Cooking, Washing and Screening): Hugh Gallinger
  Phone: (1) 250-246-6268
  Fax: (1) 250-246-6386
  Email: hugh.gallinger@catalystpaper.com
Total Employees at this Location: 530
Type of Operation: Pulp mill, Paper mill
Pulp Grades and Capacities:
  Total pulp capacity: 713,159 mt/y
  Pulp available for market: 392,700 mt/y
  Chemical Pulp: 397,937 mt/y
  Mechanical Pulp: 315,222 mt/y
Pulp Mill Data:
  Chemical Pulping Systems:
  Batch digesters: 8
  Continuous digesters: 1
  Mechanical Pulping Systems:
  TMP systems: 3
  TMP systems: 1
Pulp Lines: 6
  Bleach Plant Systems: 2
  No. 1, Type: Kraft, Sequence: DEOpDEpD, Capacity

British Columbia

181,000 admt/y
No. 2, Type: TMP, Sequence: HS/P
No. 3, Type: ATMP, Sequence: HS/P
No. 4, Type: Kraft, Sequence: DEOpDEpD, Capacity 222,000 admt/y
Chemical Recovery Equipment:
Evaporator lines: 1
Recovery boilers: 2
Lime Kiln
Pulp Dryers:
Flakt dryer 1, Fourdriniers 1, Fourdriniers 1, Other dryers 1
Paper/Paperboard Grades and Capacities:
Total paper and paperboard capacity: 340,935 mt/y
Newsprint: 340,935 mt/y
Paper and Paperboard Mill Data:
Stock Preparation:
Pulpers: 2
Refiners: 2
Paper Machines: 2
No. 2, Bel-Baie III, total capacity 146,370 mt/y, Trim width 6.23 m, Newsprint
No. 3, Bel-Baie IV, total capacity 194,565 mt/y, Trim width 7.62 m, Newsprint
Energy Data:
Power boilers: 3
Steam turbines: 1 at 40 MW
Electrical demand for mill: 3,873 MWh/D

ⓜCatalyst Paper Corporation
Port Alberni Mill
4000 Stamp Ave
Port Alberni, BC
Canada, V9Y 5J7
Phone: (1) 250-723-2161
Fax: (1) 250-724-7498
Email: contactus@catalystpaper.com
Web Address: www.catalystpaper.com
Personnel:
Gen. Mgr. (From April 2014): Harold Norlund
Phone: (1) 250-723-2161
Fax: (1) 250-724-7498
Email: harold.norlund@catalystpaper.com
Oper. Mgr.: Keith Davenport
Phone: (1) 250-723-2161
Fax: (1) 250-724-7498
Email: keith.davenport@catalystpaper.com
E/I Maint. Mgr.: Darryl Hatch
Phone: (1) 250-723-2161
Fax: (1) 250-724-7498
Email: darryl.hatch@catalystpaper.com
Reliability Maint. Supervisor: John Woodfin AScT
Phone: (1) 250-723-2161
Fax: (1) 250-724-7498
Email: john.woodfin@catalystpaper.com
Total Employees at this Location: 300
Type of Operation: Paper mill
Pulp Grades and Capacities:
Total pulp capacity: 258,806 mt/y
Mechanical Pulp: 258,806 mt/y
Pulp Mill Data:
Mechanical Pulping Systems:
CTMP systems: 1
Bleach Plant Systems: 1
Mechanical (C)TMP Pulping System, Type: Softwood, Sequence: P
Paper/Paperboard Grades and Capacities:
Total paper and paperboard capacity: 339,864 mt/y
Uncoated mechanical/groundwood: 116,025 mt/y
Coated mechanical/groundwood: 223,839 mt/y
Paper and Paperboard Mill Data:
Stock Preparation:
Pulpers: 5
Refiners: 11
Paper Machines: 2
No. 4, SpeedFormer, total capacity 116,025 mt/y, Trim width 6.4 m, Uncoated mechanical/groundwood
No. 5, SymFormer R, total capacity 223,839 mt/y, Trim width 7.6 m, Coated mechanical/groundwood

Coating Machines: 1
PM 5, total capacity 230,000 mt/y., on machine
Finishing Equipment:
Calenders: 1
Rewinders: 1
Energy Data:
Power boilers: 3
Steam turbines: 1 at 26 MW
Electrical demand for mill: 2,477 MWh/D

ⓜCatalyst Paper Corporation
Powell River Mill
5775 Ash Avenue
Powell River, BC
Canada, V8A 4R3
Mailing Address: P.O. Box 74, V0R 1R0 Crofton
Phone: (1) 604-483-3722
Fax: (1) 604-483-2951
Email: contactus@catalystpaper.com
Web Address: www.catalystpaper.com
Personnel:
VP. & Gen. Mgr. (From April 2014): Fred Chinn
Phone: (1) 604-483-3722
Fax: (1) 604-483-2951
Email: fred.chinn@catalystpaper.com
Pulp & Utilities Mgr.: Ed Antolovich
Phone: (1) 604-483-3722
Fax: (1) 604-483-2951
Email: ed.antolovich@catalystpaper.com
Environ. Mgr.: Sarah Barkowski
Phone: (1) 604-483-2850
Fax: (1) 604-483-2951
Email: sarah.barkowski@catalystpaper.com
Manuf Mgr: Bill Forrest
Phone: (1) 604-483-3722
Fax: (1) 604-483-2951
Email: bill.forrest@catalystpaper.com
Total Employees at this Location: 388
Type of Operation: Paper mill
Pulp Grades and Capacities:
Total pulp capacity: 412,742 mt/y
Mechanical Pulp: 412,742 mt/y
Pulp Mill Data:
Mechanical Pulping Systems:
CTMP systems: 5
Bleach Plant Systems: 1
Mechanical CTMP Pulping System, Type: CTMP Capacity 350,000 admt/y
Paper/Paperboard Grades and Capacities:
Total paper and paperboard capacity: 469,098 mt/y
Uncoated mechanical/groundwood: 469,098 mt/y
Paper and Paperboard Mill Data:
Stock Preparation:
Pulpers: 2
Refiners: 7
Paper Machines: 3
No. 9, Bel-Baie III, total capacity 121,380 mt/y, Trim width 6.1 m, Uncoated mechanical/groundwood
No. 10, Bel-Baie III, total capacity 160,650 mt/y, Trim width 7.7 m, Uncoated mechanical/groundwood
No. 11, Bel-Baie II, total capacity 187,068 mt/y, Trim width 7.63 m, Uncoated mechanical/groundwood
Finishing Equipment:
Calenders: 1
Energy Data:
Power boilers: 5
TMP Reboiler: 1
Steam turbines: 1 at 40 MW
Hydro turbines: 1 at 82 MW
Electrical demand for mill: 3,895 MWh/D

ⓗDaishowa-Marubeni International Ltd.
Ownership: 50% by Nippon Paper Industries Co., Ltd., 50% by Marubeni Corporation
#700, 510 Burrard Street
Vancouver, BC
Canada, V6C 3A8
Phone: (1) 604-684-4326
Fax: (1) 604-684-0512
Email: sdornbierer@dmi.ca

Web Address: www.dmi.ca
Personnel:
Pres.: Yukichi Nakamura
Phone: (1) 604-684-4326
Fax: (1) 604-684-0512
Email: ynakamura@dmi.ca
VP & Gen. Mgr. Mktg. & Transp.: Takuya Enomoto
Phone: (1) 604-684-4326
Fax: (1) 604-684-0512
Email: tenomoto@dmi.ca
Gen. Mgr. HR, Dir. of Corp. Comm.: Stuart Dornbierer
Phone: (1) 604-684-4326
Fax: (1) 604-684-0512
Email: sdornbierer@dmi.ca
Corp. Contr.: Jim McIlwain
Phone: (1) 604-684-4326
Fax: (1) 604-684-0512
Email: jmcilwain@dmi.ca
Corporate Account Mgr.: Takahiro Araki
Phone: (1) 604-684-4326
Fax: (1) 604-684-0512
Email: taraki@dmi.ca
Secretary Treas.: Shoichi Aikawa
Phone: (1) 604-684-4326
Fax: (1) 604-684-0512
Email: saikawa@dmi.ca
Total Employees of Company: 1,200
Total Employees at this Location: 17
Mill Locations:
Daishowa-Marubeni International Ltd., Peace River Pulp Division, Peace River, AB, Canada T8S 1V7, (Pulp mill)
Phone: (1) 780-624-7000
Fax: (1) 780-624-7329
Email: webmaster@dmi.ca

ⓜDomtar Corporation
Kamloops Mill
2005 Mission Flats Rd
Kamloops, BC
Canada, V2C 1A9
Mailing Address: PO Box 800, Kamloops, BC, Canada, V2C 5M7
Phone: (1) 250-434-6000
Fax: (1) 250-434-8877
Web Address: www.domtar.com
Personnel:
Mill Mgr.: Carol Lapointe
Phone: (1) 250-434-6000
Fax: (1) 250-434-8877
Email: carol.lapointe@domtar.com
Oper. Mgr.: Dennis Clare
Phone: (1) 250-434-6000
Fax: (1) 250-434-8877
Email: dennis.clare@domtar.com
Strategic Plan.: Greg Drinkwater
Phone: (1) 250-434-8813
Fax: (1) 250-434-8882
Email: greg.drinkwater@domtar.com
Maint. Leader: Bill Wade
Phone: (1) 250-434-6000
Fax: (1) 250-434-8877
Email: bill.wade@domtar.com
Bus. Mgr.: Mylene Bourgeois
Phone: (1) 250-434-6000
Fax: (1) 250-434-8877
Email: mylene.bourgeois@domtar.com
Finan. Leader: Bryan Swanton
Phone: (1) 250-434-6000
Fax: (1) 250-434-8877
Email: bryan.swanton@domtar.com
Total Employees at this Location: 300
Type of Operation: Pulp mill
Pulp Grades and Capacities:
Total pulp capacity: 374,422 mt/y
Pulp available for market: 367,353 mt/y
Chemical Pulp: 356,948 mt/y
Pulp Mill Data:
Chemical Pulping Systems:
Continuous digesters: 3
Pulp Lines: 2

British Columbia

Bleach Plant Systems: 2
Chemical Pulping System - 1, Type: Softwood, Sequence: O_2 DEoDD, Capacity 367,500 admt/y
Chemical Pulping System - 2, Type: Softwood, Sequence: DED, Capacity 115,500 admt/y
Chemical Recovery Equipment:
Evaporator lines: 1
Recovery boilers: 2
Lime Kiln
Pulp Dryers:
Flakt dryer 1, Flakt dryer 1
Energy Data:
Power boilers: 2
Steam turbines: 2 at 46, 29 MW
Electrical demand for mill: 760 MWh/D

ⒽFortress Paper Ltd.
2nd Floor, Chadwick Court
North Vancouver, BC
Canada, V7M 3K2
 Phone: (1) 888-820-3888, 604-904-2328
 Fax: (1) 604-988-5327
 Email: info@fortresspaper.com
 Web Address: www.thefortressgroup.ca, www.fortresspaper.com
Personnel:
Chmn of Bd., Pres. & CEO: Chad Wasilenkoff
 Phone: (1) 604 904 2328
 Fax: (1) 604-988-5327
 Email: cwasilenkoff@fortresspaper.com
CFO: Kurt Loewen
 Phone: (1) 604 904 2328
 Fax: (1) 604-988-5327
 Email: kloewen@fortresspaper.com
Finan. Dir & Corp. Sec.: Danial Buckle
 Phone: (1) 888-820-3888
 Fax: (1) 604-988-5327
 Email: dbuckle@fortresspaper.com
Dir.: Anil Wirasekara
 Phone: (1) 888-820-3888
 Fax: (1) 604-988-5327
Dir.: Joe Nemeth
 Phone: (1) 888-820-3888
 Fax: (1) 604-988-5327
Dir.: Per Gundersby
 Phone: (1) 888-820-3888
 Fax: (1) 604-988-5327
Dir.: Richard Whittall
 Phone: (1) 888-820-3888
 Fax: (1) 604-988-5327
Total Employees of Company: 640
Mill Locations:
Fortress Global Cellulose Ltd, Lebel-sur-Quevillon Mill, 30 Chemin du Moulin, Lebel-sur-Quevillon, QC, Canada J0Y 1X0, (Pulp mill)
 Phone: (1) 819-755-2124
 Fax: (1) 819-755-2125
Fortress Specialty Cellulose Inc., Thurso Mill, Hwy 148 E, Thurso, QC, Canada J0X 3B0, (Pulp mill)
 Phone: (1) 819-985-2233
 Fax: (1) 819-985-5023
 Email: info@fortresspaper.com, info@specialtycellulose.com
Landqart AG, Landqart Mill, Kantonsstrasse 16, CH-7302 Landquart, Switzerland, Capacity: 22,000 mt/y, (Paper mill)
 Phone: (41) 81 307 90 90
 Fax: (41) 81 307 91 41
 Email: info@landqart.com

ⒽNanaimo Forest Products Ltd
Previously Harmac Pacific Inc.
Ownership: 100% by Nanaimo Forest Products Ltd
1000 Wave Place
Nanaimo, BC
Canada, V9X 1J2
 Phone: (1) 250-722-3211
 Fax: (1) 250-722-4310
 Email: info@harmacpacific.com
 Web Address: www.harmacpacific.com
Personnel:
Pres.: Levi Sampson
 Phone: (1) 250-722-3211
 Fax: (1) 250-722-4310
 Email: lsamson@harmacpacific.com
CEO: Paul Sadler
 Phone: (1) 250-722-3211
 Fax: (1) 250-722-4310
 Email: psadler@harmacpacific.com
Dir.: Bob Smiley
 Phone: (1) 250-722-3211
 Fax: (1) 250-722-4310
 Email: bsmiley@harmacpacific.com
IT Mgr.: Bob Waldhaus
 Phone: (1) 250-722-4205
 Fax: (1) 250-722-4310
 Email: bwaldhaus@harmacpacific.com
HR Mgr.: Grant Brebber
 Phone: (1) 250-722-3211
 Fax: (1) 250-722-4310
 Email: gbrebber@harmacpacific.com
Tech. Serv. Supt.: David Bramley
 Phone: (1) 250-722-4267
 Fax: (1) 250-722-4310
 Email: dbramley@harmacpacific.com
Total Employees of Company: 285
Mill Locations:
Nanaimo Forest Products Ltd, Harmac Mill, 1000 Wave Pl, Nanaimo, BC, Canada V9X 1J2, (Pulp mill)
 Phone: (1) 250-722-3211
 Fax: (1) 250-722-4310
 Email: info@harmacpacific.com

ⓂNanaimo Forest Products Ltd
Harmac Mill
1000 Wave Pl
Nanaimo, BC
Canada, V9X 1J2
 Phone: (1) 250-722-3211
 Fax: (1) 250-722-4310
 Email: info@harmacpacific.com
 Web Address: www.harmacpacific.com
Personnel:
CEO: Paul Sadler
 Phone: (1) 250-722-3211
 Fax: (1) 250-722-4310
 Email: psadler@harmacpacific.com
Dir.: Bob Smiley
 Phone: (1) 250-722-3211
 Fax: (1) 250-722-4310
 Email: bsmiley@harmacpacific.com
Total Employees at this Location: 280
Type of Operation: Pulp mill
Pulp Grades and Capacities:
Total pulp capacity: 379,611 mt/y
Pulp available for market: 374,850 mt/y
Chemical Pulp: 379,611 mt/y
Pulp Mill Data:
  Chemical Pulping Systems:
  Batch digesters: 14
  Continuous digesters: 1
Pulp Lines: 2
Bleach Plant Systems: 3
Chemical Pulping System - A, Type: Softwood Line, Sequence: DEopDED
Chemical Pulping System - B, Type: Softwood Line, Sequence: O_2 DEopDED, Capacity 89,250 admt/y
Chemical Pulping System - C, Type: Softwood Line, Sequence: O_2 DEopDED, Capacity 285,600 admt/y
Chemical Recovery Equipment:
Evaporator lines: 1
Recovery boilers: 3
Lime Kiln
Pulp Dryers:
Flakt dryer 1, Flakt dryer 1, Flakt dryer 1, Fourdriniers 1, Fourdriniers 1, Fourdriniers 1
Energy Data:
Power boilers: 2
Steam turbines: 2 at 30, 25 MW
Electrical demand for mill: 845 MWh/D

ⒽPaper Excellence Group
Ownership: 100% by Private
#95–10551 Shellbridge Way
Richmond, BC
Canada, V6X 2W8
 Phone: (1) 604 232 2453
 Fax: (1) 604 232 2463
 Email: info@paperexcellence.com
 Web Address: www.paperexcellence.com
Personnel:
Man. Dir: Buyung Wahab
Fiber Procurement Dir.: Andreas Kammenos
Total Employees of Company: 2,600
Mill Locations:
Fibre Excellence Saint-Gaudens, St. Gaudens Mill, Blvd. du Président Saragat, BP 149, F-31803 Saint Gaudens Cedex, France, (Pulp mill)
 Phone: (33) 5 61 94 75 75
 Fax: (33) 5 61 94 75 76
Fibre Excellence Tarascon, Tarascon Mill, Route de la Cellulose, F-13156 Tarascon Cedex, France, (Pulp mill)
 Phone: (33) 4 90 91 03 00
 Fax: (33) 4 90 91 041 1/31 73
Howe Sound Pulp and Paper Corporation, Port Mellon Mill, 3838 Port Mellon Hwy, Port Mellon, BC, Canada V0N 2S0, Capacity: 239,904 mt/y, (Pulp mill, Paper mill)
 Phone: (1) 604-884-5223
 Fax: (1) 604-884-2170
 Email: info@paperexcellence.com
Mackenzie Pulp Mill, Mackenzie Mill, 1000 Coquawaldi Road, Mackenzie, BC, Canada V0J 2C0, (Pulp mill)
 Phone: (1) 250-997-2431
 Fax: (1) 250-997-2456
 Email: info@paperexcellence.com
Meadow Lake Mechanical Pulp, Meadow Lake Mill, Box 9100, Meadow Lake, SK, Canada S9X 1V7, (Pulp mill)
 Phone: (1) 306-236-2444
 Fax: (1) 306-236-4880
 Email: info@meadowlakepulp.com
Northern Pulp Nova Scotia Corporation, Pictou Mill, 260 Granton Abercrombie Branch Road, Abercrombie Point, Pictou County, NS, Canada B2H 5C6, (Pulp mill)
 Phone: (1) 902-752-8461
 Fax: (1) 902-752-9149
 Email: info@northernpulp.com
Paper Excellence Canada Holdings Corp, Skookumchuck Mill, 220 Cranbrook St, Cranbrook, BC, Canada V1C 3R2, (Pulp mill)
 Phone: (1) 250-426-6241
 Fax: (1) 250-426-3406
 Email: info@paperexcellence.com
Paper Excellence Canada Holdings Corp, Chetwynd Mill, 4181, Chetwynd Pulp, Chetwynd, BC, Canada V0C 1J0, (Pulp mill)
 Phone: (1) 250-788-7857
 Fax: (1) 250-788-7845
 Email: info@paperexcellence.com
Papierfabrik Scheufelen GmbH & Co. KG, Lenningen Mill, Adolf-Scheufelen-Str. 26, D-73252 Lenningen, Germany, Capacity: 300,000 mt/y, (Paper mill)
 Phone: (49) 7026 660
 Fax: (49) 7026 663 2701
 Email: service@scheufelen.com

ⒽⓂHowe Sound Pulp and Paper Corporation
Port Mellon Mill
Ownership: 100% by Paper Excellence Group
3838 Port Mellon Hwy
Port Mellon, BC
Canada, V0N 2S0
 Phone: (1) 604-884-5223
 Fax: (1) 604-884-2170
 Email: info@paperexcellence.com
 Web Address: www.paperexcellence.com, www.hspp.ca
Personnel:
Gen. Mgr., Fibre & Energy: Fred Forninoff

Phone: (1) 604-884-5223
Fax: (1) 604-884-2170
Email: fred.fominoff@hspp.ca
Fibre Supply Mgr.: Jeff Carwithen
Phone: (1) 604-884-5223
Fax: (1) 604-324-4023
Email: jeff.carwithen@hspp.ca
Paper Mill Mgr. & Dir. Paper Sls.: George Kosteckyj
Phone: (1) 604-884-5223
Fax: (1) 604-884-2170
Email: george.kosteckyj@hspp.ca
Maint. Superint.: Gary Fors
Phone: (1) 604-884-5223
Fax: (1) 604-884-2170
Email: gary.fors@hspp.ca
Tech. Superint.: Kim Pedersen
Phone: (1) 604-884-5223
Fax: (1) 604-884-2170
Email: kim.pedersen@hspp.ca
Total Employees of Company: 450
Total Employees at this Location: 505
Type of Operation: Pulp mill, Paper mill
Pulp Grades and Capacities:
Total pulp capacity: 678,529 mt/y
Pulp available for market: 424,830 mt/y
Chemical Pulp: 430,180 mt/y
Mechanical Pulp: 248,349 mt/y
Pulp Mill Data:
Chemical Pulping Systems:
Continuous digesters: 1
Mechanical Pulping Systems:
TMP systems: 1
Pulp Lines: 1
Bleach Plant Systems: 2
Chemical Pulping System, Type: ECF - Softwood, Sequence: O_2 DEopDED
Mechanical TMP Pulping System, Type: Softwood, Sequence: P/HS
Chemical Recovery Equipment:
Evaporator lines: 1
Recovery boilers: 1
Lime Kiln
Pulp Dryers:
Flakt dryer 1, Fourdriniers 1
Paper/Paperboard Grades and Capacities:
Total paper and paperboard capacity: 239,904 mt/y
Newsprint: 239,904 mt/y
Paper and Paperboard Mill Data:
Stock Preparation:
Refiners: 3
Paper Machines: 1
No. 1, SpeedFormer HS, total capacity 239,904 mt/y, Trim width 8.24 m, Newsprint
Finishing Equipment:
Winders: 1 at 245,000 mt/y
Rewinders: 1 at 15,000 mt/y
Energy Data:
Power boilers: 1
Steam turbines: 2 at 62.5, 50 MW
Electrical demand for mill: 2,973 MWh/D

ⓜKruger Products L.P.
New Westminster Mill
Ownership: 83.10% by Kruger Inc.
1625 Fifth Ave.
New Westminster, BC
Canada, V3M 1Z7
Mailing Address: PO Box 760, New Westminster, BC, Canada, V3L 4Z9
Phone: (1) 604-522-5711
Fax: (1) 604-520-9200
Web Address: www.krugerproducts.ca
Personnel:
Gen. Mgr. (Region West Manuf.): Chuck Stewart
Phone: (1) 604-520-9201
Fax: (1) 604-528-4542
Email: chuck.stewart@krugerproducts.ca
Mill. Mgr.: Sudhir Lamba
Phone: (1) 604-522-5711
Fax: (1) 604-520-9200

Email: sudhir.lamba@krugerproducts.ca
Maint Mgr.: Jonathan Baggett
Phone: (1) 604-522-5711
Fax: (1) 604-520-9200
Email: jon.baggett@krugerproducts.ca
Steam Serv. Mgr.: Colin Archibald
Phone: (1) 604-522-5711
Fax: (1) 604-520-9200
Email: colin.archibald@krugerproducts.ca
Papermaking Technology Mgr.: Anna-Karin Ahlman
Phone: (1) 604-520-9225
Fax: (1) 604-520-9200
Email: anna-karin.ahlman@krugerproducts.ca
Total Employees at this Location: 180
Type of Operation: Pulp mill, Paper mill
Pulp Mill Data:
Mechanical Pulping Systems:
Conventional grinders: 4
Bleach Plant Systems: 1
Mechanical Pulping system bleaching (idled-2012), Type: Hardwood, Sequence: P
Paper/Paperboard Grades and Capacities:
Total paper and paperboard capacity: 57,973 mt/y
Tissue: 57,973 mt/y
Paper and Paperboard Mill Data:
Stock Preparation:
Pulpers:
Paper Machines: 2
No. 3, crescent former, Yankee dryer, total capacity 16,194 mt/y, Trim width 3.23 m, Tissue
No. 4, crescent former, total capacity 41,779 mt/y, Trim width 4.57 m, Tissue
Energy Data:
Power boilers: 5
Electrical demand for mill: 177 MWh/D

ⓜMackenzie Pulp Mill
Mackenzie Mill
Ownership: Paper Excellence Group
1000 Coquawaldi Road
Mackenzie, BC
Canada, V0J 2C0
Mailing Address: PO Bag 6000, Mackenzie, BC, Canada, V0J 2C0
Phone: (1) 250-997-2431
Fax: (1) 250-997-2456
Email: info@paperexcellence.com
Web Address: www.paperexcellence.com/mackenzie-pulp-corp/
Personnel:
Gen. Mgr.: Terry Bradford
Phone: (1) 250-997-2432
Fax: (1) 250-997-2456
Email: tbradford@mackenziepulp.com
Fiber Supply Mgr.: Darren Carter
Phone: (1) 250-997-7754
Fax: (1) 250-997-2456
Email: dcarter@mackenziepulp.com
Special Proj. Mgr.: Kerry Morton
Phone: (1) 250-997-2449
Fax: (1) 250-997-2456
Email: kmorton@mackenziepulp.com
Prod. Supv. Kraft Area: Tony Crespeigne
Phone: (1) 250-997-2445
Fax: (1) 250-997-2456
Email: tcrespeigne@mackenziepulp.com
Total Employees at this Location: 255
Type of Operation: Pulp mill
Pulp Grades and Capacities:
Total pulp capacity: 243,360 mt/y
Pulp available for market: 239,904 mt/y
Chemical Pulp: 243,360 mt/y
Pulp Mill Data:
Chemical Pulping Systems:
Continuous digesters: 2
Pulp Lines: 1
Bleach Plant Systems: 1
No. 1, Sequence: DEopDED, Capacity 235,000 admt/y

Chemical Recovery Equipment:
Evaporator lines: 1
Recovery boilers: 1
Lime Kiln
Pulp Dryers:
Flakt dryer 1
Energy Data:
Power boilers: 1
Steam turbines: 1 at 20 MW
Electrical demand for mill: 583 MWh/D

ⓗⓜNeucel Specialty Cellulose Ltd.
Port Alice Mill
Ownership: 100% by Fulida Group Holding Co., Ltd
300 Marine Drive
Port Alice, BC
Canada, V0N 2N0
Mailing Address: PO Box 2000, Port Alice, BC, Canada, V0N 2N0
Phone: (1) 250-284-3331
Fax: (1) 250-284-7715
Email: info@neucel.com
Web Address: www.neucel.com
Personnel:
CEO: Wanli Zhao
Phone: (1) 250-284-3331
Fax: (1) 250-284-7715
Email: wzhao@neucel.com
CFO: Randy (Dongping) Liao
Phone: (1) 250-284-3331
Fax: (1) 250-284-7715
Email: rliao@neucel.com
Mill Mgr.: Lawrence Keiver
Phone: (1) 250-284-3331
Fax: (1) 250-284-7715
Email: lkeiver@neucel.com
VP & Global Sls. Mktg. Mgr.: Eric Chen
Phone: (1) 250-284-3331
Fax: (1) 250-284-7715
Email: echen@neucel.com
Purch. Agent: Michelle Reimer
Phone: (1) 250-284-3331
Fax: (1) 250-284-7715
Email: mreimer@neucel.com
Energy Mgr.: Christopher Brennan
Phone: (1) 250-284-3331
Fax: (1) 250-284-7715
Email: cbrennan@neucel.com
Total Employees of Company: 260
Total Employees at this Location: 270
Type of Operation: Pulp mill
Pulp Grades and Capacities:
Total pulp capacity: 172,623 mt/y
Pulp available for market: 162,078 mt/y
Chemical Pulp: 172,623 mt/y
Pulp Mill Data:
Chemical Pulping Systems:
Batch digesters: 11
Pulp Lines: 1
Bleach Plant Systems: 1
1, Type: vacuum washers - Softwood, Sequence: EDHD, Capacity 195,000 admt/y
Chemical Recovery Equipment:
Evaporator lines: 3
Recovery boilers: 1
Pulp Dryers:
Fourdriniers 1
Finishing Equipment:
Rewinders: 1 at 135,000 mt/y
Sheeters: 1 at 235,000 mt/y
Energy Data:
Power boilers: 3
Steam turbines: 3 at 3.5, 7.5, 16.6 MW
Hydro turbines: 1 at 2.0 MW
Electrical demand for mill: 673 MWh/D

ⓜPaper Excellence Canada Holdings Corp
Skookumchuck Mill

British Columbia

Ownership: 100% by Paper Excellence Group
220 Cranbrook St
Cranbrook, BC
Canada, V1C 3R2
Mailing Address: PO Box 4600, Cranbrook, BC, Canada, V1C 4J7
 Phone: (1) 250-426-6241
 Fax: (1) 250-426-3406
 Email: info@paperexcellence.com
 Web Address: www.paperexcellence.com
Personnel:
 Eng. & Energy Mgr.: Rene Pitre
 Phone: (1) 250-426-6241
 Fax: (1) 250-426-3406
 Main. Mgr.: Gavin Baxter
 Phone: (1) 250-426-6241
 Fax: (1) 250-426-3406
Total Employees at this Location: 280
Type of Operation: Pulp mill
Pulp Grades and Capacities:
 Total pulp capacity: 274,537 mt/y
 Pulp available for market: 269,892 mt/y
 Chemical Pulp: 274,537 mt/y
Pulp Mill Data:
 Chemical Pulping Systems:
 Continuous digesters: 1
 Pulp Lines: 1
 Bleach Plant Systems: 1
 Chemical Pulping System, Type: Softwood, Sequence: O_2 DEOpDEpD
 Chemical Recovery Equipment:
 Evaporator lines: 1
 Recovery boilers: 1
 Lime Kiln
 Pulp Dryers:
 Flakt dryer 1, Fourdriniers 1
Energy Data:
 Power boilers: 2
 Steam turbines: 2 at 17, 45 MW
 Electrical demand for mill: 702 MWh/D

ⓜPaper Excellence Canada Holdings Corp
Chetwynd Mill
Mill is idle (mill was indefinitely idled in September 2012. Paper Excellence Group plan to restart operations, possibly by January 2015.)
Ownership: 100% by Paper Excellence Group
4181, Chetwynd Pulp
Chetwynd, BC
Canada, V0C 1J0
Mailing Address: PO Box 900, Chetwynd, BC, Canada, V0C 1J0
 Phone: (1) 250-788-7857
 Fax: (1) 250-788-7845
 Email: info@paperexcellence.com
 Web Address: www.paperexcellence.com
Personnel:
 Mill Mgr.: Wayne Clement
 Phone: (1) 250-788-7857
 Fax: (1) 250-788-7845
 Woodroom & Yard Mgr.: Ceril Brewster
 Phone: (1) 250-788-7857
 Fax: (1) 250-788-7845
 Steam & Recov. Mgr.: Eli Hazelhurst
 Phone: (1) 250-788-7857
 Fax: (1) 250-788-7845
 Maint. Mgr.: Gene Fritzel
 Phone: (1) 250-788-7857
 Fax: (1) 250-788-7845
Total Employees at this Location: 160
Type of Operation: Pulp mill
Pulp Mill Data:
 Mechanical Pulping Systems:
 BCTMP systems: 1
 Bleach Plant Systems: 1
 No. 1, Sequence: P
 Pulp Dryers:
 Flash dryers 1, Flash dryers 1

Energy Data:
 Power boilers: 1
 TMP Reboiler: 1

ⓜTolko Industries Ltd.
Ownership: Thorlakson Family (Private)
3203-30th Ave.
Vernon, BC
Canada, V1T 9W9
Mailing Address: PO Box 39, Vernon, BC, Canada, V1T 6M1
 Phone: (1) 250-545-4411
 Fax: (1) 250-550-2550
 Email: tolko@tolko.com
 Web Address: www.tolko.com
Personnel:
 Pres. & CEO: Brad Thorlakson
 Phone: (1) 250-545-4411
 Fax: (1) 250-550-2550
 Email: brad.thorlakson@tolko.com
 VP Finan. & CFO: Trevor Jahnig
 Phone: (1) 250-545-4411
 Fax: (1) 250-550-2550
 Email: trevor.jahnig@tolko.com
 VP & Gen. Mgr., Solid Wood & Kraft Papers: Mike Harkies
 Phone: (1) 250-545-4411
 Fax: (1) 250-550-2550
 Email: mike.harkies@tolko.com
 VP, HR: Tanya Wick
 Phone: (1) 250-545-4411
 Fax: (1) 250-550-2550
 Email: tanya.wick@tolko.com
 VP, OSB & Kraft Papers: Jim Baskerville
 Phone: (1) 250-549-5341
 Fax: (1) 250-550-2550
 Email: jim.baskerville@tolko.com
 VP, Environ. & Forestry: Bob Fleet
 Phone: (1) 250-549-5341
 Fax: (1) 250-550-2550
 Email: bob.fleet@tolko.com
Mill Locations:
 Tolko Manitoba Kraft Papers, The Pas Mill, #10 Hwy North, The Pas, MB, Canada R9A 1L4, Capacity: 177,429 mt/y, (Pulp mill, Paper mill)
 Phone: (1) 204-623-7411
 Fax: (1) 204-623-5891
 Email: mbkraftpapers@tolko.com

ⓗⓜQuesnel River Pulp Co.
Quesnel Mill
Ownership: 100% by West Fraser Timber Co. Ltd.
1000 Finning Rd
Quesnel, BC
Canada, V2J 6A1
 Phone: (1) 250-992-8919
 Fax: (1) 250-992-2612
 Web Address: www.westfraser.com
Personnel:
 Mill Mgr. (From February 2014): Paul Dijulio
 Phone: (1) 250-992-8919
 Fax: (1) 250-992-2612
 Email: paul.dijulio@westfraser.com
 Oper. Mgr. Mech. Pulp (From February 2014): Keith Carter
 Phone: (1) 250-992-8919
 Fax: (1) 250-992-2612
 Email: keith.carter@westfraser.com
 Tech. & Strat.Capital: Mike Van Aert
 Phone: (1) 250-992-8919
 Fax: (1) 250-992-2612
 Email: mike.vanaert@westfraser.com
 Fibre Supply Mgr. for all West Fraser Canadian Operations: Ray Levac
 Phone: (1) 250-992-8919
 Fax: (1) 250-992-2612
 Email: ray.levac@westfraser.com
 Maint. and Eng. Mgr.: Vic Leblanc
 Phone: (1) 250-992-8919
 Fax: (1) 250-992-2612

 Email: vic.leblanc@westfraser.com
Total Employees at this Location: 130
Type of Operation: Pulp mill
Pulp Grades and Capacities:
 Total pulp capacity: 429,450 mt/y
 Pulp available for market: 399,840 mt/y
 Mechanical Pulp: 429,450 mt/y
Pulp Mill Data:
 Mechanical Pulping Systems:
 BCTMP systems: 1
 BCTMP systems: 1
 Pulp Lines: 3
 Bleach Plant Systems: 2
 Mechanical BCTMP Pulping System, Type: Softwood, Sequence: PP, Capacity 178,000 admt/y
 Mechanical BCTMP Pulping System, Type: Hardwood/Softwood, Sequence: PP, Capacity 178,000 admt/y
 Pulp Dryers:
 Flash dryers 1, Flash dryers 1
Energy Data:
 Power boilers: 1
 TMP Reboiler: 1
 Electrical demand for mill: 2,524 MWh/D

ⓜWeyerhaeuser Company Ltd.
Ownership: 100% by Weyerhaeuser Co.
925 W Georgia St. 5th Floor
Vancouver, BC
Canada, V6C 3L2
 Phone: (1) 604-661-8000
 Fax: (1) 604-687-2314
 Web Address: www.weyerhaeuser.com
Personnel:
 Pres., Canada: Anne E. Giardini
 Phone: (1) 604-661-8000
 Fax: (1) 604-687-2314
 Email: anne.giardini@weyerhaeuser.com
 Canadian Div. Eng.: Andy Teasell
 Phone: (1) 604-661-8000
 Fax: (1) 604-687-2314
Total Employees of Company: 2,800
Total Employees at this Location: 81
Mill Locations:
 Weyerhaeuser Company Ltd., Grande Prairie Mill, Mailbag 1020, Grande Prairie, AB, Canada T8V 3A9, (Pulp mill)
 Phone: (1) 780-539-8500
 Fax: (1) 780-539-8500

ⓜZellstoff Celgar Limited
Castlegar Mill
Ownership: 100% by Mercer International Inc.
1921 Arrow Lakes Dr
Castlegar, BC
Canada, V1N 3H9
Mailing Address: PO Box 1000, Castlegar, BC, Canada, V1N 3H9
 Phone: (1) 250-365-7211, 250-365-4238
 Fax: (1) 250-365-4211
 Email: kevina@celgar.com
 Web Address: www.mercerint.com
Personnel:
 Man. Dir.: Kevin Anderson
 Phone: (1) 250-365-7211
 Fax: (1) 250-365-4211
 Email: kevina@celgar.com
 Man. Dir. Finan.: Cherie Hanvold
 Phone: (1) 250-365-7211
 Fax: (1) 250-365-4211
 Email: cherieh@celgar.com
 HR Mgr.: John Belland
 Phone: (1) 250-365-4202
 Fax: (1) 250-365-4211
 Email: johnb@celgar.com
 Eng. & Tech. Mgr.: Douglas Sayer
 Phone: (1) 250-365-7211, 250-365-4238
 Fax: (1) 250-365-4211
 Email: dougs@celgar.com
 Maint. Mgr: Carl Sayers
 Phone: (1) 250-365-7211, 250-365-4238

Fax: (1) 250-365-4211
Email: carls@celgar.com
Snr. Process Eng.: Ralph Lunn
Phone: (1) 250-365-7211, 250-365-4238
Fax: (1) 250-365-4211
Email: ralphl@celgar.com
Fibre Mgr.: Chuck Wright
Phone: (1) 250-365-4249
Fax: (1) 250-365-4211
Email: chuckw@celgar.com
Total Employees at this Location: 396
Type of Operation: Pulp mill
Pulp Grades and Capacities:
Total pulp capacity: 527,623 mt/y
Pulp available for market: 520,149 mt/y
Chemical Pulp: 527,623 mt/y
Pulp Mill Data:
Chemical Pulping Systems:
Continuous digesters: 1
Pulp Lines: 1
Bleach Plant Systems: 1
Chemical Pulping System, Sequence: O_2 DEopDD, Capacity 495,000 admt/y
Chemical Recovery Equipment:
Evaporator lines: 1
Recovery boilers: 1
Lime Kiln
Pulp Dryers:
Air Float dryers 1, Flakt dryer 1, Fourdriniers 1, Fourdriniers 1
Energy Data:
Power boilers: 2
Steam turbines: 2 at 52, 48 MW
Electrical demand for mill: 1,010 MWh/D

MANITOBA

ⓂTolko Manitoba Kraft Papers
The Pas Mill
Ownership: 100% by Tolko Industries Ltd.
#10 Hwy North
The Pas, MB
Canada, R9A 1L4
Mailing Address: PO Box 1590, The Pas, MB, Canada, R9A 1L4
Phone: (1) 204-623-7411
Fax: (1) 204-623-5891
Email: mbkraftpapers@tolko.com
Web Address: www.tolko.com
Personnel:
Site Mgr., Manitoba Oper.: Blair Rydberg
Phone: (1) 204-623-8585
Fax: (1) 204-623-5891
Email: blair.rydberg@tolko.com
Sls & Mktg Mgr.: Peter MacLachlan
Phone: (1) 204-623-8617
Fax: (1) 204-623-5891
Email: peter.macLachlan@tolko.com
Purch. Team Ldr.: David Montgomery
Phone: (1) 204-623-8528
Fax: (1) 204-623-5891
Email: david.montgomery@tolko.com
Maint. & Eng. Mgr.: Andre Murphy
Phone: (1) 204-623-8688
Fax: (1) 204-623-5891
Email: andre.murphy@tolko.com
Prod. Mgr.: Juha Jarvinen
Phone: (1) 204-623-8688
Fax: (1) 204-623-5891
Email: juha.jarvinen@tolko.com
Total Employees at this Location: 265
Type of Operation: Pulp mill, Paper mill
Pulp Grades and Capacities:
Total pulp capacity: 186,712 mt/y
Chemical Pulp: 186,712 mt/y
Pulp Mill Data:

Chemical Pulping Systems:
Batch digesters: 5
Chemical Recovery Equipment:
Evaporator lines: 1
Recovery boilers: 1
Lime Kiln
Paper/Paperboard Grades and Capacities:
Total paper and paperboard capacity: 177,429 mt/y
Packaging papers: 177,429 mt/y
Paper and Paperboard Mill Data:
Stock Preparation:
Refiners: 5
Paper Machines: 1
No. 1, fourdrinier, total capacity 177,429 mt/y, Trim width 6.17 m, Packaging papers
Finishing Equipment:
Winders: 1 at 165,000 mt/y
Energy Data:
Power boilers: 2
Steam turbines: 1 at 23 MW
Electrical demand for mill: 569 MWh/D

NEW BRUNSWICK

ⓄⓂAV Cell Inc.
Atholville Mill
Ownership: 95% by Aditya Birla Group, 5% by Tembec Inc.
175 Mill Rd
Atholville, NB
Canada, E3N 4S7
Phone: (1) 506-575-3294
Fax: (1) 506-575-3300
Email: pschriver@avcell.com
Web Address: www.adityabirla.com, www.tembec.com
Personnel:
VP & COO: Ashley Irvine
Phone: (1) 506-575-3294
Fax: (1) 506-575-3300
Email: airvine@avcell.com
VP, Admin. & CFO: Manoj Mundra
Phone: (1) 506-575-3294
Fax: (1) 506-575-3300
Email: mmundra@avcell.com
HR Coordinator.: Line Bernard
Phone: (1) 506-575-3294
Fax: (1) 506-575-3300
Email: lbernard@avcell.com
Raw Matl. Procurement.: Marquita Martin
Phone: (1) 506-575-3294
Fax: (1) 506-575-3300
Email: mmartin@avcell.com
Recovery & Power Mgr.: Kevin Parker
Phone: (1) 506-575-3294
Fax: (1) 506-575-3300
Email: kparker@avcell.com
Total Employees of Company: 270
Total Employees at this Location: 270
Type of Operation: Pulp mill
Pulp Grades and Capacities:
Total pulp capacity: 133,188 mt/y
Pulp available for market: 124,950 mt/y
Chemical Pulp: 133,188 mt/y
Pulp Mill Data:
Chemical Pulping Systems:
Batch digesters: 7
Pulp Lines: 1
Bleach Plant Systems: 1
No. 1, Sequence: EDEopH, Capacity 116,000 admt/y
Chemical Recovery Equipment:
Evaporator lines: 1
Recovery boilers: 1
Pulp Dryers:
Air Float dryers 1, Air Float dryers 1
Energy Data:

Power boilers: 2
Steam turbines: 1 at 17.5 MW
Electrical demand for mill: 406 MWh/D

ⓄⓂAV Nackawic Inc.
Nackawic Mill
Ownership: 95% by Aditya Birla Group, 5% by Tembec Inc.
103 Pinder Rd
Nackawic, NB
Canada, E6G 1W4
Mailing Address: P.O. Box 2005, Nackawic, NB, Canada, E6G 2P2
Phone: (1) 506-575-3314
Fax: (1) 506-575-3300
Email: pat.bourgoin@avg.adityabirla.com
Web Address: www.av-group.ca, www.birlacellulose.com
Personnel:
Pres. & CEO: Alan Hitzroth
Phone: (1) 506-575-3314
Fax: (1) 506-575-3300
Email: Al.hitzroth@avg.adityabirla.com
VP, CFO: Krishna Khaitan
Phone: (1) 506-575-3314
Fax: (1) 506-575-3300
Email: krishna.k@avg.adityabirla.com
Tech. Dir.: Suresh Pai
Phone: (1) 506-575-3314
Fax: (1) 506-575-3300
Email: Suresh.pai@avg.adityabirla.com
HR Mgr.: Ginette Archambault
Phone: (1) 506-575-3314
Fax: (1) 506-575-3300
Email: ginette.archambault@avg.adityabirla.com
Exec. Assist.: Pat Bourgoin
Phone: (1) 506-575-3314
Fax: (1) 506-575-3300
Email: pat.bourgoin@avg.adityabirla.com
Total Employees of Company: 335
Total Employees at this Location: 335
Type of Operation: Pulp mill
Pulp Grades and Capacities:
Total pulp capacity: 201,684 mt/y
Pulp available for market: 188,853 mt/y
Chemical Pulp: 201,684 mt/y
Pulp Mill Data:
Chemical Pulping Systems:
Batch digesters: 6
Pulp Lines: 1
Bleach Plant Systems: 5
Chemical Pulping System - 1, Type: Hardwood, Sequence: DEopHEpD
Chemical Recovery Equipment:
Evaporator lines: 1
Recovery boilers: 1
Lime Kiln
Pulp Dryers:
Flakt dryer 1, Fourdriniers 1
Energy Data:
Power boilers: 1
Steam turbines: 1 at 25 MW
Electrical demand for mill: 563 MWh/D

ⓄJ.D. Irving, Ltd.
Ownership: 100% by JD Irving Ltd.
300 Union St
Saint John, NB
Canada, E2L 5B6
Mailing Address: PO Box 5777, Saint John, NB, Canada, E2L 4M3
Phone: (1) 506-632-7777
Fax: (1) 506-632-6415
Email: info@jdirving.com
Web Address: www.jdirving.com
Personnel:
Spruce Sls. Mgr.: Gilbert Christian
Phone: (1) 506-632-6331
Email: gilbert.christian@jdirving.com

New Brunswick

Eastern White Cedar Sls. Mgr.: John Russell
Phone: (1) 506-633-4035
Email: russell.john@jdirving.com
Eastern White Pine Sls. Mgr.: Doug Chiasson
Phone: (1) 506-632-5145
Email: chiasson.doug@jdirving.com
Gen. Mgr.: Jerome Pelletier
Phone: (1) 506-632-4111
Email: pelletier.jerome@jdirving.com
Gen. Mgr.: Daniel Couturier
Hardwood Lumber Sls.: Denis Dubé
Phone: (1) 506-992-9025
Email: dube.denis@jdirving.com
Hardwood Sls. Mgr.: Dennis Cuffley
Phone: (1) 506-992-9026
Email: cuffley.dennis@jdirving.com
Oper. Mgr.: Jason Limongelli
Pres.: James D. Irving
Phone: (1) 506-632-7777
Fax: (1) 506-632-6415
Email: irving.james@irvingforest.com
VP: Mark Mosher
Phone: (1) 506-632-5861
Email: mosher.mark@irvingforest.com
VP Commun.: Mary Keith
Phone: (1) 506-632-5122
Email: keith.mary@jdirving.com
HR: Sheri Mersereau
Phone: (1) 506-632-7777
Fax: (1) 506-632-6415
Email: sheri.mersereau@jdirving.com
VP., Corp. Dir., Purch.: Jim Jordan
Phone: (1) 506-632-7777
Fax: (1) 506-632-6415
Email: jordan.jim@irvingforest.com
VP Construction & Equipment Div.: Gilles Gagnon
Phone: (1) 506-633-3332
Email: gagnon.gilles@jdirving.com
Total Employees of Company: 15,000
Mill Locations:
Irving Paper, Saint John East Mill, 435 Bayside Dr, Saint John, NB, Canada E2J 1B2, Capacity: 419,475 mt/y, (Pulp mill, Paper mill)
Phone: (1) 506-633-3333
Fax: (1) 506-642-1688
Irving Pulp & Paper, Ltd., Saint John West Mill, Saint John, NB, Canada E2M 3H1, (Pulp mill)
Phone: (1) 506-635-6666
Fax: (1) 506-635-1059
Email: irvpulp@nbnet.nb.ca
Irving Tissue Inc., Fort Edward Mill, 1 Eddy St, Fort Edward, NY 12828, USA, Capacity: 46,961 mt/y, (Paper mill)
Phone: (1) 518-747-4151
Fax: (1) 518-747-3397
Irving Tissue Inc., Saint John Mill, 408 Mill St, Saint John, NB, Canada E2M 3H1, Capacity: 79,024 mt/y, (Paper mill)
Phone: (1) 506-635-1525, 506-632-7777
Fax: (1) 506-635-8024, 506-648-2205
Email: info@irvingtissue.ca.
Irving Tissue Inc., Toronto Mill, 1551 Weston Rd, Toronto, ON, Canada M6M 4Y4, Capacity: 96,513 mt/y, (Paper mill)
Phone: (1) 416-246-6666
Fax: (1) 416-246-6667
Lake Utopia Paper, Saint George Mill, 600 Utopia Road 785, Utopia, NB, Canada E5C 2K4, Capacity: 183,141 mt/y, (Paperboard mill)
Phone: (1) 506-755-3384
Fax: (1) 506-755-6303
Email: info@jdirving.com

ⓜIrving Paper
Saint John East Mill
Ownership: J.D. Irving, Ltd.
435 Bayside Dr
Saint John, NB
Canada, E2J 1B2
Mailing Address: PO Box 1900, Saint John, NB, Canada, E2L 4K9
Phone: (1) 506-633-3333
Fax: (1) 506-642-1688
Web Address: www.jdirving.com
Personnel:
Gen. Mgr.: Jerome Pelletier
Phone: (1) 506-633-3333
Fax: (1) 506-642-1688
Email: jerome.pelletier@irvingpaper.com
Tech. Superint. (From August 2014): Greg MacKenzie
Phone: (1) 506-633-3333
Fax: (1) 506-642-1688
Email: greg.mackenzie@irvingpaper.com
Total Employees at this Location: 320
Type of Operation: Pulp mill, Paper mill
Pulp Grades and Capacities:
Total pulp capacity: 298,226 mt/y
Mechanical Pulp: 298,226 mt/y
Pulp Mill Data:
Mechanical Pulping Systems:
TMP systems: 2
Bleach Plant Systems: 2
Mechanical TMP Pulping System, Type: Softwood, Sequence: P
Paper/Paperboard Grades and Capacities:
Total paper and paperboard capacity: 419,475 mt/y
Uncoated mechanical/groundwood: 419,475 mt/y
Paper and Paperboard Mill Data:
Stock Preparation:
Pulpers: 1
Refiners: 1
Paper Machines: 2
No. 1, SymFormer, total capacity 199,920 mt/y, Trim width 8 m, Uncoated mechanical/groundwood
No. 2, SymFormer, total capacity 219,555 mt/y, Trim width 8.2 m, Uncoated mechanical/groundwood
Finishing Equipment:
Calenders: 1
Supercalenders: 1
Energy Data:
Power boilers: 1
TMP Reboiler: 1
Electrical demand for mill: 3,103 MWh/D

ⓜIrving Pulp & Paper, Ltd.
Saint John West Mill
Ownership: J.D. Irving, Ltd.
Saint John, NB
Canada, E2M 3H1
Mailing Address: PO Box 3007, Saint John, NB, Canada, E2M 3H1
Phone: (1) 506-635-6666
Fax: (1) 506-635-1059
Email: irvpulp@nbnet.nb.ca
Web Address: www.jdirving.com
Personnel:
Mill Mgr.: Anthony Binotto
Phone: (1) 506-635-6666
Fax: (1) 506-635-1059
Email: binotto.tony@irvingpulp.com
Prod. Mgr.: Danny Mott
Phone: (1) 506-635-6666
Fax: (1) 506-635-1059
Email: mott.danny@irvingpulp.com
VP Sls & Mktg.: Kevin Chapman
Phone: (1) 506-635-6666
Fax: (1) 506-635-1059
Email: chapman.kevin@irvingpulp.com
Eng. Mgr.: Al N. Hubbard
Phone: (1) 506-635-6666
Fax: (1) 506-635-1059
Email: hubbard.al@irvingpulp.com
Mech. Reliability Superint.: Walter Bursey
Phone: (1) 506-632-4781
Fax: (1) 506-635-1059
Email: bursey.walter@irvingpulp.com
Total Employees at this Location: 350
Type of Operation: Pulp mill
Pulp Grades and Capacities:
Total pulp capacity: 340,539 mt/y
Pulp available for market: 334,866 mt/y
Chemical Pulp: 340,539 mt/y
Pulp Mill Data:
Chemical Pulping Systems:
Batch digesters: 14
Pulp Lines: 1
Bleach Plant Systems: 1
Chemical Pulping System, Type: Hardwood/Softwood, Sequence: O_2 DEopDED, Capacity 344,000 admt/y
Chemical Recovery Equipment:
Evaporator lines: 1
Recovery boilers: 1
Lime Kiln
Pulp Dryers:
Air Float dryers 1, Air Float dryers 1, Air Float dryers 1
Energy Data:
Power boilers: 2
Steam turbines: 2 at 32.5, 13 MW
Electrical demand for mill: 722 MWh/D

ⓜIrving Tissue Inc.
Saint John Mill
Ownership: J.D. Irving, Ltd.
408 Mill St
Saint John, NB
Canada, E2M 3H1
Mailing Address: PO Box 3130, Sta B, Saint John, NB, Canada, E2M 4X7
Phone: (1) 506-635-1525, 506-632-7777
Fax: (1) 506-635-8024, 506-648-2205
Email: info@irvingtissue.ca
Web Address: www.jdirving.com
Personnel:
Mill Mgr.: Dale Chaffey
Phone: (1) 506-632-5898
Fax: (1) 506-635-8024
Email: chaffey.dale@irvingpulp.com
Tech. Dir.: David Embley
Phone: (1) 506-635-1525
Fax: (1) 506-635-8024
Email: embley.david@irvingpulp.com
#1 Tissue Machine Co-ordinator: Jenna Hazelton
Phone: (1) 506-632-5886
Fax: (1) 506-635-8024
Email: hazelton.jenna@irvingpulp.com
Mech. Reliability Eng.: John Sherrard
Phone: (1) 506-635-1525
Fax: (1) 506-635-8024
Email: sherrard.john@irvingpulp.com
Maint. Mgr. & Eng. Mgr.: Trevor Downey
Phone: (1) 506-633-5280
Fax: (1) 506-635-8024
Email: downey.trevor@irvingpulp.com
Oper. Supervisor: Cameron Campbell
Phone: (1) 506-635-1525
Fax: (1) 506-635-8024
Email: campbell.cameron@irvingpulp.com
Total Employees at this Location: 105
Type of Operation: Paper mill
Paper/Paperboard Grades and Capacities:
Total paper and paperboard capacity: 79,024 mt/y
Tissue: 79,024 mt/y
Paper and Paperboard Mill Data:
Paper Machines: 2
No. 1, fourdrinier, total capacity 26,234 mt/y, Trim width 3.3 m, Tissue
No. 2, fourdrinier, total capacity 52,791 mt/y, Trim width 5.23 m, Tissue
Energy Data:
Power boilers: 1
Electrical demand for mill: 230 MWh/D

ⓜLake Utopia Paper
Ownership: J.D. Irving, Ltd.
600 Utopia Road 785
Utopia, NB
Canada, E5C 2K4
Mailing Address: PO Box 1036, Saint George, NB, Canada, E5C 3S9

Phone: (1) 506-755-3384
Fax: (1) 506-755-6303
Email: info@jdirving.com
Web Address: www.jdirving.com
Personnel:
Mill Mgr.: Tom Stewart
Phone: (1) 506-755-3384
Fax: (1) 506-755-6303
Total Employees of Company: 130
Mill Locations:
Lake Utopia Paper, Saint George Mill, 600 Utopia Road 785, Utopia, NB, Canada E5C 2K4, Capacity: 183,141 mt/y, (Paperboard mill)
Phone: (1) 506-755-3384
Fax: (1) 506-755-6303
Email: info@jdirving.com

ⓜLake Utopia Paper
Saint George Mill
Ownership: J.D. Irving, Ltd.
600 Utopia Road 785
Utopia, NB
Canada, E5C 2K4
Mailing Address: PO Box 1036, Saint George, NB, Canada, E5C 3S9
Phone: (1) 506-755-3384
Fax: (1) 506-755-6303
Email: info@jdirving.com
Web Address: www.jdirving.com
Personnel:
Mill Mgr.: Tom Stewart
Phone: (1) 506-755-3384
Fax: (1) 506-755-6303
Email: tstewart@jdirving.com
Prod. Supervisor: Jeff Ross
Phone: (1) 506-755-3384
Fax: (1) 506-755-6303
Email: jross@jdirving.com
Tech. Serv. Mgr.: Zhiqing Li
Phone: (1) 506-755-3384
Fax: (1) 506-755-6303
Email: zli@jdirving.com
Steam Plt. Superintendent: Ron Guitard
Phone: (1) 506-755-3384
Fax: (1) 506-755-6303
Email: rguitard@jdirving.com
Total Employees at this Location: 130
Type of Operation: Paperboard mill
Pulp Grades and Capacities:
Total pulp capacity: 191,356 mt/y
Chemical Pulp: 133,949 mt/y
Recycled Pulping: 57,407 mt/y
Pulp Mill Data:
Chemical Pulping Systems:
Continuous digesters: 1
Pulp Lines: 1
Recycled Fiber Treatment Lines:
Recycled packaging pulping lines: 1 at 65,000 admt/y
Paper/Paperboard Grades and Capacities:
Total paper and paperboard capacity: 183,141 mt/y
Corrugating medium/fluting: 183,141 mt/y
Paper and Paperboard Mill Data:
Paper Machines: 1
No. 1, fourdrinier, total capacity 183,141 mt/y, Trim width 4.44 m, Corrugating medium/fluting
Energy Data:
Power boilers: 3

NEWFOUNDLAND AND LABRADOR

ⓜKruger Inc.
Corner Brook Mill
Mill Road
Corner Brook, NF
Canada, A2H 6J4
Mailing Address: PO Box 2001, Corner Brook, NF, Canada, A2H 6J4
Phone: (1) 709-637-3000
Fax: (1) 709-637-3469
Email: (firstinitialandlastname@cb.kruger.com)
Web Address: www.kruger.com, www.cbppl.com
Personnel:
VP & Gen. Mgr.: Ric Tull
Phone: (1) 709-637-3000
Fax: (1) 709-637-3469
Email: richard.tull@kruger.com
Prod. Mgr.: Darren Pelley
Phone: (1) 709-637-3000
Fax: (1) 709-637-3469
Email: darren.pelley@kruger.com
Maint. Mgr.: Gary Dimmer
Phone: (1) 709-637-3000
Fax: (1) 709-637-3469
Email: gdimmer@kruger.com
Safety Mgr.: Dave Murphy
Phone: (1) 709-637-3000
Fax: (1) 709-637-3469
Email: david.murphy@kruger.com
Supt.: Michael Lacey
Phone: (1) 709-637-3000
Fax: (1) 709-637-3469
Email: michael.lacey@kruger.com
Total Employees at this Location: 350
Type of Operation: Pulp mill, Paper mill
Pulp Grades and Capacities:
Total pulp capacity: 262,396 mt/y
Mechanical Pulp: 235,785 mt/y
Recycled Pulping: 26,611 mt/y
Pulp Mill Data:
Mechanical Pulping Systems:
TMP systems: 6
Pulp Lines: 6
Bleach Plant Systems: 1
TMP, Sequence: H
Recycled Fiber Treatment Lines:
Pulpers: 1 at 50,000 admt/y
Paper/Paperboard Grades and Capacities:
Total paper and paperboard capacity: 255,255 mt/y
Newsprint: 255,255 mt/y
Paper and Paperboard Mill Data:
Stock Preparation:
Pulpers: 2
Paper Machines: 2
No. 2, Bel-Form, total capacity 108,885 mt/y, Trim width 5.51 m, Newsprint
No. 7, DuoFormer D, total capacity 146,370 mt/y, Trim width 6.6 m, Newsprint
Finishing Equipment:
Rewinders: 1
Energy Data:
Power boilers: 7
TMP Reboiler: 2
Steam turbines: 1 at 17.5 MW
Hydro turbines: 9 at 126.2 MW
Electrical demand for mill: 2,122 MWh/D

NOVA SCOTIA

ⓜNorthern Pulp Nova Scotia Corporation
Ownership: 100% by Paper Excellence Group
260 Granton Abercrombie Branch Road
Abercrombie Point, Pictou Coun, NS
Canada, B2H 5C6
Mailing Address: PO Box 549, New Glasgow, NS, Canada, B2H 5E8
Phone: (1) 902-752-8461
Fax: (1) 902-752-9149
Email: info@northernpulp.com
Web Address: www.northernpulp.ca
Personnel:
Pres., CEO & CFO: Wayne Gosse
Phone: (1) 902-752-9167
Fax: (1) 902-752-9157
Email: wgosse@northernpulp.com
VP HR & Pulp Sales: Bob Bagdon
Phone: (1) 902-752-9170
Fax: (1) 902-752-9164
Email: bbagdon@northernpulp.com
Safety Ldr.: Mike Pittoello
Phone: (1) 902-752-8461
Fax: (1) 902-752-9149
Email: mpittoello@northernpulp.com
Total Employees of Company: 230
Mill Locations:
Northern Pulp Nova Scotia Corporation, Pictou Mill, 260 Granton Abercrombie Branch Road, Abercrombie Point, Pictou County, NS, Canada B2H 5C6, (Pulp mill)
Phone: (1) 902-752-8461
Fax: (1) 902-752-9149
Email: info@northernpulp.com

ⓜNorthern Pulp Nova Scotia Corporation
Pictou Mill
Ownership: 100% by Paper Excellence Group
260 Granton Abercrombie Branch Road
Abercrombie Point, Pictou County, NS
Canada, B2H 5C6
Mailing Address: PO Box 549, New Glasgow, NS, Canada, B2H 5E8
Phone: (1) 902-752-8461
Fax: (1) 902-752-9149
Email: info@northernpulp.com
Web Address: www.northernpulp.ca
Personnel:
Tech. Mgr.: Terri Fraser
Phone: (1) 902-752-8461 Ext: 244
Fax: (1) 902-752-9149
Email: terri.fraser@northernpulp.com
Fiberline Ldr.: Ross Tugwell
Phone: (1) 902-752-8461
Fax: (1) 902-752-9149
Email: ross.tugwell@northernpulp.com
Purch. Coord.: Glenn Corbett
Phone: (1) 902-752-8461 Ext: 240
Fax: (1) 902-752-9153
Email: glenn.corbett@northernpulp.com
Oper. Mgr.: Bruce Chapman
Phone: (1) 902-752-8461
Fax: (1) 902-752-9149
Email: bchapman@northernpulp.com
Safety Ldr.: Monica Thomsen
Phone: (1) 902-752-8461
Fax: (1) 902-752-9149
Email: monica.thomsen@northernpulp.com
Environ. Mgr.: Heidi Christensen
Phone: (1) 902-752-8461 Ext: 249
Fax: (1) 902-752-9149
Email: heidi.christensen@northernpulp.com
Total Employees at this Location: 230
Type of Operation: Pulp mill
Pulp Grades and Capacities:
Total pulp capacity: 300,092 mt/y
Pulp available for market: 294,882 mt/y
Chemical Pulp: 300,092 mt/y
Pulp Mill Data:
Chemical Pulping Systems:
Continuous digesters: 1
Pulp Lines: 1
Bleach Plant Systems: 1
Chemical Pulping System, Type: Softwood, Sequence: DEoDEpD
Chemical Recovery Equipment:
Evaporator lines: 1
Recovery boilers: 1
Lime Kiln

Ontario

Pulp Dryers:
Flakt dryer 1, Fourdriniers 1
Energy Data:
Power boilers: 1
Steam turbines: 1 at 28 MW
Electrical demand for mill: 649 MWh/D

ⓑⓜPort Hawkesbury Paper
Port Hawkesbury Mill
120 Pulp Mill Rd, Point Tupper
Port Hawkesbury, NS
Canada, B0E 2V0
Mailing Address: PO Box 9500, Port Hawkesbury, NS, Canada, B9A 1A1
Phone: (1) 902-625-2460, 1-800-989-3608
Fax: (1) 902-625-1105 admn, 2955 mill, 2388 Wdlds
Email: customerservice@porthawkesburypaper.com
Web Address: www.porthawkesburypaper.com
Personnel:
Develop. Mgr. : Marc Dube
Phone: (1) 902-625-2460
Fax: (1) 902-625-1105
Email: marc.dube@porthawkesburypaper.com
Maint. Team Ldr.: Jason Spears
Phone: (1) 902-625-2460
Fax: (1) 902-625-1105
Email: jason.spears@porthawkesburypaper.com
Safety Coord.: Murdo Ferguson
Phone: (1) 902-625-2460
Fax: (1) 902-625-1105
Email: murdo.ferguson@porthawkesburypaper.com
Paper Pulp Prod. Mgr. : Mark Frith
Phone: (1) 902-625-2460
Fax: (1) 902-625-1105
Email: mark.frith@porthawkesburypaper.com
Total Employees at this Location: 330
Type of Operation: Pulp mill, Paper mill
Pulp Grades and Capacities:
Total pulp capacity: 232,843 mt/y
Mechanical Pulp: 232,843 mt/y
Pulp Mill Data:
Mechanical Pulping Systems:
TMP systems: 2
Pulp Lines: 3
Bleach Plant Systems: 1
Mechanical TMP Pulping System - 1, Type: Towers - Softwood, Sequence: H
Paper/Paperboard Grades and Capacities:
Total paper and paperboard capacity: 360,570 mt/y
Uncoated mechanical/groundwood: 360,570 mt/y
Paper and Paperboard Mill Data:
Stock Preparation:
Pulpers: 4
Refiners: 1
Paper Machines: 1
No. 2, SpeedFormer, total capacity 360,570 mt/y, Trim width 9.4 m, Uncoated mechanical/groundwood
Finishing Equipment:
Supercalenders: 2
Rewinders: 2
Energy Data:
Power boilers: 3
TMP Reboiler
Steam turbines: 1 at 80 MW
Electrical demand for mill: 2,472 MWh/D

ONTARIO

ⓑⓜAtlantic Packaging Products Ltd.
Scarborough Mill
Ownership: 100% by Private
111 Progress Ave
Scarborough, ON
Canada, M1P 2Y9
Phone: (1) 416-298-8101
Fax: (1) 416-297-2218
Web Address: www.atlantic.ca
Personnel:
Chmn.: Irving Granovsky
Phone: (1) 416-298-8101
Fax: (1) 416-297-2218
Email: irving_granovsky@atlantic.ca
Vice Chmn.: John Cherry
Phone: (1) 416-298-8101
Fax: (1) 416-297-2218
Email: john_cherry@atlantic.ca
Pres.: David (Dave) Boles
Phone: (1) 416-298-8101
Fax: (1) 416-297-2218
Email: david_boles@atlantic.ca
Snr. VP Sls. & Mktg: Bob Hagan
Phone: (1) 416-298-8101
Fax: (1) 416-297-2218
Email: bob_hagan@atlantic.ca
VP Finan. & Admin.: Paul Doyle
Phone: (1) 416-298-8101
Fax: (1) 416-297-2218
Email: paul_doyle@atlantic.ca
VP, Mills: Gerry Murray
Phone: (1) 416-298-8101
Fax: (1) 416-297-2218
Email: gerry_murray@atlantic.ca
VP, HR: Mario Sabatini
Phone: (1) 416-298-8101
Fax: (1) 416-297-2218
Email: mario_sabatini@atlantic.ca
VP, IT: Hector Navarro
Phone: (1) 416-298-8101
Fax: (1) 416-297-2218
Email: hector_navarro@atlantic.ca
Dir. of Sls.: John Pepper
Phone: (1) 416-298-5418
Fax: (1) 416-297-2218
Email: john_pepper@atlantic.ca
Procurement Mgr.: Donna Roberts
Phone: (1) 416-298-5307
Fax: (1) 416-297-2218
Email: donna_roberts@atlantic.ca
Tissue Mill Supt.: Steve Wayland
Phone: (1) 416-297-2231
Fax: (1) 416-297-2218
Email: steve_wayland@@atlantic.ca
Total Employees at this Location: 100
Type of Operation: Paperboard mill
Mill Locations:
Atlantic Packaging Products Ltd., Whitby Mill, 1900 Thickson Rd S, Whitby, ON, Canada L1N 9E1, Capacity: 272,051 mt/y, (Paper mill)
Phone: (1) 905-686-5966 / 905-686-5912
Fax: (1) 905-686-5900
New Forest Paper Mills LP, Scarborough Mill (50% owned), 333 Progress Avenue, Scarborough, ON, Canada M1P 2Y9, Capacity: 226,709 mt/y, (Paperboard mill)
Phone: (1) 416-298-8101
Fax: (1) 416-297-2218
Pulp Grades and Capacities:
Total pulp capacity: 186,242 mt/y
Recycled Pulping: 186,242 mt/y
Pulp Mill Data:
Recycled Fiber Treatment Lines:
Recycled packaging pulping lines: 1
Paper/Paperboard Grades and Capacities:
Total paper and paperboard capacity: 178,129 mt/y
Linerboard: 137,645 mt/y
Corrugating medium/fluting: 40,484 mt/y
Paper and Paperboard Mill Data:
Paper Machines: 1
No. 4, top former, total capacity 178,129 mt/y, Trim width 4.32 m, Linerboard, Corrugating medium/fluting
Energy Data:
Power boilers: 2
Electrical demand for mill: 303 MWh/D

ⓜAtlantic Packaging Products Ltd.
Whitby Mill
1900 Thickson Rd S
Whitby, ON
Canada, L1N 9E1
Phone: (1) 905-686-5966 / 905-686-5912
Fax: (1) 905-686-5900
Web Address: www.atlantic.ca
Personnel:
Site Mgr.: Ian Murray
Phone: (1) 905-686-5966
Fax: (1) 905-686-5900
Email: ian_murray@atlantic.ca
Supt. (Prod. Mgr.): Shivamurthy Modgi
Phone: (1) 905-686-5953
Fax: (1) 905-686-5900
Email: shivamurthy_modgi@atlantic.ca
Prod. Mgr.: Peter Lombardo
Phone: (1) 416-298-5322
Fax: (1) 905-686-5900
Email: peter_lombardo@atlantic.ca
Sls. Dir., Paper Mills: John Pepper
Phone: (1) 905-686-5966
Fax: (1) 905-686-5900
Email: john_pepper@atlantic.ca
Total Employees at this Location: 151
Type of Operation: Paper mill
Pulp Grades and Capacities:
Total pulp capacity: 280,931 mt/y
Recycled Pulping: 280,931 mt/y
Pulp Mill Data:
Recycled Fiber Treatment Lines:
Recycled packaging pulping lines: 1
Paper/Paperboard Grades and Capacities:
Total paper and paperboard capacity: 272,051 mt/y
Linerboard: 204,038 mt/y
Corrugating medium/fluting: 68,013 mt/y
Paper and Paperboard Mill Data:
Paper Machines: 1
No. 3, GapFormer, total capacity 272,051 mt/y, Trim width 6.45 m, Linerboard, Corrugating medium/fluting
Energy Data:
HRSG boiler
Combustion turbines: 1 at 50 MW
Electrical demand for mill: 440 MWh/D

ⓜAV Terrace Bay Pulp Inc.
Ownership: 100% by Aditya Birla Group
21 Mill Rd
Terrace Bay, ON
Canada, P0T 2W0
Phone: (1) 807-825-3211
Fax: (1) 807-825-3522
Personnel:
CEO: Giovanni Iadeluca
Phone: (1) 807-825-3211
Fax: (1) 807-825-3522
Email: giovanni.iadeluca@adityabirla.com
Mill Mgr.: Bob Bryson
Phone: (1) 807-825-9840
Fax: (1) 807-825-3522
Email: robert.bryson@adityabirla.com
Mgr., Capital Proj.: Dennis Visintin
Phone: (1) 807-825-8843
Fax: (1) 807-825-3522
Email: dennis.visintin@adityabirla.com
Total Employees of Company: 420
Mill Locations:
AV Terrace Bay Pulp Inc., Terrace Bay Mill, 21 Mill Rd, Terrace Bay, ON, Canada P0T 2W0, (Pulp mill)
Phone: (1) 807-825-3211
Fax: (1) 807-825-3522

ⓜAV Terrace Bay Pulp Inc.
Terrace Bay Mill
Ownership: 100% by Aditya Birla Group
21 Mill Rd
Terrace Bay, ON

Ontario

Canada, P0T 2W0
  Phone: (1) 807-825-3211
  Fax: (1) 807-825-3522
  Web Address: www.av-group.ca/av-terrace-bay.html, www.birlacellulose.com
Personnel:
  CEO: Giovanni Iadeluca
  Phone: (1) 807-825-3211
  Fax: (1) 807-825-3522
  Email: giovanni.iadeluca@adityabirla.com
  Mill Mgr.: Bob Bryson
  Phone: (1) 807-825-9840
  Fax: (1) 807-825-3522
  Email: robert.bryson@adityabirla.com
  Mgr., Capital Proj.: Dennis Visintin
  Phone: (1) 807-825-8843
  Fax: (1) 807-825-3522
  Email: dennis.visintin@adityabirla.com
Total Employees at this Location: 260
Type of Operation: Pulp mill
Pulp Grades and Capacities:
  Total pulp capacity: 352,302 mt/y
  Pulp available for market: 349,860 mt/y
  Chemical Pulp: 352,302 mt/y
Pulp Mill Data:
  Chemical Pulping Systems:
  Batch digesters: 18
Pulp Lines: 1
  Bleach Plant Systems: 1
  Chemical Pulping system - No. 2, Type: Softwood, Sequence: DP_CO-ODE_PD, Capacity 475,000 admt/y
  Chemical Recovery Equipment:
  Evaporator lines: 1
  Recovery boilers: 2
  Lime Kiln
  Pulp Dryers:
  Flakt dryer 1, Flakt dryer 1, Ross Dryer 1
Energy Data:
  Power boilers: 2
  Steam turbines: 1 at 55 MW
  Electrical demand for mill: 938 MWh/D

ⓜCascades Tissue Group
Scarborough Mill
Ownership: 100% by Cascades Inc.
45, Milliken Blvd.
Agincourt - Scarborough, ON
Canada, M1V 1V4
  Phone: (1) 416 329-5200
  Fax: (1) 416 329-5234
  Email: info@cascades.com
  Web Address: www.afh.cascades.com
Personnel:
  Prod. Mgr.: Tom Murray
  Phone: (1) 419-329-5200
  Fax: (1) 416 329-5234
  Email: tom_murray@cascades.com
  Maint. Mgr.: Eric Spriel
  Phone: (1) 419-329-5200
  Fax: (1) 416 329-5234
  Email: eric_spriel@cascades.com
  Storeroom Contr.: Calvin Young
  Phone: (1) 419-329-5200
  Fax: (1) 416 329-5234
  Email: calvin_young@cascades.com
  Account. Mgr.: Natasha Singh
  Phone: (1) 419-329-5200
  Fax: (1) 416 329-5234
  Email: natasha_singh@cascades.com
Total Employees at this Location: 50
Type of Operation: Paper mill
Pulp Grades and Capacities:
  Total pulp capacity: 26,776 mt/y
  Recycled Pulping: 26,776 mt/y
Pulp Mill Data:
  Recycled Fiber Treatment Lines:
  Pulpers: 1 at 25,500
Paper/Paperboard Grades and Capacities:
  Total paper and paperboard capacity: 24,938 mt/y
  Tissue: 24,938 mt/y
Paper and Paperboard Mill Data:
  Stock Preparation:
  Pulpers:
Paper Machines: 1
  No. 2, twin-wire, total capacity 24,938 mt/y, Trim width 2.64 m, Tissue
Energy Data:
  Electrical demand for mill: 107 MWh/D

ⓜCascades Tissue Group
Whitby Mill
Ownership: 100% by Cascades Inc.
1900 Thickson Road North
Whitby, ON
Canada,
  Phone: (1) 416-329-5200
  Fax: (1) 416-329-5234
  Web Address: www.afh.cascades.com
Personnel:
  Mill. Mgr.: Stephane Deshaies
  Phone: (1) 416-329-5228
  Fax: (1) 416-329-5234
  Email: stephane_deshaies@cascades.com
Total Employees at this Location: 65
Type of Operation: Paper mill
Pulp Grades and Capacities:
  Total pulp capacity: 35,494 mt/y
  Recycled Pulping: 35,494 mt/y
Pulp Mill Data:
  Bleach Plant Systems: 1
  Recycled Deinked Pulping System
  Recycled Fiber Treatment Lines:
  Flotation deinking lines: 1
Paper/Paperboard Grades and Capacities:
  Total paper and paperboard capacity: 33,035 mt/y
  Tissue: 33,035 mt/y
Paper and Paperboard Mill Data:
Paper Machines: 1
  No. 2, crescent former, total capacity 33,035 mt/y, Trim width 2.64 m, Tissue
Energy Data:
  HRSG boiler
  Combustion turbines at 50 MW
  Electrical demand for mill: 151 MWh/D

ⓜClearwater Paper Corporation
Saint Catharines Mill
45 Merritt St
Saint Catharines, ON
Canada, L2T 1J4
  Phone: (1) 905-680-3000
  Fax: (1) 905-227-1899
  Email: info@clearwaterpaper.com
  Web Address: www.clearwaterpaper.com
Personnel:
  Mill Mgr.: Steve Michalko
  Phone: (1) 905-680-3000
  Fax: (1) 905-227-1899
  Email: steve.michalko@clearwaterpaper.com
  Qlty. & IT Mgr.: Erik Dreifelds
  Phone: (1) 905-680-3000
  Fax: (1) 905-227-1899
  Email: erik.dreifelds@clearwaterpaper.com
  Process Team Ldr. PM2: Greg Nichol
  Phone: (1) 905-680-3000
  Fax: (1) 905-227-1899
  Email: greg.nichol@clearwaterpaper.com
Total Employees at this Location: 80
Type of Operation: Paper mill
Paper/Paperboard Grades and Capacities:
  Total paper and paperboard capacity: 44,370 mt/y
  Tissue: 23,643 mt/y
  Specialty and industrial: 20,728 mt/y
Paper and Paperboard Mill Data:
  Stock Preparation:
  Pulpers:
Paper Machines: 2
  No. 2, fourdrinier, total capacity 20,728 mt/y, Trim width 3.81 m, Specialty and industrial
  No. 3, TAD, total capacity 23,643 mt/y, Trim width 3.3 m, Tissue
Energy Data:
  Power boilers: 1
  Electrical demand for mill: 165 MWh/D

ⓜDomtar Corporation
Dryden Mill
1 Duke St.
Dryden, ON
Canada, P8N 3J7
Mailing Address: PO Box 3001, Dryden, ON, Canada, P8N 2Z7
  Phone: (1) 807-223-2323
  Fax: (1) 807-223-9317
  Web Address: www.domtar.com
Personnel:
  Mill Mgr.: Jim Blight
  Phone: (1) 807-223-9035
  Fax: (1) 807-223-9620
  Email: jim.blight@domtar.com
  Regional Pub. Affairs Mgr.: Bonny Skene
  Phone: (1) 807-223-9035
  Fax: (1) 807-223-9620
  Email: bonny.skene@domtar.com
  Finan. & Plan. Mgr.: Sally Sipos
  Phone: (1) 807-223-9747
  Fax: (1) 807-223-9317
  Email: sally.sipos@domtar.com
Total Employees at this Location: 340
Type of Operation: Pulp mill
Pulp Grades and Capacities:
  Total pulp capacity: 333,350 mt/y
  Pulp available for market: 328,083 mt/y
  Chemical Pulp: 333,350 mt/y
Pulp Mill Data:
  Chemical Pulping Systems:
  Continuous digesters: 1
Pulp Lines: 1
  Bleach Plant Systems: 1
  No. 1, Sequence: DWEopDED
  Chemical Recovery Equipment:
  Evaporator lines: 1
  Recovery boilers: 1
  Lime Kiln
  Pulp Dryers:
  Flakt dryer 1
Finishing Equipment:
  Sheeters: 4
Energy Data:
  Power boilers: 4
  Steam turbines: 2 at 37, 15 MW
  Electrical demand for mill: 794 MWh/D

ⓜDomtar Corporation
Espanola Mill
1 Station Rd
Espanola, ON
Canada, P5E 1R6
  Phone: (1) 705-869-2020, 705-869-2035
  Fax: (1) 705-869-5753, 705-869-5494
  Web Address: www.domtar.com
Personnel:
  Gen. Mgr.: Scott Mosher
  Phone: (1) 705-869-2020
  Fax: (1) 705-869-5753
  Email: scott.mosher@domtar.com
  Relliability Mgr.: Kim Hunt
  Phone: (1) 705-869-2020
  Fax: (1) 705-869-5753
  Email: kim.hunt@domtar.com
  Contrl.: Jodi Podlatis
  Phone: (1) 705-869-2020
  Fax: (1) 705-869-5753
  Email: jodi.podlatis@domtar.com
  Commun. Mgr.: Lynne Gibson
  Phone: (1) 705-869-2020

Ontario

Fax: (1) 705-869-5753
Email: lynne.gibson@domtar.com
Maint. Supt.: Marc Lefebvre
Phone: (1) 705-869-2020
Fax: (1) 705-869-5753
Email: marc.lefebvre@domtar.com
Total Employees at this Location: 540
Type of Operation: Pulp mill, Paper mill
Pulp Grades and Capacities:
Total pulp capacity: 350,104 mt/y
Pulp available for market: 273,819 mt/y
Chemical Pulp: 350,104 mt/y

Pulp Mill Data:
Chemical Pulping Systems:
Batch digesters: 5
Continuous digesters: 1
Pulp Lines: 2
Bleach Plant Systems: 2
Chemical Pulping System, Type: Softwood, Sequence: O_2 DEoDnD
Chemical Pulping System, Type: Hardwood, Sequence: O_2 ZDEDnD, Capacity 290,000 admt/y
Chemical Recovery Equipment:
Evaporator lines: 1
Recovery boilers: 1
Lime Kiln
Pulp Dryers:
Fourdriniers 1, Fourdriniers 1
Paper/Paperboard Grades and Capacities:
Total paper and paperboard capacity: 69,617 mt/y
Uncoated woodfree/freesheet: 13,600 mt/y
Specialty and industrial: 56,017 mt/y
Paper and Paperboard Mill Data:
Paper Machines: 2
No. 2, fourdrinier, total capacity 41,770 mt/y, Trim width 3.86 m, Uncoated woodfree/freesheet, Specialty and industrial
No. 3, Yankee dryer, total capacity 27,847 mt/y, Trim width 3.15 m, Uncoated woodfree/freesheet, Specialty and industrial
Energy Data:
Power boilers: 3
Steam turbines: 1 at 23.0 MW
Hydro turbines: 1 at 16.2 MW
Electrical demand for mill: 1,047 MWh/D

ⓘⓜGeorgia-Pacific LLC
Thorold Mill
Company is idle (in January 2014.)
Ownership: 100% by Koch Industries (Private)
319 Allanburg Rd
Thorold, ON
Canada, L2V 5C3
Phone: (1) 905-227-6651
Fax: (1) 905-227-8120
Web Address: www.gp.com
Personnel:
Plt. Mgr.: Gerry Finlayson
Phone: (1) 905-227-6651 x360
Fax: (1) 905-227-8120
Email: gffinlay@gapac.com
Snr. Process Eng.: David Burch
Phone: (1) 905-227-6651
Fax: (1) 905-227-8120
Email: dburch@gapac.com
Total Employees of Company: 35,000
Total Employees at this Location: 109
Type of Operation: Paperboard mill
Mill Locations:
G-P Gypsum LLC, San Leandro Mill, 1988 Marina Blvd, San Leandro, CA 94550, USA, Capacity: 72,871 mt/y, (Paper mill)
Phone: (1) 510-483-7580
Fax: (1) 510-483-5430
Georgia-Pacific LLC, Camas Mill, 401 NE Adams St, Camas, WA 98607-2133, USA, Capacity: 259,039 mt/y, (Pulp mill, Paper mill)
Phone: (1) 360-834-3021
Fax: (1) 360-834-8176

Georgia-Pacific LLC, Brewton Mill, 32224 US 31, Brewton, AL 36426, USA, Capacity: 453,419 mt/y, (Pulp mill, Paperboard mill)
Phone: (1) 251-867-3621
Fax: (1) 251-867-8353
GP Cellulose, LLC, Leaf River Cellulose Mill, 157 Buck Creek Rd, New Augusta, MS 39462, USA, (Pulp mill)
Phone: (1) 601-964-8411
Fax: (1) 601-964-7248
Email: info@gpcellulose.com
Georgia-Pacific LLC, Broadway Street/West Mill, 1919 S Broadway, Green Bay, WI 54304, USA, Capacity: 349,132 mt/y, (Paper mill)
Phone: (1) 920-435-8821
Fax: (1) 920-435-3703
Georgia-Pacific LLC, Big Island Mill, 9363 Lee Jackson Hwy, Big Island, VA 24526, USA, Capacity: 542,483 mt/y, (Pulp mill, Paperboard mill)
Phone: (1) 434-299-5911
Fax: (1) 434-299-5222
Georgia-Pacific LLC, Cedar Springs Mill, 12551 Georgia 273, Cedar Springs, GA 39832, USA, Capacity: 927,889 mt/y, (Paperboard mill)
Phone: (1) 229-372-5541
Fax: (1) 229-372-5191
Georgia-Pacific LLC, Wauna Mill, 92326 Taylorsville Rd, Rte 2, Box 2185, Clatskanie, OR 97016-9299, USA, Capacity: 311,887 mt/y, (Paper mill)
Phone: (1) 503-455-2221
Fax: (1) 503-455-3562
Georgia-Pacific LLC, Crossett Mill, 100 Mill Supply Rd, Crossett, AR 71635, USA, Capacity: 558,029 mt/y, (Paper mill, Paperboard mill)
Phone: (1) 870-567-8000, 870-567-5365
Fax: (1) 870-364-5123
Georgia-Pacific LLC, Day Street/East Mill, 500 Day St, Green Bay, WI 54302, USA, Capacity: 100,076 mt/y, (Paper mill)
Phone: (1) 920-433-6200
Fax: (1) 920-433-6352
Georgia-Pacific LLC, Halsey Mill, 30470 American Dr, Halsey, OR 97348, USA, Capacity: 99,428 mt/y, (Pulp mill, Paper mill)
Phone: (1) 541-369-2293
Fax: (1) 541-369-1327
Georgia-Pacific LLC, Monticello Mill, 604 NA Sandifer Rd, Monticello, MS 39654, USA, Capacity: 1,010,476 mt/y, (Paperboard mill)
Phone: (1) 601-587-7711, 601-587-3204
Fax: (1) 601-587-4532
Georgia-Pacific LLC, Muskogee Mill, 4901 Chandler Rd, Muskogee, OK 74403, USA, Capacity: 330,348 mt/y, (Paper mill)
Phone: (1) 918-683-7671
Fax: (1) 918-683-1609
Georgia-Pacific LLC, Naheola Mill, 7530 Hwy 114, Pennington, AL 36916, USA, Capacity: 525,318 mt/y, (Pulp mill, Paper mill, Paperboard mill)
Phone: (1) 205-459-1900
Fax: (1) 205-459-1303
Georgia-Pacific LLC, Plattsburgh Mill, 327 Margaret St, Plattsburgh, NY 12901, USA, Capacity: 41,132 mt/y, (Paper mill)
Phone: (1) 518-561-3500
Fax: (1) 518-562-6533
Georgia-Pacific LLC, Port Hudson Mill, 1000 West Mount Pleasant Zachary Road, Zachary, LA 70791, USA, Capacity: 746,197 mt/y, (Paper mill)
Phone: (1) 225-654-1700
Fax: (1) 225-654-7722
Georgia-Pacific LLC, Savannah River Mill, 393 Fort Howard Rd, Rincon, GA 31326, USA, Capacity: 422,975 mt/y, (Paper mill)
Phone: (1) 912-826-5216
Fax: (1) 912-806-2363
Georgia-Pacific LLC, Toledo Mill, 1400 S.E. Butler Bridge Road, Toledo, OR 97391, USA, Capacity: 811,295 mt/y, (Pulp mill, Paperboard mill)
Phone: (1) 541-336-2211
Fax: (1) 541-336-8214
Georgia-Pacific LLC, Palatka Mill, 215 County Road 216, Palatka, FL 32177, USA, Capacity: 483,539 mt/y, (Paper mill, Paperboard mill)
Phone: (1) 386-325-2001
Fax: (1) 386-325-6141
GP Cellulose, LLC, Foley Cellulose Mill (Perry Mill), One Buckeye Drive, Perry, FL 32348, USA, (Pulp mill)
Phone: (1) 850-584-1121
Fax: (1) 850-584-1722
Email: info@gpcellulose.com
GP Cellulose, LLC, Brunswick Cellulose Mill, 1400 West 9th St, Brunswick, GA 31520, USA, (Pulp mill)
Phone: (1) 912-265-5780
Fax: (1) 912-265-8060
Email: info@gpcellulose.com
GP Cellulose, LLC, Alabama River Cellulose Mill, Lena Landegger Highway, County Road 39, Perdue Hill, Claiborne, AL 36470, USA, (Pulp mill)
Phone: (1) 251-575-2000
Fax: (1) 251-743-8432
Email: info@gpcellulose.com
Industria Panameña de Papel SA, Chilibre Mill (50% owned), Milla 15, Carretera Boyd Roosevelt, 0816-02543 San Vicente, Zona Chilibre, Panama, Capacity: 29,988 mt/y, (Paper mill, Paperboard mill)
Phone: (507) 216 6555/6031
Fax: (507) 16 6766
Email: vanipel@cw.panama.net
Pulp Mill Data:
Paper/Paperboard Grades and Capacities:
Total paper and paperboard capacity: 115,000 mt/y
Boxboard/cartonboard: 115,000 mt/y
Paper and Paperboard Mill Data:
Paper Machines: 1
BM 1, (Former Type model: Ultraformer Multiple Fabrics), Ultraformer, total capacity 115,000 mt/y, Trim width 3.9 m, Boxboard/cartonboard
Energy Data:
Power boilers: 3

ⓜIrving Tissue Inc.
Toronto Mill
Ownership: J.D. Irving, Ltd.
1551 Weston Rd
Toronto, ON
Canada, M6M 4Y4
Phone: (1) 416-246-6666
Fax: (1) 416-246-6667
Web Address: www.irvingtissue.com
Personnel:
VP Oper.: Phil Viger
Phone: (1) 416-246-6666
Fax: (1) 416-246-6667
Email: phil.viger@irvingpaper.com
Paper Mill Mgr. (From November 2013): Yves L'Italien
Phone: (1) 416-246-6666
Fax: (1) 416-246-6667
Email: yves.litalien@irvingpaper.com
Machine Mgr. PM#5: Christopher Hammar
Phone: (1) 416-246-6666
Fax: (1) 416-246-6667
Email: christopher.hammar@irvingpaper.com
Total Employees at this Location: 135
Type of Operation: Paper mill
Paper/Paperboard Grades and Capacities:
Total paper and paperboard capacity: 96,513 mt/y
Tissue: 96,513 mt/y
Paper and Paperboard Mill Data:
Stock Preparation:
Pulpers:
Paper Machines: 3
No. 4, crescent former, total capacity 35,626 mt/y, Trim width 4.17 m, Tissue
No. 5, crescent former, total capacity 25,910 mt/y, Trim width 4.17 m, Tissue
No. 6, TAD, total capacity 34,978 mt/y, Trim width 4.17 m, Tissue
Energy Data:
Power boilers: 1
Electrical demand for mill: 341 MWh/D

Ontario

ⓘKimberly-Clark of Canada
Huntsville Mill
Ownership: Kimberly-Clark Corp.
570 Ravensdiffe Rd.
Huntsville, ON
Canada, P1H 2A1
  Phone: (1) 705-788-5200
  Fax: (1) 705-788-5272
  Web Address: www.kimberly-clark.com
Personnel:
  Mill Mgr. (from September 2013): Rene Landry
  Phone: (1) 705-788-5200
  Fax: (1) 705-788-5272
  Email: rlandry@kcc.com
  Team Ldr., Warehouse: Ken Parsons
  Phone: (1) 705-788-5200
  Fax: (1) 705-788-5272
  Email: ken.parsons@kcc.com
  Converting Team Ldr.: Kevin Bigelow
  Phone: (1) 705-788-5200
  Fax: (1) 705-788-5272
  Email: kbigelow@kcc.com
  Process. Eng.: Tyler Reain
  Phone: (1) 705-788-5200
  Fax: (1) 705-788-5272
  Email: tyler.reain@kcc.com
Total Employees at this Location: 70
Type of Operation: Paper mill
Paper/Paperboard Grades and Capacities:
  Total paper and paperboard capacity: 32,063 mt/y
  Tissue: 32,063 mt/y
Paper and Paperboard Mill Data:
  Stock Preparation:
  Pulpers:
Paper Machines: 1
No. 1, crescent former, total capacity 32,063 mt/y, Trim width 4.44 m, Tissue
Energy Data:
Power boilers: 2
Electrical demand for mill: 97 MWh/D

ⓘKruger Products L.P.
Ownership: 83.10% by Kruger Inc., 16.90% by KP Tissue Inc. (Public)
1900 Minnesota Ct, Suite 200
Mississauga, ON
Canada,
Mailing Address: PO Box 1500, Streetsville, ON, Canada, L5M 6A3
  Phone: (1) 905-812-6900
  Fax: (1) 905-812-6908
  Web Address: www.krugerproducts.ca
Personnel:
  CEO KPLP: Mario Gosselin
  Phone: (1) 905-812-6900
  Fax: (1) 905-812-6908
  Email: mario.gosselin@krugerproducts.ca
  CFO KPLP: Mark Holbrook
  Phone: (1) 905-812-6900
  Fax: (1) 905-812-6908
  Email: mark.holbrook@krugerproducts.ca
  Corp. VP, Manuf. & International Oper.: Glenn Taylor
  Phone: (1) 905-812-6900
  Fax: (1) 905-812-6908
  Email: glenn.taylor@krugerproducts.ca
  Corp. VP, Mktg KPLP: Nancy Marcus
  Phone: (1) 905-812-6900
  Fax: (1) 905-812-6908
  Email: nancy.marcus@krugerproducts.ca
  Corp. VP, Consumer Sls. Canada KPLP: Michel Manseau
  Phone: (1) 905-812-6900
  Fax: (1) 905-812-6908
  Email: michel.manseau@krugerproducts.ca
  Corp. VP, (AFH) Division and Strategic Planning: Rob Latter
  Phone: (1) 905-812-6900
  Fax: (1) 905-812-6908
  Email: rob.latter@krugerproducts.ca
  Corp. VP, HR & Legal KPLP: Serge Reynaud
  Phone: (1) 905-812-6900
  Fax: (1) 905-812-6908
  Email: serge.reynaud@krugerproducts.ca
  Corp. VP., Logist. KPLP: John O'Hara
  Phone: (1) 905-812-6900
  Fax: (1) 905-812-6908
  Email: john.ohara@krugerproducts.ca
  Gen. Counsel & Corp. Sec. KPLP: Wendy Kelley
  Phone: (1) 905-812-6900
  Fax: (1) 905-812-6908
  Email: wendy.kelley@krugerproducts.ca
Total Employees of Company: 2,300
Total Employees at this Location: 100
Mill Locations:
Kruger Products L.P., Crabtree Mill, 100, 1st Avenue, Crabtree, QC, Canada J0K 1B0, Capacity: 72,871 mt/y, (Pulp mill, Paper mill)
  Phone: (1) 450-754-2855
  Fax: (1) 450-754-4556
Kruger Products L.P., Gatineau Mill, 20 Laurier Street, Gatineau, QC, Canada J8X 4H3, Capacity: 91,008 mt/y, (Paper mill)
  Phone: (1) 819-595-5302
  Fax: (1) 819-595-5396
Kruger Products L.P., New Westminster Mill, 1625 Fifth Ave., New Westminster, BC, Canada V3M 1Z7, Capacity: 57,973 mt/y, (Pulp mill, Paper mill)
  Phone: (1) 604-522-5711
  Fax: (1) 604-520-9200
Kruger Products L.P., Lennoxville Mill, 2888 College St, Sherbrooke, QC, Canada J1M 1Z4, Capacity: 23,966 mt/y, (Paper mill)
  Phone: (1) 819-565-8220
  Fax: (1) 819-566-0245
Grand Bay Paper Products Ltd., Lot C Lennox Yearwood Expressway, O'Meara Industrial Estate, Arima, Trinidad and Tobago, Capacity: 32,130 mt/y, (Papermill)
  Phone: (1) 868 6432519, 868 6432520
  Fax: (1) 868 643 2522

ⓘMetro Paper Industries Tissue Group Ltd.
90 Nolan Court Unit 20
Markham, ON
Canada, L3R 4L9
  Phone: (1) 905-604-5786
  Fax: (1) 905-604-6786
Personnel:
  Pres.: Karim Jadavji
  Phone: (1) 905-604-5786 Ext: 223
  Fax: (1) 905-604-6786
  Email: karimj@mpipapermills.com
  Exec. VP: Amin Jadavji
  Phone: (1) 905-604-5786
  Fax: (1) 905-604-6786
  Email: aminj@mpipapermills.com
  CFO: Oliver Moraes
  Phone: (1) 905-604-5786
  Fax: (1) 905-604-6786
  Email: oliverm@mpipapermills.com
  Paper Mill Cust. Serv. Representative: Marsha Prince
  Phone: (1) 905-604-5786 Ext: 225
  Fax: (1) 905-604-6786
  Email: marshap@mpipapermills.com
Mill Locations:
Metro Paper Industries Tissue Group Ltd., Portneuf Mill, 200, rue Du Moulin, Portneuf, QC, Canada G0A 2Y0, Capacity: 25,910 mt/y, (Paper mill)
  Phone: (1) 418-286-3461
  Fax: (1) 418-286-6457
  Email: customerservice@metropaperindustries.com, daphnem@metropaperindustries.com

ⓘNew Forest Paper Mills LP
Scarborough Mill
Ownership: 50% by Atlantic Packaging Products Ltd., 50% by Mitchel-Lincoln
333 Progress Avenue
Scarborough, ON
Canada, M1P 2Y9
  Phone: (1) 416-298-8101
  Fax: (1) 416-297-2218
  Web Address: www.newforest.ca, www.atlantic.ca
Personnel:
  VP, Oper.: Gerry Murray
  Phone: (1) 416-298-8101
  Fax: (1) 416-297-2218
  Email: gerry_murray@atlantic.ca
  Mill Mgr.: Edward Stapleton
  Phone: (1) 416-940-1113
  Fax: (1) 416-297-2218
  Email: ed_stapleton@atlantic.ca
  Linerboard Mill Supt.: Eric Faulkner
  Phone: (1) 416-940-1112
  Fax: (1) 416-297-2218
  Email: eric_faulkner@atlantic.ca
Total Employees at this Location: 66
Type of Operation: Paperboard mill
Pulp Grades and Capacities:
  Total pulp capacity: 234,503 mt/y
  Recycled Pulping: 234,503 mt/y
Pulp Mill Data:
  Recycled Fiber Treatment Lines:
  Recycled packaging pulping lines: 1
Paper/Paperboard Grades and Capacities:
  Total paper and paperboard capacity: 226,709 mt/y
  Linerboard: 79,348 mt/y
  Corrugating medium/fluting: 147,361 mt/y
Paper and Paperboard Mill Data:
Paper Machines: 1
No. 1, fourdrinier (2), total capacity 226,709 mt/y, Trim width 5.08 m, Linerboard, Corrugating medium/fluting
Energy Data:
Power boilers: 1
Electrical demand for mill: 296 MWh/D

ⓘNorampac
Mississauga Mill
Previously Norampac Inc.
Ownership: 100% by Cascades Inc.
7447 Bramalea Rd
Mississauga, ON
Canada, L5S 1C4
  Phone: (1) 905-671-2940
  Fax: (1) 905-671-2448
  Email: mississauga_info@norampac.com
  Web Address: www.norampac.com
Personnel:
  Mill Mgr.: Joseph Zenga
  Phone: (1) 905-671-7386
  Fax: (1) 905-671-2448
  Email: joe_zenga@norampac.com
  Prod. Supervisor & Continuous Improv. Projects: Steve Goldstein
  Phone: (1) 905-671-2940
  Fax: (1) 905-671-2448
  Email: steve_goldstein@norampac.com
  Coord. Oper. Efficiency (From August 2014): Remi Beaulieu
  Phone: (1) 905-671-2940
  Fax: (1) 905-671-2448
  Email: remi_beaulieu@norampac.com
  Qlty. & Tech. Mgr.: Wendy Cerilli
  Phone: (1) 905-671-7374
  Fax: (1) 905-671-2448
  Email: wendy_cerilli@norampac.com
  Gen. Mgr. Sls & Exportation Mississauga Mill & Kingsey Fall Mill: Guy Roy
  Phone: (1) 905-671-2940
  Fax: (1) 905-671-2448
  Email: guy_roy@norampac.com
Total Employees at this Location: 114
Type of Operation: Paperboard mill
Pulp Grades and Capacities:
  Total pulp capacity: 166,829 mt/y
  Recycled Pulping: 166,829 mt/y
Pulp Mill Data:

Ontario

Recycled Fiber Treatment Lines:
Recycled packaging pulping lines: 1
Paper/Paperboard Grades and Capacities:
Total paper and paperboard capacity: 160,316 mt/y
Linerboard: 160,316 mt/y
Paper and Paperboard Mill Data:
Stock Preparation:
Pulpers: 2
Refiners: 6
Paper Machines: 1
No. 1, top former, total capacity 160,316 mt/y, Trim width 4.29 m, Linerboard
Finishing Equipment:
Winders: 1
Energy Data:
Power boilers: 1
Electrical demand for mill: 233 MWh/D

ⓜNorampac
Trenton Mill
Previously Norampac Inc.
Ownership: 100% by Cascades Inc.
300 Marmora St
Trenton, ON
Canada, K8V 5R8
Mailing Address: PO Box 807, Trenton, ON, Canada, K8V 5R8
Phone: (1) 613-392-6505
Fax: (1) 613-392-3026
Email: trentonmill@norampac.com
Web Address: www.norampac.com
Personnel:
Mill Mgr.: Michael MacNeil
Phone: (1) 613-392-6505
Fax: (1) 613-392-3026
Email: mike_macneil@norampac.com
Prod. Mgr.: Gerald Nolin
Phone: (1) 613-392-6505
Fax: (1) 613-392-3026
Email: gerald_nolin@norampac.com
Contr.: Audrey Wood
Phone: (1) 613-392-6505
Fax: (1) 613-392-3026
Email: audrey_wood@norampac.com
Tech. Coord.: Iva Sarrasin
Phone: (1) 613-392-6505
Fax: (1) 613-392-3026
Email: iva_sarrasin@norampac.com
Total Employees at this Location: 148
Type of Operation: Paperboard mill
Pulp Grades and Capacities:
Total pulp capacity: 160,633 mt/y
Chemical Pulp: 79,769 mt/y
Recycled Pulping: 80,864 mt/y
Pulp Mill Data:
Chemical Pulping Systems:
Continuous digesters: 1
Chemical Recovery Equipment:
Evaporator lines: 1
Recycled Fiber Treatment Lines:
Recycled packaging pulping lines: 1 at 106,200 admt/y
Paper/Paperboard Grades and Capacities:
Total paper and paperboard capacity: 153,515 mt/y
Corrugating medium/fluting: 153,515 mt/y
Paper and Paperboard Mill Data:
Stock Preparation:
Pulpers: 2
Refiners: 2
Paper Machines: 1
No. 1, fourdrinier, total capacity 153,515 mt/y, Trim width 5.7 m, Corrugating medium/fluting
Finishing Equipment:
Rewinders: 1
Energy Data:
Power boilers: 3
Turbines
Electrical demand for mill: 292 MWh/D

ⓜResolute Forest Products Canada Inc.
Fort Frances Mill
Mill is for sale, closed (mill idled indefinitely from January 31, 2014, permanently closed in May 2014. Sept. 2014 Expera Specialty Solutions signed a letter of intent to acquire the site.)
427 Mowat Avenue
Fort Frances, ON
Canada, P9A 1Y8
Phone: (1) 807-274-5311
Fax: (1) 807-274-8200
Email: info@resolutefp.com
Web Address: www.resolutefp.com
Personnel:
HR Mgr.: Dave Maijala
Phone: (1) 807-274-5311 EXT 1968
Fax: (1) 807-274-8200
Oper. Mgr.: Sabino Rossi
Phone: (1) 807-274-1378
Fax: (1) 807-274-8200
Safety Coord.: Richard Gruttner
Phone: (1) 807-274-5311
Fax: (1) 807-274-8200
Pulp Mill Supt.: Greg Shaw
Phone: (1) 807-274-5311
Fax: (1) 807-274-8200
Total Employees at this Location: 205
Type of Operation: Pulp mill, Paper mill
Pulp Mill Data:
Chemical Pulping Systems:
Batch digesters: 6
Mechanical Pulping Systems:
Conventional grinders: 13
Bleach Plant Systems: 2
BSKP, Sequence: DEopD
SGW, Sequence: PPY
Chemical Recovery Equipment:
Evaporator lines: 1
Recovery boilers: 1
Lime Kiln
Pulp Dryers:
Flash dryers 1
Paper and Paperboard Mill Data:
Paper Machines: 1
No. 7, Bel-Baie III, total capacity 105,315 mt/y, Trim width 5.4 m
Energy Data:
Power boilers: 2
Steam turbines: 1 at 50 MW
Hydro turbines: 12 at 27 MW

ⓜResolute Forest Products Canada Inc.
Iroquois Falls Mill
1 Park St
Iroquois Falls, ON
Canada, P0K 1E0
Phone: (1) 705-258-3931
Fax: (1) 705-258-3350
Email: info@resolutefp.com
Web Address: www.resolutefp.com
Personnel:
Gen. Mgr.: Richard Standish
Phone: (1) 705-258-3931 Ext: 4355
Fax: (1) 705-258-3350
Email: richard.standish@resolutefp.com
Prod. & Maint. Mgr.: Greg Wickens
Phone: (1) 705-258-3931
Fax: (1) 705-258-3677
Email: greg.wickens@resolutefp.com
Pulp & Utilities Mgr.: Patrick Devine
Phone: (1) 705-258-3931
Fax: (1) 705-258-3350
Email: pat.devine@resolutefp.com
Woodlands Mgr.: Robert Tomchick
Phone: (1) 705-258-3931
Fax: (1) 705-258-3350
Email: rob.tomchick@resolutefp.com
Total Employees at this Location: 304
Type of Operation: Paper mill
Pulp Grades and Capacities:
Total pulp capacity: 213,015 mt/y
Mechanical Pulp: 213,015 mt/y
Pulp Mill Data:
Mechanical Pulping Systems:
TMP systems: 2
Bleach Plant Systems: 1
Mechanical TMP Pulping System, Type: Softwood Line, Sequence: H
Paper/Paperboard Grades and Capacities:
Total paper and paperboard capacity: 207,060 mt/y
Newsprint: 207,060 mt/y
Paper and Paperboard Mill Data:
Stock Preparation:
Pulpers:
Paper Machines: 1
No. 8, SymFormer, total capacity 207,060 mt/y, Trim width 8.53 m, Newsprint
Energy Data:
Power boilers: 1
TMP Reboiler: 1
Hydro turbines at 80 MW

ⓜResolute Forest Products Canada Inc.
Thorold Mill
2 Allanburg Rd
Thorold, ON
Canada, L2V 3Z5
Mailing Address: PO Box 1040, Thorold, ON, Canada, L2V 3Z5
Phone: (1) 905-227-5000
Fax: (1) 905-227-2112
Email: info@resolutefp.com
Web Address: www.resolutefp.com
Personnel:
Gen. Mgr.: Gordon Cole
Phone: (1) 905-227-5000 Ext. 6220
Fax: (1) 905-680-3144
Email: gordon.cole@resolutefp.com
Tech. Serv. Mgr.: Henry Peters
Phone: (1) 905-227-5000 Ext. 6524
Fax: (1) 905-680-3144
Email: henry.peters@resolutefp.com
Purch. Supt.: David DeLeeuw
Phone: (1) 905-227-5000 Ext. 6962
Fax: (1) 905-227-8104
Email: david.deleeuw@resolutefp.com
Environ. Mgr.: Sue Burch
Phone: (1) 905-227-5000 Ext. 6431
Fax: (1) 905-227-2112
Email: sue.burch@resolutefp.com
Generalist, HR: Sabrina Blanchard
Phone: (1) 905-227-5000 Ext: 6302
Fax: (1) 905-680-3144
Email: sabrina.blanchard@resolutefp.com
Pulping/ETP Mgr.: Said Mozaffari
Phone: (1) 905-227-5000
Fax: (1) 905-227-2112
Email: said.mozaffari@resolutefp.com
Pulping & Environ. Superint.: Michael Wilson
Phone: (1) 905-227-5000
Fax: (1) 905-227-2112
Email: michael.wilson@resolutefp.com
Snr. Mech. Proj. Eng.: Brian Stedman
Phone: (1) 905-227-5000 Ext: 6233
Fax: (1) 905-227-2112
Email: brian.stedman@resolutefp.com
Total Employees at this Location: 245
Type of Operation: Pulp mill, Paper mill
Pulp Grades and Capacities:
Total pulp capacity: 199,887 mt/y
Recycled Pulping: 199,887 mt/y
Pulp Mill Data:
Bleach Plant Systems: 1
Recycled Deinked Pulping System, Sequence: HS
Recycled Fiber Treatment Lines:
Flotation deinking lines: 1
Paper/Paperboard Grades and Capacities:

Total paper and paperboard capacity: 192,780 mt/y
Newsprint: 192,780 mt/y
Paper and Paperboard Mill Data:
Stock Preparation:
 Pulpers: 1
Paper Machines: 1
No. 7, Bel-Baie II, total capacity 192,780 mt/y, Trim width 7.6 m, Newsprint
Finishing Equipment:
 Winders: 2 at 215,000 mt/y
 Calenders: 2
 Rewinders: 1 at 7,000 mt/y
Energy Data:
 HRSG boiler: 2
 Combustion turbines: 1 at 170 MW
 Steam turbines: 2 at 95, 9 MW
 Electrical demand for mill: 587 MWh/D

ⓂResolute Forest Products Canada Inc.
Thunder Bay Mill
2001 Neebing Ave.
Thunder Bay, ON
Canada, P7E 6S3
 Phone: (1) 807-475-2110
 Fax: (1) 807-473-8643
 Email: info@resolutefp.com
 Web Address: www.resolutefp.com
Personnel:
Gen. Mgr.: Terry Skiffington
 Phone: (1) 807-475-2149
 Fax: (1) 807-473-8643
 Email: terry.skiffington@resolutefp.com
Prod. Mgr. - Thunder Bay Woodlands: Jim Stewart
 Phone: (1) 807-475-2215
 Fax: (1) 807-473-2822
 Email: jim.stewart@resolutefp.com
HR Mgr.: Dave Halushak
 Phone: (1) 807-475-2316
 Fax: (1) 807-473-2879
 Email: dave.halushak@resolutefp.com
Reliability Paper Supt.: John Pajala
 Phone: (1) 807-475-2105
 Fax: (1) 807-473-8643
 Email: john.pajala@resolutefp.com
Forestry Mgr.: Steve Watson
 Phone: (1) 807-475-2279
 Fax: (1) 807-473-2822
 Email: steve.watson@resolutefp.com
Total Employees at this Location: 470
Type of Operation: Pulp mill, Paper mill
Pulp Grades and Capacities:
Total pulp capacity: 545,842 mt/y
Pulp available for market: 312,375 mt/y
Chemical Pulp: 318,402 mt/y
Mechanical Pulp: 222,845 mt/y
Recycled Pulping: 4,595 mt/y
Pulp Mill Data:
Chemical Pulping Systems:
 Continuous digesters
Mechanical Pulping Systems:
 RMP systems: 1
 TMP systems: 2
Pulp Lines: 3
Bleach Plant Systems: 1
 Chemical Pulping System - B Bleach, Type: Hardwood/Softwood, Sequence: DEOpDEpD
Chemical Recovery Equipment:
 Evaporator lines: 1
 Recovery boilers: 1
 Lime Kiln
Recycled Fiber Treatment Lines:
 Flotation deinking lines: 1 at 46,000 admt/y
Pulp Dryers:
 Flakt dryer 1, Fourdriniers 1
Paper/Paperboard Grades and Capacities:
Total paper and paperboard capacity: 224,910 mt/y
Newsprint: 224,910 mt/y
Paper and Paperboard Mill Data:

Paper Machines: 1
No. 5, twin-wire, total capacity 224,910 mt/y, Trim width 8.34 m, Newsprint
Finishing Equipment:
 Winders: 1 at 250,000 mt/y
Energy Data:
 Power boilers: 2
 TMP Reboiler: 1
 Steam turbines: 4 at 60, 65 MW
 Electrical demand for mill: 1,701 MWh/D

ⒽⓂSonoco Ltd.
Brantford Mill
Ownership: 100% by Sonoco Products Co.
33 Park Av E
Brantford, ON
Canada, N3T 5T5
Mailing Address: PO Box 1208, Brantford, ON, Canada, N3T 5T5
 Phone: (1) 519-752-6591
 Fax: (1) 519-752-8399
 Email: info@sonoco.com
 Web Address: www.sonoco.com
Personnel:
Mill Mgr.: Jim Maloney
 Phone: (1) 519-752-6591
 Fax: (1) 519-752-8399
 Email: jim.maloney@sonoco.com
Purch. Mgr.: John Bick
 Phone: (1) 519-752-6591
 Fax: (1) 519-752-8399
 Email: john.bick@sonoco.com
Total Employees at this Location: 120
Type of Operation: Paperboard mill
Mill Locations:
Sonoco Ltd., Trent Valley Mill, Hwy 33 North of Hwy 401, Glen Miller, ON, Canada K8V 5P6, Capacity: 113,355 mt/y, (Paperboard mill)
 Phone: (1) 613-392-1231
 Fax: (1) 613-392-2485
 Email: info@sonoco.com
Pulp Grades and Capacities:
Total pulp capacity: 52,932 mt/y
Recycled Pulping: 52,932 mt/y
Paper/Paperboard Grades and Capacities:
Total paper and paperboard capacity: 51,819 mt/y
Boxboard/cartonboard: 51,819 mt/y
Paper and Paperboard Mill Data:
Stock Preparation:
 Pulpers: 2
 Refiners: 3
Paper Machines: 1
No. 1, cylinder (9), total capacity 51,819 mt/y, Trim width 2.64 m, Boxboard/cartonboard
Finishing Equipment:
 Calenders: 1
 Rewinders: 1
Energy Data:
 Combustion turbines: 1 at 3.8 MW
 Electrical demand for mill: 78 MWh/D

ⓂSonoco Ltd.
Trent Valley Mill
Ownership: 100% by Sonoco Products Co.
Hwy 33 North of Hwy 401
Glen Miller, ON
Canada, K8V 5P6
Mailing Address: PO Box 821, Trenton, ON, Canada, K8V 5R8
 Phone: (1) 613-392-1231
 Fax: (1) 613-392-2485
 Email: info@sonoco.com
 Web Address: www.sonoco.com
Personnel:
Plt. Mgr.: Jason Giffen
 Phone: (1) 613-392-1231
 Fax: (1) 613-392-2485
 Email: jason.giffen@sonoco.com
Shift Supervisor: Jim Walt

 Phone: (1) 613-392-1231
 Fax: (1) 613-392-2485
 Email: jim.walt@sonoco.com
Total Employees at this Location: 100
Type of Operation: Paperboard mill
Pulp Grades and Capacities:
Total pulp capacity: 116,927 mt/y
Recycled Pulping: 116,927 mt/y
Pulp Mill Data:
Recycled Fiber Treatment Lines:
 Pulpers: 1 at 127,000
Paper/Paperboard Grades and Capacities:
Total paper and paperboard capacity: 113,355 mt/y
Linerboard: 80,968 mt/y
Boxboard/cartonboard: 32,387 mt/y
Paper and Paperboard Mill Data:
Stock Preparation:
 Pulpers: 1
 Refiners: 5
Paper Machines: 1
No. 3, Ultraformer, total capacity 113,355 mt/y, Trim width 4.5 m, Linerboard, Boxboard/cartonboard
Energy Data:
 HRSG boiler
 Combustion turbines: 1 at 7.8 MW
 Electrical demand for mill: 148 MWh/D

ⒽⓂStrathcona Paper LP
Napanee Mill
Ownership: 100% by Forest Resources LLC
77 County Road 16, R.R. #7
Napanee, ON
Canada, K7R 3L2
Mailing Address: PO Box 130, Napanee, ON, Canada, K7R 3L6
 Phone: (1) 613-378-6672
 Fax: (1) 613-378-6158
 Web Address: www.strathconapaper.com
Personnel:
Pres & COO, Strathcona Paper: Mark Sklar
 Phone: (1) 416-491-1701 ext.325
 Fax: (1) 416-491-0444
 Email: msklar@strathconapaper.com
Dir., HR: Barry Faubert
 Phone: (1) 613-378-6672 Ext.262
 Fax: (1) 613-378-0830
 Email: bfaubert@strathconapaper.com
Dir., Oper.: Troy T. Gibson
 Phone: (1) 613-378-6672 Ext.249
 Fax: (1) 613-378-6158
 Email: tgibson@strathconapaper.com
Supv., Environ. Research & Monitoring: Frank Dorrington
 Phone: (1) 613-378-6672 Ext.281
 Fax: (1) 613-378-6158
 Email: fdorrington@strathconapaper.com
Cust. Svc. & Mills Sls. Spcclst: Lindy Lea
 Phone: (1) 800-400-2955 Ext. 246
 Fax: (1) 613-378-0956
 Email: llea@strathconapaper.com
CSR Inside Sls.: Lisa Gammage
 Phone: (1) 416-491-1701 Ext. 27
 Fax: (1) 416-491-0444
 Email: lgammage@strathconapaper.com
Paper Machine Scheduler: Christie Perry
 Phone: (1) 613-378-6672 Ext. 269
 Fax: (1) 613-378-0956
 Email: cperry@strathconapaper.com
Finish. Supervisor: Bonnie Bailey
 Phone: (1) 613-378-6672 Ext. 273
 Fax: (1) 613-378-6158
 Email: bbailey@strathconapaper.com
Mgr., Procurement & Serv.: Michel Mongeon
 Phone: (1) 613-378-6676 Ext.244
 Fax: (1) 613-378-6158
 Email: mmongeon@strathconapaper.com
Mgr, Gen. Serv.: Glenn Owen
 Phone: (1) 613-378-6672 Ext.274
 Fax: (1) 613-378-6158
 Email: gowen@strathconapaper.com

Quebec

Total Employees of Company: 140
Total Employees at this Location: 141
Type of Operation: Paperboard mill
Pulp Grades and Capacities:
  Total pulp capacity: 93,575 mt/y
  Recycled Pulping: 93,575 mt/y
Pulp Mill Data:
  Recycled Fiber Treatment Lines:
  Pulpers: 1 at 99,700
Paper/Paperboard Grades and Capacities:
  Total paper and paperboard capacity: 96,033 mt/y
  Boxboard/cartonboard: 96,033 mt/y
Paper and Paperboard Mill Data:
  Stock Preparation:
  Pulpers: 3
  Refiners: 5
Paper Machines: 1
  No. 3, cylinder (9), total capacity 96,033 mt/y, Trim width 2.9 m, Boxboard/cartonboard
Coating Machines: 1
  No. 1, total capacity 95,000 mt/y, on machine
Finishing Equipment:
  Sheeters: 2
Energy Data:
  Power boilers: 2

ⓜTembec Inc.
Spruce Falls Mill
1 Government Rd
Kapuskasing, ON
Canada, P5N 2Y2
Mailing Address: PO Box 100, Kapuskasing, ON, Canada, P5N 2Y2
  Phone: (1) 705-337-1311
  Fax: (1) 705-337-9708
  Web Address: www.tembec.com
Personnel:
  Gen. Mgr.: André Ouimette
  Phone: (1) 705-337-1311
  Fax: (1) 705-337-9708
  Email: andre.ouimette@tembec.com
  Prod. Mgr.: Gerry Bernard
  Phone: (1) 705-337-1311
  Fax: (1) 705-337-9708
  Email: gerry.bernard@tembec.com
  Gen. Mgr Forest.: Mike Shusterman
  Phone: (1) 705-337-9784
  Fax: (1) 705-337-9785
  Email: mike.shusterman@tembec.com
  HR Mgr.: Norm Leybourne
  Phone: (1) 705-337-1311
  Fax: (1) 705-337-9708
  Email: norm.leybourne@tembec.com
Total Employees at this Location: 375
Type of Operation: Paper mill, Paper mill
Pulp Grades and Capacities:
  Total pulp capacity: 250,805 mt/y
  Mechanical Pulp: 250,805 mt/y
Pulp Mill Data:
  Mechanical Pulping Systems:
  TMP systems: 1
  TMP systems: 1
  TMP systems: 1
  Recycled Fiber Treatment Lines:
  Pulpers: 1
Paper/Paperboard Grades and Capacities:
  Total paper and paperboard capacity: 239,904 mt/y
  Newsprint: 189,924 mt/y
  Uncoated mechanical/groundwood: 49,980 mt/y
Paper and Paperboard Mill Data:
  Stock Preparation:
  Pulpers: 4
Paper Machines: 2
  No. 4, Top Flyte, total capacity 99,960 mt/y, Trim width 5.46 m, Newsprint, Uncoated mechanical/groundwood
  No. 5, Top Flyte, total capacity 139,944 mt/y, Trim width 6.24 m, Newsprint
Energy Data:
  Power boilers: 4
  TMP Reboiler: 1
  Steam turbines: 1 at 21.6 MW
  Hydro turbines at 57 MW
  Electrical demand for mill: 2,181 MWh/D

QUEBEC

ⓗCascades Inc.
Ownership: 34% by family, 58% by public, 8% by SGF Rexfor
404, rue Marie-Victorin
Kingsey Falls, QC
Canada, J0A 1B0
Mailing Address: PO Box 30, Kingsey Falls, QC, Canada
  Phone: (1) 819-363-5100
  Fax: (1) 819-363-5155
  Email: info@cascades.com
  Web Address: www.cascades.com
Personnel:
  Exec. Vice. Chmn.: Laurent Lemaire
  Phone: (1) 819-363-5113
  Fax: (1) 819-363-5166
  Dir.: Bernard Lemaire
  Phone: (1) 819-363-5112
  Fax: (1) 819-363-5166
  Email: llemaire@cascades.com
  Chmn. (May 9, 2013): Alain Lemaire
  Phone: (1) 819-363-5114
  Fax: (1) 819-363-5166
  Email: alemaire@cascades.com
  Pres. & CEO: Mario Plourde
  Phone: (1) 819-363-5133
  Fax: (1) 819-363-5155
  Email: mplourde@cascades.com
  VP. & CFO: Allan Hogg
  Phone: (1) 819-363-5100
  Fax: (1) 819-363-5155
  Email: ahogg@cascades.com
  VP, Legal Affairs & Corp. Sec.: Robert F. Hall
  Phone: (1) 819-363-5116
  Fax: (1) 819-363-5127
  Email: rhall@cascades.com
  VP, RH: Maryse Fernet
  Phone: (1) 819-363-5156
  Fax: (1) 819-363-5155
  Email: mfernet@cascades.com
  VP, IT & CIO: Dominic Doré
  Phone: (1) 450-461-8691
  Fax: (1) 450-461-8636
  Email: dominic_dore@norampac.com
  VP, Environ. Matters: Léon Marineau
  Phone: (1) 819-363-5702
  Fax: (1) 819-363-5766
  Email: leon_marineau@cascades.com
  VP, Commun. & Public Affairs: Hugo D'Amours
  Phone: (1) 819-363-5100
  Fax: (1) 819-363-5155
  Email: hugo_damours@cascades.com
  Asst. Sec.: Louise Paul
  Phone: (1) 514-282-2606
  Fax: (1) 514-282-2644
  Email: louise_paul@cascades.com
Total Employees of Company: 11,775
Total Employees at this Location: 88
Mill Locations:
Cascades Auburn Fiber, Inc., Auburn Mill, 586 Lewiston Junction Rd, Auburn, ME 04210-8847, USA, (Pulp mill)
  Phone: (1) 207-753-5300
  Fax: (1) 207-753-5333
Cascades Boxboard Group Inc., East Angus Mill, 2 Angus Nord Street, East Angus, QC, Canada J0B 1R0, Capacity: 74,970 mt/y, (Paperboard mill)
  Phone: (1) 819-832-5300
  Fax: (1) 819-832-4756
  Email: info@cascades
Cascades Boxboard Group Inc., Jonquière Mill, 4010, Chemin St-Andre, Jonquiere, QC, Canada G7S 5K5, Capacity: 144,942 mt/y, (Paperboard mill)
  Phone: (1) 418-542-9544
  Fax: (1) 418-542-5846
  Email: info@cascades.com
Cascades East Angus Inc., East Angus Mill, 248 Warner Street C.P 2000, East Angus, QC, Canada J0B 1R0, (Pulp mill, Paper mill)
  Phone: (1) 819-832-2451
  Fax: (1) 819-832-3406
  Email: info@cascades.com
Cascades SAS, La Rochette Mill, Av. Maurice Frank, F-73110 La Rochette, France, Capacity: 150,000 mt/y, (Pulp mill, Paperboard mill)
  Phone: (33) 4 79 65 32 32
  Fax: (33) 4 79 65 32 35
  Email: info@cascades-europe.com, contact@careo.biz
Cascades Lupel Inc., Trois-Rivières Mill, 700 Notre-Dame Street East C.P 23, Trois-Rivières, QC, Canada G9A 5E3, Capacity: 55,000 mt/y, (Paper mill)
  Phone: (1) 819-373-4307
  Fax: (1) 819-373-4379
  Email: lupel@cascades.com
Cascades Papier Kingsey Falls Inc., Kingsey Falls Mill, 408 Marie-Victorin Blvd., Kingsey Falls, QC, Canada J0A 1B0, Capacity: 92,820 mt/y, (Paperboard mill)
  Phone: (1) 819-363-5200
  Fax: (1) 819-363-5255
Cascades Tissue Group, Scarborough Mill, 45, Milliken Blvd., Agincourt - Scarborough, ON, Canada M1V 1V4, Capacity: 24,938 mt/y, (Paper mill)
  Phone: (1) 416 329-5200
  Fax: (1) 416 329-5234
  Email: info@cascades.com
Cascades Tissue Group, Candiac Mill, 75 Marie-Victorin Blvd, Candiac, QC, Canada J5R 1C2, Capacity: 69,956 mt/y, (Paper mill)
  Phone: (1) 450-444-6500
  Fax: (1) 450-444-0518
  Email: info@cascades.com
Cascades Tissue Group, Eau Claire Mill, 1200 Forest St, Eau Claire, WI 54703, USA, Capacity: 56,353 mt/y, (Pulp mill, Paper mill)
  Phone: (1) 715-834-3461
  Fax: (1) 715-833-3140
Cascades Tissue Group, Mechanicville Mill, 510 S Main St, Mechanicville, NY 12118, USA, Capacity: 52,467 mt/y, (Paper mill)
  Phone: (1) 518-664-8400
  Fax: (1) 518-664-7306
Cascades Tissue Group, Memphis Mill, 1535 Thomas St, Memphis, TN 38107, USA, Capacity: 41,779 mt/y, (Paper mill)
  Phone: (1) 901-523-9118
  Fax: (1) 901-526-1756
Cascades Tissue Group, Ransom Mill, 1 Main St, Ransom, PA 18653-00004, USA, Capacity: 57,001 mt/y, (Paper mill)
  Phone: (1) 570-388-6161
  Fax: (1) 570-883-4125
Cascades Tissue Group, Rockingham Mill, 805 Midway Rd, Rockingham, NC 28379, USA, Capacity: 57,001 mt/y, (Pulp mill, Paper mill)
  Phone: (1) 910-895-4033
  Fax: (1) 910-895-9887
Cascades Tissue Group, Saint Helens Mill, 1300 Kaster Rd, Saint Helens, OR 97051, USA, Capacity: 108,820 mt/y, (Paper mill)
  Phone: (1) 503-397-9372
  Fax: (1) 503-397-9440 (ofc); 9304 (shpg)
Cascades Tissue Group, Kingsey Falls Mill, 467, Marie-Victorin Blvd, Kingsey Falls, QC, Canada J0A 1B0, Capacity: 102,667 mt/y, (Paper mill)
  Phone: (1) 819-363-5600
  Fax: (1) 819-363-5655
Cascades Tissue Group, Lachute Mill, 115, Princesse Street, Lachute, QC, Canada J8H 4M3, Capacity: 38,913 mt/y, (Paper mill)
  Phone: (1) 450-562-8585

Quebec

Fax: (1) 450-562-1369
Email: info@cascades.com
Cascades Tissue Group, Whitby Mill, 1900 Thickson Road North, Whitby, ON, Canada, Capacity: 33,035 mt/y, (Paper mill)
Phone: (1) 416-329-5200
Fax: (1) 416-329-5234
Norampac, Cabano Mill, 200 Cascades Street C.P 190, Cabano, QC, Canada G0L 1E0, Capacity: 220,232 mt/y, (Pulp mill, Paperboard mill)
Phone: (1) 418-854-2803
Fax: (1) 418-854-3942
Email: cabano@norampac.com
Norampac Industries Inc., Niagara Falls Mill, 4001 Packard Rd, Niagara Falls, NY 14303, USA, Capacity: 284,682 mt/y, (Paperboard mill)
Phone: (1) 716-285-3681
Fax: (1) 716-285-3767
Email: niagarafalls_info@norampac.com
Norampac, Kingsey Falls Mill, 398, rue Marie-Victorin St, Kingsey Falls, QC, Canada J0A 1B0, Capacity: 89,064 mt/y, (Paperboard mill)
Phone: (1) 819-363-5000
Fax: (1) 819-363-5055
Email: info@norampac.com
Norampac, Mississauga Mill, 7447 Bramalea Rd, Mississauga, ON, Canada L5S 1C4, Capacity: 160,316 mt/y, (Paperboard mill)
Phone: (1) 905-671-2940
Fax: (1) 905-671-2448
Email: mississauga_info@norampac.com
Norampac, Trenton Mill, 300 Marmora St, Trenton, ON, Canada K8V 5R8, Capacity: 153,515 mt/y, (Paperboard mill)
Phone: (1) 613-392-6505
Fax: (1) 613-392-3026
Email: trentonmill@norampac.com
Reno De Medici SpA, Magenta Mill (57.60% owned), Via de Medici, 39, I-20013 Pontenuovo di Magenta, (MI), Italy, (Paperboard mill)
Phone: (39) 02 979601
Fax: (39) 02 97960323
Email: rdm.magenta@renodemedici.it, careo@pec.it
Reno De Medici SpA, Ovaro Mill (57.60% owned), Via della Cartiera 27, I-33025 Ovaro, (UD), Italy, Capacity: 110,000 mt/y, (Paperboard mill)
Phone: (39) 0433 67 241
Fax: (39) 0433 67 542
Email: info@rdmgroup.it, careo@pec.it
Reno De Medici SpA, Santa Giustina Mill (57.60% owned), Località Campo, I-32035 Santa Giustina Bellunese, (BL), Italy, Capacity: 240,000 mt/y, (Paperboard mill)
Phone: (39) 0437 8811
Fax: (39) 0437 881280
Email: rdm.santagiustina@renodemedici.it
Reno De Medici SpA, Villa Santa Lucia Mill (57.60% owned), Via Casilina Km. 134,5, I-03030 Villa Santa Lucia, (FR), Italy, Capacity: 250,000 mt/y, (Paperboard mill)
Phone: (39) 0776 37091
Fax: (39) 0776 25976
Email: rdm.vslucia@renodemedici.it, careo@pec.it

ⓘCascades Boxboard Group Inc.
Ownership: 100% by Cascades Inc.
1061, Rue Parent
St-Bruno, QC
Canada, J3V 6R7
Phone: (1) 450-461-8600
Fax: (1) 450-461-8636
Email: info@norampac.com
Web Address: www.cascades.com
Personnel:
Pres & CEO: Marc-André Dépin
Phone: (1) 450-461-8601
Fax: (1) 450-461-8636
Email: marc-andre_depin@norampac.com
VP & COO: Charles Malo
Phone: (1) 450-461-8621

Fax: (1) 450-461-8636
Email: charles_malo@norampac.com
VP, COO, Containerboard & Boxboard: Maurice Plante
Phone: (1) 450-461-8602
Fax: (1) 450-461-8636
Email: maurice_plante@norampac.com
VP, Mktg & Sustainable Dev.: Louis Lemaire
Phone: (1) 450-461-8600
Fax: (1) 450-461-8636
Email: louis_lemaire@norampac.com
Dir. Admin., Finan.: Patrick Chaperon
Phone: (1) 450-461-8641
Fax: (1) 450-461-8636
Email: patrick_champeron@norampac.com
Corp. Dir. HR: Caroline Tremblay
Phone: (1) 450-461-8600
Fax: (1) 450-461-8636
Email: caroline_tremblay@norampac.com
Total Employees at this Location: 120
Mill Locations:
Cascades Boxboard Group Inc., East Angus Mill, 2 Angus Nord Street, East Angus, QC, Canada J0B 1R0, Capacity: 74,970 mt/y, (Paperboard mill)
Phone: (1) 819-832-5300
Fax: (1) 819-832-4756
Email: info@cascades.com
Cascades Boxboard Group Inc., Jonquière Mill, 4010, Chemin St-Andre, Jonquiere, QC, Canada G7S 5K5, Capacity: 144,942 mt/y, (Paperboard mill)
Phone: (1) 418-542-9544
Fax: (1) 418-542-5846
Email: info@cascades.com
Cascades Djupafors AB, Kallinge Mill, Häggatorpsvägen 45, S-372 52 Kallinge, Sweden, Capacity: 60,000 mt/y, (Pulp mill, Paperboard mill)
Phone: (46) 457 461700
Fax: (46) 457 461710

ⓘCascades Boxboard Group Inc.
East Angus Mill
Ownership: 100% by Cascades Inc.
2 Angus Nord Street
East Angus, QC
Canada, J0B 1R0
Mailing Address: PO Box 2001, East Angus, QC, Canada, J0B 1R0
Phone: (1) 819-832-5300
Fax: (1) 819-832-4756
Email: info@cascades.com
Web Address: www.cascades.com
Personnel:
Prod. Mgr.: Carl Coulombe
Phone: (1) 819-832-5300 Ext. 5336
Fax: (1) 819-832-4756
Email: carl_coulombe@cascades.com
Total Employees at this Location: 88
Type of Operation: Paperboard mill
Pulp Grades and Capacities:
Total pulp capacity: 73,222 mt/y
Recycled Pulping: 73,222 mt/y
Pulp Mill Data:
Recycled Fiber Treatment Lines:
Recycled packaging pulping lines: 1 at 66,000
Paper/Paperboard Grades and Capacities:
Total paper and paperboard capacity: 74,970 mt/y
Boxboard/cartonboard: 74,970 mt/y
Paper and Paperboard Mill Data:
Stock Preparation:
Pulpers:
Paper Machines: 1
BM1, cylinder (7), total capacity 74,970 mt/y, Trim width 2.6 m, Boxboard/cartonboard
Coating Machines: 1
BM 1, total capacity 64,000 mt/y., on machine
Finishing Equipment:
Sheeters: 1
Energy Data:
Power boilers: 5
Electrical demand for mill: 152 MWh/D

ⓘCascades Boxboard Group Inc.
Jonquière Mill
Ownership: 100% by Cascades Inc.
4010, Chemin St-Andre
Jonquiere, QC
Canada, G7S 5K5
Mailing Address: CP 1980, Jonquiere, QC, Canada, G7S 5K5
Phone: (1) 418-542-9544
Fax: (1) 418-542-5846
Email: info@cascades.com
Web Address: www.cascades.com
Personnel:
transport, Logist., Purch. & Boiler Room Mgr.: Serge Desbiens
Phone: (1) 418-542-9544
Fax: (1) 418-542-5846
Email: serge_desbiens@cascades.com
Pulp Supervisor: Carole Gagne
Phone: (1) 418-542-9544
Fax: (1) 418-542-5846
Email: carole_gagne@cascades.com
Total Employees at this Location: 135
Type of Operation: Paperboard mill
Pulp Grades and Capacities:
Total pulp capacity: 68,581 mt/y
Mechanical Pulp: 26,482 mt/y
Recycled Pulping: 42,099 mt/y
Pulp Mill Data:
Mechanical Pulping Systems:
TMP systems: 1
Bleach Plant Systems: 1
Mechanical TMP Pulping system bleaching, Type: Softwood, Sequence: EoP
Recycled Fiber Treatment Lines:
Recycled packaging pulping lines: 1
Paper/Paperboard Grades and Capacities:
Total paper and paperboard capacity: 144,942 mt/y
Boxboard/cartonboard: 144,942 mt/y
Paper and Paperboard Mill Data:
Stock Preparation:
Pulpers: 4
Refiners: 6
Paper Machines: 1
No. 1, fourdrinier (3), total capacity 144,942 mt/y, Trim width 3.43 m, Boxboard/cartonboard
Coating Machines: 1
PM 1, total capacity 142,000 mt/y., on machine
Finishing Equipment:
Winders: 1
Rewinders: 1
Energy Data:
Power boilers: 2
Electrical demand for mill: 327 MWh/D

ⓘCascades East Angus Inc.
East Angus Mill
Mill is closed (Cascades ceased its Kraft paper manufacturing activities in East Angus on October 3, 2014)
Ownership: Cascades Inc.
248 Warner Street C.P 2000
East Angus, QC
Canada, J0B 1R0
Mailing Address: PO Box 2000, East Angus, QC, Canada, J0B 1R0
Phone: (1) 819-832-2451
Fax: (1) 819-832-3406
Email: info@cascades.com
Web Address: www.cascades.com
Personnel:
Mill Mgr.: Paul Deraiche
Phone: (1) 819-832-2451
Fax: (1) 819-832-3406
Email: paul_deraiche@cascades.com
Sls. Mgr. (will move to Kingsey Falls Eff. October 6, 2014): Yves Bienvenue
Phone: (1) 819-832-2451
Fax: (1) 819-832-3406

Quebec

Email: yves_bienvenue@cascades.com
Total Employees at this Location: 202
Type of Operation: Pulp mill, Paper mill
Pulp Mill Data:
  Chemical Pulping Systems:
  Batch digesters: 5
Pulp Lines: 1
  Chemical Recovery Equipment:
  Evaporator lines: 1
  Recovery boilers: 1
  Lime Kiln
  Recycled Fiber Treatment Lines:
  Recycled packaging pulping lines: 1 at 70,000 admt/y
Paper and Paperboard Mill Data:
  Stock Preparation:
  Pulpers: 2
  Refiners: 6
Paper Machines: 2
No. 3, fourdrinier, total capacity 47,481 mt/y, Trim width 3.69 m
No. 4, fourdrinier, total capacity 50,694 mt/y, Trim width 3.03 m
Finishing Equipment:
  Winders: 2 at 60,000 mt/y
Energy Data:
  Power boilers: 4

ⓜCascades Lupel Inc.
Trois-Rivières Mill
Ownership: Cascades Inc.
700 Notre-Dame Street East C.P 23
Trois-Rivières, QC
Canada, G9A 5E3
Mailing Address: PO Box 176, Cap-de-la-Madeleine, QC, Canada, G8T 7W2
  Phone: (1) 819-373-4307
  Fax: (1) 819-373-4379
  Email: lupel@cascades.com
  Web Address: www.cascades.com
Personnel:
  Prod. Supervisor: Julie Lafontaine
  Phone: (1) 819-373-4307
  Fax: (1) 819-373-4379
  Email: julie_lafontaine@cascades.com
  Tech. Mgr.: Normand Nadeau
  Phone: (1) 819-373-4307
  Fax: (1) 819-373-4379
  Email: normand_nadeau@cascades.com
Total Employees at this Location: 52
Type of Operation: Paper mill
Paper/Paperboard Grades and Capacities:
  Total paper and paperboard capacity: 55,000 mt/y
  Specialty and industrial: 55,000 mt/y
Paper and Paperboard Mill Data:
Paper Machines: 1
PM 1, fourdrinier, total capacity 55,000 mt/y, Trim width 3.8 m, Specialty and industrial
Coating Machines: 1
No. 1, total capacity 30,000 mt/y., on machine
Finishing Equipment:
  Winders: 1 at 50,000 mt/y
  Calenders: 1
Energy Data:
  Power boilers: 2
  Electrical demand for mill: 46 MWh/D

ⓜCascades Papier Kingsey Falls Inc.
Kingsey Falls Mill
Ownership: Cascades Inc.
408 Marie-Victorin Blvd.
Kingsey Falls, QC
Canada, J0A 1B0
Mailing Address: PO Box 150, Kingsey Falls, QC, Canada, J0A 1B0
  Phone: (1) 819-363-5200
  Fax: (1) 819-363-5255
  Web Address: www.cascades.com
Personnel:
  HR Mgr.: Isabelle Gauvreau
  Phone: (1) 819-363-5200
  Fax: (1) 819-363-5255
  Email: isabelle_gauvreau@cascades.com
Total Employees at this Location: 68
Type of Operation: Paperboard mill
Pulp Grades and Capacities:
  Total pulp capacity: 95,842 mt/y
  Recycled Pulping: 95,842 mt/y
Paper/Paperboard Grades and Capacities:
  Total paper and paperboard capacity: 92,820 mt/y
  Boxboard/cartonboard: 92,820 mt/y
Paper and Paperboard Mill Data:
  Stock Preparation:
  Pulpers: 2
  Refiners: 3
Paper Machines: 1
No. 1, cylinder (8), total capacity 92,820 mt/y, Trim width 3.35 m, Boxboard/cartonboard
Finishing Equipment:
  Calenders: 2
Energy Data:
  Power boilers
  Electrical demand for mill: 106 MWh/D

ⓜCascades Tissue Group
Ownership: 100% by Cascades Inc.
77 Marie-Victorin Blvd
Candiac, QC
Canada, J5R 1C3
  Phone: (1) 450-444-6400
  Fax: (1) 450-444-6477
  Email: info@cascades.com
  Web Address: www.afh.cascades.com
Personnel:
  COO, Pres. & CEO (Eff. August 2014): Jean Jobin
  Phone: (1) 450-444-6400
  Fax: (1) 450-444-6477
  Email: jean_jobin@cascades.com
  Snr. VP Corp. Develop. (Eff. August 2014): Suzanne Blanchet
  Phone: (1) 450-444-6400
  Fax: (1) 450-444-6477
  Email: suzanne_blanchet@cascades.com
  Exec. VP, Away-from-Home Products NA: Stéphane Rousseau
  Phone: (1) 450-444-6400
  Fax: (1) 450-444-6477
  Email: stephane_rousseau@cascades.com
  Exec. VP, Consumer Products Canada: Eric Ellyson
  Phone: (1) 450-444-6400
  Fax: (1) 450-444-6477
  Email: eric_ellyson@cascades.com
  VP Sls. Mktg.: Normand Lecours
  Phone: (1) 450-444-6403
  Fax: (1) 450-444-6477
  Email: normand_lecours@cascades.com
  Corp. Healty Safety Coord.: Jean-Francois Leblanc
  Phone: (1) 450-444-6400
  Fax: (1) 450-444-6477
  Email: jean-francois_leblanc@cascades.com
  Corp. Mgr. & HR: Sylvain Pelletier
  Phone: (1) 450-444-6406
  Fax: (1) 450-444-6477
  Email: sylvain_pelletier@cascades.com
  Dir. IT: Mario Sylvain
  Phone: (1) 450-444-6407
  Fax: (1) 450-444-6477
  Email: mario_sylvain@cascades.com
  Dir. Legal Affairs: Catherine Papineau
  Phone: (1) 450-444-6409
  Fax: (1) 450-444-6477
  Email: catherine_papineau@cascades.com
  Dir., Innovation: Nathalie Comeau
  Phone: (1) 450-444-6400
  Fax: (1) 450-444-6477
  Email: nathalie_comeau@cascades.com
Total Employees of Company: 2,200
Total Employees at this Location: 100
Mill Locations:
Cascades Tissue Group, Scarborough Mill, 45, Milliken Blvd., Agincourt - Scarborough, ON, Canada M1V 1V4, Capacity: 24,938 mt/y, (Paper mill)
  Phone: (1) 416 329-5200
  Fax: (1) 416 329-5234
  Email: info@cascades.com
Cascades Tissue Group, Candiac Mill, 75 Marie-Victorin Blvd, Candiac, QC, Canada J5R 1C2, Capacity: 69,956 mt/y, (Paper mill)
  Phone: (1) 450-444-6500
  Fax: (1) 450-444-0518
  Email: info@cascades.com
Cascades Tissue Group, Eau Claire Mill, 1200 Forest St, Eau Claire, WI 54703, USA, Capacity: 56,353 mt/y, (Pulp mill, Paper mill)
  Phone: (1) 715-834-3461
  Fax: (1) 715-833-3140
Cascades Tissue Group, Mechanicville Mill, 510 S Main St, Mechanicville, NY 12118, USA, Capacity: 52,467 mt/y, (Paper mill)
  Phone: (1) 518-664-8400
  Fax: (1) 518-664-7306
Cascades Tissue Group, Memphis Mill, 1535 Thomas St, Memphis, TN 38107, USA, Capacity: 41,779 mt/y, (Paper mill)
  Phone: (1) 901-523-9118
  Fax: (1) 901-526-1756
Cascades Tissue Group, Ransom Mill, 1 Main St, Ransom, PA 18653-00004, USA, Capacity: 57,001 mt/y, (Paper mill)
  Phone: (1) 570-388-6161
  Fax: (1) 570-883-4125
Cascades Tissue Group, Rockingham Mill, 805 Midway Rd, Rockingham, NC 28379, USA, Capacity: 57,001 mt/y, (Pulp mill, Paper mill)
  Phone: (1) 910-895-4033
  Fax: (1) 910-895-9887
Cascades Tissue Group, Saint Helens Mill, 1300 Kaster Rd, Saint Helens, OR 97051, USA, Capacity: 108,820 mt/y, (Paper mill)
  Phone: (1) 503-397-9372
  Fax: (1) 503-397-9440 (ofc); 9304 (shpg)
Cascades Tissue Group, Kingsey Falls Mill, 467, Marie-Victorin Blvd, Kingsey Falls, QC, Canada J0A 1B0, Capacity: 102,667 mt/y, (Paper mill)
  Phone: (1) 819-363-5600
  Fax: (1) 819-363-5655
Cascades Tissue Group, Lachute Mill, 115, Princesse Street, Lachute, QC, Canada J8H 4M3, Capacity: 38,913 mt/y, (Paper mill)
  Phone: (1) 450-562-8585
  Fax: (1) 450-562-1369
  Email: info@cascades.com
Cascades Tissue Group, Whitby Mill, 1900 Thickson Road North, Whitby, ON, Canada, Capacity: 33,035 mt/y, (Paper mill)
  Phone: (1) 416-329-5200
  Fax: (1) 416-329-5234

ⓜCascades Tissue Group
Candiac Mill
Ownership: 100% by Cascades Inc.
75 Marie-Victorin Blvd
Candiac, QC
Canada, J5R 1C2
  Phone: (1) 450-444-6500
  Fax: (1) 450-444-0518
  Email: info@cascades.com
  Web Address: www.afh.cascades.com
Personnel:
  VP, Oper. Efficiency: Guillaume Bouvier
  Phone: (1) 450-444-6469 Ext: 3469
  Fax: (1) 450-444-0518
  Email: guillaume_bouvier@cascades.com
  Prod. Mgr.: Benoit Rouillard
  Phone: (1) 450-444-6500
  Fax: (1) 450-444-0518
  Email: benoit_rouillard@cascades.com
Total Employees at this Location: 112
Type of Operation: Paper mill

Quebec

Pulp Grades and Capacities:
Total pulp capacity: 74,954 mt/y
Recycled Pulping: 74,954 mt/y
Pulp Mill Data:
Bleach Plant Systems: 1
DIP, Sequence: HS
Recycled Fiber Treatment Lines:
Flotation deinking lines: 1
Paper/Paperboard Grades and Capacities:
Total paper and paperboard capacity: 69,956 mt/y
Tissue: 69,956 mt/y
Paper and Paperboard Mill Data:
Stock Preparation:
Pulpers:
Paper Machines: 2
No. 1, fourdrinier, Yankee dryer, total capacity 23,319 mt/y, Trim width 3.3 m, Tissue
No. 2, ATMOS, total capacity 46,637 mt/y, Trim width 3.38 m, Tissue
Energy Data:
Power boilers: 2
Electrical demand for mill: 271 MWh/D

ⓜ Cascades Tissue Group
Kingsey Falls Mill
Ownership: 100% by Cascades Inc.
467, Marie-Victorin Blvd
Kingsey Falls, QC
Canada, J0A 1B0
Mailing Address: PO Box 210, Kingsey Falls, QC, Canada, J0A 1B0
  Phone: (1) 819-363-5600
  Fax: (1) 819-363-5655
  Web Address: www.afh.cascades.com
Personnel:
  Gen. Dir.: Paule Lavigne
  Phone: (1) 819-363-5600
  Fax: (1) 819-363-5655
  Email: paule_lavigne@cascades.com
  Prod. Supervisor: Jean-François Pion
  Phone: (1) 819-363-5608
  Fax: (1) 819-363-5655
  Email: jean-francois_pion@cascades.com
  Sls. Mgr. (Eff. October 6, 2014): Yves Bienvenue
  Phone: (1) 819-363-5600
  Fax: (1) 819-363-5655
  Email: yves_bienvenue@cascades.com
Total Employees at this Location: 150
Type of Operation: Paper mill
Pulp Grades and Capacities:
Total pulp capacity: 110,063 mt/y
Recycled Pulping: 110,063 mt/y
Pulp Mill Data:
Bleach Plant Systems: 1
Deinked Pulp Line, Sequence: PY
Recycled Fiber Treatment Lines:
Flotation deinking lines: 1
Recycled packaging pulping lines: 1
Paper/Paperboard Grades and Capacities:
Total paper and paperboard capacity: 102,667 mt/y
Tissue: 102,667 mt/y
Paper and Paperboard Mill Data:
Stock Preparation:
Pulpers: 1
Refiners: 2
Paper Machines: 3
No. 1, fourdrinier, Yankee dryer, total capacity 45,018 mt/y, Trim width 3.18 m, Tissue
No. 2, fourdrinier, Yankee dryer, total capacity 23,319 mt/y, Trim width 3.18 m, Tissue
No. 3, fourdrinier, Yankee dryer, total capacity 34,330 mt/y, Trim width 3.18 m, Tissue
Energy Data:
Combustion turbines: 1 at 31 MW
Electrical demand for mill: 416 MWh/D

ⓜ Cascades Tissue Group
Lachute Mill
Ownership: 100% by Cascades Inc.
115, Princesse Street
Lachute, QC
Canada, J8H 4M3
  Phone: (1) 450-562-8585
  Fax: (1) 450-562-1369
  Email: info@cascades.com
  Web Address: www.afh.cascades.com
Personnel:
  Mill Mgr.: Régis Arsenault
  Phone: (1) 450-566-2501, 514-978-3962 (M)
  Fax: (1) 450-562-1369
  Email: regis_arsenault@cascades.com
  Gen. Mgr. Cascades SPG - Industial Packaging: Martin Caya
  Phone: (1) 450-562-8585
  Fax: (1) 450-562-1369
  Email: martin_caya@cascades.com
  Prod. Mgr.: Alain Labelle
  Phone: (1) 450-566-2501
  Fax: (1) 450-562-1369
  Email: alain_labelle@cascades.com
Total Employees at this Location: 58
Type of Operation: Paper mill
Pulp Grades and Capacities:
Total pulp capacity: 41,479 mt/y
Recycled Pulping: 41,479 mt/y
Pulp Mill Data:
Recycled Fiber Treatment Lines:
Recycled packaging pulping lines: 1 at 41,300
Paper/Paperboard Grades and Capacities:
Total paper and paperboard capacity: 38,913 mt/y
Tissue: 38,913 mt/y
Paper and Paperboard Mill Data:
Paper Machines: 1
No. 5, fourdrinier, total capacity 38,913 mt/y, Trim width 3.05 m, Tissue
Finishing Equipment:
Rewinders: 1
Energy Data:
Power boilers: 1
Electrical demand for mill: 84 MWh/D

ⓘ Domtar Corporation
Ownership: 100% by the public
395 de Maisonneuve Blvd. West
Montreal, QC
Canada, H3A 1L6
  Phone: (1) 514-848-5555
  Fax: (1) 514-848-6850
  Email: information@domtar.com
  Web Address: www.domtar.com
Personnel:
  Chmn.: Harold Mackay
  Phone: (1) 514-848-5555
  Fax: (1) 514-848-6850
  Email: harold.mackay@domtar.com
  Pres. & CEO: John D. Williams
  Phone: (1) 514-848-5533
  Fax: (1) 514-848-6850
  Email: john.williams@domtar.com
  Pres., Pulp and Paper (Eff. May 1, 2014): Michael D. Garcia
  Phone: (1) 514-848-5555
  Fax: (1) 514-848-6850
  Snr. VP, HR: Melissa Anderson
  Phone: (1) 514-848-5555
  Fax: (1) 514-848-6850
  Email: melissa.anderson@domtar.com
  Snr. VP & CFO: Daniel Buron
  Phone: (1) 514-848-5555
  Fax: (1) 514-848-6850
  Email: daniel.buron@domtar.com
  Snr. VP, Sls. & Mktg.: Richard L. Thomas
  Phone: (1) 514-848-5555
  Fax: (1) 514-848-6850
  Email: richard.thomas@domtar.com
  Snr. VP, Personnel Care: Michael Fagan
  Phone: (1) 514-848-5555
  Fax: (1) 514-848-5638
  Email: michael.fagan@domtar.com
  Snr. VP, Law & Corp. Affairs: Zygmunt Jablonski
  Phone: (1) 514-848-5555
  Fax: (1) 514-848-5638
  Email: zygmunt.jablonski@domtar.com
  Snr. VP, Corp. Develop.: Patrick Loulou
  Phone: (1) 514-848-5555
  Fax: (1) 514-848-5638
  Mgr., Investor Rel.: Nicholas Estrela
  Phone: (1) 514-848-5555
  Fax: (1) 514-848-5638
  Email: nicholas.estrela@domtar.com
Total Employees of Company: 9,400
Mill Locations:
  Domtar Corporation, Ashdown Mill, 285 Hwy 71 South, Ashdown, AR 71822, USA, Capacity: 696,168 mt/y, (Pulp mill, Paper mill)
  Phone: (1) 870-898-2711
  Fax: (1) 870-898-4724
  Domtar Corporation, Dryden Mill, 1 Duke St., Dryden, ON, Canada P8N 3J7, (Pulp mill)
  Phone: (1) 807-223-2323
  Fax: (1) 807-223-9317
  Domtar Corporation, Espanola Mill, 1 Station Rd, Espanola, ON, Canada P5E 1R6, Capacity: 69,617 mt/y, (Pulp mill, Paper mill)
  Phone: (1) 705-869-2020, 705-869-2035
  Fax: (1) 705-869-5753, 705-869-5494
  Domtar Corporation, Hawesville Mill, Hwy. 1406, 58 Wescor Road, Hawesville, KY 42348, USA, Capacity: 518,078 mt/y, (Pulp mill, Paper mill)
  Phone: (1) 270-927-6961
  Fax: (1) 270-927-9929
  Domtar Corporation, Johnsonburg Mill, 100 Center St, Johnsonburg, PA 15845, USA, Capacity: 322,180 mt/y, (Pulp mill, Paper mill)
  Phone: (1) 814-965-2521, 800-458-4640
  Fax: (1) 814-965-6231
  Domtar Corporation, Kamloops Mill, 2005 Mission Flats Rd, Kamloops, BC, Canada V2C 1A9, (Pulp mill)
  Phone: (1) 250-434-6000
  Fax: (1) 250-434-8877
  Domtar Corporation, Kingsport Mill, 100 Clinchfield St, Kingsport, TN 37660, USA, Capacity: 375,607 mt/y, (Pulp mill, Paper mill)
  Phone: (1) 423-247-7111
  Fax: (1) 423-392-2719
  Domtar Corporation, Marlboro Mill, 585 Willamette Road, Bennettsville, SC 29512, USA, Capacity: 318,294 mt/y, (Pulp mill, Paper mill)
  Phone: (1) 843-479-0200
  Fax: (1) 843-479-0608
  Domtar Corporation, Nekoosa Mill, 301 Point Basse Ave, Nekoosa, WI 54457-1422, USA, Capacity: 135,996 mt/y, (Paper mill)
  Phone: (1) 715-886-7076/715-886-7111
  Fax: (1) 715-886-7620
  Domtar Corporation, Plymouth Mill, Highway 149, Plymouth, NC 27962, USA, (Pulp mill, Paper mill)
  Phone: (1) 252-793-8111
  Fax: (1) 252-793-8164
  Domtar Corporation, Port Huron Mill, 1700 Washington Ave., Port Huron, MI 48060, USA, Capacity: 101,997 mt/y, (Paper mill)
  Phone: (1) 810-982-0191
  Fax: (1) 810-982-7124
  Domtar Corporation, Rothschild Mill, 200 N Grand Ave, Rothschild, WI 54474-1197, USA, Capacity: 123,044 mt/y, (Pulp mill, Paper mill)
  Phone: (1) 715-359-3101
  Fax: (1) 715-355-6347
  Domtar Corporation, Windsor Mill, 609, Rang 12, Windsor, QC, Canada J1S 2L9, Capacity: 589,314 mt/y, (Pulp mill, Paper mill)
  Phone: (1) 819-845-2771
  Fax: (1) 819-845-8230/8398
  Email: (firstname.lastname@domtar.com)

ⓜ Domtar Corporation
Windsor Mill
609, Rang 12
Windsor, QC

Quebec

Canada, J1S 2L9
Mailing Address: PO Box 1010, Windsor, QC, Canada, J1S 2L9
 Phone: (1) 819-845-2771
 Fax: (1) 819-845-8230/8398
 Email: (firstname.lastname@domtar.com)
 Web Address: www.domtar.com
Personnel:
 Mill Mgr.: Eric Ashby
 Phone: (1) 819-845-2771
 Fax: (1) 819-845-8230
 Email: eric.ashby@domtar.com
 IT Mgr.: Sylvie Veilleux-Fontaine
 Phone: (1) 819-845-2771
 Fax: (1) 819-845-8230
 Email: sylvie.fontaine@domtar.com
Total Employees at this Location: 675
Type of Operation: Pulp mill, Paper mill
Pulp Grades and Capacities:
 Total pulp capacity: 412,993 mt/y
 Pulp available for market: 39,270 mt/y
 Chemical Pulp: 412,993 mt/y
Pulp Mill Data:
 Chemical Pulping Systems:
 Continuous digesters: 1
Pulp Lines: 1
 Bleach Plant Systems: 1
 Chemical Pulping System, Type: Hardwood, Sequence: DEopD
 Chemical Recovery Equipment:
 Evaporator lines: 1
 Recovery boilers: 1
 Lime Kiln
 Pulp Dryers:
 Wet Lap machine 1
Paper/Paperboard Grades and Capacities:
 Total paper and paperboard capacity: 589,314 mt/y
 Uncoated woodfree/freesheet: 589,314 mt/y
Paper and Paperboard Mill Data:
 Stock Preparation:
 Pulpers:
Paper Machines: 2
 No. 7, Bel-Baie III, total capacity 297,895 mt/y, Trim width 7.62 m, Uncoated woodfree/freesheet
 No. 8, Bel-Baie III, total capacity 291,419 mt/y, Trim width 7.62 m, Uncoated woodfree/freesheet
 Finishing Equipment:
 Sheeters: 4
Energy Data:
 Power boilers: 3
 Steam turbines: 1 at 32 MW
 Electrical demand for mill: 1,831 MWh/D

ⓗⓜF.F. Soucy SEC
Riviere du Loup Mill
Ownership: 100% by White Birch Paper Company
191 Delage St
Riviere du Loup, QC
Canada, G5R 3Z1
Mailing Address: PO Box 490, Riviere du Loup, QC, Canada, G5R 3Z1
 Phone: (1) 418-862-6941
 Fax: (1) 418-867-1134
 Web Address: www.whitebirchpaper.com
Personnel:
 HR. Mgr.: Michel Beaumont
 Phone: (1) 418-862-6941 Ext. 2263
 Fax: (1) 418-867-1134
 Email: michelbeaumont@ff.papierswhitebirch.com
 Contr.: Daniel Bérubé
 Phone: (1) 418-862-6941 Ext. 2819
 Fax: (1) 418-867-1134
 Email: danielberube@ff.papierswhitebirch.com
Total Employees of Company: 280
Total Employees at this Location: 280
Type of Operation: Paper mill
Pulp Grades and Capacities:
 Total pulp capacity: 270,887 mt/y
 Mechanical Pulp: 270,887 mt/y

Pulp Mill Data:
 Mechanical Pulping Systems:
 TMP systems: 4
 Bleach Plant Systems: 1
 Mechanical TMP Pulping System - 1, Type: Sodium hydroxide + hydrogen peroxide tower - Softwood, Sequence: P, Capacity 270,000 admt/y
Paper/Paperboard Grades and Capacities:
 Total paper and paperboard capacity: 265,965 mt/y
 Newsprint: 194,565 mt/y
 Uncoated mechanical/groundwood: 71,400 mt/y
Paper and Paperboard Mill Data:
 Stock Preparation:
 Pulpers: 1
 Refiners: 4
Paper Machines: 2
 No. 1, Dynaformer, total capacity 89,250 mt/y, Trim width 3.53 m, Newsprint, Uncoated mechanical/groundwood
 No. 2N, SymFormer, total capacity 176,715 mt/y, Trim width 6.05 m, Newsprint
 Finishing Equipment:
 Rewinders: 1
Energy Data:
 Power boilers: 2
 TMP Reboiler: 1

ⓜFortress Global Cellulose Ltd
Lebel-sur-Quevillon Mill
Mill is closed (stopped production in 2005, halted permanently in 2008. Evaluating expanding its dissolving pulp capacity by converting into a dissolving pulp mill and re-starting the cogeneration facility in 2015.)
Ownership: Fortress Paper Ltd.
30 Chemin du Moulin
Lebel-sur-Quevillon, QC
Canada, J0Y 1X0
Mailing Address: PO Box 3000, Lebel-sur-Quevillon, QC, Canada, J0Y 1X0
 Phone: (1) 819-755-2124
 Fax: (1) 819-755-2125
 Web Address: www.domtar.com
Type of Operation: Pulp mill
Pulp Mill Data:
Pulp Lines: 1
 Bleach Plant Systems: 1
 No. 1, Sequence: D/CEoWDED
 Chemical Recovery Equipment:
 Evaporator lines: 6
 Recovery boilers: 1
 Lime Kiln
 Pulp Dryers:
 Air Float dryers 1
Energy Data:
 Power boilers: 1

ⓗⓜFortress Specialty Cellulose Inc.
Thurso Mill
Ownership: Fortress Paper Ltd.
Hwy 148 E
Thurso, QC
Canada, J0X 3B0
Mailing Address: PO Box 400, Thurso, QC, Canada, J0X 3B0
 Phone: (1) 819-985-2233
 Fax: (1) 819-985-5023
 Email: info@fortresspaper.com, info@specialtycellulose.com
 Web Address: www.thefortressgroup.ca, www.fortresspaper.com, www.specialtycellulose.com
Personnel:
 CEO Fortress Paper Ltd.: Chad Wasilenkoff
 Phone: (1) 819-985-2328
 Fax: (1) 819-985-5023
 Email: chadw@fortresspaper.com cwasilenkoff@fortresspaper.com

 CFO Fortress Paper Ltd.: Kurt Loewen
 Phone: (1) 819-985-2233
 Fax: (1) 819-985-5023
 Email: kloewen@fortresspaper.com
 COO Fortress Paper Ltd.: Alain Dubuc
 Phone: (1) 819-985-2233
 Fax: (1) 819-985-5023
 Email: alain.dubuc@fortresscell.com
 VP, Bus. Develop. & Strat. Proj. Fortress Paper Ltd.: Marco Veilleux
 Phone: (1) 819-985-2233
 Fax: (1) 819-985-5023
 Email: mveilleux@fortresspaper.com
 VP., Tech. Devpt.: Vincent Byrne
 Phone: (1) 819-985-2233
 Fax: (1) 819-985-5023
 Email: vince.byrne@fortresscell.com
 Eng. Mgr.: Adam Roy
 Phone: (1) 819-985-2233
 Fax: (1) 819-985-5023
 Email: adam.roy@fortresscell.com
 Store & Purch. Mgr. (From January 2013): Patrick Roy
 Phone: (1) 819-985-2233
 Fax: (1) 819-985-5032
 Email: Patrick.Roy@fortresscell.com
Total Employees of Company: 300
Total Employees at this Location: 320
Type of Operation: Pulp mill
Pulp Grades and Capacities:
 Total pulp capacity: 237,996 mt/y
 Pulp available for market: 224,910 mt/y
 Chemical Pulp: 237,996 mt/y
Pulp Mill Data:
 Chemical Pulping Systems:
 Batch digesters: 3
Pulp Lines: 2
 Bleach Plant Systems: 1
 Chemical Pulping System - 1, Type: Hardwood, Sequence: DEopDED, Capacity 245,000 admt/y
 Chemical Recovery Equipment:
 Evaporator lines: 1
 Recovery boilers: 2
 Lime Kiln
 Pulp Dryers:
 Air Float dryers 1, Fourdriniers 1
Energy Data:
 Power boilers: 2
 Steam turbines: 1 at 24 MW
 Electrical demand for mill: 626 MWh/D

ⓗⓜGlassine Canada Inc.
Quebec City Mill
Ownership: Simkins Industries Inc.
1245 Boulevard Montmorency
Quebec City, QC
Canada, G1J 5L6
 Phone: (1) 418-522-8262
 Fax: (1) 418-648-2725
 Email: sales@glassinecanada.qc.ca, customerservice@glassinecanada.qc.ca
 Web Address: www.simkinsindustries.com, www.glassinecanada.qc.ca
Personnel:
 CEO : Claude Jean
 Phone: (1) 418-522-8262 Ext: 206
 Fax: (1) 418-648-2725
 Email: cjean@glassinecanada.qc.ca
 Pres. & Sls. Mgr.: Ronald Hermus
 Phone: (1) 418-522-8262
 Fax: (1) 418-648-2725
 Email: sales@glassinecanada.qc.ca
 Contr.: Sylvie Paradis
 Phone: (1) 418-522-8262
 Fax: (1) 418-648-2725
 Email: sparadis@glassinecanada.qc.ca
 Tech. Serv. Supt.: Denis Dumont
 Phone: (1) 418-522-8262
 Fax: (1) 418-648-2725
 Email: d.dumont@glassinecanada.qc.ca
Total Employees at this Location: 55

Quebec

Type of Operation: Paper mill
Paper/Paperboard Grades and Capacities:
 Total paper and paperboard capacity: 12,495 mt/y
 Specialty and industrial: 12,495 mt/y
Paper and Paperboard Mill Data:
 Stock Preparation:
 Pulpers: 1
 Refiners: 7
Paper Machines: 1
 No. 1, fourdrinier, total capacity 14,280 mt/y, Trim width 3 m, Specialty and industrial
Finishing Equipment:
 Supercalenders: 1
 Rewinders: 3
Energy Data:
 Power boilers

Ⓜ Kruger Inc.
Ownership: 100% by Kruger Family (Private)
3285, Chemin Bedford
Montreal, QC
Canada, H3S 1G5
 Phone: (1) 514-737-1131
 Fax: (1) 514-343-3124
 Web Address: www.kruger.com
Personnel:
Chmn. & CEO: Joseph Kruger II
 Phone: (1) 514-737-1131
 Fax: (1) 514-343-3124
 Email: jkruger@kruger.com
Exec. VP. & COO: Daniel Archambault
 Phone: (1) 514-737-1131
 Fax: (1) 514-343-3124
 Email: daniel.archambault@kruger.com
Counselor - Advisor: Pierre Duhamel
 Phone: (1) 514-737-1131
 Fax: (1) 514-343-3124
 Email: pierre.duhamel@kruger.com
Snr. VP., Containerboard/Packaging & Recycling: Michael (Mike) Lafave
 Phone: (1) 514-737-1131
 Fax: (1) 514-343-3124
 Email: michael.lafave@kruger.com
Snr. VP. & COO Kruger Energy: Jean Roy
 Phone: (1) 514-737-1131
 Fax: (1) 514-343-3124
 Email: jean.roy@kruger.com
Snr. VP., Corp Affairs & Commun.: Jean Majeau
 Phone: 1 514-343-3213
 Fax: (1) 514-343-3124
 Email: jean.majeau@kruger.com
VP., Major Projects: Jean-Yves Ouellet
 Phone: (1) 514-737-1131
 Fax: (1) 514-343-3124
 Email: jean-yves.ouellet@kruger.com
Gen. Mgr., Corp Affairs & Commun.: Chantal Chamberland
 Phone: (1) 514-343-3100 x2028
 Fax: (1) 514-343-3124
 Email: chantal.chamberland@kruger.com
Total Employees of Company: 10,000
Total Employees at this Location: 185
Mill Locations:
Papelera Inka S.A., Chincha Baja Mill (50% owned), Predio San Roque N° 2, Chincha Baja, Chincha, Peru, Capacity: 8,000 mt/y, (Paper mill)
 Phone: (51) 56 272178 /272179
 Email: ettyr@incachin.com.pe, Raul.Villavicencio@papelerainka.com.pe
Papelera Istmeña, S.A., El Dorado Mill, Apdo. 0819-08589, El Dorado, Panama, Panama, Capacity: 21,063 mt/y, (Paper mill)
 Phone: (507) 236 1611
 Fax: (507) 236 1479
 Email: lhoyos@papisa.com
Kruger Inc., Corner Brook Mill, Mill Road, Corner Brook, NF, Canada A2H 6J4, Capacity: 255,255 mt/y, (Pulp mill, Paper mill)
 Phone: (1) 709-637-3000
 Fax: (1) 709-637-3469
 Email: (firstinitiallastname@cb.kruger.com)
Kruger Inc., Bromptonville Mill, 220 Route Windsor, Sherbrooke, QC, Canada J1C 0E6, Capacity: 296,310 mt/y, (Pulp mill, Paper mill)
 Phone: (1) 819-846-2721
 Fax: (1) 819-846-8102
Kruger Inc., Place Turcot Mill, 5845 Place Turcot, Montreal, QC, Canada H4C 1V9, Capacity: 153,867 mt/y, (Paperboard mill)
 Phone: (1) 514-934-0600, 514-934-0845
 Fax: (1) 514-934-4972, 514-934-5458, 514-934-1377, 514-934-2300
 Email: imaceachen@pb.kruger.com
Kruger Inc., Trois-Rivières Mill, 3735 Gene H. Kruger Blvd, Trois-Rivières, QC, Canada G9A 6B1, Capacity: 381,990 mt/y, (Paper mill)
 Phone: (1) 819-375-1691
 Fax: (1) 819-375-3163
 Email: (firstinitiallastname@kruger.com)
K.T.G. (USA) L.P., Memphis Mill, 400 Mahannah Ave., Memphis, TN 38107-1021, USA, Capacity: 116,917 mt/y, (Paper mill)
 Phone: (1) 901-260-3900
 Fax: (1) 901-260-3910
Kruger Products L.P., Crabtree Mill (83.10% owned), 100, 1st Avenue, Crabtree, QC, Canada J0K 1B0, Capacity: 72,871 mt/y, (Pulp mill, Paper mill)
 Phone: (1) 450-754-2855
 Fax: (1) 450-754-4556
Kruger Products L.P., Gatineau Mill (83.10% owned), 20 Laurier Street, Gatineau, QC, Canada J8X 4H3, Capacity: 91,008 mt/y, (Paper mill)
 Phone: (1) 819-595-5302
 Fax: (1) 819-595-5396
Kruger Products L.P., New Westminster Mill (83.10% owned), 1625 Fifth Ave., New Westminster, BC, Canada V3M 1Z7, Capacity: 57,973 mt/y, (Pulp mill, Paper mill)
 Phone: (1) 604-522-5711
 Fax: (1) 604-520-9200
Kruger Products L.P., Lennoxville Mill (83.10% owned), 2888 College St, Sherbrooke, QC, Canada J1M 1Z4, Capacity: 23,966 mt/y, (Paper mill)
 Phone: (1) 819-565-8220
 Fax: (1) 819-566-0245
Kruger Wayagamack Inc., Trois Rivierès (Wayagamack) Mill (51% owned), PO Box 128, Trois-Rivières, QC, Canada G9A 5E9, Capacity: 253,470 mt/y, (Pulp mill, Paper mill)
 Phone: (1) 819-373-9230
 Fax: (1) 819-373-9398
Papeles Nacionales S.A., Pereira Mill (99.50% owned), Paraje La Marina, Via Cartago, Puente Bolivar, Pereira, Colombia, Capacity: 71,043 mt/y, (Paper mill)
 Phone: (57) 2 2147500
 Fax: (57) 2 2111014
 Email: servicio.cliente@papelesnacionales.com
Papeles Venezolanos CA (PAVECA), Guacara Mill, Carretera Nacional Guacara San Joaquín, Kilómetro 1, Aptdo. 003, 2201 Guacara, Venezuela, Capacity: 102,816 mt/y, (Pulp mill, Paper mill)
 Phone: (58) 245 400 3430/3280
 Fax: (58) 245 400 3601/3643
 Email: info@paveca.com, paveca@paveca.com

Ⓜ Kruger Inc.
Bromptonville Mill
220 Route Windsor
Sherbrooke, QC
Canada, J1C 0E6
Mailing Address: PO Box 100, Bromptonville, QC, Canada, J0B 1H0
 Phone: (1) 819-846-2721
 Fax: (1) 819-846-8102
 Web Address: www.kruger.ca
Personnel:
Gen. Mgr. (From September 2013): Jean Descoteaux
 Phone: (1) 819-846-2721
 Fax: (1) 819-846-8102
 Email: jean.descoteaux@kruger.com
Finan. Dir.: Gilles Daigneault
 Phone: (1) 819-846-2721
 Fax: (1) 819-846-8102
 Email: gilles.daigneault@kruger.com
HR Mgr.: Vincent Nadeau
 Phone: (1) 819-846-2721
 Fax: (1) 819-846-8102
 Email: vincent.nadeau@kruger.com
Project Mgr.: Giuseppfe Ruscigno
 Phone: (1) 819-846-2721
 Fax: (1) 819-846-8102
 Email: gruscigno@br.kruger.com
Environ. Coord.: Rene Hamel
 Phone: (1) 819-846-2721 Ext: 262
 Fax: (1) 819-846-8102
 Email: rhamel@br.kruger.com
Project Eng.: Alain Gaudet
 Phone: (1) 819-846-2721
 Fax: (1) 819-846-8102
 Email: agaudet@br.kruger.com
Process Eng.: Andre Croteau
 Phone: (1) 819-846-2721
 Fax: (1) 819-846-8102
 Email: acroteau@br.kruger.com
Total Employees at this Location: 375
Type of Operation: Pulp mill, Paper mill
Pulp Grades and Capacities:
 Total pulp capacity: 300,701 mt/y
 Mechanical Pulp: 182,319 mt/y
 Recycled Pulping: 118,381 mt/y
Pulp Mill Data:
 Mechanical Pulping Systems:
 TMP systems: 2
 Bleach Plant Lines:
 TMP, Type: Virchem Capacity 200,000 admt/y
 Recycled Fiber Treatment Lines:
 Flotation deinking lines: 2
 Pulpers: 1
Paper/Paperboard Grades and Capacities:
 Total paper and paperboard capacity: 296,310 mt/y
 Newsprint: 296,310 mt/y
Paper and Paperboard Mill Data:
Paper Machines: 3
 No. 1, Dynaformer, total capacity 93,891 mt/y, Trim width 3.76 m, Newsprint
 No. 2, Papriformer, total capacity 100,674 mt/y, Trim width 3.95 m, Newsprint
 No. 3, Bel-Baie II, total capacity 101,745 mt/y, Trim width 3.83 m, Newsprint
Energy Data:
 TMP Reboiler: 2
 Steam turbines: 1 at 23 MW
 Hydro turbines at 7.7 MW
 Electrical demand for mill: 1,966 MWh/D

Ⓜ Kruger Inc.
Place Turcot Mill
5845 Place Turcot
Montreal, QC
Canada, H4C 1V9
 Phone: (1) 514-934-0600, 514-934-0845
 Fax: (1) 514-934-4972, 514-934-5458, 514-934-1377, 514-934-2300
 Email: imaceachen@pb.kruger.com
 Web Address: www.krupack.com
Personnel:
Mill Mgr.: Benoit Painchaud
 Phone: (1) 514-934-0600 Ext. 377
 Fax: (1) 514-934-4972
 Email: benoit.painchaud@kruger.com
Gen. Sls. Mgr.: Serge Desgagnés
 Phone: (1) 514-934-0600 ext. 289
 Fax: (1) 514-934-1277
 Email: serge.desgagnes@kruger.com
Sls Mgr. USA: François Asselin
 Phone: (1) 514-934-0600 ext. 274
 Fax: (1) 514-934-1277
 Email: francois.asselin@kruger.com
Prod. Superint. (From May 2014): Anish Patel
 Phone: (1) 514-934-0600
 Fax: (1) 514-934-4972

Quebec

Email: anish.patel@kruger.com
Electric Supt.: Andre Dulude
Phone: (1) 514-934-0600
Fax: (1) 514-934-4972
Email: adulude@pb.kruger.com
Total Employees at this Location: 146
Type of Operation: Paperboard mill
Pulp Grades and Capacities:
 Total pulp capacity: 160,199 mt/y
 Recycled Pulping: 160,199 mt/y
Pulp Mill Data:
 Recycled Fiber Treatment Lines:
 Recycled packaging pulping lines: 2
Paper/Paperboard Grades and Capacities:
 Total paper and paperboard capacity: 153,867 mt/y
 Linerboard: 153,867 mt/y
Paper and Paperboard Mill Data:
 Stock Preparation:
 Pulpers: 2
 Refiners: 1
Paper Machines: 1
 No. 1, cylinder (6), total capacity 153,867 mt/y, Trim width 3.81 m, Linerboard
Finishing Equipment:
 Winders: 1 at 161,000 mt/y
 Calenders: 2
 Rewinders: 1
Energy Data:
 Power boilers: 3

ⓜKruger Inc.
Trois-Rivières Mill
3735 Gene H. Kruger Blvd
Trois-Rivières, QC
Canada, G9A 6B1
Mailing Address: PO Box 188, Trois-Rivières, QC, Canada, G9A 5P6
 Phone: (1) 819-375-1691
 Fax: (1) 819-375-3163
 Email: (firstinitiallastname@kruger.com)
 Web Address: www.kruger.com
Personnel:
 Mill Mgr.: Jean-Francois Guillot
 Phone: (1) 819-375-1691
 Fax: (1) 819-375-3163
 Email: jfguillot@tr.kruger.com
 Maint., Eng. & Supply Dir. (From March 2013): Gaétan Turner
 Phone: (1) 819-375-1695
 Fax: (1) 819-375-3163
 Email: gaetan.turner@kruger.com
 Process Eng.: Steve Carpentier
 Phone: (1) 819-375-1695
 Fax: (1) 819-375-3163
 Email: scarpentier@tr.kruger.com
Total Employees at this Location: 325
Type of Operation: Paper mill
Pulp Grades and Capacities:
 Total pulp capacity: 387,497 mt/y
 Mechanical Pulp: 387,497 mt/y
Pulp Mill Data:
 Mechanical Pulping Systems:
 Conventional grinders: 28
 TMP systems: 5
 Bleach Plant Systems: 2
 Mechanical SGW Pulping System
 Mechanical TMP Pulping System, Sequence: PY
Paper/Paperboard Grades and Capacities:
 Total paper and paperboard capacity: 381,990 mt/y
 Newsprint: 381,990 mt/y
Paper and Paperboard Mill Data:
 Stock Preparation:
 Pulpers:
Paper Machines: 2
 No. 7, twin-wire, total capacity 155,295 mt/y, Trim width 6.09 m, Newsprint
 No. 10, Bel-Baie II, total capacity 226,695 mt/y, Trim width 7.68 m, Newsprint
Coating Machines: 2
 #8, off machine
 #9, off machine
Finishing Equipment:
 Supercalenders: 7
 Rewinders: 2
Energy Data:
 Power boilers: 6

ⓜKruger Products L.P.
Crabtree Mill
Ownership: 83.10% by Kruger Inc.
100, 1st Avenue
Crabtree, QC
Canada, J0K 1B0
Mailing Address: P.O Box 500, Crabtree, QC, Canada, J0K 1B0
 Phone: (1) 450-754-2855
 Fax: (1) 450-754-4556
 Web Address: www.krugerproducts.ca
Personnel:
 Gen. Mgr. East Region (Crabtree, Gatineau, Sherbrooke) (From July 2013): Daniel Dumont
 Phone: (1) 450-754-2855
 Fax: (1) 450-754-4556
 Email: daniel.dumont@krugerproducts.ca
 Converting Mgr.: Eric Leblanc
 Phone: (1) 450-754-2855
 Fax: (1) 450-754-4556
 Email: eric.leblanc@krugerproducts.ca
 Dir. Eng. East Region (Crabtree, Gatineau, Sherbrooke): Pierre Prudhomme
 Phone: (1) 450-754-2855
 Fax: (1) 450-754-4556
 Email: pierre.prudhomme@krugerproducts.ca
Total Employees at this Location: 319
Type of Operation: Pulp mill, Paper mill
Pulp Grades and Capacities:
 Total pulp capacity: 95,442 mt/y
 Pulp available for market: 35,700 mt/y
 Recycled Pulping: 95,442 mt/y
Pulp Mill Data:
 Bleach Plant Systems: 1
 No. 1, Sequence: P
 Recycled Fiber Treatment Lines:
 Flotation deinking lines: 1
 Pulp Dryers:
 Wet Lap machine 1
Paper/Paperboard Grades and Capacities:
 Total paper and paperboard capacity: 72,871 mt/y
 Tissue: 72,871 mt/y
Paper and Paperboard Mill Data:
 Stock Preparation:
 Pulpers:
Paper Machines: 4
 No. 2, crescent former, total capacity 13,603 mt/y, Trim width 2.29 m, Tissue
 No. 3, crescent former, total capacity 11,659 mt/y, Trim width 2.29 m, Tissue
 No. 4, crescent former, total capacity 18,137 mt/y, Trim width 2.29 m, Tissue
 No. 6, crescent former, total capacity 29,472 mt/y, Trim width 2.29 m, Tissue
Energy Data:
 Power boilers: 3
 Electrical demand for mill: 300 MWh/D

ⓜKruger Products L.P.
Gatineau Mill
Ownership: 83.10% by Kruger Inc.
20 Laurier Street
Gatineau, QC
Canada, J8X 4H3
Mailing Address: PO Box 3200, Station B, Gatineau, QC, Canada, J8X 4H3
 Phone: (1) 819-595-5302
 Fax: (1) 819-595-5396
 Web Address: www.krugerproducts.ca
Personnel:
 Gen. Mgr. East Region (Gatineau, Crabtree, Sherbrooke) (From July 2013): Daniel Dumont
 Email: daniel.dumont@krugerproducts.ca
 Purch. & Stores Supervisor: Jason Larouche CSCMP
 Phone: (1) 819-595-5346
 Fax: (1) 819-595-5360
 Email: jason.larouche@krugerproducts.ca
 Proj. Mgr. & Electrical Eng.: Martin Levesque
 Phone: (1) 819-595-5346
 Fax: (1) 819-595-5360
 Email: martin.levesque@krugerproducts.ca
Total Employees at this Location: 174
Type of Operation: Paper mill
Paper/Paperboard Grades and Capacities:
 Total paper and paperboard capacity: 91,008 mt/y
 Tissue: 91,008 mt/y
Paper and Paperboard Mill Data:
 Stock Preparation:
 Pulpers:
Paper Machines: 3
 No. 3, TAD, total capacity 32,387 mt/y, Trim width 3.56 m, Tissue
 No. 4, crescent former, Yankee dryer, total capacity 28,824 mt/y, Trim width 3.56 m, Tissue
 No. 5, crescent former, Yankee dryer, total capacity 29,796 mt/y, Trim width 3.56 m, Tissue
Energy Data:
 Electrical demand for mill: 302 MWh/D

ⓜKruger Products L.P.
Lennoxville Mill
Ownership: 83.10% by Kruger Inc.
2888 College St
Sherbrooke, QC
Canada, J1M 1Z4
Mailing Address: PO Box 240, Lennoxville, QC, Canada, J1M 1Z4
 Phone: (1) 819-565-8220
 Fax: (1) 819-566-0245
 Web Address: www.krugerproducts.ca
Personnel:
 Gen. Mgr. East Region (Sherbrooke, Crabtree, Gatineau): Daniel Dumont
 Email: daniel.dumont@krugerproducts.ca
 Prod. Mgr.: Patrice Begin
 Phone: (1) 819-565-8220
 Fax: (1) 819-566-0245
 Email: patrice.begin@krugerproducts.ca
 Process Eng.: Jean Theberge
 Phone: (1) 819-565-8220
 Fax: (1) 819-566-0245
 Email: jean.theberge@krugerproducts.ca
 Maint. Mgr.: Denis Singher
 Phone: (1) 819-565-8220
 Fax: (1) 819-566-0245
 Email: denis.singher@krugerproducts.ca
Total Employees at this Location: 50
Type of Operation: Paper mill
Paper/Paperboard Grades and Capacities:
 Total paper and paperboard capacity: 23,966 mt/y
 Tissue: 23,966 mt/y
Paper and Paperboard Mill Data:
 Stock Preparation:
 Pulpers:
Paper Machines: 1
 No. 5, crescent former, Yankee dryer, total capacity 23,966 mt/y, Trim width 2.64 m, Tissue
Energy Data:
 Power boilers: 2
 Electrical demand for mill: 69 MWh/D

ⓜKruger Wayagamack Inc.
Trois Rivières (Wayagamack) Mill
Ownership: 51% by Kruger Inc., 49% by SGF Rexfor
PO Box 128
Trois-Rivières, QC
Canada, G9A 5E9
 Phone: (1) 819-373-9230
 Fax: (1) 819-373-9398

Quebec

Web Address: www.kruger.com
Personnel:
Prod. & Maint. Dir. (Paper Machine): Justin Paille
Phone: (1) 819-373-9230 Ext. 5285
Fax: (1) 819-372-4575
Email: jpaille@wa.kruger.com
Reliability Supervisor: Etienne Brisson
Phone: (1) 819-373-9230
Fax: (1) 819-373-9398
Email: ebrisson@wa.kruger.com
Mechanical Planner: Mario Milot
Phone: (1) 819-373-9230
Fax: (1) 819-373-9398
Email: mmilot@wa.kruger.com
Technician: Jacques Ayotte
Phone: (1) 819-373-9230
Fax: (1) 819-373-9398
Email: jayotte@wa.kruger.com
Operator: Stéphan Gélinas
Phone: (1) 819-373-9230
Fax: (1) 819-373-9398
Email: sgelinas@wa.kruger.com
Pulping Supt.: Denis Harvey
Phone: (1) 819-373-9230 Ext. 5217
Fax: (1) 819-373-9398
Email: denis.harvey@kruger.com
Total Employees at this Location: 360
Type of Operation: Pulp mill, Paper mill
Pulp Grades and Capacities:
Total pulp capacity: 172,003 mt/y
Chemical Pulp: 80,650 mt/y
Mechanical Pulp: 91,353 mt/y
Pulp Mill Data:
Chemical Pulping Systems:
Continuous digesters: 1
Mechanical Pulping Systems:
Conventional grinders
Bleach Plant Systems: 2
Chemical Pulping System, Type: Softwood, Sequence: CEH
Mechanical SGW Pulping System, Type: Softwood
Chemical Recovery Equipment:
Evaporator lines: 1
Recovery boilers: 1
Lime Kiln
Pulp Dryers:
Fourdriniers 1
Paper/Paperboard Grades and Capacities:
Total paper and paperboard capacity: 253,470 mt/y
Coated mechanical/groundwood: 253,470 mt/y
Paper and Paperboard Mill Data:
Stock Preparation:
Pulpers:
Paper Machines: 1
No. 4, (Former Type model: Optiformer), twin-wire, total capacity 253,470 mt/y, Trim width 7.3 m, Coated mechanical/groundwood
Coating Machines: 1
PM 4, total capacity 253,000 mt/y., on machine
Finishing Equipment:
Supercalenders: 1
Energy Data:
Power boilers: 4
Electrical demand for mill: 1,045 MWh/D

ⓘⓜ Marlboro Paper Inc.
Drummondville Mill
Ownership: Private
191 St. Henri St
Drummondville, QC
Canada, J2C 2H4
Phone: (1) 819-477-4413
Fax: (1) 819-474-4186
Email: info@papiersmarlboro.ca
Web Address: www.papiersmarlboro.ca
Personnel:
CEO, Pres.: Hugh Parenteau
Phone: (1) 819-477-4413
Fax: (1) 819-474-4186

Gen. Mgr.: Richard Parenteau
Phone: (1) 819-477-4413 Ext. 222
Fax: (1) 819-474-4186
Total Employees of Company: 35
Total Employees at this Location: 35
Type of Operation: Paper mill
Paper/Paperboard Grades and Capacities:
Total paper and paperboard capacity: 5,250 mt/y
Tissue: 5,250 mt/y
Paper and Paperboard Mill Data:
Stock Preparation:
Pulpers: 2
Refiners: 1
Paper Machines: 1
No. 1, Yankee dryer, fourdrinier, total capacity 5,250 mt/y, Trim width 2.4 m, Tissue
Finishing Equipment:
Rewinders: 2 at 15,000 mt/y
Energy Data:
Power boilers: 1

ⓜ Metro Paper Industries Tissue Group Ltd.
Portneuf Mill
200, rue Du Moulin
Portneuf, QC
Canada, G0A 2Y0
Phone: (1) 418-286-3461
Fax: (1) 418-286-6457
Email: customerservice@metropaperindustries.com, daphnem@metropaperindustries.com
Web Address: www.metropaperindustries.com
Personnel:
Paper Mill Superintendent: Daniel Thibault
Phone: (1) 416-757-2737 ext.300
Fax: (1) 418-286-6457
Email: daniel.thibault@mpiportneuf.com
Paper Mill Cust. Representative: Marsha Price
Phone: (1) 905-604-5786 Ext: 225
Fax: (1) 905-604-6786
Email: marshap@mpipapermills.com
Total Employees at this Location: 94
Type of Operation: Paper mill
Pulp Grades and Capacities:
Total pulp capacity: 27,935 mt/y
Recycled Pulping: 27,935 mt/y
Pulp Mill Data:
Recycled Fiber Treatment Lines:
Pulpers: 1 at 28,400
Paper/Paperboard Grades and Capacities:
Total paper and paperboard capacity: 25,910 mt/y
Tissue: 25,910 mt/y
Paper and Paperboard Mill Data:
Paper Machines: 2
No. 4, crescent former, Yankee dryer, total capacity 11,983 mt/y, Trim width 3.05 m, Tissue
No. 5, crescent former, total capacity 13,926 mt/y, Trim width 3.05 m, Tissue
Finishing Equipment:
Rewinders: 2
Sheeters: 2
Energy Data:
Power boilers: 5
Electrical demand for mill: 83 MWh/D

ⓘ Norampac
Ownership: 100% by Cascades Inc.
1061 Parent St.
St-Bruno, QC
Canada, J3V 6R7
Phone: (1) 450-461-8600, 866-735-2635
Fax: (1) 450-461-8636
Email: info@norampac.com
Web Address: www.norampac.com
Personnel:
Pres. & CEO: Marc-André Dépin
Phone: (1) 450-461-8601
Fax: (1) 450-461-8636
Email: marc-andre_depin@norampac.com

VP COO, Packaging: Charles Malo
Phone: (1) 450-461-8621
Fax: (1) 450-461-8636
Email: charles_malo@norampac.com
VP, COO, Containerboard & Boxboard: Maurice Plante
Phone: (1) 450-461-8602
Fax: (1) 450-461-8636
Email: maurice_plante@norampac.com
VP Legal Affairs: Lucie-Claude Lalonde
Phone: (1) 450-461-8631
Fax: (1) 450-461-8636
Email: lucie-claude_lalonde@norampac.com
VP., Finan. & Admin.: Patrick Chaperon
Phone: (1) 450-461-8641
Fax: (1) 450-461-8636
Email: patrick_champeron@norampac.com
VP., Sls. Mktg. & Innovation Containerboard & Boxboard Div.: Robert Lanthier
Phone: (1) 450-461-8600
Fax: (1) 450-461-8636
Email: robert_lanthier@norampac.com
Corp. Dir., HR: Caroline Tremblay
Phone: (1) 450-461-8651
Fax: (1) 450-461-8636
Email: caroline_tremblay@norampac.com
Total Employees of Company: 5,500
Total Employees at this Location: 120
Mill Locations:
Norampac, Cabano Mill, 200 Cascades Street C.P 190, Cabano, QC, Canada G0L 1E0, Capacity: 220,232 mt/y, (Pulp mill, Paperboard mill)
Phone: (1) 418-854-2803
Fax: (1) 418-854-3942
Email: cabano@norampac.com
Greenpac Mill, LLC, Greenpac Mill (59.70% owned), 4001 Packard Rd, Niagara Falls, NY 14303, USA, Capacity: 490,016 mt/y, (Paper mill)
Phone: (1) 716-299-0560
Norampac, Kingsey Falls Mill, 398, rue Marie-Victorin St, Kingsey Falls, QC, Canada J0A 1B0, Capacity: 89,064 mt/y, (Paperboard mill)
Phone: (1) 819-363-5000
Fax: (1) 819-363-5055
Email: info@norampac.com
Norampac, Mississauga Mill, 7447 Bramalea Rd, Mississauga, ON, Canada L5S 1C4, Capacity: 160,316 mt/y, (Paperboard mill)
Phone: (1) 905-671-2940
Fax: (1) 905-671-2448
Email: mississauga_info@norampac.com
Norampac, Trenton Mill, 300 Marmora St, Trenton, ON, Canada K8V 5R8, Capacity: 153,515 mt/y, (Paperboard mill)
Phone: (1) 613-392-6505
Fax: (1) 613-392-3026
Email: trentonmill@norampac.com

ⓜ Norampac
Cabano Mill
Previously Norampac Inc.
Ownership: 100% by Cascades Inc.
200 Cascades Street C.P 190
Cabano, QC
Canada, G0L 1E0
Phone: (1) 418-854-2803
Fax: (1) 418-854-3942
Email: cabano@norampac.com
Web Address: www.norampac.com
Personnel:
Mill Mgr.: Luc Pelletier
Phone: (1) 418-854-2803
Fax: (1) 418-854-3942
Email: luc_pelletier@norampac.com
Pulp Mill Supt.: Marco Landry
Phone: (1) 418-854-2803
Fax: (1) 418-854-3942
Email: marco_landry@norampac.com
Contr.: Nathalie Blanchet
Phone: (1) 418-854-2803
Fax: (1) 418-854-3942

Quebec

Email: nathalie_blanchet@norampac.com
Steam Plt. Supt.: Michel Dumont
Phone: (1) 418-854-2803
Fax: (1) 418-854-3942
Email: michel_dumont@norampac.com
Distribution Supervisor: Yvan Potvin
Phone: (1) 418-854-2803
Fax: (1) 418-854-3942
Email: yvan_potvin@norampac.com
Mech. Maint. Mgr.: Jean-Louis Bossé
Phone: (1) 418-854-2803
Fax: (1) 418-854-3942
Email: jean-louis_bosse@norampac.com
Elec. Maint. Mgr.: Roger Bélanger
Phone: (1) 418-854-2803
Fax: (1) 418-854-3942
Email: roger_belanger@norampac.com
Environ. Mgr.: Pascal Dubé
Phone: (1) 418-854-2803
Fax: (1) 418-854-3942
Email: pascal_dube@norampac.com
Total Employees at this Location: 140
Type of Operation: Pulp mill, Paperboard mill
Pulp Grades and Capacities:
Total pulp capacity: 230,552 mt/y
Chemical Pulp: 126,816 mt/y
Recycled Pulping: 103,736 mt/y
Pulp Mill Data:
Chemical Pulping Systems:
Continuous digesters: 1
Bleach Plant Systems: 1
No. 1
Chemical Recovery Equipment:
Recovery boilers: 1
Recycled Fiber Treatment Lines:
Pulpers: 1 at 105,000 admt/y
Paper/Paperboard Grades and Capacities:
Total paper and paperboard capacity: 220,232 mt/y
Corrugating medium/fluting: 220,232 mt/y
Paper and Paperboard Mill Data:
Stock Preparation:
Pulpers: 1
Refiners: 1
Paper Machines: 1
No. 1, fourdrinier, total capacity 220,232 mt/y, Trim width 5.7 m, Corrugating medium/fluting
Finishing Equipment:
Rewinders: 1
Energy Data:
Power boilers: 3
Electrical demand for mill: 526 MWh/D

ⓜNorampac
Kingsey Falls Mill
Previously Norampac Inc.
Ownership: 100% by Cascades Inc.
398, rue Marie-Victorin St
Kingsey Falls, QC
Canada, J0A 1B0
Mailing Address: PO Box 119, Kingsey Falls, QC,
Canada, J0A 1B0
Phone: (1) 819-363-5000
Fax: (1) 819-363-5055
Email: info@norampac.com
Web Address: www.norampac.com
Personnel:
Mill Mgr.: Luc Filiatrault
Phone: (1) 819-363-5000
Fax: (1) 819-363-5055
Email: luc_filiatrault@norampac.com
Maint. Mgr.: Gerald Kelly
Phone: (1) 819-363-5000
Fax: (1) 819-363-5055
Email: gerald_kelly@norampac.com
Total Employees at this Location: 66
Type of Operation: Paperboard mill
Pulp Grades and Capacities:
Total pulp capacity: 85,216 mt/y
Recycled Pulping: 85,216 mt/y

Pulp Mill Data:
Pulp Lines: 2
Recycled Fiber Treatment Lines:
Pulpers: 2 at 160,000 admt/y
Paper/Paperboard Grades and Capacities:
Total paper and paperboard capacity: 89,064 mt/y
Linerboard: 85,502 mt/y
Corrugating medium/fluting: 3,563 mt/y
Paper and Paperboard Mill Data:
Stock Preparation:
Pulpers: 2
Refiners: 2
Paper Machines: 1
No. 1, fourdrinier, total capacity 89,064 mt/y, Trim width 2.5 m, Linerboard, Corrugating medium/fluting
Finishing Equipment:
Winders: 1 at 150,000 mt/y
Calenders: 1
Energy Data:
Power boilers: 1
Combustion turbines: 1 at 32 MW
Electrical demand for mill: 130 MWh/D

ⓗⓜPapier Masson
Gatineau Mill
Ownership: 100% by White Birch Paper Company
2 Montreal Rd W
Gatineau, QC
Canada, J8M 2E1
Phone: (1) 819-986-4300
Fax: (1) 819-986-7331 (Admin), 819-986-6522 (Maint / Eng / Purch)
Email: resshuma@whitebirchpaper.com
Web Address: www.whitebirchpaper.com
Personnel:
Gen. Mgr.: Carol Tremblay
Phone: (1) 819-986-4300 Ext. 4307
Fax: (1) 819-986-7331 (Admin), 819-986-6522 (Maint / Eng / Purch)
Service & Paper Manuf Mgr.: Joel Gagne
Phone: (1) 819-986-4300
Fax: (1) 819-986-4326
Pulp Prod. Mgr.: Sylvain Bussière
Phone: (1) 819-986-4300
Fax: (1) 819-986-4326
Tech Mgr.: Jean Bigelow
Phone: (1) 819-986-4300
Fax: (1) 819-986-4326
Total Employees of Company: 200
Total Employees at this Location: 250
Type of Operation: Paper mill
Pulp Grades and Capacities:
Total pulp capacity: 249,381 mt/y
Mechanical Pulp: 249,381 mt/y
Pulp Mill Data:
Mechanical Pulping Systems:
TMP systems: 1
Paper/Paperboard Grades and Capacities:
Total paper and paperboard capacity: 242,760 mt/y
Newsprint: 242,760 mt/y
Paper and Paperboard Mill Data:
Stock Preparation:
Pulpers: 4
Paper Machines: 1
No. 3, Bel-Baie III, total capacity 242,760 mt/y, Trim width 8.36 m, Newsprint
Finishing Equipment:
Calenders: 1
Rewinders: 1 at 234,000 mt/y
Energy Data:
Power boilers: 2
TMP Reboiler: 1
Electrical demand for mill: 2,106 MWh/D

ⓜResolute Forest Products Canada Inc.
Alma Mill
1100, rue Melancon Ouest

Alma, QC
Canada, G8B 5W2
Phone: (1) 418-668-9400
Fax: (1) 418-662-3849
Email: info@resolutefp.com
Web Address: www.resolutefp.com
Personnel:
Gen. Mgr.: Michel Leroux
Phone: (1) 418-668-9400 Ext: 9329
Fax: (1) 418-662-3849
Email: michel.leroux@resolutefp.com
Prod. Supervisor (From January 2014): David-Nicolas Allen
Phone: (1) 418-668-9400 Ext: 9529
Fax: (1) 418-662-3849
Email: david-nicolas.allen@resolutefp.com
MIS Coord.: Réjean Côté
Phone: (1) 418-668-9400
Fax: (1) 418-662-3849
Email: rejean.cote@resolutefp.com
Total Employees at this Location: 472
Type of Operation: Paper mill
Pulp Grades and Capacities:
Total pulp capacity: 311,997 mt/y
Mechanical Pulp: 279,696 mt/y
Recycled Pulping: 32,301 mt/y
Pulp Mill Data:
Mechanical Pulping Systems:
TMP systems: 2
Bleach Plant Systems: 1
TMP, Sequence: HS
Recycled Fiber Treatment Lines:
Flotation deinking lines: 1
Paper/Paperboard Grades and Capacities:
Total paper and paperboard capacity: 344,505 mt/y
Uncoated mechanical/groundwood: 344,505 mt/y
Paper and Paperboard Mill Data:
Stock Preparation:
Pulpers: 4
Refiners: 1
Paper Machines: 3
No. 9, Top Flyte, total capacity 74,970 mt/y, Trim width 5.65 m, Uncoated mechanical/groundwood
No. 10, Top Flyte, total capacity 71,400 mt/y, Trim width 5.65 m, Uncoated mechanical/groundwood
No. 14, DuoFormer D, total capacity 198,135 mt/y, Trim width 7.68 m, Uncoated mechanical/groundwood
Coating Machines: 1
No. 1, on machine
Finishing Equipment:
Winders: 3
Calenders: 1
Rewinders: 1
Energy Data:
Power boilers: 2
TMP Reboiler: 1

ⓜResolute Forest Products Canada Inc.
Amos Mill
Mill will be idled for 30 days from October 31, 2014
801, Rue des Papetiers
Amos, QC
Canada, J9T 3X5
Phone: (1) 819-727-1515
Fax: (1) 819-727-2711
Email: info@resolutefp.com
Web Address: www.resolutefp.com
Personnel:
Gen. Mgr.: Vincent Goulet
Phone: (1) 819-727-1515 Ext: 5355
Fax: (1) 819-727-4628
Email: vincent.goulet@resolutefp.com
Contr.: Gisèle Patrice
Phone: (1) 819-727-1515 Ext. 5600
Fax: (1) 819-727-2711
Email: gisele.patrice@resolutefp.com
Supt, Finishing, Shipping: Caroline Demers
Phone: (1) 819-727-1515 Ext. 5232

Quebec

Fax: (1) 819-727-2711
Email: caroline.demers@resolutefp.com
Environ. & Continuous Improv. Coord.: Luis Urbina
Phone: (1) 819-727-1515 Ext: 5214
Fax: (1) 819-727-2711
Email: luis.urbina@resolutefp.com
HR Dir.: Jocelyne Cossette
Phone: (1) 819-727-1515 Ext: 5700
Fax: (1) 819-727-2711
Email: jocelyne.cossette@resolutefp.com
Total Employees at this Location: 166
Type of Operation: Paper mill
Pulp Grades and Capacities:
Total pulp capacity: 201,871 mt/y
Mechanical Pulp: 201,871 mt/y
Pulp Mill Data:
Mechanical Pulping Systems:
TMP systems: 4
Bleach Plant Systems: 1
Mechanical Pulping System, Type: hydrosulfite, Sequence: H
Paper/Paperboard Grades and Capacities:
Total paper and paperboard capacity: 198,135 mt/y
Newsprint: 198,135 mt/y
Paper and Paperboard Mill Data:
Stock Preparation:
Pulpers: 1
Paper Machines: 1
No. 1, Papriformer, total capacity 198,135 mt/y, Trim width 7.65 m, Newsprint
Finishing Equipment:
Calenders: 1
Rewinders: 1
Energy Data:
Power boilers: 2
Electrical demand for mill: 1,755 MWh/D

ⓘ Resolute Forest Products Canada Inc.
Baie-Comeau Mill
20, rue Marquette
Baie-Comeau, QC
Canada, G4Z 1K6
 Phone: (1) 418-296-3371
 Fax: (1) 418-296-7716
 Email: info@resolutefp.com
 Web Address: www.resolutefp.com
Personnel:
Mill Mgr.: Gaston Joncas
Phone: (1) 418-296-3371 Ext. 7686
Fax: (1) 418-296-7716
Email: gaston.joncas@resolutefp.com
Oper. & Prod. Mgr.: Michel LeClair
Phone: (1) 418-296-3371 Ext. 7261
Fax: (1) 418-296-7716
Email: michel.leclair@resolutefp.com
Pulp Supt.: Gilles Lacroix
Phone: (1) 418-296-3371 Ext. 7262
Fax: (1) 418-296-7716
Email: gilles.lacroix@resolutefp.com
Mech. Supervisor: Frédéric Dumont
Phone: (1) 418-296-3371
Fax: (1) 418-296-7716
Email: frederic.dumont@resolutefp.com
Cust. Serv.: Luc Rouleau
Phone: (1) 418-296-3371 Ext. 7589
Fax: (1) 418-296-7716
Email: luc.rouleau@resolutefp.com
Total Employees at this Location: 345
Type of Operation: Paper mill
Pulp Grades and Capacities:
Total pulp capacity: 475,572 mt/y
Mechanical Pulp: 475,572 mt/y
Pulp Mill Data:
Mechanical Pulping Systems:
TMP systems: 5
Recycled Fiber Treatment Lines:
Pulpers: 1 at 110,000
Paper/Paperboard Grades and Capacities:
Total paper and paperboard capacity: 463,029 mt/y
Newsprint: 463,029 mt/y
Paper and Paperboard Mill Data:
Stock Preparation:
Pulpers: 4
Refiners: 5
Paper Machines: 3
No. 1, Top Flyte, total capacity 131,733 mt/y, Trim width 6.06 m, Newsprint
No. 3, SpeedFormer, total capacity 132,804 mt/y, Trim width 6.04 m, Newsprint
No. 4, Bel-Baie, total capacity 198,492 mt/y, Trim width 8.88 m, Newsprint
Energy Data:
Power boilers: 8
TMP Reboiler: 1
Electrical demand for mill: 3,931 MWh/D

ⓘ Resolute Forest Products Canada Inc.
Ownership: 100% by the public
111 Duke Street, Suite 5000
Montreal, QC
Canada, H3C 2M1
Mailing Address: PO Box 69, Sta A, Montreal, QC, Canada, H3C 2R5
 Phone: (1) 514-875-2160
 Fax: (1) 514-875-6284
 Email: info@resolutefp.com
 Web Address: www.resolutefp.com
Personnel:
Pres. & CEO: Richard Garneau
Phone: (1) 514-875-2160
Fax: (1) 514-875-6284
Email: richard.garneau@resolutefp.com
Snr. VP., Pulp & Paper Oper. (From Feb 2014): André Piché
Phone: (1) 514-875-2160
Fax: (1) 514-875-6284
Snr. VP., Pulp & Paper Oper. (From Feb. 2014): Richard Tremblay
Phone: (1) 514-875-2160
Fax: (1) 514-875-6284
Snr. VP., HR: Pierre Laberge
Phone: (1) 514-875-2160
Fax: (1) 514-875-6284
Email: pierre.laberge@resolutefp.com
Snr. VP., Pulp and Paper Sls. and Mktg.: John Lafave
Phone: (1) 514-875-2160
Fax: (1) 514-875-6284
Email: john.lafave@resolutefp.com
Snr. VP., Wood Products Div., Procurement & IT: Yves LaFlamme
Phone: (1) 514-875-2160
Fax: (1) 514-875-6284
Email: yves.laflamme@resolutefp.com
Snr. VP., CFO: Jo-Ann Longworth
Phone: (1) 514-875-2160
Fax: (1) 514-875-6284
Email: jo-ann.longworth@resolutefp.com
Snr. VP., Chief Legal Officer: Jacques P. Vachon
Phone: (1) 514-875-2160
Fax: (1) 514-875-6284
Email: jacques.vachon@resolutefp.com
VP., HR. US: Becky Burris
Phone: (1) 423-336-7209
Fax: (1) 514-875-6284
Email: becky.burris@resolutefp.com
Total Employees of Company: 8,400
Mill Locations:
Resolute Paper Korea Ltd., Mokpo mill, 1694-1, Nanjeon-ri, Samho-eup, 526-892 Yeongam-gun, South Korea, Capacity: 200,000 mt/y, (Paper mill)
Phone: (82) 2-3453-7323
Fax: (82) 61 460-6158
Email: info@resolutefp.com
Ponderay Newsprint Co., Usk Mill (40% owned), 422767 State Hwy 20, Usk, WA 99180-9771, USA, Capacity: 243,831 mt/y, (Pulp mill, Paper mill)
Phone: (1) 509-445-1511
Fax: (1) 509-445-1233
Resolute Forest Products Canada Inc., Alma Mill, 1100, rue Melancon Ouest, Alma, QC, Canada G8B 5W2, Capacity: 344,505 mt/y, (Paper mill)
Phone: (1) 418-668-9400
Fax: (1) 418-662-3849
Email: info@resolutefp.com
Resolute Forest Products Canada Inc., Amos Mill, 801, Rue des Papetiers, Amos, QC, Canada J9T 3X5, Capacity: 198,135 mt/y, (Paper mill)
Phone: (1) 819-727-1515
Fax: (1) 819-727-2711
Email: info@resolutefp.com
Resolute Forest Products Canada Inc., Baie-Comeau Mill, 20, rue Marquette, Baie-Comeau, QC, Canada G4Z 1K6, Capacity: 463,029 mt/y, (Paper mill)
Phone: (1) 418-296-3371
Fax: (1) 418-296-7716
Email: info@resolutefp.com
Resolute FP US Inc., Calhoun Mill, 5020 Hwy 11 S, Calhoun, TN 37309-5249, USA, Capacity: 517,650 mt/y, (Pulp mill, Paper mill)
Phone: (1) 423-336-2211
Fax: (1) 423-336-7150/7950
Email: info@resolutefp.com
Resolute FP US Inc., Catawba Mill, 5300 Cureton Ferry Rd, Catawba, SC 29704, USA, Capacity: 529,074 mt/y, (Pulp mill, Paper mill)
Phone: (1) 803-981-8000
Fax: (1) 803-981-8181
Email: info@resolutefp.com
Resolute Forest Products Canada Inc., Clermont Mill, 100, rue Donohue, Clermont, QC, Canada G4A 1A7, Capacity: 334,152 mt/y, (Paper mill)
Phone: (1) 418-439-5300
Fax: (1) 418-439-5373
Email: info@resolutefp.com
Resolute FP US Inc., Coosa Pines Mill, 17589 Plant Rd, Coosa Pines, AL 35044-0555, USA, (Pulp mill)
Phone: (1) 256-378-5541
Fax: (1) 256-378-2165
Email: info@resolutefp.com
Resolute Forest Products Canada Inc., Dolbeau Mill, 1 Fourth Ave, Dolbeau, QC, Canada G8L 2R4, Capacity: 137,802 mt/y, (Paper mill)
Phone: (1) 418-239-2350
Fax: (1) 418-276-7067
Email: info@resolutefp.com
Resolute Forest Products Canada Inc., Fort Frances Mill, 427 Mowat Avenue, Fort Frances, ON, Canada P9A 1Y8, (Pulp mill, Paper mill)
Phone: (1) 807-274-5311
Fax: (1) 807-274-8200
Email: info@resolutefp.com
Resolute Forest Products Canada Inc., Gatineau Mill, 79 Main St, Gatineau, QC, Canada J8P 4X6, Capacity: 178,500 mt/y, (Paper mill)
Phone: (1) 819-643-7200
Fax: (1) 819-643-7229
Email: info@resolutefp.com
Resolute Forest Products Canada Inc., Laurentide Mill, 100 First St, Grand-Mere, QC, Canada G9T 7J1, (Pulp mill, Papermill, closed October 2014)
Phone: (1) 819-538-3341
Fax: (1) 819-533-6516
Email: info@resolutefp.com
Resolute FP US Inc., Grenada Mill, 1000 Papermill Rd, Grenada, MS 38901, USA, Capacity: 245,973 mt/y, (Pulp mill, Paper mill)
Phone: (1) 662-227-7900
Fax: (1) 662-227-7901
Email: info@resolutefp.com
Resolute Forest Products Canada Inc., Iroquois Falls Mill, 1 Park St, Iroquois Falls, ON, Canada P0K 1E0, Capacity: 207,060 mt/y, (Paper mill)
Phone: (1) 705-258-3931
Fax: (1) 705-258-3350
Email: info@resolutefp.com
Resolute Forest Products Canada Inc., Kenogami Mill, 3750 de Champlain, Jonquière, QC, Canada G7S 5J7, Capacity: 137,445 mt/y, (Paper mill)

Quebec

Phone: (1) 418-695-9100
Fax: (1) 418-542-1912
Email: info@resolutefp.com
Resolute Forest Products Canada Inc., Thorold Mill, 2 Allanburg Rd, Thorold, ON, Canada L2V 3Z5, Capacity: 192,780 mt/y, (Pulp mill, Paper mill)
Phone: (1) 905-227-5000
Fax: (1) 905-227-2112
Email: info@resolutefp.com
Resolute Forest Products Canada Inc., Thunder Bay Mill, 2001 Neebing Ave., Thunder Bay, ON, Canada P7E 6S3, Capacity: 224,910 mt/y, (Pulp mill, Paper mill)
Phone: (1) 807-475-2110
Fax: (1) 807-473-8643
Email: info@resolutefp.com
Resolute FP Augusta LLC, Augusta Mill (52.50% owned), 2434 Doug Bernard Pkwy, Augusta, GA 30906, USA, Capacity: 398,055 mt/y, (Pulp mill, Paper mill)
Phone: (1) 706-798-3440
Fax: (1) 706-312-6473
Email: info@resolutefp.com
Resolute Forest Products Canada Inc., St Félicien Mill, 4000, Chemin St-Eusebe, Saint-Felicien, QC, Canada G8K 2R6, (Pulp mill)
Phone: (1) 418-679-4545
Fax: (1) 418-679-8804
Resolute FP US Inc., Fairmont Mill, 702 AFR Dr, Fairmont, WV 26554, USA, (Pulp mill)
Phone: (1) 304-368-0900
Fax: (1) 304-368-2826
Resolute FP US Inc., Menominee Mill, 701 Fourth Ave., Menominee, MI 49858, USA, (Pulp mill)
Phone: (1) 906 863-9936, 906-863-8137
Fax: (1) 906-864-9108

ⓜResolute Forest Products Canada Inc.
Clermont Mill
100, rue Donohue
Clermont, QC
Canada, G4A 1A7
Phone: (1) 418-439-5300
Fax: (1) 418-439-5373
Email: info@resolutefp.com
Web Address: www.resolutefp.com
Personnel:
Mill Mgr.: Roger Leroux
Phone: (1) 418-439-5300 Ext. 3371
Fax: (1) 418-439-5373
Email: roger.leroux@resolutefp.com
Chief Eng.: Normand Parent
Phone: (1) 418-439-5300 Ext. 3228
Fax: (1) 418-439-5373
Email: normand.parent@resolutefp.com
Total Employees at this Location: 300
Type of Operation: Paper mill
Pulp Grades and Capacities:
Total pulp capacity: 342,678 mt/y
Mechanical Pulp: 342,678 mt/y
Pulp Mill Data:
Mechanical Pulping Systems:
TMP systems: 1
Bleach Plant Systems: 1
TMP, Sequence: HS
Paper/Paperboard Grades and Capacities:
Total paper and paperboard capacity: 334,152 mt/y
Newsprint: 334,152 mt/y
Paper and Paperboard Mill Data:
Paper Machines: 2
No. 4, Dynaformer, total capacity 119,952 mt/y, Trim width 5.97 m, Newsprint
No. 5, SymFormer R, total capacity 214,200 mt/y, Trim width 8.32 m, Newsprint
Energy Data:
Power boilers: 7
TMP Reboiler: 1
Electrical demand for mill: 3,027 MWh/D

ⓜResolute Forest Products Canada Inc.
Dolbeau Mill
1 Fourth Ave
Dolbeau, QC
Canada, G8L 2R4
Phone: (1) 418-239-2350
Fax: (1) 418-276-7067
Email: info@resolutefp.com
Web Address: www.resolutefp.com
Personnel:
Mill Mgr.: Martin Leclerc
Phone: (1) 418-239-2350
Fax: (1) 418-276-7067
Email: martin.leclerc@resolutefp.com
Health & Safety Superint. (From May 2013): Guy Lascelles
Phone: (1) 418-239-2350 Ext: 4003
Fax: (1) 418-276-7067
Email: guy.lascelles@resolutefp.com
Total Employees at this Location: 135
Type of Operation: Paper mill
Pulp Grades and Capacities:
Total pulp capacity: 111,459 mt/y
Mechanical Pulp: 111,459 mt/y
Pulp Mill Data:
Mechanical Pulping Systems:
TMP systems: 1
Pulp Lines: 1
Bleach Plant Lines:
No. 1, Sequence: HS-P
Paper/Paperboard Grades and Capacities:
Total paper and paperboard capacity: 137,802 mt/y
Uncoated mechanical/groundwood: 137,802 mt/y
Paper and Paperboard Mill Data:
Stock Preparation:
Pulpers:
Paper Machines: 1
No. 5, DuoFormer CFD, total capacity 137,802 mt/y, Trim width 5.8 m, Uncoated mechanical/groundwood
Finishing Equipment:
Supercalenders: 1
Energy Data:
Power boilers: 2
Steam turbines at 28 MW

ⓜResolute Forest Products Canada Inc.
Gatineau Mill
79 Main St
Gatineau, QC
Canada, J8P 4X6
Mailing Address: PO Box 1000, Gatineau, QC, Canada, J8P 4X6
Phone: (1) 819-643-7200
Fax: (1) 819-643-7229
Email: info@resolutefp.com
Web Address: www.resolutefp.com
Personnel:
Mill Mgr.: Joël Gagné
Phone: (1) 819-643-7200
Fax: (1) 819-643-7229
Email: joel.gagne@resolutefp.com
Total Employees at this Location: 130
Type of Operation: Paper mill
Pulp Grades and Capacities:
Total pulp capacity: 184,540 mt/y
Mechanical Pulp: 184,540 mt/y
Pulp Mill Data:
Mechanical Pulping Systems:
TMP systems
Paper/Paperboard Grades and Capacities:
Total paper and paperboard capacity: 178,500 mt/y
Newsprint: 178,500 mt/y
Paper and Paperboard Mill Data:
Paper Machines: 1
No. 6, Bel-Form, total capacity 178,500 mt/y, Trim width 8.98 m, Newsprint

Energy Data:
Power boilers: 1
Steam turbines: 1 at 15 MW
Electrical demand for mill: 1,604 MWh/D

ⓜResolute Forest Products Canada Inc.
Laurentide Mill
Mill is closed (on October 15, 2014.)
100 First St
Grand-Mere, QC
Canada, G9T 7J1
Mailing Address: PO Box 190, Grand-Mere, QC, Canada, G9T 7J1
Phone: (1) 819-538-3341
Fax: (1) 819-533-6516
Email: info@resolutefp.com
Web Address: www.resolutefp.com
Personnel:
Mill Mgr.: Daniel Laberge
Phone: (1) 819-538-3341 Ext. 248
Fax: (1) 819-533-6516
Email: daniel.laberge@resolutefp.com
Total Employees at this Location: 275
Type of Operation: Pulp mill, Paper mill
Pulp Mill Data:
Chemical Pulping Systems:
Continuous digesters: 2
Mechanical Pulping Systems:
Conventional grinders: 22
Bleach Plant Systems: 1
Mechanical SGW Pulping System, Type: Softwood, Sequence: H
Paper and Paperboard Mill Data:
Stock Preparation:
Pulpers:
Paper Machines: 1
No. 11, twin-wire, total capacity 223,125 mt/y, Trim width 8.46 m
Finishing Equipment:
Calenders: 4
Supercalenders: 2
Rewinders: 2
Energy Data:
Power boilers: 4

ⓜResolute Forest Products Canada Inc.
Kenogami Mill
3750 de Champlain
Jonquière, QC
Canada, G7S 5J7
Phone: (1) 418-695-9100
Fax: (1) 418-542-1912
Email: info@resolutefp.com
Web Address: www.resolutefp.com
Personnel:
Mill Mgr.: Paul Falardeau
Phone: (1) 418-695-9100
Fax: (1) 418-542-1912
Email: paul.falardeau@resolutefp.com
Prod. Mgr.: Gervais Devost
Phone: (1) 418-695-9100
Fax: (1) 418-542-1912
Email: gervais.devost@resolutefp.com
Finan. Mgr.: Remi Sirois
Phone: (1) 418-695-9211
Fax: (1) 418-542-1912
Email: remi.sirois@resolutefp.com
Total Employees at this Location: 215
Type of Operation: Paper mill
Pulp Grades and Capacities:
Total pulp capacity: 102,506 mt/y
Mechanical Pulp: 102,506 mt/y
Pulp Mill Data:
Mechanical Pulping Systems:
TMP systems: 2
Bleach Plant Systems: 1

Quebec

TMP Mechanical Pulping system bleaching, Type: Softwood, Sequence: P, Capacity 161,000 admt/y
Paper/Paperboard Grades and Capacities:
Total paper and paperboard capacity: 137,445 mt/y
Uncoated mechanical/groundwood: 137,445 mt/y
Paper and Paperboard Mill Data:
Stock Preparation:
Pulpers:
Paper Machines: 1
No. 7, SymFormer R, total capacity 137,445 mt/y, Trim width 5.6 m, Uncoated mechanical/groundwood
Finishing Equipment:
Supercalenders: 3
Energy Data:
Power boilers: 6
Hydro turbines at 90 MW

Ⓜ Resolute Forest Products Canada Inc.
St Félicien Mill
4000, Chemin St-Eusebe
Saint-Felicien, QC
Canada, G8K 2R6
  Phone: (1) 418-679-4545
  Fax: (1) 418-679-8804
  Web Address: www.resolutefp.com
Personnel:
  Mill Mgr. (from 2014): Jean Ménard
  Phone: (1) 418-679-8585 Ext: 4136
  Fax: (1) 418-679-5682
  Email: jean.menard@resolutefp.com
  Process Improvement Supt.: Roger Rousseau
  Phone: (1) 418-679-4545
  Fax: (1) 418-679-8804
  Email: roger.rousseau@resolutefp.com
  Eng. Supt.: Andre Menard
  Phone: (1) 418-679-8585 Ext. 4169
  Fax: (1) 418-679-5682
  Email: a.menard@resolutefp.com
Total Employees at this Location: 265
Type of Operation: Pulp mill
Pulp Grades and Capacities:
Total pulp capacity: 363,148 mt/y
Pulp available for market: 355,929 mt/y
Chemical Pulp: 363,148 mt/y
Pulp Mill Data:
Chemical Pulping Systems:
Continuous digesters: 1
Bleach Plant Systems: 1
Chemical Pulping System, Type: Softwood, Sequence: DEOpDEpD
Chemical Recovery Equipment:
Evaporator lines: 7
Recovery boilers: 1
Lime Kiln
Pulp Dryers:
Air Float dryers 1
Energy Data:
Power boilers: 1
Steam turbines: 3 at 30, 3.4, 9.5 MW
Electrical demand for mill: 860 MWh/D

Ⓜ RockTenn Co.
La Tuque Mill
1000 Chemin de L'Usine
La Tuque, QC
Canada, G9X 3P8
Mailing Address: PO Box 914, La Tuque, QC, Canada, G9X 3P8
  Phone: (1) 819-676-8100
  Fax: (1) 819-676-8145
  Web Address: www.rocktenn.com
Personnel:
  Gen. Mgr. La Tuque Mill & PAT - Extrusion plant Montreal: Pierre Pacarar
  Phone: (1) 819-676-8132
  Fax: (1) 819-676-8145
  Email: ppacarar@rocktenn.com
  HR Dir.: Marc Belisle
  Phone: (1) 819-676-8132
  Fax: (1) 819-676-8145
  Email: mbelisle@rocktenn.com
  Eng. Mgr.: Denis Roy
  Phone: (1) 819-676-8132
  Fax: (1) 819-676-8145
  Email: droy@rocktenn.com
Total Employees at this Location: 486
Type of Operation: Paperboard mill
Pulp Grades and Capacities:
Total pulp capacity: 434,535 mt/y
Chemical Pulp: 403,527 mt/y
Recycled Pulping: 31,008 mt/y
Pulp Mill Data:
Chemical Pulping Systems:
Batch digesters: 19
Continuous digesters: 2
Bleach Plant Systems: 1
Chemical Pulping System - 1, Type: Hardwood/Sawdust, Sequence: DEoDD, Capacity 154,000 admt/y
Chemical Pulping System - 1, Type: Softwood, Sequence: DEoDD, Capacity 182,000 admt/y
Chemical Recovery Equipment:
Evaporator lines: 1
Recovery boilers: 3
Lime Kiln
Recycled Fiber Treatment Lines:
Pulpers: 1 at 31,000
Paper/Paperboard Grades and Capacities:
Total paper and paperboard capacity: 431,719 mt/y
Linerboard: 312,859 mt/y
Boxboard/cartonboard: 118,860 mt/y
Paper and Paperboard Mill Data:
Stock Preparation:
Refiners: 6
Paper Machines: 2
No. 3, fourdrinier, total capacity 312,859 mt/y, Trim width 6.6 m, Linerboard
No. 4, fourdrinier, total capacity 118,860 mt/y, Trim width 4 m, Boxboard/cartonboard
Coating Machines: 1
PM 3, on machine
Energy Data:
Power boilers: 2
Electrical demand for mill: 1,184 MWh/D

Ⓞ Ⓜ Rolland Enterprises Inc.
Rolland Mill
455 Rolland Ave.
St. Jérôme, QC
Canada, J7Z 5S2
Mailing Address: PO Box 850, Saint-Jerome, QC, Canada, J7Z 5V6
  Phone: (1) 450-569-3900
  Fax: (1) 450-569-3988
  Email: info@rollandinc.com
  Web Address: www.rollandinc.com
Personnel:
  VP., Admin. : Guy Beaudin
  Phone: (1) 450-569-3905
  Fax: (1) 450-569-3933
  Email: gbeaudin@rollandinc.com
  Tech. Mgr.: Patrick Ager
  Phone: (1) 450-436-4140 Ext. 2439
  Fax: (1) 450-436-9722
  Email: pager@rollandinc.com
  Assist. Mgr., Commun. & Mktg.: Julie Loyer
  Phone: (1) 514-232-4022
  Email: jloyer@rollandinc.com
  Mgr.: Marc Charbonneau
  Phone: (1) 450-569-3951
  Fax: (1) 450-569-3947
  Email: mcharbonneau@rollandinc.com
  Mgr.: Pierre Guay
  Phone: (1) 450-569-3951
  Fax: (1) 450-569-3947
  Email: pguay@rollandinc.com
Total Employees at this Location: 300
Type of Operation: Paper mill
Pulp Grades and Capacities:
Total pulp capacity: 6,141 mt/y
Recycled Pulping: 6,141 mt/y
Paper/Paperboard Grades and Capacities:
Total paper and paperboard capacity: 140,853 mt/y
Uncoated woodfree/freesheet: 140,853 mt/y
Paper and Paperboard Mill Data:
Stock Preparation:
Pulpers:
Paper Machines: 3
No. 6, fourdrinier, total capacity 19,428 mt/y, Trim width 2.29 m, Uncoated woodfree/freesheet
No. 7, fourdrinier, total capacity 45,332 mt/y, Trim width 3.61 m, Uncoated woodfree/freesheet
No. 8, fourdrinier, total capacity 76,093 mt/y, Trim width 4.37 m, Uncoated woodfree/freesheet
Finishing Equipment:
Rewinders: 1
Sheeters: 2
Energy Data:
Power boilers: 6
Electrical demand for mill: 291 MWh/D
Total Employees of Company: 350
Mill Locations: Rolland Enterprises Inc. - Breakey Fibres Division, 739, av Saint-Augustin Canada
Breakeyville, QC, G0S 1E2 (Pulp mill)
  Phone: (1) 418-832-6115
  Fax: (1) 418-832-5598

Ⓜ Rolland Enterprises Inc.
Breakey Fibres Division
739, av Saint-Augustin
Breakeyville, QC
Canada, G0S 1E2
  Phone: (1) 418-832-6115
  Fax: (1) 418-832-5598
  Email: info@rollandinc.com
  Web Address: www.rollandinc.com
Personnel:
  Mill Mgr.: Richard Laramee
  Phone: (1) 418-832-6115
  Fax: (1) 418-832-5598
  Prod. Mgr.: Pascale Vachon
  Phone: (1) 418-832-6115
  Fax: (1) 418-832-5598
Total Employees at this Location: 50
Type of Operation: Pulp mill
Pulp Grades and Capacities:
Total pulp capacity: 55,113 mt/y
Pulp available for market: 54,264 mt/y
Recycled Pulping: 55,113 mt/y
Pulp Mill Data:
Pulp Lines: 1
Bleach Plant Systems: 2
DIP, Sequence: P
Recycled Fiber Treatment Lines:
Flotation deinking lines
Pulp Dryers:
Wet Lap machine 1
Energy Data:
Power boilers: 1
Electrical demand for mill: 68 MWh/D

Ⓜ Stadacona Inc.
Stadacona Mill
Ownership: 100% by White Birch Paper Company
10 Blvd des Capucins
Quebec City, QC
Canada, G1K 7H9
Mailing Address: PO Box 1487, Quebec City, QC, Canada, G1K 7H9
  Phone: (1) 418-525-2500
  Fax: (1) 418-525-2987
  Web Address: www.whitebirchpaper.com
Personnel:
  Gen. Mgr.: René Savard
  Phone: (1) 418-525-2500
  Fax: (1) 418-525-2987

Quebec

Email: rsavard@whitebirchpaper.com
Prod. Mgr.: Sylvain Girard
Phone: (1) 418-525-2500
Fax: (1) 418-525-2987
Email: sgirard@whitebirchpaper.com
Finan. Mgr.: Jocelyn Proulx
Phone: (1) 418-525-2500
Fax: (1) 418-525-2987
Email: jproulx@whitebirchpaper.com
HR Mgr: Yvon Lesage
Phone: (1) 418-525-2500 Ext. 2506
Fax: (1) 418-525-2987
Email: ylesage@whitebirchpaper.com
Total Employees at this Location: 300
Type of Operation: Paper mill
Pulp Grades and Capacities:
Total pulp capacity: 260,812 mt/y
Mechanical Pulp: 260,812 mt/y
Pulp Mill Data:
Mechanical Pulping Systems:
TMP systems: 1
Bleach Plant Systems: 1
Mechanical TMP Pulping System, Type: Softwood, Sequence: P
Recycled Fiber Treatment Lines:
Flotation deinking lines: 9
Pulpers: 1
Washing deinking lines: 3
Paper/Paperboard Grades and Capacities:
Total paper and paperboard capacity: 258,825 mt/y
Newsprint: 232,050 mt/y
Uncoated mechanical/groundwood: 26,775 mt/y
Paper and Paperboard Mill Data:
Stock Preparation:
Pulpers: 2
Paper Machines: 2
No. 3, twin-wire, total capacity 121,380 mt/y, Trim width 5.59 m, Newsprint, Uncoated mechanical/groundwood
No. 4, twin-wire, total capacity 137,445 mt/y, Trim width 5.5 m, Newsprint
Finishing Equipment:
Calenders: 4
Rewinders: 1
Energy Data:
Power boilers: 5

Technocell Canada Inc.
Drummondville Mill
Ownership: 80% by Technocell Dekor GmbH & Co. KG, 20% by Kunz Holding GmbH & Co.
3075 rue Bernier
Drummondville, QC
Canada, J2C 6Y4
 Phone: (1) 819-475-0066
 Fax: (1) 819-475-2440
 Email: myTechnocell@felix-schoeller.com
 Web Address: www.mytechnocell.com, www.technocell.com, www.felix-schoeller.com
Personnel:
Pres. & CEO: Richard Paterson Jones
Phone: (1) 819-475-0066
Fax: (1) 819-475-0055
Email: rpjones@Felix-Schoeller.com
VP Sales & Technology: Thomas Scheck
Phone: (1) 819-475-0066
Fax: (1) 819-475-0055
VP, CFO: Roland M. Belanger
Phone: (1) 819-475-0066
Fax: (1) 819-475-0055
Total Employees of Company: 146
Total Employees at this Location: 146
Type of Operation: Paper mill
Paper/Paperboard Grades and Capacities:
Total paper and paperboard capacity: 30,000 mt/y
Specialty and industrial: 30,000 mt/y
Paper and Paperboard Mill Data:
Stock Preparation:
Pulpers: 2
Refiners: 5
Paper Machines: 1
No. 19, fourdrinier, total capacity 30,000 mt/y, Trim width 3.12 m, Specialty and industrial
Energy Data:
Power boilers: 2

Tembec Inc.
Ownership: 100% by the public
800 Rene-Levesque Blvd W, Bureau 1050
Montreal, QC
Canada, H3B 1X9
 Phone: (1) 514-871-0137
 Fax: (1) 514-397-0896
 Web Address: www.tembec.com
Personnel:
Pres. & CEO: James Lopez
Phone: (1) 514-871-0137
Fax: (1) 514-397-0896
Email: james.lopez@tembec.com
Exec. VP, Specialty Cellulose: Christian Ribeyrolle
Phone: (1) 514-871-0137
Fax: (1) 514-397-0896
Email: christian.ribeyroller@tembec.com
Exec. VP., Finan. & CFO: Michel Dumas
Phone: (1) 819-627-4268
Fax: (1) 819-627-1178
Email: michel.dumas@tembec.com
Exec. VP., Forest Products, Paper & Pulp Group: Chris Black
Phone: (1) 514-871-0137
Fax: (1) 514-397-0896
Email: chris.black@tembec.com
VP., Eng., Eng. & Purch.: Mahendra Patel
Phone: (1) 514-871-0137
Fax: (1) 514-397-0896
Email: mahendra.patel@tembec.com
VP., Environ., Energy & Technology: Paul Dottori
Phone: (1) 514-871-0137
Fax: (1) 514-397-0896
Email: paul.dottori@tembec.com
VP., Gen. Counsel & Corp. Sec.: Patrick LeBel
Phone: (1) 514-871-0137
Fax: (1) 514-397-0896
Email: patrick.lebel@tembec.com
VP., HR & Corp. Affairs: Linda Coates
Phone: (1) 514-871-0137, 416-775-2819
Fax: (1) 514-397-0896
Email: linda.coates@tembec.com
Total Employees of Company: 3,500
Mill Locations:
Tembec Inc., Spruce Falls Mill, 1 Government Rd, Kapuskasing, ON, Canada P5N 2Y2, Capacity: 239,904 mt/y, (Paper mill, Paper mill)
 Phone: (1) 705-337-1311
 Fax: (1) 705-337-9708
Tembec Inc., Matane Mill, 400, rue du Port, Matane, QC, Canada G4W 3P6, (Pulp mill)
 Phone: (1) 418-562-7272
 Fax: (1) 418-566-2025
Tembec Inc., Temiscaming Mill, 33 Kipawa Rd, Temiscaming, QC, Canada J0Z3R0, Capacity: 182,070 mt/y, (Pulp mill, Paperboard mill)
 Phone: (1) 819-627-4639 (Paperboard), 819-627-3321/4207 (Temcell)
 Fax: (1) 819-627-3177
Tembec Tartas, Tartas Mill, 1154 av. du Général Leclerc, F-40400 Tartas, France, (Pulp mill)
 Phone: (33) 5 58 56 47 56
 Fax: (33) 5 58 56 47 00
 Email: tartas.adv@tembec.com

Tembec Inc.
Matane Mill
400, rue du Port
Matane, QC
Canada, G4W 3P6
Mailing Address: PO Box 640, Matane, QC, Canada, G4W 3P6
 Phone: (1) 418-562-7272
 Fax: (1) 418-566-2025
 Web Address: www.tembec.com
Personnel:
Mill Mgr.: Eric Gendreau
Phone: (1) 418-562-7272 Ext. 5001
Fax: (1) 418-566-2025
Email: eric.gendreau@tembec.com
Mech. Eng.: Eric Bernier
Phone: (1) 418-562-7272 Ext. 5014
Fax: (1) 418-562-2704
Email: eric.bernier@tembec.com
Total Employees at this Location: 140
Type of Operation: Pulp mill
Pulp Grades and Capacities:
Total pulp capacity: 253,654 mt/y
Pulp available for market: 249,900 mt/y
Mechanical Pulp: 253,654 mt/y
Pulp Mill Data:
Mechanical Pulping Systems:
CTMP systems: 1
Bleach Plant Systems: 2
Mechanical Pulping System - 1, Type: Hardwood, Sequence: P
Mechanical Pulping System - 2, Type: Hardwood, Sequence: P, Capacity 107,100 admt/y
Pulp Dryers:
Flakt dryer 1, Flakt dryer 1
Energy Data:
Power boilers: 1
TMP Reboiler: 1
Electrical demand for mill: 1,608 MWh/D

Tembec Inc.
Temiscaming Mill
33 Kipawa Rd
Temiscaming, QC
Canada, J0Z 3R0
Mailing Address: PO Box 6000, Temiscaming, QC, Canada, J0Z 3R0
 Phone: (1) 819-627-4639 (Paperboard), 819-627-3321/4207 (Temcell)
 Fax: (1) 819-627-3177
 Web Address: www.tembec.com
Personnel:
Snr. VP., Specialty Cellulose & Chem Products: Randy Fournier
Phone: (1) 819-627-4639
Fax: (1) 819-627-3177
Email: randy.fournier@tembec.com
Tech. Mgr. Specialty Cellulose: Gerard Orlowski
Phone: (1) 819-627-4493
Fax: (1) 819-627-9908
Email: gerard.orlowski@tembec.com
Chem. Prod. Mgr.: Sue Nakanishi
Phone: (1) 819-627-4639
Fax: (1) 819-627-3177
Email: sue.nakanishi@tembec.com
Tech. Serv. Mgr.: Jean Barrette
Phone: (1) 819-627-4639
Fax: (1) 819-627-3177
Email: jean.barrette@tembec.com
Mktg Mgr.: Anton Deinekin
Phone: (1) 819-627-4639
Fax: (1) 819-627-3177
Email: anton.deinekin@tembec.com
Total Employees at this Location: 900
Type of Operation: Pulp mill, Paperboard mill
Pulp Grades and Capacities:
Total pulp capacity: 485,079 mt/y
Pulp available for market: 414,834 mt/y
Chemical Pulp: 169,968 mt/y
Mechanical Pulp: 315,111 mt/y
Pulp Mill Data:
Chemical Pulping Systems:
Batch digesters: 11
Mechanical Pulping Systems:
BCTMP systems: 2
Pulp Lines: 4

Bleach Plant Systems: 7
Chemical Pulping System, Type: Oxygen and Hydrogen peroxide towers - Hardwood/Softwood, Sequence: OcDcNDH
Mechanical Pulping Lines, Type: 2 stage high density, Sequence: P
Chemical Recovery Equipment:
Evaporator lines: 1
Recovery boilers: 3
Lime Kiln
Pulp Dryers:
Flakt dryer 1, Flakt dryer 1
Paper/Paperboard Grades and Capacities:
Total paper and paperboard capacity: 182,070 mt/y
Boxboard/cartonboard: 182,070 mt/y
Paper and Paperboard Mill Data:
  Stock Preparation:
  Pulpers: 3
  Refiners: 16
Paper Machines: 1
No. 1, fourdrinier (3), total capacity 182,070 mt/y, Trim width 4.5 m, Boxboard/cartonboard
Coating Machines: 1
No. 1, total capacity 180,000 mt/y., on machine
Finishing Equipment:
  Winders: 1 at 185,000 mt/y
  Calenders: 1
Energy Data:
Power boilers: 3
Steam turbines: 1 at 9.5 MW
Electrical demand for mill: 2,767 MWh/D

SASKETCHEWAN

ⓜMeadow Lake Mechanical Pulp
Meadow Lake Mill
Ownership: 100% by Paper Excellence Group
Box 9100
Meadow Lake, SK
Canada, S9X 1V7
  Phone: (1) 306-236-2444
  Fax: (1) 306-236-4880
  Email: info@meadowlakepulp.com
  Web Address: www.meadowlakepulp.com/
Personnel:
  Gen. Mgr: Simon Imray
  Phone: (1) 306-236-2444
  Fax: (1) 306-236-4880
  Email: simray@meadowlakepulp.com
  Tech. Mgr.: Colin Schenk
  Phone: (1) 306-236-2444
  Fax: (1) 306-236-4880
  Email: cschenk@meadowlakepulp.com
  Capital Proj. Mgr. (From November 2013): Brent Dubray
  Phone: (1) 306-236-2444
  Fax: (1) 306-236-4880
  Email: bdubray@meadowlakepulp.com
  Sn. Mgr. Supply Chain: Brent McIntyre
  Phone: (1) 306-236-2444
  Fax: (1) 306-236-4880
  Email: bmcintyre@meadowlakepulp.com
  Prod. Mgr.: Rob Goozee
  Phone: (1) 306-236-2444
  Fax: (1) 306-236-4880
  Email: rgoozee@meadowlakepulp.com
  Steam Chief: Bill Easton
  Phone: (1) 306-236-2444
  Fax: (1) 306-236-4880
  Email: beaston@meadowlakepulp.com
  Finan. Mgr.: Shirley Fung
  Phone: (1) 306-236-2444
  Fax: (1) 306-236-4880
  Email: sfung@meadowlakepulp.com
  Maint. & Eng. Mgr.: Doug Chisholm
  Phone: (1) 306-236-2444
  Fax: (1) 306-236-4880
  Email: dchisholm@meadowlakepulp.com
Total Employees at this Location: 160
Type of Operation: Pulp mill
Pulp Grades and Capacities:
  Total pulp capacity: 405,600 mt/y
  Pulp available for market: 399,840 mt/y
  Mechanical Pulp: 405,600 mt/y
Pulp Mill Data:
  Mechanical Pulping Systems:
  BCTMP systems: 2
Pulp Lines: 2
  Bleach Plant Systems: 2
  Mechanical BCTMP Pulping System, Type: Two-stage towers, Sequence: PP
  Chemical Recovery Equipment:
  Evaporator lines: 1
  Pulp Dryers:
  Flash dryers 1, Flash dryers 1
Energy Data:
Power boilers: 1
TMP Reboiler: 1
Electrical demand for mill: 2,289 MWh/D

RISI's Asset Database

www.risi.com/assetdata

Developed by RISI, Conceived by Clients

RISI's Asset Database was built in partnership with our clients to deliver comprehensive mill equipment, consumption, key personnel and projects information to forest products industry professionals around the world.

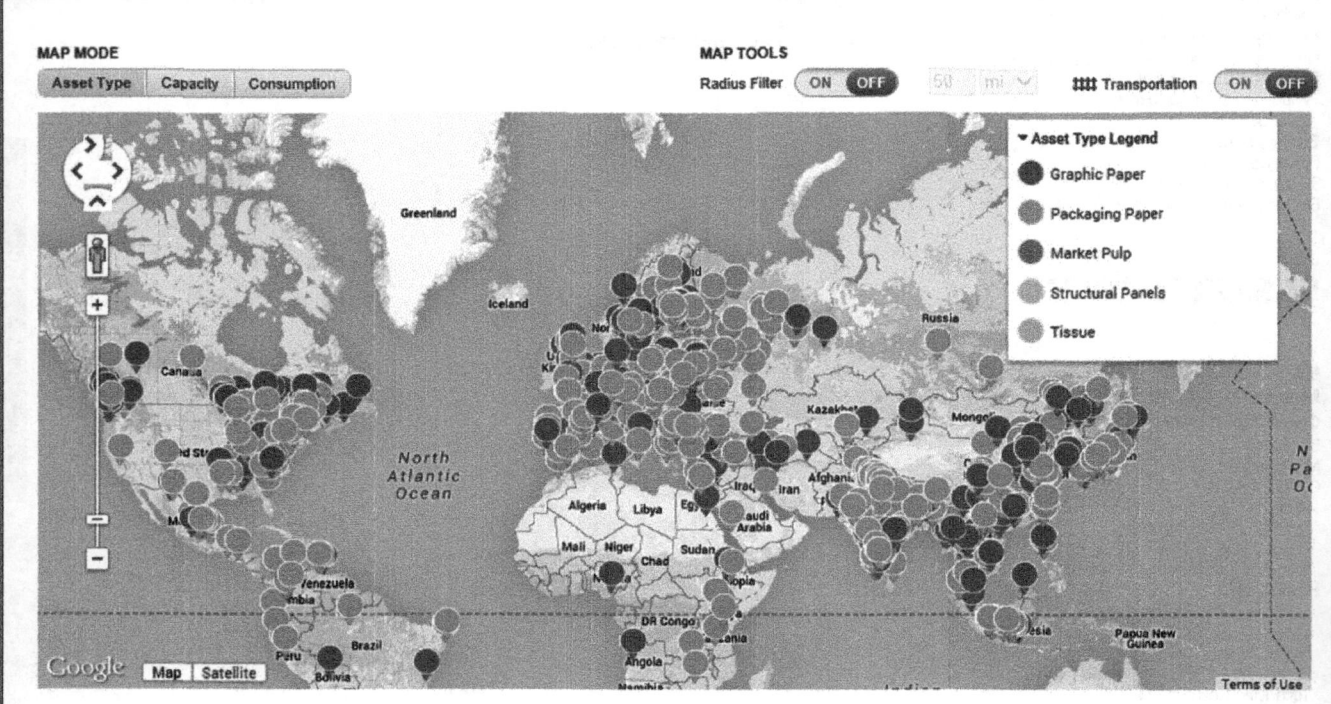

Strengthen Your Business Intelligence

Make stronger, more strategic sales and marketing decisions by better understanding what's happening at mills across global markets.

Maintain Your Competitive Advantage

Stay abreast of changes in the competitive landscape with detailed and current mill equipment, input consumption and project data.

Save Time and Resources with an Intuitive Platform

Quickly and easily customize, save and export the information you need to identify new business opportunities and threats from competition with this easy-to-use, intuitive platform.

PULP and PAPER MILLS in Europe

ALBANIA

①Edipack sh.p.k.
Lagja 15, Rr. Porto Romano
Durres
Albania
Mailing Address: P.O. Box 6665, Durres
  Phone: (355) 69 202 6111, 69 406 5104
  Fax: (355) 52 23 30 88
  Email: bbalteza@gmail.com,
  info@edipack.al,
  edipack04@yahoo.com
  Web Address: www.edipack.al
Personnel:
  Owner : Bardhyl Balteza
  Phone: (355) 69 202 6111
  Fax: (355) 52 23 30 88
  Email: bbalteza@gmail.com
  CEO & Mktg. : Admir Skonja
  Phone: (355) 69 406 5104
  Fax: (355) 52 23 30 88
  Email: info@edipack.al
  Tech. Dir.: Erti Harizi
  Phone: (355) 69 406 5102
  Fax: (355) 52 23 30 88
  Email: prodhimi@edipack.al
  Economist: Koco Mulla
  Phone: (355) 69 202 6111
  Fax: (355) 52 23 30 88
  Email: financa@edipack.al
Mill Locations:
Edipack sh.p.k., Durres Mill, Lagja 15, Rr. Porto Romano, Durres, Albania, Capacity: 22,000 mt/y, (Paperboard mill)
  Phone: (355) 68 202 61 11
  Fax: (355) 52 23 30 88
  Email: bbalteza@gmail.com, info@edipack.al, edipack04@yahoo.com

ⓜEdipack sh.p.k.
Durres Mill
Lagja 15, Rr. Porto Romano
Durres
Albania
Mailing Address: P.O. Box 6665, Durrës.
  Phone: (355) 68 202 61 11
  Fax: (355) 52 23 30 88
  Email: bbalteza@gmail.com,
  info@edipack.al,
  edipack04@yahoo.com
  Web Address: www.edipack.al
Personnel:
  Owner: Bardhyl Ballteza
  Phone: (355) 68 202 61 11
  Fax: (355) 52 23 30 88
  Email: bbalteza@gmail.com
  CEO & Mktg. : Admir Skonja
  Phone: (355) 69 406 5104
  Fax: (355) 52 23 30 88
  Email: info@edipack.al
  Tech. Dir.: Erti Harizi
  Phone: (355) 69 406 5102
  Fax: (355) 52 23 30 88
  Email: prodhimi@edipack.al
  Economist: Koco Mulla
  Phone: (355) 69 202 6111
  Fax: (355) 52 23 30 88
  Email: financa@edipack.al
Total Employees at this Location: 90
Type of Operation: Paperboard mill
Pulp Grades and Capacities:
  Total pulp capacity: 21,963 mt/y
  Recycled Pulping: 21,963 mt/y
Paper/Paperboard Grades and Capacities:
  Total paper and paperboard capacity: 22,000 mt/y
  Linerboard: 14,000 mt/y
  Corrugating medium/fluting: 8,000 mt/y
Paper and Paperboard Mill Data:
Paper Machines: 1
No. 1, fourdrinier, total capacity 22,000 mt/y, Trim width 2.5 m, Linerboard, Corrugating medium/fluting
Energy Data:
Power boilers
Electrical demand for mill: 34 MWh/D

AUSTRIA

①ⓜBrigl & Bergmeister GmbH
Niklasdorf Mill
Ownership: 100% by Roxcel Group
Proleberstr. 10
A-8712 Niklasdorf, Styria
Austria
  Phone: (43) 3842 800 0
  Fax: (43) 3842 800 213/205
  Email: marketing@brigl-bergmeister.com
  Web Address: www.brigl-bergmeister.com
Personnel:
  Man. Dir.: Ahmad Porkar
  Phone: (43) 1 401 56 143
  Fax: (43) 1 401 56 7140
  Email: ahmad.porkar@roxcel.com
  Man. Dir.: Michael Sablatnig
  Phone: (43) 3842 800 0
  Fax: (43) 3842 800 213
  Email: msablatnig@brigl-bergmeister.com
  Man. Dir.: Helmut F. Gruber
  Phone: (43) 1 401 56 0
  Fax: (43) 1 401 456 7451
  Email: helmut.gruber@roxcel.com
  Paper Mill Mgr.: Bernhard Mayer
  Phone: (43) 3842 800 300
  Fax: (43) 3842 800 213
  Email: bmayer@brigl-bergmeister.com
  Mktg. Mgr.: Robert Pachlerl
  Phone: (43) 3842 800 202
  Fax: (43) 3842 800 213
  Email: RPachlerl@brigl-bergmeister.com
  Tech. Mgr.: Franz Putz
  Phone: (43) 3842 800 355
  Fax: (43) 3842 800 213
  Email: FPutz@brigl-bergmeister.com
  Prod. Mgr.: Karl Schneller
  Phone: (43) 3842 800 215
  Fax: (43) 3842 800 213
  Email: KarlSchneller@brigl-bergmeister.com
  Sls. Dir.: Peter Cechal
  Phone: (43) 3842 800 220
  Fax: (43) 3842 800 213
  Email: PCechal@brigl-bergmeister.com
Total Employees of Company: 525
Total Employees at this Location: 254
Type of Operation: Paper mill
Paper/Paperboard Grades and Capacities:
  Total paper and paperboard capacity: 75,000 mt/y
  Specialty and industrial: 75,000 mt/y
Paper and Paperboard Mill Data:
Paper Machines: 1
No. 3, fourdrinier, total capacity 75,000 mt/y, Trim width 2.8 m, Specialty and industrial
Coating Machines: 1
PM 3, total capacity 62,000 mt/y., off machine
Finishing Equipment:
  Supercalenders: 2
  Rewinders: 2
  Sheeters: 3
Energy Data:
  Power boilers: 1
  Steam turbines: 1
  Hydro turbines: 5
  Electrical demand for mill: 150 MWh/D

①delfortgroup AG
Fabrikstrasse 20
A-4050 Traun
Austria
  Phone: (43) 7229 776-0 / 776 299
  Fax: (43) 7229 77618-100
  Email: info@delfortgroup.com
  Web Address: www.delfortgroup.com
Personnel:
  CEO: Martin Zahlbruckner
  Phone: (43) 7229 776-0
  Fax: (43) 7229 77618-100
  Email: martin.zahlbuckner@delfortgroup.com
  Man. Dir. : Saxl Heinz
  Phone: (43) 7229 776-0
  Fax: (43) 7229 77618-100
  Email: saxl.heinz@delfortgroup.com
  Head Corp. Finan.: Peter Lagler
  Phone: (43) 7229 776-0
  Fax: (43) 7229 77618-100
  Head Corp. Develop.: HockSong Lim
  Phone: (43) 43 664 88505425
  Fax: (43) 7229 77618-100
  Email: hocksong.lim@delfortgroup.com
  Head of Corp. Procurement Fiber Materials: Peter Donnabauer
  Phone: (43) 7229 776-0
  Fax: (43) 7229 77618-100
  Email: peter.donnabauer@delfortgroup.com
  Prod. Mgr.: Simon Schmee
  Phone: (43) 7229 776-0
  Fax: (43) 7229 77618-100
  Head Corporate HR: Bianca Flaschner
  Phone: (43) 7229 776-0
  Fax: (43) 7229 77618-100
  Sls. & Mktg. Mgr.: Wolfgang Mayr
  Phone: (43) 7229 776-0
  Fax: (43) 7229 77618-100
Total Employees of Company: 1,750
Mill Locations:
Dunafin Kft., Dunaujvaros Mill, Papirgyari ut. 42-46, H-2400 Dunaujvaros, Hungary, Capacity: 110,000 mt/y, (Paper mill)
  Phone: (36) 25 511 400
  Fax: (36) 25 511 415
  Email: dunafin@delfortgroup.com
Dr. Franz Feurstein GmbH, Traun Mill, Fabrikstrasse 20, A-4050 Traun, Austria, Capacity: 55,000 mt/y, (Paper mill)
  Phone: (43) 7229 7760
  Fax: (43) 7229 77618-100/660 33
  Email: feurstein@delfortgroup.com
OP Papírna s.r.o., Olšany Mill, Olšany u Šumperka 18, CZ-789 62 Olšany, Czech Republic, Capacity: 55,000 mt/y, (Paper mill)

Austria

Phone: (420) 583 384 656
Fax: (420) 583 384 854
Email: oppapirna@delfortgroup.com
Tervakoski Oy, Tervakoski Mill, Vähikkäläntie 1, FI-12400 Tervakoski, Finland, Capacity: 116,000 mt/y, (Paper mill)
Phone: (358) 19 771 1
Fax: (358) 19 771 535/537
Email: tervakoski@delfortgroup.com
Papierfabrik Wattens GmbH & Co KG, Wattens Mill, Ludwig Lassl Strasse 15, A-6112 Wattens, Austria, Capacity: 60,000 mt/y, (Paper mill)
Phone: (43) 5224 595 0
Fax: (43) 5224 595 250
Email: wattenspapier@delfortgroup.com

ⓂDuropack GmbH
Ownership: 100% by Constantia Packaging AG
Brunner Str. 75
A-1230 Vienna
Austria
Phone: (43) 1 863 000
Fax: (43) 1 863 00440
Email: duropack@duropack.eu
Web Address: www.duropack.eu
Personnel:
Man. Dir., CEO: Peter Szivacsek
Phone: (43) 1 863 00-359
Fax: (43) 1 863 00440
Email: peter.szivacsek@duropack.eu
Man. Dir., CFO: Peter Rindler
Phone: (43) 1 863 00-683
Fax: (43) 1 863 00440
Email: peter.rindler@duropack.eu
Int'l Sls. Coordinator: Reinhard Kammerhuber
Phone: (43) 1 863 00-364
Fax: (43) 1 863 00-1364
Email: kammerhuber.reinhard@duropack.eu
Head of Central Purch.: Alexander Petko
Phone: (43) 1 863 00-276
Fax: (43) 1 863 00-1276
Email: petko.alexander@durpack.eu
Fin. Dir.: Ana Stantcheva
Phone: (43) 1 863 00-726
Fax: (43) 1 863 00-1726
Email: ana.stantcheva@duropack.eu
HR & Legal Dir.: Franz-Michael Hohensinn
Phone: (43) 1 863 00-216
Fax: (43) 1 863 00-1216
Email: Franz-Michael.Hohensinn@duropack.eu
Mktg. & Commun.: Tobias Tengler
Phone: (43) 1 863 00-283
Fax: (43) 1 863 00-1283
Email: tobias.tengler@duropack.eu
Total Employees of Company: 2,762
Total Employees at this Location: 40
Mill Locations:
BELIŠCE d.d., Belišce Mill, Trg A. Starcevica 1, HR-31551 Belišce, Croatia, Capacity: 210,000 mt/y, (Pulp mill, Paperboard mill)
Phone: (385) 31 516 516
Fax: (385) 31 516 240
Email: uprava@belisce.hr
Duropack GmbH, Trakia, BG-4400 Pazardzik, Glavinitza quarter, Bulgaria, Capacity: 72,000 mt/y, (Paperboard mill)
Phone: (359) 34 401 202
Fax: (359) 34 449 000
Email: trakia@duropack.bg

ⓂDr. Franz Feurstein GmbH
Traun Mill
Ownership: 100% by delfortgroup AG
Fabrikstrasse 20
A-4050 Traun, Oberösterreich
Austria
Phone: (43) 7229 7760
Fax: (43) 7229 77618-100/660 33
Email: feurstein@delfortgroup.com
Web Address: www.delfortgroup.com
Personnel:
Man. Dir. Delfortgroup AG: Saxl Heinz
Phone: (43) 7229 7760
Fax: (43) 7229 77618-100
Email: saxl.heinz@delfortgroup.com
Head Of Financial: Stefan Scharnreitner
Phone: (43) 7229 7760
Fax: (43) 7229 77618-100
Email: stefan.scharnreitner@delfortgroup.com
Sls. Dir.: Jürgen Scheiblehner
Phone: (43) 7229 7760
Fax: (43) 7229 77618-100
Email: jurgen.scheiblehner@delfortgroup.com
Head of Quality Assurance & Develop.: Rinder Nadja
Phone: (43) 7229 7760
Fax: (43) 7229 77618-100
Email: rinder.nadja@delfortgroup.com
Cust. Service: Sonja Ringenberger
Phone: (43) 7229 7760
Fax: (43) 7229 77618-100
Total Employees at this Location: 250
Type of Operation: Paper mill
Paper/Paperboard Grades and Capacities:
Total paper and paperboard capacity: 55,000 mt/y
Uncoated woodfree/freesheet: 25,000 mt/y
Specialty and industrial: 30,000 mt/y
Paper and Paperboard Mill Data:
Stock Preparation:
Pulpers: 2
Refiners: 4
Paper Machines: 3
No. 1, fourdrinier, total capacity 5,000 mt/y, Trim width 1.46 m, Specialty and industrial
No. 2, fourdrinier, total capacity 20,000 mt/y, Trim width 2.46 m, Specialty and industrial
No. 3, DuoFormer D, total capacity 30,000 mt/y, Trim width 5 m, Uncoated woodfree/freesheet, Specialty and industrial
Finishing Equipment:
Supercalenders: 1
Rewinders: 2
Energy Data:
Power boilers: 1
Electrical demand for mill: 136 MWh/D

ⓂⓂW. Hamburger GmbH
Pitten Mill
Ownership: 100% by Prinzhorn Holding GmbH
Aspangerstr. 252
A-2823 Pitten, Niederösterreich
Austria
Phone: (43) 2627 800
Fax: (43) 2627 800 700
Email: officepitten@hamburger-containerboard.com
Web Address: www.hamburger.ag, www.hamburger-austria.com
Personnel:
Mill Mgr. & Dir. Oper.: Werner Ofenböck
Phone: (43) 2627 800 283
Fax: (43) 2627 800 710
Email: werner.ofenboeck@hamburger-containerboard.com
Conteinerboard div. Dir.: Harald Ganster
Phone: (43) 2627 800 253
Fax: (43) 2627 800 700
Email: harald.ganster@hamburger-containerboard.com
Prod. Mgr.: Gerald Steiner
Phone: (43) 2627 800 320
Fax: (43) 2627 800 710
Email: gerald.steiner@hamburger-containerboard.com
Tech. Mgr.: Josef Krenn
Phone: (43) 2627 800 302
Fax: (43) 2627 800 450
Email: jkrenn@w.hamburger.ag
Head of Central Plan. & Sls. Admin.: Marion Moitzi
Phone: (43) 2627 800 355
Fax: (43) 2627 800 400
Email: marion.moitzi@hamburger-containerboard.com
Mktg. Dir.: Manfred Lechner
Phone: (43) 2627 800 223
Fax: (43) 2627 800 700
Email: manfred.lechner@hamburger-containerboard.com
Group Contr. & Accounting Dir.: Reinhard Waldherr
Phone: (43) 2627 800 202
Fax: (43) 2627 800 300
Email: reinhard.waldherr@prinzhorn-holding.com
Lab Mgr.: Christoph Forstner
Phone: (43) 26 27 800 251
Fax: (43) 26 27 800 700
Email: christoph.forstner@hamburger-containerboard.com
Total Employees at this Location: 246
Type of Operation: Paperboard mill
Mill Locations:
W. Hamburger GmbH, Frohnleiten Mill, Peugen 1, A-8130 Frohnleiten, Austria, (Paper mill, Paperboard mill)
Phone: (43) 3126 2551 30 / 3126 2551
Fax: (43) 3126 2551 29
Email: office@hamburger-containerboard.com
Pulp Grades and Capacities:
Total pulp capacity: 373,043 mt/y
Recycled Pulping: 373,043 mt/y
Pulp Mill Data:
Recycled Fiber Treatment Lines:
Pulpers: 2
Paper/Paperboard Grades and Capacities:
Total paper and paperboard capacity: 375,000 mt/y
Linerboard: 260,000 mt/y
Corrugating medium/fluting: 115,000 mt/y
Paper and Paperboard Mill Data:
Paper Machines: 2
No. 3, SymFormer MB, total capacity 115,000 mt/y, Trim width 2.5 m, Corrugating medium/fluting
No. 4, DuoFormer Top, total capacity 260,000 mt/y, Trim width 5 m, Linerboard
Finishing Equipment:
Rewinders: 2 at 120,000 mt/y, 280,000 mt/y
Energy Data:
Power boilers: 3
Steam turbines: 1 at 7 MW
Electrical demand for mill: 446 MWh/D

ⓂW. Hamburger GmbH
Frohnleiten Mill
Mill is closed (the final closure took place on April 22, 2013)
Peugen 1
A-8130 Frohnleiten, Styria
Austria
Phone: (43) 3126 2551 30 / 3126 2551
Fax: (43) 3126 2551 29
Email: office@hamburger-containerboard.com
Web Address: www.hamburger-austria.com
Personnel:
Registered Mgr. & Paper Mill Mgr.: Michael Petschacher
Phone: (43) 3126 2551 607
Fax: (43) 3126 2551 25
Email: michael.petschacher@hamburgercontainerboard.com
Registered Mgr. & Sls. Mgr.: Martina Möstl
Phone: (43) 3126 2551 57 / 26 27 800 356
Fax: (43) 26 27 800 400
Email: martina.moestl@hamburgercontainerboard.com
Gen. Mgr.: Harald Ganster
Phone: (43) 3126 2551 30
Fax: (43) 26 27 800 700
Email: Harald.Ganster@hamburger-containerboard.com
Tech. Mgr: Georg Hammer
Phone: (43) 3126 2551 30
Fax: (43) 31 26 25 51 51
Email: Georg.Hammer@hamburger-containerboard.com
Total Employees at this Location: 105
Type of Operation: Paper mill, Paperboard mill

Austria

Pulp Mill Data:
Recycled Fiber Treatment Lines:
Pulpers: 1 at 186,000
Paper and Paperboard Mill Data:
Stock Preparation:
Pulpers: 2
Paper Machines: 2
No. 1, fourdrinier, total capacity 93,000 mt/y, Trim width 2.5 m
No. 2, fourdrinier, total capacity 78,000 mt/y, Trim width 2.5 m
Finishing Equipment:
Rewinders: 2
Energy Data:
Power boilers: 1
Steam turbines: 1 at 2.4 MW
Hydro turbines: 5 at 2.2 MW

①⑩Paul Hartmann Ges.mbH
Grimmenstein Mill
Ownership: HARTMANN international
Wechselbundesstraße 81
A-2840 Grimmenstein, Niederösterreich
Austria
Mailing Address: IZ NÖ Süd Straße 3, Ecoplus Wirtschaftspark Objekt 64, Postfach 110, A-2355 Wiener Neudorf, Austria
Phone: (43) 2644 7327/0 / 2236 64630-0
Fax: (43) 2644 2166 / 2236 64630 17
Email: office.gr@at.hartmann.info, office@at.hartmann.info
Web Address: www.at.hartmann.info
Personnel:
Gen. Mgr.: Mag. Friedrich Thomasberger
Phone: (43) 2236 64630 ext.11
Fax: (43) 2236 64630/17
Email: office@at.hartmann.info
Mill Mgr.: Prok. Herbert Baumgartner
Phone: (43) 2644 7327 ext. 20
Fax: (43) 2644 2166
Email: office.gr@at.hartmann.info
Total Employees of Company: 130
Total Employees at this Location: 76
Type of Operation: Paper mill
Pulp Grades and Capacities:
Total pulp capacity: 7,447 mt/y
Recycled Pulping: 7,447 mt/y
Pulp Mill Data:
Recycled Fiber Treatment Lines:
Flotation deinking lines: 1
Pulpers: 1 at 14,000
Paper/Paperboard Grades and Capacities:
Total paper and paperboard capacity: 10,500 mt/y
Tissue: 10,500 mt/y
Paper and Paperboard Mill Data:
Stock Preparation:
Pulpers: 1
Paper Machines: 2
No. 1, fourdrinier, Yankee dryer, total capacity 7,000 mt/y, Trim width 2.3 m, Tissue
No. 2, fourdrinier, Yankee dryer, total capacity 3,500 mt/y, Trim width 2 m, Tissue
Finishing Equipment:
Winders: 1 at 10,000 mt/y
Energy Data:
Power boilers: 2
Electrical demand for mill: 31 MWh/D

①Heinzel Holding GmbH
Ownership: 49% by EMACS Privatstiftung, 51% by Heinzel EMACS Beteiligungs AG
Wagramer Strasse 28-30
A-1223 Vienna
Austria
Mailing Address: P.O. Box 57, A-1223 Vienna
Phone: (43) 1 26011401
Fax: (43) 1 260 11402
Email: office@heinzel.com
Web Address: www.heinzel.com
Personnel:
Chairman of the Board: Wolfgang Pfarl
Phone: (43) 1 26011401
Fax: (43) 1 260 11402
Email: wolfgang.pfarl@heinzel.com
Pres.: Alfred H. Heinzel
Phone: (43) 1 26011401
Fax: (43) 1 2601155401
Email: alfred.heinzel@heinzel.com
CFO: Riia Sillave
Phone: (43) 1 26011455
Fax: (43) 1 2601155455
Email: riia.sillave@heinzel.com
VP, Strategic Planning: Sebastian Heinzel
Phone: (43) 1 26011401
Fax: (43) 1 260 11402
Email: sebastian.heinzel@heinzel.com
Head Purch. & IT: Manfred Peischler
Phone: (43) 1 26011401
Fax: (43) 1 260 11402
Email: m.peischler@zellstoff-poels.at
Head Finan. & Group Contr.: Ingrid Gruber
Phone: (43) 1 26011401
Fax: (43) 1 260 11402
Email: i.gruber@zellstoff-poels.at
Group HR.: Katharina Scheibelreiter
Phone: (43) 1 26011401
Fax: (43) 1 260 11402
Email: k.scheibelreiter@europapier.at
Total Employees of Company: 2,079
Total Employees at this Location: 4
Mill Locations:
AS Estonian Cell, Kunda Mill, Jaama 21, EE-44106 Kunda, Estonia, (Pulp mill)
Phone: (372) 687 0000
Fax: (372) 687 0099
Email: info@estoniancell.ee
Laakirchen Papier AG, Laakirchen Mill, Schillerstr. 5, A-4663 Laakirchen, Austria, Capacity: 540,000 mt/y, (Paper mill)
Phone: (43) 7613 8800 0
Fax: (43) 7613 8800 9210
Email: office@heinzelpaper.com, info@heinzel.com
Zellstoff Pöls AG, Pöls Mill, Dr. Luigi Angeli Strasse 9, A-8761 Pöls, Austria, Capacity: 80,000 mt/y, (Pulp mill, Paper mill)
Phone: (43) 3579 8181-0
Fax: (43) 3579 8181-319/8220
Email: office@zellstoff-poels.at

①⑩Laakirchen Papier AG
Laakirchen Mill
Ownership: Heinzel Holding GmbH
Schillerstr. 5
A-4663 Laakirchen, Oberösterreich
Austria
Mailing Address: Postf. 5, Laakirchen, Austria
Phone: (43) 7613 8800 0
Fax: (43) 7613 8800 9210
Email: office@heinzelpaper.com, info@heinzel.com
Web Address: www.heinzel.com
Personnel:
CEO: Dipl. Ing. Mark Lunabba
Phone: (43) 7613 8800 200
Fax: (43) 7613 8800 9210
Email: mark.lunabba@heinzelpaper.com
CFO: Franz Baldauf
Phone: (43) 7613 8800 250
Fax: (43) 7613 8800 9210
Email: franz.baldauf@heinzel.com
Prod. Mgr.: Helmut Sageder
Phone: (43) 7613 8800 300
Fax: (43) 7613 8800 9210
Email: helmut.sageder@heinzelpaper.com
Mktg. Mgr.: Stefan Eibl-Török
Phone: (43) 7613 8800 230
Fax: (43) 7613 8800 9210
Email: stefan.eibl@heinzelpaper.com
Qlty. & Develop.: Johann Brunthaler
Phone: (43) 7613 8800 366
Fax: (43) 7613 8800 9210
Email: johann.brunthaler@heinzelpaper.com
Sls. Dir.: Jurgen Nemeth
Phone: (43) 664 39 28 391
Fax: (43) 7613 8800 245/208
Email: juergen.nemeth@heinzelpaper.com
Asst. to CEO; Marketing Comm.: Brigitte Bammer
Phone: (43) 7613 8800-205
Fax: (43) 7613 8800-9205
Email: brigitte.bammer@heinzelpaper.com
Total Employees at this Location: 541
Type of Operation: Paper mill
Pulp Grades and Capacities:
Total pulp capacity: 374,254 mt/y
Mechanical Pulp: 115,758 mt/y
Recycled Pulping: 258,496 mt/y
Pulp Mill Data:
Mechanical Pulping Systems:
Conventional grinders: 14
Pulp Lines: 2
Bleach Plant Systems: 2
DIP line, Type: DIP, Sequence: P/HS, Capacity 250,000 admt/y
GW line, Type: Groundwood, Sequence: P/Y, Capacity 200,000 admt/y
Recycled Fiber Treatment Lines:
Flotation deinking lines: 1 at 250,000 admt/y
Paper/Paperboard Grades and Capacities:
Total paper and paperboard capacity: 540,000 mt/y
Uncoated mechanical/groundwood: 540,000 mt/y
Paper and Paperboard Mill Data:
Stock Preparation:
Pulpers: 1
Refiners: 6
Paper Machines: 2
No. 10, SpeedFormer HS, total capacity 255,000 mt/y, Trim width 7.24 m, Uncoated mechanical/groundwood
No. 11, DuoFormer TQv, total capacity 285,000 mt/y, Trim width 8.7 m, Uncoated mechanical/groundwood
Finishing Equipment:
Winders: 3 at 540,000 mt/y
Supercalenders: 4 at 540,000 mt/y
Rewinders: 1
Energy Data:
Power boilers: 4
HRSG boiler: 1
Combustion turbines: 1 at 40 MW
Steam turbines: 1 at 20 MW
Hydro turbines: 4 at 3 MW
Electrical demand for mill: 1,658 MWh/D

①⑩Lenzing AG
Lenzing Pulp Mill
Ownership: Public
Werkstr. 2
A-4860 Lenzing, Oberösterreich
Austria
Phone: (43) 7672 701-0
Fax: (43) 7672 701-3880
Email: office@lenzing.com
Web Address: www.lenzing.com
Personnel:
Chairman of the Supervisory: Michael Junghans
Phone: (43) 7672 701-0
Fax: (43) 7672 701-3880
Chmn. & CEO: Peter Untersperger
Phone: (43) 7672 701-0
Fax: (43) 7672 701-3880
Email: p.untersperger@lenzing.com
COO., Bd. Mbr. & VP (to step down eff. December 31, 2014): Friedrich Weninger
Phone: (43) 7672 701-0
Fax: (43) 7672 701-3880
Email: s.delorenzo@lenzing.com
Chief Commercial Officer: Robert van de Kerkhof
Phone: (43) 7672 701-2713

Austria

Fax: (43) 7672 701-3880
CFO: Thomas Riegler
Phone: (43) 7672 701-2713
Fax: (43) 7672 701-3880
Tech. Textile Mgr.: Andreas Dorner
Phone: (43) 7672 701-3025
Fax: (43) 7672 918-3025
Email: a.dorner@lenzing.com
Bus. Unit Mgr.: Wilhelm Feilmair
Phone: (43) 7672 701-2285
Fax: (43) 7672 918-2285
Email: w.feilmair@lenzing.com
Head of Investor Relations: Stephanie Kniep
Phone: (43) 7672 701-4032
Fax: (43) 7672 918 4032
Email: s.kniep@lenzing.com
Head of Corporate Commun.: Angelika Guldt
Phone: (43) 7672 701-2713
Fax: (43) 7672 701-3880
Email: a.guldt@lenzing.com
Total Employees of Company: 6,479
Total Employees at this Location: 240
Type of Operation: Pulp mill
Mill Locations:
Biocel Paskov a.s., Paskov Mill, Zahradní 762, CZ-739 21 Paskov, Czech Republic, (Pulp mill)
Phone: (420) 558 461 111
Fax: (420) 558 461 113
Email: office@biocel.cz
Lenzing Papier GmbH, Lenzing Paper Mill (40% owned), Werkstr. 2, A-4860 Lenzing, Austria, Capacity: 85,000 mt/y, (Paper mill)
Phone: (43) 7672 701-3283
Fax: (43) 7672 701-2231
Email: office@lenzingpapier.com
Pulp Grades and Capacities:
Total pulp capacity: 262,687 mt/y
Pulp available for market: 250,000 mt/y
Chemical Pulp: 262,687 mt/y

Pulp Mill Data:
Chemical Pulping Systems:
Batch digesters: 8
Bleach Plant Systems: 1
Chemical Pulping System, Type: Hardwood, Ozone process: MC, Sequence: E/OZP, Capacity 285,000 admt/y
Chemical Recovery Equipment:
Evaporator lines: 1
Recovery boilers: 4
Pulp Dryers:
Air Float dryers 1, Wet Lap machine 1
Energy Data:
Power boilers: 4
Steam turbines: 6 at 101 MW
Electrical demand for mill: 503 MWh/D

ⓂLenzing Papier GmbH
Lenzing Paper Mill
Ownership: 40% by Lenzing AG, 60% by Dachstein Papier
Werkstr. 2
A-4860 Lenzing, Oberösterreich
Austria
Phone: (43) 7672 701-3283
Fax: (43) 7672 701-2231
Email: office@lenzingpapier.com
Web Address: www.lenzingpapier.com
Personnel:
Man. Dir. (Man. Partner): Ernst Brunbauer
Phone: (43) 7672 701-3283
Fax: (43) 7672 701-2231
Email: e.brunbauer@lenzingpapier.com
Member of The Exec. Board: Franz Gstettenhofer
Phone: (43) 7672 701-3283
Fax: (43) 7672 701-2231
Email: f.gstettenhofer@lenzingpapier.com
Proj. Mgr.: Elisabeth Koudelka
Phone: (43) 7672 701-3283
Fax: (43) 7672 701-2231
Tech. Mgr.: Alexander Zacherl
Phone: (43) 7672 701-3283
Fax: (43) 7672 701-2231
Email: a.zacherl@lenzingpapier.com
Sls. & Mktg. Mgr.: Bernd Wechsler
Phone: (43) 7672 701 3160
Fax: (43) 7672 701-2231
Email: b.wechsler@lenzingpapier.com
Corporate Communications: Angelika Guldt
Phone: (43) 7672 701-2713
Fax: (43) 7672 701-2231
Email: presse@lenzing.com
Total Employees at this Location: 130
Type of Operation: Paper mill
Pulp Grades and Capacities:
Total pulp capacity: 56,420 mt/y
Recycled Pulping: 56,420 mt/y

Pulp Mill Data:
Bleach Plant Systems: 1
Recycled Pulping System, Type: DIP
Recycled Fiber Treatment Lines:
Flotation deinking lines: 3 at 100,000
Pulpers: 3 at 100,000
Paper/Paperboard Grades and Capacities:
Total paper and paperboard capacity: 85,000 mt/y
Uncoated woodfree/freesheet: 65,000 mt/y
Coated woodfree/freesheet: 15,000 mt/y
Specialty and industrial: 5,000 mt/y
Paper and Paperboard Mill Data:
Stock Preparation:
Pulpers: 1
Paper Machines: 1
No. 1, DuoFormer D, total capacity 85,000 mt/y, Trim width 4.8 m, Uncoated woodfree/freesheet, Coated woodfree/freesheet, Specialty and industrial
Coating Machines: 1
PM 1, total capacity 20,000 mt/y., on machine
Finishing Equipment:
Winders: 2
Sheeters: 2
Energy Data:
Power boilers: 6
Steam turbines: 7 at 110.0 MW
Electrical demand for mill: 194 MWh/D

ⓂMayr-Melnhof Karton AG
Ownership: Public
Brahmsplatz 6
A-1041 Vienna
Austria
Phone: (43) 1 50136 0
Fax: (43) 1 50136 91391
Email: vienna@mm-karton.com
Web Address: www.mayr-melnhof.com
Personnel:
Deputy Chairman: Romuald Bertl
Phone: (43) 1 50136 - 0
Fax: (43) 1 50136
CEO, Chrmn. of the Management Board: Dr. Wilhelm Hörmanseder
Phone: (43) 1 50136 - 0
Fax: (43) 1 50136
CFO (until March 1, 2015): Dr. Oliver Schumy
Phone: (43) 1 50136 - 0
Fax: (43) 1 50136
CFO (effective March 1, 2015): Gotthard Mayringer
Phone: (43) 1 50136 - 0
Fax: (43) 1 50136
Bd. Mbr., Sls., Mktg. MM Packaging: Dr. Andreas Blaschke
Phone: (43) 1 50136 - 0
Fax: (43) 1 50136
Member of the Management Board, (MM Karton) sales and marketing activities: Franz Rappold
Phone: (43) 1 50136 - 0
Fax: (43) 1 50136
Member of the Management Board, (MM Packaging) sales and marketing activities.: Andreas Blaschke
Phone: (43) 1 50136 - 0
Fax: (43) 1 50136
Total Employees of Company: 9,477
Mill Locations:
Baiersbronn Frischfaserkarton GmbH, Baiersbronn Mill, Sägmühleweg 18, D-72270 Baiersbronn, Germany, Capacity: 80,000 mt/y, (Pulp mill, Paperboard mill)
Phone: (49) 7442 831 0
Fax: (49) 7442 831 240
Email: sales.baiersbronn@mm-karton.com, baiersbronn@mm-karton.com
FS-Karton GmbH, Neuss Mill, Düsseldorfer Str. 182-184, D-41405 Neuss, Germany, Capacity: 350,000 mt/y, (Paperboard mill)
Phone: (49) 2131 237 0
Fax: (49) 2131 237 22162
Email: sales.neuss@mm-karton.com
Kolicevo Karton d.o.o., Kolicevo Mill, Papirniška 1, SI-1230 Domžale, Slovenia, Capacity: 240,000 mt/y, (Paperboard mill)
Phone: (386) 1 72 11 011/90 511
Fax: (386) 1 72 43 571/90 519
Email: sales.kolicevo@mm-karton.com
MMK FollaCell A.S., Folla Mill, industriveien 1, NO-7796 Follafoss, Norway, (Pulp mill)
Phone: (47) 74 12 36 00
Fax: (47) 74 12 36 01
Email: sales.follacell@mm-karton.com
Mayr-Melnhof Eerbeek BV, Eerbeek Mill, Coldenhovenseweg 4, NL-6961 ED Eerbeek, Netherlands, Capacity: 140,000 mt/y, (Pulp mill, Paperboard mill)
Phone: (31) 313 675 111
Fax: (31) 313 654 777
Email: sales.eerbeek@mm-karton.com
Mayr-Melnhof Karton GmbH, Frohnleiten Mill, Wannersdorf 80, A-8130 Frohnleiten, Austria, Capacity: 480,000 mt/y, (Pulp mill, Paperboard mill)
Phone: (43) 3126 2511-0
Fax: (43) 3126 2511-102
Email: sales.frohnleiten@mm-karton.com
Mayr-Melnhof Karton GmbH, Hirschwang Mill, Hirschwang 77, A-2651 Reichenau an der Rax, Austria, Capacity: 80,000 mt/y, (Paperboard mill)
Phone: (43) 2666 52951
Fax: (43) 2666 52951-126
Email: sales.hirschwang@mm-karton.com, hirschwang@mm-karton.com
Mayr-Melnhof Gernsbach GmbH, Gernsbach Mill, Obertsroter Strasse 9, D-76593 Gernsbach, Germany, Capacity: 250,000 mt/y, (Paperboard mill)
Phone: (49) 7224 641 0
Fax: (49) 7224 641 560/445
Email: sales.gernsbach@mm-karton.com

ⓂMayr-Melnhof Karton GmbH
Frohnleiten Mill
Ownership: Mayr-Melnhof Karton AG
Wannersdorf 80
A-8130 Frohnleiten, Styria
Austria
Phone: (43) 3126 2511-0
Fax: (43) 3126 2511-102
Email: sales.frohnleiten@mm-karton.com
Web Address: www.mm-karton.com
Personnel:
Mill Mgr.: Ing. Mag. Gernot Schleiss
Phone: (43) 3126 2511 163
Fax: (43) 3126 2511 58
Email: gernot.schleiss@mm-karton.com
Prod. Mgr.: Martin Mühlhauser
Phone: (43) 3126 2511 149
Fax: (43) 3126 2511 102
Email: martin.muehlhauser@mm-karton.com
Tech. Mgr.: Helmut Huss
Phone: (43) 3126 2511 174
Fax: (43) 3126 511 101
Email: helmut.huss@mm-karton.com
Total Employees at this Location: 530
Type of Operation: Pulp mill, Paperboard mill
Pulp Grades and Capacities:
Total pulp capacity: 431,464 mt/y
Mechanical Pulp: 79,249 mt/y

Recycled Pulping: 352,216 mt/y
Pulp Mill Data:
Mechanical Pulping Systems:
RMP systems: 1
Bleach Plant Systems: 1
Recycled Fiber Treatment Lines:
Flotation deinking lines: 1
Pulpers: 1 at 31,000
Pulpers: 1 at 393,100
Paper/Paperboard Grades and Capacities:
Total paper and paperboard capacity: 480,000 mt/y
Boxboard/cartonboard: 480,000 mt/y
Paper and Paperboard Mill Data:
Stock Preparation:
Pulpers: 4
Refiners: 8
Paper Machines: 2
No. 2, cylinder (10), total capacity 170,000 mt/y, Trim width 2.9 m, Boxboard/cartonboard
No. 3, Fourdrinier (4), total capacity 310,000 mt/y, Trim width 4.4 m, Boxboard/cartonboard
Coating Machines: 2
BM 2, total capacity 155,000 mt/y., on machine
BM 3, total capacity 310,000 mt/y., on machine
Finishing Equipment:
Winders: 2
Sheeters: 7
Energy Data:
Power boilers: 4
Combustion turbines: 1 at 4 MW
Steam turbines: 3 at 11, 13, 4 MW
Electrical demand for mill: 802 MWh/D

ⓜMayr-Melnhof Karton GmbH
Hirschwang Mill
Ownership: Mayr-Melnhof Karton AG
Hirschwang 77
A-2651 Reichenau an der Rax, Niederösterreich
Austria
  Phone: (43) 2666 52951
  Fax: (43) 2666 52951-126
  Email: sales.hirschwang@mm-karton.com,
  hirschwang@mm-karton.com
  Web Address: www.mm-karton.com
Personnel:
  Mill Dir.: Raimund Doppelreiter
  Phone: (43) 2666 52951
  Fax: (43) 2666 52951-126
  Email: raimund.doppelreiter@mm-karton.com
Total Employees at this Location: 140
Type of Operation: Paperboard mill
Pulp Grades and Capacities:
Total pulp capacity: 70,107 mt/y
Recycled Pulping: 70,107 mt/y
Pulp Mill Data:
Recycled Fiber Treatment Lines:
Pulpers: 4
Paper/Paperboard Grades and Capacities:
Total paper and paperboard capacity: 80,000 mt/y
Boxboard/cartonboard: 80,000 mt/y
Paper and Paperboard Mill Data:
Stock Preparation:
Pulpers: 4
Refiners: 6
Paper Machines: 1
No. 4, cylinder (10), Yankee dryer, total capacity 80,000 mt/y, Trim width 2.15 m, Boxboard/cartonboard
Coating Machines: 4
No. 1, on machine
No. 2, on machine
No. 3, on machine
No. 4, total capacity 70,000 mt/y., on machine
Finishing Equipment:
Rewinders: 1
Sheeters: 1
Energy Data:
Power boilers: 3
Steam turbines: 1 at 3.5 MW

Hydro turbines: 3
Electrical demand for mill: 105 MWh/D

ⓘⓜMerckens Karton- und Pappenfabrik GmbH
Schwertberg Mill
Ownership: 50% by Gerhard Merckens, 50% by Gottfried Merckens
Josefstal 10
A-4311 Schwertberg, Oberösterreich
Austria
  Phone: (43) 7262 61161-0
  Fax: (43) 7262 61161-57
  Email: pappe@merckens.at
  Web Address: www.merckens.at
Personnel:
  Chmn. & Mill Mgr.: Christoph Merckens
  Phone: (43) 7262 61161-0
  Fax: (43) 7262 611 61-57
  Email: pappe@merckens.at
  Associate, Sls. Dir.: Gottfried Merckens
  Phone: (43) 1 523 35 00
  Fax: (43) 1 526 12 28
  Email: pappe@merckens.at
  Sls. Mgr.: Bettina Viehbock
  Phone: (43) 7262 611 61-21
  Fax: (43) 7262 611 61-57
  Email: bettina.viehboeck@merckens.at
Total Employees of Company: 65
Total Employees at this Location: 65
Type of Operation: Paperboard mill
Pulp Grades and Capacities:
Total pulp capacity: 15,265 mt/y
Recycled Pulping: 15,265 mt/y
Paper/Paperboard Grades and Capacities:
Total paper and paperboard capacity: 15,000 mt/y
Boxboard/cartonboard: 15,000 mt/y
Paper and Paperboard Mill Data:
Stock Preparation:
Pulpers: 2
Paper Machines: 2
No. 1, cylinder, total capacity 10,000 mt/y, Trim width 2.4 m, Boxboard/cartonboard
No. 2, cylinder, total capacity 5,000 mt/y, Trim width 1.6 m, Boxboard/cartonboard
Coating Machines: 1
No. 1, total capacity 1,900 mt/y.
Finishing Equipment:
Calenders: 4
Energy Data:
Electrical demand for mill: 13 MWh/D

ⓘMondi Europe & International Division
Ownership: Mondi
Marxergasse 4A
A-1030 Vienna
Austria
  Phone: (43) 1 790 130
  Fax: (43) 1 790 1396
  Web Address: www.mondigroup.com
Personnel:
  Joint Chmn.: Fred Phaswana
  Phone: (43) 1 790 130
  Fax: (43) 1 790 1396
  Joint Chmn.: David Williams
  Phone: (43) 1 790 130
  Fax: (43) 1 790 1396
  CEO: David Hathorn
  Phone: (43) 1 790 130
  Fax: (43) 1 790 1396
  Email: david.hathorn@mondigroup.com
  CFO: Andrew King
  Phone: (43) 1 790 130
  Fax: (43) 1 790 1396
  Email: andrew.king@mondigroup.com
  CEO Europe & International Division: Peter Oswald
  Phone: (43) 1 790 130
  Fax: (43) 1 790 1396

  Email: peter.oswald@mondigroup.com
  CEO Uncoated Fine Paper: Peter Orisich
  Phone: (43) 1 790 130
  Fax: (43) 1 790 1396
  Email: peter.orisich@mondigroup.com
  Asst. CEO : Barbara Gaich
  Phone: (43) 1 79013-4767
  Fax: (43) 1 790 1396
  Email: barbara.gaich@mondigroup.com
  Oper. Dir: Christian Skilich
  Phone: (43) 1 790 130
  Fax: (43) 1 790 1396
  Email: christian.skilich@mondigroup.com
  Sls. & Mktg. Dir. :Johannes Klumpp
  Phone: (43) 1 790 130
  Fax: (43) 1 790 1396
  Email: johannes.klumpp@mondigroup.com
  Sls & Bus. Dev. Dir.: Fuerst Markus
  Phone: (43) 1 790 130
  Fax: (43) 1 790 1396
  HR Dir.: Helmut Raunig
  Phone: (43) 1 790 130
  Fax: (43) 1 790 1396
  Email: helmut.raunig@mondigroup.com
  Head of Commer. Excellence: Isabella Schleifer
  Phone: (43) 1 79013-4767
  Fax: (43) 1 790 1396
  Email: isabella.schleifer@mondigroup.com
  Head of Sales Middle Europe: Remco Wagner
  Phone: (43) 1 79013-4767
  Fax: (43) 1 790 1396
  Email: remco.wagner@mondigroup.com
Total Employees of Company: 866
Total Employees at this Location: 450
Mill Locations:
Mondi Dynäs AB, Väja Mill, SE-873 81 Väja, Sweden, Capacity: 250,000 mt/y, (Pulp mill, Paper mill)
  Phone: (46) 612 83000
  Fax: (46) 612 26511
  Email: info.dynas@mondigroup.com
Mondi Frantschach GmbH, Frantschach Mill, Frantschach 5, A-9413 St. Gertraud, Austria, Capacity: 289,884 mt/y, (Pulp mill, Paper mill)
  Phone: (43) 4352 530
  Fax: (43) 4352 53073
  Email: (firstname.lastname@mondigroup.com)
Mondi Neusiedler GmbH, Kematen mill, A-3331 Kematen, Austria, Capacity: 100,000 mt/y, (Pulp mill, Paper mill)
  Phone: (43) 7475 500 0
  Fax: (43) 7475 500 2259
  Email: service@mondigroup.com
Mondi Lohja Oy, Lohja Mill, Kotkantie 5, FI-08100 Lohja, Finland, Capacity: 80,000 mt/y, (Paper mill)
  Phone: (358) 2074 4611
  Fax: (358) 2074 4610
Mondi Raubling GmbH, Raubling Mill, Rosenheimer Str. 37, D-83064 Raubling, Germany, Capacity: 220,000 mt/y, (Paperboard mill)
  Phone: (49) 8035 9090
  Fax: (49) 8035 902 132
  Email: (firstname.lastname@mondigroup.com)
Mondi SCP a.s., Ružomberok Mill (51% owned), Tatranská cesta 3, SK-03417 Ružomberok, Slovakia, Capacity: 615,000 mt/y, (Pulp mill, Paper mill)
  Phone: (421) 44 436 2222/2090
  Fax: (421) 44 436 3824/2476
  Email: mondiscp@mondigroup.com
Mondi Stambolijski EAD, Stambolijski Mill, 1, Zavodska Str., BG-4210 Stambolijski, Bulgaria, Capacity: 90,000 mt/y, (Pulp mill, Paper mill)
  Phone: (359) 32 909 287
  Fax: (359) 32 909 554
Mondi Štetí, Štetí Mill, Litomerická 272, CZ-411 08 Štetí, Czech Republic, Capacity: 372,000 mt/y, (Pulp mill, Paper mill, Paperboard mill)
  Phone: (420) 416 80 2184/1111/2603
  Fax: (420) 416 80 2599 / 2233
Mondi Swiecie S.A., Swiecie Mill, Bydgoska Str. 1, PL-86100 Swiecie, Poland, Capacity: 1,399,000 mt/y, (Pulp mill, Paper mill, Paperboard mill)

Austria

Phone: (48) 52 332 1553
Fax: (48) 52 332 1931
Email: (firstname.surname@mondigroup.com), info.swiecie@mondigroup.com
Mondi Syktyvkar, Syktyvkar Mill, Burnazhnikov pr. 2, 167026 Syktyvkar, Russia, Capacity: 990,000 mt/y, (Pulp mill, Paper mill, Paperboard mill)
Phone: (7) 8212 699555
Fax: (7) 8212 620282
Email: olga.rimert@mondigroup.com
Mondi Neusiedler GmbH, Theresienthal Mill, A-3363 Ulmerfeld-Hausmening, Austria, Capacity: 287,000 mt/y, (Pulp mill, Paper mill)
Phone: (43) 7475 500 0
Fax: (43) 7475 500 2259
Email: service@mondigroup.com
Mondi Tire Kutsan Paper and Packaging Industry Inc., Tire Mill (53.56% owned), Bekleme Mevkii, TR-35900 Tire, Turkey, Capacity: 135,000 mt/y, (Paper mill, Paperboard mill)
Phone: (90) 232 5121156/1943
Fax: (90) 232 5123871/1046
Email: info@tirekutsan.com.tr

ⓂMondi Frantschach GmbH
Frantschach Mill

Ownership: Mondi Europe & International Division
Frantschach 5
A-9413 St. Gertraud
Austria
Phone: (43) 4352 530
Fax: (43) 4352 53073
Email: (firstname.lastname@mondigroup.com)
Web Address: www.mondigroup.com
Personnel:
Man. Dir.: Gottfried Joham
Phone: (43) 4352 530 355
Fax: (43) 4352 530 73
Email: gottfried.joham@mondigroup.com
Pulp Mill Mgr.: Manfred Hacker
Phone: (43) 4352 530 388
Fax: (43) 4352 530 73
Email: manfied.hacker@mondigroup.com
Procurement Mgr.: Karin Morianz
Phone: (43) 4352 530 224
Fax: (43) 4352 530 73
Email: karin.morianz@mondigroup.com
Paper Mill Mgr.: Christian Gernig
Phone: (43) 4352 530 491
Fax: (43) 4352 530 73
Email: christian.gernig@mondigroup.com
Finan. & Control Dir.: Gabriele Schallegger
Phone: (43) 4352 530
Fax: (43) 4352 530 73
Email: gabriele.schallegger@mondigroup.com
Sls. Mgr.: Gerhard Pachler
Phone: (43) 1 79 013 4920
Fax: (43) 1 79 013 951
Email: gerhard.pachler@mondigroup.com
HR Dvlpt., Commun.: Elisabeth Wuggenig
Phone: (43) 4352 530 206
Fax: (43) 4352 530 78
Email: elisabeth.wuggenig@mondigroup.com
Total Employees at this Location: 455
Type of Operation: Pulp mill, Paper mill
Pulp Grades and Capacities:
Total pulp capacity: 352,464 mt/y
Pulp available for market: 49,980 mt/y
Chemical Pulp: 352,464 mt/y

Pulp Mill Data:
Chemical Pulping Systems:
Continuous digesters: 1
Pulp Lines: 1
Chemical Recovery Equipment:
Evaporator lines: 1
Recovery boilers: 2
Lime Kiln
Pulp Dryers:
Flash dryers 1
Paper/Paperboard Grades and Capacities:
Total paper and paperboard capacity: 289,884 mt/y
Packaging papers: 259,896 mt/y
Specialty and industrial: 29,988 mt/y
Paper and Paperboard Mill Data:
Stock Preparation:
Pulpers: 1
Refiners: 10
Paper Machines: 3
No. 6, fourdrinier, total capacity 129,948 mt/y, Trim width 4.1 m, Packaging papers
No. 7, Yankee dryer, total capacity 29,988 mt/y, Trim width 3.76 m, Specialty and industrial
No. 8, fourdrinier, total capacity 129,948 mt/y, Trim width 4.3 m, Packaging papers
Finishing Equipment:
Winders: 3
Energy Data:
Power boilers: 1
Steam turbines: 4 at 30.0 MW
Electrical demand for mill: 823 MWh/D

ⓂMondi Neusiedler GmbH
Kematen mill

Ownership: Mondi Europe & International Division
A-3331 Kematen, Niederösterreich
Austria
Phone: (43) 7475 500 0
Fax: (43) 7475 500 2259
Email: service@mondigroup.com
Web Address: www.mondigroup.com
Personnel:
Man. Dir.: Karl Grill
Phone: (43) 7475 500 0
Fax: (43) 7475 500 2259
Email: karl.grill@mondigroup.com
Converting Plt & Finishing Mgr.: Thomas Novak
Phone: (43) 7475 500 0
Fax: (43) 7475 500 2259
Email: thomas.novak@mondigroup.com
Head of Finan. & Admin.: Werner Röcklinger
Phone: (43) 7475 500 0
Fax: (43) 7475 500 2259
Email: werner.roecklinger@mondigroup.com
Bus. Develop. Mgr.: Juliette Pickl
Phone: (43) 7475 500 0
Fax: (43) 7475 500 2259
Email: juliette.pickl@mondigroup.com
Mktg & Sls. Dir.: Johannes Klumpp
Phone: (43) 7475 500 0
Fax: (43) 7475 500 2259
Email: johannes.klumpp@mondigroup.com
Mktg. Mgr.: Stephanie Kienapfel
Phone: (43) 7475 500 0
Fax: (43) 7475 500 2259
Email: stephanie.kienapfel@mondigroup.com
Total Employees at this Location: 230
Type of Operation: Pulp mill, Paper mill
Pulp Grades and Capacities:
Total pulp capacity: 50,000 mt/y
Pulp available for market: 24,737 mt/y
Chemical Pulp: 50,000 mt/y
Pulp Mill Data:
Chemical Pulping Systems:
Batch digesters: 3
Pulp Lines: 1
Bleach Plant Systems: 1
No. 1, Sequence: EopP, Capacity 50,000 admt/y
Chemical Recovery Equipment:
Evaporator lines: 1
Recovery boilers: 1
Pulp Dryers:
Pulp Dryers 1, Wet Lap machine 1
Paper/Paperboard Grades and Capacities:
Total paper and paperboard capacity: 100,000 mt/y
Uncoated woodfree/freesheet: 100,000 mt/y
Paper and Paperboard Mill Data:
Stock Preparation:
Pulpers: 2
Refiners: 10
Paper Machines: 2
No. 3, DuoFormer D, total capacity 24,000 mt/y, Trim width 2.16 m, Uncoated woodfree/freesheet
No. 4, DuoFormer D, total capacity 76,000 mt/y, Trim width 2.65 m, Uncoated woodfree/freesheet
Finishing Equipment:
Winders: 4
Supercalenders: 1
Sheeters: 8
Energy Data:
Power boilers: 3
Steam turbines: 4
Hydro turbines: 9
Electrical demand for mill: 279 MWh/D

ⓂMondi Neusiedler GmbH
Theresienthal Mill

Ownership: Mondi Europe & International Division
A-3363 Ulmerfeld-Hausmening, Niederösterreich
Austria
Phone: (43) 7475 500 0
Fax: (43) 7475 500 2259
Email: service@mondigroup.com
Web Address: www.mondigroup.com
Personnel:
Man. Dir.: Karl Grill
Phone: (43) 7475 500 2250
Fax: (43) 7475 500 2259
Email: karl.grill@mondigroup.com
Total Employees at this Location: 500
Type of Operation: Pulp mill, Paper mill
Pulp Mill Data:
Pulp Lines: 1
Bleach Plant Systems: 1
Paper/Paperboard Grades and Capacities:
Total paper and paperboard capacity: 287,000 mt/y
Uncoated woodfree/freesheet: 287,000 mt/y
Paper and Paperboard Mill Data:
Paper Machines: 2
No. 5, fourdrinier, total capacity 104,000 mt/y, Trim width 4.36 m, Uncoated woodfree/freesheet
No. 6, DuoFormer CFD, total capacity 183,000 mt/y, Trim width 4.36 m, Uncoated woodfree/freesheet
Finishing Equipment:
Sheeters: 7 at 390,000 mt/y
Energy Data:
Power boilers: 1
Steam turbines: 2
Hydro turbines: 3
Electrical demand for mill: 575 MWh/D

ⓄⓂSchweighofer Fiber GmbH
Hallein Mill

Ownership: Schweighofer Holzindustrie (Private)
Salzachtalbundesstr. Süd 88
A-5400 Hallein, Salzburg
Austria
Mailing Address: Postf. 62, A-5400 Hallein, Austria
Phone: (43) 6245 890 0
Fax: (43) 6245 890 224/209
Email: office@schweighofer-fiber.at
Web Address: www.schweighofer-fiber.at
Personnel:
CEO & Mill Mgr.: Jörg Harbring
Phone: (43) 6245 890 0
Fax: (43) 6245 890 224
Email: jorg.harbring@schweighofer-fiber.at
HR. & Commun. Mgr.: Bettina Lienbacher
Phone: (43) 6245 890 201
Fax: (43) 6245 890 203
Email: bettina.lienbacher@schweighofer-fiber.at
Total Employees of Company: 230
Total Employees at this Location: 230
Type of Operation: Pulp mill
Pulp Grades and Capacities:
Total pulp capacity: 146,910 mt/y
Pulp available for market: 140,000 mt/y
Chemical Pulp: 146,910 mt/y
Pulp Mill Data:

Austria

Chemical Pulping Systems:
Batch digesters: 7
Pulp Lines: 1
Bleach Plant Lines:
Sulphite HW, Type: Eop-Z-P, Sequence: EopP, Capacity 160,000 admt/y
Chemical Recovery Equipment:
Evaporator lines: 1
Recovery boilers: 1
Pulp Dryers:
Pulp Dryers 1
Energy Data:
Power boilers: 5
Steam turbines: 8 at 54.0, 3.7 MW
Electrical demand for mill: 343 MWh/D

ⓂNorske Skog Bruck GmbH
Bruck an der Mur Mill
Ownership: Norske Skog ASA
Fabriksgasse 10
A-8600 Bruck an der Mur, Styria
Austria
Phone: (43) 3862 800-0
Fax: (43) 3862 800 300
Email: bruck@norskeskog.com,
(firstname.lastname@norskeskog.com)
Web Address: www.norskeskog.at,
www.norskeskog.com
Personnel:
Mill Mgr.: Thomas Reibelt
Phone: (43) 3862 800-0
Fax: (43) 3862 800 300
Email: thomas.reibelt@norskeskog.com
Maint. & Energy Mgr.: Karl Misslik
Phone: (43) 3862 800-0
Fax: (43) 3862 800 300
Email: karl.misslik@norskeskog.com
Pulp & Energy, Prod. Mgr., PM 3: Helmut Schwarz
Phone: (43) 3862 800-0
Fax: (43) 3862 800 300
Email: helmut.schwarz@norskeskog.com
Snr. Specialist Mech. Pulp & Continuous Improvement: Peter Kaiser
Phone: (43) 3862 800-0
Fax: (43) 3862 800 300
Email: peter.kaiser@norskeskog.com
Commun. Mgr.: Gert Pfleger
Phone: (43) 3862 800-0
Fax: (43) 3862 800 300
Email: gert.pfleger@norskeskog.com
Total Employees at this Location: 471
Type of Operation: Paper mill
Pulp Grades and Capacities:
Total pulp capacity: 290,744 mt/y
Mechanical Pulp: 87,199 mt/y
Recycled Pulping: 203,545 mt/y
Pulp Mill Data:
Mechanical Pulping Systems:
Pressurized grinders: 5
Pulp Lines: 3
Bleach Plant Systems: 1
Mechanical PGW Pulping System, Type: Softwood, Sequence: P, Capacity 90,000 admt/y
Recycled Fiber Treatment Lines:
Flotation deinking lines: 2 at 185,000 admt/y
Paper/Paperboard Grades and Capacities:
Total paper and paperboard capacity: 400,000 mt/y
Newsprint: 118,750 mt/y
Uncoated mechanical/groundwood: 6,250 mt/y
Coated mechanical/groundwood: 275,000 mt/y
Paper and Paperboard Mill Data:
Paper Machines: 2
No. 3, DuoFormer H, total capacity 125,000 mt/y, Trim width 5.23 m, Newsprint, Uncoated mechanical/groundwood
No. 4, OptiFormer, total capacity 275,000 mt/y, Trim width 6.26 m, Coated mechanical/groundwood
Coating Machines: 1
CM 1, total capacity 275,000 mt/y., on machine

Finishing Equipment:
Supercalenders: 2
Rewinders: 1
Energy Data:
Power boilers: 3
HRSG boiler: 1
Combustion turbines: 1 at 40 MW
Steam turbines: 2 at 23.0 MW
Electrical demand for mill: 1,325 MWh/D

ⓅⓂZellstoff Pöls AG
Pöls Mill
Ownership: 100% by Heinzel Holding GmbH
Dr. Luigi Angeli Strasse 9
A-8761 Pöls, Styria
Austria
Phone: (43) 3579 8181-0
Fax: (43) 3579 8181-319/8220
Email: office@zellstoff-poels.at
Web Address: www.zellstoff-poels.at
Personnel:
CEO: DI Dr. Kurt Maier
Phone: (43) 3579 8181 214
Fax: (43) 3579 8181 319
Email: k.maier@zellstoff-poels.at
CFO: DI Dr. Gunther Sames
Phone: (43) 3579 8181 223
Fax: (43) 3579 8181 319
Email: g.sames@zellstoff-poels.at
Mill Mgr.: Ing. Kurt Haberl
Phone: (43) 3579 8181 274
Fax: (43) 3579 8181 319
Email: k.haberl@zellstoff-poels.at
Head Proj. Eng.: DI Siegfried Gruber
Phone: (43) 3579 8181 290
Fax: (43) 3579 8181 319
Email: s.gruber@zellstoff-poels.at
Supervisor Integrated Management System: Franz Mayer
Phone: (43) 3579 8181 0
Fax: (43) 3579 8181 319
Email: f.mayer@zellstoff-poels.at
Head Purch. & IT: Manfred Peisler
Phone: (43) 3579 8181 222
Fax: (43) 3579 8181 319
Email: m.peischler@zellstoff-poels.at
Head Finan., Group Contr.: Ingrid Gruber
Phone: (43) 3579 8181 0
Fax: (43) 3579 8181 319
Email: i.gruber@zellstoff-poels.at
HR Dir.: Ilse Ranser
Phone: (43) 3579 8181 0
Fax: (43) 3579 8181 319
Email: i.ranser@zellstoff-poels.at
Assist. Board Management: Daniela Reicher
Phone: (43) 3579 8181 0
Fax: (43) 3579 8181 319
Email: d.reicher@zellstoff-poels.at
Maint. Mgr.: Harald Trummer
Phone: (43) 3579 8181 0
Fax: (43) 3579 8181 319
Email: h.trummer@zellstoff-poels.at
Total Employees of Company: 343
Total Employees at this Location: 349
Type of Operation: Pulp mill, Paper mill
Pulp Grades and Capacities:
Total pulp capacity: 410,048 mt/y
Pulp available for market: 340,000 mt/y
Chemical Pulp: 410,048 mt/y
Pulp Mill Data:
Chemical Pulping Systems:
Continuous digesters: 1
Pulp Lines: 1
Bleach Plant Systems: 1
Sunds, Type: Drumfilters, Sequence: O_2 DEopDD, Capacity 410,000 admt/y
Chemical Recovery Equipment:
Evaporator lines: 1
Recovery boilers: 2

Lime Kiln
Pulp Dryers:
Air Float dryers 1, Flash dryers 1
Paper/Paperboard Grades and Capacities:
Total paper and paperboard capacity: 80,000 mt/y
Packaging papers: 10,000 mt/y
Specialty and industrial: 70,000 mt/y
Paper and Paperboard Mill Data:
Stock Preparation:
Pulpers: 1
Refiners: 4
Paper Machines: 1
No. 2, hybrid former, total capacity 80,000 mt/y, Trim width 4.5 m, Specialty and industrial, Packaging papers
Finishing Equipment:
Rewinders: 1 at 16,000 mt/y
Energy Data:
Power boilers: 1
Steam turbines: 2 at 80 MW
Hydro turbines: 2 at 1.8 MW
Electrical demand for mill: 989 MWh/D

ⓅⓂPoneder Halbstoff-Fabrik GmbH
Ulmerfeld-Hausmening Mill
Ownership: 100% by Ingrid Poneder (Private)
Gunnersdorfer Str. 13
A-3363 Ulmerfeld-Hausmening, Niederösterreich
Austria
Phone: (43) 7475 523 54-0
Fax: (43) 7475 523 54-15
Email: office@poneder.at
Web Address: www.poneder.at
Personnel:
Man. Dir./Owner: Ingrid Poneder
Phone: (43) 7475 523 54-0
Prod. Mgr.: Thomas Nietsch
Phone: (43) 7475 523 54-0
Total Employees of Company: 14
Total Employees at this Location: 14
Type of Operation: Pulp mill
Pulp Grades and Capacities:
Total pulp capacity: 2,200 mt/y
Pulp available for market: 2,200 mt/y
Pulp Mill Data:
Mechanical Pulping Systems:
Conventional grinders: 4
Pulp Lines: 1
Bleach Plant Systems: 2
Paper/Paperboard Grades and Capacities:
Total paper and paperboard capacity: 4,200 mt/y
Uncoated woodfree/freesheet: 4,200 mt/y
Paper and Paperboard Mill Data:
Paper Machines: 1
PM 1, Uncoated woodfree/freesheet
Energy Data:
Electrical demand for mill: 4 MWh/D

ⓅPulp Mill Holding GesmbH
Ownership: 93% by Zinner Privatstiftung, 3% by Conrad Jacobson, 1% by A&HZ Privatstiftung, 3% by Jacob Jürgensen
Reichsratstrasse 11/3B
A-1010 Wien
Austria
Phone: (43) 1 406 2201
Fax: (43) 1 406 220120
Email: office@pulpmill.at
Web Address: www.pulpmill.at/en/index.php
Personnel:
Man. Dir.: Mr. Heinz Zinner
Phone: (43) 1 406 2201/26011 0
Fax: (43) 1 406 220120/2636363
Man. Dir.: Mr. Timur Sokolov
Phone: (43) 1 406 2201/26011 0
Fax: (43) 1 406 220120/2636363
Total Employees of Company: 6,000
Total Employees at this Location: 2
Mill Locations:

Austria

Arkhangelsk Pulp & Paper Mill, Novodvinsk (Arkhangelsk - APPM) Mill (97.50% owned), Melnikova Str., 1, 164900 Novodvinsk, Russia, Capacity: 572,000 mt/y, (Pulp mill, Paper mill, Paperboard mill)
Phone: (7) 818 52 63202, 52 63500
Fax: (7) 818 52 63231
Email: info@appm.ru

Arkhbum Tissue Group, Vorsino Mill, Vorsino, Russia, (Paper mill)

Kiev Cardboard and Paper Mill, Kiev Cardboard and Paper Mill (95% owned), vul. Kyivska, 130, 08700 Obukhiv, Ukraine, Capacity: 270,000 mt/y, (Paper mill, Paperboard mill)
Phone: (380) 4572 76300/71056/4452 09831
Fax: (380) 4572 76540/4452 09860
Email: info@papir.kiev.ua

ⓗⓜRondo Ganahl AG
Frastanz Mill
Ownership: 100% by private shareholders
Rotfarbweg 5
A-6820 Frastanz, Vorarlberg
Austria
 Phone: (43) 5522 51841 0
 Fax: (43) 5522 51841 115
 Email: paper@rondo-ganahl.com
 Web Address: www.rondo-ganahl.com
Personnel:
 CEO: Dieter Gruber
 Phone: (43) 5522 51841 0
 Fax: (43) 5522 51841 115
 Email: dieter.gruber@rondo-ganahl.com
 CTO: Michael Frey
 Phone: (43) 5522 51841 0
 Fax: (43) 5522 51841 115
 Email: michael.frey@rondo-ganahl.com
 Sls. Dir.: Peter Suppan
 Phone: (43) 5522 51841 0
 Fax: (43) 5522 51841 115
 Email: peter.suppan@rondo-ganahl.com
Total Employees of Company: 983
Total Employees at this Location: 330
Type of Operation: Paper mill, Paperboard mill
Pulp Grades and Capacities:
 Total pulp capacity: 117,373 mt/y
 Recycled Pulping: 117,373 mt/y
Pulp Mill Data:
 Recycled Fiber Treatment Lines:
 Pulpers: 3
 Recycled packaging pulping lines
Paper/Paperboard Grades and Capacities:
 Total paper and paperboard capacity: 120,000 mt/y
 Linerboard: 120,000 mt/y
Paper and Paperboard Mill Data:
 Stock Preparation:
 Pulpers:
Paper Machines: 1
 No. 2, (Suppliers: PAMA/Valmet/Voith.), DuoFormer D, total capacity 120,000 mt/y, Trim width 2.5 m, Linerboard
Finishing Equipment:
 Winders: 1
 Calenders: 1
 Rewinders: 2
Energy Data:
 Power boilers: 2
 Electrical demand for mill: 148 MWh/D

ⓗⓜSalzer Papier GmbH
Stattersdorf Mill
Ownership: Salzer family via Salzer Holding GmbH (Private)
Stattersdorfer Hauptstrasse 53
A-3100 St. Pölten, Niederösterreich
Austria
 Phone: (43) 2742 290 0
 Fax: (43) 2742 290 173
 Email: office@salzer.at
 Web Address: www.salzer.at
Personnel:
 Man. Mgr.: Thomas Salzer
 Phone: (43) 2742 290 166
 Fax: (43) 2742 290 173
 Email: thomas@salzer.at
 Man. Dir. Sls.: Dr. Harald Egger
 Phone: (43) 2742 290 101
 Fax: (43) 2742 290 173
 Email: harald.egger@salzer.at
 Prod. Mgr.: Franz Zehetner
 Phone: (43) 2742 290 132
 Fax: (43) 2742 290 173
 Email: franz.zehetner@salzer.at
 Safety, Health & Environ. Dir.: Franz Permoser
 Phone: (43) 2742 290 435
 Fax: (43) 2742 290 173
 Email: franz.permoser@salzer.at
 Asst. Management Board: Andrea Scherzer
 Phone: (43) 2742 290 166
 Fax: (43) 2742 290 173
 Email: andrea.scherzer@salzer.at
Total Employees of Company: 75
Total Employees at this Location: 75
Type of Operation: Paper mill
Paper/Paperboard Grades and Capacities:
 Total paper and paperboard capacity: 30,000 mt/y
 Uncoated woodfree/freesheet: 30,000 mt/y
Paper and Paperboard Mill Data:
 Stock Preparation:
 Pulpers: 2
 Refiners: 2
Paper Machines: 1
 No. 1, fourdrinier, total capacity 30,000 mt/y, Trim width 2.64 m, Uncoated woodfree/freesheet
Finishing Equipment:
 Winders: 1 at 28,000 mt/y
 Sheeters: 1 at 28,000 mt/y
Energy Data:
 Power boilers: 1
 Combustion turbines: 1 at 4.5 MW
 Hydro turbines: 1 at 0.15 MW
 Electrical demand for mill: 58 MWh/D

ⓜSappi Fine Paper Europe
Gratkorn Mill
Ownership: 100% by Sappi Limited
Brucker Str. 21
A-8101 Gratkorn, Styria
Austria
 Phone: (43) 3124 201 0
 Fax: (43) 3124 201 3038
 Email: gratkorn.mill@sappi.com
 Web Address: www.sappi.com
Personnel:
 Mill Dir.: Max Oberhumer
 Phone: (43) 3124 201 0
 Fax: (43) 3124 201 3038
 Email: max.oberhumer@sappi.com
 Contrl.: Michael Baumgartner
 Phone: (43) 3124 201 0
 Fax: (43) 3124 201 3038
 Email: michael.baumgartner@sappi.com
 Fibre Develop. Mgr.: Heribert Winter
 Phone: (43) 3124 201 0
 Fax: (43) 3124 201 3038
 Email: heribert.winter@sappi.com
 Paper Mill Mgr.: Manfred Tiefengruber
 Phone: (43) 3124 201 0
 Fax: (43) 3124 201 3038
 Email: manfred.tiefengruber@sappi.com
 Head, Mill Procurement: Manfred Affenberger
 Phone: (43) 3124 201 0
 Fax: (43) 3124 201 3038
 Email: manfred.affenberger@sappi.com
 Qlty. Mgr.: Peter Resch
 Phone: (43) 3124 201 0
 Fax: (43) 3124 201 3038
 Email: peter.resch@sappi.com
Total Employees at this Location: 1,400
Type of Operation: Pulp mill, Paper mill
Pulp Grades and Capacities:
 Total pulp capacity: 260,016 mt/y
 Chemical Pulp: 260,016 mt/y
Pulp Mill Data:
 Chemical Pulping Systems:
 Batch digesters
 Bleach Plant Systems: 1
 Chemical Pulping System, Type: TCF - Hardwood/Softwood
 Chemical Recovery Equipment:
 Evaporator lines: 1
 Recovery boilers: 1
Paper/Paperboard Grades and Capacities:
 Total paper and paperboard capacity: 950,000 mt/y
 Coated woodfree/freesheet: 950,000 mt/y
Paper and Paperboard Mill Data:
 Stock Preparation:
 Pulpers: 2
 Refiners: 20
Paper Machines: 2
 No. 9, DuoFormer D, total capacity 285,000 mt/y, Trim width 6.5 m, Coated woodfree/freesheet
 No. 11, DuoFormer CFD, total capacity 665,000 mt/y, Trim width 8.5 m, Coated woodfree/freesheet
Coating Machines: 4
 CM 2, total capacity 270,000 mt/y., on machine
 CM 3, off machine
 CM 11, total capacity 630,000 mt/y., off machine
 CM 11, total capacity 630,000 mt/y., on machine
Finishing Equipment:
 Winders: 4
 Supercalenders: 4
 Sheeters: 12
Energy Data:
 Power boilers: 3
 Combustion turbines: 1 at 45 MW
 Steam turbines: 3 at 36, 25, 15 MW
 Hydro turbines: 2 at 2.6 MW
 Electrical demand for mill: 1,988 MWh/D

ⓜSCA Hygiene Products GmbH
Ownership: SCA - Svenska Cellulosa Aktiebolaget
Storchengasse 1
A-1150 Vienna
Austria
 Phone: (43) 1 89901-0
 Fax: (43) 1 89901 551
 Email: office@sca.com
 Web Address: www.sca.com
Personnel:
 Country Mgr.: Thomas Strasser
 Phone: (43) 1 89901-0
 Fax: (43) 1 89901 551
 Sls. Dir.: Jurgen Nemeth
 Phone: (43) 43 664 39 28 391
 Fax: (43) 1 89901 551
 Email: juergen.nemeth@heinzelpaper.com
 Sls. Central and Eastern Europe: Ivo Spevacek
 Phone: (43) 43 1 26011 422
 Fax: (43) 1 89901 551
 Email: ivo.spevacek@austria.heinzelsales.com
 HR Mgr.: Margaret Wagenhofer
 Phone: (43) 899 01 451
 Fax: (43) 1 89901 551
 Email: margaret.wagenhofer@sca.com
Total Employees at this Location: 640
Mill Locations:
 SCA Hygiene Products GmbH, Ortmann Mill, Hauptstrasse 1, A-2763 Ortmann, Pernitz, Austria, Capacity: 128,000 mt/y, (Paper mill)
 Phone: (43) 2632 707 0
 Fax: (43) 2632 72394
 Email: office@sca.com
 SCA Hygiene Products GmbH, Witzenhausen Tissue Mill, Kasseler Landstrasse 21, D-37213 Witzenhausen, Germany, Capacity: 30,000 mt/y, (Paper mill)
 Phone: (49) 5542 509 0
 Fax: (49) 5542 509 200

Austria

ⓂSCA Hygiene Products GmbH
Ortmann Mill
Ownership: SCA - Svenska Cellulosa Aktiebolaget
Hauptstrasse 1
A-2763 Ortmann, Pernitz, Niederösterreich
Austria
  Phone: (43) 2632 707 0
  Fax: (43) 2632 72394
  Email: office@sca.com
  Web Address: www.sca.com,
  www.sca.at
Personnel:
  Mill Mgr. (Plant Mgr.): Andreas Greiner
  Phone: (43) 2632 707 0
  Fax: (43) 2632 72394
  Email: andreas.greiner@sca.com
  Environ. Mgr.: Herbert Buchinger
  Phone: (43) 26 32 707 DW 375
  Fax: (43) 26 32 72394
  Email: herbert.buchinger@sca.com
  HR Mgr.: Sabine Honcik
  Phone: (43) 2632 707 784
  Fax: (43) 2632 72394
  Email: sabine.honcik@sca.com
Total Employees at this Location: 565
Type of Operation: Paper mill
Pulp Grades and Capacities:
  Total pulp capacity: 127,929 mt/y
  Recycled Pulping: 127,929 mt/y
Pulp Mill Data:
  Recycled Fiber Treatment Lines:
  Flotation deinking lines: 1
  Pulpers: 1
  Washing deinking lines: 1
Paper/Paperboard Grades and Capacities:
  Total paper and paperboard capacity: 128,000 mt/y
  Tissue: 128,000 mt/y
Paper and Paperboard Mill Data:
  Stock Preparation:
  Pulpers: 3
  Refiners: 3
Paper Machines: 2
  No. 4, C-wrap, Yankee dryer, total capacity 90,000 mt/y, Trim width 6.98 m, Tissue
  No. 9, crescent former, Yankee dryer, total capacity 38,000 mt/y, Trim width 3.48 m, Tissue
Finishing Equipment:
  Winders: 1 at 38,000 mt/y
Energy Data:
  Power boilers: 3
  Combustion turbines: 2 at 10 MW
  Electrical demand for mill: 395 MWh/D

ⓂSmurfit Kappa Nettingsdorfer,
Nettingsdorfer Papierfabrik AG & Co.
KG
Nettingsdorfer Mill
Ownership: Smurfit Kappa Europe
Nettingsdorfer Strasse 40
A-4054 Haid bei Ansfelden, Oberösterreich
Austria
  Phone: (43) 7229 863 0
  Fax: (43) 7229 863 50 / 29 86 312
  Email: nettingsdorfer@smurfitkappa.at
  Web Address: www.smurfitkappa.at,
  www.smurfitkappa-nettingsdorfer.com
Personnel:
  Chmn. & CEO: Ferdinand Fuhrmann
  Phone: (43) 7229 863 208
  Fax: (43) 7229 863 453
  Email: ferdinand.fuhrmann@smurfitkappa.at
  Dir., Sls. Containerboard Europe: Dietmar Patric Bogensberger
  Phone: (43) 7229 863 463
  Fax: (43) 7229 863 12
  Email: dp.bogensberger@smurfitkappa.at
  Man. Dir. (Eff. Jan 1, 2014): Reinhard Reiter
  Phone: (43) 7229 863 0
  Fax: (43) 7229 863 50
  Email: reinhard.reiter@smurfitkappa.se
  Mill Mgr.: Günter Hochrathner
  Phone: (43) 7229 863 203
  Fax: (43) 7229 863 455
  Email: guenter.hochrathner@smurfitkappa.at
  Contr.: Johann Chalupar
  Phone: (43) 7229 863 210
  Fax: (43) 7229 863 12
  Email: johann.chalupar@smurfitkappa.at
  HR & Purch. Mgr.: Gerald Heidl
  Phone: (43) 7229 863 205
  Fax: (43) 7229 863 433
  Email: gerald.heidl@smurfitkappa.at
  Maint. Mgr.: Mario Mostbauer
  Phone: (43) 7229 863 206
  Fax: (43) 7229 863 455
  Email: mario.mostbauer@smurfitkappa.at
  Environ. Mgr.: Christina Ortner
  Phone: (43) 7229 863 244
  Fax: (43) 7229 863 455
  Email: christina.ortner@smurfitkappa.at
Total Employees at this Location: 360
Type of Operation: Pulp mill, Paperboard mill
Pulp Grades and Capacities:
  Total pulp capacity: 444,713 mt/y
  Chemical Pulp: 270,000 mt/y
  Recycled Pulping: 174,713 mt/y
Pulp Mill Data:
  Chemical Pulping Systems:
  Batch digesters: 4
Pulp Lines: 1
  Chemical Recovery Equipment:
  Evaporator lines: 1
  Recovery boilers: 1
  Lime Kiln
  Recycled Fiber Treatment Lines:
  Flotation deinking lines: 1
  Pulpers: 2 at 200,000 admt/y
  Recycled packaging pulping lines: 1
Paper/Paperboard Grades and Capacities:
  Total paper and paperboard capacity: 430,000 mt/y
  Linerboard: 430,000 mt/y
Paper and Paperboard Mill Data:
  Stock Preparation:
  Pulpers: 2
  Refiners: 11
Paper Machines: 1
  No. 6, fourdrinier (2), total capacity 430,000 mt/y, Trim width 7.4 m, Linerboard
Finishing Equipment:
  Winders: 2 at 430,000 mt/y
Energy Data:
  Power boilers: 1
  Steam turbines: 1 at 22.0 MW
  Electrical demand for mill: 821 MWh/D

ⓂⓄUPM-Kymmene Austria GmbH
Steyrermühl Mill
Ownership: 100% by UPM-Kymmene Corporation
Fabriksplatz 1
A-4662 Steyrermühl, Oberösterreich
Austria
  Phone: (43) 7613 89 00 0
  Fax: (43) 7613 2440
  Email: info.steyrermuhl@upm.com
  Web Address: www.upm.com
Personnel:
  CEO & Gen. Mgr.: Matthias Scharre
  Phone: (43) 7613 89 00 0
  Fax: (43) 7613 24 40
  Email: matthias.scharre@upm-kymmene.com
  Prod. Mgr.: Marko Lesiak
  Phone: (43) 7613 89 00 0
  Fax: (43) 7613 24 40
  Email: marko.lesiak@upm-kymmene.com
  Environ. & Commun. Mgr.: Christian Polzinger
  Phone: (43) 7613 89 00 509
  Fax: (43) 7613 24 40
  Email: christian.polzinger@upm-kymmene.com
  Tech. Dir.: Ernst Spitzbart
  Phone: (43) 7613 89 00 0
  Fax: (43) 7613 24 40
  Email: ernest.spitzbart@upm-kymmene.com
  Regional Buyer: Heinz Walter
  Phone: (43) 7613 89 00 0
  Fax: (43) 7613 24 40
  Email: heinz.walter@upm-kymmene.com
  HR Dir.: Josef Wiesauer
  Phone: (43) 7613 89 00 0
  Fax: (43) 7613 24 40
  Email: josef.wiesauer@upm-kymmene.com
Total Employees at this Location: 430
Type of Operation: Paper mill
Pulp Grades and Capacities:
  Total pulp capacity: 473,834 mt/y
  Mechanical Pulp: 134,173 mt/y
  Recycled Pulping: 339,661 mt/y
Pulp Mill Data:
  Mechanical Pulping Systems:
  TMP systems: 1
Pulp Lines: 2
  Bleach Plant Systems: 2
  DIP Capacity 300,000 admt/y
  TMP, Sequence: P, Capacity 160,000 admt/y
  Recycled Fiber Treatment Lines:
  Flotation deinking lines: 1 at 300,000
Paper/Paperboard Grades and Capacities:
  Total paper and paperboard capacity: 500,000 mt/y
  Newsprint: 300,000 mt/y
  Uncoated mechanical/groundwood: 200,000 mt/y
Paper and Paperboard Mill Data:
Paper Machines: 2
  No. 3, OptiFormer, total capacity 200,000 mt/y, Trim width 6.4 m, Uncoated mechanical/groundwood
  No. 4, DuoFormer C, total capacity 300,000 mt/y, Trim width 8.9 m, Newsprint
Finishing Equipment:
  Supercalenders: 1
  Rewinders: 1
Energy Data:
  Power boilers: 1
  TMP Reboiler: 1
  HRSG boiler: 1
  Combustion turbines: 1 at 40 MW
  Steam turbines: 1 at 22 MW
  Hydro turbines: 1 at 4 MW
  Electrical demand for mill: 1,995 MWh/D

ⓂPapierfabrik Wattens GmbH & Co
KG
Wattens Mill
Ownership: 100% by delfortgroup AG
Ludwig Lassl Strasse 15
A-6112 Wattens, Tyrol
Austria
Mailing Address: Postf. 29, A-6112 Wattens, Austria
  Phone: (43) 5224 595 0
  Fax: (43) 5224 595 250
  Email: wattenspapier@delfortgroup.com
  Web Address: www.delfortgroup.com
Personnel:
  R&D Mgr.: Dr. Dietmar Volgger
  Phone: (43) 5224 595 520
  Fax: (43) 5224 595 550
  Email: dietmar.volgger@delfortgroup.com
  Asst. to Mgr. Dir.: Gudrun Huber
  Phone: (43) 5224 595 220
  Fax: (43) 5224 595 250
  Email: gudrun.huber@delfortgroup.com
Total Employees at this Location: 440
Type of Operation: Paper mill
Paper/Paperboard Grades and Capacities:
  Total paper and paperboard capacity: 60,000 mt/y
  Specialty and industrial
Paper and Paperboard Mill Data:
Paper Machines: 5

Belarus

No. 1, total capacity 30,000 mt/y, Trim width 1.9 m, Specialty and industrial
No. 2, fourdrinier, Trim width 1.9 m, Specialty and industrial
No. 3, fourdrinier, Trim width 3.6 m, Specialty and industrial
No. 4, inclined, Trim width 1.9 m, Specialty and industrial
No. 5, fourdrinier, total capacity 10,000 mt/y, Specialty and industrial

BELARUS

ⓗⓜAlbertin Paperboard & Paper Mill
Slonim Mill
Ownership: 100% by mill staff
Fabrichnaya Str., 1
231793 Slonim, Grodno Region
Belarus
 Phone: (375) 1562 32058/31440
 Fax: (375) 17 2108496
 Email: albertin@mail.grodno.by, marketing@albertin.by
 Web Address: www.albertin.by
Personnel:
 Gen. Dir.: Nikolai Vladimirovich Antonik
 Phone: (375) 1562 31397
 Fax: (375) 1562 32056
 Email: albertin@mail.grodno.by
 Chief Eng.: Andrey Vladimirovich Salita
 Phone: (375) 1562 32057
 Fax: (375) 17 2108496
 Commer. Dir.: Eugenie Edvardovich Zakhozhevsky
 Phone: (375) 1562 32050
 Fax: (375) 17 2108496
 Email: sales@albertin.by
 Mktg. Mgr.: Vladimir Michailovich Urbanovich
 Phone: (375) 1562 31440
 Fax: (375) 17 2108496
 Email: marketing@albertin.by
 Economy & Finan. Mgr.: Raisa Hmarik
 Phone: (375) 1562 31146
 Fax: (375) 17 2108496
Total Employees at this Location: 1,100
Type of Operation: Pulp mill, Paper mill, Paperboard mill
Pulp Grades and Capacities:
 Total pulp capacity: 48,528 mt/y
 Recycled Pulping: 48,528 mt/y
Pulp Mill Data:
 Recycled Fiber Treatment Lines:
 Flotation deinking lines
 Recycled packaging pulping lines
Paper/Paperboard Grades and Capacities:
 Total paper and paperboard capacity: 54,000 mt/y
 Tissue: 4,000 mt/y
 Packaging papers: 3,000 mt/y
 Specialty and industrial: 1,000 mt/y
 Linerboard: 8,000 mt/y
 Corrugating medium/fluting: 4,000 mt/y
 Boxboard/cartonboard: 34,000 mt/y
Paper and Paperboard Mill Data:
 Stock Preparation:
 Pulpers: 4
Paper Machines: 4
 No. 1, cylinder, total capacity 14,000 mt/y, Trim width 1.78 m, Boxboard/cartonboard
 No. 2, cylinder, total capacity 20,000 mt/y, Trim width 1.78 m, Boxboard/cartonboard
 No. 4, fourdrinier, total capacity 4,000 mt/y, Trim width 2.1 m, Tissue
 No. 5, fourdrinier, total capacity 16,000 mt/y, Trim width 2.52 m, Specialty and industrial, Packaging papers, Linerboard, Corrugating medium/fluting
Energy Data:
 Power boilers: 3
 Combustion turbines: 1
 Electrical demand for mill: 81 MWh/D

ⓗBellesbumprom
Ownership: 80% by Ministry of State Property
K. Marx Str. 16
22030 Minsk
Belarus
 Phone: (375) 17 327 4483, 210 4445
 Fax: (375) 17 327 4483, 210 4445
 Email: info@bellesbumprom.by
 Web Address: www.bellesbumprom.by
Personnel:
 Chmn. of Group: Alexander Sergeyevich Pereslavtseva
 Phone: (375) 17 327 4483, 210 4445
 Fax: (375) 17 327 4483, 210 4445
 Chmn.: Vladimir Edvardovich Shulga
 Phone: (375) 17 2273366
 Fax: (375) 17 327 4483, 210 4445
 Vice Chmn.: Dmitriy Valentinovich Lizura
 Phone: (375) 17 227 1536
 Fax: (375) 17 327 4483, 210 4445
 Vice Chmn.: Raisa G Heifer
 Phone: (375) 17 327 4483, 210 4445
 Fax: (375) 17 327 4483, 210 4445
 Deputy Chmn.: Sergey Ivanovich Ivanov
 Phone: (375) 17 227 44 83/45
 Fax: (375) 17 227 44 83/45
 Deputy Chmn.: Viktor Dmitrievich Kharlap
 Phone: (375) 17 227 44 83/45
 Fax: (375) 17 227 44 83/45
 Chief Specialist of Informatics: Irina G Brazovsky
 Phone: (375) 17 327-59-81
 Fax: (375) 17 327 4483, 210 4445
 R&D Dir.: Vladimir Viktorovich Ukhoryenok
 Phone: (375) 17 227 1536
 Fax: (375) 17 327 4483, 210 4445
 Bus. Mgr.: Nicholas Kalyada
 Phone: (375) 17 327 4483, 210 4445
 Fax: (375) 17 327 4483, 210 4445
Total Employees at this Location: 100
Mill Locations:
Dobrushskaya Paper Mill "Geroi Truda", OJSC, Dobrush Mill, Lunacharskogo prosp., 7, 247052 Dobrush, Belarus, Capacity: 61,700 mt/y, (Paper mill)
 Phone: (375) 2333 31193/76227
 Fax: (375) 2333 76082/76337
 Email: geroytruda@tut.by
Krasnaya Zvezda, Krasnaya Zvezda Mill, Gagarina str. 20, 211156 Chashniki, Belarus, Capacity: 52,000 mt/y, (Paper mill)
 Phone: (375) 2133 28105/153/483/28434
 Fax: (375) 2133 28483
 Email: sbyt.red-star@mail.ru
Olkhovka Board Mill, JSC, Olkhovka Mill, ul. Fabrichnaya, Ostrovetskiy Distr., 231223 Olkhovka, Belarus, Capacity: 8,600 mt/y, (Paperboard mill)
 Phone: (375) 1591 33221/30
 Fax: (375) 1591 33444/459/230/459
 Email: fabrika-ol@mail.ru; lena.fabrika@mail.ru
Pukhovichskaya Paperboard Mill, Pukhovichskaya Paperboard Mill, ul. Fabrichnaya, 1, 222818 Svetly Bor, Pukhovichskiy rayon, Belarus, Capacity: 14,900 mt/y, (Paperboard mill)
 Phone: (375) 1713 60115/76676/76501
 Fax: (375) 1713 60115
 Email: belaruskarton@tut.by
Shklov Newsprint Mill (Zavod Gazetnoi Burnagi), Shklov Newsprint Mill, 9, 1st Zavodskaja str., 213010 Shklov, Mogilev region, Belarus, Capacity: 40,000 mt/y, (Paper mill)
 Phone: (375) 2239 34 997
 Fax: (375) 2239 34 996/999
 Email: reception@asnova.name
Spartak, Shklov Mill, Fabrichnaya Str., 26, 213010 Shklov, Belarus, Capacity: 58,000 mt/y, (Paper mill)
 Phone: (375) 2239 31488
 Fax: (375) 2239 34383/31704
 Email: bf-spartak@mogilev.by, info@bfs.by, sbyt@bfs.by
Svetlogorskiy Pulp and Board Mill, Svetlogorsk Mill, Zavodskaya Str., 1, 247434 Svetlogorsk, Belarus, Capacity: 130,000 mt/y, (Pulp mill, Paper mill, Paperboard mill)
 Phone: (375) 2342 224 37
 Fax: (375) 2342 235 29
 Email: sckk@mail.gomel.by, sckk@mail.ru

ⓗBelnatsionalservis
ul. Avakyana, 30a, Room 31
220065 Minsk
Belarus
 Phone: (375) 17 2205735
 Fax: (375) 17 2205735
 Email: vkliuev@tut.by
Personnel:
 Gen. Dir.: Igor Petrovich Kliuev
 Phone: (375) 17 2205735
 Fax: (375) 17 2205735
 Dir.: Oleg Igorevich Kliuev
 Phone: (375) 17 2205735
 Fax: (375) 17 2205735
 Dpty. Sls. Dir.: Vadim Vladimirovich Tokach
 Phone: (375) 17 2205735
 Fax: (375) 17 2205735
Total Employees of Company: 94
Total Employees at this Location: 9
Mill Locations:
Rayevka, Rayevka Mill, Lenina Str. 1A, Molodechenskiy Rayon, 222332 Rayevka, Belarus, Capacity: 5,000 mt/y, (Paper mill)
 Phone: (375) 1767 97 441/417
 Fax: (375) 1767 97 417
 Email: vkliuev@tut.by

ⓗⓜDobrushskaya Paper Mill "Geroi Truda", OJSC
Dobrush Mill
Ownership: 100% by Bellesbumprom
Lunacharskogo prosp., 7
247052 Dobrush, Gomel Region
Belarus
 Phone: (375) 2333 31193/76227
 Fax: (375) 2333 76082/76337
 Email: geroytruda@tut.by
 Web Address: www.geroytruda.by
Personnel:
 Branch Dir./Mill.Dir.: Aleksandr Nikolaevich Martynov
 Phone: (375) 2333 77039
 Fax: (375) 2333 76082
 Email: martynov-a-n@mail.ru
 Head of Sls. & Mktg.: Natalia Anatolievna Sokareva
 Phone: (375) 2333 77023
 Fax: (375) 2333 76082
 Email: geroytruda.market@tut.by
 Procurement Mgr.: Efirnova Tatyana
 Phone: (375) 2333 77049
 Fax: (375) 2333 76082
 Email: omts.dbf@mail.ru
 Chief Economist: Tatiana Tverdakova
 Phone: (375) 2333 76512
 Fax: (375) 2333 76082
 Email: peo@geroytruda.by
 Prod. & Development Dir.: Natalia Aleksandrovna Malashenko
 Phone: (375) 2333 77024
 Fax: (375) 2333 76082
 Email: geroytruda.pto@tut.by
 Head of Marketing: Chaika Victor
 Phone: (375) 375 (17) 2268414
 Fax: (375) 2333 76082
 Email: victor@oboi.by
 Quality Ctrl Dir.: Scherbakov Yuriy
 Phone: (375) 375 (17) 2038235
 Fax: (375) 2333 76082
 Email: kachestvo@oboi.by
Total Employees at this Location: 1,300
Type of Operation: Paper mill
Pulp Grades and Capacities:
 Total pulp capacity: 28,954 mt/y
 Recycled Pulping: 28,954 mt/y
Paper/Paperboard Grades and Capacities:
 Total paper and paperboard capacity: 61,700 mt/y
 Uncoated woodfree/freesheet: 9,700 mt/y

Belarus

Packaging papers: 10,000 mt/y
Specialty and industrial: 32,000 mt/y
Linerboard: 6,000 mt/y
Corrugating medium/fluting: 4,000 mt/y
Paper and Paperboard Mill Data:
Paper Machines: 4
No. 3, fourdrinier, total capacity 10,000 mt/y, Trim width 2.1 m, Corrugating medium/fluting, Linerboard
No. 4, fourdrinier, total capacity 6,700 mt/y, Trim width 1.81 m, Uncoated woodfree/freesheet
No. 5, fourdrinier, total capacity 10,000 mt/y, Trim width 1.85 m, Packaging papers
No. 7, fourdrinier (2), total capacity 35,000 mt/y, Trim width 2.52 m, Specialty and industrial, Uncoated woodfree/freesheet
Energy Data:
Steam turbines: 1
Electrical demand for mill: 135 MWh/D

ⓕⒺ "Myuniks" LLC
Ownership: 100% by Paperka Group
Torgovaya str. 16
222210 Smolevichi, Minsk region
Belarus
Mailing Address: 1st Poselkovaya str. 112, 220089 Minsk
Phone: (375) 17 265 1010/1111/1212 / 29 677 49 08 / 29 774 00 63
Fax: (375) 17 265 1010/1111/1212
Email: info@paperka.by
Web Address: www.paperka.by
Personnel:
CEO: Yuriy Nikolaevich Kovalev
Phone: (375) 17 265 1010/1111/1212
Fax: (375) 17 265 1010/1111/1212
Chief Eng.: Valeriy Konstantinovich Kashlyak
Phone: (375) 17 265 1010/1111/1212
Fax: (375) 17 265 1010/1111/1212
Com.Dir.: Dmitry Leonidovich Frenkel
Phone: (375) 17 265 1010/1111/1212
Fax: (375) 17 265 1010/1111/1212
Total Employees of Company: 152
Total Employees at this Location: 150
Mill Locations:
FE "Myuniks" LLC, Minsk Mill, Torgovaya str. 16, 222210 Smolevichi, Minsk region, Belarus, Capacity: 35,400 mt/y, (Paper mill)
Phone: (375) 17 265 1010/1111/1212 / 29 677 49 08 / 29 774 00 63
Fax: (375) 17 265 1010/1111/1212
Email: info@paperka.by

ⓜFE "Myuniks" LLC
Minsk Mill
Torgovaya str. 16
222210 Smolevichi, Minsk region, Minskaya obl.
Belarus
Mailing Address: 1st Poselkovaya str. 112, 220089 Minsk
Phone: (375) 17 265 1010/1111/1212 / 29 677 49 08 / 29 774 00 63
Fax: (375) 17 265 1010/1111/1212
Email: info@paperka.by
Web Address: www.paperka.by
Personnel:
Leading Sales Mngr.: Antonina Samsonovna Petrikovskaya
Phone: (375) 44 748 01 72
Fax: (375) 17 265 10 10
Email: an.p@mail.ru
Exports to CIS countries: Roman Aleksandrovich Prudnikov
Phone: (375) 29 677 49 08
Fax: (375) 17 265 10 10
Email: prudnikov_r@mail.ru
Total Employees at this Location: 150
Type of Operation: Paper mill
Paper/Paperboard Grades and Capacities:
Total paper and paperboard capacity: 35,400 mt/y
Tissue: 35,400 mt/y

Paper and Paperboard Mill Data:
Paper Machines: 3
TM 1, crescent former, total capacity 6,200 mt/y, Trim width 2.4 m, Tissue
TM 2, total capacity 15,000 mt/y, Tissue
TM 3, total capacity 14,200 mt/y, Trim width 2.53 m, Tissue

ⓞⓜUnitary Enterprise (UE) "Paper Mill of Goznak"
Borisov Mill
Zavodskaya Str. 55
222516 Borisov, Minskaya obl.
Belarus
Phone: (375) 177 781312
Fax: (375) 177 781312
Web Address: www.goznakpaper.by.com
Personnel:
Gen. Dir.: Vladimir Temrook
Phone: (7) 177 783039
Fax: (7) 177 781312
Chief Eng.: Vladimir Alekseenok
Phone: (7) 177 781396
Fax: (7) 177 781312
Commercial Mgr.: Alexander Melnikov
Phone: (375) 177 781312
Fax: (375) 177 781312
Email: melnikov@tut.by
Eng.: Yuri Nechaev
Phone: (375) 177 781312
Fax: (375) 177 781312
Email: yunechaev@gmail.com
Total Employees at this Location: 855
Type of Operation: Paper mill
Paper/Paperboard Grades and Capacities:
Total paper and paperboard capacity: 9,700 mt/y
Uncoated woodfree/freesheet: 9,700 mt/y
Specialty and industrial
Paper and Paperboard Mill Data:
Stock Preparation:
Pulpers: 2
Paper Machines: 2
PM 1, total capacity 9,000 mt/y, Trim width 2.52 m, Uncoated woodfree/freesheet, Specialty and industrial
PM 2, total capacity 700 mt/y, Trim width 0.86 m, Uncoated woodfree/freesheet
Finishing Equipment:
Supercalenders: 1
Rewinders: 3
Sheeters: 2
Energy Data:
Power boilers: 2
Electrical demand for mill: 1 MWh/D

ⓞⓜKrasnaya Zvezda
Krasnaya Zvezda Mill
Ownership: 100% by Bellesbumprom
Gagarina str. 20
211156 Chashniki, Vitebsk region
Belarus
Phone: (375) 2133 28105/153/483/28434
Fax: (375) 2133 28483
Email: sbyt.red-star@mail.ru
Web Address: www.1886red-star.by
Personnel:
Gen. Dir.: Alexandr Alexandrovich Pshenny
Phone: (375) 2133 28353
Fax: (375) 2133 28350
Chief Eng.: Anatoly Grogoryevich Myachenkov
Phone: (375) 2133 28346
Fax: (375) 2133 28357
Commer. Dir.: Teresa Antonievna Sulkovskaya
Phone: (375) 2133 28477
Fax: (375) 2133 28357
Email: sbyt.red-star@mail.ru
Manuf. Dir.: Peter Gulai
Phone: (375) 2133 28474
Fax: (375) 2133 28357
Chief Acc.: Lilia Aleksandrovna Kazyanina

Phone: (375) 2133 28103
Fax: (375) 2133 28357
Total Employees at this Location: 670
Type of Operation: Paper mill
Pulp Grades and Capacities:
Total pulp capacity: 50,587 mt/y
Recycled Pulping: 50,587 mt/y
Pulp Mill Data:
Recycled Fiber Treatment Lines:
Recycled packaging pulping lines
Paper/Paperboard Grades and Capacities:
Total paper and paperboard capacity: 52,000 mt/y
Packaging papers: 17,000 mt/y
Linerboard: 28,000 mt/y
Corrugating medium/fluting: 7,000 mt/y
Paper and Paperboard Mill Data:
Paper Machines: 3
No. 1, fourdrinier, total capacity 15,000 mt/y, Trim width 2.1 m, Corrugating medium/fluting, Packaging papers
No. 3, fourdrinier, total capacity 9,000 mt/y, Trim width 2.1 m, Corrugating medium/fluting, Packaging papers
No. 4, fourdrinier (2), total capacity 28,000 mt/y, Trim width 2.52 m, Linerboard
Energy Data:
Power boilers
Electrical demand for mill: 78 MWh/D

ⓜOlkhovka Board Mill, JSC
Olkhovka Mill
Ownership: 100% by Bellesbumprom
ul. Fabrichnaya, Ostrovetskiy Distr.
231223 Olkhovka, Grodno Region
Belarus
Phone: (375) 1591 33221/30
Fax: (375) 1591 33444/459/230/459
Email: fabrika-ol@mail.ru, lena.fabrika@mail.ru
Web Address: www.kfolh.by
Personnel:
Dir.: Rostislav Ivanovich Brazinskiy
Phone: (375) 1591 33221
Fax: (375) 1591 33230
Email: lena.fabrika@mail.ru
Chief Eng.: Nikolai Nikolaevich Sergei
Phone: (375) 1591 33248
Fax: (375) 1591 33230
Sls. Dir.: Vladimir Pavlovich Martynov
Phone: (375) 1591 33438
Fax: (375) 1591 33230
Email: denis-lokutov@mail.ru
Chief Technologist: Natalia Ivanovna Runojits
Phone: (375) 1591 33248
Fax: (375) 1591 33230
Chief Acc.: Svetlana Evgenievna Shirai
Phone: (375) 1591 33248
Fax: (375) 1591 33230
Total Employees at this Location: 246
Type of Operation: Paperboard mill
Paper/Paperboard Grades and Capacities:
Total paper and paperboard capacity: 8,600 mt/y
Linerboard: 8,600 mt/y
Paper and Paperboard Mill Data:
Paper Machines: 6
BM 1, Trim width 2.4 m, Linerboard
BM 2, Trim width 2.4 m, Linerboard
BM 3, Trim width 2.4 m, Linerboard
BM 4, Trim width 2.4 m, Linerboard
BM 5, Trim width 2.4 m, Linerboard
BM 6, Trim width 2.4 m, Linerboard
Energy Data:
Electrical demand for mill: 11 MWh/D

ⓞⓜPukhovichskaya Paperboard Mill
Pukhovichskaya Paperboard Mill
Ownership: 100% by Bellesbumprom
ul. Fabrichnaya, 1
222818 Svetly Bor, Pukhovichskiy rayon, Minskaya obl.
Belarus

Belarus

Phone: (375) 1713 60115/76676/76501
Fax: (375) 1713 60115
Email: belaruskarton@tut.by
Web Address: www.karton.by
Personnel:
Dir.: Andrei Valerevich Sokolovski
Phone: (375) 1713 76501
Fax: (375) 1713 60115
Sls. Mgr.: Ella Mikhailovna Kiseleva
Phone: (375) 1713 76676
Fax: (375) 1713 60115
Chief Eng.: Vasiliy Galuza
Phone: (375) 1713 76795
Fax: (375) 1713 60115
Tech. Mgr.: Inna Vladimirovna Stelmakh
Phone: (375) 1713 60115/76676
Fax: (375) 1713 60115
Total Employees at this Location: 190
Type of Operation: Paperboard mill
Paper/Paperboard Grades and Capacities:
Total paper and paperboard capacity: 14,900 mt/y
Boxboard/cartonboard: 14,900 mt/y
Paper and Paperboard Mill Data:
Stock Preparation:
Pulpers: 2
Paper Machines: 6
No. 1, total capacity 1,700 mt/y, Trim width 2.06 m
No. 2, total capacity 1,700 mt/y, Trim width 2.06 m
No. 3, total capacity 1,700 mt/y, Trim width 2.06 m
No. 4, total capacity 1,700 mt/y, Trim width 2.06 m
No. 5, total capacity 1,700 mt/y, Trim width 2.06 m
No. 6, (2nd hand, started October 2012), total capacity 6,400 mt/y
Finishing Equipment:
Calenders: 3
Energy Data:
Power boilers: 3
Electrical demand for mill: 8 MWh/D

ⓜRayevka
Rayevka Mill
Ownership: 100% by Belnatsionalservis
Lenina Str. 1A, Molodechenskiy Rayon
222332 Rayevka, Minskaya obl.
Belarus
Mailing Address: ul. Avakyana, 1a, 220065 Minsk, Belarus
Phone: (375) 1767 97 441/417
Fax: (375) 1767 97 417
Email: vkliuev@tut.by
Personnel:
Gen. Dir.: Igor Petrovich Kliuev
Phone: (375) 1767 97 441/417
Fax: (375) 1767 97 417
Dir.branch: Oleg Igorevich Kliuev
Phone: (375) 1767 97 441/417
Fax: (375) 1767 97 417
Chief Eng.: Aleksandr Nikolaevich Simonchik
Phone: (375) 1767 97 441
Fax: (375) 1767 97 417
Prod. Deputy Dir.: Tatiana Nikolaevna Pechan
Phone: (375) 1767 97 441
Fax: (375) 1767 97 417
Com.Dir.: Vadim V. Tolkach
Phone: (375) 017 2205942
Fax: (375) 1767 97 417
Total Employees at this Location: 68
Type of Operation: Paper mill
Paper/Paperboard Grades and Capacities:
Total paper and paperboard capacity: 5,000 mt/y
Linerboard: 3,000 mt/y
Boxboard/cartonboard: 2,000 mt/y
Paper and Paperboard Mill Data:
Paper Machines: 1
PM, total capacity 5,000 mt/y, Trim width 2.1 m, Boxboard/cartonboard, Linerboard

ⓜShklov Newsprint Mill (Zavod Gazetnoi Bumagi)
Ownership: 100% by Bellesbumprom
9, 1st Zavodskaja str.
213010 Shklov, Mogilev region
Belarus
Phone: (375) 2239 34997
Fax: (375) 2239 34997
Email: reception@asnova.name
Web Address: www.asnova.name
Personnel:
Deputy Dir. / Branch Dir.: Leonid Fedorovich Shklyar
Phone: (375) 2239 34997
Fax: (375) 2239 34997
Mill Dir.: Anatoly Vladimirovich Khmelevsky
Phone: (375) 2239 34997
Fax: (375) 2239 34997
Chief Eng.: Oleg Aleksandrovich Misiurov
Phone: (375) 2239 34997
Fax: (375) 2239 34997
Commer. Dir.: Oleg Mikhaylovich Podobed
Phone: (375) 2239 34997
Fax: (375) 2239 34997
Total Employees of Company: 600
Mill Locations:
Shklov Newsprint Mill (Zavod Gazetnoi Bumagi), Shklov Newsprint Mill, 9, 1st Zavodskaja str., 213010 Shklov, Mogilev region, Belarus, Capacity: 40,000 mt/y, (Paper mill)
Phone: (375) 2239 34 997
Fax: (375) 2239 34 996/999
Email: reception@asnova.name

ⓜShklov Newsprint Mill (Zavod Gazetnoi Bumagi)
Shklov Newsprint Mill
Ownership: 100% by Bellesbumprom
9, 1st Zavodskaja str.
213010 Shklov, Mogilev region, Mogilev Region
Belarus
Phone: (375) 2239 34 997
Fax: (375) 2239 34 996/999
Email: reception@asnova.name
Web Address: www.asnova.name
Personnel:
Mill Dir.: Anatoliy Vladimirovich Hmelevskiy
Phone: (375) 2239 34 997
Fax: (375) 2239 34 996/999
Deputy Dir. / Branch Dir.: Leonid F. Shkliar
Phone: (375) 2239 35 017
Fax: (375) 2239 34 996/999
Chief Eng.: Oleg Aleksandrovich Misiurov
Phone: (375) 2239 35 014
Fax: (375) 2239 34 996/999
Dpty. Dir. for Prod.: Yuriy Genrikhovich Luka
Phone: (375) 2239 34 988
Fax: (375) 2239 34 996/999
Prod. Mgr.: Elena Leonidovna Katashevich
Phone: (375) 2239 34 989
Fax: (375) 2239 34 996/999
Master Power Eng.: Aleksey V. Zaycev
Phone: (375) 2239 35 017
Fax: (375) 2239 34 996/999
Chief Mechanic: Vaksim G. Kazinskiy
Phone: (375) 2239 35 013
Fax: (375) 2239 34 996/999
Chief. Accountant: Svetlana A. Maruhova
Phone: (375) 2239 35 009
Fax: (375) 2239 34 996/999
Total Employees at this Location: 600
Type of Operation: Paper mill
Pulp Grades and Capacities:
Total pulp capacity: 41,179 mt/y
Mechanical Pulp: 41,179 mt/y
Pulp Mill Data:
Mechanical Pulping Systems:
TMP systems: 1
Pulp Lines: 1
Bleach Plant Systems: 1
No. 1 Capacity 50,000 admt/y
Paper/Paperboard Grades and Capacities:
Total paper and paperboard capacity: 40,000 mt/y
Newsprint: 40,000 mt/y
Paper and Paperboard Mill Data:
Paper Machines: 1
No. 1, fourdrinier, total capacity 40,000 mt/y, Trim width 2.52 m, Newsprint
Energy Data:
Power boilers
Electrical demand for mill: 311 MWh/D

ⓜSP Exclusive
Gorkogo str. 95
230005 Grodno
Belarus
Phone: (375) 152 43 22 22 / 48 44 73
Fax: (375) 152 43 22 22
Email: info@excl.by
Web Address: www.excl.by
Personnel:
CEO: Vladimir Pankevich
Phone: (375) 152 43 22 22 / 48 44 73
Fax: (375) 152 43 22 22
Chief Eng.: Vitaliy Valerievich Koltovich
Phone: (375) 152 43 22 22 / 48 44 73
Fax: (375) 152 43 22 22
Chief Acc.: Lyudmila Mikhaylovna Klosevich
Phone: (375) 152 43 22 22 / 48 44 73
Fax: (375) 152 43 22 22
Total Employees at this Location: 197
Mill Locations:
SP Exclusive, Grodno Mill, Gorkogo str. 95, 230005 Grodno, Belarus, Capacity: 7,000 mt/y, (Paper mill)
Phone: (375) 152 43 22 22 / 48 44 73
Fax: (375) 152 43 22 22
Email: info@excl.by

ⓜSP Exclusive
Grodno Mill
Gorkogo str. 95
230005 Grodno, Grodno Region
Belarus
Phone: (375) 152 43 22 22 / 48 44 73
Fax: (375) 152 43 22 22
Email: info@excl.by
Web Address: www.excl.by
Personnel:
Chief Eng.: Vitaliy Valerievich Koltovich
Phone: (375) 152 48 44 83
Fax: (375) 152 43 22 22
Chief Acc.: Lyudmila Mikhaylovna Klosevich
Phone: (375) 152 48 44 73
Fax: (375) 152 43 22 22
Com.Dir.: Mikhail Shelud'ko
Phone: (375) 152 48 44 73
Fax: (375) 152 43 22 22
HR.Dir.: Vera Vyacheslavovna Bakhmatovich
Phone: (375) 152 48 44 73
Fax: (375) 152 43 22 22
Total Employees at this Location: 197
Type of Operation: Paper mill
Paper/Paperboard Grades and Capacities:
Total paper and paperboard capacity: 7,000 mt/y
Tissue: 7,000 mt/y
Paper and Paperboard Mill Data:
Paper Machines: 1
PM 1, total capacity 7,000 mt/y, Tissue

ⓜⓜSpartak
Shklov Mill
Ownership: 100% by Bellesbumprom
Fabrichnaya Str., 26
213010 Shklov, Mogilev Region
Belarus
Phone: (375) 2239 31488
Fax: (375) 2239 34383/31704
Email: bf-spartak@mogilev.by, info@bfs.by,

sbyt@bfs.by
Web Address: www.bfs.by
Personnel:
Dir.: Serguey Mikhailovich Shumskiy
Phone: (375) 2239 31488
Fax: (375) 2239 34383/31704
Chief Eng.: Igor Vladimirovich Pobortsev
Phone: (375) 2239 31239/447187133
Fax: (375) 2239 34383/31704
Email: nfo@bfs.by
Economist (Planning Dep.): Victor Ivanovich Prodolyatchenko
Phone: (375) 2239 313 57
Fax: (375) 2239 34383/31704
Sales Dir.: Maria Petrovna Kassianova
Phone: (375) 2239 31549
Fax: (375) 2239 34383/31704
Email: sbyt@bfs.by
Total Employees at this Location: 520
Type of Operation: Paper mill
Pulp Grades and Capacities:
Total pulp capacity: 48,538 mt/y
Recycled Pulping: 48,538 mt/y
Pulp Mill Data:
Recycled Fiber Treatment Lines:
Flotation deinking lines
Recycled packaging pulping lines
Paper/Paperboard Grades and Capacities:
Total paper and paperboard capacity: 58,000 mt/y
Tissue: 20,000 mt/y
Packaging papers: 5,000 mt/y
Linerboard: 19,000 mt/y
Corrugating medium/fluting: 10,000 mt/y
Boxboard/cartonboard: 4,000 mt/y
Paper and Paperboard Mill Data:
Paper Machines: 2
No. 1, crescent former, total capacity 20,000 mt/y, Trim width 2.8 m, Tissue
No. 2, fourdrinier (2), total capacity 38,000 mt/y, Trim width 2.45 m, Linerboard, Corrugating medium/fluting, Packaging papers, Boxboard/cartonboard
Energy Data:
Power boilers: 3
Combustion turbines: 2 at 3.6 MW
Electrical demand for mill: 65 MWh/D

ⓗⓜSvetlogorskiy Pulp and Board Mill
Svetlogorsk Mill
Ownership: 100% by Bellesbumprom
Zavodskaya Str., 1
247434 Svetlogorsk, Gomel Region
Belarus
Phone: (375) 2342 224 37
Fax: (375) 2342 235 29
Email: sckk@mail.gomel.by, sckk@mail.ru
Web Address: www.sckk.by
Personnel:
Gen. Dir.: Yury Andreevich Kruk
Phone: (375) 2342 98312/22493
Fax: (375) 2342 23529
Chief. Eng.: Mikhail Ivanovich Toryansky
Phone: (375) 2342 52437
Fax: (375) 2342 23529
Pulp Mill Mgr.: Andrey Valeryevich Bogomolov
Phone: (375) 2342 98489
Fax: (375) 2342 23529
Paper Mill Mgr.: Nina Adamovna Suvalova
Phone: (375) 2342 98223
Fax: (375) 2342 23529
Vice Dir. for Commercial.: Aleksander Leonidovich Fitszner
Phone: (375) 2342 51009
Fax: (375) 2342 23529
Environ. Mgr.: Alexandr Nikolayevich Kryshnev
Phone: (375) 2342 24977
Fax: (375) 2342 23529
Finan. Dir.: Anna Alksandrovna Kashtanova
Phone: (375) 2342 23175
Fax: (375) 2342 23995

Mktg. Dir.: Olga Andreevna Beze
Phone: (375) 2342 53939/98313
Fax: (375) 2342 52480
Commercial Dir.: Alexander Vladimirovich Drozdov
Phone: (375) 2342 23635
Fax: (375) 2342 22268
Total Employees of Company: 3,272
Total Employees at this Location: 3,420
Type of Operation: Pulp mill, Paper mill, Paperboard mill
Pulp Grades and Capacities:
Total pulp capacity: 134,210 mt/y
Chemical Pulp: 74,075 mt/y
Recycled Pulping: 60,135 mt/y
Pulp Mill Data:
Chemical Pulping Systems:
Batch digesters: 4
Pulp Lines: 2
Paper/Paperboard Grades and Capacities:
Total paper and paperboard capacity: 130,000 mt/y
Packaging papers: 7,000 mt/y
Linerboard: 55,000 mt/y
Corrugating medium/fluting: 58,000 mt/y
Boxboard/cartonboard: 10,000 mt/y
Paper and Paperboard Mill Data:
Stock Preparation:
Pulpers: 7
Refiners: 7
Paper Machines: 2
No. 1, multi-wire, total capacity 65,000 mt/y, Trim width 4.2 m, Linerboard, Boxboard/cartonboard
No. 462, fourdrinier, total capacity 65,000 mt/y, Trim width 4.2 m, Packaging papers, Corrugating medium/fluting
Finishing Equipment:
Sheeters: 2 at 70,000 mt/y
Energy Data:
Power boilers: 2
TMP Reboiler: 2
Steam turbines: 1 at 4 MW
Electrical demand for mill: 292 MWh/D

BELGIUM

ⓗⓜBurgo Ardennes
Virton Mill
Ownership: Burgo Group SpA
1 Rue de la Papeterie
B-6760 Virton
Belgium
Phone: (32) 63 587111
Fax: (32) 63 587119
Email: info@burgogroup.com
Web Address: www.burgogroup.com
Personnel:
Man. Dir. & Mill Mgr.: Michel Hartman
Phone: (32) 63 587000
Fax: (32) 63 587119
Email: hartman.michel@burgo.com
Paper Mill & Prod. Mgr.: Dominique Poncelet
Phone: (32) 63 587301
Fax: (32) 63 587229
Email: poncelet.dominique@burgo.com
Pulp Mill & Prod. Mgr.: Philippe Olivy
Phone: (32) 63 587600
Fax: (32) 63 587609
Email: olivy.philippe@burgo.com
Maint. Mgr.: André Buchet
Phone: (32) 63 587770
Fax: (32) 63 587709
Email: buchet.andre@burgo.com
Environ. Mgr.: Anne Lacave
Phone: (32) 63 587770
Fax: (32) 63 587709
Email: lacave.anne@burgo.com
Purch. Mgr. & Wood Sls. Mgr.: Thierry Monaville
Phone: (32) 63 587081

Fax: (32) 63 587579
Email: monaville.thierry@burgo.com
Wood Purch. Mgr.: Eric Meurisse
Phone: (32) 63 587500
Fax: (32) 63 587509
Email: eric.meurisse@burgo.com
Admin. Mgr.: Dominique Lejeune
Phone: (32) 63 587111
Fax: (32) 63 587119
Email: dominique.lejeune@burgo.com
Mktg. Dir. & Commun. Mgr.: Philippe Corgie
Phone: (32) 63 587111
Fax: (32) 63 587119
Email: corgie.philippe@burgo.com
Total Employees at this Location: 630
Type of Operation: Pulp mill, Paper mill
Pulp Grades and Capacities:
Total pulp capacity: 360,000 mt/y
Pulp available for market: 220,729 mt/y
Chemical Pulp: 360,000 mt/y
Pulp Mill Data:
Chemical Pulping Systems:
Batch digesters: 8
Pulp Lines: 1
Bleach Plant Systems: 1
Chemical Pulping System, Type: Hardwood, Ozone process: HC, Sequence: O_2 DoEoDD, Capacity 400,000 admt/y
Chemical Recovery Equipment:
Evaporator lines: 1
Recovery boilers: 1
Lime Kiln
Pulp Dryers:
Air Float dryers 1, Air Float dryers 1
Paper/Paperboard Grades and Capacities:
Total paper and paperboard capacity: 350,000 mt/y
Coated woodfree/freesheet: 350,000 mt/y
Paper and Paperboard Mill Data:
Stock Preparation:
Pulpers: 1
Refiners: 1
Paper Machines: 1
No. 1, DuoFormer D, total capacity 350,000 mt/y, Trim width 6.9 m, Coated woodfree/freesheet
Coating Machines: 1
No. 1 & 2, total capacity 365,000 mt/y., off machine
Finishing Equipment:
Winders: 2 at 362,000 mt/y
Calenders: 2
Supercalenders: 2
Rewinders: 2
Sheeters: 6 at 302,000 mt/y
Energy Data:
Power boilers: 1
Steam turbines: 2 at 63 MW
Electrical demand for mill: 1,472 MWh/D

ⓗⓜKartonfabriek Henri Goossens
Huizingen Mill
Ownership: 100% by Family owned (private)
Torleylaan 38-40
B-1654 Huizingen
Belgium
Phone: (32) 573 346412
Fax: (32) 2 356 5480
Email: info@kartonfabriek.be
Web Address: www.kartonfabriek.be
Personnel:
Chmn.: Henri Goossens
Phone: (32) 573 346412
Fax: (32) 2 356 5480
Mill Mgr.: Jacques Vannieuwenhuyse
Phone: (32) 573 346412
Fax: (32) 2 356 5480
Total Employees of Company: 15
Total Employees at this Location: 15
Type of Operation: Paperboard mill
Paper/Paperboard Grades and Capacities:
Total paper and paperboard capacity: 5,000 mt/y

Belgium

Boxboard/cartonboard: 5,000 mt/y
Paper and Paperboard Mill Data:
Paper Machines: 1
No. 1, total capacity 5,000 mt/y, Boxboard/cartonboard

⊕⊛IdemPapers SA
Virginal Mill
2 Rue d'Asquempont
B-1460 Virginal-Samme
Belgium
  Phone: (32) 67 644211
  Fax: (32) 67 644385
  Email: info.customer@idempapers.com,
  (firstname.lastname@idempapers.com)
  Web Address: www.idempapers.com
Personnel:
  CEO: Francis Tans
  Phone: (32) 67 644211
  Fax: (32) 67 644385
  Email: francis.tans@idempapers.com
  CFO & Admin.: Emmanuel Coria
  Phone: (32) 67 644211
  Fax: (32) 67 644385
  Email: emmanuel.coria@idempapers.com
  Plt. Mgr.: Raphael Durand
  Phone: (32) 67 644211
  Fax: (32) 67 644385
  Email: raphael.durand@idempapers.com
  Dir., Supply Chain & Cust. Serv.: Marylène Vanden Berghe
  Phone: (32) 67 644211
  Fax: (32) 67 644385
  Email: marylene.vanden.berghe@idempapers.com
  Purch. Mgr.: Mr. Didier Fornini
  Phone: (32) 67 644203
  Fax: (32) 67 644385
  Email: didier.fornini@idempapers.com
  Dir. R&D Technology: Jean Bernard
  Phone: (32) 67 644202
  Fax: (32) 67 644385
  Email: jean.bernard@idempapers.com
  IT Dir.: Luc Duran
  Phone: (32) 67 644211
  Fax: (32) 67 644385
  Email: luc.duran@idempapers.com
  Dir. HR: Pierre Staquet
  Phone: (32) 67 644211
  Fax: (32) 67 644385
  Email: pierre.staquet@idempapers.com
  Gen. Counsel: Pierre Marneffe
  Phone: (32) 67 644211
  Fax: (32) 67 644385
  Email: pierre.marneffe@idempapers.com
Total Employees of Company: 400
Total Employees at this Location: 400
Type of Operation: Paper mill
Paper/Paperboard Grades and Capacities:
  Total paper and paperboard capacity: 120,000 mt/y
  Uncoated woodfree/freesheet: 80,000 mt/y
  Coated woodfree/freesheet: 5,000 mt/y
  Specialty and industrial: 35,000 mt/y
Paper and Paperboard Mill Data:
  Stock Preparation:
    Pulpers: 4
    Refiners: 10
  Paper Machines: 2
  No. 3, fourdrinier, total capacity 40,000 mt/y, Trim width 2.4 m, Uncoated woodfree/freesheet
  No. 4, fourdrinier, total capacity 80,000 mt/y, Trim width 4.9 m, Uncoated woodfree/freesheet, Specialty and industrial, Coated woodfree/freesheet
  Coating Machines: 2
  No. 3, total capacity 40,000 mt/y.
  No. 4, on machine
  Finishing Equipment:
    Rewinders: 4
    Sheeters: 1
  Energy Data:
    Power boilers: 5
    Combustion turbines: 1
    Steam turbines: 1
    Electrical demand for mill: 234 MWh/D

⊕International Paper (Europe) SA
Ownership: 100% by International Paper Co.
Chaussée de la Hulpe 166
B-1170 Brussels
Belgium
  Phone: (32) 2 774 1200 / 1211
  Fax: (32) 2 774 1299
  Email: firstname.lastname@ipaper.com
  Web Address: www.ipaper.com
Personnel:
  SVP & Pres. (E.M.E.A.): Jean Michel Ribieras
  Phone: (32) 2 774 1200
  Fax: (32) 2 774 1299
  CFO EMEA: Oliver Taudien
  Phone: (32) 2 774 1211
  Fax: (32) 2 774 1299
  Dir. Com. & Government Relations: David Higgins
  Phone: (32) 2 774 1211
  Fax: (32) 2 774 1299
  Email: david.higgins@ipaper.com
  Dir. Sourcing EMEA: Danny Pieters
  Phone: (32) 2 774 1211
  Fax: (32) 2 774 1299
  Email: danny.pieters@ipaper.com
  Dir. of Strategy EMEA: David Fulchiron
  Phone: (32) 2 774 1211
  Fax: (32) 2 774 1299
  HR Dir. EMEA: Marc Croonen
  Phone: (32) 2 774 1211
  Fax: (32) 2 774 1299
  Commun. Mgr.: Claudia Brand
  Phone: (32) 2 774 1200
  Fax: (32) 2 774 1299
  Email: claudia.brand@ipaper.com
  EMEA Area Sls. Mgr. & Regional Mktg. Lead: Voytek Sylwestrowicz
  Phone: (32) 2 477 800 440 / 2 774 1211
  Fax: (32) 2 774 1299
  Email: voytek.sylwestrowicz@ipaper.com
  Prod. Mgr.: Wim Dootselaere
  Phone: (32) 2 774 1211
  Fax: (32) 2 774 1299
Mill Locations:
  International Paper - Kwidzyn Sp. z o.o., Kwidzyn Mill, Lotnicza 1, PL-82500 Kwidzyn, Poland, Capacity: 772,500 mt/y, (Pulp mill, Paper mill, Paperboard mill)
  Phone: (48) 55 2798000
  Fax: (48) 55 2798451
  International Paper SA, Saillat Mill, Usine de Saillat, BP 1 Saillat-sur-Vienne, F-87206 Saint-Junien, France, Capacity: 240,000 mt/y, (Pulp mill, Paper mill)
  Phone: (33) 5 55 43 48 00
  Fax: (33) 5 55 43 48 65
  Email: firstname.lastname@ipaper.com
  ZAO International Paper, Svetogorsk Mill, ul. Zavodskaya 17, 188991 Svetogorsk, Russia, Capacity: 480,000 mt/y, (Pulp mill, Paper mill, Paperboard mill)
  Phone: (7) 813 7843504/5 688 4100
  Fax: (7) 813 7844 061/5 688 4900
  Email: skbf@mail.ru

⊕⊛Kartonfabriek St. Leonard NV
Huizingen Mill
Vaucampslaan 82-84
B-1654 Huizingen
Belgium
  Phone: (32) 2 356 57 89
  Fax: (32) 2 361 05 64
  Email: leonard@karton-fabriek.be
Personnel:
  Pres.: Eric Verdroncken
  Phone: (32) 2 356 57 89
  Email: leonard@karton-fabriek.be
Total Employees at this Location: 7
Type of Operation: Paperboard mill
Paper/Paperboard Grades and Capacities:
  Total paper and paperboard capacity: 3,000 mt/y
Paper and Paperboard Mill Data:
  Stock Preparation:
    Pulpers: 1
    Refiners: 1
  Paper Machines: 1
  BM 1, cylinder, Wet lap, Trim width 2.4 m

⊕Sappi Fine Paper Europe
Ownership: 100% by Sappi Limited
Glaverbel Building, 166 Chaussée de la Hulpe
B-1170 Brussels
Belgium
  Phone: (32) 2 676 9700/9784
  Fax: (32) 2 676 9601/9660/9669
  Email: communications@sappi.com
  Web Address: www.sappi.com
Personnel:
  CEO, Sappi Fine Paper Europe: Berry Wiersum
  Phone: (32) 2 676 9700
  Fax: (32) 2 676 9601/9660
  Email: Berry.Wiersum@sappi.com
  CFO, Sappi Fine Paper Europe (effective July 1, 2014): Stephen Blyth
  Phone: (32) 2 676 9700
  Fax: (32) 2 676 9601/9660
  Group Treasurer, Sappi International: Jörg Pässler
  Phone: (32) 2 676 9700
  Fax: (32) 2 676 9601/9660
  Email: Jorg.Passler@sappi.com
  Manuf. and R & D Dir., Sappi Fine Paper Europe: Mat Quaedvlieg
  Phone: (32) 2 676 9700
  Fax: (32) 2 676 9601/9660
  Corp. Comm. Mgr.: Marjolein Vile
  Phone: (32) 2 676 9786
  Fax: (32) 2 676 9669
  Email: Marjolein.Vile@sappi.com
  Oper. Plann. Dir. & Demand Man.: Rudi Barthels
  Phone: (32) 2 676 9700
  Fax: (32) 2 676 9601/9660
  Email: rudi.barthels@sappi.com
  Sls. & Mktg. Dir., Sappi Fine Paper Europe: Marco Eikelenboom
  Phone: (32) 2 676 9700
  Fax: (32) 2 676 9601/9660
  Email: marco.eikelenboom@sappi.com
  HR Dir., Sappi Fine Paper Europe: Eva De Caniere
  Phone: (32) 2 676 9700
  Fax: (32) 2 676 9601/9660
  Supply Chain Procurement & Specialties Dir.: Gregory Gettinger
  Phone: (32) 2 676 9700
  Fax: (32) 2 676 9601/9660
  Mgr, Wood Supply: Rainer Neumann
  Phone: (32) 2 676 9700
  Fax: (32) 2 676 9601/9660
  Sls. Mgr. Speciality Products, North America: Wayne Nablo
  Phone: (32) 2 676 9700
  Fax: (32) 2 676 9601/9660
Total Employees of Company: 5,838
Total Employees at this Location: 120
Mill Locations:
  Sappi Fine Paper Europe, Alfeld Mill, Mühlenmasch 1, D-31061 Alfeld (Leine), Germany, Capacity: 305,000 mt/y, (Pulp mill, Paper mill, Paperboard mill)
  Phone: (49) 5181 77-0
  Fax: (49) 5181 77208
  Email: infoalfeld@sappi.com
  Sappi Fine Paper Europe, Ehingen Mill, Biberacher Str. 73, D-89584 Ehingen, Germany, Capacity: 260,000 mt/y, (Pulp mill, Paper mill)
  Phone: (49) 7391 5010
  Fax: (49) 7391 501 315
  Email: renate.distelrath@sappi.com
  Sappi Fine Paper Europe, Gratkorn Mill, Brucker Str. 21, A-8101 Gratkorn, Austria, Capacity: 950,000 mt/y, (Pulp mill, Paper mill)
  Phone: (43) 3124 201 0
  Fax: (43) 3124 201 3038

Belgium

Email: gratkorn.mill@sappi.com
Sappi Fine Paper Europe, Kirkniemi Mill, FI-08800 Kirkniemi, Finland, Capacity: 735,000 mt/y, (Pulp mill, Paper mill)
Phone: (358) 1046 42999
Fax: (358) 1046 42411
Email: (firstname.lastname@sappi.com)
Sappi Fine Paper Europe, Lanaken Mill, Montaigneweg 2, B-3620 Lanaken, Belgium, Capacity: 500,000 mt/y, (Pulp mill, Paper mill)
Phone: (32) 89 71 9719
Fax: (32) 89 71 9222
Email: lanaken.mill@sappi.com
Sappi Fine Paper Europe, Maastricht Mill, Biesenweg 16, NL-6211 AA Maastricht, Netherlands, Capacity: 290,000 mt/y, (Paper mill)
Phone: (31) 43 382 22 22
Fax: (31) 43 382 27 31
Email: maastricht.mill@sappi.com
Sappi Fine Paper Europe, Stockstadt Mill, Obernburger Strasse 1-9, D-63811 Stockstadt am Main, Germany, Capacity: 440,000 mt/y, (Pulp mill, Paper mill)
Phone: (49) 6027 4200
Fax: (49) 6027 420 245/823
Email: stockstadt@sappi.com

ⓜSappi Fine Paper Europe
Lanaken Mill
Ownership: 100% by Sappi Limited
Montaigneweg 2
B-3620 Lanaken
Belgium
Phone: (32) 89 71 9719
Fax: (32) 89 71 9222
Email: lanaken.mill@sappi.com
Web Address: www.sappi.com
Personnel:
Mill Dir.: Peter Loubele
Phone: (32) 89 71 9719
Fax: (32) 89 71 9245
Email: Peter.Loubele@sappi.com
Finan. Mgr.: Peter Keulen
Phone: (32) 89 71 9719
Fax: (32) 89 71 9222
Email: peter.keulen@sappi.com
R & D Mgr.: Jos Daniels
Phone: (32) 89 71 9719
Fax: (32) 89 71 9222
Email: jos.daniels@sappi.com
Commun. & Training Mgr.: John Donners
Phone: (32) 89 71 9600 / 89 71 9719
Fax: (32) 89 71 9222
Email: john.donners@sappi.com
Safety & Environ. Mgr.: Carine Steegen
Phone: (32) 89 71 9719
Fax: (32) 89 71 9222
Email: carine.steegen@sappi.com
Oper. Mgr.: Paul Lauwers
Phone: (32) 89 71 9719
Fax: (32) 89 71 9222
Email: paul.lauwers@sappi.com
Prod. Mgr. PM 8: Gunther Engelen
Phone: (32) 89 71 9719
Fax: (32) 89 71 9222
Email: gunther.engelen@sappi.com
HR. Mgr.: Giel Haeldermans
Phone: (32) 89 71 9719
Fax: (32) 89 71 9222
Email: giel.haeldermans@sappi.com
Mktg. Commun. Co-ordinator: Mia Nijs
Phone: (32) 89 71 9719
Fax: (32) 89 71 9222
Email: mia.nijs@sappi.com
Total Employees at this Location: 480
Type of Operation: Pulp mill, Paper mill
Pulp Grades and Capacities:
Total pulp capacity: 191,006 mt/y
Mechanical Pulp: 191,006 mt/y

Pulp Mill Data:
Mechanical Pulping Systems:
BCTMP systems: 1
Conventional grinders: 7
Bleach Plant Systems: 1
No. 1, Sequence: P
Paper/Paperboard Grades and Capacities:
Total paper and paperboard capacity: 500,000 mt/y
Coated woodfree/freesheet: 100,000 mt/y
Coated mechanical/groundwood: 400,000 mt/y
Paper and Paperboard Mill Data:
Stock Preparation:
Pulpers: 3
Refiners: 12
Paper Machines: 2
No. 7, hybrid former, total capacity 200,000 mt/y, Trim width 4.8 m, Coated mechanical/groundwood, Coated woodfree/freesheet
No. 8, hybrid former, total capacity 300,000 mt/y, Trim width 7.4 m, Coated mechanical/groundwood
Coating Machines: 3
CM 7, off machine
PM 7, total capacity 210,000 mt/y., on machine
PM 8, total capacity 300,000 mt/y., on machine
Finishing Equipment:
Winders: 5
Supercalenders: 4
Rewinders: 2
Sheeters: 4
Energy Data:
Power boilers: 1
HRSG boiler: 1
Combustion turbines: 1 at 43.0 MW
Electrical demand for mill: 1,810 MWh/D

ⓜⓗSCA Hygiene Products S.A./N.V.
Stembert Mill
Ownership: SCA Hygiene Products SE
Rue de la Papeterie 2
B-4801 Stembert
Belgium
Phone: (32) 87 30 66 11
Fax: (32) 87 33 94 24
Email: (firstname.lastname@sca.com)
Web Address: www.sca.com
Personnel:
Site Mgr.: Jacky Dechamps
Phone: (32) 87 30 66 28
Email: jacky.dechamps@sca.com
Toilet Plant Mgr.: Alex Freart
Phone: (32) 87 30 67 35
Email: alex.freart@sca.com
PM's Plant Mgr.: Carlo Russo
Phone: (32) 87 30 66 51
Email: carlo.russo@sca.com
Investment Officer: Patrick Prégardien
Phone: (32) 87 30 66 21
Email: patrick.pregardien@sca.com
Facial Plant Mgr.: Gonzalo Castela
Phone: (32) 87 30 66 66
Email: gonzalo.castela@sca.com
HR Mgr.: Isabelle Faway
Phone: (32) 87 30 67 11
Email: isabelle.faway@sca.com
Finan. Dir.: Fabien Grégoire
Phone: (32) 87 30 67 46
Email: fabien.gregoire@sca.com
Total Employees at this Location: 290
Type of Operation: Paper mill
Paper/Paperboard Grades and Capacities:
Total paper and paperboard capacity: 75,000 mt/y
Tissue: 75,000 mt/y
Paper and Paperboard Mill Data:
Stock Preparation:
Pulpers: 4
Refiners: 6
Paper Machines: 2
No. 1, inclined, Yankee dryer, total capacity 19,000 mt/y, Trim width 2.4 m, Tissue
No. 2, C-wrap, Yankee dryer, total capacity 56,000 mt/y, Trim width 5.45 m, Tissue
Finishing Equipment:
Winders: 2 at 75,000 mt/y
Rewinders: 2 at 75,000 mt/y
Energy Data:
Power boilers: 3
Electrical demand for mill: 221 MWh/D

ⓜSofidel Benelux
Duffel Mill
Ownership: Sofidel Group
A. Stocletlaan 3
B-2570 Duffel, Antwerp
Belgium
Phone: (32) 15 30 0611
Fax: (32) 15 31 8241
Web Address: www.sofidelbenelux.lu
Personnel:
Gen. Mgr.: Ronny Baeten
Phone: (32) 15 30 0661
Fax: (32) 15 31 8241
Email: ronny.baeten@sofidelbenelux.com
Tissue Mgr.: Ericvan den Brande
Phone: (32) 15 30 0663
Fax: (32) 15 31 8241
Email: eric.vandenBrande@sofidelbenelux.com
Tech. Dir.: Victor De Boeck
Phone: (32) 15 30 0674
Fax: (32) 15 31 8241
Email: victor.deboeck@sofidelbenelux.com
Safety, Environ. & Qlty. Mgr.: Cris Beerens
Phone: (32) 15 30 0739
Fax: (32) 15 31 8241
Email: cris.beerens@sofidelbenelux.com
Total Employees at this Location: 150
Type of Operation: Paper mill
Paper/Paperboard Grades and Capacities:
Total paper and paperboard capacity: 35,000 mt/y
Tissue: 35,000 mt/y
Paper and Paperboard Mill Data:
Stock Preparation:
Pulpers: 4
Refiners: 2
Paper Machines: 1
No. 6, TAD, total capacity 35,000 mt/y, Trim width 3.4 m, Tissue
Finishing Equipment:
Rewinders: 10
Energy Data:
Power boilers: 2
Electrical demand for mill: 184 MWh/D

ⓗSonoco Alcore NV
Ownership: Sonoco Products Co.
Park Hill, Mommaertslaan 18A
B-1831 Diegem
Belgium
Phone: (32) 2 711 0900
Fax: (32) 2 675 0225/6580
Web Address: www.sonoco.com
Personnel:
VP. Industrial Europe & Corp. Officer: Adam Wood
Phone: (32) 2 711 0900
Fax: (32) 2 675 0225/6580
Email: adam.wood@sonoco.com
Finan. Dir.: Clayton Beck
Phone: (32) 2 711 0900
Fax: (32) 2 675 0225/6580
HR Dir. Europe: Toine Mutsaers
Phone: (32) 2 711 0900 Ext.: 930
Email: toine.mutsaers@sonoco.alcore.net
IT Dir.: Luc Mahy
Phone: (32) 2 711 0900
Fax: (32) 2 675 0225/6580
European Mktg. Mgr.: Timothy Stephen Morton
Phone: (32) 2 711 0900
Fax: (32) 2 675 0225/6580
Email: tim.morton@sonoco-alcore.net
Technical Product Mgr.: David Van Hove
Phone: (32) 2 711 0900
Fax: (32) 2 675 0225/6580

Bosnia &

Email: david.vanhove@sonoco.com
Mill Locations:
Sonoco Alcore-Demolli srl, Ciriè Mill, Loc. Olivetti 47, Frazione Devesi, IT-10073 Ciriè, (TO), Italy, Capacity: 65,000 mt/y, (Paper mill)
Phone: (39) 011 9225311
Fax: (39) 011 9207772
Email: cvl@demolli.it

ⓂStora Enso Printing and Reading
Langerbrugge Mill
Ownership: 100% by Stora Enso Oyj
Wondelgemkaai 200
B-9000 Gent
Belgium
Phone: (32) 9 2577211
Fax: (32) 9 2577200
Email: langerbrugge.mill@storaenso.com, (firstname.lastname@storaenso.com)
Web Address: www.storaenso.com
Personnel:
Man. Dir.: Chris De Hollander
Phone: (32) 9 2577 400
Fax: (32) 9 2577388
Email: chris.dehollander@storaenso.com
Supply Chain Mgr.: Patricia Beausaert
Phone: (32) 9 2577329
Fax: (32) 9 2577388
Email: patricia.beausaert@storaenso.com
Finan. & Purch. Mgr.: Kristof Persyn
Phone: (32) 9 2577 310
Fax: (32) 9 2577388
Email: kristof.persyn@storaenso.com
Mill Operations Mgr.: Ulrik Paulsen
Phone: (32) 9 2577 501
Fax: (32) 9 2577388
Email: ulrik.paulsen@storaenso.com
HR Mgr.: Lieven Willaert
Phone: (32) 9 2577 313
Fax: (32) 9 2577388
Email: lieven.willaert@storaenso.com
Int. & Ext. Commun.: Sylvia De Backer
Phone: (32) 9 257 7252, 486 866790
Fax: (32) 9 2577388
Email: sylvia.debacker@storaenso.com
Total Employees at this Location: 393
Type of Operation: Pulp mill, Paper mill
Pulp Grades and Capacities:
Total pulp capacity: 549,422 mt/y
Recycled Pulping: 549,422 mt/y

Pulp Mill Data:
Pulp Lines: 3
Bleach Plant Systems: 1
DIP 1, Sequence: P, Capacity 140,000 admt/y
Recycled Fiber Treatment Lines:
Flotation deinking lines: 1 at 140,000
Flotation deinking lines: 2 at 560,000
Paper/Paperboard Grades and Capacities:
Total paper and paperboard capacity: 555,000 mt/y
Newsprint: 400,000 mt/y
Uncoated mechanical/groundwood: 155,000 mt/y
Paper and Paperboard Mill Data:
Stock Preparation:
Pulpers: 4
Refiners: 6
Paper Machines: 2
No. 3, Bel-Bond, total capacity 155,000 mt/y, Trim width 5.72 m, Uncoated mechanical/groundwood
No. 4, OptiFormer, total capacity 400,000 mt/y, Trim width 10.36 m, Newsprint
Finishing Equipment:
Supercalenders: 4
Rewinders: 6 at 555,000 mt/y
Energy Data:
Power boilers: 2
Steam turbines: 2 at 10, 42 MW
Electrical demand for mill: 1,299 MWh/D

ⓄVPK Packaging Group
Ownership: Private
Kareelstraat 108
B-9300 Aalst
Belgium
Phone: (32) 52 26 12 08
Fax: (32) 53 62 80 58
Email: info@vpk.be
Web Address: www.vpk.be
Personnel:
CEO.: Pierre Macharis
Phone: (32) 52 26 12 08
Fax: (32) 53 62 80 58
Email: pierre.macharis@vpk.be
CFO: Erik Peeters
Phone: (32) 52 26 12 08
Fax: (32) 53 62 80 58
Email: eric.peeters@vpk.be
Dir.: Denis Zenner
Phone: (32) 52 26 12 08
Fax: (32) 53 62 80 58
Total Employees of Company: 3,489
Mill Locations:
Blue Paper SAS., Stracel Mill (50% owned), 4 rue Charles Friedel Port du Rhin, F-67016 Strasbourg, France, Capacity: 270,000 mt/y, (Paper mill)
Phone: (33) 3 88 417532
Fax: (33) 3 88 417598
Email: info@bluepaper.eu
VPK Paper NV, Dendermonde Mill, Oude Baan 120, B-9200 Dendermonde, Belgium, Capacity: 460,000 mt/y, (Paperboard mill)
Phone: (32) 52 26 19 11
Fax: (32) 52 21 85 05 / 52 22 55 13
Email: info.packaging@vpk.be; (firstname.surname@vpk.be)

ⓂVPK Paper NV
Dendermonde Mill
Mill is previously: Oudegem Papier NV
Ownership: VPK Packaging Group
Oude Baan 120
B-9200 Dendermonde
Belgium
Phone: (32) 52 26 19 11
Fax: (32) 52 21 85 05 / 52 22 55 13
Email: info.packaging@vpk.be, (firstname.surname@vpk.be)
Web Address: www.vpkpaper.com, wwwvpkgroup.com
Personnel:
Mill Mgr.: Alexis Zenner
Phone: (32) 52 26 19 11
Fax: (32) 52 21 85 05
Email: alexis.zenner@vpk.be
Bus. Unit Mgr. Paper: Wim Naessens
Phone: (32) 52 26 12 09
Fax: (32) 52 21 85 05 / 52 22 55 13
Email: wim.naessens@vpk.be
Prod. Mgr.: William Paepe
Phone: (32) 52 26 19 11
Fax: (32) 52 21 85 05
Email: william.paepe@vpk.be
Tech. Dir.: Bernard De Tandt
Phone: (32) 52 26 19 11
Fax: (32) 52 21 85 05
Email: bernard.de.tandt@vpk.be
Management Assist.: Martine De Wilde
Phone: (32) 52 26 19 14
Fax: (32) 52 21 85 05
Email: martine.de.wilde@vpk.be
Total Employees at this Location: 650
Type of Operation: Paperboard mill
Pulp Grades and Capacities:
Total pulp capacity: 458,062 mt/y
Recycled Pulping: 458,062 mt/y

Pulp Mill Data:
Recycled Fiber Treatment Lines:
Pulpers: 1 at 498,200

Paper/Paperboard Grades and Capacities:
Total paper and paperboard capacity: 460,000 mt/y
Linerboard: 250,000 mt/y
Corrugating medium/fluting: 140,000 mt/y
Boxboard/cartonboard: 70,000 mt/y
Paper and Paperboard Mill Data:
Stock Preparation:
Pulpers: 6
Refiners: 4
Paper Machines: 3
No. 1, fourdrinier, total capacity 70,000 mt/y, Trim width 2.9 m, Boxboard/cartonboard
No. 6, fourdrinier (2), total capacity 150,000 mt/y, Trim width 4.8 m, Linerboard
No. 7, DuoFormer Base, total capacity 240,000 mt/y, Trim width 5 m, Corrugating medium/fluting, Linerboard
Finishing Equipment:
Rewinders: 3
Sheeters: 1
Energy Data:
Power boilers: 2
Combustion turbines: 2 at 7 MW
Steam turbines: 1 at 9 MW
Electrical demand for mill: 536 MWh/D

BOSNIA & HERZEGOVINA

ⓂNatron-Hayat d.o.o.
Maglaj Mill
Ownership: 90% by Hayat Kimya A.S., 10% by Natron d.d. BiH
Lijesnica bb
74 250 Maglaj
Bosnia & Herzegovina
Phone: (387) 32 603 142
Fax: (387) 32 603 405
Email: natron-hayat@natron-hayat.ba
Web Address: www.natron-hayat.ba
Personnel:
Tech. Mgr.: Mirko Stanic
Phone: (387) 32 603 672
Fax: (387) 32 603 405
Email: mirko.stanic@natron-hayat.ba
Exec. Dir., Mktg. & Commercial Issues: Cenap Gure
Phone: (387) 32 603 352
Fax: (387) 32 603 187
Email: cenap.gure@natron-hayat.ba
Exec. Mgr. Legal Issues & HR & Liogist.: Azema Mulasmajic
Phone: (387) 32 603 142
Fax: (387) 32 603 405
Email: azema.mulasmajic@natron-hayat.ba
Exec. Mgr. Finan.: Muhamed Zahirovic
Phone: (387) 32 603 142
Fax: (387) 32 603 405
Email: muhamed.zahirovic@natron-hayat.ba
Pulp Mill Mgr.: Fuad Karahusic
Phone: (387) 32 603 142
Fax: (387) 32 603 405
Email: fuad.karahusic@natron-hayat.ba
Power Plt. Mgr.: Emir Softic
Phone: (387) 32 603 142
Fax: (387) 32 603 405
Email: emir.softic@natron-hayat.ba
Contr. Qlty. Mgr.: Mrs. Amira Tantula
Phone: (387) 32 603 142
Fax: (387) 32 603 405
Email: amira.tantula@natron-hayat.ba
Procurement Mgr.: Hakki Ucan
Phone: (387) 32 603 142
Fax: (387) 32 603 405
Email: hakki.ucan@natron-hayat.ba
Total Employees at this Location: 842
Type of Operation: Pulp mill, Paper mill, Paperboard mill

Pulp Grades and Capacities:
Total pulp capacity: 155,504 mt/y
Chemical Pulp: 89,824 mt/y
Recycled Pulping: 65,680 mt/y
Pulp Mill Data:
Chemical Pulping Systems:
Continuous digesters: 1
Pulp Lines: 1
Chemical Recovery Equipment:
Evaporator lines: 1
Recovery boilers: 1
Lime Kiln
Recycled Fiber Treatment Lines:
Recycled packaging pulping lines: 1 at 50,000 admt/y
Paper/Paperboard Grades and Capacities:
Total paper and paperboard capacity: 155,500 mt/y
Packaging papers: 74,500 mt/y
Linerboard: 63,000 mt/y
Corrugating medium/fluting: 18,000 mt/y
Paper and Paperboard Mill Data:
Paper Machines: 3
No. 1, fourdrinier (2), total capacity 56,000 mt/y, Trim width 4.25 m, Linerboard, Corrugating medium/fluting
No. 3, fourdrinier (2), Yankee dryer, total capacity 12,000 mt/y, Trim width 2.86 m, Packaging papers
No. 4, fourdrinier (2), Yankee dryer, total capacity 87,500 mt/y, Trim width 5.45 m, Packaging papers, Linerboard
Coating Machines: 1
No. 1, total capacity 6,000 mt/y., on machine
Finishing Equipment:
Rewinders: 5 at 7,500 mt/y
Sheeters: 1
Energy Data:
Power boilers: 2
Steam turbines: 2 at 25, 19 MW
Electrical demand for mill: 326 MWh/D

ⓄⓂSHP CELEX AD
Banja Luka Mill
Ownership: 70% by ECO Invest Ruzemberok, Slovakia
Veljka Mladjenovica bb, P.O.Box 142
78102 Banja Luka
Bosnia & Herzegovina
  Phone: (387) 51 332 201 / 214 / 242 / 243
  Fax: (387) 51 33 22 22 / 332 244
  Email: celex@shpgroup.eu
  Web Address: www.shpgroup.eu
Personnel:
CFO: Djordje S. Lazic
Phone: (387) 51 332 205
Fax: (387) 51 332 222
Email: djordje.lazic@shpgroup.eu
Dir.: Predrag Zgonjanin
Phone: (387) 51 33 22 01
Fax: (387) 51 33 22 50
Email: predrag.zgonjanin@shpgroup.eu
Tech. Mgr.: Milan Milakovic
Phone: (387) 51 33 22 01
Fax: (387) 51 33 22 50
Email: milan.milakovic@shpgroup.eu
Mktg. Mgr.: Željko Banjac
Phone: (387) 51 33 22 01
Fax: (387) 51 33 22 22
Email: zeljko.banjac@shpgroup.eu
Total Employees of Company: 340
Total Employees at this Location: 210
Type of Operation: Paper mill
Paper/Paperboard Grades and Capacities:
Total paper and paperboard capacity: 36,000 mt/y
Tissue: 36,000 mt/y
Paper and Paperboard Mill Data:
Stock Preparation:
Pulpers: 7
Refiners: 7
Paper Machines: 1
No. 2, twin-wire, Yankee dryer, total capacity 36,000 mt/y, Trim width 4.92 m, Tissue
Finishing Equipment:
Rewinders: 2
Energy Data:
Power boilers: 5
Electrical demand for mill: 99 MWh/D

BULGARIA

ⓂBelovo Paper Mill S.A.
Belovo Mill
Ownership: 68.07% by Zeritis Group, 28.42% by SCA - Svenska Cellulosa Aktiebolaget
1A, Dabravsko shose str.
BG-4470 Belovo
Bulgaria
  Phone: (359) 3581 2653 / 35812105-09
  Fax: (359) 3581 2110
  Email: office@belana.bg,
  belana_bg@yahoo.com
  Web Address: www.belana.bg,
  www.zeritis.gr
Personnel:
Deputy. Gen. Mgr.: Sevdalina Asparuhova
Phone: (359) 3581 2353
Fax: (359) 3581 2110
Email: office@belana.bg
Prod. Mgr.: Stefan Kiosev
Phone: (359) 3581 2105-09
Fax: (359) 3581 2110
Email: production@belana.bg
Tech.Dir.: Borislav Beltchev
Phone: (359) 3581 2105-09
Fax: (359) 3581 2110
Email: ts@belana.bg
Sales Mgr.: Gerdana Bikova
Phone: (359) 3581 2793 / 2654
Fax: (359) 3581 2794
Email: gbikova@belana.bg
Finan. Dir.: Vilma Vasileva
Phone: (359) 3581 2105-09
Fax: (359) 3581 2110
Email: vilma@belana.bg
HR Dir.: Tcvetilia Krasteva
Phone: (359) 3581 2105-09
Fax: (359) 3581 2110
Email: personnel@belana.bg
Total Employees at this Location: 380
Type of Operation: Paper mill
Pulp Grades and Capacities:
Total pulp capacity: 51,178 mt/y
Recycled Pulping: 51,178 mt/y
Pulp Mill Data:
Recycled Fiber Treatment Lines:
Pulpers: 1 at 35,000 admt/y
Pulpers: 1 at 27,400
Paper/Paperboard Grades and Capacities:
Total paper and paperboard capacity: 66,000 mt/y
Tissue: 30,000 mt/y
Packaging papers: 20,000 mt/y
Boxboard/cartonboard: 16,000 mt/y
Paper and Paperboard Mill Data:
Stock Preparation:
Pulpers: 5
Refiners: 5
Paper Machines: 4
No. 4, fourdrinier, Yankee dryer, total capacity 20,000 mt/y, Trim width 4.52 m, Tissue, Packaging papers
No. 7, DuoFormer T, Yankee dryer, total capacity 20,000 mt/y, Trim width 2.7 m, Tissue
B34, fourdrinier, total capacity 16,000 mt/y, Trim width 2.8 m, Boxboard/cartonboard
B37, fourdrinier, total capacity 10,000 mt/y, Trim width 2.8 m, Packaging papers
Finishing Equipment:
Supercalenders: 4
Rewinders: 4
Sheeters: 2
Energy Data:
Power boilers: 3
Electrical demand for mill: 151 MWh/D

ⓂDuropack GmbH
Trakia
BG-4400 Pazardzik, Glavinitza quarter
Bulgaria
  Phone: (359) 34 401 202
  Fax: (359) 34 449 000
  Email: trakia@duropack.bg
  Web Address: www.duropack.at,
  www.duropack.bg
Personnel:
Exec. Dir.: Dr. Darinka Despotova
Phone: (359) 34 401201
Fax: (359) 34 449000
Email: despotova.darinka@duropack.bg
Exec. Dir.: Eng. Atanas Kaludov
Phone: (359) 34 401203
Fax: (359) 34 449000
Email: kaludov.atanas@duropack.bg
Prod. Mgr. Paper: Eng. Georgi Nenov
Phone: (359) 34 401233
Fax: (359) 34 449000
Email: nenov.georgi@duropack.bg
Prod. Mgr. Corr' Board: Eng. Angel Georgiev
Phone: (359) 34 401495
Fax: (359) 34 449000
Email: georgiev.angel@duropack.bg
TQM-/DVP Manager: Radena Chompalova
Phone: (359) 34 401369
Fax: (359) 34 449000
Email: Chompalova.Radena@duropack.bg
Sls. Mgr.: Todor Karaboychev
Phone: (359) 34 401204
Fax: (359) 34 449000
Email: karaboychev.todor@duropack.bg
Infrastructure & Tech. serv.Mngr: Ivan Karadzhov
Phone: (359) 34 401286
Fax: (359) 34 449000
Email: Karadzhov.Ivan@duropack.bg
Fin.& Cntr. Dir.: Anna Soldatska
Phone: (359) 34 401208
Fax: (359) 34 449000
Email: Soldatska.Anna@duropack.bg
Purch.Mngr.: Milena Kumanova
Phone: (359) 34 401225
Fax: (359) 34 449000
Email: Kumanova.Milena@duropack.bg
HR Mngr.: Georgi Grozdanov
Phone: (359) 34 401321
Fax: (359) 34 449000
Email: Grozdanov.Georgi@duropack.bg
Total Employees at this Location: 513
Type of Operation: Paperboard mill
Pulp Grades and Capacities:
Total pulp capacity: 72,629 mt/y
Recycled Pulping: 72,629 mt/y
Pulp Mill Data:
Mechanical Pulping Systems:
Conventional grinders: 1
Pulp Lines: 1
Bleach Plant Systems: 1
Felder, Type: n/a Capacity 100 admt/y
Recycled Fiber Treatment Lines:
Pulpers: 1 at 100,000 admt/y
Paper/Paperboard Grades and Capacities:
Total paper and paperboard capacity: 72,000 mt/y
Linerboard: 38,000 mt/y
Corrugating medium/fluting: 34,000 mt/y
Paper and Paperboard Mill Data:
Stock Preparation:
Pulpers: 1
Refiners: 1
Paper Machines: 1
No. 23, cylinder, total capacity 72,000 mt/y, Trim width 4.4 m, Linerboard, Corrugating medium/fluting
Finishing Equipment:
Winders: 1 at 10,000 mt/y

Bulgaria

Calenders: 1 at 76,000 mt/y
Rewinders: 1 at 80,000 mt/y
Sheeters: 1 at 80,000 mt/y
Energy Data:
Power boilers: 4
Steam turbines: 1
Electrical demand for mill: 116 MWh/D

ⓄG.F.F - Nikopol AD
101 Bistritsa chaussee
BG-1444 Sofia
Bulgaria
  Phone: (359) 888 627 167
  Email: office@gffpaper.com
  Web Address: www.gffpaper.com
Personnel:
  Owner & Man. Dir.: George Freij
  Phone: (359) 888 627 167
  Email: george@gffpaper.com
  Sls. & Mktg. Dir.: Ivo Yordanov
  Phone: (359) 888 711 176
  Email: ivo@gffpaper.com
Mill Locations:
G.F.F - Nikopol AD, Nikopol Mill, Industrial Zone Nikopol, BG-5951 Cherkvitsa, Nikopol, Bulgaria, Capacity: 20,000 mt/y, (Paper mill)
Phone: (359) 885 364 123, 888 301 340
Email: factory@gffpaper.com

ⓄⓂG.F.F - Nikopol AD
Nikopol Mill
Industrial Zone Nikopol
BG-5951 Cherkvitsa, Nikopol
Bulgaria
  Phone: (359) 885 364 123, 888 301 340
  Email: factory@gffpaper.com
  Web Address: www.gffpaper.com
Personnel:
  Owner & Man. Dir.: George Freij
  Phone: (359) 888 627 167
  Email: george@gffpaper.com
  Mktg. & Sls. Dir.: Ivo Yordanov
  Phone: (359) 888 711 176
  Email: ivo@gffpaper.com
Total Employees at this Location: 80
Type of Operation: Paper mill
Pulp Grades and Capacities:
  Total pulp capacity: 15,060 mt/y
  Recycled Pulping: 15,060 mt/y
Pulp Mill Data:
  Recycled Fiber Treatment Lines:
  Flotation deinking lines: 1
Paper/Paperboard Grades and Capacities:
  Total paper and paperboard capacity: 20,000 mt/y
  Tissue: 20,000 mt/y
Paper and Paperboard Mill Data:
  Stock Preparation:
  Pulpers: 5
  Refiners: 2
Paper Machines: 1
No. 1, fourdrinier, Yankee dryer, total capacity 20,000 mt/y, Trim width 4.3 m, Tissue
Coating Machines: 1
No. 1, on machine
Finishing Equipment:
  Rewinders: 1
  Sheeters: 2
Energy Data:
Power boilers
Electrical demand for mill: 68 MWh/D

ⓄⓂKnijna Fabrika "Iskar" JSC
Paper Factory Iskar AD
Ownership: 100% by Gloria Palace
G. Iskar, 5004 Str. 1
BG-1528 Sofia
Bulgaria
  Phone: (359) 2 973 2287 / 9785177 / 9732533
  Fax: (359) 2 973 2819
  Email: kfiskar@mail.orbitel.bg

Personnel:
  Pres.: Nikolaj Bojinov
  Phone: (359) 2 973 2287
  Exec. Dir.: Violina Ilieva Takova
  Phone: (359) 2 973 2287
Total Employees of Company: 75
Total Employees at this Location: 57
Type of Operation: Paper mill, Paperboard mill
Paper/Paperboard Grades and Capacities:
  Total paper and paperboard capacity: 8,000 mt/y
  Corrugating medium/fluting: 6,000 mt/y
Paper and Paperboard Mill Data:
  Stock Preparation:
  Pulpers: 2
  Refiners: 2
Paper Machines: 1
No. 1, fourdrinier, total capacity 8,000 mt/y, Trim width 2.1 m, Corrugating medium/fluting
Finishing Equipment:
  Winders: 1
  Calenders: 1
  Rewinders: 1
  Sheeters: 1
Energy Data:
Electrical demand for mill: 2 MWh/D

ⓄⓂKostenez-HHI PLC
Kostenez Mill
Ownership: AKB Forest HJSCo
2 Saedinenie Str.
BG-2030 Kostenez
Bulgaria
  Phone: (359) 7142 2131 / 2125 / 2260
  Fax: (359) 7142 2311 / 2178
  Email: kosthhi@hhi-bg.com,
  techno@hhi-bg.com,
  marketing-spl@hhi-bg.com
  Web Address: www.hhi-bg.com
Personnel:
  Chmn. of the Board: Kiril Dimitrov Okolski
  Phone: (359) 7142 2131
  Fax: (359) 7142 3095
  Email: kiril.okolsko@hhi-bg.com
  Mill Mgr.: Dimitar Petrov
  Phone: (359) 7 142 2125
  Fax: (359) 7 142 2311
  Email: kosthhi@hhi-bg.com
  Specialist export-import: Dilyana Yordanova
  Phone: (359) 7142 2352
  Fax: (359) 7142 2311
  Email: dilyana.yordanova@hhi-bg.com
  Mech. Dept. Chief: Angel Stoev
  Phone: (359) 7142 3095
  Fax: (359) 7142 3095
  Email: angel.stoev@hhi-bg.com
  Technology Dept. Chief: Angel Spasov
  Phone: (359) 7142 2131 ext. 271
  Fax: (359) 7142 3095
  Email: technology@hhi-bg.com
  Automation Dept. Chief: Zahari Ivanov
  Phone: (359) 7142 2131 ext.201
  Fax: (359) 7142 3095
  Email: automat@hhi-bg.com
  Domestic Markets: Daniela Inkova
  Phone: (359) 7142 2260
  Fax: (359) 7142 2178
  Email: daniela.inkova@hhi-bg.com
Total Employees at this Location: 300
Type of Operation: Paper mill
Pulp Grades and Capacities:
  Total pulp capacity: 40,520 mt/y
  Recycled Pulping: 40,520 mt/y
Paper/Paperboard Grades and Capacities:
  Total paper and paperboard capacity: 60,000 mt/y
  Tissue: 26,000 mt/y
  Packaging papers: 21,000 mt/y
  Corrugating medium/fluting: 13,000 mt/y
Paper and Paperboard Mill Data:
  Stock Preparation:
  Pulpers: 4

Refiners: 12
Paper Machines: 3
No. 1, fourdrinier, total capacity 13,000 mt/y, Trim width 2.1 m, Corrugating medium/fluting
No. 2, fourdrinier, Yankee dryer, total capacity 21,000 mt/y, Trim width 4.2 m, Packaging papers
No. 3, crescent former, Yankee dryer, total capacity 26,000 mt/y, Trim width 2.75 m, Tissue
Finishing Equipment:
  Winders: 3 at 60,000 mt/y
  Rewinders: 2 at 5,000 mt/y
  Sheeters: 1 at 5,000 mt/y
Energy Data:
Power boilers: 2
Combustion turbines: 2 at 7.4 MW
Electrical demand for mill: 129 MWh/D

ⓂMondi Stambolijski EAD
Stambolijski Mill
Ownership: 100% by Mondi Europe & International Division
1, Zavodska Str.
BG-4210 Stambolijski
Bulgaria
  Phone: (359) 32 909 287
  Fax: (359) 32 909 554
  Web Address: www.mondigroup.com
Personnel:
  Exec. Man. Dir.: Alexander Krickler
  Phone: (359) 32 909 287
  Fax: (359) 32 909554
  Email: alexander.krickler@mondigroup.com
  Chief Finan.: Galina Anastasova
  Phone: (359) 32 909 311
  Fax: (359) 32 909 21
  Email: galina.anastasova@mondigroup.com
  Prod. & Tech. Mgr.: Nikola Tenov
  Phone: (359) 32 909 208
  Fax: (359) 32 909 556
  Email: nikola.tenov@mondigroup.com
  Sls. & Logist. Dir.: Kostadin Kalinkov
  Phone: (359) 32 909 281
  Fax: (359) 32 909 599
  Email: kostadin.kalinkov@mondigroup.com
Total Employees at this Location: 320
Type of Operation: Pulp mill, Paper mill
Pulp Grades and Capacities:
  Total pulp capacity: 94,313 mt/y
  Chemical Pulp: 94,313 mt/y
Pulp Mill Data:
  Chemical Pulping Systems:
  Batch digesters: 6
Pulp Lines: 2
  Chemical Recovery Equipment:
  Evaporator lines: 1
  Recovery boilers: 1
  Lime Kiln
  Recycled Fiber Treatment Lines:
  Pulpers: 2 at 17,850 admt/y
Paper/Paperboard Grades and Capacities:
  Total paper and paperboard capacity: 90,000 mt/y
  Packaging papers: 90,000 mt/y
Paper and Paperboard Mill Data:
  Stock Preparation:
  Pulpers: 2
  Refiners: 6
Paper Machines: 1
No. 2, fourdrinier, total capacity 90,000 mt/y, Trim width 4.1 m, Packaging papers
Finishing Equipment:
  Rewinders: 2 at 143,000 mt/y
Energy Data:
Power boilers: 2
Steam turbines: 2 at 4, 6 MW
Electrical demand for mill: 252 MWh/D

ⓄⓂSanitex Paper Mill Ltd.
Kostinbrod Mill
IV Lomsko Chaussee

BG-2230 Kostinbrod
Bulgaria
　Phone: (359) 721 66523
　Fax: (359) 721 66520
　Email: sanitexbg@sanitexbg.com
　Web Address: www.sanitexbg.com
Personnel:
　Sls. Dir.: Naiden Manev
　Phone: (359) 721 66523
　Fax: (359) 721 66520
　Email: nmanev@sanitexbg.com
Total Employees at this Location: 150
Type of Operation: Paper mill
Pulp Grades and Capacities:
　Total pulp capacity: 5,343 mt/y
　Recycled Pulping: 5,343 mt/y
Pulp Mill Data:
　Recycled Fiber Treatment Lines:
　Flotation deinking lines: 1
Paper/Paperboard Grades and Capacities:
　Total paper and paperboard capacity: 20,000 mt/y
　Tissue: 20,000 mt/y
Paper and Paperboard Mill Data:
　Stock Preparation:
　Pulpers: 1
Paper Machines: 2
　No. 1, crescent former, Yankee dryer, total capacity 5,000 mt/y, Trim width 2.65 m, Tissue
　No. 2, crescent former, Yankee dryer, total capacity 15,000 mt/y, Trim width 2.65 m, Tissue
Energy Data:
　Power boilers
　Electrical demand for mill: 63 MWh/D

①⑩Svilosa AD
Svilocell EAD
Ownership: 100% by Svilosa Company
Western Industrial Zone, Veliko Turnovo District
BG-5253 Svishtov
Bulgaria
　Phone: (359) 631 45277, 631 41141
　Fax: (359) 631 40104, 631 41141
　Email: svilocell@svilosa.bg
　Web Address: www.svilosa.bg
Personnel:
　CEO & Chmn. of BOD of Svilosa Company: Krassimir Dachev
　Phone: (359) 2 818 5969
　Fax: (359) 2 818 5949
　Email: kdachev@mtgbg.com
　Commer. Mgr. Svilocel: Ivan Ganev
　Phone: (359) 631 44 807
　Fax: (359) 631 48 169
　Email: i_ganev@svilosa.bg
　Exec. Dir. Svilosa Company: Michail Kolchev
　Phone: (359) 631 45 277
　Fax: (359) 631 40104
　Email: mkolchev@svilosa.bg
　Exec. Mgr. of Svilocel: Victor Zarev
　Phone: (359) 631 45277
　Fax: (359) 631 40104
　Email: vzarev@svilosa.bg
　Prod. Dir.: Plamen Petrov
　Phone: (359) 631 42781
　Fax: (359) 631 41141
　Email: ppetrov@svilosa.bg
Total Employees of Company: 440
Total Employees at this Location: 480
Type of Operation: Pulp mill
Pulp Grades and Capacities:
　Total pulp capacity: 150,446 mt/y
　Pulp available for market: 150,000 mt/y
　Chemical Pulp: 150,446 mt/y
Pulp Mill Data:
　Chemical Pulping Systems:
　Batch digesters: 7
Pulp Lines: 1
　Bleach Plant Systems: 1
　2 parallel lines, Type: ECF, Sequence: O₂ DoEopD,
　Capacity 150,000 admt/y
　Chemical Recovery Equipment:
　Evaporator lines: 2
　Recovery boilers: 1
　Lime Kiln
　Pulp Dryers:
　Air Float dryers 1, Air Float dryers 1
Energy Data:
　Power boilers: 1
　Steam turbines: 2 at 8.8, 12 MW
　Electrical demand for mill: 331 MWh/D

CROATIA

①⑩BELIŠCE d.d.
Belišce Mill
Ownership: 100% by Duropack GmbH
Trg A. Starcevica 1
HR-31551 Belišce, Salvonia
Croatia
　Phone: (385) 31 516 516
　Fax: (385) 31 516 240
　Email: uprava@belisce.hr
　Web Address: www.belisce.hr, www.duropack.at
Personnel:
　Prod. Mgr.: Damir Šaric
　Phone: (385) 31 516 568
　Fax: (385) 31 516 276
　Email: damir.saric@belisce.hr
　Purch. Mgr.: Anita Grguric
　Phone: (385) 31 516 463
　Fax: (385) 31 516 246
　Email: jandre.romic@belisce.hranita.grguric@belisce.hr
　Finan. Dir.: Gorana Špoljaric
　Phone: (385) 31 516 502
　Fax: (385) 31 516 241
　Email: gorana.spoljaric@belisce.hr
　Head of Transport Dept.: Gordana Oreškovic
　Phone: (385) 31 516 373
　Fax: (385) 31 516 291
　Email: stanko.ratkovcic@belisce.hrgordana.oreskovic@belisce.hr
Total Employees of Company: 1,200
Total Employees at this Location: 1,200
Type of Operation: Pulp mill, Paperboard mill
Pulp Grades and Capacities:
　Total pulp capacity: 211,931 mt/y
　Chemical Pulp: 68,068 mt/y
　Recycled Pulping: 143,863 mt/y
Pulp Mill Data:
　Chemical Pulping Systems:
　Continuous digesters: 2
Pulp Lines: 2
　Chemical Recovery Equipment:
　Evaporator lines: 1
　Recovery boilers: 1
　Lime Kiln
　Recycled Fiber Treatment Lines:
　Pulpers: 5 at 300,000 admt/y
　Recycled packaging pulping lines: 4 at 280,000 admt/y
Paper/Paperboard Grades and Capacities:
　Total paper and paperboard capacity: 210,000 mt/y
　Linerboard: 77,000 mt/y
　Corrugating medium/fluting: 133,000 mt/y
Paper and Paperboard Mill Data:
　Stock Preparation:
　Pulpers: 5
　Refiners: 2
Paper Machines: 2
　No. 2, fourdrinier (2), total capacity 115,000 mt/y, Trim width 5 m, Linerboard, Corrugating medium/fluting
　No. 3, fourdrinier (2), total capacity 95,000 mt/y, Trim width 4.4 m, Corrugating medium/fluting
　Finishing Equipment:
　Winders: 3 at 300,000 mt/y
　Calenders: 2
　Rewinders: 3 at 300,000 mt/y
Energy Data:
　Power boilers: 2
　Steam turbines: 2 at 31 MW
　Electrical demand for mill: 368 MWh/D

①⑩Drvenjaca d.d.
Fuzine Mill
Ownership: 100% by shareholders/workers
HR-51322 Fuzine, Gorski kotar
Croatia
　Phone: (385) 51 830 100
　Fax: (385) 51 835 487
　Email: drvenjaca@drvenjaca.hr
　Web Address: www.drvenjaca.hr
Personnel:
　CEO: Ivan Liker
　Phone: (385) 51 830 120
　Fax: (385) 51 830 190
　Email: ivan.liker@drvenjaca.hr
　CEO: Branko Liker
　Phone: (385) 51 830 111
　Fax: (385) 51 830 190
　Email: branko.liker@drvenjaca.hr
　Purch. Mgr.: Goran Mihi?
　Phone: (385) 51 830 112
　Fax: (385) 51 830 190
　Email: goran.mihic@drvenjaca.hr
　Sls. Mgr.: Sanjin Radunovic
　Phone: (385) 51 830 112
　Fax: (385) 51 830 190
　Email: sanjin.radunovic@drvenjaca.hr
　Maint. Mgr.: Žarko Blažević Eng.
　Phone: (385) 51 830 128
　Fax: (385) 51 830 190
　Email: zarko.blazevic@drvenjaca.hr
　Prod. Mgr.: Kazimir Mihaljevi?
　Phone: (385) 51 830 113
　Fax: (385) 51 830 190
　Email: kazimir.mihaljevic@drvenjaca.hr
Total Employees of Company: 186
Total Employees at this Location: 101
Type of Operation: Pulp mill
Pulp Grades and Capacities:
　Total pulp capacity: 50,846 mt/y
　Pulp available for market: 50,000 mt/y
　Mechanical Pulp: 50,846 mt/y
Pulp Mill Data:
　Mechanical Pulping Systems:
　RMP systems: 1
　Bleach Plant Systems: 1
　No. 1, Sequence: P, Capacity 50,000 admt/y
　Pulp Dryers:
　Flash dryers 1
Energy Data:
　Power boilers: 1
　Electrical demand for mill: 200 MWh/D

①⑩PAN Papirna Industrija d.o.o.
Zagreb Mill
Company is mill is scheduled to close end of 2014
Ownership: 100% by private owner
Radnicka cesta Dure Dakovica 173
HR-10000 Zagreb, Grad Zagreb
Croatia
　Phone: (385) 1 2409 333
　Fax: (385) 1 2408 022/2409 884
　Email: ured.direktora@pan-paper.hr
　Web Address: www.pan-paper.hr
Personnel:
　Prod. Mgr./Member of the board: Iva Mikuliic
　Phone: (385) 1 2409 333
　Fax: (385) 1 240 98 84
　Email: iva.mikulic@pan-paper.hr
　Mill Mgr.: Silvija Vukovic
　Phone: (385) 1 248 14 77

Czech Republic

Fax: (385) 1 240 98 84
Email: silvija.vukovic@pan-paper.hr
P.A. to Iva Mikulich: Lidia Vidasha
Email: ured.direktora@pan-paper.hr
Total Employees of Company: 1,000
Total Employees at this Location: 1,000
Type of Operation: Paper mill, Paperboard mill
Pulp Grades and Capacities:
 Total pulp capacity: 195,538 mt/y
 Recycled Pulping: 195,538 mt/y
Pulp Mill Data:
 Recycled Fiber Treatment Lines:
 Flotation deinking lines: 2 at 55,000 admt/y
 Pulpers: 6 at 155,000 admt/y
 Recycled packaging pulping lines: 2 at 155,000 admt/y
Paper/Paperboard Grades and Capacities:
 Total paper and paperboard capacity: 200,000 mt/y
 Linerboard: 100,000 mt/y
 Corrugating medium/fluting: 50,000 mt/y
 Boxboard/cartonboard: 50,000 mt/y
Paper and Paperboard Mill Data:
 Stock Preparation:
 Pulpers: 6
 Refiners: 12
Paper Machines: 1
 No. 6, multi-wire, total capacity 200,000 mt/y, Trim width 4.46 m, Corrugating medium/fluting, Linerboard, Boxboard/cartonboard
Coating Machines: 1
 No. 1, total capacity 50,000 mt/y., on machine
Finishing Equipment:
 Rewinders: 4 at 130,000 mt/y
Energy Data:
 Power boilers: 3
 Electrical demand for mill: 284 MWh/D

CZECH REPUBLIC

ⓘⓜPapírna APIS, s.r.o.
Ceská Kamenice Mill
Lužická 133
CZ-40721 Ceská Kamenice
Czech Republic
 Phone: (420) 774 584 549
 Fax: (420) 412 582 902
 Web Address: www.papirna-apis.cz
Personnel:
 Plant Dir.: Martin Cervinka
 Phone: (420) 608 248 090
 Fax: (420) 412 582 902
 Prod. Dir.: Václav Rehák
 Phone: (420) 774 584 549
 Fax: (420) 412 582 902
 Email: rehak.apis@seznam.cz
 Prod. Mgr.: Pavel Krystufek
 Phone: (420) 774584569
 Fax: (420) 412 582 902
 Email: krystufek.apis@seznam.cz
 Expedition, Warehouse, Billing: Kudrnova Lenka
 Phone: (420) 774584569
 Fax: (420) 412 582 902
 Email: kudrnova.apis@seznam.cz
Total Employees at this Location: 60
Type of Operation: Paper mill
Paper/Paperboard Grades and Capacities:
 Total paper and paperboard capacity: 18,000 mt/y
 Boxboard/cartonboard: 18,000 mt/y
Paper and Paperboard Mill Data:
Paper Machines: 1
 No. 4, fourdrinier, total capacity 18,000 mt/y, Trim width 2.6 m, Boxboard/cartonboard

ⓘⓜBiocel Paskov a.s.
Paskov Mill
Ownership: 100% by Lenzing AG
Zahradní 762
CZ-739 21 Paskov
Czech Republic
 Phone: (420) 558 461 111
 Fax: (420) 558 461 113
 Email: office@biocel.cz
 Web Address: www.biocel.cz
Personnel:
 Chmn. of the Man. Board: Dipl. Ing. Ivo Klimša
 Phone: (420) 558 462191
 Fax: (420) 558 671 331
 Email: ivo.klimsa@biocel.cz
 Member of the Man. Board: Katerina Kupkova
 Phone: (420) 558 46 2198
 Fax: (420) 558 46 1120
 Email: katerina.kupkova@biocel.cz
 Member of the Man. Board: Dipl. Ing. Vojtech Podmolik
 Phone: (420) 558 462140
 Fax: (420) 558 461113
 Email: vojtech.podmolik@biocel.cz
 Sls. Mgr.: Dipl. Ing. Jaroslav Socha
 Phone: (420) 558 462549
 Fax: (420) 558 46 1116/67 1500
 Email: jaroslav.socha@biocel.cz
 Maint. & Investment Mgr.: Dipl. Ing. Radislav Horkel
 Phone: (420) 558 462308
 Fax: (420) 558 461 113
 Email: radislav.horkel@biocel.cz
 Head of Qlty. & Environ. Protection Dept.: Dipl. Ing. Dalibor Sloncik
 Phone: (420) 558 46 3260
 Fax: (420) 558 461113
 Email: dalibor.sloncik@biocel.cz
 Finan. Mgr.: Dipl. Ing. Miroslav Mynarz
 Phone: (420) 558 461489
 Fax: (420) 558 463705
 Email: miroslav.machala@biocel.cz
 HR & Commun. Mgr.: Zdenek Kotatko
 Phone: (420) 558 46 2130
 Fax: (420) 558 46 1113
 Email: zdenek.kotatko@biocel.cz
Total Employees of Company: 400
Total Employees at this Location: 376
Type of Operation: Pulp mill
Pulp Grades and Capacities:
 Total pulp capacity: 261,271 mt/y
 Pulp available for market: 255,000 mt/y
 Chemical Pulp: 261,271 mt/y
Pulp Mill Data:
 Chemical Pulping Systems:
 Batch digesters: 9
Pulp Lines: 1
 Bleach Plant Systems: 1
 No. 1, Type: Eop-Z-P Capacity 285,000 admt/y
 Chemical Recovery Equipment:
 Evaporator lines: 1
 Recovery boilers: 1
 Pulp Dryers:
 Fourdriniers 1
Energy Data:
 Power boilers: 3
 Steam turbines: 2 at 20, 20 MW
 Electrical demand for mill: 634 MWh/D

ⓘCEREPA, a.s.
Ownership: 100% by Gaute a.s.
Cervená Recice 107
CZ-394 46 Cervená Recice
Czech Republic
 Phone: (420) 565 398 241
 Fax: (420) 565 398 247
 Web Address: www.cerepa.cz
Personnel:
 Chmn. , Dir: Vladimir Pour
 Phone: (420) 602 161 571
 Fax: (420) 565 398 307
 Email: vladimir.pour@cerepa.cz
 Sls. Dir.: Jaroslava Strapcova
 Phone: (420) 602 153 281
 Fax: (420) 565 398 307
 Email: jarka.strapcova@cerepa.cz
 HR Mgr.: Eva Chábova
 Phone: (420) 565 398 241
 Fax: (420) 565 398 247
 Email: eva.chabova@cerepa.cz
Total Employees of Company: 137
Mill Locations:
CEREPA, a.s., Cervená Recice Mill, CZ-394 46 Cervená Recice 107, Czech Republic, Capacity: 11,000 mt/y, (Paper mill)
 Phone: (420) 565 398241/ 2/3/4
 Fax: (420) 565 398247/545 398307
 Email: cerepa@cerepa.cz

ⓜCEREPA, a.s.
Cervená Recice Mill
Mill is insolvent
CZ-394 46 Cervená Recice 107
Czech Republic
 Phone: (420) 565 398241/ 2/3/4
 Fax: (420) 565 398247/545 398307
 Email: cerepa@cerepa.cz
 Web Address: www.cerepa.cz
Personnel:
 Chmn. , Dir: Vladimir Pour
 Phone: (420) 602 161 571
 Fax: (420) 565 398 307
 Email: vladimir.pour@cerepa.cz
 Technological Mgr.: Aleš Mátl
 Phone: (420) 602 161 573
 Fax: (420) 565 398 422
 Email: ales.matl@cerepa.cz
 Tech. & Prod. Dir. Vice-chairman of the Board of Directors: Miroslav Hovorka
 Phone: (420) 602 161 570
 Fax: (420) 565 398 307
 Email: miroslav.hovorka@cerepa.cz
 Sls. Dir.: Jaroslava Strapcova
 Phone: (420) 602 153 281 / 565 398 105
 Fax: (420) 565 398 307
 Email: jarka.strapcova@cerepa.cz
 HR Mgr.: Eva Chábova
 Phone: (420) 565 398 241
 Fax: (420) 565 398 247
 Email: eva.chabova@cerepa.cz
 Power Eng.: Bohuslav Hyps
 Phone: (420) 565 398 241
 Fax: (420) 565 398 422
 Email: bohuslav.hyps@cerepa.cz
Total Employees at this Location: 137
Type of Operation: Paper mill
Pulp Grades and Capacities:
 Total pulp capacity: 11,728 mt/y
 Recycled Pulping: 11,728 mt/y
Pulp Mill Data:
 Recycled Fiber Treatment Lines:
 Pulpers
Paper/Paperboard Grades and Capacities:
 Total paper and paperboard capacity: 11,000 mt/y
 Tissue: 11,000 mt/y
Paper and Paperboard Mill Data:
 Stock Preparation:
 Pulpers: 1
Paper Machines: 1
 No. 5, fourdrinier, Yankee dryer, total capacity 11,000 mt/y, Trim width 1.6 m, Tissue
Energy Data:
 Power boilers
 Electrical demand for mill: 31 MWh/D

ⓘⓜEMBA spol. s. r.o.
Paseky nad Jízerou Mill
CZ-512 47 Paseky nad Jízerou, okr. Semily
Czech Republic
 Phone: (420) 481 553 111
 Fax: (420) 481 553 163
 Email: prodej@emba.cz
 Web Address: www.emba.cz, www.archivbox.cz
Personnel:

Czech Republic

CEO: Marek Michálko
Phone: (420) 481 553 117
Fax: (420) 481 553 163
Email: michalko@emba.cz
Gen. Mgr.: Evžen Pelikán
Phone: (420) 481 553 116
Fax: (420) 481 553 168
Email: pelikan@emba.cz
Prod. Dir.: Dipl. Ing. Jiří Erben
Phone: (420) 481 533 133
Fax: (420) 481 553 163
Email: erben@emba.cz
Commercial Dir.: Dipl. Ing. Jiří Jelínek
Phone: (420) 481 553 150
Fax: (420) 481 553 163
Email: prodej@emba.cz
Prod. & Tech. Dir.: Dipl. Ing. Aleš Koucký
Phone: (420) 481 553 167
Fax: (420) 481 553 163
Email: ales.koucky@emba.cz
Head of Bus. Dept.: Renata Penickova
Phone: (420) 481 553 145
Fax: (420) 481 553 163
Email: penickova@emba.cz
Mktg. Dir.: Jiri Stastny
Phone: (420) 481 553 129
Fax: (420) 481 553 163
Email: stastny@emba.cz
Total Employees at this Location: 150
Type of Operation: Paperboard mill
Pulp Grades and Capacities:
Total pulp capacity: 12,176 mt/y
Recycled Pulping: 12,176 mt/y
Pulp Mill Data:
Recycled Fiber Treatment Lines:
Recycled packaging pulping lines: 1
Paper/Paperboard Grades and Capacities:
Total paper and paperboard capacity: 12,000 mt/y
Boxboard/cartonboard: 12,000 mt/y
Paper and Paperboard Mill Data:
Paper Machines: 2
No. 1, cylinder, total capacity 6,000 mt/y, Trim width 2.25 m, Boxboard/cartonboard
No. 2, cylinder, total capacity 6,000 mt/y, Trim width 2.34 m, Boxboard/cartonboard
Energy Data:
Power boilers
Electrical demand for mill: 11 MWh/D

ⓘⓜJIP - Papírny Vetrní, a.s.
Vetrní Mill
Papírenská cp. 2
CZ-382 11 Vetrni
Czech Republic
Phone: (420) 380 909 111
Fax: (420) 380 909 234
Email: info@jip.cz, sales@jip.cz
Web Address: www.jip.cz
Personnel:
Man. Dir. & Sls. Mgr.: Dipl. Ing. Dušan Grmolec
Phone: (420) 380 909 206
Fax: (420) 387 707 234
Email: dusan.grmolec@jip.cz
CFO: Michal Morong MBA
Phone: (420) 387 707 351
Fax: (420) 387 707 464
Email: michal.morong@jip.cz
Contr.: Petr Badán
Phone: (420) 387 707 225
Fax: (420) 387 707 464
Email: petr.badan@jip.cz
Maint. Mgr.: Karel Pavec
Phone: (420) 387 707 230
Fax: (420) 387 707 234
Email: karel.pavec@jip.cz
Energy Dir.: Miloslav Sirový
Phone: (420) 387 707 672
Fax: (420) 380 909 677
Email: miloslav.sirovy@jip.cz

Prod. & Purch. Mgr.: Jan Novák
Phone: (420) 387 707 504
Fax: (420) 380 909 274
Email: jan.novak@jip.cz
Total Employees at this Location: 460
Type of Operation: Pulp mill, Paper mill
Mill Locations:
JIP - Papírny Vetrní, a.s., Lukavice Mill, Lukavice 21, CZ-789 01 Zábreh, Czech Republic, Capacity: 27,000 mt/y, (Paper mill)
Phone: (420) 583 030 111
Fax: (420) 583 030 333
Email: info@jip.cz
Pulp Grades and Capacities:
Total pulp capacity: 36,854 mt/y
Recycled Pulping: 36,854 mt/y
Pulp Mill Data:
Recycled Fiber Treatment Lines:
Pulpers: 4 at 50,000
Paper/Paperboard Grades and Capacities:
Total paper and paperboard capacity: 51,000 mt/y
Packaging papers: 11,000 mt/y
Specialty and industrial: 40,000 mt/y
Paper and Paperboard Mill Data:
Stock Preparation:
Pulpers: 1
Paper Machines: 3
No. 6, fourdrinier, total capacity 15,000 mt/y, Trim width 4.2 m, Specialty and industrial, Packaging papers
No. 7, SymFormer MB, total capacity 30,000 mt/y, Trim width 3.85 m, Packaging papers, Specialty and industrial
No. 8, fourdrinier, total capacity 6,000 mt/y, Trim width 3.2 m, Packaging papers, Specialty and industrial
Finishing Equipment:
Winders: 4 at 100,000 mt/y
Calenders: 1
Rewinders: 3
Sheeters: 5
Energy Data:
Power boilers: 2
Combustion turbines: 2 at 12 MW
Electrical demand for mill: 126 MWh/D

ⓘJIP - Papírny Vetrní, a.s.
Lukavice Mill
Lukavice 21
CZ-789 01 Zábreh
Czech Republic
Mailing Address: Papírenská cp. 2, CZ - 382 11 Vetrní
Phone: (420) 583 030 111
Fax: (420) 583 030 333
Email: info@jip.cz
Web Address: www.jip.cz
Personnel:
Dir. Lukavice, Mill Mgr.: Vladimir Trunecka
Phone: (420) 583 030 345
Fax: (420) 583 030 333
Prod. & Technology Dir.: Vladimir Lastuvka
Phone: (420) 583 030 506
Fax: (420) 583 030 333
Total Employees at this Location: 200
Type of Operation: Paper mill
Pulp Grades and Capacities:
Total pulp capacity: 10,000 mt/y
Recycled Pulping: 10,000 mt/y
Pulp Mill Data:
Recycled Fiber Treatment Lines:
Pulpers: 1 at 12,000
Paper/Paperboard Grades and Capacities:
Total paper and paperboard capacity: 27,000 mt/y
Packaging papers: 27,000 mt/y
Paper and Paperboard Mill Data:
Stock Preparation:
Pulpers: 1
Paper Machines: 2
No. 1, fourdrinier, Yankee dryer, total capacity 12,000 mt/y, Trim width 2.7 m, Packaging papers

No. 5, Yankee dryer, total capacity 12,000 mt/y, Trim width 3.1 m, Packaging papers
Finishing Equipment:
Winders: 2
Rewinders: 1
Sheeters: 1
Energy Data:
Power boilers: 1
Steam turbines: 1 at 0.8 MW

ⓘKORONA Lochovice spol. s r.o.
Ownership: 99.99% by Berater (Central Europe) Kft., Hungary, 0.01% by CZI Group, s.r.o., Czech Republic
Lochovice cp.20
CZ-267 23 Lochovice
Czech Republic
Phone: (420) 311 545 810
Fax: (420) 311 545 852
Email: obchod@korona.cz, info@korona.cz
Web Address: www.korona.cz
Personnel:
Gen. Mgr.: Maria Truskanova
Phone: (420) 311 545 810
Fax: (420) 311 545 852
Email: truskanova@korona.cz
Export Mgr.: Radka Šterbová
Phone: (420) 311 545 814
Fax: (420) 311 545 852
Email: sterbova@korona.cz
Logistics & Procurement Mgr.: Libor Jánský
Phone: (420) 311 545 817
Fax: (420) 311 545 852
Email: jansky@korona.cz
Total Employees of Company: 172
Mill Locations:
KORONA Lochovice spol. s r.o., Lochovice Mill, Lochovice cp.20, CZ-267 23 Lochovice, Czech Republic, Capacity: 15,000 mt/y, (Paperboard mill)
Phone: (420) 311 545 810
Fax: (420) 311 545 852
Email: obchod@korona.cz, info@korona.cz

ⓘKORONA Lochovice spol. s r.o.
Lochovice Mill
Lochovice cp.20
CZ-267 23 Lochovice
Czech Republic
Phone: (420) 311 545 810
Fax: (420) 311 545 852
Email: obchod@korona.cz, info@korona.cz
Web Address: www.korona.cz
Personnel:
CEO: Ing. Maria Truskanova
Phone: (420) 311 545 810
Fax: (420) 311 545 852
Email: truskanova@korona.cz
Export Mgr.: Radka Šterbová
Phone: (420) 311 545 814
Fax: (420) 311 545 852
Email: sterbova@korona.cz
Logist. & Procurement Mgr.: Libor Jánský
Phone: (420) 311 545 817 / 602 170 745
Fax: (420) 311 545 852
Email: jansky@korona.cz
Sls. Mgr. - Domestic Market: Zdenek Dlouhy
Phone: (420) 602 354 044
Fax: (420) 311 545 852
Email: dlouhy@korona.cz
Head of Prod. Dept.: Marcel Pa?our
Phone: (420) 311 545 216
Fax: (420) 311 545 852
Email: padour@korona.cz
Mktg. & Sls. Mgr.: Václav Kade?ávek
Phone: (420) 11 545 811
Fax: (420) 311 545 852
Email: kaderavek@korona.cz
Total Employees at this Location: 172

Czech Republic

Type of Operation: Paperboard mill
Pulp Grades and Capacities:
Total pulp capacity: 15,221 mt/y
Recycled Pulping: 15,221 mt/y

Pulp Mill Data:
Recycled Fiber Treatment Lines:
Pulpers: 1 at 8,000 admt/y
Paper/Paperboard Grades and Capacities:
Total paper and paperboard capacity: 15,000 mt/y
Boxboard/cartonboard: 15,000 mt/y
Paper and Paperboard Mill Data:
Paper Machines: 1
No. 1, cylinder, total capacity 15,000 mt/y, Trim width 2.2 m, Boxboard/cartonboard
Energy Data:
Electrical demand for mill: 13 MWh/D

ⒽⓂKRPA Paper, a.s.
Krpa Papir Mill
Ownership: KRPA Group
Nádražní 266
CZ-543 71 Hostinné
Czech Republic
Phone: (420) 499 990 162
Fax: (420) 499 990 109
Email: paper@krpa.cz
Web Address: www.krpa-paper.cz
Personnel:
Man. Dir.: Ing. Milan Michael
Phone: (420) 499 990 223
Fax: (420) 499 990 109
Email: milan.michael@krpa.cz
Bus. Dev. Mgr.: Dipl.Eng. Jaroslav Lánský
Phone: (420) 499 990 390
Fax: (420) 499 990 109
Email: jaroslav.lansky@krpa.cz
Procurement Mgr.: Tomáš Novák
Phone: (420) 499 990 129
Fax: (420) 499 990 109
Email: tomas.novak@krpa.cz
Prod. Dir.: Miloslav Sir
Phone: (420) 499 990 223
Fax: (420) 499 990 109
Email: miloslav.sir@krpa.cz
Paper Prod. Mgr.: Martin Doubek
Phone: (420) 499 990 173
Fax: (420) 499 990 109
Email: martin.doubek@krpa.cz
Chief Technologist: Milos Veskrna
Phone: (420) 499 990 327
Fax: (420) 499 990 109
Email: milos.veskrna@krpa.cz
Head of Research & Technological Dept.: Dipl.Eng. David Bayer
Phone: (420) 499 990 293
Fax: (420) 499 990 109
Email: david.bayer@krpa.cz
Tech. Dir.: Milan Vachek
Phone: (420) 499 990 449
Fax: (420) 499 990 109
Email: milan.vachek@krpa.cz
Total Employees at this Location: 250
Type of Operation: Paper mill
Paper/Paperboard Grades and Capacities:
Total paper and paperboard capacity: 25,000 mt/y
Uncoated woodfree/freesheet: 18,000 mt/y
Specialty and industrial: 7,000 mt/y
Paper and Paperboard Mill Data:
Paper Machines: 1
No. 6, fourdrinier, total capacity 35,000 mt/y, Trim width 4.25 m, Specialty and industrial, Uncoated woodfree/freesheet
Finishing Equipment:
Supercalenders: 1
Rewinders: 1
Sheeters: 1
Energy Data:
Electrical demand for mill: 52 MWh/D

ⓂMELECKY a.s. závod Papírna Aloisov
Cermenská 910
CZ-749 01 Vítkov
Czech Republic
Phone: (420) 556 300 578
Fax: (420) 556 300 579
Email: info@melecky.eu
Web Address: www.melecky.eu
Personnel:
Sls. Mgr.: Melecká Jana
Phone: (420) 583 320 244, 775 293 039
Fax: (420) 583 320 280
Email: melecka.jana@melecky.cz
Business Assistant: Faltínová Jana
Phone: (420) 583 320 275
Fax: (420) 583 320 280
Email: faltinova.jana@melecky.cz
Export Mgr.: Lenoch Petr
Phone: (420) 420 602 731 022
Fax: (420) 420 556 300 579
Email: lenoch@melecky.cz
Export Mgr.: Michael Suchanka
Phone: (420) 0151 111 333 40
Fax: (420) 556 300 579
Email: suchanka@melecky.eu
Mill Locations:
MELECKY a.s. závod Papírna Aloisov, Aloisov Mill, Aloisov, CZ-789 63 Ruda nad Moravou, Czech Republic, Capacity: 9,000 mt/y, (Paper mill)
Phone: (420) 583 320 240
Fax: (420) 583 320 280
Email: stark@melecky.eu

ⓂMELECKY a.s. závod Papírna Aloisov
Aloisov Mill
Aloisov
CZ-789 63 Ruda nad Moravou
Czech Republic
Phone: (420) 583 320 240
Fax: (420) 583 320 280
Email: stark@melecky.eu
Web Address: www.melecky.cz
Personnel:
Owner: Jaromir Melecky
Mill Mgr.: Mr. Kubat
Phone: (420) 583 320 240
Fax: (420) 583 320 280
Email: kubat@melecky.eu
Sls. Dir.: Jana Melecka
Phone: (420) 583 320 244 / 775 293 039
Fax: (420) 583 320 280
Email: melecka.jana@melecky.cz
Sls. Mgr.: Pawel Benet
Phone: (420) 583 320 240, M: +48 502 100 182
Fax: (420) 556 300 579
Email: benet@melecky.eu
Export Mgr.: Dipl. Eng. Petr Lenoch
Phone: (420) 602 731 022
Fax: (420) 556 300 579
Email: lenoch@melecky.cz
Mgr. : Radislav Hruzek
Phone: (420) 583 320 240
Fax: (420) 583 320 280
Email: hruzek.radislav@melecky.cz
Total Employees at this Location: 130
Type of Operation: Paper mill
Paper/Paperboard Grades and Capacities:
Total paper and paperboard capacity: 9,000 mt/y
Uncoated woodfree/freesheet: 6,000 mt/y
Uncoated mechanical/groundwood
Linerboard: 3,000 mt/y
Paper and Paperboard Mill Data:
Stock Preparation:
Pulpers: 2
Paper Machines: 1
No. 1, fourdrinier, total capacity 9,000 mt/y, Trim width 2.1 m, Uncoated woodfree/freesheet, Uncoated mechanical/groundwood, Linerboard
Finishing Equipment:
Supercalenders: 1
Rewinders: 1
Sheeters: 2
Energy Data:
Power boilers

ⓂMondi Stetí
Štetí Mill
Ownership: Mondi Europe & International Division
Litomerická 272
CZ-411 08 Štetí
Czech Republic
Phone: (420) 416 80 2184/1111/2603
Fax: (420) 416 80 2599 / 2233
Web Address: www.mondigroup.com
Personnel:
Gen. Mgr.: Ing. Jan Žižka
Phone: (420) 416 802 211
Fax: (420) 416 802 038
Email: jan.zizka@mondigroup.com
Oper. Dir.: Ing. Zdenek Ševecek
Phone: (420) 416 802123
Fax: (420) 416 802031
Email: zdenek.sevecek@mondigroup.com
Mktg. Mgr.: Jindrich Krejcí
Phone: (420) 416 802 184
Fax: (420) 416 802 599
Email: jindrich.krejci@mondigroup.com
Capex Mgr.: Dipl. Ing. Miroslav Jùva
Phone: (420) 416 802017
Fax: (420) 416 802030
Email: miroslav.juva@mondigroup.com
Head of Sls. Office Corug. Packaging: Lukasz Szczech
Phone: (420) 725 812 566
Fax: (420) 416 802 071
Email: lukasz.szczech@mondipackaging.com
Bus. Develop. Mgr.: Zbynek Preisler
Phone: (420) 416 802 603
Fax: (420) 416 802 233
Email: zbynek.preisler@mondipackaging.com
Total Employees at this Location: 590
Type of Operation: Pulp mill, Paper mill, Paperboard mill
Pulp Grades and Capacities:
Total pulp capacity: 507,190 mt/y
Pulp available for market: 119,891 mt/y
Chemical Pulp: 440,638 mt/y
Recycled Pulping: 72,008 mt/y

Pulp Mill Data:
Chemical Pulping Systems:
Batch digesters: 4
Continuous digesters: 1
Mechanical Pulping Systems:
Conventional grinders: 8
Pulp Lines: 2
Bleach Plant Systems: 1
No. 1, Sequence: O_2 DEopDPo, Capacity 200,000 admt/y
Chemical Recovery Equipment:
Evaporator lines: 1
Recovery boilers: 1
Lime Kiln
Pulp Dryers:
Air Float dryers 1, Fourdriniers 1
Paper/Paperboard Grades and Capacities:
Total paper and paperboard capacity: 372,000 mt/y
Packaging papers: 190,000 mt/y
Specialty and industrial: 77,000 mt/y
Linerboard: 105,000 mt/y
Paper and Paperboard Mill Data:
Stock Preparation:
Pulpers: 1
Paper Machines: 4
No. 1, fourdrinier, total capacity 105,000 mt/y, Trim width 4.4 m, Linerboard
No. 3, fourdrinier, Yankee dryer, total capacity 32,000 mt/y, Trim width 4.45 m, Specialty and industrial
No. 5, fourdrinier, total capacity 190,000 mt/y, Trim width 6.45 m, Packaging papers

Czech Republic

No. 6, fourdrinier, Yankee dryer, total capacity 45,000 mt/y, Trim width 4.5 m, Specialty and industrial
Coating Machines: 1
No. 6, total capacity 45,000 mt/y., off machine
Finishing Equipment:
  Sheeters: 2
Energy Data:
Power boilers: 2
Steam turbines: 6
Electrical demand for mill: 1,323 MWh/D

ⓂOP Papírna s.r.o.
Olšany Mill
Ownership: 100% by delfortgroup AG
Olšany u Šumperka 18
CZ-789 62 Olšany
Czech Republic
  Phone: (420) 583 384 656
  Fax: (420) 583 384 854
  Email: oppapirna@delfortgroup.com
  Web Address: www.delfortgroup.com
Personnel:
Man. Dir. OP Papírna s.r.o. & Roll4you s.r.o. (member of delfortgroup): Ralf Bernd Braun
  Phone: (420) 583 384 710
  Fax: (420) 583 384 802
  Email: ralf-bernd.braun@delfortgroup.com
Finan. & Contr. Mgr.: Petr Horvát
  Phone: (420) 583 384 703
  Fax: (420) 583 384802
  Email: petr.horvat@delfortgroup.com
Sls. Mgr., Graphic Paper: Milan Petrmann
  Phone: (420) 583 384 312
  Fax: (420) 583 384 338
  Email: milan.petrmann@delfortgroup.com
Sls. Mgr., Cigarette Paper: Petr Brzobohatý
  Phone: (420) 583 384 320
  Fax: (420) 584 384 308
  Email: petr.brzobohaty@delfortgroup.com
Total Employees at this Location: 500
Type of Operation: Paper mill
Paper/Paperboard Grades and Capacities:
  Total paper and paperboard capacity: 55,000 mt/y
  Uncoated woodfree/freesheet: 45,000 mt/y
  Specialty and industrial: 10,000 mt/y
Paper and Paperboard Mill Data:
Paper Machines: 3
No. 1, fourdrinier, total capacity 10,000 mt/y, Trim width 1.9 m, Uncoated woodfree/freesheet
No. 4, fourdrinier, total capacity 10,000 mt/y, Trim width 2.5 m, Specialty and industrial
No. 5, fourdrinier, total capacity 35,000 mt/y, Trim width 4.8 m, Uncoated woodfree/freesheet
Finishing Equipment:
  Sheeters: 2
Energy Data:
Power boilers: 1
Electrical demand for mill: 128 MWh/D

ⓂOtrokovické papírny a.s.
Ownership: 100% by state
Tr. Tomáše Bati 1657
CZ-765 82 Otrokovice
Czech Republic
  Phone: (420) 577 662 241
  Fax: (420) 577 925 106
  Email: odbyt@papirny.otrokovice.cz, sekretariat@papirny.otrokovice.cz
  Web Address: www.papirny.otrokovice.cz
Personnel:
Purch. Dir.: Tomas Vrla
  Phone: (420) 577 662 369
  Fax: (420) 577 925 106
  Email: vrla@papirny.otrokovice.cz
Total Employees of Company: 100
Mill Locations:
Otrokovické papírny a.s., Otrokovice Mill, Tr. Tomáše Bati 1657, CZ-765 82 Otrokovice, Czech Republic, Capacity: 15,000 mt/y, (Paper mill)
  Phone: (420) 577 662 241
  Fax: (420) 577 925 106
  Email: odbyt@papirny.otrokovice.cz, sekretariat@papirny.otrokovice.cz

ⓂOtrokovické papírny a.s.
Otrokovice Mill
Tr. Tomáše Bati 1657
CZ-765 82 Otrokovice
Czech Republic
  Phone: (420) 577 662 241
  Fax: (420) 577 925 106
  Email: odbyt@papirny.otrokovice.cz, sekretariat@papirny.otrokovice.cz
  Web Address: www.papirny.otrokovice.cz
Personnel:
Econ. Dep. Dir.: Svatava Pikova
  Phone: (420) 577 662 235
  Fax: (420) 577 925 106
  Email: pikova@papirny.otrokovice.cz
Purch. Dir.: Tomas Vrla
  Phone: (420) 577 662 369 / 724 883 389
  Fax: (420) 577 662 369
  Email: vrla@papirny.otrokovice.cz
Total Employees at this Location: 100
Type of Operation: Paper mill
Pulp Grades and Capacities:
  Total pulp capacity: 15,332 mt/y
  Recycled Pulping: 15,332 mt/y
Pulp Mill Data:
  Recycled Fiber Treatment Lines:
  Recycled packaging pulping lines: 1
Paper/Paperboard Grades and Capacities:
  Total paper and paperboard capacity: 15,000 mt/y
  Boxboard/cartonboard: 15,000 mt/y
Paper and Paperboard Mill Data:
Paper Machines: 1
No. 1, cylinder, total capacity 15,000 mt/y, Trim width 2.25 m, Boxboard/cartonboard
Energy Data:
Power boilers
Electrical demand for mill: 16 MWh/D

ⓂPapírna APIS, s.r.o.
Ownership: 100% by private owners
Lužická 133
CZ-40721 Ceská Kamenice
Czech Republic
  Phone: (420) 774 584 549
  Fax: (420) 412 582 902
  Web Address: www.papima-apis.cz
Personnel:
Co-owner: Piotr Bloch
  Phone: (420) 774 584 549
  Fax: (420) 412 582 902
Plant Dir.: Martin Cervinka
  Phone: (420) 774 584 549
  Fax: (420) 412 582 902
Prod. Dir.: Václav Rehák
  Phone: (420) 774 584 549
  Fax: (420) 412 582 902
  Email: rehak.apis@seznam.cz
Total Employees at this Location: 60
Mill Locations:
Papírna APIS, s.r.o., Ceská Kamenice Mill, Lužická 133, CZ-40721 Ceská Kamenice, Czech Republic, Capacity: 18,000 mt/y, (Paper mill)
  Phone: (420) 774 584 549
  Fax: (420) 412 582 902

ⓄⓂPAPOS v.o.s.
Ostrov Mill
Ownership: 50% by František Volejn, 50% by Jan Rosol
Moricovská 251
CZ-362 12 Ostrov
Czech Republic
  Phone: (420) 353 439 100
  Fax: (420) 353 439 148
  Email: suroviny@papos.cz, obchodni@papos.cz
  Web Address: www.papos.cz
Personnel:
Owner & Dir.: Jan Volejník
  Phone: (420) 353 439103
  Fax: (420) 353 439 148
  Email: j.volejnik@papos.cz
CFO: Irena Horakova
  Phone: (420) 353 439 105, M: 602 455 279
  Fax: (420) 353 439 148
  Email: finance@papos.cz
commer. Mgr.: Eva Márová
  Phone: (420) 353 439 168, M: 724 294 447
  Fax: (420) 353 439 168
  Email: marova@papos.cz
Prod. Supervisor: Vlastimil Cír
  Phone: (420) 353 439 140, M: 777 768 707
  Fax: (420) 353 439 168
  Email: technolog@papos.cz
HR Mgr.: Jindra Novotná
  Phone: (420) 353 439 150, M: 777 135 178
  Fax: (420) 353 439 150
  Email: personalni@papos.cz
Purch. & Sls. Supervisor: Michaela Vadinska
  Phone: (420) 353 439 101, M: 777 819 985
  Fax: (420) 353 439 148
  Email: suroviny@papos.cz
Prod. & Quality Cntr. & Environ. & Utility Supervisor: Hana Konecna
  Phone: (420) 353 439 123, M: 775 311 076
  Fax: (420) 353 439 148
  Email: konecna@papos.cz
Total Employees of Company: 150
Total Employees at this Location: 150
Type of Operation: Paperboard mill
Pulp Grades and Capacities:
  Total pulp capacity: 13,202 mt/y
  Recycled Pulping: 13,202 mt/y
Pulp Mill Data:
  Recycled Fiber Treatment Lines:
  Recycled packaging pulping lines: 1
Paper/Paperboard Grades and Capacities:
  Total paper and paperboard capacity: 13,000 mt/y
  Boxboard/cartonboard: 13,000 mt/y
Paper and Paperboard Mill Data:
Paper Machines: 1
No. 1, fourdrinier, total capacity 13,000 mt/y, Trim width 2.1 m, Boxboard/cartonboard
Finishing Equipment:
  Rewinders: 1
  Sheeters: 1
Energy Data:
Power boilers
Electrical demand for mill: 14 MWh/D

ⓄⓂPapírna Perštejn s.r.o., Keseg & Rathouský
Perštejn nad Ohří Mill
Hlavní 20
CZ-431 63 Perštejn nad Ohří
Czech Republic
  Phone: (420) 474 394 189
  Fax: (420) 474 394 189
  Email: papirna.pernstejn@quick.cz, perstejn.papima@o2active.cz
Personnel:
Factor: Marie Rathouská
  Phone: (420) 474 394 189
Type of Operation: Paper mill
Paper/Paperboard Grades and Capacities:
  Total paper and paperboard capacity: 120 mt/y
  Specialty and industrial: 120 mt/y
Paper and Paperboard Mill Data:
Paper Machines: 1
No. 1, fourdrinier, Trim width 1.03 m, Specialty and industrial

Denmark

ⓘⓗSeveroceská papírna s.r.o.
Bystrická 29
CZ-417 31 Novosedlice
Czech Republic
  Phone: (420) 417 571 934 / 935 / 574 / 586
  Fax: (420) 417 538 257 / 530 083
  Email: obchod@papirna.cz,
  vesely@papirna.cz
  Web Address: www.papirna.cz
Personnel:
  Mill Dir.: Josef Veselý
  Phone: (420) 417 571574
  Fax: (420) 417 538 257
  Email: vesely@papirna.cz
Mill Locations:
Severoceská papírna s.r.o., Novosedlice Mill, Bystrická 29, CZ-417 31 Novosedlice, Czech Republic, Capacity: 6,000 mt/y, (Paperboard mill)
  Phone: (420) 417 571 934 / 935 / 574 / 586
  Fax: (420) 417 538 257 / 530 083
  Email: obchod@papirna.cz, vesely@papirna.cz

ⓜSeveroceská papírna s.r.o.
Novosedlice Mill
Bystrická 29
CZ-417 31 Novosedlice
Czech Republic
  Phone: (420) 417 571 934 / 935 / 574 / 586
  Fax: (420) 417 538 257 / 530 083
  Email: obchod@papirna.cz,
  vesely@papirna.cz
  Web Address: www.papirna.cz
Personnel:
  Mill Dir.: Josef Veselý
  Phone: (420) 417 571574
  Fax: (420) 417 538 257
  Email: vesely@papirna.cz
Type of Operation: Paperboard mill
Paper/Paperboard Grades and Capacities:
  Total paper and paperboard capacity: 6,000 mt/y
  Boxboard/cartonboard: 6,000 mt/y
Paper and Paperboard Mill Data:
Paper Machines: 1
No. 2, total capacity 6,000 mt/y, Trim width 1.62 m, Boxboard/cartonboard

ⓜSmurfit Kappa Morava Paper
Žimrovice Mill
Ownership: Smurfit Kappa Europe
plant Morava Paper
CZ-747 41 Žimrovice
Czech Republic
  Phone: (420) 553 753 111
  Fax: (420) 553 753 114
  Email: sales.moravapaper@smurfitkappa.cz, ludek.jurica@smurfitkappa.cz
  Web Address: www.smurfitkappa.cz
Personnel:
  Man. Dir.: Josef Vrtiska
  Phone: (420) 553 753 260
  Fax: (420) 553 753 171
  Email: josef.vrtiska@smurfitkappa.cz
  Oper. Mgr.: Ludek Jurica
  Phone: (420) 553 753 262
  Fax: (420) 553 753 114
  Email: ludek.jurica@smurfitkappa.cz
  Prod. Mgr.: Rudolf Vavra
  Phone: (420) 553 753 271
  Fax: (420) 553 753 114
  Email: rudolf.vavra@smurfitkappa.cz
Total Employees at this Location: 500
Type of Operation: Paper mill
Pulp Grades and Capacities:
  Total pulp capacity: 56,163 mt/y
  Recycled Pulping: 56,163 mt/y
Paper/Paperboard Grades and Capacities:
  Total paper and paperboard capacity: 56,000 mt/y
  Linerboard: 46,000 mt/y
  Corrugating medium/fluting: 10,000 mt/y
Paper and Paperboard Mill Data:
Stock Preparation:
  Pulpers: 1
Paper Machines: 1
No. 2, fourdrinier (2), total capacity 56,000 mt/y, Trim width 2.5 m, Linerboard, Corrugating medium/fluting
Finishing Equipment:
  Rewinders: 1 at 60,000 mt/y
Energy Data:
Electrical demand for mill: 63 MWh/D

ⓘⓜSPM - Security Paper Mill a.s.
Štetí Mill
Ownership: 9% by shareholders, 91% by Delta Capital
Litomerická 272
CZ-411 08 Štetí
Czech Republic
  Phone: (420) 326 539 111 / 122 / 123
  Fax: (420) 326 539 109 / 123 / 129
  Email: nfo@spm.cz
  Web Address: www.spm.cz
Personnel:
  Man. Dir.: Michael Broda
  Phone: (420) 326 539 111
  Fax: (420) 326 539 109
  Email: michael.broda@spm.cz
  Exec. Dir.: Václava Franceová
  Phone: (420) 326 539 111
  Fax: (420) 326 539 109
  Email: vaclava.franceova@spm.cz
Total Employees at this Location: 80
Type of Operation: Paper mill
Paper/Paperboard Grades and Capacities:
  Total paper and paperboard capacity: 2,500 mt/y
  Uncoated woodfree/freesheet: 1,250 mt/y
  Coated woodfree/freesheet: 1,250 mt/y
Paper and Paperboard Mill Data:
Stock Preparation:
  Pulpers: 2
Paper Machines: 1
No. 2, fourdrinier, total capacity 2,500 mt/y, Trim width 1.45 m, Uncoated woodfree/freesheet, Coated woodfree/freesheet
Finishing Equipment:
  Rewinders: 1 at 4,000 mt/y
  Sheeters: 1 at 2,000 mt/y

DENMARK

ⓘⓜSkjern Papirfabrik A/S
Skjern Mill
Ownership: 86% by Buur Invest, 14% by JHJ Holding
Birkvej 14
DK-6900 Skjern
Denmark
  Phone: (45) 97 351155
  Fax: (45) 97 350909
  Email: skjernpaper@skjernpaper.com
  Web Address: www.skjernpaper.com
Personnel:
  CEO: Jørgen Martin Thomsen
  Phone: (45) 96 802050
  Fax: (45) 97 350909
  Email: jt@skjernpaper.com
  CFO: John Tholstrup Nybo
  Phone: (45) 96 802056
  Fax: (45) 97 350909
  Email: jtn@skjernpaper.com
  Sls. Mgr.: Niels E. Rasmussen
  Phone: (45) 96 802052
  Fax: (45) 97 350909
  Email: nr@skjernpaper.com
  Energy & Environ. Mgr.: Søren Skærbæk
  Phone: (45) 97 351155
  Fax: (45) 97 350909
  Project Mgr.: Kurt Larsen
  Phone: (45) 96 802062
  Fax: (45) 97 354908
Total Employees of Company: 75
Total Employees at this Location: 75
Type of Operation: Paper mill, Paperboard mill
Pulp Grades and Capacities:
  Total pulp capacity: 65,717 mt/y
  Recycled Pulping: 65,717 mt/y
Pulp Mill Data:
Pulp Lines: 1
Recycled Fiber Treatment Lines:
  Pulpers: 1 at 90,000
Paper/Paperboard Grades and Capacities:
  Total paper and paperboard capacity: 65,000 mt/y
  Boxboard/cartonboard: 65,000 mt/y
Paper and Paperboard Mill Data:
Stock Preparation:
  Refiners: 3
Paper Machines: 1
No. 1, fourdrinier, total capacity 65,000 mt/y, Trim width 2.9 m, Boxboard/cartonboard
Finishing Equipment:
  Rewinders: 2
  Sheeters: 1 at 6,000 mt/y
Energy Data:
  Power boilers: 2
  Electrical demand for mill: 53 MWh/D

ESTONIA

ⓜAS Estonian Cell
Kunda Mill
Ownership: 100% by Heinzel Holding GmbH
Jaama 21
EE-44106 Kunda, Lääne-Virumaa
Estonia
  Phone: (372) 687 0000
  Fax: (372) 687 0099
  Email: info@estoniancell.ee
  Web Address: www.estoniancell.ee
Personnel:
  CFO, Member of Management Board: Siiri Lahe
  Phone: (372) 687 0011
  Fax: (372) 687 0099
  Email: siiri.lahe@estoniancell.ee
  CTO: Lauri Raid
  Phone: (372) 511 6100
  Fax: (372) 687 0099
  Email: lauri.raid@estoniancell.ee
  Maint. Mgr.: Olev Kaarlöp
  Phone: (372) 687 0000
  Fax: (372) 687 0099
  Email: olev.kaarlop@estoniancell.ee
  Environ. & Qlty. Mgr.: Kersti Luzkov
  Phone: (372) 687 0000
  Fax: (372) 687 0099
  Email: kersti.luzkov@estoniancell.ee
  Sls. Mgr.: Reeli Pärs
  Phone: (372) 687 0000
  Fax: (372) 687 0099
  Email: reeli.pars@estoniancell.ee
  Logist. Mgr.: Meelis Kuzma
  Phone: (372) 687 0000
  Fax: (372) 687 0099
  Email: meelis.kuzma@estoniancell.ee
  Office Mgr.: Kersti Tamm
  Phone: (372) 687 0000
  Fax: (372) 687 0099
  Email: kersti.tamm@estoniancell.ee
Total Employees at this Location: 84
Type of Operation: Pulp mill
Pulp Grades and Capacities:
  Total pulp capacity: 151,822 mt/y
  Pulp available for market: 150,000 mt/y
  Mechanical Pulp: 151,822 mt/y

Pulp Mill Data:
 Mechanical Pulping Systems:
 BCTMP systems: 1
Pulp Lines: 1
 Pulp Dryers:
 Flash dryers 1
Energy Data:
Power boilers: 2
TMP Reboiler: 2
Electrical demand for mill: 630 MWh/D

ⓘHorizon Pulp & Paper Ltd.
Ownership: 100% by Tolaram Group
Anija Road 10
EE-74305 Kehra
Estonia
 Phone: (372) 608 5007/4391
 Fax: (372) 608 5756/59
 Email: info@horizon.ee
 Web Address: www.horizon.ee
Personnel:
 CEO and Chairman of the Management Board:
 Bashyam Krishnan
 Phone: (372) 608 5007
 Fax: (372) 608 5756
 Email: bashyam.krishnan@horizon.ee
 CFO: Roman Bukachev
 Phone: (372) 608 5007
 Fax: (372) 608 5756
 Email: roman.bukachev@horizon.ee
 Head HR: Aime-Kersti Kelder
 Phone: (372) 608 5007
 Fax: (372) 608 5756
 Email: aime-kersti.kelder@horizon.ee
Total Employees of Company: 380
Mill Locations:
Horizon Pulp & Paper Ltd., Kehra Mill, Anija Road 10,
 EE-74305 Kehra, Estonia, Capacity: 70,000 mt/y, (Pulp mill, Paper mill)
 Phone: (372) 608 5007/4391
 Fax: (372) 608 5756/59
 Email: info@horizon.ee

ⓘHorizon Pulp & Paper Ltd.
Kehra Mill
Anija Road 10
EE-74305 Kehra
Estonia
 Phone: (372) 608 5007/4391
 Fax: (372) 608 5756/59
 Email: info@horizon.ee
 Web Address: www.horizon.ee
Personnel:
 Chief Eng.: Sergei Telepin
 Phone: (372) 608 5070
 Fax: (372) 608 5756
 Email: sergei.telepin@horizon.ee
 Proj. Mgr.: Saurabh prabhakar
 Phone: (372) 608 5007, M: 372 517 5312
 Fax: (372) 608 5756
 Email: saurabh.prabhakar@horizon.ee
Total Employees at this Location: 380
Type of Operation: Pulp mill, Paper mill
Pulp Grades and Capacities:
 Total pulp capacity: 73,767 mt/y
 Chemical Pulp: 73,767 mt/y
Pulp Mill Data:
 Chemical Pulping Systems:
 Batch digesters: 1
Pulp Lines: 1
 Chemical Recovery Equipment:
 Evaporator lines: 1
 Recovery boilers: 1
 Lime Kiln
Paper/Paperboard Grades and Capacities:
 Total paper and paperboard capacity: 70,000 mt/y
 Packaging papers: 70,000 mt/y
Paper and Paperboard Mill Data:
 Stock Preparation:
 Pulpers: 5
 Refiners: 1
Paper Machines: 3
 No. 1, fourdrinier, total capacity 27,000 mt/y, Trim width 3.66 m, Packaging papers
 No. 2, fourdrinier, total capacity 29,000 mt/y, Trim width 3.06 m, Packaging papers
 No. 3, fourdrinier, total capacity 14,000 mt/y, Trim width 2.28 m, Packaging papers
 Finishing Equipment:
 Winders: 3 at 40,800 mt/y, 45,900 mt/y, 27,200 mt/y
 Rewinders: 1 at 1,200 mt/y
Energy Data:
Power boilers: 3
Steam turbines: 2 at 6, 4 MW
Electrical demand for mill: 191 MWh/D

ⓘⓘRäpina Paberivabrik AS
Räpina Mill
Ownership: 100% by Private Estonian owners
Pargi 23
EE-64505 Räpina
Estonia
 Phone: (372) 799 8240
 Fax: (372) 799 8244
 Email: rappin@rappin.ee
 Web Address: www.rappin.ee
Personnel:
 Chmn. of the Board & Man. Dir.: Mihkel Peedirnaa
 Phone: (372) 799 8241
 Fax: (372) 799 8244
 Email: mihkel@rappin.ee
 Mktg. & Sls. Mgr.: Tiia Savimägi
 Phone: (372) 521 6860
 Fax: (372) 799 8244
 Email: tiia@rappin.ee
 Sls. Asst. Mgr.: Mrs. Kristi Seim
 Phone: (372) 799 8240
 Fax: (372) 799 8244
 tiiu@rappin.ee: Tiiu Maks
 Phone: (372) 799 8242
 Fax: (372) 799 8244
Total Employees of Company: 39
Total Employees at this Location: 39
Type of Operation: Paper mill, Paperboard mill
Paper/Paperboard Grades and Capacities:
 Total paper and paperboard capacity: 7,000 mt/y
 Boxboard/cartonboard: 7,000 mt/y
Paper and Paperboard Mill Data:
 Stock Preparation:
 Pulpers: 2
 Refiners: 1
Paper Machines: 1
 No. 1, fourdrinier, total capacity 7,000 mt/y, Trim width 1.6 m, Boxboard/cartonboard
 Finishing Equipment:
 Rewinders: 2 at 6,000 mt/y
Energy Data:
Power boilers: 1
Electrical demand for mill: 8 MWh/D

FINLAND

ⓘBillerudKorsnäs Finland Oy
Ownership: 100% by BillerudKorsnäs AB
Tulli Business Park Åkerlundinkatu 11a Building A 5th floor
331 00 Tampere
Finland
 Mailing Address: PL 346, 331 00 Tampere, Finland
 Phone: (358) 3 339 650 70
Mill Locations:
BillerudKorsnäs Finland Oy, Pietarsaari Mill,
 Larsmovägen 149, 68600 Pietarsaari, Finland,
 Capacity: 199,920 mt/y, (Paper mill)
 Phone: (358) 6 241 380 00
 Email: info@billerudkorsnas.com
BillerudKorsnäs Finland Oy, Tervasaari Mill, Tehtaankatu 7, FI-37600 Valkeakoski, Finland, Capacity: 100,000 mt/y, (Paper mill)
 Phone: (358) 3 339 266 00
 Email: info@billerudkorsnas.com

ⓘAhlstrom Corporation Oy
Alvar Aallon katu 3 C
FI-00100 Helsinki
Finland
Mailing Address: P.O. Box 329, FI-00101 Helsinki, Finland
 Phone: (358) 358 10 8880
 Fax: (358) 358 10 888 4709
 Email: (firstname.lastname@ahlstrom.com),
 investor@ahlstrom.com,
 corporate.communications@ahlstrom.com
 Web Address: www.ahlstrom.com
Personnel:
 Chrmn. of the board: Robin Ahlström
 Phone: (358) 10 8880
 Fax: (358) 10 888 4709
 Pres. & CEO (from June 16, 2014): Marco Levi
 Phone: (358) 10 8880
 Fax: (358) 10 888 4709
 CFO (as of October 24, 2014): Sakari Ahdekivi
 Phone: (358) 10 8880
 Fax: (358) 10 888 4709
 Exec. VP, HR (as of October 24, 2014): Päivi Leskinen
 Phone: (358) 10 8880
 Fax: (358) 10 888 4709
 Exec. VP., Transportation, Filteration & Sls Reg Asia. (as of October 24, 2014): Jari Koikkalainen
 Phone: (358) 10 8880
 Fax: (358) 10 888 4709
 Exec. VP., Legal (as of October 24, 2014): Ulla Bono
 Phone: (358) 10 8880
 Fax: (358) 10 888 4709
 Exec. VP., Building & Energy (as of October 24, 2014): Fulvio Capussotti
 Phone: (358) 10 888 4757
 Fax: (358) 10 888 4709
 Exec. VP., Food & Medical (as of October 24, 2014): Omar Hoek
 Phone: (358) 10 8880
 Fax: (358) 10 888 4709
 Exec. VP., Commercial Excellence (Eff. October 9, 2014): Nadia Stoykov
 Phone: (358) 10 8880
 Fax: (358) 10 888 4709
 Exec. VP., Filteration Product Develop. (reporting to Jari Koikkalainen) (as of October 24, 2014): Paul H. Stenson
 Phone: (358) 10 8880
 Fax: (358) 10 888 4709
 Email: paul.stenson@ahlstrom.com
 Exec. VP., Oper. Food & Medical (reporting to Omar Hoek) (as of October 24, 201): Roberto Boggio
 Phone: (358) 10 8880
 Fax: (358) 10 888 4709
 VP., Wallcover & Poster Bus. (reporting to Fulvio Capussotti) (as of October 24, 2014): Arnaud Raitio Marquis
 Phone: (358) 10 8880
 Fax: (358) 10 888 4709
 VP Corp. Comm.: Liisa Nyyssönen
 Phone: (358) 10 888 4757
 Fax: (358) 10 888 4709
 Email: lisa.nyyssonen@ahlstrom.com
Total Employees of Company: 3,500
Mill Locations:
Ahlstrom Binzhou, Binzhou Mill, No. 209 Huanghe Wu Rd., Binzhou 256651, China, Capacity: 10,000 mt/y, (Paper mill)
 Phone: (86) 543-340-9777
 Fax: (86) 543 340 2216
 Email: sales@puri-filter.com, filter-shi@163.com
Ahlstrom Chirnside Ltd., Duns Mill, Duns, Berwickshire TD11 3JW, United Kingdom, Capacity: 10,000 mt/y, (Paper mill)

Finland

Phone: (44) 1890 818303
Fax: (44) 1890 818256
Email: investor@ahlstrom.com, corporate.communications@ahlstrom.com
Ahlstrom Engine Filtration, L.L.C., Taylorville Mill, 1200 E Elm St, Taylorville, IL 62568, USA, Capacity: 23,587 mt/y, (Paper mill)
Phone: (1) 217-824-9611
Fax: (1) 217-824-9514
Email: investor@ahlstrom.com, corporate.communications@ahlstrom.com
Ahlstrom Chirnside Ltd., Radcliffe Mill, Mount Sion Works, Sion Road, Radcliffe M26 3SB, United Kingdom, (Pulp mill)
Phone: (44) 161 7255320
Fax: (44) 161 7249113
Email: investor@ahlstrom.com, corporate.communications@ahlstrom.com
Ahlstrom Filtration LLC, Madisonville Plant, 215 Nebo Rd, Madisonville, KY 42431, USA, Capacity: 20,865 mt/y, (Paper mill)
Phone: (1) 270-821-0140
Fax: (1) 270-824-1577
Email: investor@ahlstrom.com, corporate.communications@ahlstrom.com
Ahlstrom Filtration LLC, Mount Holly Springs Mill, 122 W Butler St, Mount Holly Springs, PA 17065, USA, Capacity: 4,990 mt/y, (Paper mill)
Phone: (1) 717-486-3438
Fax: (1) 717-486-6413
Email: investor@ahlstrom.com, corporate.communications@ahlstrom.com
Ahlstrom Korea Co., Ltd., Hyunpoong Mill, 7, Geum-ri, Yuga-myeon, Dalseong-gun, 711-882 Daegu-si, South Korea, Capacity: 27,000 mt/y, (Paper mill)
Phone: (82) 53 611-0491/92
Fax: (82) 53 611-0493
Email: investor@ahlstrom.com, corporate.communications@ahlstrom.com
Ahlstrom Brasil Indústria e Comércio de Papéis Especiais Ltda., Louveira Mill, Rua Armando Steck, 770, 13290-000 Louveira, SP, Brazil, Capacity: 9,000 mt/y, (Paper mill)
Phone: (55) 19 3878 9200
Fax: (55) 19 3878 9210
Email: willy.bordignon@ahlstrom.com, investor@ahlstrom.com, corporate.communications@ahlstrom.com
Ahlstrom Turin SpA, Turin Mill, Via Stura 98, I-10075 Mathi Canavese, (TO), Italy, Capacity: 60,000 mt/y, (Paper mill)
Phone: (39) 011 9260111
Fax: (39) 011 9269617
Email: investor@ahlstrom.com, corporate.communications@ahlstrom.com
Ahlstrom Osnabrück GmbH, Osnabrück Mill, Römereschstr. 33, D-49090 Osnabrück, Germany, Capacity: 135,000 mt/y, (Paper mill)
Phone: (49) 541 6040
Fax: (49) 541 604210
Email: investor@ahlstrom.com, corporate.communications@ahlstrom.com
Ahlstrom Packaging SA, St. Séverin Mill, Usine Le Marchais, F-16390 Saint Séverin, France, Capacity: 22,134 mt/y, (Paper mill)
Phone: (33) 5 45 98 52 21
Fax: (33) 5 45 98 52 02
Email: investor@ahlstrom.com, corporate.communications@ahlstrom.com
Ahlstrom Specialties SA, Bousbecque Mill, 5 rue de la Papeterie, BP 101, F-59166 Bousbecque, France, Capacity: 14,994 mt/y, (Paper mill)
Phone: (33) 3 20 23 46 46
Fax: (33) 3 20 23 46 10
Email: investor@ahlstrom.com, corporate.communications@ahlstrom.com
Ahlstrom Specialties SA, Pont-Audemer Mill, Rue des Papeteries, F-27501 Pont Audemer, France, Capacity: 29,988 mt/y, (Paper mill)
Phone: (33) 2 32 41 61 00
Fax: (33) 2 32 41 44 31
Email: investor@ahlstrom.com, corporate.communications@ahlstrom.com
Ahlstrom Tampere Oy, Kauttua Mill, PO Box 55, FI-27501 Kauttua, Finland, Capacity: 10,000 mt/y, (Paper mill)
Phone: (358) 10 303 200
Fax: (358) 10 303 2491
Email: investor@ahlstrom.com, corporate.communications@ahlstrom.com
Ahlstrom Yulong Specialty Paper Company Ltd., Longkou Mill (60% owned), Zhu You Guan Industrial Park, Longkou 265700, China, Capacity: 28,000 mt/y, (Paper mill)
Phone: (86) 535 8589 778
Email: investor@ahlstrom.com, corporate.communications@ahlstrom.com
Munktell & Filtrak GmbH, Bärenstein Mill, Niederschlag 1, D-09471 Bärenstein, Germany, Capacity: 2,000 mt/y, (Paper mill)
Phone: (49) 37347 8300
Fax: (49) 37347 8364
Email: filtrak@ahlstrom.com

ⓂAhlstrom Tampere Oy
Kauttua Mill
Ownership: 100% by Ahlstrom Corporation Oy
PO Box 55
FI-27501 Kauttua
Finland
Phone: (358) 10 303 200
Fax: (358) 10 303 2491
Email: investor@ahlstrom.com, corporate.communications@ahlstrom.com
Web Address: www.ahlstrom.com
Personnel:
Contrl.: Sanna Vähätalo
Phone: (358) 10 303 2522
Fax: (358) 10 303 2491
Email: sanna.vahatalo@ahlstrom.com
Prod. Mgr.: Sami Vähätalo
Phone: (358) 10 303 200
Fax: (358) 10 303 2491
Email: sami.vahatalo@ahlstrom.com
Tech. Mgr.: Jaakko Rantanen
Phone: (358) 10 303 200
Fax: (358) 10 303 2491
Email: jaakko.rantanen@ahlstrom.com
Total Employees at this Location: 23
Type of Operation: Paper mill
Paper/Paperboard Grades and Capacities:
Total paper and paperboard capacity: 10,000 mt/y
Specialty and industrial: 10,000 mt/y
Paper and Paperboard Mill Data:
Paper Machines: 1
No. 4, fourdrinier, total capacity 10,000 mt/y, Trim width 1.6 m, Specialty and industrial
Finishing Equipment:
Winders: 1 at 10,000 mt/y
Energy Data:
Electrical demand for mill: 23 MWh/D

ⓂBillerudKorsnäs Finland Oy
Pietarsaari Mill
Ownership: 100% by BillerudKorsnäs AB
Larsmovägen 149
68600 Pietarsaari
Finland
Mailing Address: PL 13, 68601 Pietarsaari, Finland
Phone: (358) 6 241 380 00
Email: info@billerudkorsnas.com
Web Address: www.billerudkorsnas.com
Personnel:
Man. Dir. Tervasaari & Pietarsaari: Risto Hovi
Phone: (358) 6 241 380 00
Email: risto.hovi@billerudkorsnas.com
Site Mgr.: Teemu Rönkkä
Phone: (358) 6 241 380 00
Email: teemu.ronkka@billerudkorsnas.com
Develop. Mgr.: Lars Asmus
Phone: (358) 6 241 380 00
Email: lars.asmus@billerudkorsnas.com
Total Employees at this Location: 100
Type of Operation: Paper mill
Paper/Paperboard Grades and Capacities:
Total paper and paperboard capacity: 199,920 mt/y
Packaging papers: 79,968 mt/y
Specialty and industrial: 119,952 mt/y
Paper and Paperboard Mill Data:
Paper Machines: 1
No. 1, fourdrinier, total capacity 199,920 mt/y, Trim width 6.4 m, Specialty and industrial, Packaging papers
Energy Data:
Electrical demand for mill: 415 MWh/D

ⒽⓂBillerudKorsnäs Finland Oy
Tervasaari Mill
Ownership: 100% by BillerudKorsnäs AB
Tehtaankatu 7
FI-37600 Valkeakoski
Finland
Mailing Address: PL 4, FI-37600 Valkeakoski, Finland
Phone: (358) 3 339 266 00
Email: info@billerudkorsnas.com
Web Address: www.billerudkorsnas.com
Personnel:
Man. Dir. Tervasaari & Pietarsaari: Risto Hovi
Phone: (358) 3 339 266 00
Email: risto.hovi@billerudkorsnas.com
Oper. Mgr.: Mikko Laakso
Phone: (358) 3 339 266 00
Email: mikko.laakso@billerudkorsnas.com
Maint. Mgr.: Juha Sipponen
Phone: (358) 3 339 266 15
Email: juha.sipponen@billerudkorsnas.com
Site Manager, PM 7: Tuomo Pappila
Phone: (358) 3 339 266 00
Email: Tuomo.pappila@billerudkorsnas.com
Total Employees at this Location: 55
Type of Operation: Paper mill
Mill Locations:
BillerudKorsnäs Finland Oy, Pietarsaari Mill, Larsmovägen 149, 68600 Pietarsaari, Finland, Capacity: 199,920 mt/y, (Paper mill)
Phone: (358) 6 241 380 00
Email: info@billerudkorsnas.com
Pulp Grades and Capacities:
Total pulp capacity: 5,210 mt/y
Recycled Pulping: 5,210 mt/y
Paper/Paperboard Grades and Capacities:
Total paper and paperboard capacity: 100,000 mt/y
Packaging papers: 50,000 mt/y
Specialty and industrial: 50,000 mt/y
Paper and Paperboard Mill Data:
Paper Machines: 1
No. 7, fourdrinier, total capacity 100,000 mt/y, Trim width 4.8 m, Specialty and industrial, Packaging papers
Energy Data:
Electrical demand for mill: 219 MWh/D

ⒽCorenso United Oy Ltd.
Company is for sale (Stora Enso has signed an agreement to divest its Corenso business operations to Powerflute Oyj. Closing is expected during Q4/2014.)
Ownership: 100% by Stora Enso Oyj
Hennalankatu 270
FI-15700 Lahti
Finland
Mailing Address: PO Box 4, FI-15701 Lahti, Finland
Phone: (358) 2046 1416
Fax: (358) 2046 48602
Web Address: www.corenso.com
Personnel:
Mill Dir. & Dir, Oper. Excellence, R&D: Ville Heikkinen
Phone: (358) 2046 1416
Fax: (358) 2046 48602
Email: ville.heikkinen@storaenso.com
Sls. Dir.: Anne Lagus
Phone: (358) 2046 1416, 2046 131
Fax: (358) 2046 21379, 2046 48602

Email: anne.lagus@storaenso.com
Sls. Dir.: Pekka Hietaranta
Phone: (358) 2046 1416, 2046 131
Fax: (358) 2046 21379, 2046 48602
Email: pekka.hietaranta@storaenso.com
Controller IT & Finance: Usko Giss
Phone: (358) 2046 1416
Fax: (358) 2046 21379, 2046 48602
Email: usko.giss@storaenso.com
Company Communications: Eeva-Maria Vainio
Phone: (358) 2046 1416
Fax: (358) 3 7831 667
Email: eeva-maria.vainio@storaenso.com
Sls. Desk Leader: Elina Puolakka
Phone: (358) 2046 1416
Fax: (358) 2046 21379, 2046 48602
Email: elina.puolakka@storaenso.com
Total Employees of Company: 1,000
Total Employees at this Location: 10
Mill Locations:
Corenso France, Soustre Mill, PO Box 4, Gours, F-33660 Saint-Seurin-Sur-L'Isle, France, Capacity: 95,000 mt/y, (Pulp mill, Paperboard mill)
Phone: (33) 5 57 56 40 00
Fax: (33) 5 57 56 40 29
Email: stephanie.claustres@storaenso.com
Corenso North America, Wisconsin Rapids Mill, 800 Fremont Street, Wisconsin Rapids, WI 54495-8050, USA, Capacity: 85,178 mt/y, (Paperboard mill)
Phone: (1) 715-422-7800
Fax: (1) 715-422-7874
Email: corenso.northamerica@storaenso.com
Corenso United Oy Ltd., Pori Coreboard Mill, Kuninkaanlahdenkatu 14, FI-28101 Pori, Finland, Capacity: 120,000 mt/y, (Paperboard mill)
Phone: (358) 2046 1416
Fax: (358) 2046 48626
Email: hannu.makela@storaenso.com

ⓂCorenso United Oy Ltd.
Pori Coreboard Mill
Mill is for sale (Powerflute has signed a conditional agreement with Stora Enso to acquire the coreboard and core manufacturer Corenso. The deal is expected to be closed in Q4 2014.)
Ownership: 100% by Stora Enso Oyj
Kuninkaanlahdenkatu 14
FI-28101 Pori
Finland
Mailing Address: PO Box 4, FI-15701 Lahti, Finland
Phone: (358) 2046 1416
Fax: (358) 2046 48626
Email: hannu.makela@storaenso.com
Web Address: www.corenso.com
Personnel:
Mill Mgr.: Mr Ville Heikkinen
Phone: (358) 2046 1416
Fax: (358) 2046 48602
Email: ville.heikkinen@storaenso.com
Total Employees at this Location: 88
Type of Operation: Paperboard mill
Pulp Grades and Capacities:
Total pulp capacity: 120,391 mt/y
Recycled Pulping: 120,391 mt/y
Pulp Mill Data:
Pulp Lines: 1
Recycled Fiber Treatment Lines:
Recycled packaging pulping lines: 1 at 142,000
Paper/Paperboard Grades and Capacities:
Total paper and paperboard capacity: 120,000 mt/y
Boxboard/cartonboard: 120,000 mt/y
Paper and Paperboard Mill Data:
Stock Preparation:
Pulpers: 2
Paper Machines: 1
No. 1, fourdrinier, total capacity 120,000 mt/y, Trim width 4.2 m, Boxboard/cartonboard
Energy Data:
Electrical demand for mill: 158 MWh/D

ⓊⓂJujo Thermal Ltd.
Kauttua Mill
Ownership: 100% by Nippon Paper Industries Co., Ltd.
Paperitehtaantie 15
FI-27500 Kauttua
Finland
Mailing Address: P.O. Box 92, FI-27501 Kauttua, Finland
Phone: (358) 10 303 200
Fax: (358) 10 303 2419, 2418
Email: jujo.thermal@jujothermal.com, jujosales@jujothermal.com
Web Address: www.jujothermal.com
Personnel:
Pres. & CEO: Sumio Miyake
Phone: (358) 2 83932600
Email: sumio.miyake@jujothermal.com
R&D Dir.: Jouko Mäkitalo
Phone: (358) 10 303 200
Fax: (358) 10 303 2419
Tech. Dir.: Matti-Pekka Vanninen
Phone: (358) 2 8393 2429
Email: matti-pekka.vanninen@jujothermal.com
HR & ICT Dir.: Marko Kallio
Phone: (358) 10 303 200
Fax: (358) 10 303 2419
Email: hr@jujothermal.com
VP, Sls & Mktg.: Jens Remmer
Phone: (358) 10 303 200
Fax: (358) 10 303 2419
Email: jens.remmer@jujothermal.com
Sls. Mgr.: Maria Kuivamaki
Phone: (358) 10 303 200
Fax: (358) 10 303 2419
Email: jujosales@jujothermal.com
IT Mgr.: Vesa Sulonen
Phone: (358) 10 303 200
Fax: (358) 10 303 2419
Prod. Planning Mgr.: Aimo Peltonen
Phone: (358) 10 303 200
Fax: (358) 10 303 2419
Tech. Mgr.: Juha-Pekka Kaivola
Phone: (358) 10 303 200
Fax: (358) 10 303 2419
Total Employees of Company: 230
Total Employees at this Location: 230
Type of Operation: Paper mill
Paper/Paperboard Grades and Capacities:
Total paper and paperboard capacity: 80,000 mt/y
Uncoated woodfree/freesheet: 60,000 mt/y
Specialty and industrial: 20,000 mt/y
Paper and Paperboard Mill Data:
Stock Preparation:
Pulpers: 1
Paper Machines: 2
No. 1, fourdrinier, total capacity 40,000 mt/y, Trim width 2.3 m, Uncoated woodfree/freesheet, Specialty and industrial
No. 2, fourdrinier, total capacity 40,000 mt/y, Trim width 2.4 m, Uncoated woodfree/freesheet
Coating Machines: 2
CM 3, total capacity 40,000 mt/y., off machine
CM 4, total capacity 40,000 mt/y., off machine
Finishing Equipment:
Winders: 5 at 90,000 mt/y
Supercalenders: 2 at 80,000 mt/y
Rewinders: 1
Energy Data:
Electrical demand for mill: 171 MWh/D

ⓊⓂKotkamills Oy
Kotka Mill
Ownership: 90% by OpenGate Capital, 10% by PowerFlute Oyj
PO Box 62-63
FI-48101 Kotka
Finland
Phone: (358) 5 210 11
Fax: (358) 5 210 1335
Email: sales@kotkamills.com.
Web Address: www.kotkamills.com
Personnel:
CEO, Kotkamills Oy: Tuija Suur-Hamari
Phone: (358) 5 210 1201
Fax: (358) 5 210 1335
Email: tuija.suur-hamari@kotkamills.com
CFO: Petri Hirvonen
Phone: (358) 5 210 1202
Fax: (358) 5 210 1335
Email: petri.hirvonen@kotkamills.com
Snr. VP, Imprex Bus. Line: Ville Seppälä
Phone: (358) 5 2101 304
Fax: (358) 5 210 1335
Email: ville.seppala@kotkamills.com
Snr. VP, Solaris Bus. Line: Pirjo Eteläinen
Phone: (358) 5 2101 204
Fax: (358) 5 210 1335
Email: pirjo.etelainen@kotkamills.com
Snr. VP., Absorbex Bus. Line: Timo Tallinen
Phone: (358) 5 210 1212
Fax: (358) 5 210 1335
Email: timo.tallinen@kotkamills.com
Snr. VP., Sawmill Bus. Line: Olli-Pekka Hakkarainen
Phone: (358) 5 2101 207
Fax: (358) 5 210 1335
Email: olli-pekka.hakkarainen@kotkamills.com
Snr. VP., Procurement & Mill Serv.: Jouni Pekonen
Phone: (358) 5 2101 203
Fax: (358) 5 210 1335
Email: jouni.pekonen@kotkamills.com
Total Employees of Company: 500
Total Employees at this Location: 420
Type of Operation: Pulp mill, Paper mill
Pulp Grades and Capacities:
Total pulp capacity: 284,500 mt/y
Chemical Pulp: 149,454 mt/y
Mechanical Pulp: 108,672 mt/y
Recycled Pulping: 26,374 mt/y
Pulp Mill Data:
Chemical Pulping Systems:
Continuous digesters: 2
Mechanical Pulping Systems:
TMP systems: 1
Pulp Lines: 3
Chemical Recovery Equipment:
Evaporator lines: 1
Recovery boilers: 1
Lime Kiln
Recycled Fiber Treatment Lines:
Pulpers: 2 at 55,000
Paper/Paperboard Grades and Capacities:
Total paper and paperboard capacity: 355,000 mt/y
Coated mechanical/groundwood: 180,000 mt/y
Packaging papers: 175,000 mt/y
Paper and Paperboard Mill Data:
Paper Machines: 2
No. 1, hybrid former, total capacity 175,000 mt/y, Trim width 5.4 m, Packaging papers
No. 2, OptiFormer, total capacity 180,000 mt/y, Trim width 5.32 m, Coated mechanical/groundwood
Coating Machines: 1
PM 2, total capacity 180,000 mt/y., on machine
Finishing Equipment:
Winders: 3 at 355,000 mt/y
Rewinders: 1 at 15,000 mt/y
Energy Data:
HRSG boiler: 1
Combustion turbines: 1 at 42 MW
Steam turbines: 1 at 30 MW
Electrical demand for mill: 1,361 MWh/D

ⓊⓂMetsä Board Kemiart Liners
Kemi Mill
Ownership: 100% by Metsä Board
FI-94200 Kemi
Finland
Phone: (358) 1046 64299

Finland

Fax: (358) 1046 61868
Email: (firstname.lastname@metsagroup.com)
Web Address: www.metsaboard.com
Personnel:
VP & Mill. Mgr.: Jari Tikkanen
Phone: (358) 1046 64299
Fax: (358) 1046 61803
Email: jari.tikkanen@metsagroup.com
Bus. Contr. Metsa Board Kemi Oy (and Metsa Board Kemi Mill): Seppo Kuismanen
Phone: (358) 1046 61494
Fax: (358) 1046 61868
Email: seppo.kuismanen@metsagroup.com
Prod. Mgr.: Pekka Marttinen
Phone: (358) 1046 61673
Fax: (358) 1046 61868
Email: pekka.marttinen@metsagroup.com
Mgr., Sls. Support & Coordin.: Ms. Leena Yliniemi
Phone: (358) 1046 61864
Fax: (358) 1046 61868
Email: leena.yliniemi@metsagroup.com
Total Employees at this Location: 100
Type of Operation: Paperboard mill
Paper/Paperboard Grades and Capacities:
Total paper and paperboard capacity: 375,000 mt/y
Linerboard: 375,000 mt/y
Paper and Paperboard Mill Data:
Paper Machines: 1
No. 1, ValFormer, total capacity 375,000 mt/y, Trim width 6.73 m, Linerboard
Coating Machines: 1
No. 1, total capacity 375,000 mt/y., on machine
Finishing Equipment:
Winders: 1
Calenders: 2
Rewinders: 1
Energy Data:
Electrical demand for mill: 437 MWh/D

ⓜMetsä Board Tako
Tako Mill
Ownership: Metsä Board
Hallituskatu 1
FI-33101 Tampere
Finland
Mailing Address: PO Box 208, FIN-33101 Tampere, Finland
Phone: (358) 1046 33999
Fax: (358) 1046 33189
Email: (firstname.lastname@metsagroup.com)
Web Address: www.metsaboard.com
Personnel:
VP & Mill Mgr.: Pertti Hietaniemi
Phone: (358) 50 598 8636
Fax: (358) 1046 33189
Email: pertti.hietaniemi@metsagroup.com
Vp., Purch.: Jani Suomalainen
Phone: (358) 50 532 0099
Fax: (358) 104 633 158
Email: jani.suomalainen@metsagroup.com
Purch. Mgr.: Mikko Koenkytö
Phone: (358) 1046 34233
Fax: (358) 1046 33189
Email: mikko.koenkyto@metsagroup.com
Development. Mgr: Kai Hellsten
Phone: (358) 1046 33707
Fax: (358) 1046 33189
Email: kai.hellsten@metsagroup.com
Prod. Dir.: Vesa Arjanmaa
Phone: (358) 1046 33048
Fax: (358) 1046 33189
Email: vesa.arjanmaa@metsagroup.com
Tech. Mgr. Cartonboard: Risto Lehtonen
Phone: (358) 50 5184612
Fax: (358) 1046 33189
Email: risto.lehtonen@metsagroup.com
Management. Asst.: Jaana Lehtinen
Phone: (358) 1046 33999
Fax: (358) 1046 33189
Email: jaana.lehtinen@metsagroup.com

Total Employees at this Location: 205
Type of Operation: Paperboard mill
Paper/Paperboard Grades and Capacities:
Total paper and paperboard capacity: 205,000 mt/y
Boxboard/cartonboard: 205,000 mt/y
Paper and Paperboard Mill Data:
Stock Preparation:
Pulpers: 9
Refiners: 32
Paper Machines: 2
No. 1, fourdrinier (3), total capacity 135,000 mt/y, Trim width 3.3 m, Boxboard/cartonboard
No. 3, fourdrinier (3), total capacity 70,000 mt/y, Trim width 3.3 m, Boxboard/cartonboard
Coating Machines: 2
No. 1, total capacity 135,000 mt/y., on machine
No. 3, total capacity 70,000 mt/y., on machine
Finishing Equipment:
Rewinders: 2 at 170,000 mt/y
Sheeters: 6 at 100,000 mt/y
Energy Data:
Power boilers: 3
Steam turbines: 2 at 14.5 MW
Hydro turbines: 2 at 6.4 MW
Electrical demand for mill: 272 MWh/D

ⓜMetsä Fibre Oy
Ownership: 24.90% by Metsä Board, 50.20% by Metsäliitto Cooperative, 24.90% by Itochu Corporation
Revontulentie 2
FI-02100 Espoo
Finland
Mailing Address: PO Box 30, FI-02020 Metsä, Finland
Phone: (358) 104 612
Fax: (358) 104 694 402
Email: (firstname.surname@metsagroup.com)
Web Address: www.metsafibre.com
Personnel:
Pres. & CEO: Ilkka Hämälä
Phone: (358) 104 612
Fax: (358) 104 694 402
Email: ikka.hamala@metsagroup.com
CFO: Mikael Westerlund
Phone: (358) 104 612
Fax: (358) 104 694 402
Email: mikael.westerlund@metsagroup.com
SVP, Prod.: Ismo Nousiainen
Phone: (358) 104 612
Fax: (358) 104 694 402
Email: ismo.nousiainen@metsagroup.com
SVP, Sls & Mktg.: Ari Harmaala
Phone: (358) 104 612
Fax: (358) 104 694 402
Email: ari.harmaala@metsagroup.com
SVP, Bus. Devlpt.: Kaija Pehu-Lehtonen
Phone: (358) 104 612
Fax: (358) 104 694 402
Email: kaija.pehu-lehtonen@metsagroup.com
Mgr. Commun, Sls & Mktg.: Saija Tuomikoski
Phone: (358) 104 612
Fax: (358) 104 694 402
Email: saija.tuomikoski@metsagroup.com
Total Employees of Company: 900
Total Employees at this Location: 30
Mill Locations:
Metsä Fibre Oy, Äänekoski Mill, FI-44100 Äänekoski, Finland, (Pulp mill)
Phone: (358) 1046 62999
Fax: (358) 1046 62550
Email: (firstname.lastname@metsagroup.com)
Metsä Fibre Oy, Joutseno Mill, FI-54120 Joutseno, Finland, (Pulp mill)
Phone: (358) 1046 65499
Fax: (358) 1046 65378
Email: (firstname.lastname@metsagroup.com)
Metsä Fibre Oy, Kemi Mill, FI-94200 Kemi, Finland, (Pulp mill)
Phone: (358) 1046 61999

Fax: (358) 1046 61876
Email: (firstname.lastname@metsagroup.com)
Metsä Fibre Oy, Rauma Mill, Maanpääntie 9, FI-26101 Rauma, Finland, (Pulp mill)
Phone: (358) 1046 68999
Fax: (358) 1046 68990
Email: (firstname.lastname@metsagroup.com)

ⓜMetsä Fibre Oy
Äänekoski Mill
Ownership: 24.90% by Metsä Board
FI-44100 Äänekoski
Finland
Phone: (358) 1046 62999
Fax: (358) 1046 62550
Email: (firstname.lastname@metsagroup.com)
Web Address: www.metsafibre.com
Personnel:
Vp. Mill Mgr.: Camilla Wikström
Phone: (358) 1046 62220
Fax: (358) 1046 62563
Email: camilla.wikstrom@metsagroup.com
Devlpt. Mgr.: Katja Konola-Manninen
Phone: (358) 1046 62999
Fax: (358) 1046 62550
Email: katja.konola-manninen@metsagroup.com
Prod. Mgr.: Matti Toivonen
Phone: (358) 1046 62999
Fax: (358) 1046 62550
Email: matti.toivonen@metsagroup.com
Total Employees at this Location: 154
Type of Operation: Pulp mill
Pulp Grades and Capacities:
Total pulp capacity: 521,980 mt/y
Pulp available for market: 520,000 mt/y
Chemical Pulp: 521,980 mt/y
Pulp Mill Data:
Chemical Pulping Systems:
Continuous digesters: 1
Pulp Lines: 1
Bleach Plant Systems: 1
HW/SW line, Type: ECF, Sequence: O_2 DEoDED, Capacity 520,000 admt/y
Chemical Recovery Equipment:
Evaporator lines: 1
Recovery boilers: 1
Lime Kiln
Pulp Dryers:
Air Float dryers 1
Energy Data:
Power boilers: 1
Steam turbines: 1 at 52 MW
Electrical demand for mill: 918 MWh/D

ⓜMetsä Fibre Oy
Joutseno Mill
Ownership: 24.90% by Metsä Board
FI-54120 Joutseno
Finland
Phone: (358) 1046 65499
Fax: (358) 1046 65378
Email: (firstname.lastname@metsagroup.com)
Web Address: www.metsafibre.com
Personnel:
Mill Mgr.: Risto Joronen
Phone: (358) 40 5773 421
Email: risto.joronen@metsagroup.com
Prod. Mgr.: Pekka Kittilä
Phone: (358) 50 5989 951
Email: pekka.kittila@metsagroup.com
Total Employees at this Location: 180
Type of Operation: Pulp mill
Pulp Grades and Capacities:
Total pulp capacity: 676,768 mt/y
Pulp available for market: 670,000 mt/y
Chemical Pulp: 676,768 mt/y
Pulp Mill Data:
Chemical Pulping Systems:

Finland

Continuous digesters: 1
Pulp Lines: 1
Bleach Plant Systems: 1
No. 1, Sequence: O$_2$ DEopD
Chemical Recovery Equipment:
Evaporator lines: 2
Recovery boilers: 1
Lime Kiln
Pulp Dryers:
Air Float dryers 1
Energy Data:
Power boilers: 1
HRSG boiler: 1
Steam turbines: 1 at 97.0 MW
Electrical demand for mill: 1,114 MWh/D

ⓜMetsä Fibre Oy
Kemi Mill
Ownership: 24.90% by Metsä Board
FI-94200 Kemi
Finland
Phone: (358) 1046 61999
Fax: (358) 1046 61876
Email: (firstname.lastname@metsagroup.com)
Web Address: www.metsafibre.com
Personnel:
VP, Mill Mgr.: Jari Tikkanen
Phone: (358) 1046 61999
Fax: (358) 1046 61876
Email: jari.tikkanen@metsagroup.com
Prod. Mgr.: Panu Räsänen
Phone: (358) 1046 61999
Fax: (358) 1046 61876
Email: panu.rasanen@metsagroup.com
Total Employees at this Location: 191
Type of Operation: Pulp mill
Pulp Grades and Capacities:
Total pulp capacity: 591,328 mt/y
Pulp available for market: 590,000 mt/y
Chemical Pulp: 591,328 mt/y
Pulp Mill Data:
Chemical Pulping Systems:
Continuous digesters: 2
Pulp Lines: 2
Bleach Plant Systems: 1
No. 1, Sequence: O$_2$ DEopDP, Capacity 460,000 admt/y
Chemical Recovery Equipment:
Evaporator lines: 3
Recovery boilers: 1
Lime Kiln
Pulp Dryers:
Flash dryers 1
Energy Data:
Power boilers: 2
Steam turbines: 1 at 100 MW
Electrical demand for mill: 1,169 MWh/D

ⓜMetsä Fibre Oy
Rauma Mill
Ownership: 24.90% by Metsä Board
Maanpääntie 9
FI-26101 Rauma
Finland
Mailing Address: P.O. Box 165, FI-26101 Rauma, Finland
Phone: (358) 1046 68999
Fax: (358) 1046 68990
Email: (firstname.lastname@metsagroup.com)
Web Address: www.metsafibre.com
Personnel:
Mill. Mgr.: Ilkka Poikolainen
Phone: (358) 10 466 8999
Fax: (358) 10 466 8990
Email: ilkka.poikolainen@metsagroup.com
Tech. Mgr.: Tuomo Niemi
Phone: (358) 1046 68999
Fax: (358) 1046 68990

Email: tuomo.niemi@metsagroup.com
VP. Tech Bus Devlpt. Dir.: Timo Merikallio
Phone: (358) 1046 68200
Fax: (358) 1046 68372
Email: timo.merikallio@metsagroup.com
Total Employees at this Location: 150
Type of Operation: Pulp mill
Pulp Grades and Capacities:
Total pulp capacity: 632,022 mt/y
Pulp available for market: 630,000 mt/y
Chemical Pulp: 632,022 mt/y
Pulp Mill Data:
Chemical Pulping Systems:
Batch digesters: 10
Pulp Lines: 1
Bleach Plant Systems: 1
No. 1, Type: SW, Sequence: O$_2$ DEopD
Chemical Recovery Equipment:
Evaporator lines: 1
Recovery boilers: 1
Lime Kiln
Pulp Dryers:
Air Float dryers 1, Fourdriniers 1, Wet Lap machine 1
Energy Data:
Power boilers
Turbines
Steam turbines: 1 at 80 MW
Electrical demand for mill: 1,152 MWh/D

ⓜMetsä Group
Ownership: Public
P.O. Box 10
FI-02020 Metsä
Finland
Phone: (358) 1046 01
Fax: (358) 1046 54400
Email: firstname.lastname@metsagroup.com
Web Address: www.metsagroup.com
Personnel:
Pres. & CEO: Kari Jordan
Phone: (358) 1046 01
Fax: (358) 1046 54400
Email: kari.jordan@metsagroup.com
CFO: Vesa-Pekka Takala
Phone: (358) 1046 01
Fax: (358) 1046 54400
Email: vesa-pekka.takala@metsagroup.com
Exec. VP, Strategy: Hannu Anttila
Phone: (358) 1046 01
Fax: (358) 1046 54400
Email: hannu.anttila@metsagroup.com
Exec. VP, Wood Supply: Juha Mäntylä
Phone: (358) 1046 01
Fax: (358) 1046 54400
Email: juha.mantyla@metsagroup.com
Snr. VP, HR: Anneli Karhula
Phone: (358) 10 465 4174
Fax: (358) 1046 54400
Email: anneli.karhula@metsagroup.com
Sen. VP, Admin. Serv.: Jukka Tuloisela
Phone: (358) 1046 01
Fax: (358) 1046 54400
Email: jukka.tuloisela@metsagroup.com
Snr. VP, Group Commun.: Reeta Kaukiainen
Phone: (358) 50 522 0924
Fax: (358) 1046 54400
Email: reeta.kaukiainen@metsagroup.com
Group VP, Risk Mngmnt.: Vesa Junes
Phone: (358) 1046 01
Fax: (358) 1046 54400
Email: vesa.junes@metsagroup.com
Total Employees of Company: 11,642
Total Employees at this Location: 500
Mill Locations:
Metsä Board Kemiart Liners, Kemi Mill, FI-94200 Kemi, Finland, Capacity: 375,000 mt/y, (Paperboard mill)
Phone: (358) 1046 64299
Fax: (358) 1046 61868
Email: (firstname.lastname@metsagroup.com)
Metsä Board Husum, Husum Mill, SE-890 35 Husum,

Sweden, Capacity: 720,000 mt/y, (Pulp mill, Paper mill)
Phone: (46) 663 18000
Fax: (46) 663 18500
Metsä Board Tako, Tako Mill, Hallituskatu 1, FI-33101 Tampere, Finland, Capacity: 205,000 mt/y, (Paperboard mill)
Phone: (358) 1046 33999
Fax: (358) 1046 33189
Email: (firstname.lastname@metsagroup.com)
Metsä Board Zanders GmbH, Zanders Gohrsmühle Mill, An der Gohrsmühle 25, D-51465 Bergisch Gladbach, Germany, Capacity: 50,000 mt/y, (Paper mill)
Phone: (49) 2202 15 0
Fax: (49) 2202 15 2806
Email: zanders@metsagroup.com
Metsä Fibre Oy, Äänekoski Mill, FI-44100 Äänekoski, Finland, (Pulp mill)
Phone: (358) 1046 62999
Fax: (358) 1046 62550
Email: (firstname.lastname@metsagroup.com)
Metsä Fibre Oy, Joutseno Mill, FI-54120 Joutseno, Finland, (Pulp mill)
Phone: (358) 1046 65499
Fax: (358) 1046 65378
Email: (firstname.lastname@metsagroup.com)
Metsä Fibre Oy, Kemi Mill, FI-94200 Kemi, Finland, (Pulp mill)
Phone: (358) 1046 61999
Fax: (358) 1046 61876
Email: (firstname.lastname@metsagroup.com)
Metsä Fibre Oy, Rauma Mill, Maanpääntie 9, FI-26101 Rauma, Finland, (Pulp mill)
Phone: (358) 1046 68999
Fax: (358) 1046 68990
Email: (firstname.lastname@metsagroup.com)
Metsä Tissue GmbH, Düren Mill, Veldener Strasse 121-131, D-52349 Düren, Germany, Capacity: 20,000 mt/y, (Paper mill)
Phone: (49) 2421 4970, 2421 4971
Fax: (49) 2421 4405 184
Email: firstname.lastname@metsagroup.com
Metsä Tissue S.A., Krapkowice Mill, ul. Opolska 103, PL-47300 Krapkowice, Poland, Capacity: 87,000 mt/y, (Paper mill)
Phone: (48) 77 541 9100/9389
Fax: (48) 77 466 1554
Email: krapkowice@metsagroup.com
Metsä Tissue GmbH, Kreuzau Mill, Theo-Strepp Strasse 2-6, D-52372 Kreuzau, Germany, Capacity: 143,000 mt/y, (Paper mill)
Phone: (49) 2422 560
Fax: (49) 2422 4940
Email: (firstname.lastname@metsagroup.com)
Metsä Tissue Corp., Mänttä Mill (70.50% owned), FI-35800 Mänttä, Finland, Capacity: 123,000 mt/y, (Paper mill)
Phone: (358) 1046 16
Fax: (358) 1046 47 700
Email: (firstname.lastname@metsagroup.com)
Metsä Tissue GmbH, Raubach Mill, D-56316 Raubach, Germany, Capacity: 50,000 mt/y, (Paper mill)
Phone: (49) 2684 6090
Fax: (49) 2684 609100/60980
Email: (firstname.lastname@metsagroup.com)
Metsä Tissue Slovakia s.r.o., Žilina (Tento) Mill, Celulózka 3494, SK-011 61 Žilina, Slovakia, Capacity: 90,000 mt/y, (Paper mill)
Phone: (421) 41 51 21 111
Fax: (421) 41 51 21 477
Email: (firstname.lastname@metsagroup.com)
Metsä Tissue GmbH, Stotzheim Mill, Adolf-Halstrickstr. 64, D-53881 Euskirchen-Stotzheim, Germany, Capacity: 23,000 mt/y, (Paper mill)
Phone: (49) 2251 8120
Fax: (49) 2251 8122233
Email: (firstname.lastname@metsagroup.com)
Metsä Board Äänekoski, Äänekoski Board Mill, P.O. Box 400, FI-44101 Äänekoski, Finland, Capacity: 240,000 mt/y, (Paperboard mill)
Phone: (358) 1046 43999

Finland

Fax: (358) 1046 43444
Email: (firstname.lastname@metsagroup.com)
Metsä Board Joutseno, Joutseno Mill, FI-54120 Joutseno, Finland, (Pulp mill)
Phone: (358) 1046 65599
Fax: (358) 1046 65590
Email: (firstname.lastname@metsagroup.com)
Metsä Board Kaskinen, Kaskinen Mill, FI-64260 Kaskinen, Finland, (Pulp mill)
Phone: (358) 1046 69501
Fax: (358) 1046 69541
Email: (firstname.lastname@metsagroup.com)
Metsä Board Kyro, Kyro Mill, Tehtaantie 9, FI-39200 Kyröskoski, Finland, Capacity: 295,000 mt/y, (Paper mill, Paperboard mill)
Phone: (358) 1046 34999
Fax: (358) 1046 34190
Email: (firstname.lastname@metsagroup.com)
Metsä Board Simpele, Simpele Mill, Kenraalintie 1, FI-56800 Simpele, Finland, Capacity: 300,000 mt/y, (Paperboard mill)
Phone: (358) 1046 48599
Fax: (358) 10465 8501
Email: (firstname.surname@metsagroup.com)

ⓗMetsä Tissue Corp.

Ownership: 70.50% by Metsä Group, 15% by Jozef Antošĺk, 8.40% by Varma Mutual Pension Insurance Company
Revontulentie 8C
FI-02100 Espoo
Finland
Mailing Address: P.O. Box 25, FI-02020 Metsä, Finland
Phone: (358) 10 4616
Fax: (358) 10 465 4199
Email: (firstname.lastname@metsagroup.com)
Web Address: www.metsatissue.com
Personnel:
Chmn.: Kari Jordan
Phone: (358) 10 4616
Fax: (358) 10 465 4199
Email: kari.jordan@metsagroup.com
Vice Chmn.: Jozef Antošĺk
Phone: (358) 10 4616
Fax: (358) 10 465 4199
Email: jozef.antosik@metsagroup.com
Pres. & CEO (moving to Metso Board 1 December 2014): Mika Joukio
Phone: (358) 10 4616
Fax: (358) 10 465 4199
Email: mika.joukio@metsagroup.com
Sec. of the Board: Juhani Pitkänen
Phone: (358) 10 4616
Fax: (358) 10 465 4199
Email: juhani.pitkanen@metsagroup.com
SVP, Brand Mktg & International Sls.: Hubert Schönbein
Phone: (358) 10 4616
Fax: (358) 10 465 4199
Email: hubert.schönbein@metsagroup.com
SVP, Baking & Cooking: Juha Tilli
Phone: (358) 10 4616
Fax: (358) 10 465 4199
Email: juha.tilli@metsagroup.com
SVP, Tissue Western Europe: Christoph Zeiler
Phone: (358) 10 4616
Fax: (358) 10 465 4199
Email: christoph.zeiler@metsagroup.com
SVP, Tissue Central Eastern Europe: Mariusz Jedrzejewski
Phone: (358) 10 4616
Fax: (358) 10 465 4199
Email: mariusz.jedrzejewski@metsagroup.com
SVP, Tissue North Eastern Europe: Jori Sahlstén
Phone: (358) 10 4616
Fax: (358) 10 465 4199
Email: jori.sahlstén@metsagroup.com
SVP, HR: Ghita Jansson-Kiuru
Phone: (358) 10 4616
Fax: (358) 10 465 4199
Email: ghita.jansson-kiuru@metsagroup.com
SVP, Tissue Scandinavia: Mark Watkins
Phone: (358) 10 4616
Fax: (358) 10 465 4199
Email: mark.watkins@metsagroup.com
SVP, Technology: Lars Warvne
Phone: (358) 10 4616
Fax: (358) 10 465 4199
Email: lars.warvne@metsagroup.com
Total Employees of Company: 3,300
Mill Locations:
Metsä Tissue GmbH, Düren Mill, Veldener Strasse 121-131, D-52349 Düren, Germany, Capacity: 20,000 mt/y, (Paper mill)
Phone: (49) 2421 4970, 2421 4971
Fax: (49) 2421 4405 184
Email: (firstname.lastname@metsagroup.com)
Metsä Tissue S.A., Krapkowice Mill, ul. Opolska 103, PL-47300 Krapkowice, Poland, Capacity: 87,000 mt/y, (Paper mill)
Phone: (48) 77 541 9100/9389
Fax: (48) 77 466 1554
Email: krapkowice@metsagroup.com
Metsä Tissue GmbH, Kreuzau Mill, Theo-Strepp Strasse 2-6, D-52372 Kreuzau, Germany, Capacity: 143,000 mt/y, (Paper mill)
Phone: (49) 2422 560
Fax: (49) 2422 4940
Email: (firstname.lastname@metsagroup.com)
Metsä Tissue Corp., Mänttä Mill, FI-35800 Mänttä, Finland, Capacity: 123,000 mt/y, (Paper mill)
Phone: (358) 1046 16
Fax: (358) 1046 47 700
Email: (firstname.lastname@metsagroup.com)
Metsä Tissue GmbH, Raubach Mill, D-56316 Raubach, Germany, Capacity: 50,000 mt/y, (Paper mill)
Phone: (49) 2684 6090
Fax: (49) 2684 609100/60980
Email: (firstname.lastname@metsagroup.com)
Metsä Tissue Slovakia s.r.o., Žilina (Tento) Mill, Celulózka 3494, SK-011 61 Žilina, Slovakia, Capacity: 90,000 mt/y, (Paper mill)
Phone: (421) 41 51 21 111
Fax: (421) 41 51 21 477
Email: (firstname.lastname@metsagroup.com)
Metsä Tissue GmbH, Stotzheim Mill, Adolf-Halstrickstr. 64, D-53881 Euskirchen-Stotzheim, Germany, Capacity: 23,000 mt/y, (Paper mill)
Phone: (49) 2251 8120
Fax: (49) 2251 8122233
Email: (firstname.lastname@metsagroup.com)

ⓜMetsä Tissue Corp.
Mänttä Mill

Ownership: 70.50% by Metsä Group
FI-35800 Mänttä
Finland
Phone: (358) 1046 16
Fax: (358) 1046 47 700
Email: (firstname.lastname@metsagroup.com)
Web Address: www.metsatissue.com
Personnel:
Mill Mgr.: Kari Karttunen
Phone: (358) 1046 16
Fax: (358) 1046 47 700
Email: kari.karttunen@metsagroup.com
Prod. Mgr.: Mikko Hänninen
Phone: (358) 1046 16
Fax: (358) 1046 47 700
Email: mikko.hanninen@metsagroup.com
Qlty. & Environ. Mgr.: Tero Alvoittu
Phone: (358) 1046 16
Fax: (358) 1046 47 700
Email: tero.alvoittu@metsagroup.com
Managemet System Coord.: Tarja Alhonen
Phone: (358) 1046 16
Fax: (358) 1046 47 700
Email: tarja.alhonen@metsagroup.com
Total Employees at this Location: 560
Type of Operation: Paper mill
Pulp Grades and Capacities:
Total pulp capacity: 65,311 mt/y
Recycled Pulping: 65,311 mt/y
Pulp Mill Data:
Bleach Plant Systems: 2
Recycled Fiber Treatment Lines:
Pulpers: 2
Washing deinking lines: 2
Pulp Dryers:
Air Float dryers 1
Paper/Paperboard Grades and Capacities:
Total paper and paperboard capacity: 123,000 mt/y
Tissue: 105,000 mt/y
Specialty and industrial: 18,000 mt/y
Paper and Paperboard Mill Data:
Paper Machines: 4
No. 1, crescent former, Yankee dryer, total capacity 35,000 mt/y, Trim width 3.3 m, Tissue
No. 7, fourdrinier, total capacity 18,000 mt/y, Trim width 5 m, Specialty and industrial
No. 9, crescent former, Yankee dryer, total capacity 26,000 mt/y, Trim width 3.3 m, Tissue
No. 10, crescent former, Yankee dryer, total capacity 44,000 mt/y, Trim width 5 m, Tissue
Finishing Equipment:
Rewinders: 12
Sheeters: 11
Energy Data:
Power boilers: 2
Steam turbines: 1 at 25 MW
Electrical demand for mill: 476 MWh/D

ⓜMondi Lohja Oy
Lohja Mill

Ownership: 100% by Mondi Europe & International Division
Kotkantie 5
FI-08100 Lohja
Finland
Phone: (358) 2074 4611
Fax: (358) 2074 4610
Web Address: www.mondigroup.com
Personnel:
Man. Dir.: Juhani Pöhö
Phone: (358) 2074 4611
Fax: (358) 2074 4610
Email: juhani.poho@mondigroup.com
Purch. & Logist. Mgr.: Irma-Liisa Byman
Phone: (358) 2074 4611
Fax: (358) 2074 4610
Email: irma-liisa.byman@mondigroup.com
Total Employees at this Location: 170
Type of Operation: Paper mill
Pulp Grades and Capacities:
Pulp available for market: 10,000 mt/y
Paper/Paperboard Grades and Capacities:
Total paper and paperboard capacity: 80,000 mt/y
Specialty and industrial: 80,000 mt/y
Paper and Paperboard Mill Data:
Paper Machines: 2
PM 1, (The machine will be shut down around June 30, 2015), Yankee dryer, twin-wire, total capacity 40,000 mt/y, Trim width 3.2 m, Specialty and industrial
PM 2, fourdrinier, total capacity 40,000 mt/y, Trim width 4.4 m, Specialty and industrial

ⓗMetsä Board

Ownership: Metsä Group
Revontulentie 6
FI-02100 Espoo
Finland
Mailing Address: PO Box 20, Metsä, Finland
Phone: (358) 10 46 11
Fax: (358) 10 465 4553
Email: (firstname.lastname@metsagroup.com)
Web Address: www.metsaboard.com
Personnel:

Finland

Chmn. of the Board: Kari Jordan
Phone: (358) 10 469 4212
Fax: (358) 10 469 4271
Email: kari.jordan@metsagroup.com
CEO (eff. 1 October 2014): Mika Joukio MBA
Phone: (358) 10 46 11
Fax: (358) 10 465 4553
Email: mika.joukio@metsagroup.com
CFO (will retire on 28 February 2015): Matti Mörsky
Phone: (358) 10 465 4913
Fax: (358) 10 465 4553
Email: matti.morsky@metsagroup.com
Group General Counsel : LL.M Miika Arola
Phone: (358) 10 46 11
Fax: (358) 10 465 4553
Email: miika.arola@metsagroup.com
Snr. VP., Head of Linerboard & Paper Bus. area: Seppo Puotinen
Phone: (358) 10 469 4655
Fax: (358) 10 469 4141
Email: seppo.puotinen@metsagroup.com
Snr. VP., Purch.: Jani Suomalainen
Phone: (358) 10 46 11
Fax: (358) 10 465 4553
Email: jani.suomalainen@metsagroup.com
SVP, Head of Cartonboard business area: Ari Kiviranta
Phone: (358) 10 46 11
Fax: (358) 10 465 4553
VP, Sls & Mktng.: Mattias Kronberg
Phone: (358) 10 46 11
Fax: (358) 10 465 4553
Email: mattias.kronberg@metsagroup.com
Snr. VP., Bus. Serv. & Develop.: Sari Pajari
Phone: (358) 10 46 11
Fax: (358) 10 465 4553
Email: sari.pajari@metsagroup.com
VP, Inv. Rel. and Commun.: Juha Laine
Phone: (358) 10 465 4335
Fax: (358) 10 465 4553
Email: juha.laine@metsagroup.com
Total Employees of Company: 3,300
Total Employees at this Location: 107
Mill Locations:
Metsä Board Kemiart Liners, Kemi Mill, FI-94200 Kemi, Finland, Capacity: 375,000 mt/y, (Paperboard mill)
Phone: (358) 1046 64299
Fax: (358) 1046 61868
Email: (firstname.lastname@metsagroup.com)
Metsä Board Husum, Husum Mill, SE-890 35 Husum, Sweden, Capacity: 720,000 mt/y, (Pulp mill, Paper mill)
Phone: (46) 663 18000
Fax: (46) 663 18500
Metsä Board Tako, Tako Mill, Hallituskatu 1, FI-33101 Tampere, Finland, Capacity: 205,000 mt/y, (Paperboard mill)
Phone: (358) 1046 33999
Fax: (358) 1046 33189
Email: (firstname.lastname@metsagroup.com)
Metsä Board Zanders GmbH, Zanders Gohrsmühle Mill, An der Gohrsmühle 25, D-51465 Bergisch Gladbach, Germany, Capacity: 50,000 mt/y, (Paper mill)
Phone: (49) 2202 15 0
Fax: (49) 2202 15 2806
Email: zanders@metsagroup.com
Metsä Fibre Oy, Äänekoski Mill (24.90% owned), FI-44100 Äänekoski, Finland, (Pulp mill)
Phone: (358) 1046 62999
Fax: (358) 1046 62550
Email: (firstname.lastname@metsagroup.com)
Metsä Fibre Oy, Joutseno Mill (24.90% owned), FI-54120 Joutseno, Finland, (Pulp mill)
Phone: (358) 1046 65499
Fax: (358) 1046 65378
Email: (firstname.lastname@metsagroup.com)
Metsä Fibre Oy, Kemi Mill (24.90% owned), FI-94200 Kemi, Finland, (Pulp mill)
Phone: (358) 1046 61999
Fax: (358) 1046 61876
Email: (firstname.lastname@metsagroup.com)
Metsä Fibre Oy, Rauma Mill (24.90% owned), Maanpääntie 9, FI-26101 Rauma, Finland, (Pulp mill)
Phone: (358) 1046 68999
Fax: (358) 1046 68990
Email: (firstname.lastname@metsagroup.com)
Metsä Board Äänekoski, Äänekoski Board Mill, P.O. Box 400, FI-44101 Äänekoski, Finland, Capacity: 240,000 mt/y, (Paperboard mill)
Phone: (358) 1046 43999
Fax: (358) 1046 43444
Email: (firstname.lastname@metsagroup.com)
Metsä Board Joutseno, Joutseno Mill, FI-54120 Joutseno, Finland, (Pulp mill)
Phone: (358) 1046 65599
Fax: (358) 1046 65590
Email: (firstname.lastname@metsagroup.com)
Metsä Board Kaskinen, Kaskinen Mill, FI-64260 Kaskinen, Finland, (Pulp mill)
Phone: (358) 1046 69501
Fax: (358) 1046 69541
Email: (firstname.lastname@metsagroup.com)
Metsä Board Kyro, Kyro Mill, Tehtaantie 9, FI-39200 Kyröskoski, Finland, Capacity: 295,000 mt/y, (Paper mill, Paperboard mill)
Phone: (358) 1046 34999
Fax: (358) 1046 34190
Email: (firstname.lastname@metsagroup.com)
Metsä Board Simpele, Simpele Mill, Kenraalintie 1, FI-56800 Simpele, Finland, Capacity: 300,000 mt/y, (Paperboard mill)
Phone: (358) 1046 48599
Fax: (358) 10465 8501
Email: (firstname.surname@metsagroup.com)

(M)Metsä Board Äänekoski
Äänekoski Board Mill
Ownership: *Metsä Board*
P.O. Box 400
FI-44101 Äänekoski
Finland
Phone: (358) 1046 43999
Fax: (358) 1046 43444
Email: (firstname.lastname@metsagroup.com)
Web Address: www.metsaboard.com
Personnel:
Mill Mgr./VP: Jouko Wacklin
Phone: (358) 1046 43350
Fax: (358) 1046 43444
Email: jouko.wacklin@metsagroup.com
Dir. Operations Planning.: Marko Koskela-Koivisto
Phone: (358) 50 5988 060
Fax: (358) 1046 43428
Email: marko.koskela-koivisto@metsagroup.com
Project Mgr.: Pentti Hyytinen
Phone: (358) 1046 43540
Fax: (358) 1046 43444
Email: pentti.hyytinen@metsagroup.com
Devlpt. Mgr.: Pekka Suokas
Phone: (358) 1046 43374
Fax: (358) 1046 43444
Email: pekka.suokas@metsagroup.com
HRD Mgr.: Pekka Nikkinen
Phone: (358) 1046 43611
Fax: (358) 1046 43444
Email: pekka.nikkinen@metsagroup.com
Commer. Dir. Food & Beverage : Nina Happonen
Phone: (358) 1046 43446
Fax: (358) 1046 43428
Email: nina.happonen@metsagroup.com
Product Mgr.: Heli Kuorikoski
Phone: (358) 1046 43085
Fax: (358) 1046 43444
Email: heli.kuorikoski@metsagroup.com
Mgr. Supply Service: Harri Karinen
Phone: (358) 1046 43999
Fax: (358) 1046 43444
Email: harri.karinen@metsagroup.com
Total Employees at this Location: 215
Type of Operation: Paperboard mill
Paper/Paperboard Grades and Capacities:
Total paper and paperboard capacity: 240,000 mt/y
Boxboard/cartonboard: 240,000 mt/y
Paper and Paperboard Mill Data:
Stock Preparation:
Pulpers: 3
Paper Machines: 1
No. 1, fourdrinier (3), Yankee dryer, total capacity 240,000 mt/y, Trim width 3.6 m, Boxboard/cartonboard
Coating Machines: 3
No. 1, on machine
No. 2, on machine
No. 3, on machine
Finishing Equipment:
Winders: 1 at 200,000 mt/y
Sheeters: 3 at 25,000 mt/y, 70,000 mt/y
Energy Data:
Electrical demand for mill: 410 MWh/D

(M)Metsä Board Joutseno
Joutseno Mill
Ownership: *Metsä Board*
FI-54120 Joutseno
Finland
Phone: (358) 1046 65599
Fax: (358) 1046 65590
Email: (firstname.lastname@metsagroup.com)
Web Address: www.metsaboard.com
Personnel:
Mill Mgr.: Veli-Pekka Kyllönen
Phone: (358) 1046 48322
Fax: (358) 1046 48501
Email: veli-pekka.kyllonen@metsagroup.com
Prod. Mgr.: Petri Vuorijärvi
Phone: (358) 50 5967 525
Email: petri.vuorijarvi@metsagroup.com
Oper.Mgr.: Miika Sinkko
Phone: (358) 50 5283 970
Email: miika.sinkko@metsagroup.com
Devlpt. Mgr.: Antti Aronen
Phone: (358) 1046 48570
Fax: (358) 1046 48501
Email: antti.aronen@metsagroup.com
Total Employees at this Location: 50
Type of Operation: Pulp mill
Pulp Grades and Capacities:
Total pulp capacity: 294,118 mt/y
Pulp available for market: 290,000 mt/y
Mechanical Pulp: 294,118 mt/y
Pulp Mill Data:
Mechanical Pulping Systems:
BCTMP systems: 2
Pulp Lines: 2
Bleach Plant Systems: 1
Andritz, Type: Two stage, high consistency, Sequence: P, Capacity 300,000 admt/y
Pulp Dryers:
Flash dryers 2
Energy Data:
HRSG boiler: 1
Electrical demand for mill: 1,236 MWh/D

(M)Metsä Board Kaskinen
Kaskinen Mill
Ownership: *Metsä Board*
FI-64260 Kaskinen
Finland
Phone: (358) 1046 69501
Fax: (358) 1046 69541
Email: (firstname.lastname@metsagroup.com)
Web Address: www.metsaboard.com
Personnel:
Mill Mgr.: Petri Jantunen
Phone: (358) 505987 523
Fax: (358) 1046 33158
Email: petri.jantunen@metsagroup.com
Total Employees at this Location: 80
Type of Operation: Pulp mill
Pulp Grades and Capacities:

Finland

Total pulp capacity: 303,767 mt/y
Pulp available for market: 300,000 mt/y
Mechanical Pulp: 303,767 mt/y
Pulp Mill Data:
Mechanical Pulping Systems:
BCTMP systems: 2
Pulp Lines: 2
Bleach Plant Systems: 1
No. 1, Sequence: P, Capacity 300,000 admt/y
Pulp Dryers:
Flash dryers 1
Paper and Paperboard Mill Data:
Stock Preparation:
Refiners: 6
Energy Data:
Power boilers: 1
TMP Reboiler: 1
Steam turbines: 1 at 55 MW
Electrical demand for mill: 1,900 MWh/D

ⓂMetsä Board Kyro
Kyro Mill
Ownership: Metsä Board
Tehtaantie 9
FI-39200 Kyröskoski
Finland
Phone: (358) 1046 34999
Fax: (358) 1046 34190
Email: (firstname.lastname@metsagroup.com)
Web Address: www.metsaboard.com
Personnel:
VP & Mill. Mgr.: Pertti Hietaniemi
Phone: (358) 1046 34999
Purch. Mgr.: Mikko Koenkytö
Phone: (358) 1046 34233
Email: mikko.koenkyto@metsagroup.com
Tech. Mgr: Raimo Salmi
Phone: (358) 1046 34999
Prod. Mgr.: Vesa Arjanmaa
Phone: (358) 1046 33048
Email: vesa.arjanmaa@metsagroup.com
HR. Mgr.: Hannu Tolonen
Phone: (358) 1046 34999
Environ. Mgr.: Sirpa Eskelinen
Phone: (358) 1046 34999
Mill Serv. Mgr.: Jarno Lehtonen
Phone: (358) 1046 34999
Total Employees at this Location: 245
Type of Operation: Paper mill, Paperboard mill
Pulp Grades and Capacities:
Total pulp capacity: 100,441 mt/y
Mechanical Pulp: 100,441 mt/y
Pulp Mill Data:
Mechanical Pulping Systems:
Conventional grinders
Pulp Lines: 1
Bleach Plant Systems: 1
SGW, Sequence: P, Capacity 100,000 admt/y
Paper/Paperboard Grades and Capacities:
Total paper and paperboard capacity: 295,000 mt/y
Specialty and industrial: 105,000 mt/y
Boxboard/cartonboard: 190,000 mt/y
Paper and Paperboard Mill Data:
Paper Machines: 2
No. 1, fourdrinier (3), total capacity 190,000 mt/y, Trim width 3.3 m, Boxboard/cartonboard
No. 3, fourdrinier, total capacity 105,000 mt/y, Trim width 3.6 m, Specialty and industrial
Coating Machines: 2
BM1, on machine
PM3, on machine
Finishing Equipment:
Sheeters: 2
Energy Data:
Power boilers: 2
Combustion turbines: 1 at 50 MW
Steam turbines: 2 at 16, 6 MW
Electrical demand for mill: 828 MWh/D

ⓂMetsä Board Simpele
Simpele Mill
Ownership: Metsä Board
Kenraalintie 1
FI-56800 Simpele
Finland
Phone: (358) 1046 48599
Fax: (358) 10465 8501
Email: (firstname.surname@metsagroup.com)
Web Address: www.metsaboard.com
Personnel:
Mill Mgr.: Veli-Pekka Kyllönen
Phone: (358) 1046 48322
Fax: (358) 1046 48501
Email: veli-pekka.kyllonen@metsagroup.com
Product Mgr.: Jari Tiainen
Phone: (358) 50 598 8913
Fax: (358) 1046 48501
Email: jari.tiainen@metsagroup.com
Devlpt. Mgr.: Antti Aronen
Phone: (358) 1046 48570
Fax: (358) 1046 48501
Email: antti.aronen@metsagroup.com
Personnel Mgr.: Vesa Vaittinen
Phone: (358) 1046 48313
Fax: (358) 1046 48501
Email: vesa.vaittinen@metsagroup.com
Regional Env. Mgr. M-real & Botnia: Mika Leino
Phone: (358) 1046 48599
Fax: (358) 1046 48502
Email: mika.leino@metsagroup.com
Total Employees at this Location: 360
Type of Operation: Paperboard mill
Pulp Grades and Capacities:
Total pulp capacity: 124,584 mt/y
Mechanical Pulp: 124,584 mt/y
Pulp Mill Data:
Mechanical Pulping Systems:
Conventional grinders: 6
Bleach Plant Lines:
No. 1, Type: SGW, Sequence: P, Capacity 100,000 admt/y
Paper/Paperboard Grades and Capacities:
Total paper and paperboard capacity: 300,000 mt/y
Boxboard/cartonboard: 300,000 mt/y
Paper and Paperboard Mill Data:
Stock Preparation:
Pulpers: 4
Refiners: 9
Paper Machines: 1
No. 3, fourdrinier (3), total capacity 300,000 mt/y, Trim width 4 m, Boxboard/cartonboard
Coating Machines: 1
No. 1, total capacity 215,000 mt/y., on machine
Finishing Equipment:
Winders: 1
Sheeters: 5 at 165,000 mt/y
Energy Data:
Power boilers: 2
Steam turbines: 2 at 19.6, 14 MW
Electrical demand for mill: 770 MWh/D

ⓅPankaboard Oy
Ruukintie 2
FI-81750 Pankakoski
Finland
Phone: (358) 1048 04600
Fax: (358) 1048 04701
Email: (firstname.lastname@pankaboard.com)
Web Address: www.pankaboard.com
Personnel:
Chmn. of the board, CEO until the end of 2013: Lauri Junnila
Phone: (358) 1048 04601
Fax: (358) 1048 04701
Email: lauri.junnila@pankaboard.com
Deputy CEO, CEO from January 1, 2014.: Ari Vouti MSc
Phone: (358) 1048 04601
Fax: (358) 1048 04701
Email: ari.vouti@pankaboard.com
CFO: Minna Dahlström
Phone: (358) 5037 25861
Fax: (358) 1048 04701
Email: minna.dahlstrom@pankaboard.com
VP, Sls. & Mktg.: Christer Nordman
Phone: (358) 1048 04623
Fax: (358) 1048 04701
Email: christer.nordman@pankaboard.com
Mill Mgr.: Petri Saastamoinen
Phone: (358) 1048 04605
Fax: (358) 1048 04701
Email: petri.saastamoinen@pankaboard.com
Sls. Dir.: Ilkka Mutka
Phone: (358) 1714 440996
Fax: (358) 1048 04701
Email: ilkka.mutka@pankaboard.com
Total Employees of Company: 160
Mill Locations:
Pankaboard Oy, Pankakoski Mill, Ruukintie 2, FI-81750 Pankakoski, Lieksa, Finland, Capacity: 100,000 mt/y, (Pulp mill, Paperboard mill)
Phone: (358) 1048 04600
Fax: (358) 1048 04701
Email: (firstname.lastname@pankaboard.com)

ⓅPankaboard Oy
Pankakoski Mill
Ruukintie 2
FI-81750 Pankakoski, Lieksa
Finland
Phone: (358) 1048 04600
Fax: (358) 1048 04701
Email: (firstname.lastname@pankaboard.com)
Web Address: www.pankaboard.com
Personnel:
Mill Mgr.: Petri Saastamoinen
Phone: (358) 1048 04605
Fax: (358) 1048 04701
Email: petri.saastamoinen@pankaboard.com
Prod. Mgr.: Ilkka Mutka
Phone: (358) 1714 440996
Fax: (358) 1048 04701
Email: ilkka.mutka@pankaboard.com
Total Employees at this Location: 160
Type of Operation: Pulp mill, Paperboard mill
Pulp Grades and Capacities:
Total pulp capacity: 103,270 mt/y
Mechanical Pulp: 103,270 mt/y
Pulp Mill Data:
Mechanical Pulping Systems:
Conventional grinders: 3
Paper/Paperboard Grades and Capacities:
Total paper and paperboard capacity: 100,000 mt/y
Boxboard/cartonboard: 100,000 mt/y
Paper and Paperboard Mill Data:
Stock Preparation:
Pulpers: 6
Refiners: 5
Paper Machines: 2
No. 2, cylinder (7), total capacity 60,000 mt/y, Trim width 3 m, Boxboard/cartonboard
No. 3, multi-wire, total capacity 40,000 mt/y, Trim width 2.3 m, Boxboard/cartonboard
Coating Machines: 1
No. 1, on machine
Finishing Equipment:
Rewinders: 3
Sheeters: 3
Energy Data:
Power boilers: 1
Electrical demand for mill: 280 MWh/D

ⓅPowerflute Oyj
Ownership: Public
P.O. Box 57
FI-70101 Kuopio
Finland
Phone: (358) 10 6606 999

Fax: (358) 10 6606 212
Email: info@powerflute.com
Web Address: www.powerflute.com

Personnel:
Chmn.: Dermot F. Smurfit
Phone: (358) 10 6606 999
Fax: (358) 10 6606 212
Email: dermot.smurfit@powerflute.com
CEO: Marco Casiraghi
Phone: (358) 10 6606 999
Fax: (358) 10 6606 212
Email: marco.casiraghi@powerflute.com
CFO: David Andrew Walton
Phone: (358) 10 6606 999
Fax: (358) 10 6606 212
Email: david.walton@powerflute.com
Management Asst.: Tiina Silvast
Phone: (358) 10 6606 205
Fax: (358) 10 6606 212
Email: tiina.silvast@powerflute.com

Total Employees of Company: 201
Mill Locations:
Savon Sellu Oy, Savon Sellu, Sorsasalo, FI-70420 Kuopio, Finland, Capacity: 275,000 mt/y, (Paperboard mill)
Phone: (358) 10 6606999
Fax: (358) 10 6606212
Email: (firstname.lastname@powerflute.com), info@powerflute.com

ⓘⓜPremium Board Finland Oy
Juankoski Board Mill
Company is idle, under bankruptcy protection (idle since December 1, 2012. Filed for Chapter 11 bankruptcy in November 2013. The company plans to resume board production in 2014 or 2015 with a focus on liquid packaging, depending on the board market situation.)
Juankoskentie 7 A
FI-73500 Juankoski
Finland
Mailing Address: P.O. Box 33, FI-73501 Juankoski, Finland
Phone: (358) 17 688641
Fax: (358) 17 612008
Email: info@premiumboard.fi
Web Address: www.premiumboard.fi

Personnel:
Chmn.: Harry Salonaho
Phone: (358) 17 688641
Fax: (358) 17 6886 564
Email: harry.salonaho@pinusconsult.fi
Man. Dir.: Mikael Abacka
Phone: (358) 400737452
Sls. & Mktg. Mgr.: Jukka Hahlanterä
Phone: (358) 17 688641
Mktg. Mgr.: Ulla Miettinen
Phone: (358) 17 688641
Prod. Dir.: Mr. Riku
Phone: (358) 505 98 7889
Purch. Mgr.: Jouko Pirinen
Phone: (358) 17 6886 435
Fax: (358) 17 6886 564
Email: jouko.pirinen@stromsdal.fi
Asst. to Man. Dir.: Tuija Lepistö
Phone: (358) 17 688641

Total Employees of Company: 200
Total Employees at this Location: 190
Type of Operation: Paperboard mill
Pulp Grades and Capacities:
Total pulp capacity: 35,000 mt/y
Mechanical Pulp: 35,000 mt/y

Pulp Mill Data:
Mechanical Pulping Systems:
Pressurized grinders: 1
Bleach Plant Systems: 1
No. 1, Sequence: P, Capacity 35,000 admt/y
Paper/Paperboard Grades and Capacities:
Total paper and paperboard capacity: 80,000 mt/y
Boxboard/cartonboard: 80,000 mt/y
Paper and Paperboard Mill Data:
Stock Preparation:
Pulpers: 3
Refiners: 8
Paper Machines: 1
No. 1, fourdrinier (3), total capacity 80,000 mt/y, Trim width 2.4 m, Boxboard/cartonboard
Coating Machines: 1
PM 1, total capacity 80,000 mt/y., off machine
Finishing Equipment:
Rewinders: 1
Sheeters: 3
Energy Data:
Power boilers: 1
Electrical demand for mill: 260 MWh/D

ⓘⓜSappi Fine Paper Europe
Kirkniemi Mill
Ownership: 100% by Sappi Limited
FI-08800 Kirkniemi
Finland
Phone: (358) 1046 42999
Fax: (358) 1046 42411
Email: (firstname.lastname@sappi.com)
Web Address: www.sappi.com

Personnel:
Mill Mgr.: Martti Savelainen
Phone: (358) 1046 42475/505987621
Fax: (358) 1046 42411
Email: martti.savelainen@sappi.com
Prod. Mgr.: Jouni Laakso
Phone: (358) 1046 42999
Fax: (358) 1046 42411
Email: jouni.laakso@sappi.com
Safety Mgr.: Jari Haijanen
Phone: (358) 1046 42999
Fax: (358) 1046 42411
Email: jari.haijanen@sappi.com

Total Employees of Company: 5,838
Total Employees at this Location: 600
Type of Operation: Pulp mill, Paper mill
Mill Locations:
Sappi Fine Paper Europe, Alfeld Mill, Mühlenmasch 1, D-31061 Alfeld (Leine), Germany, Capacity: 305,000 mt/y, (Pulp mill, Paper mill, Paperboard mill)
Phone: (49) 5181 77-0
Fax: (49) 5181 77208
Email: infoalfeld@sappi.com
Sappi Fine Paper Europe, Ehingen Mill, Biberacher Str. 73, D-89584 Ehingen, Germany, Capacity: 260,000 mt/y, (Pulp mill, Paper mill)
Phone: (49) 7391 5010
Fax: (49) 7391 501 315
Email: renate.distelrath@sappi.com
Sappi Fine Paper Europe, Gratkorn Mill, Brucker Str. 21, A-8101 Gratkorn, Austria, Capacity: 950,000 mt/y, (Pulp mill, Paper mill)
Phone: (43) 3124 201 0
Fax: (43) 3124 201 3038
Email: gratkorn.mill@sappi.com
Sappi Fine Paper Europe, Lanaken Mill, Montaigneweg 2, B-3620 Lanaken, Belgium, Capacity: 500,000 mt/y, (Pulp mill, Paper mill)
Phone: (32) 89 71 9719
Fax: (32) 89 71 9222
Email: lanaken.mill@sappi.com
Sappi Fine Paper Europe, Maastricht Mill, Biesenweg 16, NL-6211 AA Maastricht, Netherlands, Capacity: 290,000 mt/y, (Paper mill)
Phone: (31) 43 382 22 22
Fax: (31) 43 382 27 31
Email: maastricht.mill@sappi.com
Sappi Fine Paper Europe, Stockstadt Mill, Obernburger Strasse 1-9, D-63811 Stockstadt am Main, Germany, Capacity: 440,000 mt/y, (Pulp mill, Paper mill)
Phone: (49) 6027 4200
Fax: (49) 6027 420 245/823
Email: stockstadt@sappi.com

Pulp Grades and Capacities:
Total pulp capacity: 262,243 mt/y
Mechanical Pulp: 262,243 mt/y

Pulp Mill Data:
Mechanical Pulping Systems:
Conventional grinders: 12
Pressurized grinders: 6
RMP systems: 1
Bleach Plant Systems: 3
Paper/Paperboard Grades and Capacities:
Total paper and paperboard capacity: 735,000 mt/y
Coated mechanical/groundwood: 735,000 mt/y
Paper and Paperboard Mill Data:
Stock Preparation:
Refiners: 3
Paper Machines: 3
No. 1, SymFormer, total capacity 185,000 mt/y, Trim width 6.5 m, Coated mechanical/groundwood
No. 2, fourdrinier, total capacity 180,000 mt/y, Trim width 6.45 m, Coated mechanical/groundwood
No. 3, OptiFormer, total capacity 370,000 mt/y, Trim width 8.28 m, Coated mechanical/groundwood
Coating Machines: 3
CM 1, total capacity 180,000 mt/y., on machine
CM 2, total capacity 180,000 mt/y., off machine
CM 3, total capacity 380,000 mt/y., off machine
Finishing Equipment:
Winders: 5
Calenders: 1
Supercalenders: 7
Rewinders: 2
Energy Data:
Combustion turbines: 1 at 78 MW
Steam turbines: 1 at 38 MW
Electrical demand for mill: 2,603 MWh/D

ⓘⓜSavon Sellu Oy
Savon Sellu
Ownership: 100% by Powerflute Oyj
Sorsasalo
FI-70420 Kuopio
Finland
Mailing Address: P.O. Box 57, FI-70101 Kuopio, Finland
Phone: (358) 10 6606999
Fax: (358) 10 6606212
Email: (firstname.lastname@powerflute.com), info@powerflute.com
Web Address: www.powerflute.com

Personnel:
CEO, Savon Sellu: Juha Koukka
Phone: (358) 10 6606 200
Fax: (358) 10 6606 212
Email: juha.koukka@powerflute.com
Finan. Controller: Joni Päivinen
Phone: (358) 10 6606 232
Fax: (358) 10 6606 212
Email: joni.paivinen@powerflute.com
Prod. Mgr.: Antero Putkonen
Phone: (358) 10 6606 294
Fax: (358) 10 6606 212
Email: antero.putkonen@powerflute.com
R&D Mgr.: Jukka Silvennoinen
Phone: (358) 10 6606 462
Fax: (358) 10 6606 212
Email: jukka.silvennoinen@powerflute.com
VPSls. & Mktg.: Robert Vaenerberg
Phone: (358) 10 6606 220
Fax: (358) 9 2560270
Email: robert.vaenerberg@powerflute.com

Total Employees at this Location: 187
Type of Operation: Paperboard mill
Pulp Grades and Capacities:
Total pulp capacity: 279,744 mt/y
Chemical Pulp: 254,567 mt/y
Recycled Pulping: 25,177 mt/y

Pulp Mill Data:
Chemical Pulping Systems:
Continuous digesters: 2
Pulp Lines: 2
Chemical Recovery Equipment:
Evaporator lines: 1

Finland

Recovery boilers: 1
Paper/Paperboard Grades and Capacities:
Total paper and paperboard capacity: 275,000 mt/y
Corrugating medium/fluting: 275,000 mt/y
Paper and Paperboard Mill Data:
Stock Preparation:
Pulpers: 1
Refiners: 5
Paper Machines: 1
No. 1, fourdrinier, total capacity 275,000 mt/y, Trim width 6.6 m, Corrugating medium/fluting
Finishing Equipment:
Winders: 1 at 290,000 mt/y
Energy Data:
Power boilers: 1
Steam turbines: 2 at 20.0 MW
Electrical demand for mill: 554 MWh/D

ⓅⓂ SCA Tissue Finland Oy
Nokia Mill
Ownership: 100% by SCA - Svenska Cellulosa Aktiebolaget
Kerhokatu 10
FI-37101 Nokia
Finland
Mailing Address: P.O Box 1, Nokia, Finland
Phone: (358) 3 340 8111
Fax: (358) 3 340 8561
Web Address: www.sca.com
Personnel:
VP., Nordic Group Contr.: Harri Rajala
Phone: (358) 3 340 8111
Fax: (358) 3 340 8561
Mill Mgr.: Heikki Mustaniemi
Phone: (358) 3 340 8111
Fax: (358) 3 340 8561
Prod. Mgr.: Petri Huiko
Phone: (358) 3 340 8111
Fax: (358) 3 340 8561
Commer. Finan. Mgr.: Mari Puuko
Phone: (358) 3 340 8111
Fax: (358) 3 340 8561
HR Dir.: Jyri Lippo
Phone: (358) 3 340 8111
Fax: (358) 3 340 8561
Total Employees of Company: 300
Total Employees at this Location: 300
Type of Operation: Pulp mill, Paper mill
Pulp Grades and Capacities:
Total pulp capacity: 45,000 mt/y
Recycled Pulping: 45,000 mt/y
Pulp Mill Data:
Bleach Plant Lines:
No. 1, Type: DIP, Sequence: P
Recycled Fiber Treatment Lines:
Flotation deinking lines: 1
Paper/Paperboard Grades and Capacities:
Total paper and paperboard capacity: 80,000 mt/y
Tissue: 80,000 mt/y
Paper and Paperboard Mill Data:
Paper Machines: 2
No. 7, fourdrinier, Yankee dryer, total capacity 25,000 mt/y, Trim width 3.3 m, Tissue
No. 9, SpeedFormer, Yankee dryer, total capacity 55,000 mt/y, Trim width 5.21 m, Tissue
Energy Data:
Steam turbines: 1 at 30 MW
Electrical demand for mill: 283 MWh/D

Ⓜ Sonoco-Alcore Oy
Karhula Board Mill
Ownership: 100% by Sonoco Products Co.
Karhulantie 160
FI-48601 Karhula
Finland
Mailing Address: PO Box 100, FI-48601 Karhula, Finland
Phone: (358) 1023 42300
Fax: (358) 5 266 887
Email: (firstname.lastname@sonoco-alcore.net)
Web Address: www.sonoco.com
Personnel:
Mill Mgr.: Arto Lindberg
Phone: (358) 1023 42304
Fax: (358) 5 266 887
Email: arto.lindberg@sonoco-alcore.net
Tech. Mgr.: Mikko Grön
Phone: (358) 1023 42354
Fax: (358) 5 266 887
Email: mikko.gron@sonoco-alcore.net
Total Employees at this Location: 140
Type of Operation: Paperboard mill
Pulp Grades and Capacities:
Total pulp capacity: 80,825 mt/y
Recycled Pulping: 80,825 mt/y
Pulp Mill Data:
Recycled Fiber Treatment Lines:
Pulpers: 1 at 80,000
Recycled packaging pulping lines: 1 at 80,000
Paper/Paperboard Grades and Capacities:
Total paper and paperboard capacity: 80,000 mt/y
Boxboard/cartonboard: 80,000 mt/y
Paper and Paperboard Mill Data:
Stock Preparation:
Refiners: 3
Paper Machines: 1
No. 1, cylinder (6), total capacity 80,000 mt/y, Trim width 3.1 m, Boxboard/cartonboard
Finishing Equipment:
Winders: 1 at 85,000 mt/y
Rewinders: 1
Energy Data:
Electrical demand for mill: 104 MWh/D

Ⓟ Stora Enso Oyj
Ownership: 25% by Finnish State, 27% by Foundation Asset Management, 10.10% by Social Insurance Institution of Finland, 6.50% by Varma Mutual Pension Insurance Company
Kanavaranta 1
FI-00160 Helsinki
Finland
Mailing Address: PO Box 309, FI-00101 Helsinki, Finland
Phone: (358) 2046 131
Fax: (358) 2046 21471
Email: group.communications@storaenso.com
Web Address: www.storaenso.com
Personnel:
Chrmn.: Gunnar Brock
Phone: (1) 2046 21043
Fax: (1) 2046 21471
CEO (Eff. August 1, 2014): Karl-Henrik Sundström
Phone: (358) 2046 131
Fax: (358) 2046 21471
CFO : Seppo Parvi
Phone: (358) 2046 131
Fax: (358) 2046 21471
Exec. VP., Biomaterials: Juan Carlos Bueno
Phone: (358) 2046 131
Fax: (358) 2046 21471
Exec. VP., Global People and Organisation: Lars Häggström
Phone: (358) 2046 131
Fax: (358) 2046 21471
Exec. VP., Programme Director (to step down, effective March 15, 2015): Juha Vanhainen
Phone: (358) 2046 131
Fax: (358) 2046 21471
Exec. VP., Head of the Printing & Reading Div. (Eff. September 1, 2014): Kati ter Horst
Phone: (358) 2046 131
Fax: (358) 20 462 1471
Exec. VP., Building & Living Bus. (Eff. September 1, 2014): Jari Suominen
Phone: (358) 2046 131
Fax: (358) 2046 21471
Exec. VP., Global Commun. (Eff. September 1, 2014): Ulrika Lilja
Phone: (358) 2046 131
Fax: (358) 2046 21471
Exec. VP., Head of Global Responsibility (Eff. September 1, 2014): Terhi Koipijärvi
Phone: (358) 2046 131
Fax: (358) 2046 21471
Exec. VP., Sourcing (Eff. November 1, 2014): Johanna Hagelberg
Phone: (358) 2046 131
Fax: (358) 2046 21471
Snr. VP., Global Pulp Sales & Marketing: Alexandre Nicolini
Phone: (358) 2046 131
Fax: (358) 2046 21471
Sls. Dir. Finland and Germany: Tuomas Lönnroth
Phone: (358) 40 524 6111 (mobile)
Fax: (358) 20 462 1471
Email: tuomas.lonnroth@storaenso.com
Total Employees of Company: 28,000
Mill Locations:
Corenso France, Soustre Mill, PO Box 4, Gours, F-33660 Saint-Seurin-Sur-L'Isle, France, Capacity: 95,000 mt/y, (Pulp mill, Paperboard mill)
Phone: (33) 5 57 56 40 00
Fax: (33) 5 57 56 40 29
Email: stephanie.claustres@storaenso.com
Corenso North America, Wisconsin Rapids Mill, 800 Fremont Street, Wisconsin Rapids, WI 54495-8050, USA, Capacity: 85,178 mt/y, (Paperboard mill)
Phone: (1) 715-422-7800
Fax: (1) 715-422-7874
Email: corenso.northamerica@storaenso.com
Corenso United Oy Ltd., Pori Coreboard Mill, Kuninkaanlahdenkatu 14, FI-28101 Pori, Finland, Capacity: 120,000 mt/y, (Paperboard mill)
Phone: (358) 2046 1416
Fax: (358) 2046 48626
Email: hannu.makela@storaenso.com
Jiangsu Stora Enso Suzhou Paper Co. Ltd., Suzhou Mill, 600, Binhe Rd., Suzhou 215011, China, Capacity: 245,000 mt/y, (Paper mill)
Phone: (86) 512 6825 1060
Fax: (86) 512 6825 1711
Email: papyrus@public1.sz.js.cn
Montes del Plata, Punta Pereira Mill (50% owned), Zona Franca, Punta Pereira, Uruguay, (Pulp mill)
Email: contacto@montesdelplata.com.uy
Bulleh Shah Packaging (Private) Limited , Bulleh Shah Paper Mill (35% owned), Kasur Factory 11 km Kasur-Kot Radha Kishan Road, Kasur, Pakistan, Capacity: 255,000 mt/y, (Pulp mill, Paper mill, Paperboard mill)
Phone: (92) 344 413123/492 717335
Bulleh Shah Packaging (Private) Limited , Lahore Mill (35% owned), Shahrah-E-Roomi PO Amer Sidhu, 54760 Lahore, Pakistan, Capacity: 33,000 mt/y, (Pulp mill, Paper mill, Paperboard mill)
Phone: (92) 42 5811541-6/191-4
Fax: (92) 42 5811195/5820147
Email: info@packages.com.pk
Shandong Stora Enso Huatai Paper, Dawang Mill, Weigao Rd., Huatai Industrial Park, Dawang Township, Guangrao County, Dongying 257335, China, Capacity: 170,000 mt/y, (Pulp mill, Paper mill)
Phone: (86) 546 7797 200/243
Fax: (86) 546 7797 220
Stora Enso Arapoti Indústria de Papel Ltda., Arapoti Mill (80% owned), Rdv DR 01, Km 7 - Fazenda Barra Mansa, CP-11, 84990-000 Arapoti, PR, Brazil, Capacity: 185,000 mt/y, (Paper mill)
Phone: (55) 43 3512 2100
Fax: (55) 43 3512 2413
Stora Enso Renewable Packaging, Barcelona Mill, Potassi, 7, E-08755 Castellbisbal, Catalonia, Spain, Capacity: 170,000 mt/y, (Paperboard mill)
Phone: (34) 93 631 1000
Fax: (34) 93 631 1021
Email: barcelona@storaenso.com
Stora Enso Renewable Packaging, Fors Mill, Kopparforsvägen 3, SE-774 89 Fors, Sweden, Capacity: 395,000 mt/y, (Pulp mill, Paperboard mill)

Finland

Phone: (46) 1046 35000
Fax: (46) 1046 35250
Stora Enso Printing and Reading, Nymölla Mill, SE-295 80 Nymölla, Sweden, Capacity: 500,000 mt/y, (Pulp mill, Paper mill)
Phone: (46) 1046 440 00
Fax: (46) 1046 446 00
Stora Enso Printing and Reading, Oulu Mill, PO Box 196, FI-90101 Oulu, Finland, Capacity: 1,085,000 mt/y, (Pulp mill, Paper mill)
Phone: (358) 2046 124
Fax: (358) 2046 336 49
Email: (firstname.lastname@storaenso.com)
Stora Enso Biomaterials, Skutskär Pulp Mill, SE-814 81 Skutskär, Sweden, (Pulp mill)
Phone: (46) 1046 85000
Fax: (46) 1046 85015
Email: (firstname.lastname@storaenso.com)
Stora Enso Printing and Reading, Uetersen Mill, Pinnau-Allee 3, D-25436 Uetersen, Germany, Capacity: 230,000 mt/y, (Paper mill)
Phone: (49) 4122 7190
Fax: (49) 4122 719 339/222
Email: corporate.communications@storaenso.com; empfang-poststelle.uetersen.ext@storaenso.com
Stora Enso Printing and Reading, Varkaus Mill, PO Box 260, FI-78201 Varkaus, Finland, Capacity: 285,000 mt/y, (Pulp mill, Paper mill)
Phone: (358) 2046 120
Fax: (358) 2046 321 02
Stora Enso Printing and Reading, Veitsiluoto Mill, FI-94800 Kemi, Finland, Capacity: 830,000 mt/y, (Pulp mill, Paper mill)
Phone: (358) 2046 125
Fax: (358) 2046 34427 (Fine Paper), 34907 (Publication Paper)
Email: (firstname.lastname@storaenso.com)
Stora Enso Renewable Packaging, Imatra Mills (Kaukopää & Tainionkoski), FI-55800 Imatra, Finland, Capacity: 1,075,000 mt/y, (Pulp mill, Paper mill, Paperboard mill)
Phone: (358) 2046 121
Fax: (358) 2046 24701/24720
Email: (firstname.lastname@storaenso.com)
Stora Enso Biomaterials, Sunila Mill, Sunilantie, 1, FI-48900 Kotka, Finland, (Pulp mill)
Phone: (358) 2046 111
Fax: (358) 2046 20277
Email: (firstname.lastname@storaenso.fi)
Stora Enso Printing and Reading, Langerbrugge Mill, Wondelgemkaai 200, B-9000 Gent, Belgium, Capacity: 555,000 mt/y, (Pulp mill, Paper mill)
Phone: (32) 9 2577211
Fax: (32) 9 2577200
Email: langerbrugge.mill@storaenso.com, (firstname.lastname@storaenso.com)
Stora Enso Printing and Reading, Hylte Mill, SE-314 81 Hyltebruk, Sweden, Capacity: 485,000 mt/y, (Pulp mill, Paper mill)
Phone: (46) 1046 190 00
Fax: (46) 1046 188 76
Stora Enso Biomaterials, Enocell Pulp Mill, P.O. Box 2, FI-81281 Uimaharju, Finland, (Pulp mill)
Phone: (358) 2046 122
Fax: (358) 2046 28550
Email: (firstname.lastname@storaenso.com)
Stora Enso Renewable Packaging, Heinola Mill, Tampellantie 1, FI-18101 Heinola, Finland, Capacity: 300,000 mt/y, (Pulp mill, Paperboard mill)
Phone: (358) 2046 111
Fax: (358) 2046 29279
Stora Enso Renewable Packaging, Ingerois Mill, FI-46900 Kouvola, Finland, Capacity: 220,000 mt/y, (Paperboard mill)
Phone: (358) 2046 26104/117
Fax: (358) 2046 26141
Email: finland.contactcenter@storaenso.com
Stora Enso Renewable Packaging, Skoghall Mill, Udden, P.O. Box 501, SE-663 29 Skoghall, Sweden, Capacity: 725,000 mt/y, (Pulp mill, Paper mill, Paperboard mill)
Phone: (46) 1046 500 00
Fax: (46) 1046 543 44
Email: (firstname.lastname@storaenso.com)
Stora Enso Poland S.A., Ostroleka Mill (99.64% owned), ul. 1 Armii Wojska Polskiego 21, PL-07401 Ostroleka, Poland, Capacity: 640,000 mt/y, (Pulp mill, Paper mill, Paperboard mill)
Phone: (48) 29 7640000
Fax: (48) 29 7640002
Email: info.poland@storaenso.com
Stora Enso Printing and Reading, Anjala Mill, FI-46900 Kouvola, Finland, Capacity: 435,000 mt/y, (Pulp mill, Paper mill)
Phone: (358) 2046 117
Fax: (358) 2046 263 00
Email: (firstname.lastname@storaenso.com)
Stora Enso Printing and Reading, Corbehem Mill, Rue de Brébières, BP 2, F-62112 Corbehem, France, (Pulp mill, Paper mill)
Phone: (33) 3 27 92 32 00
Fax: (33) 3 27 97 99 60/92 33 31
Email: (firstname.lastname@storaenso.com)
Stora Enso Printing and Reading, Kabel Mill, Schwerter Str. 263, D-58099 Hagen, Germany, Capacity: 495,000 mt/y, (Paper mill)
Phone: (49) 2331 699 0
Fax: (49) 2331 699 516
Email: storaensokabel@storaenso.com
Stora Enso Printing and Reading, Kvarnsveden Mill, SE-781 83 Borlänge, Sweden, Capacity: 750,000 mt/y, (Pulp mill, Paper mill)
Phone: (46) 1046 650 00
Fax: (46) 1046 653 90
Stora Enso Printing and Reading, Maxau Mill, Mitscherlichstrasse, D-76187 Karlsruhe, Germany, Capacity: 530,000 mt/y, (Paper mill)
Phone: (49) 721 9566 0
Fax: (49) 721 9566 130
Email: corporate.communications@storaenso.com, (firstname.lastname@storaenso.com)
Stora Enso Printing and Reading, Sachsen Mill, Am Schanzberg 1, D-04838 Eilenburg, Germany, Capacity: 320,000 mt/y, (Pulp mill, Paper mill)
Phone: (49) 3423 650 0
Fax: (49) 3423 650 396/390
Email: sachsen.feedback@storaenso.com, (firstname.lastname@storaenso.com)
Veracel Celulose S.A., Veracel Pulp Mill (50% owned), Rodovia Fazenda Brazilândia BA 275, Km 24, Zona Rural, 45820-970 Eunápolis, BA, Brazil, (Pulp mill)
Phone: (55) 73 3166 8000
Fax: (55) 73 3166 8980
Email: veracel@veracel.com.br

Ⓜ Stora Enso Printing and Reading Oulu Mill

Ownership: 100% by Stora Enso Oyj
PO Box 196
FI-90101 Oulu
Finland
Mailing Address: PO Box 196, FI-90101 Oulu, Finland
  Phone: (358) 2046 124
  Fax: (358) 2046 336 49
  Email: (firstname.lastname@storaenso.com)
  Web Address: www.storaenso.com
Personnel:
Mill Mgr.: Jari Kärkkäinen
  Phone: (358) 2046 124
  Fax: (358) 2046 336 49
  Email: jari.karkkainen@storaenso.com
Energy Mgr.: Matti Pihko
  Phone: (358) 2046 124
  Fax: (358) 2046 336 49
  Email: matti.pihko@storaenso.com
Total Employees at this Location: 760
Type of Operation: Pulp mill, Paper mill
Pulp Grades and Capacities:
Total pulp capacity: 370,008 mt/y
Pulp available for market: 180,000 mt/y
Chemical Pulp: 370,008 mt/y
Pulp Mill Data:
Chemical Pulping Systems:
Continuous digesters: 1
Bleach Plant Systems: 1
No. 1, Type: ECF, Sequence: O_2 DEoDP, Capacity 370,000 admt/y
Chemical Recovery Equipment:
Evaporator lines: 1
Recovery boilers: 1
Lime Kiln
Pulp Dryers:
Air Float dryers 1
Paper/Paperboard Grades and Capacities:
Total paper and paperboard capacity: 1,085,000 mt/y
Coated woodfree/freesheet: 1,085,000 mt/y
Paper and Paperboard Mill Data:
Stock Preparation:
Refiners: 11
Paper Machines: 2
No. 6, SymFormer MB, total capacity 580,000 mt/y, Trim width 8.13 m, Coated woodfree/freesheet
No. 7, SpeedFormer HHS, total capacity 505,000 mt/y, Trim width 8.13 m, Coated woodfree/freesheet
Coating Machines: 3
No. 6, total capacity 580,000 mt/y., off machine
No. 7, total capacity 505,000 mt/y., off machine
PM 7, total capacity 505,000 mt/y., on machine
Finishing Equipment:
Supercalenders: 4
Rewinders: 3
Sheeters: 5
Energy Data:
Power boilers: 1
Steam turbines: 2 at 65 MW
Electrical demand for mill: 2,636 MWh/D

Ⓜ Stora Enso Printing and Reading Varkaus Mill

Ownership: 100% by Stora Enso Oyj
PO Box 260
FI-78201 Varkaus
Finland
  Phone: (358) 2046 120
  Fax: (358) 2046 321 02
  Web Address: www.storaenso.com
Personnel:
Mill Mgr.: Jarkko Tehomaa
  Phone: (358) 2046 120
  Fax: (358) 2046 321 02
  Email: jarkko.tehomaa@storaenso.com
Prod. Mgr.: Juha Hulkkonen
  Phone: (358) 2046 120
  Fax: (358) 2046 321 02
  Email: juha.hulkkonen@storaenso.com
HR Mgr.: Hannu Porasmaa
  Phone: (358) 2046 120
  Fax: (358) 2046 321 02
  Email: hannu.porasmaa@storaenso.com
Dev. Eng.: Sanna Hanhikoski
  Phone: (358) 2046 120
  Fax: (358) 2046 321 02
  Email: sanna.hanhikoski@storaenso.com
Total Employees at this Location: 314
Type of Operation: Pulp mill, Paper mill
Pulp Grades and Capacities:
Total pulp capacity: 229,687 mt/y
Pulp available for market: 5,000 mt/y
Chemical Pulp: 229,687 mt/y
Pulp Mill Data:
Chemical Pulping Systems:
Continuous digesters: 1
Pulp Lines: 1
Bleach Plant Systems: 1
No. 1, Type: Diffuser/filter MC, Sequence: O_2 DEopD, Capacity 225,000 admt/y
Chemical Recovery Equipment:
Evaporator lines: 1
Recovery boilers: 1
Lime Kiln

Finland

Pulp Dryers:
Fourdriniers 1, Pulp Dryers 1
Paper/Paperboard Grades and Capacities:
Total paper and paperboard capacity: 285,000 mt/y
Uncoated woodfree/freesheet: 285,000 mt/y
Paper and Paperboard Mill Data:
Stock Preparation:
Pulpers: 2
Refiners: 4
Paper Machines: 1
No. 3, ValFormer, total capacity 285,000 mt/y, Trim width 7.68 m, Uncoated woodfree/freesheet
Finishing Equipment:
Winders: 1
Rewinders: 1
Energy Data:
Power boilers: 3
Steam turbines: 3 at 80 MW
Hydro turbines: 4 at 5 MW
Electrical demand for mill: 913 MWh/D

ⓂStora Enso Printing and Reading
Veitsiluoto Mill
Ownership: 100% by Stora Enso Oyj
FI-94800 Kemi
Finland
  Phone: (358) 2046 125
  Fax: (358) 2046 34427 (Fine Paper), 34907 (Publication Paper)
  Email: (firstname.lastname@storaenso.com)
  Web Address: www.storaenso.com
Personnel:
  Mill Dir.: Juha Mäkimattila
  Phone: (358) 2046 125
  Fax: (358) 2046 34427
  Email: juha.makimattila@storaenso.com
  Commun. Mgr.: Taisto Saari
  Phone: (358) 2046 125
  Fax: (358) 2046 34427
  Email: taisto.saari@storaenso.com
  Pulp Mill Mgr.: Kimmo Pelander
  Phone: (358) 2046 125
  Fax: (358) 2046 34427
  Email: kimmo.pelander@storaenso.com
Total Employees at this Location: 715
Type of Operation: Pulp mill, Paper mill
Pulp Grades and Capacities:
  Total pulp capacity: 452,997 mt/y
  Chemical Pulp: 375,000 mt/y
  Mechanical Pulp: 77,997 mt/y
Pulp Mill Data:
Chemical Pulping Systems:
Continuous digesters: 1
Mechanical Pulping Systems:
Conventional grinders: 10
Pulp Lines: 2
Bleach Plant Systems: 3
No. 1, Type: Softwood groundwood, Sequence: P, Capacity 155,000 admt/y
No. 2, Type: Softwood, Sequence: O_2 (OPO)DEpD, Capacity 180,000 admt/y
No. 3, Type: Hardwood, Sequence: O_2 (OPO)DEpD, Capacity 195,000 admt/y
Chemical Recovery Equipment:
Evaporator lines
Recovery boilers: 1
Lime Kiln
Pulp Dryers:
Air Float dryers 1
Paper/Paperboard Grades and Capacities:
Total paper and paperboard capacity: 830,000 mt/y
Uncoated woodfree/freesheet: 570,000 mt/y
Coated mechanical/groundwood: 260,000 mt/y
Paper and Paperboard Mill Data:
Paper Machines: 3
No. 2, SpeedFormer HHS, total capacity 280,000 mt/y, Trim width 6.5 m, Uncoated woodfree/freesheet
No. 3, DuoFormer D, total capacity 290,000 mt/y, Trim width 6.5 m, Uncoated woodfree/freesheet
No. 5, SpeedFormer HHS, total capacity 260,000 mt/y, Trim width 7.45 m, Coated mechanical/groundwood
Coating Machines: 2
PM 1, off machine
PM 2, off machine
Finishing Equipment:
Supercalenders: 4
Rewinders: 4
Sheeters: 5 at 510,000 mt/y
Energy Data:
Power boilers: 2
Steam turbines: 3 at 93, 52 MW

ⓂStora Enso Renewable Packaging
Imatra Mills (Kaukopää & Tainionkoski)
Ownership: Stora Enso Oyj
FI-55800 Imatra
Finland
  Phone: (358) 2046 121
  Fax: (358) 2046 24701/24720
  Email: (firstname.lastname@storaenso.com)
  Web Address: www.storaenso.com
Personnel:
  Mill Dir.: Marko Pekkola
  Phone: (358) 2046 121
  Fax: (358) 2046 24720
  HR Dir.: Aimo Kettunen
  Phone: (358) 2046 121
  Fax: (358) 2046 24701
  Email: aimo.kettunen@storaenso.com
  Sls. Mgr. of Packaging Board: Jaakko Pikkarainen
  Phone: (358) 2046 26773, 358 40 515 4728
  Fax: (358) 2046 24720
  Email: jaakko.pikkarainen@storaenso.com
  Supply Chain Mgr.: Marja Jukkara
  Phone: (358) 400 374224
  Fax: (358) 2046 24720
  Email: marja.jukkara@storaenso.com
  Prod. Mgr. Kaukopää Pulp: Timo Tidenberg
  Phone: (358) 2046 121
  Fax: (358) 2046 24701
  Email: timo.tidenberg@storaenso.com
  Key Account Mgr. & Sls Mgr.: Marika Taitokari
  Phone: (358) 2046 121
  Fax: (358) 2046 24720
  Email: marika.taitokari@storaenso.com
  Sls. Mgr.: Kimmo Aulasuo
  Phone: (358) 2046 121
  Fax: (358) 2046 24720
  Email: kimmo.aulasuo@storaenso.com
  Quality & Develop. Mgr.: Mikko Nieminen
  Phone: (358) 2046 121
  Fax: (358) 2046 24701
  Email: mikko.nieminen@storaenso.com
  Prod. Mgr. BM4 and CTMP Plant: Riku Suumäkki
  Phone: (358) 2046 121
  Fax: (358) 2046 24701
  Mktg. Mgr.: Jorma K. O. Ignatius
  Phone: (358) 2046 121
  Fax: (358) 2046 24701
Total Employees at this Location: 1,000
Type of Operation: Pulp mill, Paper mill, Paperboard mill
Pulp Grades and Capacities:
  Total pulp capacity: 1,246,467 mt/y
  Pulp available for market: 304,718 mt/y
  Chemical Pulp: 1,021,385 mt/y
  Mechanical Pulp: 220,000 mt/y
  Recycled Pulping: 5,082 mt/y
Pulp Mill Data:
Chemical Pulping Systems:
Batch digesters: 8
Continuous digesters: 2
Mechanical Pulping Systems:
BCTMP systems: 1
Pulp Lines: 3
Bleach Plant Systems: 3
No. 1, Type: CTMP, Sequence: P, Capacity 200,000 admt/y
KL2, Type: SW, Sequence: O_2 DoEoEpDED, Capacity 240,000 admt/y
KL3, Type: HW, Sequence: O_2 DEopDED, Capacity 600,000 admt/y
Chemical Recovery Equipment:
Evaporator lines: 2
Recovery boilers: 2
Lime Kiln
Pulp Dryers:
Air Float dryers 1, Twin Wire 1
Paper/Paperboard Grades and Capacities:
Total paper and paperboard capacity: 1,075,000 mt/y
Packaging papers: 25,000 mt/y
Specialty and industrial: 85,000 mt/y
Boxboard/cartonboard: 965,000 mt/y
Paper and Paperboard Mill Data:
Stock Preparation:
Pulpers: 6
Paper Machines: 6
No. 1, fourdrinier (2), total capacity 175,000 mt/y, Trim width 4.4 m, Boxboard/cartonboard
No. 2, fourdrinier (3), total capacity 210,000 mt/y, Trim width 5.6 m, Boxboard/cartonboard
No. 4, fourdrinier (3), total capacity 320,000 mt/y, Trim width 6.36 m, Boxboard/cartonboard
No. 5, fourdrinier (3), total capacity 260,000 mt/y, Trim width 4.92 m, Boxboard/cartonboard
No. 6, SymFormer, total capacity 85,000 mt/y, Trim width 3.2 m, Specialty and industrial
No. 7, fourdrinier, total capacity 25,000 mt/y, Trim width 2.6 m, Packaging papers
Coating Machines: 3
BM 2, total capacity 210,000 mt/y., on machine
BM 5, total capacity 260,000 mt/y., on machine
CM6, total capacity 85,000 mt/y., on machine
Finishing Equipment:
Rewinders: 1
Sheeters: 2
Energy Data:
Power boilers: 5
HRSG boiler: 1
Steam turbines: 2 at 91.4, 64 MW
Electrical demand for mill: 4,230 MWh/D

ⓄⓂStora Enso Biomaterials
Sunila Mill
Ownership: 100% by Stora Enso Oyj
Sunilantie, 1
FI-48900 Kotka
Finland
  Phone: (358) 2046 111
  Fax: (358) 2046 20277
  Email: (firstname.lastname@storaenso.fi)
  Web Address: www.storaenso.com
Personnel:
  Mill Dir.: Olli-Pekka Reunanen
  Phone: (358) 2046 111
  Fax: (358) 2046 2027
  Email: olli-pekka.reunanen@storaenso.com
  Finan. Mgr.: Jouni Virtanen
  Phone: (358) 2046 111
  Fax: (358) 2046 2027
  Email: jouni.virtanen@storaenso.com
  Prod. Dir.: Jarmo Rinne
  Phone: (358) 2046 111
  Fax: (358) 2046 2027
  Email: jarmo.rinne@storaenso.com
  Management Assist.: Saija Kotiranta
  Phone: (358) 2046 111
  Fax: (358) 2046 2027
  Email: saija.kotiranta@storaenso.com
Total Employees at this Location: 180
Type of Operation: Pulp mill
Mill Locations:
Stora Enso Biomaterials, Skutskär Pulp Mill, SE-814 81 Skutskär, Sweden, (Pulp mill)
  Phone: (46) 1046 85000
  Fax: (46) 1046 85015
  Email: (firstname.lastname@storaenso.com)
Stora Enso Biomaterials, Enocell Pulp Mill, P.O. Box 2,

Finland

FI-81281 Uimaharju, Finland, (Pulp mill)
Phone: (358) 2046 122
Fax: (358) 2046 28550
Email: (firstname.lastname@storaenso.com)
Pulp Grades and Capacities:
Total pulp capacity: 376,121 mt/y
Pulp available for market: 370,000 mt/y
Chemical Pulp: 376,121 mt/y
Pulp Mill Data:
Chemical Pulping Systems:
Continuous digesters: 1
Pulp Lines: 1
Bleach Plant Systems: 1
No. 1, Sequence: O$_2$ DEopDP, Capacity 370,000 admt/y
Chemical Recovery Equipment:
Evaporator lines: 2
Recovery boilers: 2
Lime Kiln
Pulp Dryers:
Air Float dryers 1, Flakt dryer 1
Energy Data:
Power boilers: 1
Steam turbines: 2 at 41.0 MW
Electrical demand for mill: 750 MWh/D

ⓜStora Enso Biomaterials
Enocell Pulp Mill
Ownership: 100% by Stora Enso Oyj
P.O. Box 2
FI-81281 Uimaharju
Finland
Phone: (358) 2046 122
Fax: (358) 2046 28550
Email: (firstname.lastname@storaenso.com)
Web Address: www.storaenso.com/enocell
Personnel:
Prod. Mgr.: Sauli Purho
Phone: (358) 2046 28180
Fax: (358) 2046 28563
Email: sauli.purho@storaenso.com
Develop. Mgr.: Teppo Rovio
Phone: (358) 2046 28006
Fax: (358) 2046 28569
Email: teppo.rovio@storaenso.com
Purch. Mgr.: Petri Nevalainen
Phone: (358) 2046 28073
Fax: (358) 2046 28556
Email: petri.nevalainen@storaenso.com
Assistant, Support Functions, Commun.: Lilja Keränen
Phone: (358) 2046 28028
Fax: (358) 2046 28563
Email: lilja.keranen@storaenso.com
Total Employees at this Location: 170
Type of Operation: Pulp mill
Pulp Grades and Capacities:
Total pulp capacity: 508,906 mt/y
Pulp available for market: 500,000 mt/y
Chemical Pulp: 508,906 mt/y
Pulp Mill Data:
Chemical Pulping Systems:
Batch digesters: 10
Pulp Lines: 2
Bleach Plant Systems: 2
Chemical Pulping System, Type: Softwood, Sequence: O$_2$ DoEopDP, Capacity 400,000 admt/y
Chemical Pulping System, Type: Hardwood, Sequence: O$_2$ DoEopDP, Capacity 200,000 admt/y
Chemical Recovery Equipment:
Evaporator lines: 1
Recovery boilers: 1
Lime Kiln
Pulp Dryers:
Air Float dryers 1, Air Float dryers 1
Energy Data:
Power boilers: 1
Steam turbines: 1 at 105.0 MW
Electrical demand for mill: 1,167 MWh/D

ⓜStora Enso Renewable Packaging
Heinola Mill
Ownership: Stora Enso Oyj
Tampellantie 1
FI-18101 Heinola
Finland
Mailing Address: PO Box 5, FIN-18101 Heinola, Finland
Phone: (358) 2046 111
Fax: (358) 2046 29279
Web Address: www.storaenso.com
Personnel:
Tech. Mgr. Lahti & Heinola Mill: Jouni Lieskallio
Phone: (358) 2046 111
Fax: (358) 2046 29279
Email: jouni.lieskallio@storaenso.com
Prod. Mgr.: Kari Haapaniemi
Phone: (358) 2046 111
Fax: (358) 2046 29279
Email: kari.haapaniemi@storaenso.com
Total Employees at this Location: 200
Type of Operation: Pulp mill, Paperboard mill
Pulp Grades and Capacities:
Total pulp capacity: 305,861 mt/y
Chemical Pulp: 275,275 mt/y
Recycled Pulping: 30,586 mt/y
Pulp Mill Data:
Chemical Pulping Systems:
Continuous digesters: 4
Chemical Recovery Equipment:
Evaporator lines: 1
Recovery boilers: 1
Paper/Paperboard Grades and Capacities:
Total paper and paperboard capacity: 300,000 mt/y
Corrugating medium/fluting: 300,000 mt/y
Paper and Paperboard Mill Data:
Stock Preparation:
Pulpers: 2
Refiners: 8
Paper Machines: 1
No. 1, hybrid former, total capacity 300,000 mt/y, Trim width 6 m, Corrugating medium/fluting
Finishing Equipment:
Winders: 1
Rewinders: 1
Energy Data:
Power boilers: 2
Steam turbines: 2 at 44 MW
Electrical demand for mill: 648 MWh/D

ⓜStora Enso Renewable Packaging
Ingerois Mill
Ownership: Stora Enso Oyj
FI-46900 Kouvola
Finland
Phone: (358) 2046 26104/117
Fax: (358) 2046 26141
Email: finland.contactcenter@storaenso.com
Web Address: www.storaenso.com
Personnel:
Mill Mgr.: Taisto Nevalainen
Phone: (358) 2046 26104
Fax: (358) 2046 26141
Email: taisto.nevalainen@storaenso.com
Total Employees at this Location: 630
Type of Operation: Paperboard mill
Pulp Grades and Capacities:
Total pulp capacity: 109,762 mt/y
Mechanical Pulp: 109,762 mt/y
Pulp Mill Data:
Mechanical Pulping Systems:
Pressurized grinders: 1
TMP systems: 1
Pulp Lines: 2
Bleach Plant Lines:
PGW Mechanical pulping system bleaching
TMP Mechanical pulping system bleaching
Paper/Paperboard Grades and Capacities:
Total paper and paperboard capacity: 220,000 mt/y
Boxboard/cartonboard: 220,000 mt/y
Paper and Paperboard Mill Data:
Stock Preparation:
Pulpers: 4
Refiners: 12
Paper Machines: 1
No. 4, fourdrinier (3), total capacity 220,000 mt/y, Trim width 4.58 m, Boxboard/cartonboard
Coating Machines: 3
No. 1, on machine
No. 2, on machine
No. 3, on machine
Finishing Equipment:
Winders: 2
Sheeters: 4
Energy Data:
Electrical demand for mill: 703 MWh/D

ⓜStora Enso Printing and Reading
Anjala Mill
Ownership: 100% by Stora Enso Oyj
FI-46900 Kouvola
Finland
Phone: (358) 2046 117
Fax: (358) 2046 263 00
Email: (firstname.lastname@storaenso.com)
Web Address: www.storaenso.com
Personnel:
Mill Mgr.: Ari Johansson
Phone: (358) 2046 117
Fax: (358) 2046 263 00
Email: ari.johansson@storaenso.com
Ener. Mgr.: Ari Frantsi
Phone: (358) 2046 117
Fax: (358) 2046 263 00
Email: ari.frantsi@storaenso.com
Total Employees at this Location: 620
Type of Operation: Pulp mill, Paper mill
Pulp Grades and Capacities:
Total pulp capacity: 357,241 mt/y
Mechanical Pulp: 357,241 mt/y
Pulp Mill Data:
Mechanical Pulping Systems:
Pressurized grinders: 12
TMP systems: 2
Pulp Lines: 6
Bleach Plant Systems: 3
No. 1, Sequence: Di, Capacity 300,000 admt/y
No. 2, Sequence: P, Capacity 300,000 admt/y
Paper/Paperboard Grades and Capacities:
Total paper and paperboard capacity: 435,000 mt/y
Uncoated mechanical/groundwood: 245,000 mt/y
Coated mechanical/groundwood: 190,000 mt/y
Paper and Paperboard Mill Data:
Stock Preparation:
Pulpers: 3
Refiners: 4
Paper Machines: 2
No. 2, Tamformer, total capacity 190,000 mt/y, Trim width 5.28 m, Coated mechanical/groundwood
No. 3, SymFormer, total capacity 245,000 mt/y, Trim width 8.55 m, Uncoated mechanical/groundwood
Coating Machines: 1
PM 2, total capacity 185,000 mt/y, on machine
Finishing Equipment:
Winders: 4
Rewinders: 4
Energy Data:
Power boilers: 4
Combustion turbines: 1 at 73 MW
Steam turbines: 2 at 92 MW
Electrical demand for mill: 2,500 MWh/D

ⓜTervakoski Oy
Tervakoski Mill
Ownership: 100% by delfortgroup AG

Finland

Vähikkäläntie 1
FI-12400 Tervakoski
Finland
  Phone: (358) 19 771 1
  Fax: (358) 19 771 535/537
  Email: tervakoski@delfortgroup.com
  Web Address: www.delfortgroup.com,
  www.tervakoski.com
Personnel:
  Gen. Mgr.: Klaus Weitkaemper
  Phone: (358) 19 771 1
  Fax: (358) 19 771 535
  Email: klaus.weitkaemper@delfortgroup.com
Total Employees at this Location: 350
Type of Operation: Paper mill
Paper/Paperboard Grades and Capacities:
  Total paper and paperboard capacity: 116,000 mt/y
  Uncoated woodfree/freesheet: 22,000 mt/y
  Coated woodfree/freesheet: 56,000 mt/y
  Specialty and industrial: 38,000 mt/y
Paper and Paperboard Mill Data:
  Stock Preparation:
  Pulpers: 5
  Refiners: 29
Paper Machines: 4
  No. 3, fourdrinier, total capacity 2,000 mt/y, Trim width 1.55 m, Uncoated woodfree/freesheet
  No. 8, fourdrinier (2), total capacity 34,000 mt/y, Trim width 3.15 m, Specialty and industrial
  No. 11, fourdrinier, total capacity 24,000 mt/y, Trim width 3.45 m, Uncoated woodfree/freesheet, Specialty and industrial
  No. 12, DuoFormer, total capacity 56,000 mt/y, Trim width 4.5 m, Coated woodfree/freesheet
Coating Machines: 1
  No. 12, on machine
Finishing Equipment:
  Supercalenders: 2
  Rewinders: 16
  Sheeters: 2
Energy Data:
  Power boilers: 3
  Combustion turbines: 3 at 4 (1 idle), 4, 4 MW
  Electrical demand for mill: 283 MWh/D

ⓘUPM-Kymmene Corporation
Ownership: Public
Alvar Aallon katu 1, PO Box 380
FI-00101 Helsinki
Finland
  Phone: (358) 2041 5111
  Fax: (358) 2041 5110
  Email: inf@upm.com,
  paperinfo@upm.com
  Web Address: www.upm.com
Personnel:
  Pres. & CEO: Jussi Pesonen
  Phone: (358) 2041 5111
  Fax: (358) 2041 5110
  Email: jussi.h.pesonen@upm.com
  Exec. VP., UPM Paper ENA: Bernd Eikens
  Phone: (358) 2041 5111
  Fax: (358) 2041 5110
  Exec. VP., Stakeholder Rel.: Mrs. Pirkko Harrela
  Phone: (358) 2041 50588
  Fax: (358) 2041 50308
  Email: pirkko.harrela@upm.com
  CFO & Exec. VP., UPM Energy: Tapio Korpeinen
  Phone: (358) 2041 50004
  Fax: (358) 2041 50315
  Email: tapio.korpeinen@upm.com
  Exec. VP., Technology: Jyrki Ovaska
  Phone: (358) 2041 50564
  Fax: (358) 2041 50509
  Email: jyrki.ovaska@upm.com
  Exec. VP., UPM Biorefining: Heikki Vappula
  Phone: (358) 2041 50567
  Fax: (358) 2041 50767
  Exec. VP., HR: Ms. Riitta Savonlahti
  Phone: (358) 2041 50048
  Fax: (358) 2041 50309
  Email: riitta.savonlahti@upm.com
  Gen. Counsel: Juha Mäkelä
  Phone: (358) 2041 50407
  Fax: (358) 2041 50304/50300
  Sls. Mgr Europe. (From June 2013): Paolo Sergi
  Phone: (358) 2041 5111
  Fax: (358) 2041 5110
Total Employees of Company: 21,898
Mill Locations:
Jiangsu UPM, Changshu Paper Industry Co., Ltd., Changshu Mill, Wushi, Xingang Town, Changshu 215536, China, Capacity: 870,000 mt/y, (Paper mill)
  Phone: (86) 512 5265 1818
  Fax: (86) 512 5265 2300/2173
UPM GmbH, Augsburg Mill, Georg-Haindl-Str. 5, D-86153 Augsburg, Germany, Capacity: 500,000 mt/y, (Paper mill)
  Phone: (49) 821 3109 0
  Fax: (49) 821 3109 156/157
  Email: info.augsburg@upm.com
UPM-Kymmene (UK) Ltd., Caledonian Paper Mill, Meadowhead Rd., Irvine KA11 5AT, United Kingdom, Capacity: 280,000 mt/y, (Pulp mill, Paper mill)
  Phone: (44) 1294 312 020
  Fax: (44) 1294 314 400
  Email: caledonianpaper@upm.com
UPM, Chapelle Darblay Paper Mill, CD 3, F-76530 Grand-Couronne, France, Capacity: 380,000 mt/y, (Pulp mill, Paper mill)
  Phone: (33) 2 35 18 40 00
  Fax: (33) 2 35 18 40 40
  Email: info.chapelle@upm.com
UPM, Docelles Paper Mill, 1 rue du Grand Meix, F-88460 Docelles, France, (Paper mill)
  Phone: (33) 3 29 33 81 00
  Fax: (33) 3 29 33 81 81
  Email: info.docelles@upm.com
UPM GmbH, Ettringen Mill, Fabrikstr. 4, D-86833 Ettringen, Germany, Capacity: 280,000 mt/y, (Pulp mill, Paper mill)
  Phone: (49) 8249 802 0
  Fax: (49) 8249 802 213/119
UPM Uruguay, Fray Bentos Pulp Mill, Ruta Puente Puerto Km. 307, 65000 Fray Bentos, Uruguay, (Pulp mill)
  Phone: (598) 456 20100
  Fax: (598) 456 26971
UPM GmbH, Hürth Mill, Bertrams Jagdweg 12, D-50354 Hürth, Germany, Capacity: 310,000 mt/y, (Paper mill)
  Phone: (49) 2233 2006100
  Fax: (49) 2233 2007960
UPM-Kymmene Corporation, Jämsänkoski Mill, Tiilikantie 17, FI-42300 Jämsänkoski, Jämsä, Finland, Capacity: 880,000 mt/y, (Paper mill)
  Phone: (358) 204 16 161
  Fax: (358) 204 16 160
  Email: info.jamsai@upm.com
UPM-Kymmene Corporation, Kaipola Mill, Tehtaankatu 1, FI-42220 Kaipola, Jämsä, Finland, Capacity: 720,000 mt/y, (Paper mill)
  Phone: (358) 204 16 161
  Fax: (358) 204 16 100
  Email: info.kaipola@upm.com
UPM-Kymmene Corporation, Kaukas Mill, Kaukaantie 16, FI-53200 Lappeenranta, Finland, Capacity: 580,000 mt/y, (Pulp mill, Paper mill)
  Phone: (358) 204 15 161
  Fax: (358) 204 15 160
  Email: info.kaukas@upm.com
UPM-Kymmene Corporation, Kymi Mill, Selluntie 1, FI-45700 Kuusankoski, Kouvola, Finland, Capacity: 830,000 mt/y, (Pulp mill, Paper mill)
  Phone: (358) 204 15 121
  Fax: (358) 204 15 2552
  Email: info.kymi@upm.com
UPM North America, Madison Paper Mill, 1 Main Street, Madison, ME 04950, USA, Capacity: 219,555 mt/y, (Pulp mill, Paper mill)
  Phone: (1) 207-696-3307
  Fax: (1) 207-696-1125
UPM GmbH, Nordland Mill, Nordlandallee 1, D-26892 Dörpen, Germany, Capacity: 1,450,000 mt/y, (Paper mill)
  Phone: (49) 4963 401 00
  Fax: (49) 4963 4545
  Email: info.nordland@upm.com
UPM North America, Blandin Paper Mill, 115 First St SW, Grand Rapids, MN 55744-3699, USA, Capacity: 359,417 mt/y, (Paper mill)
  Phone: (1) 218-327-6200
  Fax: (1) 218-327-6212
  Email: info@upm-kymmene.com
UPM-Kymmene Corporation, Pietarsaari Mill, Luodontie 149, FI-68600 Pietarsaari, Finland, (Pulp mill, Paper mill)
  Phone: (358) 204 16 113
  Fax: (358) 204 16 8803
  Email: (firstname.lastname@upm-kymmene.com)
UPM GmbH, Plattling Mill, Nicolausstr. 7, D-94447 Plattling, Germany, Capacity: 780,000 mt/y, (Paper mill, Paper mill)
  Phone: (49) 9931 502-0/89606-0
  Fax: (49) 9931 502 103/255/89606 509
UPM-Kymmene Corporation, Rauma Paper Mill, Tikkalantie 1, FI-26100 Rauma, Finland, Capacity: 980,000 mt/y, (Paper mill)
  Phone: (358) 2041 4101
  Fax: (358) 2041 4100
  Email: (firstname.lastname@upm-kymmene.com), info.rauma@upm-kymmene.com
UPM-Kymmene Corporation, RaumaCell Mill, PO Box 250, FI-26101 Rauma, Finland, (Pulp mill)
  Phone: (358) 204 14101
  Fax: (358) 204 143404
  Email: info.rauma@upm-kymmene.com
UPM GmbH, Schongau Mill, Friedrich-Haindl-Str. 10, D-86956 Schongau, Germany, Capacity: 770,000 mt/y, (Paper mill)
  Phone: (49) 8861 2130
  Fax: (49) 8861 213106
  Email: info.schongau@upm.com
UPM GmbH, Schwedt Mill, Kuhheide 1, D-16303 Schwedt/Oder, Germany, Capacity: 290,000 mt/y, (Paper mill)
  Phone: (49) 3332 281 123
  Fax: (49) 3332 281 115
  Email: info.schwedt@upm-kymmene.com
UPM-Kymmene (UK) Ltd., Shotton Paper Mill, Weighbridge Road, Deeside Industrial Estate, Shotton, Deeside CH5 2LL, United Kingdom, Capacity: 500,000 mt/y, (Pulp mill, Paper mill)
  Phone: (44) 1244 280 000
  Fax: (44) 1244 280 363
  Email: info.shotton@upm.com
UPM-Kymmene Austria GmbH, Steyrermühl Mill, Fabriksplatz 1, A-4662 Steyrermühl, Austria, Capacity: 500,000 mt/y, (Paper mill)
  Phone: (43) 7613 89 00 0
  Fax: (43) 7613 2440
  Email: info.steyrermuhl@upm.com
UPM-Kymmene Corporation, Tervasaari Mill, Tehtaankatu 7, FI-37600 Valkeakoski, Finland, Capacity: 300,000 mt/y, (Pulp mill, Paper mill)
  Phone: (358) 204 16 111
  Fax: (358) 204 16 2369
  Email: info.tervasaari@upm.com

ⓘUPM-Kymmene Corporation
Jämsänkoski Mill
Tiilikantie 17
FI-42300 Jämsänkoski, Jämsä
Finland
Mailing Address: PO Box 35, FI-42301 Jämsänkoski, Finland
  Phone: (358) 204 16 161
  Fax: (358) 204 16 160
  Email: info.jamsai@upm.com
  Web Address: www.upm.com
Personnel:
  Gen. Mgr.: Markku Taavitsainen
  Phone: (358) 204 16 161
  Fax: (358) 204 16 160
  Email: markku.taavitsainen@upm.com

Finland

Specialty Papers Prod. Unit Dir. (PM3/PM4): Petri Hakanen
Phone: (358) 204 16 161
Fax: (358) 204 16 160
Email: petri.hakanen@upm.com
SC Prod. Unit Dir. (PM5/PM6): Mikko Vuori
Phone: (358) 204 16 161
Fax: (358) 204 16 160
Email: mikko.vuori@upm.com
Tech. Dir. Jämsänkoski and Kaipola Mill: Hannu Miettinen
Phone: (358) 204 16 161
Fax: (358) 204 16 160
Email: hannu.miettinen@upm.com
Total Employees at this Location: 600
Type of Operation: Paper mill
Pulp Grades and Capacities:
 Total pulp capacity: 382,651 mt/y
 Mechanical Pulp: 382,651 mt/y
Pulp Mill Data:
 Mechanical Pulping Systems:
 TMP systems: 2
 Bleach Plant Systems: 2
 No. 1, Sequence: P, Capacity 130,000 admt/y
 No. 2, Sequence: HS, Capacity 320,000 admt/y
Paper/Paperboard Grades and Capacities:
 Total paper and paperboard capacity: 880,000 mt/y
 Uncoated mechanical/groundwood: 620,000 mt/y
 Specialty and industrial: 260,000 mt/y
Paper and Paperboard Mill Data:
 Stock Preparation:
 Refiners: 28
 Paper Machines: 4
 No. 3, SymFormer MB, total capacity 140,000 mt/y, Trim width 4.12 m, Specialty and industrial
 No. 4, SymFormer R, total capacity 120,000 mt/y, Trim width 5.22 m, Specialty and industrial
 No. 5, DuoFormer TQv, total capacity 270,000 mt/y, Trim width 8.3 m, Uncoated mechanical/groundwood
 No. 6, OptiFormer, total capacity 350,000 mt/y, Trim width 9.35 m, Uncoated mechanical/groundwood
 Coating Machines: 2
 PM3, total capacity 84,000 mt/y., on machine
 PM4, total capacity 120,000 mt/y., on machine
 Finishing Equipment:
 Winders: 6
 Supercalenders: 6
 Rewinders: 4
Energy Data:
 Power boilers: 1
 TMP Reboiler: 1
 Steam turbines: 1 at 23 MW
 Hydro turbines: 2 at 2 MW
 Electrical demand for mill: 3,658 MWh/D

ⓜUPM-Kymmene Corporation
Kaipola Mill
Tehtaankatu 1
FI-42220 Kaipola, Jämsä
Finland
 Phone: (358) 204 16 161
 Fax: (358) 204 16 100
 Email: info.kaipola@upm.com
 Web Address: www.upm.com
Personnel:
 Gen. Mgr.: Markku Taavitsainen
 Phone: (358) 204 16 161
 Email: markku.taavitsainen@upm.com
 Prod. Dir.: Marko Laakkonen
 Phone: (358) 204 16 161
 Email: marko.laakkonen@upm.com
Total Employees at this Location: 500
Type of Operation: Paper mill
Pulp Grades and Capacities:
 Total pulp capacity: 556,677 mt/y
 Mechanical Pulp: 327,599 mt/y
 Recycled Pulping: 229,078 mt/y
Pulp Mill Data:
 Mechanical Pulping Systems:
 TMP systems: 2
Pulp Lines: 3
 Bleach Plant Systems: 2
 No. 1, Type: TMP, Sequence: P/Y, Capacity 400,000 admt/y
 No. 2, Type: DIP Capacity 210,000 admt/y
 Recycled Fiber Treatment Lines:
 Flotation deinking lines: 1 at 210,000 admt/y
 Pulpers: 1
Paper/Paperboard Grades and Capacities:
 Total paper and paperboard capacity: 720,000 mt/y
 Newsprint: 240,000 mt/y
 Uncoated mechanical/groundwood: 180,000 mt/y
 Coated mechanical/groundwood: 300,000 mt/y
Paper and Paperboard Mill Data:
 Stock Preparation:
 Refiners: 24
 Paper Machines: 3
 No. 4, ValFormer, total capacity 150,000 mt/y, Trim width 7.04 m, Uncoated mechanical/groundwood
 No. 6, OptiFormer, total capacity 300,000 mt/y, Trim width 8.3 m, Coated mechanical/groundwood
 No. 7, SpeedFormer HS, total capacity 270,000 mt/y, Trim width 8.4 m, Newsprint, Uncoated mechanical/groundwood
 Coating Machines: 1
 PM6, total capacity 300,000 mt/y., on machine
 Finishing Equipment:
 Supercalenders: 2
 Rewinders
Energy Data:
 Power boilers: 1
 TMP Reboiler: 1
 Steam turbines: 1 at 25 MW
 Electrical demand for mill: 3,909 MWh/D

ⓜUPM-Kymmene Corporation
Kaukas Mill
Kaukaantie 16
FI-53200 Lappeenranta
Finland
 Phone: (358) 204 15 161
 Fax: (358) 204 15 160
 Email: info.kaukas@upm.com
 Web Address: www.upm.com
Personnel:
 Gen. Mgr.: Juha Kääriäinen
 Phone: (358) 204 15 161
 Fax: (358) 204 15 160
 Email: juha.kaariainen@upm.com
 Dir. Paper Prod.: Kari Isokääntä
 Phone: (358) 204 15 161
 Fax: (358) 204 15 160
 Email: kari.isokaanta@upm.com
 Environ. Mgr.: Minna Maunus-Tiihonen
 Phone: (358) 204 15 161
 Fax: (358) 204 15 160
 Email: minna.maunus-tiihonen@upm.com
 Mgr. Labor Rel.: Hans Nyström
 Phone: (358) 204 15 161
 Fax: (358) 204 15 160
 Email: hans.nystrom@upm.com
Total Employees at this Location: 490
Type of Operation: Pulp mill, Paper mill
Pulp Grades and Capacities:
 Total pulp capacity: 698,665 mt/y
 Pulp available for market: 610,000 mt/y
 Chemical Pulp: 470,008 mt/y
 Mechanical Pulp: 228,657 mt/y
Pulp Mill Data:
 Chemical Pulping Systems:
 Batch digesters: 12
 Continuous digesters: 1
 Mechanical Pulping Systems:
 Conventional grinders: 4
 Pressurized grinders: 2
 Bleach Plant Systems: 3
 Mechanical pulp bleaching line, Type: PGW, Sequence: P, Capacity 150,000 admt/y
 NBHKP and sawdust bleaching line, Type: BHKP, Sequence: O_2 DEOpDEpD, Capacity 320,000 admt/y
 NBSKP bleaching line, Type: BSKP, Sequence: O_2 EopDPoD, Capacity 420,000 admt/y
 Chemical Recovery Equipment:
 Evaporator lines: 7
 Recovery boilers: 1
 Lime Kiln
 Pulp Dryers:
 Air Float dryers 1, Air Float dryers 1, Twin Wire 1
Paper/Paperboard Grades and Capacities:
 Total paper and paperboard capacity: 580,000 mt/y
 Coated mechanical/groundwood: 580,000 mt/y
Paper and Paperboard Mill Data:
 Paper Machines: 2
 No. 1, SpeedFormer HHS, total capacity 330,000 mt/y, Trim width 7.36 m, Coated mechanical/groundwood
 No. 2, SpeedFormer HHS, total capacity 250,000 mt/y, Trim width 7.36 m, Coated mechanical/groundwood
 Coating Machines: 3
 Coater No. 1, off machine
 Coater No. 2, off machine
 Coater No. 3, off machine
 Finishing Equipment:
 Winders: 4 at 580,000 mt/y
 Supercalenders: 5 at 580,000 mt/y
 Rewinders: 2
Energy Data:
 Power boilers: 4
 Steam turbines: 2 at 125 MW
 Electrical demand for mill: 3,532 MWh/D

ⓜUPM-Kymmene Corporation
Kymi Mill
Selluntie 1
FI-45700 Kuusankoski, Kouvola
Finland
 Phone: (358) 204 15 121
 Fax: (358) 204 15 2552
 Email: info.kymi@upm.com
 Web Address: www.upm.com
Personnel:
 Gen. Mgr. (From 2014): Markku O. Laaksonen
 Phone: (358) 204 15 121
 Fax: (358) 204 15 2552
 Email: markku.o.laaksonen@upm.com
 Dir., Pulp Mill: Teuvo Solismaa
 Phone: (358) 204 15 121
 Fax: (358) 204 15 2552
 Email: teuvo.solismaa@upm.com
Total Employees at this Location: 620
Type of Operation: Pulp mill, Paper mill
Pulp Grades and Capacities:
 Total pulp capacity: 570,000 mt/y
 Pulp available for market: 19,329 mt/y
 Chemical Pulp: 570,000 mt/y
Pulp Mill Data:
 Chemical Pulping Systems:
 Continuous digesters: 2
Pulp Lines: 2
 Bleach Plant Systems: 2
 No. 1, Type: Hardwood, Sequence: O_2 DEoDEpD, Capacity 340,000 admt/y
 No. 2, Type: Softwood, Sequence: O_2 DEopDD, Capacity 200,000 admt/y
 Chemical Recovery Equipment:
 Evaporator lines: 1
 Recovery boilers: 1
 Lime Kiln
 Pulp Dryers:
 Fourdriniers 1
Paper/Paperboard Grades and Capacities:
 Total paper and paperboard capacity: 830,000 mt/y
 Uncoated woodfree/freesheet: 400,000 mt/y
 Coated woodfree/freesheet: 430,000 mt/y
Paper and Paperboard Mill Data:
 Paper Machines: 2
 No. 8, OptiFormer, total capacity 430,000 mt/y, Trim width 9.2 m, Coated woodfree/freesheet

France

No. 9, SymFormer, total capacity 400,000 mt/y, Trim width 8.5 m, Uncoated woodfree/freesheet
Coating Machines: 1
C 3, total capacity 450,000 mt/y., off machine
Finishing Equipment:
Rewinders: 2
Sheeters: 2
Energy Data:
Power boilers: 1
Steam turbines: 2 at 80 MW
Electrical demand for mill: 2,335 MWh/D

ⓜUPM-Kymmene Corporation
Pietarsaari Mill
Luodontie 149
FI-68600 Pietarsaari
Finland
Mailing Address: PO Box 42, FI-68601 Pietarsaari/Jakobstad, Finland
Phone: (358) 204 16 113
Fax: (358) 204 16 8803
Email: (firstname.lastname@upm-kymmene.com)
Web Address: www.upm.com
Personnel:
Mill Mgr.: Veikko Petäjistö
Phone: (358) 204 16 113
Fax: (358) 204 16 8803
Email: veikko.petajisto@upm.com
Mgr., Pulp Prod.: Tero Virkkala
Phone: (358) 204 16 9424
Fax: (358) 204 16 8803
Email: tero.virkkala@upm.com
Devlpt. Dir.: Mats Backman
Phone: (358) 204 16 9776
Fax: (358) 204 16 8803
Email: mats.backman@upm.com
Commun. Mgr.: Outi Jokinen
Phone: (358) 204 16 9152
Fax: (358) 204 16 8803
Email: outi.jokinen@upm.com
Total Employees at this Location: 347
Type of Operation: Pulp mill, Paper mill
Pulp Grades and Capacities:
Total pulp capacity: 755,891 mt/y
Pulp available for market: 790,000 mt/y
Chemical Pulp: 755,891 mt/y
Pulp Mill Data:
Chemical Pulping Systems:
Batch digesters: 8
Continuous digesters: 2
Pulp Lines: 3
Bleach Plant Systems: 2
Line 1, Type: ECF/TCF, Sequence: O_2 DEopDED, Capacity 340,000 admt/y
Line 2, Type: ECF/TCF, Sequence: O_2 DEopDED, Capacity 450,000 admt/y
Chemical Recovery Equipment:
Evaporator lines: 7
Recovery boilers: 1
Lime Kiln
Pulp Dryers:
Air Float dryers 1, Air Float dryers 1, Twin Wire 1, Twin Wire 1
Energy Data:
Power boilers: 1
Steam turbines: 1 at 143 MW
Electrical demand for mill: 1,578 MWh/D

ⓜUPM-Kymmene Corporation
Rauma Paper Mill
Tikkalantie 1
FI-26100 Rauma
Finland
Mailing Address: PO Box 95, FI-26101 Rauma, Finland
Phone: (358) 2041 4101
Fax: (358) 2041 4100
Email: (firstname.lastname@upm-kymmene.com), info.rauma@upm-kymmene.com
Web Address: www.upm.com
Personnel:
VP & Gen. Mgr.: Kari Pasanen
Phone: (358) 2041 4101
Fax: (358) 2041 4100
Email: kari.pasanen@upm.com
Sec.: Jaana Kanerva
Phone: (358) 2041 43135/4002 97260
Fax: (358) 2041 43555
Email: jaana.kanerva@upm-kymmene.com
Total Employees at this Location: 580
Type of Operation: Paper mill
Pulp Grades and Capacities:
Total pulp capacity: 484,687 mt/y
Mechanical Pulp: 484,687 mt/y
Pulp Mill Data:
Mechanical Pulping Systems:
Conventional grinders: 2
TMP systems: 3
Pulp Lines: 5
Bleach Plant Systems: 2
SGW, Sequence: Di, Capacity 260,000 admt/y
TMP, Sequence: P, Capacity 380,000 admt/y
Paper/Paperboard Grades and Capacities:
Total paper and paperboard capacity: 980,000 mt/y
Uncoated mechanical/groundwood: 280,000 mt/y
Coated mechanical/groundwood: 700,000 mt/y
Paper and Paperboard Mill Data:
Paper Machines: 3
No. 1, SpeedFormer HHS, total capacity 300,000 mt/y, Trim width 8.18 m, Coated mechanical/groundwood
No. 2, OptiFormer, total capacity 280,000 mt/y, Trim width 8.4 m, Uncoated mechanical/groundwood
No. 4, OptiFormer, total capacity 400,000 mt/y, Trim width 9.2 m, Coated mechanical/groundwood
Coating Machines: 2
No. 1, total capacity 300,000 mt/y., on machine
No. 4, total capacity 410,000 mt/y., on machine
Finishing Equipment:
Supercalenders: 9
Energy Data:
Power boilers: 4
Steam turbines: 2 at 80, 25 MW
Electrical demand for mill: 5,114 MWh/D

ⓜUPM-Kymmene Corporation
RaumaCell Mill
PO Box 250
FI-26101 Rauma
Finland
Phone: (358) 204 14101
Fax: (358) 204 143404
Email: info.rauma@upm-kymmene.com
Web Address: www.upmraumacell.com
Personnel:
Dir.: Päivi Vihijärvi
Phone: (358) 2041 43502
Fax: (358) 2041 43404
Email: paivi.vihijarvi@upm.com
Mgr., Tech. Mktg: Gustaf Westberg
Phone: (358) 204 143187
Fax: (358) 204 143404
Email: gustaf.westbergo@upm.com
Mktg. Mgr.: Kirsi Suutarinen
Mktg. Mgr.: Anna Vastiala
Phone: (358) 204 143519
Email: anna.vastiala@upm.com
Total Employees at this Location: 69
Type of Operation: Pulp mill
Pulp Grades and Capacities:
Pulp available for market: 150,000 mt/y
Pulp Mill Data:
Pulp Dryers:
Other dryers 1
Energy Data:
Electrical demand for mill: 126 MWh/D

ⓜUPM-Kymmene Corporation
Tervasaari Mill
Tehtaankatu 7
FI-37600 Valkeakoski
Finland
Mailing Address: PO Box 39, F-37601 Valkeakoski, Finland
Phone: (358) 204 16 111
Fax: (358) 204 16 2369
Email: info.tervasaari@upm.com
Web Address: www.upm.com
Personnel:
Prod. Dir.: Jari Tamminen
Phone: (358) 204 16 2700
Fax: (358) 204 16 2709
Email: jari.u.tamminen@upm.com
Prod. Mgr.: Jukka Kotilainen
Phone: (358) 204 16 2705
Fax: (358) 204 16 2706
Email: jukka.kotilainen@upm.com
Prod. Sup't. PM 8: Jussi Leinonen
Phone: (358) 204 16 2734
Fax: (358) 204 16 2706
Email: jussi.x.leinonen@upm.com
Head of Supply Chain: Kaisa Aarnikoivu
Phone: (358) 20416 2563
Fax: (358) 204 16 2554
Email: kaisa.aarnikoivu@upm.com
Environ. & Safety Mgr.: Harri Hiltunen
Phone: (358) 204 16 2590
Fax: (358) 204 16 2629
Email: harri.o.hiltunen@upm.com
Develop. Mgr.: Juhani Alajoutsijärvi
Phone: (358) 204 16 2723
Fax: (358) 204 16 2369
Email: juhani.alajoutsijarvi@upm.com
Commun. Officer: Tuulikki Moisio
Phone: (358) 204 16 111
Fax: (358) 204 16 2369
Email: tuulikki.moisio@upm.com
Total Employees at this Location: 320
Type of Operation: Pulp mill, Paper mill
Paper/Paperboard Grades and Capacities:
Total paper and paperboard capacity: 300,000 mt/y
Specialty and industrial: 300,000 mt/y
Paper and Paperboard Mill Data:
Stock Preparation:
Pulpers: 4
Paper Machines: 2
No. 5, SymFormer MB, total capacity 80,000 mt/y, Trim width 4.4 m, Specialty and industrial
No. 8, SpeedFormer HHS, total capacity 220,000 mt/y, Trim width 6.5 m, Specialty and industrial
Finishing Equipment:
Supercalenders: 3
Rewinders: 3
Energy Data:
Power boilers: 4
Steam turbines: 2 at 40 MW
Hydro turbines: 1 at 4 MW
Electrical demand for mill: 851 MWh/D

FRANCE

ⓜAhlstrom Packaging SA
St. Séverin Mill
Ownership: Ahlstrom Corporation Oy
Usine Le Marchais
F-16390 Saint Séverin
France
Phone: (33) 5 45 98 52 21
Fax: (33) 5 45 98 52 02
Email: investor@ahlstrom.com, corporate.communications@ahlstrom.com
Web Address: www.ahlstrom.com
Personnel:
Mill Mgr.: Philippe Ballistreri
Phone: (33) 5 45 98 52 21
Fax: (33) 5 45 98 52 02
Email: philippe.ballistreri@ahlstrom.

France

Tech. Mgr.: Gerard Giry
Phone: (33) 5 45 98 47 54
Fax: (33) 5 45 98 52 02
Email: gerard.giry@ahlstrom.com
Prod. Mgr.: Jacky Desage
Phone: (33) 5 45 98 47 53
Fax: (33) 5 45 98 31 12
Email: jacky.desage@ahlstrom.com
HR Mgr.: Jean Marie Vieille
Phone: (33) 5 45 98 52 21
Fax: (33) 5 45 98 52 02
Email: jean-marie.vieille@ahlstrom.com
Total Employees at this Location: 70
Type of Operation: Paper mill
Paper/Paperboard Grades and Capacities:
 Total paper and paperboard capacity: 22,134 mt/y
 Specialty and industrial: 22,134 mt/y
Paper and Paperboard Mill Data:
Paper Machines: 1
 M1, fourdrinier, total capacity 22,134 mt/y, Trim width 2.46 m, Specialty and industrial
Coating Machines: 1
 CM 1, off machine
Energy Data:
 Power boilers
 Electrical demand for mill: 55 MWh/D

ⓂAhlstrom Specialties SA
Bousbecque Mill
Ownership: 100% by Ahlstrom Corporation Oy
5 rue de la Papeterie, BP 101
F-59166 Bousbecque
France
 Phone: (33) 3 20 23 46 46
 Fax: (33) 3 20 23 46 10
 Email: investor@ahlstrom.com,
  corporate.communications@ahlstrom.com
 Web Address: www.ahlstrom.com
Personnel:
 Mill Mgr.: Herve Tartar
 Phone: (33) 3 20 23 46 46
 Fax: (33) 3 20 23 46 10
 Sls. Dir. Western Europe: Eric PAROIS
 Phone: (33) 3 20 23 46 46
 Fax: (33) 3 20 23 46 10
 Supply Chain . Mgr.: Mickael Vansteenkiste
 Phone: (33) 3 20 23 46 46
 Fax: (33) 3 20 23 46 10
 Email: mickael.vansteenkiste@ahlstrom.com
 Prod. Mgr.: Clement Busslier
 Phone: (33) 3 20 23 46 46
 Fax: (33) 3 20 23 46 10
 HR Mgr. : Jean Marie Vieille
 Phone: (33) 3 20 23 46 46
 Fax: (33) 3 20 23 46 10
 Email: jean-marie.vieille@ahlstrom.com
Total Employees at this Location: 130
Type of Operation: Paper mill
Paper/Paperboard Grades and Capacities:
 Total paper and paperboard capacity: 14,994 mt/y
 Specialty and industrial: 14,994 mt/y
Paper and Paperboard Mill Data:
 Stock Preparation:
 Pulpers: 6
 Refiners: 14
Paper Machines: 1
 No. 3, fourdrinier, total capacity 14,994 mt/y, Trim width 2.4 m, Specialty and industrial
Coating Machines: 1
 No. 1, total capacity 12,000 mt/y., on machine
Finishing Equipment:
 Supercalenders: 4
 Rewinders: 4
 Sheeters: 2
Energy Data:
 Power boilers: 3
 Steam turbines: 2 at 8.3 MW

ⓂAhlstrom Specialties SA
Pont-Audemer Mill
Ownership: 100% by Ahlstrom Corporation Oy
Rue des Papeteries
F-27501 Pont Audemer
France
 Phone: (33) 2 32 41 61 00
 Fax: (33) 2 32 41 44 31
 Email: investor@ahlstrom.com,
  corporate.communications@ahlstrom.com
 Web Address: www.ahlstrom.com
Personnel:
 Mill Mgr. & Prod. Mgr.: Jean-Philippe Ponté
 Phone: (33) 2 32 41 61 01
 Email: jean-philippe.ponte@ahlstrom.com
 HR Mgr.: Jean Marie Vieille
 Phone: (33) 2 32 41 61 01
 Fax: (33) 2 32 41 44 31
 Email: jean-marie.vieille@ahlstrom.com
 Proj. Mgr.: Clémentine Boehrer
 Phone: (33) 2 32 41 61 01
 Fax: (33) 2 32 41 44 31
 Email: clementine.boehrer@ahlstrom.com
Total Employees at this Location: 75
Type of Operation: Paper mill
Pulp Mill Data:
 Recycled Fiber Treatment Lines:
 Washing deinking lines: 1
Paper/Paperboard Grades and Capacities:
 Total paper and paperboard capacity: 29,988 mt/y
 Specialty and industrial: 29,988 mt/y
Paper and Paperboard Mill Data:
Paper Machines: 1
 No. 5, fourdrinier, total capacity 29,988 mt/y, Trim width 3.7 m, Specialty and industrial
Energy Data:
 Power boilers
 Electrical demand for mill: 81 MWh/D

ⓄⓂAlamigeon SA
Ruelle sur Touvre Mill
Ownership: Oxalis
Villement
F-16600 Ruelle sur Touvre
France
 Phone: (33) 5 45 65 63 39
 Fax: (33) 5 45 65 61 58
 Email: sce.commercial@alamigeon.com
 Web Address: www.alamigeon.com
Personnel:
 CEO: Pascal Conty
 Phone: (33) 5 45 65 63 39
 Fax: (33) 5 45 65 61 58
 Pres. & Gen. Dir.: Alain Château
 Phone: (33) 5 45 65 63 39
 Fax: (33) 5 45 65 61 58
 Gen. Mgr.: Paul Julliand
 Phone: (33) 5 45 65 82 37
 Fax: (33) 5 45 65 61 58
 Commercial Export Area Mgr.: Tristan De Lestapis
 Phone: (33) 5 45 65 82 35
 Fax: (33) 5 45 65 61 58
 Method & Quality Engineer: Meije Laloi
 Phone: (33) 5 45 65 63 39
 Fax: (33) 5 45 65 61 58
Total Employees at this Location: 31
Type of Operation: Paper mill
Paper/Paperboard Grades and Capacities:
 Total paper and paperboard capacity: 14,000 mt/y
 Uncoated woodfree/freesheet: 12,000 mt/y
 Specialty and industrial: 2,000 mt/y
Paper and Paperboard Mill Data:
 Stock Preparation:
 Pulpers: 1
 Refiners: 3
Paper Machines: 1
 No. 1, fourdrinier, total capacity 14,000 mt/y, Trim width 1.7 m, Uncoated woodfree/freesheet, Specialty and industrial

Finishing Equipment:
 Rewinders: 2
 Sheeters: 1
Energy Data:
 Power boilers: 2

ⓂAllard Emballages
Ownership: 100% by The Valois Group
Av. Adrien Allard, B.P. 50510
F-19100 Brive la Gaillarde Cedex
France
 Phone: (33) 5 55 87 90 21
 Fax: (33) 5 55 88 26 69
 Email: accueil.brive@allardemballages.fr,
  contact.web@allardemballages.fr
 Web Address: www.allardemballages.fr
Personnel:
 Pres. & Gen. Mgr.: Loïc Genetay
 Phone: (33) 5 55 87 90 21
 Fax: (33) 5 55 88 26 69
 Email: loic.genetay@allardemballages.fr
 Delegated Gen. Mgr.: Paul Allard
 Phone: (33) 5 55 87 90 21
 Fax: (33) 5 55 88 26 69
 Ind. Dir., Paper Mill: Laurent Bauvais
 Phone: (33) 5 55 87 90 21
 Fax: (33) 5 55 88 26 69
 Email: laurent.bauvais@allardemballages.fr
 Sls. & Mktg. Dir. : Guillaume Alamercery
 Phone: (33) 5 55 87 90 21
 Fax: (33) 5 55 88 26 69
 Finan. Contr.: Anne Lise Claux
 Phone: (33) 5 55 87 90 21
 Fax: (33) 5 55 88 26 69
Total Employees of Company: 440
Total Employees at this Location: 180
Mill Locations:
Allard Emballages, Varennes Mill, Varennes, F-72800 Aubigné-Racan, France, Capacity: 100,000 mt/y, (Paper mill, Paperboard mill)
 Phone: (33) 2 43 46 20 56
 Fax: (33) 2 43 46 25 43
 Email: contact.web@allardemballages.fr

ⓂAllard Emballages
Varennes Mill
Varennes
F-72800 Aubigné-Racan
France
 Phone: (33) 2 43 46 20 56
 Fax: (33) 2 43 46 25 43
 Email: contact.web@allardemballages.fr
 Web Address: www.allardemballages.fr
Personnel:
 Mill Mgr. & Industrial Dir. of Allard Emballages Group: Laurent Bauvais
 Phone: (33) 2 43 46 20 56
 Fax: (33) 2 43 46 25 43
 Maint. Mgr.: Pierre Drumel
 Phone: (33) 2 43 46 20 56
 Fax: (33) 2 43 46 25 43
 Prod. Mgr.: Bruno Baril
 Phone: (33) 2 43 46 20 56
 Fax: (33) 2 43 46 25 43
 PM Mgr.: François Maigrot
 Phone: (33) 2 43 46 20 56
 Fax: (33) 2 43 46 25 43
Total Employees at this Location: 75
Type of Operation: Paper mill, Paperboard mill
Pulp Grades and Capacities:
 Total pulp capacity: 101,644 mt/y
 Recycled Pulping: 101,644 mt/y
Pulp Mill Data:
 Recycled Fiber Treatment Lines:
 Pulpers at 84,000
Paper/Paperboard Grades and Capacities:
 Total paper and paperboard capacity: 100,000 mt/y
 Linerboard: 65,000 mt/y
 Corrugating medium/fluting: 35,000 mt/y

France

Paper and Paperboard Mill Data:
Paper Machines: 1
No. 1, fourdrinier (2), total capacity 100,000 mt/y, Trim width 2.5 m, Corrugating medium/fluting, Linerboard
Energy Data:
Power boilers: 1
Electrical demand for mill: 134 MWh/D

ⓜArjowiggins SAS
Ownership: 100% by Sequana Capital (Public)
32, avenue Pierre Grenier
92517 Boulogne Billancourt Cedex
France
  Phone: (33) 1 57 75 92 12
  Fax: (33) 1 57 75 92 72
  Email: contact@arjowiggins.com
  Web Address: www.arjowiggins.com
Personnel:
  CEO: Pascal Lebard
  Phone: (33) 1 57 75 92 12
  Fax: (33) 1 57 75 92 72
  COO: Guy Léonard
  Phone: (33) 1 57 75 92 12
  Fax: (33) 1 57 75 92 72
  CFO: Alain Gourjon
  Phone: (33) 1 57 75 92 12
  Fax: (33) 1 57 75 92 72
  Man. Dir. US Coated: Douglas Osterberg
  Phone: (33) 1 57 75 92 12
  Fax: (33) 1 57 75 92 72
  Man. Dir. Graphic: Agnès Roger
  Phone: (33) 1 57 75 92 12
  Fax: (33) 1 57 75 92 72
  Man. Dir. Creative Papers: Jonathan Mitchell
  Phone: (33) 1 57 75 92 12
  Fax: (33) 1 57 75 92 72
Total Employees of Company: 4,050
Total Employees at this Location: 200
Mill Locations:
  Appleton Coated LLC, Combined Locks Mill, 540 Prospect St, Combined Locks, WI 54113, USA, Capacity: 362,655 mt/y, (Paper mill)
  Phone: (1) 920-788-3550
  Fax: (1) 920-687-3590
  Arjowiggins Papiers Couchés S.A., Aa Mill, Rue du Chocquet, F-62570 Wizernes, France, Capacity: 170,000 mt/y, (Paper mill)
  Phone: (33) 3 21 12 34 00
  Fax: (33) 3 21 12 34 99
  Email: graphic@arjowiggins.com
  Arjowiggins Papiers Couchés SAS, Bessé-sur-Braye Mill, 17 rue du 8 mai 1945, BP 3, F-72310 Bessé-sur-Braye, France, Capacity: 320,000 mt/y, (Paper mill)
  Phone: (33) 2 43 63 24 00
  Fax: (33) 2 43 63 24 10
  Email: graphic@arjowiggins.com
  Arjowiggins Le Bourray SAS, Le Bourray Mill, BP 3, Le Bourray, F-72470 Saint-Mars-la-Brière, France, Capacity: 116,000 mt/y, (Pulp mill, Paper mill)
  Phone: (33) 2 43 82 91 00
  Fax: (33) 2 43 82 91 01
  Email: norbert.michaud@arjowiggins.com, contact@bourray.com
  Arjowiggins Rives SAS, Charavines Mill, Bas Guillermet, 38 850 Charavines, France, Capacity: 22,000 mt/y, (Paper mill)
  Phone: (33) 4 76 55 76 26
  Fax: (33) 4 76 06 66 44
  Arjowiggins Chartham Ltd., Chartham Paper Mill, Station Rd., Chartham, Canterbury CT4 7JA, United Kingdom, Capacity: 8,000 mt/y, (Paper mill)
  Phone: (44) 1227 813 500
  Fax: (44) 1227 738 883
  Email: (firstname.lastname@arjowiggins.com)
  Arjowiggins Security SAS, Crèvecoeur Mill, F-77320 Jouy-sur-Morin, France, Capacity: 9,000 mt/y, (Paper mill)
  Phone: (33) 1 64 75 85 00
  Fax: (33) 1 64 75 85 10
  Arjowiggins Fine Papers Pty. Ltd., Stowford Mill, Ivybridge PL21 0AA, United Kingdom, Capacity: 14,000 mt/y, (Paper mill)
  Phone: (44) 1752 612 100
  Fax: (44) 1752 612 101
  Email: clive.wilson@arjowiggins.com
  Arjowiggins Fine Papers Pty. Ltd., Stoneywood Mill, Stoneywood Mill, Bucksburn, Aberdeen AB21 9AB, United Kingdom, Capacity: 60,000 mt/y, (Paper mill)
  Phone: (44) 1224 802 200
  Fax: (44) 1224 802 373
  Email: e-enquiries@arjowiggins.com
  Arjowiggins SAS, Palalda Mill, Route de Céret, F-66110 Amélie-les-Bains, France, Capacity: 36,000 mt/y, (Paper mill)
  Phone: (33) 4 68 87 97 00
  Fax: (33) 4 68 83 98 97
  Arjowiggins Ltda., Salto Mill, Rodovia Salto-Itu 30, 13324-195 Salto, SP, Brazil, Capacity: 26,220 mt/y, (Paper mill)
  Phone: (55) 11 4028 9200
  Fax: (55) 11 4028 9309
  Email: lina.nonaka@arjowiggins.com
  Arjowiggins Security B.V, Ugchelen Mill, Hoenderloseweg 84, NL-7339 GJ Ugchelen, Netherlands, Capacity: 5,000 mt/y, (Paper mill)
  Phone: (31) 55 533 2132
  Fax: (31) 55 533 6689
  Greenfield SAS, Château Thierry Pulp Mill, Zone Industrielle de la Grande Borne, F-02400 Château-Thierry, France, (Pulp mill)
  Phone: (33) 3 23 69 53 70
  Fax: (33) 3 23 69 53 71
  Email: contact@greenfieldsas.com, graphic@arjowiggins.com
  Guarro Casas S.A., Gelida Mill, Can Guarro s/n, E-08790 Gelida, Spain, Capacity: 7,000 mt/y, (Paper mill)
  Phone: (34) 93 7767676
  Fax: (34) 93 7767630
  Email: atencion.cliente@arjowiggins.com
  Zhejiang Halberd Paper Co., Ltd., Quzhou Mill (51% owned), No. 9 Donggang 4th Road, Donggang Industrial Zone, Quzhou 324000, China, Capacity: 5,000 mt/y, (Paper mill)
  Phone: (86) 570 888 6836/6800/ 383 2662
  Fax: (86) 570 888 6831

ⓜArjowiggins Papiers Couchés S.A.
Aa Mill
Mill is for sale (The company plan to initiate the process to sell the Wizernes mill. Would no acquirer be identified, the site is to be closed)
Ownership: Arjowiggins SAS
Rue du Chocquet
F-62570 Wizernes, Pas-de-Calais
France
  Phone: (33) 3 21 12 34 00
  Fax: (33) 3 21 12 34 99
  Email: graphic@arjowiggins.com
  Web Address: www.arjowiggins.com, www.arjowigginsgraphic.com
Personnel:
  Mill Mgr.: Olivier Avazzeri
  Phone: (33) 3 21 12 34 00
  Email: olivier.avazzeri@arjowiggins.com
  Prod. Mgr.: Patrick Désire
  Phone: (33) 3 21 12 35 50
  Email: patrick.desire@arjowiggins.com
Total Employees at this Location: 307
Type of Operation: Paper mill
Paper/Paperboard Grades and Capacities:
Total paper and paperboard capacity: 170,000 mt/y
Uncoated woodfree/freesheet: 17,000 mt/y
Coated woodfree/freesheet: 119,000 mt/y
Specialty and industrial: 34,000 mt/y
Paper and Paperboard Mill Data:
Stock Preparation:
Pulpers: 5
Refiners: 3
Paper Machines: 1
No. 5, fourdrinier, total capacity 170,000 mt/y, Trim width 3.8 m, Coated woodfree/freesheet, Uncoated woodfree/freesheet, Specialty and industrial
Coating Machines: 1
PM 5, total capacity 170,000 mt/y., off machine
Finishing Equipment:
Supercalenders: 2
Rewinders: 2
Sheeters: 3
Energy Data:
Combustion turbines: 1 at 10 MW
Electrical demand for mill: 307 MWh/D

ⓜArjowiggins Papiers Couchés SAS
Bessé-sur-Braye Mill
Ownership: Arjowiggins SAS
17 rue du 8 mai 1945, BP 3
F-72310 Bessé-sur-Braye
France
  Phone: (33) 2 43 63 24 00
  Fax: (33) 2 43 63 24 10
  Email: graphic@arjowiggins.com
  Web Address: www.arjowiggins.com, www.arjowigginsgraphic.com
Personnel:
  Mill Mgr.: Jean Cristophe Mailhan
  Phone: (33) 2 43 63 24 45
  Fax: (33) 2 43 63 24 10
  Prod. Mgr. (PM 3): Patrick Betti
  Phone: (33) 2 43 63 24 00
  Fax: (33) 2 43 63 24 10
  Email: patrick.betti@arjowiggins.com
  Prod. Mgr. (PM 2): Fabrice Fournier
  Phone: (33) 2 43 63 24 00
  Fax: (33) 2 43 63 24 10
  Email: fabrice.fournier@arjowiggins.com
  Maint. Mgr.: Jean-Yves Janvier
  Phone: (33) 2 43 63 24 00
  Fax: (33) 2 43 63 24 10
  Email: jean-yves.janvier@arjowiggins.com
  Purch. Mgr.: Gilles Leboulleux
  Phone: (33) 2 43 63 24 00
  Fax: (33) 2 43 63 24 10
  Email: gilles.leboulleux@arjowiggins.com
Total Employees at this Location: 554
Type of Operation: Paper mill
Paper/Paperboard Grades and Capacities:
Total paper and paperboard capacity: 320,000 mt/y
Coated woodfree/freesheet: 310,000 mt/y
Boxboard/cartonboard: 10,000 mt/y
Paper and Paperboard Mill Data:
Stock Preparation:
Pulpers: 3
Refiners: 4
Paper Machines: 2
No. 1, fourdrinier, total capacity 120,000 mt/y, Trim width 3.5 m, Coated woodfree/freesheet, Boxboard/cartonboard
No. 2, fourdrinier, total capacity 200,000 mt/y, Trim width 4.16 m, Coated woodfree/freesheet
Coating Machines: 3
PM 1, off machine
PM 2, off machine
No. 3, off machine
Finishing Equipment:
Supercalenders: 3
Rewinders: 3
Sheeters: 11
Energy Data:
Power boilers: 2
Combustion turbines: 1 at 43 MW
Electrical demand for mill: 541 MWh/D

ⓜArjowiggins Le Bourray SAS
Le Bourray Mill
Ownership: Arjowiggins SAS
BP 3, Le Bourray
F-72470 Saint-Mars-la-Brière
France

France

Phone: (33) 2 43 82 91 00
Fax: (33) 2 43 82 91 01
Email: norbert.michaud@arjowiggins.com,
contact@bourray.com
Web Address: www.arjowiggins.com,
www.arjowigginsgraphic.com
Personnel:
Pres.: Philippe Lacombe
Phone: (33) 2 43 82 91 00
Fax: (33) 2 43 82 91 02
Email: philippe.lacombe@arjowiggins.com
Mill Mgr.: Norbert Michaud
Phone: (33) 2 43 82 91 00
Fax: (33) 2 43 82 91 01
Email: norbert.michaud@arjowiggins.com
Prod. Mgr.: Christian Chaligné
Phone: (33) 2 43 82 91 00
Fax: (33) 2 43 82 91 01
Email: christian.chaligne@arjowiggins.com
Chief Eng. & Maint. Mgr.: Patrick Pissot
Phone: (33) 2 43 82 91 00
Fax: (33) 2 43 82 91 01
Email: patrick.pissot@arjowiggins.com
Finan. Mgr.: Olivier Lebesle
Phone: (33) 2 43 82 91 00
Fax: (33) 2 43 82 91 01
Email: olivier.lebesle@arjowiggins.com
HR. Mgr.: Christelle Dijon
Phone: (33) 2 43 82 91 00
Fax: (33) 2 43 82 91 01
Email: christelle.Dijon@arjowiggins.com
Total Employees at this Location: 275
Type of Operation: Pulp mill, Paper mill
Pulp Grades and Capacities:
Total pulp capacity: 75,472 mt/y
Recycled Pulping: 75,472 mt/y
Pulp Mill Data:
Recycled Fiber Treatment Lines:
Flotation deinking lines: 1 at 15,000 admt/y
Pulpers: 2
Washing deinking lines: 1 at 35,000 admt/y
Paper/Paperboard Grades and Capacities:
Total paper and paperboard capacity: 116,000 mt/y
Uncoated mechanical/groundwood: 13,000 mt/y
Coated mechanical/groundwood: 73,000 mt/y
Tissue: 30,000 mt/y
Paper and Paperboard Mill Data:
Stock Preparation:
Pulpers: 4
Refiners: 20
Paper Machines: 3
No. 1, (PM4, former type model: TOSCP Former), Papriformer, total capacity 86,000 mt/y, Trim width 3.6 m, Coated mechanical/groundwood, Uncoated mechanical/groundwood
No. 3, twin-wire, Yankee dryer, total capacity 8,000 mt/y, Trim width 1.85 m, Tissue
No. 4, (Former Type model: TISCO-Former), twin-wire, Yankee dryer, total capacity 22,000 mt/y, Trim width 2.75 m, Tissue
Coating Machines: 1
PM 1, total capacity 73,000 mt/y., on machine
Finishing Equipment:
Rewinders: 4
Sheeters: 1
Energy Data:
Power boilers: 1
Electrical demand for mill: 283 MWh/D

ⓜArjowiggins Rives SAS
Charavines Mill
Mill is for sale (Arjowiggins Creative Papers is considering to either sell or close mill if no buyer can be found)
Ownership: Arjowiggins SAS
Bas Guillermet
38 850 Charavines
France
Phone: (33) 4 76 55 76 26

Fax: (33) 4 76 06 66 44
Web Address: www.arjowiggins.com
Personnel:
Mill Mgr.: Daniel Triouleyre
Phone: (33) 4 76 55 76 26
Fax: (33) 4 76 06 66 44
Email: daniel.triouleyre@arjowiggins.com
Prod. Mgr.: Romain Cheradame
Phone: (33) 4 76 55 76 26
Fax: (33) 4 76 06 66 44
Email: romain.cheradame@arjowiggins.com
Maint. Mgr.: Michel Viat
Phone: (33) 4 76 55 76 26
Fax: (33) 4 76 06 66 44
Email: michel.viat@arjowiggins.com
Total Employees at this Location: 198
Type of Operation: Paper mill
Paper/Paperboard Grades and Capacities:
Total paper and paperboard capacity: 22,000 mt/y
Uncoated woodfree/freesheet: 22,000 mt/y
Paper and Paperboard Mill Data:
Paper Machines: 1
No. 2, fourdrinier, total capacity 22,000 mt/y, Trim width 2.3 m, Uncoated woodfree/freesheet
Energy Data:
Power boilers: 1
Electrical demand for mill: 49 MWh/D

ⓜArjowiggins Security SAS
Crèvecoeur Mill
Ownership: Arjowiggins SAS
F-77320 Jouy-sur-Morin
France
Phone: (33) 1 64 75 85 00
Fax: (33) 1 64 75 85 10
Web Address: www.arjowiggins.com,
www.security.arjowiggins.com
Personnel:
Tech. Services Mgr.: Pascal Barher
Phone: (33) 1 64 75 85 29
Fax: (33) 1 64 75 85 10
Email: pascal.barher@arjowiggins.com
Quality Mgr.: Patrick Quignot
Phone: (33) 1 64 75 85 16
Fax: (33) 1 64 75 85 10
Email: patrick.quignot@arjowiggins.com
Total Employees at this Location: 260
Type of Operation: Paper mill
Paper/Paperboard Grades and Capacities:
Total paper and paperboard capacity: 9,000 mt/y
Uncoated woodfree/freesheet: 9,000 mt/y
Uncoated mechanical/groundwood
Specialty and industrial
Paper and Paperboard Mill Data:
Stock Preparation:
Pulpers: 4
Refiners: 9
Paper Machines: 2
No. 4, cylinder, Trim width 2.6 m, Uncoated woodfree/freesheet, Specialty and industrial
No. 5, fourdrinier, Trim width 2.6 m, Uncoated woodfree/freesheet, Specialty and industrial
Finishing Equipment:
Rewinders: 1
Sheeters: 2

ⓜArjowiggins SAS
Palalda Mill
Route de Céret
F-66110 Amélie-les-Bains
France
Phone: (33) 4 68 87 97 00
Fax: (33) 4 68 83 98 97
Web Address: www.arjowiggins.com
Personnel:
Mill Mgr.: Fréderique Misset
Phone: (33) 4 68 87 97 00
Fax: (33) 4 68 83 98 97
Maint. Mgr.: Michel Fons

Phone: (33) 4 68 87 97 00
Fax: (33) 4 68 83 98 97
Email: michel.fons@arjowiggins.com
Asst. Mill Mgr.: Nadine Milhau
Phone: (33) 4 68 87 97 00
Fax: (33) 4 68 83 98 97
Email: nadine.milhau@arjowiggins.com
Total Employees at this Location: 250
Type of Operation: Paper mill
Paper/Paperboard Grades and Capacities:
Total paper and paperboard capacity: 36,000 mt/y
Specialty and industrial: 36,000 mt/y
Paper and Paperboard Mill Data:
Stock Preparation:
Pulpers: 3
Refiners: 14
Paper Machines: 3
No. 2, fourdrinier, total capacity 6,000 mt/y, Trim width 2.2 m, Specialty and industrial
No. 3, fourdrinier, total capacity 10,000 mt/y, Trim width 2.3 m, Specialty and industrial
No. 5, fourdrinier, total capacity 20,000 mt/y, Trim width 3 m, Specialty and industrial
Finishing Equipment:
Rewinders: 1
Sheeters: 3
Energy Data:
Power boilers: 3
Electrical demand for mill: 77 MWh/D

ⓒⓜPapeterie de la Banque de France
Vic-le-Comte Mill
Longues
F-63270 Vic-le-Comte
France
Phone: (33) 4 73 62 52 52
Fax: (33) 4 73 62 52 56
Email: infos@banque-france.fr
Personnel:
Mill Mgr.: Pascal Girnet
Phone: (33) 4 73 62 52 52
Prod. & Tech. Mgr.: Thierry Lance
Phone: (33) 4 73 62 52 52
Total Employees at this Location: 210
Type of Operation: Pulp mill, Paper mill
Pulp Grades and Capacities:
Total pulp capacity: 3,200 mt/y
Paper/Paperboard Grades and Capacities:
Total paper and paperboard capacity: 3,500 mt/y
Coated woodfree/freesheet: 3,500 mt/y
Paper and Paperboard Mill Data:
Paper Machines: 2
PM 2, fourdrinier, total capacity 2,000 mt/y, Trim width 1.26 m, Coated woodfree/freesheet
PM 6, cylinder, total capacity 1,500 mt/y, Trim width 1.26 m, Coated woodfree/freesheet
Energy Data:
Power boilers: 2
Electrical demand for mill: 80 MWh/D

ⓒⓜPapeteries de Bègles SAS
Bègles Mill
Ownership: Lafarge Platres
91 quai du Président Wilson
F-33130 Bègles
France
Phone: (33) 5 56 49 70 30
Fax: (33) 5 56 49 70 31
Personnel:
Man. Dir.: Mathieu Chateau
Phone: (33) 5 56 49 70 30
Maint. Mgr.: Eric Gresse
Phone: (33) 5 56 49 70 30
Prod. Dir.: Michel Camou
Phone: (33) 5 56 49 70 30
Total Employees of Company: 97
Total Employees at this Location: 97
Type of Operation: Pulp mill, Paperboard mill
Pulp Grades and Capacities:

France

Total pulp capacity: 76,308 mt/y
Recycled Pulping: 76,308 mt/y
Pulp Mill Data:
  Recycled Fiber Treatment Lines:
  Recycled packaging pulping lines: 2
Paper/Paperboard Grades and Capacities:
  Total paper and paperboard capacity: 77,000 mt/y
  Boxboard/cartonboard: 77,000 mt/y
Paper and Paperboard Mill Data:
  Stock Preparation:
  Pulpers: 2
  Refiners: 5
Paper Machines: 1
  No. 1, multi-fourdrinier, total capacity 77,000 mt/y, Trim width 4 m, Boxboard/cartonboard
Finishing Equipment:
  Rewinders: 1
Energy Data:
  Power boilers: 2
  Combustion turbines: 1 at 5 MW
  Electrical demand for mill: 114 MWh/D

ⓗⓜBiltube Europe Ltd.
St. Didier-en-Velay Mill
Company is idle, in liquidation (idled since March 2012, due to the market economic downturn. Placed in receivership and in liquidation since September 28, 2012)
Ownership: 100% by Biltube
Le Crouzet
F-43140 St. Didier-en-Velay
France
  Phone: (33) 6 0895 3669 / 4 7161 0591
  Fax: (33) 4 7161 0591 / 4 71 66 25 27
  Email: crouzet@biltube.com
  Web Address: www.biltube.com
Personnel:
  Mill Mgr.: Mr. Kore
  Phone: (33) 4 71 61 05 91
  Dir.: André Liogier
  Phone: (33) 4 71 61 05 91
  Tech. Mgr.: Mr. Meys
  Phone: (33) 4 71 61 05 91
  Maint. Mgr.: Mr. Meunier
  Phone: (33) 4 71 61 05 91
Total Employees at this Location: 35
Type of Operation: Paperboard mill
Paper/Paperboard Grades and Capacities:
  Total paper and paperboard capacity: 35,000 mt/y
  Boxboard/cartonboard: 35,000 mt/y
Paper and Paperboard Mill Data:
  Stock Preparation:
  Pulpers: 1
  Refiners: 1
Paper Machines: 1
  No. 1, fourdrinier, total capacity 35,000 mt/y, Trim width 2.7 m, Boxboard/cartonboard
Finishing Equipment:
  Rewinders: 1
  Sheeters: 1
Energy Data:
  Power boilers: 2

ⓗⓜBlue Paper SAS.
Stracel Mill
Ownership: 50% by Klingele Papierwerke GmbH & Co. KG, 50% by VPK Packaging Group
4 rue Charles Friedel Port du Rhin
F-67016 Strasbourg
France
Mailing Address: PO Box 79, F-67016 Strasbourg, France
  Phone: (33) 3 88 417532
  Fax: (33) 3 88 417598
  Email: info@bluepaper.eu
  Web Address: www.bluepaper.eu
Personnel:
  Dir. Gen.: François Bru
  Phone: (49) 388 417571
  Fax: (49) 388 417598
  Email: francois.bru@bluepaper.eu
  Qlty Hygiene & Environ. Mgr.: Karima Chakri
  Phone: (33) 388 417532
  Fax: (33) 388 417598
  Email: karima.chakri@bluepaper.eu
Total Employees at this Location: 140
Type of Operation: Paper mill
Pulp Grades and Capacities:
  Total pulp capacity: 267,462 mt/y
  Recycled Pulping: 267,462 mt/y
Pulp Mill Data:
  Recycled Fiber Treatment Lines:
  Recycled packaging pulping lines: 1
Paper/Paperboard Grades and Capacities:
  Total paper and paperboard capacity: 270,000 mt/y
  Linerboard: 160,000 mt/y
  Corrugating medium/fluting: 110,000 mt/y
Paper and Paperboard Mill Data:
Paper Machines: 1
  No. 1, GapFormer, total capacity 270,000 mt/y, Trim width 8.5 m, Corrugating medium/fluting, Linerboard
Energy Data:
  Power boilers
  Steam turbines: 1 at 17 MW
  Electrical demand for mill: 342 MWh/D

ⓗBolloré Thin Papers
Ownership: Republic Group
1080 Route Des Vignes Rouges, B.P. 43
74500 Thonon-les-Bains Cédex
France
  Phone: (33) 4 50 17 05 00
  Fax: (33) 4 50 17 06 32
  Web Address: www.bollorethinpapers.com
Personnel:
  Pres.: Phillipe Agut
  Phone: (33) 4 50 17 05 00
  Fax: (33) 4 50 17 06 32
  Chmn.: Michel Resseguier
  Phone: (33) 4 50 17 05 00
  Fax: (33) 4 50 17 06 32
  Gen. Mgr.: Manuel Gonzalez
  Phone: (33) 4 50 17 05 00
  Fax: (33) 4 50 17 06 32
  Sls. & Mktg. Mgr.: Bruno Delesque
  Phone: (33) 4 50 17 05 00
  Fax: (33) 4 50 17 06 32
Mill Locations:
Papeteries du Leman (PDL), Thonon-les-Bains Mill, 1080 Route d'Evian Publier, BP 43, F-74500 Thonon-les-Bains Cédex, France, Capacity: 45,000 mt/y, (Pulp mill, Paper mill)
  Phone: (33) 4 50 17 05 00
  Fax: (33) 4 50 17 06 32
  Email: marketing.pdl@pdl.fr
Papeteries des Vosges (PDV), Laval-sur-Vologne Mill, 34, rue Maurice Mougeot, BP 26, F-88600 Laval-sur-Vologne, France, Capacity: 52,500 mt/y, (Paper mill)
  Phone: (33) 3 29 53 52 00
  Fax: (33) 4 50 81 52 01
  Email: marketing.pdl@pdl.fr

ⓗⓜCartonnerie de la Boème
La Couronne
Les Beauvais
16400 La Couronne
France
  Phone: (33) 05 45 67 44 50
  Fax: (33) 05 45 67 47 05
  Email: cartonnerie-boeme@wanadoo.fr
Personnel:
  Pres & Dir. Gen (Administrative): Marcel Laurent Cohen
  Dir. Gen. (Production): Jean-Michel Cohen
Total Employees of Company: 20
Type of Operation: Paperboard mill
Paper/Paperboard Grades and Capacities:
  Total paper and paperboard capacity: 7,200 mt/y
  Boxboard/cartonboard: 7,200 mt/y
Paper and Paperboard Mill Data:
Paper Machines: 1
  No. 1, total capacity 7,200 mt/y, Boxboard/cartonboard

ⓗCanson SAS
Ownership: 10% by Hamelin Group
67 Rue Louis et Laurent Seguin
07104 Annonay
France
Mailing Address: B.P. 139, 07104 Annonay
  Phone: (33) 4 75 69 87 85
  Fax: (33) 4 75 69 89 99
  Web Address: www.hamelinbrands.com, www.canson.com
Personnel:
  CEO: Eric Joan
  Phone: (33) 4 75 69 88 00
  Fax: (33) 4 75 33 89 99
  Email: eric.joan@hamelinbrands.com
  Man. Dir.: Jacques Joly
  Phone: (33) 4 75 69 88 00
  Fax: (33) 4 75 33 89 99
  Email: Jacques.joly@hamelinbrands.com
Mill Locations:
Canson SAS, Moulin du Roy Mill, Moulin du Roy, F-07100 St. Marcel les Annonay, France, Capacity: 14,000 mt/y, (Paper mill)
  Phone: (33) 4 75 69 88 00
  Fax: (33) 4 75 33 89 99

ⓜCanson SAS
Moulin du Roy Mill
Moulin du Roy,
F-07100 St. Marcel les Annonay
France
Mailing Address: B.P. 139, 07104 Annonay, France
  Phone: (33) 4 75 69 88 00
  Fax: (33) 4 75 33 89 99
  Web Address: www.hamelinbrands.com, www.canson.com
Personnel:
  Mill Mgr.: Daniel Triouleyre
  Phone: (33) 4 75 69 88 00
  Fax: (33) 4 75 33 89 99
Total Employees at this Location: 120
Type of Operation: Paper mill
Paper/Paperboard Grades and Capacities:
  Total paper and paperboard capacity: 14,000 mt/y
  Uncoated woodfree/freesheet: 14,000 mt/y
Paper and Paperboard Mill Data:
  Stock Preparation:
  Pulpers: 4
  Refiners: 9
Paper Machines: 1
  No. 7, fourdrinier, total capacity 14,000 mt/y, Trim width 2.8 m, Uncoated woodfree/freesheet
Energy Data:
  Power boilers: 1
  Electrical demand for mill: 28 MWh/D

ⓗⓜCascades SAS
La Rochette Mill
Ownership: Cascades Inc.
Av. Maurice Frank
F-73110 La Rochette
France
Mailing Address: BP 1, F-73110 La Rochette, France
  Phone: (33) 4 79 65 32 32
  Fax: (33) 4 79 65 32 35
  Email: info@cascades-europe.com, contact@careo.biz
  Web Address: www.cascades-europe.com, www.careo.biz
Personnel:
  Mill Dir.: Jean Goulet
  Phone: (33) 4 79 65 32 32
  Fax: (33) 4 79 65 32 35

Email: jgoulet@cascades-europe.com
Oper. Mgr.: Raphaël Poullain
Phone: (33) 4 79 65 32 32
Fax: (33) 4 79 65 32 35
Email: rpoullain@cascades-europe.com
Machine Supt.: Julien Ravel
Phone: (33) 4 79 65 32 32
Fax: (33) 4 79 65 32 35
Email: jravel@cascades-europe.com
Total Employees of Company: 350
Total Employees at this Location: 350
Type of Operation: Pulp mill, Paperboard mill
Pulp Grades and Capacities:
 Total pulp capacity: 80,001 mt/y
 Mechanical Pulp: 80,001 mt/y
Pulp Mill Data:
 Mechanical Pulping Systems:
 TMP systems: 2
Paper/Paperboard Grades and Capacities:
 Total paper and paperboard capacity: 150,000 mt/y
 Boxboard/cartonboard: 150,000 mt/y
Paper and Paperboard Mill Data:
 Stock Preparation:
 Pulpers: 5
 Refiners: 10
Paper Machines: 2
 No. 2, cylinder, total capacity 55,000 mt/y, Trim width 2.4 m, Boxboard/cartonboard
 No. 3, Fourdrinier (4), total capacity 95,000 mt/y, Trim width 2.4 m, Boxboard/cartonboard
Coating Machines: 4
 No. 1, on machine
 No. 2, total capacity 6,000 mt/y., on machine
 No. 3, on machine
 No. 4, on machine
Finishing Equipment:
 Rewinders: 2
 Sheeters: 5
Energy Data:
 Power boilers: 2
 Combustion turbines: 1 at 6.0 MW
 Electrical demand for mill: 465 MWh/D

ⒽⓂPapeteries des Chatelles SAS
Raon L'Etape Mill
Ownership: 100% by Private
Les Chatelles, BP 9
F-88110 Raon L'Etape
France
 Phone: (33) 3 29 42 88 88
 Fax: (33) 3 29 41 51 98
 Web Address: www.chatelles.com
Personnel:
 Gen. Dir.: Eric Pommier
 Phone: (33) 3 29 42 88 88
 Gen.Mgr: Pierre Bertaux
 Phone: (33) 3 29 42 88 88
 Email: pierre.bertaux@chatelles.com
Total Employees of Company: 70
Total Employees at this Location: 70
Type of Operation: Paper mill
Pulp Grades and Capacities:
 Total pulp capacity: 2,635 mt/y
 Recycled Pulping: 2,635 mt/y
Paper/Paperboard Grades and Capacities:
 Total paper and paperboard capacity: 45,000 mt/y
 Uncoated woodfree/freesheet: 45,000 mt/y
Paper and Paperboard Mill Data:
Paper Machines: 1
 No. 1, fourdrinier, total capacity 45,000 mt/y, Trim width 2.62 m, Uncoated woodfree/freesheet
Energy Data:
 Power boilers: 2
 Electrical demand for mill: 99 MWh/D

ⓂPapeteries de Clairefontaine
Etival-Clairefontaine Mill
Ownership: 100% by Exacompta Clairefontaine
19 Rue de l'Abbaye
F-88480 Etival-Clairefontaine
France
 Phone: (33) 3 29 42 42 42
 Fax: (33) 3 29 42 42 00
 Email: clairefontaine.papiers@clairefontaine.com
 Web Address: www.papiers-clairefontaine.com
Personnel:
 Pres.: Frédéric Nusse
 Phone: (33) 3 29 42 42 42
 Consult. to Pres.: Jean-Marie Nusse
 Phone: (33) 3 29 42 42 42
 Gen. Dir.: Jean-Olivier Roussat
 Phone: (33) 3 29 42 42 42
 R&D Dir.: Pierre Beranger
 Phone: (33) 3 29 42 42 42
 Prod. & Tech. Mgr.: André Bauer
 Phone: (33) 6 84 97 08 44
 Fax: (33) 3 29 42 42 42
 Email: andre.bauer@clairefontaine.com
 Sls. Dir.: Michel Febvet
 Phone: (33) 3 29 42 42 42
Total Employees at this Location: 700
Type of Operation: Paper mill
Paper/Paperboard Grades and Capacities:
 Total paper and paperboard capacity: 160,000 mt/y
 Uncoated woodfree/freesheet: 160,000 mt/y
Paper and Paperboard Mill Data:
 Stock Preparation:
 Pulpers: 3
 Refiners: 10
Paper Machines: 2
 No. 5, twin former, total capacity 60,000 mt/y, Trim width 3.4 m, Uncoated woodfree/freesheet
 No. 6, Bel-Bond, total capacity 100,000 mt/y, Trim width 3.4 m, Uncoated woodfree/freesheet
Finishing Equipment:
 Rewinders: 2
 Sheeters: 4
Energy Data:
 Power boilers: 3
 Combustion turbines: 1 at 5.5 MW
 Steam turbines: 2 at 3.2, 3.2 MW
 Electrical demand for mill: 303 MWh/D

ⓂPapeteries de Condat
Condat le Lardin Mill
Ownership: 100% by Lecta S.A.
1523 avenue Georges Haupinot, BP 24
F-24570 Le Lardin St. Lazare
France
 Phone: (33) 5 53 51 43 33
 Fax: (33) 5 53 51 41 04
 Email: marketing@condat-pap.com
 Web Address: www.condat-pap.com
Personnel:
 Plt. Mgr.: Pere Canet
 Phone: (33) 5 53 51 41 09
 Fax: (33) 5 53 51 41 04
 Email: pere.canet@lecta.com
 Office Mgr.: Marta Gelis
 Phone: (33) 1 41 36 00 59
 Fax: (33) 5 53 51 41 04
 Email: marta.gelis@lecta.com
Total Employees at this Location: 519
Type of Operation: Paper mill
Paper/Paperboard Grades and Capacities:
 Total paper and paperboard capacity: 440,000 mt/y
 Coated woodfree/freesheet: 440,000 mt/y
Paper and Paperboard Mill Data:
 Stock Preparation:
 Pulpers: 6
 Refiners: 17
Paper Machines: 2
 No. 4, SymFormer MB, total capacity 210,000 mt/y, Trim width 4.6 m, Coated woodfree/freesheet
 No. 8, DuoFormer D, total capacity 230,000 mt/y, Trim width 5.1 m, Coated woodfree/freesheet
Coating Machines: 4
 PM 4, total capacity 200,000 mt/y., off machine
 PM 6, total capacity 130,000 mt/y., off machine
 PM 8, total capacity 210,000 mt/y., on machine
 No. 4, off machine
Finishing Equipment:
 Winders: 3
 Supercalenders: 3
 Sheeters: 7 at 354,000 mt/y
Energy Data:
 Power boilers: 2
 Combustion turbines: 2 at 85 MW
 Electrical demand for mill: 686 MWh/D

ⓂCorenso France
Soustre Mill
Mill is for sale (Powerflute has signed a conditional agreement with Stora Enso to acquire the coreboard and core manufacturer Corenso. The deal is expected to be closed in Q4 2014.)
Ownership: Corenso United Oy Ltd.
PO Box 4, Gours
F-33660 Saint-Seurin-Sur-L'Isle
France
Mailing Address: P.O. Box 4, F-33660 Saint-Seurin-sur-l'Isle, France
 Phone: (33) 5 57 56 40 00
 Fax: (33) 5 57 56 40 29
 Email: stephanie.claustres@storaenso.com
 Web Address: www.corenso.com
Personnel:
 Mill Dir.: Stéphanie Claustres
 Phone: (33) 5 57 56 40 00
 Fax: (33) 5 57 56 40 29
 Email: stephanie.claustres@storaenso.com
 Contrl.: Thierry Montouroy
 Phone: (33) 5 57 56 40 00
 Fax: (33) 5 57 56 40 29
 Email: thierry.montouroy@storaenso.com
 Logist. Mgr.: Patrick Maltor
 Phone: (33) 5 57 56 40 00
 Fax: (33) 5 57 56 40 29
 Email: patrick.maltor@storaenso.com
 Tech. & Maint. Mgr.: Jerome Mazet
 Phone: (33) 5 57 56 40 00
 Fax: (33) 5 57 56 40 29
 Email: jerome.mazet@storaenso.com
 Prod. Mgr.: Patrick Mesurat
 Phone: (33) 5 57 56 40 00
 Fax: (33) 5 57 56 40 29
 Email: patrick.mesurat@storaenso.com
 Environ. & Safety Mgr.: Maita Arbeloa
 Phone: (33) 5 57 56 40 00
 Fax: (33) 5 57 56 40 29
 Email: maita.arbeloa@storaenso.com
 Asst. Mill Mgr.: Karine Martinez
 Phone: (33) 5 57 56 40 00
 Fax: (33) 5 57 56 40 29
 Email: karine.martinez@storaenso.com
Total Employees at this Location: 86
Type of Operation: Pulp mill, Paperboard mill
Pulp Grades and Capacities:
 Total pulp capacity: 96,750 mt/y
 Recycled Pulping: 96,750 mt/y
Pulp Mill Data:
 Recycled Fiber Treatment Lines:
 Pulpers: 1 at 100,000
 Recycled packaging pulping lines: 1 at 100,000
Paper/Paperboard Grades and Capacities:
 Total paper and paperboard capacity: 95,000 mt/y
 Boxboard/cartonboard: 95,000 mt/y
Paper and Paperboard Mill Data:
Paper Machines: 1
 No. 1, fourdrinier, total capacity 95,000 mt/y, Trim width 2.82 m, Boxboard/cartonboard
Finishing Equipment:
 Rewinders: 1 at 90,000 mt/y
Energy Data:
 Power boilers: 1
 Electrical demand for mill: 103 MWh/D

France

ⓂDelipapier S.A.S.
Frouard Mill
Ownership: 60% by Sofidel Group
Ban la Dame, Parc d'Activités Nancy-Pompey
F-54390 Frouard
France
  Phone: (33) 3 83 49 53 53
  Fax: (33) 3 83 49 53 54
  Email: delipapier.fr@delipapier.fr,
  firstname.lastname@delipapier.fr
  Web Address: www.delipapier.fr
Personnel:
  Man. Dir.: Jean-Paul Cussenot
  Phone: (33) 3 83 49 53 53
  Fax: (33) 3 83 49 53 54
  Paper Mill Mgr.: François Lecomte
  Phone: (33) 3 83 49 53 53
  Fax: (33) 3 83 49 53 54
  Email: francois.lecomte@delipapier.fr
Total Employees at this Location: 490
Type of Operation: Paper mill
Paper/Paperboard Grades and Capacities:
  Total paper and paperboard capacity: 120,000 mt/y
  Tissue: 120,000 mt/y
Paper and Paperboard Mill Data:
  Stock Preparation:
  Pulpers: 3
Paper Machines: 2
  No. 1, crescent former, Yankee dryer, total capacity 60,000 mt/y, Trim width 5.45 m, Tissue
  No. 2, crescent former, Yankee dryer, total capacity 60,000 mt/y, Trim width 5.45 m, Tissue
Energy Data:
  Power boilers: 1
  Electrical demand for mill: 301 MWh/D

ⓂDelipapier S.A.S.
Roanne Mill
Ownership: 60% by Sofidel Group
112, Rue Mâtel
F-42335 Roanne Cédex
France
  Phone: (33) 4 77 68 82 68
  Fax: (33) 4 77 68 82 90
  Web Address: www.delipapier.fr
Personnel:
  Mill Mgr.: Mr. Vincent Domart
  Phone: (33) 4 77 68 82 68
  Fax: (33) 4 77 68 82 90
  Email: vincent.domart@delipapier.fr
  Maint. Mgr.: Antonio Pina
  Phone: (33) 4 77 68 82 68
  Fax: (33) 4 77 68 82 90
  Email: antonio.pina@delipapier.fr
  Prod. Mgr.: Patrick Stella
  Phone: (33) 4 77 68 82 68
  Fax: (33) 4 77 68 82 90
  Email: patrick.stella@delipapier.fr
Total Employees at this Location: 60
Type of Operation: Paper mill
Paper/Paperboard Grades and Capacities:
  Total paper and paperboard capacity: 30,000 mt/y
  Tissue: 30,000 mt/y
Paper and Paperboard Mill Data:
  Stock Preparation:
  Pulpers: 2
Paper Machines: 1
  No. 2, crescent former, Yankee dryer, total capacity 30,000 mt/y, Trim width 2.7 m, Tissue
Energy Data:
  Power boilers: 1
  Electrical demand for mill: 83 MWh/D

ⓄⓂDouble A (1991) Public Co., Ltd.
Alizay Mill
Ownership: 14.48% by Always Rich Holdings, 4.89% by Wiseley Managment Private, 1.99% by Other Private investors, 16.13% by Double A (1991) Public Co., Ltd., 62.51% by Double A Holdings Limited
Z.I. du Clos Pré, BP 1
F-27460 Alizay
France
  Phone: (33) 2 35 02 72 72
  Fax: (33) 2 35 02 14 60
  Email: christine.jamain@doubleapaper.eu, gaelle.louet@doubleapaper.eu
  Web Address: www.doubleapaper.com
Type of Operation: Paper mill
Pulp Mill Data:
Paper/Paperboard Grades and Capacities:
  Total paper and paperboard capacity: 300,000 mt/y
  Uncoated woodfree/freesheet: 300,000 mt/y
Paper and Paperboard Mill Data:
  Stock Preparation:
  Pulpers: 2
Paper Machines: 1
  No. 1, Bel-Baie V, total capacity 300,000 mt/y, Trim width 9.02 m, Uncoated woodfree/freesheet
Finishing Equipment:
  Rewinders: 2
  Sheeters: 3
Energy Data:
  Power boilers: 1
  Steam turbines: 1 at 12 MW
  Electrical demand for mill: 580 MWh/D

ⓂDS Smith Kaysersberg
11 Rte. Industrielle
F-68320 Kunheim
France
Mailing Address: BP 1, F-68320 Kunheim, France
  Phone: (33) 3 89 72 24 00
  Fax: (33) 3 89 72 61 54
  Email: dssmith-kaysersberg@dsskay.fr
  Web Address: www.dssmith-kaysersberg.fr
Personnel:
  Pres.: Jean Lienhardt
  Phone: (33) 3 8978 3039
  Fax: (33) 3 8947 1889
  Tech. Dir.: Alain Sirop
  Phone: (33) 3 8978 3039
  Fax: (33) 3 8947 1889
  Email: alain.sirop@dsskay.com
  Sls. & Mktg. Mgr.: Boris Hoffarth
  Phone: (33) 3 8978 3039
  Fax: (33) 3 8947 1889
  Email: boris.hoffarth@dsskay.com
  Prod. Mgr.: Philippe Bulfay
  Phone: (33) 3 8978 3039
  Fax: (33) 3 8947 1889
  Sls. Mgr.: Guillaume Maillot
  Phone: (33) 3 8978 3039
  Fax: (33) 3 8947 1889
  Head of Logist.: Vincent Weber
  Phone: (33) 3 8978 3039
  Fax: (33) 3 8947 1889
  HR. Mgr.: Patrice Durbin
  Phone: (33) 3 8978 3039
  Fax: (33) 3 8947 1889
Total Employees of Company: 1,010
Total Employees at this Location: 338
Mill Locations:
DS Smith Chouanard, Coullons Mill, Usine de la Fosse, BP 8, F-45720 Coullons, France, Capacity: 35,000 mt/y, (Paperboard mill)
  Phone: (33) 2 38 29 52 87
  Fax: (33) 2 38 29 22 38
  Email: info@dssmith.com
DS Smith Kaysersberg, Kaysersberg Mill, Route de Lapoutroie, BP 22, F-68240 Kaysersberg, France, Capacity: 170,000 mt/y, (Paperboard mill)
  Phone: (33) 3 89 78 30 00/39/43
  Fax: (33) 3 89 47 18 89
  Email: info@dssmith.com

ⓂDS Smith Packaging France
Ownership: 99% by DS Smith Plc
8, terrasse Bellini
92800 Puteaux
France
  Phone: (33) 1 49 01 48 48
  Fax: (33) 1 47 78 96 30
  Email: info@dssp.fr
  Web Address: www.dssmithpackaging.fr
Personnel:
  CEO: Mark Shaw
  Phone: (33) 1 49 01 48 48
  Fax: (33) 1 47 78 96 30
  CFO & IT Dir. France and Spain.: Philippe Hyzard
  Phone: (33) 1 49 01 48 48
  Fax: (33) 1 47 78 96 30
  Man. Dir.: Olivier Laurent
  Phone: (33) 1 49 01 48 48
  Fax: (33) 1 47 78 96 30
  Export. Dir.: Bernard Rivet
  Phone: (33) 1 49 01 48 48
  Fax: (33) 1 47 78 96 30
  Head of Communication: Christophe Furet
  Phone: (33) 1 49 01 48 48
  Fax: (33) 1 47 78 96 30
  Health & Safety Mgr.: Gouache Pascal
  Phone: (33) 1 49 01 48 48
  Fax: (33) 1 47 78 96 30
Total Employees of Company: 1,510
Total Employees at this Location: 46
Mill Locations:
DS Smith Packaging France, Contoire Hamel Mill, 39 Route Nationale, F-80500 Contoire Hamel, France, Capacity: 80,000 mt/y, (Pulp mill, Paperboard mill)
  Phone: (33) 3 22 78 77 76
  Fax: (33) 3 22 78 77 77
  Email: info@dssmith.com
DS Smith Packaging France, Nantes Mill, 33 Blvd Benoni-Goullin, F-44200 Nantes Cedex 02, France, Capacity: 53,000 mt/y, (Pulp mill, Paperboard mill)
  Phone: (33) 2 40 89 29 11
  Fax: (33) 2 40 35 21 01
  Email: info@dssmith.com

ⓂDS Smith Packaging France
Contoire Hamel Mill
Ownership: 99% by DS Smith Plc
39 Route Nationale
F-80500 Contoire Hamel
France
  Phone: (33) 3 22 78 77 76
  Fax: (33) 3 22 78 77 77
  Email: info@dssmith.com
  Web Address: www.dssmith.com
Personnel:
  Gen. Mgr.: Christian Picard
  Phone: (33) 3 22 78 77 76
  Prod. Mgr.: Thierry Vantyghem
  Phone: (33) 3 22 78 77 76
  Maint. Mgr.: Jean Claude Dupont
  Phone: (33) 3 22 78 77 76
Total Employees at this Location: 270
Type of Operation: Pulp mill, Paperboard mill
Pulp Grades and Capacities:
  Total pulp capacity: 80,433 mt/y
  Recycled Pulping: 80,433 mt/y
Pulp Mill Data:
  Recycled Fiber Treatment Lines:
  Pulpers at 90,000 admt/y
Paper/Paperboard Grades and Capacities:
  Total paper and paperboard capacity: 80,000 mt/y
  Linerboard: 50,000 mt/y
  Corrugating medium/fluting: 30,000 mt/y
Paper and Paperboard Mill Data:
  Stock Preparation:
  Refiners: 1
Paper Machines: 1
  No. 1, fourdrinier (2), total capacity 80,000 mt/y, Trim width 2.46 m, Corrugating medium/fluting, Linerboard

Energy Data:
Power boilers: 2
Electrical demand for mill: 93 MWh/D

Ⓜ DS Smith Chouanard
Coullons Mill
Ownership: DS Smith Kaysersberg
Usine de la Fosse, BP 8
F-45720 Coullons, Loiret
France
 Phone: (33) 2 38 29 52 87
 Fax: (33) 2 38 29 22 38
 Email: info@dssmith.com
 Web Address: www.dssmith.com
Personnel:
 Mill Mgr.: Serge Segura
 Phone: (33) 2 38 29 27 51
 Fax: (33) 2 38 29 22 38
 Email: serge.segura@dsskay.com
 Tech. & Maint. Mgr.: Alain Hussonnois
 Phone: (33) 2 38 29 52 87
 Fax: (33) 2 38 29 22 38
 Email: alain.hussonnois@dsskay.com
 Sls. Mgr.: Isabelle Roume
 Phone: (33) 2 38 29 52 87
 Fax: (33) 2 38 29 22 38
 Email: isabelle.roume@dsskay.com
Total Employees at this Location: 80
Type of Operation: Paperboard mill
Pulp Grades and Capacities:
 Total pulp capacity: 29,535 mt/y
 Recycled Pulping: 29,535 mt/y
Pulp Mill Data:
 Recycled Fiber Treatment Lines:
 Pulpers: 1 at 31,700
Paper/Paperboard Grades and Capacities:
 Total paper and paperboard capacity: 35,000 mt/y
 Boxboard/cartonboard: 35,000 mt/y
Paper and Paperboard Mill Data:
 Stock Preparation:
 Pulpers:
Paper Machines: 2
 No. 1, fourdrinier (2), total capacity 29,000 mt/y, Trim width 1.95 m, Boxboard/cartonboard
 No. 2, fourdrinier, total capacity 6,000 mt/y, Trim width 1.95 m, Boxboard/cartonboard
Coating Machines: 1
 PM 1, on machine
Energy Data:
 Power boilers: 1
 Electrical demand for mill: 45 MWh/D

Ⓜ DS Smith Kaysersberg
Kaysersberg Mill
Ownership: 100% by DS Smith Plc
Route de Lapoutroie, BP 22
F-68240 Kaysersberg
France
 Phone: (33) 3 89 78 30 00/39/44
 Fax: (33) 3 89 47 18 89
 Email: info@dssmith.com
 Web Address: www.dssmith.com
Personnel:
 Man Dir.: Philippe Heinrich
 Phone: (33) 3 89 78 30 32
 Fax: (33) 3 89 47 18 89
 Email: philippe.heinrich@dsskay.com
 Purch. Mgr.: Chantal Bourel
 Phone: (33) 3 89 78 31 18
 Fax: (33) 3 89 47 12 91
 Email: chantal.bourel@dsskay.com
 Sls. Mgr.: Jean-Marie Monfort
 Phone: (33) 3 89 78 30 00/39/44
 Fax: (33) 3 89 47 18 89
 Email: jean-marie.monfort@dsskay.com
 Reporting Contrl.: Élodie Loewert
 Phone: (33) 3 89 72 24 54
 Fax: (33) 3 89 47 18 89
 Email: elodie.loewert@dsskay.com
Total Employees at this Location: 200
Type of Operation: Paperboard mill
Pulp Grades and Capacities:
 Total pulp capacity: 174,073 mt/y
 Recycled Pulping: 174,073 mt/y
Pulp Mill Data:
 Recycled Fiber Treatment Lines:
 Pulpers: 1 at 183,700
Paper/Paperboard Grades and Capacities:
 Total paper and paperboard capacity: 170,000 mt/y
 Linerboard: 55,000 mt/y
 Boxboard/cartonboard: 115,000 mt/y
Paper and Paperboard Mill Data:
 Stock Preparation:
 Pulpers: 5
 Refiners: 2
Paper Machines: 2
 No. 1, cylinder (8), total capacity 40,000 mt/y, Trim width 2.2 m, Boxboard/cartonboard, Linerboard
 No. 2, cylinder (8), total capacity 130,000 mt/y, Trim width 3.4 m, Boxboard/cartonboard, Linerboard
Finishing Equipment:
 Rewinders: 3 at 200,000 mt/y
 Sheeters: 2 at 24,000 mt/y
Energy Data:
 Power boilers: 3
 Combustion turbines: 1 at 10 MW
 Steam turbines: 2 at 4 MW
 Electrical demand for mill: 212 MWh/D

Ⓜ DS Smith Packaging France
Nantes Mill
Ownership: 99% by DS Smith Plc
33 Blvd Benoni-Goullin
F-44200 Nantes Cedex 02
France
Mailing Address: BP 70113, 44201 Nantes Cedex 02, France
 Phone: (33) 2 40 89 29 11
 Fax: (33) 2 40 35 21 01
 Email: info@dssmith.com
 Web Address: www.dssmith.com
Personnel:
 Man. Dir.: Heinrich Philippe
 Phone: (33) 3 89 78 30 32
 Fax: (33) 2 40 35 21 01
 Email: philippe.heinrich@dsskay.com
 Chief. Eng.: Claire Sans
 Phone: (33) 2 40 89 29 11
 Fax: (33) 2 40 35 21 01
 Email: claire.sans@dsskay.com
 Commun. Mgr.: Christine Meul
 Phone: (33) 2 40 89 29 11
 Fax: (33) 2 40 35 21 01
 Email: christine.meul@dssmith.eu
Total Employees at this Location: 69
Type of Operation: Pulp mill, Paperboard mill
Pulp Grades and Capacities:
 Total pulp capacity: 52,372 mt/y
 Recycled Pulping: 52,372 mt/y
Pulp Mill Data:
 Recycled Fiber Treatment Lines:
 Pulpers: 2 at 70,000 admt/y
Paper/Paperboard Grades and Capacities:
 Total paper and paperboard capacity: 53,000 mt/y
 Linerboard: 53,000 mt/y
Paper and Paperboard Mill Data:
 Stock Preparation:
 Refiners: 2
Paper Machines: 1
 No. 1, fourdrinier (2), total capacity 53,000 mt/y, Trim width 2.9 m, Linerboard
Finishing Equipment:
 Winders: 1
Energy Data:
 Power boilers: 1
 Electrical demand for mill: 73 MWh/D

Ⓜ Bernard Dumas SAS
Creysse Mill
Ownership: Hokuetsu Kishu Paper Co. Ltd.
2 Rue de la Papeterie
F-24100 Creysse
France
Mailing Address: BP 3, F-24100 Creysse, France
 Phone: (33) 5 53 23 21 05
 Fax: (33) 5 53 23 37 13
 Email: bdumas@bernard-dumas.fr, tec@bernrad-dumas.com
 Web Address: www.bernard-dumas.fr
Personnel:
 Gen. Mgr., Mill Mgr.: Daniel Doillon
 Phone: (33) 5 53 23 21 05
 Email: daniel.doillon@bernard-dumas.fr
 Chief Lab.: Sylvie Bayle
 Phone: (33) 5 53 23 21 05
 Commer. Mgr.: Thierry Touzeau
 Phone: (33) 5 53 23 21 05
Total Employees at this Location: 40
Type of Operation: Paper mill
Paper/Paperboard Grades and Capacities:
 Total paper and paperboard capacity: 10,000 mt/y
 Specialty and industrial: 10,000 mt/y

Ⓜ Emin Leydier
Ownership: 100% by FINEL
Cite Internationale, 66 Quai Charles de Gaulle
F-69463 Lyon Cedex 06
France
 Phone: (33) 4 72 69 56 70
 Fax: (33) 4 72 69 56 99
 Email: direction.generale@emin-leydier.com
 Web Address: www.emin-leydier.com
Personnel:
 Chmn.: Yves Herbaut
 Phone: (33) 4 72 69 56 70
 Fax: (33) 4 72 69 56 99
 Email: yves.herbaut@emin-leydier.com
 Admin. & Finan. Dir.: Thierry Emin
 Phone: (33) 4 72 69 56 70
 Fax: (33) 4 72 69 56 99
 Email: thierry.emin@emin-leydier.com
 Ind. Dir.: Hugues Leydier
 Phone: (33) 4 72 69 56 70
 Fax: (33) 4 72 69 56 99
 Email: hugues.leydier@emin-leydier.com
 Man. Dir., Packaging Division: Christophe Souquet
 Phone: (33) 4 72 69 56 70
 Fax: (33) 4 72 69 56 99
 Email: christophe.souquet@emin-leydier.com
 HR Dir.: Didier Wurtz
 Phone: (33) 4 72 69 56 70
 Fax: (33) 4 72 69 56 99
 Email: didier.wurtz@emin-leydier.com
 Purch. Mgr.: Catherine Sarrazin
 Phone: (33) 4 72 69 56 70
 Fax: (33) 4 72 69 56 99
 Email: catherine.sarrazin@emin-leydier.com
Total Employees of Company: 1,000
Total Employees at this Location: 15
Mill Locations:
Emin Leydier, Champblain Mill, Champblain - Laveyron, BP 32, F-26241 Saint-Vallier Cedex, France, Capacity: 480,000 mt/y, (Paperboard mill)
 Phone: (33) 4 75 23 86 00
 Fax: (33) 4 75 23 86 06
 Email: papeteries@emin-leydier.com, service.relation.client@emin-leydier.com
Emin Leydier, Nogent-sur-Seine Mill, Zone Industrielle des Guignons, F-10400 Nogent-sur-Seine, France, Capacity: 300,000 mt/y, (Paperboard mill)
 Phone: (33) 3 25 21 88 15
 Fax: (33) 3 25 21 88 44

Ⓜ Emin Leydier
Champblain Mill
Champblain - Laveyron, BP 32

France

F-26241 Saint-Vallier Cedex
France
Mailing Address: BP 32, F-26241 Saint-Vallier Cedex, Drôme, France
Phone: (33) 4 75 23 86 00
Fax: (33) 4 75 23 86 06
Email: papeteries@emin-leydier.com, service.relation.client@emin-leydier.com
Web Address: www.emin-leydier.com
Personnel:
Gen. Mgr.: Vincent Chapelle
Phone: (33) 4 75 23 86 00
Industrial Dir.: Philippe Antoine
Phone: (33) 4 75 23 86 00
Sls. Mgr.: Jiri Krcmar
Phone: (33) 4 75 23 86 00
Dir. of Commun.: Patrick Aubague
Phone: (33) 4 72 69 56 70
Email: patrick.aubague@emin-leydier.com
Asst. Gen. Mgr.: Eva Ruard
Phone: (33) 4 75 23 86 00
Total Employees at this Location: 280
Type of Operation: Paperboard mill
Pulp Grades and Capacities:
Total pulp capacity: 473,715 mt/y
Recycled Pulping: 473,715 mt/y
Pulp Mill Data:
Recycled Fiber Treatment Lines:
Recycled packaging pulping lines: 1 at 540,000
Paper/Paperboard Grades and Capacities:
Total paper and paperboard capacity: 480,000 mt/y
Linerboard: 160,000 mt/y
Corrugating medium/fluting: 320,000 mt/y
Paper and Paperboard Mill Data:
Paper Machines: 2
No. 5, hybrid former, total capacity 160,000 mt/y, Trim width 5.22 m, Corrugating medium/fluting, Linerboard
No. 6, Bel-Baie, total capacity 320,000 mt/y, Trim width 7.55 m, Corrugating medium/fluting, Linerboard
Energy Data:
Power boilers: 1
Combustion turbines: 1 at 45 MW
Electrical demand for mill: 596 MWh/D

ⓂEmin Leydier
Nogent-sur-Seine Mill
Zone Industrielle des Guignons
F-10400 Nogent-sur-Seine, Aube
France
Phone: (33) 3 25 21 88 15
Fax: (33) 3 25 21 88 44
Web Address: www.emin-leydier.com
Personnel:
Plant Mgr.: Michel Hartman
Phone: (33) 3 25 21 88 32
Email: michel.hartman@emin-leydier.com
Fabrication Mgr.: Delphine Martinez
Phone: (33) 3 25 21 88 37
Email: delphine.martinez@emin-leydier.com
Maint. Mgr.: Fabien Sorgeot
Phone: (33) 3 25 21 88 18
Total Employees at this Location: 110
Type of Operation: Paperboard mill
Pulp Grades and Capacities:
Total pulp capacity: 292,216 mt/y
Recycled Pulping: 292,216 mt/y
Pulp Mill Data:
Recycled Fiber Treatment Lines:
Pulpers: 1 at 330,000 admt/y
Recycled packaging pulping lines: 1 at 330,000 admt/y
Paper/Paperboard Grades and Capacities:
Total paper and paperboard capacity: 300,000 mt/y
Linerboard: 100,000 mt/y
Corrugating medium/fluting: 200,000 mt/y
Paper and Paperboard Mill Data:
Paper Machines: 1
No. 7, GapFormer, total capacity 300,000 mt/y, Trim width 5.5 m, Corrugating medium/fluting, Linerboard

Finishing Equipment:
Winders: 1 at 330,000 mt/y
Energy Data:
Power boilers: 1
Electrical demand for mill: 346 MWh/D

ⓂEuropac Papeterie de Rouen
St. Etienne du Rouvray Mill
Ownership: 100% by Europac - Papeles y Cartones de Europa S.A.
Rue Desiré Granet, BP 30444
F-76808 St. Etienne du Rouvray Cedex
France
Phone: (33) 2 35 64 52 52/51 49
Fax: (33) 2 35 64 51 32/04 52 89
Email: www.europacgroup.com
Personnel:
Man. Dir.: José Castro
Phone: (33) 2 35 64 52 52
Fax: (33) 2 35 64 51 32
Email: jcastro@europacgroup.com
Prod. Mgr.: Mrs. Nathalie Galli
Phone: (33) 2 35 64 52 52
Fax: (33) 2 35 64 51 32
Email: ngalli@europacgroup.com
Electrical Eng.: Frederic Simon
Phone: (33) 2 35 64 52 74
Fax: (33) 2 35 64 51 32
Email: fsimon@europacgroup.com
Sls. Mgr.: Jose Luis Mestre
Phone: (33) 2 35 64 52 52
Fax: (33) 2 35 64 51 32
Email: jlmestre@europacgroup.com
Commun. Mgr.: Remi Poirson
Phone: (33) 2 35 64 52 52
Fax: (33) 2 35 64 51 32
Email: rpoirson@europacgroup.com
Total Employees at this Location: 160
Type of Operation: Pulp mill, Paperboard mill
Pulp Grades and Capacities:
Total pulp capacity: 299,946 mt/y
Recycled Pulping: 299,946 mt/y
Pulp Mill Data:
Recycled Fiber Treatment Lines:
Pulpers: 1 at 370,000 admt/y
Paper/Paperboard Grades and Capacities:
Total paper and paperboard capacity: 300,000 mt/y
Corrugating medium/fluting: 300,000 mt/y
Paper and Paperboard Mill Data:
Stock Preparation:
Pulpers: 1
Refiners: 7
Paper Machines: 1
No. 5, Bel-Baie, total capacity 300,000 mt/y, Trim width 7 m, Corrugating medium/fluting
Finishing Equipment:
Rewinders: 3 at 350,000 mt/y
Energy Data:
Power boilers: 2
Combustion turbines: 3 at 103 MW
Electrical demand for mill: 392 MWh/D

ⓄⓂEverbal
Evergnicourt Mill
Ownership: 100% by Exacompta Clairefontaine
2 route d'Avaux
F-02190 Evergnicourt
France
Phone: (33) 3 23 23 62 80 / 62 62
Fax: (33) 3 23 23 62 99
Email: everbal@everbal.fr, commercial.papier@everbal.fr
Web Address: www.exacomptaclairefontaine.fr, www.papiers-clairefontaine.com
Personnel:
Pres. & CEO: Jean-Marie Nusse
Phone: (33) 3 23 23 62 80
Gen. Mgr.: Frederic Nusse

Phone: (33) 3 23 23 62 80
Mill Mgr./Sls. Mgr./Product Devlpt. Mgr.: Hervé Deglave
Phone: (33) 3 23 23 62 80
Email: h.deglave@everbal.fr
Admin. & Finan. Dir.: Yves Appert
Phone: (33) 3 23 23 62 80
Admin Sec.: Virginie Feszezur
Phone: (33) 3 23 23 62 80
Total Employees at this Location: 130
Type of Operation: Pulp mill, Paper mill
Pulp Grades and Capacities:
Total pulp capacity: 41,554 mt/y
Recycled Pulping: 41,554 mt/y
Pulp Mill Data:
Recycled Fiber Treatment Lines:
Pulpers: 2
Paper/Paperboard Grades and Capacities:
Total paper and paperboard capacity: 40,000 mt/y
Uncoated woodfree/freesheet: 40,000 mt/y
Paper and Paperboard Mill Data:
Stock Preparation:
Pulpers: 2
Refiners: 2
Paper Machines: 1
No. 2, Bel-Bond, total capacity 40,000 mt/y, Trim width 3.1 m, Uncoated woodfree/freesheet
Finishing Equipment:
Rewinders: 4
Sheeters: 4
Energy Data:
Power boilers: 1
Electrical demand for mill: 64 MWh/D

ⓄExacompta Clairefontaine
Ownership: Public
19, rue de l'Abbaye, BP 1
F-88480 Etival-Clairefontaine
France
Phone: (33) 3 29 42 42 42
Fax: (33) 3 29 42 42 00
Email: actionnaire@clairefontaine.com
Web Address: www.exacomptaclairefontaine.fr
Personnel:
Pres. & CEO: François Nusse
Phone: (33) 1 40 40 44 44
Fax: (33) 1 42 41 09 60
Email: info@exacompta.com
Snr. VP.: Jean-Claude Gilles Nusse
Phone: (33) 1 40 40 44 70
Fax: (33) 1 45 42 30 20
Email: gilles.nusse@afa.fr
Total Employees of Company: 3,137
Total Employees at this Location: 650
Mill Locations:
Papeteries de Clairefontaine, Etival-Clairefontaine Mill, 19 Rue de l'Abbaye, F-88480 Etival-Clairefontaine, France, Capacity: 160,000 mt/y, (Paper mill)
Phone: (33) 3 29 42 42 42
Fax: (33) 3 29 42 42 00
Email: clairefontaine.papiers@clairefontaine.com
Everbal, Evergnicourt Mill, 2 route d'Avaux, F-02190 Evergnicourt, France, Capacity: 40,000 mt/y, (Pulp mill, Paper mill)
Phone: (33) 3 23 23 62 80 / 62 62
Fax: (33) 3 23 23 62 99
Email: everbal@everbal.fr, commercial.papier@everbal.fr
Papeterie de Mandeure SA, Mandeure Mill, 14 rue de la Papeterie, F-25350 Mandeure, France, Capacity: 35,000 mt/y, (Paper mill)
Phone: (33) 3 81 35 20 52
Fax: (33) 3 81 35 30 07
Email: commercial@mandeure.com
Schut Papier, Heelsum Mill, Kabeljauw 2, NL-6866 NE Heelsum, Netherlands, Capacity: 3,000 mt/y, (Paper mill)
Phone: (31) 317 31 9110
Fax: (31) 317 31 2754
Email: Info@schutpapier.com

France

ⓜFibre Excellence Saint-Gaudens
St. Gaudens Mill
Ownership: Paper Excellence Group
Blvd. du Président Saragat, BP 149
F-31803 Saint Gaudens Cedex
France
   Phone: (33) 5 61 94 75 75
   Fax: (33) 5 61 94 75 76
   Web Address: www.fibre-excellence.com
Personnel:
   Mill Mgr.: Patrick Chiron
   Phone: (33) 5 61 94 75 64
   Fax: (33) 5 61 94 75 76
   Email: patrick.chiron@fibre-excellence.com
   Qlty. & Safety & Environ. Mgr.: Jean Mazauric
   Phone: (33) 5 61 94 75 75
   Fax: (33) 5 61 94 75 76
   Email: jean.mazauric@fibre-excellence.com
Total Employees at this Location: 255
Type of Operation: Pulp mill
Pulp Grades and Capacities:
   Total pulp capacity: 306,699 mt/y
   Pulp available for market: 305,000 mt/y
   Chemical Pulp: 303,318 mt/y
Pulp Mill Data:
   Chemical Pulping Systems:
   Continuous digesters: 1
   Bleach Plant Systems: 1
   No. 1, Sequence: O$_2$ DEoDD, Capacity 320,000 admt/y
   Chemical Recovery Equipment:
   Evaporator lines: 1
   Recovery boilers: 1
   Lime Kiln
   Pulp Dryers:
   Air Float dryers 1
Energy Data:
   Power boilers: 1
   Steam turbines: 2 at 20, 20 MW
   Electrical demand for mill: 626 MWh/D

ⓜFibre Excellence Tarascon
Tarascon Mill
Ownership: Paper Excellence Group
Route de la Cellulose
F-13156 Tarascon Cedex
France
Mailing Address: BP 8, F-13150 Tarascon, France
   Phone: (33) 4 90 91 03 00
   Fax: (33) 4 90 91 041 1/31 73
   Web Address: www.fibre-excellence.com
Personnel:
   Prod. Mgr. (since 2010): Sebastien Riviere
   Phone: (33) 4 90 94 63 40
   Fax: (33) 4 90 91 04 03
   Email: sebastien.riviere@fibre-excellence.com
   Purch. Mgr.: Jeanne Murgia
   Phone: (33) 4 90 91 63 14
   Fax: (33) 4 90 91 31 73
   Email: jeanne.murgia@fibre-excellence.com
   HR Dir.: Richard Gagnac
   Phone: (33) 4 90 91 63 70
   Fax: (33) 4 90 91 63 07
   Email: richard.gagnac@fibre-excellence.com
   Environ. Mgr.: Jean-Paul Ansel
   Phone: (33) 4 90 91 63 60
   Fax: (33) 4 90 91 63 07
   Email: jean-paul.ansel@fibre-excellence.com
Total Employees at this Location: 275
Type of Operation: Pulp mill
Pulp Grades and Capacities:
   Total pulp capacity: 251,408 mt/y
   Pulp available for market: 250,000 mt/y
   Chemical Pulp: 252,781 mt/y
Pulp Mill Data:
   Chemical Pulping Systems:
   Continuous digesters: 1
Pulp Lines: 1

Bleach Plant Systems: 1
No. 1, Sequence: DEOpDEpD, Capacity 260,000 admt/y
Chemical Recovery Equipment:
Evaporator lines: 1
Evaporator lines: 1
Recovery boilers: 1
Lime Kiln
Pulp Dryers:
Air Float dryers 1
Energy Data:
Power boilers: 1
Steam turbines: 3 at 12.5, 14, 14 MW
Electrical demand for mill: 539 MWh/D

ⓗⓜPapeteries de Fures
Tullins Mill
Ownership: Guely SA
139 Blvd. Michel Perret
F-38210 Fures, Tullins
France
Mailing Address: BP 2, F-38210 Tullins, France
   Phone: (33) 4 76 07 77 77
   Fax: (33) 4 76 07 03 75
   Email: info@guely.fr
   Web Address: www.guely.fr
Personnel:
   Gen. & Sls. Mgr.: Bernard Guély
   Phone: (33) 4 76 07 77 77
   Prod. Mgr.: Gerald Sisoix
   Phone: (33) 4 76 07 77 77
   Purch./Finan. Dir.: Bruno Guély
   Phone: (33) 4 76 07 77 77
Total Employees of Company: 37
Total Employees at this Location: 37
Type of Operation: Paper mill
Paper/Paperboard Grades and Capacities:
   Total paper and paperboard capacity: 4,000 mt/y
   Packaging papers: 4,000 mt/y
Paper and Paperboard Mill Data:
   Stock Preparation:
   Pulpers: 1
   Refiners: 1
Paper Machines: 1
No. 1, table plate, total capacity 4,000 mt/y, Trim width 1.5 m, Packaging papers
Finishing Equipment:
   Supercalenders: 1
   Rewinders: 2
   Sheeters: 1
Energy Data:
   Power boilers: 1
   Electrical demand for mill: 16 MWh/D

ⓗGascogne SA
Ownership: 26.90% by Electricité et Eaux de Madagascar
650, avenue Pierre Benoit
F-40993 St. Paul-lès-Dax
France
Mailing Address: BP 98, F-40993 St. Paul les Dax Cedex, France
   Phone: (33) 5 58 56 54 00
   Fax: (33) 5 58 74 55 48
   Email: info@groupe-gascogne.com
   Web Address: www.groupe-gascogne.com
Personnel:
   Chmn. & CEO: Frédèric Doulcet
   Phone: (33) 5 58 56 54 00
   Fax: (33) 5 58 74 55 48
   Email: fdoulcet@groupe-gascogne.com
   COO: Patrick Bordessoule
   Phone: (33) 5 58 56 54 00
   Fax: (33) 5 58 74 55 48
   Email: pbordessoule@groupe-gascogne.com
   Oper. Mgr. Sack Div.: Olivier Tassel
   Phone: (33) 5 58 09 90 17
   Fax: (33) 5 58 74 55 48
   Email: otassel@groupe-gascogne.com
   Oper. Mgr. Wood Div.: Patrick Dubreil
   Phone: (33) 5 58 56 54 00
   Fax: (33) 5 58 74 55 48
   Email: pdubreil@groupe-gascogne.com
   Oper. Mgr. Laminates: Philippe Lavaud
   Phone: (33) 5 58 56 60 60
   Fax: (33) 5 58 56 60 10
   Email: plavaud@groupe-gascogne.com
   Manuf. Mgr. Paper Div.: Alain Ayral
   Phone: (33) 5 58 56 54 00
   Fax: (33) 5 58 74 55 48
   Email: aayral@groupe-gascogne.com
   HR Mgr. Paper Div.: Marie-Christine Dane
   Phone: (33) 5 58 56 54 00
   Fax: (33) 5 58 74 55 48
   Email: mcdane@groupe-gascogne.com
   Mktg. Dir.: Jean-Eric Gancille
   Phone: (33) 5 58 56 54 00
   Fax: (33) 5 58 74 55 48
   Email: jegancille@groupe-gascogne.com
   CFO Paper & Sack Div.: Williams Marquet
   Phone: (33) 5 58 56 54 00
   Email: wmarquet@groupe-gascogne.com
   Dir. Commun.: Helene Tailleur
   Phone: (33) 5 58 56 54 11
   Fax: (33) 5 58 74 55 48
   Email: htailleur@groupe-gascogne.com
Total Employees of Company: 2,125
Total Employees at this Location: 30
Mill Locations:
Gascogne Paper, Mimizan Mill, BP8, Cedex 01, F-40201 Mimizan, France, Capacity: 159,958 mt/y, (Pulp mill, Paper mill)
   Phone: (33) 5 58 09 90 00
   Fax: (33) 5 58 09 90 61
   Email: mill@gascognepaper.com

ⓜGascogne Paper
Mimizan Mill
Ownership: Gascogne SA
BP 8, Cedex 01
F-40201 Mimizan, Landes
France
   Phone: (33) 5 58 09 90 00
   Fax: (33) 5 58 09 90 61
   Email: mill@gascognepaper.com
   Web Address: www.gascognepaper.com
Personnel:
   CEO: Olivier Tassel
   Phone: (33) 5 58 09 90 00
   Fax: (33) 5 58 09 90 61
   Email: otassel@gascognepaper.com
   Mill Mgr.: Bernard Betremieux
   Phone: (33) 5 58 09 90 00
   Fax: (33) 5 58 09 90 61
   Email: bbetrmieux@gascognepaper.com
   HR Mgr.: Marie-Christine Dane
   Phone: (33) 5 58 09 90 00
   Fax: (33) 5 58 09 90 61
   Email: mcdane@gascognepaper.com
   Finan. Mgr.: Williams Marquet
   Phone: (33) 5 58 09 90 00
   Fax: (33) 5 58 09 90 61
   Email: wmarquet@gascognepaper.com
   Purch. Mgr.: Jean-Luc Mesplede
   Phone: (33) 5 58 09 90 00
   Fax: (33) 5 58 09 90 61
   Email: jlmesplede@gascognepaper.com
   Mktg & Commun. Mgr.: Aurélie Chapoton
   Phone: (33) 5 58 09 90 00
   Fax: (33) 5 58 09 90 61
   Email: achapoton@gascognepaper.com
   Sls. & Mktg. Mgr.: Jean-Eric Gancille
   Phone: (33) 5 58 09 90 00
   Fax: (33) 5 58 09 90 61
   Email: jegancille@gascognepaper.com
   R & D Mgr.: Olivier Bongrand
   Phone: (33) 5 58 09 90 00
   Fax: (33) 5 58 09 90 61

France

Email: obongrand@gascognepaper.com
Head, Log. & Cust. Serv.: Aurélie Andres
Phone: (33) 5 58 09 90 00
Fax: (33) 5 58 09 90 61
Email: aandres@gascognepaper.com
Total Employees at this Location: 470
Type of Operation: Pulp mill, Paper mill
Pulp Grades and Capacities:
Total pulp capacity: 167,734 mt/y
Chemical Pulp: 167,734 mt/y
Pulp Mill Data:
Chemical Pulping Systems:
Batch digesters: 10
Chemical Recovery Equipment:
Evaporator lines: 1
Recovery boilers: 1
Lime Kiln
Recycled Fiber Treatment Lines:
Pulpers: 4
Paper/Paperboard Grades and Capacities:
Total paper and paperboard capacity: 159,958 mt/y
Packaging papers: 55,000 mt/y
Specialty and industrial: 104,958 mt/y
Paper and Paperboard Mill Data:
Stock Preparation:
Pulpers: 4
Refiners: 28
Paper Machines: 4
No. 3, fourdrinier, Yankee dryer, total capacity 55,000 mt/y, Trim width 3.6 m, Packaging papers
No. 4, fourdrinier, Yankee dryer, total capacity 49,980 mt/y, Trim width 4.8 m, Specialty and industrial
No. 5, fourdrinier, Yankee dryer, total capacity 27,846 mt/y, Trim width 3.6 m, Specialty and industrial
No. 6, fourdrinier, Yankee dryer, total capacity 27,132 mt/y, Trim width 4.1 m, Specialty and industrial
Coating Machines: 1
No. 1, off machine
Finishing Equipment:
Winders: 5
Calenders: 1
Sheeters: 2
Energy Data:
Power boilers: 2
Steam turbines: 2 at 17.0 MW
Electrical demand for mill: 144 MWh/D

ⓗⓜGemdoubs
Novillars Mill
Rue Jean-Baptiste Weibel
F-25220 Novillars
France
Phone: (33) 3 81 55 61 12
Fax: (33) 3 81 55 61 77
Personnel:
Man. Dir.: Gérard Lasserre
Phone: (33) 3 81 55 61 12
Fax: (33) 3 81 55 61 77
Total Employees at this Location: 42
Type of Operation: Paper mill, Paperboard mill
Pulp Grades and Capacities:
Total pulp capacity: 73,427 mt/y
Recycled Pulping: 73,427 mt/y
Pulp Mill Data:
Recycled Fiber Treatment Lines:
Recycled packaging pulping lines at 70,000
Paper/Paperboard Grades and Capacities:
Total paper and paperboard capacity: 72,000 mt/y
Linerboard: 45,000 mt/y
Corrugating medium/fluting: 27,000 mt/y
Paper and Paperboard Mill Data:
Stock Preparation:
Pulpers: 1
Paper Machines: 1
No. 1, fourdrinier (2), total capacity 72,000 mt/y, Trim width 3.4 m, Linerboard, Corrugating medium/fluting
Finishing Equipment:
Rewinders: 1 at 91,250 mt/y
Energy Data:
Power boilers: 2
Electrical demand for mill: 117 MWh/D

ⓜPapeteries de Giroux SA
Giroux Mill
Ownership: 83.50% by Rossmann SAS, 11% by Independent stockholders
Giroux Gare
F-63880 Olliergues
France
Phone: (33) 4 73 80 13 46
Fax: (33) 4 73 53 55 69
Email: giroux@rossmann.com,
papgir@wanadoo.fr
Web Address: www.rossmann.com
Personnel:
Gen. Mgr.: Baudoin VanDelft
Phone: (33) 4 73 80 13 46
Fax: (33) 4 73 53 55 69
Email: b.vandelft@rossmann.com
Total Employees at this Location: 46
Type of Operation: Pulp mill, Paperboard mill
Pulp Grades and Capacities:
Total pulp capacity: 24,980 mt/y
Recycled Pulping: 24,980 mt/y
Pulp Mill Data:
Recycled Fiber Treatment Lines:
Pulpers: 1 at 25,000 admt/y
Paper/Paperboard Grades and Capacities:
Total paper and paperboard capacity: 25,000 mt/y
Linerboard: 25,000 mt/y
Paper and Paperboard Mill Data:
Stock Preparation:
Pulpers: 1
Paper Machines: 1
No. 1, fourdrinier, total capacity 25,000 mt/y, Trim width 2.45 m, Linerboard
Finishing Equipment:
Rewinders: 1
Energy Data:
Power boilers: 2
Electrical demand for mill: 35 MWh/D

ⓜGlatfelter
Scaër Mill
BP 2
F-29390 Scaër
France
Phone: (33) 2 98 66 42 00
Fax: (33) 2 98 59 09 98
Email: service.france@glatfelter.com
Web Address: www.glatfelter.com
Personnel:
Dir. Gen.: Philippe Sevoz
Phone: (33) 2 98 66 42 00
Fax: (33) 2 98 59 09 98
Email: philippe.sevoz@glatfelter.com
Eng. & Maint. Mgr.: Jean Marc Phelep
Phone: (33) 2 98 66 42 00
Fax: (33) 2 98 59 09 98
Email: jean-marc.phelep@glatfelter.com
Total Employees at this Location: 130
Type of Operation: Paper mill
Paper/Paperboard Grades and Capacities:
Total paper and paperboard capacity: 6,000 mt/y
Specialty and industrial
Paper and Paperboard Mill Data:
Stock Preparation:
Pulpers: 4
Paper Machines: 2
No. 3, inclined, Trim width 1.8 m
No. 4, inclined, Trim width 1.6 m
Finishing Equipment:
Winders: 3 at 5,700 mt/y

ⓗⓜCartonneries de Gondardennes SA
Wardrecques Mill
Ownership: Family-owned (Private)
Rue Potier
F-62120 Wardrecques, Aire-Sur-La-Lys
France
Mailing Address: BP 2, F-62120 Wardrecques, France
Phone: (33) 3 21 95 44 66
Fax: (33) 3 21 95 44 60
Email: cart.gondardennes@gondardennes.fr
Web Address: www.gondardennes.fr
Personnel:
Pres.: Max Lamiot
Phone: (33) 3 21 95 44 66
Gen. Dir.: Bertrand Helle
Phone: (33) 3 21 95 44 66
Commercial Mgr.: Mr. Smets
Phone: (33) 3 21 95 44 66
Total Employees of Company: 410
Total Employees at this Location: 410
Type of Operation: Paperboard mill
Pulp Grades and Capacities:
Total pulp capacity: 183,189 mt/y
Recycled Pulping: 183,189 mt/y
Paper/Paperboard Grades and Capacities:
Total paper and paperboard capacity: 183,500 mt/y
Linerboard: 103,500 mt/y
Corrugating medium/fluting: 80,000 mt/y
Paper and Paperboard Mill Data:
Paper Machines: 2
No. 2, fourdrinier, total capacity 80,000 mt/y, Trim width 2.5 m, Corrugating medium/fluting
No. 3, fourdrinier (2), total capacity 103,500 mt/y, Trim width 2.55 m, Linerboard
Energy Data:
Power boilers: 1
Combustion turbines: 1 at 5 MW
Electrical demand for mill: 270 MWh/D

ⓜGreenfield SAS
Château Thierry Pulp Mill
Ownership: Arjowiggins SAS
Zone Industrielle de la Grande Borne
F-02400 Château-Thierry
France
Phone: (33) 3 23 69 53 70
Fax: (33) 3 23 69 53 71
Email: contact@greenfieldsas.com,
graphic@arjowiggins.com
Web Address: www.arjowiggins.com,
www.arjowigginsgraphic.com,
www.greenfieldsas.com
Personnel:
Mill Mgr.: Laurent Benault
Phone: (33) 3 23 69 53 70
Fax: (33) 3 23 69 53 71
Email: laurent.benault@arjowiggins.com
Sls. Dir.: John Govier
Phone: (33) 3 23 69 53 70
Fax: (33) 3 23 69 53 71
Email: john.govier@arjowiggins.com
Cust. Serv. Mgr.: Christelle Thieffine
Phone: (33) 3 23 69 53 70
Fax: (33) 3 23 69 53 71
Buyer: Jo'Ann Audibert
Phone: (33) 3 23 69 53 70
Fax: (33) 3 23 69 53 71
Environ. & Qlty. Mgr.: Etienne Laurent
Phone: (33) 3 23 69 53 70
Fax: (33) 3 23 69 53 71
Email: etienne.laurent@arjowiggins.com
Pub. Rel.: Luce Catte
Phone: (33) 3 23 69 53 70
Fax: (33) 3 23 69 53 71
Email: luce.catte@arjowiggins.com
Total Employees at this Location: 79
Type of Operation: Pulp mill
Pulp Grades and Capacities:
Total pulp capacity: 142,276 mt/y
Pulp available for market: 140,000 mt/y
Recycled Pulping: 142,276 mt/y
Pulp Mill Data:
Recycled Fiber Treatment Lines:
Flotation deinking lines: 10 at 125,000 admt/y

France

Pulpers: 1 at 203,100 admt/y
Washing deinking lines: 2 at 125,000 admt/y
Pulp Dryers:
Air Float dryers 1, Flash dryers 1, Wet Lap machine 1
Energy Data:
Power boilers: 2
Electrical demand for mill: 155 MWh/D

ⓘⓂPapeterie de Gromelle
Saint-Saturnin Mill
Allée de Gromelle, P.O. Box 1
F-84450 Saint-Saturnin-les-Avignon
France
Mailing Address: BP 1, F-84450 Saint Saturnin les Avignon, France
Phone: (33) 4 90 22 66 66
Fax: (33) 4 90 22 66 67
Web Address: www.papeteries-gromelle.com
Personnel:
Pres.: Max Peyremorte
Phone: (33) 4 90 22 66 66
Gen. Mgr.: Christophe Pageau
Phone: (33) 4 90 22 66 66
Total Employees of Company: 37
Type of Operation: Paperboard mill
Paper/Paperboard Grades and Capacities:
Total paper and paperboard capacity: 17,000 mt/y
Containerboard
Boxboard/cartonboard
Paper and Paperboard Mill Data:
Paper Machines: 1
No. 1, table plate, fourdrinier, total capacity 17,000 mt/y, Trim width 2.21 m, Containerboard, Boxboard/cartonboard
Energy Data:
Power boilers: 1

ⓂICT France SAS
Montargis Mill
Ownership: 100% by ICT Italy
100, rue des Camélias, Parque Industriel "ARBORIA 2"
F-45700 Pannes, Montargis, Loiret
France
Phone: (33) 2 38 95 96 01
Fax: (33) 2 38 95 96 02
Email: reception@ictfr.eu
Web Address: www.foxy.it
Personnel:
Mill Mgr.: Michel Lecuit
Phone: (33) 2 38 95 96 01
Total Employees at this Location: 150
Type of Operation: Paper mill
Paper/Paperboard Grades and Capacities:
Total paper and paperboard capacity: 70,000 mt/y
Tissue: 70,000 mt/y
Paper and Paperboard Mill Data:
Paper Machines: 1
No. 1, Advantage DCT 200 TS, total capacity 70,000 mt/y, Trim width 5.5 m, Tissue
Energy Data:
Electrical demand for mill: 171 MWh/D

ⓂInternational Paper SA
Saillat Mill
Ownership: International Paper (Europe) SA
Usine de Saillat, BP 1 Saillat-sur-Vienne
F-87206 Saint-Junien
France
Phone: (33) 5 55 43 48 00
Fax: (33) 5 55 43 48 65
Email: firstname.lastname@ipaper.com
Web Address: www.ipaper.com
Personnel:
Mill Mgr.: Philippe D'Adhemar
Phone: (33) 5 55 43 48 00
Fax: (33) 5 55 43 48 65
Email: Philippe.DAdhemar@ipaper.com
Total Employees at this Location: 550

Type of Operation: Pulp mill, Paper mill
Pulp Grades and Capacities:
Total pulp capacity: 320,054 mt/y
Pulp available for market: 119,000 mt/y
Chemical Pulp: 320,054 mt/y
Pulp Mill Data:
Chemical Pulping Systems:
Continuous digesters: 1
Bleach Plant Systems: 2
Hardwood, Sequence: O_2 DEpD
Softwood, Sequence: O_2 DEpD
Chemical Recovery Equipment:
Evaporator lines: 2
Recovery boilers: 1
Lime Kiln
Pulp Dryers:
Air Float dryers 1
Paper/Paperboard Grades and Capacities:
Total paper and paperboard capacity: 240,000 mt/y
Uncoated woodfree/freesheet: 240,000 mt/y
Paper and Paperboard Mill Data:
Stock Preparation:
Pulpers: 1
Refiners: 11
Paper Machines: 2
No. 1, fourdrinier, total capacity 47,500 mt/y, Trim width 3.3 m, Uncoated woodfree/freesheet
No. 2, OptiFormer, total capacity 192,500 mt/y, Trim width 5.6 m, Uncoated woodfree/freesheet
Finishing Equipment:
Rewinders: 3
Sheeters: 6
Energy Data:
Power boilers: 2
Steam turbines: 3 at 47.0 MW
Electrical demand for mill: 1,036 MWh/D

ⓘCartonnerie Jean SA
Ownership: 100% by Gabriel Jean
3, le Pont à la Chatte
F-23220 Bonnat
France
Phone: (33) 5 55 62 86 50
Fax: (33) 5 55 62 96 59
Email: lacelle@carton-jean.fr
Web Address: www.carton-jean.fr
Personnel:
Pres. & Man. Dir.: Francis Durand
Phone: (33) 5 55 62 96 50
Fax: (33) 5 55 62 96 59
Email: lacelle@carton-jean.fr
Mill Mgr.: Cécile Lescop
Phone: (33) 5 55 62 11 70
Fax: (33) 5 55 81 21 37
Email: cecile.lescop@carton-jean.fr
Tech. Serv.: Christian Amoulen
Phone: (33) 5 55 62 11 70
Fax: (33) 5 55 81 21 37
Email: christian.amoulen@carton-jean.fr
Total Employees of Company: 28
Total Employees at this Location: 4
Mill Locations:
Cartonnerie Jean SA, Bonnat Mill, 3, le Pont à la Chatte, F-23220 Bonnat, France, Capacity: 9,000 mt/y, (Pulp mill, Paperboard mill)
Phone: (33) 5 55 62 11 70
Fax: (33) 5 55 81 21 37
Email: lacelle@carton-jean.fr

ⓂCartonnerie Jean SA
Bonnat Mill
3, le Pont à la Chatte
F-23220 Bonnat
France
Phone: (33) 5 55 62 11 70
Fax: (33) 5 55 81 21 37
Email: lacelle@carton-jean.fr
Web Address: www.carton-jean.fr
Personnel:

Mill Mgr.: Cécile Lescop
Phone: (33) 5 55 62 11 70
Fax: (33) 5 55 81 21 37
Email: cecile.lescop@carton-jean.fr
Tech. Service: Christian Amoulen
Phone: (33) 5 55 62 11 70
Fax: (33) 5 55 81 21 37
Email: christian.amoulen@carton-jean.fr
Total Employees at this Location: 24
Type of Operation: Pulp mill, Paperboard mill
Pulp Grades and Capacities:
Total pulp capacity: 9,116 mt/y
Recycled Pulping: 9,116 mt/y
Paper/Paperboard Grades and Capacities:
Total paper and paperboard capacity: 9,000 mt/y
Boxboard/cartonboard: 9,000 mt/y
Paper and Paperboard Mill Data:
Stock Preparation:
Pulpers: 1
Refiners: 2
Paper Machines: 2
No. 1, fourdrinier, total capacity 4,000 mt/y, Trim width 1.5 m, Boxboard/cartonboard
No. 2, fourdrinier, total capacity 5,000 mt/y, Trim width 2.4 m, Boxboard/cartonboard
Energy Data:
Power boilers: 1
Electrical demand for mill: 9 MWh/D

ⓂKimberly-Clark SAS
Sotteville-les-Rouen Mill
Ownership: Kimberly-Clark Ltd.
8 rue Antoine Lavoisier
F-76300 Sotteville-les-Rouen
France
Mailing Address: BP 264, F-76305 Sotteville-les-Rouen, France
Phone: (33) 2 35 64 38 00
Fax: (33) 2 35 65 53 74
Web Address: www.kimberly-clark.com
Personnel:
Mill Mgr.: Martial Jeannot
Phone: (33) 2 35 64 38 03
Fax: (33) 2 35 65 53 74
Email: martial.jeannot@kcc.com
Total Employees at this Location: 132
Type of Operation: Pulp mill, Paper mill
Paper/Paperboard Grades and Capacities:
Total paper and paperboard capacity: 25,000 mt/y
Tissue: 25,000 mt/y
Paper and Paperboard Mill Data:
Stock Preparation:
Pulpers: 2
Refiners: 3
Paper Machines: 1
No. 1, crescent former, total capacity 25,000 mt/y, Trim width 3.2 m, Tissue
Finishing Equipment:
Winders: 1
Energy Data:
Power boilers: 1
Electrical demand for mill: 73 MWh/D

ⓂKimberly-Clark SNC
Toul Mill
Ownership: Kimberly-Clark Ltd.
Z.A.C. de Villey-St-Etienne
F-54212 Toul
France
Phone: (33) 3 83 65 34 34
Fax: (33) 3 83 65 34 78
Web Address: www.kimberly-clark.com
Personnel:
Paper Mill Mgr.: Benoit Georges
Phone: (33) 3 83 65 34 38
Fax: (33) 3 83 65 34 78
Email: bgeorges@kcc.com
Total Employees at this Location: 250
Type of Operation: Paper mill

France

Paper/Paperboard Grades and Capacities:
Total paper and paperboard capacity: 80,000 mt/y
Tissue: 80,000 mt/y
Paper and Paperboard Mill Data:
Paper Machines: 1
No. 1, TAD, total capacity 80,000 mt/y, Trim width 5.29 m, Tissue
Energy Data:
Power boilers: 1
Electrical demand for mill: 412 MWh/D

ⒽPapeteries et Cartonneries Lacaux Frères
Ownership: 100% by IPE Group
6 Impasse Saint-Exupéry BP 87
F-87000 Limoges
France
 Phone: (33) 5 55 77 34 02
 Fax: (33) 5 55 79 27 27
 Email: contact@lacaux.com
 Web Address: www.lacaux-freres.fr
Personnel:
 Chrmn.: Yves Lacaux
 Phone: (33) 5 55 77 34 02
 Fax: (33) 5 55 79 27 27
 Pres.: Boudenne Denis
 Phone: (33) 5 55 77 34 02
 Fax: (33) 5 55 79 27 27
 Man. Dir.: Christian Morange
 Phone: (33) 5 55 77 34 02
 Fax: (33) 5 55 79 27 27
 Email: christian.morange@lacaux.com
 HR Dir.: Mr. Baylé
 Phone: (33) 5 55 77 34 02
 Fax: (33) 5 55 79 27 27
 Sls. Mgr.: Denis Sabatier
 Phone: (33) 5 55 77 34 02
 Fax: (33) 5 55 79 27 27
 Email: denis.sabatier@lacaux.com
 Production Engineer: Laurent Verhaeghe
 Phone: (33) 5 55 77 34 02
 Fax: (33) 5 55 79 27 27
Total Employees of Company: 180
Total Employees at this Location: 30
Mill Locations:
Papeteries et Cartonneries Lacaux Frères, Bosmie L'Aiguille Mill, F-87110 Bosmie L'Aiguille, France, Capacity: 60,000 mt/y, (Paperboard mill)
 Phone: (33) 5 55 39 00 19
 Fax: (33) 5 55 39 05 87
 Email: contact@lacaux.com

ⒽⓂPapeteries et Cartonneries Lacaux Frères
Bosmie L'Aiguille Mill
Ownership: 100% by IPE Group
F-87110 Bosmie L'Aiguille
France
 Phone: (33) 5 55 39 00 19
 Fax: (33) 5 55 39 05 87
 Email: contact@lacaux.com
 Web Address: www.lacaux-freres.fr
Personnel:
 Man. Dir.: Christian Morange
 Phone: (33) 5 55 39 00 19
 Mill Mgr.: Nicolas Banuls
 Phone: (33) 5 55 39 00 19
Total Employees of Company: 180
Total Employees at this Location: 150
Type of Operation: Paperboard mill
Pulp Grades and Capacities:
 Total pulp capacity: 60,666 mt/y
 Recycled Pulping: 60,666 mt/y
Pulp Mill Data:
 Recycled Fiber Treatment Lines:
 Pulpers: 1 at 71,000
Paper/Paperboard Grades and Capacities:
 Total paper and paperboard capacity: 60,000 mt/y
 Linerboard: 30,000 mt/y
 Corrugating medium/fluting: 30,000 mt/y
Paper and Paperboard Mill Data:
Paper Machines: 1
No. 1, fourdrinier (2), total capacity 60,000 mt/y, Trim width 2.92 m, Linerboard, Corrugating medium/fluting
Energy Data:
Power boilers: 1
Electrical demand for mill: 81 MWh/D

ⒽLana Papiers Speciaux
Ownership: 100% by Private
139 route de La Wantzenau, BP 10 018
F-67015 Strasbourg
France
 Phone: (33) 3 88 31 00 31
 Fax: (33) 3 88 31 57 31
 Email: info@lanapapier.fr
 Web Address: www.lanapapier.fr
Total Employees of Company: 65
Mill Locations:
Lana Papiers Speciaux, Strasbourg Mill, 139 Rte. de la Wantzenau, BP 10 018, F-67015 Strasbourg, France, Capacity: 15,000 mt/y, (Paper mill)
 Phone: (33) 3 88 31 00 31/3 88 41 57 21/1 53 25 04 80
 Fax: (33) 3 88 31 57 31/1 53 25 04 85
 Email: info@lanapapier.fr

ⓂLana Papiers Speciaux
Strasbourg Mill
139 Rte. de la Wantzenau, BP 10 018
F-67015 Strasbourg
France
 Phone: (33) 3 88 31 00 31/3 88 41 57 21/1 53 25 04 80
 Fax: (33) 3 88 31 57 31/1 53 25 04 85
 Email: info@lanapapier.fr
 Web Address: www.lanapapier.fr
Personnel:
 Mill Mgr.: Philippe Sevoz
 Phone: (33) 3 88 41 57 19
 Email: philippe.sevoz@lanapapier.fr
 Sls. Dir.: Xavier De Calbiac
 Phone: (33) 3 88 41 57 32
 Email: xavier.decalbiac@lanapapier.fr
 Operations Mgr.: Patrick Béranger
 Phone: (33) 3 88 41 57 19
Total Employees at this Location: 59
Type of Operation: Paper mill
Paper/Paperboard Grades and Capacities:
 Total paper and paperboard capacity: 15,000 mt/y
 Uncoated woodfree/freesheet: 10,000 mt/y
 Specialty and industrial: 5,000 mt/y
Paper and Paperboard Mill Data:
 Stock Preparation:
 Pulpers: 4
 Refiners: 6
Paper Machines: 2
No. 1, fourdrinier, Trim width 2.4 m
No. 4, fourdrinier, Trim width 2.1 m
Finishing Equipment:
 Supercalenders: 1
 Rewinders: 4
 Sheeters: 7
Energy Data:
Power boilers: 1
Combustion turbines: 1 at 2.0 MW

ⓂPapeteries du Leman (PDL)
Thonon-les-Bains Mill
Ownership: Bolloré Thin Papers
1080 Route d'Evian Publier, BP 43
F-74500 Thonon-les-Bains Cédex
France
Mailing Address: B.P. 43, Thonon-les-Bains, France
 Phone: (33) 4 50 17 05 00
 Fax: (33) 4 50 17 06 32
 Email: marketing.pdl@pdl.fr
 Web Address: www.bollorethinpapers.com
Personnel:
 Chrmn. & CEO: Philippe Agut
 Phone: (33) 4 50 17 05 05
 Email: p.agut@pdl.fr
 Indust. Dir.: Stéphane Barbereau
 Phone: (33) 4 50 17 05 00
 Email: s.barbereau@pdl.fr
 Gen. Mgr.: Serge Doiteaux
 Tech. Mgr.: Mr. Jochum
 Phone: (33) 4 50 17 05 00
 Dir. Supply Chain: Olivier Pisarski
 Phone: (33) 4 50 17 05 00
 Mktg. Mgr.: Virgine Prudhomme
 Phone: (33) 4 50 17 05 00
 Email: v.prudhomme@pdl.fr
Total Employees at this Location: 275
Type of Operation: Pulp mill, Paper mill
Pulp Mill Data:
Pulp Lines: 1
 Bleach Plant Systems: 1
Paper/Paperboard Grades and Capacities:
 Total paper and paperboard capacity: 45,000 mt/y
 Uncoated woodfree/freesheet: 45,000 mt/y
Paper and Paperboard Mill Data:
Paper Machines: 2
No. 4, fourdrinier, total capacity 20,000 mt/y, Trim width 3 m, Uncoated woodfree/freesheet
No. 6, fourdrinier, total capacity 25,000 mt/y, Trim width 3.8 m, Uncoated woodfree/freesheet
Energy Data:
Power boilers: 2
Steam turbines: 1
Electrical demand for mill: 133 MWh/D

ⓂLucart France SAS
Troyes Mill
Ownership: 100% by Lucart SpA
Z.I. de Torvilliers R.N. 60
F-10440 La Rivière de Corps
France
 Phone: (33) 3 25 79 06 06
 Fax: (33) 3 25 79 38 38
 Email: info@lucart.fr
 Web Address: www.lucartgroup.com
Personnel:
 Quality, Security & Environ. Eng.: Ronan Chassier
 Phone: (33) 3 25 79 06 06
 Fax: (33) 3 25 79 38 38
 Email: ronan.chassier@lucartgroup.com
 Mktg. Dir.: Mr Thomas Bricout
 Phone: (33) 3 25 79 06 06
 Fax: (33) 3 25 79 38 38
 Email: thomas.bricout@lucartgroup.com
Total Employees at this Location: 180
Type of Operation: Paper mill
Paper/Paperboard Grades and Capacities:
 Total paper and paperboard capacity: 32,000 mt/y
 Tissue: 32,000 mt/y
Paper and Paperboard Mill Data:
Paper Machines: 1
No. 8, crescent former, total capacity 32,000 mt/y, Trim width 2.88 m, Tissue
Finishing Equipment:
 Rewinders at 32,000 mt/y
Energy Data:
Power boilers: 1
Electrical demand for mill: 86 MWh/D

ⒽⓂLydall Filtration Separation SAS
Melrand Mill
Ownership: Lydall, Inc.
Saint-Rivalain
F-56310 Melrand
France
 Phone: (33) 2 97 28 53 00
 Fax: (33) 2 97 39 58 90
 Web Address: www.lydall.com

France

Personnel:
Pres. & CEO: Dale G. Barnhart
Phone: (33) 2 97 28 53 00
Fax: (33) 2 97 39 58 90
Exec. VP. & CFO: Robert K. Julian
Phone: (33) 2 97 28 53 00
Fax: (33) 2 97 39 58 90
VP. HR.: Mona G. Estey
Phone: (33) 2 97 28 53 00
Fax: (33) 2 97 39 58 90
Chief Accounting Officer & Contr.: James V. Laughlan
Phone: (33) 2 97 28 53 00
Fax: (33) 2 97 39 58 90
Oper. Mgr.: Hervé Le Port
Phone: (33) 2 97 28 53 00
Fax: (33) 2 97 39 58 90
Prod. Mgr.: Christian Desquilles
Phone: (33) 2 97 28 53 00
Fax: (33) 2 97 39 58 90
Total Employees at this Location: 68
Type of Operation: Paper mill
Paper/Paperboard Grades and Capacities:
Total paper and paperboard capacity: 3,000 mt/y
Specialty and industrial: 3,000 mt/y

ⓘⓜPapeterie de Mandeure SA
Mandeure Mill
Ownership: Exacompta Clairefontaine
14 rue de la Papeterie
F-25350 Mandeure, Doubs
France
 Phone: (33) 3 81 35 20 52
 Fax: (33) 3 81 35 30 07
 Email: commercial@mandeure.com
 Web Address: www.papmandeure.com
Personnel:
Mill Mgr.: Patrick Seigneur
Phone: (33) 3 81 35 20 52
Maint. Mgr.: Raphaël Menegain
Phone: (33) 3 81 35 20 52
Finan./Admin. Mgr.: Hervé Schlatter
Phone: (33) 3 81 35 20 52
Total Employees at this Location: 130
Type of Operation: Paper mill
Paper/Paperboard Grades and Capacities:
Total paper and paperboard capacity: 35,000 mt/y
Uncoated woodfree/freesheet: 35,000 mt/y
Paper and Paperboard Mill Data:
 Stock Preparation:
 Pulpers: 2
 Refiners: 2
Paper Machines: 1
No. 1, SymFormer MB, total capacity 35,000 mt/y, Trim width 2.12 m, Uncoated woodfree/freesheet
Finishing Equipment:
Winders: 2
Calenders: 2
Rewinders: 1
Sheeters: 2
Energy Data:
Power boilers: 1
Electrical demand for mill: 63 MWh/D

ⓘⓜPapeteries Léon Martin SA
Engomer Mill
F-09800 Engomer
France
 Phone: (33) 5 61 96 81 11
 Fax: (33) 5 61 96 19 51
 Email: info@papeteriesmartin.fr
 Web Address: www.papeteriesmartin.fr/en
Personnel:
PDG: Hélène Martin
Phone: (33) 5 61 96 81 11
Prod. Mgr.: Pascal Cantiran
Phone: (33) 5 61 96 81 11
Mktg. Mgr.: Alain Heraud
Phone: (33) 5 61 96 81 11
Total Employees of Company: 37

Type of Operation: Paper mill
Paper/Paperboard Grades and Capacities:
Total paper and paperboard capacity: 3,000 mt/y
Specialty and industrial
Paper and Paperboard Mill Data:
Paper Machines: 1
No. 1, fourdrinier, total capacity 3,000 mt/y, Trim width 2 m, Specialty and industrial
Energy Data:
Power boilers: 1
Hydro turbines: 2

ⓘⓜPapeteries de Mauduit SA
Mauduit Mill
Ownership: 100% by Schweitzer-Mauduit International Inc.
Kérisole BP 34
F-29393 Quimperlé
France
 Phone: (33) 2 98 06 20 00
 Fax: (33) 2 98 06 20 94
 Web Address: www.swmintl.com
Personnel:
Dir. (Paper Oper. France): Régis Laffont
Phone: (33) 2 98 06 20 00
Admin. Dir.: Jean-Yves Klein
Phone: (33) 2 98 06 20 00
Env. Coord. France: Michaël Ciapa
Phone: (33) 2 98 06 20 00
Sls. & Mktg. Dir. (EU Papers): Raoul Hervé
Phone: (33) 2 98 06 20 00
Total Employees at this Location: 700
Type of Operation: Pulp mill, Paper mill
Pulp Grades and Capacities:
Total pulp capacity: 15,000 mt/y
Paper/Paperboard Grades and Capacities:
Total paper and paperboard capacity: 60,000 mt/y
Specialty and industrial: 60,000 mt/y
Paper and Paperboard Mill Data:
Paper Machines: 6
No. 1, Specialty and industrial
No. 2, Specialty and industrial
No. 3, Specialty and industrial
No. 4, Specialty and industrial
No. 6, Specialty and industrial
No. 10, Specialty and industrial

ⓘPapeteries de Montségur
Ownership: 100% by Resurgence
Route de Valréas
Montségur-sur-Lauzon
France
 Phone: (33) 4 75 98 11 23
 Fax: (33) 4 75 98 16 23
 Email: info@papeteries-montsegur.com
 Web Address: www.papeteries-montsegur.com
Personnel:
Pres.: Remi Danglade
Phone: (33) 4 75 98 11 23
Fax: (33) 4 75 98 16 23
Email: r.danglade@papeteries-montsegur.com
Mgr.: Gilbert Mure
Phone: (33) 4 75 98 11 23
Fax: (33) 4 75 98 16 23
Email: g.mure@papeteries-montsegur.com
Prod. & Qual. Mgr: Hervé Pennetier
Phone: (33) 4 75 98 11 23
Fax: (33) 4 75 98 16 23
Email: h.pennetier@papeteries-montsegur.com
Commer. Mgr.: Véronique Brachet
Phone: (33) 4 75 98 11 23
Fax: (33) 4 75 98 16 23
Email: veronique@papeteries-montsegur.com
Supply Chain Asst.: Vaux Sylvie
Phone: (33) 4 75 98 11 23
Fax: (33) 4 75 98 16 23
Commer. Mktg.: Mathilde Murat
Phone: (33) 4 75 98 11 23
Fax: (33) 4 75 98 16 23

Total Employees of Company: 30
Mill Locations:
Papeteries de Montségur, Montségur-sur-Lauzon Mill, Route de Valréas, Montségur-sur-Lauzon, France, Capacity: 1,000 mt/y, (Paper mill)
Phone: (33) 4 75 98 11 23
Fax: (33) 4 75 98 16 23
Email: info@papeteries-montsegur.com

ⓜPapeteries de Montségur
Montségur-sur-Lauzon Mill
Route de Valréas
Montségur-sur-Lauzon
France
 Phone: (33) 4 75 98 11 23
 Fax: (33) 4 75 98 16 23
 Email: info@papeteries-montsegur.com
 Web Address: www.papeteries-montsegur.com
Personnel:
Pres.: Remi Danglade
Phone: (33) 4 75 98 11 23
Fax: (33) 4 75 98 16 23
Email: r.danglade@papeteries-montsegur.com
Prod. & Qlty. Mgr.: Hervé Pennetier
Phone: (33) 4 75 98 11 23
Fax: (33) 4 75 98 16 23
Email: h.pennetier@papeteries-montsegur.com
Commer. Mgr.: Véronique Brachet
Phone: (33) 4 75 98 11 23
Fax: (33) 4 75 98 16 23
Email: veronique@papeteries-montsegur.com
Total Employees at this Location: 30
Type of Operation: Paper mill
Paper/Paperboard Grades and Capacities:
Total paper and paperboard capacity: 1,000 mt/y
Packaging papers: 1,000 mt/y
Paper and Paperboard Mill Data:
Paper Machines: 1
No. 1, fourdrinier, total capacity 1,000 mt/y, Trim width 2 m, Packaging papers

ⓘⓜM.P. Hygiene, S.A.S
Annonay mill
lieu dit Pupil
07106 Annonay
France
Mailing Address: BP 159, 07106 Annonay, France
 Phone: (33) 0475 33 75 00
 Fax: (33) 0475 33 37 38
 Email: contact@mphygiene.com
 Web Address: www.mphygiene.com
Personnel:
Plant. Mgr.: François Miribel
Phone: (43) 475 33 7500
Fax: (43) 475 33 37 38
Commer. Dir.: Pierre Chataigner
Phone: (43) 475 33 7500
Fax: (43) 475 33 37 38
Total Employees at this Location: 40
Type of Operation: Paper mill
Paper/Paperboard Grades and Capacities:
Total paper and paperboard capacity: 28,000 mt/y
Tissue: 28,000 mt/y
Paper and Paperboard Mill Data:
Paper Machines: 1
No. 1, crescent former, Yankee dryer, total capacity 28,000 mt/y, Trim width 2.82 m, Tissue
Energy Data:
Electrical demand for mill: 67 MWh/D

ⓜMunksjö Arches SAS
Arches Mill
Previously Arjowiggins SAS
Ownership: Munksjö Oyj
BP 29, 48 route de Remiremont
F-88380 Arches
France
Mailing Address: BP 29, F-88380 Arches, France
 Phone: (33) 3 29 32 60 00

France

Fax: (33) 3 29 32 74 96
Email: info@munksjo.com
Web Address: www.munksjo.com
Personnel:
Mill Mgr.: Philippe Hervé
Phone: (33) 3 29 32 60 00
Fax: (33) 3 29 32 74 96
Email: philippe.herve@munksjo.com
Prod. Mgr.: Francis Prot
Phone: (33) 3 29 32 60 00
Fax: (33) 3 29 32 74 96
Email: francis.prot@munksjo.com
Total Employees at this Location: 455
Type of Operation: Paper mill
Paper/Paperboard Grades and Capacities:
Total paper and paperboard capacity: 77,000 mt/y
Uncoated woodfree/freesheet: 10,000 mt/y
Specialty and industrial: 67,000 mt/y
Paper and Paperboard Mill Data:
Stock Preparation:
Pulpers: 7
Refiners: 13
Paper Machines: 7
No. 2, cylinder, Trim width 1.3 m
No. 3, fourdrinier, Trim width 1.4 m
No. 4, multi-former, Trim width 1.7 m
No. 5, cylinder, Trim width 1.3 m
No. 6, fourdrinier, Trim width 3.4 m
No. 7, fourdrinier, Trim width 2.1 m
No. 8, multi-fourdrinier, Trim width 2.6 m
Finishing Equipment:
Supercalenders: 1
Rewinders: 7
Sheeters: 2

ⓂMunksjö LabelPack
La Gère Mill
Previously Ahlstrom LabelPack SAS
Ownership: 100% by Munksjö Oyj
Chemin Cartallier
F-38780 Pont Evêque
France
Phone: (33) 4 74161010
Fax: (33) 4 74161049
Email: info@munksjo.com
Web Address: www.munksjo.com
Personnel:
Mill Mgr.: David Beaudier
Phone: (33) 474161001
Email: david.beaudier@munksjo.com
Total Employees at this Location: 178
Type of Operation: Paper mill
Paper/Paperboard Grades and Capacities:
Total paper and paperboard capacity: 95,000 mt/y
Specialty and industrial: 95,000 mt/y
Paper and Paperboard Mill Data:
Paper Machines: 1
No. 6, fourdrinier, total capacity 95,000 mt/y, Trim width 4.62 m, Specialty and industrial
Finishing Equipment:
Supercalenders: 2
Rewinders: 2
Energy Data:
Power boilers
Electrical demand for mill: 272 MWh/D

ⓂMunksjö LabelPack
Rottersac Mill
Ownership: 100% by Munksjö Oyj
Usine de Rottersac
F-24150 Lalinde
France
Phone: (33) 5 53615400
Fax: (33) 5 53615460
Email: info@munksjo.com
Web Address: www.munksjo.com
Personnel:
Mill Mgr.: Thierry Chassagne
Phone: (33) 5 5361 5401
Fax: (33) 5 5361 5460
Email: thierry.chassagne@munksjo.com
Deputy Dir. (Maint.): Jean-François Bertrand
Phone: (33) 5 5361 5411
Fax: (33) 5 5361 5460
Total Employees at this Location: 201
Type of Operation: Paper mill
Paper/Paperboard Grades and Capacities:
Total paper and paperboard capacity: 70,000 mt/y
Specialty and industrial: 70,000 mt/y
Paper and Paperboard Mill Data:
Stock Preparation:
Pulpers: 3
Refiners: 10
Paper Machines: 2
No. 4, fourdrinier, total capacity 9,000 mt/y, Trim width 1.6 m, Specialty and industrial
No. 5, fourdrinier, total capacity 61,000 mt/y, Trim width 4 m, Specialty and industrial
Finishing Equipment:
Supercalenders: 3
Rewinders: 4
Energy Data:
Power boilers
Electrical demand for mill: 191 MWh/D

ⓂMunksjö LabelPack
Stenay Mill
Ownership: 100% by Munksjö Oyj
Usine de Stenay
F-55700 Stenay
France
Phone: (33) 3 29803010
Fax: (33) 3 29806170
Email: info@munksjo.com
Web Address: www.munksjo.com
Personnel:
Mill Mgr.: Olivier Courtaux
Phone: (33) 3 29 80 30 10
Fax: (33) 3 29 80 26 43
Email: olivier.courtaux@munksjo.com
Purch. Mgr.: Elizabeth Couvert
Phone: (33) 3 29 80 30 10
Fax: (33) 3 29 80 26 43
Maint. Mgr.: Daniel Eggerman
Phone: (33) 3 29 80 30 10
Fax: (33) 3 29 80 26 43
Prod. Mgr.: Robert Zanzen
Phone: (33) 3 29 80 30 10
Total Employees at this Location: 209
Type of Operation: Paper mill
Paper/Paperboard Grades and Capacities:
Total paper and paperboard capacity: 100,000 mt/y
Specialty and industrial: 100,000 mt/y
Paper and Paperboard Mill Data:
Paper Machines: 2
No. 1, fourdrinier, total capacity 30,000 mt/y, Trim width 3.1 m, Specialty and industrial
No. 3, fourdrinier, total capacity 70,000 mt/y, Trim width 4.1 m, Specialty and industrial
Coating Machines: 2
No. 2, total capacity 25,000 mt/y., on machine
No. 3, total capacity 70,000 mt/y., on machine
Finishing Equipment:
Supercalenders: 1
Rewinders: 2 at 25,000 mt/y, 70,000 mt/y
Energy Data:
Power boilers: 2
Electrical demand for mill: 240 MWh/D

ⓂNorpaper Avot-Vallée SAS
Blendecques Mill
Ownership: 100% by OpenGate Capital
71 rue Jean Jaurès
F-62575 Blendecques
France
Phone: (33) 3 21 98 77 00
Fax: (33) 3 21 98 77 29
Personnel:
Mill Mgr.: Laurent Glachant
Phone: (33) 3 21 98 77 20
Fax: (33) 3 21 98 77 29
Email: lglachant@norpaper.com
Prod. Mgr.: Olivier Plancq
Phone: (33) 3 21 98 77 00
Fax: (33) 3 21 98 77 29
Email: oplancq@norpaper.com
Sls. Mgr.: Joel Caus
Phone: (33) 3 21 98 77 23
Fax: (33) 3 21 98 77 29
Email: jcaus@norpaper.com
Purch. Agent: Isabelle Germain
Phone: (33) 3 21 98 77 10
Fax: (33) 3 21 98 77 29
Email: igermain@norpaper.com
Maint. Mgr.: Bruno Epifani
Phone: (33) 3 21 98 77 21
Fax: (33) 3 21 98 77 29
Email: bepifani@norpaper.com
Env. Mgr.: Frederic Flaccus
Phone: (33) 3 21 98 77 02
Fax: (33) 3 21 98 77 29
Email: fflaccus@norpaper.com
HR Mgr.: Elaine Magnier
Phone: (33) 3 21 98 77 18
Fax: (33) 3 21 98 77 29
Email: emagnier@norpaper.com
Total Employees at this Location: 165
Type of Operation: Pulp mill, Paper mill, Paperboard mill
Pulp Grades and Capacities:
Total pulp capacity: 146,161 mt/y
Recycled Pulping: 146,161 mt/y
Pulp Mill Data:
Bleach Plant Lines:
No. 1, Type: DIP Capacity 37,000 admt/y
Recycled Fiber Treatment Lines:
Flotation deinking lines: 1 at 43,000 admt/y
Pulpers: 6 at 143,000 admt/y
Paper/Paperboard Grades and Capacities:
Total paper and paperboard capacity: 151,000 mt/y
Linerboard: 151,000 mt/y
Paper and Paperboard Mill Data:
Stock Preparation:
Pulpers: 3
Paper Machines: 3
No. 2, fourdrinier (2), total capacity 48,000 mt/y, Trim width 2.5 m, Linerboard
No. 4, fourdrinier (2), total capacity 28,000 mt/y, Trim width 2.1 m, Linerboard
No. 6, fourdrinier (2), total capacity 75,000 mt/y, Trim width 2.5 m, Linerboard
Energy Data:
Power boilers: 1
Combustion turbines: 1
Steam turbines: 1 at 2.0 MW
Electrical demand for mill: 238 MWh/D

ⓄⓂNorske Skog Golbey SA
Golbey Mill
Ownership: 100% by Norske Skog ASA
Zone Industrielle III, Route Jean-Charles Pellerin
F-88194 Golbey Cedex
France
Mailing Address: BP 109, F-88194 Golbey Cedex, France
Phone: (33) 3 29 68 68 68
Fax: (33) 3 29 68 68 60
Email: dominique.bomont@norskeskog.com
Web Address: www.norske-skog.com
Personnel:
Mill Mgr.: Yves Bailly
Phone: (33) 3 29 68 68 68
Fax: (33) 3 29 68 68 60
Email: yves.bailly@norskeskog.com
Ind. Mgr.: Pascal Vignaux
Phone: (33) 3 29 68 68 68
Fax: (33) 3 29 68 68 60

Email: pascal.vignaux@norskeskog.com
Total Employees at this Location: 443
Type of Operation: Pulp mill, Paper mill
Pulp Grades and Capacities:
Total pulp capacity: 618,604 mt/y
Mechanical Pulp: 222,232 mt/y
Recycled Pulping: 396,372 mt/y
Pulp Mill Data:
Mechanical Pulping Systems:
TMP systems: 2
Bleach Plant Lines:
DIP
TMP
Recycled Fiber Treatment Lines:
Flotation deinking lines: 4 at 660,000 admt/y
Pulpers: 2 at 660,000 admt/y
Paper/Paperboard Grades and Capacities:
Total paper and paperboard capacity: 620,000 mt/y
Newsprint: 611,250 mt/y
Uncoated mechanical/groundwood: 8,750 mt/y
Paper and Paperboard Mill Data:
Paper Machines: 2
No. 1, Bel-Baie III, total capacity 270,000 mt/y, Trim width 8.67 m, Newsprint
No. 2, DuoFormer TQv, total capacity 350,000 mt/y, Trim width 9.7 m, Newsprint, Uncoated mechanical/groundwood
Finishing Equipment:
Rewinders: 2
Energy Data:
Power boilers: 5
TMP Reboiler: 1
Steam turbines: 1 at 13 MW
Electrical demand for mill: 2,925 MWh/D

ⒽⓂNovatissue SAS
Novatissue Mill
Ownership: 100% by Lucart SpA
10 rue Maurice Mougeot
F-88600 Laval-sur-Vologne
France
 Phone: (33) 3 29 55 78 78
 Fax: (33) 3 29 55 78 76
 Email: (name.surname@novatissue.fr)
 Web Address: www.lucartgroup.com
Personnel:
Pres.: Alessandro Pasquini
 Phone: (33) 3 29 55 78 78
 Fax: (33) 3 29 55 78 76
 Email: alessandro.pasquini@lucartgroup.com
Mill Mgr.: Hervé Kraemer
 Phone: (33) 3 29 55 78 78
 Fax: (33) 3 29 55 78 76
 Email: herve.kraemer@lucartgroup.com
Total Employees at this Location: 229
Type of Operation: Pulp mill, Paper mill
Pulp Grades and Capacities:
Total pulp capacity: 53,260 mt/y
Recycled Pulping: 53,260 mt/y
Pulp Mill Data:
Recycled Fiber Treatment Lines:
Flotation deinking lines at 43,000
Recycled packaging pulping lines at 12,000
Paper/Paperboard Grades and Capacities:
Total paper and paperboard capacity: 50,000 mt/y
Tissue: 50,000 mt/y
Paper and Paperboard Mill Data:
Stock Preparation:
Pulpers: 3
Paper Machines: 2
No. 2, Yankee dryer, total capacity 20,000 mt/y, Trim width 2.7 m, Tissue
No. 3, crescent former, total capacity 30,000 mt/y, Trim width 3.75 m, Tissue
Energy Data:
Power boilers: 1
Electrical demand for mill: 158 MWh/D

ⒽⓂCartonnerie Oudin
Truyes Mill
Ownership: Private
BP 1
F-37320 Truyes
France
 Phone: (33) 2 47 73 40 00
 Fax: (33) 2 47 43 02 85
 Email: oudin@cartonnerie-h-oudin.com
 Web Address: www.cartonnerie-oudin.fr
Personnel:
Chmn.: Catherine de Colbert
 Phone: (33) 2 47 73 40 00
Commercial Dir.: Georges de Tudert
 Phone: (33) 2 47 73 40 00
Industrial Mgr.: Henri de Tudert
 Phone: (33) 2 47 73 40 00
Total Employees of Company: 90
Total Employees at this Location: 90
Type of Operation: Pulp mill, Paperboard mill
Pulp Grades and Capacities:
Total pulp capacity: 30,441 mt/y
Recycled Pulping: 30,441 mt/y
Pulp Mill Data:
Recycled Fiber Treatment Lines:
Pulpers: 2
Pulp Dryers:
Air Float dryers 2
Paper/Paperboard Grades and Capacities:
Total paper and paperboard capacity: 30,000 mt/y
Boxboard/cartonboard: 30,000 mt/y
Paper and Paperboard Mill Data:
Stock Preparation:
Pulpers: 2
Paper Machines: 1
No. 1, fourdrinier, total capacity 30,000 mt/y, Trim width 2.23 m, Boxboard/cartonboard
Finishing Equipment:
Rewinders: 1 at 47,000 mt/y
Sheeters: 2 at 47,000 mt/y
Energy Data:
Power boilers: 2
Electrical demand for mill: 44 MWh/D

ⒽⓂPapeco SA
Orval Mill
Le Pont de la Roque
F-50660 Orval
France
Mailing Address: BP 228, F-50202 Coutances
Cédex, France
 Phone: (33) 2 33 76 52 10
 Fax: (33) 2 33 76 52 19
 Email: contact@papeco.fr
 Web Address: www.papeco.fr
Personnel:
Pres./Man. Dir.: G. Coulon
 Phone: (33) 2 33 76 52 14
 Email: gc.papeco@wanadoo.fr
Mill Mgr.: E. Coulon
 Phone: (33) 2 33 76 52 16
 Email: ecoulon.papeco@mac.com
Sls./Mktg. Dir.: F. Miramont
 Phone: (33) 2 33 76 52 15
Prod. Mgr.: Jean Gautier
 Phone: (33) 2 33 76 52 10
Total Employees of Company: 47
Total Employees at this Location: 47
Type of Operation: Paper mill
Pulp Grades and Capacities:
Total pulp capacity: 8,540 mt/y
Recycled Pulping: 8,540 mt/y
Paper/Paperboard Grades and Capacities:
Total paper and paperboard capacity: 8,000 mt/y
Tissue: 8,000 mt/y
Paper and Paperboard Mill Data:
Stock Preparation:
Pulpers: 1
Refiners: 1

Paper Machines: 2
No. 2, Yankee dryer, total capacity 3,000 mt/y, Trim width 1.8 m, Tissue
No. 3, Yankee dryer, total capacity 5,000 mt/y, Trim width 2.4 m, Tissue
Finishing Equipment:
Rewinders: 1
Energy Data:
Power boilers: 1
Electrical demand for mill: 25 MWh/D

ⒽPapeterie Saint Michel SAS Groupe Thiollet
Ownership: 100% by Thiollet (Private)
Avenue de l'Industrie, BP 1
F-16470 St. Michel D'Entraygues
France
 Phone: (33) 5 45 25 1725
 Fax: (33) 5 45 25 1720
 Email: papeterie@groupe-thiollet.com
 Web Address: groupe-thiollet.com/papeterie.html
Personnel:
Gen. Mgr.: Jacky Quiesse
 Phone: (33) 5 45 25 17 22
 Fax: (33) 5 45 25 17 81
Total Employees of Company: 65
Total Employees at this Location: 65
Mill Locations:
Papeterie Saint Michel SAS Groupe Thiollet, St. Michel d'Entraygues Mill, Avenue de l'Industrie, BP 1, F-16470 St. Michel d'Entraygues, France, Capacity: 90,000 mt/y, (Pulp mill, Paperboard mill)
 Phone: (33) 5 45 25 1725
 Fax: (33) 5 45 25 1720
 Email: papeterie@groupe-thiollet.com

ⓂPapeterie Saint Michel SAS Groupe Thiollet
St. Michel d'Entraygues Mill
Avenue de l'Industrie, BP 1
F-16470 St. Michel d'Entraygues
France
 Phone: (33) 5 45 25 1725
 Fax: (33) 5 45 25 1720
 Email: papeterie@groupe-thiollet.com
 Web Address: www.groupe-thiollet.com/papeterie.html
Personnel:
Gen. Mgr.: Jacky Quiesse
 Phone: (33) 5 45 25 17 22
 Fax: (33) 5 45 25 17 81
Total Employees at this Location: 65
Type of Operation: Pulp mill, Paperboard mill
Pulp Grades and Capacities:
Total pulp capacity: 90,665 mt/y
Recycled Pulping: 90,665 mt/y
Pulp Mill Data:
Paper/Paperboard Grades and Capacities:
Total paper and paperboard capacity: 90,000 mt/y
Linerboard: 60,000 mt/y
Corrugating medium/fluting: 30,000 mt/y
Paper and Paperboard Mill Data:
Stock Preparation:
Pulpers: 1
Paper Machines: 2
No. 1, fourdrinier, total capacity 30,000 mt/y, Trim width 2.06 m, Linerboard, Corrugating medium/fluting
No. 2, fourdrinier, total capacity 60,000 mt/y, Trim width 2.54 m, Linerboard, Corrugating medium/fluting
Finishing Equipment:
Rewinders: 2 at 90,000 mt/y
Energy Data:
Power boilers: 1
Electrical demand for mill: 146 MWh/D

ⒽⓂPrat Dumas & Cie.
Lalinde Mill
Couze-St-Front

France

F-24150 Lalinde
France
  Phone: (33) 5 53 61 13 33
  Fax: (33) 5 53 58 56 10
  Email: pratdumas@pratdumas.com
  Web Address: www.pratdumas.com
Personnel:
  Man. Dir.: Raymond Faura
  Phone: (33) 5 53 61 13 33
  Email: faura@pratdumas.com
  Sls. & Purch. Mgr.: Geneviève Faura
  Phone: (33) 5 53 61 13 33
  Email: gfaura@pratdumas.com
  Sls. & Qlty. Mgr.: Vanessa Roubenne
  Phone: (33) 5 53 61 13 33
  Email: vanessa.roubenne@pratdumas.com
Total Employees of Company: 12
Type of Operation: Paper mill
Paper/Paperboard Grades and Capacities:
  Total paper and paperboard capacity: 800 mt/y
  Specialty and industrial: 800 mt/y
Paper and Paperboard Mill Data:
Paper Machines: 1
  No. 1, Trim width 1.05 m, Specialty and industrial
Energy Data:
  Power boilers: 1

ⓘⓜPapeterie de Raon
Raon L'Etape Mill
Company is for sale (acquisition by the Italian kraft and specialty packaging paper manufacturer Cartiera Galliera approved. The takeover will take effect from November 1, 2014.)
Ownership: mill management
Rue Emile Zola
F-88110 Raon L'Etape, Vosges
France
Mailing Address: BP 82, F-88110 Raon L'Etape, Vosges, France
  Phone: (33) 3 29 42 61 11
  Fax: (33) 3 29 42 61 36/ 98 75
  Email: contact@papraon.com
  Web Address: www.papraon.com
Personnel:
  Owner & Pres.: Mr. Bortolloti
  Phone: (33) 3 29 42 61 11
  Prod. & Tech. Mgr.: Mr. Bertaux
  Phone: (33) 3 29 42 61 11
  Sls. Mgr.: Mr. Lesire
  Phone: (33) 3 29 42 61 11
Total Employees of Company: 100
Total Employees at this Location: 100
Type of Operation: Paper mill
Pulp Grades and Capacities:
  Total pulp capacity: 42,876 mt/y
  Recycled Pulping: 42,876 mt/y
Paper/Paperboard Grades and Capacities:
  Total paper and paperboard capacity: 42,000 mt/y
  Packaging papers: 10,000 mt/y
  Specialty and industrial: 32,000 mt/y
Paper and Paperboard Mill Data:
Paper Machines: 2
  No. 4, fourdrinier, total capacity 30,000 mt/y, Trim width 2.88 m, Packaging papers, Specialty and industrial
  No. 5, fourdrinier, total capacity 12,000 mt/y, Trim width 2.16 m, Specialty and industrial
Energy Data:
  Power boilers: 1
  Electrical demand for mill: 122 MWh/D

ⓜRDM Blendecques SAS
Blendecques Mill
Ownership: Reno De Medici SpA
Rue de l'Hermitage, BP 53006
F-62501 Blendecques, Saint Omer Cedex
France
  Phone: (33) 3 21 38 80 20
  Fax: (33) 3 21 38 80 28
  Email: contact@careo.biz

Web Address: www.careo.biz, www.renodemedici.it
Personnel:
  Man. Dir.: Benoît Rimbault
  Phone: (33) 3 21 38 80 20
  Fax: (33) 3 21 38 80 28
  Email: benoit.rimbault@rdmgroup.com
  Finishing Mgr.: Alain Florent
  Phone: (33) 3 21 38 80 20
  Fax: (33) 3 21 38 80 28
  Email: alain.florent@rdmgroup.com
  Purch. Agent: Dominique Gloriant
  Phone: (33) 3 21 38 80 20
  Fax: (33) 3 21 38 80 28
  Email: dominique.gloriant@rdmgroup.com
  Finan. Mgr.: Isabelle Lefebvre
  Phone: (33) 3 21 38 80 20
  Fax: (33) 3 21 38 80 28
  Email: isabelle.lefebvre@rdmgroup.com
Total Employees at this Location: 197
Type of Operation: Pulp mill, Paperboard mill
Pulp Grades and Capacities:
  Total pulp capacity: 95,968 mt/y
  Recycled Pulping: 95,968 mt/y
Pulp Mill Data:
Pulp Lines: 3
  Bleach Plant Systems: 1
  DIP Capacity 30,000 admt/y
  Recycled Fiber Treatment Lines:
  Flotation deinking lines: 2 at 30,000 admt/y
  Recycled packaging pulping lines: 1 at 65,000
Paper/Paperboard Grades and Capacities:
  Total paper and paperboard capacity: 105,000 mt/y
  Boxboard/cartonboard: 105,000 mt/y
Paper and Paperboard Mill Data:
Paper Machines: 1
  No. 4, multi-wire, total capacity 105,000 mt/y, Trim width 3.1 m, Boxboard/cartonboard
Coating Machines: 1
  PM 4, total capacity 105,000 mt/y., on machine
Finishing Equipment:
  Sheeters: 5
Energy Data:
  Power boilers: 2
  Combustion turbines: 2 at 6.4 MW
  Steam turbines: 2 at 6.3 MW
  Electrical demand for mill: 210 MWh/D

ⓘRepublic Group
3750 avenue Julien Panchot - BP 424
F-66004 Perpignan
France
  Phone: (33) 4 68 85 12 27
  Fax: (33) 4 68 85 65 85
  Email: contact@rpb-tech.com
  Web Address: www.republic-technologies.com
Personnel:
  Pres.: Philippe Parcevaux
  Phone: (33) 4 68 85 12 27
  Fax: (33) 4 68 85 65 85
  Dir. Oper.: Eric Guilbert
  Phone: (33) 4 68 85 12 27
  Fax: (33) 4 68 85 65 85
  Gen. Counsel: Olivier Partouche
  Phone: (33) 4 68 85 12 27
  Fax: (33) 4 68 85 65 85
  Man. Dir. Delegated: Santiago Sánchez
  Phone: (33) 4 68 85 12 27
  Fax: (33) 4 68 85 65 85
  Sls. Mgr.: Thierry Bigo
  Phone: (33) 4 68 85 12 27
  Fax: (33) 4 68 85 65 85
  Mktg. Mgr.: Valérie Amiguas
  Phone: (33) 4 68 85 12 27
  Fax: (33) 4 68 85 65 85
Mill Locations:
Papeteries du Leman (PDL), Thonon-les-Bains Mill, 1080 Route d'Evian Publier, BP 43, F-74500 Thonon-les-Bains Cédex, France, Capacity: 45,000 mt/y, (Pulp mill, Paper mill)

  Phone: (33) 4 50 17 05 00
  Fax: (33) 4 50 17 06 32
  Email: marketing.pdl@pdl.fr
Papeteries des Vosges (PDV), Laval-sur-Vologne Mill, 34, rue Maurice Mougeot, BP 26, F-88600 Laval-sur-Vologne, France, Capacity: 52,500 mt/y, (Paper mill)
  Phone: (33) 3 29 53 52 00
  Fax: (33) 4 50 81 52 01
  Email: marketing.pdl@pdl.fr

ⓘPapeteries du Rhin
Ownership: 100% by Kunert Gruppe, Paul & Co GmbH & Co. KG
Rue de la Croix de Montois
F-89100 Courtois-sur-Yonne
France
  Phone: (33) 389 61 74 47
  Fax: (33) 389 63 66 87
  Email: pdr@papeteries-du-rhin.com
  Web Address: www.kunertgruppe.com
Personnel:
  Pres.: Gaston Simonato
  Phone: (33) 3 86 97 09 38
  Fax: (33) 389 63 66 87
  Gen. Mgr.: Fabien Blanchard
  Phone: (33) 389 61 74 47
  Fax: (33) 389 63 66 87
Total Employees of Company: 71
Total Employees at this Location: 1
Mill Locations:
Papeteries du Rhin, Illzach Mill, Rue Henry de Crousaz, Ile Napoléon, BP 148, F-68110 Illzach, France, Capacity: 75,000 mt/y, (Pulp mill, Paperboard mill)
  Phone: (33) 3 89 61 74 47
  Fax: (33) 3 89 61 85 54
  Email: pdr@papeteries-du-rhin.com

ⓘPapeteries du Rhin
Illzach Mill
Ownership: 100% by Kunert Gruppe, Paul & Co GmbH & Co. KG
Rue Henry de Crousaz, Ile Napoléon, BP 148
F-68110 Illzach
France
Mailing Address: BP 148, F-68313 Illzach, France
  Phone: (33) 3 89 61 74 47
  Fax: (33) 3 89 61 85 54
  Email: pdr@papeteries-du-rhin.com
  Web Address: www.kunertgruppe.com
Personnel:
  Mill Mgr.: Fabien Blanchard
  Phone: (33) 3 89 61 74 47
  Tech. Mgr.: Pascal Crouts de Paille
  Phone: (33) 3 89 61 74 47
  Prod. Mgr.: Denis Baumann
  Phone: (33) 3 89 61 74 47
  Tech. Maint. Mgr.: Philippe Thibault
  Phone: (33) 3 89 61 74 47
  Electr. Maint. Mgr.: Mr. Manzoni
  Phone: (33) 3 89 61 74 47
Total Employees at this Location: 70
Type of Operation: Pulp mill, Paperboard mill
Pulp Grades and Capacities:
  Total pulp capacity: 74,853 mt/y
  Recycled Pulping: 74,853 mt/y
Pulp Mill Data:
  Recycled Fiber Treatment Lines:
  Recycled packaging pulping lines at 90,000 admt/y
Paper/Paperboard Grades and Capacities:
  Total paper and paperboard capacity: 75,000 mt/y
  Boxboard/cartonboard: 75,000 mt/y
Paper and Paperboard Mill Data:
Paper Machines: 1
  No. 1, fourdrinier, total capacity 75,000 mt/y, Trim width 2.45 m, Boxboard/cartonboard
Finishing Equipment:
  Rewinders: 1
Energy Data:

France

Power boilers: 1
Electrical demand for mill: 92 MWh/D

ⓂRossmann SAS
F-67602 La Vancelle Gare, Selestat
France
Mailing Address: BP 80068, Selestat Cedex, France
  Phone: (33) 3 88 57 90 77
  Fax: (33) 3 88 57 91 71
  Email: rossmann@rossmann.com
  Web Address: www.rossmann.com
Personnel:
  Chrmn.: Bernard Rossman
  Phone: (33) 3 88 57 90 77
  Fax: (33) 3 88 57 91 71
  Pres. of Dir.: Laurent Kauffmann
  Phone: (33) 3 88 57 90 77
  Fax: (33) 3 88 57 91 71
  Email: l.kauffmann@rossmann.com
  Purch. Mgr.: Laurent Barral
  Phone: (33) 3 88 57 90 77
  Fax: (33) 3 88 57 91 71
  Email: l.barral@rossmann.com
  Dir. of Health & Environ. Protection: Richard Rossmann
  Phone: (33) 3 88 57 90 77
  Fax: (33) 3 88 57 91 71
  Email: r.rossmann@rossmann.com
  Devlpt. Dir.: Ruben Alloux
  Phone: (33) 3 88 57 90 77
  Fax: (33) 3 88 57 91 71
  Email: r.alloux@rossmann.com
  Sls. Mgr.: Thierry Bouge
  Phone: (33) 3 88 57 90 77
  Fax: (33) 3 88 57 91 71
  Email: t.bouge@lavancelle.rossmann.com
  Sls. Mgr.: Thierry Walter
  Phone: (33) 3 88 57 90 77
  Fax: (33) 3 88 57 91 71
  Email: t.walter@lavancelle.rossmann.com
  Board Mill Mgr.: Alain Zumsteeg
  Phone: (33) 3 88 57 90 77
  Fax: (33) 3 88 57 91 71
  Email: a.zumsteeg@rlv.rossmann.com
Total Employees of Company: 3,000
Total Employees at this Location: 265
Mill Locations:
  Ambro SA Suceava, Suceava Mill, Calea Unirii 24, RO-720019 Suceava, Romania, Capacity: 150,000 mt/y, (Pulp mill, Paper mill)
    Phone: (40) 230 205 000
    Fax: (40) 230 205 205 / 111
    Email: office@ambro.ro
  Papeteries de Giroux SA, Giroux Mill (83.50% owned), Giroux Gare, F-63880 Olliergues, France, Capacity: 25,000 mt/y, (Pulp mill, Paperboard mill)
    Phone: (33) 4 73 80 13 46
    Fax: (33) 4 73 53 55 69
    Email: giroux@rossmann.com, papgir@wanadoo.fr
  Rossmann SAS, Ste. Croix aux Mines Mill, 6 rue de Moulin, F-68160 Ste. Croix aux Mines, France, Capacity: 40,000 mt/y, (Pulp mill, Paper mill)
    Phone: (33) 3 89 58 73 15
    Fax: (33) 3 89 58 65 63
    Email: stecroix@rossmann.com
  SICAL, Lumbres Mill (98% owned), 69 rue du Dr. Pontier, F-62380 Lumbres, France, Capacity: 36,000 mt/y, (Pulp mill, Paperboard mill)
    Phone: (33) 3 21 38 60 00
    Fax: (33) 3 21 38 60 60
    Email: sical@rossmann.com

ⓂRossmann SAS
Ste. Croix aux Mines Mill
6 rue de Moulin
F-68160 Ste. Croix aux Mines
France
  Phone: (33) 3 89 58 73 15
  Fax: (33) 3 89 58 65 63
  Email: stecroix@rossmann.com
  Web Address: www.rossmann.com
Personnel:
  Plt. Mgr.: Michel Dorlencourt
  Phone: (33) 3 89 58 73 15
  Fax: (33) 3 89 58 65 63
  Dpty. Mgr.: Alain Kretz
  Phone: (33) 3 89 58 73 15
  Fax: (33) 3 89 58 65 63
Total Employees at this Location: 50
Type of Operation: Pulp mill, Paper mill
Pulp Grades and Capacities:
  Total pulp capacity: 40,306 mt/y
  Recycled Pulping: 40,306 mt/y
Pulp Mill Data:
  Recycled Fiber Treatment Lines:
  Pulpers: 2
  Recycled packaging pulping lines at 42,000 admt/y
Paper/Paperboard Grades and Capacities:
  Total paper and paperboard capacity: 40,000 mt/y
  Linerboard: 27,000 mt/y
  Corrugating medium/fluting: 13,000 mt/y
Paper and Paperboard Mill Data:
  Stock Preparation:
  Refiners: 2
Paper Machines: 1
  No. 2, fourdrinier (2), total capacity 40,000 mt/y, Trim width 2.5 m, Corrugating medium/fluting, Linerboard
Finishing Equipment:
  Rewinders: 1
Energy Data:
  Power boilers: 1
  Electrical demand for mill: 58 MWh/D

ⓂSAICA Vénizel
Vénizel Mill
Ownership: 100% by SAICA - S.A. Industrias Celulosa Aragonesa
BP 08, rue de la Vallée
F-02200 Vénizel
France
  Phone: (33) 3 23 75 30 00/13
  Fax: (33) 3 23 75 30 01
  Web Address: www.saica.com
Personnel:
  Mill Mgr.: Renaud Guilianelli
  Phone: (33) 3 23 75 30 03
  Fax: (33) 3 23 75 6721
  Email: renaud.guilianelli@saica.com
  Prod. Mgr.: Jean-François Dupuis
  Phone: (33) 3 23 75 31 72
  Fax: (33) 3 23 75 30 01
  Email: jean-francois.dupuis@saica.com
  Finan. Dir.: Patrick Jacquemin
  Phone: (33) 3 23 75 30 04
  Fax: (33) 3 23 75 30 01
  Email: patrick.jacquemin@saica.com
Total Employees at this Location: 105
Type of Operation: Pulp mill, Paperboard mill
Pulp Grades and Capacities:
  Total pulp capacity: 250,058 mt/y
  Recycled Pulping: 250,058 mt/y
Pulp Mill Data:
Pulp Lines: 1
  Recycled Fiber Treatment Lines:
  Pulpers: 1 at 400,000 admt/y
Paper/Paperboard Grades and Capacities:
  Total paper and paperboard capacity: 250,000 mt/y
  Linerboard: 170,000 mt/y
  Corrugating medium/fluting: 80,000 mt/y
Paper and Paperboard Mill Data:
Paper Machines: 1
  No. 4, fourdrinier, total capacity 250,000 mt/y, Trim width 4.93 m, Linerboard, Corrugating medium/fluting
Finishing Equipment:
  Winders: 1
Energy Data:
  Power boilers: 2
  Electrical demand for mill: 290 MWh/D

ⓂPapeteries de Saint-Girons
Saint-Girons Mill
Ownership: 100% by Schweitzer-Mauduit International Inc.
Faubourg de la Moulasse, PO Box 20071
F-09201 Eycheil, Saint-Girons
France
Mailing Address: B.P. 71, F-09201 Saint-Girons Cedex, France
  Phone: (33) 5 34 14 35 00
  Fax: (33) 5 61 66 77 22
  Web Address: www.swmintl.com
Personnel:
  CEO & Mill Mgr.: Régis Laffont
  Phone: (33) 5 34 14 35 00
  Pulp & Paper Mill Mgr.: Jean-Louis Pfister
  Phone: (33) 5 34 14 35 00
  Tech. Mgr.: Christophe L. Bardet
  Phone: (33) 5 34 14 35 00
  Maint. Mgr.: Patrice Clanet
  Phone: (33) 5 34 14 35 00
Total Employees at this Location: 298
Type of Operation: Pulp mill, Paper mill
Pulp Grades and Capacities:
  Total pulp capacity: 10,300 mt/y
  Pulp available for market: 3,000 mt/y
  Chemical Pulp: 4,300 mt/y
Pulp Mill Data:
  Chemical Pulping Systems:
  Batch digesters: 5
  Bleach Plant Systems: 1
  No. 1, Sequence: CE, Capacity 5,000 admt/y
  Pulp Dryers:
  Air Float dryers 1
Paper/Paperboard Grades and Capacities:
  Total paper and paperboard capacity: 15,000 mt/y
  Specialty and industrial: 15,000 mt/y
Paper and Paperboard Mill Data:
  Stock Preparation:
  Pulpers: 3
  Refiners: 9
Paper Machines: 3
  No. 1, fourdrinier, total capacity 5,000 mt/y, Trim width 2.2 m, Specialty and industrial
  No. 2, fourdrinier, total capacity 9,000 mt/y, Trim width 3.6 m, Specialty and industrial
  No. 5, fourdrinier, total capacity 1,000 mt/y, Trim width 1.8 m, Specialty and industrial
Finishing Equipment:
  Rewinders: 4
  Sheeters: 1
Energy Data:
  Power boilers: 2
  Combustion turbines: 2 at 0.3 MW

ⓂSAPSO Emballages Ondulés
Bazas Mill
Ownership: SAICA - S.A. Industrias Celulosa Aragonesa
Bernos Beaulac
F-33430 Bazas
France
  Phone: (33) 5 56 65 03 00
  Fax: (33) 5 56 65 03 04
  Email: commercia.pack.beaulacl@saica.com
  Web Address: www.sapso.fr
Personnel:
  Commer. Mgr.: Franck Monestier
  Phone: (33) 5 56 65 03 00
  Mill. Mgr.: Laurent Deroo
  Phone: (33) 5 56 65 03 00
Total Employees at this Location: 150
Type of Operation: Paperboard mill
Pulp Grades and Capacities:
  Total pulp capacity: 55,774 mt/y
  Recycled Pulping: 55,774 mt/y
Pulp Mill Data:
  Recycled Fiber Treatment Lines:

France

Pulpers: 1 at 65,100
Paper/Paperboard Grades and Capacities:
Total paper and paperboard capacity: 55,000 mt/y
Corrugating medium/fluting: 55,000 mt/y
Paper and Paperboard Mill Data:
Paper Machines: 1
No. 1, fourdrinier, total capacity 55,000 mt/y, Trim width 2.5 m, Corrugating medium/fluting
Energy Data:
Power boilers: 2
Electrical demand for mill: 86 MWh/D

ⓂSCA France
Gien Mill
Formerly Georgia-Pacific France acquired by SCA, sale completed late July 2012
Ownership: 100% by SCA - Svenska Cellulosa Aktiebolaget
La Lombardie, Arrobloy 4
F-45504 Gien Cedex
France
  Phone: (33) 2 38 37 54 54
  Fax: (33) 2 38 37 54 72
  Web Address: www.sca.com
Personnel:
  Mill Mgr.: Bruno Voisin
  Phone: (33) 2 38 37 54 54
  Fax: (33) 2 38 37 54 72
  Email: bruno.voisin@sca.com
  Oper. Mgr. (Papermaking): Marc Chefson
  Phone: (33) 2 38 37 56 02
  Fax: (33) 2 38 37 54 72
  Email: marc.chefson@sca.com
  Converting Plant Mgr. & Prod. Mgr.: Christian Bourret
  Phone: (33) 2 38 37 54 54
  Fax: (33) 2 38 37 54 72
  Email: christian.bourret@sca.com
  Qlty. & Environment Mgr.: Jean-Noël Dubus
  Phone: (33) 2 38 37 54 54
  Fax: (33) 2 38 37 54 72
  Email: jean-noel.dubus@sca.com
Total Employees at this Location: 400
Type of Operation: Paper mill
Paper/Paperboard Grades and Capacities:
Total paper and paperboard capacity: 155,000 mt/y
Tissue: 155,000 mt/y
Paper and Paperboard Mill Data:
Stock Preparation:
  Pulpers: 3
  Refiners: 4
Paper Machines: 3
No. 1, twin-wire, Yankee dryer, total capacity 60,000 mt/y, Trim width 5.2 m, Tissue
No. 2, crescent former, Yankee dryer, total capacity 30,000 mt/y, Trim width 2.74 m, Tissue
No. 3, TAD, total capacity 65,000 mt/y, Trim width 5.33 m, Tissue
Finishing Equipment:
  Rewinders: 2
Energy Data:
Power boilers: 3
Electrical demand for mill: 581 MWh/D

ⓂSCA France
Hondouville Mill
Mill is Formerly Georgia-Pacific France acquired by SCA, sale completed late July 2012
Ownership: 100% by SCA - Svenska Cellulosa Aktiebolaget
Hondouville
F-27400 Louviers
France
  Phone: (33) 2 32 25 60 60
  Fax: (33) 2 32 25 61 70
  Web Address: www.sca.com
Personnel:
  Mill Mgr.: Christophe Dorin
  Phone: (33) 2 32 25 60 60
  Fax: (33) 2 32 25 61 70
  Email: christophe.dorin@sca.com
Total Employees at this Location: 620
Type of Operation: Pulp mill, Paper mill
Pulp Grades and Capacities:
Total pulp capacity: 82,056 mt/y
Recycled Pulping: 82,056 mt/y
Pulp Mill Data:
Recycled Fiber Treatment Lines:
  Flotation deinking lines: 1 at 82,100
Paper/Paperboard Grades and Capacities:
Total paper and paperboard capacity: 78,000 mt/y
Tissue: 78,000 mt/y
Paper and Paperboard Mill Data:
Stock Preparation:
  Pulpers: 1
  Refiners: 3
Paper Machines: 2
No. 1, inclined, Yankee dryer, total capacity 21,000 mt/y, Trim width 2.6 m, Tissue
No. 2, crescent former, Yankee dryer, total capacity 57,000 mt/y, Trim width 5.2 m, Tissue
Finishing Equipment:
  Rewinders: 1
Energy Data:
Power boilers: 2
Electrical demand for mill: 277 MWh/D

ⓂSCA Hygiene Products Operations SNC
Orléans Mill
Ownership: SCA Hygiene Products SE
Rue des Bouleaux, ZI de la Saussaye
F-45590 Saint Cyr en Val, Orléans
France
  Phone: (33) 2 38 49 97 97
  Fax: (33) 2 38 63 88 45
  Email: (firstname.lastname@sca.com)
  Web Address: www.sca.com
Personnel:
  Mill Mgr.: Benoist Engelhard
  Phone: (33) 238 499797
  Fax: (33) 238 638845
  Email: benoist.engelhard@sca.com
Total Employees at this Location: 115
Type of Operation: Paper mill
Paper/Paperboard Grades and Capacities:
Total paper and paperboard capacity: 35,000 mt/y
Tissue: 35,000 mt/y
Paper and Paperboard Mill Data:
Paper Machines: 1
No. 1, TAD, total capacity 35,000 mt/y, Trim width 3.6 m, Tissue
Energy Data:
Power boilers: 2
Electrical demand for mill: 182 MWh/D

ⓂSCA Hygiene Products Supply SAS
Le Theil Mill
Ownership: SCA Hygiene Products SE
Route d'Avezé, ZI Sud
F-61260 Le Theil sur Huisne
France
  Phone: (33) 2 37 53 67 00
  Fax: (33) 2 37 53 67 92
  Web Address: www.sca.com
Personnel:
  Mill Mgr.: Bertrand Malet
  Phone: (33) 2 37 53 67 90
  Prod. Mgr.: Bruno Baguin
  Phone: (33) 2 37 53 67 00
  HR Mgr.: Mrs. Chauty-Moussy
  Phone: (33) 2 37 53 67 00
Total Employees at this Location: 330
Type of Operation: Paper mill
Paper/Paperboard Grades and Capacities:
Total paper and paperboard capacity: 62,000 mt/y
Tissue: 62,000 mt/y
Paper and Paperboard Mill Data:
Paper Machines: 1
No. 1, Periformer, Yankee dryer, total capacity 62,000 mt/y, Trim width 5.3 m, Tissue
Energy Data:
Power boilers: 2
Electrical demand for mill: 160 MWh/D

ⓂSCA France
Kunheim Mill
Mill is Formerly Georgia-Pacific France acquired by SCA, sale completed late July 2012
Ownership: 100% by SCA - Svenska Cellulosa Aktiebolaget
Kunheim
F-68320 Muntzenheim
France
  Mailing Address: BP 49, F-68320 Kunheim, France
  Phone: (33) 3 89 72 23 00
  Fax: (33) 3 89 72 91 26
  Web Address: www.sca.com
Personnel:
  VP, R&D Tissue Global Hygiene Category: Remy Ruppel
  Phone: (33) 3 89 72 23 00
  Fax: (33) 3 89 72 91 26
  Email: remy.ruppel@sca.com
  Tech. Mgr.: Daniel Fleck
  Phone: (33) 3 89 72 23 00
  Fax: (33) 3 89 72 91 26
  Email: daniel.fleck@sca.com
Total Employees at this Location: 600
Type of Operation: Paper mill
Paper/Paperboard Grades and Capacities:
Total paper and paperboard capacity: 50,000 mt/y
Tissue: 50,000 mt/y
Paper and Paperboard Mill Data:
Stock Preparation:
  Pulpers: 2
  Refiners: 4
Paper Machines: 1
No. 2, inclined, Yankee dryer, total capacity 50,000 mt/y, Trim width 5.2 m, Tissue
Finishing Equipment:
  Rewinders: 2
Energy Data:
Power boilers: 3
Electrical demand for mill: 152 MWh/D

ⒽⓂSeyfert Paper S.A.S.
Descartes Mill
Ownership: 100% by Palm Group
Av. Monseigneur Roméro, BP 19
F-37160 Descartes
France
  Phone: (33) 2 47 59 76 05
  Fax: (33) 2 47 59 80 95
  Email: seyfert.paper@seyfert.fr
  Web Address: www.seyfert.fr
Personnel:
  Sls. Dir. and Finan. Dir.: T. Makaroff
  Phone: (33) 2 47 59 76 05
  Prod. Dir.: Cristophe Le Biavant
  Phone: (33) 2 47 59 76 05
  Prod. Mgr.: Patrice Boissière
  Phone: (33) 2 47 59 76 05
  Email: p.boissiere@seyfert.fr
  Asst. Mill Mgr.: Annie Proust
  Phone: (33) 2 47 59 76 05
  Maint. Mgr.: Serge Moreau
  Phone: (33) 2 47 59 84 72
  Purch. Agent: Yannick Sourisseau
  Phone: (33) 2 47 59 76 05
Total Employees of Company: 1,200
Total Employees at this Location: 117
Type of Operation: Pulp mill, Paperboard mill
Pulp Grades and Capacities:
Total pulp capacity: 207,417 mt/y
Recycled Pulping: 207,417 mt/y
Pulp Mill Data:

France

Recycled Fiber Treatment Lines:
Pulpers: 2
Recycled packaging pulping lines: 1 at 200,000 admt/y
Paper/Paperboard Grades and Capacities:
Total paper and paperboard capacity: 205,000 mt/y
Linerboard: 100,000 mt/y
Corrugating medium/fluting: 105,000 mt/y
Paper and Paperboard Mill Data:
Paper Machines: 2
No. 1, fourdrinier (2), total capacity 145,000 mt/y, Trim width 3 m, Corrugating medium/fluting, Linerboard
No. 2, fourdrinier, total capacity 60,000 mt/y, Trim width 2.9 m, Corrugating medium/fluting, Linerboard
Finishing Equipment:
Rewinders: 2
Energy Data:
Power boilers: 3
Combustion turbines: 2 at 13.4 MW
Electrical demand for mill: 269 MWh/D

ⓜSICAL
Lumbres Mill
Ownership: 98% by Rossmann SAS
69 rue du Dr. Pontier
F-62380 Lumbres
France
  Phone: (33) 3 21 38 60 00
  Fax: (33) 3 21 38 60 60
  Email: sical@rossmann.com
  Web Address: www.rossmann.com, www.sical.fr
Personnel:
  Pres. SICAL Board: Jean-Marie Paultes
  Phone: (33) 3 21 38 60 09
  Fax: (33) 3 91 38 60 36
  Email: jm.paultes@rossmann.com
  Gen. Mgr. (From May 2013): Thibault Waymel
  Phone: (33) 3 21 38 60 37
  Fax: (33) 3 21 38 60 60
  Email: t.waymel@rossmann.com
  Tech. Mgr.: Bertrand Leveugle
  Phone: (33) 3 21 38 60 34
  Fax: (33) 3 21 38 60 88
  Email: b.leveugle@sical.rossmann.com
  Commercial Mgr.: Frédéric Dufour
  Phone: (33) 3 21 38 60 29
  Fax: (33) 3 21 38 60 91
  Email: f.dufour@sical.rossmann.com
  Finan. Dir.: Fabrice Rossmann
  Phone: (33) 3 21 38 60 01
  Fax: (33) 3 91 38 60 36
  Email: f.rossmann@rossmann.com
Total Employees at this Location: 315
Type of Operation: Pulp mill, Paperboard mill
Pulp Grades and Capacities:
Total pulp capacity: 36,468 mt/y
Recycled Pulping: 36,468 mt/y
Paper/Paperboard Grades and Capacities:
Total paper and paperboard capacity: 36,000 mt/y
Linerboard: 24,000 mt/y
Corrugating medium/fluting: 12,000 mt/y
Paper and Paperboard Mill Data:
Stock Preparation:
Pulpers: 8
Paper Machines: 1
No. 2, fourdrinier, total capacity 36,000 mt/y, Trim width 2.5 m, Linerboard, Corrugating medium/fluting
Energy Data:
Electrical demand for mill: 53 MWh/D

ⓘSmurfit Kappa Europe
Ownership: 100% by Smurfit Kappa Group
2, Rue Goethe
F-75116 Paris
France
  Phone: (33) 1 49 52 32 00
  Fax: (33) 1 49 52 32 12
  Email: info-paper@smurfitkappa.com,
  marketing@smurfitkappa.fr
  Web Address: www.smurfitkappa.fr
Personnel:
  Group CEO: Gary McGann
  Phone: (33) 1 49 52 32 00
  Fax: (33) 1 49 52 32 12
  Email: gary.mcgann@smurfitkappa.com
  Group COO: Tony Smurfit
  Phone: (33) 1 49 52 32 00
  Fax: (33) 1 49 52 32 12
  Email: tony.smurfit@smurfitkappa.com
  Group CFO: Ian Curley
  Phone: (33) 1 49 52 32 00
  Fax: (33) 1 49 52 32 12
  Email: ian.curley@smurfitkappa.com
  CEO, Corr. & Converting: Roberto Villaquiran
  Phone: (33) 1 49 52 32 00
  Fax: (33) 1 49 52 32 12
  Email: roberto.villaquiran@smurfitkappa.com
  CEO, Paper & Board: Alain Baudant
  Phone: (33) 1 49 52 32 00
  Fax: (33) 1 49 52 32 12
  Email: alain.baudant@smurfitkappa.com
  VP. Finan.: John Hiscock
  Phone: (33) 1 49 52 32 00
  Fax: (33) 1 49 52 32 12
  Email: john.hiscock@smurfitkappa.com
  Group VP. HR: German Esguerra
  Phone: (33) 1 49 52 32 00
  Fax: (33) 1 49 52 32 12
  Email: german.esguerra@smurfitkappa.com
  VP. Sourcing: Dominique Binet
  Phone: (33) 1 49 52 32 00
  Fax: (33) 1 49 52 32 12
  Email: dominique.binet@smurfitkappa.com
  VP. Sls. & Mktg.: Huib Havik
  Phone: (33) 1 49 52 32 00
  Fax: (33) 1 49 52 32 12
  Email: huib.havik@smurfitkappa.com
Total Employees of Company: 27,733
Total Employees at this Location: 60
Mill Locations:
Smurfit Kappa Cellulose du Pin, Facture mill, Allée des Fougères, F-33380 Biganos, France, Capacity: 520,000 mt/y, (Pulp mill, Paperboard mill)
  Phone: (33) 5 56 03 88 00
  Fax: (33) 5 56 03 88 02
Smurfit Kappa Ania Paper, Ania Mill, Via del Mulino, I-55055 Ponte all'Ania, (LU) Italy, Capacity: 200,000 mt/y, (Paper mill, Paperboard mill)
  Phone: (39) 0583 70031
  Fax: (39) 0583 709179
  Email: ania.paper@smurfitkappa.it
Smurfit Kappa Baden Karton GmbH, Gernsbach Mill, Fabrikstrasse 1, D-76593 Gernsbach, Germany, Capacity: 145,000 mt/y, (Paperboard mill)
  Phone: (49) 7224 630
  Fax: (49) 7224 631 48
  Email: baden-karton@smurfitkappa.de
Smurfit Kappa Haupt Papier- und Pappenfabrik GmbH & Co. KG, Diemelstadt-Wrexen Mill, Orpethaler Str. 50, D-34474 Diemelstadt-Wrexen, Germany, Capacity: 320,000 mt/y, (Paper mill, Paperboard mill)
  Phone: (49) 5642 790
  Fax: (49) 5642 79177
  Email: info@cdhaupt.de
Smurfit Kappa Herzberger Papierfabrik GmbH, Herzberg Mill, Andreasberger Str. 1, D-37412 Herzberg am Harz, Germany, Capacity: 260,000 mt/y, (Paperboard mill)
  Phone: (49) 5521 82 0
  Fax: (49) 5521 82 395
  Email: info.hp@smurfitkappa.de
Smurfit Kappa Papier & Kartonfabrik Hoya, Hoya Mill, Von-dem-Bussche-Str. 1, D-27318 Hoya/Weser, Germany, Capacity: 425,000 mt/y, (Paperboard mill)
  Phone: (49) 4251 8140
  Fax: (49) 4251 814 169
  Email: info.hoya@smurfitkappa.de
Smurfit Kappa Kraftliner Piteå, Piteå Mill, SE-941 86 Piteå, Sweden, Capacity: 700,000 mt/y, (Pulp mill, Paperboard mill)
  Phone: (46) 911 97000
  Fax: (46) 911 97010
  Email: info.kraftliner@smurfitkappa.se
Smurfit Kappa Papier Recyclé France, Alfa d Avignon Mill, Route Nationale 7 - BP 56, F-84132 Le Pontet Cedex, France, Capacity: 75,000 mt/y, (Paperboard mill)
  Phone: (33) 4 90 03 98 00
  Fax: (33) 4 90 32 34 33
  Email: info-paper@smurfitkappa.com
Smurfit Kappa Mengibar Paper, Mengibar Mill, Carretera de Bailén-Motril, s/n, E-23620 Mengibar, Spain, Capacity: 200,000 mt/y, (Paper mill, Paperboard mill)
  Phone: (34) 95 337 0775
  Fax: (34) 95 337 0825
Smurfit Kappa Morava Paper, Žimrovice Mill, plant Morava Paper, CZ-747 41 Žimrovice, Czech Republic, Capacity: 56,000 mt/y, (Paper mill)
  Phone: (420) 553 753 111
  Fax: (420) 553 753 114
  Email: sales.moravapaper@smurfitkappa.cz; ludek.jurica@smurfitkappa.cz
Smurfit Kappa SSK, Birmingham Mill, Mount St., Nechells, Birmingham B7 5RE, United Kingdom, Capacity: 200,000 mt/y, (Paperboard mill)
  Phone: (44) 121 327 1381
  Fax: (44) 121 322 6300
  Email: info@smurfitkappa.co.uk
Smurfit Kappa Nervión, Iurreta Mill (99.35% owned), Bº Arriandi, s/n, E-48215 Iurreta, Spain, Capacity: 160,000 mt/y, (Pulp mill, Paper mill, Paperboard mill)
  Phone: (34) 946 205100
  Fax: (34) 946 205124
Smurfit Kappa Nettingsdorfer, Nettingsdorfer Papierfabrik AG & Co. KG, Nettingsdorfer Mill, Nettingsdorfer Strasse 40, A-4054 Haid bei Ansfelden, Austria, Capacity: 430,000 mt/y, (Pulp mill, Paperboard mill)
  Phone: (43) 7229 863 0
  Fax: (43) 7229 863 50 / 29 86 312
  Email: nettingsdorfer@smurfitkappa.at
Smurfit Kappa Papier Recyclé France, Sault-les-Rethel mill, Rue de la Petite Prée, BP 5109, F-08300 Sault-les-Rethel, France, Capacity: 68,000 mt/y, (Paperboard mill)
  Phone: (33) 3 24 39 61 81/61
  Fax: (33) 3 24 39 61 90
Smurfit Kappa Roermond Papier BV, Roermond Mill, Mijnheerkensweg 18, NL-6041 TA Roermond, Netherlands, Capacity: 590,000 mt/y, (Paperboard mill)
  Phone: (31) 475 38 44 44
  Fax: (31) 475 33 26 20
  Email: info.skrp@smurfitkappa.nl
Smurfit Kappa Sangüesa Paper, Sanguesa Mill (94.15% owned), Raimundo Lumbier, s/n, E-31400 Sangüesa, Spain, Capacity: 110,000 mt/y, (Paper mill, Paperboard mill)
  Phone: (34) 948 870000
  Fax: (34) 948 870943
Smurfit Kappa Solid Board BV, Oude Pekela Mill, W.H. Westerstraat 59, NL-9665 ZG Oude Pekela, Netherlands, Capacity: 70,000 mt/y, (Pulp mill, Paperboard mill)
  Phone: (31) 503 03 3000
  Fax: (31) 503 03 3991
  Email: sales.solidboard@smurfitkappa.nl
Smurfit Kappa Solid Board BV, Coevorden Mill, Robertweg 2, 1988 Coevorden, Netherlands, Capacity: 100,000 mt/y, (Paper mill)
  Phone: (31) 050 3033000
  Fax: (31) 050 3033399
  Email: mail.solidboard@smurfitkappa.nl; solidboard@smurfitkappa.nl
Smurfit Kappa Solid Board BV, Hoogkerk Mill, Halmstraat 1-3, NL-9745 BC Groningen-Hoogkerk, Netherlands, Capacity: 130,000 mt/y, (Paperboard mill)
  Phone: (31) 50 3033 000
  Fax: (31) 50 3033 999
  Email: mail.solidboard@smurfitkappa.nl

France

Smurfit Kappa Solid Board BV, Nieuweschans Mill, Hoofdstraat 34, 9693 AH Nieuweschans, Netherlands, Capacity: 150,000 mt/y, (Paperboard mill)
Phone: (31) 597 52 91 00
Fax: (31) 597 52 91 99
Email: mail.solidboard@smurfitkappa.nl; solidboard@smurfitkappa.nl

Smurfit Kappa Townsend Hook, Snodland Mill, Snodland ME6 5AX, United Kingdom, (Pulp mill, Paperboard mill)
Phone: (44) 1634 240 205
Fax: (44) 1634 248 046
Email: (firstname.secondname@smurfitkappa.co.uk), info@smurfitkappa.co.uk

Smurfit Kappa GmbH Viersen Papier, Viersen Mill, Krefelder Str. 175, D-41748 Viersen, Germany, Capacity: 70,000 mt/y, (Paperboard mill)
Phone: (49) 2162 249 870
Fax: (49) 2162 249 8733
Email: info.viersen@smurfitkappa.de

Smurfit Kappa Zülpich Papier GmbH, Zülpich Mill, Bessenicher Weg, D-53909 Zülpich, Germany, Capacity: 450,000 mt/y, (Paperboard mill)
Phone: (49) 2252 3060/306120
Fax: (49) 2252 306 166
Email: info.skzp@smurfitkappa.de; info.kzp@kappapackaging.com

Smurfit Kappa Papier Recyclé France, Papeteries de Saillat, Impasse des Papeteries, Saillat-sur-Vienne 2, F-87206 Saint Junien Cedex, France, Capacity: 240,000 mt/y, (Paperboard mill)
Phone: (33) 5 55 03 40 36/02 21 00
Fax: (33) 5 55 03 47 22/02 87 02

ⓂSmurfit Kappa Cellulose du Pin
Facture mill
Ownership: Smurfit Kappa Europe
Allée des Fougères
F-33380 Biganos
France
Phone: (33) 5 56 03 88 00
Fax: (33) 5 56 03 88 02
Web Address: www.smurfitkappa.com/fr
Personnel:
Mill Dir.: Nicolas Lefeuvre
Phone: (33) 5 56 03 88 10
Fax: (33) 5 56 03 88 02
Email: nicolas.lefeuvre@smurfitkappa.fr
Sls. & Mktg. Dir.: Christophe Malinge
Phone: (33) 5 56 03 89 40
Fax: (33) 5 56 03 89 02
Email: christophe.malinge@smurfitkappa.fr
SK European Paper & Pulp Sourcing Regional Mgr.: Pierre Uzureau
Phone: (33) 5 56 03 89 47
Fax: (33) 5 56 03 89 04
Email: pierre.uzureau@smurfitkappa.fr
HR Develop. & Commun. Mgr.: Mathieu Font
Phone: (33) 5 56 03 89 46
Fax: (33) 5 56 03 89 04
Email: mathieu.font@smurfitkappa.fr
Total Employees at this Location: 430
Type of Operation: Pulp mill, Paperboard mill
Pulp Grades and Capacities:
Total pulp capacity: 485,504 mt/y
Chemical Pulp: 392,040 mt/y
Recycled Pulping: 93,464 mt/y
Pulp Mill Data:
Chemical Pulping Systems:
Continuous digesters: 1
Chemical Recovery Equipment:
Evaporator lines: 1
Recovery boilers: 1
Lime Kiln
Recycled Fiber Treatment Lines:
Recycled packaging pulping lines: 1 at 110,000
Paper/Paperboard Grades and Capacities:
Total paper and paperboard capacity: 520,000 mt/y
Linerboard: 520,000 mt/y
Paper and Paperboard Mill Data:
Stock Preparation:
Pulpers: 2
Refiners: 16
Paper Machines: 2
No. 5, fourdrinier (2), Cylinder, total capacity 190,000 mt/y, Trim width 5.4 m, Linerboard
No. 6, fourdrinier (2), Cylinder, total capacity 330,000 mt/y, Trim width 6.9 m, Linerboard
Finishing Equipment:
Rewinders: 2
Energy Data:
Power boilers: 1
Steam turbines: 2 at 48 MW
Electrical demand for mill: 1,193 MWh/D

ⓂSmurfit Kappa Papier Recyclé France
Ownership: Smurfit Kappa Europe
Allée des Fougères
F-33380 Biganos
France
Phone: (33) 5 56 03 88 00
Fax: (33) 5 56 03 89 02
Web Address: www.smurfitkappa.fr
Personnel:
Pres. & CEO: Laurent Sellier
Phone: (33) 5 56 03 88 00
Fax: (33) 5 56 03 88 02
Finan. Dir.: Michèle Code
Phone: (33) 5 56 03 88 00
Fax: (33) 5 56 03 88 02
HR Dir.: Phillipe Duteil
Phone: (33) 5 56 03 88 00
Fax: (33) 5 56 03 88 02
Sls. Dir.: Christophe Malinge
Phone: (33) 5 56 03 89 40
Fax: (33) 5 56 03 89 04
Purch. Dir.: Pierre Uzureau
Phone: (33) 5 56 03 88 00
Fax: (33) 5 56 03 88 02
Email: pierre.uzureau@smurfitkappa.fr
Commun. Coordinator: Mathieu Font
Phone: (33) 5 56 03 89 46
Fax: (33) 5 56 03 89 04
Total Employees of Company: 450
Mill Locations:
Smurfit Kappa Papier Recyclé France, Alfa d Avignon Mill, Route Nationale 7 - BP 56, F-84132 Le Pontet Cedex, France, Capacity: 75,000 mt/y, (Paperboard mill)
Phone: (33) 4 90 03 98 00
Fax: (33) 4 90 32 34 33
Email: info-paper@smurfitkappa.com
Smurfit Kappa Papier Recyclé France, Sault-les-Rethel mill, Rue de la Petite Prée, BP 5109, F-08300 Sault-les-Rethel, France, Capacity: 68,000 mt/y, (Paperboard mill)
Phone: (33) 3 24 39 61 81/61
Fax: (33) 3 24 39 61 90
Smurfit Kappa Papier Recyclé France, Papeteries de Saillat, Impasse des Papeteries, Saillat-sur-Vienne 2, F-87206 Saint Junien Cedex, France, Capacity: 240,000 mt/y, (Paperboard mill)
Phone: (33) 5 55 03 40 36/02 21 00
Fax: (33) 5 55 03 47 22/02 87 02

ⓄⓂSmurfit Kappa Papier Recyclé France
Alfa d Avignon Mill
Ownership: Smurfit Kappa Europe
Route Nationale 7 - BP 56
F-84132 Le Pontet Cedex
France
Phone: (33) 4 90 03 98 00
Fax: (33) 4 90 32 34 33
Email: info-paper@smurfitkappa.com
Web Address: www.smurfitkappa.fr
Personnel:
Man. Dir. / Mill Mgr.: Olivier Chauveau
Phone: (33) 4 90 03 98 01
Fax: (33) 4 90 32 34 33
Email: olivier.chauveau@smurfitkappa.fr
Mgr.: Franck Raffier
Phone: (33) 4 90 03 98 00
Fax: (33) 4 90 32 34 33
Email: franck.raffier@smurfitkappa.fr
Total Employees of Company: 450
Total Employees at this Location: 55
Type of Operation: Paperboard mill
Mill Locations:
Smurfit Kappa Papier Recyclé France, Sault-les-Rethel mill, Rue de la Petite Prée, BP 5109, F-08300 Sault-les-Rethel, France, Capacity: 68,000 mt/y, (Paperboard mill)
Phone: (33) 3 24 39 61 81/61
Fax: (33) 3 24 39 61 90
Smurfit Kappa Papier Recyclé France, Papeteries de Saillat, Impasse des Papeteries, Saillat-sur-Vienne 2, F-87206 Saint Junien Cedex, France, Capacity: 240,000 mt/y, (Paperboard mill)
Phone: (33) 5 55 03 40 36/02 21 00
Fax: (33) 5 55 03 47 22/02 87 02
Pulp Grades and Capacities:
Total pulp capacity: 76,294 mt/y
Recycled Pulping: 76,294 mt/y
Pulp Mill Data:
Recycled Fiber Treatment Lines:
Pulpers: 2 at 84,100
Paper/Paperboard Grades and Capacities:
Total paper and paperboard capacity: 75,000 mt/y
Linerboard: 75,000 mt/y
Paper and Paperboard Mill Data:
Paper Machines: 1
No. 1, fourdrinier (2), total capacity 75,000 mt/y, Trim width 2.8 m, Linerboard
Energy Data:
Power boilers: 3
Combustion turbines: 1 at 9 MW
Electrical demand for mill: 89 MWh/D

ⓄⓂSmurfit Kappa Papier Recyclé France
Sault-les-Rethel mill
Ownership: Smurfit Kappa Europe
Rue de la Petite Prée, BP 5109
F-08300 Sault-les-Rethel
France
Phone: (33) 3 24 39 61 81/61
Fax: (33) 3 24 39 61 90
Web Address: www.smurfitgroup.com
Personnel:
Mill Mgr.: William Durnay
Phone: (33) 3 24 39 61 81
Fax: (33) 3 24 39 61 90
Email: william.durnay@smurfitkappa.fr
Maint. Mgr.: Laurent Peronnet
Phone: (33) 3 24 39 61 83
Fax: (33) 3 24 39 61 80
Email: laurent.peronnet@smurfitkappa.fr
Total Employees at this Location: 49
Type of Operation: Paperboard mill
Pulp Grades and Capacities:
Total pulp capacity: 69,714 mt/y
Recycled Pulping: 69,714 mt/y
Pulp Mill Data:
Recycled Fiber Treatment Lines:
Pulpers: 1 at 70,000 admt/y
Paper/Paperboard Grades and Capacities:
Total paper and paperboard capacity: 68,000 mt/y
Linerboard: 68,000 mt/y
Paper and Paperboard Mill Data:
Paper Machines: 1
No. 1, fourdrinier (2), total capacity 68,000 mt/y, Trim width 2.5 m, Linerboard
Finishing Equipment:
Winders: 1
Energy Data:

France

Power boilers: 1
Electrical demand for mill: 68 MWh/D

ⓂSmurfit Kappa Papier Recyclé France
Papeteries de Saillat
Ownership: Smurfit Kappa Europe
Impasse des Papeteries, Saillat-sur-Vienne 2
F-87206 Saint Junien Cedex
France
  Phone: (33) 5 55 03 40 36/02 21 00
  Fax: (33) 5 55 03 47 22/02 87 02
  Web Address: www.smurfitkappa.com
Personnel:
  Prod. Mgr.: Pierre Deveaux
  Phone: (33) 5 55 03 40 36
  Fax: (33) 5 55 03 47 22
  Email: pierre.deveaux@smurfitkappa.fr
Total Employees at this Location: 131
Type of Operation: Paperboard mill
Pulp Grades and Capacities:
  Total pulp capacity: 240,239 mt/y
  Recycled Pulping: 240,239 mt/y
Pulp Mill Data:
  Recycled Fiber Treatment Lines:
  Pulpers: 2
Paper/Paperboard Grades and Capacities:
  Total paper and paperboard capacity: 240,000 mt/y
  Linerboard: 125,000 mt/y
  Corrugating medium/fluting: 115,000 mt/y
Paper and Paperboard Mill Data:
  Stock Preparation:
  Pulpers: 2
  Refiners: 2
Paper Machines: 2
  No. 4, fourdrinier (2), total capacity 125,000 mt/y, Trim width 2.6 m, Linerboard
  No. 5, fourdrinier, total capacity 115,000 mt/y, Trim width 2.6 m, Corrugating medium/fluting
Finishing Equipment:
  Rewinders: 2
Energy Data:
  Power boilers: 2
  Steam turbines: 1 at 4.5 MW
  Hydro turbines: 2
  Electrical demand for mill: 336 MWh/D

ⓂSonoco Paper France SAS
Schweighouse Mill
Ownership: 100% by Sonoco Products Co.
5 rue de la Gare-BP 10318
F-67507 Schweighouse sur Moder
France
  Phone: (33) 3 88 72 64 00/0910
  Fax: (33) 3 88 72 64 34
  Web Address: www.sonoco.com
Personnel:
  Finan. Mgr.: Michel Jotz
  Phone: (33) 3 88 72 64 00
  Fax: (33) 3 88 72 64 34
  Email: michel.jotz@sonoco-alcore.net
  European Sls. Dir. - Paper Div.: Christophe Houdé
  Phone: (33) 3 88 72 64 00
  Fax: (33) 3 88 72 64 34
  Email: christophe.houde@sonoco-alcore.net
Total Employees at this Location: 102
Type of Operation: Pulp mill, Paper mill, Paperboard mill
Pulp Grades and Capacities:
  Total pulp capacity: 57,990 mt/y
  Recycled Pulping: 57,990 mt/y
Pulp Mill Data:
  Recycled Fiber Treatment Lines:
  Pulpers: 2 at 200 admt/y
Paper/Paperboard Grades and Capacities:
  Total paper and paperboard capacity: 86,000 mt/y
  Specialty and industrial: 29,000 mt/y
  Boxboard/cartonboard: 57,000 mt/y
Paper and Paperboard Mill Data:
  Stock Preparation:
  Pulpers: 2
  Refiners: 5
Paper Machines: 2
  No. 4, fourdrinier, Yankee dryer, total capacity 29,000 mt/y, Trim width 2.3 m, Specialty and industrial
  No. 5, multi-fourdrinier, total capacity 57,000 mt/y, Trim width 2.4 m, Boxboard/cartonboard
Finishing Equipment:
  Rewinders: 3
  Sheeters: 1
Energy Data:
  Power boilers: 1
  Combustion turbines: 1 at 1.5 MW
  Electrical demand for mill: 167 MWh/D

ⒽⓂStora Enso Printing and Reading
Corbehem Mill
Company is for sale, temporarily closed (Stora Enso halted production at the end of January 2014, while continuing to search for potential suitors interested in possibly acquiring the site)
Ownership: 100% by Stora Enso Oyj
Rue de Brébières, BP 2
F-62112 Corbehem
France
Mailing Address: 2, rue de Corbehem, F-62117 Brebières, France
  Phone: (33) 3 27 92 32 00
  Fax: (33) 3 27 97 99 60/92 33 31
  Email: (firstname.lastname@storaenso.com)
  Web Address: www.storaenso.com
Personnel:
  Mill Mgr.: Jacques Fackeure
  Phone: (33) 3 27 92 31 12
  Email: jacques.fackeure@storaenso.com
  Controller: Patrick Duchâtel
  Phone: (33) 3 27 92 33 36
  Email: patrick.duchatel@storaenso.com
Total Employees at this Location: 349
Type of Operation: Pulp mill, Paper mill
Mill Locations:
Stora Enso Printing and Reading, Nymölla Mill, SE-295 80 Nymölla, Sweden, Capacity: 500,000 mt/y, (Pulp mill, Paper mill)
  Phone: (46) 1046 440 00
  Fax: (46) 1046 446 00
Stora Enso Printing and Reading, Oulu Mill, PO Box 196, FI-90101 Oulu, Finland, Capacity: 1,085,000 mt/y, (Pulp mill, Paper mill)
  Phone: (358) 2046 124
  Fax: (358) 2046 336 49
  Email: (firstname.lastname@storaenso.com)
Stora Enso Printing and Reading, Uetersen Mill, Pinnau-Allee 3, D-25436 Uetersen, Germany, Capacity: 230,000 mt/y, (Paper mill)
  Phone: (49) 4122 7190
  Fax: (49) 4122 719 339/222
  Email: corporate.communications@storaenso.com; empfang-poststelle.uetersen.ext@storaenso.com
Stora Enso Printing and Reading, Varkaus Mill, PO Box 260, FI-78201 Varkaus, Finland, Capacity: 285,000 mt/y, (Pulp mill, Paper mill)
  Phone: (358) 2046 120
  Fax: (358) 2046 321 02
Stora Enso Printing and Reading, Veitsiluoto Mill, FI-94800 Kemi, Finland, Capacity: 830,000 mt/y, (Pulp mill, Paper mill)
  Phone: (358) 2046 125
  Fax: (358) 2046 34427 (Fine Paper), 34907 (Publication Paper)
  Email: (firstname.lastname@storaenso.com)
Stora Enso Printing and Reading, Langerbrugge Mill, Wondelgemkaai 200, B-9000 Gent, Belgium, Capacity: 555,000 mt/y, (Pulp mill, Paper mill)
  Phone: (32) 9 2577211
  Fax: (32) 9 2577200
  Email: langerbrugge.mill@storaenso.com, (firstname.lastname@storaenso.com)
Stora Enso Printing and Reading, Hylte Mill, SE-314 81 Hyltebruk, Sweden, Capacity: 485,000 mt/y, (Pulp mill, Paper mill)
  Phone: (46) 1046 190 00
  Fax: (46) 1046 188 76
Stora Enso Printing and Reading, Anjala Mill, FI-46900 Kouvola, Finland, Capacity: 435,000 mt/y, (Pulp mill, Paper mill)
  Phone: (358) 2046 117
  Fax: (358) 2046 263 00
  Email: (firstname.lastname@storaenso.com)
Stora Enso Printing and Reading, Kabel Mill, Schwerter Str. 263, D-58099 Hagen, Germany, Capacity: 495,000 mt/y, (Paper mill)
  Phone: (49) 2331 699 0
  Fax: (49) 2331 699 516
  Email: storaensokabel@storaenso.com
Stora Enso Printing and Reading, Kvarnsveden Mill, SE-781 83 Borlänge, Sweden, Capacity: 750,000 mt/y, (Pulp mill, Paper mill)
  Phone: (46) 1046 650 00
  Fax: (46) 1046 653 90
Stora Enso Printing and Reading, Maxau Mill, Mitscherlichstrasse, D-76187 Karlsruhe, Germany, Capacity: 530,000 mt/y, (Paper mill)
  Phone: (49) 721 9566 0
  Fax: (49) 721 9566 130
  Email: corporate.communications@storaenso.com, (firstname.lastname@storaenso.com)
Stora Enso Printing and Reading, Sachsen Mill, Am Schanzberg 1, D-04838 Eilenburg, Germany, Capacity: 320,000 mt/y, (Pulp mill, Paper mill)
  Phone: (49) 3423 650 0
  Fax: (49) 3423 650 396/390
  Email: sachsen.feedback@storaenso.com, (firstname.lastname@storaenso.com)
Pulp Mill Data:
  Mechanical Pulping Systems:
  TMP systems: 2
Pulp Lines: 2
  Bleach Plant Systems: 1
  TMP, Type: Andritz, Sequence: P, Capacity 195,000 admt/y
Paper and Paperboard Mill Data:
  Stock Preparation:
  Pulpers: 2
  Refiners: 6
Paper Machines: 1
  No. 5, (Suppliers: Voith/Metso.), OptiFormer, total capacity 330,000 mt/y, Trim width 8.6 m
Coating Machines: 1
  No. 1, total capacity 330,000 mt/y., on machine
Finishing Equipment:
  Winders: 2
  Supercalenders: 2
  Rewinders: 3
Energy Data:
  Power boilers: 4
  TMP Reboiler: 1

ⒽⓂTembec Tartas
Tartas Mill
Ownership: 100% by Tembec Inc.
1154 av. du Général Leclerc
F-40400 Tartas
France
  Phone: (33) 5 58 56 47 56
  Fax: (33) 5 58 56 47 00
  Email: tartas.adv@tembec.com
  Web Address: www.tartas-sa.fr
Personnel:
  Gen. Mgr.: Marise Coutou
  Phone: (33) 5 58 56 47 56
  Purch. Mgr.: Richard Descloux
  Phone: (33) 5 58 56 47 56
  Admin. & Finan. Dir.: Estelle Herel
  Phone: (33) 5 58 56 47 56
  HR Mgr.: Daniel Busin
  Phone: (33) 5 58 56 47 56
Total Employees at this Location: 300

France

Type of Operation: Pulp mill
Pulp Grades and Capacities:
  Total pulp capacity: 157,612 mt/y
  Pulp available for market: 150,000 mt/y
  Chemical Pulp: 157,612 mt/y
Pulp Mill Data:
  Chemical Pulping Systems:
  Batch digesters: 9
  Bleach Plant Systems: 1
  No. 1, Sequence: O_2 EoDEoD, Capacity 150,000 admt/y
  Chemical Recovery Equipment:
  Evaporator lines: 1
  Recovery boilers: 2
  Pulp Dryers:
  Air Float dryers 1
Energy Data:
  Power boilers: 1
  Steam turbines: 2 at 12, 8.7 MW
  Electrical demand for mill: 422 MWh/D

ⓜUPM
Ownership: UPM GmbH
134 rue Danton
F-92593 Levallois-Perret cédex
France
  Phone: (33) 1 46 39 30 00
  Fax: (33) 1 46 39 30 99
  Email: media@upm.com
  Web Address: www.upmpaper.com,
  www.upm.com
Personnel:
  Pres.: Jean-Marc Louvet
  Phone: (33) 1 46 39 30 00
  Fax: (33) 1 46 39 30 99
  VP HR.: Daniel Schwab
  Phone: (33) 1 46 39 30 00
  Fax: (33) 1 46 39 30 99
  Email: daniel.schwab@upm.com
  Responsable Environ. for the Western Europe: Geoffroy de Montmarin
  Phone: (33) 1 46 39 30 00
  Fax: (33) 1 46 39 30 99
  Tech. Sls. Mgr.: Philippe Walter
  Phone: (33) 1 46 39 30 00
  Fax: (33) 1 46 39 30 99
  Email: philippe.walter@upm.com
Mill Locations:
UPM, Chapelle Darblay Paper Mill, CD 3, F-76530 Grand-Couronne, France, Capacity: 380,000 mt/y, (Pulp mill, Paper mill)
  Phone: (33) 2 35 18 40 00
  Fax: (33) 2 35 18 40 40
  Email: info.chapelle@upm.com
UPM, Docelles Paper Mill, 1 rue du Grand Meix, F-88460 Docelles, France, (Paper mill)
  Phone: (33) 3 29 33 81 00
  Fax: (33) 3 29 33 81 81
  Email: info.docelles@upm.com

ⓜUPM
Chapelle Darblay Paper Mill
Ownership: UPM GmbH
CD 3
F-76530 Grand-Couronne
France
Mailing Address: P.O. Box 1, F-76530 Grand-Couronne, France
  Phone: (33) 2 35 18 40 00
  Fax: (33) 2 35 18 40 40
  Email: info.chapelle@upm.com
  Web Address: www.upm.com
Personnel:
  Prod. Mgr., MFS: Sébastien Finel
  Phone: (33) 2 35 18 40 00
  Fax: (33) 2 35 18 40 40
  Email: sebastien.finel@upm.com
  Prod. Mgr., Newsprint: Laurent Paon
  Phone: (33) 2 35 18 40 00
  Fax: (33) 2 35 18 40 40
  Email: laurent.paon@upm.com
  Procurement Dir. & External Relations: Philippe Carrière
  Phone: (33) 2 35 18 40 51
  Fax: (33) 2 35 18 40 30
  Email: philippe.carriere@upm-kymmene.com
  HR Mgr.: Emilie Legrand
  Phone: (33) 2 35 18 40 00
  Fax: (33) 2 35 18 40 40
  Email: emilie.legrand@upm.com
  Tech. Mgr.: Laurent Bonvalet
  Phone: (33) 2 35 18 40 00
  Fax: (33) 2 35 18 40 40
  Email: laurent.bonvalet@upm.com
Total Employees at this Location: 360
Type of Operation: Pulp mill, Paper mill
Pulp Grades and Capacities:
  Total pulp capacity: 391,788 mt/y
  Recycled Pulping: 391,788 mt/y
Pulp Mill Data:
Pulp Lines: 3
  Bleach Plant Systems: 2
  DIP 1/DIP 2, Sequence: P/Y, Capacity 233,000 admt/y
  Recycled Fiber Treatment Lines:
  Flotation deinking lines: 1 at 90,000 admt/y
  Flotation deinking lines: 1 at 143,000
  Flotation deinking lines: 1 at 410,000
  Pulpers: 3
Paper/Paperboard Grades and Capacities:
  Total paper and paperboard capacity: 380,000 mt/y
  Newsprint: 255,000 mt/y
  Uncoated mechanical/groundwood: 125,000 mt/y
Paper and Paperboard Mill Data:
Paper Machines: 2
  No. 3, SymFormer R, total capacity 130,000 mt/y, Trim width 5.2 m, Uncoated mechanical/groundwood, Newsprint
  No. 6, ValFormer, total capacity 250,000 mt/y, Trim width 8.4 m, Newsprint
Finishing Equipment:
  Winders: 4
  Rewinders: 2
Energy Data:
  Power boilers: 3
  HRSG boiler: 1
  Combustion turbines: 1 at 26 MW
  Steam turbines: 3 at 9, 3, 21 MW
  Electrical demand for mill: 1,011 MWh/D

ⓜUPM
Docelles Paper Mill
Mill is closed (permanently closed on January 24, 2014.)
Ownership: UPM GmbH
1 rue du Grand Meix
F-88460 Docelles, Vosges
France
  Phone: (33) 3 29 33 81 00
  Fax: (33) 3 29 33 81 81
  Email: info.docelles@upm.com
  Web Address: www.upm.com
Personnel:
  Gen. Dir.: Jean Kubiak
  Phone: (33) 3 29 33 81 17
  Email: jean.kubiak@upm.com
  Prod. & Tech. Mgr.: Philippe Pinard
  Phone: (33) 3 29 33 81 07
  Email: philippe.pinard@upm.com
  R&D Mgr.: Richard Jeanpierre
  Phone: (33) 3 29 33 81 49
  Email: richard.jeanpierre@upm.com
Total Employees at this Location: 161
Type of Operation: Paper mill
Paper and Paperboard Mill Data:
  Stock Preparation:
  Pulpers:
Paper Machines: 1
  No. 1, twin-wire, total capacity 160,000 mt/y, Trim width 3.84 m
Energy Data:
  Power boilers: 1
  Steam turbines: 1

ⓜVertaris/Delion France SA
Voreppe Mill
Mill is under construction, temporarily closed (stopped production mid-September 2011. The mill was due to start up de-inked market Pulp production from waste paper in late fall of 2014)
Ownership: 100% by Springwater Capital
379 rue Louis Armand, Centr'Alp, BP 125
F-38340 Voreppe
France
  Phone: (33) 4 38 26 19 40
  Fax: (33) 4 76 50 52 00/ 53 82 65
Personnel:
  Pres.: François Vessière
  Phone: (33) 4 38 26 19 50
  Logistic. & Commer. Dir.: Emmanuel Arcondara
  Phone: (33) 4 38 26 19 48
  Prod Tech. and R&D Dir.: Jean Carlos Fernandes
  Phone: (33) 4 38 26 19 49
Total Employees at this Location: 20
Type of Operation: Pulp mill, Paper mill
Paper and Paperboard Mill Data:
Paper Machines: 2
  No. 5, fourdrinier, total capacity 69,972 mt/y, Trim width 3.7 m
  No. 6, fourdrinier, total capacity 79,968 mt/y, Trim width 3.7 m
Finishing Equipment:
  Sheeters: 3 at 20 mt/y
Energy Data:
  Power boilers: 3

ⓗⓜPapeteries de Vizille (Vicat)
Vizille Mill
Ownership: Vicat
1176 avenue Aristide Briand
F-38220 Vizille
France
  Phone: (33) 4 76 68 54 00
  Fax: (33) 4 76 78 89 82
  Email: papeterie.vizille@vicat.fr
  Web Address: www.vicat.com
Personnel:
  Gen. Dir.: Mr. Jeauneau
  Phone: (33) 4 76 68 54 00
  Tech. Dir.: Alexandre Roman
  Phone: (33) 4 76 68 54 00
  Email: a.roman@vicat.fr
  Sls. Dir.: Pascal Tomasino
  Phone: (33) 4 76 68 20 55
  Email: p.tomasino@vicat.fr
Total Employees of Company: 160
Total Employees at this Location: 160
Type of Operation: Paper mill
Pulp Grades and Capacities:
  Total pulp capacity: 960 mt/y
  Mechanical Pulp: 960 mt/y
Pulp Mill Data:
  Mechanical Pulping Systems:
  RMP systems: 1
  Bleach Plant Systems: 1
  Mechanical pulp Capacity 7,000 admt/y
Paper/Paperboard Grades and Capacities:
  Total paper and paperboard capacity: 30,000 mt/y
  Uncoated woodfree/freesheet: 21,000 mt/y
  Specialty and industrial: 9,000 mt/y
Paper and Paperboard Mill Data:
  Stock Preparation:
  Pulpers: 4
  Refiners: 3
Paper Machines: 1
  No. 5, fourdrinier, total capacity 30,000 mt/y, Trim width 2.45 m, Uncoated woodfree/freesheet, Specialty and industrial

Finishing Equipment:
Rewinders: 2
Sheeters: 2
Energy Data:
Power boilers: 3
Hydro turbines: 2 at 60 MW
Electrical demand for mill: 100 MWh/D

ⓂPapeteries des Vosges (PDV)
Laval-sur-Vologne Mill
Ownership: Bolloré Thin Papers
34, rue Maurice Mougeot, BP 26
F-88600 Laval-sur-Vologne
France
Mailing Address: P.B. 26, F-88600 Laval-sur-Vologne, France
Phone: (33) 3 29 53 52 00
Fax: (33) 4 50 81 52 01
Email: marketing.pdl@pdl.fr
Web Address: www.bollorethinpapers.us
Personnel:
Gen. Dir. Bolloré Thin Papers: Philippe Agut
Phone: (33) 3 29 53 52 00
Mill Dir.: Marc Gilardi
Phone: (33) 4 50 81 52 20
Total Employees at this Location: 129
Type of Operation: Paper mill
Paper/Paperboard Grades and Capacities:
Total paper and paperboard capacity: 52,500 mt/y
Uncoated woodfree/freesheet: 52,500 mt/y
Paper and Paperboard Mill Data:
Paper Machines: 1
No. 1, hybrid former, total capacity 52,500 mt/y, Trim width 3.6 m, Uncoated woodfree/freesheet
Energy Data:
Power boilers: 1
Electrical demand for mill: 108 MWh/D

ⓅⓂWEPA Lille S.A.R.L.
Bousbecque Mill
Ownership: WEPA Hygieneprodukte GmbH
Avenue de l'Europe
F-59166 Bousbecque
France
Phone: (33) 3 20 11 57 00
Fax: (33) 3 20 25 93 33
Email: info@wepa.de
Web Address: www.wepa.de
Personnel:
Mill Mgr.: Pascal Pacaud
Phone: (33) 3 20 25 69 98
Fax: (33) 3 20 25 93 33
Email: pascal.pacaud@wepa-lucca.com
Maint. Mgr.: Pierre Tanfin
Phone: (33) 3 20 11 57 00
Fax: (33) 3 20 25 93 33
Email: pierre.tanfin@wepa-lucca.com
Total Employees at this Location: 100
Type of Operation: Paper mill
Pulp Grades and Capacities:
Total pulp capacity: 12,383 mt/y
Recycled Pulping: 12,383 mt/y
Pulp Mill Data:
Recycled Fiber Treatment Lines:
Pulpers: 1 at 17,100
Paper/Paperboard Grades and Capacities:
Total paper and paperboard capacity: 60,000 mt/y
Tissue: 60,000 mt/y
Paper and Paperboard Mill Data:
Stock Preparation:
Pulpers:
Paper Machines: 2
No. 1, (Suppliers: Erwepa/Toscotec.), crescent former, Yankee dryer, total capacity 29,000 mt/y, Trim width 2.6 m, Tissue
No. 2, crescent former, Yankee dryer, total capacity 31,000 mt/y, Trim width 2.7 m, Tissue
Energy Data:
Power boilers: 1
Electrical demand for mill: 165 MWh/D

ⓅⓂPapeterie Zuber Rieder
Boussières Mill
Ownership: 70% by Zedco
Rue Ernest Zuber
F-25320 Boussières
France
Phone: (33) 3 81 60 88 00
Fax: (33) 3 81 60 88 01
Email: info@zuberrieder.net
Web Address: www.zuberrieder.net
Personnel:
Pres. & Chmn.: Luc René Gaillet
Phone: (33) 3 81 60 88 00
Gen. Mgr. & Dir.: Alain Martz
Phone: (33) 3 81 60 88 00
Tech. Dir.: Jean-Pierre Vaudolon
Phone: (33) 3 81 60 88 22
Commer. Mgr.: Jacques Malian
Phone: (33) 3 81 60 88 13
Email: jmalian@zuberrieder.net
Purch. Dir.: Corinne Champod
Phone: (33) 3 81 60 88 00
Qlty & Env. & R&D Dir.: Olivier Goulais
Phone: (33) 3 81 60 88 00
Total Employees at this Location: 88
Type of Operation: Paper mill
Paper/Paperboard Grades and Capacities:
Total paper and paperboard capacity: 11,500 mt/y
Uncoated woodfree/freesheet: 11,500 mt/y
Paper and Paperboard Mill Data:
Stock Preparation:
Pulpers: 2
Refiners: 5
Paper Machines: 1
No. 1, fourdrinier, total capacity 11,500 mt/y, Trim width 2.1 m, Uncoated woodfree/freesheet
Finishing Equipment:
Rewinders: 1 at 11,500 mt/y
Sheeters: 2 at 10,000 mt/y
Energy Data:
Power boilers: 1

GERMANY

ⓅⓂAhlstrom Osnabrück GmbH
Osnabrück Mill
Ownership: Ahlstrom Corporation Oy
Römereschstr. 33
D-49090 Osnabrück
Germany
Mailing Address: Postf. 34 07 / 09, D-49024 Osnabrück, Germany
Phone: (49) 541 6040
Fax: (49) 541 604210
Email: investor@ahlstrom.com, corporate.communications@ahlstrom.com
Web Address: www.ahlstrom.com
Personnel:
VP & Gen. Mgr., Dir. Product Line Wallpaper/Poster base: Jürgen Oess
Phone: (49) 541 604 333
Fax: (49) 541 604 394
Email: juergen.oess@ahlstrom.com
Prod. Mgr.: Jan Witt
Phone: (49) 541 604 338
Fax: (49) 541 604210
Email: jan.witt@ahlstrom.com
Prod. Mgr. & R&D Mgr.: Holger Arnold
Phone: (49) 541 6040
Fax: (49) 541 604210
Email: holger.arnold@ahlstrom.com
HR Dir.: Bastian Thiebach
Phone: (49) 541 6040
Fax: (49) 541 604210
Email: bastian.thiebach@ahlstrom.com
Controller, Logistics and IT: Dirk Mühlenmeister
Phone: (49) 541 6040
Fax: (49) 541 604210
Email: dirk.muehlenmeister@ahlstrom.com
Total Employees of Company: 5,841
Total Employees at this Location: 359
Type of Operation: Paper mill
Paper/Paperboard Grades and Capacities:
Total paper and paperboard capacity: 135,000 mt/y
Coated woodfree/freesheet: 25,000 mt/y
Specialty and industrial: 110,000 mt/y
Paper and Paperboard Mill Data:
Stock Preparation:
Pulpers: 6
Refiners: 17
Paper Machines: 3
No. 3, fourdrinier, total capacity 22,000 mt/y, Trim width 2.3 m, Specialty and industrial
No. 4, fourdrinier, total capacity 28,000 mt/y, Trim width 2.1 m, Specialty and industrial
No. 6, DuoFormer D, total capacity 85,000 mt/y, Trim width 3.4 m, Specialty and industrial, Coated woodfree/freesheet
Coating Machines: 1
PM 6
Finishing Equipment:
Supercalenders: 3
Rewinders: 6
Energy Data:
Power boilers: 2
Combustion turbines: 2 at 5.5 MW
Electrical demand for mill: 246 MWh/D

ⓅⓂAPO Pappenfabrik Apostelmühle GmbH
Rodalben Mill
Apostelmühle 3
D-66976 Rodalben
Germany
Mailing Address: Postf. 12 61, D-66972 Rodalben, Germany
Phone: (49) 6331 23330
Fax: (49) 6331 233333
Email: IVU-Apostelmuehle@t-online.de, apo-pappenfabrik@t-online.de
Web Address: www.ivu-apo.de
Personnel:
CEO & Founder: Dipl. Ing. Manfred Schenk
Gen Mgr.: Fritz Schaaf-Tempel
Phone: (49) 6331 23330
Total Employees at this Location: 10
Type of Operation: Paperboard mill
Paper/Paperboard Grades and Capacities:
Total paper and paperboard capacity: 5,000 mt/y
Boxboard/cartonboard: 5,000 mt/y
Paper and Paperboard Mill Data:
Paper Machines: 1
No. 1, total capacity 5,000 mt/y, Trim width 4.5 m, Boxboard/cartonboard
Energy Data:
Power boilers: 1

ⓂArctic Paper Mochenwangen GmbH
Mochenwangen Mill
Ownership: 75% by Arctic Paper S.A.
Fabrikstrasse 62
D-88284 Mochenwangen, Wolpertswende
Germany
Mailing Address: Postf. 61, D-88282 Wolpertswende, Germany
Phone: (49) 7502 4010
Fax: (49) 7502 4012 16/ 4012 13
Email: info-mochenwangen@arcticpaper.com
Web Address: www.arcticpaper.com
Personnel:
Man. Dir.: Lother Burchardt
Phone: (49) 7502 4010

Germany

Fax: (49) 7502 4012 16
Email: lother.burchardt@arcticpaper.com
Man. Dir.: Michal Jarczynski
Phone: (49) 7502 4010
Fax: (49) 7502 4012 16
Finan. Mgr.: Jörg Röder
Phone: (49) 7502 4012 50
Fax: (49) 7502 4012 16
Email: joerg.roeder@arcticpaper.com
Prod. & Tech. Mgr.: Kurt Jurczik
Phone: (49) 7502 4014 01
Fax: (49) 7502 4012 16
Email: kurt.jurczik@arcticpaper.com
Purch. Mgr.: Hans-Georg Hurtig
Phone: (49) 75024013 40
Fax: (49) 45024013 20
Email: hans-georg.hurtig@arcticpaper.com
Product Mgr. Pamo & L-Print: Michael Stupp
Phone: (49) 7502 4012 56, 151 14845712
Fax: (49) 7502 4012 17
Email: michael.stupp@arcticpaper.com
HR Mgr.: Erwin Baumann
Phone: (49) 7502 4013 03
Fax: (49) 7502 4013 00
Email: erwin.baumann@arcticpaper.com
Mgr Cust. Tech. Serv.: Jörg Rogler
Phone: (49) 7502 4012 18
Fax: (49) 7502 4013 34
Email: joerg.rogler@arcticpaper.com
Total Employees at this Location: 166
Type of Operation: Paper mill
Pulp Grades and Capacities:
  Total pulp capacity: 47,062 mt/y
  Mechanical Pulp: 47,062 mt/y
Pulp Mill Data:
  Mechanical Pulping Systems:
  Pressurized grinders: 4
  Bleach Plant Systems: 1
  GW, Sequence: P/HS, Capacity 52,000 admt/y
Paper/Paperboard Grades and Capacities:
  Total paper and paperboard capacity: 105,000 mt/y
  Uncoated mechanical/groundwood: 105,000 mt/y
Paper and Paperboard Mill Data:
  Paper Machines: 2
  No. 2, hybrid former, total capacity 60,000 mt/y, Trim width 3 m, Uncoated mechanical/groundwood
  No. 3, DuoFormer D, total capacity 45,000 mt/y, Trim width 2.85 m, Uncoated mechanical/groundwood
Finishing Equipment:
  Winders: 4
  Rewinders: 1
  Sheeters: 1
Energy Data:
  Power boilers: 1
  Steam turbines: 1 at 9.5 MW
  Electrical demand for mill: 405 MWh/D

Aviretta GmbH
Ganghoferstraße 8
82131 Stockdorf, Bavaria
Germany
Mill Locations:
Aviretta GmbH, Ettringen Mill, Fabrikstr. 4, Germany, (Paperboard mill)

Aviretta GmbH
Ettringen Mill
Mill is under construction (completion expected in the second quarter of 2015)
Fabrikstr. 4
Germany
Type of Operation: Paperboard mill

Baiersbronn Frischfaserkarton GmbH
Baiersbronn Mill
Ownership: Mayr-Melnhof Karton AG
Sägmühleweg 18
D-72270 Baiersbronn
Germany
 Phone: (49) 7442 831 0
 Fax: (49) 7442 831 240
 Email: sales.baiersbronn@mm-karton.com, baiersbronn@mm-karton.com
 Web Address: www.mm-karton.com
Personnel:
Man. Dir.: Dipl. Ing. Helmut Payer
Phone: (49) 7442 831 0
Fax: (49) 7442 831 240
Email: helmut.payer@mm-karton.com
Tech. Mill Mgr.: Dipl. Ing. Stephan Klein
Phone: (49) 7442 831 0
Fax: (49) 7442 831 240
Email: stephan.klein@mm-karton.com
Sls. Mgr.: Kurt Behm
Phone: (49) 7442 831 0
Fax: (49) 7442 831 240
Email: kurt.behm@mm-karton.com
Total Employees at this Location: 160
Type of Operation: Pulp mill, Paperboard mill
Pulp Grades and Capacities:
  Total pulp capacity: 40,087 mt/y
  Mechanical Pulp: 40,087 mt/y
Pulp Mill Data:
  Mechanical Pulping Systems:
  Conventional grinders: 2
  Recycled Fiber Treatment Lines:
  Recycled packaging pulping lines
Paper/Paperboard Grades and Capacities:
  Total paper and paperboard capacity: 80,000 mt/y
  Boxboard/cartonboard: 80,000 mt/y
Paper and Paperboard Mill Data:
  Stock Preparation:
  Pulpers: 3
  Refiners: 11
Paper Machines: 1
  No. 1, fourdrinier (3), total capacity 80,000 mt/y, Trim width 2.19 m, Boxboard/cartonboard
Coating Machines: 1
  BM 1, total capacity 80,000 mt/y., on machine
Finishing Equipment:
  Rewinders: 1
  Sheeters: 2
Energy Data:
  Power boilers: 1
  Combustion turbines at 4 MW
  Steam turbines: 1 at 4.5 MW
  Electrical demand for mill: 238 MWh/D

Baron-Well GmbH
Goslar Mill
Wolfenbütteler Str. 44
D-38642 Goslar
Germany
 Phone: (49) 5321 653 49
 Fax: (49) 5321 651 64
 Email: baron-well@t-online.de
 Web Address: www.baron-well.de
Personnel:
Mill Mgr./Owner: Alexander Baron
Phone: (49) 5321 653 49
Mill Mgr./Owner: Walda Baron
Phone: (49) 5321 653 49
Total Employees of Company: 6
Type of Operation: Paperboard mill
Pulp Grades and Capacities:
  Total pulp capacity: 1,500 mt/y
Paper/Paperboard Grades and Capacities:
  Total paper and paperboard capacity: 1,500 mt/y
  Corrugating medium/fluting: 1,500 mt/y
Paper and Paperboard Mill Data:
  Paper Machines: 1
  No. 1, total capacity 1,500 mt/y, Trim width 2.1 m, Corrugating medium/fluting
Energy Data:
  Power boilers: 2
  Electrical demand for mill: 2 MWh/D

Brücher GmbH, Pappen- und Papierfabrik
Bensheim Mill
Nibelungenstr. 381
D-64625 Bensheim
Germany
 Phone: (49) 6251 69320
 Fax: (49) 6251 66226
 Email: info@bruecherpapier.de
 Web Address: www.bruecherpapier.de
Personnel:
Gen. Mgr./Owner: Friedrich Wilhelm Weil
Phone: (49) 6251 69320
Owner: Katharina Weil
Phone: (49) 6251 69320
Type of Operation: Paperboard mill
Paper/Paperboard Grades and Capacities:
  Total paper and paperboard capacity: 5,000 mt/y
  Containerboard
  Boxboard/cartonboard: 5,000 mt/y

Kartonfabrik Buchmann GmbH
Annweiler Mill
Ownership: 100% by family
Wasgaustr. 5
D-76855 Annweiler
Germany
Mailing Address: Postf. 11 48, D-76849 Annweiler, Germany
 Phone: (49) 6346 9270
 Fax: (49) 6346 9272 86
 Email: info@buchmannkarton.de
 Web Address: www.buchmannkarton.de
Personnel:
Man. Dir.: Wilhelm Weber
Phone: (49) 6346 927 342
Fax: (49) 6346 927 4342
Email: qw@buchmannkarton.de
Finan. & Accouunting Mgr.: Joachim Janssen
Phone: (49) 6346 927 201
Fax: (49) 6346 927 4201
Email: janssen@buchmannkarton.de
Gen. Mgr.: Thomas Stark
Phone: (49) 6346 9270
Fax: (49) 6346 9272 86
Email: sek.kl@buchmannkarton.de
Sls. Mgr.: Thomas Dieckhöfer
Phone: (49) 6346 9270
Fax: (49) 6346 9272 86
Email: dieckhoefer@buchmannkarton.de
HR Mgr.: Mr. Gerhard Ott
Phone: (49) 6346 927 206
Fax: (49) 6346 927 439
Email: pw@BuchmannKarton.de
Prod. Mgr.: Dip.-Ing Bernd Reinartz
Phone: (49) 6346 927 350
Fax: (49) 6346 927 4240
Email: produktion@buchmannkarton.de
Total Employees of Company: 360
Total Employees at this Location: 320
Type of Operation: Paperboard mill
Pulp Grades and Capacities:
  Total pulp capacity: 156,450 mt/y
  Mechanical Pulp: 35,124 mt/y
  Recycled Pulping: 121,326 mt/y
Pulp Mill Data:
  Mechanical Pulping Systems:
  RMP systems: 1
  Recycled Fiber Treatment Lines:
  Recycled packaging pulping lines: 1 at 120,000
Paper/Paperboard Grades and Capacities:
  Total paper and paperboard capacity: 200,000 mt/y
  Boxboard/cartonboard: 200,000 mt/y
Paper and Paperboard Mill Data:
  Stock Preparation:
  Pulpers:
Paper Machines: 2
  No. 2, fourdrinier (3), total capacity 40,000 mt/y, Trim width 2.45 m, Boxboard/cartonboard

Germany

No. 3, Fourdrinier (4), total capacity 160,000 mt/y, Trim width 4.25 m, Boxboard/cartonboard
Coating Machines: 2
No. 2, total capacity 40,000 mt/y., on machine
No. 3, total capacity 160,000 mt/y., on machine
Finishing Equipment:
Winders: 1
Sheeters: 6 at 200,000 mt/y
Energy Data:
Power boilers: 1
Combustion turbines: 1
Steam turbines: 1
Electrical demand for mill: 589 MWh/D

①⑩Büttenpapierfabrik Gmund GmbH & Co. KG
Gmund Mill
Ownership: 100% by Kohler Family
Mangfallstr. 5
D-83703 Gmund am Tegernsee
Germany
Mailing Address: Postf 11 87, D-83701 Gmund am Tegernsee, Germany
Phone: (49) 8022 75000
Fax: (49) 8022 750099
Email: info@gmund.com
Web Address: www.gmund.com
Personnel:
Mill Mgr./ Owner: Florian Kohler
Phone: (49) 8022 75000
Tech. Dir.: Stephan Treske
Phone: (49) 8022 75000
Mktg. Mgr.: Gabriele Bellendorf
Phone: (49) 8022 75000
Total Employees of Company: 100
Total Employees at this Location: 100
Type of Operation: Paper mill
Paper/Paperboard Grades and Capacities:
Total paper and paperboard capacity: 5,000 mt/y
Uncoated woodfree/freesheet: 5,000 mt/y
Paper and Paperboard Mill Data:
Stock Preparation:
Pulpers: 2
Refiners: 6
Paper Machines: 2
No. 1, fourdrinier, Trim width 2.2 m, Uncoated woodfree/freesheet
No. 2, fourdrinier, Trim width 1.56 m, Uncoated woodfree/freesheet
Coating Machines: 1
No. 1, off machine
Finishing Equipment:
Supercalenders: 1
Rewinders: 2
Sheeters: 4
Energy Data:
Power boilers: 1
Combustion turbines: 3 at 0.5 MW

①Cordier Spezialpapier GmbH
Ownership: specTra Industriekapital, Strategic Value Partners, USA
Jägerthal 6
D-67098 Bad Dürkheim
Germany
Phone: (49) 6322 9390
Fax: (49) 6322 939 174
Email: info@cordier-paper.de, geschaeftsfuehrung@cordier-paper.de
Web Address: www.cordier-paper.de
Personnel:
Gen. Mgr.: Martin Hoffmann
Phone: (49) 6322 9390
Fax: (49) 6322 939 168
Email: martin.hoffmann@cordier-paper.de
Purch. Dir.: Frank Dubberke
Phone: (49) 6322 939 219
Fax: (49) 6322 939 440
Email: frank.dubberke@cordier-paper.de
Dir. of Sls.: Robert Lamberty
Phone: (49) 6322 93 9 216
Fax: (49) 6322 93 9 481
Email: robert.lamberty@cordier-paper.de.
Finan. Mgr.: Konrad Klinger
Phone: (49) 6322 9390
Fax: (49) 6322 939 168
Sls. : Nadine Franz
Phone: (49) 6322 939 112
Fax: (49) 6322 939 497
Email: nadine.franz@cordier-paper.de
Sls.: Mirjana Mamuza
Phone: (49) 6151 509 815
Fax: (49) 6151 509 888
Email: mirjana.mamuza@cordier-paper.de
Mill Locations:
Papierfabrik Cordier, Bad Dürkheim Mill, Jägerthal 7, D-67098 Bad Dürkheim, Germany, (Paper mill)
Phone: (49) 6322 9390
Fax: (49) 6322 939269
Email: info@cordier-paper.de
Illig'sche Papierfabrik, Mühltal Mill, Rheinstr. 38, D-64367 Mühltal, Germany, Capacity: 14,000 mt/y, (Paper mill)
Phone: (49) 6151 50980
Fax: (49) 6151 509888
Email: vertrieb@cordier-paper.de
Papierfabrik Schleipen, Bad Dürkheim Mill, Kaiserslauterer Str. 405, D-67098 Bad Dürkheim, Germany, Capacity: 32,000 mt/y, (Paper mill)
Phone: (49) 6322 60080
Fax: (49) 6322 61702

⑩Papierfabrik Cordier
Bad Dürkheim Mill
Ownership: Cordier Spezialpapier GmbH
Jägerthal 7
D-67098 Bad Dürkheim
Germany
Phone: (49) 6322 9390
Fax: (49) 6322 939269
Email: info@cordier-paper.de
Web Address: www.cordier-paper.de
Personnel:
Mill Mgr.: Markus Hinkel
Phone: (49) 6322 600851-13
Email: markus.hinkel@cordier-paper.de
Tech. Mgr.: Franz Bauer
Phone: (49) 6322 600814
Email: franz.bauer@cordier-paper.de
Sales & Marketing Dir.: Thomas Wunderlich
Phone: (49) 6322 93 9 216
Fax: (49) 6322 93 9 481
Email: thomas.wunderlich@cordier-paper.de
Total Employees at this Location: 300
Type of Operation: Paper mill
Paper/Paperboard Grades and Capacities:
Specialty and industrial
Paper and Paperboard Mill Data:
Paper Machines: 1
No. 1, fourdrinier, Trim width 1.8 m, Specialty and industrial
Energy Data:
Power boilers: 1
Steam turbines: 1

⑩Delipapier GmbH
Arneburg Mill
Ownership: Sofidel Group
Schoenfelder Strasse 1
D-39596 Arneburg, Saxony-Anhalt
Germany
Phone: (49) 3932 1545 0
Fax: (49) 3932 1545 150
Email: delipapier.de@delipapier.de
Web Address: www.delipapier.de
Personnel:
Mill Mgr.: Jürgen Flickinger
Phone: (49) 3932 1545 101
Fax: (49) 3932 1545 150
Email: j.flickinger@delipapier.de
Total Employees at this Location: 250
Type of Operation: Paper mill
Paper/Paperboard Grades and Capacities:
Total paper and paperboard capacity: 60,000 mt/y
Tissue: 60,000 mt/y
Paper and Paperboard Mill Data:
Stock Preparation:
Pulpers: 3
Paper Machines: 1
No. 1, crescent former, Yankee dryer, total capacity 60,000 mt/y, Trim width 5.45 m, Tissue
Finishing Equipment:
Rewinders: 1
Energy Data:
Power boilers: 1
Electrical demand for mill: 148 MWh/D

①⑩Delkeskamp Verpackungswerke GmbH
Nortrup Mill
Ownership: Delkeskamp Family (Private)
Hauptstr. 15
D-49638 Nortrup
Germany
Phone: (49) 5436 510
Fax: (49) 5436 51284
Email: info@delkeskamp.de, sales@delkeskamp.de
Web Address: www.delkeskamp.de
Personnel:
CEO: Stefan Delkeskamp
Phone: (49) 5436 510
Tech. Dir.: Werner Surholt
Phone: (49) 5436 510
Mktg. & Sls. Mgr.: Ingo Neumann
Phone: (49) 5436 510
Finan. & Organisation Mgr.: Jürgen Werner
Phone: (49) 5436 510
Total Employees of Company: 595
Total Employees at this Location: 595
Type of Operation: Paper mill, Paperboard mill
Pulp Grades and Capacities:
Total pulp capacity: 131,668 mt/y
Recycled Pulping: 131,668 mt/y
Pulp Mill Data:
Recycled Fiber Treatment Lines:
Pulpers: 1 at 280,000
Paper/Paperboard Grades and Capacities:
Total paper and paperboard capacity: 130,000 mt/y
Linerboard: 87,000 mt/y
Corrugating medium/fluting: 43,000 mt/y
Paper and Paperboard Mill Data:
Paper Machines: 1
No. 2, fourdrinier (2), total capacity 130,000 mt/y, Trim width 2.5 m, Linerboard, Corrugating medium/fluting
Finishing Equipment:
Winders: 1 at 140,000 mt/y
Rewinders: 1
Energy Data:
Power boilers: 1
Combustion turbines: 4 at 14.9 MW
Electrical demand for mill: 168 MWh/D

①⑩Drewsen Spezialpapiere GmbH & Co. KG
Lachendorf Mill
Georg-Drewsen-Weg 2
D-29329 Lachendorf
Germany
Mailing Address: Postf. 11 51, D-29329 Lachendorf, Germany
Phone: (49) 5145 88 0
Fax: (49) 5145 2116
Email: info@drewsen.com
Web Address: www.drewsen.com
Personnel:

Germany

Joint Man. Dir.: Dr. Thomas Katzenmayer
Phone: (49) 5145 88 0
Fax: (49) 5145 2116
Email: thomas.katzenmayer@drewsen.com
Joint Man. Dir.: Dr. Matthias Rauhut
Phone: (49) 5145 88 0
Fax: (49) 5145 2116
Email: matthias.rauhut@drewsen.com
Sls. Dir., Security Papers: Antje Hensel
Phone: (49) 5145 88216
Fax: (49) 5145 2116
Email: antje.hensel@drewsen.com
Total Employees of Company: 400
Total Employees at this Location: 400
Type of Operation: Paper mill
Paper/Paperboard Grades and Capacities:
Total paper and paperboard capacity: 185,000 mt/y
Uncoated woodfree/freesheet: 165,000 mt/y
Specialty and industrial: 20,000 mt/y
Paper and Paperboard Mill Data:
Stock Preparation:
Pulpers: 3
Paper Machines: 3
No. 1, fourdrinier, total capacity 20,000 mt/y, Trim width 1.92 m, Specialty and industrial
No. 2, fourdrinier, total capacity 55,000 mt/y, Trim width 2.34 m, Uncoated woodfree/freesheet
No. 5, SymFormer MB, total capacity 110,000 mt/y, Trim width 4.8 m, Uncoated woodfree/freesheet
Energy Data:
Power boilers: 1
Combustion turbines: 1 at 6.9 MW
Steam turbines: 1 at 9.2 MW
Electrical demand for mill: 180 MWh/D

Dresden Papier GmbH
Dresden Mill
Previously Fortress Paper.
Ownership: 100% by Glatfelter Gernsbach GmbH & Co. KG
Pirnaer Str. 31-33
D-01809 Heidenau
Germany
Phone: (49) 3529 554-0
Fax: (49) 3529 554-180
Email: wallpaperbase@glatfelter.com
Web Address: www.glatfelter.com
Personnel:
Mill Mgr.: Frank Fetkenheuer
Phone: (49) 3529 554-0
Fax: (49) 3529 554 403
Email: frank.fetkenheuer@glatfelter.com
Total Employees at this Location: 117
Type of Operation: Paper mill
Pulp Grades and Capacities:
Total pulp capacity: 9,000 mt/y
Recycled Pulping: 9,000 mt/y
Pulp Mill Data:
Recycled Fiber Treatment Lines:
Flotation deinking lines: 1
Pulpers: 1
Paper/Paperboard Grades and Capacities:
Total paper and paperboard capacity: 60,000 mt/y
Specialty and industrial: 60,000 mt/y
Paper and Paperboard Mill Data:
Stock Preparation:
Pulpers: 4
Refiners: 6
Paper Machines: 1
PM 4, twin-wire, fourdrinier, total capacity 60,000 mt/y, Trim width 3.39 m, Specialty and industrial
Finishing Equipment:
Rewinders: 1
Energy Data:
Power boilers: 2
Combustion turbines: 1 at 4.2 MW
Electrical demand for mill: 100 MWh/D

DS Smith Paper Deutschland GmbH
Aschaffenburg Mill
Ownership: 100% by DS Smith Plc
Weichertstrasse 7
D-63741 Aschaffenburg
Germany
Mailing Address: Postf. 10 01 01, D-63701 Aschaffenburg, Germany
Phone: (49) 6021 400 0
Fax: (49) 6021 400 270
Email: info@dssmith.com
Web Address: www.dssmith.com
Personnel:
Man. Dir.: Bernhard Schippler
Phone: (49) 6021 400 100
Fax: (49) 6021 400 270
Email: bernhard.schippler@dssmith.com
Finan. Mgr.: Matthias Scheid
Phone: (49) 6021 400 103
Fax: (49) 6021 400 270
Email: matthias.scheid@dssmith.com
Total Employees at this Location: 200
Type of Operation: Paper mill, Paperboard mill
Pulp Grades and Capacities:
Total pulp capacity: 378,917 mt/y
Recycled Pulping: 378,917 mt/y
Pulp Mill Data:
Recycled Fiber Treatment Lines:
Pulpers: 1
Paper/Paperboard Grades and Capacities:
Total paper and paperboard capacity: 380,000 mt/y
Linerboard: 100,000 mt/y
Corrugating medium/fluting: 280,000 mt/y
Paper and Paperboard Mill Data:
Stock Preparation:
Pulpers: 1
Paper Machines: 1
No. 1, (Suppliers: Beloit/Voith.), GapFormer, total capacity 380,000 mt/y, Trim width 7.5 m, Corrugating medium/fluting, Linerboard
Finishing Equipment:
Winders: 1 at 400,000 mt/y
Rewinders: 1
Energy Data:
Power boilers: 3
Combustion turbines: 1 at 26.3 MW
Steam turbines: 1
Electrical demand for mill: 452 MWh/D

DS Smith Paper Deutschland GmbH
Witzenhausen Mill
Ownership: 100% by DS Smith Plc
Kasseler Landstr. 23
D-37213 Witzenhausen
Germany
Mailing Address: Postf. 14 44, D-37204 Witzenhausen, Germany
Phone: (49) 5542 5020
Fax: (49) 5542 502116
Email: info@dssmith.com
Web Address: www.dssmith.com
Personnel:
Mill Mgr.: Ulrich Albert
Phone: (49) 4960 21400100
Email: ulrich.albert@dssmith.com
Prod. Mgr.: Helmut Becker
Phone: (49) 5542 502 450
Fax: (49) 5542 502 409
Email: helmut.becker@dssmith.com
Total Employees at this Location: 215
Type of Operation: Paperboard mill
Pulp Grades and Capacities:
Total pulp capacity: 343,143 mt/y
Recycled Pulping: 343,143 mt/y
Paper/Paperboard Grades and Capacities:
Total paper and paperboard capacity: 340,000 mt/y
Linerboard: 120,000 mt/y
Corrugating medium/fluting: 220,000 mt/y
Paper and Paperboard Mill Data:
Stock Preparation:
Pulpers: 1
Refiners: 1
Paper Machines: 1
No. 1, fourdrinier (2), total capacity 340,000 mt/y, Trim width 7.45 m, Linerboard, Corrugating medium/fluting
Finishing Equipment:
Winders: 1 at 420,000 mt/y
Rewinders: 1 at 10,000 mt/y
Energy Data:
Power boilers: 2
Steam turbines: 1 at 22 MW
Electrical demand for mill: 402 MWh/D

Erfurt & Sohn KG
Wuppertal Mill
Ownership: 100% by Martin Erfurt & Henrik Erfurt
Hugo-Erfurt-Strasse 1
D-42399 Wuppertal
Germany
Mailing Address: Postf. 23 01 03, D-42391 Wuppertal, Germany
Phone: (49) 202 6110 0 / 6110 375
Fax: (49) 202 6110 356 / 6110 8 94 51
Email: info@erfurt.com
Web Address: www.erfurt.com
Personnel:
Gen. Mgr.: Martin Erfurt
Phone: (49) 202 61100
Gen. Mgr.: Henrik Erfurt
Phone: (49) 202 61100
Total Employees of Company: 300
Total Employees at this Location: 300
Type of Operation: Paper mill
Paper/Paperboard Grades and Capacities:
Total paper and paperboard capacity: 44,000 mt/y
Specialty and industrial: 44,000 mt/y
Paper and Paperboard Mill Data:
Paper Machines: 3
PM 1, total capacity 4,000 mt/y, Trim width 2.12 m, Specialty and industrial
PM 3, total capacity 15,000 mt/y, Trim width 3.55 m, Specialty and industrial
PM 5, total capacity 25,000 mt/y, Trim width 3.55 m, Specialty and industrial

Flexipack International Wunderlich GmbH + Co KG
Baar-Ebenhausen Mill
Äusserer Ring 40
D-85107 Baar-Ebenhausen
Germany
Mailing Address: Postf. 10 04 51, D-85004 Ingolstadt, Germany
Phone: (49) 8453 326 0
Fax: (49) 8453 326 122 / 129
Email: headoffice@flexipack.de, Verkauf@flexipack.de
Web Address: www.flexipack.de
Personnel:
Man. Dir./Partner: Dipl.-Kfm. Elfie Wunderlich-Ahmed
Phone: (49) 8453 326 0
Senior Mgr.: Bernd Huber
Phone: (49) 8453 326 0
Total Employees at this Location: 150
Type of Operation: Paperboard mill
Mill Locations:
Flexipack International Wunderlich GmbH + Co KG, Gerlingen Mill, Papiermacherstraße 2, D-57482 Wenden, Germany, Capacity: 15,000 mt/y, (Paper mill, Paperboard mill)
Phone: (49) 2762 92 670
Fax: (49) 2762 92 6711
Email: info@flexipack.de
Paper/Paperboard Grades and Capacities:
Total paper and paperboard capacity: 5,000 mt/y
Boxboard/cartonboard: 5,000 mt/y

Germany

Paper and Paperboard Mill Data:
Paper Machines: 2
No. 1, Trim width 2.1 m, Boxboard/cartonboard
No. 2, Trim width 2.4 m

ⓜFlexipack International Wunderlich GmbH + Co KG
Gerlingen Mill
Papiermacherstraße 2
D-57482 Wenden
Germany
Mailing Address: Hillmickerstr. 2, D-57482 Wenden / Gerlingen, Germany
   Phone: (49) 2762 92 670
   Fax: (49) 2762 92 6711
   Email: info@flexipack.de
   Web Address: www.flexipack.de
Total Employees at this Location: 40
Type of Operation: Paper mill, Paperboard mill
Paper/Paperboard Grades and Capacities:
   Total paper and paperboard capacity: 15,000 mt/y
   Boxboard/cartonboard: 15,000 mt/y
Paper and Paperboard Mill Data:
Paper Machines: 1
No. 1, total capacity 15,000 mt/y, Trim width 2.1 m, Boxboard/cartonboard
Energy Data:
   Steam turbines: 1
   Electrical demand for mill: 5 MWh/D

ⓜFripa Papierfabrik Albert Friedrich KG
Ownership: 100% by family
In der Mühlenau 96
D-52355 Düren
Germany
Mailing Address: Postf. 10 06 44, D-52306 Düren, Germany
   Phone: (49) 2421 96640
   Fax: (49) 2421 62655
   Email: dueren@fripa.de, info@fripa.de
   Web Address: www.fripa.de
Personnel:
   Owner: Ursula Queck
   Phone: (49) 2421 96640
   Fax: (49) 2421 62655
   Pres.: Verena Queck-Glimm
   Phone: (49) 9371 502 400
   Email: queck-glimm@fripa.de
   Man. Dir., Sls., Mktg. & Logistics: Torsten Bahl
   Phone: (49) 9371 502 501
   Email: bahl@fripa.de
Total Employees of Company: 370
Total Employees at this Location: 69
Mill Locations:
   Cartaseta-Friedrich & Co., Däniken Mill, Sandackerstrasse 3, CH-4658 Däniken, Switzerland, Capacity: 22,000 mt/y, (Paper mill)
   Phone: (41) 62 288 16 00
   Fax: (41) 62 288 16 21
   Email: info@cartaseta.ch
   Fabryka Papieru Czerwonak Sp. z o.o., Czerwonak Mill (80% owned), ul. Gdynska 131, PL-62004 Czerwonak, Poland, Capacity: 16,500 mt/y, (Paper mill)
   Phone: (48) 61 650 4800 / 4803 / 4822
   Fax: (48) 61 650 4801
   Email: biuro@fpcz.com.pl
   Fripa Papierfabrik Albert Friedrich KG, Miltenberg Mill, Grossheubacher Str. 4, D-63897 Miltenberg, Germany, Capacity: 69,000 mt/y, (Paper mill)
   Phone: (49) 9371 5020
   Fax: (49) 9371 502 401
   Email: info@fripa.de

ⓜFripa Papierfabrik Albert Friedrich KG
Miltenberg Mill
Grossheubacher Str. 4
D-63897 Miltenberg
Germany
Mailing Address: Postf. 13 80, D-63897 Miltenberg, Germany
   Phone: (49) 9371 5020
   Fax: (49) 9371 502 401
   Email: info@fripa.de
   Web Address: www.fripa.de
Personnel:
   Mill Mgr.: Andreas Noack
   Phone: (49) 9371 5020
   Fax: (49) 9371 502 401
   Email: noack@fripa.de
   Man. Dir. Sls. & Mktg.: Thorsten Bahl
   Phone: (49) 9371 5020
   Fax: (49) 9371 502 1501
   Email: bahl@fripa.de
   Head of Purch. raw material & in-house Logist.: Carmen Samorski
   Phone: (49) 9371 502 530
   Fax: (49) 9371 502 1530
   Email: samorski@fripa.de
   Head of Shipping & freight Dir.: Christiana Boettger
   Phone: (49) 9371 502 560
   Fax: (49) 9371 502 1532
   Email: boettger@fripa.de
   Head of Stock of Finished goods: Achim Kirchgaessner
   Phone: (49) 9371 502 570
   Fax: (49) 9371 502 1532
   Email: kirchgaessner@fripa.de
Total Employees at this Location: 315
Type of Operation: Paper mill
Pulp Grades and Capacities:
   Total pulp capacity: 18,131 mt/y
   Recycled Pulping: 18,131 mt/y
Pulp Mill Data:
   Recycled Fiber Treatment Lines:
   Flotation deinking lines
Paper/Paperboard Grades and Capacities:
   Total paper and paperboard capacity: 69,000 mt/y
   Tissue: 69,000 mt/y
Paper and Paperboard Mill Data:
   Stock Preparation:
   Pulpers: 3
   Refiners: 3
Paper Machines: 3
No. 1, fourdrinier, Yankee dryer, total capacity 17,000 mt/y, Trim width 2.7 m, Tissue
No. 5, C-wrap, Yankee dryer, total capacity 24,000 mt/y, Trim width 2.7 m, Tissue
No. 6, crescent former, Yankee dryer, total capacity 28,000 mt/y, Trim width 2.75 m, Tissue
Finishing Equipment:
   Rewinders: 5
Energy Data:
   Power boilers: 2
   Combustion turbines: 1 at 7.4 MW
   Electrical demand for mill: 183 MWh/D

ⓂⓂFroeb-Verpackungen GmbH
Wurzbach Mill
Lehestener Straße 63
D-07343 Wurzbach
Germany
   Phone: (49) 36652 35496-0/22316
   Fax: (49) 36652 22315
   Email: aw@froeb-verpackungen.de
   Web Address: www.froeb-verpackungen.de
Personnel:
   Man. Dir.: Norbert Froeb
   Phone: (49) 36652 35496-0
   Fax: (49) 36652 22315
   Email: n.froeb@froeb-verpackungen.de
   Sls. Mgr.: Siegmar Kunstmann
   Phone: (49) 36652 35496-17
   Fax: (49) 36652 22315
   Email: s.kunstmann@froeb-verpackungen.de
   Procurement Mgr.: Angelika Froeb
   Phone: (49) 36652 35496-12
   Fax: (49) 36652 22315
   Email: a.froeb@froeb-verpackungen.de
   Internal Sls. Serv.: Peggy Wurmehl
   Phone: (49) 36652 35496-15
   Fax: (49) 36652 22315
   Email: p.wurmehl@froeb-verpackungen.de
Type of Operation: Paper mill
Paper/Paperboard Grades and Capacities:
   Total paper and paperboard capacity: 750 mt/y
   Packaging papers: 750 mt/y
Paper and Paperboard Mill Data:
Paper Machines: 1
No. 1, total capacity 750 mt/y, Trim width 2 m, Packaging papers

ⓜFS-Karton GmbH
Neuss Mill
Ownership: Mayr-Melnhof Karton AG
Düsseldorfer Str. 182-184
D-41405 Neuss
Germany
Mailing Address: 100552, 41405 Neuss, Germany
   Phone: (49) 2131 2370
   Fax: (49) 2131 237 22162
   Email: sales.neuss@mm-karton.com
   Web Address: www.mm-karton.com
Personnel:
   Prod. Mgr. PM 5: Dieter Garztecki
   Phone: (49) 2131 237 0220
   Fax: (49) 2131 237 22162
   Email: dieter.garztecki@mm-karton.com
Total Employees at this Location: 310
Type of Operation: Paperboard mill
Pulp Grades and Capacities:
   Total pulp capacity: 314,127 mt/y
   Recycled Pulping: 314,127 mt/y
Pulp Mill Data:
   Mechanical Pulping Systems:
   RMP systems
   Bleach Plant Lines:
   DIP
   Recycled Fiber Treatment Lines:
   Flotation deinking lines
   Recycled packaging pulping lines
Paper/Paperboard Grades and Capacities:
   Total paper and paperboard capacity: 350,000 mt/y
   Linerboard: 100,000 mt/y
   Boxboard/cartonboard: 250,000 mt/y
Paper and Paperboard Mill Data:
   Stock Preparation:
   Pulpers: 6
   Refiners: 4
Paper Machines: 1
No. 5, Fourdrinier (4), total capacity 350,000 mt/y, Trim width 5.15 m, Boxboard/cartonboard, Linerboard
Coating Machines: 1
KM 5, total capacity 380,000 mt/y., on machine
Finishing Equipment:
   Winders: 1
   Sheeters: 7
Energy Data:
   Power boilers: 1
   Combustion turbines: 1
   Steam turbines: 1
   Electrical demand for mill: 531 MWh/D

ⓂⓂGlatfelter Gernsbach GmbH & Co. KG
Gernsbach Mill
Ownership: 100% by Glatfelter
Hördener Str. 5
D-76593 Gernsbach
Germany

Germany

Mailing Address: Postf. 11 55, D-76584 Gernsbach, Germany
Phone: (49) 7224 660
Fax: (49) 7224 66274
Email: composite.fibers@glatfelter.com
Web Address: www.glatfelter.com
Personnel:
Gen. Mgr. & Oper. Dir.: Dr. Reinhard Schiebeler
Phone: (49) 7224 66339
Fax: (49) 7224 66274
Email: reinhard.schiebeler@glatfelter.com
Sls & Mktg. Dir.: Mr. Fabrice Werner
Phone: (49) 7224 660
Fax: (49) 7224 66274
Email: fabrice.werner@glatfelter.com
Mktg. & Commun. Mgr.: Anne Kirse
Phone: (49) 7224 66273
Fax: (49) 7224 66323
Email: anne.kirse@glatfelter.com
Total Employees of Company: 1,400
Total Employees at this Location: 565
Type of Operation: Paper mill
Mill Locations:
Dresden Papier GmbH, Dresden Mill, Pirnaer Str. 31-33, D-01809 Heidenau, Germany, Capacity: 60,000 mt/y, (Paper mill)
Phone: (49) 3529 554-0
Fax: (49) 3529 554-180
Email: wallpaperbase@glatfelter.com
Paper/Paperboard Grades and Capacities:
Total paper and paperboard capacity: 42,000 mt/y
Specialty and industrial: 42,000 mt/y
Paper and Paperboard Mill Data:
Paper Machines: 5
No. 1, fourdrinier, Trim width 3.2 m
No. 2, fourdrinier, Trim width 3.2 m
No. 3, fourdrinier, Trim width 3.2 m
No. 9, fourdrinier, total capacity 6,000 mt/y, Specialty and industrial
No. 11, fourdrinier
Coating Machines: 1
No. 1

⊕ⓜJulius Glatz GmbH Papierfabriken
Neidenfels Mill
Staatsstrasse 37-41
D-67468 Neidenfels
Germany
Phone: (49) 6325 182 130
Fax: (49) 6325 182 248/121
Email: cigarette@glatz.de
Web Address: www.glatz.de
Personnel:
CEO: Roman Reischl
Phone: (49) 6325 182 130
Fax: (49) 6325 182 248
Email: reischl@glatz.de
Man. Dir. & Sls./Mktg.: Sylvain Epailly
Phone: (49) 6325 182 130
Fax: (49) 6325 182 248
Email: epailly@glatz.de
Purch. Mgr.: Michael Potthoff
Phone: (49) 6325 182 130
Fax: (49) 6325 182 248
Email: patthoff@glatz.de
Total Employees of Company: 380
Type of Operation: Paper mill
Mill Locations:
Julius Glatz GmbH Papierfabriken, Frankeneck Mill, Talstr., D-67468 Frankeneck, Germany, Capacity: 17,000 mt/y, (Paper mill)
Phone: (49) 6325 182-0
Fax: (49) 6325 182121
Email: finepaper@glatz.de
Glatz Finepaper Vietnam Co. Ltd., Ho Chi Minh City Mill, No. 8 Dan Chu Street, V.S.I.P II, Hoa Phu, Thu Dau Mot, Vietnam, Capacity: 12,000 mt/y, (Paper mill)
Phone: (84) 650 358 9558
Yunnan Hongta Blue Eagle Paper Co., Ltd., Honghe Mill, Zhuangzihe Village, Dongba Town, Jianshui County, Honghe District 654300, China, Capacity: 24,000 mt/y, (Paper mill)
Phone: (86) 873 765 2061/ 2341
Fax: (86) 873 765 2496/ 2061
Email: zoubaogang@ynhtbe.com, pengxingzhu@ynhtbe.com, yangfukang@ynhtbe.com
Paper/Paperboard Grades and Capacities:
Total paper and paperboard capacity: 33,000 mt/y
Uncoated mechanical/groundwood: 5,000 mt/y
Specialty and industrial: 28,000 mt/y
Paper and Paperboard Mill Data:
Stock Preparation:
Pulpers: 6
Refiners: 15
Paper Machines: 3
PM 2, fourdrinier, Trim width 1.99 m
PM 5, fourdrinier, Trim width 2.49 m
PM 6, Yankee dryer, Trim width 3.21 m
Finishing Equipment:
Rewinders: 4
Sheeters: 2

ⓜJulius Glatz GmbH Papierfabriken
Frankeneck Mill
Talstr.
D-67468 Frankeneck
Germany
Phone: (49) 6325 182-0
Fax: (49) 6325 182121
Email: finepaper@glatz.de
Web Address: www.glatz.de
Personnel:
Mill Mgr.: Freddy O. Gemlich
Phone: (49) 6325 182 251
Fax: (49) 6325 182 436
Email: gemlich@glatz.de
Type of Operation: Paper mill
Paper/Paperboard Grades and Capacities:
Total paper and paperboard capacity: 17,000 mt/y
Specialty and industrial: 17,000 mt/y
Paper and Paperboard Mill Data:
Paper Machines: 1
No. 8, fourdrinier, total capacity 17,000 mt/y, Trim width 3.4 m, Specialty and industrial

⊕Golzern Holding GmbH
Ownership: Papierfabrik Golzern
Erich-Zeigner-Allee 15
D-04229 Leipzig
Germany
Phone: (49) 49 341 984 780
Fax: (49) 49 341 984 7818
Web Address: www.golzern.biz
Personnel:
Man. Dir./Owner: Stephan Schröter
Phone: (49) 49 341 984 780
Fax: (49) 49 341 984 7818
Email: ss@golzern.biz
Man. Dir. Papierfabrik Golzern GmbH: Martin Röhrenbeck
Phone: (49) 49 3437 980 641
Fax: (49) 49 3437 980 698
Email: m.roehrenbeck@golzern-papier.de
Sls. Mgr. Papierfabrik Golzern GmbH: Peter Schindler
Phone: (7) 49 3437 980 640
Fax: (7) 49 3437 980 698
Email: p.schindler@golzern-papier.de
Mill Locations:
GrünPerga Papier GmbH, Grünhainichen Mill (20% owned), Am Güterbahnhof 3, D-09579 Grünhainichen, Germany, Capacity: 13,500 mt/y, (Paper mill)
Phone: (49) 37294 18210 / 18220
Fax: (49) 37294 18200
Email: info@gruenperga.de

⊕Gebr. Grünewald GmbH & Co. KG
Ownership: Grünewald family (Private)
Antoniusstr. 15
D-57399 Kirchhundem-Hofolpe
Germany
Mailing Address: Postf. 10 60, D-57393 Kirchhundem, Germany
Phone: (49) 2723 408 0
Fax: (49) 2723 408 125
Email: infoline@gruenewald-papier.de
Web Address: www.gruenewald-papier.de
Personnel:
Man. Dir.: Dr. Christopher Grünewald
Phone: (49) 2723 408 0
Fax: (49) 2723 408 125
Sls. & Mktg. Mgr.: Andreas Hacke
Phone: (49) 2723 408 140
Fax: (49) 2723 408 145
Email: a.hacke@gruenewald-papier.de
Total Employees of Company: 90
Mill Locations:
Gebr. Grünewald GmbH & Co. KG, Kirchhundem Mill, Antoniusstr. 15, D-57399 Kirchhundem-Hofolpe, Germany, Capacity: 44,982 mt/y, (Paper mill)
Phone: (49) 2723 408 0
Fax: (49) 2723 408 125
Email: infoline@gruenewald-papier.de

ⓜGebr. Grünewald GmbH & Co. KG
Kirchhundem Mill
Antoniusstr. 15
D-57399 Kirchhundem-Hofolpe
Germany
Mailing Address: Postf. 10 60, D-57393 Kirchhundem, Germany
Phone: (49) 2723 408 0
Fax: (49) 2723 408 125
Email: infoline@gruenewald-papier.de
Web Address: www.gruenewald-papier.de
Personnel:
Mill Mgr.: Dr. Christopher Grünewald
Phone: (49) 2723 408 0
Sls. & Mktg. Mgr.: Andreas Hacke
Phone: (49) 2723 408 140
Fax: (49) 2723 408 145
Email: a.hacke@gruenewald-papier.de
Total Employees at this Location: 75
Type of Operation: Paper mill
Pulp Grades and Capacities:
Total pulp capacity: 14,887 mt/y
Recycled Pulping: 14,887 mt/y
Pulp Mill Data:
Recycled Fiber Treatment Lines:
Pulpers: 3 at 50,000
Paper/Paperboard Grades and Capacities:
Total paper and paperboard capacity: 44,982 mt/y
Specialty and industrial: 44,982 mt/y
Paper and Paperboard Mill Data:
Stock Preparation:
Refiners: 3
Paper Machines: 1
No. 1, fourdrinier, Yankee dryer, total capacity 44,982 mt/y, Trim width 4.7 m, Specialty and industrial
Finishing Equipment:
Rewinders: 1
Energy Data:
Power boilers: 1
Electrical demand for mill: 127 MWh/D

⊕ⓜGrünPerga Papier GmbH
Grünhainichen Mill
Ownership: 20% by Golzern Holding GmbH
Am Güterbahnhof 3
D-09579 Grünhainichen
Germany
Phone: (49) 37294 18210 / 18220
Fax: (49) 37294 18200
Email: info@gruenperga.de
Web Address: www.gruenperga.de
Personnel:
Gen. Mgr.: Dipl. Ing. Ulf Ender
Phone: (49) 37294 18210

Germany

Fax: (49) 37294 18200
Email: ulf.ender@gruenperga.de
Sls. Mgr.: Sabine Irmler
Phone: (49) 37294 18210
Fax: (49) 37294 18200
Email: sabine.irmler@gruenperga.de
Total Employees of Company: 90
Total Employees at this Location: 90
Type of Operation: Paper mill
Paper/Paperboard Grades and Capacities:
Total paper and paperboard capacity: 13,500 mt/y
Specialty and industrial
Paper and Paperboard Mill Data:
Stock Preparation:
Pulpers: 4
Refiners: 10
Paper Machines: 2
PM 4, fourdrinier, Trim width 2 m, Specialty and industrial
PM 6, fourdrinier, Trim width 2 m, Specialty and industrial
Finishing Equipment:
Supercalenders: 1
Rewinders: 4
Sheeters: 1
Energy Data:
Power boilers: 3

⊕Ⓜ Hahnemühle FineArt GmbH
Dassel Mill
Hahnestr. 5
D-37586 Dassel
Germany
Mailing Address: Postfach 1361, D-37554 Dassel, Germany
Phone: (49) 5561 791 - 0 / 235 / 237
Fax: (49) 5561 791 377 / 340
Email: tfa@hahnemuehle.de,
dfa@hahnemuehle.de
Web Address: www.hahnemuehle.de
Personnel:
CEO: Friedrich Nebel
Phone: (49) 5561 791 600 / 5561 791292
Fax: (49) 5561 791 340 / 5561 791 377
Email: friedrich_nebel@hahnemuehle.de
Man. Dir.: Michael Siekiera
Phone: (49) 5561 79192
Fax: (49) 55 61 791498
Email: michael_siekiera@hahnemuehle.de
Prod. Mgr.: Volker Scheerbarth
Phone: (49) 5561 791 438
Fax: (49) 5561 791 515
Email: volker_scheerbarth@hahnemuehle.de
Purch. Dir.: Gerold Zellmann
Phone: (49) 5561 791 289
Fax: (49) 5561 791 334
Email: gerold_zellmann@hahnemuehle.de
Total Employees of Company: 150
Total Employees at this Location: 180
Type of Operation: Paper mill
Paper/Paperboard Grades and Capacities:
Total paper and paperboard capacity: 3,000 mt/y
Uncoated woodfree/freesheet: 3,000 mt/y
Coated woodfree/freesheet
Paper and Paperboard Mill Data:
Stock Preparation:
Pulpers: 2
Refiners: 2
Paper Machines: 3
PM 1, fourdrinier, total capacity 750 mt/y, Trim width 1.3 m
PM 2, cylinder mould, total capacity 2,500 mt/y, Trim width 1.26 m
PM 3, cylinder mould, total capacity 750 mt/y, Trim width 1.26 m
Finishing Equipment:
Rewinders: 4 at 1,000 mt/y
Sheeters: 4 at 2,000 mt/y
Energy Data:
Power boilers: 1

⊕Ⓜ Papierfabrik Hainsberg GmbH
Freital Mill
Ownership: 94% by Hoya Papier GmbH
Dresdner Str. 321
D-01705 Freital-Hainsberg
Germany
Phone: (49) 351 647 4223 / 351 647 0
Fax: (49) 351 647 4221
Email: kontakt@hainsberg-papier.de,
kontakthai@hainsberg-papier.de
Web Address: www.hainsberg-papier.de
Personnel:
Gen. Mgr.: Dr. Dietrich Arnhold
Phone: (49) 351 647 4390
Email: dietrich.arnhold@hainsberg-papier.de
Gen. Mgr. & Sls. Mgr.: Krystyna Saworska
Phone: (49) 351 6474380
Fax: (49) 351 6474388
Email: krystyna.saworska@hainsberg-papier.de
Purch. Dir.: Carola Gersch
Phone: (49) 351 6474211
Fax: (49) 351 6474220
Email: carola.gersch@hainsberg-papier.de
Tech. Dir.: Gunther Puschbeck
Phone: (49) 351 647 4333
Email: gunther.puschbeck@hainsberg-papier.de
Total Employees of Company: 100
Total Employees at this Location: 100
Type of Operation: Paper mill
Pulp Grades and Capacities:
Total pulp capacity: 46,131 mt/y
Recycled Pulping: 46,131 mt/y
Pulp Mill Data:
Bleach Plant Systems: 1
DIP Capacity 37,500 admt/y
Recycled Fiber Treatment Lines:
Flotation deinking lines: 1 at 37,500 admt/y
Pulpers: 1 at 7,500 admt/y
Pulpers: 1 at 58,300
Paper/Paperboard Grades and Capacities:
Total paper and paperboard capacity: 45,000 mt/y
Uncoated woodfree/freesheet: 10,000 mt/y
Uncoated mechanical/groundwood: 35,000 mt/y
Paper and Paperboard Mill Data:
Paper Machines: 1
No. 5, SymFormer MB, total capacity 45,000 mt/y, Trim width 2.64 m, Uncoated woodfree/freesheet, Uncoated mechanical/groundwood
Finishing Equipment:
Rewinders: 2
Sheeters: 1
Energy Data:
Power boilers: 1
Steam turbines: 1 at 1 MW
Electrical demand for mill: 117 MWh/D

⊕ Hakle GmbH
Ownership: 100% by Palero Capital GmbH
Bonner Straße 201
40589 Düsseldorf
Germany
Phone: (49) 0211 99 66 111
Fax: (49) 0211 99 66 109
Email: E-Mail
Web Address: www.hakle.de
Mill Locations:
Hakle GmbH, Reisholz Mill, Kappelerstr. 51, D-40597 Düsseldorf, Germany, Capacity: 50,000 mt/y, (Paper mill)
Phone: (49) 211 99 66 0
Fax: (49) 211 99 66 109
Email: service@hakle.de
Hakle GmbH, Reisholz Mill, Kappelerstr. 51, D-40597 Düsseldorf, Germany, Capacity: 50,000 mt/y, (Paper mill)
Phone: (49) 211 99 66 0
Fax: (49) 211 99 66 109
Email: consumers@hakle.de

⊕Ⓜ Hakle GmbH
Reisholz Mill
Company is previously Kimberly-Clark GmbH.
Ownership: 100% by Palero Capital GmbH
Kappelerstr. 51
D-40597 Düsseldorf
Germany
Mailing Address: Postf. 16 01 52, D-40564 Düsseldorf, Germany
Phone: (49) 211 99 66 0
Fax: (49) 211 99 66 109
Email: service@hakle.de
Web Address: www.hakle.de
Personnel:
Mill Mgr.: Peter Eickhoff
Phone: (49) 211 99 66 111
Gen.Mngr. - Europe Fin.Dir.: Renato Negro
Country Mgr.: Thomas Kaiser
PR Mgr.: Uschi Ferry
Phone: (49) 6131 6070214
Suzanna Hetkrath
Total Employees at this Location: 200
Type of Operation: Paper mill
Pulp Grades and Capacities:
Total pulp capacity: 53,522 mt/y
Recycled Pulping: 53,522 mt/y
Pulp Mill Data:
Recycled Fiber Treatment Lines:
Flotation deinking lines
Paper/Paperboard Grades and Capacities:
Total paper and paperboard capacity: 50,000 mt/y
Tissue: 50,000 mt/y
Paper and Paperboard Mill Data:
Paper Machines: 1
No. 3, DuoFormer T, Yankee dryer, total capacity 50,000 mt/y, Trim width 5.35 m, Tissue
Energy Data:
Power boilers: 1
Electrical demand for mill: 184 MWh/D

Ⓜ Hamburger Rieger GmbH & Co. KG
Spremberg-Schwarze Pumpe Mill
Ownership: 98% by Prinzhorn Holding GmbH
An der Heide B5
D-03130 Spremberg-Schwarze Pumpe, Brandenburg
Germany
Phone: (49) 3564 378 21001 / 22200 / 3564 378-0
Fax: (49) 3564 378 21090
Email: office.rieger@hamburger-spremberg.com
Web Address: www.hamburger-spremberg.com
Personnel:
Man. Dir., Mktg. Sls.: Jörg Hischemöller
Phone: (49) 3564 378 22000
Fax: (49) 3564 378 22090
Man. Dir. Production & Technology: Antje Roemer
Phone: (49) 3564 378-21100
Fax: (49) 3564 378-21190
Email: antje.roemer@hamburger-containerboard.com
Product Devlpt. & Customer Service Mgr.: Andreas Güth
Phone: (49) 3564 378 22 600
Fax: (49) 3564 378 22 090
Email: andreas.gueth@hamburger-containerboard.com
Logistics Mngr.: Torsten Linke
Phone: (49) 3564 378 22 400
Fax: (49) 3564 378 22 190
Email: Torsten.Linke@hamburger-containerboard.com
Sales Mngr.: Marlies Kupsch
Phone: (49) 3564 378 22 100
Fax: (49) 3564 378 22 190
Email: Marlies.Kupsch@hamburger-containerboard.com
Marketing & Sales Ass.: Cathleen Hoerenz
Phone: (49) 3564 378 22 001
Fax: (49) 3564 378 22 090
Email: Cathleen.Hoerenz@hamburger-containerboard.com
Total Employees at this Location: 214

Germany

Type of Operation: Paperboard mill
Pulp Grades and Capacities:
  Total pulp capacity: 318,304 mt/y
  Recycled Pulping: 318,304 mt/y
Pulp Mill Data:
Pulp Lines: 3
  Recycled Fiber Treatment Lines:
  Recycled packaging pulping lines: 3
Paper/Paperboard Grades and Capacities:
  Total paper and paperboard capacity: 330,000 mt/y
  Linerboard: 250,000 mt/y
  Boxboard/cartonboard: 80,000 mt/y
Paper and Paperboard Mill Data:
Paper Machines: 1
  No. 1, GapFormer, total capacity 330,000 mt/y, Trim width 5.4 m, Linerboard, Boxboard/cartonboard
Finishing Equipment:
  Winders: 1
  Calenders: 1
Energy Data:
  Power boilers
  Steam turbines
  Electrical demand for mill: 386 MWh/D

ⓂHamburger Rieger GmbH & Co. KG
Trostberg Mill
Ownership: 98% by Prinzhorn Holding GmbH
Riegerstr. 4
D-83308 Trostberg, Bavaria
Germany
Mailing Address: Postf. 12 63, D-83303 Trostberg, Germany
  Phone: (49) 8621 804 0
  Fax: (49) 8621 804 185
  Email: officerieger@hamburger-rieger.com
  Web Address: www.hamburger-rieger.com
Personnel:
  Mill Mgr. & Man. Dir.: Andreas Noss
  Phone: (49) 86 21804-210
  Fax: (49) 86 21804-285
  Email: officerieger@rieger-papier.com
  Commer. Dir.: Klaus H. L. Mueller
  Phone: (49) 86 21804-800
  Fax: (49) 86 21804-285
  Email: Klaus.Mueller@hamburger-containerboard.com
  Prod. Dir.: Georg Voit
  Phone: (49) 8621 804-500
  Fax: (49) 8621 804-285
  Email: Georg.Voit@hamburger-containerboard.com
  Sls. Dir.: Bernhard Dickert
  Phone: (49) 86 21804-310
  Fax: (49) 86 21804-385
  Email: Bernhardt.Dickert@hamburger-containerboard.com
  Sales Mngr.: Albert Mussner
  Phone: (49) 8621 804-320
  Fax: (49) 8621 804-385
  Email: Albert.Mussner@hamburger-containerboard.com
  Tech. Service/Product Development: Ulrich Dzinblewski
  Phone: (49) 86 21804-380
  Fax: (49) 86 21804-385
  Email: Ulrich.Dzinblewski@hamburger-containerboard.com
  Tech. Service/Product Development: Christof Huber
  Phone: (49) 86 21804-375
  Fax: (49) 86 21804-385
  Email: Christof.Huber@hamburger-containerboard.com
  Energy Mgr.: Yilmaz Gökduman
  Phone: (49) 8621 804 0
Total Employees at this Location: 200
Type of Operation: Paperboard mill
Pulp Grades and Capacities:
  Total pulp capacity: 165,900 mt/y
  Recycled Pulping: 165,900 mt/y
Pulp Mill Data:
  Recycled Fiber Treatment Lines:
  Flotation deinking lines: 1 at 22,000 admt/y
  Pulpers: 4 at 170,000 mt/y
Paper/Paperboard Grades and Capacities:
  Total paper and paperboard capacity: 171,000 mt/y
  Linerboard: 144,000 mt/y
  Boxboard/cartonboard: 27,000 mt/y
Paper and Paperboard Mill Data:
  Stock Preparation:
  Refiners: 3
Paper Machines: 2
  No. 1, cylinder (9), Yankee dryer, total capacity 27,000 mt/y, Trim width 2.3 m, Boxboard/cartonboard
  No. 2, Fourdrinier (4), Yankee dryer, total capacity 144,000 mt/y, Trim width 2.5 m, Linerboard
Coating Machines: 3
  No. 1, on machine
  No. 2, on machine
  No. 3, on machine
Finishing Equipment:
  Winders: 1
  Rewinders: 2 at 110,000 mt/y
  Sheeters: 1 at 27,000 mt/y
Energy Data:
  Power boilers: 3
  Combustion turbines: 1 at 7.3 MW
  Steam turbines: 1 at 1.2 MW
  Hydro turbines: 2 at 0.38 MW
  Electrical demand for mill: 248 MWh/D

ⒽHellbut & Co. GmbH
Ownership: Hellbut und Co. GmbH
Ilfelder Tal 1
D-99768 Ilfeld
Germany
  Phone: (49) 36331 43 73
  Fax: (49) 36331 437 45
  Email: ilfeld-papier@hellbut.com, kontakt@hellbut.com
  Web Address: www.hellbut.com
Mill Locations:
  Hellbut & Co. GmbH, Ilfeld Mill, Ilfelder Tal 1, D-99768 Ilfeld, Germany, Capacity: 5,000 mt/y, (Paper mill)
  Phone: (49) 36331 43 73
  Fax: (49) 36331 437 45
  Email: ilfeld-papier@hellbut.com; kontakt@hellbut.com

ⓂHellbut & Co. GmbH
Ilfeld Mill
Ilfelder Tal 1
D-99768 Ilfeld
Germany
  Phone: (49) 36331 43 73
  Fax: (49) 36331 437 45
  Email: ilfeld-papier@hellbut.com, kontakt@hellbut.com
  Web Address: www.hellbut.com
Personnel:
  Gen. Dir.: Christian Möhrmann
  Phone: (49) 36331 43 73
  Fax: (49) 36331 437 45
  Mill Mgr.: Jochen Gebhardt
  Phone: (49) 36331 43 73
  Fax: (49) 36331 437 45
Total Employees at this Location: 17
Type of Operation: Paper mill
Pulp Mill Data:
  Recycled Fiber Treatment Lines:
  Pulpers: 1
Paper/Paperboard Grades and Capacities:
  Total paper and paperboard capacity: 5,000 mt/y
  Corrugating medium/fluting: 5,000 mt/y
Paper and Paperboard Mill Data:
Paper Machines: 1
  No. 1, fourdrinier, total capacity 5,000 mt/y, Trim width 2.1 m, Corrugating medium/fluting
Energy Data:
  Power boilers: 1
  Electrical demand for mill: 5 MWh/D

ⒽⓂGebr. Hoffsümmer Spezialpapier GmbH & Co. KG
Düren Mill
Papiermühle 52-58
D-52349 Düren
Germany
Mailing Address: Postf. 10 09 51, D-52309 Düren, Germany
  Phone: (49) 2421 6922-0
  Fax: (49) 2421 692211
  Email: info@hoffsuemmer.de
  Web Address: www.hoffsuemmer.com
Personnel:
  Exec. Board: Roger Ruf
  Phone: (49) 2421 692 240
  Fax: (49) 2421 692 211
  Email: r.ruf@hoffsuemmer.de
  Purch. Dep. Mgr.: Tatjana Rodenbuecher
  Phone: (49) 2421 692 234
  Fax: (49) 2421 692 211
  Email: t.rodenbuecher@hoffsuemmer.de
  Sls. Dir.: Erik Schumann
  Phone: (49) 2421 692 230
  Fax: (49) 2421 692 211
  Email: e.schumann@hoffsuemmer.de
  Sls. Mgr.: Christine Dahmen
  Phone: (49) 2421 692 232
  Fax: (49) 2421 692 211
  Email: c.dahmen@hoffsuemmer.de
  Account dep. and HR Dir.: Bernadette Poll
  Phone: (49) 2421 692 236
  Fax: (49) 2421 692 211
  Email: b.poll@hoffsuemmer.de
Total Employees of Company: 100
Total Employees at this Location: 100
Type of Operation: Paper mill
Paper/Paperboard Grades and Capacities:
  Total paper and paperboard capacity: 67,000 mt/y
  Specialty and industrial: 67,000 mt/y
Paper and Paperboard Mill Data:
  Stock Preparation:
  Pulpers: 2
  Refiners: 6
Paper Machines: 3
  No. 1, fourdrinier, total capacity 35,000 mt/y, Trim width 2.75 m, Specialty and industrial
  No. 4, fourdrinier, total capacity 31,000 mt/y, Trim width 2.34 m, Specialty and industrial
  No. 5, fourdrinier, total capacity 1,000 mt/y, Trim width 1.5 m, Specialty and industrial
Finishing Equipment:
  Winders: 2
  Sheeters: 6

ⒽⓂHollingsworth & Vose GmbH
Hatzfeld Mill
Ownership: Hollingsworth & Vose Co.
Berleburgerstr. 71
D-35116 Hatzfeld
Germany
Mailing Address: Postf. 44, D-35115 Hatzfeld, Germany
  Phone: (49) 6467 801-0/4110
  Fax: (49) 6467 801 4202/4126
  Email: mail@hovo.de
  Web Address: www.hovo.com
Personnel:
  VP, Man. Dir. EMEA: Jochem Hofstetter
  Phone: (49) 6101 981 6719
  Fax: (49) 6101 981 6720
  Email: jochem.hofstetter@hovo.de
  Finan. Mgr.: Peter Fuchs
  Phone: (49) 6101 981 6729
  Fax: (49) 6467 801 4202
  Email: peter.fuchs@hovo.de
  Dir., Sls. EMEA (Europe, Middle East & Africa): Jens Hurtienne
  Phone: (49) 6101 981 6724
  Fax: (49) 6101 981 6720

Germany

Email: jens.hurtienne@hovo.de
Prod. Mgr.: Joe Kaiser
Phone: (49) 6467 801 4200
Fax: (49) 6467 801 4202
Email: jkaiser@hovo.de
Total Employees at this Location: 280
Type of Operation: Paper mill
Paper/Paperboard Grades and Capacities:
Total paper and paperboard capacity: 16,200 mt/y
Specialty and industrial
Paper and Paperboard Mill Data:
Stock Preparation:
Pulpers: 2
Paper Machines: 2
No. 2, inclined, fourdrinier, total capacity 15,000 mt/y, Trim width 2.5 m, Specialty and industrial
No. 4, fourdrinier, total capacity 1,200 mt/y, Trim width 1.6 m, Specialty and industrial
Coating Machines: 2
No. 1, off machine
No. 2, off machine
Finishing Equipment:
Rewinders: 10
Sheeters: 1
Energy Data:
Power boilers: 1

ⓜIllig'sche Papierfabrik
Mühltal Mill
Ownership: Cordier Spezialpapier GmbH
Rheinstr. 38
D-64367 Mühltal
Germany
Mailing Address: Postf. 13 01 10, D-64241 Darmstadt, Germany
Phone: (49) 6151 50980
Fax: (49) 6151 509888
Email: vertrieb@cordier-paper.de
Web Address: www.cordier-paper.de
Personnel:
Mill Mgr.: Marco Faedda
Phone: (49) 6151 5098 62
Fax: (49) 6322 9395 01
Email: marco.faedda@cordier-paper.de
Prod. Mgr.: Dirk Paeplow
Phone: (49) 6151 5098 30
Fax: (49) 6151 5098 88
Email: dirk.paeplow@cordier-paper.de
Sls. Mgr.: Mirjana Mamuza
Phone: (49) 6151 5098 15
Fax: (49) 6151 5098 88
Email: mirjana.mamuza@cordier-paper.de
Total Employees at this Location: 67
Type of Operation: Paper mill
Paper/Paperboard Grades and Capacities:
Total paper and paperboard capacity: 14,000 mt/y
Uncoated woodfree/freesheet: 14,000 mt/y
Coated woodfree/freesheet
Specialty and industrial
Paper and Paperboard Mill Data:
Paper Machines: 1
PM 1, fourdrinier, total capacity 14,000 mt/y, Trim width 2.2 m, Uncoated woodfree/freesheet, Specialty and industrial
Energy Data:
Power boilers: 1

ⓘInterface Solutions Altenkirchen GmbH
Ownership: 100% by Interface Solutions, Inc.
Koblenzer Str.
D-57610 Altenkirchen
Germany
Mailing Address: P.O. Box 12 63, D-57602 Altenkirchen, Germany
Phone: (49) 2681 8002 0
Fax: (49) 2681 8002 11
Email: (firstname.lastname@sealinfo.com)
Web Address: www.sealinfo.com
Personnel:
Gen. Mgr.: Dirk Euteneuer
Phone: (49) 2681 8002 21
Fax: (49) 2681 8002 24
Mill Mgr.: Oliver Hess
Phone: (49) 2681 800 20
Fax: (49) 2681 8002 11
Sls. Dir.: Wolfgang Schumacher
Phone: (49) 2681 8002 86
Fax: (49) 2681 8002 11
Sls. & Mktg. Mgr.: Daniel Müller
Phone: (49) 2681 8002 64
Fax: (49) 2681 8002 11
Mill Locations:
Interface Solutions Altenkirchen GmbH, Altenkirchen Mill, Koblenzer Str., D-57610 Altenkirchen, Germany, Capacity: 20,000 mt/y, (Paper mill)
Phone: (49) 2681 8002 0
Fax: (49) 2681 8002 11
Email: (firstname.lastname@sealinfo.com)

ⓜInterface Solutions Altenkirchen GmbH
Altenkirchen Mill
Koblenzer Str.
D-57610 Altenkirchen
Germany
Mailing Address: P.O. Box 12 63, D-57602 Altenkirchen, Germany
Phone: (49) 2681 8002 0
Fax: (49) 2681 8002 11
Email: (firstname.lastname@sealinfo.com)
Web Address: www.sealinfo.com
Personnel:
Gen. Mgr.: Dirk Euteneuer
Phone: (49) 2681 8002 21
Fax: (49) 2681 8002 24
Mill Mgr.: Harald Knoche
Phone: (49) 2681 8002 26
Fax: (49) 2681 8002 11
Mill Mgr.: Oliver Hess
Phone: (49) 2681 8002 0
Fax: (49) 2681 8002 11
Email: oliver.hess@sealinfo.com
Sls. Dir.: Wolfgang Schumacher
Phone: (49) 2681 8002 86
Fax: (49) 2681 8002 11
Sls. Mgr.: Werner Klak
Phone: (49) 2681 8002 38
Fax: (49) 2681 8002 11
Sls. & Mktg. Mgr.: Daniel Müller
Phone: (49) 2681 8002 64
Fax: (49) 2681 8002 11
Comm., IT and Personnel Mgr.: Stefan Weller
Phone: (49) 2681 8002 35
Fax: (49) 2681 8002 11
Total Employees at this Location: 120
Type of Operation: Paper mill
Paper/Paperboard Grades and Capacities:
Total paper and paperboard capacity: 20,000 mt/y
Specialty and industrial
Paper and Paperboard Mill Data:
Paper Machines: 2
PM 2, fourdrinier, Trim width 2.3 m, Specialty and industrial
PM 3, fourdrinier, Trim width 2.3 m, Specialty and industrial
Energy Data:
Power boilers: 1

ⓘⓜPapierfabrik Adolf Jass GmbH & Co. KG
Fulda Mill
Ownership: Jass family, Prinzhorn family
Hermann-Muth-Str. 6
D-36039 Fulda
Germany
Mailing Address: Postfach 2362, D-36013 Fulda, Germany
Phone: (49) 661 1060
Fax: (49) 661 71024
Email: info@jass.de
Web Address: www.jass.de
Personnel:
Owner: Adolf Jass
Phone: (49) 661 1060
Fax: (49) 661 106140
Email: a.jass@jass.de
Man. Dir.: Dr. Marietta Jass-Teichmann
Phone: (49) 661 1060
Fax: (49) 661 106140
Email: m.jass-teichmann@jass.de
Mill Mgr. & Tech. Mgr.: Uwe Remmert
Phone: (49) 661 1060
Fax: (49) 661 106140
Email: u.remmert@jass.de
Sls. Dir.: Christof Schnell
Phone: (49) 661 106123
Fax: (49) 661 106140
Email: c.schnell@jass.de
Commun. & Purch. Mgr.: Horst Oetke
Phone: (49) 661 1060
Fax: (49) 661 106194
Email: h.oetke@jass.de
Total Employees of Company: 407
Total Employees at this Location: 244
Type of Operation: Paperboard mill
Mill Locations:
Papierfabrik Adolf Jass GmbH & Co. KG, Rudolstadt-Schwarza Mill, Breitscheidstr. 147, D-07407 Rudolstadt-Schwarza, Germany, Capacity: 450,000 mt/y, (Paperboard mill)
Phone: (49) 3672 4770
Fax: (49) 3672 477 477
Email: info@jass-schwarza.de
Pulp Grades and Capacities:
Total pulp capacity: 506,278 mt/y
Recycled Pulping: 506,278 mt/y
Pulp Mill Data:
Recycled Fiber Treatment Lines:
Pulpers: 2 at 550,000 admt/y
Paper/Paperboard Grades and Capacities:
Total paper and paperboard capacity: 500,000 mt/y
Linerboard: 250,000 mt/y
Corrugating medium/fluting: 250,000 mt/y
Paper and Paperboard Mill Data:
Stock Preparation:
Pulpers: 2
Paper Machines: 2
No. 3, DuoFormer CFD, total capacity 250,000 mt/y, Trim width 5 m, Corrugating medium/fluting
No. 4, fourdrinier (2), total capacity 250,000 mt/y, Trim width 5 m, Linerboard
Finishing Equipment:
Winders: 2
Energy Data:
Power boilers: 2
Combustion turbines: 2 at 10 MW
Steam turbines: 2 at 25 MW
Electrical demand for mill: 747 MWh/D

ⓜPapierfabrik Adolf Jass GmbH & Co. KG
Rudolstadt-Schwarza Mill
Breitscheidstr. 147
D-07407 Rudolstadt-Schwarza, Thüringen
Germany
Phone: (49) 3672 4770
Fax: (49) 3672 477 477
Email: info@jass-schwarza.de
Web Address: www.jass.de
Personnel:
Mill Mgr.: Michael Habeck
Phone: (49) 3672 4770
Fax: (49) 3672 477477
Email: m.habeck@jass-schwarza.de
Total Employees at this Location: 163
Type of Operation: Paperboard mill
Pulp Grades and Capacities:

Germany

Total pulp capacity: 445,536 mt/y
Recycled Pulping: 445,536 mt/y
Pulp Mill Data:
Pulp Lines: 1
Recycled Fiber Treatment Lines:
Recycled packaging pulping lines: 1 at 480,000
Paper/Paperboard Grades and Capacities:
Total paper and paperboard capacity: 450,000 mt/y
Linerboard: 150,000 mt/y
Corrugating medium/fluting: 300,000 mt/y
Paper and Paperboard Mill Data:
Stock Preparation:
Pulpers: 4
Paper Machines: 1
No. 1, DuoFormer Base, total capacity 450,000 mt/y, Trim width 7.5 m, Corrugating medium/fluting, Linerboard
Finishing Equipment:
Winders: 1
Energy Data:
Steam turbines: 1 at 5.8 MW
Electrical demand for mill: 516 MWh/D

ⓗⓜKartonfabrik Kaierde GmbH & Co. Produktions KG
Delligsen Mill
Hagentalstr. 2
D-31073 Delligsen
Germany
  Phone: (49) 5187 94020
  Fax: (49) 5187 940223
  Email: info@kartonfabrikkaierde.de
  Web Address: www.kartonfabrikkaierde.de
Personnel:
Mill Mgr.: Dipl. Ing. Achim Gravenkamp
  Phone: (49) 5187 94020
  Fax: (49) 5187 9402 23
  Email: info@kartonfabrikkaierde.de
Sls. Mgr.: Stephan Gravenkamp
  Phone: (49) 5187 9402 35
  Fax: (49) 5187 9402 23
  Email: sgravenkamp@kartonfabrikkaierde.de
Total Employees at this Location: 56
Type of Operation: Paperboard mill
Pulp Grades and Capacities:
Total pulp capacity: 20,310 mt/y
Recycled Pulping: 20,310 mt/y
Pulp Mill Data:
Recycled Fiber Treatment Lines:
Pulpers: 1 at 23,800
Paper/Paperboard Grades and Capacities:
Total paper and paperboard capacity: 20,000 mt/y
Boxboard/cartonboard: 20,000 mt/y
Paper and Paperboard Mill Data:
Paper Machines: 1
No. 1, cylinder, total capacity 20,000 mt/y, Trim width 2.3 m, Boxboard/cartonboard
Energy Data:
Power boilers
Electrical demand for mill: 18 MWh/D

ⓗKämmerer GmbH
Ownership: 100% by Perusa
Römereschstrasse 33
49090 Osnabrück
Germany
  Phone: (49) 541 604-0
  Fax: (49) 541 604-210
  Email: info@kaemmerer-gmbh.de
  Web Address: www.kaemmerer-gmbh.de
Personnel:
CEO: Jürgen Oess
  Phone: (49) 541 604 333
  Fax: (49) 541 604 480
  Email: juergen.oess@kaemmerer-gmbh.de
Head of Finance: Dirk Mühlenmeister
  Phone: (49) 541 604 333
  Fax: (49) 541 604 480

Head of Prod. Dev., Mgr. Qual & Buiss.: Holger Arnold
  Phone: (49) 541 604-456
  Fax: (49) 541 604 480
  Email: holger.arnold@kaemmerer-gmbh.de
Buiss. Mgr.: Michael Peterse
  Phone: (49) 541 604-316
  Fax: (49) 541 604 480
  Email: michael.peterse@kaemmerer-gmbh.de
Head of Engineering: Matthias Pieper
  Phone: (49) 541 604 333
  Fax: (49) 541 604 480
Personnel Development/Communications: Beate Thieke
  Phone: (49) 541 604-234
  Fax: (49) 541 604-210
  Email: beate.thieke@kaemmerer-gmbh.de
Total Employees of Company: 270
Mill Locations:
Kämmerer GmbH, Osnabrück Mill, Römereschstrasse 33, 49090 Osnabrück, Germany, Capacity: 50,000 mt/y, (Paper mill)
  Phone: (49) 541 604-0
  Fax: (49) 541 604-210
  Email: info@kaemmerer-gmbh.de

ⓗⓜKämmerer GmbH
Osnabrück Mill
Ownership: 100% by Perusa
Römereschstrasse 33
49090 Osnabrück
Germany
Mailing Address: Postfach 36 67, D-49026 Osnabrück, Germany
  Phone: (49) 541 604-0
  Fax: (49) 541 604-210
  Email: info@kaemmerer-gmbh.de
  Web Address: www.kaemmerer-gmbh.de
Total Employees of Company: 270
Total Employees at this Location: 270
Type of Operation: Paper mill
Paper/Paperboard Grades and Capacities:
Total paper and paperboard capacity: 50,000 mt/y
Specialty and industrial: 50,000 mt/y
Paper and Paperboard Mill Data:
Paper Machines: 2
PM 3, (3), fourdrinier, total capacity 25,000 mt/y, Trim width 4.75 m, Specialty and industrial
PM 4, round wire, total capacity 15,000 mt/y, Trim width 2.1 m, Specialty and industrial

ⓗⓜKanzan Spezialpapiere GmbH
Neumühl Mill
Ownership: 95.20% by Oji Holdings Corporation, 4.80% by Marubeni Paper Sales Europe
Nippesstr. 5
D-52349 Düren
Germany
Mailing Address: Postf. 101141, D-52311 Düren, Germany
  Phone: (49) 2421 5924 0
  Fax: (49) 2421 5924 19
  Email: sales@kanzan.de, info@kanzan.de
  Web Address: www.kanzan.de
Personnel:
Man. Dir.: Matthias Simon
  Phone: (49) 2421 5924 0
  Fax: (49) 2421 5924 19
  Email: m.simon@kanzan.de
Head of Sls. & Mktg.: Andreas Löhr
  Phone: (49) 2421 5924 20
  Fax: (49) 2421 5924 29
  Email: a.lohr@kanzan.de
Total Employees at this Location: 300
Type of Operation: Paper mill
Paper/Paperboard Grades and Capacities:
Total paper and paperboard capacity: 60,000 mt/y
Uncoated woodfree/freesheet: 60,000 mt/y
Paper and Paperboard Mill Data:

Paper Machines: 1
No. 6, SymFormer MB, total capacity 60,000 mt/y, Trim width 3.2 m, Uncoated woodfree/freesheet
Coating Machines: 2
CM 1, total capacity 60,000 mt/y., off machine
CM 2, off machine
Finishing Equipment:
Rewinders: 5
Energy Data:
Power boilers: 3
Steam turbines: 1 at 2 MW
Electrical demand for mill: 118 MWh/D

ⓜKatz GmbH & Co. KG
Weisenbach Mill
Ownership: Papierfabrik August Koehler AG
Hauptstr. 2
D-76599 Weisenbach
Germany
Mailing Address: Postf. 40, D-76599 Weisenbach, Germany
  Phone: (49) 7224 6470
  Fax: (49) 7224 64710165
  Email: office@thekatzgroup.com
  Web Address: www.thekatzgroup.com
Personnel:
CEO: Daniel Bitton
  Phone: (49) 7224 647 131
  Fax: (49) 7224 647 10131
  Email: daniel.bitton@thekatzgroup.com
Sales Mgr.: Joe Yamamoto
  Phone: (49) 7224 647 147
  Fax: (49) 7224 647 10147
  Email: joe.yamamoto@thekatzgroup.com
Mgr. Printing Plant: Dieter Wieland
  Phone: (49) 7224 647 283
  Fax: (49) 7224 647 10283
  Email: dieter.wieland@thekatzgroup.com
Total Employees at this Location: 155
Type of Operation: Paperboard mill
Pulp Grades and Capacities:
Total pulp capacity: 28,590 mt/y
Mechanical Pulp: 25,159 mt/y
Recycled Pulping: 3,431 mt/y
Pulp Mill Data:
Mechanical Pulping Systems:
Conventional grinders: 1
Paper/Paperboard Grades and Capacities:
Total paper and paperboard capacity: 28,000 mt/y
Boxboard/cartonboard: 28,000 mt/y
Paper and Paperboard Mill Data:
Stock Preparation:
Pulpers: 2
Refiners: 4
Paper Machines: 1
No. 1, cylinder (3), total capacity 28,000 mt/y, Trim width 2.52 m, Boxboard/cartonboard
Finishing Equipment:
Rewinders: 1
Sheeters: 1
Energy Data:
Power boilers: 1
Hydro turbines: 3 at 0.55 MW
Electrical demand for mill: 112 MWh/D

ⓗⓜKimberly-Clark GmbH
Koblenz Mill
Ownership: Kimberly-Clark Corp.
Carl-Spaeter-Str. 17
D-56070 Koblenz
Germany
Mailing Address: Postf. 20 08 65, Koblenz, Germany
  Phone: (49) 261 92270
  Fax: (49) 261 9227 494 / 488
  Email: afhde@kcc.com
  Web Address: www.kcprofessional.com
Personnel:
Gen. Mgr.: Michael Kuhn

Phone: (49) 261 9227 0
Fax: (49) 261 9227 494
Email: mkuhn@kcc.com
Paper Mill Mgr.: Renato Negro
Phone: (49) 261 9227 0
Fax: (49) 261 9227 494
Email: rnegro@kcc.com
Maint. Mgr.: Wolfgang Bastian
Phone: (49) 261 1893 237
Fax: (49) 261 9227 494
Email: wbastian@kcc.com
Total Employees at this Location: 370
Type of Operation: Paper mill
Mill Locations:
Kimberly-Clark GmbH, Niederbipp Mill, Rotboden 1, CH-4704 Niederbipp, Switzerland, Capacity: 47,000 mt/y, (Paper mill)
Phone: (41) 32 633 51 11
Fax: (41) 32 633 51 00
Pulp Grades and Capacities:
Total pulp capacity: 40,478 mt/y
Recycled Pulping: 40,478 mt/y
Pulp Mill Data:
Recycled Fiber Treatment Lines:
Flotation deinking lines at 40,000
Paper/Paperboard Grades and Capacities:
Total paper and paperboard capacity: 38,000 mt/y
Tissue: 38,000 mt/y
Paper and Paperboard Mill Data:
Stock Preparation:
Pulpers: 3
Refiners: 2
Paper Machines: 1
No. 1, fourdrinier, Yankee dryer, total capacity 38,000 mt/y, Trim width 3.4 m, Tissue
Finishing Equipment:
Rewinders: 1
Energy Data:
Power boilers: 2
Electrical demand for mill: 115 MWh/D

ⓒⓜKlingele Papierwerke GmbH & Co. KG
Weener Mill
Ownership: 100% by Klingele family (Private)
Dr.-Werner-Klingele-Str. 1
D-26826 Weener
Germany
Phone: (49) 4951 303-0
Fax: (49) 4951 303-34
Email: weener@klingele.com
Web Address: www.klingele.com
Personnel:
Man. Partner: Dr. Jan Klingele
Phone: (49) 7151 701 215
Email: jan.klingele@klingele.com
Man. Dir. Paper Mill: Thilo-Hubertus Kuhl
Phone: (49) 4951 303-0
Fax: (49) 4951 303 34
Email: thilo-hubertus.kuhl@klingele.com
Power/Energy Mgr.: Thomas Tappe
Phone: (49) 4951 303-0
Fax: (49) 4951 303 34
Email: thomas.tappe@klingele.com
Tech. Mgr.: Thomas Wischeropp
Phone: (49) 4951 303 0
Fax: (49) 4951 303 34
Email: thomas.wischeropp@klingele.com
Purch. Mgr.: Günter Abheiden
Phone: (49) 4951 303 0
Fax: (49) 4951 303 34
Email: guenter.abheiden@klingele.com
Sls. Mgr.: Micha Meyer
Phone: (49) 4951 303 0
Fax: (49) 4951 303 34
Email: micha.meyer@klingele.com
Total Employees of Company: 1,250
Total Employees at this Location: 111
Type of Operation: Paper mill, Paperboard mill

Mill Locations:
Blue Paper SAS., Stracel Mill (50% owned), 4 rue Charles Friedel Port du Rhin, F-67016 Strasbourg, France, Capacity: 270,000 mt/y, (Paper mill)
Phone: (33) 3 88 417532
Fax: (33) 3 88 417598
Email: info@bluepaper.eu
Pulp Grades and Capacities:
Total pulp capacity: 250,357 mt/y
Recycled Pulping: 250,357 mt/y
Pulp Mill Data:
Recycled Fiber Treatment Lines:
Recycled packaging pulping lines: 1 at 250,000
Paper/Paperboard Grades and Capacities:
Total paper and paperboard capacity: 250,000 mt/y
Linerboard: 150,000 mt/y
Corrugating medium/fluting: 100,000 mt/y
Paper and Paperboard Mill Data:
Stock Preparation:
Pulpers: 2
Paper Machines: 1
No. 2, fourdrinier (2), total capacity 250,000 mt/y, Trim width 4.93 m, Corrugating medium/fluting, Linerboard
Finishing Equipment:
Winders: 1 at 300,000 mt/y
Energy Data:
Power boilers: 2
Steam turbines: 5 at 7.2, 9.2, 2.6 MW
Electrical demand for mill: 307 MWh/D

ⓒⓜPapierfabrik August Koehler AG
Oberkirch Mill
Ownership: Koehler Holding GmbH & Co. KG
Hauptstr. 2-4
D-77704 Oberkirch (Baden)
Germany
Mailing Address: Postf. 12 45, D-77696 Oberkirch (Baden), Germany
Phone: (49) 7802 81 0
Fax: (49) 7802 81 4330
Email: info@koehlerpaper.com
Web Address: www.koehlerpaper.com
Personnel:
CEO: Kai Michael Furler
Phone: (49) 7802 810
Fax: (49) 7802 814330
COO: Werner Ruckenbrod
Phone: (49) 7802 810
Fax: (49) 7802 814330
CFO: Frank Lendowski
Phone: (49) 7802 810
Fax: (49) 7802 814330
Dir. Corp. Commun. (Dir. Carbonless Paper Div.): Stephan Schwietzke
Phone: (49) 7802 810
Fax: (49) 7802 814330
Email: stephan.schwietzke@koehlerpaper.com
Product Mgr.: Katja Frede
Phone: (49) 7802 810
Fax: (49) 7802 814330
Email: katja.frede@koehlerpaper.com
Total Employees of Company: 1,800
Total Employees at this Location: 900
Type of Operation: Paper mill
Mill Locations:
Katz GmbH & Co. KG, Weisenbach Mill, Hauptstr. 2, D-76599 Weisenbach, Germany, Capacity: 28,000 mt/y, (Paperboard mill)
Phone: (49) 7224 6470
Fax: (49) 7224 64710165
Email: office@thekatzgroup.com
Koehler Greiz GmbH & Co. KG, Greiz Mill, Mylauer Str. 4, D-07973 Greiz, Germany, Capacity: 30,000 mt/y, (Paper mill)
Phone: (49) 3661 616 0
Fax: (49) 3661 61622 02 / 12 02
Email: info@koehlerpaper.com
Koehler Kehl GmbH, Kehl Mill, Bremerwörtstr. 4, D-77694 Kehl, Germany, Capacity: 290,000 mt/y, (Paper mill)

Phone: (49) 7851 667 000
Fax: (49) 7851 667 789
Email: info@koehlerpaper.com
Paper/Paperboard Grades and Capacities:
Total paper and paperboard capacity: 150,000 mt/y
Uncoated woodfree/freesheet: 130,000 mt/y
Specialty and industrial: 20,000 mt/y
Paper and Paperboard Mill Data:
Stock Preparation:
Pulpers: 4
Refiners: 12
Paper Machines: 3
No. 3, fourdrinier, total capacity 20,000 mt/y, Trim width 2.1 m, Specialty and industrial
No. 4, fourdrinier, total capacity 50,000 mt/y, Trim width 3.2 m, Uncoated woodfree/freesheet
No. 5, fourdrinier, total capacity 80,000 mt/y, Trim width 3.7 m, Uncoated woodfree/freesheet
Coating Machines: 1
CM 7
Finishing Equipment:
Supercalenders: 1
Rewinders: 9
Sheeters: 2
Energy Data:
Power boilers: 1
Steam turbines: 1 at 20.0 MW
Electrical demand for mill: 296 MWh/D

ⓜKoehler Greiz GmbH & Co. KG
Greiz Mill
Ownership: Papierfabrik August Koehler AG
Mylauer Str. 4
D-07973 Greiz
Germany
Phone: (49) 3661 616 0
Fax: (49) 3661 61622 02 / 12 02
Email: info@koehlerpaper.com
Web Address: www.koehlerpaper.com
Personnel:
Mill Dir.: Holger Palm
Phone: (49) 3661 616 200
Fax: (49) 3661 616 241
Email: holger.palm@koehlerpaper.com
Total Employees at this Location: 112
Type of Operation: Paper mill
Pulp Grades and Capacities:
Total pulp capacity: 30,758 mt/y
Recycled Pulping: 30,758 mt/y
Pulp Mill Data:
Bleach Plant Lines:
DIP Capacity 30,000 admt/y
Recycled Fiber Treatment Lines:
Flotation deinking lines at 30,000
Paper/Paperboard Grades and Capacities:
Total paper and paperboard capacity: 30,000 mt/y
Uncoated woodfree/freesheet: 30,000 mt/y
Paper and Paperboard Mill Data:
Stock Preparation:
Pulpers: 1
Paper Machines: 1
No. 1, top former, total capacity 30,000 mt/y, Trim width 2.74 m, Uncoated woodfree/freesheet
Finishing Equipment:
Winders: 1 at 30,000 mt/y
Sheeters: 1 at 8,000 mt/y
Energy Data:
Power boilers: 1
Steam turbines: 1 at 1.2 MW
Electrical demand for mill: 70 MWh/D

ⓜKoehler Kehl GmbH
Kehl Mill
Ownership: Papierfabrik August Koehler AG
Bremerwörtstr. 4
D-77694 Kehl
Germany

Germany

Phone: (49) 7851 667 000
Fax: (49) 7851 667 789
Email: info@koehlerpaper.com
Web Address: www.koehlerpaper.com
Personnel:
Man. Dir.: Wolfgang Furler
Phone: (49) 7851 667 000
Fax: (49) 7851 667 789
Email: wolfgang.furler@koehlerpaper.com
Tech. Mgr., Head of Reacto Carbonless Paper Div. & Head of Koehler Thermal Paper Div.: Michael Boschert
Phone: (49) 7851 667 727
Fax: (49) 7851 667 789
Email: michael.boschert@koehlerpaper.com
Dir. Thermal Paper Div.: Willy Früh
Phone: (49) 7802 814 197
Fax: (49) 7802 815 197
Email: willy.frueh@koehlerpaper.com
Total Employees at this Location: 480
Type of Operation: Paper mill
Paper/Paperboard Grades and Capacities:
  Total paper and paperboard capacity: 290,000 mt/y
  Uncoated woodfree/freesheet: 250,000 mt/y
  Specialty and industrial: 40,000 mt/y
Paper and Paperboard Mill Data:
Paper Machines: 3
  No. 1, fourdrinier, total capacity 100,000 mt/y, Trim width 4.1 m, Uncoated woodfree/freesheet
  No. 2, DuoFormer TQv, total capacity 150,000 mt/y, Trim width 4.2 m, Uncoated woodfree/freesheet
  No. 6, fourdrinier, total capacity 40,000 mt/y, Trim width 2.3 m, Specialty and industrial
Coating Machines: 2
  No. 1
  No. 2, total capacity 120,000 mt/y.
Finishing Equipment:
  Rewinders: 1
Energy Data:
Power boilers: 1
Steam turbines: 2 at 2.9, 8.6 MW
Electrical demand for mill: 563 MWh/D

ⓘⓂAlbert Köhler GmbH & Co. KG
Gengenbach Mill
Ownership: Private
Grünstr. 4
D-77723 Gengenbach
Germany
Mailing Address: Postf. 11 88, Gengenbach, Germany
  Phone: (49) 7803 8090 / 809-55 / 809-56
  Fax: (49) 7803 80950 / 80960
  Email: info@koehlerboard.com
  Web Address: www.koehlerboard.com
Personnel:
Man. Dir.: Hans-Henning Junk
Phone: (49) 7803 809 0
Fax: (49) 7803 809 50
Email: hans-henning.junk@koehlerboard.com
Head of IT: Mr. Nicola Turri
Phone: (49) 7803 8090/80955
Fax: (49) 7803 809 50
Email: nicola.turri@koehlerboard.com
Tech. Mgr.: Thomas Dörfer
Phone: (49) 7803 8090/80955
Fax: (49) 7803 809 50
Email: homas.doerfer@koethlerboard.com
Sls. Mgr.: Christian Geiger
Phone: (49) 7803 8090/80955
Fax: (49) 7803 809 50
Email: christian.geiger@koehlerboard.com
Prod. Mgr.: Rudolf Braun
Phone: (49) 7803 809 0
Fax: (49) 7803 809 50
Email: rudolf.braun@koehlerboard.com
Sls. Germany: Elke Schultis
Phone: (49) 7803 8090/80955
Fax: (49) 7803 809 50
Email: elke.schultis@koehlerboard.com
Total Employees of Company: 100

Total Employees at this Location: 100
Type of Operation: Paperboard mill
Pulp Grades and Capacities:
  Total pulp capacity: 49,635 mt/y
  Recycled Pulping: 49,635 mt/y
Pulp Mill Data:
  Recycled Fiber Treatment Lines:
  Pulpers: 1 at 50,000
  Recycled packaging pulping lines: 1 at 50,000
Paper/Paperboard Grades and Capacities:
  Total paper and paperboard capacity: 50,000 mt/y
  Boxboard/cartonboard: 50,000 mt/y
Paper and Paperboard Mill Data:
  Stock Preparation:
  Pulpers: 2
  Refiners: 2
Paper Machines: 3
  No. 1, fourdrinier, total capacity 32,000 mt/y, Trim width 1.68 m, Boxboard/cartonboard
  No. 2, cylinder, total capacity 6,000 mt/y, Trim width 3.15 m, Boxboard/cartonboard
  No. 3, cylinder, total capacity 12,000 mt/y, Trim width 3.15 m, Boxboard/cartonboard
Finishing Equipment:
  Sheeters: 1
Energy Data:
Power boilers: 1
Steam turbines: 1 at 1.5 MW
Electrical demand for mill: 62 MWh/D

ⓘⓂHans Kolb Papierfabrik GmbH & Co. KG
Kaufbeuren Mill
Ownership: 100% by Alwin Kolb GmbH & Co.
Adelindastr. 15
D-87600 Kaufbeuren
Germany
Mailing Address: Postf. 14 34, D-87574 Kaufbeuren, Germany
  Phone: (49) 8341 93630
  Fax: (49) 8341 936335
  Email: info@kolb-wellpappe.com
  Web Address: www.kolb-wellpappe.com
Personnel:
Gen. Mgr.: Dipl.-Ing. Alwin Kolb
Phone: (49) 8341 93630
Fax: (49) 8341 936335
Email: akolb@kolb-wellpappe.com
Mill Mgr.: Martin Bergner
Phone: (49) 8341 9363 45
Fax: (49) 8341 936335
Email: mbergner@kolb-wellpappe.com
Tech. Mgr.: Bernhard Bartl
Phone: (49) 8341 93630
Fax: (49) 8341 936335
Email: bbartl@kolb-wellpappe.com
Total Employees of Company: 950
Total Employees at this Location: 70
Type of Operation: Paperboard mill
Pulp Grades and Capacities:
  Total pulp capacity: 64,828 mt/y
  Recycled Pulping: 64,828 mt/y
Pulp Mill Data:
  Recycled Fiber Treatment Lines:
  Pulpers: 1 at 60,000 admt/y
Paper/Paperboard Grades and Capacities:
  Total paper and paperboard capacity: 65,000 mt/y
  Linerboard: 35,000 mt/y
  Corrugating medium/fluting: 30,000 mt/y
Paper and Paperboard Mill Data:
  Stock Preparation:
  Refiners: 1
Paper Machines: 1
  No. 4, fourdrinier, total capacity 65,000 mt/y, Trim width 2.1 m, Corrugating medium/fluting, Linerboard
Finishing Equipment:
  Winders: 1 at 60,000 mt/y
  Rewinders: 1 at 60,000 mt/y

Energy Data:
Power boilers: 1
Combustion turbines: 1 at 5.7 MW
Electrical demand for mill: 82 MWh/D

ⓘKrempel-Group
Papierfabrikstr. 4
D-71665 Vaihingen/Enz
Germany
Mailing Address: Postf. 12 40, D-71665 Vaihingen an der Enz, Germany
  Phone: (49) 7042 915-0
  Fax: (49) 7042 15985
  Email: info@krempel-group.com
  Web Address: www.krempel-group.com
Personnel:
Bd. of Directors: Torben Duer
Phone: (49) 49 7042 915-0
Fax: (49) 49 7042 15985
Man. Dir.: Uwe Assmuth
Phone: (49) 7042 915-0
Fax: (49) 7042 15985
Email: uweassmuth@krempel-group.com
Man. Dir.: Christian Reh
Phone: (49) 49 7042 915-0
Fax: (49) 49 7042 15985
Email: christianreh@krempel-group.com
Man. Dir.: Dr. Ulrich Schmidt
Phone: (49) 7042 915-0
Fax: (49) 7042 15985
Division Mgr. (Elect. Insulations Division): Tobias Zaiser
Phone: (49) 7042 915 143
Fax: (49) 7042 951 95 143
Division Mgr. & Eng. Mgr. (Composites Division): Karl-Heinz Sprenger
Phone: (49) 7042 915-185
Fax: (49) 7042 915-287
Division Mgr. (Solar Materials Division): Klaus Bernhardt
Phone: (49) 7042 915-178
Fax: (49) 7042 915-281
Application Eng. Mgr. (Solar Materials Division): Karlheinz Brust
Phone: (49) 7042 915-176
Fax: (49) 7042 915-281
Head of Sls.: Thomas Mozer
Phone: (49) 49 7042 915-0
Fax: (49) 49 7042 15985
HR. Mgr.: Silke Geiß
Phone: (49) 49 7042 915-0
Fax: (49) 49 7042 15985
Total Employees of Company: 850
Mill Locations:
  Krempel-Group, Kuppenheim Mill, Am Kanaldamm 17, D-76456 Kuppenheim, Germany, Capacity: 2,000 mt/y, (Paperboard mill)
  Phone: (49) 7222 94 56 0 / 56 100
  Fax: (49) 7222 486 06
  Email: info@ku.krempel.com
  Krempel-Group, Thalheim Mill, Bahnhofstr. 3, D-09380 Thalheim, Germany, Capacity: 5,000 mt/y, (Paper mill)
  Phone: (49) 3721 39750
  Fax: (49) 3721 397 515
  Email: presspanwerk@krempel-group.com
  Krempel-Group, Zwönitz Mill, Annaberger Str. 67, D-08297 Zwönitz, Germany, Capacity: 5,000 mt/y, (Paperboard mill)
  Phone: (49) 37754 33740
  Fax: (49) 37754 337415
  Email: info@krempel-group.com

ⓂKrempel-Group
Kuppenheim Mill
Am Kanaldamm 17
D-76456 Kuppenheim
Germany
Mailing Address: Postf. 11 23, D-76449 Kuppenheim, Germany
  Phone: (49) 7222 94 56 0 / 56 100

Pulp and Paper Mills - Europe

Germany

Fax: (49) 7222 486 06
Email: info@ku.krempel.com
Web Address: www.krempel-group.com
Personnel:
Mill Mgr.: Joachim Wachsmuth
Phone: (49) 7222 94 56 100
Fax: (49) 7222 48 60 6
Email: j.wachsmuth@krempel-group.com
Total Employees at this Location: 140
Type of Operation: Paperboard mill
Paper/Paperboard Grades and Capacities:
Total paper and paperboard capacity: 2,000 mt/y
Boxboard/cartonboard
Paper and Paperboard Mill Data:
Paper Machines: 1
PM 1, total capacity 2,000 mt/y, Boxboard/cartonboard
Energy Data:
Power boilers: 1

ⓜKrempel-Group
Thalheim Mill
Bahnhofstr. 3
D-09380 Thalheim
Germany
Mailing Address: Postf. 22, D-09377 Thalheim, Germany
Phone: (49) 3721 39750
Fax: (49) 3721 397 515
Email: presspanwerk@krempel-group.com
Web Address: www.krempel-group.com
Personnel:
Mill Mgr.: Gabriele Kretzschmar
Phone: (49) 3721 397 50
Fax: (49) 3721 397 515
Email: g.kretzschmar@krempel-group.com
Total Employees at this Location: 160
Type of Operation: Paper mill
Paper/Paperboard Grades and Capacities:
Total paper and paperboard capacity: 5,000 mt/y
Specialty and industrial: 5,000 mt/y
Paper and Paperboard Mill Data:
Stock Preparation:
Pulpers:
Refiners:
Paper Machines: 1
PM 1, total capacity 5,000 mt/y, Trim width 2 m, Boxboard/cartonboard
Finishing Equipment:
Winders
Sheeters: 1
Energy Data:
Power boilers: 1
Electrical demand for mill: 15 MWh/D

ⓜKrempel-Group
Zwönitz Mill
Annaberger Str. 67
D-08297 Zwönitz
Germany
Mailing Address: Postf. 100 05, D-08295 Zwönitz, Germany
Phone: (49) 37754 33740
Fax: (49) 37754 337415
Email: info@krempel-group.com
Web Address: www.krempel-group.com
Personnel:
Mill Mgr.: Gabriele Kretzschmar
Phone: (49) 37 2139750
Fax: (49) 37 75337415
Email: g.kretzschmar@th.krempel.com
Total Employees at this Location: 150
Type of Operation: Paperboard mill
Paper/Paperboard Grades and Capacities:
Total paper and paperboard capacity: 5,000 mt/y
Boxboard/cartonboard: 5,000 mt/y
Paper and Paperboard Mill Data:
Paper Machines: 1
PM 1, total capacity 5,000 mt/y, Trim width 2 m, Boxboard/cartonboard

Energy Data:
Power boilers: 1
Electrical demand for mill: 15 MWh/D

ⓗⓜKübler & Niethammer Papierfabrik Kriebstein AG
Kriebstein Mill
Ownership: 47% by Niethammer Family
Bauhofstr. 1 / OT Kriebethal
D-09648 Kriebstein
Germany
Phone: (49) 34327 9750
Fax: (49) 34327 97945
Email: info@k-n-paper.de
Web Address: www.k-n-paper.de
Personnel:
Chmn. and Dir.: Hubertus Burkhart
Phone: (49) 34327 9750
Fax: (49) 34327 97945
Email: hburkhart@k-n-paper.de
Supervisory Board Chrmn.: Günther Niethammer
Phone: (49) 34327 9750
Fax: (49) 34327 97945
Email: gniethammer@k-n-paper.de
Dir.: Regina Ludwig
Phone: (49) 34327 97816
Fax: (49) 34327 97755
Email: rludwig@k-n-paper.de
Mill Mgr.: Michael Moser
Phone: (49) 34327 97781
Fax: (49) 34327 97945
Email: mmoser@k-n-paper.de
Sls. & Mktg. Dir.: Herr Klaus Barth
Phone: (49) 34327 97986, 172 8054161
Fax: (49) 34327 97 934
Email: kbarth@k-n-paper.de
Sls. Mgr.: Herr Gerd Meyer
Phone: (49) 34327 97 804
Fax: (49) 34327 97 934
Email: gmeyer@k-n-paper.de
Total Employees of Company: 120
Total Employees at this Location: 135
Type of Operation: Paper mill
Pulp Grades and Capacities:
Total pulp capacity: 99,292 mt/y
Recycled Pulping: 99,292 mt/y
Pulp Mill Data:
Recycled Fiber Treatment Lines:
Flotation deinking lines: 1 at 220,000
Pulpers: 1 at 220,000
Paper/Paperboard Grades and Capacities:
Total paper and paperboard capacity: 115,000 mt/y
Coated mechanical/groundwood: 85,000 mt/y
Linerboard: 30,000 mt/y
Paper and Paperboard Mill Data:
Paper Machines: 1
No. 1, DuoFormer D, total capacity 115,000 mt/y, Trim width 3.96 m, Coated mechanical/groundwood, Linerboard
Coating Machines: 1
No. 1, total capacity 115,000 mt/y., on machine
Finishing Equipment:
Rewinders: 1 at 85,000 mt/y
Energy Data:
Power boilers: 2
Combustion turbines: 1 at 10 MW
Steam turbines: 1 at 3 MW
Electrical demand for mill: 274 MWh/D

ⓗKunert Gruppe, Paul & Co GmbH & Co. KG
Sudetenstr. 10
D-97772 Wildflecken
Germany
Phone: (49) 97 45 37-0
Fax: (49) 97 45 37-373003
Email: info@paulundco.de
Web Address: www.kunertgruppe.com
Personnel:
Man. Dir.: Manfred Kunert
Phone: (49) 97 45 37-0
Fax: (49) 97 45 37-373003
Email: manfred.kunert@paulundco.de
Exec. Dir.: Walter Kunert
Phone: (49) 97 45 37-0
Fax: (49) 97 45 37-373003
Email: walter.kunert@paulundco.de
R & D Mgr.: Christoph Schmitt
Phone: (49) 97 45 37-0
Fax: (49) 97 45 37-373003
Email: christoph.schmitt@paulundco.de
Total Employees of Company: 1,800
Mill Locations:
Carl Macher GmbH & Co. KG, Brunnenthal Mill (75% owned), Fabrikstr. 14, D-95189 Brunnenthal, Germany, Capacity: 110,000 mt/y, (Paperboard mill)
Phone: (49) 9281 70680
Fax: (49) 9281 63609
Email: info@macher.de
Papeteries du Rhin, Illzach Mill, Rue Henry de Crousaz, Ile Napoléon, BP 148, F-68110 Illzach, France, Capacity: 75,000 mt/y, (Pulp mill, Paperboard mill)
Phone: (33) 3 89 61 74 47
Fax: (33) 3 89 61 85 54
Email: pdr@papeteries-du-rhin.com

ⓗⓜKarl Kurz GmbH & Co. KG
Tullau Mill
Kocherweg 10
D-74538 Rosengarten-Tullau
Germany
Phone: (49) 791 95 55333
Fax: (49) 791 95 55344
Email: vertrieb@pappen.de, tullau@pappen.de
Web Address: www.pappen.de
Personnel:
Gen. Mgr.: Dipl. Ing. Günter Kurz
Phone: (49) 791 9555 0
Fax: (49) 791 9555 490
Email: info@pappen.de
Gen. Mgr., Tech. & Works Mgr.: Dipl. Ing. Matthias Kurz
Phone: (49) 791 95 55333
Fax: (49) 791 95 55344
Email: info@pappen.de
Sls. & Mktg. Mgr.: Angelika Munz
Phone: (49) 791 95 55313
Fax: (49) 791 95 55344
Email: munz@pappen.de
Sls. & Purch. Mgr.: Lars Henrik Meyer
Phone: (49) 791 95 55313
Fax: (49) 791 95 55344
Email: meyer@pappen.de
Logist. Mgr.: Armin Gigga
Phone: (49) 791 9555 300
Fax: (49) 791 9555 344
Email: gigga@pappen.de
Purch. Mgr.: Kirsten Kuemmerer
Phone: (49) 791 9555 220
Fax: (49) 791 9555 490
Email: kuemmerer@pappen.de
Total Employees at this Location: 42
Type of Operation: Paperboard mill
Mill Locations:
Pappenfabrik Trauchgau GmbH & Co. KG, Trauchgau Mill, Tullau Pappen®, Stockingen 2, D-87642 Halblech, Germany, Capacity: 17,000 mt/y, (Paperboard mill)
Phone: (49) 8368 9129 0
Fax: (49) 8368 9129 50
Email: vertrieb@pappen.de; gauss@pappen.de
Pulp Grades and Capacities:
Total pulp capacity: 11,171 mt/y
Recycled Pulping: 11,171 mt/y
Pulp Mill Data:
Recycled Fiber Treatment Lines:
Pulpers at 250 admt/y
Paper/Paperboard Grades and Capacities:
Total paper and paperboard capacity: 16,000 mt/y
Boxboard/cartonboard: 16,000 mt/y

Germany

Paper and Paperboard Mill Data:
Stock Preparation:
Pulpers: 5
Refiners: 3
Paper Machines: 1
No. 1, cylinder, total capacity 16,000 mt/y, Trim width 3.1 m, Boxboard/cartonboard
Finishing Equipment:
Supercalenders: 3
Sheeters: 5
Energy Data:
Power boilers: 4
Combustion turbines: 1 at 1.0 MW
Electrical demand for mill: 14 MWh/D

ⒽⓂLEIPA Georg Leinfelder GmbH
Schwedt Mill
Kuhheide 34
D-16303 Schwedt
Germany
Mailing Address: Postfach 10 01 55, D-16284 Schwedt, Germany
Phone: (49) 3332 24-00
Fax: (49) 3332 24-233
Email: kontakt.sdt@leipa.de
Web Address: www.leipa.de
Personnel:
Man. Dir.: Peter Probst
Phone: (49) 3332 24 3200
Fax: (49) 3332 24 2433
Email: peter.probst@leipa.de
Man. Dir.: Robin Huesmann
Phone: (49) 3332 24 3300
Fax: (49) 3332 24 3433
Email: robin.huesmann@leipa.de
Dir. Procurement & Logist.: Jürgen Sauter
Phone: (49) 3332 24 3240
Fax: (49) 3332 24 43224
Email: juergen.sauter@leipa.de
Mill Dir. Schwedt: Reinhard Etzel
Phone: (49) 3332 24 3042
Fax: (49) 3332 24 3229
Email: reinhard.etzel@leipa.de
Tech. Dir.: Arno Liendl
Phone: (49) 3332 24 3310
Fax: (49) 3332 24 3229
Email: arno.leindl@leipa.de
Sls. Dir. Magazine: Kai Fischer
Phone: (49) 3332 24 3280
Fax: (49) 3332 24 43280
Email: kai.fischer@leipa.de
Mktg. Dir: Marion Krüger
Phone: (49) 3332 24 3224
Fax: (49) 3332 24 43224
Email: marion.krueger@leipa.de
Total Employees of Company: 1,500
Total Employees at this Location: 750
Type of Operation: Paper mill, Paperboard mill
Mill Locations:
LEIPA Georg Leinfelder GmbH, Schrobenhausen Mill, Aichacher Strasse 8, D-86529 Schrobenhausen, Germany, Capacity: 146,000 mt/y, (Paper mill, Paperboard mill)
Phone: (49) 8252 8960
Fax: (49) 8252 8961340
Email: kontakt.sob@leipa.de
Pulp Grades and Capacities:
Total pulp capacity: 610,265 mt/y
Recycled Pulping: 610,265 mt/y
Pulp Mill Data:
Mechanical Pulping Systems:
Conventional grinders: 9
Bleach Plant Lines:
DIP, Sequence: P
Recycled Fiber Treatment Lines:
Flotation deinking lines: 2 at 450,000 admt/y
Pulpers: 8 at 430,000 admt/y
Paper/Paperboard Grades and Capacities:
Total paper and paperboard capacity: 760,000 mt/y
Coated mechanical/groundwood: 520,000 mt/y
Linerboard: 240,000 mt/y
Paper and Paperboard Mill Data:
Stock Preparation:
Pulpers: 10
Refiners: 4
Paper Machines: 3
No. 1, SpeedFormer HHS, total capacity 160,000 mt/y, Trim width 4.9 m, Coated mechanical/groundwood
No. 3, foudrinier (2), total capacity 240,000 mt/y, Trim width 4.4 m, Linerboard
No. 4, DuoFormerTQv, total capacity 360,000 mt/y, Trim width 8.05 m, Coated mechanical/groundwood
Coating Machines: 3
CM 1, total capacity 160,000 mt/y., off machine
CM 2, total capacity 216,000 mt/y., off machine
CM 3, total capacity 240,000 mt/y., on machine
Finishing Equipment:
Rewinders: 5
Sheeters: 2
Energy Data:
Power boilers: 1
Steam turbines: 1
Electrical demand for mill: 1,489 MWh/D

ⓂLEIPA Georg Leinfelder GmbH
Schrobenhausen Mill
Aichacher Strasse 8
D-86529 Schrobenhausen
Germany
Mailing Address: Postf. 11 20, D-86521 Schrobenhausen, Germany
Phone: (49) 8252 8960
Fax: (49) 8252 8961340
Email: kontakt.sob@leipa.de
Web Address: www.leipa.de
Personnel:
Mill Dir. Schrobenhausen : Martin Kaltenegger
Phone: (49) 8252 896 1456
Fax: (49) 8252 896 1468
Email: martin.kaltenegger@leipa.de
Dir., Contr.: Gerhard Fritsch
Phone: (49) 8252 896 1331
Fax: (49) 8252 896 1300
Email: gerhard.fritsch@leipa.de
Tech. Dir.: Manfred Friedl
Phone: (49) 8252 896 1377
Fax: (49) 8252 896 1340
Email: manfred.friedl@leipa.de
Environ. Mgr.: Ralf Sedlatschek
Phone: (49) 8252 896 1349
Fax: (49) 8252 896 1340
Email: ralf.sedlatschek@leipa.de
Purch. Dir.: Wolfgang Lang
Phone: (49) 8252 896 1277
Fax: (49) 8252 896 1341
Email: wolfgang.lang@leipa.de
Total Employees at this Location: 470
Type of Operation: Paper mill, Paperboard mill
Pulp Grades and Capacities:
Total pulp capacity: 148,285 mt/y
Recycled Pulping: 148,285 mt/y
Pulp Mill Data:
Recycled Fiber Treatment Lines:
Pulpers: 1 at 155,000
Paper/Paperboard Grades and Capacities:
Total paper and paperboard capacity: 146,000 mt/y
Packaging papers: 21,000 mt/y
Boxboard/cartonboard: 125,000 mt/y
Paper and Paperboard Mill Data:
Stock Preparation:
Refiners: 1
Paper Machines: 2
No. 5, foudrinier, total capacity 21,000 mt/y, Trim width 2 m, Packaging papers
No. 6, cylinder, total capacity 125,000 mt/y, Trim width 3.65 m, Boxboard/cartonboard
Finishing Equipment:
Rewinders: 6
Sheeters: 2
Energy Data:
Power boilers: 1
Steam turbines: 2 at 7.35 MW
Electrical demand for mill: 173 MWh/D

ⒽⓂPapierwerke Lenk AG
Kappelrodeck Mill
Richard-Lenk Str. 19-23
D-77876 Kappelrodeck
Germany
Mailing Address: Postf. 11 20, D-77872 Kappelrodeck, Germany
Phone: (49) 7842 801 0
Fax: (49) 7842 801 23
Email: info@lenk.de
Web Address: www.lenk.de
Personnel:
Chairman of Superv.Board: Elmar Rudolf
CEO: Sebastian Leser
Phone: (49) 1511 630 3144
Gen. Mgr., Techn.: Dirk Schuldt
Phone: (49) 7842 801-37
Email: dschuldt@lenk.de
Finan. Mgr., Personnel Mgr.: Wolfgang Ochs
Phone: (49) 7842 801-24
Email: wochs@lenk.de
Board mebr., Man.Dir.: Arun Nagwaney
Sls. & Purch. Mgr.: Wilhelm Wille
Phone: (49) 171 8068725
Fax: (49) 7842 80182
Email: wwille@lenk.de
Total Employees of Company: 135
Total Employees at this Location: 135
Type of Operation: Paper mill
Pulp Grades and Capacities:
Total pulp capacity: 10,527 mt/y
Recycled Pulping: 10,527 mt/y
Pulp Mill Data:
Paper/Paperboard Grades and Capacities:
Total paper and paperboard capacity: 40,000 mt/y
Packaging papers: 40,000 mt/y
Paper and Paperboard Mill Data:
Stock Preparation:
Pulpers: 5
Refiners: 6
Paper Machines: 2
No. 2, foudrinier, total capacity 20,000 mt/y, Trim width 2.05 m, Packaging papers
No. 4, foudrinier, total capacity 20,000 mt/y, Trim width 3.25 m, Packaging papers
Finishing Equipment:
Rewinders: 6
Sheeters: 3
Energy Data:
Power boilers: 1
Electrical demand for mill: 84 MWh/D

ⒽⓂPapierfabrik Carl Lenz GmbH & Co.
Wehr Mill
Hauptstr. 40
D-79664 Wehr
Germany
Phone: (49) 7762 9901
Fax: (49) 7762 4415
Email: info@papierfabrik-lenz.de
Web Address: www.papierfabrik-lenz.de, www.herbster.de
Personnel:
Gen. Mgr. Tech.: Michael Jenisch
Phone: (49) 7622 6871 0
Fax: (49) 7762 4415
Email: michael.jenisch@herbster.de
Gen. Mgr. Commercial: Holger Jenisch
Phone: (49) 7622 6871 0
Fax: (49) 7762 4415
Email: holger.jenisch@herbster.de
Sls. Mgr.: Wolfgang Aeckersberg
Phone: (49) 7762 9901
Fax: (49) 7762 4415

Email: wolfgang.aeckersberg@herbster.de
Total Employees of Company: 20
Total Employees at this Location: 20
Type of Operation: Paper mill
Pulp Mill Data:
  Recycled Fiber Treatment Lines:
  Pulpers: 1 at 11,000
Paper/Paperboard Grades and Capacities:
  Total paper and paperboard capacity: 7,000 mt/y
  Boxboard/cartonboard: 7,000 mt/y
Paper and Paperboard Mill Data:
Paper Machines: 1
PM 1, fourdrinier, total capacity 7,000 mt/y, Trim width 1.8 m, Boxboard/cartonboard
Finishing Equipment:
  Winders: 2 at 1 mt/y

ⓗⓜPapierfabrik Louisenthal GmbH
Gmund am Tegernsee Mill
Ownership: 100% by Giesecke & Devrient
Louisenthal 1
D-83703 Gmund am Tegernsee
Germany
Mailing Address: Postf. 11 85, D-83701 Gmund am Tegernsee, Germany
  Phone: (49) 8022 76001
  Fax: (49) 8022 76799
  Email: info@louisenthal.com
  Web Address: www.louisenthal.com
Personnel:
  Chmn.: Dr. Wolfram Seidemann
  Phone: (49) 8022 76001
  Fax: (49) 8022 760300
  Man. Dir. Oper. (Prod., Supply Chain & Support): Guido Koller
  Phone: (49) 8022 76001
  Fax: (49) 8022 76799
  Man Dir. technology and innovation: Dr. Alfred Kraxenberger
  Phone: (49) 8022 76001
  Fax: (49) 8022 76799
  Dir. Consultant: Michael Böhm
  Phone: (49) 8022 76001
  Fax: (49) 8022 760300
Total Employees of Company: 850
Type of Operation: Paper mill
Mill Locations:
  Papierfabrik Louisenthal GmbH, Königstein Mill, Bielatalstrasse 91-93, D-01824 Königstein, Germany, Capacity: 11,000 mt/y, (Paper mill)
  Phone: (49) 35021 650
  Fax: (49) 35021 686 27
  Email: sales@louisenthal.com, anja.hotning@louisenthal.com
Paper/Paperboard Grades and Capacities:
  Total paper and paperboard capacity: 5,000 mt/y
  Uncoated woodfree/freesheet: 5,000 mt/y
Paper and Paperboard Mill Data:
Paper Machines: 1
No. 1, cylinder mould, total capacity 5,000 mt/y, Uncoated woodfree/freesheet

ⓜPapierfabrik Louisenthal GmbH
Königstein Mill
Bielatalstrasse 91-93
D-01824 Königstein, Saxony
Germany
Mailing Address: Postf. 5, D-01822 Königstein, Germany
  Phone: (49) 35021 650
  Fax: (49) 35021 686 27
  Email: sales@louisenthal.com, anja.hotning@louisenthal.com
  Web Address: www.louisenthal.com
Personnel:
  Mill Mgr.: Ulrich Spiegel
  Phone: (49) 35021 650
  Commun. Mgr.: Elisabeth Wohlmannstetter
  Phone: (49) 89 41191832

Fax: (49) 89 41191140
Email: elisabeth.wohlmannstetter@louisenthal.com
Total Employees at this Location: 280
Type of Operation: Paper mill
Paper/Paperboard Grades and Capacities:
  Total paper and paperboard capacity: 11,000 mt/y
  Uncoated woodfree/freesheet: 11,000 mt/y
Paper and Paperboard Mill Data:
Paper Machines: 1
PM 4, (started up Nov. 2009), cylinder mould, total capacity 11,000 mt/y, Uncoated woodfree/freesheet

ⓗⓜLunzenauer Papier- und Pappenfabrik GmbH & Co. KG
Lunzenau Mill
Altenburger Straße 3
D-09328 Lunzenau, Saxony
Germany
  Phone: (49) 37383 690-0
  Fax: (49) 37383 690 69
  Web Address: www.papier-und-pappenfabrik.de
Personnel:
  Man. Dir.: Mr. Holger Reicher
  Phone: (49) 3 73 83 / 6 90-0
  Fax: (49) 3 73 83 / 6 90-69
Total Employees at this Location: 32
Type of Operation: Paperboard mill
Paper/Paperboard Grades and Capacities:
  Total paper and paperboard capacity: 10,000 mt/y
  Boxboard/cartonboard: 10,000 mt/y
Paper and Paperboard Mill Data:
Paper Machines: 1
No. 3, total capacity 10,000 mt/y, Trim width 2.4 m, Boxboard/cartonboard

ⓗⓜCarl Macher GmbH & Co. KG
Brunnenthal Mill
Ownership: 75% by Kunert Gruppe, Paul & Co GmbH & Co. KG, 25% by Jürgen Schaller
Fabrikstr. 14
D-95189 Brunnenthal
Germany
Mailing Address: Postf. 14 03, D-95013 Hof, Germany
  Phone: (49) 9281 70680
  Fax: (49) 9281 63609
  Email: info@macher.de
  Web Address: www.kunertgruppe.com
Personnel:
  Man. Dir. & CEO: Jüergen Schaller
  Phone: (49) 9281 7068 17
  Fax: (49) 9281 6360 9
  Email: juergen.schaller@macher.de
  Tech. Mgr.: Detlef Gabbert
  Phone: (49) 9281 70680
  Fax: (49) 9281 63609
  Email: detlef.gabbert@macher.de
  Environ. Mgr.: Bernd Fischer
  Phone: (49) 9281 706819
  Fax: (49) 9281 63609
  Email: bernd.fischer@macher.de
Total Employees of Company: 100
Total Employees at this Location: 100
Type of Operation: Paperboard mill
Pulp Grades and Capacities:
  Total pulp capacity: 111,129 mt/y
  Recycled Pulping: 111,129 mt/y
Pulp Mill Data:
  Recycled Fiber Treatment Lines:
  Pulpers: 1 at 123,400
Paper/Paperboard Grades and Capacities:
  Total paper and paperboard capacity: 110,000 mt/y
  Boxboard/cartonboard: 110,000 mt/y
Paper and Paperboard Mill Data:
Paper Machines: 1
No. 3, (Former Type model: Symformer MB), fourdrinier, total capacity 110,000 mt/y, Trim width 3.65 m, Boxboard/cartonboard
Finishing Equipment:
  Rewinders: 1
Energy Data:
  Power boilers: 2
  Combustion turbines: 2
  Electrical demand for mill: 135 MWh/D

ⓜMayr-Melnhof Gernsbach GmbH
Gernsbach Mill
Ownership: Mayr-Melnhof Karton AG
Obertsroter Strasse 9
D-76593 Gernsbach
Germany
Mailing Address: 14 61, 76587 Gernsbach, Germany
  Phone: (49) 7224 641 0
  Fax: (49) 7224 641 560/445
  Email: sales.gernsbach@mm-karton.com
  Web Address: www.mm-karton.com
Personnel:
  Man. Dir.: Hans-Joachim Stahl
  Phone: (49) 7224 641 304
  Fax: (49) 7224 641 309
  Email: hans-joachim.stahl@mm-karton.com
  Mill Mgr.: Carmine Nagel
  Phone: (49) 7224 641 520
  Fax: (49) 7224 641 309
  Email: carmine.nagel@mm-karton.com
  Prod. Mgr.: Alexander Schaefer
  Phone: (49) 7224 641 0
  Fax: (49) 7224 641 560
  Email: alexander.schaefer@mm-karton.com
Total Employees at this Location: 220
Type of Operation: Paperboard mill
Pulp Grades and Capacities:
  Total pulp capacity: 229,209 mt/y
  Recycled Pulping: 229,209 mt/y
Pulp Mill Data:
  Recycled Fiber Treatment Lines:
  Recycled packaging pulping lines at 153,000
Paper/Paperboard Grades and Capacities:
  Total paper and paperboard capacity: 250,000 mt/y
  Boxboard/cartonboard: 250,000 mt/y
Paper and Paperboard Mill Data:
  Stock Preparation:
  Pulpers: 3
  Refiners: 3
Paper Machines: 1
No. 2, Fourdrinier (4), Yankee dryer, total capacity 250,000 mt/y, Trim width 3.3 m, Boxboard/cartonboard
Coating Machines: 1
BM 1, total capacity 170,000 mt/y., on machine
Finishing Equipment:
  Rewinders: 1
  Sheeters: 3
Energy Data:
  Power boilers: 1
  Steam turbines: 1
  Electrical demand for mill: 410 MWh/D

ⓗⓜPapierfabrik Meldorf GmbH & Co. KG
Tornesch Mill
Ownership: Ownership: 100% by Panther Packaging
Esinger Strasse 5-7
D-25436 Tornesch
Germany
Mailing Address: Postf. 22 41, D-25438 Tornesch, Germany
  Phone: (49) 4122 5050/5010/50049
  Fax: (49) 4122 50569/50534/501106
  Email: info@papierfabrik-meldorf.de, info@Panther-Packaging.de
  Web Address: www.panther-packaging.com
Personnel:
  Man. Dir.: Axel Hilmer
  Phone: (49) 4122 5050
  Fax: (49) 4122 50569
  Email: a.hilmer@panther-packaging.de

Germany

Mill Mgr.: Hans-Jürgen Brenzinger
Phone: (49) 4122 5050
Fax: (49) 4122 50569
Email: hans-juergen.brenzinger@panther-packaging.de
Assist. Mill Mgr.: Joachim Brill
Phone: (49) 4122 5050
Fax: (49) 4122 50569
Email: joachim.brill@papierfabrik-meldorf.de
Mktg. Mgr.: Carin Hilmer-Brenzinger
Phone: (49) 4122 501108
Fax: (49) 4122 505 69
Email: c.hilmer-brenzinger@panther-packaging.de
Total Employees at this Location: 150
Type of Operation: Paper mill, Paperboard mill
Pulp Grades and Capacities:
Total pulp capacity: 72,082 mt/y
Recycled Pulping: 72,082 mt/y
Pulp Mill Data:
Recycled Fiber Treatment Lines:
Recycled packaging pulping lines at 72,000
Paper/Paperboard Grades and Capacities:
Total paper and paperboard capacity: 70,000 mt/y
Linerboard: 58,000 mt/y
Corrugating medium/fluting: 12,000 mt/y
Paper and Paperboard Mill Data:
Paper Machines: 2
No. 2, fourdrinier (2), total capacity 40,000 mt/y, Trim width 2.5 m, Corrugating medium/fluting, Linerboard
No. 3, fourdrinier (2), total capacity 30,000 mt/y, Trim width 2.45 m, Corrugating medium/fluting, Linerboard
Energy Data:
Power boilers: 1
Electrical demand for mill: 128 MWh/D

ⓄⓂMelitta Haushaltsprodukte GmbH & Co. KG
Minden Mill
Ringstr. 99
D-32427 Minden
Germany
Mailing Address: Postf. 12 26, D-32372 Minden, Germany
Phone: (49) 571 860
Fax: (49) 571 86810
Web Address: www.melitta.de
Personnel:
CEO Melitta Household Products Europe: Jan van Riet
Phone: (49) 571 860
Fax: (49) 571 868 10
Email: jan.vanriet@mh.melitta.de
Qlty. & Environ. Mgr.: Wolfgang Wäntig
Phone: (49) 571 861 700
Fax: (49) 571 861 560
Email: wolfgang.waentig@mh.melitta.de
Total Employees of Company: 3,300
Total Employees at this Location: 42
Type of Operation: Paper mill
Mill Locations:
CELUPA - Industrial Celulose e Papel Guaíba Ltda., Guaíba Mill, Estr. C. Ismael Chaves Barcellos, 150 - Bairro Engenho, 92500-000 Guaíba, RS, Brazil, Capacity: 30,900 mt/y, (Paper mill)
Phone: (55) 51 3480 3336 / 2101 1100
Fax: (55) 51 3480 2040 / 2101 1101
Email: celupa@melitta.com.br
Neu Kaliss Spezialpapier GmbH, Neu Kaliss Mill, Industriegebiet, Am Alten Postweg 1, D-19294 Neu Kaliss, Germany, Capacity: 15,000 mt/y, (Paper mill)
Phone: (49) 38758 550
Fax: (49) 38758 55119/55199
Email: nks@nkpaper.com
Neukölln Spezialpapier NK GmbH & Co. KG, Berlin Mill, Woermannkehre 2, D-12359 Berlin, Germany, Capacity: 25,000 mt/y, (Paper mill)
Phone: (49) 30 689807-0
Fax: (49) 30 68980781
Email: nks@nkpaper.com
Pulp Grades and Capacities:
Total pulp capacity: 9,944 mt/y
Recycled Pulping: 9,944 mt/y
Paper/Paperboard Grades and Capacities:
Total paper and paperboard capacity: 30,000 mt/y
Specialty and industrial: 30,000 mt/y
Paper and Paperboard Mill Data:
Paper Machines: 1
No. 3, fourdrinier, total capacity 30,000 mt/y, Trim width 3.15 m, Specialty and industrial
Energy Data:
Electrical demand for mill: 86 MWh/D

ⓄⓂMetsä Board Zanders GmbH
Zanders Gohrsmühle Mill
Ownership: 100% by Metsä Board
An der Gohrsmühle 25
D-51465 Bergisch Gladbach
Germany
Mailing Address: Postf. 20 09 60, D-51439 Bergisch Gladbach, Germany
Phone: (49) 2202 15 0
Fax: (49) 2202 15 2806
Email: zanders@metsagroup.com
Web Address: www.metsaboard.com, www.zanders.de
Personnel:
Oper. Controller: Stefan Weiss
Phone: (49) 2202 15 0
Fax: (49) 2202 15 2806
Email: stefan.weiss@metsagroup.com
Total Employees at this Location: 690
Type of Operation: Paper mill
Paper/Paperboard Grades and Capacities:
Total paper and paperboard capacity: 50,000 mt/y
Uncoated woodfree/freesheet: 50,000 mt/y
Paper and Paperboard Mill Data:
Paper Machines: 2
No. 2, DuoFormer D, total capacity 25,000 mt/y, Trim width 3.7 m, Uncoated woodfree/freesheet
No. 3, DuoFormer D, total capacity 25,000 mt/y, Trim width 6.6 m, Uncoated woodfree/freesheet
Coating Machines: 3
PM 3
PM 2
Specialty
Finishing Equipment:
Supercalenders: 3
Rewinders: 6
Sheeters: 13
Energy Data:
Power boilers: 1
Steam turbines: 1
Electrical demand for mill: 98 MWh/D

ⓄⓂMetsä Tissue GmbH
Kreuzau Mill
Ownership: Metsä Tissue Corp.
Theo-Strepp Strasse 2-6
D-52372 Kreuzau
Germany
Mailing Address: Postf. 11 22, D-52368 Kreuzau, Germany
Phone: (49) 2422 560
Fax: (49) 2422 4940
Email: (firstname.lastname@metsagroup.com)
Web Address: www.metsatissue.com
Personnel:
Mill Mgr. & Man. Dir.: Gero Kronen
Phone: (49) 2422 5624 4
Fax: (49) 2422 4940
Email: gero.kronen@metsagroup.com
VP., HR.: Jutta Treckmann
Phone: (49) 2422 560
Fax: (49) 2422 4940
Email: jutta.treckmann@metsagroup.com
Total Employees at this Location: 500
Type of Operation: Paper mill
Mill Locations:
Metsä Tissue GmbH, Düren Mill, Veldener Strasse 121-131, D-52349 Düren, Germany, Capacity: 20,000 mt/y, (Paper mill)
Phone: (49) 2421 4970, 2421 4971
Fax: (49) 2421 4405 184
Email: firstname.lastname@metsagroup.com
Metsä Tissue GmbH, Raubach Mill, D-56316 Raubach, Germany, Capacity: 50,000 mt/y, (Paper mill)
Phone: (49) 2684 6090
Fax: (49) 2684 609100/60980
Email: (firstname.lastname@metsagroup.com)
Metsä Tissue GmbH, Stotzheim Mill, Adolf-Halstrickstr. 64, D-53881 Euskirchen-Stotzheim, Germany, Capacity: 23,000 mt/y, (Paper mill)
Phone: (49) 2251 8120
Fax: (49) 2251 8122233
Email: (firstname.lastname@metsagroup.com)
Pulp Grades and Capacities:
Total pulp capacity: 48,375 mt/y
Recycled Pulping: 48,375 mt/y
Pulp Mill Data:
Bleach Plant Lines:
DIP Capacity 70,000 admt/y
Paper/Paperboard Grades and Capacities:
Total paper and paperboard capacity: 143,000 mt/y
Tissue: 143,000 mt/y
Paper and Paperboard Mill Data:
Paper Machines: 4
No. 1, crescent former, Yankee dryer, total capacity 28,000 mt/y, Trim width 2.76 m, Tissue
No. 3, twin-wire, Yankee dryer, total capacity 24,000 mt/y, Trim width 2.74 m, Tissue
No. 4, twin-wire, Yankee dryer, total capacity 31,000 mt/y, Trim width 2.86 m, Tissue
No. 5, crescent former, Yankee dryer, total capacity 60,000 mt/y, Trim width 5.6 m, Tissue
Finishing Equipment:
Rewinders: 4
Energy Data:
Power boilers: 1
Electrical demand for mill: 419 MWh/D

ⓂMetsä Tissue GmbH
Düren Mill
Ownership: Metsä Tissue Corp.
Veldener Strasse 121-131
D-52349 Düren
Germany
Phone: (49) 2421 4970, 2421 4971
Fax: (49) 2421 4405 184
Email: firstname.lastname@metsagroup.com
Web Address: www.metsatissue.com
Personnel:
VP. Prod. & Mill Mgr.: Michael Barth
Phone: (49) 2421 4970
Fax: (49) 2421 4405 184
Email: michael.barth@metsagroup.com
Total Employees at this Location: 104
Type of Operation: Paper mill
Paper/Paperboard Grades and Capacities:
Total paper and paperboard capacity: 20,000 mt/y
Specialty and industrial: 20,000 mt/y
Paper and Paperboard Mill Data:
Paper Machines: 1
No. 5, hybrid former, total capacity 20,000 mt/y, Trim width 3.3 m, Specialty and industrial
Energy Data:
Power boilers
Electrical demand for mill: 60 MWh/D

ⓂMetsä Tissue GmbH
Raubach Mill
Ownership: Metsä Tissue Corp.
D-56316 Raubach
Germany
Phone: (49) 2684 6090
Fax: (49) 2684 609100/60980
Email: (firstname.lastname@metsagroup.com)
Web Address: www.metsatissue.com
Personnel:
Mill Mgr.: Wilfried Oettgen

Germany

Phone: (49) 2684 609212
Fax: (49) 2684 609100
Email: wilfried.oettgen@metsagroup.com
Tech. Mgr.: Ralf Klappert
Phone: (49) 2684 609216
Fax: (49) 2684 609218
Email: ralf.klappert@metsagroup.com
Total Employees at this Location: 350
Type of Operation: Paper mill
Pulp Grades and Capacities:
Total pulp capacity: 32,545 mt/y
Recycled Pulping: 32,545 mt/y
Pulp Mill Data:
Recycled Fiber Treatment Lines:
Flotation deinking lines
Paper/Paperboard Grades and Capacities:
Total paper and paperboard capacity: 50,000 mt/y
Tissue: 50,000 mt/y
Paper and Paperboard Mill Data:
Paper Machines: 2
No. 1, fourdrinier, Yankee dryer, total capacity 25,000 mt/y, Trim width 2.75 m, Tissue
No. 3, twin-wire, Yankee dryer, total capacity 25,000 mt/y, Trim width 2.71 m, Tissue
Energy Data:
Power boilers: 1
Electrical demand for mill: 168 MWh/D

ⓜMetsä Tissue GmbH
Stotzheim Mill
Ownership: Metsä Tissue Corp.
Adolf-Halstrickstr. 64
D-53881 Euskirchen-Stotzheim
Germany
Mailing Address: Postf. 41 10-20, D-53870 Euskirchen, Germany
Phone: (49) 2251 8120
Fax: (49) 2251 8122233
Email: (firstname.lastname@metsagroup.com)
Web Address: www.metsatissue.com, www.fasana.com
Personnel:
Mill Mgr./VP, Regional Operations: Michael Päckner
Phone: (49) 2251 8120
Fax: (49) 2251 8122233
Conv. Mgr.: Christoph Alfermann
Phone: (49) 2251 8120
Fax: (49) 2251 8122233
Email: christoph.alfermann@metsagroup.com
Paper Prod. Mgr.: Klaus Zilligen
Phone: (49) 2251 8120
Fax: (49) 2251 8122233
Email: klaus.zilligen@metsagroup.com
Tech. Maint. Mgr.: Michael Hegemann
Phone: (49) 2251 8120
Fax: (49) 2251 8122233
Email: michael.hegemann@metsagroup.com
Total Employees at this Location: 306
Type of Operation: Paper mill
Paper/Paperboard Grades and Capacities:
Total paper and paperboard capacity: 23,000 mt/y
Tissue: 23,000 mt/y
Paper and Paperboard Mill Data:
Stock Preparation:
Pulpers: 3
Refiners: 2
Paper Machines: 1
No. 2, crescent former, Yankee dryer, total capacity 23,000 mt/y, Trim width 2.7 m, Tissue
Finishing Equipment:
Winders: 1
Energy Data:
Power boilers: 2
Electrical demand for mill: 61 MWh/D

ⓜMitsubishi Paper Holding (Europe) GmbH
Ownership: 100% by Mitsubishi Paper Mills Ltd.
Am Albertussee 1
D-40549 Düsseldorf
Germany
Phone: (49) 211 53 596-202
Fax: (49) 211 53 596-602
Email: info.mph@mitsubishi-paper.com
Web Address: www.mitsubishi-paper.com
Personnel:
Man. Dir. : Gerhard Schoon
Phone: (49) 49 521 2091-0
Fax: (49) 49 521 2091-41
HR Gen. Mgr. : Andreas Jastrzembowski
Phone: (49) 211 53 596-202
Fax: (49) 211 53 596-602
Marketing Mgr.: Ralf Buhl
Phone: (49) 521 2091-582
Fax: (49) 521 2091-610
Email: ralf.buhl@mitsubishi-paper.com
Total Employees of Company: 700

ⓜMitsubishi HiTec Paper Europe GmbH
Ownership: Mitsubishi Paper Mills Ltd.
Niedernholz 23
D-33699 Bielefeld
Germany
Mailing Address: Postf. 18 01 03, D-33691 Bielefeld, Germany
Phone: (49) 49 521 2091-0, 49 521 2091 582
Fax: (49) 49 521 2091 411, 49 521 2091 610
Email: info.mpe@mitsubishi-paper.com
Web Address: www.mitsubishi-paper.com
Personnel:
Man. Dir. : Gerhard Schoon
Phone: (49) 49 521 2091-0
Fax: (49) 49 521 2091-41
IT., Logist., Planning., Procurement & Strategy Gen.Mgr.: Holger Palandt
Phone: (49) 49 521 2091-0
Fax: (49) 49 521 2091-41
Mktg. Mgr. : Ralf Buhl
Phone: (49) 521 2091-582
Fax: (49) 521 2091-610
Email: ralf.buhl@mitsubishi-paper.com
HR Gen. Mgr. : Andreas Jastrzembowski
Phone: (49) 49 521 2091-0
Fax: (49) 49 521 2091-41
Eng. & Maint. Mgr. : Andreas Flada
Phone: (49) 49 521 2091-0
Fax: (49) 49 521 2091-41
Sls. & Mktg. Mgr.: Claudia Vogel
Phone: (49) 49 521 2091-673
Fax: (49) 521 2091-688
Email: claudia.vogel@mitsubishi-paper.com
Area Sls. Mgr. : Monika Stubbe
Phone: (49) 49 521 2091-0
Fax: (49) 49 521 2091-41
Head of Purchasing: Jörg Dittombee
Phone: (49) 49 521 2091-0
Fax: (49) 49 521 2091-41
Head of Production: Christian Elsner
Phone: (49) 49 521 2091-0
Fax: (49) 49 521 2091-41
Total Employees of Company: 712
Mill Locations:
Mitsubishi HiTec Paper Europe GmbH, Bielefeld Mill, Niedernholz 23, D-33699 Bielefeld, Germany, Capacity: 150,000 mt/y, (Paper mill)
Phone: (49) 521 20910
Fax: (49) 521 2091411
Email: info.mpe@mitsubishi-paper.com
Mitsubishi HiTec Paper Europe GmbH, Flensburg Mill, Husumer Str. 12, D-24941 Flensburg, Germany, Capacity: 35,000 mt/y, (Paper mill)
Phone: (49) 461 8695 0
Fax: (49) 461 8695500
Email: info.mpe@mitsubishi-paper.com

ⓜMitsubishi HiTec Paper Europe GmbH
Bielefeld Mill
Ownership: Mitsubishi Paper Mills Ltd.
Niedernholz 23
D-33699 Bielefeld
Germany
Mailing Address: Postf. 18 01 03, D-33691 Bielefeld, Germany
Phone: (49) 521 20910
Fax: (49) 521 2091411
Email: info.mpe@mitsubishi-paper.com
Web Address: www.mitsubishi-paper.com
Personnel:
Man. Dir.: Gerhard Schoon
Phone: (49) 521 2091 0
Fax: (49) 521 2091 411
Email: gerhard.schoon@mitsubishi-paper.com
Mktg. Mgr.: Ralf Buhl
Phone: (49) 521 2091 582
Fax: (49) 521 2091 611
Email: ralf.buhl@mitsubishi-paper.com
Purch. Mgr.: Jörg Dittombee
Phone: (49) 521 2091 223
Fax: (49) 521 2091 411
Email: joerg.dittombee@mitsubishi-paper.com
Total Employees at this Location: 430
Type of Operation: Paper mill
Paper/Paperboard Grades and Capacities:
Total paper and paperboard capacity: 150,000 mt/y
Uncoated woodfree/freesheet: 150,000 mt/y
Paper and Paperboard Mill Data:
Stock Preparation:
Pulpers:
Paper Machines: 1
No. 3, DuoFormer D, total capacity 150,000 mt/y, Trim width 5.8 m, Uncoated woodfree/freesheet
Coating Machines: 4
No. 1
No. 2
No. 3
No. 4, on machine
Energy Data:
Power boilers: 3
Combustion turbines: 2 at 14, 14 MW
Steam turbines: 1 at 9.5 MW
Electrical demand for mill: 294 MWh/D

ⓜMitsubishi HiTec Paper Europe GmbH
Flensburg Mill
Ownership: Mitsubishi Paper Mills Ltd.
Husumer Str. 12
D-24941 Flensburg
Germany
Mailing Address: Postf. 15 62, D-24905 Flensburg, Germany
Phone: (49) 461 8695 0
Fax: (49) 461 8695500
Email: info.mpe@mitsubishi-paper.com
Web Address: www.mitsubishi-paper.com
Personnel:
Mill Dir.: Wolfgang Theis
Phone: (49) 461 8695 418
Fax: (49) 461 8695 417
Email: wolfgang.theis@mitsubishi-paper.com
Head of Sales: Martin Klingenschmid
Phone: (49) 461 8695
Fax: (49) 461 8695 460
Email: martin.klingenschmid@mitsubishi-paper.com
Total Employees at this Location: 250
Type of Operation: Paper mill
Paper/Paperboard Grades and Capacities:
Total paper and paperboard capacity: 35,000 mt/y
Uncoated woodfree/freesheet: 35,000 mt/y
Paper and Paperboard Mill Data:
Stock Preparation:
Pulpers: 2
Refiners: 8

Germany

Paper Machines: 1
No. 1, fourdrinier, total capacity 35,000 mt/y, Trim width 2.3 m, Uncoated woodfree/freesheet
Coating Machines: 2
No. 1, off machine
No. 2, on machine
Finishing Equipment:
Rewinders: 3
Energy Data:
Power boilers: 2
Steam turbines: 1
Electrical demand for mill: 71 MWh/D

ⓜMondi Raubling GmbH
Raubling Mill
Ownership: Mondi Europe & International Division
Rosenheimer Str. 37
D-83064 Raubling
Germany
Phone: (49) 8035 9090
Fax: (49) 8035 902 132
Email: (firstname.lastname@mondigroup.com)
Web Address: www.mondigroup.com
Personnel:
Tech. Mgr.: Robert Gebhart
Phone: (49) 8035 909 0
Fax: (49) 8035 902 132
Email: robert.gebhart@mondigroup.com
Total Employees at this Location: 150
Type of Operation: Paperboard mill
Pulp Grades and Capacities:
Total pulp capacity: 194,801 mt/y
Recycled Pulping: 194,801 mt/y
Paper/Paperboard Grades and Capacities:
Total paper and paperboard capacity: 220,000 mt/y
Linerboard: 150,000 mt/y
Corrugating medium/fluting: 70,000 mt/y
Paper and Paperboard Mill Data:
Paper Machines: 2
No. 5, fourdrinier (2), total capacity 85,000 mt/y, Trim width 2.5 m, Linerboard
No. 7, fourdrinier (2), total capacity 135,000 mt/y, Trim width 2.5 m, Corrugating medium/fluting, Linerboard
Energy Data:
Power boilers: 1
Combustion turbines: 1 at 14 MW
Steam turbines: 1
Electrical demand for mill: 293 MWh/D

ⓜⓜMunksjö Dettingen GmbH
Dettingen Mill
Company is previously Arjowiggins Deutschland GmbH
Ownership: Munksjö Paper AB
Schwalbenstadt 1
D-72581 Dettingen an der Erms
Germany
Mailing Address: Postf. 12 62, D-72576 Dettingen an der Erms, Germany
Phone: (49) 7123 977-0
Fax: (49) 7123 977 113
Email: info.dettingen@munksjo.com, info@munksjo.com
Web Address: www.munksjo.com
Personnel:
Man. Dir. & Mill Mgr.: Gerd Häensel
Phone: (49) 7123 977 111
Fax: (49) 7123 977 117
Email: gerd.haensel@munksjo.com
Contrl.: Mr. Andreas Braun
Phone: (49) 7123 977 0
Fax: (49) 7123 977 113
Email: andreas.braun@munksjo.com
Total Employees at this Location: 190
Type of Operation: Paper mill
Pulp Grades and Capacities:
Total pulp capacity: 3,477 mt/y
Recycled Pulping: 3,477 mt/y
Paper/Paperboard Grades and Capacities:
Total paper and paperboard capacity: 60,000 mt/y
Uncoated woodfree/freesheet: 40,000 mt/y
Specialty and industrial: 20,000 mt/y
Paper and Paperboard Mill Data:
Stock Preparation:
Pulpers: 2
Refiners: 8
Paper Machines: 2
No. 1, fourdrinier, total capacity 40,000 mt/y, Trim width 3.9 m, Uncoated woodfree/freesheet
No. 4, fourdrinier, total capacity 20,000 mt/y, Trim width 2.7 m, Specialty and industrial
Finishing Equipment:
Rewinders: 3 at 60,000 mt/y
Sheeters: 2 at 20,000 mt/y
Energy Data:
Power boilers: 3
Electrical demand for mill: 85 MWh/D

ⓜⓜMunksjö Paper GmbH
Unterkochen Mill
Ownership: Munksjö Oyj
Waldhäuser Str. 41
D-73432 Aalen-Unterkochen
Germany
Mailing Address: Postf. 91 52, D-73416 Aalen/Unterkochen, Germany
Phone: (49) 7361 5060
Fax: (49) 7361 506 248
Email: marketing@de.munksjo.com, info@de.munksjo.com
Web Address: www.munksjo.com
Personnel:
Man. Dir. & Plt. Mgr.: Michael Schirle
Phone: (49) 7361 506 0
Fax: (49) 7361 506 248
Email: michael.schirle@munksjo.com
Supply Chain Mgr.: Uwe Albersmeier
Phone: (49) 7361 506 339
Fax: (49) 7361 984 045
Email: uwe.albersmeier@munksjo.com
Total Employees at this Location: 242
Type of Operation: Paper mill
Paper/Paperboard Grades and Capacities:
Total paper and paperboard capacity: 90,000 mt/y
Specialty and industrial: 90,000 mt/y
Paper and Paperboard Mill Data:
Stock Preparation:
Pulpers: 3
Refiners: 21
Paper Machines: 3
No. 1, fourdrinier, total capacity 30,000 mt/y, Trim width 2.24 m
No. 2, fourdrinier, total capacity 20,000 mt/y, Trim width 1.65 m
No. 3, fourdrinier, total capacity 40,000 mt/y, Trim width 2.84 m, Specialty and industrial
Finishing Equipment:
Rewinders: 2
Energy Data:
Steam turbines: 1 at 7.2 MW

ⓜⓜMunktell & Filtrak GmbH
Bärenstein Mill
Ownership: 100% by Ahlstrom Corporation Oy
Niederschlag 1
D-09471 Bärenstein
Germany
Phone: (49) 37347 8300
Fax: (49) 37347 8364
Email: filtrak@ahlstrom.com
Web Address: www.munktell.com
Personnel:
Man. Dir., Group CEO : Gustav Kyrk
Phone: (46) 37347 83 0
Fax: (46) 37347 8364
Email: gustav.kyrk@munktell.com
Total Employees of Company: 48
Total Employees at this Location: 48
Type of Operation: Paper mill
Paper/Paperboard Grades and Capacities:
Total paper and paperboard capacity: 2,000 mt/y
Specialty and industrial: 2,000 mt/y
Paper and Paperboard Mill Data:
Paper Machines: 2
No. 1, fourdrinier, Trim width 1.6 m, Specialty and industrial
No. 2, fourdrinier, Trim width 1.2 m, Specialty and industrial

ⓜNeenah Gessner GmbH
Bruckmühl Mill
Ownership: Neenah Paper, Inc.
Otto-von-Steinbeis-Str. 14b
D-83052 Bruckmühl
Germany
Phone: (49) 8062 7030
Fax: (49) 8062 703255
Web Address: www.neenah.com, www.neenah-gessner.de/en/home.html
Personnel:
Mill Mgr.: Holger Baumgartner
Phone: (49) 8062 7030
Fax: (49) 8062 703255
Email: h.baumgartner@neenah.de
Total Employees at this Location: 193
Type of Operation: Paper mill
Paper/Paperboard Grades and Capacities:
Total paper and paperboard capacity: 25,000 mt/y
Specialty and industrial
Paper and Paperboard Mill Data:
Stock Preparation:
Pulpers: 4
Refiners: 8
Paper Machines: 1
PM 1, fourdrinier, Trim width 2.15 m, Specialty and industrial
Coating Machines: 1
No. 1+2, off machine
Finishing Equipment:
Winders: 2
Rewinders: 3
Sheeters: 1
Energy Data:
Power boilers: 3
Hydro turbines: 5
Electrical demand for mill: 96 MWh/D

ⓜNeenah Gessner GmbH
Feldkirchen-Westerham Mill
Ownership: Neenah Paper, Inc.
Weidacher Str. 30
D-83620 Feldkirchen-Westerham
Germany
Mailing Address: Postf. 11 16, D-83618 Feldkirchen-Westerham, Germany
Phone: (49) 8062 703 0
Fax: (49) 8062 703 461
Email: c.koegl@neenah.de
Web Address: www.neenah.de
Personnel:
Mill Mgr.: Holger Baumgartner
Phone: (49) 8062703408
Fax: (49) 8062703461
Email: h.baumgartner@neenah.de
Head of Eng./Maint.: Bernd Ernhart
Phone: (49) 8062 703 0
Fax: (49) 8062703461
Email: b.ernhart@neenah.de
Purch. Mgr.: Henning Dinges
Phone: (49) 8062 703 0
Fax: (49) 8062703461
Email: h.dinges@neenah.de
R&D and Innovations: Dr.Juergen Nientiedt
Phone: (49) 8062 703 0
Fax: (49) 8062703461
Email: j.nientiedt@neenah.de
Total Employees at this Location: 340

Type of Operation: Paper mill
Paper/Paperboard Grades and Capacities:
Total paper and paperboard capacity: 30,000 mt/y
Specialty and industrial: 30,000 mt/y
Paper and Paperboard Mill Data:
Stock Preparation:
Pulpers: 1
Refiners: 3
Paper Machines: 2
PM 3, inclined, total capacity 15,000 mt/y, Trim width 1.56 m, Specialty and industrial
PM 5, inclined, total capacity 15,000 mt/y, Trim width 1.85 m, Specialty and industrial
Coating Machines: 3
No. 1, off machine
No. 2, off machine
No. 3
Finishing Equipment:
Rewinders: 6
Energy Data:
Power boilers: 3
Electrical demand for mill: 170 MWh/D

ⓜNeenah Lahnstein
Lahnstein Mill
Ownership: Neenah Paper, Inc.
Auf Brühl 15-27
D-56112 Lahnstein
Germany
Mailing Address: Postf. 21 78, D-56108 Lahnstein, Germany
   Phone: (49) 2621 1770
   Fax: (49) 2621 177609
   Email: lahnstein@neenah.de
   Web Address: www.neenah-lahnstein.de
Personnel:
   Gen. Mgr.: Detlef Stoltefaut
   Phone: (49) 2621 1770
   Fax: (49) 2621 177609
   Email: d.stoltefaut@neenah.de
   Product Mgr. Printmedia: Rainer Joeken
   Phone: (49) 2621 177610
   Fax: (49) 2621 177609
   Email: r.joeken@neenah.de
   Sls Service.: Marisa Minor
   Phone: (49) 2621 177 612
   Fax: (49) 2621 177 49612
   Email: m.minor@neenah.de
Total Employees at this Location: 220
Type of Operation: Paper mill
Paper/Paperboard Grades and Capacities:
Total paper and paperboard capacity: 17,000 mt/y
Specialty and industrial
Paper and Paperboard Mill Data:
Paper Machines: 1
PM 6, inclined, Specialty and industrial

ⓜPapierfabrik Nettemühle GmbH & Co. KG
Mayen Mill
Polcher Strasse 107
D-56727 Mayen
Germany
Mailing Address: Postf. 16 54, D-56706 Mayen, Germany
   Phone: (49) 2651 9886 0
   Fax: (49) 2651 9886 24
   Email: info@nettemuehle.net
   Web Address: www.nettemuehle.net
Personnel:
   Man. Dir./Owner: Manfred Sax
   Phone: (49) 2651 9886 0
Total Employees at this Location: 45
Type of Operation: Paper mill
Pulp Mill Data:
Recycled Fiber Treatment Lines:
Pulpers: 1 at 10,950
Paper/Paperboard Grades and Capacities:
Total paper and paperboard capacity: 6,000 mt/y
Tissue: 6,000 mt/y
Paper and Paperboard Mill Data:
Paper Machines: 1
No. 1, Yankee dryer, total capacity 6,000 mt/y, Tissue
Finishing Equipment:
Winders: 2
Sheeters: 1
Energy Data:
Electrical demand for mill: 120 MWh/D

ⓞⓜNeu Kaliss Spezialpapier GmbH
Neu Kaliss Mill
Ownership: 100% by Melitta Haushaltsprodukte GmbH & Co. KG
Industriegebiet, Am Alten Postweg 1
D-19294 Neu Kaliss
Germany
   Phone: (49) 38758 550
   Fax: (49) 38758 55119/55199
   Email: nks@nkpaper.com
   Web Address: www.nkpaper.com
Personnel:
   Man. Dir. Mktg. & Sls.: Paul Fender
   Phone: (49) 38758 550
   Fax: (49) 38758 55119
   Email: fender@nkpaper.com
   Man Dir, Prod., Eng., Develop. & Technology Mgr.: Ing. Dieter Kirchner
   Phone: (49) 38758 550
   Fax: (49) 38758 55119
   Email: kirchner@nkpaper.com
   Finan., Purch., HR Mgr.: Dipl. Oec. Gernold Stier
   Phone: (49) 38758 550
   Fax: (49) 38758 55119
   Email: stier@nkpaper.com
   Quality Cntr. Mgr.: Birgit Gebert
   Phone: (49) 38758 550
   Fax: (49) 38758 55119
   Email: gebert@nkpaper.com
   Sls. Mgr.: Raimo Reincke
   Phone: (49) 38758 550
   Fax: (49) 38758 55119
   Email: reincke@nkpaper.com
Total Employees of Company: 135
Total Employees at this Location: 135
Type of Operation: Paper mill
Paper/Paperboard Grades and Capacities:
Total paper and paperboard capacity: 15,000 mt/y
Specialty and industrial
Paper and Paperboard Mill Data:
Paper Machines: 1
PM 6, fourdrinier, inclined, total capacity 15,000 mt/y, Trim width 2.25 m, Specialty and industrial
Finishing Equipment:
Rewinders: 3
Sheeters: 1

ⓜNeukölln Spezialpapier NK GmbH & Co. KG
Berlin Mill
Ownership: 100% by Melitta Haushaltsprodukte GmbH & Co. KG
Woermannkehre 2
D-12359 Berlin
Germany
   Phone: (49) 30 689807-0
   Fax: (49) 30 68980781
   Email: nks@nkpaper.com
   Web Address: www.nkpaper.com, www.melitta.de
Personnel:
   Tech. Dir.: Martin Ostermayer
   Phone: (49) 30 689807 0
   Fax: (49) 30 689807 81
   Email: martin.ostermayer@nkpaper.com
   Head of Finan., Contrl & IT: Matthias Helm
   Phone: (49) 30 689807 0
   Fax: (49) 30 689807 81
   Email: matthias.helm@nkpaper.com

Total Employees at this Location: 83
Type of Operation: Paper mill
Paper/Paperboard Grades and Capacities:
Total paper and paperboard capacity: 25,000 mt/y
Specialty and industrial: 25,000 mt/y
Paper and Paperboard Mill Data:
Paper Machines: 1
PM 4, fourdrinier, total capacity 25,000 mt/y, Trim width 3.15 m, Specialty and industrial

ⓜAbelan Board and Packaging Solutions
Viersen Mill
Grefrather Strasse 120
D-41749 Viersen
Germany
Mailing Address: Narzissenweg 15, D-40723 Hilden, Germany
   Phone: (49) 2162 89640/896420
   Fax: (49) 2162 89569/896442
   Web Address: www.abelan.com/home
Personnel:
   Gen. Mgr.: Jan H. Bos
   Phone: (49) 2162 8964-0
   Prod. Mgr.: Mr. Land
   Phone: (49) 2162 8964-0
   Sls. Mgr.: Mr. Lennerkaerf
   Phone: (49) 2162 8964-0
   Purch. Mgr.: Mr. Graupeter
   Phone: (49) 2162 8964-0
   Prod. & Quality Mgr.: Mario Nelkes
   Phone: (49) 2162 8964-0
Total Employees at this Location: 65
Type of Operation: Paperboard mill
Pulp Grades and Capacities:
Total pulp capacity: 60,889 mt/y
Recycled Pulping: 60,889 mt/y
Pulp Mill Data:
Recycled Fiber Treatment Lines:
Recycled packaging pulping lines
Paper/Paperboard Grades and Capacities:
Total paper and paperboard capacity: 60,000 mt/y
Boxboard/cartonboard: 60,000 mt/y
Paper and Paperboard Mill Data:
Stock Preparation:
Pulpers: 2
Refiners: 4
Paper Machines: 1
No. 2, multi-fourdrinier, total capacity 60,000 mt/y, Trim width 2.2 m, Boxboard/cartonboard
Energy Data:
Power boilers
Electrical demand for mill: 101 MWh/D

ⓞⓜPapierfabrik Niederauer Mühle GmbH
Kreuzau and Niederau Mills
Windener Weg 1
D-52372 Kreuzau
Germany
Mailing Address: Postf. 13 40, D-52370, Kreuzau, Germany
   Phone: (49) 2422 94940
   Fax: (49) 2422 949410
   Email: mail@niederauer-muehle.de
   Web Address: www.niederauer-muehle.de
Personnel:
   Man. Dir.: Holger Autenrieb
   Phone: (49) 2422 94940
   Email: h.autenrieb@niederauer-muehle.de
   Man. Dir.: Stephanie Autenrieb
   Phone: (49) 2422 94940
   Email: s.autenrieb@niederauer-muehle.de
   Man. Dir.: Harald Ensmann
   Phone: (49) 2422 94940
   Email: h.ensmann@niederauer-muehle.de
   Prod. Mgr.: Mr. Peter Czoski
   Phone: (49) 2422 9494-658
   Email: p.czoski@niederauer-muehle.de

Germany

Tech. Mgr.: Mr. T. Fischer
Phone: (49) 2422 9494-69
Fax: (49) 2422 9494-60
Total Employees of Company: 155
Total Employees at this Location: 70
Type of Operation: Paperboard mill
Pulp Grades and Capacities:
  Total pulp capacity: 302,084 mt/y
  Recycled Pulping: 302,084 mt/y
Paper/Paperboard Grades and Capacities:
  Total paper and paperboard capacity: 300,000 mt/y
  Linerboard: 250,000 mt/y
  Corrugating medium/fluting: 50,000 mt/y
Paper and Paperboard Mill Data:
Paper Machines: 3
No. 1, multi-wire, total capacity 25,000 mt/y, Trim width 2.5 m, Linerboard
No. 2, fourdrinier (2), total capacity 25,000 mt/y, Trim width 2.75 m, Linerboard
No. 3, DuoFormer CFD, total capacity 250,000 mt/y, Trim width 5.3 m, Linerboard, Corrugating medium/fluting
Energy Data:
  Power boilers: 1
  Electrical demand for mill: 375 MWh/D

ⓂⓂPappenfabrik Nierfeld, J. Piront GmbH & Co. KG
Schleiden Mill
Ownership: 100% by Uhlmann Family
Luxemburger Str. 16
D-53937 Schleiden
Germany
Mailing Address: Postf. 12 50, D-53930 Schleiden, Germany
  Phone: (49) 2444 91290
  Fax: (49) 2444 912910
  Email: info@nierfeld-pappe.de
  Web Address: www.nierfeld-pappe.de
Personnel:
  Man. Dir.: Martin Uhlmann
  Phone: (49) 2444 91290
  Email: martin.uhlmann@nierfeld-pappe.de
  Man. Dir.: Detlef Hahn
  Phone: (49) 2444 91290
  Email: detlef.hahn@nierfeld-pappe.de
  Mill Mgr.: Willi Kratz
  Phone: (49) 2444 91290
  Email: willi.kratz@nierfeld-pappe.de
  Sls. Mgr.: Wolfgang Üdelhofen
  Phone: (49) 2444 91290
  Email: wolfgang.uedelhofen@nierfeld-pappe.de
  Admin. Dir.: Alexandra Milz
  Phone: (49) 2444 91290
  Email: alexandra.milz@nierfeld-pappe.de
Total Employees of Company: 30
Total Employees at this Location: 30
Type of Operation: Paperboard mill
Pulp Grades and Capacities:
  Total pulp capacity: 8,646 mt/y
  Recycled Pulping: 8,646 mt/y
Pulp Mill Data:
  Recycled Fiber Treatment Lines:
  Pulpers: 1 at 24,000
Paper/Paperboard Grades and Capacities:
  Total paper and paperboard capacity: 8,500 mt/y
  Boxboard/cartonboard: 8,500 mt/y
Paper and Paperboard Mill Data:
  Stock Preparation:
  Refiners: 2
Paper Machines: 1
No. 1, cylinder, total capacity 8,500 mt/y, Trim width 2.4 m, Boxboard/cartonboard
Finishing Equipment:
  Supercalenders: 1
  Sheeters: 2
Energy Data:
  Power boilers: 1
  Electrical demand for mill: 7 MWh/D

ⓂNorske Skog Walsum GmbH
Walsum Mill
Ownership: Norske Skog ASA
Theodor-Heuss-Strasse 228
D-47179 Duisburg
Germany
Mailing Address: Postf. 18 03 20, D-47173 Duisburg, Germany
  Phone: (49) 203 49920
  Fax: (49) 203 4992180
  Web Address: www.norskeskog.com
Personnel:
  Gen. Mgr.: Trond Sverre Flaten
  Phone: (49) 203 49920
  Fax: (49) 203 4992180
  Email: trond.sverre.flaten@norskeskog.com
  Chief Eng.: Klaus Borowski
  Phone: (49) 203 4992352
  Fax: (49) 203 4992180
  Email: klaus.borowski@norskeskog.com
  Sustainability Mgr.: Frank Hamacher
  Phone: (49) 203 4992277
  Fax: (49) 203 4992180
  Email: frank.hamacher@norskeskog.com
Total Employees at this Location: 260
Type of Operation: Pulp mill, Paper mill
Pulp Grades and Capacities:
  Total pulp capacity: 82,234 mt/y
  Mechanical Pulp: 82,234 mt/y
Pulp Mill Data:
  Mechanical Pulping Systems:
  TMP systems: 1
Pulp Lines: 4
  Bleach Plant Systems: 2
  No. 1, Sequence: P/Di, Capacity 125,000 admt/y
  No. 2, Sequence: P, Capacity 125,000 admt/y
  Recycled Fiber Treatment Lines:
  Pulpers: 1 at 20,000 admt/y
Paper/Paperboard Grades and Capacities:
  Total paper and paperboard capacity: 200,000 mt/y
  Coated mechanical/groundwood: 200,000 mt/y
Paper and Paperboard Mill Data:
  Stock Preparation:
  Pulpers: 3
  Refiners: 10
Paper Machines: 1
No. 10, DuoFormer CF, total capacity 200,000 mt/y, Trim width 7.25 m, Coated mechanical/groundwood
Coating Machines: 2
CM 4, total capacity 220,000 mt/y., off machine
CM 10, total capacity 200,000 mt/y., off machine
Finishing Equipment:
  Winders: 4 at 430,000 mt/y
  Supercalenders: 5 at 430,000 mt/y
  Rewinders: 2 at 50,000 mt/y
Energy Data:
  TMP Reboiler: 1
  Electrical demand for mill: 1,071 MWh/D

ⓂⓂPappenfabrik A. Obenauf GmbH & Co. KG
Bad Harzburg Mill
Eckertal
D-38667 Bad Harzburg
Germany
  Phone: (49) 5322 558 930
  Fax: (49) 5322 558 9329
  Email: info@obenauf-pappe.de
  Web Address: www.obenauf-pappe.de
Personnel:
  Mill Mgr.: Tobias Neidhardt
  Phone: (49) 5322 50522
  Email: t.neidhardt@obenauf-pappe.de
  Mill Mgr.: Christoph Wigger
  Phone: (49) 5322 50521
Total Employees of Company: 48
Total Employees at this Location: 48
Type of Operation: Paperboard mill
Paper/Paperboard Grades and Capacities:
  Total paper and paperboard capacity: 15,000 mt/y
  Boxboard/cartonboard: 15,000 mt/y
Paper and Paperboard Mill Data:
  Stock Preparation:
  Pulpers: 1
  Refiners: 1
Paper Machines: 2
No. 1, cylinder, total capacity 7,500 mt/y, Trim width 2.85 m, Boxboard/cartonboard
No. 2, cylinder, total capacity 7,500 mt/y, Trim width 3.4 m, Boxboard/cartonboard
Coating Machines: 1
No. 1, on machine
Energy Data:
  Power boilers: 1
  Electrical demand for mill: 14 MWh/D

ⓂⓂSpezialpapierfabrik Oberschmitten GmbH
Nidda/Ober-Schmitten Mill
Ownership: Glatfelter
Rhönstr. 13
D-63667 Nidda/Ober-Schmitten
Germany
Mailing Address: Postf. 13 30, D-63660 Nidda, Germany
  Phone: (49) 6043 80801
  Fax: (49) 6043 8081 00
  Email: info@spo-gmbh.de
  Web Address: www.spo-gmbh.de
Personnel:
  Man. Dir.: Hagen Knodt
  Phone: (49) 6043 80801
  Fax: (49) 6043 808300
  Email: knodt@spo-kopafilm.de
  Mgr. of Operations: Dipl. Ing. Klaus Deuchert
  Phone: (49) 6043 808219
  Fax: (49) 6043 808223
  Email: deuchert@spo-kopafilm.de
  Production Paper: Norbert Freymann
  Phone: (49) 6043 808156
  Fax: (49) 6043 808223
  Email: freymann@spo-kopafilm.de
  Leader Management System (Qlty., Hygiene, Env.): Ralf Grün
  Phone: (49) 6043 808 221
  Fax: (49) 6043 808 119
  Email: ralf.gruen@spo-gmbh.de
  Gen. Sls. Mgr.: Ulrich Becker
  Phone: (49) 6043 808 131
  Email: ulrich.becker@spo-gmbh.de
  Mktg. Asst.: Tamara Eberhard
  Phone: (49) 6043 808208
  Fax: (49) 6043 808100
  Email: tamara.eberhard@spo-kopafilm.de
Total Employees of Company: 240
Total Employees at this Location: 65
Type of Operation: Paper mill
Paper/Paperboard Grades and Capacities:
  Total paper and paperboard capacity: 12,495 mt/y
  Specialty and industrial: 12,495 mt/y
Paper and Paperboard Mill Data:
  Stock Preparation:
  Pulpers: 3
  Refiners: 20
Paper Machines: 4
No. 1, fourdrinier, total capacity 2,856 mt/y, Trim width 1.5 m, Specialty and industrial
No. 2, fourdrinier, total capacity 3,213 mt/y, Trim width 1.7 m, Specialty and industrial
No. 3, fourdrinier, total capacity 3,570 mt/y, Trim width 1.9 m, Specialty and industrial
No. 4, fourdrinier, total capacity 4,284 mt/y, Trim width 2.1 m, Specialty and industrial
Finishing Equipment:
  Supercalenders: 3
  Rewinders: 17
  Sheeters: 2
Energy Data:

Germany

Power boilers: 1
Steam turbines: 1 at 2.5 MW

ⓗⓜPAKA Glashütter Pappen- und Kartonagenfabrik GmbH
Glashütte Mill
Altenberger Str. 25
D-01768 Glashütte
Germany
Phone: (49) 35053 4140
Fax: (49) 35053 42802
Email: info@paka-gmbh.de
Web Address: www.paka-gmbh.de

Personnel:
Man. Dir., Sls.: Eckehart Klemm
Phone: (49) 35053 4140
Fax: (49) 35053 42802
Email: eckehart.klemm@paka-gmbh.de
Man. Dir., Mktg.: Joachim Möschke
Phone: (49) 35053 4140
Fax: (49) 35053 42802
Email: joachim.moschke@paka-gmbh.de
Man. Dir., Sls.: Christoph Klemm
Phone: (49) 35053 41419
Fax: (49) 35053 42802
Email: christoph.klemm@paka-gmbh.de
Tech. Mgr.: Christian Bobe
Phone: (49) 35053 41435
Fax: (49) 35053 42802
Email: christian.bobe@paka-gmbh.de
Chief Accountant: Baerbel Tittel
Phone: (49) 35053 41418
Fax: (49) 35053 42802
Email: baerbel.tittel@paka-gmbh.de
Sls. Mgr.: Halina Wojtek
Phone: (49) 35053 41413
Fax: (49) 35053 42802
Email: halina.wojtek@paka-gmbh.de
Purch. Mgr.: Monika Kroll
Phone: (49) 35053 41414
Fax: (49) 35053 42802
Email: monika.kroll@paka-gmbh.de
Offers/Quotes Mngr.: Katrin Schrom
Phone: (49) 35053 41432
Fax: (49) 35053 41420
Email: katrin.schrom@paka-gmbh.de
Total Employees of Company: 60
Total Employees at this Location: 60
Type of Operation: Paperboard mill
Pulp Grades and Capacities:
Total pulp capacity: 10,147 mt/y
Recycled Pulping: 10,147 mt/y
Pulp Mill Data:
Recycled Fiber Treatment Lines:
Pulpers: 1 at 11,900
Paper/Paperboard Grades and Capacities:
Total paper and paperboard capacity: 10,000 mt/y
Boxboard/cartonboard: 10,000 mt/y
Paper and Paperboard Mill Data:
Paper Machines: 2
No. 1, cylinder, total capacity 4,500 mt/y, Trim width 2.6 m, Boxboard/cartonboard
No. 2, cylinder, total capacity 5,500 mt/y, Trim width 2.6 m, Boxboard/cartonboard
Finishing Equipment:
Sheeters: 2
Energy Data:
Power boilers: 1
Electrical demand for mill: 9 MWh/D

ⓗPalm Group
Neukochen 10
D-73432 Aalen-Neukochen
Germany
Phone: (49) 7361 5770
Fax: (49) 7361 577298
Email: vertrieb@papierfabrik-palm.de, einkauf@papierfabrik-palm.de
Web Address: www.papierfabrik-palm.de

Personnel:
CEO: Wolfgang Palm
Phone: (49) 7361 5770
Fax: (49) 7361 577298
Man. Dir.: Artur Stöckler
Phone: (49) 7361 5770
Fax: (49) 7361 577298
COO, Man.Dir.: Joachim Lange
Phone: (49) 7361 5770
Fax: (49) 7361 577298
Mill Mgr.: Stefan Lübsen
Phone: (49) 7361 5770
Fax: (49) 7361 577298
Email: stefan.luebsen@papierfabrik-palm.de
Finan. Dir.: Roland Bauman
Phone: (49) 7361 5770
Fax: (49) 7361 577298
Dir., Technology: Volker Schuberth
Phone: (49) 7361 577205
Fax: (49) 7361 577298
Email: volker.schuberth@papierfabrik-palm.de
Total Employees of Company: 4,200
Mill Locations:
Palm Paper Limited, King's Lynn Mill, Poplar Avenue, Saddlebow Industrial Estate, King's Lynn PE34 3AL, United Kingdom, Capacity: 450,000 mt/y, (Pulp mill, Paper mill)
Phone: (44) 1553 782 222
Fax: (44) 1553 782 223
Email: info@palmpaper.co.uk
Papierfabrik Palm GmbH & Co KG, Aalen Mill, Neukochen 10, D-73432 Aalen-Neukochen, Germany, Capacity: 330,000 mt/y, (Paper mill, Paperboard mill)
Phone: (49) 7361 5770
Fax: (49) 7361 577298
Email: vertrieb@papierfabrik-palm.de, einkauf@papierfabrik-palm.de
Palm Group, Eltmann Mill, Industriestr. 23, D-97483 Eltmann, Germany, Capacity: 540,000 mt/y, (Paper mill)
Phone: (49) 9522 9250
Fax: (49) 9522 925100
Email: vertrieb@papierfabrik-palm.de, eltmann@papierfabrik-palm.de
Palm Group, Wörth Mill, Am Oberwald 2, D-76744 Wörth am Rhein, Germany, Capacity: 650,000 mt/y, (Paperboard mill)
Phone: (49) 7271 9790
Fax: (49) 7271 979300
Seyfert Paper S.A.S., Descartes Mill, Av. Monseigneur Roméro, BP 19, F-37160 Descartes, France, Capacity: 205,000 mt/y, (Pulp mill, Paperboard mill)
Phone: (33) 2 47 59 76 05
Fax: (33) 2 47 59 80 95
Email: seyfert.paper@seyfert.fr

ⓗⓜPapierfabrik Palm GmbH & Co KG
Aalen Mill
Ownership: 100% by Palm Group
Neukochen 10
D-73432 Aalen-Neukochen
Germany
Mailing Address: Postf. 16 05, D-73406 Aalen, Germany
Phone: (49) 7361 5770
Fax: (49) 7361 577298
Email: vertrieb@papierfabrik-palm.de, einkauf@papierfabrik-palm.de
Web Address: www.papierfabrik-palm.de

Personnel:
CEO: Dr. Wolfgang Palm
Phone: (49) 7361 577 102/104
Fax: (49) 7361 577 298
Email: w.palm@papierfabrik-palm.de
Man. Dir.: Artur Stöckler
Phone: (49) 7361 5770
Fax: (49) 7361 577298
Email: artur.stoeckler@papierfabrik-palm.de
COO, Man. Dir.: Joachim Lange
Phone: (49) 7361 5770
Fax: (49) 7361 577298
Email: joachim.lange@papierfabrik-palm.de
Mill Mgr.: Stefan Lübsen
Phone: (49) 7361 5770
Fax: (49) 7361 577298
Email: s.luebsen@papierfabrik-palm.de
Dir., Technology: Volker Schuberth
Phone: (49) 7361 5770
Fax: (49) 7361 577298
Email: volker.schuberth@papierfabrik-palm.de
Total Employees of Company: 3,000
Total Employees at this Location: 700
Type of Operation: Paper mill, Paperboard mill
Pulp Grades and Capacities:
Total pulp capacity: 333,737 mt/y
Recycled Pulping: 333,737 mt/y
Pulp Mill Data:
Bleach Plant Lines:
DIP
Recycled Fiber Treatment Lines:
Flotation deinking lines
Recycled packaging pulping lines
Paper/Paperboard Grades and Capacities:
Total paper and paperboard capacity: 330,000 mt/y
Newsprint: 90,000 mt/y
Linerboard: 135,000 mt/y
Corrugating medium/fluting: 105,000 mt/y
Paper and Paperboard Mill Data:
Stock Preparation:
Pulpers: 10
Refiners: 13
Paper Machines: 3
No. 2, DuoFormer D, total capacity 90,000 mt/y, Trim width 4.56 m, Newsprint
No. 4, fourdrinier, total capacity 105,000 mt/y, Trim width 4.3 m, Corrugating medium/fluting
No. 5, fourdrinier (2), total capacity 135,000 mt/y, Trim width 5 m, Linerboard
Energy Data:
Power boilers: 3
Steam turbines: 3 at 20.0 MW
Electrical demand for mill: 510 MWh/D

ⓜPalm Group
Eltmann Mill
Industriestr. 23
D-97483 Eltmann
Germany
Phone: (49) 9522 9250
Fax: (49) 9522 925100
Email: vertrieb@papierfabrik-palm.de, eltmann@papierfabrik-palm.de
Web Address: www.papierfabrik-palm.de

Personnel:
Mill Mgr.: Andreas Reichert
Phone: (49) 9522 9250
Fax: (49) 9522 925100
Email: andreas.reichert@papierfabrik-palm.de
Total Employees at this Location: 250
Type of Operation: Paper mill
Pulp Grades and Capacities:
Total pulp capacity: 554,245 mt/y
Recycled Pulping: 554,245 mt/y
Pulp Mill Data:
Bleach Plant Systems: 1
DIP Capacity 554,000 admt/y
Recycled Fiber Treatment Lines:
Flotation deinking lines: 1 at 554,000
Paper/Paperboard Grades and Capacities:
Total paper and paperboard capacity: 540,000 mt/y
Newsprint: 540,000 mt/y
Paper and Paperboard Mill Data:
Paper Machines: 2
No. 1, DuoFormer CFD, total capacity 200,000 mt/y, Trim width 5.68 m, Newsprint
No. 3, DuoFormer TQv, total capacity 340,000 mt/y, Trim width 8.12 m, Newsprint
Energy Data:
Power boilers: 1

Germany

HRSG boiler: 1
Combustion turbines: 1 at 55 MW
Electrical demand for mill: 1,277 MWh/D

ⓂPalm Group
Wörth Mill
Am Oberwald 2
D-76744 Wörth am Rhein
Germany
  Phone: (49) 7271 9790
  Fax: (49) 7271 979300
  Web Address: www.papierfabrik-palm.de
Personnel:
  Mill Mgr.: Jürgen Kosse
  Phone: (49) 7271 979 301
  Fax: (49) 7271 979 300
  Email: juergen.kosse@papierfabrik-palm.de
  Oper. Mgr.: Christian Mück
  Phone: (49) 7271 979 0
  Fax: (49) 7271 979 300
  Email: christian.mueck@papierfabrik-palm.de
Total Employees at this Location: 150
Type of Operation: Paperboard mill
Pulp Grades and Capacities:
  Total pulp capacity: 648,732 mt/y
  Recycled Pulping: 648,732 mt/y
Pulp Mill Data:
  Recycled Fiber Treatment Lines:
  Recycled packaging pulping lines: 1 at 635,000
Paper/Paperboard Grades and Capacities:
  Total paper and paperboard capacity: 650,000 mt/y
  Linerboard: 350,000 mt/y
  Corrugating medium/fluting: 300,000 mt/y
Paper and Paperboard Mill Data:
  Stock Preparation:
  Pulpers: 2
  Refiners:
Paper Machines: 1
  No. 6, OptiFormer, total capacity 650,000 mt/y, Trim width 10.3 m, Linerboard, Corrugating medium/fluting
Coating Machines: 1
  No. 1
Finishing Equipment:
  Winders: 2 at 600,000 mt/y
Energy Data:
  Power boilers: 1
  Combustion turbines: 1 at 44 MW
  Steam turbines: 1 at 18 MW
  Electrical demand for mill: 672 MWh/D

ⓉWellkistenfabrik Fritz Peters GmbH & Co. KG
Ownership: 100% by Angela and Roman Peters
Industriestrasse 5
D-47447 Moers
Germany
Mailing Address: Postf. 20 03 40, D-47423 Moers, Germany
  Phone: (49) 2841 601-0
  Fax: (49) 2841 601 234
  Email: info@peters-packaging.de
  Web Address: www.peters-packaging.de
Personnel:
  Owner & Gen. Mgr.: Roman Peters
  Phone: (49) 2841 601-0
  Fax: (49) 2841 601 234
  Email: roman.peters@peters-packaging.de
  Gen. Mgr.: Angela Peters
  Phone: (49) 2841 601-0
  Fax: (49) 2841 601 234
  Email: angela.peters@peters-packaging.de
  Man. Dir.: Winfried Flemmer
  Phone: (49) 2841 601-0
  Fax: (49) 2841 601 234
  Email: winfried.flemmer@peters-packaging.de
  Mill Mgr.: Jakob Koch
  Phone: (49) 2841 601-0
  Fax: (49) 2841 601 234
  Email: jakob.koch@peters-packaging.de
  Sls. Mgr.: Peter Ingenleuf
  Phone: (49) 2841 601-0
  Fax: (49) 2841 601 234
  Email: peter.ingenleuf@peters-packaging.de
  Supply Chain Mgr.: Christine Thissen
  Phone: (49) 2841 601 303
  Fax: (49) 2841 601 295/303
  Email: christine.thissen@peters-packaging.de
  Sls. Mgr.: Andreas Jeske
  Phone: (49) 2841 601 304
  Fax: (49) 2841 601 306
  Email: andreas.jeske@peters-packaging.de

ⓂPapierfabrik Fritz Peters GmbH & Co. KG
Gelsenkirchen Mill
Ownership: 100% by Prinzhorn Holding GmbH
Alfred-Zingler-Strasse 15
D-45881 Gelsenkirchen
Germany
Mailing Address: Postf. 10 20 52, D-45820 Gelsenkirchen, Germany
  Phone: (49) 209 80 040
  Fax: (49) 209 80 04119
  Email: info@peters-gelsenkirchen.de
  Web Address: www.peters-gelsenkirchen.de
Personnel:
  Owner, Pres.: Volkmar Peters
  Phone: (49) 2841 601 0
  Fax: (49) 2841 601 115
  Email: volkmar.peters@peters-beteiligung.de
  Man. Dir.: Christoph Deinhard
  Email: Christoph.Deinhard@peters-gelsenkirchen.de
  Sales Dir.: Heinz Breucker
  Phone: (49) 209 8004-114
  Fax: (49) 209 8004 119
  Email: heinz.breucker@peters-gelsenkirchen.de
  Prod. Mgr.: Andreas Hußing
  Email: Andreas.Hussing@peters-gelsenkirchen.de
  Prod. Mgr.-Testliner: Dietmar Kampka
  Phone: (49) 209 8004-151
  Fax: (49) 209 8004-159
  Email: dietmar.kampka@peters-gelsenkirchen.de
  Prod. Mgr., Plasterboard liner: Klaus Bründel
  Phone: (49) 209 8004-142
  Fax: (49) 209 8004-158
  Email: klaus.bruendel@peters-gelsenkirchen.de
  Tech. Dir.: Huub Haas
  Phone: (49) 209 8004 115
  Fax: (49) 209 8004 119
  Email: huub.haas@peters-gelsenkirchen.de
Total Employees at this Location: 140
Type of Operation: Paperboard mill
Pulp Grades and Capacities:
  Total pulp capacity: 249,535 mt/y
  Recycled Pulping: 249,535 mt/y
Pulp Mill Data:
  Recycled Fiber Treatment Lines:
  Recycled packaging pulping lines at 226,000
Paper/Paperboard Grades and Capacities:
  Total paper and paperboard capacity: 250,000 mt/y
  Linerboard: 135,000 mt/y
  Corrugating medium/fluting: 25,000 mt/y
  Boxboard/cartonboard: 90,000 mt/y
Paper and Paperboard Mill Data:
  Stock Preparation:
  Pulpers: 2
  Refiners: 3
Paper Machines: 1
  No. 1, fourdrinier (2), total capacity 250,000 mt/y, Trim width 5.4 m, Boxboard/cartonboard, Linerboard, Corrugating medium/fluting
Finishing Equipment:
  Winders: 1 at 180,000 mt/y
Energy Data:
  Power boilers: 3
  Electrical demand for mill: 332 MWh/D

ⓄⓂPfleiderer Spezialpapiere
Teisnach Mill
Adolf-Pfleiderer-Strasse 19
D-94244 Teisnach
Germany
Mailing Address: Postfach 11 20, D-94240 Teisnach, Germany
  Phone: (49) 9923 290
  Fax: (49) 9923 29125
  Email: k.augustin@pfleiderer-spezialpapiere.de
  Web Address: www.pfleiderer-spezialpapiere.de
Personnel:
  Man. Dir.: Manfred Brückl
  Phone: (49) 9923 290
  Email: m.brueckl@pfleiderer-spezialpapiere.de
  Paper Mill Mgr.: Sebastian Arnold
  Phone: (49) 9923 29111
  Fax: (49) 9923 29170
  Email: s.arnold@pfleiderer-spezialpapiere.de
  Sls. Dir.: Karl Augustin
  Phone: (49) 9923 29100
  Fax: (49) 9923 29125
  Email: k.augustin@pfleiderer-spezialpapiere.de
  Tech. Purch. Mgr.: Herbert Saller
  Phone: (49) 9923 29164
  Fax: (49) 9923 29170
  Email: h.saller@pfleiderer-spezialpapiere.de
  Purch. Mgr.: Karl-Heinz Pfeffer
  Phone: (49) 9923 29112
  Fax: (49) 9923 29170
  Email: h.pfeffer@pfleiderer-spezialpapiere.de
Total Employees of Company: 210
Total Employees at this Location: 210
Type of Operation: Paper mill
Paper/Paperboard Grades and Capacities:
  Total paper and paperboard capacity: 37,842 mt/y
  Specialty and industrial: 37,842 mt/y
Paper and Paperboard Mill Data:
  Stock Preparation:
  Pulpers: 4
  Refiners: 8
Paper Machines: 3
  No. 1, fourdrinier, total capacity 13,923 mt/y, Trim width 2.25 m, Specialty and industrial
  No. 2, fourdrinier, total capacity 13,923 mt/y, Trim width 2.25 m, Specialty and industrial
  No. 4, Yankee dryer, total capacity 9,996 mt/y, Trim width 2.25 m, Specialty and industrial
Finishing Equipment:
  Rewinders: 4
  Sheeters: 3
Energy Data:
  Power boilers: 1
  Electrical demand for mill: 93 MWh/D

ⓄⓂPapierfabrik Poerringer GmbH & Co. KG
Annweiler Mill
Zweibrückerstr. 53
D-76855 Annweiler am Trifels
Germany
Mailing Address: Postf. 12 47, D-76850 Annweiler, Germany
  Phone: (49) 6346 8495
  Fax: (49) 6346 1024
  Email: wachtelmuehle@t-online.de
Personnel:
  Gen. Mgr. / Mill Mgr.: Ursula Poerringer
  Phone: (49) 6346 8495
  Com. Mngr.: Hubert Schmitz
Total Employees of Company: 30
Total Employees at this Location: 30
Type of Operation: Paper mill
Paper/Paperboard Grades and Capacities:
  Total paper and paperboard capacity: 1,500 mt/y
  Specialty and industrial
  Boxboard/cartonboard
Paper and Paperboard Mill Data:
Paper Machines: 2

No. 1, cylinder mould, Trim width 1.3 m, Specialty and industrial, Boxboard/cartonboard
No. 2, fourdrinier, Trim width 1.56 m, Specialty and industrial, Boxboard/cartonboard
Energy Data:
Power boilers: 1

ⓂKartonfabrik Porstendorf GmbH
Porstendorf Mill
Fabrikstr. 1
D-07778 Porstendorf
Germany
Phone: (49) 36427 874 100 / 210
Fax: (49) 36427 874 101 / 102
Email: contact@kartonfabrik.de
Web Address: www.kartonfabrik.de
Personnel:
Gen. Mgr.: Andreas Prahl
Phone: (49) 36427 874 160
Fax: (49) 36427 874 101
Email: andreas.prahl@kartonfabrik.de
Mill Mgr.: Frank Tilch
Phone: (49) 36427 874 100
Fax: (49) 36427 874 101
Email: frank.tilch@kartonfabrik.de
Sls. Mgr.: Christian Bretzing
Phone: (49) 36427 874 100
Fax: (49) 36427 874 101
Email: christian.bretzing@kartonfabrik.de
Total Employees at this Location: 70
Type of Operation: Paperboard mill
Pulp Grades and Capacities:
Total pulp capacity: 50,508 mt/y
Recycled Pulping: 50,508 mt/y
Pulp Mill Data:
Recycled Fiber Treatment Lines:
Flotation deinking lines: 1 at 60,000
Pulpers: 1 at 60,000
Paper/Paperboard Grades and Capacities:
Total paper and paperboard capacity: 50,000 mt/y
Boxboard/cartonboard: 50,000 mt/y
Paper and Paperboard Mill Data:
Paper Machines: 1
No. 1, cylinder, total capacity 50,000 mt/y, Trim width 2.3 m, Boxboard/cartonboard
Finishing Equipment:
Sheeters: 1 at 55,000 mt/y
Energy Data:
Electrical demand for mill: 62 MWh/D

ⓂProgroup AG
Ownership: BWK (partly owned)
Horstring 12
D-76829 Landau
Germany
Phone: (49) 63 41 55 76-0
Fax: (49) 6348 6109-109
Email: heindl@progroup.ag, info@progroup.ag
Web Address: www.progroup.ag
Personnel:
CEO: Jürgen Heindl
Phone: (49) 6348 6109-100
Fax: (49) 6348 6109-109
Email: heindl@progroup.ag
CFO: Frank Gumbinger
Phone: (49) 6348 6109-100
Fax: (49) 6348 6109-109
Email: gumbinger@progroup.ag
Head of The Paper Division: Götz Herold
Phone: (49) 63 4155 76-0
Fax: (49) 63 4155 76-109
Email: herold@propapier.de
Head of The Corrugated Board Div.: Jürgen Lemke
Phone: (49) 63 4155 76-0
Fax: (49) 63 4155 76-109
Sls. Dir.: Gerd Rinderhagen
Phone: (49) 6348 6109-100
Fax: (49) 6348 6109-109
Head of Mktg.: Stephan Göckler

Phone: (49) 63 4155 76-0
Fax: (49) 63 4155 76-109
Exec. Asst. Mktg. & Support IT Mgt : Swaantje Katz
Phone: (49) 63 4155 76-0
Fax: (49) 63 4155 76-109
Total Employees of Company: 830
Mill Locations:
Propapier PM 1 GmbH, Burg Mill, Lindenallee 28, D-39288 Burg, Germany, Capacity: 320,000 mt/y, (Paperboard mill)
Phone: (49) 3921 45 66-5000
Fax: (49) 3921 45 66-5009
Email: (lastname@propapier.de), info.pm1@propapier.de
Propapier PM 2 GmbH & Co. KG, Eisenhüttenstadt Mill, Oderlandstraße 110, D-15890 Eisenhüttenstadt, Germany, Capacity: 650,000 mt/y, (Paperboard mill)
Phone: (49) 3364 77277 10
Fax: (49) 3364 77277 19
Email: info.pm2@propapier.de

ⓂPropapier PM 1 GmbH
Burg Mill
Ownership: 100% by Progroup AG
Lindenallee 28
D-39288 Burg
Germany
Phone: (49) 3921 45 66-5000
Fax: (49) 3921 45 66-5009
Email: (lastname@propapier.de), info.pm1@propapier.de
Web Address: www.propapier.de, www.prowell.de
Personnel:
Mill Mgr.: Götz Herold
Phone: (49) 3921 4566-5002
Email: herold@propapier.de
Sls. Mgr.: Günter J. Hornik
Phone: (49) 6348 6109 120
Email: hornik@prowell.de
Prod. Mgr.: Peter Resvanis
Phone: (49) 3921 4566-5200
Email: resvanis@propapier.de
Prod. Mgr.: Torsten Möbes
Phone: (49) 33921 4566 5200
Email: moebes@propapier.de
Project Team: Thomas Müller
Phone: (49) 3921 4566-5113
Total Employees at this Location: 100
Type of Operation: Paperboard mill
Pulp Grades and Capacities:
Total pulp capacity: 320,772 mt/y
Recycled Pulping: 320,772 mt/y
Pulp Mill Data:
Recycled Fiber Treatment Lines:
Recycled packaging pulping lines: 1 at 350,000
Paper/Paperboard Grades and Capacities:
Total paper and paperboard capacity: 320,000 mt/y
Linerboard: 256,000 mt/y
Corrugating medium/fluting: 64,000 mt/y
Paper and Paperboard Mill Data:
Stock Preparation:
Pulpers: 1
Paper Machines: 1
No. 1, Gap former (2), total capacity 320,000 mt/y, Trim width 5.83 m, Linerboard, Corrugating medium/fluting
Finishing Equipment:
Winders: 1 at 320,000 mt/y
Energy Data:
Power boilers: 4
Combustion turbines: 1 at 0.75 MW
Electrical demand for mill: 360 MWh/D

ⓂPropapier PM 2 GmbH & Co. KG
Eisenhüttenstadt Mill
Ownership: 100% by Progroup AG
Oderlandstraße 110
D-15890 Eisenhüttenstadt, Brandenburg
Germany

Germany

Phone: (49) 3364 77277 10
Fax: (49) 3364 77277 19
Email: info.pm2@propapier.de
Web Address: www.progroup.ag
Personnel:
Mill Mgr.: Götz Herold
Phone: (49) 3364 77277 10
Prod. Mgr.: Peter Resvanis
Phone: (49) 3364 7712 2110
Energy Mgr.: Mr. Otto
Phone: (49) 3364 77277 10
Total Employees at this Location: 130
Type of Operation: Paperboard mill
Pulp Grades and Capacities:
Total pulp capacity: 645,877 mt/y
Recycled Pulping: 645,877 mt/y
Pulp Mill Data:
Recycled Fiber Treatment Lines:
Recycled packaging pulping lines: 1 at 850,000 admt/y
Paper/Paperboard Grades and Capacities:
Total paper and paperboard capacity: 650,000 mt/y
Linerboard: 130,000 mt/y
Corrugating medium/fluting: 520,000 mt/y
Paper and Paperboard Mill Data:
Paper Machines: 1
No. 2, OptiConcept, total capacity 650,000 mt/y, Trim width 10.2 m, Corrugating medium/fluting, Linerboard
Finishing Equipment:
Winders: 1 at 650,000 mt/y
Energy Data:
Power boilers: 2
Steam turbines: 1 at 28 MW
Electrical demand for mill: 750 MWh/D

ⓂⓂPucaro Elektro-Isolierstoffe GmbH
Roigheim Mill
Ownership: ABB
Pucarostrasse 1
D-74255 Roigheim
Germany
Mailing Address: Postf. 1, D-74255 Roigheim, Germany
Phone: (49) 6298 27 0
Fax: (49) 6298 27 820/204
Email: info@pucaro.de, pucaro@pucaro.de
Web Address: www.pucaro.de
Personnel:
Man. Dir.: Tomas Arenius
Phone: (49) 6298 27 0
Finan. & Controlling Mgr.: Jochen Strauss
Phone: (49) 6298 27 0
Tech. Mgr.: Mark Czernuschka
Phone: (49) 6298 27 0
Email: mark.czernuschka@de.abb.com
Div. Mgr.: Harald Gieser
Phone: (49) 6298 27 0
Div. Mgr.: Karl-Heinz Keim
Phone: (49) 6298 27 0
Purch. Mgr: Thomas Gilke
Phone: (49) 6298 27 0
Total Employees at this Location: 400
Type of Operation: Paper mill, Paperboard mill
Paper/Paperboard Grades and Capacities:
Total paper and paperboard capacity: 20,000 mt/y
Specialty and industrial
Boxboard/cartonboard: 5,000 mt/y
Paper and Paperboard Mill Data:
Stock Preparation:
Pulpers: 2
Refiners: 7
Paper Machines: 2
No. 1, cylinder, Trim width 2.3 m
No. 2, cylinder, Trim width 1.3 m
Finishing Equipment:
Rewinders: 6
Sheeters: 1

Germany

Energy Data:
Power boilers: 1

ⓄⓂReflex Premium Papier AG
Reflex Mill
Ownership: 50% by company management and other private investors, 50% by Hahnemühle FineArt GmbH
Veldener Strasse 121-131
D-52349 Düren
Germany
Mailing Address: Postf. 10 19 61, D-52319 Düren, Germany
Phone: (49) 2421 497-0
Fax: (49) 2421 497 421 / 437
Email: info@zanders-premium.de
Web Address: www.zanders-premium.com
Personnel:
Sales & Mktg. Dir.: Thomas Kohls
Phone: (49) 172 291 4894
Fax: (49) 242 149 7421
Email: thomas.kohls@zanders-premium.de
Prod. Mgr.: Heinz Moritz
Phone: (49) 242 149 7378, 172 293 8947
Fax: (49) 242 149 7421
Email: heinz.moritz@zanders-premium.de
Member of board of directors: Jörg Gollnick
Phone: (49) 242 149 7497, 172 299
Fax: (49) 242 149 7421
Assist. Plt. Mgr.: Brigitte Kraus
Phone: (49) 242 149 7216
Fax: (49) 242 149 7421
Email: brigitte.kraus@zanders-premium.de
Total Employees at this Location: 102
Type of Operation: Paper mill
Paper/Paperboard Grades and Capacities:
Total paper and paperboard capacity: 20,000 mt/y
Uncoated woodfree/freesheet: 20,000 mt/y
Paper and Paperboard Mill Data:
Stock Preparation:
Pulpers: 9
Refiners: 37
Paper Machines: 3
No. 1, fourdrinier, total capacity 5,000 mt/y, Trim width 2.2 m, Uncoated woodfree/freesheet
No. 3, fourdrinier, total capacity 10,000 mt/y, Trim width 2 m, Uncoated woodfree/freesheet
No. 4, fourdrinier, total capacity 5,000 mt/y, Trim width 1.7 m, Uncoated woodfree/freesheet
Coating Machines: 1
No. 1, total capacity 75,000 mt/y., on machine
Finishing Equipment:
Supercalenders: 2
Rewinders: 10
Sheeters: 7
Energy Data:
Power boilers
Electrical demand for mill: 40 MWh/D

ⓄⓂReinsberger Spezialpapier GmbH
Reinsberg Mill
Ownership: Private
Muldenweg 1
D-09629 Reinsberg
Germany
Phone: (49) 37324 7214
Fax: (49) 37324 7215
Email: reipa@t-online.de
Web Address: www.kreppfabrik.de
Personnel:
Gen. Mgr.: Gerald Gotthardt
Phone: (49) 172351 3034
Total Employees of Company: 34
Total Employees at this Location: 34
Type of Operation: Paper mill
Pulp Mill Data:
Recycled Fiber Treatment Lines:
Pulpers: 2 at 5,000

Paper/Paperboard Grades and Capacities:
Total paper and paperboard capacity: 2,500 mt/y
Paper and Paperboard Mill Data:
Paper Machines: 1
No. 1, fourdrinier, total capacity 2,500 mt/y, Trim width 1.7 m
Finishing Equipment:
Sheeters: 1 at 1,500 mt/y
Energy Data:
Power boilers: 2
Electrical demand for mill: 5 MWh/D

ⓂReno De Medici Arnsberg GmbH
Arnsberg Mill
Ownership: Reno De Medici SpA
Hellefelder Str. 51
D-59821 Arnsberg
Germany
Mailing Address: Postf. 52 51, D-59821 Arnsberg, Germany
Phone: (49) 2931 851
Fax: (49) 2931 85201
Email: info@rdmgroup.com
Web Address: www.renodemedici.it
Personnel:
Man. Dir.: Dirk Verschueren
Phone: (49) 2931 85309
Fax: (49) 2931 85204
Email: dirk.verschueren@rdmgroup.com
Prod. Mgr.: Joachim Corthum
Phone: (49) 2931 851
Fax: (49) 2931 85201
Email: joachim.corthum@renodemedici.it
Qlty. & Devlpt. Mgr.: Rainer Sandrock
Phone: (49) 2931 851
Fax: (49) 2931 85201
Email: rainer.sandrock@renodemedici.it
Purch. Mgr.: Andreas Krekeler
Phone: (49) 2931 85318
Fax: (49) 2931 85201
Email: andreas.krekeler@rdmgroup.com
Tech. Mgr.: Norbert Kokot
Phone: (49) 2931 851
Fax: (49) 2931 85201
Email: norbert.kokot@renodemedici.it
Finishing Dept. Mgr.: Peter Dierig
Phone: (49) 2931 851
Fax: (49) 2931 85201
Email: peter.dierig@renodemedici.it
Total Employees at this Location: 315
Type of Operation: Paperboard mill
Pulp Grades and Capacities:
Total pulp capacity: 206,197 mt/y
Recycled Pulping: 206,197 mt/y
Pulp Mill Data:
Bleach Plant Lines:
DIP
Recycled Fiber Treatment Lines:
Flotation deinking lines
Pulpers
Washing deinking lines
Paper/Paperboard Grades and Capacities:
Total paper and paperboard capacity: 230,000 mt/y
Boxboard/cartonboard: 230,000 mt/y
Paper and Paperboard Mill Data:
Stock Preparation:
Pulpers: 5
Refiners: 8
Paper Machines: 1
No. 3, multi-fourdrinier, Yankee dryer, total capacity 230,000 mt/y, Trim width 3.5 m, Boxboard/cartonboard
Coating Machines: 1
No. 3, total capacity 230,000 mt/y., on machine
Finishing Equipment:
Winders: 1
Sheeters: 6
Energy Data:
Power boilers: 2

Steam turbines: 3 at 19.6 MW
Electrical demand for mill: 307 MWh/D

ⓄⓂCarta Riedenburg GmbH
Riedenburg Mill
Neuenkehrsdorf 14 - 18
D-93339 Riedenburg
Germany
Mailing Address: Postfach 7, D-93337 Riedenburg, Germany
Phone: (49) 9442 92050
Fax: (49) 9442 920535
Total Employees at this Location: 40
Type of Operation: Paperboard mill
Paper/Paperboard Grades and Capacities:
Total paper and paperboard capacity: 15,000 mt/y
Boxboard/cartonboard
Paper and Paperboard Mill Data:
Stock Preparation:
Pulpers: 1
Paper Machines: 2
No. 1, cylinder, Trim width 2.3 m, Boxboard/cartonboard
No. 2, cylinder, Trim width 1.5 m
Finishing Equipment:
Supercalenders: 4
Sheeters: 2
Energy Data:
Power boilers: 2
Combustion turbines: 2 at 0.2 MW
Electrical demand for mill: 14 MWh/D

ⓂSappi Fine Paper Europe
Alfeld Mill
Ownership: 100% by Sappi Limited
Mühlenmasch 1
D-31061 Alfeld (Leine)
Germany
Phone: (49) 5181 77-0
Fax: (49) 5181 77208
Email: infoalfeld@sappi.com
Web Address: www.sappi.com
Personnel:
Mill Dir.: Dr. Stefan Karrer
Phone: (49) 5181 77200
Fax: (49) 5181 77190
Email: stefan.karrer@sappi.com
Pulp & Services Mgr.: Richard Huster
Phone: (49) 5181 77161
Fax: (49) 5181 77163
Email: richard.huster@sappi.com
Total Employees at this Location: 925
Type of Operation: Pulp mill, Paper mill, Paperboard mill
Pulp Grades and Capacities:
Total pulp capacity: 120,007 mt/y
Chemical Pulp: 120,007 mt/y
Pulp Mill Data:
Chemical Pulping Systems:
Batch digesters: 5
Pulp Lines: 1
Bleach Plant Systems: 1
Other Chemical Pulping System, Type: TCF, Sequence: PP, Capacity 125,000 admt/y
Chemical Recovery Equipment:
Evaporator lines: 1
Recovery boilers: 1
Paper/Paperboard Grades and Capacities:
Total paper and paperboard capacity: 305,000 mt/y
Specialty and industrial: 240,000 mt/y
Linerboard: 5,000 mt/y
Boxboard/cartonboard: 60,000 mt/y
Paper and Paperboard Mill Data:
Stock Preparation:
Pulpers: 1
Paper Machines: 5
No. 1, fourdrinier, total capacity 60,000 mt/y, Trim width 3.3 m, Boxboard/cartonboard
No. 2, DuoFormer D, total capacity 135,000 mt/y, Trim width 4.6 m, Specialty and industrial, Linerboard

Germany

No. 3, fourdrinier, Yankee dryer, total capacity 35,000 mt/y, Trim width 4.8 m, Specialty and industrial
No. 4, fourdrinier, Yankee dryer, total capacity 40,000 mt/y, Trim width 3.3 m, Specialty and industrial
No. 5, fourdrinier, Yankee dryer, total capacity 35,000 mt/y, Trim width 4.8 m, Specialty and industrial
Coating Machines: 4
SM 1, total capacity 35,000 mt/y., on machine
SM 2, total capacity 60,000 mt/y., off machine
SM 3, total capacity 215,000 mt/y., off machine
SM 4, total capacity 45,000 mt/y., on machine
Finishing Equipment:
  Winders: 5
  Supercalenders: 2
  Rewinders: 9
  Sheeters: 7
Energy Data:
Power boilers: 6
Steam turbines: 3 at 8, 11, 17 MW
Electrical demand for mill: 827 MWh/D

ⓜSappi Fine Paper Europe
Ehingen Mill
Ownership: 100% by Sappi Limited
Biberacher Str. 73
D-89584 Ehingen
Germany
Mailing Address: Postf. 13 65, D-89573 Ehingen, Germany
  Phone: (49) 7391 5010
  Fax: (49) 7391 501 315
  Email: renate.distelrath@sappi.com
  Web Address: www.sappi.com
Personnel:
Mill Dir.: Dr. Steffen Wurdinger
  Phone: (49) 7391 501 230
  Fax: (49) 7391 501 315
  Email: steffen.wurdinger@sappi.com
Tech. Mgr.: Wolfgang Schmidt
  Phone: (49) 7391 501 338
  Fax: (49) 7391 501 315
  Email: wolfgang.schmidt@sappi.com
Environ. Dir.: Markus Hilpert
  Phone: (49) 7391 501 0
  Fax: (49) 7391 501 315
  Email: markus.hilpert@sappi.com
Chief Eng.: Richard Zuefle
  Phone: (49) 7391 501 0
  Fax: (49) 7391 501 315
  Email: richard.zuefle@sappi.com
Total Employees at this Location: 551
Type of Operation: Pulp mill, Paper mill
Pulp Grades and Capacities:
  Total pulp capacity: 135,000 mt/y
  Pulp available for market: 18,343 mt/y
  Chemical Pulp: 135,000 mt/y
Pulp Mill Data:
Chemical Pulping Systems:
Batch digesters: 8
Bleach Plant Systems: 1
Chemical Pulping System, Type: TCF - Hardwood/Softwood
Chemical Recovery Equipment:
Evaporator lines: 1
Recovery boilers: 2
Pulp Dryers:
Air Float dryers 1, Fourdriniers 1
Paper/Paperboard Grades and Capacities:
  Total paper and paperboard capacity: 260,000 mt/y
  Coated woodfree/freesheet: 260,000 mt/y
Paper and Paperboard Mill Data:
Paper Machines: 1
No. 6, hybrid former, total capacity 260,000 mt/y, Trim width 5.65 m, Coated woodfree/freesheet
Coating Machines: 1
CM 6, total capacity 260,000 mt/y., off machine
Finishing Equipment:
  Sheeters: 6
Energy Data:
Power boilers: 5
Steam turbines: 3 at 23 MW
Electrical demand for mill: 684 MWh/D

ⓜSappi Fine Paper Europe
Stockstadt Mill
Ownership: 100% by Sappi Limited
Obernburger Strasse 1-9
D-63811 Stockstadt am Main
Germany
Mailing Address: Postf. 60, D-63809 Stockstadt am Main, Germany
  Phone: (49) 6027 4200
  Fax: (49) 6027 420 245/823
  Email: stockstadt@sappi.com
  Web Address: www.sappi.com
Personnel:
Mill Dir.: Christian Dietershagen
  Phone: (49) 6027 420 355
  Fax: (49) 6027 420 589
  Email: christian.dietershagen@sappi.com
Pulp Mill Mgr.: Matthias Liebich
  Phone: (49) 6027 420 509
  Fax: (49) 6027 420 823
  Email: matthias.liebich@sappi.com
Pulp & Utilities Proj.: Berthold Fath
  Phone: (49) 6027 420 326
  Fax: (49) 6027 420 646
  Email: berthold.fath@sappi.com
PR/Commun. Mgr.: Kerstin Kalajian
  Phone: (49) 60 27 420 280
  Fax: (49) 60 27 420 9280
  Email: kerstin.kalajian@sappi.com
Total Employees at this Location: 720
Type of Operation: Pulp mill, Paper mill
Pulp Grades and Capacities:
  Total pulp capacity: 160,000 mt/y
  Pulp available for market: 43,963 mt/y
  Chemical Pulp: 160,000 mt/y
Pulp Mill Data:
Chemical Pulping Systems:
Batch digesters: 7
Bleach Plant Systems: 1
No. 1, Sequence: EopP, Capacity 165,000 admt/y
Chemical Recovery Equipment:
Evaporator lines: 2
Recovery boilers: 4
Pulp Dryers:
Other dryers 1
Paper/Paperboard Grades and Capacities:
  Total paper and paperboard capacity: 440,000 mt/y
  Uncoated woodfree/freesheet: 210,000 mt/y
  Coated woodfree/freesheet: 230,000 mt/y
Paper and Paperboard Mill Data:
Stock Preparation:
Pulpers: 2
Refiners: 12
Paper Machines: 2
No. 1, DuoFormer D, total capacity 210,000 mt/y, Trim width 5.6 m, Uncoated woodfree/freesheet
No. 2, DuoFormer D, total capacity 230,000 mt/y, Trim width 5.6 m, Coated woodfree/freesheet
Coating Machines: 1
PM 2, total capacity 230,000 mt/y., off machine
Finishing Equipment:
  Winders: 2
  Calenders: 1
  Sheeters: 6
Energy Data:
Power boilers: 1
Combustion turbines: 5 at 60.0 MW
Electrical demand for mill: 1,096 MWh/D

ⓑSCA Hygiene Products SE
Ownership: SCA - Svenska Cellulosa Aktiebolaget
Terminalstrasse Mitte 18 (MAC)
D-85336 München-Flughafen
Germany
Mailing Address: PO Box 24 15 40, D-85356 München-Flughafen, Germany
  Phone: (49) 89 97006 0
  Fax: (49) 89 97006 204
  Email: info@sca.com
  Web Address: www.sca.com
Personnel:
Bd. Mbr.: Gernot Wiedenbrüg
  Phone: (49) 89 97006 0
  Fax: (49) 89 97006 204
COO, SCA Global Hygiene: Mats Berencreutz
  Phone: (49) 89 97006 0
  Fax: (49) 89 97006 204
Pres., SCA Tissue Europe: Magnus Groth
  Phone: (49) 89 97006 0
  Fax: (49) 89 97006 204
Pres. Global Hygiene Supply: William Ledger
  Phone: (49) 89 97006 0
  Fax: (49) 89 97006 204
VP Consumer Tissue Sls. & Mktg.: Bernhard Riede
  Phone: (49) 89 97006 0
  Fax: (49) 89 97006 204
VP Commun.: Stefanie Christmann
  Phone: (49) 89 97006 - 223
  Fax: (49) 89 97006 204
  Email: stefanie.christmann@sca.com
Commun. Dir.: Cherry Harris-Bayer
  Phone: (49) 89 97006 - 205
  Fax: (49) 89 97006 412
  Email: cherry.harris-bayer@sca.com
Proj. Mgr.: Niamh Walsh
  Phone: (49) 89 97006 0
  Fax: (49) 89 97006 204
Manager Service Management: Michael Dumproff
  Phone: (49) 89 97006 0
  Fax: (49) 89 97006 204
Total Employees at this Location: 76
Mill Locations:
SCA Hygiene Products SpA, Altopascio Mill, Via Proviciale Romana, I-55010 Altopascio, Loc. Badia Pozzeveri, (LU), Italy, Capacity: 25,000 mt/y, (Paper mill)
  Phone: (39) 0583 2791
  Fax: (39) 0583 279250
SCA Hygiene Products S.L., La Riba Mill, Cardenal Gomá 16, E-43450 La Riba, Spain, Capacity: 26,000 mt/y, (Paper mill)
  Phone: (34) 977 87 6749/ 977 87 6745
  Fax: (34) 977 87 6025
SCA Hygiene Products SE, Goytside Mill, Goytside Road, Chesterfield S40 2PH, United Kingdom, Capacity: 31,000 mt/y, (Paper mill)
  Phone: (44) 1246 558 557
  Fax: (44) 1246 552 556
SCA Hygiene Products AB, Edet Mill, Emil Haegers väg 21, SE-463 81 Lilla Edet, Sweden, Capacity: 110,000 mt/y, (Paper mill)
  Phone: (46) 520 659 000
  Fax: (46) 520 659 302
SCA Hygiene Products SE, Mainz-Kostheim Mill, Hauptstrasse 1, D-55246 Mainz-Kostheim, Germany, Capacity: 166,000 mt/y, (Paper mill)
  Phone: (49) 6134 608 202/0
  Fax: (49) 6134 608 387/400
  Email: info.hygiene@sca.com, torkmaster@sca.com
SCA Hygiene Products Manchester Ltd., Manchester (Trafford Park) Mill, Trafford Park Road, Trafford Park, Manchester M17 1EQ, United Kingdom, Capacity: 60,000 mt/y, (Paper mill)
  Phone: (44) 161 888 6002
  Fax: (44) 161 888 6195
SCA Hygiene Products SE, Mannheim Mill, Sandhofer Str. 176, D-68305 Mannheim, Germany, Capacity: 350,000 mt/y, (Pulp mill, Paper mill)
  Phone: (49) 621 778 0
  Fax: (49) 621 778 3146/3141/2248
  Email: (firstname.surname@sca.com)
SCA Hygiene Products S.L., Mediona Mill, Carretera de la Llacuna, E-08773 Mediona, Spain, Capacity: 45,000 mt/y, (Paper mill)
  Phone: (34) 93 898 5570
  Fax: (34) 93 898 5820

Germany

SCA Hygiene Products SE, Neuss Mill, Floßhafenstraße 16, D-41460 Neuss, Germany, Capacity: 105,000 mt/y, (Paper mill)
Phone: (49) 2131 296 0
Fax: (49) 2131 296 104/111

SCA Hygiene Products SE, Oakenholt Mill, Chester Road, Oakenholt, Flint CH6 5PU, United Kingdom, Capacity: 68,000 mt/y, (Paper mill)
Phone: (44) 1352 732 101
Fax: (44) 1352 732 760

SCA Hygiene Products Operations SNC, Orléans Mill, Rue des Bouleaux, ZI de la Saussaye, F-45590 Saint Cyr en Val, Orléans, France, Capacity: 35,000 mt/y, (Paper mill)
Phone: (33) 2 38 49 97 97
Fax: (33) 2 38 63 88 45
Email: (firstname.lastname@sca.com)

SCA Hygiene Products, Collodi Mill, Via delle Cartiere 13, I-51014 Collodi, (PT), Italy, Capacity: 42,000 mt/y, (Paper mill)
Phone: (39) 0572 429090
Fax: (39) 0572 426335

SCA Hygiene Products Supply SAS, Le Theil Mill, Route d'Avezé, ZI Sud, F-61260 Le Theil sur Huisne, France, Capacity: 62,000 mt/y, (Paper mill)
Phone: (33) 2 37 53 67 00
Fax: (33) 2 37 53 67 92

SCA Hygiene Products SpA, Lucca 1 Tissue Mill, Via del Frizzone, I-55016 Porcari, (LU), Italy, Capacity: 140,000 mt/y, (Paper mill)
Phone: (39) 0583 21241
Fax: (39) 0583 297575
Email: info@sca.com

SCA Hygiene Products SE, Prudhoe Mill, Princess Way, Prudhoe NE42 6HE, United Kingdom, Capacity: 90,000 mt/y, (Pulp mill, Paper mill)
Phone: (44) 1661 806000
Fax: (44) 1661 806001

SCA Hygiene Products Russia LLC, Sovetsk Mill, Molodyozhnaya Str. 9, 301205 Sovetsk, Shchekino Distr., Russia, Capacity: 30,000 mt/y, (Paper mill)
Phone: (7) 48751 746 66 / 751 36/41
Email: ekaterina.serezhnikova@sca.com

SCA Hygiene Products S.A./N.V., Stembert Mill, Rue de la Papeterie 2, B-4801 Stembert, Belgium, Capacity: 75,000 mt/y, (Paper mill)
Phone: (32) 87 30 66 11
Fax: (32) 87 33 94 24
Email: (firstname.lastname@sca.com)

SCA Hygiene Products Russia LLC, Svetogorsk Mill, ul. Zavodskaya 21, 188991 Svetogorsk, Russia, Capacity: 43,000 mt/y, (Paper mill)
Phone: (7) 812 320 4834
Fax: (7) 812 320 4835
Email: info@scacompany.com, svetogorsk@sca.com, tissue@mail.ru

SCA Hygiene Products S.L., Puigpelat (Valls) Mill, Ctra. Valls-Puigpelat, Km 2, E-43812 Puigpelat, Spain, Capacity: 120,000 mt/y, (Paper mill)
Phone: (34) 977 030 600
Fax: (34) 977 605 554

SCA Hygiene Products SE, Stubbins Mill, Stubbins Lane, Ramsbottom, Bury BL0 0NH, United Kingdom, Capacity: 117,000 mt/y, (Pulp mill, Paper mill)
Phone: (44) 1706 283 000
Fax: (44) 1706 283 001

ⓜSCA Hygiene Products SE
Mainz-Kostheim Mill

Ownership: SCA - Svenska Cellulosa Aktiebolaget
Hauptstrasse 1
D-55246 Mainz-Kostheim
Germany
Mailing Address: Postf. 11 61, D-55240 Mainz-Kostheim, Germany
Phone: (49) 6134 608 202/0
Fax: (49) 6134 608 387/400
Email: info.hygiene@sca.com, torkmaster@sca.com
Web Address: www.sca.com

Personnel:
Gen. Mgr.: Thomas Wüst
Phone: (49) 6134 608 202/0
Fax: (49) 6134 608-387
Email: thomas.wust@sca.com
Mill Mgr.: Ulrich Beltz
Phone: (49) 6134 608 202/0
Fax: (49) 6134 608-387
Email: ulrich.beltz@sca.com
Prod. Mgr.: Markus Klenk
Phone: (49) 6134 608 372
Fax: (49) 6134 608-387
Email: markus.klenk@sca.com
Total Employees at this Location: 500
Type of Operation: Paper mill
Pulp Grades and Capacities:
Total pulp capacity: 98,662 mt/y
Recycled Pulping: 98,662 mt/y
Pulp Mill Data:
Recycled Fiber Treatment Lines:
Flotation deinking lines
Paper/Paperboard Grades and Capacities:
Total paper and paperboard capacity: 166,000 mt/y
Tissue: 166,000 mt/y
Paper and Paperboard Mill Data:
Paper Machines: 4
No. 1, fourdrinier, Yankee dryer, total capacity 14,000 mt/y, Trim width 2.22 m, Tissue
No. 3, fourdrinier, Yankee dryer, total capacity 27,000 mt/y, Trim width 2.54 m, Tissue
No. 4, C-wrap, Yankee dryer, total capacity 65,000 mt/y, Trim width 5.23 m, Tissue
No. 5, ATMOS, Yankee dryer, total capacity 60,000 mt/y, Trim width 5.5 m, Tissue
Energy Data:
Power boilers: 1
Steam turbines: 1 at 5.5 MW
Electrical demand for mill: 128 MWh/D

ⓜSCA Hygiene Products SE
Mannheim Mill

Ownership: SCA - Svenska Cellulosa Aktiebolaget
Sandhofer Str. 176
D-68305 Mannheim
Germany
Mailing Address: Postf. 31 04 20, D-68264 Mannheim, Germany
Phone: (49) 621 778 0
Fax: (49) 621 778 3146/3141/2248
Email: (firstname.surname@sca.com)
Web Address: www.sca.com

Personnel:
Mill Mgr.: Mr. Roger Schilling
Phone: (49) 621 778 0
Fax: (49) 621 778 3146
Email: roger.schilling@sca.com
Man. Dir. Regional Central: Bernhard Riede
Phone: (49) 621 778 0
Fax: (49) 621 778 3146
Email: bernhard.riede@sca.com
Admin. Mgr., GBS Regional Director, Europe Central: Thomas Wüst
Phone: (49) 621 778 2229
Fax: (49) 621 778 3146
Email: thomas.wust@sca.com
Total Employees at this Location: 2,000
Type of Operation: Pulp mill, Paper mill
Pulp Grades and Capacities:
Total pulp capacity: 220,000 mt/y
Chemical Pulp: 220,000 mt/y
Pulp Mill Data:
Chemical Pulping Systems:
Batch digesters: 12
Continuous digesters: 1
Bleach Plant Systems: 3
No. 1, Sequence: EP, Capacity 120 admt/y
No. 2, Sequence: PMgOA, Capacity 130 admt/y
No. 3, Sequence: PMgOA, Capacity 450 admt/y
Chemical Recovery Equipment:
Evaporator lines: 1
Recovery boilers: 2
Pulp Dryers:
Air Float dryers 1
Paper/Paperboard Grades and Capacities:
Total paper and paperboard capacity: 350,000 mt/y
Tissue: 290,000 mt/y
Packaging papers: 30,000 mt/y
Specialty and industrial: 30,000 mt/y
Paper and Paperboard Mill Data:
Stock Preparation:
Pulpers: 2
Refiners: 13
Paper Machines: 7
No. 2, DuoFormer T, Yankee dryer, total capacity 50,000 mt/y, Trim width 5.04 m, Tissue
No. 3, crescent former, Yankee dryer, total capacity 55,000 mt/y, Trim width 5.27 m, Tissue
No. 4, Periformer, Yankee dryer, total capacity 60,000 mt/y, Trim width 5.27 m, Tissue
No. 5, DuoFormer T, Yankee dryer, total capacity 60,000 mt/y, Trim width 5.3 m, Tissue
No. 6, TAD, total capacity 65,000 mt/y, Trim width 5.34 m, Tissue
PM 6, fourdrinier, total capacity 30,000 mt/y, Trim width 3.08 m, Specialty and industrial
PM 9, fourdrinier, Yankee dryer, total capacity 30,000 mt/y, Trim width 3.2 m, Packaging papers
Finishing Equipment:
Rewinders: 7
Sheeters: 1
Energy Data:
Power boilers: 3
Steam turbines: 2 at 54 MW
Electrical demand for mill: 151 MWh/D

ⓜSCA Hygiene Products SE
Neuss Mill

Ownership: SCA - Svenska Cellulosa Aktiebolaget
Floßhafenstraße 16
D-41460 Neuss
Germany
Mailing Address: Postf. 10 15 62, D-41415 Neuss, Germany
Phone: (49) 2131 296 0
Fax: (49) 2131 296 104/111
Web Address: www.sca.com, www.tempo-web.de

Personnel:
Mill Mgr.: Bernd Bichbeimer
Phone: (49) 2131 296 0
Fax: (49) 2131 296-104
Email: bernd.bichbeimer@sca.com
Total Employees at this Location: 455
Type of Operation: Paper mill
Paper/Paperboard Grades and Capacities:
Total paper and paperboard capacity: 105,000 mt/y
Tissue: 105,000 mt/y
Paper and Paperboard Mill Data:
Stock Preparation:
Pulpers: 5
Refiners: 5
Paper Machines: 2
No. 1, crescent former, Yankee dryer, total capacity 50,000 mt/y, Trim width 5.17 m, Tissue
No. 2, twin-wire, Yankee dryer, total capacity 55,000 mt/y, Trim width 5.17 m, Tissue
Finishing Equipment:
Rewinders: 5
Energy Data:
Power boilers: 3
Electrical demand for mill: 280 MWh/D

ⓜSCA Hygiene Products GmbH
Witzenhausen Tissue Mill

Ownership: SCA - Svenska Cellulosa Aktiebolaget
Kasseler Landstrasse 21
D-37213 Witzenhausen
Germany

Mailing Address: P.O. Box 11 52, D-37201 Witzenhausen, Germany
  Phone: (49) 5542 509 0
  Fax: (49) 5542 509 200
  Web Address: www.sca.com
Personnel:
  Mill Mgr.: Dietmar Haschke
  Phone: (49) 5542 509 0
  Email: dietmar.haschke@sca.com
  Sls & Mktg Mgr & Develop. Mgr: Alexander Merkel
  Phone: (49) 621 778 2280
  Email: alexander.merkel@sca.com
Total Employees at this Location: 264
Type of Operation: Paper mill
Paper/Paperboard Grades and Capacities:
  Total paper and paperboard capacity: 30,000 mt/y
  Tissue: 30,000 mt/y
Paper and Paperboard Mill Data:
Paper Machines: 1
  No. 1, C-wrap, Yankee dryer, total capacity 30,000 mt/y, Trim width 2.73 m, Tissue
Energy Data:
  Electrical demand for mill: 81 MWh/D

ⒽⓂPapierfabrik Scheufelen GmbH & Co. KG
Lenningen Mill
Ownership: 100% by Paper Excellence Group
Adolf-Scheufelen-Str. 26
D-73252 Lenningen, Baden-Württemberg
Germany
Mailing Address: Postfach 11 04, D-73250 Lenningen, Germany
  Phone: (49) 7026 660
  Fax: (49) 7026 663 2701
  Email: service@scheufelen.com
  Web Address: www.scheufelen.com
Personnel:
  Man. Dir - CEO: Peter L. Bright
  Phone: (49) 7026 660
  Fax: (49) 7026 663 2701
  Man. Dir.: Peter H. Wardhana
  Phone: (49) 7026 660
  Fax: (49) 7026 663 2701
  Head of Finan. & Contrl.: Claus-Jürgen Zimmer
  Phone: (49) 7026 660
  Fax: (49) 7026 663 2701
  Email: claus.zimmer@scheufelen.de
  Head of Purch.: Jörg Schall
  Phone: (49) 7026 662 231
  Fax: (49) 7026 663 2701
  Email: joerg.schall@scheufelen.de
  Head of Prod.: Filip Sundholm
  Phone: (49) 7026 660
  Fax: (49) 7026 663 2701
  Email: filip.sundholm@scheufelen.de
  Head of Mktg. & Commun.: Irmgard Glanz
  Phone: (49) 7026 662 554
  Fax: (49) 7026 663 2701
  Email: irmgard.glanz@scheufelen.de
  Dir., CSO Sls. & Mktg.: Horst Lamparter
  Phone: (49) 7026 662 436
  Fax: (49) 7026 663 2701
  Email: horst.lamparter@scheufelen.de
  Head of HR.: Christine Schilling
  Phone: (49) 7026 662 358
  Fax: (49) 7026 663 2701
  Email: christine.schilling@scheufelen.de
Total Employees at this Location: 522
Type of Operation: Paper mill
Paper/Paperboard Grades and Capacities:
  Total paper and paperboard capacity: 300,000 mt/y
  Coated woodfree/freesheet: 300,000 mt/y
Paper and Paperboard Mill Data:
  Stock Preparation:
  Pulpers: 4
  Refiners: 8
Paper Machines: 2

  No. 5, DuoFormer D, total capacity 140,000 mt/y, Trim width 3.6 m, Coated woodfree/freesheet
  No. 6, DuoFormer F, total capacity 160,000 mt/y, Trim width 4 m, Coated woodfree/freesheet
Coating Machines: 5
  No. 1, off machine
  No. 2, off machine
  No. 3, off machine
  No. 4, off machine
  No. 5, off machine
Finishing Equipment:
  Supercalenders: 6
  Rewinders: 10
  Sheeters: 18
Energy Data:
  Power boilers: 4
  Steam turbines: 5 at 15 MW
  Hydro turbines: 1
  Electrical demand for mill: 558 MWh/D

ⓂPapierfabrik Schleipen
Bad Dürkheim Mill
Ownership: Cordier Spezialpapier GmbH
Kaiserslauterer Str. 405
D-67098 Bad Dürkheim
Germany
  Phone: (49) 6322 60080
  Fax: (49) 6322 61702
  Web Address: www.cordier-paper.de
Personnel:
  Paper Mill Mgr.: Markus Henkel
  Phone: (49) 6322 600851
  Fax: (49) 6322 939520
  Email: markus.henkel@cordier-paper.de
Total Employees at this Location: 85
Type of Operation: Paper mill
Paper/Paperboard Grades and Capacities:
  Total paper and paperboard capacity: 32,000 mt/y
  Uncoated woodfree/freesheet: 6,400 mt/y
  Uncoated mechanical/groundwood: 25,600 mt/y
Paper and Paperboard Mill Data:
  Stock Preparation:
  Pulpers: 4
  Refiners: 3
Paper Machines: 1
  No. 1, fourdrinier, total capacity 32,000 mt/y, Trim width 2.55 m, Uncoated mechanical/groundwood, Uncoated woodfree/freesheet
Finishing Equipment:
  Winders: 1
  Sheeters: 1
Energy Data:
  Power boilers: 2
  Steam turbines: 1 at 0.3 MW
  Electrical demand for mill: 70 MWh/D

ⒽⓂTechnocell Dekor GmbH & Co. KG
Osnabrück Mill
Ownership: Felix Schoeller Jr. GmbH & Co. KG
Burg Gretesch
D-49086 Osnabrück
Germany
Mailing Address: Postf. 36 67, D-49026 Osnabrück, Germany
  Phone: (49) 541 38 00 0
  Fax: (49) 541 38 00 425
  Email: technocell@felix-schoeller.com
  Web Address: www.technocell.com
Personnel:
  VP., PR Mgr.: Dr. Friederike Texter
  Phone: (49) 541 3800 453
  Fax: (49) 541 3800-121
  Email: ftexter@felix-schoeller.com
Total Employees of Company: 2,270
Total Employees at this Location: 600
Type of Operation: Paper mill
Mill Locations:
OAO Mayak Technocell, Penza Mill, Burnazhnikov Str., 1, 440007 Penza, Russia, Capacity: 92,000 mt/y, (Paper mill)
  Phone: (7) 8412 522353
  Fax: (7) 8412 590858
  Email: mayak@sura.ru
Felix Schoeller Jr. Foto & Spezialpapiere GmbH, Weissenborn Mill, Fabrikstr. 1, Berthelsdorf, D-09600 Weissenborn, Germany, Capacity: 105,000 mt/y, (Paper mill)
  Phone: (49) 3731 792-0
  Fax: (49) 3731 792 444
  Email: weissenborn@felix-schoeller.com; Digital_Imaging@Felix-Schoeller.com
Technocell Canada Inc., Drummondville Mill, 3075 rue Bernier, Drummondville, QC, Canada J2C 6Y4, Capacity: 30,000 mt/y, (Paper mill)
  Phone: (1) 819-475-0066
  Fax: (1) 819-475-2440
  Email: myTechnocell@felix-schoeller.com
Technocell Dekor GmbH & Co. KG, Günzach Mill, Nicolausstr. 10, D-87634 Günzach, Germany, Capacity: 59,000 mt/y, (Paper mill)
  Phone: (49) 8372 910 0
  Fax: (49) 8372 910 123
  Email: technocell@felix-schoeller.com
Technocell Dekor GmbH & Co. KG, Neustadt Mill, Donaueschinger Str. 18, D-79822 Titisee-Neustadt, Germany, Capacity: 27,000 mt/y, (Paper mill)
  Phone: (49) 7651 202 0
  Fax: (49) 7651 202 301/190
  Email: technocell@felix-schoeller.com
Technocell Dekor GmbH & Co. KG, Penig Mill, Flinschstrasse 7-11, D-09322 Penig, Germany, Capacity: 30,000 mt/y, (Paper mill)
  Phone: (49) 37381 88 0
  Fax: (49) 37381 802 96
  Email: technocell@felix-schoeller.com
Paper/Paperboard Grades and Capacities:
  Total paper and paperboard capacity: 107,500 mt/y
  Uncoated woodfree/freesheet: 14,600 mt/y
  Specialty and industrial: 92,900 mt/y
Paper and Paperboard Mill Data:
Paper Machines: 2
  No. 1, twin-wire, total capacity 73,000 mt/y, Trim width 4.75 m, Uncoated woodfree/freesheet, Specialty and industrial
  No. 15, fourdrinier, total capacity 34,500 mt/y, Trim width 2.9 m, Specialty and industrial
Energy Data:
  Electrical demand for mill: 210 MWh/D

ⓂFelix Schoeller Jr. Foto & Spezialpapiere GmbH
Weissenborn Mill
Ownership: 100% by Felix Schoeller Jr. GmbH & Co. KG
Fabrikstr. 1, Berthelsdorf
D-09600 Weissenborn
Germany
  Phone: (49) 3731 792-0
  Fax: (49) 3731 792 444
  Email: weissenborn@felix-schoeller.com, Digital_Imaging@Felix-Schoeller.com
  Web Address: www.felix-schoeller.com, www.Felix-Schoeller-DI.com
Personnel:
  Mill Mgr.: Volker Barth
  Phone: (49) 3731 792-0
  Fax: (49) 3731 792 444
  Email: vbarth@felix-schoeller.com
  Comm. Mgr.: Andrea Hoffmann
  Phone: (49) 541 3800 208
  Fax: (49) 541 3800 170
  Email: Digital_Imaging@Felix-Schoeller.com
Total Employees at this Location: 758
Type of Operation: Paper mill
Paper/Paperboard Grades and Capacities:
  Total paper and paperboard capacity: 105,000 mt/y
  Uncoated woodfree/freesheet: 105,000 mt/y
Paper and Paperboard Mill Data:
Paper Machines: 1

Germany

No. 4, DuoFormer D, total capacity 105,000 mt/y, Trim width 3.5 m, Uncoated woodfree/freesheet
Coating Machines: 4
No. 1
No. 2
No. 5, off machine
No. 6
Energy Data:
Power boilers: 1
Combustion turbines: 2 at 10.7 MW
Steam turbines: 1 at 3.2 MW
Electrical demand for mill: 202 MWh/D

⊕ⓜPapierfabrik Schoellershammer
Düren Mill
Ownership: 100% by Heinr. Aug. Schoeller Söhne GmbH & Co. KG
Kreuzauerstr. 18
D-52355 Düren
Germany
Mailing Address: Postfach 10 19 46, D-52319 Düren, Germany
Phone: (49) 2421 557 0
Fax: (49) 2421 557 110
Email: info@schoellershammer.de
Web Address: www.schoellershammer.de
Personnel:
Man. Partner: Dr. Detlef Rhodius
Phone: (49) 2421 557 112
Fax: (49) 2421 557 111
Email: iboltersdorf@schoellershammer.de
Man. Dir.: Alexander Stern
Phone: (49) 2421 557 122
Fax: (49) 2421 557 6122
Man. Dir. Eng., Production Packaging Paper: Armin Vetter
Phone: (49) 2421 557 112
Fax: (49) 2421 557 111
Email: iboltersdorf@schoellershammer.de
Man. Dir. Sales and Materials: Bernd Scholbrock
Phone: (49) 2421 557 121
Fax: (49) 2421 557 111
Sen. Sls. Mgr., Corr. Board Base Paper: Dirk van Meerbeck
Phone: (49) 2421 557 125
Fax: (49) 2421 557 6125
Email: dvanmeerbeek@schoellershammer.de
Sen. Sls. Mgr., Central Europe, Fine Papers: Rolf-Bernhard Schlee
Phone: (49) 2421 557 199
Fax: (49) 2421 557 6199
Email: rbschlee@schoellershammer.de
Sen. Sls. Mgr. Export, Fine Papers: Helmut Kessel
Phone: (49) 2421 557 137
Fax: (49) 2421 557 6137
Email: hkessel@schoellershammer.de
Prod. Mgr.: Konrad Franken
Phone: (49) 2421 557 112
Fax: (49) 2421 557 111
Total Employees of Company: 235
Type of Operation: Paper mill, Paperboard mill
Pulp Grades and Capacities:
Total pulp capacity: 230,818 mt/y
Recycled Pulping: 230,818 mt/y
Pulp Mill Data:
Recycled Fiber Treatment Lines:
Recycled packaging pulping lines
Paper/Paperboard Grades and Capacities:
Total paper and paperboard capacity: 240,000 mt/y
Uncoated woodfree/freesheet: 20,000 mt/y
Linerboard: 90,000 mt/y
Corrugating medium/fluting: 130,000 mt/y
Paper and Paperboard Mill Data:
Stock Preparation:
Pulpers: 3
Refiners: 9
Paper Machines: 3
No. 1, fourdrinier, total capacity 8,000 mt/y, Trim width 1.9 m, Uncoated woodfree/freesheet
No. 3, fourdrinier, total capacity 12,000 mt/y, Trim width 2.2 m, Uncoated woodfree/freesheet
No. 5, GapFormer, total capacity 220,000 mt/y, Trim width 5.5 m, Corrugating medium/fluting, Linerboard
Finishing Equipment:
Supercalenders: 1
Rewinders: 4
Sheeters: 2
Energy Data:
Power boilers: 4
Steam turbines: 2 at 8.0 MW
Electrical demand for mill: 319 MWh/D

⊕ⓜSchönfelder Papierfabrik GmbH
Annaberg-Buchholz Mill
Tannenberger Str. 4
D-09456 Annaberg-Buchholz
Germany
Phone: (49) 3733 56 38 0
Fax: (49) 3733 56 38 33
Email: kontakt@schoenfelder-papierfabrik.de
Web Address: www.schoenfelder-papierfabrik.de
Personnel:
Gen. Mgr.: Dipl.-Ing. Volker Cordier
Phone: (49) 3733 56 38 0
Gen. Mgr.: Dipl. Ing. Felix Cordier
Phone: (49) 3733 5638 0
Fax: (49) 3733 5638 99
Gen. Mgr. (Tech.): Holger Hampel
Phone: (49) 3733 56 38 0
ICT and Comm. Mngr.: Frank Liebig
Email: frank.liebig@schoenfelder-papierfabrik.de
Total Employees of Company: 85
Total Employees at this Location: 81
Type of Operation: Paper mill
Pulp Grades and Capacities:
Total pulp capacity: 48,191 mt/y
Recycled Pulping: 48,191 mt/y
Pulp Mill Data:
Bleach Plant Systems: 1
DIP
Recycled Fiber Treatment Lines:
Flotation deinking lines
Paper/Paperboard Grades and Capacities:
Total paper and paperboard capacity: 50,000 mt/y
Newsprint: 5,000 mt/y
Uncoated woodfree/freesheet: 25,000 mt/y
Uncoated mechanical/groundwood: 20,000 mt/y
Paper and Paperboard Mill Data:
Stock Preparation:
Pulpers: 1
Paper Machines: 1
No. 1, (Film Press), SymFormer MB, total capacity 50,000 mt/y, Trim width 3.24 m, Uncoated woodfree/freesheet, Newsprint, Uncoated mechanical/groundwood
Finishing Equipment:
Rewinders: 1
Energy Data:
Power boilers
Steam turbines
Electrical demand for mill: 124 MWh/D

⊕ⓜJulius Schulte Söhne GmbH & Co. KG
Düsseldorf Mill
Ownership: 100% by private owner
Fruchtstr. 28
D-40223 Düsseldorf
Germany
Mailing Address: Postf. 25 01 43, D-40093 Düsseldorf, Germany
Phone: (49) 211 310 83 0
Fax: (49) 211 310 83 55
Email: info@schulte-duesseldorf.de, sales@schulte-duesseldorf.de
Web Address: www.jssd.de, www.schulte-papier.de
Personnel:
Member Management Team Develop. & Technology: Dipl.-Ing. Georg Pingen
Phone: (49) 211 310 83 0
Fax: (49) 211 310 83 55
Email: gpingen@schulte-duesseldorf.de
Gen. Mgr.: Jörg Kober
Phone: (49) 211 310 83 0
Fax: (49) 211 310 83 55
Email: jkober@schulte-duesseldorf.de
Member management team / Sls.: Stefan Brüggen
Phone: (49) 211 310 83 16
Fax: (49) 211 310 83 55
Email: sbrueggen@schulte-duesseldorf.de
Total Employees at this Location: 105
Type of Operation: Paper mill
Mill Locations:
Julius Schulte Trebsen GmbH & Co. KG, Trebsen Mill, Pauschwitzer Str. 45, D-04687 Trebsen, Germany, Capacity: 170,000 mt/y, (Paper mill, Paperboard mill)
Phone: (49) 34383 970
Fax: (49) 34383 97237
Email: info@schulte-trebsen.de; Verkauf-Trebsen@Schulte-Trebsen.de
Pulp Grades and Capacities:
Total pulp capacity: 109,105 mt/y
Recycled Pulping: 109,105 mt/y
Pulp Mill Data:
Recycled Fiber Treatment Lines:
Pulpers: 1 at 70,000
Pulpers: 1 at 50,000
Paper/Paperboard Grades and Capacities:
Total paper and paperboard capacity: 105,000 mt/y
Packaging papers: 15,000 mt/y
Boxboard/cartonboard: 90,000 mt/y
Paper and Paperboard Mill Data:
Stock Preparation:
Pulpers: 2
Refiners: 2
Paper Machines: 2
No. 2, hybrid former, total capacity 45,000 mt/y, Trim width 2.2 m, Packaging papers, Boxboard/cartonboard
No. 3, hybrid former, total capacity 60,000 mt/y, Trim width 2.4 m, Packaging papers, Boxboard/cartonboard
Finishing Equipment:
Calenders: 2
Rewinders: 2 at 80,000 mt/y, 50,000 mt/y
Energy Data:
Power boilers: 2
Combustion turbines: 1 at 3.575 MW
Steam turbines: 1 at 1.925 MW
Electrical demand for mill: 133 MWh/D

ⓜJulius Schulte Trebsen GmbH & Co. KG
Trebsen Mill
Ownership: Julius Schulte Söhne GmbH & Co. KG
Pauschwitzer Str. 45
D-04687 Trebsen
Germany
Phone: (49) 34383 970
Fax: (49) 34383 97237
Email: info@schulte-trebsen.de, Verkauf-Trebsen@Schulte-Trebsen.de
Web Address: www.schulte-trebsen.de, www.schulte-papier.de
Personnel:
Gen. Mgr.: Matthias Gerstung
Phone: (49) 34383 970
Gen. Mgr.: Jörg Kober
Phone: (49) 34383 970
Sls. Mgr.: Martin Hild
Phone: (49) 34383 97 205
Fax: (49) 34383 97 226
Email: mhild@schulte-papier.de
Prod. Planning: Margit Schäfer
Phone: (49) 34383 97 214
Fax: (49) 34383 97 226
Email: mschaefer@schulte-papier.de
Total Employees at this Location: 90

Germany

Type of Operation: Paper mill, Paperboard mill
Pulp Grades and Capacities:
  Total pulp capacity: 171,891 mt/y
  Recycled Pulping: 171,891 mt/y
Pulp Mill Data:
  Recycled Fiber Treatment Lines:
  Pulpers: 1 at 100,000 admt/y
Paper/Paperboard Grades and Capacities:
  Total paper and paperboard capacity: 170,000 mt/y
  Linerboard: 110,000 mt/y
  Corrugating medium/fluting: 60,000 mt/y
Paper and Paperboard Mill Data:
  Stock Preparation:
  Pulpers: 1
  Refiners: 2
Paper Machines: 1
  No. 3, fourdrinier (2), total capacity 170,000 mt/y, Trim width 4.2 m, Linerboard, Corrugating medium/fluting
Finishing Equipment:
  Rewinders: 1
Energy Data:
  Power boilers: 3
  Electrical demand for mill: 246 MWh/D

ⓗSchumacher Packaging GmbH
Ownership: 100% by Björn Schumacher
Friesendorfer Str. 4
D-96237 Ebersdorf
Germany
Phone: (49) 9562 383-0
Fax: (49) 9562 383-299
Email: ebersdorf@schumacher-packaging.com
Web Address: www.schumacher-packaging.com
Personnel:
  Owner: Björn Schumacher
  Phone: (49) 9562 383-0
  Fax: (49) 9562 383-299
Total Employees of Company: 2,200
Mill Locations:
  Schumacher Packaging Zaklad Grudziadz Sp. z o.o., Grudziadz Mill, ul. Parkowa 56, PL-86300 Grudziadz, Poland, Capacity: 80,000 mt/y, (Paperboard mill)
    Phone: (48) 56 450 3810
    Fax: (48) 56 462 1376
    Email: grudziadz@schumacher-packaging.com
  Schumacher Packaging GmbH, Schwarzenberg Mill, Raschauer Weg 30, D-08340 Schwarzenberg, Germany, Capacity: 45,000 mt/y, (Paperboard mill)
    Phone: (49) 3774 171-0 / 15 80-0
    Fax: (49) 3774 86275 / 8 11 81
    Email: info@kartonagen-szb.de, schwarzenberg@schumacher-packaging.com

ⓜSchumacher Packaging GmbH
Schwarzenberg Mill
Raschauer Weg 30
D-08340 Schwarzenberg
Germany
Phone: (49) 3774 171-0 / 15 80-0
Fax: (49) 3774 86275 / 8 11 81
Email: info@kartonagen-szb.de, schwarzenberg@schumacher-packaging.com
Web Address: www.kartonagen-szb.de, www.schumacher-packaging.com
Personnel:
  Gen. Mgr.: Dipl. Ing. Christian Bleyl
  Phone: (49) 3774 171-0
  Gen. Mgr.: Hendrik Schumacher
  Phone: (49) 3774 171-0
  Gen. Mgr.: Björn Schumacher
  Phone: (49) 3774 171-0
  Sls. Mnr.: Christina Kühne
  Phone: (49) 3774 / 1 71-173
  Email: christina.kuehne@schumacher-packaging.com
  Sls. Dir.: Ronny Wuestling
  Phone: (49) 3774 171-0
  Email: ronny.wuestling@schumacher-packaging.com
Total Employees at this Location: 120
Type of Operation: Paperboard mill
Pulp Grades and Capacities:
  Total pulp capacity: 45,276 mt/y
  Recycled Pulping: 45,276 mt/y
Paper/Paperboard Grades and Capacities:
  Total paper and paperboard capacity: 45,000 mt/y
  Boxboard/cartonboard: 45,000 mt/y
Paper and Paperboard Mill Data:
Paper Machines: 1
  No. 1, cylinder (10), total capacity 45,000 mt/y, Trim width 2.1 m, Boxboard/cartonboard
Energy Data:
  Electrical demand for mill: 41 MWh/D

ⓗⓜFeinpappenwerk Gebr. Schuster GmbH & Co. KG
Dachau Mill
Krautgartenstrasse 36
D-85241 Hebertshausen, Dachau
Germany
Mailing Address: Postf. 12 20, D-85202 Hebertshausen, Dachau, Germany
Phone: (49) 8131 2940
Fax: (49) 8131 294 168/110
Email: info@schuster-karton.de
Web Address: www.fgs-heb.de, www.schuster-karton.de
Personnel:
  CEO: Claus Palm
  Phone: (49) 8131 2941 28
  Fax: (49) 8131 2941 10
  Email: claus.palm@schuster-karton.de
  Mill Mgr. (Head Tech. Unit): Martin Jung
  Phone: (49) 8131 2942 07
  Fax: (49) 8131 2942 41
  Email: martin.jung@schuster-karton.de
  Exec. Man. Assistant: Anja Neumayer
  Phone: (49) 8131 2941 28
  Fax: (49) 8131 2941 10
  Email: anja.neumayer@schuster-karton.de
  Unit Mgr. Sls.: Olav Schecker
  Phone: (49) 8131 2942 31
  Fax: (49) 8131 2136 3
  Email: olav.schecker@schuster-karton.de
  Purch. Mgr.: Christian Grössler
  Phone: (49) 8131 2942 56
  Fax: (49) 8131 2942 57
  Email: christian.groessler@schuster-karton.de
  HR. Mgr.: Sabine Kaes
  Phone: (49) 8131 2941 38
  Fax: (49) 8131 2941 95
  Email: sabine.kaes@schuster-karton.de
Total Employees at this Location: 120
Type of Operation: Paperboard mill
Pulp Grades and Capacities:
  Total pulp capacity: 48,807 mt/y
  Recycled Pulping: 48,807 mt/y
Pulp Mill Data:
  Recycled Fiber Treatment Lines:
  Pulpers: 1 at 52,400
Paper/Paperboard Grades and Capacities:
  Total paper and paperboard capacity: 48,000 mt/y
  Boxboard/cartonboard: 48,000 mt/y
Paper and Paperboard Mill Data:
  Stock Preparation:
  Pulpers: 1
  Refiners: 4
Paper Machines: 1
  No. 1, cylinder (9), total capacity 48,000 mt/y, Trim width 2.25 m, Boxboard/cartonboard
Finishing Equipment:
  Rewinders: 1
Energy Data:
  Power boilers: 2
  Electrical demand for mill: 57 MWh/D

ⓗⓜSchwarzwald Papierwerke AG
Titisee-Neustadt
Donaueschingerstr. 18
D-79822 Titisee-Neustadt
Germany
Phone: (49) 7842 801-0
Fax: (49) 7842 801-23
Email: info@lenk.de
Personnel:
  Man. Dir.: Dirk Schuldt
  Phone: (49) 7842 801-0
  Fax: (49) 7842 801-23
  Sls. Mgr.: J. Wender
  Phone: (49) 7842 801-14
  Fax: (49) 7842 801-86
  Email: jwender@lenk.de
  Man. Dir.: Sebastian Leser
  Phone: (49) 7842 801-0
  Fax: (49) 7842 801-23
Total Employees of Company: 35
Total Employees at this Location: 35
Type of Operation: Paper mill
Paper/Paperboard Grades and Capacities:
  Total paper and paperboard capacity: 25,000 mt/y
  Specialty and industrial: 25,000 mt/y
Paper and Paperboard Mill Data:
Paper Machines: 1
  PM 17, fourdrinier, total capacity 25,000 mt/y, Trim width 2.25 m, Specialty and industrial

ⓜSmurfit Kappa Baden Karton GmbH
Gernsbach Mill
Ownership: Smurfit Kappa Europe
Fabrikstrasse 1
D-76593 Gernsbach
Germany
Mailing Address: Postf. 14 34, D-76587 Gernsbach, Germany
Phone: (49) 7224 630
Fax: (49) 7224 631 48
Email: baden-karton@smurfitkappa.de
Web Address: www.smurfitkappa.de
Personnel:
  Plt. Mgr.: Lars Gerlach
  Phone: (49) 7224 63 231
  Fax: (49) 7224 631 48
  Email: lars.gerlach@smurfitkappa.de
  Contr.: Stefan Böll
  Phone: (49) 7224 632 09
  Fax: (49) 7224 631 48
  Email: stefan.boell@smurfitkappa.de
  Purch. Agent: Torsten Schlate
  Phone: (49) 7224 631 03
  Fax: (49) 7224 631 48
  Email: torsten.schlate@smurfitkappa.de
Total Employees at this Location: 166
Type of Operation: Paperboard mill
Pulp Grades and Capacities:
  Total pulp capacity: 126,944 mt/y
  Recycled Pulping: 126,944 mt/y
Pulp Mill Data:
  Recycled Fiber Treatment Lines:
  Pulpers: 4 at 150,000 admt/y
Paper/Paperboard Grades and Capacities:
  Total paper and paperboard capacity: 145,000 mt/y
  Boxboard/cartonboard: 145,000 mt/y
Paper and Paperboard Mill Data:
  Stock Preparation:
  Pulpers: 4
Paper Machines: 1
  No. 2, cylinder, total capacity 145,000 mt/y, Trim width 3.3 m, Boxboard/cartonboard
Coating Machines: 1
  PM 2, total capacity 145,000 mt/y., on machine
Finishing Equipment:
  Rewinders: 1
  Sheeters: 2
Energy Data:
  Power boilers: 1
  Combustion turbines: 1 at 4.6 MW
  Steam turbines: 1 at 6.4 MW
  Electrical demand for mill: 178 MWh/D

Germany

ⓜSmurfit Kappa Haupt Papier- und Pappenfabrik GmbH & Co. KG
Diemelstadt-Wrexen Mill
Ownership: Smurfit Kappa Europe
Orpethaler Str. 50
D-34474 Diemelstadt-Wrexen
Germany
 Phone: (49) 5642 790
 Fax: (49) 5642 79177
 Email: info@cdhaupt.de
 Web Address: www.smurfitkappa-cdhaupt.com
Personnel:
 Tech. Mgr.: Mark Kettmann
 Phone: (49) 5642 790
 Fax: (49) 5642 79177
 Email: mark.kettmann@smurfitkappa.de
 CFO: Antje Steinborn
 Phone: (49) 5642 790
 Fax: (49) 5642 79177
 Email: antje.steinborn@smurfitkappa.de
 Commer. Mgr.: Manfred Misselwitz
 Phone: (49) 5642 79 115
 Fax: (49) 5642 79 178
 Email: manfred.misselwitz@smurfitkappa.de
 Sls. Dir. Graphic Board: Gerwin Poschmann
 Phone: (49) 5642 79 160
 Fax: (49) 5642 79 254
 Email: gerwin.poschmann@smurfitkappa.de
Total Employees at this Location: 270
Type of Operation: Paper mill, Paperboard mill
Pulp Grades and Capacities:
 Total pulp capacity: 265,055 mt/y
 Recycled Pulping: 265,055 mt/y
Pulp Mill Data:
 Recycled Fiber Treatment Lines:
 Recycled packaging pulping lines
Paper/Paperboard Grades and Capacities:
 Total paper and paperboard capacity: 320,000 mt/y
 Linerboard: 230,000 mt/y
 Corrugating medium/fluting: 10,000 mt/y
 Boxboard/cartonboard: 80,000 mt/y
Paper and Paperboard Mill Data:
 Stock Preparation:
 Pulpers: 3
 Refiners: 2
Paper Machines: 2
 No. 2, fourdrinier, total capacity 80,000 mt/y, Trim width 2.3 m, Boxboard/cartonboard
 No. 3, fourdrinier, total capacity 240,000 mt/y, Trim width 4.9 m, Linerboard, Corrugating medium/fluting
Finishing Equipment:
 Rewinders: 3
 Sheeters: 2
Energy Data:
 Power boilers: 2
 Steam turbines: 1 at 9.87 MW
 Electrical demand for mill: 278 MWh/D

ⓗⓜSmurfit Kappa Herzberger Papierfabrik GmbH
Herzberg Mill
Ownership: Smurfit Kappa Europe
Andreasberger Str. 1
D-37412 Herzberg am Harz
Germany
Mailing Address: Postf. 11 69, D-37401 Herzberg am Harz, Germany
 Phone: (49) 5521 820
 Fax: (49) 5521 82395
 Email: info.hp@smurfitkappa.de
 Web Address: www.smurfitkappa.com, www.smurfitkappa.com/vHome/de/HerzbergPapier/Seiten/Default.aspx
Personnel:
 CFO Solid Board Packaging Germany: Holger Grotheer
 Phone: (49) 5521 820
 Fax: (49) 5521 82395
 Email: holger.grotheer@smurfitkappa.de
 Sls. Dir. Packaging Board: Peer Heinecke
 Phone: (49) 5521 82319
 Fax: (49) 5521 82395
 Email: peer.heinecke@smurfitkappa.de
 Sls. Dir. Converting: Rolf Bierwirth
 Phone: (49) 5521 82338
 Fax: (49) 5521 82395
 Email: rolf.bierwirth@smurfitkappa.de
Total Employees at this Location: 600
Type of Operation: Paperboard mill
Pulp Grades and Capacities:
 Total pulp capacity: 258,720 mt/y
 Recycled Pulping: 258,720 mt/y
Paper/Paperboard Grades and Capacities:
 Total paper and paperboard capacity: 260,000 mt/y
 Boxboard/cartonboard: 260,000 mt/y
Paper and Paperboard Mill Data:
Paper Machines: 2
 No. 1, combination, size press, total capacity 160,000 mt/y, Trim width 3.2 m, Boxboard/cartonboard
 No. 3, fourdrinier (2), total capacity 100,000 mt/y, Trim width 3.2 m, Boxboard/cartonboard
Energy Data:
 Power boilers: 1
 Combustion turbines: 1 at 9 MW
 Hydro turbines: 1
 Electrical demand for mill: 269 MWh/D

ⓜSmurfit Kappa Papier & Kartonfabrik Hoya
Hoya Mill
Ownership: Smurfit Kappa Europe
Von-dem-Bussche-Str. 1
D-27318 Hoya/Weser
Germany
Mailing Address: Postf. 11 54, D-27314 Hoya, Germany
 Phone: (49) 4251 8140
 Fax: (49) 4251 814 169
 Email: info.hoya@smurfitkappa.de
 Web Address: www.smurfitkappa-hoya.de
Personnel:
 Man. Dir.: Armin Buschmann
 Phone: (49) 4251 814 200
 Fax: (49) 4251 814 169
 Email: armin.buschmann@smurfitkappa.de
 Tech. & Maint. Mgr.: Pride Schmidt
 Phone: (49) 4251 814 0 Ext. 157
 Fax: (49) 4251 814 169
 Email: pride.schmidt@smurfitkappa.de
Total Employees at this Location: 390
Type of Operation: Paperboard mill
Pulp Grades and Capacities:
 Total pulp capacity: 411,326 mt/y
 Recycled Pulping: 411,326 mt/y
Pulp Mill Data:
 Recycled Fiber Treatment Lines:
 Pulpers: 5 at 300,000 admt/y
Paper/Paperboard Grades and Capacities:
 Total paper and paperboard capacity: 425,000 mt/y
 Linerboard: 136,000 mt/y
 Corrugating medium/fluting: 204,000 mt/y
 Boxboard/cartonboard: 85,000 mt/y
Paper and Paperboard Mill Data:
 Stock Preparation:
 Pulpers: 5
 Refiners:
Paper Machines: 2
 No. 2, fourdrinier (2), total capacity 340,000 mt/y, Trim width 7.5 m, Linerboard, Corrugating medium/fluting
 No. 4, cylinder (9), total capacity 85,000 mt/y, Trim width 2.3 m, Boxboard/cartonboard
Coating Machines: 1
 PM 4, total capacity 85,000 mt/y., on machine
Finishing Equipment:
 Winders: 2
 Sheeters: 3
Energy Data:
 Power boilers: 5
 Combustion turbines: 1 at 4.5 MW
 Steam turbines: 2 at 3.1, 3.8 MW
 Electrical demand for mill: 490 MWh/D

ⓜSmurfit Kappa GmbH Viersen Papier
Viersen Mill
Ownership: Smurfit Kappa Europe
Krefelder Str. 175
D-41748 Viersen
Germany
Mailing Address: Postf. 10 04 46, D-41704 Viersen, Germany
 Phone: (49) 2162 249 870
 Fax: (49) 2162 249 8733
 Email: info.viersen@smurfitkappa.de
 Web Address: www.smurfitkappa-viersen.com
Personnel:
 Mill Mgr.: Stefan Beck
 Phone: (49) 172 218 55 65
 Fax: (49) 2252 306 166
 Email: stefan.beck@smurfitkappa.de
 Prod. Mgr.: Jochen Theis
 Phone: (49) 2162 249 870
 Fax: (49) 2252 306 166
 Email: jochen.theis@smurfitkappa.de
 Contr.: Ralf Koenzgen
 Phone: (49) 2162 249 870
 Fax: (49) 2252 306 166
 Email: ralf.koenzgen@smurfitkappa.de
 Oper. Mgr.: Joachim Rall
 Phone: (49) 2162 249 870
 Fax: (49) 2252 306 166
 Email: joachim.rall@smurfitkappa.de
Total Employees at this Location: 60
Type of Operation: Paperboard mill
Pulp Grades and Capacities:
 Total pulp capacity: 69,624 mt/y
 Recycled Pulping: 69,624 mt/y
Paper/Paperboard Grades and Capacities:
 Total paper and paperboard capacity: 70,000 mt/y
 Linerboard: 20,000 mt/y
 Corrugating medium/fluting: 50,000 mt/y
Paper and Paperboard Mill Data:
 Stock Preparation:
 Pulpers: 1
Paper Machines: 1
 No. 1, fourdrinier, total capacity 70,000 mt/y, Trim width 2.3 m, Corrugating medium/fluting, Linerboard
Finishing Equipment:
 Winders: 1
Energy Data:
 Power boilers: 4
 Electrical demand for mill: 65 MWh/D

ⓗⓜSmurfit Kappa Zülpich Papier GmbH
Zülpich Mill
Ownership: Smurfit Kappa Europe
Bessenicher Weg
D-53909 Zülpich
Germany
Mailing Address: Postf. 13 53, D-53905 Zülpich, Germany
 Phone: (49) 2252 3060/306120
 Fax: (49) 2252 306 166
 Email: info.skzp@smurfitkappa.de, info.kzp@kappapackaging.com
 Web Address: www.kappa-containerboard.com, www.smurfitkappa-zuelpich.com
Personnel:
 Man. Dir./Paper Mill Mgr.: Dr. Peter Kramp
 Phone: (49) 2252 306 0
 Fax: (49) 2252 306 166
 Email: peter.kramp@smurfitkappa.de
 Tech. Mgr.: Rolf Thelen
 Phone: (49) 2252 306 0
 Fax: (49) 2252 306 166
 Email: rolf.thelen@smurfitkappa.de
 Purch. Mgr.: Ralf Bädorf

Pulp and Paper Mills - Europe

Germany

Phone: (49) 2252 306 116
Fax: (49) 2252 306 166
Email: ralf.baedorf@smurfitkappa.de
Qlty. & Environ., Safety & Health Mgr.: Dr. Josef Herberz
Phone: (49) 2252 306 170
Fax: (49) 2252 306 210
Email: josef.herberz@smurfitkappa.de
Finan. & Admin. Mgr.: Herbert Weber
Phone: (49) 2252 306 0
Fax: (49) 2252 306 166
Email: herbert.weber@smurfitkappa.de
Total Employees at this Location: 202
Type of Operation: Paperboard mill
Pulp Grades and Capacities:
  Total pulp capacity: 450,737 mt/y
  Recycled Pulping: 450,737 mt/y
Pulp Mill Data:
  Recycled Fiber Treatment Lines:
  Recycled packaging pulping lines: 1 at 440,000 admt/y
Paper/Paperboard Grades and Capacities:
  Total paper and paperboard capacity: 450,000 mt/y
  Linerboard: 200,000 mt/y
  Corrugating medium/fluting: 250,000 mt/y
Paper and Paperboard Mill Data:
Paper Machines: 2
  No. 4, fourdrinier, total capacity 150,000 mt/y, Trim width 4.9 m, Corrugating medium/fluting
  No. 6, DuoFormer CFD, total capacity 300,000 mt/y, Trim width 5 m, Corrugating medium/fluting, Linerboard
Finishing Equipment:
  Winders: 2
Energy Data:
  Power boilers: 1
  Combustion turbines: 3
  Steam turbines: 1 at 17 MW
  Electrical demand for mill: 527 MWh/D

⑪Sprick GmbH Bielefelder Papier- und Wellpappenwerke & Co.
Ownership: 100% by family
Hanfstr. 23
D-33607 Bielefeld
Germany
Mailing Address: Postf. 10 26 29, Bielefeld, Germany
  Phone: (49) 521 932050
  Fax: (49) 521 9320511
  Email: info@papier-sprick.de
  Web Address: www.papier-sprick.de
Personnel:
  Owner & Gen. Mgr.: Dr. Stephan Sprick-Schütte
  Phone: (49) 521 932050
  Fax: (49) 521 9320510
  Owner & Gen. Mgr.: Andreas Sprick-Schütte
  Phone: (49) 521 932050
  Fax: (49) 521 9320510
  Owner: Peter Sprick-Schütte
  Phone: (49) 521 932050
  Fax: (49) 521 9320510
  Gen. Dir.: Norbert Drauschke
  Phone: (49) 521 932050
  Fax: (49) 521 9320510
  Email: n.drauschke@papier-sprick.de
  Regional Sales Dir.: Thomas Halt
  Phone: (49) 521-9320542
  Email: t.halt@papier-sprick.de
  Sales Director – Bielefeld: Christian Drauschke
  Phone: (49) 521-93 205 17
  Email: c.drauschke@papier-sprick.de
  Prod. Mgr.: Oliver Schmidt
  Phone: (49) 176-10123369
  Email: o.schmidt@papier-sprick.de
Total Employees of Company: 160
Total Employees at this Location: 20
Mill Locations:
  Sprick GmbH & Co., Mitte Mill, Orpethaler Str. 26, D-34474 Diemelstadt, Germany, Capacity: 70,000 mt/y, (Paperboard mill)
  Phone: (49) 5642 98010

Fax: (49) 5642 980110
Email: info@papier-sprick.de

⑪Ⓜ Sprick GmbH & Co.
Mitte Mill
Ownership: Sprick GmbH Bielefelder Papier- und Wellpappenwerke & Co.
Orpethaler Str. 26
D-34474 Diemelstadt
Germany
Mailing Address: Postf. 11 67, D-34472 Diemelstadt, Germany
  Phone: (49) 5642 98010
  Fax: (49) 5642 980110
  Email: info@papier-sprick.de
  Web Address: www.papier-sprick.de
Personnel:
  Mill Mgr.: Dipl.-Ing. Andreas Sprick-Schütte
  Phone: (49) 5642 98010
  Sls. Dir.: Manfred Thill
  Phone: (49) 5642 98010
  Email: m.thill@papier-sprick.de
Total Employees at this Location: 110
Type of Operation: Paperboard mill
Pulp Grades and Capacities:
  Total pulp capacity: 71,659 mt/y
  Recycled Pulping: 71,659 mt/y
Pulp Mill Data:
  Recycled Fiber Treatment Lines:
  Recycled packaging pulping lines: 1
Paper/Paperboard Grades and Capacities:
  Total paper and paperboard capacity: 70,000 mt/y
  Packaging papers: 35,000 mt/y
  Linerboard: 20,000 mt/y
  Corrugating medium/fluting: 15,000 mt/y
Paper and Paperboard Mill Data:
Paper Machines: 1
  No. 1, fourdrinier, total capacity 70,000 mt/y, Trim width 2.5 m, Packaging papers, Corrugating medium/fluting, Linerboard
Energy Data:
  Power boilers: 2
  Electrical demand for mill: 101 MWh/D

⑪Ⓜ Steinbeis Papier Glückstadt GmbH & Co. KG
Glückstadt Mill
Stadtstr. 20
D-25348 Glückstadt
Germany
Mailing Address: Postf. 12 20, D-25343 Glückstadt, Germany
  Phone: (49) 4124 911 0
  Fax: (49) 4124 911 210/201
  Email: info@stp.de
  Web Address: www.stp.de
Personnel:
  CEO: Michael Söffge
  Phone: (49) 4124 911 01
  Fax: (49) 4124 911 210
  Email: michael.soffge@stp.de
  Head, Supply Chain Management: Hans-Gerd Lachmann
  Phone: (49) 4124 911 0
  Fax: (49) 4124 911 210
  Email: hans-ger.lachmann@stp.de
  Head, Mktg. & Sls.: Torsten Froh
  Phone: (49) 4124 911 0
  Fax: (49) 4124 911 210
  Email: torsten.froh@stp.de
  Head, Finan., Accounting & Contrl.: Jörg Warnke
  Phone: (49) 4124 911 0
  Fax: (49) 4124 911 210
  Email: jorg.warnke@stp.de
  Head, R & D: Dr. Volker Gehr
  Phone: (49) 4124 911 0
  Fax: (49) 4124 911 210
  Email: volker.gehr@stp.de
  Head, Prod.: Dr. Michael Hunold

Phone: (49) 4124 911 0
Fax: (49) 4124 911 210
Email: michael.hunold@stp.de
Head, Plt. Eng.: Werner Reinhold
Phone: (49) 4124 911 0
Fax: (49) 4124 911 210
Email: werner.reinhold@stp.de
Head, HR & Gen. Admin.: Hans-Rüdiger Bruchmann
Phone: (49) 4124 911 366
Fax: (49) 4124 911 204
Email: h-r.bruchmann@stp.de
HR Mgr.: Ann-Kathrin Stoldt
Phone: (49) 4124 911 238
Fax: (49) 4124 911 204
Email: ann-kathrin.stoldt@stp.de
Div. Mgr. Office Paper: Benjamin Hoeckendorf
Phone: (49) 4124 911 290
Fax: (49) 4124 911 623
Email: Benjamin.Hoeckendorf@stp.de
Total Employees of Company: 329
Total Employees at this Location: 329
Type of Operation: Paper mill
Pulp Grades and Capacities:
  Total pulp capacity: 216,495 mt/y
  Recycled Pulping: 216,495 mt/y
Pulp Mill Data:
  Bleach Plant Systems: 1
  DIP
  Recycled Fiber Treatment Lines:
  Flotation deinking lines at 265,000
Paper/Paperboard Grades and Capacities:
  Total paper and paperboard capacity: 275,000 mt/y
  Uncoated woodfree/freesheet: 110,000 mt/y
  Coated mechanical/groundwood: 165,000 mt/y
Paper and Paperboard Mill Data:
  Stock Preparation:
  Pulpers: 4
Paper Machines: 2
  No. 4, fourdrinier, total capacity 165,000 mt/y, Trim width 4.6 m, Uncoated woodfree/freesheet, Coated mechanical/groundwood
  No. 6, DuoFormer H, total capacity 110,000 mt/y, Trim width 3.7 m, Coated mechanical/groundwood
Coating Machines: 2
  PM 4, total capacity 56,000 mt/y., on machine
  PM 6, total capacity 110,000 mt/y., on machine
Finishing Equipment:
  Rewinders: 2 at 250,000 mt/y
  Sheeters: 2 at 110,000 mt/y
Energy Data:
  Power boilers: 5
  Steam turbines: 3 at 33 MW
  Electrical demand for mill: 647 MWh/D

Ⓜ Zellstoff Stendal GmbH
Stendal Mill
Ownership: 74.90% by Mercer International Inc., 25.10% by E&Z Industrie-Lösungen GmbH
Goldbecker Strasse 1
D-39596 Arneburg, Saxony-Anhalt
Germany
  Phone: (49) 39321 55 0
  Fax: (49) 39321 55108
  Email: info@zellstoff-stendal.de, bewerbung@zellstoff-stendal.de
  Web Address: www.zellstoff-stendal.de
Personnel:
  Man. Dir.: Dr. Niklaus Grünenfelder
  Phone: (49) 39321 55 0
  Fax: (49) 39321 551 08
  Mill Mgr.: Thomas Sjögren
  Phone: (49) 39321 55 0
  Fax: (49) 39321 551 08
  Mktg. Mgr.: Sabine Schrader
  Phone: (49) 39321 55472, 176 163 03 280
  Fax: (49) 39321 55129
  Email: sabine.schrader@zellstoff--stendal.de
  HR Mngr.: Peter Heinemann
  Phone: (49) 39321 554 28

Germany

Fax: (49) 39321 551 08
Email: peter.heinemann@zellstoff-stendal.de
Total Employees at this Location: 595
Type of Operation: Pulp mill
Pulp Grades and Capacities:
Total pulp capacity: 646,034 mt/y
Pulp available for market: 645,000 mt/y
Chemical Pulp: 646,034 mt/y
Pulp Mill Data:
Chemical Pulping Systems:
Batch digesters: 10
Pulp Lines: 1
Bleach Plant Systems: 1
No. 1, Type: ECF, Sequence: O_2 (OP)-D/Q-(PO), Capacity 645,000 admt/y
No. 2, Type: TCF, Sequence: O_2 QOPPAA/QPO
Chemical Recovery Equipment:
Evaporator lines: 1
Recovery boilers: 1
Lime Kiln
Pulp Dryers:
Air Float dryers 1
Energy Data:
Power boilers: 2
Steam turbines: 1 at 100 MW
Electrical demand for mill: 1,273 MWh/D

ⓂStora Enso Printing and Reading
Uetersen Mill

Mill is for sale (Stora Enso will evaluate its options, which may include divestment or restructuring of the Uetersen Mill.)
Ownership: 100% by Stora Enso Oyj
Pinnau-Allee 3
D-25436 Uetersen
Germany
Mailing Address: Postf. 11 44, D-25429 Uetersen, Germany
Phone: (49) 4122 7190
Fax: (49) 4122 719 339/222
Email: corporate.communications@storaenso.com, empfang-poststelle.uetersen.ext@storaenso.com
Web Address: www.storaenso.com
Personnel:
VP., Speciality Papers: Eckhard Kallies
Phone: (49) 4122 719 680
Fax: (49) 4122 719 697
Man. Dir.: Mr. Thomas Rajcsanyi
Phone: (49) 4122 7190
Fax: (49) 4122 719 339
Email: thomas.rajcsanyi@storaenso.com
Sec.: Ulrike Johns
Phone: (49) 4122 7190
Fax: (49) 4122 719 339
Email: ulrike.johns@storaenso.com
Total Employees at this Location: 416
Type of Operation: Paper mill
Paper/Paperboard Grades and Capacities:
Total paper and paperboard capacity: 230,000 mt/y
Coated woodfree/freesheet: 165,000 mt/y
Specialty and industrial: 50,000 mt/y
Linerboard: 5,000 mt/y
Boxboard/cartonboard: 10,000 mt/y
Paper and Paperboard Mill Data:
Paper Machines: 2
No. 1, fourdrinier, total capacity 50,000 mt/y, Trim width 2.85 m, Specialty and industrial
No. 2, DuoFormer D, total capacity 180,000 mt/y, Trim width 3.75 m, Coated woodfree/freesheet, Boxboard/cartonboard, Linerboard
Coating Machines: 1
No. 2, off machine
Finishing Equipment:
Winders: 3
Sheeters: 7 at 250,000 mt/y
Energy Data:
Power boilers: 2
Steam turbines: 1 at 6 MW
Electrical demand for mill: 435 MWh/D

ⓂStora Enso Printing and Reading
Kabel Mill

Ownership: 100% by Stora Enso Oyj
Schwerter Str. 263
D-58099 Hagen
Germany
Mailing Address: Postf. 26 29, D-58026 Hagen, Germany
Phone: (49) 2331 699 0
Fax: (49) 2331 699 516
Email: storaensokabel@storaenso.com
Web Address: www.storaenso.com
Personnel:
Mill Mgr.: Christian Schürmann
Phone: (49) 2331 699 0
Email: christian.schuermann@storaenso.com
Mktg. Mgr.: Mareike Weber
Phone: (49) 2331 699 219
Fax: (49) 233 699 874
Email: mareike.weber@storaenso.com
Total Employees at this Location: 595
Type of Operation: Paper mill
Pulp Grades and Capacities:
Total pulp capacity: 165,884 mt/y
Mechanical Pulp: 165,884 mt/y
Pulp Mill Data:
Mechanical Pulping Systems:
Conventional grinders: 11
Pulp Lines: 2
Bleach Plant Systems: 2
SGW, Sequence: P/Y, Capacity 200,000 admt/y
Paper/Paperboard Grades and Capacities:
Total paper and paperboard capacity: 495,000 mt/y
Coated mechanical/groundwood: 495,000 mt/y
Paper and Paperboard Mill Data:
Stock Preparation:
Pulpers: 4
Refiners: 12
Paper Machines: 2
No. 4, SpeedFormer HHS, total capacity 200,000 mt/y, Trim width 7.2 m, Coated mechanical/groundwood
No. 5, SpeedFormer HHS, total capacity 295,000 mt/y, Trim width 7.2 m, Coated mechanical/groundwood
Coating Machines: 2
No. 4, total capacity 200,000 mt/y., off machine
No. 5, total capacity 295,000 mt/y., off machine
Finishing Equipment:
Calenders
Supercalenders: 6
Rewinders: 8
Sheeters: 4
Energy Data:
Power boilers: 3
Steam turbines: 1 at 7 MW
Electrical demand for mill: 1,680 MWh/D

ⒽⓂStora Enso Printing and Reading
Maxau Mill

Ownership: 100% by Stora Enso Oyj
Mitscherlichstrasse
D-76187 Karlsruhe
Germany
Phone: (49) 721 9566 0
Fax: (49) 721 9566 130
Email: corporate.communications@storaenso.com, (firstname.lastname@storaenso.com)
Web Address: www.storaenso.com
Personnel:
Man. Dir.: Joachim Grünewald
Phone: (49) 721 9566 0
Fax: (49) 721 9566 130
Email: joachim.grunewald@storaenso.com
Environ. Mgr.: Ingrid Ebert
Phone: (49) 721 9566 306
Fax: (49) 721 9566 130
Email: ingrid.ebert@storaenso.com
Total Employees at this Location: 604
Type of Operation: Paper mill
Mill Locations:

Stora Enso Printing and Reading, Nymölla Mill, SE-295 80 Nymölla, Sweden, Capacity: 500,000 mt/y, (Pulp mill, Paper mill)
Phone: (46) 1046 440 00
Fax: (46) 1046 446 00
Stora Enso Printing and Reading, Oulu Mill, PO Box 196, FI-90101 Oulu, Finland, Capacity: 1,085,000 mt/y, (Pulp mill, Paper mill)
Phone: (358) 2046 124
Fax: (358) 2046 336 49
Email: (firstname.lastname@storaenso.com)
Stora Enso Printing and Reading, Uetersen Mill, Pinnau-Allee 3, D-25436 Uetersen, Germany, Capacity: 230,000 mt/y, (Paper mill)
Phone: (49) 4122 7190
Fax: (49) 4122 719 339/222
Email: corporate.communications@storaenso.com; empfang-poststelle.uetersen.ext@storaenso.com
Stora Enso Printing and Reading, Varkaus Mill, PO Box 260, FI-78201 Varkaus, Finland, Capacity: 285,000 mt/y, (Pulp mill, Paper mill)
Phone: (358) 2046 120
Fax: (358) 2046 321 02
Stora Enso Printing and Reading, Veitsiluoto Mill, FI-94800 Kemi, Finland, Capacity: 830,000 mt/y, (Pulp mill, Paper mill)
Phone: (358) 2046 125
Fax: (358) 2046 34427 (Fine Paper), 34907 (Publication Paper)
Email: (firstname.lastname@storaenso.com)
Stora Enso Printing and Reading, Langerbrugge Mill, Wondelgemkaai 200, B-9000 Gent, Belgium, Capacity: 555,000 mt/y, (Pulp mill, Paper mill)
Phone: (32) 9 2577211
Fax: (32) 9 2577200
Email: langerbrugge.mill@storaenso.com, (firstname.lastname@storaenso.com)
Stora Enso Printing and Reading, Hylte Mill, SE-314 81 Hyltebruk, Sweden, Capacity: 485,000 mt/y, (Pulp mill, Paper mill)
Phone: (46) 1046 190 00
Fax: (46) 1046 188 76
Stora Enso Printing and Reading, Anjala Mill, FI-46900 Kouvola, Finland, Capacity: 435,000 mt/y, (Pulp mill, Paper mill)
Phone: (358) 2046 117
Fax: (358) 2046 263 00
Email: (firstname.lastname@storaenso.com)
Stora Enso Printing and Reading, Corbehem Mill, Rue de Brébières, BP 2, F-62112 Corbehem, France, (Pulp mill, Paper mill)
Phone: (33) 3 27 92 32 00
Fax: (33) 3 27 97 99 60/92 33 31
Email: (firstname.lastname@storaenso.com)
Stora Enso Printing and Reading, Kabel Mill, Schwerter Str. 263, D-58099 Hagen, Germany, Capacity: 495,000 mt/y, (Paper mill)
Phone: (49) 2331 699 0
Fax: (49) 2331 699 516
Email: storaensokabel@storaenso.com
Stora Enso Printing and Reading, Kvarnsveden Mill, SE-781 83 Borlänge, Sweden, Capacity: 750,000 mt/y, (Pulp mill, Paper mill)
Phone: (46) 1046 650 00
Fax: (46) 1046 653 90
Stora Enso Printing and Reading, Sachsen Mill, Am Schanzberg 1, D-04838 Eilenburg, Germany, Capacity: 320,000 mt/y, (Pulp mill, Paper mill)
Phone: (49) 3423 650 0
Fax: (49) 3423 650 396/390
Email: sachsen.feedback@storaenso.com, (firstname.lastname@storaenso.com)
Pulp Grades and Capacities:
Total pulp capacity: 413,552 mt/y
Mechanical Pulp: 117,212 mt/y
Recycled Pulping: 296,341 mt/y
Pulp Mill Data:
Mechanical Pulping Systems:
Conventional grinders
Pressurized grinders
TMP systems

Germany

Bleach Plant Systems: 3
DIP, Sequence: P
SGW, Sequence: P/Y
TMP, Sequence: P/Y
Recycled Fiber Treatment Lines:
Flotation deinking lines: 3 at 300,000 admt/y
Paper/Paperboard Grades and Capacities:
Total paper and paperboard capacity: 530,000 mt/y
Uncoated mechanical/groundwood: 530,000 mt/y
Paper and Paperboard Mill Data:
Stock Preparation:
Pulpers: 2
Refiners: 4
Paper Machines: 2
No. 6, DuoFormer TQv, total capacity 270,000 mt/y, Trim width 7.2 m, Uncoated mechanical/groundwood
No. 8, SpeedFormer HS, total capacity 260,000 mt/y, Trim width 7.2 m, Uncoated mechanical/groundwood
Finishing Equipment:
Supercalenders: 3
Rewinders: 8
Energy Data:
Power boilers: 4
TMP Reboiler: 1
Steam turbines: 4 at 57, 41 MW
Electrical demand for mill: 1,816 MWh/D

ⓂStora Enso Printing and Reading
Sachsen Mill
Ownership: 100% by Stora Enso Oyj
Am Schanzberg 1
D-04838 Eilenburg, Saxony
Germany
Mailing Address: Postf. 1334, D-04833 Eilenburg, Germany
Phone: (49) 3423 650 0
Fax: (49) 3423 650 396/390
Email: sachsen.feedback@storaenso.com, (firstname.lastname@storaenso.com)
Web Address: www.storaenso.com/sachsen/de
Personnel:
Mill Mgr.: Dr. Ulrich Höke
Phone: (49) 3423 650331
Fax: (49) 3423 650200
Email: ulrich.hoeke@storaenso.com
Total Employees at this Location: 302
Type of Operation: Pulp mill, Paper mill
Pulp Grades and Capacities:
Total pulp capacity: 401,732 mt/y
Pulp available for market: 70,000 mt/y
Recycled Pulping: 401,732 mt/y
Pulp Mill Data:
Bleach Plant Systems: 1
Recycled Fiber Treatment Lines:
Flotation deinking lines: 2 at 430,000 admt/y
Pulp Dryers:
Air Float dryers 1, Twin Wire 1
Paper/Paperboard Grades and Capacities:
Total paper and paperboard capacity: 320,000 mt/y
Newsprint: 304,000 mt/y
Uncoated mechanical/groundwood: 16,000 mt/y
Paper and Paperboard Mill Data:
Paper Machines: 1
No. 1, OptiFormer, total capacity 320,000 mt/y, Trim width 9.2 m, Newsprint, Uncoated mechanical/groundwood
Finishing Equipment:
Rewinders: 2
Energy Data:
Power boilers: 2
Combustion turbines: 1 at 32 MW
Steam turbines: 1 at 17 MW
Electrical demand for mill: 902 MWh/D

ⓄⓂPapierwerk Sundern GmbH
Sundern Mill
Hauptstrasse 20
D-59846 Sundern
Germany
Mailing Address: Postf. 13 53, D-59833 Sundern, Germany
Phone: (49) 2933 984 0
Fax: (49) 2933 984 472
Email: info@papierwerk-sundern.de
Web Address: papierwerk-sundern.de
Personnel:
Man. Dir.: Andreas Ramthun
Phone: (49) 2933 984 0
Man. Dir.: Frank Röhling
Phone: (49) 2933 984 0
Email: r.rohling@papierwerk-sundern.de
Export Mgr.: Bernard Hansknecht
Phone: (49) 2933 984 0
Total Employees at this Location: 50
Type of Operation: Paper mill
Pulp Grades and Capacities:
Total pulp capacity: 13,334 mt/y
Recycled Pulping: 13,334 mt/y
Pulp Mill Data:
Recycled Fiber Treatment Lines:
Recycled packaging pulping lines: 1 at 13,000
Paper/Paperboard Grades and Capacities:
Total paper and paperboard capacity: 22,000 mt/y
Tissue: 22,000 mt/y
Paper and Paperboard Mill Data:
Stock Preparation:
Pulpers: 2
Refiners: 3
Paper Machines: 2
No. 3, Yankee dryer, total capacity 12,000 mt/y, Trim width 2.5 m, Tissue
No. 4, Yankee dryer, total capacity 10,000 mt/y, Trim width 2.5 m, Tissue
Finishing Equipment:
Rewinders: 3
Sheeters: 3
Energy Data:
Power boilers: 2
Electrical demand for mill: 74 MWh/D

ⓂTechnocell Dekor GmbH & Co. KG
Günzach Mill
Ownership: Felix Schoeller Jr. GmbH & Co. KG
Nicolausstr. 10
D-87634 Günzach
Germany
Phone: (49) 8372 910 0
Fax: (49) 8372 910 123
Email: technocell@felix-schoeller.com
Web Address: www.technocell.com
Total Employees at this Location: 250
Type of Operation: Paper mill
Paper/Paperboard Grades and Capacities:
Total paper and paperboard capacity: 59,000 mt/y
Specialty and industrial: 59,000 mt/y
Paper and Paperboard Mill Data:
Paper Machines: 3
PM 11, fourdrinier, Trim width 2.28 m
PM 12, fourdrinier, Trim width 2.28 m, Specialty and industrial
PM 14, fourdrinier, Trim width 2.26 m

ⓂTechnocell Dekor GmbH & Co. KG
Neustadt Mill
Ownership: Felix Schoeller Jr. GmbH & Co. KG
Donaueschinger Str. 18
D-79822 Titisee-Neustadt
Germany
Mailing Address: Postf. 11 20, D-79811 Titisee-Neustadt, Germany
Phone: (49) 7651 202 0
Fax: (49) 7651 202 301/190
Email: technocell@felix-schoeller.com
Web Address: www.technocell.com
Personnel:
Mill Mgr.: Jens Lategahn
Phone: (49) 541 3800459
Fax: (49) 541 3800588
Email: jlategahn@felix-schoeller.com
Total Employees at this Location: 154
Type of Operation: Paper mill
Paper/Paperboard Grades and Capacities:
Total paper and paperboard capacity: 27,000 mt/y
Specialty and industrial: 27,000 mt/y
Paper and Paperboard Mill Data:
Paper Machines: 1
PM 18, total capacity 27,000 mt/y, Trim width 3.25 m, Specialty and industrial

ⓂTechnocell Dekor GmbH & Co. KG
Penig Mill
Ownership: Felix Schoeller Jr. GmbH & Co. KG
Flinschstrasse 7-11
D-09322 Penig
Germany
Phone: (49) 37381 88 0
Fax: (49) 37381 802 96
Email: technocell@felix-schoeller.com
Web Address: www.technocell.com
Total Employees at this Location: 100
Type of Operation: Paper mill
Paper/Paperboard Grades and Capacities:
Total paper and paperboard capacity: 30,000 mt/y
Specialty and industrial: 30,000 mt/y
Paper and Paperboard Mill Data:
Paper Machines: 1
PM 16, fourdrinier, total capacity 30,000 mt/y, Trim width 2.6 m, Specialty and industrial

ⓄⓂTexon Möckmühl GmbH
Möckmühl Mill
Roigheimer Str. 69-72
D-74219 Möckmühl
Germany
Mailing Address: Postf. 12 05, D-74216 Möckmühl, Germany
Phone: (49) 6298 209-0
Fax: (49) 6298 209 122
Email: sales.texon.de@texon.com
Web Address: www.texon.com
Personnel:
Gen. Mngr./ Mill & Purch. Mngr.: Helmut Lenz
Gen. Mngr.: Neil Fleming
Marketing Mngr.: Manfred Höreth
Prod. Mgr.: M. Schmelzer
Phone: (49) 6298 209168
Sales Mngr.: Jörg Gaberdann
Sales Mngr.: Dieter Hernd
Total Employees of Company: 87
Total Employees at this Location: 87
Type of Operation: Paper mill
Paper/Paperboard Grades and Capacities:
Total paper and paperboard capacity: 15,000 mt/y
Specialty and industrial: 15,000 mt/y
Paper and Paperboard Mill Data:
Paper Machines: 2
PM 1, Trim width 1.5 m, Specialty and industrial
PM 2, Trim width 3 m, Specialty and industrial

ⓂThüringer Hygiene Papier GmbH
Thüringer Mill
Ownership: 100% by Sofidel Group
OT Wernshausen, Unterm Bahnhof 10
D-98574 Schmalkalden
Germany
Phone: (49) 36848 385 0
Fax: (49) 36848 385 410
Email: info@werrapapier.de
Web Address: www.sofidel.it, www.werrapapier.de
Personnel:
Gen. Mgr.: Mr. Bertolotti
Phone: (49) 36848 385 0
Exec. Dir.: Emi Stefani

Germany

Total Employees at this Location: 120
Type of Operation: Paper mill
Paper/Paperboard Grades and Capacities:
  Total paper and paperboard capacity: 34,000 mt/y
  Tissue: 34,000 mt/y
Paper and Paperboard Mill Data:
Paper Machines: 1
No. 2, crescent former, Yankee dryer, total capacity 34,000 mt/y, Trim width 2.75 m, Tissue
Energy Data:
Power boilers: 1
Electrical demand for mill: 84 MWh/D

ⓂFa. Katharina Tillmann Papier- und Wellpappenfabrik e.K.
Ownership: 100% by Katharina Tillmann
Im Karweg 14
D-59846 Sundem-Stockum
Germany
  Phone: (49) 2933 2038/9716-0
  Fax: (49) 2933 6871/9716-66
  Email: info@tillmann-wellpappe.de
  Web Address: www.tillmann-wellpappe.de
Personnel:
  Pres/Owner: Mrs. Tillmann
  Phone: (49) 2933 2038/9716-0
  Fax: (49) 2933 6871/971666
  Mill Mgr.: Matthias Ostrop
  Phone: (49) 2933 2038/9716-0
  Fax: (49) 2933 6871/971666
  Email: matthias.ostrop@tillmann-wellpappe.de
  Sls. Mgr.: Bernhard Weber
  Phone: (49) 2933 9716-27
  Email: bernhard.weber@tillmann-wellpappe.de
Total Employees of Company: 465
Total Employees at this Location: 400
Mill Locations:
Papierfabrik Tillmann, Zülpich-Sinzenich Mill, Kommerner Str. 78, D-53909 Zülpich-Sinzenich, Germany, Capacity: 66,000 mt/y, (Paperboard mill)
  Phone: (49) 2252 83610
  Fax: (49) 2252 836120
  Email: info@papierfabrik-tillmann.de

ⓂPapierfabrik Tillmann
Zülpich-Sinzenich Mill
Ownership: Fa. Katharina Tillmann Papier- und Wellpappenfabrik e.K.
Kommerner Str. 78
D-53909 Zülpich-Sinzenich
Germany
  Phone: (49) 2252 83610
  Fax: (49) 2252 836120
  Email: info@papierfabrik-tillmann.de
  Web Address: www.tillmann-wellpappe.de
Personnel:
  Mill Mgr., Tech.: Hans-Josef Hellwich
  Phone: (49) 2252 83610
  Email: hans-josef.hellwich@papierfabriktillmann.de
  Purch. Mgr.: Eduard Lippertz
  Phone: (49) 2252 836 112
  Email: eduard.lippertz@papierfabriktillmann.de
  Sls. Mgr.: Bernhard Weber
  Phone: (49) 2933 971627
Total Employees at this Location: 50
Type of Operation: Paperboard mill
Pulp Grades and Capacities:
  Total pulp capacity: 66,239 mt/y
  Recycled Pulping: 66,239 mt/y
Pulp Mill Data:
  Recycled Fiber Treatment Lines:
  Pulpers: 1 at 70,000
  Recycled packaging pulping lines: 1 at 70,000
Paper/Paperboard Grades and Capacities:
  Total paper and paperboard capacity: 66,000 mt/y
  Linerboard: 41,000 mt/y
  Corrugating medium/fluting: 25,000 mt/y
Paper and Paperboard Mill Data:
Paper Machines: 1
No. 1, fourdrinier (2), total capacity 66,000 mt/y, Trim width 2.45 m, Corrugating medium/fluting, Linerboard
Energy Data:
Power boilers
Combustion turbines: 1
Electrical demand for mill: 86 MWh/D

ⓄⓂJ. Tönnesmann & Vogel, Papierfabrik Hönnetal GmbH
Menden Mill
Company is idle, under bankruptcy protection (production was suspended from March 2013. The company filed for bankruptcy at same time)
Hönnetalstr. 53
D-58710 Menden
Germany
  Mailing Address: Postf. 12 80, D-58695 Menden, Germany
  Phone: (49) 2373 98980
  Fax: (49) 2373 989898
  Email: info@toennesmann-vogel.de
  Web Address: www.toennesmann-vogel.de
Personnel:
  Owner & Gen. Mgr.: J. C. Tönnesmann
  Phone: (49) 2373 98980
  Fax: (49) 2373 98 98 98
  Email: c.toennesmann@toennesmann-vogel.de
  Vice Gen. Mgr.: Günter Paul
  Phone: (49) 2373 98980
  Fax: (49) 2373 98 98 98
  Email: g.paul@toennesmann-vogel.de
  Tech. Mgr.: Rolf Schruba
  Phone: (49) 2373 98980
  Email: r.schruba@toennesmann-vogel.de
  Sales Mngr.: Ms. D. Rennebaum
  Phone: (49) 2373 98 98 20
  Email: D.Rennebaum@toennesmann-vogel.de
  Purch. Mngr.: Ms. S. Wulf
  Phone: (49) 2373 98 98 29
  Email: S.Wulf@toennesmann-vogel.de
  Distr. Mngr: Mr. M. Gaisbauer
  Phone: (49) 2373 98 98 10
  Email: M.Gaisbauer@toennesmann-vogel.de
Total Employees of Company: 49
Total Employees at this Location: 49
Type of Operation: Paper mill
Pulp Grades and Capacities:
  Total pulp capacity: 20,000 mt/y
Pulp Mill Data:
  Recycled Fiber Treatment Lines:
  Pulpers: 1 at 20,000
Paper/Paperboard Grades and Capacities:
  Total paper and paperboard capacity: 20,000 mt/y
  Uncoated woodfree/freesheet: 5,000 mt/y
  Packaging papers: 10,000 mt/y
  Specialty and industrial: 5,000 mt/y
Paper and Paperboard Mill Data:
Paper Machines: 1
PM 1, fourdrinier, total capacity 20,000 mt/y, Trim width 1.82 m, Uncoated woodfree/freesheet, Packaging papers, Specialty and industrial
Energy Data:
Power boilers: 1
Electrical demand for mill: 33 MWh/D

ⓂPappenfabrik Trauchgau GmbH & Co. KG
Trauchgau Mill
Ownership: Karl Kurz GmbH & Co. KG
Tullau Pappen®, Stockingen 2
D-87642 Halblech
Germany
  Phone: (49) 8368 9129 0
  Fax: (49) 8368 9129 50
  Email: vertrieb@pappen.de, gauss@pappen.de
  Web Address: www.pappen.de
Personnel:
  Mill Mgr.: Jörg Gauss
  Phone: (49) 8368 9129 42
  Fax: (49) 8368 9129 50
  Email: gauss@pappen.de
Total Employees at this Location: 50
Type of Operation: Paperboard mill
Pulp Grades and Capacities:
  Total pulp capacity: 17,250 mt/y
  Recycled Pulping: 17,250 mt/y
Pulp Mill Data:
  Recycled Fiber Treatment Lines:
  Pulpers: 1 at 20,000
Paper/Paperboard Grades and Capacities:
  Total paper and paperboard capacity: 17,000 mt/y
  Boxboard/cartonboard: 17,000 mt/y
Paper and Paperboard Mill Data:
Paper Machines: 1
No. 1, cylinder, total capacity 17,000 mt/y, Trim width 2.65 m, Boxboard/cartonboard
Finishing Equipment:
  Winders: 1
  Sheeters: 1
Energy Data:
Power boilers: 1
Steam turbines: 1 at 2 MW
Electrical demand for mill: 15 MWh/D

ⓄⓂUPM GmbH
Augsburg Mill
Ownership: 100% by UPM-Kymmene Corporation
Georg-Haindl-Str. 5
D-86153 Augsburg
Germany
  Phone: (49) 821 3109 0
  Fax: (49) 821 3109 156/157
  Email: info.augsburg@upm.com
  Web Address: www.upm-kymmene.de
Personnel:
  Gen. Mgr.: Wolfgang Ohnesorg
  Phone: (49) 821 3109 462
  Fax: (49) 821 3109 156
  Email: wolfgang.ohnesorg@upm.com
  Mill Service Dir.: Josef Kovacs
  Phone: (49) 821 3109215
  Fax: (49) 821 3109 156
  Email: josef.kovacs@upm.com
  Eng. Dir.: Markus Rausch
  Phone: (49) 821 3109 601
  Fax: (49) 821 3109 156
  Email: markus.rausch@upm.com
  Prod. Mgr. PM2: Markus Messmer
  Phone: (49) 821 3109 0
  Fax: (49) 821 3109 156
  Email: markus.messmer@upm.com
  Prod. Mgr. PM3: Karl-Heinz Hannen
  Phone: (49) 821 3109 0
  Fax: (49) 821 3109 156
  Email: karl-heinz.hannen@upm.com
  Oper. Dir.: Gerhard Mayer
  Phone: (49) 821 3109 0
  Fax: (49) 821 3109 156
  Email: gerhard.mayer@upm.com
  OHS & Environ. Mgr.: Eva Männer
  Phone: (49) 21 3109 249
  Fax: (49) 821 3109 156
Total Employees at this Location: 450
Type of Operation: Paper mill
Mill Locations:
UPM, Chapelle Darblay Paper Mill, CD 3, F-76530 Grand-Couronne, France, Capacity: 380,000 mt/y, (Pulp mill, Paper mill)
  Phone: (33) 2 35 18 40 00
  Fax: (33) 2 35 18 40 40
  Email: info.chapelle@upm.com
UPM, Docelles Paper Mill, 1 rue du Grand Meix, F-88460 Docelles, France, (Paper mill)
  Phone: (33) 3 29 33 81 00
  Fax: (33) 3 29 33 81 81
  Email: info.docelles@upm.com

Germany

UPM GmbH, Ettringen Mill, Fabrikstr. 4, D-86833 Ettringen, Germany, Capacity: 280,000 mt/y, (Pulp mill, Paper mill)
Phone: (49) 8249 802 0
Fax: (49) 8249 802 213/119

UPM GmbH, Hürth Mill, Bertrams Jagdweg 12, D-50354 Hürth, Germany, Capacity: 310,000 mt/y, (Paper mill)
Phone: (49) 2233 2006100
Fax: (49) 2233 2007960

UPM GmbH, Nordland Mill, Nordlandallee 1, D-26892 Dörpen, Germany, Capacity: 1,450,000 mt/y, (Paper mill)
Phone: (49) 4963 401 00
Fax: (49) 4963 4545
Email: info.nordland@upm.com

UPM GmbH, Plattling Mill, Nicolausstr. 7, D-94447 Plattling, Germany, Capacity: 780,000 mt/y, (Paper mill, Paper mill)
Phone: (49) 9931 502-0/89606-0
Fax: (49) 9931 502 103/255/89606 509

UPM GmbH, Schongau Mill, Friedrich-Haindl-Str. 10, D-86956 Schongau, Germany, Capacity: 770,000 mt/y, (Paper mill)
Phone: (49) 8861 2130
Fax: (49) 8861 213106
Email: info.schongau@upm.com

UPM GmbH, Schwedt Mill, Kuhheide 1, D-16303 Schwedt/Oder, Germany, Capacity: 290,000 mt/y, (Paper mill)
Phone: (49) 3332 281 123
Fax: (49) 3332 281 115
Email: info.schwedt@upm-kymmene.com

Pulp Grades and Capacities:
Total pulp capacity: 267,727 mt/y
Mechanical Pulp: 127,630 mt/y
Recycled Pulping: 140,097 mt/y

Pulp Mill Data:
Mechanical Pulping Systems:
Conventional grinders: 11
Pulp Lines: 2
Bleach Plant Systems: 2
DIP, Sequence: P, Capacity 140,000 admt/y
SGW, Sequence: P, Capacity 135,000 admt/y
Recycled Fiber Treatment Lines:
Flotation deinking lines: 1 at 140,000
Pulpers: 1 at 220,000 admt/y

Paper/Paperboard Grades and Capacities:
Total paper and paperboard capacity: 500,000 mt/y
Uncoated mechanical/groundwood: 100,000 mt/y
Coated mechanical/groundwood: 400,000 mt/y

Paper and Paperboard Mill Data:
Stock Preparation:
Pulpers: 1
Refiners: 10
Paper Machines: 2
No. 2, DuoFormer CFD, total capacity 100,000 mt/y, Trim width 4.6 m, Uncoated mechanical/groundwood
No. 3, OptiFormer, total capacity 400,000 mt/y, Trim width 9.6 m, Coated mechanical/groundwood
Coating Machines: 1
No. 1, total capacity 395,000 mt/y, on machine
Finishing Equipment:
Winders: 2
Supercalenders: 2
Rewinders: 1
Energy Data:
Power boilers: 1
Steam turbines: 2 at 30.0 MW
Electrical demand for mill: 1,590 MWh/D

ⓜ UPM GmbH
Ettringen Mill
Ownership: 100% by UPM-Kymmene Corporation
Fabrikstr. 4
D-86833 Ettringen, Bavaria
Germany
Phone: (49) 8249 802 0
Fax: (49) 8249 802 213/119
Web Address: www.upm.com

Personnel:
Gen. Mgr.: Caius Murtola
Phone: (49) 8249 802 0
Fax: (49) 8249 802 213/119
Man. Dir.: Henrik Björnberg
Phone: (49) 8131 6699506
Fax: (49) 8131 6699505
Finan. Dir.: Josef Gropper
Phone: (49) 8249 802101
Fax: (49) 8249 802247
Mktg. & Sls. Mgr.: Thomas Doiwa
Phone: (49) 8249 802208
Fax: (49) 8249802314
Tech. Planning Mgr.: Rudolf Schreivogel
Phone: (49) 8249 802416
Fax: (49) 8249 802314
Eng. Dir.: Markus Rausch
Phone: (49) 821 3109 601
Fax: (49) 8249802314
Email: markus.rausch@upm.com

Total Employees at this Location: 220
Type of Operation: Pulp mill, Paper mill

Pulp Grades and Capacities:
Total pulp capacity: 244,930 mt/y
Mechanical Pulp: 39,739 mt/y
Recycled Pulping: 205,191 mt/y

Pulp Mill Data:
Mechanical Pulping Systems:
Conventional grinders: 1
Pulp Lines: 2
Bleach Plant Systems: 2
DIP, Sequence: P/Y, Capacity 350,000 admt/y
SGW, Sequence: Di, Capacity 80,000 admt/y
Recycled Fiber Treatment Lines:
Flotation deinking lines: 1 at 314,000
Pulpers: 1 at 357,000

Paper/Paperboard Grades and Capacities:
Total paper and paperboard capacity: 280,000 mt/y
Newsprint: 15,000 mt/y
Uncoated mechanical/groundwood: 265,000 mt/y

Paper and Paperboard Mill Data:
Paper Machines: 1
No. 5, DuoFormer TQv, total capacity 280,000 mt/y, Trim width 8.1 m, Uncoated mechanical/groundwood, Newsprint
Finishing Equipment:
Winders: 2 at 280,000 mt/y
Supercalenders: 1 at 280,000 mt/y
Energy Data:
Power boilers: 3
Steam turbines: 2 at 4.5, 6.5 MW
Hydro turbines: 2
Electrical demand for mill: 842 MWh/D

ⓜ UPM GmbH
Hürth Mill
Ownership: 100% by UPM-Kymmene Corporation
Bertrams Jagdweg 12
D-50354 Hürth
Germany
Phone: (49) 2233 2006100
Fax: (49) 2233 2007960
Web Address: www.upm.com

Personnel:
Gen. Mgr.: Juha Ebeling
Phone: (49) 2233 2006100
Fax: (49) 2233 2007960
Sec.: Renate Stolle
Phone: (49) 2233 2006102
Fax: (49) 2233 2007960

Total Employees at this Location: 125
Type of Operation: Paper mill

Pulp Grades and Capacities:
Total pulp capacity: 321,650 mt/y
Recycled Pulping: 321,650 mt/y

Pulp Mill Data:
Pulp Lines: 1
Recycled Fiber Treatment Lines:
Flotation deinking lines: 1 at 320,000

Paper/Paperboard Grades and Capacities:
Total paper and paperboard capacity: 310,000 mt/y
Newsprint: 310,000 mt/y

Paper and Paperboard Mill Data:
Paper Machines: 1
No. 1, DuoFormer TQv, total capacity 310,000 mt/y, Trim width 8.1 m, Newsprint
Finishing Equipment:
Winders: 2 at 310,000 mt/y
Rewinders: 1 at 310,000 mt/y
Energy Data:
Electrical demand for mill: 756 MWh/D

ⓜ UPM GmbH
Nordland Mill
Ownership: 100% by UPM-Kymmene Corporation
Nordlandallee 1
D-26892 Dörpen
Germany
Mailing Address: Postf. 11 60, D-26888 Dörpen, Germany
Phone: (49) 4963 401 00
Fax: (49) 4963 4545
Email: info.nordland@upm.com
Web Address: www.upm.com

Personnel:
Mill Mgr.: Klaus Reimann
Phone: (49) 4963 401 00
Fax: (49) 4963 454 5
Specialist Logistics Invoicing Central Europe: Mechthild Wübben
Phone: (49) 4963 401 2409
Fax: (49) 4963 401 962100
Email: mechthild.wubben@upm.com

Total Employees at this Location: 1,185
Type of Operation: Paper mill

Paper/Paperboard Grades and Capacities:
Total paper and paperboard capacity: 1,450,000 mt/y
Uncoated woodfree/freesheet: 500,000 mt/y
Coated woodfree/freesheet: 950,000 mt/y

Paper and Paperboard Mill Data:
Stock Preparation:
Pulpers: 3
Refiners: 23
Paper Machines: 4
No. 1, SymFormer MB, total capacity 300,000 mt/y, Trim width 4.7 m, Coated woodfree/freesheet
No. 2, SymFormer F, total capacity 200,000 mt/y, Trim width 4.7 m, Uncoated woodfree/freesheet
No. 3, OptiFormer, total capacity 300,000 mt/y, Trim width 6.4 m, Uncoated woodfree/freesheet
No. 4, OptiFormer, total capacity 650,000 mt/y, Trim width 9.4 m, Coated woodfree/freesheet
Coating Machines: 3
CM 1, total capacity 280,000 mt/y., off machine
CM 2, total capacity 560,000 mt/y., off machine
CM 3, total capacity 300,000 mt/y.
Finishing Equipment:
Supercalenders: 4
Rewinders: 12
Sheeters: 20 at 970,000 mt/y, 220,000 mt/y
Energy Data:
Power boilers: 2
Steam turbines: 1 at 14 MW
Electrical demand for mill: 2,613 MWh/D

ⓜ UPM GmbH
Plattling Mill
Ownership: 100% by UPM-Kymmene Corporation
Nicolausstr. 7
D-94447 Plattling
Germany
Phone: (49) 9931 502-0/89606-0
Fax: (49) 9931 502 103/255/89606 509
Web Address: www.upm.com

Personnel:
Gen. Mgr.: Wolfgang Ohnesorg
Phone: (49) 9931 89606-500
Fax: (49) 9931 502 103/255/89606 509

Germany

Email: wolfgang.ohnesorg@upm.com
Oper. Dir.: Mika Kämpe
Phone: (49) 9931 502-0/89606-0
Fax: (49) 9931 502 103/255/89606 509
Email: mika.kampe@upm.com
Mill Service Dir.: Josef Kovacs
Phone: (49) 9931 89606 700
Fax: (49) 9931 502 103/255/89606 509
Email: josef.kovacs@upm.com
Eng. Dir.: Markus Rausch
Phone: (49) 821 3109 601
Email: markus.rausch@upm.com
Total Employees at this Location: 550
Type of Operation: Paper mill, Paper mill
Pulp Grades and Capacities:
Total pulp capacity: 401,414 mt/y
Mechanical Pulp: 359,025 mt/y
Recycled Pulping: 42,390 mt/y
Pulp Mill Data:
Mechanical Pulping Systems:
Conventional grinders: 9
Pressurized grinders: 8
Pulp Lines: 3
Bleach Plant Systems: 3
1, Sequence: P, Capacity 250,000 admt/y
10, Sequence: P, Capacity 50,000 admt/y
11, Sequence: P, Capacity 80,000 admt/y
Recycled Fiber Treatment Lines:
Flotation deinking lines: 1 at 60,000 admt/y
Pulpers: 1 at 60,000 admt/y
Paper/Paperboard Grades and Capacities:
Total paper and paperboard capacity: 780,000 mt/y
Uncoated mechanical/groundwood: 380,000 mt/y
Coated mechanical/groundwood: 400,000 mt/y
Paper and Paperboard Mill Data:
Stock Preparation:
Pulpers: 2
Refiners: 3
Paper Machines: 3
No. 1, OptiFormer, total capacity 380,000 mt/y, Trim width 10.5 m, Uncoated mechanical/groundwood
No. 10, fourdrinier, total capacity 150,000 mt/y, Trim width 5.9 m, Coated mechanical/groundwood
No. 11, OptiFormer, total capacity 250,000 mt/y, Trim width 7.6 m, Coated mechanical/groundwood
Coating Machines: 2
No. 10, total capacity 150,000 mt/y., off machine
No. 11, total capacity 250,000 mt/y., off machine
Finishing Equipment:
Winders: 6 at 400,000 mt/y, 380,000 mt/y
Supercalenders: 4 at 400,000 mt/y
Rewinders: 4
Sheeters: 2 at 100,000 mt/y
Energy Data:
Power boilers: 5
HRSG boiler: 1
Combustion turbines: 1 at 80 MW
Steam turbines: 1 at 40 MW
Electrical demand for mill: 3,680 MWh/D

ⓜUPM GmbH
Schongau Mill
Ownership: 100% by UPM-Kymmene Corporation
Friedrich-Haindl-Str. 10
D-86956 Schongau
Germany
Mailing Address: 12 50, D-86952 Schongau, Germany
Phone: (49) 8861 2130
Fax: (49) 8861 213 106
Email: info.schongau@upm.com
Web Address: www.upm-kymmene.de
Personnel:
Gen. Mgr.: Caius Murtola
Phone: (49) 8249 802 0
Fax: (49) 8861 213 130
Dir. Mill Service: Markus Rausch
Phone: (49) 821 3109 601
Fax: (49) 8861 213 106

Email: markus.rausch@upm.com
Oper. Dir.: Rainer Eichner
Phone: (49) 8861 2130
Fax: (49) 8861 213106
Email: rainer.eichner@upm.com
Total Employees at this Location: 530
Type of Operation: Paper mill
Pulp Grades and Capacities:
Total pulp capacity: 717,197 mt/y
Mechanical Pulp: 104,832 mt/y
Recycled Pulping: 612,364 mt/y
Pulp Mill Data:
Mechanical Pulping Systems:
TMP systems
Pulp Lines: 2
Bleach Plant Systems: 2
DIP, Sequence: P, Capacity 350,000 admt/y
TMP, Sequence: P, Capacity 105,000 admt/y
Recycled Fiber Treatment Lines:
Flotation deinking lines: 5 at 560,000 admt/y
Paper/Paperboard Grades and Capacities:
Total paper and paperboard capacity: 770,000 mt/y
Newsprint: 310,000 mt/y
Uncoated mechanical/groundwood: 460,000 mt/y
Paper and Paperboard Mill Data:
Stock Preparation:
Pulpers: 2
Refiners: 2
Paper Machines: 3
No. 6, DuoFormer CF, total capacity 195,000 mt/y, Trim width 5.9 m, Uncoated mechanical/groundwood
No. 7, DuoFormer C, total capacity 310,000 mt/y, Trim width 8.5 m, Newsprint
No. 9, DuoFormerTQv, total capacity 265,000 mt/y, Trim width 6 m, Uncoated mechanical/groundwood
Finishing Equipment:
Rewinders: 5
Energy Data:
Power boilers: 5
TMP Reboiler: 1
Steam turbines: 4 at 100.0 MW
Hydro turbines: 1 at 7 MW
Electrical demand for mill: 2,402 MWh/D

ⓜUPM GmbH
Schwedt Mill
Ownership: 100% by UPM-Kymmene Corporation
Kuhheide 1
D-16303 Schwedt/Oder
Germany
Phone: (49) 3332 281 123
Fax: (49) 3332 281 115
Email: info.schwedt@upm-kymmene.com
Web Address: www.upm-kymmene.com
Total Employees at this Location: 245
Type of Operation: Paper mill
Pulp Grades and Capacities:
Total pulp capacity: 299,530 mt/y
Recycled Pulping: 299,530 mt/y
Pulp Mill Data:
Recycled Fiber Treatment Lines:
Flotation deinking lines: 1 at 400,000 admt/y
Paper/Paperboard Grades and Capacities:
Total paper and paperboard capacity: 290,000 mt/y
Newsprint: 290,000 mt/y
Paper and Paperboard Mill Data:
Paper Machines: 1
No. 11, DuoFormer CFD, total capacity 290,000 mt/y, Trim width 8.5 m, Newsprint
Coating Machines: 1
No. 1
Finishing Equipment:
Rewinders: 2 at 300,000 mt/y
Energy Data:
Steam turbines: 1 at 10.0 MW
Electrical demand for mill: 720 MWh/D

ⒽⓜPapier- und Kartonfabrik Varel GmbH & Co. KG
Varel Mill
Ownership: 100% by private owner
Dangaster Strasse 38
D-26316 Varel, Niedersachsen
Germany
Mailing Address: Postf. 13 40, D-26303 Varel, Niedersachsen, Germany
Phone: (49) 4451 138 0
Fax: (49) 4451 810 46
Email: info@pkvarel.de, papierverkauf@pkvarel.de
Web Address: www.pkvarel.de
Personnel:
Gen. Mgr.: Ralf Schu
Phone: (49) 4451 138 0
Fax: (49) 4451 810 46
Email: r.schu@pkvarel.de
Gen. Mgr.: Uwe Wollschläger
Phone: (49) 4451 138 265
Fax: (49) 4451 13825 265
Email: u.wollschlaeger@pkvarel.de
Gen. Mgr. Board: Klaus Schnitger
Phone: (49) 4451 138 105
Fax: (49) 4451 13825 105
Email: k.schnitger@pkvarel.de
Internal Sls. Admin.: Stefan Schäfer
Phone: (49) 4451 138 172
Fax: (49) 4451 13825 172
Email: s.schaefer@pkvarel.de
Qlty. & Environ. Mgr.: Martin Krasa
Phone: (49) 4451 138 0
Fax: (49) 4451 810 46
Email: m.krasa@pkvarel.de
Total Employees of Company: 440
Total Employees at this Location: 440
Type of Operation: Paperboard mill
Pulp Grades and Capacities:
Total pulp capacity: 812,944 mt/y
Recycled Pulping: 812,944 mt/y
Pulp Mill Data:
Pulp Lines: 3
Bleach Plant Systems: 1
DIP
Recycled Fiber Treatment Lines:
Flotation deinking lines: 1
Pulpers: 1
Recycled packaging pulping lines: 1 at 600
Paper/Paperboard Grades and Capacities:
Total paper and paperboard capacity: 850,000 mt/y
Linerboard: 300,000 mt/y
Corrugating medium/fluting: 300,000 mt/y
Boxboard/cartonboard: 250,000 mt/y
Paper and Paperboard Mill Data:
Paper Machines: 4
No. 2, cylinder (10), Yankee dryer, total capacity 100,000 mt/y, Trim width 2.75 m, Boxboard/cartonboard
No. 3, cylinder (8), Yankee dryer, total capacity 150,000 mt/y, Trim width 2.95 m, Boxboard/cartonboard
No. 4, fourdrinier (2), Cylinder, total capacity 300,000 mt/y, Trim width 5.1 m, Linerboard, Corrugating medium/fluting
No. 5, DuoFormer Base, Cylinder, total capacity 300,000 mt/y, Trim width 5.6 m, Linerboard, Corrugating medium/fluting
Coating Machines: 1
PM 3, on machine
Energy Data:
Power boilers: 3
Combustion turbines: 4
Steam turbines: 3 at 13 (1) MW
Electrical demand for mill: 989 MWh/D

ⒽⓜPapierfabrik Vreden GmbH
Vreden Mill
Ownership: 50% by Straub Braunlingen, 50% by Wellpappenfabrik Sausenheim

Ausbachstr. 9
D-48691 Vreden
Germany
Mailing Address: Postf. 12 45, D-48685 Vreden, Germany
  Phone: (49) 2564 3990
  Fax: (49) 2564 39929
  Email: infok@papierfabrik-vreden.de
  Web Address: www.papierfabrik-vreden.de
Personnel:
Man. Dir.: Frank Brauckmann
  Phone: (49) 2564 3990
  Email: frank.brauckmann@papierfabrik-vreden.de
Tech. Mgr.: Jens Bussmann
  Phone: (49) 2564 399 18
  Email: jens.bussmann@papierfabrik-vreden.de
Accountant: Heinz G. Terhürne
  Phone: (49) 2564 3990
  Email: heinz-georg.terhuerne@papierfabrik-vreden.de
Total Employees of Company: 70
Total Employees at this Location: 70
Type of Operation: Paper mill, Paperboard mill
Pulp Grades and Capacities:
Total pulp capacity: 94,316 mt/y
Recycled Pulping: 94,316 mt/y
Pulp Mill Data:
Recycled Fiber Treatment Lines:
Recycled packaging pulping lines: 1 at 120,000
Paper/Paperboard Grades and Capacities:
Total paper and paperboard capacity: 94,000 mt/y
Linerboard: 33,000 mt/y
Corrugating medium/fluting: 61,000 mt/y
Paper and Paperboard Mill Data:
Paper Machines: 2
No. 1, fourdrinier, total capacity 45,000 mt/y, Trim width 2.5 m, Corrugating medium/fluting
No. 3, fourdrinier, total capacity 49,000 mt/y, Trim width 2.5 m, Corrugating medium/fluting, Linerboard
Finishing Equipment:
Winders: 2 at 80,000 mt/y
Energy Data:
Power boilers: 2
Steam turbines: 1
Electrical demand for mill: 117 MWh/D

⊕ⓜMoritz J. Weig GmbH & Co. KG
Mayen Mill
Polcher Strasse 113
D-56727 Mayen
Germany
Mailing Address: Postf. 21 60, D-56724 Mayen, Germany
  Phone: (49) 2651 84 0
  Fax: (49) 2651 84 490/329
  Email: info@weig-karton.de, service@weig-karton.de
  Web Address: www.weig-karton.de
Personnel:
Chmn. & Gen. Mgr.: Dipl. Kfm. Moritz Weig
  Phone: (49) 2651 84200
  Fax: (49) 2651 84355
  Email: mweig@weig-karton.de
Gen. Mgr.: Dipl. Ing. Xaver Weig
  Phone: (49) 2651 84200
  Fax: (49) 2651 84355
  Email: xweig@weig-karton.de
Finan. Mgr.: Michael Buchner
  Phone: (49) 2651 84175
  Fax: (49) 2651 84355
  Email: mbuchner@weig-karton.de
Tech. Dir.: Gerd Alef
  Phone: (49) 2651 84339
  Fax: (49) 2651 84355
  Email: galef@weig-karton.de
Prod. Mgr.: Henning Dippel
  Phone: (49) 2651 84365
  Fax: (49) 2651 8444365
  Email: hdippel@weig-karton.de
Head of tech. Purch.: Torsten Asch
  Phone: (49) 2651 84 233
  Fax: (49) 2651 84 490
  Email: torsten.asch@weig-karton.de
Sls. Mgr.: Reinhard Wölwer
  Phone: (49) 2651 84 313
  Fax: (49) 2651 84 490
  Email: reinhard.woelwer@weig-karton.de
Total Employees of Company: 700
Total Employees at this Location: 700
Type of Operation: Paperboard mill
Mill Locations:
Kartotec - Papeles Técnicos-, Villeta Mill, Calle Amambay 39, Zona Industrial Sur, Villeta, Paraguay, Capacity: 69,972 mt/y, (Paperboard mill)
  Phone: (595) 225 952 680, 952 679
  Fax: (595) 225 952 682
  Email: ventas@kartotec.com.py
Pulp Grades and Capacities:
Total pulp capacity: 572,561 mt/y
Recycled Pulping: 572,561 mt/y
Pulp Mill Data:
Bleach Plant Systems: 1
Recycled Fiber Treatment Lines:
Flotation deinking lines
Recycled packaging pulping lines
Paper/Paperboard Grades and Capacities:
Total paper and paperboard capacity: 610,000 mt/y
Linerboard: 40,000 mt/y
Boxboard/cartonboard: 570,000 mt/y
Paper and Paperboard Mill Data:
Stock Preparation:
Pulpers: 9
Refiners: 7
Paper Machines: 2
No. 3, cylinder (9), total capacity 260,000 mt/y, Trim width 4.2 m, Boxboard/cartonboard
No. 6, fourdrinier (3), total capacity 350,000 mt/y, Trim width 5.3 m, Linerboard, Boxboard/cartonboard
Coating Machines: 1
No. 1, total capacity 260,000 mt/y., on machine
Finishing Equipment:
Winders: 3
Sheeters: 5
Energy Data:
Power boilers: 2
Combustion turbines: 1
Steam turbines: 1
Electrical demand for mill: 777 MWh/D

⊕ⓜWEPA Hygieneprodukte GmbH
Arnsberg Mill
Ownership: 32% by Marsberger Kraftwerkgesellschaft mbH, 68% by Krengel family
Rönkhauser Strasse 26
D-59757 Arnsberg-Müschede
Germany
Mailing Address: Postf. 30 40, 59757 Arnsberg, Germany
  Phone: (49) 2932 307 0
  Fax: (49) 2932 307 179
  Email: info@wepa.de
  Web Address: www.wepa.de
Personnel:
CEO and Chairman: Martin Krengel
  Phone: (49) 2932 307 0
  Fax: (49) 2932 307 179
  Email: martin.krengel@wepa.de
Man. Dir.: Manfred Meier
  Phone: (49) 2932 307 0
  Fax: (49) 2932 307 179
  Email: manfred.meier@wepa.de
Man. Dir. Wepa Professional: Martin Rohde
  Phone: (49) 2932 307 0
  Fax: (49) 2932 307 179
  Email: martin.rohde@wepa.de
Head of Energy & Environ.: Hans-Michael Fraikin
  Phone: (49) 2932 307 8391
  Fax: (49) 2932 307 728391
  Email: hans.fraikin@wepa.de
Mktg & Product Mgr.: Matthias Post
  Phone: (49) 2932 900 5980 11
  Fax: (49) 2932 307 179
  Email: matthias.post@wepa.de
Commun. Mgr.: Silvia Kerwin
  Phone: (49) 2931 786 5811 4
  Fax: (49) 2932 307 179
  Email: silvia.kerwin@wepa.de
Total Employees of Company: 2,700
Total Employees at this Location: 500
Type of Operation: Paper mill
Mill Locations:
Northwood & Wepa Limited, Llangynwyd (Bridgend) Mill (50% owned), Llangynwyd, Bridgend CF34 9RS, United Kingdom, Capacity: 55,000 mt/y, (Pulp mill, Paper mill)
  Phone: (44) 1656 684 500
  Fax: (44) 1656 684 501/689
WEPA Lucca Srl, Cassino Mill, Via Contrada Cerasola, 28, I-03043 Cassino, (FR), Italy, Capacity: 55,000 mt/y, (Paper mill)
  Phone: (39) 0776 3961
  Fax: (39) 0776 302076
  Email: info@wepa.de
WEPA Lucca Srl, Fosso Raletta Mill, Via Carlotti, 32, I-55016 Porcari, (LU), Italy, Capacity: 60,000 mt/y, (Paper mill)
  Phone: (39) 0583 448399
  Fax: (39) 0583 448350
  Email: info@wepa.de
WEPA Hygieneprodukte GmbH, Marsberg-Giershagen Mill, Unterm Klausknapp 5, D-34431 Marsberg-Giershagen, Germany, Capacity: 89,000 mt/y, (Paper mill)
  Phone: (49) 2991 7210
  Fax: (49) 2991 721-309
  Email: info@wepa.de
WEPA Leuna GmbH, Leuna Mill, An der B91, Alter Maienweg, D-06237 Leuna, Spergau, Germany, Capacity: 60,000 mt/y, (Paper mill)
  Phone: (49) 3461 4314 00 /4314 51
  Fax: (49) 3461 431499
  Email: manja.keiser@wepa.de
WEPA Lille S.A.R.L., Bousbecque Mill, Avenue de l'Europe, F-59166 Bousbecque, France, Capacity: 60,000 mt/y, (Paper mill)
  Phone: (33) 3 20 11 57 00
  Fax: (33) 3 20 25 93 33
  Email: info@wepa.de
WEPA Hygieneprodukte GmbH, Mainz Mill, Gassnerallee 45-47, D-55120 Mainz, Germany, Capacity: 60,000 mt/y, (Paper mill)
  Phone: (49) 6131 9724 0
  Fax: (49) 6131 9724 228 / 9724 267
  Email: info@wepa.de
WEPA Papierfabrik Sachsen GmbH, Kriebethal Mill, An der Zschopau 2, D-09648 Kriebethal, Germany, Capacity: 85,000 mt/y, (Paper mill)
  Phone: (49) 34327 66660
  Fax: (49) 34327 66669
  Email: info@wepa.de
WEPA Professional Piechowice S.A., Piechowice Mill, ul. Tysiaclecia 49, PL-58573 Piechowice, Poland, Capacity: 25,000 mt/y, (Paper mill)
  Phone: (48) 75 7547 800
  Fax: (48) 75 7547 855
  Email: info@wepro.com.pl
Pulp Grades and Capacities:
Total pulp capacity: 70,000 mt/y
Pulp available for market: 10,893 mt/y
Recycled Pulping: 70,000 mt/y
Pulp Mill Data:
Recycled Fiber Treatment Lines:
Flotation deinking lines: 1
Pulp Dryers:
Wet Lap machine 1
Paper/Paperboard Grades and Capacities:
Total paper and paperboard capacity: 64,000 mt/y
Tissue: 64,000 mt/y
Paper and Paperboard Mill Data:

Germany

Paper Machines: 2
No. 6, crescent former, Yankee dryer, total capacity 29,000 mt/y, Trim width 2.68 m, Tissue
No. 8, crescent former, Yankee dryer, total capacity 35,000 mt/y, Trim width 2.68 m, Tissue
Energy Data:
Power boilers: 1
Electrical demand for mill: 219 MWh/D

ⓜWEPA Hygieneprodukte GmbH
Marsberg-Giershagen Mill
Ownership: WEPA Hygieneprodukte GmbH
Unterm Klausknapp 5
D-34431 Marsberg-Giershagen
Germany
  Phone: (49) 2991 7210
  Fax: (49) 2991 721-309
  Email: info@wepa.de
  Web Address: www.wepa-professional.de
Personnel:
  Mill Mgr.: Frank Folcz
  Phone: (49) 2991 721 0
  Fax: (49) 2991 721 309
  Email: frank.folcz@wepa.de
  Sls. Mgr. North / East Germany: Torsten Reiher
  Phone: (49) 2932 307 0, 1715631253
  Fax: (49) 2991 721 309
  Email: torsten.reiher@wepa.de
Total Employees at this Location: 380
Type of Operation: Paper mill
Pulp Grades and Capacities:
  Total pulp capacity: 69,710 mt/y
  Recycled Pulping: 69,710 mt/y
Pulp Mill Data:
  Recycled Fiber Treatment Lines:
  Flotation deinking lines at 77,000
  Pulp Dryers:
  Wet Lap machine 1
Paper/Paperboard Grades and Capacities:
  Total paper and paperboard capacity: 89,000 mt/y
  Tissue: 89,000 mt/y
Paper and Paperboard Mill Data:
Paper Machines: 3
No. 4, crescent former, Yankee dryer, total capacity 29,000 mt/y, Trim width 2.68 m, Tissue
No. 5, crescent former, Yankee dryer, total capacity 30,000 mt/y, Trim width 2.71 m, Tissue
No. 7, crescent former, Yankee dryer, total capacity 30,000 mt/y, Trim width 2.68 m, Tissue
Energy Data:
Power boilers: 1
Combustion turbines: 1
Steam turbines: 1
Electrical demand for mill: 268 MWh/D

ⓜWEPA Leuna GmbH
Leuna Mill
Ownership: WEPA Hygieneprodukte GmbH
An der B91, Alter Maienweg
D-06237 Leuna, Spergau
Germany
Mailing Address: Postf. 11 11, D-06234 Leuna, Germany
  Phone: (49) 3461 4314 00 / 4314 51
  Fax: (49) 3461 431499
  Email: manja.keiser@wepa.de
  Web Address: www.wepa.de
Personnel:
  Gen. Mgr.: Lars Helge Peters
  Phone: (49) 3461 431451
  Fax: (49) 3461 431499
  Email: lars-helge.peters@wepa.de
  Chief Eng.: Dirk Barten
  Phone: (49) 3461 431451
  Fax: (49) 3461 431499
  Email: dirk.barten@wepa.de
  Prod. Mgr.: Tim Hesselbarth
  Phone: (49) 3461 431506

  Fax: (49) 3461 431419
  Email: tim.hesselbarth@wepa.de
Total Employees at this Location: 175
Type of Operation: Paper mill
Paper/Paperboard Grades and Capacities:
  Total paper and paperboard capacity: 60,000 mt/y
  Tissue: 60,000 mt/y
Paper and Paperboard Mill Data:
Paper Machines: 1
No. 1, crescent former, Yankee dryer, total capacity 60,000 mt/y, Trim width 5.4 m, Tissue
Energy Data:
Electrical demand for mill: 147 MWh/D

ⓜWEPA Hygieneprodukte GmbH
Mainz Mill
Ownership: WEPA Hygieneprodukte GmbH
Gassnerallee 45-47
D-55120 Mainz
Germany
Mailing Address: Postf. 22 60, D-55012 Mainz, Germany
  Phone: (49) 6131 9724 0
  Fax: (49) 6131 9724 228 / 9724 267
  Email: info@wepa.de
  Web Address: www.wepa.de
Personnel:
  Mill Mgr.: Franz Weber
  Phone: (49) 6131 9724 0
  Fax: (49) 6131 9724 228
  Email: franz.weer@wepa.de
Total Employees at this Location: 200
Type of Operation: Paper mill
Pulp Grades and Capacities:
  Total pulp capacity: 63,736 mt/y
  Recycled Pulping: 63,736 mt/y
Pulp Mill Data:
  Recycled Fiber Treatment Lines:
  Flotation deinking lines at 63,000
Paper/Paperboard Grades and Capacities:
  Total paper and paperboard capacity: 60,000 mt/y
  Tissue: 60,000 mt/y
Paper and Paperboard Mill Data:
Paper Machines: 1
No. 1, DuoFormerT, Yankee dryer, total capacity 60,000 mt/y, Trim width 5.35 m, Tissue
Energy Data:
Power boilers: 1
Electrical demand for mill: 211 MWh/D

ⓜWEPA Papierfabrik Sachsen GmbH
Kriebethal Mill
Ownership: 100% by WEPA Hygieneprodukte GmbH
An der Zschopau 2
D-09648 Kriebethal
Germany
  Phone: (49) 34327 66660
  Fax: (49) 34327 66669
  Email: info@wepa.de
  Web Address: www.wepa.de
Personnel:
  Mill Mgr.: Andreas Weise
  Phone: (49) 34327 66660
  Fax: (49) 34327 66669
  Email: andreas.weise@wepa.de
Total Employees at this Location: 180
Type of Operation: Paper mill
Paper/Paperboard Grades and Capacities:
  Total paper and paperboard capacity: 85,000 mt/y
  Tissue: 85,000 mt/y
Paper and Paperboard Mill Data:
Paper Machines: 2
No. 3, crescent former, Yankee dryer, total capacity 30,000 mt/y, Trim width 2.7 m, Tissue
No. 9, crescent former, Yankee dryer, total capacity 55,000 mt/y, Trim width 5.4 m, Tissue
Energy Data:

Power boilers: 1
Electrical demand for mill: 214 MWh/D

ⓞⓜW & M Pappen GmbH & Co. KG
Elbrinxen Mill
Ownership: Family - owned (Private)
Pappmühle 2/3
D-32676 Lügde / Elbrinxen
Germany
  Phone: (49) 5283 9806 0
  Fax: (49) 5283 9806 47
  Email: info@wm-pappen.de
  Web Address: www.wm-pappen.de
Personnel:
  Gen. Mgr., Sales & Mktg.: Michael Werner
  Phone: (49) 5283 9806 0
  Gen. Mgr. & Mill Mgr.: Frank Moschinski
  Phone: (49) 5283 9806 0
  Sls. Mgr.: Sigrid Wenneker
  Phone: (49) 5283 9806 0
  Finan. Mgr.: Sigrid Moschinski
  Phone: (49) 5283 9806 0
Total Employees of Company: 16
Total Employees at this Location: 16
Type of Operation: Paperboard mill
Paper/Paperboard Grades and Capacities:
  Total paper and paperboard capacity: 8,000 mt/y
  Boxboard/cartonboard: 8,000 mt/y
Paper and Paperboard Mill Data:
Paper Machines: 1
No. 1, total capacity 8,000 mt/y, Trim width 1.93 m, Boxboard/cartonboard
Energy Data:
Power boilers: 1
Electrical demand for mill: 9 MWh/D

ⓞⓜWerra Papier
Omega Mill
Ownership: 100% by Sofidel Group
OT Wernshausen, Unterm Bahnhof 10
D-98574 Wernshausen
Germany
  Phone: (49) 36848 385 0
  Fax: (49) 36848 385 410 / 385 36
  Email: info@werrapapier.de
  Web Address: www.werrapapier.de, www.sofidel.it/werraPapier.php
Personnel:
  Mktg. Assist.: Christina Gräfenhan
  Phone: (49) 36848 385 243
  Fax: (49) 36848 385 410
  Email: christina.graefenhan@werrapapier.de
Total Employees of Company: 430
Total Employees at this Location: 430
Type of Operation: Paper mill
Pulp Grades and Capacities:
  Total pulp capacity: 89,063 mt/y
  Recycled Pulping: 89,063 mt/y
Paper/Paperboard Grades and Capacities:
  Total paper and paperboard capacity: 84,000 mt/y
  Tissue: 84,000 mt/y
Paper and Paperboard Mill Data:
Paper Machines: 3
No. 1, crescent former, Yankee dryer, total capacity 40,000 mt/y, Trim width 3.45 m, Tissue
No. 4, fourdrinier, Yankee dryer, total capacity 12,000 mt/y, Trim width 2.3 m, Tissue
No. 5, fourdrinier, Yankee dryer, total capacity 32,000 mt/y, Trim width 2.75 m, Tissue
Energy Data:
Power boilers: 1
Electrical demand for mill: 234 MWh/D

ⓞⓜPapierfabrik Zerkall Renker & Söhne GmbH & Co. KG
Hürtgenwald-Zerkall Mill
Ownership: Family-owned (Private)
Gustav-Renker-Str. 5

D-52393 Hürtgenwald-Zerkall
Germany
Phone: (49) 2427 9406 0
Fax: (49) 2427 9406 79
Email: info@zerkall.com
Web Address: www.zerkall.com
Personnel:
Man. Dir.: Felix A. Renker
Phone: (49) 2427 9406 0
Man. Dir.: Stefan Renker
Phone: (49) 2427 9406 0
Total Employees of Company: 95
Total Employees at this Location: 95
Type of Operation: Paper mill
Pulp Grades and Capacities:
Paper/Paperboard Grades and Capacities:
Total paper and paperboard capacity: 10,000 mt/y
Uncoated woodfree/freesheet: 10,000 mt/y
Uncoated mechanical/groundwood
Coated woodfree/freesheet
Paper and Paperboard Mill Data:
Stock Preparation:
Pulpers: 2
Refiners: 2
Paper Machines: 2
No. 1, cylinder, Trim width 1.5 m, Uncoated woodfree/freesheet
No. 2, cylinder, Trim width 1.6 m, Uncoated woodfree/freesheet
Finishing Equipment:
Winders: 1
Sheeters: 1

ⓘⓜZPR, Zellstoff- und Papierfabrik Rosenthal GmbH
Rosenthal Mill
Ownership: Mercer International Inc.
Hauptstrasse 16
D-07366 Blankenstein
Germany
Phone: (49) 36642 8-0
Fax: (49) 36642 8 2000 / 2020
Email: info@zpr.de
Web Address: www.zpr.de
Personnel:
Man. Dir.: Leonhard Nossol
Phone: (49) 36642 8 2166
Fax: (49) 36642 8 2000
Email: leonhard.nossol@zpr.de
Mill & Prod Mgr.: Dr. Christian Sörgel
Phone: (49) 36642 8 2278
Fax: (49) 36642 8 2000
Email: christian.soergel@zpr.de
Oper. Mgr.: Hans-Jörg Krieg
Phone: (49) 36642 8 2328
Fax: (49) 36642 8 2088
Email: hansjoerg.krieg@zpr.de
Head of Prod.: Dr. Klaus Dietrich
Phone: (49) 36642 8 2443
Fax: (49) 36642 8 2010
Email: klaus.dietrich@zpr.de
Finan. Dir.: Katrin Stöcker
Phone: (49) 36642 8 2105
Fax: (49) 36642 8 2000
Sls. Dir.: Christine Rennert
Phone: (49) 36642 8 2261
Fax: (49) 36642 8 2020
Email: christine.rennert@zpr.de
Env. Dir.: Uwe Fleischmann
Phone: (49) 36642 82128
Fax: (49) 36642 8 2000
Email: uwe.fleischmann@zpr.de
HR Mngr.: Angelika Zimmermann
Phone: (49) 36642 8 2249
Fax: (49) 36642 8 2000
Sec. to Mr. Nossol: Katja Grundig
Phone: (49) 36642 8 2166
Fax: (49) 36642 8 2270
Email: katja.grundig@zpr.de
Total Employees at this Location: 445

Type of Operation: Pulp mill
Pulp Grades and Capacities:
Total pulp capacity: 345,899 mt/y
Pulp available for market: 345,000 mt/y
Chemical Pulp: 345,899 mt/y
Pulp Mill Data:
Chemical Pulping Systems:
Continuous digesters: 1
Pulp Lines: 1
Bleach Plant Systems: 1
Softwood Pulp Line, Type: ~75%, Sequence: O_2 Q Op D/Q Po/P, Capacity 360,000 admt/y
Softwood Pulp Line, Type: ~25%, Sequence: O_2 Q Op/QZ/Po/P
Chemical Recovery Equipment:
Evaporator lines: 1
Recovery boilers: 1
Lime Kiln
Pulp Dryers:
Air Float dryers 1
Energy Data:
Power boilers: 1
Steam turbines: 1 at 57.0 MW
Electrical demand for mill: 731 MWh/D

GREECE

ⓜAthens Paper Mill SA
Athens Mill
Ownership: Bolton Hellas
1 Chartergaton st., Votanikos
GR-11855 Athens
Greece
Mailing Address: "Acteon" Building, 2, Irinis Street, Neo Faliro, GR-18547 Athens, Greece
Phone: (30) 210 3466 015 / 210 4897800
Fax: (30) 210 3451970 / 210 4897831
Email: exports@apm.boltongroup.gr, mail@apm.boltongroup.gr
Web Address: www.boltongroup.net
Personnel:
Prod. Dir.: Eng. Makis Ktenas
Phone: (30) 210 3466 015
Finan. Dir.: S. Bostatsoglou
Phone: (30) 210 3466 015
Total Employees at this Location: 180
Type of Operation: Paper mill
Paper/Paperboard Grades and Capacities:
Total paper and paperboard capacity: 50,000 mt/y
Tissue: 50,000 mt/y
Paper and Paperboard Mill Data:
Stock Preparation:
Pulpers: 12
Refiners: 9
Paper Machines: 2
No. 8, inclined, Yankee dryer, total capacity 25,000 mt/y, Trim width 5 m, Tissue
No. 9, inclined, Yankee dryer, total capacity 25,000 mt/y, Trim width 5 m, Tissue
Finishing Equipment:
Supercalenders: 2
Rewinders: 2
Sheeters: 2
Energy Data:
Power boilers: 1
Electrical demand for mill: 140 MWh/D

ⓘBolton Hellas
Ownership: Bolton Group
Acteon Building, 2, Irinis Street
GR-18547 Neo Faliro, Athens
Greece
Phone: (30) 210 4897800
Fax: (30) 210 4897831
Email: mail@boltonhellas.boltongroup.gr
Web Address: www.boltongroup.net

Personnel:
Gen. Mgr.: Stelios Tsakalakis
Phone: (30) 210 4897800
Fax: (30) 210 4897831
Brand Mgr.: George Katsikaronis
Phone: (30) 210 4897800
Fax: (30) 210 4897831
Category Develop. Mgr.: George Tsakalakis
Phone: (30) 210 4897800
Fax: (30) 210 4897831
Admin. & Finan. Mgr.: Dimitris Avrasoglou
Phone: (30) 210 4897800
Fax: (30) 210 4897831
Key Account Mgr.: Emmanouil Xenoudakis
Phone: (30) 210 4897800
Fax: (30) 210 4897831
Purch. Correspondant: P. Togias
Phone: (30) 210 4897877
Email: ptogias@boltonhellas.boltongroup.gr
Sls. Mgr., Athens Paper Mill: Rafail Rafailidis
Phone: (30) 210 489 7874
Fax: (30) 210 489 7884
Email: rrafailidis@apm.boltongroup.gr
Total Employees at this Location: 100
Mill Locations:
Athens Paper Mill SA, Athens Mill, 1 Chartergaton st., Votanikos, GR-11855 Athens, Greece, Capacity: 50,000 mt/y, (Paper mill)
Phone: (30) 210 3466 015 / 210 4897800
Fax: (30) 210 3451970 / 210 4897831
Email: exports@apm.boltongroup.gr, mail@apm.boltongroup.gr

ⓘFthiotis Paper Mill SA
Ownership: El Pack S.A. (majority)
Orizomilon 5
GR-12244 Egaleo
Greece
Phone: (30) 210 5693240-1/5613101
Fax: (30) 210 5450863
Email: fthiapapermill@elpack.gr, fthiapapermill@otenet.gr
Web Address: www.elpack.gr
Personnel:
COO of El Pack Group: Vangelis Spirakis
Phone: (30) 210 5693240-1/5613101
Fax: (30) 210 5450863
Email: elpack@elpack.gr
Finan. Planner & Contr. of El Pack Group: Ioanna Labrinou
Phone: (30) 210 5693240-1/5613101
Fax: (30) 210 5450863
Email: elpack@elpack.gr
Purch. Mgr.: Elena Spiraki
Phone: (30) 210 5693240-1/5613101
Fax: (30) 210 5450863
Email: elspiraki@elpack.gr
Total Employees of Company: 61
Total Employees at this Location: 8
Mill Locations:
Fthiotis Paper Mill SA, Damasta Mill, GR-35100 Damasta, Greece, Capacity: 45,000 mt/y, (Paperboard mill)
Phone: (30) 22310 81211
Email: fthiapapermill@elpack.gr, fthiapapermill@otenet.gr

ⓜFthiotis Paper Mill SA
Damasta Mill
GR-35100 Damasta, Lamia
Greece
Phone: (30) 22310 81211
Email: fthiapapermill@elpack.gr, fthiapapermill@otenet.gr
Web Address: www.elpack.gr/siteold/fthiotis/indexf.htm
Personnel:
Mill Mgr.: Eng. Telis Christodoulopoulos
Phone: (30) 69 481 18710
Total Employees at this Location: 53
Type of Operation: Paperboard mill

Greece

Pulp Grades and Capacities:
Total pulp capacity: 45,839 mt/y
Recycled Pulping: 45,839 mt/y
Pulp Mill Data:
Recycled Fiber Treatment Lines:
Recycled packaging pulping lines: 1
Paper/Paperboard Grades and Capacities:
Total paper and paperboard capacity: 45,000 mt/y
Linerboard: 25,000 mt/y
Corrugating medium/fluting: 10,000 mt/y
Boxboard/cartonboard: 10,000 mt/y
Paper and Paperboard Mill Data:
Stock Preparation:
Pulpers: 3
Refiners: 8
Paper Machines: 1
No. 2, fourdrinier, total capacity 45,000 mt/y, Trim width 2.95 m, Corrugating medium/fluting, Linerboard, Boxboard/cartonboard
Coating Machines: 1
No. 1, total capacity 10,000 mt/y., on machine
Finishing Equipment:
Rewinders: 1
Sheeters: 1
Energy Data:
Power boilers
Electrical demand for mill: 72 MWh/D

ⓂA. Vl. Koliopoulos S.A. Pako
57 Ag. Polykarpou St.
GR-11855 Athens
Greece
  Phone: (30) 210 3467006
  Fax: (30) 210 3471281
  Email: info@pako.gr
  Web Address: www.pako.gr
Personnel:
  Chmn.: Eleni Koliopoulos
  Phone: (30) 210 3467006
  Fax: (30) 210 3471281
  Email: lenak@otenet.gr
  Man. Mgr.: Thomas Batavanis
  Phone: (30) 210 3467006
  Fax: (30) 210 3471281
  Email: batavanis@pako.gr
  Tech. Dir.: Pantelis Sarantos
  Phone: (30) 210 3467006
  Fax: (30) 210 3471281
  Email: sarantos@pako.gr
  Electrical & Computer Science Eng.: Thodoris Nikolaou
  Phone: (30) 210 3467006
  Fax: (30) 210 3471281
Total Employees of Company: 400
Total Employees at this Location: 50
Mill Locations:
A. Vl. Koliopoulos S.A. Pako, Korinthias Mill, GR-20002 Velo, Greece, Capacity: 10,000 mt/y, (Paper mill)
  Phone: (30) 27420 32385
  Fax: (30) 27420 30121
  Email: info@pako.gr
A. Vl. Koliopoulos S.A. Pako, Pelasghia Mill, GR-35013 Pelasghia, Greece, Capacity: 60,000 mt/y, (Paperboard mill)
  Phone: (30) 22380 51270/370
  Fax: (30) 22380 51262

ⓂA. Vl. Koliopoulos S.A. Pako
Korinthias Mill
GR-20002 Velo, Korinthias
Greece
  Phone: (30) 27420 32385
  Fax: (30) 27420 30121
  Email: info@pako.gr
  Web Address: www.pako.gr
Personnel:
  Mill Mgr.: Apostoles Steriopoulos
  Phone: (30) 27420 32385
  Fax: (30) 27420 30121
Total Employees at this Location: 50
Type of Operation: Paper mill
Paper/Paperboard Grades and Capacities:
Total paper and paperboard capacity: 10,000 mt/y
Linerboard: 10,000 mt/y
Paper and Paperboard Mill Data:
Stock Preparation:
Pulpers: 2
Refiners: 2
Paper Machines: 1
PM 2, cylinder, total capacity 10,000 mt/y, Trim width 2.2 m, Linerboard
Energy Data:
Power boilers: 2

ⓂA. Vl. Koliopoulos S.A. Pako
Pelasghia Mill
GR-35013 Pelasghia, Phtiotidos
Greece
  Phone: (30) 22380 51270/370
  Fax: (30) 22380 51262
Personnel:
  Mill Mgr.: Charilaos Karagounis
  Phone: (30) 6948 112277
  Fax: (30) 22380 51262
Total Employees at this Location: 250
Type of Operation: Paperboard mill
Pulp Grades and Capacities:
Total pulp capacity: 61,410 mt/y
Recycled Pulping: 61,410 mt/y
Paper/Paperboard Grades and Capacities:
Total paper and paperboard capacity: 60,000 mt/y
Linerboard: 37,000 mt/y
Corrugating medium/fluting: 23,000 mt/y
Paper and Paperboard Mill Data:
Stock Preparation:
Pulpers: 4
Refiners: 10
Paper Machines: 2
No. 3, fourdrinier, total capacity 24,000 mt/y, Trim width 2.3 m, Corrugating medium/fluting, Linerboard
No. 4, fourdrinier, total capacity 36,000 mt/y, Trim width 2.4 m, Corrugating medium/fluting, Linerboard
Energy Data:
Power boilers: 2
Electrical demand for mill: 96 MWh/D

ⓂⓂKomotini Papermill SA - Elina
Elina Mill
Industrial Area PO Box 57
GR-69100 Komotini
Greece
  Phone: (30) 25310 82216
  Fax: (30) 25310 82217/19
  Email: elinapm@otenet.gr, info@komotinipaper.gr
  Web Address: komotinipaper.gr
Personnel:
  Chmn.: George Gravouniotis
  Phone: (30) 25310 82216
  Fax: (30) 25310 82217
  Email: gg@komotinipaper.gr
  CEO: Dr. Paris Gravouniotis
  Phone: (30) 25310 82216
  Fax: (30) 25310 82217
  Email: pg@komotinipaper.gr
  Prod. Mgr.: Christos Papageorgiou
  Phone: (30) 69444 66726
  Fax: (30) 25310 82217
  Email: cp@komotinipaper.gr
  Tech. Mgr. : Margaritis Kapsalas
  Phone: (30) 25310 82216
  Fax: (30) 25310 82217
  Email: mk@komotinipaper.gr
  Sls. Mgr.: Chrysa Nestoridou
  Phone: (30) 25310 82216
  Fax: (30) 25310 82217
  Email: cn@komotinipaper.gr
Total Employees at this Location: 142
Type of Operation: Paper mill
Pulp Grades and Capacities:
Total pulp capacity: 3,188 mt/y
Recycled Pulping: 3,188 mt/y
Paper/Paperboard Grades and Capacities:
Total paper and paperboard capacity: 15,000 mt/y
Tissue: 15,000 mt/y
Paper and Paperboard Mill Data:
Stock Preparation:
Pulpers: 3
Refiners: 5
Paper Machines: 2
No. 1, fourdrinier, Yankee dryer, total capacity 3,000 mt/y, Trim width 1.8 m, Tissue
No. 2, crescent former, Yankee dryer, total capacity 12,000 mt/y, Trim width 2.1 m, Tissue
Finishing Equipment:
Rewinders: 3
Energy Data:
Power boilers: 3
Electrical demand for mill: 42 MWh/D

ⓂⓂMAXI S.A.
Katerini Mill
1st klm. O.R. Katerini - Thessaloniki
601 00 Katerini
Greece
  Phone: (30) 23510 31322
  Fax: (30) 23510 31143
  Web Address: www.maxi.gr
Personnel:
  Mill Eng.: Iordanis Samlidis
  Phone: (30) 23510 31322
  Fax: (30) 23510 31143
Total Employees of Company: 150
Total Employees at this Location: 150
Type of Operation: Paper mill
Paper/Paperboard Grades and Capacities:
Total paper and paperboard capacity: 23,000 mt/y
Tissue: 23,000 mt/y
Paper and Paperboard Mill Data:
Paper Machines: 1
No. 1, crescent former, Yankee dryer, total capacity 23,000 mt/y, Trim width 2.75 m, Tissue
Energy Data:
Power boilers
Electrical demand for mill: 60 MWh/D

ⓂⓂMel Macedonian Paper Mills S.A.
Thessaloniki Mill
Ownership: 100% by Pak Group
Kato Gefyra
GR-57011 Thessaloniki
Greece
  Phone: (30) 2310 728000
  Fax: (30) 2310 715351
  Email: info@melpaper.com, admin1@melpaper.com
  Web Address: www.melpaper.com
Personnel:
  Chmn./Pres./Man. Dir.: Kyriakos Economou
  Phone: (30) 2310 728102
  Fax: (30) 2310 715351
  Email: admin1@melpaper.com
  Mill Mgr.: George Georgiadis
  Phone: (30) 2310 728159
  Fax: (30) 2310 715351
  Email: g.georgiadis@melpaper.com
  Tech. Mgr.: Theothoros Pirdelis
  Phone: (30) 2310 728000
  Fax: (30) 2310 715351
  Email: techdpt@melpaper.com
Total Employees at this Location: 220
Type of Operation: Paperboard mill
Pulp Grades and Capacities:
Total pulp capacity: 88,524 mt/y
Recycled Pulping: 88,524 mt/y
Pulp Mill Data:
Recycled Fiber Treatment Lines:
Flotation deinking lines: 1

Greece

Paper/Paperboard Grades and Capacities:
Total paper and paperboard capacity: 95,000 mt/y
Boxboard/cartonboard: 95,000 mt/y
Paper and Paperboard Mill Data:
Stock Preparation:
Pulpers: 5
Refiners: 4
Paper Machines: 1
No. 1, cylinder (6), total capacity 95,000 mt/y, Trim width 3.6 m, Boxboard/cartonboard
Coating Machines: 3
No. 1, on machine
No. 2, on machine
No. 3, on machine
Finishing Equipment:
Rewinders: 2
Sheeters: 5
Energy Data:
Power boilers: 1
Electrical demand for mill: 115 MWh/D

ⓂPapyros Paper Mill S.A.
Papyros Mill
Ownership: 100% by Sofidel Group
1st km Old Nat. Road Katerini-Thessaloniki
GR-60100 Katerini
Greece
Phone: (30) 23 510 79500
Fax: (30) 23 510 79501
Email: info@papyros-pm.com
Web Address: www.sofidel.com
Personnel:
Tech. & Mill Mgr.: Eng. Nikos Batzios
Phone: (30) 69 702 65110
Fax: (30) 23 510 79501
Prod. Plan.: Efthymia Bakaimi
Phone: (30) 23 510 79500
Fax: (30) 23 510 79501
Total Employees at this Location: 36
Type of Operation: Paper mill
Paper/Paperboard Grades and Capacities:
Total paper and paperboard capacity: 25,000 mt/y
Tissue: 25,000 mt/y
Paper and Paperboard Mill Data:
Stock Preparation:
Pulpers: 2
Refiners: 2
Paper Machines: 1
No. 1, crescent former, Yankee dryer, total capacity 25,000 mt/y, Trim width 2.75 m, Tissue
Energy Data:
Power boilers
Electrical demand for mill: 65 MWh/D

ⓂⓂPatras Paper Mills SA
Patras Mill
Kria Iteon
GR-26333 Patras, Achaia
Greece
Phone: (30) 2610 520398/522324
Fax: (30) 2610 523584
Email: admin@elite.gr
Web Address: www.elite.gr
Personnel:
Pres.: George Triantafillopoulos
Phone: (30) 2610 520398
Fax: (30) 2610 523584
Email: george@elite.gr
Mill Mgr.: Eng. Michael Androulakis
Phone: (30) 2610 520398
Fax: (30) 2610 523584
Email: mandroulakis@elite.gr
Total Employees at this Location: 70
Type of Operation: Paper mill
Paper/Paperboard Grades and Capacities:
Total paper and paperboard capacity: 10,000 mt/y
Tissue: 10,000 mt/y
Paper and Paperboard Mill Data:
Stock Preparation:
Pulpers: 1
Refiners: 3
Paper Machines: 1
No. 1, fourdrinier, Yankee dryer, total capacity 10,000 mt/y, Trim width 2 m, Tissue
Finishing Equipment:
Rewinders: 1
Energy Data:
Power boilers: 2
Electrical demand for mill: 30 MWh/D

ⓂSCA Patras
Patras Mill
Ownership: 100% by SCA - Svenska Cellulosa Aktiebolaget
Industrial Area of Patras, PO Box 150
GR-25018 Ag. Stefanos - Patras, Achaia
Greece
Phone: (30) 2610 242200
Fax: (30) 2610 647216
Web Address: www.sca.com
Personnel:
Mill Mgr.: George Placogiannakis
Phone: (30) 2610 242200
Fax: (30) 2610 647216
Email: george.placogiannakis@sca.com
Total Employees at this Location: 72
Type of Operation: Paper mill
Paper/Paperboard Grades and Capacities:
Total paper and paperboard capacity: 20,000 mt/y
Tissue: 20,000 mt/y
Paper and Paperboard Mill Data:
Stock Preparation:
Pulpers: 1
Refiners: 2
Paper Machines: 1
No. 1, twin-wire, Yankee dryer, total capacity 20,000 mt/y, Trim width 2.55 m, Tissue
Finishing Equipment:
Rewinders: 1
Energy Data:
Power boilers: 2
Electrical demand for mill: 56 MWh/D

ⓂⓂSER.PA.M S.A.
Serres Mill
22 L. Papadovlou St., Neohori
GR-62100 Serres
Greece
Phone: (30) 23210 76000
Fax: (30) 23210 76004
Email: info@serpam.gr
Web Address: www.serpam.gr
Personnel:
Owner & Tech. Mgr. Eng.: Eng. Angelo Cavalli
Phone: (30) 6944550618
Total Employees at this Location: 50
Type of Operation: Paper mill
Paper/Paperboard Grades and Capacities:
Total paper and paperboard capacity: 3,000 mt/y
Specialty and industrial: 3,000 mt/y
Paper and Paperboard Mill Data:
Paper Machines: 1
No. 1, (second hand), total capacity 3,000 mt/y, Trim width 2.5 m

ⓂSonoco Hellas
Stavrohori Mill
Ownership: 100% by Sonoco Products Co.
10.5 km Kilkis Doirani National Road
GR-61100 Stavrohori, Kilkis
Greece
Mailing Address: P.O. Box 85, GR-61100 Stavrohori, Kilkis, Greece
Phone: (30) 23 41051558
Fax: (30) 23 41051267
Web Address: www.sonoco.com
Personnel:
Mill Mgr.: Yiannis Tsakiridis
Phone: (30) 23 41051558, 69 72039916
Fax: (30) 23 41051267
Email: yiannis.tsakiridis@sonoco-alcore.net
Finan. Mgr.: Anna Karakasi
Phone: (30) 23 41051558
Fax: (30) 23 41051267
Email: anna.karakasi@sonoco.com
Accountant: Dafni Stefanidou
Phone: (30) 23 41051558
Fax: (30) 23 41051267
Email: dafni.stefanidou@sonoco.com
Total Employees at this Location: 47
Type of Operation: Paper mill, Paperboard mill
Pulp Grades and Capacities:
Total pulp capacity: 25,160 mt/y
Recycled Pulping: 25,160 mt/y
Paper/Paperboard Grades and Capacities:
Total paper and paperboard capacity: 25,000 mt/y
Boxboard/cartonboard: 25,000 mt/y
Paper and Paperboard Mill Data:
Stock Preparation:
Pulpers: 1
Refiners: 2
Paper Machines: 1
No. 1, multi-fourdrinier, total capacity 25,000 mt/y, Trim width 2.2 m, Boxboard/cartonboard
Finishing Equipment:
Calenders: 1
Rewinders: 1 at 30,000 mt/y
Energy Data:
Power boilers: 1
Electrical demand for mill: 41 MWh/D

ⓉTechnocart SA
Ownership: 40% by Haitoglou-Hartel SA, 60% by Lagos Family
6 Aghias Sophias St., Nea Smirni
GR-17123 Athens
Greece
Phone: (30) 210 935 5043/4
Fax: (30) 210 935 5040
Email: info@technocart.gr
Web Address: www.technocart.gr
Personnel:
Man. Dir./Sls.& Mktg. Dir.: Dimitris Lagos
Phone: (30) 210 935 5043/4
Fax: (30) 210 935 5040
Email: dlagos@technocart.gr
Total Employees of Company: 40
Total Employees at this Location: 6
Mill Locations:
Technocart SA, Tripolis Mill, Industrial Area of Tripolis, GR-22100 Tripolis, Greece, Capacity: 26,000 mt/y, (Paper mill)
Phone: (30) 2710 239 250
Fax: (30) 2710 233 373
Email: info@technocart.gr

ⓂTechnocart SA
Tripolis Mill
Industrial Area of Tripolis
GR-22100 Tripolis
Greece
Phone: (30) 2710 239 250
Fax: (30) 2710 233 373
Email: info@technocart.gr
Web Address: www.technocart.gr
Personnel:
Mill Mgr.: Nikos Lagos
Phone: (30) 2710 239 250
Fax: (30) 2710 233 373
Email: nlagos@technocart.gr
Tech. Mgr.: Vasilis Angelopoulos
Phone: (30) 2710 239 250
Fax: (30) 2710 233 373
Email: angelopoulos@technocart.gr
Qlty. Assur. & Environ. Mgr.: Panagiotis Frontistis
Phone: (30) 2710 239 250
Fax: (30) 2710 233 373
Email: frontistis@technocart.gr

Greece

Total Employees at this Location: 38
Type of Operation: Paper mill
Pulp Grades and Capacities:
  Total pulp capacity: 23,346 mt/y
  Recycled Pulping: 23,346 mt/y
Pulp Mill Data:
  Recycled Fiber Treatment Lines:
  Recycled packaging pulping lines: 2
Paper/Paperboard Grades and Capacities:
  Total paper and paperboard capacity: 26,000 mt/y
  Packaging papers: 2,000 mt/y
  Linerboard: 16,000 mt/y
  Corrugating medium/fluting: 8,000 mt/y
Paper and Paperboard Mill Data:
  Stock Preparation:
  Pulpers: 2
  Refiners: 3
Paper Machines: 1
  No. 1, fourdrinier (2), total capacity 26,000 mt/y, Trim width 2.5 m, Corrugating medium/fluting, Linerboard, Packaging papers
Finishing Equipment:
  Calenders: 1
  Rewinders: 1 at 25,000 mt/y
Energy Data:
  Power boilers: 1
  Electrical demand for mill: 33 MWh/D

ⓂThrace Paper Mill S.A.
Thrace (Diana) Mill
Ownership: 100% by Zeritis Group
17th km Xanthi-Magana Road
67100 Xanthi
Greece
  Phone: (30) 25 410 94002/94024/29040
  Fax: (30) 25 410 94168/94146
  Email: sales@diana.gr
  Web Address: www.zeritis.gr/diana/index.html
Personnel:
  Mill Mgr.: Stephanos Charalamboglou
  Phone: (30) 25 410 94002/94024/29040
  Paper Mill Mgr.: Christos Dimitriadis
  Phone: (30) 25 410 94002/94024/29040
  Environmental Dir.: Nikos Mattheos
  Phone: (30) 25 410 94002/94024/29040
Total Employees at this Location: 118
Type of Operation: Pulp mill, Paper mill
Pulp Grades and Capacities:
  Total pulp capacity: 36,000 mt/y
  Recycled Pulping: 36,000 mt/y
Pulp Mill Data:
  Recycled Fiber Treatment Lines:
  Flotation deinking lines: 1 at 36,000 admt/y
  Pulpers: 1 at 36,000 admt/y
  Washing deinking lines: 1 at 36,000 admt/y
Paper/Paperboard Grades and Capacities:
  Total paper and paperboard capacity: 50,000 mt/y
  Tissue: 50,000 mt/y
Paper and Paperboard Mill Data:
  Stock Preparation:
  Pulpers: 3
  Refiners: 6
Paper Machines: 2
  No. 2, fourdrinier, Yankee dryer, total capacity 22,000 mt/y, Trim width 2.55 m, Tissue
  No. 3, crescent former, Yankee dryer, total capacity 28,000 mt/y, Trim width 2.55 m, Tissue
Energy Data:
  Power boilers
  Electrical demand for mill: 164 MWh/D

ⓂViochartiki Paper Mill SA
Ownership: Anastasios Voutselas
19 Themidos St., Rentis
GR-18233 Piraeus
Greece
  Phone: (30) 210 4825411-19
  Fax: (30) 210 4819001
  Email: sales@viochartiki.gr, info@viochartiki.gr
  Web Address: www.viochartiki.gr
Personnel:
  Sales Mngr.: Tiannis Argiropoulos
  Phone: (30) 210 4825411-19
  Fax: (30) 210 4819001
  Email: sales@viochartiki.gr
  Secretary: Viki Zgura
  Phone: (30) 210 557 1310
  Fax: (30) 210 4823936
  Email: personnel@viochartiki.gr
Total Employees of Company: 150
Total Employees at this Location: 20
Mill Locations:
Viochartiki Paper Mill SA, Aspropirgos Mill, Drassara Point, GR-19300 Aspropirgos, Greece, Capacity: 61,000 mt/y, (Paper mill)
  Phone: (30) 210 5571310-15
  Fax: (30) 210 5575432
  Email: info@viochartiki.gr; papermill@viochartiki.gr

ⓂViochartiki Paper Mill SA
Aspropirgos Mill
Drassara Point
GR-19300 Aspropirgos, Attica
Greece
  Phone: (30) 210 5571310-15
  Fax: (30) 210 5575432
  Email: info@viochartiki.gr, papermill@viochartiki.gr
  Web Address: www.viochartiki.gr
Personnel:
  Owner, Chmn. Man. Dir., Mill Mgr., Purch. Mgr.: Dimitrious Voutselas
  Phone: (30) 210 5571310-15
  Maint. Mgr.: Thanasis Bourandas
  Phone: (30) 210 5571310-15
  Email: mechanical@viochartiki.gr
  Prod. Mgr.: Kyriakos Psalikides
  Phone: (30) 210 5571310-15
  Sec.: Viki Zgura
  Phone: (30) 210 4825411-19
Total Employees at this Location: 130
Type of Operation: Paper mill
Pulp Grades and Capacities:
  Total pulp capacity: 63,353 mt/y
  Recycled Pulping: 63,353 mt/y
Pulp Mill Data:
  Recycled Fiber Treatment Lines:
  Pulpers: 2
Paper/Paperboard Grades and Capacities:
  Total paper and paperboard capacity: 61,000 mt/y
  Tissue: 16,000 mt/y
  Packaging papers: 45,000 mt/y
Paper and Paperboard Mill Data:
  Stock Preparation:
  Pulpers: 4
  Refiners: 3
Paper Machines: 2
  No. 1, fourdrinier, total capacity 45,000 mt/y, Trim width 2.45 m, Packaging papers
  No. 2, fourdrinier, Yankee dryer, total capacity 16,000 mt/y, Trim width 2.85 m, Tissue
Finishing Equipment:
  Supercalenders: 1
  Rewinders: 3
  Sheeters: 3
Energy Data:
  Power boilers: 3
  Electrical demand for mill: 142 MWh/D

ⓂVIS Containers Manufacturing SA
Ownership: Filippou family, 67.50% by IOFIL S.A.
G. Genimatas Ave.
GR-190 16 Magoula, Attica
Greece
  Phone: (30) 210 6161300
  Fax: (30) 210 6161399
  Email: info@vis.gr, sales@vis.gr
  Web Address: www.vis.gr
Personnel:
  Chmn. & Man. Dir.: Dimitrios Filippou
  Phone: (30) 210 6161300
  Fax: (30) 210 6161499
  CEO & VP of the Board: George Hadjivassileiou
  Phone: (30) 210 61 61 300
  Fax: (30) 210 61 61 399
  CFO & Bd. Mbr.: Kyriakos Soupionas
  Phone: (30) 210 61 61 300
  Fax: (30) 210 61 61 399
  Email: k.soupionas@omphalio.gr
  Purch. Dir./Corporate Controlling Dir.: Dimitris Karatzas
  Phone: (30) 210 6161 105
  Fax: (30) 210 6161499
  Email: d.karatzas@omphalio.gr
  Sls./Mktg. Dir.: Christos Zablakos
  Phone: (30) 210 6161 228
  Fax: (30) 210 61 61 399
  Email: c.zablakos@vis.gr
Total Employees at this Location: 240
Mill Locations:
VIS Containers Manufacturing SA, Volos Mill, Volos Industrial Zone, GR-385 00 Volos, Greece, Capacity: 23,000 mt/y, (Pulp mill, Paper mill, Paperboard mill)
  Phone: (30) 24210 95334
  Fax: (30) 210 6161399
  Email: info@vis.gr

ⓂVIS Containers Manufacturing SA
Volos Mill
Volos Industrial Zone
GR-385 00 Volos
Greece
Mailing Address: 4 Gravias Street, GR-15121 Maroussi, Greece
  Phone: (30) 24210 95334
  Fax: (30) 210 6161399
  Email: info@vis.gr
  Web Address: www.vis.gr
Personnel:
  Plt. Dir.: Athanasios Tzitzaras
  Phone: (30) 24210 95334
  Fax: (30) 21061 61399
  Email: a.tzitzaras@vis.gr
  R&D Mgr. & Quality Control Mgr.: Konstantinos Karagiannis
  Phone: (30) 24210 95334
  Fax: (30) 21061 61399
  Email: c.karagiannis@vis.gr
Total Employees at this Location: 40
Type of Operation: Pulp mill, Paper mill, Paperboard mill
Pulp Grades and Capacities:
  Total pulp capacity: 23,357 mt/y
  Recycled Pulping: 23,357 mt/y
Pulp Mill Data:
  Recycled Fiber Treatment Lines:
  Pulpers: 2 at 25,000 admt/y
Paper/Paperboard Grades and Capacities:
  Total paper and paperboard capacity: 23,000 mt/y
  Linerboard: 23,000 mt/y
Paper and Paperboard Mill Data:
  Stock Preparation:
  Pulpers: 2
  Refiners: 5
Paper Machines: 2
  No. 1, fourdrinier, total capacity 13,000 mt/y, Trim width 2.2 m, Linerboard
  No. 2, cylinder, total capacity 10,000 mt/y, Trim width 2.2 m, Linerboard
Finishing Equipment:
  Rewinders: 2
Energy Data:
  Power boilers: 1
  Electrical demand for mill: 29 MWh/D

Hungary

⊕Zeritis Group
Iera Odos 150
GR-12242 Athens
Greece
 Phone: (30) 210 6248700
 Fax: (30) 210 8071469
 Email: zeritis@zeritis.gr
 Web Address: www.zeritis.gr, www.diana.gr
Personnel:
 Chmn. & Pres.: Panos Zeritis
 Phone: (30) 210 6248700
 Fax: (30) 210 8071469
 Sls. Mgr.: George Sofianopoulos
 Phone: (30) 210 6248700
 Fax: (30) 210 8071469
 Purch. Dir.: John Frangopoulos
 Phone: (30) 210 6248700
 Fax: (30) 210 8071469
Total Employees of Company: 2,500
Total Employees at this Location: 250
Mill Locations:
 Belovo Paper Mill S.A., Belovo Mill (68.07% owned), 1A, Dabravsko shose str., BG-4470 Belovo, Bulgaria, Capacity: 66,000 mt/y, (Paper mill)
 Phone: (359) 3581 2653 / 35812105-09
 Fax: (359) 3581 2110
 Email: office@belana.bg, belana_bg@yahoo.com
 Pyramids Paper Mills S.A.E. - Flora, 6th October City Mill (62.50% owned), Plot no. 194/195, 1st Industrial Zone, 6th October City, Egypt, Capacity: 55,000 mt/y, (Paper mill)
 Phone: (20) 23 833 1400
 Fax: (20) 23 833 1010/0500
 Email: ppm@flora.com.eg
 Thrace Paper Mill S.A., Thrace (Diana) Mill, 17th km Xanthi-Magana Road, 67100 Xanthi, Greece, Capacity: 50,000 mt/y, (Pulp mill, Paper mill)
 Phone: (30) 25 410 94002/94024/29040
 Fax: (30) 25 410 94168/94146
 Email: sales@diana.gr

HUNGARY

⊕Diósgyöri Papírgyár Rt.
Ownership: 100% by Penzjegynyomda
Hegyalja út 203/1 Miskolc, H-3535
Miskolc
Hungary
Mailing Address: Postf. 540, H-3510 Miskolc, Hungary
 Phone: (36) 46 530 890
 Fax: (36) 46 530 810
 Email: dipa@dipa.hu
 Web Address: www.dipa.hu
Personnel:
 CEO: András Kassai
 Phone: (36) 46 530 800
 Fax: (36) 46 530 810
 CFO: Gizella Ráczkövy
 Phone: (36) 46 530 800
 Fax: (36) 46 530 810
 Sls. & Mktg. Dir.: István Garai
 Phone: (36) 46 530 800
 Fax: (36) 46 530 810
 Email: garai.istvan@dipa.hu
Total Employees of Company: 150
Mill Locations:
 Diósgyöri Papírgyár Rt, Miskolc Mill, Hegyalja út 203/1, H-3535 Miskolc, Hungary, Capacity: 1,000 mt/y, (Paper mill)
 Phone: (36) 46 530 890
 Fax: (36) 46 530 810
 Email: dipa@dipa.hu

⊕Diósgyöri Papírgyár Rt.
Miskolc Mill
Hegyalja út 203/1
H-3535 Miskolc
Hungary
Mailing Address: Postf. 540, H-3510 Miskolc, Hungary
 Phone: (36) 46 530 890
 Fax: (36) 46 530 810
 Email: dipa@dipa.hu
 Web Address: www.dipa.hu
Personnel:
 Gen. Dir.: Gyula Juhász
 Phone: (36) 46 530 800
 Contr.: Mónika Tóth
 Phone: (36) 46 530 821
 Fax: (36) 46 530 840
 Email: tothnenagy.monika@dipa.hu
 Tech. Dir.: István Mida
 Phone: (36) 46 530 871
 Fax: (36) 46 530 870
 Email: mida.istvan@dipa.hu
 Sls. Mgr.: Gyöngyi Kerekes
 Phone: (36) 46 530 847
 Fax: (36) 46 530 840
 Email: kerekes.gyongyi@dipa.hu
 R&D Dir.: Ildikó Zákány
 Phone: (36) 46 530 828
 Fax: (36) 46 530 880
 Email: zakany.ildiko@dipa.hu
 Qlty. Assurance Dir.: Edit Fülöp Török
 Phone: (36) 46 530 829
 Fax: (36) 46 530 880
 Email: toroknefulop.edit@dipa.hu
Total Employees at this Location: 150
Type of Operation: Paper mill
Paper/Paperboard Grades and Capacities:
 Total paper and paperboard capacity: 1,000 mt/y
 Uncoated woodfree/freesheet: 1,000 mt/y
 Specialty and industrial
Paper and Paperboard Mill Data:
 Stock Preparation:
 Pulpers: 1
 Refiners: 3
Paper Machines: 1
 No. 2, cylinder mould, fourdrinier, total capacity 1,000 mt/y, Trim width 1 m, Uncoated woodfree/freesheet, Specialty and industrial
Finishing Equipment:
 Supercalenders: 1 at 5,000 mt/y
 Rewinders: 2 at 1,000 mt/y, 12,000 mt/y
 Sheeters: 1 at 1,000 mt/y
Energy Data:
 Power boilers: 2

⊕Dunafin Kft.
Dunaujvaros Mill
Ownership: 100% by delfortgroup AG
Papirgyari ut. 42-46
H-2400 Dunaujvaros
Hungary
 Phone: (36) 25 511 400
 Fax: (36) 25 511 415
 Email: dunafin@delfortgroup.com
 Web Address: www.delfortgroup.com
Personnel:
 Contr.: Éva Pajor
 Phone: (36) 25 511 400
 Fax: (36) 25 511 415
 Email: eva.pajor@delfortgroup.com
 Finan. Mgr.: Anikó Somodi
 Phone: (36) 25 511 400
 Fax: (36) 25 511 415
 Email: aniko.somodi@delfortgroup.com
 Assist. Mill Mgr.: Ágnes Pintér
 Phone: (36) 25 511 400
 Fax: (36) 25 511 415
 Email: agnes.pinter@delfortgroup.com
Total Employees at this Location: 150
Type of Operation: Paper mill
Pulp Mill Data:
 Bleach Plant Systems: 1
 Chemical Recovery Equipment:
 Evaporator lines: 2
 Recovery boilers: 2
Paper/Paperboard Grades and Capacities:
 Total paper and paperboard capacity: 110,000 mt/y
 Specialty and industrial: 110,000 mt/y
Paper and Paperboard Mill Data:
 Stock Preparation:
 Pulpers: 5
 Refiners: 4
Paper Machines: 1
 No. 9, SymFormer MB, total capacity 110,000 mt/y, Trim width 4.3 m, Specialty and industrial
Finishing Equipment:
 Supercalenders: 1
 Rewinders: 2 at 100,000 mt/y
 Sheeters: 2 at 65,000 mt/y
Energy Data:
 Power boilers: 1
 Electrical demand for mill: 297 MWh/D

⊕⊕Hamburger Hungaria Ltd
Dunaújváros Mill
Ownership: 100% by Prinzhorn Holding GmbH
Papírgyári út 42-46
H-2400 Dunaújváros
Hungary
Mailing Address: PO BOX 552, H-2401 Dunaújváros, Hungary
 Phone: (36) 25 557 200/700
 Fax: (36) 25 557 286/777
 Email: office@hamburger-hungaria.com
 Web Address: www.hamburger-hungaria.com
Personnel:
 Man. Dir. / Head of Oper.: Attila Bencs
 Phone: (36) 25 55 7701
 Fax: (36) 25 55 7777
 Email: attila.bencs@hamburger-hungaria.com
 MD, Hamburger Hungaria Power: Dr. Zoltan Szikla
 Phone: (36) 25 557 200
 Fax: (36) 25 557 286
 Email: zoltan.szikla@hamburger-hungaria.com
 Head of Contr. & Admin.: Eva Forgo
 Phone: (36) 25 557 702
 Fax: (36) 25 557 739
 Email: eva.forgo@hamburger-hungaria.com
 Prod. Mgr.: Gyorgy Szilas
 Phone: (36) 25 55 7705
 Fax: (36) 25 55 7700
 Email: gyorgy.szilas@hamburger-hungaria.com
 Head of Sls. Central Eastern Europe (CEE): Antal Braunecker
 Phone: (36) 25 55 7703
 Fax: (36) 25 55 7749
 Email: antal.braunecker@hamburger-hungaria.com
 Head of Tech. Purch. & Logist.: Jeno Vass
 Phone: (36) 25 55 7790
 Fax: (36) 25 55 7320
 Email: kornelia.kaiser@hamburger-hungaria.com
 HR Leader: Anna Szalai
 Phone: (36) 25 55 7730
 Fax: (36) 25 55 7733
 Email: anna.szalai@hamburger-hungaria.com
Total Employees at this Location: 280
Type of Operation: Paperboard mill
Pulp Grades and Capacities:
 Total pulp capacity: 571,821 mt/y
 Recycled Pulping: 571,821 mt/y
Pulp Mill Data:
 Recycled Fiber Treatment Lines:
 Pulpers: 6
Paper/Paperboard Grades and Capacities:
 Total paper and paperboard capacity: 580,000 mt/y
 Linerboard: 250,000 mt/y
 Corrugating medium/fluting: 330,000 mt/y
Paper and Paperboard Mill Data:
Paper Machines: 2
 No. 3, fourdrinier, total capacity 180,000 mt/y, Trim width 4.32 m, Corrugating medium/fluting, Linerboard

Ireland

No. 7, DuoFormer Base, total capacity 400,000 mt/y, Trim width 7.8 m, Corrugating medium/fluting, Linerboard
Energy Data:
Power boilers: 4
Steam turbines: 1 at 12.0 MW
Electrical demand for mill: 676 MWh/D

Higi Papersoft Co. Ltd.
Szolnok Mill
Piroskai Ut. 16
H-5000 Szolnok
Hungary
Mailing Address: Piroskai Ut. 16, H-5000 Szolnok, Hungary
Phone: (36) 706300159 /5652 1160 /709421492
Fax: (36) 5652 1161
Email: sales@higipapir.com
Personnel:
Tech. Mgr.: Zoltan Harsanyi
Phone: (36) 7063 00159
Fax: (36) 5652 1161
HR Mgr.: Krisztina Nagy
Phone: (36) 1 3519665
Fax: (36) 5652 1161
Technologist: Istvan Foldes
Phone: (36) 7063 00159
Fax: (36) 5652 1161
Chief Electrician: Laszlo Povedak
Phone: (36) 7063 00159
Fax: (36) 5652 1161
Total Employees at this Location: 160
Type of Operation: Paper mill
Paper/Paperboard Grades and Capacities:
Total paper and paperboard capacity: 30,000 mt/y
Tissue: 30,000 mt/y
Paper and Paperboard Mill Data:
Paper Machines: 1
No. 1, OVER Former-CR, Yankee dryer, total capacity 29,988 mt/y, Trim width 2.9 m, Tissue
Energy Data:
Power boilers
Electrical demand for mill: 75 MWh/D

IRELAND

Smurfit Kappa Group
Ownership: 8.74% by Norges Bank, Public
Beech Hill, Clonskeagh
Dublin 4
Ireland
Phone: (353) 1 2027000
Fax: (353) 1 2694481
Email: info@smurfitkappa.com
Web Address: www.smurfitkappa.com
Personnel:
CEO: Gary McGann
Phone: (353) 1 2027000
Fax: (353) 1 2694481
Email: gary.mcgann@smurfitkappa.com
COO: Antony Smurfit
Phone: (353) 1 2027000
Fax: (353) 1 2694481
Email: anthony.smurfit@smurfitkappa.com
CFO: Ian J. Curley
Phone: (353) 1 2027000
Fax: (353) 1 2694481
Email: ian.curley@smurfitkappa.com
Group Company Sec.: Michael O'Riordan
Phone: (353) 1 2027000
Fax: (353) 1 2694481
Email: michael.oriordan@smurfitkappa.com
Group Finan. Contrl.: Ken Bowles
Phone: (353) 1 2027000
Fax: (353) 1 2694481
Email: ken.bowles@smurfitkappa.com
Group Corp. Planner: Ray Murphy
Phone: (353) 1 2027000
Fax: (353) 1 2694481
Email: ray.murphy@smurfitkappa.com
Total Employees of Company: 41,000
Total Employees at this Location: 50
Mill Locations:
PAPELSA - Papeles y Cartones SA, Barbosa Mill, Troncal del Nordeste km 1, Via Porce, Barbosa, Colombia, Capacity: 64,260 mt/y, (Paper mill, Paperboard mill)
Phone: (57) 4 405 7000
Fax: (57) 4 406 2788
Email: alvaro.henao@papelsa.com
Smurfit Kappa Cellulose du Pin, Facture mill, Allée des Fougères, F-33380 Biganos, France, Capacity: 520,000 mt/y, (Pulp mill, Paperboard mill)
Phone: (33) 5 56 03 88 00
Fax: (33) 5 56 03 88 02
Smurfit Kappa Cartón y Papel de México S.A. de C.V., Cerro Gordo Mill, Km. 15.5 Carr. Mexico-Laredo, 55540 Santa Clara Coatitla, Ecatepec de Morelos, Mexico, Capacity: 269,892 mt/y, (Pulp mill, Paperboard mill)
Phone: (52) 55 5729 2300
Fax: (52) 55 3067 5233
Email: juancarlos.benavides@smurfitkappa.com.mx
Smurfit Kappa Ania Paper, Ania Mill, Via del Mulino, I-55055 Ponte all'Ania, (LU), Italy, Capacity: 200,000 mt/y, (Paper mill, Paperboard mill)
Phone: (39) 0583 70031
Fax: (39) 0583 709179
Email: ania.paper@smurfitkappa.it
Smurfit Kappa de Argentina S.A., Bernal Mill (80% owned), Espora 200, 1876 Bernal, Argentina, Capacity: 62,832 mt/y, (Paper mill, Paperboard mill)
Phone: (54) 11 4259 6990/5253 7000
Fax: (54) 11 4259 9995/4259 3134
Smurfit Kappa de Argentina S.A., Coronel Suárez Mill (80% owned), Av. M. Lloveras 531, 7540 Coronel Suárez, Argentina, Capacity: 49,980 mt/y, (Paperboard mill)
Phone: (54) 292 643 1700
Fax: (54) 292 642 4188
Smurfit Kappa Baden Karton GmbH, Gernsbach Mill, Fabrikstrasse 1, D-76593 Gernsbach, Germany, Capacity: 145,000 mt/y, (Paperboard mill)
Phone: (49) 7224 630
Fax: (49) 7224 631 48
Email: baden-karton@smurfitkappa.de
Smurfit Kappa Cartón de Venezuela S.A., Caracas Mill (78% owned), Final Calle El Hatillo, 1070-A Petare, Caracas, Venezuela, Capacity: 23,919 mt/y, (Paperboard mill)
Phone: (58) 212 219 1100/01
Fax: (58) 212 219 1243
Smurfit Kappa Cartón de Colombia SA, Barranquilla Mill (70% owned), Via 40 # 85 - 695 Las Flores, Barranquilla, Colombia, Capacity: 58,905 mt/y, (Paperboard mill)
Phone: (57) 5 373 4500/ 5373 4579
Fax: (57) 5 373 4579
Email: cesar.valencia@smurfitkappa.com.co
Smurfit Kappa Cartón de Colombia SA, Yumbo Mill (70% owned), Antigua Carretera a Yumbo Km. 15, Cali, Colombia, Capacity: 251,685 mt/y, (Pulp mill, Paper mill, Paperboard mill)
Phone: (57) 2 691 4000
Fax: (57) 2 691 4199
Email: comunicaciones@smurfitkappa.com.co
Smurfit Kappa Haupt Papier- und Pappenfabrik GmbH & Co. KG, Diemelstadt-Wrexen Mill, Orpethaler Str. 50, D-34474 Diemelstadt-Wrexen, Germany, Capacity: 320,000 mt/y, (Paper mill, Paperboard mill)
Phone: (49) 5642 790
Fax: (49) 5642 79177
Email: info@cdhaupt.de
Smurfit Kappa Herzberger Papierfabrik GmbH, Herzberg Mill, Andreasberger Str. 1, D-37412 Herzberg am Harz, Germany, Capacity: 260,000 mt/y, (Paperboard mill)
Phone: (49) 5521 82 0
Fax: (49) 5521 82 395
Email: info.hp@smurfitkappa.de
Smurfit Kappa Papier & Kartonfabrik Hoya, Hoya Mill, Von-dem-Bussche-Str. 1, D-27318 Hoya/Weser, Germany, Capacity: 425,000 mt/y, (Paperboard mill)
Phone: (49) 4251 8140
Fax: (49) 4251 814 169
Email: info.hoya@smurfitkappa.de
Smurfit Kappa Kraftliner Piteå, Piteå Mill, SE-941 86 Piteå, Sweden, Capacity: 700,000 mt/y, (Pulp mill, Paperboard mill)
Phone: (46) 911 97000
Fax: (46) 911 97010
Email: info.kraftliner@smurfitkappa.se
Smurfit Kappa Papier Recyclé France, Alfa d Avignon Mill, Route Nationale 7 - BP 56, F-84132 Le Pontet Cedex, France, Capacity: 75,000 mt/y, (Paperboard mill)
Phone: (33) 4 90 03 98 00
Fax: (33) 4 90 32 34 33
Email: info-paper@smurfitkappa.com
Smurfit Kappa Mengibar Paper, Mengibar Mill, Carretera de Bailén-Motril, s/n, E-23620 Mengibar, Spain, Capacity: 200,000 mt/y, (Paper mill, Paperboard mill)
Phone: (34) 95 337 0775
Fax: (34) 95 337 0825
Smurfit Kappa Morava Paper, Žimrovice Mill, plant Morava Paper, CZ-747 41 Žimrovice, Czech Republic, Capacity: 56,000 mt/y, (Paper mill)
Phone: (420) 553 753 111
Fax: (420) 553 753 114
Email: sales.moravapaper@smurfitkappa.cz; ludek.jurica@smurfitkappa.cz
Smurfit Kappa SSK, Birmingham Mill, Mount St., Nechells, Birmingham B7 5RE, United Kingdom, Capacity: 200,000 mt/y, (Paperboard mill)
Phone: (44) 121 327 1381
Fax: (44) 121 322 6300
Email: info@smurfitkappa.co.uk
Smurfit Kappa Nervión, Iurreta Mill, B° Arriandi, s/n, E-48215 Iurreta, Spain, Capacity: 160,000 mt/y, (Pulp mill, Paper mill, Paperboard mill)
Phone: (34) 946 205100
Fax: (34) 946 205124
Smurfit Kappa Nettingsdorfer, Nettingsdorfer Papierfabrik AG & Co. KG, Nettingsdorfer Mill, Nettingsdorfer Strasse 40, A-4054 Haid bei Ansfelden, Austria, Capacity: 430,000 mt/y, (Pulp mill, Paperboard mill)
Phone: (43) 7229 863 0
Fax: (43) 7229 863 50 / 29 86 312
Email: nettingsdorfer@smurfitkappa.at
Smurfit Kappa Orange County, Forney Mill, 855 East Hwy 80, Forney, TX 75126, USA, Capacity: 305,086 mt/y, (Paperboard mill)
Phone: (1) 214-515-6400, 888-870-4582
Fax: (1) 214-515-6499
Smurfit Kappa Papier Recyclé France, Sault-les-Rethel mill, Rue de la Petite Prée, BP 5109, F-08300 Sault-les-Rethel, France, Capacity: 68,000 mt/y, (Paperboard mill)
Phone: (33) 3 24 39 61 81/61
Fax: (33) 3 24 39 61 90
Smurfit Kappa Roermond Papier BV, Roermond Mill, Mijnheerkensweg 18, NL-6041 TA Roermond, Netherlands, Capacity: 590,000 mt/y, (Paperboard mill)
Phone: (31) 475 38 44 44
Fax: (31) 475 33 26 20
Email: info.skrp@smurfitkappa.nl
Smurfit Kappa Cartón de Venezuela S.A., San Felipe Mill (78% owned), Carretera Morón-San Felipe, Zona Carbonero, 1010-A San Felipe, Venezuela, Capacity: 134,946 mt/y, (Pulp mill, Paperboard mill)
Phone: (58) 254 600 7215/6
Fax: (58) 254 600 7383
Smurfit Kappa Sangüesa Paper, Sanguesa Mill, Raimundo Lumbier, s/n, E-31400 Sangüesa, Spain, Capacity: 110,000 mt/y, (Paper mill, Paperboard mill)
Phone: (34) 948 870000
Fax: (34) 948 870943
Smurfit Kappa Solid Board BV, Oude Pekela Mill, W.H. Westerstraat 59, NL-9665 ZG Oude Pekela,

Netherlands, Capacity: 70,000 mt/y, (Pulp mill, Paperboard mill)
Phone: (31) 503 03 3000
Fax: (31) 503 03 3991
Email: sales.solidboard@smurfitkappa.nl
Smurfit Kappa Solid Board BV, Coevorden Mill, Robertweg 2, 1988 Coevorden, Netherlands, Capacity: 100,000 mt/y, (Paper mill)
Phone: (31) 050 3033000
Fax: (31) 050 3033399
Email: mail.solidboard@smurfitkappa.nl; solidboard@smurfitkappa.nl
Smurfit Kappa Solid Board BV, Hoogkerk Mill, Halmstraat 1-3, NL-9745 BC Groningen-Hoogkerk, Netherlands, Capacity: 130,000 mt/y, (Paperboard mill)
Phone: (31) 50 3033 000
Fax: (31) 50 3033 999
Email: mail.solidboard@smurfitkappa.nl
Smurfit Kappa Solid Board BV, Nieuweschans Mill, Hoofdstraat 34, 9693 AH Nieuweschans, Netherlands, Capacity: 150,000 mt/y, (Paperboard mill)
Phone: (31) 597 52 91 00
Fax: (31) 597 52 91 99
Email: mail.solidboard@smurfitkappa.nl; solidboard@smurfitkappa.nl
Smurfit Kappa Townsend Hook, Snodland Mill, Snodland ME6 5AX, United Kingdom, (Pulp mill, Paperboard mill)
Phone: (44) 1634 240 205
Fax: (44) 1634 248 046
Email: (firstname.secondname@smurfitkappa.co.uk), info@smurfitkappa.co.uk
Smurfit Kappa Cartón de Venezuela S.A., Valencia Mill (78% owned), Aptdo. Postal 448, Ave. Domingo Olavarria, Zona Industrial Sur, 2003 Valencia, Venezuela, Capacity: 80,682 mt/y, (Paperboard mill)
Phone: (58) 241 813 0401
Fax: (58) 241 813 0477
Smurfit Kappa GmbH Viersen Papier, Viersen Mill, Krefelder Str. 175, D-41748 Viersen, Germany, Capacity: 70,000 mt/y, (Paperboard mill)
Phone: (49) 2162 249 870
Fax: (49) 2162 249 8733
Email: info.viersen@smurfitkappa.de
Smurfit Kappa Zülpich Papier GmbH, Zülpich Mill, Bessenicher Weg, D-53909 Zülpich, Germany, Capacity: 450,000 mt/y, (Paperboard mill)
Phone: (49) 2252 3060/306120
Fax: (49) 2252 306 166
Email: info.skzp@smurfitkappa.de; info.kzp@kappapackaging.com
Smurfit Kappa Papier Recyclé France, Papeteries de Saillat, Impasse des Papeteries, Saillat-sur-Vienne 2, F-87206 Saint Junien Cedex, France, Capacity: 240,000 mt/y, (Paperboard mill)
Phone: (33) 5 55 03 40 36/02 21 00
Fax: (33) 5 55 03 47 22/02 87 02
Smurfit Cartón y Papel de México S.A. de C.V., Los Reyes Mill, Av. Presidente Juarez No 2030, 54090 Col. Los Reyes Iztacala, Tlalnepantla, Mexico, Capacity: 77,112 mt/y, (Paperboard mill)
Phone: (52) 55 5729 2300
Fax: (52) 55 3067 5204
Email: josecarlos.nocetti@smurfitkappa.com.mx
Smurfit Cartón y Papel de México S.A. de C.V., Monterrey Mill, Carlos Salazar 1821 Oriente, 64010 Monterrey, BCA, Mexico, Capacity: 35,700 mt/y, (Paper mill, Paperboard mill)
Phone: (52) 81 83545080
Fax: (52) 81 83541990
Email: ricardo.garcia@smurfitkappa.com.mx

ITALY

⊕ⓜCartiera dell' Adda SpA
Calolziocorte Mill
Ownership: 100% by Cima family
Via Cavour 63
I-23801 Calolziocorte, (LC)
Italy
Phone: (39) (0)341 635511
Fax: (39) (0)341 635599
Email: info@cartieradelladda.com
Web Address: www.cartieradelladda.com
Personnel:
Chmn.: Giulio Cima
Phone: (39) 0341 635511
Fax: (39) 0341 635599
Pres. & CEO: Giuseppe Cima
Phone: (39) 0341 635511
Fax: (39) 0341 635599
Mill Mgr.: Amedeo Valeri
Phone: (39) 0341 635511
Fax: (39) 0341 635599
Email: valeri@cartieradelladda.com
Tech. Mgr. & Commerc. Mgr.: Mario Rossi
Phone: (39) 0341 635511
Fax: (39) 0341 635599
Email: rossi@cartieradelladda.com
Total Employees of Company: 70
Total Employees at this Location: 70
Type of Operation: Paperboard mill
Pulp Grades and Capacities:
Total pulp capacity: 141,828 mt/y
Recycled Pulping: 141,828 mt/y
Pulp Mill Data:
Recycled Fiber Treatment Lines:
Pulpers: 1 at 180,000
Paper/Paperboard Grades and Capacities:
Total paper and paperboard capacity: 140,000 mt/y
Boxboard/cartonboard: 140,000 mt/y
Paper and Paperboard Mill Data:
Stock Preparation:
Refiners: 1
Paper Machines: 1
No. 1, cylinder, total capacity 140,000 mt/y, Trim width 4.4 m, Boxboard/cartonboard
Finishing Equipment:
Winders: 1 at 180,000 mt/y
Energy Data:
Power boilers: 2
HRSG boiler: 1
Combustion turbines: 1 at 6.5 MW
Electrical demand for mill: 173 MWh/D

⊕ⓜAdda Ondulati SpA
Annone di Brianza Mill
Via Repubblica 6
I-23841 Annone di Brianza, (LC)
Italy
Phone: (39) 0341 266211
Fax: (39) 0341 577682
Email: addaondulati@addaondulati.com
Web Address: www.addaondulati.com
Personnel:
Prod. Mgr.: Stefano Sita
Phone: (39) 0341 266211
Fax: (39) 0341 577682
Email: stefano.sita@addaondulati.com
Sls. Mgr.: Luciano Manzoni
Phone: (39) 0341 266211
Fax: (39) 0341 577682
Email: luciano.manzoni@addaondulati.com
Total Employees of Company: 170
Total Employees at this Location: 40
Type of Operation: Paperboard mill
Pulp Grades and Capacities:
Total pulp capacity: 28,744 mt/y
Recycled Pulping: 28,744 mt/y
Pulp Mill Data:
Recycled Fiber Treatment Lines:
Recycled packaging pulping lines: 1 at 33,000 admt/y
Paper/Paperboard Grades and Capacities:
Total paper and paperboard capacity: 28,000 mt/y
Corrugating medium/fluting: 28,000 mt/y
Paper and Paperboard Mill Data:
Paper Machines: 1
No. 1, fourdrinier, total capacity 28,000 mt/y, Trim width 2.4 m, Corrugating medium/fluting
Energy Data:
Power boilers
Electrical demand for mill: 42 MWh/D

⊕ⓜAhlstrom Turin SpA
Turin Mill
Ownership: Ahlstrom Corporation Oy
Via Stura 98
I-10075 Mathi Canavese, (TO)
Italy
Phone: (39) 011 9260111
Fax: (39) 011 9269617
Email: investor@ahlstrom.com, corporate.communications@ahlstrom.com
Web Address: www.ahlstrom.com
Personnel:
Exec. VP: Fulvio Capussotti
Phone: (39) 011 9260111
Fax: (39) 011 9269617
Email: fulvio.capussotti@ahlstrom.com
VP, Supply Chain & Label: Giorgio Mirone
Phone: (39) 011 9260111
Fax: (39) 011 9269617
Email: giorgio.mirone@ahlstrom.com
Purch. Dir.: Fabio Bellio
Phone: (39) 011 9260111
Fax: (39) 011 9269617
Email: fabio.bellio@ahlstrom.com
Commer. Dir.: Alessandro Visca
Phone: (39) 011 9260111
Fax: (39) 011 9269617
Finan. Mgr.: Sergio Calandrina
Phone: (39) 011 9260111
Fax: (39) 011 9269617
HR. Mgr.: Flavio Menon
Phone: (39) 011 9260111
Fax: (39) 011 9269617
Email: flavio.menon@ahlstrom.com
Prod. Mgr.: Monica Cappello
Phone: (39) 011 9260111
Fax: (39) 011 9269617
Sls. Mgr.: Paolo Rocchi
Phone: (39) 011 9260111
Fax: (39) 011 9269617
Email: paolo.rocchi@ahlstrom.com
Total Employees at this Location: 325
Type of Operation: Paper mill
Paper/Paperboard Grades and Capacities:
Total paper and paperboard capacity: 60,000 mt/y
Specialty and industrial: 60,000 mt/y
Paper and Paperboard Mill Data:
Paper Machines: 4
No. 1, Trim width 1.6 m, Specialty and industrial
No. 3, fourdrinier, Trim width 1.6 m, Specialty and industrial
No. 4, fourdrinier, Trim width 2.3 m, Specialty and industrial
No. 5, fourdrinier, Trim width 2.3 m, Specialty and industrial

⊕ⓜNuova F.lli Alimonti srl
Castelmadama Mill
Via Empolitana Km. 9,800
I-00024 Castelmadama, (RM)
Italy
Phone: (39) 0774 447556
Fax: (39) 0774 447452
Email: info@fratelli-alimonti.it
Personnel:
Gen. Mgr.: Mr. Andrea Alimonti
Phone: (39) 0774 447556
Prod. Mgr.: Mr. Umberto Alimonti
Phone: (39) 0774 447556
Total Employees at this Location: 4
Type of Operation: Paperboard mill
Paper/Paperboard Grades and Capacities:
Total paper and paperboard capacity: 2,000 mt/y

Italy

Boxboard/cartonboard: 2,000 mt/y
Paper and Paperboard Mill Data:
Paper Machines: 1
No. 1, fourdrinier, total capacity 2,000 mt/y, Trim width 2.4 m, Boxboard/cartonboard
Energy Data:
Power boilers: 1

ⓘⓜCartiera Ferdinando Amatruda di Amatruda Antonietta
Amalfi Mill
Via delle Cartiere 100
I-84011 Amalfi, (SA)
Italy
 Phone: (39) 089 871315
 Fax: (39) 089 8304233
 Email: info@amatruda.it
 Web Address: www.amatruda.it
Personnel:
 Mgr.: Antonietta Amatruda
 Phone: (39) 089 871315
Total Employees at this Location: 9
Type of Operation: Paper mill
Paper/Paperboard Grades and Capacities:
 Total paper and paperboard capacity: 1,000 mt/y
 Uncoated woodfree/freesheet
Paper and Paperboard Mill Data:
Paper Machines: 1
No. 1, Trim width 1.2 m, Uncoated woodfree/freesheet
Energy Data:
Power boilers: 1
Electrical demand for mill: 1 MWh/D

ⓘAriete Srl
Riviera di Chiaia 256
I-80121 Napoli, (NA)
Italy
 Phone: (39) 089 463882-463955-340323
 Fax: (39) 089 34114
 Web Address: www.cartieraariete.it
Personnel:
 Chmn.: Nicola Salsano
 Phone: (39) 089 463882
 Fax: (39) 089 341144
 Email: nicolasalsano@cartieraariete.it
 CEO: Salvatore Salsano
 Phone: (39) 089 463882
 Fax: (39) 089 341144
 Email: salvatoresalsano@cartieraariete.it
Total Employees of Company: 23
Mill Locations:
 Ariete Srl, Cava Dè Tirreni Mill, Via G. Palumbo, 37, I-84013 Cava Dè Tirreni, (SA), Italy, Capacity: 16,000 mt/y, (Paper mill)
 Phone: (39) 089 463955
 Fax: (39) 089 341144

ⓜAriete Srl
Cava Dè Tirreni Mill
Via G. Palumbo, 37
I-84013 Cava Dè Tirreni, (SA)
Italy
 Phone: (39) 089 463955
 Fax: (39) 089 341144
 Web Address: www.cartieraariete.it
Personnel:
 Prod. Mgr.: Rino Di Stasio
 Phone: (39) 089 463955
 Fax: (39) 089 341144
 Email: rinodistasio@cartieraariete.it
 Admin. & Safety Mgr.: Massimiliano Iapicca
 Phone: (39) 089 463955
 Fax: (39) 089 341144
 Email: salvatoresalsano@cartieraariete.it massimilianoiapicca@cartieraariete.it
 Tech. Dir.: Demonico Fasolino
 Phone: (39) 089 463955
 Fax: (39) 089 341144
 Email: ufficiotecnico@cartieraariete.it

Logist. Mgr.: Francesco Desiderio
 Phone: (39) 089 463955
 Fax: (39) 089 341144
 Email: logistica@cartieraariete.it
Total Employees at this Location: 23
Type of Operation: Paper mill
Paper/Paperboard Grades and Capacities:
 Total paper and paperboard capacity: 16,000 mt/y
 Tissue: 16,000 mt/y
Paper and Paperboard Mill Data:
 Stock Preparation:
 Pulpers: 3
Paper Machines: 1
No. 1, C-wrap, Yankee dryer, total capacity 16,000 mt/y, Trim width 2.7 m, Tissue
Finishing Equipment:
 Winders: 1 at 16,000 mt/y
Energy Data:
Power boilers: 1
Electrical demand for mill: 43 MWh/D

ⓘⓜBartoli F.lli SpA
Carraia Mill
Via Traversa di Parezzana 12-14-16
I-55012 Carraia, (LU)
Italy
 Phone: (39) 0583 980196
 Fax: (39) 0583 980878
 Email: info@bartolispa.it
 Web Address: www.bartolispa.it
Personnel:
 Mill Mgr.: Luca Rugani
 Phone: (39) 0583 980196
 Fax: (39) 0583 980878
 Email: lrugani@bartolispa.it
 Admin. Mgr.: Marco Franceschini
 Phone: (39) 0583 980196
 Fax: (39) 0583 980878
 Email: mfranceschini@bartolispa.it
 Sls. & Mktg. Dept.: Carla Bandoni
 Phone: (39) 0583 980196
 Fax: (39) 0583 980878
 Email: cbandoni@bartolispa.it
Total Employees at this Location: 50
Type of Operation: Pulp mill, Paperboard mill
Pulp Grades and Capacities:
 Total pulp capacity: 20,279 mt/y
 Recycled Pulping: 20,279 mt/y
Pulp Mill Data:
 Recycled Fiber Treatment Lines:
 Recycled packaging pulping lines: 1
Paper/Paperboard Grades and Capacities:
 Total paper and paperboard capacity: 20,000 mt/y
 Boxboard/cartonboard: 20,000 mt/y
Paper and Paperboard Mill Data:
 Stock Preparation:
 Pulpers: 1
 Refiners: 4
Paper Machines: 2
No. 1, cylinder, total capacity 8,000 mt/y, Trim width 3.6 m, Boxboard/cartonboard
No. 2, cylinder, total capacity 12,000 mt/y, Trim width 3.6 m, Boxboard/cartonboard
Finishing Equipment:
 Supercalenders: 5
 Sheeters: 3
Energy Data:
Power boilers
Electrical demand for mill: 22 MWh/D

ⓜCartiera Della Basilica SRL
Bagni di Lucca Mill
14, Via Rotabile di Lugliano, Ponte e Serraglio
I-55022 Bagni di Lucca, (LU)
Italy
 Phone: (39) 0583 805093
 Fax: (39) 0583 87893
 Email: info@eurovast.com
 Web Address: www.eurovast.com

Personnel:
 Mill Mgr.: Mr. Stefano Orsi
 Phone: (39) 0583 805093
 Fax: (39) 0583 87893
 Email: stefano.orsi@eurovast.com
 Mgr.: Gianfranco Bocci
 Phone: (39) 0583 805093
 Fax: (39) 0583 87893
 Email: gianfranco.bocci@eurovast.com
Total Employees at this Location: 20
Type of Operation: Paper mill
Paper/Paperboard Grades and Capacities:
 Total paper and paperboard capacity: 9,000 mt/y
 Tissue: 9,000 mt/y
Paper and Paperboard Mill Data:
 Stock Preparation:
 Pulpers: 2
Paper Machines: 1
No. 1, fourdrinier, Yankee dryer, total capacity 9,000 mt/y, Trim width 2.65 m, Tissue
Energy Data:
Power boilers
Electrical demand for mill: 26 MWh/D

ⓘⓜCartiera Della Basilica SRL
Villa Basilica Mill
Ownership: Eurovast SpA
Via delle Cartiere 153
I-55010 Botticino, (LU)
Italy
 Phone: (39) 0572 461030
 Fax: (39) 0572 434 52
 Email: info@eurovast.com
 Web Address: www.eurovast.com
Personnel:
 Mill Mgr.: Simone Lucchesini
 Phone: (39) 0572 461030
 Fax: (39) 0572 434 52
 Email: simone.lucchesini@eurovast.com
 Commercial Mgr.: Stefano Ambrogi
 Phone: (39) 0572 461030
 Fax: (39) 0572 434 52
 Email: stefano.ambrogi@eurovast.com
 Qlty. Mgr.: Ruben Massari
 Phone: (39) 0572 461030
 Fax: (39) 0572 434 52
 Email: ruben.massari@eurovast.com
 Purch. Mgr.: Melania Calissi
 Phone: (39) 0572 461030
 Fax: (39) 0572 434 52
 Email: melania.calissi@eurovast.com
Total Employees of Company: 50
Total Employees at this Location: 25
Type of Operation: Paper mill
Mill Locations:
 Cartiera Della Basilica SRL, Bagni di Lucca Mill, 14, Via Rotabile di Lugliano, Ponte e Serraglio, I-55022 Bagni di Lucca, (LU), Italy, Capacity: 9,000 mt/y, (Paper mill)
 Phone: (39) 0583 805093
 Fax: (39) 0583 87893
 Email: info@eurovast.com
Paper/Paperboard Grades and Capacities:
 Total paper and paperboard capacity: 13,000 mt/y
 Tissue: 13,000 mt/y
Paper and Paperboard Mill Data:
 Stock Preparation:
 Pulpers: 2
Paper Machines: 1
No. 1, twin-wire, Yankee dryer, total capacity 13,000 mt/y, Trim width 2.75 m, Tissue
Energy Data:
Power boilers: 1
Electrical demand for mill: 35 MWh/D

ⓘMauro Benedetti S.p.A.
Via Pievaiola 164/M
I-06132 Zona Industriale Sant'Andrea delle Fratte, (PG)
Italy
 Phone: (39) 075 52 751

Fax: (39) 075 5275237
Email: staff@maurobenedetti.it
Web Address: www.maurobenedetti.it
Personnel:
 Owner: Francesca Benedetti
 Phone: (39) 075 52 751
 Fax: (39) 075 5275237
 CEO: Renato Perovich
 Phone: (39) 075 52 751
 Fax: (39) 075 5275237
 Vice Gen. Dir. : Roberto Ceccotti
 Phone: (39) 075 52 751
 Fax: (39) 075 5275237
 Oper. Dir. : Paolo Moschini
 Phone: (39) 075 52 751
 Fax: (39) 075 5275237
 European Key Account Mgr.: Andrea Cocchieri
 Phone: (39) 075 52 751
 Fax: (39) 075 5275237
 Area Sls. Mgr.: Stefano Bibi
 Phone: (39) 075 52 751
 Fax: (39) 075 5275237
Total Employees at this Location: 32
Mill Locations:
 Cartiera di Salerno di Mauro Benedetti, Salerno Mill, Via dei Carrari 24, I-84100 Salerno, (SA), Italy, Capacity: 50,000 mt/y, (Paperboard mill)
 Phone: (39) 089 301327
 Fax: (39) 089 301327
 Email: salerno@maurobenedetti.it

ⓜCartiera di Salerno di Mauro Benedetti
Salerno Mill
Ownership: Mauro Benedetti S.p.A.
Via dei Carrari 24
I-84100 Salerno, (SA)
Italy
 Phone: (39) 089 301327
 Fax: (39) 089 301327
 Email: salerno@maurobenedetti.it
 Web Address: www.maurobenedetti.it
Personnel:
 Mill Dir.: Ing. Roberto Versiglioni
 Phone: (39) 089 301327
Total Employees at this Location: 34
Type of Operation: Paperboard mill
Pulp Grades and Capacities:
 Total pulp capacity: 50,370 mt/y
 Recycled Pulping: 50,370 mt/y
Pulp Mill Data:
 Recycled Fiber Treatment Lines:
 Flotation deinking lines: 2
 Pulpers: 1 at 70,000
Paper/Paperboard Grades and Capacities:
 Total paper and paperboard capacity: 50,000 mt/y
 Linerboard: 15,000 mt/y
 Corrugating medium/fluting: 35,000 mt/y
Paper and Paperboard Mill Data:
Paper Machines: 1
 No. 1, fourdrinier, total capacity 50,000 mt/y, Trim width 2.45 m, Corrugating medium/fluting, Linerboard
Finishing Equipment:
 Winders: 1
 Rewinders: 1
Energy Data:
 Power boilers: 1
 HRSG boiler: 1
 Combustion turbines: 1 at 4.2 MW
 Electrical demand for mill: 72 MWh/D

ⓗⓜCartiera Bocci Ponte di Gemolano Srl
Pescia Mill
Via Mammianese 283
I-51010 Pescia, (PT)
Italy
 Phone: (39) 0572 408195
 Fax: (39) 0572 408907
 Email: pontedigemolano@cartierebocci.it
 Web Address: www.cartierebocci.it
Personnel:
 Mill Mgr.: Paolo Bocci
 Phone: (39) 0572 408195
Total Employees of Company: 6
Type of Operation: Paper mill
Paper/Paperboard Grades and Capacities:
 Total paper and paperboard capacity: 3,000 mt/y
 Packaging papers: 3,000 mt/y
Paper and Paperboard Mill Data:
 Stock Preparation:
 Pulpers: 1
 Refiners: 1
Paper Machines: 1
 No. 1, fourdrinier, total capacity 3,000 mt/y, Trim width 2.35 m, Packaging papers
Energy Data:
 Power boilers: 1
 Electrical demand for mill: 3 MWh/D

ⓗⓜBormio SpA
Ponte Lambro Mill
Via Fiume 40
I-22037 Ponte Lambro, (CO)
Italy
 Phone: (39) 031 620384
 Fax: (39) 031 620384
 Email: bormiospa@bormioco.191.it
Personnel:
 Admin. Mgr.: Stefano Mazza
 Phone: (39) 031 620384
 Tech. Mgr.: Stefano Sita
 Phone: (39) 031 620384
Total Employees at this Location: 30
Type of Operation: Paperboard mill
Pulp Grades and Capacities:
 Total pulp capacity: 28,579 mt/y
 Recycled Pulping: 28,579 mt/y
Pulp Mill Data:
 Recycled Fiber Treatment Lines:
 Pulpers: 1 at 32,500
Paper/Paperboard Grades and Capacities:
 Total paper and paperboard capacity: 28,000 mt/y
 Linerboard: 18,000 mt/y
 Corrugating medium/fluting: 10,000 mt/y
Paper and Paperboard Mill Data:
Paper Machines: 1
 No. 1, fourdrinier, total capacity 28,000 mt/y, Trim width 2.4 m, Linerboard, Corrugating medium/fluting
Energy Data:
 Power boilers
 Electrical demand for mill: 41 MWh/D

ⓗⓜCartiera di Bosco Marengo SpA
Alessandria Mill
Ownership: 100% by Ghigliotti Family
Via Casalcermelli, 11
I-15062 Bosco Marengo , Alessandria
Italy
 Phone: (39) 0131 299 284
 Fax: (39) 0131 289 649
 Email: cartboscoma.sede@tiscalinet.it, info@cartieraboscomarengo.it
 Web Address: www.cartieraboscomarengo.it
Personnel:
 Gen. Mgr.: Guido Ghigliotti
 Phone: (39) 0131 299 284
 Fax: (39) 0131 289 649
 Email: info@cartieraboscomarengo.it
Total Employees of Company: 37
Total Employees at this Location: 37
Type of Operation: Paperboard mill
Pulp Grades and Capacities:
 Total pulp capacity: 90,507 mt/y
 Recycled Pulping: 90,507 mt/y
Paper/Paperboard Grades and Capacities:
 Total paper and paperboard capacity: 90,000 mt/y
 Boxboard/cartonboard: 90,000 mt/y
Paper and Paperboard Mill Data:
Paper Machines: 1
 No. 2, fourdrinier, total capacity 90,000 mt/y, Trim width 2.4 m, Boxboard/cartonboard
Energy Data:
 Electrical demand for mill: 114 MWh/D

ⓗBurgo Group SpA
Ownership: Private
Via Piave 1
I-36077 Altavilla Vicentina, (VI)
Italy
 Phone: (39) 0444 396811
 Fax: (39) 0444 396888
 Email: info@burgogroup.com
 Web Address: www.burgogroup.com
Personnel:
 Chmn.: Girolamo Marchi
 Phone: (39) 0444 396811
 Fax: (39) 0444 396888
 Vice Chmn. : Giorgio Cefis
 Phone: (39) 0444 396811
 Fax: (39) 0444 396888
 CEO : Paolo Mattei
 Phone: (39) 0444 396811
 Fax: (39) 0444 396888
 Dir.: Alessandro Bertani
 Phone: (39) 0444 396811
 Fax: (39) 0444 396888
Total Employees of Company: 4,629
Total Employees at this Location: 120
Mill Locations:
 Burgo Ardennes, Virton Mill, 1 Rue de la Papeterie, B-6760 Virton, Belgium, Capacity: 350,000 mt/y, (Pulp mill, Paper mill)
 Phone: (32) 63 587111
 Fax: (32) 63 587119
 Email: info@burgogroup.com
 Burgo Group SpA, Avezzano Mill, Via Leonardo da Vinci 1, I-67051 Avezzano, (AQ), Italy, (Paper mill)
 Phone: (39) 0863 4271
 Fax: (39) 0863 509347
 Email: info@burgogroup.com
 Burgo Group SpA, Duino Mill, Frazione S. Giovanni Di Duino 24/D, I-34013 Duino, (TS), Italy, Capacity: 300,000 mt/y, (Pulp mill, Paper mill)
 Phone: (39) 040 209 9111
 Fax: (39) 040 209 9132
 Email: info@burgogroup.com
 Mosaico Speciality Papers, Lugo di Vicenza Mill, Via Privata Cartiera 1, I-36030 Lugo di Vicenza, (VI), Italy, Capacity: 65,000 mt/y, (Paper mill)
 Phone: (39) 0445 329 511
 Fax: (39) 0445 860 988
 Email: infomosaico@burgogroup.com
 Burgo Group SpA, Sarego Mill, Via Guido Salvagnini 70, I-36040 Sarego, (VI), italy, Capacity: 150,000 mt/y, (Paper mill)
 Phone: (39) 0444 726411
 Fax: (39) 0444 726499
 Email: info@burgogroup.com
 Burgo Group SpA, Sora Mill, Via San Domenico 83, I-03039 Sora, (FR), Italy, Capacity: 280,000 mt/y, (Paper mill)
 Phone: (39) 0776 85221
 Fax: (39) 0776 813503
 Email: info@burgogroup.com
 Mosaico Speciality Papers, Tolmezzo Mill, Via Pier Francesco Calvi 15, I-33028 Tolmezzo, (UD), Italy, Capacity: 165,000 mt/y, (Pulp mill, Paper mill)
 Phone: (39) 0433 4801
 Fax: (39) 0433 480287
 Email: infomosaico@burgogroup.com
 Burgo Group SpA, Toscolano Mill, Via A. Vespucci 28, I-25088 Toscolano Maderno, (BS), Italy, Capacity: 130,000 mt/y, (Pulp mill, Paper mill)
 Phone: (39) 0365 5491
 Fax: (39) 0365 641536
 Email: info@burgogroup.com
 Mosaico Speciality Papers, Treviso Mill, Via Duca D'Aosta

Italy

109 - Loc. Mignagola, I-31030 Carbonera, (TV), Italy,
Capacity: 39,984 mt/y, (Paper mill)
Phone: (39) 0422 691200
Fax: (39) 0422 691290
Email: infomosaico@burgogroup.com
Mosaico Speciality Papers, Chiampo Mill, Via Arzignano 38, I-36072 Chiampo, (VI), Italy, Capacity: 39,984 mt/y, (Paper mill)
Phone: (39) 0444 422200/624288
Fax: (39) 0444 624130
Email: infomosaico@burgogroup.com
Burgo Group SpA, Verzuolo Mill, Via Roma 26, I-12039 Verzuolo, (CN), Italy, Capacity: 565,000 mt/y, (Pulp mill, Paper mill)
Phone: (39) 0175 280111
Fax: (39) 0175 280180
Email: info@burgogroup.com
Burgo Group SpA, Villorba Mill, Via Roma 212, I-31050 Villorba, (TV), Italy, Capacity: 200,000 mt/y, (Paper mill)
Phone: (39) 0422 6281
Fax: (39) 0422 928756
Email: info@burgogroup.com

ⓜBurgo Group SpA
Avezzano Mill
Mill is closed (Burgo permanently ceased UWF manufacturing at Avezzano mill from August 25, 2014)
Via Leonardo da Vinci 1
I-67051 Avezzano, (AQ)
Italy
  Phone: (39) 0863 4271
  Fax: (39) 0863 509347
  Email: info@burgogroup.com
  Web Address: www.burgogroup.com
Personnel:
  Sustainability & Qlty. System Mgr.: Carlotta Priola
  Phone: (39) 0863 4271
  Fax: (39) 0863 509347
  Email: priola.carlotta@burgo.com
Total Employees at this Location: 291
Type of Operation: Paper mill
Paper and Paperboard Mill Data:
  Stock Preparation:
  Pulpers: 4
  Refiners: 10
Paper Machines: 1
No. 2, SymFormer MB, total capacity 150,000 mt/y, Trim width 5.3 m
Coating Machines: 1
No. 2, total capacity 155,000 mt/y, off machine
Finishing Equipment:
  Supercalenders: 2 at 125,000 mt/y, 155,000 mt/y
Energy Data:
Power boilers: 1
HRSG boiler: 2
Combustion turbines: 2 at 26.8, 26.8 MW
Steam turbines: 2 at 30.2, 7.4 MW
Hydro turbines: 1 at 12 MW

ⓜBurgo Group SpA
Duino Mill
Frazione S. Giovanni Di Duino 24/D
I-34013 Duino, (TS)
Italy
  Phone: (39) 040 209 9111
  Fax: (39) 040 209 9132
  Email: info@burgogroup.com
  Web Address: www.burgogroup.com
Personnel:
  Mill Mgr.: Alberto Sorge
  Phone: (39) 040 209 9111
  Fax: (39) 040 209 9132
  Email: sorge.alberto@burgo.com
  Environ. Mgr.: Dr. Roberto Bettella
  Phone: (39) 040 209 9111
  Fax: (39) 040 209 9132
  Email: bettella.roberto@burgo.com
  Technology Mgr.: Mr Enrico Crida
  Phone: (39) 040 209 9111
  Fax: (39) 040 209 9132
  Email: crida.enrico@burgo.com
Total Employees at this Location: 460
Type of Operation: Pulp mill, Paper mill
Pulp Grades and Capacities:
  Total pulp capacity: 109,383 mt/y
  Pulp available for market: 12,000 mt/y
  Mechanical Pulp: 109,383 mt/y
Pulp Mill Data:
  Mechanical Pulping Systems:
  Conventional grinders: 8
  Bleach Plant Systems: 2
  No. 1, Sequence: P, Capacity 140,000 admt/y
  Pulp Dryers:
  Twin Wire 1
Paper/Paperboard Grades and Capacities:
  Total paper and paperboard capacity: 300,000 mt/y
  Coated mechanical/groundwood: 300,000 mt/y
Paper and Paperboard Mill Data:
Paper Machines: 2
No. 2, hybrid former, total capacity 100,000 mt/y, Trim width 5.28 m, Coated mechanical/groundwood
No. 3, Bel-Baie III, total capacity 200,000 mt/y, Trim width 8.45 m, Coated mechanical/groundwood
Coating Machines: 2
OMC 2, total capacity 130,000 mt/y., off machine
OMC 3, total capacity 220,000 mt/y., off machine
Finishing Equipment:
  Supercalenders: 5
Energy Data:
HRSG boiler: 2
Combustion turbines: 2 at 46, 46 MW
Steam turbines: 3 at 40, 3.5, 4 MW
Electrical demand for mill: 1,111 MWh/D

ⓜMosaico Speciality Papers
Lugo di Vicenza Mill
Ownership: 100% by Burgo Group SpA
Via Privata Cartiera 1
I-36030 Lugo di Vicenza, (VI)
Italy
  Phone: (39) 0445 329 511
  Fax: (39) 0445 860 988
  Email: infomosaico@burgogroup.com
  Web Address: mosaico.burgogroup.com
Personnel:
  Mill Mgr.: Ernesto Giuseppe Polga
  Phone: (39) 0445 329 511
  Fax: (39) 0445 860 988
  Email: polga.ernesto@burgo.com
  Assist. Prod. Mgr.: Ciprian Hanga
  Phone: (39) 0445 329 511
  Fax: (39) 0445 860 988
  Email: hanga.ciprian@burgo.com
Total Employees at this Location: 260
Type of Operation: Paper mill
Paper/Paperboard Grades and Capacities:
  Total paper and paperboard capacity: 65,000 mt/y
  Coated woodfree/freesheet: 20,000 mt/y
  Specialty and industrial: 35,000 mt/y
  Boxboard/cartonboard: 10,000 mt/y
Paper and Paperboard Mill Data:
Paper Machines: 2
No. 1, fourdrinier, total capacity 30,000 mt/y, Trim width 2.16 m, Coated woodfree/freesheet, Boxboard/cartonboard
No. 5, fourdrinier, Yankee dryer, total capacity 35,000 mt/y, Trim width 2.76 m, Specialty and industrial
Coating Machines: 4
No. 1
No. 2
No. 3, off machine
No. 4, on machine
Finishing Equipment:
  Sheeters: 3 at 50,000 mt/y
Energy Data:
Power boilers: 1
Steam turbines: 3 at 7.33 MW
Electrical demand for mill: 35 MWh/D

ⓜBurgo Group SpA
Sarego Mill
Via Guido Salvagnini 70
I-36040 Sarego, (VI)
Italy
  Phone: (39) 0444 726411
  Fax: (39) 0444 726499
  Email: info@burgogroup.com
  Web Address: www.burgogroup.com
Personnel:
  Mill Mgr.: Roberto Giatti
  Phone: (39) 0444 726411
  Fax: (39) 0444 726499
  Email: giatti.roberto@burgo.com
  Mgr.: Mauro Rigoni
  Phone: (39) 0444 726404
  Fax: (39) 0444 726499
  Email: rigoni.mauro@burgo.com
  Admin. Mgr.: Mariagrazia Ferraretto
  Phone: (39) 0444 726411
  Fax: (39) 0444 726499
  Email: ferraretto.mariagrazia@burgo.com
Total Employees at this Location: 229
Type of Operation: Paper mill
Pulp Grades and Capacities:
  Total pulp capacity: 8,694 mt/y
  Recycled Pulping: 8,694 mt/y
Paper/Paperboard Grades and Capacities:
  Total paper and paperboard capacity: 150,000 mt/y
  Coated woodfree/freesheet: 150,000 mt/y
Paper and Paperboard Mill Data:
  Stock Preparation:
  Pulpers: 1
  Refiners: 5
Paper Machines: 1
No. 1, fourdrinier, total capacity 150,000 mt/y, Trim width 3.36 m, Coated woodfree/freesheet
Coating Machines: 1
No. 1, total capacity 150,000 mt/y., on machine
Finishing Equipment:
  Supercalenders: 2
  Rewinders: 2
  Sheeters: 5
Energy Data:
Power boilers: 1
HRSG boiler: 1
Combustion turbines: 1 at 5.2 MW
Steam turbines: 1 at 2.5 MW
Electrical demand for mill: 228 MWh/D

ⓜBurgo Group SpA
Sora Mill
Via San Domenico 83
I-03039 Sora, (FR)
Italy
  Phone: (39) 0776 85221
  Fax: (39) 0776 813503
  Email: info@burgogroup.com
  Web Address: www.burgogroup.com
Personnel:
  Mill Mgr.: Ing. Fiorenzo Pesenti
  Phone: (39) 0776 85221
  Fax: (39) 0776 813503
  Email: pesenti.fiorenzo@burgo.com
  Qlty. & Envir. Mgr.: Recchia Domenico
  Phone: (39) 0776 85221
  Fax: (39) 0776 813503
  Email: recchia.domenico@burgo.com
Total Employees at this Location: 380
Type of Operation: Paper mill
Pulp Grades and Capacities:
  Total pulp capacity: 4,605 mt/y
  Recycled Pulping: 4,605 mt/y
Paper/Paperboard Grades and Capacities:
  Total paper and paperboard capacity: 280,000 mt/y
  Coated woodfree/freesheet: 280,000 mt/y
Paper and Paperboard Mill Data:

Italy

Paper Machines: 2
No. 1, DuoFormer D, total capacity 105,000 mt/y, Trim width 3.65 m, Coated woodfree/freesheet
No. 2, Bel-Bond, total capacity 175,000 mt/y, Trim width 3.8 m, Coated woodfree/freesheet
Coating Machines: 3
1, on machine
No. 2, total capacity 240,000 mt/y., off machine
No. 3, on machine
Finishing Equipment:
Supercalenders: 4
Rewinders: 3
Sheeters: 5 at 1,100 mt/y
Energy Data:
Power boilers: 1
Combustion turbines: 1 at 33.3 MW
Steam turbines: 2 at 3, 8.8 MW
Electrical demand for mill: 509 MWh/D

ⓜMosaico Speciality Papers
Tolmezzo Mill
Ownership: 100% by Burgo Group SpA
Via Pier Francesco Calvi 15
I-33028 Tolmezzo, (UD)
Italy
  Phone: (39) 0433 4801
  Fax: (39) 0433 480287
  Email: infomosaico@burgogroup.com
  Web Address: mosaico.burgogroup.com
Personnel:
  Mill Mgr.: Ing. Furio Azzopardo
  Phone: (39) 0433 480111
  Fax: (39) 0433 480287
  Email: azzopardo.furio@burgo.com
  Mgr.: Ing. Pietro Armellini
  Phone: (39) 0433 480216
  Fax: (39) 0433 480287
  Email: armellini.pietro@burgo.com
  H&S Environ. Mgr.: Dssa. Claudia Fachin
  Phone: (39) 0433 480210
  Fax: (39) 0433 480287
  Email: fachin.claudia@burgo.com
Total Employees at this Location: 305
Type of Operation: Pulp mill, Paper mill
Pulp Grades and Capacities:
  Total pulp capacity: 40,003 mt/y
  Chemical Pulp: 40,003 mt/y
Pulp Mill Data:
  Chemical Pulping Systems:
  Batch digesters: 3
  Pulp Lines: 1
  Bleach Plant Systems: 1
  Sulfite Pulping System Capacity 43,000 admt/y
  Chemical Recovery Equipment:
  Evaporator lines: 2
Paper/Paperboard Grades and Capacities:
  Total paper and paperboard capacity: 165,000 mt/y
  Uncoated woodfree/freesheet: 140,000 mt/y
  Packaging papers: 5,000 mt/y
  Specialty and industrial: 20,000 mt/y
Paper and Paperboard Mill Data:
  Stock Preparation:
  Pulpers: 5
  Refiners: 10
Paper Machines: 2
No. 1, fourdrinier, Yankee dryer, total capacity 25,000 mt/y, Trim width 3.36 m, Specialty and industrial, Packaging papers
No. 3, Bel-Bond, total capacity 140,000 mt/y, Trim width 4.54 m, Uncoated woodfree/freesheet
Finishing Equipment:
  Rewinders: 6 at 160,000 mt/y
  Sheeters: 4 at 110,000 mt/y
Energy Data:
  Power boilers: 4
  Steam turbines: 3 at 6, 1.85, 3 MW
  Electrical demand for mill: 309 MWh/D

ⓜBurgo Group SpA
Toscolano Mill
Via A. Vespucci 28
I-25088 Toscolano Maderno, (BS)
Italy
  Phone: (39) 0365 5491
  Fax: (39) 0365 641536
  Email: info@burgogroup.com
  Web Address: www.burgogroup.com
Personnel:
  Mill Mgr.: Italo Scian
  Phone: (39) 0365 5492 58
  Fax: (39) 0365 6415 36
  Email: scian.italo@burgo.com
Total Employees at this Location: 212
Type of Operation: Pulp mill, Paper mill
Pulp Grades and Capacities:
  Total pulp capacity: 49,587 mt/y
  Mechanical Pulp: 9,742 mt/y
  Recycled Pulping: 39,845 mt/y
Pulp Mill Data:
  Mechanical Pulping Systems:
  CTMP systems: 1
  Pulp Lines: 1
  Bleach Plant Systems: 1
  CMP Pulping System, Sequence: P/Y, Capacity 15,000 admt/y
  Recycled Fiber Treatment Lines:
  Pulpers: 1
Paper/Paperboard Grades and Capacities:
  Total paper and paperboard capacity: 130,000 mt/y
  Coated woodfree/freesheet: 26,000 mt/y
  Coated mechanical/groundwood: 104,000 mt/y
Paper and Paperboard Mill Data:
  Stock Preparation:
  Pulpers: 2
  Refiners: 2
Paper Machines: 1
No. 10, DuoFormer D, total capacity 130,000 mt/y, Trim width 3.7 m, Coated mechanical/groundwood, Coated woodfree/freesheet
Coating Machines: 3
No. 1, total capacity 130,000 mt/y., off machine
No. 2, on machine
No. 3, on machine
Finishing Equipment:
  Winders: 3
  Supercalenders: 3
  Rewinders: 1
  Sheeters: 4
Energy Data:
  Power boilers: 1
  Combustion turbines: 2 at 7, 7 MW
  Steam turbines: 3 at 9.2, 3, 3.9 MW
  Electrical demand for mill: 263 MWh/D

ⓜMosaico Speciality Papers
Treviso Mill
Ownership: 100% by Burgo Group SpA
Via Duca D'Aosta 109 - Loc. Mignagola
I-31030 Carbonera, (TV)
Italy
  Phone: (39) 0422 691200
  Fax: (39) 0422 691290
  Email: infomosaico@burgogroup.com
  Web Address: mosaico.burgogroup.com
Personnel:
  Mill Mgr.: Ing. Roberto De Bortoli
  Phone: (39) 0422 691201
  Email: debortoli.roberto@burgo.com
  Chief Eng.: Ing. Zefferino Gava
  Phone: (39) 0422 691208
  Email: gava.zefferino@burgo.com
Total Employees at this Location: 190
Type of Operation: Paper mill
Paper/Paperboard Grades and Capacities:
  Total paper and paperboard capacity: 39,984 mt/y
  Specialty and industrial: 39,984 mt/y
Paper and Paperboard Mill Data:
  Stock Preparation:
  Pulpers: 3
  Refiners: 3
Paper Machines: 1
No. 6, fourdrinier, Yankee dryer, total capacity 39,984 mt/y, Trim width 3.28 m, Specialty and industrial
Finishing Equipment:
  Winders: 1 at 40,000 mt/y
Energy Data:
  Power boilers: 1
  Electrical demand for mill: 103 MWh/D

ⓜMosaico Speciality Papers
Chiampo Mill
Ownership: 100% by Burgo Group SpA
Via Arzignano 38
I-36072 Chiampo, (VI)
Italy
  Phone: (39) 0444 422200/624288
  Fax: (39) 0444 624130
  Email: infomosaico@burgogroup.com
  Web Address: mosaico.burgogroup.com
Personnel:
  Mill Mgr.: Ing. Alberto Gasbarrini
  Phone: (39) 0444 422200
  Fax: (39) 0444 624130
  Email: gasbarrini.alberto@burgo.com
Total Employees at this Location: 122
Type of Operation: Paper mill
Paper/Paperboard Grades and Capacities:
  Total paper and paperboard capacity: 39,984 mt/y
  Specialty and industrial: 39,984 mt/y
Paper and Paperboard Mill Data:
  Stock Preparation:
  Pulpers: 1
  Refiners: 3
Paper Machines: 1
No. 1, fourdrinier, Yankee dryer, total capacity 39,984 mt/y, Trim width 2.4 m, Specialty and industrial
Coating Machines: 1
PM 1, total capacity 50,000 mt/y., on machine
Finishing Equipment:
  Calenders: 1
  Rewinders: 1
  Sheeters: 2
Energy Data:
  Power boilers: 2
  Steam turbines: 1
  Electrical demand for mill: 105 MWh/D

ⓜBurgo Group SpA
Verzuolo Mill
Via Roma 26
I-12039 Verzuolo, (CN)
Italy
  Phone: (39) 0175 280111
  Fax: (39) 0175 280180
  Email: info@burgogroup.com
  Web Address: www.burgogroup.com
Personnel:
  Mill Mgr.: Raffaele Marinucci
  Phone: (39) 0175 280 130
  Fax: (39) 0175 280 180
  Email: marinucci.raffaele@burgo.com
  Energy Mgr.: Maurilio Martina
  Phone: (39) 0175 280 200
  Fax: (39) 0175 280 180
  Email: martina.maurilio@burgo.com
Total Employees at this Location: 440
Type of Operation: Pulp mill, Paper mill
Pulp Grades and Capacities:
  Total pulp capacity: 225,541 mt/y
  Mechanical Pulp: 225,541 mt/y
Pulp Mill Data:
  Mechanical Pulping Systems:
  Conventional grinders: 4
  Pressurized grinders: 6
  Bleach Plant Systems: 2
  PGW Pulping System, Sequence: P, Capacity 160,000 admt/y

Italy

SGW Pulping System, Sequence: P, Capacity 50,000 admt/y
Paper/Paperboard Grades and Capacities:
Total paper and paperboard capacity: 565,000 mt/y
Coated mechanical/groundwood: 565,000 mt/y
Paper and Paperboard Mill Data:
Stock Preparation:
Pulpers: 2
Refiners: 6
Paper Machines: 2
No. 8, Bel-Baie IV, total capacity 165,000 mt/y, Trim width 6.1 m, Coated mechanical/groundwood
No. 9, OptiFormer, total capacity 400,000 mt/y, Trim width 9.6 m, Coated mechanical/groundwood
Coating Machines: 2
No. 8, total capacity 165,000 mt/y., off machine
No. 9, on machine
Finishing Equipment:
Winders: 3 at 565,000 mt/y
Calenders: 2
Supercalenders: 2 at 565,000 mt/y
Rewinders: 2 at 100,000 mt/y
Energy Data:
Power boilers: 1
HRSG boiler: 1
Combustion turbines: 2 at 40, 40 MW
Steam turbines: 1 at 40 MW
Electrical demand for mill: 2,125 MWh/D

ⓜBurgo Group SpA
Villorba Mill
Via Roma 212
I-31050 Villorba, (TV)
Italy
Phone: (39) 0422 6281
Fax: (39) 0422 928756
Email: info@burgogroup.com
Web Address: www.burgogroup.com
Personnel:
Dir.: Massimo Beltrame
Phone: (39) 0422 6281
Fax: (39) 0422 928756
Email: beltrame.massimo@burgo.com
Resp. for Maint.: Ing. Danilo Mendolia
Phone: (39) 0422 6282 58
Fax: (39) 0422 928756
Email: mendolia.danilo@burgo.com
Total Employees at this Location: 176
Type of Operation: Paper mill
Pulp Mill Data:
Paper/Paperboard Grades and Capacities:
Total paper and paperboard capacity: 200,000 mt/y
Coated mechanical/groundwood: 200,000 mt/y
Paper and Paperboard Mill Data:
Paper Machines: 1
No. 8, DuoFormer D, total capacity 200,000 mt/y, Trim width 4.4 m, Coated mechanical/groundwood
Coating Machines: 1
No. 1, total capacity 190,000 mt/y., off machine
Finishing Equipment:
Winders: 2
Supercalenders: 2
Rewinders: 1
Energy Data:
HRSG boiler: 1
Combustion turbines: 2 at 6, 6 MW
Steam turbines: 1 at 7.7 MW
Electrical demand for mill: 332 MWh/D

ⓗⓜC & C Srl
Broccostella Mill
Via Ferrazza 16
I-03030 Broccostella, (FR)
Italy
Phone: (39) 0776 890150
Fax: (39) 0776 890878
Email: elmacart@virgilio.it,
cec.carta@virgilio.it
Personnel:

CEO: Dr. Ettore Ciaffoni
Phone: (39) 0776 890150
Prod. Mgr.: Massimo Casinelli
Phone: (39) 0776 890150
Total Employees of Company: 33
Total Employees at this Location: 60
Type of Operation: Paperboard mill
Pulp Grades and Capacities:
Total pulp capacity: 55,944 mt/y
Recycled Pulping: 55,944 mt/y
Pulp Mill Data:
Recycled Fiber Treatment Lines:
Recycled packaging pulping lines: 1
Paper/Paperboard Grades and Capacities:
Total paper and paperboard capacity: 55,000 mt/y
Linerboard: 41,000 mt/y
Corrugating medium/fluting: 14,000 mt/y
Paper and Paperboard Mill Data:
Paper Machines: 1
No. 1, fourdrinier, total capacity 55,000 mt/y, Trim width 2.53 m, Corrugating medium/fluting, Linerboard
Energy Data:
Power boilers: 1
Electrical demand for mill: 80 MWh/D

ⓜCartiera di Cagliari Srl
Assemini (Sardinia) Mill
Ownership: 100% by Pro-Gest S.p.A.
5a Strada Traversa Localita Macchiareddu Grogastu
I-09032 Assemini, (CA)
Italy
Phone: (39) 070 247632
Fax: (39) 070 247632
Web Address: www.pro-gestspa.it
Personnel:
Mgr.: Evenio Vanzo
Phone: (39) 070 247632
Fax: (39) 070 247632
Email: assemini.ca@gmail.com
Total Employees at this Location: 40
Type of Operation: Paper mill
Paper/Paperboard Grades and Capacities:
Total paper and paperboard capacity: 22,000 mt/y
Tissue: 22,000 mt/y
Paper and Paperboard Mill Data:
Paper Machines: 1
No. 1, crescent former, Yankee dryer, total capacity 22,000 mt/y, Trim width 3.22 m, Tissue
Energy Data:
Power boilers: 1
Electrical demand for mill: 56 MWh/D

ⓗⓜCalcarta S.R.L.
Chifenti Mill
551/A Via Pizzorna
55026 Chifenti, Borgo a Mozzano, (LU)
Italy
Phone: (39) 0583 805320
Fax: (39) 0583 87596
Email: info@cartieracalcarta.it
Web Address: www.cartieracalcarta.it
Personnel:
Mill Mgr.: Marcello Calamari
Phone: (39) 0583 805320
Total Employees of Company: 30
Total Employees at this Location: 30
Type of Operation: Paper mill
Pulp Grades and Capacities:
Total pulp capacity: 18,123 mt/y
Recycled Pulping: 18,123 mt/y
Pulp Mill Data:
Recycled Fiber Treatment Lines:
Pulpers: 1 at 24,200
Paper/Paperboard Grades and Capacities:
Total paper and paperboard capacity: 17,000 mt/y
Tissue: 17,000 mt/y
Paper and Paperboard Mill Data:
Paper Machines: 1

No. 1, fourdrinier, Yankee dryer, total capacity 17,000 mt/y, Trim width 2.7 m, Tissue
Energy Data:
Power boilers: 1
Electrical demand for mill: 48 MWh/D

ⓜCartiera Cama S.R.L.
Via Matteo Gianolio 31
I-27029 Vigevano, (PV)
Italy
Phone: (39) 0381 71498
Fax: (39) 0381 83247
Email: cama@cartieracama.it,
info@cartieracama.it
Web Address: www.cartieracama.it
Personnel:
Account & Finan. Mgr.: Paolo Colombo
Phone: (39) 0381 71498
Fax: (39) 0381 83247
Email: paolo.colombo@cartieracama.it
Total Employees at this Location: 7
Mill Locations:
Cartiera Cama S.R.L., Lallio Mill, Via Centrale 1, I-24040 Lallio, (BG), Italy, Capacity: 29,500 mt/y, (Paperboard mill)
Phone: (39) 035 691080/055
Fax: (39) 035 200505
Email: giovanni.mina@cartieracama.it

ⓜCartiera Cama S.R.L.
Lallio Mill
Via Centrale 1
I-24040 Lallio, (BG)
Italy
Phone: (39) 035 691080/055
Fax: (39) 035 200505
Email: giovanni.mina@cartieracama.it
Web Address: www.cartieracama.it
Personnel:
Prod. Mgr.: Giovanni Mina
Phone: (39) 035 691080
Fax: (39) 035 200505
Email: giovanni.mina@cartieracama.it
Total Employees at this Location: 52
Type of Operation: Paperboard mill
Pulp Grades and Capacities:
Total pulp capacity: 29,802 mt/y
Recycled Pulping: 29,802 mt/y
Pulp Mill Data:
Recycled Fiber Treatment Lines:
Recycled packaging pulping lines at 30,000 admt/y
Paper/Paperboard Grades and Capacities:
Total paper and paperboard capacity: 29,500 mt/y
Boxboard/cartonboard: 29,500 mt/y
Paper and Paperboard Mill Data:
Paper Machines: 1
No. 1, cylinder, total capacity 29,500 mt/y, Trim width 2.4 m, Boxboard/cartonboard
Energy Data:
Combustion turbines: 1
Electrical demand for mill: 26 MWh/D

ⓗCamose Srl
Via Guerrazzi, 4
I-56025 Pontedera, (PI)
Italy
Phone: (39) 0587 723163
Fax: (39) 0587 723164
Email: camose@tiscalinet.it
Personnel:
Man. Dir.: Anacleto Pozzi
Phone: (39) 0587 723163
Fax: (39) 0587 723164
Sls. Dir.: Rosita Di Martella
Phone: (39) 0587 723163
Fax: (39) 0587 723164
Total Employees at this Location: 7
Mill Locations:
Camose Srl, del Serra Mill, Via di Costa 1, I-56032 Buti,

Italy

(PI), Italy, Capacity: 1,700 mt/y, (Paper mill)
Phone: (39) 0587 723163
Fax: (39) 0587 723164
Email: info@camosesrl.com

ⓂCamose Srl
del Serra Mill
Via di Costa 1
I-56032 Buti, (PI)
Italy
Phone: (39) 0587 723163
Fax: (39) 0587 723164
Email: info@camosesrl.com
Web Address: www.camosesrl.com
Personnel:
Man. Dir.: Anacleto Pozzi
Phone: (39) 0587 723163
Total Employees at this Location: 9
Type of Operation: Paper mill
Paper/Paperboard Grades and Capacities:
Total paper and paperboard capacity: 1,700 mt/y
Specialty and industrial
Paper and Paperboard Mill Data:
Stock Preparation:
Pulpers: 1
Refiners: 1
Paper Machines: 1
No. 1, cylinder, Trim width 1.6 m, Specialty and industrial
Coating Machines: 2
No. 1
No. 2
Finishing Equipment:
Rewinders: 2
Energy Data:
Power boilers: 1

ⒽⓂCartiera Capostrada SpA
Tullio Carrara Mill
Ownership: Sant'Andrea Spa
Via dei Barbi 32
I-51000 Capostrada, (PT)
Italy
Phone: (39) 0573 401135
Fax: (39) 0573 401215
Email: info@cartieracapostrada.com
Web Address: www.cartieracapostrada.com
Personnel:
Mill Mgr.: Alessandro Carrara
Phone: (39) 0573 401135
Fax: (39) 0573 401215
Email: alessandrocarrara@cartieracapostrada.com
Total Employees of Company: 20
Total Employees at this Location: 20
Type of Operation: Paper mill
Paper/Paperboard Grades and Capacities:
Total paper and paperboard capacity: 7,000 mt/y
Tissue: 7,000 mt/y
Paper and Paperboard Mill Data:
Paper Machines: 1
No. 1, crescent former, Yankee dryer, total capacity 7,000 mt/y, Trim width 1.75 m, Tissue
Energy Data:
Electrical demand for mill: 21 MWh/D

ⓂCartiera di Carbonera SpA
Camposampiero Mill
Ownership: Pro-Gest S.p.A.
Via Borgo Padova, 67
I-35012 Camposampiero, (PD)
Italy
Phone: (39) 049 5790744
Fax: (39) 049 5793492
Email: cartieradicarbonera@pro-gestspa.it
Web Address: www.pro-gestspa.it
Personnel:
Mill Mgr.: Mr. Giancarlo Giacomin
Phone: (39) 049 5790744
Fax: (39) 049 5793492

Email: giancarlo.giacomin@pro-gestspa.it
Mgr.: Mr. Francesco Zago
Phone: (39) 049 5790744
Fax: (39) 049 5793492
Email: francesco.zago@pro-gestspa.it
Total Employees at this Location: 80
Type of Operation: Paper mill, Paperboard mill
Pulp Grades and Capacities:
Total pulp capacity: 75,904 mt/y
Recycled Pulping: 75,904 mt/y
Pulp Mill Data:
Recycled Fiber Treatment Lines:
Pulpers: 1 at 89,000
Paper/Paperboard Grades and Capacities:
Total paper and paperboard capacity: 115,000 mt/y
Tissue: 20,000 mt/y
Linerboard: 95,000 mt/y
Paper and Paperboard Mill Data:
Stock Preparation:
Pulpers: 2
Paper Machines: 2
No. 1, fourdrinier (2), total capacity 95,000 mt/y, Trim width 2.65 m, Linerboard
No. 2, fourdrinier, Yankee dryer, total capacity 20,000 mt/y, Trim width 2.75 m, Tissue
Energy Data:
Power boilers: 1
Combustion turbines: 2 at 24 MW
Electrical demand for mill: 160 MWh/D

ⒽⓂCartiera Carmenta
Carmignano di Brenta Mill
Ownership: Cartiera Mantovana S.R.L.
Via Provinciale 45
I-35010 Carmignano di Brenta, (PD)
Italy
Phone: (39) 049 9430000
Fax: (39) 049 5958821
Email: cariolaro@cariolaro.com
Web Address: www.cariolaro.com
Personnel:
Pres., Prod.: Ing. Federico Cariolaro
Phone: (39) 049 9430000
Fax: (39) 049 5958821
Email: cariolaro.federico@cariolaro.com
VP, Sls., Mktg. & Purch.: Dr. Giorgio Cariolaro
Phone: (39) 049 9430000
Fax: (39) 049 5958821
Email: giorgio.cariolaro@cariolaro.com
Total Employees of Company: 107
Total Employees at this Location: 85
Type of Operation: Paper mill
Pulp Grades and Capacities:
Total pulp capacity: 60,145 mt/y
Recycled Pulping: 60,145 mt/y
Pulp Mill Data:
Bleach Plant Systems: 1
DIP Capacity 53,000 admt/y
Recycled Fiber Treatment Lines:
Flotation deinking lines: 1 at 68,000
Paper/Paperboard Grades and Capacities:
Total paper and paperboard capacity: 65,000 mt/y
Uncoated woodfree/freesheet: 30,000 mt/y
Coated woodfree/freesheet: 25,000 mt/y
Packaging papers: 10,000 mt/y
Paper and Paperboard Mill Data:
Paper Machines: 1
No. 2, hybrid former, total capacity 65,000 mt/y, Trim width 2.4 m, Coated woodfree/freesheet, Uncoated woodfree/freesheet, Packaging papers
Coating Machines: 1
PM 2, total capacity 32,500 mt/y., on machine
Finishing Equipment:
Calenders
Energy Data:
Power boilers: 1
Combustion turbines: 2 at 5.2, 6.3 MW
Hydro turbines
Electrical demand for mill: 141 MWh/D

ⒽⓂCartiera Carma Srl
Pistoia Mill
Ownership: Sant'Andrea Spa
Via Val di Forfora 27
I-51010 Pescia-Pietrabuona, (PT)
Italy
Phone: (39) 0572 405505/06
Fax: (39) 0572 405405
Email: info@carma.it
Web Address: www.carma.it
Personnel:
Chmn.: Massimo Carrara
Phone: (39) 0572 405505
Fax: (39) 0572 405405
Email: m.carrara@carma.it
Commer. Dir.: Giacomo Sandri
Phone: (39) 0572 405505
Fax: (39) 0572 405405
Email: g.sandri@carma.it
Export Sls. Mgr.: Giuliana Benigni
Phone: (39) 0572 405505
Fax: (39) 0572 405405
Email: giuliana.benigni@carma.it
Sls. Mgr. Italy: Alfredo Mazzanti
Phone: (39) 0572 405505
Fax: (39) 0572 405405
Email: a.mazzanti@carma.it
Commer. Mgr.: Manuela Rossi
Phone: (39) 0583 9851
Fax: (39) 0572 405405
Email: manuela.rossi@carma.it
Total Employees at this Location: 60
Type of Operation: Paper mill
Mill Locations:
Cartiera Carma Srl, Pratovecchio Mill, Via Dante Alighieri, 26/A, I-52015 Pratovecchio, (AR), Italy, Capacity: 22,500 mt/y, (Paper mill)
Phone: (39) 0575 582204
Fax: (39) 0575 582201
Email: info@carma.it
Paper/Paperboard Grades and Capacities:
Total paper and paperboard capacity: 31,000 mt/y
Tissue: 31,000 mt/y
Paper and Paperboard Mill Data:
Paper Machines: 2
No. 1, fourdrinier, Yankee dryer, total capacity 13,000 mt/y, Trim width 2.8 m, Tissue
No. 2, crescent former, Yankee dryer, total capacity 18,000 mt/y, Trim width 2.65 m, Tissue
Energy Data:
Power boilers: 1
Electrical demand for mill: 82 MWh/D

ⓂCartiera Carma Srl
Pratovecchio Mill
Ownership: Sant'Andrea Spa
Via Dante Alighieri, 26/A
I-52015 Pratovecchio, (AR)
Italy
Phone: (39) 0575 582204
Fax: (39) 0575 582201
Email: info@carma.it
Web Address: www.carma.it
Personnel:
Mill Mgr.: Luca Chiappini
Phone: (39) 0575 582204
Fax: (39) 0575 582201
Email: l.chiappini@carma.it
Energy Supt.: Francesco Fabbri
Phone: (39) 0575 582204
Fax: (39) 0575 582201
Email: f.fabbri@carma.it
Total Employees at this Location: 128
Type of Operation: Paper mill
Paper/Paperboard Grades and Capacities:
Total paper and paperboard capacity: 22,500 mt/y
Tissue: 22,500 mt/y
Paper and Paperboard Mill Data:
Paper Machines: 1

Italy

No. 1, C-wrap, total capacity 22,500 mt/y, Trim width 2.75 m, Tissue
Energy Data:
Power boilers: 2
Combustion turbines: 2 at 6.6 MW
Electrical demand for mill: 63 MWh/D

ⓄⓂCartesar SpA
Pellezano Mill
Ownership: De Iulliis Group
Via delle Fratte, 3 - Frazione Coperchia
I-84080 Pellezano, (SA)
Italy
Phone: (39) 089 568601
Fax: (39) 089 566375
Email: info@cartesar.it
Web Address: www.cartesar.it
Personnel:
Chmn.: Luigi Perna
Phone: (39) 089 568601
CEO: Luigi Ferrara
Phone: (39) 089 568601
Man. Dir./Mill Mgr.: Felice De Iuliis
Phone: (39) 089 568601
Tech./Prod. Mgr.: Luigi De Iuliis
Phone: (39) 89 568677
R&D Mgr.: Dr. Pietro Giuliano
Phone: (39) 89 568 621
Total Employees at this Location: 45
Type of Operation: Paperboard mill
Pulp Grades and Capacities:
Total pulp capacity: 85,013 mt/y
Recycled Pulping: 85,013 mt/y
Pulp Mill Data:
Recycled Fiber Treatment Lines:
Recycled packaging pulping lines: 1 at 85,000
Paper/Paperboard Grades and Capacities:
Total paper and paperboard capacity: 85,000 mt/y
Linerboard: 57,000 mt/y
Corrugating medium/fluting: 28,000 mt/y
Paper and Paperboard Mill Data:
Stock Preparation:
Pulpers: 2
Refiners: 2
Paper Machines: 1
No. 1, fourdrinier (2), total capacity 85,000 mt/y, Trim width 2.7 m, Corrugating medium/fluting, Linerboard
Finishing Equipment:
Winders: 1 at 85,000 mt/y
Energy Data:
Power boilers: 1
Combustion turbines: 2 at 3.5, 3.5 MW
Electrical demand for mill: 116 MWh/D

ⓄⓂCartiera Logudoro S.r.l.
Sassari Mill
Via Caniga 65
07100 Sassari
Italy
Phone: (39) 079 319-064
Fax: (39) 079 319-013
Total Employees of Company: 19
Type of Operation: Paper mill
Paper/Paperboard Grades and Capacities:
Total paper and paperboard capacity: 16,000 mt/y
Specialty and industrial: 16,000 mt/y
Paper and Paperboard Mill Data:
Paper Machines: 1
PM 1, total capacity 16,000 mt/y, Trim width 1.5 m, Specialty and industrial

ⓂCartitalia S.r.l.
Cartitalia Mill
Ownership: 100% by Pro-Gest S.p.A.
Via Motte 50
I-44026 Mesola, (FE)
Italy
Phone: (39) 0533 993 571
Fax: (39) 0533 993 566
Email: cartitalia@pro-gestspa.it
Web Address: www.pro-gestspa.it
Personnel:
Mill Mgr. Camposampiero Mill & Cartitalia Mill: Giancarlo Giacomin
Email: giancarlo.giacomin@pro-gestspa.it
Total Employees at this Location: 60
Type of Operation: Paper mill, Paperboard mill
Pulp Grades and Capacities:
Total pulp capacity: 125,771 mt/y
Recycled Pulping: 125,771 mt/y
Paper/Paperboard Grades and Capacities:
Total paper and paperboard capacity: 125,000 mt/y
Linerboard: 85,000 mt/y
Corrugating medium/fluting: 40,000 mt/y
Paper and Paperboard Mill Data:
Paper Machines: 1
No. 1, fourdrinier, total capacity 125,000 mt/y, Trim width 2.65 m, Corrugating medium/fluting, Linerboard
Energy Data:
Power boilers: 1
Combustion turbines: 1
Steam turbines: 1
Electrical demand for mill: 151 MWh/D

ⓄⓂCarval Cartiera Di Valletrompia Srl.
Concesio Mill
Via G. Sangervasio 28
I-25062 Concesio, (BS)
Italy
Phone: (39) 030 2180859
Fax: (39) 030 2180258
Email: info@carvalnet.it
Web Address: www.monteverdinet.it
Personnel:
Man. Dir.: Loisia Morinelli
Phone: (39) 030 2180859
Mill Mgr.: Aristide Bontempi
Phone: (39) 030 2180859
Total Employees of Company: 29
Total Employees at this Location: 29
Type of Operation: Paperboard mill
Pulp Grades and Capacities:
Total pulp capacity: 10,140 mt/y
Recycled Pulping: 10,140 mt/y
Pulp Mill Data:
Recycled Fiber Treatment Lines:
Recycled packaging pulping lines: 1
Paper/Paperboard Grades and Capacities:
Total paper and paperboard capacity: 10,000 mt/y
Boxboard/cartonboard: 10,000 mt/y
Paper and Paperboard Mill Data:
Paper Machines: 1
No. 1, cylinder, total capacity 10,000 mt/y, Trim width 1.6 m, Boxboard/cartonboard
Energy Data:
Power boilers: 1
Steam turbines: 1 at 1 MW
Electrical demand for mill: 8 MWh/D

ⓂCasalino Carta S.r.l.
Localitá Malvista
I-15078 Roccagrimalda
Italy
Phone: (39) 0143 841149
Fax: (39) 0143 882507
Email: info@casalinocarta.it
Web Address: www.casalinocarta.it
Personnel:
Co-Owner & Sls. Mgr.: Ambrogio Casalino
Phone: (39) 0143 841149
Fax: (39) 0143 882507
Email: info@casalinocarta.it
Mill Locations:
Casalino Carta S.r.l., Mele Mill, Via Biscaccia 97, I-16010 Mele, (GE), Italy, Capacity: 3,500 mt/y, (Paper mill)
Phone: (39) 010 631 9062
Fax: (39) 010 611 9095/014 388
Email: info@casalinocarta.it

ⓂCasalino Carta S.r.l.
Mele Mill
Via Biscaccia 97
I-16010 Mele, (GE)
Italy
Phone: (39) 010 631 9062
Fax: (39) 010 611 9095/014 388
Email: info@casalinocarta.it
Web Address: www.casalinocarta.it
Personnel:
Co-own./Sls.: Ambrogio Casalino
Phone: (39) 010 631 9062
Fax: (39) 010 611 9095
Email: info@casalinocarta.it
Total Employees at this Location: 10
Type of Operation: Paper mill
Pulp Grades and Capacities:
Total pulp capacity: 3,752 mt/y
Recycled Pulping: 3,752 mt/y
Pulp Mill Data:
Recycled Fiber Treatment Lines:
Pulpers: 1
Paper/Paperboard Grades and Capacities:
Total paper and paperboard capacity: 3,500 mt/y
Tissue: 3,500 mt/y
Paper and Paperboard Mill Data:
Paper Machines: 1
No. 1, fourdrinier, Yankee dryer, total capacity 3,500 mt/y, Trim width 1.3 m, Tissue
Energy Data:
Power boilers: 1
Electrical demand for mill: 9 MWh/D

ⓄⓂCartiera Enrico Cassina SNC
Pinerolo Mill
Piazza Frairia Sisto 4
I-10064 Pinerolo, (TO)
Italy
Phone: (39) 0121 397 297
Fax: (39) 0121 74 293
Email: cartierecassina@libero.it
Web Address: www.cartierecassina.com
Personnel:
Mill Mgr.: Giorgio Cassina
Phone: (39) 0121 397 297
Fax: (39) 0121 74 293
Email: produzione@cartierecassina.com
Total Employees of Company: 20
Total Employees at this Location: 20
Type of Operation: Paper mill
Pulp Grades and Capacities:
Total pulp capacity: 20,143 mt/y
Recycled Pulping: 20,143 mt/y
Pulp Mill Data:
Recycled Fiber Treatment Lines:
Flotation deinking lines: 1
Pulpers: 2
Recycled packaging pulping lines: 1
Paper/Paperboard Grades and Capacities:
Total paper and paperboard capacity: 20,000 mt/y
Corrugating medium/fluting: 20,000 mt/y
Paper and Paperboard Mill Data:
Stock Preparation:
Refiners: 2
Paper Machines: 1
No. 1, fourdrinier, total capacity 20,000 mt/y, Trim width 2.51 m, Corrugating medium/fluting
Finishing Equipment:
Winders: 1
Energy Data:
Power boilers: 1
Electrical demand for mill: 26 MWh/D

Italy

ⓞⓜC.C.R. - Cartiera Cooperativa Rivalta
Rivalta Veronese Mill
Via Don Cesare Scala, 51
I-37020 Brentino-Belluno, (VR)
Italy
  Phone: (39) 045 6284063
  Fax: (39) 045 6284096
  Email: info@cartierarivalta.com
  Web Address: www.cartierarivalta.com
Personnel:
  Man. Dir.: Roberto Stella
  Phone: (39) 045 6284063
  Fax: (39) 045 6284096
  Email: r.stella@cartierarivalta.com
Total Employees of Company: 22
Total Employees at this Location: 22
Type of Operation: Paper mill
Pulp Grades and Capacities:
  Total pulp capacity: 25,180 mt/y
  Recycled Pulping: 25,180 mt/y
Paper/Paperboard Grades and Capacities:
  Total paper and paperboard capacity: 25,000 mt/y
  Corrugating medium/fluting: 25,000 mt/y
Paper and Paperboard Mill Data:
Paper Machines: 1
  No. 1, fourdrinier, total capacity 25,000 mt/y, Trim width 2.4 m, Corrugating medium/fluting
Energy Data:
  Power boilers: 1
  Electrical demand for mill: 31 MWh/D

ⓞCeltex S.p.a
Via Trav. Del Marginone 21/23
55015 Montecarlo, (LU)
Italy
  Phone: (39) 39 0583 27 41
  Fax: (39) 39 0583 277 777
  Email: info@celtex.it
  Web Address: www.celtex.it
Personnel:
  CEO: Andrea Bernacchi
  Phone: (39) 0583 27 41
  Fax: (39) 0583 277 777
  Dir.: Luca Perini
  Phone: (39) 0583 27 41
  Fax: (39) 0583 277 777
  Export Sls. Mgr.: Alessia Filidei
  Phone: (39) 0583 27 41
  Fax: (39) 0583 277 777
Total Employees of Company: 150
Mill Locations:
  Celtex S.p.a, Pracando Mill, Via delle Cartiere 203, I-55010 Pracando Villa Basilica, (LU), Italy, Capacity: 23,000 mt/y, (Paper mill)
  Cartiera San Lorenzo S.R.L., Gassano Mill, Via Molino, 1, I-54020 Gassano, (MS), Italy, Capacity: 20,000 mt/y, (Paper mill)
  Phone: (39) 0585 998045
  Fax: (39) 0585 99214
  Email: info@cartierasanlorenzo.it

ⓞCeltex S.p.a
Pracando Mill
Via delle Cartiere 203
I-55010 Pracando Villa Basilica, (LU)
Italy
  Web Address: www.celtex.it
Total Employees at this Location: 30
Type of Operation: Paper mill
Paper/Paperboard Grades and Capacities:
  Total paper and paperboard capacity: 23,000 mt/y
  Tissue: 23,000 mt/y
Paper and Paperboard Mill Data:
Paper Machines: 1
  No. 1, crescent former, Yankee dryer, total capacity 23,000 mt/y, Trim width 2.75 m, Tissue
Energy Data:
  Power boilers: 1
  Electrical demand for mill: 58 MWh/D

ⓞⓜCartiera Cerrone Francescantonio SpA
Cerrone Mill
Via delle Antichita 1
I-03031 Aquino, (FR)
Italy
  Phone: (39) 0776 728012
  Fax: (39) 0776 728426
  Email: cartiera.cerrone@tin.it, clientserv@tin.it
  Web Address: www.cartierafrancescantoniocerrone.it
Personnel:
  Man. Dir.: Francesco Antonio Cerrone
  Phone: (39) 0776 728012
  Fax: (39) 0776 728426
  Email: cartiera.cerrone@tin.it
  Sls. Mgr.: Mr. Rocco Giannitelli
  Phone: (39) 0776 728012
  Fax: (39) 0776 728426
  Email: cartiera.cerrone@tin.it
Total Employees at this Location: 50
Type of Operation: Paperboard mill
Pulp Grades and Capacities:
  Total pulp capacity: 39,844 mt/y
  Recycled Pulping: 39,844 mt/y
Pulp Mill Data:
  Recycled Fiber Treatment Lines:
  Pulpers: 2
Paper/Paperboard Grades and Capacities:
  Total paper and paperboard capacity: 40,000 mt/y
  Boxboard/cartonboard: 40,000 mt/y
Paper and Paperboard Mill Data:
Paper Machines: 1
  No. 1, cylinder, total capacity 40,000 mt/y, Trim width 2.4 m, Boxboard/cartonboard
Coating Machines: 1
  PM1, off machine
Finishing Equipment:
  Rewinders: 1
Energy Data:
  Power boilers: 1
  Electrical demand for mill: 57 MWh/D

ⓞⓜCham Paper Group Italia S.p.A.
Carmignano Mill
Ownership: 100% by Cham Paper Group Schweiz AG
Via Roma 67
I-35010 Carmignano di Brenta, (PD)
Italy
  Phone: (39) 049 942 3600
  Fax: (39) 049 942 3700
  Email: mail.carmignano@cham-group.com
  Web Address: www.champaper.com
Personnel:
  CEO: Peter Struder
  Phone: (39) 049 942 3600
  Site Mgr.: Marcello Di Giacomo
  Eng. & Prod. Mgr.: Gianluca Scaglioni
  Phone: (39) 049 942 3600
  Finan./Admin. Dir.: Corrado Martignago
  Phone: (39) 049 942 3600
  Quality Mgr.: Dr. Mario Moretto
  Phone: (39) 049 942 3600
Total Employees of Company: 330
Total Employees at this Location: 220
Type of Operation: Paper mill
Mill Locations:
  Cham Paper Group Italia S.p.A., Condino Mill, Via Roma 153, I-38083 Condino, (TN), Italy, Capacity: 45,000 mt/y, (Paper mill)
  Phone: (39) 0465 622 511
  Fax: (39) 0465 622 540
  Email: mail.condino@cham-group.com
Paper/Paperboard Grades and Capacities:
  Total paper and paperboard capacity: 100,000 mt/y
  Specialty and industrial: 100,000 mt/y
Paper and Paperboard Mill Data:
Paper Machines: 2
  No. 4, fourdrinier, total capacity 70,000 mt/y, Trim width 3.3 m, Specialty and industrial
  No. 6, fourdrinier, total capacity 30,000 mt/y, Trim width 3.3 m, Specialty and industrial
Coating Machines: 2
  No. 1, total capacity 60,000 mt/y, off machine
  No. 2, total capacity 30,000 mt/y, on machine
Finishing Equipment:
  Winders: 2
  Supercalenders: 2
  Rewinders: 2
Energy Data:
  Power boilers: 1
  Combustion turbines: 1
  Steam turbines: 1
  Electrical demand for mill: 236 MWh/D

ⓜCham Paper Group Italia S.p.A.
Condino Mill
Ownership: 100% by Cham Paper Group Schweiz AG
Via Roma 153
I-38083 Condino, (TN)
Italy
  Phone: (39) 0465 622 511
  Fax: (39) 0465 622 540
  Email: mail.condino@cham-group.com
  Web Address: www.cham-group.com
Personnel:
  Mill Mgr.: Gerold Zuegg
  Phone: (39) 0465 622 511
  Fax: (39) 0465 622 540
  Email: gerold.zuegg@cham-group.com
  Mgr.: Mario Moretto
  Phone: (39) 0465 622 511
  Fax: (39) 0465 622 540
  Email: mario.moretto@cham-group.com
Total Employees at this Location: 117
Type of Operation: Paper mill
Paper/Paperboard Grades and Capacities:
  Total paper and paperboard capacity: 45,000 mt/y
  Specialty and industrial: 45,000 mt/y
Paper and Paperboard Mill Data:
  Stock Preparation:
  Pulpers: 2
  Refiners: 5
Paper Machines: 1
  No. 5, fourdrinier, total capacity 45,000 mt/y, Trim width 3.3 m, Specialty and industrial
Coating Machines: 1
  CM1 (idle), total capacity 100,000 mt/y, off machine
Finishing Equipment:
  Supercalenders: 2
  Rewinders: 2
Energy Data:
  Power boilers: 2
  Steam turbines: 2 at 11.0 MW
  Electrical demand for mill: 128 MWh/D

ⓞⓜCartiera del Chiese SpA
Montichiari Mill
Via Tito Speri 61
I-25018 Montichiari, (BS)
Italy
  Phone: (39) 030 9653711
  Fax: (39) 030 96 44 44
  Email: cartieradelchiese@cartieradelchiese.it
  Web Address: www.cartieradelchiese.it
Personnel:
  Man. Dir. & Prod. Mgr.: Enzo Fenotti
  Phone: (39) 030 9653711
  Fax: (39) 030 964444
  Email: enzo.fenotti@cartieradelchiese.it
  Technology Mgr.: Giuseppe Carsana
  Phone: (39) 030 9653711
  Fax: (39) 030 964444
  Email: giuseppe.carsana@cartieradelchiese.it
  Sls. Dir.: Enrico Fenotti
  Phone: (39) 030 9653711

Italy

Fax: (39) 030 964444
Email: enrico.fenotti@cartieradelchiese.it
Total Employees of Company: 100
Total Employees at this Location: 100
Type of Operation: Paper mill
Pulp Grades and Capacities:
  Total pulp capacity: 58,608 mt/y
  Recycled Pulping: 58,608 mt/y
Paper/Paperboard Grades and Capacities:
  Total paper and paperboard capacity: 58,000 mt/y
  Packaging papers: 58,000 mt/y
Paper and Paperboard Mill Data:
Paper Machines: 1
  No. 1, fourdrinier, total capacity 58,000 mt/y, Trim width 2.34 m, Packaging papers
Coating Machines: 1
  No. 1, on machine
Energy Data:
  Combustion turbines: 1
  Electrical demand for mill: 114 MWh/D

ⓗⓜCartiera di Cologno SpA
Cologno Monzese Mill
Ownership: 100% by Masotina Group
Via Guzzina 135
I-20093 Cologno Monzese, (MI)
Italy
  Phone: (39) 02 2539 0824
  Fax: (39) 02 2539 0403
  Email: cartieradicologno@cartieradicologno.it
  Web Address: www.gruppomasotina.it
Personnel:
  Pres.: Francesco Masotina
  Phone: (39) 02 2539 0824
  Fax: (39) 02 2539 0403
  Mgr.: Agostino Righetti
  Phone: (39) 02 2539 0824
  Fax: (39) 02 2539 0403
Total Employees at this Location: 33
Type of Operation: Paper mill, Paperboard mill
Pulp Grades and Capacities:
  Total pulp capacity: 50,401 mt/y
  Recycled Pulping: 50,401 mt/y
Pulp Mill Data:
  Recycled Fiber Treatment Lines:
  Pulpers: 1 at 55,000
Paper/Paperboard Grades and Capacities:
  Total paper and paperboard capacity: 50,000 mt/y
  Corrugating medium/fluting: 50,000 mt/y
Paper and Paperboard Mill Data:
  Stock Preparation:
  Pulpers: 2
  Refiners: 4
Paper Machines: 1
  No. 1, fourdrinier, total capacity 50,000 mt/y, Trim width 2.5 m, Corrugating medium/fluting
Finishing Equipment:
  Rewinders: 1
Energy Data:
  Power boilers
  Combustion turbines
  Steam turbines
  Electrical demand for mill: 72 MWh/D

ⓗCartiera Confalone S.R.L.
Via San Pietro 147
I-84010 Maiori, (SA)
Italy
  Phone: (39) 089 877059
  Fax: (39) 089 851516
  Email: info@confalone.it
  Web Address: www.confalone.it
Personnel:
  Admin., Sls., Finan. Dir.: Dr. Giusseppe Confalone
  Phone: (39) 089 877059
  Fax: (39) 089 851516
  Email: giuconf@confalone.it
  Comm., Prod. Dir.: Rag. Gaetano Confalone
  Phone: (39) 089 877059

Fax: (39) 089 851516
Email: gaeconf@confalone.it
Total Employees of Company: 58
Mill Locations:
Cartiera Confalone S.R.L., Salerno Mill, Via San Pietro 147, I-84010 Maiori, (SA), Italy, Capacity: 20,000 mt/y, (Paper mill)
Phone: (39) 089 877059
Fax: (39) 089 851516
Email: info@confalone.it

ⓜCartiera Confalone S.R.L.
Salerno Mill
Via San Pietro 147
I-84010 Maiori, (SA)
Italy
  Phone: (39) 089 877059
  Fax: (39) 089 851516
  Email: info@confalone.it
  Web Address: www.confalone.it
Personnel:
  Sls. Mgr.: Gaetano Confalone
  Phone: (39) 089 274841
Total Employees at this Location: 51
Type of Operation: Paper mill
Paper/Paperboard Grades and Capacities:
  Total paper and paperboard capacity: 20,000 mt/y
  Tissue: 20,000 mt/y
Paper and Paperboard Mill Data:
  Stock Preparation:
  Pulpers: 2
Paper Machines: 1
  No. 1, crescent former, Yankee dryer, total capacity 20,000 mt/y, Trim width 2.7 m, Tissue
Energy Data:
  Power boilers
  Electrical demand for mill: 53 MWh/D

ⓗGruppo Cordenons SpA
Ownership: Bilberti Ferrucio
Via Niccolò Machiavelli 38
I-20145 Milano, (MI)
Italy
  Phone: (39) 02 467 101
  Fax: (39) 02 481 8507
  Email: cordenons@gruppocordenons.com
  Web Address: www.gruppocordenons.com
Personnel:
  Pres. Chmn.: Ferruccio Gilberti
  Phone: (39) 02 467 101
  Fax: (39) 02 481 8507
  Email: f.gilberti@gruppocordenons.com
  Man. Dir.: Ottavio Zucca
  Phone: (39) 02 467 101
  Fax: (39) 02 481 8507
  Email: o.zucca@gruppocordenons.com
  Tech. Dir.: Christoph Kalbhenn
  Phone: (39) 02 467 101
  Fax: (39) 02 481 8507
  Email: c.kalbhenn@gruppocordenons.com
  Sls. Dir.: Massimiliano Zicchittella
  Phone: (39) 02 467 101
  Fax: (39) 02 481 8507
  Commer. Dir.: Marc Geelen
  Phone: (39) 02 467 101
  Fax: (39) 02 481 8507
  Email: m.geelen@gruppocordenons.com
  Purch. & Logist. Dir.: Giovanni Pelis
  Phone: (39) 02 467 101
  Fax: (39) 02 481 8507
  Email: g.pelis@gruppocordenons.com
  Export Mgr. & Branch Dir.: Philippe Virey
  Phone: (39) 02 467 101
  Fax: (39) 02 481 8507
  Email: p.virey@gruppocordenons.com
  Sls. Area Mgr.: Giovanni Gilberti
  Phone: (39) 02 467 101
  Fax: (39) 02 481 8507
Total Employees of Company: 282
Total Employees at this Location: 50

Mill Locations:
Gruppo Cordenons SpA, Cordenons Mill, Via Pasch 95, I-33084 Cordenons, (PN), Italy, Capacity: 35,000 mt/y, (Paper mill)
Phone: (39) 0434 586 811
Fax: (39) 0434 932 120
Email: cordenons@gruppocordenons.com
Gruppo Cordenons SpA, Scurelle Mill, Via Beniamino Donzelli 48/1, I-38050 Scurelle, (TN), Italy, Capacity: 15,000 mt/y, (Paper mill)
Phone: (39) 0461 762238
Fax: (39) 0461 763587
Email: cordenons@gruppocordenons.com

ⓜGruppo Cordenons SpA
Cordenons Mill
Via Pasch 95
I-33084 Cordenons, (PN)
Italy
  Phone: (39) 0434 586 811
  Fax: (39) 0434 932 120
  Email: cordenons@gruppocordenons.com
  Web Address: www.gruppocordenons.com
Personnel:
  Maint. Mgr.: Giampaolo Passarin
  Phone: (39) 0434 586 822
  Fax: (39) 0434 932120
  Email: g.passarin@gruppocordenons.com
  Qlty. Mgr.: Francesco Guidi
  Phone: (39) 0434 586 819
  Fax: (39) 0434 932120
  Email: f.guidi@gruppocordenons.com
Total Employees at this Location: 175
Type of Operation: Paper mill
Pulp Grades and Capacities:
  Total pulp capacity: 1,516 mt/y
  Recycled Pulping: 1,516 mt/y
Paper/Paperboard Grades and Capacities:
  Total paper and paperboard capacity: 35,000 mt/y
  Uncoated woodfree/freesheet: 32,500 mt/y
  Specialty and industrial: 2,500 mt/y
Paper and Paperboard Mill Data:
  Stock Preparation:
  Pulpers: 4
  Refiners: 12
Paper Machines: 2
  No. 1, fourdrinier, total capacity 17,500 mt/y, Trim width 1.63 m, Uncoated woodfree/freesheet, Specialty and industrial
  No. 2, fourdrinier, total capacity 17,500 mt/y, Trim width 1.63 m, Uncoated woodfree/freesheet
Coating Machines: 2
  No. 1, total capacity 7,500 mt/y., off machine
  No. 2, total capacity 9,000 mt/y., off machine
Finishing Equipment:
  Winders: 2 at 10,000 mt/y
  Sheeters: 6 at 20,000 mt/y
Energy Data:
  Power boilers: 3
  HRSG boiler: 1
  Combustion turbines: 1 at 5 MW
  Electrical demand for mill: 62 MWh/D

ⓜGruppo Cordenons SpA
Scurelle Mill
Via Beniamino Donzelli 48/1
I-38050 Scurelle, (TN)
Italy
  Phone: (39) 0461 762238
  Fax: (39) 0461 763587
  Email: cordenons@gruppocordenons.com
  Web Address: www.gruppocordenons.com
Personnel:
  Central Technical Dir.: Giorgio Monacelli
  Phone: (39) 0461 762238
  Fax: (39) 0434 932120
  Email: g.monacelli@gruppocordenons.com
  Qlty. Mgr.: Olivo Olivi
  Phone: (39) 0461 762238
  Fax: (39) 0461 763587

Italy

Email: o.olivi@gruppocordenons.com
R&D Mgr. & Tech. Dir. Assist.: Luca Monacelli
Phone: (39) 0434 586 852
Fax: (39) 0434 932120
Email: l.monacelli@gruppocordenons.com
Qlty. Management Assist.: Alex (Alessandro) Garutti
Phone: (39) 0434 586850
Fax: (39) 0434 932120
Email: a.garutti@gruppocordenons.com
Total Employees at this Location: 45
Type of Operation: Paper mill
Paper/Paperboard Grades and Capacities:
Total paper and paperboard capacity: 15,000 mt/y
Uncoated woodfree/freesheet: 15,000 mt/y
Paper and Paperboard Mill Data:
Stock Preparation:
Pulpers: 2
Refiners: 4
Paper Machines: 1
No. 3, fourdrinier, total capacity 15,000 mt/y, Trim width 1.6 m, Uncoated woodfree/freesheet
Finishing Equipment:
Winders: 1 at 5,000 mt/y
Sheeters: 2 at 6,000 mt/y
Energy Data:
Power boilers: 3
Hydro turbines: 1 at 0.2 MW
Electrical demand for mill: 28 MWh/D

ⓗⓜDelicarta SpA
Porcari Mill
Ownership: 100% by Sofidel Group
Via di Lucia 9
I-55016 Porcari, (LU)
Italy
Phone: (39) 0583 2681
Fax: (39) 0583 299898
Email: delicarta@sofidel.it
Web Address: www.sofidel.it
Personnel:
Maint. Mgr.: Leandro Campagna
Phone: (39) 3469 419615
Fax: (39) 0583 246128
Email: leandro.campagna@sofidel.it
Purch. Mgr.: Riccardo Lena
Phone: (39) 0583 2681
Fax: (39) 0583 299898
Email: riccardo.lena@sofidel.it
Total Employees of Company: 380
Total Employees at this Location: 160
Type of Operation: Paper mill
Mill Locations:
Delicarta SpA, Monfalcone Mill, Via Grota del Diau Zot, I-34074 Monfalcone, (GO), Italy, Capacity: 30,000 mt/y, (Paper mill)
Phone: (39) 0481 791596
Fax: (39) 0481 791589
Delicarta SpA, Valdottavo Mill, Via Provinciale Ludovica, I-55067 Valdottavo di Borgo a Mozzano, (LU), Italy, Capacity: 28,000 mt/y, (Paper mill)
Phone: (39) 0583 2681
Fax: (39) 0583 246240
Email: imbalpaper@sofidel.it
Paper/Paperboard Grades and Capacities:
Total paper and paperboard capacity: 125,000 mt/y
Tissue: 125,000 mt/y
Paper and Paperboard Mill Data:
Stock Preparation:
Pulpers: 4
Refiners: 6
Paper Machines: 3
No. 1, twin-wire, Yankee dryer, total capacity 30,000 mt/y, Trim width 2.7 m, Tissue
No. 2, crescent former, Yankee dryer, total capacity 35,000 mt/y, Trim width 2.7 m, Tissue
No. 3, crescent former, Yankee dryer, total capacity 60,000 mt/y, Trim width 5.2 m, Tissue
Finishing Equipment:
Rewinders: 3 at 125,000 mt/y
Energy Data:

Power boilers: 11
Combustion turbines: 2 at 8 MW
Electrical demand for mill: 321 MWh/D

ⓜDelicarta SpA
Monfalcone Mill
Previously Cartiera di Monfalcone SpA.
Ownership: 100% by Sofidel Group
Via Grota del Diau Zot
I-34074 Monfalcone, (GO)
Italy
Phone: (39) 0481 791596
Fax: (39) 0481 791589
Web Address: www.sofidel.it
Personnel:
Mill Mgr.: Alessandro Zampar
Phone: (39) 0481 791596
Fax: (39) 0481 791589
Email: alessandro.zampar@sofidel.it
Mgr.: Linda Kuzmicki
Phone: (39) 0481 791596
Fax: (39) 0481 791589
Email: linda.kuzmicki@sofidel.it
Total Employees at this Location: 40
Type of Operation: Paper mill
Paper/Paperboard Grades and Capacities:
Total paper and paperboard capacity: 30,000 mt/y
Tissue: 30,000 mt/y
Paper and Paperboard Mill Data:
Stock Preparation:
Pulpers: 1
Refiners: 2
Paper Machines: 1
No. 1, crescent former, Yankee dryer, total capacity 30,000 mt/y, Trim width 2.85 m, Tissue
Finishing Equipment:
Winders: 1 at 30,000 mt/y
Energy Data:
Power boilers: 1
Electrical demand for mill: 74 MWh/D

ⓜDelicarta SpA
Valdottavo Mill
Ownership: 100% by Sofidel Group
Via Provinciale Ludovica
I-55067 Valdottavo di Borgo a Mozzano, (LU)
Italy
Phone: (39) 0583 2681
Fax: (39) 0583 246240
Email: imbalpaper@sofidel.it
Web Address: www.sofidel.it
Personnel:
Plt. Mgr.: Fabio Franceschi
Phone: (39) 0583 268629
Fax: (39) 0583 246240
Email: fabio.franceschi@sofidel.it
Total Employees at this Location: 86
Type of Operation: Paper mill
Paper/Paperboard Grades and Capacities:
Total paper and paperboard capacity: 28,000 mt/y
Tissue: 28,000 mt/y
Paper and Paperboard Mill Data:
Paper Machines: 1
No. 1, crescent former, Yankee dryer, total capacity 28,000 mt/y, Trim width 2.75 m, Tissue
Energy Data:
Power boilers: 1
Electrical demand for mill: 75 MWh/D

ⓗⓜCartiera Delle Alpi S.r.l.
Guardabosone Mill
Ownership: Ownership: Bresi S.P.A.
Via Molino 6
I-13010 Guardabosone, (VC)
Italy
Phone: (39) 015 7697 056
Fax: (39) 015 7697 509
Personnel:

Mill Mgr.: Ing. Nicola Cozzolino
Phone: (39) 015 76 81 53
Total Employees at this Location: 20
Type of Operation: Paper mill
Pulp Mill Data:
Recycled Fiber Treatment Lines:
Flotation deinking lines: 1 at 7,200 admt/y
Paper/Paperboard Grades and Capacities:
Total paper and paperboard capacity: 13,000 mt/y
Paper and Paperboard Mill Data:
Stock Preparation:
Pulpers: 1
Refiners: 4
Paper Machines: 1
No. 1, fourdrinier, total capacity 13,000 mt/y, Trim width 1.6 m
Finishing Equipment:
Winders: 1 at 13,000 mt/y
Energy Data:
Power boilers: 1
Electrical demand for mill: 53 MWh/D

ⓜDS Smith Packaging Italia S.p.A.
Lucca Mill
Ownership: 100% by DS Smith Plc
Via del Frizzone
I-55016 Porcari, (LU)
Italy
Phone: (39) 0583 2961
Fax: (39) 0583 296657
Email: info@dssmith.com
Web Address: www.dssmith.com
Personnel:
Gen. Mgr.: Michele Bianchi
Phone: (39) 0583 296664
Fax: (39) 0583 296657
Email: michele.bianchi@dssmith.com
Tech. Mgr.: Stefano Andreotti
Phone: (39) 0583 296616
Fax: (39) 0583 296600
Email: stefano.andreotti@dssmith.com
Purch. Agt.: Paolo Cardarelli
Phone: (39) 0583 2961
Fax: (39) 0583 296673
Email: paolo.cardarelli@dssmith.com
Sls. Mgr.: Maurizio Fini
Phone: (39) 0583 296622
Fax: (39) 0583 296685
Email: maurizio.fini@dssmith.eu
HR Mgr.: Alessandro Rosellini
Phone: (39) 0583 296615
Fax: (39) 0583 296600
Email: alessandro.rosellini@dssmith.com
Logist. & Purch. Mgr.: Marcello Lembi
Phone: (39) 0583 2961
Fax: (39) 0583 296657
Email: marcello.lembi@dssmith.eu
Finance Dept.: Luca Castrucci
Phone: (39) 0583 296662
Fax: (39) 0583 296673
Email: luca.castrucci@dssmith.com
Total Employees at this Location: 170
Type of Operation: Paperboard mill
Pulp Grades and Capacities:
Total pulp capacity: 419,966 mt/y
Recycled Pulping: 419,966 mt/y
Pulp Mill Data:
Recycled Fiber Treatment Lines:
Flotation deinking lines: 1 at 134,000
Pulpers: 6 at 400,000 admt/y
Paper/Paperboard Grades and Capacities:
Total paper and paperboard capacity: 420,000 mt/y
Linerboard: 262,000 mt/y
Corrugating medium/fluting: 158,000 mt/y
Paper and Paperboard Mill Data:
Stock Preparation:
Pulpers: 6
Refiners: 15
Paper Machines: 2

Italy

No. 1, fourdrinier (2), total capacity 170,000 mt/y, Trim width 4.6 m, Linerboard, Corrugating medium/fluting
No. 2, GapFormer, total capacity 250,000 mt/y, Trim width 5 m, Linerboard, Corrugating medium/fluting
Finishing Equipment:
 Winders: 2 at 420,000 mt/y
 Rewinders: 2 at 370,000 mt/y
Energy Data:
Combustion turbines
Electrical demand for mill: 577 MWh/D

ⓗⓜEFW Tuscania Srl
Tuscania Mill
Strada Cartiera 2
I-01017 Tuscania, (VT)
Italy
 Phone: (39) 0761 435248
 Fax: (39) 0761 435272
 Email: amministrazione@efwtuscania.com
Personnel:
 Admin. Mgr.: Olena Zharikova
 Phone: (39) 0761 443 544
Total Employees of Company: 35
Total Employees at this Location: 35
Type of Operation: Paperboard mill
Pulp Grades and Capacities:
 Total pulp capacity: 40,183 mt/y
 Recycled Pulping: 40,183 mt/y
Pulp Mill Data:
 Recycled Fiber Treatment Lines:
 Recycled packaging pulping lines: 1
Paper/Paperboard Grades and Capacities:
 Total paper and paperboard capacity: 40,000 mt/y
 Corrugating medium/fluting: 40,000 mt/y
Paper and Paperboard Mill Data:
Paper Machines: 1
No. 1, fourdrinier, total capacity 40,000 mt/y, Trim width 2.2 m, Corrugating medium/fluting
Energy Data:
Power boilers: 1
Electrical demand for mill: 53 MWh/D

ⓗⓜCartiere Ermolli S.p.a.
Moggio Udinese Mill
Ownership: Gruppo Ermolli
Via Giorgio Ermolli 62
I-33015 Moggio Udinese, (UD)
Italy
 Phone: (39) 0433 5553
 Fax: (39) 0433 51022
 Email: mocom@ermolli.it
 Web Address: www.ermolli.it
Personnel:
 Chmn. & Finan. Dir.: Giuseppe Tobia
 Phone: (39) 0433 5553
 Fax: (39) 0433 51022
 Email: giuseppetobia@ermolli.it
 Man. Dir. & Sls. Dir.: Gilio Munaro
 Phone: (39) 0433 5553
 Fax: (39) 0433 51022
 Email: giliomunaro@ermolli.it
 R&D Mgr.: Mara Blasutto
 Phone: (39) 0433 5553
 Fax: (39) 0433 51022
 Email: marablasutto@ermolli.it
 Sls. Office Mgr.: Magda Moschitz
 Phone: (39) 0433 555241
 Fax: (39) 0433 51022
 Email: magdamoschitz@ermolli.it
Total Employees at this Location: 180
Type of Operation: Paper mill
Paper/Paperboard Grades and Capacities:
 Total paper and paperboard capacity: 44,000 mt/y
 Uncoated woodfree/freesheet: 5,000 mt/y
 Specialty and industrial: 39,000 mt/y
Paper and Paperboard Mill Data:
 Stock Preparation:
 Pulpers: 3
Paper Machines: 3
No. 1, fourdrinier, Twin HSM, total capacity 18,000 mt/y, Trim width 2.24 m, Specialty and industrial
No. 2, fourdrinier, Yankee dryer, total capacity 8,000 mt/y, Trim width 2.1 m, Specialty and industrial
No. 3, fourdrinier, total capacity 18,000 mt/y, Trim width 2.12 m, Specialty and industrial, Uncoated woodfree/freesheet
Finishing Equipment:
 Supercalenders: 4 at 35,000 mt/y
 Rewinders: 4 at 48,000 mt/y
Energy Data:
Power boilers: 1
Combustion turbines: 2
Steam turbines: 1 at 3 MW
Hydro turbines: 5
Electrical demand for mill: 126 MWh/D

ⓗⓜEurocartiera
Pietramelara Mill
Ownership: 25% by Antonio Pieri, 50% by Pasquale Liguori, 25% by Prodi Group
Contrada Pantano
I-81051 Pietramelara, (CE)
Italy
 Phone: (39) 0823 987590
 Fax: (39) 0823 987595
 Email: eurocartiera@libero.it
Personnel:
 Admin.: Pascale Liguori
 Phone: (39) 0823 987590
 Prod. Mgr.: Domenico Liguori
 Phone: (39) 0823 987590
 Accountant: Antonio Bosco
 Phone: (39) 0823 987590
Total Employees of Company: 30
Total Employees at this Location: 30
Type of Operation: Paper mill
Paper/Paperboard Grades and Capacities:
 Total paper and paperboard capacity: 30,000 mt/y
 Tissue: 30,000 mt/y
Paper and Paperboard Mill Data:
 Stock Preparation:
 Pulpers:
Paper Machines: 1
No. 1, crescent former, Yankee dryer, total capacity 30,000 mt/y, Trim width 2.75 m, Tissue
Energy Data:
Power boilers: 1
Electrical demand for mill: 76 MWh/D

ⓗⓜCartiera Europaper SpA
Monzone-Fivizzano Mill
Ownership: ICT Italy
Via Pian di Molino
I-54013 Monzone-Fivizzano, (MS)
Italy
 Phone: (39) 0585 97910
 Fax: (39) 0585 97918
 Email: info@europaperspa.it
 Web Address: www.europaper.it
Personnel:
 Mill Mgr.: Giuseppe Poli
 Phone: (39) 0585 97910
 Fax: (39) 0585 97918
 Email: g.poli@europaperspa.it
Total Employees at this Location: 33
Type of Operation: Paper mill
Paper/Paperboard Grades and Capacities:
 Total paper and paperboard capacity: 27,000 mt/y
 Tissue: 27,000 mt/y
Paper and Paperboard Mill Data:
Paper Machines: 1
No. 1, crescent former, Yankee dryer, total capacity 27,000 mt/y, Trim width 2.7 m, Tissue
Energy Data:
Power boilers: 1
Electrical demand for mill: 71 MWh/D

ⓜCartiera Eurotec srl.
Fabbriche di Vallico Mill
Mill is mill was idled by WEPA in mid-2012, restarted tissue production in May 2014 as Cartiera Eurotec srl.
Località Gnocconi
I-55020 Fabbriche di Vallico, (LU)
Italy
 Phone: (39) 0583 448 930
 Fax: (39) 0583 709 578
Total Employees at this Location: 16
Type of Operation: Paper mill
Paper and Paperboard Mill Data:
Paper Machines: 1
No. 1, fourdrinier, Yankee dryer, total capacity 17,000 mt/y, Trim width 2.7 m
Energy Data:
Power boilers: 1

ⓗⓜFavini Spa
Rossano Veneto Mill
Ownership: 62% by OI-Paper, 4% by Favini management, 21% by Credit Agricole, 13% by Lacim
Via Alcide de Gasperi 26
I-36028 Rossano Veneto, (VI)
Italy
 Phone: (39) 0424 547711
 Fax: (39) 0424 540684
 Email: rossano@favini.com
 Web Address: www.favini.com
Personnel:
 CEO: Mr. Andrea Nappa
 Phone: (39) 0424 54771
 Fax: (39) 0424 547793
 Gen. Mgr.: Eugenio Eger
 Phone: (39) 0424 547707
 Fax: (39) 0424 547897
 Email: eugenio.eger@favini.com
 Mill Mgr.: Flavio Stragliotto
 Phone: (39) 0424 547888
 Fax: (39) 0424 848668
 Email: flavio.stragliotto@favini.com
 Direct Mktg., Sls. Central Europe: Christopher Braun
 Phone: (39) 0424 54771
 Fax: (39) 0424 547793
 Tech. Mgr.: Giuseppe Zurlo
 Phone: (39) 0424 54771
 Fax: (39) 0424 547793
 Sls. Dir., Italy: Marco Bertolo
 Phone: (39) 0424 54771
 Fax: (39) 0424 547793
 Export Sls Dir.: Andrea Favini
 Phone: (39) 0424 547738
 Fax: (39) 0424 547793
 Email: andrea.favini@favini.com
Total Employees of Company: 500
Total Employees at this Location: 230
Type of Operation: Paper mill
Mill Locations:
Favini Spa, Crusinallo Mill, Via IV Novembre 276, I-28882 Crusinallo di Omegna, (VB), Italy, Capacity: 20,000 mt/y, (Paper mill)
 Phone: (39) 0323 882300
 Fax: (39) 0323 882399
 Email: crusinallo@favini.com
Pulp Grades and Capacities:
 Total pulp capacity: 5,327 mt/y
 Recycled Pulping: 5,327 mt/y
Paper/Paperboard Grades and Capacities:
 Total paper and paperboard capacity: 60,000 mt/y
 Uncoated woodfree/freesheet: 60,000 mt/y
Paper and Paperboard Mill Data:
 Stock Preparation:
 Pulpers: 2
Paper Machines: 2
No. 1, fourdrinier, total capacity 10,000 mt/y, Trim width 1.48 m, Uncoated woodfree/freesheet
No. 3, fourdrinier, total capacity 50,000 mt/y, Trim width 2.48 m, Uncoated woodfree/freesheet

Finishing Equipment:
 Sheeters: 3
Energy Data:
 Power boilers: 1
 Combustion turbines: 1 at 1.0 MW
 Electrical demand for mill: 122 MWh/D

ⓜFavini Spa
Crusinallo Mill
Previously Favini Srl
Via IV Novembre 276
I-28882 Crusinallo di Omegna, (VB)
Italy
 Phone: (39) 0323 882300
 Fax: (39) 0323 882399
 Email: crusinallo@favini.com
 Web Address: www.favini.com
Personnel:
 Mill Mgr.: Ferdinando Galli
 Phone: (39) 0323 882300
 Fax: (39) 0323 882399
 Email: ferdinando.galli@favini.com
Total Employees at this Location: 270
Type of Operation: Paper mill
Paper/Paperboard Grades and Capacities:
 Total paper and paperboard capacity: 20,000 mt/y
 Uncoated woodfree/freesheet: 20,000 mt/y
Paper and Paperboard Mill Data:
Paper Machines: 1
 No. 1, fourdrinier, total capacity 20,000 mt/y, Trim width 2.2 m, Uncoated woodfree/freesheet
Finishing Equipment:
 Rewinders: 6
Energy Data:
 Power boilers
 Combustion turbines: 1 at 1 MW
 Hydro turbines: 2
 Electrical demand for mill: 44 MWh/D

ⓜFedrigoni S.P.A.
Ownership: Family-owned (Private)
Viale Piave 3
I-37135 Verona, (VR)
Italy
 Phone: (39) 045 808 7888
 Fax: (39) 045 200 9015 / 045 800 9015
 Email: info@fedrigoni.it,
 info@fedrigoni.com
 Web Address: www.fedrigonicartiere.com,
 www.fedrigoni.com
Personnel:
 Chmn.: Alessandro Fedrigoni
 Phone: (39) 045 808 7888
 Fax: (39) 045 800 9015
 Depty. Chmn.: Massimiliano Pancera
 Phone: (39) 045 808 7888
 Fax: (39) 045 800 9015
 CEO: Claudio Alfonsi
 Phone: (39) 045 808 7888
 Fax: (39) 045 800 9015
 Email: claudio.alfonsi@fedrigoni.com
 Mktg. Dir.: Chiara Medioli
 Phone: (39) 045 808 7888
 Fax: (39) 045 800 9015
 Email: chiara.medioli@fedrigoni.com
 Purch. Dir.: Vitaliano Vantini
 Phone: (39) 045 808 7888
 Fax: (39) 045 800 9015
 Email: vitaliano.vantini@fedrigoni.com
 Sls. Mgr.: Alfonsi Gabriele
 Phone: (39) 045 808 7888
 Fax: (39) 045 800 9015
 Email: alfonsi.gabriele@fedrigoni.com
 Sls. Mgr.: Antoci Sergio
 Phone: (39) 045 808 7888
 Fax: (39) 045 8011701
 Environ., Health & Safety Mgr.: Azzolini Paolo
 Phone: (39) 045 808 7888
 Fax: (39) 045 8011701
 HR Specialist: Paola Cordioli
 Phone: (39) 045 808 7888
 Fax: (39) 045 8011701
Total Employees of Company: 2,000
Total Employees at this Location: 100
Mill Locations:
 Fedrigoni S.P.A., Arco Mill, Via Linfano 16, I-38062 Arco, (TN), Italy, Capacity: 130,000 mt/y, (Paper mill)
 Phone: (39) 0464 516 456
 Fax: (39) 0464 519 111
 Email: info@fedrigoni.com
 Fedrigoni S.P.A., Fabriano Mill, Via XIII Luglio 91/A, I-60044 Fabriano, (AN), Italy, Capacity: 168,493 mt/y, (Paper mill)
 Phone: (39) 0732 7021
 Fax: (39) 0732 702333
 Email: direzione.fabriano@fabriano.com
 Fedrigoni S.P.A., Pioraco Mill, Via L. Eustacchi, 29, I-62025 Pioraco, (MC), Italy, Capacity: 55,000 mt/y, (Paper mill)
 Phone: (39) 0732 7021/611782
 Fax: (39) 0737 611727
 Email: direzione.fabriano@fabriano.com
 Fedrigoni S.P.A., Varone Mill, Via Nuova 2, I-38066 Riva del Garda, Frazione Varone, (TN), Italy, Capacity: 42,000 mt/y, (Paper mill)
 Phone: (39) 0464 521 444
 Fax: (39) 0464 520 645
 Email: info@fedrigoni.com
 Fedrigoni S.P.A., Verona Mill, Via Tombetta 5, I-37135 Verona, (VR), Italy, Capacity: 70,000 mt/y, (Paper mill)
 Phone: (39) 045 808 7753
 Fax: (39) 045 808 7800
 Email: info@fedrigoni.com

ⓜFedrigoni S.P.A.
Arco Mill
Via Linfano 16
I-38062 Arco, (TN)
Italy
 Phone: (39) 0464 516 456
 Fax: (39) 0464 519 111
 Email: info@fedrigoni.com
 Web Address: www.fedrigoni.com
Personnel:
 Mill Mgr.: Augusto Mascher
 Phone: (39) 0464 516 456
 Fax: (39) 0464 519 1111
 Email: augusto.mascher@fedrigoni.com
 Mgr.: Marco Canova
 Phone: (39) 0464 516 456
 Fax: (39) 0464 519 1111
 Email: marco.canova@fedrigoni.com
Total Employees at this Location: 180
Type of Operation: Paper mill
Pulp Grades and Capacities:
 Total pulp capacity: 3,646 mt/y
 Recycled Pulping: 3,646 mt/y
Paper/Paperboard Grades and Capacities:
 Total paper and paperboard capacity: 130,000 mt/y
 Coated woodfree/freesheet: 130,000 mt/y
Paper and Paperboard Mill Data:
 Stock Preparation:
 Pulpers: 2
 Refiners: 4
Paper Machines: 1
 No. 1, fourdrinier, total capacity 130,000 mt/y, Trim width 3.3 m, Coated woodfree/freesheet
Coating Machines: 1
 No. 1, total capacity 120,000 mt/y., on machine
Energy Data:
 Power boilers: 1
 Combustion turbines: 1 at 7 MW
 Hydro turbines
 Electrical demand for mill: 175 MWh/D

ⓜFedrigoni S.P.A.
Fabriano Mill
Via XIII Luglio 91/A
I-60044 Fabriano, (AN)
Italy
 Phone: (39) 0732 7021
 Fax: (39) 0732 702333
 Email: direzione.fabriano@fabriano.com
 Web Address: www.fedrigoni.com,
 www.fabriano.com
Personnel:
 Mill Mgr. (since 2013) & Tech. Dir. Arche Area Factories: Ivo Planeta
 Phone: (39) 0732 7021
 Fax: (39) 0732 702333
 Email: ivo.planeta@fabriano.com
Total Employees at this Location: 269
Type of Operation: Paper mill
Pulp Grades and Capacities:
 Total pulp capacity: 12,613 mt/y
 Recycled Pulping: 12,613 mt/y
Paper/Paperboard Grades and Capacities:
 Total paper and paperboard capacity: 168,493 mt/y
 Uncoated woodfree/freesheet: 150,000 mt/y
 Specialty and industrial: 18,493 mt/y
Paper and Paperboard Mill Data:
 Stock Preparation:
 Pulpers:
Paper Machines: 4
 No. 3, DuoFormer D, total capacity 150,000 mt/y, Trim width 4.4 m, Uncoated woodfree/freesheet
 No. 6, fourdrinier, total capacity 1,499 mt/y, Trim width 1.7 m, Specialty and industrial
 No. 7, cylinder, total capacity 2,499 mt/y, Trim width 1.7 m, Specialty and industrial
 No. 8, cylinder, total capacity 7,997 mt/y, Trim width 2.8 m, Specialty and industrial
Finishing Equipment:
 Sheeters: 2
Energy Data:
 Power boilers: 1
 Combustion turbines: 2 at 7.34, 7.34 MW
 Steam turbines: 1 at 14 MW
 Hydro turbines: 2
 Electrical demand for mill: 322 MWh/D

ⓜFedrigoni S.P.A.
Pioraco Mill
Via L. Eustacchi, 29
I-62025 Pioraco, (MC)
Italy
 Phone: (39) 0732 7021/611782
 Fax: (39) 0737 611727
 Email: direzione.fabriano@fabriano.com
 Web Address: www.fedrigoni.com
Personnel:
 Environ. & Quality & Safety Coord.: Dssa. Maria Falcone
 Phone: (39) 0732 702267
 Fax: (39) 0737 611727
 Email: maria.falcone@fabriano.com
Total Employees at this Location: 144
Type of Operation: Paper mill
Paper/Paperboard Grades and Capacities:
 Total paper and paperboard capacity: 55,000 mt/y
 Uncoated woodfree/freesheet: 55,000 mt/y
Paper and Paperboard Mill Data:
 Stock Preparation:
 Pulpers:
Paper Machines: 2
 No. 1, fourdrinier, total capacity 15,000 mt/y, Trim width 1.55 m, Uncoated woodfree/freesheet
 No. 2, fourdrinier, total capacity 40,000 mt/y, Trim width 2.2 m, Uncoated woodfree/freesheet
Finishing Equipment:
 Sheeters: 3
Energy Data:
 Power boilers: 2
 Steam turbines: 1 at 2.5 MW
 Hydro turbines: 3
 Electrical demand for mill: 97 MWh/D

ⓜFedrigoni S.P.A.
Varone Mill
Via Nuova 2

Italy

I-38066 Riva del Garda, Frazione Varone, (TN)
Italy
 Phone: (39) 0464 521 444
 Fax: (39) 0464 520 645
 Email: info@fedrigoni.com
 Web Address: www.fedrigoni.com
Personnel:
 Mill Mgr.: Bruno Giuliani
 Phone: (39) 0464 521 444
 Fax: (39) 0464 520 645
 Email: bruno.giuliani@fedrigoni.com
Total Employees at this Location: 171
Type of Operation: Paper mill
Pulp Grades and Capacities:
 Total pulp capacity: 4,447 mt/y
 Recycled Pulping: 4,447 mt/y
Paper/Paperboard Grades and Capacities:
 Total paper and paperboard capacity: 42,000 mt/y
 Uncoated woodfree/freesheet: 42,000 mt/y
Paper and Paperboard Mill Data:
 Stock Preparation:
 Pulpers: 2
 Refiners: 5
Paper Machines: 2
No. 1, fourdrinier, total capacity 32,000 mt/y, Trim width 1.6 m, Uncoated woodfree/freesheet
No. 2, fourdrinier, total capacity 10,000 mt/y, Trim width 2.3 m, Uncoated woodfree/freesheet
Energy Data:
Power boilers: 1
Steam turbines: 2 at 2.2, 1.2 MW
Hydro turbines
Electrical demand for mill: 87 MWh/D

Ⓜ Fedrigoni S.P.A.
Verona Mill
Via Tombetta 5
I-37135 Verona, (VR)
Italy
 Phone: (39) 045 808 7753
 Fax: (39) 045 808 7800
 Email: info@fedrigoni.com
 Web Address: www.fedrigoni.com
Personnel:
 Mill Mgr. (Since May 2013): Marzio Miori
 Phone: (39) 045 808 7753
 Fax: (39) 045 8087800
 Email: marzio.miori@fedrigoni.com
Total Employees at this Location: 263
Type of Operation: Paper mill
Pulp Grades and Capacities:
 Total pulp capacity: 3,019 mt/y
 Recycled Pulping: 3,019 mt/y
Paper/Paperboard Grades and Capacities:
 Total paper and paperboard capacity: 70,000 mt/y
 Uncoated woodfree/freesheet: 70,000 mt/y
Paper and Paperboard Mill Data:
 Stock Preparation:
 Pulpers: 4
 Refiners: 6
Paper Machines: 2
No. 1, fourdrinier, total capacity 38,000 mt/y, Trim width 2.3 m, Uncoated woodfree/freesheet
No. 3, fourdrinier, total capacity 32,000 mt/y, Trim width 2.3 m, Uncoated woodfree/freesheet
Energy Data:
Power boilers: 1
Combustion turbines: 1 at 7.5 MW
Steam turbines: 1 at 2.05 MW
Electrical demand for mill: 118 MWh/D

ⓄⓂ Industria Cartaria Fenili S.p.A.
Coselli Capannori Mill
Via Sottomonte-Coselli 2/4
I-55060 Coselli Capannori, (LU)
Italy
 Phone: (39) 0583 947736
 Fax: (39) 0583 403053
 Email: info@icfenili.com
 Web Address: www.industriacartaria.it
Personnel:
 Prod. Mgr.: Fernando Tuzi
 Phone: (39) 0583 947736
 Fax: (39) 0583 403053
 Email: f.tuzi@icfenili.it
 Prod. & Planning Mgr.: Mr. Mirko Bechelli
 Phone: (39) 0583 947736
 Fax: (39) 0583 403053
 Email: m.bechelli@icfenili.it
Total Employees of Company: 35
Total Employees at this Location: 35
Type of Operation: Paper mill
Pulp Grades and Capacities:
 Total pulp capacity: 5,714 mt/y
 Recycled Pulping: 5,714 mt/y
Paper/Paperboard Grades and Capacities:
 Total paper and paperboard capacity: 18,000 mt/y
 Tissue: 18,000 mt/y
Paper and Paperboard Mill Data:
Paper Machines: 1
No. 1, fourdrinier, total capacity 18,000 mt/y, Trim width 2.7 m, Tissue
Finishing Equipment:
Rewinders: 1
Energy Data:
Power boilers: 1
Electrical demand for mill: 53 MWh/D

ⓄⓂ Cartiera di Ferrara SpA
Ferrara Mill
Via Marconi 69
I-44100 Ferrara, (FE)
Italy
 Phone: (39) 0532 772323
 Fax: (39) 0532 56642
 Email: info@cartieradiferrara.com
 Web Address: www.cartieradiferrara.com
Personnel:
 Export Mgr.: Carlotta Piva
 Phone: (39) 0532 772323
 Fax: (39) 0532 56642
 Email: export@cartieradiferrara.com
Total Employees of Company: 63
Total Employees at this Location: 63
Type of Operation: Paperboard mill
Pulp Grades and Capacities:
 Total pulp capacity: 69,198 mt/y
 Recycled Pulping: 69,198 mt/y
Paper/Paperboard Grades and Capacities:
 Total paper and paperboard capacity: 70,000 mt/y
 Boxboard/cartonboard: 70,000 mt/y
Paper and Paperboard Mill Data:
 Stock Preparation:
 Pulpers: 1
Paper Machines: 1
No. 1, fourdrinier, total capacity 70,000 mt/y, Trim width 2.6 m, Boxboard/cartonboard
Finishing Equipment:
Rewinders: 2 at 50,000 mt/y, 70,000 mt/y
Energy Data:
Power boilers: 1
Combustion turbines: 2 at 2 MW
Electrical demand for mill: 84 MWh/D

Ⓜ Fibrocellulosa S.p.A
Bagni di Lucca Mill
Ownership: 100% by Sofidel Group
Via Fegana 38 - Loc. Fornoli
I-55026 Bagni di Lucca, (LU)
Italy
 Phone: (39) 0583 2681
 Fax: (39) 0583 809374
 Email: moena.biagioni@sofidel.it, fibrocellulosa@sofidel.it
 Web Address: www.sofidel.it
Personnel:
 Man. Dir.: Piero Buchignani
 Phone: (39) 0583 2681
 Fax: (39) 0583 809374
 Email: piero.buchignani@sofidel.it
Total Employees at this Location: 31
Type of Operation: Paper mill
Paper/Paperboard Grades and Capacities:
 Total paper and paperboard capacity: 18,000 mt/y
 Tissue: 18,000 mt/y
Paper and Paperboard Mill Data:
Paper Machines: 1
No. 1, fourdrinier, Yankee dryer, total capacity 18,000 mt/y, Trim width 2.75 m, Tissue
Finishing Equipment:
Rewinders: 1
Energy Data:
Power boilers: 1
Hydro turbines
Electrical demand for mill: 48 MWh/D

ⓄⓂ Cartiera Fornaci SpA
Fagnano Olona Mill
Via Fornaci 16
I-21054 Fagnano Olona, (VA)
Italy
 Phone: (39) 0331 617164/610549
 Fax: (39) 0331 611211
 Email: info@cartierafornaci.it
 Web Address: www.cartierafornaci.com
Personnel:
 Sls. Dir.: Ugo Cattaneo
 Phone: (39) 0331 617164/610549
 Purch. Mgr.: Massimo Cattaneo
 Phone: (39) 0331 617164/610549
Total Employees of Company: 50
Total Employees at this Location: 50
Type of Operation: Paperboard mill
Pulp Grades and Capacities:
 Total pulp capacity: 60,776 mt/y
 Recycled Pulping: 60,776 mt/y
Pulp Mill Data:
 Recycled Fiber Treatment Lines:
 Pulpers: 2 at 60,000
Paper/Paperboard Grades and Capacities:
 Total paper and paperboard capacity: 60,000 mt/y
 Boxboard/cartonboard: 60,000 mt/y
Paper and Paperboard Mill Data:
 Stock Preparation:
 Pulpers:
Paper Machines: 1
No. 1, cylinder, total capacity 60,000 mt/y, Trim width 1.93 m, Boxboard/cartonboard
Energy Data:
Power boilers: 1
Electrical demand for mill: 64 MWh/D

ⓄⓂ Cartiera Galliera srl
Galliera Veneta Mill
Via I Maggio 21
I-35015 Galliera Veneta, (PD)
Italy
 Phone: (39) 049 9413777
 Fax: (39) 049 9440020
 Email: info@cartieragalliera.it
 Web Address: www.cartieragalliera.it
Personnel:
 CEO: Alberto Marenghi
 Phone: (39) 049 9413777
 Fax: (39) 049 9440020
 Email: alberto.marenghi@cartieragalliera.it
 Sls. Dir.: Fabio Maiani
 Phone: (39) 049 9413777
 Fax: (39) 049 9440020
 Email: fabio.maiani@cartieragalliera.it
Total Employees of Company: 30
Total Employees at this Location: 30
Type of Operation: Paper mill
Pulp Grades and Capacities:
 Total pulp capacity: 18,493 mt/y
 Recycled Pulping: 18,493 mt/y
Pulp Mill Data:

Recycled Fiber Treatment Lines:
Recycled packaging pulping lines: 2
Paper/Paperboard Grades and Capacities:
Total paper and paperboard capacity: 27,000 mt/y
Packaging papers: 23,000 mt/y
Specialty and industrial: 2,000 mt/y
Linerboard: 2,000 mt/y
Paper and Paperboard Mill Data:
Paper Machines: 1
No. 1, fourdrinier, Yankee dryer, total capacity 30,000 mt/y, Trim width 2.5 m, Packaging papers, Linerboard, Specialty and industrial
Coating Machines: 1
No. 1
Energy Data:
Power boilers: 3
Electrical demand for mill: 42 MWh/D

⊕⊚Cartiere del Garda SpA
Riva del Garda Mill
Ownership: 100% by Lecta S.A.
Viale Rovereto 15
I-38066 Riva del Garda, (TN)
Italy
  Phone: (39) 0464 579 111
  Fax: (39) 0464 521706
  Email: info@gardacartiere.it
  Web Address: www.gardacartiere.it
Personnel:
  CEO of Cartiere Del Garda Spa : Paolo Mattei
  Phone: (39) 0464 579 111
  Fax: (39) 0464 521706
  Prd. Mgr.: Antonio Di Blas
  Phone: (39) 0464 579 580
  Fax: (39) 0464 579 595
  Email: antonio.diblas@lecta.com
  HR Mgr.: Fabio Tomaselli
  Phone: (39) 0464 579514
  Fax: (39) 0464 522046
  Email: fabio.tomaselli@lecta.com
  Ind. Gen. Mgr.: Giovanni Lo Presti
  Phone: (39) 0464 579508
  Fax: (39) 0464 579509
  Email: giovanni.lopresti@lecta.com.it
  Commer. Gen. Mgr.: Maurizio Molina
  Phone: (39) 0464 579 540
  Fax: (39) 0464 521706
  Email: maurizio.molina@lecta.com
  Asst. to Ind. Gen. Mgr.: Sonia Zampedri
  Phone: (39) 0464 579 456
  Fax: (39) 0464 579 509
  Email: sonia.zampedri@lecta.com
  Exp. Sales Mgr.: Alessandro Nardelli
  Phone: (39) 0464 555
  Fax: (39) 0464 521 706
  Email: alessandro.nardelli@lecta.com
Total Employees of Company: 505
Total Employees at this Location: 500
Type of Operation: Paper mill
Pulp Grades and Capacities:
  Total pulp capacity: 9,720 mt/y
  Recycled Pulping: 9,720 mt/y
Paper/Paperboard Grades and Capacities:
  Total paper and paperboard capacity: 345,000 mt/y
  Coated woodfree/freesheet: 345,000 mt/y
Paper and Paperboard Mill Data:
  Stock Preparation:
  Pulpers: 3
  Refiners: 8
Paper Machines: 2
  No. 2, fourdrinier, total capacity 155,000 mt/y, Trim width 3.2 m, Coated woodfree/freesheet
  No. 3, DuoFormer D, total capacity 190,000 mt/y, Trim width 3.6 m, Coated woodfree/freesheet
Coating Machines: 3
  No. 1, total capacity 180,000 mt/y., off machine
  No. 2, total capacity 165,000 mt/y., off machine
  No. 5
Finishing Equipment:
  Supercalenders: 3

Rewinders: 4
Sheeters: 6
Energy Data:
HRSG boiler: 1
Combustion turbines: 1 at 46.9 MW
Steam turbines: 1 at 12.3 MW
Electrical demand for mill: 556 MWh/D

⊕⊚Cartiera Giacosa SpA
Front Canavese Mill
Via Rivera 2
I-10070 Front Canavese, (TO)
Italy
  Phone: (39) 011 9250111
  Fax: (39) 011 9251681
  Email: info@cartieragiacosa.it
  Web Address: www.cartieragiacosa.it
Personnel:
  Pres.: Vittorio Roscio
  Phone: (39) 011 9250111
  Fax: (39) 011 9251681
  Gen. Mgr./Admin.: Rag. Sergio Grosso
  Phone: (39) 011 9250111
  Fax: (39) 011 9251681
  Prod. Mgr.: Graziano Giannotti
  Phone: (39) 011 9250111
  Fax: (39) 011 9251681
  Tech. Serv. Mgr.: Fabio Pia
  Phone: (39) 011 9250111
  Fax: (39) 011 9251681
  Email: ufficiotecnico@cartieragiacosa.it
Total Employees of Company: 90
Total Employees at this Location: 90
Type of Operation: Paper mill
Pulp Grades and Capacities:
  Total pulp capacity: 46,050 mt/y
  Recycled Pulping: 46,050 mt/y
Pulp Mill Data:
  Recycled Fiber Treatment Lines:
  Flotation deinking lines: 1
  Recycled packaging pulping lines: 1
Paper/Paperboard Grades and Capacities:
  Total paper and paperboard capacity: 45,000 mt/y
  Packaging papers: 15,000 mt/y
  Specialty and industrial: 5,000 mt/y
  Linerboard: 25,000 mt/y
Paper and Paperboard Mill Data:
Paper Machines: 2
  No. 1, fourdrinier, total capacity 20,000 mt/y, Trim width 2.1 m, Packaging papers, Specialty and industrial
  No. 2, fourdrinier, total capacity 25,000 mt/y, Trim width 3 m, Linerboard
Energy Data:
Power boilers
Electrical demand for mill: 69 MWh/D

⊕⊚Cartiera G.I.C. S.r.l.
Francavilla di Sicilia Mill
Ownership: 50% by A. Latorre, 50% by A. Puglisi
Contrada Santa Caterina
I-98034 Francavilla di Sicilia, (ME)
Italy
  Phone: (39) 0942 982 155
  Fax: (39) 0942 982 036
  Email: cartieragic@tiscali.it
Personnel:
  Pres.: Sig. Lanzafame
  Phone: (39) 0942 982 155
Type of Operation: Paper mill
Paper/Paperboard Grades and Capacities:
  Total paper and paperboard capacity: 3,000 mt/y
  Packaging papers: 3,000 mt/y
Paper and Paperboard Mill Data:
Paper Machines: 1
No. 1, fourdrinier, total capacity 3,000 mt/y, Packaging papers

⊕⊚Cartiera Giorgione SpA
Castelfranco Veneto Mill
Via Borgo Padova 112
I-31033 Castelfranco Veneto, (TV)
Italy
  Phone: (39) 0423 491 221/6
  Fax: (39) 0423 498 778
  Email: info@cartieragiorgione.it
  Web Address: www.cartieragiorgione.com
Personnel:
  Pres.: Franco Bordignon
  Phone: (39) 0423 491 221
  Fax: (39) 0423 498 778
  Email: f.bordignon@cartieragiorgione.it
  Mill Mgr.: Walter Vighesso
  Phone: (39) 0423 491 221
  Fax: (39) 0423 498 778
  Email: w.vighesso@cartieragiorgione.it
Total Employees of Company: 62
Total Employees at this Location: 62
Type of Operation: Paperboard mill
Pulp Grades and Capacities:
  Total pulp capacity: 97,980 mt/y
  Recycled Pulping: 97,980 mt/y
Pulp Mill Data:
  Recycled Fiber Treatment Lines:
  Pulpers: 2 at 106,000
Paper/Paperboard Grades and Capacities:
  Total paper and paperboard capacity: 100,000 mt/y
  Linerboard: 100,000 mt/y
Paper and Paperboard Mill Data:
  Stock Preparation:
  Pulpers: 2
  Refiners: 4
Paper Machines: 1
  No. 1, (FormerType model: DuoFormer Base), fourdrinier (2), total capacity 100,000 mt/y, Trim width 2.45 m, Linerboard
Energy Data:
Power boilers: 1
Combustion turbines: 1 at 7.5 MW
Electrical demand for mill: 120 MWh/D

⊕⊚Cartiera Giusta Srl
Pracando Mill
Via delle Cartiere 213
I-55019 Pracando-Villa Basilica, (LU)
Italy
  Phone: (39) 0572 43078/413
  Fax: (39) 0572 43530
  Email: cdm@cdm-group.com
Personnel:
  Mill Mgr.: Piero Pieri
  Phone: (39) 0572 43078
  Fax: (39) 0572 43530
  Email: p.pieri@cartieragiusta.it
  Sls. Mgr.: Antonio Pieri
  Phone: (39) 0572 43078
  Fax: (39) 0572 43530
  Email: a.pieri@cartieragiusta.it
  Mgr.: Edoardo Sari
  Phone: (39) 0572 43078
  Fax: (39) 0572 43530
  Email: e.sari@cartieragiusta.it
Total Employees of Company: 30
Total Employees at this Location: 30
Type of Operation: Paper mill
Paper/Paperboard Grades and Capacities:
  Total paper and paperboard capacity: 20,000 mt/y
  Tissue: 20,000 mt/y
Paper and Paperboard Mill Data:
Paper Machines: 1
No. 1, crescent former, Yankee dryer, total capacity 20,000 mt/y, Trim width 2.62 m, Tissue
Finishing Equipment:
  Rewinders: 1
Energy Data:
Power boilers
Electrical demand for mill: 54 MWh/D

Italy

ⓗⓜCartiera Grillo sas di Giuseppe e Domenico Grillo
Genova-Voltri Mill
Via Acquasanta 20
I-16158 Genova-Voltri, (GE)
Italy
  Phone: (39) 010 6136630/6631
  Fax: (39) 010 613 3809
  Email: info@cartieragrillo.it
  Web Address: www.cartieragrillo.com
Personnel:
  Pres.: Domenico Grillo
  Phone: (39) 010 6136630
  Fax: (39) 010 613 3809
  Email: domenicogrillo@cartieragrillo.it
  Prod. Mgr.: Alberto Grillo
  Phone: (39) 010 6136630
  Fax: (39) 010 613 3809
  Email: albertogrillo@cartieragrillo.it
  Sls. Mgr.: Enrico Grillo
  Phone: (39) 010 6136630
  Fax: (39) 010 613 3809
  Email: enricogrillo@cartieragrillo.it
Total Employees at this Location: 34
Type of Operation: Paper mill
Pulp Grades and Capacities:
  Total pulp capacity: 8,195 mt/y
  Recycled Pulping: 8,195 mt/y
Pulp Mill Data:
  Recycled Fiber Treatment Lines:
  Recycled packaging pulping lines: 2
Paper/Paperboard Grades and Capacities:
  Total paper and paperboard capacity: 20,000 mt/y
  Packaging papers: 20,000 mt/y
Paper and Paperboard Mill Data:
Paper Machines: 1
  No. 1, fourdrinier, Yankee dryer, total capacity 20,000 mt/y, Trim width 2.1 m, Packaging papers
Energy Data:
  Power boilers
  Electrical demand for mill: 32 MWh/D

ⓗⓜCartiera di Guarcino S.p.A.
Guarcino Mill
Via Madonna di Loreto, 2
I-03016 Guarcino, (FR)
Italy
  Phone: (39) 0775 4891
  Fax: (39) 0775 46609
  Email: info@cdgspa.com
  Web Address: www.cdgspa.com
Personnel:
  CEO (Gen. Man. Dir.): Mr. Massimo Giorgilli
  Phone: (39) 0775 4891
  Fax: (39) 0775 46609
  Email: m.giorgilli@cdgspa.com
  Manuf. & Technology Man. Dir.: Mr. Nazzareno Serafini
  Phone: (39) 0775 4891
  Fax: (39) 0775 46609
  Email: n.serafini@cdgspa.com
  Sls. Man. Dir.: Mr Christian Molteni
  Phone: (39) 0775 4891
  Fax: (39) 0775 46609
  Email: c.molteni@cdgspa.com
Total Employees of Company: 130
Total Employees at this Location: 130
Type of Operation: Paper mill
Paper/Paperboard Grades and Capacities:
  Total paper and paperboard capacity: 65,000 mt/y
  Specialty and industrial: 65,000 mt/y
Paper and Paperboard Mill Data:
  Stock Preparation:
  Pulpers: 2
  Refiners: 3
Paper Machines: 2
  No. 1, fourdrinier, Yankee dryer, total capacity 25,000 mt/y, Trim width 2.9 m, Specialty and industrial
  No. 2, fourdrinier, Yankee dryer, total capacity 40,000 mt/y, Trim width 2.9 m, Specialty and industrial

Finishing Equipment:
  Rewinders: 3
Energy Data:
  Power boilers: 3
  Combustion turbines: 1 at 2 MW
  Electrical demand for mill: 139 MWh/D

ⓗⓜICO-Industria Cartone Ondulato Srl
San Giovanni Teatino Mill
Via Amendola 150
I-66020 San Giovanni Teatino, (CH)
Italy
  Phone: (39) 085 444481
  Fax: (39) 199152171111
  Email: ico@ico.it
  Web Address: www.ico.it
Personnel:
  CEO & Mill Mgr.: Leonida Lancia
  Phone: (39) 085 444481
  Fax: (39) 199152171111
  Email: leonida.lancia@ico.it
  Oper. Mgr.: Manlio Cocchini
  Phone: (39) 085 444481
  Fax: (39) 199152171111
  Email: manlio.cocchini@ico.it
  Sls. Mgr.: Pasquale Arfé
  Phone: (39) 085 444481
  Fax: (39) 199152171111
  Email: pasquale.arfe@ico.it
  Prod. Dir.: Maurizio Gualdi
  Phone: (39) 085 444819/335 121 4148
  Fax: (39) 199152171111
  Email: maurizio.gualdi@ico.it
Total Employees at this Location: 180
Type of Operation: Paperboard mill
Pulp Grades and Capacities:
  Total pulp capacity: 65,379 mt/y
  Recycled Pulping: 65,379 mt/y
Pulp Mill Data:
  Recycled Fiber Treatment Lines:
  Pulpers: 1 at 72,000
  Recycled packaging pulping lines: 1 at 65,000
Paper/Paperboard Grades and Capacities:
  Total paper and paperboard capacity: 65,000 mt/y
  Linerboard: 25,000 mt/y
  Corrugating medium/fluting: 40,000 mt/y
Paper and Paperboard Mill Data:
Paper Machines: 1
  No. 1, fourdrinier (2), total capacity 65,000 mt/y, Trim width 2.4 m, Corrugating medium/fluting, Linerboard
Finishing Equipment:
  Winders: 1 at 100,000 mt/y
Energy Data:
  Power boilers: 1
  Combustion turbines: 1
  Electrical demand for mill: 92 MWh/D

ⓗICT Italy
Località Baccanella
I-55020 Diecimo, (LU)
Italy
  Phone: (39) 0583 888888
  Fax: (39) 0583 888990
  Email: ict@tronchetti.com
  Web Address: www.foxy.it
Personnel:
  Pres./CEO: Sauro Tronchetti
  Phone: (39) 0583 888888
  Fax: (39) 0583 888990
  Chmn.: Massimo Tronchetti
  Phone: (39) 0583 888888
  Fax: (39) 0583 888990
  Exec. Dir.: Rico Baccelli
  Phone: (39) 0583 888888
  Fax: (39) 0583 888990
  Gen. Mgr.: Walter Bordi
  Phone: (39) 0583 888888
  Fax: (39) 0583 888990
  Paper Mills Div. Dir. : Mauro Tempini

  Phone: (39) 0583 888888
  Fax: (39) 0583 888990
  Plant Mgr. Converting Diecimo Lucca: Sergio Bertoncello
  Phone: (39) 0583 888888
  Fax: (39) 0583 888990
  Plant Mgr., Converting Diecimo: Luca Ulivi
  Phone: (39) 0583 888888
  Fax: (39) 0583 888990
  HR Mgr. : Nadio Crudeli
  Phone: (39) 0583 888888
  Fax: (39) 0583 888990
  Senior Mktg. Prod. Mgr. : Simone Biagini
  Phone: (39) 0583 888888
  Fax: (39) 0583 888990
  Quality Mgr.: Fabio Timperi
  Phone: (39) 0583 888888
  Fax: (39) 0583 888990
  Tech. Mgr. : Marco Cortopassi
  Phone: (39) 0583 888888
  Fax: (39) 0583 888990
  Commun. Mgr.: Badera Vergassola
  Phone: (39) 0583 888888
  Fax: (39) 0583 888990
  Email: b.vergassola@ictit.eu
Total Employees at this Location: 80
Mill Locations:
  Cartiera Europaper SpA, Monzone-Fivizzano Mill, Via Pian di Molino, I-54013 Monzone-Fivizzano, (MS), Italy, Capacity: 27,000 mt/y, (Paper mill)
  Phone: (39) 0585 97910
  Fax: (39) 0585 97918
  Email: info@europaperspa.it
  ICT France SAS, Montargis Mill, 100, rue des Camélias, Parque Industriel "ARBORIA 2", F-45700 Pannes, Montargis, France, Capacity: 70,000 mt/y, (Paper mill)
  Phone: (33) 2 38 95 96 01
  Fax: (33) 2 38 95 96 02
  Email: reception@ictfr.eu
  ICT Ibérica, S.L.U, El Burgo de Ebro Mill, Carretera Castellon Km 216, Camino de la Cañada Real, Las Peñas, E-50730 El Burgo de Ebro, Spain, Capacity: 70,000 mt/y, (Paper mill)
  Phone: (34) 97 6104672
  Fax: (34) 97 6104673
  Email: info@ictes.eu
  ICT Italy, Piano della Rocca Mill, Piano della Rocca, I-55023 Borgo a Mozzano, (LU), Italy, Capacity: 57,000 mt/y, (Paper mill)
  Phone: (39) 0583 833161
  Fax: (39) 0583 833200
  Email: ict@ictit.eu
  ICT Italy, Piano di Coreglia Mill, Località al Fontanone, I-55028 Piano di Coreglia, (LU), Italy, Capacity: 90,000 mt/y, (Paper mill)
  Phone: (39) 0583 73901
  Fax: (39) 0583 739 045/032
  Email: ict@tronchetti.com
  ICT Poland Sp. z o.o., Kostrzyn Mill, Wloska 3, PL-66470 Kostrzyn, Poland, Capacity: 140,000 mt/y, (Paper mill)
  Phone: (48) 95 733 6800
  Fax: (48) 95 733 6801
  Email: recepcja@ictpoland.pl

ⓜICT Italy
Piano della Rocca Mill
Piano della Rocca
I-55023 Borgo a Mozzano, (LU)
Italy
  Phone: (39) 0583 833161
  Fax: (39) 0583 833200
  Email: ict@ictit.eu
  Web Address: www.foxy.it
Personnel:
  Man. Dir.: Michele Scipioni
  Phone: (39) 0583 833161
  Fax: (39) 0583 833200
  Email: m.scipioni@ictit.eu
Total Employees at this Location: 60
Type of Operation: Paper mill
Paper/Paperboard Grades and Capacities:

Total paper and paperboard capacity: 57,000 mt/y
Tissue: 57,000 mt/y
Paper and Paperboard Mill Data:
Paper Machines: 2
No. 1, twin-wire, Yankee dryer, total capacity 22,000 mt/y, Trim width 2.65 m, Tissue
No. 2, crescent former, Yankee dryer, total capacity 35,000 mt/y, Trim width 2.65 m, Tissue
Energy Data:
Power boilers: 1
Electrical demand for mill: 157 MWh/D

ⓜICT Italy
Piano di Coreglia Mill
Località al Fontanone
I-55028 Piano di Coreglia, (LU)
Italy
Phone: (39) 0583 73901
Fax: (39) 0583 739 045/032
Email: ict@tronchetti.com
Web Address: www.foxy.it
Personnel:
Mill Mgr.: Mr. Valter Vanni
Phone: (39) 0583 739 01
Fax: (39) 0583 739 032
Email: v.vanni@ictit.eu
Total Employees at this Location: 70
Type of Operation: Paper mill
Paper/Paperboard Grades and Capacities:
Total paper and paperboard capacity: 90,000 mt/y
Tissue: 90,000 mt/y
Paper and Paperboard Mill Data:
Paper Machines: 2
No. 3, crescent former, total capacity 30,000 mt/y, Trim width 2.7 m, Tissue
No. 4, crescent former, total capacity 60,000 mt/y, Trim width 5.4 m, Tissue
Finishing Equipment:
Rewinders: 2 at 2 mt/y
Energy Data:
Power boilers: 2
Electrical demand for mill: 230 MWh/D

ⓘⓜIdeal Cart SpA
Sermoneta Mill
Via del Murillo, Km. 3,500
I-04013 Sermoneta, (LT)
Italy
Phone: (39) 0773 318037
Fax: (39) 0773 319075
Email: info@idealcartspa.it
Personnel:
Mill. Mgr.: Rossano Caldaroni
Phone: (39) 0773 318037
Fax: (39) 0773 319075
Email: rossano.caldaroni@idealcartspa.it
Prod. Mgr.: Ing. Luca Loccia
Phone: (39) 0773 318037
Fax: (39) 0773 319075
Email: luca.loccia@idealcartspa.it
Total Employees of Company: 29
Total Employees at this Location: 29
Type of Operation: Paper mill
Paper/Paperboard Grades and Capacities:
Total paper and paperboard capacity: 19,000 mt/y
Tissue: 19,000 mt/y
Paper and Paperboard Mill Data:
Stock Preparation:
Pulpers: 1
Paper Machines: 1
No. 2, twin-wire, Yankee dryer, total capacity 19,000 mt/y, Trim width 2.75 m, Tissue
Finishing Equipment:
Rewinders: 2
Energy Data:
Power boilers: 1
Electrical demand for mill: 51 MWh/D

ⓘⓜCartiera Francesco Imperato e Figli SNC
Palermo Mill
Via Guadagna 51
I-90124 Palermo, (PA)
Italy
Phone: (39) 091 441260
Fax: (39) 091 444064
Email: cartimperato@tin.it
Web Address: www.cartimperato.it
Personnel:
Pres.: Giovanni Imperato
Phone: (39) 091 441260
Man. Dir.: Domenico Imperato
Phone: (39) 091 441260
Sls. Dir. Exports: Antonio Imperato
Phone: (39) 091 441260
Total Employees of Company: 20
Total Employees at this Location: 20
Type of Operation: Paper mill
Pulp Grades and Capacities:
Total pulp capacity: 2,444 mt/y
Recycled Pulping: 2,444 mt/y
Pulp Mill Data:
Recycled Fiber Treatment Lines:
Flotation deinking lines: 1
Pulpers: 1
Washing deinking lines: 1
Paper/Paperboard Grades and Capacities:
Total paper and paperboard capacity: 12,000 mt/y
Tissue: 12,000 mt/y
Paper and Paperboard Mill Data:
Paper Machines: 1
No. 1, fourdrinier, Yankee dryer, total capacity 12,000 mt/y, Trim width 2.6 m, Tissue
Finishing Equipment:
Winders: 1
Rewinders: 1
Sheeters: 2
Energy Data:
Power boilers: 1
Electrical demand for mill: 33 MWh/D

ⓘⓜIstituto Poligrafico e Zecca dello Stato
Foggia Mill
Viale Leone XIII 333
I-71100 Foggia, (FG)
Italy
Phone: (39) 0881 796 111
Fax: (39) 0881 777529
Email: informazioni@ipzs.it, stabilimentofg@ipzs.it
Web Address: www.ipzs.it
Personnel:
Tech. Mgr.: Luigi Savoia
Phone: (39) 0881 796 111
Chief Eng.: Guido Picucci
Phone: (39) 0881 796 111
Total Employees at this Location: 597
Type of Operation: Pulp mill, Paper mill
Pulp Grades and Capacities:
Total pulp capacity: 20,001 mt/y
Recycled Pulping: 20,001 mt/y
Pulp Mill Data:
Chemical Pulping Systems:
Continuous digesters: 2
Bleach Plant Systems: 2
No. 1, Sequence: H, Capacity 15,000 admt/y
Chemical Recovery Equipment:
Evaporator lines: 1
Recovery boilers: 1
Recycled Fiber Treatment Lines:
Flotation deinking lines: 1
Pulpers: 1
Pulp Dryers:
Air Float dryers 1
Paper/Paperboard Grades and Capacities:
Total paper and paperboard capacity: 33,500 mt/y
Uncoated mechanical/groundwood: 33,500 mt/y
Paper and Paperboard Mill Data:
Stock Preparation:
Pulpers: 4
Refiners: 5
Paper Machines: 1
No. 1, fourdrinier, total capacity 33,500 mt/y, Trim width 2.7 m, Uncoated mechanical/groundwood
Coating Machines: 1
No. 1, total capacity 44,000 mt/y.
Finishing Equipment:
Rewinders: 2
Sheeters: 2
Energy Data:
Power boilers: 2
Steam turbines: 1 at 26.0 MW
Electrical demand for mill: 81 MWh/D

ⓘⓜCartiera Italiana Srl.
Serravalle Sesia Mill
Via alla Cartiera 16
I-13037 Serravalle Sesia, (VC)
Italy
Phone: (39) 0163 450201
Fax: (39) 0163 450203
Email: cartieraitaliana@libero.it
Personnel:
Mill Mgr.: Adriano Pizzi
Phone: (39) 0163 450201
Fax: (39) 0163 450203
Sls. Mgr.: Mr. R. Sanzari
Phone: (39) 0163 450201
Fax: (39) 0163 450203
Email: cartieraitaliana.sanzari@libero.it
Total Employees at this Location: 25
Type of Operation: Pulp mill
Pulp Grades and Capacities:
Total pulp capacity: 25,699 mt/y
Pulp available for market: 25,000 mt/y
Mechanical Pulp: 25,699 mt/y
Pulp Mill Data:
Mechanical Pulping Systems:
Conventional grinders: 1
Pulp Dryers:
Flash dryers 1
Paper and Paperboard Mill Data:
Stock Preparation:
Pulpers: 2
Refiners: 4
Coating Machines: 1
No. 1, total capacity 25,000 mt/y., off machine
Finishing Equipment:
Rewinders: 2
Energy Data:
Power boilers
Combustion turbines: 10
Electrical demand for mill: 115 MWh/D

ⓘKimberly-Clark Srl
Ownership: Kimberly-Clark Ltd.
Via della Rocca 49
I-10123 Torino, (TO)
Italy
Phone: (39) 01188141, 800-379009, 800-804030
Fax: (39) 011 889120
Email: info@kimberly-clark.it, communications.europe@kcc.com
Web Address: www.kimberly-clark.com
Personnel:
CEO: Filippo Pinori
Phone: (39) 011 88141
Fax: (39) 011 889120
Man. Dir.: Domenico Lovallo
Phone: (39) 011 88141
Fax: (39) 011 889120
Customer Mktg. Dir.: Roberta Campio
Phone: (39) 011 88141
Fax: (39) 011 889120

Italy

Email: roberta.campio@kcc.com
Mktg. Dir.: Enrico Castellani
Phone: (39) 800-379009/804030
Fax: (39) 011 889120
Email: enrico.castellani@kcc.com
Prod. Mgr. (South of Europe): Marco Querzoli
Phone: (39) 011 88141
Fax: (39) 011 889120
HR Mgr.: Livia Birolo
Phone: (39) 01188141
Fax: (39) 011 889120
Mill Locations:
Kimberly-Clark Srl, Alanno Scalo Mill, Località S. Emidio, I-65020 Alanno Scalo, (PE), Italy, Capacity: 40,000 mt/y, (Paper mill)
Phone: (39) 085 854 0800
Fax: (39) 085 854 2849
Kimberly-Clark Srl, Romagnano Sesia Mill, Via S. Martino 16, I-28078 Romagnano Sesia, (NO), Italy, Capacity: 115,000 mt/y, (Paper mill)
Phone: (39) 0163 821200
Fax: (39) 0163 821202

ⓂKimberly-Clark Srl
Alanno Scalo Mill
Ownership: Kimberly-Clark Ltd.
Località S. Emidio
I-65020 Alanno Scalo, (PE)
Italy
Phone: (39) 085 854 0800
Fax: (39) 085 854 2849
Web Address: www.kimberly-clark.com
Total Employees at this Location: 211
Type of Operation: Paper mill
Paper/Paperboard Grades and Capacities:
Total paper and paperboard capacity: 40,000 mt/y
Tissue: 40,000 mt/y
Paper and Paperboard Mill Data:
Paper Machines: 1
No. 1, TAD, total capacity 40,000 mt/y, Trim width 3.54 m, Tissue
Energy Data:
Power boilers: 1
Electrical demand for mill: 214 MWh/D

ⓂKimberly-Clark Srl
Romagnano Sesia Mill
Ownership: Kimberly-Clark Ltd.
Via S. Martino 16
I-28078 Romagnano Sesia, (NO)
Italy
Phone: (39) 0163 821200
Fax: (39) 0163 821202
Web Address: www.kimberly-clark.com
Personnel:
Finance Mgr.: Philippe Manfredi
Phone: (39) 0163 821200
Fax: (39) 0163 821202
Total Employees at this Location: 310
Type of Operation: Paper mill
Paper/Paperboard Grades and Capacities:
Total paper and paperboard capacity: 115,000 mt/y
Tissue: 115,000 mt/y
Paper and Paperboard Mill Data:
Paper Machines: 2
No. 1, twin-wire, Yankee dryer, total capacity 45,000 mt/y, Trim width 5.2 m, Tissue
No. 2, TAD, total capacity 70,000 mt/y, Trim width 5.2 m, Tissue
Energy Data:
Power boilers: 1
Electrical demand for mill: 473 MWh/D

ⒽⓂLucart SpA
Porcari Mill
Company is previously Cartiera Lucchese SpA
Via Ciarpi 77
I-55016 Porcari, (LU)
Italy
Phone: (39) 0583 2140
Fax: (39) 0583 299 051
Web Address: www.lucartgroup.com
Personnel:
CEO: Rag. Massimo Pasquini
Phone: (39) 0583 2140
Fax: (39) 0583 2990 51
Email: massimo.pasquini@lucartgroup.com
Plan. & Contr. Dir.: Sandro Pasquini
Phone: (39) 0583 2140
Fax: (39) 0583 2990 51
Email: sandro.pasquini@lucartgroup.com
CTO (Chief Technology Officer): Franco Pasquini
Phone: (39) 0583 2140
Fax: (39) 0583 2990 51
Email: franco.pasquini@lucartgroup.com
Purch. Mgr.: Lorenzo Pasquini
Phone: (39) 0583 2140
Fax: (39) 0583 2990 51
Email: lorenzo.pasquini@lucartgroup.com
Sls. Mgr. B2B: Giorgio Bresciani
Phone: (39) 0583 2140
Fax: (39) 0583 2990 51
Email: giorgio.bresciani@lucartgroup.com
Purch. Mgr. (Raw Material): Luigi Trombetta
Phone: (39) 0583 2140
Fax: (39) 0583 2990 51
Email: luigi.trombetta@lucartgroup.com
Total Employees of Company: 1,400
Total Employees at this Location: 250
Type of Operation: Paper mill
Mill Locations:
Lucart SpA, Castelnuovo Mill, Via Enrico Fermi 13, I-55032 Castelnuovo di Garfagnana, (LU), Italy, Capacity: 45,000 mt/y, (Paper mill)
Phone: (39) 0583 6401
Fax: (39) 0583 658893
Lucart SpA, Diecimo Mill, Via Ludovica - Z.I., I-55020 Diecimo, (LU), Italy, Capacity: 98,000 mt/y, (Paper mill)
Phone: (39) 0583 83701
Fax: (39) 0583 838262
Email: info@lucartgroup.com
Lucart France SAS, Troyes Mill, Z.I. de Torvilliers R.N. 60, F-10440 La Rivière de Corps, France, Capacity: 32,000 mt/y, (Paper mill)
Phone: (33) 3 25 79 06 06
Fax: (33) 3 25 79 38 38
Email: info@lucart.fr
Novatissue SAS, Novatissue Mill, 10 rue Maurice Mougeot, F-88600 Laval-sur-Vologne, France, Capacity: 50,000 mt/y, (Pulp mill, Paper mill)
Phone: (33) 3 29 55 78 78
Fax: (33) 3 29 55 78 76
Email: (name.surname@novatissue.fr)
Pulp Grades and Capacities:
Total pulp capacity: 85,680 mt/y
Recycled Pulping: 85,680 mt/y
Pulp Mill Data:
Recycled Fiber Treatment Lines:
Flotation deinking lines: 1
Paper/Paperboard Grades and Capacities:
Total paper and paperboard capacity: 120,000 mt/y
Tissue: 35,000 mt/y
Packaging papers: 13,000 mt/y
Specialty and industrial: 72,000 mt/y
Paper and Paperboard Mill Data:
Stock Preparation:
Pulpers: 5
Refiners: 9
Paper Machines: 3
No. 2, fourdrinier, Yankee dryer, total capacity 32,000 mt/y, Trim width 4.2 m, Packaging papers, Specialty and industrial
No. 3, fourdrinier, Yankee dryer, total capacity 68,000 mt/y, Trim width 5.4 m, Packaging papers, Specialty and industrial, Tissue
No. 4, twin-wire, Yankee dryer, total capacity 20,000 mt/y, Trim width 2.7 m, Tissue
Finishing Equipment:
Rewinders: 4
Sheeters: 2
Energy Data:
Power boilers: 2
Combustion turbines: 2 at 10.4, 5.3 MW
Steam turbines: 1 at 1.8 MW
Electrical demand for mill: 377 MWh/D

ⓂLucart SpA
Castelnuovo Mill
Previously Airtissue srl
Via Enrico Fermi 13
I-55032 Castelnuovo di Garfagnana, (LU)
Italy
Phone: (39) 0583 6401
Fax: (39) 0583 658893
Web Address: www.lucartgroup.com
Personnel:
Qlty. Mgr. (Castelnuovo & Diecimo Mills): Lucilla Ribezzi
Phone: (39) 0583 6401
Fax: (39) 0583 658893
Email: lucilla.ribezzi@lucartgroup.com
Total Employees at this Location: 150
Type of Operation: Paper mill
Paper/Paperboard Grades and Capacities:
Total paper and paperboard capacity: 45,000 mt/y
Tissue: 45,000 mt/y
Paper and Paperboard Mill Data:
Stock Preparation:
Pulpers: 2
Paper Machines: 1
No. 4, twin-wire, Yankee dryer, total capacity 45,000 mt/y, Trim width 4.7 m, Tissue
Finishing Equipment:
Rewinders: 1 at 45,000 mt/y
Energy Data:
Power boilers: 1
Combustion turbines: 1 at 7.5 MW
Electrical demand for mill: 120 MWh/D

ⓂLucart SpA
Diecimo Mill
Mill is was Cartiera Lucchese SpA
Via Ludovica - Z.I.
I-55020 Diecimo, (LU)
Italy
Phone: (39) 0583 83701
Fax: (39) 0583 838262
Email: info@lucartgroup.com
Web Address: www.lucartgroup.com
Personnel:
Mill Mgr.: Marco Dallara
Phone: (39) 0583 83701
Fax: (39) 0583 838262
Email: marco.dallara@lucartgroup.com
Total Employees at this Location: 355
Type of Operation: Paper mill
Pulp Grades and Capacities:
Total pulp capacity: 59,756 mt/y
Recycled Pulping: 59,756 mt/y
Pulp Mill Data:
Bleach Plant Systems: 1
DIP
Recycled Fiber Treatment Lines:
Flotation deinking lines: 1
Paper/Paperboard Grades and Capacities:
Total paper and paperboard capacity: 98,000 mt/y
Tissue: 98,000 mt/y
Paper and Paperboard Mill Data:
Paper Machines: 3
No. 5, crescent former, Yankee dryer, total capacity 21,000 mt/y, Trim width 2.7 m, Tissue
No. 6, crescent former, Yankee dryer, total capacity 21,000 mt/y, Trim width 2.7 m, Tissue
No. 7, crescent former, Yankee dryer, total capacity 56,000 mt/y, Trim width 5.4 m, Tissue
Energy Data:

Italy

Power boilers: 1
Combustion turbines: 1 at 10.5 MW
Electrical demand for mill: 289 MWh/D

ⓘⓜM.C.LIRI S.R.L.
Isola del Liri Mill
Via Aldo Moro 87
03100 Frosinone, (FR)
Italy
  Phone: (39) 0776 808 848
  Fax: (39) 0776 806 703
  Email: m.c.liri@gmail.com
Personnel:
  Mill Mgr.: Luigi Pennacchia
  Phone: (39) 0776 808 848
Total Employees of Company: 27
Total Employees at this Location: 27
Type of Operation: Paper mill
Pulp Grades and Capacities:
  Total pulp capacity: 14,240 mt/y
  Recycled Pulping: 14,240 mt/y
Pulp Mill Data:
  Recycled Fiber Treatment Lines:
  Pulpers: 2 at 20,000
Paper/Paperboard Grades and Capacities:
  Total paper and paperboard capacity: 14,000 mt/y
  Boxboard/cartonboard: 14,000 mt/y
Paper and Paperboard Mill Data:
Paper Machines: 1
  No. 1, cylinder, total capacity 14,000 mt/y, Trim width 1.7 m, Boxboard/cartonboard
Energy Data:
Power boilers: 1
Electrical demand for mill: 13 MWh/D

ⓘⓜMagnani Srl
Pescia Mill
Località Calamari
I-51017 Pescia, (PT)
Italy
  Phone: (39) 0572 405486
  Fax: (39) 0572 405523
Personnel:
  CEO: Ing. Renzo Angelo Cardini
  Phone: (39) 0572 405486
  Fax: (39) 0572 405523
  Prod. Mgr.: Fabrizio Stiavelli
  Phone: (39) 0572 405486
  Fax: (39) 0572 405523
Total Employees at this Location: 27
Type of Operation: Paper mill
Pulp Grades and Capacities:
Paper/Paperboard Grades and Capacities:
  Total paper and paperboard capacity: 2,500 mt/y
  Uncoated woodfree/freesheet

ⓘCartiera Mantovana S.R.L.
Via Principe Amedeo di Savoia 17
I-46100 Mantova, (MN)
Italy
  Phone: (39) 0376 688216
  Fax: (39) 0376 686760
  Email: info@cartieramantovana.it
  Web Address: www.cartieramantovana.it
Personnel:
  Man. Dir.: Alberto Marenghi
  Phone: (39) 0376 688216
  Fax: (39) 0376 686760
  Email: alberto@cartieramantovana.it
Total Employees of Company: 30
Mill Locations:
Cartiera Carmenta, Carmignano di Brenta Mill, Via Provinciale 45, I-35010 Carmignano di Brenta, (PD), Italy, Capacity: 65,000 mt/y, (Paper mill)
  Phone: (39) 049 9430000
  Fax: (39) 049 5958821
  Email: info@cartieracarmenta.it
Cartiera Mantovana S.R.L., Maglio di Goito Mill, Piazza Franco Marenghi, 18, I-46044 Maglio di Goito, (MN),

Italy, Capacity: 20,000 mt/y, (Paper mill)
  Phone: (39) 0376 688216
  Fax: (39) 0376 686760
  Email: info@cartieramantovana.it

ⓜCartiera Mantovana S.R.L.
Maglio di Goito Mill
Piazza Franco Marenghi, 18
I-46044 Maglio di Goito, (MN)
Italy
  Phone: (39) 0376 688216
  Fax: (39) 0376 686760
  Email: info@cartieramantovana.it
  Web Address: www.cartieramantovana.it
Personnel:
  Man. Dir.: Alberto Marenghi
  Phone: (39) 0376 688216
  Fax: (39) 0376 686760
  Email: alberto@cartieramantovana.it
Total Employees at this Location: 30
Type of Operation: Paper mill
Pulp Grades and Capacities:
  Total pulp capacity: 20,386 mt/y
  Recycled Pulping: 20,386 mt/y
Paper/Paperboard Grades and Capacities:
  Total paper and paperboard capacity: 20,000 mt/y
  Packaging papers: 20,000 mt/y
Paper and Paperboard Mill Data:
Paper Machines: 1
  No. 1, fourdrinier, total capacity 20,000 mt/y, Trim width 2 m, Packaging papers
Energy Data:
Hydro turbines: 1
Electrical demand for mill: 30 MWh/D

ⓘCartiera Marchigiana Srl
Via Matteo Gianolio 31
I-27029 Vigevano, (PV)
Italy
  Phone: (39) 0381 79790
  Fax: (39) 0381 83121/247
  Email: marchigiana@isemgroup.it
  Web Address: www.cartieracama.it/ds_marchigiana.htm
Personnel:
  CEO & Mill Mgr.: Nedo Aristei
  Phone: (39) 0381 79790
  Fax: (39) 0381 83121
  Email: nedo.aristei@cartieracama.it
  Finan. Mgr.: Marzio Albani
  Phone: (39) 0381 79790
  Fax: (39) 0381 83121
  Email: marzio.albani@cartieracama.it
Total Employees of Company: 52
Total Employees at this Location: 2
Mill Locations:
Cartiera Marchigiana Srl, Montelupone Mill, Via Enrico Fermi 29-31, I-62010 Montelupone, (MC), Italy, Capacity: 20,000 mt/y, (Paperboard mill)
  Phone: (39) 0733 224006
  Fax: (39) 0733 224020
  Email: info@cartieramarchigiana.it

ⓘⓜCartiera Marchigiana Srl
Montelupone Mill
Via Enrico Fermi 29-31
I-62010 Montelupone, (MC)
Italy
  Phone: (39) 0733 224006
  Fax: (39) 0733 224020
  Email: info@cartieramarchigiana.it
  Web Address: www.cartieracama.it/ds_marchigiana.htm
Personnel:
  CEO & Mill Mgr.: Nedo Aristei
  Phone: (39) 0381 79790
  Fax: (39) 0381 83121
  Email: nedo.aristei@cartieracama.it
  Finan. Mgr.: Marzio Albani
  Phone: (39) 0381 79790

  Fax: (39) 0381 83121
  Email: marzio.albani@cartieracama.it
Total Employees of Company: 52
Total Employees at this Location: 50
Type of Operation: Paperboard mill
Pulp Grades and Capacities:
  Total pulp capacity: 20,280 mt/y
  Recycled Pulping: 20,280 mt/y
Paper/Paperboard Grades and Capacities:
  Total paper and paperboard capacity: 20,000 mt/y
  Boxboard/cartonboard: 20,000 mt/y
Paper and Paperboard Mill Data:
Paper Machines: 1
  No. 1, cylinder, total capacity 20,000 mt/y, Trim width 2.3 m, Boxboard/cartonboard
Energy Data:
Power boilers: 1
Electrical demand for mill: 18 MWh/D

ⓜMC Tissue SpA
Tassignano Mill
Ownership: Sant'Andrea Spa
Via del Casalino, 8
I-55012 Tassignano/Capannori, (LU)
Italy
  Phone: (39) 0583 93031
  Fax: (39) 0583 936724
  Email: info@mctissue.it
  Web Address: www.mctissue.it
Personnel:
  Mill Mgr.: Fabio Mariani
  Phone: (39) 0583 93031
  Fax: (39) 0583 936724
  Email: fabio.mariani@mctissue.it
  Administrator: Massimo Carrara
  Phone: (39) 0583 93031
  Fax: (39) 0583 936724
  Email: massimo.carrara@mctissue.it
  Prod. Mgr.: Alfredo Bonfanti
  Phone: (39) 0583 93031
  Fax: (39) 0583 936724
  Email: alfredo.bonfanti@mctissue.it
  Mgr.: Corrado Vannucci
  Phone: (39) 0583 93031
  Fax: (39) 0583 936724
  Email: corrado.vannucci@mctissue.it
Total Employees at this Location: 100
Type of Operation: Paper mill
Paper/Paperboard Grades and Capacities:
  Total paper and paperboard capacity: 55,000 mt/y
  Tissue: 55,000 mt/y
Paper and Paperboard Mill Data:
Paper Machines: 2
  No. 1, crescent former, Yankee dryer, total capacity 25,000 mt/y, Trim width 2.71 m, Tissue
  No. 3, crescent former, Yankee dryer, total capacity 30,000 mt/y, Trim width 2.85 m, Tissue
Energy Data:
Power boilers: 1
Electrical demand for mill: 137 MWh/D

ⓘⓜA. Merati - Cartiera di Laveno SpA
Laveno Mombello Mill
Via Silvio Pellico 5
I-21014 Laveno Mombello, (VA)
Italy
  Phone: (39) 0332 658011
  Fax: (39) 0332 667085
  Email: marco.merati@cartiera-merati.com, info@cartiera-merati.com
  Web Address: www.cartiera-merati.com
Personnel:
  Man. Dir.: Enrico Merati
  Phone: (39) 0332 658011-12
  Fax: (39) 0332 667085
  Email: info@cartiera-merati.com
  Man. Dir.: Franco Merati
  Phone: (39) 0332 658011-12
  Fax: (39) 0332 667085

Italy

Email: info@cartiera-merati.com
Man. Dir.: Marco Merati
Phone: (39) 0332 658011-12
Fax: (39) 0332 667085
Email: marco.merati@cartiera-merati.com
Man. Dir.: Marco Filauro
Phone: (39) 0332 658011-12
Fax: (39) 0332 667085
Email: marco.filauro@cartiera-merati.com
Accountant: Anna Maria Variani
Phone: (39) 0332 658018
Fax: (39) 0332 667085
Email: info@cartiera-merati.com
Total Employees at this Location: 80
Type of Operation: Paperboard mill
Pulp Grades and Capacities:
Total pulp capacity: 143,363 mt/y
Recycled Pulping: 143,363 mt/y
Pulp Mill Data:
Recycled Fiber Treatment Lines:
Pulpers: 1 at 125,350
Paper/Paperboard Grades and Capacities:
Total paper and paperboard capacity: 140,000 mt/y
Boxboard/cartonboard: 140,000 mt/y
Paper and Paperboard Mill Data:
Stock Preparation:
Pulpers: 2
Refiners: 1
Paper Machines: 1
No. 1, fourdrinier, total capacity 140,000 mt/y, Trim width 3.35 m, Boxboard/cartonboard
Energy Data:
Power boilers: 2
Steam turbines: 2 at 3 MW
Electrical demand for mill: 112 MWh/D

ⓗⓜCartiere Modesto Cardella SpA
San Pietro a Vico Mill
Via Acquacalda, Seconda Traversa N 20
I-55100 San Pietro a Vico, (LU)
Italy
Phone: (39) 0583 998701
Fax: (39) 0583 998704
Email: info@cartierecardella.it
Web Address: www.cartierecardella.it
Personnel:
Pres.: Mario Cardella
Phone: (39) 0583 998701
Fax: (39) 0583 998704
Email: m.cardella@cartierecardella.it
Mill Mgr.: Andrea Moretti
Phone: (39) 0583 998701
Fax: (39) 0583 998704
Email: a.moretti@cartierecardella.it
Finan. Mgr.: Andrea Bortoli
Phone: (39) 0583 998701
Fax: (39) 0583 998704
Email: a.bortoli@cartierecardella.it
Total Employees of Company: 95
Total Employees at this Location: 95
Type of Operation: Paper mill, Paperboard mill
Pulp Grades and Capacities:
Total pulp capacity: 161,141 mt/y
Recycled Pulping: 161,141 mt/y
Pulp Mill Data:
Recycled Fiber Treatment Lines:
Recycled packaging pulping lines: 1 at 160,000
Paper/Paperboard Grades and Capacities:
Total paper and paperboard capacity: 160,000 mt/y
Corrugating medium/fluting: 160,000 mt/y
Paper and Paperboard Mill Data:
Stock Preparation:
Pulpers: 2
Refiners: 5
Paper Machines: 2
No. 3, fourdrinier, total capacity 75,000 mt/y, Trim width 2.5 m, Corrugating medium/fluting
No. 4, GapFormer, total capacity 85,000 mt/y, Trim width 2.7 m, Corrugating medium/fluting

Energy Data:
Power boilers: 1
Combustion turbines: 1 at 7 MW
Steam turbines: 1 at 5.0 MW
Electrical demand for mill: 226 MWh/D

ⓗⓜCartiera di Momo SpA
Momo Mill
Via Valsesia 22
I-28015 Momo, (NO)
Italy
Phone: (39) 0321 990100
Fax: (39) 0321 990152/150
Email: info@cartieramomo.com
Web Address: www.cartieramomo.com
Personnel:
CEO: Ugo Dell' Aria Burani
Phone: (39) 0321 990109
Fax: (39) 0321 990152
Email: dellariaburani@cartieramomo.com
Prod. Mgr.: Piero Pitzalis
Phone: (39) 0321 990100
Fax: (39) 0321 990152
Email: pitzalis@cartieramomo.com
Qlty Mgr.: Antonio Bergamaschi
Phone: (39) 0321 990100
Fax: (39) 0321 990152
Email: bergamaschi@cartieramomo.com
Admin. Mgr.: Giuseppe Albertinazzi
Phone: (39) 0321 990100
Fax: (39) 0321 990152
Email: albertinazzi@cartieramomo.com
Total Employees of Company: 99
Total Employees at this Location: 99
Type of Operation: Paperboard mill
Pulp Grades and Capacities:
Total pulp capacity: 46,910 mt/y
Recycled Pulping: 46,910 mt/y
Pulp Mill Data:
Recycled Fiber Treatment Lines:
Pulpers: 1 at 52,000
Paper/Paperboard Grades and Capacities:
Total paper and paperboard capacity: 55,000 mt/y
Boxboard/cartonboard: 55,000 mt/y
Paper and Paperboard Mill Data:
Stock Preparation:
Pulpers: 1
Paper Machines: 1
No. 1, cylinder, total capacity 55,000 mt/y, Trim width 2.6 m, Boxboard/cartonboard
Coating Machines: 2
No. 1, on machine
No. 2-3
Finishing Equipment:
Sheeters
Energy Data:
Power boilers
Electrical demand for mill: 72 MWh/D

ⓗⓜMondialcarta SpA
Diecimo Mill
Ownership: 100% by Gruppo Puccetti Spa
Loc. Renaccio
I-55023 Diecimo, (LU)
Italy
Phone: (39) 0583 8207
Fax: (39) 0583 838205
Email: info@mondialcarta.com
Web Address: www.mondialcarta.com
Personnel:
Chmn.: Edo Puccetti
Phone: (39) 583 8207
Fax: (39) 583 838205
Email: edo.puccetti@mondialcarta.com
CEO: Giuliano Gaddini
Phone: (39) 0583 820803
Fax: (39) 0583 838205
Email: giuliano.gaddini@mondialcarta.com
Tech. & Prod. Mgr.: Mario Luvisi

Phone: (39) 0583 820801
Fax: (39) 0583 838205
Email: mario.luvisi@mondialcarta.com
Total Employees of Company: 55
Total Employees at this Location: 55
Type of Operation: Paper mill, Paperboard mill
Pulp Grades and Capacities:
Total pulp capacity: 115,463 mt/y
Recycled Pulping: 115,463 mt/y
Pulp Mill Data:
Recycled Fiber Treatment Lines:
Pulpers: 1 at 135,600 admt
Recycled packaging pulping lines: 1 at 135,600 admt/y
Paper/Paperboard Grades and Capacities:
Total paper and paperboard capacity: 115,000 mt/y
Linerboard: 115,000 mt/y
Paper and Paperboard Mill Data:
Stock Preparation:
Refiners: 3
Paper Machines: 1
No. 1, fourdrinier (2), total capacity 115,000 mt/y, Trim width 2.61 m, Linerboard
Finishing Equipment:
Winders: 1 at 115,000 mt/y
Rewinders: 1 at 120,000 mt/y
Sheeters: 2
Energy Data:
Power boilers: 1
Combustion turbines: 1 at 5.2 MW
Electrical demand for mill: 154 MWh/D

ⓗⓜMunksjö Italia S.p.A.
Turin Mill
Ownership: 100% by Munksjö Oyj
Via Stura 98
I-10075 Mathi Canavese, (TO)
Italy
Phone: (39) 011 9260111
Fax: (39) 011 9269617
Email: info@munksjo.com
Web Address: www.munksjo.com
Personnel:
Mill Mgr.: Tamara Quatrano
Phone: (39) 011 92 60 111
Fax: (39) 011 92 69 617
Email: tamara.quatrano@munksjo.com
Prod. Supervisor.: Davide D'Amore
Phone: (39) 011 9260376
Fax: (39) 011 9260162
Email: davide.damore@munksjo.com
Production Engineer: Paolo Guagliumi
Phone: (39) 011 92 60 347
Fax: (39) 011 92 60 162
Email: paolo.guagliumi@munksjo.com
Total Employees of Company: 1,100
Total Employees at this Location: 275
Type of Operation: Paper mill
Paper/Paperboard Grades and Capacities:
Total paper and paperboard capacity: 120,000 mt/y
Specialty and industrial: 120,000 mt/y
Paper and Paperboard Mill Data:
Stock Preparation:
Pulpers: 7
Refiners: 15
Paper Machines: 1
No. 8, fourdrinier, total capacity 120,000 mt/y, Trim width 4.65 m, Specialty and industrial
Coating Machines: 1
No. 1, on machine
Finishing Equipment:
Supercalenders: 2
Rewinders: 9
Energy Data:
Power boilers: 1
Combustion turbines: 1 at 12.5 MW
Steam turbines: 1 at 6 MW
Electrical demand for mill: 341 MWh/D

Italy

ⓘⓂCartiera di Nave SpA
Caino Mill
Via Nazionale 6
I-25070 Caino, (BS)
Italy
  Phone: (39) 030 6830561
  Fax: (39) 030 6830562
  Email: info@cartieradinave.com,
  amministrazione@cartieradinave.com
  Web Address: www.cartieradinave.com
Personnel:
  Pres.: Ugo Fenotti
  Phone: (39) 030 6830561
  Email: amministrazione@cartieradinave.com
Total Employees of Company: 45
Total Employees at this Location: 45
Type of Operation: Paperboard mill
Pulp Grades and Capacities:
  Total pulp capacity: 10,140 mt/y
  Recycled Pulping: 10,140 mt/y
Pulp Mill Data:
  Recycled Fiber Treatment Lines:
  Recycled packaging pulping lines: 1
Paper/Paperboard Grades and Capacities:
  Total paper and paperboard capacity: 10,000 mt/y
  Boxboard/cartonboard: 10,000 mt/y
Paper and Paperboard Mill Data:
Paper Machines: 1
No. 1, cylinder, total capacity 10,000 mt/y, Trim width 2.4 m, Boxboard/cartonboard
Energy Data:
  Power boilers: 1
  Electrical demand for mill: 9 MWh/D

ⓘⓂCartiera di Nebbiuno S.R.L.
Nebbiuno Mill
Ownership: 100% by Family-owned (Private)
Via Privata Cartiera
I-28010 Nebbiuno, (NO)
Italy
  Phone: (39) 0322 58103
  Fax: (39) 0322 589784
  Email: info@cartieranebbiuno.it,
  dino@cartieranebbiuno.it
  Web Address: www.cartieranebbiuno.it
Personnel:
  Pres. & Man. Dir. & Tech. Dir. & Mill Mgr.: Luigi Donati
  Phone: (39) 0322 58103
  Fax: (39) 0322 589784
  Sls. Dir.: Dino Donati
  Phone: (39) 0322 58103
  Fax: (39) 0322 589784
  Email: dino@cartieranebbiuno.it
  Sls. Mgr.: Paolo Buzio
  Phone: (39) 0322 58103, 329 4614060 (Mobile)
  Fax: (39) 0322 589784
  Email: paolo@cartieranebbiuno.it
  Finan. & HR Mgr.: Elena Simonotti
  Phone: (39) 0322 58103
  Fax: (39) 0322 589784
  Email: elena@cartieranebbiuno.it
  Account. & Purch. Mgr.: Laura Decesari
  Phone: (39) 0322 58103
  Fax: (39) 0322 589784
  Email: laura@cartieranebbiuno.it
Total Employees of Company: 30
Total Employees at this Location: 30
Type of Operation: Paper mill
Paper/Paperboard Grades and Capacities:
  Total paper and paperboard capacity: 2,200 mt/y
  Packaging papers: 2,200 mt/y
Paper and Paperboard Mill Data:
  Stock Preparation:
  Pulpers: 2
  Refiners: 4
Paper Machines: 1
No. 1, total capacity 2,200 mt/y, Trim width 1.75 m, Packaging papers
Finishing Equipment:
  Rewinders: 3 at 1,300 mt/y
Energy Data:
  Combustion turbines: 2 at 0.25 MW
  Electrical demand for mill: 7 MWh/D

ⓘⓂCartiera Nuova So.Car.Pi. S.r.l.
Piteglio Mill
Via Pesciatina 2, Frazine Lanciole
I-51020 Piteglio, (PT)
Italy
  Phone: (39) 0573 628000, 628065
  Fax: (39) 0573 628065
  Email: n.socarpi@dada.it
Personnel:
  Pres.: Antonio Bocci
  Phone: (39) 0573 628000
  Fax: (39) 0573 628065
  Mill Mgr.: Lara Bocci
  Phone: (39) 0573 628000
  Fax: (39) 0573 628065
Total Employees of Company: 21
Total Employees at this Location: 21
Type of Operation: Paper mill
Pulp Grades and Capacities:
  Total pulp capacity: 12,869 mt/y
  Recycled Pulping: 12,869 mt/y
Paper/Paperboard Grades and Capacities:
  Total paper and paperboard capacity: 15,000 mt/y
  Tissue: 15,000 mt/y
Paper and Paperboard Mill Data:
Paper Machines: 1
No. 1, inclined, Yankee dryer, total capacity 15,000 mt/y, Trim width 2.7 m, Tissue
Finishing Equipment:
  Rewinders: 1 at 12,000 mt/y
Energy Data:
  Power boilers: 1
  Electrical demand for mill: 43 MWh/D

ⓘⓂCartiera Olona Sas di Belvisi Dr. Davide & C.
Gorla Minore Mill
Via Galileo Galilei 6
I-21055 Gorla Minore, (VA)
Italy
  Phone: (39) 0331 601101
  Fax: (39) 0331 601173
  Email: colona@tin.it,
  info@cartiraolona.it
  Web Address: www.cartieraolona.it
Personnel:
  Chmn.: Davide Belvisi
  Phone: (39) 0331 601101
  Prod. Mgr.: Giorgio Tenti
  Phone: (39) 0331 601101
  Sls. Mgr.: Gianluigi Paglieri
  Phone: (39) 0331 601101
Total Employees of Company: 50
Total Employees at this Location: 50
Type of Operation: Paperboard mill
Pulp Grades and Capacities:
  Total pulp capacity: 30,726 mt/y
  Recycled Pulping: 30,726 mt/y
Paper/Paperboard Grades and Capacities:
  Total paper and paperboard capacity: 30,000 mt/y
  Boxboard/cartonboard: 30,000 mt/y
Paper and Paperboard Mill Data:
  Stock Preparation:
  Pulpers: 1
  Refiners: 2
Paper Machines: 1
No. 1, cylinder, total capacity 30,000 mt/y, Trim width 2.3 m, Boxboard/cartonboard
Finishing Equipment:
  Rewinders: 1
Energy Data:
  Power boilers: 1
  Electrical demand for mill: 36 MWh/D

ⓘOmniafibre srl
Ownership: Omniafiltra SpA
Via Matteotti 1
I-81011 Alife, (CE)
Italy
  Phone: (39) 0823 918234
  Fax: (39) 0823 918559, 787304
  Email: info@omniafibre.it
  Web Address: www.omniafibre.it
Personnel:
  Pres.: Vittorio Civitillo
  Phone: (39) 0823-918234
  Fax: (39) 0823-787304
  Email: vcivitillo@serihg.com
  Man. Dir. & Bus. Develop.: Dr. Gino Fronzoni
  Phone: (39) 0823 918234
  Fax: (39) 0823 787304
  Email: gfronzoni@omniafibre.it
  Administration: Dr. Domenico Di Monaco
  Phone: (39) 0823 918234
  Fax: (39) 0823 787304
  Email: administration@omniafibre.it
  Sls. Mgr.: Drs. Angela Ridolfi
  Phone: (39) 0823 918234
  Fax: (39) 0823 787304
  Email: sales@omniafibre.it
  Purch. Mgr.: Gianni Polverino
  Phone: (39) 0823 918234
  Fax: (39) 0823 787304
  Email: purchase@omniafibre.it
  R & D Mgr.: Antonio Di Muccio
  Phone: (39) 0823 918234
  Fax: (39) 0823 787304
  Email: rs@omniafibre.it
  Cust. Service Mgr.: Teresa Catalano
  Phone: (39) 0823 918234
  Fax: (39) 0823 787304
  Email: customerservice@omniafibre.it
Mill Locations:
  Omniafibre srl, Alife Mill, Via Matteotti 1, I-81011 Alife, (CE), Italy, Capacity: 30,000 mt/y, (Paper mill)
  Phone: (39) 0823 918234
  Fax: (39) 0823 918559
  Email: info@omniafibre.it

ⓂOmniafibre srl
Alife Mill
Via Matteotti 1
I-81011 Alife, (CE)
Italy
  Phone: (39) 0823 918234
  Fax: (39) 0823 918559
  Email: info@omniafibre.it
  Web Address: www.omniafibre.it
Personnel:
  Pres.: Vittorio Civitillo
  Phone: (39) 0823 918234
  Fax: (39) 0823 787304
  Email: vcivitillo@serihg.com
  Man. Dir. & Bus. Develop.: Gino Fronzoni
  Phone: (39) 0823 918234
  Fax: (39) 0823 787304
  Email: gfronzoni@omniafibre.it
  Admin. Mgr.: Domenico Di Monaco
  Phone: (39) 0823 918234
  Fax: (39) 0823 787304
  Email: administration@omniafibre.it
  Sls. Mgr.: Angela Ridolfi
  Phone: (39) 0823 918234
  Fax: (39) 0823 787304
  Email: sales@omniafibre.it
  Purch. Mgr.: Gianni Polverino
  Phone: (39) 0823 918234
  Fax: (39) 0823 787304
  Email: purchase@omniafibre.it
  R & D Mgr.: Antonio Di Muccio
  Phone: (39) 0823 918234
  Fax: (39) 0823 787304
  Email: rs@omniafibre.it
  Cust. Serv. Mgr.: Teresa Catalano

Italy

Phone: (39) 0823 918234
Fax: (39) 0823 787304
Email: customerservice@omniafibre.it
Type of Operation: Paper mill
Pulp Grades and Capacities:
 Total pulp capacity: 9,000 mt/y
Paper/Paperboard Grades and Capacities:
 Total paper and paperboard capacity: 30,000 mt/y
 Specialty and industrial
Paper and Paperboard Mill Data:
Paper Machines: 2
No. 1, cylinder mould, Trim width 1.23 m, Specialty and industrial
No. 2, cylinder mould, Trim width 2.3 m, Specialty and industrial

ⓄⓂCartiere Panigada S.R.L.
Piteglio Mill
Via Pesciatina 8, Frazione Lanciole
I-51020 Piteglio, (PT)
Italy
 Phone: (39) 0573 628146
 Fax: (39) 0573 628193
 Email: cartierepanigada@libero.it
Personnel:
 Gen. Mgr.: Stefano Panigada
 Phone: (39) 0573 628146
 Fax: (39) 0573 628193
 Email: info@cartierepanigada.com
Total Employees at this Location: 25
Type of Operation: Paper mill
Paper/Paperboard Grades and Capacities:
 Total paper and paperboard capacity: 10,000 mt/y
 Specialty and industrial: 10,000 mt/y
Paper and Paperboard Mill Data:
Paper Machines: 2
No. 1, cylinder, Trim width 1.7 m, Specialty and industrial
No. 2, cylinder, Trim width 3 m, Specialty and industrial

Ⓞpapergroup® SpA
Via Tazio Nuvolari, 23
I-55061 Carraia - Capannori, (LU)
Italy
 Phone: (39) 0583 98221
 Fax: (39) 0583 982292
 Email: info@papergroup.it
 Web Address: www.tenerella.it, www.papergroup.it
Personnel:
 Owner: Famiglia Vamberti
 Phone: (39) 0583 98221
 Fax: (39) 0583 982 292
 Chmn.: Antonio Vamberti
 Phone: (39) 0583 98221
 Fax: (39) 0583 982 292
 CEO & Man. Dir.: Daniele Vamberti
 Phone: (39) 0583 98221
 Fax: (39) 0583 982 292
 Export Area Sls. Mgr.: Ivan Mancini
 Phone: (39) 0583 98221
 Fax: (39) 0583 982 292
 Sls. Mgr.: Ivan Mancini
 Phone: (39) 0583 98221
 Fax: (39) 0583 982 292
 Email: ivan.mancini@papergroup.it
Total Employees of Company: 120
Total Employees at this Location: 70
Mill Locations:
papergroup® SpA, San Gennaro Mill, Localita San Gennaro, I-55010 Capannori, (LU), Italy, Capacity: 30,000 mt/y, (Paper mill)
 Phone: (39) 0583 4461
 Fax: (39) 0583 982298
 Email: info@papergroup.it

Ⓜpapergroup® SpA
San Gennaro Mill
Localita San Gennaro
I-55010 Capannori, (LU)
Italy
 Phone: (39) 0583 4461
 Fax: (39) 0583 982298
 Email: info@papergroup.it
 Web Address: www.papergroup.it
Personnel:
 Sls. Mgr.: Chiara Lazzari
 Phone: (39) 0583 4461
 Fax: (39) 0583 982298
 Email: chiara.lazzari@papergroup.it
Total Employees at this Location: 30
Type of Operation: Paper mill
Paper/Paperboard Grades and Capacities:
 Total paper and paperboard capacity: 30,000 mt/y
 Tissue: 30,000 mt/y
Paper and Paperboard Mill Data:
 Stock Preparation:
 Pulpers: 2
 Refiners: 5
Paper Machines: 1
No. 2, crescent former, Yankee dryer, total capacity 30,000 mt/y, Trim width 3.13 m, Tissue
Finishing Equipment:
 Rewinders: 2
 Sheeters: 2
Energy Data:
Power boilers: 1
Electrical demand for mill: 80 MWh/D

ⓄⓂPapiro Sarda S.R.L.
Assemini mill
Zona Industriale - 10a Strada Macchiareddu Grogastu
I-09032 Assemini, (CO)
Italy
 Phone: (39) 070 247248
 Fax: (39) 070 247169
 Email: papirosarda@tiscali.it
Personnel:
 Mgr./Admin.: Giulio Barsanti
 Phone: (39) 070 247248
Total Employees of Company: 11
Total Employees at this Location: 20
Type of Operation: Paper mill, Paperboard mill
Pulp Grades and Capacities:
 Total pulp capacity: 20,090 mt/y
 Recycled Pulping: 20,090 mt/y
Pulp Mill Data:
 Recycled Fiber Treatment Lines:
 Recycled packaging pulping lines at 20,000 admt/y
Paper/Paperboard Grades and Capacities:
 Total paper and paperboard capacity: 20,000 mt/y
 Corrugating medium/fluting: 20,000 mt/y
Paper and Paperboard Mill Data:
Paper Machines: 1
No. 1, fourdrinier, total capacity 20,000 mt/y, Trim width 2.61 m, Corrugating medium/fluting
Finishing Equipment:
 Rewinders: 1
Energy Data:
Power boilers: 1
Electrical demand for mill: 26 MWh/D

ⓄⓂPapiro Sud Srl
Scafati Mill
Company is closed, in liquidation (in liquidation from late 2012, closed in September 2013)
Via Madonnelle, 2
I-84018 Scafati, (SA)
Italy
 Phone: (39) 081 8638090
 Fax: (39) 081 8633896
 Email: info@papirosud.it
 Web Address: www.papirosud.it
Personnel:
 Owner: Renato Scarlato
 Phone: (39) 081 8638090
 Fax: (39) 081 8633896
 CEO: Corrado Scarlato
 Phone: (39) 081 8638090
 Fax: (39) 081 8633896
 Mill Mgr.: Ing. Cosmo Di Feo
 Phone: (39) 081 8638090
 Fax: (39) 081 8633896
Total Employees at this Location: 33
Type of Operation: Paper mill
Pulp Grades and Capacities:
 Total pulp capacity: 50,487 mt/y
 Recycled Pulping: 50,487 mt/y
Pulp Mill Data:
 Recycled Fiber Treatment Lines:
 Pulpers: 2
Paper/Paperboard Grades and Capacities:
 Total paper and paperboard capacity: 50,000 mt/y
 Corrugating medium/fluting: 50,000 mt/y
Paper and Paperboard Mill Data:
Paper Machines: 1
No. 1, fourdrinier, total capacity 50,000 mt/y, Trim width 2.6 m, Corrugating medium/fluting
Finishing Equipment:
 Rewinders: 1
Energy Data:
Power boilers: 2
Combustion turbines: 1 at 3.6 MW
Electrical demand for mill: 68 MWh/D

ⓄⓂCartiera Partenope S.r.l
Arzano Mill
Corso Salvatore D'Amato, 3
I-80022 Arzano, (NA)
Italy
 Phone: (39) 081 7312998
 Fax: (39) 081 7316927
 Email: info@cartierapartenope.it
 Web Address: www.cartierapartenope.it
Personnel:
 Associate & Gen. Mgr.: Umberto Serrao
 Phone: (39) 081 7312998
 Associate & Prod. Mgr.: Ciro Serrao
 Phone: (39) 081 7312998
 Associate & Sls. Mgr.: Giovanni Serrao
 Phone: (39) 081 7312998
 Maint. Mgr.: Luigi Palmini
 Phone: (39) 081 7312998
 R&D Mgr.: Francesco Giusti
 Phone: (39) 081 7312998
Total Employees of Company: 60
Total Employees at this Location: 60
Type of Operation: Paper mill
Pulp Grades and Capacities:
 Total pulp capacity: 53,174 mt/y
 Recycled Pulping: 53,174 mt/y
Pulp Mill Data:
 Chemical Recovery Equipment:
 Recovery boilers: 2
 Recycled Fiber Treatment Lines:
 Pulpers: 2 at 50,000 admt/y
 Recycled packaging pulping lines: 2 at 50,000 admt/y
Paper/Paperboard Grades and Capacities:
 Total paper and paperboard capacity: 50,000 mt/y
 Tissue: 25,000 mt/y
 Packaging papers: 25,000 mt/y
Paper and Paperboard Mill Data:
 Stock Preparation:
 Refiners: 2
Paper Machines: 2
No. 1, fourdrinier, Yankee dryer, total capacity 25,000 mt/y, Trim width 3.2 m, Packaging papers
No. 2, crescent former, Yankee dryer, total capacity 25,000 mt/y, Trim width 3.2 m, Tissue
Finishing Equipment:
 Rewinders: 2 at 100,000 mt/y
Energy Data:
Power boilers: 2
Electrical demand for mill: 127 MWh/D

ⓄⓂCartiera Pasquini Srl
Bagni di Lucca Mill
Ownership: 100% by Family-owned (Private)

Via Letizia 52
I-55021 Bagni di Lucca, (LU)
Italy
  Phone: (39) 0583 872 74
  Fax: (39) 0583 867 728
  Email: info@cartierapasquini.it
  Web Address: www.cartierapasquini.it
Personnel:
  CEO: Sig. Stefano Pasquini
  Phone: (39) 0583 872 74
  Fax: (39) 0583 867 728
  Email: stefano@cartierapasquini.it
  Foreign Sls. & Admin. Mgr.: Laura Gigliotti
  Phone: (39) 0583 872 74
  Fax: (39) 0583 867 728
  Email: laura@cartierapasquini.it
Total Employees of Company: 40
Total Employees at this Location: 40
Type of Operation: Paper mill
Pulp Grades and Capacities:
  Total pulp capacity: 37,174 mt/y
  Recycled Pulping: 37,174 mt/y
Pulp Mill Data:
  Recycled Fiber Treatment Lines:
  Recycled packaging pulping lines: 2
Paper/Paperboard Grades and Capacities:
  Total paper and paperboard capacity: 35,000 mt/y
  Tissue: 2,000 mt/y
  Packaging papers: 33,000 mt/y
Paper and Paperboard Mill Data:
Paper Machines: 1
No. 1, fourdrinier, Yankee dryer, total capacity 35,000 mt/y, Trim width 2.85 m, Packaging papers, Tissue
Energy Data:
Power boilers: 1
Electrical demand for mill: 91 MWh/D

ⓘCartiera Pieretti SpA
Via dei Masini 95/97
I-55014 Marlia-Capannori, (LU)
Italy
  Phone: (39) 0583 407575
  Fax: (39) 0583 407444
  Email: commerciale@cartierapieretti.it
  Web Address: www.cartierapieretti.it
Personnel:
  Man. Dir. : Leonardo Pieretti
  Phone: (39) 0583 407575
  Fax: (39) 0583 407444
  Admin.: Liliana Lenzini
  Phone: (39) 0583 407575
  Fax: (39) 0583 407444
  Sls. Dir.: Barbara Pesi
  Phone: (39) 0583 407575
  Fax: (39) 0583 407444
  Email: barbara.pesi@cartierapieretti.it
Total Employees of Company: 75
Mill Locations:
Cartiera Pieretti SpA, Marlia-Capannori Mill, Via dei Masini 95/97, I-55014 Marlia-Capannori, (LU), Italy, Capacity: 60,000 mt/y, (Paperboard mill)
  Phone: (39) 0583 407575
  Fax: (39) 0583 407444
  Email: commerciale@cartierapieretti.it

ⓘⓂIndustria Cartaria Pieretti SpA (ICP)
Marlia Mill
Ownership: 100% by Pieretti Family
Via del Fanuccio 128
I-55014 Marlia di Capannori, (LU)
Italy
  Phone: (39) 0583 30891
  Fax: (39) 0583 308930
  Email: icp@pieretti.it
  Web Address: www.pieretti.it
Personnel:
  Pres.: Graziano Pieretti
  Phone: (39) 0583 30891

Fax: (39) 0583 308930
  Email: graziano@pieretti.it
  VP, Paper Mill Dir.: Luisiano Pieretti
  Phone: (39) 0583 30891
  Fax: (39) 0583 308930
  Email: luisiano@pieretti.it
  Man. Dir.: Tiziano Pieretti
  Phone: (39) 0583 30891
  Fax: (39) 0583 308930
  Email: tiziano@pieretti.it
  Mill Mgr.: Lio Giannasi
  Phone: (39) 0583 30891
  Fax: (39) 0583 308930
  Email: lio.giannasi@pieretti.it
  Finan. Dir.: Carmen Pieretti
  Phone: (39) 0583 30891
  Fax: (39) 0583 308930
  Email: carmen@pieretti.it
  Export Mgr.: Sonia Bernicchi
  Phone: (39) 0583 30891
  Fax: (39) 0583 308930
  Email: sonia.bernicchi@pieretti.it
Total Employees of Company: 97
Total Employees at this Location: 97
Type of Operation: Paper mill
Pulp Grades and Capacities:
  Total pulp capacity: 142,644 mt/y
  Recycled Pulping: 142,644 mt/y
Pulp Mill Data:
  Recycled Fiber Treatment Lines:
  Pulpers: 3 at 154,000 admt/y
Paper/Paperboard Grades and Capacities:
  Total paper and paperboard capacity: 140,000 mt/y
  Linerboard: 35,000 mt/y
  Corrugating medium/fluting: 20,000 mt/y
  Boxboard/cartonboard: 85,000 mt/y
Paper and Paperboard Mill Data:
  Stock Preparation:
  Pulpers: 4
  Refiners: 15
Paper Machines: 2
No. 1, cylinder, total capacity 30,000 mt/y, Trim width 1.6 m, Boxboard/cartonboard
No. 2, fourdrinier, total capacity 110,000 mt/y, Trim width 2.6 m, Corrugating medium/fluting, Linerboard, Boxboard/cartonboard
Finishing Equipment:
  Winders: 3 at 150,000 mt/y
Energy Data:
Power boilers: 3
Combustion turbines: 1 at 7.5 MW
Electrical demand for mill: 161 MWh/D

ⓂCartiera Pieretti SpA
Marlia-Capannori Mill
Via dei Masini 95/97
I-55014 Marlia-Capannori, (LU)
Italy
  Phone: (39) 0583 407575
  Fax: (39) 0583 407444
  Email: commerciale@cartierapieretti.it
  Web Address: www.cartierapieretti.it
Personnel:
  Admin.: Liliana Lenzini
  Phone: (39) 0583 407575
  Sls. Dir.: Barbara Pesi
  Phone: (39) 0583 407575
  Email: barbara.pesi@cartierapieretti.it
Total Employees at this Location: 75
Type of Operation: Paperboard mill
Pulp Grades and Capacities:
  Total pulp capacity: 60,880 mt/y
  Recycled Pulping: 60,880 mt/y
Pulp Mill Data:
  Recycled Fiber Treatment Lines:
  Recycled packaging pulping lines: 1
Paper/Paperboard Grades and Capacities:
  Total paper and paperboard capacity: 60,000 mt/y
  Linerboard: 55,000 mt/y

Boxboard/cartonboard: 5,000 mt/y
Paper and Paperboard Mill Data:
  Stock Preparation:
  Pulpers: 2
Paper Machines: 1
No. 1, cylinder, total capacity 60,000 mt/y, Trim width 2.65 m, Boxboard/cartonboard, Linerboard
Energy Data:
Power boilers: 1
Combustion turbines: 1
Electrical demand for mill: 78 MWh/D

ⓘⓂCartiere del Polesine Spa
Loreo Mill
Viale Stazione 1
I-45017 Loreo, (RO)
Italy
  Phone: (39) 0426 334533
  Fax: (39) 0426 334313
  Email: info@cartieredelpolesine.it
  Web Address: www.cartieredelpolesine.it
Personnel:
  Raw Material Buyer: Enrico Scantamburlo
  Phone: (39) 0426 334533
  Fax: (39) 0426 334313
  Email: enrico.scantamburlo@cartieredelpolesine.it
Total Employees of Company: 156
Total Employees at this Location: 55
Type of Operation: Paper mill, Paperboard mill
Mill Locations:
Cartiere del Polesine Spa, Adria Mill, Loc. Cavanella Po - Zona A.I.A., I-45010 Adria, (RO), Italy, Capacity: 205,000 mt/y, (Paperboard mill)
  Phone: (39) 0426 949508/334533
  Fax: (39) 0426 944085
  Email: info@cartieredelpolesine.it
Pulp Grades and Capacities:
  Total pulp capacity: 75,380 mt/y
  Recycled Pulping: 75,380 mt/y
Pulp Mill Data:
  Recycled Fiber Treatment Lines:
  Pulpers: 1 at 82,000
Paper/Paperboard Grades and Capacities:
  Total paper and paperboard capacity: 75,000 mt/y
  Corrugating medium/fluting: 75,000 mt/y
Paper and Paperboard Mill Data:
Paper Machines: 2
No. 1, fourdrinier, total capacity 30,000 mt/y, Trim width 2.2 m, Corrugating medium/fluting
No. 2, fourdrinier, total capacity 45,000 mt/y, Trim width 2.4 m, Corrugating medium/fluting
Energy Data:
Power boilers: 2
Combustion turbines: 1
Electrical demand for mill: 108 MWh/D

ⓂCartiere del Polesine Spa
Adria Mill
Loc. Cavanella Po - Zona A.I.A.
I-45010 Adria, (RO)
Italy
  Phone: (39) 0426 949508/334533
  Fax: (39) 0426 944085
  Email: info@cartieredelpolesine.it
  Web Address: www.cartieredelpolesine.it
Total Employees at this Location: 100
Type of Operation: Paperboard mill
Pulp Grades and Capacities:
  Total pulp capacity: 204,505 mt/y
  Recycled Pulping: 204,505 mt/y
Pulp Mill Data:
  Recycled Fiber Treatment Lines:
  Recycled packaging pulping lines at 200,000
Paper/Paperboard Grades and Capacities:
  Total paper and paperboard capacity: 205,000 mt/y
  Linerboard: 115,000 mt/y
  Corrugating medium/fluting: 90,000 mt/y
Paper and Paperboard Mill Data:
Paper Machines: 2

Italy

No. 3, fourdrinier, total capacity 80,000 mt/y, Trim width 2.8 m, Linerboard, Corrugating medium/fluting
No. 4, OVER Former, total capacity 125,000 mt/y, Trim width 2.8 m, Linerboard, Corrugating medium/fluting
Energy Data:
Power boilers: 1
Combustion turbines: 1
Steam turbines: 1
Electrical demand for mill: 263 MWh/D

ⓗⓜCartiera Ponte A Villa s.r.l.
Villa Basilica Mill
Via Delle Cartiere 8
I-55019 Villa Basilica, (LU)
Italy
 Phone: (39) 0572 43575
 Fax: (39) 0572 43529
 Email: cartpvilla@bcc.tin.it
Personnel:
 CEO: Mariantonietta Berardi
 Phone: (39) 0572 43575
Total Employees at this Location: 20
Type of Operation: Paper mill
Pulp Grades and Capacities:
 Total pulp capacity: 9,631 mt/y
 Recycled Pulping: 9,631 mt/y
Pulp Mill Data:
 Recycled Fiber Treatment Lines:
 Pulpers: 1
Paper/Paperboard Grades and Capacities:
 Total paper and paperboard capacity: 9,000 mt/y
 Tissue: 9,000 mt/y
Paper and Paperboard Mill Data:
Paper Machines: 1
No. 1, fourdrinier, Yankee dryer, total capacity 9,000 mt/y, Trim width 2.6 m, Tissue
Energy Data:
Power boilers: 1
Electrical demand for mill: 27 MWh/D

ⓗⓜCartiera Ponte d'Oro Ansalcarta Srl
Pracando Mill
Via delle Cartiere 271
I-55010 Pracando Villa Basilica, (LU)
Italy
 Phone: (39) 0572 43034
 Fax: (39) 0572 43518
 Email: cpdans@tin.it
Personnel:
 Mill Mgr.: Armando Ansaldi
 Phone: (39) 0572 43034
Total Employees of Company: 22
Total Employees at this Location: 22
Type of Operation: Paper mill
Paper/Paperboard Grades and Capacities:
 Total paper and paperboard capacity: 12,000 mt/y
 Tissue: 10,500 mt/y
 Specialty and industrial: 1,500 mt/y
Paper and Paperboard Mill Data:
Paper Machines: 2
No. 1, fourdrinier, Yankee dryer, total capacity 10,500 mt/y, Trim width 2.76 m, Tissue
No. 2, fourdrinier, Yankee dryer, total capacity 1,500 mt/y, Trim width 1.5 m, Specialty and industrial
Energy Data:
Power boilers: 1
Electrical demand for mill: 32 MWh/D

ⓗⓜCartiera di Ponzano Srl
Ponzano Veneto Mill
Via Colombera 25
I-31050 Ponzano Veneto, (TV)
Italy
 Phone: (39) 0422 969076
 Fax: (39) 0422 969181
 Email: info@cartieradiponzano.com
Personnel:
 Mill Mgr.: Gaetano Biffanti
 Phone: (39) 0422 969076
 Sls. Mgr.: Matteo Biffanti
 Phone: (39) 0422 969076
Total Employees of Company: 10
Total Employees at this Location: 10
Type of Operation: Paper mill
Pulp Grades and Capacities:
 Total pulp capacity: 4,272 mt/y
 Recycled Pulping: 4,272 mt/y
Paper/Paperboard Grades and Capacities:
 Total paper and paperboard capacity: 5,000 mt/y
 Tissue: 5,000 mt/y
Paper and Paperboard Mill Data:
Paper Machines: 1
No. 1, twin-wire, Yankee dryer, total capacity 5,000 mt/y, Trim width 1.85 m, Tissue
Energy Data:
Power boilers: 2
Combustion turbines: 1
Electrical demand for mill: 14 MWh/D

ⓗⓜCartiera di Porporano Srl
Porporano Mill
Via Mario Pemis 23/A
I-43123 Porporano, (PR)
Italy
 Phone: (39) 0521 641146
 Fax: (39) 0521 641146
 Email: cartieraporporano@libero.it
Personnel:
 Mill Mgr.: Paolo Villani
 Phone: (39) 0521 641146
 Mill Mgr.: Pietro Villani
 Phone: (39) 0521 641146
Total Employees of Company: 13
Total Employees at this Location: 13
Type of Operation: Paperboard mill
Pulp Grades and Capacities:
 Total pulp capacity: 14,000 mt/y
 Recycled Pulping: 14,000 mt/y
Paper/Paperboard Grades and Capacities:
 Total paper and paperboard capacity: 15,000 mt/y
 Linerboard: 10,000 mt/y
 Corrugating medium/fluting: 5,000 mt/y
Paper and Paperboard Mill Data:
Paper Machines: 1
No. 1, total capacity 15,000 mt/y, Trim width 2.51 m, Linerboard, Corrugating medium/fluting
Finishing Equipment:
 Rewinders: 1 at 14,000 mt/y
Energy Data:
Power boilers: 1
Electrical demand for mill: 15 MWh/D

ⓗⓜPortonogaro S.a.s. di Raffin Mario & C.
Casarsa della Delizia Mill
Ownership: 100% by Biofibre SRL.
Via Romana 1
I-33072 Casarsa della Delizia, (PN)
Italy
 Phone: (39) 0434 870688
 Fax: (39) 0434 979895
 Email: info@biofibre.it
 Web Address: www.biofibre.it
Personnel:
 Owner, Man. Dir.: Claudia Raffin
 Phone: (39) 0434 870688
 Fax: (39) 0434 979895
 Email: claudia.raffin@portonogaro.it
Total Employees of Company: 40
Total Employees at this Location: 40
Type of Operation: Pulp mill
Pulp Grades and Capacities:
 Total pulp capacity: 35,000 mt/y
 Pulp available for market: 35,000 mt/y
 Mechanical Pulp: 35,000 mt/y
Pulp Mill Data:
Pulp Lines: 1
 Pulp Dryers:
 Flash dryers 1
Energy Data:
Power boilers

ⓗPro-Gest S.p.A.
Via Castellna, 90
I-31036 Ospedaletto d'Istrana, (TV)
Italy
 Phone: (39) 0422 832336
 Fax: (39) 0422 832288/730739
 Email: info@pro-gestspa.it
 Web Address: www.pro-gestspa.it
Personnel:
 CEO & Pres.: Bruno Zago
 Phone: (39) 0422 832336
 Fax: (39) 0422 832288/730739
 Email: bruno.zago@pro-gestspa.it
 Man. Dir.: Benedetta Zago
 Phone: (39) 0422 832336
 Fax: (39) 0422 832288/730739
 Email: benedetta.zago@pro-gestspa.it
Total Employees at this Location: 44
Mill Locations:
Cartiera di Cagliari Srl, Assemini (Sardinia) Mill, 5a Strada Traversa Localita Macchiareddu Grogastu, I-09032 Assemini, (CA), Italy, Capacity: 22,000 mt/y, (Paper mill)
 Phone: (39) 070 247632
 Fax: (39) 070 247632
Cartiera di Carbonera SpA, Camposampiero Mill, Via Borgo Padova, 67, I-35012 Camposampiero, (PD), Italy, Capacity: 115,000 mt/y, (Paper mill, Paperboard mill)
 Phone: (39) 049 5790744
 Fax: (39) 049 5793492
 Email: cartieradicarbonera@pro-gestspa.it
Cartitalia S.r.l., Cartitalia Mill, Via Motte 50, I-44026 Mesola, (FE), Italy, Capacity: 125,000 mt/y, (Paper mill, Paperboard mill)
 Phone: (39) 0533 993 571
 Fax: (39) 0533 993 566
 Email: cartitalia@pro-gestspa.it
Tolentino S.r.l., Tolentino Mill, Via Borgo Cartiere 20, I-62029 Tolentino, (MC), Italy, Capacity: 150,000 mt/y, (Paper mill, Paperboard mill)
 Phone: (39) 0733 956601
 Fax: (39) 0733 966401
 Email: tolentino@pro-gestspa.it
Cartiere Villa Lagarina Spa, Trento Mill, Via Pesenti 1, I-38060 Trento, (TN), Italy, Capacity: 285,700 mt/y, (Paper mill, Paperboard mill)
 Phone: (39) 0464 411511
 Fax: (39) 0464 410400
 Email: cvl@pro-gestspa.it

ⓗCartiera Puglisi SRL
Contrada S. Caterina
I-98034 Francavilla di Sicilia, (ME)
Italy
 Phone: (39) 0942 982061
 Fax: (39) 0942 982032
 Email: cartierapuglisi@cartierapuglisi.191.it
Personnel:
 Owner: Giuseppe Puglisi
 Phone: (39) 0942 982061
 Fax: (39) 0942 982032
 Pres.: Carmela Raffa
 Phone: (39) 0942 982061
 Fax: (39) 0942 982032
Total Employees of Company: 25
Mill Locations:
Cartiera Puglisi SRL, Castiglione di Sicilia Mill, Contrada-Macca 2, I-95012 Castiglione di Sicilia, (CT), Italy, Capacity: 18,000 mt/y, (Paper mill)
 Phone: (39) 0942 981 129
 Fax: (39) 0942 982032
 Email: cartierapuglisi@cartierapuglisi.191.it

Italy

ⓂCartiera Puglisi SRL
Castiglione di Sicilia Mill
Contrada-Macca 2
I-95012 Castiglione di Sicilia, (CT)
Italy
 Phone: (39) 0942 981 129
 Fax: (39) 0942 982032
 Email: cartierapuglisi@cartierapuglisi.191.it
Personnel:
 Owner: Giuseppe Puglisi
 Phone: (39) 0942 981 129
Total Employees at this Location: 25
Type of Operation: Paper mill
Pulp Grades and Capacities:
 Total pulp capacity: 17,928 mt/y
 Recycled Pulping: 17,928 mt/y
Pulp Mill Data:
 Recycled Fiber Treatment Lines:
 Recycled packaging pulping lines: 1
Paper/Paperboard Grades and Capacities:
 Total paper and paperboard capacity: 18,000 mt/y
 Packaging papers: 18,000 mt/y
Paper and Paperboard Mill Data:
Paper Machines: 1
 No. 1, fourdrinier, Yankee dryer, total capacity 18,000 mt/y, Trim width 2.7 m, Packaging papers
Energy Data:
 Power boilers: 1
 Electrical demand for mill: 33 MWh/D

ⓄⓂRaipaper S.r.l.
Isola del Liri Mill
Via Napoli 187
I-03036 Isola del Liri, (FR)
Italy
 Phone: (39) 0776 808972 / 809859
 Fax: (39) 0776 807440
 Email: info@alcart.eu, alcartsas@libero.it
 Web Address: www.alcart.eu
Personnel:
 Pres.: Maurizio Gaudiosi
 Phone: (39) 0776 808972
 Mill Mgr.: Salvatore Alleva
 Phone: (39) 0776 808972
 Tech. Dir.: Antonio Alleva
 Phone: (39) 0776 808972
 Foreign Market Mgr. & Accounting Mgr.: Daniele Bernardelli
 Phone: (39) 0776 808972
Total Employees at this Location: 36
Type of Operation: Paper mill
Pulp Grades and Capacities:
 Total pulp capacity: 9,206 mt/y
 Recycled Pulping: 9,206 mt/y
Pulp Mill Data:
 Recycled Fiber Treatment Lines:
 Pulpers: 1 at 8,000
Paper/Paperboard Grades and Capacities:
 Total paper and paperboard capacity: 9,000 mt/y
 Packaging papers: 9,000 mt/y
Paper and Paperboard Mill Data:
Paper Machines: 1
 No. 1, fourdrinier, total capacity 9,000 mt/y, Trim width 2.4 m, Packaging papers
Finishing Equipment:
 Winders: 2 at 8,000 mt/y
Energy Data:
 Power boilers: 1
 Electrical demand for mill: 12 MWh/D

ⓄⓂCartiere Rodolfo Reguzzoni SRL
Giaveno Mill
Ownership: 100% by Family-owned (Private)
Via Canonico Pio Rolle, 78
I-10094 Giaveno, (TO)
Italy
 Phone: (39) 011 9376112/8869
 Fax: (39) 011 9378584
 Email: commerciale@cartierereguzzoni.it
 Web Address: www.cartierereguzzoni.it
Personnel:
 Gen. Man.: Wanda Reguzzoni
 Phone: (39) 011 9376112/8869
 Mgr.: Ing. Claudio Perazzini
 Phone: (39) 011 9376112/8869
Total Employees of Company: 11
Total Employees at this Location: 11
Type of Operation: Paper mill
Paper/Paperboard Grades and Capacities:
 Total paper and paperboard capacity: 10,000 mt/y
Paper and Paperboard Mill Data:
Paper Machines: 1
 PM 1, total capacity 10,000 mt/y, Trim width 1.5 m, Packaging papers

ⓂReno De Medici SpA
Ownership: 57.60% by Cascades Inc., 42.40% by Industria e Innovazione
Via Durini 16/18
I-20122 Milano
Italy
 Phone: (39) 02 89966 111
 Fax: (39) 02 89966 200
 Email: info@rdmgroup.com
 Web Address: www.renodemedici.it
Personnel:
 Chmn.: Christian Dubé
 Phone: (39) 02 89966 111
 Fax: (39) 02 89966 200
 Chmn.: Robert Hall
 Phone: (39) 02 89966 111
 Fax: (39) 02 89966 200
 Deputy Chmn.: Giuseppe Garofano
 Phone: (39) 02 89966 111
 Fax: (39) 02 89966 200
 CEO: Ignazio Capuano
 Phone: (39) 02 89966 111
 Fax: (39) 02 89966 200
 Email: ignazio.capuano@renodemedici.it
 CFO: Stefano Moccagatta
 Phone: (39) 02 89966 111
 Fax: (39) 02 89966 200
 COO: Manfred Draxler
 Phone: (39) 02 89966 111
 Fax: (39) 02 89966 200
 Sls. Dir.: Davide Cusani
 Phone: (39) 02 89966 111
 Fax: (39) 02 89966 200
 Procurement & Logist. Mgr.: Guido Giuseppe Vigorelli
 Phone: (39) 02 89966 111
 Fax: (39) 02 89966 200
 Email: guido.vigorelli@renodemedici.it
 IT Mgr.: Daniele Gatti
 Phone: (39) 02 89966 111
 Fax: (39) 02 89966 200
 HR Mgr.: Marita Lovera
 Phone: (39) 02 89966 111
 Fax: (39) 02 89966 200
Total Employees of Company: 1,430
Total Employees at this Location: 117
Mill Locations:
 RDM Blendecques SAS, Blendecques Mill, Rue de l'Hermitage, BP 53006, F-62501 Blendecques, Saint Omer Cedex, France, Capacity: 105,000 mt/y, (Pulp mill, Paperboard mill)
 Phone: (33) 3 21 38 80 20
 Fax: (33) 3 21 38 80 28
 Email: contact@careo.biz
 Reno De Medici, Iberica S.L.U., Almazán Mill, Carretera de Gomara km 14, E-2200 Almazán, Spain, Capacity: 40,000 mt/y, (Paperboard mill)
 Phone: (34) 975 310144
 Fax: (34) 975 300041
 Email: jaraso@sarrio.es
 Reno De Medici Arnsberg GmbH, Arnsberg Mill, Hellefelder Str. 51, D-59821 Arnsberg, Germany, Capacity: 230,000 mt/y, (Paperboard mill)
 Phone: (49) 2931 851
 Fax: (49) 2931 85201
 Email: info@rdmgroup.com
 Reno De Medici SpA, Magenta Mill, Via de Medici, 39, I-20013 Pontenuovo di Magenta, (MI), Italy, (Paperboard mill)
 Phone: (39) 02 979601
 Fax: (39) 02 97960323
 Email: rdm.magenta@renodemedici.it, careo@pec.it
 Reno De Medici SpA, Ovaro Mill, Via della Cartiera 27, I-33025 Ovaro, (UD), Italy, Capacity: 110,000 mt/y, (Paperboard mill)
 Phone: (39) 0433 67 241
 Fax: (39) 0433 67 542
 Email: info@rdmgroup.it , careo@pec.it
 Reno De Medici SpA, Santa Giustina Mill, Località Campo, I-32035 Santa Giustina Bellunese, (BL), Italy, Capacity: 240,000 mt/y, (Paperboard mill)
 Phone: (39) 0437 8811
 Fax: (39) 0437 881280
 Email: rdm.santagiustina@renodemedici.it
 Reno De Medici SpA, Villa Santa Lucia Mill, Via Casilina Km. 134,5, I-03030 Villa Santa Lucia, (FR), Italy, Capacity: 250,000 mt/y, (Paperboard mill)
 Phone: (39) 0776 37091
 Fax: (39) 0776 25976
 Email: rdm.vslucia@renodemedici.it, careo@pec.it

ⓂReno De Medici SpA
Magenta Mill
Ownership: 57.60% by Cascades Inc.
Via de Medici, 39
I-20013 Pontenuovo di Magenta, (MI)
Italy
 Phone: (39) 02 979601
 Fax: (39) 02 97960323
 Email: rdm.magenta@renodemedici.it, careo@pec.it
 Web Address: www.renodemedici.it
Personnel:
 Mill Dir.: Ing. Alessandro Magnoni
 Phone: (39) 02 979601
 Fax: (39) 02 97960323
 Email: alessandro.magnoni@rdmgroup.com
 Maint. Mgr.: Ing. Luca Boz
 Phone: (39) 02 979 601
 Fax: (39) 02 97960323
 Email: luca.boz@renodemedici.it
Total Employees at this Location: 183
Type of Operation: Paperboard mill
Paper and Paperboard Mill Data:
 Stock Preparation:
 Pulpers: 9
 Refiners: 8
Paper Machines: 1
 No. 2, Fourdrinier (5), total capacity 145,000 mt/y, Trim width 3.6 m
Coating Machines: 1
 No. 1-3, total capacity 145,000 mt/y., on machine
Finishing Equipment:
 Rewinders: 1
 Sheeters: 5 at 160,000 mt/y
Energy Data:
 Power boilers: 1
 Steam turbines: 1 at 11 MW

ⓂReno De Medici SpA
Ovaro Mill
Ownership: 57.60% by Cascades Inc.
Via della Cartiera 27
I-33025 Ovaro, (UD)
Italy
 Phone: (39) 0433 67 241
 Fax: (39) 0433 67 542
 Email: info@rdmgroup.it, careo@pec.it
 Web Address: www.renodemedici.it
Personnel:
 Mill Dir.: Silvano Giorgis

Italy

Phone: (39) 0433 67 241
Fax: (39) 0433 67 542
Email: silvano.giorgis@renodemedici.it
Prod. Mgr.: Alvise Stefani
Phone: (39) 0433 67 241
Fax: (39) 0433 67 542
Email: alvise.stefani@renodemedici.it
Converting Plant Mgr.: Giuseppe Ardizzone
Phone: (39) 0433 67 241
Fax: (39) 0433 67 542
Email: giuseppe.ardizzone@renodemedici.it
Total Employees at this Location: 150
Type of Operation: Paperboard mill
Pulp Grades and Capacities:
Total pulp capacity: 113,149 mt/y
Recycled Pulping: 113,149 mt/y
Paper/Paperboard Grades and Capacities:
Total paper and paperboard capacity: 110,000 mt/y
Boxboard/cartonboard: 110,000 mt/y
Paper and Paperboard Mill Data:
Stock Preparation:
Pulpers: 4
Refiners: 2
Paper Machines: 2
No. 1, cylinder (8), Yankee dryer, total capacity 50,000 mt/y, Trim width 2.3 m, Boxboard/cartonboard
No. 2, fourdrinier, total capacity 60,000 mt/y, Trim width 2.3 m, Boxboard/cartonboard
Coating Machines: 1
PM 1, total capacity 40,000 mt/y., on machine
Finishing Equipment:
Rewinders: 2
Sheeters: 2 at 130,000 mt/y
Energy Data:
Power boilers: 1
Combustion turbines: 1 at 3.2 MW
Steam turbines: 1 at 4.8 MW
Electrical demand for mill: 134 MWh/D

ⓜReno De Medici SpA
Santa Giustina Mill
Ownership: 57.60% by Cascades Inc.
Località Campo
I-32035 Santa Giustina Bellunese, (BL)
Italy
Phone: (39) 0437 8811
Fax: (39) 0437 881280
Email: rdm.santagiustina@renodemedici.it
Web Address: www.renodemedici.it
Personnel:
Mill Mgr.: Francesco Canal
Phone: (39) 0437 8811
Fax: (39) 0437 881280
Email: francesco.canal@rdmgroup.com
Tech. Mgr.: Massimo Marcer
Phone: (39) 0437 8811
Fax: (39) 0437 881280
Email: massimo.marcer@renodemedici.it
Total Employees at this Location: 240
Type of Operation: Paperboard mill
Pulp Grades and Capacities:
Total pulp capacity: 204,607 mt/y
Recycled Pulping: 204,607 mt/y
Pulp Mill Data:
Recycled Fiber Treatment Lines:
Flotation deinking lines: 1
Recycled packaging pulping lines: 1
Paper/Paperboard Grades and Capacities:
Total paper and paperboard capacity: 240,000 mt/y
Boxboard/cartonboard: 240,000 mt/y
Paper and Paperboard Mill Data:
Stock Preparation:
Pulpers: 5
Refiners: 5
Paper Machines: 1
No. 1, combination, total capacity 240,000 mt/y, Trim width 4.6 m, Boxboard/cartonboard
Coating Machines: 3
No. 1, on machine

No. 2, on machine
No. 3, on machine
Finishing Equipment:
Rewinders: 2 at 240,000 mt/y
Sheeters: 6 at 240,000 mt/y
Energy Data:
Power boilers: 2
Steam turbines: 1 at 10 MW
Electrical demand for mill: 330 MWh/D

ⓜReno De Medici SpA
Villa Santa Lucia Mill
Ownership: 57.60% by Cascades Inc.
Via Casilina Km. 134,5
I-03030 Villa Santa Lucia, (FR)
Italy
Phone: (39) 0776 37091
Fax: (39) 0776 25976
Email: rdm.vslucia@renodemedici.it, careo@pec.it
Web Address: www.renodemedici.it
Personnel:
Mill Dir.: Minoleo Marucci
Phone: (39) 0776 37091
Fax: (39) 0776 25976
Email: minoleo.marucci@rdmgroup.com
Prod. Mgr.: Franco D'Orazio
Phone: (39) 0776 37091
Fax: (39) 0776 25976
Email: franco.dorazio@renodemedici.it
Total Employees at this Location: 214
Type of Operation: Paperboard mill
Pulp Grades and Capacities:
Total pulp capacity: 287,486 mt/y
Recycled Pulping: 287,486 mt/y
Pulp Mill Data:
Recycled Fiber Treatment Lines:
Recycled packaging pulping lines at 202,000
Paper/Paperboard Grades and Capacities:
Total paper and paperboard capacity: 250,000 mt/y
Boxboard/cartonboard: 250,000 mt/y
Paper and Paperboard Mill Data:
Paper Machines: 1
No. 1, fourdrinier, total capacity 250,000 mt/y, Trim width 4.4 m, Boxboard/cartonboard
Coating Machines: 1
PM 1, total capacity 250,000 mt/y., on machine
Finishing Equipment:
Sheeters: 5
Energy Data:
Power boilers: 1
Combustion turbines: 1 at 7 MW
Steam turbines: 1 at 4 MW
Electrical demand for mill: 336 MWh/D

ⓞⓜCartiera di Rivignano SpA
Rivignano Mill
Ownership: 100% by Bolzonella Bros.
Via Giordano Bruno 32
I-33050 Rivignano, (UD)
Italy
Phone: (39) 0432 772811
Fax: (39) 0432 772828
Email: info@rivignano.com
Web Address: www.rivignano.com
Personnel:
Chmn.: Cesare Bolzonella
Phone: (39) 0432 772811
Purch. Dir.: Mario Bolzonella
Phone: (39) 0432 772811
Sls. Mgr.: Barbara Bolzonella
Phone: (39) 0432 772811
Email: sales@rivignano.com
Total Employees of Company: 68
Total Employees at this Location: 68
Type of Operation: Paper mill
Paper/Paperboard Grades and Capacities:
Total paper and paperboard capacity: 19,000 mt/y
Boxboard/cartonboard

Paper and Paperboard Mill Data:
Paper Machines: 1
PM 1, fourdrinier, total capacity 19,000 mt/y, Trim width 2.3 m
Coating Machines: 1
No. 1

ⓜRoto-cart SpA
Via Mussà, 30
I-35017 Piombino Dese, (PD)
Italy
Phone: (39) 049 9365511
Fax: (39) 049 9365118
Email: info@rotocart.com
Web Address: www.rotocart.it
Personnel:
Mgr.: Paolo Scattolon
Phone: (39) 049 9365511
Fax: (39) 049 9365118
Email: paolo.scattolon@rotocart.com
Mill Locations:
Roto-cart SpA, Piano della Rocca (Lunata) Mill, Località La Madonnina, I-55010 Lunata, (LU), Italy, Capacity: 31,000 mt/y, (Paper mill)
Phone: (39) 0583 4481
Fax: (39) 0583 448667
Email: info@rotocart.com

ⓜRoto-cart SpA
Piano della Rocca (Lunata) Mill
Località La Madonnina
I-55010 Lunata, (LU)
Italy
Phone: (39) 0583 4481
Fax: (39) 0583 448667
Email: info@rotocart.com
Web Address: www.rotocart.com
Personnel:
COO: Paolo Scattolon
Phone: (39) 0583 4481
Fax: (39) 0583 448667
Email: paolo.scattolon@rotocart.com
Total Employees at this Location: 48
Type of Operation: Paper mill
Paper/Paperboard Grades and Capacities:
Total paper and paperboard capacity: 31,000 mt/y
Tissue: 31,000 mt/y
Paper and Paperboard Mill Data:
Paper Machines: 1
No. 1, crescent former, total capacity 31,000 mt/y, Trim width 2.75 m, Tissue
Energy Data:
Power boilers: 1
Electrical demand for mill: 85 MWh/D

ⓞⓜCartiera S.A.C.C.A. SpA
Calatabiano Mill
Via Pasteria, 17/19
I-95011 Calatabiano, (CT)
Italy
Phone: (39) 095 645 522
Fax: (39) 095 645 240
Email: amministrazione@saccaspa.com
Web Address: www.saccaspa.com
Personnel:
Chmn.: Gianpaolo Alberici
Phone: (39) 095 645 522
Admin.: Antonio La Spada
Phone: (39) 095 645 522
Filippo Tati
Total Employees at this Location: 18
Type of Operation: Paperboard mill
Pulp Grades and Capacities:
Total pulp capacity: 14,280 mt/y
Recycled Pulping: 14,280 mt/y
Paper/Paperboard Grades and Capacities:
Total paper and paperboard capacity: 14,000 mt/y
Corrugating medium/fluting: 14,000 mt/y
Paper and Paperboard Mill Data:

Italy

Paper Machines: 1
No. 1, fourdrinier, total capacity 14,000 mt/y, Trim width 2.4 m, Corrugating medium/fluting
Energy Data:
Power boilers: 1
Electrical demand for mill: 20 MWh/D

ⓂⓂCartiera Sacchettificio Bonino
Borgaro Torinese Mill
Via Stroppiana 9/11
I-10071 Borgaro Torinese, (TO)
Italy
  Phone: (39) 011 4701055
  Fax: (39) 011 4503855
  Email: fvgcr@tin.it, cartierabonino@hotmail.com
Personnel:
  Mill Mgr.: Pietro Bonino
  Phone: (39) 011 4701055
Total Employees of Company: 28
Total Employees at this Location: 28
Type of Operation: Paper mill
Paper/Paperboard Grades and Capacities:
  Total paper and paperboard capacity: 17,500 mt/y
  Uncoated woodfree/freesheet: 10,000 mt/y
  Packaging papers: 7,500 mt/y
Paper and Paperboard Mill Data:
Paper Machines: 1
No. 1, fourdrinier, total capacity 17,500 mt/y, Uncoated woodfree/freesheet, Packaging papers
Energy Data:
Power boilers: 2

ⓂⓂCartiere SACI SpA
Verona Mill
Strada della Ferriera, 17
I-37100 Cà di David, (VR)
Italy
  Phone: (39) 045 8550077/17
  Fax: (39) 045 8550024/8568260
  Email: vendite@cartieresaci.com
  Web Address: www.cartieresaci.com
Personnel:
  CEO: Lorenzo Poli
  Phone: (39) 045 8550077
  Fax: (39) 045 8550024
  Email: lorenzo.poli@cartieresaci.com
  Tech. Mgr.: Ing. Volker Tippelmann
  Phone: (39) 045 8550077
  Fax: (39) 045 8550024
  Email: tippelmann@cartieresaci.com
  Admin. Mgr.: Pierangelo Minozzo
  Phone: (39) 045 8550077
  Fax: (39) 045 8550024
  Email: pierangelo.minozzo@cartieresaci.com
  Commercial Mgr.: Gualtiero Giacopuzzi
  Phone: (39) 045 8550077
  Fax: (39) 045 8550024
  Email: gualtiero@cartieresaci.com
  Purch. Mgr.: Giovanni Scalia
  Phone: (39) 045 8550077
  Fax: (39) 045 8550024
  Email: g.scalia@cartieresaci.com
Total Employees at this Location: 95
Type of Operation: Paper mill
Pulp Grades and Capacities:
  Total pulp capacity: 80,552 mt/y
  Recycled Pulping: 80,552 mt/y
Pulp Mill Data:
  Recycled Fiber Treatment Lines:
  Pulpers: 4
Paper/Paperboard Grades and Capacities:
  Total paper and paperboard capacity: 80,000 mt/y
  Packaging papers: 31,000 mt/y
  Corrugating medium/fluting: 49,000 mt/y
Paper and Paperboard Mill Data:
  Stock Preparation:
  Refiners: 3
Paper Machines: 2
No. 1, fourdrinier, Yankee dryer, total capacity 31,000 mt/y, Trim width 2.4 m, Packaging papers
No. 2, OptiFormer, total capacity 49,000 mt/y, Trim width 2.51 m, Corrugating medium/fluting
Finishing Equipment:
  Rewinders: 3
Energy Data:
Power boilers: 1
Steam turbines: 1 at 2.7 MW
Electrical demand for mill: 115 MWh/D

ⓂⓂCartiera San Felice SpA
San Felice Mill
Ownership: 100% by Sant'Andrea Spa
Via Calabbiana, 1
I-51110 Piteccio, (PT)
Italy
  Phone: (39) 0573 99871
  Fax: (39) 0573 41468
  Email: cartiera@cartierasanfelice.com
Personnel:
  Mgr.: Arianna Tacchini
  Phone: (39) 0573 99871
  Fax: (39) 0573 41468
  Email: arianna.tacchini@cartierasanfelice.com
Total Employees of Company: 81
Total Employees at this Location: 80
Type of Operation: Paperboard mill
Pulp Grades and Capacities:
  Total pulp capacity: 40,595 mt/y
  Recycled Pulping: 40,595 mt/y
Paper/Paperboard Grades and Capacities:
  Total paper and paperboard capacity: 40,000 mt/y
  Boxboard/cartonboard: 40,000 mt/y
Paper and Paperboard Mill Data:
Paper Machines: 2
No. 2, fourdrinier, total capacity 18,000 mt/y, Trim width 3 m, Boxboard/cartonboard
No. 3, fourdrinier, total capacity 22,000 mt/y, Trim width 2.6 m, Boxboard/cartonboard
Energy Data:
Power boilers: 1
Electrical demand for mill: 46 MWh/D

ⓂⓂCartiera San Giorgio S.r.l.
Genova-Voltri Mill
Via Vincenzo Malenchini 13
I-16158 Genova-Voltri, (GE)
Italy
  Phone: (39) 010 639159
  Fax: (39) 010 639153
  Email: info@cartierasangiorgio.it
  Web Address: www.cartierasangiorgio.it
Personnel:
  Man. Dir.: Alessandro Ardinghi
  Phone: (39) 010 639159
  Fax: (39) 010 639153
  Email: alessandro.ardinghi@cartierasangiorgio.it
  Man. Dir.: Antonio Ardinghi
  Phone: (39) 010 639159
  Fax: (39) 010 639153
  Email: antonio.ardinghi@cartierasangiorgio.it
Total Employees of Company: 25
Total Employees at this Location: 25
Type of Operation: Paper mill
Pulp Grades and Capacities:
  Total pulp capacity: 10,551 mt/y
  Recycled Pulping: 10,551 mt/y
Pulp Mill Data:
  Recycled Fiber Treatment Lines:
  Flotation deinking lines: 1 at 20,000
Paper/Paperboard Grades and Capacities:
  Total paper and paperboard capacity: 16,500 mt/y
  Tissue: 16,500 mt/y
Paper and Paperboard Mill Data:
Paper Machines: 1
No. 1, fourdrinier, Yankee dryer, total capacity 16,500 mt/y, Trim width 2.42 m, Tissue
Energy Data:
Power boilers: 1
Electrical demand for mill: 43 MWh/D

ⓂⓂCartiera S. Giovanni di Figli di Checchi G. S.R.L.
Pietrabuona di Pescia Mill
Via Mammianese Nord 148
I-51017 Pietrabuona di Pescia, (PT)
Italy
  Phone: (39) 0572 408068
  Fax: (39) 0572 408055
  Email: info@cartierasangiovanni.it
  Web Address: www.cartierasangiovanni.it
Personnel:
  Pres.: Goffredo Checchi
  Phone: (39) 0572 408068
  Fax: (39) 0572 408055
  Email: info@cartierasangiovanni.it
Total Employees of Company: 15
Total Employees at this Location: 13
Type of Operation: Paperboard mill
Paper/Paperboard Grades and Capacities:
  Total paper and paperboard capacity: 6,000 mt/y
  Specialty and industrial
  Boxboard/cartonboard
Paper and Paperboard Mill Data:
Paper Machines: 1
No. 1, Specialty and industrial, Boxboard/cartonboard
Energy Data:
Power boilers: 1

ⓂⓂCartiera San Lorenzo S.R.L.
Gassano Mill
Ownership: 100% by Celtex S.p.a
Via Molino, 1
I-54020 Gassano, (MS)
Italy
  Phone: (39) 0585 998045
  Fax: (39) 0585 99214
  Email: info@cartierasanlorenzo.it
  Web Address: www.celtex.it
Personnel:
  Mgr.: Roberta Martinelli
  Phone: (39) 0585 998045
  Fax: (39) 0585 99214
  Email: roberta@cartierasanlorenzo.it
Total Employees of Company: 30
Total Employees at this Location: 30
Type of Operation: Paper mill
Pulp Grades and Capacities:
  Total pulp capacity: 1,803 mt/y
  Recycled Pulping: 1,803 mt/y
Paper/Paperboard Grades and Capacities:
  Total paper and paperboard capacity: 20,000 mt/y
  Tissue: 20,000 mt/y
Paper and Paperboard Mill Data:
Paper Machines: 1
No. 1, twin-wire, Yankee dryer, total capacity 20,000 mt/y, Trim width 3.2 m, Tissue
Energy Data:
Power boilers: 1
Electrical demand for mill: 54 MWh/D

ⓂⓂCartiera San Martino SpA
Broccostella Mill
Via Ferrazza 15/a
I-03030 Broccostella, (FR)
Italy
  Phone: (39) 0776 891242/244
  Fax: (39) 0776 890461
  Email: info@cartierasanmartino.it
  Web Address: www.cartierasanmartino.it
Personnel:
  Tech. Dir.: Olimpio Cerrone
  Phone: (39) 0776 891242
  Fax: (39) 0776 890461
  Email: o.cerrone@cartierasanmartino.it
  Sls. Dir.: Giancarlo Cerrone

Italy

Phone: (39) 0776 891242
Fax: (39) 0776 890461
Email: g.cerrone@cartierasanmartino.it
Admin. Dir.: Rita Mancini
Phone: (39) 0776 891242
Fax: (39) 0776 890461
Email: r.mancini@cartierasanmartino.it
Total Employees of Company: 63
Total Employees at this Location: 63
Type of Operation: Paperboard mill
Pulp Grades and Capacities:
Total pulp capacity: 28,323 mt/y
Recycled Pulping: 28,323 mt/y

Pulp Mill Data:
Recycled Fiber Treatment Lines:
Recycled packaging pulping lines: 1
Paper/Paperboard Grades and Capacities:
Total paper and paperboard capacity: 27,500 mt/y
Boxboard/cartonboard: 27,500 mt/y
Paper and Paperboard Mill Data:
Paper Machines: 2
No. 1, cylinder, total capacity 10,000 mt/y, Trim width 1.6 m, Boxboard/cartonboard
No. 2, cylinder, total capacity 17,500 mt/y, Trim width 2.25 m, Boxboard/cartonboard
Energy Data:
Power boilers
Electrical demand for mill: 38 MWh/D

ⓘCartiera San Rocco SpA
Via delle Cartiere 76, Loc. Botticino
I-55019 Villa Basilica, (LU)
Italy
Phone: (39) 0572 43017
Fax: (39) 0572 43446
Email: info@cartierasrocco.it
Web Address: www.cartierasrocco.it
Personnel:
Admin. Mgr.: Monica Lurci
Phone: (39) 0572 43017
Fax: (39) 0572 43446
Email: monica@cartierasrocco.it
Safety and Environ. Mgr.: Osvaldo Domenici
Phone: (39) 0572 43017
Fax: (39) 0572 43446
Email: info@cartierasrocco.it
Sls. Mgr.: Alessandra Pasquini
Phone: (39) 0572 43017
Fax: (39) 0572 43446
Email: alessandra@cartierasrocco.it
Accounting Mgr.: Anna Pasquini
Phone: (39) 0572 43017
Fax: (39) 0572 43446
Email: anna@cartierasrocco.it
Purch. Mgr.: Giancarlo Poinziani
Phone: (39) 0572 43017
Fax: (39) 0572 43446
Email: giancarlo@cartierasrocco.it
Total Employees of Company: 32
Mill Locations:
Cartiera San Rocco SpA, Villa Basilica Mill, Via delle Cartiere 76, Loc. Botticino, I-55019 Villa Basilica, (LU), Italy, Capacity: 25,000 mt/y, (Paper mill)
Phone: (39) 0572 43017
Fax: (39) 0572 43446
Email: info@cartierasrocco.it

ⓘCartiera San Rocco SpA
Villa Basilica Mill
Via delle Cartiere 76, Loc. Botticino
I-55019 Villa Basilica, (LU)
Italy
Phone: (39) 0572 43017
Fax: (39) 0572 43446
Email: info@cartierasrocco.it
Web Address: www.cartierasrocco.it
Personnel:
Mill Mgr.: Pasquini Alessandra
Phone: (39) 0572 43017
Fax: (39) 0572 43446
Email: info@cartierasrocco.it
Total Employees at this Location: 32
Type of Operation: Paper mill
Pulp Grades and Capacities:
Total pulp capacity: 17,503 mt/y
Recycled Pulping: 17,503 mt/y

Pulp Mill Data:
Recycled Fiber Treatment Lines:
Pulpers: 1 at 25,400
Paper/Paperboard Grades and Capacities:
Total paper and paperboard capacity: 25,000 mt/y
Tissue: 25,000 mt/y
Paper and Paperboard Mill Data:
Stock Preparation:
Pulpers:
Paper Machines: 1
No. 1, twin-wire, Yankee dryer, total capacity 25,000 mt/y, Trim width 2.85 m, Tissue
Energy Data:
Power boilers
Electrical demand for mill: 71 MWh/D

ⓘⓂCartonificio Sandreschi S.R.L.
Villa Basilica Mill
Via delle Cartiere 1
I-55019 Villa Basilica, (LU)
Italy
Phone: (39) 0572 43033/43472
Fax: (39) 0572 43504
Email: info@sandreschi.it
Web Address: www.sandreschi.it
Personnel:
Man. Dir.: Ernesto Sandreschi
Phone: (39) 0572 43033/43472
Sls. Dir.: Benedetto Sandreschi
Phone: (39) 0572 43033/43472
Total Employees of Company: 55
Total Employees at this Location: 55
Type of Operation: Paperboard mill
Pulp Grades and Capacities:
Total pulp capacity: 36,464 mt/y
Recycled Pulping: 36,464 mt/y

Pulp Mill Data:
Recycled Fiber Treatment Lines:
Recycled packaging pulping lines: 1
Paper/Paperboard Grades and Capacities:
Total paper and paperboard capacity: 35,000 mt/y
Boxboard/cartonboard: 35,000 mt/y
Paper and Paperboard Mill Data:
Paper Machines: 1
No. 1, cylinder, total capacity 35,000 mt/y, Trim width 2.6 m, Boxboard/cartonboard
Energy Data:
Power boilers: 1
Electrical demand for mill: 46 MWh/D

ⓘSant'Andrea Spa
Ownership: 100% by Carrara Group
Via Franchetti 11
I-51100 Pistoia, (PT)
Italy
Phone: (39) 0573 368154
Fax: (39) 0573 368566
Email: sa@santandreaspa.net
Personnel:
Chmn.: Paolo Carrara
Phone: (39) 0573 368154
Fax: (39) 0573 368566
Mill Locations:
Cartiera Capostrada SpA, Tullio Carrara Mill, Via dei Barbi 32, I-51000 Capostrada, (PT), Italy, Capacity: 7,000 mt/y, (Paper mill)
Phone: (39) 0573 401135
Fax: (39) 0573 401215
Email: info@cartieracapostrada.com
Cartiera Carma Srl, Pistoia Mill, Via Val di Forfora 27, I-51010 Pescia-Pietrabuona, (PT), Italy, Capacity: 31,000 mt/y, (Paper mill)

Phone: (39) 0572 405505/06
Fax: (39) 0572 405405
Email: info@carma.it
Cartiera Carma Srl, Pratovecchio Mill, Via Dante Alighieri, 26/A, I-52015 Pratovecchio, (AR), Italy, Capacity: 22,500 mt/y, (Paper mill)
Phone: (39) 0575 582204
Fax: (39) 0575 582201
Email: info@carma.it
MCTissue SpA, Tassignano Mill, Via del Casalino, 8, I-55012 Tassignano/Capannori, (LU), Italy, Capacity: 55,000 mt/y, (Paper mill)
Phone: (39) 0583 93031
Fax: (39) 0583 936724
Email: info@mctissue.it
Cartiera San Felice SpA, San Felice Mill, Via Calabbiana, 1, I-51110 Piteccio, (PT), Italy, Capacity: 40,000 mt/y, (Paperboard mill)
Phone: (39) 0573 99871
Fax: (39) 0573 41468
Email: cartiera@cartierasanfelice.com

ⓘSCA Hygiene Products SpA
Altopascio Mill
Ownership: SCA Hygiene Products SE
Via Proviciale Romana
I-55010 Altopascio, Loc. Badia Pozzeveri, (LU)
Italy
Phone: (39) 0583 2791
Fax: (39) 0583 279250
Web Address: www.sca.com
Personnel:
Mill Mgr.: Emiliano Mazzola
Phone: (39) 0583 2791
Fax: (39) 0583 279250
Email: emiliano.mazzola@sca.com
Total Employees at this Location: 176
Type of Operation: Paper mill
Paper/Paperboard Grades and Capacities:
Total paper and paperboard capacity: 25,000 mt/y
Tissue: 25,000 mt/y
Paper and Paperboard Mill Data:
Paper Machines: 1
No. 1, C-wrap, Yankee dryer, total capacity 25,000 mt/y, Trim width 2.7 m, Tissue
Energy Data:
Power boilers: 1
Combustion turbines: 1
Electrical demand for mill: 74 MWh/D

ⓘSCA Hygiene Products
Collodi Mill
Ownership: SCA Hygiene Products SE
Via delle Cartiere 13
I-51014 Collodi, (PT)
Italy
Phone: (39) 0572 429090
Fax: (39) 0572 426335
Web Address: www.scaconsumertissue.com
Personnel:
Prod. Mgr.: Emilio Biagini
Phone: (39) 0572 429090
Total Employees at this Location: 65
Type of Operation: Paper mill
Paper/Paperboard Grades and Capacities:
Total paper and paperboard capacity: 42,000 mt/y
Tissue: 42,000 mt/y
Paper and Paperboard Mill Data:
Paper Machines: 2
No. 1, crescent former, Yankee dryer, total capacity 20,000 mt/y, Trim width 2.8 m, Tissue
No. 2, crescent former, Yankee dryer, total capacity 22,000 mt/y, Trim width 2.85 m, Tissue
Energy Data:
Power boilers: 1
Electrical demand for mill: 108 MWh/D

Italy

Ⓜ SCA Hygiene Products SpA
Lucca 1 Tissue Mill
Ownership: SCA Hygiene Products SE
Via del Frizzone
I-55016 Porcari, (LU)
Italy
  Phone: (39) 0583 21241
  Fax: (39) 0583 297575
  Email: info@sca.com
  Web Address: www.scaconsumertissue.com
Personnel:
  Mill Mgr.: Massimo Santolini
  Phone: (39) 0583 21241
  Fax: (39) 0583 297575
  Email: massimo.santolini@sca.com
Total Employees at this Location: 130
Type of Operation: Paper mill
Paper/Paperboard Grades and Capacities:
  Total paper and paperboard capacity: 140,000 mt/y
  Tissue: 140,000 mt/y
Paper and Paperboard Mill Data:
Paper Machines: 4
  No. 1, crescent former, Yankee dryer, total capacity 22,000 mt/y, Trim width 2.7 m, Tissue
  No. 2, OVER Former, Yankee dryer, total capacity 18,000 mt/y, Trim width 2.7 m, Tissue
  No. 3, OVER Former, Yankee dryer, total capacity 50,000 mt/y, Trim width 5.45 m, Tissue
  No. 4, crescent former, Yankee dryer, total capacity 50,000 mt/y, Trim width 5.4 m, Tissue
Energy Data:
  Power boilers: 2
  Combustion turbines: 1 at 10 MW
  Electrical demand for mill: 340 MWh/D

Ⓗ Ⓜ Cartiera Sicars S.R.L.
Aci Bonaccorsi Mill
Via Calcara 27
I-95020 Aci Bonaccorsi, (CT)
Italy
  Phone: (39) 095 7899485
  Fax: (39) 095 7890248
  Email: info@cartieradisicilia.it
Personnel:
  Sls. Mgr.: Michele Sciuto
  Phone: (39) 095 7899485
  Mgr.: Patrizia Renata Santonocito
  Phone: (39) 095 7899485
Total Employees at this Location: 14
Type of Operation: Paper mill
Paper/Paperboard Grades and Capacities:
  Total paper and paperboard capacity: 5,000 mt/y
  Specialty and industrial: 5,000 mt/y

Ⓗ Ⓜ Sicem-Saga SpA
Ciano di Canossa Mill
Via delle Industrie, 58
I-42026 Ciano d'Enza, (RE)
Italy
  Phone: (39) 0522 242811
  Fax: (39) 0522 242568/878944
  Email: vendite@sicemsaga.com
  Web Address: www.sicemsaga.com
Personnel:
  Chmn. & Purch. Dir.: Dr. Filippo Gazza
  Phone: (39) 0522 242811
  Fax: (39) 0522 242568
  Email: fgazza@sicemsaga.com
  Mill Mgr. & Tech. Dir.: Ing. Gianluca Gazza
  Phone: (39) 0522 242811
  Fax: (39) 0522 242568
  Email: ggazza@sicemsaga.com
  Sls. Dir.: Dr. Savino Gazza
  Phone: (39) 0522 242811
  Fax: (39) 0522 242568
  Email: sgazza@sicemsaga.com
  Export Mgr.: Claudio Menzio
  Phone: (39) 0522 242811
  Fax: (39) 0522 242568
  Email: cmenzio@sicemsaga.com
  Sls. Mgr.: Marco Brugnoli
  Phone: (39) 0522 242811
  Fax: (39) 0522 242568
  Email: mbrugnoli@sicemsaga.com
Total Employees at this Location: 74
Type of Operation: Pulp mill
Pulp Grades and Capacities:
  Total pulp capacity: 131,632 mt/y
  Pulp available for market: 130,000 mt/y
  Mechanical Pulp: 131,632 mt/y
Pulp Mill Data:
  Mechanical Pulping Systems:
  BCTMP systems: 1
  Bleach Plant Systems: 1
  No. 1, Sequence: P
  Pulp Dryers:
  Flash dryers 1
Energy Data:
  Power boilers: 1
  Combustion turbines: 2 at 10 MW
  Electrical demand for mill: 356 MWh/D

Ⓜ Smurfit Kappa Ania Paper
Ania Mill
Ownership: Smurfit Kappa Europe
Via del Mulino
I-55055 Ponte all'Ania, (LU)
Italy
  Phone: (39) 0583 70031
  Fax: (39) 0583 709179
  Email: ania.paper@smurfitkappa.it
  Web Address: www.smurfitkappa-ania.com
Personnel:
  Man. Dir. & Oper. Mgr. (Alfa d'Avignon Mill, Rethel Mill, Saillat Mill): Jean Bernard Latour
  Phone: (39) 0583 70031
  Fax: (39) 0583 709179
  Email: jean-bernard.latour@smurfitkappa.it
  Gen. Mgr.: Massimiliano Listi
  Phone: (39) 0583 70031
  Fax: (39) 0583 709179
  Email: massimiliano.listi@smurfitkappa.it
  Tech. Mgr.: Marino Donati
  Phone: (39) 0583 70031
  Fax: (39) 0583 709179
  Email: marino.donati@smurfitkappa.it
Total Employees at this Location: 130
Type of Operation: Paper mill, Paperboard mill
Pulp Grades and Capacities:
  Total pulp capacity: 200,719 mt/y
  Recycled Pulping: 200,719 mt/y
Pulp Mill Data:
Paper/Paperboard Grades and Capacities:
  Total paper and paperboard capacity: 200,000 mt/y
  Linerboard: 50,000 mt/y
  Corrugating medium/fluting: 150,000 mt/y
Paper and Paperboard Mill Data:
  Stock Preparation:
  Pulpers: 1
Paper Machines: 2
  No. 2, fourdrinier, total capacity 85,000 mt/y, Trim width 2.45 m, Corrugating medium/fluting
  No. 3, fourdrinier (2), total capacity 115,000 mt/y, Trim width 2.6 m, Corrugating medium/fluting, Linerboard
Finishing Equipment:
  Winders: 2 at 300,000 mt/y
Energy Data:
  Power boilers: 1
  Steam turbines: 1 at 6.1 MW
  Electrical demand for mill: 206 MWh/D

Ⓗ Ⓜ Socarpi S.R.L.
Villa Basilica Mill
Ownership: Fabrizio Bocci
Via dell Torbola, 33
I-55019 Villa Basilica, (LU)
Italy
  Phone: (39) 0572 43066
  Fax: (39) 0572 461032
  Email: socarpi1@tin.it
Personnel:
  Pres.: Armando Ansaldi
  Phone: (39) 0572 43066
Total Employees at this Location: 35
Type of Operation: Paper mill
Pulp Grades and Capacities:
  Total pulp capacity: 12,786 mt/y
  Recycled Pulping: 12,786 mt/y
Pulp Mill Data:
  Recycled Fiber Treatment Lines:
  Flotation deinking lines: 1
Paper/Paperboard Grades and Capacities:
  Total paper and paperboard capacity: 30,000 mt/y
  Tissue: 30,000 mt/y
Paper and Paperboard Mill Data:
Paper Machines: 1
  No. 1, crescent former, Yankee dryer, total capacity 30,000 mt/y, Trim width 2.75 m, Tissue
Finishing Equipment:
  Rewinders: 1
Energy Data:
  Power boilers: 1
  Electrical demand for mill: 81 MWh/D

Ⓜ Soffass S.p.A.
Soffass Mill
Ownership: 100% by Sofidel Group
Via di Leccio, 19
I-55016 Porcari, (LU)
Italy
  Phone: (39) 0583 2681
  Fax: (39) 0583 297645
  Email: soffass.cartiera@sofidel.it
  Web Address: www.sofidel.it
Personnel:
  Plant Mgr.: Enrico Belmonte
  Phone: (39) 0583 2681
  Fax: (39) 0583 290967
  Email: enrico.belmonte@sofidel.it
  Mktg. Mgr.: Rolando Figaia
  Phone: (39) 0583 2681
  Email: rolando.figaia@sofidel.it
  Sls. Mgr.: Giovanni Carnazza
  Phone: (39) 3498 195942
  Fax: (39) 0583 246290
  Email: giovanni.carnazza@sofidel.it
Total Employees at this Location: 105
Type of Operation: Paper mill
Paper/Paperboard Grades and Capacities:
  Total paper and paperboard capacity: 70,000 mt/y
  Tissue: 70,000 mt/y
Paper and Paperboard Mill Data:
  Stock Preparation:
  Pulpers: 4
  Refiners: 3
Paper Machines: 2
  No. 2, Yankee dryer, total capacity 15,000 mt/y, Trim width 1.95 m, Tissue
  No. 3, crescent former, Yankee dryer, total capacity 55,000 mt/y, Trim width 5.4 m, Tissue
Finishing Equipment:
  Rewinders: 3
Energy Data:
  Power boilers: 1
  Combustion turbines: 1 at 4.5 MW
  Electrical demand for mill: 196 MWh/D

Ⓗ Sofidel Group
Ownership: Public
Via di Lucia, 23
I-55016 Porcari, (LU)
Italy
  Phone: (39) 0583 2907/2681
  Fax: (39) 0583 295474
  Email: sofidel@sofidel.it
  Web Address: www.sofidel.it

Italy

Personnel:
CEO & Owner: Luigi Lazzareschi
Phone: (39) 0583 2681
Fax: (39) 0583 295474
Pres.: Mr. Erni Stefani
Phone: (39) 584.08429690414
Fax: (39) 0583 295474
Man. Dir.: Alessandro Nanni
Phone: (39) 584.08429690414
Fax: (39) 0583 295474
Email: alessandro.nanni@sofidel.it
Advisor: Edilio Stefani
Phone: (39) 584.08429690414
Fax: (39) 0583 295474
Bus. Line Dir.: Garzelli Giorgio
Phone: (39) 0583 2681
Fax: (39) 0583 295474
Mktg. & Sls. Dir.: Luca Benedetto
Phone: (39) 0583 2681
Fax: (39) 0583 295474
Corp. HR Mgr.: Roberto Berti
Phone: (39) 0583 2681
Fax: (39) 0583 295474
Total Employees of Company: 5,064
Total Employees at this Location: 180
Mill Locations:
S.C. Comceh S. A., Comceh Mill (30% owned), 1, Prelungirea Bucuresti St., RO-910161 Calarasi Judet, Romania, Capacity: 37,000 mt/y, (Paper mill)
Phone: (40) 242 312 942
Fax: (40) 242 315 723
Email: office@comceh.ro
Delicarta SpA, Porcari Mill, Via di Lucia 9, I-55016 Porcari, (LU), Italy, Capacity: 125,000 mt/y, (Paper mill)
Phone: (39) 0583 2681
Fax: (39) 0583 299898
Email: delicarta@sofidel.it
Delicarta SpA, Monfalcone Mill, Via Grota del Diau Zot, I-34074 Monfalcone, (GO), Italy, Capacity: 30,000 mt/y, (Paper mill)
Phone: (39) 0481 791596
Fax: (39) 0481 791589
Delicarta SpA, Valdottavo Mill, Via Provinciale Ludovica, I-55067 Valdottavo di Borgo a Mozzano, (LU), Italy, Capacity: 28,000 mt/y, (Paper mill)
Phone: (39) 0583 2681
Fax: (39) 0583 246240
Email: imbalpaper@sofidel.it
Delipapier GmbH, Arneburg Mill, Schoenfelder Strasse 1, D-39596 Arneburg, Germany, Capacity: 60,000 mt/y, (Paper mill)
Phone: (49) 3932 1545 0
Fax: (49) 3932 1545 150
Email: delipapier.de@delipapier.de
Delipapier S.A.S., Frouard Mill (60% owned), Ban la Dame, Parc d'Activités Nancy-Pompey, F-54390 Frouard, France, Capacity: 120,000 mt/y, (Paper mill)
Phone: (33) 3 83 49 53 53
Fax: (33) 3 83 49 53 54
Email: delipapier.fr@delipapier.fr, firstname.lastname@delipapier.fr
Delipapier S.A.S., Roanne Mill (60% owned), 112, Rue Mâtel, F-42335 Roanne Cédex, France, Capacity: 30,000 mt/y, (Paper mill)
Phone: (33) 4 77 68 82 68
Fax: (33) 4 77 68 82 90
Delitissue Sp. z.o.o., Ciechanow Mill (60% owned), ul. Mleczarska 31, PL-06 400 Ciechanow, Poland, Capacity: 35,000 mt/y, (Paper mill)
Phone: (48) 23 6743100
Fax: (48) 23 6739400
Email: delitissue.pl@delitissue.pl
Fibrocellulosa S.p.A, Bagni di Lucca Mill, Via Fegana 38 - Loc. Fornoli, I-55026 Bagni di Lucca, (LU), Italy, Capacity: 18,000 mt/y, (Paper mill)
Phone: (39) 0583 2681
Fax: (39) 0583 809374
Email: moena.biagioni@sofidel.it, fibrocellulosa@sofidel.it
Ibertissue S.L.U., Buñuel Mill, Pol. Industrial, S/N, E-31540 Buñuel, Spain, Capacity: 30,000 mt/y, (Paper mill)
Phone: (34) 948 832 080
Fax: (34) 948 823 028
Email: ibertissue@centralita.es, ibertissue@ibertissue.es
Intertissue Ltd., Port Talbot Mill, Brunel Way, Baglan Energy Park, Briton Ferry, Neath SA11 2HZ, United Kingdom, Capacity: 60,000 mt/y, (Paper mill)
Phone: (44) 1639 825 380
Fax: (44) 1639 825 381
Email: info@intertissue.co.uk, intertissue.uk@intertissue.co.uk
Papyros Paper Mill S.A., Papyros Mill, 1st km Old Nat. Road Katerini-Thessaloniki, GR-60100 Katerini, Greece, Capacity: 25,000 mt/y, (Paper mill)
Phone: (30) 23 510 79500
Fax: (30) 23 510 79501
Email: info@papyros-pm.com
Soffass S.p.A., Soffass Mill, Via di Leccio, 19, I-55016 Porcari, (LU), Italy, Capacity: 70,000 mt/y, (Paper mill)
Phone: (39) 0583 2681
Fax: (39) 0583 297645
Email: soffass.cartiera@sofidel.it
Sofidel Benelux, Duffel Mill, A. Stocdetlaan 3, B-2570 Duffel, Belgium, Capacity: 35,000 mt/y, (Paper mill)
Phone: (32) 15 30 0611
Fax: (32) 15 31 8241
Sofidel America Corporation, Haines City Mill, 1006 Marley Drive, Haines City, FL 33844, USA, Capacity: 68,013 mt/y, (Paper mill)
Phone: (1) 800-443-6099
Fax: (1) 863-547-1101
Sofidel Group, Kamns Mill, Waterside Road, Hamilton Industrial Park, Leicester LE5 1TZ, United Kingdom, Capacity: 75,000 mt/y, (Paper mill)
Phone: (44) 1162 460 888
Fax: (44) 1162 460 222/304 271
Sofidel Group, Lancaster Mill, Lansil Industrial Estate, Lansil Way, Caton Road, Lancaster LA1 3QY, United Kingdom, Capacity: 30,000 mt/y, (Paper mill)
Phone: (44) 1524 844 600
Fax: (44) 1524 842 800
Swedish Tissue AB, Kisa Mill, SE-590 40 Kisa, Sweden, Capacity: 62,000 mt/y, (Paper mill)
Phone: (46) 494 15000
Fax: (46) 494 15040
Email: info@swedishtissue.se
Thüringer Hygiene Papier GmbH, Thüringer Mill, OT Wernshausen, Unterm Bahnhof 10, D-98574 Schmalkalden, Germany, Capacity: 34,000 mt/y, (Paper mill)
Phone: (49) 36848 385 0
Fax: (49) 36848 385 410
Email: info@werrapapier.de
Werra Papier, Omega Mill, OT Wernshausen, Unterm Bahnhof 10, D-98574 Wernshausen, Germany, Capacity: 84,000 mt/y, (Paper mill)
Phone: (49) 36848 385 0
Fax: (49) 36848 385 410 / 385 36
Email: info@werrapapier.de

ⓘSonoco Alcore-Demolli srl

Ownership: 100% by Sonoco Alcore NV
Via Urago 10
I-22038 Tavernerio, (CO)
Italy
Phone: (39) 031 429811
Fax: (39) 031 427720
Email: info.italia@sonoco-alcore.net
Web Address: www.sonocoalcore.it
Personnel:
CEO & Gen. Mgr. Italy, Turkey & Middle East: Stamatios Trantas
Phone: (39) 031 429811
Fax: (39) 031 427720
Finan. Dir.: Bruno Cilenti
Phone: (39) 031 429811
Fax: (39) 031 427720
Email: bruno.cilenti@sonoco-alcore.net
HR Mgr. Italy: Marianna Sonvico
Phone: (39) 031 429811
Fax: (39) 031 427720
Inside Sls. Mgr.: Andrea Pistoni
Phone: (39) 031 429811
Fax: (39) 031 427720
Mill Mgr., Sls. Mgr.: Alessandro Castelletti
Phone: (39) 011 9225311
Fax: (39) 011 9207772
Email: alessandro.castelletti@sonoco-alcore.net
Purch. Mgr: Davide Faborelli
Phone: (39) 031 429811
Fax: (39) 031 427720
Prod. Mgr.: Ing. Massimo Basta
Phone: (39) 011 9225311
Fax: (39) 011 9207772
Email: massimo.basta@sonoco-alcore.net
Quality Dept.: Cristina Borgogno
Phone: (39) 011 9225311
Fax: (39) 011 9207772
Email: cristina.borgogno@sonoco-alcore.net
IT Mgr.: Monica Fontana
Phone: (39) 031 429811
Fax: (39) 031 427720
Total Employees of Company: 130
Total Employees at this Location: 58
Mill Locations:
Sonoco Alcore-Demolli srl, Ciriè Mill, Loc. Olivetti 47, Frazione Devesi, IT-10073 Ciriè, (TO), Italy, Capacity: 65,000 mt/y, (Paper mill)
Phone: (39) 011 9225311
Fax: (39) 011 9207772
Email: cvl@demolli.it

ⓘSonoco Alcore-Demolli srl
Ciriè Mill

Ownership: 100% by Sonoco Alcore NV
Loc. Olivetti 47, Frazione Devesi
IT-10073 Ciriè, (TO)
Italy
Phone: (39) 011 9225311
Fax: (39) 011 9207772
Email: cvl@demolli.it
Web Address: www.sonoco.com
Personnel:
Mill Mgr.: Alessandro Castelletti
Phone: (39) 011 9225311
Fax: (39) 011 9207772
Email: alessandro.castelletti@sonoco-alcore.net
Tech. Mgr.: Ing. Massimo Basta
Phone: (39) 011 9225311
Fax: (39) 011 9207772
Email: massimo.basta@sonoco-alcore.net
Total Employees at this Location: 51
Type of Operation: Paper mill
Pulp Grades and Capacities:
Total pulp capacity: 66,354 mt/y
Recycled Pulping: 66,354 mt/y
Paper/Paperboard Grades and Capacities:
Total paper and paperboard capacity: 65,000 mt/y
Boxboard/cartonboard: 65,000 mt/y
Paper and Paperboard Mill Data:
Paper Machines: 1
No. 1, fourdrinier, total capacity 65,000 mt/y, Trim width 2.5 m, Boxboard/cartonboard
Energy Data:
Combustion turbines: 1 at 4.5 MW
Electrical demand for mill: 84 MWh/D

ⓘⓘCartiera S. Stefano Di Sodini Davide & C. SAS
Collodi Mill

Via delle Cartiera 84
51017 Collodi
Italy
Phone: (39) 0572429122
Fax: (39) 0572429722
Email: info@linepaper.it
Web Address: www.cartierasantostefano.it
Personnel:
Mgr.: Elisa Giuliani
Phone: (39) 0572429122
Fax: (39) 0572429722
Email: elisa.giuliani@linepaper.it

Italy

Type of Operation: Paper mill
Paper/Paperboard Grades and Capacities:
Total paper and paperboard capacity: 2,200 mt/y
Packaging papers: 2,200 mt/y
Paper and Paperboard Mill Data:
Paper Machines: 1
No. 1, fourdrinier, total capacity 2,200 mt/y, Trim width 1.2 m, Packaging papers
Finishing Equipment:
Winders

⊕⊛Nuova Cartiera Sordini S.R.L.
Foligno Mill
Via Trinità 2 -Frazione Pale
I-06030 Foligno, (PG)
Italy
 Phone: (39) 0742 660859
 Fax: (39) 0742 661226
 Email: info@nuovacartierasordini.it, nuovacartierasordini@libero.it
Personnel:
 Pres.: Alessandro Sordini
 Phone: (39) 0742 660859
 Mill Mgr.: Ferdinando Allegrini
 Phone: (39) 0742 660859
 Man. Dir.: Giovanni Severi
 Phone: (39) 0742 660859
Total Employees at this Location: 17
Type of Operation: Paper mill
Paper/Paperboard Grades and Capacities:
Total paper and paperboard capacity: 3,000 mt/y
Boxboard/cartonboard: 3,000 mt/y
Paper and Paperboard Mill Data:
Paper Machines: 1
No. 1, fourdrinier, total capacity 3,000 mt/y, Trim width 1.55 m, Boxboard/cartonboard
Energy Data:
Power boilers: 1

⊕⊛Nuove Cartiere di Tivoli S.R.L.
Villa Adriana Mill
Ownership: The Gallotti Group
Strada di Paterno
I-00010 Villa Adriana, (RM)
Italy
Mailing Address: Via Nazionale Tiburtina 156,
I-00010 Villa Adriana, Italy
 Phone: (39) 0774 530808
 Fax: (39) 0774 534118
 Email: gallotticrt@gmail.com
Personnel:
 Owner: Giuseppe Gallotti
 Phone: (39) 0774 530808
 Email: gallotticrt@tiscalinet.it
 Mill Mgr.: Rag. Adriano Giocondi
 Phone: (39) 0774 530808
Total Employees at this Location: 140
Type of Operation: Paper mill
Pulp Grades and Capacities:
Total pulp capacity: 161,468 mt/y
Recycled Pulping: 161,468 mt/y
Pulp Mill Data:
Recycled Fiber Treatment Lines:
Recycled packaging pulping lines: 1
Paper/Paperboard Grades and Capacities:
Total paper and paperboard capacity: 185,000 mt/y
Tissue: 25,000 mt/y
Packaging papers: 20,000 mt/y
Linerboard: 65,000 mt/y
Corrugating medium/fluting: 75,000 mt/y
Paper and Paperboard Mill Data:
Paper Machines: 4
No. 1, fourdrinier, total capacity 30,000 mt/y, Trim width 2.1 m, Packaging papers, Corrugating medium/fluting
No. 2, fourdrinier (2), total capacity 65,000 mt/y, Trim width 2.4 m, Linerboard
No. 3, fourdrinier, total capacity 65,000 mt/y, Trim width 2.5 m, Corrugating medium/fluting

No. 4, crescent former, Yankee dryer, total capacity 25,000 mt/y, Trim width 2.7 m, Tissue
Energy Data:
Power boilers
Combustion turbines: 1 at 11.0 MW
Electrical demand for mill: 276 MWh/D

⊕⊛Tolentino S.r.l.
Tolentino Mill
Ownership: Pro-Gest S.p.A.
Via Borgo Cartiere 20
I-62029 Tolentino, (MC)
Italy
 Phone: (39) 0733 956601
 Fax: (39) 0733 966401
 Email: tolentino@pro-gestspa.it
 Web Address: www.pro-gestspa.it
Personnel:
 Mill Dir.: Mr. Novello Cantolacqua
 Phone: (39) 0733 956601
 Fax: (39) 0733 966401
 Email: novello.cantolacqua@pro-gestspa.it
Total Employees at this Location: 44
Type of Operation: Paper mill, Paperboard mill
Pulp Grades and Capacities:
Total pulp capacity: 150,763 mt/y
Recycled Pulping: 150,763 mt/y
Pulp Mill Data:
Recycled Fiber Treatment Lines:
Recycled packaging pulping lines at 150,000 admt/y
Paper/Paperboard Grades and Capacities:
Total paper and paperboard capacity: 150,000 mt/y
Linerboard: 100,000 mt/y
Corrugating medium/fluting: 50,000 mt/y
Paper and Paperboard Mill Data:
Stock Preparation:
Pulpers: 2
Refiners:
Paper Machines: 1
No. 1, DuoFormer, total capacity 150,000 mt/y, Trim width 3.3 m, Corrugating medium/fluting, Linerboard
Finishing Equipment:
Winders: 2
Energy Data:
Power boilers: 1
Combustion turbines: 1
Steam turbines: 1
Electrical demand for mill: 186 MWh/D

⊕⊛Cartiera Torre Mondovi
Cartiera Torre Mondovi
Ownership: 100% by Ghigliotti Family
Via Bosso, 3
I-12080 Torre Mondovi, (CN)
Italy
 Phone: (39) 0174 329 003
 Fax: (39) 0174 327 900
 Web Address: www.cartieratorremondovi.com
Personnel:
 Man. Dir.: Alberto Ghigliotti
 Phone: (48) 0174 329 003
 Fax: (48) 0174 327 900
Total Employees of Company: 25
Total Employees at this Location: 25
Type of Operation: Paperboard mill
Pulp Grades and Capacities:
Total pulp capacity: 25,534 mt/y
Recycled Pulping: 25,534 mt/y
Pulp Mill Data:
Recycled Fiber Treatment Lines:
Recycled packaging pulping lines: 1
Paper/Paperboard Grades and Capacities:
Total paper and paperboard capacity: 25,000 mt/y
Boxboard/cartonboard: 25,000 mt/y
Paper and Paperboard Mill Data:
Paper Machines: 1
No. 1, fourdrinier, total capacity 25,000 mt/y, Trim width 1.5 m, Boxboard/cartonboard

Energy Data:
Power boilers
Electrical demand for mill: 34 MWh/D

⊕⊛Nuova Cartiera della Toscana SpA
Villa Basilica Mill
Via delle Cartiere 25
I-55019 Villa Basilica, (LU)
Italy
 Phone: (39) 0572 432 81
 Fax: (39) 0572 432 54
 Email: ibarsi@credit.tin.it
Personnel:
 Mill Mgr.: Andrea Barsi
 Phone: (39) 0572 432 81
Total Employees at this Location: 25
Type of Operation: Paper mill
Paper/Paperboard Grades and Capacities:
Total paper and paperboard capacity: 18,000 mt/y
Tissue: 18,000 mt/y
Paper and Paperboard Mill Data:
Paper Machines: 1
No. 1, twin-wire, Yankee dryer, total capacity 18,000 mt/y, Trim width 2.5 m, Tissue
Energy Data:
Power boilers
Electrical demand for mill: 49 MWh/D

⊕⊛Toscopaper SpA
Ponte a Moriano Mill
Via del Brennero 6143
I-55100 Ponte a Moriano, (LU)
Italy
 Phone: (39) 0583 406341
 Fax: (39) 0583 578341
 Email: info@toscopaper.it
Personnel:
 Resp. Secur. & Envir.: Mr. Nicola Toschi
 Phone: (39) 0583 406341
 Fax: (39) 0583 578341
 Email: nicolatoschi@toscopaper.it
Total Employees at this Location: 28
Type of Operation: Paperboard mill
Pulp Grades and Capacities:
Total pulp capacity: 24,914 mt/y
Recycled Pulping: 24,914 mt/y
Pulp Mill Data:
Recycled Fiber Treatment Lines:
Recycled packaging pulping lines
Paper/Paperboard Grades and Capacities:
Total paper and paperboard capacity: 25,000 mt/y
Corrugating medium/fluting: 25,000 mt/y
Paper and Paperboard Mill Data:
Paper Machines: 1
No. 1, fourdrinier, total capacity 25,000 mt/y, Trim width 2.61 m, Corrugating medium/fluting
Energy Data:
Power boilers: 1
Steam turbines: 1 at 2 MW
Electrical demand for mill: 11 MWh/D

⊕⊛Cartiere di Trevi SpA
Trevi Mill
Ownership: 100% by Graziosi family (Private)
Via Clitunno 4
I-06039 Trevi, (PG)
Italy
 Phone: (39) 0742 38511
 Fax: (39) 0742 385130
 Email: contact@cartieredirevi.com
 Web Address: www.cartieredirevi.com
Personnel:
 Pres.: Guido Graziosi
 Phone: (39) 0742 38511
 Fax: (39) 0742 385130
 Email: ggraziosi@cartieredirevi.com
 Commercial Mgr.: Francesco Lusenti
 Phone: (39) 0742 385134
 Fax: (39) 0742 385130

Italy

Email: commerciale@cartiereditrevi.com
Tech. Director (Prod. Dir.): Marco Loreti
Phone: (39) 0742 385191
Fax: (39) 0742 385130
Email: mloreti@cartiereditrevi.com
Purch. Dir.: Franco Graziosi
Phone: (39) 0742 385152
Fax: (39) 0742 385130
Email: acquisti@cartiereditrevi.com
Total Employees of Company: 49
Total Employees at this Location: 49
Type of Operation: Paper mill, Paperboard mill
Pulp Grades and Capacities:
Total pulp capacity: 65,566 mt/y
Recycled Pulping: 65,566 mt/y
Pulp Mill Data:
Recycled Fiber Treatment Lines:
Recycled packaging pulping lines at 65,000
Paper/Paperboard Grades and Capacities:
Total paper and paperboard capacity: 65,000 mt/y
Corrugating medium/fluting: 20,000 mt/y
Boxboard/cartonboard: 45,000 mt/y
Paper and Paperboard Mill Data:
Paper Machines: 1
No. 1, fourdrinier, total capacity 65,000 mt/y, Trim width 2.31 m, Corrugating medium/fluting, Boxboard/cartonboard
Energy Data:
HRSG boiler: 2
Combustion turbines: 2 at 2 MW
Electrical demand for mill: 92 MWh/D

ⓗⓜCartiera Val di Lima S.R.L.
Bagni di Lucca Mill
Via di Renaio 9, Ponte a Serraglio
I-55021 Bagni di Lucca, (LU)
Italy
Phone: (39) 0583 87270
Fax: (39) 0583 867865
Email: valdilima@libero.it
Personnel:
Dir.: Leo Stefani
Phone: (39) 0583 87270
Total Employees at this Location: 14
Type of Operation: Paper mill
Paper/Paperboard Grades and Capacities:
Total paper and paperboard capacity: 7,000 mt/y
Tissue: 7,000 mt/y
Paper and Paperboard Mill Data:
Paper Machines: 1
No. 1, fourdrinier, total capacity 7,000 mt/y, Trim width 2.55 m, Tissue
Energy Data:
Power boilers: 1
Electrical demand for mill: 8 MWh/D

ⓗⓜCartiera del Vignaletto Srl
Santa Maria di Zevio Mill
Ownership: Cartiera di Conselice Srl
Località Tre Ponti 8
I-37050 Santa Maria di Zevio, (VR)
Italy
Phone: (39) 045 606 9014/9005
Fax: (39) 045 606 9116
Email: info@vignaletto.com
Web Address: www.vignaletto.com
Personnel:
Pres. & Mill Mgr.: Mario Lovato
Phone: (39) 045 606 9005
Fax: (39) 045 606 9116
Email: mariol@vignaletto.com
Tech. Mgr.: Claudio Lovato
Phone: (39) 045 606 9005
Fax: (39) 045 606 9116
Email: claudiol@vignaletto.com
Maint. Mgr.: Paolo Lovato
Phone: (39) 045 606 9005
Fax: (39) 045 606 9116
Email: paolol@vignaletto.com

Total Employees of Company: 63
Total Employees at this Location: 63
Type of Operation: Paper mill
Paper/Paperboard Grades and Capacities:
Total paper and paperboard capacity: 41,000 mt/y
Tissue: 41,000 mt/y
Paper and Paperboard Mill Data:
Stock Preparation:
Pulpers: 2
Paper Machines: 2
No. 4, crescent former, Yankee dryer, total capacity 18,000 mt/y, Trim width 2.7 m, Tissue
No. 5, crescent former, Yankee dryer, total capacity 23,000 mt/y, Trim width 2.7 m, Tissue
Energy Data:
Power boilers: 2
Combustion turbines: 1 at 5.5 MW
Electrical demand for mill: 115 MWh/D

ⓜCartiere Villa Lagarina Spa
Trento Mill
Ownership: 100% by Pro-Gest S.p.A.
Via Pesenti 1
I-38060 Trento, (TN)
Italy
Phone: (39) 0464 411511
Fax: (39) 0464 410400
Email: cvl@pro-gestspa.it
Web Address: www.pro-gestspa.it
Personnel:
Mill Mgr.: Mauro Dorigatti
Phone: (39) 0464 411511
Fax: (39) 0464 410400
Email: mauro.dorigatti@pro-gestspa.it
Logist. & Sls. Mgr.: Gianmario Sterni
Phone: (39) 0464 411511
Fax: (39) 0464 410400
Email: gianmario.sterni@pro-gestspa.it
Total Employees at this Location: 220
Type of Operation: Paper mill, Paperboard mill
Pulp Grades and Capacities:
Total pulp capacity: 248,094 mt/y
Recycled Pulping: 248,094 mt/y
Pulp Mill Data:
Recycled Fiber Treatment Lines:
Recycled packaging pulping lines at 300,000 admt/y
Paper/Paperboard Grades and Capacities:
Total paper and paperboard capacity: 285,700 mt/y
Tissue: 35,700 mt/y
Linerboard: 150,000 mt/y
Corrugating medium/fluting: 100,000 mt/y
Paper and Paperboard Mill Data:
Paper Machines: 2
No. 2, twin-wire, total capacity 250,000 mt/y, Trim width 5.25 m, Linerboard, Corrugating medium/fluting
No. 3, crescent former, total capacity 35,700 mt/y, Trim width 2.8 m, Tissue
Finishing Equipment:
Winders
Energy Data:
Power boilers: 1
Combustion turbines: 3 at 7, 7, 7 MW
Steam turbines: 1 at 7 MW
Electrical demand for mill: 361 MWh/D

ⓜWEPA Lucca Srl
Ownership: WEPA Hygieneprodukte GmbH
Localita Salanetti, Frazione Lunata
I-55012 Capannori
Italy
Phone: (39) 0583 448 1
Fax: (39) 0583 448 846
Email: info@wepa.de
Web Address: www.wepa.de, www.wepa-lucca.com
Personnel:
Mgr.: Giulio Marsili
Phone: (39) 0583 448 1
Fax: (39) 0583 448 846

Sls. & Mktg. Dir.: Hector Bermejo
Phone: (39) 0583 448 1
Fax: (39) 0583 448 846
Adm. Mgr.: Annalisa Benetti
Phone: (39) 0583 448 1
Fax: (39) 0583 448 846
Purch. Mgr.: Massimo Serafini
Phone: (39) 0583 448 1
Fax: (39) 0583 448 846
HR Mgr.: Fernando Destri
Phone: (39) 0583 448 1
Fax: (39) 0583 448 846
National Account Mgr.: Francesco Scilio
Phone: (39) 0583 448 1
Fax: (39) 0583 448 846
Total Employees of Company: 500
Mill Locations:
WEPA Lucca Srl, Cassino Mill, Via Contrada Cerasola, 28, I-03043 Cassino, (FR), Italy, Capacity: 55,000 mt/y, (Paper mill)
Phone: (39) 0776 3961
Fax: (39) 0776 302076
Email: info@wepa.de
WEPA Lucca Srl, Fosso Raletta Mill, Via Carlotti, 32, I-55016 Porcari, (LU), Italy, Capacity: 60,000 mt/y, (Paper mill)
Phone: (39) 0583 448399
Fax: (39) 0583 448350
Email: info@wepa.de

ⓜWEPA Lucca Srl
Cassino Mill
Ownership: WEPA Hygieneprodukte GmbH
Via Contrada Cerasola, 28
I-03043 Cassino, (FR)
Italy
Phone: (39) 0776 3961
Fax: (39) 0776 302076
Email: info@wepa.de
Web Address: www.wepa.de
Personnel:
Mill Mgr.: Maurizio Lattanzi
Phone: (39) 0776 396 1
Fax: (39) 0776 302076
Email: maurizio.lattanzi@wepa.de
Total Employees at this Location: 150
Type of Operation: Paper mill
Paper/Paperboard Grades and Capacities:
Total paper and paperboard capacity: 55,000 mt/y
Tissue: 55,000 mt/y
Paper and Paperboard Mill Data:
Paper Machines: 1
No. 1, crescent former, Yankee dryer, total capacity 55,000 mt/y, Trim width 5.4 m, Tissue
Energy Data:
Power boilers: 1
Combustion turbines: 1
Electrical demand for mill: 141 MWh/D

ⓜWEPA Lucca Srl
Fosso Raletta Mill
Ownership: WEPA Hygieneprodukte GmbH
Via Carlotti, 32
I-55016 Porcari, (LU)
Italy
Phone: (39) 0583 448399
Fax: (39) 0583 448350
Email: info@wepa.de
Web Address: www.wepa.de
Personnel:
Plt. Mgr.: Riccardo Consani
Phone: (39) 0583 448399
Fax: (39) 0583 448350
Email: riccardo.consani@wepa-lucca.com
Total Employees at this Location: 75
Type of Operation: Paper mill
Paper/Paperboard Grades and Capacities:
Total paper and paperboard capacity: 60,000 mt/y
Tissue: 60,000 mt/y

Paper and Paperboard Mill Data:
Paper Machines: 2
No. 1, twin-wire, total capacity 29,000 mt/y, Trim width 2.7 m, Tissue
No. 2, twin-wire, total capacity 31,000 mt/y, Trim width 2.7 m, Tissue
Energy Data:
Power boilers: 1
Combustion turbines: 1
Electrical demand for mill: 160 MWh/D

LATVIA

ⓘⓂPapirfabrika Ligatne Ltd.
Ligatne Mill
Ownership: 49.23% by Baltic Investment Fund III L.P., 20.99% by Guntis P?r?gs, 20.99% by Valts Klucis, 8.79% by Netherlands registered the "Baltic Investmment Fund III CV

Pilsonu 1
LV-4110 Ligatne
Latvia
 Phone: (371) 641 533 37
 Fax: (371) 641 533 30
 Email: birojs@pf-ligatne.lv
 Web Address: www.pf-ligatne.lv
Personnel:
 Dir.: Normondes Deserve
 Phone: (371) 64153337
 Email: birojs@pf-ligatne.lv
 Owner: Valts Klucis
 Phone: (371) 2920 7743
 Owner: Gundas Pirak
 Phone: (371) 641 533 37
 Prod. Mgr.: Anna Chernaya
 Phone: (371) 2652 1978
 Tech. Dir.: Gints Stipniks
 Phone: (371) 261 62249
 Sls. Mgr.: Valeris Matyuks
 Phone: (371) 2886 26898
Total Employees of Company: 150
Total Employees at this Location: 85
Type of Operation: Paper mill
Pulp Grades and Capacities:
 Total pulp capacity: 14,118 mt/y
 Recycled Pulping: 14,118 mt/y
Pulp Mill Data:
 Recycled Fiber Treatment Lines:
 Recycled packaging pulping lines: 1
Paper/Paperboard Grades and Capacities:
 Total paper and paperboard capacity: 14,000 mt/y
 Linerboard: 3,000 mt/y
 Corrugating medium/fluting: 1,500 mt/y
 Boxboard/cartonboard: 9,500 mt/y
Paper and Paperboard Mill Data:
 Stock Preparation:
 Pulpers: 3
 Refiners: 3
Paper Machines: 1
No. 1, fourdrinier, total capacity 14,000 mt/y, Trim width 2 m, Boxboard/cartonboard, Linerboard, Corrugating medium/fluting
Energy Data:
Power boilers: 1
Electrical demand for mill: 19 MWh/D

LITHUANIA

ⓘCJSC ESEIRA
Paliuniškio g. 13
LT-38031 Panevezys
Lithuania
 Phone: (370) 370 45 592103, 370 699 99543
 Fax: (370) 370 45 500317
 Email: esveras@mail.lt
 Web Address: www.eseira.lt
Personnel:
 Gen. Dir.: Erlandas Simaitis
 Phone: (370) 45 592103
 Fax: (370) 45 500317
 Email: eseira@delfi.lt
 Paper Prod. Dept. Dir.: Stasys Jencius
 Phone: (370) 45 592103
 Fax: (370) 45 500317
 Mktg. Dept.: Nerijus Keras
 Phone: (370) 45 592103
 Fax: (370) 45 500317
Mill Locations:
CJSC ESEIRA, Panevezys Mill, Paliuniškio g. 13, LT-38031 Panevezys, Lithuania, Capacity: 1,800 mt/y, (Paper mill)
 Phone: (370) 45 592103
 Fax: (370) 45 500317
 Email: esveras@mail.lt

ⓜCJSC ESEIRA
Panevezys Mill
Paliuniškio g. 13
LT-38031 Panevezys
Lithuania
 Phone: (370) 45 592103
 Fax: (370) 45 500317
 Email: esveras@mail.lt
Personnel:
 Gen. Dir.: Erlandas Simaitis
 Phone: (370) 45 592103
 Email: eseira@delfi.lt
 Paper Prod. Dept. Dir.: Stasys Jencius
 Phone: (370) 45 592103
 Mktg. Dept.: Nerijus Keras
 Phone: (370) 45 592103
 Email: nerijus@eseira.lt
Type of Operation: Paper mill
Paper/Paperboard Grades and Capacities:
 Total paper and paperboard capacity: 1,800 mt/y
 Tissue: 1,800 mt/y
Paper and Paperboard Mill Data:
Paper Machines: 1
PM 1, Yankee dryer, total capacity 1,800 mt/y, Trim width 1.7 m, Tissue
Finishing Equipment:
 Rewinders: 2
Energy Data:
Power boilers: 1

ⓘⓂJSC Grigiskes
Vilnius Mill
Ownership: 100% by private owners
Vilniaus 10, Grigiskes
LT-27101 Vilnius
Lithuania
 Phone: (370) 5 243 5801
 Fax: (370) 5 243 5802
 Email: info@grigiskes.lt
 Web Address: www.grigiskes.lt, www.grite.lt
Personnel:
 Pres.: Gintautas Pangonis
 Phone: (370) 5 2 435 800
 Fax: (370) 5 2 435 802
 Email: gintautas.pangonis@grigiskes.lt
 VP., Bus. Develop.: Vigmantas Kažukauskas
 Phone: (370) 5 243 5933
 Fax: (370) 5 243 5802
 Email: vigmantas.kazukauskas@grigiskes.lt
 VP., Purch. & Logist.: Vytautas Juška
 Phone: (370) 5 243 5901
 Fax: (370) 5 243 5802
 Email: vytautas.juska@grigiskes.lt
 VP., Finan.: Nina Sileriene
 Phone: (370) 5 243 5801
 Fax: (370) 5 2435903
 Email: nina.sileriene@grigiskes.lt
 Sls. Dir.: Sarunas Luksys
 Phone: (370) 5 2435989
 Fax: (370) 5 2435850
 Email: sarunas.luksys@grigiskes.lt
 HR Dir.: Edita Vilkiene
 Phone: (370) 5 2435811
 Fax: (370) 5 2435802
 Email: edita.vilkiene@grigiskes.lt
Total Employees of Company: 440
Total Employees at this Location: 270
Type of Operation: Paper mill
Mill Locations:
Klaipedos Kartonas, Klaipeda Mill, Nemuno 2, LT-91199 Klaipeda, Lithuania, Capacity: 100,000 mt/y, (Pulp mill, Paperboard mill)
 Phone: (370) 46 395601
 Fax: (370) 46 395600
 Email: info@kartonas.lt
Pulp Grades and Capacities:
 Total pulp capacity: 20,122 mt/y
 Recycled Pulping: 20,122 mt/y
Pulp Mill Data:
 Chemical Recovery Equipment:
 Recovery boilers
Paper/Paperboard Grades and Capacities:
 Total paper and paperboard capacity: 25,000 mt/y
 Tissue: 25,000 mt/y
Paper and Paperboard Mill Data:
 Stock Preparation:
 Pulpers: 6
 Refiners: 2
Paper Machines: 3
No. 2, fourdrinier, Yankee dryer, total capacity 4,000 mt/y, Trim width 2.2 m, Tissue
No. 3, fourdrinier, Yankee dryer, total capacity 4,000 mt/y, Trim width 2.2 m, Tissue
No. 5, crescent former, Yankee dryer, total capacity 17,000 mt/y, Trim width 2.7 m, Tissue
Finishing Equipment:
 Rewinders: 4
Energy Data:
Power boilers: 2
Steam turbines: 2 at 5.0 MW
Electrical demand for mill: 74 MWh/D

ⓜKlaipedos Kartonas
Klaipeda Mill
Ownership: JSC Grigiskes
Nemuno 2
LT-91199 Klaipeda
Lithuania
 Phone: (370) 46 395601
 Fax: (370) 46 395600
 Email: info@kartonas.lt
 Web Address: www.kartonas.lt
Personnel:
 Member of the Board: Arūnas Pasvenskas
 Phone: (370) 46 395607
 Fax: (370) 46 395600
 Email: a.pasvenskas@kartonas.lt
 Man. Dir.: Vidas Berzonskis
 Phone: (370) 46 395608
 Fax: (370) 46 395600
 Email: v.berzonskis@kartonas.lt
 Sls. Dir.: Gitana Sersnioviene
 Phone: (370) 46 395620/65691931
 Fax: (370) 46 395637
 Email: g.sersnioviene@kartonas.lt
 Deputy Tech. Dir.: Rimantas Bieliauskas
 Phone: (370) 46 395662
 Fax: (370) 46 395600
 Email: r.bieliauskas@kartonas.lt
Total Employees at this Location: 194
Type of Operation: Pulp mill, Paperboard mill
Pulp Grades and Capacities:
 Total pulp capacity: 100,693 mt/y
 Recycled Pulping: 100,693 mt/y
Pulp Mill Data:
 Mechanical Pulping Systems:

Macedonia

Conventional grinders
Recycled Fiber Treatment Lines:
 Pulpers: 3 at 120,000 admt/y
Paper/Paperboard Grades and Capacities:
 Total paper and paperboard capacity: 100,000 mt/y
 Linerboard: 55,000 mt/y
 Corrugating medium/fluting: 45,000 mt/y
Paper and Paperboard Mill Data:
 Stock Preparation:
 Pulpers: 3
 Refiners: 6
Paper Machines: 1
 No. 3, Inverformer, total capacity 100,000 mt/y, Trim width 4.2 m, Linerboard, Corrugating medium/fluting
Finishing Equipment:
 Rewinders: 4
Energy Data:
 Power boilers: 2
 Electrical demand for mill: 148 MWh/D

MACEDONIA

Ⓗ Ⓜ Hartija Ko DOO
Kochani Mill
Ownership: 100% by Aleksprom
29. Noemvri 36
MA-2030 Kochani
Macedonia
 Phone: (389) 33 278 181/185
 Fax: (389) 33 278 181/185
 Email: contact@hartijako.com.mk,
 aleksprom@mt.net.mk,
 hartijako@yahoo.com
Personnel:
 Gen. Mgr.: Alexander Markovic
 Phone: (389) 22 551 588
 Paper Mill Mgr.: Kiril Ivanov
 Phone: (389) 33 278 181/185
 Maint. Mgr.: Oliver Tasov
 Phone: (389) 33 278 181/185
Total Employees at this Location: 120
Type of Operation: Pulp mill, Paper mill
Pulp Grades and Capacities:
 Total pulp capacity: 13,500 mt/y
 Chemical Pulp: 7,500 mt/y
Pulp Mill Data:
 Chemical Pulping Systems:
 Batch digesters: 1
 Bleach Plant Systems: 1
Paper/Paperboard Grades and Capacities:
 Total paper and paperboard capacity: 16,000 mt/y
 Uncoated woodfree/freesheet: 16,000 mt/y
Paper and Paperboard Mill Data:
 Stock Preparation:
 Pulpers: 2
 Refiners: 3
Paper Machines: 1
 PM 1, fourdrinier, total capacity 16,000 mt/y, Trim width 2.57 m, Uncoated woodfree/freesheet
Finishing Equipment:
 Calenders
 Supercalenders: 1
 Rewinders: 1
 Sheeters: 1
Energy Data:
 Power boilers: 1

NETHERLANDS

Ⓜ Arjowiggins Security B.V
Ugchelen Mill
Ownership: Arjowiggins SAS
Hoenderloseweg 84
NL-7339 GJ Ugchelen
Netherlands
Mailing Address: Postb. 648, NL-7300 AP Apeldoorn, Netherlands
 Phone: (31) 55 533 2132
 Fax: (31) 55 533 6689
 Web Address: www.security.arjowiggins.com
Personnel:
 Mill Mgr., Prod. Mgr.: H. van de Kamp
 Phone: (31) 55 533 2132
 Fax: (31) 55 533 6689
 Logistics Mgr.: Mrs. Margreet H. Weenink-Keus
 Phone: (31) 55 533 2132
 Fax: (31) 55 533 6689
 Maint. & ICT Manager: Ton Reinten
 Phone: (31) 55 533 2132
 Fax: (31) 55 533 6689
 Email: ton.reinten@arjowiggins.com
 Safety & Qlty. Mgr.: Henk Baas
 Phone: (31) 55 533 2132
 Fax: (31) 55 533 6689
 Email: henk.baas@arjowiggins.com
 Technology & QHSE Mgr.: Duward Sikkens
 Phone: (31) 55 533 2132
 Fax: (31) 55 533 6689
 Email: duward.sikkens@arjowiggins.com
 Supply Chain: Wendy Oostenbrugge
 Phone: (31) 55 533 2132
 Fax: (31) 55 533 6689
 Email: wendy.oostenbrugge@arjowiggins.com
Total Employees at this Location: 150
Type of Operation: Paper mill
Pulp Grades and Capacities:
Paper/Paperboard Grades and Capacities:
 Total paper and paperboard capacity: 5,000 mt/y
 Uncoated woodfree/freesheet: 5,000 mt/y
Paper and Paperboard Mill Data:
Paper Machines: 2
 No. 1, cylinder mould, Trim width 1.6 m, Uncoated woodfree/freesheet
 No. 2, cylinder mould, Trim width 2.5 m, Uncoated woodfree/freesheet

Ⓗ Ⓜ Coldenhove Papier
Eerbeek Mill
Ownership: Family-owned (Private)
D.W. van Vreeswijklaan 9
NL-6961 LG Eerbeek
Netherlands
Mailing Address: P.O.Box 6, NL-6960 AA Eerbeek, Netherlands
 Phone: (31) 313 670 670
 Fax: (31) 313 670 680
 Email: info@coldenhove.com
 Web Address: www.coldenhove.com
Personnel:
 Man. Dir.: K. Herder
 Phone: (31) 313 670 635
 Fax: (31) 313 670 680
 Key Account Mgr.: Hans Huiskamp
 Phone: (31) 313 670 670
 Fax: (31) 313 670 680
 Email: hans.huiskamp@coldenhove.com
 Innovation & Develpt. Mgr.: Ron Sportel
 Phone: (31) 313 670 656
 Fax: (31) 313 670 680
 Email: ron.sportel@coldenhove.com
 Sls. & Mktg. Mgr.: Hans Kiewiet
 Phone: (31) 313 670 641
 Fax: (31) 313 670 680
 Email: hans.kiewiet@coldenhove.com
Total Employees of Company: 130
Total Employees at this Location: 130
Type of Operation: Paper mill, Paperboard mill
Pulp Grades and Capacities:
 Total pulp capacity: 8,429 mt/y
 Recycled Pulping: 8,429 mt/y
Pulp Mill Data:
 Recycled Fiber Treatment Lines:
 Pulpers: 1 at 9,520
Paper/Paperboard Grades and Capacities:
 Total paper and paperboard capacity: 30,000 mt/y
 Uncoated woodfree/freesheet: 10,000 mt/y
 Packaging papers: 5,000 mt/y
 Boxboard/cartonboard: 15,000 mt/y
Paper and Paperboard Mill Data:
 Stock Preparation:
 Pulpers:
Paper Machines: 2
 No. 1, fourdrinier, total capacity 15,000 mt/y, Trim width 2.5 m, Boxboard/cartonboard
 No. 2, fourdrinier, total capacity 15,000 mt/y, Trim width 3.5 m, Uncoated woodfree/freesheet, Packaging papers
Coating Machines: 1
 No. 1, on machine
Finishing Equipment:
 Winders: 2
 Rewinders: 5
 Sheeters: 2
Energy Data:
 Power boilers
 Combustion turbines: 1
 Electrical demand for mill: 41 MWh/D

Ⓗ Ⓜ Crown Van Gelder NV
Velsen-Noord Mill
Company is for sale (Private investor group Andlinger have made a recommended all-cash full public offer to acquire Crown Van Gelder. The Offer is intended to be settled in the second quarter of 2015.)
Eendrachtsstraat 30, Postb. 30
NL-1950 AA Velsen-Noord
Netherlands
 Phone: (31) 251 262 270
 Fax: (31) 251 221 399
 Email: info@cvg.nl
 Web Address: www.cvg.nl
Personnel:
 CEO: Miklas Dronkers
 Phone: (31) 251 262 270
 Fax: (31) 251 221 399
 Supply Chain Mgr.: Gea Kortekaas
 Phone: (31) 251 262 270
 Fax: (31) 251 221 399
 snr. Buyer: Jos de Vries
 Phone: (31) 251 262 227
 Fax: (31) 251 221 399
 Email: jos.de.vries@cvg.nl
 Area Manager Benelux, Sls. Mgr.: Sylvo van den Broek
 Phone: (31) 251 262 212
 Fax: (31) 251 262 398
 Sls & Mktng. Dir: Hans Ekelmans
 Phone: (31) 251 262 270
 Fax: (31) 251 221 399
Total Employees of Company: 280
Type of Operation: Paper mill
Paper/Paperboard Grades and Capacities:
 Total paper and paperboard capacity: 225,000 mt/y
 Uncoated woodfree/freesheet: 225,000 mt/y
Paper and Paperboard Mill Data:
 Stock Preparation:
 Pulpers: 4
 Refiners: 10
Paper Machines: 2
 No. 1, DuoFormer D, total capacity 90,000 mt/y, Trim width 3.6 m, Uncoated woodfree/freesheet
 No. 2, DuoFormer D, total capacity 135,000 mt/y, Trim width 4.8 m, Uncoated woodfree/freesheet
Coating Machines: 2
 No. 1, on machine
 No. 2, on machine
Finishing Equipment:
 Rewinders: 2
Energy Data:
 Power boilers: 1
 Combustion turbines: 1 at 21 MW
 Steam turbines: 1 at 7 MW
 Electrical demand for mill: 436 MWh/D

Netherlands

ⓘPapierfabriek Doetinchem BV
Ownership: 100% by Papier-Mettler Group
Terborgseweg 52
NL-7005 BB Doetinchem
Netherlands
Mailing Address: Postb. 42, NL-7000 AA Doetinchem, Netherlands
Phone: (31) 314 347 911
Fax: (31) 314 347 611/711
Email: info@papierfabriekdoetinchem.nl
Web Address: www.papierfabriekdoetinchem.nl
Personnel:
Man. Dir.: G. W. Broens
Phone: (31) 314 347 911
Fax: (31) 314 347 611/711
Finan. Dir.: B. Broens
Phone: (31) 314 347 911
Fax: (31) 314 347 611/711
Commer. Dir.: Hans de Heus
Phone: (31) 314 347 911
Fax: (31) 314 347 611/711
Email: hans.de.heus@papierfabriekdoetinchem.nl
Tech. Mgr.: Klaas Knol
Phone: (31) 314 347 911
Fax: (31) 314 347 611/711
HR Exec.: Simone Wenneker
Phone: (31) 314 347 911
Fax: (31) 314 347 611/711
Email: simone.wenneker@papierfabriekdoetinchem.nl
Bus. Analyst: Jaap Buijs
Phone: (31) 314 347 911
Fax: (31) 314 347 611/711
Total Employees of Company: 150
Mill Locations:
Papierfabriek Doetinchem BV, Doetinchem Mill, Terborgseweg 52, NL-7005 BB Doetinchem, Netherlands, Capacity: 72,000 mt/y, (Paper mill)
Phone: (31) 314 347 911
Fax: (31) 314 347 611/711
Email: info@papierfabriekdoetinchem.nl

ⓜPapierfabriek Doetinchem BV
Doetinchem Mill
Terborgseweg 52
NL-7005 BB Doetinchem
Netherlands
Mailing Address: Postb. 42, NL-7000 AA Doetinchem, Netherlands
Phone: (31) 314 347 911
Fax: (31) 314 347 611/711
Email: info@papierfabriekdoetinchem.nl
Web Address: www.papierfabriekdoetinchem.nl
Personnel:
Advisor: G. Wim Broens
Phone: (31) 314 347 911
Fax: (31) 314 347 611
Email: w.broens@wrij.nl
Oper. Dir.: B. G. Broens
Phone: (31) 314 347 911
Fax: (31) 314 347 611
Commercial Director: Hans de Heus
Phone: (31) 314 347 911
Fax: (31) 314 347 611
Email: hans.de.heus@papierfabriekdoetinchem.nl
Tech. Mgr.: Klaas Knol
Phone: (31) 314 347 911
Fax: (31) 314 347 611
Email: klaas.knol@papierfabriekdoetinchem.nl
Total Employees at this Location: 150
Type of Operation: Paper mill
Pulp Grades and Capacities:
Total pulp capacity: 76,143 mt/y
Recycled Pulping: 76,143 mt/y
Pulp Mill Data:
Recycled Fiber Treatment Lines:
Pulpers: 1 at 15,100
Pulpers: 1 at 86,100
Paper/Paperboard Grades and Capacities:
Total paper and paperboard capacity: 72,000 mt/y
Tissue: 10,000 mt/y
Packaging papers: 62,000 mt/y
Paper and Paperboard Mill Data:
Stock Preparation:
Pulpers: 5
Paper Machines: 4
No. 1, fourdrinier, Yankee dryer, total capacity 10,000 mt/y, Trim width 1.74 m, Tissue
No. 2, fourdrinier, Yankee dryer, total capacity 13,000 mt/y, Trim width 2.2 m, Packaging papers
No. 3, fourdrinier, Yankee dryer, total capacity 19,000 mt/y, Trim width 2.6 m, Packaging papers
No. 4, fourdrinier, Yankee dryer, total capacity 30,000 mt/y, Trim width 3.4 m, Packaging papers
Finishing Equipment:
Rewinders: 5
Sheeters: 2
Energy Data:
Power boilers: 3
Combustion turbines: 1 at 4.0 MW
Electrical demand for mill: 141 MWh/D

ⓘⓜDS Smith Packaging Benelux B.V.
Eerbeek Mill
Ownership: 100% by DS Smith Plc
Harderwijkerweg 41
NL-6961 GH Eerbeek
Netherlands
Mailing Address: Postb. 96, NL-6960 AB Eerbeek, Netherlands
Phone: (31) 313 677 922
Fax: (31) 313 654 745
Email: info@dssmith.com
Web Address: www.dssmith.com
Personnel:
Man. Dir.: Henk Lingbeek
Phone: (31) 313 677 500
Fax: (31) 313 654 745
Email: henk.lingbeek@dssmith.eu
Purch. & Logist. Mgr.: Alex Zweekhorst
Phone: (31) 313 677 592
Fax: (31) 313 654 745
Email: alex.zweekhorst@dssmith.eu
Oper Mgr. - Maint.: Willy Vonk
Phone: (31) 313 677 505
Fax: (31) 313 677 927
Email: willy.vonk@dssmith.eu
Total Employees of Company: 49,531
Total Employees at this Location: 215
Type of Operation: Paper mill, Paperboard mill
Pulp Grades and Capacities:
Total pulp capacity: 356,220 mt/y
Recycled Pulping: 356,220 mt/y
Pulp Mill Data:
Recycled Fiber Treatment Lines:
Pulpers: 3 at 385,000 admt/y
Paper/Paperboard Grades and Capacities:
Total paper and paperboard capacity: 355,000 mt/y
Linerboard: 255,000 mt/y
Corrugating medium/fluting: 100,000 mt/y
Paper and Paperboard Mill Data:
Stock Preparation:
Refiners: 2
Paper Machines: 2
No. 4, (PM4 single-ply Fourdrinier machine), fourdrinier, total capacity 100,000 mt/y, Trim width 4.6 m, Corrugating medium/fluting
No. 5, (PM5 triple-ply Gapformer - Fourdrinier machine), GapFormer, total capacity 255,000 mt/y, Trim width 4.6 m, Linerboard
Finishing Equipment:
Winders: 2
Energy Data:
Power boilers: 3
Combustion turbines: 2 at 50 MW
Steam turbines: 1 at 25 MW
Electrical demand for mill: 390 MWh/D

ⓜEska Graphic Board BV
Hoogezand Mill
M. Veningastraat 114-116
NL-9601 KJ Hoogezand
Netherlands
Mailing Address: P.O. Box 90, NL-9610 AB Sappemeer, Netherlands
Phone: (31) 598 318911
Fax: (31) 598 396627
Email: sales@eskagraphicboard.com
Web Address: www.eskagraphicboard.com
Personnel:
CEO: Kees van Zijderveld
Phone: (31) 598 318911
CFO: Henk Steenwijk
Phone: (31) 598 318911
Mgr. Tech. Operations: Rene Zwaan
Phone: (31) 598 318911
Commer. Dir.: Gert van der Veen
Phone: (31) 598 318911
HR Mgr.: Femmie Slomp
Phone: (31) 598 318911
Mgr. Logistics: Gert van der Wenden
Phone: (31) 598 318911
Commun. Mgr.: Ms. Gea Voort
Phone: (31) 598 318911
Fax: (31) 598 396627
Email: g.voort@eskagraphicboard.com
Total Employees at this Location: 200
Type of Operation: Pulp mill, Paper mill, Paperboard mill
Pulp Grades and Capacities:
Total pulp capacity: 166,516 mt/y
Recycled Pulping: 166,516 mt/y
Pulp Mill Data:
Recycled Fiber Treatment Lines:
Recycled packaging pulping lines: 1 at 150,000 admt/y
Paper/Paperboard Grades and Capacities:
Total paper and paperboard capacity: 160,000 mt/y
Boxboard/cartonboard: 160,000 mt/y
Paper and Paperboard Mill Data:
Stock Preparation:
Pulpers: 1
Paper Machines: 2
No. 7, fourdrinier, total capacity 80,000 mt/y, Trim width 2.8 m, Boxboard/cartonboard
No. 8, fourdrinier, total capacity 80,000 mt/y, Trim width 2.8 m, Boxboard/cartonboard
Energy Data:
Power boilers: 2
Combustion turbines: 2 at 7.5 MW
Electrical demand for mill: 155 MWh/D

ⓘⓜEska Graphic Board BV
Sappemeer Mill
Ownership: 100% by Andlinger & Company
Noorderstraat 394
9611 AW Sappemeer
Netherlands
Mailing Address: Postb. 90, NL-9611 AW Sappemeer, Netherlands
Phone: (31) 598 318911
Fax: (31) 598 396627
Email: sales@eskagraphicboard.com
Web Address: www.eskagraphicboard.com
Personnel:
CEO: Kees van Zijderveld
Phone: (31) 598 318911
Fax: (31) 598 396627
Email: k.vanzijderveld@eskagraphicboard.com
CFO: Henk Steenwijk
Phone: (31) 598 318911
Fax: (31) 598 396627
Email: h.steenwijk@eskagraphicboard.com
HR Mgr.: Femmie Slomp
Phone: (31) 598 318911
Fax: (31) 598 396627
Email: f.slomp@eskagraphicboard.com

Netherlands

Mgr. Logistics: Gert van der Wenden
Phone: (31) 598 318911
Fax: (31) 598 396627
Email: g.vanderwenden@eskagraphicboard.com
Mgr. Tech. Oper.: René W. Zwaan
Phone: (31) 598 318911
Fax: (31) 598 396627
Email: r.zwaan@eskagraphicboard.com
Commer. Dir.: Gert Van der Veen
Phone: (31) 598 318911
Fax: (31) 598 396627
Email: g.vanderveen@eskagraphicboard.com
Comm. Mgr.: Gea Voort
Phone: (31) 598 318911
Fax: (31) 598 396627
Email: g.voort@eskagraphicboard.com
Total Employees of Company: 450
Total Employees at this Location: 200
Type of Operation: Pulp mill, Paperboard mill
Mill Locations:
Eska Graphic Board BV, Hoogezand Mill, M. Veningastraat 114-116, NL-9601 KJ Hoogezand, Netherlands, Capacity: 160,000 mt/y, (Pulp mill, Paper mill, Paperboard mill)
Phone: (31) 598 318911
Fax: (31) 598 396627
Email: sales@eskagraphicboard.com
Pulp Grades and Capacities:
Total pulp capacity: 146,336 mt/y
Recycled Pulping: 146,336 mt/y
Pulp Mill Data:
Recycled Fiber Treatment Lines:
Recycled packaging pulping lines: 1 at 216,000 admt/y
Paper/Paperboard Grades and Capacities:
Total paper and paperboard capacity: 140,000 mt/y
Boxboard/cartonboard: 140,000 mt/y
Paper and Paperboard Mill Data:
Stock Preparation:
Pulpers: 2
Paper Machines: 3
No. 1, twin-wire, total capacity 35,000 mt/y, Trim width 2.8 m, Boxboard/cartonboard
No. 2, twin-wire, total capacity 35,000 mt/y, Trim width 2.8 m, Boxboard/cartonboard
No. 8, fourdrinier, total capacity 70,000 mt/y, Trim width 2.8 m, Boxboard/cartonboard
Energy Data:
Power boilers: 1
Combustion turbines: 1
Electrical demand for mill: 127 MWh/D

ⓘ Innovio Papers
Ownership: 100% by American Industrial Acquisition Corporation ("AIAC")
Ambachtsweg 2
NL-6541 DB Nijmegen
Netherlands
Phone: (31) 24 371 0911
Fax: (31) 24 371 0746
Total Employees of Company: 192
Total Employees at this Location: 192
Mill Locations:
Innovio Papers, Nijmegen Mill, Ambachtsweg 2, NL-6541 DB Nijmegen, Netherlands, Capacity: 240,000 mt/y, (Paper mill)
Phone: (31) 24 371 0911
Fax: (31) 24 371 0746

ⓘⓜ Innovio Papers
Nijmegen Mill
Ambachtsweg 2
NL-6541 DB Nijmegen
Netherlands
Mailing Address: PO Box 4, NL-6500 AA Nijmegen, Netherlands
Phone: (31) 24 371 0911
Fax: (31) 24 371 0746
Personnel:
Mill Dir.: Wayne Thomas
Phone: (31) 24 371 0600
Fax: (31) 24 371 0840
Email: wayne.thomas@innoviopapers.com
Process & Technology Mgr.: Cees van Esch
Phone: (31) 24 371 0634
Fax: (31) 24 371 0785
Email: cees.vanesch@innoviopapers.com
Prod. Mgr.: Rene van Wieringen
Phone: (31) 24 371 0911
Fax: (31) 24 371 0746
Commun. Mgr.: Ellen Bouwmeester
Phone: (31) 24 371 0601
Fax: (31) 24 371 0840
Email: ellen.bouwmeester@innoviopapers.com
Total Employees at this Location: 192
Type of Operation: Paper mill
Paper/Paperboard Grades and Capacities:
Total paper and paperboard capacity: 240,000 mt/y
Coated woodfree/freesheet: 240,000 mt/y
Paper and Paperboard Mill Data:
Stock Preparation:
Pulpers: 2
Refiners: 7
Paper Machines: 1
No. 7, Bel-Form, total capacity 240,000 mt/y, Trim width 4.9 m, Coated woodfree/freesheet
Coating Machines: 1
PM 7, total capacity 240,000 mt/y, on machine
Finishing Equipment:
Supercalenders: 2 at 200,000 mt/y
Rewinders: 1 at 300,000 mt/y
Energy Data:
Power boilers: 4
Combustion turbines: 1 at 5.0 MW
Steam turbines: 1 at 10.0 MW
Electrical demand for mill: 421 MWh/D

ⓜ Mayr-Melnhof Eerbeek BV
Eerbeek Mill
Ownership: Mayr-Melnhof Karton AG
Coldenhovenseweg 12
NL-6961 ED Eerbeek
Netherlands
Mailing Address: Postb. 3, NL-6960 AA Eerbeek, Netherlands
Phone: (31) 313 675 111
Fax: (31) 313 654 777
Email: sales.eerbeek@mm-karton.com
Web Address: www.mm-karton.com
Personnel:
Man. Dir.: Dipl. Eng. Helmut Payer
Phone: (31) 313 675 111
Mill Mgr.: A. Steinkellner
Phone: (31) 313 675 111
Email: august.steinkellner@mm-karton.com
Chief Eng.: Mr Jonker
Phone: (31) 313 675 111
Env. Mgr.: Mr. Tripp
Phone: (31) 313 675 111
Mill Service Manager: Herman Van den Nieuwendijk
Phone: (31) 313 675 111
Total Employees at this Location: 170
Type of Operation: Pulp mill, Paperboard mill
Pulp Grades and Capacities:
Total pulp capacity: 86,052 mt/y
Mechanical Pulp: 34,678 mt/y
Recycled Pulping: 51,374 mt/y
Pulp Mill Data:
Mechanical Pulping Systems:
RMP systems: 1
Bleach Plant Systems: 1
Recycled DIP Pulping System
Recycled Fiber Treatment Lines:
Pulpers: 1 at 62,300
Paper/Paperboard Grades and Capacities:
Total paper and paperboard capacity: 140,000 mt/y
Boxboard/cartonboard: 140,000 mt/y
Paper and Paperboard Mill Data:
Stock Preparation:
Pulpers: 4
Refiners: 10
Paper Machines: 1
No. 3, fourdrinier (3), total capacity 140,000 mt/y, Trim width 3.26 m, Boxboard/cartonboard
Coating Machines: 3
BM 3, total capacity 120,000 mt/y., on machine
No. 2
No. 3
Finishing Equipment:
Winders: 1 at 120,000 mt/y
Sheeters: 2 at 120,000 mt/y
Energy Data:
Power boilers: 2
Combustion turbines: 1 at 5.5 MW
Steam turbines: 1 at 4 MW
Electrical demand for mill: 314 MWh/D

ⓘⓜ Meerssen Papier BV
Meerssen Mill
Weert 78
NL-6231 SB Meerssen
Netherlands
Mailing Address: PO Box 2, NL-6230 AA Meerssen, Netherlands
Phone: (31) 43 3663500
Fax: (31) 43 3663501
Email: info@meerssen-papier.com
Web Address: www.meerssen-papier.com
Personnel:
Man. Dir.: Jack Giesen
Phone: (31) 43 3663434
Fax: (31) 43 3663501
Email: jack.giesen@meerssen-papier.com
Total Employees of Company: 71
Total Employees at this Location: 71
Type of Operation: Paper mill
Pulp Grades and Capacities:
Total pulp capacity: 3,225 mt/y
Recycled Pulping: 3,225 mt/y
Paper/Paperboard Grades and Capacities:
Total paper and paperboard capacity: 35,000 mt/y
Uncoated woodfree/freesheet: 35,000 mt/y
Paper and Paperboard Mill Data:
Paper Machines: 3
No. 2, fourdrinier, total capacity 11,500 mt/y, Trim width 2.1 m, Uncoated woodfree/freesheet
No. 3, fourdrinier, total capacity 11,500 mt/y, Trim width 2.1 m, Uncoated woodfree/freesheet
No. 4, fourdrinier, total capacity 12,000 mt/y, Trim width 2.01 m, Uncoated woodfree/freesheet
Finishing Equipment:
Supercalenders: 1
Rewinders: 3
Sheeters: 3
Energy Data:
Power boilers: 1
Steam turbines: 1
Electrical demand for mill: 55 MWh/D

ⓘ Parenco B.V.
Ownership: 100% by H2 Equity Partners
Industrieterrein Veerweg 1
NL-6871 AV Renkum
Netherlands
Phone: (31) 31 736 1911
Fax: (31) 31 731 7645
Email: info@parenco.com
Web Address: www.parenco.com
Personnel:
CEO: Geert Wassens
Phone: (31) 31 736 1911
Fax: (31) 31 731 7645
Gen. Mgr.: Kees Bleeker
Phone: (31) 31 736 1911
Fax: (31) 31 731 7645
Oper. Mgr.: Yan Vassart
Phone: (31) 31 736 1911
Fax: (31) 31 731 7645

Netherlands

Mktg. & Sls. Dir.: Marleen van den Berg
Phone: (31) 31 736 1911
Fax: (31) 31 731 7645
Supply & Logist. Dir.: Raymond Jolink
Phone: (31) 31 736 1911
Fax: (31) 31 731 7645
Finan. & IT Dir.: Comelis Feiter
Phone: (31) 31 736 1911
Fax: (31) 31 731 7645
Bus. Develop. Mgr.: Joris Spaan
Phone: (31) 31 736 1911
Fax: (31) 31 731 7645
HR. Mgr. & Gen. Serv.: Wim Steijven
Phone: (31) 31 736 1911
Fax: (31) 31 731 7645
Office Mgr.: Sabine Broekman
Phone: (31) 31 736 1911
Fax: (31) 31 731 7645
Total Employees of Company: 265
Mill Locations:
Parenco B.V., Renkum Mill, Industrieterrein Veerweg 1, NL-6871 AV Renkum, Netherlands, Capacity: 265,000 mt/y, (Pulp mill, Paper mill)
Phone: (31) 31 736 1911
Fax: (31) 31 731 7645
Email: info@parenco.com

ⓜParenco B.V.
Renkum Mill
Previously Norske Skog Parenco B.V.
Industrieterrein Veerweg 1
NL-6871 AV Renkum
Netherlands
Phone: (31) 31 736 1911
Fax: (31) 31 731 7645
Email: info@parenco.com
Web Address: www.parenco.com
Personnel:
CEO: Geert Wassens
Phone: (31) 31 736 1911
Fax: (31) 31 731 7645
Gen. Mgr.: Kees Bleeker
Phone: (31) 31 736 1911
Fax: (31) 31 731 7645
Oper. Mgr.: Yan Vassart
Phone: (31) 31 736 1911
Fax: (31) 31 731 7645
Mktg. & Sls. Dir.: Marleen van den Berg
Phone: (31) 31 736 1911
Fax: (31) 31 731 7645
Supply & Logist. Dir.: Raymond Jolink
Phone: (31) 31 736 1911
Fax: (31) 31 731 7645
Finan. & IT Dir.: Comelis Feiter
Phone: (31) 31 736 1911
Fax: (31) 31 731 7645
HR. Mgr. & Gen. Serv.: Wim Steijven
Phone: (31) 31 736 1911
Fax: (31) 31 731 7645
Office Mgr.: Sabine Broekman
Phone: (31) 31 736 1911
Fax: (31) 31 731 7645
Total Employees at this Location: 243
Type of Operation: Pulp mill, Paper mill
Pulp Grades and Capacities:
Total pulp capacity: 262,711 mt/y
Recycled Pulping: 262,711 mt/y
Pulp Mill Data:
Bleach Plant Systems: 2
DIP4, Type: Oxydative, Sequence: P, Capacity 110,000 admt/y
DIP6, Type: Oxydative, Sequence: P, Capacity 190,000 admt/y
Recycled Fiber Treatment Lines:
Flotation deinking lines: 2 at 300,000 admt/y
Pulpers: 2 at 300,000 admt/y
Paper/Paperboard Grades and Capacities:
Total paper and paperboard capacity: 265,000 mt/y
Uncoated mechanical/groundwood: 265,000 mt/y
Paper and Paperboard Mill Data:
Paper Machines: 1
No. 1, DuoFormer CFD, total capacity 265,000 mt/y, Trim width 8.4 m, Uncoated mechanical/groundwood
Finishing Equipment:
Winders: 2 at 270,000 mt/y
Calenders: 2
Energy Data:
Power boilers: 3
Combustion turbines: 1 at 24.0 MW
Steam turbines: 1 at 16.0 MW
Electrical demand for mill: 807 MWh/D

ⓜSappi Fine Paper Europe
Maastricht Mill
Ownership: 100% by Sappi Limited
Biesenweg 16
NL-6211 AA Maastricht
Netherlands
Phone: (31) 43 382 22 22
Fax: (31) 43 382 27 31
Email: maastricht.mill@sappi.com
Web Address: www.sappi.com
Personnel:
Mill Dir.: Peter Loubele
Phone: (31) 43 382 22 22
Fax: (31) 43 382 27 31
Email: peter.loubele@sappi.com
Safety Mgr.: Harrie Nievergeld
Phone: (31) 43 382 22 22
Fax: (31) 43 382 27 31
Email: harrie.nievergeld@sappi.com
Sheet Finishing & Logist. Mgr.: Veenerick Luijten
Phone: (31) 43 382 23 55
Fax: (31) 43 382 27 31
Email: veenerick.luijten@sappi.com
Mill Contr.: Nico van Holsteijn
Phone: (31) 43 382 22 22
Fax: (31) 43 382 27 31
Email: nico.vanholsteijn@sappi.com
Environ. Mgr.: Wim Quint
Phone: (31) 43 382 22 22
Fax: (31) 43 382 27 31
Email: wim.quint@sappi.com
Total Employees at this Location: 450
Type of Operation: Paper mill
Paper/Paperboard Grades and Capacities:
Total paper and paperboard capacity: 290,000 mt/y
Coated woodfree/freesheet: 290,000 mt/y
Paper and Paperboard Mill Data:
Stock Preparation:
Pulpers: 4
Paper Machines: 1
No. 6, Bel-Bond, total capacity 290,000 mt/y, Trim width 4.3 m, Coated woodfree/freesheet
Coating Machines: 2
CM 6, total capacity 300,000 mt/y., off machine
PM 6, total capacity 300,000 mt/y., on machine
Finishing Equipment:
Winders: 2
Supercalenders: 2
Sheeters: 8
Energy Data:
Power boilers: 2
Combustion turbines: 2 at 40, 24 MW
Steam turbines: 1 at 22 MW
Electrical demand for mill: 515 MWh/D

ⓜSCA Nederlands BV
Cuijk Mill
Mill is Formerly Georgia-Pacific Netherlands acquired by SCA, sale completed late July 2012
Ownership: 100% by SCA - Svenska Cellulosa Aktiebolaget
Lange Linden 22
NL- 5433 NC Katwijk, Cuijk
Netherlands
Mailing Address: P.O. Box 90, NL- 5430 AB Cuijk, Netherlands
Phone: (31) 48 533 9339
Fax: (31) 48 533 9449
Personnel:
Man. Dir.: Ron van den Heuvel
Phone: (31) 48 533 9339
Manuf. Dir.: Ferdinand Koster
Phone: (31) 48 533 9339
Purch. Mgr.: George Cordewener
Phone: (31) 48 533 9339
Sen. Comm. Mngr.: Sabine Henssler
Phone: (31) 48 533 9339
Total Employees at this Location: 500
Type of Operation: Pulp mill, Paper mill
Pulp Grades and Capacities:
Total pulp capacity: 66,426 mt/y
Recycled Pulping: 66,426 mt/y
Pulp Mill Data:
Recycled Fiber Treatment Lines:
Flotation deinking lines: 2 at 45,000 admt/y
Pulpers: 5
Washing deinking lines: 2 at 45,000 admt/y
Paper/Paperboard Grades and Capacities:
Total paper and paperboard capacity: 65,000 mt/y
Tissue: 65,000 mt/y
Paper and Paperboard Mill Data:
Stock Preparation:
Pulpers: 5
Refiners: 2
Paper Machines: 2
No. 2, crescent former, total capacity 30,000 mt/y, Trim width 2.7 m, Tissue
No. 4, (Supplier: Chantrenne.), crescent former, total capacity 35,000 mt/y, Trim width 3.71 m, Tissue
Finishing Equipment:
Winders: 2
Energy Data:
Power boilers: 4
Electrical demand for mill: 223 MWh/D

ⓜSchut Papier
Heelsum Mill
Ownership: 100% by Exacompta Clairefontaine
Kabeljauw 2
NL-6866 NE Heelsum
Netherlands
Mailing Address: Postbus 1, NL-6866 ZG Heelsum, Netherlands
Phone: (31) 317 31 9110
Fax: (31) 317 31 2754
Email: Info@schutpapier.com
Web Address: www.schutpapier.nl
Personnel:
Mill Mgr.: Rene Korg
Phone: (31) 317 31 9110
Sales & Marketing Dir.: R. R. J. Künne
Email: Sales@schutpapier.com
Sls. Mgr.: Jele Tabois
Phone: (31) 317 31 9110
Email: Sales@schutpapier.com
Purch. & Syst. Mgr.: Edwin Vermaes
Total Employees at this Location: 40
Type of Operation: Paper mill
Paper/Paperboard Grades and Capacities:
Total paper and paperboard capacity: 3,000 mt/y
Uncoated woodfree/freesheet: 3,000 mt/y
Coated woodfree/freesheet
Specialty and industrial
Paper and Paperboard Mill Data:
Paper Machines: 1
No. 1, hybrid former, total capacity 3,000 mt/y, Trim width 2 m, Uncoated woodfree/freesheet, Specialty and industrial

ⓜSmurfit Kappa Roermond Papier BV
Roermond Mill
Ownership: Smurfit Kappa Europe
Mijnheerkensweg 18
NL-6041 TA Roermond
Netherlands

Netherlands

Mailing Address: Postb. 1225, NL-6040 KE Roermond, Netherlands
Phone: (31) 475 38 44 44
Fax: (31) 475 33 26 20
Email: info.skrp@smurfitkappa.nl
Web Address: www.smurfitkappa-roermondpapier.com
Personnel:
Man. Dir.: Jo Cox
Phone: (31) 475 38 44 44
Fax: (31) 475 33 26 20
Email: jo.cox@smurfitkappa.nl
Oper. Mgr.: Wouter Lap
Phone: (31) 475 38 44 44
Fax: (31) 475 33 26 20
Email: wouter.lap@smurfitkappa.nl
Bus. Controller: Ed Halmans
Phone: (31) 475 38 44 44
Fax: (31) 475 33 26 20
Email: ed.halmans@smurfitkappa.nl
Total Employees at this Location: 250
Type of Operation: Paperboard mill
Pulp Grades and Capacities:
Total pulp capacity: 594,320 mt/y
Recycled Pulping: 594,320 mt/y
Pulp Mill Data:
Recycled Fiber Treatment Lines:
Pulpers: 1
Recycled packaging pulping lines
Paper/Paperboard Grades and Capacities:
Total paper and paperboard capacity: 590,000 mt/y
Linerboard: 240,000 mt/y
Corrugating medium/fluting: 350,000 mt/y
Paper and Paperboard Mill Data:
Paper Machines: 3
No. 1, Bel-Bond, total capacity 240,000 mt/y, Trim width 5.4 m, Linerboard, Corrugating medium/fluting
No. 2, fourdrinier, total capacity 50,000 mt/y, Trim width 2.5 m, Corrugating medium/fluting
No. 3, Bel-Bond, total capacity 300,000 mt/y, Trim width 5 m, Corrugating medium/fluting, Linerboard
Finishing Equipment:
Rewinders: 4
Energy Data:
HRSG boiler: 4
Combustion turbines: 4 at 3.5, 3.5, 3.5, 3.5 MW
Electrical demand for mill: 430 MWh/D

ⓂSmurfit Kappa Solid Board BV
Oude Pekela Mill
Ownership: Smurfit Kappa Europe
W.H. Westerstraat 59
NL-9665 ZG Oude Pekela
Netherlands
Mailing Address: P.O. Box 5, NL-9693 ZG Nieuweschans, Netherlands
Phone: (31) 503 03 3000
Fax: (31) 503 03 3991
Email: sales.solidboard@smurfitkappa.nl
Web Address: www.smurfitkappa-specialties.com, www.solidboard.com
Personnel:
Mill Mgr.: Peter Nijland
Phone: (31) 503 03 3000
Fax: (31) 503 03 3991
Email: peter.nijland@smurfitkappa.nl
Total Employees at this Location: 100
Type of Operation: Pulp mill, Paperboard mill
Pulp Grades and Capacities:
Total pulp capacity: 70,975 mt/y
Recycled Pulping: 70,975 mt/y
Pulp Mill Data:
Recycled Fiber Treatment Lines:
Recycled packaging pulping lines at 120,000
Paper/Paperboard Grades and Capacities:
Total paper and paperboard capacity: 70,000 mt/y
Boxboard/cartonboard: 70,000 mt/y
Paper and Paperboard Mill Data:
Paper Machines: 1
No. 4, fourdrinier, total capacity 70,000 mt/y, Trim width 2.35 m, Boxboard/cartonboard
Energy Data:
Power boilers: 1
Combustion turbines: 2 at 7.0 MW
Electrical demand for mill: 67 MWh/D

ⓂSmurfit Kappa Solid Board BV
Coevorden Mill
Ownership: Smurfit Kappa Europe
Robertweg 2
1988 Coevorden
Netherlands
Phone: (31) 050 3033000
Fax: (31) 050 3033399
Email: mail.solidboard@smurfitkappa.nl, solidboard@smurfitkappa.nl
Web Address: www.solidboard.com
Personnel:
Mill Mgr.: Wim Bos
Phone: (31) 050 303 3000
Fax: (31) 050 303 3399
Email: wim.bos@smurfitkappa.nl
Bus. Unit Mgr. Graphic Board: Jouke de Vries
Phone: (31) 050 303 3888
Fax: (31) 050 303 3991
Email: jouke.de.vries@smurfitkappa.nl
Total Employees at this Location: 100
Type of Operation: Paper mill
Pulp Grades and Capacities:
Total pulp capacity: 101,476 mt/y
Recycled Pulping: 101,476 mt/y
Pulp Mill Data:
Recycled Fiber Treatment Lines:
Recycled packaging pulping lines at 100,000
Paper/Paperboard Grades and Capacities:
Total paper and paperboard capacity: 100,000 mt/y
Boxboard/cartonboard: 100,000 mt/y
Paper and Paperboard Mill Data:
Paper Machines: 1
No. 4, (Former: Multi-Cylinder.), cylinder, Yankee dryer, total capacity 100,000 mt/y, Trim width 2.4 m, Boxboard/cartonboard
Energy Data:
Power boilers: 1
Steam turbines: 1
Electrical demand for mill: 75 MWh/D

ⓂSmurfit Kappa Solid Board BV
Hoogkerk Mill
Ownership: Smurfit Kappa Europe
Halmstraat 1-3
NL-9745 BC Groningen-Hoogkerk
Netherlands
Mailing Address: Postb. 2, NL-9693 ZG Nieuweschans, Netherlands
Phone: (31) 50 3033 000
Fax: (31) 50 3033 999
Email: mail.solidboard@smurfitkappa.nl
Web Address: www.smurfitkappa.com/nl
Personnel:
Mill Mgr.: Wim Bos
Phone: (31) 503 03 3000
Fax: (31) 503 03 3991
Email: wim.bos@smurfitkappa.nl
Paper Mill Mgr.: Hans Arends
Phone: (31) 503 03 3000
Fax: (31) 503 03 3991
Email: hans.arends@smurfitkappa.nl
Purch. Mgr.: Cobi Komduur
Phone: (31) 503 03 3000
Fax: (31) 503 03 3991
Email: cobi.komduur@smurfitkappa.n
Sls. Mgr.: Bert Blaauw
Phone: (31) 503 03 3000
Fax: (31) 503 03 3991
Email: bert.blaauw@smurfitkappa.nl
Total Employees at this Location: 520
Type of Operation: Paperboard mill
Pulp Grades and Capacities:
Total pulp capacity: 131,489 mt/y
Recycled Pulping: 131,489 mt/y
Pulp Mill Data:
Recycled Fiber Treatment Lines:
Pulpers: 2
Paper/Paperboard Grades and Capacities:
Total paper and paperboard capacity: 130,000 mt/y
Boxboard/cartonboard: 130,000 mt/y
Paper and Paperboard Mill Data:
Stock Preparation:
Pulpers: 2
Paper Machines: 2
No. 1, fourdrinier (2), total capacity 65,000 mt/y, Trim width 2.3 m, Boxboard/cartonboard
No. 4, fourdrinier (2), total capacity 65,000 mt/y, Trim width 2.75 m, Boxboard/cartonboard
Finishing Equipment:
Rewinders: 1
Sheeters: 2
Energy Data:
Power boilers: 4
Electrical demand for mill: 99 MWh/D

ⓂSmurfit Kappa Solid Board BV
Nieuweschans Mill
Ownership: Smurfit Kappa Europe
Hoofdstraat 34
9693 AH Nieuweschans
Netherlands
Mailing Address: PO Box 5, NL-9693 ZG Nieuweschans, Netherlands
Phone: (31) 597 52 91 00
Fax: (31) 597 52 91 99
Email: mail.solidboard@smurfitkappa.nl, solidboard@smurfitkappa.nl
Web Address: www.smurfitkappa-specialties.com, www.solidboard.com
Personnel:
CEO: Jelte Bouma
Phone: (31) 597 52 91 00
Fax: (31) 597 52 91 99
Email: jelte.bouma@smurfitkappa.com
ICT Mgr.: Erik Mulder
Phone: (31) 597 52 91 00
Fax: (31) 597 52 91 99
Email: erik.mulder@smurfitkappa.nl
Bus. Unit Mg. Graphic Board: Jouke de Vries
Phone: (31) 503 03 38 88
Fax: (31) 503 03 39 91
Email: jouke.de.vries@smurfitkappa.nl
Total Employees at this Location: 295
Type of Operation: Paperboard mill
Pulp Grades and Capacities:
Total pulp capacity: 151,503 mt/y
Recycled Pulping: 151,503 mt/y
Pulp Mill Data:
Recycled Fiber Treatment Lines:
Recycled packaging pulping lines at 150,000
Paper/Paperboard Grades and Capacities:
Total paper and paperboard capacity: 150,000 mt/y
Boxboard/cartonboard: 150,000 mt/y
Paper and Paperboard Mill Data:
Paper Machines: 2
No. 2, cylinder, total capacity 75,000 mt/y, Trim width 3.38 m, Boxboard/cartonboard
No. 3, cylinder, total capacity 75,000 mt/y, Trim width 3.38 m, Boxboard/cartonboard
Energy Data:
Power boilers: 1
Combustion turbines: 1 at 6.0 MW
Electrical demand for mill: 129 MWh/D

ⓄⓂSolidpack B.V.
Loenen Mill
Ownership: Private
Kanaal Zuid 492
7371 Loenen, Gelderland
Netherlands

Mailing Address: Postbus 43, 7370 Loenen, Gelderland, Netherlands
 Phone: (31) 55 505 8222
 Fax: (31) 55 505 8272
 Email: info@solidpack.eu
 Web Address: www.solidpack.eu
Personnel:
 Gen. Mgr: Dirk Schut
 Phone: (31) 55 505 8222
 Fax: (31) 55 505 8272
 Plant & Mill Mgr.: Rob Broere
 Phone: (31) 55 505 8222
 Fax: (31) 55 505 8272
 Sls. Mgr.: J.L Van Ommeren
 Phone: (31) 55 505 8222
 Fax: (31) 55 505 8272
 Email: bert.van.ommeren@solidpack.eu
 Management Asst.: Sharon Reulink
 Phone: (31) 55 505 8222
 Fax: (31) 55 505 8272
Total Employees of Company: 170
Total Employees at this Location: 170
Type of Operation: Paperboard mill
Pulp Grades and Capacities:
 Total pulp capacity: 71,320 mt/y
 Recycled Pulping: 71,320 mt/y
Pulp Mill Data:
 Recycled Fiber Treatment Lines:
 Recycled packaging pulping lines: 1
Paper/Paperboard Grades and Capacities:
 Total paper and paperboard capacity: 70,000 mt/y
 Boxboard/cartonboard: 70,000 mt/y
Paper and Paperboard Mill Data:
 Paper Machines: 1
 No. 1, total capacity 70,000 mt/y, Trim width 2.08 m, Boxboard/cartonboard
Energy Data:
 Power boilers
 Electrical demand for mill: 69 MWh/D

ⓗⓜVan Houtum BV
Swalmen Mill
Ownership: Henk van Houtum, Mill management
Boutestraat 125
NL-6071 JR Swalmen
Netherlands
Mailing Address: Postb. 9013, NL-6070 AA Swalmen, Netherlands
 Phone: (31) 475 50 73 00
 Fax: (31) 475 50 73 01
 Email: info@vanhoutum.nl
 Web Address: www.vanhoutum.nl
Personnel:
 Man. Dir., Owner: Henk P. Van Houtum
 Phone: (31) 475 50 73 00
 Fax: (31) 475 50 73 01
 Email: henk.vanhoutum@vanhoutum.nl
 Finan. Mgr.: Jos Rutten
 Phone: (31) 475 50 73 00
 Fax: (31) 475 50 73 01
 Email: jos.rutten@vanhoutum.nl
 Man. Dir.: Bas Gehlen
 Phone: (31) 475 50 73 00
 Fax: (31) 475 50 73 01
 Email: bas.gehlen@vanhoutum.nl
 Prod. Mgr.: Ronald Kok
 Phone: (31) 475 50 73 00
 Fax: (31) 475 50 73 01
 Email: ronald.kok@vanhoutum.nl
 Sls. Mgr.: Toin Van der Velden
 Phone: (31) 475 50 73 00
 Fax: (31) 475 50 73 01
 Email: toin.vandervelden@vanhoutum.nl
 Export Mgr.: Rob Didden
 Phone: (31) 475 50 73 00
 Fax: (31) 475 50 73 01
 Email: rob.didden@vanhoutum.nl
 CSR Mgr.: Nick Op den Buijsch
 Phone: (31) 475 50 73 00
 Fax: (31) 475 50 73 01
 Email: nick.opdenbuijsch@vanhoutum.nl
 Office Mgr.: Marleen Gommans
 Phone: (31) 475 50 73 00
 Fax: (31) 475 50 73 01
 Email: marleen.gommans@vanhoutum.nl
Total Employees of Company: 190
Total Employees at this Location: 190
Type of Operation: Paper mill
Pulp Grades and Capacities:
 Total pulp capacity: 51,047 mt/y
 Recycled Pulping: 51,047 mt/y
Pulp Mill Data:
 Recycled Fiber Treatment Lines:
 Flotation deinking lines: 2 at 50,000 admt/y
 Pulpers: 2 at 50,000 admt/y
 Washing deinking lines: 2 at 50,000 admt/y
Paper/Paperboard Grades and Capacities:
 Total paper and paperboard capacity: 48,000 mt/y
 Tissue: 48,000 mt/y
Paper and Paperboard Mill Data:
 Stock Preparation:
 Pulpers: 2
 Paper Machines: 2
 No. 3, fourdrinier, Yankee dryer, total capacity 23,000 mt/y, Trim width 2.3 m, Tissue
 No. 4, crescent former, Yankee dryer, total capacity 25,000 mt/y, Trim width 2.7 m, Tissue
Energy Data:
 Power boilers: 1
 Combustion turbines: 1 at 4.2 MW
 Electrical demand for mill: 164 MWh/D

NORWAY

ⓗⓜBorregaard ChemCell
Sarpsborg Mill
Ownership: Public
Hjalmar Wessels vei 10
NO-1701 Sarpsborg
Norway
Mailing Address: P.O. Box 162, NO-1701 Sarpsborg, Norway
 Phone: (47) 69 118 000
 Fax: (47) 69 118 770
 Email: borregaard@borregaard.com
 Web Address: www.chemcell.com, www.borregaard.com
Personnel:
 Pres. & CEO: Per A. Sørlie
 Phone: (47) 69 118 000
 Fax: (47) 69 118 770
 CFO: Per Bjarne Lyngstad
 Phone: (47) 69 118 000
 Fax: (47) 69 118 770
 Email: per.bjarne.lyngstad@borregaard.com
 Exec. VP, Borregaard ChemCell: Tom Erik Foss-Jacobsen
 Phone: (47) 69 118 000
 Fax: (47) 69 118 770
 Email: tom.erik.foss-jacobsen@borregaard.com
 Mill Mgr.: Ole Gunnar Jakobsen
 Phone: (47) 69 118 000
 Fax: (47) 69 118 770
 Email: ole.gunnar.jakobsen@borregaard.com
 SVP, Bus. Dvlpt.: Gisle Lohre Johansen
 Phone: (47) 69 118 000
 Fax: (47) 69 118 770
 Email: gisle.lohre.johansen@borregaard.com
 SVP Commun. & HR & Pub. Rel.: Dag Arthur Aasbø
 Phone: (47) 69 118 216
 Fax: (47) 69 118 770
 Email: dag.arthur.aasbo@borregaard.com
 Commun. Mgr: Tone Horvei Bredal
 Phone: (47) 69 118 165
 Fax: (47) 69 118 770
 Email: tone.horvei.bredal@borregaard.com
Total Employees of Company: 1,025
Total Employees at this Location: 750
Type of Operation: Pulp mill
Pulp Grades and Capacities:
 Total pulp capacity: 168,859 mt/y
 Pulp available for market: 160,800 mt/y
 Chemical Pulp: 168,859 mt/y
Pulp Mill Data:
 Chemical Pulping Systems:
 Batch digesters: 9
 Pulp Lines: 1
 Bleach Plant Systems: 1
 No. 1, Sequence: EOP, Capacity 160,800 admt/y
 Chemical Recovery Equipment:
 Evaporator lines: 1
 Pulp Dryers:
 Fourdriniers 1
Energy Data:
 Power boilers: 1
 Steam turbines: 2
 Electrical demand for mill: 409 MWh/D

ⓗⓜHellefoss Paper
Hokksund Mill
Ownership: 100% by Heva Holding
Hellefossveien 113
NO-3300 Hokksund
Norway
 Phone: (47) 32 252 200
 Fax: (47) 32 252 299
 Email: sales@hellefoss.com
 Web Address: www.hellefoss.com
Personnel:
 Chmn.: Terje Haglund
 Phone: (47) 32 252 200
 Fax: (47) 32 252 299
 Email: terje.haglund@hellefoss.no
 Pres.: Roar Paulsrud
 Phone: (47) 32 252 200
 Fax: (47) 32 252 299
 Email: roar.paulsrud@hellefoss.no
 Mill Mgr.: Trond Lindborg
 Phone: (47) 90 773 607
 Fax: (47) 32 252 299
 Email: trond.lindborg@hellefoss.no
 Prod. Mgr.: Ketil Borgevad
 Phone: (47) 48 113 358
 Fax: (47) 32 252 299
 Email: ketil.borgevad@hellefoss.no
 Sls. & Mktg. Mgr.: Vicky Doleman
 Phone: (44) 1784 430822
 Fax: (44) 1784 430823
 Email: vicky.doleman@hellefoss.no
 Purch. Dir.: Arnfinn Kroken
 Phone: (47) 95 132 148
 Fax: (47) 32 252 299
 Email: arnfinn.kroken@hellefoss.no
 Qlty. Mgr.: Roy Anders Kristofersen
 Phone: (47) 48 147 958
 Fax: (47) 32 252 299
 Email: roy.anders.kristofersen@hellefoss.no
 HR. Mgr.: Jarle Borgersen
 Phone: (47) 93 446 418
 Fax: (47) 32 252 299
 Email: jarle.borgersen@hellefoss.no
Total Employees of Company: 75
Total Employees at this Location: 77
Type of Operation: Paper mill
Pulp Grades and Capacities:
 Total pulp capacity: 43,914 mt/y
 Mechanical Pulp: 43,914 mt/y
Pulp Mill Data:
 Mechanical Pulping Systems:
 Conventional grinders: 2
 Bleach Plant Lines:
 Mechanical pulping system bleaching, Sequence: P
Paper/Paperboard Grades and Capacities:
 Total paper and paperboard capacity: 50,000 mt/y
 Uncoated mechanical/groundwood: 50,000 mt/y
Paper and Paperboard Mill Data:

Norway

Stock Preparation:
Pulpers: 1
Refiners: 2
Paper Machines: 1
No. 1, twin-wire, total capacity 50,000 mt/y, Trim width 3.78 m, Uncoated mechanical/groundwood
Finishing Equipment:
Rewinders: 1
Energy Data:
Power boilers: 3
Electrical demand for mill: 321 MWh/D

ⒽⓂMMK FollaCell A.S.
Folla Mill
Ownership: Mayr-Melnhof Karton AG
Industriveien 1
NO-7796 Follafoss
Norway
Mailing Address: Ostre Strandvei 52, NO-3482 Tofte, Norway
 Phone: (47) 74 12 36 00
 Fax: (47) 74 12 36 01
 Email: sales.follacell@mm-karton.com
 Web Address: www.mm-karton.com/en/company/mills/follacell.html
Personnel:
 CEO: Wilhelm Hörmanseder
 Phone: (47) 74 1236 00
 Fax: (47) 74 1236 01
 CFO: Oliver Schumy
 Phone: (47) 74 1236 00
 Fax: (47) 74 1236 01
 Bd. Mbr.: Andreas Blaschke
 Phone: (47) 74 1236 00
 Fax: (47) 74 1236 01
 Bd. Mbr. & Mktg & Sls. Cartonboard: Franz Rappold
 Phone: (47) 74 1236 00
 Fax: (47) 74 1236 01
 Head of Marketing: Horst Bittermann
 Phone: (47) 74 1236 00
 Fax: (47) 74 1236 01
Total Employees at this Location: 50
Type of Operation: Pulp mill
Pulp Grades and Capacities:
 Total pulp capacity: 132,469 mt/y
 Pulp available for market: 130,000 mt/y
 Mechanical Pulp: 132,469 mt/y

Pulp Mill Data:
 Mechanical Pulping Systems:
 CTMP systems: 1
 Bleach Plant Systems: 1
 No. 1, Sequence: P, Capacity 100,000 admt/y
 Pulp Dryers:
 Flash dryers 1
 Energy Data:
 Power boilers: 2
 Electrical demand for mill: 651 MWh/D

ⒽⓂNordic Paper Greåker AS
Greåker Mill
Ownership: Nordic Paper Holding AB
NO-1720 Greåker
Norway
Mailing Address: P.O. Box 155, NO-1720 Greåker, Norway
 Phone: (47) 69 138 500
 Fax: (47) 69 141 102
 Email: info@nordic-paper.com
 Web Address: www.nordic-paper.com
Personnel:
 Chmn. of the Board: Richard Heiberg
 Phone: (47) 69 138 601
 Fax: (47) 69 141 102
 Email: richard.heiberg@nordic-paper.com
 CEO: Jan Runo
 Phone: (47) 53 382 484
 Email: jan.runo@nordic-paper.com
 CFO, Dpty CEO: Frederik Høye
 Phone: (47) 69 138 500
 Fax: (47) 69 141 102
 Email: frederik.hoye@nordic-paper.com
 Dir., Sls. & Mktg.: Ake Wallman
 Phone: (47) 53 38 20 00
 Fax: (47) 53 38 20 08
 Email: ake.wallman@nordic-paper.com
 HR. Dir.: Lars Lofquist
 Phone: (47) 69 138 500
 Fax: (47) 69 141 102
 Email: lars.lofquist@nordic-paper.com
 Dir. Purch & Log.: Per Knatterod
 Phone: (47) 69 138 500
 Fax: (47) 69 141 102
 Email: per.knatterod@nordic-paper.com
Total Employees at this Location: 124
Type of Operation: Paper mill
Paper/Paperboard Grades and Capacities:
 Total paper and paperboard capacity: 29,988 mt/y
 Specialty and industrial: 29,988 mt/y
Paper and Paperboard Mill Data:
 Stock Preparation:
 Pulpers:
 Paper Machines: 2
 No. 1, fourdrinier, total capacity 9,996 mt/y, Trim width 4.7 m, Specialty and industrial
 No. 4, fourdrinier, total capacity 19,992 mt/y, Trim width 2.8 m, Specialty and industrial
 Finishing Equipment:
 Rewinders: 1
 Sheeters: 1
 Energy Data:
 Power boilers: 1
 Electrical demand for mill: 147 MWh/D

ⒽNorske Skog ASA
Ownership: 50% by foreign shareholders, 19% by Forest Owners' Association, 5.78% by Unionen AS
Karenslyst allé 49
NO-0278 Skøyen, Oslo
Norway
Mailing Address: PB 294, NO-0213 Skøyen, Oslo, Norway
 Phone: (47) 22 51 20 20
 Fax: (47) 22 51 20 21
 Email: (firstname.lastname@norskeskog.com)
 Web Address: www.norskeskog.com
Personnel:
 Pres. & CEO : Sven Ombudstvedt
 Phone: (47) 22 51 20 20
 Fax: (47) 22 51 20 21
 Email: sven.ombudstvedt@norskeskog.com
 COO : Roar Ødelien
 Phone: (47) 22 51 20 20
 Fax: (47) 22 51 20 21
 CFO: Rune Sollie
 Phone: (47) 22 51 20 20
 Fax: (47) 22 51 20 21
 Email: rune.sollie@norskeskog.com
 Snr. VP., Corp. Strat. & Legal: Lars P. Sperre
 Phone: (47) 22 51 20 20
 Fax: (47) 22 51 20 21
 Snr. VP, Commercial Oper. & Log.: Jan H. Clasen
 Phone: (47) 22 51 20 20
 Fax: (47) 22 51 20 21
 Email: jan.clasen@norskeskog.com
 VP. Corp. Affair: Carsten Dybevig
 Phone: (47) 917 63 117
 Fax: (47) 22 51 20 21
 Email: carsten.dybevig@norskeskog.com
Total Employees of Company: 3,274
Total Employees at this Location: 127
Mill Locations:
Malaysian Newsprint Industries Sdn. Bhd., Mentakab Mill (34% owned), Lot 3771 Jalan Lencongan Mentakab-Temerloh, Temerloh Industrial Pahang, 28400 Mentakab, Malaysia, Capacity: 280,245 mt/y, (Paper mill)
 Phone: (60) 6 09 2779898
 Fax: (60) 6 092715115
 Email: mni_mill@tm.net.my
Norske Skog (Australia), Albury Mill, Hume Highway, Ettamogah via Albury, NSW 2640, Australia, Capacity: 267,750 mt/y, (Pulp mill, Paper mill)
 Phone: (61) 2 6058 3111 / 2 60583181
 Fax: (61) 2 6058 3080
 Email: contactalbury@norskeskog.com; (firstname.lastname@norske-skog.com.au)
Norske Skog (Australia), Boyer Mill, Boyer, TAS 7140, Australia, Capacity: 305,000 mt/y, (Pulp mill, Paper mill)
 Phone: (61) 3 6261 0111
 Fax: (61) 3 6261 3274
 Email: (firstname.lastname@norskeskog.com)
Norske Skog Bruck GmbH, Bruck an der Mur Mill, Fabriksgasse 10, A-8600 Bruck an der Mur, Austria, Capacity: 400,000 mt/y, (Paper mill)
 Phone: (43) 3862 800-0
 Fax: (43) 3862 800 300
 Email: bruck@norskeskog.com, (firstname.lastname@norskeskog.com)
Norske Skog Golbey SA, Golbey Mill, Zone Industrielle III, Route Jean-Charles Pellerin, F-88194 Golbey Cedex, France, Capacity: 620,000 mt/y, (Pulp mill, Paper mill)
 Phone: (33) 3 29 68 68 68
 Fax: (33) 3 29 68 68 60
 Email: dominique.bomont@norskeskog.com
Norske Skog ASA, Saugbrugs Mill, NO-1756 Halden, Norway, Capacity: 550,000 mt/y, (Pulp mill, Paper mill)
 Phone: (47) 69 174 000
 Fax: (47) 69 174 330
 Email: (firstname.lastname@norskeskog.com)
Norske Skog ASA, Skogn Mill, NO-7620 Skogn, Norway, Capacity: 550,000 mt/y, (Pulp mill, Paper mill)
 Phone: (47) 74 087 000
 Fax: (47) 74 087 109
 Email: (firstname.lastname@norskeskog.com)
Norske Skog Tasman, Tasman Mill, Private Bag, Fletcher Avenue, 3169 Kawerau, New Zealand, Capacity: 154,938 mt/y, (Paper mill)
 Phone: (64) 7 323 3999
 Fax: (64) 7 323 3790
 Email: (firstname.surname@norskeskog.com)
Norske Skog Walsum GmbH, Walsum Mill, Theodor-Heuss-Strasse 228, D-47179 Duisburg, Germany, Capacity: 200,000 mt/y, (Pulp mill, Paper mill)
 Phone: (49) 203 49920
 Fax: (49) 203 4992180

ⒽⓂNorske Skog ASA
Saugbrugs Mill
NO-1756 Halden
Norway
Mailing Address: P.O. Box 68, N-1756 Halden, Norway
 Phone: (47) 69 174 000
 Fax: (47) 69 174 330
 Email: (firstname.lastname@norskeskog.com)
 Web Address: www.norske-skog.com
Personnel:
 Gen. Mgr.: Roy Vardheim
 Phone: (47) 69 174 000
 Fax: (47) 69 174 330
 Email: roy.vardheim@norskeskog.com
 Finan. Dir.: Svein Ove Njåstad
 Phone: (47) 69 174 000
 Fax: (47) 69 174 330
 Email: svein.njastad@norskeskog.com
Total Employees at this Location: 524
Type of Operation: Pulp mill, Paper mill
Pulp Grades and Capacities:
 Total pulp capacity: 359,329 mt/y
 Mechanical Pulp: 359,329 mt/y

Pulp Mill Data:
 Mechanical Pulping Systems:
 TMP systems: 2
 TMP systems: 1
 Pulp Lines: 2
 Bleach Plant Systems: 3
 TMP bleaching, Sequence: P, Capacity 400,000 admt/y

Norway

Paper/Paperboard Grades and Capacities:
Total paper and paperboard capacity: 550,000 mt/y
Uncoated mechanical/groundwood: 550,000 mt/y
Paper and Paperboard Mill Data:
Paper Machines: 3
No. 4, SymFormer R, total capacity 125,000 mt/y, Trim width 4.6 m, Uncoated mechanical/groundwood
No. 5, SpeedFormer HHS, total capacity 125,000 mt/y, Trim width 6.2 m, Uncoated mechanical/groundwood
No. 6, OptiFormer, total capacity 300,000 mt/y, Trim width 8.62 m, Uncoated mechanical/groundwood
Finishing Equipment:
Winders: 4 at 300,000 mt/y, 250,000 mt/y
Supercalenders: 3 at 300,000 mt/y
Energy Data:
Power boilers: 6
TMP Reboiler: 1
Steam turbines: 1 at 15.4 MW
Electrical demand for mill: 3,893 MWh/D

ⓜNorske Skog ASA
Skogn Mill
NO-7620 Skogn
Norway
Phone: (47) 74 087 000
Fax: (47) 74 087 109
Email: (firstname.lastname@norskeskog.com)
Web Address: www.norskeskog.com
Personnel:
Mill. Mgr.: Amund Saxrud
Phone: (47) 74 087 000
Fax: (47) 74 087 109
Email: amund.saxrud@norskeskog.com
Prod. Mgr.: Arild Hegdal
Phone: (47) 74 087 000
Fax: (47) 74 087 109
Email: arild.hegdal@norskeskog.com
Tech. Mgr.: Knut Dreier
Phone: (47) 74 087 000
Fax: (47) 74 087 109
Email: knut.dreier@norskeskog.com
Total Employees at this Location: 405
Type of Operation: Pulp mill, Paper mill
Pulp Grades and Capacities:
Total pulp capacity: 530,867 mt/y
Mechanical Pulp: 365,950 mt/y
Recycled Pulping: 164,917 mt/y
Pulp Mill Data:
Mechanical Pulping Systems:
TMP systems: 2
Bleach Plant Systems: 1
Recycled Fiber Treatment Lines:
Flotation deinking lines: 1 at 180,000
Pulpers: 1 at 180,000
Paper/Paperboard Grades and Capacities:
Total paper and paperboard capacity: 550,000 mt/y
Newsprint: 498,400 mt/y
Uncoated mechanical/groundwood: 51,600 mt/y
Paper and Paperboard Mill Data:
Stock Preparation:
Refiners: 18
Paper Machines: 3
No. 1, DuoFormer D, total capacity 172,000 mt/y, Trim width 6.67 m, Newsprint, Uncoated mechanical/groundwood
No. 2, SymFormer R, total capacity 136,000 mt/y, Trim width 6.7 m, Newsprint
No. 3, SpeedFormer HS, total capacity 242,000 mt/y, Trim width 8.47 m, Newsprint
Finishing Equipment:
Winders: 5
Rewinders: 1
Energy Data:
Power boilers: 3
TMP Reboiler: 3
Steam turbines: 1 at 10 MW
Electrical demand for mill: 3,477 MWh/D

ⓜPeterson Packaging AS
Ownership: 100% by The Pemco Group
Olav Haraldssonsgate 99
1707 Sarpsborg
Norway
Mailing Address: Postboks 40, 1701 Sarpsborg
Phone: (47) 815 30 444
Fax: (47) 69 15 62 70
Email: kundeservice@peterson.no
Web Address: www.petersonpackaging.no
Personnel:
Chmn. of the Board: Olav Kjell Holtan
Phone: (47) 47 815 30 444
Fax: (47) 47 691 56 270
Email: olav.holtan@peterson.no
CFO: Jan Erik Skovdahl
Phone: (47) 47 815 30 444
Fax: (47) 47 691 56 270
Man. Dir.: Pontus Lindblom
Phone: (47) 47 815 30 444
Fax: (47) 47 691 56 270
Email: pontus.lindblom@peterson.no
Sls Dir.: Tommy Prøitz
Phone: (47) 47 958 99 047
Fax: (47) 47 691 56 270
Email: tommy.proitz@peterson.no
Key Account Mgr.: Kenneth Vassdal
Phone: (47) 47 928 14 834
Fax: (47) 47 691 56 270
Email: kenneth.vassdal@peterson.no
Mktg. Mgr.: Sofie Ritzén
Phone: (47) 46 112 82 360
Fax: (47) 47 691 56 270
Email: sofie.ritzen@petersonpackaging.se
Maint. Mgr.: David Weber
Phone: (47) 47 815 30 444
Fax: (47) 47 691 56 270
Total Employees of Company: 1,600
Mill Locations:
Peterson Packaging AS, Ranheim Mill, Peder Myhres veg 19, NO-7492 Ranheim, Trondheim, Norway, Capacity: 110,000 mt/y, (Pulp mill, Paperboard mill)
Phone: (47) 73 57 70 00
Fax: (47) 73 57 70 01
Email: info@peterson.no

ⓜPeterson Packaging AS
Ranheim Mill
Peder Myhres veg 19
NO-7492 Ranheim, Trondheim
Norway
Phone: (47) 73 57 70 00
Fax: (47) 73 57 70 01
Email: info@peterson.no
Web Address: www.petersonpackaging.no
Personnel:
Plt. Mgr.: Arve Torset
Phone: (47) 97 58 71 45
Fax: (47) 73 57 70 01
Email: arve.torset@peterson.no
Sls. Mgr.: Geir Knutsen
Phone: (47) 97 17 42 30
Fax: (47) 73 57 70 01
Email: geir.knutsen@peterson.no
Plt. Mgr. Paper: Jean-Francois Larosa
Phone: (47) 98 22 90 84
Fax: (47) 73 57 70 01
Email: jean-francois.larosa@peterson.no
Total Employees at this Location: 115
Type of Operation: Pulp mill, Paperboard mill
Pulp Grades and Capacities:
Total pulp capacity: 110,616 mt/y
Recycled Pulping: 110,616 mt/y
Pulp Mill Data:
Recycled Fiber Treatment Lines:
Pulpers: 3 at 130,000 admt/y
Recycled packaging pulping lines at 130,000 admt/y
Paper/Paperboard Grades and Capacities:
Total paper and paperboard capacity: 110,000 mt/y
Linerboard: 55,000 mt/y
Boxboard/cartonboard: 55,000 mt/y
Paper and Paperboard Mill Data:
Stock Preparation:
Refiners: 6
Paper Machines: 2
No. 5, fourdrinier, total capacity 40,000 mt/y, Trim width 3.5 m, Boxboard/cartonboard
No. 6, fourdrinier, total capacity 70,000 mt/y, Trim width 4 m, Boxboard/cartonboard, Linerboard
Finishing Equipment:
Winders: 2
Energy Data:
Power boilers: 2
Electrical demand for mill: 154 MWh/D

ⓜⓜRygene-Smith & Thommesen AS
Rykene Mill
NO-4821 Rykene
Norway
Phone: (47) 37 05 84 00
Fax: (47) 37 01 02 50
Email: mail@rygene.no
Web Address: www.rygene.no
Personnel:
Chmn.: Christian B. Herlofson
Phone: (47) 37 05 84 00
Fax: (47) 37 01 02 50
Man. Dir./Pres. & Mill Mgr.: Kristen Eltvedt Hagestad
Phone: (47) 37 05 84 00
Fax: (47) 37 01 02 50
Email: keh@rygene.no
Total Employees at this Location: 20
Type of Operation: Pulp mill
Pulp Grades and Capacities:
Total pulp capacity: 61,202 mt/y
Pulp available for market: 60,000 mt/y
Mechanical Pulp: 61,202 mt/y
Pulp Mill Data:
Mechanical Pulping Systems:
TMP systems: 2
Bleach Plant Systems: 1
Hy-Brite Capacity 60,000 admt/y
Pulp Dryers:
Flash dryers 1
Energy Data:
Power boilers: 1
TMP Reboiler: 1
Electrical demand for mill: 380 MWh/D

ⓜSödra Cell Tofte
Tofte Mill
Mill is closed (Södra ceased production August, 25, 2013.)
Ownership: Södra Cell AB
Østre Strandvei 52
NO-3482 Tofte
Norway
Mailing Address: P.O. Box 83, N-3481 Tofte, Norway
Phone: (47) 32 799 000
Fax: (47) 32 799 001
Web Address: www.sodra.com
Personnel:
Man. Dir.: Christen Gronvold-Hansen
Phone: (47) 32 799 000
Mill. Mgr.: Per Åenarsloberg
Phone: (47) 32 799 000
Email: per.aenarsloberg@sodra.com
Prod. Mgr.: Espen Eriksen
Phone: (47) 32 799 240
Maint. Mgr.: Jan Carlsson
Economy Mgr.: Berit Helgefen
Phone: (47) 32 799 000
Total Employees at this Location: 300
Type of Operation: Pulp mill
Pulp Mill Data:
Chemical Pulping Systems:
Continuous digesters: 2
Bleach Plant Systems: 1
No. 1, Sequence: DEopDED, Capacity 400,000 admt/y

Poland

Chemical Recovery Equipment:
Evaporator lines: 1
Recovery boilers: 1
Lime Kiln
Pulp Dryers:
Air Float dryers 1, Air Float dryers 1, Air Float dryers 1
Energy Data:
Power boilers: 2
Steam turbines: 2 at 50 MW

⑪Vafos Pulp
Kragerø Mill
Kragerøveien 698
NO-3770 Kragerø
Norway
Mailing Address: Sannidalsveien 120, NO-3770 Kragerø, Norway
Phone: (47) 35 986 400
Fax: (47) 35 990 765
Email: hm@vafos.no
Web Address: www.vafos.no
Personnel:
Purch. Mgr.: Arnfinn Kroken
Phone: (47) 35 986 400
Fax: (47) 35 990 765
Email: arnfinn.kroken@hellefoss.no
Total Employees at this Location: 35
Type of Operation: Pulp mill
Pulp Grades and Capacities:
Total pulp capacity: 81,776 mt/y
Pulp available for market: 80,000 mt/y
Mechanical Pulp: 81,776 mt/y
Pulp Mill Data:
Mechanical Pulping Systems:
Conventional grinders: 3
Bleach Plant Systems: 1
Pulp Dryers:
Flash dryers 1
Energy Data:
Power boilers: 1
Electrical demand for mill: 363 MWh/D

⑪Vafos Pulp
Ownership: 100% by Heva Holding
Kragerøveien 698
NO-3770 Kragerø
Norway
Phone: (47) 35 986 400
Fax: (47) 35 990 765
Email: hm@vafos.no
Web Address: www.vafos.no
Personnel:
Chmn. of the Board: Terje Haglund
Phone: (47) 35 986 400
Fax: (47) 35 990 765
Man. Dir.: Trond Alexander Lindborg
Phone: (47) 35 986 400
Fax: (47) 35 990 765
Prod. Mgr.: Jan Sundbø
Phone: (47) 35 986 400
Fax: (47) 35 990 765
Purch. Mgr.: Arnfinn Kroken
Phone: (47) 35 986 400
Fax: (47) 35 990 765
Total Employees of Company: 45
Mill Locations:
Vafos Pulp, Kragerø Mill, Kragerøveien 698, NO-3770 Kragerø, Norway, (Pulp mill)
Phone: (47) 35 986 400
Fax: (47) 35 990 765
Email: hm@vafos.no

⑪⑩Vajda-Papir Scandinavia AS
Drammen Mill
Ownership: 100% by Vajda Papír Ltd
Nedre Eikervei 48
NO-3045 Drammen
Norway
Mailing Address: P.O. Box 2273, Strømsø, N-3045 Drammen, Norway
Phone: (47) 32 80 95 00
Fax: (47) 32 83 22 12
Email: info@vajdapapir.hu
Web Address: www.vajdapapir.hu
Personnel:
Man. Dir./Mill Mgr.: Hege G. Eizenberger
Phone: (47) 32 80 95 00, 91 33 91 15
Fax: (47) 32 83 22 12
Email: hege.g.eizenberger@vajdapapir.com
Reg. Commercial Mgr.: Ulf Andersson
Phone: (47) 32 80 95 00, +46 (0) 70 975 1950
Fax: (47) 32 83 22 12
Email: ulf.andersson@vajdapapir.com
Total Employees at this Location: 81
Type of Operation: Pulp mill, Paper mill
Pulp Grades and Capacities:
Total pulp capacity: 23,468 mt/y
Recycled Pulping: 23,468 mt/y
Pulp Mill Data:
Recycled Fiber Treatment Lines:
Pulpers: 1 at 27,500 admt/y
Washing deinking lines: 1 at 27,500 admt/y
Paper/Paperboard Grades and Capacities:
Total paper and paperboard capacity: 22,000 mt/y
Tissue: 22,000 mt/y
Paper and Paperboard Mill Data:
Stock Preparation:
Pulpers: 2
Refiners: 3
Paper Machines: 1
No. 4, twin-wire, total capacity 22,000 mt/y, Trim width 2.7 m, Tissue
Finishing Equipment:
Rewinders: 2
Energy Data:
Power boilers: 2
Electrical demand for mill: 91 MWh/D

POLAND

⑪A & B Paper Ltd.
Ownership: 100% by private
Kaweczyn 1a Dobrzejewice, k/Torunia, PL-87123
Dobrzejewice, k/Torunia
Poland
Phone: (48) 56 674 6190 -92
Fax: (48) 56 674 6190
Email: abpaper@abpaper.com.pl
Personnel:
Pres.: Grazyna Ruminska
Phone: (48) 48 56 6746191
Fax: (48) 48 56 6746190
Email: abpaper@abpaper.com.pl
Management Advisor: Jacek Krzynkowski
Phone: (48) 48 56 6746191
Fax: (48) 48 56 6746190
Prod. Mgr.: Cezary Duk
Phone: (48) 48 56 6746191
Fax: (48) 48 56 6746190
Total Employees of Company: 40
Mill Locations:
A & B Paper Ltd., Dobrzejewice k/Torunia Mill, Kaweczyn 1a, PL-87123 Dobrzejewice, k/Torunia, Poland, Capacity: 4,000 mt/y, (Paper mill)
Phone: (48) 56 674 6190 /91/92
Fax: (48) 56 674 6190

⑪A & B Paper Ltd.
Dobrzejewice k/Torunia Mill
Kaweczyn 1a
PL-87123 Dobrzejewice, k/Torunia
Poland
Phone: (48) 56 674 6190 /91/92
Fax: (48) 56 674 6190

Personnel:
Pres.: Grazyna Ruminska
Phone: (48) 56 6746191
Fax: (48) 56 6746190
Management Advisor: Jacek Krzynkowski
Phone: (48) 56 674 6190/6191/9192
Prod. Mgr.: Cezary Duk
Phone: (48) 56 674 6190/6191/9192
Total Employees at this Location: 40
Type of Operation: Paper mill
Pulp Grades and Capacities:
Total pulp capacity: 4,274 mt/y
Recycled Pulping: 4,274 mt/y
Pulp Mill Data:
Recycled Fiber Treatment Lines:
Pulpers: 1
Paper/Paperboard Grades and Capacities:
Total paper and paperboard capacity: 4,000 mt/y
Tissue: 4,000 mt/y
Paper and Paperboard Mill Data:
Stock Preparation:
Pulpers: 1
Refiners: 1
Paper Machines: 1
No. 1, fourdrinier, Yankee dryer, total capacity 4,000 mt/y, Trim width 2.15 m, Tissue
Finishing Equipment:
Winders: 1 at 3,400 mt/y
Calenders: 2
Rewinders: 1
Energy Data:
Power boilers: 2
Electrical demand for mill: 12 MWh/D

⑪⑩P.W. "APIS" S.J.
Chodecz Mill
Ownership: 100% by private
ul. Kaliska 11
PL-87 860 Chodecz
Poland
Phone: (48) 54 284 8519
Fax: (48) 54 284 8520
Email: apis@pwapis.pl
Web Address: www.pwapis.pl
Personnel:
Gen. Mgr. & Owner: Henryk Andrzej Fijalkowski
Phone: (48) 54 284 8519
Fax: (48) 54 284 8520
Prod. Mgr.: Leszek Czerwinski
Phone: (48) 600 874445
Total Employees at this Location: 25
Type of Operation: Paper mill
Mill Locations:
P.W. "APIS" S.J., Nowa Bystrzyca Mill, Filia Nowa Bystrzyca, PL-57 516 Stara Bystrzyca, Poland, Capacity: 13,000 mt/y, (Paperboard mill)
Phone: (48) 74 811 1610
Fax: (48) 74 811 1610
Email: bystrzyca@pwapis.pl
Pulp Grades and Capacities:
Total pulp capacity: 7,459 mt/y
Recycled Pulping: 7,459 mt/y
Pulp Mill Data:
Recycled Fiber Treatment Lines:
Pulpers: 1
Paper/Paperboard Grades and Capacities:
Total paper and paperboard capacity: 7,000 mt/y
Tissue: 7,000 mt/y
Paper and Paperboard Mill Data:
Paper Machines: 1
No. 1, fourdrinier, Yankee dryer, total capacity 7,000 mt/y, Trim width 2.5 m, Tissue
Energy Data:
Power boilers
Electrical demand for mill: 21 MWh/D

⑪P.W. "APIS" S.J.
Nowa Bystrzyca Mill
Filia Nowa Bystrzyca

Poland

PL-57 516 Stara Bystrzyca
Poland
  Phone: (48) 74 811 1610
  Fax: (48) 74 811 1610
  Email: bystrzyca@pwapis.pl
  Web Address: www.pwapis.pl
Personnel:
  Gen. Mgr.: Andrzej Michalski
  Phone: (48) 606 244468
  Prod. Mgr.: Piotr Bloch
  Phone: (48) 660 760206
Total Employees at this Location: 30
Type of Operation: Paperboard mill
Pulp Grades and Capacities:
  Total pulp capacity: 13,125 mt/y
  Recycled Pulping: 13,125 mt/y
Pulp Mill Data:
  Recycled Fiber Treatment Lines:
  Recycled packaging pulping lines: 1
Paper/Paperboard Grades and Capacities:
  Total paper and paperboard capacity: 13,000 mt/y
  Corrugating medium/fluting: 13,000 mt/y
Paper and Paperboard Mill Data:
Paper Machines: 1
  No. 1, fourdrinier, total capacity 13,000 mt/y, Trim width 2 m, Corrugating medium/fluting
Energy Data:
  Power boilers
  Electrical demand for mill: 19 MWh/D

ⓂⓅP.W. "APIS" S.J.
Szczecin (Skolwin) Mill
Company is under construction, closed (Brownfield redevelopment of the mill, planning to restart with production of recycling fluting and testliner at the end of 2014)
ul. Stolczynska 100
PL-71869 Szczecin, district Skolwin
Poland
  Phone: (48) 91 453 8793/423 1210
  Fax: (48) 91 4538143/8533
  Email: apis@pwapis.pl
  Web Address: www.pwapis.pl
Personnel:
  Pres.: Dariusz Sabalski
  Phone: (48) 91 453 8793/423 1210
  Email: dariusz.sabalski@skolwin.com.pl
  Prod. Dir.: Marcin Ratajczyk
  Phone: (48) 91 453 8793/423 1210
  Email: marcin.ratajczyk@skolwin.com.pl
  Advisor to Tech./Prod. Dir.: Jan Gorski
  Phone: (48) 601 935 083 (GSM)
  Email: jan.gorski@skolwin.com.pl
  Logist. Mgr.: Aneta Borowska
  Phone: (48) 91 453 85 33
  Email: aneta.borowska@skolwin.com.pl
  Sls. Dir.: Magdalena Roggenbuck-Herges
  Phone: (48) 91 423 0216
  Email: Magdalena.herges@skolwin.com.pl
  Prod. Ass.: Katarzyna Czyzewska
  Phone: (48) 91 453 87 93, 606 494649 (GSM)
  Email: katarzyna.czyzewska@skolwin.com.pl
Total Employees at this Location: 250
Type of Operation: Pulp mill, Paper mill
Pulp Mill Data:
  Mechanical Pulping Systems:
  Conventional grinders: 8
  Recycled Fiber Treatment Lines:
  Flotation deinking lines: 2 at 410 admt/y
  Pulpers: 1 at 195 admt/y
Paper and Paperboard Mill Data:
Paper Machines: 1
  No. 1, total capacity 57,120 mt/y, Trim width 5.46 m
Finishing Equipment:
  Rewinders: 2 at 100,000 mt/y
  Sheeters: 2 at 7,500 mt/y
Energy Data:
  Power boilers: 3
  Combustion turbines: 1
  Steam turbines: 2 at 24.0 MW

ⓅArctic Paper S.A.
Ownership: Public
ul. J.H. Dabrowskiego 334A
PL-60 406 Poznan
Poland
  Phone: (48) 61 62 62 000
  Fax: (48) 61 62 62 001
  Email: biuro@arcticpaper.com
  Web Address: www.arcticpaper.com
Personnel:
  CEO & Pres. of the Management Board: Wolfgang Lübbert
  Phone: (49) 40 51 48 53 10
  COO & Member of the Management Board: Per Skoglund
  Phone: (46) 31 63 17 03
  Email: per.skoglund@arcticpaper.com
  CFO & Member of the Management Board: Malgorzata Majewska-Sliwa
  Phone: (48) 61 62 62 00
  Fax: (48) 61 62 62 001
  Chief Procurement Officer & Member of the Management Board: Jacek Ireneusz Los
  Phone: (48) 61 62 62 003
  Fax: (48) 61 62 62 001
  Email: jacek.los@arcticpaper.com
  Sls. Dir. & Member of the Management Member (From 2014): Michal Sawka
  Phone: (48) 95 72 10 500
  Fax: (48) 61 62 62 001
  Email: henryk.derejczyk@arcticpaper.com
Total Employees of Company: 1,830
Total Employees at this Location: 6
Mill Locations:
  Arctic Paper Kostrzyn S.A., Kostrzyn Mill (75% owned), ul. Fabryczna 1, PL-66 470 Kostrzyn n/Odra, Poland, Capacity: 279,000 mt/y, (Paper mill)
  Phone: (48) 95 7210 600
  Fax: (48) 95 7524 196
  Email: info-pl@arcticpaper.com; info-kostrzyn@arcticpaper.com
  Arctic Paper Grycksbo AB, Grycksbo Mill (75% owned), SE-790 20 Grycksbo, Sweden, Capacity: 265,000 mt/y, (Paper mill)
  Phone: (46) 23 68000
  Fax: (46) 23 68350
  Email: grycksbo@arcticpaper.com
  Arctic Paper Mochenwangen GmbH, Mochenwangen Mill (75% owned), Fabrikstrasse 62, D-88284 Mochenwangen, Wolpertswende, Germany, Capacity: 105,000 mt/y, (Paper mill)
  Phone: (49) 7502 4010
  Fax: (49) 7502 4012 16/ 4012 13
  Email: info-mochenwangen@arcticpaper.com
  Arctic Paper Munkedals AB, Munkedal Mill (75% owned), SE-455 81 Munkedal, Sweden, Capacity: 160,000 mt/y, (Paper mill)
  Phone: (46) 770 110 120
  Fax: (46) 524 12533
  Email: info-munkedals@arcticpaper.com
  Rottneros Bruk AB, Rottneros Mill, SE-686 94 Rottneros, Sweden, (Pulp mill)
  Phone: (46) 565 17600
  Fax: (46) 565 17680
  Email: info@rottneros.com
  Rottneros, Vallviks Bruk AB, Vallvik Mill, SE-820 21 Vallvik, Sweden, (Pulp mill)
  Phone: (46) 270 62000
  Fax: (46) 270 69210/69420
  Email: info@rottneros.com

ⓂArctic Paper Kostrzyn S.A.
Kostrzyn Mill
Ownership: 75% by Arctic Paper S.A.
ul. Fabryczna 1
PL-66 470 Kostrzyn n/Odra
Poland
Mailing Address: ul. Biskupia 39, PL-04-216 Warszava, Poland
  Phone: (48) 95 7210 600
  Fax: (48) 95 7524 196
  Email: info-pl@arcticpaper.com, info-kostrzyn@arcticpaper.com
  Web Address: www.arcticpaper.com
Personnel:
  Man. Dir.: Henryk Derejczyk
  Phone: (48) 95 7210550
  Fax: (48) 95 7524196
  Email: henryk.derejczyk@arcticpaper.com
  Purch. Mgr.: Jacek Los
  Phone: (48) 95 7210577 / 601 398 321
  Fax: (48) 95 7524196
  Email: jacek.los@arcticpaper.com
  Shipping Team Mgr.: Piotr Kowalski
  Phone: (48) 95 7210581 / 601 438302
  Fax: (48) 95 7524133
  Email: piotr.kowalski@arcticpaper.com
  Prod. Plan. Mgr.: Piotr Stolowski
  Phone: (48) 95 7210668 / 603 136473
  Fax: (48) 95 7524 196
  Email: piotr.stolowski@arcticpaper.com
  Tech. Support: Pawel Piotrowski
  Phone: (48) 95 7210558
  Fax: (48) 95 7524 196
  Email: pawel.piotrowski@arcticpaper.com
Total Employees at this Location: 425
Type of Operation: Paper mill
Paper/Paperboard Grades and Capacities:
  Total paper and paperboard capacity: 279,000 mt/y
  Uncoated woodfree/freesheet: 279,000 mt/y
Paper and Paperboard Mill Data:
  Stock Preparation:
  Pulpers: 5
  Refiners: 12
Paper Machines: 2
  No. 1, SymFormer, total capacity 127,000 mt/y, Trim width 5.25 m, Uncoated woodfree/freesheet
  No. 2, DuoFormer D, total capacity 152,000 mt/y, Trim width 5.25 m, Uncoated woodfree/freesheet
Finishing Equipment:
  Winders: 2
  Rewinders: 1
  Sheeters: 4 at 125,000 mt/y
Energy Data:
  Power boilers: 2
  Combustion turbines: 2 at 10.9, 10.9 MW
  Steam turbines: 2 at 6.5, 12.11 MW
  Electrical demand for mill: 511 MWh/D

ⓂⓅFabryka Papieru i Tektury "BESKIDY" S.A.
Wadowice Mill
Ownership: joint stock company
ul. Chopina 1a
PL-34100 Wadowice
Poland
  Phone: (48) 33 8735010
  Fax: (48) 33 8735011
  Email: handlowy@beskidy-wadowice.pl, sekretariat@beskidy-wadowice.pl
  Web Address: beskidy-wadowice.pl
Personnel:
  Chmn. of the Board: Beniamin Szczur
  Phone: (48) 33 873 5010
  Fax: (48) 33 873 5011
  Email: b.szczur@estena.pl
  Tech. Mgr.: Marek Olesinski
  Phone: (48) 33 8735010
  Fax: (48) 33 8735011
  Email: m.olesinski@estena.pl
  Purch. Mgr.: Jacek Rapacz
  Phone: (48) 501 065 485
  Email: j.rapacz@estena.pl
  Finan. Dir.: Mateusz Data
  Phone: (48) 501 421 593
  Email: m.data@estena.pl
  Sls. Mgr.: Piotr Gadek
  Phone: (48) 515 033 890
  Fax: (48) 338 735 011
  Email: p.gadek@estena.pl

Poland

Total Employees of Company: 100
Total Employees at this Location: 100
Type of Operation: Paperboard mill
Pulp Grades and Capacities:
  Total pulp capacity: 31,249 mt/y
  Recycled Pulping: 31,249 mt/y
Pulp Mill Data:
  Recycled Fiber Treatment Lines:
  Pulpers: 2
Paper/Paperboard Grades and Capacities:
  Total paper and paperboard capacity: 30,000 mt/y
  Tissue: 15,000 mt/y
  Boxboard/cartonboard: 15,000 mt/y
Paper and Paperboard Mill Data:
Paper Machines: 3
No. 1, fourdrinier, total capacity 8,000 mt/y, Trim width 2 m, Boxboard/cartonboard
No. 2, fourdrinier, total capacity 7,000 mt/y, Trim width 2 m, Boxboard/cartonboard
No. 3, fourdrinier, Yankee dryer, total capacity 15,000 mt/y, Trim width 2.15 m, Tissue
Finishing Equipment:
  Sheeters: 1 at 2,500 mt/y
Energy Data:
  Power boilers: 2
  Electrical demand for mill: 59 MWh/D

ⓘⓜFabryka Papieru Czerwonak Sp. z o.o.
Czerwonak Mill
Ownership: 80% by Fripa Papierfabrik Albert Friedrich KG
ul. Gdynska 131
PL-62004 Czerwonak
Poland
  Phone: (48) 61 650 4800 / 4803 / 4822
  Fax: (48) 61 650 4801
  Email: biuro@fpcz.com.pl
  Web Address: www.fpcz.com.pl
Personnel:
Pres./Mill Mgr./Chmn.: Claus Queck
  Phone: (48) 61 650 4800
  Fax: (48) 61 650 4801
Finan. Dir.: Kasper Vencken
  Phone: (48) 61 650 4800
  Fax: (48) 61 650 4801
Total Employees of Company: 98
Total Employees at this Location: 98
Type of Operation: Paper mill
Pulp Grades and Capacities:
  Total pulp capacity: 17,589 mt/y
  Recycled Pulping: 17,589 mt/y
Pulp Mill Data:
  Recycled Fiber Treatment Lines:
  Pulpers: 1 at 23,400
Paper/Paperboard Grades and Capacities:
  Total paper and paperboard capacity: 16,500 mt/y
  Tissue: 16,500 mt/y
Paper and Paperboard Mill Data:
Paper Machines: 1
No. 2, fourdrinier, Yankee dryer, total capacity 16,500 mt/y, Trim width 2.7 m, Tissue
Energy Data:
  Power boilers: 1
  Electrical demand for mill: 47 MWh/D

ⓘⓜFabryka Papieru Sp. z.o.o. w Dabrowicy
Jelenia Gora Mill
Ownership: 100% by limited liability company
PL-58500 Jelenia Gora
Poland
  Phone: (48) 75 713 0058
  Fax: (48) 75 752 2071
  Email: sekretariat@fabryka-papieru.pl, sprzedaz@fabryka-papieru.pl
  Web Address: www.fabryka-papieru.pl

Personnel:
Pres. & Gen. Mgr.: Jerzy Czarnecki
  Phone: (48) 75 713 0058
  Fax: (48) 75 752 2071
  Email: jerzy.czarnecki@fabryka-papieru.pl
Prod. Mgr.: Witold Roczon
  Phone: (48) 75 713 0058 ext 27
  Fax: (48) 75 752 2071
  Email: w.roczon@fabryka-papieru.pl
Maint. Mgr.: Slawomir Gadzina
  Email: s.gadzina@fabryka-papieru.pl
Finan. Dir.: Maria Krypner
  Phone: (48) 75 713 0058
  Fax: (48) 75 752 2071
  Email: m.krypner@fabryka-papieru.pl
Sls. Mgr.: Ewa Wilk
  Phone: (48) 75 713 0058
  Fax: (48) 75 752 2071
  Email: e.wilk@fabryka-papieru.pl
Supply Mgr.: Stanislaw Jarzynski
  Phone: (48) 75 713 0058
  Fax: (48) 75 752 2071
  Email: s.jarzynski@fabryka-papieru.pl
Total Employees of Company: 100
Total Employees at this Location: 100
Type of Operation: Paper mill
Paper/Paperboard Grades and Capacities:
  Total paper and paperboard capacity: 9,600 mt/y
  Packaging papers: 9,600 mt/y
Paper and Paperboard Mill Data:
  Stock Preparation:
  Pulpers: 4
  Refiners: 6
Paper Machines: 2
No. 1, fourdrinier, total capacity 6,100 mt/y, Trim width 2.03 m, Packaging papers
No. 2, fourdrinier, total capacity 3,500 mt/y, Trim width 2.05 m, Packaging papers
Finishing Equipment:
  Winders: 2 at 5,000 mt/y
  Sheeters: 1 at 12,000 mt/y
Energy Data:
  Power boilers: 2
  Hydro turbines: 1 at 0.4 MW
  Electrical demand for mill: 30 MWh/D

ⓜDelitissue Sp. z.o.o.
Ciechanow Mill
Ownership: 60% by Sofidel Group
ul. Mleczarska 31
PL-06 400 Ciechanow
Poland
  Phone: (48) 23 6743100
  Fax: (48) 23 6739400
  Email: delitissue.pl@delitissue.pl
  Web Address: www2.sofidel.it, www.delitissue.pl
Personnel:
Gen. Dir.: Marcello Marzano
  Phone: (48) 23 6743100
  Fax: (48) 23 6739400
  Email: marcello.marzano@delitissue.pl
PR Dir.: Janusz Kolwinski
  Phone: (48) 23 6743100
  Fax: (48) 23 6739400
  Email: janusz.kolwinski@delitissue.pl
Total Employees at this Location: 295
Type of Operation: Paper mill
Paper/Paperboard Grades and Capacities:
  Total paper and paperboard capacity: 35,000 mt/y
  Tissue: 35,000 mt/y
Paper and Paperboard Mill Data:
  Stock Preparation:
  Pulpers: 3
Paper Machines: 1
No. 1, crescent former, total capacity 35,000 mt/y, Trim width 2.75 m, Tissue
Energy Data:
  Power boilers: 1
  Electrical demand for mill: 86 MWh/D

ⓜWPT Eko-Klan Sp. z o.o.
Margonin Mill
Margonska Wies 34A
PL-64830 Margonin
Poland
  Phone: (48) 67 2846097
  Fax: (48) 67 2846097
  Email: marketing.ekoklan@interia.pl, biuro@eko-klan.com.pl
  Web Address: www.eko-klan.com.pl
Personnel:
Owner/Pres.: Pawel Smektala
  Phone: (48) 60 028 2998 (GSM)
  Fax: (48) 67 2846097
  Email: prezes@eko-klan.com.pl
Tech. Dir.: Grzegorz Smektala
  Phone: (48) 60 495 2271
  Fax: (48) 67 2846097
  Email: biuro@eko-klan.com.pl
Sls. & Mktg. Mgr.: Tomasz Janeczko
  Phone: (48) 66 214 2206
  Fax: (48) 67 284 6097
  Email: marketing.ekoklan@interia.pl
Total Employees at this Location: 40
Type of Operation: Paper mill
Pulp Grades and Capacities:
  Total pulp capacity: 4,265 mt/y
  Recycled Pulping: 4,265 mt/y
Pulp Mill Data:
  Recycled Fiber Treatment Lines:
  Pulpers: 1
Paper/Paperboard Grades and Capacities:
  Total paper and paperboard capacity: 4,000 mt/y
  Tissue: 4,000 mt/y
Paper and Paperboard Mill Data:
Paper Machines: 1
No. 1, fourdrinier, Yankee dryer, total capacity 4,000 mt/y, Trim width 2.1 m, Tissue
Energy Data:
  Power boilers
  Electrical demand for mill: 12 MWh/D

ⓘⓜElpap
Krakow Mill
1 Ujastek Road
PL-30969 Krakow
Poland
  Phone: (48) 12 425 8200 GSM: 696 48 2199
  Management GSM: 606 75 0744
  Fax: (48) 12 425 8200
  Email: kontat@elpap.pl, elpap@elpap.pl
Total Employees at this Location: 20
Type of Operation: Paper mill
Pulp Grades and Capacities:
  Total pulp capacity: 8,519 mt/y
  Recycled Pulping: 8,519 mt/y
Pulp Mill Data:
  Recycled Fiber Treatment Lines:
  Pulpers: 1
Paper/Paperboard Grades and Capacities:
  Total paper and paperboard capacity: 8,000 mt/y
  Tissue: 8,000 mt/y
Paper and Paperboard Mill Data:
Paper Machines: 1
No. 1, fourdrinier, Yankee dryer, total capacity 8,000 mt/y, Trim width 2.2 m, Tissue
Energy Data:
  Power boilers
  Electrical demand for mill: 23 MWh/D

ⓘFabryka Papieru Kaczory Sp. z o.o.
Ownership: 100% by private shareholders
ul. Dziembowska 20
PL-64810 Kaczory
Poland
  Phone: (48) 67 2842128
  Fax: (48) 67 2842113

Poland

Email: info@fabrykapapieru.pl
Web Address: www.fabrykapapieru.pl
Personnel:
Pres.: Stanislaw Cierzniak
Phone: (48) 67 2842128
Fax: (48) 67 2842113
Email: prezes@fabrykapapieru.pl
Tech. Dir.: Eugeniusz Cierzniak
Phone: (48) 67 2842128
Fax: (48) 67 2842113
Email: cierzniak.e@fabrykapapieru.pl
Sls. & HR Mgr.: Janina Malinska
Phone: (48) 67 2842128
Fax: (48) 67 2842113
Email: info@fabrykapapieru.pl
Total Employees of Company: 64
Mill Locations:
Fabryka Papieru Kaczory Sp. z o.o., Margonin Mill, ul.Strzelecka 15, 64-830 Margonin, Poland, Capacity: 21,000 mt/y, (Paper mill)
Phone: (48) 67 350 75 57
Fax: (48) 67 28 42 113
Email: info@fabrykapapieru.pl
Fabryka Papieru Kaczory Sp. z o.o., Kaczory Mill, ul. Dziembowska 20, PL-64810 Kaczory, Poland, Capacity: 7,000 mt/y, (Paper mill)
Phone: (48) 67 2842128
Fax: (48) 67 2842113
Email: info@fabrykapapieru.pl

ⓘⓜFabryka Papieru Kaczory Sp. z o.o.
Margonin Mill
Company is under construction (was due to start Q3, 2013 but having problems with power, no start up date given)
Ownership: 100% by private shareholders
ul.Strzelecka 15
64-830 Margonin
Poland
Phone: (48) 67 350 75 57
Fax: (48) 67 28 42 113
Email: info@fabrykapapieru.pl
Web Address: www.FabrykaPapieru.pl, www.sklep.fabrykapapieru.pl
Personnel:
Chrmn. of the board: Cierzniak Stanislaw
Phone: (48) 67 350 75 57
Fax: (48) 67 28 42 113
Email: prezes@fabrykapapieru.pl
Vice President: Malgorzata Walczak
Phone: (48) 67 350 75 57
Fax: (48) 67 28 42 113
Email: wiceprezes@fabrykapapieru.pl
Total Employees of Company: 64
Type of Operation: Paper mill
Mill Locations:
Fabryka Papieru Kaczory Sp. z o.o., Kaczory Mill, ul. Dziembowska 20, PL-64810 Kaczory, Poland, Capacity: 7,000 mt/y, (Paper mill)
Phone: (48) 67 2842128
Fax: (48) 67 2842113
Email: info@fabrykapapieru.pl
Paper/Paperboard Grades and Capacities:
Total paper and paperboard capacity: 21,000 mt/y
Tissue: 21,000 mt/y
Paper and Paperboard Mill Data:
Paper Machines: 1
PM 2, (2nd hand, due to start Q3 2013), Yankee dryer, crescent former, total capacity 21,000 mt/y, Trim width 3.1 m, Tissue

ⓘⓜFPHU "Filar" Sp. Jawna
Sadlno Mill
Ownership: 100% by Public
Zaryn 46
PL-62 619 Sadlno, Gm Wierzbinek
Poland
Phone: (48) 63 261 4884/4883/4700
Fax: (48) 63 261 4884
Email: filar@filar.info.pl
Web Address: www.filar.info.pl
Personnel:
Mill Dir.: Andrzej Rakowski
Phone: (48) 60 243 9991
Fax: (48) 63 261 4884
Email: andrzej.rakowski@filar.info.pl
Prod. Dir.: Marek Ulanski
Phone: (48) 60 240 9565
Fax: (48) 63 261 4884
Email: marekulanski@interia.pl
Mktg. Mgr.: Artur Ratajczyk
Phone: (48) 69 861 3720
Fax: (48) 63 261 4884
Email: artur.ratajczyk@filar.info.pl
Total Employees at this Location: 125
Type of Operation: Paper mill
Pulp Grades and Capacities:
Total pulp capacity: 12,765 mt/y
Recycled Pulping: 12,765 mt/y
Paper/Paperboard Grades and Capacities:
Total paper and paperboard capacity: 12,000 mt/y
Tissue: 12,000 mt/y
Paper and Paperboard Mill Data:
Paper Machines: 2
No. 1, fourdrinier, Yankee dryer, total capacity 5,000 mt/y, Trim width 2.2 m, Tissue
No. 2, fourdrinier, Yankee dryer, total capacity 7,000 mt/y, Trim width 2.2 m, Tissue
Energy Data:
Electrical demand for mill: 36 MWh/D

ⓘⓜGlucholaskie Zaklady Papiernicze Sp. z o.o.
Glucholazy Mill
Ownership: 100% by employees
ul. Gen. Andersa 32
PL-48340 Glucholazy
Poland
Phone: (48) 77 439 1911/1912
Fax: (48) 77 439 1875
Email: gzp@gzp.com.pl
Web Address: www.gzp.com.pl
Personnel:
Pres. & Mill Mgr. & Chmn.: Miroslaw Stokowski
Phone: (48) 77 4391915
Fax: (48) 77 439 1875
Email: m.stokowski@gzp.com.pl
VP.: Janusz Momot
Phone: (48) 77 4391915
Fax: (48) 77 439 1875
Email: janusz.momot@gzp.com.pl
Sls. Mgr.: Krzysztof Szajwaj
Phone: (48) 77 4391210
Fax: (48) 77 4391210
Email: k.szajwaj@gzp.com.pl
Tech. Mgr.: Ryszard Skubinski
Phone: (48) 77 4392505
Fax: (48) 77 439 1875
Email: rskubinski@gzp.com.pl
Economic Dir. - Main Bookkeeper: Zbigniew Koziol
Phone: (48) 77 4391915
Fax: (48) 77 439 1875
Email: z.koziol@gzp.com.pl
Head Qlty. Contr. & Environ.: Elizabeth M. Szoldra
Phone: (48) 77 439 1911
Fax: (48) 77 439 1875
Email: eszoldra@gzp.com.pl
Prod. Dir.: Miroslaw Englot
Phone: (48) 77 4391 210 / 4393 210
Fax: (48) 77 439 1875
Email: produkcja@gzp.com.pl
Total Employees of Company: 270
Total Employees at this Location: 170
Type of Operation: Paper mill
Mill Locations:
Glucholaskie Zaklady Papiernicze Sp. z o.o., Niedomice Mill, ul. Niedomicka 45, PL-33132 Niedomice, Poland, Capacity: 15,000 mt/y, (Paper mill)
Phone: (48) 14 645 8715/8716
Fax: (48) 14 645 8717
Email: kwiazewicz@gzp.com.pl
Pulp Grades and Capacities:
Total pulp capacity: 42,164 mt/y
Recycled Pulping: 42,164 mt/y
Pulp Mill Data:
Recycled Fiber Treatment Lines:
Pulpers: 2
Paper/Paperboard Grades and Capacities:
Total paper and paperboard capacity: 40,000 mt/y
Tissue: 21,000 mt/y
Packaging papers: 7,000 mt/y
Corrugating medium/fluting: 12,000 mt/y
Paper and Paperboard Mill Data:
Stock Preparation:
Pulpers: 4
Paper Machines: 4
No. 1, fourdrinier, Yankee dryer, total capacity 6,000 mt/y, Trim width 2.25 m, Tissue
No. 2, fourdrinier, Yankee dryer, total capacity 7,500 mt/y, Trim width 2.25 m, Tissue
No. 3, fourdrinier, total capacity 19,000 mt/y, Trim width 2.27 m, Corrugating medium/fluting, Packaging papers
No. 5, fourdrinier, Yankee dryer, total capacity 7,500 mt/y, Trim width 2.25 m, Tissue
Finishing Equipment:
Supercalenders: 1
Rewinders: 1 at 12,000 mt/y
Sheeters: 2 at 200 mt/y
Energy Data:
Power boilers: 2
Steam turbines: 2 at 3.5 MW
Electrical demand for mill: 88 MWh/D

ⓜGlucholaskie Zaklady Papiernicze Sp. z o.o.
Niedomice Mill
ul. Niedomicka 45
PL-33132 Niedomice
Poland
Phone: (48) 14 645 8715/8716
Fax: (48) 14 645 8717
Email: kwiazewicz@gzp.com.pl
Web Address: www.gzp.com.pl
Personnel:
Niedomicach Mill. Dir.: Karol Wiazewicz
Phone: (48) 14 645 8715 Ext: 201
Fax: (48) 14 645 8717
Email: kwiazewicz@gzp.com.pl
Total Employees at this Location: 70
Type of Operation: Paper mill
Paper/Paperboard Grades and Capacities:
Total paper and paperboard capacity: 15,000 mt/y
Tissue: 13,000 mt/y
Packaging papers: 2,000 mt/y
Paper and Paperboard Mill Data:
Paper Machines: 1
No. 1, fourdrinier, Yankee dryer, total capacity 15,000 mt/y, Trim width 3.2 m, Tissue, Packaging papers
Energy Data:
Electrical demand for mill: 42 MWh/D

ⓘⓜHanke Tissue Spólka z o.o.
Kostrzyn Mill
Ownership: 87.30% by MBB Industries AG
ul. Fabryczna 1
PL-66470 Kostrzyn
Poland
Phone: (48) 95 720 8600
Fax: (48) 95 752 3560
Email: hanke.tissue@hanketissue.com.pl
Web Address: www.hanketissue.com.pl
Personnel:
Pres.: Robert Szczepkowski
Phone: (48) 95 720 8600
Fax: (48) 95 752 3560
Email: rs@hanketissue.com.pl
Prod. Logistics Mgr.: Mariusz Lehmann
Phone: (48) 95 720 8668

Poland

Fax: (48) 95 752 3560
Email: mariusz.lehmann@hanketissue.com.pl
Sls. Mgr. (domestic): Zofia Kalinowska
Phone: (48) 95 720 8610
Fax: (48) 95 752 2057
Email: zofia.kalinowska@hanketissue.com.pl
Sls. Mgr. (export): Tomasz Molczyk
Phone: (48) 95 720 8670
Fax: (48) 95 752 3560
Email: tomasz.molczyk@hanketissue.com.pl
Total Employees of Company: 145
Total Employees at this Location: 145
Type of Operation: Paper mill
Paper/Paperboard Grades and Capacities:
Total paper and paperboard capacity: 15,000 mt/y
Tissue: 15,000 mt/y
Paper and Paperboard Mill Data:
Stock Preparation:
Pulpers: 1
Refiners: 2
Paper Machines: 1
No. 1, foundrinier, Yankee dryer, total capacity 15,000 mt/y, Trim width 3.2 m, Tissue
Finishing Equipment:
Rewinders: 1 at 13,000 mt/y
Energy Data:
Power boilers: 1
Electrical demand for mill: 43 MWh/D

ⓂICT Poland Sp. z o.o.
Kostrzyn Mill
Ownership: ICT Italy
Wloska 3
PL-66470 Kostrzyn
Poland
Phone: (48) 95 733 6800
Fax: (48) 95 733 6801
Email: recepcja@ictpoland.pl
Web Address: www.ictpoland.pl, www.foxy.com.pl
Personnel:
Gen. Mgr. - Board Member: Michal Wrembel
Phone: (48) 95 733 6800
Fax: (48) 95 733 6801
Email: m.wrembel@ictpoland.pl
Total Employees at this Location: 394
Type of Operation: Paper mill
Paper/Paperboard Grades and Capacities:
Total paper and paperboard capacity: 140,000 mt/y
Tissue: 140,000 mt/y
Paper and Paperboard Mill Data:
Paper Machines: 2
No. 11, crescent former, total capacity 70,000 mt/y, Trim width 5.55 m, Tissue
No. 12, crescent former, total capacity 70,000 mt/y, Trim width 5.55 m, Tissue
Energy Data:
Power boilers: 1
Electrical demand for mill: 345 MWh/D

ⓘInpol-Papier Sp. z o.o.
Ownership: 100% by Rafal Vitek
Czarnohucka 3
PL-42600 Tarnowskie Gory
Poland
Phone: (48) 32 4500 400
Fax: (48) 32 4500 499
Email: ip@inpolpapier.pl
Web Address: www.inpolpapier.pl
Personnel:
Owner: Rafal Witek
Phone: (48) 32 284 1834, 32 4500 400
Fax: (48) 32 384 3505, 32 4500 499
Mill Locations:
Inpol-Papier Sp. z o.o., Bardo Mill, ul. Fabryczna 18, PL-57256 Bardo, Poland, Capacity: 20,000 mt/y, (Paper mill)
Phone: (48) 74 8171 970
Fax: (48) 74 8171 960
Email: tektura@inpolpapier.pl

ⓂInpol-Papier Sp. z o.o.
Bardo Mill
ul. Fabryczna 18
PL-57256 Bardo
Poland
Phone: (48) 74 8171 970
Fax: (48) 74 8171 960
Email: tektura@inpolpapier.pl
Web Address: www.inpolpapier.pl
Personnel:
Owner: Rafal Vitek
Phone: (48) 32 4500 400
Fax: (48) 32 4500 499
Email: ip@inpolpapier.pl
Mgr.: Agnieszka Nowak
Phone: (48) 32 4500 400
Fax: (48) 32 4500 499
Email: agnieszka.nowak@inpolpapier.pl
Total Employees at this Location: 110
Type of Operation: Paper mill
Pulp Grades and Capacities:
Total pulp capacity: 20,175 mt/y
Recycled Pulping: 20,175 mt/y
Pulp Mill Data:
Recycled Fiber Treatment Lines:
Recycled packaging pulping lines: 1
Paper/Paperboard Grades and Capacities:
Total paper and paperboard capacity: 20,000 mt/y
Linerboard: 12,000 mt/y
Corrugating medium/fluting: 8,000 mt/y
Paper and Paperboard Mill Data:
Paper Machines: 1
No. 1, foundrinier, total capacity 20,000 mt/y, Trim width 3.2 m, Corrugating medium/fluting, Linerboard
Energy Data:
Power boilers: 2
Electrical demand for mill: 29 MWh/D

ⓂInternational Paper - Kwidzyn Sp. z o.o.
Kwidzyn Mill
Ownership: International Paper (Europe) SA
Lotnicza 1
PL-82500 Kwidzyn
Poland
Phone: (48) 55 2798000
Fax: (48) 55 2798451
Web Address: www.internationalpaper.com.pl, www.ipaper.com.pl
Personnel:
Mill Gen. Dir.: Marek Krzykowski
Phone: (48) 55 2798000
Fax: (48) 55 2798451
Email: marek.krzykowski@ipaper.com
Mgr.: Monika Zulma
Phone: (48) 55 2798000
Fax: (48) 55 2798451
Email: monika.zulma@ipaper.com
Total Employees at this Location: 1,550
Type of Operation: Pulp mill, Paper mill, Paperboard mill
Pulp Grades and Capacities:
Total pulp capacity: 593,455 mt/y
Chemical Pulp: 400,019 mt/y
Mechanical Pulp: 76,800 mt/y
Recycled Pulping: 116,636 mt/y
Pulp Mill Data:
Chemical Pulping Systems:
Batch digesters: 6
Mechanical Pulping Systems:
CTMP systems: 1
Pulp Lines: 1
Bleach Plant Systems: 3
CTMP, Sequence: P, Capacity 72,600 admt/y
DIP, Sequence: P, Capacity 120,000 admt/y
Kraft, Sequence: O_2 DEopDP, Capacity 400,000 admt/y
Chemical Recovery Equipment:
Evaporator lines: 1
Recovery boilers: 1
Lime Kiln
Recycled Fiber Treatment Lines:
Flotation deinking lines: 2 at 120,000 admt/y
Pulpers: 2 at 120,000 admt/y
Pulp Dryers:
Flakt dryer 1, Wet Lap machine 2
Paper/Paperboard Grades and Capacities:
Total paper and paperboard capacity: 772,500 mt/y
Newsprint: 112,500 mt/y
Uncoated woodfree/freesheet: 420,000 mt/y
Boxboard/cartonboard: 240,000 mt/y
Paper and Paperboard Mill Data:
Stock Preparation:
Pulpers: 7
Refiners: 36
Paper Machines: 4
No. 1, DuoFormer D, total capacity 200,000 mt/y, Trim width 5.3 m, Uncoated woodfree/freesheet
No. 2, DuoFormer D, total capacity 220,000 mt/y, Trim width 5.3 m, Uncoated woodfree/freesheet
No. 3, Bel-Baie II, total capacity 112,500 mt/y, Trim width 5.3 m, Newsprint
No. 4, Fourdrinier (4), Yankee dryer, total capacity 240,000 mt/y, Trim width 4.3 m, Boxboard/cartonboard
Coating Machines: 1
CM 1, total capacity 216,700 mt/y., on machine
Finishing Equipment:
Rewinders
Sheeters: 13
Energy Data:
Power boilers: 5
TMP Reboiler: 1
Steam turbines: 3 at 80 MW
Electrical demand for mill: 2,451 MWh/D

ⓘⓂPPH Izopaper Sp. z o.o.
Chelmza Mill
Ownership: 100% by Private
Mala Grzywna
PL-87 140 Chelmza
Poland
Phone: (48) 56 675 2273
Fax: (48) 56 675 2272
Email: izopaper@op.pl
Web Address: www.izopaper.pl
Personnel:
Gen. Mgr.: Grzegorz Mocny
Phone: (48) 56 675 2272
Total Employees at this Location: 36
Type of Operation: Paper mill
Pulp Grades and Capacities:
Total pulp capacity: 6,393 mt/y
Recycled Pulping: 6,393 mt/y
Pulp Mill Data:
Recycled Fiber Treatment Lines:
Pulpers: 1
Paper/Paperboard Grades and Capacities:
Total paper and paperboard capacity: 6,000 mt/y
Tissue: 6,000 mt/y
Paper and Paperboard Mill Data:
Paper Machines: 2
No. 1, fourdrinier, Yankee dryer, total capacity 3,000 mt/y, Trim width 2.2 m, Tissue
No. 2, fourdrinier, Yankee dryer, total capacity 3,000 mt/y, Trim width 2.2 m, Tissue
Energy Data:
Power boilers
Electrical demand for mill: 18 MWh/D

ⓘⓂJack-Pol Sp. z o.o.
Olawa Mill
ul. Portowa 1B
PL-55200 Olawa
Poland
Phone: (48) 71 3133861 / 303 30 36 / 303 52 87
Fax: (48) 71 3035290
Email: biuro@jack-pol.pl,

Poland

kadry@jack-pol.pl
Web Address: www.jack-pol.pl
Personnel:
Pres.: Jacek Wozniak
Phone: (48) 71 303 30396
Fax: (48) 71 303 5290
Email: biuro@jack-pol.pl
Dir.: Piotr Bartoszek
Phone: (48) 71 313 3861
Fax: (48) 71 303 5290
Email: logistyka@jack-pol.pl
Total Employees at this Location: 120
Type of Operation: Paper mill
Pulp Grades and Capacities:
Total pulp capacity: 18,677 mt/y
Recycled Pulping: 18,677 mt/y
Pulp Mill Data:
Recycled Fiber Treatment Lines:
Pulpers: 1
Paper/Paperboard Grades and Capacities:
Total paper and paperboard capacity: 17,500 mt/y
Tissue: 17,500 mt/y
Paper and Paperboard Mill Data:
Paper Machines: 1
No. 1, fourdrinier, Yankee dryer, total capacity 17,500 mt/y, Trim width 2.85 m, Tissue
Energy Data:
Power boilers: 1
Electrical demand for mill: 50 MWh/D

⑪Fabryka Papieru Kaczory Sp. z o.o.
Kaczory Mill
ul. Dziembowska 20
PL-64810 Kaczory
Poland
Phone: (48) 67 2842128
Fax: (48) 67 2842113
Email: info@fabrykapapieru.pl
Web Address: www.fabrykapapieru.pl
Personnel:
Pres.: Stanislaw Cierzniak
Phone: (48) 67 2842128
Fax: (48) 67 2842113
Email: prezes@fabrykapapieru.pl
VP: Malgorzata Walczak
Phone: (48) 67 2842128
Fax: (48) 67 2842113
Email: wiceprezes@fabrykapapieru.pl
Tech. Dir.: Eugeniusz Cierzniak
Phone: (48) 67 2842128
Fax: (48) 67 2842113
Email: cierzniak.e@fabrykapapieru.pl
Prod. Mgr.: Stefan Kozak
Phone: (48) 67 2842128
Fax: (48) 67 2842113
Email: kozak@fabrykapapieru.pl
Sls. & HR Mgr.: Janina Malinska
Phone: (48) 67 2842128
Fax: (48) 67 2842113
Email: info@fabrykapapieru.pl
Total Employees at this Location: 64
Type of Operation: Paper mill
Pulp Grades and Capacities:
Total pulp capacity: 14,533 mt/y
Recycled Pulping: 14,533 mt/y
Paper/Paperboard Grades and Capacities:
Total paper and paperboard capacity: 7,000 mt/y
Tissue: 7,000 mt/y
Paper and Paperboard Mill Data:
Stock Preparation:
Pulpers: 1
Paper Machines: 1
No. 1, fourdrinier, Yankee dryer, total capacity 7,000 mt/y, Trim width 2.5 m, Tissue
Energy Data:
Power boilers: 1
Electrical demand for mill: 20 MWh/D

⑪PPHU 'KARAS'
Ownership: 100% by Mieczyslaw Karasinski
Wolnosci 23
PL- 58-260 Bielawa
Poland
Phone: (48) 71 313 3021/3022 / 74 836 53 98 / 505 079 447
Fax: (48) 71 313 9868/3222 / 74 836 53 98
Email: karas.paper@wp.pl
Personnel:
Pres. & Owner: Mieczyslaw Karasinski
Phone: (48) 74 645 6334
Fax: (48) 71 313 9868
Prod. Mgr.: Miroslaw Wybaczyk
Phone: (48) 71 313 3021
Fax: (48) 71 313 9868
Total Employees of Company: 34
Mill Locations:
PPHU 'KARAS', Olawa Mill, ul. Zwierzyniec Duzy 6, PL-55200 Olawa, Poland, Capacity: 5,000 mt/y, (Paper mill)
Phone: (48) 71 313 3021/3022 / 74 836 53 98 / 505 079 447
Fax: (48) 71 313 9868/3222 / 74 836 53 98
Email: karas.paper@wp.pl

⑪PPHU 'KARAS'
Olawa Mill
ul. Zwierzyniec Duzy 6
PL-55200 Olawa
Poland
Mailing Address: Wolnosci 23, PL- 58-260 Bielawa, Poland
Phone: (48) 71 313 3021/3022 / 74 836 53 98 / 505 079 447
Fax: (48) 71 313 9868/3222 / 74 836 53 98
Email: karas.paper@wp.pl
Personnel:
Pres. & Owner: Mieczyslaw Karasinski
Phone: (48) 74 645 6334
Prod. Mgr.: Miroslaw Wybaczyk
Phone: (48) 71 313 3021
Total Employees at this Location: 34
Type of Operation: Paper mill
Pulp Grades and Capacities:
Total pulp capacity: 5,379 mt/y
Recycled Pulping: 5,379 mt/y
Paper/Paperboard Grades and Capacities:
Total paper and paperboard capacity: 5,000 mt/y
Tissue: 5,000 mt/y
Paper and Paperboard Mill Data:
Stock Preparation:
Pulpers: 2
Refiners: 2
Paper Machines: 1
No. 2, fourdrinier, Yankee dryer, total capacity 5,000 mt/y, Trim width 2.7 m, Tissue
Finishing Equipment:
Rewinders: 5
Sheeters: 4
Energy Data:
Power boilers: 1
Electrical demand for mill: 16 MWh/D

⑪Lamix
Ownership: 100% by Miroslaw Laszko
ul. Papiernicza 1
PL-66460 Witnica
Poland
Phone: (48) 95 751 7000
Fax: (48) 95 751 7009
Email: lamix@lamix.pl
Web Address: www.lamix.pl
Personnel:
Gen. Dir./Owner: Miroslaw Laszko
Phone: (48) 95 751 7000
Fax: (48) 95 751 7009
Email: mlaszko@lamix.pl
Chief Acc.: Krzysztof Brodnicki
Phone: (48) 95 751 7000
Fax: (48) 95 751 7009
Email: kbrodnicki@lamix.pl
Sls. & Logist. Dir.: Dariusz Czulada
Phone: (48) 95 751 7000
Fax: (48) 95 751 7009
Email: dczulada@lamix.pl
Total Employees at this Location: 140
Mill Locations:
Lamix, Witnica Mill, ul. Papiernicza 1, PL-66460 Witnica, Poland, Capacity: 22,000 mt/y, (Paper mill)
Phone: (48) 95 751 7000
Fax: (48) 95 751 7009
Email: lamix@lamix.pl

⑪Lamix
Witnica Mill
ul. Papiernicza 1
PL-66460 Witnica
Poland
Phone: (48) 95 751 7000
Fax: (48) 95 751 7009
Email: lamix@lamix.pl
Web Address: www.lamix.pl
Personnel:
Gen. Dir./Owner: Miroslaw Laszko
Phone: (48) 95 751 7000
Fax: (48) 95 751 7009
Email: mlaszko@lamix.pl
Paper Mill Mgr.: Roman Buczynski
Phone: (48) 95 751 7014
Fax: (48) 95 751 7009
Email: rbuczynski@lamix.pl
Export & Mktg. Mgr.: Dariusz Kukiel
Phone: (48) 95 751 7011
Fax: (48) 95 751 7009
Email: dkukiel@lamix.pl
Sls. & Logist. Dir.: Dariusz Czulada
Phone: (48) 95 751 7007
Fax: (48) 95 751 7009
Email: dczulada@lamix.pl
Energy Mgr.: Roman Lisiecki
Phone: (48) 95 751 70 16
Fax: (48) 95 751 7009
Email: rlisiecki@lamix.pl
Chief Acc.: Krzysztof Brodnicki
Phone: (48) 95 751 7006
Fax: (48) 95 751 7009
Email: kbrodnicki@lamix.pl
Total Employees at this Location: 140
Type of Operation: Paper mill
Pulp Grades and Capacities:
Total pulp capacity: 23,379 mt/y
Recycled Pulping: 23,379 mt/y
Pulp Mill Data:
Recycled Fiber Treatment Lines:
Pulpers
Paper/Paperboard Grades and Capacities:
Total paper and paperboard capacity: 22,000 mt/y
Tissue: 22,000 mt/y
Paper and Paperboard Mill Data:
Paper Machines: 1
No. 1, fourdrinier, Yankee dryer, total capacity 22,000 mt/y, Trim width 2.55 m, Tissue
Energy Data:
Power boilers: 2
Electrical demand for mill: 62 MWh/D

⑪Firma "W. Lewandowski" P.H.U.
Ownership: 100% by Wieslaw Lewandowski
ul. Kopernika 5
PL-90 509 Lodz
Poland
Phone: (48) 42 633 7212/639 1072
Fax: (48) 42 632 4064
Email: lewandowski@lewandowski.com.pl, marketing@lewandowski.com.pl
Web Address: www.lewandowski.com.pl
Personnel:
Owner: Wieslaw Lewandowski

Poland

Phone: (48) 42 639 1072
Fax: (48) 42 632 4064
Vice Mgr.: Jadwiga Furgalska
Phone: (48) 42 633 6930/7212
Fax: (48) 42 632 4064
Email: jadzia@lewandowski.com.pl
Head of Marketing and Supply: Michael Drzazga
Phone: (48) 42 639 1073
Fax: (48) 42 632 4064
Email: michal@lewandowski.com.pl
Purch. Specialist: Barbara Szpakowska
Phone: (48) 42 639 1075
Fax: (48) 42 632 4064
Email: basia@lewandowski.com.pl
Head of Purch. Waste Paper: Jacek Galdecki
Phone: (48) 42 611 1509
Fax: (48) 42 611 1509
Email: hurtownia@lewandowski.com.pl
Total Employees of Company: 157
Total Employees at this Location: 17
Mill Locations:
Firma "W. Lewandowski" P.H.U., Wloclawek Mill, ul. Legska 12, PL-87 800 Wloclawek, Poland, Capacity: 15,000 mt/y, (Paper mill)
Phone: (48) 54 232 7359/413 7112
Fax: (48) 54 232 3964
Email: lewandowski@lewandowski.com.pl

ⓜFirma "W. Lewandowski" P.H.U.
Wloclawek Mill
ul. Legska 12
PL-87 800 Wloclawek
Poland
Phone: (48) 54 232 7359/413 7112
Fax: (48) 54 232 3964
Email: lewandowski@lewandowski.com.pl
Web Address: www.lewandowski.com.pl
Personnel:
Mill Mgr.: Leszek Zasada
Phone: (48) 54 232 7359
Fax: (48) 54 232 3964
Total Employees at this Location: 100
Type of Operation: Paper mill
Pulp Grades and Capacities:
Total pulp capacity: 15,970 mt/y
Recycled Pulping: 15,970 mt/y
Pulp Mill Data:
Recycled Fiber Treatment Lines:
Pulpers: 1
Paper/Paperboard Grades and Capacities:
Total paper and paperboard capacity: 15,000 mt/y
Tissue: 15,000 mt/y
Paper and Paperboard Mill Data:
Paper Machines: 1
No. 1, fourdrinier, Yankee dryer, total capacity 15,000 mt/y, Trim width 2.22 m, Tissue
Energy Data:
Power boilers
Electrical demand for mill: 43 MWh/D

ⓗⓜFabryka Papieru Malta Decor S.A.
Poznan Mill
Ownership: 100% by Kronospan Holdings Ltd.
ul. Wolkowyska 32
PL-61132 Poznan
Poland
Phone: (48) 61 8735400
Fax: (48) 61 8735401
Email: office.malta@kronospan.pl
Web Address: www.maltadecor.pl
Personnel:
Paper Mill Mgr.: Miroslaw Wronski
Phone: (48) 61 8735400
Fax: (48) 61 8735401
Email: m.wronski@kronospan.pl
Paper Mill Mgr.: Ralf Piederstorfer
Phone: (48) 61 8735400
Fax: (48) 61 8735401
Email: r.piederstorfer@kronospan.pl

Mgr.: Tomasz Zgórecki
Phone: (48) 61 8735426
Fax: (48) 61 8735401
Email: t.zgorecki@kronospan.pl
Total Employees at this Location: 300
Type of Operation: Paper mill
Mill Locations:
Fabryka Papieru Malta Decor S.A., Rudawa Mill, PL-48 330 Nowy Swietów, Poland, Capacity: 24,000 mt/y, (Paper mill)
Phone: (48) 77 439 1901
Fax: (48) 77 439 1902
Paper/Paperboard Grades and Capacities:
Total paper and paperboard capacity: 63,000 mt/y
Specialty and industrial: 63,000 mt/y
Paper and Paperboard Mill Data:
Stock Preparation:
Pulpers: 3
Refiners: 13
Paper Machines: 3
PM 1, fourdrinier, Trim width 2.12 m, Specialty and industrial
PM 2, fourdrinier, Trim width 2.52 m, Specialty and industrial
PM 4, Trim width 2.64 m, Specialty and industrial
Coating Machines: 1
No. 1, off machine
Finishing Equipment:
Rewinders: 3
Energy Data:
Power boilers: 4
Combustion turbines: 1 at 1.5 MW

ⓜFabryka Papieru Malta Decor S.A.
Rudawa Mill
PL-48 330 Nowy Swietów
Poland
Phone: (48) 77 439 1901
Fax: (48) 77 439 1902
Personnel:
Pres.: Peter Kaindl
Phone: (48) 77 439 1901
Type of Operation: Paper mill
Paper/Paperboard Grades and Capacities:
Total paper and paperboard capacity: 24,000 mt/y
Specialty and industrial: 24,000 mt/y
Paper and Paperboard Mill Data:
Paper Machines: 1
PM 3, fourdrinier, Trim width 2.12 m, Specialty and industrial

ⓜMetsä Tissue S.A.
Krapkowice Mill
Ownership: 100% by Metsä Tissue Corp.
ul. Opolska 103
PL-47300 Krapkowice
Poland
Phone: (48) 77 541 9100/9389
Fax: (48) 77 466 1554
Email: krapkowice@metsagroup.com
Web Address: www.metsatissue.com
Personnel:
VP Prod. & Mill Mgr.: Peter Simo
Phone: (48) 69 446 6797
Fax: (48) 77 466 1554
Email: peter.simo@metsagroup.com
Total Employees at this Location: 250
Type of Operation: Paper mill
Pulp Grades and Capacities:
Total pulp capacity: 40,342 mt/y
Recycled Pulping: 40,342 mt/y
Pulp Mill Data:
Recycled Fiber Treatment Lines:
Flotation deinking lines: 1
Paper/Paperboard Grades and Capacities:
Total paper and paperboard capacity: 87,000 mt/y
Tissue: 87,000 mt/y
Paper and Paperboard Mill Data:
Stock Preparation:

Pulpers: 3
Refiners: 8
Paper Machines: 3
No. 6, twin-wire, Yankee dryer, total capacity 17,000 mt/y, Trim width 3.3 m, Tissue
No. 7, crescent former, Yankee dryer, total capacity 35,000 mt/y, Trim width 2.75 m, Tissue
No. 8, crescent former, Yankee dryer, total capacity 35,000 mt/y, Trim width 2.75 m, Tissue
Energy Data:
Power boilers
Steam turbines: 2 at 4.5 MW
Electrical demand for mill: 243 MWh/D

ⓜMondi Swiecie S.A.
Swiecie Mill
Ownership: Mondi Europe & International Division
Bydgoska Str. 1
PL-86100 Swiecie
Poland
Phone: (48) 52 332 1553
Fax: (48) 52 332 1931
Email: (firstname.surname@mondigroup.com), info.swiecie@mondigroup.com
Web Address: www.mondigroup.com
Personnel:
Man. Dir. & COO Containerboard Europe & International: Maciej Kunda
Phone: (48) 52 332 1553
Fax: (48) 52 332 1931
Email: maciej.kunda@mondigroup.com
Paper Prod. Mgr.: Sebastian Rzepa Olejniczak
Phone: (48) 52 332 1553
Fax: (48) 52 332 1931
Email: sebastian.rzepa@mondigroup.com
Head of Fiber Preparation: Ryszard Maciejak
Phone: (48) 52 332 1664
Fax: (48) 52 332 1992
Email: ryszard.maciejak@mondigroup.com
Finan. Dir. & Member of Mangm. Board: Boguslaw Bielecki
Phone: (48) 52 332 1553
Fax: (48) 52 332 1910
Email: boguslaw.bielecki@mondigroup.com
Mktg. & Technical Service: Marek Motylewski
Phone: (48) 52 332 1553
Fax: (48) 52 332 1931
Email: marek.motylewski@mondigroup.com
Head of Energy Containerboard Europe & International: Henryk Drechnowicz
Phone: (48) 52 332 1602
Fax: (48) 52 332 1833
Email: henryk.drechnowicz@mondigroup.com
Prod. Dir.: Tomasz Katewicz
Phone: (48) 52 332 15 05
Fax: (48) 52 332 19 22
Email: tomasz.katewicz@mondigroup.com
Wood & Biofuels Procurement Dir.: Jacek Kulis
Phone: (48) 52 332 1553
Fax: (48) 52 332 1931
Email: jacek.kulis@mondigroup.com
Head of Purch.: Marcin Witkowski
Phone: (48) 52 332 1149
Fax: (48) 52 332 1854
Email: marcin.witkowski@mondigroup.com
Total Employees at this Location: 1,100
Type of Operation: Pulp mill, Paper mill, Paperboard mill
Pulp Grades and Capacities:
Total pulp capacity: 1,432,922 mt/y
Chemical Pulp: 537,363 mt/y
Recycled Pulping: 895,558 mt/y
Pulp Mill Data:
Chemical Pulping Systems:
Continuous digesters: 2
Chemical Recovery Equipment:
Evaporator lines: 1
Recovery boilers: 1
Lime Kiln
Recycled Fiber Treatment Lines:

Poland

Pulpers: 8 at 348,170 admt/y
Recycled packaging pulping lines: 3
Pulp Dryers:
Air Float dryers 1, Wet Lap machine 1
Paper/Paperboard Grades and Capacities:
Total paper and paperboard capacity: 1,399,000 mt/y
Packaging papers: 35,000 mt/y
Linerboard: 875,000 mt/y
Corrugating medium/fluting: 489,000 mt/y
Paper and Paperboard Mill Data:
Paper Machines: 6
No. 1, GapFormer, total capacity 162,000 mt/y, Trim width 5.3 m, Linerboard, Packaging papers
No. 2, fourdrinier (2), total capacity 227,000 mt/y, Trim width 4.45 m, Linerboard
No. 3, fourdrinier (2), total capacity 128,000 mt/y, Trim width 4.45 m, Linerboard
No. 4, fourdrinier, total capacity 179,000 mt/y, Trim width 4.4 m, Corrugating medium/fluting
No. 5, fourdrinier (2), total capacity 218,000 mt/y, Trim width 5.25 m, Linerboard
No. 7, OptiFormer, total capacity 485,000 mt/y, Trim width 7.8 m, Corrugating medium/fluting, Linerboard
Energy Data:
Power boilers: 4
Steam turbines: 4 at 122 MW
Electrical demand for mill: 2,585 MWh/D

ⓘⓜFabryka Papieru Myszków Sp. z o.o.
Myszkow Mill
Ownership: 95% by Green House Project, 5% by Polish government
ul. Pulaskiego 6
PL-42300 Myszkow
Poland
  Phone: (48) 34 313 1022/ 7236
  Fax: (48) 34 313 1135
  Email: papiernia@papiernia.pl
  Web Address: www.papiernia.pl
Personnel:
Gen. Mgr.: Ireneusz Grabowski
Phone: (48) 34 313 1022
Fax: (48) 34 313 1135
Environ .Dir.: Dominika Prokop
Phone: (48) 34 313 1022
Fax: (48) 34 313 1135
Email: dominika.prokop@papiernia.pl
Chief Acc.: Barbara Leszczynska
Phone: (48) 34 313 1022
Fax: (48) 34 313 1135
Email: barbara.leszczynska@papiernia.pl
Dir. Tech. & Prod.: Jerzy Wysocki
Phone: (48) 34 313 1022
Fax: (48) 34 313 1135
Email: jerzy.wysocki@papiernia.pl
Total Employees of Company: 315
Total Employees at this Location: 315
Type of Operation: Pulp mill, Paper mill
Pulp Grades and Capacities:
Total pulp capacity: 95,963 mt/y
Mechanical Pulp: 47,010 mt/y
Recycled Pulping: 48,953 mt/y
Pulp Mill Data:
Mechanical Pulping Systems:
Conventional grinders: 8
Bleach Plant Lines:
SGW, Sequence: P
Recycled Fiber Treatment Lines:
Flotation deinking lines: 1 at 70,000
Paper/Paperboard Grades and Capacities:
Total paper and paperboard capacity: 95,000 mt/y
Newsprint: 57,000 mt/y
Uncoated mechanical/groundwood: 38,000 mt/y
Paper and Paperboard Mill Data:
Stock Preparation:
Pulpers: 4
Refiners: 8
Paper Machines: 1
No. 6, fourdrinier, total capacity 95,000 mt/y, Trim width 5.36 m, Newsprint, Uncoated mechanical/groundwood
Finishing Equipment:
Supercalenders: 2
Rewinders: 2
Sheeters: 2
Energy Data:
Power boilers: 3
Electrical demand for mill: 384 MWh/D

ⓜPabianicka Fabryka Papieru Sp. z.o.o.
Pabianice Mill
Mill is under construction (Original mill was scrapped in April 2011. New mill on adjacent site being constructed, production is supposed to start at the end of 2014)
ul. Marszalka J. Pilsudskiego 7
PL-95200 Pabianice
Poland
  Phone: (48) 42 215 3063
  Fax: (48) 42 215 2532
  Email: info@pfp.net.pl
  Web Address: www.pfp.net.pl
Personnel:
Chmn. of the Board: Romuald Starosielec
Phone: (48) 42 215 3016
Email: starosielec.r@pfp.net.pl
Type of Operation: Paper mill, Paperboard mill
Paper and Paperboard Mill Data:
Paper Machines: 2
PM 1, (2nd hand, due to start for the end of 2014), total capacity 52,500 mt/y, Trim width 2.9 m
PM 2, (2nd hand, due to start in the beginning of 2015), total capacity 77,000 mt/y, Trim width 2.85 m, Boxboard/cartonboard
Energy Data:
Power boilers: 3

ⓘPabianicka Fabryka Papieru Sp. z.o.o.
ul Syreny 14
PL-01-132 Warsaw
Poland
  Phone: (48) 42 227 15 23, 42 215 30 63
  Fax: (48) 42 215 2532
  Email: info@pfp.net.pl
  Web Address: www.pfp.net.pl
Personnel:
Pres.: Romuald Starosielec
Phone: (48) 42 215 30 16
Email: starosielec.r@pfp.net.pl
Proj. Mgr.: Piotr Nowakowski
Phone: (48) 42 215 30 16
Mill Locations:
Pabianicka Fabryka Papieru Sp. z.o.o., Pabianice Mill, ul. Marszalka J. Pilsudskiego 7, PL-95200 Pabianice, Poland, (Paper mill, Paperboard mill)
Phone: (48) 42 215 3063
Fax: (48) 42 215 2532
Email: info@pfp.net.pl

ⓘⓜPackprofil Sp. z o.o.
Kolonowskie Mill
Ownership: 100% by private shareholders
ul. Zakladowa 3
PL-47 110 Kolonowskie 1
Poland
  Phone: (48) 77 461 1115/ 400 4350
  Fax: (48) 77 461 1485
  Email: info@packprofil.pl
  Web Address: www.packprofil.pl
Personnel:
CEO: Wojciech Serafin
Phone: (48) 77 400 4350
Fax: (48) 77 461 1485
Email: wserafin@packprofil.pl
Tech. Mgr.: Grzegorz Walaszek
Phone: (48) 77 400 4350 ext. 62
Fax: (48) 77 461 1485
Email: walaszek@packprofil.pl
Sls. Mgr.: Rafal Swierczok
Phone: (48) 77 400 4354
Fax: (48) 77 461 1485
Email: rswierczok@packprofil.pl
Qlty. Contr. Dir.: Malgorzata Golombek
Phone: (48) 77 400 4359
Fax: (48) 77 461 1485
Email: golabek@packprofil.pl
Environ. Dir.: Damian Czok
Phone: (48) 77 400 43 58
Fax: (48) 77 461 1485
Email: czok@packprofil.pl
Chief Acc.: Renata Czupala
Phone: (48) 77 400 43 53
Fax: (48) 77 461 1485
Email: rczupala@packprofil.pl
Total Employees at this Location: 120
Type of Operation: Paper mill
Pulp Grades and Capacities:
Total pulp capacity: 12,266 mt/y
Recycled Pulping: 12,266 mt/y
Pulp Mill Data:
Recycled Fiber Treatment Lines:
Recycled packaging pulping lines: 1
Paper/Paperboard Grades and Capacities:
Total paper and paperboard capacity: 12,000 mt/y
Boxboard/cartonboard: 12,000 mt/y
Paper and Paperboard Mill Data:
Stock Preparation:
Pulpers: 1
Paper Machines: 1
No. 2, cylinder, total capacity 12,000 mt/y, Trim width 2.1 m, Boxboard/cartonboard
Finishing Equipment:
Winders: 1 at 19,200 mt/y
Rewinders: 1 at 20,000 mt/y
Energy Data:
Power boilers: 2
Electrical demand for mill: 14 MWh/D

ⓘPapiernia Sieroslawice
Ownership: 100% by Marcin Markiewicz
PL-46220 Byczyna
Poland
  Phone: (48) 77 417 6205
  Fax: (48) 77 417 6205
  Email: info@papierniasieroslawice.pl
Personnel:
Owner: Marcin Markiewicz
Phone: (48) 601 822 467
Mill Mgr.: Waclaw Winiarski
Phone: (48) 696 753 764
Total Employees of Company: 20
Mill Locations:
Papiernia Sieroslawice, Byczyna Mill, PL-46220 Byczyna, Poland, Capacity: 8,000 mt/y, (Paper mill)
Phone: (48) 77 417 6205
Fax: (48) 77 417 6205
Email: info@papierniasieroslawice.pl

ⓜPapiernia Sieroslawice
Byczyna Mill
PL-46220 Byczyna
Poland
  Phone: (48) 77 417 6205
  Fax: (48) 77 417 6205
  Email: info@papierniasieroslawice.pl
Personnel:
Owner: Marcin Markiewicz
Phone: (48) 601 822 467
Mill Mgr.: Waclaw Winiarski
Phone: (48) 696 753 764
Total Employees at this Location: 20
Type of Operation: Paper mill
Pulp Grades and Capacities:
Total pulp capacity: 8,574 mt/y
Recycled Pulping: 8,574 mt/y

Poland

Paper/Paperboard Grades and Capacities:
Total paper and paperboard capacity: 8,000 mt/y
Tissue: 8,000 mt/y
Paper and Paperboard Mill Data:
Paper Machines: 1
No. 1, fourdrinier, Yankee dryer, total capacity 8,000 mt/y, Trim width 2.15 m, Tissue
Energy Data:
Electrical demand for mill: 24 MWh/D

ⒽPaptol, Zaklad Produkcji Papieru Toaletowego
ul. Deszczowa 10
31-985 Kraków
Poland
  Phone: (48) 12 645 0808
  Fax: (48) 12 626 9761
  Email: paptol@xl.wp.pl
Personnel:
  Dir.: Ludwik Stefaniszyn
  Phone: (48) 12 645 0808
  Fax: (48) 12 626 9761
Total Employees at this Location: 15
Mill Locations:
Paptol, Zaklad Produkcji Papieru Toaletowego, Kraków Mill, ul. Deszczowa 10, 31-985 Kraków, Poland, Capacity: 2,000 mt/y, (Paper mill)
Phone: (48) 12 645 0808
Fax: (48) 12 626 9761
Email: paptol@xl.wp.pl

ⓂPaptol, Zaklad Produkcji Papieru Toaletowego
Kraków Mill
ul. Deszczowa 10
31-985 Kraków
Poland
  Phone: (48) 12 645 0808
  Fax: (48) 12 626 9761
  Email: paptol@xl.wp.pl
Personnel:
  Director: Ludwik Stefaniszyn
  Phone: (48) 12 645 0808
Total Employees at this Location: 15
Type of Operation: Paper mill
Pulp Grades and Capacities:
  Total pulp capacity: 2,135 mt/y
  Recycled Pulping: 2,135 mt/y
Paper/Paperboard Grades and Capacities:
  Total paper and paperboard capacity: 2,000 mt/y
  Tissue: 2,000 mt/y
Paper and Paperboard Mill Data:
Paper Machines: 1
No. 1, fourdrinier, Yankee dryer, total capacity 2,000 mt/y, Trim width 2.6 m, Tissue
Energy Data:
Electrical demand for mill: 6 MWh/D

ⓂPolska Wytwornia Papierow Wartosciowych S.A.
Warsaw Mill
ul. Romana Sanguszki 1
PL-00222 Warsaw
Poland
  Phone: (48) 22 530 2000
  Fax: (48) 22 530 2450
  Email: pwpw@pwpw.pl
  Web Address: www.pwpw.pl
Personnel:
  Chmn. of the Board: Krzysztof Zamotal
  Phone: (48) 22 530 2000
  Member of the Board: Krzysztof Czyz
  Phone: (48) 22 635 1481
  Member of the Board: Andrzej Bogun
  Phone: (48) 22 635 1481
  Member of the Board: Maciej Flemming
  Phone: (48) 22 635 1481
  Sls. Mgr. - Banknotes & Secured Prints: Sylwia Barylska
  Phone: (48) 22 235 2816
  Fax: (48) 22 530 2450
  Email: s.barylska@pwpw.pl
  Commun. Dir.: Arkadiusz Slodkowski
  Phone: (48) 60 703 0311 GSM
  Fax: (48) 22 530 2450
  Email: aslodkowski@profitsystem.pl
Type of Operation: Paper mill
Paper/Paperboard Grades and Capacities:
  Total paper and paperboard capacity: 1,500 mt/y
  Uncoated woodfree/freesheet
  Specialty and industrial

ⒽPolska Wytwornia Papierow Wartosciowych S.A.
Ownership: 100% by State Treasury
ul. Romana Sanguszki 1
PL-00222 Warsaw
Poland
  Phone: (48) 22 530 2000
  Fax: (48) 22 530 2450
  Email: pwpw@pwpw.pl
  Web Address: www.pwpw.pl
Personnel:
  Chmn. of Bd.: Krzysztof Zamotal
  Phone: (48) 22 530 2000
  Fax: (48) 22 530 2450
  Bd. Mbr.: Krzysztof Czyz
  Phone: (48) 22 530 2000
  Fax: (48) 22 530 2450
  Bd. Mbr.: Andrzej Bogun
  Phone: (48) 22 530 2000
  Fax: (48) 22 530 2450
  Bd. Mbr.: Maciej Flemming
  Phone: (48) 22 530 2000
  Fax: (48) 22 530 2450
Total Employees at this Location: 160
Mill Locations:
Polska Wytwornia Papierow Wartosciowych S.A., Warsaw Mill, ul. Romana Sanguszki 1, PL-00222 Warsaw, Poland, Capacity: 1,500 mt/y, (Paper mill)
Phone: (48) 22 530 2000
Fax: (48) 22 530 2450
Email: pwpw@pwpw.pl

ⒽⓂPPHU Rolls Sp. z o.o.
Wloclawek Mill
Ownership: 100% by limited liability company
ul. Stefana Wyszynskiego 26
PL-87800 Wloclawek
Poland
  Phone: (48) 54 236 2605, 54 413 1014
  Fax: (48) 54 236 2806
  Email: info@rollspap.com.pl
  Web Address: www.rollspap.com.pl
Personnel:
  Chmn.: Krzysztof Mikolajczyk
  Phone: (48) 54 236 9958
  Email: krzmik@onet.pl
  Advisor of Board: Wieslaw Czernik
  Phone: (48) 54 413 1014 int. 22
  Email: info@rollspap.com.pl
Total Employees of Company: 96
Total Employees at this Location: 96
Type of Operation: Paper mill
Pulp Grades and Capacities:
  Total pulp capacity: 15,957 mt/y
  Recycled Pulping: 15,957 mt/y
Paper/Paperboard Grades and Capacities:
  Total paper and paperboard capacity: 15,000 mt/y
  Tissue: 15,000 mt/y
Paper and Paperboard Mill Data:
Paper Machines: 2
No. 1, fourdrinier, Yankee dryer, total capacity 7,000 mt/y, Trim width 2.23 m, Tissue
No. 2, fourdrinier, Yankee dryer, total capacity 8,000 mt/y, Trim width 2.2 m, Tissue
Energy Data:
Electrical demand for mill: 43 MWh/D

ⒽⓂSchumacher Packaging Zaklad Grudziadz Sp.z o.o.
Grudziadz Mill
Ownership: Schumacher Packaging GmbH
ul. Parkowa 56
PL-86300 Grudziadz
Poland
  Phone: (48) 56 450 3810
  Fax: (48) 56 462 1376
  Email: grudziadz@schumacher-packaging.com
  Web Address: www.schumacher-packaging.com
Personnel:
  Pres.: Björn Schumacher
  Phone: (48) 56 450 3810
Total Employees at this Location: 250
Type of Operation: Paperboard mill
Pulp Grades and Capacities:
  Total pulp capacity: 81,301 mt/y
  Recycled Pulping: 81,301 mt/y
Paper/Paperboard Grades and Capacities:
  Total paper and paperboard capacity: 80,000 mt/y
  Linerboard: 50,000 mt/y
  Corrugating medium/fluting: 30,000 mt/y
Paper and Paperboard Mill Data:
Paper Machines: 1
No. 1, fourdrinier, total capacity 80,000 mt/y, Trim width 2.8 m, Corrugating medium/fluting, Linerboard
Energy Data:
Electrical demand for mill: 97 MWh/D

ⒽⓂStora Enso Poland S.A.
Ostroleka Mill
Ownership: 99.64% by Stora Enso Oyj
ul. 1 Armii Wojska Polskiego 21
PL-07401 Ostroleka
Poland
  Phone: (48) 29 7640000
  Fax: (48) 29 7640002
  Email: info.poland@storaenso.com
  Web Address: www.storaenso.com/poland
Personnel:
  Pres. & Man. Dir.: Jerzy Janowicz
  Phone: (48) 29 7640350
  Fax: (48) 29 7640002
  Email: jerzy.janowicz@storaenso.com
  VP Corrugated Packaging Central Europe: Tomasz Zebrowski
  Phone: (48) 29 7640000
  Fax: (48) 29 7640002
  Email: tomasz.zebrowski@storaenso.com
  Oper. Dir. Corrugated Board & Boxes Central Europe: Tomasz Darniecki
  Phone: (48) 29 7640000
  Fax: (48) 29 7640002
  Email: tomasz.darniecki@storaenso.com
  Dir. of sack mill: Robert Biwald
  Phone: (48) 29 7640000
  Fax: (48) 29 7640002
  Email: robert.biwald@storaenso.com
  Dir. Corrugated Board & Boxes Mill: Marek Sygula
  Phone: (48) 29 7640557
  Fax: (48) 29 7640002
  Email: marek.sygula@storaenso.com
  Pulp & Paper Mill Dir.: Krzysztof Zeranski
  Phone: (48) 29 7640722
  Fax: (48) 29 7640002
  Email: krzysztof.zeranski@storaenso.com
Total Employees of Company: 1,040
Total Employees at this Location: 1,040
Type of Operation: Pulp mill, Paper mill, Paperboard mill
Pulp Grades and Capacities:
  Total pulp capacity: 639,653 mt/y
  Chemical Pulp: 92,054 mt/y
  Recycled Pulping: 547,599 mt/y
Pulp Mill Data:
  Chemical Pulping Systems:
  Batch digesters: 5

Poland

Chemical Recovery Equipment:
Evaporator lines: 1
Recovery boilers: 1
Lime Kiln
Recycled Fiber Treatment Lines:
Pulpers: 2 at 165,000 admt/y
Paper/Paperboard Grades and Capacities:
Total paper and paperboard capacity: 640,000 mt/y
Packaging papers: 70,800 mt/y
Specialty and industrial: 18,200 mt/y
Linerboard: 400,000 mt/y
Corrugating medium/fluting: 151,000 mt/y
Paper and Paperboard Mill Data:
Paper Machines: 4
No. 1, fourdrinier, total capacity 63,000 mt/y, Trim width 4.4 m, Packaging papers
No. 3, fourdrinier, total capacity 26,000 mt/y, Trim width 4.4 m, Specialty and industrial, Packaging papers
No. 4, fourdrinier, Yankee dryer, total capacity 96,000 mt/y, Trim width 4.4 m, Corrugating medium/fluting
No. 5, GapFormer, total capacity 455,000 mt/y, Trim width 7.8 m, Corrugating medium/fluting, Linerboard
Energy Data:
Power boilers: 1
Steam turbines: 2 at 37, 7 MW
Electrical demand for mill: 799 MWh/D

⊕ⓂTektura Sp. z o.o.
Mikolow Mill
Ownership: 100% by Private
ul. Rybnicka 5
PL-43190 Mikolow
Poland
 Phone: (48) 32 226 2325
 Fax: (48) 32 226 2293
 Email: tektura@tektura.com.pl
 Web Address: www.tektura.com.pl
Personnel:
 Pres.: Piotr Caban
 Phone: (48) 603 928 736 (gsm)
 Fax: (48) 32 226 2293
 VP: Dariusz Zalewski
 Phone: (48) 32 226 2325
 Sls. Specialist: Mieczyslawa Sroczynska
 Phone: (48) 32 226 2324 / 601 878 861
 Email: handel@tektura.com.pl
Total Employees at this Location: 120
Type of Operation: Paper mill
Paper/Paperboard Grades and Capacities:
 Total paper and paperboard capacity: 10,000 mt/y
 Containerboard: 5,000 mt/y
 Boxboard/cartonboard: 5,000 mt/y
Paper and Paperboard Mill Data:
Paper Machines: 1
No. 2, fourdrinier, total capacity 10,000 mt/y, Trim width 2.1 m, Containerboard, Boxboard/cartonboard
Energy Data:
Power boilers: 2

ⓂTOP S.A.
Katowice Mill
ul. Checinskiego 10
PL-40750 Katowice
Poland
 Phone: (48) 32 209 4769
 Fax: (48) 32 209 4767
 Email: kostuchna@topsa.pl
 Web Address: www.topsa.pl
Personnel:
 Sls Mgr. - Dept. Solid & Glued Cardboard: Agata Szojda
 Phone: (48) 32 209 4769
 Fax: (48) 32 209 4767
 Email: aszojda@topsa.pl
Total Employees at this Location: 60
Type of Operation: Paperboard mill
Pulp Grades and Capacities:
 Total pulp capacity: 20,378 mt/y
 Recycled Pulping: 20,378 mt/y
Pulp Mill Data:
Recycled Fiber Treatment Lines:
 Recycled packaging pulping lines: 1
Paper/Paperboard Grades and Capacities:
 Total paper and paperboard capacity: 20,000 mt/y
 Boxboard/cartonboard: 20,000 mt/y
Paper and Paperboard Mill Data:
Paper Machines: 1
No. 1, cylinder, total capacity 20,000 mt/y, Trim width 2 m, Boxboard/cartonboard
Energy Data:
Power boilers
Electrical demand for mill: 29 MWh/D

⊕ⓂTOP S.A.
Tychy Mill
ul. Katowicka 182
PL-43100 Tychy
Poland
 Phone: (48) 32 3257300
 Fax: (48) 32 219 8065
 Email: office@topsa.pl
 Web Address: www.topsa.pl
Personnel:
 Pres., Strategy, Bus. Develop, Investment, Technology & Eng. & Owner: Andrej Kowalczyk
 Phone: (48) 32 325 7300
 Fax: (48) 32 219 8065
 Email: akowalczyk@topsa.pl
 VP, Sls. & Acquisition: Marek Kosewski
 Phone: (48) 32 325 7300
 Fax: (48) 32 219 8065
 Email: mkosewski@topsa.pl
 Environ. Mgr.: Kamila Cwikla
 Phone: (48) 32 325 7392
 Fax: (48) 32 219 7377
 Email: kcwikla@topsa.pl
Total Employees at this Location: 100
Type of Operation: Paper mill
Mill Locations:
TOP S.A., Katowice Mill, ul. Checinskiego 10, PL-40750 Katowice, Poland, Capacity: 20,000 mt/y, (Paperboard mill)
 Phone: (48) 32 209 4769
 Fax: (48) 32 209 4767
 Email: kostuchna@topsa.pl
Pulp Grades and Capacities:
 Total pulp capacity: 40,832 mt/y
 Recycled Pulping: 40,832 mt/y
Pulp Mill Data:
Recycled Fiber Treatment Lines:
 Recycled packaging pulping lines: 1
Paper/Paperboard Grades and Capacities:
 Total paper and paperboard capacity: 40,000 mt/y
 Linerboard: 25,000 mt/y
 Corrugating medium/fluting: 15,000 mt/y
Paper and Paperboard Mill Data:
Paper Machines: 2
No. 4, fourdrinier, total capacity 28,000 mt/y, Trim width 2.22 m, Corrugating medium/fluting, Linerboard
No. 5, cylinder, total capacity 12,000 mt/y, Trim width 1.8 m, Linerboard
Energy Data:
Power boilers
Electrical demand for mill: 65 MWh/D

⊕Velvet CARE sp. z o.o.
Ownership: 100% by Avallon MBO Fund
Klucze-Osada 3
Klucze
Poland
 Phone: (48) 32 75 87 100
 Fax: (48) 32 75 87 102
 Email: kontakt@velvetcare.pl
 Web Address: www.velvetcare.pl
Personnel:
 CEO: Artur Pielak
 Phone: (48) 32 75 87 100
 Fax: (48) 32 75 87 102
 Email: artur.pielak@velvetcare.pl
 Man. Dir.: Marek Sciazko
 Phone: (48) 32 75 87 100
 Fax: (48) 32 75 87 102
 Email: marek.sciazko@velvetcare.pl
Total Employees of Company: 300
Mill Locations:
Velvet CARE sp. z o.o., Klucze Mill, Klucze - Osada 3, PL-32310 Klucze, Poland, Capacity: 32,000 mt/y, (Paper mill)
 Phone: (48) 32 758 7100/7101
 Fax: (48) 32 6428410
 Email: kontakt@velvetcare.pl

⊕Velvet CARE sp. z o.o.
Klucze Mill
Klucze - Osada 3
PL-32310 Klucze
Poland
 Phone: (48) 32 758 7100/7101
 Fax: (48) 32 6428410
 Email: kontakt@velvetcare.pl
 Web Address: www.velvetcare.pl
Personnel:
 Man. Dir.: Marek Sciazko
 Phone: (48) 32 75 87 101
 Fax: (48) 32 75 87 102
 Email: marek.sciazko@velvetcare.pl
 Mgr.: Marian Kafel
 Phone: (48) 32 75 87 100
 Fax: (48) 32 75 87 102
 Email: marian.kafel@velvetcare.pl
Total Employees at this Location: 239
Type of Operation: Paper mill
Paper/Paperboard Grades and Capacities:
 Total paper and paperboard capacity: 32,000 mt/y
 Tissue: 32,000 mt/y
Paper and Paperboard Mill Data:
Stock Preparation:
 Pulpers: 1
 Refiners: 5
Paper Machines: 1
No. 6, fourdrinier, Yankee dryer, total capacity 32,000 mt/y, Trim width 3.45 m, Tissue
Finishing Equipment:
 Rewinders: 1 at 18,800 mt/y
Energy Data:
Power boilers
Electrical demand for mill: 95 MWh/D

⊕WARTER - Fabryka Papieru i Tektury
Ownership: 100% by Wojciech Rychlik
Ul. Koralowa 60
PL-02967 Warsaw
Poland
 Phone: (48) 22 756 8530
 Fax: (48) 22 885 4400
 Email: biuro@warter.pl, sekretariat@warter.pl
 Web Address: www.fabryka-tektury.pl
Personnel:
 Plant Dir. & CEO: Henryk Bednarek
 Phone: (48) 78 589 7132
 Fax: (48) 22 885 4400
 Email: dyrektor@warter.pl
 Exec. Board: Agnieszka Galazka
 Phone: (48) 22 756 8530
 Fax: (48) 22 885 4400
 Email: biuro@warter.pl
 Com. Sec.: Edyta Gazarkiewicz
 Phone: (48) 67 266 4001
 Fax: (48) 22 885 4400
 Email: sekretariat@warter.pl
 Billing Dept.: Grazyna Paciepnik
 Phone: (48) 67 266 4097
 Fax: (48) 22 885 4400
 Email: grazyna.paciepnik@warter.pl
Mill Locations:
WARTER - Fabryka Papieru i Tektury, Tarnowka Mill, Oddzial Tarnowka, PL-77416 Tarnowka, Poland, Capacity: 11,000 mt/y, (Paperboard mill)

Poland

Phone: (48) 67 266 4001
Fax: (48) 67 266 4300
Email: sekretariat@warter.pl

ⓜWARTER - Fabryka Papieru i Tektury
Tarnowka Mill
Oddzial Tarnowka
PL-77416 Tarnowka
Poland
Phone: (48) 67 266 4001
Fax: (48) 67 266 4300
Email: sekretariat@warter.pl
Web Address: www.fabryka-tektury.pl
Personnel:
Plt. Dir. & CEO: Henryk Bednarek
Phone: (48) 78 589 7132
Fax: (48) 22 885 4400
Email: dyrektor@warter.pl
Prod. Mgr.: Jacek Bednarek
Phone: (48) 72 648 4826
Fax: (48) 67 266 4300
Email: tektura2@warter.pl
Sls. Mgr.: Krzysztof Pauk
Phone: (48) 67 266 4097
Fax: (48) 67 266 4300
Email: krzysztof.pauk@warter.pl
Transportation: Szymon Sredzki
Phone: (48) 67 266 4001
Fax: (48) 67 266 4300
Email: tektura1@warter.pl
Total Employees at this Location: 100
Type of Operation: Paperboard mill
Pulp Grades and Capacities:
Total pulp capacity: 14,400 mt/y
Recycled Pulping: 14,400 mt/y
Paper/Paperboard Grades and Capacities:
Total paper and paperboard capacity: 11,000 mt/y
Boxboard/cartonboard: 11,000 mt/y
Paper and Paperboard Mill Data:
Paper Machines: 2
No. 1, multi-cylinder, Trim width 1.7 m, Boxboard/cartonboard
No. 2, multi-cylinder, Trim width 2.2 m, Boxboard/cartonboard
Energy Data:
Power boilers: 1
Combustion turbines: 1 at 0.4 MW

ⓜWELMAX Zaklad Produkcyjno-Handlowy Wieslaw Adamowicz
Wohyn Mill
ul. Bezwolska 18 A (POM Bezwola)
PL-21310 Wohyń
Poland
Phone: (48) 83 353 0410/0383
Fax: (48) 83 353 0383
Email: welmax@post.pl
Web Address: www.welmax.eu
Personnel:
Regional Sls. Mgr. - North Region: Robert Sawicki
Phone: (48) 83 353 0410
Fax: (48) 83 353 0383
Email: robert.sawicki@welmax.eu
Regional Sls. Mgr. - Southern Region: Marcin Soko?owski
Phone: (48) 83 353 0410
Fax: (48) 83 353 0383
Email: marcin.sokolowski@welmax.eu
Total Employees at this Location: 25
Type of Operation: Paper mill
Pulp Grades and Capacities:
Total pulp capacity: 6,388 mt/y
Recycled Pulping: 6,388 mt/y
Pulp Mill Data:
Recycled Fiber Treatment Lines:
Pulpers: 1
Paper/Paperboard Grades and Capacities:
Total paper and paperboard capacity: 6,000 mt/y
Tissue: 6,000 mt/y
Paper and Paperboard Mill Data:
Paper Machines: 1
No. 1, fourdrinier, total capacity 6,000 mt/y, Trim width 2.2 m, Tissue
Energy Data:
Power boilers
Electrical demand for mill: 17 MWh/D

ⓜWELMAX Zaklad Produkcyjno-Handlowy Wieslaw Adamowicz
Ownership: 100% by Wieslaw Adamowicz
ul. Bezwolska 18 A (POM Bezwola)
PL-21310 Wohyń
Poland
Phone: (48) 83 353 0410/0383
Fax: (48) 83 353 0383
Email: welmax@post.pl
Web Address: www.welmax.eu
Personnel:
Regional Sls. Mgr. - North region: Robert Sawicki
Phone: (48) 83 353 0410
Fax: (48) 83 353 0383
Email: robert.sawicki@welmax.eu
Regional Sls. Mgr. - Southern Division: Marcin Soko?owski
Phone: (48) 83 353 0410
Fax: (48) 83 353 0383
Email: marcin.sokolowski@welmax.eu
Mill Locations:
WELMAX Zaklad Produkcyjno-Handlowy Wieslaw Adamowicz, Wohyn Mill, ul. Bezwolska 18 A (POM Bezwola), PL-21310 Wohyń, Poland, Capacity: 6,000 mt/y, (Paper mill)
Phone: (48) 83 353 0410/0383
Fax: (48) 83 353 0383
Email: welmax@post.pl

ⓜⓜWEPA Professional Piechowice S.A.
Piechowice Mill
Ownership: WEPA Hygieneprodukte GmbH
ul. Tysiaclecia 49
PL-58573 Piechowice
Poland
Phone: (48) 75 7547 800
Fax: (48) 75 7547 855
Email: info@wepro.com.pl
Web Address: www.wepro.com.pl
Personnel:
Pres. & Gen. Mgr.: Janusz Brylinski
Phone: (48) 75 7617 387
Fax: (48) 75 7547 855
Email: jbrylinski@wepro.com.pl
Paper Mill Mgr.: Wojciech Figiel
Phone: (48) 75 7617 387
Fax: (48) 75 7547 855
Email: wfigiel@wepro.com.pl
Prod. Dir.: Teodor Frys
Phone: (48) 75 7617 387
Fax: (48) 75 7547 855
Email: tfrys@wepro.com.pl
Tech. Dir.: Zbigniew Kulakowski
Phone: (48) 75 7547 800
Fax: (48) 75 7547 855
Email: zbigniew.kulakowski@wepro.com.pl
Key Acc.Mgr. & Environ. Dir.: Piotr Nieradzik
Phone: (48) 75 7547 800
Fax: (48) 75 7547 855
Email: piotr.nieradzik@wepa.de
Total Employees at this Location: 340
Type of Operation: Paper mill
Pulp Grades and Capacities:
Total pulp capacity: 26,446 mt/y
Recycled Pulping: 26,446 mt/y
Paper/Paperboard Grades and Capacities:
Total paper and paperboard capacity: 25,000 mt/y
Tissue: 25,000 mt/y
Paper and Paperboard Mill Data:
Stock Preparation:
Pulpers: 1

Paper Machines: 1
No. 1, fourdrinier, Yankee dryer, total capacity 25,000 mt/y, Trim width 3.2 m, Tissue
Finishing Equipment:
Rewinders: 1
Energy Data:
Power boilers: 2
Electrical demand for mill: 71 MWh/D

ⓜWPT Eko-Klan Sp. z o.o.
Ownership: 100% by Pawel Smektala
Margonska Wies 34A
PL-64830 Margonin
Poland
Phone: (48) 67 2846097
Fax: (48) 67 2846097
Email: marketing.ekoklan@interia.pl, biuro@eko-klan.com.pl
Web Address: www.eko-klan.com.pl
Personnel:
Owner/Pres.: Pawel Smektala
Phone: (48) 67 2846097
Fax: (48) 67 2846097
Email: prezes@eko-klan.com.pl
Tech. Dir.: Grzegorz Smektala
Phone: (48) 67 2846097
Fax: (48) 67 2846097
Email: biuro@eko-klan.com.pl
Sls. & Mktg. Mgr.: Tomasz Janeczko
Phone: (48) 67 2846097
Fax: (48) 67 2846097
Email: marketing.ekoklan@interia.pl
Total Employees at this Location: 40
Mill Locations:
WPT Eko-Klan Sp. z o.o., Margonin Mill, Margonska Wies 34A, PL-64830 Margonin, Poland, Capacity: 4,000 mt/y, (Paper mill)
Phone: (48) 67 2846097
Fax: (48) 67 2846097
Email: marketing.ekoklan@interia.pl, biuro@eko-klan.com.pl

ⓜⓜZywieckie Zaklady Papiernicze "SOLALI" S.A.
Zywiec Mill
Ownership: 100% by private shareholders
Ks. Pralata St. Slonki 24
PL-34300 Zywiec
Poland
Phone: (48) 33 8620831
Fax: (48) 33 8620888
Email: solali@solali.com.pl, marketing@solali.com.pl
Web Address: www.solali.com.pl
Personnel:
Pres.: Jerzy Miekisz
Phone: (48) 33 862 0831
Fax: (48) 33 862 0888
Email: jerzy.miekisz@solali.com.pl
Mill Mgr.: Stanislaw Mrowiec
Phone: (48) 33 862 0831 ext. 112-113
Fax: (48) 33 862 0888
Email: s.mrowiec@solali.com.pl
Tech. Dir.: Slawomir Boczek
Phone: (48) 33 862 0831 ext. 135-136
Fax: (48) 33 862 0888
Email: slawomir.boczek@solali.com.pl
Mgr.: Piotr Niewdana
Phone: (48) 33 862 0831 Ext. 110
Fax: (48) 33 862 0888
Email: p.niewdana@solali.com.pl
Total Employees at this Location: 300
Type of Operation: Paper mill
Paper/Paperboard Grades and Capacities:
Total paper and paperboard capacity: 12,000 mt/y
Tissue: 9,000 mt/y
Specialty and industrial: 3,000 mt/y
Paper and Paperboard Mill Data:
Paper Machines: 2

No. 4, foudrinier, Yankee dryer, total capacity 9,000 mt/y, Trim width 3 m, Tissue
No. 5, foudrinier, Yankee dryer, total capacity 3,000 mt/y, Trim width 3 m, Specialty and industrial
Finishing Equipment:
Supercalenders: 1
Rewinders: 4
Sheeters: 2
Energy Data:
Power boilers: 2
Electrical demand for mill: 32 MWh/D

PORTUGAL

ⓘⓜAMS - Gomà Camps S.A.
Vila Velha de Ródão Mill
Ownership: 30% by Grupo Gopaca, 30% by Grupo Mateus
Estrada Nacional 241, Zona Industrial
6030-245 Vila Velha de Ródão
Portugal
  Phone: (351) 272 549 020
  Fax: (351) 272 549 049
  Email: info@ams-gomacamps.eu
  Web Address: ams-gomacamps.eu
Personnel:
CEO and Gen. Mgr.: José Miranda
 Phone: (351) 272 549 031
 Fax: (351) 272 549 049
 Email: jose.miranda@ams-gomacamps.eu
Finan. Mgr.: Paulo Santos
 Phone: (351) 272 549 026
 Fax: (351) 272 549 049
 Email: paulo.santos@ams-gomacamps.eu
Commercial Mgr.: António Almeida
 Phone: (351) 935 806 528
 Fax: (351) 272 549 049
 Email: antonio.almeida@ams-gomacamps.eu
Purch. Mgr.: Manuel Fernandes
 Phone: (351) 272 549 038
 Fax: (351) 272 549 049
 Email: manuel.fernandes@ams-gomacamps.eu
Total Employees at this Location: 155
Type of Operation: Paper mill
Paper/Paperboard Grades and Capacities:
Total paper and paperboard capacity: 33,000 mt/y
Tissue: 33,000 mt/y
Paper and Paperboard Mill Data:
Paper Machines: 1
No. 1, crescent former, Yankee dryer, total capacity 33,000 mt/y, Trim width 2.82 m, Tissue
Energy Data:
Power boilers
Electrical demand for mill: 80 MWh/D

ⓘⓜFábrica de Papel Aveirense Lda.
Esgueira Mill
Quinta do Simão, Aptdo. 3076
3801-101 Esgueira, Aveiro
Portugal
  Phone: (351) 234 312491
  Fax: (351) 234 315154
Personnel:
Owner: Mário de Rocha Martins
 Phone: (351) 234 312491
Total Employees at this Location: 25
Type of Operation: Paper mill
Paper/Paperboard Grades and Capacities:
Total paper and paperboard capacity: 1,100 mt/y
Paper and Paperboard Mill Data:
Stock Preparation:
Pulpers: 1
Refiners: 1
Paper Machines: 1
No. 1, cylinder, total capacity 1,100 mt/y, Trim width 1.6 m

Finishing Equipment:
Calenders: 1
Rewinders: 1
Energy Data:
Power boilers: 1

ⓘⓜCaima-Indústria de Celulose S.A.
Constância Mill
Ownership: 100% by Altri Group
Bairro Caima
P-2250-058 Constância
Portugal
  Phone: (351) 249 730 000
  Fax: (351) 249 736 126
  Web Address: www.altri.pt
Personnel:
Pres.: Paulo Proença Fernandes
 Phone: (351) 249 730 000
Gen. Mgr./Mill Mgr.: Agostinho Dolores Ferreira
 Phone: (351) 249 730 000
 Email: dolores.ferreira@altri.pt
Prod. Mill Mgr.: Gualter Vasco
 Phone: (351) 249 730 000
 Email: gvasco@altri.pt
Maint. Mgr.: Santos Pinto
 Phone: (351) 249 730 000
 Email: spinto@altri.pt
Quality & Dev. Mgr.: António Prates
 Phone: (351) 249 730 000
 Email: aprates@altri.pt
Gen. Mgr. Sec.: Cláudia Pombo
 Phone: (351) 249 730 000
Total Employees at this Location: 205
Type of Operation: Pulp mill
Mill Locations:
Celtejo - Empresa de Celulose do Tejo, S.A., Celtejo Mill, P-6030-223 Vila Velha de Rodão, Portugal, (Pulp mill)
 Phone: (351) 272 540 100
 Fax: (351) 272 540 111/130
 Email: info@celtejo.com
Pulp Grades and Capacities:
Total pulp capacity: 109,648 mt/y
Pulp available for market: 105,000 mt/y
Chemical Pulp: 109,648 mt/y
Pulp Mill Data:
Chemical Pulping Systems:
Batch digesters: 5
Bleach Plant Systems: 1
No. 1, Sequence: EopP
Chemical Recovery Equipment:
Evaporator lines: 1
Recovery boilers: 1
Pulp Dryers:
Air Float dryers 1
Energy Data:
Power boilers: 1
Steam turbines: 3 at 16.0 MW
Electrical demand for mill: 227 MWh/D

ⓘⓜCelulose Beira Industrial (Celbi) S.A.
Celbi Mill
Ownership: 99.96% by Altri Group
Leirosa
P-3081-853 Figueira da Foz
Portugal
  Phone: (351) 233 955 600
  Fax: (351) 233 955 667
  Web Address: www.celbi.pt
Personnel:
Pres. of the Admin. Board: Paulo Fernandes
 Phone: (351) 233 955 600
 Fax: (351) 233 955 667
CFO: Nogueira Santos
 Phone: (351) 233 955 600
 Fax: (351) 233 955 667
 Email: nogueira.santos@altri.pt
Prod. Mgr.: João Rebola
 Phone: (351) 233 955 600
 Fax: (351) 233 955 667
 Email: joao.rebola@altri.pt
Eng. Mgr.: João Mota
 Phone: (351) 233 955 600
 Fax: (351) 233 955 667
 Email: Joao.mota@altri.pt
Industrial Mgr.: Carlos Vanveller
 Phone: (351) 233 955 600
 Fax: (351) 233 955 667
 Email: carlos.vanveller@celbi.pt
Pulp Prod. Mgr.: Vítor Lucas
 Phone: (351) 233 955 600
 Fax: (351) 233 955 667
 Email: vitor.lucas@altri.pt
HR Mgr.: Silva Tavares
 Phone: (351) 233 955 600
 Fax: (351) 233 955 667
 Email: silva.tavares@celbi.pt
Admin. Sec.: Fátima Furet
 Phone: (351) 233 955 600
 Fax: (351) 233 955 667
 Email: fatima.furet@celbi.pt
Total Employees of Company: 236
Total Employees at this Location: 210
Type of Operation: Pulp mill
Pulp Grades and Capacities:
Total pulp capacity: 671,118 mt/y
Pulp available for market: 667,000 mt/y
Chemical Pulp: 671,118 mt/y
Pulp Mill Data:
Chemical Pulping Systems:
Continuous digesters: 1
Pulp Lines: 1
Bleach Plant Systems: 1
1, Type: ECF, Sequence: O_2 DEOpDEpD, Capacity 667,000 admt/y
Chemical Recovery Equipment:
Evaporator lines: 7
Recovery boilers: 1
Lime Kiln
Pulp Dryers:
Air Float dryers 1, Twin Wire 1
Energy Data:
Power boilers: 1
Steam turbines: 2 at 70, 30 MW
Electrical demand for mill: 1,074 MWh/D

ⓘⓜCeltejo - Empresa de Celulose do Tejo, S.A.
Celtejo Mill
Ownership: Caima-Indústria de Celulose S.A.
P-6030-223 Vila Velha de Rodão
Portugal
  Phone: (351) 272 540 100
  Fax: (351) 272 540 111/130
  Email: info@celtejo.com
  Web Address: www.altri.pt
Personnel:
Admin. Mgr.: Eng. Francisco Silva Gomes
 Phone: (351) 272 540 100
Mgr.: Eng. Agostinho Dolores Ferreira
 Phone: (351) 272 540 100
Qlty. Mgr.: Eng. Manuel Soares Goncalves
 Phone: (351) 272 540 100
Prod. Mgr.: Eng. Carlos Coelho
 Phone: (351) 272 540 100
Maint. Mgr.: Eng. Miguel Bernardo
 Phone: (351) 272 540 100
Finan. Dir.: Dr. Nogueira Santos
 Phone: (351) 272 540 100
HR Mgr.: Dra. Isabel Proenca
 Phone: (351) 272 540 100
Sec.: Maria do Céu Barata
 Phone: (351) 272 540 100
 Email: ceu.barata@celtejo.com
Total Employees at this Location: 193
Type of Operation: Pulp mill
Pulp Grades and Capacities:

Portugal

Total pulp capacity: 190,918 mt/y
Pulp available for market: 190,000 mt/y
Chemical Pulp: 190,918 mt/y
Pulp Mill Data:
Chemical Pulping Systems:
Continuous digesters: 1
Pulp Lines: 1
Bleach Plant Lines:
No. 1, Type: Ze-D-P, Sequence: ZED
No. 2, Type: ECF, Ze-P-P, Sequence: O_2 ZeD1D2, Capacity 190,000 admt/y
Chemical Recovery Equipment:
Evaporator lines: 1
Recovery boilers: 1
Lime Kiln
Pulp Dryers:
Flakt dryer 1
Energy Data:
Power boilers: 2
Steam turbines: 2 at 75 MW
Electrical demand for mill: 439 MWh/D

ⓘEuropac Portugal
Ownership: 100% by Europac - Papeles y Cartones de Europa S.A.
Rua do Monte Grande, n.3, Guilhabreu
4485-255 Vila do Conde
Portugal
Phone: (351) 22 987 1302/300
Fax: (351) 22 987 1305
Email: eugenia.costa@gescartao.pt
Web Address: www.europac.es
Personnel:
Pres.: Fernando Padron Estarriol
Phone: (351) 22 987 1302/300
Fax: (351) 22 987 1305
Country Mgr. Portugal: Tiago Domingues
Phone: (351) 22 987 1302/300
Fax: (351) 22 987 1305
Plant Mgr.: Nuno Cunha
Phone: (351) 22 987 1302/300
Fax: (351) 22 987 1305
Sec.: Eugenia Costa
Phone: (351) 22 987 1302/300
Fax: (351) 22 987 1305
Email: eugenia.costa@gescartao.pt
HR Country Mgr.: Vera Mouta
Phone: (351) 22 987 1302/300
Fax: (351) 22 987 1305
Prod. Mgr.: Paula Quevedo Costa
Phone: (48) 22 987 1302/300
Fax: (48) 22 987 1305
Purch. Mgr.: António Luís Coelho
Phone: (351) 22 987 1302/300
Fax: (351) 22 987 1305
Mill Locations:
Europac Kraft Viana, Viana do Castelo Mill, P.O. Box 550, Deocriste, P-4901-852 Viana do Castelo, Portugal, Capacity: 375,000 mt/y, (Pulp mill, Paperboard mill)
Phone: (351) 258 739600
Fax: (351) 258 731914
Email: portucel.viana@gescartao.pt

ⓂEuropac Kraft Viana
Viana do Castelo Mill
Ownership: Europac Portugal
P.O. Box 550, Deocriste
P-4901-852 Viana do Castelo
Portugal
Phone: (351) 258 739600
Fax: (351) 258 731914
Email: portucel.viana@gescartao.pt
Web Address: www.europac.es
Personnel:
Man. Dir.: Mario Amaral
Phone: (351) 258 739600
Fax: (351) 258 731914
Email: mamaral@europacgroup.com
Prod. Mgr.: Pedro Campos
Phone: (351) 258 739600
Fax: (351) 258 731914
Email: pcampos@europacgroup.com
Proj. Mgr.: Manuel F. Domingues
Phone: (351) 258 739600
Fax: (351) 258 731914
Email: mdomingues@europacgroup.com
Total Employees at this Location: 300
Type of Operation: Pulp mill, Paperboard mill
Pulp Grades and Capacities:
Total pulp capacity: 385,999 mt/y
Chemical Pulp: 215,000 mt/y
Recycled Pulping: 170,999 mt/y
Pulp Mill Data:
Chemical Pulping Systems:
Continuous digesters: 1
Pulp Lines: 1
Chemical Recovery Equipment:
Evaporator lines: 1
Recovery boilers: 1
Lime Kiln
Recycled Fiber Treatment Lines:
Pulpers: 2 at 89,250 admt/y
Recycled packaging pulping lines: 1 at 138,873 admt/y
Paper/Paperboard Grades and Capacities:
Total paper and paperboard capacity: 375,000 mt/y
Linerboard: 375,000 mt/y
Paper and Paperboard Mill Data:
Stock Preparation:
Refiners: 9
Paper Machines: 1
No. 1, fourdrinier (2), total capacity 375,000 mt/y, Trim width 6.4 m, Linerboard
Finishing Equipment:
Winders: 1
Calenders: 1
Rewinders: 1
Energy Data:
Power boilers: 1
Combustion turbines: 2 at 30, 30 MW
Steam turbines: 2 at 10, 26 MW
Electrical demand for mill: 726 MWh/D

ⓘⓂFábrica de Papel de Medros, Lda.
Travessa de Bento Antas da Cruz n.81 Barcelinhos, Barcelos, P-4755-064
Barcelos
Portugal
Phone: (351) 253 833 264/831 370
Fax: (351) 253 821 621
Email: fpmedros@iol.pt
Personnel:
Man. Dir.: Elisio Pereira da Silva
Phone: (351) 253 833 264/831 370
Fax: (351) 253 821 621
Man. Dir.: Elisio Jorge T. F. Silva
Phone: (351) 253 833 264/831 370
Fax: (351) 253 821 621
Man. Dir.: Liliena T.C.F. Silva
Phone: (351) 253 833 264/831 370
Fax: (351) 253 821 621
Mill Locations:
Fábrica de Papel de Medros, Lda., Barcelinhos Mill, Travessa de Bento Antas da Cruz n.81, P-4755-064 Barcelinhos, Portugal, Capacity: 5,000 mt/y, (Paper mill)
Phone: (351) 253 833 264/831 370
Fax: (351) 253 821 621

ⓘⓂFAPAJAL - Fábrica de Papel de Tojal S.A.
São Julião do Tojal Mill
Ownership: 100% by Dinamis - Gestão e Serviços SGPS
Rua Arq. Dias Coelho
P-2670-842 São Julião do Tojal
Portugal
Phone: (351) 21 9738150
Fax: (351) 21 9748104
Email: fapajal@fapajal.pt
Web Address: www.fapajal.pt
Personnel:
Co-Gen. Mgr.: Luis Pereira da Cunha
Phone: (351) 21 9738150
Fax: (351) 21 9748104
Email: luis.cunha@fapajal.pt
Co-Gen. Mgr.: Helen G. de Castro
Phone: (351) 21 9738150
Fax: (351) 21 9748104
Email: hgcastro@fapajal.pt
Tech. Mgr.: Victor da Silva
Phone: (351) 93 974 8575
Fax: (351) 21 9748104
Email: victor.silva@fapajal.pt
Total Employees of Company: 115
Total Employees at this Location: 113
Type of Operation: Paper mill
Pulp Grades and Capacities:
Total pulp capacity: 7,974 mt/y
Recycled Pulping: 7,974 mt/y
Pulp Mill Data:
Recycled Fiber Treatment Lines:
Pulpers: 1 at 13,000
Paper/Paperboard Grades and Capacities:
Total paper and paperboard capacity: 30,000 mt/y
Tissue: 28,000 mt/y
Packaging papers: 2,000 mt/y
Paper and Paperboard Mill Data:
Stock Preparation:
Pulpers:
Paper Machines: 3
No. 1, fourdrinier, Yankee dryer, total capacity 2,000 mt/y, Trim width 1.8 m, Packaging papers
No. 2, fourdrinier, Yankee dryer, total capacity 8,000 mt/y, Trim width 2.34 m, Tissue
No. 3, crescent former, Yankee dryer, total capacity 20,000 mt/y, Trim width 2.7 m, Tissue
Energy Data:
Power boilers: 2
Combustion turbines: 2 at 1.3, 1.1 MW
Steam turbines: 1
Electrical demand for mill: 85 MWh/D

ⓘⓂFábrica de Papel de Fontes Lda.
Grijó Mill
Rua N.ª Sr.ª Fontes
4410-047 Serzedo VNG Porto - Vila Nova de Gaia
Portugal
Mailing Address: Aptdo. 1013, P-4416-801 Grijó, Portugal
Phone: (351) 22 753 7170
Fax: (351) 22 753 7179
Email: info@papelfontes.com
Web Address: www.papelfontes.com
Personnel:
Owner: Maria Brabetz
Phone: (351) 22 753 7170
Owner: Giulio Brabetz
Phone: (351) 22 753 7170
Total Employees of Company: 60
Total Employees at this Location: 60
Type of Operation: Paper mill
Paper/Paperboard Grades and Capacities:
Total paper and paperboard capacity: 2,400 mt/y
Uncoated woodfree/freesheet
Paper and Paperboard Mill Data:
Paper Machines: 1
PM 1, Uncoated woodfree/freesheet

ⓘFábrica de Papel da Lapa Lda.
Rua Comendador Sá Couto, 902
P-4535-439 São Paio de Oleiros
Portugal
Mailing Address: Feira Norte, P-4535 São Paio de Oleiros
Phone: (351) 227 642 186, 227 649 410
Fax: (351) 227 642 920
Email: fplapa@fplapa.pt,
fabrica@lapa3.com

Portugal

Web Address: www.lapa.com.pt
Personnel:
 Chmn. & Dir.: Belmiro Rosas Couto
 Phone: (351) 227 642 186
 Fax: (351) 227 642 920
 Pres. & Dir. : José Manuel Alves Couto
 Phone: (351) 227 642 186
 Fax: (351) 227 642 920
 CFO: Pedro Ribas
 Phone: (351) 227 642 186
 Fax: (351) 227 642 920
 Purch. Dir.: Maria Emilia Alves Couto
 Phone: (351) 227 642 186
 Fax: (351) 227 642 920
 Mgr.: Manuela Couto
 Phone: (351) 227 642 186
 Fax: (351) 227 642 920
 Mill Mgr.: Saul Filipe R. Couto
 Phone: (351) 227 642 186
 Fax: (351) 227 642 920
Mill Locations:
Fábrica de Papel da Lapa Lda., São Paio de Oleiros Mill, Rua Comendador Sá Couto, 902, P-4535-439 São Paio de Oleiros, Portugal, Capacity: 12,000 mt/y, (Paper mill)
 Phone: (351) 227 642 186
 Fax: (351) 227 642 920
 Email: fplapa@fplapa.pt

ⓜFábrica de Papel da Lapa Lda.
São Paio de Oleiros Mill
Rua Comendador Sá Couto, 902
P-4535-439 São Paio de Oleiros
Portugal
Mailing Address: Feira Norte, P-4535 São Paio de Oleiros, Portugal
 Phone: (351) 227 642 186
 Fax: (351) 227 642 920
 Email: fplapa@fplapa.pt
 Web Address: www.lapa.com.pt
Personnel:
 Dir.: Belmiro Rosas Couto
 Phone: (351) 227 642 186
 Fax: (351) 227 642 920
 Dir.: José Manuel Alves Couto
 Phone: (351) 227 642 186
 Fax: (351) 227 642 920
 Mill Mgr.: Saul Filipe R. Couto
 Phone: (351) 227 642 186
 Fax: (351) 227 642 920
 Purch. Dir.: Maria Emilia Alves Couto
 Phone: (351) 227 642 186
 Fax: (351) 227 642 920
 Office Mgr.: Manuela Couto
 Phone: (351) 227 642 186
 Fax: (351) 227 642 920
 Sec.: Sara Couto
 Phone: (351) 227 642 186
 Fax: (351) 227 642 920
Total Employees at this Location: 40
Type of Operation: Paper mill
Pulp Grades and Capacities:
 Total pulp capacity: 12,358 mt/y
 Recycled Pulping: 12,358 mt/y
Pulp Mill Data:
 Recycled Fiber Treatment Lines:
 Recycled packaging pulping lines: 1
Paper/Paperboard Grades and Capacities:
 Total paper and paperboard capacity: 12,000 mt/y
 Packaging papers: 5,000 mt/y
 Linerboard: 4,000 mt/y
 Corrugating medium/fluting: 3,000 mt/y
Paper and Paperboard Mill Data:
Paper Machines: 1
No. 1, fourdrinier (2), total capacity 12,000 mt/y, Trim width 2 m, Packaging papers, Corrugating medium/fluting, Linerboard
Energy Data:
Power boilers
Electrical demand for mill: 16 MWh/D

ⓜFábrica de Papel de Medros, Lda.
Barcelinhos Mill
Travessa de Bento Antas da Cruz n.81
P-4755-064 Barcelinhos, Barcelos
Portugal
 Phone: (351) 253 833 264/831 370
 Fax: (351) 253 821 621
Personnel:
 Man. Dir.: Elisio Pereira da Silva
 Phone: (351) 253 833 264/831 370
 Fax: (351) 253 821 621
 Man. Dir.: Elisio Jorge T. F. Silva
 Phone: (351) 253 833 264/831 370
 Fax: (351) 253 821 621
 Man. Dir.: Liliena T.C.F. Silva
 Phone: (351) 253 833 264/831 370
 Fax: (351) 253 821 621
 Sec.: Isaura Mandim
 Phone: (351) 253 833 264/831 370
 Fax: (351) 253 821 621
Type of Operation: Paper mill
Paper/Paperboard Grades and Capacities:
 Total paper and paperboard capacity: 5,000 mt/y
 Specialty and industrial: 5,000 mt/y
Paper and Paperboard Mill Data:
Paper Machines: 1
No. 1, Trim width 2.2 m, Specialty and industrial

ⓜNatural - Indústria de Papel, Lda.
E.N. 16 - Vila Meã
3505-252 Povolide, Viseu
Portugal
 Phone: (351) 232 930000
 Fax: (351) 232 932285
 Email: mail@natural.com.pt, depto.comercial@natural.com.pt
 Web Address: www.natural.com.pt
Personnel:
 CEO: Carlos Manuel Castro Silva
 Phone: (351) 232 930000
 Fax: (351) 232 932285
 Email: castro.silva@natural.com.pt
 Finan. Mgr.: Álvaro Ribeiro
 Phone: (351) 232 930000
 Fax: (351) 232 932285
 Email: alvaro.ribeiro@natural.com.pt
Mill Locations:
Natural - Indústria de Papel, Lda., Povolide (Viseu) Mill, E.N. 16 - Vila Meã, 3505-252 Povolide, Viseu, Portugal, Capacity: 11,000 mt/y, (Paper mill)
 Phone: (351) 232 930000
 Fax: (351) 232 932285
 Email: mail@natural.com.pt, depto.comercial@natural.com.pt

ⓜNatural - Indústria de Papel, Lda.
Povolide (Viseu) Mill
E.N. 16 - Vila Meã
3505-252 Povolide, Viseu
Portugal
 Phone: (351) 232 930000
 Fax: (351) 232 932285
 Email: mail@natural.com.pt, depto.comercial@natural.com.pt
 Web Address: www.natural.com.pt
Personnel:
 CEO: Carlos Manuel Castro Silva
 Phone: (351) 232 930000
 Fax: (351) 232 932285
 Email: castro.silva@natural.com.pt
 Finan. Mgr.: Álvaro Ribeiro
 Phone: (351) 232 930000
 Fax: (351) 232 932285
 Email: depto.financeiro@natural.com.pt alvaro.ribeiro@natural.com.pt
Total Employees at this Location: 92
Type of Operation: Paper mill
Paper/Paperboard Grades and Capacities:
 Total paper and paperboard capacity: 11,000 mt/y
 Tissue: 11,000 mt/y
Paper and Paperboard Mill Data:
Paper Machines: 1
No. 1, fourdrinier, Yankee dryer, total capacity 11,000 mt/y, Trim width 2 m, Tissue
Energy Data:
Electrical demand for mill: 32 MWh/D

ⓟⓜOliveira Santos & Irmão, Lda.
Paços de Brandão Mill
Ownership: Fábrica de Papel e Cartão da Zarrinha, S.A.
Calçada Rio Maior, 228 Apartado 19
P-4536-906 Paços de Brandão, Santa Maria da Feira
Portugal
 Phone: (351) 22 744 2113 / 22 747 2070
 Fax: (351) 22 744 2391
 Email: osil@netvisao.pt
Personnel:
 Dir.: Orlando Santos
 Phone: (351) 22 7472070
Total Employees at this Location: 30
Type of Operation: Paperboard mill
Pulp Grades and Capacities:
 Total pulp capacity: 20,246 mt/y
 Recycled Pulping: 20,246 mt/y
Pulp Mill Data:
 Recycled Fiber Treatment Lines:
 Recycled packaging pulping lines: 1
Paper/Paperboard Grades and Capacities:
 Total paper and paperboard capacity: 20,000 mt/y
 Linerboard: 20,000 mt/y
Paper and Paperboard Mill Data:
Paper Machines: 1
No. 1, fourdrinier, total capacity 20,000 mt/y, Trim width 2.2 m, Linerboard
Energy Data:
Power boilers
Electrical demand for mill: 27 MWh/D

ⓟⓜFábrica de Papel de Ponte Redonda S.A.
Silvalde, Espinho Mill
Ownership: 100% by Loureiro
Rua de Ponte Redonda, 2700
4500-832 Silvalde, Espinho
Portugal
Mailing Address: Apartado 2, 4501-851 Espinho, Portugal
 Phone: (351) 227 330 800
 Fax: (351) 227 330 801
 Email: geral@ponteredonda.com
 Web Address: www.ponteredonda.com
Personnel:
 Gen. Dir.: Américo Pais Loureiro
 Phone: (351) 227 330 800
 Fax: (351) 227 330 801
 Email: americo.loureiro@ponteredonda.com
 Paper Prod. Mgr.: Pedro Loureiro
 Phone: (351) 227 330 800
 Fax: (351) 227 330 801
 Email: p.loureiro@ponteredonda.com
 Finan. Dir.: Rui Morteira
 Phone: (351) 227 330 800
 Fax: (351) 227 330 801
 Email: rui.morteira@ponteredonda.com
 Paper Bags Prod. Dir.: Raul Loureiro
 Phone: (351) 227 330 800
 Fax: (351) 227 330 801
 Email: raul.loureiro@ponteredonda.com
Total Employees of Company: 135
Total Employees at this Location: 135
Type of Operation: Paper mill, Paperboard mill
Paper/Paperboard Grades and Capacities:
 Total paper and paperboard capacity: 10,000 mt/y
 Packaging papers: 1,300 mt/y
 Linerboard: 1,650 mt/y
 Corrugating medium/fluting: 7,000 mt/y
 Boxboard/cartonboard: 50 mt/y

Portugal

Paper and Paperboard Mill Data:
Stock Preparation:
 Pulpers: 3
 Refiners: 6
Paper Machines: 2
 No. 1, cylinder, total capacity 8,700 mt/y, Trim width 1.7 m, Packaging papers
 No. 2, fourdrinier, Trim width 2.65 m
Finishing Equipment:
 Rewinders: 7
 Sheeters: 1
Energy Data:
 Power boilers: 1
 Electrical demand for mill: 10 MWh/D

ⓜGrupo Portucel Soporcel
Fábrica de Cacia
Rua dos Bombeiros da Celulose, Beira Litoral
P-3800-536 Cacia, Aveiro
Portugal
 Phone: (351) 234 910 600
 Fax: (351) 234 910 619
 Email: portucel.cacia@portucelsoporcel.com
 Web Address: www.portucelsoporcel.com
Personnel:
 Mill. Mgr: José Manuel Namorado Nordeste
 Phone: (351) 234 910 600
 Fax: (351) 234 910 619
 Email: namorado.nordeste@portucelsoporcel.com
 Prod. Mgr.: António Gomes
 Phone: (351) 234 910 600
 Fax: (351) 234 910 619
 Email: antonio.gomes@portucelsoporcel.com
 Sec.: Rosa Maria Nogueira
 Phone: (351) 234 910 610
 Fax: (351) 234 910 619
 Email: rosa.maria.nogueira@portucelsoporcel.com
 HR Mgr.: António Mendes
 Phone: (351) 234 910 600
 Fax: (351) 234 910 619
 Email: antonio.mendes@portucelsoporcel.com
Total Employees at this Location: 181
Type of Operation: Pulp mill, Paper mill
Pulp Grades and Capacities:
 Total pulp capacity: 288,353 mt/y
 Pulp available for market: 285,000 mt/y
 Chemical Pulp: 288,353 mt/y
Pulp Mill Data:
Chemical Pulping Systems:
 Batch digesters: 4
 Continuous digesters: 1
Pulp Lines: 2
Bleach Plant Systems: 2
 Line 1, Type: ECF, Sequence: DEopDED, Capacity 95,000 admt/y
 Line 2, Type: ECF, Sequence: DEopDED, Capacity 190,000 admt/y
Chemical Recovery Equipment:
 Evaporator lines: 2
 Recovery boilers: 1
 Lime Kiln
Pulp Dryers:
 Flakt dryer 1, Flakt dryer 1, Twin Wire 1
Energy Data:
 Power boilers: 3
 Steam turbines: 3 at 33, 15 MW
 Electrical demand for mill: 612 MWh/D

ⓜⓜGrupo Portucel Soporcel
Figueira da Foz Mill
Ownership: 75.90% by Semapa
Lavos - PO Box/ Apartado 5
P-3081 851 Figueira da Foz, Coimbra
Portugal
 Phone: (351) 233 900 100/134
 Fax: (351) 233 940 007
 Email: info@soporcel.pt
 Web Address: www.portucelsoporcel.com
Personnel:
 Mill Mgr.: Carlos Vieira
 Phone: (351) 233 900 100
 Fax: (351) 233 940 007
 Email: carlos.vieira@portucelsoporcel.com
 Eng. Mgr.: Guilherme Pedroso
 Phone: (351) 233 900 100
 Fax: (351) 233 940 007
 Email: guilherme.pedroso@portucelsoporcel.com
 Dir. Purch.: José Freire
 Phone: (351) 233 900 100
 Fax: (351) 233 940 007
 Email: jose.freire@portucelsoporcel.com
 Sls. Mgr.: Porto Monteiro
 Phone: (351) 233 900 100
 Fax: (351) 233 940 007
 Email: porto.monteiro@portucelsoporcel.com
 Commun. Mgr.: Ana Nery
 Phone: (351) 233 900 100
 Fax: (351) 233 940 007
 Email: ana.nery@portucelsoporcel.com
Total Employees of Company: 2,288
Total Employees at this Location: 850
Type of Operation: Pulp mill, Paper mill
Mill Locations:
 Grupo Portucel Soporcel, Fábrica de Cacia, Rua dos Bombeiros da Celulose, Beira Litoral, P-3800-536 Cacia, Portugal, (Pulp mill, Paper mill)
 Phone: (351) 234 910 600
 Fax: (351) 234 910 619
 Email: portucel.cacia@portucelsoporcel.com
 Grupo Portucel Soporcel, Setúbal Mill, Península da Mitrena, Apartado 55, P-2901-861 Setúbal, Portugal, Capacity: 800,000 mt/y, (Pulp mill, Paper mill)
 Phone: (351) 265 709 000/790 600
 Fax: (351) 265 101 355
 Email: dic@portucelsoporcel.com
Pulp Grades and Capacities:
 Total pulp capacity: 560,005 mt/y
 Chemical Pulp: 560,005 mt/y
Pulp Mill Data:
Chemical Pulping Systems:
 Continuous digesters: 1
Pulp Lines: 1
Bleach Plant Systems: 1
 No. 1, Sequence: DEoDED, Capacity 560,000 admt/y
Chemical Recovery Equipment:
 Evaporator lines: 1
 Recovery boilers: 1
 Lime Kiln
Pulp Dryers:
 Air Float dryers
Paper/Paperboard Grades and Capacities:
 Total paper and paperboard capacity: 830,000 mt/y
 Uncoated woodfree/freesheet: 830,000 mt/y
Paper and Paperboard Mill Data:
Stock Preparation:
 Pulpers: 2
 Refiners: 9
Paper Machines: 2
 No. 1, SymFormer, total capacity 370,000 mt/y, Trim width 8.6 m, Uncoated woodfree/freesheet
 No. 2, DuoFormer TQv, total capacity 460,000 mt/y, Trim width 8.65 m, Uncoated woodfree/freesheet
Finishing Equipment:
 Sheeters: 10 at 450,000 mt/y, 240,000 mt/y
Energy Data:
 Power boilers: 3
 Combustion turbines: 1 at 66.0 MW
 Steam turbines: 3 at 56.0 MW
 Electrical demand for mill: 2,384 MWh/D

ⓜⓜGrupo Portucel Soporcel
Setúbal Mill
Ownership: 75.90% by Semapa
Península da Mitrena, Apartado 55
P-2901-861 Setúbal
Portugal
 Phone: (351) 265 709 000/790 600
 Fax: (351) 265 101 355
 Email: dic@portucelsoporcel.com
 Web Address: www.portucelsoporcel.com
Personnel:
 Board member: Luís Alberto Caldeira Deslandes
 Phone: (351) 265 709 000
 Fax: (351) 265 101 355
 CEO (as of April 1st 2014): Diogo António Rodrigues da Silveira
 Phone: (351) 265 709 000
 Fax: (351) 265 101 355
 Chmn.: Pedro Mendonça de Queiroz Pereira
 Phone: (351) 265 709 000
 Fax: (351) 265 101 355
 Mill Mgr.: Eng. Carlos Bras
 Phone: (351) 265 709 000
 Fax: (351) 265 101 355
 Email: carlos.bras@portucelsoporcel.com
 Purch. Dir.: José Freire
 Phone: (351) 265 709 000
 Fax: (351) 265 101 355
 Email: jose.freire@portucelsoporcel.com
 Finan. Dir.: Manuel Arouca
 Phone: (351) 265 709 000
 Fax: (351) 265 101 355
 Email: manuel.arouca@portucelsoporcel.com
 Environ. Dir.: Julieta Sansana
 Phone: (351) 265 709 000
 Fax: (351) 265 101 355
 Email: julieta.sansana@portucelsoporcel.com
 Plan. & Contrl. Mgr.: Jorge Peixoto
 Phone: (351) 265 709 000
 Fax: (351) 265 101 355
 Email: jorge.peixoto@portucelsoporcel.com
Total Employees of Company: 2,288
Total Employees at this Location: 925
Type of Operation: Pulp mill, Paper mill
Mill Locations:
 Grupo Portucel Soporcel, Fábrica de Cacia, Rua dos Bombeiros da Celulose, Beira Litoral, P-3800-536 Cacia, Portugal, (Pulp mill, Paper mill)
 Phone: (351) 234 910 600
 Fax: (351) 234 910 619
 Email: portucel.cacia@portucelsoporcel.com
 Grupo Portucel Soporcel, Figueira da Foz Mill, Lavos - PO Box/ Apartado 5, P-3081 851 Figueira da Foz, Portugal, Capacity: 830,000 mt/y, (Pulp mill, Paper mill)
 Phone: (351) 233 900 100/134
 Fax: (351) 233 940 007
 Email: info@soporcel.pt
Pulp Grades and Capacities:
 Total pulp capacity: 530,004 mt/y
 Chemical Pulp: 530,004 mt/y
Pulp Mill Data:
Chemical Pulping Systems:
 Continuous digesters: 2
Pulp Lines: 2
Bleach Plant Systems: 5
 No. 1, Sequence: DEOpDEpD
Chemical Recovery Equipment:
 Evaporator lines: 2
 Recovery boilers: 1
 Lime Kiln
Pulp Dryers:
 Other dryers 1
Paper/Paperboard Grades and Capacities:
 Total paper and paperboard capacity: 800,000 mt/y
 Uncoated woodfree/freesheet: 800,000 mt/y
Paper and Paperboard Mill Data:
Paper Machines: 4
 No. 1, fourdrinier, total capacity 85,000 mt/y, Trim width 3.8 m, Uncoated woodfree/freesheet
 No. 2, fourdrinier, total capacity 25,000 mt/y, Trim width 2.2 m, Uncoated woodfree/freesheet
 No. 3, DuoFormer D, total capacity 190,000 mt/y, Trim width 4.5 m, Uncoated woodfree/freesheet
 No. 4, OptiFormer, total capacity 500,000 mt/y, Trim width 10.4 m, Uncoated woodfree/freesheet
Finishing Equipment:
 Sheeters: 8 at 110,000 mt/y, 320,000 mt/y, 180,000 mt/y

Portugal

Energy Data:
Power boilers: 3
HRSG boiler: 2
Combustion turbines: 2 at 65 MW
Steam turbines: 1
Electrical demand for mill: 2,209 MWh/D

ⓗⓜPapeleira Portuguesa S.A.
São Paio de Oleiros Mill
Rua Comendador Sá Couto, 829
4535-439 São Paio de Oleiros
Portugal
Phone: (351) 22 7471760
Fax: (351) 22 7641717
Email: geral@papeleira-sa.pt
Web Address: www.papeleira.pt
Personnel:
Chief Eng./Purch. Agent: Aires Ferreira
Phone: (351) 22 7471760
Fax: (351) 22 7641717
Email: aires.ferreira@papeleira-sa.pt
Comm. & Sales Mgr.: João Pedro Castro
Phone: (351) 22 7471760
Fax: (351) 22 7641717
Email: comercial@papeleira-sa.pt
Total Employees of Company: 58
Total Employees at this Location: 58
Type of Operation: Paperboard mill
Pulp Grades and Capacities:
Total pulp capacity: 30,789 mt/y
Recycled Pulping: 30,789 mt/y

Pulp Mill Data:
Recycled Fiber Treatment Lines:
Pulpers: 2
Paper/Paperboard Grades and Capacities:
Total paper and paperboard capacity: 30,000 mt/y
Linerboard: 10,000 mt/y
Corrugating medium/fluting: 5,000 mt/y
Boxboard/cartonboard: 15,000 mt/y
Paper and Paperboard Mill Data:
Stock Preparation:
Pulpers: 2
Refiners: 2
Paper Machines: 1
No. 1, fourdrinier (2), total capacity 30,000 mt/y, Trim width 2.5 m, Boxboard/cartonboard, Corrugating medium/fluting, Linerboard
Finishing Equipment:
Rewinders: 3 at 40,000 mt/y
Sheeters: 1
Energy Data:
Power boilers
Electrical demand for mill: 37 MWh/D

ⓜPrado-Cartolinas da Lousã S.A.
Lousã Mill
Ownership: 100% by Prado Karton S.A.
Penedo - Apartado 1
3200-901 Lousã
Portugal
Phone: (351) 239 990 100
Fax: (351) 239 992 347
Email: lousa@papeldoprado.com
Web Address: www.papeldoprado.com
Personnel:
Industrial Dir.: Manuel Caetano Pedro
Phone: (351) 239 990 105
Fax: (351) 239 992 347
Email: c.pedro@papeldoprado.com
Commer. Dir.: Filomena Teixeira
Phone: (351) 239 990 100
Fax: (351) 239 992 347
Email: f.teixeira@papeldoprado.com
Total Employees at this Location: 123
Type of Operation: Paper mill
Pulp Grades and Capacities:
Total pulp capacity: 22,220 mt/y
Recycled Pulping: 22,220 mt/y
Paper/Paperboard Grades and Capacities:

Total paper and paperboard capacity: 25,500 mt/y
Boxboard/cartonboard: 25,500 mt/y
Paper and Paperboard Mill Data:
Stock Preparation:
Pulpers: 2
Refiners: 2
Paper Machines: 1
No. 1, fourdrinier, total capacity 25,500 mt/y, Trim width 2.1 m, Boxboard/cartonboard
Finishing Equipment:
Rewinders: 1
Sheeters: 1
Energy Data:
Power boilers: 2
Electrical demand for mill: 35 MWh/D

ⓗⓜPrado Karton S.A.
Tomar Mill
Ownership: 95% by Finpro, private investors
Lugar do Prado
2304-909 Tomar
Portugal
Mailing Address: Apartado 36, 2305-556 Pedreira, Tomar, Portugal
Phone: (351) 249 320200
Fax: (351) 249 322046
Email: prado.geral@pradocartonboard.com, dir.com@pradocartonboard.com
Web Address: www.pradocartonboard.com
Personnel:
Industrial Dir.: Ing. Fernando Antunes Rosa
Phone: (351) 249 320200
Fax: (351) 249 322046
Email: a.rosa@pradocartonboard.com
Comm. Dir.: Dr. José Maria Ferreira da Silva
Phone: (351) 249 320257
Fax: (351) 249 322046
Email: f.silva@pradocartonboard.com
Qlty. Mgr.: Antonio S. Cardoso
Phone: (351) 249 320200
Fax: (351) 249 322046
Email: a.cardoso@pradocartonboard.com
Total Employees at this Location: 117
Type of Operation: Paperboard mill
Mill Locations:
Prado-Cartolinas da Lousã S.A., Lousã Mill, Penedo - Apartado 1, 3200-901 Lousã, Portugal, Capacity: 25,500 mt/y, (Paper mill)
Phone: (351) 239 990 100
Fax: (351) 239 992 347
Email: lousa@papeldoprado.com
Pulp Grades and Capacities:
Total pulp capacity: 14,635 mt/y
Recycled Pulping: 14,635 mt/y
Paper/Paperboard Grades and Capacities:
Total paper and paperboard capacity: 40,000 mt/y
Boxboard/cartonboard: 40,000 mt/y
Paper and Paperboard Mill Data:
Stock Preparation:
Pulpers: 4
Refiners: 4
Paper Machines: 1
No. 1, cylinder (7), total capacity 40,000 mt/y, Trim width 2.48 m, Boxboard/cartonboard
Coating Machines: 3
No. 1, on machine
No. 2, on machine
No. 3, on machine
Finishing Equipment:
Rewinders: 2
Sheeters: 2
Energy Data:
Power boilers: 3
Steam turbines: 1 at 0.235 MW
Electrical demand for mill: 56 MWh/D

ⓗⓜRenova - Fábrica de Papel do Almonda S.A.
Torres Novas Mill
Ownership: Almonda, S.G.P.S.
Renova
P-2354-001 Torres Novas
Portugal
Phone: (351) 249 830200
Fax: (351) 249 830201
Email: info@renova.pt
Web Address: www.renova.pt
Personnel:
Brd. Mbr.: António de Andrade Tavares
Phone: (351) 249 830200
Fax: (351) 249 830201
Email: antonio.tavares@renova.pt
Brd. Mbr.: Carlos Fernando Pedro dos Santos
Phone: (351) 249 830200
Fax: (351) 249 830201
Email: carlos.santos@renova.pt
Brd. Mbr.: João Clara
Phone: (351) 249 830200
Fax: (351) 249 830201
Email: joao.clara@renova.pt
Brd. Mbr.: João de Andrade Tavares
Phone: (351) 249 830200
Fax: (351) 249 830201
Email: joao.tavares@renova.pt
Commer. Dir.: João Palmeira
Phone: (351) 249 830200
Fax: (351) 249 830201
Email: joao.palmeira@renova.pt
Mktg. Dir.: Luís Saramago
Phone: (351) 249 830 294
Fax: (351) 249 830201
Email: luis.saramago@renova.pt
Total Employees at this Location: 600
Type of Operation: Paper mill
Pulp Grades and Capacities:
Total pulp capacity: 35,000 mt/y
Pulp available for market: 9,223 mt/y
Recycled Pulping: 35,000 mt/y
Pulp Mill Data:
Pulp Lines: 1
Bleach Plant Systems: 1
Recycled Fiber Treatment Lines:
Flotation deinking lines: 1 at 35,000
Pulp Dryers:
Twin Wire 1
Paper/Paperboard Grades and Capacities:
Total paper and paperboard capacity: 95,000 mt/y
Uncoated woodfree/freesheet: 5,000 mt/y
Coated woodfree/freesheet: 5,000 mt/y
Tissue: 80,000 mt/y
Packaging papers: 5,000 mt/y
Paper and Paperboard Mill Data:
Stock Preparation:
Pulpers: 7
Refiners: 17
Paper Machines: 5
No. 1, fourdrinier, size press, total capacity 10,000 mt/y, Trim width 2.1 m, Uncoated woodfree/freesheet, Coated woodfree/freesheet
No. 2, fourdrinier, size press, total capacity 5,000 mt/y, Trim width 2.3 m, Packaging papers
No. 4, fourdrinier, Yankee dryer, total capacity 10,000 mt/y, Trim width 2.7 m, Tissue
No. 5, crescent former, Yankee dryer, total capacity 35,000 mt/y, Trim width 2.85 m, Tissue
No. 6, Periformer, Yankee dryer, total capacity 35,000 mt/y, Trim width 2.85 m, Tissue
Finishing Equipment:
Supercalenders: 1
Rewinders: 7
Sheeters: 2
Energy Data:
Power boilers: 1
Combustion turbines: 1 at 13 MW
Electrical demand for mill: 279 MWh/D

Romania

ⓘⓂFábrica de Papel de Torres Novas Lda.
Torres Novas Mill
Ownership: Private
Ribeira Branca
P-2354-909 Torres Novas
Portugal
Mailing Address: Apt. 2, Ribeira Branca, 2354-909 Torres Novas, Portugal
  Phone: (351) 249 830890
  Fax: (351) 249 831694
  Email: papeltorres@clix.pt, geral@fptn.pt
  Web Address: fabricadepapeltorresnovas.pai.pt
Personnel:
  Mgr.: Teresa Alexandre
  Phone: (351) 249 830 890
  Fax: (351) 249 831 694
Total Employees of Company: 60
Total Employees at this Location: 60
Type of Operation: Paperboard mill
Pulp Grades and Capacities:
  Total pulp capacity: 20,616 mt/y
  Recycled Pulping: 20,616 mt/y
Pulp Mill Data:
  Recycled Fiber Treatment Lines:
  Pulpers: 1 at 23,400
Paper/Paperboard Grades and Capacities:
  Total paper and paperboard capacity: 20,000 mt/y
  Packaging papers: 5,000 mt/y
  Linerboard: 5,000 mt/y
  Corrugating medium/fluting: 5,000 mt/y
  Boxboard/cartonboard: 5,000 mt/y
Paper and Paperboard Mill Data:
Paper Machines: 1
  No. 1, fourdrinier, total capacity 20,000 mt/y, Trim width 2.35 m, Packaging papers, Corrugating medium/fluting, Linerboard, Boxboard/cartonboard
Energy Data:
  Power boilers
  Electrical demand for mill: 27 MWh/D

ⓘFábrica de Papel e Cartão da Zarrinha, S.A.
Ownership: Zarrinha Group
Rua da Estação, 26
4520-467 Rio Meão
Portugal
Mailing Address: Apt. 19, 4536-906 Paços de Brandão, Portugal
  Phone: (351) 22 747 20 70
  Fax: (351) 22 744 48 47
  Email: info@zarrinha.pt
  Web Address: www.zarrinha.pt
Personnel:
  CEO: Orlando Oliveira Santos
  Phone: (351) 22 747 20 70
  Fax: (351) 22 744 48 47
  Pres. of Gen. Assembly: Maria Alzira Marques Costa
  Phone: (351) 22 747 20 70
  Fax: (351) 22 744 48 47
  Admin./Finan. Dir.: Marieta Costa Oliveira Santos
  Phone: (351) 22 747 20 70
  Fax: (351) 22 744 48 47
  Admin.: Orlando Bóris Costa Oliveira Santos
  Phone: (351) 22 747 20 70
  Fax: (351) 22 744 48 47
Mill Locations:
  Oliveira Santos & Irmão, Lda., Paços de Brandão Mill, Calçada Rio Maior, 228 Apartado 19, P-4536-906 Paços de Brandão, Portugal, Capacity: 20,000 mt/y, (Paperboard mill)
  Phone: (351) 22 744 2113 / 22 747 2070
  Fax: (351) 22 744 2391
  Email: osil@netvisao.pt
  Fábrica de Papel e Cartão da Zarrinha, S.A., Rio Meão Mill, Rua da Estação, 26, 4520-467 Rio Meão, Portugal, Capacity: 20,000 mt/y, (Paper mill, Paperboard mill)
  Phone: (351) 22 747 20 70
  Fax: (351) 22 744 48 47
  Email: info@zarrinha.pt, vendas@zarrinha.pt

ⓜFábrica de Papel e Cartão da Zarrinha, S.A.
Rio Meão Mill
Rua da Estação, 26
4520-467 Rio Meão
Portugal
Mailing Address: Apt. 19, 4536-906 Paços de Brandão, Portugal
  Phone: (351) 22 747 20 70
  Fax: (351) 22 744 48 47
  Email: info@zarrinha.pt, vendas@zarrinha.pt
  Web Address: www.zarrinha.pt
Personnel:
  Admin. Asst.: Nuno Pinto
  Phone: (351) 22 747 20 70
  Fax: (351) 22 744 48 47
  Email: nunopinto@zarrinha.pt
  Admin. Sec.: Deolinda Albergaria
  Phone: (351) 22 747 20 70
  Fax: (351) 22 744 48 47
  Email: administracao@zarrinha.pt
Total Employees at this Location: 35
Type of Operation: Paper mill, Paperboard mill
Pulp Grades and Capacities:
  Total pulp capacity: 20,256 mt/y
  Recycled Pulping: 20,256 mt/y
Pulp Mill Data:
  Recycled Fiber Treatment Lines:
  Pulpers: 3
Paper/Paperboard Grades and Capacities:
  Total paper and paperboard capacity: 20,000 mt/y
  Corrugating medium/fluting: 20,000 mt/y
Paper and Paperboard Mill Data:
  Stock Preparation:
  Pulpers: 3
  Refiners: 4
Paper Machines: 2
  No. 1, fourdrinier, total capacity 10,000 mt/y, Trim width 2.3 m, Corrugating medium/fluting
  No. 2, fourdrinier, total capacity 10,000 mt/y, Trim width 2.4 m, Corrugating medium/fluting
Finishing Equipment:
  Rewinders: 2
Energy Data:
  Power boilers: 1
  Electrical demand for mill: 27 MWh/D

ROMANIA

ⓜAmbro SA Suceava
Suceava Mill
Ownership: 100% by Rossmann SAS
Calea Unirii 24
RO-720019 Suceava
Romania
  Phone: (40) 230 205 000
  Fax: (40) 230 205 205 / 111
  Email: office@ambro.ro
  Web Address: www.rossmann.com
Personnel:
  Tech. Mgr.: Ing. Mihai Banu
  Phone: (40) 230 205 103
  Fax: (40) 230 205 205
  Email: mihai.banu@ambro.ro
  Purch. Mgr.: Dipl. Ing. Florin Negriuc
  Phone: (40) 230 205 000
  Fax: (40) 230 205 205
  Email: florin.negriuc@ambro.ro
  Finan. Mgr.: Ec. Angela Nistor
  Phone: (40) 230 205 104
  Fax: (40) 230 205 205
  Email: angela.nistor@ambro.ro
  Environ. Dir.: Dipl. Ing. Marilena Vlaic
  Phone: (40) 230 205 127
  Fax: (40) 230 205 205
  Email: marilena.vlaic@ambro.ro
  Commercial Mgr. Paper Div.: Ing. Dan Semenciuc
  Phone: (40) 230 205 000
  Fax: (40) 230 205 205
  Email: dan.semenciuc@ambro.ro
Total Employees at this Location: 366
Type of Operation: Pulp mill, Paper mill
Pulp Grades and Capacities:
  Total pulp capacity: 151,581 mt/y
  Recycled Pulping: 151,581 mt/y
Pulp Mill Data:
Pulp Lines: 1
  Recycled Fiber Treatment Lines:
  Pulpers: 1 at 150,000 admt/y
  Pulpers: 1 at 70,000
  Recycled packaging pulping lines: 1 at 150,000 admt/y
Paper/Paperboard Grades and Capacities:
  Total paper and paperboard capacity: 150,000 mt/y
  Linerboard: 93,000 mt/y
  Corrugating medium/fluting: 57,000 mt/y
Paper and Paperboard Mill Data:
  Stock Preparation:
  Pulpers: 2
  Refiners: 4
Paper Machines: 1
  No. 1, fourdrinier (2), total capacity 149,940 mt/y, Trim width 5.2 m, Corrugating medium/fluting, Linerboard
Energy Data:
  Power boilers: 3
  Steam turbines: 2 at 17 MW
  Electrical demand for mill: 201 MWh/D

ⓘⓜCeprohart SA
Braila Mill
Ownership: 30% by Financial Investment Company of Moldova, 10% by private shareholders, 58% by public property fund
3 Al. I. Cuza
RO-810019 Braila
Romania
  Phone: (40) 239 619733
  Fax: (40) 239 680280
  Email: office@ceprohart.ro
  Web Address: www.ceprohart.ro
Personnel:
  Gen. Dir.: Dipl. Ing. Dan Buteica
  Phone: (40) 239 619741
  Fax: (40) 239 680280
  Email: dan.buteica@ceprohart.ro
  Research Dir.: Dipl. Ing. Ghiorhe Gore
  Phone: (40) 239 619733
  Fax: (40) 239 680280
  Email: ghiorghe.gore@ceprohart.ro
  Tech. Dir.: Dipl. Ing. Boris Andronic
  Phone: (40) 239 619734
  Fax: (40) 239 680280
  Email: boris.andronic@ceprohart.ro
  Sls. Dir.: Dipl. Econ Pena Botez
  Phone: (40) 239 611725
  Fax: (40) 239 680280
  Email: pena.botez@ceprohart.ro
Total Employees of Company: 125
Total Employees at this Location: 125
Type of Operation: Paperboard mill
Paper/Paperboard Grades and Capacities:
  Total paper and paperboard capacity: 2,000 mt/y
  Uncoated woodfree/freesheet: 1,000 mt/y
  Boxboard/cartonboard: 1,000 mt/y
Paper and Paperboard Mill Data:
  Stock Preparation:
  Pulpers: 2
  Refiners: 3
Paper Machines: 1

Romania

No. 1, fourdrinier, total capacity 2,000 mt/y, Trim width 1.65 m, Uncoated woodfree/freesheet, Boxboard/cartonboard
Finishing Equipment:
Winders: 1
Sheeters: 1
Energy Data:
Power boilers: 1
Electrical demand for mill: 20 MWh/D

ⓂS.C. Comceh S. A.
Comceh Mill
Ownership: 30% by Sofidel Group
1, Prelungirea Bucuresti St.
RO-910161 Calarasi Judet
Romania
Phone: (40) 242 312 942
Fax: (40) 242 315 723
Email: office@comceh.ro
Web Address: www.comceh.ro
Personnel:
Gen. Mgr.: Carlo Ferrero
Phone: (40) 242 312 942
Fax: (40) 242 315 723
Email: carlo.ferrero@comceh.ro
Prod. Mgr.: Eng. Marius Radu
Phone: (40) 242 312 942
Fax: (40) 242 315 723
Email: marius.radu@comceh.ro
Environ. Dir.: Dipl. Eng. Neculai Floranz
Phone: (40) 242 312 942
Fax: (40) 242 315 723
Email: neculai.floranz@comceh.ro
Purch. Mgr.: Dipl. Eng. Georgiana Reitu
Phone: (40) 242 307 600
Fax: (40) 242 307 757
Email: georgiana.reitu@comceh.ro
Total Employees at this Location: 260
Type of Operation: Paper mill
Pulp Grades and Capacities:
Total pulp capacity: 25,297 mt/y
Recycled Pulping: 25,297 mt/y
Pulp Mill Data:
Recycled Fiber Treatment Lines:
Flotation deinking lines: 1 at 30,000 admt/y
Pulpers: 1
Washing deinking lines: 1 at 30,000 admt/y
Paper/Paperboard Grades and Capacities:
Total paper and paperboard capacity: 37,000 mt/y
Tissue: 37,000 mt/y
Paper and Paperboard Mill Data:
Stock Preparation:
Pulpers: 2
Refiners: 6
Paper Machines: 1
No. 2, crescent former, Yankee dryer, total capacity 37,000 mt/y, Trim width 4.54 m, Tissue
Finishing Equipment:
Rewinders: 4 at 66,000 mt/y
Sheeters: 2 at 60,000 mt/y
Energy Data:
Power boilers: 2
Steam turbines: 2 at 12.0 MW
Electrical demand for mill: 106 MWh/D

ⓂS.C. EcoPaper S.A.
Ownership: 97% by SC Ecopack SA Ghimbav
str. 13 Decembrie, nr. 18 Zarnesti, RO-505800
Zarnesti
Romania
Phone: (40) 268 223139, 223140, 223147, 223148
Fax: (40) 268 220311
Email: office@ecopaper.ro
Web Address: www.ecopaper.ro
Personnel:
Mill Mgr. & Econ. Dir.: Aronica Oncioiu
Phone: (40) 268 223139
Fax: (40) 268 220311
Maint. Mgr.: Gh. Bejenariu
Phone: (40) 268 223139
Fax: (40) 268 220311
Control Qlty. & Env.: Mirela Iana
Phone: (40) 268 223139
Fax: (40) 268 220311
Total Employees of Company: 158
Mill Locations:
S.C. EcoPaper S.A., Zarnesti Mill, str. 13 Decembrie, nr. 18, RO-505800 Zarnesti, Romania, Capacity: 80,000 mt/y, (Pulp mill, Paper mill)
Phone: (40) 268 220 341
Fax: (40) 268 220 311
Email: office@ecopaper.ro

ⓂS.C. EcoPaper S.A.
Zarnesti Mill
str. 13 Decembrie, nr. 18
RO-505800 Zarnesti
Romania
Phone: (40) 268 220 341
Fax: (40) 268 220 311
Email: office@ecopaper.ro
Web Address: www.ecopaper.ro
Personnel:
Mill Mgr. & Econ. Dir.: Dipl. Ec. Aronica Oncioiu
Phone: (40) 268 220341
Maint. Mgr.: Dipl. Ing. Gh. Bejenariu
Phone: (40) 268 220926
Control Qlty. & Env.: Dipl. Ing. Mirela Iana
Phone: (40) 268 220926
Purch. Agent: Dipl. Ing. Stefan Stroie
Phone: (40) 268 220926
Paper Mill Mgr.: Eng. Marian Burcoman
Phone: (40) 268 220 341
Total Employees at this Location: 158
Type of Operation: Pulp mill, Paper mill
Pulp Grades and Capacities:
Total pulp capacity: 79,955 mt/y
Recycled Pulping: 79,955 mt/y
Pulp Mill Data:
Recycled Fiber Treatment Lines:
Pulpers: 1
Recycled packaging pulping lines: 1 at 100,000 admt/y
Paper/Paperboard Grades and Capacities:
Total paper and paperboard capacity: 80,000 mt/y
Linerboard: 50,000 mt/y
Corrugating medium/fluting: 30,000 mt/y
Paper and Paperboard Mill Data:
Stock Preparation:
Pulpers: 1
Refiners: 1
Paper Machines: 1
No. 6, fourdrinier, total capacity 80,000 mt/y, Trim width 4.2 m, Corrugating medium/fluting, Linerboard
Energy Data:
Power boilers: 1
Electrical demand for mill: 108 MWh/D

ⓂSC Metalicplas Impex SRL
Dej Mill
Henri Coanda Street, No. 4A
405200 Dej, Judet Cluj
Romania
Phone: (40) 0264-213.091 / 0264-222.207
Email: office@metalicplas.ro
Web Address: www.metalicplas.ro
Total Employees at this Location: 50
Type of Operation: Paper mill
Paper/Paperboard Grades and Capacities:
Total paper and paperboard capacity: 25,000 mt/y
Tissue: 25,000 mt/y
Paper and Paperboard Mill Data:
Paper Machines: 1
No. 1, crescent former, Yankee dryer, total capacity 25,000 mt/y, Trim width 2.82 m, Tissue
Energy Data:
Power boilers
Electrical demand for mill: 63 MWh/D

ⓂSC Metalicplas Impex SRL
Ownership: 100% by MG Tec Group
Str. 1 Mai nr. 113
Dej, Judet Cluj
Romania
Phone: (40) 0264 211 168
Fax: (40) 0264 211 967
Email: office@metalicplas.ro
Web Address: www.metalicplas.ro
Mill Locations:
SC Metalicplas Impex SRL, Dej Mill, Henri Coanda Street, No. 4A, 405200 Dej, Romania, Capacity: 25,000 mt/y, (Paper mill)
Phone: (40) 0264-213.091 / 0264-222.207
Email: office@metalicplas.ro

ⓂPehart Tec SA Petresti
Petresti Mill
Petresti Judet Alba Str. 1 Mai nr. 1
RO-515850 Petresti-Sebes
Romania
Phone: (40) 258 743624
Fax: (40) 258 743625
Email: marketing@peharttec.ro
Web Address: www.peharttec.ro
Personnel:
Mill Gen. Mgr.: Dipl. Ing. Gabriel Stanciu
Phone: (40) 258 743615
Fax: (40) 258 743625
Email: gabriel_stanciu@peharttec.ro
Tech. Mgr.: Dipl. Ing. Cristian Silas
Phone: (40) 258 743626
Fax: (40) 258 743625
Email: cristian_silas@peharttec.ro
Finan. Mgr.: Ec. Ancuta Irimie
Phone: (40) 258 743624
Fax: (40) 258 743625
Email: ancuta_irimie@peharttec.ro
Commer. Mgr.: Borza Pompeiu
Phone: (40) 258 743624
Fax: (40) 258 743625
Email: borza_pompeiu@peharttec.ro
Environ. & Qlty. Dir.: Dipl. Ing. Liana Pastina
Phone: (40) 258 743624
Fax: (40) 258 743625
Email: liana_pastina@peharttec.ro
Mktg. Rep.: Elena Silas
Phone: (40) 745 533 421
Fax: (40) 258 743625
Email: elena_silas@peharttec.ro
Total Employees at this Location: 363
Type of Operation: Paper mill
Pulp Grades and Capacities:
Total pulp capacity: 3,187 mt/y
Recycled Pulping: 3,187 mt/y
Pulp Mill Data:
Recycled Fiber Treatment Lines:
Pulpers: 2 at 10,000 admt/y
Paper/Paperboard Grades and Capacities:
Total paper and paperboard capacity: 57,000 mt/y
Tissue: 57,000 mt/y
Paper and Paperboard Mill Data:
Stock Preparation:
Pulpers: 4
Refiners: 3
Paper Machines: 3
No. 5, fourdrinier, Yankee dryer, total capacity 3,000 mt/y, Trim width 2.1 m, Tissue
No. 6, crescent former, Yankee dryer, total capacity 20,000 mt/y, Trim width 2.5 m, Tissue
No. 7, crescent former, Yankee dryer, total capacity 34,000 mt/y, Trim width 2.75 m, Tissue
Finishing Equipment:
Winders: 3 at 25,900 mt/y
Calenders: 1
Rewinders: 2 at 22,900 mt/y
Sheeters: 1 at 7,900 mt/y
Energy Data:
Power boilers: 2
Electrical demand for mill: 145 MWh/D

Romania

ⓘPehart Tec SA Petresti
Ownership: 100% by Metalicplas Group
Petresti Judet Alba Str. 1 Mai nr. 1
RO-515850 Petresti-Sebes
Romania
 Phone: (40) 258 743624
 Fax: (40) 258 743625
 Email: marketing@peharttec.ro
 Web Address: www.peharttec.ro
Personnel:
 Mill Gen. Mgr.: Gabriel Stanciu
 Phone: (40) 258 743615
 Fax: (40) 258 743625
 Email: gabriel_stanciu@peharttec.ro
 Tech. Mgr.: Cristian Silas
 Phone: (40) 258 743626
 Fax: (40) 258 743625
 Email: cristian_silas@peharttec.ro
 Finan. Mgr.: Ancuta Irimie
 Phone: (40) 258 743624
 Fax: (40) 258 743625
 Email: ancuta_irimie@peharttec.ro
Total Employees of Company: 363
Mill Locations:
 Pehart Tec SA Petresti, Petresti Mill, Petresti Judet Alba Str. 1 Mai nr. 1, RO-515850 Petresti-Sebes, Romania, Capacity: 57,000 mt/y, (Paper mill)
 Phone: (40) 258 743624
 Fax: (40) 258 743625
 Email: marketing@peharttec.ro

ⓜPetrocart SA
Piatra Neamt Mill
170 Bicaz Str.
RO-611070 Piatra Neamt
Romania
Mailing Address: Strada Decebal nr. 171, RO-610052 Piatra Neamt
 Phone: (40) 233 218330 / 237881
 Fax: (40) 233 218330 / 237881
 Email: office@petrocart.ro
 Web Address: www.petrocart.ro
Personnel:
 CEO & Gen. Dir.: Dipl. Ing. Adrian Vais
 Phone: (40) 233 210 621
 Fax: (40) 233 218 330
 Email: avais@petrocart.ro
 CFO: Dipl. Ing. Adriana Dascalu
 Phone: (40) 233 218 330
 Fax: (40) 233 218 330
 Email: adascalu@petrocart.ro
 Chief Eng.: Dipl. Ing. Vasile Nafareanu
 Phone: (40) 233 210 621
 Fax: (40) 233 218 330
 Email: tehnic@petrocart.ro
 Sls. Dir.: Ec. Oana Afloarei
 Phone: (40) 233 210 620
 Fax: (40) 233 218 330
 Email: desfacere@petrocart.ro
 Mktg. Mgr.: Calin Leahu
 Phone: (40) 233 210 620
 Fax: (40) 233 218 330
 Email: marketing@petrocart.ro
 Import Export Mgr.: Stefan Milea
 Phone: (40) 233 210 620
 Fax: (40) 233 218 330
 Email: impex@petrocart.ro
 Energetics Mgr.: Virgil Odagescu
 Phone: (40) 233 218 330
 Fax: (40) 233 218 330
 Email: energetic@petrocart.ro
Total Employees at this Location: 319
Type of Operation: Pulp mill, Paper mill, Paperboard mill

Pulp Mill Data:
 Recycled Fiber Treatment Lines:
 Pulpers: 3 at 12,000 admt/y
Paper/Paperboard Grades and Capacities:
 Total paper and paperboard capacity: 32,500 mt/y
 Tissue: 25,000 mt/y
 Boxboard/cartonboard: 7,500 mt/y
Paper and Paperboard Mill Data:
Paper Machines: 4
 PM 2, (closed in April 2014, replaced by new PM 4), Yankee dryer, total capacity 10,000 mt/y, Trim width 2.2 m, Tissue
 PM 3, cylinder, total capacity 5,000 mt/y, Trim width 2.2 m, Boxboard/cartonboard
 PM 4, (started May 2014), total capacity 25,000 mt/y, Trim width 2.85 m, Tissue
 PM 5, multi-wire, total capacity 2,500 mt/y, Trim width 3.2 m, Boxboard/cartonboard
Energy Data:
 Power boilers: 1
 Steam turbines: 1 at 3.0 MW
 Electrical demand for mill: 50 MWh/D

ⓘPetrocart SA
Ownership: 43% by employees, 29% by private property fund, 28% by private shareholders
170 Bicaz Str.
RO-611070 Piatra Neamt
Romania
Mailing Address: Strada Decebal nr. 171, RO-610052 Piatra Neamt
 Phone: (40) 233 218330 / 237881
 Fax: (40) 233 213513
 Email: office@petrocart.ro
 Web Address: www.petrocart.ro
Personnel:
 CEO: Adrian Vais
 Phone: (40) 233 218330, 233 213 513
 Fax: (40) 233 218330
 Email: avais@petrocart.ro
 CFO: Adriana Dascalu
 Phone: (40) 233 218330, 233 213 513
 Fax: (40) 233 218330
 Email: adascalu@petrocart.ro
 Chief Eng.: Vasile Nafareanu
 Phone: (40) 233 218330, 233 213 513
 Fax: (40) 233 218330
 Email: tehnic@petrocart.ro
 Mktg. Mgr.: Calin Leahu
 Phone: (40) 233 218330, 233 213 513
 Fax: (40) 233 218330
 Email: marketing@petrocart.ro
Total Employees of Company: 319
Mill Locations:
 Petrocart SA, Piatra Neamt Mill, 170 Bicaz Str., RO-611070 Piatra Neamt, Romania, Capacity: 32,500 mt/y, (Pulp mill, Paper mill, Paperboard mill)
 Phone: (40) 233 218330 / 237881
 Fax: (40) 233 218330 / 237881
 Email: office@petrocart.ro

ⓘSC Monte Bianco SA
Str. Fructelor nr. 5
RO-135800 Pucioasa Targoviste
Romania
 Phone: (40) 245 206 296/297 / 722 577 771
 Fax: (40) 245 606 286
 Email: montebianco@montebianco.ro
 Web Address: www.montebianco.ro
Personnel:
 Tech. & Prod. Mgr.: Mihai Petrica
 Phone: (40) 245 206 296
 Fax: (40) 245 606 286
 Email: mihai.petrica@montebianco.ro
 Converting Plt. Mgr.: Rozina Sandulescu
 Phone: (40) 245 206 296
 Fax: (40) 245 606 286
 Email: rozina.sandulescu@montebianco.ro
Total Employees of Company: 198
Mill Locations:
 SC Monte Bianco SA, Targoviste Mill, Str. Fructelor nr. 5, Pucioasa, RO-135800 Targoviste, Romania, Capacity: 7,000 mt/y, (Paper mill)
 Phone: (40) 245 206 296/297 / 722 577 771
 Fax: (40) 245 606 286
 Email: montebianco@montebianco.ro

ⓜSC Monte Bianco SA
Targoviste Mill
Str. Fructelor nr. 5, Pucioasa
RO-135800 Targoviste
Romania
 Phone: (40) 245 206 296/297 / 722 577 771
 Fax: (40) 245 606 286
 Email: montebianco@montebianco.ro
 Web Address: www.montebianco.ro
Personnel:
 Gen. Mgr.: Osman Yelmer
 Phone: (40) 245 206 296
 Fax: (40) 245 606 286
 Email: osman.yelmer@montebianco.ro
 Converting Plt. Mgr.: Rozina Sandulescu
 Phone: (40) 245 206 296
 Fax: (40) 245 606 286
 Email: rozina.sandulescu@montebianco.ro
 Tech. & Prod. Mgr.: Mihai Petrica
 Phone: (40) 245 206 296
 Fax: (40) 245 606 286
 Email: mihai.petrica@montebianco.ro
Total Employees at this Location: 198
Type of Operation: Paper mill
Paper/Paperboard Grades and Capacities:
 Total paper and paperboard capacity: 7,000 mt/y
 Tissue: 7,000 mt/y
Paper and Paperboard Mill Data:
Paper Machines: 1
 No. 1, fourdrinier, Yankee dryer, total capacity 7,000 mt/y, Trim width 2.3 m, Tissue
Energy Data:
 Power boilers: 1
 Electrical demand for mill: 19 MWh/D

ⓘSomes SA Dej
Ownership: 19.11% by MFCC Commodities, 10.57% by Private shareholders, 55.63% by SCR investment company, 14.69% by SIF Banat Crisana
Str. Bistritei 63
RO-405200 Dej
Romania
 Phone: (40) 264 211 331 / 223417 / 222097 / 222700
 Fax: (40) 264 222 182 / 222700
 Email: office@somes.ro, marketing@somes.ro
 Web Address: www.somes.ro
Personnel:
 Gen. Mgr.: Grigore Craciun
 Phone: (40) 264 211 331 / 223417
 Fax: (40) 264 222 182 / 222700
 Finan. Dir.: Radu Maricel Stir
 Phone: (40) 264 211 331 / 223417
 Fax: (40) 264 222 182 / 222700
 Com. Dir.: Crisan Alexandru
 Phone: (40) 264 211 331 / 223417
 Fax: (40) 264 222 182 / 222700
 Tech. & Prod. Mgr.: Gheorghe Dutuc
 Phone: (40) 264 211 331 / 223417
 Fax: (40) 264 222 182 / 222700
Total Employees at this Location: 118
Mill Locations:
 Somes SA Dej, Dej Mill, Str. Bistritei 63, RO-405200 Dej, Romania, Capacity: 50,000 mt/y, (Pulp mill, Paper mill)
 Phone: (40) 264 223 417
 Fax: (40) 264 222 182
 Email: office@somes.ro

ⓜSomes SA Dej
Dej Mill
Mill is idle (production was idled from sometime mid-2010, general bankruptcy proceedings opened on December 10, 2013.)
Str. Bistritei 63

RO-405200 Dej, Judet Cluj
Romania
  Phone: (40) 264 223 417
  Fax: (40) 264 222 182
  Email: office@somes.ro
  Web Address: www.somes.ro
Personnel:
  Gen. Mgr.: Ing. Grigore Craciun
  Phone: (40) 264 211 331
  Fax: (40) 264 222182
  Tech. & Prod. Mgr.: Ing. Gheorghe Dutuc
  Phone: (40) 264 211 331
  Fax: (40) 264 222182
  Finan. Dir.: Ec. Radu Maricel Stir
  Phone: (40) 264 211 331
  Fax: (40) 264 222 098
  Com. Dir.: Crisan Alexandru
  Phone: (40) 264 211 331
  Env. Mgr.: Eng. Angela Vlasin
  Phone: (40) 264 211 331
Total Employees at this Location: 118
Type of Operation: Pulp mill, Paper mill
Pulp Mill Data:
  Chemical Pulping Systems:
  Continuous digesters: 1
  Pulp Lines: 1
  Bleach Plant Systems: 1
  Conventional, Sequence: CECEHD, Capacity 60,000 admt/y
  Chemical Recovery Equipment:
  Evaporator lines: 2
  Recovery boilers: 1
  Lime Kiln
  Pulp Dryers:
  Fourdriniers 1
Paper/Paperboard Grades and Capacities:
  Total paper and paperboard capacity: 50,000 mt/y
  Packaging papers: 50,000 mt/y
Paper and Paperboard Mill Data:
  Stock Preparation:
  Pulpers: 2
  Refiners: 5
Paper Machines: 1
  PM 1, fourdrinier, total capacity 50,000 mt/y, Trim width 4.4 m, Packaging papers
Finishing Equipment:
  Winders: 1 at 60,000 mt/y
  Calenders: 1
  Rewinders
  Sheeters: 1 at 15,000 mt/y
Energy Data:
  Power boilers: 4
  Steam turbines: 3 at 15 MW
  Electrical demand for mill: 130 MWh/D

ⓘVrancart SA
Ownership: 96.66% by Private Property Fund, 3.34% by Private Shareholders, Sif Banar Crisano
Str. Ecaterina Teodoroiu 17
RO-625100 Adjud
Romania
  Phone: (40) 237-640800, 741-816512
  Fax: (40) 237-641720
  Email: vrancart@vrancart.ro
  Web Address: www.vrancart.ro
Personnel:
  Chmn. & Gen. Mgr.: Mihai Marcel Botez
  Phone: (40) 237 641 902/640 800
  Fax: (40) 237 641 720
  Economic Dir.: Tatiana Botez
  Phone: (40) 237 641 902/640 800
  Fax: (40) 237 641 720
  Env. Resp.: Lidia Tofan
  Phone: (40) 237 641 902/640 800
  Fax: (40) 237 641 720
  Containerboard Mill Mgr.: Cristian Banarie
  Phone: (40) 237 641 902/640 800
  Fax: (40) 237 641 720
Total Employees of Company: 1,085
Mill Locations:
  Vrancart SA, Adjud Mill, Str. Ecaterina Teodoroiu 17, RO-625100 Adjud, Romania, Capacity: 80,000 mt/y, (Paper mill, Paperboard mill)
  Phone: (40) 237-640800, 0741-816512
  Fax: (40) 237 641720
  Email: vrancart@vrancart.ro

ⓘVrancart SA
Adjud Mill
Str. Ecaterina Teodoroiu 17
RO-625100 Adjud, Vrancea
Romania
  Phone: (40) 237-640800, 0741-816512
  Fax: (40) 237 641720
  Email: vrancart@vrancart.ro
  Web Address: www.vrancart.ro
Personnel:
  Gen. Mgr. & Chairman: Ec. Mihai Marcel Botez
  Phone: (40) 237 640800
  Containerboard Mill Mgr.: Dr. Eng. Cristian Banarie
  Phone: (40) 237 641 902/640 800
  Tissue Mill Mgr.: Dipl. Eng. Dima Dorian
  Phone: (40) 237 641 902/640 800
  Sls. Mgr.: Dipl. Econ Tatiana Mitrofan
  Phone: (40) 237 640800
  Dev. Mgr.: Dipl. Ing. Romeo Sava
  Phone: (40) 237 640800
  Purch. Mgr.: Dipl. Ing. Dan Vintila
  Phone: (40) 237 640800
  Utilities Mgr.: Dipl. Ing. Vasile Matcasu
  Phone: (40) 237 641 902/640 800
  Env. Resp.: Dipl. Ing. Lidia Tofan
  Phone: (40) 237 641 902/640 800
Total Employees at this Location: 432
Type of Operation: Paper mill, Paperboard mill
Pulp Grades and Capacities:
  Total pulp capacity: 76,752 mt/y
  Recycled Pulping: 76,752 mt/y
Pulp Mill Data:
  Recycled Fiber Treatment Lines:
  Pulpers: 3 at 100,000 admt/y
  Recycled packaging pulping lines: 1 at 40,000 admt/y
Paper/Paperboard Grades and Capacities:
  Total paper and paperboard capacity: 80,000 mt/y
  Tissue: 20,000 mt/y
  Packaging papers: 5,000 mt/y
  Linerboard: 30,000 mt/y
  Corrugating medium/fluting: 20,000 mt/y
  Boxboard/cartonboard: 5,000 mt/y
Paper and Paperboard Mill Data:
  Stock Preparation:
  Pulpers: 3
Paper Machines: 2
  No. 1, fourdrinier, total capacity 60,000 mt/y, Trim width 4.2 m, Linerboard, Corrugating medium/fluting, Boxboard/cartonboard, Packaging papers
  No. 2, fourdrinier, Yankee dryer, total capacity 20,000 mt/y, Trim width 4.6 m, Tissue
Finishing Equipment:
  Winders
  Rewinders: 5
Energy Data:
  Power boilers: 3
  Electrical demand for mill: 146 MWh/D

RUSSIA

ⓘZAO NPP Filter Materials
Ownership: closed shareholding company
Tsentralnaya ul. 4
187330 Otradnoye, Kirovskaya Obl.
Russia
  Phone: (7)   813 6241938/812 4485920
  Fax: (7) 813 6241938/812 4485920
  Email: info@filter-m.ru
  Web Address: www.filtermaterials.ru
Personnel:
  Dir.: Aleksandr Evgenyevich
  Phone: (7) 813 6241938
  Fax: (7) 812 4485920
Total Employees of Company: 70
Mill Locations:
  ZAO NPP Filter Materials, Otradnoye Mill, Tsentralnaya ul. 4, 187330 Otradnoye, Russia, Capacity: 3,000 mt/y, (Paper mill)
  Phone: (7) 813 6241938/812 4485920
  Fax: (7) 813 6241938/812 4485920
  Email: info@filter-m.ru

ⓘZAO Uralskaya Bumaga
Beregovaya Str. 5
624803 Sukhoy Log
Russia
  Phone: (7) 34373 42 701/42 925/42614
  Fax: (7) 34373 42 391/42614
  Email: uralbumaga@list.ru
  Web Address: www.urbum.narod.ru
Personnel:
  Gen. Dir: Vladislav Viktorovich Chepulanis
  Phone: (7) 34373 42 701/42925
  Fax: (7) 34373 42 391/42614
  Com.Dir: Aleksey Sergeevich Napalkov
  Phone: (7) 34373 42 701/42925
  Fax: (7) 34373 42 391/42614
  Chief Eng.: Yuriy Demyanenko
  Phone: (7) 34373 42 701/42925
  Fax: (7) 34373 42 391/42614
  Commer. Mgr.: Valentina Vladimirovna Neustroyeva
  Phone: (7) 34373 42 701/42925
  Fax: (7) 34373 42 391/42614
Total Employees at this Location: 140
Mill Locations:
  ZAO Uralskaya Bumaga, Sukhoy Log Mill, Beregovaya Str. 5, 624803 Sukhoy Log, Russia, Capacity: 4,000 mt/y, (Paper mill)
  Phone: (7) 34373 42 701/42 925/42614
  Fax: (7) 34373 42 391/42614
  Email: uralbumaga@list.ru

ⓘⓘAdischevskaya Board Mill
Adischevo Mill
Ownership: 100% by Lad-M Ltd.
Dzerzhinskogo str.2
157921 Adischevo, Ostrovsky District, Kostroma Region
Russia
Mailing Address: Dzerzhinskogo str.2, 157921 Adischevo, Ostrovsky District, Kostroma Region, Russia
  Phone: (7) 49438 26460/31219/4997242461
  Fax: (7) 49438 31219/26460
  Email: tdbumaga@mail.ru, abftb@mail.ru
  Web Address: www.tual-bum.ru
Personnel:
  Chief Engineer: Dmitry Kurochkin
  Phone: (7) 49438 31219
  Dir.: Svetlana Pavlovna Smirnova
  Phone: (7) 49438 31220/26413
  Fax: (7) 49438 26460
  Tech. Dir.: Alexander Sergeev
  Phone: (7) 49438 26491
  Financial Manager: Elena Smirnova
  Phone: (7) 49438 26460
Total Employees at this Location: 180
Type of Operation: Paper mill
Pulp Grades and Capacities:
  Total pulp capacity: 8,516 mt/y
  Recycled Pulping: 8,516 mt/y
Pulp Mill Data:
  Recycled Fiber Treatment Lines:
  Pulpers: 1
Paper/Paperboard Grades and Capacities:
  Total paper and paperboard capacity: 8,000 mt/y
  Tissue: 8,000 mt/y
Paper and Paperboard Mill Data:
Paper Machines: 4

Russia

No. 1, fourdrinier, Yankee dryer, total capacity 2,000 mt/y, Trim width 1.68 m, Tissue
No. 2, fourdrinier, Yankee dryer, total capacity 2,000 mt/y, Trim width 1.68 m, Tissue
No. 3, fourdrinier, Yankee dryer, total capacity 2,000 mt/y, Trim width 1.68 m, Tissue
No. 4, fourdrinier, Yankee dryer, total capacity 2,000 mt/y, Trim width 1.68 m, Tissue
Energy Data:
Power boilers: 1
Electrical demand for mill: 24 MWh/D

ⓞⓜAlatyrskaya Paper Mill
Alatyr Mill
Yaroslavskaya Str. 19
429827 Alatyr, Chuvashkaya Republic
Russia
 Phone: (7) 83531 61189
 Fax: (7) 83531 28223
 Email: ooo-abf@rambler.ru, ooo-abf@mail.ru, oooabf@mail.ru
 Web Address: www.alatyrbumaga.ru
Personnel:
 Dir.: Sergey Venyaminovich Aleksandrov
 Phone: (7) 83531 61189
 Email: info@alatyrbumaga.ru
 Chief Eng.: Andrey Viktorovich Tremasov
 Phone: (7) 83531 28931
 Deputy Commercial Dir.: Aleksandr Yurievich Stepantsov
 Phone: (7) 83531 61119
 Fax: (7) 83531 28560
 Email: sbyt@alatyrbumaga.ru
Total Employees at this Location: 430
Type of Operation: Paper mill
Pulp Grades and Capacities:
 Total pulp capacity: 39,443 mt/y
 Recycled Pulping: 39,443 mt/y
Pulp Mill Data:
 Recycled Fiber Treatment Lines:
 Recycled packaging pulping lines: 1
Paper/Paperboard Grades and Capacities:
 Total paper and paperboard capacity: 39,000 mt/y
 Packaging papers: 5,000 mt/y
 Linerboard: 20,000 mt/y
 Corrugating medium/fluting: 14,000 mt/y
Paper and Paperboard Mill Data:
Paper Machines: 2
No. 1, fourdrinier (2), total capacity 25,000 mt/y, Trim width 3.2 m, Linerboard, Packaging papers
No. 2, fourdrinier, total capacity 14,000 mt/y, Trim width 1.68 m, Corrugating medium/fluting
Energy Data:
Power boilers: 1
Electrical demand for mill: 54 MWh/D

ⓜOAO Aleksandrovbumprom (ABP)
Krasnopolyanskij Paperboard Mill
Ul. Lugavaya 18
157912 Pos. Krasnaya Polyana, Ostrovskiy rayon, Kostroma Region
Russia
 Phone: (7) 49438 26691/31217
 Fax: (7) 49438 31217
 Email: skbf@bk.ru
Personnel:
 Gen. Dir.: Mikhail Moiseevich Sedov
 Phone: (7) 49438.8550148957
 Sls. Mgr., Ass. Gen. Dir.: Tatiana Yuryevna Chikhvatova
 Phone: (7) 49438.8550148957
 Chief Acc.: Elena Nikolaevna Stchiraya
 Chief.Technolog: Rida Romashova
Total Employees at this Location: 80
Type of Operation: Paperboard mill
Paper/Paperboard Grades and Capacities:
 Total paper and paperboard capacity: 5,000 mt/y
 Boxboard/cartonboard: 5,000 mt/y
Paper and Paperboard Mill Data:
Paper Machines: 1
No. 1, total capacity 5,000 mt/y, Boxboard/cartonboard
Energy Data:
Electrical demand for mill: 11 MWh/D

ⓞⓜAleksinskaya Board & Paper Mill, CJSC
Aleksin Mill
Ownership: 100% by SFT Group
Aleksin Square Pobedy 19 a
301340 Aleksin, Tula Region
Russia
 Phone: (7) 48753 41888/42653
 Fax: (7) 48753 42590
 Email: fabrika@aleksinkarton.ru
 Web Address: www.aleksinkarton.ru
Personnel:
 Man. Dir.: Vladimir Vasilevich Velichko
 Phone: (7) 48753 41888/42653
 Fax: (7) 48753 42590
 Email: v_velichko@aleksinkarton.ru
 Sls. Dir.: Lyudmila Nikolaevna Krendeleva
 Phone: (7) 48753 41038
 Fax: (7) 48753 42590
 Email: l_krendeleva@aleksinkarton.ru
 Chief Eng.: Igor Nikolaevich Belyaev
 Phone: (7) 48753 40443
 Fax: (7) 48753 42590
 Email: i_belyaev@aleksinkarton.ru
 Commercial Dir.: Natalia Nikolaevna Tavkin
 Phone: (7) 48753 41516
 Fax: (7) 48753 42590
 Email: n_tavkin@aleksinkarton.ru
 Finan. Dir. and Chief Account.: Natalia Sergeevna Vasileva
 Phone: (7) 48753 42137
 Fax: (7) 48753 42590
 Email: n_vasileva@aleksinkarton.ru
Total Employees at this Location: 370
Type of Operation: Paperboard mill
Pulp Grades and Capacities:
 Total pulp capacity: 120,888 mt/y
 Recycled Pulping: 120,888 mt/y
Pulp Mill Data:
 Recycled Fiber Treatment Lines:
 Recycled packaging pulping lines: 1
Paper/Paperboard Grades and Capacities:
 Total paper and paperboard capacity: 120,000 mt/y
 Boxboard/cartonboard: 120,000 mt/y
Paper and Paperboard Mill Data:
Paper Machines: 1
No. 1, cylinder (7), total capacity 120,000 mt/y, Trim width 4.2 m, Boxboard/cartonboard
Energy Data:
Power boilers
Electrical demand for mill: 117 MWh/D

ⓞⓜZAO Altaykrovlya
Novoaltaysk Mill
ul. Vagonostroitelnaya, 9
658087 Novoaltaysk, Altaisky Kraý
Russia
 Phone: (7) 38532 61129/61152/61385
 Fax: (7) 38532 61225/61159
 Email: reklama@altkrov.ru
 Web Address: www.altkrov.ru, www.tosa-rpp.ru
Personnel:
 Gen. Dir.: Evgeniy Nikolaevich Ryzhak
 Phone: (7) 38532 61129/51
 Fax: (7) 38532 61159
 Commercial Dir.: Tatiana Yurievna Pashkevich
 Phone: (7) 38532 61581
 Fax: (7) 38532 61159
 Chief Tech.: Lyudmila Alexeevna Orlova
 Phone: (7) 38532 61597
 Fax: (7) 38532 61159
 Prod. Mgr.: Konstantin Anatolyevich Alexandrov
 Phone: (7) 38532 61129/61152/61385
 Fax: (7) 38532 61159
 Dep.Tech.Director: Natalia Kinsel
 Phone: (7) 38532 61129
 Fax: (7) 38532 61159
Total Employees at this Location: 1,907
Type of Operation: Paper mill
Pulp Grades and Capacities:
 Total pulp capacity: 60,842 mt/y
 Recycled Pulping: 60,842 mt/y
Pulp Mill Data:
 Recycled Fiber Treatment Lines:
 Recycled packaging pulping lines: 1
Paper/Paperboard Grades and Capacities:
 Total paper and paperboard capacity: 68,000 mt/y
 Tissue: 8,000 mt/y
 Linerboard: 27,000 mt/y
 Corrugating medium/fluting: 27,000 mt/y
 Boxboard/cartonboard: 6,000 mt/y
Paper and Paperboard Mill Data:
Paper Machines: 2
No. 1, fourdrinier, Yankee dryer, total capacity 60,000 mt/y, Trim width 4.2 m, Corrugating medium/fluting, Linerboard, Boxboard/cartonboard
No. 3, total capacity 8,000 mt/y, Trim width 2.2 m, Tissue
Energy Data:
Power boilers: 1
Electrical demand for mill: 115 MWh/D

ⓞⓜArkhangelsk Pulp & Paper Mill
Novodvinsk (Arkhangelsk - APPM) Mill
Ownership: 97.50% by Pulp Mill Holding GesmbH
Melnikova Str., 1
164900 Novodvinsk, Arkhangelsk Region
Russia
 Phone: (7) 818 52 63202, 52 63500
 Fax: (7) 818 52 63231
 Email: info@appm.ru
 Web Address: www.appm.ru
Personnel:
 Pres. & Chmn. of Board: Heinz Zinner
 Phone: (7) 81852 63202
 Fax: (7) 818 52 63231
 Sls. Dir.: Aleksey Dyachenko
 Phone: (7) 81852 63187
 Fax: (7) 818 52 63231
 Email: dyachenko.aleksey@appm.ru
 Head of Mktg.: Margarita Kuznetsova
 Phone: (7) 81852 63197
 Fax: (7) 818 52 63231
 Email: kuznetsova.margarita@appm.ru
 Transport & Logist. Mgr.: Alexei Izhmyakov
 Phone: (7) 81852 63198
 Fax: (7) 818 52 63231
 Email: izhmyakov.aleksey@appm.ru
Total Employees of Company: 4,000
Total Employees at this Location: 4,000
Type of Operation: Pulp mill, Paper mill, Paperboard mill
Mill Locations:
Arkhbum Tissue Group, Vorsino Mill, Vorsino, Russia, (Paper mill)
Pulp Grades and Capacities:
 Total pulp capacity: 850,401 mt/y
 Pulp available for market: 265,000 mt/y
 Chemical Pulp: 850,401 mt/y
Pulp Mill Data:
 Chemical Pulping Systems:
 Batch digesters: 2
 Continuous digesters: 1
 Pulp Lines: 2
 Bleach Plant Lines:
 Chemical Pulping System - Hardwood, Type: ECF, Sequence: DEDED
 Chemical Pulping System - Softwood, Type: ECF, Sequence: DEDED
 Chemical Recovery Equipment:
 Evaporator lines: 1
 Recovery boilers: 2

Lime Kiln
Pulp Dryers:
Air Float dryers 1
Paper/Paperboard Grades and Capacities:
Total paper and paperboard capacity: 572,000 mt/y
Uncoated woodfree/freesheet: 70,500 mt/y
Packaging papers: 6,500 mt/y
Specialty and industrial: 10,000 mt/y
Linerboard: 345,000 mt/y
Corrugating medium/fluting: 140,000 mt/y
Paper and Paperboard Mill Data:
Paper Machines: 5
No. 1, fourdrinier, total capacity 290,000 mt/y, Trim width 6.3 m, Linerboard
No. 2, fourdrinier, total capacity 195,000 mt/y, Trim width 6.3 m, Corrugating medium/fluting, Linerboard
No. 3, fourdrinier, total capacity 27,000 mt/y, Trim width 3.16 m, Uncoated woodfree/freesheet
No. 4, fourdrinier, total capacity 43,500 mt/y, Trim width 4.2 m, Uncoated woodfree/freesheet
No. 6, fourdrinier, Yankee dryer, total capacity 16,500 mt/y, Trim width 4.2 m, Packaging papers, Specialty and industrial
Energy Data:
Power boilers: 5
Steam turbines: 4 at 194 MW
Electrical demand for mill: 2,234 MWh/D

ⓘⓜArkhbum Tissue Group
Vorsino Mill
Company is under construction (new tissue mill, scheduled for completion in 2015)
Ownership: Arkhangelsk Pulp & Paper Mill
Vorsino, Kaluga Region
Russia
Type of Operation: Paper mill
Paper and Paperboard Mill Data:
Paper Machines: 1
TM 1, (scheduled for completion in 2015), total capacity 35,000 mt/y, Tissue

ⓜOOO Astrakhanskaya Paperboard Mill
Solyanka Mill
ul. Optovaya 2
416130 Solyanka
Russia
Phone: (7) 8512 581285/6
Fax: (7) 8512 581285
Email: akf-pap@yandex.ru
Type of Operation: Paperboard mill
Paper/Paperboard Grades and Capacities:
Total paper and paperboard capacity: 2,450 mt/y
Linerboard
Corrugating medium/fluting
Paper and Paperboard Mill Data:
Paper Machines: 1
No. 1, Trim width 1.4 m, Linerboard, Corrugating medium/fluting
Energy Data:
Electrical demand for mill: 12 MWh/D

ⓘⓜZAO ATMSS
Kazan Mill
Zalesnaya Str. 30
420076 Kazan, Tatarstan Republic
Russia
Phone: (7) 843 5559363/53
Fax: (7) 843 555 9665/9353
Email: info@paper-avenue.com, info@nega-paper.com
Personnel:
Gen. Dir.: Erik Fagmievich Akchurin
Phone: (7) 843 555 9363
Fax: (7) 843 555 9665
Email: erik@nega-paper.com
Total Employees at this Location: 250
Type of Operation: Paper mill

Paper/Paperboard Grades and Capacities:
Total paper and paperboard capacity: 7,000 mt/y
Tissue: 7,000 mt/y
Paper and Paperboard Mill Data:
Paper Machines: 1
No. 1, fourdrinier, Yankee dryer, total capacity 7,000 mt/y, Trim width 2.52 m, Tissue
Energy Data:
Power boilers
Electrical demand for mill: 20 MWh/D

ⓘⓜBaikalskiy Pulp and Paper Mill (Baikal)
Baikalsk Mill
Company is closed (On September 8 2013, the mill stopped its production of bleached pulp.)
Ownership: 50.25% by Continental Invest, 49% by Federal Property Fund
Promploshadka, Sljudyansk District
665932 Baikalsk, Irkutsk Region
Russia
Phone: (7) 39542 61103/61101
Fax: (7) 35942 61240/61387
Email: bcbk@bcbk.ru
Web Address: www.bcbk.ru
Personnel:
Gen. Dir.: Konstantin Proshkin
Phone: (7) 39542 61103/61101
Sales Dir.: Alexandr Viktorovich Nepomnyaschikh
Phone: (7) 39542 61128 / 61281
Email: NepomniashchikhAV@bcbk.ru
Total Employees at this Location: 1,605
Type of Operation: Pulp mill, Paper mill, Paperboard mill
Pulp Mill Data:
Chemical Pulping Systems:
Batch digesters: 24
Pulp Lines: 2
Bleach Plant Systems: 2
No. 1, Sequence: O$_2$ C/DE$_0$HDED
No. 2, Sequence: O$_2$ C/DE$_0$HDED
Chemical Recovery Equipment:
Evaporator lines: 7
Recovery boilers: 5
Lime Kiln
Pulp Dryers:
Air Float dryers 1, Pulp Dryers 1
Paper and Paperboard Mill Data:
Stock Preparation:
Pulpers: 2
Refiners: 5
Paper Machines: 1
No. 2, cylinder, total capacity 12,000 mt/y, Trim width 2.5 m
Energy Data:
Power boilers: 13
Steam turbines: 5 at 109.0 MW

ⓘⓜBrianskaya Paper Mill
Belye Berega Mill
Ownership: 100% by private owners
Proletarskaya Str., 1a
241902 Pos. Belye Berega, Bryansk Region
Russia
Phone: (7) 4832 714007/714507/714058
Fax: (7) 4832 714072/714058
Email: market@bumfabrika.ru, rva@bumfabrika.ru, info@bumfabrika.ru
Web Address: www.bumfabrika.ru
Personnel:
Gen. Dir.: Sergey Anatolyevich Zabelin
Phone: (7) 4832 714507
Fax: (7) 4832 714072
Chief Prod. Dir.: Michail Konstantinovich Karzhkov
Phone: (7) 4832 714007/714507/714058
Chief Eng.: Sergei Mikhailovich Bisarev
Phone: (7) 4832 714507

Commer. Dir.: Vladimir Pavlovich Kovalev
Phone: (7) 4832 714007/714507/714058
Total Employees of Company: 410
Total Employees at this Location: 410
Type of Operation: Paper mill, Paperboard mill
Pulp Grades and Capacities:
Total pulp capacity: 27,347 mt/y
Recycled Pulping: 27,347 mt/y
Paper/Paperboard Grades and Capacities:
Total paper and paperboard capacity: 27,000 mt/y
Packaging papers: 5,000 mt/y
Linerboard: 13,000 mt/y
Corrugating medium/fluting: 9,000 mt/y
Paper and Paperboard Mill Data:
Paper Machines: 1
No. 1, fourdrinier, total capacity 27,000 mt/y, Trim width 3.2 m, Linerboard, Packaging papers, Corrugating medium/fluting
Energy Data:
Power boilers: 1
Electrical demand for mill: 37 MWh/D

ⓜOOO Bumy
Lyskovo Mill
Engelsa Str. 1
606210 Lyskovo, Nizhny Novgorod
Russia
Phone: (7) 83149 28896/50632
Fax: (7) 83149 50632
Email: bumy@nm.ru
Personnel:
Chmn./ Com.Dir.: Oleg Konstantinovich Zavarzin
Phone: (7) 83149 28896/50632
Gen. Dir.: Ivan Aleksandrovich Averin
Phone: (7) 83149 59652
Type of Operation: Paper mill
Paper/Paperboard Grades and Capacities:
Total paper and paperboard capacity: 2,500 mt/y
Tissue: 2,500 mt/y
Paper and Paperboard Mill Data:
Paper Machines: 2
PM 1, Trim width 1.6 m, Tissue
PM 2, Trim width 2.1 m, Tissue
Energy Data:
Electrical demand for mill: 2 MWh/D

ⓜOOO Buprom-Pokrov
Pokrov, Petushinskiy rayon Mill
Franz Shtolverk Str. 18
601135 Pokrov, Petushinskiy rayon
Russia
Phone: (7) 49243 64284 / 64153/64194
Fax: (7) 49243 64284
Email: buprom.pokrov@mail.ru
Personnel:
Dir.: Andrey Aleksandrovich Titov
Phone: (7) 49243 64153
Chief. Eng.: Vyacheslav Petrovich Inyushin
Phone: (7) 49243 64153
Prod. Mgr.: Vladimir Sergeevich Tertychnik
Phone: (7) 9038336725
Sls. Dep. Mgr.: Lyudmila Evgenievna Klimova
Total Employees at this Location: 150
Type of Operation: Paper mill
Pulp Grades and Capacities:
Total pulp capacity: 7,318 mt/y
Recycled Pulping: 7,318 mt/y
Pulp Mill Data:
Recycled Fiber Treatment Lines:
Pulpers: 2
Paper/Paperboard Grades and Capacities:
Total paper and paperboard capacity: 8,000 mt/y
Tissue: 8,000 mt/y
Paper and Paperboard Mill Data:
Paper Machines: 1
No. 1, fourdrinier, Yankee dryer, total capacity 8,000 mt/y, Trim width 1.85 m, Tissue
Energy Data:
Power boilers: 2
Electrical demand for mill: 24 MWh/D

Russia

ⒽChaltyr Paper Mill
Promzona
346800 Chaltyr
Russia
 Phone: (7) 863 49 31291
 Fax: (7) 863 49 23242
 Email: prototrade@chlat.donpak.ru
 Web Address: www.paper.chalt.ru
Personnel:
 Commer. Dir.: Sergei Arshakovich Kutulian
 Phone: (7) 863 49 23241
 Fax: (7) 863 49 23242
 Email: kut-ser@mail.ru
Total Employees of Company: 230
Mill Locations:
 Chaltyr Paper Mill, Chaltyr Mill, Promzona, 346800 Chaltyr, Russia, Capacity: 13,000 mt/y, (Paper mill)
 Phone: (7) 86349 23241
 Fax: (7) 86349 23242
 Email: prototrade@chlat.donpak.ru

ⓂChaltyr Paper Mill
Chaltyr Mill
Promzona
346800 Chaltyr
Russia
 Phone: (7) 86349 23241
 Fax: (7) 86349 23242
 Email: prototrade@chlat.donpak.ru
 Web Address: www.paper.chalt.ru
Personnel:
 Dir.: Serguey Khorenovich Dagldyan
 Phone: (7) 863 49 21515
 Fax: (7) 863 49 23242
 Email: prototrade@chalt.donpak.ru
 Commer. Dir.: Sergei Arshakovich Kutulian
 Phone: (7) 863 49 23241
 Fax: (7) 863 49 23242
 Email: kut-ser@mail.ru
Total Employees at this Location: 160
Type of Operation: Paper mill
Pulp Grades and Capacities:
 Total pulp capacity: 7,449 mt/y
 Recycled Pulping: 7,449 mt/y
Pulp Mill Data:
 Recycled Fiber Treatment Lines:
 Flotation deinking lines: 1
Paper/Paperboard Grades and Capacities:
 Total paper and paperboard capacity: 13,000 mt/y
 Tissue: 13,000 mt/y
Paper and Paperboard Mill Data:
Paper Machines: 2
 No. 1, total capacity 6,000 mt/y, Trim width 2.1 m, Tissue
 No. 2, total capacity 7,000 mt/y, Trim width 2.1 m, Tissue
Energy Data:
 Power boilers: 1
 Steam turbines: 1
 Electrical demand for mill: 38 MWh/D

ⒽConsolidated Paper Mills PLC
Business Park "Roumyantsevo", 1km Kievskoe shosse, building 1, office 901 A
142784 Moscow
Russia
 Phone: (7) 495 5140324
 Fax: (7) 495 5140324
 Email: com@ukobf.com, com@pzbf.com
 Web Address: www.ukobf.com
Personnel:
 CEO: Dmitry Aleksandrovich Dulkin
 Phone: (7) 495 514 0324
 Fax: (7) 495 514 0324
 Exec. VP: Inna Yevgenyevna Belousova
 Phone: (7) 495 514 0324
 Fax: (7) 495 514 0324
 Deputy Gen. Dir.: Alexander Vladimirovich Sinchuk
 Phone: (7) 495 514 0324
 Fax: (7) 495 514 0324
 Chief Technical Officer: Nikolai Ivanovich Popov
 Phone: (7) 495 514 0324
 Fax: (7) 495 514 0324
 Commer. Dir.: Andrey Kuzmin
 Phone: (7) 495 514 0324
 Fax: (7) 495 514 0324
Mill Locations:
 OAO Poligrafkarton, Balakhna Mill, Prospekt Revolutsii 93, 606400 Balakhna, Russia, Capacity: 115,000 mt/y, (Pulp mill, Paperboard mill)
 Phone: (7) 83144 62289/62284
 Fax: (7) 83144 62289
 Email: polygrafkarton@yandex.ru
 Polotnyano-Zavodskaya Paper Mill, Polotnyany Zavod Mill, Trudovaya Str., 2, 249844 Polotnyany Zavod, Russia, Capacity: 72,000 mt/y, (Paper mill)
 Phone: (7) 48434 32043/74598
 Fax: (7) 48434 46319/33824
 Email: sales@pzbf.com, pzbf@pzbf.ru
 Sukhonsky Pulp and Paper Mill, Sokol Mill, 129 Sovetskaya Str., 162135 Sokol, Russia, Capacity: 100,000 mt/y, (Paperboard mill)
 Phone: (7) 81733 32687/32877 / 31052
 Fax: (7) 81733 31892 / 32203
 Email: scbk@suhona.com, com-paper@yandex.ru

ⒽContinental Management Plc
Rochdelskaya Str. 15
123022 Moscow
Russia
 Phone: (7) 495 775 3566
 Fax: (7) 495 775 1788
 Email: info@lpk-km.ru
Personnel:
 CEO: Serguey Khvostikov
 Phone: (7) 495 775 3566
 Fax: (7) 495 775 1788
 Deputy Gen. Dir. for Economics and Finance: Marina Bugakova
 Phone: (7) 495 775 3566
 Fax: (7) 495 775 1788
 Dir. of Legal Affairs: Alexander Fedorov
 Phone: (7) 495 775 3566
 Fax: (7) 495 775 1788
 Head of Infrastructure Projects: Konstantin Gerasimov
 Phone: (7) 495 775 3566
 Fax: (7) 495 775 1788
 Deputy Gen. Dir. of Prod. & Develop.: Alexei Panshin
 Phone: (7) 495 775 3566
 Fax: (7) 495 775 1788
 HR. Dir.: Eugene Nertik
 Phone: (7) 495 775 3566
 Fax: (7) 495 775 1788
 Commer. Dir.: Andrew Bulsunaeva
 Phone: (7) 495 775 3566
 Fax: (7) 495 775 1788
 Public Relations Mgr.: Marina Savchenkova
 Phone: (7) 495 775 3566
 Fax: (7) 495 775 1788
 Email: marinavsa@basel.ru
Mill Locations:
 JSC 'Kondrovskaya Paper company', Kondrovskaya Paper Company Mill, ul. Pushkina, 1, 249833 Kondrovo, Russia, Capacity: 37,000 mt/y, (Paper mill)
 Phone: (7) 48434 32158/33115
 Fax: (7) 48434 33365
 Email: kpc@kaluga.ru
 Ojsc 'Troitskaya Paper Mill', Troitskaya Mill, Mayakovskogo Str., 1, 249834 Kondrovo, Russia, Capacity: 20,000 mt/y, (Paper mill)
 Phone: (7) 48434 33221/32504/46238/33743
 Fax: (7) 48434 32504/33221/46238
 Email: export@tbf.ru, tbf@kaluga.ru

ⒽDalkrovlya
Ownership: *100% by private owners*
Khalturina Str., 3a Khabarovsk, 680015
Khabarovsk
Russia
 Phone: (7) 4212 527711, 527716
 Fax: (7) 4212 524551, 525440
 Email: zavod@krz.khv.ru
 Web Address: www.dalkrovl.khv.ru
Personnel:
 Gen. Dir.: Alexandr Nikolaevich Konnov
 Phone: (7) 4212 527711
 Fax: (7) 4212 524551
 Chief Eng.: Ivan Timofeevich Dumanskiy
 Phone: (7) 4212 527711
 Fax: (7) 4212 524551
Total Employees of Company: 350
Mill Locations:
 Dalkrovlya, Khabarovsk Mill, Khalturina Str., 3a, 680015 Khabarovsk, Russia, Capacity: 20,000 mt/y, (Paper mill, Paperboard mill)
 Phone: (7) 4212 527711/527716
 Fax: (7) 4212 524551/525440
 Email: zavod@krz.khv.ru

ⓂDalkrovlya
Khabarovsk Mill
Khalturina Str., 3a
680015 Khabarovsk
Russia
 Phone: (7) 4212 527711/527716
 Fax: (7) 4212 524551/525440
 Email: zavod@krz.khv.ru
 Web Address: www.dalkrovl.khv.ru
Personnel:
 Gen. Dir.: Alexandr Nikolaevich Konnov
 Phone: (7) 4212 527711/527716
 Chief Eng.: Ivan Timofeevich Dumanskiy
 Phone: (7) 4212 527711/527716
Total Employees at this Location: 200
Type of Operation: Paper mill, Paperboard mill
Pulp Grades and Capacities:
 Total pulp capacity: 20,749 mt/y
 Recycled Pulping: 20,749 mt/y
Pulp Mill Data:
 Recycled Fiber Treatment Lines:
 Recycled packaging pulping lines: 1
Paper/Paperboard Grades and Capacities:
 Total paper and paperboard capacity: 20,000 mt/y
 Packaging papers: 1,000 mt/y
 Boxboard/cartonboard: 19,000 mt/y
Paper and Paperboard Mill Data:
Paper Machines: 1
 No. 2, fourdrinier, total capacity 20,000 mt/y, Trim width 2.75 m, Packaging papers, Boxboard/cartonboard
Energy Data:
 Power boilers: 1
 Electrical demand for mill: 25 MWh/D

ⒽⓂDonskaya Gofrotara
Rostov na Donu Mill
Ownership: *mill staff*
Bolshaya Sadovaya Str., 1
344082 Rostov na Donu
Russia
Mailing Address: 1st Lugovaya street, 2, 344002 Rostov na Donu, Russia
 Phone: (7) 863 2402462/8256
 Fax: (7) 863 2404599
 Email: contact@rostovbumaga.ru, sekretar_dgt@grain.ru
 Web Address: www.rostovbumaga.ru
Personnel:
 CEO: Aleksandr Arturovich Koval
 Fin. Dir.: Galina Nikolaevna Voronkova
 Chief Eng.: Igor Alexandrovich Ivashchenko
Total Employees of Company: 400
Total Employees at this Location: 400
Type of Operation: Paper mill
Pulp Grades and Capacities:
 Total pulp capacity: 59,888 mt/y
 Recycled Pulping: 59,888 mt/y
Pulp Mill Data:

Russia

Recycled Fiber Treatment Lines:
Recycled packaging pulping lines: 1
Paper/Paperboard Grades and Capacities:
Total paper and paperboard capacity: 60,000 mt/y
Linerboard: 35,000 mt/y
Corrugating medium/fluting: 25,000 mt/y
Paper and Paperboard Mill Data:
Paper Machines: 1
No. 3, fourdrinier (2), total capacity 60,000 mt/y, Trim width 2.2 m, Corrugating medium/fluting, Linerboard
Energy Data:
Power boilers
Electrical demand for mill: 85 MWh/D

⊕Ecologicheskie Tekhnologii Ltd
Ownership: 100% by Grigoriy Sverdlik
Ezhny Novgorod, 606400
Nizhny Novgorod
Russia
Phone: (7) 83144 76035/76036
Fax: (7) 83144 76036
Email: eco_bumaga@list.ru, office@ecopaper.ru
Web Address: ecopapers.ru
Personnel:
Dir.: Grigoriy Vladimirovich Sverdlik
Phone: (7) 83144 76035/76036
Fax: (7) 83144 76036
Commer. Dir.: Vladimir Vladimirovich Pankin
Phone: (7) 83144 76035/76036
Fax: (7) 83144 76036
Chief Eng.: Yuriy Vladimirovich Moroz
Phone: (7) 83144 76035/76036
Fax: (7) 83144 76036
Total Employees of Company: 130
Mill Locations:
Ecologicheskie Tekhnologii Ltd, Balakhna Mill, Elizarova 1, 606400 Balakhna, Russia, Capacity: 13,000 mt/y, (Paper mill)
Phone: (7) 83144 76035/76036
Fax: (7) 83144 76036
Email: eco_bumaga@list.ru, office@ecopaper.ru

ⓂEcologicheskie Tekhnologii Ltd
Balakhna Mill
Elizarova 1
606400 Balakhna, Nizhny Novgorod
Russia
Phone: (7) 83144 76035/76036
Fax: (7) 83144 76036
Email: eco_bumaga@list.ru, office@ecopaper.ru
Web Address: ecopapers.ru
Personnel:
Dir.: Grigoriy Vladimirovich Sverdlik
Phone: (7) 8312 233402
Commer. Dir.: Vladimir Vladimirovich Pankin
Phone: (7) 8314 476035/476036
Total Employees at this Location: 130
Type of Operation: Paper mill
Paper/Paperboard Grades and Capacities:
Total paper and paperboard capacity: 13,000 mt/y
Specialty and industrial: 6,000 mt/y
Linerboard: 5,000 mt/y
Corrugating medium/fluting: 2,000 mt/y
Paper and Paperboard Mill Data:
Paper Machines: 1
No. 1, Yankee dryer, total capacity 13,000 mt/y, Trim width 2.85 m, Specialty and industrial, Linerboard, Corrugating medium/fluting
Energy Data:
Electrical demand for mill: 17 MWh/D

⊕Elikon
Ownership: mill staff
Fabrichnaya Str. 1 Murygino, Kirovskaya Obl., 613641
Kirovskaya
Russia
Phone: (7) 83366 27870 / 27200 / 274 62 / 27142
Fax: (7) 83366 27870
Email: elikon@paper.kirov.ru
Personnel:
CEO, Gen.Dir.: Vladimir Ivanovich Okulov
Phone: (7) 83366 27870 /27200
Fax: (7) 83366 27870
Chief Acc.: Irina Valerievna Rumyantseva
Phone: (7) 83366 27870 /27200
Fax: (7) 83366 27870
Chief Eng.: Aleks Urevich
Phone: (7) 83366 27870 /27200
Fax: (7) 83366 27870
Commer. Dir.: Natalya Valentinovna Plotnikova
Phone: (7) 83366 27870 /27200
Fax: (7) 83366 27870
Total Employees of Company: 520
Mill Locations:
Elikon, Murygino Mill, Fabrichnaya Str. 1, 613641 Murygino, Russia, Capacity: 60,000 mt/y, (Paper mill)
Phone: (7) 83366 27870 / 27200 / 274 62 / 27142
Fax: (7) 83366 27870
Email: elikon@paper.kirov.ru

ⓂElikon
Murygino Mill
Fabrichnaya Str. 1
613641 Murygino, Kirovskaya Obl.
Russia
Phone: (7) 83366 27870 / 27200 / 274 62 / 27142
Fax: (7) 83366 27870
Email: elikon@paper.kirov.ru
Personnel:
Chief Acc.: Irina Valerievna Rumyantseva
Phone: (7) 8332 678485/83366 27254
Chief Eng.: Aleks Urevich
Phone: (7) 83366 27140
Commer. Dir.: Natalya Valentinovna Plotnikova
Phone: (7) 8332 678485/83366 27254
Total Employees at this Location: 520
Type of Operation: Paper mill
Pulp Grades and Capacities:
Paper/Paperboard Grades and Capacities:
Total paper and paperboard capacity: 60,000 mt/y
Tissue: 3,800 mt/y
Packaging papers
Specialty and industrial
Containerboard: 20,000 mt/y
Paper and Paperboard Mill Data:
Paper Machines: 11
PM 2, total capacity 2,275 mt/y, Trim width 2.49 m, Specialty and industrial
PM 3, total capacity 1,900 mt/y, Trim width 2.49 m, Tissue
PM 4, total capacity 1,900 mt/y, Trim width 2.49 m, Tissue
PM 5, total capacity 12,250 mt/y, Trim width 2 m, Specialty and industrial, Linerboard
PM 6, total capacity 12,250 mt/y, Trim width 2 m
PM 7, total capacity 2,160 mt/y, Trim width 2.49 m, Specialty and industrial
PM 8, total capacity 1,200 mt/y, Trim width 2.49 m, Uncoated woodfree/freesheet
PM 9, total capacity 2,100 mt/y, Trim width 2.49 m, Specialty and industrial
PM 11, total capacity 1,875 mt/y, Trim width 2.49 m, Uncoated woodfree/freesheet, Specialty and industrial
PM 12, total capacity 1,875 mt/y, Trim width 2.49 m
PM 14, total capacity 1,750 mt/y, Trim width 2.49 m

⊕ⓂSSYMB BM12
SSYMB BM12
Vochanskaya 141
308017 Belgorod
Russia
Phone: (7) 4722 21-52-38
Fax: (7) 4722 21-39-46, 4722 27-36-17
Email: info@gofrobel.ru, gt.marketing@mail.ru
Web Address: www.gofrobel.ru
Type of Operation: Paperboard mill
Mill Locations:
Gofrotara OOO, Belgorod Mill, Vochanskaya 141, 308017 Belgorod, Russia, Capacity: 15,000 mt/y, (Paperboard mill)
Phone: (7) 4722 21-52-38
Fax: (7) 4722 21-39-46, 4722 27-36-17
Email: info@gofrobel.ru, gt.marketing@mail.ru

⊕ⓂGofrotara OOO
Belgorod Mill
Vochanskaya 141
308017 Belgorod, Belgorodskaya Region
Russia
Phone: (7) 4722 21-52-38
Fax: (7) 4722 21-39-46, 4722 27-36-17
Email: info@gofrobel.ru, gt.marketing@mail.ru
Web Address: www.gofrobel.ru
Personnel:
Man. Dir.: Aleksandr Lagutin
Phone: (7) 4722 21-52-38
Comm. Dir.: Sergey Blazhyevskiy
Phone: (7) 4722 21-52-38
Type of Operation: Paperboard mill
Paper/Paperboard Grades and Capacities:
Total paper and paperboard capacity: 15,000 mt/y
Corrugating medium/fluting: 15,000 mt/y
Paper and Paperboard Mill Data:
Paper Machines: 1
PM 1, (2nd hand, started 2006), total capacity 15,000 mt/y, Trim width 2.2 m, Corrugating medium/fluting

⊕Ilim Group
Ownership: private shareholders, 50% by International Paper Co.
Marata Street 17
191025 St. Petersburg
Russia
Phone: (7) 812 718 6050
Fax: (7) 812 718 6006
Email: office@ilimgroup.ru, sales@ilimgroup.ru
Web Address: www.ilimgroup.ru
Personnel:
Ilim Group Chairman: Zakhar Smushkin
Phone: (7) 812 718 6050
Fax: (7) 812 718 6006
CEO: Franz Josef Marx
Phone: (7) 812 718 6055
Fax: (7) 812 718 6006
Email: franz.marx@ilimgroup.ru
VP., Finan.: Alexander Emdin
Phone: (7) 812 718 6040
Fax: (7) 812 718 6006
VP., Strategy & Product Management.: Vladimir Tuzov
Phone: (7) 812 718 6050
Fax: (7) 812 718 6006
VP., Procurement & Supply Chain Management (SCM): Redmond de Burgh
Phone: (7) 812 718 6050
Fax: (7) 812 718 6006
VP., Manuf.: Brett Mosley
Phone: (7) 812 718 6050
Fax: (7) 812 718 6006
VP., Legal Officer: Alexey Lomko
Phone: (7) 812 718 6050
Fax: (7) 812 718 6006
Email: alexey.lomko@ilimgroup.ru
VP., HR.: Ekaterina Serebrenikova
Phone: (7) 812 718 6050
Fax: (7) 812 718 6006
Email: evgeniy.dymkin@ilimgroup.ru
VP., sales: Timofei Sokolenko
Phone: (7) 812 718 6050
Fax: (7) 812 718 6006
Email: timofei.sokolenko@ilimgroup.ru
Total Employees of Company: 19,000
Total Employees at this Location: 500
Mill Locations:
Bratsk Branch of Ilim Group, Bratsk Mill (50% owned),

Russia

1 Mira Street, Mail box 467, 665718 Bratsk, Russia, Capacity: 240,000 mt/y, (Pulp mill, Paperboard mill)
Phone: (7) 3953 340106/47/04
Fax: (7) 3953 340448
Email: office@brk.ilimgroup.ru
Koryazhma Branch of Ilim Group, Kotlas Pulp and Paper Mill (50% owned), 42, Dybtsyna St., 165651 Koryazhma, Russia, Capacity: 1,000,000 mt/y, (Pulp mill, Paper mill, Paperboard mill)
Phone: (7) 81850 45103
Fax: (7) 81850 33327
Email: office@krm.ilimgroup.ru
Ust-Ilimsk Branch of Ilim Group, Ust-Ilimsk Mill (50% owned), PO Box 353, 666684 Ust-Ilimsk, Russia, (Pulp mill)
Phone: (7) 39535 92266
Fax: (7) 39535 71505
Email: office@usk.ilimgroup.ru

ⓜBratsk Branch of Ilim Group
Bratsk Mill
Ownership: 50% by Ilim Group, 50% by International Paper Co.
1 Mira Street, Mail box 467
665718 Bratsk, Irkutsk Region
Russia
Phone: (7) 3953 340106/47/04
Fax: (7) 3953 340448
Email: office@brk.ilimgroup.ru
Web Address: www.ilimgroup.ru
Personnel:
VP. & Man Dir. : Alexander Pozdnyakov
Phone: (7) 3953 340106
Fax: (7) 3953 340448
Branch Dir.: Vladimir Nikolaevich Batischev
Phone: (7) 3953 340106
Fax: (7) 3953 340448
Prod. Mgr.: Lev Nesterovich Heikkinen
Phone: (7) 3953 340106
Fax: (7) 3953 340448
Tech. Dir.: Nikolay Anatolyevich Kozyaev
Phone: (7) 3953 340193
Fax: (7) 3953 340448
Pulp Prod. Mgr.: Vasiliy Mikhaylovich Basov
Phone: (7) 3953 340106
Fax: (7) 3953 340448
Email: vasiliy.basov@ilimgroup.ru
Paperboard Prod. Mgr.: Oleg Alekseevich Tikhonov
Phone: (7) 3953 340106
Fax: (7) 3953 340448
Sls. Mgr.: Vladimir Anatolyevich Timofeev
Phone: (7) 3953 340106
Fax: (7) 3953 340448
Environ. Mgr.: Nikolay Trofimovich Sikov
Phone: (7) 3953 340106
Fax: (7) 3953 340448
Email: nikolay.sikov@brk.ilimgroup.ru
Total Employees at this Location: 3,087
Type of Operation: Pulp mill, Paperboard mill
Pulp Grades and Capacities:
Total pulp capacity: 1,026,073 mt/y
Pulp available for market: 770,000 mt/y
Chemical Pulp: 1,026,073 mt/y
Pulp Mill Data:
Chemical Pulping Systems:
Continuous digesters: 2
Pulp Lines: 2
Bleach Plant Systems: 2
hardwood, Type: ECF, Sequence: O_2 DEDED, Capacity 270,000 admt/y
softwood, Type: ECF, Sequence: O_2 DEoDED, Capacity 655,000 admt/y
Chemical Recovery Equipment:
Evaporator lines: 1
Recovery boilers: 2
Lime Kiln
Pulp Dryers:
Air Float dryers 1, Air Float dryers 1, Fourdriniers 1
Paper/Paperboard Grades and Capacities:
Total paper and paperboard capacity: 240,000 mt/y
Linerboard: 240,000 mt/y
Paper and Paperboard Mill Data:
Stock Preparation:
Refiners: 6
Paper Machines: 1
No. 1, fourdrinier (2), Cylinder, total capacity 240,000 mt/y, Trim width 6.3 m, Linerboard
Finishing Equipment:
Calenders: 1
Sheeters: 1
Energy Data:
Power boilers: 3
Steam turbines: 10 at 72 MW
Electrical demand for mill: 2,635 MWh/D

ⓜKoryazhma Branch of Ilim Group
Kotlas Pulp and Paper Mill
Ownership: 50% by Ilim Group, 50% by International Paper Co.
42, Dybtsyna St.
165651 Koryazhma, Arkhangelsk Region
Russia
Phone: (7) 81850 45103
Fax: (7) 81850 33327
Email: office@krm.ilimgroup.ru
Web Address: www.ilimgroup.ru
Personnel:
West Region Mills Deputy Dir.: Aleksandr Pozdnyakov
Phone: (7) 81850 45103
Branch Dir./ Board Mill Mgr.: Valerij Valerievich Antonishin
Phone: (7) 81850 45103
Finan. Dir.: Elena Inokentievna Popova
Phone: (7) 81850 45103
Region HR Dr.: Denis Vasilievich Svetlugin
Phone: (7) 81850 45103
Tech. Dir.: Ludvik Belovich Krakovski
Phone: (7) 81850 30521/45409
Dpty Dir. on Tech. Devlpt.: Pavel Vasilyevich Kushmerev
Phone: (7) 81850 45103
Admin. Dir.: Nikolai Balakshin
Phone: (7) 81850 45103
Chief Technology: Yurij Nikolaevich Konovalov
Phone: (7) 81850 45342
Env. Dir.: Nikolaj Ryabov
Phone: (7) 81850 45103
Total Employees at this Location: 3,328
Type of Operation: Pulp mill, Paper mill, Paperboard mill
Pulp Grades and Capacities:
Total pulp capacity: 1,154,843 mt/y
Pulp available for market: 200,000 mt/y
Chemical Pulp: 1,154,843 mt/y
Pulp Mill Data:
Chemical Pulping Systems:
Continuous digesters: 3
Bleach Plant Lines:
No. 1, Sequence: DEoDED
Chemical Recovery Equipment:
Evaporator lines: 1
Recovery boilers: 1
Lime Kiln
Pulp Dryers:
Air Float dryers 1
Paper/Paperboard Grades and Capacities:
Total paper and paperboard capacity: 1,000,000 mt/y
Uncoated woodfree/freesheet: 250,000 mt/y
Coated woodfree/freesheet: 90,000 mt/y
Packaging papers: 90,000 mt/y
Specialty and industrial: 40,000 mt/y
Linerboard: 295,000 mt/y
Corrugating medium/fluting: 235,000 mt/y
Paper and Paperboard Mill Data:
Stock Preparation:
Pulpers: 19
Refiners: 59
Paper Machines: 7
No. 1, fourdrinier, total capacity 150,000 mt/y, Trim width 4.3 m, Corrugating medium/fluting
No. 2, fourdrinier, total capacity 140,000 mt/y, Trim width 4.3 m, Packaging papers, Corrugating medium/fluting
No. 3, fourdrinier (2), total capacity 160,000 mt/y, Trim width 4.2 m, Linerboard, Corrugating medium/fluting
No. 4, fourdrinier (2), total capacity 170,000 mt/y, Trim width 4.2 m, Linerboard
No. 5, fourdrinier, total capacity 60,000 mt/y, Trim width 4.2 m, Uncoated woodfree/freesheet
No. 6, fourdrinier, total capacity 80,000 mt/y, Trim width 4.2 m, Uncoated woodfree/freesheet, Specialty and industrial
No. 7, DuoFormer, total capacity 240,000 mt/y, Trim width 6.84 m, Uncoated woodfree/freesheet, Coated woodfree/freesheet
Coating Machines: 1
No. 7, total capacity 220,000 mt/y., off machine
Finishing Equipment:
Supercalenders: 1
Rewinders: 6
Energy Data:
Power boilers: 1
Steam turbines: 1
Electrical demand for mill: 3,296 MWh/D

ⓜUst-Ilimsk Branch of Ilim Group
Ust-Ilimsk Mill
Ownership: 50% by Ilim Group, 50% by International Paper Co.
PO Box 353
666684 Ust-Ilimsk, Irkutsk Region
Russia
Phone: (7) 39535 92266
Fax: (7) 39535 71505
Email: office@usk.ilimgroup.ru
Web Address: www.ilimgroup.ru
Personnel:
Branch Dir.: Nikolay Yuryevich Naumov
Phone: (7) 39535 92266
Fax: (7) 39535 71505
Tech. Dir.: Andrey Alekseevich Tarabanenko
Phone: (7) 39535 92265
Pulp Mill Mgr.: Sergey Evgenyevich Sizov
Phone: (7) 39535 92286
Bus. Devlpt. Mgr.: Evgeniy Inokentievich Kuklin
Phone: (7) 39535 92266
Environ, Health & Safety Mgr.: Irina Gennadievna Sizykh
Phone: (7) 39535 92266
Total Employees at this Location: 2,245
Type of Operation: Pulp mill
Pulp Grades and Capacities:
Total pulp capacity: 672,664 mt/y
Pulp available for market: 660,000 mt/y
Chemical Pulp: 672,664 mt/y
Pulp Mill Data:
Chemical Pulping Systems:
Continuous digesters: 3
Pulp Lines: 3
Bleach Plant Systems: 2
No. 1, Sequence: O_2 C/DEoHDED, Capacity 315,000 admt/y
Chemical Recovery Equipment:
Evaporator lines: 2
Recovery boilers: 3
Lime Kiln
Pulp Dryers:
Air Float dryers 1, Air Float dryers 1, Flash dryers 1
Energy Data:
Power boilers: 5
Steam turbines: 5 at 12, 12, 12, 6, 6 MW
Electrical demand for mill: 1,612 MWh/D

ⓜNicol-Pack Imperial Co. Ltd.
Murom (Imperial) Mill
Ownership: 100% by Nicol-Pack Corporation
ul. Moskovskaya 90
602256 Murom, Vladimir oblast
Russia
Phone: (7) 49234 22238

Russia

Fax: (7) 49234 22227
Email: info@nicol-pack.ru
Web Address: nicol-pack.ru
Personnel:
Gen. Dir.: Dmitry Nikolaevich Semikin
Phone: (7) 49234 22238
Fax: (7) 49234 22227
Email: semikin@nicol-pack.ru
Total Employees at this Location: 160
Type of Operation: Paperboard mill
Pulp Grades and Capacities:
Total pulp capacity: 20,375 mt/y
Recycled Pulping: 20,375 mt/y
Pulp Mill Data:
Recycled Fiber Treatment Lines:
Recycled packaging pulping lines: 1
Paper/Paperboard Grades and Capacities:
Total paper and paperboard capacity: 20,000 mt/y
Boxboard/cartonboard: 20,000 mt/y
Paper and Paperboard Mill Data:
Paper Machines: 1
No. 1, cylinder, total capacity 20,000 mt/y, Trim width 2 m, Boxboard/cartonboard
Energy Data:
Power boilers: 3
Electrical demand for mill: 25 MWh/D

ⓂZAO International Paper
Svetogorsk Mill
Ownership: International Paper (Europe) SA
ul. Zavodskaya 17
188991 Svetogorsk, Leningrad Region
Russia
Phone: (7) 813 7843504/5 688 4100
Fax: (7) 813 7844 061/5 688 4900
Email: skbf@mail.ru
Web Address: www.internationalpaper.com/RUSSIA
Personnel:
Pres.: Ksenia Sosnina
Phone: (7) 812 334 4130
Fax: (7) 813 7844 061/5 688 4900
Email: ksenia.sosnina@ipaper.com
VP, Manufacturing IP EMEA: Pat Wilczynski
Phone: (7) 812 334 4403
Fax: (7) 813 7844 061/5 688 4900
Email: pat.wilczynski@ipaper.com
Mill Mgr.: Luis Claudio Pereira
Phone: (7) 812 334 4130
Fax: (7) 813 7844 061/5 688 4900
Email: luis.pereira@ipaper.com
Oper. Dir.: David Hunt
Phone: (7) 813 7843504/5 688 4100
Fax: (7) 813 7844 061/5 688 4900
Email: david.hunt@ipaper.com
Exec. Asst to Pat Wilczynski : Marina Ivanova
Phone: (7) 812 334 5739
Fax: (7) 812 334 5740
Email: marina.ivanova@ipaper.com
Total Employees of Company: 56,100
Total Employees at this Location: 3,200
Type of Operation: Pulp mill, Paper mill, Paperboard mill
Pulp Grades and Capacities:
Total pulp capacity: 578,570 mt/y
Pulp available for market: 183,000 mt/y
Chemical Pulp: 379,038 mt/y
Mechanical Pulp: 199,532 mt/y
Pulp Mill Data:
Chemical Pulping Systems:
Batch digesters: 20
Mechanical Pulping Systems:
BCTMP systems: 1
Bleach Plant Lines:
Hardwood, Sequence: O_2 DEoD, Capacity 250,000 admt/y
Softwood, Sequence: DEoDED, Capacity 130,000 admt/y
Chemical Recovery Equipment:
Evaporator lines: 1
Recovery boilers: 2
Lime Kiln
Pulp Dryers:
Air Float dryers 1
Paper/Paperboard Grades and Capacities:
Total paper and paperboard capacity: 480,000 mt/y
Uncoated woodfree/freesheet: 360,000 mt/y
Boxboard/cartonboard: 120,000 mt/y
Paper and Paperboard Mill Data:
Paper Machines: 2
No. 1, fourdrinier, total capacity 120,000 mt/y, Trim width 4.2 m, Boxboard/cartonboard
No. 4, SymFormer F, total capacity 360,000 mt/y, Trim width 8.4 m, Uncoated woodfree/freesheet
Coating Machines: 1
PM 1, total capacity 120,000 mt/y., on machine
Finishing Equipment:
Sheeters: 4
Energy Data:
Power boilers: 1
TMP Reboiler: 1
Combustion turbines: 1 at 25 MW
Steam turbines: 1
Electrical demand for mill: 2,479 MWh/D

ⓘInvestlesprom
Company is for sale
Ownership: 90% by LLC Segezha Managing Company, 10% by Norekom Segezha Investment Ltd.
Petrovsky-Razumovsky passage, Street 28 (Dmitrovskaja)
127287 Moscow
Russia
Phone: (7) 7 499 962 8200
Fax: (7) 7 499 962 8200, 7 499 418 0000
Email: smi@scbk.ru
Web Address: www.investlesprom.ru
Personnel:
Chmn.: Mikhail Busygiun
Phone: (7) 7 499 962 8200
Fax: (7) 7 499 962 8200
Gen. Dir. : AG Zavalkovsky
Phone: (7) 499 962 8200
Fax: (7) 499 962 8200
Dir., Pulp&Paper Industry Division: Vasily Preminin
Phone: (7) 7 499 962 8200
Fax: (7) 7 499 962 8200
Sls. Dir.: Alexey A. Vdovin
Phone: (7) 495 500 3051/499 418 0051
Fax: (7) 495 500 3051
Email: vdovin_aa@investlesprom.ru
Head of Marketing Dept. : Sergey F. Novikov
Phone: (7) 7 499 962 8200 ext. 2080
Fax: (7) 7 499 418 0000
Email: novikov_sf@investlesprom.ru
Responsible for Russia Sale of Bags: Valery Zakharov
Phone: (7) 499 962 8200 ext. 2125
Fax: (7) 499 962 8200
Email: zaharov_vv@investlesprom.ru

ⓘKama Pulp & Paper Mill
Ownership: 100% by Private Investors
Shosseynaya Str., 11
Krasnokarnsk, Perm Region
Russia
Phone: (7) 34273 95388
Fax: (7) 34273 95385
Email: kcbk@permonline.ru, office@cbk-kama.ru
Total Employees of Company: 700
Mill Locations:
Kama Pulp & Paper Mill, Krasnokarnsk Mill, Shosseynaya Str., 11, 617060 Krasnokarnsk, Russia, Capacity: 86,000 mt/y, (Pulp mill, Paper mill)
Phone: (7) 34273 95388
Fax: (7) 34273 95385
Email: kcbk@permonline.ru, office@cbk-kama.ru

ⓂKama Pulp & Paper Mill
Krasnokamsk Mill
Shosseynaya Str., 11
617060 Krasnokamsk, Perm Region
Russia
Phone: (7) 34273 95388
Fax: (7) 34273 95385
Email: kcbk@permonline.ru, office@cbk-kama.ru
Web Address: cbk-kama.ru
Personnel:
Exec. Dir.: Grigoriy Yurive Bandovskiy
Phone: (7) 34273 95388
Chief Technologist: Yuriy Prokopyevich Dedik
Phone: (7) 34273 95369
PR Mgr.: Vladimir Borisovich Pavlov
Phone: (7) 34273 45772/40660/44034/95388
Chief Eng.: Aliksey Nikolaevich Kudrov
Phone: (7) 34273 95356
Com. Dir.: Anastasia Sergeyevna Chebotkova
Phone: (7) 34273 95394
Dep.Dir.Econ.Affairs: Olga Ivanovna Bushurova
Phone: (7) 34273 95378
Chief Eng.: Irina Vasiljevna Golovleva
Phone: (7) 34273 95355
Tech. Mgr.: Nadezhda Ivanovna Rodcheva
Phone: (7) 34273 45772/40660/44034/95388
Chief Electr. Eng.: Ilya Vladimirovich Kobernik
Phone: (7) 34273 45772/40660/44034/95388
Chief Energy Tech.: Azat Klimovich Basyrov
Phone: (7) 34273 45772/40660/44034/95388
HR Dir.: Alla Antolievna Chestakova
Phone: (7) 34273 95360
Total Employees at this Location: 700
Type of Operation: Pulp mill, Paper mill
Pulp Grades and Capacities:
Total pulp capacity: 48,459 mt/y
Mechanical Pulp: 48,459 mt/y
Pulp Mill Data:
Mechanical Pulping Systems:
BCTMP systems: 1
TMP systems: 1
Pulp Lines: 2
Bleach Plant Lines:
No. 1, Sequence: O_2 P
Paper/Paperboard Grades and Capacities:
Total paper and paperboard capacity: 86,000 mt/y
Coated mechanical/groundwood: 86,000 mt/y
Paper and Paperboard Mill Data:
Stock Preparation:
Refiners: 2
Paper Machines: 1
No. 7, DuoFormer, total capacity 86,000 mt/y, Trim width 3.36 m, Coated mechanical/groundwood
Coating Machines: 1
No. 7, on machine
Energy Data:
Power boilers: 1
TMP Reboiler: 1
Electrical demand for mill: 352 MWh/D

ⓘⓂKamenskaya Board & Paper Mill, OJSC
Kuvshinovo Mill
Ownership: SFT Group
Oktyabrskaya Str., 5
172110 Kuvshinovo, Tver Region
Russia
Phone: (7) 48257 45246
Fax: (7) 48257 44456/45392
Email: kbkf@kbkf.ru
Web Address: www.kbkf.ru
Personnel:
Man. Dir.: Gennadiy Nikolaevich Gladyshev
Phone: (7) 48257 44109
Fax: (7) 48257 44456
Email: ggladyshev@kbkf.ru
Prod. Mgr.: Sergey Valerievich Volkov
Phone: (7) 48257 45 363

Russia

Fax: (7) 4825744456
Email: svolkov@kbkf.ru
Chief Eng.: Yuriy Konstantinovich Bazanov
Phone: (7) 4825745318
Fax: (7) 4825744456
Email: ybazanov@kbkf.ru
Sls. & Mktg. Mgr.: Liliya Izotovna Smirnova
Phone: (7) 4825745391
Fax: (7) 4825744456
Email: lsmirnova@kbkf.ru
PR Dir.: Galina Alekseevna Skaptsova
Phone: (7) 4825745246
Fax: (7) 4825744456
Email: gskaptsova@kbkf.ru
Total Employees at this Location: 1,100
Type of Operation: Paper mill, Paperboard mill
Pulp Grades and Capacities:
  Total pulp capacity: 293,406 mt/y
  Recycled Pulping: 293,406 mt/y
Pulp Mill Data:
  Recycled Fiber Treatment Lines:
  Recycled packaging pulping lines: 1
Paper/Paperboard Grades and Capacities:
  Total paper and paperboard capacity: 292,000 mt/y
  Linerboard: 173,000 mt/y
  Corrugating medium/fluting: 119,000 mt/y
Paper and Paperboard Mill Data:
Paper Machines: 5
No. 1, fourdrinier, total capacity 11,000 mt/y, Trim width 2.1 m, Corrugating medium/fluting
No. 2, fourdrinier, total capacity 12,000 mt/y, Trim width 2.1 m, Linerboard
No. 5, fourdrinier, total capacity 11,000 mt/y, Trim width 1.9 m, Linerboard
No. 6, fourdrinier, total capacity 8,000 mt/y, Trim width 1.9 m, Corrugating medium/fluting
No. 7, fourdrinier (2), total capacity 250,000 mt/y, Trim width 4.6 m, Corrugating medium/fluting, Linerboard
Energy Data:
Power boilers
Electrical demand for mill: 356 MWh/D

⊕ⓂKaravaevo
Karavaevo Mill
Ownership: 70% by mill staff, 30% by State
p/o Bolshoe Bunkovo
142438 Pos. Karavaevo, Moscow Region
Russia
Mailing Address: P.O. Box Bolshoe Bunkovo, 142438 Noginsky rayon, Moscow Region, Russia
  Phone: (7) (495) 7879271, (49651) 20551
  Fax: (7) 495 993 2798/2330
  Email: inform@karavaevo.ru
  Web Address: www.karavaevo.ru
Personnel:
  Tech. Dir.: Valeriy Ivanovich Borets
  Gen. Dir.: Valerii Borisovich Zaytsev
  Phone: (7) 495 7879271
  Mill Dir.: Luka Yurievich Erstenyuk
  Chief Acc.: Irina Aleksandrovna Rakitina
Total Employees at this Location: 500
Type of Operation: Paper mill
Pulp Grades and Capacities:
  Total pulp capacity: 37,050 mt/y
  Recycled Pulping: 37,050 mt/y
Pulp Mill Data:
  Recycled Fiber Treatment Lines:
  Recycled packaging pulping lines: 2
Paper/Paperboard Grades and Capacities:
  Total paper and paperboard capacity: 36,000 mt/y
  Packaging papers: 5,000 mt/y
  Linerboard: 17,000 mt/y
  Corrugating medium/fluting: 10,000 mt/y
  Boxboard/cartonboard: 4,000 mt/y
Paper and Paperboard Mill Data:
Paper Machines: 2
No. 1, fourdrinier (2), total capacity 21,000 mt/y, Trim width 2.1 m, Linerboard, Boxboard/cartonboard
No. 2, fourdrinier, total capacity 15,000 mt/y, Trim width 2.1 m, Packaging papers, Corrugating medium/fluting
Energy Data:
Electrical demand for mill: 52 MWh/D

⊕ⓂKartontara
Velikie Luki Mill
Ownership: mill staff
Kornienko Str., 5
182100 Velikie Luki, Pskov obl.
Russia
  Phone: (7) 81153 73939/ 73929 / 71767
  Fax: (7) 81153 73929
  Email: kartontara@rbcmail.ru
Personnel:
  Gen. Dir.: Valeriy Bokavchuk
  Phone: (7) 81153 73939
  Prod. Dir. & Tech. Dir.: Vladimir Kovenkov
  Phone: (7) 81153 73932
Total Employees at this Location: 120
Type of Operation: Paperboard mill
Paper/Paperboard Grades and Capacities:
  Total paper and paperboard capacity: 5,000 mt/y
  Boxboard/cartonboard: 5,000 mt/y
Paper and Paperboard Mill Data:
Paper Machines: 2
No. 1, total capacity 2,500 mt/y, Trim width 1.17 m
No. 2, total capacity 2,500 mt/y, Trim width 1.17 m
Energy Data:
Electrical demand for mill: 4 MWh/D

⊕Kartontol
Obukhovskoi Oborony Prosp., 72
192029 St. Petersburg
Russia
  Phone: (7) 812 412 7188/2063
  Fax: (7) 812 412 7181
  Email: sekretar@kartontol.ru
  Web Address: www.kartontol.ru
Personnel:
  Dir.: Sergei Rybakov
  Phone: (7) 812 412 7188/2063
  Fax: (7) 812 412 7181
  Prod. Mgr.: Aleksandr Leonidovich Prosuzhikh
  Phone: (7) 812 412 7188/2063
  Fax: (7) 812 412 7181
  Tech. Dir.: Sergey Valentinovich Vinogradov
  Phone: (7) 812 412 7188/2063
  Fax: (7) 812 412 7181
  Sls. Dir.: Andrey Evgenievich Anisimov
  Phone: (7) 812 412 7188/2063
  Fax: (7) 812 412 7181
Total Employees at this Location: 160
Mill Locations:
Kartontol, St. Petersburg Mill, Obukhovskoi Oborony Prosp., 72, 192029 St. Petersburg, Russia, Capacity: 24,000 mt/y, (Paperboard mill)
  Phone: (7) 812 412 7188/2063
  Fax: (7) 812 412 7181
  Email: sekretar@kartontol.ru

⊕Kartontol
St. Petersburg Mill
Obukhovskoi Oborony Prosp., 72
192029 St. Petersburg
Russia
  Phone: (7) 812 412 7188/2063
  Fax: (7) 812 412 7181
  Email: sekretar@kartontol.ru
  Web Address: www.kartontol.ru
Personnel:
  Dir.: Sergei Rybakov
  Phone: (7) 812 412 7188
  Prod. Mgr.: Aleksandr Leonidovich Prosuzhikh
  Phone: (7) 812 412 2063
  Tech. Dir.: Sergey Valentinovich Vinogradov
  Phone: (7) 812 412 7188
  Sls. Dir.: Andrey Evgenievich Anisimov
  Phone: (7) 812 412 7188

Total Employees at this Location: 180
Type of Operation: Paperboard mill
Pulp Grades and Capacities:
  Total pulp capacity: 24,262 mt/y
  Recycled Pulping: 24,262 mt/y
Pulp Mill Data:
  Recycled Fiber Treatment Lines:
  Recycled packaging pulping lines: 1
Paper/Paperboard Grades and Capacities:
  Total paper and paperboard capacity: 24,000 mt/y
  Packaging papers: 2,000 mt/y
  Corrugating medium/fluting: 3,000 mt/y
  Boxboard/cartonboard: 19,000 mt/y
Paper and Paperboard Mill Data:
Paper Machines: 2
No. 1, cylinder (7), total capacity 14,000 mt/y, Trim width 2.1 m, Boxboard/cartonboard
No. 2, cylinder (7), total capacity 10,000 mt/y, Trim width 2.1 m, Boxboard/cartonboard, Corrugating medium/fluting, Packaging papers
Finishing Equipment:
  Sheeters: 2
Energy Data:
Power boilers: 3
Electrical demand for mill: 29 MWh/D

⊕KBK Ltd
Ownership: Tuymazinskaya Bumazhnaya
ul Fabrichnaya 1
452754 Tuymazy
Russia
  Phone: (7) 34782 78100 / 58900
  Fax: (7) 34782 70422 / 58910
  Email: kbk@tkbk.ru
Personnel:
  Gen. Dir.: Sergey Alexandrovich Smorodin
  Phone: (7) 34782 78100 / 58900
  Fax: (7) 34782 70422 / 58910
  Deputy Tech. Dir.: Vadim Olegovich Karpenko
  Phone: (7) 34782 78100 / 58900
  Fax: (7) 34782 70422 / 58910
  Mktg. Mgr.: Igor Nikolaevich Garmash
  Phone: (7) 34782 78100 / 58900
  Fax: (7) 34782 70422 / 58910
Total Employees at this Location: 550
Mill Locations:
KBK Ltd, Tuymazy Mill, ul Fabrichnaya 1, 452754 Tuymazy, Russia, Capacity: 45,000 mt/y, (Paper mill)
  Phone: (7) 34782 78100 / 58900
  Fax: (7) 34782 70422 / 58910
  Email: kbk@tkbk.ru

ⓂKBK Ltd
Tuymazy Mill
ul Fabrichnaya 1
452754 Tuymazy, Respublika Bashkortostan
Russia
  Phone: (7) 34782 78100 / 58900
  Fax: (7) 34782 70422 / 58910
  Email: kbk@tkbk.ru
Personnel:
  Gen. Dir.: Sergey Alexandrovich Smorodin
  Phone: (7) 34782 78100
  Deputy Tech. Dir.: Vadim Olegovich Karpenko
  Phone: (7) 34782 78100
  Marketing Mngr: Igor Nikolaevich Garmash
  Phone: (7) 812 326 0832
  Vice Director (Commerce): Sergey Tyutin
Total Employees at this Location: 600
Type of Operation: Paper mill
Pulp Grades and Capacities:
  Total pulp capacity: 45,617 mt/y
  Recycled Pulping: 45,617 mt/y
Pulp Mill Data:
  Recycled Fiber Treatment Lines:
  Pulpers
Paper/Paperboard Grades and Capacities:
  Total paper and paperboard capacity: 45,000 mt/y
  Tissue: 5,000 mt/y

Russia

Linerboard: 24,000 mt/y
Corrugating medium/fluting: 16,000 mt/y
Paper and Paperboard Mill Data:
Paper Machines: 2
No. 1, fourdrinier, total capacity 40,000 mt/y, Trim width 3.15 m, Corrugating medium/fluting, Linerboard
No. 2, Yankee dryer, total capacity 5,000 mt/y, Trim width 1.96 m, Tissue
Energy Data:
Power boilers
Electrical demand for mill: 69 MWh/D

⊕Ⓜ Kommunar Paper Mill
Kommunar Mill
Ownership: 29.93% by ArktikInKom, Arkhangelsk, 53.03% by KhimTekhnoServis-Taloil
Fabrichnaya Str., 1
188320 Kommunar, Leningrad Region
Russia
Phone: (7) 812 460 1095 /3090 / 5243
Fax: (7) 812 460 1095
Email: marketing@kommunar.ru,
paper@kommunar.com.ru
Web Address: www.kommunar.ru
Personnel:
Gen. Dir.: Alexey Pavlovich Kirilyuk
Phone: (7) 812 460 1095
Fax: (7) 812 460 1095
Email: alexey@kommunar.ru
Dir.: Igor Anatoylevich Dikunets
Phone: (7) 812 460 1095
Fax: (7) 812 460 1095
Email: igor@kommunar.ru
Project Eng.: Vladislava Shutyak
Phone: (7) 812 460 1095 Ext. 114
Fax: (7) 812 460 1095
Email: vladislava@kommunar.ru
Tech. Dir.: Viktor Petrovich Poslanichenko
Phone: (7) 812 460 1095
Fax: (7) 812 460 1095
Email: viktor@kommunar.ru
Mgr.: Ivanova Tatyana
Phone: (7) 812 460 1095
Fax: (7) 812 460 1095
Email: ivanova@kommunar.ru
Total Employees at this Location: 450
Type of Operation: Paper mill
Pulp Grades and Capacities:
Total pulp capacity: 58,213 mt/y
Recycled Pulping: 58,213 mt/y
Pulp Mill Data:
Recycled Fiber Treatment Lines:
Recycled packaging pulping lines: 1
Paper/Paperboard Grades and Capacities:
Total paper and paperboard capacity: 78,000 mt/y
Packaging papers: 10,000 mt/y
Specialty and industrial: 23,000 mt/y
Linerboard: 25,000 mt/y
Corrugating medium/fluting: 20,000 mt/y
Paper and Paperboard Mill Data:
Paper Machines: 4
No. 7, fourdrinier, total capacity 25,000 mt/y, Trim width 2.5 m, Linerboard, Corrugating medium/fluting
No. 8, fourdrinier, total capacity 20,000 mt/y, Trim width 2.5 m, Specialty and industrial
No. 9, fourdrinier, total capacity 9,000 mt/y, Trim width 2.5 m, Specialty and industrial
No. 10, fourdrinier, total capacity 30,000 mt/y, Trim width 2.5 m, Linerboard, Corrugating medium/fluting, Packaging papers
Energy Data:
Power boilers
Electrical demand for mill: 132 MWh/D

⊕Ⓜ Kondopoga
Kondopoga Mill
Ownership: 27% by Bumazhnik, 26% by Conrad Jacobson, GmbH, 15% by Moscow Bank, ZAO, 18% by LLC Falcon, 8% by 21 vek, 6% by other Investors
ul. Promyshlennaya 2
186220 Kondopoga, Karelia
Russia
Phone: (7) 81451 79285/36500
Fax: (7) 81451 36083
Email: kbk@kbk.onego.ru
Web Address: oaokondopoga.ru
Personnel:
Chmn & Advisor to Gen. Mgr.: Vladimir Bibilov
Phone: (7) 81451 79285/36500
Fax: (7) 81451 36083
Mill Mgr.: Andrei Shutilov
Phone: (7) 81451 79285
Fax: (7) 81451 36083
Mktg. Dir.: Yury Shinderov
Phone: (7) 81451 79285/36500
Fax: (7) 81451 36083
Tech. Dir.: Viktor Tolstov
Phone: (7) 81451 79285/36500
Fax: (7) 81451 36083
Chief Technology: Sergey Leontyev
Phone: (7) 8145136630
Total Employees of Company: 5,540
Total Employees at this Location: 5,540
Type of Operation: Pulp mill, Paper mill
Pulp Grades and Capacities:
Total pulp capacity: 723,377 mt/y
Chemical Pulp: 130,888 mt/y
Mechanical Pulp: 592,489 mt/y
Pulp Mill Data:
Chemical Pulping Systems:
Batch digesters: 10
Mechanical Pulping Systems:
Conventional grinders: 20
Pulp Lines: 2
Bleach Plant Lines:
No. 1, Type: ECF
Chemical Recovery Equipment:
Evaporator lines: 1
Recovery boilers: 1
Paper/Paperboard Grades and Capacities:
Total paper and paperboard capacity: 766,500 mt/y
Newsprint: 750,000 mt/y
Packaging papers: 16,500 mt/y
Paper and Paperboard Mill Data:
Paper Machines: 7
No. 1, Bel-Form, total capacity 55,000 mt/y, Trim width 4.62 m, Newsprint
No. 3, fourdrinier, total capacity 16,500 mt/y, Trim width 2.5 m, Packaging papers
No. 4, Bel-Form, total capacity 110,000 mt/y, Trim width 6.72 m, Newsprint
No. 7, Bel-Form, total capacity 110,000 mt/y, Trim width 6.72 m, Newsprint
No. 8, DuoFormer C, total capacity 185,000 mt/y, Trim width 8.4 m, Newsprint
No. 9, Bel-Form, total capacity 110,000 mt/y, Trim width 6.72 m, Newsprint
No. 10, Bel-Baie IV, total capacity 180,000 mt/y, Trim width 7.4 m, Newsprint
Energy Data:
Power boilers: 1
Combustion turbines: 1 at 30 MW
Steam turbines: 6 at 70 MW
Electrical demand for mill: 4,330 MWh/D

⊕Ⓜ JSC 'Kondrovskaya Paper company'
Kondrovskaya Paper Company Mill
Ownership: Continental Management Plc, 29.47% by Bravelink Limtied, 24% by OOO "ASG Profit", 24% by OOO "Gorizont", 9% by ZAO "TransKom"
ul. Pushkina, 1
249833 Kondrovo, Kaluga Region
Russia
Phone: (7) 48434 32158/33115
Fax: (7) 48434 33365
Email: kpc@kaluga.ru
Web Address: www.kpc.ru
Personnel:
Gen. Dir.: Sergey Ivanovich Shakhov
Phone: (7) 48434 32158/33115
Chief Eng.: Vladimir Viktorovich Loginov
Phone: (7) 964 144 2393
Com. Dir.: Natalia Bocharova
Phone: (7) 48434 32561
Finan. Dir.: Irina Anatolievna Fedorova
Phone: (7) 48434 32158/33115
Total Employees at this Location: 1,100
Type of Operation: Paper mill
Pulp Grades and Capacities:
Total pulp capacity: 25,960 mt/y
Recycled Pulping: 25,960 mt/y
Pulp Mill Data:
Recycled Fiber Treatment Lines:
Flotation deinking lines: 1 at 13,000
Recycled packaging pulping lines: 1 at 13,000
Paper/Paperboard Grades and Capacities:
Total paper and paperboard capacity: 37,000 mt/y
Tissue: 24,000 mt/y
Linerboard: 8,000 mt/y
Corrugating medium/fluting: 5,000 mt/y
Paper and Paperboard Mill Data:
Paper Machines: 2
No. 4, total capacity 13,000 mt/y, Trim width 2.5 m, Corrugating medium/fluting, Linerboard
No. 6, fourdrinier, Yankee dryer, total capacity 24,000 mt/y, Trim width 4.2 m, Tissue
Energy Data:
Power boilers: 5
Steam turbines: 1
Electrical demand for mill: 95 MWh/D

Ⓜ Kosino Paper Mill
Kosino Mill
ul. Kommuny, 1
612425 Kosino, Zuevskiy rayon, Kirovskaya Obl.
Russia
Phone: (7) 83337 27 295 / 467 / 451
Fax: (7) 83337 27 295 /541/467
Email: cosa@kbf.kirov.ru
Personnel:
Gen. Dir.: Nikolay Mikhaylovich Bakin
Phone: (7) 83337 27 541 / 2 40
Exec. Dir.: Sergey Vladimirovich Polyakov
Prod. Dir.: Maryana Viktorovna Gorinova
Finan. Dir.: Natalia Sergeevna Shulepova
Com. Dir.: Vladislav Davidovich Rodinskiy
Total Employees at this Location: 147
Type of Operation: Paperboard mill
Paper/Paperboard Grades and Capacities:
Total paper and paperboard capacity: 10,500 mt/y
Specialty and industrial: 5,250 mt/y
Boxboard/cartonboard: 5,250 mt/y
Paper and Paperboard Mill Data:
Stock Preparation:
Refiners: 0
Paper Machines: 2
BM2, total capacity 5,250 mt/y, Trim width 1.62 m, Specialty and industrial
BM3, total capacity 5,250 mt/y, Trim width 1.72 m, Boxboard/cartonboard
Finishing Equipment:
Rewinders: 2
Sheeters: 1
Energy Data:
Power boilers: 3

⊕ Kosino Paper Mill
Ownership: 100% by private owner
ul. Kommuny, 1
612425 Kosino, Zuevskiy rayon
Russia
Phone: (7) 83337 27 295 / 467 / 451
Fax: (7) 83337 27 295 /541/467
Email: cosa@kbf.kirov.ru
Personnel:
Gen. Dir.: Nikolay Mikhaylovich Bakin

Russia

Phone: (7) 83337 27 541 / 2 40
Exec. Dir.: Sergey Vladimirovich Polyakov
Phone: (7) 83337 27 541 / 2 40
Finan. Dir.: Natalia Sergeevna Shulepova
Phone: (7) 83337 27 541 / 2 40
Prod. Dir.: Maryana Viktorovna Gorinova
Phone: (7) 83337 27 541 / 2 40
Total Employees at this Location: 147
Mill Locations:
Kosino Paper Mill, Kosino Mill, ul. Kommuny, 1, 612425 Kosino, Zuevskiy rayon, Russia, Capacity: 10,500 mt/y, (Paperboard mill)
Phone: (7) 83337 27 295 / 467 / 451
Fax: (7) 83337 27 295 /541/467
Email: cosa@kbf.kirov.ru

ⓜKPK St. Petersburg OOAO

Ownership: 91% by Knauf International GmbH, 9% by minority owners
Pavloskaya Str. 9
188320 Kommunar, Leningrad Region
Russia
Mailing Address: P.O Box 51, 196620 Pavlovsk, Russia
Phone: (7) 812 460 2278
Fax: (7) 812 460 2287
Email: kpk@kpk.ru, info@kpk.com.ru
Web Address: www.knauf.com
Personnel:
Gen. Dir.: Sergey Sergeevich Kuznetsov
Phone: (7) 812 460 2778
Fax: (7) 812 460 2287
Chrm. of the board: Yanis Kraulis
Phone: (7) 812 460 2778
Fax: (7) 812 460 2287
Vice Gen. Dir.: Vadim Sukhuv
Phone: (7) 812 460 2778
Fax: (7) 812 460 2287
Finan. Mgr.: Oleg Besdenychish
Phone: (7) 812 460 2778
Fax: (7) 812 460 2287
Total Employees of Company: 1,320
Mill Locations:
KPKSt. Petersburg OOAO, Kommunar Mill, Pavloskaya Str. 9, 188320 Kommunar, Russia, Capacity: 250,000 mt/y, (Paperboard mill)
Phone: (7) 812 460 2278
Fax: (7) 812 460 2287
Email: kpk@kpk.ru, info@kpk.com.ru

ⓜKrasnokamskaya Paper Mill Goznak
Krasnokamsk Mill

Shkolnaya Str., 13
617060 Krasnokamsk, Perm Region
Russia
Phone: (7) 34273 28199/28119
Fax: (7) 34273 28100/28101
Email: kbfg@kbfg.ru
Web Address: www.kbfg.ru
Personnel:
Dir.: Aleksandr Nikolaevich Birichevskiy
Phone: (7) 34273 28199
Chief Eng.: Vladimir Viktorovich Nikishin
Phone: (7) 34273 28191
Mktg. Dir.: Larisa Viktorovna Bolshakova
Phone: (7) 34273 28-119
Deputy Econ. and Finance Dir.: Nikolay Andreevich Shafranskiy
Phone: (7) 34273 28193
Com.Dir.: Nail' Ismagilovich Sayfutdinov
Phone: (7) 34273 28192
Total Employees at this Location: 1,200
Type of Operation: Paper mill
Paper/Paperboard Grades and Capacities:
Total paper and paperboard capacity: 59,976 mt/y
Uncoated woodfree/freesheet: 59,976 mt/y
Specialty and industrial
Paper and Paperboard Mill Data:
Paper Machines: 6

No. 1, cylinder, Trim width 2.54 m, Specialty and industrial
No. 2, fourdrinier, total capacity 14,994 mt/y, Trim width 3.2 m, Uncoated woodfree/freesheet
No. 3, fourdrinier, total capacity 29,988 mt/y, Trim width 3.2 m, Uncoated woodfree/freesheet
No. 4, fourdrinier, total capacity 14,994 mt/y, Trim width 3.2 m, Uncoated woodfree/freesheet
No. 5, Trim width 1.8 m, Specialty and industrial
No. 6, cylinder, Trim width 1.85 m, Specialty and industrial
Energy Data:
Power boilers: 1
Electrical demand for mill: 167 MWh/D

ⓜKrasnokamskaya Paper Mill Goznak

Ownership: 100% by state
Shkolnaya Str., 13
617060 Krasnokamsk
Russia
Phone: (7) 34273 28199/28119
Fax: (7) 34273 28100/28101
Email: kbfg@kbfg.ru
Web Address: www.kbfg.ru
Personnel:
Dir.: Aleksandr Nikolaevich Birichevskiy
Phone: (7) 34273 28199
Deputy Econ. and Finance Dir.: Nikolay Andreevich Shafranskiy
Phone: (7) 34273 28193
Chief Eng.: Vladimir Viktorovich Nikishin
Phone: (7) 34273 28191
Total Employees at this Location: 1,200
Mill Locations:
Krasnokamskaya Paper Mill Goznak, Krasnokamsk Mill, Shkolnaya Str., 13, 617060 Krasnokamsk, Russia, Capacity: 59,976 mt/y, (Paper mill)
Phone: (7) 34273 28199/28119
Fax: (7) 34273 28100/28101
Email: kbfg@kbfg.ru

ⓜOOO KubanPapir
Krasnodar Mill

Kalinina Str. 1
350039 Krasnodar
Russia
Phone: (7) 8612 281709 / 1692 / 1978
Fax: (7) 8612 281709
Email: kubanpapir@rambler.ru, papir-yg@rambler.ru
Web Address: tissue-bumaga.ru
Personnel:
Gen. Dir.: Kirill Gennadiyevich Minin
Phone: (7) 8612 281709
Man. Dir. & PapirJug Sls. Dir.: Andrey Yurievich Lysenko
Phone: (7) 8612 281709
Chief Eng.: Andrey Vasiliyevich Nikulin
Phone: (7) 8612 282028
Total Employees at this Location: 100
Type of Operation: Paper mill, Paperboard mill
Pulp Grades and Capacities:
Total pulp capacity: 10,000 mt/y
Paper/Paperboard Grades and Capacities:
Total paper and paperboard capacity: 10,000 mt/y
Tissue: 10,000 mt/y
Paper and Paperboard Mill Data:
Paper Machines: 1
PM 2, (second-hand, started up January 2011), total capacity 10,000 mt/y, Trim width 2.7 m, Tissue
Energy Data:
Power boilers: 1
Electrical demand for mill: 10 MWh/D

ⓞⓜKuzbasskiy Skarabey
Kemerovo Mill

Ownership: 100% by private
Zapadniy proezd 4
650021 Kemerovo
Russia
Phone: (7) 3842 571717/570408

Fax: (7) 3842 570402
Email: mail@ckarabey.ru, kuz_ckarabey@mail.ru, market@ckarabey.ru, director@ckarabey.ru
Personnel:
Com.Director: Yulia Leonidovna Knyazeva
Phone: (7) 3842 570128
Gen. Dir.: Igor Vladimirovich Kosinov
Phone: (7) 3842 57 17 17
Exec. Dir.: Dmitriy Aleksandrovich Razuvaev
Phone: (7) 3842 57 17 17
Chief Eng.: Denis Alexandrovich Kushnevets
Phone: (7) 3842 57 17 17
Total Employees of Company: 219
Total Employees at this Location: 200
Type of Operation: Paperboard mill
Pulp Grades and Capacities:
Total pulp capacity: 24,136 mt/y
Recycled Pulping: 24,136 mt/y
Pulp Mill Data:
Recycled Fiber Treatment Lines:
Recycled packaging pulping lines: 1
Paper/Paperboard Grades and Capacities:
Total paper and paperboard capacity: 24,000 mt/y
Linerboard: 7,000 mt/y
Corrugating medium/fluting: 16,000 mt/y
Boxboard/cartonboard: 1,000 mt/y
Paper and Paperboard Mill Data:
Paper Machines: 1
No. 3, fourdrinier, total capacity 24,000 mt/y, Trim width 2.1 m, Boxboard/cartonboard, Corrugating medium/fluting, Linerboard
Energy Data:
Power boilers
Electrical demand for mill: 35 MWh/D

ⓞⓜLalskaya Paper Mill
Lalsk Mill

Ownership: 100% by private
Gagarina Str., 36, pos. Fabrichny
613967 Lalsk, Kirovskaya Obl.
Russia
Phone: (7) 83346 31601/31131 / 31505/24200
Fax: (7) 83346 31505/31133
Email: lalskbum@yandex.ru
Personnel:
Dir.: Olga Viktorovna Pupysheva
Phone: (7) 83346 31131
Chief Acct.: Tatyana Vladiminovna Korekina
Phone: (7) 83347.0150974912
Com.Dir.: Tatyana Nikolaevna Gaysina
Phone: (7) 83347.0150974912
Total Employees at this Location: 150
Type of Operation: Paper mill
Paper/Paperboard Grades and Capacities:
Total paper and paperboard capacity: 10,000 mt/y
Tissue: 5,000 mt/y
Packaging papers
Specialty and industrial: 5,000 mt/y
Paper and Paperboard Mill Data:
Paper Machines: 2
PM 1, total capacity 4,500 mt/y, Trim width 1.52 m, Specialty and industrial
PM 2, total capacity 5,500 mt/y, Trim width 1.68 m, Tissue, Packaging papers
Energy Data:
Power boilers: 1
Electrical demand for mill: 7 MWh/D

ⓞⓜLLC Pulp Invest
Kazan Mill

ulitsa Vosstaniya 100
Kazan, Tatarstan Republic
Russia
Total Employees at this Location: 250
Type of Operation: Paper mill
Paper/Paperboard Grades and Capacities:
Total paper and paperboard capacity: 30,000 mt/y

Tissue: 30,000 mt/y
Paper and Paperboard Mill Data:
Paper Machines: 1
No. 1, crescent former, Yankee dryer, total capacity 30,000 mt/y, Trim width 2.8 m, Tissue
Energy Data:
Power boilers
Electrical demand for mill: 74 MWh/D

ⓒⓜMarisky Pulp & Paper Mill
Volzhsk Mill
Ownership: 87.10% by Liga Promyshlennikov, Ltd
K. Marksa Str., 10
425000 Volzhsk, Mari El Republic
Russia
Phone: (7) 83631 69791
Fax: (7) 83631 49965/69791
Email: info@marbum.ru, marbum@mail.ru
Web Address: www.marbum.ru
Personnel:
Gen. Dir.: Alexandr Mihailovich Stashkevich
Phone: (7) 83631 51010
Email: info@marbum.ru
Chief Eng.: Alexei Vasilyevich Feshchenko
Phone: (7) 83631 49985
Email: oborud@marbum.ru
Commer. Dir.: Eugeny Novikov
Phone: (7) 83631 68790
Email: sale@marbum.ru
Chief Acc: Klavdiya Viktorovna Korneeva
Phone: (7) 83631 49972
Total Employees at this Location: 2,000
Type of Operation: Pulp mill, Paper mill, Paperboard mill
Pulp Grades and Capacities:
Total pulp capacity: 225,726 mt/y
Pulp available for market: 50,000 mt/y
Chemical Pulp: 127,203 mt/y
Recycled Pulping: 98,524 mt/y
Pulp Mill Data:
Chemical Pulping Systems:
Batch digesters: 11
Pulp Lines: 2
Recycled Fiber Treatment Lines:
Recycled packaging pulping lines: 1 at 80,000
Pulp Dryers:
Air Float dryers 1, Air Float dryers 1, Fourdriniers 1
Paper/Paperboard Grades and Capacities:
Total paper and paperboard capacity: 168,000 mt/y
Packaging papers: 11,000 mt/y
Specialty and industrial: 9,500 mt/y
Linerboard: 86,500 mt/y
Corrugating medium/fluting: 61,000 mt/y
Paper and Paperboard Mill Data:
Paper Machines: 6
No. 1, fourdrinier, total capacity 18,000 mt/y, Trim width 2.52 m, Linerboard, Packaging papers
No. 2, fourdrinier, total capacity 18,000 mt/y, Trim width 2.52 m, Corrugating medium/fluting
No. 3, fourdrinier, total capacity 43,000 mt/y, Trim width 2.52 m, Corrugating medium/fluting
No. 4, fourdrinier, total capacity 7,000 mt/y, Trim width 2.52 m, Specialty and industrial
No. 6, fourdrinier, total capacity 64,000 mt/y, Trim width 4.2 m, Linerboard
No. 7, fourdrinier, total capacity 18,000 mt/y, Trim width 2.52 m, Linerboard, Specialty and industrial
Energy Data:
Steam turbines: 6 at 48 MW
Electrical demand for mill: 463 MWh/D

ⓒⓜOAO Mayak Technocell
Penza Mill
Ownership: 40% by Technocell Dekor GmbH & Co. KG, 60% by OAO Mayak
Burnazhnikov Str., 1
440007 Penza
Russia
Phone: (7) 8412 522353
Fax: (7) 8412 590858
Email: mayak@sura.ru
Web Address: www.mayak-penza.ru
Personnel:
Gen. Dir.: Vasily Alexeevich Vdonin
Phone: (7) 8412 522353
Prod. Dir.: Vladimir Vasilyevich Vdonin
Phone: (7) 8412 56 06 02
Finan. Dir.: Tatyana Alexandrovna Tulyupa
Phone: (7) 8412 522353
Mktg. & Sls. Dir.: Dmitri Vladimirovich Kuznetsov
Phone: (7) 8412 560934
Email: mayakexport@sura.ru
R&D Mgr.: Vladimir Alexandrovich Kazantsev
Phone: (7) 8412 56 35 13
Co-founder: Wolfgang Janssen
Phone: (7) 8412 522353
Co-founder: Stephen Igel
Phone: (7) 8412 522353
Total Employees at this Location: 700
Type of Operation: Paper mill
Pulp Grades and Capacities:
Total pulp capacity: 47,483 mt/y
Recycled Pulping: 47,483 mt/y
Pulp Mill Data:
Recycled Fiber Treatment Lines:
Flotation deinking lines: 1
Recycled packaging pulping lines: 1
Paper/Paperboard Grades and Capacities:
Total paper and paperboard capacity: 92,000 mt/y
Specialty and industrial: 62,000 mt/y
Linerboard: 18,000 mt/y
Corrugating medium/fluting: 12,000 mt/y
Paper and Paperboard Mill Data:
Paper Machines: 5
No. 1, fourdrinier, total capacity 8,500 mt/y, Trim width 1.9 m, Specialty and industrial
No. 2, fourdrinier, total capacity 8,500 mt/y, Trim width 1.9 m, Specialty and industrial
No. 3, fourdrinier, total capacity 15,000 mt/y, Trim width 1.9 m, Specialty and industrial
No. 4, fourdrinier, total capacity 30,000 mt/y, Trim width 2.52 m, Linerboard, Corrugating medium/fluting
No. 5, fourdrinier, total capacity 30,000 mt/y, Trim width 2.3 m, Specialty and industrial
Energy Data:
Power boilers
Electrical demand for mill: 174 MWh/D

ⓒⓜKartontara, CJSC
Maykop Mill
Ownership: 100% by SFT Group
per. Profsoyuzny 2
385012 Maykop, Adygheya Republic
Russia
Phone: (7) 8772 548455
Fax: (7) 8772 548820
Email: secretary@kartontara.ru
Personnel:
Man. Dir.: Sergey Petrovich Pogodin
Phone: (7) 8772 548455
Fax: (7) 8772 548820
Chief Acc.: Lyudmila Viktorovna Strueva
Phone: (7) 8772 548455
Fax: (7) 8772 548820
Prod. Dir.: Andrey Vasilyevich Nosachev
Phone: (7) 8772 548002
Fax: (7) 8772 548820
Tech. Dir.: Sergey Vasilievich Romanenko
Phone: (7) 8772 548466
Fax: (7) 8772 548820
Sls. Dir.: Alexei Yuryevich Glushko
Phone: (7) 8772 548862
Fax: (7) 8772 548820
Email: alexei@kartontara.ru
Commer. Dir.: Alexei Alexandrovich Kosenko
Phone: (7) 8772 548455
Fax: (7) 8772 548820
Chief Technology: Tamara Alexandrovna Sotnikova
Phone: (7) 8772 545616
Fax: (7) 8772 548820
Total Employees at this Location: 1,200
Type of Operation: Pulp mill, Paperboard mill
Pulp Grades and Capacities:
Total pulp capacity: 107,574 mt/y
Chemical Pulp: 41,257 mt/y
Recycled Pulping: 66,316 mt/y
Pulp Mill Data:
Chemical Pulping Systems:
Continuous digesters: 1
Recycled Fiber Treatment Lines:
Recycled packaging pulping lines: 1 at 55,000 admt/y
Paper/Paperboard Grades and Capacities:
Total paper and paperboard capacity: 105,000 mt/y
Linerboard: 50,000 mt/y
Corrugating medium/fluting: 55,000 mt/y
Paper and Paperboard Mill Data:
Stock Preparation:
Pulpers: 4
Refiners: 7
Paper Machines: 1
No. 1, fourdrinier, total capacity 105,000 mt/y, Trim width 4.2 m, Corrugating medium/fluting, Linerboard
Finishing Equipment:
Supercalenders: 2
Rewinders: 1
Energy Data:
Power boilers: 3
Steam turbines: 2 at 12.0 MW
Electrical demand for mill: 179 MWh/D

ⓜMondi Syktyvkar
Syktyvkar Mill
Ownership: 100% by Mondi Europe & International Division
Burnazhnikov pr. 2
167026 Syktyvkar, Komi Republic
Russia
Phone: (7) 8212 699555
Fax: (7) 8212 620282
Email: olga.rimert@mondigroup.com
Web Address: www.mondigroup.com
Personnel:
Man. Dir.: Klaus Peller
Phone: (7) 8212 699555
Fax: (7) 8212 620282
Email: klaus.peller@mondigroup.com
Sls. Dir. Containerboard: Natalia Shamina
Phone: (7) 495 783 5286
Fax: (7) 495 514 0450
Email: natalia.shamina@mondigroup.com
Corp. Commun. Mgr.: Ekaterima Edapina
Phone: (7) 8212 699533
Fax: (7) 8212 620282
Email: ekaterina.edapina@mondigroup.com
Total Employees at this Location: 8,200
Type of Operation: Pulp mill, Paper mill, Paperboard mill
Pulp Grades and Capacities:
Total pulp capacity: 915,650 mt/y
Chemical Pulp: 720,782 mt/y
Mechanical Pulp: 194,868 mt/y
Pulp Mill Data:
Chemical Pulping Systems:
Continuous digesters: 3
Mechanical Pulping Systems:
CTMP systems: 1
TMP systems: 1
Pulp Lines: 2
Bleach Plant Lines:
BHKP, Sequence: DoEOPDD
BSKP, Sequence: DEpDEpD
Chemical Recovery Equipment:
Evaporator lines: 1
Recovery boilers: 1
Lime Kiln
Paper/Paperboard Grades and Capacities:
Total paper and paperboard capacity: 990,000 mt/y

Russia

Newsprint: 204,000 mt/y
Uncoated woodfree/freesheet: 506,000 mt/y
Linerboard: 270,000 mt/y
Boxboard/cartonboard: 10,000 mt/y
Paper and Paperboard Mill Data:
Paper Machines: 4
No. 11, fourdrinier, total capacity 150,000 mt/y, Trim width 6.3 m, Uncoated woodfree/freesheet
No. 14, fourdrinier, total capacity 356,000 mt/y, Trim width 8.4 m, Uncoated woodfree/freesheet
No. 15, fourdrinier, total capacity 204,000 mt/y, Trim width 8.4 m, Newsprint
No. 21, fourdrinier (2), total capacity 280,000 mt/y, Trim width 6.3 m, Linerboard, Boxboard/cartonboard
Finishing Equipment:
Sheeters: 3
Energy Data:
Power boilers: 1
TMP Reboiler: 1
Steam turbines: 1 at 100 MW
Electrical demand for mill: 3,719 MWh/D

ⓘZAO MPK KRZ - Multibranch Production Company KRZ
Company is previously Ryazansky Paperboard & Asphalt Board
Ownership: mill staff
ul. Druzhnaya, 18
390017 Ryazan
Russia
Phone: (7) 4912 242043
Fax: (7) 4912 242033
Email: krz@krz.ru,
kadr@krz.ru,
region@krz.ru
Web Address: www.krz.ru
Personnel:
Gen. Dir.: Konstantin Nikolaevich Meerevitch
Phone: (7) 4912 242043
Fax: (7) 4912 242033
Commer. Dir.: Aleksandr Sergeevich Semchenkov
Phone: (7) 4912 249860
Fax: (7) 4912 242033
Bus. Devlpt. & Mktg. Dir.: Yuriy Alekseevich Grishkin
Phone: (7) 4912 249844
Fax: (7) 4912 242033
Email: reklama@krz.ru
Total Employees of Company: 800
Mill Locations:
ZAO MPK KRZ - Multibranch Production Company KRZ, Ryazan Mill, ul. Druzhnaya, 18, 390017 Ryazan, Russia, Capacity: 68,000 mt/y, (Paperboard mill)
Phone: (7) 4912 242043
Fax: (7) 4912 242033
Email: krz@krz.ru, kadr@krz.ru, region@krz.ru

ⓘZAO MPK KRZ - Multibranch Production Company KRZ
Ryazan Mill
ul. Druzhnaya, 18
390017 Ryazan
Russia
Phone: (7) 4912 242043
Fax: (7) 4912 242033
Email: krz@krz.ru,
kadr@krz.ru,
region@krz.ru
Web Address: www.krz.ru
Personnel:
Gen. Dir.: Konstantin Nikolaevich Meerevitch
Phone: (7) 4912 242043
Fax: (7) 4912 242033
Head of Logist.: Skvortsov Maxim
Phone: (7) 4912 249814
Fax: (7) 4912 242033
Email: snab.ms@krz.ru
Chief power Eng.: Averkina Svetlana
Phone: (7) 4912 249800
Fax: (7) 4912 242033

Email: energo@krz.ru
Tech. Dir.: Dmitri Mikhaylovich Sychev
Phone: (7) 4912 242044
Fax: (7) 4912 242033
Chief Mech.: Andrey Vasilievich Eremin
Phone: (7) 4912 249884
Fax: (7) 4912 242033
Email: meh@krz.ru
Head of Sls.: Golikov S. Svyatoslav
Phone: (7) 4912 242040
Fax: (7) 4912 242033
Email: gss@krz.ru
Chief Technology: Irina Yurievna Koblova
Phone: (7) 4912 249890
Fax: (7) 4912 242033
Advertising Mgr.: Tatiana Ashcheulova
Phone: (7) 4912 249844
Fax: (7) 4912 242033
Email: reklama@krz.ru
Total Employees at this Location: 800
Type of Operation: Paperboard mill
Pulp Grades and Capacities:
Total pulp capacity: 68,525 mt/y
Recycled Pulping: 68,525 mt/y
Pulp Mill Data:
Recycled Fiber Treatment Lines:
Flotation deinking lines: 1
Recycled packaging pulping lines: 1
Paper/Paperboard Grades and Capacities:
Total paper and paperboard capacity: 68,000 mt/y
Tissue: 7,000 mt/y
Packaging papers: 5,000 mt/y
Linerboard: 21,000 mt/y
Corrugating medium/fluting: 15,000 mt/y
Boxboard/cartonboard: 20,000 mt/y
Paper and Paperboard Mill Data:
Paper Machines: 3
No. 1, fourdrinier, Yankee dryer, total capacity 7,000 mt/y, Trim width 2.1 m, Tissue
BM 1, multi-wire, total capacity 31,000 mt/y, Trim width 2.1 m, Boxboard/cartonboard, Linerboard
BM 3, fourdrinier (2), total capacity 30,000 mt/y, Trim width 2.1 m, Corrugating medium/fluting, Linerboard, Packaging papers
Energy Data:
Power boilers: 1
Electrical demand for mill: 112 MWh/D

ⓘMyagkaya Krovlya
ul. Belgorodskaya 1
443017 Samara
Russia
Phone: (7) 846 261 8722/7640
Fax: (7) 846 261 7090/7364
Email: krovlya@mkrovlya.ru
Web Address: www.mkrovlya.ru
Personnel:
Sls. Dir.: Olga Antonova
Phone: (7) 846 261 8722/7640
Fax: (7) 846 261 7090/7364
Email: antonova@mkrovlya.ru
Total Employees of Company: 620
Mill Locations:
Myagkaya Krovlya, Samara Mill, ul. Belgorodskaya 1, 443017 Samara, Russia, Capacity: 35,000 mt/y, (Paperboard mill)
Phone: (7) 846 261 8722/7640
Fax: (7) 846 261 7090/7364
Email: krovlya@mkrovlya.ru

ⓜMyagkaya Krovlya
Samara Mill
ul. Belgorodskaya 1
443017 Samara
Russia
Phone: (7) 846 261 8722/7640
Fax: (7) 846 261 7090/7364
Email: krovlya@mkrovlya.ru
Web Address: www.mkrovlya.ru
Personnel:

Sls. Dir.: Olga Antonova
Phone: (7) 846 261 8722
Fax: (7) 846 261 7090
Email: antonova@mkrovlya.ru
Logist. & Purch. Mgr.: Natalya Marinova
Phone: (7) 846 261 1111
Fax: (7) 846 261 1111
Email: marinova@mkrovlya.ru
Total Employees at this Location: 610
Type of Operation: Paperboard mill
Pulp Grades and Capacities:
Total pulp capacity: 35,700 mt/y
Recycled Pulping: 35,700 mt/y
Pulp Mill Data:
Recycled Fiber Treatment Lines:
Pulpers: 2 at 38,500
Paper/Paperboard Grades and Capacities:
Total paper and paperboard capacity: 35,000 mt/y
Boxboard/cartonboard: 35,000 mt/y
Paper and Paperboard Mill Data:
Paper Machines: 2
No. 1, cylinder, total capacity 20,000 mt/y, Trim width 2.05 m, Boxboard/cartonboard
No. 2, cylinder, total capacity 15,000 mt/y, Trim width 2.05 m, Boxboard/cartonboard
Energy Data:
Power boilers
Electrical demand for mill: 43 MWh/D

ⓘⓜNaberezhnye Chelny Paper & Board Mill
Naberezhnye Chelny Mill
Ownership: mill staff
423800 Naberezhnye Chelny, Tatarstan Republic
Russia
Phone: (7) 8552 468495/791955
Fax: (7) 8552 460597
Email: nkbk@nkbk.ru
Web Address: www.nkbk.ru
Personnel:
Gen. Dir.: Vladimir Ivanovich Bestolkov
Phone: (7) 8552 791910
Chief Eng.: Mikhail Fedorovich Nokhrin
Phone: (7) 8552 791915
Commercial Dir.: Vladimir Dmitrievich Zubkov
Phone: (7) 8552 465600
1st Depty. Dir. External Economic issues: Andrey Gennadiyevich Khomyachev
Phone: (7) 8552 791952
Total Employees at this Location: 1,880
Type of Operation: Paper mill, Paperboard mill
Pulp Grades and Capacities:
Total pulp capacity: 195,785 mt/y
Recycled Pulping: 195,785 mt/y
Pulp Mill Data:
Recycled Fiber Treatment Lines:
Flotation deinking lines: 1
Recycled packaging pulping lines: 1
Paper/Paperboard Grades and Capacities:
Total paper and paperboard capacity: 191,000 mt/y
Tissue: 56,000 mt/y
Linerboard: 95,000 mt/y
Corrugating medium/fluting: 40,000 mt/y
Paper and Paperboard Mill Data:
Paper Machines: 2
No. 1, DuoFormer, Yankee dryer, total capacity 56,000 mt/y, Trim width 4.2 m, Tissue
BM 1, cylinder (7), total capacity 135,000 mt/y, Trim width 4.2 m, Corrugating medium/fluting, Linerboard
Energy Data:
Power boilers: 1
Electrical demand for mill: 374 MWh/D

ⓘNeman Pulp & Paper Mill
Ownership: 100% by Private
Podgornaya Str., 3
238710 Neman, Kaliningrad Region
Russia

Russia

Phone: (7) 40162 23034
Fax: (7) 40162 22189
Email: office@ncbk.koenig.ru
Mill Locations:
Neman Pulp & Paper Mill, Neman Mill, Podgornaya Str., 3, 238710 Neman, Russia, Capacity: 60,000 mt/y, (Pulp mill, Paper mill)
Phone: (7) 40162 23034
Fax: (7) 40162 22189
Email: office@ncbk.koenig.ru

ⓂNeman Pulp & Paper Mill
Neman Mill
Mill is for sale, bankrupt (bankrupt from May 2008, only one PM operating)
Podgornaya Str., 3
238710 Neman, Kaliningrad Region
Russia
Phone: (7) 40162 23034
Fax: (7) 40162 22189
Email: office@ncbk.koenig.ru
Personnel:
Gen. Mgr. Bidding: Dmitriy Andreevich Shurakov
Phone: (7) 40162 23034
Chief Eng.: Serguey Nikolaevich Percherin
Phone: (7) 40162 23034
Comm. Mgr.: Tatiana Victorovna Zhemekhkiv
Phone: (7) 40162 23275
HR Mgr.: Natalia Ivanovna Zyubina
Phone: (7) 40162 23034
Total Employees at this Location: 440
Type of Operation: Pulp mill, Paper mill
Pulp Grades and Capacities:
Total pulp capacity: 47,598 mt/y
Chemical Pulp: 47,598 mt/y
Pulp Mill Data:
Chemical Pulping Systems:
Continuous digesters: 1
Pulp Lines: 1
Chemical Recovery Equipment:
Evaporator lines: 1
Recovery boilers: 1
Lime Kiln
Paper/Paperboard Grades and Capacities:
Total paper and paperboard capacity: 60,000 mt/y
Uncoated woodfree/freesheet: 60,000 mt/y
Paper and Paperboard Mill Data:
Stock Preparation:
Pulpers: 7
Paper Machines: 1
No. 9, fourdrinier, total capacity 60,000 mt/y, Trim width 3.65 m, Uncoated woodfree/freesheet
Finishing Equipment:
Supercalenders: 5
Rewinders: 8
Energy Data:
Power boilers: 5
Steam turbines
Electrical demand for mill: 197 MWh/D

ⓄNicol-Pack Corporation
Promploschadka, 5-b, bldg. 4 p/b 28
140204 Voskresensk, Moscow Region
Russia
Phone: (7) 495 956 2265
Fax: (7) 495 956 2196
Email: uk@nicol-pack.ru
Web Address: nicol-pack.ru
Personnel:
Mgr.: Valery Mirzin
Phone: (7) 495 956 2265
Fax: (7) 495 956 2196
Total Employees of Company: 490
Mill Locations:
Nicol-Pack Imperial Co. Ltd., Murom (Imperial) Mill, ul. Moskovskaya 90, 602256 Murom, Russia, Capacity: 20,000 mt/y, (Paperboard mill)
Phone: (7) 49234 22238
Fax: (7) 49234 22227

Email: info@nicol-pack.ru
Nicol-Pack Corporation, Uchaly Mill, Krovelnaya Str. 1, 453700 Uchaly, Russia, Capacity: 120,000 mt/y, (Paperboard mill)
Phone: (7) 34791 41376/79
Fax: (7) 34791 41360/76
Email: nicolpack@uch.tn.ru
Nizhegorodsky Board & Asphalt Board Mill, Nizhegorodsky Mill, Sportsmensky Per., 11, 603028 Nizhny Novgorod, Russia, Capacity: 25,000 mt/y, (Paperboard mill)
Phone: (7) 831 2411364/2597 710 / 2416 962 / 2416 322
Fax: (7) 831 2412220
Email: sekretar@nn.tn.ru; info@nn.tn.ru

ⓂNicol-Pack Corporation
Uchaly Mill
Krovelnaya Str. 1
453700 Uchaly, Respublika Bashkortostan
Russia
Phone: (7) 34791 41376/79
Fax: (7) 34791 41360/76
Email: nicolpack@uch.tn.ru
Web Address: nicol-pack.ru, www.tn.ru
Personnel:
Gen. Dir.: Valeriy Borisovich Kovtun
Phone: (7) 34791 41376
Fax: (7) 34791 41360
Email: kovtun@uch.tn.ru
Total Employees at this Location: 175
Type of Operation: Paperboard mill
Pulp Grades and Capacities:
Total pulp capacity: 106,501 mt/y
Recycled Pulping: 106,501 mt/y
Pulp Mill Data:
Recycled Fiber Treatment Lines:
Recycled packaging pulping lines: 1
Paper/Paperboard Grades and Capacities:
Total paper and paperboard capacity: 120,000 mt/y
Linerboard: 70,000 mt/y
Corrugating medium/fluting: 40,000 mt/y
Boxboard/cartonboard: 10,000 mt/y
Paper and Paperboard Mill Data:
Paper Machines: 1
No. 1, fourdrinier (2), total capacity 120,000 mt/y, Trim width 4.03 m, Corrugating medium/fluting, Linerboard, Boxboard/cartonboard
Energy Data:
Power boilers: 1
Electrical demand for mill: 161 MWh/D

ⓄⓂOOO Nikmas
Chelyabinsk Mill
1-ya Potrebitelskaya Str. 24
454053 Chelyabinsk
Russia
Phone: (7) 351 262 3259/3368/3991
Fax: (7) 351 262 3259/3368/3991
Email: mail@nikmas.ru, operator@nikmas.ru
Web Address: www.nikmas.ru
Personnel:
Gen. Dir.: Aleksandr Pazyak
Phone: (7) 351 262 3259
Fax: (7) 351 262 3259
Prod. Mgr.: Aleksandr Arsentievich Izotov
Phone: (7) 351 262 3259
Fax: (7) 351 262 3259
Email: izotov@nikmas.ru
Head of Sls.: Natalia Makhmutova
Phone: (7) 951 799 7898
Fax: (7) 351 262 3259
Email: machmutova@nikmas.ru
Sls. Mgr.: Veronica V. Inozemtseva
Phone: (7) 908 044 7569
Fax: (7) 351 262 3259
Email: inozemceva@nikmas.ru

Mktg. Dir.: Alex Y. Isakov
Phone: (7) 912 317 9371
Fax: (7) 351 262 3259
Email: isakov@nikmas.ru
Total Employees at this Location: 300
Type of Operation: Paper mill
Pulp Grades and Capacities:
Total pulp capacity: 11,635 mt/y
Recycled Pulping: 11,635 mt/y
Pulp Mill Data:
Recycled Fiber Treatment Lines:
Recycled packaging pulping lines: 1
Paper/Paperboard Grades and Capacities:
Total paper and paperboard capacity: 25,000 mt/y
Tissue: 25,000 mt/y
Paper and Paperboard Mill Data:
Paper Machines: 3
No. 1, fourdrinier, Yankee dryer, total capacity 5,500 mt/y, Trim width 1.7 m, Tissue
No. 2, fourdrinier, Yankee dryer, total capacity 5,500 mt/y, Trim width 1.7 m, Tissue
No. 3, twin-wire, Yankee dryer, total capacity 14,000 mt/y, Trim width 2.1 m, Tissue
Energy Data:
Power boilers: 4
Combustion turbines: 1
Electrical demand for mill: 73 MWh/D

ⓂNizhegorodsky Board & Asphalt Board Mill
Nizhegorodsky Mill
Ownership: Nicol-Pack Corporation, Techno Nikol
Sportsmensky Per., 11
603028 Nizhny Novgorod
Russia
Phone: (7) 831 2411364/2597 710 / 2416 962 / 2416 322
Fax: (7) 831 2412220
Email: sekretar@nn.tn.ru, info@nn.tn.ru
Web Address: www.nkrz.ru
Personnel:
Gen. Dir.: Alex Yurievich Sulimov
Phone: (7) 831 2411364
Fax: (7) 831 2412220
Email: sulimov@nn.tn.ru
HR Dir.: Natalia L. Voroshylova
Phone: (7) 831 2597710
Fax: (7) 831 2778030
Email: kostileva@nn.tn.ru
Logist. Mgr.: Svetlana Astaf'eva
Phone: (7) 831 2778036
Fax: (7) 831 2778036
Email: astafeva@nn.tn.ru
Total Employees at this Location: 170
Type of Operation: Paperboard mill
Pulp Grades and Capacities:
Total pulp capacity: 25,470 mt/y
Recycled Pulping: 25,470 mt/y
Pulp Mill Data:
Recycled Fiber Treatment Lines:
Recycled packaging pulping lines: 1
Paper/Paperboard Grades and Capacities:
Total paper and paperboard capacity: 25,000 mt/y
Boxboard/cartonboard: 25,000 mt/y
Paper and Paperboard Mill Data:
Paper Machines: 1
No. 1, cylinder, total capacity 25,000 mt/y, Trim width 2 m, Boxboard/cartonboard
Energy Data:
Power boilers: 3
Electrical demand for mill: 31 MWh/D

ⓂZAO NPP Filter Materials
Otradnoye Mill
Tsentralnaya ul. 4
187330 Otradnoye
Russia

Russia

Phone: (7) 813 6241938/812 4485920
Fax: (7) 813 6241938/812 4485920
Email: info@filter-m.ru
Web Address: www.filtermaterials.ru
Personnel:
Dir.: Aleksandr Evgenyevich Orachev
Phone: (7) 812 4485920
Fax: (7) 812 4485920
Tech. Dir.: Anna Leonidovna Trukhtenkova
Phone: (7) 812 448 5922
Fax: (7) 812 4485920
Email: a.trukhtenkova@gmail.com
Prod. Dir.: Olga Leonidovna Shanina
Phone: (7) 813 6241938
Fax: (7) 812 4485920
Chief Eng.: Vladimir Leonidovich Mezencev
Phone: (7) 813 6241938
Fax: (7) 812 4485920
Vice Dir.Commerce: Andrey Yurievich Gorbunov
Phone: (7) 813 6241938
Fax: (7) 812 4485920
Chief Acc.: Olga Alekseevna Sychava
Phone: (7) 813 6241938
Fax: (7) 812 4485920
Total Employees at this Location: 70
Type of Operation: Paper mill
Paper/Paperboard Grades and Capacities:
Total paper and paperboard capacity: 3,000 mt/y
Specialty and industrial: 3,000 mt/y
Paper and Paperboard Mill Data:
Stock Preparation:
Pulpers: 2
Refiners: 2
Paper Machines: 1
No. 1, inclined, total capacity 3,000 mt/y, Trim width 1.6 m, Specialty and industrial
Energy Data:
Electrical demand for mill: 6 MWh/D

ⓂOAO Aleksandrovbumprom (ABP)
Ul. Lugavaya 18
157912 Pos. Krasnaya Polyana
Russia
Phone: (7) 49438 26691/31217
Fax: (7) 49438 31217
Email: skbf@bk.ru
Personnel:
Gen. Dir.: Mikhail Moiseevich Sedov
Phone: (7) 49438 26691/31217
Fax: (7) 49438 31217
Sls. Mgr., Ass. Gen. Dir.: Tatiana Yuryevna Chikhvatova
Phone: (7) 49438 26691/31217
Fax: (7) 49438 31217
Chief Acc.: Elena Nikolaevna Stchiraya
Phone: (7) 49438 26691/31217
Fax: (7) 49438 31217
Total Employees of Company: 80
Total Employees at this Location: 80
Mill Locations:
OAO Aleksandrovbumprom (ABP), Krasnopolyanskij Paperboard Mill, Ul. Lugavaya 18, 157912 Pos. Krasnaya Polyana, Ostrovskiy rayon, Russia, Capacity: 5,000 mt/y, (Paperboard mill)
Phone: (7) 49438 26691/31217
Fax: (7) 49438 31217
Email: skbf@bk.ru

ⓂOmskkrovlya
Omsk Mill
ul. Kombinatskaya 38, PO Box 544
644040 Omsk
Russia
Phone: (7) 3812 652061/691630
Fax: (7) 3812 652061
Email: adm@okrz.sibintercom.ru,
sbyt@sibintercom.ru,
admkrz.su@mail.ru
Web Address: www.krz.su
Personnel:
Tech. Dir.: Tatiana Timofeevna Savchenko

Phone: (7) 3812 691612
Tech. Mech. Dir.: Igor Petrovich Struchaev
Phone: (7) 3812 691326
Chief Acc.: Elena Timofeevna Kopteva
Phone: (7) 3812 691347
Gen. Dir.: Andrei Mikhailovich Laskovets
Phone: (7) 3812 652061
Prod. Mgr.: Vyacheslav Aleksandrovich Sychikhin
Phone: (7) 3812 691603
Chief Eng.: Anatoliy Nikolaevich Chyarvyanzev
Phone: (7) 3812 691603
Sls. Dir.: Roman Leonidovich Aleksandrov
Phone: (7) 3812 652061
Email: krz.su@mail.ru
Total Employees at this Location: 283
Type of Operation: Paperboard mill
Paper/Paperboard Grades and Capacities:
Total paper and paperboard capacity: 18,000 mt/y
Boxboard/cartonboard: 18,000 mt/y
Paper and Paperboard Mill Data:
Paper Machines: 1
No. 1, total capacity 18,000 mt/y, Trim width 2.1 m, Boxboard/cartonboard
Energy Data:
Electrical demand for mill: 30 MWh/D

ⓂOkulovka P&P Mill Ltd.
Ownership: private investors
Ul. Chelieva 13, Business Center "MacTower"
193230 Saint-Petersburg
Russia
Phone: (7) 812 336 2718
Fax: (7) 812 336 2718
Email: secretar@fluting.ru,
info@adress.ru
Web Address: www.fluting.ru
Personnel:
Branch Dir.: Petr Markovich Kogan
Phone: (7) 816 572 3012
Email: Kogan@fluting.ru
Mill Locations:
Okulovka P&P Mill Ltd., Okulovka Mill, Tsentralnaya Str., 5, 174350 Okulovka, Russia, Capacity: 85,000 mt/y, (Paper mill)
Phone: (7) 81657 23012/812 336 2701
Fax: (7) 812 336 2718/812 336 2718
Email: secretar@fluting.ru

ⓂOkulovka P&P Mill Ltd.
Okulovka Mill
Tsentralnaya Str., 5
174350 Okulovka, Novgorod Region
Russia
Phone: (7) 81657 23012/812 336 2701
Fax: (7) 812 336 2718/812 336 2718
Email: secretar@fluting.ru
Web Address: www.fluting.ru
Personnel:
Branch Dir.: Petr Markovich Kogan
Phone: (7) 816 572 3012
Fax: (7) 812 336 2718
Email: Kogan@fluting.ru
Dpty. Dir., Pulp Prod.: Andrey Olegovich Isaev
Phone: (7) 816 572 3012
Fax: (7) 812 336 2718
Email: isaev@fluting.ru
Tech. Dir.: Sergey Alexeevich Samsonov
Phone: (7) 816 572 3783
Fax: (7) 812 336 2718
Email: samsonov@fluting.ru
Chief Mechanic: Sergey Kazimirovich Shtukel
Phone: (7) 816 572 3012
Fax: (7) 812 336 2718
Email: shtukel@fluting.ru
Chief Eng.: Vladislav Valeryevich Travkin
Phone: (7) 816 572 3012
Fax: (7) 812 336 2718
Email: travkin@fluting.ru
Total Employees at this Location: 270
Type of Operation: Paper mill

Pulp Grades and Capacities:
Total pulp capacity: 85,853 mt/y
Recycled Pulping: 85,853 mt/y
Pulp Mill Data:
Recycled Fiber Treatment Lines:
Recycled packaging pulping lines: 1
Paper/Paperboard Grades and Capacities:
Total paper and paperboard capacity: 85,000 mt/y
Linerboard: 50,000 mt/y
Corrugating medium/fluting: 35,000 mt/y
Paper and Paperboard Mill Data:
Paper Machines: 2
No. 6, fourdrinier, total capacity 34,000 mt/y, Trim width 2.1 m, Linerboard, Corrugating medium/fluting
No. 7, fourdrinier, total capacity 51,000 mt/y, Trim width 2.5 m, Linerboard, Corrugating medium/fluting
Energy Data:
Power boilers: 2
Electrical demand for mill: 115 MWh/D

ⓂOmsk Paper Mill
Dachnaya Str. 1
644516 Klyuchi
Russia
Phone: (7) 3812 340324 / 487884
Fax: (7) 3812 246806 / 3812 399695
Email: obz@bk.ru
Web Address: www.ombz.ru
Personnel:
CEO: Kurbangaly Sakhrutdinov
Phone: (7) 3812 340324 / 487884
Fax: (7) 3812 246806
Chief Eng.: Igor' Tuyurov
Phone: (7) 3812 340324 / 487884
Fax: (7) 3812 246806
Admin. Mgr.: Maria Serdyuk
Phone: (7) 3812 340324 / 487884
Fax: (7) 3812 246806
Total Employees at this Location: 80
Mill Locations:
Omsk Paper Mill, Klyuchi Mill, Dachnaya Str. 1, 644516 Klyuchi, Russia, Capacity: 700 mt/y, (Paper mill)
Phone: (7) 3812 340324 / 487884
Fax: (7) 3812 246806 / 3812 399695
Email: obz@bk.ru

ⓂOmsk Paper Mill
Klyuchi Mill
Dachnaya Str. 1
644516 Klyuchi
Russia
Phone: (7) 3812 340324 / 487884
Fax: (7) 3812 246806 / 3812 399695
Email: obz@bk.ru
Web Address: www.ombz.ru
Personnel:
CEO: Kurbangaly Sakhrutdinov
Chief Eng.: Igor' Tuyurov
Total Employees at this Location: 80
Type of Operation: Paper mill
Paper/Paperboard Grades and Capacities:
Total paper and paperboard capacity: 700 mt/y
Tissue: 700 mt/y
Paper and Paperboard Mill Data:
Paper Machines: 1
No. 1, Trim width 1.2 m, Tissue
Energy Data:
Electrical demand for mill: 4 MWh/D

ⓂOmskkrovlya
Ownership: 40.30% by Mitra
ul. Kombinatskaya 38, PO Box 544
644040 Omsk
Russia
Phone: (7) 3812 652061/691630
Fax: (7) 3812 652061
Email: adm@okrz.sibintercom.ru,
sbyt@sibintercom.ru,
admkrz.su@mail.ru

Russia

Web Address: www.krz.su
Personnel:
Gen. Dir.: Andrei Mikhailovich Laskovets
Phone: (7) 3812 652061/691630
Fax: (7) 3812 652061
Prod. Mgr.: Vyacheslav Aleksandrovich Sychikhin
Phone: (7) 3812 652061/691630
Fax: (7) 3812 652061
Chief Eng.: Anatoliy Nikolaevich Chyarvyanzev
Phone: (7) 3812 652061/691630
Fax: (7) 3812 652061
Total Employees at this Location: 283
Mill Locations:
Omskkrovlya, Omsk Mill, ul. Kombinatskaya 38, PO Box 544, 644040 Omsk, Russia, Capacity: 18,000 mt/y, (Paperboard mill)
Phone: (7) 3812 652061/691630
Fax: (7) 3812 652061
Email: adm@okrz.sibintercom.ru, sbyt@sibintercom.ru; admkrz.su@mail.ru

⊕OOO Astrakhanskaya Paperboard Mill
ul. Optovaya 2
416130 Solyanka
Russia
Phone: (7) 8512 581285/6
Fax: (7) 8512 581285
Email: akf-pap@yandex.ru
Mill Locations:
OOO Astrakhanskaya Paperboard Mill, Solyanka Mill, ul. Optovaya 2, 416130 Solyanka, Russia, Capacity: 2,450 mt/y, (Paperboard mill)
Phone: (7) 8512 581285/6
Fax: (7) 8512 581285
Email: akf-pap@yandex.ru

⊕OOO Bumy
Engelsa Str. 1
606210 Lyskovo
Russia
Phone: (7) 83149 28896/50632
Fax: (7) 83149 50632
Email: bumy@nm.ru
Web Address: www.bumy.nm.ru
Personnel:
Chmn., Com.Dir.: Oleg Konstantinovich Zavarzin
Phone: (7) 83149 28896/50632
Fax: (7) 83149 50632
Gen. Dir.: Ivan Aleksandrovich Averin
Phone: (7) 83149 28896/50632
Fax: (7) 83149 50632
Chief Eng.: Vladimir Aleksandrovich Korobkov
Phone: (7) 83149 28896/50632
Fax: (7) 83149 50632
Chief Acc.: Valentina Ivanovna Komendantov
Phone: (7) 83149 28896/50632
Fax: (7) 83149 50632
Total Employees at this Location: 134
Mill Locations:
OOO Bumy, Lyskovo Mill, Engelsa Str. 1, 606210 Lyskovo, Russia, Capacity: 2,500 mt/y, (Paper mill)
Phone: (7) 83149 28896/50632
Fax: (7) 83149 50632
Email: bumy@nm.ru

⊕OOO Buprom-Pokrov
Franz Shtolverk Str. 18
601135 Pokrov, Petushinskiy rayon
Russia
Phone: (7) 49243 64284 / 64153/64194
Fax: (7) 49243 64284
Email: buprom.pokrov@mail.ru
Web Address: www.buprom-pokrov.ru
Personnel:
Dir.: Andrey Aleksandrovich Titov
Phone: (7) 49243 64284 / 64153/64194
Fax: (7) 49243 64284
Chief Eng.: Vyacheslav Petrovich Inyushin
Phone: (7) 49243 64284 / 64153/64194

Fax: (7) 49243 64284
Prod. Mgr.: Vladimir Sergeevich Tertychnik
Phone: (7) 49243 64284 / 64153/64194
Fax: (7) 49243 64284
Total Employees of Company: 118
Mill Locations:
OOO Buprom-Pokrov, Pokrov, Petushinskiy rayon Mill, Franz Shtolverk Str. 18, 601135 Pokrov, Petushinskiy rayon, Russia, Capacity: 8,000 mt/y, (Paper mill)
Phone: (7) 49243 64284 / 64153/64194
Fax: (7) 49243 64284
Email: buprom.pokrov@mail.ru

⊕OOO KubanPapir
Ownership: OOO Tissue Bumaga
Kalinina Str. 1
350039 Krasnodar
Russia
Phone: (7) 8612 281709 / 1692 / 1978
Fax: (7) 8612 281709
Email: kubanpapir@rambler.ru, papir-yg@rambler.ru
Web Address: tissue-bumaga.ru
Personnel:
Gen. Dir.: Kirill Gennadiyevich Minin
Phone: (7) 8612 281709
Fax: (7) 8612 281709
Man. Dir. & Sls. Dir.: Andrey Yurievich Lysenko
Phone: (7) 8612 281709
Fax: (7) 8612 281709
Chief Eng.: Andrey Vasiliyevich Nikulin
Phone: (7) 8612 282028
Fax: (7) 8612 281709
Total Employees of Company: 100
Mill Locations:
OOO KubanPapir, Krasnodar Mill, Kalinina Str. 1, 350039 Krasnodar, Russia, Capacity: 10,000 mt/y, (Paper mill, Paperboard mill)
Phone: (7) 8612 281709 / 1692 / 1978
Fax: (7) 8612 281709
Email: kubanpapir@rambler.ru; papir-yg@rambler.ru

⊕OOO Tissue-Bumaga
Putevaya Str. 68
350038 Krasnodar
Russia
Phone: (7) 861 274 18 36 / 0267
Fax: (7) 861 274 06 15/43/13
Email: tissu-bumaga@rambler.ru
Web Address: tissue-bumaga.ru
Personnel:
Gen. Dir.: Kirill Gennadievich Minin
Phone: (7) 861 274 18 36 / 0267
Fax: (7) 861 274 06 15/43/13
Tech. Dir.: Alexey Gennadievich Alexandri'n
Phone: (7) 861 274 18 36 / 0267
Fax: (7) 861 274 06 15/43/13
Depty. Dir.: Alla Petrovna Kliop
Phone: (7) 861 274 18 36 / 0267
Fax: (7) 861 274 06 15/43/13
Total Employees of Company: 130
Total Employees at this Location: 130
Mill Locations:
OOO Tissue-Bumaga, Krasnodar Mill, Putevaya Str. 68, 350038 Krasnodar, Russia, Capacity: 5,000 mt/y, (Paper mill)
Phone: (7) 861 274 18 36 / 0267
Fax: (7) 861 274 06 15/43/13
Email: tissu-bumaga@rambler.ru

⊕OOO Triton-M
Promyshlenny proezd, 4
170028 Tver
Russia
Phone: (7) 4822 430222/430333
Fax: (7) 4822 430333/430222
Email: ale-belov@mail.ru
Web Address: www.tritonm.ru
Personnel:
Gen. Dir.: Anatoliy Egorovich Belov

Phone: (7) 4822 430222/430333
Fax: (7) 4822 430333/430222
Mgr.: Alexandr Anatolievich Belov
Phone: (7) 4822 430222/430333
Fax: (7) 4822 430333/430222
Chief Acc.: Olga Sergeevna Smirnova
Phone: (7) 4822 430222/430333
Fax: (7) 4822 430333/430222
Total Employees at this Location: 140
Mill Locations:
OOO Triton-M, Tver Mill, Promyshlenny proezd, 4, 170028 Tver, Russia, Capacity: 7,000 mt/y, (Paper mill)
Phone: (7) 4822 430222/430333
Fax: (7) 4822 430333/430222
Email: ale-belov@mail.ru

⊕⓾Perm Pulp and Paper Mill
Perm Mill
Bumazhnikov Str., 1
614037 Perm
Russia
Phone: (7) 342 263 9090
Fax: (7) 342 263 9250
Email: pcbk@pcbk.perm.ru
Web Address: pcbk.perm.ru
Personnel:
Gen. Dir.: Alexander Boychenko
Phone: (7) 342 263 9090
Fax: (7) 342 263 9250
Email: boychenko@pcbk.perm.ru
Exec. Dir.: Evgeniy Andreevich Glezman
Phone: (7) 342 263 9090
Fax: (7) 342 263 9250
Email: glezman@pcbk.perm.ru
Tech. Dir.: Sergei Serebrennikov
Phone: (7) 342 263 9090
Fax: (7) 342 263 9250
Email: serebrennikov@pcbk.perm.ru
Chief Eng.: Mikhail Nikolaevich Spasennikov
Phone: (7) 342 263 9090
Fax: (7) 342 263 9250
Email: spasennikov@pcbk.perm.ru
Total Employees at this Location: 2,000
Type of Operation: Pulp mill, Paper mill, Paperboard mill
Pulp Grades and Capacities:
Total pulp capacity: 191,219 mt/y
Chemical Pulp: 82,722 mt/y
Recycled Pulping: 108,498 mt/y
Pulp Mill Data:
Chemical Pulping Systems:
Continuous digesters: 1
Recycled Fiber Treatment Lines:
Recycled packaging pulping lines: 1
Paper/Paperboard Grades and Capacities:
Total paper and paperboard capacity: 186,000 mt/y
Linerboard: 106,000 mt/y
Corrugating medium/fluting: 80,000 mt/y
Paper and Paperboard Mill Data:
Paper Machines: 3
BM 1, fourdrinier, total capacity 72,000 mt/y, Trim width 4.2 m, Linerboard
BM 2, fourdrinier, total capacity 65,000 mt/y, Trim width 2.3 m, Corrugating medium/fluting, Linerboard
PM 1, fourdrinier, total capacity 49,000 mt/y, Trim width 4.2 m, Corrugating medium/fluting
Energy Data:
Power boilers: 5
Steam turbines: 2
Electrical demand for mill: 342 MWh/D

⊕⓾OAO Pitkyaranta Pulp Mill
Pitkyaranta Mill
Company is under bankruptcy protection
Ownership: Marlin Enterprise Ltd.
186810 Pitkyaranta, Karelia
Russia
Phone: (7) 81433 40 101 / 102
Fax: (7) 84133 40101 / 143
Email: office@pitzavod.ru

Russia

Personnel:
Gen.Dir.: Alexandr Evgenievich Soventsov
Deputy Gen. Dir.: Zajtuna Andreevna Sorval
Phone: (7) 81433 45057/44157
Advisor of Gen. Dir.: Mikhail Ivanovich Selyuzhitsky
Phone: (7) 81433 45057/44157
Commer. Dir.: Andrey Nikolaevich Bezverkhiy
Phone: (7) 81433 43051
Prod. Quality Dir.: Igor Anatolyevich Grigoryev
Asst. of Gen. Dir.: Elena Vasilyevna Yakovleva
Phone: (7) 81433 40106
Total Employees of Company: 1,042
Total Employees at this Location: 1,042
Type of Operation: Pulp mill
Pulp Grades and Capacities:
Total pulp capacity: 110,801 mt/y
Pulp available for market: 110,000 mt/y
Chemical Pulp: 110,801 mt/y
Pulp Mill Data:
Chemical Pulping Systems:
Batch digesters: 8
Pulp Dryers:
Air Float dryers 1
Energy Data:
Power boilers: 2
Electrical demand for mill: 241 MWh/D

ⓘⓜOAO Poligrafkarton
Balakhna Mill
Company is filed for bankruptcy in the Nizhny Novgorod arbitration court in June 2014.
Ownership: Consolidated Paper Mills PLC
Prospekt Revolutsii 93
606400 Balakhna, Nizhny Novgorod
Russia
Phone: (7) 83144 62289/62284
Fax: (7) 83144 62289
Email: polygrafkarton@yandex.ru
Web Address: www.ukobf.com
Personnel:
CEO: Dmitriy Evgenyevich Kashtirev
Phone: (7) 83144 62288
Fax: (7) 83144 62289
Gen. Mgr.: Dmitry Aleksandrovich Dulkin
Phone: (7) 83144 62290
Fax: (7) 83144 62289
Chief Eng.: Vladimir Vasilyevich Fokin
Phone: (7) 83144 62289
Fax: (7) 83144 62289
Chief Mech.: Vladimir Vasilyevich Fokin
Phone: (7) 83144 62289
Fax: (7) 83144 62289
Chief Acc.: Olga Yurievna Voroshina
Phone: (7) 83144 62289
Fax: (7) 83144 62289
Commer. Dir. & Exec.Dir.: Tatiana Valerievna Yablokova
Phone: (7) 83144 62289
Fax: (7) 83144 62289
Office Mgr.: Maria Letova
Phone: (7) 83144 62289
Fax: (7) 83144 62289
Total Employees of Company: 900
Total Employees at this Location: 900
Type of Operation: Pulp mill, Paperboard mill
Pulp Grades and Capacities:
Total pulp capacity: 115,871 mt/y
Recycled Pulping: 115,871 mt/y
Pulp Mill Data:
Chemical Pulping Systems:
Continuous digesters: 1
Chemical Recovery Equipment:
Evaporator lines: 1
Recovery boilers: 1
Recycled Fiber Treatment Lines:
Recycled packaging pulping lines: 1
Paper/Paperboard Grades and Capacities:
Total paper and paperboard capacity: 115,000 mt/y
Corrugating medium/fluting: 70,000 mt/y
Boxboard/cartonboard: 45,000 mt/y

Paper and Paperboard Mill Data:
Paper Machines: 2
No. 1, cylinder (7), total capacity 45,000 mt/y, Trim width 3.2 m, Boxboard/cartonboard
No. 2, fourdrinier, total capacity 70,000 mt/y, Trim width 2.5 m, Corrugating medium/fluting
Energy Data:
Power boilers
Steam turbines
Electrical demand for mill: 146 MWh/D

ⓘⓜPolotnyano-Zavodskaya Paper Mill
Polotnyany Zavod Mill
Ownership: Consolidated Paper Mills PLC
Trudovaya Str., 2
249844 Polotnyany Zavod, Kaluga Region
Russia
Phone: (7) 48434 32043/74598
Fax: (7) 48434 46319/33824
Email: sales@pzbf.com, pzbf@pzbf.ru
Web Address: www.pzbf.com, www.ukobf.com
Personnel:
Gen. Dir.: Valentina Mironova
Phone: (7) 48434 32043/74693/74598
Chief Eng.: Serguey Finozhenkov
Phone: (7) 48434 32043/74693/74598
Chief Acc.: Elena Nikolaevna Amelina
Total Employees of Company: 534
Total Employees at this Location: 534
Type of Operation: Paper mill
Pulp Grades and Capacities:
Total pulp capacity: 73,079 mt/y
Recycled Pulping: 73,079 mt/y
Paper/Paperboard Grades and Capacities:
Total paper and paperboard capacity: 72,000 mt/y
Linerboard: 44,000 mt/y
Corrugating medium/fluting: 28,000 mt/y
Paper and Paperboard Mill Data:
Paper Machines: 2
No. 1, fourdrinier, total capacity 44,000 mt/y, Trim width 2.45 m, Linerboard
No. 2, fourdrinier, total capacity 28,000 mt/y, Trim width 2.1 m, Corrugating medium/fluting
Energy Data:
Power boilers: 2
Steam turbines
Electrical demand for mill: 100 MWh/D

ⓘPolymerkrovlya
Pos. Verkhnedneprovsky
215750 Dorogobuzhskiy Rayon
Russia
Phone: (7) 48144 53993

ⓘⓜJSC Primsnabcontract Ussurijsk Paperboard Mill
Ussurijsk Mill
Ownership: Primsnabkombinat (main share)
Rakovskoye Shosse, 1
692527 Ussurijsk
Russia
Phone: (7) 4234 231579/61/62/77
Fax: (7) 4234 231563
Email: primsnabkontrakt@mail.ru, ukk@primsk.ru
Web Address: www.primsk.ru
Personnel:
Gen. Dir.: Evgeniy Borisovich Dolnikov
Phone: (7) 4234 231579
Fax: (7) 4234 231563
Email: dolnikov@primsk.ru
Chief Acc.: Olga Vladimirovna Komarova
Phone: (7) 4234 231579
Fax: (7) 4234 231563
Email: komarova@primsk.ru

Exec. Dir.: Aleksandr Aleksandrovich Dmitrichenko
Phone: (7) 4234 2313579
Fax: (7) 4234 231563
Email: dmitrichenko@primsk.ru
Tech. Dir.: Leonid Reokatovich Kytmanov
Phone: (7) 4234 231577
Fax: (7) 4234 231563
Email: kytmanov@primsk.ru
PR Mgr.: Eugeniy Aleksandrovich Savenkov
Phone: (7) 4234 231578
Fax: (7) 4234 231563
Email: savenkov@primsk.ru
Prod. Mgr.: Igor Mikhaylovich Boyko
Phone: (7) 4234 231563
Fax: (7) 4234 231563
Email: boyko@primsk.ru
Sls. Mgr.: Lyudmila Dmitrievna Drozd
Phone: (7) 4234 231572
Fax: (7) 4234 231563
Email: drozd@primsk.ru
Total Employees at this Location: 780
Type of Operation: Paperboard mill
Pulp Grades and Capacities:
Total pulp capacity: 100,851 mt/y
Recycled Pulping: 100,851 mt/y
Pulp Mill Data:
Recycled Fiber Treatment Lines:
Pulpers: 3
Paper/Paperboard Grades and Capacities:
Total paper and paperboard capacity: 100,000 mt/y
Linerboard: 60,000 mt/y
Corrugating medium/fluting: 40,000 mt/y
Paper and Paperboard Mill Data:
Paper Machines: 1
No. 1, fourdrinier (2), total capacity 100,000 mt/y, Trim width 4.2 m, Linerboard, Corrugating medium/fluting
Finishing Equipment:
Calenders: 1
Energy Data:
Power boilers: 5
Electrical demand for mill: 121 MWh/D

ⓘⓜProletariy, JSC
Surazh Mill
Ownership: 100% by mill staff
Fabrichnaya Str., 1
243500 Surazh, Bryansk Region
Russia
Phone: (7) 48330 21995
Fax: (7) 48330 21442
Email: info@proletarii.ru
Web Address: www.proletarii.ru
Personnel:
Gen. Dir.: Viktor Aleksandrovich Tanich
Phone: (7) 48330 21995
Chief Eng.: Aleksandr Ivanovich Sokolov
Phone: (7) 48330 21268
Total Employees of Company: 1,170
Total Employees at this Location: 1,170
Type of Operation: Paper mill, Paperboard mill
Pulp Grades and Capacities:
Total pulp capacity: 76,674 mt/y
Recycled Pulping: 76,674 mt/y
Pulp Mill Data:
Recycled Fiber Treatment Lines:
Recycled packaging pulping lines: 1
Paper/Paperboard Grades and Capacities:
Total paper and paperboard capacity: 75,000 mt/y
Packaging papers: 5,000 mt/y
Linerboard: 10,000 mt/y
Corrugating medium/fluting: 10,000 mt/y
Boxboard/cartonboard: 50,000 mt/y
Paper and Paperboard Mill Data:
Paper Machines: 5
No. 1, cylinder, total capacity 12,500 mt/y, Trim width 1 m, Boxboard/cartonboard
No. 2, cylinder, total capacity 12,500 mt/y, Trim width 2.15 m, Boxboard/cartonboard

Russia

No. 3, cylinder, total capacity 12,500 mt/y, Trim width 1.65 m, Boxboard/cartonboard
No. 4, cylinder, total capacity 12,500 mt/y, Trim width 2.1 m, Boxboard/cartonboard
No. 5, fourdrinier, total capacity 25,000 mt/y, Trim width 4.2 m, Corrugating medium/fluting, Linerboard, Packaging papers
Energy Data:
Power boilers: 7
Electrical demand for mill: 95 MWh/D

ⓜKPK St. Petersburg OOAO
Kommunar Mill
Pavloskaya Str. 9
188320 Kommunar, Leningrad Region
Russia
Mailing Address: P.O Box 51, 196620 Pavlovsk, Russia
Phone: (7) 812 460 2278
Fax: (7) 812 460 2287
Email: kpk@kpk.ru,
info@kpk.com.ru
Web Address: www.knauf.com
Personnel:
Gen. Dir.: Sergey Sergeevich Kuznetsov
Phone: (7) 812 4602778
Vice Gen. Dir.: Vadim Sukhuv
Phone: (7) 812 460 2278
Finan. Mgr.: Oleg Besdenychish
Phone: (7) 812 460 2278
Tech. Dir.: Dmitriy Ivanovich Menshikov
Phone: (7) 812 4602778
Mktg. Dir.: Vitaly Vasilyevich Ryndin
Phone: (7) 812 460 1748
Total Employees at this Location: 1,320
Type of Operation: Paperboard mill
Pulp Grades and Capacities:
Total pulp capacity: 225,473 mt/y
Recycled Pulping: 225,473 mt/y
Paper/Paperboard Grades and Capacities:
Total paper and paperboard capacity: 250,000 mt/y
Linerboard: 20,000 mt/y
Boxboard/cartonboard: 230,000 mt/y
Paper and Paperboard Mill Data:
Paper Machines: 2
No. 1, multi-wire, total capacity 125,000 mt/y, Trim width 4.2 m, Boxboard/cartonboard, Linerboard
No. 2, multi-wire, total capacity 125,000 mt/y, Trim width 4.2 m, Boxboard/cartonboard
Coating Machines: 1
No. 1, total capacity 70,000 mt/y., off machine
Energy Data:
Electrical demand for mill: 390 MWh/D

ⓜSCA Hygiene Products Russia LLC
Sovetsk Mill
Ownership: SCA Hygiene Products SE
Molodyozhnaya Str. 9
301205 Sovetsk, Shchekino Distr., Tula Region
Russia
Phone: (7) 48751 746 66 / 751 36/41
Email: ekaterina.serezhnikova@sca.com
Web Address: www.sca.ru,
www.sca.com
Personnel:
Mill Dir.: Artem Lebedev
Phone: (7) 48751 7 51 41
Fax: (7) 48751 7 50 25
Email: artem.lebedev@sca.com
Office Mgr.: Ekaterina Serezhnikova
Phone: (7) 48751 7 51 41
Fax: (7) 48751 7 50 25
Email: ekaterina.serezhnikova@sca.com
HR Director Global Hygiene Supply: Anna Stepanova
Phone: (7) 89 97006 600
Fax: (7) 48751 7 50 25
Email: anna.stepanova@sca.com
HR Mgr.: Oksana Vityugina
Phone: (7) 48751 7 51 41

Email: oksana.vityugina@sca.com
Total Employees at this Location: 230
Type of Operation: Paper mill
Pulp Grades and Capacities:
Total pulp capacity: 31,619 mt/y
Recycled Pulping: 31,619 mt/y
Pulp Mill Data:
Recycled Fiber Treatment Lines:
Flotation deinking lines: 1
Paper/Paperboard Grades and Capacities:
Total paper and paperboard capacity: 30,000 mt/y
Tissue: 30,000 mt/y
Paper and Paperboard Mill Data:
Paper Machines: 1
No. 1, (started November 2009), crescent former, total capacity 30,000 mt/y, Trim width 2.8 m, Tissue
Energy Data:
Power boilers: 1
Electrical demand for mill: 95 MWh/D

ⓜSCA Hygiene Products Russia LLC
Svetogorsk Mill
Ownership: SCA Hygiene Products SE
ul. Zavodskaya 21
188991 Svetogorsk, Leningrad Region
Russia
Mailing Address: P. Box 54, 188990 Svetogorsk, Leningrad Region, Russia
Phone: (7) 812 320 4834
Fax: (7) 812 320 4835
Email: info@scacompany.com,
svetogorsk@sca.com,
tissue@mail.ru
Web Address: www.sca.ru,
www.sca.com
Personnel:
Dir.: Dmitri Konstantinovich Adamov
Phone: (7) 81278 45962
Chief Eng.: Vladimir Viktorovich Yakovlev
Phone: (7) 81278 45451
Deputy Gen. Dir. - Production: Yuriy Anatolievich Mitin
Phone: (7) 812 320 4834
Sls. Distr. Dir.: Yuriy Arkadeevich Pavlov
Phone: (7) 812 320 4834
HR Dir.: Sergey Vasiliev
Phone: (7) 812 320 4834
HR Mgr.: Natalia Nikolaevna Zimina
Phone: (7) 812 320 4834
Total Employees at this Location: 450
Type of Operation: Paper mill
Pulp Grades and Capacities:
Total pulp capacity: 45,832 mt/y
Recycled Pulping: 45,832 mt/y
Pulp Mill Data:
Recycled Fiber Treatment Lines:
Flotation deinking lines: 1 at 77,350
Paper/Paperboard Grades and Capacities:
Total paper and paperboard capacity: 43,000 mt/y
Tissue: 43,000 mt/y
Paper and Paperboard Mill Data:
Paper Machines: 1
No. 1, (Former Type model: SpeedFormer T), SpeedFormer, total capacity 43,000 mt/y, Trim width 4.35 m, Tissue
Finishing Equipment:
Rewinders: 1 at 35,000 mt/y
Energy Data:
Electrical demand for mill: 139 MWh/D

ⓒⓜSegezha Pulp & Paper Mill
Segezha Mill
Ownership: 100% by AFK Sistema subsidiary Lesinvest
Zavodskaya Str., 1
186420 Segezha, Karelia
Russia
Phone: (7) 81431 43311/34420/34645/34989
Fax: (7) 81431 42663/34222

Email: office@scbk.ru
Web Address: www.scbk.ru
Personnel:
Gen. Dir.: Aleksandr Uvarov
Phone: (7) 81431 43311/34420/34645/34989
Fax: (7) 81431 34340
Tech. Dir.: Alexander Ivanov
Phone: (7) 81431 43311/34420/34645/34989
Finan. Dir.: Lilia Zhigalova
Phone: (7) 81431 43311/34420/34645/34989
Pulp Div. Mgr.: Vladimir Nokhrin
Phone: (7) 81431 43311/34420/34645/34989
Paper Div. Mgr.: Alexei Shevtsov
Phone: (7) 81431 43311/34420/34645/34989
Commun. Mgr.: Nikolay Gabalov
Phone: (7) 81431 34024
Email: smi@scbk.ru
Total Employees of Company: 3,600
Total Employees at this Location: 3,600
Type of Operation: Pulp mill, Paper mill
Pulp Grades and Capacities:
Total pulp capacity: 245,466 mt/y
Chemical Pulp: 245,466 mt/y
Pulp Mill Data:
Chemical Pulping Systems:
Continuous digesters: 2
Pulp Lines: 4
Chemical Recovery Equipment:
Evaporator lines: 1
Recovery boilers: 3
Lime Kiln
Paper/Paperboard Grades and Capacities:
Total paper and paperboard capacity: 235,000 mt/y
Packaging papers: 235,000 mt/y
Paper and Paperboard Mill Data:
Paper Machines: 2
No. 9, fourdrinier, total capacity 90,000 mt/y, Trim width 6.3 m, Packaging papers
No. 10, fourdrinier, total capacity 145,000 mt/y, Trim width 6.3 m, Packaging papers
Energy Data:
Power boilers: 1
Steam turbines: 6 at 54 MW
Electrical demand for mill: 594 MWh/D

ⓒⓜSelenginsky Pulp & Board Mill
Selenginsk Mill
Ownership: 66% by Baikal Forest Company, 34% by Continental Management Plc
671247 Selenginsk, Buryatia Republic
Russia
Phone: (7) 30138 74579
Fax: (7) 30138 74175
Email: sckk@sckkbur.ru,
sbyt@sckkbur.ru
Web Address: www.sckkbur.ru
Personnel:
Gen. Dir.: Deeva Liliya
Phone: (7) 30138 74579
Fax: (7) 30138 74175
Email: sckk@sckkbur.ru
Logist. & Supply Dir.: Alexandr Mikhaylovich Lukyanov
Phone: (7) 30138 73975
Fax: (7) 30138 74175
Email: LAlexandrM@sckkbur.ru
Head of Pub. Rel.: Snezhana Viktorovna Lukyanova
Phone: (7) 30138 74551
Fax: (7) 30138 74579
Email: LSnejanaV@sckkbur.ru
Total Employees at this Location: 2,150
Type of Operation: Pulp mill, Paperboard mill
Pulp Grades and Capacities:
Total pulp capacity: 125,028 mt/y
Chemical Pulp: 122,833 mt/y
Recycled Pulping: 2,195 mt/y
Pulp Mill Data:
Chemical Pulping Systems:
Batch digesters: 10
Chemical Recovery Equipment:

Russia

Evaporator lines: 1
Recovery boilers: 1
Lime Kiln
Paper/Paperboard Grades and Capacities:
Total paper and paperboard capacity: 120,000 mt/y
Packaging papers: 10,000 mt/y
Linerboard: 110,000 mt/y
Paper and Paperboard Mill Data:
Paper Machines: 1
No. 1, fourdrinier, total capacity 120,000 mt/y, Trim width 4.2 m, Packaging papers, Linerboard
Coating Machines: 1
PM1, off machine
Energy Data:
Power boilers: 3
Steam turbines
Electrical demand for mill: 292 MWh/D

ⓗⓜSerpukhovskaya Paper Mill
Serpukhov Mill
Ownership: 100% by mill staff
Proletarskaya Str., 134
142201 Serpukhov, Moscow Region
Russia
  Phone: (7) 4967 727867 / 725438
  Fax: (7) 4967 727867 / 725438
  Email: serp@voskhod-group.ru
Personnel:
  Gen. Dir.: Oleg Petrovich Lazarev
  Deputy Prod. Dir.: Vladimir Vasilievich Ilyuxin
  Chief Acc.: Svetlana Yurievna Pavlova
  Com.Dir.: Elena Maksimova
  Phone: (7) 926 5303906
  Email: maksimova@voskhod-group.ru
  Sales Mngr.: Elena Larkina
  Phone: (7) 926 5303908
  Email: larkina@voskhod-group.ru
Total Employees at this Location: 150
Type of Operation: Paper mill
Paper/Paperboard Grades and Capacities:
Total paper and paperboard capacity: 39,000 mt/y
Uncoated woodfree/freesheet: 7,000 mt/y
Coated woodfree/freesheet: 2,000 mt/y
Specialty and industrial
Paper and Paperboard Mill Data:
Paper Machines: 4
BM 1, total capacity 7,000 mt/y
BM 2, total capacity 7,000 mt/y
PM 1, total capacity 10,000 mt/y, Trim width 1.2 m
PM 2, total capacity 15,000 mt/y, Trim width 1.8 m

ⓗⓜSeverny Kommunar
Sivinskiy Mill
Ownership: mill staff
Lenina Str., 13
617252 Severny Kommunar, Sivinskiy rayon, Perm Region
Russia
  Phone: (7) 34277 23100/23309/23430
  Fax: (7) 34277 23100/23309
  Email: severkommunar@list.ru
Personnel:
  Depty. Dir.: Daniil Sergeefvich Vlasov
  Phone: (7) 3422 101922
  Chief Eng.: Zinaida Nikolaevna Korbunova
  Phone: (7) 34277 23100/23309/23430
Total Employees at this Location: 200
Type of Operation: Paperboard mill
Paper/Paperboard Grades and Capacities:
Total paper and paperboard capacity: 7,200 mt/y
Boxboard/cartonboard: 7,200 mt/y
Paper and Paperboard Mill Data:
Paper Machines: 4
No. 1, total capacity 1,800 mt/y, Trim width 2.4 m, Boxboard/cartonboard
No. 2, total capacity 1,800 mt/y, Trim width 2.4 m, Boxboard/cartonboard
k206, total capacity 1,800 mt/y, Trim width 2.4 m, Boxboard/cartonboard
k217, total capacity 1,800 mt/y, Trim width 2.4 m, Boxboard/cartonboard

ⓗSFT Group
Trubnikovsky per. 13, bldg. 1
121069 Moscow
Russia
  Phone: (7) 495 925 7656
  Fax: (7) 495 925 7650
  Email: secretar@sftgroup.ru
  Web Address: www.sftgroup.ru
Personnel:
  Chairman of Advisory Board: Anatoly Schteinberg
  Phone: (7) 495 925 7656
  Fax: (7) 495 925 7650
  CEO: Stepan Khomyakov
  Phone: (7) 495 925 7656
  Fax: (7) 495 925 7650
  Email: stepan.khomyakov@sftgroup.ru
  First Depty. CEO: Anatoliy Safronov
  Phone: (7) 495 925 7656
  Fax: (7) 495 925 7650
  Email: anatoly.safronov@sftgroup.ru
  Gen. Mgr.: Hamsters Stepan A.
  Phone: (7) 495 925 7656
  Fax: (7) 495 925 7650
  Email: Stepan.Khomyakov@sftgroup.ru
  Tech. Dir.: Vishnjakov Oleg
  Phone: (7) 495 925 7656
  Fax: (7) 495 925 7650
  Email: Oleg.Vishniakov@sftgroup.ru
  Finan. Dir.: Krupin Sergey
  Phone: (7) 495 925 7656
  Fax: (7) 495 925 7650
  Email: sergey.krupina@sftgroup.ru
  HR Dir.: Oksana Smirnova
  Phone: (7) 495 925 7656
  Fax: (7) 495 925 7650
  Email: o.smirnova@sftgroup.ru
  Dir. of Investments: Roman A. Steinberg
  Phone: (7) 495 925 7656
  Fax: (7) 495 925 7650
  Email: Roman.Steinberg@sftgroup.ru
  Bus. Mgr.: Smirnova Tatiana V.
  Phone: (7) 495 925 7656
  Fax: (7) 495 925 7650
  Email: T.Smirnova@sftgroup.ru
Total Employees of Company: 2,400
Total Employees at this Location: 10
Mill Locations:
Aleksinskaya Board & Paper Mill, CJSC, Aleksin Mill, Aleksin Square Pobedy 19 a, 301340 Aleksin, Russia, Capacity: 120,000 mt/y, (Paperboard mill)
  Phone: (7) 48753 41888/42653
  Fax: (7) 48753 42590
  Email: fabrika@aleksinkarton.ru
Kamenskaya Board & Paper Mill, OJSC, Kuvshinovo Mill, Oktyabrskaya Str., 5, 172110 Kuvshinovo, Russia, Capacity: 292,000 mt/y, (Paper mill, Paperboard mill)
  Phone: (7) 48257 45246
  Fax: (7) 48257 44456/45392
  Email: kbkf@kbkf.ru
Kartontara, CJSC, Maykop Mill, per. Profsoyuzny 2, 385012 Maykop, Russia, Capacity: 105,000 mt/y, (Pulp mill, Paperboard mill)
  Phone: (7) 8772 548455
  Fax: (7) 8772 548820
  Email: secretary@kartontara.ru

ⓗⓜSokolsky Pulp & Paper Mill
Sokol Mill
Ownership: 100% by AFK Sistema subsidiary Lesinvest
Sovetsky Prosp., 8
162130 Sokol, Vologodskaya obl.
Russia
  Phone: (7) 81733 92100/92694
  Fax: (7) 81733 22244
  Email: delo@sokolmill.ru, sbit@sokolmill.ru
  Web Address: www.sokolmill.ru
Personnel:
  Gen. Dir.: Ekaterina Andreevna Kosova
  Phone: (7) 81733 22535
  Email: delo@sokolmill.ru
  Chief Eng.: Yuriy Aleksandrovich Kuzmin
  Phone: (7) 81733 22996
  Commer. Dir.: Sergey Vasilyevich Sokolov
  Phone: (7) 81733 23674
  Oper. Mgr.: Evgeniy Alexandrovich Kuzminov
  Phone: (7) 81733 92555
  Finan. Dir.: Svetlana Vladimirovna Kharakh
  Phone: (7) 81733 92100/92694
  Com.Dep.Dir.: Evgeniy Vladimirovich Gomzyakov
  Email: sbit@sokolmill.ru
Total Employees at this Location: 600
Type of Operation: Pulp mill, Paper mill
Pulp Grades and Capacities:
Total pulp capacity: 37,521 mt/y
Chemical Pulp: 37,521 mt/y
Pulp Mill Data:
Chemical Pulping Systems:
Batch digesters: 6
Paper/Paperboard Grades and Capacities:
Total paper and paperboard capacity: 36,000 mt/y
Packaging papers: 36,000 mt/y
Paper and Paperboard Mill Data:
Paper Machines: 1
No. 10, fourdrinier, total capacity 36,000 mt/y, Trim width 2.52 m, Packaging papers
Energy Data:
Power boilers: 8
Steam turbines: 5 at 6 MW
Electrical demand for mill: 93 MWh/D

ⓗⓜJSC Solikamskbumprom
Solikamsk Mill
Ownership: 100% by mill staff
Kommunisticheskaya Str., 21
618540 Solikamsk, Perm Region
Russia
  Phone: (7) 34253 64663
  Fax: (7) 34253 47433/48130
  Email: pochta@solbum.ru
  Web Address: www.solbum.ru
Personnel:
  Pres.: Victor Ivanovich Baranov
  Phone: (7) 34253 64663
  Fax: (7) 34253 47433/48130
  Head of Mill Dev.: Yuriy Vezner
  Phone: (7) 34253 64895
  Commer. Dir.: Anatoly Sergeevich Naumov
  Phone: (7) 34253 64448
  Commun. Dir.: Nina Alexandrovna Musikhina
  Phone: (7) 34253 64743
  Prod. Dir.: Aleksandr Mikhaylovich Litvinenko
  Phone: (7) 34253 64656
  Legal & Corp. Relation Dir.: Valerij Alexandrovich Pisotskij
  Phone: (7) 34253 64663
  Fax: (7) 34253 47433/48130
  HR Dir.: Evgeniya Petrovna Pisotskaya
  Phone: (7) 34253 64663
  Fax: (7) 34253 47433/48130
  Finan. & Econ. Dir.: Olga Vasilievna Tokhtueva
  Phone: (7) 34253 64663
  Fax: (7) 34253 47433/48130
Total Employees at this Location: 3,000
Type of Operation: Paper mill
Pulp Grades and Capacities:
Total pulp capacity: 585,144 mt/y
Chemical Pulp: 117,029 mt/y
Mechanical Pulp: 468,115 mt/y
Pulp Mill Data:
Chemical Pulping Systems:
Batch digesters: 10
Mechanical Pulping Systems:
Conventional grinders
TMP systems

Russia

Pulp Lines: 3
Bleach Plant Systems: 2
Sulfite
Chemical Recovery Equipment:
Evaporator lines: 1
Recovery boilers: 1
Paper/Paperboard Grades and Capacities:
Total paper and paperboard capacity: 560,000 mt/y
Newsprint: 560,000 mt/y
Paper and Paperboard Mill Data:
Stock Preparation:
Refiners: 2
Paper Machines: 4
No. 1, DuoFormer D, total capacity 155,000 mt/y, Trim width 6.7 m, Newsprint
No. 2, DuoFormer D, total capacity 155,000 mt/y, Trim width 6.7 m, Newsprint
No. 3, fourdrinier, total capacity 125,000 mt/y, Trim width 6.7 m, Newsprint
No. 4, fourdrinier, total capacity 125,000 mt/y, Trim width 6.7 m, Newsprint
Energy Data:
Power boilers: 1
TMP Reboiler: 1
Steam turbines: 1
Electrical demand for mill: 3,759 MWh/D

ⓘSolombalales Managing Company
Ownership: 7.33% by Anna Milchenko, 6.66% by Elena Malkova, 6.77% by OOO Central Investment Company, 6.77% by OOO KART, 10.06% by OOO Norwood, OOO Solombalales, 17.52% by OOO YuristKonsult, 13.33% by Vladimir Nechaev
Kirovskaya Str., 4
163059 Arkhangelsk
Russia
  Phone: (7) 8182 679-679
  Fax: (7) 8182 679-700
  Email: office@soles.ru
  Web Address: www.solombala.com
Personnel:
Chmn. of Bd. of Directors: Nikolai Lvov
  Phone: (7) 8182 679-679
  Fax: (7) 8182 679-700
Chmn. of the Bd. Pulp & Paper Mill: Alexander PLastinin
  Phone: (7) 8182 679-679
  Fax: (7) 8182 679-700
Gen. Dir.: Ivan Albertovich Borodin
  Phone: (7) 8182 679-679
  Fax: (7) 8182 679-700
Dir. Pulp & Paper Division: Anatoly P. Dratchev
  Phone: (7) 8182 679-679
  Fax: (7) 8182 679-700
Dir. of Timber-Harvesting: Vladimir Drochkov
  Phone: (7) 8182 679-679
  Fax: (7) 8182 679-700
Finan. Dir.: Dmitriy Anatolyevich Drachev
  Phone: (7) 8182 679-679
  Fax: (7) 8182 679-700
Asst. Gen. Dir., Commer. Affairs: Dmitry S. Milchenko
  Phone: (7) 8182 679-679
  Fax: (7) 8182 679-700
Mill Locations:
Solombalsky Pulp & Paper Mill, Arkhangelsk Mill, Kirovskaya str., 4, 163059 Arkhangelsk, Russia, Capacity: 8,200 mt/y, (Pulp mill, Paper mill)
  Phone: (7) 8182 679 142/394/110/125
  Fax: (7) 8182 679 700/696/697/230430
  Email: office@soles.ru

ⓘSolombalsky Pulp & Paper Mill
Arkhangelsk Mill
Mill is closed (From January 2013 Solombalsky pulp paper mill closed due to unfavorable market conditions, as well as technological challenges. At present there are only shop biological treatment of industrial wastewater, as well as some support services at the site.)

Ownership: Solombalales Managing Company
Kirovskaya str., 4
163059 Arkhangelsk
Russia
  Phone: (7) 8182 679 142/394/110/125
  Fax: (7) 8182 679 700/696/697/230430
  Email: office@soles.ru
  Web Address: www.solombala.com
Personnel:
Gen. Dir., Chrm.: Anatoly Drachev
  Phone: (7) 8182 679679
Gen. Dir. of Solombalales: Ivan Albertovich Borodin
  Phone: (7) 8182 679 142/394/110/125
CEO: Alexandr Viktorovich Plastinin
  Phone: (7) 8182 679 142/394/110/125
Commer. Dir.: Dmitry Milchenko
  Phone: (7) 8182 679640
Prod. Mgr.: Aleksandr Vyacheslavovich Antrushin
  Phone: (7) 8182 679113
Maint. Mgr.: Viktor Svetlakov
  Phone: (7) 8182 679 142/394/110/125
Env. Dir.: Tatyana Drobeshkina
  Phone: (7) 8182 299622
PR: Alexandr Perepelkin
  Phone: (7) 8182 679 101
  Fax: (7) 8182 679 700
  Email: soles@list.ru
Total Employees at this Location: 2,243
Type of Operation: Pulp mill, Paper mill
Pulp Grades and Capacities:
Total pulp capacity: 234,701 mt/y
Pulp available for market: 220,000 mt/y
Chemical Pulp: 234,701 mt/y
Pulp Mill Data:
Chemical Pulping Systems:
Batch digesters: 6
Continuous digesters: 2
Pulp Lines: 1
Chemical Recovery Equipment:
Evaporator lines: 1
Recovery boilers: 2
Pulp Dryers:
Air Float dryers 1
Paper/Paperboard Grades and Capacities:
Total paper and paperboard capacity: 8,200 mt/y
Packaging papers: 8,200 mt/y
Paper and Paperboard Mill Data:
Paper Machines: 1
No. 1, fourdrinier, Yankee dryer, total capacity 8,200 mt/y, Trim width 2.52 m, Packaging papers
Energy Data:
Power boilers: 5
Steam turbines: 4 at 36.0 MW
Electrical demand for mill: 496 MWh/D

ⓘⓜSt. Petersburg Paper Mill Goznak
St. Petersburg Mill
Ownership: 100% by state
Nab. Reki Fontanki 144
190103 St. Petersburg
Russia
  Phone: (7) 812 331 78 88/99/ 2510034
  Fax: (7) 812 2514646
  Email: goznak@goznak.spb.ru,
  marketing@goznak.spb.ru
  Web Address: www.goznak.spb.ru
Personnel:
Dir.: Aleksandr Olegovich Balunov
  Phone: (7) 812 331 78 88/2510034
Chief Eng.: Mikhail Evgenyevich Yakuba
  Phone: (7) 812 2512718
Commer. Dir.: Nikolay Mikhailovich Kudryashov
  Phone: (7) 812 2515973
Mktg. Dir.: Aleksey Vladimirovich Filippov
  Phone: (7) 812 331 78 88/2510034
Chief Account.: Vladimir Mikhaylovich Sharshakov
  Phone: (7) 812 331 78 88/2510034
Chief Technologist: Alexandr Ivanovich Pianykh
  Phone: (7) 812 331 78 88/2510034

Chief Technologist: Vitaliy Artemov
  Phone: (7) 812 331 78 88/2510034
Depty. Dir. of Prod.: Vitaliy Artemov
  Phone: (7) 812 331 78 88/2510034
Depty. Dir. of Prod.: Evgeniy Rasikhovich Khabibulin
  Phone: (7) 812 331 78 88/2510034
Depty. Dir. of Sls.: Pavel Karpushev
  Phone: (7) 812 331 78 88/2510034
Depty. Dir. of Quality: Alina Mikhaylovna Neverovich
  Phone: (7) 812 331 78 88/2510034
Total Employees at this Location: 1,100
Type of Operation: Paper mill
Paper/Paperboard Grades and Capacities:
Total paper and paperboard capacity: 24,000 mt/y
Uncoated woodfree/freesheet: 10,000 mt/y
Coated woodfree/freesheet: 4,000 mt/y
Specialty and industrial
Boxboard/cartonboard
Paper and Paperboard Mill Data:
Paper Machines: 3
PM 1, (Former Type: Rundsieb/Rundsiebformer.), Trim width 1.68 m
PM 2, Trim width 2.4 m
PM 3, fourdrinier, Trim width 2.54 m
Coating Machines: 1
No. 1

ⓘSukhonsky Pulp and Paper Mill
Sokol Mill
Ownership: 100% by Consolidated Paper Mills PLC
129 Sovetskaya Str.
162135 Sokol, Vologodskaya obl.
Russia
  Phone: (7) 81733 32687/32877 / 31052
  Fax: (7) 81733 31892 / 32203
  Email: scbk@suhona.com,
  com-paper@yandex.ru
  Web Address: www.ukobf.com,
  www.suhona.com
Personnel:
Gen. Dir.: Dmitry Alexandrovich Dulkin
  Phone: (7) 81733 32687/32877
Commer. & Logistics Dir.: Olga Ivanovna Yaroshkina
  Phone: (7) 495 514 0324
Exec. Dir.: Lyudmila Anatolyevna Yuzhaninova
  Phone: (7) 81733 32687/32877
Technologist: Igor Lavrov
  Phone: (7) 81733 32687/32877
Prod. Dir.: Olga Ivanovna Blinushova
  Phone: (7) 81733 32687/32877
Tech. Dir.: Yuriy Alexandrovich Blinushov
  Phone: (7) 81733 32687/32877
Exec. Prod. Dir: Anna Romova
  Phone: (7) 81733 32877
Total Employees at this Location: 1,069
Type of Operation: Paperboard mill
Pulp Grades and Capacities:
Total pulp capacity: 100,781 mt/y
Recycled Pulping: 100,781 mt/y
Paper/Paperboard Grades and Capacities:
Total paper and paperboard capacity: 100,000 mt/y
Linerboard: 66,000 mt/y
Corrugating medium/fluting: 34,000 mt/y
Paper and Paperboard Mill Data:
Paper Machines: 2
No. 1, fourdrinier, total capacity 44,000 mt/y, Trim width 3.15 m, Corrugating medium/fluting, Linerboard
No. 2, fourdrinier, total capacity 56,000 mt/y, Trim width 2.52 m, Corrugating medium/fluting, Linerboard
Energy Data:
Power boilers: 2
Steam turbines: 4
Electrical demand for mill: 168 MWh/D

ⓘⓜZAO Suoyarvi Paperboard Mill
Suoyarvi Mill
Nuhi Idrisova Str., 24
186870 Suoyarvi, Karelia
Russia

Russia

Phone: (7) 81457 53605/53038
Email: suokf@mail.ru
Personnel:
Dir. Gen.: Yuriy Ivanovich Ivanov
Phone: (7) 81457 53605/53038
Mill Mgr.: Viktor Petrovich Savelyev
Phone: (7) 81457 53605/921 4582121
Prod. Dir.: Aleksandr Ivanovich Vorobyev
Phone: (7) 81457 53605/53038
Email: aiv4444@mail.ru
Total Employees at this Location: 230
Type of Operation: Paperboard mill
Pulp Grades and Capacities:
Total pulp capacity: 24,339 mt/y
Recycled Pulping: 24,339 mt/y
Pulp Mill Data:
Recycled Fiber Treatment Lines:
Recycled packaging pulping lines: 1
Paper/Paperboard Grades and Capacities:
Total paper and paperboard capacity: 24,000 mt/y
Boxboard/cartonboard: 24,000 mt/y
Paper and Paperboard Mill Data:
Paper Machines: 1
No. 2, cylinder, total capacity 24,000 mt/y, Trim width 2.1 m, Boxboard/cartonboard
Energy Data:
Power boilers
Electrical demand for mill: 28 MWh/D

ⓘSyassky Pulp & Paper Mill
Kirochnaya Str. 11
191014 St. Petersburg
Russia
Phone: (7) 812 301 9100, 813 63 52551, 813 63 56444
Fax: (7) 813 63 53052
Email: market@syas.ru, sales@syas.ru
Web Address: www.syas.ru
Personnel:
Sls. Mgr.: Alexey Makarov
Phone: (7) 812 301 9100
Fax: (7) 813 63 53052
Email: alexxx_m@mail.ru
Proj. Tech. Mgr.: Dmitry Epifanov
Phone: (7) 813 63 52551
Fax: (7) 813 63 53052

ⓘⓜSyassky Pulp & Paper Mill
Syasstroy Mill
Ownership: LTR (majority of shares)
Zavodskaya Str., 1
187420 Syasstroy, Volkhovskiy rayon, Leningrad Region
Russia
Phone: (7) 81363 56444/56218
Fax: (7) 81363 53080/52388
Email: sppm@syas.ru, market@syas.ru
Web Address: www.syas.ru
Personnel:
Chmn.: Alexandr Semenovich Utevskiy
Phone: (7) 81363 52488
Exec. & Gen. Dir.: Lyudmila Valentinovna Epifanova
Phone: (7) 81263 56534
Finan. Mgr.: Kirill Vladimirovich Rogal
Phone: (7) 81363 52812
Chief Eng.: Sergey Valentinovich Katin
Phone: (7) 81363 56677
Email: supply@syas.ru
Total Employees at this Location: 2,400
Type of Operation: Pulp mill, Paper mill
Pulp Grades and Capacities:
Total pulp capacity: 205,000 mt/y
Pulp available for market: 115,330 mt/y
Chemical Pulp: 120,000 mt/y
Mechanical Pulp: 85,000 mt/y
Pulp Mill Data:
Chemical Pulping Systems:
Batch digesters: 7
Mechanical Pulping Systems:
Conventional grinders: 1
Bleach Plant Systems: 2
Chemical Pulping System
Mechanical Pulping System, Type: CMP, Sequence: P
Pulp Dryers:
Fourdriniers 1, Fourdriniers 1, Fourdriniers 1
Paper/Paperboard Grades and Capacities:
Total paper and paperboard capacity: 85,000 mt/y
Tissue: 85,000 mt/y
Paper and Paperboard Mill Data:
Paper Machines: 3
No. 2, crescent former, Yankee dryer, total capacity 38,000 mt/y, Trim width 4.2 m, Tissue
No. 3, fourdrinier, Yankee dryer, total capacity 20,000 mt/y, Trim width 4.2 m, Tissue
No. 5, crescent former, Yankee dryer, total capacity 27,000 mt/y, Trim width 2.75 m, Tissue
Energy Data:
Power boilers
Electrical demand for mill: 754 MWh/D

ⓜSyktyvkar Tissue Group, LLC
Syktyvkar Mill
Pr. Bumazhnikov 4
167026 Syktyvkar
Russia
Phone: (7) 8212 620220/0224
Fax: (7) 8212 620222
Email: mail@sgbi.ru
Web Address: www.sgbi.ru
Personnel:
Gen. Dir.: Mark Abramovich Reznik
Phone: (7) 8212 620220/0224
Finan. Dir.: Tatyana Nikolaevna Sokolova
Phone: (7) 8212 620220/0224
Prod. Dir.: Anatoly Aleksandrovich Cherniyatiev
Phone: (7) 8212 620224
Total Employees at this Location: 230
Type of Operation: Paper mill
Pulp Grades and Capacities:
Total pulp capacity: 21,298 mt/y
Recycled Pulping: 21,298 mt/y
Pulp Mill Data:
Recycled Fiber Treatment Lines:
Pulpers: 1
Paper/Paperboard Grades and Capacities:
Total paper and paperboard capacity: 50,000 mt/y
Tissue: 50,000 mt/y
Paper and Paperboard Mill Data:
Paper Machines: 2
No. 1, fourdrinier, Yankee dryer, total capacity 20,000 mt/y, Trim width 2.65 m, Tissue
No. 2, Advantage DCT 100, Yankee dryer, total capacity 30,000 mt/y, Trim width 2.7 m, Tissue
Energy Data:
Power boilers: 1
Electrical demand for mill: 138 MWh/D

ⓘSyktyvkar Tissue Group, LLC
Ownership: Mir Tissue Ltd.
Pr. Bumazhnikov 4
167026 Syktyvkar
Russia
Phone: (7) 8212 620220/0224
Fax: (7) 8212 620222
Web Address: www.sgbi.ru
Personnel:
Gen. Dir.: Mark Abramovich Reznik
Phone: (7) 8212 620220
Fax: (7) 8212 620222
Finan. Dir.: Tatyana Nikolaevna Sokolova
Phone: (7) 8212 620220
Fax: (7) 8212 620222
Prod. Dir.: Anatoly Aleksandrovich Cherniyatiev
Phone: (7) 8212 620220
Fax: (7) 8212 620222
Total Employees of Company: 430
Mill Locations:
Syktyvkar Tissue Group, LLC, Syktyvkar Mill, Pr. Bumazhnikov 4, 167026 Syktyvkar, Russia, Capacity: 50,000 mt/y, (Paper mill)
Phone: (7) 8212 620220/0224
Fax: (7) 8212 620222
Email: mail@sgbi.ru
Syktyvkar Tissue Group, LLC, Semibratovo Mill, Semibratovo, Russia, Capacity: 40,000 mt/y, (Paper mill)
Phone: (7) 4853 691600
Email: mail@sgbi.ru

ⓘⓜSyktyvkar Tissue Group, LLC
Semibratovo Mill
Ownership: Mir Tissue Ltd.
Semibratovo, Yaroslavl obl.
Russia
Phone: (7) 4853 691600
Email: mail@sgbi.ru
Web Address: www.sgbi.ru
Total Employees of Company: 430
Type of Operation: Paper mill
Mill Locations:
Syktyvkar Tissue Group, LLC, Syktyvkar Mill, Pr. Bumazhnikov 4, 167026 Syktyvkar, Russia, Capacity: 50,000 mt/y, (Paper mill)
Phone: (7) 8212 620220/0224
Fax: (7) 8212 620222
Email: mail@sgbi.ru
Pulp Mill Data:
Recycled Fiber Treatment Lines:
Recycled packaging pulping lines: 1 at 40,000
Paper/Paperboard Grades and Capacities:
Total paper and paperboard capacity: 40,000 mt/y
Tissue: 40,000 mt/y
Paper and Paperboard Mill Data:
Paper Machines: 1
PM 1, (started September 2014), Advantage DCT 100 HS, Yankee dryer, total capacity 40,000 mt/y, Trim width 2.7 m, Tissue

ⓘⓜOAO Technicheskaya Bumaga
Rybinskiy rayon Mill
ul. Molodezhnaya 20, pos. Iskra Oktyabrya
152973 Rybinskiy rayon, Yaroslavl obl.
Russia
Phone: (7) 4855 236181-3
Fax: (7) 4855 287951
Email: techbum@techbum.ru, mail@techbum.ru
Web Address: www.techbum.ru
Personnel:
Gen. Dir.: Dmitry Anastasovich Romanov
Phone: (7) 4855 236183
Sls. Dir.: Vyacheslav Mikhaylovich Smyslov
Phone: (7) 4855 236185 / 8-910 811 43 43
Commer. Dir.: Alexander Ivanovich Murashov
Phone: (7) 4855 236184 / 8 901 999 62 09
Total Employees at this Location: 180
Type of Operation: Paper mill, Paperboard mill
Mill Locations:
Yaroslavl Paper ZAO, Yaroslavl Mill, prospekt Oktyabrya 85., 150044 Yaroslavl, Russia, Capacity: 50,000 mt/y, (Paperboard mill)
Phone: (7) 4852 73 53 13
Fax: (7) 4852 73 53 13
Paper/Paperboard Grades and Capacities:
Total paper and paperboard capacity: 28,000 mt/y
Packaging papers: 6,500 mt/y
Linerboard: 13,000 mt/y
Corrugating medium/fluting: 8,500 mt/y
Boxboard/cartonboard
Paper and Paperboard Mill Data:
Paper Machines: 2
No. 1, total capacity 10,000 mt/y, Packaging papers, Linerboard, Boxboard/cartonboard
No. 2, (started up in September 2011), fourdrinier, total capacity 18,000 mt/y, Trim width 2.52 m
Energy Data:
Power boilers: 2

Russia

ⓜOOO Tissue-Bumaga
Krasnodar Mill
Putevaya Str. 68
350038 Krasnodar
Russia
  Phone: (7) 861 274 18 36 / 0267
  Fax: (7) 861 274 06 15/43/13
  Email: tissu-bumaga@rambler.ru
  Web Address: tissue-bumaga.ru
Personnel:
  Gen. Dir.: Kirill Gennadievich Minin
  Phone: (7) 861 274 0615
  Tech. Dir.: Alexey Gennadievich Alexandri'n
  Phone: (7) 861 274 18 36
  Depty. Dir.: Alla Petrovna Kliop
  Phone: (7) 861 274 18 36
  Sales Mngr.: Vladimir Nikolaevich Ryabenko
Type of Operation: Paper mill
Paper/Paperboard Grades and Capacities:
  Total paper and paperboard capacity: 5,000 mt/y
  Tissue: 5,000 mt/y
Paper and Paperboard Mill Data:
Paper Machines: 1
  PM 1, Yankee dryer, total capacity 5,000 mt/y, Trim width 2.8 m, Tissue
Energy Data:
  Power boilers: 1
  Combustion turbines: 1

ⓜTolyatti Paper Mill (TPM)
Tolyatti Mill
Mill is under construction (scheduled to start up in late 2015)
Tolyatti, near Samara
Russia
Type of Operation: Paperboard mill

ⓜOOO Triton-M
Tver Mill
Promyshlenny proezd, 4
170028 Tver
Russia
  Phone: (7) 4822 430222/430333
  Fax: (7) 4822 430333/430222
  Email: ale-belov@mail.ru
  Web Address: www.tritonm.ru
Personnel:
  Gen. Dir.: Anatoliy Egorovich Belov
  Phone: (7) 4822 430222/430333
  Mgr.: Alexandr Anatolievich Belov
  Phone: (7) 4822 430222/430333
  Prod. Dir.: Viktor Ivanovich Ushkov
  Phone: (7) 4822 430222/430333
  Sls. & Mktg. Mgr.: Olga Valerievna Zabolueva
  Phone: (7) 4822 430222/430333
  Chief Account.: Olga Sergeevna Smirnova
  Phone: (7) 4822 430222/430333
Total Employees at this Location: 140
Type of Operation: Paper mill
Pulp Grades and Capacities:
  Total pulp capacity: 7,447 mt/y
  Recycled Pulping: 7,447 mt/y
Pulp Mill Data:
  Recycled Fiber Treatment Lines:
  Pulpers: 1
Paper/Paperboard Grades and Capacities:
  Total paper and paperboard capacity: 7,000 mt/y
  Tissue: 7,000 mt/y
Paper and Paperboard Mill Data:
Paper Machines: 1
  No. 1, fourdrinier, Yankee dryer, total capacity 7,000 mt/y, Trim width 2.8 m, Tissue
Energy Data:
  Power boilers: 3
  Electrical demand for mill: 21 MWh/D

ⓘⓜOjsc 'Troitskaya Paper Mill'
Troitskaya Mill
Ownership: Continental Management Plc
Mayakovskogo Str., 1
249834 Kondrovo, Kaluga Region
Russia
  Phone: (7) 48434 33221/32504/46238/33743
  Fax: (7) 48434 32504/33221/46238
  Email: export@tbf.ru, tbf@kaluga.ru
  Web Address: www.tbf.ru
Personnel:
  Gen. Dir.: Konstantin Vladimirovich Koltsov
  Phone: (7) 48434 33 743
  Fax: (7) 48434 32 504
  CFO: Irina E. Belin
  Phone: (7) 48434 32 323
  Fax: (7) 48434 32 504
  Tech. Dir.: Vitaliy Vasilievich Lemtse
  Phone: (7) 48434 32 843
  Fax: (7) 48434 32 504
  Chief Technologist: Lyudmila Pavlovna Berezina
  Phone: (7) 48434 32 054
  Fax: (7) 48434 32 504
  Purch. & Logist. Dir.: Eugene V. Platonov
  Phone: (7) 48434 33 233
  Fax: (7) 48434 32 504
Total Employees at this Location: 300
Type of Operation: Paper mill
Paper/Paperboard Grades and Capacities:
  Total paper and paperboard capacity: 20,000 mt/y
  Specialty and industrial: 20,000 mt/y
Paper and Paperboard Mill Data:
Paper Machines: 2
  No. 1, fourdrinier, total capacity 26,000 mt/y, Trim width 2.52 m, Specialty and industrial
  No. 2, fourdrinier, total capacity 20,000 mt/y, Trim width 2.52 m, Specialty and industrial
Energy Data:
  Power boilers
  Electrical demand for mill: 59 MWh/D

ⓘⓜTurinsky Pulp & Paper Mill
Turinsk Mill
Ownership: 100% by mill staff
Dzerhinskogo Str., 2
623900 Turinsk, Sverdlovskaya obl.
Russia
  Phone: (7) 34349 24452
  Fax: (7) 34349 24375
  Email: info@tcbz.uraltc.ru, mar@tcbz.uralct.ru, sdv@tcbz.uraltc.ru
  Web Address: www.tcbz.ru
Personnel:
  Gen. Dir.: Nikolai Nikolaevich Gerasimov
  Phone: (7) 34349 23747
  Fax: (7) 34349 24375
  Email: komdir@tcbz.uraltc.ru
  Dpty. Gen. Dir. - Commerce: Marushenko Alexander
  Phone: (7) 34349 24030
  Fax: (7) 34349 24375
  Email: sbyt@tcbz.uraltc.ru
  Head of Procurement: Nikolay Nikolaevich Urusov
  Phone: (7) 34349 21039
  Fax: (7) 34349 24375
  Email: ol@tcbz.uraltc.ru
  Dpty. Gen. Dir. - Exec. Dir.: Vadim Andreevich Bychkov
  Phone: (7) 34349 24302
  Fax: (7) 34349 24375
Total Employees at this Location: 1,500
Type of Operation: Pulp mill, Paper mill
Pulp Grades and Capacities:
  Total pulp capacity: 20,627 mt/y
  Chemical Pulp: 20,627 mt/y
Pulp Mill Data:
  Chemical Pulping Systems:
  Batch digesters: 4
  Bleach Plant Systems: 1
  No. 1, Sequence: DEopD
  Chemical Recovery Equipment:
  Evaporator lines: 1
  Recovery boilers: 1
Paper/Paperboard Grades and Capacities:
  Total paper and paperboard capacity: 22,134 mt/y
  Uncoated woodfree/freesheet: 22,134 mt/y
Paper and Paperboard Mill Data:
  Stock Preparation:
  Pulpers: 2
  Refiners: 7
Paper Machines: 1
  No. 2, fourdrinier, total capacity 22,134 mt/y, Trim width 2.52 m, Uncoated woodfree/freesheet
Energy Data:
  Power boilers: 1
  Electrical demand for mill: 70 MWh/D

ⓜZAO Uralskaya Bumaga
Sukhoy Log Mill
Beregovaya Str. 5
624803 Sukhoy Log, Sverdlovskaya obl.
Russia
  Phone: (7) 34373 42 701/42 925 /42614
  Fax: (7) 34373 42 391 /42614
  Email: uralbumaga@list.ru
  Web Address: www.urbum.narod.ru
Personnel:
  Gen. Dir.: Vladislav Viktorovich Chepulanis
  Phone: (7) 34373 42 701/42 925
  Commer. Mgr.: Valentina Vladimirovna Neustroyeva
  Phone: (7) 34373 42925
  Com.Dir: Aleksey Sergeevich Napalkov
  Phone: (7) 34373 32691
  Chief Eng.: Yuriy Demyanenko
  Phone: (7) 34373 42962
Total Employees at this Location: 140
Type of Operation: Paper mill
Paper/Paperboard Grades and Capacities:
  Total paper and paperboard capacity: 4,000 mt/y
  Tissue: 4,000 mt/y
Paper and Paperboard Mill Data:
Paper Machines: 1
  PM 1, total capacity 4,000 mt/y, Trim width 1.67 m, Tissue
Energy Data:
  Power boilers: 2
  Electrical demand for mill: 10 MWh/D

ⓘⓜVelgiiskaya Paper Mill
Borovichi Mill
Ownership: mill staff
Kommunisticheskaya Str., 20
174400 Borovichi, Novgorod Region
Russia
  Phone: (7) 81664 48255/262
  Fax: (7) 81664 48263/255
  Email: bvbf@mail.natm.ru
  Web Address: www.bvbf.natm.ru
Personnel:
  Gen. Dir.: Victor Viktorovich Chernikov
  Phone: (7) 81664 48259
  Fax: (7) 81664 48263
  Chief Eng.: Nikolay Pavlovich Rosadkin
  Phone: (7) 81664 48255
  Fax: (7) 81664 48263
  Commer. Dir.: Alexsey Vasilievich Repichev
  Phone: (7) 81664 48261
  Fax: (7) 81664 48263
  Chief Acc.: Tatiana Yurievna Bessonova
  Phone: (7) 81664 48257
  Fax: (7) 81664 48263
  Mktg. Dir.: Olga Viktorovna Semenova
  Phone: (7) 81664 48262
  Fax: (7) 81664 48263
Total Employees at this Location: 430
Type of Operation: Paper mill
Paper/Paperboard Grades and Capacities:
  Total paper and paperboard capacity: 14,200 mt/y
  Tissue: 13,000 mt/y
  Packaging papers: 200 mt/y
Paper and Paperboard Mill Data:

San Marino

Paper Machines: 2
PM 1, Trim width 2.06 m, Tissue
PM 2, fourdrinier, Trim width 2 m, Tissue
Energy Data:
Electrical demand for mill: 35 MWh/D

ⓗⓜVolga
Balakhna Mill
Ownership: 43% by Alfa-Bank, 56% by Ost-West Group, 1% by other minor shareholders
Gorky Str., 1
606407 Balakhna, Nizhny Novgorod
Russia
 Phone: (7) 831 44 41010
 Fax: (7) 831 44 45393/41011
 Email: info@volga-paper.ru
 Web Address: www.volga-paper.ru
Personnel:
Gen. Dir.: Stanislavski Malyshev
Phone: (7) 831 44 41010
Fax: (7) 831 44 41011
Email: malyshev@volga-paper.ru
Sls. Dir.: Andrey Miller
Phone: (7) 831 44 40366
Fax: (7) 831 44 45393
Email: info@volga-paper.ru
Prod. Dir.: Andrey Gurylev
Phone: (7) 831 44 93979
Fax: (7) 831 44 45393
Email: gurylev@volga-paper.ru
Purch. Mgr.: Natalia Alexandrovna Shainskaya
Phone: (7) 831 449 3273
Fax: (7) 831 44 45393
Email: shainskaya@volga-paper.ru
Chief Eng.: Alexey Kanatal
Phone: (7) 831 44 93445
Fax: (7) 831 44 45393
Email: info@volga-paper.ru
Total Employees at this Location: 2,500
Type of Operation: Paper mill
Pulp Grades and Capacities:
Total pulp capacity: 522,479 mt/y
Mechanical Pulp: 509,972 mt/y
Recycled Pulping: 12,507 mt/y
Pulp Mill Data:
Mechanical Pulping Systems:
Conventional grinders: 1
TMP systems: 4
Bleach Plant Systems: 1
SGW Mechanical Pulp, Sequence: P, Capacity 120,000 admt/y
Recycled Fiber Treatment Lines:
Recycled packaging pulping lines: 1
Paper/Paperboard Grades and Capacities:
Total paper and paperboard capacity: 577,000 mt/y
Newsprint: 565,000 mt/y
Packaging papers: 12,000 mt/y
Paper and Paperboard Mill Data:
Stock Preparation:
Refiners: 10
Paper Machines: 5
No. 4, fourdrinier, total capacity 12,000 mt/y, Trim width 2.34 m, Packaging papers
No. 5, fourdrinier, total capacity 105,000 mt/y, Trim width 5.64 m, Newsprint
No. 6, fourdrinier, total capacity 95,000 mt/y, Trim width 6.72 m, Newsprint
No. 7, fourdrinier, total capacity 95,000 mt/y, Trim width 6.72 m, Newsprint
No. 8, GapFormer, total capacity 270,000 mt/y, Trim width 9.08 m, Newsprint
Energy Data:
Power boilers: 1
TMP Reboiler: 1
Electrical demand for mill: 3,695 MWh/D

ⓗⓜVyborgskaya Cellulose, JSC
Sovetsky Mill
Ownership: 87% by Alcem UK Ltd.
Zavodskaya Str., 2
188918 Vyborg, Sovetsky, Leningrad Region
Russia
 Phone: (7) 81378 73400 / 71848
 Fax: (7) 81378 746 46
 Email: vybcell@beltele.com,
  email@vybcell.ru,
  export@vybcell.ru
 Web Address: vybcell.ru/en.html
Personnel:
Pres.: Aleksey Sergeevich Kazmin
Phone: (7) 81378 73400/219 17/71848
Gen. Dir.: Mikhail Yuryevich Shalayev
Phone: (7) 81378 73400/219 17/71848
Email: vybpulp@yandex.ru
Sls. Dept. Chief: Lyudmila Fyodorovna Kunts
Phone: (7) 81378 73400/219 17/71848
Email: sale@vybcell.ru
Paper Prod. Dir.: Andrey Yalmorovich Kuningas
Phone: (7) 81378 73400/219 17/71848
Pulp Prod. Mgr.: Nikolay Yurievich Sitnikov
Phone: (7) 81378 73400/219 17/71848
Tech. Mgr.: Andrey Borisovich Karpov
Phone: (7) 81378 73400/219 17/71848
Total Employees at this Location: 1,350
Type of Operation: Pulp mill, Paper mill
Pulp Grades and Capacities:
Total pulp capacity: 122,350 mt/y
Chemical Pulp: 62,864 mt/y
Recycled Pulping: 59,486 mt/y
Pulp Mill Data:
Chemical Pulping Systems:
Batch digesters: 5
Pulp Lines: 5
Recycled Fiber Treatment Lines:
Recycled packaging pulping lines: 1
Paper/Paperboard Grades and Capacities:
Total paper and paperboard capacity: 154,000 mt/y
Specialty and industrial: 40,000 mt/y
Linerboard: 114,000 mt/y
Paper and Paperboard Mill Data:
Stock Preparation:
Pulpers: 2
Refiners: 7
Paper Machines: 1
No. 2, fourdrinier (2), total capacity 154,000 mt/y, Trim width 4.41 m, Linerboard, Specialty and industrial
Coating Machines: 1
No. 1
Finishing Equipment:
Calenders: 1
Supercalenders: 1 at 30,000 mt/y
Energy Data:
Power boilers: 4
Electrical demand for mill: 289 MWh/D

ⓜYaroslavl Paper ZAO
Yaroslavl Mill
Ownership: OAO Technicheskaya Bumaga
prospekt Oktyabrya 85.
150044 Yaroslavl, Yaroslavl obl.
Russia
 Phone: (7) 4852 73 53 13
 Fax: (7) 4852 73 53 13
Personnel:
Dir. Gen: Aleksandr Kuzmin
Tech. Dir.: Nikolay Popov
Total Employees at this Location: 160
Type of Operation: Paperboard mill
Pulp Grades and Capacities:
Total pulp capacity: 50,661 mt/y
Recycled Pulping: 50,661 mt/y
Pulp Mill Data:
Recycled Fiber Treatment Lines:
Recycled packaging pulping lines: 1
Paper/Paperboard Grades and Capacities:
Total paper and paperboard capacity: 50,000 mt/y
Packaging papers: 5,000 mt/y
Linerboard: 27,000 mt/y
Corrugating medium/fluting: 18,000 mt/y
Paper and Paperboard Mill Data:
Paper Machines: 1
No. 1, fourdrinier, total capacity 50,000 mt/y, Trim width 2.45 m, Packaging papers, Corrugating medium/fluting, Linerboard
Energy Data:
Power boilers
Electrical demand for mill: 72 MWh/D

ⓗⓜYenisey Pulp and Paper Mill Inc.
Yenisey Pulp and Paper Mill
Company is for sale, closed (Yeniseyskiy pulp and paper mill's owner Basic Element (BasEl) looking into the possibility of finding a partner to run the mill or else selling it. High production costs had led to the mill's stoppage in December 2013.)
Ownership: 100% by Basic Element (BasEl)
26 Bakinskikh Komissarov Str., 8
660004 Krasnoyarsk
Russia
 Phone: (7) 391 2649012/2649313
 Fax: (7) 39102649240
 Email: lytkina@ecbk.ru,
  info@cbk.ktk.ru
Personnel:
Man. Dir.: Vladimir Filippov
Phone: (7) 391 264 9012
Fax: (7) 39102649240
Email: lytkina@ecbk.ru
Qlty. Mgr.: Olga Nikolaevna Dityateva
Phone: (7) 391 2649012/2649313
Finan. Dir.: Vera Nikolaevna Akhmadieva
Phone: (7) 391 2649310
Tech. Dir.: Sergey Nikolaevich Zamkin
Phone: (7) 391 2649749
Total Employees at this Location: 800
Type of Operation: Pulp mill, Paper mill, Paperboard mill
Pulp Grades and Capacities:
Total pulp capacity: 104,853 mt/y
Chemical Pulp: 104,853 mt/y
Pulp Mill Data:
Chemical Recovery Equipment:
Evaporator lines: 1
Recovery boilers: 1
Paper/Paperboard Grades and Capacities:
Total paper and paperboard capacity: 229,449 mt/y
Newsprint: 94,962 mt/y
Specialty and industrial: 16,993 mt/y
Corrugating medium/fluting: 102,000 mt/y
Boxboard/cartonboard: 15,494 mt/y
Paper and Paperboard Mill Data:
Paper Machines: 5
No. 1, (Idle.), total capacity 54,978 mt/y, Trim width 4.2 m, Newsprint
No. 2, (Idle.), total capacity 39,984 mt/y, Trim width 4.2 m, Newsprint
No. 3, (Idle.), total capacity 16,993 mt/y, Trim width 2.52 m, Specialty and industrial
BM 1, (Idle.), total capacity 15,494 mt/y, Trim width 2.52 m, Boxboard/cartonboard
BM 2, fourdrinier, total capacity 102,000 mt/y, Trim width 6.3 m, Corrugating medium/fluting
Energy Data:
Power boilers: 1
Electrical demand for mill: 259 MWh/D

SAN MARINO

ⓗⓜCartiera Ciacci S.a.
San Marino Mill
Via F. da Montebello 29
I-47892 Gualdicciolo, San Marino
San Marino
 Phone: (378) 0549 999 201 / +378 999201

Fax: (378) 0549 999 406
Email: gianfranco.diluca@cartieraciacci.sm
Web Address: www.cartieraciacci.sm
Personnel:
Man. Dir.: Dr. Emanuele Rossini
Phone: (378) 0549 999 201
Fax: (378) 0549 999 406
Email: emanuele.rossini@cartieraciacci.sm
Sls. Mgr.: Ambrogio Rossini
Phone: (378) 0549 999 201
Fax: (378) 0549 999 406
Email: ambrogio.rossini@cartieraciacci.sm
Admin. Dir.: Gianfranco Di Luca
Phone: (378) 0549 999 201
Fax: (378) 0549 999 406
Email: gianfranco.diluca@cartieraciacci.sm
Mgr.: Adriano Zampetti
Phone: (378) 0549 999 201
Fax: (378) 0549 999 406
Email: adriano.zampetti@cartieraciacci.sm
Total Employees of Company: 48
Total Employees at this Location: 48
Type of Operation: Paperboard mill
Pulp Grades and Capacities:
Total pulp capacity: 111,208 mt/y
Recycled Pulping: 111,208 mt/y
Pulp Mill Data:
Pulp Lines: 1
Recycled Fiber Treatment Lines:
Recycled packaging pulping lines: 1
Paper/Paperboard Grades and Capacities:
Total paper and paperboard capacity: 110,000 mt/y
Corrugating medium/fluting: 110,000 mt/y
Paper and Paperboard Mill Data:
Paper Machines: 1
No. 1, fourdrinier, total capacity 110,000 mt/y, Trim width 2.61 m, Corrugating medium/fluting
Energy Data:
Power boilers: 1
Electrical demand for mill: 155 MWh/D

SERBIA

⊕Drenik A.D.
Pancevacki put 69
11000 Belgrade
Serbia
Phone: (381) 11 20 72 000
Fax: (381) 11 331 8293
Email: drenik@drenik.net
Web Address: www.dreniknd.com
Personnel:
Owner/VP: Igor Peric
Phone: (381) 11 20 72 000
Email: igor@drenik.net
Owner/Gen. Mgr.: Nebojsa Djordjevic
Email: nebojsa@drenik.net
Total Employees of Company: 50
Mill Locations:
Drenik A.D., Belgrade Mill, Pancevacki put 69, 11000 Belgrade, Serbia, Capacity: 40,000 mt/y, (Paper mill)
Phone: (381) 11 20 72 000
Fax: (381) 11 331 8293
Email: drenik@drenik.net

⊕Drenik A.D.
Belgrade Mill
Pancevacki put 69
11000 Belgrade
Serbia
Phone: (381) 11 20 72 000
Fax: (381) 11 331 8293
Email: drenik@drenik.net
Web Address: www.dreniknd.com
Personnel:
Owner/VP: Igor Peric
Phone: (381) 11 207 2000

Fax: (381) 11 331 8293
Email: igor@drenik.net
Owner/Gen. Mgr.: Nebojsa Djordjevic
Phone: (381) 11 207 2000
Fax: (381) 11 331 8293
Email: nebojsa@drenik.net
Chief Technologist: Marina Stanic
Phone: (381) 11 207 2000
Fax: (381) 11 331 8293
Email: marista@drenik.net
Total Employees at this Location: 50
Type of Operation: Paper mill
Paper/Paperboard Grades and Capacities:
Total paper and paperboard capacity: 40,000 mt/y
Tissue: 40,000 mt/y
Paper and Paperboard Mill Data:
Stock Preparation:
Pulpers: 2
Refiners: 2
Paper Machines: 2
No. 1, crescent former, Yankee dryer, total capacity 14,000 mt/y, Trim width 2.75 m, Tissue
No. 2, crescent former, Yankee dryer, total capacity 26,000 mt/y, Trim width 2.85 m, Tissue
Energy Data:
Power boilers
Electrical demand for mill: 100 MWh/D

⊕⊕Fabrika Hartije - PAP - DP
Beogradska Mill
Ownership: 83.90% by KappaStar Holding Group, 16.10% by State
Prilazni put Ada Huji 9
11000 Beograde
Serbia
Phone: (381) 11 3316 501
Fax: (381) 11 2771 322
Email: info@fabrikahartije.rs
Web Address: www.fabrikahartije.rs
Personnel:
Gen Mgr.: Dejan Eric
Phone: (381) 11 3316 501
Fax: (381) 11 2771 322
Email: dejan.eric@fabrikahartije.rs
Mgr.: Tatjana Mladenovic
Phone: (381) 11 3316 501
Fax: (381) 11 2771 322
Email: tatjana.mladenovic@fabrikahartije.rs
Total Employees of Company: 100
Total Employees at this Location: 100
Type of Operation: Paper mill
Pulp Grades and Capacities:
Total pulp capacity: 69,894 mt/y
Recycled Pulping: 69,894 mt/y
Pulp Mill Data:
Recycled Fiber Treatment Lines:
Recycled packaging pulping lines: 1
Paper/Paperboard Grades and Capacities:
Total paper and paperboard capacity: 70,000 mt/y
Linerboard: 45,000 mt/y
Corrugating medium/fluting: 25,000 mt/y
Paper and Paperboard Mill Data:
Stock Preparation:
Pulpers: 4
Refiners: 7
Paper Machines: 1
No. 4, fourdrinier, total capacity 70,000 mt/y, Trim width 5 m, Corrugating medium/fluting, Linerboard
Finishing Equipment:
Winders: 2
Supercalenders: 1
Sheeters: 1
Energy Data:
Power boilers: 3
Electrical demand for mill: 101 MWh/D

⊕⊕Lepenka AD
Novi Knezevac Mill
Ownership: Lepenka

Lepenka d.o.o, Cara Dusana 45
23 330 Novi Knezevac, Vojvodina
Serbia
Phone: (381) 230 81 202
Fax: (381) 230 81 610
Email: lepenka@gmail.com
Web Address: www.lepenka.co.rs
Personnel:
Gen. Mgr.: Aleksandar Ivosevic
Phone: (381) 230 81 202
Tech. Mgr.: Z. Lazarevic
Phone: (381) 230 81 202
Finan. Mgr.: B. Brkljac
Phone: (381) 230 81 202
Bus. Mgr.: V. Radovic
Phone: (381) 230 81 202
Paper Mill Mgr.: B. Surbatovic
Phone: (381) 230 81 202
Maint. Mgr.: M. Tkalac
Phone: (381) 230 81 202
Total Employees at this Location: 135
Type of Operation: Pulp mill, Paper mill, Paperboard mill
Pulp Grades and Capacities:
Total pulp capacity: 30,643 mt/y
Recycled Pulping: 15,862 mt/y
Other Pulp: 14,780 mt/y
Pulp Mill Data:
Chemical Pulping Systems:
Continuous digesters: 3
Paper/Paperboard Grades and Capacities:
Total paper and paperboard capacity: 30,000 mt/y
Linerboard: 8,000 mt/y
Corrugating medium/fluting: 16,000 mt/y
Boxboard/cartonboard: 6,000 mt/y
Paper and Paperboard Mill Data:
Stock Preparation:
Pulpers: 3
Refiners: 1
Paper Machines: 2
No. 1, fourdrinier (2), total capacity 24,000 mt/y, Trim width 2.5 m, Linerboard, Corrugating medium/fluting
No. 2, cylinder, total capacity 6,000 mt/y, Trim width 2.2 m, Boxboard/cartonboard
Finishing Equipment:
Rewinders: 1
Energy Data:
Power boilers: 3
Electrical demand for mill: 63 MWh/D

⊕⊕Mladost Cuprija A.D.G.D.
Cuprija Mill
Ownership: Zivkovic DOO, Serbia
Kneza Milosa
35 230 Cuprija
Serbia
Phone: (381) 35 471 022
Fax: (381) 35 471 727
Email: mladostcuprija@ptt.yu
Personnel:
Owner/Gen. Mgr.: Dragoslav Jovanovic
Phone: (381) 35 471 022
Bus. Mgr.: M. Andrejic
Phone: (381) 35 471 022
Finan. Mgr.: N. Jocic
Phone: (381) 35 471 022
Board Mill Mgr.: V. Zivanovic
Phone: (381) 35 471 022
Tech. Mgr.: Mrs. D. Andrejic
Phone: (381) 35 471 022
Total Employees at this Location: 128
Type of Operation: Paperboard mill
Paper/Paperboard Grades and Capacities:
Total paper and paperboard capacity: 3,500 mt/y
Boxboard/cartonboard: 3,500 mt/y
Paper and Paperboard Mill Data:
Stock Preparation:
Pulpers: 2
Refiners: 1
Paper Machines: 1

Slovakia

BM, total capacity 3,500 mt/y, Trim width 2.1 m, Boxboard/cartonboard
Energy Data:
Power boilers: 1

ⓘⓜPapirpak D. O. O. Preduzece za proizvodnju i promet papirne konfekcije
Ownership: 100% by Jovanovic Family
Cacak-Preljina
32000
Serbia
  Phone: (381) 32 381 835
  Fax: (381) 32 381 751
  Email: papirpak@yu1.net
Personnel:
  Gen. Mgr.: M. Jovanovic
  Phone: (381) 32 381 835
  Fax: (381) 32 381 751
  Tech. Mgr.: S. Petrovic
  Phone: (381) 32 381 835
  Fax: (381) 32 381 751
  Bus. Mgr.: R. Jovanovic
  Phone: (381) 32 381 835
  Fax: (381) 32 381 751
  Finan. Mgr.: M. Brkovic
  Phone: (381) 32 381 835
  Fax: (381) 32 381 751
Mill Locations:
Papirpak D. O. O. Preduzece za proizvodnju i promet papirne konfekcije, Cacak-Preljina Mill, 32 000 Cacak-Preljina, Serbia, Capacity: 10,000 mt/y, (Paper mill)
  Phone: (381) 32 381 835
  Fax: (381) 32 381 751
  Email: papirpak@yu1.net, papirpak@diva.co.yu

ⓘⓜPapirpak D. O. O. Preduzece za proizvodnju i promet papirne konfekcije
Cacak-Preljina Mill
32 000 Cacak-Preljina
Serbia
  Phone: (381) 32 381 835
  Fax: (381) 32 381 751
  Email: papirpak@yu1.net, papirpak@diva.co.yu
Personnel:
  Gen. Mgr.: M. Jovanovic
  Phone: (381) 32 381 835
  Tech. Mgr.: S. Petrovic
  Phone: (381) 32 381 835
  Bus. Mgr.: R. Jovanovic
  Phone: (381) 32 381 835
  Finan. Mgr.: M. Brkovic
  Phone: (381) 32 381 835
  Mant. Dir.: V. Bugarcic
  Phone: (381) 32 381 835
Total Employees at this Location: 170
Type of Operation: Paper mill
Paper/Paperboard Grades and Capacities:
Total paper and paperboard capacity: 10,000 mt/y
Tissue: 10,000 mt/y
Paper and Paperboard Mill Data:
  Stock Preparation:
  Pulpers: 2
  Refiners: 3
Paper Machines: 2
PM 1, Yankee dryer, total capacity 4,000 mt/y, Trim width 1.9 m, Tissue
PM 2, (second hand), Yankee dryer, total capacity 6,000 mt/y, Trim width 1.9 m, Tissue
Energy Data:
Power boilers: 2

ⓘStragarit
Ownership: Belege, Serbia
D. Jokovica 4
34 323 Stragari
Serbia
  Phone: (381) 34 522 147
  Fax: (381) 34 522 097/133
Personnel:
  Gen. Mgr.: M. Minic
  Phone: (381) 34 522 147
  Fax: (381) 34 522 097/133
Mill Locations:
Stragarit, Stragari Mill, D. Jokovica 4, 34 323 Stragari, Serbia, Capacity: 22,000 mt/y, (Paper mill, Paperboard mill)
  Phone: (381) 34 522 147
  Fax: (381) 34 522 097/133

ⓘStragarit
Stragari Mill
D. Jokovica 4
34 323 Stragari
Serbia
  Phone: (381) 34 522 147
  Fax: (381) 34 522 097/133
Personnel:
  Gen. Mgr.: M. Minic
  Phone: (381) 63 8269 269
Total Employees at this Location: 120
Type of Operation: Paper mill, Paperboard mill
Paper/Paperboard Grades and Capacities:
Total paper and paperboard capacity: 22,000 mt/y
Corrugating medium/fluting: 13,000 mt/y
Paper and Paperboard Mill Data:
  Stock Preparation:
  Pulpers: 4
Paper Machines: 2
BM 1, fourdrinier, total capacity 13,000 mt/y, Trim width 4 m, Corrugating medium/fluting
BM 2, total capacity 9,000 mt/y, Trim width 3 m
Energy Data:
Power boilers: 2

ⓘⓜUmka AD, Fabrika Kartona
Umka Mill
Ownership: Kappa Star, Serbia
13. Oktobra br.1
11260 Umka, Belgrade
Serbia
  Phone: (381) 11 3602 600 / 699, 11 8025 119
  Fax: (381) 11 3026 995 / 11 8025 151
  Email: umka@umka.rs, prodaja@umka.rs
  Web Address: www.umka.rs
Personnel:
  Gen. Mgr.: Milos Ljusic
  Phone: (381) 11 3062 699
  Fax: (381) 11 8026 955
  Email: milos.ljusic@umka.rs
  Qlty. Contr. & R&D Dir.: Danijela Ošap
  Phone: (381) 11 3602 600
  Fax: (381) 11 3026 995
  Email: danijela.osap@umka.rs
Total Employees at this Location: 215
Type of Operation: Paperboard mill
Pulp Grades and Capacities:
Total pulp capacity: 75,035 mt/y
Recycled Pulping: 75,035 mt/y
Pulp Mill Data:
  Recycled Fiber Treatment Lines:
  Recycled packaging pulping lines: 1
Paper/Paperboard Grades and Capacities:
Total paper and paperboard capacity: 88,000 mt/y
Boxboard/cartonboard: 88,000 mt/y
Paper and Paperboard Mill Data:
  Stock Preparation:
  Pulpers: 7
  Refiners: 10
Paper Machines: 1
No. 1, cylinder (7), total capacity 88,000 mt/y, Trim width 3.2 m, Boxboard/cartonboard
Coating Machines: 4
No. 1, on machine
No. 2, on machine
No. 3, on machine
No. 4, on machine
Finishing Equipment:
  Rewinders: 1
  Sheeters: 2
Energy Data:
Power boilers: 3
Electrical demand for mill: 144 MWh/D

ⓘⓜVISKOZA
Loznica Mill
Ownership: 100% by state
Gradiliste bb
15 300 Loznica
Serbia
  Phone: (381) 15 874 710
  Fax: (381) 15 874 741
  Email: viskoza@isp.b92.net, viskoza@ptt.yu
Personnel:
  Gen. Mgr.: Dr. M. Blagojevic
  Phone: (381) 15 874 710
  Pulp Mill Mgr.: S. Perisic
  Phone: (381) 15 874 710
  Busn. Mgr.: S. Nikolic
  Phone: (381) 15 874 710
Total Employees at this Location: 450
Type of Operation: Pulp mill
Pulp Grades and Capacities:
Total pulp capacity: 10,000 mt/y
Chemical Pulp: 10,000 mt/y
Pulp Mill Data:
  Chemical Pulping Systems:
  Batch digesters: 7
  Bleach Plant Systems: 1
  Chemical Recovery Equipment:
  Evaporator lines: 1
  Recovery boilers: 1
  Pulp Dryers:
  Flash dryers 1

SLOVAKIA

ⓘⓜBUKOCEL, a.s.
Hencovce Mill
Ownership: 100% by Bukóza Holding
Hencovská 2073
SK-093 02 Hencovce
Slovakia
  Phone: (421) 57 441 1111, 3008, 2511
  Fax: (421) 57 44 12563
  Email: predajbunicin@bukoza.sk
  Web Address: www.bukoza.sk
Personnel:
  Chmn.: Ing. Jaroslav Fic
  Phone: (421) 57 441 3002
  Fax: (421) 57 441 2563
  Email: jaroslav.fic@bukoza.sk
  Pulp Mill Mgr.: Ing. Peter Pavelko
  Phone: (421) 57 441 3032
  Fax: (421) 57 441 2563
  Email: peter.pavelko@bukoza.sk
  Tech. Invest. Dir.: Ing. Rudolf Pánis
  Phone: (421) 57 441 3040
  Fax: (421) 57 441 2561
  Email: rudolf.panis@bukoza.sk
Total Employees of Company: 955
Total Employees at this Location: 357
Type of Operation: Pulp mill
Pulp Grades and Capacities:
Total pulp capacity: 155,460 mt/y
Pulp available for market: 155,000 mt/y
Chemical Pulp: 155,460 mt/y
Pulp Mill Data:
  Chemical Pulping Systems:

Slovakia

Batch digesters: 5
Pulp Lines: 1
Bleach Plant Systems: 1
No. 1, Sequence: O_2 C/DEpDHD, Capacity 155,000 admt/y
Chemical Recovery Equipment:
Evaporator lines: 1
Recovery boilers: 1
Lime Kiln
Pulp Dryers:
Air Float dryers 1, Fourdriniers 1
Energy Data:
Power boilers: 3
Steam turbines: 3 at 45 MW
Electrical demand for mill: 343 MWh/D

ⓂMetsä Tissue Slovakia s.r.o.
Žilina (Tento) Mill
Ownership: 100% by Metsä Tissue Corp.
Celulózka 3494
SK-011 61 Žilina
Slovakia
  Phone: (421) 41 51 21 111
  Fax: (421) 41 51 21 477
  Email: (firstname.lastname@metsagroup.com)
  Web Address: www.metsatissue.com,
  www.tento.eu,
  www.lambi.com
Personnel:
VP Prod. & Mill Mgr.: Lubomír Kotuláč
Phone: (421) 41 512 1320
Fax: (421) 41 512 1509
Email: lubomir.kotulac@metsagroup.com
VP Supply Chain: Zsolt Tóth
Phone: (421) 41 512 1260
Fax: (421) 41 512 1257
Email: zsolt.toth@metsagroup.com
Sls. Dir.: Igor Malík
Phone: (421) 41 512 1481
Fax: (421) 41 512 1477
Email: igor.malik@metsagroup.com
Qlty. & Environ. Mgr.: Eva Chochlíková
Phone: (421) 41 512 1130
Fax: (421) 41 51 21 477
Email: eva.chochlikova@metsagroup.com
Safety & Protection Mgr.: Katarína Rolková
Phone: (421) 41 512 1247
Fax: (421) 41 51 21 477
Email: katarina.rolkova@metsagroup.com
Brand Dir.: Miroslava Šibíková
Phone: (421) 41 512 1467
Fax: (421) 41 512 1477
Email: miroslava.sibikova@metsagroup.com
Total Employees of Company: 3,400
Total Employees at this Location: 402
Type of Operation: Paper mill
Pulp Grades and Capacities:
Total pulp capacity: 63,916 mt/y
Recycled Pulping: 63,916 mt/y
Pulp Mill Data:
Bleach Plant Systems: 1
DIP Capacity 58,000 admt/y
Recycled Fiber Treatment Lines:
Flotation deinking lines: 1 at 90,000 admt/y
Pulpers: 2 at 90,000 admt/y
Washing deinking lines: 1 at 82,000 admt/y
Pulp Dryers:
Air Float dryers 1
Paper/Paperboard Grades and Capacities:
Total paper and paperboard capacity: 90,000 mt/y
Tissue: 90,000 mt/y
Paper and Paperboard Mill Data:
Stock Preparation:
Pulpers: 2
Refiners: 6
Paper Machines: 2
No. 1, crescent former, Yankee dryer, total capacity 30,000 mt/y, Trim width 2.87 m, Tissue
No. 2, Periformer, Yankee dryer, total capacity 60,000 mt/y, Trim width 5.28 m, Tissue
Finishing Equipment:
Calenders: 1
Rewinders: 2
Energy Data:
Electrical demand for mill: 280 MWh/D

ⓂMondi SCP a.s.
Ružomberok Mill
Ownership: 51% by Mondi Europe & International Division, 49% by ECO-Invest a.s.
Tatranská cesta 3
SK-03417 Ružomberok
Slovakia
  Phone: (421) 44 436 2222/2090
  Fax: (421) 44 436 3824/2476
  Email: mondiscp@mondigroup.com
  Web Address: www.mondigroup.com
Personnel:
Man. Dir. Fine paper: Roman Senecký
Phone: (421) 44 436 1111
Fax: (421) 44 436 3824
Email: alena.kelovska@mondigroup.com
Oper. Mgr.: Vladimír Krajci
Phone: (421) 44 436 2350
Fax: (421) 44 436 6321
Email: vladimir.krajci@mondigroup.com
Eng. Mgr.: Peter Svajciak
Phone: (421) 44 436 3345
Fax: (421) 44 436 6900
Email: peter.svajciak@mondigroup.com
Procurement Mgr.: Martin Huska
Phone: (421) 44 436 2500
Fax: (421) 44 436 6726
Email: martin.huska@mondigroup.com
Total Employees at this Location: 1,400
Type of Operation: Pulp mill, Paper mill
Pulp Grades and Capacities:
Total pulp capacity: 500,000 mt/y
Pulp available for market: 40,312 mt/y
Chemical Pulp: 500,000 mt/y
Pulp Mill Data:
Chemical Pulping Systems:
Batch digesters: 8
Pulp Lines: 1
Bleach Plant Systems: 1
No. 1, Type: ZEop-D-P HW/SW, Sequence: O_2 ZEoD, Capacity 500,000 admt/y
Chemical Recovery Equipment:
Evaporator lines: 1
Recovery boilers: 2
Lime Kiln
Pulp Dryers:
Air Float dryers 1
Paper/Paperboard Grades and Capacities:
Total paper and paperboard capacity: 615,000 mt/y
Uncoated woodfree/freesheet: 550,000 mt/y
Packaging papers: 65,000 mt/y
Paper and Paperboard Mill Data:
Stock Preparation:
Pulpers: 4
Refiners: 14
Paper Machines: 4
No. 1, fourdrinier, total capacity 65,000 mt/y, Trim width 2.5 m, Packaging papers
No. 16, Bel-Bond, total capacity 50,000 mt/y, Trim width 2.16 m, Uncoated woodfree/freesheet
No. 17, Bel-Bond, total capacity 140,000 mt/y, Trim width 4.26 m, Uncoated woodfree/freesheet
No. 18, DuoFormer, total capacity 360,000 mt/y, Trim width 6.56 m, Uncoated woodfree/freesheet
Finishing Equipment:
Winders: 2
Calenders: 1
Supercalenders: 1
Rewinders: 1
Energy Data:
Power boilers: 3
Combustion turbines: 2 at 34.0 MW
Steam turbines: 5 at 66.5 MW
Electrical demand for mill: 1,857 MWh/D

ⓘⓂSHP Harmanec, a.s.
Harmanec Mill
Ownership: 100% by Eco-Invest
SK-976 03 Harmanec
Slovakia
  Phone: (421) 48 4322111
  Fax: (421) 48 4198105
  Email: harmanec@shpgroup.eu
  Web Address: www.shpgroup.eu
Personnel:
Chief Prod. Officer: Jozef Horák
Phone: (421) 484 322210
Fax: (421) 484 322502
Email: jozef.horak@shpgroup.eu
Internal Auditor: Martin Michálik
Phone: (421) 48 4322140
Fax: (421) 48 4198105
Email: martin.michalik@shpgroup.eu
Total Employees at this Location: 300
Type of Operation: Paper mill
Pulp Grades and Capacities:
Total pulp capacity: 28,941 mt/y
Recycled Pulping: 28,941 mt/y
Pulp Mill Data:
Bleach Plant Lines:
No. 1
Recycled Fiber Treatment Lines:
Flotation deinking lines: 1 at 65,700
Pulpers: 2 at 61,000 admt/y
Paper/Paperboard Grades and Capacities:
Total paper and paperboard capacity: 46,000 mt/y
Tissue: 46,000 mt/y
Paper and Paperboard Mill Data:
Stock Preparation:
Pulpers: 2
Refiners: 3
Paper Machines: 1
No. 7, C-wrap, Yankee dryer, total capacity 46,000 mt/y, Trim width 4.48 m, Tissue
Finishing Equipment:
Winders: 1 at 40,000 mt/y
Energy Data:
Power boilers: 2
Electrical demand for mill: 123 MWh/D

ⓘⓂSHP Slavošovce, a.s.
Slavošovce Mill
Ownership: 100% by ECO-Invest
SK-049 36 Slavošovce
Slovakia
  Phone: (421) 58 7770 275
  Fax: (421) 58 7770 276
  Email: slavosovce@shpgroup.eu
  Web Address: www.shpgroup.eu
Total Employees of Company: 233
Total Employees at this Location: 165
Type of Operation: Paper mill
Pulp Mill Data:
Bleach Plant Lines:
No. 1
Paper/Paperboard Grades and Capacities:
Total paper and paperboard capacity: 20,000 mt/y
Tissue: 20,000 mt/y
Paper and Paperboard Mill Data:
Stock Preparation:
Pulpers: 1
Refiners: 3
Paper Machines: 1
No. 8, fourdrinier, Yankee dryer, total capacity 20,000 mt/y, Trim width 3.26 m, Tissue
Finishing Equipment:
Rewinders: 1 at 20,000 mt/y
Sheeters: 9
Energy Data:

Power boilers: 1
Electrical demand for mill: 58 MWh/D

SLOVENIA

ⓘⓜGoricane, tovarna papirja Medvode, d.d.
Medvode Mill
Ownership: 10.96% by Papirus, Slovenia, 85.53% by Papigor, Slovenia, 3.09% by Employees and Former Employees, 0.42% by Goricane, Slovenia
Ladja 10
SI-1215 Medvode
Slovenia
  Phone: (386) 1 58 23400
  Fax: (386) 1 36 12804/ 3613 319
  Email: goricane@goricane.si
  Web Address: www.goricane.si
Personnel:
  Man. Dir.: Andraz Stegu
  Phone: (386) 1 58 23 402
  Fax: (386) 1 36 12804
  Email: andraz.stegu@goricane.si
  Prod. Dir.: Klemen Burgar
  Phone: (386) 1 58 23 447
  Fax: (386) 1 36 12 904
  Email: klemen.burgar@goricane.si
  Sls. Dir.: Andrej Gradisek
  Phone: (386) 1 58 23 413
  Fax: (386) 1 36 13 319
  Email: andrej.gradisek@goricane.si
  Power Plant Mgr.: Marko Žiberna
  Phone: (386) 1 58 23 480
  Fax: (386) 1 36 12 800
  Email: marko.ziberna@goricane.si
  Tech. Mgr.: Janez Gale
  Phone: (386) 1 58 23 483
  Fax: (386) 1 36 12 800
  Email: janez.gale@goricane.si
  Develpt. & Qlty. Mgr.: Jemeja Pecnik
  Phone: (386) 1 58 23 422
  Fax: (386) 1 36 12 904
  Email: okolje@goricane.si
Total Employees at this Location: 220
Type of Operation: Paper mill
Paper/Paperboard Grades and Capacities:
  Total paper and paperboard capacity: 80,000 mt/y
  Uncoated woodfree/freesheet: 50,000 mt/y
  Coated woodfree/freesheet: 25,000 mt/y
  Specialty and industrial: 5,000 mt/y
Paper and Paperboard Mill Data:
  Stock Preparation:
  Pulpers: 3
  Refiners: 5
Paper Machines: 1
  No. 1, DuoFormer D, total capacity 80,000 mt/y, Trim width 3.68 m, Coated woodfree/freesheet, Uncoated woodfree/freesheet, Specialty and industrial
Coating Machines: 1
  PM 1, total capacity 50,000 mt/y., on machine
Finishing Equipment:
  Winders: 2 at 85,000 mt/y
  Calenders: 1
  Sheeters: 2 at 30,000 mt/y
Energy Data:
  Power boilers: 2
  Steam turbines: 1 at 6.4 MW
  Hydro turbines: 1 at 0.4 MW
  Electrical demand for mill: 135 MWh/D

ⓘⓜKolicevo Karton d.o.o.
Kolicevo Mill
Ownership: 100% by Mayr-Melnhof Karton AG
Papirniška 1
SI-1230 Domžale
Slovenia
  Phone: (386) 1 72 11 011/90 511
  Fax: (386) 1 72 43 571/90 519
  Email: sales.kolicevo@mm-karton.com
  Web Address: www.mm-karton.com
Personnel:
  Gen. Mgr.: Branko Rozic
  Phone: (386) 1 7241 309
  Fax: (386) 1 7212 750
  Email: branko.rozic@mm-karton.com
  Sls. Dir.: Peter Ziberna
  Phone: (386) 1 72 90 561
  Fax: (386) 1 72 90 567
  Email: peter.ziberna@mm-karton.com
Total Employees at this Location: 306
Type of Operation: Paperboard mill
Pulp Grades and Capacities:
  Total pulp capacity: 148,507 mt/y
  Mechanical Pulp: 29,207 mt/y
  Recycled Pulping: 119,300 mt/y
Pulp Mill Data:
  Mechanical Pulping Systems:
  Conventional grinders
  Recycled Fiber Treatment Lines:
  Recycled packaging pulping lines: 1
Paper/Paperboard Grades and Capacities:
  Total paper and paperboard capacity: 240,000 mt/y
  Linerboard: 10,000 mt/y
  Boxboard/cartonboard: 230,000 mt/y
Paper and Paperboard Mill Data:
  Stock Preparation:
  Pulpers: 7
  Refiners: 3
Paper Machines: 2
  No. 2, multi-fourdrinier, total capacity 40,000 mt/y, Trim width 2.2 m, Boxboard/cartonboard
  No. 3, fourdrinier (3), total capacity 200,000 mt/y, Trim width 4.4 m, Boxboard/cartonboard, Linerboard
Coating Machines: 3
  No. 1, on machine
  No. 2, on machine
  No. 3, on machine
Finishing Equipment:
  Rewinders: 2 at 260,000 mt/y
  Sheeters: 7 at 250,000 mt/y
Energy Data:
  Power boilers: 2
  Steam turbines: 2 at 10.0 MW
  Electrical demand for mill: 401 MWh/D

ⓘⓜLepenka
Trzic Mill
Ownership: Krater Group, private owner
Slap 8
SI-4290 Trzic
Slovenia
  Phone: (386) 4 5963 044 / 547 / 133
  Fax: (386) 4 5963538
  Email: lepenka@lepenka.si
  Web Address: www.lepenka.si
Personnel:
  CEO, Dir.: Gregor Repic
  Phone: (386) 4 5963 044
  Fax: (386) 4 5963538
  Email: lepenka@lepenka.si
Total Employees at this Location: 94
Type of Operation: Paper mill, Paperboard mill
Mill Locations:
  Lepenka AD, Novi Knezevac Mill, Lepenka d.o.o, Cara Dusana 45, 23 330 Novi Knezevac, Serbia, Capacity: 30,000 mt/y, (Pulp mill, Paper mill, Paperboard mill)
  Phone: (381) 230 81 202
  Fax: (381) 230 81 610
  Email: lepenka@gmail.com
Pulp Grades and Capacities:
  Total pulp capacity: 20,835 mt/y
  Recycled Pulping: 20,835 mt/y
Pulp Mill Data:
  Mechanical Pulping Systems:
  Conventional grinders
Paper/Paperboard Grades and Capacities:
  Total paper and paperboard capacity: 20,000 mt/y
  Tissue: 8,000 mt/y
  Boxboard/cartonboard: 12,000 mt/y
Paper and Paperboard Mill Data:
Paper Machines: 2
  No. 1, fourdrinier, Yankee dryer, total capacity 8,000 mt/y, Trim width 2.7 m, Tissue
  No. 2, cylinder, total capacity 12,000 mt/y, Trim width 2.2 m, Boxboard/cartonboard
Energy Data:
  Electrical demand for mill: 37 MWh/D

ⓘⓜPaloma-Sladkogorska Tovarna Papirja d.d. Sladki Vrh
Sladki Vrh Mill
Ownership: 29.03% by others, 70.97% by Posebna Družba Za Preoblikovanje
Sladki Vrh 1
SI-2214 Sladki Vrh
Slovenia
  Phone: (386) 2 6457 100
  Fax: (386) 2 6457 107
  Email: info@paloma.si
  Web Address: www.paloma.si
Personnel:
  Pres. Board Management: Tadej Gosak
  Phone: (386) 2 6457 100
  Fax: (386) 2 6457 107
  Email: tadej.gosak@paloma.si
  Representative, Management Bus. Systems & Qlty. & Ecology Systems: Jasna Bauman
  Phone: (386) 2 6457 100
  Fax: (386) 2 6457 107
  Email: jasna.bauman@paloma.si
  Prod. & Tech. Dep. Mgr.: Boris Jancic
  Phone: (386) 2 6457 301
  Fax: (386) 2 6457 302
  Email: boris.jancic@paloma.si
  Finan. & Economics Mgr.: Tatjana Intihar
  Phone: (386) 2 6457 100
  Fax: (386) 2 6457 107
  Email: Tatjana.intihar@paloma.si
  HR Dir.: Zora Kirbis
  Phone: (386) 2 6457 100
  Fax: (386) 2 6457 107
  Email: zora.kirbis@paloma.si
Total Employees of Company: 850
Total Employees at this Location: 755
Type of Operation: Paper mill
Pulp Grades and Capacities:
  Total pulp capacity: 25,022 mt/y
  Recycled Pulping: 25,022 mt/y
Pulp Mill Data:
  Recycled Fiber Treatment Lines:
  Flotation deinking lines: 1
Paper/Paperboard Grades and Capacities:
  Total paper and paperboard capacity: 73,000 mt/y
  Tissue: 73,000 mt/y
Paper and Paperboard Mill Data:
Paper Machines: 4
  No. 3, fourdrinier, Yankee dryer, total capacity 20,000 mt/y, Trim width 2.5 m, Tissue
  No. 4, fourdrinier, Yankee dryer, total capacity 18,000 mt/y, Trim width 2.5 m, Tissue
  No. 5, fourdrinier, Yankee dryer, total capacity 16,000 mt/y, Trim width 2.5 m, Tissue
  No. 6, inclined, Yankee dryer, total capacity 38,000 mt/y, Trim width 5.2 m, Tissue
Energy Data:
  Power boilers: 3
  Steam turbines: 1 at 4.6 MW
  Electrical demand for mill: 212 MWh/D

ⓘⓜRadece Papir Nova
Radece Mill
Ownership: 100% by Emkaam Investment
Njivice 7

SI-1433 Radece Zidani most
Slovenia
 Phone: (386) 3 568 0500
 Fax: (386) 3 568 0501
 Email: info@radecepapir.si
 Web Address: www.radecepapir.si
Personnel:
 Chmn.: Peter Tevž
 Phone: (386) 3 568 0500
 Man. Dir.: Janez Pelhan
 Phone: (386) 3 568 0500
 Gen. Mgr.: George Savdijec Berbberi
 Phone: (386) 3 568 0500
 Sls. Mgr.: Bostjan Robida
 Phone: (386) 3 568 04 08
 Tech. Mgr.: Marjan Kocjancic
 Phone: (386) 45 03568053
 Email: marjan.kocjancic@radecepapir.si
 Maint. Mgr.: Andrej Hrup
 Phone: (386) 3 568 04 00
 Email: andrej.hrup@radecepapir.si
 R&D Dir.: Sergej Knez
 Phone: (386) 3 568 03 80
 Email: sergej.knez@radecepapir.si
 Energy Mgr.: Pavel Znidarsic
 Phone: (386) 3 568 0500
 Email: pavel.znidarsic@radecepapir.si
Total Employees of Company: 370
Total Employees at this Location: 126
Type of Operation: Paper mill
Paper/Paperboard Grades and Capacities:
 Total paper and paperboard capacity: 45,000 mt/y
 Uncoated woodfree/freesheet: 36,000 mt/y
 Specialty and industrial: 9,000 mt/y
Paper and Paperboard Mill Data:
Paper Machines: 2
 No. 4, fourdrinier, total capacity 36,000 mt/y, Trim width 2.2 m, Uncoated woodfree/freesheet
 No. 5, combination, total capacity 9,000 mt/y, Trim width 2.4 m, Specialty and industrial
Coating Machines: 1
 No. 1, total capacity 10,000 mt/y., off machine
Finishing Equipment:
 Sheeters: 4 at 50,000 mt/y
Energy Data:
 Power boilers: 1
 Steam turbines: 1 at 5 MW
 Electrical demand for mill: 91 MWh/D

ⓘⓜPapirnica Vevce d.o.o.
Vevce Mill
Ownership: 100% by Roxcel Group
Papirniška pot 25
SI-1261 Ljubljana-Dobrunje
Slovenia
 Phone: (386) 1 58 77 200
 Fax: (386) 1 52 85 450
 Email: info@papir-vevce.si
 Web Address: www.papir-vevce.si
Personnel:
 Tech. Mgr. & Paper Mill Mgr.: Marko Jagodic
 Phone: (386) 1 5877 201
 Fax: (386) 1 52 85 450
 Email: marko.jagodic@papir-vevce.si
 Maint. Mgr.: Bostjan Smrekar
 Phone: (386) 1 5877 300
 Fax: (386) 1 5284 300
 Email: bostjan.smrekar@papir-vevce.si
 Sls. Dept.: Mitja Bregar
 Phone: (386) 1 5877 410
 Fax: (386) 1 52 85 450
 Email: mitja.bregar@papir-vevce.si
Total Employees at this Location: 270
Type of Operation: Paper mill
Paper/Paperboard Grades and Capacities:
 Total paper and paperboard capacity: 90,000 mt/y
 Coated woodfree/freesheet: 36,000 mt/y
 Specialty and industrial: 54,000 mt/y
Paper and Paperboard Mill Data:
 Stock Preparation:
  Pulpers: 6
  Refiners: 7
Paper Machines: 1
 No. 5, fourdrinier, total capacity 90,000 mt/y, Trim width 3.66 m, Coated woodfree/freesheet, Specialty and industrial
Coating Machines: 1
 PM 5, on machine
Finishing Equipment:
 Winders: 2 at 90,000 mt/y
 Calenders: 2
 Rewinders: 2 at 90,000 mt/y
 Sheeters: 2 at 90,000 mt/y
Energy Data:
 Power boilers: 3
 Steam turbines: 1 at 6.3 MW
 Hydro turbines: 5 at 2.2 MW
 Electrical demand for mill: 163 MWh/D

ⓘⓜVipap Videm Krško d.d.
Krško Mill
Ownership: 96.50% by Ministry of Finance of the Czech Republic, 3.50% by Company Treasury
Tovarniska 18
SI-8270 Krško, Ljubljana
Slovenia
 Phone: (386) 7 481 1100
 Fax: (386) 7 492 1115/2077
 Email: vipap@vipap.si
 Web Address: www.vipap.si
Personnel:
 Chmn. & Gen. Mgr.: Miloš Habrnál
 Phone: (386) 7 481 1122
 Fax: (386) 7 492 0038
 Email: milos.habrnal@vipap.si
 Paper Prod. Mgr.: Dragan Kranjc
 Phone: (386) 7 481 1325
 Fax: (386) 7 492 0038
 Email: dragan.kranjc@vipap.si
 Finan. Mgr. & Bd. Mbr.: Jožica Stegne
 Phone: (386) 7 481 1151
 Fax: (386) 7 492 0038
 Email: jozica.stegne@vipap.si
 Sls. Mgr.: Boris Macur
 Phone: (386) 7 481 1191
 Fax: (386) 7 492 0038
 Email: boris.macur@vipap.si
 Purch. Mgr.: Milena Humar
 Phone: (386) 7 481 1209
 Fax: (386) 7 492 2739
 Email: milena.humar@vipap.si
 R&D Mgr.: Danijel Oštir
 Phone: (386) 7 481 1331
 Fax: (386) 7 492 2403
 Email: danijel.ostir@vipap.si
 Chief Eng.: Darko Ribic
 Phone: (386) 7 481 1383
 Fax: (386) 7 492 2065
 Email: darko.ribic@vipap.si
 Environ. Mgr.: Justina Šepetavc
 Phone: (386) 7 481 1370
 Fax: (386) 7 492 2403
 Email: justina.sepetavc@vipap.si
 Maint. Mgr.: Janko Ganc
 Phone: (386) 7 481 1400
 Fax: (386) 7 492 2630
 Email: janko.ganc@vipap.si
Total Employees at this Location: 382
Type of Operation: Paper mill
Pulp Grades and Capacities:
 Total pulp capacity: 199,090 mt/y
 Mechanical Pulp: 22,159 mt/y
 Recycled Pulping: 176,931 mt/y
Pulp Mill Data:
 Mechanical Pulping Systems:
  Conventional grinders: 1
Pulp Lines: 2
 Bleach Plant Systems: 2
  1, Type: DIP, Sequence: P/Y, Capacity 160,000 admt/y
  1, Type: TGW, Sequence: P/Y, Capacity 60,000 admt/y
Recycled Fiber Treatment Lines:
 Flotation deinking lines: 1 at 180,000
 Pulpers: 1 at 180,000 admt/y
Paper/Paperboard Grades and Capacities:
 Total paper and paperboard capacity: 212,000 mt/y
 Newsprint: 154,000 mt/y
 Uncoated mechanical/groundwood: 3,000 mt/y
 Coated mechanical/groundwood: 55,000 mt/y
Paper and Paperboard Mill Data:
Paper Machines: 3
 No. 1, Bel-Form, total capacity 70,000 mt/y, Trim width 4.17 m, Coated mechanical/groundwood, Uncoated mechanical/groundwood, Newsprint
 No. 2, hybrid former, total capacity 70,000 mt/y, Trim width 4.17 m, Newsprint
 No. 3, Vertiformer, total capacity 72,000 mt/y, Trim width 3.8 m, Newsprint
Coating Machines: 1
 No. 1, total capacity 61,000 mt/y., on machine
Finishing Equipment:
 Winders: 3 at 201,000 mt/y
 Sheeters: 1 at 72,000 mt/y
Energy Data:
 Power boilers: 3
 Steam turbines: 2 at 6.3 MW
 Electrical demand for mill: 528 MWh/D

SPAIN

ⓘAbelan Board and Packaging Solutions
Ownership: 100% by Phi Industrial Acquisitions
Balmes 200, 5th & 6th
E-08006 Barcelona
Spain
 Phone: (34) 93 415 15 22
 Fax: (34) 93 415 44 52
 Email: catalana@abelan.com, catalana.export@abelan.com
 Web Address: www.abelan.com
Personnel:
 Gen. Mgr.: Jaime Llopis
 Phone: (34) 93 415 15 22
 Fax: (34) 93 415 44 52
 Export Sls. Mgr.: José Manuel Pelayo
 Phone: (34) 93 415 15 22
 Fax: (34) 93 415 44 52
 Iberian Sls. Mgr.: Ignacio Ruiz
 Phone: (34) 93 415 15 22
 Fax: (34) 93 415 44 52
 Finan. Dir.: Ernesto Riera Juliá
 Phone: (34) 93 415 15 22
 Fax: (34) 93 415 44 52
Total Employees of Company: 230
Total Employees at this Location: 22
Mill Locations:
Abelan Board and Packaging Solutions, Alcover Mill, Carr. Salou-Ponts, Km. 26, E-43460 Alcover, Spain, Capacity: 70,000 mt/y, (Paperboard mill)
 Phone: (34) 34 93 415 1522
 Fax: (34) 34 93 415 4452, 34 93 415 6300
 Email: catalana@abelan.com, catalana.export@abelan.com
Abelan Board and Packaging Solutions, Villava Mill, San Andrés S/N, E-31610 Villava, Spain, Capacity: 120,000 mt/y, (Paper mill, Paperboard mill)
 Phone: (34) 948 16 83 00
 Fax: (34) 948 16 83 01
 Email: jlzubiete@tngeu.com, sanandres@abelan.com
Abelan Board and Packaging Solutions, Viersen Mill, Grefrather Strasse 120, D-41749 Viersen, Germany, Capacity: 60,000 mt/y, (Paperboard mill)
 Phone: (49) 2162 89640/896420
 Fax: (49) 2162 89569/896442

Spain

ⓂAbelan Board and Packaging Solutions
Alcover Mill
Carr. Salou-Ponts, Km. 26
E-43460 Alcover, Tarragona
Spain
 Phone: (34) 34 93 415 1522
 Fax: (34) 34 93 415 4452, 34 93 415 6300
 Email: catalana@abelan.com,
 catalana.export@abelan.com
 Web Address: www.abelan.com
Personnel:
 Factory Dir. : Antonio Cordova
 Phone: (34) 34 93 415 1522
 Fax: (34) 34 93 415 4452
 Ind. Dir.: Alfonso Bello
 Phone: (34) 977 600461
 Fax: (34) 34 93 415 4452
 Prod. Mgr.: Luis Rodriguez
 Phone: (34) 977 600461
 Fax: (34) 34 93 415 4452
 Email: lfrodriguez@tngeu.com
 Maint. Mgr.: Yusep Albaiges
 Phone: (34) 977 600461
 Fax: (34) 34 93 415 4452
 Email: yalbaiges@tngeu.com
 Gen. Sec.: Sara Castaño
 Phone: (34) 977 600461
 Fax: (34) 34 93 415 4452
 Email: scastano@tngeu.com
Total Employees at this Location: 190
Type of Operation: Paperboard mill
Pulp Grades and Capacities:
 Total pulp capacity: 71,247 mt/y
 Recycled Pulping: 71,247 mt/y
Pulp Mill Data:
 Recycled Fiber Treatment Lines:
 Recycled packaging pulping lines: 1 at 70,000
Paper/Paperboard Grades and Capacities:
 Total paper and paperboard capacity: 70,000 mt/y
 Boxboard/cartonboard: 70,000 mt/y
Paper and Paperboard Mill Data:
 Stock Preparation:
 Pulpers: 3
Paper Machines: 2
 No. 1, fourdrinier, total capacity 20,000 mt/y, Trim width 1.9 m, Boxboard/cartonboard
 No. 2, fourdrinier, total capacity 50,000 mt/y, Trim width 2.3 m, Boxboard/cartonboard
Energy Data:
 Power boilers: 1
 Combustion turbines: 1 at 4.8 MW
 Electrical demand for mill: 94 MWh/D

ⓂAbelan Board and Packaging Solutions
Villava Mill
San Andrés S/N
E-31610 Villava, Navarra
Spain
 Phone: (34) 948 16 83 00
 Fax: (34) 948 16 83 01
 Email: jlzubiete@tngeu.com,
 sanandres@abelan.com
 Web Address: www.abelan.com/home
Personnel:
 Gen. Dir. Abelan South : Jorge Beschinsky
 Phone: (34) 948 16 83 00
 Fax: (34) 948 16 83 01
 Mill Mgr.: Juan L. Zubiete
 Phone: (34) 948 16 83 00
 Fax: (34) 948 16 83 01
 Email: jlzubiete@tngeu.com
 Gen. Mgr.: Jaime Llopis
 Phone: (34) 948 16 83 00
 Fax: (34) 948 16 83 01
 Email: jllopis@tngeu.com
 Prod. Chief: E. Uriz
 Phone: (34) 948 16 83 00
 Fax: (34) 948 16 83 01
 Email: euriz@tngeu.com
 Maint. Chief: M. A. Plazza
 Phone: (34) 948 16 83 00
 Fax: (34) 948 16 83 01
 Email: maplaza@tngeu.com
 Chief, Raw Material Buyer: F. Gardeazabal
 Phone: (34) 948 16 83 00
 Fax: (34) 948 16 83 01
 Process Chief: J. Valdazo
 Phone: (34) 948 16 83 00
 Fax: (34) 948 16 83 01
 Email: jvaldazo@tngeu.com
Total Employees at this Location: 154
Type of Operation: Paper mill, Paperboard mill
Pulp Grades and Capacities:
 Total pulp capacity: 123,010 mt/y
 Recycled Pulping: 123,010 mt/y
Pulp Mill Data:
 Recycled Fiber Treatment Lines:
 Pulpers: 4 at 120,000 admt/y
Paper/Paperboard Grades and Capacities:
 Total paper and paperboard capacity: 120,000 mt/y
 Boxboard/cartonboard: 120,000 mt/y
Paper and Paperboard Mill Data:
 Stock Preparation:
 Pulpers: 4
 Refiners: 5
Paper Machines: 2
 No. 1, multi-fourdrinier, total capacity 40,000 mt/y, Trim width 1.7 m, Boxboard/cartonboard
 No. 2, pressure former, total capacity 80,000 mt/y, Trim width 2.3 m, Boxboard/cartonboard
Finishing Equipment:
 Rewinders: 2
 Sheeters: 1
Energy Data:
 Power boilers: 1
 Combustion turbines: 1 at 5 MW
 Steam turbines: 1 at 1.6 MW
 Electrical demand for mill: 153 MWh/D

ⓂAlier S.A.
Ownership: 100% by Private
Diputación, 238, 5°- 8°
E-08007 Barcelona
Spain
 Phone: (34) 93 304 28 60
 Fax: (34) 93 301 44 81
 Email: alier@aliersa.com
 Web Address: www.aliersa.com
Personnel:
 Pres.: Pedro Alier Gasull
 Phone: (34) 93 304 28 60
 Fax: (34) 93 301 44 81
 Chmn./Man. Dir.: Florentino Nespereira Salgado
 Phone: (34) 93 304 28 60
 Fax: (34) 93 301 44 81
 Email: nespereira@aliersa.com
 Fin. Dir.: Julio Berdejo Homedes
 Phone: (34) 93 304 28 60
 Fax: (34) 93 301 44 81
 Email: j.berdejo@aliersa.com
 Sls. Dir.: Francisco Lluis Riba
 Phone: (34) 93 304 28 60
 Fax: (34) 93 301 44 81
 Email: f.lluis@aliersa.com
 Purch. Dir.: Robert Banyeres Gasol
 Phone: (34) 973 73 2705
 Fax: (34) 973 73 0362
 Email: alierlle@aliersa.com
 Commer. Dir.: Juan Lopez
 Phone: (34) 93 304 28 60
 Fax: (34) 93 301 44 81
 Exec. Sec.: Helena Valls
 Phone: (34) 93 304 28 60
 Fax: (34) 93 301 44 81
 Email: h.valls@aliersa.com
 Mill. Mgr.: Igor Garcia
 Phone: (34) 973 73 2705
 Fax: (34) 973 73 0362
 Email: i.garcia@aliersa.com
 Area Mgr. : Joan Ribas Ferrer
 Phone: (34) 93 304 28 60
 Fax: (34) 93 301 44 81
 Sls. Export Area Mgr. : Albert Gimeno
 Phone: (34) 93 304 28 60
 Fax: (34) 93 301 44 81
 Admin. & Finan. Dept.: Gemma Pallarols Taylor
 Phone: (34) 93 304 28 60
 Fax: (34) 93 301 44 81
Total Employees of Company: 146
Total Employees at this Location: 12
Mill Locations:
 Alier S.A., Roselló Mill, Afueras s/n, E-25125 Roselló, Spain, Capacity: 143,000 mt/y, (Paper mill, Paperboard mill)
 Phone: (34) 973 732705/ 933042871
 Fax: (34) 973 730362/933014481
 Email: alierlle@aliersa.com

ⓂAlier S.A.
Roselló Mill
Mill is filed for voluntary insolvency proceedings in April 2014
Afueras s/n
E-25125 Roselló, Lérida
Spain
 Phone: (34) 973 732705/ 933042871
 Fax: (34) 973 730362/933014481
 Email: alierlle@aliersa.com
 Web Address: www.aliersa.com
Personnel:
 Man. Dir.: Alessandro Aldighieri
 Phone: (34) 973 732705
 Fax: (34) 973 730362
 Tech. Dir.: José Pulido
 Phone: (34) 973 732705
 Fax: (34) 973 730362
 Purch. Dir: Robert Banyeres Gasol
 Phone: (34) 973 732705/ 933042871
 Fax: (34) 973 730362
 Email: alierlle@aliersa.com
 Mill Mgr.: Igor Garcia Sala
 Phone: (34) 973 732705/ 933042871
 Fax: (34) 973 730362
 Email: i.garcia@aliersa.com
Total Employees at this Location: 155
Type of Operation: Paper mill, Paperboard mill
Pulp Grades and Capacities:
 Total pulp capacity: 144,186 mt/y
 Recycled Pulping: 144,186 mt/y
Pulp Mill Data:
 Recycled Fiber Treatment Lines:
 Pulpers: 4 at 144,400 admt/y
Paper/Paperboard Grades and Capacities:
 Total paper and paperboard capacity: 143,000 mt/y
 Packaging papers: 63,000 mt/y
 Boxboard/cartonboard: 80,000 mt/y
Paper and Paperboard Mill Data:
 Stock Preparation:
 Pulpers: 4
 Refiners: 5
Paper Machines: 2
 No. 2, fourdrinier (2), total capacity 80,000 mt/y, Trim width 2.52 m, Boxboard/cartonboard
 No. 3, fourdrinier, total capacity 63,000 mt/y, Trim width 3.54 m, Packaging papers
Finishing Equipment:
 Winders: 1
 Rewinders: 2
Energy Data:
 Power boilers: 4
 Combustion turbines: 1 at 21 MW
 Steam turbines: 1 at 3 MW
 Electrical demand for mill: 212 MWh/D

ⓂPapelera de la Alqueria S.L.
Cl San Lorenzo 2
E-03829 Alqueria de Aznar, Alicante
Spain

Spain

Phone: (34) 96 6516128
Fax: (34) 96 5531421
Email: edari@palqueria.com
Personnel:
Mgr.: Pablo Sanz
Phone: (34) 96 6516128
Fax: (34) 96 5531421
Email: pablo.sanz@palqueria.com
Mill Locations:
Papelera de la Alqueria S.L., Alicante Mill, Cl San Lorenzo 2, E-03829 Alqueria de Aznar, Alicante, Spain, Capacity: 100,000 mt/y, (Paper mill, Paperboard mill)
Phone: (34) 96 6516128
Fax: (34) 96 5531421
Email: edari@palqueria.com

ⓂPapelera de la Alqueria S.L.
Alicante Mill
Cl San Lorenzo 2
E-03829 Alqueria de Aznar, Alicante
Spain
Phone: (34) 96 6516128
Fax: (34) 96 5531421
Email: edari@palqueria.com
Personnel:
Mgr.: Pablo Sanz
Phone: (34) 96 6516128
Fax: (34) 96 5531421
Email: pablo.sanz@palqueria.com
Total Employees at this Location: 50
Type of Operation: Paper mill, Paperboard mill
Pulp Grades and Capacities:
  Total pulp capacity: 99,533 mt/y
  Recycled Pulping: 99,533 mt/y
Pulp Mill Data:
  Recycled Fiber Treatment Lines:
  Recycled packaging pulping lines: 1 at 100,000
Paper/Paperboard Grades and Capacities:
  Total paper and paperboard capacity: 100,000 mt/y
  Linerboard: 65,000 mt/y
  Corrugating medium/fluting: 35,000 mt/y
Paper and Paperboard Mill Data:
  Stock Preparation:
  Pulpers: 2
  Refiners: 2
Paper Machines: 1
No. 1, fourdrinier, total capacity 100,000 mt/y, Trim width 3.24 m, Linerboard, Corrugating medium/fluting
Finishing Equipment:
  Winders: 1 at 60,000 mt/y
Energy Data:
Power boilers: 3
Combustion turbines: 1 at 5 MW
Electrical demand for mill: 139 MWh/D

ⓞⓂPapel Aralar S.A.
Amezqueta Mill
Calle San Bartolomé 40
E-20268 Amezqueta, Gipúzcoa
Spain
Phone: (34) 943 653 050
Fax: (34) 943 653 161
Email: info@papelaralar.com
Web Address: www.papelaralar.com
Personnel:
Gen. Dir.: Mr. Senen Amunarriz
Phone: (34) 943 653 050
Fax: (34) 943 653 161
Email: senen@papelaralar.com
Total Employees of Company: 150
Total Employees at this Location: 144
Type of Operation: Paper mill
Paper/Paperboard Grades and Capacities:
  Total paper and paperboard capacity: 100,000 mt/y
  Coated woodfree/freesheet: 12,300 mt/y
  Specialty and industrial: 87,700 mt/y
Paper and Paperboard Mill Data:
  Stock Preparation:
  Pulpers: 3

Refiners: 5
Paper Machines: 3
No. 1, fourdrinier, total capacity 46,000 mt/y, Trim width 2.6 m, Specialty and industrial, Coated woodfree/freesheet
No. 2, fourdrinier, total capacity 18,000 mt/y, Trim width 3.42 m, Specialty and industrial
No. 3, fourdrinier, total capacity 36,000 mt/y, Trim width 4.4 m, Specialty and industrial, Coated woodfree/freesheet
Coating Machines: 3
No. 1, total capacity 25,000 mt/y., on machine
No. 2, off machine
No. 3, on machine
Finishing Equipment:
  Calenders: 4
  Rewinders: 3
Energy Data:
Power boilers
HRSG boiler
Combustion turbines: 1 at 15 MW
Hydro turbines: 3
Electrical demand for mill: 220 MWh/D

ⓞⓂPapeleras del Arlanzón, S.A
Burgos Mill
Bº de Villayuda, s/n
E-09007 Burgos
Spain
Phone: (34) 947 483 268
Fax: (34) 947 480 416
Email: arlanzon@papelerasdelarlanzon.es
Web Address: www.papelerasdelarlanzon.es
Personnel:
Sls. Mgr.: Javier Castas
Phone: (34) 915777553
Total Employees at this Location: 25
Type of Operation: Paperboard mill
Pulp Grades and Capacities:
  Total pulp capacity: 39,349 mt/y
  Recycled Pulping: 39,349 mt/y
Pulp Mill Data:
  Recycled Fiber Treatment Lines:
  Recycled packaging pulping lines: 1
Paper/Paperboard Grades and Capacities:
  Total paper and paperboard capacity: 39,000 mt/y
  Linerboard: 39,000 mt/y
Paper and Paperboard Mill Data:
Paper Machines: 1
No. 1, fourdrinier (2), total capacity 39,000 mt/y, Trim width 2.6 m, Linerboard
Energy Data:
Power boilers
Combustion turbines: 1
Electrical demand for mill: 57 MWh/D

ⓞⓂAgustín Barral, S.A.
Barcelona Mill
Ownership: 100% by A. Agustín Barral
Afueras, s/n
E-08696 La Pobla de Lillet (Barcelona)
Spain
Phone: (34) 93 8236028
Fax: (34) 93 8236611
Email: agustinbarral@gmail.com,
agustin_barral@teleline.es
Personnel:
Mgr.: Agustín Barral
Phone: (34) 93 8236028
Fax: (34) 93 8236611
Mill Dir.: José Colomer
Phone: (34) 93 8236028
Fax: (34) 93 8236611
Accountant: Miguel Giner
Phone: (34) 93 4147600
Total Employees at this Location: 30
Type of Operation: Pulp mill, Paperboard mill
Pulp Grades and Capacities:
  Total pulp capacity: 20,140 mt/y

Recycled Pulping: 20,140 mt/y
Pulp Mill Data:
Pulp Lines: 1
  Recycled Fiber Treatment Lines:
  Pulpers: 1 at 20,000 admt/y
Paper/Paperboard Grades and Capacities:
  Total paper and paperboard capacity: 20,000 mt/y
  Linerboard: 14,000 mt/y
  Corrugating medium/fluting: 2,000 mt/y
  Boxboard/cartonboard: 4,000 mt/y
Paper and Paperboard Mill Data:
  Stock Preparation:
  Pulpers: 3
  Refiners: 2
Paper Machines: 1
No. 1, fourdrinier (2), total capacity 20,000 mt/y, Trim width 2.46 m, Corrugating medium/fluting, Linerboard, Boxboard/cartonboard
Energy Data:
Power boilers
Hydro turbines: 1 at 0.3 MW
Electrical demand for mill: 27 MWh/D

ⓞⓂPapelera de Brandia S.A.
La Coruña Mill
Paseo de Amaia N 2
E-15706 Santiago de Compostela, La Coruña
Spain
Phone: (34) 981 522133
Fax: (34) 981 521927
Email: info@brandia.com
Web Address: www.brandia.com
Personnel:
Man. Dir.: Gaspar D. Barreras
Phone: (34) 981 522133
Fax: (34) 981 521927
Email: gaspar.barreras@brandia.com
Qlty. Mgr.: Javier Santos
Phone: (34) 981 522133
Fax: (34) 981 521927
Email: javier.santos@brandia.com
Total Employees of Company: 65
Total Employees at this Location: 59
Type of Operation: Paper mill
Paper/Paperboard Grades and Capacities:
  Total paper and paperboard capacity: 30,000 mt/y
  Packaging papers: 5,000 mt/y
  Specialty and industrial: 25,000 mt/y
Paper and Paperboard Mill Data:
Paper Machines: 1
No. 1, fourdrinier, Yankee dryer, total capacity 30,000 mt/y, Trim width 2.52 m, Specialty and industrial, Packaging papers
Energy Data:
Power boilers: 1
Combustion turbines: 5 at 4.9 MW
Electrical demand for mill: 71 MWh/D

ⓞCEL Technologies & Systems, S.L.
Ownership: 100% by Indarkia SL, Basc Government
Barrio Barroetaguren s/n
E-01474 Arceniega
Spain
Phone: (34) 945 398100
Fax: (34) 945 398101
Web Address: www.celtechno.es
Personnel:
Mgr.: Begoña Arechabala
Phone: (34) 945 398122
Fax: (34) 945 398101
Email: begona.arechavala@celtechno.com
Total Employees of Company: 185
Mill Locations:
CEL Technologies & Systems, S.L., Arceniega Mill, Barrio Barroetaguren s/n, E-01474 Arceniega, Spain, Capacity: 30,000 mt/y, (Paper mill)
Phone: (34) 945 398122 / 398100
Fax: (34) 945 398101

Spain

CEL Technologies & Systems, S.L., Aranguren Mill, Bo Aranguren, s/n, E-48850 Calle Nicola Urgoiti, Spain, Capacity: 40,000 mt/y, (Pulp mill, Paper mill)
Phone: (34) 94 667 0000
Fax: (34) 94 639 0985

ⓜCEL Technologies & Systems, S.L.
Arceniega Mill
Barrio Barroetaguren s/n
E-01474 Arceniega, Alava
Spain
Phone: (34) 945 398122 / 398100
Fax: (34) 945 398101
Web Address: celtechno.com
Personnel:
Mgr.: Begoña Arechabala
Phone: (34) 945 398122
Fax: (34) 945 398101
Email: begona.arechavala@celtechno.com
Total Employees at this Location: 95
Type of Operation: Paper mill
Paper/Paperboard Grades and Capacities:
Total paper and paperboard capacity: 30,000 mt/y
Tissue: 30,000 mt/y

ⓜCEL Technologies & Systems, S.L.
Aranguren Mill
Bo Aranguren, s/n
E-48850 Calle Nicola Urgoiti, Vizcaya
Spain
Phone: (34) 94 667 0000
Fax: (34) 94 639 0985
Web Address: celtechno.com
Personnel:
Mill Mgr.: Eduardo Larrea
Phone: (34) 94 667 0000
Fax: (34) 94 639 0985
Email: eduardo.larrea@celtechno.com
Eng. & Maint. Mgr.: Luis Abajo
Phone: (34) 94 667 0000
Fax: (34) 94 639 0985
Email: luis.abajo@ecofibras.es
Total Employees at this Location: 90
Type of Operation: Pulp mill, Paper mill
Pulp Grades and Capacities:
Total pulp capacity: 38,545 mt/y
Recycled Pulping: 38,545 mt/y
Pulp Mill Data:
Bleach Plant Systems: 1
DIF Sequence: P/HS
Recycled Fiber Treatment Lines:
Flotation deinking lines: 2
Pulp Dryers:
Wet Lap machine 1
Paper/Paperboard Grades and Capacities:
Total paper and paperboard capacity: 40,000 mt/y
Tissue: 40,000 mt/y
Paper and Paperboard Mill Data:
Paper Machines: 2
No. 2, fourdrinier, Yankee dryer, total capacity 10,000 mt/y, Trim width 3.3 m, Tissue
No. 5, inclined, Yankee dryer, total capacity 30,000 mt/y, Trim width 2.6 m, Tissue
Energy Data:
Power boilers: 1
Electrical demand for mill: 134 MWh/D

ⓞⓜCotton South S.L. (CELSUR)
Fonelas Mill
Ownership: 70% by Celulosas Del Sur S.C.A., 30% by Inversiones Progranada S.A.
Carretera de Benalúa - Fonelas, Km. 3
E-18515 Fonelas, Granada
Spain
Phone: (34) 958 684 400
Fax: (34) 958 684 409
Email: lmg@celsur.es
Personnel:
Gen. Dir.: Miguel Segura Jimenez
Phone: (34) 958 684 402
Fax: (34) 958 684 409
Email: m.segura@celsur.es
Mill Mgr.: Fernando Molina Sabio
Phone: (34) 958 684 405
Fax: (34) 958 684 409
Email: f.molina@celsur.es
Qlty. Contr. Mgr.: Miguel Ángel Martínez Guirado
Phone: (34) 958 684 404
Fax: (34) 958 684 409
Email: m.martinez@celsur.es
Finan. Mgr.: Manuel Ortiz Lorente
Phone: (34) 958 684 406
Fax: (34) 958 684 409
Email: m.ortiz@celsur.es
Sls. & Mktg. Mgr.: Luis Maria García Garijo
Phone: (34) 958 684 407
Fax: (34) 958 684 409
Email: lmg@celsur.es
Purch. Mgr.: Luis García Tejada
Phone: (34) 958 684 403
Fax: (34) 958 684 409
Email: lgarcia@celsur.es
Total Employees of Company: 65
Total Employees at this Location: 65
Type of Operation: Pulp mill
Pulp Grades and Capacities:
Total pulp capacity: 13,000 mt/y
Pulp available for market: 13,000 mt/y
Pulp Mill Data:
Chemical Pulping Systems:
Batch digesters: 5
Pulp Lines: 1
Bleach Plant Lines:
No. 1 Capacity 13,000 admt/y
Chemical Recovery Equipment:
Evaporator lines: 1
Recovery boilers: 1
Lime Kiln
Pulp Dryers:
Fourdriniers 1

ⓜCelulosas de Asturias S.A. (CEASA)
Navia Mill
Ownership: 100% by ENCE Energia y Celulosa SA
Armental, s/n
E-33710 Navia, Asturias
Spain
Phone: (34) 9 85 630 200
Fax: (34) 9 85 473 280/630686
Email: info@ence.es
Web Address: www.ence.es
Personnel:
Mill Mgr.: Eduardo Garcia
Phone: (34) 9 85 630 200
Email: egarcia@ence.es
Dir.: David Valdés Heugas
Phone: (34) 9 85 630 200
Head of Admin.: Ramón Díaz Martínez
Phone: (34) 9 85 630 200
Fax: (34) Ext. 320
Email: rdiaz@ence.es
Dir. Sec.: María Ester García Mendez
Phone: (34) 9 85 630 200 Ext. 101
Email: mgarcia@ence.es
Total Employees at this Location: 350
Type of Operation: Pulp mill
Pulp Grades and Capacities:
Total pulp capacity: 503,860 mt/y
Pulp available for market: 500,000 mt/y
Chemical Pulp: 503,860 mt/y
Pulp Mill Data:
Chemical Pulping Systems:
Continuous digesters: 1
Pulp Lines: 1
Bleach Plant Systems: 1
Line 1, Type: ECF, Sequence: O_2 DEopD, Capacity 500,000 admt/y
Chemical Recovery Equipment:
Evaporator lines: 7
Recovery boilers: 1
Lime Kiln
Pulp Dryers:
Flakt dryer 1, Twin Wire 1
Energy Data:
Power boilers: 1
Steam turbines: 2 at 77 MW
Electrical demand for mill: 840 MWh/D

ⓞⓜClariana S.A.
Vila-Real Mill
Ownership: 100% by individual shareholders
Avda. Alemania 48
E-12540 Vila-Real, Castellón
Spain
Phone: (34) 964 521950
Fax: (34) 964 530554 / 964531385
Email: clariana@clariana.com
Web Address: www.clariana.com
Personnel:
COO: Miguel Goenaga
Phone: (34) 964 521950
Fax: (34) 964 530554
Email: mgoenaga@clariana.com
Export Dir.: Ms Amparo Boltes
Phone: (34) 964 531386
Fax: (34) 964 531385
Email: aboltes@clariana.com
Total Employees of Company: 99
Total Employees at this Location: 99
Type of Operation: Paper mill
Pulp Mill Data:
Chemical Recovery Equipment:
Recovery boilers: 1
Paper/Paperboard Grades and Capacities:
Total paper and paperboard capacity: 25,000 mt/y
Uncoated woodfree/freesheet: 25,000 mt/y
Paper and Paperboard Mill Data:
Stock Preparation:
Pulpers: 2
Refiners: 3
Paper Machines: 1
No. 2, hybrid former, total capacity 25,000 mt/y, Trim width 2.2 m, Uncoated woodfree/freesheet
Finishing Equipment:
Rewinders: 1 at 25,000 mt/y
Sheeters: 2 at 12,000 mt/y, 12,000 mt/y
Energy Data:
Power boilers: 2
Combustion turbines: 1 at 5 MW
Steam turbines: 1 at 1.2 MW
Electrical demand for mill: 50 MWh/D

ⓞⓜCartones Compactos S.L.
Barberá del Vallés Mill
C/ Molí Den Gall, S/N Nave 3
E-08210 Barberá del Vallés, Barcelona
Spain
Phone: (34) 937 122045
Fax: (34) 937 124119
Email: info@cartonescompactos.com
Web Address: www.cartonescompactos.com
Personnel:
Dir. & Mill Mgr.: Gabriel Llonch
Phone: (34) 937 122045
Accountant: Sónia Llado
Phone: (34) 937 122045
Email: contabilidad@cartonescompactos.com
Total Employees at this Location: 20
Type of Operation: Paper mill, Paperboard mill
Pulp Mill Data:
Recycled Fiber Treatment Lines:
Recycled packaging pulping lines: 1
Paper/Paperboard Grades and Capacities:
Total paper and paperboard capacity: 250 mt/y
Boxboard/cartonboard

Spain

Paper and Paperboard Mill Data:
Paper Machines: 2
PM 1, Trim width 0.8 m
PM 2, Trim width 0.8 m, Packaging papers
Energy Data:
Electrical demand for mill: 1,500 MWh/D

ⓘⓜ DICEPA Papelera de Enate S.L.
Enate Mill
Ctra. de Barbastro a Francia, Km 7,700
E-22312 Enate, Huesca
Spain
  Phone: (34) 974 312400
  Fax: (34) 974 312199
  Email: dicepa@dicepa.com, info@dicepa.com
  Web Address: www.dicepa.com
Personnel:
  Chmn. of Bd.: Ramón Mor Fernandez
  Phone: (34) 974 312400
  Vice Chmn. of Bd.: Teresa Pera Cases
  Phone: (34) 974 312400
  Gen. Dir.: Juan Ramón Mor
  Phone: (34) 974 311628
  Prod. Mgr.: Ismael Amal
  Phone: (34) 974 312400
  Finan. Dir.: Antonio Nogués
  Phone: (34) 974 312400
Total Employees of Company: 45
Total Employees at this Location: 45
Type of Operation: Paper mill
Pulp Grades and Capacities:
  Total pulp capacity: 38,312 mt/y
  Recycled Pulping: 38,312 mt/y
Pulp Mill Data:
  Recycled Fiber Treatment Lines:
  Pulpers: 1 at 58,300
Paper/Paperboard Grades and Capacities:
  Total paper and paperboard capacity: 36,000 mt/y
  Tissue: 15,000 mt/y
  Packaging papers: 21,000 mt/y
Paper and Paperboard Mill Data:
  Stock Preparation:
  Pulpers: 2
Paper Machines: 1
No. 1, fourdrinier, Yankee dryer, total capacity 36,000 mt/y, Trim width 2.53 m, Tissue, Packaging papers
Energy Data:
  Power boilers: 2
  Combustion turbines: 1
  Electrical demand for mill: 116 MWh/D

ⓘⓜ Papelera Ecker S.A.
Beniparrell Mill
Partida del Palacio s/n
E-46469 Beniparrell, Valencia
Spain
  Phone: (34) 96 121 2476 / 120 3005
  Fax: (34) 96 121 1944
  Email: comercial@papelera-ecker.es
Personnel:
  Admin. Dir.: Ricardo Galan
  Phone: (34) 96 121 2476
  Gen. Mgr.: Mrs. Amparo García Chapa
  Phone: (34) 96 121 2476
Total Employees at this Location: 34
Type of Operation: Paper mill
Paper/Paperboard Grades and Capacities:
  Total paper and paperboard capacity: 14,000 mt/y
Paper and Paperboard Mill Data:
Paper Machines: 4
No. 1, Trim width 2.5 m
No. 2, Trim width 2.5 m
No. 3, Trim width 2.5 m
No. 4, Trim width 2.25 m

ⓜ ENCE Energia y Celulosa SA
Ownership: 20.40% by Alcor Holding, 5% by Atalaya Inversiones, 42.40% by free float, 22.16% by Retos Operativos XXI, 5% by Caja de Ahorros de Asturias, 5% by Fidalser, S.L.
Paseo de la Castellana 35
E-28036 Madrid
Spain
  Phone: (34) 91 337 8500
  Fax: (34) 91 337 8602
  Email: comunicacion@ence.es, rrhh@ence.es
  Web Address: www.ence.es
Personnel:
  Chmn. & Exec. Dir.: Juan Luis Arregui Ciarsolo
  Phone: (34) 91 337 8500
  Fax: (34) 91 337 8601
  CEO & Exec. Dir.: Ignacio de Colmenares y Brunet
  Phone: (34) 91 337 8500
  Fax: (34) 91 337 8601
  CFO: Diego Maus Lizariturry
  Phone: (34) 91 337 8500
  Fax: (34) 91 337 8601
  Gen. Mgr. Energy Bus. Unit: Jacinto Lobo Morán
  Phone: (34) 91 337 8500
  Fax: (34) 91 337 8602
  Gen. Mgr. Commun. & Institutional Rel.: Luis Carlos Martínez Martín
  Phone: (34) 91 337 8500
  Fax: (34) 91 337 8602
  Gen. Mgr. Pulp Bus. Unit: Guillermo Medina Ors
  Phone: (34) 91 337 8500
  Fax: (34) 91 337 8602
  HR Mgr.: Maria José Zueras Saludas
  Phone: (34) 91 337 8500
  Fax: (34) 91 337 8601
Total Employees of Company: 1,057
Mill Locations:
Celulosas de Asturias S.A. (CEASA), Navia Mill, Armental, s/n, E-33710 Navia, Spain, (Pulp mill)
  Phone: (34) 9 85 630 200
  Fax: (34) 9 85 473 280/630686
  Email: info@ence.es
ENCE Energia y Celulosa SA, Huelva Mill, Carretera A-472, Km. 79, Apartado 223, E-21007 Huelva, Spain, (Pulp mill)
  Phone: (34) 959 367700
  Fax: (34) 959 367628
  Email: comunicacionsur@ence.es
ENCE Energia y Celulosa SA, Pontevedra Mill, Marisma de Lourizán, s/n Aptdo. 157, E-36080 Pontevedra, Spain, (Pulp mill)
  Phone: (34) 986 856000
  Fax: (34) 986 847774
  Email: info@ence.es

ⓜ ENCE Energia y Celulosa SA
Huelva Mill
Mill is closed (Huelva bleached eucalyptus kraft (BEK) pulp mill in Spain definitively shut from October 19, 2014)
Carretera A-472, Km. 79, Apartado 223
E-21007 Huelva
Spain
  Phone: (34) 959 367700
  Fax: (34) 959 367628
  Email: comunicacionsur@ence.es
  Web Address: www.ence.es
Personnel:
  Mill Mgr.: Ernesto García
  Phone: (34) 959 367700
  Email: egarcia@ence.es
  Prod. Chief: Jorge del Toro
  Phone: (34) 959 367700
  Email: jtoroma@ence.es
  Sec.: Imaculada Lopez
  Phone: (34) 959 367 726
  Fax: (34) 959 367 628
  Email: ilopez@ence.es
Total Employees at this Location: 294
Type of Operation: Pulp mill
Pulp Grades and Capacities:
  Total pulp capacity: 411,308 mt/y
  Pulp available for market: 410,000 mt/y
  Chemical Pulp: 411,308 mt/y
Pulp Mill Data:
  Chemical Pulping Systems:
  Batch digesters: 10
  Continuous digesters: 1
  Bleach Plant Systems: 1
  No. 1, Sequence: O_2 DEoD
  Chemical Recovery Equipment:
  Evaporator lines: 1
  Recovery boilers: 2
  Lime Kiln
  Pulp Dryers:
  Flash dryers 1, Flash dryers 1
Energy Data:
  Power boilers: 2
  Steam turbines: 1 at 27.0 MW
  Electrical demand for mill: 750 MWh/D

ⓘⓜ ENCE Energia y Celulosa SA
Pontevedra Mill
Ownership: 20.40% by Alcor Holding, 5% by Atalaya Inversiones, 42.40% by free float, 22.16% by Retos Operativos XXI, 5% by Caja de Ahorros de Asturias, 5% by Fidalser, S.L.
Marisma de Lourizán, s/n Aptdo. 157
E-36080 Pontevedra
Spain
  Phone: (34) 986 856000
  Fax: (34) 986 847774
  Email: info@ence.es
  Web Address: www.ence.es
Personnel:
  Mill Mgr.: Antonio Casal Lago
  Phone: (34) 986 856000
  Quality & Environ. Mgr.: Carlos Casas
  Phone: (34) 986 856000
  Mill Mgr. Sec.: Clara Arza
  Phone: (34) 986 856000
  Email: claraag@ence.es
Total Employees of Company: 1,057
Total Employees at this Location: 320
Type of Operation: Pulp mill
Mill Locations:
Celulosas de Asturias S.A. (CEASA), Navia Mill, Armental, s/n, E-33710 Navia, Spain, (Pulp mill)
  Phone: (34) 9 85 630 200
  Fax: (34) 9 85 473 280/630686
  Email: info@ence.es
ENCE Energia y Celulosa SA, Huelva Mill, Carretera A-472, Km. 79, Apartado 223, E-21007 Huelva, Spain, (Pulp mill)
  Phone: (34) 959 367700
  Fax: (34) 959 367628
  Email: comunicacionsur@ence.es
Pulp Grades and Capacities:
  Total pulp capacity: 443,625 mt/y
  Pulp available for market: 440,000 mt/y
  Chemical Pulp: 443,625 mt/y
Pulp Mill Data:
  Chemical Pulping Systems:
  Batch digesters: 9
Pulp Lines: 1
  Bleach Plant Systems: 1
  Line 1, Type: TCF, Sequence: O_2 QPo, Capacity 440,000 admt/y
  Chemical Recovery Equipment:
  Evaporator lines: 6
  Recovery boilers: 1
  Lime Kiln
  Pulp Dryers:
  Flakt dryer 1, Flakt dryer 1, Fourdriniers 1, Twin Wire 1, Twin Wire 1
Energy Data:
  Power boilers: 1

Spain

Steam turbines: 2 at 35 MW
Electrical demand for mill: 752 MWh/D

ⓞEuropac - Papeles y Cartones de Europa S.A.
Ownership: 5.17% by Norges Bank
Avenida de Fuencarral, 98.
E- 28108 Alcobendas, Madrid
Spain
Phone: (34) 91 490 2160
Fax: (34) 91 662 4717
Email: dcri@europacgroup.com
Web Address: www.europac.es
Personnel:
Chmn.: D.José Miguel Isidro Corner
Phone: (34) 91 490 2160
Fax: (34) 91 662 4717
CEO: D. Enrique Isidro
Phone: (34) 91 490 2160
Fax: (34) 91 662 4717
Gen. Mgr. Paper: Fernando Pinto
Phone: (34) 91 490 2160
Fax: (34) 91 662 4717
Gen. Mgr. Packaging: Carlos Larriba
Phone: (34) 91 490 2160
Fax: (34) 91 662 4717
Gen. Mgr. Resource Div.: Fernando Aranguren
Phone: (34) 91 490 2160
Fax: (34) 91 662 4717
Total Employees of Company: 2,012
Total Employees at this Location: 60
Mill Locations:
Europac Alcolea de Cinca, Alcolea Mill, Ctra. de Fraga s/n, E-22410 Alcolea de Cinca, Spain, Capacity: 90,000 mt/y, (Paper mill, Paperboard mill)
Phone: (34) 97 446 8011/41
Fax: (34) 97 446 8293
Email: webpage@europac.es
Europac Papel Dueñas, Dueñas Mill, Carretera Burgos-Portugal, Km. 96, E-34210 Dueñas, Spain, Capacity: 230,000 mt/y, (Paper mill, Paperboard mill)
Phone: (34) 97 9761413
Fax: (34) 97 9761570
Email: europac.duenas@europac.es
Europac Kraft Viana, Viana do Castelo Mill, P.O. Box 550, Deocriste, P-4901-852 Viana do Castelo, Portugal, Capacity: 375,000 mt/y, (Pulp mill, Paperboard mill)
Phone: (351) 258 739600
Fax: (351) 258 731914
Email: portucel.viana@gescartao.pt
Europac Papeterie de Rouen, St. Etienne du Rouvray Mill, Rue Desiré Granet, BP 30444, F-76808 St. Etienne du Rouvray Cedex, France, Capacity: 300,000 mt/y, (Pulp mill, Paperboard mill)
Phone: (33) 2 35 64 52 52/51 49
Fax: (33) 2 35 64 51 32/04 52 89
Email: www.europacgroup.com

ⓜEuropac Alcolea de Cinca
Alcolea Mill
Ownership: 100% by Europac - Papeles y Cartones de Europa S.A.
Ctra. de Fraga s/n
E-22410 Alcolea de Cinca, Huesca
Spain
Phone: (34) 97 446 8011/41
Fax: (34) 97 446 8293
Email: webpage@europac.es
Web Address: www.europac.es
Personnel:
Mill Mgr.: Rafael Lacasa Cebollero
Phone: (34) 97 446 8011
Fax: (34) 97 446 8293
Email: rlacasa@europacgroup.com
Total Employees at this Location: 140
Type of Operation: Paper mill, Paperboard mill
Pulp Grades and Capacities:
Total pulp capacity: 87,672 mt/y
Recycled Pulping: 87,672 mt/y
Pulp Mill Data:
Recycled Fiber Treatment Lines:
Recycled packaging pulping lines: 1
Paper/Paperboard Grades and Capacities:
Total paper and paperboard capacity: 90,000 mt/y
Corrugating medium/fluting: 90,000 mt/y
Paper and Paperboard Mill Data:
Stock Preparation:
Pulpers: 1
Refiners: 18
Paper Machines: 1
No. 3, fourdrinier, total capacity 90,000 mt/y, Trim width 2.5 m, Corrugating medium/fluting
Finishing Equipment:
Winders: 1 at 90,000 mt/y
Energy Data:
Power boilers: 3
Combustion turbines: 2 at 10 MW
Electrical demand for mill: 126 MWh/D

ⓞⓜEuropac Papel Duenas
Dueñas Mill
Ownership: 100% by Europac - Papeles y Cartones de Europa S.A.
Carretera Burgos-Portugal, Km. 96
E-34210 Dueñas, Castilla y León
Spain
Phone: (34) 97 9761413
Fax: (34) 97 9761570
Email: europac.duenas@europac.es
Web Address: www.europac.es
Personnel:
Mill Mgr.: Agustín Arribas
Phone: (34) 97 9761413
Fax: (34) 97 9761570
Email: aarribas@europac.es
Commer. Dept: Carmen Perez
Phone: (34) 97 9761413
Fax: (34) 97 9761570
Email: cperez@europac.es
Total Employees at this Location: 300
Type of Operation: Paper mill, Paperboard mill
Pulp Grades and Capacities:
Total pulp capacity: 224,608 mt/y
Recycled Pulping: 224,608 mt/y
Pulp Mill Data:
Recycled Fiber Treatment Lines:
Recycled packaging pulping lines: 1
Paper/Paperboard Grades and Capacities:
Total paper and paperboard capacity: 230,000 mt/y
Linerboard: 230,000 mt/y
Paper and Paperboard Mill Data:
Stock Preparation:
Pulpers: 4
Refiners: 6
Paper Machines: 2
No. 1, fourdrinier (2), total capacity 95,000 mt/y, Trim width 2.35 m, Linerboard
No. 2, fourdrinier (2), total capacity 135,000 mt/y, Trim width 2.6 m, Linerboard
Finishing Equipment:
Winders: 1
Energy Data:
Power boilers: 4
Combustion turbines: 3 at 10, 25 MW
Steam turbines: 1 at 10 MW
Electrical demand for mill: 312 MWh/D

ⓞⓜFábrica Nacional de Moneda y Timbre-FNMT
Burgos Mill
Ownership: 100% by Ministry of Finance
Avda. Costa Rica 2
E-09001 Burgos
Spain
Phone: (34) 947 46 20 10
Fax: (34) 947 46 08 75
Email: fcapapel@fnmt.es
Web Address: www.fnmt.es
Personnel:
Paper Mill Man. Dir.: Antonio Olmos
Phone: (34) 947 46 20 05
Fax: (34) 947 46 08 75
Email: aolmos@fnmt.es
Prod. Mgr.: Javier Baraja
Phone: (34) 947 46 20 10
Fax: (34) 947 46 08 75
Email: jbaraja@fnmt.es
Product & Develop. Mgr.: Vicente Garcia-Juez
Phone: (34) 947 46 21 36
Fax: (34) 947 46 08 75
Email: vgjuez@fnmt.es
Qlty & Environ. Mgr.: Miguel Angel Riberas
Phone: (34) 947 46 20 10
Fax: (34) 947 46 08 75
Email: mariberas@fnmt.es
Maint. & Eng. Mgr.: José Mendía Aguilar
Phone: (34) 947 46 21 45
Fax: (34) 947 46 08 75
Email: jmendia@fnmt.es
Total Employees of Company: 178
Total Employees at this Location: 178
Type of Operation: Pulp mill, Paper mill
Pulp Grades and Capacities:
Paper/Paperboard Grades and Capacities:
Total paper and paperboard capacity: 2,500 mt/y
Uncoated woodfree/freesheet
Uncoated mechanical/groundwood
Coated woodfree/freesheet
Specialty and industrial

ⓞFiltros Anoia, S.A.
Camí de Baix, s/n
E-08776 Sant Pere de Riudebitlles, Barcelona
Spain
Phone: (34) 93 899 50 36
Fax: (34) 93 899 71 72
Email: fanoia@fanoia.com
Web Address: www.fanoia.com
Personnel:
Pres.: Enric Pérez Brignardelli
Phone: (34) 93 899 50 36
Fax: (34) 93 899 71 72
Email: fanoia@fanoia.com
Tech. Mgr.: Mrs. Engracia Sabate
Phone: (34) 93 899 50 36
Fax: (34) 93 899 71 72
Email: engracia@fanoia.com
Commer. Mgr.: Antonio Mesquida
Phone: (34) 93 899 50 36
Fax: (34) 93 899 71 72
Email: antonio@fanoia.com
Mill Locations:
Filtros Anoia, S.A., Sant Pere de Riudebitlles Mill, Camí de Baix, s/n, E-08776 Sant Pere de Riudebitlles, Spain, Capacity: 3,000 mt/y, (Paper mill)
Phone: (34) 93 899 50 36
Fax: (34) 93 899 71 72
Email: fanoia@fanoia.com

ⓜFiltros Anoia, S.A.
Sant Pere de Riudebitlles Mill
Camí de Baix, s/n
E-08776 Sant Pere de Riudebitlles, Barcelona
Spain
Phone: (34) 93 899 50 36
Fax: (34) 93 899 71 72
Email: fanoia@fanoia.com
Web Address: www.fanoia.com
Personnel:
Pres.: Enric Pérez Brignardelli
Phone: (34) 93 899 50 36
Fax: (34) 93 899 71 72
Email: fanoia@fanoia.com
Tech. Mgr.: Mrs. Engracia Sabate
Phone: (34) 93 899 50 36
Fax: (34) 93 899 71 72
Email: engracia@fanoia.com

Spain

Commer. & Mktg. Dir.: Antonio Mesquida
Phone: (34) 93 899 50 36
Fax: (34) 93 899 71 72
Email: antonio@fanoia.com
Export Assistant: Joana Sellares
Phone: (34) 93 899 50 36
Fax: (34) 93 899 71 72
Email: export@fanoia.com
Total Employees at this Location: 25
Type of Operation: Paper mill
Paper/Paperboard Grades and Capacities:
Total paper and paperboard capacity: 3,000 mt/y
Specialty and industrial
Paper and Paperboard Mill Data:
Paper Machines: 1
No. 1, Trim width 1.8 m, Specialty and industrial

ⓄⓂGomà-Camps S.A.U.
La Riba Mill
Cardenal Gomá, 29
E-43450 La Riba, Tarragona
Spain
Phone: (34) 977 876 800
Fax: (34) 977 876 241
Email: info@gomacamps.com
Web Address: www.gomacamps.com
Personnel:
Gen. Mgr.: Matias Gomà-Camps Reboltós
Phone: (34) 977 876 800
Fax: (34) 977 876 241
Tech. Mgr.: Jordi Gomà-Camps Llorens
Phone: (34) 977 876 801
Fax: (34) 977 876 241
Email: jordi@gomacamps.com
Maint. Head: Jaume Olle
Phone: (34) 977 876 800
Fax: (34) 977 876 241
Email: jaolle@gomacamps.com
Env. Head: Emma Marine
Phone: (34) 977 876 800
Fax: (34) 977 876 241
Email: emarine@gomacamps.com
Prod. Mgr.: Jordi Gomà-Camps Travé
Phone: (34) 977 876 800
Fax: (34) 977 876 241
Total Employees of Company: 425
Total Employees at this Location: 165
Type of Operation: Paper mill
Pulp Grades and Capacities:
Total pulp capacity: 33,945 mt/y
Recycled Pulping: 33,945 mt/y
Pulp Mill Data:
Bleach Plant Systems: 1
DIP
Recycled Fiber Treatment Lines:
Flotation deinking lines: 1
Paper/Paperboard Grades and Capacities:
Total paper and paperboard capacity: 65,000 mt/y
Tissue: 65,000 mt/y
Paper and Paperboard Mill Data:
Paper Machines: 2
No. 5, crescent former, Yankee dryer, total capacity 35,000 mt/y, Trim width 2.85 m, Tissue
No. 6, crescent former, Yankee dryer, total capacity 30,000 mt/y, Trim width 2.86 m, Tissue
Energy Data:
Power boilers: 2
Electrical demand for mill: 181 MWh/D

ⓄⓂGuarro Casas S.A.
Gelida Mill
Ownership: Arjowiggins SAS
Can Guarro s/n
E-08790 Gelida
Spain
Phone: (34) 93 7767676
Fax: (34) 93 7767630
Email: atencion.cliente@arjowiggins.com
Web Address: www.guarrocasas.com
Personnel:
Man. Dir.: Jordi Sauras
Phone: (34) 93 7767676
Fax: (34) 93 7767630
Email: jsauras@guarro.com
HR Mgr.: Albert Torné
Phone: (34) 93 776 7688
Fax: (34) 93 7767630
Email: atorne@guarro.com
Tech, R&D Mgr.: Jordi Sau
Phone: (34) 93 776 7698
Fax: (34) 93 7767630
Email: jsau@guarro.com
Finan. Mgr.: Gustavo Barredo
Phone: (34) 93 776 7672
Fax: (34) 93 7767630
Email: gbarredo@guarro.com
Export Sls. Mgr.: Miguel Alarcon
Phone: (34) 93 776 7674
Fax: (34) 93 7767630
Email: malarcon@guarro.com
National Sls. Mgr.: Antonio Piñol
Phone: (34) 93 776 7655
Fax: (34) 93 7767630
Email: apinol@guarro.com
Maint. Mgr.: Pierre Bertheas
Phone: (34) 93 776 7623
Fax: (34) 93 7767630
Email: pbertheas@guarro.com
Technical Papers: Carles Seuma
Phone: (34) 93 7767676
Fax: (34) 93 7767630
Email: cseuma@guarro.com
Technical Papers: Jon Lander Iraola
Phone: (34) 93 776 7682
Fax: (34) 93 7767630
Email: jiraola@guarro.com
Total Employees of Company: 8,094
Total Employees at this Location: 200
Type of Operation: Paper mill
Paper/Paperboard Grades and Capacities:
Total paper and paperboard capacity: 7,000 mt/y
Uncoated woodfree/freesheet: 7,000 mt/y
Paper and Paperboard Mill Data:
Paper Machines: 1
PM 2, total capacity 7,000 mt/y, Trim width 1.6 m, Uncoated woodfree/freesheet

ⓂPapelera Guipuzcoana de Zicuñaga S.A.
Hernani Mill
Ownership: 100% by Iberpapel
Barrio de Zicuñaga, s/n
E-20120 Hernani, Gipúzcoa
Spain
Mailing Address: Apartado 226, E-20080 San Sebastián, Guipúzcoa, Spain
Phone: (34) 94 3551100/3462600
Fax: (34) 94 3557728/3463681
Email: zicunaga@iberpapel.es
Web Address: www.iberpapel.es
Personnel:
Pres.: Iñigo Echevarria Canales
Phone: (34) 94 3551100
Fax: (34) 94 3557728
Gen. Mgr.: Fermin Urtasun
Phone: (34) 94 3551100
Fax: (34) 94 3557728
Email: zicupro.pgz@iberpapel.es
Sec.: Ana Frade
Phone: (34) 94 3551100
Fax: (34) 94 3557728
Email: dpgz@iberpapel.es
Total Employees at this Location: 285
Type of Operation: Pulp mill, Paper mill
Pulp Grades and Capacities:
Total pulp capacity: 175,879 mt/y
Chemical Pulp: 175,879 mt/y
Pulp Mill Data:
Chemical Pulping Systems:
Continuous digesters: 1
Pulp Lines: 1
Bleach Plant Systems: 1
No. 1, Type: ECF, Sequence: DEopD, Capacity 185,000 admt/y
Chemical Recovery Equipment:
Evaporator lines: 1
Recovery boilers: 1
Recovery boilers: 1
Lime Kiln
Paper/Paperboard Grades and Capacities:
Total paper and paperboard capacity: 237,750 mt/y
Uncoated woodfree/freesheet: 215,000 mt/y
Packaging papers: 10,500 mt/y
Specialty and industrial: 12,250 mt/y
Paper and Paperboard Mill Data:
Paper Machines: 3
No. 1, DuoFormer D, total capacity 35,000 mt/y, Trim width 2.2 m, Packaging papers, Specialty and industrial
No. 3, SymFormer, total capacity 65,000 mt/y, Trim width 2.3 m, Uncoated woodfree/freesheet
No. 4, Bel-Bond, total capacity 150,000 mt/y, Trim width 4.5 m, Uncoated woodfree/freesheet
Finishing Equipment:
Winders: 6 at 250,000 mt/y
Sheeters: 1
Energy Data:
Power boilers: 3
HRSG boiler: 2
Combustion turbines: 2 at 12, 42 MW
Steam turbines: 2 at 5, 7.5 MW
Electrical demand for mill: 780 MWh/D

ⓂHolmen Paper Madrid S.L.
Madrid Mill
Ownership: 100% by Holmen AB
P.I. La Cantueña, c/ del Papel, 1
E-28947 Fuenlabrada, Madrid
Spain
Phone: (34) 91 6420603
Fax: (34) 91 6422470
Email: madrid@holmenpaper.com
Web Address: www.holmenpaper.com
Personnel:
Mill Dir.: Juha Paulin
Phone: (34) 91 4958724, 680 653 277
Fax: (34) 91 6422470
Email: juha.paulin@holmenpaper.com
Prod. Dir.: Oscar García
Phone: (34) 91 6420603
Fax: (34) 91 6422470
Email: oscar.garcia@holmenpaper.com
Cogeneration Plant Dir.: Javier González
Phone: (34) 91 6420603
Fax: (34) 91 6422470
Admin. & Finan. Mgr.: Ignacio Paja
Phone: (34) 91 4958716
Fax: (34) 91 6422470
Email: ignacio.paja@holmenpaper.com
HR Dir.: Cristina Tocino
Phone: (34) 91 6420603 (649), 648 747 811
Fax: (34) 91 6422470
Email: cristina.tocino@holmenpaper.com
Purch. Logist. Mgr.: Joseba Goñi
Phone: (34) 91 6420603
Fax: (34) 91 6422470
Total Employees at this Location: 188
Type of Operation: Pulp mill, Paper mill
Pulp Grades and Capacities:
Total pulp capacity: 332,587 mt/y
Recycled Pulping: 332,587 mt/y
Pulp Mill Data:
Pulp Lines: 1
Recycled Fiber Treatment Lines:
Flotation deinking lines: 1 at 390,000 admt/y
Pulpers: 1 at 390,000 admt/y
Paper/Paperboard Grades and Capacities:
Total paper and paperboard capacity: 330,000 mt/y

Spain

Newsprint: 313,500 mt/y
Uncoated mechanical/groundwood: 16,500 mt/y
Paper and Paperboard Mill Data:
Stock Preparation:
Pulpers: 1
Refiners:
Paper Machines: 1
No. 62, DuoFormer TQv, total capacity 330,000 mt/y, Trim width 8.9 m, Newsprint, Uncoated mechanical/groundwood
Finishing Equipment:
Winders: 4 at 500,000 mt/y
Rewinders: 1
Sheeters: 1
Energy Data:
Power boilers: 4
HRSG boiler: 2
Combustion turbines: 2 at 30, 40 MW
Steam turbines: 1 at 8 MW
Electrical demand for mill: 832 MWh/D

⊕Iberpapel
Av. Sancho Sabio 2, 1st floor
E-20010 San Sebastián
Spain
Phone: (34) 91 564 0720
Fax: (34) 91 564 9716
Email: atencion.al.accionista@iberpapel.es
Web Address: www.iberpapel.es
Personnel:
Chmn.: Iñigo Echevarria Canales
Phone: (34) 91 564 0720
Fax: (34) 91 564 9716
Vice Chmn.: Néstor Basterra Larroude
Phone: (34) 91 564 0720
Fax: (34) 91 564 9716
Dir.: Baltasar Errazti Navarro
Phone: (34) 91 564 0720
Fax: (34) 91 564 9716
Gen. Dir.: Fermin Urtasum Erro
Phone: (34) 94 551 100
Fax: (34) 94 346 3681
Env. Dir.: Martin Arregui Gonzalo
Phone: (34) 94 355 1100
Fax: (34) 91 564 9716
Comp. Sec.: Joaquín Manso Ramón
Phone: (34) 91 564 0720
Fax: (34) 91 564 9716
Contr.: Luis Gonzalez Gutierrez
Phone: (34) 91 564 0720
Fax: (34) 91 564 9716
Email: lgonzalezg@iberpapel.es
Total Employees of Company: 349
Mill Locations:
Papelera Guipuzcoana de Zicuñaga S.A., Hernani Mill, Bario de Zicuñaga, s/n, E-20120 Hernani, Spain, Capacity: 237,750 mt/y, (Pulp mill, Paper mill)
Phone: (34) 94 3551100/3462600
Fax: (34) 94 3557728/3463681
Email: zicunaga@iberpapel.es

⊕Ibertissue S.L.U.
Buñuel Mill
Ownership: 100% by Sofidel Group
Pol. Industrial, S/N
E-31540 Buñuel, Navarra
Spain
Phone: (34) 948 832 080
Fax: (34) 948 823 028
Email: ibertissue@centralita.es, ibertissue@ibertissue.es
Web Address: www.sofidel.it
Personnel:
Gen. Mgr.: Javier Apecechea
Phone: (34) 948 832 080
Fax: (34) 948 823 028
Email: javier.apecechea@ibertissue.es
Mill Mgr.: Clemente Bonet
Phone: (34) 948 832 080
Fax: (34) 948 823 028

Email: clemente.bonet@ibertissue.es
Purch. Mgr.: Rosana Martínez
Phone: (34) 948 832 080
Fax: (34) 948 823 028
Email: rosana.martinez@ibertissue.es
Total Employees at this Location: 140
Type of Operation: Paper mill
Paper/Paperboard Grades and Capacities:
Total paper and paperboard capacity: 30,000 mt/y
Tissue: 30,000 mt/y
Paper and Paperboard Mill Data:
Paper Machines: 1
No. 1, crescent former, Yankee dryer, total capacity 30,000 mt/y, Trim width 2.71 m, Tissue
Energy Data:
Power boilers: 1
Electrical demand for mill: 74 MWh/D

⊕ICT Ibérica, S.L.U
El Burgo de Ebro Mill
Ownership: ICT Italy
Carretera Castellon Km 216, Camino de la Cañada Real, Las Peñas
E-50730 El Burgo de Ebro, Zaragoza
Spain
Phone: (34) 97 6104672
Fax: (34) 97 6104673
Email: info@ictes.eu
Web Address: www.foxy.it
Personnel:
Gen. Mgr.: José Luis Pérez Quintana
Phone: (34) 97 6104672
Fax: (34) 97 6104673
Email: p.quintana@ictes.eu
Prod. Dir.: Agustin Maronda
Phone: (34) 97 6104672
Fax: (34) 97 6104673
Email: a.maronda@ictes.eu
Dir., Converting: Ramon Clofent Ruiz
Phone: (34) 97 6104672
Fax: (34) 97 6104673
Email: r.clofent@ictes.eu
Finan. Dir.: Fernando Andolz
Phone: (34) 97 6104672
Fax: (34) 97 6104673
Email: f.andolz@ictes.eu
Logist. Dir.: Francisco Gil
Phone: (34) 97 6104672
Fax: (34) 97 6104673
Email: f.gil@ictes.eu
Total Employees at this Location: 180
Type of Operation: Paper mill
Paper/Paperboard Grades and Capacities:
Total paper and paperboard capacity: 70,000 mt/y
Tissue: 70,000 mt/y
Paper and Paperboard Mill Data:
Stock Preparation:
Refiners: 3
Paper Machines: 1
No. 1, crescent former, total capacity 70,000 mt/y, Trim width 5.55 m, Tissue
Energy Data:
Power boilers: 1
Electrical demand for mill: 170 MWh/D

⊕Isma 2000 (Ismaeco Group)
C/ Celleters,117,132, C/Ollers, 92, Pol. Ind. C'an Rubiol
07141 Marratxi
Spain
Phone: (34) 971604596
Fax: (34) 971604632
Email: info@ismaeco.com
Web Address: www.ismaeco.com/index.htm
Personnel:
Mill Mgr.: Fernando Luz
Phone: (34) 971604596
Fax: (34) 971604632
Email: nando@ismaeco.com
Mill Locations:
Isma 2000 (Ismaeco Group), Marratxi Mill, C/ Celleters,117,132, C/Ollers, 92, Pol. Ind. C'an Rubiol, 07141 Marratxi, Spain, Capacity: 2,000 mt/y, (Pulp mill, Paper mill)
Phone: (34) 971604596
Fax: (34) 971604632
Email: info@ismaeco.com

⊕Isma 2000 (Ismaeco Group)
Marratxi Mill
C/ Celleters,117,132, C/Ollers, 92, Pol. Ind. C'an Rubiol
07141 Marratxi
Spain
Phone: (34) 971604596
Fax: (34) 971604632
Email: info@ismaeco.com
Web Address: www.ismaeco.com
Personnel:
Mill Mgr.: Fernando Luz
Phone: (34) 971604596
Fax: (34) 971604632
Email: nando@ismaeco.com
Total Employees at this Location: 12
Type of Operation: Pulp mill, Paper mill
Pulp Grades and Capacities:
Total pulp capacity: 2,127 mt/y
Recycled Pulping: 2,127 mt/y
Pulp Mill Data:
Recycled Fiber Treatment Lines:
Pulpers: 1
Paper/Paperboard Grades and Capacities:
Total paper and paperboard capacity: 2,000 mt/y
Tissue: 2,000 mt/y
Paper and Paperboard Mill Data:
Paper Machines: 1
No. 1, fourdrinier, Yankee dryer, total capacity 2,000 mt/y, Trim width 2.1 m, Tissue
Energy Data:
Power boilers
Electrical demand for mill: 6 MWh/D

⊕Jofel Industrial S.A.
Ownership: 35% by Private, 65% by Mercapital
Pol. Ind. Las Atalayas, C/. Del Franco, s/n.
03114 Alicante
Spain
Phone: (34) 96 5104533
Fax: (34) 96 5104588
Email: jofel@jofel.com
Web Address: www.jofel.es
Personnel:
Pres. & Gen. Dir.: Luis Gomez Sierra
Phone: (34) 96 5104533
Fax: (34) 96 5104588
Admin. Dir.: Vicente Juan Salcedo
Phone: (34) 96 5104533
Fax: (34) 96 5104588
Purch. Dir.: Ricardo Zaragoza
Phone: (34) 96 5104533
Fax: (34) 96 5104588
Finan. Mgr.: Manuel Cruz
Phone: (34) 96 5104533
Fax: (34) 96 5104588
Finan. Contr.: Jairo Castro
Phone: (34) 96 5104533
Fax: (34) 96 5104588
Email: jcastro@jofel.es
Purch.Mgr.: Ricardo Paton
Phone: (34) 96 5104533
Fax: (34) 96 5104588
Email: rpaton@jofel.com
International Sls. Area: Emilio Marijuan
Phone: (34) 96 5104533
Fax: (34) 96 5104588
Admin.: Silvia Jiménez Moreta
Phone: (34) 96 5104533
Fax: (34) 96 5104588
Total Employees of Company: 200
Total Employees at this Location: 50
Mill Locations:

Spain

Virtisú S.L., Capellades Mill, C/ Torre Baixa, s/n, 08789 La Torre de Claramunt, Spain, Capacity: 22,000 mt/y, (Paper mill)
Phone: (34) 93 801 0723
Fax: (34) 93 801 0375
Email: iazcon@jofel.com

ⓘKartogroup España S.L.
Ownership: 100% by Cominter Inversiones
Passeig de Gràcia, 42, 2n
E-08007 Barcelona, Barcelona
Spain
Phone: (34) 934 670 650
Fax: (34) 964 51 696
Email: comercial@cominterpaper.com
Web Address: www.cominterpaper.com
Personnel:
Gen. Mgr.: Pascual Goméz
Email: pascual.gomez@kartogroup.es
Total Employees of Company: 500
Mill Locations:
Kartogroup España S.L., Castellòn Mill, Camino Xamussa, 0 S/N, E-12530 Burriana, Castellòn, Spain, Capacity: 38,000 mt/y, (Paper mill)
Phone: (34) 964 57 70 53
Fax: (34) 964 51 69 61
Email: comercial@cominterpaper.com

ⓘKartogroup España S.L.
Castellòn Mill
Camino Xamussa, 0 S/N
E-12530 Burriana, Castellòn
Spain
Phone: (34) 964 57 70 53
Fax: (34) 964 51 69 61
Email: comercial@cominterpaper.com
Web Address: www.cominterpaper.com
Personnel:
Gen. Mgr.: Pascual Goméz
Phone: (34) 964 51 03 54
Fax: (34) 964 51 69 61
Email: pascual.gomez@kartogroup.es
Tech. Dir.: Anton Clara
Phone: (34) 964 51 03 54
Fax: (34) 964 51 69 61
Email: anton.clara@kartogroup.es
Admin. Mgr.: Carmina Alonso
Phone: (34) 964 51 03 54
Fax: (34) 964 51 69 61
Email: carmina.alonso@kartogroup.es
Total Employees at this Location: 175
Type of Operation: Paper mill
Pulp Grades and Capacities:
Total pulp capacity: 11,854 mt/y
Recycled Pulping: 11,854 mt/y
Pulp Mill Data:
Recycled Fiber Treatment Lines:
Flotation deinking lines: 1
Paper/Paperboard Grades and Capacities:
Total paper and paperboard capacity: 38,000 mt/y
Tissue: 38,000 mt/y
Paper and Paperboard Mill Data:
Paper Machines: 2
No. 1, fourdrinier, Yankee dryer, total capacity 11,000 mt/y, Trim width 2.45 m, Tissue
No. 2, crescent former, Yankee dryer, total capacity 27,000 mt/y, Trim width 2.65 m, Tissue
Energy Data:
Power boilers: 1
Electrical demand for mill: 101 MWh/D

ⓘKimberly-Clark S.A.
Ownership: 100% by Kimberly-Clark Corp.
Calle Juan Esplandiu 11-13
E-28007 Madrid
Spain
Phone: (34) 91 504 3136, 91 557 9728, 91 557 9700
Fax: (34) 91 5579701
Email: kcpes@kcc.com, contacta.spain@kcc.com, productos.spain@kcc.com
Web Address: www.kcc.com, www.kimberlyclark.es
Personnel:
Dir. KC Latin America: David Campos
Phone: (34) 91 557 9728/9700
Fax: (34) 91 5579701
Country Mgr. Spain & Portugal: Daniel Isart
Phone: (34) 91 557 9728/9700
Fax: (34) 91 5579701
Email: daniel.isart@kcc.com
Key Account Mgr.: Begona Gonzalez Galarza
Phone: (34) 91 557 9728/9700
Fax: (34) 91 5579701
Trade Mktg. & Category Mgr.: Nieves Genovese
Phone: (34) 91 557 9728/9700
Fax: (34) 91 5579701
Email: nieves.genovese@kcc.com
Total Employees of Company: 58,000
Mill Locations:
Kimberly-Clark S.A., Bernal Mill, Espora 50, 1876 Bernal, Argentina, Capacity: 34,986 mt/y, (Paper mill)
Phone: (54) 11 4365 7209
Fax: (54) 11 4365 7244
Email: gustavo.magnani@kcc.com
Kimberly-Clark S.A., Salamanca Mill, Carr. Florida de Liébana, km. 3,8, E-37120 Doñinos, Spain, Capacity: 50,000 mt/y, (Paper mill)
Phone: (34) 92 333 0011
Fax: (34) 92 333 0030/0115

ⓘKimberly-Clark S.A.
Salamanca Mill
Ownership: 100% by Kimberly-Clark Corp.
Carr. Florida de Liébana, km. 3,8
E-37120 Doñinos, Salamanca
Spain
Phone: (34) 92 333 0011
Fax: (34) 92 333 0030/0115
Web Address: www.kcc.com
Personnel:
Dir.: Andres Calle
Phone: (34) 92 333 0011
Fax: (34) 92 333 0030
Email: acalle@kcc.com
Total Employees at this Location: 190
Type of Operation: Paper mill
Paper/Paperboard Grades and Capacities:
Total paper and paperboard capacity: 50,000 mt/y
Tissue: 50,000 mt/y
Paper and Paperboard Mill Data:
Paper Machines: 1
No. 1, crescent former, Yankee dryer, total capacity 50,000 mt/y, Trim width 5.28 m, Tissue
Energy Data:
Power boilers: 1
Electrical demand for mill: 132 MWh/D

ⓘⓘLC Paper 1881, S.A.
Besalú Mill
Ctra. de Besalú-Figueres, km 62
E-17850 Besalú, Girona
Spain
Phone: (34) 972 59 02 51
Fax: (34) 972 59 12 54
Email: info@lcpaper.net
Web Address: www.lcpaper.net
Personnel:
CEO: Joan Vila
Phone: (34) 972 59 02 51
Fax: (34) 972 59 12 54
Email: jvila@ecopaper.net
Assmpcio Vila
Phone: (34) 972 59 02 51
Fax: (34) 972 59 12 54
Chief Sls. Officer: Xavier Puig
Phone: (34) 972 59 02 51
Fax: (34) 972 59 12 54
Chief of Energy: Candy Jordan
Phone: (34) 972 59 02 51
Fax: (34) 972 59 12 54
Chief Maint. Officer: Josep Font
Phone: (34) 972 59 02 51
Fax: (34) 972 59 12 54
Total Employees at this Location: 150
Type of Operation: Paper mill
Pulp Grades and Capacities:
Total pulp capacity: 17,344 mt/y
Recycled Pulping: 17,344 mt/y
Pulp Mill Data:
Recycled Fiber Treatment Lines:
Recycled packaging pulping lines: 1
Paper/Paperboard Grades and Capacities:
Total paper and paperboard capacity: 60,000 mt/y
Tissue: 37,000 mt/y
Packaging papers: 23,000 mt/y
Paper and Paperboard Mill Data:
Stock Preparation:
Pulpers: 2
Refiners: 2
Paper Machines: 2
No. 2, fourdrinier, Yankee dryer, total capacity 23,000 mt/y, Trim width 3.3 m, Packaging papers
No. 3, crescent former, Yankee dryer, total capacity 37,000 mt/y, Trim width 2.8 m, Tissue
Finishing Equipment:
Supercalenders: 1
Rewinders: 2
Energy Data:
Power boilers: 1
Combustion turbines: 1 at 12 MW
Electrical demand for mill: 143 MWh/D

ⓘLecta S.A.
Ownership: 100% by CVC Capital Partners (Private)
Llull, 331
08019 Barcelona
Spain
Phone: (34) 93 482 10 00
Fax: (34) 93 482 11 70
Email: info@lecta.com
Web Address: www.lecta.com
Personnel:
Chmn. & CEO: Santiago Ramirez Larrauri
Phone: (33) 1 46 01 70 70/1 41 36 00 60
Fax: (33) 1 46 01 70 71/1 41 36 00 59
Email: sramirez@lecta.com
CFO: Andrea Minguzzi
Phone: (33) 1 46 01 70 70/1 41 36 00 60
Fax: (33) 1 46 01 70 71/1 41 36 00 59
Email: aminguzzi@lecta.com
Group Controller: Denis Cramazou
Phone: (33) 1 46 01 70 70/1 41 36 00 60
Fax: (33) 1 46 01 70 71/1 41 36 00 59
Email: dcramazou@lecta.com
Total Employees of Company: 3,752
Mill Locations:
Papeteries de Condat, Condat le Lardin Mill, 1523 avenue Georges Haupinot, BP 24, F-24570 Le Lardin St. Lazare, France, Capacity: 440,000 mt/y, (Paper mill)
Phone: (33) 5 53 51 43 33
Fax: (33) 5 53 51 41 04
Email: marketing@condat-pap.com
Cartiere del Garda SpA, Riva del Garda Mill, Viale Rovereto 15, I-38066 Riva del Garda, (TN), Italy, Capacity: 345,000 mt/y, (Paper mill)
Phone: (39) 0464 579 111
Fax: (39) 0464 521706
Email: info@gardacartiere.it
Torraspapel S.A., Motril Mill, Camino de la Via s/n, E-18600 Motril, Spain, Capacity: 243,000 mt/y, (Pulp mill, Paper mill)
Phone: (34) 958 832000
Fax: (34) 958 832030
Email: infomot@torraspapel.com
Torraspapel S.A., Sant Joan les Fonts Mill, Avda. Paperera. Torras s/n, E-17857 Sant Joan les Fonts, Spain, Capacity: 147,000 mt/y, (Paper mill)

Spain

Phone: (34) 972 277700
Fax: (34) 972 277701
Email: slvicens@torraspapel.es
Torraspapel S.A., Sarriá de Ter Mill, Avda. Josep Flores, s/n°, E-17840 Sarriá de Ter, Spain, Capacity: 85,000 mt/y, (Paper mill)
Phone: (34) 972 187300
Fax: (34) 972 187350
Torraspapel S.A., Uranga Mill, Carretera Tolosa s/n, E-20493 Berrobi, Tolosa, Spain, (Paper mill)
Phone: (34) 943 683409
Fax: (34) 943 683220
Torraspapel S.A., Zaragoza Mill, Avenida de Montañana, 429, E-50059 Zaragoza, Spain, Capacity: 189,000 mt/y, (Pulp mill, Paper mill)
Phone: (34) 976 01 70 00
Fax: (34) 976 01 70 50

ⓘⓜCelulosa de Levante S.A. (CELESA)
Tortosa Mill
Ownership: Miquel y Costas & Miquel S.A.
Carretera C-42, Km 8.5
E-43500 Tortosa, Tarragona
Spain
 Phone: (34) 977 44 9050/9137
 Fax: (34) 977 44 9135
 Email: celesa@celesa-pulp.com
 Web Address: www.celesa-pulp.com
Personnel:
 Man. Dir.: Jordi Bernardo
 Phone: (34) 977 44 9050
 Fax: (34) 977 44 9135
 Email: jbernardo@celesa-pulp.com
 Mill Mgr.: Josep M. Gras
 Phone: (34) 977 44 9050
 Fax: (34) 977 44 9135
 Email: gras@celesa-pulp.com
 Mktg. & Sls. Dir.: Miguel Martinez
 Phone: (34) 977 44 9050
 Fax: (34) 977 44 9135
 Email: mmartinez@celesa-pulp.com
 Purch. Dir.: Joan Arqué Alcové
 Phone: (34) 977 44 9155
 Fax: (34) 977 44 9135
 Email: arque@celesa-pulp.com
 Assist. to Man. Dir.: Maria José Audí
 Phone: (34) 977 44 9141
 Fax: (34) 997 44 9128
 Email: mjaudi@celesa-pulp.com
Total Employees of Company: 95
Total Employees at this Location: 95
Type of Operation: Pulp mill
Pulp Grades and Capacities:
 Total pulp capacity: 14,000 mt/y
Pulp Mill Data:
Pulp Lines: 1
 Bleach Plant Lines:
 No. 1

ⓘMatias Gomá Tomás S.A.
Afores s/n
43450 La Riba
Spain
 Phone: (34) 97 787 6040
 Fax: (34) 97 787 6039
Personnel:
 Owner: Carlos Gomá Lladó
 Phone: (34) 977 87 6040
 Fax: (34) 977 87 6039
 CEO: Xavier Gomà Segur
 Phone: (34) 977 87 6040
 Fax: (34) 977 87 6039
 Plant. Dir.: Josep Paretas Fabrellas
 Phone: (34) 977 87 6040
 Fax: (34) 977 87 6039
 Tech. Dir & Sls. Mgr.: Enric Fuster Ventosa
 Phone: (34) 977 87 6040
 Fax: (34) 977 87 6039
Mill Locations:
 Matias Gomá Tomás S.A., La Riba Mill, Afores s/n, 43450 La Riba, Spain, Capacity: 40,000 mt/y, (Paperboard mill)
 Phone: (34) 97 787 6040
 Fax: (34) 97 787 6039

ⓜMatias Gomá Tomás S.A.
La Riba Mill
Afores s/n
43450 La Riba
Spain
 Phone: (34) 97 787 6040
 Fax: (34) 97 787 6039
Personnel:
 Owner: Carlos Gomá Lladó
 Phone: (34) 97 787 6040
 Owner: Ramon Guillamat Ferré
 Phone: (34) 97 787 6040
Total Employees at this Location: 32
Type of Operation: Paperboard mill
Pulp Grades and Capacities:
 Total pulp capacity: 40,513 mt/y
 Recycled Pulping: 40,513 mt/y
Pulp Mill Data:
 Recycled Fiber Treatment Lines:
 Recycled packaging pulping lines: 1
Paper/Paperboard Grades and Capacities:
 Total paper and paperboard capacity: 40,000 mt/y
 Linerboard: 24,000 mt/y
 Corrugating medium/fluting: 16,000 mt/y
Paper and Paperboard Mill Data:
Paper Machines: 1
 No. 1, fourdrinier, total capacity 40,000 mt/y, Trim width 4.7 m, Corrugating medium/fluting, Linerboard
Energy Data:
 Power boilers
 Electrical demand for mill: 57 MWh/D

ⓘⓜMB Papeles Especiales
La Pobla de Claramunt Mill
Ownership: 100% by Miquel y Costas & Miquel S.A.
Carretera de Carme, Km. 1
E-08787 La Pobla de Claramunt, Barcelona
Spain
 Phone: (34) 93 808 7100
 Fax: (34) 93 808 6627/93 808 7727
 Email: mbpapers@mbpapers.com
 Web Address: www.mbpapers.com
Personnel:
 Man. Dir.: Josep Payola
 Phone: (34) 93 808 7100
 Fax: (34) 93 808 6627
 Email: jpayola@mbpapers.com
 Mill Mgr. Papeles Especiales and Terranova Papers: Joan Guma
 Phone: (34) 93 808 7100
 Fax: (34) 93 808 6627
 Email: jguma@mbpapers.com
 Purch. Mgr.: Joan Reynes
 Phone: (34) 93 808 7100
 Fax: (34) 93 808 6627
 Email: jreynes@mbpapers.com
 Sls. Mgr.: Olga Brufau
 Phone: (34) 93 808 7100
 Fax: (34) 93 808 6627
 Email: obrufau@mbpapers.com
Total Employees at this Location: 93
Type of Operation: Paper mill
Paper/Paperboard Grades and Capacities:
 Total paper and paperboard capacity: 16,000 mt/y
 Specialty and industrial: 16,000 mt/y
Paper and Paperboard Mill Data:
Paper Machines: 2
 No. 1, fourdrinier, Trim width 1.45 m, Specialty and industrial
 No. 2, fourdrinier, Trim width 2.2 m, Specialty and industrial
Finishing Equipment:
 Winders: 3
 Rewinders: 2
Energy Data:
 Power boilers: 2

ⓘMiquel y Costas & Miquel S.A.
Tuset 8-10
E-08006 Barcelona, Barcelona
Spain
 Phone: (34) 93 290 6100
 Fax: (34) 93 290 6126
 Web Address: www.miquelycostas.com
Personnel:
 Pres.: Jorge Mercader Miró
 Phone: (34) 93 290 6100
 Fax: (34) 93 290 6128
 Gen. Mgr.: Jorge Mercader Barata
 Phone: (34) 93 290 6100
 Fax: (34) 93 290 6128
 Exec. Dir. & Secretary: Fracisco Javier Basanez Villaluenga
 Phone: (34) 93 290 6100
 Fax: (34) 93 290 6128
 Dir. Factory: Javier Adriaca Colomer
 Phone: (34) 93 290 6100
 Fax: (34) 93 290 6128
 Dir. Booklets Division: Javier Garcia Blasco
 Phone: (34) 93 290 6100
 Fax: (34) 93 290 6128
 Dir. Plant Manipulated: Joan Calbó
 Phone: (34) 93 290 6100
 Fax: (34) 93 290 6128
 Purch. Dir.: Antonio Hita Martinez
 Phone: (34) 93 290 6100
 Fax: (34) 93 290 6128
 Paper Plant Mgr.: Alfonso Perez Llorente
 Phone: (34) 93 290 6100
 Fax: (34) 93 290 6128
Total Employees at this Location: 45
Mill Locations:
 Celulosa de Levante S.A. (CELESA), Tortosa Mill, Carretera C-42, Km 8.5, E-43500 Tortosa, Spain, (Pulp mill)
 Phone: (34) 977 44 9050/9137
 Fax: (34) 977 44 9135
 Email: celesa@celesa-pulp.com
 MB Papeles Especiales, La Pobla de Claramunt Mill, Carretera de Carme, Km. 1, E-08787 La Pobla de Claramunt, Spain, Capacity: 16,000 mt/y, (Paper mill)
 Phone: (34) 93 808 7100
 Fax: (34) 93 808 6627/93 808 7727
 Email: mbpapers@mbpapers.com
 Miquel y Costas & Miquel S.A., de Besos mill, P° Santa Coloma 125, E-08030 Barcelona, Spain, Capacity: 17,000 mt/y, (Paper mill)
 Phone: (34) 93 2906115
 Fax: (34) 93 2906112 / 2906113
 Terranova Papers, La Pobla de Claramunt Mill, Carretera de Carme, km 1, 08787 La Pobla de Claramunt, Spain, Capacity: 18,000 mt/y, (Paper mill)
 Phone: (34) 93 808 71 00
 Fax: (34) 93 808 77 27
 Miquel y Costas & Miquel S.A., Mislata mill, C/San Antonio 18, E-46920 Mislata, Spain, Capacity: 24,000 mt/y, (Paper mill)
 Phone: (34) 96 3790500
 Fax: (34) 96 3790504

ⓜMiquel y Costas & Miquel S.A.
de Besos mill
P° Santa Coloma 125
E-08030 Barcelona
Spain
 Phone: (34) 93 2906115
 Fax: (34) 93 2906112 / 2906113
Personnel:
 Mill Mgr.: José Maria Masifern
 Phone: (34) 93 2906115
 Fax: (34) 93 2906112
 Email: jmasifern@miquelycostas.com
Total Employees at this Location: 219
Type of Operation: Paper mill

Spain

Paper/Paperboard Grades and Capacities:
Total paper and paperboard capacity: 17,000 mt/y
Specialty and industrial: 17,000 mt/y
Paper and Paperboard Mill Data:
Paper Machines: 2
No. 3, fourdrinier, Trim width 2 m, Specialty and industrial
No. 5, fourdrinier, Trim width 2.9 m, Specialty and industrial
Finishing Equipment:
Rewinders: 2

ⓜTerranova Papers
La Pobla de Claramunt Mill
Ownership: Miquel y Costas & Miquel S.A.
Carretera de Carme, km 1
08787 La Pobla de Claramunt, Barcelona
Spain
Phone: (34) 93 808 71 00
Fax: (34) 93 808 77 27
Web Address: terranovapapers.com
Personnel:
Prod. Dir.: Tilo Herrmann
Phone: (34) 93 808 71 00
Fax: (34) 93 808 77 27
Email: thermann@miquelycostas.com
Type of Operation: Paper mill
Paper/Paperboard Grades and Capacities:
Total paper and paperboard capacity: 18,000 mt/y
Specialty and industrial: 18,000 mt/y
Paper and Paperboard Mill Data:
Paper Machines: 1
PM 3, (started December 2012), total capacity 18,000 mt/y, Trim width 3.3 m, Specialty and industrial

ⓜMiquel y Costas & Miquel S.A.
Mislata mill
C/San Antonio 18
E-46920 Mislata, Valencia
Spain
Phone: (34) 96 3790500
Fax: (34) 96 3790504
Web Address: www.miquelycostas.com
Personnel:
Mill Mgr.: Javier Ardiaca Colomer
Phone: (34) 96 3790500
Fax: (34) 96 3790504
Total Employees at this Location: 84
Type of Operation: Paper mill
Paper/Paperboard Grades and Capacities:
Total paper and paperboard capacity: 24,000 mt/y
Uncoated woodfree/freesheet: 11,500 mt/y
Specialty and industrial: 12,500 mt/y
Paper and Paperboard Mill Data:
Paper Machines: 1
No. 7, fourdrinier, total capacity 24,000 mt/y, Trim width 3.4 m, Uncoated woodfree/freesheet, Specialty and industrial

ⓜMunksjö Paper S.A.
Tolosa Mill
Ownership: Munksjö Oyj
Barrio de Eldua s/n
E-20492 Berástegui, Gipúzcoa
Spain
Mailing Address: Apartado 15, 20400 Berástegui, Spain
Phone: (34) 943 683 032
Fax: (34) 943 683 398
Email: info@munksjo.com
Web Address: www.munksjo.com
Personnel:
Mill Mgr.: Juan Antonio Navalpotro
Phone: (34) 943 683 032
Fax: (34) 943 683 398
Email: juan-antonio.navalpotro@munksjo.com
Sls. Mgr.: Amaia Muñoz
Phone: (34) 943 683 032
Fax: (34) 943 683 398
Email: amaia.munoz@munksjo.com
Finan. Mgr.: Aitziber Larrañaga
Phone: (34) 943 683032
Fax: (34) 943 683 484
Email: aitziber.larranaga@munksjo.com
Prod. Mgr.: Juan José Odriozola
Phone: (34) 943 683 032
Fax: (34) 943 683 398
Email: juan-jose.odriozola@munksjo.com
Environ. & Safety Mgr.: Aitor Mier
Phone: (34) 943 683 032
Fax: (34) 943 683 398
Email: aitor.mier@munksjo.com
Total Employees at this Location: 167
Type of Operation: Paper mill
Paper/Paperboard Grades and Capacities:
Total paper and paperboard capacity: 40,000 mt/y
Specialty and industrial: 40,000 mt/y
Paper and Paperboard Mill Data:
Stock Preparation:
Pulpers: 2
Refiners: 12
Paper Machines: 2
No. 11, fourdrinier, total capacity 7,000 mt/y, Trim width 1.6 m, Specialty and industrial
No. 12, fourdrinier, total capacity 33,000 mt/y, Trim width 2.7 m, Specialty and industrial
Finishing Equipment:
Winders: 2 at 45,000 mt/y
Rewinders: 2
Energy Data:
Power boilers: 2

ⓞⓜPapelera Munné S.A.
Capellades Mill
Ownership: 100% by J. Vilaseca S.A.
Antoni Mª Claret, 7-9
E-08786 Capellades, Barcelona
Spain
Phone: (34) 93 8011081
Fax: (34) 93 8012929
Email: munne@papeleramunne.com
Web Address: www.papeleramunne.com
Total Employees of Company: 17
Total Employees at this Location: 20
Type of Operation: Paper mill, Paperboard mill
Paper/Paperboard Grades and Capacities:
Total paper and paperboard capacity: 7,200 mt/y
Specialty and industrial
Boxboard/cartonboard
Paper and Paperboard Mill Data:
Stock Preparation:
Pulpers: 2
Refiners: 2
Paper Machines: 1
No. 1, twin-wire, Trim width 1.6 m, Boxboard/cartonboard
Finishing Equipment:
Rewinders: 1

ⓞⓜPapelera del Oria, S.A.
Zizurkil Mill
Barrio Elbarrena, 26
E-20150 Zizurkil, Gipúzcoa
Spain
Phone: (34) 943 696200
Fax: (34) 943 691550
Email: oficina@papeleradeloria.es, tecnico@papeleradeloria.es, ventas@papeleradeloria.es
Web Address: www.papeleradeloria.es
Personnel:
Gen. Dir.: Luis Fernando Ruiz Arrúe
Phone: (34) 943 696200 Ext. 218
Fax: (34) 943 691550
Email: lf.ruiz@papeleradeloria.es
Mgr.: Javier Lopez Castano
Phone: (34) 943 696200
Fax: (34) 943 691550
Email: javier.lopez@papeleradeloria.es
Total Employees at this Location: 92
Type of Operation: Paper mill
Paper/Paperboard Grades and Capacities:
Total paper and paperboard capacity: 60,000 mt/y
Uncoated woodfree/freesheet: 60,000 mt/y
Paper and Paperboard Mill Data:
Paper Machines: 1
No. 1, hybrid former, total capacity 60,000 mt/y, Trim width 2.68 m, Uncoated woodfree/freesheet
Finishing Equipment:
Rewinders: 1
Sheeters: 2
Energy Data:
HRSG boiler: 2
Combustion turbines: 2 at 3.7, 4.0 MW
Steam turbines: 1 at 1.5 MW
Electrical demand for mill: 112 MWh/D

ⓞⓜPapertech S.L.
Tudela Mill
Ownership: Sonoco Products Co., Conitex Sonoco Holding, BV, Texpack Group
Aptdo. 18 / Carr. de Pamplona, 2
E-31500 Tudela, Navarra
Spain
Phone: (34) 948 823400
Fax: (34) 948 827756
Email: comercial@papertech.com
Web Address: www.papertech.com
Personnel:
VP, Paper Manuf.: Fernando Martinez
Phone: (34) 948 823400
Fax: (34) 948 827756
Email: fmartinez@papertech.com
Gen. Mgr.: David Rubio
Phone: (34) 948 823400
Fax: (34) 948 827756
Email: drubio@papertech.com
Prod. Dir.: José Antonio Martinez
Phone: (34) 948 823400
Fax: (34) 948 827756
Email: jmartinez@papertech.com
Tech. Mgr.: António Sola
Phone: (34) 948 823400
Fax: (34) 948 827756
Email: asola@papertech.com
Commercial Dir.: Joan Gimenez
Phone: (34) 948 823400
Fax: (34) 948 827756
Email: jgimenez@papertech.com
Purch., Proj., Qlty. & Environ. Dir.: Luis Miguel Calvo
Phone: (34) 948 402190
Fax: (34) 948 827756
Email: lmcalvo@papertech.com
Total Employees at this Location: 68
Type of Operation: Paperboard mill
Mill Locations:
PT Papertech Indonesia, Subang Mill, Jln. Raya Cipeundeuy Km 1, Desa Cipeundeuy, 41272 Subang, Indonesia, Capacity: 60,000 mt/y, (Paper mill)
Phone: (62) 260 710645
Fax: (62) 260 710644
Email: pti@id.papertech.com
PT Papertech Indonesia, Blabak Mill, Jalan Sanggrahan Gatak No.23, 56511 Blabak, Mungkid, Indonesia, Capacity: 26,000 mt/y, (Paperboard mill)
PT Papertech Indonesia, Unit II, Kabupaten Magelang, Jl. Sanggrahan Gatak No. 23, Desa Mungkid, 56511 Kecamatan Mungkid, Kabupaten Magelang, Indonesia, Capacity: 17,500 mt/y, (Paperboard mill)
Phone: (62) 293 327231
Fax: (62) 293 327230
Email: pti@id.papertech.com
Pulp Grades and Capacities:
Total pulp capacity: 55,507 mt/y
Recycled Pulping: 55,507 mt/y
Pulp Mill Data:
Pulp Dryers:

Spain

Air Float dryers 1
Paper/Paperboard Grades and Capacities:
Total paper and paperboard capacity: 55,000 mt/y
Boxboard/cartonboard: 55,000 mt/y
Paper and Paperboard Mill Data:
Stock Preparation:
Pulpers: 1
Paper Machines: 1
No. 1, fourdrinier, total capacity 55,000 mt/y, Trim width 2 m, Boxboard/cartonboard
Finishing Equipment:
Rewinders: 2
Energy Data:
Power boilers: 1
Electrical demand for mill: 55 MWh/D

ⓄⓂPapresa, S.L.
Rentería Mill
Ownership: 100% by KKR
Avda. Martires de la Libertad 6
E-20100 Rentería, Gipúzcoa
Spain
Phone: (34) 943 344342
Fax: (34) 943 344251
Email: direc@papresa.es, comercial@papresa.es
Web Address: www.papresa.es
Personnel:
Gen. Mgr.: José Maria Argote
Phone: (34) 943 344252
Fax: (34) 943 344261
Email: jmargote@papresa.es
Mill Dir.: Lourdes Marquet Imaz
Phone: (34) 943 344252
Fax: (34) 943 344261
Email: lmarquet@papresa.es
Finan. Mgr.: Jose Maria Arruabarrena
Phone: (34) 943 344342
Fax: (34) 943 344261
Email: jmarruabarrena@papresa.es
Mgr.: Lorenza Alzaga
Phone: (34) 943 344342
Fax: (34) 943 344251
Email: lalzaga@papresa.es
Total Employees at this Location: 214
Type of Operation: Pulp mill, Paper mill
Pulp Grades and Capacities:
Total pulp capacity: 390,073 mt/y
Recycled Pulping: 390,073 mt/y
Pulp Mill Data:
Pulp Lines: 3
Bleach Plant Systems: 2
Voith Capacity 125,000 admt/y
Voith Capacity 175,000 admt/y
Recycled Fiber Treatment Lines:
Flotation deinking lines: 1 at 125,000 admt/y
Flotation deinking lines: 1 at 175,000
Flotation deinking lines: 1 at 30,000
Paper/Paperboard Grades and Capacities:
Total paper and paperboard capacity: 375,000 mt/y
Newsprint: 355,500 mt/y
Uncoated mechanical/groundwood: 19,500 mt/y
Paper and Paperboard Mill Data:
Stock Preparation:
Pulpers: 14
Refiners: 9
Paper Machines: 3
No. 4, SymFormer, total capacity 85,000 mt/y, Trim width 3.9 m, Newsprint, Uncoated mechanical/groundwood
No. 5, DuoFormer H, total capacity 110,000 mt/y, Trim width 5.3 m, Newsprint, Uncoated mechanical/groundwood
No. 6, DuoFormer TQv, total capacity 180,000 mt/y, Trim width 5.4 m, Newsprint
Finishing Equipment:
Winders: 3 at 180,000 mt/y, 110,000 mt/y, 85,000 mt/y
Rewinders: 2
Energy Data:
Power boilers: 2
Steam turbines: 1 at 7 MW
Electrical demand for mill: 865 MWh/D

ⓄⓂPapelera del Principado, S.A. (Paprinsa)
Mollerussa Mill
Enlace Autovía L-200, s/n
E-25230 Mollerussa, Lérida
Spain
Phone: (34) 973 600050
Fax: (34) 973 603431
Email: paprinsa@paprinsa.com
Web Address: www.paprinsa.es
Personnel:
Gen. Mgr.: Fco. Javier Farré Domingo
Phone: (34) 973 600050
Fax: (34) 973 603431
Email: javierfarre@paprinsa.com
Tech. Dir.: Felix Escauriaza
Phone: (34) 973 600050
Fax: (34) 973 710998
Email: felixescauriaza@paprinsa.com
Chief Eng.: Ramón Buixade Salvia
Phone: (34) 973 600050
Fax: (34) 973 603431
Email: ramonbuixade@paprinsa.com
Purch. Agent: Salvador Oriola Rey
Phone: (34) 973 600050
Fax: (34) 973 603431
Email: salvadororiola@paprinsa.com
Mgr.: Ramon Puig
Phone: (34) 973 600050
Fax: (34) 973 603431
Email: ramonroig@paprinsa.com
Total Employees at this Location: 94
Type of Operation: Paperboard mill
Pulp Grades and Capacities:
Total pulp capacity: 75,684 mt/y
Recycled Pulping: 75,684 mt/y
Pulp Mill Data:
Recycled Fiber Treatment Lines:
Pulpers: 4
Paper/Paperboard Grades and Capacities:
Total paper and paperboard capacity: 80,000 mt/y
Boxboard/cartonboard: 80,000 mt/y
Paper and Paperboard Mill Data:
Stock Preparation:
Pulpers: 4
Refiners: 2
Paper Machines: 1
No. 1, cylinder, total capacity 80,000 mt/y, Trim width 4.8 m, Boxboard/cartonboard
Coating Machines: 2
BM 1, total capacity 80,000 mt/y., on machine
BM 2, total capacity 80,000 mt/y., on machine
Finishing Equipment:
Rewinders: 1
Sheeters: 3
Energy Data:
Power boilers: 2
Combustion turbines: 2 at 6.8, 4.7 MW
Electrical demand for mill: 106 MWh/D

ⓄPere Valls S.A.
Dissemina s/n
E-08776 Sant Pere de Riudebiltes
Spain
Phone: (34) 938 995 176, 938 995 762
Fax: (34) 938 996 032
Email: perevalls@perevalls.es, info@perevalls.es
Web Address: www.perevalls.es
Personnel:
Mill Mgr.: Ramón Valls Amat
Phone: (34) 938 995 176
Fax: (34) 938 996 032
Commer. Dir.: Pere Valls Amat
Phone: (34) 938 995 176
Fax: (34) 938 996 032
Mill Locations:
Pere Valls S.A., Sant Pere de Riudebiltes Mill, Afores s/n - Cal Jan, E-08776 Sant Pere de Riudebiltes, Spain, Capacity: 15,000 mt/y, (Paperboard mill)
Phone: (34) 938 995176/ 938 995 762
Fax: (34) 938 996 032
Email: perevalls@perevalls.es, info@perevalls.es

ⓂPere Valls S.A.
Sant Pere de Riudebiltes Mill
Afores s/n - Cal Jan
E-08776 Sant Pere de Riudebiltes, Barcelona
Spain
Phone: (34) 938 995176/ 938 995 762
Fax: (34) 938 996 032
Email: perevalls@perevalls.es, info@perevalls.es
Web Address: www.perevalls.es
Personnel:
Mill Mgr.: Ramón Valls Amat
Phone: (34) 938 995 176
Fax: (34) 938 996 032
Commer. Dir.: Pere Valls Amat
Phone: (34) 938 995 176
Fax: (34) 938 996 032
Type of Operation: Paperboard mill
Paper/Paperboard Grades and Capacities:
Total paper and paperboard capacity: 15,000 mt/y
Linerboard: 15,000 mt/y
Paper and Paperboard Mill Data:
Paper Machines: 1
No. 1, total capacity 15,000 mt/y, Trim width 2.5 m, Linerboard

ⓄⓂPrietopapel
Murcia Mill
Company is for sale, idle (idle since late March 2012.)
Carretera Nacional 301, km. 363, Blanca
30540 Murcia
Spain
Mailing Address: Apt. 28, Blanca, 30540 Murcia, Spain
Phone: (34) 968 45 91 38/44
Fax: (34) 968 45 92 60
Email: prietopapel@prietopapel.com, info@prietopapel.com
Web Address: www.prietopapel.com
Type of Operation: Paper mill
Paper/Paperboard Grades and Capacities:
Total paper and paperboard capacity: 15,000 mt/y
Tissue: 15,000 mt/y
Paper and Paperboard Mill Data:
Paper Machines: 1
PM 1, total capacity 15,000 mt/y, Tissue

ⓄⓂProductos Celulosicos S.A. - Procesa
Azuqueca de Henares Mill
Ownership: 100% by Genaro Malo
Calle de Plástico 12, Poligono Industrial Miralcampo 11
19200 Azuqueca de Henares
Spain
Phone: (34) 949 262 469
Fax: (34) 9 49263319
Email: prcel@procesa.e.telefonica.net
Personnel:
Owner & Pres.: Genaro Malo
Phone: (34) 9 4956 2469
Pres. Sec.: Miriam Salgado
Phone: (34) 9 4956 2469
Total Employees at this Location: 14
Type of Operation: Paper mill
Paper/Paperboard Grades and Capacities:
Total paper and paperboard capacity: 7,000 mt/y
Tissue: 7,000 mt/y
Paper and Paperboard Mill Data:
Paper Machines: 1

Spain

No. 1, crescent former, Yankee dryer, total capacity 7,000 mt/y, Trim width 2.7 m, Tissue
Energy Data:
Power boilers
Combustion turbines: 1
Electrical demand for mill: 19 MWh/D

ⓂPROTISA, Productos Tinerfeños S.A.
Poligono Industrial Valle Güimar, Manzana 11, Parcela 2-3, Arafo
38509 Santa Cruz de Tenerife
Spain
 Phone: (34) 922 501 363
 Fax: (34) 922 501 536
 Email: protisa@protisa.eu
 Web Address: www.protisa.eu
Personnel:
 Dir. & CEO: Raquel Malo Serisa
 Phone: (34) 922 501363 / 922 506152
 Fax: (34) 922501536
 Prod. Mgr.: Antonio Suarez Dominguez
 Phone: (34) 922 501363
 Fax: (34) 922501536
 Administrative Accounting: Francesca Maria Weeks Leon
 Phone: (34) 922 501363
 Fax: (34) 922501536
Mill Locations:
PROTISA, Productos Tinerfeños S.A., Santa Cruz de Tenerife Mill, Poligono Industrial Valle Güimar, Manzana 11, Parcela 2-3, Arafo, 38509 Santa Cruz de Tenerife, Spain, Capacity: 5,000 mt/y, (Paper mill)
 Phone: (34) 922 501 363
 Fax: (34) 922 501 536
 Email: protisa@protisa.eu

ⓂPROTISA, Productos Tinerfeños S.A.
Santa Cruz de Tenerife Mill
Poligono Industrial Valle Güimar, Manzana 11, Parcela 2-3, Arafo
38509 Santa Cruz de Tenerife
Spain
 Phone: (34) 922 501 363
 Fax: (34) 922 501 536
 Email: protisa@protisa.eu
 Web Address: www.protisa.eu
Personnel:
 Mgr.: Raquel Malo
 Phone: (34) 922 501 363
Total Employees at this Location: 27
Type of Operation: Paper mill
Pulp Grades and Capacities:
 Total pulp capacity: 5,320 mt/y
 Recycled Pulping: 5,320 mt/y
Paper/Paperboard Grades and Capacities:
 Total paper and paperboard capacity: 5,000 mt/y
 Tissue: 5,000 mt/y
Paper and Paperboard Mill Data:
Paper Machines: 1
 No. 1, fourdrinier, Yankee dryer, total capacity 5,000 mt/y, Trim width 2.7 m, Tissue
Energy Data:
Electrical demand for mill: 15 MWh/D

ⓂReno De Medici, Iberica S.L.U.
Ownership: 100% by Reno De Medici SpA
Calle Selva n° 2
E-08820 El Prat de Llobregat, Barcelona
Spain
 Phone: (34) 93 4759100
 Fax: (34) 93 4759144
 Email: renodemedici@sarrio.es
 Web Address: www.renodemedici.it
Personnel:
 Chmn.: Christian Dubé
 Phone: (34) 93 4759100
 Fax: (34) 93 4759144
 Chmn.: Robert Hall
 Phone: (34) 93 4759100

CEO: Ignazio Capuano
 Phone: (34) 93 4759100
 Fax: (34) 93 4759144
CFO: Stefano Moccagata
 Phone: (34) 93 4759100
 Fax: (34) 93 4759144
Finan. Dir. Spain: Robert Nogueras
 Phone: (34) 93 4759100
 Fax: (34) 93 4759144
 Email: rnogueras@sarrio.es
Sls. Mgr.: Juan Barbera Gimenez
 Phone: (34) 93 475 9134
 Fax: (34) 93 478 2643
 Email: juan.barbera@careo.biz
Tech. Coordinator: Miguel Figuera
 Phone: (34) 93 4759100
 Fax: (34) 93 4759144
Total Employees of Company: 1,635
Total Employees at this Location: 114
Mill Locations:
Reno De Medici, Iberica S.L.U., Almazán Mill, Carretera de Gomara km 14, E-2200 Almazán, Spain, Capacity: 40,000 mt/y, (Paperboard mill)
 Phone: (34) 975 310144
 Fax: (34) 975 300041
 Email: jaraso@sarrio.es

ⓂReno De Medici, Iberica S.L.U.
Almazán Mill
Ownership: 100% by Reno De Medici SpA
Carretera de Gomara km 14
E-2200 Almazán, Soria
Spain
 Phone: (34) 975 310144
 Fax: (34) 975 300041
 Email: jaraso@sarrio.es
 Web Address: www.renodemedici.it
Personnel:
 Mill Mgr.: José Antonio Raso Garin
 Phone: (34) 975 318060
 Fax: (34) 975 300041
 Prod. Mgr.: Justo Tarancon
 Phone: (34) 975 310144
 Fax: (34) 975 300041
 Email: jtaranson@sarrio.es
 Purch. & Logist. Mgr.: Antonio Martínez Peregrina
 Phone: (34) 975 318063
 Fax: (34) 975 300041
 Email: amartinez@sarrio.es
 Maint. & Env. Mgr.: Carlos Tarancón Garijo
 Phone: (34) 975 318065
 Fax: (34) 975 300041
 Email: ctarancon@sarrio.es
Total Employees at this Location: 93
Type of Operation: Paperboard mill
Pulp Grades and Capacities:
 Total pulp capacity: 66,460 mt/y
 Recycled Pulping: 66,460 mt/y
Pulp Mill Data:
 Recycled Fiber Treatment Lines:
 Recycled packaging pulping lines: 1
Paper/Paperboard Grades and Capacities:
 Total paper and paperboard capacity: 40,000 mt/y
 Boxboard/cartonboard: 40,000 mt/y
Paper and Paperboard Mill Data:
 Stock Preparation:
 Pulpers: 4
 Refiners: 3
Paper Machines: 1
 No. 1, cylinder (4), total capacity 40,000 mt/y, Trim width 2.25 m, Boxboard/cartonboard
Coating Machines: 3
 No. 1, on machine
 No. 2, on machine
 No. 3
Finishing Equipment:
 Rewinders: 1 at 33,720 mt/y
 Sheeters: 3 at 40,000 mt/y

Energy Data:
Power boilers: 1
Electrical demand for mill: 75 MWh/D

ⓂSAICA - S.A. Industrias Celulosa Aragonesa
Ownership: 100% by private owners
San Juan de la Peña 144
E-50015 Zaragoza
Spain
 Phone: (34) 976 10 3100, 3101
 Fax: (34) 976 10 3110, 3111
 Email: webpaper@saica.com
 Web Address: www.saica.com
Personnel:
 Pres.: Joaquin Herrero Balet
 Phone: (34) 976 10 3100, 3101
 Fax: (34) 976 10 3110, 3111
 Email: mlgamo@saica.es
 Deputy Man. Dir. SAICA Group: Federico Asensio Balet
 Phone: (34) 976 10 3100, 3101
 Fax: (34) 976 10 3110, 3111
 Email: Isabel.sienes@saica.com
 Man. Dir. Group SAICA: Pedro Gascón
 Phone: (34) 976 10 3100, 3101
 Fax: (34) 976 10 3110, 3111
 Man. Dir. SAICA Paper: Enrique De Yraolagoitia
 Phone: (34) 976 10 3100, 3101
 Fax: (34) 976 10 3110, 3111
 Email: eyraolagoitia@saica.com
 Man. Dir. SAICA Pack: Ramon Alejandro Balet
 Phone: (34) 976 10 3100, 3101
 Fax: (34) 976 10 3110, 3111
 Deputy HR Dir. SAICA Pack: Joaquin Solanas Rivas
 Phone: (34) 976 10 3100, 3101
 Fax: (34) 976 10 3110, 3111
 Group HR & Commun. Dir.: Pilar Franca
 Phone: (34) 976 10 3100, 3101
 Fax: (34) 976 10 3110, 3111
 Commer. Dir. SAICA Group: Ignacio Guallart
 Phone: (34) 976 10 3100, 3101
 Fax: (34) 976 10 3110, 3111
 Email: ignacio.guallart@saica.com
 Sls. Dir. SAICA Group: Fernando Angulo
 Phone: (34) 976 10 3100, 3101
 Fax: (34) 976 10 3110, 3111
 Email: fernando.angulo@saica.com
 Asst. Man. Dir.: Margarita Rama
 Phone: (34) 976 10 3100, 3101
 Fax: (34) 976 10 3110, 3111
 Email: margarita.rama@saica.com
 Regional Mgr. SAICA Group: Joaquín Balet
 Phone: (34) 976 10 3100, 3101
 Fax: (34) 976 10 3110, 3111
Total Employees of Company: 9,000
Mill Locations:
SAICA Paper UK Ltd., Partington Mill, 144 Manchester Road, Carrington, Manchester M31 4QN, United Kingdom, Capacity: 400,000 mt/y, (Paperboard mill)
 Phone: (44) 161 776 7000
 Email: web.paper.pm11@saica.com
SAICA - S.A. Industrias Celulosa Aragonesa, Fábrica I - Zaragoza Mill, Avda. San Juan de la Peña, 144, E-50015 Zaragoza, Spain, Capacity: 525,000 mt/y, (Pulp mill, Paperboard mill)
 Phone: (34) 976 10 3100/1
 Fax: (34) 976 10 3110
 Email: web.paper@saica.com
SAICA - S.A. Industrias Celulosa Aragonesa, Fábrica II, III & IV - El Burgo de Ebro Mill, Polígono El Espartal Ctra. Castellón, Km. 21, E-50730 El Burgo de Ebro, Spain, Capacity: 1,230,000 mt/y, (Pulp mill, Paper mill, Paperboard mill)
 Phone: (34) 976 103102
 Fax: (34) 976 103112
SAICA Vénizel, Vénizel Mill, BP 08, rue de la Vallée, F-02200 Vénizel, France, Capacity: 250,000 mt/y, (Pulp mill, Paperboard mill)
 Phone: (33) 3 23 75 30 00/13

Spain

Fax: (33) 3 23 75 30 01
SAPSO Emballages Ondulés, Bazas Mill, Bernos Beaulac, F-33430 Bazas, France, Capacity: 55,000 mt/y, (Paperboard mill)
Phone: (33) 5 56 65 03 00
Fax: (33) 5 56 65 03 04
Email: commercia.pack.beaulacl@saica.com

ⓜSAICA - S.A. Industrias Celulosa Aragonesa
Fábrica I - Zaragoza Mill
Avda. San Juan de la Peña, 144
E-50015 Zaragoza
Spain
Phone: (34) 976 10 3100/1
Fax: (34) 976 10 3110
Email: web.paper@saica.com
Web Address: www.saica.com
Personnel:
Gen. Dir.: Pedro Gutierrez
Phone: (34) 976 10 3100
Fax: (34) 976 10 3110
Email: pedro.gutierrez@saica.com
Sec. to Gen. Dir.: Margarita Rama
Phone: (34) 976 10 3100
Fax: (34) 976 10 3110
Email: margarita.rama@saica.com
Total Employees at this Location: 250
Type of Operation: Pulp mill, Paperboard mill
Pulp Grades and Capacities:
Total pulp capacity: 524,682 mt/y
Recycled Pulping: 524,682 mt/y
Pulp Mill Data:
Recycled Fiber Treatment Lines:
Recycled packaging pulping lines: 1 at 520,000
Paper/Paperboard Grades and Capacities:
Total paper and paperboard capacity: 525,000 mt/y
Linerboard: 100,000 mt/y
Corrugating medium/fluting: 425,000 mt/y
Paper and Paperboard Mill Data:
Stock Preparation:
Pulpers: 3
Refiners: 5
Paper Machines: 2
No. 6, Bel-Bond, total capacity 200,000 mt/y, Trim width 4.6 m, Linerboard, Corrugating medium/fluting
No. 7, DuoFormer D, total capacity 325,000 mt/y, Trim width 6.7 m, Corrugating medium/fluting
Finishing Equipment:
Winders: 2
Energy Data:
Power boilers: 1
Combustion turbines: 1 at 37 MW
Steam turbines: 2 at 11 MW
Electrical demand for mill: 595 MWh/D

ⓜSAICA - S.A. Industrias Celulosa Aragonesa
Fábrica II, III & IV - El Burgo de Ebro Mill
Polígono El Espartal Ctra. Castellón, Km. 21
E-50730 El Burgo de Ebro, Zaragoza
Spain
Phone: (34) 976 103102
Fax: (34) 976 103112
Web Address: www.saica.com
Personnel:
Mill Mgr., SAICA 3: José Manuel Barroso
Phone: (34) 976 103102
Fax: (34) 976 103112
Email: jose.barroso@saica.com
Sls. Dir. & Export Mgr.: Agustin Sauras
Phone: (34) 976 103 216
Fax: (34) 976 103 246
Email: agustin.sauras@saica.com
Total Employees at this Location: 100
Type of Operation: Pulp mill, Paper mill, Paperboard mill
Pulp Grades and Capacities:
Total pulp capacity: 1,213,095 mt/y
Recycled Pulping: 1,213,095 mt/y
Pulp Mill Data:
Bleach Plant Systems: 1
DIP
Recycled Fiber Treatment Lines:
Flotation deinking lines: 1
Pulpers: 2
Recycled packaging pulping lines: 1
Paper/Paperboard Grades and Capacities:
Total paper and paperboard capacity: 1,230,000 mt/y
Linerboard: 600,000 mt/y
Corrugating medium/fluting: 630,000 mt/y
Paper and Paperboard Mill Data:
Stock Preparation:
Pulpers: 2
Refiners: 5
Paper Machines: 3
No. 8, fourdrinier (2), total capacity 380,000 mt/y, Trim width 7.3 m, Linerboard
No. 9, DuoFormer Base, total capacity 410,000 mt/y, Trim width 7.5 m, Corrugating medium/fluting
No. 10, DuoFormer Base, total capacity 440,000 mt/y, Trim width 7.8 m, Linerboard, Corrugating medium/fluting
Finishing Equipment:
Winders: 1
Energy Data:
Power boilers: 4
Combustion turbines: 3 at 38, 40, 33 MW
Steam turbines: 1 at 10 MW
Electrical demand for mill: 1,473 MWh/D

ⓜSCA Spain
Allo Mill
Mill is Former Georgia-Pacific Sprl mill acquired by SCA, sale completed late July 2012
Ownership: 100% by SCA - Svenska Cellulosa Aktiebolaget
Poligono Industrial Mirabete
E-31262 Allo, Navarra
Spain
Phone: (34) 948 54 8305
Fax: (34) 948 54 8308
Web Address: www.colhogar.com, www.sca.com
Personnel:
Oper. Mgr.: Romà Calvo Martínez
Phone: (34) 948 54 8305
Fax: (34) 948 54 8308
Shift Mgr.: Alberto Fauste González
Phone: (34) 948 54 8305
Fax: (34) 948 54 8308
Nat. Account Mgr.: Marc Balcells
Phone: (34) 948 54 8305
Fax: (34) 948 54 8308
Dir., HR: Serafín Borreguero
Phone: (34) 948 54 8305
Fax: (34) 948 54 8308
Dir., Mktg.: Ignasi Martin
Phone: (34) 948 54 8305
Fax: (34) 948 54 8308
Product & Market Mgr.: Montserrat Burgues
Phone: (34) 948 54 8305
Fax: (34) 948 54 8308
Prod. Mgr.: Miguel Angel Casanova Gomez
Phone: (34) 948 54 8305
Fax: (34) 948 54 8308
Total Employees at this Location: 273
Type of Operation: Paper mill
Paper/Paperboard Grades and Capacities:
Total paper and paperboard capacity: 175,000 mt/y
Tissue: 175,000 mt/y
Paper and Paperboard Mill Data:
Stock Preparation:
Pulpers: 3
Refiners: 4
Paper Machines: 3
No. 1, crescent former, Yankee dryer, total capacity 50,000 mt/y, Trim width 5.4 m, Tissue
No. 2, crescent former, Yankee dryer, total capacity 60,000 mt/y, Trim width 5.4 m, Tissue
No. 3, crescent former, Yankee dryer, total capacity 65,000 mt/y, Trim width 5.4 m, Tissue
Finishing Equipment:
Rewinders: 1
Energy Data:
Power boilers: 2
Combustion turbines: 2 at 15 MW
Electrical demand for mill: 445 MWh/D

ⓜSCA Hygiene Products S.L.
La Riba Mill
Ownership: SCA Hygiene Products SE
Cardenal Gomá 16
E-43450 La Riba, Tarragona
Spain
Phone: (34) 977 87 6749 / 977 87 6745
Fax: (34) 977 87 6025
Web Address: www.sca.com
Personnel:
Mill Mgr.: Marc Rodriguez
Phone: (34) 977 87 6086
Email: marc.rodriguez@sca.com
Prod. Mgr.: Sergio Alvarez
Phone: (34) 977 87 6086
Total Employees at this Location: 35
Type of Operation: Paper mill
Paper/Paperboard Grades and Capacities:
Total paper and paperboard capacity: 26,000 mt/y
Tissue: 26,000 mt/y
Paper and Paperboard Mill Data:
Paper Machines: 1
No. 3, DuoFormer T, Yankee dryer, total capacity 26,000 mt/y, Trim width 2.65 m, Tissue
Finishing Equipment:
Winders
Calenders
Energy Data:
Power boilers: 1
Electrical demand for mill: 75 MWh/D

ⓜSCA Hygiene Products S.L.
Mediona Mill
Ownership: SCA Hygiene Products SE
Carretera de la Llacuna,
E-08773 Mediona, Barcelona
Spain
Phone: (34) 93 898 5570
Fax: (34) 93 898 5820
Web Address: www.sca.com
Personnel:
Mill Mgr.: Marc Rodriguez
Phone: (34) 93 898 5570
Email: marc.rodriguez@sca.com
HR Mgr.: Marina Sanchez
Phone: (34) 618 29 18 19
Email: marina.sanchez@sca.com
Asst. Mill Mgr.: Fatima Santos
Phone: (34) 93 898 5574
Fax: (34) 93 898 5820
Email: fatima.santos@sca.com
Total Employees at this Location: 200
Type of Operation: Paper mill
Paper/Paperboard Grades and Capacities:
Total paper and paperboard capacity: 45,000 mt/y
Tissue: 45,000 mt/y
Paper and Paperboard Mill Data:
Paper Machines: 2
No. 1, crescent former, total capacity 21,000 mt/y, Trim width 2.65 m, Tissue
No. 2, crescent former, total capacity 24,000 mt/y, Trim width 2.65 m, Tissue
Energy Data:
Power boilers: 1
Electrical demand for mill: 120 MWh/D

Spain

ⓜSCA Hygiene Products S.L.
Puigpelat (Valls) Mill
Ownership: SCA Hygiene Products SE
Ctra. Valls-Puigpelat, Km 2
E-43812 Puigpelat, Tarragona
Spain
  Phone: (34) 977 030 600
  Fax: (34) 977 605 554
  Web Address: www.sca.com
Personnel:
  Mill Mgr.: Toni Mata
  Phone: (34) 977 030 600
  Email: toni.mata@sca.com
  Country Mgr.: José Ramón Iracheta
  Phone: (34) 977 030 600
  Email: jose.iracheta@sca.com
  Paper Mill Mgr.: Jordi Miró
  Phone: (34) 977 030 600
  Email: jordi.miro@sca.com
  Prod. Leader: Marta Manresa
  Phone: (34) 977 030 600
  Email: marta.manresa@sca.com
Total Employees at this Location: 400
Type of Operation: Paper mill
Paper/Paperboard Grades and Capacities:
  Total paper and paperboard capacity: 120,000 mt/y
  Tissue: 120,000 mt/y
Paper and Paperboard Mill Data:
Paper Machines: 2
  No. 5, crescent former, Yankee dryer, total capacity 60,000 mt/y, Trim width 5.45 m, Tissue
  No. 6, crescent former, Yankee dryer, total capacity 60,000 mt/y, Trim width 5.45 m, Tissue
Energy Data:
  Power boilers: 1
  Electrical demand for mill: 301 MWh/D

ⓜSmurfit Kappa Mengibar Paper
Mengibar Mill
Ownership: Smurfit Kappa Europe
Carretera de Bailén-Motril , s/n
E-23620 Mengibar, Jaén
Spain
  Phone: (34) 95 337 0775
  Fax: (34) 95 337 0825
  Web Address: www.smurfitkappa.com
Personnel:
  Mill Mgr.: Ramón Callejo
  Phone: (34) 95 337 0775
  Fax: (34) 95 337 0825
  Email: ramon.callejo@smurfitkappa.es
  Sec.: Ana Beltran
  Phone: (34) 95 337 4226
  Fax: (34) 95 337 0825
  Email: ana.beltran@smurfitkappa.es
Total Employees at this Location: 120
Type of Operation: Paper mill, Paperboard mill
Pulp Grades and Capacities:
  Total pulp capacity: 200,937 mt/y
  Recycled Pulping: 200,937 mt/y
Pulp Mill Data:
  Recycled Fiber Treatment Lines:
  Pulpers: 3 at 350,000 admt/y
Paper/Paperboard Grades and Capacities:
  Total paper and paperboard capacity: 200,000 mt/y
  Linerboard: 90,000 mt/y
  Corrugating medium/fluting: 110,000 mt/y
Paper and Paperboard Mill Data:
  Stock Preparation:
  Pulpers: 3
  Refiners: 5
Paper Machines: 1
  No. 1, fourdrinier (2), total capacity 200,000 mt/y, Trim width 5 m, Corrugating medium/fluting, Linerboard
Finishing Equipment:
  Winders: 1 at 200,000 mt/y
  Calenders: 1
  Rewinders
  Sheeters

Energy Data:
Power boilers: 1
Combustion turbines: 1 at 21 MW
Steam turbines: 1 at 4 MW
Electrical demand for mill: 294 MWh/D

ⓜSmurfit Kappa Nervión
Iurreta Mill
Ownership: 99.35% by Smurfit Kappa Europe
B° Arriandi, s/n
E-48215 Iurreta, Vizcaya
Spain
  Phone: (34) 946 205100
  Fax: (34) 946 205124
  Web Address: www.smurfitkappa.com
Personnel:
  Gen. Mgr.: Rafael Sarrionandia
  Phone: (34) 946 205100
  Fax: (34) 946 205124
  Email: rafael.sarrionandia@smurfitkappa.es
  Sls. Mgr.: Ignacio Telleria
  Phone: (34) 946 205100
  Fax: (34) 946 205124
  Email: ignacio.telleria@smurfitkappa.es
  Contr.: Marcelino Iriondo
  Phone: (34) 946 205100
  Fax: (34) 946 205124
  Email: marcelino.iriondo@smurfitkappa.es
  Paper Product Mgr.: Oscar Elorriaga
  Phone: (34) 946 205100
  Fax: (34) 946 205124
  Email: oscar.elorriaga@smurfitkappa.es
  Qlty. & Environ. Mgr.: Francisco Javier Pérez Ruiz
  Phone: (34) 946 205168
  Fax: (34) 946 205124
  Email: francisco-javier.perez@smurfitkappa.es
Total Employees at this Location: 231
Type of Operation: Pulp mill, Paper mill, Paperboard mill
Pulp Grades and Capacities:
  Total pulp capacity: 140,287 mt/y
  Chemical Pulp: 140,287 mt/y
Pulp Mill Data:
  Chemical Pulping Systems:
  Batch digesters: 4
Pulp Lines: 1
  Chemical Recovery Equipment:
  Evaporator lines: 1
  Recovery boilers: 1
  Lime Kiln
Paper/Paperboard Grades and Capacities:
  Total paper and paperboard capacity: 160,000 mt/y
  Packaging papers: 160,000 mt/y
Paper and Paperboard Mill Data:
Paper Machines: 2
  No. 1, fourdrinier, total capacity 30,000 mt/y, Trim width 2.2 m, Packaging papers
  No. 2, fourdrinier, total capacity 130,000 mt/y, Trim width 4.8 m, Packaging papers
Energy Data:
  Power boilers: 1
  Steam turbines: 1 at 13.5 MW
  Electrical demand for mill: 456 MWh/D

ⓜSmurfit Kappa Sangüesa Paper
Sanguesa Mill
Ownership: 94.15% by Smurfit Kappa Europe
Raimundo Lumbier, s/n
E-31400 Sangüesa, Navarra
Spain
  Phone: (34) 948 870000
  Fax: (34) 948 870943
  Web Address: www.smurfitkappa.com
Personnel:
  Gen. Mgr.: Javier Rivas
  Phone: (34) 948 870000
  Fax: (34) 948 870943
  Email: javier.rivas@smurfitkappa.es

  Residentl Mgr.: Ricardo Ballestar
  Phone: (34) 948 870000
  Fax: (34) 948 870943
  Email: ricardo.ballestar@smurfitkappa.es
  Pulp Mill Mgr.: Javier Saenz
  Phone: (34) 948 870000
  Fax: (34) 948 870943
  Email: javier.saenz@smurfitkappa.es
  Prod. Mgr.: Javier Figueroa
  Phone: (34) 948 870000
  Fax: (34) 948 870943
  Email: javier.figueroa@smurfitkappa.es
  Qlty. Mgr.: Joaquin Latasa
  Phone: (34) 948 870000
  Fax: (34) 948 870943
  Email: joaquin.latasa@smurfitkappa.es
  Dir., Maint. : José Luis Vaquero
  Phone: (34) 948 870000
  Fax: (34) 948 870943
  Email: jose-luis.vaquero@smurfitkappa.es
  Environ. Dir.: Daniel Oscariz
  Phone: (34) 948 870000
  Fax: (34) 948 870943
  Email: daniel.oscariz@smurfitkappa.es
  Sls. Mgr.: Ivan Medrano
  Phone: (34) 948 870000
  Fax: (34) 948 870943
  Email: ivan.medrano@smurfitkappa.es
Total Employees at this Location: 231
Type of Operation: Paper mill, Paperboard mill
Pulp Grades and Capacities:
  Total pulp capacity: 115,661 mt/y
  Chemical Pulp: 77,873 mt/y
  Recycled Pulping: 37,788 mt/y
Pulp Mill Data:
  Chemical Pulping Systems:
  Batch digesters: 1
  Chemical Recovery Equipment:
  Evaporator lines: 1
  Recovery boilers: 1
  Lime Kiln
  Recycled Fiber Treatment Lines:
  Pulpers: 1 at 46,000 admt
  Recycled packaging pulping lines: 1 at 60,000
Paper/Paperboard Grades and Capacities:
  Total paper and paperboard capacity: 110,000 mt/y
  Packaging papers: 30,000 mt/y
  Specialty and industrial: 20,000 mt/y
  Linerboard: 60,000 mt/y
Paper and Paperboard Mill Data:
  Stock Preparation:
  Pulpers: 3
  Refiners: 6
Paper Machines: 3
  No. 1, fourdrinier (2), total capacity 60,000 mt/y, Trim width 2.4 m, Linerboard
  No. 2, fourdrinier, Yankee dryer, total capacity 30,000 mt/y, Trim width 2.4 m, Packaging papers, Specialty and industrial
  No. 3, fourdrinier, Yankee dryer, total capacity 20,000 mt/y, Trim width 2.4 m, Packaging papers, Specialty and industrial
Finishing Equipment:
  Rewinders: 3
Energy Data:
  Power boilers: 2
  Steam turbines: 1 at 8 MW
  Electrical demand for mill: 358 MWh/D

ⓞSniace S.A.
Avenida de Burgos 12, 4°
E-28036 Madrid
Spain
  Phone: (34) 91 768 4070
  Fax: (34) 91 383 2986
  Email: sniace@sniace.com,
  comercial@sniace.com
  Web Address: www.sniace.com
Personnel:
  Pres.: Blas Mezquita

Spain

Phone: (34) 91 768 4070
Fax: (34) 91 383 2986
Proj. & Invest. Dir.: Fernando Gomez De Liaño
Phone: (34) 91 768 4070
Fax: (34) 91 383 2986
Sls. & Mktg. Dir.: Francisco Lorenzo
Phone: (34) 91 768 4070
Fax: (34) 91 383 2986
Email: plorenzo@sniace.com, comercial@sniace.com
Service Dir.: José González Payno
Phone: (34) 91 768 4070
Fax: (34) 91 383 2986
Comp. Sec.: Marie Lazinier
Phone: (34) 91 768 4070
Fax: (34) 91 383 2986
Head of Dept. Eng.: Alain Blanco Menendez
Phone: (34) 91 768 4070
Fax: (34) 91 383 2986
Project Engineer: María Velázquez Pereda
Phone: (34) 91 768 4070
Fax: (34) 91 383 2986
Total Employees of Company: 595
Total Employees at this Location: 20
Mill Locations:
Sniace S.A., Torrelavega Mill, Carretera de Ganzo s/n, E-39300 Torrelavega, Spain, (Pulp mill)
Phone: (34) 942 835400
Fax: (34) 942 806166
Email: sniace@sniace.com

ⓂSniace S.A.
Torrelavega Mill
Mill is temporarily closed (On October 25, 2013 Sniace and its subsidiaries Viscocel and Celltech were declared bankrupt with retroactive effect from September 6. Production at standstill from early July 2013.)
Carretera de Ganzo s/n
E-39300 Torrelavega, Cantabria
Spain
  Phone: (34) 942 835400
  Fax: (34) 942 806166
  Email: sniace@sniace.com
  Web Address: www.sniace.com
Personnel:
  Chrmn.: Blas Mezquita Saez
  Phone: (34) 942 835400
  Oper. Dir.: José Francisco Gonzalez Payno
  Phone: (34) 942 835400
  Email: jpayno@sniace.com
Total Employees at this Location: 200
Type of Operation: Pulp mill
Pulp Mill Data:
  Chemical Pulping Systems:
  Batch digesters: 1
Pulp Lines: 1
  Bleach Plant Systems: 1
  No. 1, Type: Sulphite, Sequence: ZEP, Capacity 85,000 admt/y
  Chemical Recovery Equipment:
  Evaporator lines: 1
  Pulp Dryers:
  Pulp Dryers 1
Energy Data:
  Power boilers: 3
  Combustion turbines: 2 at 80 MW
  Steam turbines: 1 at 20 MW

ⓂⓂStora Enso Renewable Packaging
Barcelona Mill
Ownership: Stora Enso Oyj
Potassi, 7
E-08755 Castellbisbal, Catalonia
Spain
  Phone: (34) 93 631 1000
  Fax: (34) 93 631 1021
  Email: barcelona@storaenso.com
  Web Address: www.storaenso.com
Personnel:
  Mill Mgr.: Juan Vila
  Phone: (34) 93 631 1101
  Fax: (34) 93 631 1097
  Email: juan.vila@storaenso.com
  Prod. Mgr.: Juan Ardiaca
  Phone: (34) 93 631 1000
  Fax: (34) 93 631 1021
  Email: juan.ardiaca@storaenso.com
  Purch. Mgr.: Francisco Galindo
  Phone: (34) 93 631 1063
  Fax: (34) 93 631 1188
  Email: francisco.galindo@storaenso.com
  Environ. Mgr.: Nuria Ayats
  Phone: (34) 93 631 1000
  Fax: (34) 93 631 1021
  Email: nuria.ayats@storaenso.com
  HR Mgr.: Juan Navarrete
  Phone: (34) 93 631 1000
  Fax: (34) 93 631 1021
  Email: juan.navarrete@storaenso.com
  Dir., Regional Sls. - Iberia: Juan Torras
  Phone: (34) 93 631 1000
  Fax: (34) 93 631 1021
  Email: juan.torras@storaenso.com
  Mill Supply Chain Mgr. (from January 1, 2014): Julio López
  Phone: (34) 93 631 1000
  Fax: (34) 93 631 1021
  Email: julio.lopez@storaenso.com
Total Employees at this Location: 260
Type of Operation: Paperboard mill
Mill Locations:
Stora Enso Renewable Packaging, Fors Mill, Kopparforsvägen 3, SE-774 89 Fors, Sweden, Capacity: 395,000 mt/y, (Pulp mill, Paperboard mill)
  Phone: (46) 1046 35000
  Fax: (46) 1046 35250
Stora Enso Renewable Packaging, Imatra Mills (Kaukopää & Tainionkoski), FI-55800 Imatra, Finland, Capacity: 1,075,000 mt/y, (Pulp mill, Paper mill, Paperboard mill)
  Phone: (358) 2046 121
  Fax: (358) 2046 24701/24720
  Email: (firstname.lastname@storaenso.com)
Stora Enso Renewable Packaging, Heinola Mill, Tampellantie 1, FI-18101 Heinola, Finland, Capacity: 300,000 mt/y, (Pulp mill, Paperboard mill)
  Phone: (358) 2046 111
  Fax: (358) 2046 29279
Stora Enso Renewable Packaging, Ingerois Mill, FI-46900 Kouvola, Finland, Capacity: 220,000 mt/y, (Paperboard mill)
  Phone: (358) 2046 26104/117
  Fax: (358) 2046 26141
  Email: finland.contactcenter@storaenso.com
Stora Enso Renewable Packaging, Skoghall Mill, Udden, P.O. Box 501, SE-663 29 Skoghall, Sweden, Capacity: 725,000 mt/y, (Pulp mill, Paper mill, Paperboard mill)
  Phone: (46) 1046 500 00
  Fax: (46) 1046 543 44
  Email: (firstname.lastname@storaenso.com)
Pulp Grades and Capacities:
  Total pulp capacity: 134,313 mt/y
  Recycled Pulping: 134,313 mt/y
Pulp Mill Data:
Pulp Lines: 6
  Recycled Fiber Treatment Lines:
  Recycled packaging pulping lines: 6
Paper/Paperboard Grades and Capacities:
  Total paper and paperboard capacity: 170,000 mt/y
  Boxboard/cartonboard: 170,000 mt/y
Paper and Paperboard Mill Data:
  Stock Preparation:
  Pulpers: 6
  Refiners: 11
Paper Machines: 1
No. 1, fourdrinier (3), total capacity 170,000 mt/y, Trim width 4 m, Boxboard/cartonboard
Coating Machines: 2
No. 1, on machine
No. 2, on machine
Finishing Equipment:
  Winders: 1 at 170,000 mt/y
  Rewinders: 1
  Sheeters: 5 at 155,000 mt/y
Energy Data:
  Power boilers: 1
  Combustion turbines: 1 at 42 MW
  Steam turbines: 1 at 7 MW
  Electrical demand for mill: 256 MWh/D

ⓂTorraspapel S.A.
Ownership: 100% by Lecta S.A.
C/Llull 331
E-08019 Barcelona
Spain
  Phone: (34) 93 482 1000, 93 482 1300
  Fax: (34) 93 482 1170, 93 482 0910
  Email: info@torraspapel.com
  Web Address: www.torraspapel.com
Personnel:
  CEO of Torraspapel Sa: Francisco Rudilla Molina
  Phone: (34) 93 482 1000
  Fax: (34) 93 482 1170
  International Branch Dir.: Ramses Linan
  Phone: (34) 93 482 1000
  Fax: (34) 93 482 1170
  Gen. Dir. HR: Joan Ribas Casas
  Phone: (34) 93 482 1000
  Fax: (34) 93 482 1170
  Mktg. Dir.: Ricard Miró
  Phone: (34) 93 482 1000
  Fax: (34) 93 482 1170
  Indus. Dir.: Guinart Joan
  Phone: (34) 93 482 1000
  Fax: (34) 93 482 1170
  Commercial Gen. Dir.: Eduardo Querol
  Phone: (34) 93 482 1000
  Fax: (34) 93 482 1170
  Finan. Gen. Dir.: José Llongueras
  Phone: (34) 93 482 1000
  Fax: (34) 93 482 1170
  Prod. Mgr.: Miguel F. Segura Medina
  Phone: (34) 93 482 1000
  Fax: (34) 93 482 1170
  International Export Mgr.: Magda Chancosa Spacek
  Phone: (34) 93 482 1000
  Fax: (34) 93 482 1170
Total Employees of Company: 1,809
Mill Locations:
Torraspapel S.A., Motril Mill, Camino de la Vía s/n, E-18600 Motril, Spain, Capacity: 243,000 mt/y, (Pulp mill, Paper mill)
  Phone: (34) 958 832000
  Fax: (34) 958 832030
  Email: infomot@torraspapel.com
Torraspapel S.A., Sant Joan les Fonts Mill, Avda. Paperera. Torras s/n, E-17857 Sant Joan les Fonts, Spain, Capacity: 147,000 mt/y, (Paper mill)
  Phone: (34) 972 277700
  Fax: (34) 972 277701
  Email: slvicens@torraspapel.es
Torraspapel S.A., Sarriá de Ter Mill, Avda. Josep Flores, s/n°, E-17840 Sarriá de Ter, Spain, Capacity: 85,000 mt/y, (Paper mill, closed October 2014)
  Phone: (34) 972 187300
  Fax: (34) 972 187350
Torraspapel S.A., Uranga Mill, Carretera Tolosa s/n, E-20493 Berrobi, Tolosa, Spain, (Paper mill)
  Phone: (34) 943 683409
  Fax: (34) 943 683220
Torraspapel S.A., Zaragoza Mill, Avenida de Montañana, 429, E-50059 Zaragoza, Spain, Capacity: 189,000 mt/y, (Pulp mill, Paper mill)
  Phone: (34) 976 01 70 00
  Fax: (34) 976 01 70 50

ⓂTorraspapel S.A.
Motril Mill
Ownership: 100% by Lecta S.A.

Spain

Camino de la Vía s/n
E-18600 Motril, Granada
Spain
  Phone: (34) 958 832000
  Fax: (34) 958 832030
  Email: infomot@torraspapel.com
  Web Address: www.torraspapel.com
Personnel:
  Mill Dir.: José Rodriguez
  Phone: (34) 958 832000
  Fax: (34) 958 832030
  Email: jose.rodriguez@lecta.com
Total Employees at this Location: 384
Type of Operation: Pulp mill, Paper mill
Paper/Paperboard Grades and Capacities:
  Total paper and paperboard capacity: 243,000 mt/y
  Coated woodfree/freesheet: 193,000 mt/y
  Specialty and industrial: 50,000 mt/y
Paper and Paperboard Mill Data:
Paper Machines: 2
  No. 1, fourdrinier, total capacity 110,000 mt/y, Trim width 3.2 m, Coated woodfree/freesheet, Specialty and industrial
  No. 2, DuoFormer D, total capacity 133,000 mt/y, Trim width 3.2 m, Coated woodfree/freesheet, Specialty and industrial
Coating Machines: 2
  No. 1, on machine
  No. 2, total capacity 120,000 mt/y., off machine
Energy Data:
  Power boilers: 1
  Combustion turbines: 1 at 41 MW
  Steam turbines: 1 at 7 MW
  Electrical demand for mill: 380 MWh/D

ⓜTorraspapel S.A.
Sant Joan les Fonts Mill
Ownership: 100% by Lecta S.A.
Avda. Paperera. Torras s/n
E-17857 Sant Joan les Fonts, Girona
Spain
  Phone: (34) 972 277700
  Fax: (34) 972 277701
  Email: slvicens@lecta.es
  Web Address: www.torraspapel.com
Personnel:
  Paper Mill Mgr.: Javier Garcia
  Phone: (34) 972 277700
  Fax: (34) 972 277701
  Email: javier.garcia@lecta.com
  Tech. Mgr.: Luis Vicents
  Phone: (34) 972 277700
  Fax: (34) 972 277701
  Email: luis.vicents@lecta.com
  Purch. Mgr.: Rosa Maria Gayola
  Phone: (34) 972 277700
  Fax: (34) 972 277701
  Email: rosa.gayola@lecta.com
Total Employees at this Location: 266
Type of Operation: Paper mill
Paper/Paperboard Grades and Capacities:
  Total paper and paperboard capacity: 147,000 mt/y
  Coated woodfree/freesheet: 147,000 mt/y
Paper and Paperboard Mill Data:
  Stock Preparation:
  Pulpers: 5
  Refiners: 3
Paper Machines: 1
  No. 1, fourdrinier, total capacity 147,000 mt/y, Trim width 3.3 m, Coated woodfree/freesheet
Coating Machines: 1
  No. 1, total capacity 145,000 mt/y., off machine
Finishing Equipment:
  Winders: 1 at 145,000 mt/y
  Supercalenders: 2
  Rewinders: 1
  Sheeters: 3
Energy Data:
  Power boilers: 2
  Combustion turbines: 1 at 22.4 MW
  Steam turbines: 1 at 2.5 MW
  Electrical demand for mill: 242 MWh/D

ⓜTorraspapel S.A.
Sarriá de Ter Mill
Mill is closed, as of late October 2014
Ownership: 100% by Lecta S.A.
Avda. Josep Flores, s/n°
E-17840 Sarriá de Ter, Girona
Spain
  Phone: (34) 972 187300
  Fax: (34) 972 187350
  Web Address: www.torraspapel.com
Personnel:
  Mill Dir.: Josep Casellas Macao
  Phone: (34) 972 187300
  Fax: (34) 972 187350
  Email: sjcasell@torraspapel.com
  Paper Division Dir.: Jordi Serra
  Phone: (34) 972 187300
  Fax: (34) 972 187350
  Email: jjserra@torraspapel.com
Total Employees at this Location: 146
Type of Operation: Paper mill
Paper/Paperboard Grades and Capacities:
  Total paper and paperboard capacity: 85,000 mt/y
  Uncoated woodfree/freesheet: 85,000 mt/y
Paper and Paperboard Mill Data:
  Stock Preparation:
  Pulpers: 7
  Refiners: 15
Paper Machines: 1
  No. 4, DuoFormer D, total capacity 85,000 mt/y, Trim width 3.2 m, Uncoated woodfree/freesheet
Finishing Equipment:
  Winders: 2
  Calenders: 1
  Supercalenders: 1
  Rewinders: 2
  Sheeters: 2
Energy Data:
  Power boilers: 1
  Combustion turbines: 1 at 21 MW
  Steam turbines: 1 at 3 MW
  Electrical demand for mill: 160 MWh/D

ⓜTorraspapel S.A.
Uranga Mill
Mill is for sale, closed (Production was stopped on January 31, 2014. Owners Lecta announced plans to sell the site in April 2014.)
Ownership: 100% by Lecta S.A.
Carretera Tolosa s/n
E-20493 Berrobi, Tolosa, Gipúzcoa
Spain
  Phone: (34) 943 683409
  Fax: (34) 943 683220
  Web Address: www.torraspapel.com
Personnel:
  Mill Dir.: Ivon Antolin
  Phone: (34) 943 683409
  Maint. Mgr.: Pedro Gomez
  Phone: (34) 943 683409
  Maint. Mgr.: Daniel Marcos
  Phone: (34) 943 683409
Total Employees at this Location: 80
Type of Operation: Paper mill
Paper and Paperboard Mill Data:
Paper Machines: 1
  No. 2, fourdrinier, total capacity 25,000 mt/y, Trim width 2.2 m
Energy Data:
  Power boilers: 1

ⓘⓜTorraspapel S.A.
Zaragoza Mill
Ownership: 100% by Lecta S.A.
Avenida de Montañana, 429
E-50059 Zaragoza
Spain
  Phone: (34) 976 01 70 00
  Fax: (34) 976 01 70 50
  Web Address: www.torraspapel.com
Personnel:
  Mill Dir.: Primitivo Prados
  Phone: (34) 976 01 70 09
  Fax: (34) 976 01 70 60
  Email: gpprados@torraspapel.com
  Paper Mill Mgr.: Juan F. Miramón
  Phone: (34) 976 01 70 54
  Fax: (34) 976 01 70 50
  Email: wmiramon@torraspapel.es
  Environ. Dir.: Ana Diez
  Phone: (34) 976 01 70 19
  Fax: (34) 976 01 70 40
  Email: wadiez@torraspapel.com
Total Employees of Company: 1,809
Total Employees at this Location: 521
Type of Operation: Pulp mill, Paper mill
Mill Locations:
  Torraspapel S.A., Motril Mill, Camino de la Vía s/n, E-18600 Motril, Spain, Capacity: 243,000 mt/y, (Pulp mill, Paper mill)
  Phone: (34) 958 832000
  Fax: (34) 958 832030
  Email: infomot@torraspapel.com
  Torraspapel S.A., Sant Joan les Fonts Mill, Avda. Paperera. Torras s/n, E-17857 Sant Joan les Fonts, Spain, Capacity: 147,000 mt/y, (Paper mill)
  Phone: (34) 972 277700
  Fax: (34) 972 277701
  Email: slvicens@torraspapel.es
  Torraspapel S.A., Sarriá de Ter Mill, Avda. Josep Flores, s/n°, E-17840 Sarriá de Ter, Spain, Capacity: 85,000 mt/y, (Paper mill, closed October 2014)
  Phone: (34) 972 187300
  Fax: (34) 972 187350
  Torraspapel S.A., Uranga Mill, Carretera Tolosa s/n, E-20493 Berrobi, Tolosa, Spain, (Paper mill)
  Phone: (34) 943 683409
  Fax: (34) 943 683220
Pulp Grades and Capacities:
  Total pulp capacity: 230,472 mt/y
  Pulp available for market: 145,000 mt/y
  Chemical Pulp: 230,472 mt/y
Pulp Mill Data:
  Chemical Pulping Systems:
  Continuous digesters: 2
Pulp Lines: 2
  Bleach Plant Systems: 2
  No. 1, Sequence: O_2 DoEopD
  No. 2, Sequence: O_2 DEopD
  Chemical Recovery Equipment:
  Evaporator lines: 2
  Recovery boilers: 2
  Lime Kiln
  Pulp Dryers:
  Wet Lap machine 1, Wet Lap machine 1
Paper/Paperboard Grades and Capacities:
  Total paper and paperboard capacity: 189,000 mt/y
  Uncoated woodfree/freesheet: 31,000 mt/y
  Coated woodfree/freesheet: 158,000 mt/y
Paper and Paperboard Mill Data:
  Stock Preparation:
  Pulpers: 3
  Refiners: 7
Paper Machines: 2
  No. 4, fourdrinier, total capacity 158,000 mt/y, Trim width 3.3 m, Coated woodfree/freesheet
  No. 6, Bel-Bond, total capacity 31,000 mt/y, Trim width 2.2 m, Uncoated woodfree/freesheet
Coating Machines: 1
  No. 1, total capacity 158,000 mt/y., off machine
Finishing Equipment:
  Winders: 3 at 150,000 mt/y
  Supercalenders: 2 at 150,000 mt/y
  Rewinders: 2 at 150,000 mt/y
  Sheeters: 4 at 150,000 mt/y

Spain

Energy Data:
Power boilers: 2
Combustion turbines: 1 at 22 MW
Steam turbines: 1 at 20 MW
Electrical demand for mill: 470 MWh/D

ⓇUnión Industrial Papelera S.A. (UIPSA)
Pas Blau s/n
E-08787 La Pobla de Claramunt, Barcelona
Spain
  Phone: (34) 93 8086262/80
  Fax: (34) 93 8086550
  Email: uipsa@uipsa.com
Personnel:
  Gen. Mgr: Ramon Bruquetas
  Phone: (34) 93 8086262
  Fax: (34) 93 8086550
  Email: r.bruquetas@uipsa.com
Mill Locations:
  Unión Industrial Papelera S.A. (UIPSA), La Pobla de Claramunt Mill, Pas Blau s/n, E-08787 La Pobla de Claramunt, Spain, Capacity: 200,000 mt/y, (Paper mill, Paperboard mill)
  Phone: (34) 93 8086262/80
  Fax: (34) 93 8086550
  Email: uipsa@uipsa.com

ⓂUnión Industrial Papelera S.A. (UIPSA)
La Pobla de Claramunt Mill
Pas Blau s/n
E-08787 La Pobla de Claramunt, Barcelona
Spain
  Phone: (34) 93 8086262/80
  Fax: (34) 93 8086550
  Email: uipsa@uipsa.com
Personnel:
  Gen. Mgr: Ramon Bruquetas
  Phone: (34) 93 8086262
  Fax: (34) 93 8086550
  Email: r.bruquetas@uipsa.com
  Mill Mgr.: Miguel Petit
  Phone: (34) 93 8086262
  Fax: (34) 93 8086550
  Email: mp@uipsa.com
  Qlty. & Environ. Mgr.: Meritxell Marcet
  Phone: (34) 93 8086262
  Fax: (34) 93 8086550
  Email: mm@uipsa.com
Total Employees at this Location: 100
Type of Operation: Paper mill, Paperboard mill
Pulp Grades and Capacities:
  Total pulp capacity: 200,793 mt/y
  Recycled Pulping: 200,793 mt/y
Pulp Mill Data:
  Recycled Fiber Treatment Lines:
  Recycled packaging pulping lines: 1
Paper/Paperboard Grades and Capacities:
  Total paper and paperboard capacity: 200,000 mt/y
  Linerboard: 135,000 mt/y
  Corrugating medium/fluting: 65,000 mt/y
Paper and Paperboard Mill Data:
Paper Machines: 1
No. 1, fourdrinier (2), total capacity 200,000 mt/y, Trim width 5 m, Corrugating medium/fluting, Linerboard
Energy Data:
Power boilers: 1
Combustion turbines: 1 at 28 MW
Steam turbines: 1 at 7 MW
Electrical demand for mill: 283 MWh/D

ⓇJ. Vilaseca S.A.
Ownership: 11% by SIGNE S.A, 12% by Fábrica Nacional de Moneda y Timbre, 76% by Torredemer Corporation
Plaza Urquinaona 6, Planta 20
E-08010 Barcelona, Barcelona
Spain
Phone: (34) 93 412 4689 / 0709/0658
Fax: (34) 93 317 5284
Email: jv@jvilaseca.es
Web Address: www.jvilaseca.es
Personnel:
Pres.: Juan Torredemer Riu
Phone: (34) 93 412 4689
Fax: (34) 93 317 5284
Finan. Dir.: Jose Torredemer Galles
Phone: (34) 93 412 0658
Fax: (34) 93 317 5284
Tech. Dir.: Antonio Coronas
Phone: (34) 93 412 0658
Fax: (34) 93 317 5284
Commer. Dir.: Carlos Torredemer
Phone: (34) 93 412 0658
Fax: (34) 93 317 5284
Gen. Mgr.: Jaime Batllori
Phone: (34) 93 412 4689
Fax: (34) 93 317 5284
Export Mgr.: Miquel Redorta Olalla
Phone: (34) 93 412 0658
Fax: (34) 93 317 5284
Area Mgr.: Gonzalo Turell Silva
Phone: (34) 93 412 0658
Fax: (34) 93 317 5284
Head of Plant: Joan Farran
Phone: (34) 93 412 0658
Fax: (34) 93 317 5284
Purch. Pulp Mgr.: Isabel Moran
Phone: (34) 93 412 0383
Fax: (34) 93 481 3710
Email: imoran@jvilaseca.es
Comm. Mgr.: Jema Serra
Phone: (34) 93 412 4689
Fax: (34) 93 317 5284
Mill Locations:
Papelera Munné S.A., Capellades Mill, Antoni Mª Claret, 7-9, E-08786 Capellades, Spain, Capacity: 7,200 mt/y, (Paper mill, Paperboard mill)
Phone: (34) 93 8011081
Fax: (34) 93 8012929
Email: munne@papeleramunne.com
J. Vilaseca S.A., Capellades Mill, Calle Amador Romani s/n, 49, E-08786 Capellades, Spain, Capacity: 63,000 mt/y, (Paper mill, Paperboard mill)
Phone: (34) 93 801 1510
Fax: (34) 93 801 1526
Email: jv@jvilaseca.es

ⓂJ. Vilaseca S.A.
Capellades Mill
Calle Amador Romani s/n, 49
E-08786 Capellades, Barcelona
Spain
Phone: (34) 93 801 1510
Fax: (34) 93 801 1526
Email: jv@jvilaseca.es
Web Address: www.jvilaseca.es
Personnel:
Mill Dir.: Pablo Osorno
Phone: (34) 93 801 1510
Fax: (34) 93 801 1526
Email: posorno@jvilaseca.es
Purch. Mgr.: Xavier Torredemer
Phone: (34) 93 801 1510
Fax: (34) 93 801 1526
Email: xtorredemer@jvilaseca.es
Maint. Mgr.: José María Martinez
Phone: (34) 93 801 1523
Fax: (34) 96 481 1527
Email: jmartinez@jvilaseca.es
Purch. Pulp Mgr.: Isabel Moran
Phone: (34) 93 412 0383
Fax: (34) 93 481 3710
Email: imoran@jvilaseca.es
Tech. Office Mgr.: Josep Soler
Phone: (34) 93 801 1523
Fax: (34) 96 481 1527
Email: jsoler@jvilaseca.es
Total Employees at this Location: 210
Type of Operation: Paper mill, Paperboard mill
Pulp Grades and Capacities:
  Total pulp capacity: 15,737 mt/y
  Recycled Pulping: 15,737 mt/y
Pulp Mill Data:
Pulp Lines: 1
  Bleach Plant Systems: 1
  DIP
  Recycled Fiber Treatment Lines:
  Flotation deinking lines: 1 at 50,000
  Pulpers: 1 at 50,000
Paper/Paperboard Grades and Capacities:
  Total paper and paperboard capacity: 63,000 mt/y
  Uncoated woodfree/freesheet: 58,000 mt/y
  Specialty and industrial: 5,000 mt/y
Paper and Paperboard Mill Data:
  Stock Preparation:
  Pulpers: 4
  Refiners: 7
Paper Machines: 2
No. 1, twin-wire, total capacity 15,000 mt/y, Trim width 1.62 m, Uncoated woodfree/freesheet, Specialty and industrial
No. 2, fourdrinier, total capacity 48,000 mt/y, Trim width 3.33 m, Uncoated woodfree/freesheet
Coating Machines: 1
No. 1, total capacity 6,000 mt/y., off machine
Finishing Equipment:
  Winders
  Calenders: 1
  Rewinders: 5
  Sheeters: 3 at 30,000 mt/y
Energy Data:
Power boilers: 2
Combustion turbines: 1 at 6 MW
Electrical demand for mill: 86 MWh/D

ⓂVirtisú S.L.
Capellades Mill
Ownership: Jofel Industrial S.A.
C/ Torre Baixa, s/n
08789 La Torre de Claramunt, Barcelona
Spain
  Phone: (34) 93 801 0723
  Fax: (34) 93 801 0375
  Email: iazcon@jofel.com
  Web Address: www.jofel.es
Personnel:
  Mill Mgr.: Pedro Mendarozketa
  Phone: (34) 93 801 0723
  Fax: (34) 93 801 0375
  Email: pmendarozketa@jofel.com
  Mill Contr.: Marc Moli
  Phone: (34) 93 801 0723
  Fax: (34) 93 801 0375
  Email: mmoli@jofel.com
Total Employees at this Location: 80
Type of Operation: Paper mill
Paper/Paperboard Grades and Capacities:
  Total paper and paperboard capacity: 22,000 mt/y
  Tissue: 22,000 mt/y
Paper and Paperboard Mill Data:
Paper Machines: 1
No. 1, twin-wire, Yankee dryer, total capacity 22,000 mt/y, Trim width 2.65 m, Tissue
Energy Data:
Power boilers
Electrical demand for mill: 61 MWh/D

ⓇⓂZubialde S.A.
Aizarnazabal Mill
Barrio Etxezarreta s/n
E-20749 Aizarnazabal, Gipúzcoa
Spain
  Phone: (34) 943 14 76 40/2
  Fax: (34) 943 14 76 43
  Email: zubialde@zubialde.com
  Web Address: www.zubialde.com

Personnel:
Gen. Mgr.: Felix Garciandia
Phone: (34) 943 14 76 40
Fax: (34) 943 14 76 43
Email: fgarciandia@zubialde.com
Mgr.: Ana Hurtado
Phone: (34) 943 14 76 40
Fax: (34) 943 14 76 43
Email: sgi@zubialde.com
Total Employees at this Location: 70
Type of Operation: Pulp mill
Pulp Grades and Capacities:
Total pulp capacity: 101,667 mt/y
Pulp available for market: 100,000 mt/y
Mechanical Pulp: 101,667 mt/y
Pulp Mill Data:
Mechanical Pulping Systems:
Conventional grinders: 4
RMP systems: 1
TMP systems: 2
Bleach Plant Systems: 1
No. 1, Sequence: P, Capacity 100,000 admt/y
Pulp Dryers:
Flash dryers 1
Energy Data:
Power boilers: 1
TMP Reboiler: 1
Electrical demand for mill: 544 MWh/D

SWEDEN

ⓂArctic Paper Grycksbo AB
Grycksbo Mill
Ownership: 75% by Arctic Paper S.A.
SE-790 20 Grycksbo
Sweden
Mailing Address: Box 1, Grycksbo, Sweden
Phone: (46) 23 68000
Fax: (46) 23 68350
Email: grycksbo@arcticpaper.com
Web Address: www.grycksbopaper.com, www.arcticpaper.com
Personnel:
Man. Dir.: Anders Nygårds
Phone: (46) 23 68100
Fax: (46) 23 68350
Email: anders.nygards@arcticpaper.com
Finan. Mgr.: Anna Gåsste
Phone: (46) 23 68020
Fax: (46) 23 68350
Email: anna.gasste@arcticpaper.com
Prod. Mgr.: Magnus Nerpin
Phone: (46) 23 68196
Fax: (46) 23 68350
Email: magnus.nerpin@arcticpaper.com
Product Mgr.: Jaana Ahlroos
Phone: (46) 23 68039
Fax: (46) 23 68350
Email: jaana.ahlroos@arcticpaper.com
Purch. Mgr: Göran Axelsson
Phone: (46) 23 68080
Fax: (46) 23 68350
Email: goran.axelsson@arcticpaper.com
Total Employees at this Location: 430
Type of Operation: Paper mill
Paper/Paperboard Grades and Capacities:
Total paper and paperboard capacity: 265,000 mt/y
Coated woodfree/freesheet: 235,000 mt/y
Specialty and industrial: 10,000 mt/y
Linerboard: 15,000 mt/y
Boxboard/cartonboard: 5,000 mt/y
Paper and Paperboard Mill Data:
Stock Preparation:
Pulpers: 2
Refiners: 15
Paper Machines: 3
No. 7, fourdrinier, total capacity 50,000 mt/y, Trim width 2.36 m, Coated woodfree/freesheet
No. 9, fourdrinier, total capacity 55,000 mt/y, Trim width 2.52 m, Coated woodfree/freesheet, Linerboard, Boxboard/cartonboard
No. 10, DuoFormer D, total capacity 160,000 mt/y, Trim width 3.86 m, Coated woodfree/freesheet, Specialty and industrial
Coating Machines: 3
PM 10, total capacity 160,000 mt/y., on machine
PM 7, total capacity 50,000 mt/y., on machine
PM 9, total capacity 55,000 mt/y., on machine
Finishing Equipment:
Rewinders: 3
Sheeters: 5 at 190,000 mt/y
Energy Data:
Power boilers: 2
Steam turbines: 1 at 6 MW
Electrical demand for mill: 566 MWh/D

ⓂArctic Paper Munkedals AB
Munkedal Mill
Ownership: 75% by Arctic Paper S.A.
SE-455 81 Munkedal
Sweden
Phone: (46) 770 110 120
Fax: (46) 524 12533
Email: info-munkedals@arcticpaper.com
Web Address: www.arcticpaper.com
Personnel:
Mill Mgr.: Göran Lindqvist
Phone: (46) 524 171 24
Fax: (46) 524 173 68
Email: goran.lindqvist@arcticpaper.com
Finan. Mgr.: Magnus Hultman
Phone: (46) 524 17148
Fax: (46) 524 12533
Email: magnus.hultman@arcticpaper.com
Prod. Mgr.: Mattias Wigelius
Phone: (46) 524 17172
Fax: (46) 524 71983
Email: mattias.wigelius@arcticpaper.com
Purch. Mgr.: Thomas Asehäll
Phone: (46) 524 17167
Fax: (46) 524 12533
Email: thomas.asehall@arcticpaper.com
Env. & Devlpt. Mgr.: Ulf Johannesson
Phone: (46) 524 171 08
Fax: (46) 524 719 83
Email: ulf.johannesson@arcticpaper.com
Total Employees at this Location: 320
Type of Operation: Paper mill
Paper/Paperboard Grades and Capacities:
Total paper and paperboard capacity: 160,000 mt/y
Uncoated woodfree/freesheet: 130,000 mt/y
Uncoated mechanical/groundwood: 30,000 mt/y
Paper and Paperboard Mill Data:
Stock Preparation:
Pulpers: 3
Refiners: 9
Paper Machines: 2
No. 5, DuoFormer D, total capacity 75,000 mt/y, Trim width 3.22 m, Uncoated woodfree/freesheet
No. 8, DuoFormer D, total capacity 85,000 mt/y, Trim width 3.96 m, Uncoated woodfree/freesheet, Uncoated mechanical/groundwood
Finishing Equipment:
Winders: 2
Sheeters: 5 at 25,000 mt/y
Energy Data:
Power boilers: 2
Steam turbines: 1
Electrical demand for mill: 868 MWh/D

ⓂBillerudKorsnäs AB
Ownership: Fourth Swedish National Pension Fund (AP4), Norges Bank, Sweden AMF, other Investment funds, Alecta
Gustav III boulevard 18
Solna
Sweden
Mailing Address: P.O. Box 703, SE-169 27 Solna, Sweden
Phone: (46) 8 553 335 00
Fax: (46) 8 553 335 60
Email: info@billerudkorsnas.com
Web Address: www.billerudkorsnas.com
Personnel:
Pres. & CEO: Per Lindberg
Phone: (46) 8 553 335 00
Fax: (46) 8 553 335 60
Email: per.lindberg@billerud.com
Exec. VP. & COO: Christer Simrén
Phone: (46) 8 553 335 00
Fax: (46) 8 553 335 60
Email: christer.simren@billerud.com
CFO: Susanne Lithander
Phone: (46) 8 553 335 00
Fax: (46) 8 553 335 60
Email: susanne.lithander@billerud.com
Snr. VP., Packaging Paper: Johan Nellbeck
Phone: (46) 8 553 335 00
Fax: (46) 8 553 335 60
Email: johan.nellbeck@billerud.com
Snr. VP., Containerboard: Lennart Eberleh
Phone: (46) 8 553 335 00
Fax: (46) 8 553 335 60
Email: lennart.eberled@billerud.com
SnrVP., Corp. HR.: Karin Hågfeldt
Phone: (46) 8 553 335 00
Fax: (46) 8 553 335 60
Email: karin.hagfeldt@billerud.com
Snr. VP., Technology & Strategic Develop.: Magnus Wikström
Phone: (46) 8 553 335 00
Fax: (46) 8 553 335 60
Email: magnus.wikstrom@billerud.com
Total Employees of Company: 4,270
Total Employees at this Location: 40
Mill Locations:
BillerudKorsnäs AB, Rockhammar Mill, SE - 71880 Frövi, Sweden, (Pulp mill)
Phone: (46) 261 510 00
Email: info@billerudkorsnas.com
BillerudKorsnäs AB, Beetham Mill, Beetham, Milnthorpe LA7 7AR, United Kingdom, Capacity: 44,982 mt/y, (Paper mill)
Phone: (44) 1539 565 000
Fax: (44) 1539 565 033
Email: info@billerudkorsnas.com
BillerudKorsnäs Finland Oy, Pietarsaari Mill, Larsmovägen 149, 68600 Pietarsaari, Finland, Capacity: 199,920 mt/y, (Paper mill)
Phone: (358) 6 241 380 00
Email: info@billerudkorsnas.com
BillerudKorsnäs AB, Frövi Mill, SE-718 80 Frövi, Sweden, Capacity: 420,000 mt/y, (Pulp mill, Paperboard mill)
Phone: (46) 261 510 00
Email: (firstname.lastname@billerudkorsnas.com)
BillerudKorsnäs AB, Gruvön Mill, SE-664 28 Grums, Sweden, Capacity: 593,000 mt/y, (Pulp mill, Paper mill, Paperboard mill)
Phone: (46) 555 410 00
Fax: (46) 555 416 90
Email: info@billerudkorsnas.com
BillerudKorsnäs AB, Karlsborg Mill, Strandvagen 3, SE-952 83 Karlsborg, Sweden, Capacity: 130,000 mt/y, (Pulp mill, Paper mill)
Phone: (46) 923 660 00
Fax: (46) 923 203 48
Email: info@billerudkorsnas.com
BillerudKorsnäs AB, Skärblacka Mill, SE-617 10 Skärblacka, Sweden, Capacity: 350,000 mt/y, (Pulp mill, Paper mill, Paperboard mill)
Phone: (46) 11 245 300
Fax: (46) 11 57502
Email: info@billerudkorsnas.com
BillerudKorsnäs Finland Oy, Tervasaari Mill, Tehtaankatu 7, FI-37600 Valkeakoski, Finland, Capacity: 100,000 mt/y, (Paper mill)

Sweden

Phone: (358) 3 339 266 00
Email: info@billerudkorsnas.com
BillerudKorsnäs AB, Gävle Mill, SE-801 81 Gävle,
Sweden, Capacity: 630,000 mt/y, (Pulp mill, Paper mill, Paperboard mill)
Phone: (46) 26 151000
Fax: (46) 26 152240
Email: info@billerudkorsnas.com

ⓜBillerudKorsnäs AB
Rockhammar Mill
SE - 71880 Frövi
Sweden
Phone: (46) 261 510 00
Email: info@billerudkorsnas.com
Web Address: www.billerudkorsnas.com
Personnel:
Prod. Mgr : Peter Juntti
Phone: (46) 261 510 00
Email: peter.juntti@billerudkorsnas.com
Total Employees at this Location: 42
Type of Operation: Pulp mill
Pulp Grades and Capacities:
Total pulp capacity: 90,492 mt/y
Pulp available for market: 90,000 mt/y
Mechanical Pulp: 90,492 mt/y

Pulp Mill Data:
Mechanical Pulping Systems:
CTMP systems: 2
Bleach Plant Systems: 1
No. 1, Sequence: P, Capacity 90,000 admt/y
Pulp Dryers:
Flash dryers 1
Energy Data:
Power boilers: 1
Hydro turbines: 1
Electrical demand for mill: 274 MWh/D

ⓜBillerudKorsnäs AB
Frövi Mill
SE-718 80 Frövi
Sweden
Phone: (46) 261 510 00
Email: (firstname.lastname@billerudkorsnas.com)
Web Address: www.billerudkorsnas.com
Personnel:
Mill Dir.: Håkan Krantz
Phone: (46) 261 510 00
Email: hakan.krantz@billerudkorsnas.com
Pulp Mill Mgr.: Hans Jennsjö
Phone: (46) 261 510 00
Email: hans.Jennsjo@billerudkorsnas.com
Proj. Mgr.: Agneta Funke
Phone: (46) 261 510 00
Email: agneta.funke@billerudkorsnas.com
Total Employees at this Location: 560
Type of Operation: Pulp mill, Paperboard mill
Pulp Grades and Capacities:
Total pulp capacity: 274,529 mt/y
Chemical Pulp: 274,529 mt/y

Pulp Mill Data:
Chemical Pulping Systems:
Batch digesters: 3
Continuous digesters: 1
Pulp Lines: 2
Bleach Plant Systems: 1
hard- and softwood, Type: TCF, Sequence: O_2 QQPoPo, Capacity 130,000 admt/y
Chemical Recovery Equipment:
Evaporator lines: 1
Recovery boilers: 1
Lime Kiln
Paper/Paperboard Grades and Capacities:
Total paper and paperboard capacity: 420,000 mt/y
Boxboard/cartonboard: 420,000 mt/y
Paper and Paperboard Mill Data:
Stock Preparation:
Pulpers: 2
Refiners: 16

Paper Machines: 1
No. 5, Fourdrinier (4), total capacity 420,000 mt/y, Trim width 6.6 m, Boxboard/cartonboard
Coating Machines: 2
No. 1, on machine
No. 2, on machine
Finishing Equipment:
Winders: 1 at 450,000 mt/y
Calenders: 3
Rewinders: 1
Sheeters: 2 at 60,000 mt/y
Energy Data:
Power boilers: 1
Steam turbines: 1 at 26 MW
Electrical demand for mill: 1,052 MWh/D

ⓜBillerudKorsnäs AB
Gruvön Mill
SE-664 28 Grums
Sweden
Mailing Address: PO Box 500, SE-664 28 Grums, Sweden
Phone: (46) 555 410 00
Fax: (46) 555 416 90
Email: info@billerudkorsnas.com
Web Address: www.billerudkorsnas.com
Personnel:
Mill Mgr.: Fredrik Turzik
Phone: (46) 730 811591
Fax: (46) 555 416 90
Email: fredrik.turzik@billerudkorsnas.com
Prod. Mgr.: Alf Sondell
Phone: (46) 555 410 00
Fax: (46) 555 416 90
Email: alf.sondell@billerudkorsnas.com
Tech. Mgr.: Eva Söfting
Phone: (46) 555 410 00
Fax: (46) 555 416 90
Email: eva.softing@billerudkorsnas.com
Maint. Mgr.: Inge Carlsson
Phone: (46) 555 410 00
Fax: (46) 555 416 90
Email: inge.carlsson@billerudkorsnas.com
HR Mgr.: Claes Hansson
Phone: (46) 555 411 22
Fax: (46) 555 416 90
Email: claes.hansson@billerudkorsnas.com
Commun. Dir.: Marianne Jonsson
Phone: (46) 555 416 99
Fax: (46) 555 416 90
Email: marianne.jonsson@billerudkorsnas.com
Total Employees at this Location: 840
Type of Operation: Pulp mill, Paper mill, Paperboard mill
Pulp Grades and Capacities:
Total pulp capacity: 726,860 mt/y
Pulp available for market: 115,000 mt/y
Chemical Pulp: 726,860 mt/y

Pulp Mill Data:
Chemical Pulping Systems:
Continuous digesters: 3
Pulp Lines: 3
Bleach Plant Systems: 2
Hardwood, Sequence: O_2 DEpD, Capacity 100,000 admt/y
Softwood, Sequence: O_2 DEOpDEpD, Capacity 340,000 admt/y
Chemical Recovery Equipment:
Evaporator lines: 1
Recovery boilers: 3
Lime Kiln
Pulp Dryers:
Flash dryers 1, Flash dryers 1, Fourdriniers 1, Fourdriniers 1
Paper/Paperboard Grades and Capacities:
Total paper and paperboard capacity: 593,000 mt/y
Packaging papers: 75,000 mt/y
Specialty and industrial: 63,000 mt/y
Linerboard: 170,000 mt/y
Corrugating medium/fluting: 260,000 mt/y

Boxboard/cartonboard: 25,000 mt/y
Paper and Paperboard Mill Data:
Stock Preparation:
Pulpers: 1
Refiners: 15
Paper Machines: 5
No. 1, fourdrinier (2), total capacity 95,000 mt/y, Trim width 4.3 m, Linerboard, Boxboard/cartonboard
No. 2, fourdrinier (2), total capacity 90,000 mt/y, Trim width 4.3 m, Packaging papers, Linerboard, Specialty and industrial
No. 4, fourdrinier (2), total capacity 110,000 mt/y, Trim width 5.2 m, Linerboard, Packaging papers, Boxboard/cartonboard, Specialty and industrial
No. 5, fourdrinier, Yankee dryer, total capacity 38,000 mt/y, Trim width 4.6 m, Specialty and industrial
No. 6, fourdrinier, total capacity 260,000 mt/y, Trim width 6.7 m, Corrugating medium/fluting
Coating Machines: 1
No. 1, off machine
Finishing Equipment:
Winders: 7
Sheeters: 1
Energy Data:
Power boilers: 1
Steam turbines: 2 at 49 MW
Electrical demand for mill: 2,151 MWh/D

ⓜBillerudKorsnäs AB
Karlsborg Mill
Strandvagen 3
SE-952 83 Karlsborg
Sweden
Phone: (46) 923 660 00
Fax: (46) 923 203 48
Email: info@billerudkorsnas.com
Web Address: www.billerudkorsnas.com
Personnel:
Paper Mill Mgr.: Ove Lindstrom
Phone: (46) 923 661 60
Fax: (46) 923 203 48
Email: ove.lindstrom@billerudkorsnas.com
Maint. Mgr.: Anders Ejerlund
Phone: (46) 923 660 00
Fax: (46) 923 203 48
Email: anders.ejerlund@billerudkorsnas.com
Tech. Mgr.: Lars Erik Johansson
Phone: (46) 923 663 42
Fax: (46) 923 204 04
Email: lars-erik.johansson@billerudkorsnas.com
Total Employees at this Location: 390
Type of Operation: Pulp mill, Paper mill
Pulp Grades and Capacities:
Total pulp capacity: 302,976 mt/y
Pulp available for market: 170,000 mt/y
Chemical Pulp: 302,976 mt/y

Pulp Mill Data:
Chemical Pulping Systems:
Batch digesters: 8
Pulp Lines: 1
Bleach Plant Systems: 1
Line 1, Type: ECF, Sequence: O_2 DEoDD, Capacity 300,000 admt/y
Chemical Recovery Equipment:
Evaporator lines: 1
Recovery boilers: 1
Lime Kiln
Pulp Dryers:
Air Float dryers 1
Paper/Paperboard Grades and Capacities:
Total paper and paperboard capacity: 130,000 mt/y
Packaging papers: 110,000 mt/y
Specialty and industrial: 20,000 mt/y
Paper and Paperboard Mill Data:
Stock Preparation:
Pulpers: 2
Refiners: 8
Paper Machines: 1

Sweden

No. 2, SymFormer MB, total capacity 130,000 mt/y, Trim width 4.5 m, Packaging papers, Specialty and industrial
Coating Machines: 1
No. 1, total capacity 40,000 mt/y., off machine
Finishing Equipment:
  Rewinders: 2 at 5,000 mt/y
Energy Data:
Power boilers: 1
Steam turbines: 1 at 42 MW
Electrical demand for mill: 866 MWh/D

BillerudKorsnäs AB
Skärblacka Mill
SE-617 10 Skärblacka
Sweden
  Phone: (46) 11 245 300
  Fax: (46) 11 57502
  Email: info@billerudkorsnas.com
  Web Address: www.billerudkorsnas.com
Personnel:
  Mill Mgr.: Tor Lundqvist
  Phone: (46) 11 245 300
  Fax: (46) 11 575 02
  Email: tor.lundqvist@billerudkorsnas.com
  Finan. Mgr.: Per-Olof Kiellarson
  Phone: (46) 11 245 300
  Fax: (46) 11 575 02
  Email: per-olof.kiellarson@billerudkorsnas.com
  Tech. Mgr.: Margaretha Öhm
  Phone: (46) 11 24 5554
  Fax: (46) 11 575 02
  Email: margareta.ohm@billerudkorsnas.com
  Purch. Dir.: Rickard Björsten
  Phone: (46) 11 245 300
  Fax: (46) 11 575 02
  Email: rickard.bjorsten@billerudkorsnas.com
  Commun. Mgr.: Monica Lundgren
  Phone: (46) 11 24 5301
  Fax: (46) 11 575 02
  Email: monica.lundgren@billerudkorsnas.com
Total Employees at this Location: 625
Type of Operation: Pulp mill, Paper mill, Paperboard mill
Pulp Grades and Capacities:
  Total pulp capacity: 424,262 mt/y
  Pulp available for market: 58,277 mt/y
  Chemical Pulp: 400,715 mt/y
  Recycled Pulping: 23,547 mt/y
Pulp Mill Data:
  Chemical Pulping Systems:
  Batch digesters: 6
  Continuous digesters: 2
Pulp Lines: 3
  Bleach Plant Systems: 1
  Chemical Batch Digester, Sequence: O_2 DEoDD
  Chemical Recovery Equipment:
  Evaporator lines: 3
  Recovery boilers: 2
  Lime Kiln
  Recycled Fiber Treatment Lines:
  Pulpers: 1 at 25,000
  Pulp Dryers:
  Air Float dryers 1, Twin Wire 1
Paper/Paperboard Grades and Capacities:
  Total paper and paperboard capacity: 350,000 mt/y
  Packaging papers: 160,000 mt/y
  Specialty and industrial: 100,000 mt/y
  Corrugating medium/fluting: 90,000 mt/y
Paper and Paperboard Mill Data:
  Stock Preparation:
  Pulpers: 2
  Refiners: 11
Paper Machines: 4
No. 4, fourdrinier, total capacity 90,000 mt/y, Trim width 4.4 m, Corrugating medium/fluting
No. 7, fourdrinier, Yankee dryer, total capacity 55,000 mt/y, Trim width 4.7 m, Specialty and industrial
No. 8, fourdrinier, Yankee dryer, total capacity 45,000 mt/y, Trim width 5.1 m, Specialty and industrial
No. 9, fourdrinier, total capacity 160,000 mt/y, Trim width 6.4 m, Packaging papers
Finishing Equipment:
  Winders: 2
Energy Data:
Power boilers: 2
Steam turbines: 1 at 48 MW
Electrical demand for mill: 1,342 MWh/D

Cascades Djupafors AB
Kallinge Mill
Company is closed (Production at the mill ceased on June 30, 2014)
Ownership: *Cascades Boxboard Group Inc.*
Häggatorpsvägen 45
S-372 52 Kallinge
Sweden
Mailing Address: PO Box 501, SE-37 225 Ronneby, Sweden
  Phone: (46) 457 461700
  Fax: (46) 457 461710
  Web Address: www.careo.biz,
    www.cascades-europe.com
Total Employees of Company: 130
Total Employees at this Location: 130
Type of Operation: Pulp mill, Paperboard mill
Pulp Grades and Capacities:
  Total pulp capacity: 33,886 mt/y
  Mechanical Pulp: 33,886 mt/y
Pulp Mill Data:
  Mechanical Pulping Systems:
  Conventional grinders: 2
Paper/Paperboard Grades and Capacities:
  Total paper and paperboard capacity: 60,000 mt/y
  Boxboard/cartonboard: 60,000 mt/y
Paper and Paperboard Mill Data:
  Stock Preparation:
  Pulpers: 3
  Refiners: 5
Paper Machines: 1
No. 1, combination, total capacity 60,000 mt/y, Trim width 2.8 m, Boxboard/cartonboard
Coating Machines: 2
No. 1, on machine
No. 2, on machine
Finishing Equipment:
  Rewinders: 1
  Sheeters: 2
Energy Data:
Power boilers: 2
Electrical demand for mill: 218 MWh/D

Crane AB
Tumba Mill
Ownership: *100% by Crane & Co., Inc.*
Tumbavägen 5
SE-147 82 Tumba
Sweden
  Phone: (46) 8 57869500
  Fax: (46) 8 57869800
  Email: info@cranecurrency.com
  Web Address: www.crane.se
Personnel:
  Chmn.: C. Kittredge
  Phone: (46) 8 57869500
  Man. Dir.: Timothy Crane
  Phone: (46) 8 57869500
  Paper Mill Mgr.: Sixten Jansson
  Phone: (46) 8 57869500
  Purch. Mgr.: Henrik Andersson
  Phone: (46) 8 57869500
  Purch. Agent: Tomas Aggefors
  Phone: (46) 8 57869500
  Tech. Mgr.: Claes-Göran Hedström
  Phone: (46) 8 57869500
  Sls. Dir.: T. Gustafsson
  Phone: (46) 8 57869500
Total Employees of Company: 240
Total Employees at this Location: 240
Type of Operation: Paper mill
Paper/Paperboard Grades and Capacities:
  Total paper and paperboard capacity: 7,000 mt/y
  Uncoated woodfree/freesheet: 7,000 mt/y
Paper and Paperboard Mill Data:
  Stock Preparation:
  Pulpers: 2
  Refiners: 5
Paper Machines: 1
No. 2, total capacity 7,000 mt/y, Trim width 2.7 m, Uncoated woodfree/freesheet
Finishing Equipment:
  Rewinders: 2
  Sheeters: 2
Energy Data:
Power boilers: 2

Domsjö Fabriker
Örnsköldsvik Mill
Ownership: *Aditya Birla Group*
SE-891 86 Örnsköldsvik
Sweden
  Phone: (46) 660 75600
  Fax: (46) 660 75990
  Email: info@domsjoe.com
  Web Address: www.domsjoe.com
Personnel:
  CEO: Lars Winter
  Phone: (46) 660 75600
  Fax: (46) 660 75990
  Email: lars.winter@domsjoe.com
  Project Dir.: Lars Ahlenius
  Phone: (46) 660 75674
  Fax: (46) 660 75990
  Email: lars.ahlenius@domsjoe.com
  Finan. Dir.: Carola Hägglund
  Phone: (46) 660 75623
  Fax: (46) 660 75990
  Email: carola.hagglund@domsjoe.com
  Purch. Agent: Lars-Olof Lögdström
  Phone: (46) 660 75627
  Fax: (46) 660 75628
  Email: lars-olof.logdstrom@domsjoe.com
  Maint. Mgr.: Jan Crone
  Phone: (46) 660 75690
  Fax: (46) 660 75990
  Email: jan.crone@domsjoe.com
  Prod. Mgr.: Christin Norberg
  Phone: (46) 660 75756
  Fax: (46) 660 75990
  Email: christin.norberg@domsjoe.com
  Env. Mgr.: Patrik Svensson
  Phone: (46) 660 75570
  Fax: (46) 660 75990
  Email: patrik.svensson@domsjoe.com
  Mgr. Prod. Dvlpt. Cellulose: Magnus Lundmark
  Phone: (46) 660 75544
  Fax: (46) 660 75990
  Commun. Mgr.: Sören Back
  Phone: (46) 660 75780
  Fax: (46) 660 75990
  Mgr. Eng. Unit: Björn Edström
  Phone: (46) 660 75576
  Fax: (46) 660 75990
  Email: bjorn.edstrom@domsjoe.com
  Mgr. HR: Billy Nordin
  Phone: (46) 660 75610
  Fax: (46) 660 75990
  Email: billy.nordin@domsjoe.com
Total Employees of Company: 405
Total Employees at this Location: 395
Type of Operation: Pulp mill
Pulp Grades and Capacities:
  Total pulp capacity: 267,984 mt/y
  Pulp available for market: 255,000 mt/y
  Chemical Pulp: 267,984 mt/y
Pulp Mill Data:
  Chemical Pulping Systems:
  Batch digesters: 14

Sweden

Pulp Lines: 1
  Bleach Plant Systems: 1
    No. 1, Sequence: EopP, Capacity 230,300 admt/y
  Chemical Recovery Equipment:
    Evaporator lines: 5
    Recovery boilers: 2
  Pulp Dryers:
    Air Float dryers 1
Energy Data:
  Power boilers: 1
  Combustion turbines: 1 at 15.0 MW
  Electrical demand for mill: 690 MWh/D

ⓜDuni AB
Ownership: 100% by public company
Östra Varvsgatan 9
SE-211 73 Malmö
Sweden
Mailing Address: Box 237, SE-201 22 Malmö
  Phone: (46) 40 106200
  Fax: (46) 40 396630
  Email: info@duni.com
  Web Address: www.duni.com
Personnel:
  Chmn.: Anders Bülow
  Phone: (46) 40 106200
  Fax: (46) 40 396630
  Email: anders.bulow@duni.com
  Pres. & CEO: Thomas Gustafsson
  Phone: (46) 40 106445
  Fax: (46) 40 106469
  Email: thomas.gustafsson@duni.com
  CFO: Mats Lindroth
  Phone: (46) 40 106375
  Fax: (46) 40 106262
  Email: mats.lindroth@duni.com
  Sls. Dir.: Leendert Amersfoort
  Phone: (46) 40 106200
  Fax: (46) 40 396630
  Email: leendert.amersfoort@duni.com
  Bus. Develop. Dir.: Patrik Söderstjerna
  Phone: (46) 40 106200
  Fax: (46) 40 396630
  Email: patrik.söderstjerna@duni.com
  Prod. & Supply Dir.: Ulfert Rott
  Phone: (46) 40 106200
  Fax: (46) 40 396630
  Email: ulfert.rott@duni.com
  Bus. Area Professional (Table Top) Dir.: Maria Wahlgren
  Phone: (46) 40 106200
  Fax: (46) 40 396630
  Email: maria.wahlgren@duni.com
  Bus. Area Professional (Meal Service) Dir.: Linus Lemark
  Phone: (46) 40 106200
  Fax: (46) 40 396630
  Email: linus.lemark@duni.com
  Bus. Area Consumer Dir.: Robert Dackeskog
  Phone: (46) 40 106200
  Fax: (46) 40 396630
  Email: robert.dackeskog@duni.com
  Dir., Corp. Mktg & Commun.: Tina Andersson
  Phone: (46) 40 106200
  Fax: (46) 40 396630
Total Employees of Company: 1,875
Total Employees at this Location: 100
Mill Locations:
  Rexcell Tissue & Airlaid AB, Skåpafors Mill, SE-666 25 Bengtsfors, Sweden, Capacity: 50,000 mt/y, (Paper mill)
  Phone: (46) 531 728 00
  Fax: (46) 531 122 83
  Email: info@rexcell.se

ⓜⓜFiskeby Board AB
Norrköping Mill
Ownership: 100% by Coors Family Trust (Private)
PO Box 1, Fiskeby
SE-601 02 Norrköping
Sweden
  Phone: (46) 11 15 57 00
  Fax: (46) 11 15 59 95
  Web Address: www.fiskeby.com
Personnel:
  CEO: Torbjörn Hansen
  Phone: (46) 11 15 57 30
  Fax: (46) 11 15 59 95
  Email: torbjorn.hansen@fiskeby.com
  Mill Mgr.: Hans Hagdahl
  Phone: (46) 11 15 58 13
  Fax: (46) 11 15 59 95
  Email: hans.hagdahl@fiskeby.com
  Develop. Mgr.: Corrina Fogelberg
  Phone: (46) 11 15 59 03
  Fax: (46) 11 15 59 95
  Email: corrina.fogelberg@fiskeby.com
  Sls. & Mktg. Mgr.: Anders Nyren
  Phone: (46) 11 15 59 12
  Fax: (46) 11 15 59 95
  Strat. Supply: Sten Christoffersson
  Phone: (46) 11 15 57 13
  Fax: (46) 11 15 59 95
  Email: sten.christoffersson@fiskeby.com
  HR Mgr.: Åke Pettersson
  Phone: (46) 11 15 57 48
  Fax: (46) 11 15 59 95
  Admin. Mgr.: Michael Nilsson
  Phone: (46) 11 15 57 63
  Fax: (46) 11 15 59 95
  Email: michael.nilsson@fiskeby.com
Total Employees of Company: 300
Total Employees at this Location: 300
Type of Operation: Paperboard mill
Pulp Grades and Capacities:
  Total pulp capacity: 154,495 mt/y
  Recycled Pulping: 154,495 mt/y
Pulp Mill Data:
  Recycled Fiber Treatment Lines:
    Recycled packaging pulping lines: 1
Paper/Paperboard Grades and Capacities:
  Total paper and paperboard capacity: 170,000 mt/y
  Boxboard/cartonboard: 170,000 mt/y
Paper and Paperboard Mill Data:
  Stock Preparation:
    Pulpers: 4
Paper Machines: 1
  No. 1, Fourdrinier (4), total capacity 170,000 mt/y, Trim width 3.7 m, Boxboard/cartonboard
Coating Machines: 2
  No. 1, on machine
  No. 2, on machine
Finishing Equipment:
  Winders: 2
  Sheeters: 4 at 132,000 mt/y
Energy Data:
  Power boilers: 1
  Steam turbines: 1 at 10 MW
  Electrical demand for mill: 391 MWh/D

ⓜHolmen AB
Ownership: Public
Strandvägen 1
SE-114 84 Stockholm
Sweden
Mailing Address: PO Box 5407, SE-11484 Stockholm, Sweden
  Phone: (46) 8 666 2100
  Fax: (46) 8 666 2130
  Email: info@holmen.com
  Web Address: www.holmen.com
Personnel:
  Chmn.: Fredrik Lundberg
  Phone: (46) 8 666 2100
  Fax: (46) 8 666 2130
  Pres. & CEO: Henrik Sjölund
  Phone: (46) 8 666 2105
  Fax: (46) 8 666 2130
  Email: henrik.sjolund@holmen.com
  CFO: Anders Jernhall
  Phone: (46) 8 666 2122
  Fax: (46) 8 666 2130
  Email: anders.jernhall@holmen.com
  Exec. VP., Sls. & Spanish Oper. (From May 2014): Juha Paulin
  Phone: (46) 8 666 2100
  Fax: (46) 8 666 2130
  Dir., Mktg. & Sls.: Karolina Svensson
  Phone: (46) 8 666 2100
  Fax: (46) 8 666 2130
  Tech. Dir.: Staffan Jonsson
  Phone: (46) 8 666 2100
  Fax: (46) 8 666 2130
  Email: staffan.jonsson@holmen.com
  Dir. Legal Affairs: Lars Ericson
  Phone: (46) 8 666 2110
  Fax: (46) 8 666 2180
  Email: lars.ericson@holmen.com
  Dir. Commun.: Ingela Carlsson
  Phone: (46) 8 666 2115
  Fax: (46) 8 666 2130
  Email: ingela.carlsson@holmen.com
  CEO Holmen Energy: Arne Wallin
  Phone: (46) 8 666 2157
  Fax: (46) 8 666 2130
  Email: arne.wallin@holmen.com
  Dir. Bus. Develop. & Innovation: Dr. Ola Schultz-Eklund
  Phone: (46) 8 666 2100
  Fax: (46) 8 666 2130
Total Employees of Company: 3,718
Total Employees at this Location: 30
Mill Locations:
  Holmen AB, Braviken Paper Mill, Östra Bravikenvägen 20, SE-601 88 Norrköping, Sweden, Capacity: 600,000 mt/y, (Pulp mill, Paper mill)
  Phone: (46) 11 23 50 00
  Fax: (46) 11 23 66 30
  Email: info@holmenpaper.com
  Holmen AB, Hallsta Mill, SE-763 81 Hallstavik, Sweden, Capacity: 550,000 mt/y, (Pulp mill, Paper mill)
  Phone: (46) 175 26000
  Fax: (46) 175 26401
  Email: hallsta@holmenpaper.com
  Holmen Paper Madrid S.L., Madrid Mill, P.I. La Cantueña, c/ del Papel, 1, E-28947 Fuenlabrada, Spain, Capacity: 330,000 mt/y, (Pulp mill, Paper mill)
  Phone: (34) 91 6420603
  Fax: (34) 91 6422470
  Email: madrid@holmenpaper.com
  Iggesund Paperboard AB, Iggesund Mill, SE-825 80 Iggesund, Sweden, Capacity: 340,000 mt/y, (Pulp mill, Paperboard mill)
  Phone: (46) 650 28000
  Fax: (46) 650 28830
  Email: info@iggesund.com
  Iggesund Paperboard (Workington) Ltd., Workington Mill, Siddick, Workington CA14 1JX, United Kingdom, Capacity: 200,000 mt/y, (Pulp mill, Paperboard mill)
  Phone: (44) 1900 601 000
  Fax: (44) 1900 605 000

ⓜHolmen AB
Braviken Paper Mill
Östra Bravikenvägen 20
SE-601 88 Norrköping
Sweden
  Phone: (46) 11 23 50 00
  Fax: (46) 11 23 66 30
  Email: info@holmenpaper.com
  Web Address: www.holmen.com
Personnel:
  Mill Mgr. (Eff. April 1, 2014): Fredrik Holgersson
  Phone: (46) 11 23 50 00
  Fax: (46) 11 23 66 30
  Finan. Dir.: Peter Kjell-Berger
  Phone: (46) 11 23 64 33, 702 44 42 84
  Fax: (46) 11 23 66 30
  Email: peter.kjell-berger@holmenpaper.com
  Prod. Mgr. (PM 51 & 52): Torbjörn Westerlund
  Phone: (46) 11 23 50 00
  Fax: (46) 11 23 66 30
  Prod. Mgr. (PM 53): Jenny Melander

Sweden

Phone: (46) 11 23 50 00
Fax: (46) 11 23 66 30
Develop. Mgr.: Magnus Revland
Phone: (46) 11 23 50 00
Fax: (46) 11 23 66 30
Economy & Purch. Agent: Johan Engberg
Phone: (46) 11 23 63 74
Fax: (46) 11 23 66 30
Email: johan.engberg@holmenpaper.com
HR Mgr.: Britt-Inger Eliasson
Phone: (46) 11 23 63 17, 705 13 31 78
Fax: (46) 11 23 66 30
Email: britt-inger.eliasson@holmenpaper.com
Total Employees at this Location: 390
Type of Operation: Pulp mill, Paper mill
Pulp Grades and Capacities:
Total pulp capacity: 594,040 mt/y
Mechanical Pulp: 453,242 mt/y
Recycled Pulping: 140,797 mt/y
Pulp Mill Data:
Mechanical Pulping Systems:
TMP systems: 4
Pulp Lines: 6
Bleach Plant Systems: 2
DIP
TMP, Type: Softwood, Sequence: P
Recycled Fiber Treatment Lines:
Flotation deinking lines: 2 at 320,000
Paper/Paperboard Grades and Capacities:
Total paper and paperboard capacity: 600,000 mt/y
Newsprint: 305,000 mt/y
Uncoated mechanical/groundwood: 295,000 mt/y
Paper and Paperboard Mill Data:
Stock Preparation:
Pulpers: 1
Refiners: 4
Paper Machines: 2
No. 52, DuoFormer TQv, total capacity 290,000 mt/y, Trim width 8.55 m, Newsprint, Uncoated mechanical/groundwood
No. 53, DuoFormer CFD, total capacity 310,000 mt/y, Trim width 8.9 m, Newsprint, Uncoated mechanical/groundwood
Finishing Equipment:
Rewinders: 4
Energy Data:
Power boilers: 2
TMP Reboiler: 1
Steam turbines: 1 at 13.6 MW
Electrical demand for mill: 4,130 MWh/D

ⓘⓜ Holmen AB
Hallsta Mill
SE-763 81 Hallstavik
Sweden
Phone: (46) 175 26000
Fax: (46) 175 26401
Email: hallsta@holmenpaper.com
Web Address: www.holmenpaper.com
Personnel:
Mill. Mgr.: Daniel Peltonen
Phone: (46) 175 26000
Fax: (46) 175 26401
Email: daniel.peltonen@holmenpaper.com
Develop. Mgr.: Mikael Wahlgren
Phone: (46) 175 26108, 73 2594075
Fax: (46) 175 26401
Email: mikael.wahlgren@holmenpaper.com
Develop. Mgr.: Göran Starck
Phone: (46) 175 26000
Fax: (46) 175 26401
Total Employees at this Location: 600
Type of Operation: Pulp mill, Paper mill
Pulp Grades and Capacities:
Total pulp capacity: 524,518 mt/y
Mechanical Pulp: 524,518 mt/y
Pulp Mill Data:
Mechanical Pulping Systems:
Conventional grinders: 8
TMP systems: 1
TMP systems: 1
Pulp Lines: 2
Bleach Plant Lines:
No. 1, Type: TMP Peroxide line, Sequence: P, Capacity 365,000 admt/y
No. 2, Type: TMP Hydrosulfite line, Sequence: HS, Capacity 275,000 admt/y
Paper/Paperboard Grades and Capacities:
Total paper and paperboard capacity: 550,000 mt/y
Uncoated mechanical/groundwood: 550,000 mt/y
Paper and Paperboard Mill Data:
Stock Preparation:
Refiners:
Paper Machines: 2
No. 11, OptiFormer, total capacity 330,000 mt/y, Trim width 8.6 m, Uncoated mechanical/groundwood
No. 12, OptiFormer, total capacity 220,000 mt/y, Trim width 8.5 m, Uncoated mechanical/groundwood
Finishing Equipment:
Winders: 3
Supercalenders: 2
Energy Data:
Power boilers: 4
TMP Reboiler: 1
Steam turbines: 2 at 28.0 MW
Electrical demand for mill: 4,538 MWh/D

ⓘⓜ Iggesund Paperboard AB
Iggesund Mill
Ownership: 100% by Holmen AB
SE-825 80 Iggesund
Sweden
 Phone: (46) 650 28000
 Fax: (46) 650 28830
 Email: info@iggesund.com
 Web Address: www.iggesund.com
Personnel:
CEO (from 1 October 2013): Annica Bresky
Phone: (46) 650 28000
Fax: (46) 650 28830
Mill Mgr: Olov Winblad von Walter
Phone: (46) 650 28532
Fax: (46) 650 28830
Email: olov.winbaldvonwalter@iggesund.com
Fin. Dir.: Tobias Bäärnman
Phone: (46) 650 28000
Fax: (46) 650 28830
Pulp Mill Mgr.: Hans Eriksson
Phone: (46) 650 28455
Fax: (46) 650 28681
Email: hans.eriksson@iggesund.com
Maint. Mgr.: Bo Larsson
Phone: (46) 650 28495
Fax: (46) 650 28740
Email: bo.larsson@iggesund.com
Global Sls. & Mktg.: Arvid Sundblad
Phone: (46) 650 28000
Fax: (46) 650 28830
Total Employees of Company: 1,500
Type of Operation: Pulp mill, Paperboard mill
Pulp Grades and Capacities:
Total pulp capacity: 361,203 mt/y
Pulp available for market: 50,000 mt/y
Chemical Pulp: 361,203 mt/y
Pulp Mill Data:
Chemical Pulping Systems:
Continuous digesters: 2
Pulp Lines: 2
Bleach Plant Systems: 2
Hardwood, Sequence: DEOpDEpD, Capacity 223,125 admt/y
Softwood, Sequence: O$_2$ DEopDD, Capacity 160,650 admt/y
Chemical Recovery Equipment:
Evaporator lines: 2
Recovery boilers: 2
Lime Kiln
Pulp Dryers:
Air Float dryers 1
Paper/Paperboard Grades and Capacities:
Total paper and paperboard capacity: 340,000 mt/y
Boxboard/cartonboard: 340,000 mt/y
Paper and Paperboard Mill Data:
Paper Machines: 2
No. 1, Multi-wire (4), total capacity 150,000 mt/y, Trim width 3.86 m, Boxboard/cartonboard
No. 2, Multi-wire (5), total capacity 190,000 mt/y, Trim width 4.65 m, Boxboard/cartonboard
Coating Machines: 2
PM 1, total capacity 145,000 mt/y., on machine
PM 2, total capacity 185,000 mt/y., on machine
Finishing Equipment:
Winders: 2 at 30 mt/y
Sheeters: 6 at 112 mt/y
Energy Data:
Power boilers: 2
Steam turbines: 3 at 20, 21, 14 MW
Electrical demand for mill: 1,014 MWh/D

ⓘⓜ BillerudKorsnäs AB
Gävle Mill
Ownership: Fourth Swedish National Pension Fund (AP4), Norges Bank, Sweden AMF, other Investment funds, Alecta
SE-801 81 Gävle
Sweden
 Phone: (46) 26 151000
 Fax: (46) 26 152240
 Email: info@billerudkorsnas.com
 Web Address: www.billerudkorsnas.com
Personnel:
Mill Dir.: Ulf Eliasson
Phone: (46) 26 151000
Fax: (46) 26 152240
Email: ulf.eliasson@billerudkorsnas.com
Snr. Project Mgr. Asset Management: Mats Tornkvist
Phone: (46) 26 151000
Fax: (46) 26 152240
Email: mats.tornkvist@billerudkorsnas.com
Total Employees of Company: 4,270
Total Employees at this Location: 977
Type of Operation: Pulp mill, Paper mill, Paperboard mill
Mill Locations:
BillerudKorsnäs AB, Rockhammar Mill, SE - 71880 Frövi, Sweden, (Pulp mill)
Phone: (46) 261 510 00
Email: info@billerudkorsnas.com
BillerudKorsnäs AB, Beetham Mill, Beetham, Milnthorpe LA7 7AR, United Kingdom, Capacity: 44,982 mt/y, (Paper mill)
Phone: (44) 1539 565 000
Fax: (44) 1539 565 033
Email: info@billerudkorsnas.com
BillerudKorsnäs Finland Oy, Pietarsaari Mill, Larsmovägen 149, 68600 Pietarsaari, Finland, Capacity: 199,920 mt/y, (Paper mill)
Phone: (358) 6 241 380 00
Email: info@billerudkorsnas.com
BillerudKorsnäs AB, Frövi Mill, SE-718 80 Frövi, Sweden, Capacity: 420,000 mt/y, (Pulp mill, Paperboard mill)
Phone: (46) 261 510 00
Email: (firstname.lastname@billerudkorsnas.com)
BillerudKorsnäs AB, Gruvön Mill, SE-664 28 Grums, Sweden, Capacity: 593,000 mt/y, (Pulp mill, Paper mill, Paperboard mill)
Phone: (46) 555 410 00
Fax: (46) 555 416 90
Email: info@billerudkorsnas.com
BillerudKorsnäs AB, Karlsborg Mill, Strandvagen 3, SE-952 83 Karlsborg, Sweden, Capacity: 130,000 mt/y, (Pulp mill, Paper mill)
Phone: (46) 923 660 00
Fax: (46) 923 203 48
Email: info@billerudkorsnas.com
BillerudKorsnäs AB, Skärblacka Mill, SE-617 10 Skärblacka, Sweden, Capacity: 350,000 mt/y, (Pulp mill, Paper mill, Paperboard mill)

Sweden

Phone: (46) 11 245 300
Fax: (46) 11 57502
Email: info@billerudkorsnas.com
BillerudKorsnäs Finland Oy, Tervasaari Mill, Tehtaankatu 7, FI-37600 Valkeakoski, Finland, Capacity: 100,000 mt/y, (Paper mill)
Phone: (358) 3 339 266 00
Email: info@billerudkorsnas.com
Pulp Grades and Capacities:
 Total pulp capacity: 680,768 mt/y
 Pulp available for market: 73,486 mt/y
 Chemical Pulp: 680,768 mt/y
Pulp Mill Data:
 Chemical Pulping Systems:
 Continuous digesters: 3
Pulp Lines: 2
 Bleach Plant Systems: 1
 Chemical Pulping System, Type: Hardwood/Softwood, Sequence: O_2 DEPP, Capacity 360,000 admt/y
 Chemical Recovery Equipment:
 Evaporator lines: 1
 Recovery boilers: 2
 Lime Kiln
 Pulp Dryers:
 Air Float dryers 1
Paper/Paperboard Grades and Capacities:
 Total paper and paperboard capacity: 630,000 mt/y
 Linerboard: 154,000 mt/y
 Boxboard/cartonboard: 476,000 mt/y
Paper and Paperboard Mill Data:
 Stock Preparation:
 Pulpers: 2
Paper Machines: 2
 No. 4, multi-fourdrinier, total capacity 265,000 mt/y, Trim width 7.4 m, Linerboard, Boxboard/cartonboard
 No. 5, fourdrinier (3), total capacity 365,000 mt/y, Trim width 7 m, Boxboard/cartonboard
Coating Machines: 2
 PM 4, total capacity 265,000 mt/y., on machine
 PM 5, total capacity 365,000 mt/y., on machine
Finishing Equipment:
 Rewinders: 4
Energy Data:
 Power boilers: 1
 Steam turbines: 3 at 5, 43, 85 MW
 Electrical demand for mill: 2,039 MWh/D

ⓜLessebo Paper
Ownership: Lessebo Finance
Storgatan 79
SE-360 50 Lessebo
Sweden
 Phone: (46) 478 47600
 Fax: (46) 478 10758
 Email: info@lessebobruk.se
 Web Address: www.lessebobruk.se
Personnel:
 Chmn. Lessebo: Björn Knappskog
 Phone: (46) 478 47600
 Fax: (46) 478 10758
 Email: bjorn.knappskog@lessebobruk.se
 Man. Dir.: Terje Haglund
 Phone: (46) 478 47601
 Fax: (46) 478 10758
 Email: terje.haglund@lessebobruk.se
 Mill Mgr.: Øistein Vedahl
 Phone: (46) 478 47760
 Fax: (46) 478 10758
 Email: oistein.vedahl@lessebobruk.se
 Product Develop. Mgr.: Kjell Andersson
 Phone: (46) 478 47630
 Fax: (46) 478 10758
 Email: kjell.andersson@lessebobruk.se
 Indoor Salesman: Ing-Britt Norlin
 Phone: (46) 478 47622
 Fax: (46) 478 10758
 Email: ing-britt.norlin@lessebobruk.se
Total Employees of Company: 245
Mill Locations:
Lessebo Paper, Lessebo Paper Mill, Storgatan 79, SE-360 50 Lessebo, Sweden, Capacity: 42,000 mt/y, (Pulp mill, Paper mill)
Phone: (46) 478 47600
Fax: (46) 478 10758
Email: info@lessebobruk.se

ⓜLessebo Pulp
Lessebo Pulp Mill
Mill is temporarily closed (Pulp production idled from December 18, 2013. No timeline for when a restart could take place)
Ownership: Lessebo Finance
Storgatan 79
SE-360 50 Lessebo
Sweden
 Phone: (46) 478 47600
 Fax: (46) 478 10758
 Email: info@lessebobruk.se
 Web Address: www.lessebobruk.se
Personnel:
 Pulp Mill Mgr.: Thomas Lindroos
 Phone: (46) 478 47600
 Fax: (46) 478 10758
 Email: thomas.lindroosinfo@lessebobruk.se
Type of Operation: Pulp mill
Pulp Grades and Capacities:
 Total pulp capacity: 27,000 mt/y
 Pulp available for market: 27,000 mt/y
 Other Pulp: 27,000 mt/y
Pulp Mill Data:
 Chemical Pulping Systems:
 Batch digesters: 2
Pulp Lines: 1
 Bleach Plant Systems: 1
 1, Type: TCF, Sequence: PP, Capacity 27,000 admt/y
 Chemical Recovery Equipment:
 Evaporator lines: 4
 Recovery boilers: 1
 Pulp Dryers:
 Cylinder Dryer 1, Fourdriniers 1
Energy Data:
 Power boilers: 2

ⓜLessebo Paper
Lessebo Paper Mill
Storgatan 79
SE-360 50 Lessebo
Sweden
 Phone: (46) 478 47600
 Fax: (46) 478 10758
 Email: info@lessebobruk.se
 Web Address: www.lessebobruk.se
Personnel:
 Man. Dir.: Terje Haglund
 Phone: (46) 478 47601
 Fax: (46) 478 10758
 Email: terje.haglund@lessebobruk.se
 Mill Mgr.: Øistein Vedahl
 Phone: (46) 478 47760
 Fax: (46) 478 10758
 Email: oistein.vedahl@lessebobruk.se
 Plan. Mgr.: Pär Johnsson
 Phone: (46) 478 47634
 Fax: (46) 478 10758
 Email: par.johnsson@lessebobruk.se
 Sls. & Mktg. Mgr.: Max Peters
 Phone: (44) 478 47602
 Fax: (44) 478 10758
 Email: max.peters@lessebobruk.se
 Product Develop. Mgr.: Kjell Andersson
 Phone: (46) 478 47630
 Fax: (46) 478 10758
 Email: kjell.andersson@lessebobruk.se
Total Employees at this Location: 100
Type of Operation: Pulp mill, Paper mill
Pulp Mill Data:
Pulp Lines: 1
Paper/Paperboard Grades and Capacities:
Total paper and paperboard capacity: 42,000 mt/y
Uncoated woodfree/freesheet: 42,000 mt/y
Paper and Paperboard Mill Data:
 Stock Preparation:
 Pulpers: 6
 Refiners: 9
Paper Machines: 2
 No. 1, fourdrinier, total capacity 15,000 mt/y, Trim width 2.25 m, Uncoated woodfree/freesheet
 No. 2, fourdrinier, total capacity 27,000 mt/y, Trim width 2.3 m, Uncoated woodfree/freesheet
Finishing Equipment:
 Supercalenders: 2
 Rewinders: 3
 Sheeters: 5
Energy Data:
 Electrical demand for mill: 86 MWh/D

ⓜMetsä Board Husum
Husum Mill
Ownership: 100% by Metsä Board
SE-890 35 Husum
Sweden
 Phone: (46) 663 18000
 Fax: (46) 663 18500
 Web Address: www.metsaboard.com
Personnel:
 Snr. VP., Pulp & Paper: Seppo Puotinen
 Phone: (46) 663 18102
 Fax: (46) 663 18500
 Email: seppo.puotinen@metsagroup.com
 VP., Mill Mgr.: Anders Ek
 Phone: (46) 663 18860
 Fax: (46) 663 18500
 Email: anders.ek@metsagroup.com
 Purch. Mgr.: David Hjelm
 Phone: (46) 663 18415
 Fax: (46) 663 18500
 Email: david.hjelm@metsagroup.com
 HR Mgr.: Anna Edblad
 Phone: (46) 663 18172
 Fax: (46) 663 18021
 Email: anna.edblad@metsagroup.com
 Environ., Energy & Laboratory Mgr.: Lars Salomonsson
 Phone: (46) 663 18190
 Fax: (46) 663 18500
 Email: lars.salomonsson@metsagroup.com
 Mill Mgr. Office: Carin Enevang
 Phone: (46) 663 18110
 Fax: (46) 663 18500
 Email: carin.enevang@metsagroup.com
Total Employees at this Location: 800
Type of Operation: Pulp mill, Paper mill
Pulp Grades and Capacities:
 Total pulp capacity: 739,929 mt/y
 Pulp available for market: 292,000 mt/y
 Chemical Pulp: 739,929 mt/y
Pulp Mill Data:
 Chemical Pulping Systems:
 Batch digesters: 12
 Continuous digesters: 1
Pulp Lines: 2
 Bleach Plant Systems: 2
 Hardwood, Type: ECF, Sequence: O_2 DEpDP, Capacity 340,000 admt/y
 Softwood, Type: ECF, Sequence: O_2 DEpDP, Capacity 380,000 admt/y
 Chemical Recovery Equipment:
 Evaporator lines: 1
 Recovery boilers: 2
 Lime Kiln
 Pulp Dryers:
 Air Float dryers 1, Air Float dryers 1
Paper/Paperboard Grades and Capacities:
 Total paper and paperboard capacity: 720,000 mt/y
 Uncoated woodfree/freesheet: 350,000 mt/y
 Coated woodfree/freesheet: 290,000 mt/y
 Linerboard: 80,000 mt/y
Paper and Paperboard Mill Data:

Sweden

Stock Preparation:
Pulpers: 2
Refiners: 15
Paper Machines: 3
No. 6, SymFormer, total capacity 190,000 mt/y, Trim width 6.5 m, Uncoated woodfree/freesheet, Linerboard
No. 7, DuoFormer, total capacity 240,000 mt/y, Trim width 6.5 m, Uncoated woodfree/freesheet
No. 8, OptiFormer, total capacity 290,000 mt/y, Trim width 6.5 m, Coated woodfree/freesheet
Coating Machines: 1
PM 8, total capacity 275,000 mt/y., off machine
Finishing Equipment:
Winders: 4
Rewinders: 3
Sheeters: 4
Energy Data:
Power boilers: 1
Steam turbines: 3 at 25, 10, 26 MW
Electrical demand for mill: 2,664 MWh/D

ⓘⓜMetsä Tissue AB
Katrinefors Mill
Holländaregatan 4
SE-542 88 Mariestad
Sweden
Phone: (46) 501 27 50 00
Fax: (46) 501 103 10
Web Address: www.metsatissue.com
Personnel:
Snr. VP., Tissue Scandinavia: Mark Watkins
Phone: (46) 501 27 50 00
Fax: (46) 501 103 10
Email: mark.watkins@metsagroup.com
Mill Mgr.: Peter Lindgren
Phone: (46) 501 27 50 00
Fax: (46) 501 103 10
Email: peter.lindgren@metsagroup.com
Maint. Mgr.: Yngve Larsson
Phone: (46) 501 27 50 00
Fax: (46) 501 103 10
Email: yngve.larsson@metsagroup.com
Total Employees of Company: 500
Total Employees at this Location: 310
Type of Operation: Paper mill
Mill Locations:
Metsä Tissue AB, Nyboholm Mill (Småland Mills), SE-570 16 Kvillsfors, Sweden, Capacity: 24,000 mt/y, (Paper mill)
Phone: (46) 501 27 50 00
Fax: (46) 383 27 54 97
Email: (firstname.lastname@metsagroup.com)
Metsä Tissue AB, Paulistöm Mill (Småland Mills), SE-570 19 Paulistöm, Sweden, Capacity: 24,000 mt/y, (Paper mill)
Phone: (46) 501 27 50 00
Fax: (46) 501 27 54 97
Email: (firstname.lastname@metsagroup.com)
Pulp Grades and Capacities:
Total pulp capacity: 55,039 mt/y
Recycled Pulping: 55,039 mt/y
Pulp Mill Data:
Bleach Plant Systems: 1
DIP
Recycled Fiber Treatment Lines:
Flotation deinking lines: 1
Pulpers: 2 at 65,000 admt/y
Paper/Paperboard Grades and Capacities:
Total paper and paperboard capacity: 81,000 mt/y
Tissue: 81,000 mt/y
Paper and Paperboard Mill Data:
Paper Machines: 2
No. 35, crescent former, Yankee dryer, total capacity 40,000 mt/y, Trim width 3.4 m, Tissue
No. 36, Advantage DCT, Yankee dryer, total capacity 41,000 mt/y, Trim width 3.4 m, Tissue
Energy Data:
Power boilers
Electrical demand for mill: 270 MWh/D

ⓜMetsä Tissue AB
Nyboholm Mill (Småland Mills)
SE-570 16 Kvillsfors
Sweden
Phone: (46) 501 27 50 00
Fax: (46) 383 27 54 97
Email: (firstname.lastname@metsagroup.com)
Web Address: www.metsatissue.com
Personnel:
Mill Mgr.: Håkan Johansson
Phone: (46) 501 27 50 00
Fax: (46) 383 27 54 97
Email: hakan.johansson@metsagroup.com
Total Employees at this Location: 832
Type of Operation: Paper mill
Pulp Grades and Capacities:
Total pulp capacity: 16,064 mt/y
Recycled Pulping: 16,064 mt/y
Paper/Paperboard Grades and Capacities:
Total paper and paperboard capacity: 24,000 mt/y
Tissue: 24,000 mt/y
Paper and Paperboard Mill Data:
Paper Machines: 2
No. 3, fourdrinier, Yankee dryer, total capacity 9,000 mt/y, Trim width 2.7 m, Tissue
No. 5, crescent former, Yankee dryer, total capacity 15,000 mt/y, Trim width 2.7 m, Tissue
Energy Data:
Power boilers: 1
Electrical demand for mill: 66 MWh/D

ⓜMetsä Tissue AB
Paulistöm Mill (Småland Mills)
SE-570 19 Paulistöm
Sweden
Phone: (46) 501 27 50 00
Fax: (46) 501 27 54 97
Email: (firstname.lastname@metsagroup.com)
Web Address: www.metsatissue.com
Personnel:
Mill Mgr.: Håkan Johansson
Phone: (46) 501 27 50 00
Fax: (46) 383 27 54 97
Email: hakan.johansson@metsagroup.com
Total Employees at this Location: 200
Type of Operation: Paper mill
Paper/Paperboard Grades and Capacities:
Total paper and paperboard capacity: 24,000 mt/y
Tissue: 24,000 mt/y
Paper and Paperboard Mill Data:
Stock Preparation:
Pulpers: 2
Refiners: 2
Paper Machines: 1
No. 1, twin-wire, Yankee dryer, total capacity 24,000 mt/y, Trim width 2.7 m, Tissue
Energy Data:
Power boilers: 1
Steam turbines: 2 at 3 MW
Electrical demand for mill: 68 MWh/D

ⓜMondi Dynäs AB
Väja Mill
Ownership: Mondi Europe & International Division
SE-873 81 Väja
Sweden
Phone: (46) 612 83000
Fax: (46) 612 26511
Email: info.dynas@mondigroup.com
Web Address: www.mondigroup.com
Personnel:
Man. Dir.: Robin de Jong
Phone: (46) 612 83111
Fax: (46) 612 83030
Email: robin.dejong@mondigroup.com
Prod. Mgr.: Mats Jakobsson
Phone: (46) 612 83000
Fax: (46) 612 83030
Email: mats.jakobsson@mondigroup.com
R&D Mgr., Tech Mgr., Env. Mgr.: Mikael Björklund
Phone: (46) 612 83240
Email: mikael.bjorklund@mondigroup.com
Mktg. Mgr.: Lars-Göran Berglund
Phone: (46) 612 83333
Fax: (46) 612 83300
Email: lasse.berglund@mondigroup.com
Total Employees at this Location: 300
Type of Operation: Pulp mill, Paper mill
Pulp Grades and Capacities:
Total pulp capacity: 259,661 mt/y
Chemical Pulp: 259,661 mt/y
Pulp Mill Data:
Chemical Pulping Systems:
Batch digesters: 5
Pulp Lines: 1
Chemical Recovery Equipment:
Evaporator lines: 1
Recovery boilers: 1
Lime Kiln
Paper/Paperboard Grades and Capacities:
Total paper and paperboard capacity: 250,000 mt/y
Packaging papers: 250,000 mt/y
Paper and Paperboard Mill Data:
Stock Preparation:
Pulpers: 1
Refiners: 12
Paper Machines: 2
No. 5, fourdrinier, total capacity 86,000 mt/y, Trim width 4.5 m, Packaging papers
No. 6, fourdrinier, total capacity 164,000 mt/y, Trim width 6.4 m, Packaging papers
Finishing Equipment:
Winders: 2
Energy Data:
Power boilers: 1
Steam turbines: 1 at 21 MW
Electrical demand for mill: 710 MWh/D

ⓜMunksjö Oyj
Ownership: 100% by EQT III Fund
Klarabergsviadukten 70 D5
SE-107 24 Stockholm
Sweden
Mailing Address: P.O. Box 70365
Phone: (46) 10 250 1000
Fax: (46) 36 129058
Email: info@munksjo.com
Web Address: www.munksjo.com
Personnel:
CEO: Jan Åström
Phone: (46) 36 303300
Fax: (46) 36 162633
Email: jan.astrom@munksjo.com
Exec. VP. & CFO (to resign during Q 1, 2015): Kim Hendriksson
Phone: (46) 36 303300
Fax: (46) 36 162633
Email: kim.hendriksson@munksjo.com
Dep. Chmn. of the Board: Fredrik Cappelen
Phone: (46) 36 303300
Fax: (46) 36 162633
Email: fredrik.cappelen@munksjo.com
Snr. VP., HR & Commun.: Åsa Fredriksson
Phone: (46) 36 303300
Fax: (46) 36 162633
Email: asa.fredriksson@munksjo.com
Snr. VP., Strategic Develop.: Anna Bergquist
Phone: (46) 36 303300
Fax: (46) 36 162633
Email: anna.bergquist@munksjo.com
Snr. VP & Gen Counsel: Gustav Adlercreutz
Phone: (46) 36 303300
Fax: (46) 36 162633
Email: gustav.adlercreutz@munksjo.com
Total Employees of Company: 3,000
Total Employees at this Location: 11
Mill Locations:
Munksjö Dettingen GmbH, Dettingen Mill, Schwalbenstadt 1, D-72581 Dettingen an der Erms,

Sweden

Germany, Capacity: 60,000 mt/y, (Paper mill)
Phone: (49) 7123 977-0
Fax: (49) 7123 977 113
Email: info.dettingen@munksjo.com; info@munksjo.com
Munksjö Arches SAS, Arches Mill, BP 29, 48 route de Remiremont, F-88380 Arches, France, Capacity: 77,000 mt/y, (Paper mill)
Phone: (33) 3 29 32 60 00
Fax: (33) 3 29 32 74 96
Email: info@munksjo.com
Munksjö Aspa Bruk AB, Aspabruk Mill, SE-696 80 Aspabruk, Sweden, (Pulp mill)
Phone: (46) 583 81500
Fax: (46) 583 503 35
Email: info@munksjo.com
Munksjö Paper AB, Billingsfors Mill, Strandvägen 7, S-66011 Billingsfors, Sweden, Capacity: 50,000 mt/y, (Pulp mill, Paper mill)
Phone: (46) 531 37600
Fax: (46) 531 30517, 531 31248
Email: info.spx@munksjo.com, virke.billingsfors@munksjo.com
Munksjö Brasil Industria e Comercio de Comercio de papeis especiais Ltda., Jacareí Paper Mill, Rdv. Gen. Euryale de Jesus Zerbini, km 84, 12340-010 Jacareí, SP, Brazil, Capacity: 109,956 mt/y, (Paper mill)
Phone: (55) 12 2127 9300
Fax: (55) 12 2127 9330
Email: info@munksjo.com
Munksjö LabelPack, La Gère Mill, Chemin Cartallier, F-38780 Pont Evêque, France, Capacity: 95,000 mt/y, (Paper mill)
Phone: (33) 4 74161010
Fax: (33) 4 74161049
Email: info@munksjo.com
Munksjö LabelPack, Rottersac Mill, Usine de Rottersac, F-24150 Lalinde, France, Capacity: 70,000 mt/y, (Paper mill)
Phone: (33) 5 53615400
Fax: (33) 5 53615460
Email: info@munksjo.com
Munksjö LabelPack, Stenay Mill, Usine de Stenay, F-55700 Stenay, France, Capacity: 100,000 mt/y, (Paper mill)
Phone: (33) 3 29803010
Fax: (33) 3 29806170
Email: info@munksjo.com
Munksjö Paper S.A., Tolosa Mill, Barrio de Eldua s/n, E-20492 Berástegui, Spain, Capacity: 40,000 mt/y, (Paper mill)
Phone: (34) 943 683 032
Fax: (34) 943 683 398
Email: info@munksjo.com
Munksjö Paper GmbH, Unterkochen Mill, Waldhäuser Str. 41, D-73432 Aalen-Unterkochen, Germany, Capacity: 90,000 mt/y, (Paper mill)
Phone: (49) 7361 5060
Fax: (49) 7361 506 248
Email: marketing@de.munksjo.com, info@de.munksjo.com
Munksjö Paper AB, Jönköping mill, Barnarpsgatan, SE-55118 Jönköping, Sweden, Capacity: 35,000 mt/y, (Paper mill)
Phone: (46) 36 303300
Fax: (46) 36 303380
Email: info@munksjo.com, paperinfo@munksjo.com
Munksjö Italia S.p.A., Turin Mill, Via Stura 98, I-10075 Mathi Canavese, (TO), Italy, Capacity: 120,000 mt/y, (Paper mill)
Phone: (39) 011 9260111
Fax: (39) 011 9269617
Email: info@munksjo.com

ⓂMunksjö Paper AB
Ownership: 100% by Munksjö Oyj
Barnarpsgatan 41
Jönköping
Sweden
Mailing Address: Box 624, 551 18 Jönköping, Sweden
Phone: (46) 36 30 33 00
Fax: (46) 36 30 33 80
Email: paperinfo@munksjo.com
Web Address: www.munksjo.com
Personnel:
VP Strategy: Martin Hindemark
Phone: (46) 46 36 30 33 00
Fax: (46) 46 36 30 33 80
Email: investors@munksjo.com
Senior VP HR & Commun.: Åsa Fredriksson
Phone: (46) 46 10 250 10 03
Fax: (46) 46 730 45 49 29
Email: asa.fredriksson@munksjo.com
Mill Mgr.: Mats Flood
Phone: (46) 46 36 30 33 00
Fax: (46) 46 36 30 33 80
Email: mats.flood@munksjo.com
Corporate Communications: Cecilia Strath
Phone: (46) 46 36 30 33 00
Fax: (46) 46 36 30 33 80
Mill Locations:
Munksjö Dettingen GmbH, Dettingen Mill, Schwalbenstadt 1, D-72581 Dettingen an der Erms, Germany, Capacity: 60,000 mt/y, (Paper mill)
Phone: (49) 7123 977-0
Fax: (49) 7123 977 113
Email: info.dettingen@munksjo.com; info@munksjo.com
Munksjö Paper AB, Billingsfors Mill, Strandvägen 7, S-66011 Billingsfors, Sweden, Capacity: 50,000 mt/y, (Pulp mill, Paper mill)
Phone: (46) 531 37600
Fax: (46) 531 30517, 531 31248
Email: info.spx@munksjo.com, virke.billingsfors@munksjo.com
Munksjö Paper AB, Jönköping mill, Barnarpsgatan, SE-55118 Jönköping, Sweden, Capacity: 35,000 mt/y, (Paper mill)
Phone: (46) 36 303300
Fax: (46) 36 303380
Email: info@munksjo.com, paperinfo@munksjo.com

ⓂMunksjö Aspa Bruk AB
Aspabruk Mill
Ownership: Munksjö Oyj
SE-696 80 Aspabruk
Sweden
Phone: (46) 583 81500
Fax: (46) 583 503 35
Email: info@munksjo.com
Web Address: www.munksjo.com
Personnel:
Man. Dir.: Bengt Lindqvist
Phone: (46) 583 815 01
Fax: (46) 583 501 11
Email: bengt.lindqvist@munksjo.com
Prod. Mgr.: Michael Berggren
Phone: (46) 583 815 00
Fax: (46) 583 503 35
Email: michael.berggren@munksjo.com
Maint. Mgr: Lennart Jönsson
Phone: (46) 583 815 00
Fax: (46) 583 503 35
Email: lennart.jonsson@munksjo.com
Tech. and Environ. Manager: Dan Björk
Phone: (46) 583 815 00
Fax: (46) 583 503 35
Email: dan.bjork@munksjo.com
Tech. Customer Support: Thomas Eriksson
Phone: (46) 583 815 16
Fax: (46) 583 503 35
Email: thomas.eriksson@munksjo.com
Total Employees at this Location: 169
Type of Operation: Pulp mill
Pulp Grades and Capacities:
Total pulp capacity: 201,623 mt/y
Pulp available for market: 200,000 mt/y
Chemical Pulp: 201,623 mt/y
Pulp Mill Data:
Chemical Pulping Systems:
Continuous digesters: 1
Pulp Lines: 1
Bleach Plant Systems: 1
Softwood, Type: ECF/TCF, Sequence: O$_2$ DEopDEPP, Capacity 200,000 admt/y
Chemical Recovery Equipment:
Evaporator lines: 1
Recovery boilers: 1
Lime Kiln
Pulp Dryers:
Air Float dryers 1
Energy Data:
Steam turbines: 2 at 26 MW
Electrical demand for mill: 371 MWh/D

ⓂMunksjö Paper AB
Billingsfors Mill
Ownership: 100% by Munksjö Oyj
Strandvägen 7
S-66011 Billingsfors
Sweden
Phone: (46) 531 37600
Fax: (46) 531 30517, 531 31248
Email: info.spx@munksjo.com, virke.billingsfors@munksjo.com
Web Address: www.munksjo.com
Personnel:
Mill Mgr.: Ulf Maxén
Phone: (46) 531 37617
Fax: (46) 531 30517
Email: ulf.maxen@munksjo.com
Tech. Mgr.: Sven Strand
Phone: (46) 531 37623
Fax: (46) 531 30982
Email: sven.strand@munksjo.com
Paper Mill Prod. Mgr.: Lars-Eric Aronsson
Phone: (46) 531 37652
Fax: (46) 531 30517
Email: lars-eric.aronsson@munksjo.com
Purch. Mgr.: Peter Lundström
Phone: (46) 531 37634
Fax: (46) 531 30517
Email: peter.lundstrom@munksjo.com
Total Employees at this Location: 272
Type of Operation: Pulp mill, Paper mill
Pulp Grades and Capacities:
Total pulp capacity: 61,790 mt/y
Pulp available for market: 15,000 mt/y
Chemical Pulp: 61,790 mt/y
Pulp Mill Data:
Chemical Pulping Systems:
Batch digesters: 4
Pulp Lines: 1
Chemical Recovery Equipment:
Evaporator lines: 1
Recovery boilers: 1
Pulp Dryers:
Wet Lap machine 1
Paper/Paperboard Grades and Capacities:
Total paper and paperboard capacity: 50,000 mt/y
Specialty and industrial: 50,000 mt/y
Paper and Paperboard Mill Data:
Stock Preparation:
Pulpers: 2
Refiners: 12
Paper Machines: 3
No. 2, fourdrinier, Yankee dryer, total capacity 12,000 mt/y, Trim width 3.26 m, Specialty and industrial
No. 5, fourdrinier, total capacity 14,000 mt/y, Trim width 3.12 m, Specialty and industrial
No. 6, fourdrinier, Yankee dryer, total capacity 24,000 mt/y, Trim width 5.05 m, Specialty and industrial
Coating Machines: 1
BM 1, total capacity 2,000 mt/y., off machine
Finishing Equipment:
Rewinders: 2 at 15,000 mt/y
Sheeters: 4 at 3,300 mt/y

Sweden

Energy Data:
Power boilers: 1
Steam turbines: 1 at 3 MW
Electrical demand for mill: 133 MWh/D

ⓘMunksjö Paper AB
Jönköping mill
Ownership: 100% by Munksjö Oyj
Barnarpsgatan
SE-55118 Jönköping
Sweden
Mailing Address: PO Box 624, SE-55118 Jönköping, Sweden
Phone: (46) 36 303300
Fax: (46) 36 303380
Email: info@munksjo.com, paperinfo@munksjo.com
Web Address: www.munksjo.com
Personnel:
Div. Mgr.: Mats Flood
Phone: (46) 36 303399
Fax: (46) 36 303380
Email: mats.flood@munksjo.com
Sls. Mgr.: Anders Hellstadius
Phone: (46) 36 303402
Fax: (46) 36 303380
Email: anders.hellstadius@munksjo.com
Finan. Mgr.: Andre Jonsson
Phone: (46) 36 303389
Fax: (46) 36 303380
Email: andre.jonsson@munksjo.com
Prod. Mgr.: Jörgen Almén
Phone: (46) 36 303404
Fax: (46) 36 303413
Email: jorgen.almen@munksjo.com
Total Employees at this Location: 110
Type of Operation: Paper mill
Pulp Grades and Capacities:
Total pulp capacity: 60,000 mt/y
Chemical Pulp: 60,000 mt/y
Paper/Paperboard Grades and Capacities:
Total paper and paperboard capacity: 35,000 mt/y
Specialty and industrial: 35,000 mt/y
Paper and Paperboard Mill Data:
Stock Preparation:
Pulpers: 3
Refiners: 4
Paper Machines: 1
PM 13, fourdrinier, multi-cylinder, total capacity 35,000 mt/y, Trim width 3.2 m, Specialty and industrial
Finishing Equipment:
Rewinders: 1 at 35,000 mt/y

ⓘNordic Paper Åmotfors
Åmotfors Bruk Mill
Ownership: Nordic Paper Holding AB
SE-670 40 Åmotfors
Sweden
Phone: (46) 571 308 00/12800
Fax: (46) 571 310 10
Email: info@nordic-paper.com
Web Address: www.nordic-paper.com
Personnel:
Mill Mgr.: Jonas Lindqvist
Phone: (46) 571 128 72
Fax: (46) 571 310 10
Email: jonas.lindqvist@nordic-paper.com
Total Employees at this Location: 65
Type of Operation: Paper mill
Paper/Paperboard Grades and Capacities:
Total paper and paperboard capacity: 55,000 mt/y
Specialty and industrial: 55,000 mt/y
Paper and Paperboard Mill Data:
Stock Preparation:
Pulpers: 2
Paper Machines: 2
No. 1, hybrid former, total capacity 25,000 mt/y, Trim width 3.6 m, Specialty and industrial
No. 6, fourdrinier, total capacity 30,000 mt/y, Trim width 4.3 m, Specialty and industrial
Finishing Equipment:
Winders: 2
Rewinders: 1
Sheeters: 1
Energy Data:
Power boilers: 3
Electrical demand for mill: 153 MWh/D

ⓘNordic Paper Bäckhammar
Bäckhammars Bruk Mill
Ownership: Nordic Paper Holding AB
SE-681 83 Kristinehamn
Sweden
Mailing Address: PO Box 1003, Kristinehamn, Sweden
Phone: (46) 550 34500
Fax: (46) 550 34501
Email: info@nordic-paper.com
Web Address: www.nordic-paper.com
Personnel:
Man. Dir.: Jan Runo
Phone: (46) 550 34500
Fax: (46) 550 34501
Email: jan.runo@nordic-paper.com
Prod. Mgr.: Lars Rosén
Phone: (46) 550 34500
Fax: (46) 550 34501
Email: lars.rosen@nordic-paper.com
Maint. Mgr.: Peter Bergkvist
Phone: (46) 550 34500
Fax: (46) 550 34501
Email: peter.bergkvist@nordic-paper.com
Environ. Mgr. Bäckhammar and –Åmotfors Mills: Tarjei Svensen
Phone: (46) 550 345 51
Fax: (46) 550 34501
Email: tarjei.svensen@nordic-paper.com
HMS coord.: Roger Johansson
Phone: (46) 550 345 34
Fax: (46) 550 34501
Email: roger.johansson@nordic-paper.com
Total Employees at this Location: 230
Type of Operation: Pulp mill, Paper mill
Pulp Grades and Capacities:
Total pulp capacity: 200,024 mt/y
Pulp available for market: 63,000 mt/y
Chemical Pulp: 200,024 mt/y
Pulp Mill Data:
Chemical Pulping Systems:
Continuous digesters: 1
Chemical Recovery Equipment:
Evaporator lines: 2
Recovery boilers: 1
Lime Kiln
Pulp Dryers:
Flakt dryer 1, Fourdriniers 1, Wet Lap machine 1
Paper/Paperboard Grades and Capacities:
Total paper and paperboard capacity: 130,000 mt/y
Packaging papers: 110,000 mt/y
Specialty and industrial: 20,000 mt/y
Paper and Paperboard Mill Data:
Stock Preparation:
Refiners: 4
Paper Machines: 2
No. 4, fourdrinier, Yankee dryer, total capacity 40,000 mt/y, Trim width 4.6 m, Specialty and industrial, Packaging papers
No. 5, fourdrinier, total capacity 90,000 mt/y, Trim width 4.7 m, Packaging papers
Finishing Equipment:
Winders: 2
Rewinders: 1
Energy Data:
Power boilers: 2
Steam turbines: 1 at 16.4 MW
Electrical demand for mill: 553 MWh/D

ⓘNordic Paper Holding AB
Company is for sale (Private investment funds to acquire 60% stake in Nordic Paper Holding)
Ownership: 7.64% by JSR Invest AB, 1.71% by Hartvig Wennberg AS, 50.41% by Petek GmbH, Germany, 32.60% by NorgesInvestor 111 AS
Bäckhammars Bruk
SE-681 83 Kristinehamn
Sweden
Phone: (46) 550 345 00
Fax: (46) 550 345 01
Email: info@nordic-paper.com
Web Address: www.nordic-paper.com
Personnel:
Chmn. of the Board: Richard Heiberg
Phone: (46) 69 138 601
Fax: (46) 69 141 102
Email: richard.heiberg@nordic-paper.com
CEO: Jan Runo
Phone: (46) 53 382 484
Fax: (46) 69 141 102
Email: jan.runo@nordic-paper.com
CFO, Dpty CEO: Frederik Høye
Phone: (46) 69 138 500
Fax: (46) 69 141 102
Email: frederik.hoye@nordic-paper.com
Dir., Sls. & Mktg.: Ake Wallman
Phone: (46) 53 38 20 00
Fax: (46) 53 38 20 08
Email: ake.wallman@nordic-paper.com
Total Employees of Company: 650
Mill Locations:
Nordic Paper Åmotfors, Åmotfors Bruk Mill, SE-670 40 Åmotfors, Sweden, Capacity: 55,000 mt/y, (Paper mill)
Phone: (46) 571 308 00/12800
Fax: (46) 571 310 10
Email: info@nordic-paper.com
Nordic Paper Bäckhammar, Bäckhammars Bruk Mill, SE-681 83 Kristinehamn, Sweden, Capacity: 130,000 mt/y, (Pulp mill, Paper mill)
Phone: (46) 550 34500
Fax: (46) 550 34501
Email: info@nordic-paper.com
Nordic Paper Greåker AS, Greåker Mill, NO-1720 Greåker, Norway, Capacity: 29,988 mt/y, (Paper mill)
Phone: (47) 69 138 500
Fax: (47) 69 141 102
Email: info@nordic-paper.com
Nordic Paper Seffle, Säffle Mill, PO Box 610, SE-661 29 Säffle, Sweden, Capacity: 29,988 mt/y, (Pulp mill, Paper mill)
Phone: (46) 533 82000
Fax: (46) 533 82090/08

ⓘNordic Paper Seffle
Säffle Mill
Ownership: Nordic Paper Holding AB
PO Box 610
SE-661 29 Säffle
Sweden
Phone: (46) 533 82000
Fax: (46) 533 82090/08
Web Address: www.nordic-paper.com
Personnel:
Prod. Mgr.: Mats Nordling
Phone: (46) 533 82000
Fax: (46) 533 82090
Email: mats.nordling@nordic-paper.com
Total Employees at this Location: 220
Type of Operation: Pulp mill, Paper mill
Pulp Grades and Capacities:
Total pulp capacity: 50,566 mt/y
Pulp available for market: 18,921 mt/y
Chemical Pulp: 50,566 mt/y
Pulp Mill Data:
Chemical Pulping Systems:
Batch digesters: 4
Bleach Plant Lines:

Sweden

No. 1, Sequence: ZEP, Capacity 36,000 admt/y
Chemical Recovery Equipment:
Evaporator lines: 1
Recovery boilers: 1
Pulp Dryers:
Wet Lap machine 1
Paper/Paperboard Grades and Capacities:
Total paper and paperboard capacity: 29,988 mt/y
Specialty and industrial: 29,988 mt/y
Paper and Paperboard Mill Data:
Stock Preparation:
Pulpers: 1
Refiners: 12
Paper Machines: 2
No. 2, fourdrinier, total capacity 17,136 mt/y, Trim width 4.2 m, Specialty and industrial
No. 3, fourdrinier, total capacity 12,852 mt/y, Trim width 3.25 m, Specialty and industrial
Coating Machines: 2
No. 2, on machine
No. 3, on machine
Finishing Equipment:
Rewinders: 3
Sheeters: 2
Energy Data:
Electrical demand for mill: 222 MWh/D

ⓂRexcell Tissue & Airlaid AB
Skåpafors Mill
Ownership: 100% by Duni AB
SE-666 25 Bengtsfors
Sweden
  Phone: (46) 531 728 00
  Fax: (46) 531 122 83
  Email: info@rexcell.se
  Web Address: www.rexcell.se
Personnel:
  CEO & Site Mgr.: Patrik Söderstjerna
  Phone: (46) 531 72801
  Email: patrik.soderstjerna@rexcell.se
  Oper. Mgr. Tissue: Stefan Åbom
  Phone: (46) 531 72840
  Fax: (46) 531 12443
  Email: stefan.abom@rexcell.se
  Oper. Mgr. Airlaid: Karsten Thomsen
  Phone: (46) 531 72813
  Email: karsten.thomsen@rexcell.se
  Purch. & Logistics Mgr.: Ulf Rundlof
  Phone: (46) 531 72818
  Fax: (46) 531 12916
  Email: ulf.rundlof@rexcell.se
  Env. Mgr.: Monica Johansson
  Phone: (46) 531 72838
  Fax: (46) 531 12443
  Email: monica.b.johansson@rexcell.se
  Fin. Mgr.: Rolf Andersson
  Phone: (46) 531 72811
  Fax: (46) 531 61524
  Email: rolf.andersson@rexcell.se
  VP Sls. & Mktg.: Andreas Normén
  Phone: (46) 531 72810
  Fax: (46) 531 61529
  Email: andreas.normen@rexcell.se
Total Employees at this Location: 260
Type of Operation: Paper mill
Paper/Paperboard Grades and Capacities:
Total paper and paperboard capacity: 50,000 mt/y
Tissue: 50,000 mt/y
Paper and Paperboard Mill Data:
Stock Preparation:
Pulpers: 3
Refiners: 4
Paper Machines: 2
No. 1, fourdrinier, Yankee dryer, total capacity 25,000 mt/y, Trim width 2.7 m, Tissue
No. 2, Periformer, Yankee dryer, total capacity 25,000 mt/y, Trim width 2.7 m, Tissue
Finishing Equipment:
Calenders: 1
Rewinders: 2 at 60,000 mt/y

Energy Data:
Power boilers: 1
Electrical demand for mill: 154 MWh/D

ⓂRottneros AB
Ownership: 51.30% by Arctic Paper S.A., Public, 11.05% by Bronstädet
SE-820 2 Vallvik
Sweden
  Phone: (46) 270 62000
  Fax: (46) 270 69210
  Email: info@rottneros.com
  Web Address: www.rottneros.com
Personnel:
  acting CEO: Per Lundeen
  Phone: (46) 70 546 52 09
  Fax: (46) 270 69210
  Email: per.lundeen@rottneros.com
  CFO: Tomas Hedström
  Phone: (46) 270 62000
  Fax: (46) 270 69210
  Email: tomas.hedstrom@rottneros.com
  Chrmn. of the board: Rune Ingvarsson
  Phone: (46) 270 62000
  Fax: (46) 270 69210
  Man. Dir. Rottneros Mill: Olle Dahlin
  Phone: (46) 270 62000
  Fax: (46) 270 69210
  Email: olle.dahlin@rotternos.com
  Tech. Dir.: Ragnar Lundberg
  Phone: (46) 270 62000
  Fax: (46) 270 69210
  Email: ragnar.lundberg@rottnernos.com
  Dir., Wood Procurement: Ingemar Eliasson
  Phone: (46) 270 62000
  Fax: (46) 270 69210
  Email: ingemar.eliasson@rottnernos.com
  Exec. Sec.: Hella Wopfner
  Phone: (46) 270 62000
  Fax: (46) 270 69210
  Email: hella.wopfner@rottneros.com
Total Employees of Company: 275
Total Employees at this Location: 10
Mill Locations:
Rottneros Bruk AB, Rottneros Mill, SE-686 94 Rottneros, Sweden, (Pulp mill)
  Phone: (46) 565 17600
  Fax: (46) 565 17680
  Email: info@rottneros.com
Rottneros, Vallviks Bruk AB, Vallvik Mill, SE-820 21 Vallvik, Sweden, (Pulp mill)
  Phone: (46) 270 62000
  Fax: (46) 270 69210/69420
  Email: info@rottneros.com

ⓂRottneros Bruk AB
Rottneros Mill
Ownership: Rottneros AB
SE-686 94 Rottneros
Sweden
  Phone: (46) 565 17600
  Fax: (46) 565 17680
  Email: info@rottneros.com
  Web Address: www.rottneros.com
Personnel:
  Man. Dir.: Olle Dahlin
  Phone: (46) 565 17610
  Fax: (46) 565 17680
  Email: olle.dahlin@rottneros.com
  Prod. Mgr.: Per-Anders Broström
  Phone: (46) 565 17630
  Fax: (46) 565 17680
  Email: peranders.brostrom@rottneros.com
  Purch. Mgr.: Ingemar Eliasson
  Phone: (46) 565 17600
  Fax: (46) 565 17680
  Email: ingemar.eliasson@rottneros.com
Total Employees at this Location: 100
Type of Operation: Pulp mill

Pulp Grades and Capacities:
Total pulp capacity: 172,939 mt/y
Pulp available for market: 170,000 mt/y
Mechanical Pulp: 172,939 mt/y
Pulp Mill Data:
Mechanical Pulping Systems:
Conventional grinders: 6
CTMP systems: 1
Pulp Lines: 2
Bleach Plant Systems: 2
No. 1, Sequence: P, Capacity 170,000 admt/y
Pulp Dryers:
Flash dryers 1, Flash dryers 1
Energy Data:
Power boilers: 2
TMP Reboiler: 1
Electrical demand for mill: 846 MWh/D

ⓂRottneros, Vallviks Bruk AB
Vallvik Mill
Ownership: 100% by Rottneros AB
SE-820 21 Vallvik
Sweden
  Phone: (46) 270 62000
  Fax: (46) 270 69210/69420
  Email: info@rottneros.com
  Web Address: www.rottneros.com
Personnel:
  Man. Dir.: Robert Jensen
  Phone: (46) 270 62111
  Fax: (46) 270 69210
  Email: robert.jensen@rottneros.com
  VP, Mktg. & Sls.: Magnus Persson
  Phone: (46) 270 62010
  Fax: (46) 565 176 80
  Email: magnus.persson@rottneros.com
  Deputy Finan. Mgr: Eva Bostrom
  Phone: (46) 270 62106
  Fax: (46) 270 69210
  Email: eva.bostrom@rottneros.com
Total Employees at this Location: 160
Type of Operation: Pulp mill
Pulp Grades and Capacities:
Total pulp capacity: 241,337 mt/y
Pulp available for market: 240,000 mt/y
Chemical Pulp: 241,337 mt/y
Pulp Mill Data:
Chemical Pulping Systems:
Continuous digesters: 1
Pulp Lines: 1
Bleach Plant Systems: 1
No. 1, Sequence: O_2 DPoDP, Capacity 240,000 admt/y
Chemical Recovery Equipment:
Evaporator lines: 5
Recovery boilers: 1
Lime Kiln
Pulp Dryers:
Flash dryers 1, Flash dryers 1
Energy Data:
Power boilers: 1
Steam turbines: 1 at 28 MW
Electrical demand for mill: 422 MWh/D

ⓄSCA - Svenska Cellulosa Aktiebolaget
Ownership: Public
Klarabergsviadukten 63
SE-103 97 Stockholm
Sweden
Mailing Address: 200, SE-101 23 Stockholm, Sweden
  Phone: (46) 8 788 5100
  Fax: (46) 8 788 5380
  Email: info@sca.com
  Web Address: www.sca.com
Personnel:
  Chrmn.: Sverker Martin-Löf

Sweden

Phone: (46) 8 788 5151
Fax: (46) 8 788 5380
Email: sverker.martin-lof@sca.com
Pres. & CEO: Jan Johansson
Phone: (46) 8 788 5125
Fax: (46) 8 788 5380
Email: jan.c.johansson@sca.com
Pres. SCA Asia Pacific: Ulf Söderström
Phone: (46) 8 788 5100
Fax: (46) 8 788 5380
Email: ulf.soderstrom@sca.com
Pres. SCA Global Hygiene: Christoph Michalski
Phone: (46) 8 788 5100
Fax: (46) 8 788 5380
Email: christoph.michalski@sca.com
Exec. VP. & CFO (will retire on July 1, 2014): Lennart Persson
Phone: (46) 8 788 5122
Fax: (46) 8 788 5380
Email: lennart.persson@sca.com
Exec. VP. & CFO (from July 1, 2014): Fredrik Rystedt
Phone: (46) 8 788 5122
Fax: (46) 8 788 5380
Snr. VP., Group treasurer: Johan Rydin
Phone: (46) 8 788 5131
Fax: (46) 8 788 5380
Email: johan.rydin@sca.com
Snr. VP., Group Function Global Strat. & Bus. Develop., Global Bus. Serv. & IT: Robert Sjöström
Phone: (46) 8 788 5100
Fax: (46) 8 788 5380
Email: robert.sjostrom@sca.com
Snr. VP, Group Function Commun.: Joséphine Edwall-Björklund
Phone: (46) 8 788 5100
Fax: (46) 8 788 5380
Email: josephine.edwall-bjorklund@sca.com
Snr. VP., Group Finction HR: Gordana Landén
Phone: (46) 8 788 5191
Fax: (46) 8 788 5380
Email: gordana.landen@sca.com
Snr. VP. & General Counsel: Mikael Schmidt
Phone: (46) 8 788 5100
Fax: (46) 8 788 5380
Email: mikael.schmidt@sca.com
Snr. VP., Group Function Sustainability: Kersti Strandqvist
Phone: (46) 8 788 5100
Fax: (46) 8 788 5380
Email: kersti.strandqvist@sca.com
VP. Invest. Rel.: Johan Karlsson
Phone: (46) 8 788 5130
Fax: (46) 8 788 5380
Email: johan.ir.karlsson@sca.com
Total Employees of Company: 33,535
Total Employees at this Location: 120
Mill Locations:
Beijing Vinda Paper (Beijing) Co., Ltd., Beijing Mill, No. 16, Hangyu Street, Binhe Industrial Park, Pinggu, Beijing 100023, China, Capacity: 30,000 mt/y, (Paper mill)
Phone: (86) 10 5822 0818
Fax: (86) 10 5822 0802
Productos Familia Sancela del Ecuador S.A., Lasso Mill (50% owned), Panamericana Norte, Km. 20, Lasso, Ecuador, Capacity: 24,990 mt/y, (Paper mill)
Phone: (593) 3 271 8253 / 22484 352
Fax: (593) 22484 357/2484356-57
Guangdong Vinda Paper Co., Ltd., Sanjiang Mill, Baimiao Industrial Park, Sanjiang County, Xinhui District, Jiangmen 529100, China, Capacity: 107,250 mt/y, (Paper mill)
Guangdong Vinda Paper (Guangdong) Co., Ltd., Xinhui Mill, Donghou Industrial Zone, Huicheng Town, Xinhui 529100, China, Capacity: 57,000 mt/y, (Paper mill)
Phone: (86) 750 6122 846/6168 333
Fax: (86) 750 6120 239
Email: vd-computer@chinavinda.com
Guangdong Vinda Paper (Jiangmen) Co., Ltd., Jiangmen Mill, Yingbin Ave., Shuangshui Town, Xinhui Zone, Jiangmen 529100, China, Capacity: 120,000 mt/y, (Paper mill)

Phone: (86) 86 750 641 3111
Fax: (86) 86 750 641 3068
Hubei Vinda Paper (Hubei) Co., Ltd., Xiaogan Mill, Nanda Industry & Development Zone, Xiaonan District, Xiaogan 432100, China, Capacity: 180,000 mt/y, (Paper mill)
Phone: (86) 712 2519 099/ 007
Fax: (86) 712 2519 089
Papeles Industriales S.A. (PISA), Lampa Mill, Panamericana Norte, 22550 Lampa, Chile, Capacity: 61,047 mt/y, (Paper mill)
Phone: (56) 800 200 973, 2640 5200/5021/5270
Fax: (56) 2 733 1103/1031/1108
Email: contacto@pisa.cl, infochile@sca.com
Productos Familia SA, Medellin Mill (50% owned), Calle 9 Sur, 35160 Medellín, Colombia, Capacity: 39,270 mt/y, (Paper mill)
Phone: (57) 4 360 9500 /9600 ,360 9522
Fax: (57) 4 361 3010, 4 360 9578
Email: servicioaldientemedellin@familia.com.co, margaritamm@familia.com.co
Productos Familia SA, Cajica Mill (50% owned), Km 7.5 Via Cajicá Zipaquirá, Cajica, Colombia, Capacity: 74,970 mt/y, (Paper mill)
Phone: (57) 1593 84 84/43609500
SCA Consumidor México y Centroamérica S.A. de C.V., Sahagun Tissue Mill, Carretera Federal Ciudad Sahagún – Emiliano Zapata Km. 6.5, Comunidad Irolo, Municipio, 43991 Tepeapulco, Mexico, Capacity: 57,120 mt/y, (Paper mill)
Phone: (52) 79 1913 5456
Email: comunicacion.scamexico@sca.com
SCA Spain, Allo Mill, Poligono Industrial Mirabete, E-31262 Allo, Spain, Capacity: 175,000 mt/y, (Paper mill)
Phone: (34) 948 54 8305
Fax: (34) 948 54 8308
SCA Hygiene Products SpA, Altopascio Mill, Via Proviciale Romana, I-55010 Altopascio, Loc. Badia Pozzeveri, (LU), Italy, Capacity: 25,000 mt/y, (Paper mill)
Phone: (39) 0583 2791
Fax: (39) 0583 279250
SCA Hygiene Products Australasia, Box Hill Mill (50% owned), Ailsa St., Box Hill, VIC 3128, Australia, Capacity: 54,000 mt/y, (Paper mill)
Phone: (61) 3 9258 0555
Fax: (61) 3 9258 0785
Email: (firstname.surname@sca.com), info@sca.com
SCA Nederlands BV, Cuijk Mill, Lange Linden 22, NL-5433 NC Katwijk, Cuijk, Netherlands, Capacity: 65,000 mt/y, (Pulp mill, Paper mill)
Phone: (31) 48 533 9339
Fax: (31) 48 533 9449
SCA Tissue Finland Oy, Nokia Mill, Kerhokatu 10, FI-37101 Nokia, Finland, Capacity: 80,000 mt/y, (Pulp mill, Paper mill)
Phone: (358) 3 340 8111
Fax: (358) 3 340 8561
SCA France, Gien Mill, La Lombardie, Arrobloy 4, F-45504 Gien Cedex, France, Capacity: 155,000 mt/y, (Paper mill)
Phone: (33) 2 38 37 54 54
Fax: (33) 2 38 37 54 72
SCA France, Hondouville Mill, Hondouville, F-27400 Louviers, France, Capacity: 78,000 mt/y, (Pulp mill, Paper mill)
Phone: (33) 2 32 25 60 60
Fax: (33) 2 32 25 61 70
SCA GraphicSundsvall AB, Ortviken Mill, PO Box 846, SE-851 23 Sundsvall, Sweden, Capacity: 900,000 mt/y, (Pulp mill, Paper mill)
Phone: (46) 60 194000
Fax: (46) 60 152450
SCA GraphicSundsvall AB, Östrand Pulp Mill, Östrands Massafabrik, SE-861 81 Timrå, Sweden, (Pulp mill)
Phone: (46) 60 16 40 00
Fax: (46) 60 57 43 28
Email: info@sca.com
SCA Hygiene Products S.L., La Riba Mill, Cardenal Gomá 16, E-43450 La Riba, Spain, Capacity: 26,000 mt/y, (Paper mill)

Phone: (34) 977 87 6749/ 977 87 6745
Fax: (34) 977 87 6025
SCA Hygiene Products SE, Goytside Mill, Goytside Road, Chesterfield S40 2PH, United Kingdom, Capacity: 31,000 mt/y, (Paper mill)
Phone: (44) 1246 558 557
Fax: (44) 1246 552 556
SCA Hygiene Products AB, Edet Mill, Emil Haegers väg 21, SE-463 81 Lilla Edet, Sweden, Capacity: 110,000 mt/y, (Paper mill)
Phone: (46) 520 659 000
Fax: (46) 520 659 302
SCA Hygiene Products SE, Mainz-Kostheim Mill, Hauptstrasse 1, D-55246 Mainz-Kostheim, Germany, Capacity: 166,000 mt/y, (Paper mill)
Phone: (49) 6134 608 202/0
Fax: (49) 6134 608 387/400
Email: info.hygiene@sca.com, torkmaster@sca.com
SCA Hygiene Products Manchester Ltd., Manchester (Trafford Park) Mill, Trafford Park Road, Trafford Park, Manchester M17 1EQ, United Kingdom, Capacity: 60,000 mt/y, (Paper mill)
Phone: (44) 161 888 6002
Fax: (44) 161 888 6195
SCA Hygiene Products SE, Mannheim Mill, Sandhofer Str. 176, D-68305 Mannheim, Germany, Capacity: 350,000 mt/y, (Pulp mill, Paper mill)
Phone: (49) 621 778 0
Fax: (49) 621 778 3146/3141/2248
Email: (firstname.surname@sca.com)
SCA Hygiene Products S.L., Mediona Mill, Carretera de la Llacuna, E-08773 Mediona, Spain, Capacity: 45,000 mt/y, (Paper mill)
Phone: (34) 93 898 5570
Fax: (34) 93 898 5820
SCA Hygiene Products SE, Neuss Mill, Floßhafenstraße 16, D-41460 Neuss, Germany, Capacity: 105,000 mt/y, (Paper mill)
Phone: (49) 2131 296 0
Fax: (49) 2131 296 104/111
SCA Hygiene Products SE, Oakenholt Mill, Chester Road, Oakenholt, Flint CH6 5PU, United Kingdom, Capacity: 68,000 mt/y, (Paper mill)
Phone: (44) 1352 732 101
Fax: (44) 1352 732 760
SCA Hygiene Products Operations SNC, Orléans Mill, Rue des Bouleaux, ZI de la Saussaye, F-45590 Saint Cyr en Val, Orléans, France, Capacity: 35,000 mt/y, (Paper mill)
Phone: (33) 2 38 49 97 97
Fax: (33) 2 38 63 88 45
Email: (firstname.lastname@sca.com)
SCA Hygiene Products GmbH, Ortmann Mill, Hauptstrasse 1, A-2763 Ortmann, Pernitz, Austria, Capacity: 128,000 mt/y, (Paper mill)
Phone: (43) 2632 707 0
Fax: (43) 2632 72394
Email: office@sca.com
SCA Hygiene Products, Collodi Mill, Via delle Cartiere 13, I-51014 Collodi, (PT), Italy, Capacity: 42,000 mt/y, (Paper mill)
Phone: (39) 0572 429090
Fax: (39) 0572 426335
SCA Hygiene Products Supply SAS, Le Theil Mill, Route d'Avezé, ZI Sud, F-61260 Le Theil sur Huisne, France, Capacity: 62,000 mt/y, (Paper mill)
Phone: (33) 2 37 53 67 00
Fax: (33) 2 37 53 67 92
SCA Hygiene Products SpA, Lucca 1 Tissue Mill, Via del Frizzone, I-55016 Porcari, (LU), Italy, Capacity: 140,000 mt/y, (Paper mill)
Phone: (39) 0583 21241
Fax: (39) 0583 297575
Email: info@sca.com
SCA Hygiene Products SE, Prudhoe Mill, Princess Way, Prudhoe NE42 6HE, United Kingdom, Capacity: 90,000 mt/y, (Pulp mill, Paper mill)
Phone: (44) 1661 806000
Fax: (44) 1661 806001
SCA Hygiene Products Russia LLC, Sovetsk Mill, Molodyozhnaya Str. 9, 301205 Sovetsk, Shchekino

Sweden

Distr., Russia, Capacity: 30,000 mt/y, (Paper mill)
Phone: (7) 48751 746 66 / 751 36/41
Email: ekaterina.serezhnikova@sca.com
SCA Hygiene Products S.A./N.V., Stembert Mill, Rue de la Papeterie 2, B-4801 Stembert, Belgium, Capacity: 75,000 mt/y, (Paper mill)
Phone: (32) 87 30 66 11
Fax: (32) 87 33 94 24
Email: (firstname.lastname@sca.com)
SCA Hygiene Products Russia LLC, Svetogorsk Mill, ul. Zavodskaya 21, 188991 Svetogorsk, Russia, Capacity: 43,000 mt/y, (Paper mill)
Phone: (7) 812 320 4834
Fax: (7) 812 320 4835
Email: info@scacompany.com, svetogorsk@sca.com, tissue@mail.ru
SCA Hygiene Products S.L., Puigpelat (Valls) Mill, Ctra. Valls-Puigpelat, Km 2, E-43812 Puigpelat, Spain, Capacity: 120,000 mt/y, (Paper mill)
Phone: (34) 977 030 600
Fax: (34) 977 605 554
SCA Hygiene Products GmbH, Witzenhausen Tissue Mill, Kasseler Landstrasse 21, D-37213 Witzenhausen, Germany, Capacity: 30,000 mt/y, (Paper mill)
Phone: (49) 5542 509 0
Fax: (49) 5542 509 200
SCA Hygiene Products Australasia, Kawerau Mill (50% owned), Fletcher Avenue, 3169 Kawerau, New Zealand, Capacity: 57,000 mt/y, (Paper mill)
Phone: (64) 7 323 9899
Fax: (64) 7 323 6601
Email: (firstname.lastname@sca.com)
SCA France, Kunheim Mill, Kunheim, F-68320 Muntzenheim, France, Capacity: 50,000 mt/y, (Paper mill)
Phone: (33) 3 89 72 23 00
Fax: (33) 3 89 72 91 26
SCA Consumidor México y Centroamérica S.A. de C.V., Monterrey Tissue Mill, Avenida San Nicolás #300, Colonia Cuauthémoc, 66450 San Nicolas de los Garza, Mexico, Capacity: 59,976 mt/y, (Paper mill)
Phone: (52) 81 5000 7300
Fax: (52) 81 8 305 7317
Email: comunicacion.scamexico@sca.com
SCA Munksund AB, Piteå Mill, Munksundsvägen, SE-941 87 Piteå, Sweden, Capacity: 365,000 mt/y, (Pulp mill, Paperboard mill)
Phone: (46) 911 98000
Fax: (46) 911 98220
SCA Obbola AB, Obbola Mill, Linjevägen 33, SE-913 80 Obbola, Sweden, Capacity: 435,000 mt/y, (Pulp mill, Paperboard mill)
Phone: (46) 90 154000
Fax: (46) 90 154200
Email: obbola@sca.com
SCA Patras, Patras Mill, Industrial Area of Patras, PO Box 150, GR-25018 Ag. Stefanos - Patras, Greece, Capacity: 20,000 mt/y, (Paper mill)
Phone: (30) 2610 242200
Fax: (30) 2610 647216
SCA Tissue North America, L.L.C., Encore Paper, 1 River St, South Glens Falls, NY 12803, USA, Capacity: 80,644 mt/y, (Paper mill)
Phone: (1) 518-793-5684
Fax: (1) 518-793-2650
Email: torkusa@sca.com
SCA Hygiene Products SE, Stubbins Mill, Stubbins Lane, Ramsbottom, Bury BL0 0NH, United Kingdom, Capacity: 117,000 mt/y, (Pulp mill, Paper mill)
Phone: (44) 1706 283 000
Fax: (44) 1706 283 001
SCA Tissue North America, L.L.C., Barton Mill, 1834 Haley Dr., Cherokee, AL 35616, USA, Capacity: 159,020 mt/y, (Paper mill)
Phone: (1) 256-370-8100
Fax: (1) 256-370-8195
SCA Tissue North America, L.L.C., Flagstaff Mill, 1600 E Butler Av, Flagstaff, AZ 86001, USA, Capacity: 56,030 mt/y, (Paper mill)
Phone: (1) 928-774-7375
Fax: (1) 928-774-9546
Email: americas@sca.com
SCA Tissue North America, L.L.C., Menasha Mill, 190 Tayco Street, Menasha, WI 54952, USA, Capacity: 190,112 mt/y, (Paper mill)
Phone: (1) 920-727-2910
Fax: (1) 920-727-2902
Email: info@sca.com
SCA Consumidor México y Centroamérica S.A. de C.V., Uruapan Tissue Mill, Boulevard Industrial No. 3201, Col. La Cofradía, 60221 Uruapan, Mexico, Capacity: 34,986 mt/y, (Pulp mill, Paper mill)
Phone: (52) 452 527 5200
Fax: (52) 452 527 5249
Email: comunicacion.scamexico@sca.com
Vinda Paper (Sichuan) Co. Ltd., Deyang Mill, No. 19, three District, South Longquan Rd., Deyang 618000, China, Capacity: 45,000 mt/y, (Paper mill)
Phone: (86) 838 290 6199
Fax: (86) 838 290 6311
Vinda Paper (Shandong) Co., Ltd., Laiwu Mill, Laiwu Wenyang Industrial Park, Laiwu, China, Capacity: 50,000 mt/y, (Paper mill)
Phone: (86) 634 5628 881
Vinda Paper (Liaoning) Co., Ltd., Anshan Mill, Anshan Dadaowan Industry & Development Park, Anshan 114013, China, Capacity: 54,000 mt/y, (Paper mill)
Vinda Paper (Zhejiang) Co., Ltd., Quzhou Mill, No.9, Fengkun Rd., Longyou Industry Park, Longyou County, Quzhou 324000, China, Capacity: 90,000 mt/y, (Paper mill)
Phone: (86) 570 7788 888/808
Fax: (86) 570 7608 202

ⓜⓜSCA Graphic Sundsvall AB Ortviken Mill

Ownership: 100% by SCA - Svenska Cellulosa Aktiebolaget

PO Box 846
SE-851 23 Sundsvall
Sweden
Phone: (46) 60 194000
Fax: (46) 60 152450
Web Address: www.sca.se, www.forestproducts.sca.com

Personnel:
Mill Mgr: Kristina Enander
Phone: (46) 60 194000
Fax: (46) 60 152450
Email: kristina.enander@sca.com
VP Sls Mktg, Pulp Paper & Containerboard.: Rolf Johannesson
Phone: (46) 60 1941 52
Fax: (46) 60 1935 65
Email: rolf.johannesson@sca.com
Bus. Group Management: Alvar Andersson
Phone: (46) 705674098

Total Employees of Company: 49,531
Total Employees at this Location: 700
Type of Operation: Pulp mill, Paper mill
Mill Locations:
SCA Graphic Sundsvall AB, Östrand Pulp Mill, Östrands Massafabrik, SE-861 81 Timrå, Sweden, (Pulp mill)
Phone: (46) 60 16 40 00
Fax: (46) 60 57 43 28
Email: info@sca.com

Pulp Grades and Capacities:
Total pulp capacity: 587,190 mt/y
Mechanical Pulp: 587,190 mt/y

Pulp Mill Data:
Mechanical Pulping Systems:
TMP systems: 2
Pulp Lines: 2
Bleach Plant Systems: 3
1, Sequence: P, Capacity 300,000 admt/y
2, Sequence: P, Capacity admt/y
3, Sequence: P, Capacity admt/y

Paper/Paperboard Grades and Capacities:
Total paper and paperboard capacity: 900,000 mt/y
Newsprint: 200,000 mt/y
Uncoated mechanical/groundwood: 130,000 mt/y
Coated mechanical/groundwood: 495,000 mt/y
Specialty and industrial: 50,000 mt/y
Linerboard: 25,000 mt/y

Paper and Paperboard Mill Data:
Stock Preparation:
Pulpers: 2
Refiners: 5

Paper Machines: 4
No. 1, SymFormer R, total capacity 220,000 mt/y, Trim width 6.39 m, Coated mechanical/groundwood, Specialty and industrial, Linerboard
No. 2, Bel-Baie III, total capacity 140,000 mt/y, Trim width 6.56 m, Uncoated mechanical/groundwood, Specialty and industrial, Linerboard
No. 4, DuoFormer CFD, total capacity 290,000 mt/y, Trim width 7.74 m, Coated mechanical/groundwood
No. 5, Bel-Baie IV, total capacity 250,000 mt/y, Trim width 8.68 m, Newsprint, Uncoated mechanical/groundwood

Coating Machines: 2
CM 1, total capacity 210,000 mt/y., off machine
PM 4, total capacity 280,000 mt/y., on machine

Finishing Equipment:
Winders: 7
Supercalenders: 2

Energy Data:
Power boilers: 6
TMP Reboiler: 3
Combustion turbines: 1 at 20 MW
Steam turbines: 2 at 29 MW
Electrical demand for mill: 6,002 MWh/D

ⓜSCA Graphic Sundsvall AB Östrand Pulp Mill

Ownership: 100% by SCA - Svenska Cellulosa Aktiebolaget

Östrands Massafabrik
SE-861 81 Timrå
Sweden
Mailing Address: SCA Forest Products AB, S-85188 Sundsvall, Sweden, Sweden
Phone: (46) 60 16 40 00
Fax: (46) 60 57 43 28
Email: info@sca.com
Web Address: www.sca.com, www.pulp.sca.com

Personnel:
Mill Mgr.: Ingela Ekebro
Phone: (46) 60 16 40 53
Fax: (46) 60 57 43 28
Email: ingela.ekebro@sca.com
Sls & Mktg Mgr.: Stefan Sjöström
Phone: (46) 60 16 40 00
Fax: (46) 60 57 43 28
Email: stefan.sjostrom@sca.com
Purch.: Billy Norberg
Phone: (46) 60 16 41 41
Fax: (46) 60 57 43 28
Email: billy.norberg@sca.com
Maint. Mgr.: Trond Norman
Phone: (46) 60 16 40 33
Fax: (46) 60 57 43 28
Environ.: Christer Fält
Phone: (46) 60 16 41 09
Fax: (46) 60 57 43 28
Email: christer.falt@sca.com
Pulp Prod. Mgr.: Mikael Hjärpe
Phone: (46) 60 16 40 00
Fax: (46) 60 57 43 28
Email: mikael.hjarpe@sca.com
HR. Mgr.: Jonas Nilsson
Phone: (46) 60 16 40 00
Fax: (46) 60 57 43 28

Total Employees at this Location: 410
Type of Operation: Pulp mill
Pulp Grades and Capacities:
Total pulp capacity: 529,329 mt/y
Pulp available for market: 520,000 mt/y
Chemical Pulp: 432,264 mt/y
Mechanical Pulp: 97,066 mt/y

Sweden

Pulp Mill Data:
Chemical Pulping Systems:
Continuous digesters
Mechanical Pulping Systems:
BCTMP systems
Bleach Plant Systems: 2
BCTMP Mechanical Pulping system bleaching,
Sequence: P
Continuous Digester system bleaching, Type: SW
- Ozone process: HC, Sequence: O_2 QOpDZPoP,
Capacity 446,300 admt/y
Chemical Recovery Equipment:
Recovery boilers: 1
Lime Kiln
Pulp Dryers:
Flakt dryer 1, Flash dryers 1, Flash dryers 1
Finishing Equipment:
Sheeters
Energy Data:
Power boilers: 1
TMP Reboiler: 1
Steam turbines: 1 at 75 MW
Electrical demand for mill: 1,451 MWh/D

ⓜSCA Hygiene Products AB
Edet Mill

Ownership: SCA Hygiene Products SE
Emil Haegers väg 21
SE-463 81 Lilla Edet
Sweden
Phone: (46) 520 659 000
Fax: (46) 520 659 302
Web Address: www.sca.com
Personnel:
Mill Mgr.: Robert Fuhrmann
Phone: (46) 520 659 000
Fax: (46) 520 659 302
Email: robert.fuhrmann@sca.com
Prod. Mgr. PM: Stefan Montarius
Phone: (46) 520 659 000
Fax: (46) 520 659 302
Email: stefan.montarius@sca.com
Qual. & Env. Mgr.: Per-Anders Holmgren
Phone: (46) 520 659 000
Fax: (46) 520 659 302
Prod. Mgr PP/PM: Isabell Ljusberg
Phone: (46) 520 65 94 50
Fax: (46) 520 659 302
Email: isabell.ljusberg@sca.com
Conv. Plant Mgr.: Pierre Magnusson
Phone: (46) 520 65 90 00
Fax: (46) 520 659 302
Email: pierre.magnusson@sca.com
Plann. Mgr.: Kamilla Nilsson
Phone: (46) 31 746 10 58
Fax: (46) 520 659 302
Email: kamilla.nilsson@sca.com
Purch. Mgr.: Mikael Ståhl
Phone: (46) 520 659 000
Fax: (46) 520 659 302
Email: mikael.stahl@sca.com
Total Employees at this Location: 450
Type of Operation: Paper mill
Pulp Grades and Capacities:
Total pulp capacity: 92,606 mt/y
Recycled Pulping: 92,606 mt/y

Pulp Mill Data:
Bleach Plant Systems: 1
DIP
Recycled Fiber Treatment Lines:
Flotation deinking lines at 20,000 admt/y
Pulpers: 2 at 300 admt/y
Washing deinking lines at 50,000 admt/y
Paper/Paperboard Grades and Capacities:
Total paper and paperboard capacity: 110,000 mt/y
Tissue: 110,000 mt/y
Paper and Paperboard Mill Data:
Stock Preparation:
Pulpers: 6
Refiners: 6
Paper Machines: 3
No. 5, fourdrinier, Yankee dryer, total capacity 30,000 mt/y, Trim width 3.4 m, Tissue
No. 7, C-wrap, Yankee dryer, total capacity 35,000 mt/y, Trim width 3.4 m, Tissue
No. 8, crescent former, Yankee dryer, total capacity 45,000 mt/y, Trim width 3.56 m, Tissue
Energy Data:
Power boilers: 2
Steam turbines: 1 at 2.2 MW
Electrical demand for mill: 506 MWh/D

ⓜSCA Munksund AB
Piteå Mill

Ownership: 100% by SCA - Svenska Cellulosa Aktiebolaget
Munksundsvägen
SE-941 87 Piteå
Sweden
Phone: (46) 911 98000
Fax: (46) 911 98220
Web Address: www.scacontainerboard.com
Personnel:
Man. Dir.: Per Embertsén
Phone: (46) 46 911 98 207
Fax: (46) 911 98220
Email: per.embertsen@sca.com
Project Mgr.: Per-Håkan Stoltz
Phone: (46) 911 98000
Fax: (46) 911 98220
Maint. Mgr.: Tomas Westerlund
Phone: (46) 911 98000
Fax: (46) 911 98220
Total Employees at this Location: 300
Type of Operation: Pulp mill, Paperboard mill
Pulp Grades and Capacities:
Total pulp capacity: 367,276 mt/y
Chemical Pulp: 288,640 mt/y
Recycled Pulping: 78,636 mt/y

Pulp Mill Data:
Chemical Pulping Systems:
Continuous digesters: 2
Bleach Plant Systems: 1
hardwood, Type: TCF Capacity 50,000 admt/y
Chemical Recovery Equipment:
Evaporator lines: 2
Recovery boilers: 1
Lime Kiln
Recycled Fiber Treatment Lines:
Pulpers: 1 at 100,000 admt/y
Paper/Paperboard Grades and Capacities:
Total paper and paperboard capacity: 365,000 mt/y
Linerboard: 365,000 mt/y
Paper and Paperboard Mill Data:
Stock Preparation:
Refiners: 4
Paper Machines: 1
No. 1, fourdrinier (2), total capacity 365,000 mt/y, Trim width 6.4 m, Linerboard
Finishing Equipment:
Winders: 1
Calenders: 1
Energy Data:
Power boilers: 1
Steam turbines: 1 at 25 MW
Electrical demand for mill: 968 MWh/D

ⓜSCA Obbola AB
Obbola Mill

Ownership: SCA - Svenska Cellulosa Aktiebolaget
Linjevägen 33
SE-913 80 Obbola
Sweden
Phone: (46) 90 154000
Fax: (46) 90 154200
Email: obbola@sca.com
Web Address: www.sca.com/containerboard
Personnel:
Man. Dir.: Per Strand
Phone: (46) 90 154001
Fax: (46) 90 154200
Email: per.strand@sca.com
Maint. Mgr.: Mats Backeström
Phone: (46) 90 154000
Fax: (46) 90 154200
Email: mats.backestrom@sca.com
Tech. Mgr.: Susanne Rutqvist
Phone: (46) 90 154000
Fax: (46) 90 154200
Email: susanne.rutqvist@sca.com
Finan. Mgr.: Ranko Kaljevic
Phone: (46) 90 154000
Fax: (46) 90 154200
Email: ranko.kaljevic@sca.com
Commun. Asst. & HR: Annika Persson
Phone: (46) 90 154117
Fax: (46) 90 154200
Email: annika.persson@sca.com
Total Employees at this Location: 300
Type of Operation: Pulp mill, Paperboard mill
Pulp Grades and Capacities:
Total pulp capacity: 448,706 mt/y
Chemical Pulp: 246,000 mt/y
Recycled Pulping: 202,706 mt/y

Pulp Mill Data:
Chemical Pulping Systems:
Batch digesters: 8
Chemical Recovery Equipment:
Evaporator lines: 2
Recovery boilers: 1
Lime Kiln
Recycled Fiber Treatment Lines:
Recycled packaging pulping lines: 1
Paper/Paperboard Grades and Capacities:
Total paper and paperboard capacity: 435,000 mt/y
Linerboard: 435,000 mt/y
Paper and Paperboard Mill Data:
Stock Preparation:
Pulpers: 2
Refiners: 9
Paper Machines: 1
No. 1, fourdrinier (2), total capacity 435,000 mt/y, Trim width 9.4 m, Linerboard
Finishing Equipment:
Winders: 1
Energy Data:
Power boilers: 1
Steam turbines: 1 at 15.0 MW
Electrical demand for mill: 907 MWh/D

ⓜSmurfit Kappa Kraftliner Piteå
Piteå Mill

Ownership: Smurfit Kappa Europe
SE-941 86 Piteå
Sweden
Phone: (46) 911 97000
Fax: (46) 911 97010
Email: info.kraftliner@smurfitkappa.se
Web Address: www.smurfitkappa-kraftliner.com
Personnel:
Man. Dir. (transfer to Nettingsdorf late 2014): Reinhard Reiter
Phone: (46) 911 97510
Fax: (46) 911 97010
Email: reinhard.reiter@smurfitkappa.se
Mill Mgr. (Man. Dir. from Jan. 1, 2015): Per Swärd
Phone: (46) 911 97322
Fax: (46) 911 97010
Email: per.sward@smurfitkappa.se
Tech. Mgr.: Bo Johansson
Phone: (46) 911 97339
Fax: (46) 911 97010
Email: bo.johansson@smurfitkappa.se
Mill Mgr. (eff Jan. 1, 2015): Ulf Aili
Phone: (46) 911 97322
Fax: (46) 911 97010

Sweden

Purch. Mgr.: Lina Danielsson
Phone: (46) 911 97148
Fax: (46) 911 97010
Email: lina.danielsson@smurfitkappa.se
Total Employees at this Location: 530
Type of Operation: Pulp mill, Paperboard mill
Pulp Grades and Capacities:
  Total pulp capacity: 701,688 mt/y
  Chemical Pulp: 550,000 mt/y
  Recycled Pulping: 151,688 mt/y
Pulp Mill Data:
  Chemical Pulping Systems:
  Continuous digesters: 3
Pulp Lines: 3
  Bleach Plant Systems: 1
  No. 1, Sequence: O_2 QPo, Capacity 200,000 admt/y
  Chemical Recovery Equipment:
  Evaporator lines: 2
  Recovery boilers: 1
  Lime Kiln
  Recycled Fiber Treatment Lines:
  Pulpers: 1 at 150,000 admt/y
Paper/Paperboard Grades and Capacities:
  Total paper and paperboard capacity: 700,000 mt/y
  Linerboard: 700,000 mt/y
Paper and Paperboard Mill Data:
  Stock Preparation:
  Pulpers: 2
  Refiners: 8
Paper Machines: 2
  No. 1, fourdrinier (2), total capacity 360,000 mt/y, Trim width 6.5 m, Linerboard
  No. 2, DuoFormer DK, total capacity 340,000 mt/y, Trim width 6.5 m, Linerboard
Coating Machines: 1
  No. 1, off machine
Finishing Equipment:
  Winders: 2
Energy Data:
  Power boilers: 1
  Steam turbines: 2 at 27, 26 MW
  Electrical demand for mill: 1,752 MWh/D

ⓂSödra Cell AB
Ownership: Private
Skogsudden
S-351 89 Växjö
Sweden
Phone: (46) 470 89000
Fax: (46) 470 89402
Email: (firstname.lastname@sodra.com)
Web Address: www.sodra.com
Personnel:
Chmn.: Christer Segerstéen
Phone: (46) 470 89000
Fax: (46) 470 89402
Pres & CEO - Södra Group: Lars Idermark
Phone: (46) 470 89437
Fax: (46) 470 89402
Email: lars.idermark@sodra.com
Pres. Södra Cell business area: Gunilla Saltin
Phone: (46) 470 85591
Fax: (46) 470 89424
Email: gunilla.saltin@sodra.com
CFO & Dir. HR: Carina Olson
Phone: (46) 470 89000
Fax: (46) 470 89402
Pres. Sodra Interior: Ulf Edman
Phone: (46) 470 89000
Fax: (46) 470 89402
Email: ulf.edman@sodra.com
Pres. Sodra Cell International: Magnus Björkman
Phone: (46) 470 89422
Fax: (46) 470 89402
Email: magnus.bjorkman@sodra.com
Bus. Area Mgr. Printing Paper & Specialities: Henrik Wettergren
Phone: (46) 470 89452
Fax: (46) 470 89402

Email: henrik.wettergren@sodra.com
Tech. Prod. Mgr. Printing paper Sodra Cell International: Ann Nilsson
Phone: (46) 454 59807
Fax: (46) 454 55056
Email: ann.nilsson@sodra.com
Mktg. Dir.: Marcus Hellberg
Phone: (46) 470 85584
Fax: (46) 470 89402
Email: marcus.hellberg@sodra.com
HR Director: Christer Thörn
Phone: (46) 470 89000
Fax: (46) 470 89402
Email: christer.thorn@sodra.com
Total Employees of Company: 1,444
Total Employees at this Location: 30
Mill Locations:
Södra Cell AB, Mönsterås Mill, SE-383 25 Mönsterås, Sweden, (Pulp mill)
Phone: (46) 499 150 00
Fax: (46) 499 154 60
Email: msb@sodra.com
Södra Cell AB, Mörrum Mill, SE-375 86 Mörrum, Sweden, (Pulp mill)
Phone: (46) 454 550 00
Fax: (46) 454 550 50
Email: (firstname.lastname@sodra.com)
Södra Cell Tofte, Tofte Mill, Østre Strandvei 52, NO-3482 Tofte, Norway, (Pulp mill)
Phone: (47) 32 799 000
Fax: (47) 32 799 001
Södra Cell AB, Värö Mill, SE-430 24 Väröbacka, Sweden, (Pulp mill)
Phone: (46) 340 6280 00
Fax: (46) 340 6280 01
Email: (firstname.lastname@sodra.com)

ⓂSödra Cell AB
Mönsterås Mill
SE-383 25 Mönsterås
Sweden
  Phone: (46) 499 150 00
  Fax: (46) 499 154 60
  Email: msb@sodra.com
  Web Address: www.sodra.se
Personnel:
Mill Mgr.: Carsten Wieger
Phone: (46) 499 15264
Fax: (46) 499 15460
Email: carsten.wieger@sodra.com
Tech. & Energy Mgr.: Jörgen Agebjörn
Phone: (46) 499 15124
Fax: (46) 499 15460
Email: jorgen.agebjorn@sodra.com
Prod. Mgr.: Johan Sjögren
Phone: (46) 499 15125
Fax: (46) 499 15460
Email: johan.sjogren@sodra.com
Maint. Mgr.: Thomas Håkansson
Phone: (46) 499 15147
Fax: (46) 499 15460
Email: thomas.hakansson@sodra.com
Process Mgr.: Tobias Runesson
Phone: (46) 499 15155
Fax: (46) 499 15460
Email: tobias.runesson@sodra.com
Total Employees at this Location: 372
Type of Operation: Pulp mill
Pulp Grades and Capacities:
  Total pulp capacity: 752,164 mt/y
  Pulp available for market: 750,000 mt/y
  Chemical Pulp: 752,164 mt/y
Pulp Mill Data:
  Chemical Pulping Systems:
  Continuous digesters: 3
  Bleach Plant Systems: 2
  Chemical Pulping System - Hardwood, Sequence: O_2 QOPPAA/QPO, Capacity 305,400 admt/y
  Chemical Pulping System - Softwood, Sequence: O_2 QOPPAA/QPO, Capacity 450,000 admt/y

  Chemical Recovery Equipment:
  Evaporator lines: 2
  Recovery boilers: 1
  Lime Kiln
  Pulp Dryers:
  Air Float dryers 1, Air Float dryers 1, Fourdriniers 1
Energy Data:
  Power boilers: 1
  Steam turbines: 4 at 135 MW
  Wind turbines: 6 at 30 MW
  Electrical demand for mill: 1,620 MWh/D

ⓂSödra Cell AB
Mörrum Mill
SE-375 86 Mörrum
Sweden
  Phone: (46) 454 550 00
  Fax: (46) 454 550 50
  Email: (firstname.lastname@sodra.com)
  Web Address: www.sodra.se
Personnel:
Mill Mgr.: Stefan Sandberg
Phone: (46) 702657522
Fax: (46) 454 550 50
Email: stefan.sandberg@sodra.com
Prod. Mgr.: Leif Andersson
Phone: (46) 454 550 00
Fax: (46) 454 550 50
Email: leif.andersson@sodra.com
Tech. Mgr.: Annica Ahlstedt
Phone: (46) 454 550 00
Fax: (46) 454 550 50
Email: annica.ahlstedt@sodra.com
Fin. Mgr.: Ulf Svensson
Phone: (46) 454 550 00
Fax: (46) 454 550 50
Email: ulf.svensson@sodra.com
Maint. Mgr.: Lars-Göran Svensson
Phone: (46) 454 550 00
Fax: (46) 454 550 50
Email: lars-goran.svensson@sodra.com
Total Employees at this Location: 399
Type of Operation: Pulp mill
Pulp Grades and Capacities:
  Total pulp capacity: 440,128 mt/y
  Pulp available for market: 430,000 mt/y
  Chemical Pulp: 440,128 mt/y
Pulp Mill Data:
  Chemical Pulping Systems:
  Batch digesters: 10
Pulp Lines: 2
  Bleach Plant Systems: 2
  Hardwood Pulp Line, Type: ECF/TCF
  Softwood Pulp Line, Type: ECF/TCF
  Chemical Recovery Equipment:
  Evaporator lines: 2
  Recovery boilers: 2
  Lime Kiln
  Pulp Dryers:
  Air Float dryers 1, Air Float dryers 1
Energy Data:
  Power boilers: 1
  Steam turbines: 3 at 11, 22, 23 MW
  Electrical demand for mill: 941 MWh/D

ⓂSödra Cell AB
Värö Mill
SE-430 24 Väröbacka
Sweden
  Phone: (46) 340 6280 00
  Fax: (46) 340 6280 01
  Email: (firstname.lastname@sodra.com)
  Web Address: www.sodra.se
Personnel:
Mill Mgr.: Jonas Eriksson
Phone: (46) 340 628102
Fax: (46) 340 628100
Email: jonas.eriksson@sodra.com
Prod. Mgr.: Marcus Åsgärde

Sweden

Phone: (46) 340 628103
Fax: (46) 340 628100
Email: marcus.asgarde@sodra.com
Tech. & Environ. Mgr.: Knut Omholt
Phone: (46) 340 633503
Fax: (46) 340 628100
Email: knut.omholt@sodra.com
Maint. Mgr.: Ola Walin
Phone: (46) 340 633535
Fax: (46) 340 628001
Email: ola.walin@sodra.com
Total Employees at this Location: 340
Type of Operation: Pulp mill
Pulp Grades and Capacities:
Total pulp capacity: 427,391 mt/y
Pulp available for market: 425,000 mt/y
Chemical Pulp: 427,391 mt/y

Pulp Mill Data:
Chemical Pulping Systems:
Batch digesters: 10
Pulp Lines: 1
Bleach Plant Systems: 1
No. 1, Type: TCF Capacity 425,000 admt/y
Chemical Recovery Equipment:
Evaporator lines: 1
Recovery boilers: 1
Lime Kiln
Pulp Dryers:
Flakt dryer 1, Flash dryers 1, Fourdriniers 1
Energy Data:
Power boilers: 1
Steam turbines: 1 at 63 MW
Electrical demand for mill: 859 MWh/D

ⓜStora Enso Renewable Packaging
Fors Mill
Ownership: Stora Enso Oyj
Kopparforsvägen 3
SE-774 89 Fors
Sweden
Phone: (46) 1046 35000
Fax: (46) 1046 35250
Web Address: www.storaenso.com
Personnel:
Mill Dir.: Cecilia Carter
Phone: (46) 1046 35000
Fax: (46) 1046 35250
Email: cecilia.carter@storaenso.com
HR. Mgr.: Ulla Hunting
Phone: (46) 1046 35000
Fax: (46) 1046 35250
Email: ulla.hunting@storaenso.com
Total Employees at this Location: 530
Type of Operation: Pulp mill, Paperboard mill
Pulp Grades and Capacities:
Total pulp capacity: 369,665 mt/y
Mechanical Pulp: 185,000 mt/y

Pulp Mill Data:
Mechanical Pulping Systems:
BCTMP systems: 2
Bleach Plant Systems: 1
Mechanical BCTMP Pulping System, Type: Softwood, Sequence: P
Paper/Paperboard Grades and Capacities:
Total paper and paperboard capacity: 395,000 mt/y
Boxboard/cartonboard: 395,000 mt/y
Paper and Paperboard Mill Data:
Stock Preparation:
Pulpers: 4
Paper Machines: 2
No. 2, fourdrinier (3), total capacity 135,000 mt/y, Trim width 3.71 m, Boxboard/cartonboard
No. 3, fourdrinier (3), total capacity 260,000 mt/y, Trim width 5.43 m, Boxboard/cartonboard
Coating Machines: 2
PM 2, total capacity 135,000 mt/y., on machine
PM 3, total capacity 260,000 mt/y., on machine
Finishing Equipment:
Winders: 2 at 20,000 mt/y
Sheeters: 6
Energy Data:
Power boilers: 4
TMP Reboiler: 1
Steam turbines: 1 at 10 MW
Electrical demand for mill: 1,447 MWh/D

ⓜStora Enso Printing and Reading
Nymölla Mill
Ownership: 100% by Stora Enso Oyj
SE-295 80 Nymölla
Sweden
Phone: (46) 1046 440 00
Fax: (46) 1046 446 00
Web Address: www.storaenso.com/nymolla
Personnel:
Mill Dir.: Jens Christian Lamprecht
Phone: (46) 1046 440 00
Fax: (46) 1046 446 00
Email: jens-christian.lamprecht@storaenso.com
Prod. Mgr. Pulp Mill: Per-Ola Nilsson
Phone: (46) 1046 440 00
Fax: (46) 1046 446 00
Prod. Mgr., Paper: Erik Mänssen
Phone: (46) 1046 440 00
Fax: (46) 1046 446 00
Email: erik.manssen@storaenso.com
Mill Controller: Lisbeth Nilsson
Phone: (46) 1046 440 00
Fax: (46) 1046 446 00
Email: lisbeth.nilsson@storaenso.com
R&D Mgr.: Philip Håkansson
Phone: (46) 7059 361 71
Fax: (46) 1046 446 00
Email: philip.hakansson@storaenso.com
Purch. Mgr.: Christer Olsen
Phone: (46) 1046 440 00
Fax: (46) 1046 446 00
Email: christer.olsen@storaenso.com
Total Employees at this Location: 520
Type of Operation: Pulp mill, Paper mill
Pulp Grades and Capacities:
Total pulp capacity: 335,000 mt/y
Pulp available for market: 10,000 mt/y
Chemical Pulp: 335,000 mt/y

Pulp Mill Data:
Chemical Pulping Systems:
Batch digesters: 9
Pulp Lines: 1
Bleach Plant Systems: 2
No. 1, Type: TCF, Sequence: O_2 EoQP, Capacity 335,000 admt/y
Chemical Recovery Equipment:
Evaporator lines: 3
Recovery boilers: 1
Recovery boilers: 1
Pulp Dryers:
Air Float dryers 1
Paper/Paperboard Grades and Capacities:
Total paper and paperboard capacity: 500,000 mt/y
Uncoated woodfree/freesheet: 500,000 mt/y
Paper and Paperboard Mill Data:
Stock Preparation:
Pulpers: 1
Refiners: 8
Paper Machines: 2
No. 1, DuoFormer D, total capacity 250,000 mt/y, Trim width 6.5 m, Uncoated woodfree/freesheet
No. 2, SymFormer, total capacity 250,000 mt/y, Trim width 6.7 m, Uncoated woodfree/freesheet
Finishing Equipment:
Winders: 3
Sheeters: 4
Energy Data:
Power boilers: 1
Steam turbines: 2 at 30 MW
Electrical demand for mill: 1,447 MWh/D

ⓜStora Enso Biomaterials
Skutskär Pulp Mill
Ownership: 100% by Stora Enso Oyj
SE-814 81 Skutskär
Sweden
Phone: (46) 1046 85000
Fax: (46) 1046 85015
Email: (firstname.lastname@storaenso.com)
Web Address: www.storaenso.com
Personnel:
Mill Dir.: Tommy Lodin
Phone: (46) 1046 75001
Fax: (46) 1046 85015
Email: tommy.lodin@storaenso.com
Prod. Mgr.: Geenny Bergstrom
Phone: (46) 1046 85000
Fax: (46) 1046 85015
Email: geenny.bergstrom@storaenso.com
Maint. Mgr.: Matts Hockman
Phone: (46) 1046 85000
Fax: (46) 1046 85015
Email: Matts.Hockman@storaenso.com
Mgr. Market Support: Marie Gower
Phone: (46) 1046 85000
Fax: (46) 1046 85015
Email: marie.gower@storaenso.com
Total Employees at this Location: 377
Type of Operation: Pulp mill
Pulp Grades and Capacities:
Total pulp capacity: 558,945 mt/y
Pulp available for market: 550,000 mt/y
Chemical Pulp: 558,945 mt/y

Pulp Mill Data:
Chemical Pulping Systems:
Continuous digesters: 2
Pulp Lines: 2
Bleach Plant Systems: 3
bleach plant 1, Sequence: O_2 DEopDED
bleach plant 3, Sequence: O_2 DEOpDEpD
bleach plant 4, Sequence: O_2 DQ(B)PO
Chemical Recovery Equipment:
Evaporator lines: 2
Recovery boilers: 2
Lime Kiln
Pulp Dryers:
Air Float dryers 1, Air Float dryers 1, Air Float dryers 1, Air Float dryers 1
Energy Data:
Power boilers: 1
Steam turbines: 1 at 46 MW
Wind turbines: 3 at 2, 2, 2 MW
Electrical demand for mill: 1,211 MWh/D

ⓜStora Enso Printing and Reading
Hylte Mill
Ownership: 100% by Stora Enso Oyj
SE-314 81 Hyltebruk
Sweden
Phone: (46) 1046 190 00
Fax: (46) 1046 188 76
Web Address: www.storaenso.com
Personnel:
Mill Mgr: Kenneth Ohlsson
Phone: (46) 1046 190 00
Fax: (46) 1046 188 76
Email: kenneth.ohlsson@storaenso.com
Snr. Mgr. Master Plan.: Jorgen Andersson
Phone: (46) 1046 190 00
Fax: (46) 1046 188 76
Email: jorgen.andersson@storaenso.com
Mgr. Process Develop.: Elisabet Tullander
Phone: (46) 1046 190 00
Fax: (46) 1046 188 76
Email: elisabet.tullander@storaenso.com
Total Employees at this Location: 470
Type of Operation: Pulp mill, Paper mill
Pulp Grades and Capacities:
Total pulp capacity: 500,299 mt/y
Mechanical Pulp: 250,251 mt/y

Sweden

Recycled Pulping: 250,251 mt/y
Pulp Mill Data:
Mechanical Pulping Systems:
TMP systems: 1
Pulp Lines: 2
Bleach Plant Systems: 2
DIP, Sequence: P
TMP, Sequence: P/Y
Recycled Fiber Treatment Lines:
Flotation deinking lines: 1 at 280,000
Paper/Paperboard Grades and Capacities:
Total paper and paperboard capacity: 485,000 mt/y
Newsprint: 485,000 mt/y
Paper and Paperboard Mill Data:
Paper Machines: 2
No. 3, SpeedFormer HS, total capacity 230,000 mt/y, Trim width 8.4 m, Newsprint
No. 4, Bel-Baie III, total capacity 255,000 mt/y, Trim width 8.4 m, Newsprint
Energy Data:
Power boilers: 4
HRSG boiler
Steam turbines: 1 at 28 MW
Electrical demand for mill: 2,428 MWh/D

Ⓜ Stora Enso Renewable Packaging
Skoghall Mill
Ownership: Stora Enso Oyj
Udden, P.O. Box 501
SE-663 29 Skoghall
Sweden
  Phone: (46) 1046 500 00
  Fax: (46) 1046 543 44
  Email: (firstname.lastname@storaenso.com)
  Web Address: www.storaenso.com
Personnel:
  Mill Mgr.: Carl-Johan Albinsson
  Phone: (46) 1046 500 00
  Fax: (46) 1046 543 44
  Email: carl-johan.albinsson@storaenso.com
  Tech. Mgr.: Thomas Olsson
  Phone: (46) 1046 73175
  Fax: (46) 1046 543 44
  Email: thomas.olsson@storaenso.com
  Commun. Mgr.: Kjell Kumlin
  Phone: (46) 1046 54303
  Fax: (46) 1046 543 44
  Email: kjell.kumlin@storaenso.com
  Env. Mgr.: Margareta Sandström
  Phone: (46) 1046 500 00
  Fax: (46) 1046 543 44
  Email: margareta.sandstrom@storaenso.com
Total Employees at this Location: 984
Type of Operation: Pulp mill, Paper mill, Paperboard mill
Pulp Grades and Capacities:
  Total pulp capacity: 559,611 mt/y
  Chemical Pulp: 320,531 mt/y
  Mechanical Pulp: 239,080 mt/y
Pulp Mill Data:
Chemical Pulping Systems:
  Continuous digesters: 1
Mechanical Pulping Systems:
  CTMP systems: 1
Bleach Plant Systems: 2
  CTMP, Sequence: P, Capacity 200,000 admt/y
  Kraft pulp, Type: OP)DQ(PO) Capacity 250,000 admt/y
Chemical Recovery Equipment:
  Evaporator lines: 2
  Recovery boilers: 1
  Lime Kiln
Paper/Paperboard Grades and Capacities:
  Total paper and paperboard capacity: 725,000 mt/y
  Linerboard: 80,000 mt/y
  Boxboard/cartonboard: 645,000 mt/y
Paper and Paperboard Mill Data:
Stock Preparation:
  Pulpers: 2
  Refiners: 28
Paper Machines: 2
No. 7, Bel-Bond, total capacity 300,000 mt/y, Trim width 5.4 m, Boxboard/cartonboard
No. 8, SymFormer, total capacity 425,000 mt/y, Trim width 8.1 m, Boxboard/cartonboard, Linerboard
Coating Machines: 2
PM 7, total capacity 300,000 mt/y., on machine
PM 8, total capacity 425,000 mt/y., on machine
Finishing Equipment:
Winders: 2
Energy Data:
Power boilers: 2
Steam turbines: 2 at 58, 19 MW
Electrical demand for mill: 2,736 MWh/D

Ⓜ Stora Enso Printing and Reading
Kvarnsveden Mill
Ownership: 100% by Stora Enso Oyj
SE-781 83 Borlänge
Sweden
  Phone: (46) 1046 650 00
  Fax: (46) 1046 653 90
  Web Address: www.storaenso.com
Personnel:
  Mill Mgr.: Mikko Jokio
  Phone: (46) 1046 650 00
  Fax: (46) 1046 653 90
  Email: mikko.jokio@storaenso.com
  Prod. Mgr. (Pulp): Per Skyttner
  Phone: (46) 1046 650 00
  Fax: (46) 1046 653 90
  Email: per.skyttner@storaenso.com
  Prod. Mgr. (paper): Anders Nordell
  Phone: (46) 1046 650 00
  Fax: (46) 1046 653 90
  Email: anders.e.nordell@storaenso.com
  Environ. Mgr.: Maria Edling-Hansson
  Phone: (46) 1046 650 00
  Fax: (46) 1046 653 90
  Email: maria.edling-hansson@storaenso.com
Total Employees at this Location: 524
Type of Operation: Pulp mill, Paper mill
Pulp Grades and Capacities:
  Total pulp capacity: 522,933 mt/y
  Mechanical Pulp: 522,933 mt/y
Pulp Mill Data:
Mechanical Pulping Systems:
  Conventional grinders: 1
  TMP systems: 3
Pulp Lines: 4
Bleach Plant Systems: 2
  SGW, Sequence: P, Capacity 100,000 admt/y
  TMP, Sequence: P/Y, Capacity 800,000 admt/y
Paper/Paperboard Grades and Capacities:
  Total paper and paperboard capacity: 750,000 mt/y
  Uncoated mechanical/groundwood: 750,000 mt/y
Paper and Paperboard Mill Data:
Stock Preparation:
  Pulpers: 3
  Refiners: 14
Paper Machines: 3
No. 8, SpeedFormer, total capacity 120,000 mt/y, Trim width 5.4 m, Uncoated mechanical/groundwood
No. 10, SpeedFormer HS, total capacity 210,000 mt/y, Trim width 8.4 m, Uncoated mechanical/groundwood
No. 12, OptiConcept, total capacity 420,000 mt/y, Trim width 10.4 m, Uncoated mechanical/groundwood
Finishing Equipment:
  Winders: 6 at 1,020,000 mt/y
  Supercalenders: 4 at 120,000 mt/y, 400,000 mt/y
Energy Data:
Power boilers: 3
TMP Reboiler: 1
Steam turbines: 1 at 15 MW
Electrical demand for mill: 4,986 MWh/D

ⒽⓂ Svanskog Bruk AB
Svanskog Mill
Ownership: Panier Pappenerzeunis HgmbH
SE-662 03 Svanskog
Sweden
  Phone: (46) 532 616 60
  Fax: (46) 532 300 50
  Email: info@svanskogbruk.se
  Web Address: www.svanskogbruk.se
Personnel:
  Mgr.: Anders Lind
  Phone: (46) 532 616 60
  Fax: (46) 532 300 50
  Email: a.lind@svanskogbruk.se
Total Employees of Company: 29
Total Employees at this Location: 29
Type of Operation: Paperboard mill
Paper/Paperboard Grades and Capacities:
  Total paper and paperboard capacity: 14,000 mt/y
  Boxboard/cartonboard: 14,000 mt/y
Paper and Paperboard Mill Data:
Paper Machines: 1
No. 1, multi-wire, total capacity 14,000 mt/y, Trim width 2 m, Boxboard/cartonboard
Finishing Equipment:
  Sheeters
Energy Data:
Power boilers
Electrical demand for mill: 14 MWh/D

ⒽⓂ Svenska Pappersbruket
Klippan Mill
Bruksallen 9
SE-264 39 Klippan
Sweden
  Phone: (46) 435 29100
  Fax: (46) 435 13915
  Email: info@klippans-bruk.se
  Web Address: www.colourtissue.com
Personnel:
  Owner: Bengt Thomasson
  Phone: (46) 706 568216
  Email: bengt.thomasson@meccom.se
  Owner, Man. Dir.: Olle Grundberg
  Phone: (46) 706 544420
  Email: olle.grundberg@bredband.net
  Mill Mgr.: Ronnie Pålsson
  Phone: (46) 435 29100
  Fax: (46) 435 13915
  Email: ronnie.palsson@klippansbruk.se
Total Employees at this Location: 36
Type of Operation: Paper mill
Paper/Paperboard Grades and Capacities:
  Total paper and paperboard capacity: 10,000 mt/y
  Tissue: 10,000 mt/y
Paper and Paperboard Mill Data:
Stock Preparation:
  Pulpers: 1
  Refiners: 1
Paper Machines: 1
No. 9, Advantage DCT, Yankee dryer, total capacity 10,000 mt/y, Trim width 1.66 m, Tissue
Finishing Equipment:
  Winders: 1
Energy Data:
Power boilers: 1
Electrical demand for mill: 29 MWh/D

Ⓜ Swedish Tissue AB
Kisa Mill
Ownership: 100% by Sofidel Group
SE-590 40 Kisa
Sweden
  Phone: (46) 494 15000
  Fax: (46) 494 15040
  Email: info@swedishtissue.se
  Web Address: www.swedishtissue.se
Personnel:
  Man. Dir.: Lorenzo Bianchi
  Phone: (46) 494 15000
  Fax: (46) 494 15040
  Email: lorenzo.bianchi@sofidel.it

Mill Mgr.: Lars Sjögren
Phone: (46) 494 15041
Fax: (46) 494 15045
Email: lars.sjogren@swedishtissue.se
Finan. Mgr.: Mikael Hermansson
Phone: (46) 494 15003
Fax: (46) 494 15040
Email: mikael.hermansson@swedishtissue.se
Purch. Officer: Jesper Banck
Phone: (46) 494 15023
Fax: (46) 494 15040
Email: jesper.banck@swedishtissue.se
Total Employees at this Location: 140
Type of Operation: Paper mill
Paper/Paperboard Grades and Capacities:
Total paper and paperboard capacity: 62,000 mt/y
Tissue: 62,000 mt/y
Paper and Paperboard Mill Data:
Paper Machines: 2
No. 3, crescent former, Yankee dryer, total capacity 40,000 mt/y, Trim width 3.37 m, Tissue
No. 4, crescent former, Yankee dryer, total capacity 22,000 mt/y, Trim width 2.64 m, Tissue
Energy Data:
Electrical demand for mill: 165 MWh/D

ⓘSwedPaper AB
Ownership: 100% by Private Investors
Korsnäsverken
SE-801 81 Gävle
Sweden
Email: info.sweden@ekmangroup.com
Web Address: www.swedpaper.com
Personnel:
Man. Dir.: Lars-Åke Brännström
Phone: (46) 70 580 23 37
Email: lars-ake.brannstrom@swedpaper.com
Prod. Mgr.: Per-Olov Welde
Phone: (46) 70 795 16 74
Email: per-olov.welde@swedpaper.com
Technology Mgr.: Peder Johansson
Phone: (46) 70 795 10 85
Email: peder.johansson@swedpaper.com
Sls. Mgr.: Annika Lenströmer
Phone: (46) 70 795 10 07
Email: annika.lenstromer@swedpaper.com
Mill Locations:
SwedPaper AB, Gävle Mill, Korsnäsverken, SE-801 81 Gävle, Sweden, Capacity: 70,000 mt/y, (Paper mill)
Email: info.sweden@ekmangroup.com

ⓘSwedPaper AB
Gävle Mill
Korsnäsverken
SE-801 81 Gävle
Sweden
Email: info.sweden@ekmangroup.com
Web Address: www.swedpaper.com
Personnel:
Man. Dir.: Lars-Åke Brännström
Phone: (46) 70 580 23 37
Email: lars-ake.brannstrom@swedpaper.com
Prod. Mgr.: Per-Olov Welde
Phone: (46) 70 795 16 74
Email: per-olov.welde@swedpaper.com
Technology Mgr.: Peder Johansson
Phone: (46) 70 795 10 85
Email: peder.johansson@swedpaper.com
Sls. Mgr.: Annika Lenströmer
Phone: (46) 70 795 10 07
Email: annika.lenstromer@swedpaper.com
Total Employees at this Location: 60
Type of Operation: Paper mill
Paper/Paperboard Grades and Capacities:
Total paper and paperboard capacity: 70,000 mt/y
Packaging papers: 70,000 mt/y
Paper and Paperboard Mill Data:
Paper Machines: 1
No. 2, fourdrinier, total capacity 70,000 mt/y, Trim width 5.2 m, Packaging papers

Energy Data:
Electrical demand for mill: 104 MWh/D

ⓘⓜWaggeryd Cell AB
Waggeryd Mill
Ownership: 100% by ATA Holding
PO Box 7
SE-567 21 Vaggeryd
Sweden
Phone: (46) 393 36200
Fax: (46) 393 36225
Email: mail@waggerydcell.se
Web Address: www.ata.nu, www.waggerydcell.se
Personnel:
Man. Dir. & CEO: Ulf Karlsson
Phone: (46) 393 36200
Fax: (46) 393 36225
Email: ulf.k@waggerydcell.se
Mktg. Mgr. & Commodity Purchases: Thomas Sandstedt
Phone: (46) 393 36208
Fax: (46) 393 36225
Email: thomas.s@waggerydcell.se
Total Employees of Company: 45
Total Employees at this Location: 45
Type of Operation: Pulp mill
Pulp Grades and Capacities:
Total pulp capacity: 137,217 mt/y
Pulp available for market: 135,000 mt/y
Mechanical Pulp: 137,217 mt/y
Pulp Mill Data:
Mechanical Pulping Systems:
BCTMP systems: 1
Bleach Plant Systems: 1
No. 1, Sequence: P, Capacity 175,000 admt/y
Pulp Dryers:
Flash dryers 1
Energy Data:
Power boilers: 1
TMP Reboiler: 1
Electrical demand for mill: 468 MWh/D

SWITZERLAND

ⓘAarepapier AG
Ownership: 100% by Model Holding AG
Langackerstr. 2
CH-5013 Niedergösgen
Switzerland
Phone: (41) 62 858 5151
Fax: (41) 62 858 5477
Web Address: www.modelgroup.com
Personnel:
Oper. Mgr.: Simon Schäfer
Phone: (41) 62 858 5151
Fax: (41) 62 858 5477
Finan. & HR: Andreas Wermuth
Phone: (41) 62 858 5151
Fax: (41) 62 858 5477
Total Employees of Company: 90
Mill Locations:
Aarepapier AG, Niedergösgen Mill, Langackerstr. 2, CH-5013 Niedergösgen, Switzerland, Capacity: 185,000 mt/y, (Paperboard mill)
Phone: (41) 62 858 5151
Fax: (41) 62 858 5477
Email: info.apn@modelgroup.com

ⓘAarepapier AG
Niedergösgen Mill
Langackerstr. 2
CH-5013 Niedergösgen
Switzerland
Phone: (41) 62 858 5151
Fax: (41) 62 858 5477
Email: info.apn@modelgroup.com

Web Address: www.modelgroup.com
Personnel:
Oper. Mgr.: Simon Schäfer
Phone: (41) 62 858 5151
Fax: (41) 62 858 5477
Finan. & HR: Andreas Wermuth
Phone: (41) 62 858 5151
Fax: (41) 62 858 5477
Total Employees at this Location: 90
Type of Operation: Paperboard mill
Pulp Grades and Capacities:
Total pulp capacity: 185,763 mt/y
Recycled Pulping: 185,763 mt/y
Pulp Mill Data:
Recycled Fiber Treatment Lines:
Pulpers: 2
Paper/Paperboard Grades and Capacities:
Total paper and paperboard capacity: 185,000 mt/y
Linerboard: 120,000 mt/y
Corrugating medium/fluting: 65,000 mt/y
Paper and Paperboard Mill Data:
Stock Preparation:
Pulpers: 3
Paper Machines: 1
No. 2, DuoFormer Base, total capacity 185,000 mt/y, Trim width 5.1 m, Linerboard, Corrugating medium/fluting
Finishing Equipment:
Winders: 1 at 160,000 mt/y
Energy Data:
Electrical demand for mill: 241 MWh/D

ⓘⓜCartaseta-Friedrich & Co.
Däniken Mill
Ownership: Fripa Papierfabrik Albert Friedrich KG
Sandackerstrasse 3
CH-4658 Däniken
Switzerland
Phone: (41) 62 288 16 00
Fax: (41) 62 288 16 21
Email: info@cartaseta.ch
Web Address: www.cartaseta.ch
Personnel:
Finan. Mgr.: Erika Christ
Phone: (41) 62 288 1622
Fax: (41) 62 288 1626
Email: christ@cartaseta.ch
Sls. Mgr.: Roberto Todaro
Phone: (41) 62 288 16 00
Fax: (41) 62 288 16 21
Email: todaro@cartaseta.ch
Total Employees of Company: 70
Total Employees at this Location: 70
Type of Operation: Paper mill
Pulp Grades and Capacities:
Total pulp capacity: 852 mt/y
Recycled Pulping: 852 mt/y
Pulp Mill Data:
Recycled Fiber Treatment Lines:
Pulpers: 1
Paper/Paperboard Grades and Capacities:
Total paper and paperboard capacity: 22,000 mt/y
Tissue: 22,000 mt/y
Paper and Paperboard Mill Data:
Stock Preparation:
Pulpers: 2
Refiners: 2
Paper Machines: 1
No. 3, crescent former, Yankee dryer, total capacity 22,000 mt/y, Trim width 2.7 m, Tissue
Finishing Equipment:
Rewinders: 1 at 22,000 mt/y
Energy Data:
Power boilers: 2
Electrical demand for mill: 57 MWh/D

ⓜKimberly-Clark GmbH
Niederbipp Mill
Ownership: Kimberly-Clark Corp.

Switzerland

Rotboden 1
CH-4704 Niederbipp
Switzerland
Mailing Address: Postfach 189, CH-4704 Niederbipp, Switzerland
 Phone: (41) 32 633 51 11
 Fax: (41) 32 633 51 00
 Web Address: www.kimberly-clark.com
Personnel:
 Mill Mgr.: Reinhard Waas
 Phone: (41) 32 633 52 20
 Fax: (41) 32 633 51 20
 Email: reinhard.waas@kcc.com
Total Employees at this Location: 330
Type of Operation: Paper mill
Pulp Grades and Capacities:
 Total pulp capacity: 40,000 mt/y
 Pulp available for market: 11,000 mt/y
 Recycled Pulping: 40,000 mt/y
Pulp Mill Data:
 Bleach Plant Systems: 1
 deinked pulp
 Recycled Fiber Treatment Lines:
 Flotation deinking lines: 1
 Pulp Dryers:
 Wet Lap machine 1
Paper/Paperboard Grades and Capacities:
 Total paper and paperboard capacity: 47,000 mt/y
 Tissue: 47,000 mt/y
Paper and Paperboard Mill Data:
Paper Machines: 2
 No. 1, twin-wire, Yankee dryer, total capacity 22,000 mt/y, Trim width 2.4 m, Tissue
 No. 2, twin-wire, Yankee dryer, total capacity 25,000 mt/y, Trim width 2.42 m, Tissue
Energy Data:
 Power boilers: 1
 Steam turbines: 1 at 12 MW
 Electrical demand for mill: 164 MWh/D

ⓜLandqart AG
Landqart Mill
Ownership: Fortress Paper Ltd.
Kantonsstrasse 16
CH-7302 Landquart
Switzerland
 Phone: (41) 81 307 90 90
 Fax: (41) 81 307 91 41
 Email: info@landqart.com
 Web Address: www.landqart.com
Personnel:
 CEO (Eff. July 1, 2013): Axel Wappler
 Phone: (41) 81 307 9090
 Fax: (41) 81 307 9141
 Email: axel.wappler@landqart.com
 Assistant Management Team: Susi Borghi
 Phone: (41) 81 307 9203
 Fax: (41) 81 307 9141
 Email: susi.borghi@landqart.com
Total Employees at this Location: 250
Type of Operation: Paper mill
Paper/Paperboard Grades and Capacities:
 Total paper and paperboard capacity: 22,000 mt/y
 Uncoated woodfree/freesheet: 22,000 mt/y
Paper and Paperboard Mill Data:
Paper Machines: 2
 No. 1, fourdrinier, total capacity 10,000 mt/y, Uncoated woodfree/freesheet
 No. 2, (machine only operates when additional capacity is required), total capacity 12,000 mt/y, Uncoated woodfree/freesheet

ⓘⓜPapierfabrik Netstal AG
Netstal Mill
Ownership: 100% by G.T. Mandl Ltd.
Industrie Kleinzaun
CH-8754 Netstal, Glarus
Switzerland
Mailing Address: Postf. 135, CH-8754 Netstal, Glarus, Switzerland
 Phone: (41) 55 645 70 80
 Fax: (41) 55 645 70 81
 Email: info@pfn.ch
 Web Address: www.pfn.ch
Personnel:
 Man. Dir.: Christian Höpper
 Phone: (41) 55 645 7090
 Fax: (41) 55 645 70 81
 Email: christian.hoepper@pfn.ch
 Plt. Mgr.: Volker Greschner
 Phone: (41) 55 645 70 85
 Fax: (41) 55 645 70 81
 Email: volker.greschner@pfn.ch
 Prod. Mgr.: Anton Rajkovic
 Phone: (41) 55 645 70 82
 Fax: (41) 55 645 70 81
 Email: anton.rajkovic@pfn.ch
 Sls. Mgr.: Andreas Zindel
 Phone: (41) 55 645 70 99
 Fax: (41) 55 645 70 81
 Email: andreas.zindel@pfn.ch
Total Employees of Company: 30
Total Employees at this Location: 30
Type of Operation: Paper mill
Paper/Paperboard Grades and Capacities:
 Total paper and paperboard capacity: 20,000 mt/y
 Tissue: 2,500 mt/y
 Specialty and industrial: 17,500 mt/y
Paper and Paperboard Mill Data:
 Stock Preparation:
 Pulpers: 1
 Refiners: 3
Paper Machines: 1
 No. 1, fourdrinier, total capacity 20,000 mt/y, Trim width 2.25 m, Specialty and industrial, Tissue
Finishing Equipment:
 Rewinders: 2
 Sheeters: 1
Energy Data:
 Power boilers: 1
 Hydro turbines: 1 at 1.1 MW
 Electrical demand for mill: 47 MWh/D

ⓘPapierfabrik Utzenstorf AG
Ownership: 100% by management
Postfach, Fabrikstrasse
CH-3427 Utzenstorf
Switzerland
 Phone: (41) 32 671 4545
 Fax: (41) 32 671 4555
 Email: info@utzenstorf-papier.ch
 Web Address: www.utzenstorf-papier.ch
Personnel:
 Pres.: Bernhard Ludwig
 Phone: (41) 32 671 4600
 Fax: (41) 32 671 4712
 Email: bernhard.ludwig@utzenstorf-papier.ch
 Man. Dir.: Stefan Endras
 Phone: (41) 32 671 4502
 Fax: (41) 32 671 4712
 Email: stefan.endras@utzenstorf-papier.ch
 Finan. Mgr.: Riccardo Incerti
 Phone: (41) 32 671 4604
 Fax: (41) 32 671 4555
 Email: riccardo.incerti@utzenstorf-papier.ch
 Sls. & Mktg. Mgr.: Alfonso Sciullo
 Phone: (41) 32 671 46 30
 Fax: (41) 32 671 45 55
 Email: alfonso.sciullo@utzenstorf-papier.ch
 Head of Service & PaperWork: Alain Probst
 Phone: (41) 32 671 49 24
 Fax: (41) 32 671 45 55
 Email: alain.probst@utzenstorf-papier.ch
 Prod. Mgr.: Jonas Loud
 Phone: (41) 32 671 48 59
 Fax: (41) 32 671 45 55
 Email: jonas.lauter@utzenstorf-papier.ch
 Head Sales Office: Thomas Keller
 Phone: (41) 32 671 46 33
 Fax: (41) 32 671 45 55
 Email: thomas.keller@utzenstorf-papier.ch
 HR Mgr.: Hanspeter Ryser
 Phone: (41) 32 671 46 52
 Fax: (41) 32 671 45 55
 Email: hanspeter.ryser@utzenstorf-papier.ch
 Marketing & Communications: Andrea Morone
 Phone: (41) 32 671 47 02
 Fax: (41) 32 671 45 55
 Email: andrea.morone@utzenstorf-papier.ch
Total Employees of Company: 250
Total Employees at this Location: 230
Mill Locations:
 Papierfabrik Utzenstorf AG, Utzenstorf Mill, Postfach, Fabrikstrasse, CH-3427 Utzenstorf, Switzerland, Capacity: 210,000 mt/y, (Pulp mill, Paper mill)
 Phone: (41) 32 671 4545
 Fax: (41) 32 671 4555
 Email: info@utzenstorf-papier.ch

ⓘPapierfabrik Utzenstorf AG
Utzenstorf Mill
Postfach, Fabrikstrasse
CH-3427 Utzenstorf
Switzerland
 Phone: (41) 32 671 4545
 Fax: (41) 32 671 4555
 Email: info@utzenstorf-papier.ch
 Web Address: www.utzenstorf-papier.ch
Personnel:
 Pres.: Bernhard Ludwig
 Phone: (41) 32 671 4600
 Fax: (41) 32 671 4712
 Email: bernhard.ludwig@utzenstorf-papier.ch
 Man. Dir.: Stefan Endras
 Phone: (41) 32 671 4502
 Fax: (41) 32 671 4712
 Email: stefan.endras@utzenstorf-papier.ch
 Finan. Mgr.: Riccardo Incerti
 Phone: (41) 32 671 4604
 Fax: (41) 32 671 4555
 Email: riccardo.incerti@utzenstorf-papier.ch
 Sls. & Mktg. Mgr.: Alonso Sciullo
 Phone: (41) 32 671 4630
 Fax: (41) 32 671 4555
 Email: alonso.sciullo@utzenstorf-papier.ch
Total Employees at this Location: 260
Type of Operation: Pulp mill, Paper mill
Pulp Grades and Capacities:
 Total pulp capacity: 216,009 mt/y
 Mechanical Pulp: 17,490 mt/y
 Recycled Pulping: 198,519 mt/y
Pulp Mill Data:
 Mechanical Pulping Systems:
 Conventional grinders: 8
 Bleach Plant Systems: 2
 Recycled Fiber Treatment Lines:
 Flotation deinking lines: 2 at 235,000 admt/y
 Pulpers: 2 at 235,000 admt/y
Paper/Paperboard Grades and Capacities:
 Total paper and paperboard capacity: 210,000 mt/y
 Newsprint: 131,250 mt/y
 Uncoated mechanical/groundwood: 78,750 mt/y
Paper and Paperboard Mill Data:
Paper Machines: 2
 No. 1, DuoFormer, total capacity 105,000 mt/y, Trim width 4.16 m, Newsprint, Uncoated mechanical/groundwood
 No. 2, DuoFormer, total capacity 105,000 mt/y, Trim width 4.16 m, Newsprint, Uncoated mechanical/groundwood
Finishing Equipment:
 Winders: 3 at 210,000 mt/y
 Rewinders: 1 at 3,500 mt/y
Energy Data:
 Power boilers: 3
 Steam turbines: 1 at 5.5 MW
 Hydro turbines: 1 at 0.4 MW
 Electrical demand for mill: 577 MWh/D

Switzerland

ⓄⓂPerlen Papier AG
Perlen Mill
Ownership: 100% by CPH Chemie & Perlen Holding AG
Dorfstrasse
CH-6035 Perlen
Switzerland
  Phone: (41) 41 455 80 00
  Fax: (41) 41 455 80 01
  Email: info@perlen.ch
  Web Address: www.perlen.ch
Personnel:
Chmn.: Peter Schaub
  Phone: (41) 41 4558000
  Fax: (41) 41 4558004
  Email: peter.schaub@perlen.ch
CEO: Klemens Gottstein
  Phone: (41) 41 4558056
  Fax: (41) 41 4558004
  Email: klemens.gottstein@perlen.ch
CFO: Markus Keller
  Phone: (41) 41 4558062
  Fax: (41) 41 4558004
  Email: markus.keller@perlen.ch
Paper Mill Dir.: Ansgar Tiller
  Phone: (41) 41 4558122
  Fax: (41) 41 4558013
  Email: ansgar.tiller@perlen.ch
Technology & Energy: Dirk Breuer
  Phone: (41) 41 4558405
  Fax: (41) 41 4558002
  Email: dirk.breuer@perlen.ch
Sls. & Mktg. Mgr.: Andreas Straub
  Phone: (41) 41 4558000
  Fax: (41) 41 455 8001
  Email: andreas.straub@perlen.ch
Prod. Mgr.: Karsten von Malottki
  Phone: (41) 41 4558000
  Fax: (41) 41 455 8001
  Email: karsten.vonMalottki@perlen.ch
Total Employees of Company: 385
Total Employees at this Location: 380
Type of Operation: Pulp mill, Paper mill
Pulp Grades and Capacities:
  Total pulp capacity: 497,987 mt/y
  Mechanical Pulp: 126,523 mt/y
  Recycled Pulping: 371,463 mt/y
Pulp Mill Data:
  Mechanical Pulping Systems:
  TMP systems: 1
Pulp Lines: 3
  Bleach Plant Systems: 2
  Deinked pulp, Sequence: HS-P, Capacity 430,000 admt/y
  TMP, Sequence: HS-P, Capacity 135,000 admt/y
  Recycled Fiber Treatment Lines:
  Flotation deinking lines: 1 at 170,000 admt/y
  Flotation deinking lines: 1 at 260,000
Paper/Paperboard Grades and Capacities:
  Total paper and paperboard capacity: 549,986 mt/y
  Newsprint: 287,986 mt/y
  Uncoated mechanical/groundwood: 72,000 mt/y
  Coated mechanical/groundwood: 190,000 mt/y
Paper and Paperboard Mill Data:
  Stock Preparation:
  Pulpers: 1
Paper Machines: 2
No. 4, DuoFormer TQv, total capacity 190,000 mt/y, Trim width 5.32 m, Coated mechanical/groundwood
No. 7, DuoFormer TQv, total capacity 360,000 mt/y, Trim width 9.6 m, Newsprint, Uncoated mechanical/groundwood
Coating Machines: 1
PM 4, total capacity 190,000 mt/y., on machine
Energy Data:
Power boilers: 3
TMP Reboiler: 1
Steam turbines: 2
Hydro turbines: 1 at 1 MW
Electrical demand for mill: 1,845 MWh/D

ⓂSaber Swiss Quality Paper AG
Balsthal Mill
Ownership: Saber Group
Tiergartenstr. 1
CH-4710 Balsthal
Switzerland
  Phone: (41) 62 386 4111
  Fax: (41) 62 386 4123
  Email: info@swissqualitypaper.com
  Web Address: www.swissqualitypaper.com
Personnel:
CEO: Thomas Bichler
  Phone: (41) 62 386 4267
  Fax: (41) 62 386 4121
  Email: thomas.bichler@swissqualitypaper.com
Head of Sls. & Mktg.: Sascha Spielmann
  Phone: (41) 62 386 4271
  Fax: (41) 62 386 4123
  Email: sascha.spielmann@swissqualitypaper.com
Head of Prod.: Roland Zieri
  Phone: (41) 62 386 4111
  Fax: (41) 62 386 4121
  Email: roland.zieri@swissqualitypaper.com
Tech. Mgr.: Rolf Künzler
  Phone: (41) 62 386 4111
  Fax: (41) 62 386 4121
  Email: rolf.kuenzler@swissqualitypaper.com
Chief Eng. & Environ. Mgr.: Franz-Ulrich Seydel
  Phone: (41) 62 386 4111
  Fax: (41) 62 386 4121
  Email: ulrich.seydel@swissqualitypaper.com
R&D Mgr.: Laurence Jungo
  Phone: (41) 62 386 4320
  Fax: (41) 62 386 4121
  Email: laurence.jungo@swissqualitypaper.com
Total Employees at this Location: 113
Type of Operation: Paper mill
Pulp Mill Data:
  Recycled Fiber Treatment Lines:
  Pulpers: 1 at 50,000 admt/y
Paper/Paperboard Grades and Capacities:
  Total paper and paperboard capacity: 37,000 mt/y
  Tissue: 9,000 mt/y
  Specialty and industrial: 28,000 mt/y
Paper and Paperboard Mill Data:
  Stock Preparation:
  Pulpers: 3
  Refiners: 3
Paper Machines: 1
PM 3, Yankee dryer, total capacity 28,000 mt/y, Trim width 3.1 m, Specialty and industrial
Finishing Equipment:
  Rewinders: 3 at 40,000 mt/y

ⓄⓂThurpapier, Model AG
Weinfelden Mill
Industriestr. 30
CH-8570 Weinfelden
Switzerland
  Phone: (41) 71 626 76 21
  Fax: (41) 71 626 76 22
  Email: nfo.moh@modelgroup.com
  Web Address: www.modelgroup.com
Personnel:
Chmn.: Daniel Model
  Phone: (41) 71 626 7777
  Fax: (41) 71 626 7788
  Email: daniel.model@modelgroup.com
Mill Mgr.: Andreas Klumpp
  Phone: (41) 71 626 7299
  Fax: (41) 71 626 7622
  Email: andreas.klumpp@modelgroup.com
Papertrading Mgr.: Stephan Schad
  Phone: (41) 71 626 7239
  Fax: (41) 71 626 7622
  Email: stephan.schad@modelgroup.com
Prod. Plann. Mgr.: Ernst Hess
  Phone: (41) 71 626 7251
  Fax: (41) 71 626 7622
  Email: ernst.hess@modelgroup.com
Tech. Mgr.: Ernst Herzog
  Phone: (41) 71 626 7777
  Fax: (41) 71 626 7788
  Email: ernst.herzog@modelgroup.com
Total Employees of Company: 100
Total Employees at this Location: 100
Type of Operation: Paperboard mill
Pulp Grades and Capacities:
  Total pulp capacity: 160,712 mt/y
  Recycled Pulping: 160,712 mt/y
Pulp Mill Data:
  Recycled Fiber Treatment Lines:
  Recycled packaging pulping lines: 1
Paper/Paperboard Grades and Capacities:
  Total paper and paperboard capacity: 160,000 mt/y
  Linerboard: 80,000 mt/y
  Corrugating medium/fluting: 80,000 mt/y
Paper and Paperboard Mill Data:
  Stock Preparation:
  Pulpers: 2
Paper Machines: 2
No. 1, fourdrinier, total capacity 50,000 mt/y, Trim width 2.5 m, Corrugating medium/fluting, Linerboard
No. 2, fourdrinier (2), total capacity 110,000 mt/y, Trim width 2.5 m, Corrugating medium/fluting, Linerboard
Finishing Equipment:
  Rewinders: 2
Energy Data:
Power boilers: 2
Steam turbines: 1 at 1.2 MW
Electrical demand for mill: 192 MWh/D

ⓂWeidmann Electrical Technology AG
Rapperswil Mill
Ownership: 100% by Wicor Group
Neue Jonastr. 60
CH-8640 Rapperswil
Switzerland
  Phone: (41) 55 221 4103
  Fax: (41) 55 221 4674
  Email: sales.wetag@wicor.com
  Web Address: www.weidmann-electrical.com
Personnel:
CEO: Marcel Sutter
  Phone: (41) 55 221 43 72
  Email: marcel.sutter@wicor.com
Technol. Mgr.: Christoph Krause
  Phone: (41) 55 221 4490
  Fax: (41) 55 222 8376
  Email: christoph.krause@wicor.com
Qlty. Mgr.: Rolf Eberle
  Phone: (41) 55 221 4331
  Email: rolf.eberle@wicor.com
Total Employees at this Location: 500
Type of Operation: Paperboard mill
Paper/Paperboard Grades and Capacities:
  Total paper and paperboard capacity: 20,000 mt/y
  Boxboard/cartonboard: 20,000 mt/y
Paper and Paperboard Mill Data:
Paper Machines: 3
BM 5, fourdrinier, Trim width 2.4 m, Boxboard/cartonboard
BM 6, cylinder, Trim width 3.2 m, Boxboard/cartonboard
BM 9, cylinder
Finishing Equipment:
  Supercalenders: 3

ⓄWicor Group
Ownership: 100% by private owner
Neue Jonastr. 60
CH-8640 Rapperswil
Switzerland
  Phone: (41) 55 221 4109, 55 221 4152
  Fax: (41) 55 221 4160
  Email: sales.wetag@wicor.com, wicor.info@wicor.com
  Web Address: www.wicor.com
Personnel:

Ukraine

Chmn.: Prof. Dr. Ulrich W. Suter
Phone: (41) 55 221 4109
Fax: (41) 55 221 41 60
CEO: Franziska Sauber Tschudi
Phone: (41) 55 221 41 52
Fax: (41) 55 221 41 60
Email: franziska.tschudi@wicor.com
Bd. Mbr.: Dr. Rudolf Huber
Phone: (41) 55 221 4109
Fax: (41) 55 221 41 60
Bd. Mbr.: Dean A. Yannucci
Phone: (41) 55 221 4109
Fax: (41) 55 221 41 60
CFO: Oliver Kopp
Phone: (41) 55 221 4109
Fax: (41) 55 221 41 60
Man. Dir.: Jürg Brunner
Phone: (41) 55 221 4111
Fax: (41) 55 221 4681
Email: jurg.brunner@wicor.com
Mktg. Dir.: Gianni Heldmaier
Phone: (41) 55 221 4111
Fax: (41) 55 221 4681
Email: gianni.heldmaier@wicor.com
Prod. Mgr. (Components): Reto Caspani
Phone: (41) 55 221 4111
Fax: (41) 55 221 4681
Email: reto.caspani@wicor.com
Prod. Mgr. (Board Mill): Andreas Uecker
Phone: (41) 55 221 4111
Fax: (41) 55 221 4681
Email: andreas.uecker@wicor.com
Total Employees of Company: 3,740
Mill Locations:
Jiangsu Taizhou Weidmann High Voltage Insulation Co. Ltd, Taizhou Mill (50% owned), No.40 Haiyang Rd., Taizhou 225300, China, Capacity: 7,500 mt/y, (Paper mill)
Phone: (86) 523 8656 6972/8655 9379/8284 8691
Fax: (86) 523 8656 0610
Email: michael.xu@weidmann.com.hk; xuluping@weidmann.com.cn
Malyn - Weidmann Paper Mill VAT, Malyn Mill (95% owned), vul. Prikhodska 66, 11602 Malyn, Ukraine, Capacity: 17,800 mt/y, (Paper mill, Paperboard mill)
Phone: (380) 4133 67222
Fax: (380) 4133 53343
Email: mpf@malin.zt.ua, info@wicor.com, info.wmpm@wicor.com, wicor@wicor.kiev.ua
Weidmann Electrical Technology AG, Rapperswil Mill, Neue Jonastr. 60, CH-8640 Rapperswil, Switzerland, Capacity: 20,000 mt/y, (Paperboard mill)
Phone: (41) 55 221 4103
Fax: (41) 55 221 4674
Email: sales.wetag@wicor.com
Weidmann Electrical Technology Inc., Saint Johnsbury Mill, One Gordon Mills Way, Saint Johnsbury, VT 05819, USA, Capacity: 13,608 mt/y, (Paperboard mill)
Phone: (1) 802-748-3936
Fax: (1) 802-748-3897
Email: service.weti@wicor.com
Weidmann Electrical Technology Inc., Howard Mill, 700 W Court St, Urbana, OH 43078, USA, (Paper mill)
Phone: (1) 937 652 1220
Fax: (1) 937-652-1722
Email: service.weti@wicor.com
Weidmann Whiteley Ltd., Otley Mill, Pool-in-Wharfedale, Otley LS21 1RP, United Kingdom, Capacity: 12,500 mt/y, (Paperboard mill)
Phone: (44) 113 202 7000
Fax: (44) 113 284 2272
Email: sales.whiteley@wicor.com

①⑩Ziegler Papier AG
Grellingen Mill
Ownership: 100% by Kuttler-Frey family
Bahnhofstr. 21
CH-4203 Grellingen
Switzerland
Phone: (41) 61 745 12 12
Fax: (41) 61 745 12 66
Email: info@zieglerpapier.com
Web Address: www.zieglerpapier.com
Personnel:
CEO & Man. Dir.: Philipp Kuttler
Phone: (41) 61 745 12 12
Fax: (41) 61 745 12 66
Email: philipp.kuttler@zieglerpapier.com
CFO & Man. Dir.: Isabel Frey Kuttler
Phone: (41) 61 745 12 12
Fax: (41) 61 745 12 66
Email: isabel.kuttler@zieglerpapier.com
Head of Sls.: Susanne Oste
Phone: (41) 61 745 12 50
Fax: (41) 61 745 12 66
Email: susanne.oste@zieglerpapier.com
Prod. Mgr.: Dr. Jens Besser
Phone: (41) 61 745 13 07
Fax: (41) 61 745 12 66
Email: jens.besser@zieglerpapier.com
Eng. Mgr.: René Thoma
Phone: (41) 61 745 13 41
Fax: (41) 61 745 12 66
Email: rene.thoma@zieglerpapier.com
Head of Technology: Dr. Andreas Schüssele
Phone: (41) 61 745 12 33
Fax: (41) 61 745 12 66
Email: andreas.schuessele@zieglerpapier.com
Total Employees of Company: 182
Total Employees at this Location: 182
Type of Operation: Paper mill
Paper/Paperboard Grades and Capacities:
Total paper and paperboard capacity: 75,000 mt/y
Uncoated woodfree/freesheet: 75,000 mt/y
Paper and Paperboard Mill Data:
Stock Preparation:
Pulpers: 2
Refiners: 4
Paper Machines: 1
No. 3, hybrid former, total capacity 75,000 mt/y, Trim width 3.31 m, Uncoated woodfree/freesheet
Finishing Equipment:
Rewinders: 1 at 60,000 mt/y
Sheeters: 1 at 25,000 mt/y
Energy Data:
Power boilers: 1
Combustion turbines: 1 at 4.0 MW
Hydro turbines: 4 at 1.5 MW
Electrical demand for mill: 122 MWh/D

UKRAINE

①Albatros Paper Mill
Stroitelei Str. 60 Dnepropetrovsk, 49089
Dnepropetrovsk
Ukraine
Mailing Address: 4572, 49085 Dnepropetrovsk, Ukraine
Phone: (380) 562 341 899/790 5040,44,46
Fax: (380) 562 340 589
Email: albatros_info@mail.ru, albatros_burnaga@i.ua
Web Address: www.albatros.com.ua
Personnel:
Mill Dir.: Serguey Katsyuba
Phone: (213) 380 562 34 18 99
Fax: (213) 567 905040
Tech. Dir.: Alexei Tcherniak
Phone: (213) 380 562 34 18 99
Fax: (213) 567 905040
Technol. Mgr.: Alexei Tkachenko
Phone: (213) 380 562 34 18 99
Fax: (213) 567 905040
Total Employees of Company: 75
Mill Locations:
Albatros Paper Mill, Dnepropetrovsk Mill, Stroitelei Str. 60, 49089 Dnepropetrovsk, Ukraine, Capacity: 12,000 mt/y, (Paper mill)
Phone: (380) 562 341 899/790 5040,44,46
Fax: (380) 562 340 589
Email: albatros_info@mail.ru, albatros_burnaga@i.ua

①⑩Albatros Paper Mill
Dnepropetrovsk Mill
Stroitelei Str. 60
49089 Dnepropetrovsk
Ukraine
Mailing Address: 4572, 49085 Dnepropetrovsk, Ukraine
Phone: (380) 562 341 899/790 5040,44,46
Fax: (380) 562 340 589
Email: albatros_info@mail.ru, albatros_burnaga@i.ua
Web Address: www.albatros.com.ua
Personnel:
Mill Dir.: Serguey Katsyuba
Phone: (380) 562 34 18 99/567 905040
Tech. Dir.: Alexei Tcherniak
Phone: (380) 562 34 18 99/567 905040
Email: albatros_burnaga@i.ua
Technology Mgr./PM 1: Alexei Tkachenko
Phone: (380) 562 34 18 99/567 905040
Total Employees at this Location: 75
Type of Operation: Paper mill
Paper/Paperboard Grades and Capacities:
Total paper and paperboard capacity: 12,000 mt/y
Tissue: 12,000 mt/y
Paper and Paperboard Mill Data:
Paper Machines: 1
PM 1, fourdrinier, Trim width 3.4 m, Tissue
Energy Data:
Combustion turbines: 3
Electrical demand for mill: 25 MWh/D

①⑩OOO Ametist
Chernigov Mill
Industrialnaya Str. 11
14001 Chernigov
Ukraine
Mailing Address: Ushinskogo Str. 4, 14014 Chernigov, Ukraine
Phone: (380) 462 973365
Fax: (380) 462 973467
Email: pametist@rambler.ru
Personnel:
Mgr.: Valery Radchenko
Phone: (380) 503 130131
Total Employees at this Location: 47
Type of Operation: Paper mill
Paper/Paperboard Grades and Capacities:
Total paper and paperboard capacity: 3,000 mt/y
Tissue: 3,000 mt/y

①⑩OOO ASS-Korostyshiv Paper Mill
Korostyshiv Mill
vul. Proletarska 31
12500 Korostyshiv
Ukraine
Phone: (380) 4130 52189 / 52188
Fax: (380) 4130 52189 / 52188
Email: korostishev@accworld.com.ua
Personnel:
Sales Mngr.: Natalia Alekseevna Gutovskaya
Dir.: Yuriy Frankovich Krishikha
Phone: (380) 4130 35323/29
Chief Eng.: Vitaliy Anatoliyovych Shkabara
Phone: (380) 4130 35323/29
Chief. Tech.: Olga Mykolayivna Budnik
Phone: (380) 4130 35323/29
Sls. Mgr.: Oleh Viktorovych Kovalchuk
Phone: (380) 4130 32196
Total Employees at this Location: 166
Type of Operation: Paper mill
Paper/Paperboard Grades and Capacities:
Total paper and paperboard capacity: 6,000 mt/y
Uncoated woodfree/freesheet: 6,000 mt/y

Ukraine

Paper and Paperboard Mill Data:
Paper Machines: 1
No. 1, total capacity 6,000 mt/y, Trim width 1.68 m, Uncoated woodfree/freesheet

ⓜBanknote Paper Mill
ul. Prikhodko, 62 Malin, Zhitomirskaya obl., 11602
Zhitomirskaya obl.
Ukraine
  Phone: (380) 4133 52773/52407
  Fax: (380) 4133 52407
  Email: info@fpb.bank.gov.ua
Personnel:
  Dir.: Vasiliy Ischenko
  Phone: (380) 4133 52773
  Fax: (380) 4133 52407
Total Employees of Company: 400
Mill Locations:
  Banknote Paper Mill, Malin Mill, ul. Prikhodko, 62, 11602 Malin, Ukraine, Capacity: 20,000 mt/y, (Paper mill)
  Phone: (380) 4133 52773/52407
  Fax: (380) 4133 52407
  Email: info@fpb.bank.gov.ua

ⓜBanknote Paper Mill
Malin Mill
ul. Prikhodko, 62
11602 Malin, Zhitomirskaya obl.
Ukraine
  Phone: (380) 4133 52773/52407
  Fax: (380) 4133 52407
  Email: info@fpb.bank.gov.ua
Personnel:
  Dir.: Vasiliy Ischenko
  Phone: (380) 4133 51366
Total Employees at this Location: 400
Type of Operation: Paper mill
Paper/Paperboard Grades and Capacities:
  Total paper and paperboard capacity: 20,000 mt/y
  Uncoated woodfree/freesheet: 20,000 mt/y
Paper and Paperboard Mill Data:
Paper Machines: 1
  PM 1, (Former Type model: Rundsieb/Rundsiebformer.), round former, total capacity 20,000 mt/y, Trim width 1.84 m, Uncoated woodfree/freesheet
Energy Data:
  Combustion turbines: 1
  Electrical demand for mill: 40 MWh/D

ⓜOOO Bely Kamen Paper Mill
Bely Kamen Mill
80710 Bely Kamen
Ukraine
  Phone: (380) 32 65 5 87 30 / 32 939644 / 32 939643
  Fax: (380) 3265 5 87 30
Personnel:
  Gen.Dir.: Mikhail Tkachishyn
  Phone: (380) 32 939644 / 32 939643
Type of Operation: Paper mill
Paper/Paperboard Grades and Capacities:
  Total paper and paperboard capacity: 8,000 mt/y
  Tissue: 8,000 mt/y
Paper and Paperboard Mill Data:
Paper Machines: 2
  PM 1, Trim width 2.1 m, Tissue
  PM 2, Trim width 2.1 m, Tissue

ⓜChizhovskaya Paper Mill
Novograd-Volynskiy Mill
Tarasa Shevchenka Str. 16
11725 Chizhovka, Novograd-Volynskiy rayon, Zhitomirskaya obl.
Ukraine
  Phone: (380) 4141 68435, 67 2353561 (GSM)
  Fax: (380) 4141 68435
  Email: karton@i.ua
Personnel:
  Chmn. & Man. Dir.: Aleksandr Ivanovich Basov
  Phone: (380) 4141 68435, 67 2353561 (GSM)
Total Employees at this Location: 160
Type of Operation: Paper mill
Paper/Paperboard Grades and Capacities:
  Total paper and paperboard capacity: 12,000 mt/y
  Linerboard: 4,000 mt/y
  Corrugating medium/fluting: 8,000 mt/y
Paper and Paperboard Mill Data:
Paper Machines: 1
  No. 1, total capacity 12,000 mt/y, Trim width 1.8 m, Linerboard, Corrugating medium/fluting
Energy Data:
  Hydro turbines: 1

ⓜChizhovskaya Paper Mill
Tarasa Shevchenka Str. 16 Chizhovka, Novograd-Volynskiy rayon, Zhitomirskaya obl., 11725
Novograd-Volynskiy
Ukraine
  Phone: (380) 4141 68435, 67 2353561
  Fax: (380) 4141 68435
  Email: karton@i.ua
Personnel:
  Chmn. & Man. Dir.: Aleksandr Ivanovich Basov
  Phone: (380) 4141 68435, 67 2353561
  Fax: (380) 4141 68435
Total Employees of Company: 160
Mill Locations:
  Chizhovskaya Paper Mill, Novograd-Volynskiy Mill, Tarasa Shevchenka Str. 16, 11725 Chizhovka, Novograd-Volynskiy rayon, Ukraine, Capacity: 12,000 mt/y, (Paper mill)
  Phone: (380) 4141 68435, 67 2353561 (GSM)
  Fax: (380) 4141 68435
  Email: karton@i.ua

ⓜDnepropetrovsk Paper Mill, Ltd.
Ownership: 100% by ComputerLand
ul. Kaspijskaya 2
49034 Dnepropetrovsk
Ukraine
  Phone: (380) 5672 50405/50660
  Fax: (380) 5672 50405/50660
  Email: dbf@dbf.com.ua, sales@dbf.com.ua
  Web Address: www.dbf.com.ua
Personnel:
  Dir.: Sergey Petrovich Sak
  Phone: (380) 5672 50405/50660
  Fax: (380) 5672 50405
  Prod. Dir.: Ivan Vasilievich Ponomarenko
  Phone: (380) 56 7250384
  Fax: (380) 5672 50405
  Export Sls. Dir.: Aleksey Krivosheev
  Phone: (380) 56 725 0660, 979208268
  Fax: (380) 5672 50405
  Deputy Tech. Dir.: Vladimir Mikhailovich Obukhov
  Phone: (380) 5672 50405/50660
  Fax: (380) 5672 50405
  Tech. Mgr.: Dmitriy Vladimirovich Khudeev
  Phone: (380) 56 7250384
  Fax: (380) 5672 50405
  Export Sls Mgr. Toilet Paper Roll: Kalaychyan Vartan Dzhivanovich
  Phone: (380) 63 470 88 46
  Fax: (380) 56 725 0660
  Email: vartan@dbf.com.ua
  Head of QA: Kozhumnyaka Victoria V.
  Phone: (380) 56 725 0405
  Fax: (380) 56 725 0660
Total Employees of Company: 540
Total Employees at this Location: 540
Mill Locations:
  Dnepropetrovsk Paper Mill, Ltd., Dnepropetrovsk Mill, ul. Kaspijskaya 2, 49034 Dnepropetrovsk, Ukraine, Capacity: 61,000 mt/y, (Paper mill)
  Phone: (380) 5672 50405/50660
  Fax: (380) 5672 50405
  Email: dbf@dbf.com.ua, sales@dbf.com.ua

ⓜDnepropetrovsk Paper Mill, Ltd.
Dnepropetrovsk Mill
ul. Kaspijskaya 2
49034 Dnepropetrovsk
Ukraine
  Phone: (380) 5672 50405/50660
  Fax: (380) 5672 50405
  Email: dbf@dbf.com.ua, sales@dbf.com.ua
  Web Address: www.dbf.com.ua
Personnel:
  Dir.: Sergey Petrovich Sak
  Phone: (380) 5672 50405/50660
  Prod. Dir.: Ivan Vasilievich Ponomarenko
  Phone: (380) 63 798 19 43
  Export Sls. Dir.: Aleksey Krivosheev
  Phone: (380) 56 725 0660, 979208268
  Deputy Tech. Dir.: Vladimir Mikhailovich Obukhov
  Phone: (380) 5672 50405/50660
  Tech. Mgr.: Dmitriy Vladimirovich Khludeev
  Phone: (380) 63 796 10 45
  Email: hludeev@dbf.com.ua
  Sales Mngr.: Yulia Aleksandrovna Moroz
  Phone: (380) 93 780 98 84
  Email: julia.moroz@dbf.com.ua
Total Employees at this Location: 540
Type of Operation: Paper mill
Pulp Grades and Capacities:
  Total pulp capacity: 45,883 mt/y
  Recycled Pulping: 45,883 mt/y
Pulp Mill Data:
  Recycled Fiber Treatment Lines:
  Flotation deinking lines: 1
  Recycled packaging pulping lines: 1
Paper/Paperboard Grades and Capacities:
  Total paper and paperboard capacity: 61,000 mt/y
  Uncoated woodfree/freesheet: 16,500 mt/y
  Tissue: 24,000 mt/y
  Packaging papers: 2,000 mt/y
  Linerboard: 10,000 mt/y
  Corrugating medium/fluting: 8,500 mt/y
Paper and Paperboard Mill Data:
Paper Machines: 3
  No. 1, fourdrinier, total capacity 16,500 mt/y, Trim width 2.2 m, Uncoated woodfree/freesheet
  No. 2, fourdrinier (2), total capacity 20,500 mt/y, Trim width 2.8 m, Corrugating medium/fluting, Linerboard, Packaging papers
  No. 5, twin-wire, Yankee dryer, total capacity 24,000 mt/y, Trim width 3.2 m, Tissue
Energy Data:
  Power boilers
  Electrical demand for mill: 138 MWh/D

ⓜDonetsk-Vtorma Ltd.
Krasnogvardeyskiy pr., 46 Donetsk, 83076
Donetsk
Ukraine
  Phone: (380) 62 382 9408/8744/8742
  Fax: (380) 62 382 9362
  Email: dkbf@vtorma.com, info@vtorma.com
  Web Address: www.vtorma.com
Personnel:
  Gen. Dir.: Vladlen Markovich Golbert
  Phone: (380) 62 382 9408
  Fax: (380) 62 386 9362
  Email: golbert@vtorma.com
  Commer. Dir.: Dmitriy Olegovich Romanov
  Phone: (380) 62 382 9408
  Fax: (380) 62 386 9362
  Email: paper@vtorma.com
Total Employees of Company: 180
Mill Locations:
  Donetsk-Vtorma Ltd., Donetsk Mill, Krasnogvardeyskiy pr., 46, 83076 Donetsk, Ukraine, Capacity: 43,000 mt/y, (Paperboard mill)
  Phone: (380) 62 382 9408/8744/8742
  Fax: (380) 62 382 9362
  Email: dkbf@vtorma.com, info@vtorma.com

Ukraine

ⓂDonetsk-Vtorma Ltd.
Donetsk Mill
Krasnogvardeyskiy pr., 46
83076 Donetsk
Ukraine
Phone: (380) 62 382 9408/8744/8742
Fax: (380) 62 382 9362
Email: dkbf@vtorma.com,
info@vtorma.com
Web Address: www.vtorma.com
Personnel:
Gen. Dir.: Vladlen Markovich Golbert
Phone: (380) 62 382 9928
Fax: (380) 62 382 9362
Email: golbert@vtorma.com
Commer. Mgr.: Romanov Olegovich Dmitry
Phone: (380) 62 382 9408
Fax: (380) 62 382 9362
Email: paper@vtorma.com
Prod. Mgr.: Egor Kuznetsov
Phone: (380) 050 476 2693
Fax: (380) 62 382 9362
Email: egor@vtorma.com
Mktg. Mgr.: Alexandr Anatolievich Kukushkin
Phone: (380) 62 382 8744
Fax: (380) 62 382 9362
Email: sales@vtorma.com
Energy Dir.: Alexei Bakhmut
Phone: (380) 62 382 9408
Fax: (380) 62 382 9362
Email: bakhmut@vtorma.com
Tech. Dir.: Pavel Petrovich Shlyahov
Phone: (380) 62 382 9408
Fax: (380) 62 382 9362
Email: shlyahov@vtorma.com
Total Employees at this Location: 180
Type of Operation: Paperboard mill
Pulp Grades and Capacities:
Total pulp capacity: 40,700 mt/y
Recycled Pulping: 40,700 mt/y
Pulp Mill Data:
Recycled Fiber Treatment Lines:
Recycled packaging pulping lines: 1
Paper/Paperboard Grades and Capacities:
Total paper and paperboard capacity: 43,000 mt/y
Linerboard: 26,000 mt/y
Corrugating medium/fluting: 17,000 mt/y
Paper and Paperboard Mill Data:
Stock Preparation:
Pulpers: 2
Refiners: 3
Paper Machines: 1
No. 1, fourdrinier (2), total capacity 43,000 mt/y, Trim width 2.1 m, Corrugating medium/fluting, Linerboard
Finishing Equipment:
Winders: 1 at 30,000 mt/y
Energy Data:
Power boilers: 2
Electrical demand for mill: 56 MWh/D

ⓄⓂOOO First Donetsk Paper Mill
Donetsk Mill
Universitetskaya Str. 8/22
83008 Donetsk
Ukraine
Phone: (380) 62 345 9116
Fax: (380) 62 304 6687
Personnel:
Dir.: Vyacheslav Dvoyrin
Phone: (380) 62 345 9116
HR Dir.: Valentina Vasilyevna Parkhomenko
Total Employees at this Location: 75
Type of Operation: Paper mill
Paper/Paperboard Grades and Capacities:
Total paper and paperboard capacity: 5,000 mt/y
Tissue: 5,000 mt/y
Paper and Paperboard Mill Data:
Paper Machines: 1
PM 1, (second hand), total capacity 5,000 mt/y, Trim width 1.85 m, Tissue
Energy Data:
Power boilers: 1

ⓄⓂGorlovskaya Paper Mill OOO
Gorlovka Mill
Gagarina Str. 32
84601 Gorlovka
Ukraine
Phone: (380) 624 55 2059
Fax: (380) 624 552059
Email: info@gbf.com.ua
Personnel:
Dir.: Sergey Sergeevich Stanislavishin
Phone: (380) 624 55 3288/3634
Chief Eng.: Sergey Stepanovich Stanislavishin
Phone: (380) 624 55 3288/3634
Total Employees at this Location: 90
Type of Operation: Paper mill
Paper/Paperboard Grades and Capacities:
Total paper and paperboard capacity: 14,000 mt/y
Tissue: 14,000 mt/y
Paper and Paperboard Mill Data:
Paper Machines: 1
PM 1
Energy Data:
Power boilers: 1

ⓄⓂOOO Interecoline
Kharkiv Mill
ul. Klochkovskaya, 345-a
61051 Kharkiv
Ukraine
Phone: (380) 57 7548503 / 57 773 2278
Fax: (380) 57 7732278
Email: ecoline2006@mail.ru
Web Address: www.interecoline.com
Personnel:
Dir.: Yulia Ivanovna Kostenko
Phone: (380) 57 7548503
Chief Eng.: Aleksandr Vasilievich Melnikov
Phone: (380) 57 7548503
Sls. Mgr.: Svetlana Sergeevna Pokusaj
Phone: (380) 57 7548503
Total Employees at this Location: 40
Type of Operation: Paper mill
Paper/Paperboard Grades and Capacities:
Total paper and paperboard capacity: 1,000 mt/y
Tissue: 1,000 mt/y
Paper and Paperboard Mill Data:
Paper Machines: 1
No. 1, total capacity 1,000 mt/y, Trim width 1.6 m, Tissue
Energy Data:
Power boilers: 1
Electrical demand for mill: 2 MWh/D

ⓄIzmail Pulp & Paperboard Combine
ul. Nachimova, 300
68603 Izmail, Odesskaya obl.
Ukraine
Phone: (380) 48 41 70591/70583
Fax: (380) 48 41 70586
Email: info@ckk.izmail.com.ua,
info@osnova.ua,
ckk@te.net.ua
Web Address: www.ckk.com.ua,
www.osnova.ua
Personnel:
CEO, Chairman: Fedor Mikhaylovich Cheban
Phone: (380) 48 41 70591
Fax: (380) 48 41 70586
Tech. Mgr.: Igor Nikolaevich Dubyk
Phone: (380) 48 41 70580
Commer. Mgr.: Roman Gonchar
Phone: (380) 48 41 70586
Total Employees of Company: 580
Mill Locations:
Izmail Pulp & Paperboard Combine, Izmail Mill, ul. Nachimova, 300, 68603 Izmail, Ukraine, Capacity: 30,000 mt/y, (Paperboard mill)
Phone: (380) 48 41 70591/70583
Fax: (380) 48 41 70586
Email: info@ckk.izmail.com.ua, info@osnova.ua, ckk@te.net.ua,

ⓄIzmail Pulp & Paperboard Combine
Izmail Mill
ul. Nachimova, 300
68603 Izmail, Odesskaya obl.
Ukraine
Phone: (380) 48 41 70591/70583
Fax: (380) 48 41 70586
Email: info@ckk.izmail.com.ua,
info@osnova.ua,
ckk@te.net.ua
Web Address: www.ckk.com.ua,
www.osnova.ua
Personnel:
CEO, Chairman: Fedor Mikhaylovich Cheban
Phone: (380) 48 41 70591/70583
Tech. Mgr.: Igor Nikolaevich Dubyk
Phone: (380) 4841 70580
CFO: Inga Anatolievna Zelenova
Phone: (380) 48 41 70591/70583
Commer. Mgr.: Roman Gonchar
Phone: (380) 4841 25535
Prod.Dir.: Sergey Evgenievich Volkov
Total Employees at this Location: 580
Type of Operation: Paperboard mill
Pulp Grades and Capacities:
Total pulp capacity: 28,392 mt/y
Recycled Pulping: 28,392 mt/y
Pulp Mill Data:
Recycled Fiber Treatment Lines:
Recycled packaging pulping lines: 1
Paper/Paperboard Grades and Capacities:
Total paper and paperboard capacity: 30,000 mt/y
Linerboard: 18,000 mt/y
Corrugating medium/fluting: 12,000 mt/y
Paper and Paperboard Mill Data:
Paper Machines: 1
No. 2, fourdrinier (2), total capacity 30,000 mt/y, Trim width 3.5 m, Corrugating medium/fluting, Linerboard
Energy Data:
Power boilers
Electrical demand for mill: 43 MWh/D

ⓄⓂKiev Cardboard and Paper Mill
Kiev Cardboard and Paper Mill
Ownership: 95% by Pulp Mill Holding GesmbH
vul. Kyivska, 130
08700 Obukhiv, Kyivska obl.
Ukraine
Phone: (380) 4572 76300/71056/4452 09831
Fax: (380) 4572 76540/4452 09860
Email: info@papir.kiev.ua
Web Address: www.papir.kiev.ua
Personnel:
Gen. Dir.: Vitaly Aleksandrovich Basko
Phone: (380) 4452 09831
Fax: (380) 4472 67300
Email: office@papir.kiev.ua
Dir., Corrugated Packaging Plt.: Aleksey Aleksandrovich Katyshev
Phone: (380) 4572 76115
Fax: (380) 4452 09873
Email: gofra@papir.kiev.ua
Chief Eng.: Aleksandr Petrovich Yakovina
Phone: (380) 4452 09856
Fax: (380) 4472 67300
Email: alex_py@papir.kiev.ua
Purch. Dir.: Alexandr Nikolaevich Bykovets
Phone: (380) 4572 76042
Fax: (380) 4572 76113
Email: alex_nb@papir.kiev.ua
Dir., IT: Alexandr Pavlovich Dudarenko
Phone: (380) 4449 44040
Fax: (380) 4572 76307

Ukraine

Email: sasha.dou@papir.kiev.ua
Total Employees at this Location: 1,900
Type of Operation: Paper mill, Paperboard mill
Pulp Grades and Capacities:
Total pulp capacity: 220,016 mt/y
Recycled Pulping: 220,016 mt/y

Pulp Mill Data:
Recycled Fiber Treatment Lines:
Pulpers: 7

Paper/Paperboard Grades and Capacities:
Total paper and paperboard capacity: 270,000 mt/y
Tissue: 70,000 mt/y
Linerboard: 60,000 mt/y
Corrugating medium/fluting: 40,000 mt/y
Boxboard/cartonboard: 100,000 mt/y

Paper and Paperboard Mill Data:
Stock Preparation:
Pulpers: 11
Refiners: 7

Paper Machines: 4
BM 1, cylinder (4), total capacity 100,000 mt/y, Trim width 4.2 m, Boxboard/cartonboard
BM 2, cylinder (4), total capacity 100,000 mt/y, Trim width 4.2 m, Corrugating medium/fluting, Linerboard
PM 1, twin-wire, Yankee dryer, total capacity 40,000 mt/y, Trim width 4.2 m, Tissue
PM 2, twin-wire, Yankee dryer, total capacity 30,000 mt/y, Trim width 4.2 m, Tissue

Coating Machines: 1
No. 1, total capacity 60,000 mt/y., on machine

Finishing Equipment:
Rewinders: 1

Energy Data:
Power boilers: 3
Combustion turbines: 3 at 39 MW
Electrical demand for mill: 458 MWh/D

ⓗⓜOAO Kohavinska Paper Mill
Gnizdychiv Mill
Ownership: 100% by Private owners
Konovaltsa Str. 6
81740 Gnizdychiv, Zhydachivsky rayon
Ukraine
Phone: (380) 3239 48348
Fax: (380) 3239 48377
Email: info@kpf.ua,
sales@kpf.ua
Web Address: www.kpf.ua

Personnel:
Chief Accountant: Olga Petrovna Pirog
Phone: (380) 3239 48376
Chmn. Bd.: Roman V. Pirog
Phone: (380) 3239 48348
Prod. & Tech. Dir.: Mikhail Fedorovich Tytykalo
Phone: (380) 3239 48348
Head of Papermaking: Taras Orestovich Medved
Phone: (380) 3239 48348
Head of Sales: Orest Nikolaevich Kostur
Phone: (380) 3239 48348
Email: sales@kpf.ua
Finan. Dir.: Roman Chebotarev
Phone: (380) 3239 48348
Email: findirector@kpf.ua
Env. Mgr.: Alyona Mihaylovna Yurchishin
Phone: (380) 3239 48348
Total Employees at this Location: 236
Type of Operation: Paper mill

Paper/Paperboard Grades and Capacities:
Total paper and paperboard capacity: 18,500 mt/y
Tissue: 18,500 mt/y

Paper and Paperboard Mill Data:
Stock Preparation:
Pulpers: 1

Paper Machines: 2
PM 1, total capacity 10,000 mt/y, Trim width 2.3 m, Tissue
PM 2, total capacity 8,500 mt/y, Trim width 2.1 m, Tissue

Energy Data:
Power boilers: 2
Electrical demand for mill: 31 MWh/D

ⓜKronex-Ukraina, Ltd.
Zmiev Mill
ul. Fabrichnaya 11
63403 Zmiev, Kharkovskaya Obl.
Ukraine
Phone: (380) 5747 33 888/171/450/500/485
Fax: (380) 5747 33 888
Email: pstv@zm.kh.ua,
ir_pavlenko@ukr.net

Personnel:
Gen. Dir.: Alina Viktorovna Sych
Phone: (380) 5770 32017
Chief Engineer: Petr Grigorievich Vysotsky
Chief Acc.: Olesya Kovalchuk
Type of Operation: Paper mill

Paper/Paperboard Grades and Capacities:
Total paper and paperboard capacity: 5,000 mt/y
Newsprint: 1,000 mt/y
Uncoated woodfree/freesheet: 4,000 mt/y
Packaging papers

Paper and Paperboard Mill Data:
Paper Machines: 1
No. 1, (switch machine between kraft and graphic paper), Trim width 2.1 m, Newsprint, Uncoated woodfree/freesheet, Packaging papers

Energy Data:
Electrical demand for mill: 15 MWh/D

ⓗKronex-Ukraina, Ltd.
ul. Fabrichnaya 11
63403 Zmiev
Ukraine
Phone: (380) 5747 33 888/171/450/500/485
Fax: (380) 5747 33 888
Email: pstv@zm.kh.ua,
ir_pavlenko@ukr.net

Personnel:
Gen. Dir.: Alina Viktorovna Sych
Phone: (380) 5770 32017
Exec. Dir.: Sergey Borisovich Kochuk
Phone: (380) 5747 33 888/171
Chief Acc.: Olesya Kovalchuk
Phone: (380) 5747 33 888/171
Chief Eng.: Petr Grigorievich Vysotsky
Phone: (380) 5747 33 888/171
Total Employees at this Location: 152
Mill Locations:
Kronex-Ukraina, Ltd., Zmiev Mill, ul. Fabrichnaya 11, 63403 Zmiev, Ukraine, Capacity: 5,000 mt/y, (Paper mill)
Phone: (380) 5747 33 888/171/450/500/485
Fax: (380) 5747 33 888
Email: pstv@zm.kh.ua, ir_pavlenko@ukr.net

ⓗKrymbumaga
Moskovskoye shosse, 11 km
95493 Simferopol
Ukraine
Phone: (380) 652 227367/262685
Fax: (380) 652 227367
Email: krymbumaga@mail.ru

Personnel:
Gen. Dir.: Samvel Aramovich Akopyan
Phone: (380) 652 227367/262685
Fax: (380) 652 227367
Prod. Mgr.: Avak Liparitovich Tsaturyan
Phone: (380) 652 227367/26268550 5889363
Fax: (380) 652 227367
Total Employees at this Location: 200
Mill Locations:
Krymbumaga, Simferopol Mill, Moskovskoye shosse, 11 km, 95493 Simferopol, Ukraine, Capacity: 7,500 mt/y, (Paper mill)
Phone: (380) 652 227367/262685
Fax: (380) 652 227367
Email: krymbumaga@mail.ru

ⓜKrymbumaga
Simferopol Mill
Moskovskoye shosse, 11 km
95493 Simferopol
Ukraine
Phone: (380) 652 227367/262685
Fax: (380) 652 227367
Email: krymbumaga@mail.ru

Personnel:
Gen. Dir.: Samvel Aramovich Akopyan
Phone: (380) 652 227367/262685
Prod. Mgr.: Avak Liparitovich Tsaturyan
Phone: (380) 50 5889363
Total Employees at this Location: 200
Type of Operation: Paper mill

Pulp Mill Data:
Recycled Fiber Treatment Lines:
Pulpers: 1 at 10,000 admt/y

Paper/Paperboard Grades and Capacities:
Total paper and paperboard capacity: 7,500 mt/y
Tissue: 7,500 mt/y

Paper and Paperboard Mill Data:
Paper Machines: 2
PM 1, total capacity 7,500 mt/y, Tissue
PM 2, (under construction, due to start up in Q3, 2011), total capacity 10,000 mt/y

Energy Data:
Power boilers: 2
Electrical demand for mill: 14 MWh/D

ⓗⓜLutsky KRK
Lutsk Mill
Ownership: 24.52% by AFK "Sistema" (Kiev), 44.14% by Agenstvo "Svit" (Kiev), 17.14% by Bureau of Investment Technologies (Kiev)
vul. Karbysheva, 3
43023 Lutsk
Ukraine
Phone: (380) 332 7870 31
Fax: (380) 332 7870 31
Email: info@lkrk.com.ua,
krk@fk.lutsk.ua,
krk13@fk.lutsk.ua
Web Address: www.lkrk.com.ua

Personnel:
Gen. Dir.: Olexandr Leonidovych Sharaev
Phone: (380) 332 78 70 32
Fax: (380) 332 7870 31
Email: sharaev@lkrk.com.ua
Chief Mech. Eng.: Yuriy Perevedenets
Phone: (380) 332 7870 38
Fax: (380) 332 7870 31
Email: perevedenets@lkrk.com.ua
Chief Eng.: Andriy Viktorovych Gusev
Phone: (380) 332 7870 42
Fax: (380) 332 7870 31
Email: gusev@lkrk.com.ua
Finan. Dir.: Sergey Korenyev
Phone: (380) 332 7870 31
Fax: (380) 332 7870 31
Email: korenyev@lkrk.com.ua
Prod. Dir.: Sergey Ligoskiy
Phone: (380) 332 7870 31
Fax: (380) 332 7870 31
Email: ligoskiy@lkrk.com.ua
Total Employees of Company: 1,200
Total Employees at this Location: 400
Type of Operation: Paperboard mill
Pulp Grades and Capacities:
Total pulp capacity: 50,768 mt/y
Recycled Pulping: 50,768 mt/y

Pulp Mill Data:
Recycled Fiber Treatment Lines:
Recycled packaging pulping lines: 1

Paper/Paperboard Grades and Capacities:
Total paper and paperboard capacity: 50,000 mt/y
Packaging papers: 5,000 mt/y
Linerboard: 18,000 mt/y
Corrugating medium/fluting: 12,000 mt/y
Boxboard/cartonboard: 15,000 mt/y

Paper and Paperboard Mill Data:
Paper Machines: 1

Ukraine

No. 1, cylinder, total capacity 50,000 mt/y, Trim width 4.1 m, Corrugating medium/fluting, Linerboard, Boxboard/cartonboard, Packaging papers
Energy Data:
Power boilers
Electrical demand for mill: 65 MWh/D

ⓂⓄLvivkartonplast
Lviv Mill
Ownership: Tema Company
vul. Kovelskaya 109
79056 Lviv
Ukraine
 Phone: (380) 322 939640/93 4142
 Fax: (380) 322 939 640/41
 Email: office@lvivkp.com.ua,
 karton@svitonline.com
 Web Address: www.paperandboard.com.ua,
 www.lvivkp.com.ua
Personnel:
 Gen.Dir.: Yaroslav Evgenovych Poshyvailo
 Phone: (380) 322 939640/93 4142
 Tech. Dir.: Igor Stepanovych Enets
 Phone: (380) 322 939640/93 4142
 Head of Paperboard Sls. Dept.: Yuriy Ivanovych Shymanskyi
 Phone: (380) 322 939640/93 4142
Total Employees at this Location: 260
Type of Operation: Paperboard mill
Pulp Grades and Capacities:
 Total pulp capacity: 34,257 mt/y
 Recycled Pulping: 34,257 mt/y
Pulp Mill Data:
 Recycled Fiber Treatment Lines:
 Recycled packaging pulping lines: 2
Paper/Paperboard Grades and Capacities:
 Total paper and paperboard capacity: 41,000 mt/y
 Tissue: 12,000 mt/y
 Boxboard/cartonboard: 29,000 mt/y
Paper and Paperboard Mill Data:
Paper Machines: 2
 BM 2, cylinder, total capacity 29,000 mt/y, Trim width 2.1 m, Boxboard/cartonboard
 PM 1, fourdrinier, Yankee dryer, total capacity 12,000 mt/y, Trim width 2.3 m, Tissue
Energy Data:
Power boilers: 4
Electrical demand for mill: 70 MWh/D

ⓂMalyn - Weidmann Paper Mill VAT
Malyn Mill
Ownership: 95% by Wicor Group
vul. Prikhodska 66
11602 Malyn, Zhitomirskaya obl.
Ukraine
 Phone: (380) 4133 67222
 Fax: (380) 4133 53343
 Email: mpf@malin.zt.ua,
 info@wicor.com,
 info.wmpm@wicor.com,
 wicor@wicor.kiev.ua
 Web Address: www.weidmann-electrical.com
Personnel:
 Member of the Supervisory Board: Vyacheslav Grigorovych Pokotylo
 Phone: (380) 4133 67201
 Fax: (380) 4133 53343
 Email: vyacheslav.pokotylo@wicor.com
Total Employees at this Location: 585
Type of Operation: Paper mill, Paperboard mill
Paper/Paperboard Grades and Capacities:
 Total paper and paperboard capacity: 17,800 mt/y
 Specialty and industrial: 13,300 mt/y
 Boxboard/cartonboard: 4,500 mt/y
Paper and Paperboard Mill Data:
Paper Machines: 5
No. 13, total capacity 2,800 mt/y, Trim width 2.52 m, Specialty and industrial
No. 15, total capacity 5,250 mt/y, Trim width 2.52 m, Specialty and industrial
No. 16, total capacity 2,450 mt/y, Trim width 2.1 m, Specialty and industrial
No. 17, total capacity 2,800 mt/y, Trim width 3.1 m, Specialty and industrial
BM, total capacity 4,500 mt/y, Trim width 3.2 m, Boxboard/cartonboard

ⓂMier
vul. Technicnna, 10/6
79000 Lviv
Ukraine
 Phone: (380) 32 2949430/4
 Fax: (380) 32 2949435
 Email: shpylyk_sasha@ukr.net,
 com-dep-mier@rambler.ru
Personnel:
 Gen. Dir.: Igor Olegovych Mykhaylyshyn
 Phone: (380) 32 2949430/4
 Fax: (380) 32 2949435
 Chief Acc.: Olena Fedorivna Stchukina
 Phone: (380) 32 2949430/4
 Fax: (380) 32 2949435
 Tech. Dir./Chief Eng.: Olexandr Volodymyrovych Shpylyk
 Phone: (380) 32 2949430/4
 Fax: (380) 32 2949435
Total Employees at this Location: 70
Mill Locations:
Mier, Lviv Mill, vul. Technicnna, 10/6, 79000 Lviv, Ukraine, Capacity: 2,200 mt/y, (Paper mill)
 Phone: (380) 32 2949430/4
 Fax: (380) 32 2949435
 Email: shpylyk_sasha@ukr.net, com-dep-mier@rambler.ru

ⓂMier
Lviv Mill
vul. Technicnna, 10/6
79000 Lviv
Ukraine
 Phone: (380) 32 2949430/4
 Fax: (380) 32 2949435
 Email: shpylyk_sasha@ukr.net,
 com-dep-mier@rambler.ru
Personnel:
 Gen. Dir.: Igor Olegovych Mykhaylyshyn
 Phone: (380) 32 2949430
 Tech. Dir./Chief Eng.: Olexandr Volodymyrovych Shpylyk
 Phone: (380) 32 2949430/4
 Sls. Mgr.: Valeriy Masesov
 Phone: (380) 32 2949430/4
 Sls. Mgr.: Andriy Leonidovych Sydorenko
 Phone: (380) 32 2949430/4
Type of Operation: Paper mill
Pulp Mill Data:
 Recycled Fiber Treatment Lines:
 Pulpers: 1 at 10,500 admt/y
Paper/Paperboard Grades and Capacities:
 Total paper and paperboard capacity: 2,200 mt/y
 Packaging papers: 900 mt/y
 Linerboard: 1,300 mt/y
 Corrugating medium/fluting
Paper and Paperboard Mill Data:
 Stock Preparation:
 Refiners: 2
Paper Machines: 1
No. 1, total capacity 2,200 mt/y, Trim width 1.15 m, Linerboard, Packaging papers, Corrugating medium/fluting
Energy Data:
Power boilers: 2
Electrical demand for mill: 7 MWh/D

ⓂⓄOAO Miropol Paper Mill
Miropol Mill
Ownership: 80% by Kharkivs'ky Karton, Ltd.
vul. Fabrychna 1
13033 Miropol, Romanovskiy rayon, Zhitomirskaya obl.
Ukraine
 Phone: (380) 4146 9300 00 / 02 / 07
 Fax: (380) 4146 93007
 Email: vat.mpf@dz.zt.ukrtel.net
Personnel:
 Chmn.: Viktor Petrovich Kondratyuk
 Phone: (380) 4146 93007
 Prod. Dir.: Ludmyla Il'ivna
 Phone: (380) 4146 93000
 Chief Eng.: Mikhaylo Vasilyoviych Lesko
 Phone: (380) 4146 93007
 Dpty. Dir.: Andriy Vasylyovych Levchuk
 Phone: (380) 4146 93007
Total Employees of Company: 258
Total Employees at this Location: 200
Type of Operation: Paper mill, Paperboard mill
Paper/Paperboard Grades and Capacities:
 Total paper and paperboard capacity: 14,400 mt/y
 Corrugating medium/fluting: 14,000 mt/y
Paper and Paperboard Mill Data:
Paper Machines: 1
No. 3, total capacity 14,400 mt/y, Trim width 2.52 m, Corrugating medium/fluting
Energy Data:
Electrical demand for mill: 19 MWh/D

ⓂMokvynska Paper Mill, Ltd.
Mokvyn Mill
Ownership: ZAO Kiev Packaging & Board, ZAO UkrTara Holding
Bereznivskiy rayon
34634 Mokvyn
Ukraine
 Phone: (380) 3653 51540
 Fax: (380) 3653 51544/40
 Email: info@mpapir.com
Personnel:
 Mill Dir.: Mykhaylo Vasylyovych Nykytyuk
 Phone: (380) 3653 51540
 Chief Acc.: Nataliya Mykolaivna Shponyak
 Phone: (380) 3653 51540
 Sls. Dir.: Volodymyr Galaguz
 Phone: (380) 3653 51544
Type of Operation: Paper mill
Paper/Paperboard Grades and Capacities:
 Total paper and paperboard capacity: 5,500 mt/y
 Tissue: 3,000 mt/y
 Packaging papers: 2,500 mt/y
Paper and Paperboard Mill Data:
Paper Machines: 2
No. 1, fourdrinier, total capacity 3,000 mt/y, Trim width 1.68 m, Tissue
No. 2, total capacity 2,500 mt/y, Trim width 1.68 m

ⓄTOV Novy Kyiv (New Kiev) Paper Mill
ul. Blagovestnaya 169, 51
18000 Cherkassy
Ukraine
Mill Locations:
TOV Novy Kyiv (New Kiev) Paper Mill, Raketnaya Mill, ul. Okruzhnaya 4, Raketnaya, Ukraine, Capacity: 12,000 mt/y, (Paper mill)
 Phone: (380) 0472 502052 / 552084 / 067 4721169
 Fax: (380) 0472 502052 / 552084
 Email: info@nov.kiev.ua

ⓄTOV Novy Kyiv (New Kiev) Paper Mill
Raketnaya Mill
ul. Okruzhnaya 4
Raketnaya
Ukraine
Mailing Address: Lutsenka strret 7, p/o box 3562, 18007 Cherkassy
 Phone: (380) 0472 502052 / 552084 / 067 4721169
 Fax: (380) 0472 502052 / 552084
 Email: info@nov.kiev.ua

Ukraine

Web Address: www.nov.kiev.ua
Personnel:
Gen. Dir.: Tatiana Vladimirovna Lavrichenko
Phone: (380) 067 4703434
Fax: (380) 472 719935
Prod. Dir.: Andrey Loentyevich Pervanyuk
Phone: (380) 472 7199385/4562 61214
Sls. Mgr.: Aleksandr Vladimirovich Kobylyanskiy
Phone: (380) 472 7199385/4562 61214
Type of Operation: Paper mill
Pulp Mill Data:
Recycled Fiber Treatment Lines:
Pulpers: 1 at 12,000 admt/y
Paper/Paperboard Grades and Capacities:
Total paper and paperboard capacity: 12,000 mt/y
Tissue: 12,000 mt/y
Paper and Paperboard Mill Data:
Stock Preparation:
Refiners: 1
Paper Machines: 1
No. 1, total capacity 12,000 mt/y, Trim width 2.1 m, Tissue
Energy Data:
Power boilers: 2
Electrical demand for mill: 11 MWh/D

ⓄⓂPapir-Mal
Malin Mill
vul. Nemanykhina, 2
11602 Malin, Zhitomirskaya obl.
Ukraine
Phone: (380) 4133 32279/32261
Fax: (380) 4133 32261
Email: papir-mal@ukr.net,
info@papir-mal.com.ua
Web Address: www.papir-mal.com.ua
Personnel:
Fin. Dir.: Irina Stepanovna Proharenko
Mill Mgr.: Alexandr Grigoryevich Timoshenko
Phone: (380) 4134.00055794923
Tech. Dir.: Alexandr Petrovich Filonenko
Phone: (380) 4134.00055794923
Prod. Dir.: Maxim Petrovich Maydanovich
Phone: (380) 4134.00055794923
Email: snab@papir-mal.com.ua
Prod. Mgr.: Alexey Alexeevich Kleschov
Phone: (380) 4134.00055794923
Sls. Mgr.: Sergey Nikolaevich Bykovets
Phone: (380) 4134.00055794923
Total Employees of Company: 280
Total Employees at this Location: 280
Type of Operation: Paper mill
Pulp Grades and Capacities:
Total pulp capacity: 51,531 mt/y
Recycled Pulping: 51,531 mt/y
Pulp Mill Data:
Recycled Fiber Treatment Lines:
Recycled packaging pulping lines: 2
Paper/Paperboard Grades and Capacities:
Total paper and paperboard capacity: 51,000 mt/y
Tissue: 8,000 mt/y
Packaging papers: 3,000 mt/y
Linerboard: 24,000 mt/y
Corrugating medium/fluting: 16,000 mt/y
Paper and Paperboard Mill Data:
Paper Machines: 2
BM 1, fourdrinier (2), total capacity 43,000 mt/y, Trim width 2.32 m, Corrugating medium/fluting, Linerboard, Packaging papers
PM 1, fourdrinier, Yankee dryer, total capacity 8,000 mt/y, Trim width 2.5 m, Tissue
Energy Data:
Power boilers: 3
Electrical demand for mill: 81 MWh/D

ⓄⓂTOV Poninki Cardboard and Paper Mill
Poninka Mill
Ownership: Ukranian investment companies
vul. Peremogy, 34
30511 Poninka, Polonsky rayon, Khmelnitska obl.
Ukraine
Phone: (380) 3843 72141
Fax: (380) 3843 72141
Email: tovpkpk@gmail.com
Personnel:
Dir.: Petro Yosypovych Samchyshyn
Phone: (380) 67 311 2700
Depty. Dir./ Chief Eng.: Victor Evgenovych Ignatyuk
Phone: (380) 67 311 2707
Depty. Dir.: Grygory Ischenko
Phone: (380) 67 311 2712
Office Manager: Iryna Valentynivna Reber
Total Employees at this Location: 350
Type of Operation: Paper mill, Paperboard mill
Pulp Grades and Capacities:
Total pulp capacity: 25,272 mt/y
Recycled Pulping: 25,272 mt/y
Pulp Mill Data:
Recycled Fiber Treatment Lines:
Recycled packaging pulping lines: 1
Paper/Paperboard Grades and Capacities:
Total paper and paperboard capacity: 25,000 mt/y
Linerboard: 14,000 mt/y
Corrugating medium/fluting: 11,000 mt/y
Paper and Paperboard Mill Data:
Stock Preparation:
Pulpers: 1
Paper Machines: 2
No. 1, fourdrinier (2), total capacity 14,000 mt/y, Trim width 2.52 m, Corrugating medium/fluting, Linerboard
No. 4, fourdrinier (2), total capacity 11,000 mt/y, Trim width 2.1 m, Corrugating medium/fluting, Linerboard
Energy Data:
Power boilers
Electrical demand for mill: 35 MWh/D

ⓄⓂRogan Paperboard Mill
Rogan Mill
Lenin Str. 57
62481 Rogan, Kharkovskaya Obl.
Ukraine
Phone: (380) 57740 7275/7191
Fax: (380) 57740 7172
Email: secretar@rkf.com.ua,
mail@rkf.com.ua,
marketing@rkf.com.ua,
sbut_karton@rkf.com.ua
Web Address: www.rkf.com.ua
Personnel:
Chmn. & CEO: Gennadiy Vladimirovich Ladyzhinskiy
Phone: (380) 57740 7290
Fax: (380) 57740 7172
Email: lgv@rkf.com.ua
Sls. & Mktg. Dir.: Olga Vladimirovna Metko
Phone: (380) 57740 7108
Fax: (380) 57740 7172
Email: marketing@rkf.com.ua
Total Employees at this Location: 140
Type of Operation: Paperboard mill
Paper/Paperboard Grades and Capacities:
Total paper and paperboard capacity: 10,000 mt/y
Boxboard/cartonboard: 10,000 mt/y
Paper and Paperboard Mill Data:
Paper Machines: 1
KDM, total capacity 10,000 mt/y, Trim width 2.05 m, Boxboard/cartonboard
Energy Data:
Power boilers: 1
Electrical demand for mill: 20 MWh/D

ⓄⓂRubezhansky Cardboard and Packaging Mill
Rubezhnoye Mill
Ownership: 49.60% by DS Smith Plc, Invest Consulting, overseas investor
ul. Mendeleeva, 67
93006 Rubezhnoye, Lugansk obl.
Ukraine
Phone: (380) 6453 92210/92260
Fax: (380) 6453 70415/92407
Email: info@rktk.com.ua,
rktk@svitonline.com
Web Address: www.rktk.com.ua
Personnel:
Man. Dir./Mill Mgr.: Gennady Mihailovich Minin
Phone: (380) 6453 92210/92260
Paper Mill Mgr.: Nikolay Nikolaevich Semiryazhko
Phone: (380) 6453 92210/92260
Tech. Dir.: Vladimir Ignatyevich Latsko
Phone: (380) 6453 9 22 20
Service Centre Dir.: Viktor Stepanovych Ismanitskiy
Phone: (380) 6453 9 2260
Total Employees at this Location: 1,300
Type of Operation: Paperboard mill
Pulp Grades and Capacities:
Total pulp capacity: 266,042 mt/y
Recycled Pulping: 266,042 mt/y
Pulp Mill Data:
Recycled Fiber Treatment Lines:
Recycled packaging pulping lines: 1
Paper/Paperboard Grades and Capacities:
Total paper and paperboard capacity: 290,000 mt/y
Linerboard: 200,000 mt/y
Corrugating medium/fluting: 90,000 mt/y
Paper and Paperboard Mill Data:
Stock Preparation:
Pulpers: 4
Refiners: 8
Paper Machines: 3
No. 1, fourdrinier (3), total capacity 100,000 mt/y, Trim width 4.2 m, Linerboard
No. 2, fourdrinier, total capacity 70,000 mt/y, Trim width 2.54 m, Corrugating medium/fluting
No. 3, fourdrinier (2), total capacity 120,000 mt/y, Trim width 2.85 m, Corrugating medium/fluting, Linerboard
Finishing Equipment:
Winders: 1
Energy Data:
Power boilers: 2
Combustion turbines: 1 at 15 MW
Steam turbines: 1 at 6.0 MW
Electrical demand for mill: 399 MWh/D

ⓄⓂSlavuta-Papir, JSC
Slavuta Mill
Ownership: 100% by private
ul. Khmelnitskogo, 144
30070 Slavuta
Ukraine
Phone: (380) 3842 71759
Fax: (380) 3842 22095
Email: slavpap@mail.ru
Personnel:
Chmn.: Volodymyr Romanoyich Filinyuk
Phone: (380) 3842 71759
Dir.: Yaroslav Volodymyrovych Levchouk
Phone: (380) 3842 70543
Tech. Dir.: Viktor Oleksiyovych Klimchouk
Phone: (380) 3842 22971
Paper Prod. Mgr.: Svitlana Pavlivna Krotyuk
Phone: (380) 3842 71759
Sls. Mgr.: Valentyna Grigorievna Tymoschuk
Phone: (380) 3842 71759
Environ. Mgr.: Olena Vasilievna Yaskova
Phone: (380) 3842 71759
Total Employees of Company: 120
Total Employees at this Location: 200
Type of Operation: Paper mill
Pulp Grades and Capacities:
Total pulp capacity: 92,782 mt/y
Recycled Pulping: 92,782 mt/y
Pulp Mill Data:
Recycled Fiber Treatment Lines:
Recycled packaging pulping lines: 1
Paper/Paperboard Grades and Capacities:

United Kingdom

Total paper and paperboard capacity: 92,000 mt/y
Packaging papers: 6,000 mt/y
Linerboard: 43,000 mt/y
Corrugating medium/fluting: 43,000 mt/y
Paper and Paperboard Mill Data:
Stock Preparation:
Pulpers: 2
Paper Machines: 3
No. 1, fourdrinier, total capacity 6,000 mt/y, Trim width 2.1 m, Packaging papers
No. 7, fourdrinier, total capacity 43,000 mt/y, Trim width 2.5 m, Linerboard
No. 10, fourdrinier, total capacity 43,000 mt/y, Trim width 2.7 m, Corrugating medium/fluting
Energy Data:
Power boilers: 1
Electrical demand for mill: 133 MWh/D

ⓞTsyurupinsk Paper Company
Ownership: 100% by ABH GmbH
ul. Gvardeiskaya, 103
75101 Tsyurupinsk, Kherson obl.
Ukraine
Phone: (380) 5542 45347/45201
Fax: (380) 5542 45347
Email: refns1@tpm.com.ua
Web Address: www.tpm.com.ua
Personnel:
Gen. Dir.: Sergey Vasilievich Sokolskiy
Phone: (380) 5542 45347/45201
Fax: (380) 5542 45347
Deputy Dir.: Lyudmila Nikolaevna Kudryavtseva
Phone: (380) 5542 45347/45201
Fax: (380) 5542 45347
Email: kln1@tpm.com.ua
Commer. Dir.: Sergei Eduardovich Basov
Phone: (380) 5542 45347/45201
Fax: (380) 5542 45347
Email: reg@tpm.com.ua
Prod. Dir.: Juriy Gennadyevich Shipilov
Phone: (380) 5542 45347/45201
Fax: (380) 5542 45347
Email: sug@tpm.com.ua
Total Employees at this Location: 276
Mill Locations:
Tsyurupinsk Paper Company, Tsyurupinsk Mill, ul. Gvardeiskaya, 103, 75101 Tsyurupinsk, Kherson obl., Ukraine, Capacity: 10,000 mt/y, (Paper mill)
Phone: (380) 5542 45347/45201
Fax: (380) 5542 45347
Email: refns1@tpm.com.ua

ⓜTsyurupinsk Paper Company
Tsyurupinsk Mill
ul. Gvardeiskaya, 103
75101 Tsyurupinsk, Kherson obl.
Ukraine
Phone: (380) 5542 45347/45201
Fax: (380) 5542 45347
Email: refns1@tpm.com.ua
Web Address: www.tpm.com.ua
Personnel:
Gen. Dir.: Sergey Vasilievich Sokolskiy
Deputy Dir.: Lyudmila Nikolaevna Kudryavtseva
Phone: (380) 5542 45347/45201
Email: kln1@tpm.com.ua
Commer. Dir.: Sergei Eduardovich Basov
Phone: (380) 05542 45212
Email: reg@tpm.com.ua
Prod. Dir.: Juriy Gennadyevich Shipilov
Phone: (380) 5542 45201
Email: sug@tpm.com.ua
Chief of Sls. Dept.: Eugeniya Michailovna Burenko
Phone: (380) 5542 45347
Email: snab@tpm.com.ua
Total Employees at this Location: 276
Type of Operation: Paper mill
Paper/Paperboard Grades and Capacities:
Total paper and paperboard capacity: 10,000 mt/y
Specialty and industrial: 10,000 mt/y

Paper and Paperboard Mill Data:
Paper Machines: 1
B-46, total capacity 10,000 mt/y, Specialty and industrial
Energy Data:
Electrical demand for mill: 3 MWh/D

ⓞⓜOOO Yarovoy
Cherkassy Mill
Engelsa 170
18000 Cherkassy
Ukraine
Phone: (380) 472 64 84 00
Fax: (380) 472 64 84 00
Email: yaroviy@ukr.net
Personnel:
Gen. Dir.: Roman Mikhaylovich Yarovoy
Phone: (380) 472 64 84 00
Gen. Dir.: Petr Mikhaylovich Yarovoy
Phone: (380) 472 64 84 00
Total Employees at this Location: 50
Type of Operation: Paper mill
Paper/Paperboard Grades and Capacities:
Total paper and paperboard capacity: 3,000 mt/y
Tissue: 3,000 mt/y
Paper and Paperboard Mill Data:
Paper Machines: 1
No. 1, total capacity 3,000 mt/y, Tissue

ⓞⓜZhydachiv Pulp & Paper Mill
Zhydachiv Mill
vul. Fabrychna, 4
81700 Zhydachiv, Lviv obl.
Ukraine
Phone: (380) 3239 31832/21420
Fax: (380) 3239 21046/31832
Email: gck@zppf.com, (mill),
info@osnova.ua
Web Address: www.paper.com.ua, www.osnova.ua
Personnel:
Chmn.: Mykola Mykolayovych Korsunskyi
Phone: (380) 3240.48608776844
Commer. Mgr.: Vitali Vytalevych Grytsak
Phone: (380) 3240.48608776844
Finan. Dir.: Volodymyr Iosypovych Pigul
Phone: (380) 3240.48608776844
Tech. Dir.: Olexandr Vasilovych Teletkov
Phone: (380) 3239 31809
Head of the Tech. Department: Mariya Yaroslavivna Donetska
Phone: (380) 3239 21168
Mariya
Phone: (380) 3239 31809
Total Employees at this Location: 100
Type of Operation: Pulp mill, Paper mill
Pulp Grades and Capacities:
Total pulp capacity: 30,036 mt/y
Recycled Pulping: 30,036 mt/y
Pulp Mill Data:
Mechanical Pulping Systems:
Conventional grinders
Pulp Lines: 2
Recycled Fiber Treatment Lines:
Recycled packaging pulping lines: 1
Paper/Paperboard Grades and Capacities:
Total paper and paperboard capacity: 32,000 mt/y
Packaging papers: 2,000 mt/y
Linerboard: 18,000 mt/y
Corrugating medium/fluting: 10,000 mt/y
Boxboard/cartonboard: 2,000 mt/y
Paper and Paperboard Mill Data:
Paper Machines: 1
No. 2, fourdrinier (2), total capacity 32,000 mt/y, Trim width 3.5 m, Corrugating medium/fluting, Linerboard, Boxboard/cartonboard, Packaging papers
Energy Data:
Power boilers

Steam turbines: 2 at 6, 12 MW
Electrical demand for mill: 44 MWh/D

ⓞⓜZhytomyr Paperboard Mill
Zhytomyr Mill
Maydan Stanishivskyj 7
12009 Zhytomyr
Ukraine
Phone: (380) 412 343561/375054 #8
Fax: (380) 412 343561
Email: ztkk@zt.ukrtel.net
Web Address: www.ztkk.net.ua
Personnel:
Gen. Dir.: Oleh Oleksandrovych Karpeka
Phone: (380) 412 343561/375054
Sls. Dir.: Viktor Vasilyevich Chegeyda
Phone: (380) 412 343561/375054
Fax: (380) 412 519833
Email: victor@ztkk.net.ua
Chief Eng.: Alexandr Borysovich Yergidzey
Phone: (380) 412 343561/375054
Prod. Mgr.: Oleksandr Anatoliyovych Palashkevych
Phone: (380) 412 343561/375054
Tech. Dir.: Alexey Evgenievich Kovtonyuk
Phone: (380) 412 343561/375054
Chief of Prod.: Svetlana Ivanova Kuznetsova
Phone: (380) 412 343561/375054
Envir. Mgr.: Olga Nikolaevna Lysak
Phone: (380) 412 343561/375054
Total Employees at this Location: 390
Type of Operation: Paperboard mill
Pulp Grades and Capacities:
Total pulp capacity: 53,915 mt/y
Recycled Pulping: 53,915 mt/y
Pulp Mill Data:
Recycled Fiber Treatment Lines:
Recycled packaging pulping lines: 1
Paper/Paperboard Grades and Capacities:
Total paper and paperboard capacity: 54,000 mt/y
Linerboard: 34,000 mt/y
Corrugating medium/fluting: 20,000 mt/y
Paper and Paperboard Mill Data:
Stock Preparation:
Pulpers: 2
Refiners: 4
Paper Machines: 1
No. 1, fourdrinier, total capacity 54,000 mt/y, Trim width 2.6 m, Corrugating medium/fluting, Linerboard
Energy Data:
Power boilers: 4
Electrical demand for mill: 73 MWh/D

UNITED KINGDOM

ⓞⓜAhlstrom Chirnside Ltd.
Duns Mill
Ownership: 100% by Ahlstrom Corporation Oy
Duns, Berwickshire, TD11 3JW
United Kingdom
Phone: (44) 1890 818303
Fax: (44) 1890 818256
Email: investor@ahlstrom.com, corporate.communications@ahlstrom.com
Web Address: www.ahlstrom.com
Personnel:
Mill Mgr.: Stuart Nixon
Phone: (44) 1890 818303
Fax: (44) 1890 818256
HR Mgr.: Martin Tennant
Phone: (44) 1890 818303
Fax: (44) 1890 818256
Email: martin.tennant@ahlstrom.com
Type of Operation: Paper mill
Mill Locations:
Ahlstrom Chirnside Ltd., Radcliffe Mill, Mount Sion Works, Sion Road, Radcliffe M26 3SB, United

Kingdom, (Pulp mill)
Phone: (44) 161 7255320
Fax: (44) 161 7249113
Email: investor@ahlstrom.com, corporate.
communications@ahlstrom.com
Paper/Paperboard Grades and Capacities:
Total paper and paperboard capacity: 10,000 mt/y
Specialty and industrial: 10,000 mt/y
Paper and Paperboard Mill Data:
Paper Machines: 2
No. 21, fourdrinier, Specialty and industrial
No. 22, fourdrinier, Specialty and industrial

ⓐⓜAhlstrom Chirnside Ltd.
Radcliffe Mill
Ownership: 100% by Ahlstrom Corporation Oy
Mount Sion Works, Sion Road
Radcliffe, Manchester M26 3SB
United Kingdom
Phone: (44) 161 7255320
Fax: (44) 161 7249113
Email: investor@ahlstrom.com,
corporate.communications@ahlstrom.com
Web Address: www.ahlstrom.com
Personnel:
Gen. Mgr.: Geoff Lott
Phone: (44) 161 7255320
Fax: (44) 161 7249113
Regulatory Affairs Manager: Stuart Fraser
Phone: (44) 161 7255320
Fax: (44) 161 7249113
Email: stuart.fraser@ahlstrom.com
Plant. Mgr.: Stuart Nixon
Phone: (44) 161 7255320
Fax: (44) 161 7249113
Email: stuart.nixon@ahlstrom.com
HR Mgr.: Martin Tennant
Phone: (44) 161 7255320
Fax: (44) 161 7249113
Email: martin.tennant@ahlstrom.com
Continuous Improvement Mgr.: Andrew Gorvett
Phone: (44) 161 7255320
Fax: (44) 161 7249113
Email: andrew.gorvett@ahlstrom.com
Total Employees at this Location: 24
Type of Operation: Pulp mill
Mill Locations:
Ahlstrom Chirnside Ltd., Duns Mill, Duns, Berwickshire TD11 3JW, United Kingdom, Capacity: 10,000 mt/y, (Paper mill)
Phone: (44) 1890 818303
Fax: (44) 1890 818256
Email: investor@ahlstrom.com, corporate.
communications@ahlstrom.com
Pulp Grades and Capacities:
Total pulp capacity: 10,000 mt/y

ⓜArjowiggins Chartham Ltd.
Chartham Paper Mill
Ownership: Arjowiggins SAS
Station Rd.
Chartham, Canterbury, Kent CT4 7JA
United Kingdom
Phone: (44) 1227 813 500
Fax: (44) 1227 738 883
Email: (firstname.lastname@arjowiggins.com)
Web Address: www.arjowiggins-tracingpapers.com,
www.arjowiggins.com
Personnel:
Mill Mgr.: Mark Hobday
Phone: (44) 1227 813 500
Fax: (44) 1227 738 883
Email: mark.hobday@arjowiggins.com
Tech. Mgr.: Jim C. Body
Phone: (44) 1227 813 500
Fax: (44) 1227 738 883
Email: jim.body@arjowiggins.com
Prod. Mgr. PM3: Caron Brislee
Phone: (44) 1227 813 500
Fax: (44) 1227 738 883
Email: caron.brislee@arjowiggins.com
Converting Plant Mgr.: Mick Tuss
Phone: (44) 1227 813 500
Fax: (44) 1227 738 883
Email: mick.tuff@arjowiggins.com
Sales & Mktg. Mgr.: James Barclay
Phone: (44) 1227 813 520
Fax: (44) 1227 738 883
Email: james.barclay@arjowiggins.com
Total Employees at this Location: 104
Type of Operation: Paper mill
Paper/Paperboard Grades and Capacities:
Total paper and paperboard capacity: 8,000 mt/y
Uncoated woodfree/freesheet: 8,000 mt/y
Paper and Paperboard Mill Data:
Stock Preparation:
Pulpers: 2
Refiners: 18
Paper Machines: 1
No. 3, fourdrinier, total capacity 8,000 mt/y, Trim width 2.9 m, Uncoated woodfree/freesheet
Finishing Equipment:
Rewinders: 2
Sheeters: 1
Energy Data:
Power boilers: 2
Combustion turbines: 1 at 4.5 MW
Steam turbines: 1 at 1.5 MW

ⓜArjowiggins Fine Papers Pty. Ltd.
Stowford Mill
Mill is closed (closed at the end of 2013)
Ownership: Arjowiggins SAS
Ivybridge, Devon PL21 0AA
United Kingdom
Phone: (44) 1752 612 100
Fax: (44) 1752 612 101
Email: clive.wilson@arjowiggins.com
Web Address: www.arjowiggins.com
Personnel:
Mill Mgr.: Clive N. Wilson
Phone: (44) 1752 612 100
Email: clive.wilson@arjowiggins.com
Manuf. Mgr.: Andrew Dykes
Phone: (44) 1752 612 100
Prod. Mgr.: John Belcher
Phone: (44) 1752 612 100
Total Employees at this Location: 103
Type of Operation: Paper mill
Pulp Grades and Capacities:
Paper/Paperboard Grades and Capacities:
Total paper and paperboard capacity: 14,000 mt/y
Uncoated woodfree/freesheet: 14,000 mt/y
Specialty and industrial
Paper and Paperboard Mill Data:
Stock Preparation:
Pulpers: 3
Refiners: 7
Paper Machines: 2
No. 2, fourdrinier, Trim width 1.8 m
No. 3, fourdrinier, Trim width 1.8 m
Finishing Equipment:
Rewinders: 2
Sheeters: 3
Energy Data:
Power boilers

ⓜArjowiggins Fine Papers Pty. Ltd.
Stoneywood Mill
Ownership: Arjowiggins SAS
Stoneywood Mill, Bucksburn
Aberdeen, Scotland AB21 9AB
United Kingdom
Phone: (44) 1224 802 200
Fax: (44) 1224 802 373
Email: e-enquiries@arjowiggins.com
Web Address: www.arjowiggins.com,
www.arjowiggins-castingpapers.com
Personnel:
Mill Mgr.: Angus MacSween
Phone: (44) 1224 802 200
Fax: (44) 1224 802 373
Email: angus.macsween@arjowiggins.com
Buyer: Ryan Coutts
Phone: (44) 1224 802 200
Fax: (44) 1224 802 373
Project Eng.: David Stewart
Phone: (44) 1224 802 200
Fax: (44) 1224 802 373
Total Employees at this Location: 441
Type of Operation: Paper mill
Paper/Paperboard Grades and Capacities:
Total paper and paperboard capacity: 60,000 mt/y
Uncoated woodfree/freesheet: 60,000 mt/y
Paper and Paperboard Mill Data:
Stock Preparation:
Pulpers: 7
Refiners: 14
Paper Machines: 4
No. 2, fourdrinier, total capacity 10,000 mt/y, Trim width 1.9 m, Uncoated woodfree/freesheet
No. 8, fourdrinier, total capacity 20,000 mt/y, Trim width 2.8 m, Uncoated woodfree/freesheet
No. 9, hybrid former, total capacity 20,000 mt/y, Trim width 2.3 m, Uncoated woodfree/freesheet
No. 10, fourdrinier, total capacity 10,000 mt/y, Trim width 2.2 m, Uncoated woodfree/freesheet
Coating Machines: 2
No. 1, on machine
No. 2
Finishing Equipment:
Supercalenders: 1
Rewinders: 6
Sheeters: 4
Energy Data:
Power boilers
Combustion turbines: 1 at 10 MW
Steam turbines: 1 at 2.7 MW
Electrical demand for mill: 129 MWh/D

ⓐⓜAylesford Newsprint Ltd.
Aylesford Mill
Ownership: 100% by Martland Holdings (Private)
Newsprint House, Bellingham Way
Aylesford, Kent ME20 7DL
United Kingdom
Phone: (44) 1622 796 000
Fax: (44) 1622 796 001
Email: info@aylesford-newsprint.co.uk
Web Address: www.aylesford-newsprint.co.uk
Personnel:
Man. Dir. (From August 2014): Landry Kouakou
Phone: (44) 1622 796 342
Fax: (44) 1622 796 001
Email: landry.kouakou@aylnews.com
Proj. Mgr.: Richard Hornewood
Phone: (44) 1622 796 000
Fax: (44) 1622 796 001
Email: richard.hornewood@aylnews.com
Head recycling department: Gemma Barratt
Phone: (44) 1622 796 372
Fax: (44) 1622 796 001
Email: gemma.stapeley@aylesford-newsprint.co.uk
Head of UK Sls.: Terry Worby
Phone: (44) 1622 796 314
Fax: (44) 1622 796 001
Email: terry.worby@aylesford-newsprint.co.uk
Secondary Products Manager: Rachel Bain
Phone: (44) 1622 796 252
Fax: (44) 1622 796 001
Email: rachel.bain@aylesford-newsprint.co.uk
Total Employees of Company: 350
Total Employees at this Location: 285
Type of Operation: Pulp mill, Paper mill
Pulp Grades and Capacities:
Total pulp capacity: 411,587 mt/y
Recycled Pulping: 411,587 mt/y

United Kingdom

Pulp Mill Data:
Recycled Fiber Treatment Lines:
Flotation deinking lines: 2 at 500,000 admt/y
Pulpers: 2 at 500,000 admt/y
Paper/Paperboard Grades and Capacities:
Total paper and paperboard capacity: 400,000 mt/y
Newsprint: 400,000 mt/y
Paper and Paperboard Mill Data:
Stock Preparation:
Pulpers: 2
Paper Machines: 2
No. 13, Top Flyte, total capacity 100,000 mt/y, Trim width 5.2 m, Newsprint
No. 14, OptiFormer, total capacity 300,000 mt/y, Trim width 9.3 m, Newsprint
Finishing Equipment:
Rewinders: 3
Energy Data:
HRSG boiler: 2
Combustion turbines: 2 at 78 MW
Steam turbines: 1 at 20 MW
Electrical demand for mill: 1,014 MWh/D

ⓂBillerudKorsnäs AB
Beetham Mill
Beetham
Milnthorpe, Cumbria LA7 7AR
United Kingdom
Phone: (44) 1539 565 000
Fax: (44) 1539 565 033
Email: info@billerudkorsnas.com
Web Address: www.billerudkorsnas.com
Personnel:
Mill & Oper. Mgr.: Ying Sou
Phone: (44) 1539 565 000
Fax: (44) 1539 565 033
Email: ying.sou@billerudkorsnas.com
Finan. & Admin. & Purch. Mgr.: Wit Lazurek
Phone: (44) 1539 565 000
Fax: (44) 1539 565 033
Email: wit.lazurek@billerudkorsnas.com
Tech. Mgr.: David Shaw
Phone: (44) 1539 565 000
Fax: (44) 1539 565 033
Email: david.shaw@billerudkorsnas.com
Tech. Mgr. Sls.: Cherry Archer
Phone: (44) 1539 565 000
Fax: (44) 1539 565 033
Email: cherry.archer@billerudkorsnas.com
Total Employees at this Location: 141
Type of Operation: Paper mill
Paper/Paperboard Grades and Capacities:
Total paper and paperboard capacity: 44,982 mt/y
Specialty and industrial: 44,982 mt/y
Paper and Paperboard Mill Data:
Stock Preparation:
Pulpers: 3
Refiners: 9
Paper Machines: 2
No. 1, Yankee dryer, total capacity 22,491 mt/y, Trim width 2.6 m, Specialty and industrial
No. 2, Yankee dryer, total capacity 22,491 mt/y, Trim width 2.6 m, Specialty and industrial
Coating Machines: 2
PM1, on machine
PM2, on machine
Finishing Equipment:
Winders: 1
Calenders: 1
Energy Data:
Power boilers: 2
Hydro turbines: 1
Electrical demand for mill: 112 MWh/D

ⓄⓂJames Cropper
Kendal Mill
Company is formerly James Cropper Speciality Papers
Ownership: 100% by James Cropper PLC
Burneside Mills
Kendal, Cumbria LA9 6PZ
United Kingdom
Phone: (44) 1539 722 002
Fax: (44) 1539 728 088
Email: info@cropper.com
Web Address: www.jamescropper.com, www.cropper.com
Personnel:
Chrmn.: Mark A. J. Cropper
Phone: (44) 1539 722 002
Fax: (44) 1539 728 088
CEO: Phil I. Wild
Phone: (44) 1539 722 002
Fax: (44) 1539 728 088
COO: Dave Watson
Phone: (44) 1539 722 002
Fax: (44) 1539 728088
Email: dave.watson@cropper.com
Man. Dir. of Technical Fibre Products Limited: Martin Thompson
Phone: (44) 1539 722 002
Fax: (44) 1539 728 088
Email: martin.thompson@cropper.com
Comm. Dir.: Chris Brown
Phone: (44) 1539 818 214
Fax: (44) 1539 728 088
Email: chris.brown@cropper.com
Finan. Dir.: Isabelle M. Maddock
Phone: (44) 1539 722 002
Fax: (44) 1539 728 088
Email: isabelle.maddock@cropper.com
Chief Technology Officer (from January 2014): Patrick Willink
Phone: (44) 1539 722 002
Fax: (44) 1539 728 088
Email: patrick.willink@cropper.com
Total Employees of Company: 486
Total Employees at this Location: 486
Type of Operation: Paper mill
Paper/Paperboard Grades and Capacities:
Total paper and paperboard capacity: 60,000 mt/y
Uncoated woodfree/freesheet: 30,000 mt/y
Specialty and industrial: 30,000 mt/y
Paper and Paperboard Mill Data:
Stock Preparation:
Pulpers: 4
Refiners: 10
Paper Machines: 4
No. 1, twin-wire, total capacity 10,000 mt/y, Trim width 1.95 m, Uncoated woodfree/freesheet
No. 2, twin-wire, total capacity 15,000 mt/y, Trim width 2.15 m, Uncoated woodfree/freesheet, Specialty and industrial
No. 3, fourdrinier, total capacity 15,000 mt/y, Trim width 3.2 m, Uncoated woodfree/freesheet, Specialty and industrial
No. 4, twin-wire, total capacity 20,000 mt/y, Trim width 2.54 m, Specialty and industrial
Finishing Equipment:
Rewinders: 5
Sheeters: 4
Energy Data:
Power boilers: 1
Combustion turbines: 1 at 7.0 MW
Electrical demand for mill: 119 MWh/D

ⓄDe La Rue plc
Ownership: public
De La Rue House, Jays Close
Basingstoke, Hampshire RG22 4BS
United Kingdom
Phone: (44) 1256 605000
Fax: (44) 1256 605004
Email: sales@uk.delarue.com
Web Address: www.delarue.com
Personnel:
Chrmn.: Philip Rogerson
Phone: (44) 1256 605000
Fax: (44) 1256 605004
Email: philip.rogerson@uk.delarue.com
CEO (Eff. October 13, 2014): Martin Sutherland
Phone: (44) 1256 605000
Fax: (44) 1256 605004
Group Finan. Dir. & COO: Colin Child
Phone: (44) 1256 605000
Fax: (44) 1256 605004
Email: colin.child@uk.delarue.com
Chrmn. of the Audit Committee: Warren East CBE
Phone: (44) 1256 605000
Fax: (44) 1256 605004
Chrmn. of the Remuneration Committee: Gill Rider
Phone: (44) 1256 605000
Fax: (44) 1256 605004
Group Dir. of Communications: Rob Hutchison
Phone: (44) 1256 605000
Fax: (44) 1256 605004
Total Employees of Company: 4,000
Mill Locations:
De La Rue Currency, Overton Mill, Overton, Basingstoke RG25 3JG, United Kingdom, Capacity: 8,700 mt/y, (Paper mill)
Phone: (44) 1256 771990/770770
Fax: (44) 1256 771738/770937
Email: sales@uk.delarue.com
De La Rue Security Papers, Bathford Paper Mill, Bathford, Bath, Avon BA1 7QG, United Kingdom, Capacity: 2,000 mt/y, (Paper mill)
Phone: (44) 1225 859 903
Fax: (44) 1225 852 128
Email: security.print@uk.delarue.com; firstname.lastname@uk.delarue.com

ⓄⓂDe La Rue Currency
Overton Mill
Ownership: De La Rue plc
Overton
Basingstoke, Hampshire RG25 3JG
United Kingdom
Phone: (44) 1256 771990/770770
Fax: (44) 1256 771738/770937
Email: sales@uk.delarue.com
Web Address: www.delarue.com
Personnel:
Group Dir., Strategy & Bus. Develop.: Constance Baroudel
Phone: (44) 1256 770 770
Fax: (44) 1256 770 937
Email: constance.baroudel@uk.delarue.com
Group Dir., HR: Andy Kemp
Phone: (44) 1256 770 770
Fax: (44) 1256 770 937
Email: andy.kemp@uk.delarue.com
Man. Dir., Supply Chain: Rupert Middleton
Phone: (44) 1256 770 770
Fax: (44) 1256 770 937
Email: rupert.middleton@uk.delarue.com
Gen. Counsel & Corp. Secretary: Ed Peppiatt
Phone: (44) 1256 770 770
Fax: (44) 1256 770 937
Email: ed.peppiatt@uk.delarue.com
Total Employees of Company: 4,000
Total Employees at this Location: 600
Type of Operation: Paper mill
Paper/Paperboard Grades and Capacities:
Total paper and paperboard capacity: 8,700 mt/y
Uncoated woodfree/freesheet: 8,700 mt/y

ⓂDe La Rue Security Papers
Bathford Paper Mill
Ownership: De La Rue plc
Bathford
Bath, Avon, Somerset BA1 7QG
United Kingdom
Phone: (44) 1225 859 903
Fax: (44) 1225 852 128
Email: security.print@uk.delarue.com, firstname.lastname@uk.delarue.com
Web Address: www.delarue.com
Personnel:

United Kingdom

Gen. Mgr.: Laura Redman-Thomas
Phone: (44) 1225 859 903
Prod. Mgr.: Andrew Nash
Phone: (44) 1225 859 903
Sls. Mgr.: Melanie Huttunen
Phone: (44) 1225 859 903
Total Employees at this Location: 110
Type of Operation: Paper mill
Paper/Paperboard Grades and Capacities:
Total paper and paperboard capacity: 2,000 mt/y
Uncoated woodfree/freesheet: 2,000 mt/y
Paper and Paperboard Mill Data:
Paper Machines: 1
No. 1, cylinder mould, total capacity 2,000 mt/y, Uncoated woodfree/freesheet

①⑩Devon Valley Ltd.
Devon Valley Mill
Ownership: Purico Group Ltd.
Hele, Exeter, Devon EX5 4JP
United Kingdom
Phone: (44) 1392 881 731
Fax: (44) 1392 883 550
Email: info@devonvalleymill.com,
sales@cromptonpapers.com
Web Address: www.purico.com,
www.devonvalleymill.com
Personnel:
Chmn: Anil Puri
Phone: (44) 1159 013 000
CEO: Eddie Holt
Phone: (44) 1204 526 241
Gen. Mgr./Dir./VP: Horst Blum
Phone: (44) 1392 883 501
Fax: (44) 1392 883 550
Email: hblum@devonvalleymill.com
Total Employees of Company: 48
Total Employees at this Location: 48
Type of Operation: Paper mill
Paper/Paperboard Grades and Capacities:
Total paper and paperboard capacity: 12,000 mt/y
Specialty and industrial: 12,000 mt/y
Paper and Paperboard Mill Data:
Stock Preparation:
Pulpers: 2
Refiners: 3
Paper Machines: 2
PM 5, fourdrinier, inclined, total capacity 6,000 mt/y, Trim width 2.3 m, Specialty and industrial
PM 6, fourdrinier, total capacity 6,000 mt/y, Trim width 1.86 m, Specialty and industrial
Finishing Equipment:
Rewinders: 2
Energy Data:
Power boilers

①⑩Disley Tissue Ltd.
Disley Mill
Ownership: Northwood Group
Waterside
Disley, North Stockport, Cheshire SK12 2HW
United Kingdom
Phone: (44) 1663 762 701
Fax: (44) 1663 762 421
Web Address: www.northwoodpaper.com,
www.connecthygiene.co.uk/
Personnel:
Mill Mgr.: Chris Wickham
Phone: (44) 1663 762 701
Email: chris.wickham@connecthygiene.co.uk
Oper. Mgr.: Michael Mallouris
Phone: (44) 1663 762 701
Prod. Mgr.: Craig Galloway
Phone: (44) 1663 762 701
Total Employees at this Location: 150
Type of Operation: Pulp mill, Paper mill
Pulp Grades and Capacities:
Total pulp capacity: 33,000 mt/y
Pulp available for market: 6,375 mt/y
Recycled Pulping: 33,000 mt/y
Pulp Mill Data:
Recycled Fiber Treatment Lines:
Flotation deinking lines: 2 at 37,485 admt/y
Pulpers: 4 at 119,595 admt/y
Washing deinking lines: 2 at 53,550 admt/y
Pulp Dryers:
Wet Lap machine 1
Paper/Paperboard Grades and Capacities:
Total paper and paperboard capacity: 25,000 mt/y
Tissue: 25,000 mt/y
Paper and Paperboard Mill Data:
Stock Preparation:
Pulpers: 4
Refiners: 6
Paper Machines: 1
No. 1, crescent former, Yankee dryer, total capacity 25,000 mt/y, Trim width 2.8 m, Tissue
Finishing Equipment:
Rewinders: 1
Energy Data:
Power boilers: 3
Electrical demand for mill: 90 MWh/D

①⑩DS Smith Paper
Kemsley Mill
Ownership: 100% by DS Smith Plc
Kemsley, Sittingbourne, Kent ME10 2TD
United Kingdom
Phone: (44) 1795 518 900
Fax: (44) 1795 514 305
Email: info@dssmith.com
Web Address: www.dssmith.com
Personnel:
Chmn.: Gareth Davies
Phone: (44) 1795 518 900
Fax: (44) 1795 514 305
CEO: Miles Roberts
Phone: (44) 1795 518 900
Fax: (44) 1795 514 305
Gen. Mgr. Kemsley Mill: Niels Flierman
Phone: (44) 1795 514 025
Fax: (44) 1795 514 305
Email: niels.flierman@dssmith.com
Sls. & Mktg. Dir.: Nick Britton
Phone: (44) 1795 518 900
Fax: (44) 1795 514 305
Man. Dir. DS Smith Paper: Chris Rosser
Phone: (44) 1795 518 900
Fax: (44) 1795 514 305
Reliability Mgr.: Richard Usher
Phone: (44) 1795 518 900
Fax: (44) 1795 514 305
Purch. Mgr.: Keith Back
Phone: (44) 1795 518 900
Fax: (44) 1795 514 305
Oper. Mgr.: Kerri Baldwin
Phone: (44) 1795 518 900
Fax: (44) 1795 514 305
Site Prod. Mgr.: Rogier Gerritsen
Phone: (44) 1795 518 900
Fax: (44) 1795 514 305
Tech. Mgr.: Guy Lacey
Phone: (44) 1795 518 900
Fax: (44) 1795 514 305
Total Employees at this Location: 400
Type of Operation: Pulp mill, Paperboard mill
Mill Locations:
DS Smith Paper, Wansbrough Paper Mill, Watchet TA23 0AY, United Kingdom, Capacity: 162,000 mt/y, (Paper mill, Paperboard mill)
Phone: (44) 1984 631 456
Fax: (44) 1984 634 123
Email: info@dssmith.com
Pulp Grades and Capacities:
Total pulp capacity: 880,564 mt/y
Pulp available for market: 72,800 mt/y
Recycled Pulping: 880,564 mt/y
Pulp Mill Data:
Bleach Plant Systems: 1
Recycled Fiber Treatment Lines:
Flotation deinking lines: 1
Recycled packaging pulping lines: 1
Pulp Dryers:
Air Float dryers 1
Paper/Paperboard Grades and Capacities:
Total paper and paperboard capacity: 810,000 mt/y
Linerboard: 328,000 mt/y
Corrugating medium/fluting: 352,000 mt/y
Boxboard/cartonboard: 130,000 mt/y
Paper and Paperboard Mill Data:
Stock Preparation:
Pulpers: 3
Refiners: 3
Paper Machines: 3
No. 3, fourdrinier (3), total capacity 325,000 mt/y, Trim width 5.4 m, Boxboard/cartonboard, Linerboard
No. 4, fourdrinier, total capacity 220,000 mt/y, Trim width 6 m, Corrugating medium/fluting
No. 6, (Former Type model: DuoFormer D), twin-wire, total capacity 265,000 mt/y, Trim width 6.8 m, Corrugating medium/fluting, Linerboard
Finishing Equipment:
Winders: 4
Energy Data:
Power boilers: 2
Combustion turbines: 1
Steam turbines: 1
Electrical demand for mill: 1,293 MWh/D

①DS Smith Plc
Ownership: Public, Norges Bank
7th Floor, 350 Euston Road, Regent's Place
London, NW1 3AX
United Kingdom
Phone: (44) 20 7756 1800
Email: ir@dssmith.co.uk
Web Address: www.dssmith.com
Personnel:
Chmn. of the Board: Gareth Davis
Phone: (44) 20 7756 1800
Exec. Dir. & Group Chief Exec.: Miles Roberts
Phone: (44) 20 7756 1800
Group Finan. Dir.: Adrian Marsh
Phone: (44) 20 7756 1800
Paper CEO: Stefano Rossi
Phone: (44) 20 7756 1800
Email: stefano.rossi@dssmith.com
Man. Dir. UK packaging division.: Gareth Jenkins
Phone: (44) 20 7756 1800
Non-Exec. Dir.: Christopher Bunker
Phone: (44) 20 7756 1800
Head of Inv. Relations & Commun. Mgr.: Rachel Stevens
Phone: (44) 20 7756 1800
Email: ir@dssmith.co.uk
Chief Procurement Officer: Paul Harridine
Phone: (44) 20 7756 1800
HR Dir.: Brian Wark
Phone: (44) 20 7756 1800
Email: head.office@dssp.com
Total Employees of Company: 21,500
Total Employees at this Location: 45
Mill Locations:
DS Smith Paper, Kemsley Mill, Kemsley, Sittingbourne ME10 2TD, United Kingdom, Capacity: 810,000 mt/y, (Pulp mill, Paperboard mill)
Phone: (44) 1795 518 900
Fax: (44) 1795 514 305
Email: info@dssmith.com
DS Smith Paper Deutschland GmbH, Aschaffenburg Mill, Weichertstrasse 7, D-63741 Aschaffenburg, Germany, Capacity: 380,000 mt/y, (Paper mill, Paperboard mill)
Phone: (49) 6021 400 0
Fax: (49) 6021 400 270
Email: info@dssmith.com
DS Smith Packaging France, Contoire Hamel Mill (99% owned), 39 Route Nationale, F-80500 Contoire

United Kingdom

Hamel, France, Capacity: 80,000 mt/y, (Pulp mill, Paperboard mill)
Phone: (33) 3 22 78 77 76
Fax: (33) 3 22 78 77 77
Email: info@dssmith.com

DS Smith Chouanard, Coullons Mill, Usine de la Fosse, BP 8, F-45720 Coullons, France, Capacity: 35,000 mt/y, (Paperboard mill)
Phone: (33) 2 38 29 52 87
Fax: (33) 2 38 29 22 38
Email: info@dssmith.com

DS Smith Packaging Benelux B.V., Eerbeek Mill, Harderwijkerweg 41, NL-6961 GH Eerbeek, Netherlands, Capacity: 355,000 mt/y, (Paper mill, Paperboard mill)
Phone: (31) 313 677 922
Fax: (31) 313 654 745
Email: info@dssmith.com

DS Smith Paper, Hollins Paper Mill, Hollins Road, Darwen BB3 0BE, United Kingdom, (Paper mill, Paperboard mill)
Phone: (44) 1254 702 728
Fax: (44) 1254 873 358
Email: info@dssmith.com

DS Smith Kaysersberg, Kaysersberg Mill, Route de Lapoutroie, BP 22, F-68240 Kaysersberg, France, Capacity: 170,000 mt/y, (Paperboard mill)
Phone: (33) 3 89 78 30 00/39/44
Fax: (33) 3 89 47 18 89
Email: info@dssmith.com

DS Smith Packaging Italia S.p.A., Lucca Mill, Via del Frizzone, I-55016 Porcari, (LU), Italy, Capacity: 420,000 mt/y, (Paperboard mill)
Phone: (39) 0583 2961
Fax: (39) 0583 296657
Email: info@dssmith.com

DS Smith Packaging France, Nantes Mill (99% owned), 33 Blvd Benoni-Goullin, F-44200 Nantes Cedex 02, France, Capacity: 53,000 mt/y, (Pulp mill, Paperboard mill)
Phone: (33) 2 40 89 29 11
Fax: (33) 2 40 35 21 01
Email: info@dssmith.com

DS Smith Paper, Wansbrough Paper Mill, Watchet TA23 0AY, United Kingdom, Capacity: 162,000 mt/y, (Paper mill, Paperboard mill)
Phone: (44) 1984 631 456
Fax: (44) 1984 634 123
Email: info@dssmith.com

DS Smith Paper Deutschland GmbH, Witzenhausen Mill, Kasseler Landstr. 23, D-37213 Witzenhausen, Germany, Capacity: 340,000 mt/y, (Paperboard mill)
Phone: (49) 5542 5020
Fax: (49) 5542 502116
Email: info@dssmith.com

Rubezhansky Cardboard and Packaging Mill, Rubezhnoye Mill (49.60% owned), ul. Mendeleeva, 67, 93006 Rubezhnoye, Ukraine, Capacity: 290,000 mt/y, (Paperboard mill)
Phone: (380) 6453 92210/92260
Fax: (380) 6453 70415/92407
Email: info@rktk.com.ua, rktk@svitonline.com

Selkasan Kagit ve Paketleme Malzemeleri Imalati San. ve Tic. AS, Manisa Mill, Organize Sanayi Bölgesi, PK.199, 45001 Manisa, Turkey, Capacity: 170,000 mt/y, (Paper mill)
Phone: (90) 236 213 02 73-77
Fax: (90) 236 213 0278
Email: selkasan@superonline.com

Ⓜ DS Smith Paper
Wansbrough Paper Mill
Ownership: 100% by DS Smith Plc

Watchet, Somerset TA23 0AY
United Kingdom
 Phone: (44) 1984 631 456
 Fax: (44) 1984 634 123
 Email: info@dssmith.com
 Web Address: www.dssmith.com
Personnel:
Gen. Mgr. & Technology & Manuf. Dir.: Craig Nicol
 Phone: (44) 1984 639 704
 Fax: (44) 1984 634 123
 Email: craig.nicol@dssmith.com
Chief Accountant: Jane Trunks
 Phone: (44) 1984 631 456
 Fax: (44) 1984 634 123
 Email: jane.trunks@dssmith.com
Oper. Mgr.: Chris Kellaway
 Phone: (44) 1984 639 745
 Fax: (44) 1984 634 123
 Email: chris.kellaway@dssmith.com
Total Employees at this Location: 168
Type of Operation: Paper mill, Paperboard mill
Pulp Grades and Capacities:
Total pulp capacity: 164,521 mt/y
Recycled Pulping: 164,521 mt/y
Pulp Mill Data:
Recycled Fiber Treatment Lines:
Recycled packaging pulping lines: 1
Paper/Paperboard Grades and Capacities:
Total paper and paperboard capacity: 162,000 mt/y
Packaging papers: 37,000 mt/y
Linerboard: 35,000 mt/y
Boxboard/cartonboard: 90,000 mt/y
Paper and Paperboard Mill Data:
Stock Preparation:
Pulpers: 4
Refiners: 4
Paper Machines: 2
No. 1, fourdrinier, Yankee dryer, total capacity 37,000 mt/y, Trim width 3.4 m, Packaging papers
No. 5, fourdrinier, total capacity 125,000 mt/y, Trim width 3.2 m, Boxboard/cartonboard, Linerboard
Finishing Equipment:
Winders: 4
Energy Data:
Power boilers: 3
Steam turbines: 1 at 5.5 MW
Electrical demand for mill: 194 MWh/D

ⓘⓂ Fourstones Paper Mill Co. Ltd.
Sapphire Mills

Glenwood Road
Leslie, Scotland KY6 3AB
United Kingdom
 Phone: (44) 1592 746 000, 1592 328 652
 Fax: (44) 1592 743 888, 1592 328 652
 Email: team@fourstonespapermill.co.uk
 Web Address: www.fourstonespapermill.co.uk
Personnel:
Man.Dir.: Peter Duxbury
 Phone: (44) 07879441958
 Fax: (44) 1592 328 652
 Email: peter.duxbury@fourstonespapermill.co.uk
Mill Mgr.: John French
 Phone: (44) 1592 743 888
 Fax: (44) 1592 328 652
Type of Operation: Pulp mill, Paper mill
Pulp Grades and Capacities:
Total pulp capacity: 8,056 mt/y
Recycled Pulping: 8,056 mt/y
Paper/Paperboard Grades and Capacities:
Total paper and paperboard capacity: 15,000 mt/y
Tissue: 15,000 mt/y
Paper and Paperboard Mill Data:
Stock Preparation:
Pulpers: 5
Refiners: 6
Paper Machines: 1
No. 2, fourdrinier, Yankee dryer, total capacity 15,000 mt/y, Trim width 2.64 m, Tissue
Finishing Equipment:
Rewinders: 5
Sheeters: 2
Energy Data:
Power boilers
Steam turbines: 2 at 3.5 MW
Electrical demand for mill: 41 MWh/D

ⓘⓂ Fourstones Paper Mill Co. Ltd.
South Tyne Mill

Fourstones
Hexham, Northumberland NE46 3SD
United Kingdom
 Phone: (44) 1434 602 444
 Fax: (44) 1434 607 046
 Email: team@fourstonespapermill.co.uk, sales@fourstonespapermill.co.uk
 Web Address: www.fourstonespapermill.co.uk
Personnel:
Man. Dir.: Peter Duxbury
 Phone: (44) 1434 602 444
 Fax: (44) 1434 607 046
 Email: peter.duxbury@fourstonespapermill.co.uk
Mill Mgr.: Ken Skate
 Phone: (44) 1434 602 444
 Fax: (44) 1434 607 046
Sales Mgr.: Rob Pennington
 Phone: (44) 1434 602 444
 Fax: (44) 1434 607 046
 Email: rob.pennington@fourstonespapermill.co.uk
Purch.Mgr.: Pauline Duxbury
 Phone: (44) 1434 602 444
 Fax: (44) 1434 607 046
 Email: pauline.duxbury@fourstonespapermill.co.uk
Total Employees at this Location: 46
Type of Operation: Paper mill
Mill Locations:
Fourstones Paper Mill Co. Ltd., Sapphire Mills, Glenwood Road, Leslie KY6 3AB, United Kingdom, Capacity: 15,000 mt/y, (Pulp mill, Paper mill)
 Phone: (44) 1592 743 888
 Fax: (44) 1592 328 652
 Email: team@fourstonespapermill.co.uk
Pulp Grades and Capacities:
Total pulp capacity: 5,180 mt/y
Recycled Pulping: 5,180 mt/y
Pulp Mill Data:
Recycled Fiber Treatment Lines:
Pulpers: 2
Paper/Paperboard Grades and Capacities:
Total paper and paperboard capacity: 7,000 mt/y
Tissue: 7,000 mt/y
Paper and Paperboard Mill Data:
Stock Preparation:
Pulpers: 2
Refiners: 2
Paper Machines: 1
No. 1, fourdrinier, total capacity 7,000 mt/y, Trim width 2.34 m, Tissue
Finishing Equipment:
Rewinders: 2
Energy Data:
Power boilers: 1
Electrical demand for mill: 17 MWh/D

Ⓜ Glatfelter UK Ltd.
Lydney Paper Mill
Ownership: Glatfelter

Church Rd.
Lydney, Gloucestershire GL15 5EJ
United Kingdom
 Phone: (44) 1594 842 235
 Fax: (44) 1594 844 213
 Email: info@glatfelter.com, uksales@glatfelter.com
 Web Address: www.glatfelter.com
Personnel:
Man. Dir.: Amy Wannemacher
 Phone: (44) 1594 842 235
 Fax: (44) 1594 844 213
 Email: amy.wannemacher@glatfelter.com
Mill Mgr.: David Foulds
 Phone: (44) 1594 842 235
 Fax: (44) 1594 844 213
 Email: david.foulds@glatfelter.com
Prod. Mgr.: Andy Durdif
 Phone: (44) 1594 842 235

United Kingdom

Fax: (44) 1594 844 213
Email: andy.durdif@glatfelter.com
Total Employees at this Location: 276
Type of Operation: Paper mill
Paper/Paperboard Grades and Capacities:
Total paper and paperboard capacity: 15,000 mt/y
Specialty and industrial: 15,000 mt/y
Paper and Paperboard Mill Data:
Paper Machines: 3
PM 7, Trim width 4.2 m, Specialty and industrial
PM 8, Trim width 2.2 m, Specialty and industrial
PM 9, Trim width 3.2 m, Specialty and industrial

ⓘⓜPeter Grant Papers Limited
Ownership: 100% by Northwood Group
Stafford Park 12
Telford, TF3 3BJ
United Kingdom
 Phone: (44) 1952 292 200
 Fax: (44) 1952 291 108
 Email: info@petergrantpapers.com,
 sales@petergrantpapers.com
 Web Address: www.petergrantpapers.com
Personnel:
 Man. Dir.: Adrian Jones
 Phone: (44) 1952 292 200
 Fax: (44) 1952 291 108
 Sales & Mktg. Dir.: Paul Weddle
 Phone: (44) 1952 292 200
 Fax: (44) 1952 291 108
 Email: paul.weddle@petergrantpapers.com
 Mktg. Mgr.: Maria Smallcombe
 Phone: (44) 1952 292 200
 Fax: (44) 1952 291 108
 Bus. Develop. Mgr.: Stones Graham
 Phone: (44) 1952 292 200
 Fax: (44) 1952 291 108
 Account Mgr.: Kevin Westbury
 Phone: (44) 1952 292 200
 Fax: (44) 1952 291 108
 Purch. Mgr.: Ann Short
 Phone: (44) 1952 292 200
 Fax: (44) 1952 291 108
 Oper. Mgr.: Mike Speller
 Phone: (44) 1952 292 200
 Fax: (44) 1952 291 108
Total Employees of Company: 170
Mill Locations:
Peter Grant Papers Limited, Lancaster Mill, Lansil Way, Caton Rd., Lancaster LA1 3PQ, United Kingdom, Capacity: 8,000 mt/y, (Paper mill)
 Phone: (44) 1524 843 678
 Fax: (44) 1524 843 644
 Email: sales@petergrantpapers.com

ⓜPeter Grant Papers Limited
Lancaster Mill
Ownership: 100% by Northwood Group
Lansil Way, Caton Rd.
Lancaster, Lancashire LA1 3PQ
United Kingdom
 Phone: (44) 1524 843 678
 Fax: (44) 1524 843 644
 Email: sales@petergrantpapers.com
 Web Address: www.petergrant-papers.com
Personnel:
 Man. Dir.: Adrian Jones
 Phone: (44) 1952 292 200
 Fax: (44) 1952 291 108
 Dir.: Adam Fecher
 Phone: (44) 1524 843 678
 Fax: (44) 1524 843 644
 Sls. & Mktg. Dir.: Paul Weddle
 Phone: (44) 1952 292 200
 Fax: (44) 1952 291 108
 Email: paul.weddle@petergrantpapers.com
 Mill Mgr.: James McDougall Gordon
 Phone: (44) 1524 843 678
 Fax: (44) 1524 843 644
 Mktg. Mgr.: Maria Smallcombe

Phone: (44) 1952 292 200
Fax: (44) 1952 291 108
Email: sales@petergrantpapers.com
Account Mgr. (National & International): Phil d'Arcy
Phone: (44) 1524 843 678
Fax: (44) 1524 843 644
Total Employees at this Location: 32
Type of Operation: Paper mill
Pulp Grades and Capacities:
Total pulp capacity: 8,501 mt/y
Recycled Pulping: 8,501 mt/y
Pulp Mill Data:
Recycled Fiber Treatment Lines:
Flotation deinking lines: 1
Paper/Paperboard Grades and Capacities:
Total paper and paperboard capacity: 8,000 mt/y
Tissue: 8,000 mt/y
Paper and Paperboard Mill Data:
Paper Machines: 1
No. 1, Yankee dryer, total capacity 8,000 mt/y, Trim width 2.7 m, Tissue
Energy Data:
Power boilers: 1
Electrical demand for mill: 25 MWh/D

ⓘⓜJohn Hargreaves (C&S) Ltd.
Stalybridge Mill
Ownership: Hargreaves Family (Private)
Tameside Paper Mills, Knowl Street
Stalybridge, Cheshire, Greater Manchester SK15 3AJ
United Kingdom
 Phone: (44) 1613 386 011
 Fax: (44) 1613 384 194
 Email: general@john-hargreaves.co.uk,
 mt@john-hargreaves.co.uk
 Web Address: www.john-hargreaves.co.uk
Personnel:
 Chmn. & Man. Dir.: John M.P. Hargreaves
 Phone: (44) 1613 386 011
 Mill Mgr.: M. Thompson
 Phone: (44) 1613 386 011
 Sls. Mgr.: G. Tootle
 Phone: (44) 1613 386 011
 Oper. Dir.: A. N. Hargreaves
 Phone: (44) 1613 386 011
Total Employees of Company: 47
Total Employees at this Location: 47
Type of Operation: Paperboard mill
Paper/Paperboard Grades and Capacities:
Total paper and paperboard capacity: 15,000 mt/y
Linerboard: 15,000 mt/y
Paper and Paperboard Mill Data:
Paper Machines: 1
PM 1, total capacity 15,000 mt/y, Trim width 2.15 m, Linerboard

ⓘⓜHigher Kings Mill Ltd
Higher Kings Mill
Cullompton, Devon EX15 1QJ
United Kingdom
 Phone: (44) 1884 836 300
 Fax: (44) 1884 836 333 / 330
 Email: hkm.sales@higherkings.co.uk
 Web Address: www.higherkings.co.uk
Personnel:
 Oper. Dir.: Mark Broom
 Phone: (44) 1884 836 300, (M) 772 068 1163
 Fax: (44) 1884 836 333
 Email: mark.broom@higherkings.co.uk
 Energy & Proj. Mgr.: Adam Appleby
 Phone: (44) 1884 836 311
 Fax: (44) 1884 836 333
 Email: adam.appleby@higherkings.co.uk
 Mgr.: Dean Hutter
 Phone: (44) 1884 836 300
 Fax: (44) 1884 836 333
 Email: dean.hutter@higherkings.co.uk
Total Employees at this Location: 120
Type of Operation: Paper mill

Pulp Grades and Capacities:
Total pulp capacity: 35,617 mt/y
Recycled Pulping: 35,617 mt/y
Pulp Mill Data:
Bleach Plant Systems: 1
Paper/Paperboard Grades and Capacities:
Total paper and paperboard capacity: 36,000 mt/y
Uncoated woodfree/freesheet: 36,000 mt/y
Paper and Paperboard Mill Data:
Stock Preparation:
Pulpers: 2
Refiners: 2
Paper Machines: 1
No. 1, fourdrinier, total capacity 36,000 mt/y, Trim width 2.3 m, Uncoated woodfree/freesheet
Finishing Equipment:
Rewinders: 1
Sheeters: 3
Energy Data:
Power boilers: 2
Electrical demand for mill: 99 MWh/D

ⓘⓜHollingsworth & Vose Co. Ltd.
Postlip Mills
Ownership: 100% by Hollingsworth & Vose Co.
Winchcombe
Cheltenham, Gloucestershire GL54 5BB
United Kingdom
 Phone: (44) 1242 602 227
 Fax: (44) 1242 604 099
 Email: hollingsworth@hovo.co.uk
 Web Address: www.hollingsworth-vose.com
Personnel:
 President & CEO: Valentine III Hollingsworth
 Ops. Dir.: J. Patterson
 Phone: (44) 1242 602 227
 Sls. Mgr.: H. Jones
 Phone: (44) 1242 602 227
 Sls. Mgr.: P. Smith
 Phone: (44) 1242 602 227
 Co Secretary: Eileen Margaret Swain
Total Employees at this Location: 134
Type of Operation: Pulp mill, Paper mill
Pulp Grades and Capacities:
Total pulp capacity: 10,000 mt/y
Paper/Paperboard Grades and Capacities:
Total paper and paperboard capacity: 10,000 mt/y
Specialty and industrial: 10,000 mt/y
Paper and Paperboard Mill Data:
Stock Preparation:
Pulpers: 3
Refiners: 3
Paper Machines: 2
No. 1, fourdrinier, total capacity 6,000 mt/y, Trim width 1.8 m, Specialty and industrial
No. 2, Rotoformer, total capacity 4,000 mt/y, Trim width 1.5 m, Specialty and industrial
Finishing Equipment:
Rewinders: 3
Sheeters: 1

ⓘⓜIggesund Paperboard (Workington) Ltd.
Workington Mill
Ownership: 100% by Holmen AB
Siddick
Workington, Cumbria CA14 1JX
United Kingdom
 Phone: (44) 1900 601 000
 Fax: (44) 1900 605 000
 Web Address: www.iggesund.com
Personnel:
 Man. Dir.: Ulf Löfgren
 Phone: (44) 1900 601 115
 Fax: (44) 1900 605 000
 Email: ulf.lofgren@iggesund.com
 Head of HR: Jonny Lowe
 Phone: (44) 1900 601 128

United Kingdom

Fax: (44) 1900 605 000
Email: jonny.lowe@iggesund.com
Head of Cust. Serv. & Dev. Centre: Ian Black
Phone: (44) 1900 601 000
Fax: (44) 1900 605 000
Email: ian.black@iggesund.com
Prod. Mgr.: Bengt Löfroth
Phone: (44) 1900 601 000
Fax: (44) 1900 605 000
Email: bengt.lofroth@iggesund.com
Eng. & Maint. Mngr: Jan Svensson
Phone: (44) 1900 600242
Fax: (44) 1900 605 000
Email: jan.svensson@iggesund.com
Total Employees at this Location: 405
Type of Operation: Pulp mill, Paperboard mill
Pulp Grades and Capacities:
Total pulp capacity: 108,823 mt/y
Mechanical Pulp: 108,823 mt/y
Pulp Mill Data:
Mechanical Pulping Systems:
RMP systems: 1
Bleach Plant Systems: 1
RMP, Sequence: P
Paper/Paperboard Grades and Capacities:
Total paper and paperboard capacity: 200,000 mt/y
Boxboard/cartonboard: 200,000 mt/y
Paper and Paperboard Mill Data:
Stock Preparation:
Pulpers: 5
Refiners: 3
Paper Machines: 1
No. 2, Multi-wire (5), total capacity 200,000 mt/y, Trim width 5.65 m, Boxboard/cartonboard
Coating Machines: 1
No. 2, total capacity 200,000 mt/y., on machine
Finishing Equipment:
Winders: 1 at 200,000 mt/y
Calenders: 1
Rewinders: 2
Sheeters: 5
Energy Data:
Power boilers: 1
Combustion turbines: 1 at 42 MW
Steam turbines: 1 at 7 MW
Electrical demand for mill: 741 MWh/D

ⓂIntertissue Ltd.
Port Talbot Mill
Ownership: 100% by Sofidel Group
Brunel Way, Baglan Energy Park
Briton Ferry, Neath, Wales SA11 2HZ
United Kingdom
Phone: (44) 1639 825 380
Fax: (44) 1639 825 381
Email: info@intertissue.co.uk,
intertissue.uk@intertissue.co.uk
Web Address: www.intertissue.eu,
www.sofidel.it
Personnel:
Country Mgr. & Interim Plt. Mgr.: Giuseppe Munari
Phone: (44) 1639 825 380
Fax: (44) 1639 825 381
Email: giuseppe.munari@sofidel.it
Dir., Mktg. & Sls.: Massimo Nicosia
Phone: (44) 1639 825 380
Fax: (44) 1639 825 381
Email: massimo.nicosia@sofidel.it
Exec. Dir.: Erni Stefani
Phone: (39) 1639 825 380
Fax: (39) 1639 825 381
Email: erni.stefani@sofidel.it
Total Employees at this Location: 293
Type of Operation: Paper mill
Paper/Paperboard Grades and Capacities:
Total paper and paperboard capacity: 60,000 mt/y
Tissue: 60,000 mt/y
Paper and Paperboard Mill Data:
Stock Preparation:
Pulpers: 2
Refiners: 3
Paper Machines: 1
No. 1, crescent former, Yankee dryer, total capacity 60,000 mt/y, Trim width 5.4 m, Tissue
Finishing Equipment:
Rewinders: 1 at 60,000 mt/y
Energy Data:
Power boilers: 1
Electrical demand for mill: 148 MWh/D

ⓂKimberly-Clark Ltd.
Ownership: 100% by Kimberly-Clark Corp.
1 Tower View, Kings Hill
West Malling, Kent ME19 4HA
United Kingdom
Phone: (44) 1732 594 000 / 1737 736119 / 0800 269470
Fax: (44) 1732 594 001 / 1732 594150
Email: consumeruk@kcc.com,
communications.europe@kcc.com,
kcpuk@kcc.com
Web Address: www.kimberly-clark.com
Personnel:
CEO & Chairman: Thomas J. Falk
Phone: (44) 1732 594 000
Fax: (44) 1732 594 001
Audit Committee Chairman: John R. Alm
Phone: (44) 0800 269470
Fax: (44) 1732 594150
Man. Dev. & Compensation Committee Chrmn: James M. Jenness
Phone: (44) 0800 269470
Fax: (44) 1732 594150
VP Europe, Middle East & Africa: Donna McPherson
Phone: (44) 0800 269470
Fax: (44) 1732 594150
Sls. Dir. Europe, Middle East & Africa: Marc Besson
Phone: (44) 0800 269470
Fax: (44) 1732 594150
Email: mbesson@kcc.com
Corporate Comms Mgr.: Stuart Lawton-Davies
Phone: (44) 1732 594 000
Fax: (44) 1732 594 001
Email: communications.europe@kcc.com
Total Employees of Company: 57,000
Mill Locations:
Kimberly-Clark Srl, Alanno Scalo Mill, Località S. Emidio, I-65020 Alanno Scalo, (PE), Italy, Capacity: 40,000 mt/y, (Paper mill)
Phone: (39) 085 854 0800
Fax: (39) 085 854 2849
Kimberly-Clark Ltd., Barrow-in-Furness Mill, PO Box 25, Barrow-in-Furness LA14 4QX, United Kingdom, Capacity: 130,000 mt/y, (Pulp mill, Paper mill)
Phone: (44) 1229 495 000
Fax: (44) 1229 495 001
Kimberly-Clark Ltd., Coleshill Mill, Flint Site, Aber Road, Flint CH6 5EX, United Kingdom, Capacity: 29,000 mt/y, (Paper mill)
Phone: (44) 1352 805 000
Fax: (44) 1352 805 001
Kimberly-Clark Ltd., Delyn Mill, Flint Site, Aber Road, Flint CH6 5EX, United Kingdom, Capacity: 30,000 mt/y, (Paper mill)
Phone: (44) 1352 805 000
Fax: (44) 1352 805 001
Kimberly-Clark Ltd., Northfleet Mill, Thames House, Crete Hall Rd., Northfleet, Gravesend DA11 9AD, United Kingdom, Capacity: 75,000 mt/y, (Pulp mill, Paper mill)
Phone: (44) 1474 336 000
Fax: (44) 1474 336 478
Kimberly-Clark Srl, Romagnano Sesia Mill, Via S. Martino 16, I-28078 Romagnano Sesia, (NO), Italy, Capacity: 115,000 mt/y, (Paper mill)
Phone: (39) 0163 821200
Fax: (39) 0163 821202
Kimberly-Clark SAS, Sotteville-les-Rouen Mill, 8 rue Antoine Lavoisier, F-76300 Sotteville-les-Rouen, France, Capacity: 25,000 mt/y, (Pulp mill, Paper mill)
Phone: (33) 2 35 64 38 00
Fax: (33) 2 35 65 53 74
Kimberly-Clark SNC, Toul Mill, Z.A.C. de Villey-St.-Etienne, F-54212 Toul, France, Capacity: 80,000 mt/y, (Paper mill)
Phone: (33) 3 83 65 34 34
Fax: (33) 3 83 65 34 78

ⓂKimberly-Clark Ltd.
Barrow-in-Furness Mill
Ownership: 100% by Kimberly-Clark Corp.
PO Box 25
Barrow-in-Furness, Cumbria LA14 4QX
United Kingdom
Phone: (44) 1229 495 000
Fax: (44) 1229 495 001
Web Address: www.kimberly-clark.com
Personnel:
Mill Mgr.: Simon Woods
Phone: (44) 1229 495 000
Fax: (44) 1229 495 001
SQE Manager: Geoff Pilling
Phone: (44) 1229 495 000
Fax: (44) 1229 495 001
Total Employees at this Location: 400
Type of Operation: Pulp mill, Paper mill
Pulp Grades and Capacities:
Total pulp capacity: 17,865 mt/y
Recycled Pulping: 17,865 mt/y
Pulp Mill Data:
Bleach Plant Systems: 1
Recycled Fiber Treatment Lines:
Flotation deinking lines: 1
Paper/Paperboard Grades and Capacities:
Total paper and paperboard capacity: 130,000 mt/y
Tissue: 130,000 mt/y
Paper and Paperboard Mill Data:
Stock Preparation:
Pulpers: 7
Paper Machines: 3
No. 1, TAD, Yankee dryer, total capacity 40,000 mt/y, Trim width 3.4 m, Tissue
No. 3, crescent former, Yankee dryer, total capacity 45,000 mt/y, Trim width 5.4 m, Tissue
No. 4, inclined, Yankee dryer, total capacity 45,000 mt/y, Trim width 5.4 m, Tissue
Finishing Equipment:
Rewinders: 1
Energy Data:
Power boilers: 5
Electrical demand for mill: 474 MWh/D

ⓂKimberly-Clark Ltd.
Coleshill Mill
Ownership: 100% by Kimberly-Clark Corp.
Flint Site, Aber Road
Flint, CH6 5EX
United Kingdom
Phone: (44) 1352 805 000
Fax: (44) 1352 805 001
Web Address: www.kimberly-clark.com
Personnel:
Mill Mgr.: Euan Anderson
Phone: (44) 1352 805 000
Fax: (44) 1352 805 001
Total Employees at this Location: 280
Type of Operation: Paper mill
Pulp Grades and Capacities:
Total pulp capacity: 30,990 mt/y
Recycled Pulping: 30,990 mt/y
Pulp Mill Data:
Recycled Fiber Treatment Lines:
Flotation deinking lines: 1 at 30,000
Paper/Paperboard Grades and Capacities:
Total paper and paperboard capacity: 29,000 mt/y
Tissue: 29,000 mt/y
Paper and Paperboard Mill Data:

United Kingdom

Paper Machines: 1
No. 1, crescent former, Yankee dryer, total capacity 29,000 mt/y, Trim width 3.1 m, Tissue
Finishing Equipment:
Rewinders
Energy Data:
Power boilers: 1
Electrical demand for mill: 103 MWh/D

ⓂKimberly-Clark Ltd.
Delyn Mill
Mill is closed (production ceased May 2013, permanently closed September 2013)
Ownership: 100% by Kimberly-Clark Corp.
Flint Site, Aber Road
Flint, CH6 5EX
United Kingdom
  Phone: (44) 1352 805 000
  Fax: (44) 1352 805 001
  Web Address: www.kcprofessional.com/uk, www.kimberly-clark.com
Total Employees at this Location: 50
Type of Operation: Paper mill
Pulp Grades and Capacities:
Total pulp capacity: 31,777 mt/y
Recycled Pulping: 31,777 mt/y
Pulp Mill Data:
Recycled Fiber Treatment Lines:
Flotation deinking lines: 1
Paper/Paperboard Grades and Capacities:
Total paper and paperboard capacity: 30,000 mt/y
Tissue: 30,000 mt/y
Paper and Paperboard Mill Data:
Paper Machines: 1
No. 1, fourdrinier, Yankee dryer, total capacity 30,000 mt/y, Trim width 3.1 m, Tissue
Energy Data:
Power boilers: 1
Electrical demand for mill: 79 MWh/D

ⓂKimberly-Clark Ltd.
Northfleet Mill
Ownership: 100% by Kimberly-Clark Corp.
Thames House, Crete Hall Rd.
Northfleet, Gravesend, Kent DA11 9AD
United Kingdom
  Phone: (44) 1474 336 000
  Fax: (44) 1474 336 478
  Web Address: www.kimberly-clark.com
Personnel:
Mill Mgr.: Steve Monks
  Phone: (44) 1474 336 000
  Fax: (44) 1474 336 478
Tech. Mgr.: Suzanne Tarr
  Phone: (44) 1474 336 000
  Fax: (44) 1474 336 478
Chief Eng.: Bob Ramsay
  Phone: (44) 1474 336 000
  Fax: (44) 1474 336 478
Maint. Mgr.: Steve Baxter
  Phone: (44) 1474 336 000
  Fax: (44) 1474 336 478
  Email: steve.baxter@kcc.com
Conv. Plant Mgr.: Stuart Anderson
  Phone: (44) 1474 336 000
  Fax: (44) 1474 336 478
Total Employees at this Location: 300
Type of Operation: Pulp mill, Paper mill
Paper/Paperboard Grades and Capacities:
Total paper and paperboard capacity: 75,000 mt/y
Tissue: 75,000 mt/y
Paper and Paperboard Mill Data:
Stock Preparation:
Pulpers: 4
Refiners: 8
Paper Machines: 3
No. 1, inclined, Yankee dryer, total capacity 25,000 mt/y, Trim width 3.35 m, Tissue
No. 2, inclined, Yankee dryer, total capacity 23,000 mt/y, Trim width 3.35 m, Tissue
No. 3, inclined, Yankee dryer, total capacity 27,000 mt/y, Trim width 3.35 m, Tissue
Finishing Equipment:
Rewinders: 5
Energy Data:
Power boilers: 4
Electrical demand for mill: 216 MWh/D

ⓂNorthwood & Wepa Limited
Llangynwyd (Bridgend) Mill
Ownership: 50% by WEPA Hygieneprodukte GmbH, 50% by Northwood Group
Llangynwyd
Bridgend, Wales CF34 9RS
United Kingdom
  Phone: (44) 1656 684 500
  Fax: (44) 1656 684 501/689
Personnel:
Man. Dir.: Michael Thompson
  Phone: (44) 1656 684 500
Mill Mngr.: E. F. Marker
Total Employees at this Location: 250
Type of Operation: Pulp mill, Paper mill
Paper/Paperboard Grades and Capacities:
Total paper and paperboard capacity: 55,000 mt/y
Tissue: 55,000 mt/y
Paper and Paperboard Mill Data:
Stock Preparation:
Pulpers: 5
Refiners: 10
Paper Machines: 1
No. 6, twin-wire, Yankee dryer, total capacity 55,000 mt/y, Trim width 5.03 m, Tissue
Finishing Equipment:
Supercalenders: 1
Rewinders: 3
Sheeters: 1
Energy Data:
Power boilers: 2
Electrical demand for mill: 161 MWh/D

ⓘNorthwood Group
4 Warner House, Harrovian Business Village, Bessborough Road
Harrow, HA1 3EX
United Kingdom
  Phone: (44) 020 8423 0100
  Fax: (44) 020 8423 8880
  Email: nps@northwoodpaper.com
  Web Address: www.northwoodpaper.com/
Personnel:
Chrmn.: Paul Fecher
Total Employees of Company: 350
Mill Locations:
Disley Tissue Ltd., Disley Mill, Waterside, Disley, North Stockport SK12 2HW, United Kingdom, Capacity: 25,000 mt/y, (Pulp mill, Paper mill)
  Phone: (44) 1663 762 701
  Fax: (44) 1663 762 421
Peter Grant Papers Limited, Lancaster Mill, Lansil Way, Caton Rd., Lancaster LA1 3PQ, United Kingdom, Capacity: 8,000 mt/y, (Paper mill)
  Phone: (44) 1524 843 678
  Fax: (44) 1524 843 644
  Email: sales@petergrantpapers.com
Northwood & Wepa Limited, Llangynwyd (Bridgend) Mill (50% owned), Llangynwyd, Bridgend CF34 9RS, United Kingdom, Capacity: 55,000 mt/y, (Pulp mill, Paper mill)
  Phone: (44) 1656 684 500
  Fax: (44) 1656 684 501/689

ⓂPalm Paper Limited
King's Lynn Mill
Ownership: 100% by Palm Group
Poplar Avenue, Saddlebow Industrial Estate
King's Lynn, PE34 3AL
United Kingdom
  Phone: (44) 1553 782 222
  Fax: (44) 1553 782 223
  Email: info@palmpaper.co.uk
  Web Address: www.palmpaper.co.uk
Personnel:
Man. Dir., Business & Admin.: Derek Harman
  Phone: (44) 1553 782 250
  Fax: (44) 1553 782 223
  Email: derek.harman@palmpaper.co.uk
HR Dir.: Mick Beckett
  Phone: (44) 1553 782 222
  Fax: (44) 1553 782 223
  Email: mick.beckett@palmpaper.co.uk
Total Employees at this Location: 157
Type of Operation: Pulp mill, Paper mill
Pulp Grades and Capacities:
Total pulp capacity: 465,399 mt/y
Recycled Pulping: 465,399 mt/y
Pulp Mill Data:
Pulp Lines: 2
Bleach Plant Systems: 1
DIP bleaching line, Type: ECF, Sequence: P, Capacity 595,000 admt/y
Recycled Fiber Treatment Lines:
Flotation deinking lines: 2 at 595,000
Paper/Paperboard Grades and Capacities:
Total paper and paperboard capacity: 450,000 mt/y
Newsprint: 360,000 mt/y
Uncoated mechanical/groundwood: 90,000 mt/y
Paper and Paperboard Mill Data:
Paper Machines: 1
No. 1, DuoFormer TQv, total capacity 450,000 mt/y, Trim width 10.6 m, Newsprint, Uncoated mechanical/groundwood
Finishing Equipment:
Winders: 2 at 400,000 mt/y
Calenders: 2 at 400,000 mt/y
Energy Data:
Power boilers: 2
Electrical demand for mill: 1,010 MWh/D

ⓘPreston Board and Packaging Ltd.
Ownership: 50% by Charles Ingham, 50% by David Hardman
Greenbank St.
Preston, Lancashire, Lancashire PR1 7JS
United Kingdom
  Phone: (44) 1772 254 187
  Fax: (44) 1772 253 264
  Email: sales@prestonboard.co.uk
  Web Address: www.prestonboard.co.uk
Personnel:
Man. Dir., Owner: Charles Ingham
  Phone: (44) 1772 254 187
  Fax: (44) 1772 253 264
Man. Dir., Owner: David Hardman
  Phone: (44) 1772 254 187
  Fax: (44) 1772 253 264
Gen. Mgr.: Stanley Struszczak
  Phone: (44) 1772 254 187, 0777 164 1320
  Fax: (44) 1772 253 264
  Email: stan@prestonboard.co.uk
Sls. Mgr.: Chris Ingham
  Phone: (44) 1772 254 187, 0777 164 1319
  Fax: (44) 1772 253 264
  Email: stan@prestonboard.co.uk
Total Employees of Company: 150
Total Employees at this Location: 48
Mill Locations:
Romiley Board Mill, Stockport Mill, Oakwood Road, Romiley, Stockport, Greater Manchester SK6 4DZ, United Kingdom, Capacity: 43,000 mt/y, (Paperboard mill)
  Phone: (44) 1614 306 061
  Fax: (44) 1614 066 114
  Email: info@romileyboard.co.uk

United Kingdom

ⓂPurico Group Ltd.
Ownership: 100% by Nathu Ram Puri
Environment House, 6 Union Road
Nottingham, NG3 1FH
United Kingdom
 Phone: (44) 1159 013 000
 Fax: (44) 1159 013 100/3003
 Email: sales@purico.co.uk
 Web Address: www.purico.com
Personnel:
 Owner: Nathu Ram Puri
 Phone: (44) 115 901 3000
 Fax: (44) 115 901 3100/3003
 Chmn.: Mr. Anil Puri
 Phone: (44) 115 901 3000
 Fax: (44) 115 901 3100/3003
 Chmn. Sec.: Sue Lee
 Phone: (44) 115 901 3000
 Fax: (44) 115 901 3100/3003
 Email: sales@purico.co.uk
 Comp. Dir. of Subsidiary Companies: Mary McGowan
 Phone: (44) 115 901 3000
 Fax: (44) 115 901 3100/3003
 Sls. & Mktg. Dir.: Michael Black
 Phone: (44) 115 901 3000
 Fax: (44) 115 901 3100/3003
 Email: sales@purico.co.uk
 Paper Company Contact: P. Tyler
 Phone: (44) 115 901 3000
 Fax: (44) 115 901 3100/3003
 Email: sales@purico.co.uk
 Legal Counsel: John Gossage
 Phone: (44) 115 901 3000
 Fax: (44) 115 901 3100/3003
Total Employees of Company: 3,000
Total Employees at this Location: 9
Mill Locations:
 Devon Valley Ltd., Devon Valley Mill, Hele, Exeter EX5 4JP, United Kingdom, Capacity: 12,000 mt/y, (Paper mill)
 Phone: (44) 1392 881 731
 Fax: (44) 1392 883 550
 Email: info@devonvalleymill.com, sales@cromptonpapers.com
 Union Papertech, Simpson Clough Paper Mill, Ashworth Rd., Heywood OL10 4BE, United Kingdom, Capacity: 6,000 mt/y, (Paper mill)
 Phone: (44) 1706 362 600/364 121
 Fax: (44) 1706 624 944 / 1706 624 678
 Email: sales@upapertech.com
 Zhejiang Minfeng Robert Special Paper Co., Ltd., Jiaxing Mill, 70, Luli Street, Jiaxing 314001, China, Capacity: 12,000 mt/y, (Paper mill)
 Phone: (86) 573 283 9600/9057
 Fax: (86) 573 281 9766/2821027
 Email: jb@minfengrobert.com
 Zhejiang Purico Speciality Paper Company Limited, Jiaxing Mill, 70 Luli Street, Jiaxing 314000, China, Capacity: 10,000 mt/y, (Paper mill)
 Phone: (86) 573 8283 9600/ 8282 0799
 Fax: (86) 573 8282 0700/ 8281 7677
 Email: jb@minfengrobert.com, info@purico.cn

ⓄⓂRomiley Board Mill
Stockport Mill
Ownership: 100% by Preston Board and Packaging Ltd.
Oakwood Road, Romiley
Stockport, Greater Manchester, Cheshire SK6 4DZ
United Kingdom
 Phone: (44) 1614 306 061
 Fax: (44) 1614 066 114
 Email: info@romileyboard.co.uk
 Web Address: www.romileyboard.co.uk
Personnel:
 Gen. Mgr.: John Johnson
 Phone: (44) 1614 301 156, (M): 7747 840292
 Fax: (44) 1614 066 114
 Email: john.johnson@romileyboard.co.uk
 Commer. Mgr.: Nick Hardman
 Phone: (44) 1614 301 153, (M): 7880 738409
 Fax: (44) 1614 066 114
 Email: nick.hardman@romileyboard.co.uk
Total Employees of Company: 100
Total Employees at this Location: 100
Type of Operation: Paperboard mill
Pulp Grades and Capacities:
 Total pulp capacity: 43,443 mt/y
 Recycled Pulping: 43,443 mt/y
Pulp Mill Data:
Recycled Fiber Treatment Lines:
 Pulpers: 1 at 50,000 admt/y
Paper/Paperboard Grades and Capacities:
 Total paper and paperboard capacity: 43,000 mt/y
 Boxboard/cartonboard: 43,000 mt/y
Paper and Paperboard Mill Data:
Stock Preparation:
 Pulpers: 1
 Refiners: 1
Paper Machines: 1
 No. 1, cylinder, total capacity 43,000 mt/y, Trim width 2.1 m, Boxboard/cartonboard
Finishing Equipment:
 Rewinders: 1
 Sheeters: 1
Energy Data:
 Power boilers: 4
 Electrical demand for mill: 48 MWh/D

ⓂSAICA Paper UK Ltd.
Partington Mill
Previously SAICA Containerboard UK Ltd.
Ownership: 100% by SAICA - S.A. Industrias Celulosa Aragonesa
144 Manchester Road
Carrington, Manchester, Greater Manchester M31 4QN
United Kingdom
 Phone: (44) 161 776 7000
 Email: web.paper.pm11@saica.com
 Web Address: www.saica.com
Personnel:
 Plt. Mgr.: Pasi Hayrynen
 Phone: (44) 0800 849 1117
 Email: Pasi.hayrynen@saica.com
Total Employees at this Location: 120
Type of Operation: Paperboard mill
Pulp Grades and Capacities:
 Total pulp capacity: 392,254 mt/y
 Recycled Pulping: 392,254 mt/y
Pulp Mill Data:
Recycled Fiber Treatment Lines:
 Recycled packaging pulping lines: 1
Paper/Paperboard Grades and Capacities:
 Total paper and paperboard capacity: 400,000 mt/y
 Linerboard: 200,000 mt/y
 Corrugating medium/fluting: 200,000 mt/y
Paper and Paperboard Mill Data:
Paper Machines: 1
 No. 11, (started up January 2012), OptiFormer, total capacity 400,000 mt/y, Trim width 7.6 m, Linerboard, Corrugating medium/fluting
Finishing Equipment:
 Winders: 1
Energy Data:
 Power boilers
 Combustion turbines: 1
 Steam turbines: 1
 Electrical demand for mill: 448 MWh/D

ⓂSCA Hygiene Products SE
Goytside Mill
Ownership: SCA - Svenska Cellulosa Aktiebolaget
Goytside Road
Chesterfield, Derbyshire S40 2PH
United Kingdom
 Phone: (44) 1246 558 557
 Fax: (44) 1246 552 556
 Web Address: www.sca.com
Personnel:
 Mill Mgr.: James Lang
 Phone: (44) 1246 558557
 Fax: (44) 1246 558556
 Email: james.lang@sca.com
Total Employees at this Location: 43
Type of Operation: Paper mill
Pulp Grades and Capacities:
 Total pulp capacity: 32,982 mt/y
 Recycled Pulping: 32,982 mt/y
Pulp Mill Data:
Recycled Fiber Treatment Lines:
 Pulpers: 1 at 55,200
Paper/Paperboard Grades and Capacities:
 Total paper and paperboard capacity: 31,000 mt/y
 Tissue: 31,000 mt/y
Paper and Paperboard Mill Data:
Paper Machines: 1
 No. 1, crescent former, total capacity 31,000 mt/y, Trim width 3.4 m, Tissue
Energy Data:
 Power boilers: 1
 Electrical demand for mill: 97 MWh/D

ⓂSCA Hygiene Products Manchester Ltd.
Manchester (Trafford Park) Mill
Ownership: SCA Hygiene Products SE
Trafford Park Road, Trafford Park
Manchester, M17 1EQ
United Kingdom
 Phone: (44) 161 888 6002
 Fax: (44) 161 888 6195
 Web Address: www.sca.com
Personnel:
 Mill Mgr.: Colin Popplewell
 Phone: (44) 161 888 6002
 Fax: (44) 161 888 6195
 Email: colin.Popplewell@sca.com
Total Employees at this Location: 160
Type of Operation: Paper mill
Paper/Paperboard Grades and Capacities:
 Total paper and paperboard capacity: 60,000 mt/y
 Tissue: 60,000 mt/y
Paper and Paperboard Mill Data:
Paper Machines: 1
 No. 1, TAD, total capacity 60,000 mt/y, Trim width 5.16 m, Tissue
Energy Data:
 Power boilers: 1
 Electrical demand for mill: 304 MWh/D

ⓂSCA Hygiene Products SE
Oakenholt Mill
Ownership: SCA - Svenska Cellulosa Aktiebolaget
Chester Road
Oakenholt, Flint, Wales CH6 5PU
United Kingdom
 Phone: (44) 1352 732 101
 Fax: (44) 1352 732 760
 Web Address: www.sca.com
Personnel:
 Mill Mgr.: James Lang
 Phone: (44) 1352 732 101
 Fax: (44) 1352 732 760
 Email: james.lang@sca.com
Total Employees at this Location: 85
Type of Operation: Paper mill
Paper/Paperboard Grades and Capacities:
 Total paper and paperboard capacity: 68,000 mt/y
 Tissue: 68,000 mt/y
Paper and Paperboard Mill Data:
Paper Machines: 2
 No. 1, crescent former, total capacity 22,000 mt/y, Trim width 2.7 m, Tissue
 No. 2, crescent former, total capacity 46,000 mt/y, Trim width 5.4 m, Tissue
Energy Data:

United Kingdom

Power boilers: 1
Electrical demand for mill: 161 MWh/D

ⓂSCA Hygiene Products SE
Prudhoe Mill
Ownership: SCA - Svenska Cellulosa Aktiebolaget
Princess Way
Prudhoe, Northumberland NE42 6HE
United Kingdom
  Phone: (44) 1661 806000
  Fax: (44) 1661 806001
  Web Address: www.sca.com
Personnel:
  Factory & Site Mgr.: Tony Richards
  Phone: (44) 1661 806000
  Fax: (44) 1661 806 001
  Email: tony.richards@sca.com
  VP Product Supply Tissue Europe.: Andy Woodburn
  Phone: (44) 49 89 9 70 06 690
  Email: andy.woodburn@sca.com
Total Employees at this Location: 350
Type of Operation: Pulp mill, Paper mill
Pulp Grades and Capacities:
  Total pulp capacity: 70,000 mt/y
  Recycled Pulping: 70,000 mt/y
Pulp Mill Data:
Pulp Lines: 1
  Recycled Fiber Treatment Lines:
  Flotation deinking lines: 1
Paper/Paperboard Grades and Capacities:
  Total paper and paperboard capacity: 90,000 mt/y
  Tissue: 90,000 mt/y
Paper and Paperboard Mill Data:
Paper Machines: 2
  No. 1, crescent former, Yankee dryer, total capacity 45,000 mt/y, Trim width 5.04 m, Tissue
  No. 2, TAD, total capacity 45,000 mt/y, Trim width 4.96 m, Tissue
Energy Data:
Power boilers: 1
Electrical demand for mill: 382 MWh/D

ⓂSCA Hygiene Products SE
Stubbins Mill
Mill is Former Georgia-Pacific UK Ltd. acquired by SCA, sale completed late July 2012
Ownership: SCA - Svenska Cellulosa Aktiebolaget
Stubbins Lane
Ramsbottom, Bury, Lancashire BL0 0NH
United Kingdom
  Phone: (44) 1706 283 000
  Fax: (44) 1706 283 001
  Web Address: www.sca.com
Total Employees at this Location: 200
Type of Operation: Pulp mill, Paper mill
Pulp Grades and Capacities:
  Total pulp capacity: 125,187 mt/y
  Recycled Pulping: 125,187 mt/y
Pulp Mill Data:
  Recycled Fiber Treatment Lines:
  Pulpers: 1 at 203,000
Paper/Paperboard Grades and Capacities:
  Total paper and paperboard capacity: 117,000 mt/y
  Tissue: 117,000 mt/y
Paper and Paperboard Mill Data:
  Stock Preparation:
  Pulpers:
Paper Machines: 3
  No. 1, inclined, Yankee dryer, total capacity 35,000 mt/y, Trim width 3.37 m, Tissue
  No. 2, Periformer, Yankee dryer, total capacity 27,000 mt/y, Trim width 2.54 m, Tissue
  No. 3, C-wrap, Yankee dryer, total capacity 55,000 mt/y, Trim width 5.23 m, Tissue
Energy Data:
Power boilers: 1
Electrical demand for mill: 444 MWh/D

ⓅⓂSmurfit Kappa SSK
Birmingham Mill
Ownership: Smurfit Kappa Europe
Mount St.
Nechells, Birmingham, West Midlands B7 5RE
United Kingdom
  Phone: (44) 121 327 1381
  Fax: (44) 121 322 6300
  Email: info@smurfitkappa.co.uk
  Web Address: www.smurfitkappa.com
Personnel:
  CEO, Smurfit Kappa Paper UK: Chris Allen
  Phone: (44) 1634 240 205
  Fax: (44) 121 322 6300
  Email: chris.allen@smurfitkappa.co.uk
  CEO, Smurfit Kappa Corrugated UK: Clive Bowers
  Phone: (44) 121 327 1381
  Fax: (44) 121 322 6300
  Email: clive.bowers@smurfitkappa.co.uk
  Oper. Dir.: Paul Freeman
  Phone: (44) 121 327 1381
  Fax: (44) 121 322 6300
  Email: paul.freeman@smurfitkappa.co.uk
  Prod. Mgr.: Nigel Pontin
  Phone: (44) 121 327 1381
  Fax: (44) 121 322 6300
  Email: nigel.pontin@smurfitkappa.co.uk
  Sls. Dir.: Martin Ferrari
  Phone: (44) 121 327 1381
  Fax: (44) 121 322 6300
  Email: martin.ferrari@smurfitkappa.co.uk
  Supply Chain Dir.: Paul Lythgoe
  Phone: (44) 121 327 1381
  Fax: (44) 121 322 6300
  Email: paul.lythgoe@smurfitkappa.co.uk
  Logist. Mgr.: Keith Hughes
  Phone: (44) 121 327 1381
  Fax: (44) 121 322 6300
  Email: keith.hughes@smurfitkappa.co.uk
Total Employees at this Location: 110
Type of Operation: Paperboard mill
Pulp Grades and Capacities:
  Total pulp capacity: 201,427 mt/y
  Recycled Pulping: 201,427 mt/y
Pulp Mill Data:
  Recycled Fiber Treatment Lines:
  Pulpers: 1 at 224,500
Paper/Paperboard Grades and Capacities:
  Total paper and paperboard capacity: 200,000 mt/y
  Linerboard: 155,000 mt/y
  Corrugating medium/fluting: 45,000 mt/y
Paper and Paperboard Mill Data:
  Stock Preparation:
  Pulpers: 2
  Refiners: 1
Paper Machines: 1
  No. 4, (Suppliers: Beloit/Voith/Valmet), fourdrinier (2), total capacity 200,000 mt/y, Trim width 4.8 m, Corrugating medium/fluting, Linerboard
Finishing Equipment:
  Winders: 1 at 250,000 mt/y
Energy Data:
Power boilers: 3
Combustion turbines: 2 at 3.5, 4.5 MW
Electrical demand for mill: 195 MWh/D

ⓂSmurfit Kappa Townsend Hook
Snodland Mill
Mill is temporarily closed (temporarily closed at the end of June 2013, and is scheduled to re-start in the fourth quarter of 2014)
Ownership: Smurfit Kappa Europe
Snodland, Kent ME6 5AX
United Kingdom
  Phone: (44) 1634 240 205
  Fax: (44) 1634 248 046
  Email: (firstname.secondname@smurfitkappa.co.uk), info@smurfitkappa.co.uk
  Web Address: www.smurfitkappa.com

Personnel:
  CEO: Chris Allen
  Phone: (44) 1634 248 101
  Email: chris.allen@smurfitkappa.co.uk
  CFO: Colin Shepherd
  Phone: (44) 1827 892100
  Email: colin.shepherd@smurfitkappa.co.uk
  Projects Dir.: Geoff Brooks
  Phone: (44) 1634 248152
  Email: geoff.brooks@smurfitkappa.co.uk
  Acting Oper. Dir.: Peter Kitto
  Phone: (44) 1634 248 118
  Email: peter.kitto@smurfitkappa.co.uk
  Tech. Services Dir.: R. M. Huelin
  Phone: (44) 1634 248 118
  Email: bob.huelin@smurfitkappa.co.uk
  Energy Mgr.: Graham D. Peters
  Phone: (44) 1634 248 180
  Email: graham.peters@smurfitkappa.co.uk
  Sls., Mktg. & Sustain. Dir.: Martin Ferrari
  Phone: (44) 1634 248 095
  Email: martin.ferrari@smurfitkappa.co.uk
  Supply Chain Dir.: Paul Lythgoe
  Phone: (44) 1634 240 205
  Email: paul.lythgoe@smurfitkappa.co.uk
  Sustain. Mgr.: Monika Maciejewska
  Phone: (44) 1634 248144
  Email: monika.maciejewska@smurfitkappa.co.uk
  P.A. to CEO: Jackie Huggett
  Phone: (44) 1634 248 101
  Email: jackie.huggett@smurfitkappa.co.uk
Total Employees at this Location: 170
Type of Operation: Pulp mill, Paperboard mill
Pulp Mill Data:
  Recycled Fiber Treatment Lines:
  Recycled packaging pulping lines: 1
Paper and Paperboard Mill Data:
  Stock Preparation:
  Pulpers: 5
Paper Machines: 2
  No. 7, fourdrinier, total capacity 70,000 mt/y, Trim width 4 m
  No. 8, fourdrinier, total capacity 180,000 mt/y, Trim width 4.4 m
Energy Data:
Power boilers: 7
Combustion turbines: 1 at 40.0 MW
Steam turbines: 1 at 12.0 MW

ⓅⓂSofidel Group
Kamns Mill
Ownership: Public
Waterside Road, Hamilton Industrial Park
Leicester, LE5 1TZ
United Kingdom
  Phone: (44) 0116 2460 888
  Fax: (44) 0116 2460 222/304 271
  Email: info@sofideluk.co.uk
  Web Address: www.sofideluk.co.uk
Personnel:
  Man. Dir. International Division: Richard Poole
  Phone: (44) 1162 460 888
  Fax: (44) 1162 460 222
  Mill Mgr.: David Lynn
  Phone: (44) 1162 460 888
  Fax: (44) 1162 460 222
  Bus. Mgr.: Dean Hopper
  Phone: (44) 1162 460 888
  Fax: (44) 1162 460 222
  Prod. Mgr.: Kalpesh Vadgama
  Phone: (44) 1162 460 888
  Fax: (44) 1162 460 222
  Purch. Dept.: Pravin Rayarela
  Phone: (44) 1162 460 888
  Fax: (44) 1162 460 222
Total Employees of Company: 1,200
Total Employees at this Location: 750
Type of Operation: Paper mill
Paper/Paperboard Grades and Capacities:
  Total paper and paperboard capacity: 75,000 mt/y

United Kingdom

Tissue: 75,000 mt/y
Paper and Paperboard Mill Data:
Paper Machines: 2
No. 1, crescent former, Yankee dryer, total capacity 25,000 mt/y, Trim width 2.7 m, Tissue
No. 2, crescent former, Yankee dryer, total capacity 50,000 mt/y, Trim width 5.4 m, Tissue
Energy Data:
Power boilers: 1
Electrical demand for mill: 196 MWh/D

ⓜSofidel Group
Lancaster Mill
Mill is former Northern Tissue Group, acquired by Sofidel October 1, 2013
Lansil Industrial Estate, Lansil Way, Caton Road
Lancaster, Lancashire LA1 3QY
United Kingdom
  Phone: (44) 1524 844 600
  Fax: (44) 1524 842 800
  Web Address: www.sofideluk.co.uk
Personnel:
  Man. Dir.: Piero Ceccon
  Phone: (44) 1524 844 600
  Fax: (44) 1524 842 800
  Snr Eng. Mgr.: Stefano Marengo
  Phone: (44) 1524 844 600
  Fax: (44) 1524 842 800
  Finan. Dir.: Garry Scott Walker
  Phone: (44) 1524 844 600
  Fax: (44) 1524 842 800
Total Employees at this Location: 50
Type of Operation: Paper mill
Pulp Grades and Capacities:
  Total pulp capacity: 19,135 mt/y
  Recycled Pulping: 19,135 mt/y
Paper/Paperboard Grades and Capacities:
  Total paper and paperboard capacity: 30,000 mt/y
  Tissue: 30,000 mt/y
Paper and Paperboard Mill Data:
Paper Machines: 1
No. 1, crescent former, Yankee dryer, total capacity 30,000 mt/y, Trim width 3.56 m, Tissue
Finishing Equipment:
  Rewinders: 1 at 30,000 mt/y
Energy Data:
Power boilers: 1
Electrical demand for mill: 80 MWh/D

ⓜSonoco Board Mills Ltd.
Stainland Mill
Ownership: 100% by Sonoco Products Co.
Stainland, Holywell Green
Halifax, West Yorkshire HX4 9PY
United Kingdom
Mailing Address: Station Road, Milnrow, Rochdale Lancashire, Lancashire OL16 4HQ, United Kingdom
  Phone: (44) 1422 374 741
  Fax: (44) 1422 311 725 / 1422 371 495
  Web Address: www.sonoco.com
Personnel:
  Prod. Mgr.: Nigel Rhodes
  Phone: (44) 1422 374 741
  Fax: (44) 1422 311 725
  Email: nigel.rhodes@sonoco.com
  Mill Eng.: Paul Hindley
  Phone: (44) 1422 374 741
  Fax: (44) 1422 311 725
  Email: paul.hindley@sonoco.com
Total Employees at this Location: 78
Type of Operation: Paperboard mill
Pulp Grades and Capacities:
  Total pulp capacity: 66,726 mt/y
  Recycled Pulping: 66,726 mt/y
Paper/Paperboard Grades and Capacities:
  Total paper and paperboard capacity: 65,000 mt/y
  Boxboard/cartonboard: 65,000 mt/y
Paper and Paperboard Mill Data:
  Stock Preparation:
    Pulpers: 1
    Refiners: 4
Paper Machines: 1
No. 2, cylinder, total capacity 65,000 mt/y, Trim width 2.9 m, Boxboard/cartonboard
Finishing Equipment:
  Rewinders: 2
Energy Data:
Power boilers
Electrical demand for mill: 72 MWh/D

ⓜSt Cuthberts Mill Limited
HAYBRIDGE
Wells, BA5 1AG
United Kingdom
  Phone: (44) 1749 672 015
  Fax: (44) 1749 678 844
  Email: sales@stcuthbertsmill.com
  Web Address: www.stcuthbertsmill.com
Personnel:
  CEO: Colin Andre Stott
  Phone: (44) 1749 672015
  Fax: (44) 1749 678844
  Man. Dir.: Martin Bell
  Phone: (44) 1749 672015
  Fax: (44) 1749 678844
  Mill Mgr.: Dave Veater
  Phone: (44) 1749 672015
  Fax: (44) 1749 678844
  Quality Control Mgr.: Steve Gardner
  Phone: (44) 1749 672015
  Fax: (44) 1749 678844
  Tech. Supervisor: Stephen Carroll
  Phone: (44) 1749 672015
  Fax: (44) 1749 678844
Total Employees of Company: 41
Mill Locations:
St Cuthberts Mill Limited, St. Cuthbert's Paper Mill, Haybridge, Wells BA5 1AG, United Kingdom, Capacity: 2,000 mt/y, (Paper mill)
  Phone: (44) 1749 672 015
  Fax: (44) 1749 678 844
  Email: sales@stcuthbertsmill.com

ⓜSt Cuthberts Mill Limited
St. Cuthbert's Paper Mill
Haybridge
Wells, Somerset BA5 1AG
United Kingdom
  Phone: (44) 1749 672 015
  Fax: (44) 1749 678 844
  Email: sales@stcuthbertsmill.com
  Web Address: www.stcuthbertsmill.com
Personnel:
  CEO: Colin Andre Stott
  Phone: (44) 1749 672015
  Mill Mgr.: Dave Veater
  Phone: (44) 1749 672015
Total Employees at this Location: 41
Type of Operation: Paper mill
Pulp Grades and Capacities:
Paper/Paperboard Grades and Capacities:
  Total paper and paperboard capacity: 2,000 mt/y
  Uncoated woodfree/freesheet: 2,000 mt/y
Paper and Paperboard Mill Data:
  Stock Preparation:
    Pulpers: 2
    Refiners: 2
Paper Machines: 1
No. 2, total capacity 2,000 mt/y, Trim width 1.54 m, Uncoated woodfree/freesheet
Finishing Equipment:
  Rewinders: 2
  Sheeters: 1
Energy Data:
Power boilers: 1

ⓞⓜTullis Russell Papermakers Ltd.
Markinch Mill
Ownership: 30% by Family - owned, 70% by Employees - owned
Markinch, Glenrothes, Scotland KY7 6PB
United Kingdom
  Phone: (44) 1592 753 311
  Fax: (44) 1592 755 872
  Email: paperandboard@tullisrussell.com
  Web Address: www.tullisrussell.com
Personnel:
  CEO: Chris Parr
  Phone: (44) 1592 753 311
  Fax: (44) 1592 755 872
  Email: chris.parr@tullisrussell.com
  Man. Dir. (From September 2014): Niall MacDonald
  Phone: (44) 1592 753 311
  Fax: (44) 1592 755 872
  Email: niall.macdonald@tullisrussell.com
  HR. Mgr.: Linda Brailsford
  Phone: (44) 1592 753 311
  Fax: (44) 1592 755 872
  Email: linda.brailsford@tullisrussell.com
  Mktg. Mgr.: Amanda Treend
  Phone: (44) 1592 761 285
  Fax: (44) 1592 755 872
  Email: amanda.treend@tullisrussell.com
  Safety, Health & Environ.: Ken McDougall
  Phone: (44) 1592 753 311
  Fax: (44) 1592 755 872
  Email: ken.mcdougall@tullisrussell.com
  Pub. Rel. Mgr.: Derek Guthrie
  Phone: (44) 1592 761 261
  Fax: (44) 1592 755 872
  Email: derek.guthrie@tullisrussell.com
Total Employees of Company: 744
Total Employees at this Location: 500
Type of Operation: Paper mill, Paperboard mill
Paper/Paperboard Grades and Capacities:
  Total paper and paperboard capacity: 170,000 mt/y
  Uncoated woodfree/freesheet: 60,000 mt/y
  Specialty and industrial: 20,000 mt/y
  Boxboard/cartonboard: 90,000 mt/y
Paper and Paperboard Mill Data:
  Stock Preparation:
    Pulpers: 8
    Refiners: 28
Paper Machines: 3
No. 1, fourdrinier (2), total capacity 90,000 mt/y, Trim width 3.8 m, Boxboard/cartonboard
No. 4, fourdrinier (2), total capacity 40,000 mt/y, Trim width 3.4 m, Uncoated woodfree/freesheet
No. 5, fourdrinier (2), total capacity 40,000 mt/y, Trim width 2.6 m, Uncoated woodfree/freesheet, Specialty and industrial
Coating Machines: 2
No. 1, total capacity 100,000 mt/y., off machine
No. 2, total capacity 7,000 mt/y., off machine
Finishing Equipment:
  Supercalenders: 3
  Rewinders: 6
  Sheeters: 7
Energy Data:
Power boilers
Steam turbines: 3 at 20 MW
Electrical demand for mill: 304 MWh/D

ⓜUnion Papertech
Simpson Clough Paper Mill
Ownership: Purico Group Ltd.
Ashworth Rd.
Heywood, Lancashire OL10 4BE
United Kingdom
Mailing Address: 6 Union Road, NG3 1FH Nottingham
  Phone: (44) 1706 362 600 / 364 121
  Fax: (44) 1706 624 944 / 1706 624 678
  Email: sales@upapertech.com
  Web Address: www.purico.com, www.unionpapertech.co.uk
Personnel:
  Man. Dir.: Stephen Todd
  Dir. & Gen. Mgr.: Alastair James White Hume

United Kingdom

Phone: (44) 1706 362 600/364 121
Fin.Dir.: Garry Johnson
Tech. Mgr.: W.J. Atherden
Phone: (44) 1706 362 600/364 121
Chief Eng.: S. Sherlock
Phone: (44) 1706 362 600/364 121
Oper. Mgr.: Steve Hall
Phone: (44) 1706 362 616
Email: shall@upapertech.com
Total Employees at this Location: 102
Type of Operation: Paper mill
Paper/Paperboard Grades and Capacities:
Total paper and paperboard capacity: 6,000 mt/y
Specialty and industrial: 6,000 mt/y
Paper and Paperboard Mill Data:
Stock Preparation:
Pulpers: 4
Refiners: 8
Paper Machines: 2
PM 1, fourdrinier, Specialty and industrial
PM 2, fourdrinier, Specialty and industrial
Finishing Equipment:
Rewinders: 4

ⓘⓜUPM-Kymmene (UK) Ltd.
Caledonian Paper Mill
Ownership: 100% by UPM-Kymmene Corporation
Meadowhead Rd.
Irvine, Scotland KA11 5AT
United Kingdom
Phone: (44) 1294 312 020
Fax: (44) 1294 314 400
Email: caledonianpaper@upm.com
Web Address: www.upm.com
Personnel:
Bus. Develop. Mgr.: Simon Walker
Phone: (44) 1294 312 020
Fax: (44) 1294 314 400
Email: simon.walker@upm.com
Purch. Mgr.: Justin Playford
Phone: (44) 1294 312 020
Fax: (44) 1294 314 400
Email: justin.playford@upm.com
National Sourcing Mgr.: Mike Burgess
Phone: (44) 1294 312 020
Fax: (44) 1294 314 400
Email: mike.burgess@upm.com
Total Employees at this Location: 295
Type of Operation: Pulp mill, Paper mill
Pulp Grades and Capacities:
Total pulp capacity: 121,856 mt/y
Mechanical Pulp: 121,856 mt/y
Pulp Mill Data:
Mechanical Pulping Systems:
Pressurized grinders: 4
Pulp Lines: 1
Bleach Plant Systems: 1
PGW line, Type: Softwood, Sequence: P, Capacity 100,000 admt/y
Paper/Paperboard Grades and Capacities:
Total paper and paperboard capacity: 280,000 mt/y
Coated mechanical/groundwood: 280,000 mt/y
Paper and Paperboard Mill Data:
Stock Preparation:
Pulpers: 1
Refiners: 2
Paper Machines: 1
No. 1, SymFormer, total capacity 280,000 mt/y, Trim width 8.2 m, Coated mechanical/groundwood
Coating Machines: 1
PM 1, total capacity 280,000 mt/y., off machine
Finishing Equipment:
Supercalenders: 2
Rewinders: 2
Energy Data:
Power boilers: 1
Steam turbines: 1 at 26 MW
Electrical demand for mill: 1,087 MWh/D

ⓘⓜUPM-Kymmene (UK) Ltd.
Shotton Paper Mill
Ownership: 100% by UPM-Kymmene Corporation
Weighbridge Road, Deeside Industrial Estate
Shotton, Deeside, Wales CH5 2LL
United Kingdom
Phone: (44) 1244 280 000
Fax: (44) 1244 280 363
Email: info.shotton@upm.com
Web Address: www.upm.com
Personnel:
Mgr. of Pulp & Paper Prod.: David Green
Phone: (44) 1244 280 000
Fax: (44) 1244 280 363
Email: david.green@upm.com
Commun. Controller: Paula Andrews
Phone: (44) 1244 280 000
Fax: (44) 1244 280 363
Email: paula.andrews@upm.com
Total Employees at this Location: 360
Type of Operation: Pulp mill, Paper mill
Mill Locations:
UPM-Kymmene (UK) Ltd., Caledonian Paper Mill, Meadowhead Rd., Irvine KA11 5AT, United Kingdom, Capacity: 280,000 mt/y, (Pulp mill, Paper mill)
Phone: (44) 1294 312 020
Fax: (44) 1294 314 400
Email: caledonianpaper@upm.com
Pulp Grades and Capacities:
Total pulp capacity: 514,271 mt/y
Recycled Pulping: 514,271 mt/y
Pulp Mill Data:
Pulp Lines: 3
Bleach Plant Systems: 1
Recycled Fiber Treatment Lines:
Flotation deinking lines: 3 at 640,000 admt/y
Pulpers: 3 at 640,000 admt/y
Paper/Paperboard Grades and Capacities:
Total paper and paperboard capacity: 500,000 mt/y
Newsprint: 500,000 mt/y
Paper and Paperboard Mill Data:
Stock Preparation:
Pulpers: 2
Refiners: 16
Paper Machines: 2
No. 1, SymFormer R, total capacity 240,000 mt/y, Trim width 8.6 m, Newsprint
No. 2, SpeedFormer HS, total capacity 260,000 mt/y, Trim width 8.7 m, Newsprint
Finishing Equipment:
Rewinders: 3
Energy Data:
Power boilers: 2
Steam turbines: 1 at 20 MW
Electrical demand for mill: 1,400 MWh/D

ⓘⓜWeidmann Whiteley Ltd.
Otley Mill
Ownership: 100% by Wicor Group
Pool-in-Wharfedale
Otley, West Yorkshire LS21 1RP
United Kingdom
Phone: (44) 113 202 7000
Fax: (44) 113 284 2272
Email: sales.whiteley@wicor.com
Web Address: www.weidmann-electrical.com/en/about-us/electrical-technology/great-britain
Personnel:
Fabrication Bus. Mgr.: Tim Johnson
Phone: (44) 113 284 2121
Fax: (44) 113 284 2272
Email: tim.johnson@wicor.com
Sls. Mgr. & Cust. Serv. Mgr.: Toby Albrecht
Phone: (44) 113 202 7003
Fax: (44) 113 284 2272
Email: toby.albrecht@wicor.com
Finan. Dir.: John Stephen Briggs
Phone: (44) 113 284 2121
Fax: (44) 113 284 2272
Email: john.briggs@wicor.com
Total Employees at this Location: 110
Type of Operation: Paperboard mill
Paper/Paperboard Grades and Capacities:
Total paper and paperboard capacity: 12,500 mt/y
Boxboard/cartonboard: 12,500 mt/y
Paper and Paperboard Mill Data:
Stock Preparation:
Pulpers: 4
Refiners: 7
Paper Machines: 1
PM 1, cylinder, total capacity 12,500 mt/y, Trim width 3.4 m, Boxboard/cartonboard
Coating Machines: 1
No. 1, off machine
Finishing Equipment:
Supercalenders: 2
Rewinders: 7
Energy Data:
Power boilers

ⓘⓜWhatman International Ltd.
Springfield Mill
Ownership: GE Healthcare
James Whatman Way
Maidstone, Kent ME14 2LE
United Kingdom
Phone: (44) 1622 676 670 / 800 515 313
Fax: (44) 1622 691 425 / 800 616 927
Email: whatmaninfo@ge.com, whatmaninformation@ge.com, custservuk@ge.com
Web Address: www.whatman.com
Personnel:
Gen. Mgr.: Vic Wells
Phone: (44) 1295 702411
Fin. Mgr.: Stewart Margerum
Phone: (44) 1622 626 226
Prod. Mgr.: Paul Highsted
Phone: (44) 1622 676 670
Email: paul.highsted@ge.com
Eng. Mgr.: Dave Bower
Phone: (44) 1622 626 479
R&D Mgr.: Mark Green
Phone: (44) 1622 626 344
Safety Off.: M. Banfield
Phone: (44) 1622 626 243
Total Employees of Company: 200
Total Employees at this Location: 200
Type of Operation: Paper mill
Paper/Paperboard Grades and Capacities:
Total paper and paperboard capacity: 6,000 mt/y
Uncoated woodfree/freesheet
Coated woodfree/freesheet
Specialty and industrial
Paper and Paperboard Mill Data:
Stock Preparation:
Pulpers: 3
Refiners: 2
Paper Machines: 4
No. 1, fourdrinier, Trim width 1.5 m
No. 2, cylinder mould, Trim width 1 m
No. 3, cylinder mould, Trim width 1.5 m
No. 4, cylinder mould, Trim width 0.5 m
Coating Machines: 1
No. 1, off machine
Finishing Equipment:
Supercalenders: 1
Rewinders: 5
Sheeters: 2

UPCOMING RISI EVENTS

RISI hosts worldwide events throughout the year. These events are exclusive gatherings of decision-makers from throughout the forest products industry, featuring high-quality programs with expert speakers from a variety of sectors. They also provide an excellent opportunity to network with key industry players and to showcase your company's product(s) or service(s) through our various sponsorship options.

RISI's European Conference
March 9-11, 2015
Amsterdam, Netherlands

Forest Products and Timberland Investments Conference
March 31-April 1, 2015
New York, USA

China Paper Packaging Summit
April 2015
Shanghai, China

Asia Pacific Nonwovens Symposium
May 11-12, 2015
Shanghai, China

RISI's Asian Conference
June 2015
Shanghai, China

PPI Transport Symposium 21
October 19-21, 2015
Bremen, Germany

Latin American Paper Packaging Conference
November 2015
Miami, Florida

**Visit www.risi.com/events
to learn more about these events**

|R|S|

PULP and PAPER MILLS in Asia and Oceania

ARMENIA

ⓘArbumprom-Kartontara, LLC
Ownership: Grand Holding
ul Aeratsiya 1
375085 Yerevan, Gorod Yerevan
Armenia
 Phone: (374) 9140 6993 / 1046 7986 / 1042 8882
 Fax: (374) 1046 7986
 Email: tuxtard@inbox.ru,
 info@arbumprom.am
 Web Address: www.arbumprom.am
Mill Locations:
Arbumprom-Kartontara, LLC, Yerevan Mill, ul Aeratsiya 1, 375085 Yerevan, Armenia, Capacity: 15,000 mt/y, (Paperboard mill)
 Phone: (374) 9140 6993 / 1046 7986 / 1042 8882
 Fax: (374) 1046 7986
 Email: tuxtard@inbox.ru; info@arbumprom.am

ⓜArbumprom-Kartontara, LLC
Yerevan Mill
ul Aeratsiya 1
375085 Yerevan, Gorod Yerevan
Armenia
 Phone: (374) 9140 6993 / 1046 7986 / 1042 8882
 Fax: (374) 1046 7986
 Email: tuxtard@inbox.ru,
 info@arbumprom.am
 Web Address: www.arbumprom.am
Personnel:
 Gen. Mgr.: Mr. Garegin Orbikovich Issaxanyan
 Phone: (374) 91 20 39 87 (GSM)
 Fax: (374) 10 46 79 86
 Tech. Dir.: Grair Movsesyan
 Phone: (374) 9140 6993, 1046 7986
 Chief Eng.: Grair Asatryan
 Phone: (374) 9140 6993, 1046 7986
 Deputy Dir. / Tech.Dir.: Rafael Georgievich Vardanyan
Total Employees at this Location: 150
Type of Operation: Paperboard mill
Paper/Paperboard Grades and Capacities:
 Total paper and paperboard capacity: 15,000 mt/y
 Linerboard: 15,000 mt/y
Paper and Paperboard Mill Data:
Paper Machines: 1
 PM 1, total capacity 15,000 mt/y, Trim width 1.4 m, Linerboard
Energy Data:
 Electrical demand for mill: 48 MWh/D

ⓘⓜGrand Holding Mill
Yerevan Mill
Yerevan, Gorod Yerevan
Armenia
Personnel:
 Gen. Mgr.: Grant Vardanyan
Type of Operation: Paperboard mill
Paper/Paperboard Grades and Capacities:
 Total paper and paperboard capacity: 3,600 mt/y
 Linerboard: 3,600 mt/y
 Corrugating medium/fluting
Paper and Paperboard Mill Data:
Paper Machines: 1
 No. 1, total capacity 3,600 mt/y, Linerboard, Corrugating medium/fluting

AUSTRALIA

ⓘⓜABC Tissue Products Pty. Ltd.
Wetherill Park Mill
34-36 Redfern Street, Wetherill Park
Fairfield, Sydney, NSW, 2164
Australia
 Phone: (61) 2 8787 2222
 Fax: (61) 2 8787 2280
 Email: henry.ngai@abctissue.com
 Web Address: www.abctissue.com
Personnel:
 Owner, Man. Dir. & CEO: Henry Ngai
 Phone: (61) 2 8787 2222
 Fax: (61) 2 8787 2280
 Email: henryngai@abctissue.com
 Mktg. Dir.: Sunny Ngai
 Phone: (61) 2 8787 2222
 Fax: (61) 2 8787 2280
 Email: sunnyngai@abctissue.com
 Gen. Mgr.: Ming Ly
 Phone: (61) 2 8787 2232
 Fax: (61) 2 8787 2280
 Email: mingly@abctissue.com
 Bus. Dev. Mgr.: Maurice O'Meagher
 Phone: (61) 2 8787 2222
 Fax: (61) 2 8787 2280
 Email: mauriceomeagher@abctissue.com
 Prod. Mgr. : Frank Fan
 Phone: (61) 2 8787 2222
 Fax: (61) 2 8787 2280
 Email: frankfan@abctissue.com
Total Employees of Company: 500
Total Employees at this Location: 80
Type of Operation: Paper mill
Mill Locations:
Queensland Tissue Products, Carole Park Mill, Corner Antimony and Emery Street, Carole Park, Brisbane, QLD 4300, Australia, Capacity: 21,000 mt/y, (Paper mill)
 Phone: (61) 7 3271 2288
 Fax: (61) 7 3271 2299
 Email: gordon.sutton@abctissue.com, johnrea@softex.net.au
Paper/Paperboard Grades and Capacities:
 Total paper and paperboard capacity: 34,000 mt/y
 Tissue: 34,000 mt/y
Paper and Paperboard Mill Data:
Paper Machines: 1
 No. 1, crescent former, total capacity 34,000 mt/y, Trim width 3.4 m, Tissue, Uncoated woodfree/freesheet
Energy Data:
 Power boilers
 Electrical demand for mill: 95 MWh/D

ⓘAustralian Paper
Ownership: Nippon Paper Industries Co., Ltd.
307 Ferntree Gully Rd
Mt Waverley, VIC, 3149
Australia
Mailing Address: Private Bag 87, Mt Waverley, 3149, Australia
 Phone: (61) 3 8540 2211
 Fax: (61) 3 8540 2280
 Email: (firstname.lastname@australianpaper.com.au)
 Web Address: www.australianpaper.com.au
Personnel:
 Acting CEO: Hirofumi Fujimori
 Phone: (61) 3 8540 2211
 Fax: (61) 3 8540 2280
 CFO: Peter Williams
 Phone: (61) 3 8540 2211
 Fax: (61) 3 8540 2280
 Group Gen. Mgr. Corp. Planner: Jon Ryder
 Phone: (61) 3 8540 2211
 Fax: (61) 3 8540 2280
 Group Gen. Mgr., Supply Chain: Julian Matthers
 Phone: (61) 3 8540 2211
 Fax: (61) 3 8540 2280
 Group Gen. Mgr., HR: Mark Nelson
 Phone: (61) 3 8540 2211
 Fax: (61) 3 8540 2280
 Snr. Mktg. Mgr. Sustainability: Craig Dunn
 Phone: (61) 4 0812 2408
 Email: craig.dunn@australianpaper.com.au
Total Employees of Company: 1,400
Mill Locations:
Australian Paper, Maryvale Mill, Maryvale Road, Morwell, VIC 3840, Australia, Capacity: 605,000 mt/y, (Pulp mill, Paper mill, Paperboard mill)
 Phone: (61) 3 5136 0360
 Fax: (61) 3 5134 6127
 Email: (firstname.surname@australianpaper.com.au)
Australian Paper, Shoalhaven Mill, 340 Bolong Road, Bomaderry, NSW 2541, Australia, Capacity: 16,000 mt/y, (Pulp mill, Paper mill, Paperboard mill)
 Phone: (61) 2 4428 6444
 Fax: (61) 2 4423 1066
 Email: (firstname.lastname@australianpaper.com.au)

ⓜAustralian Paper
Maryvale Mill
Ownership: Nippon Paper Industries Co., Ltd.
Maryvale Road
Morwell, VIC, 3840
Australia
Mailing Address: PO Box 37, Morwell, 3840, Australia
 Phone: (61) 3 5136 0360
 Fax: (61) 3 5134 6127
 Email: (firstname.surname@australianpaper.com.au)
 Web Address: www.australianpaper.com.au
Personnel:
 Gen. Mgr., Maryvale: Howard Lovell
 Phone: (61) 3 5136 0360
 Fax: (61) 3 5134 6127
 Email: howard.lovell@australianpaper.com.au
 Tech. Mgr.: Lachlan Mclean
 Phone: (61) 3 5136 0446
 Fax: (61) 3 5134 6127
 Email: lachlan.mclean@australianpaper.com.au
 Gen. Mgr. Proj.: Gavin Jones
 Phone: (61) 3 5136 0360
 Fax: (61) 3 5134 6127
 Email: gavin.jones@australianpaper.com.au
 HR Gen. Mgr.: Rod Beales
 Phone: (61) 3 5136 0360
 Fax: (61) 3 5134 6127
Total Employees at this Location: 820
Type of Operation: Pulp mill, Paper mill, Paperboard mill
Pulp Grades and Capacities:
 Total pulp capacity: 539,213 mt/y
 Chemical Pulp: 493,456 mt/y
 Recycled Pulping: 45,757 mt/y
Pulp Mill Data:
 Chemical Pulping Systems:
 Batch digesters: 9
 Continuous digesters: 2

Australia

Pulp Lines: 3
Bleach Plant Systems: 1
No. 1, Type: (ZD)-Eop-D, Sequence: O_2 ZDoEopD, Capacity 250,000 admt/y
Chemical Recovery Equipment:
Evaporator lines: 2
Recovery boilers: 2
Lime Kiln
Recycled Fiber Treatment Lines:
Pulpers: 1 at 100,000 admt/y
Pulp Dryers:
Wet Lap machine 1
Paper/Paperboard Grades and Capacities:
Total paper and paperboard capacity: 605,000 mt/y
Uncoated woodfree/freesheet: 280,500 mt/y
Packaging papers: 94,500 mt/y
Linerboard: 230,000 mt/y
Paper and Paperboard Mill Data:
Stock Preparation:
Pulpers: 5
Paper Machines: 5
M1, fourdrinier, total capacity 60,000 mt/y, Trim width 4.8 m, Packaging papers
M2, fourdrinier, total capacity 30,000 mt/y, Trim width 4.8 m, Packaging papers
M3, twin-wire, total capacity 90,000 mt/y, Trim width 5.2 m, Uncoated woodfree/freesheet, Packaging papers
M4, twin-wire, total capacity 230,000 mt/y, Trim width 6.6 m, Linerboard
M5, twin-wire, total capacity 195,000 mt/y, Trim width 6.8 m, Uncoated woodfree/freesheet
Finishing Equipment:
Rewinders: 2
Sheeters: 2
Energy Data:
Power boilers: 3
Steam turbines: 4 at 12, 12, 12, 18.5 MW
Electrical demand for mill: 1,514 MWh/D

(M) Australian Paper
Shoalhaven Mill
Ownership: Nippon Paper Industries Co., Ltd.
340 Bolong Road
Bomaderry, NSW, 2541
Australia
Mailing Address: PO Box 149, Bomaderry, NSW 2541, Australia
Phone: (61) 2 4428 6444
Fax: (61) 2 4423 1066
Email: (firstname.lastname@australianpaper.com.au)
Web Address: www.australianpaper.com.au
Personnel:
Mill Mgr.: Bruce Borchardt
Phone: (61) 2 4428 6444
Fax: (61) 2 4423 1066
Email: bruce.borchardt@australianpaper.com.au
Eng. Mgr.: John Bishop
Phone: (61) 2 4428 6452
Fax: (61) 2 4428 6472
Email: john.bishop@australianpaper.com.au
Bus. & Process Develop. Mgr.: Alan Barnes
Phone: (61) 2 4428 6461, 0419 003 307
Fax: (61) 2 4423 1066
Email: alan.barnes@australianpaper.com.au
Total Employees at this Location: 95
Type of Operation: Pulp mill, Paper mill, Paperboard mill
Paper/Paperboard Grades and Capacities:
Total paper and paperboard capacity: 16,000 mt/y
Uncoated woodfree/freesheet: 16,000 mt/y
Paper and Paperboard Mill Data:
Stock Preparation:
Pulpers: 5
Refiners: 19
Paper Machines: 1
No. 3, fourdrinier, total capacity 16,000 mt/y, Trim width 2.1 m, Uncoated woodfree/freesheet
Finishing Equipment:
Winders: 3
Sheeters: 5
Energy Data:
Power boilers: 1
Electrical demand for mill: 37 MWh/D

(M) Encore Tissue
Ownership: 100% by Private (Holckner family)
37-41 Gilbertson Road
Laverton North, VIC, 3026
Australia
Phone: (61) 3 9931 1488
Fax: (61) 3 9931 1433
Email: sales@encoretissue.com.au
Web Address: www.encoretissue.com.au
Personnel:
CFO: Miranda Payet
Phone: (61) 3 9931 1488
Fax: (61) 3 9931 1433
Email: miranda.payet@encoretissue.com.au
Bus. Develop. Mgr.: John Frantzis
Phone: (61) 3 9931 1488
Fax: (61) 3 9931 1433
Email: johnf@encoretissue.com.au
Log. Supervisor: Daniel Modica
Phone: (61) 3 9931 1488
Fax: (61) 3 9931 1433
Email: daniel.modica@encoretissue.com.au
Mill Locations:
Encore Tissue, Laverton North Mill, 37-41 Gilbertson Road, Laverton North, VIC 3026, Australia, Capacity: 20,000 mt/y, (Paper mill)
Phone: (61) 3 9931 1488
Fax: (61) 3 9931 1433
Email: david@encoretissue.com.au

(M) Encore Tissue
Laverton North Mill
37-41 Gilbertson Road
Laverton North, VIC, 3026
Australia
Phone: (61) 3 9931 1488
Fax: (61) 3 9931 1433
Email: david@encoretissue.com.au
Web Address: www.encoretissue.com.au
Personnel:
Mill Mgr.: Hugo Rust
Phone: (61) 3 9948 4104
Fax: (61) 3 9931 1433
Email: hugor@encoretissue.com.au
Total Employees at this Location: 65
Type of Operation: Paper mill
Pulp Grades and Capacities:
Total pulp capacity: 21,338 mt/y
Recycled Pulping: 21,338 mt/y
Pulp Mill Data:
Recycled Fiber Treatment Lines:
Pulpers: 1
Paper/Paperboard Grades and Capacities:
Total paper and paperboard capacity: 20,000 mt/y
Tissue: 20,000 mt/y
Paper and Paperboard Mill Data:
Paper Machines: 1
No. 1, twin-wire, total capacity 20,000 mt/y, Trim width 2.75 m, Tissue
Energy Data:
Power boilers: 1
Electrical demand for mill: 57 MWh/D

(M) Kimberly-Clark Australia Pty Ltd.
Millicent Mill
Ownership: Kimberly-Clark Corp.
Princes Highway
Millicent, SA, 5280
Australia
Mailing Address: P.O. Box 156, Millicent, 5280, Australia
Phone: (61) 8 8721 4200
Fax: (61) 8 8723 2253
Web Address: www.kca.com.au
Personnel:
Mill Mgr.: Scott Whicker
Phone: (61) 8 8721 4200
Fax: (61) 8 8723 2253
Tech. & Prod. Mgr.: Stuart Blizzard
Phone: (61) 8 8721 4200
Fax: (61) 8 8723 2253
Oper. Support Mgr.: Darren Williams
Phone: (61) 8 8721 4555
Fax: (61) 8 8721 2251
Email: darren.j.williams@kcc.com
Plan. Mgr.: John Ryan
Phone: (61) 8 8721 4200
Fax: (61) 8 8723 2253
Proj. Mgr.: Graham Burch
Phone: (61) 8 8721 4200
Fax: (61) 8 8723 2253
Total Employees at this Location: 200
Type of Operation: Paper mill
Pulp Grades and Capacities:
Total pulp capacity: 10,378 mt/y
Mechanical Pulp: 10,378 mt/y
Pulp Mill Data:
Mechanical Pulping Systems:
TMP systems: 1
Bleach Plant Systems: 1
Mechanical Pulping System, Type: Softwood, Sequence: P
Paper/Paperboard Grades and Capacities:
Total paper and paperboard capacity: 90,000 mt/y
Tissue: 90,000 mt/y
Paper and Paperboard Mill Data:
Stock Preparation:
Pulpers: 2
Refiners: 5
Paper Machines: 2
No. 4, Yankee dryer, total capacity 40,000 mt/y, Trim width 5.25 m, Tissue
No. 5, TAD, total capacity 50,000 mt/y, Trim width 5.4 m, Tissue
Energy Data:
Power boilers: 1
Steam turbines
Electrical demand for mill: 363 MWh/D

(M) Norske Skog (Australia)
Albury Mill
Ownership: 100% by Norske Skog ASA
Hume Highway
Ettamogah via Albury, NSW, 2640
Australia
Mailing Address: Private Bag, Lavington, 2641, Australia
Phone: (61) 2 6058 3111 / 2 60583181
Fax: (61) 2 6058 3080
Email: contactalbury@norskeskog.com,
(firstname.lastname@norske-skog.com.au)
Web Address: www.norske-skog.com
Personnel:
Mill Mgr.: Ernie Hacker
Phone: (61) 2 6058 3111
Fax: (61) 2 6058 3080
Email: ernie.hacker@norskeskog.com
Environ. & Bus. Develop. Mgr.: Michael Machin
Phone: (61) 2 6058 3089 / 3254
Fax: (61) 2 6058 3080
Email: michael.machin@norskeskog.com
Paper & Finishing Mgr.: Bob Bright
Phone: (61) 2 6058 3195
Fax: (61) 2 6058 3080
Email: bob.bright@norskeskog.com
Maint. Mgr.: John McPherson
Phone: (61) 2 6058 3111
Fax: (61) 2 6058 3080
Email: john.mcpherson@norskeskog.com
HR, Safety Mgr.: Nathan Bright
Phone: (61) 2 5058 3168

Fax: (61) 2 6058 3080
Email: nathan.bright@norskeskog.com
Admin. Officer: Melissa Bright
Phone: (61) 2 6058 3130
Fax: (61) 2 6058 3080
Email: melissa.bright@norskeskog.com
Total Employees at this Location: 188
Type of Operation: Pulp mill, Paper mill
Pulp Grades and Capacities:
Total pulp capacity: 273,756 mt/y
Mechanical Pulp: 191,630 mt/y
Recycled Pulping: 82,127 mt/y
Pulp Mill Data:
Mechanical Pulping Systems:
TMP systems: 4
Pulp Lines: 2
Bleach Plant Systems: 1
Mechanical Pulping System - Softwood TMP, Type: Softwood TMP, Sequence: H
Recycled Fiber Treatment Lines:
Flotation deinking lines: 2 at 100,000 admt/y
Pulpers: 1 at 170,000 admt/y
Pulp Dryers:
Wet Lap machine 1
Paper/Paperboard Grades and Capacities:
Total paper and paperboard capacity: 267,750 mt/y
Newsprint: 267,750 mt/y
Paper and Paperboard Mill Data:
Paper Machines: 1
No. 1, twin-wire, total capacity 267,750 mt/y, Trim width 8.49 m, Newsprint
Finishing Equipment:
Winders: 2 at 220,000 mt/y, 220,000 mt/y
Rewinders: 1
Energy Data:
Power boilers: 2
TMP Reboiler: 1
Electrical demand for mill: 1,907 MWh/D

ⓂNorske Skog (Australia)
Boyer Mill
Ownership: 100% by Norske Skog ASA
Boyer, TAS, 7140
Australia
Phone: (61) 3 6261 0111
Fax: (61) 3 6261 3274
Email: (firstname.lastname@norskeskog.com)
Web Address: www.norske-skog.com
Personnel:
Mill Mgr.: Rod Bender
Phone: (61) 3 6261 0111
Fax: (61) 3 6261 3304
Email: rod.bender@norskeskog.com
Supply & Logistics Mgr.: Arnold Willems
Phone: (61) 3 6261 0184
Fax: (61) 3 6261 3247
Email: arnold.willems@norskeskog.com
Eng. & Maint. Mgr.: Patrick Dooley
Phone: (61) 3 6261 0465
Fax: (61) 3 6261 3549
Email: patrick.dooley@norskeskog.com
Paper Performance Mgr.: Michael Browning
Phone: (61) 3 6261 0102
Fax: (61) 3 6261 3304
Email: michael.browning@norskeskog.com
Prod. Mgr.: Mark Hutchinson
Phone: (61) 3 6261 0111
Fax: (61) 3 6261 3304
Email: mark.hutchinson@norskeskog.com
Pulp Performance Mgr.: Roger Hare
Phone: (61) 3 6261 0111
Fax: (61) 3 6261 3304
Email: roger.hare@norskeskog.com
Product & Bus. Support Mgr.: Vaughn Coleman
Phone: (61) 3 6261 0111
Fax: (61) 3 6261 3247
Email: vaughn.coleman@norskeskog.com
Total Employees at this Location: 300
Type of Operation: Pulp mill, Paper mill

Pulp Grades and Capacities:
Total pulp capacity: 257,985 mt/y
Mechanical Pulp: 257,985 mt/y
Pulp Mill Data:
Mechanical Pulping Systems:
TMP systems: 3
Pulp Lines: 3
Bleach Plant Lines:
Andritz, Metso/HCBP Capacity 320 admt/y
Paper/Paperboard Grades and Capacities:
Total paper and paperboard capacity: 305,000 mt/y
Newsprint: 95,000 mt/y
Uncoated mechanical/groundwood: 70,000 mt/y
Coated mechanical/groundwood: 140,000 mt/y
Paper and Paperboard Mill Data:
Stock Preparation:
Pulpers: 2
Refiners: 2
Paper Machines: 2
No. 2, twin-wire, total capacity 140,000 mt/y, Trim width 5.85 m, Coated mechanical/groundwood
No. 3, GapFormer, total capacity 165,000 mt/y, Trim width 6.6 m, Newsprint, Uncoated mechanical/groundwood
Finishing Equipment:
Winders: 2 at 150,000 mt/y
Calenders: 2
Rewinders: 1 at 5,000 mt/y
Energy Data:
Power boilers: 3
TMP Reboiler: 1
Electrical demand for mill: 2,282 MWh/D

ⓂOrora Ltd
109 Burwood Road
Hawthorn, Melbourne, VIC, 3122
Australia
Phone: (61) 3 9811 7111
Web Address: www.ororagroup.com
Personnel:
Man. Dir. & CEO: Nigel Garrard
Email: nigel.garrard@ororagroup.com
Group Gen. Mgr. (Cartons and Sacks): David Berry
Email: david.berry@ororagroup.com
Group Gen. Mgr. (Paper and Recycling): Sonny Coleiro
Email: sonny.coleiro@ororagroup.com
CFO: Stuart Hutton
Email: stuart.hutton@ororagroup.com
Mill Locations:
Orora Ltd, Botany Mill, 1891 Botany Rd., Matraville, NSW 2036, Australia, Capacity: 320,000 mt/y, (Paper mill, Paperboard mill)
Phone: (61) 2 9695 3472, 2 9695 3434
Fax: (61) 2 9666 3048

ⓂOrora Ltd
Botany Mill
1891 Botany Rd.
Matraville, NSW, 2036
Australia
Phone: (61) 2 9695 3472, 2 9695 3434
Fax: (61) 2 9666 3048
Web Address: www.ororagroup.com
Personnel:
Gen. Mgr. Oper. B9: Karl Achleitner
Phone: (61) 2 9695 3483, M:417 866 925
Fax: (61) 2 9666 3048
OHSE Mgr.: Melissa Pollock
Phone: (61) 2 9695 3472
Fax: (61) 2 9666 3048
Tech. Mgr.: Jacob Chretien
Phone: (61) 2 9695 3472
Fax: (61) 2 9666 3048
Cust. Support Mgr.: Cathy Parra
Phone: (61) 2 9695 3472
Fax: (61) 2 9666 3048
Total Employees at this Location: 150
Type of Operation: Paper mill, Paperboard mill

Pulp Grades and Capacities:
Total pulp capacity: 320,215 mt/y
Recycled Pulping: 320,215 mt/y
Pulp Mill Data:
Recycled Fiber Treatment Lines:
Pulpers: 2 at 260,000 admt/y
Paper/Paperboard Grades and Capacities:
Total paper and paperboard capacity: 320,000 mt/y
Linerboard: 192,000 mt/y
Corrugating medium/fluting: 128,000 mt/y
Paper and Paperboard Mill Data:
Stock Preparation:
Pulpers: 2
Paper Machines: 1
B9, Gap former (2), total capacity 320,000 mt/y, Trim width 5.66 m, Linerboard, Corrugating medium/fluting
Finishing Equipment:
Rewinders: 2
Energy Data:
Power boilers: 1
Electrical demand for mill: 375 MWh/D

ⓂQueensland Tissue Products
Carole Park Mill
Ownership: 100% by ABC Tissue Products Pty. Ltd.
Corner Antimony and Emery Street, Carole Park
Brisbane, QLD, 4300
Australia
Phone: (61) 7 3271 2288
Fax: (61) 7 3271 2299
Email: gordon.sutton@abctissue.com,
johnrea@softex.net.au
Web Address: www.abctissue.com
Personnel:
Gen. Mgr.: Desmond Lau
Phone: (61) 7 3271 2288
Fax: (61) 7 3271 2299
Email: desmondlau@abctissue.com
Total Employees at this Location: 88
Type of Operation: Paper mill
Pulp Grades and Capacities:
Total pulp capacity: 22,498 mt/y
Recycled Pulping: 22,498 mt/y
Pulp Mill Data:
Bleach Plant Systems: 1
Recyled Pulping System, Type: Deinked
Recycled Fiber Treatment Lines:
Pulpers: 1
Paper/Paperboard Grades and Capacities:
Total paper and paperboard capacity: 21,000 mt/y
Tissue: 21,000 mt/y
Paper and Paperboard Mill Data:
Paper Machines: 2
No. 1, Yankee dryer, total capacity 7,500 mt/y, Trim width 2.65 m, Tissue
No. 2, crescent former, total capacity 13,500 mt/y, Trim width 2.65 m, Tissue
Energy Data:
Power boilers: 4
Electrical demand for mill: 61 MWh/D

ⓉⓂSCA Hygiene Products Australasia
Box Hill Mill
Ownership: 50% by SCA - Svenska Cellulosa Aktiebolaget, 50% by Pacific Equity Partners
Ailsa St.
Box Hill, VIC, 3128
Australia
Mailing Address: PO Box 117, Box Hill, 3128, Australia
Phone: (61) 3 9258 0555
Fax: (61) 3 9258 0785
Email: (firstname.surname@sca.com),
info@sca.com
Web Address: www.sca.com/australasia,
www.sca.com
Personnel:
Pres.: Peter Diplaris

Australia

Phone: (61) 3 9258 0555
Fax: (61) 3 9258 0785
CFO: Paul Townsend
Phone: (61) 3 9258 0555
Fax: (61) 3 9258 0785
Exec. Gen. Mgr. Oper.: Willie Wiese
Phone: (61) 3 9258 0555
Fax: (61) 3 9258 0785
Exec. Gen. Mgr. HR.: David Griss
Phone: (61) 3 9258 0555
Fax: (61) 3 9258 0785
CIO: Andrea Bell
Phone: (61) 3 9258 0555
Fax: (61) 3 9258 0785
Gen. Mgr. Technical: Scott Wightwick
Phone: (61) 3 9258 0555
Fax: (61) 3 9258 0785
Eng. & Maint. Systems: John McMillan
Phone: (61) 3 9258 0555
Fax: (61) 3 9258 0785
Mgr, Sustainability: Andrew Taylor
Phone: (61) 3 9258 0751
Fax: (61) 3 9258 0785
Email: andrew.taylor@sca.com
Total Employees of Company: 1,300
Total Employees at this Location: 147
Type of Operation: Paper mill
Mill Locations:
SCA Hygiene Products Australasia, Kawerau Mill, Fletcher Avenue, 3169 Kawerau, New Zealand, Capacity: 57,000 mt/y, (Paper mill)
Phone: (64) 7 323 9899
Fax: (64) 7 323 6601
Email: (firstname.lastname@sca.com)
Paper/Paperboard Grades and Capacities:
Total paper and paperboard capacity: 54,000 mt/y
Tissue: 54,000 mt/y
Paper and Paperboard Mill Data:
Stock Preparation:
Pulpers: 7
Refiners: 5
Paper Machines: 2
No. 3 fourdrinier, total capacity 27,000 mt/y, Trim width 3.4 m, Tissue, Uncoated woodfree/freesheet
No. 4 TAD, total capacity 27,000 mt/y, Trim width 3.5 m, Tissue
Finishing Equipment:
Rewinders: 4
Energy Data:
Electrical demand for mill: 178 MWh/D

ⓜVisy Pulp & Paper
Ownership: 100% by Pratt family
13 Reo Crescent
Campbellfield, VIC, 3062
Australia
Mailing Address: Locked Bag 65, Somerton Business Centre, Campbellfield, 3062, Australia
Phone: (61) 3 9247 4450
Fax: (61) 3 9247 4460
Email: paper@visy.com.au, info@visy.com.au
Web Address: www.visy.com.au
Personnel:
Exec. Chmn.: Anthony Pratt
Phone: (61) 3 9247 4450
Fax: (61) 3 9247 4460
Email: anthony.pratt@visy.com.au
COO: Gus Carfi
Phone: (61) 3 9247 4450
Fax: (61) 3 9247 4460
Email: gus.carfi@visy.com.au
Gen. Mgr. Operations and Capital: Stephen Deane
Phone: (61) 3 9247 4450
Fax: (61) 3 9247 4460
Email: stephen.deane@visy.com.au
Dir., Sust. & Corp. Commun.: Tony Gray
Phone: (61) 3 9247 4450
Fax: (61) 3 9247 4460
Email: tony.gray@visy.com.au

Nat. Reliability & Manuf. Mgr.: Grant Crosley
Phone: (61) 3 9247 4450
Fax: (61) 3 9247 4460
Email: grant.crosley@visy.com.au
Total Employees of Company: 5,500
Mill Locations:
Pratt Industries (USA), Conyers Mill, 1800 A Sarasota Business Parkway, Conyers, GA 30013, USA, Capacity: 331,967 mt/y, (Paper mill, Paperboard mill)
Phone: (1) 770-922-5400, 770-918-5678
Fax: (1) 770-922-7572
Email: info@prattindustries.com
Pratt Industries (USA), Shreveport Mill, 10429 Richard Pratt Drive, Shreveport, LA 71115, USA, Capacity: 340,064 mt/y, (Paperboard mill)
Phone: (1) 318-797-7375
Pratt Industries (USA), Staten Island Mill, 4435 Victory Blvd, Staten Island, NY 10314, USA, Capacity: 338,445 mt/y, (Paper mill, Paperboard mill)
Phone: (1) 718-355-6754
Fax: (1) 718-370-1115
Visy Pulp & Paper, Tumut, VPP9, 436 Gadara Road, Tumut, NSW 2720, Australia, Capacity: 700,000 mt/y, (Pulp mill, Paperboard mill)
Phone: (61) 2 6947 7900
Fax: (61) 2 6947 5315
Visy Pulp & Paper, Coolaroo Mill, 13 Reo Crescent, Campbellfield, VIC 3061, Australia, Capacity: 253,113 mt/y, (Paper mill, Paperboard mill)
Phone: (61) 3 9247 4400
Fax: (61) 3 9247 4444
Email: (firstname.surname@visy.com.au)
Visy Pulp & Paper, Gibson Island, VPP8, 168 Paringa Road, Gibson Island, QLD 4172, Australia, Capacity: 169,000 mt/y, (Paperboard mill)
Phone: (61) 7 3259 2444
Fax: (61) 7 3259 2455
Email: paper@visy.com.au
Visy Pulp & Paper, VPP2, Reservoir Mill, 22 Radford Rd., Reservoir, VIC 3073, Australia, Capacity: 100,500 mt/y, (Paperboard mill)
Phone: (61) 3 9247 4296
Fax: (61) 3 9247 4076
Visy Pulp & Paper, VPP3/6, Smithfield Mill, 158-160 McCredie Rd., Smithfield, NSW 2164, Australia, Capacity: 255,000 mt/y, (Paperboard mill)
Phone: (61) 2 9794 3120
Fax: (61) 2 9794 3150

ⓜVisy Pulp & Paper
Tumut, VPP9
436 Gadara Road
Tumut, NSW, 2720
Australia
Mailing Address: PO Box 98, Tumut, 2720, Australia
Phone: (61) 2 6947 7900
Fax: (61) 2 6947 5315
Web Address: www.visy.com.au
Personnel:
Gen. Mgr.: Jean-Yves Nouaze
Phone: (61) 2 6947 7900
Fax: (61) 2 6947 5315
Email: jeanyves.nouaze@visy.com.au
Manuf. Mgr.: Johan Stoltz
Phone: (61) 2 6947 7900
Fax: (61) 2 6947 5315
Email: johan.stoltz@visy.com.au
Environ. Mgr.: Matthew O'Donovan
Phone: (61) 2 6947 7900
Fax: (61) 2 6947 5315
Email: matthew.o'donovan@visi.com.au
Maint. & Reliability Mgr.: Grant Crosley
Phone: (61) 2 6947 7900
Fax: (61) 2 6947 5315
Email: grant.crosley@visy.com.au
Total Employees at this Location: 216
Type of Operation: Pulp mill, Paperboard mill
Pulp Grades and Capacities:
Total pulp capacity: 708,574 mt/y
Chemical Pulp: 566,859 mt/y
Recycled Pulping: 141,715 mt/y

Pulp Mill Data:
Chemical Pulping Systems:
Continuous digesters: 1
Pulp Lines: 2
Chemical Recovery Equipment:
Evaporator lines: 2
Recovery boilers: 2
Lime Kiln
Recycled Fiber Treatment Lines:
Pulpers: 1
Paper/Paperboard Grades and Capacities:
Total paper and paperboard capacity: 700,000 mt/y
Linerboard: 700,000 mt/y
Paper and Paperboard Mill Data:
Paper Machines: 2
No. 9, twin-wire, total capacity 300,000 mt/y, Trim width 5.3 m, Linerboard
No. 10, fourdrinier (3), total capacity 400,000 mt/y, Trim width 7.49 m, Linerboard
Energy Data:
Power boilers: 1
Steam turbines: 1 at 20 MW
Electrical demand for mill: 1,489 MWh/D

ⓜVisy Pulp & Paper
Coolaroo Mill
13 Reo Crescent
Campbellfield, VIC, 3061
Australia
Mailing Address: Locked Bag 65, Somerton Business Centre, Cambellfield, 3062, Australia
Phone: (61) 3 9247 4400
Fax: (61) 3 9247 4444
Email: (firstname.surname@visy.com.au)
Web Address: www.visy.com.au
Personnel:
Plant Mgr. VP4: Peter Whittingham
Phone: (61) 3 9247 4400
Fax: (61) 3 9247 4444
Email: peter.whittingham@visy.com.au
Plant Mgr. VP5: Chris Martin
Phone: (61) 3 9247 4500
Fax: (61) 3 9247 4540
Email: chris.martin@visy.com.au
Gen. Mgr. Finan.: Anthony Pasceri
Phone: (61) 3 9247 4400
Fax: (61) 3 9247 4444
Email: anthony.pasceri@visy.com.au
Total Employees at this Location: 112
Type of Operation: Paper mill, Paperboard mill
Pulp Grades and Capacities:
Total pulp capacity: 260,049 mt/y
Recycled Pulping: 260,049 mt/y
Pulp Mill Data:
Bleach Plant Systems: 1
Recycled Pulping System, Type: Deinked
Recycled Fiber Treatment Lines:
Flotation deinking lines: 1 at 140,000 admt/y
Pulpers: 4 at 250,000 admt/y
Washing deinking lines: 1 at 140,000 admt/y
Paper/Paperboard Grades and Capacities:
Total paper and paperboard capacity: 253,113 mt/y
Linerboard: 126,378 mt/y
Corrugating medium/fluting: 39,270 mt/y
Boxboard/cartonboard: 87,465 mt/y
Paper and Paperboard Mill Data:
Stock Preparation:
Pulpers: 4
Refiners: 4
Paper Machines: 2
No. 4, twin-wire, total capacity 123,165 mt/y, Trim width 2.5 m, Linerboard, Boxboard/cartonboard
No. 5, twin-wire, total capacity 129,948 mt/y, Trim width 2.8 m, Linerboard, Corrugating medium/fluting
Coating Machines: 1
No. 1, off machine
Energy Data:
Power boilers: 3
Electrical demand for mill: 426 MWh/D

ⓜVisy Pulp & Paper
Gibson Island, VPP8
168 Paringa Road
Gibson Island, QLD, 4172
Australia
Phone: (61) 7 3259 2444
Fax: (61) 7 3259 2455
Email: paper@visy.com.au
Web Address: www.visy.com.au
Personnel:
Oper. Mgr.: Lee Taylor
Phone: (61) 7 3259 2444
Fax: (61) 7 3259 2455
Email: lee.taylor@visy.com.au
Prod. Mgr.: Peter van Buuren
Phone: (61) 7 3259 2444
Fax: (61) 7 3259 2455
Email: peter.vanbuuren@visy.com.au
Maint. & Reliability Mgr.: Nathan Campbell
Phone: (61) 7 3259 2403, 0429 347 178
Fax: (61) 7 3259 2456
Email: nathan.campbell@visy.com.au
Total Employees at this Location: 89
Type of Operation: Paperboard mill
Pulp Grades and Capacities:
Total pulp capacity: 171,157 mt/y
Recycled Pulping: 171,157 mt/y
Pulp Mill Data:
Recycled Fiber Treatment Lines:
Recycled packaging pulping lines
Paper/Paperboard Grades and Capacities:
Total paper and paperboard capacity: 169,000 mt/y
Linerboard: 79,000 mt/y
Corrugating medium/fluting: 90,000 mt/y
Paper and Paperboard Mill Data:
Paper Machines: 1
No. 8, GapFormer, total capacity 169,000 mt/y, Trim width 2.8 m, Linerboard, Corrugating medium/fluting
Finishing Equipment:
Winders: 1 at 160,000 mt/y
Energy Data:
Power boilers: 1
Steam turbines: 1 at 2 MW
Electrical demand for mill: 197 MWh/D

ⓜVisy Pulp & Paper
VPP2, Reservoir Mill
22 Radford Rd.
Reservoir, VIC, 3073
Australia
Phone: (61) 3 9247 4296
Fax: (61) 3 9247 4076
Web Address: www.visy.com.au
Personnel:
Mill Mgr.: Dale Hopkins
Phone: (61) 3 9247 4296
Fax: (61) 3 9247 4076
Email: dale.hopkins@visy.com.au
Reliability Mgr.: Ajamal Safar
Phone: (61) 3 9247 4296
Fax: (61) 3 9247 4076
Email: ajamal.safar@visy.com.au
Total Employees at this Location: 51
Type of Operation: Paperboard mill
Pulp Grades and Capacities:
Total pulp capacity: 101,925 mt/y
Recycled Pulping: 101,925 mt/y
Pulp Mill Data:
Recycled Fiber Treatment Lines:
Pulpers: 3 at 80,000 admt/y
Paper/Paperboard Grades and Capacities:
Total paper and paperboard capacity: 100,500 mt/y
Linerboard: 36,000 mt/y
Corrugating medium/fluting: 52,000 mt/y
Boxboard/cartonboard: 12,500 mt/y
Paper and Paperboard Mill Data:
Stock Preparation:
Pulpers: 3
Paper Machines: 1
No. 2, fourdrinier, total capacity 100,500 mt/y, Trim width 2.78 m, Linerboard, Corrugating medium/fluting, Boxboard/cartonboard
Finishing Equipment:
Rewinders: 1
Energy Data:
Power boilers: 3
Electrical demand for mill: 119 MWh/D

ⓜVisy Pulp & Paper
VPP3/6, Smithfield Mill
158-160 McCredie Rd.
Smithfield, NSW, 2164
Australia
Phone: (61) 2 9794 3120
Fax: (61) 2 9794 3150
Web Address: www.visy.com.au
Personnel:
Oper. Mgr.: Christopher McComb
Phone: (61) 2 9794 3120
Fax: (61) 2 9794 3150
Email: christopher.mccomb@visy.com.au
Prod. Mgr.: Chris Marshall
Phone: (61) 2 9794 3120
Fax: (61) 2 9794 3150
Email: chris.marshall@visy.com.au
Nat. Continuous Improve. Mgr.: Mark Dixon
Phone: (61) 2 9794 3120
Fax: (61) 2 9794 3150
Email: mark.dixon@visy.com.au
Eng. Mgr.: Pramil Agrawal
Phone: (61) 2 9794 3120
Fax: (61) 2 9794 3150
Email: pramil.agrawal@visy.com.au
Total Employees at this Location: 113
Type of Operation: Paperboard mill
Pulp Grades and Capacities:
Total pulp capacity: 258,583 mt/y
Recycled Pulping: 258,583 mt/y
Pulp Mill Data:
Recycled Fiber Treatment Lines:
Recycled packaging pulping lines: 2
Paper/Paperboard Grades and Capacities:
Total paper and paperboard capacity: 255,000 mt/y
Linerboard: 140,250 mt/y
Corrugating medium/fluting: 114,750 mt/y
Paper and Paperboard Mill Data:
Stock Preparation:
Pulpers: 2
Refiners: 4
Paper Machines: 2
No. 3, fourdrinier (3), total capacity 140,000 mt/y, Trim width 2.52 m, Linerboard, Corrugating medium/fluting
No. 6, GapFormer, total capacity 115,000 mt/y, Trim width 2.52 m, Corrugating medium/fluting, Linerboard
Finishing Equipment:
Rewinders: 3
Energy Data:
Power boilers: 3
Electrical demand for mill: 300 MWh/D

AZERBAIJAN

ⓞⓜQafqaz Kagit Sanaye, Caucasus Paper Industry
Baku Mill
Darnagul, 108
Baku, Binagadi District
Azerbaijan
Phone: (994) 12 448 06 82/436 06 58
Fax: (994) 12 448 06 83
Email: info@azersun.com
Web Address: qafqazkagiz.az/indexEn.html
Type of Operation: Paper mill
Paper/Paperboard Grades and Capacities:
Total paper and paperboard capacity: 2,500 mt/y
Tissue: 2,500 mt/y

BAHRAIN

ⓜOlayan Kimberly-Clark (Bahrain) W.L.L.
Isa Town Mill
Ownership: Kimberly-Clark Corp., Olayan Saudi Holding
South Alba Industrial Area
Isa Town, Bahrain
Bahrain
Mailing Address: P.O. Box 33124, Isa Town, Bahrain
Phone: (973) 17 830-688
Fax: (973) 17 830-449
Email: okb@olayangroup.com, kuginm@kcc.com
Web Address: www.olayan.com
Personnel:
Man. Dir.: Rudy Mirran
Phone: (973) 17 830-688
Fax: (973) 17 830-449
Email: rudy.mirran@kcc.com
Oper. Dir.: Kugin Matu
Phone: (973) 17 830-688
Fax: (973) 17 830-449
Email: kugin.muthu@kcc.com
Finan. Dir.: Ameer Hamza
Phone: (973) 17 830-688
Fax: (973) 17 830-449
Email: ameer.hamza@kcc.com
Total Employees at this Location: 200
Type of Operation: Paper mill
Paper/Paperboard Grades and Capacities:
Total paper and paperboard capacity: 47,000 mt/y
Tissue: 47,000 mt/y
Paper and Paperboard Mill Data:
Paper Machines: 2
No. 1, twin-wire, Yankee dryer, total capacity 15,000 mt/y, Trim width 2.7 m, Tissue, Uncoated woodfree/freesheet
No. 2, crescent former, Yankee dryer, total capacity 32,000 mt/y, Trim width 2.85 m, Tissue
Energy Data:
Power boilers
Electrical demand for mill: 120 MWh/D

BANGLADESH

ⓞⓜAnanta Paper Mills Pvt. Ltd
Rupgonj Mill
Ownership: 100% by Younus Group
Mithabo, Narayanganj Sadar
Rupgonj, Narayanganj
Bangladesh
Total Employees of Company: 196
Total Employees at this Location: 196
Type of Operation: Paper mill
Paper/Paperboard Grades and Capacities:
Total paper and paperboard capacity: 7,300 mt/y
Newsprint
Packaging papers
Paper and Paperboard Mill Data:
Paper Machines: 1
No. 1, total capacity 7,300 mt/y, Newsprint, Packaging papers
Energy Data:
Steam turbines

ⓜBangladesh Chemical Industries Corp.
Ownership: 100% by Govt. of Bangladesh
BCIC Bhaban, 30-31, Dilkusha C.A.
1000 Dhaka
Bangladesh
Phone: (880) 2 955281-82/9562140-41/9559286

Bangladesh

Fax: (880) 2 9564120
Email: bcic_comp@bangla.net
Web Address: www.bcic.gov.bd
Personnel:
Chmn.: Md Mahbubur Rahman
Phone: (880) 2 9564153
Fax: (880) 2 9564180
Finan. Dir.: A.S.M Rashidul Hai
Phone: (880) 2 9509395
Fax: (880) 2 956180
Plan & Impl. Div.: Raficu Islam
Phone: (880) 2 9554043
Fax: (880) 2 9556624
Commercial Dir.: Mostafizur Rahman
Phone: (880) 2 9564135
Fax: (880) 2 9564120
Proc. & Eng. Dir.: Zahid Kabir
Phone: (880) 2 9565691
Sec. Mohammad Abdul Rab
Phone: (880) 2 9559392
Total Employees of Company: 11,307
Total Employees at this Location: 656
Mill Locations:
Karnaphuli Paper Mills Ltd., Chandraghona Mill, 92 Sadarghat Road, 4531 Chandraghona of Kaptai, Bangladesh, Capacity: 30,000 mt/y, (Pulp mill, Paper mill)
Phone: (880) 31 619768/630150/616215
Fax: (880) 31 612833
Email: kpm@globalctg.net

ⓘBangladesh Monospool Paper Mfg. Co. Ltd. (MPMC)
Ownership: Bangladesh Development Group
Sreerampur, Dhamrai
Dhaka, Dhaka
Bangladesh
Phone: (880) 2 95 65413/57962
Fax: (880) 2 9564192
Email: mpmc@bdg.com.bd
Web Address: www.mpmc.com.bd, www.bdg.com.bd
Personnel:
IT Mgr.: Zillur Rahman
Total Employees of Company: 40
Mill Locations:
Bangladesh Monospool Paper Mfg. Co. Ltd. (MPMC), Dhaka Mill, Sreerampur, Dhamrai, 1212 Dhaka, Bangladesh, Capacity: 18,000 mt/y, (Paper mill)
Phone: (880) 2 95 65413/57962
Fax: (880) 2 9564192
Email: mpmc@bdg.com.bd

ⓜBangladesh Monospool Paper Mfg. Co. Ltd. (MPMC)
Dhaka Mill
Sreerampur, Dhamrai
1212 Dhaka, Dhaka
Bangladesh
Phone: (880) 2 95 65413/57962
Fax: (880) 2 9564192
Email: mpmc@bdg.com.bd
Web Address: www.mpmc.com.bd, www.bdg.com.bd
Personnel:
IT Mgr.: Zillur Rahman
Phone: (880) 2 95 65413/57962
Total Employees at this Location: 40
Type of Operation: Paper mill

ⓘBashundhara Paper Mills Ltd.
Ownership: 100% by Private Limited Company
Road-03, Block-G, Umme Kulsum Road, Bashundhara R/A
1229 Dhaka
Bangladesh
Phone: (880) 2 8402008
Fax: (880) 2 8401522
Email: info@bg.com.bd
Web Address: www.bashundharagroup.com

Personnel:
Chmn.: Mr. Ahmed Akbar Sobhan Shah Alam
Phone: (880) 2 8119006
Fax: (880) 2 8158612
Email: chairman@bg.com.bd
Man. Dir.: Mr. Sayem Sobhan Anvir
Phone: (880) 2 8119006
Fax: (880) 2 8158612
DMD: Mr. M. Mustafizur Rahman
Phone: (880) 2 8119006
Fax: (880) 2 8158612
Email: dmd@bg.com.bd
Dir., Foreign Procurement, Paper sector: Mr. Abdullah Md. Eusuf (Parash)
Phone: (880) 2 8119006
Fax: (880) 2 8158612
Email: eusuf.parash@bg.com.bd
Total Employees at company: 1,000
Mill Locations:
Bashundhara Paper Mills Ltd., Unit 1, Meghnaghat, Sonargaon, Baranagar, Bangladesh, (Paper mill)
Bashundhara Paper Mills Ltd., Unit 2, Meghnaghat, Sonargaon, New Town, Bangladesh, Capacity: 73,500 mt/y, (Paper mill)
Phone: (880) 1199 865814
Fax: (880) 11 93 43415
Bashundhara Paper Mills Ltd., Unit 3, Anarpura, Gazaria, Bangladesh, Capacity: 54,000 mt/y, (Paper mill)
Phone: (880) 1199855694
Fax: (880) 4476001562
Email: bpml.unit3@bg.com.bd

ⓘⓜBashundhara Paper Mills Ltd.
Unit 1
Ownership: 100% by Private Limited Company
Meghnaghat
Sonargaon, Baranagar, Narayanganj
Bangladesh
Web Address: www.bashundharapapermill.com
Personnel:
Man. Dir.: Mr. Sayem Sobhan Anvir
Email: md@bg.com.bd
DMD: Mr. M. Mustafizur Rahman
Email: dmd@bg.com.bd
Exec. Dir. - Prod.: Engr. Shah Alam
Email: bpml.unit1@bg.com.bd
Total Employees at this Location: 500
Type of Operation: Paper mill
Mill Locations:
Bashundhara Paper Mills Ltd., Unit 2, Meghnaghat, Sonargaon, New Town, Bangladesh, Capacity: 73,500 mt/y, (Paper mill)
Phone: (880) 1199 865814
Fax: (880) 11 93 43415
Bashundhara Paper Mills Ltd., Unit 3, Anarpura, Gazaria, Bangladesh, Capacity: 54,000 mt/y, (Paper mill)
Phone: (880) 1199855694
Fax: (880) 4476001562
Email: bpml.unit3@bg.com.bd
Paper/Paperboard Grades and Capacities:
Newsprint
Uncoated woodfree/freesheet
Specialty and industrial
Paper and Paperboard Mill Data:
Paper Machines: 2
PM 1
PM 3
Coating Machines: 1
No. 1, total capacity 6,000 mt/y.

ⓜBashundhara Paper Mills Ltd.
Unit 2
Meghnaghat
Sonargaon, New Town, Narayanganj
Bangladesh
Phone: (880) 1199 865814
Fax: (880) 11 93 43415
Web Address: bashundharagroup.com, www.bashundharapapermill.com

Personnel:
Man. Dir.: Mr. Sayem Sobhan Anvir
Phone: (880) 1199 865814
Email: md@bg.com.bd
DMD (Mgr.): Mr. M. Mustafizur Rahman
Email: dmd@bg.com.bd
Project Head: Engr. ABM Easin
Email: abm.easin@bg.com.bd
Total Employees at this Location: 300
Type of Operation: Paper mill
Pulp Grades and Capacities:
Total pulp capacity: 69,597 mt/y
Chemical Pulp: 15,098 mt/y
Recycled Pulping: 54,499 mt/y
Pulp Mill Data:
Chemical Pulping Systems:
Batch digesters
Bleach Plant Systems: 1
Chemical Pulping System, Type: ECF
Recycled Fiber Treatment Lines:
Flotation deinking lines: 1
Pulpers: 2
Recycled packaging pulping lines: 1
Paper/Paperboard Grades and Capacities:
Total paper and paperboard capacity: 73,500 mt/y
Newsprint: 18,750 mt/y
Uncoated woodfree/freesheet: 18,750 mt/y
Packaging papers: 7,200 mt/y
Linerboard: 14,400 mt/y
Boxboard/cartonboard: 14,400 mt/y
Paper and Paperboard Mill Data:
Stock Preparation:
Refiners: 4
Paper Machines: 2
No. 1, fourdrinier, total capacity 36,000 mt/y, Trim width 3.25 m, Boxboard/cartonboard, Linerboard, Packaging papers
No. 2, fourdrinier, total capacity 37,500 mt/y, Trim width 3.6 m, Uncoated woodfree/freesheet, Newsprint
Coating Machines: 1
No. 1, on machine
Energy Data:
Power boilers: 1
HRSG boiler: 2
Combustion turbines: 2 at 13.8 MW
Electrical demand for mill: 137 MWh/D

ⓜBashundhara Paper Mills Ltd.
Unit 3
Anarpura
Gazaria, Munshigonj
Bangladesh
Phone: (880) 1199855694
Fax: (880) 4476001562
Email: bpml.unit3@bg.com.bd
Web Address: www.bashundharagroup.com, www.bashundharapapermill.com
Personnel:
Man. Dir.: Mr. Sayem Sobhan Anvir
Email: md@bg.com.bd
DMD: Mr. M. Mustafizur Rahman
Email: dmd@bg.com.bd
Project Head: Engr. Mozammel Hossain
Email: mozammel.hossain@bg.com.bd
Head of Division - Prod.: Engr. A.K.M. Kamal Uddin
Email: bpml.unit3@bg.com
Total Employees at this Location: 500
Type of Operation: Paper mill
Paper/Paperboard Grades and Capacities:
Total paper and paperboard capacity: 54,000 mt/y
Tissue: 30,000 mt/y
Packaging papers
Specialty and industrial
Paper and Paperboard Mill Data:
Paper Machines: 5
PM 1, fourdrinier, Trim width 2.2 m, Tissue, Packaging papers
PM 2, fourdrinier, total capacity 15,750 mt/y, Trim width 2.4 m, Tissue, Specialty and industrial

Bangladesh

PM 3, Tissue
PM 4, Tissue
PM 5, (started September 2010), crescent former, total capacity 25,000 mt/y, Trim width 2.2 m, Tissue
Finishing Equipment:
Rewinders: 2
Sheeters: 2
Energy Data:
Power boilers: 1
Combustion turbines: 4 at 1.03 MW

ⓒCapital Paper & Pulp Industries Ltd.
House-57, Road-28, Gulshan
Dhaka, Dhaka
Bangladesh
  Phone: (880) 2 8821 358/8813 183/989 5370/882 7877
Personnel:
  Gen. Mgr.: Zaglul Khan Majlis
  Phone: (880) 2 8821 358/8813 183/989 5370/882 7877
Mill Locations:
Capital Paper & Pulp Industries Ltd., Dhaka Mill, House-57, Road-28, Gulshan, Dhaka, Bangladesh, Capacity: 3,000 mt/y, (Paper mill)
  Phone: (880) 2 8821 358/8813 183/989 5370/882 7877

ⓜCapital Paper & Pulp Industries Ltd.
Dhaka Mill
House-57, Road-28, Gulshan
Dhaka, Dhaka
Bangladesh
  Phone: (880) 2 8821 358/8813 183/989 5370/882 7877
Personnel:
  Gen. Mgr.: Zaglul Khan Majlis
  Phone: (880) 2 8821 358/8813 183/989 5370/882 7877
Type of Operation: Paper mill
Paper/Paperboard Grades and Capacities:
  Total paper and paperboard capacity: 3,000 mt/y
  Tissue: 3,000 mt/y

ⓒCreative Paper Mills Ltd
Amin Court, 1 st, 2nd and 3rd Floor, 62-63
Motijeel, Dhaka
Bangladesh
Mailing Address: MOTIJHEEL
  Phone: (880) 880-2-9571410-11
  Fax: (880) 880-2-9571409
  Email: creative@cel.com.bd
  Web Address: www.creative-engrs.com
Mill Locations:
Creative Paper Mills Ltd, Rupganj Mill, Tarabo, Rupganj, Bangladesh, Capacity: 80,000 mt/y, (Paper mill)
  Phone: (880) 02-9561926, 9571410-11
  Fax: (880) 02-9561927, 9571409
  Email: creative@cel.com.bd

ⓜCreative Paper Mills Ltd
Rupganj Mill
Tarabo
Rupganj, Narayanganj
Bangladesh
  Phone: (880) 02-9561926, 9571410-11
  Fax: (880) 02-9561927, 9571409
  Email: creative@cel.com.bd
  Web Address: www.creative-engrs.com/Sister.html
Personnel:
  Dir.: Feroz Ahmed
Total Employees at this Location: 242
Type of Operation: Paper mill
Pulp Grades and Capacities:
  Total pulp capacity: 60,732 mt/y
  Recycled Pulping: 60,732 mt/y
Pulp Mill Data:
  Recycled Fiber Treatment Lines:
  Recycled packaging pulping lines: 1

Paper/Paperboard Grades and Capacities:
  Total paper and paperboard capacity: 80,000 mt/y
  Uncoated woodfree/freesheet: 20,000 mt/y
  Linerboard: 60,000 mt/y
Paper and Paperboard Mill Data:
Paper Machines: 2
  No. 1, fourdrinier, total capacity 20,000 mt/y, Trim width 2.45 m, Uncoated woodfree/freesheet
  No. 2, fourdrinier, total capacity 60,000 mt/y, Trim width 2.55 m, Linerboard
Energy Data:
Power boilers: 1
Combustion turbines: 5 at 5 MW
Electrical demand for mill: 128 MWh/D

ⓒⓜHussain Pulp, Paper & Board Mills Ltd.
Dhaka Mill
Ownership: 100% by Hussain family and others
263 Tejgaon Industrial Area
1208 Dhaka, Dhaka
Bangladesh
  Phone: (880) 2 8822294-95
  Fax: (880) 2 8827501
  Email: husgrind@bol-online.com
Personnel:
  Man. Dir.: Mr. Syed Mehdi Hussain
  Phone: (880) 2 8822294-95
  Gen. Mgr.: Mr. M. Quadir Khan
  Phone: (880) 2 88 22294-95
  Dir. Chemical: Zakir Hussein
  Phone: (880) 2 8822294-95
  Exec. Officer: Zubair Panni
  Phone: (880) 2 8822294-95
  Dir. HPPML: Mr. Azizul Karim
  Phone: (880) 2 8822294-5
Total Employees of Company: 157
Type of Operation: Pulp mill, Paperboard mill
Paper/Paperboard Grades and Capacities:
  Total paper and paperboard capacity: 20,000 mt/y
  Specialty and industrial: 3,500 mt/y
Paper and Paperboard Mill Data:
Paper Machines: 2
  PM 1, total capacity 3,500 mt/y
  PM 2, total capacity 16,500 mt/y

ⓜKarnaphuli Paper Mills Ltd.
Chandraghona Mill
Ownership: Bangladesh Chemical Industries Corp.
92 Sadarghat Road
4531 Chandraghona of Kaptai, Chittagong
Bangladesh
Mailing Address: PO Box 25, Bangladesh
  Phone: (880) 31 619768/630150/616215
  Fax: (880) 31 612833
  Email: kpm@globalctg.net
Personnel:
  Man. Dir.: Mir. Muzaffar Ali
  Phone: (880) 31 619768/630150/616215
  Gen. Mgr. (Oper.): Md. Abdur Razzaque
  Phone: (880) 31 619768/630150/616215
  Gen. Mgr. (Tech.): S.M. Mizanur Rahman
  Phone: (880) 31 619768/630150/616215
  Gen. Mgr. (MTS): Nurul Islam
  Phone: (880) 31 619768/630150/616215
  R&D: Dr. K. Bhowmick
  Phone: (880) 31 619768/630150/616215
  Paper Mill Mgr.: Mr. Sk. Md. Humayun Kabir
  Phone: (880) 31 619768/630150/616215
  Pulp Mill Mgr.: Mr. B. K. Bismas
  Phone: (880) 31 619768/630150/616215
  Account. Mgr. (Recovery): Mr. Aynul Haque
  Phone: (880) 31 619768/630150/616215
  Chief Admin. Mgr.: Md. Jahangir Alam
  Phone: (880) 31 619768/630150/616215
  Maint. Mgr.: Mr. A.U.M Zubair
  Phone: (880) 31 619768/630150/616215
  Chief Forest Mgr.: M. A. Baten
  Phone: (880) 31 619768/630150/616215

Total Employees at this Location: 2,368
Type of Operation: Pulp mill, Paper mill
Pulp Grades and Capacities:
  Total pulp capacity: 23,000 mt/y
  Pulp available for market: 6,000 mt/y
  Chemical Pulp: 5,600 mt/y

Pulp Mill Data:
  Chemical Pulping Systems:
  Batch digesters: 5
  Pulp Lines: 2
  Bleach Plant Systems: 1
  No. 1, Sequence: CEHEH, Capacity 24,000 admt/y
  No. 2, Sequence: CEHEHD, Capacity 5,700 admt/y
  Chemical Recovery Equipment:
  Evaporator lines: 8
  Recovery boilers: 1
  Lime Kiln
Paper/Paperboard Grades and Capacities:
  Total paper and paperboard capacity: 30,000 mt/y
  Uncoated woodfree/freesheet: 24,000 mt/y
  Packaging papers: 5,300 mt/y
  Corrugating medium/fluting: 700 mt/y
Paper and Paperboard Mill Data:
  Stock Preparation:
  Pulpers: 6
  Refiners: 17
Paper Machines: 3
  No. 1, fourdrinier, total capacity 12,000 mt/y, Trim width 3 m, Uncoated woodfree/freesheet
  No. 2, fourdrinier, total capacity 12,000 mt/y, Trim width 3 m, Uncoated woodfree/freesheet
  No. 3, Yankee dryer, total capacity 6,000 mt/y, Trim width 3 m, Packaging papers, Corrugating medium/fluting
Finishing Equipment:
  Supercalenders: 1
  Rewinders: 2
  Sheeters: 2
Energy Data:
Power boilers: 4
Steam turbines: 3 at 21 MW
Electrical demand for mill: 192 MWh/D

ⓒⓜMAF Newsprint Mills Ltd (MAF NFL)
Chittagong Mill
Ownership: 100% by TK Group
83, Khatungonj
Chittagong, Chittagong
Bangladesh
  Phone: (880) 31 670321/ 618095-6
  Fax: (880) 31 636381
Personnel:
  Chrmn.: Hasnat Md Abu Obida
  Phone: (880) 31 670321/ 618095-6
Total Employees at this Location: 200
Type of Operation: Paper mill
Pulp Grades and Capacities:
  Total pulp capacity: 49,032 mt/y
  Recycled Pulping: 49,032 mt/y

Pulp Mill Data:
Pulp Lines: 2
  Bleach Plant Systems: 1
  Recycled Pulping System, Type: DIP
  Recycled Fiber Treatment Lines:
  Flotation deinking lines: 1
Paper/Paperboard Grades and Capacities:
  Total paper and paperboard capacity: 102,000 mt/y
  Newsprint: 51,000 mt/y
  Uncoated woodfree/freesheet: 51,000 mt/y
Paper and Paperboard Mill Data:
Paper Machines: 1
  No. 7, fourdrinier, total capacity 102,000 mt/y, Trim width 6.1 m, Newsprint, Uncoated woodfree/freesheet
Energy Data:
Power boilers
Steam turbines
Electrical demand for mill: 238 MWh/D

Bangladesh

ⓘMagura Group
Ownership: 100% by Bangladesh Development Group
SW(C)-14, 7, Gulshan-1
1212 Dhaka
Bangladesh
 Phone: (880) 2 9894963/9895363/8814841/8829935
 Fax: (880) 2 8821192
 Email: info@maguragroup.com
Personnel:
 Chmn.: Mustafa Kamal Mohiuddin
 Phone: (880) 2 9894963/9895363/8814841/8829935
 Fax: (880) 2 8821192
 Vice Chmn.: Mrs. Dilara Mustafa
 Phone: (880) 2 9894963/9895363/8814841/8829935
 Fax: (880) 2 8821192
 Corp. Sec.: Md. Mustafizur Rahman
 Phone: (880) 2 9894963/9895363/8814841/8829935
 Fax: (880) 2 8821192
Mill Locations:
Magura Paper Mills Ltd., Narayanganj Mill, Meghnaghat, Sonargaon, Narayanganj, Bangladesh, Capacity: 22,000 mt/y, (Pulp mill, Paper mill)
 Phone: (880) 2 7647734
 Fax: (880) 2 7647734
 Email: magurapapermills@yahoo.com

ⓘMagura Paper Mills Ltd.
Narayanganj Mill
Ownership: Magura Group
Meghnaghat, Sonargaon
Narayanganj, Narayanganj
Bangladesh
 Phone: (880) 2 7647734
 Fax: (880) 2 7647734
 Email: magurapapermills@yahoo.com
Personnel:
 Chmn.: Mustafa Kamal Mohiuddin
 Phone: (880) 2 894963/9895363
 Fax: (880) 2 8821192
 Email: info@maguragroup.com
 Man. Dir.: Abul Basher Amirul Miah
 Phone: (880) 1712953072
 Fax: (880) 2 7647734
 Email: abmiah@yahoo.co.uk
 Paper Mill Mgr.: Md. Selim Akber
 Phone: (880) 1711321503
 Fax: (880) 2 7648012
 Prod. Mgr.: Md. Mahbubul Ahsan
 Phone: (880) 1711571014
 Fax: (880) 2 7647734
 Email: mahbubul_012@ymail.com
Type of Operation: Pulp mill, Paper mill
Pulp Grades and Capacities:
Pulp Mill Data:
 Recycled Fiber Treatment Lines:
 Pulpers: 3 at 5,000 admt/y
 Recycled packaging pulping lines: 2 at 25,000 admt/y
Paper/Paperboard Grades and Capacities:
 Total paper and paperboard capacity: 22,000 mt/y
 Packaging papers: 7,000 mt/y
 Linerboard: 15,000 mt/y
 Corrugating medium/fluting
Paper and Paperboard Mill Data:
 Stock Preparation:
 Pulpers: 3
 Refiners: 6
Paper Machines: 2
 2, cylinder (4), total capacity 7,000 mt/y, Trim width 2.4 m, Packaging papers
 No. 1, fourdrinier, total capacity 15,000 mt/y, Trim width 2.54 m, Packaging papers, Corrugating medium/fluting, Linerboard
Finishing Equipment:
 Winders: 1 at 22,000 mt/y
 Calenders: 5
 Rewinders: 1 at 20,000 mt/y
 Sheeters: 1 at 9,000 mt/y
Energy Data:
 Power boilers: 2

ⓘⓂMostafa Paper
Chittagong Mill
M. Rahman Chambers, 277 Khatungonj
4000 Chittagong, Chittagong
Bangladesh
 Phone: (880) 31 615 815/818
 Fax: (880) 31 610 152
 Email: mostafagroupctg@yahoo.com, mostafagroup@dick-online.net
 Web Address: www.mostafagroup.com
Personnel:
 Gen. Mgr.: Ranjan Kanti
 Phone: (880) 31 615 815/818
Type of Operation: Pulp mill, Paper mill
Pulp Grades and Capacities:
 Total pulp capacity: 59,663 mt/y
 Recycled Pulping: 59,663 mt/y
Paper/Paperboard Grades and Capacities:
 Total paper and paperboard capacity: 63,000 mt/y
 Newsprint: 27,000 mt/y
 Uncoated woodfree/freesheet: 27,000 mt/y
 Packaging papers: 9,000 mt/y
Paper and Paperboard Mill Data:
Paper Machines: 2
 No. 1, fourdrinier, total capacity 9,000 mt/y, Packaging papers
 No. 2, fourdrinier, total capacity 54,000 mt/y, Uncoated woodfree/freesheet, Newsprint

ⓘPearl Paper & Board Mills Ltd.
Dhamrai Mill
Ownership: 100% by Bangladesh Development Group
Sreerampur
Dhamrai, Dhaka
Bangladesh
 Email: pearlpapermill@gmail.com
 Web Address: www.bdg.com.bd
Personnel:
 Project Mgr.: Eng. Motlubar Rahman
 Phone: (880) 1713 144729
 Gen. Mgr., Oper. Mgr.: Dr. Mamunur Rashid
 Phone: (880) 1713 1447
 Email: mamunpulp@gmail.com
 Addl. Chief Eng.: Sk. Omar Faruq
 Phone: (880) 1711 951530
 Tech. Dir.: Eng. M. Akhtar UzZaman
 Phone: (880) 1713 144702
 Email: zaaman09@gmail.com
 Prod. Mgr.: Ashraf Uddin Ahmed
 Phone: (880) 1726 863148
Total Employees at this Location: 190
Type of Operation: Paper mill
Pulp Mill Data:
 Recycled Fiber Treatment Lines:
 Pulpers: 2 at 10,000 admt/y
Paper/Paperboard Grades and Capacities:
 Total paper and paperboard capacity: 7,500 mt/y
 Uncoated woodfree/freesheet: 7,000 mt/y
Paper and Paperboard Mill Data:
 Stock Preparation:
 Pulpers: 2
 Refiners: 6
Paper Machines: 1
 No. 1, fourdrinier, total capacity 7,500 mt/y, Trim width 1.5 m, Uncoated woodfree/freesheet
Finishing Equipment:
 Winders: 1 at 7,500 mt/y
 Calenders: 1
 Supercalenders: 1 at 7,500 mt/y
 Rewinders: 1 at 9,000 mt/y
 Sheeters: 2 at 9,000 mt/y
Energy Data:
 Power boilers: 1
 Combustion turbines: 3 at 2 MW
 Electrical demand for mill: 30 MWh/D

ⓘSadeque Paper & Board Mills Ltd.
Ownership: 50% by public, 50% by sponsors
Shafipur
Kaliakoir, Gazipur, Gazipur
Bangladesh
 Phone: (880) 171 946545
 Email: mail@sadequepaper.com, sadequepaper@yahoo.com
Mill Locations:
Sadeque Paper & Board Mills Ltd., Kaliakoir, Gazipur Mill, Shafipur, Kaliakoir, Gazipur, Bangladesh, Capacity: 8,000 mt/y, (Paperboard mill)
 Phone: (880) 171 946545
 Email: mail@sadequepaper.com, sadequepaper@yahoo.com

ⓘSadeque Paper & Board Mills Ltd.
Kaliakoir, Gazipur Mill
Shafipur
Kaliakoir, Gazipur, Gazipur
Bangladesh
 Phone: (880) 171 946545
 Email: mail@sadequepaper.com, sadequepaper@yahoo.com
Personnel:
 Chmn.: Ms. Ayesha Khatoon
 Phone: (880) 171 946545
 Man. Dir. & CEO: Asif Sadeque
 Phone: (880) 171 946545
 Email: asif@sadequepaper.com
 Prod. Mgr.: Dewan Abdul Karim
 Phone: (880) 171 946545
 Sls. Dir.: Sabbir Sadeque
 Phone: (880) 171 946545
 Email: sabbir_s@yahoo.com
 Advisor: Mr. P. C. Talukdar
 Phone: (880) 171 946545
Total Employees at this Location: 125
Type of Operation: Paperboard mill
Pulp Grades and Capacities:
 Total pulp capacity: 3,225 mt/y
Pulp Mill Data:
 Chemical Pulping Systems:
 Batch digesters
Paper/Paperboard Grades and Capacities:
 Total paper and paperboard capacity: 8,000 mt/y
 Linerboard
 Boxboard/cartonboard: 8,000 mt/y
Paper and Paperboard Mill Data:
 Stock Preparation:
 Pulpers: 2
 Refiners: 2
Paper Machines: 2
 No. 1, cylinder, Trim width 2 m
 No. 2
Finishing Equipment:
 Rewinders: 1 at 35 mt/y
 Sheeters: 1 at 18 mt/y

ⓘⓂSonali Paper & Board Mills Ltd.
Dhaka Mill
Ownership: 20% by Islamic Development Bank, 80% by Younus Group
Printers Bldg., 5 Rajuk Ave.
1000 Dhaka, Dhaka
Bangladesh
 Phone: (880) 2 8621735
 Fax: (880) 2 8613965
Personnel:
 Chmn.: Mansur Alam.
Total Employees at this Location: 550
Type of Operation: Paper mill, Paperboard mill
Pulp Mill Data:
 Chemical Pulping Systems:

Batch digesters
Bleach Plant Systems: 1
Paper/Paperboard Grades and Capacities:
Total paper and paperboard capacity: 34,200 mt/y
Uncoated woodfree/freesheet: 18,200 mt/y
Paper and Paperboard Mill Data:
Stock Preparation:
Pulpers: 6
Refiners: 13
Paper Machines: 2
No. 1, multi-cylinder, total capacity 16,000 mt/y, Trim width 2.5 m
No. 2, fourdrinier, total capacity 18,200 mt/y, Trim width 2.9 m, Uncoated woodfree/freesheet
Finishing Equipment:
Rewinders: 2
Sheeters: 2
Energy Data:
Power boilers
Combustion turbines: 6 at 4.5 MW

ⓘT. K. Paper Products Ltd.
Ownership: 100% by T. K. Group of Industries
T. K. Bhaban (2nd Floor) 13, Kawran Bazar
1215 Dhaka
Bangladesh
  Phone: (880) 02-9115210, 9144136, 9115210
  Fax: (880) 02-9143211
  Email: info@tkgroupbd.com
  Web Address: www.tkgroupbd.net
Personnel:
  Chrmn.: Mohammmed Abu Tayab
  Phone: (880) 2-9115210
  Fax: (880) 2-9143211
  Man. Dir.: Mohammed Abul Kalam
  Phone: (880) 2-9115210
  Fax: (880) 2-9143211
Total Employees of Company: 5,500
Mill Locations:
T. K. Paper Products Ltd., Chittagong mill, 83 Khatungonj Rd, Boalkhali, Chittagong, Bangladesh, Capacity: 106,000 mt/y, (Paper mill)
Phone: (880) 31-636245, 618095-6, 617837, 620984
Fax: (880) 31-636381, 631583
Email: infoctg@tkgroupbd.com

ⓘT. K. Paper Products Ltd.
Chittagong mill
Ownership: 100% by T. K. Group of Industries
83 Khatungonj Rd, Boalkhali
Chittagong, Chittagong
Bangladesh
  Phone: (880) 31-636245, 618095-6, 617837, 620984
  Fax: (880) 31-636381, 631583
  Email: infoctg@tkgroupbd.com
  Web Address: www.tkgroupbd.com
Personnel:
  Proj. Dir. : Md. Reazul Hoque
  Phone: (880) 01819313724
  Email: tkccl@colbd.com
Type of Operation: Paper mill
Pulp Grades and Capacities:
Total pulp capacity: 39,290 mt/y
Recycled Pulping: 39,290 mt/y
Paper/Paperboard Grades and Capacities:
Total paper and paperboard capacity: 106,000 mt/y
Uncoated woodfree/freesheet: 66,000 mt/y
Linerboard: 40,000 mt/y
Paper and Paperboard Mill Data:
Paper Machines: 6
No. 1, fourdrinier, total capacity 25,000 mt/y, Trim width 2 m, Uncoated woodfree/freesheet
No. 2, fourdrinier, total capacity 20,000 mt/y, Trim width 2 m, Uncoated woodfree/freesheet
No. 3, fourdrinier, total capacity 7,000 mt/y, Trim width 1.2 m, Uncoated woodfree/freesheet
No. 4, fourdrinier, total capacity 7,000 mt/y, Trim width 1.2 m, Uncoated woodfree/freesheet
No. 5, fourdrinier, total capacity 40,000 mt/y, Trim width 1.7 m, Linerboard
No. 6, fourdrinier, total capacity 7,000 mt/y, Trim width 1 m, Uncoated woodfree/freesheet
Energy Data:
Electrical demand for mill: 167 MWh/D

ⓘⓜYounus Paper Mills Ltd.
Rupgonj Mill
Ownership: 100% by Younus Group
Jatramura, Rupgonj
Bangladesh
  Phone: (880) 02-8621735-8, 02-8611434
  Fax: (880) 02-8613965, 02-8615683
  Email: info@younusgroup.com
  Web Address: www.younusgroup.com
Total Employees of Company: 326
Total Employees at this Location: 326
Type of Operation: Paper mill
Paper/Paperboard Grades and Capacities:
Total paper and paperboard capacity: 47,400 mt/y
Newsprint: 18,000 mt/y
Uncoated woodfree/freesheet: 29,400 mt/y
Paper and Paperboard Mill Data:
Paper Machines: 3
PM 1, total capacity 18,000 mt/y, Newsprint
PM 2, total capacity 10,800 mt/y, Uncoated woodfree/freesheet
PM 3, total capacity 18,600 mt/y, Uncoated woodfree/freesheet

CHINA

ANHUI

ⓜAnhui Bilun Tissue Paper Co. Ltd.
Maanshan Mill
Ownership: 100% by Guangdong Guangzhou Smile Daily Necessities Co., Ltd.
Dangtu Industry Park
Maanshan, Anhui, 243100
China
  Phone: (86) 555 675 8368
Personnel:
  Pres.: Junyi Wang
  Phone: (86) 555 675 8368
Total Employees at this Location: 85
Type of Operation: Paper mill
Paper/Paperboard Grades and Capacities:
Total paper and paperboard capacity: 18,000 mt/y
Tissue: 18,000 mt/y
Paper and Paperboard Mill Data:
Paper Machines: 1
No. 1, crescent former, Yankee dryer, total capacity 18,000 mt/y, Trim width 2.82 m, Tissue
Energy Data:
Power boilers: 1
Electrical demand for mill: 42 MWh/D

ⓜAnhui Chaohu Jinhe Paper Co. Ltd
Chaohu Mill
Ownership: 100% by Shandong Huajin Paper Group
East Tianmen Rd., Xiliangshan District, Baiqiao Town, He County
Chaohu, Anhui, 238267
China
  Phone: (86) 565 589 6888
  Fax: (86) 565 589 6999
  Email: daynow@163.com
  Web Address: www.huajinpaper.com
Personnel:
  Chmn.: Shangdong Xin
  Phone: (86) 565 589 6888
Total Employees at this Location: 200
Type of Operation: Paperboard mill
Paper/Paperboard Grades and Capacities:
Total paper and paperboard capacity: 165,000 mt/y
Uncoated woodfree/freesheet: 15,000 mt/y
Boxboard/cartonboard: 150,000 mt/y
Paper and Paperboard Mill Data:
Paper Machines: 2
PM 1, cylinder, total capacity 15,000 mt/y, Trim width 1.76 m, Uncoated woodfree/freesheet
PM 3, Fourdrinier (4), total capacity 150,000 mt/y, Trim width 3.4 m
Energy Data:
Power boilers: 2

ⓘⓜAnhui Hefei Jinzhong Paper Co. Ltd.
Hefei Mill
Ownership: 100% by shareholders
No. 1 Youfang Rd., Daxing Town
Hefei, Anhui, 230011
China
  Phone: (86) 551 453 4116/2820/8650
  Fax: (86) 551 4532820
  Email: hejzzy@mail.hf.ah.cn
Personnel:
  Pres.: Zhengyang Zhong
  Phone: (86) 551 453 4116/2820/8650
  Vice Pres.: Xiang Wang
  Phone: (86) 551 453 4116/2820/8650
Total Employees at this Location: 550
Type of Operation: Paperboard mill
Pulp Grades and Capacities:
Total pulp capacity: 131,297 mt/y
Recycled Pulping: 131,297 mt/y
Pulp Mill Data:
Pulp Lines: 5
Recycled Fiber Treatment Lines:
Recycled packaging pulping lines: 5 at 160,000 admt/y
Paper/Paperboard Grades and Capacities:
Total paper and paperboard capacity: 129,948 mt/y
Corrugating medium/fluting: 69,972 mt/y
Boxboard/cartonboard: 59,976 mt/y
Paper and Paperboard Mill Data:
Paper Machines: 5
No. 1, total capacity 9,996 mt/y, Trim width 1.58 m, Boxboard/cartonboard
No. 2, total capacity 9,996 mt/y, Trim width 1.76 m, Boxboard/cartonboard
No. 3, total capacity 9,996 mt/y, Trim width 1.76 m, Boxboard/cartonboard
No. 4, total capacity 29,988 mt/y, Trim width 2.4 m, Boxboard/cartonboard
No. 6, (Supplier: Wuzhou Light Industry.), fourdrinier, total capacity 69,972 mt/y, Trim width 4.2 m, Corrugating medium/fluting
Energy Data:
Power boilers: 5
Steam turbines
Electrical demand for mill: 190 MWh/D

ⓘAnhui Hefei Xingdong Paper Co., Ltd.
Ownership: 100% by private owners
Daxing Industry Park
Hefei, Anhui, 230069
China
  Phone: (86) 551 452 5707/ 453 5383/ 3438
  Fax: (86) 551 452 5707
  Email: sgh74@163.com
  Web Address: www.xingdongpaper.com
Personnel:
  Chrmn. & Gen. Mgr.: Hongcheng Shang
  Sls. Mgr.: Chuanlian Xia
  Mktg. Mgr.: Youjun Zhong
Mill Locations:

China

Anhui Hefei Xingdong Paper Co., Ltd., Hefei Mill, Daxing Industry Park, Hefei 230069, China, Capacity: 61,404 mt/y, (Paperboard mill)
Phone: (86) 551 452 5707/ 453 5383/ 3438
Fax: (86) 551 452 5707
Email: sgh74@163.com

ⓜAnhui Hefei Xingdong Paper Co., Ltd.
Hefei Mill
Daxing Industry Park
Hefei, Anhui, 230069
China
Phone: (86) 551 452 5707/ 453 5383/ 3438
Fax: (86) 551 452 5707
Email: sgh74@163.com
Web Address: www.xingdongpaper.com
Personnel:
Chmn. & Gen. Mgr.: Hongcheng Shang
Phone: (86) 551 452 5707/ 453 5383/ 3438
Sls. Mgr.: Chuanlian Xia
Phone: (86) 551 452 5707/ 453 5383/ 3438
Mktg. Mgr.: Youjun Zhong
Phone: (86) 551 452 5707/ 453 5383/ 3438
Total Employees at this Location: 200
Type of Operation: Paperboard mill
Pulp Grades and Capacities:
Total pulp capacity: 60,310 mt/y
Recycled Pulping: 60,310 mt/y
Pulp Mill Data:
Pulp Lines: 2
Recycled Fiber Treatment Lines:
Recycled packaging pulping lines: 2 at 61,000 admt/y
Paper/Paperboard Grades and Capacities:
Total paper and paperboard capacity: 61,404 mt/y
Corrugating medium/fluting: 48,552 mt/y
Boxboard/cartonboard: 12,852 mt/y
Paper and Paperboard Mill Data:
Paper Machines: 3
No. 1, cylinder, total capacity 21,420 mt/y, Trim width 2.8 m, Corrugating medium/fluting
No. 2, cylinder, total capacity 27,132 mt/y, Trim width 3.2 m, Corrugating medium/fluting
No. 3, cylinder, total capacity 12,852 mt/y, Trim width 1.8 m, Boxboard/cartonboard
Energy Data:
Power boilers
Electrical demand for mill: 81 MWh/D

ⓜAnhui HengAn Wuhu Paper Co., Ltd
Wuhu Mill
Ownership: Fujian Hengan International Group
Linjiang Industrial Park, Sanshan Economic Development Zone
Wuhu , Anhui, 241080
China
Phone: (86) 553 3916 595/320
Web Address: www.hengan.com
Total Employees at this Location: 320
Type of Operation: Paper mill
Paper/Paperboard Grades and Capacities:
Total paper and paperboard capacity: 120,000 mt/y
Tissue: 120,000 mt/y
Paper and Paperboard Mill Data:
Paper Machines: 2
No. 13, crescent former, Yankee dryer, total capacity 60,000 mt/y, Trim width 5.6 m, Tissue, Uncoated woodfree/freesheet
No. 14, crescent former, Yankee dryer, total capacity 60,000 mt/y, Trim width 5.6 m, Tissue, Uncoated woodfree/freesheet
Energy Data:
Electrical demand for mill: 340 MWh/D

ⓜAnhui Huatai Forest Pulp & Paper Co., Ltd.
Anqing (Anhui Huatai) Mill
Ownership: 85% by Shandong Huatai Group Co., Ltd., 15% by Anhui Anqing Development & Investment (Group) Co., Ltd.
Xihu, Laofeng town, Yingjiang dist.
Anqing, Anhui, 246003
China
Phone: (86) 86-556-597 9326
Fax: (86) 86-556-597 9279
Web Address: www.huatai.com
Personnel:
Chmn.: Mr. Jianhua Li
Vice Chmn.: Mr. Wanliang Zhu
Gen. Mgr.: Mr. Gang Li
Total Employees at this Location: 600
Type of Operation: Pulp mill, Paper mill
Pulp Grades and Capacities:
Total pulp capacity: 121,261 mt/y
Pulp available for market: 120,000 mt/y
Chemical Pulp: 121,261 mt/y
Pulp Mill Data:
Chemical Pulping Systems:
Continuous digesters: 1
Pulp Lines: 1
Bleach Plant Systems: 1
Chemical Pulping System (Hardwood), Type: Hardwood: OO-ECF Capacity 150,000 admt/y
Chemical Recovery Equipment:
Evaporator lines: 1
Recovery boilers: 1
Pulp Dryers:
Fourdriniers 1
Paper/Paperboard Grades and Capacities:
Total paper and paperboard capacity: 140,000 mt/y
Uncoated woodfree/freesheet: 140,000 mt/y
Paper and Paperboard Mill Data:
Paper Machines: 1
No. 1, fourdrinier, total capacity 140,000 mt/y, Trim width 4.45 m, Uncoated woodfree/freesheet
Energy Data:
Power boilers: 1
Steam turbines: 1 at 45 MW
Electrical demand for mill: 581 MWh/D

ⓜAnhui Huoshan County Chenfeng Paper Co., Ltd
Ownership: 100% by private owners
LuoErling Town
Huoshan County, LiuAn, Anhui, 237283
China
Phone: (86) 564 556 6248
Fax: (86) 564 556 6144
Mill Locations:
Anhui Huoshan County Chenfeng Paper Co., Ltd, LiuAn Mill, LuoErling Town, Huoshan County, LiuAn 237283, China, Capacity: 30,000 mt/y, (Paper mill, Paperboard mill)
Phone: (86) 564 556 6248
Fax: (86) 564 556 6144

ⓜAnhui Huoshan County Chenfeng Paper Co., Ltd
LiuAn Mill
LuoErling Town, Huoshan County
LiuAn, Anhui, 237283
China
Phone: (86) 564 556 6248
Fax: (86) 564 556 6144
Personnel:
Gen. Mgr.: Feng Xiao
Phone: (86) 564 556 6248
Total Employees at this Location: 550
Type of Operation: Paper mill, Paperboard mill
Pulp Grades and Capacities:
Total pulp capacity: 25,000 mt/y
Recycled Pulping: 25,000 mt/y
Pulp Mill Data:
Pulp Lines: 2
Recycled Fiber Treatment Lines:
Recycled packaging pulping lines: 2 at 25,000 admt/y
Paper/Paperboard Grades and Capacities:
Total paper and paperboard capacity: 30,000 mt/y
Packaging papers: 5,000 mt/y
Linerboard: 18,000 mt/y
Boxboard/cartonboard: 7,000 mt/y
Paper and Paperboard Mill Data:
Paper Machines: 6
PM 1-2, multi-cylinder, total capacity 3,500 mt/y, Trim width 1.09 m, Boxboard/cartonboard
PM 3-4, (PM 3-4 was idled in July 2011), cylinder, total capacity 9,000 mt/y, Trim width 1.58 m, Linerboard
PM 5-6, fourdrinier, total capacity 2,500 mt/y, Trim width 1.76 m, Packaging papers

ⓜAnhui Jingfeng Paper Co., Ltd.
Huainan Mill
Ownership: 70% by Zhejiang Jingxing Paper Joint Stock Co., Ltd., 30% by Purico Group Ltd.
West Zhenxing Rd., Huainan Economy & Technology Park
Huainan, Anhui, 232008
China
Phone: (86) 554 3312 663
Fax: (86) 554 3312 663
Web Address: www.purico.com
Personnel:
Chmn.: Jing Gao
Phone: (86) 554 3312 663
Total Employees at this Location: 120
Type of Operation: Paper mill
Paper/Paperboard Grades and Capacities:
Total paper and paperboard capacity: 10,000 mt/y
Specialty and industrial: 10,000 mt/y
Paper and Paperboard Mill Data:
Paper Machines: 1
PM 1, fourdrinier, total capacity 10,000 mt/y, Trim width 3.8 m, Specialty and industrial

ⓜAnhui Jing County Xuanzhi Mill
Ownership: 100% by shareholders
Wuxi, Láng Qiáo Zhèn
Jingxian, Anhui, 242511
China
Phone: (86) 563 560 1218/560 0008/560 0006
Fax: (86) 563 560 1040/560 0353
Email: xuan_paper@163.com, hxxzxsb@hongxingxuanpaper.com.cn
Web Address: www.hongxingxuanpaper.com.cn
Mill Locations:
Anhui Jing County Xuanzhi Mill, Jingxian Mill, Wuxi, Láng Qiáo Zhèn, Jingxian 242511, China, Capacity: 600 mt/y, (Paper mill)
Phone: (86) 563 560 1218/560 0008/560 0006
Fax: (86) 563 560 1040/560 0353
Email: xuan_paper@163.com, hxxzxsb@hongxingxuanpaper.com.cn

ⓜAnhui Jing County Xuanzhi Mill
Jingxian Mill
Wuxi, Láng Qiáo Zhèn
Jingxian, Anhui, 242511
China
Phone: (86) 563 560 1218/560 0008/560 0006
Fax: (86) 563 560 1040/560 0353
Email: xuan_paper@163.com, hxxzxsb@hongxingxuanpaper.com.cn
Web Address: www.hongxingxuanpaper.com.cn
Personnel:
Pres./Mill Mgr.: Wansheng Cao
Phone: (86) 563 502 2652/509 6008
Total Employees at this Location: 1,200
Type of Operation: Paper mill
Pulp Mill Data:
Chemical Pulping Systems:
Batch digesters: 2
Paper/Paperboard Grades and Capacities:
Total paper and paperboard capacity: 600 mt/y
Uncoated woodfree/freesheet: 600 mt/y

ⓜAnhui Kailai Paper Co., Ltd.
Bengbu Mill
Huaiyuan Industrial Park
Bengbu, Anhui
China
  Phone: (86) 552 8501 799
  Web Address: www.kailaipaper.com
Type of Operation: Paper mill
Paper/Paperboard Grades and Capacities:
  Total paper and paperboard capacity: 70,000 mt/y
  Boxboard/cartonboard: 70,000 mt/y
Paper and Paperboard Mill Data:
Paper Machines: 2
  PM 1, Multi-wire (3), total capacity 25,000 mt/y, Trim width 1.8 m, Boxboard/cartonboard
  PM 2, Multi-wire (3), total capacity 45,000 mt/y, Trim width 2.6 m, Boxboard/cartonboard

ⓞⓜAnhui Linping Paper Co., Ltd
Suzhou Mill
North City, Shengquan Town, Xiao county
Suzhou, Anhui
China
Total Employees at this Location: 370
Type of Operation: Paperboard mill
Pulp Grades and Capacities:
  Total pulp capacity: 96,683 mt/y
  Recycled Pulping: 96,683 mt/y
Pulp Mill Data:
  Recycled Fiber Treatment Lines:
  Recycled packaging pulping lines
Paper/Paperboard Grades and Capacities:
  Total paper and paperboard capacity: 99,603 mt/y
  Corrugating medium/fluting: 99,603 mt/y
Paper and Paperboard Mill Data:
Paper Machines: 2
  No. 1, (Anhui Keija), fourdrinier, total capacity 51,051 mt/y, Trim width 3.6 m, Corrugating medium/fluting
  No. 2, (Changshu Gaoxin), fourdrinier, total capacity 48,552 mt/y, Trim width 4.1 m, Corrugating medium/fluting
Energy Data:
Power boilers: 1
Steam turbines
Electrical demand for mill: 156 MWh/D

ⓞⓜAnhui Mikitoku Paper Co., Ltd
Anqing Mill
Ownership: 65% by Miki Tokushu Paper Mfg. Co., Ltd., 35% by Anhui Gaohe Paper Co., Ltd.
No. 36, Gaobu Road, Gaohe Town
Anqing, Anhui
China
  Phone: (86) 556 485 6888/461 6888
  Fax: (86) 556 461 6288
Total Employees at this Location: 310
Type of Operation: Paper mill
Paper/Paperboard Grades and Capacities:
  Total paper and paperboard capacity: 2,856 mt/y
  Specialty and industrial: 2,856 mt/y
Paper and Paperboard Mill Data:
Paper Machines: 2
  PM 1, cylinder, total capacity 1,428 mt/y, Trim width 1.6 m, Specialty and industrial
  PM 2, cylinder, total capacity 1,428 mt/y, Trim width 1.18 m, Specialty and industrial

ⓞⓜAnhui Ningguo Zhaofeng Paper Co., Ltd.
Ningguo Mill
Wangxi Industrial Park
Ningguo, Anhui, 242300
China
  Phone: (86) 563 444 1598/1679/0777
  Fax: (86) 563 444 1589
  Web Address: www.chinazf.com.cn
Type of Operation: Paper mill
Paper/Paperboard Grades and Capacities:
  Total paper and paperboard capacity: 6,000 mt/y
  Tissue: 6,000 mt/y
Paper and Paperboard Mill Data:
Paper Machines: 5
  PM 1-5, total capacity 1,200 mt/y, Tissue

ⓞAnhui Shanying Paper No. 1 Mill
Ownership: 86.98% by other private owners, 7.50% by Shanying Group, 5.52% by Maanshan Industry Investment Company
No. 3 Qinjian Rd.
Maanshan, Anhui, 243021
China
  Phone: (86) 555 281 0395/ 282 6310/ 281 0496
  Fax: (86) 555 281 0496/7277
  Email: fics@shanyingpaper.com, information@shanyingpaper.com
  Web Address: www.shanyingpaper.com
Personnel:
  Gen. Mgr.: Yongquan Tang
  Phone: (86) 555 281 0395
  Fax: (86) 555 281 0496
  Finan. Mgr.: Jiayu He
  Phone: (86) 555 281 0395
  Fax: (86) 555 281 0496
Total Employees of Company: 1,538
Mill Locations:
Anhui Shanying Paper No. 1 Mill, Maanshan (No. 1) Mill, No. 3 Qinjian Rd., Maanshan 243021, China, Capacity: 623,679 mt/y, (Pulp mill, Paperboard mill)
Phone: (86) 555 281 0395/ 282 6310/ 281 0496
Fax: (86) 555 281 0496/7277
Email: fics@shanyingpaper.com, information@shanyingpaper.com

ⓜAnhui Shanying Paper No. 1 Mill
Maanshan (No. 1) Mill
No. 3 Qinjian Rd.
Maanshan, Anhui, 243021
China
  Phone: (86) 555 281 0395/ 282 6310/ 281 0496
  Fax: (86) 555 281 0496/7277
  Email: fics@shanyingpaper.com, information@shanyingpaper.com
  Web Address: www.shanyingpaper.com
Personnel:
  Chmn.: Lin Xia
  Phone: (86) 555 281 0395/ 282 6310/ 281 0496
  Gen. Mgr.: Yongquan Tang
  Phone: (86) 555 281 0395/ 282 6310/ 281 0496
  Finan. Mgr.: Jiayu He
  Phone: (86) 555 281 0395/ 282 6310/ 281 0496
  Dpty. Gen. Mgr.: Yichuan Yang
  Phone: (86) 555 281 0395/ 282 6310/ 281 0496
  Dpty. Gen. Mgr.: Lin Xia
  Phone: (86) 555 281 0395/ 282 6310/ 281 0496
  Dpty. Gen. Mgr.: Xiaoqing Shen
  Phone: (86) 555 281 0395/ 282 6310/ 281 0496
  Dpty. Gen. Mgr.: Min Fang
  Phone: (86) 555 281 0395/ 282 6310/ 281 0496
  Dpty. Gen. Mgr.: Zhaojin Lu
  Phone: (86) 555 281 0395/ 282 6310/ 281 0496
  Dpty. Gen. Mgr.: Hounian Sun
  Phone: (86) 555 281 0395/ 282 6310/ 281 0496
  Board Sec.: Ms. Hongli Sun
  Phone: (86) 555 2826 275
  Fax: (86) 555 2826 369
  Email: stock@shanyingpaper.com
Total Employees at this Location: 1,538
Type of Operation: Pulp mill, Paperboard mill
Pulp Grades and Capacities:
  Total pulp capacity: 616,082 mt/y
  Recycled Pulping: 616,082 mt/y
Pulp Mill Data:
Pulp Lines: 4
  Recycled Fiber Treatment Lines:
  Recycled packaging pulping lines: 4 at 655,000
Paper/Paperboard Grades and Capacities:
  Total paper and paperboard capacity: 623,679 mt/y
  Linerboard: 599,403 mt/y
  Boxboard/cartonboard: 24,276 mt/y
Paper and Paperboard Mill Data:
Paper Machines: 5
  No. 3, multi-wire, total capacity 342,363 mt/y, Trim width 6.1 m, Linerboard
  No. 4, Ultraformer, total capacity 110,670 mt/y, Trim width 4.2 m, Linerboard
  No. 6, Ultraformer, total capacity 58,548 mt/y, Trim width 2.8 m, Linerboard
  No. 7, Multi-wire (3), total capacity 87,822 mt/y, Trim width 3.15 m, Linerboard
  No. 8, cylinder (8), total capacity 24,276 mt/y, Trim width 1.76 m, Boxboard/cartonboard
Energy Data:
Power boilers: 5
Steam turbines: 4 at 15, 12, 12, 12 MW
Electrical demand for mill: 1,042 MWh/D

ⓞⓜAnhui Shanying Paper No. 2 Mill
Maanshan (No. 2) Mill
Ownership: 59.95% by individual shareholders, 13.88% by Shanying Group, 14.17% by state, 12% by Cheng Loong Corporation
No. 68 Changjiang Rd.
Maanshan, Anhui, 243021
China
  Phone: (86) 555 282 6300
  Fax: (86) 555 282 6418
  Email: infomation@shanyingpaper.com
  Web Address: www.shanyingpaper.com
Personnel:
  Chmn.: Dexian Wang
  Phone: (86) 555 282 6300
  Pres.: Yongquan Tang
  Phone: (86) 555 282 6300
  VP: Lin Xia
  Phone: (86) 555 282 6300
  Vice Gen. Mgr.: Zhao Jin Lu
  Phone: (86) 555 282 6300
Total Employees at this Location: 440
Type of Operation: Paper mill, Paperboard mill
Pulp Grades and Capacities:
  Total pulp capacity: 439,921 mt/y
  Recycled Pulping: 439,921 mt/y
Pulp Mill Data:
Pulp Lines: 2
  Recycled Fiber Treatment Lines:
  Recycled packaging pulping lines: 1 at 250,000 admt/y
  Washing deinking lines: 1 at 180,000 admt/y
Paper/Paperboard Grades and Capacities:
  Total paper and paperboard capacity: 446,250 mt/y
  Newsprint: 196,350 mt/y
  Linerboard: 249,900 mt/y
Paper and Paperboard Mill Data:
Paper Machines: 2
  No. 1, Multi-wire (3), total capacity 249,900 mt/y, Trim width 5.02 m, Linerboard
  No. 2, OptiConcept, total capacity 196,350 mt/y, Trim width 6.05 m, Newsprint
Energy Data:
Power boilers: 2
Steam turbines: 1 at 60 MW
Electrical demand for mill: 978 MWh/D

ⓞAnhui Shanying Paper Industry Co., Ltd.
Ownership: 12.40% by State, 34.05% by Fujian Taisheng, 53.55% by Individual Shareholders
Thrift Road ICP
Maanshan, Anhui, 243021
China
  Phone: (86) 0555-2826360
  Email: sale@shanyingpaper.com
  Web Address: www.shanyingpaper.com
Personnel:

China

Chmn: Mingwu Wu
Phone: (86) 0555-2826360
Gen. Mgr., Dir.: Yongquan Tang
Phone: (86) 0555-2826360
Dpty. Gen. Mgr., Dir.: Ruoyi Lin
Phone: (86) 0555-2826360
Dpty. Gen. Mgr., Dir.: Jintang Pan
Phone: (86) 0555-2826360
Dir.: Guangxian Huang
Phone: (86) 0555-2826360
Dir.: Wenxin Lin
Phone: (86) 0555-2826360
Finan. Dir.: Jiayu He
Phone: (86) 0555-2826360
Total Employees of Company: 4,510
Mill Locations:
Anhui Shanying Paper Industry Co., Ltd., Maanshan Mill, Maanshan 243021, China, Capacity: 780,000 mt/y, (Paperboard mill)
Zhejiang JiAn Paper Package Co., Ltd., Jiaxing Mill (99.85% owned), No. A 5 Rd., Economy Develoment District, Haiyan County, Jiaxing 314300, China, Capacity: 1,650,000 mt/y, (Paperboard mill)
Phone: (86) 573 8696 6188/ 686 1265
Fax: (86) 573 8686 1333
Email: man@zjjian.com

ⓂAnhui Shanying Paper Industry Co., Ltd.
Maanshan Mill
Maanshan, Anhui, 243021
China
Type of Operation: Paperboard mill
Pulp Grades and Capacities:
Total pulp capacity: 759,738 mt/y
Recycled Pulping: 759,738 mt/y
Paper/Paperboard Grades and Capacities:
Total paper and paperboard capacity: 780,000 mt/y
Linerboard: 367,500 mt/y
Corrugating medium/fluting: 412,500 mt/y
Paper and Paperboard Mill Data:
Paper Machines: 2
No. 5, foudrinier (3), total capacity 367,500 mt/y, Trim width 8.6 m, Linerboard
No. 6, GapFormer, total capacity 412,500 mt/y, Trim width 8.6 m, Corrugating medium/fluting
Energy Data:
Electrical demand for mill: 953 MWh/D

ⓂAnhui Snow Dragon Fiber Technology Co., Ltd.
No.318, South Huaiyuan Rd.
Suzhou, Anhui, 234000
China
Phone: (86) 557 3928 275/220/3903 355
Fax: (86) 557 3900 500
Email: xlhq@vip.sina.com
Web Address: www.xlhx.com
Total Employees at this Location: 800
Mill Locations:
Anhui Snow Dragon Fiber Technology Co., Ltd., Suzhou Mill, No.318, South Huaiyuan Rd., Suzhou 234000, China, (Pulp mill)
Phone: (86) 557 3928 275/220/3903 355
Fax: (86) 557 3900 500
Email: xlhq@vip.sina.com

ⓂAnhui Snow Dragon Fiber Technology Co., Ltd.
Suzhou Mill
No.318, South Huaiyuan Rd.
Suzhou, Anhui, 234000
China
Phone: (86) 557 3928 275/220/3903 355
Fax: (86) 557 3900 500
Email: xlhq@vip.sina.com
Web Address: www.xlhx.com
Total Employees at this Location: 231
Type of Operation: Pulp mill
Pulp Grades and Capacities:
Total pulp capacity: 20,259 mt/y
Pulp available for market: 35,000 mt/y
Chemical Pulp: 20,259 mt/y
Pulp Mill Data:
Chemical Pulping Systems:
Batch digesters: 2
Pulp Lines: 3
Bleach Plant Systems: 3
Chemical Pulping System, Type: Cotton Linter
Chemical Pulping System, Type: Cotton
Chemical Pulping System, Type: Cotton
Pulp Dryers:
Fourdriniers 1, Fourdriniers 1, Fourdriniers 1
Energy Data:
Power boilers: 5
Electrical demand for mill: 52 MWh/D

ⓂAnhui Weilun Industry & Trade Co., Ltd.
Ownership: 100% by private owners
No. 8 Changjiang Rd., Panji District
Huainan, Anhui, 232082
China
Phone: (86) 554 498 2718
Fax: (86) 554 498 2718
Mill Locations:
Anhui Weilun Industry & Trade Co., Ltd., Huainan Mill, No. 8 Changjiang Rd., Panji District, Huainan 232082, China, Capacity: 13,000 mt/y, (Paper mill)
Phone: (86) 554 498 2718
Fax: (86) 554 498 2718

ⓂAnhui Weilun Industry & Trade Co., Ltd.
Huainan Mill
No. 8 Changjiang Rd., Panji District
Huainan, Anhui, 232082
China
Phone: (86) 554 498 2718
Fax: (86) 554 498 2718
Personnel:
Chmn.: Ms. Huailan Xu
Phone: (86) 554 498 2718
Gen. Mgr.: Kaihuai Yang
Phone: (86) 554 498 2718
Sls. Mgr.: Qilin Yang
Phone: (86) 554 498 2718
Total Employees at this Location: 120
Type of Operation: Paper mill
Pulp Grades and Capacities:
Total pulp capacity: 10,000 mt/y
Recycled Pulping: 10,000 mt/y
Pulp Mill Data:
Pulp Lines: 2
Recycled Fiber Treatment Lines:
Flotation deinking lines: 2 at 10,000 admt/y
Paper/Paperboard Grades and Capacities:
Total paper and paperboard capacity: 13,000 mt/y
Tissue: 13,000 mt/y
Paper and Paperboard Mill Data:
Paper Machines: 4
PM 1-2, cylinder, total capacity 3,250 mt/y, Trim width 1.58 m, Tissue
PM 3-4, cylinder, total capacity 3,250 mt/y, Trim width 1.58 m, Tissue
Energy Data:
Power boilers: 1

ⓂAnhui Winbon Gaosen Paper Manufacture Co., Ltd.
Anqing Mill
Ownership: Zhejiang Welbon Pulp & Paper Group
No. 36 Gaobu Rd., Gaohe Town, Huaining County
Anqing, Anhui, 246121
China
Phone: (86) 556 4616 019/040/080
Fax: (86) 556 461 7888
Email: vivienne@welbon.com
Web Address: www.welbon-paper.com
Personnel:
Vice Chmn.: Xiaoyan Hu
Vice Gen. Mgr.: Min Li
Total Employees at this Location: 301
Type of Operation: Paper mill
Paper/Paperboard Grades and Capacities:
Total paper and paperboard capacity: 12,000 mt/y
Specialty and industrial: 12,000 mt/y
Paper and Paperboard Mill Data:
Paper Machines: 4
PM 1, cylinder, total capacity 2,000 mt/y, Trim width 1.58 m, Specialty and industrial
PM 2, fourdrinier, total capacity 2,000 mt/y, Trim width 1.58 m, Specialty and industrial
PM 3, cylinder, total capacity 4,000 mt/y, Trim width 1.88 m, Specialty and industrial
PM 4, cylinder, total capacity 4,000 mt/y, Trim width 1.88 m, Specialty and industrial

ⓂAnhui Huabon Specialty Paper Co. Ltd.
Huangshan Mill
Ownership: Zhejiang Welbon Pulp & Paper Group
North Xu Village, She County
Huangshan, Anhui, 245200
China
Phone: (86) 559 652 3166/ 3131
Fax: (86) 559 652 3588
Email: vivienne@welbon.com
Web Address: www.welbon-paper.com/www.welbon.com
Personnel:
Chmn.: Shunhu Xu
Total Employees at this Location: 90
Type of Operation: Paper mill
Paper/Paperboard Grades and Capacities:
Total paper and paperboard capacity: 25,000 mt/y
Specialty and industrial: 25,000 mt/y
Paper and Paperboard Mill Data:
Paper Machines: 2
PM 1, fourdrinier, total capacity 12,500 mt/y, Trim width 1.88 m, Specialty and industrial
PM 2, total capacity 12,500 mt/y, Specialty and industrial

ⓂHefei Jiadong Paper Co., Ltd.
No.2 Miaogang Rd., Yaohai District
Hefei, Anhui, 230000
China
Phone: (86) 551 6453 3152
Mill Locations:
Hefei Jiadong Paper Co., Ltd., Hefei Mill, No.2 Miaogang Rd., Yaohai District, Hefei 230000, China, Capacity: 11,000 mt/y, (Paper mill)
Phone: (86) 551 6453 3152

ⓂHefei Jiadong Paper Co., Ltd.
Hefei Mill
No.2 Miaogang Rd., Yaohai District
Hefei, Anhui, 230000
China
Phone: (86) 551 6453 3152
Type of Operation: Paper mill
Paper/Paperboard Grades and Capacities:
Total paper and paperboard capacity: 11,000 mt/y
Tissue: 11,000 mt/y
Paper and Paperboard Mill Data:
Paper Machines: 7
PM 1, total capacity 1,200 mt/y, Trim width 1.58 m, Tissue
PM 2, total capacity 1,200 mt/y, Trim width 1.58 m, Tissue
PM 3, total capacity 1,500 mt/y, Trim width 1.88 m, Tissue
PM 4, total capacity 1,500 mt/y, Trim width 1.88 m, Tissue
PM 5, total capacity 1,500 mt/y, Trim width 1.88 m, Tissue
PM 6, total capacity 1,500 mt/y, Trim width 1.88 m, Tissue
PM 7, total capacity 2,600 mt/y, Trim width 2.4 m, Tissue

China

ⓜLiuan Zihao Paper Co., Ltd.
Longjing Industrial Park, Dushan Town, Yuan District
Liuan, Anhui, 237131
China
 Phone: (86) 564 2910 107
 Web Address: www.ahzhzy.com
Mill Locations:
Liuan Zihao Paper Co., Ltd., Liuan Mill, Longjing Industrial
 Park, Dushan Town, Yuan District, Liuan 237131 , China,
 Capacity: 4,000 mt/y, (Paper mill)
 Phone: (86) 564 2910 107

ⓜLiuan Zihao Paper Co., Ltd.
Liuan Mill
Longjing Industrial Park, Dushan Town, Yuan District
Liuan, Anhui, 237131
China
 Phone: (86) 564 2910 107
 Web Address: www.ahzhzy.com
Type of Operation: Paper mill
Paper/Paperboard Grades and Capacities:
 Total paper and paperboard capacity: 4,000 mt/y
 Tissue: 4,000 mt/y
Paper and Paperboard Mill Data:
Paper Machines: 1
 PM 1, total capacity 4,000 mt/y, Trim width 2.4 m, Tissue

BEIJING

ⓜBeijing Paper Mill No. 7 Co., Ltd.
Ownership: 100% by state
No. 126 Binhe Rd., Tongzhou District
Beijing, Beijing, 101149
China
 Phone: (86) 10 6156 3101/ 2898/ 6150 1805
 Fax: (86) 10 6156 3376
 Email: bj7@bjhbzy.com
 Web Address: www.bjhbzy.com
Total Employees of Company: 500
Mill Locations:
Beijing Paper Mill No. 7 Co., Ltd., Beijing Mill, No. 126
 Binhe Rd., Tongzhou District, Beijing 101149, China,
 Capacity: 48,000 mt/y, (Paper mill)
 Phone: (86) 10 6156 3101/ 2898/ 6150 1805
 Fax: (86) 10 6156 3376
 Email: bj7@bjhbzy.com

ⓜBeijing Paper Mill No. 7 Co., Ltd.
Beijing Mill
No. 126 Binhe Rd., Tongzhou District
Beijing, Beijing, 101149
China
 Phone: (86) 10 6156 3101/ 2898/ 6150 1805
 Fax: (86) 10 6156 3376
 Email: bj7@bjhbzy.com
 Web Address: www.bjhbzy.com
Personnel:
 Gen. Mgr.: Fanyi Kong
 Phone: (86) 10 6156 3101/ 2898/ 6150 1805
Total Employees at this Location: 500
Type of Operation: Paper mill
Pulp Grades and Capacities:
 Total pulp capacity: 60,000 mt/y
 Recycled Pulping: 60,000 mt/y
Pulp Mill Data:
Pulp Lines: 2
 Recycled Fiber Treatment Lines:
 Recycled packaging pulping lines: 2 at 60,000 admt/y
Paper/Paperboard Grades and Capacities:
 Total paper and paperboard capacity: 48,000 mt/y
 Boxboard/cartonboard: 48,000 mt/y
Paper and Paperboard Mill Data:
Paper Machines: 3
 PM 2, multi-cylinder, total capacity 10,000 mt/y, Trim
 width 1.76 m, Boxboard/cartonboard
 PM 3, cylinder, total capacity 10,000 mt/y, Trim width
 1.76 m, Boxboard/cartonboard
 PM 4, cylinder, total capacity 10,000 mt/y, Trim width
 1.88 m, Boxboard/cartonboard
Energy Data:
Power boilers: 2

ⓜBeijing Vinda Paper (Beijing) Co., Ltd.
Beijing Mill
Ownership: Vinda International Holdings Limited.
No. 16, Hangyu Street, Binhe Industrial Park, Pinggu
Beijing, Beijing, 100023
China
 Phone: (86) 10 5822 0818
 Fax: (86) 10 5822 0802
 Web Address: www.vindapaper.com
Personnel:
 Chmn: Mr. Zhaowang Li
 Vice Chmn: Miss Yifang Yu
 CEO: Miss Dongfang Zhang
 Tech. Dir.: Mr. Yiping Dong
Total Employees at this Location: 160
Type of Operation: Paper mill
Paper/Paperboard Grades and Capacities:
 Total paper and paperboard capacity: 30,000 mt/y
 Tissue: 30,000 mt/y
Paper and Paperboard Mill Data:
Paper Machines: 3
 No. 1, BF-10, total capacity 10,000 mt/y, Trim width 2.66
 m, Tissue, Uncoated woodfree/freesheet
 No. 2, BF-10, total capacity 10,000 mt/y, Trim width 2.66
 m, Tissue, Uncoated woodfree/freesheet
 No. 3, BF-10, total capacity 10,000 mt/y, Trim width
 2.66 m, Tissue, Uncoated woodfree/freesheet
Energy Data:
Power boilers: 2
Electrical demand for mill: 55 MWh/D

ⓜBeijing Xinghe Paper Co., Ltd.
Beijing Mill
Erjie Village, Liulihe Town, Fangshan District
Beijing, Beijing, 102403
China
 Phone: (86) 10 6236 1616/ 8938 1498
 Fax: (86) 10 6236 0903
 Email: bjxhzyyxgs@163.com
 Web Address: xinghezhiye.com
Type of Operation: Paper mill
Paper/Paperboard Grades and Capacities:
 Total paper and paperboard capacity: 15,000 mt/y
 Tissue: 15,000 mt/y
Paper and Paperboard Mill Data:
Paper Machines: 2
 No. 1, total capacity 7,500 mt/y, Tissue
 No. 2, total capacity 7,500 mt/y, Tissue

ⓜChina Chengtong Holding Group Ltd.
Building 17, Section 6, No.188 Nansihuanxilu
Fengtai District, Beijing, 100070
China
 Phone: (86) 10 8367 3030/88
 Web Address: www.cctgroup.com.cn
Personnel:
 Chmn.: Zhengwu Ma
 Phone: (86) 10 8367 3030
 Vice Gen.Mgr.: Kaiming Qi
 Phone: (86) 10 8367 3030
 Vice Gen. Mgr.: Guiru Cai
 Phone: (86) 10 8367 3030
 Vice Gen. Mgr.: Yousheng Li
 Phone: (86) 10 8367 3030
 CFO: Zhen Xu
Mill Locations:
Guangdong Foshan Chengtong Paper Co., Ltd., Foshan
 Mill, No.17 Hebin Rd., Foshan 528000, China,
 (Paperboard mill)
 Phone: (86) 757 8281 6867/ 8280 3823/ 8280
 3848
 Fax: (86) 757 82813 125/ 8281 3125
 Email: huafeng.0000@yahoo.com.cn
Guangdong Zhuhai S.E.Z. Hongta Renheng Paper Co.
 Ltd., Zhuhai (Gaolangang) Mill, Riverside Road No.
 17, Zhuhai 528000, China, Capacity: 300,000 mt/y,
 (Paperboard mill)
 Phone: (86) 757 8281 6867/ 8281 2282
 Fax: (86) 757 8281 3125/ 8281 0459
Guangdong Zhuhai S.E.Z. Hongta Renheng Paper
 Co. Ltd., Zhuhai (Qianshan) Mill, 508 West Jinji Rd.,
 Qianshan District, Zhuhai 519070, China, Capacity:
 300,000 mt/y, (Paper mill, Paperboard mill)
 Phone: (86) 756 866 6888
 Fax: (86) 756 861 5037
 Email: zhhtrh@htrh-paper.com
Hunan Tiger Forest & Paper Group Yueyang Paper Co.,
 Ltd., Yueyang Mill, Chenglingji, Yueyang 414002,
 China, Capacity: 834,996 mt/y, (Pulp mill, Paper mill,
 Paperboard mill)
 Phone: (86) 730 859 0241/ 856 6443/ 856 3139/
 856 1622/ 859 0456
 Fax: (86) 730 856 1262
 Email: office@yypaper.com, yzmzhxxx@sina.com
Hunan Tiger Forest & Paper Group Hongjiang Paper
 Co., Ltd, Hongjiang Mill, 45 Luobowan, Hebin Rd.,
 Hongjiang District, Huaihua 418201, China, Capacity:
 35,700 mt/y, (Paper mill)
 Phone: (86) 745 769 1750
 Fax: (86) 745 769 1858
Hunan Juntai Pulp & Paper Co., Ltd, Huaihua Mill,
 Industry Park, Zhongfang Town, Huaihua 418005,
 China, (Pulp mill)
 Phone: (86) 745 2837 009
 Fax: (86) 745 2837 009
 Email: lqh1005@126.com
Hunan Tiger Forest & Paper Group Yuanjiang Paper
 Co., Ltd., Yuanjiang Mill, 358 Shuyuan Rd., Yuanjiang
 413100, China, Capacity: 159,641 mt/y, (Pulp mill,
 Paper mill)
 Phone: (86) 737 285 0000/0254
 Fax: (86) 737 285 0258
 Email: dzb@yj-paper.com
Hunan Tiger Forest & Paper Group Co., Ltd, Yongzhou
 Mill (55.92% owned), No. 105, Xiahexian Rd.,
 Lengshuitan District, Yongzhou 425000, China,
 Capacity: 202,062 mt/y, (Pulp mill, Paper mill)
 Phone: (86) 746 847 0536/ 1448/ 0529
 Fax: (86) 746 847 1569/ 0498
 Email: webmaster@xjpaper.com
Kyrgyz-Chinese Paper Mill, Chuj-Tokmok Mill, Promzona,
 724919 Chuj-Tokmok, Kyrgyzstan, Capacity: 11,000
 mt/y, (Paper mill)
 Phone: (996) 3138 55655
 Fax: (996) 3138 55650
MCC Meili Paper Industry Co., Ltd., Zhongwei Mill,
 Rouyuan District, Zhongwei 755000, China, Capacity:
 257,040 mt/y, (Pulp mill, Paper mill, Paperboard mill)
 Phone: (86) 955 767 9339
 Fax: (86) 955 767 9438
 Email: mlzy@china-meili.com
MCC Meili Paper (Laishan) Co., Ltd., Qionglai Mill,
 YangAn Town, Qionglai 611543, China, (Pulp mill)
 Phone: (86) 28 8875 8559/ 8330/ 8895
MCC Paper Yinhe Co., Ltd., Linqing Mill, No. 297, Ximenli
 Street, Linqing 252600, China, Capacity: 817,000 mt/y,
 (Pulp mill, Paper mill, Paperboard mill)
 Phone: (86) 635 243 3886/ 3348/ 7949
 Fax: (86) 635 243 7251/ 3346/ 6952
 Email: yinhe@yinhepaper.com, info@yinhepaper.com

ⓜMCC Paper Group Co., Ltd.
Ownership: 100% by China Chengtong Holding Group Ltd.
No. 11 Gaoliangqiao Xiejie
Chaoyang District, Beijing, Beijing, 100080
China
 Mailing Address: No. 28 West Shuguang Street
 Phone: (86) 10 5986 8622
 Fax: (86) 10 5986 8622
 Web Address: www.mccpapergroup.com
Total Employees of Company: 50,000
Mill Locations:
Kyrgyz-Chinese Paper Mill, Chuj-Tokmok Mill (72.50%

China

owned), Promzona, 724919 Chuj-Tokmok, Kyrgyzstan, Capacity: 11,000 mt/y, (Paper mill)
Phone: (996) 3138 55655
Fax: (996) 3138 55650

MCC Meili Paper Industry Co., Ltd., Zhongwei Mill (26.91% owned), Rouyuan District, Zhongwei 755000, China, Capacity: 257,040 mt/y, (Pulp mill, Paper mill, Paperboard mill)
Phone: (86) 955 767 9339
Fax: (86) 955 767 9438
Email: mlzy@china-meili.com

MCC Meili Paper (Laishan) Co., Ltd., Qionglai Mill, YangAn Town, Qionglai 611543, China, (Pulp mill)
Phone: (86) 28 8875 8559/8330/8895

MCC Paper Yinhe Co., Ltd., Linqing Mill, No. 297, Ximenli Street, Linqing 252600, China, Capacity: 817,000 mt/y, (Pulp mill, Paper mill, Paperboard mill)
Phone: (86) 635 243 3886/3348/7949
Fax: (86) 635 243 7251/3346/6952
Email: yinhe@yinhepaper.com, info@yinhepaper.com

ⓂYuen Foong Yu Inc.
Beijing Mill
No.1, East Park of Mafang Industrial Park, Pinggu District
Beijing, Beijing, 101204
China
Phone: (86) 10 6099 9688
Fax: (86) 10 6099 9611
Web Address: www.yfy.com
Personnel:
Gen. Mgr.: Xuejian Zhang
Phone: (86) 8008104686
Total Employees at this Location: 63
Type of Operation: Paper mill
Paper/Paperboard Grades and Capacities:
Total paper and paperboard capacity: 15,000 mt/y
Tissue, 15,000 mt/y
Paper and Paperboard Mill Data:
Paper Machines: 1
No. 1, crescent former, Yankee dryer, total capacity 15,000 mt/y, Trim width 2.4 m, Tissue, Uncoated woodfree/freesheet
Energy Data:
Power boilers: 1
Electrical demand for mill: 45 MWh/D

CHONGQING

ⓂChongqing HengAn Paper Co., Ltd.
Chongqing Mill
Ownership: Fujian Hengan International Group
No.8 Hongguang Rd., Banan District
Chongqing, Chongqing
China
Phone: (86) 23 6259 9622/8129/5333
Web Address: www.hengan.com
Total Employees at this Location: 365
Type of Operation: Paper mill
Paper/Paperboard Grades and Capacities:
Total paper and paperboard capacity: 120,000 mt/y
Tissue, 120,000 mt/y
Paper and Paperboard Mill Data:
Paper Machines: 2
No. 11, crescent former, Yankee dryer, total capacity 60,000 mt/y, Trim width 5.6 m, Tissue, Uncoated woodfree/freesheet
No. 12, crescent former, Yankee dryer, total capacity 60,000 mt/y, Trim width 5.6 m, Tissue, Uncoated woodfree/freesheet
Energy Data:
Power boilers
Steam turbines: 1
Electrical demand for mill: 355 MWh/D

ⓂChongqing Lee & Man Paper Co., Ltd.
Chongqing Mill
Ownership: 100% by Lee & Man Paper Manufacturing Ltd.
Zhutuo Town, Yongchuan
Chongqing, Chongqing, 402191
China
Phone: (86) 23 4960 3333
Fax: (86) 23 4960 3188
Web Address: www.leemanpaper.com
Total Employees at this Location: 1,180
Type of Operation: Pulp mill, Paper mill, Paperboard mill
Pulp Grades and Capacities:
Total pulp capacity: 1,037,800 mt/y
Pulp available for market: 140,000 mt/y
Chemical Pulp: 50,060 mt/y
Recycled Pulping: 897,632 mt/y
Other Pulp: 90,108 mt/y
Pulp Mill Data:
Chemical Pulping Systems:
Batch digesters
Pulp Lines: 2
Bleach Plant Lines:
No. 1, Sequence: DoEopD
Chemical Recovery Equipment:
Evaporator lines
Recovery boilers: 1
Lime Kiln
Recycled Fiber Treatment Lines:
Flotation deinking lines: 13 at 300,000 admt/y
Pulp Dryers:
Air Float dryers 1
Paper/Paperboard Grades and Capacities:
Total paper and paperboard capacity: 920,000 mt/y
Linerboard: 920,000 mt/y
Paper and Paperboard Mill Data:
Paper Machines: 3
No. 13, fourdrinier (3), total capacity 300,000 mt/y, Trim width 5.5 m, Linerboard
No. 16, fourdrinier (3), total capacity 300,000 mt/y, Trim width 5.5 m, Linerboard
No. 20, OptiConcept, total capacity 320,000 mt/y, Trim width 7.25 m, Linerboard
Energy Data:
Power boilers: 2
Steam turbines: 1 at 75 MW
Electrical demand for mill: 1,399 MWh/D

ⓂChongqing Lee & Man Tissue Manufacturing Ltd.
Chongqing Mill
Ownership: Chongqing Lee & Man Paper Co., Ltd.
Gangqiao Industrial Park, Zhutuo Town, Yongchuan
Chongqing, Chongqing, 404100
China
Phone: (86) 23 4960 3333
Web Address: www.leemanpaper.com
Type of Operation: Paper mill
Paper/Paperboard Grades and Capacities:
Total paper and paperboard capacity: 30,000 mt/y
Tissue: 30,000 mt/y
Paper and Paperboard Mill Data:
Paper Machines: 2
No. 1, total capacity 15,000 mt/y, Trim width 2.76 m, Tissue
No. 2, total capacity 15,000 mt/y, Trim width 2.76 m, Tissue

ⓂChongqing Longjing Paper
Fengdu Industrial Park
Fengdu county, Chongqing, 400039
China
Phone: (86) 23 67769301
Fax: (86) 23 67769257
Email: longjinghzy@126.com
Web Address: www.longjingpaper.com
Mill Locations:
Chongqing Longjing Paper, Chongqing Mill, Fengdu Industrial Park, Fengdu County, Chongqing 400039, China, Capacity: 24,000 mt/y, (Paper mill)
Phone: (86) 23 67769301
Fax: (86) 23 67769257
Email: longjinghzy@126.com

ⓂChongqing Longjing Paper
Chongqing Mill
Fengdu Industrial Park, Fengdu County
Chongqing, Chongqing, 400039
China
Phone: (86) 23 67769301
Fax: (86) 23 67769257
Email: longjinghzy@126.com
Web Address: www.longjingpaper.com
Personnel:
Chmn. & CEO: Yun Zhang
Phone: (86) 23 67769301
Sls. Mgr.: Eason Ma
Phone: (86) 15909321949
Fax: (86) 23 67769257
Total Employees at this Location: 165
Type of Operation: Paper mill
Pulp Mill Data:
Chemical Pulping Systems:
Continuous digesters: 1
Bleach Plant Systems: 1
Chemical Pulping System, Type: Bamboo
Chemical Recovery Equipment:
Recovery boilers
Paper/Paperboard Grades and Capacities:
Total paper and paperboard capacity: 24,000 mt/y
Tissue: 24,000 mt/y
Paper and Paperboard Mill Data:
Paper Machines: 2
No. 1, BF-10 EX, total capacity 12,000 mt/y, Trim width 2.66 m, Tissue, Uncoated woodfree/freesheet
No. 2, BF-10 EX, total capacity 12,000 mt/y, Trim width 2.66 m, Tissue, Uncoated woodfree/freesheet
Energy Data:
Power boilers: 2
Electrical demand for mill: 40 MWh/D

ⓂChongqing Longzhang Paper Co., Ltd.
Ownership: Chongqing Light Industry & Textile Holding Group
No. 27, Gongnong Street, Xiquan Village, Hufeng Town
Tongliang County, Chongqing, Chongqing, 402568
China
Phone: (86) 23 4558 9811/9808/9801
Fax: (86) 23 4558 0042
Personnel:
Chmn.: Guiyuan Pu
Sls. Mgr.: Ms. Zhengxiang Hu
Chief. Eng.: Yanlong He
Total Employees at this Location: 600
Mill Locations:
Chongqing Longzhang Paper Co., Ltd., Chongqing Mill, No. 27, Gongnong Street, Xiquan Village, Hufeng Town, Tongliang County, Chongqing 402568, China, (Pulp mill, Paper mill, Paperboard mill)
Phone: (86) 23 4558 9811/9808/9801
Fax: (86) 23 4558 0042

ⓂChongqing Longzhang Paper Co., Ltd.
Chongqing Mill
Mill is closed (from early 2013)
No. 27, Gongnong Street, Xiquan Village, Hufeng Town, Tongliang County
Chongqing, Chongqing, 402568
China
Phone: (86) 23 4558 9811/9808/9801
Fax: (86) 23 4558 0042
Personnel:
Chmn.: Guiyuan Pu
Phone: (86) 23 4558 9811/9808/9801
Sls. Mgr.: Ms. Zhengxiang Hu
Phone: (86) 23 4558 9811/9808/9801
Chief. Eng.: Yanlong He
Phone: (86) 23 4558 9811/9808/9801
Total Employees at this Location: 600
Type of Operation: Pulp mill, Paper mill, Paperboard mill

Pulp Mill Data:
  Chemical Pulping Systems:
  Batch digesters: 1
Pulp Lines: 1
  Bleach Plant Lines:
  No. 1, Type: ECF
  Chemical Recovery Equipment:
  Evaporator lines
  Recovery boilers: 2
  Lime Kiln
  Pulp Dryers:
  Fourdriniers 1
Paper and Paperboard Mill Data:
Paper Machines: 2
  No. 2, fourdrinier, total capacity 10,710 mt/y, Trim width 1.76 m, Uncoated woodfree/freesheet
  No. 3, fourdrinier, total capacity 14,280 mt/y, Trim width 1.76 m, Uncoated woodfree/freesheet
Energy Data:
  Power boilers: 3

ⓂChongqing Qianzheng Paper Co., Ltd.
Chongqing Mill
Zhengyang Industrial Park, Qianjiang District
Chongqing, Chongqing, 409000
China
Type of Operation: Paper mill
Paper/Paperboard Grades and Capacities:
  Total paper and paperboard capacity: 19,200 mt/y
  Tissue: 19,200 mt/y
Paper and Paperboard Mill Data:
Paper Machines: 12
  PM 1, total capacity 1,600 mt/y, Trim width 1.88 m, Tissue
  PM 2, total capacity 1,600 mt/y, Trim width 1.88 m, Tissue
  PM 3, total capacity 1,600 mt/y, Trim width 1.88 m, Tissue
  PM 4, total capacity 1,600 mt/y, Trim width 1.88 m, Tissue
  PM 5, total capacity 1,600 mt/y, Trim width 1.88 m, Tissue
  PM 6, total capacity 1,600 mt/y, Trim width 1.88 m, Tissue
  PM 7, total capacity 1,600 mt/y, Trim width 1.88 m, Tissue
  PM 8, total capacity 1,600 mt/y, Trim width 1.88 m, Tissue
  PM 9, total capacity 1,600 mt/y, Trim width 1.88 m, Tissue
  PM 10, total capacity 1,600 mt/y, Trim width 1.88 m, Tissue
  PM 11, total capacity 1,600 mt/y, Trim width 1.88 m, Tissue
  PM 12, total capacity 1,600 mt/y, Trim width 1.88 m, Tissue

ⓂChongqing Wei Er Mei Paper
Chongqing Mill
Ownership: Jiangsu Huaji Zhangjiagang Huaxing Papermaking Co. Ltd.
Industrial Park, Tongnan County
Chongqing, Chongqing
China
  Phone: (86) 23 6789 9888
  Web Address: www.wellmindpaper.com.cn
Total Employees at this Location: 190
Type of Operation: Paper mill
Paper/Paperboard Grades and Capacities:
  Total paper and paperboard capacity: 54,000 mt/y
  Tissue: 54,000 mt/y
Paper and Paperboard Mill Data:
Paper Machines: 3
  No. 1, BF-10 EX, total capacity 12,000 mt/y, Trim width 2.76 m, Tissue, Uncoated woodfree/freesheet
  No. 2, BF-10 EX, total capacity 12,000 mt/y, Trim width 2.76 m, Tissue, Uncoated woodfree/freesheet
  No. 3, crescent former, total capacity 30,000 mt/y, Trim width 2.85 m, Tissue, Uncoated woodfree/freesheet
Energy Data:
  Power boilers: 1
  Steam turbines
  Electrical demand for mill: 116 MWh/D

ⓂNine Dragons Paper Industries (Chongqing) Co., Ltd.
Chongqing Mill
Ownership: Guangdong Dongguan Nine Dragons Paper Industries Co., Ltd.
Luohuang Industrial Park, Jiangjin Industry Park
Chongqing, Chongqing, 402279
China
  Phone: (86) 23 6555 8888
  Fax: (86) 23 6555 8999
  Email: info_cq@ndpaper.com
  Web Address: www.ndpaper.com
Total Employees at this Location: 1,150
Type of Operation: Paperboard mill
Pulp Grades and Capacities:
  Total pulp capacity: 1,195,258 mt/y
  Recycled Pulping: 1,195,258 mt/y
Pulp Mill Data:
Pulp Lines: 2
  Bleach Plant Systems: 1
  Recycled Pulping System
  Recycled Fiber Treatment Lines:
  Flotation deinking lines: 1
  Recycled packaging pulping lines: 2 at 868,000 admt/y
Paper/Paperboard Grades and Capacities:
  Total paper and paperboard capacity: 1,350,000 mt/y
  Linerboard: 450,000 mt/y
  Corrugating medium/fluting: 350,000 mt/y
  Boxboard/cartonboard: 550,000 mt/y
Paper and Paperboard Mill Data:
Paper Machines: 3
  No. 22, (Metso/Voith 3-Ply), fourdrinier (3), total capacity 450,000 mt/y, Trim width 6.66 m, Linerboard
  No. 23, (Metso/Voith), DuoFormer, total capacity 350,000 mt/y, Trim width 6.76 m, Corrugating medium/fluting
  No. 33, (Multi-ply(4)+DuoFormer), Fourdrinier (4), total capacity 550,000 mt/y, Trim width 6.66 m, Boxboard/cartonboard
Coating Machines: 1
  PM33, on machine
Energy Data:
  Power boilers: 2
  Steam turbines: 2 at 60, 60 MW
  Electrical demand for mill: 1,974 MWh/D

FUJIAN

ⒽFujian Annuo Group
Ownership: 100% by private owners
Floor 15, Jinsanqiao Plaza, No. 558 North Liuyi Rd.
Fuzhou, Fujian, 350011
China
  Phone: (86) 591 8743 1156
  Fax: (86) 591 8743 1166
Mill Locations:
Fujian Annuo Paper (Fujian) Co., Ltd., Fuding Mill, Lengcheng Annuo Industry Park, Qinyu Town, Fuding 350011, China, Capacity: 30,000 mt/y, (Paper mill)
  Phone: (86) 593 720 3333/ 789 7816/ 7812/ 7815
  Fax: (86) 593 789 7777
  Email: scb@anjt.com.cn, xsb@anjt.com.cn, ht@anjt.com.cn

ⓂFujian Annuo Paper (Fujian) Co., Ltd.
Fuding Mill
Ownership: Fujian Annuo Group
Lengcheng Annuo Industry Park, Qinyu Town
Fuding, Fujian, 350011
China
  Phone: (86) 593 720 3333/ 789 7816/ 7812/ 7815
  Fax: (86) 593 789 7777
  Email: scb@anjt.com.cn,
  xsb@anjt.com.cn,
  ht@anjt.com.cn
  Web Address: www.anjt.com.cn
Personnel:
  Pres.: Shimei Zhou
  Phone: (86) 593 720 3333/ 789 7816/ 7812/ 7815
Total Employees at this Location: 500
Type of Operation: Paper mill
Paper/Paperboard Grades and Capacities:
  Total paper and paperboard capacity: 30,000 mt/y
  Tissue: 30,000 mt/y
Paper and Paperboard Mill Data:
Paper Machines: 10
  PM 1, fourdrinier, total capacity 3,000 mt/y, Trim width 2.8 m, Tissue
  PM 2, fourdrinier, total capacity 3,000 mt/y, Trim width 2.8 m, Tissue
  PM 3, total capacity 3,000 mt/y, Trim width 2.8 m, Tissue
  PM 4, total capacity 3,000 mt/y, Trim width 2.8 m, Tissue
  PM 5, total capacity 3,000 mt/y, Trim width 2.8 m, Tissue
  PM 6, total capacity 3,000 mt/y, Trim width 2.8 m, Tissue
  PM 7, total capacity 3,000 mt/y, Trim width 2.8 m, Tissue
  PM 8, total capacity 3,000 mt/y, Trim width 2.8 m, Tissue
  PM 9, total capacity 3,000 mt/y, Trim width 2.8 m, Tissue
  PM 10, total capacity 3,000 mt/y, Trim width 2.8 m, Tissue
Energy Data:
  Power boilers: 1
  Turbines

ⒽFujian Dongxin (Zhangzhou) Paper Co., Ltd.
Ownership: 100% by private owners
Guanshan Industry Park, Changtai County
Zhangzhou, Fujian, 363900
China
  Phone: (86) 596 8313 678
  Fax: (86) 596 8313 207
  Email: dxpapers@ypcn.net
  Web Address: www.dxpapers.ypcn.net
Mill Locations:
Fujian Dongxin (Zhangzhou) Paper Co., Ltd., Zhangzhou Mill, Guanshan Industry Park, Changtai County, Zhangzhou 363900, China, Capacity: 69,972 mt/y, (Pulp mill, Paperboard mill)
  Phone: (86) 596 8313 678
  Fax: (86) 596 8313 207
  Email: dxpapers@ypcn.net

ⓂFujian Dongxin (Zhangzhou) Paper Co., Ltd.
Zhangzhou Mill
Guanshan Industry Park, Changtai County
Zhangzhou, Fujian, 363900
China
  Phone: (86) 596 8313 678
  Fax: (86) 596 8313 207
  Email: dxpapers@ypcn.net
  Web Address: www.dxpapers.ypcn.net
Personnel:
  Gen. Mgr.: Shaohe Wei
  Phone: (86) 596 8313 678
Total Employees at this Location: 200
Type of Operation: Pulp mill, Paperboard mill
Pulp Grades and Capacities:
  Total pulp capacity: 70,607 mt/y
  Recycled Pulping: 70,607 mt/y
Pulp Mill Data:
Pulp Lines: 2
  Recycled Fiber Treatment Lines:
  Recycled packaging pulping lines
Paper/Paperboard Grades and Capacities:
  Total paper and paperboard capacity: 69,972 mt/y
  Corrugating medium/fluting: 69,972 mt/y
Paper and Paperboard Mill Data:
Paper Machines: 2
  No. 1, multi-ply, total capacity 29,988 mt/y, Trim width 2.9 m, Corrugating medium/fluting
  No. 2, multi-ply, total capacity 39,984 mt/y, Trim width 3.3 m, Corrugating medium/fluting
Energy Data:
  Power boilers: 3
  Electrical demand for mill: 113 MWh/D

ⒽFujian Dunxin Group
Ownership: 100% by private owners
Guanshan Industry Park, Changtai County
Zhangzhou, Fujian, 363900
China

China

Phone: (86) 596 831 3999/ 828 8316
Email: zdm@dxwj.com
Web Address: www.dxwj.com
Total Employees of Company: 1,000
Mill Locations:
Fujian Dunxin Paper Co., Ltd., Zhangzhou Mill, Guanshan Industry Park, Changtai County, Zhangzhou 363900, China, Capacity: 79,968 mt/y, (Paperboard mill)
Phone: (86) 596 8313 999
Fax: (86) 596 8313 998

ⓂFujian Dunxin Paper Co., Ltd.
Zhangzhou Mill
Ownership: Fujian Dunxin Group
Guanshan Industry Park, Changtai County
Zhangzhou, Fujian, 363900
China
Phone: (86) 596 8313 999
Fax: (86) 596 8313 998
Web Address: www.dxwj.com
Personnel:
Gen. Mgr.: Guomu Zhen
Phone: (86) 596 8313 999
Total Employees at this Location: 1,000
Type of Operation: Paperboard mill
Pulp Grades and Capacities:
Total pulp capacity: 72,987 mt/y
Recycled Pulping: 72,987 mt/y
Pulp Mill Data:
Pulp Lines: 1
Recycled Fiber Treatment Lines:
Recycled packaging pulping lines at 66,000
Paper/Paperboard Grades and Capacities:
Total paper and paperboard capacity: 79,968 mt/y
Linerboard: 79,968 mt/y
Paper and Paperboard Mill Data:
Paper Machines: 1
No. 1, (This machine can also produce white top linerboard.), multi-ply, total capacity 79,968 mt/y, Trim width 4 m, Linerboard
Energy Data:
Electrical demand for mill: 125 MWh/D

ⓂFujian Nan'an Hengli Paper Products Co., Ltd.
Ownership: Fujian Heng Li Group. Co.
Shengxin Industry Zone Nanan
Nanan City, Fujian, 362300
China
Phone: (86) 595 8625 2666
Fax: (86) 595 8625 2099
Email: qingbo57@pub2.qz.fj.cn
Web Address: www.fjhl.com.cn/
Personnel:
Chmn.: Jiahe Wu
Total Employees at this Location: 300
Mill Locations:
Fujian Nan'an Hengli Paper Products Co., Ltd., Nanan Mill, Shengxin Industry Zone Nanan, Nanan 362300, China, Capacity: 90,000 mt/y, (Paper mill)
Phone: (86) 595 8625 2666/5880
Fax: (86) 595 8625 2099
Email: hengli@fjhl.com.cn, purchasing@fjhl.com.cn

ⓂFujian Nan'an Hengli Paper Products Co., Ltd.
Nanan Mill
Shengxin Industry Zone Nanan
Nanan, Fujian, 362300
China
Phone: (86) 595 8625 2666/5880
Fax: (86) 595 8625 2099
Email: hengli@fjhl.com.cn, purchasing@fjhl.com.cn
Web Address: www.fjhl.com.cn
Personnel:
Chmn.: Jiahe Wu
Phone: (86) 595 8625 2666
Total Employees at this Location: 300
Type of Operation: Paper mill
Paper/Paperboard Grades and Capacities:
Total paper and paperboard capacity: 90,000 mt/y
Tissue: 90,000 mt/y
Paper and Paperboard Mill Data:
Paper Machines: 2
No. 1, Advantage DCT 100, total capacity 30,000 mt/y, Trim width 2.8 m, Tissue, Uncoated woodfree/freesheet
No. 2, Advantage DCT 200 HS, Yankee dryer, total capacity 60,000 mt/y, Trim width 5.6 m, Tissue
Finishing Equipment:
Rewinders: 2
Energy Data:
Power boilers: 1
Electrical demand for mill: 251 MWh/D

ⓗFujian Hengan International Group
Ownership: 100% by Shareholders (Public)
Hengan Industrial City, Anhai Town
Jinjiang, Fujian, 362261
China
Phone: (86) 595 8570 8888
Fax: (86) 595 8570 8666
Web Address: www.hengan.com
Personnel:
Exec. Chmn.: Man Bok Sze
Phone: (86) 595 8570 8888
Fax: (86) 595 8570 8666
CEO: Chit Hui Lin
Phone: (86) 595 8570 8888
Fax: (86) 595 8570 8666
Dpty. CEO, COO, Exec. Dir.: Shui Shen Xu
Phone: (86) 595 8570 8888
Fax: (86) 595 8570 8666
CFO, Company Sec., Exec. Dir.: Hong Shing Loo
Phone: (86) 595 8570 8888
Fax: (86) 595 8570 8666
VP., HR: Ying Liu
Phone: (86) 595 8570 8888
Fax: (86) 595 8570 8666
Exec. Dir: Ching Shan Hung
Phone: (86) 595 8570 8888
Fax: (86) 595 8570 8666
Exec. Dir.: Chun Man Xu
Phone: (86) 595 8570 8888
Fax: (86) 595 8570 8666
Group Dpty. Dir.- Finan., Exec. Dir.: Da Zuo Xu
Phone: (86) 595 8570 8888
Fax: (86) 595 8570 8666
Total Employees of Company: 34,000
Total Employees at this Location: 5,210
Mill Locations:
Anhui HengAn Wuhu Paper Co., Ltd, Wuhu Mill, Linjiang Industrial Park, Sanshan Economic Development Zone, Wuhu 241080, China, Capacity: 120,000 mt/y, (Paper mill)
Phone: (86) 553 3916 595/320
Chongqing HengAn Paper Co., Ltd., Chongqing Mill, No.8 Hongguang Rd., Banan District, Chongqing, China, Capacity: 120,000 mt/y, (Paper mill)
Phone: (86) 23 6259 9622/8129/5333
Fujian HengAn (China) Paper Co., Ltd., Jinjiang Mill, Hengan Industrial City, Anhai Town, Jinjiang 362200, China, Capacity: 300,000 mt/y, (Paper mill)
Phone: (86) 595 8570 8888
Fax: (86) 595 8572 2992
Hunan Changde HengAn Paper Co., Ltd., Changde Mill, Tao Lin Road, Laishan Industrial Zone, Changde 415100, China, Capacity: 280,000 mt/y, (Paper mill)
Phone: (86) 736 731 8489
Fax: (86) 736 730 0322
Email: ceha@hengan.com
Shandong Weifang HengAn Paper Co. Ltd., Weifang Mill, Beihai Rd., Fangzi District, Weifang 261200, China, Capacity: 189,996 mt/y, (Paper mill)
Phone: (86) 536 776 1889/ 766 6888
Fax: (86) 536 776 1889/ 751 5603

ⓂFujian HengAn (China) Paper Co., Ltd.
Jinjiang Mill
Ownership: Fujian Hengan International Group
Hengan Industrial City, Anhai Town
Jinjiang, Fujian, 362200
China
Phone: (86) 595 8570 8888
Fax: (86) 595 8572 2992
Web Address: www.hengan.com
Personnel:
Chmn.: Wenbo Shi
Phone: (86) 595 8570 8888
Vice Chmn., CEO: Lianjie Xu
Phone: (86) 595 8570 8888
Total Employees at this Location: 420
Type of Operation: Paper mill
Pulp Mill Data:
Pulp Lines: 2
Paper/Paperboard Grades and Capacities:
Total paper and paperboard capacity: 300,000 mt/y
Tissue: 300,000 mt/y
Paper and Paperboard Mill Data:
Paper Machines: 5
No. 4, Advantage DCT 200 TS, Yankee dryer, total capacity 60,000 mt/y, Trim width 5.55 m, Tissue, Uncoated woodfree/freesheet
No. 6, Advantage DCT 200 TS, Yankee dryer, total capacity 60,000 mt/y, Trim width 5.55 m, Tissue, Uncoated woodfree/freesheet
No. 9, crescent former, Yankee dryer, total capacity 60,000 mt/y, Trim width 5.6 m, Tissue
No. 15, crescent former, Yankee dryer, total capacity 60,000 mt/y, Trim width 5.6 m, Tissue, Uncoated woodfree/freesheet
No. 16, crescent former, Yankee dryer, total capacity 60,000 mt/y, Trim width 5.6 m, Tissue, Uncoated woodfree/freesheet
Energy Data:
Electrical demand for mill: 908 MWh/D

ⓗFujian Huafa (Fujian) Industrial Co., Ltd.
Ownership: 100% by shareholders
Dongyuan Industry Zone
Longhai City, Fujian, 363102
China
Phone: (86) 596 670 9888
Fax: (86) 596 670 9891/9811
Email: lhyf@wellfit.com.cn
Web Address: www.wellfit.com.cn
Personnel:
Pres. & Gen. Mgr.: Wenyu Shi
Mill Locations:
Fujian Huafa (Fujian) Industrial Co., Ltd., Longhai Mill, Dongyuan Industry Zone, Longhai 363102, China, Capacity: 83,538 mt/y, (Paperboard mill)
Phone: (86) 596 670 9888
Fax: (86) 596 670 9891/9811
Email: lhyf@wellfit.com.cn

ⓂFujian Huafa (Fujian) Industrial Co., Ltd.
Longhai Mill
Dongyuan Industry Zone
Longhai, Fujian, 363102
China
Phone: (86) 596 670 9888
Fax: (86) 596 670 9891/9811
Email: lhyf@wellfit.com.cn
Web Address: www.wellfit.com.cn
Personnel:
Pres. & Gen. Mgr.: Wenyu Shi
Phone: (86) 596 670 8555/8700/9731
Total Employees at this Location: 350
Type of Operation: Paperboard mill
Pulp Grades and Capacities:
Total pulp capacity: 79,542 mt/y
Recycled Pulping: 79,542 mt/y

Pulp Mill Data:
Pulp Lines: 2
Recycled Fiber Treatment Lines:
Recycled packaging pulping lines: 1
Paper/Paperboard Grades and Capacities:
Total paper and paperboard capacity: 83,538 mt/y
Corrugating medium/fluting: 83,538 mt/y
Paper and Paperboard Mill Data:
Paper Machines: 4
No. 1, cylinder, total capacity 5,712 mt/y, Trim width 1.88 m, Corrugating medium/fluting
No. 2, cylinder, total capacity 16,422 mt/y, Trim width 2.64 m, Corrugating medium/fluting
No. 3, cylinder, total capacity 20,706 mt/y, Trim width 2.9 m, Corrugating medium/fluting
No. 4, fourdrinier, total capacity 40,698 mt/y, Trim width 4.2 m, Corrugating medium/fluting
Energy Data:
Power boilers: 2
Electrical demand for mill: 112 MWh/D

⊕Fujian Huamin Paper Co., Ltd.
Futang Industrial Park, Datian County
Sanming, Fujian, 366100
China
 Phone: (86) 598 7260 618
 Fax: (86) 598 7222 143
 Email: hmzy2000@163.cn
 Web Address: www.chinafjhm.com
Mill Locations:
Fujian Huamin Paper Co., Ltd., Sanming Mill, Futang Industrial Park, Datian County, Sanming 366100, China, Capacity: 28,000 mt/y, (Paper mill)
Phone: (86) 598 7260 618
Fax: (86) 598 7222 143
Email: hmzy2000@163.cn

ⓜFujian Huamin Paper Co., Ltd.
Sanming Mill
Futang Industrial Park, Datian County
Sanming, Fujian, 366100
China
 Phone: (86) 598 7260 618
 Fax: (86) 598 7222 143
 Email: hmzy2000@163.cn
Type of Operation: Paper mill
Paper/Paperboard Grades and Capacities:
Total paper and paperboard capacity: 28,000 mt/y
Tissue: 8,000 mt/y
Specialty and industrial: 20,000 mt/y
Paper and Paperboard Mill Data:
Paper Machines: 7
PM 1, total capacity 1,300 mt/y, Trim width 1.58 m, Tissue
PM 2, total capacity 1,300 mt/y, Trim width 1.58 m, Tissue
PM 3, total capacity 1,300 mt/y, Trim width 1.58 m, Tissue
PM 4, total capacity 1,300 mt/y, Trim width 1.58 m, Tissue
PM 5, total capacity 1,300 mt/y, Trim width 1.58 m, Tissue
PM 6, total capacity 1,300 mt/y, Trim width 1.58 m, Tissue
PM 7, total capacity 20,000 mt/y, Trim width 3.2 m, Specialty and industrial

⊕Fujian Jian'ou Hengfeng Paper Co., Ltd.
Ownership: 100% by private owners
Lianhuaping Industry Park, Dongfeng Town
Jian'ou, Fujian, 353100
China
 Phone: (86) 599 359 1588
 Fax: (86) 599 359 1933
 Email: fjqzwjb@126.com
 Web Address: johf-paper.com
Mill Locations:
Fujian Jian'ou Hengfeng Paper Co., Ltd., Jian'ou Mill, Lianhuaping Industry Park, Dongfeng Town, Jian'ou 353100, China, Capacity: 15,000 mt/y, (Paper mill)
Phone: (86) 599 359 1588
Fax: (86) 599 359 1933
Email: fjqzwjb@126.com

ⓜFujian Jian'ou Hengfeng Paper Co., Ltd.
Jian'ou Mill
Lianhuaping Industry Park, Dongfeng Town
Jian'ou, Fujian, 353100
China
 Phone: (86) 599 359 1588
 Fax: (86) 599 359 1933
 Email: fjqzwjb@126.com
Personnel:
Chmn. & Pres.: Jianbing Wei
 Phone: (86) 599 359 1588
Sls. Mgr.: Chengsheng Zhang
 Phone: (86) 599 359 1588
Total Employees at this Location: 100
Type of Operation: Paper mill
Paper/Paperboard Grades and Capacities:
Total paper and paperboard capacity: 15,000 mt/y
Tissue: 15,000 mt/y
Paper and Paperboard Mill Data:
Paper Machines: 3
PM 1, fourdrinier, total capacity 5,000 mt/y, Trim width 1.88 m, Tissue
PM 2, total capacity 5,000 mt/y, Trim width 1.88 m, Tissue
PM 3, total capacity 5,000 mt/y, Trim width 1.88 m, Tissue
Energy Data:
Power boilers: 1

⊕ⓜFujian Jian'ou Taipingyang Paper Mill
Jian'ou Mill
Taiping Industry Zone, Nanya Town
Jian'ou, Fujian, 353101
China
 Phone: (86) 599 352 0188/0338/698
 Fax: (86) 599 3520 358
Total Employees at this Location: 100
Type of Operation: Paperboard mill
Pulp Grades and Capacities:
Total pulp capacity: 21,493 mt/y
Recycled Pulping: 21,493 mt/y
Paper/Paperboard Grades and Capacities:
Total paper and paperboard capacity: 25,000 mt/y
Boxboard/cartonboard: 25,000 mt/y
Paper and Paperboard Mill Data:
Paper Machines: 1
No. 1, multi-fourdrinier, total capacity 25,000 mt/y, Trim width 2.4 m, Boxboard/cartonboard
Energy Data:
Electrical demand for mill: 31 MWh/D

⊕Fujian Liansheng Paper (Zhangzhou) Co., Ltd.
Ownership: 100% by private owners
Guanshan Industry Zone, Changtai County
Zhangzhou, Fujian, 363900
China
 Phone: (86) 596 831 3788/835 5349
 Fax: (86) 596 831 3766
 Email: suker2683@163.com
Personnel:
VP, Technol. Mgr.: Zhiwei Yang
Total Employees at this Location: 200
Mill Locations:
Fujian Liansheng Paper (Zhangzhou) Co., Ltd., Zhangzhou Mill, Guanshan Industry Zone, Changtai County, Zhangzhou 363900, China, Capacity: 850,000 mt/y, (Paperboard mill)
Phone: (86) 596 831 3788/835 5349
Fax: (86) 596 831 3766
Email: suker2683@163.com

ⓜFujian Liansheng Paper (Zhangzhou) Co., Ltd.
Zhangzhou Mill
Guanshan Industry Zone, Changtai County
Zhangzhou, Fujian, 363900
China
 Phone: (86) 596 831 3788/835 5349
 Fax: (86) 596 831 3766
 Email: suker2683@163.com
Personnel:
VP, Technol. Mgr.: Zhiwei Yang
 Phone: (86) 596 831 3788/835 5349
Total Employees at this Location: 850
Type of Operation: Paperboard mill
Pulp Grades and Capacities:
Total pulp capacity: 838,491 mt/y
Recycled Pulping: 838,491 mt/y
Pulp Mill Data:
Pulp Lines: 2
Recycled Fiber Treatment Lines:
Recycled packaging pulping lines: 1 at 150,000 admt/y
Recycled packaging pulping lines: 1 at 350,000 admt/y
Paper/Paperboard Grades and Capacities:
Total paper and paperboard capacity: 850,000 mt/y
Linerboard: 300,000 mt/y
Corrugating medium/fluting: 550,000 mt/y
Paper and Paperboard Mill Data:
Paper Machines: 4
No. 1, fourdrinier (2), total capacity 150,000 mt/y, Trim width 4.8 m, Corrugating medium/fluting
No. 2, fourdrinier (3), total capacity 300,000 mt/y, Trim width 5.8 m, Linerboard
No. 3, fourdrinier, total capacity 300,000 mt/y, Trim width 6.4 m, Corrugating medium/fluting
No. 4, fourdrinier, total capacity 100,000 mt/y, Trim width 4.2 m, Corrugating medium/fluting
Energy Data:
Power boilers: 2
Steam turbines: 2 at 15, 18 MW
Electrical demand for mill: 1,007 MWh/D

⊕ⓜFujian Liansheng Paper (Longhai) Co., Ltd
Longhai Mill
Ownership: Fujian Liansheng Paper Industry Co., Ltd
Jiaomei Industrial Park
Longhai City, Fujian, 363107
China
Total Employees at this Location: 800
Type of Operation: Paper mill
Pulp Grades and Capacities:
Total pulp capacity: 1,218,042 mt/y
Recycled Pulping: 1,218,042 mt/y
Pulp Mill Data:
Recycled Fiber Treatment Lines:
Pulpers: 1 at 350,000
Pulpers: 1 at 350,000
Pulpers: 1 at 300,000
Paper/Paperboard Grades and Capacities:
Total paper and paperboard capacity: 1,300,000 mt/y
Linerboard: 430,000 mt/y
Corrugating medium/fluting: 210,000 mt/y
Boxboard/cartonboard: 660,000 mt/y
Paper and Paperboard Mill Data:
Paper Machines: 4
No. 5, hybrid former, total capacity 360,000 mt/y, Trim width 7.25 m, Linerboard
No. 6, fourdrinier, total capacity 280,000 mt/y, Trim width 7.25 m, Corrugating medium/fluting, Linerboard
No. 7, Fourdrinier (4), total capacity 240,000 mt/y, Trim width 5.8 m, Boxboard/cartonboard
No. 8, Fourdrinier (4), total capacity 420,000 mt/y, Trim width 6.6 m, Boxboard/cartonboard
Energy Data:
Power boilers
Steam turbines: 2 at 130 MW

⊕Fujian Lishu Pulp & Paper Co., Ltd.
Ownership: 100% by private owners
Xingning Industry Zone
Jianou City, Fujian, 353100
China

China

Phone: (86) 599 373 3278/3378
Fax: (86) 599 373 8901
Mill Locations:
Fujian Lishu Pulp & Paper Co., Ltd., Jianou Mill, Xingning Industry Zone, Jianou 353100, China, Capacity: 82,824 mt/y, (Pulp mill, Paperboard mill)
Phone: (86) 599 373 3278/3378
Fax: (86) 599 373 8901

ⓂFujian Lishu Pulp & Paper Co., Ltd.
Jianou Mill
Xingning Industry Zone
Jianou, Fujian, 353100
China
Phone: (86) 599 373 3278/3378
Fax: (86) 599 373 8901
Personnel:
Pres. & Gen. Mgr.: Jianhua Zhu
Phone: (86) 599 373 3278/3378
Sls. Mgr.: Guirong Tang
Phone: (86) 599 373 3278/3378
Total Employees at this Location: 400
Type of Operation: Pulp mill, Paperboard mill
Pulp Grades and Capacities:
Total pulp capacity: 80,389 mt/y
Recycled Pulping: 80,389 mt/y
Pulp Mill Data:
Pulp Lines: 1
Recycled Fiber Treatment Lines:
Recycled packaging pulping lines
Paper/Paperboard Grades and Capacities:
Total paper and paperboard capacity: 82,824 mt/y
Corrugating medium/fluting: 82,824 mt/y
Paper and Paperboard Mill Data:
Paper Machines: 1
No. 2, fourdrinier, total capacity 82,824 mt/y, Trim width 4.8 m, Corrugating medium/fluting
Energy Data:
Power boilers: 1
Steam turbines: 1 at 3 MW
Electrical demand for mill: 128 MWh/D

ⓒFujian Luoyuan Xiongfeng Paper Mill
Ownership: 100% by private owners
Lane No. 38 Zhan Jin Xiang
Cang Shan District, Fuzhou, Fujian
China
Phone: (86) 0591 83488288/388
Fax: (86) 0591 83302435
Email: xfjinxiu@yahoo.com.cn
Web Address: www.xfzy.net
Mill Locations:
Fujian Luoyuan Xiongfeng Paper Mill, Fuzhou Mill, Jiulongban, Luoyuan County, Fuzhou 350600, China, (Paper mill)
Phone: (86) 591 3865 6888/6808
Fax: (86) 591 3865 6858
Email: xiaoshou@xfzy.net

ⓂFujian Luoyuan Xiongfeng Paper Mill
Fuzhou Mill
Mill is closed, from sometime in early 2014
Jiulongban, Luoyuan County
Fuzhou, Fujian, 350600
China
Phone: (86) 591 3865 6888/6808
Fax: (86) 591 3865 6858
Email: xiaoshou@xfzy.net
Web Address: www.xfzy.net
Personnel:
Chmn. & Gen. Mgr.: Xiongqi Lin
Phone: (86) 591 2687 5309/5319/ 2687 2202
Sls. Mgr.: Ms. Qing Chen
Phone: (86) 591 2687 5309/5319/ 2687 2202
Total Employees at this Location: 500
Type of Operation: Paper mill

Pulp Mill Data:
Pulp Lines: 2
Recycled Fiber Treatment Lines:
Recycled packaging pulping lines: 2 at 120,000 admt/y
Energy Data:
Power boilers: 2

ⓒFujian Nanjing County Youlida Co., Ltd.
Ownership: 100% by shareholders
Fengtian Industry Zone, Nanjing County
Zhangzhou, Fujian, 363600
China
Phone: (86) 596 7672 666
Fax: (86) 596 7672 669
Mill Locations:
Fujian Nanjing County Youlida Co., Ltd., Zhangzhou Mill, Fengtian Industry Zone, Nanjing County, Zhangzhou 363600, China, Capacity: 154,482 mt/y, (Paperboard mill)
Phone: (86) 596 7672 666
Fax: (86) 596 7672 669

ⓂFujian Nanjing County Youlida Co., Ltd.
Zhangzhou Mill
Fengtian Industry Zone, Nanjing County
Zhangzhou, Fujian, 363600
China
Phone: (86) 596 7672 666
Fax: (86) 596 7672 669
Total Employees at this Location: 160
Type of Operation: Paperboard mill
Pulp Grades and Capacities:
Total pulp capacity: 150,000 mt/y
Recycled Pulping: 150,000 mt/y
Pulp Mill Data:
Pulp Lines: 1
Recycled Fiber Treatment Lines:
Recycled packaging pulping lines: 1 at 150,000 admt/y
Paper/Paperboard Grades and Capacities:
Total paper and paperboard capacity: 154,482 mt/y
Corrugating medium/fluting: 154,482 mt/y
Paper and Paperboard Mill Data:
Paper Machines: 1
No. 1, fourdrinier, total capacity 154,482 mt/y, Trim width 4.8 m, Corrugating medium/fluting
Finishing Equipment:
Winders: 1
Energy Data:
Power boilers: 1
Steam turbines: 1 at 6 MW
Electrical demand for mill: 227 MWh/D

ⓂFujian Nanping Paper Co. Ltd.
Nanping Mill
177#, Binjiang Northen Rd.
Nanping, Fujian, 353000
China
Phone: (86) 599 880 8888/8101/8102/8579/8214/8521
Fax: (86) 599 880 8312/0721/1353/8580
Email: webmaster@nanping-paper.com, nzzqb@public.npptt.fj.cn
Web Address: www.nanpingpaper.com
Personnel:
Chmn.: Mr. Jinbiao Huang
Phone: (86) 599 880 1888/8806
Vice Chmn.: Mr. Xiaobang Lin
Phone: (86) 599 880 1888/8806
CFO: Ms. Bingxia Lin
Phone: (86) 599 880 1888/8806
Total Employees at this Location: 1,800
Type of Operation: Pulp mill, Paper mill
Pulp Grades and Capacities:
Total pulp capacity: 189,473 mt/y

Mechanical Pulp: 15,158 mt/y
Recycled Pulping: 174,315 mt/y
Pulp Mill Data:
Chemical Pulping Systems:
Batch digesters: 1
Mechanical Pulping Systems:
Conventional grinders: 1
Pulp Lines: 4
Bleach Plant Systems: 2
No. 1
Chemical Recovery Equipment:
Evaporator lines
Recovery boilers: 1
Recycled Fiber Treatment Lines:
Flotation deinking lines: 1 at 107,100 admt/y
Flotation deinking lines: 1 at 178,500 admt/y
Pulp Dryers:
Fourdriniers 1, Fourdriniers 1
Paper/Paperboard Grades and Capacities:
Total paper and paperboard capacity: 389,210 mt/y
Newsprint: 189,210 mt/y
Uncoated woodfree/freesheet: 200,000 mt/y
Paper and Paperboard Mill Data:
Paper Machines: 2
No. 5, OptiFormer, total capacity 189,210 mt/y, Trim width 5.56 m, Newsprint
No. 6, ValFormer, total capacity 200,000 mt/y, Trim width 5.8 m, Uncoated woodfree/freesheet
Finishing Equipment:
Rewinders: 4
Energy Data:
Power boilers: 5
Steam turbines: 4 at 6, 12, 25, 25 MW
Electrical demand for mill: 1,015 MWh/D

ⓒFujian Nanyang Paper Co., Ltd.
Ownership: 100% by private owners
Guangyang Industry District
Fuding, Fujian, 355215
China
Phone: (86) 593 763 7988
Fax: (86) 593 763 7288
Email: nanyangzhiye@126.com
Web Address: www.nanyangzy.com
Mill Locations:
Fujian Nanyang Paper Co., Ltd., Fuding Mill, Guangyang Industry District, Fuding 355215, China, Capacity: 12,000 mt/y, (Paper mill)
Phone: (86) 593 763 7988
Fax: (86) 593 763 7288
Email: nanyangzhiye@126.com

ⓂFujian Nanyang Paper Co., Ltd.
Fuding Mill
Guangyang Industry District
Fuding, Fujian, 355215
China
Phone: (86) 593 763 7988
Fax: (86) 593 763 7288
Email: nanyangzhiye@126.com
Web Address: www.nanyangzy.com
Personnel:
Gen. Mgr.: Liyuan Chen
Phone: (86) 593 763 7988
Total Employees at this Location: 263
Type of Operation: Paper mill
Paper/Paperboard Grades and Capacities:
Total paper and paperboard capacity: 12,000 mt/y
Tissue: 12,000 mt/y
Paper and Paperboard Mill Data:
Paper Machines: 11
No. 1, cylinder, total capacity 1,090 mt/y, Trim width 1.58 m, Tissue
No. 2, total capacity 1,090 mt/y, Trim width 1.58 m, Tissue
No. 3, total capacity 1,090 mt/y, Trim width 1.58 m, Tissue
No. 4, total capacity 1,090 mt/y, Trim width 1.58 m, Tissue
No. 5, total capacity 1,090 mt/y, Trim width 1.58 m, Tissue
No. 6, total capacity 1,090 mt/y, Trim width 1.58 m, Tissue
No. 7, total capacity 1,090 mt/y, Trim width 1.58 m, Tissue

No. 8, total capacity 1,090 mt/y, Trim width 1.58 m, Tissue
No. 9, total capacity 1,090 mt/y, Trim width 1.58 m, Tissue
No. 10, total capacity 1,090 mt/y, Trim width 1.58 m, Tissue
No. 11, total capacity 1,090 mt/y, Trim width 1.58 m, Tissue
Energy Data:
Power boilers: 2

ⓂFujian Naoshan Paper Group Co. Ltd
Ownership: 100% by shareholders
No. 20 Taxia Road
Jianning County, Fujian, 354501
China
 Phone: (86) 598 398 2712/8840
 Fax: (86) 598 398 2705
 Email: info@chinatissuepaper.com
 Web Address: www.chinesetissuepaper.com
Mill Locations:
Fujian Naoshan Paper Group Co. Ltd, Sanming Mill, No. 20 Taxia Road, Jianning County, Sanming 354501, China, Capacity: 50,000 mt/y, (Paper mill)
 Phone: (86) 598 398 2712/8840
 Fax: (86) 598 398 2705
 Email: info@chinatissuepaper.com

ⓂFujian Naoshan Paper Group Co. Ltd
Sanming Mill
No. 20 Taxia Road, Jianning County
Sanming, Fujian, 354501
China
 Phone: (86) 598 398 2712/8840
 Fax: (86) 598 398 2705
 Email: info@chinatissuepaper.com
 Web Address: www.nspaper.com
Personnel:
 Chmn & Pres.: Xiaoming Gao
 Phone: (86) 598 398 2712/8840
Total Employees at this Location: 1,000
Type of Operation: Paper mill
Paper/Paperboard Grades and Capacities:
 Total paper and paperboard capacity: 50,000 mt/y
 Specialty and industrial: 50,000 mt/y
Paper and Paperboard Mill Data:
Paper Machines: 20
PM 1-2, fourdrinier, total capacity 1,000 mt/y, Trim width 1.09 m, Specialty and industrial
PM 18, fourdrinier, total capacity 2,500 mt/y, Trim width 1.58 m, Specialty and industrial
PM 19, fourdrinier, total capacity 4,000 mt/y, Trim width 2.64 m, Specialty and industrial
PM 20, fourdrinier, total capacity 6,000 mt/y, Trim width 1.88 m, Specialty and industrial
PM 3-17, fourdrinier, total capacity 2,400 mt/y, Trim width 1.88 m, Specialty and industrial
Finishing Equipment:
 Calenders
 Supercalenders: 3
Energy Data:
Power boilers: 2

ⓗⓂFujian Qingshan Paper Industry Co., Ltd.
Qingzhou Mill
Ownership: 100% by shareholders
Qingzhou, Sha County
Qingzhou, Fujian, 365506
China
 Phone: (86) 598 565 8518/8888/759 1043/8 336 7773
 Fax: (86) 598 565 3336/8 711 0973
 Email: qszy@qspaper.com, jplin@sohu.com
 Web Address: www.qingshanpaper.com
Personnel:
 Chmn. & Pres.: Shiying Pan
 Vice Chmn.: Xiaohan Lan
 CFO: Junqing Guo
 Chief Eng.: Jinguan Huang
Total Employees of Company: 2,437
Total Employees at this Location: 1,700

Type of Operation: Pulp mill, Paperboard mill
Pulp Grades and Capacities:
 Total pulp capacity: 290,934 mt/y
 Pulp available for market: 100,000 mt/y
 Chemical Pulp: 238,275 mt/y
 Recycled Pulping: 52,659 mt/y
Pulp Mill Data:
 Chemical Pulping Systems:
 Batch digesters: 6
 Continuous digesters: 1
Pulp Lines: 5
 Bleach Plant Systems: 1
 No. 1, Type: ECF, Sequence: DEopDP
 Chemical Recovery Equipment:
 Evaporator lines
 Recovery boilers: 2
 Lime Kiln
 Recycled Fiber Treatment Lines:
 Recycled packaging pulping lines: 3 at 500,000 admt/y
 Pulp Dryers:
 Air Float dryers 1, Fourdriniers 1
Paper/Paperboard Grades and Capacities:
 Total paper and paperboard capacity: 185,000 mt/y
 Packaging papers: 185,000 mt/y
Paper and Paperboard Mill Data:
Paper Machines: 2
No. 1, multi-wire, total capacity 90,000 mt/y, Trim width 4.18 m, Packaging papers
No. 2, Multi-wire (3), total capacity 95,000 mt/y, Trim width 5.3 m, Packaging papers
Energy Data:
Power boilers: 5
Steam turbines: 6 at 25, 5, 5, 5, 15, 20 MW
Electrical demand for mill: 649 MWh/D

ⓂFujian Qingshan Youxi Paper Co., Ltd.
Sanming Mill
Ownership: 80% by Huang jiacheng
Qiwu Road, Putou Village, Youxi County
Sanming, Fujian, 365100
China
 Phone: (86) 598 632 1089
Total Employees at this Location: 10
Type of Operation: Paper mill
Paper/Paperboard Grades and Capacities:
 Total paper and paperboard capacity: 25,000 mt/y
 Coated woodfree/freesheet: 25,000 mt/y
Paper and Paperboard Mill Data:
Paper Machines: 1
PM 1, (leased out to another company), total capacity 25,000 mt/y, Trim width 2.48 m, Coated woodfree/freesheet

ⓂFujian Quanzhou Guige Paper Co. Ltd.
Ownership: 100% by Youbisheng Green Paper AG
Fonei Industy Zone, Matou Town, Nan-An
Quanzhou City, Fujian, 362311
China
 Phone: (86) 595 8646 1222/ 1333
 Fax: (86) 596 8645 1988/ 1188
Personnel:
 Pres. & Gen. Mgr.: Haiming Huang
 Sls. Mgr.: Zeqing Zhuang
Total Employees of Company: 307
Mill Locations:
Fujian Quanzhou Guige Paper Co. Ltd., Quanzhou Mill, Fonei Industy Zone, Matou Town, Nan-An, Quanzhou 362311, China, Capacity: 149,940 mt/y, (Paperboard mill)
 Phone: (86) 595 8646 1222/ 1333
 Fax: (86) 596 8645 1988/ 1188
 Email: guige@vip.163.com

ⓂFujian Quanzhou Guige Paper Co. Ltd.
Quanzhou Mill
Fonei Industy Zone, Matou Town, Nan-An
Quanzhou, Fujian, 362311
China

 Phone: (86) 595 8646 1222/ 1333
 Fax: (86) 596 8645 1988/ 1188
 Email: guige@vip.163.com
 Web Address: www.guigepaper.com, www.youbisheng-greenpaper.de
Personnel:
 Pres. & Gen. Mgr.: Haiming Huang
 Phone: (86) 595 8646 1222/ 1333
 Sls. Mgr.: Zeqing Zhuang
 Phone: (86) 595 8646 1222/ 1333
Total Employees at this Location: 307
Type of Operation: Paperboard mill
Pulp Grades and Capacities:
 Total pulp capacity: 111,067 mt/y
 Recycled Pulping: 111,067 mt/y
Pulp Mill Data:
 Recycled Fiber Treatment Lines:
 Recycled packaging pulping lines
Paper/Paperboard Grades and Capacities:
 Total paper and paperboard capacity: 149,940 mt/y
 Linerboard: 139,944 mt/y
 Boxboard/cartonboard: 9,996 mt/y
Paper and Paperboard Mill Data:
Paper Machines: 3
No. 1, multi-ply, total capacity 49,980 mt/y, Trim width 2.4 m, Linerboard
No. 2, multi-ply, total capacity 89,964 mt/y, Trim width 2.88 m, Linerboard
No. 3, total capacity 9,996 mt/y, Trim width 1.76 m, Boxboard/cartonboard
Energy Data:
Power boilers: 1
Steam turbines: 1 at 12 MW
Electrical demand for mill: 241 MWh/D

ⓗFujian Quanzhou Jingyu Paper Co., Ltd.
Ownership: 100% by private owners
No. 43 Chengguan Huqian Rd., Dehua County
Quanzhou, Fujian, 362500
China
 Phone: (86) 595 2358 3188/ 2352 3693
 Fax: (86) 595 2355 5968
 Web Address: www.qzjyzy.com
Personnel:
 Chmn.: Yutang Deng
 Phone: (86) 595 2358 3188/ 2352 3693
 Fax: (86) 595 2355 5968
Mill Locations:
Fujian Quanzhou Jingyu Paper Mill, Quanzhou Mill, Tuban Village, Xunzhong Town, Dehua County, Quanzhou 362500, China, Capacity: 24,990 mt/y, (Paperboard mill)
 Phone: (86) 595 2356 8999/ 9777
 Fax: (86) 595 2356 9988
 Email: info@qzjyzy.com

ⓂFujian Quanzhou Jingyu Paper Mill
Quanzhou Mill
Ownership: Fujian Quanzhou Jingyu Paper Co., Ltd.
Tuban Village, Xunzhong Town, Dehua County
Quanzhou, Fujian, 362500
China
 Phone: (86) 595 2356 8999/ 9777
 Fax: (86) 595 2356 9988
 Email: info@qzjyzy.com
 Web Address: www.qzjyzy.com
Personnel:
 Chmn. & Gen. Mgr.: Yutang Deng
 Phone: (86) 595 2356 8999/ 9777
Total Employees at this Location: 145
Type of Operation: Paperboard mill
Pulp Grades and Capacities:
 Total pulp capacity: 25,030 mt/y
 Recycled Pulping: 25,030 mt/y
Pulp Mill Data:
Pulp Lines: 2

China

Recycled Fiber Treatment Lines:
 Recycled packaging pulping lines: 1
Paper/Paperboard Grades and Capacities:
 Total paper and paperboard capacity: 24,990 mt/y
 Linerboard: 16,065 mt/y
 Corrugating medium/fluting: 8,925 mt/y
Paper and Paperboard Mill Data:
Paper Machines: 2
 No. 1, cylinder, total capacity 8,925 mt/y, Trim width 1.58 m, Corrugating medium/fluting
 No. 2, cylinder, total capacity 16,065 mt/y, Trim width 2.88 m, Linerboard
Energy Data:
 Power boilers: 2
 Electrical demand for mill: 36 MWh/D

ⒽⓂFujian Tengrongda Pulp Co., Ltd
Sanming Mill
No. 26, Guishan North Rd., Guyong Town, Jiangle County
Sanming, Fujian
China
 Phone: (86) 598 233 9778
 Fax: (86) 598 233 9566
Total Employees at this Location: 260
Type of Operation: Pulp mill
Pulp Grades and Capacities:
 Total pulp capacity: 50,710 mt/y
 Pulp available for market: 49,980 mt/y
 Mechanical Pulp: 50,710 mt/y
Pulp Mill Data:
 Mechanical Pulping Systems:
 BCTMP systems: 1
 Pulp Lines: 1
 Pulp Dryers:
 Cylinder Dryer 1, Fourdriniers 1
Energy Data:
 Power boilers: 1
 Electrical demand for mill: 295 MWh/D

ⒽFujian Xinlida Paper Co., Ltd.
Ownership: 100% by private owners
Dumei Village, Jinshan Town, Nanjing County
Zhangzhou, Fujian, 363603
China
 Phone: (86) 596 7563 666
 Fax: (86) 596 7563 666
Mill Locations:
Fujian Xinlida Paper Co., Ltd., Zhangzhou Mill, Dumei Village, Jinshan Town, Nanjing County, Zhangzhou, 363603, China, Capacity: 60,333 mt/y, (Paperboard mill)
 Phone: (86) 596 7563 666
 Fax: (86) 596 7563 666

ⓂFujian Xinlida Paper Co., Ltd.
Zhangzhou Mill
Dumei Village, Jinshan Town, Nanjing County
Zhangzhou, Fujian, 363603
China
 Phone: (86) 596 7563 666
 Fax: (86) 596 7563 666
Personnel:
 Pres. & Gen. Mgr.: Zhixiong Hong
 Phone: (86) 596 7563 666
 Prod. Mgr.: Baoguo Miao
 Phone: (86) 596 7563 666
Total Employees at this Location: 120
Type of Operation: Paperboard mill
Pulp Grades and Capacities:
 Total pulp capacity: 58,767 mt/y
 Recycled Pulping: 58,767 mt/y
Pulp Mill Data:
Pulp Lines: 3
 Recycled Fiber Treatment Lines:
 Recycled packaging pulping lines: 3 at 70,000 admt/y
Paper/Paperboard Grades and Capacities:
 Total paper and paperboard capacity: 60,333 mt/y
 Linerboard: 60,333 mt/y
Paper and Paperboard Mill Data:
Paper Machines: 2
 No. 1, cylinder (3), total capacity 12,852 mt/y, Trim width 2.75 m, Linerboard
 No. 2, cylinder (3), total capacity 47,481 mt/y, Trim width 4.6 m, Linerboard
Energy Data:
 Power boilers: 1
 Electrical demand for mill: 98 MWh/D

ⓂFujian Xiyuan Paper Co., Ltd.
Longhai Mill
Ownership: 10% by Youyuan International Holding Limited
Wuzhai Industrial Park, Jiaomei
Longhai, Fujian
China
 Phone: (86) 596 6383 3357/3366
 Web Address: www.youyuan.com.hk
Type of Operation: Paper mill
Pulp Mill Data:
Pulp Lines: 1
 Recycled Fiber Treatment Lines:
 Flotation deinking lines: 1 at 60,000
Paper/Paperboard Grades and Capacities:
 Total paper and paperboard capacity: 99,000 mt/y
 Specialty and industrial: 99,000 mt/y
Paper and Paperboard Mill Data:
Paper Machines: 10
 PM 1, total capacity 7,000 mt/y, Trim width 2.64 m, Specialty and industrial
 PM 2, total capacity 7,000 mt/y, Trim width 2.64 m, Specialty and industrial
 PM 3, total capacity 7,000 mt/y, Trim width 2.64 m, Specialty and industrial
 PM 4, total capacity 7,000 mt/y, Trim width 2.64 m, Specialty and industrial
 PM 5, total capacity 7,000 mt/y, Trim width 2.64 m, Specialty and industrial
 PM 6, total capacity 7,000 mt/y, Trim width 2.64 m, Specialty and industrial
 PM 7, total capacity 7,000 mt/y, Trim width 2.64 m, Specialty and industrial
 PM 8, total capacity 7,000 mt/y, Trim width 2.64 m, Specialty and industrial
 PM 9, total capacity 8,000 mt/y, Trim width 3.3 m, Specialty and industrial
 PM 10, total capacity 35,000 mt/y, Trim width 2.8 m, Specialty and industrial

ⒽFujian Youlanfa Group
Ownership: 100% by Youyuan International Holding Limited
Xibin Nongchang Industry Zone
Jinjiang, Fujian, 362221
China
 Phone: (86) 595 8512 3889/ 3891
 Fax: (86) 595 8512 3861
 Web Address: www.youyuan.com.hk
Personnel:
 Chmn.: Wentuo Ke
 Phone: (86) 595 8512 3889/ 3891
 Fax: (86) 595 8512 3861
 CEO: Jixiang Ke
 Phone: (86) 595 8512 3889/ 3891
 Fax: (86) 595 8512 3861
Total Employees of Company: 600
Mill Locations:
Fujian Youlanfa Group, Jinjiang Mill, Xibin Nongchang Industry Zone, Jinjiang 362221, China, Capacity: 100,000 mt/y, (Paperboard mill)
 Phone: (86) 595 8512 3879
 Fax: (86) 595 8512 3861

ⓂFujian Youlanfa Group
Jinjiang Mill
Ownership: 100% by Youyuan International Holding Limited
Xibin Nongchang Industry Zone
Jinjiang, Fujian, 362221
China
 Phone: (86) 595 8512 3879
 Fax: (86) 595 8512 3861
 Web Address: www.youyuan.com.hk
Total Employees at this Location: 600
Type of Operation: Paperboard mill
Paper/Paperboard Grades and Capacities:
 Total paper and paperboard capacity: 100,000 mt/y
 Uncoated woodfree/freesheet: 15,000 mt/y
 Tissue: 10,000 mt/y
 Specialty and industrial: 75,000 mt/y
Paper and Paperboard Mill Data:
Paper Machines: 10
 PM 5, total capacity 10,000 mt/y, Trim width 2.64 m, Tissue
 PM 6, (yoshire paper), total capacity 6,000 mt/y, Trim width 2.64 m, Specialty and industrial
 PM 7, (yoshire paper), total capacity 6,000 mt/y, Trim width 2.8 m, Specialty and industrial
 PM 8, total capacity 20,000 mt/y, Trim width 2.4 m, Specialty and industrial
 PM 9, (yoshire paper), fourdrinier, total capacity 8,000 mt/y, Trim width 2.64 m, Specialty and industrial
 PM 10, total capacity 15,000 mt/y, Trim width 2.88 m, Specialty and industrial
 PM 11, total capacity 15,000 mt/y, Trim width 2.4 m, Uncoated woodfree/freesheet
 PM 12, (yoshire paper), total capacity 5,000 mt/y, Trim width 1.88 m, Specialty and industrial
 PM 13, (yoshire paper), total capacity 5,000 mt/y, Trim width 1.88 m, Specialty and industrial
 PM 15, (yoshire paper), total capacity 10,000 mt/y, Trim width 2.64 m, Specialty and industrial

ⒽFujian Zhangzhou Gangxing Group Gangxing Paper Co., Ltd
Ownership: shareholders
Long Shan Industrial Zone, Nanjing County
Zhangzhou, Fujian, 363602
China
 Phone: (86) 596 757 8067/8092/8043
 Fax: (86) 596 757 9182
Mill Locations:
Fujian Zhangzhou Gangxing Group Gangxing Paper Co., Ltd, Zhangzhou Mill, Long Shan Industrial Zone, Nanjing County, Zhangzhou 363602, China, Capacity: 209,916 mt/y, (Paper mill, Paperboard mill)
 Phone: (86) 596 757 8067/8092/8043
 Fax: (86) 596 757 9182

ⓂFujian Zhangzhou Gangxing Group Gangxing Paper Co., Ltd
Zhangzhou Mill
Long Shan Industrial Zone, Nanjing County
Zhangzhou, Fujian, 363602
China
 Phone: (86) 596 757 8067/8092/8043
 Fax: (86) 596 757 9182
Personnel:
 Chmn.: Jiajv Wu
 Phone: (86) 596 757 8067/8092/8043
 Pres./Mill Mgr.: Linghui Zhou
 Phone: (86) 596 757 8067/8092/8043
Total Employees at this Location: 400
Type of Operation: Paper mill, Paperboard mill
Pulp Mill Data:
Pulp Lines: 2
 Recycled Fiber Treatment Lines:
 Recycled packaging pulping lines: 2 at 250,000 admt/y
Paper/Paperboard Grades and Capacities:
 Total paper and paperboard capacity: 209,916 mt/y
 Linerboard: 209,916 mt/y
Paper and Paperboard Mill Data:
Paper Machines: 2

China

No. 1, multi-ply, total capacity 49,980 mt/y, Trim width 3 m, Linerboard
No. 2, multi-ply, total capacity 159,936 mt/y, Trim width 4.5 m, Linerboard
Energy Data:
Power boilers: 3
Steam turbines
Hydro turbines at 6 MW
Electrical demand for mill: 331 MWh/D

ⓂFujian Lvjin Huamei Paper Co., Ltd.
Fuqing Mill
Mill is under construction (was due to start Q3 2014, delayed)
Ownership: 100% by Guangxi Huamei Paper Group Co., Ltd.
Jiangyin Industrial Park
Fuqing, Fujian
China
 Phone: (86) 591 8596 2177
 Fax: (86) 591 8596 5133
 Web Address: www.hmpaper.cn
Type of Operation: Paper mill
Paper and Paperboard Mill Data:
Paper Machines: 4
PM 1, (due to start up in Q3 of 2014), crescent former, total capacity 30,000 mt/y, Trim width 2.8 m, Tissue
PM 2, (due to start Q3 2014), crescent former, total capacity 30,000 mt/y, Trim width 2.8 m, Tissue
PM 3, (due to start Q4 2014), total capacity 30,000 mt/y, Trim width 2.8 m, Tissue
PM 4, (due to start Q4 2014), total capacity 30,000 mt/y, Trim width 2.8 m, Tissue

ⓂKing Paper(Xiamen) Co., Ltd.
Xiamen Mill
Ownership: Ching Mei Paper Co., Ltd.
No. 66 Xiafei Rd., Xinyang Industrial Park, Haicang
Xiamen, Fujian, 361022
China
 Phone: (86) 592 651 2288
 Fax: (86) 592 651 2277
 Email: service@kpp.com.tw
 Web Address: www.kingpaper.com.cn
Type of Operation: Paperboard mill
Pulp Grades and Capacities:
Total pulp capacity: 58,484 mt/y
Recycled Pulping: 58,484 mt/y
Paper/Paperboard Grades and Capacities:
Total paper and paperboard capacity: 60,000 mt/y
Boxboard/cartonboard: 60,000 mt/y
Paper and Paperboard Mill Data:
Paper Machines: 1
No. 1, multi-fourdrinier, total capacity 60,000 mt/y, Trim width 2.64 m, Boxboard/cartonboard
Energy Data:
Electrical demand for mill: 67 MWh/D

ⓂMax Fortune (FZ) Paper Products
Fuzhou Mill
No.39, Tieling Industrial Area Phase 2, Minhou County
Fuzhou, Fujian
China
 Phone: (86) 591 2207 0288
 Fax: (86) 591 2207 0388
 Web Address: www.max-fortune.com/cn2/index.php
Type of Operation: Paper mill
Paper/Paperboard Grades and Capacities:
Total paper and paperboard capacity: 60,000 mt/y
Tissue: 60,000 mt/y
Paper and Paperboard Mill Data:
Paper Machines: 1
PM 1, (started late 2012), Yankee dryer, total capacity 60,000 mt/y, Trim width 5.6 m

ⓂNine Dragons Paper Industries (Quanzhou) Co., Ltd.
Quanzhou Mill
Ownership: Nine Dragons Paper (Holdings) Ltd.
Quanzhou, Fujian
China
 Email: info_group@ndpaper.com
 Web Address: www.ndpaper.com
Personnel:
 Dep. Gen Mgr.: Xin Gang
Total Employees at this Location: 600
Type of Operation: Paperboard mill
Pulp Grades and Capacities:
Total pulp capacity: 654,559 mt/y
Recycled Pulping: 654,559 mt/y
Pulp Mill Data:
Recycled Fiber Treatment Lines:
Recycled packaging pulping lines
Paper/Paperboard Grades and Capacities:
Total paper and paperboard capacity: 650,000 mt/y
Linerboard: 650,000 mt/y
Paper and Paperboard Mill Data:
Paper Machines: 2
No. 35, fourdrinier, total capacity 350,000 mt/y, Trim width 6.66 m, Linerboard
No. 36, fourdrinier (2), total capacity 300,000 mt/y, Trim width 6.66 m, Linerboard
Energy Data:
Power boilers: 2
Steam turbines: 3 at 155 MW
Electrical demand for mill: 827 MWh/D

ⓂQuanzhou Huaxiang Paper Co., Ltd.
Jinjiang Mill
Ownership: 100% by Youyuan International Holding Limited
Xibin Industrial Park
Jinjiang, Fujian
China
 Phone: (86) 595 8512 3518
 Web Address: www.youyuan.com.hk
Type of Operation: Paper mill
Paper/Paperboard Grades and Capacities:
Total paper and paperboard capacity: 136,000 mt/y
Uncoated woodfree/freesheet: 44,000 mt/y
Tissue: 22,000 mt/y
Specialty and industrial: 70,000 mt/y
Paper and Paperboard Mill Data:
Paper Machines: 13
PM 1, total capacity 7,000 mt/y, Trim width 2.64 m, Specialty and industrial
PM 2, total capacity 7,000 mt/y, Trim width 2.64 m, Specialty and industrial
PM 3, total capacity 7,000 mt/y, Trim width 2.64 m, Specialty and industrial
PM 4, total capacity 7,000 mt/y, Trim width 2.64 m, Specialty and industrial
PM 5, total capacity 7,000 mt/y, Trim width 2.64 m, Specialty and industrial
PM 6, total capacity 7,000 mt/y, Trim width 2.64 m, Specialty and industrial
PM 7, total capacity 22,000 mt/y, Trim width 3.25 m, Uncoated woodfree/freesheet
PM 8, total capacity 22,000 mt/y, Trim width 3.25 m, Uncoated woodfree/freesheet
PM 9, total capacity 22,000 mt/y, Trim width 2.88 m, Tissue
PM 10, total capacity 22,000 mt/y, Trim width 2.88 m, Tissue
PM 11, total capacity 7,000 mt/y, Trim width 2.64 m, Specialty and industrial
PM 12, total capacity 7,000 mt/y, Trim width 2.64 m, Specialty and industrial
PM 13, total capacity 7,000 mt/y, Trim width 2.64 m, Specialty and industrial
Energy Data:
Power boilers: 3

ⓂXiamen Xinyang Paper
Ownership: Xiamen Construction & Development Group Co., Ltd, Xiamen Shun-Cheng Asset Management Co., Ltd, Xiamen Haicang Investment Group Co., Ltd, Nanping Paper Co., Ltd
No. 288, West Sunshine Rd., Haicang District
Xiamen, Fujian
China
 Phone: (86) 592 6197 666/2226 672
 Fax: (86) 592 6197 676/2226 673
 Email: xmxyzy@163.com,
 xyzyscb@163.com
 Web Address: www.xinyangpaper.com
Mill Locations:
Xiamen Xinyang Paper, Xiamen Mill, No. 288, West Sunshine Rd., Haicang District, Xiamen 361026, China, Capacity: 60,000 mt/y, (Paper mill)
 Phone: (86) 592 6197 666/2226 672
 Fax: (86) 592 6197 676/2226 673
 Email: xmxyzy@163.com, xyzyscb@163.com

ⓂXiamen Xinyang Paper
Xiamen Mill
No. 288, West Sunshine Rd., Haicang District
Xiamen, Fujian, 361026
China
 Phone: (86) 592 6197 666/2226 672
 Fax: (86) 592 6197 676/2226 673
 Email: xmxyzy@163.com,
 xyzyscb@163.com
 Web Address: www.xinyangpaper.com
Type of Operation: Paper mill
Paper/Paperboard Grades and Capacities:
Total paper and paperboard capacity: 60,000 mt/y
Tissue: 60,000 mt/y
Paper and Paperboard Mill Data:
Paper Machines: 1
PM 1, (started September 2012), total capacity 60,000 mt/y, Trim width 5.6 m, Tissue

ⓂZhangzhou Xinyan Environmental Protection Products Co. Ltd
Zhanzhou Mill
NO.55, Gutang Rd., Mingcheng District
Zhangzhou, Fujian, 363000
China
 Phone: (86) 596 2993 667/556
 Fax: (86) 596 2991 916
 Web Address: www.myo-e.com
Type of Operation: Paper mill
Paper/Paperboard Grades and Capacities:
Total paper and paperboard capacity: 6,000 mt/y
Tissue: 6,000 mt/y
Paper and Paperboard Mill Data:
Paper Machines: 5
PM 1-5, total capacity 1,200 mt/y, Tissue

GANSU

ⓄGansu Hanfu Dongfang Paper Co., Ltd.
Ownership: 100% by private owners
No. 168 Houjia Village, Nanhe Chuan, Beidao District
Tianshui, Gansu, 741027
China
 Phone: (86) 938 2821 318
 Fax: (86) 938 2821 318
Personnel:
 Gen. Mgr.: Yongfang Zhang
Mill Locations:
Gansu Hanfu Dongfang Paper Co., Ltd., Tianshui Mill, No. 168 Houjia Village, Nanhe Chuan, Beidao District, Tianshui 741027, China, Capacity: 29,988 mt/y, (Paperboard mill)
 Phone: (86) 938 2821 318
 Fax: (86) 938 2821 318

China

ⓂGansu Hanfu Dongfang Paper Co., Ltd.
Tianshui Mill
No. 168 Houjia Village, Nanhe Chuan, Beidao District
Tianshui, Gansu, 741027
China
  Phone: (86) 938 2821 318
  Fax: (86) 938 2821 318
Personnel:
  Gen. Mgr.: Yongfang Zhang
  Phone: (86) 938 2821 318
Total Employees at this Location: 300
Type of Operation: Paperboard mill
Pulp Grades and Capacities:
  Total pulp capacity: 29,224 mt/y
  Recycled Pulping: 29,224 mt/y
Pulp Mill Data:
Pulp Lines: 2
  Recycled Fiber Treatment Lines:
  Recycled packaging pulping lines: 2 at 50,000 admt/y
Paper/Paperboard Grades and Capacities:
  Total paper and paperboard capacity: 29,988 mt/y
  Corrugating medium/fluting: 29,988 mt/y
Paper and Paperboard Mill Data:
Paper Machines: 1
  No. 1, multi-wire, total capacity 29,988 mt/y, Trim width 3.6 m, Corrugating medium/fluting
Energy Data:
  Power boilers: 1
  Electrical demand for mill: 44 MWh/D

ⓂGansu Jingning HengDa Paper Co., Ltd.
Pingliang Mill
Bali Industrial Park, Chengguan Town, Jingning County
Pingliang, Gansu, 743400
China
  Phone: (86) 933 2587 689
Type of Operation: Paper mill
Pulp Grades and Capacities:
  Total pulp capacity: 284,159 mt/y
  Recycled Pulping: 284,159 mt/y
Paper/Paperboard Grades and Capacities:
  Total paper and paperboard capacity: 288,000 mt/y
  Linerboard: 160,000 mt/y
  Corrugating medium/fluting: 110,000 mt/y
  Boxboard/cartonboard: 18,000 mt/y
Paper and Paperboard Mill Data:
Paper Machines: 6
  No. 1, multi-wire, total capacity 18,000 mt/y, Trim width 2.85 m, Boxboard/cartonboard
  No. 2, multi-wire, total capacity 20,000 mt/y, Trim width 2.85 m, Corrugating medium/fluting
  No. 3, multi-wire, total capacity 20,000 mt/y, Trim width 2.85 m, Linerboard
  No. 4, multi-wire, total capacity 20,000 mt/y, Trim width 2.85 m, Linerboard
  No. 5, fourdrinier, total capacity 90,000 mt/y, Trim width 3.8 m, Corrugating medium/fluting
  No. 6, fourdrinier (3), total capacity 120,000 mt/y, Trim width 3.8 m, Linerboard

ⓂGansu Tianshui Xuanyuan Paper Co., Ltd.
Ownership: 100% by shareholders
Hongpu Industry Park, Qingshui County
Tianshui, Gansu, 741400
China
  Phone: (86) 938 738 1710
  Fax: (86) 938 738 1710
Mill Locations:
  Gansu Tianshui Xuanyuan Paper Co., Ltd., Tianshui Mill, Hongpu Industry Park, Qingshui County, Tianshui 741400, China, Capacity: 49,980 mt/y, (Paperboard mill)
  Phone: (86) 938 738 1710
  Fax: (86) 938 738 1710

ⓂGansu Tianshui Xuanyuan Paper Co., Ltd.
Tianshui Mill
Hongpu Industry Park, Qingshui County
Tianshui, Gansu, 741400
China
  Phone: (86) 938 738 1710
  Fax: (86) 938 738 1710
Personnel:
  Gen. Mgr.: Bing He
  Phone: (86) 938 738 1710
Total Employees at this Location: 230
Type of Operation: Paperboard mill
Pulp Grades and Capacities:
  Total pulp capacity: 48,310 mt/y
  Recycled Pulping: 48,310 mt/y
Pulp Mill Data:
  Recycled Fiber Treatment Lines:
  Recycled packaging pulping lines: 1 at 50,000 admt/y
Paper/Paperboard Grades and Capacities:
  Total paper and paperboard capacity: 49,980 mt/y
  Corrugating medium/fluting: 49,980 mt/y
Paper and Paperboard Mill Data:
Paper Machines: 1
  No. 1, fourdrinier, total capacity 49,980 mt/y, Trim width 4 m, Corrugating medium/fluting
Energy Data:
  Power boilers: 1
  Electrical demand for mill: 79 MWh/D

ⓂⓂGansu Xinglong Paper Co., Ltd
Lingtai Mill
No. 81, South Town street
Lingtai, Gansu
China
  Phone: (86) 933 3625 350
Total Employees at this Location: 70
Type of Operation: Paperboard mill
Pulp Grades and Capacities:
  Total pulp capacity: 14,626 mt/y
  Recycled Pulping: 14,626 mt/y
Pulp Mill Data:
  Recycled Fiber Treatment Lines:
  Recycled packaging pulping lines: 1
Paper/Paperboard Grades and Capacities:
  Total paper and paperboard capacity: 15,000 mt/y
  Corrugating medium/fluting: 15,000 mt/y
Paper and Paperboard Mill Data:
Paper Machines: 1
  No. 1, cylinder, total capacity 15,000 mt/y, Trim width 3.4 m, Corrugating medium/fluting
Energy Data:
  Power boilers: 1
  Electrical demand for mill: 17 MWh/D

ⓂGansu Zhangye City Mingyang Paper Mill
Ownership: 100% by private owners
West Railway Station
Zhangye, Gansu, 734000
China
  Phone: (86) 936 8433 777
  Fax: (86) 936 8433 777
  Web Address: www.gsmyzy.com
Mill Locations:
  Gansu Zhangye City Mingyang Paper Mill, Zhangye Mill, West of Dongquan Village, Ganzhou District, Zhangye 734000, China, (Pulp mill, Paper mill)
  Phone: (86) 936 6922 396/388/377

ⓂGansu Zhangye City Mingyang Paper Mill
Zhangye Mill
West of Dongquan Village, Ganzhou District
Zhangye, Gansu, 734000
China
  Phone: (86) 936 6922 396/388/377

  Web Address: www.gsmygroup.com
Personnel:
  Pres.: Kesong Li
  Phone: (86) 936 6922 399
  Gen. Mgr.: Kefeng Li
  Phone: (86) 936 6922 777
Total Employees at this Location: 657
Type of Operation: Pulp mill, Paper mill
Pulp Grades and Capacities:
  Total pulp capacity: 80,000 mt/y
  Pulp available for market: 80,000 mt/y
Pulp Mill Data:
  Chemical Pulping Systems:
  Batch digesters: 2
Pulp Lines: 2
  Pulp Dryers:
  Fourdriniers 2
Energy Data:
  Steam turbines: 1 at 1.5 MW

ⓂPingliang Xiamen Paper Co., Ltd.
Pingliang Mill
Baipo Village, Xiamen Town, Kongtong District
Pingliang, Gansu, 744024
China
  Phone: (86) 933 857 0035/0036
Total Employees at this Location: 400
Type of Operation: Paper mill
Paper/Paperboard Grades and Capacities:
  Total paper and paperboard capacity: 35,000 mt/y
  Tissue: 35,000 mt/y
Paper and Paperboard Mill Data:
Paper Machines: 18
  PM 1-16, total capacity 1,500 mt/y, Trim width 1.88 m, Tissue
  PM 17-18, total capacity 5,500 mt/y, Trim width 3.2 m, Tissue

GUANGDONG

ⓂBaoda Paper
Ownership: 100% by private owners
Xinyuan Industry Park, Deze Town, Xinhui District
Jiangmen, Guangdong, 529161
China
  Phone: (86) 750 689 9428/ 9438
  Fax: (86) 750 689 9252
  Email: baoda@baodapaper.com, sale@baodapaper.com
  Web Address: www.baodapaper.com
Mill Locations:
  Baoda Paper, Jiangmen Mill, Xinyuan Industry Park, Deze Town, Xinhui District, Jiangmen 529161, China, Capacity: 24,000 mt/y, (Paper mill)
  Phone: (86) 750 689 9428/ 9438
  Fax: (86) 750 689 9252
  Email: baoda@baodapaper.com, sale@baodapaper.com

ⓂBaoda Paper
Jiangmen Mill
Xinyuan Industry Park, Deze Town, Xinhui District
Jiangmen, Guangdong, 529161
China
  Phone: (86) 750 689 9428/ 9438
  Fax: (86) 750 689 9252
  Email: baoda@baodapaper.com, sale@baodapaper.com
  Web Address: www.baodapaper.com
Personnel:
  Pres., Gen. Mgr.: Weiping Yu
  Phone: (86) 750 689 9428/ 9438
Total Employees at this Location: 150
Type of Operation: Paper mill
Paper/Paperboard Grades and Capacities:
  Total paper and paperboard capacity: 24,000 mt/y
  Tissue: 24,000 mt/y

China

Paper and Paperboard Mill Data:
Paper Machines: 2
No. 1, (Supplier: Foshan Baotuo Japanese SaSaki.), four-drinier, Yankee dryer, total capacity 12,000 mt/y, Trim width 2.66 m, Tissue, Uncoated woodfree/freesheet
No. 2, (Supplier: Foshan Baotuo Japanese SaSaki.), four-drinier, Yankee dryer, total capacity 12,000 mt/y, Trim width 2.66 m, Tissue, Uncoated woodfree/freesheet
Energy Data:
Electrical demand for mill: 63 MWh/D

ⓂⒸC&S Paper Co., Ltd.
Zhongshan Mill
Ownership: 100% by shareholders
Hi-tech Exploiting Area, Shalang, West District
Zhongshan, Guangdong, 528411
China
Phone: (86) 760 855 3333/3008
Fax: (86) 760 855 3028/3006
Email: sales@zhongshungroup.com,
zhshco@public.zhongshan.gd.cn,
dsh@zhongshungroup.com
Web Address: www.zhongshungroup.com
Personnel:
Pres, Chmn.: Yingzhong Deng
Phone: (86) 760 855 3333/3008
Member of Board/Mill. Mgr.: Guanbiao Deng
Phone: (86) 760 855 3333/3008
CFO/Asst. Mgr.: Lin Li
Phone: (86) 760 855 3333/3008
Asst. Mgr.: Yuwu Liu
Phone: (86) 760 855 3333/3008
Asst. Mgr.: Yong Yue
Phone: (86) 760 855 3333/3008
Board Sec.: Haijun Zhang
Phone: (86) 0760-87885678
Fax: (86) 0760-87885677
Email: dsh@zhongshungroup.com
Total Employees at this Location: 480
Type of Operation: Paper mill
Mill Locations:
Sichuan Zhongshun Tiantian Paper Co., Ltd., Chengdu Mill, Mudan Avenue Industry Park, Pengzhou, Chengdu 611930, China, Capacity: 47,996 mt/y, (Paper mill)
Phone: (86) 28 8373 5698/5266
Fax: (86) 28 8380 6666
C&S Paper Co., Ltd., Jiangmen Mill, Yinzhouhu Paper Making Base, Shuangshui Town, Xinhui District, Jiangmen 529153, China, Capacity: 155,000 mt/y, (Paper mill)
Phone: (86) 750 640 8888
C&S Paper Co., Ltd., Jiaxing Mill, No. 222 Weisan Rd., Zhapu Town, Jiaxing 313301, China, Capacity: 22,500 mt/y, (Paper mill)
Phone: (86) 573 8558 1109/1101/6005/3180
Fax: (86) 573 8558 1101
C&S Paper Co., Ltd., Tangshan Mill, Donggao qiao, Yutian county, Tangshan 063000, China, Capacity: 25,000 mt/y, (Paper mill)
Phone: (86) 315 633 0999/0991
Fax: (86) 315 655 0606
Email: jiangxuhui1985@163.com
C&S Paper Co., Ltd., Xiaogan Mill, No. 8 Xiaowu Ave., Xiaonan Economic Development Zone, Xiaogan 431200, China, Capacity: 22,500 mt/y, (Paper mill)
Phone: (86) 712 2515 512/ 507
Fax: (86) 712 2515 508
C&S Paper Co., Ltd., Yunfu Mill, Shuangdong Industrial Park, Luoding City, Yunfu, China, Capacity: 60,000 mt/y, (Paper mill)
Phone: (86) 766 3903 888
Fax: (86) 766 3902 966
Paper/Paperboard Grades and Capacities:
Total paper and paperboard capacity: 21,285 mt/y
Tissue: 21,285 mt/y
Paper and Paperboard Mill Data:
Paper Machines: 44
No. 1, BF-10, total capacity 10,000 mt/y, Trim width 2.66 m, Tissue, Uncoated woodfree/freesheet
No. 2, total capacity 10,000 mt/y, Trim width 2.4 m, Tissue, Uncoated woodfree/freesheet
No. 3, total capacity 1,285 mt/y, Trim width 1.58 m, Tissue
No. 4, Trim width 1.58 m, Tissue
No. 5, Trim width 1.58 m, Tissue
No. 6, Trim width 1.58 m, Tissue
No. 7, Trim width 1.58 m, Tissue
No. 8, Trim width 1.58 m, Tissue
No. 9, Trim width 1.58 m, Tissue
No. 10, Trim width 1.58 m, Tissue
No. 11, Trim width 1.58 m, Tissue
No. 12, Trim width 1.58 m, Tissue
No. 14, Trim width 1.58 m, Tissue
No. 15, Trim width 1.58 m, Tissue
No. 16, Trim width 1.58 m, Tissue
No. 17, Trim width 1.58 m, Tissue
No. 18, Trim width 1.58 m, Tissue
No. 19, Trim width 1.58 m, Tissue
No. 20, Trim width 1.58 m, Tissue
No. 21, Trim width 1.58 m, Tissue
No. 22, Trim width 1.58 m, Tissue
No. 23, Trim width 1.58 m, Tissue
No. 24, Trim width 1.58 m, Tissue
No. 25, Trim width 1.58 m, Tissue
No. 26, Trim width 1.58 m, Tissue
No. 27, Trim width 1.58 m, Tissue
No. 28, Trim width 1.58 m, Tissue
No. 29, Trim width 1.58 m, Tissue
No. 30, Trim width 1.58 m, Tissue
No. 31, Trim width 1.58 m, Tissue
No. 32, Trim width 1.58 m, Tissue
No. 33, Trim width 1.58 m, Tissue
No. 34, Trim width 1.58 m, Tissue
No. 35, Trim width 1.58 m, Tissue
No. 36, Trim width 1.58 m, Tissue
No. 37, Trim width 1.58 m, Tissue
No. 38, Trim width 1.58 m, Tissue
No. 39, Trim width 1.58 m, Tissue
No. 40, Trim width 1.58 m, Tissue
No. 41, Trim width 1.58 m, Tissue
No. 42, Trim width 1.58 m, Tissue
No. 43, Trim width 1.58 m, Tissue
No. 44, Trim width 1.58 m, Tissue
No. 45, Trim width 1.58 m, Tissue
Energy Data:
Power boilers
Steam turbines
Electrical demand for mill: 92 MWh/D

ⓂC&S Paper Co., Ltd.
Jiangmen Mill
Yinzhouhu Paper Making Base, Shuangshui Town, Xinhui District
Jiangmen, Guangdong, 529153
China
Phone: (86) 750 640 8888
Web Address: www.zhongshungroup.com
Personnel:
Chmn.: Yinzhong Deng
Phone: (86) 750 640 8888
Total Employees at this Location: 350
Type of Operation: Paper mill
Paper/Paperboard Grades and Capacities:
Total paper and paperboard capacity: 155,000 mt/y
Tissue: 155,000 mt/y
Paper and Paperboard Mill Data:
Paper Machines: 8
No. 1, BF-10, total capacity 10,000 mt/y, Trim width 2.66 m, Tissue
No. 2, BF-10 a, total capacity 12,000 mt/y, Trim width 2.73 m, Tissue
No. 3, BF-10 a, total capacity 12,000 mt/y, Trim width 2.73 m, Tissue
No. 4, (Supplier: Kgong Yong Machinery (S. Korea).), crescent former, total capacity 15,000 mt/y, Trim width 2.68 m, Tissue
No. 5, crescent former, total capacity 25,000 mt/y, Trim width 3.5 m, Tissue
No. 6, crescent former, total capacity 25,000 mt/y, Trim width 3.5 m, Tissue
No. 7, crescent former, total capacity 28,000 mt/y, Trim width 3.6 m, Tissue
No. 8, crescent former, total capacity 28,000 mt/y, Trim width 3.6 m, Tissue
Energy Data:
Electrical demand for mill: 348 MWh/D

ⓂC&S Paper Co., Ltd.
Yunfu Mill
Shuangdong Industrial Park, Luoding City
Yunfu, Guangdong
China
Phone: (86) 766 3903 888
Fax: (86) 766 3902 966
Web Address: www.zhongshungroup.com
Type of Operation: Paper mill
Paper/Paperboard Grades and Capacities:
Total paper and paperboard capacity: 60,000 mt/y
Tissue: 60,000 mt/y
Paper and Paperboard Mill Data:
Paper Machines: 2
PM 1, Yankee dryer, total capacity 60,000 mt/y, Trim width 5.56 m, Tissue
PM 2, (was due to start in August 2014, but has been delayed with no completion date given), Yankee dryer, total capacity 60,000 mt/y, Trim width 5.56 m, Tissue
Energy Data:
Power boilers: 3
Steam turbines: 2 at 3, 10 MW

ⓂChina Tobacco Mauduit (Jiangmen) Paper Industry Company Ltd.
Jiangmen Mill
Ownership: 50% by Schweitzer-Mauduit International Inc., 50% by China Tobacco
Aizia Ling, Fengsheng Industrial Base West Zone, Tangxia Township
Jiangmen, Guangdong, 529085
China
Phone: (86) 750 3132 300/ 3626 262
Fax: (86) 750 3385 228
Email: hr@ct-pdm.com,
lihuining@ct-pdm.com
Personnel:
Gen. Mgr.: Steve Jiang
Phone: (86) 750 3132 300/ 3626 262
Sales Mgr.: Huining Li
Phone: (86) 750 3132 300/ 3626 262
Type of Operation: Paper mill
Paper/Paperboard Grades and Capacities:
Total paper and paperboard capacity: 18,000 mt/y
Specialty and industrial: 18,000 mt/y
Paper and Paperboard Mill Data:
Paper Machines: 2
PM 1, fourdrinier, total capacity 12,000 mt/y, Trim width 4.25 m, Specialty and industrial
PM 2, fourdrinier, total capacity 6,000 mt/y, Trim width 3 m, Specialty and industrial

ⓂⓂDongguan Dalin Paper
Dongguan Mill
Xinsha, Chajiao Village, Zhongtang Town
Dongguan, Guangdong
China
Phone: (86) 769 8888 7388/1788
Fax: (86) 769 8812 1882
Web Address: www.dalinpaper.com
Total Employees at this Location: 100
Type of Operation: Paper mill
Pulp Grades and Capacities:
Total pulp capacity: 15,827 mt/y
Recycled Pulping: 15,827 mt/y
Pulp Mill Data:
Pulp Lines: 1
Bleach Plant Systems: 1
DIP
Recycled Fiber Treatment Lines:
Flotation deinking lines: 1

China

Paper/Paperboard Grades and Capacities:
Total paper and paperboard capacity: 20,000 mt/y
Tissue: 20,000 mt/y
Paper and Paperboard Mill Data:
Paper Machines: 2
No. 1 fourdrinier, total capacity 10,000 mt/y, Trim width 2.8 m, Tissue
No. 2 fourdrinier, total capacity 10,000 mt/y, Trim width 2.8 m, Tissue
Energy Data:
Power boilers: 2
Turbines
Electrical demand for mill: 35 MWh/D

ⓜDongguan Enxing Paper Co., Ltd.
Dongguan
No.2, Qingfeng First Rd., Wanjiang District
Dongguan, Guangdong, 523039
China
 Phone: (86) 769 2227 5923
Type of Operation: Paper mill
Paper/Paperboard Grades and Capacities:
Total paper and paperboard capacity: 15,000 mt/y
Tissue: 15,000 mt/y
Paper and Paperboard Mill Data:
Paper Machines: 15
No. 1 total capacity 1,000 mt/y, Tissue
No. 2 total capacity 1,000 mt/y, Tissue
No. 3 total capacity 1,000 mt/y, Tissue
No. 4 total capacity 1,000 mt/y, Tissue
No. 5 total capacity 1,000 mt/y, Tissue
No. 6 total capacity 1,000 mt/y, Tissue
No. 7 total capacity 1,000 mt/y, Tissue
No. 8 total capacity 1,000 mt/y, Tissue
No. 9 total capacity 1,000 mt/y, Tissue
No. 10, total capacity 1,000 mt/y, Tissue
No. 11, total capacity 1,000 mt/y, Tissue
No. 12, total capacity 1,000 mt/y, Tissue
No. 13, total capacity 1,000 mt/y, Tissue
No. 14, total capacity 1,000 mt/y, Tissue
No. 15, total capacity 1,000 mt/y, Tissue

ⓜDongguan Huaixing Paper Co., Ltd.
Dongguan Mill
Dani Village, Shatian Town
Dongguan, Guangdong, 523993
China
 Phone: (86) 769 8868 6832
Type of Operation: Paper mill
Paper/Paperboard Grades and Capacities:
Total paper and paperboard capacity: 36,000 mt/y
Boxboard/cartonboard: 36,000 mt/y
Paper and Paperboard Mill Data:
Paper Machines: 3
PM 1, total capacity 10,000 mt/y, Trim width 1.58 m, Boxboard/cartonboard
PM 2, total capacity 10,000 mt/y, Trim width 1.58 m, Boxboard/cartonboard
PM 3, total capacity 16,000 mt/y, Trim width 2.4 m, Boxboard/cartonboard

ⓜDongguan Huaxing Paper Co., Ltd.
Dongguan
Wanjiang Jiaolian Industrial Park
Dongguan, Guangdong, 523046
China
 Phone: (86) 769 2218 0322/9034
 Fax: (86) 769 2227 5919
 Email: hxzy@huaxing-dg.com
 Web Address: www.huaxing-dg.com/link.htm
Type of Operation: Paper mill
Paper/Paperboard Grades and Capacities:
Total paper and paperboard capacity: 8,000 mt/y
Tissue: 8,000 mt/y
Paper and Paperboard Mill Data:
Paper Machines: 6
No. 1, total capacity 1,300 mt/y, Tissue
No. 2, total capacity 1,300 mt/y, Tissue
No. 3, total capacity 1,300 mt/y, Tissue
No. 4, total capacity 1,300 mt/y, Tissue
No. 5, total capacity 1,300 mt/y, Tissue
No. 6, total capacity 1,300 mt/y, Tissue

ⓘDongguan Weihong Paper Co., Ltd.
Duwu Village, Wangniudun Town
Dongguan, Guangdong, 523200
China
 Phone: (86) 769 8855 8198
Mill Locations:
Dongguan Weihong Paper Co., Ltd., Dongguan Mill, Duwu Village, Wangniudun Town, Dongguan 523200, China, Capacity: 12,000 mt/y, (Paper mill)
 Phone: (86) 769 8855 8198

ⓜDongguan Weihong Paper Co., Ltd.
Dongguan Mill
Duwu Village, Wangniudun Town
Dongguan, Guangdong, 523200
China
 Phone: (86) 769 8855 8198
Type of Operation: Paper mill
Paper/Paperboard Grades and Capacities:
Total paper and paperboard capacity: 12,000 mt/y
Tissue: 12,000 mt/y
Paper and Paperboard Mill Data:
Paper Machines: 7
PM 1, total capacity 1,300 mt/y, Trim width 1.76 m, Tissue
PM 2, total capacity 1,300 mt/y, Trim width 1.76 m, Tissue
PM 3, total capacity 1,300 mt/y, Trim width 1.76 m, Tissue
PM 4, total capacity 1,300 mt/y, Trim width 1.76 m, Tissue
PM 5, total capacity 1,300 mt/y, Trim width 1.76 m, Tissue
PM 6, total capacity 1,300 mt/y, Trim width 1.76 m, Tissue
PM 7, total capacity 4,200 mt/y, Trim width 2.4 m, Tissue

ⓘⓜDongguan Xuantong Paper
Dongguan Mill
Dongxiang Industrial Park, Zhongtang Town
Dongguan, Guangdong
China
 Phone: (86) 769 8802 8808
 Fax: (86) 769 8802 8818/8828
Total Employees at this Location: 300
Type of Operation: Paper mill
Paper/Paperboard Grades and Capacities:
Total paper and paperboard capacity: 45,000 mt/y
Tissue: 45,000 mt/y
Paper and Paperboard Mill Data:
Paper Machines: 14
PM 1-10, Trim width 2.85 m, Tissue
PM 11-14, Trim width 1.76 m, Tissue

ⓜDongguan Youngsun Paper Co., Ltd.
Dongguan Mill
Dayou Industrial Park, Dalang Town
Dongguan, Guangdong, 523796
China
 Phone: (86) 769 8282 6651
 Web Address: www.yspaper.com
Type of Operation: Paper mill
Paper/Paperboard Grades and Capacities:
Total paper and paperboard capacity: 100,000 mt/y
Boxboard/cartonboard: 100,000 mt/y
Paper and Paperboard Mill Data:
Paper Machines: 2
PM 1, total capacity 45,000 mt/y, Trim width 2.4 m, Boxboard/cartonboard
PM 2, total capacity 55,000 mt/y, Trim width 3.2 m, Boxboard/cartonboard

ⓘDongguan Zhongqiao Paper Co., Ltd.
Beiwang Rd., Zhongtang Town
Dongguan, Guangdong
China
 Phone: (86) 769 8812 7866
 Fax: (86) 769 8812 7966
 Web Address: www.zhongqiaopaper.cn
Mill Locations:
Dongguan Zhongqiao Paper Co., Ltd., Dongguan Mill, Beiwang Rd., Zhongtang Town, Dongguan, China, Capacity: 30,000 mt/y, (Paper mill)
 Phone: (86) 769 8812 7866
 Fax: (86) 769 8812 7966

ⓜDongguan Zhongqiao Paper Co., Ltd.
Dongguan Mill
Beiwang Rd., Zhongtang Town
Dongguan, Guangdong
China
 Phone: (86) 769 8812 7866
 Fax: (86) 769 8812 7966
 Web Address: www.zhongqiaopaper.cn
Type of Operation: Paper mill
Paper/Paperboard Grades and Capacities:
Total paper and paperboard capacity: 30,000 mt/y
Tissue: 30,000 mt/y
Paper and Paperboard Mill Data:
Paper Machines: 23
PM 1, cylinder, total capacity 1,300 mt/y, Trim width 1.58 m, Tissue
PM 2, total capacity 1,300 mt/y, Trim width 1.58 m, Tissue
PM 3, total capacity 1,300 mt/y, Trim width 1.58 m, Tissue
PM 4, cylinder, total capacity 1,300 mt/y, Trim width 1.58 m, Tissue
PM 5, cylinder, total capacity 1,300 mt/y, Trim width 1.58 m, Tissue
PM 6, cylinder, total capacity 1,300 mt/y, Trim width 1.58 m, Tissue
PM 7, cylinder, total capacity 1,300 mt/y, Trim width 1.58 m, Tissue
PM 8, cylinder, total capacity 1,300 mt/y, Trim width 1.58 m, Tissue
PM 9, cylinder, total capacity 1,300 mt/y, Trim width 1.58 m, Tissue
PM 10, cylinder, total capacity 1,300 mt/y, Trim width 1.58 m, Tissue
PM 11, cylinder, total capacity 1,300 mt/y, Trim width 1.58 m, Tissue
PM 12, cylinder, total capacity 1,300 mt/y, Trim width 1.58 m, Tissue
PM 13, cylinder, total capacity 1,300 mt/y, Trim width 1.58 m, Tissue
PM 14, cylinder, total capacity 1,300 mt/y, Trim width 1.58 m, Tissue
PM 15, cylinder, total capacity 1,300 mt/y, Trim width 1.58 m, Tissue
PM 16, cylinder, total capacity 1,300 mt/y, Trim width 1.58 m, Tissue
PM 17, cylinder, total capacity 1,300 mt/y, Trim width 1.58 m, Tissue
PM 18, cylinder, total capacity 1,300 mt/y, Trim width 1.58 m, Tissue
PM 19, cylinder, total capacity 1,300 mt/y, Trim width 1.58 m, Tissue
PM 20, cylinder, total capacity 1,300 mt/y, Trim width 1.58 m, Tissue
PM 21, cylinder, total capacity 1,300 mt/y, Trim width 1.58 m, Tissue
PM 22, cylinder, total capacity 1,300 mt/y, Trim width 1.58 m, Tissue
PM 23, cylinder, total capacity 1,300 mt/y, Trim width 1.58 m, Tissue

ⓘFoshan Gold Rich Union Paper Industry Co., Ltd.
Ownership: 100% by Guangdong Gold Rich (Lushi) Group Co., Ltd.
No. 111 Nanbian Industry Ave., Sanshui District
Foshan, Guangdong, 528135
China
 Phone: (86) 757 8731 1888/ 3688
 Fax: (86) 757 8731 1777
 Email: caijinlu@goldrich.com.cn, jianronglv@goldrich.com.cn
 Web Address: www.goldrich.com.cn
Mill Locations:
Foshan Gold Rich Union Paper Industry Co., Ltd., Foshan Mill, No. 111 Nanbian Industry Ave., Sanshui District,

Foshan 528135, China, Capacity: 178,500 mt/y, (Paperboard mill)
Phone: (86) 757 8731 1888/ 3688
Fax: (86) 757 8731 1777
Email: caijinlu@goldrich.com.cn, jianronglv@goldrich.com.cn

ⓂFoshan Gold Rich Union Paper Industry Co., Ltd.
Foshan Mill
No. 111 Nanbian Industry Ave., Sanshui District
Foshan, Guangdong, 528135
China
Phone: (86) 757 8731 1888/ 3688
Fax: (86) 757 8731 1777
Email: caijinlu@goldrich.com.cn, jianronglv@goldrich.com.cn
Web Address: www.goldrich.com.cn
Personnel:
Chmn.: Lie Lu
Phone: (86) 757 8731 1888/ 3688
Gen. Mgr.: Jianrong Lv
Phone: (86) 757 8731 1888/ 3688
Gen. Mgr., Dpty. Mgr., Sls. Mgr.: Guangrong Chen
Phone: (86) 757 8731 1888/ 3688
Total Employees at this Location: 400
Type of Operation: Paperboard mill
Pulp Grades and Capacities:
Total pulp capacity: 173,373 mt/y
Recycled Pulping: 173,373 mt/y

Pulp Mill Data:
Recycled Fiber Treatment Lines:
Recycled packaging pulping lines: 3 at 156,000 admt/y
Paper/Paperboard Grades and Capacities:
Total paper and paperboard capacity: 178,500 mt/y
Corrugating medium/fluting: 178,500 mt/y
Paper and Paperboard Mill Data:
Paper Machines: 2
No. 1, fourdrinier, total capacity 77,826 mt/y, Trim width 3.9 m, Corrugating medium/fluting
No. 2, (started in June 2011), fourdrinier, total capacity 100,674 mt/y, Trim width 4.6 m, Corrugating medium/fluting
Energy Data:
Power boilers: 1
Steam turbines
Electrical demand for mill: 271 MWh/D

ⓂAsia Symbol (Guangdong) Paper Co., Ltd.
Jiangmen Mill
Ownership: Asia Pacific Resources International - APRIL
No.1, Ruifeng Industrial Park, Shalu Village, Shuangshui Town, Xinhui district
Jiangmen, Guangdong, 529153
China
Phone: (86) 750 650 3000/3150
Fax: (86) 750 650 3166
Web Address: asiasymbol.com, www.rgei.com.cn
Total Employees at this Location: 400
Type of Operation: Paper mill
Paper/Paperboard Grades and Capacities:
Total paper and paperboard capacity: 450,000 mt/y
Uncoated woodfree/freesheet: 450,000 mt/y
Paper and Paperboard Mill Data:
Paper Machines: 1
No. 11, OptiFormer, total capacity 450,000 mt/y, Trim width 8.65 m, Uncoated woodfree/freesheet
Finishing Equipment:
Sheeters: 4
Energy Data:
Power boilers: 1
Steam turbines: 1 at 60 MW
Electrical demand for mill: 838 MWh/D

ⓗGuangdong Baoli Paper Co., Ltd.
Ownership: 100% by private owners
Meisha Village, Hexi Industry Ave.
Hongmei Town, Dongguan, Guangdong, 523000
China
Phone: (86) 769 8884 6368/ 6999/ 6238
Fax: (86) 769 8884 3178
Web Address: www.baoli.net.8hy.cn
Mill Locations:
Guangdong Baoli Paper Co., Ltd., Dongguan Mill, Meisha Village, Hexi Industry Ave., Hongmei Town, Dongguan 523000, China, Capacity: 72,004 mt/y, (Paperboard mill)
Phone: (86) 769 8884 6368/ 6999/ 6238
Fax: (86) 769 8884 3178

ⓂGuangdong Baoli Paper Co., Ltd.
Dongguan Mill
Meisha Village, Hexi Industry Ave., Hongmei Town
Dongguan, Guangdong, 523000
China
Phone: (86) 769 8884 6368/ 6999/ 6238
Fax: (86) 769 8884 3178
Web Address: www.baoli.net.8hy.cn
Personnel:
Gen. Mgr.: Shurong Liang
Phone: (86) 769 8884 6368/ 6999/ 6238
Total Employees at this Location: 350
Type of Operation: Paperboard mill
Pulp Grades and Capacities:
Total pulp capacity: 71,743 mt/y
Recycled Pulping: 71,743 mt/y
Paper/Paperboard Grades and Capacities:
Total paper and paperboard capacity: 72,004 mt/y
Boxboard/cartonboard: 72,004 mt/y
Paper and Paperboard Mill Data:
Paper Machines: 2
No. 1, multi-fourdrinier, total capacity 32,000 mt/y, Trim width 2.4 m, Boxboard/cartonboard
No. 2, multi-fourdrinier, total capacity 40,000 mt/y, Trim width 3.2 m, Boxboard/cartonboard
Energy Data:
Electrical demand for mill: 80 MWh/D

ⓂGuangdong Dingfeng Paper Corporation
Zhaoqing Mill
Ownership: 73% by Yuen Foong Yu Inc., 27% by Chung Hwa Pulp Corporation
Shouyue, South Street, Guangning
Zhaoqing, Guangdong, 526300
China
Phone: (86) 758 865 6436/9000/6808
Fax: (86) 758 865 6450/9168
Email: dingfung@gddfpaper.com
Web Address: www.gddfpaper.com
Personnel:
Chmn.: Qingxiong Guo
Phone: (86) 758 865 6436/9000/6808
Gen. Mgr.: Mingfeng Zhang
Phone: (86) 758 865 6436/9000/6808
Total Employees at this Location: 375
Type of Operation: Pulp mill
Pulp Grades and Capacities:
Total pulp capacity: 116,312 mt/y
Pulp available for market: 116,000 mt/y
Chemical Pulp: 93,049 mt/y
Other Pulp: 23,262 mt/y
Pulp Mill Data:
Pulp Lines: 1
Bleach Plant Systems: 1
No. 1, Sequence: O₂ DEoD, Capacity 120,000 admt/y
Chemical Recovery Equipment:
Recovery boilers: 1
Recovery boilers: 1
Pulp Dryers:
Fourdriniers 1, Twin Wire 1
Energy Data:

Power boilers: 3
Steam turbines: 3 at 6, 6, 6 MW
Electrical demand for mill: 242 MWh/D

ⓗⓂGuangdong Dongguan Baojian Paper Co., Ltd.
Dongguan Mill
Ownership: 100% by private owners
No. 1 Baojian Rd., Jianshanzhuo, Wanjiang District
Dongguan, Guangdong, 523062
China
Phone: (86) 769 2218 6695/ 2227 0703
Fax: (86) 769 2218 9689
Web Address: www.baojianpaper.com.cn
Personnel:
Chmn.: Baoming Hu
Phone: (86) 769 2218 6695/ 2227 0703
Sls. Mgr.- Exp.: Lei Liu
Phone: (86) 13316600100
Total Employees at this Location: 300
Type of Operation: Paper mill
Mill Locations:
Guangdong Dongguan Yongchang Paper Co., Ltd., Dongguan Mill, Liuyongwei Industry Park, Wanjiang District, Dongguan 523051, China, Capacity: 50,000 mt/y, (Paper mill)
Phone: (86) 769 2218 6695
Fax: (86) 769 2218 9689
Paper/Paperboard Grades and Capacities:
Total paper and paperboard capacity: 32,400 mt/y
Tissue: 32,400 mt/y
Paper and Paperboard Mill Data:
Paper Machines: 18
No. 1, cylinder, total capacity 1,800 mt/y, Trim width 1.58 m, Tissue
No. 2, cylinder, total capacity 1,800 mt/y, Trim width 1.58 m, Tissue
No. 3, cylinder, total capacity 1,800 mt/y, Trim width 1.58 m, Tissue
No. 4, cylinder, total capacity 1,800 mt/y, Trim width 1.58 m, Tissue
No. 5, cylinder, total capacity 1,800 mt/y, Trim width 1.58 m, Tissue
No. 6, cylinder, total capacity 1,800 mt/y, Trim width 1.58 m, Tissue
No. 7, cylinder, total capacity 1,800 mt/y, Trim width 1.58 m, Tissue
No. 8, cylinder, total capacity 1,800 mt/y, Trim width 1.58 m, Tissue
No. 9, cylinder, total capacity 1,800 mt/y, Trim width 1.58 m, Tissue
No. 10, cylinder, total capacity 1,800 mt/y, Trim width 1.58 m, Tissue
No. 11, cylinder, total capacity 1,800 mt/y, Trim width 1.58 m, Tissue
No. 12, cylinder, total capacity 1,800 mt/y, Trim width 1.58 m, Tissue
No. 13, cylinder, total capacity 1,800 mt/y, Trim width 1.58 m, Tissue
No. 14, cylinder, total capacity 1,800 mt/y, Trim width 1.58 m, Tissue
No. 15, cylinder, total capacity 1,800 mt/y, Trim width 1.58 m, Tissue
No. 16, cylinder, total capacity 1,800 mt/y, Trim width 1.58 m, Tissue
No. 17, cylinder, total capacity 1,800 mt/y, Trim width 1.58 m, Tissue
No. 18, cylinder, total capacity 1,800 mt/y, Trim width 1.58 m, Tissue

ⓗGuangdong Dongguan Dongfa Paper Industry Co., Ltd.
Ownership: 100% by private owners
Daluosha Industry Park, Daojiao Town
Dongguan, Guangdong, 523856
China
Phone: (86) 769 8883 9018
Fax: (86) 769 8883 0627
Web Address: www.dfzz888.com

China

Mill Locations:
Guangdong Dongguan Dongfa Paper Industry Co., Ltd.,
 Dongguan Mill, Daluosha Industry Park, Daojiao Town,
 Dongguan 523856, China, Capacity: 180,000 mt/y,
 (Paperboard mill)
 Phone: (86) 769 8883 9018
 Fax: (86) 769 8883 0627

ⓜGuangdong Dongguan Dongfa Paper Industry Co., Ltd.
Dongguan Mill
Daluosha Industry Park, Daojiao Town
Dongguan, Guangdong, 523856
China
 Phone: (86) 769 8883 9018
 Fax: (86) 769 8883 0627
 Web Address: www.dfzz888.com
Personnel:
 Gen. Mgr.: Shuxian Fang
 Phone: (86) 769 8883 9018
Total Employees at this Location: 500
Type of Operation: Paperboard mill
Paper/Paperboard Grades and Capacities:
 Total paper and paperboard capacity: 180,000 mt/y
 Boxboard/cartonboard: 180,000 mt/y
Paper and Paperboard Mill Data:
Paper Machines: 4
 PM 1, multi-wire, total capacity 34,000 mt/y, Trim width 2.1 m, Boxboard/cartonboard
 PM 2, multi-wire, total capacity 41,000 mt/y, Trim width 2.92 m, Boxboard/cartonboard
 PM 3, multi-wire, total capacity 45,000 mt/y, Trim width 3.25 m, Boxboard/cartonboard
 PM 4, multi-wire, total capacity 60,000 mt/y, Trim width 3.45 m, Boxboard/cartonboard
Energy Data:
 Power boilers: 3
 Steam turbines: 1 at 6 MW

ⓞⓜGuangdong Dongguan Duorong Paper Co., Ltd
Dongguan Mill
Beizhou Industrial District, Daojiao County
Dongguan, Guangdong
China
 Phone: (86) 769 8838 0718
 Fax: (86) 769 8838 0628
Total Employees at this Location: 265
Type of Operation: Paperboard mill
Pulp Grades and Capacities:
 Total pulp capacity: 121,519 mt/y
 Recycled Pulping: 121,519 mt/y
Paper/Paperboard Grades and Capacities:
 Total paper and paperboard capacity: 124,950 mt/y
 Corrugating medium/fluting: 124,950 mt/y
Paper and Paperboard Mill Data:
Paper Machines: 3
 No. 1, fourdrinier, total capacity 84,252 mt/y, Trim width 4.6 m, Corrugating medium/fluting
 No. 2, fourdrinier, total capacity 20,349 mt/y, Trim width 2.36 m, Corrugating medium/fluting
 No. 3, fourdrinier, total capacity 20,349 mt/y, Trim width 2.36 m, Corrugating medium/fluting
Energy Data:
 Power boilers
 Electrical demand for mill: 197 MWh/D

ⓞGuangdong Dongguan Gaobu Qiangan Paper Mill
Ownership: 100% by private owners
Baoanwei Village, Gaobu Town
Dongguan, Guangdong, 523270
China
 Phone: (86) 769 8887 6118
 Fax: (86) 769 8887 6119/ 6188
Mill Locations:
Guangdong Dongguan Gaobu Qiangan Paper Mill,
 Dongguan Mill, Baoanwei Village, Gaobu Town,
 Dongguan 523270, China, Capacity: 80,000 mt/y,
 (Paperboard mill)
 Phone: (86) 769 8887 6118
 Fax: (86) 769 8887 6119/ 6188

ⓜGuangdong Dongguan Gaobu Qiangan Paper Mill
Dongguan Mill
Baoanwei Village, Gaobu Town
Dongguan, Guangdong, 523270
China
 Phone: (86) 769 8887 6118
 Fax: (86) 769 8887 6119/ 6188
Total Employees at this Location: 200
Type of Operation: Paperboard mill
Pulp Grades and Capacities:
 Total pulp capacity: 81,200 mt/y
 Recycled Pulping: 81,200 mt/y
Pulp Mill Data:
 Recycled Fiber Treatment Lines:
 Recycled packaging pulping lines: 1
Paper/Paperboard Grades and Capacities:
 Total paper and paperboard capacity: 80,000 mt/y
 Linerboard: 80,000 mt/y
Paper and Paperboard Mill Data:
Paper Machines: 3
 No. 1, fourdrinier, total capacity 15,000 mt/y, Trim width 2.92 m, Linerboard
 No. 2, fourdrinier, total capacity 15,000 mt/y, Trim width 2.92 m, Linerboard
 No. 3, fourdrinier, total capacity 50,000 mt/y, Trim width 3.8 m, Linerboard
Energy Data:
 Power boilers: 1
 Electrical demand for mill: 90 MWh/D

ⓜGuangdong Dongguan Hongmei Lee & Man Paper Co., Ltd.
Dongguan (Hongmei) Mill
Ownership: 100% by Lee & Man Paper Manufacturing Ltd.
He Xi Industrial Park, Hongmei Town
Dongguan, Guangdong, 523160
China
 Phone: (86) 769 8843 2168
 Fax: (86) 769 8843 2188
 Web Address: www.leemanpaper.com
Personnel:
 Chmn.: Wenjun Li
 CFO: Guoqiang Zhang
Total Employees at this Location: 1,500
Type of Operation: Paperboard mill
Pulp Grades and Capacities:
 Total pulp capacity: 2,057,111 mt/y
 Recycled Pulping: 2,057,111 mt/y
Pulp Mill Data:
 Bleach Plant Systems: 1
 Recycled Pulping System
 Recycled Fiber Treatment Lines:
 Flotation deinking lines: 1
 Recycled packaging pulping lines: 2
Paper/Paperboard Grades and Capacities:
 Total paper and paperboard capacity: 2,175,000 mt/y
 Linerboard: 1,499,400 mt/y
 Corrugating medium/fluting: 285,600 mt/y
 Boxboard/cartonboard: 390,000 mt/y
Paper and Paperboard Mill Data:
Paper Machines: 6
 No. 7, fourdrinier (3), total capacity 428,400 mt/y, Trim width 6.65 m, Linerboard
 No. 9, fourdrinier (3), total capacity 428,400 mt/y, Trim width 6.65 m, Linerboard
 No. 11, fourdrinier (3), total capacity 285,600 mt/y, Trim width 5.5 m, Linerboard
 No. 12, top former, total capacity 357,000 mt/y, Trim width 6.65 m, Linerboard
 No. 15, fourdrinier (3), total capacity 285,600 mt/y, Trim width 6.8 m, Corrugating medium/fluting
 No. 17, ValFormer, total capacity 390,000 mt/y, Trim width 6.75 m, Boxboard/cartonboard
Coating Machines: 1
 PM# 17, on machine
Energy Data:
 Power boilers: 4
 Combustion turbines: 2 at 200 MW
 Electrical demand for mill: 2,958 MWh/D

ⓞGuangdong Dongguan Jianhua Paper Co. Ltd.
Ownership: 100% by Huangchong Paper Development Corp. (Group)
Huangchong Zone, Zhongtang Town
Dongguan, Guangdong, 523221
China
 Phone: (86) 769 8818 1288
 Fax: (86) 769 8818 1277
Personnel:
 Chmn.: Zuqiu Li
 Pres. & Purch. Mgr.: Canhui Li
Mill Locations:
Guangdong Dongguan Jianhua Paper Co. Ltd.,
 Dongguan Mill, Huangchong Zone, Zhongtang Town,
 Dongguan 523221, China, Capacity: 104,601 mt/y,
 (Paperboard mill)
 Phone: (86) 769 8818 1288
 Fax: (86) 769 8818 1277

ⓜGuangdong Dongguan Jianhua Paper Co. Ltd.
Dongguan Mill
Huangchong Zone, Zhongtang Town
Dongguan, Guangdong, 523221
China
 Phone: (86) 769 8818 1288
 Fax: (86) 769 8818 1277
Personnel:
 Chmn.: Zuqiu Li
 Phone: (86) 769 8818 1288
 Pres. & Purch. Mgr.: Canhui Li
 Phone: (86) 769 8818 1288
Total Employees at this Location: 410
Type of Operation: Paperboard mill
Pulp Grades and Capacities:
 Total pulp capacity: 104,180 mt/y
 Recycled Pulping: 104,180 mt/y
Pulp Mill Data:
Pulp Lines: 2
 Recycled Fiber Treatment Lines:
 Recycled packaging pulping lines: 2 at 130,000 admt/y
Paper/Paperboard Grades and Capacities:
 Total paper and paperboard capacity: 104,601 mt/y
 Linerboard: 53,193 mt/y
 Corrugating medium/fluting: 51,408 mt/y
Paper and Paperboard Mill Data:
Paper Machines: 5
 No. 1, cylinder, total capacity 12,495 mt/y, Trim width 2.1 m, Linerboard
 No. 2, cylinder, total capacity 12,495 mt/y, Trim width 2.1 m, Linerboard
 No. 3, fourdrinier, total capacity 28,203 mt/y, Trim width 3.05 m, Linerboard
 No. 4, fourdrinier, total capacity 25,704 mt/y, Trim width 3.05 m, Corrugating medium/fluting
 No. 5, fourdrinier, total capacity 25,704 mt/y, Trim width 3.05 m, Corrugating medium/fluting
Energy Data:
 Electrical demand for mill: 150 MWh/D

ⓞGuangdong Dongguan Jianhui Paper
Ownership: 100% by Huangyong Industrial
Huangchong Village
Zhongtang Town, Dongguan City, Guangdong,
Zhongtang
China
 Phone: (86) 769 8888 8363

China

Fax: (86) 769 8818 7777/0918
Email: jhzy@dgjhzy.com,
wfwilliam@123.com
Personnel:
Pres.: Zuqiu Li
Dir./VP: Huihua Li
Gen. Mgr., Sls: Shugao Li
Phone: (86) 769 8888 8363 Ext. 8333
Fax: (86) 769 8818 7777
Email: sales@dgjhzy.com
Gen. Mgr., Purch.Mgr: Zhiheng He
Phone: (86) 769 8818 3377
Fax: (86) 769 8818 0918
Oper. Mgr., Tech. Mgr., Mill Mgr.: Po Chen
Phone: (86) 769 8888 8363
Fax: (86) 769 8818 3833
Email: jhzy@dgjhzy.com
Sls. Mgr.: William Wu
Phone: (86) 769 8888 8363
Fax: (86) 769 8818 7777/0918
Email: wfwilliam@123.com
Total Employees of Company: 1,465
Mill Locations:
Guangdong Dongguan Jianhui Paper, Dongguan Mill, Huangchong Village, Zhongtang Town, Dongguan 523221, China, Capacity: 1,110,000 mt/y, (Paperboard mill)
Phone: (86) 769 8888 8363
Fax: (86) 769 8818 7777/0918
Email: jhzy@dgjhzy.com, wfwilliam@123.com

ⓜGuangdong Dongguan Jianhui Paper
Dongguan Mill
Huangchong Village, Zhongtang Town
Dongguan, Guangdong, 523221
China
Phone: (86) 769 8888 8363
Fax: (86) 769 8818 7777/0918
Email: jhzy@dgjhzy.com,
wfwilliam@123.com
Personnel:
Pres.: Zuqiu Li
Phone: (86) 769 8888 8363
Dir./VP: Huihua Li
Phone: (86) 769 8888 8363
Gen. Mgr., Sls: Shugao Li
Phone: (86) 769 8888 8363 Ext. 8333
Fax: (86) 769 8818 7777
Email: sales@dgjhzy.com
Gen. Mgr., Purch.: Zhiheng He
Phone: (86) 769 8818 3377
Fax: (86) 769 8818 0918
VP Oper., Technology, Eng.: Po Chen
Phone: (86) 769 8888 8363
Fax: (86) 769 8818 3833
Email: jhzy@dgjhzy.com
Sls. Mgr.: William Wu
Phone: (86) 769 8888 8363
Fax: (86) 769 8818 7777/0918
Total Employees at this Location: 1,465
Type of Operation: Paperboard mill
Pulp Grades and Capacities:
Total pulp capacity: 977,349 mt/y
Recycled Pulping: 977,349 mt/y
Pulp Mill Data:
Bleach Plant Systems: 1
DIP
Recycled Fiber Treatment Lines:
Flotation deinking lines: 1
Recycled packaging pulping lines: 2
Paper/Paperboard Grades and Capacities:
Total paper and paperboard capacity: 1,110,000 mt/y
Linerboard: 360,000 mt/y
Boxboard/cartonboard: 750,000 mt/y
Paper and Paperboard Mill Data:
Stock Preparation:
Pulpers: 5
Refiners: 6
Paper Machines: 4
No. 1, SymFormer MB, total capacity 330,000 mt/y, Trim width 4.5 m, Boxboard/cartonboard
No. 2, Fourdrinier (5), total capacity 420,000 mt/y, Trim width 4.5 m, Boxboard/cartonboard
No. 3, Multi-wire (3), total capacity 180,000 mt/y, Trim width 4.6 m, Linerboard
No. 4, Multi-wire (3), total capacity 180,000 mt/y, Trim width 4.6 m, Linerboard
Coating Machines: 2
PM 1, total capacity 310,600 mt/y., on machine
PM 2, total capacity 350,000 mt/y., on machine
Energy Data:
Power boilers: 5
Steam turbines: 3 at 60, 18, 18 MW
Electrical demand for mill: 1,726 MWh/D

ⓜGuangdong Dongguan Jintian Paper Co., Ltd.
Dongguan Mill
Ownership: Guangdong Dongguan White Swan Paper Co, Ltd., Dongguan Goltia Real Estate Co., Ltd.
Dafen Jintian Industry Zone, Wanfen Area
Dongguan, Guangdong, 518053
China
Phone: (86) 769 2228 0688
Fax: (86) 769 2277 2255
Web Address: www.jintianpaper.com
Personnel:
Chmn.: Yi Yuan
Phone: (86) 769 2228 0688
Gen. Mgr.: Zhong Ouyang
Phone: (86) 769 2228 0688
Vice Sls. Mgr.: Yanfu Chu
Phone: (86) 769 2228 0688
Sls. & Mktg. Mgr.: Jason Wang
Phone: (86) 769 2228 0688
Total Employees at this Location: 800
Type of Operation: Paperboard mill
Pulp Grades and Capacities:
Total pulp capacity: 250,000 mt/y
Recycled Pulping: 250,000 mt/y
Pulp Mill Data:
Pulp Lines: 6
Recycled Fiber Treatment Lines:
Recycled packaging pulping lines: 6 at 250,000 admt/y
Paper/Paperboard Grades and Capacities:
Total paper and paperboard capacity: 800,000 mt/y
Boxboard/cartonboard: 800,000 mt/y
Paper and Paperboard Mill Data:
Paper Machines: 5
PM 1, multi-wire, total capacity 150,000 mt/y, Trim width 2.8 m, Boxboard/cartonboard
PM 2, fourdrinier (3), total capacity 100,000 mt/y, Trim width 3.4 m, Boxboard/cartonboard
PM 3, fourdrinier (3), total capacity 250,000 mt/y, Trim width 5.6 m, Boxboard/cartonboard
PM 4, multi-fourdrinier, total capacity 150,000 mt/y, Trim width 3.4 m, Boxboard/cartonboard
PM 5, multi-fourdrinier, total capacity 150,000 mt/y, Trim width 3.4 m, Boxboard/cartonboard
Energy Data:
Power boilers: 3
Steam turbines: 1 at 60 MW

ⓜGuangdong Dongguan Jinzhou Paper Co., Ltd.
Ownership: 100% by Huangchong Paper Development Corp.
Huangchong Dist., Zhongtang Town
Dongguan City, Guangdong, 523221
China
Phone: (86) 769 88181288
Fax: (86) 769 88181277/88880126
Email: jzzy@dgjzzy.com
Web Address: www.jinzhoupaper.com
Personnel:
Chmn.: Shikang Li
CEO & Pres.: Jingjun Li
VP, Technology, Chief Eng.: Chaoyue Su
VP, Operation: Hong Lin Yang
Total Employees at this Location: 600
Mill Locations:
Guangdong Dongguan Jinzhou Paper Co., Ltd., Dongguan Mill, Huangchong Dist., Zhongtang Town, Dongguan 523221, China, Capacity: 679,014 mt/y, (Paperboard mill)
Phone: (86) 769 8818 1288
Fax: (86) 769 8818 1277/8888 0126
Email: jzzy@dgjzzy.com

ⓜGuangdong Dongguan Jinzhou Paper Co., Ltd.
Dongguan Mill
Huangchong Dist., Zhongtang Town
Dongguan, Guangdong, 523221
China
Phone: (86) 769 8818 1288
Fax: (86) 769 8818 1277/8888 0126
Email: jzzy@dgjzzy.com
Web Address: www.jinzhoupaper.com
Personnel:
Chmn.: Shikang Li
Phone: (86) 769 88181288
CEO & Pres.: Jingjun Li
Phone: (86) 769 88181288
VP, Technology, Chief Eng.: Chaoyue Su
Phone: (86) 769 88181288
VP, Operation: Hong Lin Yang
Phone: (86) 769 88181288
Total Employees at this Location: 600
Type of Operation: Paperboard mill
Pulp Grades and Capacities:
Total pulp capacity: 642,634 mt/y
Recycled Pulping: 642,634 mt/y
Pulp Mill Data:
Pulp Lines: 1
Recycled Fiber Treatment Lines:
Recycled packaging pulping lines: 1 at 350,000 admt/y
Paper/Paperboard Grades and Capacities:
Total paper and paperboard capacity: 679,014 mt/y
Linerboard: 357,714 mt/y
Corrugating medium/fluting: 321,300 mt/y
Paper and Paperboard Mill Data:
Paper Machines: 4
No. 1, fourdrinier, total capacity 160,650 mt/y, Trim width 4.4 m, Corrugating medium/fluting
No. 2, fourdrinier, total capacity 160,650 mt/y, Trim width 4.4 m, Corrugating medium/fluting
No. 3, fourdrinier (3), total capacity 178,857 mt/y, Trim width 4.6 m, Linerboard
No. 4, fourdrinier (3), total capacity 178,857 mt/y, Trim width 4.6 m, Linerboard
Energy Data:
Power boilers: 2
Steam turbines: 1 at 20 MW
Electrical demand for mill: 881 MWh/D

ⓜDongguan Landsing (Lianxing) Packaging Co., Ltd.
Dongguan Mill
Jiangnan Middle Road, Xihu District, Shilong Town
Dongguan, Guangdong, 523325
China
Phone: (86) 769 8849 6066/ 6089/ 6086
Fax: (86) 769 8611 0138
Email: sales@landsing-paperpackaging.com
Web Address: www.landsingpaper.com, www.landsing-paperpackaging.com
Type of Operation: Paper mill
Paper/Paperboard Grades and Capacities:
Total paper and paperboard capacity: 20,000 mt/y
Packaging papers: 20,000 mt/y
Paper and Paperboard Mill Data:
Paper Machines: 2

China

No. 1, Trim width 1.88 m
No. 2, Trim width 2.4 m

ⓂGuangdong Dongguan Lee & Man Paper Co., Ltd.
Dongguan (Huangyong) Mill
Ownership: 100% by Lee & Man Manufacturing Ltd.
Huangyong Dist., Zhongtang Town
Dongguan, Guangdong, 523221
China
 Phone: (86) 769 8888 8168
 Fax: (86) 769 8889 9101/8888 5188
 Email: info@leeman.com.hk
 Web Address: www.leemanpaper.com
Personnel:
 Chrmn.: Wenjun Li
 CFO: Guoqiang Zhang
 Sls. Mgr.: Xiuping Lan
 Purch. Mgr.: Baigang Xie
Total Employees at this Location: 750
Type of Operation: Paperboard mill
Pulp Grades and Capacities:
 Total pulp capacity: 652,331 mt/y
 Recycled Pulping: 652,331 mt/y
Pulp Mill Data:
Pulp Lines: 4
 Recycled Fiber Treatment Lines:
 Pulpers at 120,000 admt/y
 Recycled packaging pulping lines: 4 at 530,000 admt/y
Paper/Paperboard Grades and Capacities:
 Total paper and paperboard capacity: 670,000 mt/y
 Linerboard: 620,000 mt/y
 Corrugating medium/fluting: 50,000 mt/y
Paper and Paperboard Mill Data:
Paper Machines: 4
 No. 1, fourdrinier, total capacity 50,000 mt/y, Trim width 2.8 m, Corrugating medium/fluting
 No. 2, twin-wire, total capacity 50,000 mt/y, Trim width 4 m, Linerboard
 No. 3, Multi-wire (3), total capacity 220,000 mt/y, Trim width 5.6 m, Linerboard
 No. 4, twin-wire, total capacity 350,000 mt/y, Trim width 5.5 m, Linerboard
Energy Data:
 Power boilers: 3
 Steam turbines: 2 at 3.3, 3.3 MW
 Electrical demand for mill: 1,013 MWh/D

ⒽⓂGuangdong Dongguan Nine Dragons Paper Industries Co., Ltd.
Dongguan Mill
Ownership: Nine Dragons Paper (Holdings) Ltd.
Xinsha Port Industrial Zone, Mayong Town
Dongguan, Guangdong, 523147
China
 Phone: (86) 769 8823 4888
 Fax: (86) 769 8882 8111/4198
 Email: info@ndpaper.com, sales@ndpaper.com
 Web Address: www.ndpaper.com
Personnel:
 Chairman of the Corporate Governance Committee of the Board: Kwong Man Fok
 Phone: (86) 769 8823 4888
 Fax: (86) 769 8882 8111/4198
 CEO: Ming Chung Liu
 Phone: (86) 769 8823 4888
 Fax: (86) 769 8882 8111/4198
 Exec. Dir. & Deputy CEO: Cheng Fei Zhang
 Phone: (86) 769 8823 4888
 Fax: (86) 769 8882 8111/4198
 Member of Corporate Governance Committee. : Yan Cheung
 Phone: (86) 769 8823 4888
 Fax: (86) 769 8882 8111/4198
 Exec. Dir.: Zhang Yuanfu
 Phone: (86) 769 8823 4888
 Fax: (86) 769 8882 8111/4198
 Exec. Dir.: Jing Gao
 Phone: (86) 769 8823 4888
 Fax: (86) 769 8882 8111/4198
Total Employees at this Location: 3,500
Type of Operation: Paperboard mill
Mill Locations:
 ChengYang Paper Mill Co., Ltd., Ben Cat Dist. (Cheng Yang Paper) Mill (60% owned), D 15, My Phuoc Industrial Park, Ben Cat Dist., Vietnam, Capacity: 108,000 mt/y, (Paperboard mill)
 Phone: (84) 650 3558006-8
 Fax: (84) 650 3558009
 Jiangsu Nine Dragons Paper Industries, Taicang Mill, JiuLong Road, Taicang Port Development Area, Taicang, China, Capacity: 3,021,291 mt/y, (Paperboard mill)
 Phone: (86) 512 5370 3399
 Fax: (86) 512 5370 3800/ 3751
 Email: ndpaper@ndpaper.com.cn
 Nine Dragons Pulp & Paper (Leshan) Co., Ltd., Leshan Mill, YanZhi Village, QingXi Town, Qianwei County, Leshan 614005, China, Capacity: 311,700 mt/y, (Paper mill)
 Phone: (86) 833 2299 999
 Fax: (86) 833 2299 666
 Nine Dragons Paper Industries (Chongqing) Co., Ltd., Chongqing Mill, Luohuang Industrial Park, Jiangjin Industry Park, Chongqing 402279, China, Capacity: 1,350,000 mt/y, (Paperboard mill)
 Phone: (86) 23 6555 8888
 Fax: (86) 23 6555 8999
 Email: info_cq@ndpaper.com
 Nine Dragons Paper (Tianjin) Co., Ltd., Tianjin Mill, Jiulong Rd., Economy & Development Zone, Ninghe County, Tianjin 301500, China, Capacity: 1,976,352 mt/y, (Paperboard mill)
 Phone: (86) 22 6955 8585
 Fax: (86) 22 6922 2139
 Email: info@ndpaper.com, sales@ndpaper.com
 Nine Dragons XingAn Paper Co., Ltd. (Inner Mongolia), Zhalantun Mill (55% owned), No. 33, Zhijiang Street, Zhalantun 162650, China, Capacity: 14,994 mt/y, (Pulp mill, Paper mill)
 Phone: (86) 470 330 2447
 Fax: (86) 470 330 3820
Pulp Grades and Capacities:
 Total pulp capacity: 4,662,307 mt/y
 Recycled Pulping: 4,632,964 mt/y
Pulp Mill Data:
Pulp Lines: 6
 Recycled Fiber Treatment Lines:
 Flotation deinking lines: 1 at 100,000 admt/y
 Recycled packaging pulping lines: 5 at 360,000 admt/y
Paper/Paperboard Grades and Capacities:
 Total paper and paperboard capacity: 5,474,406 mt/y
 Uncoated woodfree/freesheet: 249,900 mt/y
 Linerboard: 2,290,512 mt/y
 Corrugating medium/fluting: 1,419,600 mt/y
 Boxboard/cartonboard: 1,514,394 mt/y
Paper and Paperboard Mill Data:
Paper Machines: 15
 No. 1, fourdrinier (3), total capacity 240,975 mt/y, Trim width 5.43 m, Linerboard
 No. 2, fourdrinier (3), total capacity 399,840 mt/y, Trim width 5.56 m, Linerboard
 No. 3, fourdrinier, total capacity 399,840 mt/y, Trim width 5.95 m, Linerboard
 No. 4, SymFormer MB, total capacity 405,552 mt/y, Trim width 5.65 m, Boxboard/cartonboard
 No. 6, (second hand), fourdrinier, total capacity 249,900 mt/y, Trim width 5.6 m, Corrugating medium/fluting
 No. 7, (second hand), fourdrinier, total capacity 249,900 mt/y, Trim width 5.6 m, Corrugating medium/fluting
 No. 9, fourdrinier, total capacity 249,900 mt/y, Trim width 5.6 m, Corrugating medium/fluting
 No. 10, fourdrinier, total capacity 249,900 mt/y, Trim width 5.6 m, Corrugating medium/fluting
 No. 11, DuoFormer D, total capacity 558,348 mt/y, Trim width 5.65 m, Boxboard/cartonboard
 No. 12, fourdrinier (3), total capacity 399,840 mt/y, Trim width 7.2 m, Linerboard
 No. 13, fourdrinier (3), total capacity 399,840 mt/y, Trim width 7.2 m, Linerboard
 No. 18, DuoFormer Base, total capacity 420,000 mt/y, Trim width 6.6 m, Corrugating medium/fluting
 No. 19, fourdrinier (3), total capacity 450,177 mt/y, Trim width 6.6 m, Linerboard
 No. 27, (started August 2011), Fourdrinier (4), total capacity 550,494 mt/y, Trim width 6.6 m, Boxboard/cartonboard
 No. 28, (started July 2011), DuoFormer Base, total capacity 249,900 mt/y, Trim width 6.6 m, Uncoated woodfree/freesheet
Coating Machines: 3
 PM 11, total capacity 558,000 mt/y., on machine
 PM 27, total capacity 550,000 mt/y., on machine
 PM 4, total capacity 406,000 mt/y., on machine
Finishing Equipment:
 Supercalenders: 2
 Rewinders: 1
 Sheeters: 4
Energy Data:
 Power boilers: 6
 Steam turbines: 6 at 25, 6, 30, 30, 50, 210 MW
 Electrical demand for mill: 8,000 MWh/D

ⒽGuangdong Dongguan Shenlian Paper Making Co., Ltd.
Ownership: 100% by private owners
Chajiaoxinsha Industry Park, Zhongtang Town
Dongguan, Guangdong, 523231
China
 Phone: (86) 769 8881 8778/ 8418
 Fax: (86) 769 8881 3428
Mill Locations:
 Guangdong Dongguan Shenlian Paper Making Co., Ltd., Dongguan Mill, Chajiaoxinsha Industry Park, Zhongtang Town, Dongguan 523231, China, Capacity: 200,277 mt/y, (Paperboard mill)
 Phone: (86) 769 8881 8778/ 8418
 Fax: (86) 769 8881 3428

ⓂGuangdong Dongguan Shenlian Paper Making Co., Ltd.
Dongguan Mill
Chajiaoxinsha Industry Park, Zhongtang Town
Dongguan, Guangdong, 523231
China
 Phone: (86) 769 8881 8778/ 8418
 Fax: (86) 769 8881 3428
Personnel:
 Gen. Mgr.: Ruiliang Chen
 Phone: (86) 769 8881 8778/ 8418
 Sls. Mgr.: Mr. Li
 Phone: (86) 769 8881 8778/ 8418
Total Employees at this Location: 700
Type of Operation: Paperboard mill
Pulp Grades and Capacities:
 Total pulp capacity: 197,125 mt/y
 Recycled Pulping: 197,125 mt/y
Pulp Mill Data:
Pulp Lines: 4
 Recycled Fiber Treatment Lines:
 Recycled packaging pulping lines: 4 at 107,000 admt/y
Paper/Paperboard Grades and Capacities:
 Total paper and paperboard capacity: 200,277 mt/y
 Corrugating medium/fluting: 200,277 mt/y
Paper and Paperboard Mill Data:
Paper Machines: 5
 No. 1, fourdrinier, total capacity 22,848 mt/y, Trim width 2.64 m, Corrugating medium/fluting
 No. 2, fourdrinier, total capacity 20,349 mt/y, Trim width 2.36 m, Corrugating medium/fluting
 No. 3, fourdrinier, total capacity 28,560 mt/y, Trim width 3.2 m, Corrugating medium/fluting

China

No. 4, fourdrinier, total capacity 28,560 mt/y, Trim width 3.2 m, Corrugating medium/fluting
No. 5, fourdrinier, total capacity 99,960 mt/y, Trim width 4.6 m, Corrugating medium/fluting
Energy Data:
Power boilers: 3
Steam turbines: 2 at 3, 6 MW
Electrical demand for mill: 314 MWh/D

ⒽGuangdong Dongguan Shuangzhou Paper Co., Ltd.
Ownership: 100% by private owners
Wujiachong No. 2 Industry District
Zhongtang Town, Dongguan, Guangdong, 523221
China
Phone: (86) 769 8811 1678/8818 2628
Mill Locations:
Guangdong Dongguan Shuangzhou Paper Co., Ltd., Dongguan Mill, Wujiachong No. 2 Industry District, Zhongtang Town, Dongguan 523221, China, Capacity: 406,980 mt/y, (Paperboard mill)
Phone: (86) 769 8811 1678/8818 2628

ⓂGuangdong Dongguan Shuangzhou Paper Co., Ltd.
Dongguan Mill
Wujiachong No. 2 Industry District, Zhongtang Town
Dongguan, Guangdong, 523221
China
Phone: (86) 769 8811 1678/8818 2628
Personnel:
Pres.: Youyin Wu
Phone: (86) 769 8811 1678/8818 2628
Sls. Mgr.: Lianxiong Liu
Phone: (86) 769 8811 1678/8818 2628
Total Employees at this Location: 765
Type of Operation: Paperboard mill
Pulp Grades and Capacities:
Total pulp capacity: 395,540 mt/y
Recycled Pulping: 395,540 mt/y

Pulp Mill Data:
Pulp Lines: 3
Recycled Fiber Treatment Lines:
Recycled packaging pulping lines: 3 at 400,000
Paper/Paperboard Grades and Capacities:
Total paper and paperboard capacity: 406,980 mt/y
Corrugating medium/fluting: 406,980 mt/y
Paper and Paperboard Mill Data:
Paper Machines: 5
No. 1, fourdrinier, total capacity 52,836 mt/y, Trim width 3.8 m, Corrugating medium/fluting
No. 2, fourdrinier, total capacity 52,836 mt/y, Trim width 3.8 m, Corrugating medium/fluting
No. 3, fourdrinier, total capacity 52,836 mt/y, Trim width 3.8 m, Corrugating medium/fluting
No. 4, fourdrinier, total capacity 124,236 mt/y, Trim width 4.6 m, Corrugating medium/fluting
No. 5, fourdrinier, total capacity 124,236 mt/y, Trim width 4.6 m, Corrugating medium/fluting
Energy Data:
Power boilers: 3
Steam turbines: 3 at 22.5 MW
Electrical demand for mill: 645 MWh/D

ⒽⓂGuangdong Dongguan Shunyu Paper Co., Ltd
Dongguan Mill
Wangniudun Zhupingsha Industry Zone
Dongguan, Guangdong, 523213
China
Phone: (86) 769 8855 3923
Fax: (86) 769 8856 0007
Total Employees at this Location: 600
Type of Operation: Paperboard mill
Pulp Grades and Capacities:
Total pulp capacity: 292,389 mt/y
Recycled Pulping: 292,389 mt/y

Pulp Mill Data:
Pulp Lines: 2
Recycled Fiber Treatment Lines:
Recycled packaging pulping lines: 1
Paper/Paperboard Grades and Capacities:
Total paper and paperboard capacity: 295,596 mt/y
Corrugating medium/fluting: 295,596 mt/y
Paper and Paperboard Mill Data:
Paper Machines: 4
No. 1, fourdrinier, total capacity 22,848 mt/y, Trim width 2.36 m, Corrugating medium/fluting
No. 2, fourdrinier, total capacity 22,848 mt/y, Trim width 2.36 m, Corrugating medium/fluting
No. 3, fourdrinier, total capacity 99,960 mt/y, Trim width 4.8 m, Corrugating medium/fluting
No. 4, fourdrinier, total capacity 149,940 mt/y, Trim width 5.8 m, Corrugating medium/fluting
Energy Data:
Power boilers: 3
Steam turbines: 3 at 15 MW
Electrical demand for mill: 456 MWh/D

ⒽGuangdong Dongguan Taichang Paper Co., Ltd.
Ownership: 100% by private owners
Xiazao Village, Wangniudun Town
Dongguan, Guangdong, 523219
China
Phone: (86) 769 8885 2607
Fax: (86) 769 8885 1169
Mill Locations:
Guangdong Dongguan Taichang Paper Co., Ltd., Dongguan Mill, Xiazao Village, Wangniudun Town, Dongguan 523219, China, Capacity: 204,918 mt/y, (Paperboard mill)
Phone: (86) 769 8885 2607
Fax: (86) 769 8885 1169

ⓂGuangdong Dongguan Taichang Paper Co., Ltd.
Dongguan Mill
Xiazao Village, Wangniudun Town
Dongguan, Guangdong, 523219
China
Phone: (86) 769 8885 2607
Fax: (86) 769 8885 1169
Total Employees at this Location: 600
Type of Operation: Paperboard mill
Pulp Grades and Capacities:
Total pulp capacity: 208,742 mt/y
Recycled Pulping: 208,742 mt/y

Pulp Mill Data:
Recycled Fiber Treatment Lines:
Recycled packaging pulping lines
Paper/Paperboard Grades and Capacities:
Total paper and paperboard capacity: 204,918 mt/y
Linerboard: 204,918 mt/y
Paper and Paperboard Mill Data:
Paper Machines: 2
No. 7, fourdrinier (3), total capacity 72,828 mt/y, Trim width 3.4 m, Linerboard
No. 8, fourdrinier (3), total capacity 132,090 mt/y, Trim width 4.8 m, Linerboard
Energy Data:
Power boilers
Steam turbines: 1 at 15.5 MW
Electrical demand for mill: 376 MWh/D

ⒽGuangdong Dongguan White Swan Paper Co, Ltd.
Ownership: 100% by Dongguan Jiamin Indus. Co
Guyong Indus. Zone, Wanjiang
Dongguan, Guangdong, 523047
China
Phone: (86) 769 2217 2118/ 2128
Fax: (86) 769 2218 1226
Email: bte@whiteswanpaper.com
Web Address: www.dgbte.com
Personnel:
Chmn. & Gen. Mgr.: Baoxiang Lu
Mill Locations:
Guangdong Dongguan Jintian Paper Co., Ltd., Dongguan Mill, Dafen Jintian Industry Zone, Wanfen Area, Dongguan 518053, China, Capacity: 800,000 mt/y, (Paperboard mill)
Phone: (86) 769 2228 0688
Fax: (86) 769 2277 2255
Guangdong Dongguan White Swan Paper Co, Ltd., Dongguan Mill, Guyong Indus. Zone, Wanjiang, Dongguan 523047, China, Capacity: 20,000 mt/y, (Paper mill)
Phone: (86) 769 2217 2118/ 2128
Fax: (86) 769 2218 1226
Email: bte@whiteswanpaper.com

ⓂGuangdong Dongguan White Swan Paper Co, Ltd.
Dongguan Mill
Guyong Indus. Zone, Wanjiang
Dongguan, Guangdong, 523047
China
Phone: (86) 769 2217 2118/ 2128
Fax: (86) 769 2218 1226
Email: bte@whiteswanpaper.com
Web Address: www.dgbte.com
Personnel:
Chmn. & Gen. Mgr.: Baoxiang Lu
Phone: (86) 769 2217 2118/ 2128
Total Employees at this Location: 390
Type of Operation: Paper mill
Paper/Paperboard Grades and Capacities:
Total paper and paperboard capacity: 20,000 mt/y
Tissue: 20,000 mt/y
Paper and Paperboard Mill Data:
Paper Machines: 32
No. 11, cylinder, Trim width 1.58 m, Tissue
No. 12, cylinder, Trim width 1.58 m, Tissue
No. 13, cylinder, Trim width 1.58 m, Tissue
No. 14, cylinder, Trim width 1.58 m, Tissue
No. 15, cylinder, Trim width 1.58 m, Tissue
No. 16, cylinder, Trim width 1.58 m, Tissue
No. 17, cylinder, Trim width 1.58 m, Tissue
No. 18, cylinder, Trim width 1.58 m, Tissue
No. 19, cylinder, Trim width 1.58 m, Tissue
No. 20, cylinder, Trim width 1.58 m, Tissue
No. 21, cylinder, Trim width 1.58 m, Tissue
No. 22, cylinder, Trim width 1.58 m, Tissue
No. 23, cylinder, Trim width 1.58 m, Tissue
No. 24, cylinder, Trim width 1.58 m, Tissue
No. 25, cylinder, Trim width 1.58 m, Tissue
No. 26, cylinder, Trim width 1.58 m, Tissue
No. 27, cylinder, Trim width 1.58 m, Tissue
No. 28, cylinder, Trim width 1.58 m, Tissue
No. 29, cylinder, Trim width 1.58 m, Tissue
No. 30, cylinder, Trim width 1.58 m, Tissue
No. 31, cylinder, Trim width 1.58 m, Tissue
No. 32, cylinder, Trim width 1.58 m, Tissue
No. 33, cylinder, Trim width 1.58 m, Tissue
No. 34, cylinder, Trim width 1.58 m, Tissue
No. 35, cylinder, Trim width 1.58 m, Tissue
No. 36, cylinder, Trim width 1.58 m, Tissue
No. 37, cylinder, Trim width 1.58 m, Tissue
No. 38, cylinder, Trim width 1.58 m, Tissue
No. 39, cylinder, Trim width 1.58 m, Tissue
No. 40, cylinder, Trim width 1.58 m, Tissue
TM1, (Supplier: Guiyang Light Industry/Hangzhou Light Industy), cylinder, total capacity 10,000 mt/y, Trim width 2.8 m, Tissue
TM2, (Supplier: Guiyang Light Industry/Hangzhou Light Industy), cylinder, total capacity 10,000 mt/y, Trim width 2.8 m, Tissue
Energy Data:
Power boilers: 1
Steam turbines: 2 at 1.5, 1.5 MW
Electrical demand for mill: 81 MWh/D

China

ⓜGuangdong Dongguan Huangyong Yinzhou Paper Industry Ltd.
Ownership: 100% by Huangchong Paper Development Corp. (Group)
Huangyong Zone, Zhong Tang Town
Dongguan, Guangdong, 523221
China
 Phone: (86) 769 88899113
 Fax: (86) 769 88180293
 Email: sales@dgyzzy.com
 Web Address: en.dgyzzy.com/index.html
Personnel:
 Chmn. & Pres.: Zuqiu Li
 Pres.: Xikang Li
 VP: Huihua Li
 VP, Sls. & Mktg. Mgr: Weier Li
 VP: Chenglai Li
 VP: Jinghui Li
 Asst. VP: Jingjun Li
 VP-Technology: Chaorui Su
 Chief Eng.: Wenlin Tang
 Mill Mgr.: Heqiu Li
 Mill Mgr.: Jianxiong Li
 Mill Mgr.: Wenhui Li
 Mill Mgr.: Yucheng Li
 Mill Mgr.: Zhentao Wang
 Mgr. Power Plant: Guangxin Zhu
Mill Locations:
Guangdong Dongguan Huangyong Yinzhou Paper Industry Ltd., Dongguan Mill, Huangyong Zone, Zhong Tang Town, Dongguan 523221, China, Capacity: 559,776 mt/y, (Paperboard mill)
 Phone: (86) 769 8818 1288/ 8888 1033
 Fax: (86) 769 8818 1277/8888 0126
 Email: jzzy@96326.com

ⓜGuangdong Dongguan Huangyong Yinzhou Paper Industry Ltd.
Dongguan Mill
Huangyong Zone, Zhong Tang Town
Dongguan, Guangdong, 523221
China
 Phone: (86) 769 8818 1288/ 8888 1033
 Fax: (86) 769 8818 1277/8888 0126
 Email: jzzy@96326.com
Personnel:
 Chmn. & Pres.: Zuqiu Li
 Phone: (86) 769 8818 1288/ 8888 1033
 Pres.: Xikang Li
 Phone: (86) 769 8818 1288/ 8888 1033
 VP: Huihua Li
 Phone: (86) 769 8818 1288/ 8888 1033
 VP, Sls. & Mktg. Mgr: Weier Li
 Phone: (86) 769 8818 1288/ 8888 1033
 VP: Chenglai Li
 Phone: (86) 769 8818 1288/ 8888 1033
 VP: Jinghui Li
 Phone: (86) 769 8818 1288/ 8888 1033
 Asst. VP: Jingjun Li
 Phone: (86) 769 8818 1288/ 8888 1033
 VP-Technology: Chaorui Su
 Phone: (86) 769 8818 1288/ 8888 1033
 Chief Eng.: Wenlin Tang
 Phone: (86) 769 8818 1288/ 8888 1033
 Mill Mgr.: Heqiu Li
 Phone: (86) 769 8818 1288/ 8888 1033
 Mill Mgr.: Jianxiong Li
 Phone: (86) 769 8818 1288/ 8888 1033
 Mill Mgr.: Wenhui Li
 Phone: (86) 769 8818 1288/ 8888 1033
 Mill Mgr.: Yucheng Li
 Phone: (86) 769 8818 1288/ 8888 1033
 Mill Mgr.: Zhentao Wang
 Phone: (86) 769 8818 1288/ 8888 1033
 Mgr. Power Plant: Guangxin Zhu
 Phone: (86) 769 8818 1288/ 8888 1033
Total Employees at this Location: 1,600
Type of Operation: Paperboard mill
Pulp Grades and Capacities:
 Total pulp capacity: 561,283 mt/y
 Recycled Pulping: 561,283 mt/y
Pulp Mill Data:
 Recycled Fiber Treatment Lines:
 Flotation deinking lines: 1 at 350,000 admt/y
 Pulpers: 15 at 400,000 admt/y
Paper/Paperboard Grades and Capacities:
 Total paper and paperboard capacity: 559,776 mt/y
 Linerboard: 299,880 mt/y
 Corrugating medium/fluting: 259,896 mt/y
Paper and Paperboard Mill Data:
Paper Machines: 14
No. 1, multi-ply, total capacity 149,940 mt/y, Trim width 4.7 m, Linerboard
No. 2, multi-ply, total capacity 149,940 mt/y, Trim width 4.7 m, Linerboard
No. 9, total capacity 9,996 mt/y, Trim width 1.09 m, Corrugating medium/fluting
No. 10, total capacity 19,992 mt/y, Trim width 2.4 m, Corrugating medium/fluting
No. 11, total capacity 19,992 mt/y, Trim width 2.4 m, Corrugating medium/fluting
No. 12, total capacity 19,992 mt/y, Trim width 2.4 m, Corrugating medium/fluting
No. 13, total capacity 19,992 mt/y, Trim width 2.4 m, Corrugating medium/fluting
No. 14, total capacity 19,992 mt/y, Trim width 2.4 m, Corrugating medium/fluting
No. 15, total capacity 19,992 mt/y, Trim width 2.4 m, Corrugating medium/fluting
No. 16, total capacity 19,992 mt/y, Trim width 2.4 m, Corrugating medium/fluting
No. 17, total capacity 19,992 mt/y, Trim width 2.4 m, Corrugating medium/fluting
No. 18, total capacity 19,992 mt/y, Trim width 2.4 m, Corrugating medium/fluting
No. 19, total capacity 19,992 mt/y, Trim width 2.63 m, Corrugating medium/fluting
No. 20, total capacity 49,980 mt/y, Trim width 3.1 m, Corrugating medium/fluting
Energy Data:
Power boilers: 5
Combustion turbines: 3 at 6, 10, 10 MW
Electrical demand for mill: 917 MWh/D

ⓞⓜGuangdong Dongguan Yongan Paper Co., Ltd
Dongguan Mill
11, Taian Street, Yongtou Village, Changan Town
Dongguan, Guangdong
China
 Phone: (86) 769 2217 7467
Total Employees at this Location: 500
Type of Operation: Paperboard mill
Pulp Grades and Capacities:
 Total pulp capacity: 227,989 mt/y
 Recycled Pulping: 227,989 mt/y
Pulp Mill Data:
 Recycled Fiber Treatment Lines:
 Recycled packaging pulping lines
Paper/Paperboard Grades and Capacities:
 Total paper and paperboard capacity: 228,123 mt/y
 Corrugating medium/fluting: 228,123 mt/y
Paper and Paperboard Mill Data:
Paper Machines: 6
No. 1, fourdrinier, total capacity 16,779 mt/y, Trim width 1.8 m, Corrugating medium/fluting
No. 2, fourdrinier, total capacity 21,777 mt/y, Trim width 2.36 m, Corrugating medium/fluting
No. 3, fourdrinier, total capacity 21,777 mt/y, Trim width 2.36 m, Corrugating medium/fluting
No. 4, fourdrinier, total capacity 30,702 mt/y, Trim width 3.3 m, Corrugating medium/fluting
No. 5, fourdrinier, total capacity 30,702 mt/y, Trim width 3.3 m, Corrugating medium/fluting
No. 6, fourdrinier, total capacity 106,386 mt/y, Trim width 4.6 m, Corrugating medium/fluting
Energy Data:
Power boilers
Steam turbines: 2 at 3, 3 MW
Electrical demand for mill: 357 MWh/D

ⓜGuangdong Dongguan Yongchang Paper Co., Ltd.
Dongguan Mill
Ownership: 100% by Guangdong Dongguan Baojian Paper Co., Ltd.
Liuyongwei Industry Park, Wanjiang District
Dongguan, Guangdong, 523051
China
 Phone: (86) 769 2218 6695
 Fax: (86) 769 2218 9689
Personnel:
 Pres.: Baoming Hu
 Phone: (86) 769 2218 6695
 Gen. Mgr.: Wenbiao He
 Phone: (86) 769 2218 6695
 Dir.: Jijian Hu
 Phone: (86) 769 2218 6695
Total Employees at this Location: 140
Type of Operation: Paper mill
Paper/Paperboard Grades and Capacities:
 Total paper and paperboard capacity: 50,000 mt/y
 Tissue: 50,000 mt/y
Paper and Paperboard Mill Data:
Paper Machines: 2
No. 1, BF-12, total capacity 20,000 mt/y, Trim width 2.7 m, Tissue, Uncoated woodfree/freesheet
No. 2, BF-12 EX, total capacity 30,000 mt/y, Trim width 3.4 m, Tissue, Uncoated woodfree/freesheet
Finishing Equipment:
 Rewinders: 1 at 15,000 mt/y
Energy Data:
Electrical demand for mill: 83 MWh/D

ⓞⓜGuangdong Dongguan Zhonglian Paper Co., Ltd.
Dongguan Mill
Ownership: 100% by private owners
Guansui Rd., Zhongtang County
Dongguan, Guangdong, 523220
China
 Phone: (86) 769 8881 1027/1028
 Fax: (86) 769 8881 1705
 Email: webmaster@zhonglianpaper.com
Personnel:
 Chmn. & Gen. Mgr.: Haobing Wu
 Phone: (86) 769 8881 1027/1028
Total Employees at this Location: 530
Type of Operation: Paperboard mill
Pulp Grades and Capacities:
 Total pulp capacity: 240,380 mt/y
 Recycled Pulping: 240,380 mt/y
Pulp Mill Data:
 Recycled Fiber Treatment Lines:
 Recycled packaging pulping lines
Paper/Paperboard Grades and Capacities:
 Total paper and paperboard capacity: 239,904 mt/y
 Linerboard: 169,932 mt/y
 Corrugating medium/fluting: 69,972 mt/y
Paper and Paperboard Mill Data:
Paper Machines: 5
No. 1, total capacity 34,986 mt/y, Trim width 2.8 m, Corrugating medium/fluting
No. 2, total capacity 34,986 mt/y, Trim width 2.8 m, Linerboard
No. 3, total capacity 34,986 mt/y, Trim width 3.2 m, Corrugating medium/fluting
No. 4, total capacity 34,986 mt/y, Trim width 3.2 m, Linerboard
No. 5, total capacity 99,960 mt/y, Trim width 4.6 m, Linerboard
Energy Data:
Power boilers: 1
Steam turbines: 3 at 3, 3, 6 MW
Electrical demand for mill: 397 MWh/D

ⓗGuangdong Donta Group Co., Ltd.
Ownership: 100% by shareholders
8 Guangzhang Rd., Dongcheng Dist.
Dongguan, Guangdong, 523120
China
  Phone: (86) 769 2261 1888
  Fax: (86) 769 2261 2888
  Web Address: www.dongtanggroup.com
Personnel:
  Chmn.: Xiaoshen Yan
  Phone: (86) 769 2261 1888
  Fax: (86) 769 2261 2888
Total Employees of Company: 2,632
Mill Locations:
  Guangdong Donta Group Dongwen Paper Mill, Dongguan Mill, Zhongtang Town, Dongguan 523243, China, Capacity: 20,000 mt/y, (Pulp mill, Paper mill)
  Phone: (86) 769 8881 7300
  Fax: (86) 769 8881 7718/ 2817
  Guangxi Laibin Donta Paper Co., Ltd., Laibin Mill, Datianping, Putian Village, Chengxiang County, Xinbin District, Laibin 546100, China, Capacity: 18,433 mt/y, (Pulp mill, Paper mill)
  Phone: (86) 772 406 6669/6666
  Fax: (86) 772 406 6889

ⓜGuangdong Donta Group Dongwen Paper Mill
Dongguan Mill
Ownership: 100% by Guangdong Donta Group Co., Ltd.
Zhongtang Town
Dongguan, Guangdong, 523243
China
  Phone: (86) 769 8881 7300
  Fax: (86) 769 8881 7718/ 2817
  Web Address: www.donta.com.cn
Personnel:
  Chmn.: Yaoshen Chen
  Phone: (86) 769 8881 7300
  VP: Yongan Liang
  Phone: (86) 769 8881 7300
  Chmn. & Pres.: Wujiao Ye
  Phone: (86) 769 8881 7300
  Paper Mill Mgr.: Rujie Chao
  Phone: (86) 769 8881 7300
  Asst. Mill Mgr.: Guiheng Li
  Phone: (86) 769 8881 7300
  Tech. Mgr.: Weidong Zhong
  Phone: (86) 769 8881 7300
  Eng.: Guangqing Shi
  Phone: (86) 769 8881 7300
  Asst. Eng.: Liu Li
  Phone: (86) 769 8881 7300
  Purch. Agent: Shu Zhu
  Phone: (86) 769 8881 7300
Total Employees at this Location: 200
Type of Operation: Pulp mill, Paper mill
Pulp Grades and Capacities:
  Total pulp capacity: 20,000 mt/y
  Recycled Pulping: 20,000 mt/y
Pulp Mill Data:
  Chemical Pulping Systems:
  Batch digesters: 1
Pulp Lines: 2
Paper/Paperboard Grades and Capacities:
  Total paper and paperboard capacity: 20,000 mt/y
  Corrugating medium/fluting: 20,000 mt/y
Paper and Paperboard Mill Data:
  Stock Preparation:
  Pulpers: 1
  Refiners: 4
Paper Machines: 2
  PM 1, cylinder, total capacity 11,000 mt/y, Trim width 2.46 m, Corrugating medium/fluting
  PM 2, cylinder, total capacity 9,000 mt/y, Trim width 2.1 m, Corrugating medium/fluting
Finishing Equipment:
  Rewinders: 2

Energy Data:
Power boilers: 5
Combustion turbines: 5 at 0.2 MW
Steam turbines: 5 at 0.2 MW

ⓗⓜGuangdong Foshan Chengtong Paper Co., Ltd.
Foshan Mill
Company is closed (indefinitely closed from February 2014. Site is being re-purposed for some urban construction projects.)
Ownership: China Paper Corporation
No.17 Hebin Rd.
Foshan, Guangdong, 528000
China
  Phone: (86) 757 8281 6867/8280 3823/ 8280 3848
  Fax: (86) 757 82813 125/8281 3125
  Email: huafeng.0000@yahoo.com.cn
  Web Address: www.fshxp.com
Personnel:
  Chmn.: Qi Wang
  Phone: (86) 757 8281 6867/8280 3823/ 8280 3848
  Pres.: Tan Shanghui
  Phone: (86) 757 8281 6867/8280 3823/ 8280 3848
  VP, Sls.: Ji Fu
  Phone: (86) 757 8281 6867/8280 3823/ 8280 3848
  Asst. Gen. Mgr.: Mr. Liu
  Phone: (86) 757 8281 6867/8280 3823/ 8280 3848
  Paper Mill Mgr.: Xiaochu Chen
  Phone: (86) 757 8281 6867/8280 3823/ 8280 3848
  Pulp Mill Mgr.: Pinhu Liang
  Phone: (86) 757 8281 6867/8280 3823/ 8280 3848
  Chief Eng.: Jiaping Huang
  Phone: (86) 757 8281 6867/8280 3823/ 8280 3848
  Maint. Mgr.: Sheng Cao
  Phone: (86) 757 8281 6867/8280 3823/ 8280 3848
  Exp. Mgr.: Qingdong Li
  Phone: (86) 757 820 3823
  Fax: (86) 757 820 3990
  Email: huafeng.0000@yahoo.com.cn
Total Employees at this Location: 800
Type of Operation: Paperboard mill
Pulp Mill Data:
  Recycled Fiber Treatment Lines:
  Flotation deinking lines
  Pulpers
Paper and Paperboard Mill Data:
  Stock Preparation:
  Pulpers: 7
  Refiners: 7
Paper Machines: 2
  No. 1, cylinder, total capacity 19,992 mt/y, Trim width 1.6 m, Boxboard/cartonboard
  No. 2, fourdrinier, total capacity 130,305 mt/y, Trim width 4.6 m, Boxboard/cartonboard
Coating Machines: 2
  PM 1, total capacity 20,000 mt/y., on machine
  PM 2, total capacity 130,000 mt/y., on machine
Energy Data:
Power boilers: 2
Steam turbines: 2 at 6, 6 MW
Electrical demand for mill: 236 MWh/D

ⓗⓜGuangdong Foshan City Gaoming Hongyuan Paper Co., Ltd.
Foshan Mill
Ownership: 100% by private owners
Binjia Rd., Sanzhu, Gaoming District
Foshan, Guangdong, 528511
China
  Phone: (86) 757 8862 2228
  Fax: (86) 757 8862 6886
  Email: 88622228n@163.com
  Web Address: www.hy-paper.com.cn
Personnel:
  Pres. & Gen. Mgr.: Yongjian Huang
  Phone: (86) 757 8862 2228

Total Employees at this Location: 400
Type of Operation: Paper mill
Mill Locations:
  Guangxi Fangchenggang Hongyuan Pulp & Paper Co., Ltd., Fangchenggang Mill, Maoling Industry Park, Fangcheng District, Fangchenggang 538023, China, (Pulp mill)
  Phone: (86) 770 309 2918/3168
  Fax: (86) 770 309 2918
Paper/Paperboard Grades and Capacities:
  Total paper and paperboard capacity: 99,960 mt/y
  Uncoated woodfree/freesheet: 99,960 mt/y
Paper and Paperboard Mill Data:
Paper Machines: 5
  No. 1, fourdrinier, total capacity 9,996 mt/y, Trim width 1.76 m, Uncoated woodfree/freesheet
  No. 2, fourdrinier, total capacity 9,996 mt/y, Trim width 1.76 m, Uncoated woodfree/freesheet
  No. 3, fourdrinier, total capacity 9,996 mt/y, Trim width 1.76 m, Uncoated woodfree/freesheet
  No. 4, fourdrinier, total capacity 9,996 mt/y, Trim width 1.76 m, Uncoated woodfree/freesheet
  No. 5, fourdrinier, total capacity 59,976 mt/y, Trim width 2.8 m, Uncoated woodfree/freesheet
Energy Data:
Electrical demand for mill: 190 MWh/D

ⓗGuangdong Foshan Gaoming Super Trans Paper Co., Ltd.
Ownership: 100% by shareholders
No. 127 Yanjiang Rd., Gaoming District
Foshan, Guangdong, 528500
China
  Phone: (86) 757 8882 1628/8863 0773/8868 2626
  Fax: (86) 757 8888 1723
  Web Address: richuangpaper.cn.alibaba.com
Mill Locations:
  Guangdong Foshan Gaoming Super Trans Paper Co., Ltd., Foshan Mill, No. 127 Yanjiang Rd., Gaoming District, Foshan 528500, China, Capacity: 30,710 mt/y, (Paper mill)
  Phone: (86) 757 8882 1628/8863 0773/8868 2626
  Fax: (86) 757 8888 1723

ⓜGuangdong Foshan Gaoming Super Trans Paper Co., Ltd.
Foshan Mill
No. 127 Yanjiang Rd., Gaoming District
Foshan, Guangdong, 528500
China
  Phone: (86) 757 8882 1628/8863 0773/8868 2626
  Fax: (86) 757 8888 1723
Personnel:
  Chmn.: Jinhong Huang
  Phone: (86) 757 8882 1628/8863 0773/8868 2626
  Gen. Mgr.: Jinming Wu
  Phone: (86) 757 8882 1628/8863 0773/8868 2626
Total Employees at this Location: 290
Type of Operation: Paper mill
Paper/Paperboard Grades and Capacities:
  Total paper and paperboard capacity: 30,710 mt/y
  Tissue: 30,710 mt/y
Paper and Paperboard Mill Data:
Paper Machines: 8
  No. 1, total capacity 2,499 mt/y, Trim width 1.76 m, Tissue, Uncoated woodfree/freesheet
  No. 2, total capacity 2,499 mt/y, Trim width 1.76 m, Tissue, Uncoated woodfree/freesheet
  No. 3, total capacity 4,998 mt/y, Trim width 2.56 m, Tissue, Uncoated woodfree/freesheet
  No. 4, total capacity 4,998 mt/y, Trim width 2.56 m, Tissue, Uncoated woodfree/freesheet
  No. 5, total capacity 4,998 mt/y, Trim width 2.56 m, Tissue, Uncoated woodfree/freesheet
  No. 6, total capacity 4,998 mt/y, Trim width 2.56 m, Tissue, Uncoated woodfree/freesheet

China

No. 7, BF-12, Yankee dryer, total capacity 10,000 mt/y, Trim width 2.68 m, Tissue, Uncoated woodfree/freesheet
No. 8, BF-12, Yankee dryer, total capacity 10,000 mt/y, Trim width 2.68 m, Tissue, Uncoated woodfree/freesheet

Energy Data:
Power boilers
Electrical demand for mill: 43 MWh/D

⊕ⓂGuangdong Foshan Shanshui Kelun Paper Co., Ltd
Foshan Mill
Hekou Shunda Industrial Park, Sanshui District
Foshan, Guangdong, 528133
China
 Phone: (86) 757 8767 0000
Type of Operation: Paper mill

ⓂGuangdong Green Forest (QingXin) Paper Industrial Limited
Qingyuan Mill
Ownership: 100% by Hop Fung Group Holdings Limited
Green Forest Industrial Town, Taihe Industrial District, Qingxin County
Qingyuan, Guangdong, 511850
China
 Phone: (86) 763 538 3348/ 3999
 Fax: (86) 763 538 3358
 Email: fkhf@hopfunggroup.com, gfgx@hopfunggroup.com.cn
 Web Address: www.hopfunggroup.com
Personnel:
 Chmn. & CEO: Hui Sum Kwok
 Phone: (86) 763 538 3348/ 3999
Total Employees at this Location: 180
Type of Operation: Paperboard mill
Pulp Grades and Capacities:
 Total pulp capacity: 330,423 mt/y
 Recycled Pulping: 330,423 mt/y
Pulp Mill Data:
 Recycled Fiber Treatment Lines:
 Recycled packaging pulping lines
Paper/Paperboard Grades and Capacities:
 Total paper and paperboard capacity: 349,860 mt/y
 Linerboard: 229,908 mt/y
 Corrugating medium/fluting: 119,952 mt/y
Paper and Paperboard Mill Data:
Paper Machines: 2
No. 1, multi-ply, total capacity 119,952 mt/y, Trim width 4.4 m, Corrugating medium/fluting
No. 2, multi-ply, total capacity 229,908 mt/y, Trim width 4.86 m, Linerboard
Energy Data:
Power boilers: 4
Steam turbines: 1 at 18 MW
Electrical demand for mill: 556 MWh/D

⊕ⓂGuangdong Guangzhou Panyu Lianhuashan Paper-Making Co., Ltd.
Guangzhou Mill
Ownership: 100% by shareholders
No. 80 East Lianhua Rd., Lianhuashan Town, Panyu Dist.
Guangzhou, Guangdong, 511400
China
 Phone: (86) 20 8486 1315/ 1371/ 1362
 Fax: (86) 20 8486 3686/ 0433
 Email: lhspaper@21cn.com, guoxiang97@163.com
Personnel:
 Pres. & Gen. Mgr.: Zhuohui He
 Phone: (86) 20 8486 1315/ 1371/ 1362
 Vice. Gen. Mgr.: Yanping Xu
 Phone: (86) 20 8486 1315/ 1371/ 1362
 Sls. Mgr.: Guoxiang Liang
 Phone: (86) 20 8486 1315/ 1371/ 1362

 Email: guoxiang97@163.com
Total Employees at this Location: 500
Type of Operation: Paper mill
Mill Locations:
Guangxi Nanning Lianli Paper Co., Ltd, Nanning Mill, Donghailin Rd., Xinqiao Town, Binyang County, Nanning 530401, China, Capacity: 5,000 mt/y, (Paper mill)
 Phone: (86) 771 8484 008
 Fax: (86) 771 8484 008
Guangxi Xiangzhou Liangui Paper Co., Ltd., Laibin Mill, Tulan Village, Shilong Town, Xiangzhou County, Laibin 545801, China, Capacity: 20,000 mt/y, (Paper mill)
 Phone: (86) 772 439 4988/ 4982
 Fax: (86) 772 439 4989
Pulp Grades and Capacities:
 Recycled Pulping
Paper/Paperboard Grades and Capacities:
 Total paper and paperboard capacity: 14,800 mt/y
 Tissue: 14,800 mt/y
Paper and Paperboard Mill Data:
Paper Machines: 21
No. 1, cylinder, total capacity 500 mt/y, Trim width 1.58 m, Tissue
No. 2, cylinder, total capacity 500 mt/y, Trim width 1.58 m, Tissue
No. 3, cylinder, total capacity 500 mt/y, Trim width 1.58 m, Tissue
No. 4, cylinder, total capacity 500 mt/y, Trim width 1.58 m, Tissue
No. 5, cylinder, total capacity 500 mt/y, Trim width 1.58 m, Tissue
No. 6, cylinder, total capacity 500 mt/y, Trim width 1.58 m, Tissue
No. 7, cylinder, total capacity 500 mt/y, Trim width 1.58 m, Tissue
No. 8, cylinder, total capacity 500 mt/y, Trim width 1.58 m, Tissue
No. 9, cylinder, total capacity 500 mt/y, Trim width 1.58 m, Tissue
No. 10, cylinder, total capacity 500 mt/y, Trim width 1.58 m, Tissue
No. 11, cylinder, total capacity 500 mt/y, Trim width 1.58 m, Tissue
No. 12, cylinder, total capacity 500 mt/y, Trim width 1.58 m, Tissue
No. 13, cylinder, total capacity 500 mt/y, Trim width 1.58 m, Tissue
No. 14, cylinder, total capacity 500 mt/y, Trim width 1.58 m, Tissue
No. 15, cylinder, total capacity 500 mt/y, Trim width 1.58 m, Tissue
No. 16, cylinder, total capacity 500 mt/y, Trim width 1.58 m, Tissue
No. 17, cylinder, total capacity 500 mt/y, Trim width 1.58 m, Tissue
No. 18, cylinder, total capacity 500 mt/y, Trim width 1.58 m, Tissue
No. 19, cylinder, total capacity 500 mt/y, Trim width 1.58 m, Tissue
No. 20, cylinder, total capacity 500 mt/y, Trim width 1.58 m, Tissue
No. 21, fourdrinier, total capacity 4,800 mt/y, Trim width 2.4 m, Tissue
Energy Data:
Power boilers: 2

⊕ⓂGuangdong Guangzhou Smile Daily Necessities Co., Ltd.
Guangzhou Mill
Ownership: 100% by private owners
No. 2193 East Guangyuan Rd., Tianhe District
Guangzhou, Guangdong, 510500
China
 Phone: (86) 20 2282 2188
 Fax: (86) 20 2282 2198
 Email: kidabs@126.com
 Web Address: www.smile-gz.com, www.ho-comfort.com
Personnel:
 Gen. Mgr.: Xiaojian Xu
 Phone: (86) 20 2282 2188
 Email: kidabs@126.com
Total Employees at this Location: 500
Type of Operation: Paper mill
Mill Locations:
Anhui Bilun Tissue Paper Co. Ltd., Maanshan Mill, Dangtu Industry Park, Maanshan 243100, China, Capacity: 18,000 mt/y, (Paper mill)
 Phone: (86) 555 675 8368
Paper/Paperboard Grades and Capacities:
 Total paper and paperboard capacity: 30,000 mt/y
 Tissue: 30,000 mt/y
Paper and Paperboard Mill Data:
Paper Machines: 20
No. 1, cylinder, total capacity 1,500 mt/y, Trim width 1.58 m, Tissue
No. 2, cylinder, total capacity 1,500 mt/y, Trim width 1.58 m, Tissue
No. 3, cylinder, total capacity 1,500 mt/y, Trim width 1.58 m, Tissue
No. 4, cylinder, total capacity 1,500 mt/y, Trim width 1.58 m, Tissue
No. 5, cylinder, total capacity 1,500 mt/y, Trim width 1.58 m, Tissue
No. 6, cylinder, total capacity 1,500 mt/y, Trim width 1.58 m, Tissue
No. 7, cylinder, total capacity 1,500 mt/y, Trim width 1.58 m, Tissue
No. 8, cylinder, total capacity 1,500 mt/y, Trim width 1.58 m, Tissue
No. 9, cylinder, total capacity 1,500 mt/y, Trim width 1.58 m, Tissue
No. 10, cylinder, total capacity 1,500 mt/y, Trim width 1.58 m, Tissue
No. 11, cylinder, total capacity 1,500 mt/y, Trim width 1.58 m, Tissue
No. 12, cylinder, total capacity 1,500 mt/y, Trim width 1.58 m, Tissue
No. 13, cylinder, total capacity 1,500 mt/y, Trim width 1.58 m, Tissue
No. 14, cylinder, total capacity 1,500 mt/y, Trim width 1.58 m, Tissue
No. 15, cylinder, total capacity 1,500 mt/y, Trim width 1.58 m, Tissue
No. 16, cylinder, total capacity 1,500 mt/y, Trim width 1.58 m, Tissue
No. 17, cylinder, total capacity 1,500 mt/y, Trim width 1.58 m, Tissue
No. 18, cylinder, total capacity 1,500 mt/y, Trim width 1.58 m, Tissue
No. 19, cylinder, total capacity 1,500 mt/y, Trim width 1.58 m, Tissue
No. 20, cylinder, total capacity 1,500 mt/y, Trim width 1.58 m, Tissue

⊕Guangdong Guanhao High-Tech Co., LTD.
Ownership: 29.08% by China Chengtong Holding Group Ltd.
No.6 Leyi Rd., Zhanjiang Economy & Technology Development Zone
Zhanjiang, Guangdong
China
 Phone: (86) 759 3399 898
 Fax: (86) 759 3382 109
 Email: guanhao@guanhao.com
 Web Address: www.guanhao.com/cn
Mill Locations:
Guangdong Guanhao High-Tech Co., LTD., Donghai Island Mill, No.6, Leyi Road, Zhanjiang Economy & Technology Development Zone, Donghai Island, Zhanjiang 524022, China, Capacity: 125,000 mt/y, (Paper mill)
 Phone: (86) 0759-3399898
 Fax: (86) 0759-3382109
 Email: guanhao@guanhao.com
Guangdong Zhanjiang Guanlong Paper Co., Ltd., Zhanjiang Mill, Taiping Town, Mazhang Dist., Zhanjiang 524084, China, Capacity: 60,000 mt/y, (Paper mill)

Phone: (86) 759 273 8001/8019/8020/8059
Fax: (86) 759 273 8009/8068/2865706
Email: guanlong@glpaper.com
Tianjin Zhongchao Paper Co. Ltd., Tianjin Mill (24.93% owned), No. 38 Xinghua Ave., Xiqing Economy & Development District, Tianjin 300381, China, Capacity: 6,100 mt/y, (Paper mill)
Phone: (86) 22 6037 0931/ 2396 0572
Fax: (86) 22 2396 1457
Email: zhagnchaoliushulin@163.com

ⓜGuangdong Guanhao High-Tech Co., LTD.
Donghai Island Mill
No.6, Leyi Road, Zhanjiang Economy & Technology Development Zone, Donghai Island
Zhanjiang, Guangdong, 524022
China
  Phone: (86) 0759-3399898
  Fax: (86) 0759-3382109
  Email: guanhao@guanhao.com
  Web Address: www.guanhao.com
Type of Operation: Paper mill
Paper/Paperboard Grades and Capacities:
  Total paper and paperboard capacity: 125,000 mt/y
  Uncoated woodfree/freesheet: 125,000 mt/y
Paper and Paperboard Mill Data:
Paper Machines: 1
No. 1, (started production by end of June 2014), total capacity 125,000 mt/y, Trim width 5.33 m, Uncoated woodfree/freesheet

ⓜGuangdong Heshan Paper Co., Ltd.
Ownership: 100% by shareholders
No. 2002 Jiezhou Industry Zone, Shaping Town
Heshan, Guangdong, 529700
China
  Phone: (86) 750 882 1389
  Fax: (86) 750 882 1288
Personnel:
  Sls. Mgr.: Jun Cao
Mill Locations:
Guangdong Heshan Paper Co., Ltd., Heshan Mill, No. 2002 Jiezhou Industry Zone, Shaping Town, Heshan 529700, China, Capacity: 43,911 mt/y, (Paperboard mill)
Phone: (86) 750 882 1389
Fax: (86) 750 882 1288

ⓜGuangdong Heshan Paper Co., Ltd.
Heshan Mill
No. 2002 Jiezhou Industry Zone, Shaping Town
Heshan, Guangdong, 529700
China
  Phone: (86) 750 882 1389
  Fax: (86) 750 882 1288
Personnel:
  Sls. Mgr.: Jun Cao
  Phone: (86) 750 882 1389
Total Employees at this Location: 362
Type of Operation: Paperboard mill
Pulp Grades and Capacities:
  Total pulp capacity: 44,727 mt/y
  Recycled Pulping: 44,727 mt/y
Pulp Mill Data:
  Chemical Recovery Equipment:
  Recovery boilers
  Recycled Fiber Treatment Lines:
  Recycled packaging pulping lines: 1 at 50,000 admt/y
Paper/Paperboard Grades and Capacities:
  Total paper and paperboard capacity: 43,911 mt/y
  Linerboard: 43,911 mt/y
Paper and Paperboard Mill Data:
Paper Machines: 4
No. 1, cylinder, total capacity 6,426 mt/y, Trim width 1.58 m, Linerboard
No. 2, cylinder, total capacity 6,426 mt/y, Trim width 1.58 m, Linerboard
No. 3, cylinder, total capacity 7,140 mt/y, Trim width 1.76 m, Linerboard
No. 4, cylinder, total capacity 23,919 mt/y, Trim width 2.36 m, Linerboard
Energy Data:
Power boilers: 1
Steam turbines: 1 at 6 MW
Electrical demand for mill: 61 MWh/D

ⓜGuangdong Huizhou Fook Woo Paper Co., Ltd.
Huizhou Mill
Ownership: Fook Woo Group
Liangwu District, Boluo County, Yuanzhou Town
Huizhou, Guangdong, 516123
China
  Phone: (86) 752 681 2888
  Fax: (86) 752 681 2628
  Web Address: www.fookwoo.com
Personnel:
  Pres.: Qiquan Liang
  Phone: (86) 752 681 2888
  Gen. Mgr.: Dabiao Liang
  Phone: (86) 752 681 2888
  Sls. Mgr.: Zhengqiang Zheng
  Phone: (86) 752 681 2888
Total Employees at this Location: 365
Type of Operation: Paper mill
Pulp Grades and Capacities:
  Total pulp capacity: 37,132 mt/y
  Recycled Pulping: 37,132 mt/y
Pulp Mill Data:
Pulp Lines: 3
  Bleach Plant Systems: 1
  Recycled Fiber Treatment Lines:
  Flotation deinking lines: 3 at 89,000 admt/y
Paper/Paperboard Grades and Capacities:
  Total paper and paperboard capacity: 55,000 mt/y
  Tissue: 55,000 mt/y
Paper and Paperboard Mill Data:
Paper Machines: 5
No. 22, fourdrinier, total capacity 5,750 mt/y, Trim width 2.8 m, Tissue
No. 23, fourdrinier, total capacity 5,750 mt/y, Trim width 2.8 m, Tissue
No. 24, fourdrinier, total capacity 3,500 mt/y, Trim width 2.8 m, Tissue
No. 25, Advantage DCT 60, total capacity 20,000 mt/y, Trim width 2.85 m, Tissue
No. 26, Advantage DCT 60, total capacity 20,000 mt/y, Trim width 2.85 m, Tissue
Energy Data:
Power boilers: 3
Steam turbines: 3 at 20, 30, 60 MW
Electrical demand for mill: 166 MWh/D

ⓜGuangdong Jiangmen City Qiaoyu Paper Co., Ltd.
Ownership: 100% by private owners
Shaqiao, Dongnan Village, Yamen Town
Jiangmen, Guangdong, 529000
China
  Phone: (86) 750 644 0088/ 1330
  Fax: (86) 750 644 1333
  Web Address: www.qiaoyupaper.com
Mill Locations:
Guangdong Jiangmen City Qiaoyu Paper Co., Ltd., Jiangmen Mill, Shaqiao, Dongnan Village, Yamen Town, Jiangmen 529000, China, Capacity: 80,325 mt/y, (Paperboard mill)
Phone: (86) 750 644 0088/ 1330
Fax: (86) 750 644 1333

ⓜGuangdong Jiangmen City Qiaoyu Paper Co., Ltd.
Jiangmen Mill
Shaqiao, Dongnan Village, Yamen Town
Jiangmen, Guangdong, 529000
China
  Phone: (86) 750 644 0088/ 1330
  Fax: (86) 750 644 1333
  Web Address: www.qiaoyupaper.com
Personnel:
  Pres. & Gen. Mgr.: Jiankang Yang
  Phone: (86) 750 644 0088/ 1330
Total Employees at this Location: 237
Type of Operation: Paperboard mill
Pulp Grades and Capacities:
  Total pulp capacity: 78,089 mt/y
  Recycled Pulping: 78,089 mt/y
Pulp Mill Data:
Pulp Lines: 1
  Recycled Fiber Treatment Lines:
  Recycled packaging pulping lines
Paper/Paperboard Grades and Capacities:
  Total paper and paperboard capacity: 80,325 mt/y
  Corrugating medium/fluting: 80,325 mt/y
Paper and Paperboard Mill Data:
Paper Machines: 1
No. 1, fourdrinier, total capacity 80,325 mt/y, Trim width 4.2 m, Corrugating medium/fluting
Energy Data:
Power boilers: 1
Steam turbines: 1 at 6 MW
Electrical demand for mill: 125 MWh/D

ⓜGuangdong Jiangmen City Xinlong Paper Co., Ltd.
Ownership: 100% by private owners
Baimiao Industrial Park, Sanjiang Town, Xinhui District
Jiangmen City, Guangdong, 529142
China
  Phone: (86) 750 620 8668
  Fax: (86) 750 621 1278
  Email: gmo@youranpaper.com
  Web Address: www.youranpaper.com
Mill Locations:
Guangdong Jiangmen City Xinlong Paper Co., Ltd., Jiangmen Mill, Baimiao Industrial Park, Sanjiang Town, Xinhui District, Jiangmen 529142, China, Capacity: 16,400 mt/y, (Paper mill)
Phone: (86) 750 620 8668
Fax: (86) 750 621 1278
Email: gmo@youranpaper.com

ⓜGuangdong Jiangmen City Xinlong Paper Co., Ltd.
Jiangmen Mill
Baimiao Industrial Park, Sanjiang Town, Xinhui District
Jiangmen, Guangdong, 529142
China
  Phone: (86) 750 620 8668
  Fax: (86) 750 621 1278
  Email: gmo@youranpaper.com
  Web Address: www.youranpaper.com
Personnel:
  Pres.: Huabiao Liang
  Phone: (86) 750 620 8668
Total Employees at this Location: 120
Type of Operation: Paper mill
Paper/Paperboard Grades and Capacities:
  Total paper and paperboard capacity: 16,400 mt/y
  Tissue: 16,400 mt/y
Paper and Paperboard Mill Data:
Paper Machines: 10
PM 1-4, cylinder, total capacity 1,200 mt/y, Trim width 1.58 m, Tissue
PM 5-8, cylinder, total capacity 1,500 mt/y, Trim width 1.58 m, Tissue
PM 9-10, (idled since July 2008, operating occasionally), cylinder, total capacity 2,800 mt/y, Trim width 2.4 m, Tissue
Energy Data:
Power boilers: 1

China

ⓘGuangdong Jiangmen Jingang Paper Co., Ltd.
Ownership: 100% by private owners
89 Wenchangsha, Jianghai District
Jiangmen, Guangdong, 529020
China
 Phone: (86) 750 327 6381
 Fax: (86) 750 333 0893
 Email: jmzze@pub.jiangmen.gd.cn

ⓘGuangdong Jiangmen Renke Lvzhou Paper Industry Co., Ltd.
Ownership: Hong Kong Boli Luzhou Paper Co., Ltd., Jiangmen Boli Luzhou Packaging Co., Ltd., Xinhui Renke Electric
Yinzhouhu Paper Industry Base, Shuangshui Town
Xinhui District, Jiangmen, Guangdong, 529153
China
 Phone: (86) 750 6419 188
 Fax: (86) 750 6416 666
 Email: xz@sivlake.com
 Web Address: www.sivlake.com
Personnel:
 Chmn & Gen. Mgr.: Hongyan Xu
Total Employees of Company: 110
Mill Locations:
Guangdong Jiangmen Renke Lvzhou Paper Industry Co., Ltd., Jiangmen Mill, Yinzhouhu Paper Industry Base, Shuangshui Town, Xinhui District, Jiangmen 529153, China, Capacity: 20,000 mt/y, (Paper mill)
 Phone: (86) 750 6419 188
 Fax: (86) 750 6416 666
 Email: xz@sivlake.com

ⓜGuangdong Jiangmen Renke Lvzhou Paper Industry Co., Ltd.
Jiangmen Mill
Yinzhouhu Paper Industry Base, Shuangshui Town, Xinhui District
Jiangmen, Guangdong, 529153
China
 Phone: (86) 750 6419 188
 Fax: (86) 750 6416 666
 Email: xz@sivlake.com
 Web Address: www.sivlake.com
Personnel:
 Chmn & Gen. Mgr.: Hongyan Xu
 Phone: (86) 750 6419 188
Total Employees at this Location: 100
Type of Operation: Paper mill
Paper/Paperboard Grades and Capacities:
 Total paper and paperboard capacity: 20,000 mt/y
 Tissue: 20,000 mt/y
Paper and Paperboard Mill Data:
Paper Machines: 1
No. 1, BF-12, total capacity 20,000 mt/y, Trim width 3.4 m, Tissue
Energy Data:
Electrical demand for mill: 31 MWh/D

ⓘGuangdong Jiangmen Zhenlong Paper Mill Co., Ltd.
Ownership: 100% by private owners
Complex Development Area, Shuangshui Town
Xinhui District, Jiangmen, Guangdong, 529100
China
 Phone: (86) 750 640 7928
 Fax: (86) 750 640 7999
 Email: ahson921@163.com, ahson921@126.com
Mill Locations:
Guangdong Jiangmen Zhenlong Paper Mill Co., Ltd., Jiangmen Mill, Complex Development Area, Shuangshui Town, Xinhui District, Jiangmen 529100, China, Capacity: 90,000 mt/y, (Paperboard mill)
 Phone: (86) 750 640 7928
 Fax: (86) 750 640 7999
 Email: ahson921@163.com, ahson921@126.com

ⓜGuangdong Jiangmen Zhenlong Paper Mill Co., Ltd.
Jiangmen Mill
Complex Development Area, Shuangshui Town, Xinhui District
Jiangmen, Guangdong, 529100
China
 Phone: (86) 750 640 7928
 Fax: (86) 750 640 7999
 Email: ahson921@163.com, ahson921@126.com
Personnel:
 Asst. Mgr.: Sai Ming (Matthew) Ho
 Phone: (86) 750 6870 4890
 Email: ahson921@126.com
Total Employees at this Location: 230
Type of Operation: Paperboard mill
Pulp Grades and Capacities:
 Total pulp capacity: 84,895 mt/y
 Recycled Pulping: 84,895 mt/y
Paper/Paperboard Grades and Capacities:
 Total paper and paperboard capacity: 90,000 mt/y
 Linerboard: 90,000 mt/y
Paper and Paperboard Mill Data:
Paper Machines: 1
No. 1, Multi-wire (5), total capacity 90,000 mt/y, Trim width 3.2 m, Linerboard
Energy Data:
Electrical demand for mill: 113 MWh/D

ⓜGuangdong Jiangnan Paper Co. Ltd.
Zhaoqing Mill
Ownership: Guangdong Regall Group Co., Ltd.
Hengjiang Industrial District, Guangning County
Zhaoqing, Guangdong, 526343
China
 Phone: (86) 758 871 6365/6917
 Fax: (86) 758 871 6798
Personnel:
 Chmn.: Touxian He
 Phone: (86) 758 871 6365/6917
 Chief Eng.: Kefu Ling
 Phone: (86) 758 871 6365/6917
Total Employees at this Location: 500
Type of Operation: Paper mill
Paper/Paperboard Grades and Capacities:
 Total paper and paperboard capacity: 68,544 mt/y
 Uncoated woodfree/freesheet: 49,980 mt/y
 Coated woodfree/freesheet: 18,564 mt/y
Paper and Paperboard Mill Data:
Paper Machines: 3
No. 1, fourdrinier, total capacity 24,990 mt/y, Trim width 1.76 m, Uncoated woodfree/freesheet
No. 2, fourdrinier, total capacity 24,990 mt/y, Trim width 1.76 m, Uncoated woodfree/freesheet
No. 3, fourdrinier, total capacity 18,564 mt/y, Trim width 2.64 m, Coated woodfree/freesheet
Coating Machines: 1
CM 1, total capacity 15,000 mt/y.
Finishing Equipment:
 Supercalenders: 2
Energy Data:
Power boilers: 1
Steam turbines: 1 at 1.5 MW
Electrical demand for mill: 129 MWh/D

ⓘGuangdong Jieyang City Xinda Paper Co., Ltd.
Ownership: 100% by private owners
Yang Mei Village
Jieyang, Guangdong, 522000
China
 Phone: (86) 663 877 1738/8782928
 Fax: (86) 663 877 2738/ 8782283
 Email: xinda@xinda-paper.com
 Web Address: www.xinda-paper.com
Mill Locations:
Guangdong Jieyang City Xinda Paper Co., Ltd., Jieyang Mill, Yang Mei Village, Jieyang 522000, China, Capacity: 10,000 mt/y, (Paper mill)
 Phone: (86) 663 877 1738/8782928
 Fax: (86) 663 877 2738/ 8782283
 Email: xinda@xinda-paper.com

ⓜGuangdong Jieyang City Xinda Paper Co., Ltd.
Jieyang Mill
Yang Mei Village
Jieyang, Guangdong, 522000
China
 Phone: (86) 663 877 1738/8782928
 Fax: (86) 663 877 2738/ 8782283
 Email: xinda@xinda-paper.com
 Web Address: www.xinda-paper.com
Personnel:
 Pres.: Huailin Li
 Phone: (86) 663 877 1738
Total Employees at this Location: 200
Type of Operation: Paper mill
Paper/Paperboard Grades and Capacities:
 Total paper and paperboard capacity: 10,000 mt/y
 Tissue: 10,000 mt/y
Paper and Paperboard Mill Data:
Paper Machines: 10
PM 1-10, cylinder, total capacity 1,000 mt/y, Trim width 1.58 m, Tissue
Energy Data:
Power boilers: 1
Steam turbines: 2 at 1.5, 1.5 MW

ⓘGuangdong Junye Paper Co., Ltd.
Ownership: 100% by private owners
Nanya Village, Weiwu Industry District
Zaojiao Town, Dongguan, Guangdong, 523187
China
 Phone: (86) 769 8838 0833/ 8883 0822
 Fax: (86) 769 8832 3502
Mill Locations:
Guangdong Junye Paper Co., Ltd., Dongguan Mill, Nanya Village, Weiwu Industry District, Zaojiao Town, Dongguan 523187, China, Capacity: 255,255 mt/y, (Paperboard mill)
 Phone: (86) 769 8838 0833/ 8883 0822
 Fax: (86) 769 8832 3502

ⓜGuangdong Junye Paper Co., Ltd.
Dongguan Mill
Nanya Village, Weiwu Industry District, Zaojiao Town
Dongguan, Guangdong, 523187
China
 Phone: (86) 769 8838 0833/ 8883 0822
 Fax: (86) 769 8832 3502
Personnel:
 Pres.: Jiongtai Wu
 Phone: (86) 769 8838 0833/ 8883 0822
Total Employees at this Location: 1,000
Type of Operation: Paperboard mill
Pulp Grades and Capacities:
 Total pulp capacity: 259,311 mt/y
 Recycled Pulping: 259,311 mt/y
Pulp Mill Data:
 Recycled Fiber Treatment Lines:
 Recycled packaging pulping lines at 235,000
Paper/Paperboard Grades and Capacities:
 Total paper and paperboard capacity: 255,255 mt/y
 Linerboard: 139,230 mt/y
 Corrugating medium/fluting: 116,025 mt/y
Paper and Paperboard Mill Data:
Paper Machines: 5
No. 1, fourdrinier, total capacity 22,491 mt/y, Trim width 2.1 m, Corrugating medium/fluting
No. 2, fourdrinier, total capacity 17,136 mt/y, Trim width 1.76 m, Corrugating medium/fluting
No. 3, fourdrinier, total capacity 24,633 mt/y, Trim width 2.1 m, Corrugating medium/fluting

China

No. 4, fourdrinier, total capacity 51,765 mt/y, Trim width 3.8 m, Corrugating medium/fluting
No. 5, fourdrinier (3), total capacity 139,230 mt/y, Trim width 4.6 m, Linerboard
Energy Data:
Power boilers: 3
Steam turbines: 2 at 6, 6 MW
Electrical demand for mill: 401 MWh/D

ⓜGuangdong Mingxing Paper Co., Ltd.
Ownership: 100% by private owners
Muzhou Town, Xinhui District
Jiangmen, Guangdong, 510115
China
 Phone: (86) 750 622 7288/ 2828/ 7328
Personnel:
 Gen. Mgr.: Yizheng Mo
 Phone: (86) 750 622 7288/ 2828/ 7328
 Sls. Mgr.: Xianyang Zhang
 Phone: (86) 750 622 7288/ 2828/ 7328
Mill Locations:
Guangdong Mingxing Paper Co., Ltd., Jiangmen Mill, No.1 Fengda Rd., Muzhou Town, Xinhui District, Jiangmen 510115, China, Capacity: 140,000 mt/y, (Paperboard mill)
 Phone: (86) 750 6222 422/ 653 9800/ 9801-9812
 Fax: (86) 750 622 2965
 Email: bussiness@sspaper.com

ⓜGuangdong Mingxing Paper Co., Ltd.
Jiangmen Mill
No.1 Fengda Rd., Muzhou Town, Xinhui District
Jiangmen, Guangdong, 510115
China
 Phone: (86) 750 6222 422/ 653 9800/ 9801-9812
 Fax: (86) 750 622 2965
 Email: bussiness@sspaper.com
 Web Address: www.sspaper.com
Personnel:
 Gen. Mgr.: Zhaojin Zhao
 Phone: (86) 750 622 7288/ 2828/ 7328
Total Employees at this Location: 400
Type of Operation: Paperboard mill
Pulp Grades and Capacities:
 Total pulp capacity: 133,162 mt/y
 Recycled Pulping: 133,162 mt/y
Pulp Mill Data:
Pulp Lines: 2
 Recycled Fiber Treatment Lines:
 Recycled packaging pulping lines: 2 at 100,000 admt/y
Paper/Paperboard Grades and Capacities:
 Total paper and paperboard capacity: 140,000 mt/y
 Linerboard: 120,000 mt/y
 Corrugating medium/fluting: 20,000 mt/y
Paper and Paperboard Mill Data:
Paper Machines: 5
No. 1, Multi-wire (4), total capacity 70,000 mt/y, Trim width 4.4 m, Linerboard
No. 2, multi-wire, total capacity 10,000 mt/y, Trim width 2.1 m, Corrugating medium/fluting
No. 4, multi-wire, total capacity 10,000 mt/y, Trim width 2.1 m, Corrugating medium/fluting
No. 5, multi-wire, total capacity 15,000 mt/y, Trim width 2.36 m, Linerboard
No. 6, Ultraformer, total capacity 35,000 mt/y, Trim width 3.2 m, Linerboard
Energy Data:
Power boilers: 1
Steam turbines: 1 at 6 MW
Electrical demand for mill: 186 MWh/D

ⓜGuangdong Regall Group Co., Ltd.
Ownership: 100% by private owners
Yuejing Industry Park, 823 Maogang Rd., Huangpu District
Guangzhou, Guangdong, 510700
China
 Phone: (86) 20 3238 9898/ 6295 9898
 Fax: (86) 20 3238 8681
 Web Address: www.regall.cn
Personnel:
 Chmn.: Qinghua Li
 Phone: (86) 20 3238 9898/ 6295 9898
 Fax: (86) 20 3238 8681
Total Employees of Company: 2,000
Mill Locations:
Guangdong Jiangnan Paper Co. Ltd., Zhaoqing Mill, Hengjiang Industrial District, Guangning County, Zhaoqing 526343, China, Capacity: 68,544 mt/y, (Paper mill)
 Phone: (86) 758 871 6365/ 6917
 Fax: (86) 758 871 6798
Heilongjiang Yuejing Pulp & Paper Co., Ltd., Harbin Mill, Dongxing Street, Tonghe Town, Tonghe County, Harbin 105900, China, (Pulp mill)
 Phone: (86) 451 5742 0669
 Fax: (86) 451 5742 7978

ⓜGuangzhou Ronglong Paper Co., Ltd.
Xialuo Village, Jiangpu Town, Conghua City
Guangzhou, Guangdong, 510925
China
 Phone: (86) 20 8799 2130
 Fax: (86) 20 8799 2886
Mill Locations:
Guangzhou Ronglong Paper Co., Ltd., Guangzhou Mill, Xialuo Village, Jiangpu Town, Conghua City, Guangzhou 510925, China, Capacity: 24,000 mt/y, (Paper mill)
 Phone: (86) 20 8799 2130
 Fax: (86) 20 8799 2886

ⓜGuangzhou Ronglong Paper Co., Ltd.
Guangzhou Mill
Xialuo Village, Jiangpu Town, Conghua City
Guangzhou, Guangdong, 510925
China
 Phone: (86) 20 8799 2130
 Fax: (86) 20 8799 2886
Type of Operation: Paper mill
Paper/Paperboard Grades and Capacities:
 Total paper and paperboard capacity: 24,000 mt/y
 Tissue: 24,000 mt/y
Paper and Paperboard Mill Data:
Paper Machines: 9
PM 1, total capacity 1,500 mt/y, Trim width 1.76 m, Tissue
PM 2, total capacity 1,500 mt/y, Trim width 1.76 m, Tissue
PM 3, total capacity 1,500 mt/y, Trim width 1.76 m, Tissue
PM 4, total capacity 1,500 mt/y, Trim width 1.76 m, Tissue
PM 5, total capacity 1,500 mt/y, Trim width 1.76 m, Tissue
PM 6, total capacity 1,500 mt/y, Trim width 1.76 m, Tissue
PM 7, total capacity 1,500 mt/y, Trim width 1.76 m, Tissue
PM 8, total capacity 1,500 mt/y, Trim width 1.76 m, Tissue
PM 9, total capacity 12,000 mt/y, Trim width 3.5 m, Tissue

ⓜGuangdong Shantou City WanAn Paper Co., Ltd.
Ownership: 100% by private owners
Daxue Rd., Shengping Industry Park
Shantou, Guangdong, 515000
China
 Phone: (86) 754 8251 6877
 Fax: (86) 754 8251 1877
 Email: wananpaper@tom.com
 Web Address: www.wananpaper.com
Personnel:
 Chmn.: Kangju Zhen
 Phone: (86) 754 8251 6877
 Fax: (86) 754 8251 1877
 Gen. Mgr.: Kangrong Zhen
 Phone: (86) 754 8251 6877
 Fax: (86) 754 8251 1877
 Sls. Mgr.: Weijia Lin
 Phone: (86) 754 8251 6877
 Fax: (86) 754 8251 1877
Total Employees at this Location: 650
Mill Locations:
Sichuan WanAn Paper Co., Ltd., Leshan Mill, Xinmin Industry Park, Ganjiang Town, Jiajiang County, Leshan 614102, China, Capacity: 15,000 mt/y, (Paper mill)
 Phone: (86) 833 577 0878/ 2516
 Fax: (86) 833 577 0878
 Email: sc-wananzhiye@263.net

ⓜGuangdong Shantou Huashi Paper Industrial Co., Ltd.
Ownership: 100% by private owners
Jinxin Rd., Xinxi Town, Longhu District
Shantou, Guangdong, 515800
China
 Phone: (86) 754 8620 0033
 Fax: (86) 754 8620 0055
Mill Locations:
Guangdong Shantou Huashi Paper Industrial Co., Ltd., Shantou Mill, Jinxin Rd., Xinxi Town, Longhu District, Shantou 515800, China, Capacity: 79,254 mt/y, (Paperboard mill)
 Phone: (86) 754 8620 0033
 Fax: (86) 754 8620 0055

ⓜGuangdong Shantou Huashi Paper Industrial Co., Ltd.
Shantou Mill
Jinxin Rd., Xinxi Town, Longhu District
Shantou, Guangdong, 515800
China
 Phone: (86) 754 8620 0033
 Fax: (86) 754 8620 0055
Personnel:
 Gen. Mgr.: Shaoxiong Chen
 Phone: (86) 754 8620 0033
Total Employees at this Location: 499
Type of Operation: Paperboard mill
Pulp Grades and Capacities:
 Total pulp capacity: 77,944 mt/y
 Recycled Pulping: 77,944 mt/y
Pulp Mill Data:
Pulp Lines: 2
 Recycled Fiber Treatment Lines:
 Recycled packaging pulping lines: 2 at 90,000 admt/y
Paper/Paperboard Grades and Capacities:
 Total paper and paperboard capacity: 79,254 mt/y
 Corrugating medium/fluting: 79,254 mt/y
Paper and Paperboard Mill Data:
Paper Machines: 3
No. 1, cylinder, total capacity 7,497 mt/y, Trim width 2.82 m, Corrugating medium/fluting
No. 2, (idle since March 2008), cylinder, total capacity 7,497 mt/y, Trim width 2.82 m, Corrugating medium/fluting
No. 3, fourdrinier, total capacity 64,260 mt/y, Trim width 3.8 m, Corrugating medium/fluting
Energy Data:
Power boilers: 2
Electrical demand for mill: 124 MWh/D

ⓜGuangdong Shaoneng Group
No. 38 Nanxiong Rd.
Nanxiong, Guangdong, 512400
China
 Phone: (86) 751 382 0896
 Fax: (86) 751 387 0018
 Web Address: www.snzjp.com
Personnel:
 Pres.: Bing Xu
 Gen. Mgr.: Liexi Liu
Total Employees of Company: 200
Mill Locations:
Guangdong Shaoneng Group, Nanxiong Mill, No. 38 Nanxiong Rd., Nanxiong 512400, China, Capacity: 25,000 mt/y, (Paper mill)
 Phone: (86) 751 382 0896
 Fax: (86) 751 387 0018

China

ⓜGuangdong Shaoneng Group
Nanxiong Mill
No. 38 Nanxiong Rd.
Nanxiong, Guangdong, 512400
China
  Phone: (86) 751 382 0896
  Fax: (86) 751 387 0018
  Web Address: www.shaoneng.com.cn
Personnel:
  Pres.: Bing Xu
  Phone: (86) 751 382 0896
  Gen. Mgr.: Liexi Liu
  Phone: (86) 751 382 0896
Total Employees at this Location: 200
Type of Operation: Paper mill
Pulp Grades and Capacities:
  Total pulp capacity: 21,666 mt/y
  Other Pulp: 21,666 mt/y
Pulp Mill Data:
  Chemical Recovery Equipment:
    Recovery boilers: 1
Paper/Paperboard Grades and Capacities:
  Total paper and paperboard capacity: 25,000 mt/y
  Uncoated woodfree/freesheet: 25,000 mt/y
Paper and Paperboard Mill Data:
Paper Machines: 3
No. 1, cylinder, total capacity 4,300 mt/y, Trim width 1.58 m, Uncoated woodfree/freesheet
No. 2, fourdrinier, total capacity 8,000 mt/y, Trim width 1.88 m, Uncoated woodfree/freesheet
No. 3, fourdrinier, total capacity 12,700 mt/y, Trim width 2.36 m, Uncoated woodfree/freesheet
Energy Data:
Power boilers: 3
Electrical demand for mill: 78 MWh/D

ⓗGuangdong Shunde Sugar Co., Ltd.
Shatou Daliang, Shunde District
Foshan, Guangdong, 528333
China
  Phone: (86) 757 2229 2281/ 2232 6123/ 1775
  Fax: (86) 757 2232 1711
  Email: shuntang@163.com
  Web Address: www.gdsdtc.com
Personnel:
  Chmn. & Pres.: Zhiqiang Feng
  Phone: (86) 757 2229 2281/ 2232 6123/ 1775
  VP/Sls. & Mktg. Mgr.: Weiqiang Ou
  Phone: (86) 757 2229 2281/ 2232 6123/ 1775
  VP, Tech. Dir.: Xianben Kong
  Phone: (86) 757 2229 2281/ 2232 6123/ 1775
Mill Locations:
Guangdong Shunde Sugar Co., Ltd., Foshan Mill, Shatou Daliang, Shunde District, Foshan 528333, China, Capacity: 150,000 mt/y, (Paperboard mill)
  Phone: (86) 757 2229 2281/ 2232 6123/ 1775
  Fax: (86) 757 2232 1711
  Email: shuntang@163.com

ⓜGuangdong Shunde Sugar Co., Ltd.
Foshan Mill
Shatou Daliang, Shunde District
Foshan, Guangdong, 528333
China
  Phone: (86) 757 2229 2281/ 2232 6123/ 1775
  Fax: (86) 757 2232 1711
  Email: shuntang@163.com
  Web Address: www.shuntang.com
Personnel:
  Chmn. & Pres.: Zhiqiang Feng
  Phone: (86) 757 2229 2281/ 2232 6123/ 1775
  VP/Sls. & Mktg. Mgr.: Weiqiang Ou
  Phone: (86) 757 2229 2281/ 2232 6123/ 1775
  VP, Tech. Dir.: Xianben Kong
  Phone: (86) 757 2229 2281/ 2232 6123/ 1775
Total Employees at this Location: 530
Type of Operation: Paperboard mill
Paper/Paperboard Grades and Capacities:
  Total paper and paperboard capacity: 150,000 mt/y
  Linerboard: 80,000 mt/y
  Corrugating medium/fluting: 70,000 mt/y
Paper and Paperboard Mill Data:
Paper Machines: 6
PM 1, cylinder, total capacity 10,000 mt/y, Trim width 2.1 m, Corrugating medium/fluting
PM 2, cylinder, total capacity 15,000 mt/y, Trim width 2.36 m, Corrugating medium/fluting
PM 3, cylinder, total capacity 25,000 mt/y, Trim width 2.88 m, Corrugating medium/fluting
PM 4, cylinder, total capacity 30,000 mt/y, Trim width 2.88 m, Linerboard
PM 5, cylinder, total capacity 50,000 mt/y, Trim width 3.4 m, Linerboard
PM 6, cylinder, total capacity 20,000 mt/y, Trim width 2.36 m, Corrugating medium/fluting

ⓗGuangdong Taiyuan Paper Co., Ltd.
Ownership: 100% by private owners
Baimiao Industry Park, Sanjiang Town, Xinhui
Jiangmen, Guangdong, 529142
China
  Phone: (86) 750 620 6933/8968/6966
  Fax: (86) 750 620 6995
Mill Locations:
Guangdong Taiyuan Paper Co., Ltd., Jiangmen Mill, Baimiao Industry Park, Sanjiang Town, Xinhui, Jiangmen 529142, China, Capacity: 90,321 mt/y, (Paperboard mill)
  Phone: (86) 750 620 6933/8968/6966
  Fax: (86) 750 620 6995

ⓜGuangdong Taiyuan Paper Co., Ltd.
Jiangmen Mill
Baimiao Industry Park, Sanjiang Town, Xinhui
Jiangmen, Guangdong, 529142
China
  Phone: (86) 750 620 6933/8968/6966
  Fax: (86) 750 620 6995
Personnel:
  Chmn. & Pres.: Yinglai Liu
  Phone: (86) 750 620 6933/8968/6966
Total Employees at this Location: 300
Type of Operation: Paperboard mill
Pulp Grades and Capacities:
  Total pulp capacity: 87,771 mt/y
  Recycled Pulping: 87,771 mt/y
Pulp Mill Data:
Pulp Lines: 1
  Recycled Fiber Treatment Lines:
    Recycled packaging pulping lines: 1 at 100,000 admt/y
Paper/Paperboard Grades and Capacities:
  Total paper and paperboard capacity: 90,321 mt/y
  Corrugating medium/fluting: 90,321 mt/y
Paper and Paperboard Mill Data:
Paper Machines: 1
No. 1, fourdrinier, total capacity 90,321 mt/y, Trim width 3.6 m, Corrugating medium/fluting
Energy Data:
Power boilers: 1
Steam turbines: 1 at 6 MW
Electrical demand for mill: 137 MWh/D

ⓗⓜGuangdong Vinda Paper Co., Ltd.
Sanjiang Mill
Ownership: Vinda International Holdings Limited.
Baimiao Industrial Park, Sanjiang County, Xinhui District
Jiangmen, Guangdong, 529100
China
  Web Address: www.vindapaper.com
Total Employees at this Location: 330
Type of Operation: Paper mill
Paper/Paperboard Grades and Capacities:
  Total paper and paperboard capacity: 107,250 mt/y
  Tissue: 107,250 mt/y
Paper and Paperboard Mill Data:
Paper Machines: 6
No. 1, crescent former, Yankee dryer, total capacity 20,000 mt/y, Trim width 2.8 m, Tissue, Uncoated woodfree/freesheet
No. 2, crescent former, Yankee dryer, total capacity 20,000 mt/y, Trim width 2.8 m, Tissue, Uncoated woodfree/freesheet
No. 3, crescent former, Yankee dryer, total capacity 20,000 mt/y, Trim width 2.8 m, Tissue, Uncoated woodfree/freesheet
No. 4, crescent former, Yankee dryer, total capacity 20,000 mt/y, Trim width 2.8 m, Tissue, Uncoated woodfree/freesheet
No. 5, crescent former, Yankee dryer, total capacity 25,000 mt/y, Trim width 2.7 m, Uncoated woodfree/freesheet, Tissue
No. 6, crescent former, Yankee dryer, total capacity 25,000 mt/y, Trim width 2.7 m, Tissue, Uncoated woodfree/freesheet
Energy Data:
Power boilers: 1

ⓜGuangdong Vinda Paper (Guangdong) Co., Ltd.
Xinhui Mill
Ownership: Vinda International Holdings Limited.
Donghou Industrial Zone, Huicheng Town
Xinhui, Guangdong, 529100
China
  Phone: (86) 750 6122 846/6168 333
  Fax: (86) 750 6120 239
  Email: vd-computer@chinavinda.com
  Web Address: www.vindapaper.com
Personnel:
  Chmn.: Zhaowang Li
  Vice Chmn.: Yifang Yu
  Tech. Dir.: Yiping Dong
  CEO: Ms. Dongfang Zhang
Total Employees at this Location: 1,100
Type of Operation: Paper mill
Paper/Paperboard Grades and Capacities:
  Total paper and paperboard capacity: 57,000 mt/y
  Tissue: 57,000 mt/y
Paper and Paperboard Mill Data:
  Stock Preparation:
    Pulpers: 9
    Refiners: 4
Paper Machines: 3
No. 2, cylinder, total capacity 8,000 mt/y, Trim width 2.38 m, Tissue
No. 3, cylinder, total capacity 12,000 mt/y, Trim width 2.66 m, Tissue
No. 4, crescent former, total capacity 37,000 mt/y, Trim width 2.75 m, Tissue
Finishing Equipment:
  Rewinders: 6
  Sheeters: 3
Energy Data:
Power boilers: 2
Electrical demand for mill: 99 MWh/D

ⓜGuangdong Vinda Paper (Jiangmen) Co., Ltd.
Jiangmen Mill
Ownership: Vinda International Holdings Limited.
Yingbin Ave., Shuangshui Town, Xinhui Zone
Jiangmen, Guangdong, 529100
China
  Phone: (86) 86 750 641 3111
  Fax: (86) 86 750 641 3068
  Web Address: www.vindapaper.com
Total Employees at this Location: 450
Type of Operation: Paper mill
Paper/Paperboard Grades and Capacities:
  Total paper and paperboard capacity: 120,000 mt/y
  Tissue: 120,000 mt/y
Paper and Paperboard Mill Data:
Paper Machines: 6

No. 1, BF-12, Yankee dryer, total capacity 20,000 mt/y, Trim width 3.4 m, Tissue
No. 2, BF-12, Yankee dryer, total capacity 20,000 mt/y, Trim width 3.4 m, Tissue
No. 3, BF-12, Yankee dryer, total capacity 20,000 mt/y, Trim width 3.4 m, Tissue
No. 4, BF-12, Yankee dryer, total capacity 20,000 mt/y, Trim width 3.4 m, Tissue, Uncoated woodfree/freesheet
No. 5, BF-12, Yankee dryer, total capacity 20,000 mt/y, Trim width 3.4 m, Tissue, Uncoated woodfree/freesheet
No. 6, BF-12, Yankee dryer, total capacity 20,000 mt/y, Trim width 3.4 m, Tissue, Uncoated woodfree/freesheet
Energy Data:
Electrical demand for mill: 223 MWh/D

ⓘGuangdong Wanlida Paper
Ownership: Hong Kong Weng Yiu Group (joint venture)
Dongzhou District, Xintang Town
Zengcheng City, Guangdong, 511340
China
Phone: (86) 20 8268 2666/8279 4291
Fax: (86) 20 8277 6892
Mill Locations:
Guangdong Wanlida Paper, Guangzhou Mill, Dongzhou District, Xintang Town, Zengcheng City, Guangdong 511340, China, Capacity: 887,502 mt/y, (Paperboard mill)
Phone: (86) 20 8268 2666/8279 4291
Fax: (86) 20 8277 6892

ⓜGuangdong Wanlida Paper
Guangzhou Mill
Dongzhou District, Xintang Town, Zengcheng City
Guangzhou, Guangdong, 511340
China
Phone: (86) 20 8268 2666/8279 4291
Fax: (86) 20 8277 6892
Personnel:
Chmn./CEO/Pres.: Haoxin Zhong
Phone: (86) 20 8268 2666/8279 4291
CEO & Pres.: Zhixin Zhong
Phone: (86) 20 8268 2666/8279 4291
Gen. Mgr.: Runhao Li
Phone: (86) 20 8268 2666/8279 4291
VP, Technol. Mgr., Chief Eng.: Yuxiang Chen
Phone: (86) 20 8268 2666/8279 4291
Purch. Mgr.: Zhanyang Zhong
Phone: (86) 20 8268 2666/8279 4291
Total Employees at this Location: 1,200
Type of Operation: Paperboard mill
Pulp Grades and Capacities:
Total pulp capacity: 859,577 mt/y
Recycled Pulping: 859,577 mt/y
Pulp Mill Data:
Recycled Fiber Treatment Lines:
Recycled packaging pulping lines at 775,000
Paper/Paperboard Grades and Capacities:
Total paper and paperboard capacity: 887,502 mt/y
Linerboard: 567,630 mt/y
Corrugating medium/fluting: 319,872 mt/y
Paper and Paperboard Mill Data:
Paper Machines: 5
No. 1, multi-ply, total capacity 124,950 mt/y, Trim width 3.4 m, Linerboard
No. 2, multi-ply, total capacity 142,800 mt/y, Trim width 3.5 m, Linerboard
No. 3, multi-ply, total capacity 299,880 mt/y, Trim width 5.7 m, Linerboard
No. 4, multi-ply, total capacity 159,936 mt/y, Trim width 5.6 m, Corrugating medium/fluting
No. 5, multi-ply, total capacity 159,936 mt/y, Trim width 5.6 m, Corrugating medium/fluting
Energy Data:
Power boilers: 6
Steam turbines: 3 at 25, 50, 12 MW
Electrical demand for mill: 1,437 MWh/D

ⓘGuangdong Zhanjiang Guanlong Paper Co., Ltd.
Ownership: Guangdong Guanhao High-Tech Co., LTD.
Taiping Town, Mazhang Dist.
Zhanjiang, Guangdong, 524084
China
Phone: (86) 759 273 8001/8019/8020/8059
Fax: (86) 759 273 8009/8068/2865706
Email: guanlong@glpaper.com
Web Address: www.glpaper.com
Personnel:
Chmn.: Yangxu Huang
VP: Mr. Haibin Zhan
Total Employees at this Location: 370
Mill Locations:
Guangdong Zhanjiang Guanlong Paper Co., Ltd., Zhanjiang Mill, Taiping Town, Mazhang Dist., Zhanjiang 524084, China, Capacity: 60,000 mt/y, (Paper mill)
Phone: (86) 759 273 8001/8019/8020/8059
Fax: (86) 759 273 8009/8068/2865706
Email: guanlong@glpaper.com

ⓜGuangdong Zhanjiang Guanlong Paper Co., Ltd.
Zhanjiang Mill
Ownership: Guangdong Guanhao High-Tech Co., LTD.
Taiping Town, Mazhang Dist.
Zhanjiang, Guangdong, 524084
China
Phone: (86) 759 273 8001/8019/8020/8059
Fax: (86) 759 273 8009/8068/2865706
Email: guanlong@glpaper.com
Web Address: www.glpaper.com
Personnel:
Chmn.: Lairning Tong
Phone: (86) 759 273 8001/8019/8020/8059
Gen. Mgr.: Yangxu Huang
Total Employees at this Location: 370
Type of Operation: Paper mill
Paper/Paperboard Grades and Capacities:
Total paper and paperboard capacity: 60,000 mt/y
Uncoated woodfree/freesheet: 60,000 mt/y
Paper and Paperboard Mill Data:
Paper Machines: 1
No. 1, fourdrinier, total capacity 60,000 mt/y, Trim width 3.3 m, Uncoated woodfree/freesheet
Energy Data:
Power boilers: 1
Steam turbines: 3 at 3, 3, 3 MW
Electrical demand for mill: 170 MWh/D

ⓘⓜGuangdong Zhaoqing Kelun Paper Co., Ltd
Zhaoqing Mill
Dawang Development Zone
Zhaoqing, Guangdong
China
Total Employees at this Location: 150
Type of Operation: Paper mill
Paper/Paperboard Grades and Capacities:
Total paper and paperboard capacity: 99,960 mt/y
Packaging papers: 99,960 mt/y
Paper and Paperboard Mill Data:
Paper Machines: 1
No. 1, (second hand, started May 2011), fourdrinier, total capacity 99,960 mt/y, Trim width 4.2 m, Packaging papers
Energy Data:
Electrical demand for mill: 196 MWh/D

ⓘGuangdong Zhongshan Polly Paper Manufacture Co., Ltd.
Ownership: 100% by private owners
No. 38 Kunshan Rd., Haizhou, Guzhen Town
Zhongshan, Guangdong, 528422
China
Phone: (86) 760 2313 388/ 385
Fax: (86) 760 2313 389
Email: polly@zsnet.net.cn
Web Address: www.zspolly.com
Mill Locations:
Guangdong Zhongshan Polly Paper Manufacture Co., Ltd., Zhongshan Mill, No. 38 Kunshan Rd., Haizhou, Guzhen Town, Zhongshan 528422, China, Capacity: 20,000 mt/y, (Paper mill)
Phone: (86) 760 2313 388/ 385
Fax: (86) 760 2313 389
Email: polly@zsnet.net.cn

ⓜGuangdong Zhongshan Polly Paper Manufacture Co., Ltd.
Zhongshan Mill
No. 38 Kunshan Rd., Haizhou, Guzhen Town
Zhongshan, Guangdong, 528422
China
Phone: (86) 760 2313 388/ 385
Fax: (86) 760 2313 389
Email: polly@zsnet.net.cn
Web Address: zspolly.cn.gongchang.com
Personnel:
Gen. Mgr.: Zhaoyuan Huang
Phone: (86) 760 2313 388/ 385
Total Employees at this Location: 500
Type of Operation: Paper mill
Paper/Paperboard Grades and Capacities:
Total paper and paperboard capacity: 20,000 mt/y
Tissue: 20,000 mt/y
Paper and Paperboard Mill Data:
Paper Machines: 15
PM 1-11, cylinder, total capacity 1,250 mt/y, Trim width 1.58 m, Tissue
PM 12-15, cylinder, total capacity 1,600 mt/y, Trim width 1.76 m, Tissue
Energy Data:
Power boilers: 3
Steam turbines: 1 at 20 MW

ⓘGuangdong Zhongshan Sanjiao Paper Manufacture Co., Ltd.
Ownership: 100% by private owners
Aiguo Industrial Zone, Sanjiao Town
Zhongshan, Guangdong, 528445
China
Phone: (86) 760 2338 9328/8554 1208
Fax: (86) 760 8554 1038
Email: sanjiao@sjpaper.com
Mill Locations:
Guangdong Zhongshan Sanjiao Paper Manufacture Co., Ltd., Zhongshan Mill, Aiguo Industrial Zone, Sanjiao Town, Zhongshan 528445, China, Capacity: 37,000 mt/y, (Paper mill)
Phone: (86) 760 2338 9328/8554 1208
Fax: (86) 760 8554 1038
Email: sanjiao@sjpaper.com

ⓜGuangdong Zhongshan Sanjiao Paper Manufacture Co., Ltd.
Zhongshan Mill
Mill is temporarily closed (since Oct. 2008 for shortage of fund)
Aiguo Industrial Zone, Sanjiao Town
Zhongshan, Guangdong, 528445
China
Phone: (86) 760 2338 9328/8554 1208
Fax: (86) 760 8554 1038
Email: sanjiao@sjpaper.com
Personnel:
Gen. Mgr.: Fakun Yang
Phone: (86) 760 2338 9328/8554 1208
Total Employees at this Location: 1,000
Type of Operation: Paper mill
Paper/Paperboard Grades and Capacities:
Total paper and paperboard capacity: 37,000 mt/y
Tissue: 37,000 mt/y

China

Paper and Paperboard Mill Data:
Paper Machines: 60
PM 1-20, cylinder, total capacity 250 mt/y, Trim width 1.22 m, Tissue
PM 21-50, cylinder, total capacity 800 mt/y, Trim width 1.76 m, Tissue
Energy Data:
Power boilers: 3

ⓂGuangdong Zhongshan Yajieli Paper Co., Ltd.
Qunfu Industrial Park, Gangkou Town
Zhongshan, Guangdong, 528447
China
  Phone: (86) 760 8483 633
  Fax: (86) 760 8412 688
Mill Locations:
Guangdong Zhongshan Yajieli Paper Co., Ltd., Zhongshan Mill, Qunfu Industrial Park, Gangkou Town, Zhongshan 528447, China, Capacity: 15,000 mt/y, (Paper mill)
  Phone: (86) 760 8483 633
  Fax: (86) 760 8412 688

ⓂGuangdong Zhongshan Yajieli Paper Co., Ltd.
Zhongshan Mill
Qunfu Industrial Park, Gangkou Town
Zhongshan, Guangdong, 528447
China
  Phone: (86) 760 8483 633
  Fax: (86) 760 8412 688
Type of Operation: Paper mill
Paper/Paperboard Grades and Capacities:
  Total paper and paperboard capacity: 15,000 mt/y
  Tissue: 15,000 mt/y
Paper and Paperboard Mill Data:
Paper Machines: 11
PM 1, total capacity 1,400 mt/y, Trim width 1.58 m, Tissue
PM 2, total capacity 1,400 mt/y, Trim width 1.58 m, Tissue
PM 3, total capacity 1,400 mt/y, Trim width 1.58 m, Tissue
PM 4, total capacity 1,400 mt/y, Trim width 1.58 m, Tissue
PM 5, total capacity 1,400 mt/y, Trim width 1.58 m, Tissue
PM 6, total capacity 1,400 mt/y, Trim width 1.58 m, Tissue
PM 7, total capacity 1,400 mt/y, Trim width 1.58 m, Tissue
PM 8, total capacity 1,400 mt/y, Trim width 1.58 m, Tissue
PM 9, total capacity 1,400 mt/y, Trim width 1.58 m, Tissue
PM 10, total capacity 1,400 mt/y, Trim width 1.58 m, Tissue
PM 11, total capacity 1,400 mt/y, Trim width 1.58 m, Tissue

ⓂGuangdong Zhongshan Yongfa Paper Co., Ltd.
Ownership: 100% by Zhengye International Holdings Company Limited
Zhongshan Tangchangnei, Huangpu Town
Zhongshan, Guangdong, 528400
China
  Phone: (86) 760 2397 3117/ 2322 0773
  Fax: (86) 760 2332 5474
  Web Address: www.zhengye-cn.com
Personnel:
  Gen. Mgr.: Zheng Hu
  Phone: (86) 760 2397 3117/ 2322 0773
Mill Locations:
Guangdong Zhongshan Rengo Hung Hing Paper Mfg. Co. Ltd., Zhongshan Mill (58.70% owned), Westside of Zhongshan 3rd Bridge, No.105 National Rd., Zhongshan 528471, China, Capacity: 400,000 mt/y, (Paperboard mill)
  Phone: (86) 760 8779 6524/ 0563
  Fax: (86) 760 8779 6222
  Email: pmco@zsrghh.com, zsllj@163.com
Guangdong Zhongshan Yongfa Paper Co., Ltd., Zhongshan Mill, Zhongshan Tangchangnei, Huangpu Town, Zhongshan 528400, China, Capacity: 350,000 mt/y, (Paperboard mill)
  Phone: (86) 760 2397 3117/ 2322 0773
  Fax: (86) 760 2332 5474

ⓂGuangdong Zhongshan Yongfa Paper Co., Ltd.
Zhongshan Mill
Zhongshan Tangchangnei, Huangpu Town
Zhongshan, Guangdong, 528400
China
  Phone: (86) 760 2397 3117/ 2322 0773
  Fax: (86) 760 2332 5474
  Web Address: www.zhengye-cn.com
Personnel:
  Chmn.: Zheng Hu
  Phone: (86) 760 2397 3117/ 2322 0773
Total Employees at this Location: 1,200
Type of Operation: Paperboard mill
Pulp Grades and Capacities:
  Total pulp capacity: 346,532 mt/y
  Recycled Pulping: 346,532 mt/y
Pulp Mill Data:
  Recycled Fiber Treatment Lines:
  Recycled packaging pulping lines at 265,000
Paper/Paperboard Grades and Capacities:
  Total paper and paperboard capacity: 350,000 mt/y
  Corrugating medium/fluting: 350,000 mt/y
Paper and Paperboard Mill Data:
Paper Machines: 4
No. 1, fourdrinier, total capacity 70,000 mt/y, Trim width 3.6 m, Corrugating medium/fluting
No. 2, fourdrinier, total capacity 100,000 mt/y, Trim width 4 m, Corrugating medium/fluting
No. 3, fourdrinier, total capacity 100,000 mt/y, Trim width 4.6 m, Corrugating medium/fluting
No. 5, fourdrinier, total capacity 80,000 mt/y, Trim width 4 m, Corrugating medium/fluting
Energy Data:
Power boilers: 1
Steam turbines at 33 MW
Electrical demand for mill: 440 MWh/D

ⓂGuangdong Zhongshan Rengo Hung Hing Paper Mfg. Co. Ltd.
Zhongshan Mill
Ownership: 58.70% by Guangdong Yongfa Paper Co., Ltd., 30% by Rengo, 3.80% by Hong Kong Hung Hing Printing Group Ltd., 7.50% by Guangdong Zhongshan Packaging
Westside of Zhongshan 3rd Bridge, No.105 National Rd.
Zhongshan, Guangdong, 528471
China
  Phone: (86) 760 8779 6524/ 0563
  Fax: (86) 760 8779 6222
  Email: pmco@zsrghh.com, zsllj@163.com
  Web Address: www.zsrghh.com/introduction.htm
Personnel:
  Chmn., CEO & Pres.: Haoming Ren
  Phone: (86) 760 8779 6524/ 0563
  Gen. Mgr.: Guowei Li
  Phone: (86) 760 8779 6524/ 0563
  VP-Technology/Chief Eng.: Shinoka Hiroaki
  Phone: (86) 760 8779 6524/ 0563
  VP - Operations, Mill Mgr.: Zhaopei Deng
  Phone: (86) 760 8779 6524/ 0563
  Sls. Mgr.: Dayue Sun
  Phone: (86) 760 779 6524
  Email: zsllj@163.com
Total Employees at this Location: 955
Type of Operation: Paperboard mill
Pulp Grades and Capacities:
  Total pulp capacity: 388,434 mt/y
  Recycled Pulping: 388,434 mt/y
Pulp Mill Data:
  Recycled Fiber Treatment Lines:
  Recycled packaging pulping lines
Paper/Paperboard Grades and Capacities:
  Total paper and paperboard capacity: 400,000 mt/y
  Linerboard: 200,000 mt/y
  Corrugating medium/fluting: 200,000 mt/y
Paper and Paperboard Mill Data:
Paper Machines: 3
No. 1, fourdrinier, total capacity 100,000 mt/y, Trim width 4 m, Corrugating medium/fluting
No. 3, Multi-wire (3), total capacity 200,000 mt/y, Trim width 5.5 m, Linerboard
No. 4, twin-wire, total capacity 100,000 mt/y, Trim width 4 m, Corrugating medium/fluting
Finishing Equipment:
  Rewinders: 4
  Sheeters: 2
Energy Data:
  Power boilers: 2
  Combustion turbines: 2 at 24 MW
  Electrical demand for mill: 505 MWh/D

ⓄⓂGuangdong Zhongsheng Paper Co., Ltd
Zhaoqing Mill
Shouyue Village, Nanjie Town, Guangning County
Zhaoqing, Guangdong
China
  Phone: (86) 758 8657 470
Personnel:
  Chmn.: Yaoxin Zhong
Type of Operation: Paper mill
Paper/Paperboard Grades and Capacities:
  Total paper and paperboard capacity: 110,000 mt/y
  Uncoated woodfree/freesheet: 110,000 mt/y
Paper and Paperboard Mill Data:
Paper Machines: 4
PM 1, total capacity 20,000 mt/y, Trim width 1.76 m, Uncoated woodfree/freesheet
PM 2, total capacity 20,000 mt/y, Trim width 1.76 m, Uncoated woodfree/freesheet
PM 3, fourdrinier, total capacity 35,000 mt/y, Trim width 2.64 m, Uncoated woodfree/freesheet
PM 4, fourdrinier, total capacity 35,000 mt/y, Trim width 2.64 m, Uncoated woodfree/freesheet

ⓄGuangdong Zhuhai S.E.Z. Hongta Renheng Paper Co. Ltd.
Ownership: China Chengtong Holding Group Ltd., 41.97% by Foshan Huaxin Packaging Co., Ltd, 11.60% by Longbang International Limited, 13.93% by Singapore Renheng Investment Corp., 32.50% by Yunnan Hongta Group
508 West Jinji Rd., Qianshan District
Zhuhai, Guangdong, 519070
China
  Phone: (86) 756 866 6888
  Fax: (86) 756 861 5037
  Email: zhhtrh@htrh-paper.com
  Web Address: www.htrh-paper.com
Personnel:
  Gen. Mgr.: Xiandong Ji
  COO: Linong Zhang
  Tech. Mgr., VP, Chief. Eng: Jiang Wu
  Sls Mgr.: Minghui Peng
  Phone: (86) 756 866 8888
  Fax: (86) 756 861 5037
Total Employees at this Location: 1,576
Mill Locations:
Guangdong Zhuhai S.E.Z. Hongta Renheng Paper Co. Ltd., Zhuhai (Gaolangang) Mill, Riverside Road No. 17, Zhuhai 528000, China, Capacity: 300,000 mt/y, (Paperboard mill)
  Phone: (86) 757 8281 6867/ 8281 2282
  Fax: (86) 757 8281 3125/ 8281 0459
Guangdong Zhuhai S.E.Z. Hongta Renheng Paper Co. Ltd., Zhuhai (Qianshan) Mill, 508 West Jinji Rd., Qianshan District, Zhuhai 519070, China, Capacity: 300,000 mt/y, (Paper mill, Paperboard mill)
  Phone: (86) 756 866 6888
  Fax: (86) 756 861 5037
  Email: zhhtrh@htrh-paper.com

China

ⓜGuangdong Zhuhai S.E.Z. Hongta Renheng Paper Co. Ltd.
Zhuhai (Gaolangang) Mill
Ownership: China Chengtong Holding Group Ltd.
Riverside Road No. 17
Zhuhai, Guangdong, 528000
China
 Phone: (86) 757 8281 6867/ 8281 2282
 Fax: (86) 757 8281 3125/ 8281 0459
 Web Address: www.hfpaper.cn
Personnel:
 Vice. Gen. Mgr.: Fu Ji
 Phone: (86) 756 7713291
Total Employees at this Location: 680
Type of Operation: Paperboard mill
Paper/Paperboard Grades and Capacities:
 Total paper and paperboard capacity: 300,000 mt/y
 Boxboard/cartonboard: 300,000 mt/y
Paper and Paperboard Mill Data:
Paper Machines: 1
 No. 3, fourdrinier, total capacity 300,000 mt/y, Trim width 4.65 m, Boxboard/cartonboard
Coating Machines: 1
 PM 3, total capacity 300,000 mt/y., on machine
Energy Data:
 Power boilers: 2
 Steam turbines: 2 at 15, 15 MW

ⓜGuangdong Zhuhai S.E.Z. Hongta Renheng Paper Co. Ltd.
Zhuhai (Qianshan) Mill
Ownership: China Chengtong Holding Group Ltd.
508 West Jinji Rd., Qianshan District
Zhuhai, Guangdong, 519070
China
 Phone: (86) 756 866 6888
 Fax: (86) 756 861 5037
 Email: zhhtrh@htrh-paper.com
 Web Address: www.htrh-paper.com
Personnel:
 Gen. Mgr., Dpty. Mgr: Yun Lin
 Phone: (86) 756 866 6888
 COO: Linong Zhang
 Phone: (86) 756 866 6888
 Tech. Mgr., VP, Chief. Eng: Jiang Wu
 Phone: (86) 756 866 6888
 Sls Mgr.: Minghui Peng
 Phone: (86) 756 866 8888
 Fax: (86) 756 861 5037
Total Employees at this Location: 896
Type of Operation: Paper mill, Paperboard mill
Pulp Mill Data:
 Chemical Recovery Equipment:
  Recovery boilers
Paper/Paperboard Grades and Capacities:
 Total paper and paperboard capacity: 300,000 mt/y
 Boxboard/cartonboard: 300,000 mt/y
Paper and Paperboard Mill Data:
 Stock Preparation:
  Pulpers: 17
  Refiners: 9
Paper Machines: 2
 No. 1, fourdrinier (3), total capacity 70,000 mt/y, Trim width 2.4 m, Boxboard/cartonboard
 No. 2, fourdrinier (3), total capacity 230,000 mt/y, Trim width 4.2 m, Boxboard/cartonboard
Finishing Equipment:
 Rewinders: 2
 Sheeters: 2
Energy Data:
 Power boilers: 5

ⓘGuangdong Zhuhai Jiangqiao Special Paper Co. Ltd.
Ownership: 100% by shareholders
No. 2 Honghui Rd., Hongqi Town, Jinwan Dist.
Zhuhai, Guangdong, 519090
China
 Phone: (86) 756 336 2277
 Fax: (86) 756 336 4719
Mill Locations:
 Guangdong Zhuhai Jiangqiao Special Paper Co. Ltd., Zhuhai Mill, No. 2 Honghui Rd., Hongqi Town, Jinwan Dist., Zhuhai 519090, China, Capacity: 15,000 mt/y, (Paper mill)
 Phone: (86) 756 336 2277
 Fax: (86) 756 336 4719

ⓜGuangdong Zhuhai Jiangqiao Special Paper Co. Ltd.
Zhuhai Mill
No. 2 Honghui Rd., Hongqi Town, Jinwan Dist.
Zhuhai, Guangdong, 519090
China
 Phone: (86) 756 336 2277
 Fax: (86) 756 336 4719
Personnel:
 Gen. Mgr.: Shikai Zhang
 Phone: (86) 756 336 2277
Total Employees at this Location: 300
Type of Operation: Paper mill
Paper/Paperboard Grades and Capacities:
 Total paper and paperboard capacity: 15,000 mt/y
 Uncoated woodfree/freesheet: 15,000 mt/y
Paper and Paperboard Mill Data:
Paper Machines: 1
 PM 1, fourdrinier, total capacity 15,000 mt/y, Trim width 2.64 m, Uncoated woodfree/freesheet
Finishing Equipment:
 Winders

ⓘGuangzhou Hongjieda Paper Co., Ltd.
No.127 Sansha Street, Lingshan Town, Fanyu District
Guangzhou, Guangdong, 511483
China
 Phone: (86) 20 8492 8128
 Fax: (86) 20 8492 7398
Mill Locations:
 Guangzhou Hongjieda Paper Co., Ltd., Guangzhou Mill, No.127 Sansha Street, Lingshan Town, Fanyu District, Guangzhou 511483, China, Capacity: 8,000 mt/y, (Paper mill)
 Phone: (86) 20 8492 8128
 Fax: (86) 20 8492 7398

ⓜGuangzhou Hongjieda Paper Co., Ltd.
Guangzhou Mill
No.127 Sansha Street, Lingshan Town, Fanyu District
Guangzhou, Guangdong, 511483
China
 Phone: (86) 20 8492 8128
 Fax: (86) 20 8492 7398
Type of Operation: Paper mill
Paper/Paperboard Grades and Capacities:
 Total paper and paperboard capacity: 8,000 mt/y
 Tissue: 8,000 mt/y
Paper and Paperboard Mill Data:
Paper Machines: 7
 PM 1, total capacity 1,150 mt/y, Trim width 1.58 m, Tissue
 PM 2, total capacity 1,150 mt/y, Trim width 1.58 m, Tissue
 PM 3, total capacity 1,150 mt/y, Trim width 1.58 m, Tissue
 PM 4, total capacity 1,150 mt/y, Trim width 1.58 m, Tissue
 PM 5, total capacity 1,150 mt/y, Trim width 1.58 m, Tissue
 PM 6, total capacity 1,150 mt/y, Trim width 1.58 m, Tissue
 PM 7, total capacity 1,150 mt/y, Trim width 1.58 m, Tissue

ⓜGuangzhou Paper Group Ltd. (Nansha)
Guangzhou Mill
Ownership: Guangzhou Paper Group Ltd.
No. 29, Xinguang Rd., Nansha District
Guangzhou, Guangdong, 511462
China
 Phone: (86) 20 3466 3302
 Fax: (86) 20 8494 6051
 Email: gzzc@gzpaper.cn
 Web Address: www.gzpaper.com.cn
Total Employees at this Location: 400
Type of Operation: Paper mill
Pulp Grades and Capacities:
 Total pulp capacity: 550,365 mt/y
 Recycled Pulping: 550,365 mt/y
Pulp Mill Data:
Pulp Lines: 1
 Bleach Plant Systems: 1
  No. 1
 Recycled Fiber Treatment Lines:
  Flotation deinking lines
Paper/Paperboard Grades and Capacities:
 Total paper and paperboard capacity: 600,000 mt/y
 Newsprint: 600,000 mt/y
Paper and Paperboard Mill Data:
Paper Machines: 3
 No. 1, OptiConcept, total capacity 150,000 mt/y, Trim width 5.3 m, Newsprint
 No. 5, total capacity 50,000 mt/y, Trim width 3.94 m, Newsprint
 No. 9, OptiConcept, total capacity 400,000 mt/y, Trim width 10.2 m, Newsprint
Energy Data:
 Power boilers: 2
 Steam turbines: 1
 Electrical demand for mill: 1,625 MWh/D

ⓜGuangzhou Qiming Paper Co., Ltd.
Guangzhou Mill
No.2 Third Zhutang Rd., Nansha District
Guangzhou, Guangdong, 511462
China
 Phone: (86) 20 8494 9777
 Fax: (86) 20 8452 5050
Type of Operation: Paper mill
Paper/Paperboard Grades and Capacities:
 Total paper and paperboard capacity: 18,000 mt/y
 Tissue: 18,000 mt/y

ⓜGuangzhou Victorgo Industry Co., Ltd.
Guangzhou (Guangzhou Victorgo) Mill
Ownership: Guangzhou Paper Group Ltd.
No. 29, Xinguang Rd., Nansha District
Guangzhou, Guangdong, 511462
China
 Phone: (86) 020 3466 3302
 Fax: (86) 020 8494 6051
 Email: gzzc@gzpaper.cn
 Web Address: www.gzpaper.com.cn
Personnel:
 Chmn.: Chunfu Chen
 Phone: (86) 020 8430 8993/ 2772/ 8494 5043
 CEO/Pres.: Weixing Chen
 Phone: (86) 020 8430 8993/ 2772/ 8494 5043
Total Employees at this Location: 800
Type of Operation: Paperboard mill
Pulp Grades and Capacities:
 Total pulp capacity: 149,543 mt/y
 Recycled Pulping: 149,543 mt/y
Pulp Mill Data:
 Recycled Fiber Treatment Lines:
  Flotation deinking lines: 1
  Recycled packaging pulping lines: 1
Paper/Paperboard Grades and Capacities:
 Total paper and paperboard capacity: 178,500 mt/y
 Boxboard/cartonboard: 178,500 mt/y
Paper and Paperboard Mill Data:
Paper Machines: 1
 No. 1, DuoFormer D, total capacity 178,500 mt/y, Trim width 3.45 m, Boxboard/cartonboard
Coating Machines: 1
 CM 1, total capacity 170,000 mt/y., on machine
Energy Data:
 Power boilers: 2
 Steam turbines: 3 at 6, 6, 6 MW
 Electrical demand for mill: 292 MWh/D

China

ⓗGuangzhou Zhujiang Specialty Paper Co. ,Ltd.
Ownership: 100% by shareholders
Wuheng Rd., Yuan Village, Tianhe District
Guangzhou, Guangdong, 510655
China
　Phone: (86) 20 8553 8904/8552 4155
　Fax: (86) 20 8552 4827/8554 2497
　Email: psppaper@163.com
　Web Address: www.psppaper.com
Mill Locations:
　Guangzhou Zhujiang Specialty Paper Co. ,Ltd., Guangzhou Mill, Wuheng Rd., Yuan Village, Tianhe District, Guangzhou 510655, China, Capacity: 10,000 mt/y, (Paper mill)
　Phone: (86) 20 8553 2324/8552 4200/5149/4155
　Fax: (86) 20 8552 4827/8554 2497
　Email: pspzhi@163.com

ⓜGuangzhou Zhujiang Specialty Paper Co. ,Ltd.
Guangzhou Mill
Wuheng Rd., Yuan Village, Tianhe District
Guangzhou, Guangdong, 510655
China
　Phone: (86) 20 8553 2324/8552 4200/5149/4155
　Fax: (86) 20 8552 4827/8554 2497
　Email: pspzhi@163.com
　Web Address: www.pspzhujiang.com
Personnel:
　Chmn. & Pres.: Guangrui Zhong
　Phone: (86) 20 8553 8904/8552 4155
　Chief. Eng.: Shinan Xiao
　Phone: (86) 20 8553 8904/8552 4155
Total Employees at this Location: 230
Type of Operation: Paper mill
Pulp Mill Data:
　Chemical Pulping Systems:
　Batch digesters: 5
　Continuous digesters: 1
Paper/Paperboard Grades and Capacities:
　Total paper and paperboard capacity: 10,000 mt/y
　Specialty and industrial: 10,000 mt/y
Paper and Paperboard Mill Data:
Paper Machines: 1
　PM 2, fourdrinier, total capacity 10,000 mt/y, Trim width 1.58 m, Specialty and industrial

ⓗⓜJiangmen Hongxiang Paper Co. Ltd (YY Group)
Jiangmen Mill
No.8, Ziyun Rd., Huicheng, Xinhui District
Jiangmen, Guangdong
China
　Phone: (86) 750 6680 726
　Fax: (86) 750 6680 716
　Web Address: www.yygroup.cn/hx
Total Employees of Company: 80
Total Employees at this Location: 80
Type of Operation: Paper mill
Paper/Paperboard Grades and Capacities:
　Total paper and paperboard capacity: 10,000 mt/y
　Tissue: 10,000 mt/y
Paper and Paperboard Mill Data:
Paper Machines: 3
　PM 1-3, (Local papermachine), total capacity 10,000 mt/y, Trim width 1.76 m, Tissue
Energy Data:
　Power boilers

ⓗJiangmen Rijia Paper Co., Ltd.
No.1, Chaolian Merchants Industrial Park
Jiangmen, Guangdong, 529090
China
　Phone: (86) 750 3727 816
　Fax: (86) 750 3726 328
Mill Locations:
　Jiangmen Rijia Paper Co., Ltd., Jiangmen Mill, No.1, Chaolian Merchants Industrial Park, Jiangmen 529090, China, Capacity: 12,000 mt/y, (Paper mill)
　Phone: (86) 750 3727 816
　Fax: (86) 750 3726 328

ⓜJiangmen Rijia Paper Co., Ltd.
Jiangmen Mill
No.1, Chaolian Merchants Industrial Park
Jiangmen, Guangdong, 529090
China
　Phone: (86) 750 3727 816
　Fax: (86) 750 3726 328
Type of Operation: Paper mill
Paper/Paperboard Grades and Capacities:
　Total paper and paperboard capacity: 12,000 mt/y
　Tissue: 12,000 mt/y

ⓗⓜJiangmen Xinghui Paper Mill Co., Ltd
Jiangmen Mill
Ownership: 60% by Hokuetsu Kishu Paper Co. Ltd., 10% by Mitsubishi Corporation, 30% by Hop Cheong Paper
Yinzhouhu Paper Making Park, Shuangshui Town, Xinhui District
Jiangmen, Guangdong
China
Type of Operation: Paper mill
Pulp Grades and Capacities:
　Total pulp capacity: 205,272 mt/y
　Recycled Pulping: 205,272 mt/y
Paper/Paperboard Grades and Capacities:
　Total paper and paperboard capacity: 240,000 mt/y
　Boxboard/cartonboard: 240,000 mt/y
Paper and Paperboard Mill Data:
Paper Machines: 1
　No. 1, Fourdrinier (4), total capacity 240,000 mt/y, Trim width 4.36 m, Boxboard/cartonboard
Energy Data:
　Electrical demand for mill: 312 MWh/D

ⓜShandong Huatai Group Co., Ltd.
Jiangmen Mill
Lingtou Industrial Park, Shuangshui Town, Xinhui District
Jiangmen, Guangdong, 529153
China
　Phone: (86) 750 3411 768/728
　Web Address: www.huatai.com
Total Employees at this Location: 185
Type of Operation: Paper mill
Pulp Grades and Capacities:
　Total pulp capacity: 180,328 mt/y
　Recycled Pulping: 180,328 mt/y
Pulp Mill Data:
　Bleach Plant Systems: 1
　Recycled Pulping System, Type: Deinked
　Recycled Fiber Treatment Lines:
　Flotation deinking lines: 1
Paper/Paperboard Grades and Capacities:
　Total paper and paperboard capacity: 200,000 mt/y
　Newsprint: 200,000 mt/y
Paper and Paperboard Mill Data:
Paper Machines: 1
　No. 1, OptiFormer, total capacity 200,000 mt/y, Trim width 5.56 m, Newsprint
Energy Data:
　Electrical demand for mill: 590 MWh/D

ⓗShantou Piaohe Paper Co., Ltd.
Juding Industrial Park, Jinping District
Shantou, Guangdong, 515061
China
　Phone: (86) 754 8827 9165/8253 0777/8253 3777
　Fax: (86) 754 8251 5777/8254 3324
　Email: piaohep1660@sina.com
　Web Address: www.piaohe.cn
Mill Locations:
　Shantou Piaohe Paper Co., Ltd., Shantou Mill, Juding Industrial Park, Jinping District, Shantou 515061, China, Capacity: 68,000 mt/y, (Paper mill)
　Phone: (86) 754 8827 9165/8253 0777/8253 3777
　Fax: (86) 754 8251 5777/8254 3324
　Email: piaohep1660@sina.com

ⓜShantou Piaohe Paper Co., Ltd.
Shantou Mill
Juding Industrial Park, Jinping District
Shantou, Guangdong, 515061
China
　Phone: (86) 754 8827 9165/8253 0777/8253 3777
　Fax: (86) 754 8251 5777/8254 3324
　Email: piaohep1660@sina.com
　Web Address: www.piaohe.cn
Type of Operation: Paper mill
Paper/Paperboard Grades and Capacities:
　Total paper and paperboard capacity: 68,000 mt/y
　Tissue: 68,000 mt/y
Paper and Paperboard Mill Data:
Paper Machines: 17
　PM 1, total capacity 4,000 mt/y, Trim width 2.85 m, Tissue
　PM 2, total capacity 4,000 mt/y, Trim width 2.85 m, Tissue
　PM 3, total capacity 4,000 mt/y, Trim width 2.85 m, Tissue
　PM 4, total capacity 4,000 mt/y, Trim width 2.85 m, Tissue
　PM 5, total capacity 4,000 mt/y, Trim width 2.85 m, Tissue
　PM 6, total capacity 4,000 mt/y, Trim width 2.85 m, Tissue
　PM 7, total capacity 4,000 mt/y, Trim width 2.85 m, Tissue
　PM 8, total capacity 4,000 mt/y, Trim width 2.85 m, Tissue
　PM 9, total capacity 4,000 mt/y, Trim width 2.85 m, Tissue
　PM 10, cylinder, total capacity 4,000 mt/y, Trim width 2.95 m, Tissue
　PM 11, cylinder, total capacity 4,000 mt/y, Trim width 2.95 m, Tissue
　PM 12, cylinder, total capacity 4,000 mt/y, Trim width 2.95 m, Tissue
　PM 13, cylinder, total capacity 4,000 mt/y, Trim width 2.95 m, Tissue
　PM 14, cylinder, total capacity 4,000 mt/y, Trim width 2.95 m, Tissue
　PM 15, cylinder, total capacity 4,000 mt/y, Trim width 2.95 m, Tissue
　PM 16, cylinder, total capacity 4,000 mt/y, Trim width 2.95 m
　PM 17, total capacity 4,000 mt/y, Trim width 2.95 m, Tissue

ⓜZhanjiang Chenming Paper Pulp Co., Ltd.
Zhanjiang (Zhanjiang Chenming Pulp & Paper) Mill
Ownership: 100% by Chenming Paper Holdings Ltd.
Zhanjiang, Guangdong
China
　Phone: (86) 759 8216 086/087
　Web Address: www.chenmingpaper.com
Personnel:
　Dir. & Dep. Gen. Mgr.: Geng GuangLin
Total Employees at this Location: 1,250
Type of Operation: Pulp mill, Paper mill
Pulp Grades and Capacities:
　Total pulp capacity: 850,000 mt/y
　Pulp available for market: 413,564 mt/y
　Chemical Pulp: 850,000 mt/y
Pulp Mill Data:
　Chemical Pulping Systems:
　Continuous digesters: 1
Pulp Lines: 1
　Bleach Plant Systems: 1
　Chemical Pulping System - Hardwood, Type: Hardwood - ECF, Sequence: O_2 DEopDPo
　Chemical Recovery Equipment:
　Evaporator lines: 1
　Recovery boilers: 1
　Lime Kiln
　Pulp Dryers:
　Other dryers 1
Paper/Paperboard Grades and Capacities:
　Total paper and paperboard capacity: 649,820 mt/y

Uncoated woodfree/freesheet: 649,820 mt/y
Paper and Paperboard Mill Data:
Paper Machines: 1
No. 1, GapFormer, total capacity 649,820 mt/y, Trim width 10.5 m, Uncoated woodfree/freesheet
Finishing Equipment:
Sheeters: 2
Energy Data:
Power boilers: 3
Steam turbines: 3 at 180 MW
Electrical demand for mill: 2,563 MWh/D

GUANGXI

Guangxi Baise Hezhong Paper Co., Ltd.
Longjing Community, Youjiang District
Baise, Guangxi, 533000
China
Phone: (86) 776 2786 073
Mill Locations:
Guangxi Baise Hezhong Paper Co., Ltd., Baise Mill, Longjing Community, Youjiang District, Baise 533000, China, Capacity: 32,000 mt/y, (Paper mill)
Phone: (86) 776 2786 073

Guangxi Baise Hezhong Paper Co., Ltd.
Baise Mill
Longjing Community, Youjiang District
Baise, Guangxi, 533000
China
Phone: (86) 776 2786 073
Type of Operation: Paper mill
Paper/Paperboard Grades and Capacities:
Total paper and paperboard capacity: 32,000 mt/y
Tissue: 32,000 mt/y
Paper and Paperboard Mill Data:
Paper Machines: 16
PM 1-14, total capacity 1,430 mt/y, Trim width 1.58 m, Tissue
PM 15-16, total capacity 6,000 mt/y, Trim width 3.9 m, Tissue

Guangxi Binyang Daqiao Paper Co., Ltd.
Nanning (Binyang Daqiao) Mill
Ownership: Guangxi Yongkai Sugar and Paper Group
No. 167 Nanwu Str., Daqiao Town, Binyang County
Nanning, Guangxi, 530408
China
Phone: (86) 771 8111 511
Fax: (86) 771 8111 007
Email: dqbgs@yongkai.com.cn
Web Address: www.yksugar.com
Total Employees at this Location: 350
Type of Operation: Paper mill
Paper/Paperboard Grades and Capacities:
Total paper and paperboard capacity: 199,920 mt/y
Uncoated woodfree/freesheet: 199,920 mt/y
Paper and Paperboard Mill Data:
Paper Machines: 2
No. 1, hybrid former, total capacity 99,960 mt/y, Trim width 4.5 m, Uncoated woodfree/freesheet
No. 2, hybrid former, total capacity 99,960 mt/y, Trim width 4.5 m, Uncoated woodfree/freesheet
Finishing Equipment:
Sheeters: 2
Energy Data:
Power boilers: 2
Steam turbines at 25 MW
Electrical demand for mill: 389 MWh/D

Guangxi Binyang Jiangnan Paper Co., Ltd.
Xinqiao Industrial Park, Binyang County
Nanning, Guangxi, 530401
China
Phone: (86) 771 8481 038
Mill Locations:
Guangxi Binyang Jiangnan Paper Co., Ltd., Nanning Mill, Xinqiao Industrial Park, Binyang County, Nanning 530401, China, Capacity: 13,000 mt/y, (Paper mill)
Phone: (86) 771 8481 038
Guangxi Heng County Jiangnan Paper Co., Ltd., Nanning Mill, Liujing Industrial Park, Heng County, Nanning 530313, China, Capacity: 20,000 mt/y, (Paper mill)
Phone: (86) 771 8481 038

Guangxi Binyang Jiangnan Paper Co., Ltd.
Nanning Mill
Xinqiao Industrial Park, Binyang County
Nanning, Guangxi, 530401
China
Phone: (86) 771 8481 038
Type of Operation: Paper mill
Paper/Paperboard Grades and Capacities:
Total paper and paperboard capacity: 13,000 mt/y
Tissue: 13,000 mt/y
Paper and Paperboard Mill Data:
Paper Machines: 3
PM 1, cylinder, total capacity 3,000 mt/y, Trim width 1.65 m, Tissue
PM 2, fourdrinier, total capacity 5,000 mt/y, Trim width 2.1 m, Tissue
PM 3, fourdrinier, total capacity 5,000 mt/y, Trim width 2.1 m, Tissue

Guangxi Boguan Paper Co., Ltd.
Hechi Mill
Luodong Industrial Park, Yizhou City
Hechi, Guangxi
China
Phone: (86) 778 3978 075
Fax: (86) 778 3978 057
Web Address: www.gxboguan.com
Total Employees at this Location: 35
Type of Operation: Pulp mill
Pulp Grades and Capacities:
Total pulp capacity: 68,000 mt/y
Pulp available for market: 68,000 mt/y
Other Pulp: 68,000 mt/y
Pulp Mill Data:
Chemical Pulping Systems:
Continuous digesters: 1
Pulp Lines: 1
Bleach Plant Lines:
No. 1, Type: TCF, Sequence: O₂ OQEpP, Capacity 68,000 admt/y
Energy Data:
Electrical demand for mill: 107 MWh/D

Guangxi Chongzuo Daming Paper Co., Ltd.
Zuojiang Economic Development Zone, Zuojiang District
Chongzuo, Guangxi, 532206
China
Phone: (86) 771 7958 888
Web Address: www.cndmgroup.com
Mill Locations:
Guangxi Chongzuo Daming Paper Co., Ltd., Chongzuo Mill, Zuojiang Economic Development Zone, Zuojiang District, Chongzuo 532206, China, Capacity: 24,000 mt/y, (Paper mill)
Phone: (86) 771 7958 888

Guangxi Chongzuo Daming Paper Co., Ltd.
Chongzuo Mill
Zuojiang Economic Development Zone, Zuojiang District
Chongzuo, Guangxi, 532206
China
Phone: (86) 771 7958 888
Type of Operation: Paper mill
Paper/Paperboard Grades and Capacities:
Total paper and paperboard capacity: 24,000 mt/y
Tissue: 24,000 mt/y

Guangxi Chongzuo Huamei Paper Co., Ltd.
Chongzuo Mill
Ownership: Guangxi Huamei Paper Group Co., Ltd.
Light Industrial Park Of Candy, City Industrial Zone
Chongzuo, Guangxi, 532200
China
Phone: (86) 771 7965 877/7963 579
Fax: (86) 771 7965 977
Web Address: www.hmpaper.cn
Total Employees at this Location: 500
Type of Operation: Paper mill
Paper/Paperboard Grades and Capacities:
Total paper and paperboard capacity: 60,000 mt/y
Tissue: 60,000 mt/y
Paper and Paperboard Mill Data:
Paper Machines: 40
No. 1, (Local PMs), cylinder, total capacity 1,200 mt/y, Trim width 1.88 m, Tissue
No. 2, (Local PMs), cylinder, total capacity 1,200 mt/y, Trim width 1.88 m, Tissue
No. 3, (Local PMs), cylinder, total capacity 1,200 mt/y, Trim width 1.88 m, Tissue
No. 4, (Local PMs), cylinder, total capacity 1,200 mt/y, Trim width 1.88 m, Tissue
No. 5, (Local PMs), cylinder, total capacity 1,200 mt/y, Trim width 1.88 m, Tissue
No. 6, (Local PMs), cylinder, total capacity 1,200 mt/y, Trim width 1.88 m, Tissue
No. 7, (Local PMs), cylinder, total capacity 1,200 mt/y, Trim width 1.88 m, Tissue
No. 8, (Local PMs), cylinder, total capacity 1,200 mt/y, Trim width 1.88 m, Tissue
No. 9, (Local PMs), cylinder, total capacity 1,200 mt/y, Trim width 1.88 m, Tissue
No. 10, (Local PMs), total capacity 1,200 mt/y, Trim width 1.88 m, Tissue
No. 11, (Local PMs), cylinder, total capacity 1,200 mt/y, Trim width 1.88 m, Tissue
No. 12, (Local PMs), cylinder, total capacity 1,200 mt/y, Trim width 1.88 m, Tissue
No. 13, (Local PMs), cylinder, total capacity 1,200 mt/y, Trim width 1.88 m, Tissue
No. 14, (Local PMs), cylinder, total capacity 1,200 mt/y, Trim width 1.88 m, Tissue
No. 15, (Local PMs), cylinder, total capacity 1,200 mt/y, Trim width 1.88 m, Tissue
No. 16, (Local PMs), cylinder, total capacity 1,200 mt/y, Trim width 1.88 m, Tissue
No. 17, (Local PMs), cylinder, total capacity 1,200 mt/y, Trim width 1.88 m, Tissue
No. 18, (Local PMs), cylinder, total capacity 1,200 mt/y, Trim width 1.88 m, Tissue
No. 19, cylinder, total capacity 1,200 mt/y, Trim width 1.88 m, Tissue
No. 20, (Local PMs), cylinder, total capacity 1,200 mt/y, Trim width 1.88 m, Tissue
No. 21, (Local PMs), cylinder, total capacity 1,200 mt/y, Trim width 1.88 m, Tissue
No. 22, (Local PMs), cylinder, total capacity 1,200 mt/y, Trim width 1.88 m, Tissue
No. 23, (Local PMs), cylinder, total capacity 1,200 mt/y, Trim width 1.88 m, Tissue
No. 24, (Local PMs), cylinder, total capacity 1,200 mt/y, Trim width 1.88 m, Tissue

China

No. 25, (Local PMs), cylinder, total capacity 1,200 mt/y, Trim width 1.88 m, Tissue
No. 26, (Local PMs), cylinder, total capacity 2,000 mt/y, Trim width 3.48 m, Tissue
No. 27, (Local PMs), cylinder, total capacity 2,000 mt/y, Trim width 3.48 m, Tissue
No. 28, (Local PMs), cylinder, total capacity 2,000 mt/y, Trim width 3.48 m, Tissue
No. 29, (Local PMs), cylinder, total capacity 2,000 mt/y, Trim width 3.48 m, Tissue
No. 30, (Local PMs), cylinder, total capacity 2,000 mt/y, Trim width 3.48 m, Tissue
No. 31, (Local PMs), cylinder, total capacity 2,000 mt/y, Trim width 3.48 m, Tissue
No. 32, (Local PMs), cylinder, total capacity 2,000 mt/y, Trim width 3.48 m, Tissue
No. 33, (Local PMs), cylinder, total capacity 2,000 mt/y, Trim width 3.48 m, Tissue
No. 34, (Local PMs), cylinder, total capacity 2,000 mt/y, Trim width 3.48 m, Tissue
No. 35, (Local PMs), cylinder, total capacity 2,000 mt/y, Trim width 3.48 m, Tissue
No. 36, (Local PMs), cylinder, total capacity 2,000 mt/y, Trim width 3.48 m, Tissue
No. 37, (Local PMs), cylinder, total capacity 2,000 mt/y, Trim width 3.48 m, Tissue
No. 38, (Local PMs), cylinder, total capacity 2,000 mt/y, Trim width 3.48 m, Tissue
No. 39, (Local PMs), cylinder, total capacity 2,000 mt/y, Trim width 3.48 m, Tissue
No. 40, (Local PMs), cylinder, total capacity 2,000 mt/y, Trim width 3.48 m, Tissue
Energy Data:
Power boilers: 1

ⓂGuangxi East Asia Paper Co., Ltd.
Chongyou City Industry Park
Nanning, Guangxi, 530022
China
  Phone: (86) 771 550 5612/ 5609
  Fax: (86) 771 550 8552
  Web Address: www.easugar.com
Personnel:
  Gen. Mgr.: Zhuoming Ma
  Phone: (86) 771 550 5612/ 5609
Mill Locations:
  Guangxi East Asia Paper Co., Ltd., Chongzuo Mill, Chongzuo City Industry Park, Chongzuo 530022, China, Capacity: 60,000 mt/y, (Pulp mill, Paper mill)
  Phone: (86) 771 7848 016/012

ⓂGuangxi East Asia Paper Co., Ltd.
Chongzuo Mill
Chongzuo City Industry Park
Chongzuo, Guangxi, 530022
China
  Phone: (86) 771 7848 016/012
  Web Address: www.easugar.com
Personnel:
  Gen. Mgr.: Zhuoming Ma
  Phone: (86) 771 550 5612/ 5609
Total Employees at this Location: 500
Type of Operation: Pulp mill, Paper mill
Pulp Grades and Capacities:
  Total pulp capacity: 60,800 mt/y
  Pulp available for market: 10,000 mt/y
  Other Pulp: 60,800 mt/y
Pulp Mill Data:
Pulp Lines: 1
  Chemical Recovery Equipment:
  Recovery boilers: 1
Paper/Paperboard Grades and Capacities:
  Total paper and paperboard capacity: 60,000 mt/y
  Packaging papers: 20,000 mt/y
  Boxboard/cartonboard: 40,000 mt/y
Paper and Paperboard Mill Data:
Paper Machines: 2
No. 1, fourdrinier, total capacity 30,000 mt/y, Trim width 2.64 m, Boxboard/cartonboard, Packaging papers
No. 2, fourdrinier, total capacity 30,000 mt/y, Trim width 2.64 m, Boxboard/cartonboard, Packaging papers
Energy Data:
Power boilers: 2
Combustion turbines: 2 at 6, 6 MW
Electrical demand for mill: 151 MWh/D

ⓂGuangxi Fangchenggang Hongyuan Pulp & Paper Co., Ltd.
Fangchenggang Mill
Ownership: Guangdong Foshan City Gaoming Hongyuan Paper Co., Ltd.
Maoling Industry Park, Fangcheng District
Fangchenggang, Guangxi, 538023
China
  Phone: (86) 770 309 2918/3168
  Fax: (86) 770 309 2918
Personnel:
  Pres. & Gen. Mgr.: Yongjian Huang
  Phone: (86) 770 309 2918/3168
Total Employees at this Location: 368
Type of Operation: Pulp mill
Pulp Grades and Capacities:
  Total pulp capacity: 50,036 mt/y
  Pulp available for market: 50,000 mt/y
  Chemical Pulp: 40,029 mt/y
  Other Pulp: 10,007 mt/y
Pulp Mill Data:
  Chemical Pulping Systems:
  Batch digesters: 2
Pulp Lines: 2
  Bleach Plant Systems: 1
  Chemical Pulping System, Type: Hardwood - CEHQP, Sequence: CEH, Capacity 80,000 admt/y
  Chemical Recovery Equipment:
  Evaporator lines: 1
  Recovery boilers: 2
  Pulp Dryers:
  Fourdriniers 1, Fourdriniers 1
Energy Data:
Power boilers: 3
Steam turbines: 1 at 6 MW
Electrical demand for mill: 110 MWh/D

ⓂGuangxi Fengtang Luzhai Paper Co., Ltd.
Luzhai Industrial Park
Liuzhou, Guangxi
China
  Phone: (86) 772 6828 968/969/6829 575
Mill Locations:
  Guangxi Fengtang Luzhai Paper Co., Ltd., Liuzhou Mill, Luzhai Industrial Park, Luxin Rd., Liuzhou, China, (Pulp mill)
  Phone: (86) 772 6828 968/969/6829 575

ⓂGuangxi Fengtang Luzhai Paper Co., Ltd.
Liuzhou Mill
Luzhai Industrial Park, Luxin Rd.
Liuzhou, Guangxi
China
  Phone: (86) 772 6828 968/969/6829 575
Total Employees at this Location: 300
Type of Operation: Pulp mill
Pulp Grades and Capacities:
  Total pulp capacity: 50,000 mt/y
  Pulp available for market: 50,000 mt/y
  Other Pulp: 50,000 mt/y
Pulp Mill Data:
  Chemical Pulping Systems:
  Continuous digesters: 1
Pulp Lines: 1
  Bleach Plant Systems: 1
  Chemical Pulping System, Type: ECF
  Chemical Recovery Equipment:
  Evaporator lines
  Recovery boilers
Energy Data:
Power boilers
Electrical demand for mill: 79 MWh/D

ⓂGuangxi Gold Zhuyuan Paper Co., Ltd.
Ownership: Guangxi Dongsheng Paper Group
Chengdong Rd., Wuxuan Town, Wuxuan County
Laibin, Guangxi, 546100
China
  Phone: (86) 772 5222 118
Mill Locations:
  Guangxi Gold Zhuyuan Paper Co., Ltd., Laibin Mill, Chengdong Rd., Wuxuan Town, Wuxuan County, Laibin 546100, China, (Pulp mill)
  Phone: (86) 772 5222 118

ⓂGuangxi Gold Zhuyuan Paper Co., Ltd.
Laibin Mill
Chengdong Rd., Wuxuan Town, Wuxuan County
Laibin, Guangxi, 546100
China
  Phone: (86) 772 5222 118
Total Employees at this Location: 315
Type of Operation: Pulp mill
Pulp Grades and Capacities:
  Total pulp capacity: 68,000 mt/y
  Pulp available for market: 68,000 mt/y
  Other Pulp: 68,000 mt/y
Pulp Mill Data:
  Chemical Pulping Systems:
  Continuous digesters: 1
Pulp Lines: 1
  Bleach Plant Systems: 1
  No. 1, Sequence: CEH
  Chemical Recovery Equipment:
  Evaporator lines: 1
  Recovery boilers: 1
Energy Data:
Power boilers: 1
Electrical demand for mill: 107 MWh/D

ⓂGuangxi Guangui Sugar Co., Ltd.
Xie Wei, Heng County
Nanning, Guangxi, 530300
China
  Phone: (86) 771 7382 533
Total Employees of Company: 446
Mill Locations:
  Guangxi Guangui Sugar Co., Ltd., Nanning, Xie Wei, Heng County, Nanning 530300, China, (Pulp mill)
  Phone: (86) 771 7382 533

ⓂGuangxi Guangui Sugar Co., Ltd.
Nanning
Xie Wei, Heng County
Nanning, Guangxi, 530300
China
  Phone: (86) 771 7382 533
Total Employees at this Location: 446
Type of Operation: Pulp mill
Pulp Grades and Capacities:
  Total pulp capacity: 128,000 mt/y
  Pulp available for market: 128,000 mt/y
  Other Pulp: 128,000 mt/y
Pulp Mill Data:
  Chemical Pulping Systems:
  Continuous digesters: 2
Pulp Lines: 2
  Bleach Plant Systems: 2
  No. 1, Sequence: CEH
  Chemical Recovery Equipment:
  Evaporator lines
  Recovery boilers
Energy Data:
Power boilers
Steam turbines: 1 at 12 MW
Electrical demand for mill: 201 MWh/D

ⓘGuangxi Guigang Hongqi Paper Mill
Ownership: Hong Kong Shunhe Waste Paper Co., Ltd.
West Renmin Rd.
Guigang, Guangxi, 537100
China
  Phone: (86) 775 426 3407
  Fax: (86) 775 426 3407
  Personnel:
  Pres. & Gen. Mgr.: Jianbin Li
  Phone: (86) 775 426 3407
  Sls. Mgr.: Zhenming Shao
  Phone: (86) 775 426 3407
  Mill Locations:
  Guangxi Guigang Hongqi Paper Mill, Guigang mill, West Renmin Rd., Guigang 537100, China, Capacity: 47,838 mt/y, (Paperboard mill)
  Phone: (86) 775 426 3087
  Fax: (86) 775 426 3407

ⓜGuangxi Guigang Hongqi Paper Mill
Guigang mill
West Renmin Rd.
Guigang, Guangxi, 537100
China
  Phone: (86) 775 426 3087
  Fax: (86) 775 426 3407
  Personnel:
  Pres. & Gen. Mgr.: Jianbin Li
  Phone: (86) 775 426 3407
  Sls. Mgr.: Zhenming Shao
  Phone: (86) 775 426 3407
Total Employees at this Location: 260
Type of Operation: Paperboard mill
Pulp Grades and Capacities:
  Total pulp capacity: 47,372 mt/y
  Recycled Pulping: 47,372 mt/y
Paper/Paperboard Grades and Capacities:
  Total paper and paperboard capacity: 47,838 mt/y
  Corrugating medium/fluting: 47,838 mt/y
Paper and Paperboard Mill Data:
Paper Machines: 4
No. 4, cylinder, total capacity 9,996 mt/y, Trim width 2.1 m, Corrugating medium/fluting
No. 5, multi-wire, total capacity 17,850 mt/y, Trim width 2.36 m, Corrugating medium/fluting
No. 7, multi-wire, total capacity 9,996 mt/y, Trim width 2.1 m, Corrugating medium/fluting
No. 8, multi-wire, total capacity 9,996 mt/y, Trim width 2.1 m, Corrugating medium/fluting
Energy Data:
Power boilers: 1
Steam turbines: 2 at 6, 3 MW
Electrical demand for mill: 66 MWh/D

ⓘGuangxi Guilin Paper Inc.
Ownership: 90% by shareholders, 10% by state
Yulei Bay, Licheng Town
Lipu, Guangxi, 546600
China
  Phone: (86) 773 723 3098
  Fax: (86) 773 723 3397
  Web Address: www.guilnpaperinc.com
  Personnel:
  Chmn., CEO: Fangde Zhang
  Phone: (86) 773 723 3098
  Fax: (86) 773 723 3397
  CFO: Mingzhu Zhang
  Phone: (86) 773 723 3098
  Fax: (86) 773 723 3397
  Secr.: Jinhua Shu
  Phone: (86) 773 723 3098
  Fax: (86) 773 723 3397
Total Employees at this Location: 100
Mill Locations:
Guangxi Forest Lipu Paper Co., Ltd., Lipu Mill, Yulei Bay, Licheng Town, Lipu 546600, China, Capacity: 126,000 mt/y, (Paperboard mill)
Phone: (86) 773 721 3098/ 3398
Fax: (86) 773 722 2397
Email: eva@guilinpaperinc.com

ⓜGuangxi Forest Lipu Paper Co., Ltd.
Lipu Mill
Ownership: Guangxi Guilin Paper Inc.
Yulei Bay, Licheng Town
Lipu, Guangxi, 546600
China
  Phone: (86) 773 721 3098/ 3398
  Fax: (86) 773 722 2397
  Email: eva@guilinpaperinc.com
  Web Address: www.glcpc.com/GYQY/lplyzc/lyxc.htm
  Personnel:
  Pres., CEO, Gen. Mgr.: Fangde Zhang
  Phone: (86) 773 721 3098/ 3398
  Vice Gen. Mgr.: Jiajie Chen
  Phone: (86) 773 721 3098/ 3398
  Sls. Mgr.: Shaoqiu Li
  Phone: (86) 773 721 3098/ 3398
  Prod. Mgr.: Jianqiang Peng
  Phone: (86) 773 721 3098/ 3398
Total Employees at this Location: 600
Type of Operation: Paperboard mill
Pulp Grades and Capacities:
  Total pulp capacity: 94,341 mt/y
  Chemical Pulp: 53,032 mt/y
  Recycled Pulping: 41,309 mt/y
Pulp Mill Data:
Pulp Lines: 3
Paper/Paperboard Grades and Capacities:
  Total paper and paperboard capacity: 126,000 mt/y
  Packaging papers: 42,000 mt/y
  Specialty and industrial: 44,400 mt/y
  Linerboard: 39,600 mt/y
Paper and Paperboard Mill Data:
Paper Machines: 8
No. 1, cylinder, total capacity 6,000 mt/y, Trim width 1.09 m, Specialty and industrial
No. 2, cylinder, total capacity 9,600 mt/y, Trim width 1.58 m, Linerboard
No. 3, cylinder, total capacity 10,800 mt/y, Trim width 1.58 m, Specialty and industrial
No. 4, fourdrinier, total capacity 12,000 mt/y, Trim width 2.2 m, Packaging papers
No. 5, cylinder, total capacity 7,200 mt/y, Trim width 1.58 m, Specialty and industrial
No. 6, fourdrinier, total capacity 10,800 mt/y, Trim width 2.36 m, Specialty and industrial
No. 7, fourdrinier (3), total capacity 60,000 mt/y, Trim width 2.64 m, Packaging papers, Linerboard
No. 8, cylinder, total capacity 9,600 mt/y, Trim width 1.7 m, Specialty and industrial
Energy Data:
Power boilers: 1
Steam turbines: 2 at 3, 6 MW

ⓘGuangxi Guilin No. 2 Paper Mill
Ownership: 100% by state
No. 2, Tingjiang Road
Guilin, Guangxi, 541001
China
  Phone: (86) 773 260 4012/ 3234
  Fax: (86) 773 260 4498
  Mill Locations:
Guangxi Guilin No. 2 Paper Mill, Guilin Mill, No. 2, Tingjiang Road, Guilin 541001, China, Capacity: 3,000 mt/y, (Paper mill)
Phone: (86) 773 260 4012/ 3234
Fax: (86) 773 260 4498

ⓜGuangxi Guilin No. 2 Paper Mill
Guilin Mill
No. 2, Tingjiang Road
Guilin, Guangxi, 541001
China
  Phone: (86) 773 260 4012/ 3234
  Fax: (86) 773 260 4498
  Personnel:
  Sls. Mgr.: Zhifeng He
  Phone: (86) 773 260 4012/ 3234
Total Employees at this Location: 200
Type of Operation: Paper mill
Paper/Paperboard Grades and Capacities:
  Total paper and paperboard capacity: 3,000 mt/y
  Specialty and industrial: 3,000 mt/y
Paper and Paperboard Mill Data:
Paper Machines: 2
PM 1, cylinder, total capacity 1,500 mt/y, Trim width 1.88 m, Specialty and industrial
PM 2, cylinder, total capacity 1,500 mt/y, Trim width 1.88 m, Specialty and industrial

ⓘGuangxi Guilin Qifeng Paper Co., Ltd.
Ownership: 100% by state
Fulong industrial park, Suqiao economic development zone
Guilin, Guangxi, 541805
China
  Phone: (86) 773 360 2593/ 3693
  Fax: (86) 773 360 5388
  Email: glpaper@guilinpaper.com
  Web Address: www.guilinpaper.com
  Mill Locations:
Guangxi Guilin Qifeng Paper Co., Ltd., Guilin Mill, Fulong industrial park, Suqiao economic development zone, Guilin 541805, China, Capacity: 25,000 mt/y, (Paper mill)
Phone: (86) 773 360 2593/ 3693
Fax: (86) 773 360 5388
Email: glpaper@guilinpaper.com

ⓜGuangxi Guilin Qifeng Paper Co., Ltd.
Guilin Mill
Fulong industrial park, Suqiao economic development zone
Guilin, Guangxi, 541805
China
  Phone: (86) 773 360 2593/ 3693
  Fax: (86) 773 360 5388
  Email: glpaper@guilinpaper.com
  Web Address: www.guilinpaper.com
  Personnel:
  Pres.: Jie Peng
  Phone: (86) 773 360 2593/ 3693
Total Employees at this Location: 1,000
Type of Operation: Paper mill
Paper/Paperboard Grades and Capacities:
  Total paper and paperboard capacity: 25,000 mt/y
  Specialty and industrial: 25,000 mt/y
Paper and Paperboard Mill Data:
Paper Machines: 18
No. 1, cylinder, total capacity 400 mt/y, Trim width 1.09 m, Specialty and industrial
No. 2, cylinder, total capacity 500 mt/y, Trim width 1.58 m, Specialty and industrial
No. 3, cylinder, total capacity 500 mt/y, Trim width 1.58 m, Specialty and industrial
No. 4, cylinder, total capacity 500 mt/y, Trim width 1.58 m, Specialty and industrial
No. 5, cylinder, total capacity 500 mt/y, Trim width 1.58 m, Specialty and industrial
No. 6, cylinder, total capacity 500 mt/y, Trim width 1.58 m, Specialty and industrial
No. 7, cylinder, total capacity 500 mt/y, Trim width 1.58 m, Specialty and industrial
No. 8, cylinder, total capacity 500 mt/y, Trim width 1.58 m, Specialty and industrial
No. 9, fourdrinier, total capacity 780 mt/y, Trim width 1.6 m, Specialty and industrial
No. 10, cylinder, total capacity 780 mt/y, Trim width 1.6 m, Specialty and industrial
No. 11, fourdrinier, total capacity 800 mt/y, Trim width 1.76 m, Specialty and industrial
No. 12, fourdrinier, total capacity 800 mt/y, Trim width 1.76 m, Specialty and industrial
No. 13, fourdrinier, total capacity 2,000 mt/y, Trim width 2.3 m, Specialty and industrial

China

No. 14, fourdrinier, total capacity 2,000 mt/y, Trim width 2.3 m, Specialty and industrial
No. 15, fourdrinier, total capacity 3,500 mt/y, Trim width 2.36 m, Specialty and industrial
No. 16, fourdrinier, total capacity 3,500 mt/y, Trim width 2.36 m, Specialty and industrial
No. 17, cylinder, total capacity 3,500 mt/y, Trim width 2.36 m, Specialty and industrial
No. 18, cylinder, total capacity 3,500 mt/y, Trim width 2.36 m, Specialty and industrial
Coating Machines: 1
No. 1

ⓂGuangxi Guitang Paper Group Co., Ltd.
Ownership: 100% by shareholders
No.100 Xinfu Rd.
Guigang City, Guangxi, 537102
China
   Phone: (86) 755 420 1997/426 0268
   Fax: (86) 755 426 0088
   Email: zhaomeiyuan@guitang.com
   Web Address: www.guitang.com
Personnel:
   Chmn.: Zhenbiao Huang
   Phone: (86) 755 420 1997/426 0268
   Fax: (86) 755 426 0088
   Pres. & Gen. Mgr.: Jiaju Huang
   Phone: (86) 755 420 1997/426 0268
   Fax: (86) 755 426 0088
   Dir.: Chaohui Li
   Phone: (86) 755 420 1997/426 0268
   Fax: (86) 755 426 0088
   Vice Gen. Mgr.: Shouchong Chen
   Phone: (86) 755 420 1997/426 0268
   Fax: (86) 755 426 0088
Total Employees of Company: 3,000
Mill Locations:
   Guangxi Guitang (Group) Stock Co., Ltd, Guigang Mill, No. 100 Xingfu Road, Guigang 537102, China, Capacity: 163,863 mt/y, (Paper mill, Paperboard mill)
   Phone: (86) 775 420 1380/1504/1445/1456/0268
   Fax: (86) 775 426 0088
   Guangxi Jeanper Paper Co., Ltd. (Jiebao Paper), Guiping Mill, Tangchang Road, Guigang 537102, China, Capacity: 65,500 mt/y, (Paper mill)
   Phone: (86) 775 426 2863/771 5739 689
   Fax: (86) 775 426 2182
   Email: jeanperhr@163.com, hrm@jeanper.com

ⓂGuangxi Guitang (Group) Stock Co., Ltd
Guigang Mill
Ownership: Guangxi Guitang Paper Group Co., Ltd.
No. 100 Xingfu Road
Guigang, Guangxi, 537102
China
   Phone: (86) 775 420 1380/1504/1445/1456/0268
   Fax: (86) 775 426 0088
   Web Address: www.guitang.com
Personnel:
   Chmn.: Zhenbiao Huang
   Phone: (86) 755 420 1380/1504/1445/1456/0268
   CFO, Dpty. Gen. Mgr., Board Secretary, Dir.: Zheng Yang
   Phone: (86) 755 420 1380/1504/1445/1456/0268
   Gen. Mgr.: Jian Chen
   Phone: (86) 755 420 1380/1504/1445/1456/0268
   Dpty. Gen. Mgr.: Shouchong Chen
   Phone: (86) 755 420 1380/1504/1445/1456/0268
   Dpty. Gen. Mgr.: Guixin Huang
   Phone: (86) 755 420 1380/1504/1445/1456/0268
   Gen. Mgr., Dir.: Jiaju Huang
   Phone: (86) 755 420 1380/1504/1445/1456/0268
   Dir.: Zhaohui Li
   Phone: (86) 755 420 1380/1504/1445/1456/0268
   Dir.: Jun Ning
   Phone: (86) 755 420 1380/1504/1445/1456/0268
   Indep. Dir.: Zailiang Xu
   Phone: (86) 755 420 1380/1504/1445/1456/0268
   Indep. Dir.: Lansong Deng
   Phone: (86) 755 420 1380/1504/1445/1456/0268
   Chief Accounting Officer: Zhu Fu
   Phone: (86) 755 420 1380/1504/1445/1456/0268
   Chief Eng.: Xianzhou Lan
   Phone: (86) 755 420 1380/1504/1445/1456/0268
Total Employees at this Location: 1,250
Type of Operation: Paper mill, Paperboard mill
Pulp Grades and Capacities:
   Total pulp capacity: 119,397 mt/y
   Chemical Pulp: 119,397 mt/y
Pulp Mill Data:
Chemical Pulping Systems:
   Batch digesters: 18
Pulp Lines: 1
Bleach Plant Systems: 1
   Chemical Pulping System, Type: Bagasse, Sequence: CEH, Capacity 100,000 admt/y
Chemical Recovery Equipment:
   Recovery boilers: 4
Paper/Paperboard Grades and Capacities:
   Total paper and paperboard capacity: 163,863 mt/y
   Uncoated woodfree/freesheet: 108,885 mt/y
   Tissue: 49,980 mt/y
   Corrugating medium/fluting: 4,998 mt/y
Paper and Paperboard Mill Data:
Paper Machines: 14
No. 6, fourdrinier, total capacity 8,925 mt/y, Trim width 1.76 m, Uncoated woodfree/freesheet
No. 7, fourdrinier, total capacity 5,712 mt/y, Trim width 1.76 m, Uncoated woodfree/freesheet
No. 8, fourdrinier, total capacity 5,712 mt/y, Trim width 1.76 m, Uncoated woodfree/freesheet
No. 10, cylinder, total capacity 4,998 mt/y, Trim width 1.58 m, Corrugating medium/fluting
No. 11, (second hand), fourdrinier, total capacity 35,700 mt/y, Trim width 2.64 m, Uncoated woodfree/freesheet
No. 12, fourdrinier, total capacity 35,700 mt/y, Trim width 2.64 m, Uncoated woodfree/freesheet
No. 6 PMs, cylinder, total capacity 17,136 mt/y, Trim width 1.58 m, Uncoated woodfree/freesheet
TM1, crescent former, total capacity 24,990 mt/y, Trim width 2.7 m, Tissue, Uncoated woodfree/freesheet
TM2, crescent former, total capacity 24,990 mt/y, Trim width 2.7 m, Tissue, Uncoated woodfree/freesheet
Energy Data:
Power boilers: 1
Steam turbines: 3 at 12, 12, 12 MW
Electrical demand for mill: 516 MWh/D

ⓂGuangxi Guofa Forest & Paper Co. Ltd.
Liuzhou (Guangxi Guofa Forest & Paper) Mill
Ownership: 100% by Asia Pulp & Paper (APP)
No.2 Miyuan Rd. Luorong Town, Yufeng District
Liuzhou, Guangxi, 545616
China
   Phone: (86) 772 8255 676/697
   Fax: (86) 772 8255 668/6511 006
   Email: gxgflz@appjg.com.cn
   Web Address: www.gxpaper.cn
Personnel:
   Chmn.: Mingming An
   Phone: (86) 772 6666999/899/888/971/6996444
   Chief Eng.: Huiying Xian
   Phone: (86) 772 6666999/899/888/971/6996444
   VP - Sls. & Mktg.: Jun Lu
   Phone: (86) 772 6666999/899/888/971/6996444
Total Employees at this Location: 700
Type of Operation: Pulp mill, Pulp mill, Paper mill
Pulp Grades and Capacities:
   Total pulp capacity: 80,000 mt/y
   Chemical Pulp: 80,000 mt/y
Pulp Mill Data:
Chemical Recovery Equipment:
   Recovery boilers: 2
Paper/Paperboard Grades and Capacities:
   Total paper and paperboard capacity: 120,000 mt/y
   Uncoated woodfree/freesheet: 50,000 mt/y
   Linerboard: 30,000 mt/y
   Boxboard/cartonboard: 20,000 mt/y
Paper and Paperboard Mill Data:
Paper Machines: 8
No. 1, cylinder, Trim width 1.09 m
No. 6, cylinder, Trim width 2.88 m
No. 7, fourdrinier, Trim width 2.36 m
No. 8, fourdrinier, Trim width 2.4 m
No. 2-3, cylinder, Trim width 1.58 m
No. 4-5, cylinder, Trim width 2.36 m
Energy Data:
Steam turbines: 1 at 10 MW

ⓂGuangxi Haolin Paper Co., Ltd.
Ownership: Guangxi Fufeng Group
Liujing Industrial Park
Nanning, Guangxi, 530313
China
   Phone: (86) 771 7265 826
   Fax: (86) 771 7265 836
   Web Address: www.fufeng.com.cn
Mill Locations:
   Guangxi Haolin Paper Co., Ltd., Nanning Mill, Liujing Industrial Park, Nanning 530313, China, Capacity: 10,000 mt/y, (Paper mill)
   Phone: (86) 771 7265 826
   Fax: (86) 771 7265 836

ⓂGuangxi Haolin Paper Co., Ltd.
Nanning Mill
Liujing Industrial Park
Nanning, Guangxi, 530313
China
   Phone: (86) 771 7265 826
   Fax: (86) 771 7265 836
   Web Address: www.fufeng.com.cn
Type of Operation: Paper mill
Paper/Paperboard Grades and Capacities:
   Total paper and paperboard capacity: 10,000 mt/y
   Tissue: 10,000 mt/y
Paper and Paperboard Mill Data:
Paper Machines: 8
PM 1, total capacity 1,250 mt/y, Trim width 1.58 m, Tissue
PM 2, total capacity 1,250 mt/y, Trim width 1.58 m, Tissue
PM 3, total capacity 1,250 mt/y, Trim width 1.58 m, Tissue
PM 4, total capacity 1,250 mt/y, Trim width 1.58 m, Tissue
PM 5, total capacity 1,250 mt/y, Trim width 1.58 m, Tissue
PM 6, total capacity 1,250 mt/y, Trim width 1.58 m, Tissue
PM 7, total capacity 1,250 mt/y, Trim width 1.58 m, Tissue
PM 8, total capacity 1,250 mt/y, Trim width 1.58 m, Tissue

ⓂGuangxi Heda Paper Co. Ltd.
Hezhou Mill
Ownership: Guangxi Huamei Paper Group Co., Ltd.
150 Bada Rd., Babu Town
Hezhou, Guangxi, 542800
China
   Phone: (86) 774 510 0081/0142
   Fax: (86) 774 512 5154/528 3054
   Web Address: www.hmpaper.cn
Personnel:
   Chmn.: Bin Huang
   Phone: (86) 774 510 0081/1172/510
   Pres.: Xianlu Tang
   Phone: (86) 774 510 0081/1172/510
   VP, Tech. Mgr.: Shangui Liu
   Phone: (86) 774 510 0081/1172/510
   Dir.: Yimo Liu
   Phone: (86) 774 510 0081/1172/510
Total Employees at this Location: 820
Type of Operation: Pulp mill
Pulp Grades and Capacities:
   Total pulp capacity: 80,229 mt/y
   Pulp available for market: 80,000 mt/y
   Chemical Pulp: 64,183 mt/y

Other Pulp: 16,046 mt/y
Pulp Mill Data:
Chemical Pulping Systems:
Batch digesters: 5
Pulp Lines: 1
Bleach Plant Systems: 1
No. 1, Sequence: O_2 D/CEopD, Capacity 80,000 admt/y
Chemical Recovery Equipment:
Recovery boilers: 1
Pulp Dryers:
Fourdriniers 1
Energy Data:
Power boilers: 1
TMP Reboiler: 1
Steam turbines: 2 at 7, 7 MW
Electrical demand for mill: 176 MWh/D

ⓜGuangxi Heng County Jiabao Paper Co., Ltd.
Ownership: Guangxi Nanning Jiabao Paper, Guangxi Dongsheng Paper Group
Hengzhou Town, Heng County
Nanning, Guangxi, 530300
China
Phone: (86) 771 7382219
Mill Locations:
Guangxi Heng County Jiabao Paper Co., Ltd., Nanning Mill, Hengzhou Town, Heng County, Nanning 530300, China, Capacity: 20,000 mt/y, (Paper mill)
Phone: (86) 771 7382219

ⓜGuangxi Heng County Jiabao Paper Co., Ltd.
Nanning Mill
Hengzhou Town, Heng County
Nanning, Guangxi, 530300
China
Phone: (86) 771 7382219
Type of Operation: Paper mill
Paper/Paperboard Grades and Capacities:
Total paper and paperboard capacity: 20,000 mt/y
Tissue: 20,000 mt/y
Paper and Paperboard Mill Data:
Paper Machines: 10
PM 1, total capacity 2,000 mt/y, Trim width 1.88 m, Tissue
PM 2, total capacity 2,000 mt/y, Trim width 1.88 m, Tissue
PM 3, total capacity 2,000 mt/y, Trim width 1.88 m, Tissue
PM 4, total capacity 2,000 mt/y, Trim width 1.88 m, Tissue
PM 5, total capacity 2,000 mt/y, Trim width 1.88 m, Tissue
PM 6, total capacity 2,000 mt/y, Trim width 1.88 m, Tissue
PM 7, total capacity 2,000 mt/y, Trim width 1.88 m, Tissue
PM 8, total capacity 2,000 mt/y, Trim width 1.88 m, Tissue
PM 9, total capacity 2,000 mt/y, Trim width 1.88 m, Tissue
PM 10, total capacity 2,000 mt/y, Trim width 1.88 m, Tissue

ⓜGuangxi Heng County Jiangnan Paper Co., Ltd.
Nanning Mill
Ownership: Guangxi Binyang Jiangnan Paper Co., Ltd.
Liujing Industrial Park, Heng County
Nanning, Guangxi, 530313
China
Phone: (86) 771 8481 038
Type of Operation: Paper mill
Paper/Paperboard Grades and Capacities:
Total paper and paperboard capacity: 20,000 mt/y
Tissue: 20,000 mt/y
Paper and Paperboard Mill Data:
Paper Machines: 1
PM 1, fourdrinier, total capacity 20,000 mt/y, Trim width 3.5 m, Tissue

ⓒGuangxi Huaken Paper
Laibin, Guangxi
China
Web Address: www.gxnkty.com

Mill Locations:
Guangxi Huaken Paper, Laibin Mill, Honghe Farm, Xingbin District, Laibin 546128, China, Capacity: 200,634 mt/y, (Pulp mill, Paper mill)
Phone: (86) 772 4713 608/525

ⓜGuangxi Huaken Paper
Laibin Mill
Honghe Farm, Xingbin District
Laibin, Guangxi, 546128
China
Phone: (86) 772 4713 608/525
Web Address: www.gxnkty.com
Total Employees at this Location: 400
Type of Operation: Pulp mill, Paper mill
Pulp Mill Data:
Chemical Pulping Systems:
Continuous digesters: 1
Pulp Lines: 1
Bleach Plant Lines:
No. 1, Sequence: DEpD
Paper/Paperboard Grades and Capacities:
Total paper and paperboard capacity: 200,634 mt/y
Uncoated woodfree/freesheet: 200,634 mt/y
Paper and Paperboard Mill Data:
Paper Machines: 6
No. 1, (started up Q4 2011), fourdrinier, total capacity 53,193 mt/y, Trim width 2.73 m, Uncoated woodfree/freesheet
No. 2, (started up Q4 2011), fourdrinier, total capacity 53,193 mt/y, Trim width 2.73 m, Uncoated woodfree/freesheet
No. 3, (started up Q4 2011), fourdrinier, total capacity 23,562 mt/y, Trim width 3.6 m, Uncoated woodfree/freesheet
No. 4, (started up Q4 2011), fourdrinier, total capacity 23,562 mt/y, Trim width 3.6 m, Uncoated woodfree/freesheet
No. 5, fourdrinier, total capacity 23,562 mt/y, Trim width 3.6 m, Uncoated woodfree/freesheet
No. 6, fourdrinier, total capacity 23,562 mt/y, Trim width 3.6 m, Uncoated woodfree/freesheet
Energy Data:
Power boilers: 1
Electrical demand for mill: 372 MWh/D

ⓒGuangxi Huayi Paper Co., Ltd.
Ownership: 100% by private owners
Gangnan Industry District
Guigang, Guangxi, 537132
China
Phone: (86) 775 459 2299/ 2008
Fax: (86) 775 459 2299
Mill Locations:
Guangxi Huayi Paper Co., Ltd., Guigang Mill, Gangnan Industry District, Guigang 537132, China, Capacity: 100,000 mt/y, (Paper mill)
Phone: (86) 775 459 2299/ 2008
Fax: (86) 775 459 2299

ⓜGuangxi Huayi Paper Co., Ltd.
Guigang Mill
Gangnan Industry District
Guigang, Guangxi, 537132
China
Phone: (86) 775 459 2299/ 2008
Fax: (86) 775 459 2299
Web Address: www.gxhuayi.com
Personnel:
Chmn. & Pres.: Shihui Huang
Phone: (86) 775 459 2299/ 2008
Total Employees at this Location: 700
Type of Operation: Paper mill
Paper/Paperboard Grades and Capacities:
Total paper and paperboard capacity: 100,000 mt/y
Tissue: 100,000 mt/y
Paper and Paperboard Mill Data:
Paper Machines: 30

No. 1, fourdrinier, total capacity 2,100 mt/y, Trim width 1.88 m, Tissue
No. 2, fourdrinier, total capacity 2,100 mt/y, Trim width 1.88 m, Tissue
No. 3, fourdrinier, total capacity 2,100 mt/y, Trim width 1.88 m, Tissue
No. 4, fourdrinier, total capacity 2,100 mt/y, Trim width 1.88 m, Tissue
No. 5, fourdrinier, total capacity 2,100 mt/y, Trim width 1.88 m, Tissue
No. 6, fourdrinier, total capacity 2,100 mt/y, Trim width 1.88 m, Tissue
No. 7, cylinder, total capacity 2,100 mt/y, Trim width 1.88 m, Tissue
No. 8, fourdrinier, total capacity 2,100 mt/y, Trim width 1.88 m, Tissue
No. 9, fourdrinier, total capacity 2,100 mt/y, Trim width 1.88 m, Tissue
No. 10, fourdrinier, total capacity 2,100 mt/y, Trim width 1.88 m, Tissue
No. 11, fourdrinier, total capacity 2,100 mt/y, Trim width 1.88 m, Tissue
No. 12, fourdrinier, total capacity 2,100 mt/y, Trim width 1.88 m, Tissue
No. 13, fourdrinier, total capacity 3,500 mt/y, Trim width 3 m, Tissue
No. 14, fourdrinier, total capacity 3,500 mt/y, Trim width 3 m, Tissue
No. 15, (Liaoyang Allideas Papertech Company, Ltd.), crescent former, Trim width 2.8 m, Tissue
No. 16, (Liaoyang Allideas Papertech Company, Ltd.), crescent former, Trim width 2.8 m, Tissue
No. 17, (Liaoyang Allideas Papertech Company, Ltd.), crescent former, Trim width 2.8 m, Tissue
No. 18, (Liaoyang Allideas Papertech Company, Ltd.), crescent former, Trim width 2.8 m, Tissue
No. 19, (Liaoyang Allideas Papertech Company, Ltd.), crescent former, Trim width 2.8 m, Tissue
No. 20, (Liaoyang Allideas Papertech Company, Ltd.), crescent former, Trim width 2.8 m, Tissue
No. 21, (Liaoyang Allideas Papertech Company, Ltd.), crescent former, Trim width 2.8 m, Tissue
No. 22, (Liaoyang Allideas Papertech Company, Ltd.), crescent former, Trim width 2.8 m, Tissue
No. 23, Trim width 1.58 m, Tissue
No. 24, Trim width 1.58 m, Tissue
No. 25, Trim width 1.58.m, Tissue
No. 26, Trim width 1.58 m, Tissue
No. 27, Trim width 1.76 m, Tissue
No. 28, Trim width 1.76 m, Tissue
No. 29, Trim width 1.76 m, Tissue
No. 30, Trim width 1.76 m, Tissue

ⓒGuangxi Hwagain Group
Ownership: 100% by shareholders
Floor 29 Yahang Finance Center, No. 55 Jinhu Rd.
Guangning, Guangxi, 530028
China
Phone: (86) 771 5568 819
Fax: (86) 771 5533 953
Email: hwagain@hwagain.com
Web Address: www.hwagain.com
Personnel:
Pres.: Jun Ning
Phone: (86) 771 5568 819
Fax: (86) 771 5533 953
Total Employees of Company: 3,500
Mill Locations:
Guangxi Hwagain Group, Nanning Mill, Liangqing Town, Liangqing District, Nanning 530028, China, Capacity: 60,400 mt/y, (Paper mill)
Phone: (86) 771 556 8819-5362/5380
Fax: (86) 771 475 1302
Email: gxnz@hwagain.com
Jiangxi Ganzhou Hwagain Paper Co., Ltd, Ganzhou Mill, No. 168, Sangyanxia, Shuixi Town, Ganzhou 341000, China, Capacity: 205,000 mt/y, (Paper mill)
Phone: (86) 797 8251 388/ 771 5568 819
Fax: (86) 797 8253 018/ 8257 111
Email: jxnz@hwagain.com

China

ⓘⓂ Guangxi Hwagain Group
Nanning Mill
Company is closed (closed due to environmental concerns, stopped production in late August 2014)
Ownership: *100% by shareholders*
Liangqing Town, Liangqing District
Nanning, Guangxi, 530028
China
 Phone: (86) 771 556 8819-5362/5380
 Fax: (86) 771 475 1302
 Email: gxnz@hwagain.com
 Web Address: www.hwagain.com
Personnel:
 Vice Chmn.: Peihe Yan
 VP: Yeling Xie
 Gen.Mgr.: Gaoqiang Huang
Total Employees of Company: 3,500
Total Employees at this Location: 1,100
Type of Operation: Paper mill
Mill Locations:
 Jiangxi Ganzhou Hwagain Paper Co., Ltd., Ganzhou Mill, No. 168, Sangyanxia, Shuixi Town, Ganzhou 341000, China, Capacity: 205,000 mt/y, (Paper mill)
 Phone: (86) 797 8251 388/ 771 5568 819
 Fax: (86) 797 8253 018/ 8257 111
 Email: jxnz@hwagain.com
Pulp Grades and Capacities:
 Total pulp capacity: 50,000 mt/y
Pulp Mill Data:
Pulp Lines: 1
 Chemical Recovery Equipment:
 Recovery boilers: 1
Paper/Paperboard Grades and Capacities:
 Total paper and paperboard capacity: 60,400 mt/y
 Uncoated woodfree/freesheet: 34,800 mt/y
 Tissue: 25,600 mt/y
Paper and Paperboard Mill Data:
Paper Machines: 16
 No. 1, cylinder, total capacity 1,600 mt/y, Trim width 1.58 m, Tissue
 No. 2, cylinder, total capacity 1,600 mt/y, Trim width 1.58 m, Tissue
 No. 3, cylinder, total capacity 1,600 mt/y, Trim width 1.58 m, Tissue
 No. 4, cylinder, total capacity 1,600 mt/y, Trim width 1.58 m, Tissue
 No. 5, cylinder, total capacity 1,600 mt/y, Trim width 1.58 m, Tissue
 No. 6, cylinder, total capacity 1,600 mt/y, Trim width 1.58 m, Tissue
 No. 7, cylinder, total capacity 1,600 mt/y, Trim width 1.58 m, Tissue
 No. 8, cylinder, total capacity 1,600 mt/y, Trim width 1.58 m, Tissue
 No. 9, cylinder, total capacity 1,600 mt/y, Trim width 1.58 m, Tissue
 No. 10, cylinder, total capacity 1,600 mt/y, Trim width 1.58 m, Tissue
 No. 11, cylinder, total capacity 1,600 mt/y, Trim width 1.58 m, Tissue
 No. 12, cylinder, total capacity 1,600 mt/y, Trim width 1.58 m, Tissue
 No. 13, cylinder, total capacity 1,600 mt/y, Trim width 1.58 m, Tissue
 No. 14, cylinder, total capacity 1,600 mt/y, Trim width 1.58 m, Tissue
 No. 15, cylinder, total capacity 1,600 mt/y, Trim width 1.58 m, Tissue
 No. 16, cylinder, total capacity 1,600 mt/y, Trim width 1.58 m, Tissue
Energy Data:
 Power boilers: 1

Ⓜ Guangxi Jeanper Paper Co., Ltd. (Jiebao Paper)
Guiping Mill
Ownership: *100% by Guangxi Guitang Paper Group Co., Ltd.*
Tangchang Road
Guigang, Guangxi, 537102
China
 Phone: (86) 775 426 2863/771 5739 689
 Fax: (86) 775 426 2182
 Email: jeanperhr@163.com, hrm@jeanper.com
 Web Address: www.jeanper.com
Personnel:
 Pres. & Gen. Mgr.: Chaohui Li
 Phone: (86) 775 420 1800/426 2863
 Sls. Mgr.: Zhihui Zhang
 Phone: (86) 775 420 1800/426 2863
 HR Mgr.: Sufeng Ji
 Phone: (86) 775 420 1800/426 2863
Total Employees at this Location: 700
Type of Operation: Paper mill
Paper/Paperboard Grades and Capacities:
 Total paper and paperboard capacity: 65,500 mt/y
 Tissue: 65,500 mt/y
Paper and Paperboard Mill Data:
Paper Machines: 23
 PM 1-8, cylinder, total capacity 1,250 mt/y, Trim width 1.58 m, Tissue
 PM 15-23, total capacity 4,800 mt/y, Trim width 1.88 m, Tissue
 PM 9-14, cylinder, total capacity 2,500 mt/y, Trim width 1.88 m, Tissue

ⓘ Guangxi Jiayi Paper Co., Ltd.
Ownership: *100% by Hong Kong Jiafu International Group*
No. 11, Dongsun Rd., Youjiang District
Baise City, Guangxi, 533000
China
 Phone: (86) 776 267 1066/ 1088
 Fax: (86) 776 267 1088
Mill Locations:
 Guangxi Jiayi Paper Co., Ltd., Baise Mill, No. 11, Dongsun Rd., Youjiang District, Baise 533000, China, Capacity: 60,000 mt/y, (Pulp mill, Paper mill, Paperboard mill)
 Phone: (86) 776 267 1066/1088
 Fax: (86) 776 267 1088

Ⓜ Guangxi Jiayi Paper Co., Ltd.
Baise Mill
No. 11, Dongsun Rd., Youjiang District
Baise, Guangxi, 533000
China
 Phone: (86) 776 267 1066/1088
 Fax: (86) 776 267 1088
Personnel:
 Chmn.: Wanjian Chen
 Phone: (86) 776 267 1066/ 1088
 Gen. Mgr.: Cheng Huang
 Phone: (86) 776 267 1066/ 1088
Total Employees at this Location: 648
Type of Operation: Pulp mill, Paper mill, Paperboard mill
Pulp Grades and Capacities:
 Total pulp capacity: 95,000 mt/y
 Pulp available for market: 18,000 mt/y
 Recycled Pulping: 35,000 mt/y
Pulp Mill Data:
Pulp Lines: 2
 Recycled Fiber Treatment Lines:
 Recycled packaging pulping lines: 1 at 35,000 admt/y
 Pulp Dryers:
 Other dryers 3
Paper/Paperboard Grades and Capacities:
 Total paper and paperboard capacity: 60,000 mt/y
 Uncoated woodfree/freesheet: 25,000 mt/y
 Corrugating medium/fluting: 35,000 mt/y
Paper and Paperboard Mill Data:
Paper Machines: 4
 No. 4, cylinder, total capacity 7,500 mt/y, Trim width 1.76 m, Uncoated woodfree/freesheet
 No. 5, cylinder, total capacity 7,500 mt/y, Trim width 1.76 m, Uncoated woodfree/freesheet
 No. 6, cylinder, total capacity 10,000 mt/y, Trim width 1.88 m, Uncoated woodfree/freesheet
 No. 7, multi-ply, total capacity 35,000 mt/y, Trim width 3.4 m, Corrugating medium/fluting

ⓘ Guangxi Jindaxing Paper Group Co., Ltd.
Ownership: *90% by Foshan Jindaxing Paper Industry Co., Ltd., 10% by Guangxi Lianlin Paper Mill*
No. 59 Jinhu Rd.
Nanning, Guangxi, 530021
China
 Phone: (86) 771 6162 888/ 666
 Fax: (86) 771 5592 626
 Web Address: www.jingdaxing.com
Personnel:
 Chmn.: Jinsong Liu
 Phone: (86) 771 6162 888/ 666
 Fax: (86) 771 5592 626
Total Employees at this Location: 300
Mill Locations:
 Guangxi Jindaxing Paper Group Co., Ltd., Baise Mill, No. 5 Xinchangpian, Leli Town, Tianlin County, Baise 533300, China, Capacity: 120,000 mt/y, (Paper mill)
 Phone: (86) 776 720 1316/ 1329
 Fax: (86) 776 720 1336/ 1288
 Guangxi Nanning Jindaxing Pulp & Paper Co., Ltd., Nanning Mill, Liujing Industry Park, Heng County, Nanning, China, Capacity: 171,360 mt/y, (Pulp mill, Paper mill)
 Phone: (86) 771 559 9766

Ⓜ Guangxi Jindaxing Paper Group Co., Ltd.
Baise Mill
Mill is idle (being rebuild to produce printing and writing paper)
No. 5 Xinchangpian, Leli Town, Tianlin County
Baise, Guangxi, 533300
China
 Phone: (86) 776 720 1316/ 1329
 Fax: (86) 776 720 1336/ 1288
 Web Address: www.jingdaxing.com
Personnel:
 Chmn. & Pres.: Jinsong Liu
 Phone: (86) 13307766228
 Chief Eng.: Zhixiang Cai
 Phone: (86) 776 720 1316/ 1329
 VP: Yuhe Gan
 Phone: (86) 776 720 1316/ 1329
 Asst. Mgr.: Sijin Gan
 Phone: (86) 776 720 1316/ 1329
 Sls. Mgr.: Jieyin Zeng
 Phone: (86) 757 8339 1733
 Fax: (86) 757 8338 8818
 Email: jdx_zjy@yahoo.com.cn
Total Employees at this Location: 600
Type of Operation: Paper mill
Pulp Grades and Capacities:
 Total pulp capacity: 110,595 mt/y
 Recycled Pulping: 110,595 mt/y
Pulp Mill Data:
Pulp Lines: 1
 Bleach Plant Systems: 1
 No. 1, Type: peroxide, Sequence: P
 Recycled Fiber Treatment Lines:
 Flotation deinking lines
Paper/Paperboard Grades and Capacities:
 Total paper and paperboard capacity: 120,000 mt/y
 Newsprint: 120,000 mt/y
Paper and Paperboard Mill Data:
Paper Machines: 2
 No. 1, GapFormer, total capacity 60,000 mt/y, Trim width 3.25 m, Newsprint
 No. 2, GapFormer, total capacity 60,000 mt/y, Trim width 3.25 m, Newsprint
Energy Data:
 Power boilers: 1
 Electrical demand for mill: 337 MWh/D

China

ⓂGuangxi Jingui Pulp & Paper Co., Ltd.
Qinzhou (Guangxi Jingui Pulp & Paper) Mill
Ownership: Asia Pulp & Paper (APP)
Dalanping Industry Park, Linhai Industry District
Qinzhou, Guangxi, 535000
China
　Phone: (86) 777 3698 606/022/012/3696 205
　Web Address: www.appjg.com.cn
Total Employees at this Location: 1,400
Type of Operation: Pulp mill, Paperboard mill
Pulp Grades and Capacities:
　Total pulp capacity: 787,020 mt/y
　Pulp available for market: 294,314 mt/y
　Mechanical Pulp: 600,000 mt/y
Pulp Mill Data:
　Mechanical Pulping Systems:
　APMP Systems: 1
　APMP Systems: 1
Pulp Lines: 2
　Chemical Recovery Equipment:
　Recovery boilers: 1
　Lime Kiln
　Pulp Dryers:
　Flash dryers 1
Paper/Paperboard Grades and Capacities:
　Total paper and paperboard capacity: 1,000,000 mt/y
　Boxboard/cartonboard: 1,000,000 mt/y
Paper and Paperboard Mill Data:
Paper Machines: 1
No. 5, fourdrinier (3), total capacity 1,000,000 mt/y, Trim width 8.1 m, Boxboard/cartonboard
Coating Machines: 1
PM5, on machine
Energy Data:
Power boilers: 2
TMP Reboiler: 1
Steam turbines: 2 at 300 MW
Electrical demand for mill: 4,150 MWh/D

ⓂGuangxi Jinrong Paper Co., Ltd.
Silin Town Industrial Park, Tiandong Town
Baise, Guangxi, 531504
China
　Phone: (86) 776 5151 808/5152 869
　Fax: (86) 776 5151 808/5152 668
　Web Address: www.jinrongpaper.com
Mill Locations:
Guangxi Jinrong Paper Co., Ltd., Baise Mill, Silin Town Industrial Park, Tiandong Town, Baise 531504, China, Capacity: 180,000 mt/y, (Pulp mill, Paper mill)
Phone: (86) 776 5151 808/5152 869
Fax: (86) 776 5151 808/5152 668

ⓂGuangxi Jinrong Paper Co., Ltd.
Baise Mill
Silin Town Industrial Park, Tiandong Town
Baise, Guangxi, 531504
China
　Phone: (86) 776 5151 808/5152 869
　Fax: (86) 776 5151 808/5152 668
　Web Address: www.jinrongpaper.com
Type of Operation: Pulp mill, Paper mill
Pulp Grades and Capacities:
　Total pulp capacity: 179,745 mt/y
　Recycled Pulping: 133,015 mt/y
　Other Pulp: 46,730 mt/y
Pulp Mill Data:
　Chemical Pulping Systems:
　Not Given: 1
Pulp Lines: 1
　Chemical Recovery Equipment:
　Recovery boilers: 1
Paper/Paperboard Grades and Capacities:
　Total paper and paperboard capacity: 180,000 mt/y
　Tissue: 30,000 mt/y
　Corrugating medium/fluting: 150,000 mt/y
Paper and Paperboard Mill Data:
Paper Machines: 19
No. 1, fourdrinier, total capacity 60,000 mt/y, Trim width 3.2 m, Corrugating medium/fluting
No. 2, fourdrinier, total capacity 90,000 mt/y, Trim width 4.6 m, Corrugating medium/fluting
No. 3, cylinder, total capacity 1,765 mt/y, Trim width 1.88 m, Tissue
No. 4, cylinder, total capacity 1,765 mt/y, Trim width 1.88 m, Tissue
No. 5, cylinder, total capacity 1,765 mt/y, Trim width 1.88 m, Tissue
No. 6, cylinder, total capacity 1,765 mt/y, Trim width 1.88 m, Tissue
No. 7, cylinder, total capacity 1,765 mt/y, Trim width 1.88 m, Tissue
No. 8, cylinder, total capacity 1,765 mt/y, Trim width 1.88 m, Tissue
No. 9, cylinder, total capacity 1,765 mt/y, Trim width 1.88 m, Tissue
No. 10, cylinder, total capacity 1,765 mt/y, Trim width 1.88 m, Tissue
No. 11, cylinder, total capacity 1,765 mt/y, Trim width 1.88 m, Tissue
No. 12, cylinder, total capacity 1,765 mt/y, Trim width 1.88 m, Tissue
No. 13, cylinder, total capacity 1,765 mt/y, Trim width 1.88 m, Tissue
No. 14, cylinder, total capacity 1,765 mt/y, Trim width 1.88 m, Tissue
No. 15, cylinder, total capacity 1,765 mt/y, Trim width 1.88 m, Tissue
No. 16, cylinder, total capacity 1,765 mt/y, Trim width 1.88 m, Tissue
No. 17, cylinder, total capacity 1,765 mt/y, Trim width 1.88 m, Tissue
No. 18, cylinder, total capacity 1,765 mt/y, Trim width 1.88 m, Tissue
No. 19, cylinder, total capacity 1,765 mt/y, Trim width 1.88 m, Tissue
Energy Data:
Power boilers: 2
Steam turbines: 1 at 12 MW
Electrical demand for mill: 309 MWh/D

ⓂGuangxi Laibin Donta Paper Co., Ltd.
Laibin Mill
Ownership: Guangdong Donta Group Co., Ltd.
Datianping, Putian Village, Chengxiang County, Xinbin District
Laibin, Guangxi, 546100
China
　Phone: (86) 772 406 6669/6666
　Fax: (86) 772 406 6889
　Web Address: www.donta.com.cn
Personnel:
　Chmn. & Gen. Mgr.: Jingshen Li
　Phone: (86) 772 406 6669
　Chief Eng.: Yuedong Lv
　Phone: (86) 772 406 6669
Total Employees at this Location: 1,407
Type of Operation: Pulp mill, Paper mill
Pulp Grades and Capacities:
　Total pulp capacity: 87,229 mt/y
　Pulp available for market: 87,229 mt/y
　Other Pulp: 87,229 mt/y
Pulp Mill Data:
　Chemical Pulping Systems:
　Batch digesters
　Bleach Plant Systems: 1
　No. 1, Sequence: CEopHP
　Chemical Recovery Equipment:
　Evaporator lines
　Recovery boilers: 1
　Recovery boilers: 1
Paper/Paperboard Grades and Capacities:
　Total paper and paperboard capacity: 18,433 mt/y
　Tissue: 18,433 mt/y
Paper and Paperboard Mill Data:
Paper Machines: 12
T10, cylinder, total capacity 1,535 mt/y, Trim width 1.88 m, Tissue
T11, cylinder, total capacity 1,535 mt/y, Trim width 1.88 m, Tissue
T12, cylinder, total capacity 1,535 mt/y, Trim width 1.88 m, Tissue
T13, cylinder, total capacity 1,535 mt/y, Trim width 1.88 m, Tissue
T2, cylinder, total capacity 1,547 mt/y, Trim width 1.88 m, Tissue
T3, cylinder, total capacity 1,535 mt/y, Trim width 1.88 m, Tissue
T4, cylinder, total capacity 1,535 mt/y, Trim width 1.88 m, Tissue
T5, cylinder, total capacity 1,535 mt/y, Trim width 1.88 m, Tissue
T6, cylinder, total capacity 1,535 mt/y, Trim width 1.88 m, Tissue
T7, cylinder, total capacity 1,535 mt/y, Trim width 1.88 m, Tissue
T8, cylinder, total capacity 1,535 mt/y, Trim width 1.88 m, Tissue
T9, cylinder, total capacity 1,535 mt/y, Trim width 1.88 m, Tissue
Energy Data:
Power boilers: 1
Steam turbines: 1 at 6 MW
Electrical demand for mill: 128 MWh/D

ⓂⓂGuangxi Laibin Huamei Paper Co., Ltd
Laibin Mill
Ownership: Guangxi Huamei Paper Group Co., Ltd.
Henan Industrial Park
Laibin, Guangxi, 546100
China
　Phone: (86) 772 4201 888/006
　Fax: (86) 772 4201 666
　Web Address: www.hmpaper.cn
Total Employees at this Location: 500
Type of Operation: Paper mill
Paper/Paperboard Grades and Capacities:
　Total paper and paperboard capacity: 130,000 mt/y
　Tissue: 130,000 mt/y
Paper and Paperboard Mill Data:
Paper Machines: 42
No. 31-42, total capacity 3,500 mt/y, Trim width 4.2 m, Tissue
PM 1-24, total capacity 3,000 mt/y, Trim width 3.48 m, Tissue
PM 25-26, total capacity 3,000 mt/y, Trim width 3.48 m, Tissue
PM 27-30, total capacity 2,500 mt/y, Trim width 2.88 m, Tissue

ⓂGuangxi Liangmianzhen Paper Co., Ltd.
Liuzhou Mill
Ownership: Zhongzhu Paper Group
Luofu Town
Liuzhou, Guangxi, 545011
China
　Phone: (86) 772 2068 369/351
　Fax: (86) 772 275 0177/0784
　Email: liujiangpaper@163.com
　Web Address: www.lmzzy.com.cn
Personnel:
　Pres./Mill Mgr.: Yanmin Zheng
　Phone: (86) 772 275 0335
　Chief Eng.: Qingrong Hong
　Phone: (86) 772 275 0335
Total Employees at this Location: 575
Type of Operation: Pulp mill, Paper mill
Pulp Grades and Capacities:
　Total pulp capacity: 65,000 mt/y
　Pulp available for market: 65,000 mt/y
　Chemical Pulp: 55,250 mt/y
　Other Pulp: 9,750 mt/y

China

Pulp Mill Data:
Chemical Pulping Systems:
Batch digesters: 3
Continuous digesters: 1
Pulp Lines: 2
Bleach Plant Systems: 2
wood-bamboo pulping system, Sequence: C/D-E/O-H-D, Capacity 70,000 admt/y
wood-bamboo pulping system, Sequence: CEpH, Capacity 35,000 admt/y
Chemical Recovery Equipment:
Recovery boilers: 2
Pulp Dryers:
Wet Lap machine 3
Finishing Equipment:
Supercalenders: 1
Rewinders: 1
Sheeters: 1
Energy Data:
Power boilers: 3
Steam turbines: 3 at 3, 6, 12 MW
Electrical demand for mill: 108 MWh/D

ⓗGuangxi Liuzhou Guizhong Paper Co., Ltd.
Luzhai County Industrial Park
Liuzhou, Guangxi, 545600
China
Phone: (86) 772 3596 660
Mill Locations:
Guangxi Liuzhou Guizhong Paper Co., Ltd., Liuzhou Mill, Luzhai County Industrial Park, Liuzhou 545600, China, Capacity: 12,000 mt/y, (Paper mill)
Phone: (86) 772 3596 660

ⓜGuangxi Liuzhou Guizhong Paper Co., Ltd.
Liuzhou Mill
Luzhai County Industrial Park
Liuzhou, Guangxi, 545600
China
Phone: (86) 772 3596 660
Type of Operation: Paper mill
Paper/Paperboard Grades and Capacities:
Total paper and paperboard capacity: 12,000 mt/y
Tissue: 12,000 mt/y

ⓗGuangxi Liuzhou Liulin Paper Co., Ltd.
Luzhai County Industrial Park
Liuzhou, Guangxi, 545600
China
Mill Locations:
Guangxi Liuzhou Liulin Paper Co., Ltd., Liuzhou Mill, Luzhai County Industrial Park, Liuzhou 545600, China, Capacity: 15,000 mt/y, (Paper mill)

ⓜGuangxi Liuzhou Liulin Paper Co., Ltd.
Liuzhou Mill
Luzhai County Industrial Park
Liuzhou, Guangxi, 545600
China
Type of Operation: Paper mill
Paper/Paperboard Grades and Capacities:
Total paper and paperboard capacity: 15,000 mt/y
Tissue: 15,000 mt/y
Paper and Paperboard Mill Data:
Paper Machines: 10
PM 1, total capacity 1,500 mt/y, Trim width 1.76 m, Tissue
PM 2, total capacity 1,500 mt/y, Trim width 1.76 m, Tissue
PM 3, total capacity 1,500 mt/y, Trim width 1.76 m, Tissue
PM 4, total capacity 1,500 mt/y, Trim width 1.76 m, Tissue
PM 5, total capacity 1,500 mt/y, Trim width 1.76 m, Tissue
PM 6, total capacity 1,500 mt/y, Trim width 1.76 m, Tissue
PM 7, total capacity 1,500 mt/y, Trim width 1.76 m, Tissue
PM 8, total capacity 1,500 mt/y, Trim width 1.76 m, Tissue
PM 9, total capacity 1,500 mt/y, Trim width 1.76 m, Tissue
PM 10, total capacity 1,500 mt/y, Trim width 1.76 m, Tissue

ⓗGuangxi Liuzhou Zhongdi Paper Co., Ltd.
Luorong Industrial Park, Luzhai County
Liuzhou, Guangxi
China
Phone: (86) 772 6510 368
Mill Locations:
Guangxi Liuzhou Zhongdi Paper Co., Ltd., Liuzhou Mill, Luorong Industrial Park, Luzhai County, Liuzhou, China, Capacity: 10,000 mt/y, (Paper mill)
Phone: (86) 772 6510 368

ⓜGuangxi Liuzhou Zhongdi Paper Co., Ltd.
Liuzhou Mill
Luorong Industrial Park, Luzhai County
Liuzhou, Guangxi
China
Phone: (86) 772 6510 368
Type of Operation: Paper mill
Paper/Paperboard Grades and Capacities:
Total paper and paperboard capacity: 10,000 mt/y
Tissue: 10,000 mt/y

ⓜGuangxi Longzhou Nanhua Paper Co., Ltd.
Chongzuo Mill
Ownership: Guangxi Yangpu Nanhua Sugar Industry Group Co., Ltd.
Longzhou County
Chongzuo, Guangxi
China
Phone: (86) 771 8833 458
Total Employees at this Location: 350
Type of Operation: Pulp mill
Pulp Grades and Capacities:
Total pulp capacity: 95,000 mt/y
Pulp available for market: 95,000 mt/y
Other Pulp: 95,000 mt/y
Pulp Mill Data:
Chemical Pulping Systems:
Batch digesters: 1
Pulp Lines: 1
Bleach Plant Systems: 1
No. 1, Sequence: DEpD
Chemical Recovery Equipment:
Evaporator lines: 1
Recovery boilers: 1
Energy Data:
Power boilers
Steam turbines
Electrical demand for mill: 151 MWh/D

ⓜGuangxi Nanning Huaze Pulp & Paper Co., Ltd.
Nanning Mill
Baisha Rd., Jiangnan District
Nanning, Guangxi
China
Phone: (86) 771 4300 895
Type of Operation: Paper mill
Paper/Paperboard Grades and Capacities:
Total paper and paperboard capacity: 15,000 mt/y
Tissue: 15,000 mt/y
Paper and Paperboard Mill Data:
Paper Machines: 12
No. 1, total capacity 1,000 mt/y, Trim width 1.58 m, Tissue
No. 2, total capacity 1,000 mt/y, Trim width 1.58 m, Tissue
No. 3, total capacity 1,000 mt/y, Trim width 1.58 m, Tissue
No. 4, total capacity 1,000 mt/y, Trim width 1.58 m, Tissue
No. 5, total capacity 1,000 mt/y, Trim width 1.58 m, Tissue
No. 6, total capacity 1,000 mt/y, Trim width 1.58 m, Tissue
No. 7, total capacity 1,500 mt/y, Trim width 1.88 m, Tissue
No. 8, total capacity 1,500 mt/y, Trim width 1.88 m, Tissue
No. 9, total capacity 1,500 mt/y, Trim width 1.88 m, Tissue
No. 10, total capacity 1,500 mt/y, Trim width 1.88 m, Tissue
No. 11, total capacity 1,500 mt/y, Trim width 1.88 m, Tissue
No. 12, total capacity 1,500 mt/y, Trim width 1.88 m, Tissue
Energy Data:
Power boilers: 1

ⓗGuangxi Nanning Jiabao Paper Co., Ltd.
Youyi Rd., Jiangnan District
Nanning, Guangxi, 530000
China
Phone: (86) 771 4842 929
Mill Locations:
Guangxi Nanning Jiabao Paper Co., Ltd., Nanning Mill, Youyi Rd., Jiangnan District, Nanning 530000, China, Capacity: 20,000 mt/y, (Paper mill)
Phone: (86) 771 4842 929

ⓜGuangxi Nanning Jiabao Paper Co., Ltd.
Nanning Mill
Youyi Rd., Jiangnan District
Nanning, Guangxi, 530000
China
Phone: (86) 771 4842 929
Type of Operation: Paper mill
Paper/Paperboard Grades and Capacities:
Total paper and paperboard capacity: 20,000 mt/y
Tissue: 20,000 mt/y

ⓗGuangxi Nanning Jiada Paper
Lo Wei Yan Oi Street Park in Xinbin road (Lu Wei industrial zone)
Binyang county, Nanning city, Guangxi
China
Phone: (86) 077182816888/285/688
Fax: (86) 07718283288
Email: tf@gxnnzy.cn
Web Address: www.gxnnzy.cn
Mill Locations:
Guangxi Nanning Jiada Paper, Nanning Mill, Lo Wei Yan Oi Street Park in Xinbin road (Lu Wei industrial zone), Binyang County, Nanning, China, Capacity: 26,000 mt/y, (Paper mill)
Phone: (86) 771 8281 688/8285 688
Fax: (86) 771 8283 288
Email: tf@gxnnzy.cn

ⓜGuangxi Nanning Jiada Paper
Nanning Mill
Lo Wei Yan Oi Street Park in Xinbin road (Lu Wei industrial zone), Binyang County
Nanning, Guangxi
China
Phone: (86) 771 8281 688/8285 688
Fax: (86) 771 8283 288
Email: tf@gxnnzy.cn
Web Address: www.gxnnzy.cn
Total Employees at this Location: 120
Type of Operation: Paper mill
Paper/Paperboard Grades and Capacities:
Total paper and paperboard capacity: 26,000 mt/y
Tissue: 26,000 mt/y
Paper and Paperboard Mill Data:
Paper Machines: 2
No. 1, (Supplier: Foshan Baotuo SF-12.), cylinder, total capacity 13,000 mt/y, Trim width 2.66 m, Tissue, Uncoated woodfree/freesheet
No. 2, (Supplier: Foshan Baotuo SF-12.), cylinder, total capacity 13,000 mt/y, Trim width 2.66 m, Tissue, Uncoated woodfree/freesheet
Energy Data:
Power boilers: 2
Steam turbines
Electrical demand for mill: 58 MWh/D

ⓜGuangxi Nanning Jindaxing Pulp & Paper Co., Ltd.
Nanning Mill
Ownership: Guangxi Jindaxing Paper Group Co., Ltd.

Liujing Industry Park, Heng County
Nanning, Guangxi
China
 Phone: (86) 771 559 9766
 Web Address: www.jingdaxing.com
Personnel:
 Chmn.: Jinsong Liu
 Phone: (86) 771 559 9766
Total Employees at this Location: 300
Type of Operation: Pulp mill, Paper mill
Pulp Mill Data:
 Chemical Pulping Systems:
 Batch digesters: 1
Pulp Lines: 1
Paper/Paperboard Grades and Capacities:
 Total paper and paperboard capacity: 171,360 mt/y
 Uncoated woodfree/freesheet: 171,360 mt/y
Paper and Paperboard Mill Data:
Paper Machines: 1
No. 1, (2nd hand, started up September 2011), DuoFormer D, total capacity 171,360 mt/y, Trim width 5.8 m, Uncoated woodfree/freesheet
Energy Data:
Electrical demand for mill: 332 MWh/D

ⓂGuangxi Nanning Lianli Paper Co., Ltd
Nanning Mill
Ownership: 100% by Guangdong Guangzhou Panyu Lianhuashan Paper-Making Co., Ltd.
Donghailin Rd., Xinqiao Town, Binyang County
Nanning, Guangxi, 530401
China
 Phone: (86) 771 8484 008
 Fax: (86) 771 8484 008
Personnel:
 Gen. Mgr.: Xiao Huang
 Phone: (86) 771 8484 008
 Sls. Mgr.: Daqi Han
 Phone: (86) 771 8484 008
 Purch. Mgr.: Faqiang Lin
 Phone: (86) 771 8484 008
Total Employees at this Location: 200
Type of Operation: Paper mill
Paper/Paperboard Grades and Capacities:
 Total paper and paperboard capacity: 5,000 mt/y
 Tissue: 5,000 mt/y
Paper and Paperboard Mill Data:
Paper Machines: 1
PM 1-4, fourdrinier, total capacity 1,250 mt/y, Trim width 1.58 m, Tissue

ⓂGuangxi Nanning Phoenix Pulp & Paper Co. Ltd.
Ownership: 100% by shareholders
158 Xingguang Rd.
Nanning, Guangxi, 530031
China
 Phone: (86) 771 459 0200 / 0261/ 0229/ 0255/ 0312
 Fax: (86) 771 459 0236/ 0268/ 451 6683
 Email: phoenix@nppc.cn
 Web Address: www.nppc.cn
Personnel:
 Chmn.: Xiaoming Duan
 Email: duanxm@nppc.cn
 Gen. Mgr.: Deshan Huang
 Sls. Mgr.: Shengkang Pan
Total Employees at this Location: 869
Mill Locations:
Guangxi Nanning Phoenix Pulp & Paper Co. Ltd., Nanning Mill, 158 Xingguang Rd., Nanning 530031, China, Capacity: 74,863 mt/y, (Pulp mill, Paper mill)
Phone: (86) 771 459 0200 / 0261 / 0229/ 0255/ 0312
Fax: (86) 771 459 0236/ 0268/ 451 6683
Email: phoenix@nppc.cn

ⓂGuangxi Nanning Phoenix Pulp & Paper Co. Ltd.
Nanning Mill
158 Xingguang Rd.
Nanning, Guangxi, 530031
China
 Phone: (86) 771 459 0200 / 0261/ 0229/ 0255/ 0312
 Fax: (86) 771 459 0236/ 0268/ 451 6683
 Email: phoenix@nppc.cn
 Web Address: www.nppc.cn
Personnel:
 Chmn.: Xiaoming Duan
 Phone: (86) 771 459 0206/136 0771 5733
 Email: duanxm@nppc.cn
 Gen. Mgr.: Deshan Huang
 Phone: (86) 771 459 0200 / 0261/ 0229/ 0255/ 0312
 Sls. Mgr.: Shengkang Pan
 Phone: (86) 771 459 0200 / 0261/ 0229/ 0255/ 0312
Total Employees at this Location: 631
Type of Operation: Pulp mill, Paper mill
Pulp Grades and Capacities:
 Total pulp capacity: 125,693 mt/y
 Pulp available for market: 104,601 mt/y
 Chemical Pulp: 125,693 mt/y
Pulp Mill Data:
 Chemical Pulping Systems:
 Continuous digesters: 1
 Bleach Plant Systems: 1
 No. 1, Sequence: O_2 DEopDD
 Chemical Recovery Equipment:
 Evaporator lines
 Recovery boilers: 1
 Lime Kiln
 Pulp Dryers:
 Flakt dryer 1, Flakt dryer 1
Paper/Paperboard Grades and Capacities:
 Total paper and paperboard capacity: 74,863 mt/y
 Tissue: 74,863 mt/y
Paper and Paperboard Mill Data:
Paper Machines: 14
No. 1, cylinder, total capacity 1,321 mt/y, Trim width 1.58 m, Tissue
No. 2, cylinder, total capacity 1,321 mt/y, Trim width 1.58 m, Tissue
No. 3, cylinder, total capacity 1,321 mt/y, Trim width 1.58 m, Tissue
No. 4, cylinder, total capacity 1,321 mt/y, Trim width 1.58 m, Tissue
No. 5, cylinder, total capacity 1,321 mt/y, Trim width 1.58 m, Tissue
No. 6, cylinder, total capacity 1,321 mt/y, Trim width 1.58 m, Tissue
No. 7, cylinder, total capacity 1,321 mt/y, Trim width 1.58 m, Tissue
No. 8, cylinder, total capacity 1,321 mt/y, Trim width 1.58 m, Tissue
No. 9, cylinder, total capacity 1,321 mt/y, Trim width 1.58 m, Tissue
No. 10, cylinder, total capacity 1,321 mt/y, Trim width 1.58 m, Tissue
No. 11, cylinder, total capacity 1,321 mt/y, Trim width 1.58 m, Tissue
TM 1, BF-10 a, total capacity 9,996 mt/y, Trim width 2.66 m, Tissue
TM 2, BF-12, total capacity 20,349 mt/y, Trim width 3.4 m, Tissue, Uncoated woodfree/freesheet
TM 3, crescent former, total capacity 29,988 mt/y, Trim width 3.65 m, Tissue, Uncoated woodfree/freesheet
Energy Data:
Power boilers: 2
Steam turbines: 1 at 20 MW
Electrical demand for mill: 425 MWh/D

ⓂGuangxi Nanning Tianran Paper Co., Ltd.
Nanning Mill
Mill is leased to Nanning Meina from March 1, 2013 to February 28, 2018

Ownership: 79% by Guangxi Nanning Sugar and Paper Mill
Gongye Rd., Wuming County
Nanning, Guangxi, 530105
China
 Phone: (86) 771 630 1420/ 1278
 Fax: (86) 771 630 1423
 Web Address: www.nnsugar.com
Personnel:
 Chmn. & Gen. Mgr.: Han Pan
 Phone: (86) 771 630 1420/ 1278
 Asst. Gen. Mgr.: Zhen Yang
 Phone: (86) 771 630 1420/ 1278
Total Employees at this Location: 532
Type of Operation: Paper mill
Paper/Paperboard Grades and Capacities:
 Total paper and paperboard capacity: 40,000 mt/y
 Tissue: 40,000 mt/y
Paper and Paperboard Mill Data:
Paper Machines: 28
PM 1-20, cylinder, total capacity 1,400 mt/y, Trim width 1.58 m, Tissue
PM 21-28, fourdrinier, total capacity 1,500 mt/y, Trim width 1.88 m, Tissue

ⓂGuangxi Paiji Paper Co., Ltd.
Ownership: Nanda(Zhejiang) EP Technology
No.48 Tinghong Rd., Jiangnan District
Nanning, Guangxi, 530031
China
 Phone: (86) 771 4925 951
 Email: paiji@zjnd.com
 Web Address: www.zjnd.com
Mill Locations:
Guangxi Paiji Paper Co., Ltd., Nanning Mill, No.48 Tinghong Rd., Jiangnan District, Nanning 530031, China, Capacity: 90,000 mt/y, (Paperboard mill)
Phone: (86) 771 4925 951
Email: paiji@zjnd.com

ⓂGuangxi Paiji Paper Co., Ltd.
Nanning Mill
No.48 Tinghong Rd., Jiangnan District
Nanning, Guangxi, 530031
China
 Phone: (86) 771 4925 951
 Email: paiji@zjnd.com
 Web Address: www.zjnd.com
Total Employees at this Location: 370
Type of Operation: Paperboard mill
Pulp Grades and Capacities:
 Total pulp capacity: 82,131 mt/y
 Other Pulp: 82,131 mt/y
Pulp Mill Data:
 Chemical Pulping Systems:
 Batch digesters: 1
 Bleach Plant Systems: 1
 Chemical Pulping System
 Chemical Recovery Equipment:
 Evaporator lines: 1
 Recovery boilers: 1
Paper/Paperboard Grades and Capacities:
 Total paper and paperboard capacity: 90,000 mt/y
 Boxboard/cartonboard: 90,000 mt/y
Paper and Paperboard Mill Data:
Paper Machines: 2
No. 1, Multi-wire (3), total capacity 35,000 mt/y, Trim width 1.76 m, Boxboard/cartonboard
No. 2, Multi-wire (4), total capacity 55,000 mt/y, Trim width 2.76 m, Boxboard/cartonboard
Energy Data:
Power boilers
Steam turbines

ⓂGuangxi Pumiao Paper Co., Ltd.
Nanning Mill
East Industry Park, Yongning District
Nanning, Guangxi, 530200
China

China

Phone: (86) 771 470 1582/ 1003
Fax: (86) 771 470 0287/ 0768
Web Address: www.nnsugar.com
Personnel:
Chmn.: Ling Xiao
Gen. Mgr.: Runsheng Ding
Total Employees at this Location: 1,300
Type of Operation: Pulp mill
Pulp Grades and Capacities:
Total pulp capacity: 130,000 mt/y
Pulp available for market: 105,000 mt/y
Pulp Mill Data:
Chemical Pulping Systems:
Batch digesters: 1
Pulp Lines: 1
Bleach Plant Systems: 1
No. 1, Sequence: O_2 DEopD

ⓗGuangxi Sky Power Natural Material Co., Ltd.
Liujing Industrial Park
Nanning, Guangxi, 530313
China
Phone: (86) 771 737 1999
Fax: (86) 771 726 5779
Web Address: www.tlfpaper.com
Total Employees at this Location: 200
Mill Locations:
Guangxi Sky Power Natural Material Co., Ltd., Nanning Mill, Liujing Industrial Park, Nanning 530313, China, Capacity: 25,000 mt/y, (Paper mill)
Phone: (86) 771 737 1999
Fax: (86) 771 726 5779

ⓜGuangxi Sky Power Natural Material Co., Ltd.
Nanning Mill
Liujing Industrial Park
Nanning, Guangxi, 530313
China
Phone: (86) 771 737 1999
Fax: (86) 771 726 5779
Web Address: www.tlfpaper.com
Total Employees at this Location: 200
Type of Operation: Paper mill
Paper/Paperboard Grades and Capacities:
Total paper and paperboard capacity: 25,000 mt/y
Tissue: 25,000 mt/y
Paper and Paperboard Mill Data:
Paper Machines: 12
PM 1, total capacity 1,200 mt/y, Trim width 1.58 m, Tissue
PM 2, total capacity 1,200 mt/y, Trim width 1.58 m, Tissue
PM 3, total capacity 1,200 mt/y, Trim width 1.58 m, Tissue
PM 4, total capacity 1,200 mt/y, Trim width 1.58 m, Tissue
PM 5, total capacity 1,200 mt/y, Trim width 1.58 m, Tissue
PM 6, total capacity 1,500 mt/y, Trim width 1.88 m, Tissue
PM 7, total capacity 1,500 mt/y, Trim width 1.88 m, Tissue
PM 8, total capacity 1,500 mt/y, Trim width 1.88 m, Tissue
PM 9, total capacity 1,500 mt/y, Trim width 1.88 m, Tissue
PM 10, total capacity 1,500 mt/y, Trim width 1.88 m, Tissue
PM 11, total capacity 1,500 mt/y, Trim width 1.88 m, Tissue
PM 12, total capacity 10,000 mt/y, Trim width 2.8 m, Tissue

ⓗGuangxi Tianlin County Lisen Paper Co., Ltd.
Ownership: 100% by private owners
No. 188 Huancheng Rd.
Tianlin County, Baise, Guangxi, 533300
China
Phone: (86) 776 720 3748
Fax: (86) 776 720 3958
Web Address: mmsky0776.kmip.net
Mill Locations:
Guangxi Tianlin County Lisen Paper Co., Ltd., Baise Mill, No. 188 Huancheng Rd., Tianlin County, Baise 533300, China, Capacity: 10,000 mt/y, (Paper mill)
Phone: (86) 776 720 3748
Fax: (86) 776 720 3958

ⓜGuangxi Tianlin County Lisen Paper Co., Ltd.
Baise Mill
No. 188 Huancheng Rd., Tianlin County
Baise, Guangxi, 533300
China
Phone: (86) 776 720 3748
Fax: (86) 776 720 3958
Personnel:
Chmn.: Ruipeng Tan
Phone: (86) 776 720 3748
Total Employees at this Location: 245
Type of Operation: Paper mill
Paper/Paperboard Grades and Capacities:
Total paper and paperboard capacity: 10,000 mt/y
Tissue: 10,000 mt/y
Paper and Paperboard Mill Data:
Paper Machines: 5
No. 1, fourdrinier, total capacity 1,650 mt/y, Trim width 1.58 m, Tissue
No. 2, fourdrinier, total capacity 1,650 mt/y, Trim width 1.58 m, Tissue
No. 3, fourdrinier, total capacity 1,650 mt/y, Trim width 1.58 m, Tissue
No. 4, cylinder, total capacity 2,500 mt/y, Trim width 1.58 m, Tissue
No. 5, cylinder, total capacity 2,500 mt/y, Trim width 1.58 m, Tissue
Energy Data:
Power boilers: 1

ⓗGuangxi Tianyang Huamei Paper Co., Lt.d
Ownership: Guangxi Huamei Paper Group Co., Ltd.
Tangzhi Industry Park, Honglingpo, Tianyang County
Baise, Guangxi, 533600
China
Phone: (86) 776 323 6838/ 6599/ 6891
Fax: (86) 776 323 6333
Email: linruicai@163.com, huamei200808@163.com
Web Address: www.hmpaper.cn
Personnel:
Gen. Mgr.: Ruicai Lin
Phone: (86) 776 323 6838/ 6599
Mill Locations:
Guangxi Tianyang Huamei Paper Co., Lt.d, Tianyang Mill, Tangzhi Industry Park, Honglingpo, Tianyang County, Baise 533600, China, Capacity: 70,000 mt/y, (Paper mill)
Phone: (86) 776 323 6838/6788/ 6891
Fax: (86) 776 323 6333
Email: linruicai@163.com, huamei200808@163.com

ⓜGuangxi Tianyang Huamei Paper Co., Lt.d
Tianyang Mill
Ownership: Guangxi Huamei Paper Group Co., Ltd.
Tangzhi Industry Park, Honglingpo, Tianyang County
Baise, Guangxi, 533600
China
Phone: (86) 776 323 6838/6788/ 6891
Fax: (86) 776 323 6333
Email: linruicai@163.com, huamei200808@163.com
Web Address: www.hmpaper.cn
Personnel:
Gen. Mgr.: Ruicai Lin
Phone: (86) 776 323 6838/ 6599
Total Employees at this Location: 700
Type of Operation: Paper mill
Paper/Paperboard Grades and Capacities:
Total paper and paperboard capacity: 70,000 mt/y
Tissue: 70,000 mt/y
Paper and Paperboard Mill Data:
Paper Machines: 51
PM 1-18, cylinder, total capacity 20,000 mt/y, Trim width 1.57 m, Tissue
PM 19-43, cylinder, total capacity 30,000 mt/y, Trim width 1.88 m, Tissue
PM 44-51, cylinder, total capacity 20,000 mt/y, Trim width 3.48 m, Tissue

ⓗⓜGuangxi Tianyang Nanhua Paper Co., Ltd
Baise Mill
Ownership: Guangxi Yangpu Nanhua Sugar Industry Group Co., Ltd.
Tianyang County
Baise, Guangxi
China
Phone: (86) 776 323 6366
Total Employees at this Location: 600
Type of Operation: Pulp mill, Paper mill
Pulp Grades and Capacities:
Total pulp capacity: 133,651 mt/y
Pulp available for market: 100,000 mt/y
Other Pulp: 133,651 mt/y
Pulp Mill Data:
Chemical Pulping Systems:
Batch digesters: 1
Pulp Lines: 1
Bleach Plant Systems: 1
No. 1, Type: Nonwood, Sequence: CEpH
Chemical Recovery Equipment:
Evaporator lines: 1
Recovery boilers: 1
Lime Kiln
Paper/Paperboard Grades and Capacities:
Total paper and paperboard capacity: 50,000 mt/y
Uncoated woodfree/freesheet: 50,000 mt/y
Paper and Paperboard Mill Data:
Paper Machines: 2
No. 1, fourdrinier, total capacity 25,000 mt/y, Trim width 1.88 m, Uncoated woodfree/freesheet
No. 2, fourdrinier, total capacity 25,000 mt/y, Trim width 1.88 m, Uncoated woodfree/freesheet
Energy Data:
Power boilers: 2
Steam turbines: 1 at 6 MW
Electrical demand for mill: 282 MWh/D

ⓜGuangxi Xiangzhou Liangui Paper Co., Ltd.
Laibin Mill
Ownership: Guangdong Guangzhou Panyu Lianhuashan Paper-Making Co., Ltd.
Tulan Village, Shilong Town, Xiangzhou County
Laibin, Guangxi, 545801
China
Phone: (86) 772 439 4988/ 4982
Fax: (86) 772 439 4989
Personnel:
Pres. & Gen. Mgr.: Zhiqiang Xian
Phone: (86) 772 439 4988/ 4982
VP - Sls.: Fulin Chen
Phone: (86) 772 439 4988/ 4982
Total Employees at this Location: 700
Type of Operation: Paper mill
Paper/Paperboard Grades and Capacities:
Total paper and paperboard capacity: 20,000 mt/y
Tissue: 20,000 mt/y
Paper and Paperboard Mill Data:
Paper Machines: 12
PM 1-8, fourdrinier, total capacity 1,875 mt/y, Trim width 1.58 m, Tissue
PM 9-12, cylinder, total capacity 1,250 mt/y, Trim width 1.58 m, Tissue

ⓗGuangxi Xinrui Paper Co., Ltd.
Liujing Industrial Park, Heng County
Nanning, Guangxi, 530313
China
Phone: (86) 771 7082 050/7265 896
Mill Locations:
Guangxi Xinrui Paper Co., Ltd., Nanning Mill, Liujing

Industrial Park, Heng County, Nanning 530313, China, Capacity: 50,000 mt/y, (Paper mill)
Phone: (86) 771 7082 050/7265 896

ⓜGuangxi Xinrui Paper Co., Ltd.
Nanning Mill
Liujing Industrial Park, Heng County
Nanning, Guangxi, 530313
China
Phone: (86) 771 7082 050/7265 896
Web Address: www.gxxrpc.com
Type of Operation: Paper mill
Paper/Paperboard Grades and Capacities:
Total paper and paperboard capacity: 50,000 mt/y
Tissue: 50,000 mt/y
Paper and Paperboard Mill Data:
Paper Machines: 8
PM 1, total capacity 5,000 mt/y, Trim width 2.9 m, Tissue
PM 2, total capacity 5,000 mt/y, Trim width 2.9 m, Tissue
PM 3, total capacity 5,000 mt/y, Trim width 2.9 m, Tissue
PM 4, total capacity 5,000 mt/y, Trim width 2.9 m, Tissue
PM 5, total capacity 5,000 mt/y, Trim width 2.9 m, Tissue
PM 6, total capacity 5,000 mt/y, Trim width 2.9 m, Tissue
PM 7, total capacity 10,000 mt/y, Trim width 2.9 m, Tissue
PM 8, total capacity 10,000 mt/y, Trim width 2.9 m, Tissue
Energy Data:
Power boilers: 1

ⓜGuangxi Yongkai Sugar and Paper Co., Ltd.
Nanning(liujing) Mill
Ownership: Guangxi Yongkai Sugar and Paper Group
Jingtai Rd., Liujing Industrial Park, Heng County
Nanning, Guangxi
China
Phone: (86) 771 2385 588
Email: tybgs@yongkai.com.cn
Web Address: www.yksugar.com, yongkaitangzhi.smenn.com.cn
Total Employees at this Location: 307
Type of Operation: Pulp mill
Pulp Grades and Capacities:
Total pulp capacity: 95,000 mt/y
Pulp available for market: 95,000 mt/y
Other Pulp: 95,000 mt/y
Pulp Mill Data:
Chemical Pulping Systems:
Continuous digesters: 1
Pulp Lines: 1
Bleach Plant Systems: 1
Chemical Pulping System, Type: ECF, Sequence: DEpD
Chemical Recovery Equipment:
Evaporator lines
Recovery boilers
Energy Data:
Power boilers: 2
Steam turbines: 3 at 33 MW
Electrical demand for mill: 141 MWh/D

ⓜGuangxi Yongxin Huatang Group Laibin Paper Co., Ltd.
No. 401, Tianranqiao Rd.
Laibin, Guangxi, 546100
China
Email: yxlbzy@163.com
Web Address: www.yxsugar.com
Mill Locations:
Guangxi Yongxin Huatang Group Laibin Paper Co., Ltd., Laibin Mill, No. 401, Tianranqiao Rd., Laibin 546100, China, (Pulp mill)
Email: yxlbzy@163.com

ⓜGuangxi Yongxin Huatang Group Laibin Paper Co., Ltd.
Laibin Mill
No. 401, Tianranqiao Rd.
Laibin, Guangxi, 546100
China
Email: yxlbzy@163.com
Web Address: www.yxsugar.com
Total Employees at this Location: 350
Type of Operation: Pulp mill
Pulp Grades and Capacities:
Total pulp capacity: 120,000 mt/y
Pulp available for market: 120,000 mt/y
Other Pulp: 120,000 mt/y
Pulp Mill Data:
Chemical Pulping Systems:
Continuous digesters: 1
Pulp Lines: 1
Bleach Plant Systems: 1
Bleached bagasse pulp line, Sequence: DEopD, Capacity 120,000 admt/y
Chemical Recovery Equipment:
Evaporator lines: 1
Recovery boilers: 1
Energy Data:
Power boilers
Steam turbines
Electrical demand for mill: 166 MWh/D

GUIZHOU

ⓜGuizhou Chitianhua Paper Industrial Co., Ltd
Chishui Mill
No. 1, Litai Road
Chishui, Guizhou, 564707
China
Phone: (86) 852 287 9721/6246
Fax: (86) 852 287 9729
Email: cth_sales@sina.com, chthzhiye@163.com
Web Address: www.cthzhiye.cn
Personnel:
Chmn.: Caiyou Zheng
Gen. Mgr.: Yong Tian
CFO: Shanhua Wu
Total Employees at this Location: 550
Type of Operation: Pulp mill
Pulp Grades and Capacities:
Total pulp capacity: 250,250 mt/y
Pulp available for market: 250,000 mt/y
Other Pulp: 250,250 mt/y
Pulp Mill Data:
Chemical Pulping Systems:
Continuous digesters
Pulp Lines: 1
Bleach Plant Systems: 1
Chemical Pulping System, Sequence: O_2 Q Op D/Q Po/P
Chemical Recovery Equipment:
Evaporator lines: 1
Recovery boilers: 1
Lime Kiln
Pulp Dryers:
Fourdriniers 1
Energy Data:
Power boilers
Steam turbines: 1 at 38 MW
Electrical demand for mill: 517 MWh/D

HAINAN

ⓜHainan Gold Hongye Paper Co., Ltd.
Yangpu (Gold Hongye Paper) Mill
Ownership: 100% by Asia Pulp & Paper (APP)
D12, Yangpu Eco. Deve. Zone
Haikou, Hainan, 578101
China
Phone: (86) 898 28822288
Fax: (86) 898 28821260
Web Address: www.appjh.com.cn
Total Employees at this Location: 300
Type of Operation: Paper mill
Paper/Paperboard Grades and Capacities:
Total paper and paperboard capacity: 409,218 mt/y
Tissue: 409,218 mt/y
Paper and Paperboard Mill Data:
Paper Machines: 10
No. 1, crescent former, total capacity 28,203 mt/y, Trim width 2.8 m, Tissue
No. 2, crescent former, total capacity 28,203 mt/y, Trim width 2.8 m, Tissue
No. 3, crescent former, total capacity 28,203 mt/y, Trim width 2.8 m, Tissue
No. 4, crescent former, total capacity 28,203 mt/y, Trim width 2.8 m, Tissue
No. 5, crescent former, total capacity 28,203 mt/y, Trim width 2.8 m, Tissue
No. 6, crescent former, total capacity 28,203 mt/y, Trim width 2.8 m, Tissue
No. 21, crescent former, total capacity 60,000 mt/y, Trim width 5.6 m, Tissue
No. 22, crescent former, total capacity 60,000 mt/y, Trim width 5.6 m, Tissue
No. 23, crescent former, total capacity 60,000 mt/y, Trim width 5.6 m, Tissue
No. 24, crescent former, total capacity 60,000 mt/y, Trim width 5.6 m, Tissue
Energy Data:
Electrical demand for mill: 558 MWh/D

ⓜHainan Gold Shengpu Paper Co., Ltd.
Haikou (Gold Shengpu Paper) Mill
Ownership: 100% by Asia Pulp & Paper (APP)
D12, Yangpu Eco. Deve. Zone
Haikou, Hainan, 578101
China
Phone: (86) 898 28822288
Fax: (86) 898 28821260
Web Address: www.appjh.com.cn
Personnel:
Pres. Dir: Liu Han Hung
Phone: (86) 898 28821251
Email: hhliu@appjh.com.cn
Total Employees at this Location: 200
Type of Operation: Paper mill
Paper/Paperboard Grades and Capacities:
Total paper and paperboard capacity: 202,062 mt/y
Tissue: 202,062 mt/y
Paper and Paperboard Mill Data:
Paper Machines: 10
No. 7, fourdrinier, total capacity 19,992 mt/y, Trim width 2.8 m, Tissue
No. 8, fourdrinier, total capacity 19,992 mt/y, Trim width 2.8 m, Tissue
No. 9, fourdrinier, total capacity 19,992 mt/y, Trim width 2.8 m, Tissue
No. 10, fourdrinier, total capacity 19,992 mt/y, Trim width 2.8 m, Tissue
No. 11, fourdrinier, total capacity 19,992 mt/y, Trim width 2.8 m, Tissue
No. 12, fourdrinier, total capacity 19,992 mt/y, Trim width 2.8 m, Tissue
No. 17, fourdrinier, total capacity 19,992 mt/y, Trim width 2.8 m, Tissue
No. 18, fourdrinier, total capacity 19,992 mt/y, Trim width 2.8 m, Tissue
No. 19, fourdrinier, total capacity 19,992 mt/y, Trim width 2.8 m, Tissue
No. 20, fourdrinier, total capacity 19,992 mt/y, Trim width 2.8 m, Tissue
Energy Data:
Electrical demand for mill: 330 MWh/D

ⓜHainan Jinhai Pulp & Paper Industry Co., Ltd.
Yangpu (Hainan Jinhai Pulp & Paper Industry) Mill

China

Ownership: 100% by Asia Pulp & Paper (APP)
D12, Yangpu Eco. Deve. Zone
Haikou, Hainan, 578101
China
  Phone: (86) 898 28822288/28821513
  Fax: (86) 898 28821260
  Web Address: www.appjh.com.cn
Personnel:
  Pres. Dir.: Liu Han Hung
  Phone: (86) 898 28821251
  Fax: (86) 898 2882 3623
  Email: hhliu@appjh.com.cn
Total Employees at this Location: 1,887
Type of Operation: Pulp mill, Paper mill
Pulp Grades and Capacities:
  Total pulp capacity: 1,248,672 mt/y
  Pulp available for market: 859,847 mt/y
  Chemical Pulp: 1,248,672 mt/y
Pulp Mill Data:
  Chemical Pulping Systems:
  Continuous digesters: 1
  Pulp Lines: 1
  Bleach Plant Systems: 1
  Chemical Pulping System - Hardwood, Sequence: O₂ DEopDD
  Chemical Recovery Equipment:
  Evaporator lines
  Recovery boilers: 1
  Recovery boilers: 1
  Lime Kiln
  Pulp Dryers:
  Flakt dryer 1
Paper/Paperboard Grades and Capacities:
  Total paper and paperboard capacity: 1,035,300 mt/y
  Coated woodfree/freesheet: 1,035,300 mt/y
Paper and Paperboard Mill Data:
  Paper Machines: 1
  No. 2, DuoFormer TQv, total capacity 1,035,300 mt/y, Trim width 11.2 m, Coated woodfree/freesheet
  Coating Machines: 1
  PM 2, total capacity 1,035,000 mt/y, off machine
  Finishing Equipment:
  Supercalenders: 2
  Rewinders: 14
Energy Data:
  Power boilers: 2
  Steam turbines: 4 at 120, 120, 90, 90 MW
  Electrical demand for mill: 3,615 MWh/D

HEBEI

ⓘⓜBaoding Aisen Paper Co., Ltd
Baoding Mill
Daceying Paper Making Industry Park, Mancheng
Baoding, Hebei
China
Total Employees of Company: 250
Total Employees at this Location: 250
Type of Operation: Paper mill
Paper/Paperboard Grades and Capacities:
  Total paper and paperboard capacity: 30,000 mt/y
  Tissue

ⓘBaoding Jinboshi Paper Co., Ltd.
DaMancheng County
Baoding, Hebei, 072150
China
  Phone: (86) 312 7021 036
  Fax: (86) 312 5578 388
  Email: hbjbs7021036@126.com
  Web Address: www.jbspaper.com
Mill Locations:
Baoding Jinboshi Paper Co., Ltd., Baoding Mill, DaMancheng County, Baoding 072150, China, Capacity: 22,800 mt/y, (Paper mill)
  Phone: (86) 312 7021 036
  Fax: (86) 312 5578 388
  Email: hbjbs7021036@126.com

ⓘⓜBaoding Jinboshi Paper Co., Ltd.
Baoding Mill
DaMancheng County
Baoding, Hebei, 072150
China
  Phone: (86) 312 7021 036
  Fax: (86) 312 5578 388
  Email: hbjbs7021036@126.com
  Web Address: www.jbspaper.com
Type of Operation: Paper mill
Paper/Paperboard Grades and Capacities:
  Total paper and paperboard capacity: 22,800 mt/y
  Tissue: 22,800 mt/y
Paper and Paperboard Mill Data:
  Paper Machines: 6
  PM 1, total capacity 2,400 mt/y, Trim width 2.8 m, Tissue
  PM 2, total capacity 2,400 mt/y, Trim width 2.8 m, Tissue
  PM 3, total capacity 4,500 mt/y, Trim width 3.5 m, Tissue
  PM 4, total capacity 4,500 mt/y, Trim width 3.5 m, Tissue
  PM 5, total capacity 4,500 mt/y, Trim width 3.5 m, Tissue
  PM 6, total capacity 4,500 mt/y, Trim width 3.5 m, Tissue

ⓘⓜBaoding City Jinneng Sanitary Products Co., Ltd.
Baoding Mill
Beigoutou Industrial Zone, South Chaoyang Street
Baoding, Hebei, 071000
China
  Phone: (86) 312-2151998
  Fax: (86) 312-2152998
Total Employees of Company: 250
Total Employees at this Location: 250
Type of Operation: Paper mill
Paper/Paperboard Grades and Capacities:
  Total paper and paperboard capacity: 20,000 mt/y
  Tissue

ⓘⓜBaoding Yazi Paper Co., Ltd.
Baoding Mill
Luzhuang Village, Hengxiang North Street
Baoding, Hebei, 071051
China
  Phone: (86) 312 3184 992
Type of Operation: Paper mill
Paper/Paperboard Grades and Capacities:
  Total paper and paperboard capacity: 9,000 mt/y
  Tissue: 9,000 mt/y
Paper and Paperboard Mill Data:
  Paper Machines: 2
  PM 1, total capacity 4,500 mt/y, Trim width 3.5 m, Tissue
  PM 2, total capacity 4,500 mt/y, Trim width 3.5 m, Tissue

ⓘⓜBaoding Yusen Hygiene Products Co., Ltd
Baoding Yusen Hygiene Products Co., Ltd
Daceying Paper Making Industry Park, Mancheng
Baoding, Hebei, 072150
China
  Phone: (86) 312 5578100
  Fax: (86) 312 5572100
  Email: yusen@yusenpaper.com
  Web Address: www.yusenpaper.com
Total Employees at this Location: 400
Type of Operation: Paper mill
Paper/Paperboard Grades and Capacities:
  Total paper and paperboard capacity: 50,000 mt/y
  Tissue

ⓜBotou Longda Paper Co., Ltd.
Cangzhou Mill
Yingbin Rd., Botou
Cangzhou, Hebei, 062150
China
  Phone: (86) 317 818 5878/831 8556
  Fax: (86) 317 831 8655
  Email: suyanqiusss@163.com
Type of Operation: Paper mill
Pulp Grades and Capacities:
  Total pulp capacity: 50,048 mt/y
  Recycled Pulping: 50,048 mt/y
Paper/Paperboard Grades and Capacities:
  Total paper and paperboard capacity: 50,000 mt/y
  Corrugating medium/fluting: 50,000 mt/y
Paper and Paperboard Mill Data:
  Paper Machines: 2
  No. 1, fourdrinier, total capacity 18,000 mt/y, Trim width 2.4 m, Corrugating medium/fluting
  No. 2, fourdrinier, total capacity 32,000 mt/y, Trim width 3.6 m, Corrugating medium/fluting
Energy Data:
  Power boilers: 1
  Electrical demand for mill: 58 MWh/D

ⓜC&S Paper Co., Ltd.
Tangshan Mill
Donggao qiao, Yutian county
Tangshan, Hebei, 063000
China
  Phone: (86) 315 633 0999/0991
  Fax: (86) 315 655 0606
  Email: jiangxuhui1985@163.com
  Web Address: www.zhongshungroup.com
Total Employees at this Location: 125
Type of Operation: Paper mill
Paper/Paperboard Grades and Capacities:
  Total paper and paperboard capacity: 25,000 mt/y
  Tissue: 25,000 mt/y
Paper and Paperboard Mill Data:
  Paper Machines: 1
  No. 9, crescent former, Yankee dryer, total capacity 25,000 mt/y, Trim width 3.48 m, Tissue
Energy Data:
  Power boilers
  Electrical demand for mill: 62 MWh/D

ⓘFengyuan (Xingtai) Specialty Paper Co., Ltd.
Yang Village, Wangjiazhuang Town, Baixiang County
Xingtai, Hebei
China
  Phone: (86) 319 770 1166/1179
Personnel:
  Chmn.: Bingqiang Lv
  Phone: (86) 319 770 1166/1179
Mill Locations:
Fengyuan (Xingtai) Specialty Paper Co., Ltd., Xingtai Mill, Yang Village, Wangjiazhuang Town, Baixiang County, Xingtai, China, (Pulp mill)
  Phone: (86) 319 770 1166/1179

ⓘFengyuan (Xingtai) Specialty Paper Co., Ltd.
Xingtai Mill
Yang Village, Wangjiazhuang Town, Baixiang County
Xingtai, Hebei
China
  Phone: (86) 319 770 1166/1179
Type of Operation: Pulp mill
Pulp Grades and Capacities:
  Total pulp capacity: 10,000 mt/y
  Pulp available for market: 10,000 mt/y
Pulp Mill Data:
  Pulp Lines: 1

ⓘHebei Baoding Banknote Paper Mill
Ownership: 100% by state
No. 98, West Shengxing Rd.
Baoding City, Hebei, 071071
China
  Phone: (86) 312 317 6416/ 319 8052
  Fax: (86) 312 317 8167
  Email: baochao@bdcpzc.com
  Web Address: www.cbpmc.com.cn
Mill Locations:
Hebei Baoding Banknote Paper Mill, Baoding Mill, No. 98, West Shengxing Rd., Baoding 071071, China,

Capacity: 35,000 mt/y, (Paper mill)
Phone: (86) 312 317 6416/ 319 8052
Fax: (86) 312 317 8167
Email: baochao@bdcpzc.com

ⓜHebei Baoding Banknote Paper Mill
Baoding Mill
No. 98, West Shengxing Rd.
Baoding, Hebei, 071071
China
Phone: (86) 312 317 6416/ 319 8052
Fax: (86) 312 317 8167
Email: baochao@bdcpzc.com
Web Address: www.cbpmc.com.cn
Personnel:
Mill Mgr.: Congbiao Zhou
Phone: (86) 312 317 6416/ 319 8052
Tech. Dir.: Shuhai Jin
Phone: (86) 312 317 6416/ 319 8052
Total Employees at this Location: 2,842
Type of Operation: Paper mill
Pulp Mill Data:
Chemical Pulping Systems:
Batch digesters: 10
Paper/Paperboard Grades and Capacities:
Total paper and paperboard capacity: 35,000 mt/y
Uncoated woodfree/freesheet

ⓜHebei Baoding Baojie Paper Co., Ltd.
Daceying Paper Making Industrial Park, Mancheng County
Baoding, Hebei
China
Phone: (86) 312 7021 228
Mill Locations:
Hebei Baoding Baojie Paper Co., Ltd., Baoding Mill, Daceying Paper Making Industrial Park, Mancheng County, Baoding, China, Capacity: 5,000 mt/y, (Paper mill)
Phone: (86) 312 7021 228

ⓜHebei Baoding Baojie Paper Co., Ltd.
Baoding Mill
Daceying Paper Making Industrial Park, Mancheng County
Baoding, Hebei
China
Phone: (86) 312 7021 228
Type of Operation: Paper mill
Paper/Paperboard Grades and Capacities:
Total paper and paperboard capacity: 5,000 mt/y
Tissue: 5,000 mt/y
Paper and Paperboard Mill Data:
Paper Machines: 1
PM 1, total capacity 5,000 mt/y, Trim width 3.5 m, Tissue

ⓜHebei Baoding Chenguang Paper Co., Ltd.
Ownership: 100% by private owners
North Ring Road No. 699
Baoding, Hebei, 071000
China
Phone: (86) 312 310 4888/ 317 1036
Fax: (86) 312 317 2452
Email: chenguangzhiye@126.com
Web Address: www.chgzy.com.cn
Mill Locations:
Hebei Baoding Chenguang Paper Co., Ltd., Baoding Mill, North Ring Road No. 699, Baoding 071000, China, Capacity: 18,000 mt/y, (Paper mill)
Phone: (86) 312 310 4888/ 317 1036
Fax: (86) 312 317 2452
Email: chenguangzhiye@126.com

ⓜHebei Baoding Chenguang Paper Co., Ltd.
Baoding Mill
North Ring Road No. 699
Baoding, Hebei, 071000
China
Phone: (86) 312 310 4888/ 317 1036
Fax: (86) 312 317 2452
Email: chenguangzhiye@126.com
Web Address: www.chgzy.com.cn
Personnel:
Chmn.: Jinming Hou
Phone: (86) 312 317 1036/ 9815
Gen. Mgr.: Fuyin Hou
Phone: (86) 312 317 1036/ 9815
Total Employees at this Location: 400
Type of Operation: Paper mill
Paper/Paperboard Grades and Capacities:
Total paper and paperboard capacity: 18,000 mt/y
Tissue: 18,000 mt/y
Paper and Paperboard Mill Data:
Paper Machines: 5
No. 1, cylinder, total capacity 2,550 mt/y, Trim width 1.58 m, Tissue
No. 2, cylinder, total capacity 2,550 mt/y, Trim width 1.58 m, Tissue
No. 3, cylinder, total capacity 2,550 mt/y, Trim width 1.58 m, Tissue
No. 4, total capacity 5,300 mt/y, Trim width 2.8 m, Tissue
No. 5, total capacity 5,300 mt/y, Trim width 2.8 m, Tissue
Energy Data:
Power boilers

ⓜHebei Baoding Dayi Paper Co., Ltd.
Wangjiaguan Industrial Park, Shunping County
Baoding, Hebei, 072250
China
Phone: (86) 312 7656 888
Fax: (86) 312 7656 888
Email: dayizhiye@163.com
Web Address: www.bddyzy.com
Mill Locations:
Hebei Baoding Dayi Paper Co., Ltd., Baoding Mill, Wangjiaguan Industrial Park, Shunping County, Baoding 072250, China, Capacity: 70,000 mt/y, (Paper mill)
Phone: (86) 312 7656 888
Fax: (86) 312 7656 888
Email: dayizhiye@163.com

ⓜHebei Baoding Dayi Paper Co., Ltd.
Baoding Mill
Wangjiaguan Industrial Park, Shunping County
Baoding, Hebei, 072250
China
Phone: (86) 312 7656 888
Fax: (86) 312 7656 888
Email: dayizhiye@163.com
Web Address: www.bddyzy.com
Type of Operation: Paper mill
Paper/Paperboard Grades and Capacities:
Total paper and paperboard capacity: 70,000 mt/y
Tissue: 70,000 mt/y
Paper and Paperboard Mill Data:
Paper Machines: 15
PM 1, total capacity 4,000 mt/y, Trim width 2.8 m, Tissue
PM 2, total capacity 4,000 mt/y, Trim width 2.8 m, Tissue
PM 3, total capacity 4,000 mt/y, Trim width 2.8 m, Tissue
PM 4, total capacity 4,000 mt/y, Trim width 2.8 m, Tissue
PM 5, total capacity 4,000 mt/y, Trim width 2.8 m, Tissue
PM 6, total capacity 4,000 mt/y, Trim width 2.8 m, Tissue
PM 7, total capacity 3,500 mt/y, Trim width 2.4 m, Tissue
PM 8, total capacity 3,500 mt/y, Trim width 2.4 m, Tissue
PM 9, total capacity 3,500 mt/y, Trim width 2.4 m, Tissue
PM 10, total capacity 3,500 mt/y, Trim width 2.4 m, Tissue
PM 11, total capacity 3,500 mt/y, Trim width 2.4 m, Tissue
PM 12, total capacity 3,500 mt/y, Trim width 2.4 m, Tissue
PM 13, total capacity 3,500 mt/y, Trim width 2.4 m, Tissue
PM 14, total capacity 3,500 mt/y, Trim width 2.4 m, Tissue
PM 15, fourdrinier, total capacity 18,000 mt/y, Trim width 2.85 m, Tissue

ⓜHebei Baoding Dongsheng Hygiene Products Co., Ltd.
Ownership: 100% by shareholders
Dongsheng Paper Industry Zone, Daceying
Mancheng County, Baoding, Hebei, 071051
China
Phone: (86) 312 557 8886/ 8899
Fax: (86) 312 557 2790
Email: xsb@dshpaper.com.cn, mail@dshpaper.com.cn
Web Address: www.dshpaper.com.cn
Mill Locations:
Hebei Baoding Dongsheng Hygiene Products Co., Ltd., Baoding Mill, Dongsheng Paper Industry Zone, Daceying, Baoding 071051, China, Capacity: 50,000 mt/y, (Paper mill)
Phone: (86) 312 557 8886/ 8899
Fax: (86) 312 557 2790
Email: xsb@dshpaper.com.cn, mail@dshpaper.com.cn

ⓜHebei Baoding Dongsheng Hygiene Products Co., Ltd.
Baoding Mill
Dongsheng Paper Industry Zone, Daceying
Baoding, Hebei, 071051
China
Phone: (86) 312 557 8886/ 8899
Fax: (86) 312 557 2790
Email: xsb@dshpaper.com.cn, mail@dshpaper.com.cn
Web Address: www.dshpaper.com.cn
Personnel:
Chmn.: Zhiwu Zhang
Phone: (86) 312 557 8886/ 8899
Gen. Mgr.: Jie Zhang
Phone: (86) 312 557 8886/ 8899
Total Employees at this Location: 2,000
Type of Operation: Paper mill
Paper/Paperboard Grades and Capacities:
Total paper and paperboard capacity: 50,000 mt/y
Tissue: 50,000 mt/y
Paper and Paperboard Mill Data:
Paper Machines: 20
PM 16-30, cylinder, Trim width 1.58 m, Tissue
PM 31-35, total capacity 10,000 mt/y, Trim width 2.88 m, Tissue

ⓜHebei Baoding Gangxing Paper Co., Ltd.
Ownership: 100% by private owners
Daceying Papermaking Industry Park, Mancheng County
Baoding, Hebei, 072150
China
Phone: (86) 312 702 1908/ 3908
Fax: (86) 312 702 1728
Email: qiaobaoru@mainone.cn, bdlibang@163.com
Web Address: www.libangnet.cn
Mill Locations:
Hebei Baoding Gangxing Paper Co., Ltd., Baoding Mill, Daceying Papermaking Industry Park, Mancheng County, Baoding 071000, China, Capacity: 73,980 mt/y, (Paper mill)
Phone: (86) 312 702 1908/ 3908
Fax: (86) 312 702 1728
Email: bdlibang@163.com

ⓜHebei Baoding Gangxing Paper Co., Ltd.
Baoding Mill
Daceying Papermaking Industry Park, Mancheng County
Baoding, Hebei, 071000
China
Phone: (86) 312 702 1908/ 3908
Fax: (86) 312 702 1728
Email: bdlibang@163.com

China

Personnel:
Chmn.: Emiu Zhang
Phone: (86) 312 702 1908/ 3908
Gen. Mgr.: Santao Zhang
Phone: (86) 312 702 1908/ 3908
Mill Mgr.: Siche Zhang
Phone: (86) 312 702 1908/ 3908
Total Employees at this Location: 420
Type of Operation: Paper mill
Paper/Paperboard Grades and Capacities:
Total paper and paperboard capacity: 73,980 mt/y
Tissue: 73,980 mt/y
Paper and Paperboard Mill Data:
Paper Machines: 18
No. 11, cylinder, total capacity 1,357 mt/y, Trim width 1.58 m, Tissue
No. 12, cylinder, total capacity 1,357 mt/y, Trim width 1.58 m, Tissue
No. 13, cylinder, total capacity 1,357 mt/y, Trim width 1.58 m, Tissue
No. 14, cylinder, total capacity 1,357 mt/y, Trim width 1.58 m, Tissue
No. 15, cylinder, total capacity 1,357 mt/y, Trim width 1.58 m, Tissue
No. 16, cylinder, total capacity 1,357 mt/y, Trim width 1.58 m, Tissue
No. 17, cylinder, total capacity 1,357 mt/y, Trim width 1.58 m, Tissue
No. 18, cylinder, total capacity 1,357 mt/y, Trim width 1.58 m, Tissue
No. 19, cylinder, total capacity 4,998 mt/y, Trim width 2.66 m, Tissue
No. 20, cylinder, total capacity 4,998 mt/y, Trim width 2.66 m, Tissue
No. 21, cylinder, total capacity 4,998 mt/y, Trim width 2.66 m, Tissue
No. 22, cylinder, total capacity 4,998 mt/y, Trim width 2.66 m, Tissue
No. 23, cylinder, total capacity 4,998 mt/y, Trim width 2.66 m, Tissue
No. 24, cylinder, total capacity 4,998 mt/y, Trim width 2.66 m, Tissue
No. 25, cylinder, total capacity 4,998 mt/y, Trim width 2.66 m, Tissue
No. 26, cylinder, total capacity 4,998 mt/y, Trim width 2.66 m, Tissue
No. 27, BF-10 EX, Yankee dryer, total capacity 12,000 mt/y, Trim width 2.76 m, Tissue
No. 28, BF-10 EX, Yankee dryer, total capacity 12,000 mt/y, Trim width 2.76 m, Tissue
Energy Data:
Power boilers
Electrical demand for mill: 32 MWh/D

ⓜHebei Baoding Haofeng Paper Co., Ltd.
Daceying Paper Making Industrial Park, Mancheng County
Baoding, Hebei, 072150
China
Phone: (86) 312 7021 038
Fax: (86) 312 7026 369
Web Address: www.fuerya.com.cn
Mill Locations:
Hebei Baoding Haofeng Paper Co., Ltd., Baoding Mill, Daceying Paper Making Industrial Park, Mancheng County, Baoding 072150, China, Capacity: 2,400 mt/y, (Paper mill)
Phone: (86) 312 7021 038
Fax: (86) 312 7026 369

ⓜHebei Baoding Haofeng Paper Co., Ltd.
Baoding Mill
Daceying Paper Making Industrial Park, Mancheng County
Baoding, Hebei, 072150
China
Phone: (86) 312 7021 038
Fax: (86) 312 7026 369
Web Address: www.fuerya.com.cn
Type of Operation: Paper mill
Paper/Paperboard Grades and Capacities:
Total paper and paperboard capacity: 2,400 mt/y
Tissue: 2,400 mt/y
Paper and Paperboard Mill Data:
Paper Machines: 1
PM 1, total capacity 2,400 mt/y, Trim width 2.8 m, Tissue

ⓜHebei Baoding Hengfa Paper Co., Ltd.
Ownership: 100% by private owners
Daceying Paper Making Industry Park, Mancheng County
Baoding, Hebei, 072150
China
Phone: (86) 312 7023 621
Mill Locations:
Hebei Baoding Hengfa Paper Co., Ltd., Baoding Mill, Daceying Paper Making Industry Park, Mancheng County, Baoding 072150, China, Capacity: 5,000 mt/y, (Paper mill)
Phone: (86) 13703285502
Fax: (86) 03127026662
Email: hengfa-paper@163.com

ⓜHebei Baoding Hengfa Paper Co., Ltd.
Baoding Mill
Daceying Paper Making Industry Park, Mancheng County
Baoding, Hebei, 072150
China
Phone: (86) 13703285502
Fax: (86) 03127026662
Email: hengfa-paper@163.com
Web Address: www.hengfazy.com
Personnel:
Chmn.: Hengfa Zhang
Phone: (86) 312 7023 621
Total Employees at this Location: 100
Type of Operation: Paper mill
Paper/Paperboard Grades and Capacities:
Total paper and paperboard capacity: 5,000 mt/y
Tissue: 5,000 mt/y
Paper and Paperboard Mill Data:
Paper Machines: 5
No. 1, cylinder, total capacity 500 mt/y, Trim width 1.09 m, Tissue
No. 2, cylinder, total capacity 500 mt/y, Trim width 1.09 m, Tissue
No. 3, cylinder, total capacity 500 mt/y, Trim width 1.09 m, Tissue
No. 4, cylinder, total capacity 1,750 mt/y, Trim width 2.4 m, Tissue
No. 5, cylinder, total capacity 1,750 mt/y, Trim width 2.4 m, Tissue
Energy Data:
Power boilers: 2

ⓜHebei Baoding Hengtai Paper Co., Ltd.
Ownership: 100% by private owners
Daceying Industry Park, Mancheng County
Baoding, Hebei, 072150
China
Phone: (86) 312 702 3888
Fax: (86) 312 702 2666
Mill Locations:
Hebei Baoding Hengtai Paper Co., Ltd., Baoding Mill, Daceying Industry Park, Mancheng County, Baoding 072150, China, Capacity: 12,000 mt/y, (Paper mill)
Phone: (86) 312 702 3888
Fax: (86) 312 702 2666

ⓜHebei Baoding Hengtai Paper Co., Ltd.
Baoding Mill
Daceying Industry Park, Mancheng County
Baoding, Hebei, 072150
China
Phone: (86) 312 702 3888
Fax: (86) 312 702 2666
Personnel:
Chmn.: Yue Wang
Phone: (86) 312 702 3888
Type of Operation: Paper mill
Paper/Paperboard Grades and Capacities:
Total paper and paperboard capacity: 12,000 mt/y
Tissue: 12,000 mt/y
Paper and Paperboard Mill Data:
Paper Machines: 7
No. 1, fourdrinier, total capacity 2,000 mt/y, Trim width 1.58 m, Tissue
No. 2, fourdrinier, total capacity 2,000 mt/y, Trim width 1.58 m, Tissue
No. 3, fourdrinier, total capacity 2,000 mt/y, Trim width 1.58 m, Tissue
No. 4, fourdrinier, total capacity 2,000 mt/y, Trim width 1.58 m, Tissue
No. 5, fourdrinier, total capacity 2,000 mt/y, Trim width 1.58 m, Tissue
No. 6, cylinder, total capacity 2,000 mt/y, Trim width 1.58 m, Tissue
No. 7, (delivery date is 2013.12), total capacity 16,000 mt/y, Trim width 2.76 m, Tissue

ⓜHebei Baoding Mancheng Donggou Paper Mill
Ownership: 100% by private owners
Nanhancun Town, Mancheng County
Baoding, Hebei, 072150
China
Phone: (86) 312 703 3988
Fax: (86) 312 703 6668
Mill Locations:
Hebei Baoding Mancheng Donggou Paper Mill, Baoding Mill, Nanhancun Town, Mancheng County, Baoding 072150, China, Capacity: 1,800 mt/y, (Paper mill)
Phone: (86) 312 703 3988
Fax: (86) 312 703 6668

ⓜHebei Baoding Mancheng Donggou Paper Mill
Baoding Mill
Nanhancun Town, Mancheng County
Baoding, Hebei, 072150
China
Phone: (86) 312 703 3988
Fax: (86) 312 703 6668
Personnel:
Chmn.: Baoping Shi
Phone: (86) 312 703 3988
Total Employees at this Location: 40
Type of Operation: Paper mill
Paper/Paperboard Grades and Capacities:
Total paper and paperboard capacity: 1,800 mt/y
Tissue: 1,800 mt/y
Paper and Paperboard Mill Data:
Paper Machines: 1
PM 1, cylinder, total capacity 1,800 mt/y, Trim width 1.09 m, Tissue

ⓜHebei Baoding Mancheng Fukang Paper Co., Ltd.
Ownership: 100% by private owners
Xiaobei Village, Mancheng County
Baoding, Hebei, 072150
China
Phone: (86) 312 7019 229
Fax: (86) 312 7019 229
Mill Locations:
Hebei Baoding Mancheng Fukang Paper Co., Ltd., Baoding Mill, Xiaobei Village, Mancheng County, Baoding 072150, China, Capacity: 6,000 mt/y, (Paper mill)
Phone: (86) 312 7019 229
Fax: (86) 312 7019 229

ⓜHebei Baoding Mancheng Fukang Paper Co., Ltd.
Baoding Mill
Xiaobei Village, Mancheng County
Baoding, Hebei, 072150
China
 Phone: (86) 312 7019 229
 Fax: (86) 312 7019 229
Personnel:
 Chmn.: Changhai Li
 Phone: (86) 312 7019 229
 Mill Mgr.: Changhe Li
 Phone: (86) 312 7019 229
Total Employees at this Location: 200
Type of Operation: Paper mill
Paper/Paperboard Grades and Capacities:
 Total paper and paperboard capacity: 6,000 mt/y
 Tissue: 6,000 mt/y
Paper and Paperboard Mill Data:
Paper Machines: 5
 No. 1, cylinder, total capacity 850 mt/y, Trim width 1.09 m, Tissue
 No. 2, cylinder, total capacity 850 mt/y, Trim width 1.09 m, Tissue
 No. 3, fourdrinier, total capacity 850 mt/y, Trim width 1.09 m, Tissue
 No. 4, cylinder, total capacity 1,750 mt/y, Trim width 1.58 m, Tissue
 No. 5, cylinder, total capacity 1,750 mt/y, Trim width 1.58 m, Tissue
Energy Data:
 Power boilers: 1

ⓜHebei Baoding Mancheng Guanquan Paper Co., Ltd.
Ownership: *100% by private owners*
Gangtou Village, Mancheng County
Baoding, Hebei, 072150
China
 Phone: (86) 312 702 1892
 Fax: (86) 312 702 1892
Mill Locations:
Hebei Baoding Mancheng Guanquan Paper Co., Ltd., Baoding Mill, Gangtou Village, Mancheng County, Baoding 072150, China, Capacity: 6,500 mt/y, (Paper mill)
 Phone: (86) 312 702 1892
 Fax: (86) 312 702 1982

ⓜHebei Baoding Mancheng Guanquan Paper Co., Ltd.
Baoding Mill
Gangtou Village, Mancheng County
Baoding, Hebei, 072150
China
 Phone: (86) 312 702 1892
 Fax: (86) 312 702 1982
Personnel:
 Chmn. & Mill Mgr.: Changyuan Nie
 Phone: (86) 312 702 1892
 Sls. Mgr.: Changshun Nie
 Phone: (86) 312 702 1892
Total Employees at this Location: 215
Type of Operation: Paper mill
Pulp Grades and Capacities:
 Total pulp capacity: 1,700 mt/y
 Recycled Pulping: 1,700 mt/y
Pulp Mill Data:
 Recycled Fiber Treatment Lines:
 Flotation deinking lines: 1 at 1,700 admt/y
Paper/Paperboard Grades and Capacities:
 Total paper and paperboard capacity: 6,500 mt/y
 Tissue: 6,500 mt/y
Paper and Paperboard Mill Data:
Paper Machines: 4
 No. 1, cylinder, total capacity 850 mt/y, Trim width 1.09 m, Tissue
 No. 2, cylinder, total capacity 850 mt/y, Trim width 1.09 m, Tissue
 No. 3, fourdrinier, total capacity 2,400 mt/y, Trim width 2.4 m, Tissue
 No. 4, fourdrinier, total capacity 2,400 mt/y, Trim width 2.4 m, Tissue
Energy Data:
 Power boilers: 1

ⓜHebei Baoding Mancheng Huifeng Paper Co., Ltd.
Ownership: *100% by private owners*
Daceying Papermaking Industry Park, Mancheng County
Baoding, Hebei, 072150
China
 Phone: (86) 312 702 1568
 Fax: (86) 312 702 6339
Mill Locations:
Hebei Baoding Mancheng Huifeng Paper Co., Ltd., Baoding Mill, Daceying Papermaking Industry Park, Mancheng County, Baoding 072150, China, Capacity: 10,000 mt/y, (Paper mill)
 Phone: (86) 312 702 1568
 Fax: (86) 312 702 6339

ⓜHebei Baoding Mancheng Huifeng Paper Co., Ltd.
Baoding Mill
Daceying Papermaking Industry Park, Mancheng County
Baoding, Hebei, 072150
China
 Phone: (86) 312 702 1568
 Fax: (86) 312 702 6339
Personnel:
 Chmn.: Zhenlin Zhao
 Phone: (86) 312 702 1568
Type of Operation: Paper mill
Paper/Paperboard Grades and Capacities:
 Total paper and paperboard capacity: 10,000 mt/y
 Tissue: 10,000 mt/y
Paper and Paperboard Mill Data:
Paper Machines: 6
 No. 1, cylinder, total capacity 1,600 mt/y, Trim width 1.57 m, Tissue
 No. 2, cylinder, total capacity 1,600 mt/y, Trim width 1.57 m, Tissue
 No. 3, cylinder, total capacity 1,600 mt/y, Trim width 1.57 m, Tissue
 No. 4, cylinder, total capacity 1,600 mt/y, Trim width 1.57 m, Tissue
 No. 5, cylinder, total capacity 1,600 mt/y, Trim width 1.57 m, Tissue
 No. 6, cylinder, total capacity 1,600 mt/y, Trim width 1.57 m, Tissue
Energy Data:
 Power boilers: 1

ⓜHebei Baoding Mancheng Jifa Paper Co., Ltd.
Ownership: *100% by shareholders*
Daceying Papermaking Industry Park, Mancheng County
Baoding, Hebei, 072150
China
 Phone: (86) 312 702 6882
 Fax: (86) 312 702 6887
 Email: jfzy88@126.com
 Web Address: www.jfzy.net
Mill Locations:
Hebei Baoding Mancheng Jifa Paper Co., Ltd., Baoding Mill, Daceying Papermaking Industry Park, Mancheng County, Baoding 072150, China, Capacity: 10,000 mt/y, (Paper mill)
 Phone: (86) 312 702 6882
 Fax: (86) 312 702 6887
 Email: jfzy88@126.com

ⓜHebei Baoding Mancheng Jifa Paper Co., Ltd.
Baoding Mill
Daceying Papermaking Industry Park, Mancheng County
Baoding, Hebei, 072150
China
 Phone: (86) 312 702 6882
 Fax: (86) 312 702 6887
 Email: jfzy88@126.com
 Web Address: www.jfzy.net
Personnel:
 Chmn.: Xilin Bao
 Phone: (86) 312 702 6882
 Mill Mgr.: Zhihai Cui
 Phone: (86) 1350 3223 526
Type of Operation: Paper mill
Paper/Paperboard Grades and Capacities:
 Total paper and paperboard capacity: 10,000 mt/y
 Tissue: 10,000 mt/y
Paper and Paperboard Mill Data:
Paper Machines: 8
 No. 1, cylinder, total capacity 1,000 mt/y, Trim width 1.09 m, Tissue
 No. 2, cylinder, total capacity 1,000 mt/y, Trim width 1 m, Tissue
 No. 3, cylinder, total capacity 1,000 mt/y, Trim width 1.09 m, Tissue
 No. 4, cylinder, total capacity 1,000 mt/y, Trim width 1.09 m, Tissue
 No. 5, cylinder, total capacity 1,500 mt/y, Trim width 1.58 m, Tissue
 No. 6, cylinder, total capacity 1,500 mt/y, Trim width 1.58 m, Tissue
 No. 7, cylinder, total capacity 1,500 mt/y, Trim width 1.58 m, Tissue
 No. 8, cylinder, total capacity 1,500 mt/y, Trim width 1.58 m, Tissue
Energy Data:
 Power boilers: 2

ⓜHebei Baoding Mancheng Lida Paper Mill
Ownership: *100% by private owners*
Shitou Village, Shenxing Town, Mancheng County
Baoding, Hebei, 072150
China
 Phone: (86) 312 706 5712
 Fax: (86) 312 701 0858
Mill Locations:
Hebei Baoding Mancheng Lida Paper Mill, Baoding Mill, Shitou Village, Shenxing Town, Mancheng County, Baoding 072150, China, Capacity: 15,000 mt/y, (Paper mill)
 Phone: (86) 312 706 5712
 Fax: (86) 312 701 0858

ⓜHebei Baoding Mancheng Lida Paper Mill
Baoding Mill
Shitou Village, Shenxing Town, Mancheng County
Baoding, Hebei, 072150
China
 Phone: (86) 312 706 5712
 Fax: (86) 312 701 0858
Personnel:
 Chmn.: Michen Fan
 Phone: (86) 312 706 5712
 Mill Mgr.: Dayong Fan
 Phone: (86) 312 706 5712
Type of Operation: Paper mill
Paper/Paperboard Grades and Capacities:
 Total paper and paperboard capacity: 15,000 mt/y
 Tissue: 15,000 mt/y
Paper and Paperboard Mill Data:
Paper Machines: 8
 PM 5-8, fourdrinier, total capacity 1,800 mt/y, Trim width 1.76 m, Tissue

China

PM 9-12, total capacity 2,100 mt/y, Trim width 2.8 m, Tissue
Energy Data:
Power boilers: 1

ⓂHebei Baoding Mancheng Yikang Paper Co., Ltd.
Ownership: 100% by private owners
Daceying Paper Making Industry Park, Mancheng County
Baoding, Hebei, 072150
China
 Phone: (86) 312 702 1050
 Fax: (86) 312 702 6801
Mill Locations:
Hebei Baoding Mancheng Yikang Paper Co., Ltd., Baoding Mill, Daceying Paper Making Industry Park, Mancheng County, Baoding 072150, China, Capacity: 6,000 mt/y, (Paper mill)
 Phone: (86) 312 702 1050
 Fax: (86) 312 702 6801

ⓂHebei Baoding Mancheng Yikang Paper Co., Ltd.
Baoding Mill
Daceying Paper Making Industry Park, Mancheng County
Baoding, Hebei, 072150
China
 Phone: (86) 312 702 1050
 Fax: (86) 312 702 6801
Personnel:
 Chmn. & Gen. Mgr.: Daniu Zhang
 Phone: (86) 312 702 1050
Type of Operation: Paper mill
Paper/Paperboard Grades and Capacities:
 Total paper and paperboard capacity: 6,000 mt/y
 Tissue: 6,000 mt/y
Paper and Paperboard Mill Data:
Paper Machines: 6
No. 1, cylinder, total capacity 600 mt/y, Trim width 1.09 m, Tissue
No. 2, cylinder, total capacity 600 mt/y, Trim width 1.09 m, Tissue
No. 3, cylinder, total capacity 600 mt/y, Trim width 1.09 m, Tissue
No. 4, cylinder, total capacity 1,400 mt/y, Trim width 1.58 m, Tissue
No. 5, cylinder, total capacity 1,400 mt/y, Trim width 1.58 m, Tissue
No. 6, cylinder, total capacity 1,400 mt/y, Trim width 1.58 m, Tissue
Energy Data:
Power boilers: 2

ⓂHebei Baoding Mancheng Yongxing Paper Mill
Ownership: 100% by private owners
Daceying Paper Making Industry Park, Mancheng County
Baoding, Hebei, 072150
China
 Phone: (86) 312 702 1019
 Fax: (86) 312 702 2288
Mill Locations:
Hebei Baoding Mancheng Yongxing Paper Mill, Baoding Mill, Daceying Paper Making Industry Park, Mancheng County, Baoding 072150, China, Capacity: 1,440 mt/y, (Paper mill)
 Phone: (86) 312 702 1019
 Fax: (86) 312 702 2288

ⓂHebei Baoding Mancheng Yongxing Paper Mill
Baoding Mill
Daceying Paper Making Industry Park, Mancheng County
Baoding, Hebei, 072150
China
 Phone: (86) 312 702 1019
 Fax: (86) 312 702 2288
Personnel:
 Chmn.: Xichun He
 Phone: (86) 312 702 1019
Type of Operation: Paper mill
Paper/Paperboard Grades and Capacities:
 Total paper and paperboard capacity: 1,440 mt/y
 Tissue: 1,440 mt/y
Paper and Paperboard Mill Data:
Paper Machines: 2
No. 1, cylinder, total capacity 720 mt/y, Trim width 1.09 m, Tissue
No. 2, cylinder, total capacity 720 mt/y, Trim width 1.09 m, Tissue
Energy Data:
Power boilers: 1

ⓂHebei Baoding Mancheng Yuexing Paper Mill
Ownership: 100% by private owners
Daceying Papermaking Industry Park, Mancheng County
Baoding, Hebei, 072150
China
 Phone: (86) 312 702 1898
 Fax: (86) 312 702 2288
Mill Locations:
Hebei Baoding Mancheng Yuexing Paper Mill, Baoding Mill, Daceying Papermaking Industry Park, Mancheng County, Baoding 072150, China, Capacity: 8,000 mt/y, (Paper mill)
 Phone: (86) 312 702 1898
 Fax: (86) 312 702 2288

ⓂHebei Baoding Mancheng Yuexing Paper Mill
Baoding Mill
Daceying Papermaking Industry Park, Mancheng County
Baoding, Hebei, 072150
China
 Phone: (86) 312 702 1898
 Fax: (86) 312 702 2288
Personnel:
 Chmn. & Mill Mgr.: Zheng Zhao
 Phone: (86) 312 702 1898
Type of Operation: Paper mill
Paper/Paperboard Grades and Capacities:
 Total paper and paperboard capacity: 8,000 mt/y
 Tissue: 8,000 mt/y
Paper and Paperboard Mill Data:
Paper Machines: 4
No. 1, total capacity 2,000 mt/y, Trim width 1.75 m, Tissue
No. 2, total capacity 2,000 mt/y, Trim width 1.75 m, Tissue
No. 3, total capacity 2,000 mt/y, Trim width 1.75 m, Tissue
No. 4, total capacity 2,000 mt/y, Trim width 1.75 m, Tissue
Energy Data:
Power boilers: 1

ⓂHebei Baoding No. 5 Paper Mill
Ownership: 100% by private owners
No. 110 Fuchang Rd.
Baoding, Hebei, 071051
China
 Phone: (86) 312 323 2205/ 322 8286
 Fax: (86) 312 322 3687
 Email: yushengyong668899@126.com
 Web Address: www.bddwzzc.cn
Mill Locations:
Hebei Baoding No. 5 Paper Mill, Baoding Mill, No. 110 Fuchang Rd., Baoding 071051, China, Capacity: 5,000 mt/y, (Paper mill)
 Phone: (86) 312 323 2205/ 322 8286
 Fax: (86) 312 322 3687
 Email: yushengyong668899@126.com

ⓂHebei Baoding No. 5 Paper Mill
Baoding Mill
No. 110 Fuchang Rd.
Baoding, Hebei, 071051
China
 Phone: (86) 312 323 2205/ 322 8286
 Fax: (86) 312 322 3687
 Email: yushengyong668899@126.com
 Web Address: www.bddwzzc.cn
Personnel:
 Chmn.: Zhongxi Li
 Phone: (86) 312 323 2205/ 322 8286
 Gen. Mgr.: Shengyong Yu
 Phone: (86) 312 323 2205/ 322 8286
Total Employees at this Location: 500
Type of Operation: Paper mill
Paper/Paperboard Grades and Capacities:
 Total paper and paperboard capacity: 5,000 mt/y
 Tissue: 5,000 mt/y
Paper and Paperboard Mill Data:
Paper Machines: 6
No. 1, cylinder, total capacity 500 mt/y, Trim width 1.09 m, Tissue
No. 2, cylinder, total capacity 500 mt/y, Trim width 1.09 m, Tissue
No. 3, cylinder, total capacity 500 mt/y, Trim width 1.09 m, Tissue
No. 4, cylinder, total capacity 500 mt/y, Trim width 1.09 m, Tissue
No. 5, cylinder, total capacity 1,500 mt/y, Trim width 1.58 m, Tissue
No. 6, cylinder, total capacity 1,500 mt/y, Trim width 1.58 m, Tissue
Energy Data:
Power boilers: 1

ⓄⓂHebei Baoding Orient Paper Co., Ltd.
Baoding Mill
Ownership: 100% by shareholders
North 3 Km. Nanhuan Rd., Xushui County
Baoding, Hebei, 072250
China
 Phone: (86) 312 860 5508/ 869 8217/ 8213
 Fax: (86) 312 860 5530/ 5301
 Email: info@orientpaperinc.com
 Web Address: www.orientpaperinc.com
Personnel:
 Chmn. & CEO: Zhenyong Liu
 Phone: (86) 136 0324 5198
 Fax: (86) 312 860 5530
 CFO (Eff. November 1, 2014): Jing Hao
 Phone: (86) 312 860 5508
 Fax: (86) 312 860 5530
 Gen. Eng.: Zhongmin Ma
 Phone: (86) 312 860 5530
 Fax: (86) 312 860 5530
 Vice. Gen. Mgr.: Xiaodong Liu
 Phone: (86) 312 860 5508
 Fax: (86) 312 860 5530
 VP., Oper.: Fuzeng Liu
 Phone: (86) 312 860 5508
 Fax: (86) 312 860 5530
 VP., Sls.: Gengqi Yang
 Phone: (86) 312 860 5508
 Fax: (86) 312 860 5530
Total Employees at this Location: 580
Type of Operation: Paper mill, Paperboard mill
Mill Locations:
Hebei Baoding Orient Paper Milling Co., Ltd, Baoding Mill, Wei County Industrial Park, Baoding, China, (Paper mill)
Pulp Grades and Capacities:
 Total pulp capacity: 374,706 mt/y
 Recycled Pulping: 374,706 mt/y
Pulp Mill Data:
Recycled Fiber Treatment Lines:
Pulpers
Recycled packaging pulping lines

Paper/Paperboard Grades and Capacities:
Total paper and paperboard capacity: 390,000 mt/y
Uncoated woodfree/freesheet: 90,000 mt/y
Corrugating medium/fluting: 300,000 mt/y
Paper and Paperboard Mill Data:
Paper Machines: 4
No. 1, fourdrinier, total capacity 50,000 mt/y, Trim width 3.2 m, Corrugating medium/fluting
No. 2, fourdrinier, total capacity 50,000 mt/y, Trim width 3.4 m, Uncoated woodfree/freesheet
No. 3, fourdrinier, total capacity 40,000 mt/y, Trim width 3.4 m, Uncoated woodfree/freesheet
No. 6, fourdrinier, total capacity 250,000 mt/y, Trim width 5.6 m, Corrugating medium/fluting
Energy Data:
Power boilers: 5

ⓂHebei Baoding Orient Paper Milling Co., Ltd
Baoding Mill
Mill is under construction (due to start in the second half of 2015)
Ownership: Hebei Baoding Orient Paper Co., Ltd.
Wei County Industrial Park
Baoding, Hebei
China
Type of Operation: Paper mill
Paper and Paperboard Mill Data:
Paper Machines: 2
PM 8, (scheduled for completion by the second half of 2015), total capacity 15,000 mt/y, Tissue
PM 9, (Scheduled to roll out production by the second half of 2015), total capacity 15,000 mt/y, Tissue

ⓂHebei Baoding Ruifeng Paper Co., Ltd.
Ownership: 100% by private owners
Daceying Paper Making Industry Park, Mancheng County
Baoding, Hebei, 072150
China
 Phone: (86) 312 3186 252
Personnel:
 Chmn.: Fusheng Zhao
 Phone: (86) 312 702 1904
 Sls. Mgr.: Junying Yang
 Phone: (86) 312 702 1904
Mill Locations:
Hebei Baoding Ruifeng Paper Co., Ltd., Baoding Mill, Daceying Paper Making Industry Park, Mancheng County, Baoding 072150, China, Capacity: 6,000 mt/y, (Paper mill)
 Phone: (86) 312 3186 252

ⓂHebei Baoding Ruifeng Paper Co., Ltd.
Baoding Mill
Daceying Paper Making Industry Park, Mancheng County
Baoding, Hebei, 072150
China
 Phone: (86) 312 3186 252
Personnel:
 Chmn.: Fusheng Zhao
 Phone: (86) 312 702 1904
 Sls. Mgr.: Junying Yang
 Phone: (86) 312 702 1904
Type of Operation: Paper mill
Paper/Paperboard Grades and Capacities:
Total paper and paperboard capacity: 6,000 mt/y
Tissue: 6,000 mt/y
Paper and Paperboard Mill Data:
Paper Machines: 8
No. 1, cylinder, total capacity 570 mt/y, Trim width 1.09 m, Tissue
No. 2, cylinder, total capacity 570 mt/y, Trim width 1.09 m, Tissue
No. 3, cylinder, total capacity 570 mt/y, Trim width 1.09 m, Tissue
No. 4, cylinder, total capacity 570 mt/y, Trim width 1.09 m, Tissue
No. 5, cylinder, total capacity 570 mt/y, Trim width 1.09 m, Tissue
No. 6, cylinder, total capacity 1,050 mt/y, Trim width 1.58 m, Tissue
No. 7, cylinder, total capacity 1,050 mt/y, Trim width 1.58 m, Tissue
No. 8, cylinder, total capacity 1,050 mt/y, Trim width 1.58 m, Tissue
Energy Data:
Power boilers: 3

ⓂHebei Baoding Sanlian Paper Co., Ltd.
Ownership: 100% by shareholders
Southern Section, West Waihuan Rd.
Baoding City, Hebei, 071051
China
 Phone: (86) 312 323 9070
 Fax: (86) 312 325 0899
 Email: slzy@bdslzy.com, bdslzy@126.com
 Web Address: www.bdslzy.com
Mill Locations:
Hebei Baoding Sanlian Paper Co., Ltd., Baoding Mill, Southern Section, West Waihuan Rd., Baoding 071051, China, Capacity: 170,289 mt/y, (Paperboard mill)
 Phone: (86) 312 323 9070
 Fax: (86) 312 325 0899
 Email: slzy@bdslzy.com, bdslzy@126.com

ⓂHebei Baoding Sanlian Paper Co., Ltd.
Baoding Mill
Southern Section, West Waihuan Rd.
Baoding, Hebei, 071051
China
 Phone: (86) 312 323 9070
 Fax: (86) 312 325 0899
 Email: slzy@bdslzy.com, bdslzy@126.com
Personnel:
 Chmn. & Pres.: Dhonghai Zhang
 Phone: (86) 312 323 9070
Total Employees at this Location: 620
Type of Operation: Paperboard mill
Pulp Grades and Capacities:
Total pulp capacity: 169,751 mt/y
Recycled Pulping: 169,751 mt/y
Paper/Paperboard Grades and Capacities:
Total paper and paperboard capacity: 170,289 mt/y
Linerboard: 170,289 mt/y
Paper and Paperboard Mill Data:
Paper Machines: 6
No. 1, cylinder (3), total capacity 19,635 mt/y, Trim width 2.85 m, Linerboard
No. 2, cylinder (3), total capacity 19,635 mt/y, Trim width 2.85 m, Linerboard
No. 3, cylinder (3), total capacity 19,635 mt/y, Trim width 2.85 m, Linerboard
No. 4, Fourdrinier (4), total capacity 39,627 mt/y, Trim width 3.4 m, Linerboard
No. 5, fourdrinier (3), total capacity 13,566 mt/y, Trim width 2.2 m, Linerboard
No. 6, (second-hand), fourdrinier (3), total capacity 58,191 mt/y, Trim width 3.6 m, Linerboard
Energy Data:
Power boilers: 8
Electrical demand for mill: 310 MWh/D

ⓂHebei Baoding Xiangyu Paper Co., Ltd.
Baoding Mill
North of Hongchang Rd., Mancheng County
Baoding, Hebei, 071000
China
 Phone: (86) 312 7078 875
Type of Operation: Paper mill
Pulp Grades and Capacities:
Total pulp capacity: 109,804 mt/y
Recycled Pulping: 109,804 mt/y
Paper/Paperboard Grades and Capacities:
Total paper and paperboard capacity: 110,000 mt/y
Linerboard: 48,000 mt/y
Corrugating medium/fluting: 32,000 mt/y
Boxboard/cartonboard: 30,000 mt/y
Paper and Paperboard Mill Data:
Paper Machines: 2
No. 1, multi-wire, total capacity 30,000 mt/y, Trim width 1.88 m, Boxboard/cartonboard
No. 2, fourdrinier, total capacity 80,000 mt/y, Trim width 4.4 m, Linerboard, Corrugating medium/fluting
Energy Data:
Electrical demand for mill: 136 MWh/D

ⓂHebei Baoding Xinghua Paper Mill
Ownership: 100% by private owners
Nanqi Town, Xinshi District
Baoding City, Hebei, 071051
China
 Phone: (86) 312 317 4425/319 7398
 Fax: (86) 312 317 8911
 Email: xhua@xinghuazaozhi.com.cn
 Web Address: www.xinghuazaozhi.com.cn
Mill Locations:
Hebei Baoding Xinghua Paper Mill, Baoding Mill, Nanqi Town, Xinshi District, Baoding 071000, China, Capacity: 16,800 mt/y, (Paper mill, Paperboard mill)
 Phone: (86) 312 317 4425/319 7398
 Fax: (86) 312 317 8911
 Email: xhua@xinghuazaozhi.com.cn

ⓂHebei Baoding Xinghua Paper Mill
Baoding Mill
Nanqi Town, Xinshi District
Baoding, Hebei, 071000
China
 Phone: (86) 312 317 4425/319 7398
 Fax: (86) 312 317 8911
 Email: xhua@xinghuazaozhi.com.cn
 Web Address: www.xinghuazaozhi.com.cn
Personnel:
 Mill Mgr.: Guozhu Pan
 Phone: (86) 312 317 4425/319 7398
 Sls. Mgr.: Zhishui Qi
 Phone: (86) 312 317 4425/319 7398
Total Employees at this Location: 220
Type of Operation: Paper mill, Paperboard mill
Paper/Paperboard Grades and Capacities:
Total paper and paperboard capacity: 16,800 mt/y
Tissue: 1,800 mt/y
Boxboard/cartonboard: 15,000 mt/y
Paper and Paperboard Mill Data:
Paper Machines: 5
PM 1, cylinder, total capacity 7,000 mt/y, Trim width 1.58 m, Boxboard/cartonboard
PM 2, fourdrinier, total capacity 8,000 mt/y, Trim width 1.76 m, Boxboard/cartonboard
PM 3, cylinder, total capacity 600 mt/y, Trim width 1.09 m, Tissue
PM 4, cylinder, total capacity 600 mt/y, Trim width 1.09 m, Tissue
PM 5, cylinder, total capacity 600 mt/y, Trim width 1.09 m, Tissue

ⓂHebei Baoding Xingji Specialty Paper Mill
Ownership: 100% by shareholders
No. 68 Liming Rd.
Baoding City, Hebei, 071000
China
 Phone: (86) 312 211 3318 /0518
 Fax: (86) 312 211 6666
 Email: xingji@hexingji.com.cn
 Web Address: www.hexingji.com.cn
Mill Locations:
Hebei Baoding Xingji Specialty Paper Mill, Baoding Mill, No. 68 Liming Rd., Baoding 071000, China, Capacity: 19,000 mt/y, (Paper mill)
 Phone: (86) 312 211 3318 /0518

China

Fax: (86) 312 211 6666
Email: xingji@hexingji.com.cn

ⓜHebei Baoding Xingji Specialty Paper Mill
Baoding Mill
No. 68 Liming Rd.
Baoding, Hebei, 071000
China
  Phone: (86) 312 211 3318 /0518
  Fax: (86) 312 211 6666
  Email: xingji@hexingji.com.cn
  Web Address: www.hexingji.com.cn
Personnel:
  Chmn.: Hua Liu
  Phone: (86) 312 211 3318 /0518
  Mill Mgr.: Xintian Duan
  Phone: (86) 312 211 3318 /0518
  VP, Tech. Dir.: Cai Liu
  Phone: (86) 312 211 3318 /0518
Total Employees at this Location: 230
Type of Operation: Paper mill
Paper/Paperboard Grades and Capacities:
  Total paper and paperboard capacity: 19,000 mt/y
  Specialty and industrial: 3,000 mt/y
Paper and Paperboard Mill Data:
Paper Machines: 2
  PM 1, fourdrinier, total capacity 9,000 mt/y, Trim width 1.88 m, Uncoated woodfree/freesheet, Specialty and industrial
  PM 2, fourdrinier, total capacity 10,000 mt/y, Trim width 1.88 m, Specialty and industrial

ⓘHebei Baoding Zhengda Paper Co., Ltd.
Shangfang Village, Daceying Town, Mancheng County
Baoding, Hebei, 072150
China
  Phone: (86) 312 7021 068
  Fax: (86) 312 7027 258
  Email: bdzhengda@163.com
  Web Address: www.bdzhengda.net/pel/index.asp
Mill Locations:
Hebei Baoding Zhengda Paper Co., Ltd., Baoding Mill, Shangfang Village, Daceying Town, Mancheng County, Baoding 072150, China, Capacity: 10,000 mt/y, (Paper mill)
  Phone: (86) 312 7021 068
  Fax: (86) 312 7027 258
  Email: bdzhengda@163.com

ⓜHebei Baoding Zhengda Paper Co., Ltd.
Baoding Mill
Shangfang Village, Daceying Town, Mancheng County
Baoding, Hebei, 072150
China
  Phone: (86) 312 7021 068
  Fax: (86) 312 7027 258
  Email: bdzhengda@163.com
  Web Address: www.bdzhengda.net
Type of Operation: Paper mill
Paper/Paperboard Grades and Capacities:
  Total paper and paperboard capacity: 10,000 mt/y
  Tissue: 10,000 mt/y

ⓘHebei Birou Paper Co., Ltd.
Mancheng
Baoding, Hebei, 071000
China
  Phone: (86) 312 2068 811
  Fax: (86) 312 7062 880
Mill Locations:
Hebei Birou Paper Co., Ltd., Baoding Mill, Mancheng, Baoding 071000, China, Capacity: 21,000 mt/y, (Paper mill)
  Phone: (86) 312 2068 811
  Fax: (86) 312 7062 880

ⓜHebei Birou Paper Co., Ltd.
Baoding Mill
Mancheng
Baoding, Hebei, 071000
China
  Phone: (86) 312 2068 811
  Fax: (86) 312 7062 880
Type of Operation: Paper mill
Paper/Paperboard Grades and Capacities:
  Total paper and paperboard capacity: 21,000 mt/y
  Tissue: 21,000 mt/y
Paper and Paperboard Mill Data:
Paper Machines: 6
  PM 1, total capacity 3,500 mt/y, Trim width 3.5 m, Tissue
  PM 2, total capacity 3,500 mt/y, Trim width 3.5 m, Tissue
  PM 3, total capacity 3,500 mt/y, Trim width 3.5 m, Tissue
  PM 4, total capacity 3,500 mt/y, Trim width 3.5 m, Tissue
  PM 5, total capacity 3,500 mt/y, Trim width 3.5 m, Tissue
  PM 6, total capacity 3,500 mt/y, Trim width 3.5 m, Tissue

ⓘHebei Changtai Paper
Ownership: Hebei Tangshan Guotai Paper Co., Ltd.
Yutian county, Hebei, 064000
China
  Phone: (86) 315 776 0089/0096/0052
  Fax: (86) 315 776 0088/0051
  Email: tsguotaizhiye@163.com
  Web Address: gtpaper.cn
Mill Locations:
Hebei Changtai Paper, Yutian Mill, Yutian county 064000, China, Capacity: 430,000 mt/y, (Paper mill)
  Phone: (86) 315 776 0089/0096/0052
  Fax: (86) 315 776 0088/0051
  Email: tsguotaizhiye@163.com

ⓜHebei Changtai Paper
Yutian Mill
Ownership: Hebei Tangshan Guotai Paper Co., Ltd.
Yutian county, Hebei, 064000
China
  Phone: (86) 315 776 0089/0096/0052
  Fax: (86) 315 776 0088/0051
  Email: tsguotaizhiye@163.com
Type of Operation: Paper mill
Pulp Grades and Capacities:
  Total pulp capacity: 429,441 mt/y
  Recycled Pulping: 429,441 mt/y
Pulp Mill Data:
  Bleach Plant Systems: 1
  Recycled Pulping System, Type: DIP
  Recycled Fiber Treatment Lines:
  Flotation deinking lines: 1
  Recycled packaging pulping lines: 1
Paper/Paperboard Grades and Capacities:
  Total paper and paperboard capacity: 430,000 mt/y
  Linerboard: 250,000 mt/y
  Boxboard/cartonboard: 180,000 mt/y
Paper and Paperboard Mill Data:
Paper Machines: 2
  No. 1, Fourdrinier (4), total capacity 180,000 mt/y, Trim width 3.8 m, Boxboard/cartonboard
  No. 2, fourdrinier (3), total capacity 250,000 mt/y, Trim width 5.6 m, Linerboard
Energy Data:
  Power boilers
  Steam turbines: 2 at 55 MW
  Electrical demand for mill: 548 MWh/D

ⓜHebei Chengda Paper Co., Ltd.
Tangshan Mill
Ownership: Hebei Kangda Paper Group
West No. 8 Farm Middle School, Tanghai County
Tangshan, Hebei, 063207
China
  Phone: (86) 315 879 0388/ 0312
  Fax: (86) 315 879 0312
Personnel:
  Chmn. & Gen. Mgr.: Zhenfeng Zhen
  Phone: (86) 315 879 0388/ 0312
  Sls. Mgr.: Xijiao Sun
  Phone: (86) 315 879 0388/ 0312
  CFO: Fengguo Zhen
  Phone: (86) 315 879 0388/ 0312
Total Employees at this Location: 278
Type of Operation: Paper mill
Pulp Grades and Capacities:
  Total pulp capacity: 18,000 mt/y
  Recycled Pulping: 18,000 mt/y
Pulp Mill Data:
  Pulp Lines: 3
Paper/Paperboard Grades and Capacities:
  Total paper and paperboard capacity: 17,000 mt/y
  Uncoated woodfree/freesheet: 17,000 mt/y
Paper and Paperboard Mill Data:
Paper Machines: 3
  No. 1, fourdrinier, total capacity 7,000 mt/y, Trim width 1.76 m, Uncoated woodfree/freesheet
  No. 2, fourdrinier, total capacity 7,000 mt/y, Trim width 1.76 m, Uncoated woodfree/freesheet
  No. 3, cylinder, total capacity 3,000 mt/y, Trim width 1.8 m, Uncoated woodfree/freesheet

ⓘHebei Dafa Paper Co., Ltd.
Dongniu Village, Rongcheng County
Baoding, Hebei, 071700
China
  Phone: (86) 312 5692 818/288
  Fax: (86) 312 5692 838
  Email: www.dafapaper.com
Mill Locations:
Hebei Dafa Paper Co., Ltd., Baoding Mill, Dongniu Village, Rongcheng County, Baoding 071700, China, Capacity: 6,000 mt/y, (Paper mill)
  Phone: (86) 312 5692 818/288
  Fax: (86) 312 5692 838

ⓜHebei Dafa Paper Co., Ltd.
Baoding Mill
Dongniu Village, Rongcheng County
Baoding, Hebei, 071700
China
  Phone: (86) 312 5692 818/288
  Fax: (86) 312 5692 838
  Web Address: www.dafapaper.com
Type of Operation: Paper mill
Paper/Paperboard Grades and Capacities:
  Total paper and paperboard capacity: 6,000 mt/y
  Tissue: 6,000 mt/y
Paper and Paperboard Mill Data:
Paper Machines: 2
  PM 1, total capacity 3,000 mt/y, Trim width 2.4 m, Tissue
  PM 2, total capacity 3,000 mt/y, Trim width 2.4 m, Tissue

ⓘHebei Daiyu Paper Co., Ltd.
Ownership: 100% by private owners
Daiyu Industry Park, Orient Food Town, Longrao County
Xingtai, Hebei, 055350
China
  Phone: (86) 319 659 2098
  Fax: (86) 319 659 9616
  Web Address: www.daiyuzy.com.cn
Mill Locations:
Hebei Daiyu Paper Co., Ltd., Xingtai Mill, Daiyu Industry Park, Orient Food Town, Longrao County, Xingtai 055350, China, Capacity: 6,000 mt/y, (Paper mill)
  Phone: (86) 319 659 2098
  Fax: (86) 319 659 9616

ⓜHebei Daiyu Paper Co., Ltd.
Xingtai Mill
Daiyu Industry Park, Orient Food Town, Longrao County
Xingtai, Hebei, 055350
China
  Phone: (86) 319 659 2098
  Fax: (86) 319 659 9616
  Web Address: www.daiyuzy.com.cn

China

Personnel:
Chmn.: Luzhou Fan
Phone: (86) 319 659 2098
Gen. Mgr.: Jiafu Wen
Phone: (86) 319 659 2098
Type of Operation: Paper mill
Paper/Paperboard Grades and Capacities:
Total paper and paperboard capacity: 6,000 mt/y
Tissue: 6,000 mt/y
Paper and Paperboard Mill Data:
Paper Machines: 4
PM 1-2, fourdrinier, total capacity 1,300 mt/y, Trim width 1.58 m, Tissue
PM 3-4, fourdrinier, total capacity 1,700 mt/y, Trim width 1.58 m, Tissue

ⓂHebei Dazhong Baolai Paper Co., Ltd.
Ownership: 100% by private owners
Paper-making Industry Park, Dajiatun Village,
Sanshuitou Town
Yutian County, Tangshan, Hebei, 064105
China
  Phone: (86) 315 6557 858
  Fax: (86) 315 6559 858
Personnel:
Gen. Mgr.: Aihua Bo
Phone: (86) 315 6557 858
Mill Locations:
Hebei Dazhong Baolai Paper Co., Ltd., Tangshan Mill, Paper-making Industry Park, Dajiatun Village, Sanshuitou Town, Yutian County, Tangshan 064105, China, Capacity: 71,400 mt/y, (Paperboard mill)
Phone: (86) 315 6557 858
Fax: (86) 315 6559 858

ⓂHebei Dazhong Baolai Paper Co., Ltd.
Tangshan Mill
Paper-making Industry Park, Dajiatun Village,
Sanshuitou Town, Yutian County
Tangshan, Hebei, 064105
China
  Phone: (86) 315 6557 858
  Fax: (86) 315 6559 858
Personnel:
Gen. Mgr.: Aihua Bo
Phone: (86) 315 6557 858
Total Employees at this Location: 300
Type of Operation: Paperboard mill
Pulp Grades and Capacities:
Total pulp capacity: 72,451 mt/y
Recycled Pulping: 72,451 mt/y
Pulp Mill Data:
Pulp Lines: 3
Recycled Fiber Treatment Lines:
Recycled packaging pulping lines: 3 at 90,000 admt/y
Paper/Paperboard Grades and Capacities:
Total paper and paperboard capacity: 71,400 mt/y
Linerboard: 36,057 mt/y
Boxboard/cartonboard: 35,343 mt/y
Paper and Paperboard Mill Data:
Paper Machines: 2
No. 1, multi-wire, total capacity 35,343 mt/y, Trim width 2.64 m, Boxboard/cartonboard
No. 3, fourdrinier (3), total capacity 36,057 mt/y, Trim width 4.1 m, Linerboard
Energy Data:
Electrical demand for mill: 105 MWh/D

ⓂHebei Haotong Paper Co., Ltd.
Daceying Paper Making Industrial Park, Mancheng County
Baoding, Hebei
China
  Phone: (86) 312 7023 939
Mill Locations:
Hebei Haotong Paper Co., Ltd., Baoding Mill, Daceying Paper Making Industrial Park, Mancheng County, Baoding, China, Capacity: 7,000 mt/y, (Paper mill)
Phone: (86) 312 7023 939

ⓂHebei Haotong Paper Co., Ltd.
Baoding Mill
Daceying Paper Making Industrial Park, Mancheng County
Baoding, Hebei
China
  Phone: (86) 312 7023 939
Type of Operation: Paper mill
Paper/Paperboard Grades and Capacities:
Total paper and paperboard capacity: 7,000 mt/y
Tissue: 7,000 mt/y
Paper and Paperboard Mill Data:
Paper Machines: 6
PM 1, total capacity 1,400 mt/y, Trim width 1.58 m, Tissue
PM 2, total capacity 1,400 mt/y, Trim width 1.58 m, Tissue
PM 3, total capacity 1,400 mt/y, Trim width 1.58 m, Tissue
PM 4, total capacity 1,400 mt/y, Trim width 1.58 m, Tissue
PM 5, total capacity 1,400 mt/y, Trim width 1.58 m, Tissue
PM 6, total capacity 1,400 mt/y, Trim width 1.58 m, Tissue

ⓂHebei Hongli Chenggong Paper Co., Ltd.
Ownership: 100% by private owners
Paper-making Industry Park, Daijiatun Village,
Shanshuitou Town
Yutai County, Tangshan, Hebei, 064105
China
  Phone: (86) 315 6399 768
  Fax: (86) 315 6399 768
Personnel:
Gen. Mgr.: Li Yang
Phone: (86) 315 6399 768
Mill Locations:
Hebei Hongli Chenggong Paper Co., Ltd., Tangshan Mill, Paper-making Industry Park, Daijiatun Village, Shanshuitou Town, Yutai County, Tangshan 064105, China, Capacity: 15,000 mt/y, (Paperboard mill)
Phone: (86) 315 639 6539/9768
Fax: (86) 315 6399 768

ⓂHebei Hongli Chenggong Paper Co., Ltd.
Tangshan Mill
Paper-making Industry Park, Daijiatun Village,
Shanshuitou Town, Yutai County
Tangshan, Hebei, 064105
China
  Phone: (86) 315 639 6539/9768
  Fax: (86) 315 6399 768
Personnel:
Gen. Mgr.: Li Yang
Phone: (86) 315 6399 768
Total Employees at this Location: 45
Type of Operation: Paperboard mill
Pulp Grades and Capacities:
Total pulp capacity: 13,404 mt/y
Recycled Pulping: 13,404 mt/y
Pulp Mill Data:
Pulp Lines: 1
Recycled Fiber Treatment Lines:
Recycled packaging pulping lines: 1 at 30,000 admt/y
Paper/Paperboard Grades and Capacities:
Total paper and paperboard capacity: 15,000 mt/y
Linerboard: 15,000 mt/y
Paper and Paperboard Mill Data:
Paper Machines: 1
No. 1, multi-wire, total capacity 15,000 mt/y, Trim width 3.2 m, Linerboard
Energy Data:
Electrical demand for mill: 19 MWh/D

ⒽⓂHebei Hengwei Paper Co., Ltd
Cangzhou Mill
Nanxinfang Village, Liuhe Twon, Qing County
Cangzhou, Hebei
China
  Phone: (86) 317 417 1141/428 1627
Total Employees at this Location: 100
Type of Operation: Paperboard mill
Pulp Grades and Capacities:
Total pulp capacity: 51,483 mt/y
Recycled Pulping: 51,483 mt/y
Paper/Paperboard Grades and Capacities:
Total paper and paperboard capacity: 53,000 mt/y
Corrugating medium/fluting: 53,000 mt/y
Paper and Paperboard Mill Data:
Paper Machines: 1
No. 1, fourdrinier, total capacity 53,000 mt/y, Trim width 4.2 m, Corrugating medium/fluting
Energy Data:
Electrical demand for mill: 55 MWh/D

ⓂHebei Hualin Textile Raw Materials Co., Ltd.
West of Development Rd., Qiu County
Handan, Hebei, 057450
China
  Phone: (86) 310 8351 665
Mill Locations:
Hebei Hualin Textile Raw Materials Co., Ltd., Handan Mill, West of Development Rd., Qiu County, Handan 057450, China, (Pulp mill)
Phone: (86) 310 8351 665

ⓂHebei Hualin Textile Raw Materials Co., Ltd.
Handan Mill
West of Development Rd., Qiu County
Handan, Hebei, 057450
China
  Phone: (86) 310 8351 665
Type of Operation: Pulp mill
Pulp Grades and Capacities:
Total pulp capacity: 50,000 mt/y
Pulp available for market: 50,000 mt/y
Pulp Mill Data:
Pulp Lines: 1

ⒽⓂHebei Huashuo Paper Co., Ltd.
Baoding Mill
East of Botanic Garden, North Second Ring Rd.,
Baoding, Hebei, 071051
China
  Phone: (86) 312 5951 626
Type of Operation: Paper mill
Paper/Paperboard Grades and Capacities:
Total paper and paperboard capacity: 2,400 mt/y
Tissue: 2,400 mt/y
Paper and Paperboard Mill Data:
Paper Machines: 2
PM 1, total capacity 1,200 mt/y, Trim width 1.58 m, Tissue
PM 2, total capacity 1,200 mt/y, Trim width 1.58 m, Tissue

ⓂHebei Huatong Paper Co., Ltd.
Ownership: 100% by private owners
South Wangzhuangzi Rd., Bazhou
Langfang, Hebei, 065700
China
  Phone: (86) 316 7412 222
  Fax: (86) 316 7412 328
  Email: htmy@cnhtwood.com,
  wqx@cnhtwood.com
  Web Address: cnhtwood.cn.gongchang.com
Mill Locations:
Hebei Huatong Paper Co., Ltd., Langfang Mill, South Wangzhuangzi Rd., Bazhou, Langfang 065700, China, Capacity: 141,015 mt/y, (Paperboard mill)
Phone: (86) 316 7412 222
Fax: (86) 316 7412 328
Email: htmy@cnhtwood.com, wqx@cnhtwood.com

ⓂHebei Huatong Paper Co., Ltd.
Langfang Mill
South Wangzhuangzi Rd., Bazhou
Langfang, Hebei, 065700
China

China

Phone: (86) 316 7412 222
Fax: (86) 316 7412 328
Email: htmy@cnhtwood.com,
wqx@cnhtwood.com
Web Address: cnhtwood.cn.gongchang.com
Personnel:
Gen. Mgr.: Quanxi Wang
Phone: (86) 316 7412 222
Total Employees at this Location: 200
Type of Operation: Paperboard mill
Pulp Grades and Capacities:
Total pulp capacity: 137,531 mt/y
Recycled Pulping: 137,531 mt/y
Pulp Mill Data:
Recycled Fiber Treatment Lines:
Recycled packaging pulping lines: 2 at 80,000 admt/y
Paper/Paperboard Grades and Capacities:
Total paper and paperboard capacity: 141,015 mt/y
Corrugating medium/fluting: 141,015 mt/y
Paper and Paperboard Mill Data:
Paper Machines: 3
No. 1, cylinder, total capacity 30,345 mt/y, Trim width 2.8 m, Corrugating medium/fluting
No. 2, fourdrinier, total capacity 50,337 mt/y, Trim width 3.2 m, Corrugating medium/fluting
No. 3, (started up 2009), fourdrinier, total capacity 60,333 mt/y, Trim width 3.2 m, Corrugating medium/fluting
Energy Data:
Power boilers: 2
Electrical demand for mill: 224 MWh/D

ⓜHebei Huatai Paper Co., Ltd.
Shijiazhuang Mill
Ownership: Shandong Huatai Group Co., Ltd.
No.164, First Industry St., West Shita Rd., Zhao County
Shijiazhuang, Hebei, 051530
China
Phone: (86) 311 84955555/7899300/4911710
Fax: (86) 311 8495 5520/4911710/4945663/7897051
Web Address: www.huatai.com
Personnel:
Gen. Mgr.: Julong Tian
Phone: (86) 311 84955555/7899300/4911710
Senior Operation Manager: Anquan Zhang
Phone: (86) 311 84955555/7899300/4911710
Mill Mgr.: Yibin Nie
Phone: (86) 311 84955555/7899300/4911710
Total Employees at this Location: 285
Type of Operation: Paper mill
Pulp Grades and Capacities:
Total pulp capacity: 273,275 mt/y
Recycled Pulping: 273,275 mt/y
Pulp Mill Data:
Pulp Lines: 1
Bleach Plant Systems: 1
DIP
Recycled Fiber Treatment Lines:
Flotation deinking lines
Paper/Paperboard Grades and Capacities:
Total paper and paperboard capacity: 300,000 mt/y
Newsprint: 300,000 mt/y
Paper and Paperboard Mill Data:
Paper Machines: 1
No. 1, OptiConcept, total capacity 300,000 mt/y, Trim width 7.8 m, Newsprint
Energy Data:
Power boilers
Electrical demand for mill: 780 MWh/D

ⓜHebei Huixing Paper Co., Ltd.
Ownership: 100% by private owner
Gancheng Village
Shunping County, Baoding City, Hebei, 072250
China
Phone: (86) 312 762 5317
Fax: (86) 312 762 5317
Email: huixing@huixing-paper.com
Mill Locations:
Hebei Huixing Paper Co., Ltd., Baoding Mill, Gancheng Village, Baoding 072250, China, Capacity: 22,500 mt/y, (Paper mill)
Phone: (86) 312 762 5317
Fax: (86) 312 762 5317
Email: huixing@huixing-paper.com

ⓜHebei Huixing Paper Co., Ltd.
Baoding Mill
Gancheng Village
Baoding, Hebei, 072250
China
Phone: (86) 312 762 5317
Fax: (86) 312 762 5317
Email: huixing@huixing-paper.com
Personnel:
Chmn. & Gen. Mgr.: Kemin Wang
Phone: (86) 312 762 5317
Total Employees at this Location: 200
Type of Operation: Paper mill
Paper/Paperboard Grades and Capacities:
Total paper and paperboard capacity: 22,500 mt/y
Specialty and industrial: 22,500 mt/y
Paper and Paperboard Mill Data:
Paper Machines: 2
PM 1, fourdrinier, total capacity 12,500 mt/y, Trim width 2.64 m, Specialty and industrial
PM 2, cylinder, total capacity 10,000 mt/y, Trim width 1.76 m, Specialty and industrial
Finishing Equipment:
Calenders: 1

ⓜHebei Jigao Chemical Fiber Co., Ltd.
Gaocheng Mill
Ownership: Jilin Chemical Fiber Group Co., Ltd.
No.2, Dongning Rd.
Gaocheng, Hebei, 052160
China
Phone: (86) 311 8804 2886/1472/8812 8044
Fax: (86) 311 8804 8224/3526/8815 8590/
Email: jghx@jghx.cn
Web Address: www.jghx.cn
Total Employees at this Location: 580
Type of Operation: Pulp mill
Pulp Grades and Capacities:
Total pulp capacity: 50,175 mt/y
Pulp available for market: 50,000 mt/y
Chemical Pulp: 50,175 mt/y
Pulp Mill Data:
Pulp Lines: 7
Bleach Plant Lines:
Chemical Pulping System, Type: Cotton Linter
Chemical Pulping System, Type: Cotton Linter
Chemical Pulping System, Type: Cotton Linter
Chemical Pulping System, Type: Unbleached bamboo Pulp
Pulp Dryers:
Fourdriniers 1, Fourdriniers 1, Fourdriniers 1, Pulp Dryers 1, Pulp Dryers 1, Pulp Dryers 1
Energy Data:
Power boilers: 2
Steam turbines: 3 at 6, 6, 3 MW
Electrical demand for mill: 73 MWh/D

ⓘHebei Jurun Paper Co., Ltd.
Yeshan Village, Mancheng County
Baoding, Hebei, 072150
China
Phone: (86) 312 7065 498
Mill Locations:
Hebei Jurun Paper Co., Ltd., Baoding Mill, Yeshan Village, Mancheng County, Baoding 072150, China, Capacity: 25,200 mt/y, (Paper mill)
Phone: (86) 312 7065 498

ⓜHebei Jurun Paper Co., Ltd.
Baoding Mill
Yeshan Village, Mancheng County
Baoding, Hebei, 072150
China
Phone: (86) 312 7065 498
Type of Operation: Paper mill
Paper/Paperboard Grades and Capacities:
Total paper and paperboard capacity: 25,200 mt/y
Tissue: 25,200 mt/y
Paper and Paperboard Mill Data:
Paper Machines: 9
PM 1, total capacity 1,200 mt/y, Trim width 1.58 m, Tissue
PM 2, total capacity 1,200 mt/y, Trim width 1.58 m, Tissue
PM 3, total capacity 1,200 mt/y, Trim width 1.58 m, Tissue
PM 4, total capacity 1,200 mt/y, Trim width 1.58 m, Tissue
PM 5, total capacity 1,200 mt/y, Trim width 1.58 m, Tissue
PM 6, total capacity 1,200 mt/y, Trim width 1.58 m, Tissue
PM 7, total capacity 6,000 mt/y, Trim width 2.8 m, Tissue
PM 8, total capacity 6,000 mt/y, Trim width 2.8 m, Tissue
PM 9, total capacity 6,000 mt/y, Trim width 2.8 m, Tissue

ⓜHebei Kaishide Specialty Paper Co., Ltd.
Zhangjiakou Mill
No.29, Binhe Street, Xuanhua
Zhangjiakou, Hebei, 075000
China
Phone: (86) 313 5960 099/020/033
Fax: (86) 313 5960 011
Web Address: www.ksdpaper.com
Total Employees at this Location: 400
Type of Operation: Paper mill
Paper/Paperboard Grades and Capacities:
Total paper and paperboard capacity: 50,000 mt/y
Specialty and industrial: 50,000 mt/y
Paper and Paperboard Mill Data:
Paper Machines: 1
PM 1, total capacity 50,000 mt/y, Trim width 2.64 m, Specialty and industrial

ⓘHebei Kangda Paper Group
Ownership: 100% by private owners
No. 8 Farm, Tanghai County
Tangshan, Hebei, 063207
China
Phone: (86) 86 13363201168
Web Address: www.kdpaper.com
Personnel:
Chmn.: Jian Tan
Phone: (86) 86 13363201168
Mill Locations:
Hebei Chengda Paper Co., Ltd., Tangshan Mill, West No. 8 Farm Middle School, Tanghai County, Tangshan 063207, China, Capacity: 17,000 mt/y, (Paper mill)
Phone: (86) 315 879 0388/ 0312
Fax: (86) 315 879 0312
Hebei Tanghai Chenguang Paper Co., Ltd., Tangshan Mill, West Sluice, No. 3 Farm, Tanghai County, Tangshan 063207, China, Capacity: 35,000 mt/y, (Paperboard mill)
Phone: (86) 315 888 8002/ 0100
Fax: (86) 315 888 8002

ⓘHebei Linhai Paper Co., Ltd.
Middle North Outer Ring Rd., Mancheng
Baoding, Hebei, 072150
China
Phone: (86) 312 701 2999
Fax: (86) 312 701 2666
Web Address: www.bdlhzy.com.cn
Mill Locations:
Hebei Linhai Paper Co., Ltd., Baoding Mill, Middle North Outer Ring Rd., Mancheng, Baoding 072150, China, Capacity: 6,000 mt/y, (Paper mill)
Phone: (86) 312 701 2999
Fax: (86) 312 701 2666

China

ⓂHebei Linhai Paper Co., Ltd.
Baoding Mill
Middle North Outer Ring Rd., Mancheng
Baoding, Hebei, 072150
China
  Phone: (86) 312 701 2999
  Fax: (86) 312 701 2666
  Web Address: www.bdlhzy.com.cn
Personnel:
  Chmn.: Guoli Dong
  Phone: (86) 312 701 2999
Total Employees at this Location: 260
Type of Operation: Paper mill
Paper/Paperboard Grades and Capacities:
  Total paper and paperboard capacity: 6,000 mt/y
  Tissue: 6,000 mt/y
Paper and Paperboard Mill Data:
Paper Machines: 8
No. 1, cylinder, total capacity 400 mt/y, Trim width 1.09 m, Tissue
No. 2, cylinder, total capacity 400 mt/y, Trim width 1.09 m, Tissue
No. 3, cylinder, total capacity 400 mt/y, Trim width 1.09 m, Tissue
No. 4, cylinder, total capacity 400 mt/y, Trim width 1.09 m, Tissue
No. 5, cylinder, total capacity 400 mt/y, Trim width 1.09 m, Tissue
No. 6, cylinder, total capacity 400 mt/y, Trim width 1.09 m, Tissue
No. 7, fourdrinier, total capacity 1,800 mt/y, Trim width 2.04 m, Tissue
No. 8, fourdrinier, total capacity 1,800 mt/y, Trim width 2.04 m, Tissue

ⓄHebei Longyuan Paper Co., Ltd.
Dapang Village, Suicheng Town, Xushui County
Baoding, Hebei, 072550
China
  Phone: (86) 312 8968 999/838
Mill Locations:
Hebei Longyuan Paper Co., Ltd., Baoding Mill, Dapang Village, Suicheng Town, Xushui County, Baoding 072550, China, Capacity: 25,000 mt/y, (Paper mill)
  Phone: (86) 312 8968 999/838

ⓂHebei Longyuan Paper Co., Ltd.
Baoding Mill
Dapang Village, Suicheng Town, Xushui County
Baoding, Hebei, 072550
China
  Phone: (86) 312 8968 999/838
Type of Operation: Paper mill
Paper/Paperboard Grades and Capacities:
  Total paper and paperboard capacity: 25,000 mt/y
  Tissue: 25,000 mt/y
Paper and Paperboard Mill Data:
Paper Machines: 8
PM 1, total capacity 1,200 mt/y, Trim width 1.58 m, Tissue
PM 2, total capacity 1,200 mt/y, Trim width 1.58 m, Tissue
PM 3, total capacity 1,200 mt/y, Trim width 1.58 m, Tissue
PM 4, total capacity 1,200 mt/y, Trim width 1.58 m, Tissue
PM 5, total capacity 5,000 mt/y, Trim width 3.4 m, Tissue
PM 6, total capacity 5,000 mt/y, Trim width 3.5 m, Tissue
PM 7, total capacity 5,000 mt/y, Trim width 3.5 m, Tissue
PM 8, total capacity 5,000 mt/y, Trim width 3.5 m, Tissue

ⓂHebei Lu Quan Shunfa Industrial Co., Ltd.
Luquan Mill
Ownership: 100% by Hebei Qu Zhai Group
Qu Zhai Industry Zone, Dahe Town
Luquan, Hebei, 050200
China
  Phone: (86) 311 8229 4878/ 7253/ 6227
  Fax: (86) 311 8229 4959
  Email: quzhaizhiye@163.com
Personnel:
  Chmn.: Jicheng Hu
  Phone: (86) 311 8229 4878/ 7253/ 6227
  Gen. Mgr.: Dongxi Guo
  Phone: (86) 311 8229 4878/ 7253/ 6227
  Mill Mgr.: Wenhui Niu
  Phone: (86) 311 8229 4878/ 7253/ 6227
Total Employees at this Location: 1,500
Type of Operation: Paper mill, Paperboard mill
Pulp Grades and Capacities:
  Total pulp capacity: 71,011 mt/y
  Recycled Pulping: 71,011 mt/y
Paper/Paperboard Grades and Capacities:
  Total paper and paperboard capacity: 72,000 mt/y
  Newsprint: 12,000 mt/y
  Linerboard: 60,000 mt/y
Paper and Paperboard Mill Data:
Paper Machines: 7
No. 1, cylinder, total capacity 8,000 mt/y, Trim width 1.6 m, Linerboard
No. 2, cylinder, total capacity 8,000 mt/y, Trim width 1.6 m, Linerboard
No. 3, cylinder, total capacity 8,000 mt/y, Trim width 1.6 m, Linerboard
No. 4, cylinder, total capacity 8,000 mt/y, Trim width 1.6 m, Linerboard
No. 8, fourdrinier, total capacity 10,000 mt/y, Trim width 1.76 m, Linerboard
No. 10, fourdrinier, total capacity 18,000 mt/y, Trim width 2.2 m, Linerboard
No. 11, multi-wire, total capacity 12,000 mt/y, Trim width 2.4 m, Newsprint
Energy Data:
Electrical demand for mill: 104 MWh/D

ⓂHebei Luquan Yuanda Industrial Co., Ltd.
Luquan Mill
Ownership: 100% by Hebei Qu Zhai Group
Qu Zhai Industry Zone, Dahe Town
Luquan, Hebei, 050200
China
  Phone: (86) 311 8229 2057/ 5756/ 5506/ 5708/ 5887
  Fax: (86) 311 8229 2057/ 5706
  Email: qz599@163.com
Personnel:
  Chmn.: Jicheng Hu
  Phone: (86) 311 8229 2057/ 5756/ 5506/ 5708/ 5887
  Gen. Mgr.: Dongxin Gao
  Phone: (86) 311 8229 2057/ 5756/ 5506/ 5708/ 5887
  Mill Mgr.: Wenhui Niu
  Phone: (86) 311 8229 2057/ 5756/ 5506/ 5708/ 5887
Total Employees at this Location: 200
Type of Operation: Paperboard mill
Pulp Grades and Capacities:
  Total pulp capacity: 91,869 mt/y
  Recycled Pulping: 91,869 mt/y
Pulp Mill Data:
  Bleach Plant Systems: 1
  Recycled Pulping System, Type: 1
  Recycled Fiber Treatment Lines:
  Flotation deinking lines: 1
  Recycled packaging pulping lines: 1 at 100,000 admt/y
Paper/Paperboard Grades and Capacities:
  Total paper and paperboard capacity: 100,000 mt/y
  Boxboard/cartonboard: 100,000 mt/y
Paper and Paperboard Mill Data:
Paper Machines: 1
No. 1, Multi-wire (4), total capacity 100,000 mt/y, Trim width 3.8 m, Boxboard/cartonboard
Coating Machines: 1
PM 1, on machine
Energy Data:
Electrical demand for mill: 157 MWh/D

ⓄHebei Mancheng Anxin Paper Co., Ltd.
Mancheng
Baoding, Hebei, 072150
China
  Phone: (86) 312 7026 716
Mill Locations:
Hebei Mancheng Anxin Paper Co., Ltd., Baoding Mill, Mancheng, Baoding 072150, China, Capacity: 21,000 mt/y, (Paper mill)
  Phone: (86) 312 7026 716

ⓂHebei Mancheng Anxin Paper Co., Ltd.
Baoding Mill
Mancheng
Baoding, Hebei, 072150
China
  Phone: (86) 312 7026 716
Type of Operation: Paper mill
Paper/Paperboard Grades and Capacities:
  Total paper and paperboard capacity: 21,000 mt/y
  Tissue: 21,000 mt/y
Paper and Paperboard Mill Data:
Paper Machines: 8
PM 1, total capacity 1,400 mt/y, Trim width 1.86 m, Tissue
PM 2, total capacity 1,400 mt/y, Trim width 1.86 m, Tissue
PM 3, total capacity 1,400 mt/y, Trim width 1.86 m, Tissue
PM 4, total capacity 1,400 mt/y, Trim width 1.86 m, Tissue
PM 5, total capacity 1,400 mt/y, Trim width 1.86 m, Tissue
PM 6, total capacity 5,000 mt/y, Trim width 3.5 m, Tissue
PM 7, total capacity 5,000 mt/y, Trim width 3.4 m, Tissue
PM 8, total capacity 5,000 mt/y, Trim width 3.5 m, Tissue

ⓄHebei Mancheng Changfa Paper Co., Ltd.
Ownership: 100% by private owners
Fangshang Industry Park, Daceying Town, Mancheng
Baoding, Hebei, 072150
China
  Phone: (86) 312 702 1716
Mill Locations:
Hebei Mancheng Changfa Paper Co., Ltd., Baoding Mill, Fangshang Industry Park, Daceying Town, Mancheng, Baoding 072150, China, Capacity: 8,400 mt/y, (Paper mill)
  Phone: (86) 312 702 1716

ⓂHebei Mancheng Changfa Paper Co., Ltd.
Baoding Mill
Fangshang Industry Park, Daceying Town, Mancheng
Baoding, Hebei, 072150
China
  Phone: (86) 312 702 1716
Personnel:
  Chmn.: Lianying Zhao
  Phone: (86) 312 702 1716
Type of Operation: Paper mill
Paper/Paperboard Grades and Capacities:
  Total paper and paperboard capacity: 8,400 mt/y
  Tissue: 8,400 mt/y
Paper and Paperboard Mill Data:
Paper Machines: 3
No. 1, total capacity 2,000 mt/y, Trim width 1.75 m, Tissue
No. 2, total capacity 2,000 mt/y, Trim width 1.75 m, Tissue
No. 3, total capacity 4,400 mt/y, Trim width 3.5 m, Tissue
Energy Data:
Power boilers: 1

ⓄHebei Mancheng Chenggong Paper Co., Ltd.
Fangshang Industry Park, Daceying Town, Mancheng County
Baoding, Hebei, 072150
China
  Phone: (86) 312 702 1302
  Fax: (86) 312 702 3518
Mill Locations:
Hebei Mancheng Chenggong Paper Co., Ltd., Baoding Mill, Fangshang Industry Park, Daceying Town,

China

Mancheng County, Baoding 072150, China, Capacity: 18,000 mt/y, (Paper mill)
Phone: (86) 312 702 1302
Fax: (86) 312 702 3518

ⓂHebei Mancheng Chenggong Paper Co., Ltd.
Baoding Mill
Fangshang Industry Park, Daceying Town, Mancheng County
Baoding, Hebei, 072150
China
 Phone: (86) 312 702 1302
 Fax: (86) 312 702 3518
Personnel:
 Chmn.: Shengli Li
 Phone: (86) 312 702 1302
 Sls. Mgr.: Mr. Gao
 Phone: (86) 312 702 1302
Total Employees at this Location: 300
Type of Operation: Paper mill
Paper/Paperboard Grades and Capacities:
 Total paper and paperboard capacity: 18,000 mt/y
 Tissue: 18,000 mt/y
Paper and Paperboard Mill Data:
Paper Machines: 7
No. 1, (Rebuilt from 1092 PMs), cylinder, total capacity 2,000 mt/y, Trim width 2.4 m, Tissue
No. 2, (Rebuilt from 1092 PMs), cylinder, total capacity 2,000 mt/y, Trim width 2.4 m, Tissue
No. 3, (Rebuilt from 1092 PMs), cylinder, total capacity 2,000 mt/y, Trim width 2.4 m, Tissue
No. 4, (Rebuilt from 1575 PMs), cylinder, total capacity 3,000 mt/y, Trim width 2.88 m, Tissue
No. 5, (Rebuilt from 1575 PMs), cylinder, total capacity 3,000 mt/y, Trim width 2.88 m, Tissue
No. 6, (Rebuilt from 1575 PMs), cylinder, total capacity 3,000 mt/y, Trim width 2.88 m, Tissue
No. 7, (Rebuilt from 1575 PMs), cylinder, total capacity 3,000 mt/y, Trim width 2.88 m, Tissue
Energy Data:
Power boilers: 1

ⓂHebei Mancheng Chengxin Paper Co., Ltd.
Ownership: 100% by shareholders
Daceying Papermaking Industry Park, Mancheng County
Baoding, Hebei, 072150
China
 Phone: (86) 312 702 6699
 Fax: (86) 312 702 0123
 Email: chengxin@chengxinpaper.com
 Web Address: www.chengxinpaper.com
Mill Locations:
Hebei Mancheng Chengxin Paper Co., Ltd., Baoding Mill, Daceying Papermaking Industry Park, Mancheng County, Baoding 072150, China, Capacity: 12,000 mt/y, (Paper mill)
 Phone: (86) 312 702 6699
 Fax: (86) 312 702 0123
 Email: chengxin@chengxinpaper.com

ⓂHebei Mancheng Chengxin Paper Co., Ltd.
Baoding Mill
Daceying Papermaking Industry Park, Mancheng County
Baoding, Hebei, 072150
China
 Phone: (86) 312 702 6699
 Fax: (86) 312 702 0123
 Email: chengxin@chengxinpaper.com
 Web Address: www.chengxinpaper.com
Personnel:
 Gen. Mgr.: Ms. Baojiang Han
 Phone: (86) 312 702 6699
Total Employees at this Location: 800
Type of Operation: Paper mill
Paper/Paperboard Grades and Capacities:
 Total paper and paperboard capacity: 12,000 mt/y
 Tissue: 12,000 mt/y
Paper and Paperboard Mill Data:
Paper Machines: 6
No. 1, cylinder, total capacity 2,000 mt/y, Trim width 3.5 m, Tissue
No. 2, cylinder, total capacity 2,000 mt/y, Trim width 3.5 m, Tissue
No. 3, cylinder, total capacity 2,000 mt/y, Trim width 3.5 m, Tissue
No. 4, cylinder, total capacity 2,000 mt/y, Trim width 3.5 m, Tissue
No. 5, cylinder, total capacity 2,000 mt/y, Trim width 3.5 m, Tissue
No. 6, cylinder, total capacity 2,000 mt/y, Trim width 3.5 m, Tissue

ⓂHebei Mancheng Chenyu Paper Co., Ltd.
Daceying Industrial Park, Mancheng County
Baoding, Hebei, 072150
China
 Phone: (86) 312 7021 011
Mill Locations:
Hebei Mancheng Chenyu Paper Co., Ltd., Baoding Mill, Daceying Industrial Park, Mancheng County, Baoding 072150, China, Capacity: 15,000 mt/y, (Paper mill)
 Phone: (86) 312 7021 011

ⓂHebei Mancheng Chenyu Paper Co., Ltd.
Baoding Mill
Daceying Industrial Park, Mancheng County
Baoding, Hebei, 072150
China
 Phone: (86) 312 7021 011
Type of Operation: Paper mill
Paper/Paperboard Grades and Capacities:
 Total paper and paperboard capacity: 15,000 mt/y
 Tissue: 15,000 mt/y
Paper and Paperboard Mill Data:
Paper Machines: 3
PM 1, total capacity 5,000 mt/y, Trim width 3.5 m, Tissue
PM 2, total capacity 5,000 mt/y, Trim width 3.5 m, Tissue
PM 3, total capacity 5,000 mt/y, Trim width 3.5 m, Tissue

ⓂHebei Mancheng Hongda Paper Co., Ltd.
Ownership: 100% by private owners
Shenxing Paper Making Industry Park, Mancheng County
Baoding, Hebei, 072150
China
 Phone: (86) 312 705 6268
 Fax: (86) 312 705 6668
Mill Locations:
Hebei Mancheng Hongda Paper Co., Ltd., Baoding Mill, Shenxing Paper Making Industry Park, Mancheng County, Baoding 072150, China, Capacity: 10,000 mt/y, (Paper mill)
 Phone: (86) 312 705 6268
 Fax: (86) 312 705 6668
 Email: bdhdzy@163.com

ⓂHebei Mancheng Hongda Paper Co., Ltd.
Baoding Mill
Shenxing Paper Making Industry Park, Mancheng County
Baoding, Hebei, 072150
China
 Phone: (86) 312 705 6268
 Fax: (86) 312 705 6668
 Email: bdhdzy@163.com
 Web Address: www.hongdazhiye.com
Personnel:
 Chmn.: Ms. Qiulai Li
 Phone: (86) 312 705 6268
Total Employees at this Location: 150
Type of Operation: Paper mill
Paper/Paperboard Grades and Capacities:
 Total paper and paperboard capacity: 10,000 mt/y
 Tissue: 10,000 mt/y
Paper and Paperboard Mill Data:
Paper Machines: 10
No. 1, cylinder, total capacity 1,000 mt/y, Trim width 1.09 m, Tissue
No. 2, cylinder, total capacity 1,000 mt/y, Trim width 1.09 m, Tissue
No. 3, cylinder, total capacity 1,000 mt/y, Trim width 1.09 m, Tissue
No. 4, cylinder, total capacity 1,000 mt/y, Trim width 1.09 m, Tissue
No. 5, cylinder, total capacity 1,000 mt/y, Trim width 1.09 m, Tissue
No. 6, cylinder, total capacity 1,000 mt/y, Trim width 1.09 m, Tissue
No. 7, cylinder, total capacity 1,000 mt/y, Trim width 1.09 m, Tissue
No. 8, cylinder, total capacity 1,000 mt/y, Trim width 1.09 m, Tissue
No. 9, cylinder, total capacity 1,000 mt/y, Trim width 1.09 m, Tissue
No. 10, cylinder, total capacity 1,000 mt/y, Trim width 1.09 m, Tissue

ⓂHebei Mancheng Hongsheng Paper Co., Ltd.
Baoding Mill
Daceying Paper Making Industry Park, Mancheng County
Baoding, Hebei, 072150
China
 Phone: (86) 312 702 1889
 Fax: (86) 312 702 6900
Personnel:
 Chmn.: Hailiang Liu
 Phone: (86) 312 702 1889
Total Employees at this Location: 300
Type of Operation: Paper mill
Paper/Paperboard Grades and Capacities:
 Total paper and paperboard capacity: 12,000 mt/y
 Tissue: 12,000 mt/y
Paper and Paperboard Mill Data:
Paper Machines: 7
No. 1, cylinder, total capacity 1,500 mt/y, Trim width 1.58 m, Tissue
No. 2, cylinder, total capacity 1,500 mt/y, Trim width 1.58 m, Tissue
No. 3, cylinder, total capacity 1,500 mt/y, Trim width 1.58 m, Tissue
No. 4, cylinder, total capacity 1,500 mt/y, Trim width 1.58 m, Tissue
No. 5, cylinder, total capacity 1,500 mt/y, Trim width 1.58 m, Tissue
No. 6, fourdrinier, total capacity 2,000 mt/y, Trim width 1.58 m, Tissue
No. 7, cylinder, total capacity 2,000 mt/y, Trim width 1.58 m, Tissue
Energy Data:
Power boilers: 2

ⓂHebei Mancheng Jinguang Paper Co., Ltd.
Ownership: 100% by private owners
Shangfang Village, Daceying Town, Mancheng County
Baoding, Hebei, 072150
China
 Phone: (86) 312 702 1707
 Fax: (86) 312 702 1899
Mill Locations:
Hebei Mancheng Jinguang Paper Co., Ltd., Baoding Mill, Shangfang Village, Daceying Town, Mancheng County, Baoding 072150, China, Capacity: 2,900 mt/y, (Paper mill)

China

Phone: (86) 312 702 1707
Fax: (86) 312 702 1899

ⓜHebei Mancheng Jinguang Paper Co., Ltd.
Baoding Mill
Shangfang Village, Daceying Town, Mancheng County
Baoding, Hebei, 072150
China
 Phone: (86) 312 702 1707
 Fax: (86) 312 702 1899
 Web Address: www.maowangpaper.cn
Personnel:
 Chmn.: Baoquan Han
 Phone: (86) 312 702 1707
Total Employees at this Location: 108
Type of Operation: Paper mill
Paper/Paperboard Grades and Capacities:
 Total paper and paperboard capacity: 2,900 mt/y
 Tissue: 2,900 mt/y
Paper and Paperboard Mill Data:
Paper Machines: 3
 No. 1, cylinder, total capacity 700 mt/y, Trim width 1.09 m, Tissue
 No. 2, cylinder, total capacity 700 mt/y, Trim width 1.09 m, Tissue
 No. 3, cylinder, total capacity 1,500 mt/y, Trim width 1.76 m, Tissue

ⓜHebei Mancheng Jinli Paper Co., Ltd.
Daceying Town, Mancheng County
Baoding, Hebei, 072150
China
 Phone: (86) 312 7021 669
Mill Locations:
 Hebei Mancheng Jinli Paper Co., Ltd., Baoding Mill, Daceying Town, Mancheng County, Baoding 072150, China, Capacity: 7,000 mt/y, (Paper mill)
 Phone: (86) 312 7021 669

ⓜHebei Mancheng Jinli Paper Co., Ltd.
Baoding Mill
Daceying Town, Mancheng County
Baoding, Hebei, 072150
China
 Phone: (86) 312 7021 669
Type of Operation: Paper mill
Paper/Paperboard Grades and Capacities:
 Total paper and paperboard capacity: 7,000 mt/y
 Tissue: 7,000 mt/y
Paper and Paperboard Mill Data:
Paper Machines: 4
 PM 1, total capacity 2,000 mt/y, Trim width 1.88 m, Tissue
 PM 2, total capacity 2,000 mt/y, Trim width 1.88 m
 PM 3, total capacity 1,600 mt/y, Trim width 1.76 m, Tissue
 PM 4, total capacity 1,400 mt/y, Trim width 1.58 m, Tissue

ⓜHebei Mancheng Shunli Paper Co., Ltd.
Ownership: 100% by private owners
Daceying Industry Park, Mancheng County
Baoding, Hebei, 072150
China
 Phone: (86) 312 702 2127/ 1633/ 0666
 Fax: (86) 312 702 2601
Mill Locations:
 Hebei Mancheng Shunli Paper Co., Ltd., Baoding Mill, Daceying Industry Park, Mancheng County, Baoding 072150, China, Capacity: 10,000 mt/y, (Paper mill)
 Phone: (86) 312 702 2127/ 1633/ 0666
 Fax: (86) 312 702 2601

ⓜHebei Mancheng Shunli Paper Co., Ltd.
Baoding Mill
Daceying Industry Park, Mancheng County
Baoding, Hebei, 072150
China
 Phone: (86) 312 702 2127/ 1633/ 0666
 Fax: (86) 312 702 2601
Personnel:
 Chmn.: Ms. Xiangzhan Zhao
 Phone: (86) 312 702 2127/ 1633/ 0666
 Gen. Mgr.: Yaqing Zhao
 Phone: (86) 312 702 2127/ 1633/ 0666
 Dir.: Ms. Jie Chang
 Phone: (86) 312 702 2127/ 1633/ 0666
Total Employees at this Location: 500
Type of Operation: Paper mill
Paper/Paperboard Grades and Capacities:
 Total paper and paperboard capacity: 10,000 mt/y
 Tissue: 10,000 mt/y
Paper and Paperboard Mill Data:
Paper Machines: 8
 No. 1, cylinder, total capacity 1,250 mt/y, Trim width 1.09 m, Tissue
 No. 2, cylinder, total capacity 1,250 mt/y, Trim width 1.09 m, Tissue
 No. 3, cylinder, total capacity 1,250 mt/y, Trim width 1.09 m, Tissue
 No. 4, cylinder, total capacity 1,250 mt/y, Trim width 1.09 m, Tissue
 No. 5, cylinder, total capacity 1,250 mt/y, Trim width 1.09 m, Tissue
 No. 6, cylinder, total capacity 1,250 mt/y, Trim width 1.09 m, Tissue
 No. 7, cylinder, total capacity 1,250 mt/y, Trim width 1.09 m, Tissue
 No. 8, cylinder, total capacity 1,250 mt/y, Trim width 1.09 m, Tissue

ⓜHebei Mancheng Shuntong Paper Co., Ltd.
Baoding Mill
Dazhuang Village, Mancheng County
Baoding, Hebei, 072150
China
 Phone: (86) 312 7018 440
Type of Operation: Paper mill
Paper/Paperboard Grades and Capacities:
 Total paper and paperboard capacity: 21,600 mt/y
 Tissue: 21,600 mt/y
Paper and Paperboard Mill Data:
Paper Machines: 10
 PM 1, total capacity 1,800 mt/y, Trim width 2.4 m, Tissue
 PM 2, total capacity 1,800 mt/y, Trim width 2.4 m, Tissue
 PM 3, total capacity 1,800 mt/y, Trim width 2.4 m, Tissue
 PM 4, total capacity 1,800 mt/y, Trim width 2.4 m, Tissue
 PM 5, total capacity 1,800 mt/y, Tissue
 PM 6, total capacity 1,800 mt/y, Trim width 2.4 m, Tissue
 PM 7, total capacity 1,800 mt/y, Trim width 2.4 m, Tissue
 PM 8, total capacity 2,000 mt/y, Trim width 2.64 m, Tissue
 PM 9, total capacity 3,500 mt/y, Trim width 3.5 m, Tissue
 PM 10, total capacity 3,500 mt/y, Trim width 3.5 m, Tissue

ⓜHebei Mancheng Xinyu Paper Co., Ltd.
Gangtou Village, Daceying Town, Mancheng County
Baoding, Hebei, 072150
China
 Phone: (86) 312 7021 901
Mill Locations:
 Hebei Mancheng Xinyu Paper Co., Ltd., Baoding Mill, Gangtou Village, Daceying Town, Mancheng County, Baoding 072150, China, Capacity: 15,000 mt/y, (Paper mill)
 Phone: (86) 312 7021 901

ⓜHebei Mancheng Xinyu Paper Co., Ltd.
Baoding Mill
Gangtou Village, Daceying Town, Mancheng County
Baoding, Hebei, 072150
China
 Phone: (86) 312 7021 901
Type of Operation: Paper mill
Paper/Paperboard Grades and Capacities:
 Total paper and paperboard capacity: 15,000 mt/y
 Tissue: 15,000 mt/y
Paper and Paperboard Mill Data:
Paper Machines: 15
 PM 1, total capacity 1,000 mt/y, Trim width 1.58 m, Tissue
 PM 2, total capacity 1,000 mt/y, Trim width 1.58 m, Tissue
 PM 3, total capacity 1,000 mt/y, Trim width 1.58 m, Tissue
 PM 4, total capacity 1,000 mt/y, Trim width 1.58 m, Tissue
 PM 5, total capacity 1,000 mt/y, Trim width 1.58 m, Tissue
 PM 6, total capacity 1,000 mt/y, Trim width 1.58 m, Tissue
 PM 7, total capacity 1,000 mt/y, Trim width 1.58 m, Tissue
 PM 8, total capacity 1,000 mt/y, Trim width 1.58 m, Tissue
 PM 9, total capacity 1,000 mt/y, Trim width 1.58 m, Tissue
 PM 10, total capacity 1,000 mt/y, Trim width 1.58 m, Tissue
 PM 11, total capacity 1,000 mt/y, Trim width 1.58 m, Tissue
 PM 12, total capacity 1,000 mt/y, Trim width 1.58 m, Tissue
 PM 13, total capacity 1,000 mt/y, Trim width 1.58 m, Tissue
 PM 14, total capacity 1,000 mt/y, Trim width 1.58 m, Tissue
 PM 15, total capacity 1,000 mt/y, Trim width 1.58 m, Tissue

ⓜHebei Mancheng Yiyuan Paper Mill
Ownership: 100% by private owners
Daceying Paper Making Industry Park, Mancheng County
Baoding, Hebei, 072150
China
 Phone: (86) 312 702 1012/ 557 8868
 Fax: (86) 312 702 6285
Mill Locations:
 Hebei Mancheng Yiyuan Paper Mill, Baoding Mill, Daceying Paper Making Industry Park, Mancheng County, Baoding 072150, China, Capacity: 8,000 mt/y, (Paper mill)
 Phone: (86) 312 702 1012/ 557 8868
 Fax: (86) 312 702 6285

ⓜHebei Mancheng Yiyuan Paper Mill
Baoding Mill
Daceying Paper Making Industry Park, Mancheng County
Baoding, Hebei, 072150
China
 Phone: (86) 312 702 1012/ 557 8868
 Fax: (86) 312 702 6285
Personnel:
 Chmn.: Shangjun Zhang
 Phone: (86) 312 702 1012/ 557 8868
 Mill Mgr.: Yuzhu Zhang
 Phone: (86) 312 702 1012/ 557 8868
 Sls. Mgr.: Yuhai Liu
 Phone: (86) 312 702 1012/ 557 8868
Total Employees at this Location: 200
Type of Operation: Paper mill
Paper/Paperboard Grades and Capacities:
 Total paper and paperboard capacity: 8,000 mt/y
 Tissue: 8,000 mt/y
Paper and Paperboard Mill Data:
Paper Machines: 4
 PM 3, fourdrinier, total capacity 2,400 mt/y, Trim width 1.8 m, Tissue
 PM 4, total capacity 3,200 mt/y, Trim width 3.5 m, Tissue
 PM 1-2, cylinder, total capacity 600 mt/y, Trim width 1.58 m, Tissue
Energy Data:
 Power boilers: 1

ⓜHebei Mancheng Yongfa Paper Co., Ltd.
Ownership: 100% by private owners
Gangtou Village, Daceying Town, Mancheng County
Baoding, Hebei, 072150
China
 Phone: (86) 312 702 1333
 Fax: (86) 312 702 5777
Mill Locations:
 Hebei Mancheng Yongfa Paper Co., Ltd., Baoding Mill, Gangtou Village, Daceying Town, Mancheng County, Baoding 072150, China, Capacity: 15,000 mt/y, (Paper mill)
 Phone: (86) 312 702 1333
 Fax: (86) 312 702 5777

China

(m)Hebei Mancheng Yongfa Paper Co., Ltd.
Baoding Mill
Gangtcu Village, Daceying Town, Mancheng County
Baoding, Hebei, 072150
China
  Phone: (86) 312 702 1333
  Fax: (86) 312 702 5777
Personnel:
  Chmn.: Liansuo Gou
  Phone: (86) 312 702 1333
  Mill Mgr.: Lianjin Gou
  Phone: (86) 312 702 1333
Total Employees at this Location: 316
Type of Operation: Paper mill
Paper/Paperboard Grades and Capacities:
  Total paper and paperboard capacity: 15,000 mt/y
  Tissue: 15,000 mt/y
Paper and Paperboard Mill Data:
Paper Machines: 6
No. 1, fourdrinier, total capacity 2,500 mt/y, Trim width 2.4 m, Tissue
No. 2, fourdrinier, total capacity 2,500 mt/y, Trim width 2.4 m, Tissue
No. 3, fourdrinier, total capacity 2,500 mt/y, Trim width 2.4 m, Tissue
No. 4, fourdrinier, total capacity 2,500 mt/y, Trim width 2.4 m, Tissue
No. 5, fourdrinier, total capacity 2,500 mt/y, Trim width 2.4 m, Tissue
No. 6, fourdrinier, total capacity 2,500 mt/y, Trim width 2.4 m, Tissue
Energy Data:
Power boilers: 1

(1)Hebei Qinhuangdao Fengman Paper Co., Ltd.
Ownership: 100% by shareholders
Liushouying Town, Funing County
Qinghuangdao, Hebei, 066300
China
  Phone: (86) 335 604 6075/ 6289
  Fax: (86) 335 604 6706
  Email: fmght@tom.com,
  fmqhtqhd@sina.com
  Web Address: www.fengmanqhd.com
Mill Locations:
Hebei Qinhuangdao Fengman Paper Co., Ltd., Qinghuangdao Mill, Liushouying Town, Funing County, Qinghuangdao 066300, China, Capacity: 180,000 mt/y, (Paper mill, Paperboard mill)
  Phone: (86) 335 604 6075/ 6289
  Fax: (86) 335 604 6706
  Email: fmght@tom.com, fmqhtqhd@sina.com

(m)Hebei Qinhuangdao Fengman Paper Co., Ltd.
Qinghuangdao Mill
Liushouying Town, Funing County
Qinghuangdao, Hebei, 066300
China
  Phone: (86) 335 604 6075/ 6289
  Fax: (86) 335 604 6706
  Email: fmght@tom.com,
  fmqhtqhd@sina.com
  Web Address: www.fengmanqhd.com
Personnel:
  Gen. Mgr.: Yuchang Guo
  Phone: (86) 335 604 6075/ 6289
Total Employees at this Location: 360
Type of Operation: Paper mill, Paperboard mill
Pulp Grades and Capacities:
  Total pulp capacity: 177,463 mt/y
  Recycled Pulping: 177,463 mt/y
Pulp Mill Data:
Pulp Lines: 2
  Recycled Fiber Treatment Lines:
  Recycled packaging pulping lines: 1

Paper/Paperboard Grades and Capacities:
  Total paper and paperboard capacity: 180,000 mt/y
  Linerboard: 100,000 mt/y
  Corrugating medium/fluting: 80,000 mt/y
Paper and Paperboard Mill Data:
Paper Machines: 2
No. 1, Ultraformer, total capacity 100,000 mt/y, Trim width 4.2 m, Linerboard
No. 2, fourdrinier, total capacity 80,000 mt/y, Trim width 4.2 m, Corrugating medium/fluting
Energy Data:
Power boilers: 1
Steam turbines at 1.5 MW
Electrical demand for mill: 228 MWh/D

(1)Hebei Qinhuangdao Haofeng Enterprise Group
Ownership: 100% by private owners
Liushouying, North Beidai River
Qinhuangdao, Hebei, 066301
China
  Phone: (86) 335 6045 948/ 6046 145/ 6046 125
  Fax: (86) 335 6046 145/ 6045 948
  Email: haofeng558@163.com
Mill Locations:
Hebei Qinhuangdao Haofeng Enterprise Group, Qinhuangdao Mill, Liushouying, North Beidai River, Qinhuangdao 066301, China, Capacity: 36,000 mt/y, (Paper mill)
  Phone: (86) 335 6045 948/ 6046 145/ 6046 125
  Fax: (86) 335 6046 145/ 6045 948
  Email: haofeng558@163.com

(m)Hebei Qinhuangdao Haofeng Enterprise Group
Qinhuangdao Mill
Liushouying, North Beidai River
Qinhuangdao, Hebei, 066301
China
  Phone: (86) 335 6045 948/ 6046 145/ 6046 125
  Fax: (86) 335 6046 145/ 6045 948
  Email: haofeng558@163.com
Personnel:
  Chmn.: Xiaofeng Chen
  Phone: (86) 335 6045 948/ 6046 145/ 6046 125
  Sls. Mgr.: Heng Gao
  Phone: (86) 335 6045 948/ 6046 145/ 6046 125
Total Employees at this Location: 600
Type of Operation: Paper mill
Pulp Grades and Capacities:
  Total pulp capacity: 40,000 mt/y
  Recycled Pulping: 40,000 mt/y
Pulp Mill Data:
  Recycled Fiber Treatment Lines:
  Flotation deinking lines: 3 at 40,000 admt/y
Paper/Paperboard Grades and Capacities:
  Total paper and paperboard capacity: 36,000 mt/y
  Newsprint: 10,000 mt/y
  Packaging papers: 26,000 mt/y
Paper and Paperboard Mill Data:
Paper Machines: 4
PM 7, cylinder, total capacity 8,000 mt/y, Trim width 1.76 m, Packaging papers
PM 8, fourdrinier, total capacity 18,000 mt/y, Trim width 2.64 m, Packaging papers
PM 5-6, cylinder, total capacity 5,000 mt/y, Trim width 1.58 m, Newsprint

(1)Hebei Qu Zhai Group
Ownership: 100% by state
Qu Zhai Industry Zone, Dahe Town
Luquan, Hebei, 050200
China
  Phone: (86) 311 8229 1038/ 3951/ 3953/ 6995
  Email: hbqzjt@hbqzjt.cn
  Web Address: www.hbqzjt.cn
Personnel:
  Chmn.: Jicheng Hu
  Phone: (86) 311 8229 1038/ 3951/ 3953/ 6995
  Gen. Mgr.: Dongxin Gao
  Phone: (86) 311 8229 1038/ 3951/ 3953/ 6995
Total Employees of Company: 5,300
Mill Locations:
Hebei Lu Quan Shunfa Industrial Co., Ltd., Luquan Mill, Qu Zhai Industry Zone, Dahe Town, Luquan 050200, China, Capacity: 72,000 mt/y, (Paper mill, Paperboard mill)
  Phone: (86) 311 8229 4878/ 7253/ 6227
  Fax: (86) 311 8229 4959
  Email: quzhaizhiye@163.com
Hebei Luquan Yuanda Industrial Co., Ltd., Luquan Mill, Qu Zhai Industry Zone, Dahe Town, Luquan 050200, China, Capacity: 100,000 mt/y, (Paperboard mill)
  Phone: (86) 311 8229 2057/ 5756/ 5506/ 5708/ 5887
  Fax: (86) 311 8229 2057/ 5706
  Email: qz599@163.com

(1)Hebei Sanhe City Jingdong Shuhe Paper Mill
Ownership: 100% by private owners
Dongchengzi Village, Huangtuzhuang Town
Sanhe, Hebei, 065200
China
  Phone: (86) 316 317 0241
Mill Locations:
Hebei Sanhe City Jingdong Shuhe Paper Mill, Sanhe Mill, Dongchengzi Village, Huangtuzhuang Town, Sanhe 065200, China, Capacity: 1,800 mt/y, (Paper mill)
  Phone: (86) 316 317 0241

(m)Hebei Sanhe City Jingdong Shuhe Paper Mill
Sanhe Mill
Dongchengzi Village, Huangtuzhuang Town
Sanhe, Hebei, 065200
China
  Phone: (86) 316 317 0241
Personnel:
  Chmn.: Fuhe Liu
  Phone: (86) 316 317 0241
Type of Operation: Paper mill
Pulp Grades and Capacities:
  Total pulp capacity: 1,800 mt/y
  Recycled Pulping: 1,800 mt/y
Pulp Mill Data:
Pulp Lines: 1
  Recycled Fiber Treatment Lines:
  Pulpers: 1 at 1,800 admt/y
Paper/Paperboard Grades and Capacities:
  Total paper and paperboard capacity: 1,800 mt/y
  Tissue: 1,800 mt/y
Paper and Paperboard Mill Data:
Paper Machines: 2
PM 1, cylinder, total capacity 700 mt/y, Trim width 1.09 m, Tissue
PM 2, cylinder, total capacity 1,100 mt/y, Trim width 1.58 m, Tissue
Energy Data:
Power boilers: 1

(1)Hebei Sanhe City Youyi Paper Mill
Ownership: 100% by private owners
Dazhao Village, Yang Town
Sanhe, Hebei, 065200
China
  Phone: (86) 316 321 2996
  Fax: (86) 316 321 4929
Mill Locations:
Hebei Sanhe City Youyi Paper Mill, Sanhe Mill, Dazhao Village, Yang Town, Sanhe 065200, China, Capacity: 1,800 mt/y, (Paper mill)
  Phone: (86) 316 321 2996
  Fax: (86) 316 321 4929

Hebei Sanhe City Youyi Paper Mill
Sanhe Mill
Dazhao Village, Yang Town
Sanhe, Hebei, 065200
China
  Phone: (86) 316 321 2996
  Fax: (86) 316 321 4929
Personnel:
  Chmn.: Delong Gao
  Phone: (86) 316 321 2996
  Mill Mgr.: Yun Gao
  Phone: (86) 316 321 2996
Type of Operation: Paper mill
Pulp Grades and Capacities:
  Total pulp capacity: 2,000 mt/y
  Recycled Pulping: 2,000 mt/y
Pulp Mill Data:
  Recycled Fiber Treatment Lines:
  Washing deinking lines: 1 at 2,000 admt/y
Paper/Paperboard Grades and Capacities:
  Total paper and paperboard capacity: 1,800 mt/y
  Tissue: 1,800 mt/y
Paper and Paperboard Mill Data:
Paper Machines: 2
  PM 1-2, cylinder, total capacity 900 mt/y, Trim width 1.09 m, Tissue
Energy Data:
  Power boilers: 1

Hebei Sanhe Xingwang Paper Mill
Ownership: 100% by private owners
Zhaotu Village, Juyang Town
Sanhe, Hebei, 065200
China
  Phone: (86) 316 316 1069
Mill Locations:
Hebei Sanhe Xingwang Paper Mill, Sanhe Mill, Zhaotu Village, Juyang Town, Sanhe 065200, China, Capacity: 2,100 mt/y, (Paper mill)
  Phone: (86) 316 316 1069

Hebei Sanhe Xingwang Paper Mill
Sanhe Mill
Zhaotu Village, Juyang Town
Sanhe, Hebei, 065200
China
  Phone: (86) 316 316 1069
Personnel:
  Chmn.: Ziliang Cai
  Phone: (86) 316 316 1069
Type of Operation: Paper mill
Pulp Grades and Capacities:
  Total pulp capacity: 2,100 mt/y
  Recycled Pulping: 2,100 mt/y
Pulp Mill Data:
Pulp Lines: 1
  Recycled Fiber Treatment Lines:
  Pulpers: 1 at 2,100 admt/y
Paper/Paperboard Grades and Capacities:
  Total paper and paperboard capacity: 2,100 mt/y
  Tissue: 2,100 mt/y
Paper and Paperboard Mill Data:
Paper Machines: 3
  PM 1-3, cylinder, total capacity 700 mt/y, Trim width 1.58 m, Tissue
Energy Data:
  Power boilers: 1

Hebei Sanhe Yangzhuang Dawotou Paper Mill
Ownership: 100% by private owners
Dawotou Village, Yangzhuang Town
Sanhe, Hebei, 065200
China
  Phone: (86) 316 365 0254
Mill Locations:
Hebei Sanhe Yangzhuang Dawotou Paper Mill, Sanhe Mill, Dawotou Village, Yangzhuang Town, Sanhe 065200, China, Capacity: 3,000 mt/y, (Paper mill)
  Phone: (86) 316 365 0254

Hebei Sanhe Yangzhuang Dawotou Paper Mill
Sanhe Mill
Dawotou Village, Yangzhuang Town
Sanhe, Hebei, 065200
China
  Phone: (86) 316 365 0254
Personnel:
  Chmn.: Changsheng Wang
  Phone: (86) 316 365 0254
Total Employees at this Location: 50
Type of Operation: Paper mill
Pulp Grades and Capacities:
  Total pulp capacity: 2,000 mt/y
  Recycled Pulping: 2,000 mt/y
Pulp Mill Data:
Pulp Lines: 1
Paper/Paperboard Grades and Capacities:
  Total paper and paperboard capacity: 3,000 mt/y
  Tissue: 3,000 mt/y
Paper and Paperboard Mill Data:
Paper Machines: 4
  PM 1-4, cylinder, total capacity 750 mt/y, Trim width 1.58 m, Tissue
Energy Data:
  Power boilers: 1

Hebei Sanhe Yanling Paper Mill
Ownership: 100% by private owners
Zhaotu Village, Juyang Town
Sanhe, Hebei, 065200
China
  Phone: (86) 316 316 1021
  Fax: (86) 316 316 1021
Mill Locations:
Hebei Sanhe Yanling Paper Mill, Sanhe Mill, Zhaotu Village, Juyang Town, Sanhe 065200, China, Capacity: 1,500 mt/y, (Paper mill)
  Phone: (86) 316 316 1021
  Fax: (86) 316 316 1021

Hebei Sanhe Yanling Paper Mill
Sanhe Mill
Zhaotu Village, Juyang Town
Sanhe, Hebei, 065200
China
  Phone: (86) 316 316 1021
  Fax: (86) 316 316 1021
Personnel:
  Chmn.: Guanghui Tian
  Phone: (86) 316 316 1021
Type of Operation: Paper mill
Pulp Grades and Capacities:
  Total pulp capacity: 1,500 mt/y
  Recycled Pulping: 1,500 mt/y
Pulp Mill Data:
Pulp Lines: 1
  Recycled Fiber Treatment Lines:
  Pulpers: 1 at 1,500 admt/y
Paper/Paperboard Grades and Capacities:
  Total paper and paperboard capacity: 1,500 mt/y
  Tissue: 1,500 mt/y
Paper and Paperboard Mill Data:
Paper Machines: 2
  PM 1-2, cylinder, total capacity 750 mt/y, Trim width 1.09 m, Tissue
Energy Data:
  Power boilers: 1

Hebei Sanhe Zhaotuzhuang Aimin Paper Mill
Ownership: 100% by private owners
Zaotu Village, Xunyang Town
Sanhe, Hebei, 065200
China
  Phone: (86) 312 316 1020
Mill Locations:
Hebei Sanhe Zhaotuzhuang Aimin Paper Mill, Sanhe Mill, Zaotu Village, Xunyang Town, Sanhe 065200, China, Capacity: 2,000 mt/y, (Paper mill)
  Phone: (86) 312 316 1020

Hebei Sanhe Zhaotuzhuang Aimin Paper Mill
Sanhe Mill
Zaotu Village, Xunyang Town
Sanhe, Hebei, 065200
China
  Phone: (86) 312 316 1020
Personnel:
  Chmn.: Aiming Tian
  Phone: (86) 312 316 1020
  Prod. Mgr.: Shengli Zhang
  Phone: (86) 312 316 1020
Total Employees at this Location: 50
Type of Operation: Paper mill
Pulp Grades and Capacities:
  Total pulp capacity: 2,500 mt/y
  Recycled Pulping: 2,500 mt/y
Pulp Mill Data:
Pulp Lines: 1
Paper/Paperboard Grades and Capacities:
  Total paper and paperboard capacity: 2,000 mt/y
  Tissue: 2,000 mt/y
Paper and Paperboard Mill Data:
Paper Machines: 2
  PM 1-2, cylinder, total capacity 1,000 mt/y, Trim width 1.09 m, Tissue
Energy Data:
  Power boilers: 1

Hebei Tangshan Guotai Paper Co., Ltd.
Ownership: 100% by private owners
Guotai Street, Fengrun Yinxi Industry Park
Tangshan, Hebei, 063035
China
  Phone: (86) 315 7760 089/096
  Fax: (86) 315 7760 088
  Email: tsguotaizhiye@163.com
  Web Address: www.gtpaper.cn
Personnel:
  Chmn.: Guochang Peng
  Phone: (86) 315 7760 089/096
  Gen. Mgr.: Jianxun Xiao
  Phone: (86) 315 7760 089/096
  Prod. Mgr.: Yulong Zhang
  Phone: (86) 315 7760 089/096
Mill Locations:
Hebei Changtai Paper, Yutian Mill, Yutian county 064000, China, Capacity: 430,000 mt/y, (Paper mill)
  Phone: (86) 315 776 0089/0096/0052
  Fax: (86) 315 776 0088/0051
  Email: tsguotaizhiye@163.com
Hebei Tangshan Guotai Paper Co., Ltd., Tangshan Mill, Guotai Street, Fengrun Yinxi Industry Park, Tangshan 063035, China, Capacity: 120,666 mt/y, (Paperboard mill)
  Phone: (86) 315 7760 089/096
  Fax: (86) 315 7760 088
  Email: tsguotaizhiye@163.com

Hebei Tangshan Guotai Paper Co., Ltd.
Tangshan Mill
Guotai Street, Fengrun Yinxi Industry Park
Tangshan, Hebei, 063035
China
  Phone: (86) 315 7760 089/096
  Fax: (86) 315 7760 088
  Email: tsguotaizhiye@163.com
  Web Address: www.gtpaper.cn
Personnel:
  Chmn.: Guochang Peng

China

Phone: (86) 315 7760 089/096
Gen. Mgr.: Jianxun Xiao
Phone: (86) 315 7760 089/096
Prod. Mgr.: Yulong Zhang
Phone: (86) 315 7760 089/096
Total Employees at this Location: 500
Type of Operation: Paperboard mill
Pulp Grades and Capacities:
 Total pulp capacity: 110,187 mt/y
 Recycled Pulping: 110,187 mt/y
Pulp Mill Data:
Pulp Lines: 2
 Bleach Plant Systems: 1
 Recycled Fiber Treatment Lines:
 Flotation deinking lines
 Recycled packaging pulping lines
Paper/Paperboard Grades and Capacities:
 Total paper and paperboard capacity: 120,666 mt/y
 Corrugating medium/fluting: 50,337 mt/y
 Boxboard/cartonboard: 70,329 mt/y
Paper and Paperboard Mill Data:
Paper Machines: 2
 No. 1, multi-wire, total capacity 70,329 mt/y, Trim width 3.35 m, Boxboard/cartonboard
 No. 2, fourdrinier, total capacity 50,337 mt/y, Trim width 3.4 m, Corrugating medium/fluting
Energy Data:
 Electrical demand for mill: 211 MWh/D

ⓂHebei Tanghai Chenguang Paper Co., Ltd.
Tangshan Mill
Ownership: Hebei Kangda Paper Group
West Sluice, No. 3 Farm, Tanghai County
Tangshan, Hebei, 063207
China
 Phone: (86) 315 888 8002/ 0100
 Fax: (86) 315 888 8002
Personnel:
 Chmn.: Jian Tan
 Phone: (86) 315 888 8002/ 0100
 Mill Mgr.: Youfu Zhen
 Phone: (86) 315 888 8002/ 0100
 Sls. Mgr.: Xujian Sun
 Phone: (86) 315 888 8002/ 0100
 CFO: Ruifen Li
 Phone: (86) 315 888 8002/ 0100
Total Employees at this Location: 200
Type of Operation: Paperboard mill
Pulp Grades and Capacities:
 Total pulp capacity: 30,000 mt/y
 Recycled Pulping: 30,000 mt/y
Pulp Mill Data:
Pulp Lines: 2
Paper/Paperboard Grades and Capacities:
 Total paper and paperboard capacity: 35,000 mt/y
 Linerboard: 15,000 mt/y
 Corrugating medium/fluting: 10,000 mt/y
 Boxboard/cartonboard: 10,000 mt/y
Paper and Paperboard Mill Data:
Paper Machines: 3
 PM 1, multi-wire, total capacity 15,000 mt/y, Trim width 3.2 m, Linerboard
 PM 2, multi-wire, total capacity 10,000 mt/y, Trim width 3.2 m, Corrugating medium/fluting
 PM 3, fourdrinier, total capacity 10,000 mt/y, Trim width 2.1 m, Boxboard/cartonboard
Coating Machines: 1
 CM 1, total capacity 10,000 mt/y., off machine

ⓗHebei Tangshan Boda Paper Mill Co., Ltd.
Ownership: 100% by private owners
Industry Park, Pingqing Rd., Qian An
Thangshan, Hebei, 064400
China
 Phone: (86) 315 596 6965
 Email: wenbin.hua@163.com

 Web Address: www.bodapaper.com
Personnel:
 Gen. Mgr.: Wenbin Hua
 Phone: (86) 137 0100 2341
 Email: wenbin.hua@163.com
Mill Locations:
 Hebei Tangshan Boda Paper Mill Co., Ltd., Thangshan Mill, Industry Park, Pingqing Rd., Qian An, Thangshan 064400, China, Capacity: 30,000 mt/y, (Paper mill)
 Phone: (86) 315 596 6965
 Email: wenbin.hua@163.com

ⓂHebei Tangshan Boda Paper Mill Co., Ltd.
Thangshan Mill
Industry Park, Pingqing Rd., Qian An
Thangshan, Hebei, 064400
China
 Phone: (86) 315 596 6965
 Email: wenbin.hua@163.com
Personnel:
 Gen. Mgr.: Wenbin Hua
 Phone: (86) 137 0100 2341
Total Employees at this Location: 160
Type of Operation: Paper mill
Paper/Paperboard Grades and Capacities:
 Total paper and paperboard capacity: 30,000 mt/y
 Tissue: 30,000 mt/y
Paper and Paperboard Mill Data:
Paper Machines: 17
 PM 1-4, fourdrinier, total capacity 1,000 mt/y, Trim width 2.36 m, Tissue
 PM 13-16, fourdrinier, total capacity 1,500 mt/y, Trim width 1.58 m, Tissue
 PM 17, fourdrinier, total capacity 8,000 mt/y, Trim width 1.88 m, Tissue
 PM 5-8, fourdrinier, total capacity 1,500 mt/y, Trim width 1.58 m, Tissue
 PM 9-12, fourdrinier, total capacity 1,500 mt/y, Trim width 1.58 m, Tissue

ⓗHebei Xiaorenguo Paper Co., Ltd.
Ownership: 100% by private owners
West 100 meter Jianguo Rd.
Baoding, Hebei
China
 Phone: (86) 312 217 7997
 Fax: (86) 312 217 3636
Mill Locations:
 Hebei Xiaorenguo Paper Co., Ltd., Baoding Mill, West 100 meter Jianguo Rd., Baoding 071000, China, Capacity: 12,000 mt/y, (Paper mill)
 Phone: (86) 312 217 7997
 Fax: (86) 312 217 3636

ⓂHebei Xiaorenguo Paper Co., Ltd.
Baoding Mill
West 100 meter Jianguo Rd.
Baoding, Hebei, 071000
China
 Phone: (86) 312 217 7997
 Fax: (86) 312 217 3636
 Web Address: www.hbxiaorenguo.com
Personnel:
 Chmn.: Guoyi Shao
 Phone: (86) 312 217 7997
 Mill Mgr.: Li Yang
 Phone: (86) 312 217 7997
 Sls. Mgr.: Jiansheng Wu
 Phone: (86) 312 217 7997
Total Employees at this Location: 350
Type of Operation: Paper mill
Paper/Paperboard Grades and Capacities:
 Total paper and paperboard capacity: 12,000 mt/y
 Tissue: 12,000 mt/y
Paper and Paperboard Mill Data:
Paper Machines: 8
 No. 1, cylinder, total capacity 1,000 mt/y, Trim width 1.58 m, Tissue

 No. 2, cylinder, total capacity 1,000 mt/y, Trim width 1.58 m, Tissue
 No. 3, cylinder, total capacity 1,000 mt/y, Trim width 1.58 m, Tissue
 No. 4, cylinder, total capacity 1,000 mt/y, Trim width 1.58 m, Tissue
 No. 5, cylinder, total capacity 1,000 mt/y, Trim width 1.58 m, Tissue
 No. 6, cylinder, total capacity 2,300 mt/y, Trim width 1.58 m, Tissue
 No. 7, cylinder, total capacity 2,300 mt/y, Trim width 1.58 m, Tissue
 No. 8, cylinder, total capacity 2,300 mt/y, Trim width 1.58 m, Tissue
Energy Data:
 Power boilers: 1

ⓗHebei Xierman Nengwei Paper Co., Ltd.
Beizhang Village, Nanqi Town, Xinshi District
Baoding, Hebei, 071051
China
 Phone: (86) 312 3177 389
 Fax: (86) 312 3177 665
 Email: yaonianxue@sina.com
 Web Address: www.xemnwpaper.com
Mill Locations:
 Hebei Xierman Nengwei Paper Co., Ltd., Baoding Mill, Beizhang Village, Nanqi Town, Xinshi District, Baoding 071051, China, Capacity: 25,000 mt/y, (Paper mill)
 Phone: (86) 312 3177 389
 Fax: (86) 312 3177 665
 Email: yaonianxue@sina.com

ⓂHebei Xierman Nengwei Paper Co., Ltd.
Baoding Mill
Beizhang Village, Nanqi Town, Xinshi District
Baoding, Hebei, 071051
China
 Phone: (86) 312 3177 389
 Fax: (86) 312 3177 665
 Email: yaonianxue@sina.com
 Web Address: www.xemnwpaper.com
Type of Operation: Paper mill
Paper/Paperboard Grades and Capacities:
 Total paper and paperboard capacity: 25,000 mt/y
 Tissue: 25,000 mt/y
Paper and Paperboard Mill Data:
Paper Machines: 9
 PM 1, total capacity 1,250 mt/y, Trim width 1.58 m, Tissue
 PM 2, total capacity 1,250 mt/y, Trim width 1.58 m, Tissue
 PM 3, total capacity 1,250 mt/y, Trim width 1.58 m, Tissue
 PM 4, total capacity 1,250 mt/y, Trim width 1.58 m, Tissue
 PM 5, total capacity 1,250 mt/y, Trim width 1.58 m, Tissue
 PM 6, total capacity 1,250 mt/y, Trim width 1.58 m, Tissue
 PM 7, total capacity 1,250 mt/y, Trim width 1.58 m, Tissue
 PM 8, total capacity 1,250 mt/y, Trim width 1.58 m, Tissue
 PM 9, total capacity 15,000 mt/y, Trim width 3.6 m, Tissue

ⓗⓂHebei Xingchang Paper Co., Ltd
Qinghuangdao Mill
Zhugezhuang
Qinghuangdao, Hebei
China
 Phone: (86) 335 299 6222
Total Employees at this Location: 170
Type of Operation: Paperboard mill
Pulp Grades and Capacities:
 Total pulp capacity: 85,925 mt/y
 Recycled Pulping: 85,925 mt/y
Pulp Mill Data:
 Recycled Fiber Treatment Lines:
 Recycled packaging pulping lines
Paper/Paperboard Grades and Capacities:
 Total paper and paperboard capacity: 87,822 mt/y
 Corrugating medium/fluting: 87,822 mt/y
Paper and Paperboard Mill Data:

China

Paper Machines: 2
No. 1, cylinder, total capacity 17,850 mt/y, Trim width 3.2 m, Corrugating medium/fluting
No. 2, fourdrinier, total capacity 69,972 mt/y, Trim width 4.2 m, Corrugating medium/fluting
Energy Data:
Power boilers: 2
Electrical demand for mill: 139 MWh/D

ⓘHebei Xuesong Paper Co., Ltd.
Ownership: 100% by shareholders
Papermaking Industrial Zone, Da Ce Ying Town
Mancheng County, Baoding City, Hebei, 072150
China
  Phone: (86) 312 702 1606/ 0048/ 1512
  Fax: (86) 312 702 0869/ 1512
Mill Locations:
Hebei Xuesong Paper Co., Ltd., Baoding Mill, Papermaking Industrial Zone, Da Ce Ying Town, Baoding 072150, China, Capacity: 80,000 mt/y, (Paper mill)
  Phone: (86) 312 702 1606/ 0048/ 1512
  Fax: (86) 312 702 0869/ 1512
  Email: xuesonghb@126.com

ⓜHebei Xuesong Paper Co., Ltd.
Baoding Mill
Papermaking Industrial Zone, Da Ce Ying Town
Baoding, Hebei, 072150
China
  Phone: (86) 312 702 1606/ 0048/ 1512
  Fax: (86) 312 702 0869/ 1512
  Email: xuesonghb@126.com
  Web Address: www.hbxuesong.cn
Personnel:
  Pres. & Mill Mgr.: Baojiang Zhao
  Phone: (86) 312 702 1606/ 0048/ 1512
Total Employees at this Location: 320
Type of Operation: Paper mill
Paper/Paperboard Grades and Capacities:
  Total paper and paperboard capacity: 80,000 mt/y
  Tissue: 80,000 mt/y
Paper and Paperboard Mill Data:
Paper Machines: 25
PM 1-24, cylinder, total capacity 2,440 mt/y, Trim width 1.58 m, Tissue
PM 25, (started April 28, 2014), Yankee dryer, total capacity 25,000 mt/y, Trim width 2.85 m, Tissue
Energy Data:
Power boilers: 6

ⓘHebei Yaguang Paper Co., Ltd.
Ownership: 100% by private owners
Mancheng Industry District
Baoding, Hebei, 072150
China
  Phone: (86) 312 702 1008
  Fax: (86) 312 702 1609
Mill Locations:
Hebei Yaguang Paper Co., Ltd., Baoding Mill, Mancheng Industry District, Baoding 072150, China, Capacity: 12,000 mt/y, (Paper mill)
  Phone: (86) 312 702 1008
  Fax: (86) 312 702 1609

ⓜHebei Yaguang Paper Co., Ltd.
Baoding Mill
Mancheng Industry District
Baoding, Hebei, 072150
China
  Phone: (86) 312 702 1008
  Fax: (86) 312 702 1609
Personnel:
  Pres. & Mill Mgr.: Fusheng Zhang
  Phone: (86) 312 702 1008
Type of Operation: Paper mill
Paper/Paperboard Grades and Capacities:
  Total paper and paperboard capacity: 12,000 mt/y
  Tissue: 12,000 mt/y
Paper and Paperboard Mill Data:
Paper Machines: 10
No. 1, cylinder, total capacity 550 mt/y, Trim width 1.09 m, Tissue
No. 2, cylinder, total capacity 550 mt/y, Trim width 1.09 m, Tissue
No. 3, cylinder, total capacity 550 mt/y, Trim width 1.09 m, Tissue
No. 4, cylinder, total capacity 550 mt/y, Trim width 1.09 m, Tissue
No. 5, cylinder, total capacity 1,200 mt/y, Trim width 1.58 m, Tissue
No. 6, cylinder, total capacity 1,200 mt/y, Trim width 1.58 m, Tissue
No. 7, cylinder, total capacity 1,200 mt/y, Trim width 1.58 m, Tissue
No. 8, cylinder, total capacity 1,200 mt/y, Trim width 1.58 m, Tissue
No. 9, cylinder, total capacity 2,500 mt/y, Trim width 1.76 m, Tissue
No. 10, cylinder, total capacity 2,500 mt/y, Trim width 1.76 m, Tissue

ⓜHebei Yihoucheng Commodity Co. Ltd
Baoding Mill
No.131 Yunshan Rd., Xinshi District
Baoding, Hebei, 071000
China
  Phone: (86) 312 3327 600/609
  Fax: (86) 312 3327 610
  Web Address: www.hbyhc.com
Personnel:
  Gen. Mgr.: Tian Yuwei
  Phone: (86) 312 3327 600/609
  Fax: (86) 312 3327 610
Type of Operation: Paper mill
Paper/Paperboard Grades and Capacities:
  Total paper and paperboard capacity: 25,000 mt/y
  Tissue: 25,000 mt/y
Paper and Paperboard Mill Data:
Paper Machines: 1
No. 1, (started up late May 2014), Yankee dryer, crescent former, total capacity 25,000 mt/y, Trim width 2.85 m, Tissue

ⓜHebei Yongxin Paper Co., Ltd.
Tangshan (Hebei Yongxin) Mill
Ownership: 78.13% by Nine Dragons Paper (Holdings) Ltd.
No. 88 Guanxin Rd., Luannan County
Tangshan, Hebei, 063500
China
  Phone: (86) 315 411 0424
  Fax: (86) 315 412 3486
  Web Address: www.ndpaper.com
Personnel:
  Chmn.: Yin Zhang
  CEO: Mingzhong Liu
  CFO: Yuanfu Zhang
  Phone: (86) 315 411 0424
Total Employees at this Location: 810
Type of Operation: Paperboard mill
Pulp Grades and Capacities:
  Total pulp capacity: 507,620 mt/y
  Recycled Pulping: 507,620 mt/y
Pulp Mill Data:
Pulp Lines: 3
  Recycled Fiber Treatment Lines:
  Recycled packaging pulping lines: 3 at 960,000 admt/y
Paper/Paperboard Grades and Capacities:
  Total paper and paperboard capacity: 499,800 mt/y
  Linerboard: 349,146 mt/y
  Boxboard/cartonboard: 150,654 mt/y
Paper and Paperboard Mill Data:
Paper Machines: 2
No. 5, multi-wire, total capacity 150,654 mt/y, Trim width 4.2 m, Boxboard/cartonboard
No. 6, fourdrinier, total capacity 349,146 mt/y, Trim width 5.6 m, Linerboard
Energy Data:
Power boilers: 3
Steam turbines: 2 at 12, 12 MW
Electrical demand for mill: 853 MWh/D

ⓘHebei Yuanshi County Jinpeng Paper Co., Ltd.
Ownership: 100% by private owners
South Section, Jiahui Street, Yuanshi County
Shijiazhuang, Hebei, 051130
China
  Phone: (86) 311 8462 3867/ 2756/ 1775
  Fax: (86) 311 8460 3101
  Email: jpzy@jpzy.cn
Mill Locations:
Hebei Yuanshi County Jinpeng Paper Co., Ltd., Shijiazhuang Mill, South Section, Jiahui Street, Yuanshi County, Shijiazhuang 051130, China, Capacity: 94,248 mt/y, (Paper mill)
  Phone: (86) 311 8462 3867/ 2756/ 1775
  Fax: (86) 311 8460 3101
  Email: jpzy@jpzy.cn

ⓜHebei Yuanshi County Jinpeng Paper Co., Ltd.
Shijiazhuang Mill
South Section, Jiahui Street, Yuanshi County
Shijiazhuang, Hebei, 051130
China
  Phone: (86) 311 8462 3867/ 2756/ 1775
  Fax: (86) 311 8460 3101
  Email: jpzy@jpzy.cn
  Web Address: www.jpzy.cn
Personnel:
  Pres. & Gen. Mgr.: Yingqi Liu
  Phone: (86) 311 8462 3867/ 2756/ 1775
Total Employees at this Location: 600
Type of Operation: Paper mill
Pulp Grades and Capacities:
  Total pulp capacity: 90,766 mt/y
  Recycled Pulping: 90,766 mt/y
Pulp Mill Data:
Pulp Lines: 2
Paper/Paperboard Grades and Capacities:
  Total paper and paperboard capacity: 94,248 mt/y
  Corrugating medium/fluting: 94,248 mt/y
Paper and Paperboard Mill Data:
Paper Machines: 2
No. 1, fourdrinier, total capacity 29,988 mt/y, Trim width 2.64 m, Corrugating medium/fluting
No. 2, fourdrinier, total capacity 64,260 mt/y, Trim width 3.2 m, Corrugating medium/fluting
Energy Data:
Power boilers: 3
Electrical demand for mill: 149 MWh/D

ⓘHebei Yutian Shunfa Paper Co., Ltd.
Ownership: 100% by private owners
Daijiatun, Yutian County
Tangshan, Hebei, 064105
China
  Phone: (86) 315 656 9700
Mill Locations:
Hebei Yutian Shunfa Paper Co., Ltd., Tangshan Mill, Daijiatun, Yutian County, Tangshan 064105, China, Capacity: 80,000 mt/y, (Paperboard mill)
  Phone: (86) 315 656 9700

ⓜHebei Yutian Shunfa Paper Co., Ltd.
Tangshan Mill
Daijiatun, Yutian County
Tangshan, Hebei, 064105
China
  Phone: (86) 315 656 9700

China

Total Employees at this Location: 80
Type of Operation: Paperboard mill
Pulp Grades and Capacities:
Total pulp capacity: 68,130 mt/y
Recycled Pulping: 68,130 mt/y
Pulp Mill Data:
Pulp Lines: 1
Recycled Fiber Treatment Lines:
Recycled packaging pulping lines: 1 at 100,000 admt/y
Paper/Paperboard Grades and Capacities:
Total paper and paperboard capacity: 80,000 mt/y
Linerboard: 80,000 mt/y
Paper and Paperboard Mill Data:
Paper Machines: 1
No. 1, Multi-wire (4), total capacity 80,000 mt/y, Trim width 3.6 m, Linerboard
Energy Data:
Electrical demand for mill: 106 MWh/D

ⓂHebei Zhongxin Paper Co., Ltd.
Ownership: 100% by private owners
Daceying Paper Making Industry District, Mancheng County
Baoding, Hebei, 072150
China
Phone: (86) 312 702 1807/713 1212
Fax: (86) 312 702 2988
Email: zx@zhongxinpaper.com
Web Address: www.zhongxinpaper.com
Personnel:
Chmn.: Jianzhong Li
Phone: (86) 312 702 6600/1807/6100
Fax: (86) 312 702 2988
Gen. Mgr.: Congfeng Li
Phone: (86) 312 702 6600/1807/6100
Fax: (86) 312 702 2988
Sls. Mgr.: Hongliang Fan
Phone: (86) 312 702 6600/1807/6100
Fax: (86) 312 702 2988
Total Employees at this Location: 350
Mill Locations:
Hebei Zhongxin Paper Co., Ltd., Baoding Mill, Daceying Paper Making Industry District, Mancheng County, Baoding 072150, China, Capacity: 12,000 mt/y, (Paper mill)
Phone: (86) 312 702 1807/713 1212
Fax: (86) 312 702 2988
Email: zx@zhongxinpaper.com

ⓂHebei Zhongxin Paper Co., Ltd.
Baoding Mill
Daceying Paper Making Industry District, Mancheng County
Baoding, Hebei, 072150
China
Phone: (86) 312 702 1807/713 1212
Fax: (86) 312 702 2988
Email: zx@zhongxinpaper.com
Web Address: www.zhongxinpaper.com
Personnel:
Chmn.: Jianzhong Li
Phone: (86) 312 702 6600/1807/6100
Gen. Mgr.: Congfeng Li
Phone: (86) 312 702 6600/1807/6100
Sls. Mgr.: Hongliang Fan
Phone: (86) 312 702 6600/1807/6100
Total Employees at this Location: 350
Type of Operation: Paper mill
Paper/Paperboard Grades and Capacities:
Total paper and paperboard capacity: 12,000 mt/y
Tissue: 12,000 mt/y
Paper and Paperboard Mill Data:
Paper Machines: 8
No. 1, cylinder, total capacity 1,200 mt/y, Trim width 1.58 m, Tissue
No. 2, cylinder, total capacity 1,200 mt/y, Trim width 1.58 m, Tissue
No. 3, cylinder, total capacity 1,200 mt/y, Trim width 1.58 m, Tissue
No. 4, cylinder, total capacity 1,200 mt/y, Trim width 1.58 m, Tissue
No. 5, cylinder, total capacity 1,200 mt/y, Trim width 1.58 m, Tissue
No. 6, cylinder, total capacity 1,200 mt/y, Trim width 1.58 m, Tissue
No. 7, fourdrinier, total capacity 2,400 mt/y, Trim width 2.4 m, Tissue
No. 8, fourdrinier, total capacity 2,400 mt/y, Trim width 2.4 m, Tissue
Energy Data:
Power boilers: 2

ⓘTangshan Sanyou Group
No.1 Guanzhou Rd., Dongguang
Cangzhou, Hebei, 061600
China
Phone: (86) 317 779 8311
Fax: (86) 317 766 5566
Web Address: www.sanyou-group.com.cn/jtweb/contents/520/2681.html
Mill Locations:
Tangshan Sanyou Group, Cangzhou Mill, No.1 Guanzhou Rd., Dongguang, Cangzhou 061600, China, (Pulp mill)
Phone: (86) 317 779 8311
Fax: (86) 317 766 5566

ⓂTangshan Sanyou Group
Cangzhou Mill
No.1 Guanzhou Rd., Dongguang
Cangzhou, Hebei, 061600
China
Phone: (86) 317 779 8311
Fax: (86) 317 766 5566
Web Address: www.sanyou-group.com.cn/jtweb/contents/520/2681.html
Total Employees at this Location: 650
Type of Operation: Pulp mill
Pulp Grades and Capacities:
Total pulp capacity: 89,590 mt/y
Pulp available for market: 90,000 mt/y
Chemical Pulp: 89,590 mt/y
Pulp Mill Data:
Chemical Pulping Systems:
Batch digesters: 3
Pulp Lines: 3
Bleach Plant Systems: 3
Chemical Pulping System, Type: Cotton Linter
Chemical Pulping System, Type: Cotton Linter
Chemical Pulping System, Type: Cotton Linter
Pulp Dryers:
Pulp Dryers 1, Pulp Dryers 1, Pulp Dryers 1
Energy Data:
Power boilers
Electrical demand for mill: 119 MWh/D

ⓘXingtai Jinbai Pulp Co., Ltd.
Baixiang County
Xingtai, Hebei, 055450
China
Personnel:
Gen. Mgr.: Qiusheng Wei
Mill Locations:
Xingtai Jinbai Pulp Co., Ltd., Xingtai Mill, Baixiang County, Xingtai 055450, China, (Pulp mill)

ⓂXingtai Jinbai Pulp Co., Ltd.
Xingtai Mill
Baixiang County
Xingtai, Hebei, 055450
China
Type of Operation: Pulp mill
Pulp Grades and Capacities:
Total pulp capacity: 35,000 mt/y

HEILONGJIANG

ⓂDuerbote Mongolian Autonomous County Haida Paper Co., Ltd.
Daqing Mill
Ownership: Daqing Haida Paper Co., Ltd.
No.1 East Ring Rd., Taikang Town, Duerbote Mongolian Autonomous County
Daqing, Heilongjiang, 166200
China
Phone: (86) 459 342 2993/9633
Fax: (86) 459 343 9685
Web Address: www.haidapaper.com
Type of Operation: Pulp mill, Paper mill
Pulp Grades and Capacities:
Total pulp capacity: 420,000 mt/y
Pulp Mill Data:
Pulp Lines: 1
Paper/Paperboard Grades and Capacities:
Total paper and paperboard capacity: 50,000 mt/y
Uncoated woodfree/freesheet: 50,000 mt/y
Paper and Paperboard Mill Data:
Paper Machines: 3
No. 1, total capacity 25,000 mt/y, Trim width 2.73 m, Uncoated woodfree/freesheet
No. 2, total capacity 12,500 mt/y, Trim width 1.76 m, Uncoated woodfree/freesheet
No. 3, total capacity 12,500 mt/y, Trim width 1.76 m, Uncoated woodfree/freesheet

ⓂHeilongjiang Fuyu Chenming Paper Co., Ltd.
Qiqihar (Heilongjiang Fuyu Chenming Paper) Mill
Ownership: 100% by Chenming Paper Holdings Ltd.
Fuyu County
Qiqihar, Heilongjiang, 161021
China
Phone: (86) 452 3102 256/ 401/ 267
Email: www.chenmingpaper.com
Total Employees at this Location: 800
Type of Operation: Paper mill
Pulp Grades and Capacities:
Total pulp capacity: 71,510 mt/y
Chemical Pulp: 71,510 mt/y
Pulp Mill Data:
Chemical Pulping Systems:
Continuous digesters: 1
Pulp Lines: 1
Chemical Recovery Equipment:
Recovery boilers
Lime Kiln
Paper/Paperboard Grades and Capacities:
Total paper and paperboard capacity: 69,972 mt/y
Packaging papers: 69,972 mt/y
Paper and Paperboard Mill Data:
Paper Machines: 2
No. 7, fourdrinier, total capacity 53,550 mt/y, Trim width 3.15 m, Packaging papers
No. 8, fourdrinier (2), total capacity 16,422 mt/y, Trim width 2.36 m, Packaging papers
Energy Data:
Power boilers: 4
Steam turbines: 3 at 15 MW
Electrical demand for mill: 198 MWh/D

ⓘHeilongjiang Kaifeng Paper Produce Co., Ltd.
Ownership: 100% by shareholders
Yama Industry Zone, Tuanjie Street, Zhaozhou Town
Zhaozhou County, Daqing, Heilongjiang, 166400
China
Phone: (86) 459 851 6701/ 6702
Fax: (86) 459 851 8106

Email: kaifeng@kfzy.cn
Web Address: www.kfzy.cn
Mill Locations:
Heilongjiang Kaifeng Paper Produce Co., Ltd., Daqing Mill, Yama Industry Zone, Tuanjie Street, Zhaozhou County, Daqing 166400, China, Capacity: 15,000 mt/y, (Paper mill)
Phone: (86) 459 851 6701/ 6702
Fax: (86) 459 851 8106
Email: kaifeng@kfzy.cn

ⓂHeilongjiang Kaifeng Paper Produce Co., Ltd.
Daqing Mill
Yama Industry Zone, Tuanjie Street, Zhaozhou County
Daqing, Heilongjiang, 166400
China
Phone: (86) 459 851 6701/ 6702
Fax: (86) 459 851 8106
Email: kaifeng@kfzy.cn
Web Address: www.kfzy.cn
Personnel:
Chmn.: Weifeng Wang
Phone: (86) 459 851 6701/ 6702
Total Employees at this Location: 230
Type of Operation: Paper mill
Paper/Paperboard Grades and Capacities:
Total paper and paperboard capacity: 15,000 mt/y
Tissue: 15,000 mt/y
Paper and Paperboard Mill Data:
Paper Machines: 10
No. 1, cylinder, total capacity 1,500 mt/y, Trim width 1.58 m, Tissue
No. 2, cylinder, total capacity 1,500 mt/y, Trim width 1.58 m, Tissue
No. 3, cylinder, total capacity 1,500 mt/y, Trim width 1.58 m, Tissue
No. 4, cylinder, total capacity 1,500 mt/y, Trim width 1.58 m, Tissue
No. 5, cylinder, total capacity 1,500 mt/y, Trim width 1.58 m, Tissue
No. 6, cylinder, total capacity 1,500 mt/y, Trim width 1.58 m, Tissue
No. 7, cylinder, total capacity 1,500 mt/y, Trim width 1.58 m, Tissue
No. 8, cylinder, total capacity 1,500 mt/y, Trim width 1.58 m, Tissue
No. 9, cylinder, total capacity 1,500 mt/y, Trim width 1.58 m, Tissue
No. 10, cylinder, total capacity 1,500 mt/y, Trim width 1.58 m, Tissue
Energy Data:
Power boilers: 2

ⓂHeilongjiang Longjiangfu Pulp & Paper Co., Ltd.
Ownership: ARC International Material Co., Ltd., China International Tourism & Trade Co., Ltd. (CITTC)
306, Guangfu Road
Jiamusi, Heilongjiang, 154005
China
Phone: (86) 454 6066885
Email: lilell@163.com
Personnel:
Chmn.: Hai Lan
Phone: (86) 454 6066885
Mill Locations:
Heilongjiang Longjiangfu Pulp & Paper Co., Ltd., Jiamusi Mill, 306, Guangfu Road, Dongfeng District, Jiamusi 154005, China, Capacity: 14,994 mt/y, (Paper mill)
Phone: (86) 454 6066 885/773/211
Fax: (86) 454 6066 987
Email: lilell@163.com

ⓂHeilongjiang Longjiangfu Pulp & Paper Co., Ltd.
Jiamusi Mill
306, Guangfu Road, Dongfeng District
Jiamusi, Heilongjiang, 154005
China
Phone: (86) 454 6066 885/773/211
Fax: (86) 454 6066 987
Email: lilell@163.com
Web Address: www.ljfjz.com
Personnel:
Chmn.: Hai Lan
Phone: (86) 454 6066885
Total Employees at this Location: 300
Type of Operation: Paper mill
Pulp Grades and Capacities:
Pulp Mill Data:
Chemical Pulping Systems:
Batch digesters: 2
Pulp Lines: 2
Chemical Recovery Equipment:
Evaporator lines
Recovery boilers: 1
Lime Kiln
Paper/Paperboard Grades and Capacities:
Total paper and paperboard capacity: 14,994 mt/y
Packaging papers: 14,994 mt/y
Paper and Paperboard Mill Data:
Paper Machines: 2
No. 1, fourdrinier, total capacity 14,994 mt/y, Trim width 2.52 m, Packaging papers
No. 3, fourdrinier, Trim width 5.5 m, Packaging papers
Energy Data:
Electrical demand for mill: 22 MWh/D

ⓂHeilongjiang Mudanjiang Daewoo Paper Mfg. Co. Ltd.
Mudanjiang Mill
Ownership: 39.95% by Heilongjiang Mudanjiang Hengfeng Paper Group Co., Ltd., 39.16% by Daewoo (China), 20.76% by Daewoo International
No. 8 Guanghua Street
Yangming District, Mudanjiang, Heilongjiang, 157013
China
Phone: (86) 453 632 5718
Fax: (86) 453 633 3577
Email: postmaster@daewoopaper.com
Web Address: www.daewoopaper.com
Personnel:
Pres.: Douyong Hong
Phone: (86) 453 632 5718
Vic. Pres.: Xingjiang Guan
Phone: (86) 453 632 5718
Sls. Mgr.: Lehong Chen
Phone: (86) 453 632 5718
Fax: (86) 453 633 3557/ 632 5737
Email: chenlh9@hotmail.com
Total Employees at this Location: 520
Type of Operation: Pulp mill, Paper mill
Pulp Mill Data:
Chemical Recovery Equipment:
Recovery boilers: 4
Paper/Paperboard Grades and Capacities:
Total paper and paperboard capacity: 82,500 mt/y
Coated woodfree/freesheet: 82,500 mt/y
Paper and Paperboard Mill Data:
Paper Machines: 1
No. 1, fourdrinier, total capacity 82,500 mt/y, Trim width 2.64 m, Coated woodfree/freesheet
Coating Machines: 1
CM 1, total capacity 100,000 mt/y., off machine
Finishing Equipment:
Supercalenders: 1
Rewinders: 1
Sheeters: 1
Energy Data:
Electrical demand for mill: 151 MWh/D

ⓂHeilongjiang Mudanjiang Hengfeng Paper Group Co., Ltd.
Mudanjiang Mill
No. 11, Zaozhi Road, Guanghua Street, Yangming District
Mudanjiang, Heilongjiang, 157013
China
Phone: (86) 453 633 1111/1333
Fax: (86) 453 633 1063
Email: hfzyjt@263.net
Web Address: www.hengfengpaper.com
Personnel:
Chmn.: Xiang Xu
Phone: (86) 453 633 1111/1333
Vice Chmn., Gen. Mgr.: Yingchun Li
Phone: (86) 453 633 1111/1333
Vice Gen. Mgr.: Quanli Pan
Phone: (86) 453 633 1111/1333
CFO: Ms. Qiushi Fu
Phone: (86) 453 633 1111/1333
Finan. Mgr.: Jun Liu
Phone: (86) 453 633 1111/1333
Chief Eng.: Jinsong Li
Phone: (86) 453 633 1111/1333
Total Employees of Comany: 1,953
Type of Operation: Pulp mill, Paper mill
Mill Locations:
Heilongjiang Mudanjiang Daewoo Paper Mfg. Co. Ltd., Mudanjiang Mill (39.95% owned), No. 8 Guanghua Street, Yangming District, Mudanjiang 157013, China, Capacity: 82,500 mt/y, (Pulp mill, Paper mill)
Phone: (86) 453 632 5718
Fax: (86) 453 633 3577
Email: postmaster@daewoopaper.com
Hubei Hengfeng Paper Co., Ltd., Xianning Mill (65.32% owned), Mabai Rd., Xian'an District, Xianning, China, Capacity: 6,000 mt/y, (Paper mill)
Pulp Grades and Capacities:
Total pulp capacity: 3,000 mt/y
Pulp Mill Data:
Chemical Pulping Systems:
Batch digesters: 8
Pulp Lines: 1
Paper/Paperboard Grades and Capacities:
Total paper and paperboard capacity: 115,200 mt/y
Specialty and industrial: 115,200 mt/y
Paper and Paperboard Mill Data:
Paper Machines: 16
PM 3, fourdrinier, total capacity 4,000 mt/y, Trim width 2.5 m, Specialty and industrial
PM 4, fourdrinier, total capacity 4,000 mt/y, Trim width 1.88 m, Specialty and industrial
PM 8, total capacity 4,000 mt/y, Trim width 1.88 m, Specialty and industrial
PM 9, cylinder, total capacity 1,000 mt/y, Trim width 1.58 m, Specialty and industrial
PM 10, fourdrinier, total capacity 6,000 mt/y, Trim width 2.36 m, Specialty and industrial
PM 11, fourdrinier, total capacity 4,000 mt/y, Trim width 2.5 m, Specialty and industrial
PM 12, fourdrinier, total capacity 12,000 mt/y, Trim width 3.15 m, Specialty and industrial
PM 13, total capacity 10,000 mt/y, Trim width 2.87 m, Specialty and industrial
PM 14, inclined, total capacity 5,000 mt/y, Trim width 1.88 m, Specialty and industrial
PM 15, fourdrinier, total capacity 20,000 mt/y, Trim width 3.86 m, Specialty and industrial
PM 16, (started mid-June 2011), fourdrinier, total capacity 15,000 mt/y, Trim width 3.3 m, Specialty and industrial
PM 17, fourdrinier, total capacity 17,000 mt/y, Trim width 3.3 m, Specialty and industrial
T1, cylinder, total capacity 1,200 mt/y, Trim width 1.25 m, Specialty and industrial
T2, cylinder, total capacity 2,000 mt/y, Trim width 1.25 m, Specialty and industrial
T3, cylinder, total capacity 6,000 mt/y, Trim width 2.36 m, Specialty and industrial

China

T4, total capacity 4,000 mt/y, Trim width 1.88 m, Specialty and industrial
Energy Data:
Power boilers: 3
Steam turbines: 4 at 15, 3, 1.5, 1.5 MW

ⓂHeilongjiang Xinhua Hygiene & Specialty Paper Co., Ltd.
Ownership: 100% by private owners
Xinhua 2 Rd.
Acheng, Heilongjiang, 150300
China
  Phone: (86) 451 5376 1432
  Fax: (86) 451 5372 2503
Mill Locations:
Heilongjiang Xinhua Hygiene & Specialty Paper Co., Ltd., Acheng Mill, Xinhua 2 Rd., Acheng 150300, China, Capacity: 1,800 mt/y, (Paper mill)
  Phone: (86) 451 5376 1432
  Fax: (86) 451 5372 2503

ⓂHeilongjiang Xinhua Hygiene & Specialty Paper Co., Ltd.
Acheng Mill
Xinhua 2 Rd.
Acheng, Heilongjiang, 150300
China
  Phone: (86) 451 5376 1432
  Fax: (86) 451 5372 2503
Personnel:
  Chmn.: Wenzhi Lu
  Phone: (86) 451 5376 1432
  Gen. Mgr.: Ms. Fengying Lu
  Phone: (86) 451 5376 1432
  Sls. Mgr.: Guochuan Zhang
  Phone: (86) 451 5376 1432
Type of Operation: Paper mill
Paper/Paperboard Grades and Capacities:
  Total paper and paperboard capacity: 1,800 mt/y
  Tissue: 1,800 mt/y
Paper and Paperboard Mill Data:
Paper Machines: 6
No. 1, cylinder, total capacity 300 mt/y, Trim width 1.09 m, Tissue
No. 2, cylinder, total capacity 300 mt/y, Trim width 1.09 m, Tissue
No. 3, cylinder, total capacity 300 mt/y, Trim width 1.09 m, Tissue
No. 4, cylinder, total capacity 300 mt/y, Trim width 1.09 m, Tissue
No. 5, cylinder, total capacity 300 mt/y, Trim width 1.09 m, Tissue
No. 6, cylinder, total capacity 1 mt/y, Tissue
Energy Data:
Power boilers: 3

ⓂHeilongjiang Yuejing Pulp & Paper Co., Ltd.
Harbin Mill
Ownership: Guangdong Regall Group Co., Ltd.
Dongxing Street, Tonghe Town, Tonghe County
Harbin, Heilongjiang, 105900
China
  Phone: (86) 451 5742 0669
  Fax: (86) 451 5742 7978
  Web Address: www.regall.cn
Personnel:
  Pres. & Gen. Mgr.: Fuan Zhao
  Phone: (86) 451 5742 0669
Total Employees at this Location: 400
Type of Operation: Pulp mill
Pulp Grades and Capacities:
  Total pulp capacity: 35,000 mt/y
  Chemical Pulp: 35,000 mt/y
Pulp Mill Data:
Pulp Lines: 4
Energy Data:
Power boilers: 4
Steam turbines: 3 at 3, 3, 3 MW

ⓂHeilongjiang Dongshun Paper Co., Ltd
Zhaodong Mill
11 Km Stone, Zhaochang Rd.
Zhaodong, Heilongjiang, 151100
China
  Phone: (86) 455 7923 338
  Web Address: www.dongshunpaper.com
Type of Operation: Paper mill
Paper/Paperboard Grades and Capacities:
  Total paper and paperboard capacity: 28,000 mt/y
  Tissue: 28,000 mt/y
Paper and Paperboard Mill Data:
Paper Machines: 2
PM 1, (started up in Nov.2012), BF-10 EX, total capacity 12,000 mt/y, Trim width 2.76 m, Tissue
PM 2, total capacity 16,000 mt/y, Trim width 2.76 m, Tissue

ⓂLindian Haida Paper Co., Ltd.
Daqing Mill
Ownership: Daqing Haida Paper Co., Ltd.
Lindian County, Lindian County
Daqing, Heilongjiang, 166200
China
  Phone: (86) 459 331 8233/332 3544
  Fax: (86) 459 331 8133/343 9685
  Web Address: www.haidapaper.com
Total Employees at this Location: 498
Type of Operation: Paper mill
Paper/Paperboard Grades and Capacities:
  Total paper and paperboard capacity: 50,000 mt/y
  Tissue: 50,000 mt/y
Paper and Paperboard Mill Data:
Paper Machines: 4
No. 1, total capacity 12,500 mt/y, Trim width 2.1 m, Tissue
No. 2, total capacity 12,500 mt/y, Trim width 2.1 m, Tissue
No. 3, total capacity 12,500 mt/y, Trim width 2.1 m, Tissue
No. 4, total capacity 12,500 mt/y, Trim width 2.1 m, Tissue

ⓂMudanjiang Sandu Specialty Paper Co., Ltd.
Mudanjiang Mill
No.19, Daqing Street, Aimin District
Mudanjiang, Heilongjiang, 157009
China
  Phone: (86) 451 8229 5611
  Fax: (86) 451 8229 5610
  Email: WebMaster@sandu.net.cn
  Web Address: www.sandu.net.cn
Personnel:
  Chmn.: Yong Liu
Type of Operation: Paper mill
Paper/Paperboard Grades and Capacities:
  Total paper and paperboard capacity: 25,000 mt/y
  Tissue: 25,000 mt/y
Paper and Paperboard Mill Data:
Paper Machines: 1
PM 1, total capacity 5,000 mt/y, Trim width 2.64 m, Tissue

HENAN

ⓄHenan Anyang Huaxian Paper
No.140 Daocheng Rd., Daokou Town, Huaxian
Anyang, Henan, 456400
China
Total Employees at this Location: 100
Mill Locations:
Henan Anyang Huaxian Paper, Anyang Mill, No.140 Daocheng Rd., Daokou Town, Huaxian, Anyang 456400, China, Capacity: 15,000 mt/y, (Paper mill)

ⓂHenan Anyang Huaxian Paper
Anyang Mill
No.140 Daocheng Rd., Daokou Town, Huaxian
Anyang, Henan, 456400
China
Total Employees at this Location: 100
Type of Operation: Paper mill
Paper/Paperboard Grades and Capacities:
  Total paper and paperboard capacity: 15,000 mt/y
  Uncoated woodfree/freesheet
Paper and Paperboard Mill Data:
Paper Machines: 2
PM 1, Trim width 1.76 m, Uncoated woodfree/freesheet
PM 2, Trim width 1.88 m, Uncoated woodfree/freesheet

ⓂHenan Anyang Senyuan Paper Co., Ltd.
Hua County
Anyang, Henan
China
  Phone: (86) 372 8622 222
  Fax: (86) 372 8621 555
Mill Locations:
Henan Anyang Senyuan Paper Co., Ltd., Anyang Mill, Hua County, Anyang, China, Capacity: 10,000 mt/y, (Paper mill)
  Phone: (86) 372 8622 222
  Fax: (86) 372 8621 555

ⓂHenan Anyang Senyuan Paper Co., Ltd.
Anyang Mill
Hua County
Anyang, Henan
China
  Phone: (86) 372 8622 222
  Fax: (86) 372 8621 555
Type of Operation: Paper mill
Paper/Paperboard Grades and Capacities:
  Total paper and paperboard capacity: 10,000 mt/y
  Tissue: 10,000 mt/y
Paper and Paperboard Mill Data:
Paper Machines: 6
PM 1, total capacity 1,700 mt/y, Trim width 1.88 m, Tissue
PM 2, total capacity 1,700 mt/y, Trim width 1.88 m, Tissue
PM 3, total capacity 1,700 mt/y, Trim width 1.88 m, Tissue
PM 4, total capacity 1,700 mt/y, Trim width 1.88 m, Tissue
PM 5, total capacity 1,700 mt/y, Trim width 1.88 m, Tissue
PM 6, total capacity 1,700 mt/y, Trim width 1.88 m, Tissue

ⓄⓂHenan Aobo Paper Co., Ltd
Xinxiang Mill
Aobo Paper Park, Zhaogu Town, Hui County
Xinxiang, Henan, 453600
China
  Phone: (86) 373 695 6900/5976
  Fax: (86) 373 695 5561
  Web Address: hnabo.com
Total Employees of Company: 1,000
Total Employees at this Location: 1,000
Type of Operation: Paper mill
Paper/Paperboard Grades and Capacities:
  Total paper and paperboard capacity: 50,000 mt/y
  Tissue: 50,000 mt/y
Paper and Paperboard Mill Data:
Paper Machines: 4
No. 1, crescent former, total capacity 12,500 mt/y, Trim width 2.8 m, Tissue, Uncoated woodfree/freesheet
No. 2, crescent former, total capacity 12,500 mt/y, Trim width 2.8 m, Tissue, Uncoated woodfree/freesheet
No. 3, crescent former, total capacity 12,500 mt/y, Trim width 2.8 m, Tissue, Uncoated woodfree/freesheet
No. 4, crescent former, total capacity 12,500 mt/y, Trim width 2.8 m, Tissue, Uncoated woodfree/freesheet
Energy Data:
Power boilers: 1
Steam turbines: 2 at 16 MW
Electrical demand for mill: 138 MWh/D

China

ⓂHenan Chenyang Paper Co., Ltd.
Xuchang Mill
Ownership: 100% by Henan Hongteng Paper Group Co., Ltd.
Caoqiao, Weidu District
Xuchang, Henan, 461000
China
  Phone: (86) 374 431 0088
  Fax: (86) 374 431 0298
Type of Operation: Paperboard mill
Paper/Paperboard Grades and Capacities:
  Total paper and paperboard capacity: 40,000 mt/y
  Linerboard: 40,000 mt/y

ⓘHenan Dahe Paper Co., Ltd.
Ownership: Henan Investment Group
No.41 Nongye Rd.
Zhengzhou, Henan
China
  Phone: (86) 371 6951 5191
  Fax: (86) 371 6951 5194
  Email: dhzy@dahepaper.com
  Web Address: www.dahepaper.com
Mill Locations:
Henan Jiaozuo Ruifeng Paper Co., Ltd., Jiaozuo (Jiaozuo Ruifeng) Mill, South Yingbin Rd., Wuzhi County, Jiaozuo 454000, China, (Pulp mill)
  Phone: (86) 391 726 8650/ 8605
  Fax: (86) 391 726 8710/ 8176
  Email: jzrfzy@163.com
Henan Puyang Longfeng Paper Co. Ltd, Puyang (Puyang Longfeng) Mill, West Shengli Rd., Puyang 457000, China, Capacity: 300,000 mt/y, (Pulp mill, Paper mill)
  Phone: (86) 393 462 7569/ 899 0895/ 896 1988
  Fax: (86) 393 896 1906
  Email: pylf@pylfzy.com
Henan Zhumadian City Baiyun Paper Co., Ltd., Zhumadian (Zhumadian Baiyun) Mill, North Worker Rd., Suiping County, Zhumadian 463100, China, Capacity: 294,000 mt/y, (Pulp mill, Paper mill)
  Phone: (86) 396 490 2206/2211/2218
  Fax: (86) 396 491 4805/490 2299/2211/ 2251
  Email: byzy@dahepaper.com

ⓘⓂHenan Dongsheng Paper Co.,Ltd.
Xinmi Mill
Xinhua Rd.
Xinmi, Henan, 452370
China
  Phone: (86) 371 6978 6848
Personnel:
  Mill Mgr.: Zhicheng Zhang
  Phone: (86) 371 6978 6848
Total Employees of Company: 550
Total Employees at this Location: 550
Type of Operation: Paperboard mill
Pulp Grades and Capacities:
  Total pulp capacity: 142,064 mt/y
  Recycled Pulping: 142,064 mt/y
Pulp Mill Data:
  Recycled Fiber Treatment Lines:
  Recycled packaging pulping lines
Paper/Paperboard Grades and Capacities:
  Total paper and paperboard capacity: 169,575 mt/y
  Corrugating medium/fluting: 145,299 mt/y
  Boxboard/cartonboard: 24,276 mt/y
Paper and Paperboard Mill Data:
Paper Machines: 6
No. 1, fourdrinier, total capacity 60,690 mt/y, Trim width 4.2 m, Corrugating medium/fluting
No. 2, fourdrinier, total capacity 49,266 mt/y, Trim width 3.8 m, Corrugating medium/fluting
No. 3, fourdrinier, total capacity 35,343 mt/y, Trim width 2.64 m, Corrugating medium/fluting
No. 6, multi-former, total capacity 7,140 mt/y, Trim width 1.58 m, Boxboard/cartonboard
No. 4-5, multi-former, total capacity 17,136 mt/y, Trim width 1.88 m, Boxboard/cartonboard

Energy Data:
Electrical demand for mill: 259 MWh/D

ⓘHenan Fangzheng Paper Co., Ltd.
Xinye County
Nanyang, Henan
China
Mill Locations:
Henan Fangzheng Paper Co., Ltd., Nanyang Mill, Xinye County, Nanyang, China, Capacity: 11,000 mt/y, (Paper mill)

ⓂHenan Fangzheng Paper Co., Ltd.
Nanyang Mill
Xinye County
Nanyang, Henan
China
Type of Operation: Paper mill
Paper/Paperboard Grades and Capacities:
  Total paper and paperboard capacity: 11,000 mt/y
  Tissue: 11,000 mt/y
Paper and Paperboard Mill Data:
Paper Machines: 6
PM 1, total capacity 1,800 mt/y, Trim width 1.88 m, Tissue
PM 2, total capacity 1,800 mt/y, Trim width 1.88 m, Tissue
PM 3, total capacity 1,800 mt/y, Trim width 1.88 m, Tissue
PM 4, total capacity 1,800 mt/y, Trim width 1.88 m, Tissue
PM 5, total capacity 1,800 mt/y, Trim width 1.88 m, Tissue
PM 6, total capacity 1,800 mt/y, Trim width 1.88 m, Tissue

ⓘHenan Feida Group
Ownership: 100% by shareholders
Hejie Industry Park
Xuchang, Henan, 461000
China
  Phone: (86) 374 566 6666
  Fax: (86) 374 566 8888
  Email: fdgroup@126.com
  Web Address: www.fdgroup.com.cn
Personnel:
  Chmn.: Zhijie Xu
  Phone: (86) 374 566 6666
  Fax: (86) 374 566 8888
Total Employees of Company: 1,200
Mill Locations:
Henan Xuchang Feida Paper Co., Ltd., Xuchang Mill, Hejie Industry Park, Xuchang 461000, China, Capacity: 202,000 mt/y, (Paper mill, Paperboard mill)
  Phone: (86) 374 566 8188
  Fax: (86) 374 566 8888

ⓘⓂHenan Fengyuan Paper Co., Ltd
Shangqiu Mill
Beihuan Rd.
Shangqiu, Henan
China
Total Employees at this Location: 475
Type of Operation: Paperboard mill
Pulp Grades and Capacities:
  Total pulp capacity: 78,341 mt/y
  Recycled Pulping: 78,341 mt/y
Pulp Mill Data:
  Recycled Fiber Treatment Lines:
  Recycled packaging pulping lines: 1
Paper/Paperboard Grades and Capacities:
  Total paper and paperboard capacity: 80,682 mt/y
  Corrugating medium/fluting: 80,682 mt/y
Paper and Paperboard Mill Data:
Paper Machines: 1
No. 1, fourdrinier, total capacity 80,682 mt/y, Trim width 4.4 m, Corrugating medium/fluting
Energy Data:
Electrical demand for mill: 125 MWh/D

ⓘHenan Haiyang Chemical Fiber Group Co., Ltd.
North Section of Xuesong Road, High-New Development Zone, Zhengzhou, Henan, 450000, China
  Web Address: www.hyfiber.com
Mill Locations:
Henan Weierte Chemical Fiber Co., Ltd., Sanmenxia Mill, Lvjiaya, Xiwentang Town, Sanmenxia 472000, China, (Pulp mill)
  Phone: (86) 398 2223 219
Henan Xinxiang Runyang Chemical Fiber Co., Ltd., Xinxiang Mill, Xiaodian Industrial Park, Yanjin County, Xinxiang 453200, China, (Pulp mill)
  Phone: (86) 373 3689 708
Jiujiang Hengsheng Chemical Fiber Co., Ltd., Jiujiang Mill, Gutang Town, Lushan District, Jiujiang 332011, China, (Pulp mill)
  Phone: (86) 792 8316 891
Xingping Jinlong Chemical Fiber Co., Ltd., Xingping Mill, Donghuan Rd., Xingping City, Xianyang, China, (Pulp mill)
  Phone: (86) 29 3882 2014
Zhenjiang Wanfa Chemical Fiber Co., Ltd., Zhenjiang Mill, Gaoqiao Town, Dantu District, Zhejiang, China, (Pulp mill)
  Phone: (86) 511 85572828

ⓘHenan Hebi Ruizhou Paper Co., Ltd.
No.66, Qiexi Industrial Rd., Qi County
Hebi, Henan, 456750
China
  Phone: (86) 392 7277 688
  Fax: (86) 392 7277 000
  Email: ruizhou2006@163.com
  Web Address: www.rzpaper.com
Mill Locations:
Henan Hebi Ruizhou Paper Co., Ltd., Hebi Mill, No.66, Qiexi Industrial Rd., Qi County, Hebi 456750, China, Capacity: 36,400 mt/y, (Paper mill)
  Phone: (86) 392 7277 688
  Fax: (86) 392 7277 000
  Email: ruizhou2006@163.com

ⓂHenan Hebi Ruizhou Paper Co., Ltd.
Hebi Mill
No.66, Qiexi Industrial Rd., Qi County
Hebi, Henan, 456750
China
  Phone: (86) 392 7277 688
  Fax: (86) 392 7277 000
  Email: ruizhou2006@163.com
  Web Address: www.rzpaper.com
Type of Operation: Paper mill
Paper/Paperboard Grades and Capacities:
  Total paper and paperboard capacity: 36,400 mt/y
  Uncoated woodfree/freesheet: 24,400 mt/y
  Tissue: 12,000 mt/y
Paper and Paperboard Mill Data:
Paper Machines: 12
PM 1, total capacity 1,200 mt/y, Trim width 1.88 m, Tissue
PM 2, total capacity 1,200 mt/y, Trim width 1.88 m, Tissue
PM 3, total capacity 1,200 mt/y, Trim width 1.88 m, Tissue
PM 4, total capacity 1,200 mt/y, Trim width 1.88 m, Tissue
PM 5, total capacity 1,800 mt/y, Trim width 2.4 m, Tissue
PM 6, total capacity 1,800 mt/y, Trim width 2.4 m, Tissue
PM 7, total capacity 1,800 mt/y, Trim width 2.4 m, Tissue
PM 8, total capacity 1,800 mt/y, Trim width 2.4 m, Tissue
PM 9, total capacity 3,600 mt/y, Trim width 1.76 m, Uncoated woodfree/freesheet
PM 10, total capacity 4,400 mt/y, Trim width 1.88 m, Uncoated woodfree/freesheet
PM 11, total capacity 4,400 mt/y, Trim width 1.88 m, Uncoated woodfree/freesheet
PM 12, total capacity 1,200 mt/y, Trim width 3.4 m, Uncoated woodfree/freesheet

China

ⓂHenan Hongteng Paper Group Co., Ltd.
Ownership: 100% by private owners
Science and Technology Zone, Weidu District
Xuchang, Henan, 461000
China
  Phone: (86) 374 431 0088
  Fax: (86) 374 431 0298
  Email: hongteng_renli@126.com
  Web Address: www.htzy.com.cn
Personnel:
  Chmn.: Jianshe Dai
  Phone: (86) 374 431 0088
  Fax: (86) 374 431 0298
  Gen. Mgr.: Lihui Fang
  Phone: (86) 374 431 0088
  Fax: (86) 374 431 0298
  Sls. Mgr.: Youping Liu
  Phone: (86) 374 431 0088
  Fax: (86) 374 431 0298
Total Employees of Company: 1,400
Mill Locations:
  Henan Chenyang Paper Co., Ltd., Xuchang Mill, Caoqiao, Weidu District, Xuchang 461000, China, Capacity: 40,000 mt/y, (Paperboard mill)
  Phone: (86) 374 431 0088
  Fax: (86) 374 431 0298
  Henan Hongteng Paper Group Co., Ltd., Xuchang Mill, Science and Technology Zone, Weidu District, Xuchang 461000, China, Capacity: 159,222 mt/y, (Paper mill, Paperboard mill)
  Phone: (86) 374 832 6918
  Fax: (86) 374 832 6939
  Email: hongteng_renli@126.com

ⓂHenan Hongteng Paper Group Co., Ltd.
Xuchang Mill
Science and Technology Zone, Weidu District
Xuchang, Henan, 461000
China
  Phone: (86) 374 832 6918
  Fax: (86) 374 832 6939
  Email: hongteng_renli@126.com
Personnel:
  Chmn.: Jianshe Dai
  Phone: (86) 374 832 6918
  Gen. Mgr.: Lihui Fang
  Phone: (86) 374 832 6918
Total Employees at this Location: 400
Type of Operation: Paper mill, Paperboard mill
Pulp Grades and Capacities:
  Total pulp capacity: 159,532 mt/y
  Recycled Pulping: 159,532 mt/y
Pulp Mill Data:
Pulp Lines: 4
  Recycled Fiber Treatment Lines:
  Recycled packaging pulping lines: 1
Paper/Paperboard Grades and Capacities:
  Total paper and paperboard capacity: 159,222 mt/y
  Linerboard: 97,818 mt/y
  Corrugating medium/fluting: 61,404 mt/y
Paper and Paperboard Mill Data:
Paper Machines: 2
  No. 1, Multi-wire (4), total capacity 97,818 mt/y, Trim width 3.6 m, Linerboard
  No. 2, fourdrinier, total capacity 61,404 mt/y, Trim width 3.6 m, Corrugating medium/fluting
Energy Data:
Power boilers: 2
Electrical demand for mill: 260 MWh/D

ⓅⓂHenan Hongwei Paper Co., Ltd
Xuchang Mill
North of Laodong Rd, Mingying Technology Park, Weidu District
Xuchang, Henan, 461000
China
  Phone: (86) 374 738 6618/6612
  Fax: (86) 374 451 6497/6438
  Email: hongweigroup@126.com
Total Employees at this Location: 1,600
Type of Operation: Paperboard mill
Pulp Grades and Capacities:
  Total pulp capacity: 213,967 mt/y
  Recycled Pulping: 213,967 mt/y
Paper/Paperboard Grades and Capacities:
  Total paper and paperboard capacity: 221,200 mt/y
  Linerboard: 156,000 mt/y
  Corrugating medium/fluting: 58,000 mt/y
  Boxboard/cartonboard: 7,200 mt/y
Paper and Paperboard Mill Data:
Paper Machines: 4
  No. 1, cylinder, total capacity 7,200 mt/y, Trim width 1.76 m, Boxboard/cartonboard
  No. 3, multi-wire, total capacity 66,000 mt/y, Trim width 3.6 m, Linerboard
  No. 4, Fourdrinier (4), total capacity 90,000 mt/y, Trim width 3.8 m, Linerboard
  No. 5, fourdrinier, total capacity 58,000 mt/y, Trim width 3.8 m, Corrugating medium/fluting
Energy Data:
Electrical demand for mill: 286 MWh/D

ⓂHenan Huifeng Paper Co., Ltd.
Ownership: 100% by private owners
East Jianshe Rd.
Zhoukou City, Henan, 466001
China
  Phone: (86) 371 6925 1051/ 6369 1682
  Fax: (86) 371 6369 1680
Mill Locations:
  Henan Huifeng Paper Co., Ltd., Zhoukou Mill, East Jianshe Rd., Zhoukou 466001, China, Capacity: 26,000 mt/y, (Paper mill)
  Phone: (86) 371 6925 1051/ 6369 1682
  Fax: (86) 371 6369 1680

ⓂHenan Huifeng Paper Co., Ltd.
Zhoukou Mill
East Jianshe Rd.
Zhoukou, Henan, 466001
China
  Phone: (86) 371 6925 1051/ 6369 1682
  Fax: (86) 371 6369 1680
Personnel:
  Chmn. & Gen. Mgr.: Haichang Zhong
  Phone: (86) 371 6925 1051/ 6369 1682
  Sls. Mgr.: Chunting Zhang
  Phone: (86) 371 6925 1051/ 6369 1682
Total Employees at this Location: 260
Type of Operation: Paper mill
Paper/Paperboard Grades and Capacities:
  Total paper and paperboard capacity: 26,000 mt/y
  Specialty and industrial: 26,000 mt/y
Paper and Paperboard Mill Data:
Paper Machines: 4
  PM 2, fourdrinier, total capacity 4,000 mt/y, Trim width 1.09 m, Specialty and industrial
  PM 3, fourdrinier, total capacity 6,000 mt/y, Trim width 1.88 m, Specialty and industrial
  PM 4, fourdrinier, total capacity 7,000 mt/y, Trim width 1.88 m, Specialty and industrial
  PM 5, fourdrinier, total capacity 9,000 mt/y, Trim width 1.88 m, Specialty and industrial

ⓅⓂHenan Hulijia Industry Co. Ltd.
Zhoukou Mill
Chengdong Economic Development Zone, Luyi County
Zhoukou, Henan, 477200
China
  Phone: (86) 394 749 0998
  Fax: (86) 394 749 1168
  Web Address: www.hulijia.com
Total Employees at this Location: 140
Type of Operation: Paper mill
Paper/Paperboard Grades and Capacities:
  Total paper and paperboard capacity: 30,000 mt/y
  Tissue: 30,000 mt/y
Paper and Paperboard Mill Data:
Paper Machines: 2
  No. 1, crescent former, total capacity 15,000 mt/y, Trim width 2.85 m, Tissue
  No. 2, crescent former, total capacity 15,000 mt/y, Trim width 2.85 m, Tissue
Energy Data:
Power boilers: 2
Steam turbines
Electrical demand for mill: 84 MWh/D

ⓂHenan Jianghe Paper Co., Ltd.
Ownership: 100% by shareholders
Chengdong Development Zone, Wushe County
Jiaozuo, Henan, 454950
China
  Phone: (86) 391 726 8890/ 8160
  Fax: (86) 391 726 8181
  Web Address: www.jianghe.com
Personnel:
  Gen. Mgr.: Fengwei Jiang
  Phone: (86) 391 726 8890/ 8160
Mill Locations:
  Henan Jianghe Paper Co., Ltd., Jiaozuo Mill, Chengdong Development Zone, Wuzhi County, Jiaozuo 454950, China, Capacity: 442,000 mt/y, (Paper mill)
  Phone: (86) 391 726 8890/ 8160, 3917231008
  Fax: (86) 391 726 8181, 391 7268991
  Shandong Jianghe Paper Co., Ltd., Qihe Mill, No.1 Chenming Road, Qihe County, Dezhou 251100, China, Capacity: 349,800 mt/y, (Pulp mill, Paper mill, Paperboard mill)
  Phone: (86) 534 5028 600/5028 501
  Email: 5qhcmbz@dz-public.sd.cninfo.net, qhbzc@163.net

ⓂHenan Jianghe Paper Co., Ltd.
Jiaozuo Mill
Chengdong Development Zone, Wuzhi County
Jiaozuo, Henan, 454950
China
  Phone: (86) 391 726 8890/ 8160, 3917231008
  Fax: (86) 391 726 8181, 391 7268991
  Web Address: www.jianghe.com
Personnel:
  Gen. Mgr.: Fengwei Jiang
  Phone: (86) 391 726 8890/ 8160
Total Employees at this Location: 2,000
Type of Operation: Paper mill
Paper/Paperboard Grades and Capacities:
  Total paper and paperboard capacity: 442,000 mt/y
  Uncoated woodfree/freesheet: 442,000 mt/y
Paper and Paperboard Mill Data:
Paper Machines: 6
  No. 1, hybrid former, total capacity 40,000 mt/y, Trim width 2.64 m, Uncoated woodfree/freesheet
  No. 2, hybrid former, total capacity 70,000 mt/y, Trim width 3.27 m, Uncoated woodfree/freesheet
  No. 3, fourdrinier, total capacity 48,000 mt/y, Trim width 3.2 m, Uncoated woodfree/freesheet
  No. 4, hybrid former, total capacity 58,000 mt/y, Trim width 3.2 m, Uncoated woodfree/freesheet
  No. 5, fourdrinier, total capacity 26,000 mt/y, Trim width 3.2 m, Uncoated woodfree/freesheet
  No. 6, hybrid former, total capacity 200,000 mt/y, Trim width 5.8 m, Uncoated woodfree/freesheet
Energy Data:
Power boilers: 4
Steam turbines: 2 at 35, 35 MW
Electrical demand for mill: 885 MWh/D

ⓂHenan Jiaozuo Ruifeng Paper Co., Ltd.
Jiaozuo (Jiaozuo Ruifeng) Mill
Ownership: Henan Dahe Paper Co., Ltd.
South Yingbin Rd., Wuzhi County

Jiaozuo, Henan, 454000
China
  Phone: (86) 391 726 8650/ 8605
  Fax: (86) 391 726 8710/ 8176
  Email: jzrfzy@163.com
  Web Address: www.ruifengpaper.com
Personnel:
  Gen. Mgr.: Changning Xu
  Phone: (86) 188 3911 6969
Total Employees at this Location: 360
Type of Operation: Pulp mill
Pulp Grades and Capacities:
  Total pulp capacity: 152,131 mt/y
  Pulp available for market: 149,940 mt/y
  Mechanical Pulp: 152,131 mt/y
Pulp Mill Data:
  Mechanical Pulping Systems:
  APMP Systems: 1
  Pulp Lines: 1
  Pulp Dryers:
  Twin Wire 1
Energy Data:
  Steam turbines: 4 at 0.5 MW

ⓘHenan Jiyuan Tengsheng Paper Co., Ltd.
West of Xizhicheng Village, Zhicheng Town
Jiyuan, Henan, 454672
China
  Phone: (86) 391 6081 666/6095 626
  Fax: (86) 391 6095 666
  Email: jystszy@163.com
  Web Address: www.jytszy.com
Personnel:
  Gen. Mgr.: Mingzhao Ma
  Phone: (86) 391 6081 666/6095 626
  Fax: (86) 391 6095 666
  Vice Gen. Mgr.: Dianbo Sun
  Phone: (86) 391 6081 666/6095 626
  Fax: (86) 391 6095 666
  Prod. Mgr.: Chaobo Wang
  Phone: (86) 391 6081 666/6095 626
  Fax: (86) 391 6095 666
Total Employees at this Location: 200
Mill Locations:
  Henan Jiyuan Tengsheng Paper Co., Ltd., Jiyuan Mill, West of Xizhicheng Village, Zhicheng Town, Jiyuan 454672, China, Capacity: 100,000 mt/y, (Paper mill)
  Phone: (86) 391 6081 666/6095 626
  Fax: (86) 391 6095 666
  Email: jystszy@163.com

ⓜHenan Jiyuan Tengsheng Paper Co., Ltd.
Jiyuan Mill
West of Xizhicheng Village, Zhicheng Town
Jiyuan, Henan, 454672
China
  Phone: (86) 391 6081 666/6095 626
  Fax: (86) 391 6095 666
  Email: jystszy@163.com
Total Employees at this Location: 200
Type of Operation: Paper mill
Pulp Grades and Capacities:
  Total pulp capacity: 97,099 mt/y
  Recycled Pulping: 97,099 mt/y
Paper/Paperboard Grades and Capacities:
  Total paper and paperboard capacity: 100,000 mt/y
  Corrugating medium/fluting: 100,000 mt/y
Paper and Paperboard Mill Data:
  Paper Machines: 1
  No. 1, fourdrinier, total capacity 100,000 mt/y, Trim width 4.2 m, Corrugating medium/fluting
Energy Data:
  Electrical demand for mill: 118 MWh/D

ⓘHenan Longquan Group Co., Ltd.
Longquan Village, Qiliying Town, Xinxiang County
Xinxiang, Henan, 453731
China
  Phone: (86) 373 13569845145
  Fax: (86) 373 565 1372
  Web Address: lqjtgs5651.cn.busytrade.com
Personnel:
  Chmn.: Xiaowei Xu
  Phone: (86) 373 13569845145
  Fax: (86) 373 565 1372
  Sales Mgr.: Jie Liang
  Phone: (86) 373 13569845145
  Fax: (86) 373 565 1372
Total Employees of Company: 2,200
Mill Locations:
  Henan Longquan Group Yubei Co., Ltd., Xinxiang Mill, Longquan Industry Zone, Xinxiang County, Xinxiang 453731, China, Capacity: 78,000 mt/y, (Paper mill)
  Phone: (86) 373 5651 952/988
  Fax: (86) 373 565 1627
  Email: liangzhengpeil@163.com

ⓜHenan Longquan Group Yubei Co., Ltd.
Xinxiang Mill
Ownership: 100% by Henan Longquan Group Co., Ltd.
Longquan Industry Zone, Xinxiang County
Xinxiang, Henan, 453731
China
  Phone: (86) 373 5651 952/988
  Fax: (86) 373 565 1627
  Email: liangzhengpeil@163.com
  Web Address: www.yubeizhiye.com
Personnel:
  Chmn.: Xiaowei Wu
  Phone: (86) 373 565 1952/1627
  Gen. Mgr.: Yan Li
  Phone: (86) 373 565 1952/1627
Total Employees at this Location: 1,600
Type of Operation: Paper mill
Paper/Paperboard Grades and Capacities:
  Total paper and paperboard capacity: 78,000 mt/y
  Uncoated woodfree/freesheet: 72,000 mt/y
  Uncoated mechanical/groundwood: 6,000 mt/y
Paper and Paperboard Mill Data:
  Paper Machines: 6
  No. 1, total capacity 12,000 mt/y, Trim width 1.88 m, Uncoated woodfree/freesheet
  PM 5, fourdrinier, total capacity 12,000 mt/y, Trim width 2.64 m, Uncoated mechanical/groundwood, Uncoated woodfree/freesheet
  PM 6, fourdrinier, total capacity 12,000 mt/y, Trim width 3.2 m, Uncoated woodfree/freesheet
  PM 7, fourdrinier, total capacity 12,000 mt/y, Trim width 3.2 m, Uncoated woodfree/freesheet
  PM 9, total capacity 12,000 mt/y, Trim width 3.2 m, Uncoated woodfree/freesheet
  PM 10, total capacity 18,000 mt/y, Trim width 2.36 m, Uncoated woodfree/freesheet

ⓘHenan Longquan Group Qilong Co., Ltd.
Longquan Village, Qiliying Town, Xinxiang County
Xinxiang, Henan, 453731
China
  Phone: (86) 373 5682 629
  Web Address: www.longquanjituan.com
Total Employees at this Location: 200
Mill Locations:
  Henan Longquan Group Qilong Co., Ltd., Xinxiang Mill, Longquan Village, Qiliying Town, Xinxiang County, Xinxiang 453731, China, Capacity: 80,000 mt/y, (Paperboard mill)
  Phone: (86) 373 5682 629

ⓜHenan Longquan Group Qilong Co., Ltd.
Xinxiang Mill
Longquan Village, Qiliying Town, Xinxiang County
Xinxiang, Henan, 453731
China
  Phone: (86) 373 5682 629
  Web Address: www.longquanjt.com
Total Employees at this Location: 200
Type of Operation: Paperboard mill
Pulp Grades and Capacities:
  Total pulp capacity: 77,734 mt/y
  Recycled Pulping: 77,734 mt/y
Pulp Mill Data:
  Recycled Fiber Treatment Lines:
  Recycled packaging pulping lines: 1
Paper/Paperboard Grades and Capacities:
  Total paper and paperboard capacity: 80,000 mt/y
  Corrugating medium/fluting: 80,000 mt/y
Paper and Paperboard Mill Data:
  Paper Machines: 2
  No. 1, fourdrinier, total capacity 30,000 mt/y, Trim width 3.4 m, Corrugating medium/fluting
  No. 2, fourdrinier, total capacity 50,000 mt/y, Trim width 4.3 m, Corrugating medium/fluting
Energy Data:
  Electrical demand for mill: 97 MWh/D

ⓘHenan Longyuan Paper Co., Ltd.
Ownership: 100% by private owners
No. 38 Xinhongchen
Zhengzhou, Henan, 450011
China
  Phone: (86) 371 6579 8929
  Email: longyouzhiye@sina.com
  Web Address: www.hnlyzy.com
Personnel:
  Pres.: Xinfang Feng
  Phone: (86) 371 6579 8929
Total Employees of Company: 1,300
Mill Locations:
  Henan Longyuan Paper Co., Ltd., Zhengzhou Mill, West Erhuan Rd., Industry Park, Taikang County, Zhengzhou 461400, China, Capacity: 239,904 mt/y, (Paperboard mill)
  Phone: (86) 394 691 5909/5837/5906
  Fax: (86) 394 691 5908
  Email: longyouzhiye@sina.com
  Henan Luoyang City Longxiang Paper Co., Ltd., Luoyang Mill, No. 2 Luoyi Rd., Luoyang 471000, China, Capacity: 20,000 mt/y, (Paperboard mill)
  Phone: (86) 371 6579 8929
  Fax: (86) 379 6551 2640
  Email: lxzhiye@sina.com
  Henan Ningling County Longyuan Paper Co., Ltd., Zhengzhou Mill, North Erhuan Rd. Industry Park, Ningling County, Zhengzhou 476000, China, Capacity: 13,000 mt/y, (Paperboard mill)
  Phone: (86) 370 7810 517
  Fax: (86) 370 7827 312

ⓜHenan Longyuan Paper Co., Ltd.
Zhengzhou Mill
Ownership: Henan Longyuan Paper Co., Ltd.
West Erhuan Rd., Industry Park, Taikang County
Zhengzhou, Henan, 461400
China
  Phone: (86) 394 691 5909/5837/5906
  Fax: (86) 394 691 5908
  Email: longyouzhiye@sina.com
  Web Address: www.hnlyzy.com
Personnel:
  Gen. Mgr.: Jianxin Feng
  Phone: (86) 394 691 5909/5837/5906
Total Employees at this Location: 475
Type of Operation: Paperboard mill
Pulp Grades and Capacities:
  Total pulp capacity: 235,476 mt/y
  Recycled Pulping: 235,476 mt/y
Pulp Mill Data:
  Recycled Fiber Treatment Lines:
  Recycled packaging pulping lines: 2 at 170,000 admt/y
Paper/Paperboard Grades and Capacities:
  Total paper and paperboard capacity: 239,904 mt/y

China

Corrugating medium/fluting: 239,904 mt/y
Paper and Paperboard Mill Data:
Paper Machines: 3
No. 1, fourdrinier, total capacity 53,550 mt/y, Trim width 3.6 m, Corrugating medium/fluting
No. 2, fourdrinier, total capacity 78,540 mt/y, Trim width 4.05 m, Corrugating medium/fluting
No. 3, fourdrinier, total capacity 107,814 mt/y, Trim width 4.4 m, Corrugating medium/fluting
Energy Data:
Power boilers: 3
Electrical demand for mill: 386 MWh/D

ⓂHenan Luohe Paperboard Mill
Ownership: 100% by state
Dongfeng Xiang, West Renmin Rd., Yuanhui dist.
Luohe City, Henan, 462000
China
  Phone: (86) 395 212 2554
  Fax: (86) 395 212 1519/2624495
  Email: lhjia@21cn.com
Mill Locations:
Henan Luohe Paperboard Mill, Luohe Mill, Dongfeng Xiang, West Renmin Rd., Yuanhui dist., Luohe 462000, China, Capacity: 20,000 mt/y, (Paper mill, Paperboard mill)
  Phone: (86) 395 212 2554
  Fax: (86) 395 212 1519/2624495
  Email: lhjia@21cn.com

ⓂHenan Luohe Paperboard Mill
Luohe Mill
Dongfeng Xiang, West Renmin Rd., Yuanhui dist.
Luohe, Henan, 462000
China
  Phone: (86) 395 212 2554
  Fax: (86) 395 212 1519/2624495
  Email: lhjia@21cn.com
Personnel:
  Chmn.: Yuxiang Chen
  Phone: (86) 395 212 2554
  VP/Tech.: Fuliang Pei
  Phone: (86) 395 212 2554
  VP/Bus.: Yue Zhang
  Phone: (86) 395 212 2554
  Sales Mgr.: Xia Zhu
  Phone: (86) 395 212 2554
Total Employees at this Location: 700
Type of Operation: Paper mill, Paperboard mill
Paper/Paperboard Grades and Capacities:
  Total paper and paperboard capacity: 20,000 mt/y
  Containerboard: 20,000 mt/y
Paper and Paperboard Mill Data:
Paper Machines: 5
No. 1-2, Trim width 1.58 m, Containerboard
No. 3-5, Trim width 1.88 m, Containerboard
Finishing Equipment:
  Rewinders: 10
  Sheeters: 2
Energy Data:
Power boilers: 1

ⓂHenan Luohe Yinge Specialty Paper Co., Ltd.
Luohe (Yinge Specialty) Mill
Ownership: 25% by Marubeni Corporation, 75% by Henan Energy and Chemical Industry Group Co., Ltd.
Renmin Rd. & Donghuan Rd.
Luohe, Henan, 462000
China
  Phone: (86) 395 2355 797
  Fax: (86) 395 2355 797
  Web Address: www.yinge.com.cn
Total Employees at this Location: 190
Type of Operation: Paper mill
Paper/Paperboard Grades and Capacities:
  Total paper and paperboard capacity: 69,972 mt/y

Uncoated woodfree/freesheet: 69,972 mt/y
Paper and Paperboard Mill Data:
Paper Machines: 2
No. 1, (second-hand), fourdrinier, total capacity 19,992 mt/y, Trim width 2.25 m, Uncoated woodfree/freesheet
No. 2, (started up in Sep. 2009), hybrid former, total capacity 49,980 mt/y, Trim width 3.8 m, Uncoated woodfree/freesheet
Energy Data:
Power boilers
Steam turbines
Electrical demand for mill: 151 MWh/D

ⓂHenan Luohe Yinge Tissue Paper Industry Co., Ltd.
Luohe (Yinge Tissue) Mill
Ownership: 99.75% by Henan Yinge Industrial Investment Co. Ltd.
No. 2 East Xiangjiang Rd.
Luohe, Henan, 462000
China
  Phone: (86) 395 266 8315/ 263 5700/5531
  Fax: (86) 395 268 7700
  Email: zsb555@126.com
  Web Address: www.yinge.com.cn
Personnel:
  Chmn.: Wei Wang
Total Employees at this Location: 1,900
Type of Operation: Paper mill
Paper/Paperboard Grades and Capacities:
  Total paper and paperboard capacity: 160,000 mt/y
  Tissue: 160,000 mt/y
Paper and Paperboard Mill Data:
Paper Machines: 5
No. 10, inclined, total capacity 10,000 mt/y, Trim width 2.65 m, Tissue
No. 11, inclined, total capacity 15,000 mt/y, Trim width 2.8 m, Tissue
No. 12, inclined, total capacity 15,000 mt/y, Trim width 2.8 m, Tissue
T1, (started March 2012), crescent former, total capacity 60,000 mt/y, Trim width 5.6 m, Tissue
T2, (started December 2012), crescent former, total capacity 60,000 mt/y, Trim width 5.6 m, Tissue
Energy Data:
Power boilers: 1
Steam turbines: 1
Electrical demand for mill: 435 MWh/D

ⓗⓂHenan Luoshan Hengyuan Paper Co., Ltd
Luoshan Mill
Tangwan, Liuli Village, Longshan Town
Luoshan, Henan, 464200
China
  Phone: (86) 376 215 5888
  Fax: (86) 376 215 5999
  Email: lsxhyzy@126.com
Personnel:
  Jian Dong
Total Employees at this Location: 345
Type of Operation: Paperboard mill
Pulp Grades and Capacities:
  Total pulp capacity: 98,112 mt/y
  Recycled Pulping: 98,112 mt/y
Paper/Paperboard Grades and Capacities:
  Total paper and paperboard capacity: 101,031 mt/y
  Corrugating medium/fluting: 101,031 mt/y
Paper and Paperboard Mill Data:
Paper Machines: 2
No. 1, multi-wire, total capacity 44,268 mt/y, Trim width 3.6 m, Corrugating medium/fluting
No. 2, Multi-wire (2), total capacity 56,763 mt/y, Trim width 3.6 m, Corrugating medium/fluting
Energy Data:
Power boilers
Electrical demand for mill: 162 MWh/D

ⓂHenan Luoyang City Longxiang Paper Co., Ltd.
Luoyang Mill
Ownership: 100% by Henan Longyuan Paper Co., Ltd.
No. 2 Luoyi Rd.
Luoyang, Henan, 471000
China
  Phone: (86) 371 6579 8929
  Fax: (86) 379 6551 2640
  Email: lxzhiye@sina.com
  Web Address: www.hnlyzy.com
Personnel:
  Gen. Mgr.: Qingsong Zhang
  Phone: (86) 371 6579 8929
Type of Operation: Paperboard mill
Paper/Paperboard Grades and Capacities:
  Total paper and paperboard capacity: 20,000 mt/y
  Linerboard: 20,000 mt/y
Paper and Paperboard Mill Data:
Paper Machines: 3
PM 1, total capacity 5,000 mt/y, Trim width 1.09 m, Linerboard
PM 2, total capacity 7,000 mt/y, Trim width 1.58 m, Linerboard
PM 3, total capacity 8,000 mt/y, Trim width 1.58 m, Linerboard

ⓗHenan Mintong Huarui Paper Co., Ltd.
Taiqian County
Puyang, Henan, 457600
China
  Phone: (86) 393 2733 777/888
  Email: bnmintong@126.com
  Web Address: www.mthr.biz
Total Employees at this Location: 336
Mill Locations:
Henan Mintong Huarui Paper Co., Ltd., Puyang Mill, Taiqian County, Puyang 457600, China, Capacity: 45,000 mt/y, (Paper mill)
  Phone: (86) 393 2733 777/888
  Email: bnmintong@126.com

ⓂHenan Mintong Huarui Paper Co., Ltd.
Puyang Mill
Taiqian County
Puyang, Henan, 457600
China
  Phone: (86) 393 2733 777/888
  Email: bnmintong@126.com
  Web Address: www.mthr.biz
Total Employees at this Location: 336
Type of Operation: Paper mill
Paper/Paperboard Grades and Capacities:
  Total paper and paperboard capacity: 45,000 mt/y
  Uncoated mechanical/groundwood: 45,000 mt/y
Paper and Paperboard Mill Data:
Paper Machines: 3
PM 1, total capacity 10,000 mt/y, Trim width 1.76 m, Uncoated mechanical/groundwood
PM 2, total capacity 10,000 mt/y, Trim width 1.76 m, Uncoated mechanical/groundwood
PM 9, total capacity 25,000 mt/y, Trim width 2.64 m, Uncoated mechanical/groundwood

ⓂHenan Neixiang Xianhe Special Paper & Pulp Co., Ltd.
Nanyang Mill
Ownership: Zhejiang Xianhe Specialty Paper
Neixiang County Industry District, Neixiang County
Nanyang, Henan, 473000
China
  Phone: (86) 377 6532 7302/ 6531 3171
  Fax: (86) 377 6531 5570
  Web Address: www.nxxhzy.com
Personnel:
  Gen. Mgr.: Mingliang Wang
  Phone: (86) 377 6532 7302/ 6531 3171

China

Chief Eng.: Jiaming Zhang
Phone: (86) 377 6532 7302/ 6531 3171
Sls. Dir.: Xiwen Sun
Phone: (86) 377 6532 7302/ 6531 3171
Sls. Mgr.: Haiji Du
Phone: (86) 377 6532 7302/ 6531 3171
Total Employees at this Location: 600
Type of Operation: Pulp mill, Paper mill
Pulp Grades and Capacities:
Total pulp capacity: 32,449 mt/y
Other Pulp: 32,449 mt/y
Pulp Mill Data:
Chemical Pulping Systems:
Continuous digesters: 2
Pulp Lines: 2
Bleach Plant Systems: 1
No. 1, Type: TCF
Chemical Recovery Equipment:
Evaporator lines
Recovery boilers: 1
Paper/Paperboard Grades and Capacities:
Total paper and paperboard capacity: 99,960 mt/y
Uncoated woodfree/freesheet: 79,968 mt/y
Specialty and industrial: 19,992 mt/y
Paper and Paperboard Mill Data:
Paper Machines: 3
No. 1, fourdrinier, total capacity 19,992 mt/y, Trim width 2.88 m, Specialty and industrial
No. 2, fourdrinier, total capacity 39,984 mt/y, Trim width 2.88 m, Uncoated woodfree/freesheet
No. 3, fourdrinier, total capacity 39,984 mt/y, Trim width 2.88 m, Uncoated woodfree/freesheet
Energy Data:
Power boilers: 2
Steam turbines: 2 at 12, 12 MW
Electrical demand for mill: 253 MWh/D

ⓜHenan Ningling County Longyuan Paper Co., Ltd.
Zhengzhou Mill
Ownership: Henan Longyuan Paper Co., Ltd.
North Erhuan Rd. Industry Park, Ningling County
Zhengzhou, Henan, 476000
China
Phone: (86) 370 7810 517
Fax: (86) 370 7827 312
Web Address: www.hnlyzy.com
Personnel:
Gen. Mgr.: Chuanyong Ren
Phone: (86) 370 7810 517
Type of Operation: Paperboard mill
Pulp Grades and Capacities:
Total pulp capacity: 13,000 mt/y
Recycled Pulping: 13,000 mt/y
Pulp Mill Data:
Pulp Lines: 1
Recycled Fiber Treatment Lines:
Recycled packaging pulping lines: 1 at 13,000 admt/y
Paper/Paperboard Grades and Capacities:
Total paper and paperboard capacity: 13,000 mt/y
Linerboard: 13,000 mt/y
Paper and Paperboard Mill Data:
Paper Machines: 1
PM 1, total capacity 13,000 mt/y, Trim width 1.76 m, Linerboard

ⓜHenan Puyang City Tongyu Paper Co., Ltd.
Ownership: 100% by shareholders
Gongmao District, Wanglou Village, Fan County
Puyang, Henan, 457500
China
Phone: (86) 393 597 2218/ 597 2068/597 2369
Fax: (86) 393 597 2188/ 597 2078
Email: pytyzy@163.com
Web Address: www.pytyzy.com
Personnel:
Chmn.: Meiling Shi
Phone: (86) 393 597 2218/ 597 2068/597 2369
Sls. Mgr. - P&W: Hongsheng Shi
Phone: (86) 393 597 2218/ 597 2068/597 2369
Sls. Mgr. - Tissue Paper: Hongbing Zhang
Phone: (86) 393 597 2218/ 597 2068/597 2369
Mill Locations:
Henan Puyang City Tongyu Paper Co., Ltd., Puyang Mill, Gongmao District, Wanglou Village, Fan County, Puyang 457500, China, Capacity: 50,000 mt/y, (Paper mill)
Phone: (86) 393 597 2218/ 597 2068/597 2369
Fax: (86) 393 597 2188/ 597 2078
Email: pytyzy@163.com

ⓜHenan Puyang City Tongyu Paper Co., Ltd.
Puyang Mill
Gongmao District, Wanglou Village, Fan County
Puyang, Henan, 457500
China
Phone: (86) 393 597 2218/ 597 2068/597 2369
Fax: (86) 393 597 2188/ 597 2078
Email: pytyzy@163.com
Personnel:
Chmn.: Meiling Shi
Phone: (86) 393 597 2218/ 597 2068/597 2369
Sls. Mgr. - P&W: Hongsheng Shi
Phone: (86) 393 597 2218/ 597 2068/597 2369
Sls. Mgr. - Tissue Paper: Hongbing Zhang
Phone: (86) 393 597 2218/ 597 2068/597 2369
Total Employees at this Location: 475
Type of Operation: Paper mill
Pulp Mill Data:
Recycled Fiber Treatment Lines:
Recycled packaging pulping lines: 1
Paper/Paperboard Grades and Capacities:
Total paper and paperboard capacity: 50,000 mt/y
Uncoated mechanical/groundwood: 50,000 mt/y
Tissue
Paper and Paperboard Mill Data:
Paper Machines: 7
No. 1, fourdrinier, total capacity 10,000 mt/y, Trim width 2.64 m, Uncoated mechanical/groundwood
No. 2, (Idle since 2011), cylinder, total capacity 3,927 mt/y, Trim width 1.88 m, Tissue
No. 3, (Idle since 2011), cylinder, total capacity 3,927 mt/y, Trim width 1.88 m, Tissue
No. 4, (Idle since 2011), cylinder, total capacity 3,927 mt/y, Trim width 1.88 m, Tissue
No. 5, (Idle since 2011), cylinder, total capacity 3,927 mt/y, Trim width 1.88 m, Tissue
No. 6, fourdrinier, total capacity 20,000 mt/y, Trim width 2.64 m, Uncoated mechanical/groundwood
No. 7, fourdrinier, total capacity 20,000 mt/y, Trim width 2.64 m, Uncoated mechanical/groundwood
Energy Data:
Power boilers: 3
Electrical demand for mill: 97 MWh/D

ⓜHenan Puyang Longfeng Paper Co. Ltd
Puyang (Puyang Longfeng) Mill
Ownership: Henan Dahe Paper Co., Ltd.
West Shengli Rd.
Puyang, Henan, 457000
China
Phone: (86) 393 462 7569/ 899 0895/ 896 1988
Fax: (86) 393 896 1906
Email: pylf@pylfzy.com
Web Address: www.pylfzy.com
Personnel:
Chmn. & Gen. Mgr.: Haiquan Guo
Phone: (86) 393 462 7569/ 899 0895/ 896 1988
Vice Gen. Mgr.: Yongjun Cao
Phone: (86) 393 462 7569/ 899 0895/ 896 1988
Total Employees at this Location: 900
Type of Operation: Pulp mill, Paper mill
Pulp Grades and Capacities:
Total pulp capacity: 41,889 mt/y
Mechanical Pulp: 41,889 mt/y
Pulp Mill Data:
Mechanical Pulping Systems:
APMP Systems: 1
Pulp Lines: 1
Bleach Plant Systems: 1
Paper/Paperboard Grades and Capacities:
Total paper and paperboard capacity: 300,000 mt/y
Uncoated woodfree/freesheet: 204,000 mt/y
Coated woodfree/freesheet: 96,000 mt/y
Paper and Paperboard Mill Data:
Paper Machines: 1
No. 1, OptiFormer, total capacity 300,000 mt/y, Trim width 7.22 m, Coated woodfree/freesheet, Uncoated woodfree/freesheet
Coating Equipment: 1
PM 1, total capacity 165,000 mt/y., on machine
Finishing Equipment:
Supercalenders: 1
Energy Data:
Power boilers: 3
Steam turbines: 2 at 55, 25 MW
Electrical demand for mill: 731 MWh/D

ⓜHenan Qinyang Haolin Paper Co., Ltd.
Ownership: 100% by private owners
No. 1 Tuntou Industry District
Qinyang, Jiaozuo, Henan, 454550
China
Phone: (86) 391 5066 392
Fax: (86) 391 5066 132
Personnel:
Gen. Mgr.: Xiangwen v
Phone: (86) 391 5066 392
Sls. Mgr.: Lijiang Li
Phone: (86) 391 5066 392
Mill Locations:
Henan Qinyang Haolin Paper Co., Ltd., Qinyang Mill, No. 1 Tuntou Industry District, Qinyang, Jiaozuo 454550, China, Capacity: 36,000 mt/y, (Paperboard mill)
Phone: (86) 391 5066 392
Fax: (86) 391 5066 132

ⓜHenan Qinyang Haolin Paper Co., Ltd.
Qinyang Mill
No. 1 Tuntou Industry District, Qinyang
Jiaozuo, Henan, 454550
China
Phone: (86) 391 5066 392
Fax: (86) 391 5066 132
Personnel:
Gen. Mgr.: Xiangwen Ma
Phone: (86) 391 5066 392
Sls. Mgr.: Lijiang Li
Phone: (86) 391 5066 392
Total Employees at this Location: 250
Type of Operation: Paperboard mill
Pulp Grades and Capacities:
Total pulp capacity: 35,083 mt/y
Recycled Pulping: 35,083 mt/y
Pulp Mill Data:
Chemical Pulping Systems:
Not Given: 1
Pulp Lines: 1
Paper/Paperboard Grades and Capacities:
Total paper and paperboard capacity: 36,000 mt/y
Corrugating medium/fluting: 36,000 mt/y
Paper and Paperboard Mill Data:
Paper Machines: 1
No. 1, multi-wire, total capacity 36,000 mt/y, Trim width 3.2 m, Corrugating medium/fluting
Energy Data:
Power boilers: 1
Electrical demand for mill: 45 MWh/D

ⓜHenan Shangqiu Xinhao Paper Co., Ltd.
Shangqiu Mill
Ownership: 100% by China Haoran Investment Co., Ltd.

China

Northern City Industrial Zone
Shangqiu, Henan, 476900
China
　Phone: (86) 370 3116/177/176/230
　Fax: (86) 370 8152 777
　Web Address: www.xinhaopaper.com
Total Employees at this Location: 285
Type of Operation: Paperboard mill
Paper/Paperboard Grades and Capacities:
　Total paper and paperboard capacity: 100,000 mt/y
　Boxboard/cartonboard: 100,000 mt/y
Paper and Paperboard Mill Data:
Paper Machines: 1
No. 5, fourdrinier (3), total capacity 100,000 mt/y, Trim width 3.2 m, Boxboard/cartonboard
Coating Machines: 1
PM 5, total capacity 120,000 mt/y., on machine
Energy Data:
Power boilers
Electrical demand for mill: 148 MWh/D

ⓂHenan Shangqiu Xinrong Paper Co., Ltd.
Shangqiu (Xinrong Paper) Mill
Ownership: Henan Shangqiu Xinhao Paper Co., Ltd.
Sui County Industrial Park
Shangqiu, Henan
China
　Phone: (86) 370 3116 177/176/230
　Fax: (86) 370 8152 777
　Web Address: www.xinhaopaper.com
Type of Operation: Paper mill
Paper/Paperboard Grades and Capacities:
　Total paper and paperboard capacity: 70,000 mt/y
　Boxboard/cartonboard: 70,000 mt/y
Paper and Paperboard Mill Data:
Paper Machines: 1
No. 1, Multi-wire (5), total capacity 70,000 mt/y, Trim width 2.4 m, Boxboard/cartonboard
Energy Data:
Electrical demand for mill: 104 MWh/D

ⓂHenan Shengyuan Paper Co., Ltd.
Luoyang Mill
Mill is under construction (due to start early 2015)
Industrial Park in Gaolong Town, Yanshi City
Luoyang, Henan, 471943
China
　Phone: (86) 379 6523 3288
　Fax: (86) 379 6593 9779
　Email: lysyzy@yeah.net
　Web Address: www.hnsyzy.com.cn
Type of Operation: Paperboard mill
Paper/Paperboard Grades and Capacities:
　Total paper and paperboard capacity: 400,000 mt/y
Paper and Paperboard Mill Data:
Paper Machines: 1
No. 1, (Startup is scheduled for early 2015), total capacity 400,000 mt/y, Trim width 6.6 m, Linerboard

ⓘHenan No. 1 Sub-factory of Huixian City Paper Mill
Ownership: 100% by shareholders
Mengzhuang Town, Hui County
Xinxiang, Henan, 453621
China
　Phone: (86) 373 609 3812
　Fax: (86) 373 609 0312
Personnel:
　Mill Mgr.: Lianzhu Ma
　Phone: (86) 373 609 3812
Mill Locations:
Henan No. 1 Sub-factory of Huixian City Paper Mill, Xinxiang Mill, Mengzhuang Town, Hui County, Xinxiang 453621, China, Capacity: 23,562 mt/y, (Paper mill)
　Phone: (86) 373 609 3812
　Fax: (86) 373 609 0312

ⓂHenan No. 1 Sub-factory of Huixian City Paper Mill
Xinxiang Mill
Mengzhuang Town, Hui County
Xinxiang, Henan, 453621
China
　Phone: (86) 373 609 3812
　Fax: (86) 373 609 0312
Personnel:
　Mill Mgr.: Lianzhu Ma
　Phone: (86) 373 609 3812
Total Employees at this Location: 200
Type of Operation: Paper mill
Pulp Grades and Capacities:
　Total pulp capacity: 22,215 mt/y
　Recycled Pulping: 22,215 mt/y
Pulp Mill Data:
Pulp Lines: 2
Paper/Paperboard Grades and Capacities:
　Total paper and paperboard capacity: 23,562 mt/y
　Corrugating medium/fluting: 23,562 mt/y
Paper and Paperboard Mill Data:
Paper Machines: 2
No. 7, cylinder, total capacity 11,781 mt/y, Trim width 1.86 m, Corrugating medium/fluting
No. 8, cylinder, total capacity 11,781 mt/y, Trim width 1.86 m, Corrugating medium/fluting
Energy Data:
Power boilers: 2
Electrical demand for mill: 30 MWh/D

ⓂHenan Tengfei Paper Co., Ltd.
Xinxiang
Huojia County
Xinxiang, Henan
China
　Phone: (86) 373 4778 166
　Fax: (86) 373 4778 299
　Email: tengfeizhiye@126.com
　Web Address: www.xxtfzy.com
Type of Operation: Paper mill
Paper/Paperboard Grades and Capacities:
　Total paper and paperboard capacity: 50,000 mt/y
　Uncoated woodfree/freesheet: 50,000 mt/y
Paper and Paperboard Mill Data:
Paper Machines: 1
PM 1, total capacity 50,000 mt/y, Trim width 3.3 m, Uncoated woodfree/freesheet

ⓘHenan Tianbang Group Paper Co., Ltd.
East Erhuan Rd., Changcun Town
Huxian, Henan, 463600
China
　Phone: (86) 373 685 5118/ 5333
　Fax: (86) 373 685 5299
Personnel:
　Sls. Mgr.: Wenyi Li
　Phone: (86) 373 685 5118/ 5333
Mill Locations:
Henan Tianbang Group Paper Co., Ltd., Xinxiang Mill, East Second Ring Rd., Changcun Town, Hui County, Xinxiang 463600, China, Capacity: 130,000 mt/y, (Paper mill)
　Phone: (86) 373 685 5118/ 5333
　Fax: (86) 373 685 5299

ⓂHenan Tianbang Group Paper Co., Ltd.
Xinxiang Mill
East Second Ring Rd., Changcun Town, Hui County
Xinxiang, Henan, 463600
China
　Phone: (86) 373 685 5118/ 5333
　Fax: (86) 373 685 5299
　Web Address: www.hntbsy.cn
Personnel:
　Sls. Mgr.: Wenyi Li
　Phone: (86) 373 685 5118/ 5333
Total Employees at this Location: 325
Type of Operation: Paper mill
Paper/Paperboard Grades and Capacities:
　Total paper and paperboard capacity: 130,000 mt/y
　Uncoated woodfree/freesheet: 130,000 mt/y
Paper and Paperboard Mill Data:
Paper Machines: 2
No. 1, top former, total capacity 68,000 mt/y, Trim width 3.52 m, Uncoated woodfree/freesheet
No. 2, fourdrinier, total capacity 62,000 mt/y, Trim width 3.95 m, Uncoated woodfree/freesheet
Energy Data:
Electrical demand for mill: 258 MWh/D

ⓂHenan Weierte Chemical Fiber Co., Ltd.
Sanmenxia Mill
Ownership: Henan Haiyang Chemical Fiber Group Co., Ltd.
Lvjiaya, Xiwentang Town
Sanmenxia, Henan, 472000
China
　Phone: (86) 398 2223 219
　Web Address: www.hyfiber.com
Type of Operation: Pulp mill
Pulp Grades and Capacities:
　Total pulp capacity: 60,000 mt/y
　Pulp available for market: 60,000 mt/y

ⓂHenan Wugang Qunwang Paper Co., Ltd.
Pingdingshan Mill
Wugang
Pingdingshan, Henan, 462500
China
　Phone: (86) 375 8388 458
Type of Operation: Paper mill
Paper/Paperboard Grades and Capacities:
　Total paper and paperboard capacity: 170,000 mt/y
　Boxboard/cartonboard: 170,000 mt/y
Paper and Paperboard Mill Data:
Paper Machines: 3
No. 1, total capacity 25,000 mt/y, Trim width 1.76 m, Boxboard/cartonboard
No. 2, total capacity 25,000 mt/y, Trim width 1.76 m, Boxboard/cartonboard
No. 3, total capacity 120,000 mt/y, Trim width 3.6 m, Boxboard/cartonboard
Energy Data:
Power boilers: 3
Steam turbines: 1 at 6 MW

ⓘⓂHenan Wuzhi Guangyuan Paper Mill
Jiaozuo Mill
No. 28, Hongqi Rd., Mucheng Town, Wuzhi County
Jiaozuo, Henan, 454950
China
　Phone: (86) 391 764 5818
　Fax: (86) 391 764 5577
Personnel:
　Gen. Mgr./ Mill Mgr.: Tongzheng Xu
　Phone: (86) 391 764 0342
　Sls. Mgr.: Fuquan Song
　Phone: (86) 391 764 0342
Total Employees at this Location: 700
Type of Operation: Paper mill
Paper/Paperboard Grades and Capacities:
　Total paper and paperboard capacity: 25,000 mt/y
　Uncoated woodfree/freesheet: 25,000 mt/y
Paper and Paperboard Mill Data:
Paper Machines: 6
No. 15, cylinder, total capacity 3,000 mt/y, Trim width 1.58 m, Uncoated woodfree/freesheet
No. 16, cylinder, total capacity 3,000 mt/y, Trim width 1.58 m, Uncoated woodfree/freesheet
No. 17, cylinder, total capacity 3,000 mt/y, Trim width 1.58 m, Uncoated woodfree/freesheet
No. 18, cylinder, total capacity 3,000 mt/y, Trim width 1.58 m, Uncoated woodfree/freesheet

China

No. 19, cylinder, total capacity 3,000 mt/y, Trim width 1.58 m, Uncoated woodfree/freesheet
No. 20, fourdrinier, total capacity 10,000 mt/y, Trim width 1.76 m, Uncoated woodfree/freesheet
Finishing Equipment:
Rewinders: 8
Sheeters: 6

⑪Henan Xinxiang Hengli Paper Co., Ltd.
Ownership: 100% by private owners
Zhoubo Village, Changcun Town
Huixian, Henan, 453613
China
  Phone: (86) 373 689 7666
  Fax: (86) 373 689 8999
Mill Locations:
Henan Xinxiang Hengli Paper Co., Ltd., Huixian Mill, Zhoubo Village, Changcun Town, Huixian 453613, China, Capacity: 106,743 mt/y, (Paperboard mill)
  Phone: (86) 373 689 7666
  Fax: (86) 373 689 8999

⑪Henan Xinxiang Hengli Paper Co., Ltd.
Huixian Mill
Zhoubo Village, Changcun Town
Huixian, Henan, 453613
China
  Phone: (86) 373 689 7666
  Fax: (86) 373 689 8999
  Web Address: www.xxhengli.com
Personnel:
  Gen. Mgr.: Jianjun Guo
  Phone: (86) 373 689 7666
Total Employees at this Location: 180
Type of Operation: Paperboard mill
Pulp Grades and Capacities:
  Total pulp capacity: 104,025 mt/y
  Recycled Pulping: 104,025 mt/y
Pulp Mill Data:
  Recycled Fiber Treatment Lines:
  Recycled packaging pulping lines: 1
Paper/Paperboard Grades and Capacities:
  Total paper and paperboard capacity: 106,743 mt/y
  Corrugating medium/fluting: 106,743 mt/y
Paper and Paperboard Mill Data:
Paper Machines: 1
No. 1, twin-wire, total capacity 106,743 mt/y, Trim width 4.8 m, Corrugating medium/fluting
Energy Data:
Power boilers: 2
Combustion turbines: 1 at 12 MW
Electrical demand for mill: 163 MWh/D

⑪⑪Henan Xinxiang Hongda Paper Co., Ltd.
Xinxiang Mill
Xinyan Rd., Guzhai Town, Xinxiang County
Xinxiang, Henan, 453700
China
  Phone: (86) 373 575 0153/1153/380 0318
  Fax: (86) 373 575 0452
Personnel:
  Pres. & Gen. Mgr.: Hongjun Zhang
  Phone: (86) 373 575 0153
Total Employees at this Location: 729
Type of Operation: Paperboard mill
Pulp Grades and Capacities:
  Total pulp capacity: 73,870 mt/y
  Recycled Pulping: 73,870 mt/y
Pulp Mill Data:
Pulp Lines: 2
Paper/Paperboard Grades and Capacities:
  Total paper and paperboard capacity: 77,469 mt/y
  Corrugating medium/fluting: 77,469 mt/y
Paper and Paperboard Mill Data:
Paper Machines: 2
No. 6, cylinder, total capacity 27,489 mt/y, Trim width 3.2 m, Corrugating medium/fluting
No. 7, fourdrinier, total capacity 49,980 mt/y, Trim width 4 m, Corrugating medium/fluting
Energy Data:
Power boilers: 2
Steam turbines: 1 at 9 MW
Electrical demand for mill: 106 MWh/D

⑪Henan Xinxiang Hongtai Paper Co., Ltd.
Ownership: 100% by private owners
Hongtai Ave., Qupo Town, Xinxiang County
Xinxiang, Henan, 453700
China
  Phone: (86) 373 559 7490
  Fax: (86) 373 558 6269
  Email: ssq@chinapaper.net
  Web Address: www.hongtaizy.com
Mill Locations:
Henan Xinxiang Hongtai Paper Co., Ltd., Xinxiang Mill, Hongtai Ave., Qupo Town, Xinxiang County, Xinxiang 453700, China, Capacity: 60,000 mt/y, (Paper mill)
  Phone: (86) 373 558 4630
  Fax: (86) 373 558 6269
  Email: htzy1@126.com

⑪Henan Xinxiang Hongtai Paper Co., Ltd.
Xinxiang Mill
Hongtai Ave., Qupo Town, Xinxiang County
Xinxiang, Henan, 453700
China
  Phone: (86) 373 558 4630
  Fax: (86) 373 558 6269
  Email: htzy1@126.com
  Web Address: www.htzygroup.com
Personnel:
  Pres. & Gen. Mgr.: Shigong Shi
  Phone: (86) 373 559 7490
  Sls. Mgr.: Yaoqiang Shi
  Phone: (86) 373 559 7490
Total Employees at this Location: 1,000
Type of Operation: Paper mill
Pulp Grades and Capacities:
  Total pulp capacity: 120,000 mt/y
  Recycled Pulping: 120,000 mt/y
Pulp Mill Data:
Pulp Lines: 2
Paper/Paperboard Grades and Capacities:
  Total paper and paperboard capacity: 60,000 mt/y
  Uncoated woodfree/freesheet: 46,000 mt/y
  Uncoated mechanical/groundwood: 14,000 mt/y
Paper and Paperboard Mill Data:
Paper Machines: 12
No. 1, cylinder, total capacity 1,350 mt/y, Trim width 1.58 m, Uncoated mechanical/groundwood
No. 2, cylinder, total capacity 1,350 mt/y, Trim width 1.58 m, Uncoated mechanical/groundwood
No. 3, cylinder, total capacity 1,350 mt/y, Trim width 1.58 m, Uncoated mechanical/groundwood
No. 4, cylinder, total capacity 2,000 mt/y, Trim width 1.76 m, Uncoated mechanical/groundwood
No. 5, cylinder, total capacity 2,000 mt/y, Trim width 1.76 m, Uncoated mechanical/groundwood
No. 6, cylinder, total capacity 2,000 mt/y, Trim width 1.76 m, Uncoated mechanical/groundwood
No. 7, cylinder, total capacity 2,000 mt/y, Trim width 1.76 m, Uncoated mechanical/groundwood
No. 8, cylinder, total capacity 2,000 mt/y, Trim width 1.76 m, Uncoated mechanical/groundwood
No. 9, fourdrinier, total capacity 5,000 mt/y, Trim width 1.88 m, Uncoated woodfree/freesheet
No. 10, fourdrinier, total capacity 5,000 mt/y, Trim width 1.88 m, Uncoated woodfree/freesheet
No. 11, fourdrinier, total capacity 18,000 mt/y, Trim width 3.2 m, Uncoated woodfree/freesheet
No. 12, fourdrinier, total capacity 18,000 mt/y, Trim width 3.2 m, Uncoated woodfree/freesheet

⑪Henan Xinxiang Runyang Chemical Fiber Co., Ltd.
Xinxiang Mill
Ownership: Henan Haiyang Chemical Fiber Group Co., Ltd.
Xiaodian Industrial Park, Yanjin County
Xinxiang, Henan, 453200
China
  Phone: (86) 373 3689 708
  Web Address: www.hyfiber.com
Type of Operation: Pulp mill
Pulp Grades and Capacities:
  Total pulp capacity: 60,000 mt/y
Pulp Mill Data:
Pulp Lines: 1

⑪Henan Xinxiang Xinya Paper Group Co., Ltd.
Xinzhuang Village, Qiliying Town
Xinxiang County, Henan, 453731
China
  Phone: (86) 373 568 9017/1188
  Fax: (86) 373 568 0286
  Email: xinyapaper@163.com
  Web Address: www.xinyapaper.cn
Personnel:
  Chmn.: Jingzhi Song
  Phone: (86) 373 568 9017/1188
  Fax: (86) 373 568 0286
Total Employees of Company: 5,000
Mill Locations:
Henan Xinxiang Xinya Paper Group Co., Ltd., Xinxiang No. 1 Mill, Xinzhuang Village, Qiliying Town, Xinxiang County, Xinxiang 453731, China, Capacity: 147,441 mt/y, (Paperboard mill)
  Phone: (86) 373 568 9017/ 9166/ 0286
  Fax: (86) 373 568 0286
  Email: xinyajituan@371.net
Henan Xinxiang Xinya Paper Group Co., Ltd., Xinxiang No. 2 Mill, Xinzhuang Village, Qiliying Town, Xinxiang County, Xinxiang 453731, China, Capacity: 125,000 mt/y, (Paperboard mill)
  Phone: (86) 373 568 9017/ 9166/ 0286
  Fax: (86) 373 568 0286
Henan Xinxiang Xinya Paper Group Co., Ltd., Xinxiang No. 3 Mill, Xinzhuang Village, Qiliying Town, Xinxiang County, Xinxiang 453731, China, Capacity: 32,155 mt/y, (Paper mill)
  Phone: (86) 373 568 9017/ 9166/ 0286
  Fax: (86) 373 568 0286
  Email: xinyajituan@371.net
Henan Xinxiang Xinya Paper Group Co., Ltd., Xinxiang No. 4 Mill, Xinzhuang Village, Qiliying Town, Xinxiang County, Xinxiang 453731, China, Capacity: 78,000 mt/y, (Paperboard mill)
  Phone: (86) 373 569 7666
  Fax: (86) 373 568 0286
Henan Xinxiang Xinya Paper Group Co., Ltd., Xinxiang No. 5 Mill, Xinzhuang Village, Qiliying Town, Xinxiang County, Xinxiang 453731, China, Capacity: 28,228 mt/y, (Paper mill)
  Phone: (86) 373 568 9017/ 9166/ 0286
  Fax: (86) 373 568 0286
  Email: xinyajituan@371.net
Henan Xinxiang Xinya Paper Group Co., Ltd., Xinxiang No. 6 Mill, Xinzhuang Village, Qiliying Town, Xinxiang County, Xinxiang 453731, China, Capacity: 82,856 mt/y, (Paper mill)
  Phone: (86) 373 569 9688
  Fax: (86) 373 568 0286
Henan Xinxiang Xinya Paper Group Co., Ltd., Xinxiang Mill, Xingzhuang Village, Qiliying Town, Xinxiang County, Xinxiang 453731, China, Capacity: 200,000 mt/y, (Paperboard mill)
  Phone: (86) 373 568 1188
  Fax: (86) 373 568 0286

China

ⓂHenan Xinxiang Xinya Paper Group Co., Ltd.
Xinxiang No. 1 Mill
Xinzhuang Village, Qiliying Town, Xinxiang County
Xinxiang, Henan, 453731
China
 Phone: (86) 373 568 9017/ 9166/ 0286
 Fax: (86) 373 568 0286
 Email: xinyajituan@371.net
 Web Address: www.xinyapaper.cn
Personnel:
 Pres./Mill Mgr.: Jingzhi Song
 Phone: (86) 373 568 9017/ 9166/ 0286
 Chief Eng.: Guoqiang Wang
 Phone: (86) 373 568 9017/ 9166/ 0286
 VP - Oper.: Xixiang Li
 Phone: (86) 373 568 9017/ 9166/ 0286
Total Employees at this Location: 560
Type of Operation: Paperboard mill
Pulp Grades and Capacities:
 Total pulp capacity: 143,422 mt/y
 Recycled Pulping: 100,395 mt/y
 Other Pulp: 43,026 mt/y
Pulp Mill Data:
 Chemical Pulping Systems:
 Batch digesters
Pulp Lines: 1
 Chemical Recovery Equipment:
 Evaporator lines: 1
 Recovery boilers: 1
 Recycled Fiber Treatment Lines:
 Recycled packaging pulping lines: 1
Paper/Paperboard Grades and Capacities:
 Total paper and paperboard capacity: 147,441 mt/y
 Corrugating medium/fluting: 147,441 mt/y
Paper and Paperboard Mill Data:
Paper Machines: 7
 No. 1, fourdrinier, total capacity 33,558 mt/y, Trim width 3.2 m, Corrugating medium/fluting
 No. 2, fourdrinier, total capacity 33,558 mt/y, Trim width 3.2 m, Corrugating medium/fluting
 No. 3, cylinder, total capacity 16,065 mt/y, Trim width 3.2 m, Corrugating medium/fluting
 No. 4, cylinder, total capacity 16,065 mt/y, Trim width 3.2 m, Corrugating medium/fluting
 No. 5, cylinder, total capacity 16,065 mt/y, Trim width 3.2 m, Corrugating medium/fluting
 No. 6, cylinder, total capacity 16,065 mt/y, Trim width 3.2 m, Corrugating medium/fluting
 No. 7, cylinder, total capacity 16,065 mt/y, Trim width 3.2 m, Corrugating medium/fluting
Energy Data:
 Power boilers: 4
 Electrical demand for mill: 272 MWh/D

ⓂHenan Xinxiang Xinya Paper Group Co., Ltd.
Xinxiang No. 2 Mill
Xinzhuang Village, Qiliying Town, Xinxiang County
Xinxiang, Henan, 453731
China
 Phone: (86) 373 568 9017/ 9166/ 0286
 Fax: (86) 373 568 0286
 Web Address: www.xinyapaper.cn
Personnel:
 Exective Director: Yeqi Yan
 Phone: (86) (86) 373 568 9017
 Fax: (86) (86) 373 568 0286
Type of Operation: Paperboard mill
Pulp Grades and Capacities:
 Total pulp capacity: 38,028 mt/y
 Other Pulp: 38,028 mt/y
Pulp Mill Data:
Pulp Lines: 1
Paper/Paperboard Grades and Capacities:
 Total paper and paperboard capacity: 125,000 mt/y
 Uncoated woodfree/freesheet: 75,000 mt/y
 Boxboard/cartonboard: 50,000 mt/y

Paper and Paperboard Mill Data:
Paper Machines: 3
 No. 1, fourdrinier, total capacity 20,000 mt/y, Trim width 3.15 m, Uncoated woodfree/freesheet
 No. 2, fourdrinier, total capacity 55,000 mt/y, Trim width 3.52 m, Uncoated woodfree/freesheet
 No. 3, Multi-wire (3), total capacity 50,000 mt/y, Trim width 3.2 m, Boxboard/cartonboard
Energy Data:
 Electrical demand for mill: 275 MWh/D

ⓂHenan Xinxiang Xinya Paper Group Co., Ltd.
Xinxiang No. 3 Mill
Xinzhuang Village, Qiliying Town, Xinxiang County
Xinxiang, Henan, 453731
China
 Phone: (86) 373 568 9017/ 9166/ 0286
 Fax: (86) 373 568 0286
 Email: xinyajituan@371.net
 Web Address: www.xinyapaper.cn
Personnel:
 Pres. & Gen. Mgr.: Jingzhi Song
 Phone: (86) 373 568 9017/ 9166/ 0286
Total Employees at this Location: 600
Type of Operation: Paper mill
Pulp Grades and Capacities:
 Total pulp capacity: 40,000 mt/y
Pulp Mill Data:
Pulp Lines: 1
Paper/Paperboard Grades and Capacities:
 Total paper and paperboard capacity: 32,155 mt/y
 Uncoated woodfree/freesheet: 26,800 mt/y
 Tissue: 5,355 mt/y
Paper and Paperboard Mill Data:
Paper Machines: 6
 No. 1, fourdrinier, total capacity 6,700 mt/y, Trim width 1.88 m, Uncoated woodfree/freesheet
 No. 2, fourdrinier, total capacity 6,700 mt/y, Trim width 1.88 m, Uncoated woodfree/freesheet
 No. 3, fourdrinier, total capacity 6,700 mt/y, Trim width 1.88 m, Uncoated woodfree/freesheet
 No. 4, fourdrinier, total capacity 6,700 mt/y, Trim width 1.88 m, Uncoated woodfree/freesheet
 No. 5, cylinder, total capacity 5,355 mt/y, Trim width 2.9 m, Tissue
 No. 6, cylinder, total capacity 5,355 mt/y, Trim width 2.9 m, Tissue

ⓂHenan Xinxiang Xinya Paper Group Co., Ltd.
Xinxiang No. 4 Mill
Xinzhuang Village, Qiliying Town, Xinxiang County
Xinxiang, Henan, 453731
China
 Phone: (86) 373 569 7666
 Fax: (86) 373 568 0286
 Web Address: www.xinyapaper.cn
Personnel:
 Exective Director: Yeqi Yan
 Phone: (86) (86) 373 568 9017
 Fax: (86) (86) 373 568 0286
Total Employees at this Location: 400
Type of Operation: Paperboard mill
Pulp Grades and Capacities:
 Total pulp capacity: 76,625 mt/y
 Recycled Pulping: 37,879 mt/y
 Other Pulp: 38,746 mt/y
Pulp Mill Data:
 Chemical Pulping Systems:
 Continuous digesters: 1
 Bleach Plant Systems: 1
 Chemical Pulping System, Type: straw - 4 stages
 Chemical Recovery Equipment:
 Evaporator lines: 1
 Recovery boilers: 1
 Recycled Fiber Treatment Lines:
 Recycled packaging pulping lines: 1
Paper/Paperboard Grades and Capacities:

 Total paper and paperboard capacity: 78,000 mt/y Tissue
 Corrugating medium/fluting: 78,000 mt/y
Paper and Paperboard Mill Data:
Paper Machines: 10
 No. 1, cylinder, total capacity 19,000 mt/y, Trim width 3.2 m, Corrugating medium/fluting
 No. 2, cylinder, total capacity 19,000 mt/y, Trim width 3.2 m, Corrugating medium/fluting
 No. 3, cylinder, total capacity 20,000 mt/y, Trim width 3.2 m, Corrugating medium/fluting
 No. 4, cylinder, total capacity 20,000 mt/y, Trim width 3.2 m, Corrugating medium/fluting
 No. 5, cylinder, total capacity 2,680 mt/y, Trim width 2.9 m, Tissue
 No. 6, cylinder, total capacity 2,680 mt/y, Trim width 2.9 m, Tissue
 No. 7, cylinder, total capacity 2,680 mt/y, Trim width 2.9 m, Tissue
 No. 8, cylinder, total capacity 2,680 mt/y, Trim width 2.9 m, Tissue
 No. 9, cylinder, total capacity 2,680 mt/y, Trim width 2.9 m, Tissue
 No. 10, cylinder, total capacity 2,680 mt/y, Trim width 2.9 m, Tissue
Energy Data:
 Power boilers: 4
 Steam turbines at 75 MW
 Electrical demand for mill: 120 MWh/D

ⓂHenan Xinxiang Xinya Paper Group Co., Ltd.
Xinxiang No. 5 Mill
Xinzhuang Village, Qiliying Town, Xinxiang County
Xinxiang, Henan, 453731
China
 Phone: (86) 373 568 9017/ 9166/ 0286
 Fax: (86) 373 568 0286
 Email: xinyajituan@371.net
 Web Address: www.xinyapaper.cn
Personnel:
 Pres. & Gen. Mgr.: Jingzhi Song
 Phone: (86) 373 568 9017/ 9166/ 0286
Total Employees at this Location: 610
Type of Operation: Paper mill
Pulp Grades and Capacities:
 Total pulp capacity: 40,000 mt/y
Pulp Mill Data:
Pulp Lines: 1
Paper/Paperboard Grades and Capacities:
 Total paper and paperboard capacity: 28,228 mt/y
 Uncoated woodfree/freesheet: 26,800 mt/y
 Tissue: 1,428 mt/y
Paper and Paperboard Mill Data:
Paper Machines: 5
 No. 1, fourdrinier, total capacity 6,700 mt/y, Trim width 1.88 m, Uncoated woodfree/freesheet
 No. 2, fourdrinier, total capacity 6,700 mt/y, Trim width 1.88 m, Uncoated woodfree/freesheet
 No. 3, fourdrinier, total capacity 6,700 mt/y, Trim width 1.88 m, Uncoated woodfree/freesheet
 No. 4, fourdrinier, total capacity 6,700 mt/y, Trim width 1.88 m, Uncoated woodfree/freesheet
 No. 5, total capacity 1,500 mt/y, Trim width 1.58 m, Tissue

ⓂHenan Xinxiang Xinya Paper Group Co., Ltd.
Xinxiang No. 6 Mill
Xinzhuang Village, Qiliying Town, Xinxiang County
Xinxiang, Henan, 453731
China
 Phone: (86) 373 569 9688
 Fax: (86) 373 568 0286
 Web Address: www.xinyapaper.cn
Personnel:
 Exective Director: Yeqi Yan
 Phone: (86) (86) 373 568 9017
 Fax: (86) (86) 373 568 0286
Total Employees at this Location: 500

Type of Operation: Paper mill
Pulp Grades and Capacities:
Total pulp capacity: 45,678 mt/y
Other Pulp: 45,678 mt/y
Pulp Mill Data:
Chemical Pulping Systems:
Continuous digesters
Pulp Lines: 1
Bleach Plant Systems: 1
No. 1, Type: 4-stage
Chemical Recovery Equipment:
Evaporator lines
Recovery boilers
Paper/Paperboard Grades and Capacities:
Total paper and paperboard capacity: 82,856 mt/y
Uncoated woodfree/freesheet: 80,000 mt/y
Tissue: 2,856 mt/y
Paper and Paperboard Mill Data:
Paper Machines: 4
No. 1, top former, total capacity 40,000 mt/y, Trim width 2.64 m, Uncoated woodfree/freesheet
No. 2, top former, total capacity 40,000 mt/y, Trim width 2.64 m, Uncoated woodfree/freesheet
No. 3, total capacity 1,428 mt/y, Trim width 1.58 m, Tissue
No. 4, total capacity 1,428 mt/y, Tissue
Energy Data:
Power boilers: 3
Steam turbines: 3 at 30, 30, 15 MW
Electrical demand for mill: 219 MWh/D

ⓜHenan Xinxiang Xinya Paper Group Co., Ltd.
Xinxiang Mill
Xingzhuang Village, Qiliying Town, Xinxiang County
Xinxiang, Henan, 453731
China
Phone: (86) 373 568 1188
Fax: (86) 373 568 0286
Web Address: www.xinyapaper.cn
Personnel:
Chmn.: Jingzhi Song
Phone: (86) 373 568 1188
Total Employees at this Location: 500
Type of Operation: Paperboard mill
Pulp Grades and Capacities:
Total pulp capacity: 95,745 mt/y
Mechanical Pulp: 95,745 mt/y
Pulp Mill Data:
Mechanical Pulping Systems:
Conventional grinders: 1
Pulp Lines: 1
Bleach Plant Lines:
APMP Mechanical pulp system bleaching, Sequence: P
Chemical Recovery Equipment:
Evaporator lines
Recovery boilers: 1
Paper/Paperboard Grades and Capacities:
Total paper and paperboard capacity: 200,000 mt/y
Boxboard/cartonboard: 200,000 mt/y
Paper and Paperboard Mill Data:
Paper Machines: 1
No. 1, fourdrinier (3), total capacity 200,000 mt/y, Trim width 4.26 m, Boxboard/cartonboard
Coating Machines: 1
PM 1, total capacity 206,000 mt/y., on machine
Energy Data:
Power boilers: 2
TMP Reboiler: 1
Steam turbines: 2 at 12, 25 MW
Electrical demand for mill: 747 MWh/D

ⓜHenan Xuchang Feida Paper Co., Ltd.
Xuchang Mill
Ownership: Henan Feida Group
Hejie Industry Park
Xuchang, Henan, 461000
China
Phone: (86) 374 566 8188
Fax: (86) 374 566 8888
Web Address: www.fdgroup.com.cn
Personnel:
Chmn. & Pres.: Zhijie Xu
Phone: (86) 374 566 8188
Sls. Mgr.: Huaijiang Chang
Phone: (86) 374 566 8188
Total Employees at this Location: 400
Type of Operation: Paper mill, Paperboard mill
Pulp Grades and Capacities:
Total pulp capacity: 201,025 mt/y
Recycled Pulping: 201,025 mt/y
Pulp Mill Data:
Bleach Plant Systems: 1
DIP
Recycled Fiber Treatment Lines:
Flotation deinking lines: 1
Recycled packaging pulping lines: 1
Paper/Paperboard Grades and Capacities:
Total paper and paperboard capacity: 202,000 mt/y
Linerboard: 166,000 mt/y
Corrugating medium/fluting: 36,000 mt/y
Paper and Paperboard Mill Data:
Paper Machines: 3
No. 1, fourdrinier, total capacity 36,000 mt/y, Trim width 3.6 m, Corrugating medium/fluting
No. 2, Multi-wire (2), total capacity 66,000 mt/y, Trim width 3.8 m, Linerboard
No. 3, Multi-wire (4), total capacity 100,000 mt/y, Trim width 4 m, Linerboard
Coating Machines: 1
PM3, on machine
Energy Data:
Power boilers
Electrical demand for mill: 300 MWh/D

ⓜHenan Yilin Paper Co., Ltd.
Ownership: 100% by private owners
No. 5 Gongnong Rd.
Xuchang, Henan, 461000
China
Phone: (86) 374 3126 868/ 5736 367
Fax: (86) 374 312 6868
Email: hnyl126@163.com
Web Address: www.hnyilin.com
Total Employees at this Location: 600
Mill Locations:
Henan Yilin Paper Co., Ltd., Xuchang Mill, No. 5 Gongnong Rd., Xuchang 461000, China, Capacity: 179,944 mt/y, (Paper mill)
Phone: (86) 374 3126 868/ 5736 367
Fax: (86) 374 3126 868
Email: hnyl126@163.com

ⓜHenan Yilin Paper Co., Ltd.
Xuchang Mill
No. 5 Gongnong Rd.
Xuchang, Henan, 461000
China
Phone: (86) 374 3126 868/ 5736 367
Fax: (86) 374 3126 868
Email: hnyl126@163.com
Personnel:
Chmn. & Pres.: Jinggang Li
Phone: (86) 374 331 0384/ 312 6876
Total Employees at this Location: 600
Type of Operation: Paper mill
Pulp Grades and Capacities:
Total pulp capacity: 54,382 mt/y
Chemical Pulp: 27,191 mt/y
Other Pulp: 27,191 mt/y
Pulp Mill Data:
Chemical Pulping Systems:
Batch digesters
Continuous digesters
Pulp Lines: 2
Bleach Plant Systems: 2
No. 1, Type: hardwood, Sequence: CEH
No. 2, Type: nonwood, Sequence: CEH
Chemical Recovery Equipment:
Evaporator lines
Recovery boilers: 2
Paper/Paperboard Grades and Capacities:
Total paper and paperboard capacity: 179,944 mt/y
Uncoated woodfree/freesheet: 179,944 mt/y
Paper and Paperboard Mill Data:
Paper Machines: 6
No. 1, fourdrinier, total capacity 19,992 mt/y, Trim width 1.88 m, Uncoated woodfree/freesheet
No. 3, fourdrinier, total capacity 15,000 mt/y, Trim width 1.76 m, Uncoated woodfree/freesheet
No. 6, fourdrinier, total capacity 25,000 mt/y, Trim width 2.73 m, Uncoated woodfree/freesheet
No. 8, fourdrinier, total capacity 9,996 mt/y, Trim width 2.73 m, Uncoated woodfree/freesheet
No. 9, fourdrinier, total capacity 9,996 mt/y, Trim width 2.73 m, Uncoated woodfree/freesheet
No. 10, fourdrinier, total capacity 99,960 mt/y, Trim width 3.75 m, Uncoated woodfree/freesheet
Energy Data:
Power boilers: 6
Steam turbines: 2 at 12 MW
Electrical demand for mill: 416 MWh/D

ⓜHenan Yingbo Paper Co., Ltd.
Ownership: 100% by private owners
Xiangzi Industry Park, East Huanghe Ave.
Mengzhou, Henan, 454750
China
Phone: (86) 391 386 9999
Fax: (86) 391 819 3000
Mill Locations:
Henan Yingbo Paper Co., Ltd., Mengzhou Mill, Xiangzi Industry Park, East Huanghe Ave., Mengzhou 454750, China, Capacity: 15,000 mt/y, (Paper mill)
Phone: (86) 391 386 9999
Fax: (86) 391 819 3000

ⓜHenan Yingbo Paper Co., Ltd.
Mengzhou Mill
Xiangzi Industry Park, East Huanghe Ave.
Mengzhou, Henan, 454750
China
Phone: (86) 391 386 9999
Fax: (86) 391 819 3000
Personnel:
Chmn. & Pres.: Guanghui Liu
Phone: (86) 391 386 9999
Gen. Mgr.: Xiangmin Zhang
Phone: (86) 391 386 9999
Type of Operation: Paper mill
Pulp Grades and Capacities:
Total pulp capacity: 15,000 mt/y
Recycled Pulping: 15,000 mt/y
Pulp Mill Data:
Pulp Lines: 1
Recycled Fiber Treatment Lines:
Flotation deinking lines: 1 at 15,000 admt/y
Paper/Paperboard Grades and Capacities:
Total paper and paperboard capacity: 15,000 mt/y
Newsprint: 15,000 mt/y
Paper and Paperboard Mill Data:
Paper Machines: 1
PM 1, fourdrinier, total capacity 15,000 mt/y, Trim width 2.36 m, Newsprint
Energy Data:
Power boilers: 1

ⓞⓜHenan Yinge Industrial Investment Co. Ltd.
Luohe (Yinge Industrial Investment) Mill
Mill is closed (in Sep. 2014)
Ownership: 100% by shareholders
No. 95, Renmin Donglu
Luohe, Henan, 46200
China
Phone: (86) 395 235 5680/5681

China

Fax: (86) 395 235 5117
Web Address: www.yinge.com.cn
Personnel:
 Chmn.: Lianggang Jia
 Phone: (86) 395 235 5680
 Fax: (86) 395 235 5117
 Vice Chmn., Vice Gen. Mgr.: Shijin Zhang
 Phone: (86) 395 235 5680
 Fax: (86) 395 235 5117
 Vice Chmn.: Jichao Wang
 Phone: (86) 395 235 5680
 Fax: (86) 395 235 5117
 Gen. Mgr.: Wenpu Zhou
 Phone: (86) 395 235 5680
 Fax: (86) 395 235 5117
 Dpty. Gen. Mgr.: Hui Dong
 Phone: (86) 395 235 5680
 Fax: (86) 395 235 5117
 CFO: Yingkuo Geng
 Phone: (86) 395 235 5680
 Fax: (86) 395 235 5117
Total Employees of Company: 5,682
Total Employees at this Location: 4,773
Type of Operation: Pulp mill, Paper mill
Mill Locations:
 Henan Luohe Yinge Tissue Paper Industry Co., Ltd., Luohe (Yinge Tissue) Mill (99.75% owned), No. 2 East Xiangjiang Rd., Luohe 462000, China, Capacity: 160,000 mt/y, (Paper mill)
 Phone: (86) 395 266 8315/ 263 5700/5531
 Fax: (86) 395 268 7700
 Email: zsb555@126.com
 Henan Yinge Packaging Paper Industry Co., Ltd., Luohe (Yinge Packaging Paper) Mill, Renmin Rd., & Donghuan Rd., Luohe 462000, China, Capacity: 360,000 mt/y, (Paperboard mill)
 Phone: (86) 395 235 5638/ 5639
 Fax: (86) 395 235 5139
 Sichuan Yinge Bamboo Pulp & Paper Co., Ltd., Luzhou (Sichuan Yinge) Mill (40% owned), Shuangqiao, Quba Town, Naxi District, Luzhou 646300, China, Capacity: 66,000 mt/y, (Paper mill)
 Phone: (86) 830 439 0999/0192/0555
 Fax: (86) 830 439 0777
Pulp Grades and Capacities:
 Total pulp capacity: 129,940 mt/y
 Other Pulp: 129,940 mt/y
Pulp Mill Data:
 Chemical Pulping Systems:
 Continuous digesters: 2
 Pulp Lines: 3
 Chemical Recovery Equipment:
 Evaporator lines
 Recovery boilers: 2
 Recycled Fiber Treatment Lines:
 Recycled packaging pulping lines: 1
Paper/Paperboard Grades and Capacities:
 Total paper and paperboard capacity: 219,900 mt/y
 Uncoated woodfree/freesheet: 219,900 mt/y
Paper and Paperboard Mill Data:
 Paper Machines: 18
 No. 1, fourdrinier, total capacity 12,000 mt/y, Trim width 1.76 m, Uncoated woodfree/freesheet
 No. 2, fourdrinier, total capacity 12,000 mt/y, Trim width 1.76 m, Uncoated woodfree/freesheet
 No. 3, fourdrinier, total capacity 8,000 mt/y, Trim width 1.76 m, Uncoated woodfree/freesheet
 No. 4, fourdrinier, total capacity 15,000 mt/y, Trim width 3.6 m, Uncoated woodfree/freesheet
 No. 5, fourdrinier, total capacity 15,000 mt/y, Trim width 3.6 m, Uncoated woodfree/freesheet
 No. 6, fourdrinier, total capacity 15,000 mt/y, Trim width 3.6 m, Uncoated woodfree/freesheet
 No. 7, fourdrinier, total capacity 8,300 mt/y, Trim width 1.76 m, Uncoated woodfree/freesheet
 No. 8, fourdrinier, total capacity 8,300 mt/y, Trim width 1.76 m, Uncoated woodfree/freesheet
 No. 9, fourdrinier, total capacity 8,300 mt/y, Trim width 1.76 m, Uncoated woodfree/freesheet
 No. 10, fourdrinier, total capacity 25,000 mt/y, Trim width 2.64 m, Uncoated woodfree/freesheet
 No. 11, fourdrinier, total capacity 25,000 mt/y, Trim width 2.64 m, Uncoated woodfree/freesheet
 No. 12, fourdrinier, total capacity 8,250 mt/y, Trim width 1.76 m, Uncoated woodfree/freesheet
 No. 13, fourdrinier, total capacity 8,250 mt/y, Trim width 1.76 m, Uncoated woodfree/freesheet
 No. 14, fourdrinier, total capacity 8,250 mt/y, Trim width 1.76 m, Uncoated woodfree/freesheet
 No. 15, fourdrinier, total capacity 8,250 mt/y, Trim width 1.76 m, Uncoated woodfree/freesheet
 No. 16, fourdrinier, total capacity 19,000 mt/y, Trim width 3.6 m, Uncoated woodfree/freesheet
 No. 17, fourdrinier, total capacity 8,000 mt/y, Trim width 1.88 m, Uncoated woodfree/freesheet
 No. 18, fourdrinier, total capacity 8,000 mt/y, Trim width 1.88 m, Uncoated woodfree/freesheet
Energy Data:
 Power boilers: 4
 Steam turbines at 22 MW
 Electrical demand for mill: 628 MWh/D

⑩Henan Yinge Packaging Paper Industry Co., Ltd.
Luohe (Yinge Packaging Paper) Mill
Ownership: 100% by Henan Yinge Industrial Investment Co. Ltd.
Renmin Rd., & Donghuan Rd.
Luohe, Henan, 462000
China
 Phone: (86) 395 235 5638/ 5639
 Fax: (86) 395 235 5139
 Web Address: www.yinge.com.cn
Personnel:
 Chmn.: Wei Wang
 Phone: (86) 395 235 5638/ 5639
Total Employees at this Location: 500
Type of Operation: Paperboard mill
Pulp Grades and Capacities:
 Total pulp capacity: 357,123 mt/y
 Recycled Pulping: 357,123 mt/y
Pulp Mill Data:
 Recycled Fiber Treatment Lines:
 Recycled packaging pulping lines: 2 at 400,000 admt/y
Paper/Paperboard Grades and Capacities:
 Total paper and paperboard capacity: 360,000 mt/y
 Linerboard: 360,000 mt/y
Paper and Paperboard Mill Data:
 Paper Machines: 2
 No. 20, Multi-wire (3), total capacity 160,000 mt/y, Trim width 4.4 m, Linerboard
 No. 21, Multi-wire (3), total capacity 200,000 mt/y, Trim width 4.8 m, Linerboard
Energy Data:
 Electrical demand for mill: 450 MWh/D

⑩Henan Yuzhou Shengxuan Paper Co., Ltd.
Ownership: 100% by private owners
No. 1 Shengxuan Rd., Economic & Development Zone
Liangbei Town, Yuzhou, Henan, 461600
China
 Phone: (86) 374 888 5999/5006
 Fax: (86) 374 888 5666
 Email: sxpapercto@163.com,
 xinsui0374@163.com
 Web Address: www.papercto.com
Mill Locations:
 Henan Yuzhou Shengxuan Paper Co., Ltd., Yuzhou Mill, No. 1 Shengxuan Rd., Economic & Development Zone, Liangbei Town, Yuzhou 461600, China, Capacity: 30,000 mt/y, (Paper mill)
 Phone: (86) 374 888 5999/5006
 Fax: (86) 374 888 5666
 Email: sxpapercto@163.com, xinsui0374@163.com

⑩Henan Yuzhou Shengxuan Paper Co., Ltd.
Yuzhou Mill
No. 1 Shengxuan Rd., Economic & Development Zone, Liangbei Town
Yuzhou, Henan, 461600
China
 Phone: (86) 374 888 5999/5006
 Fax: (86) 374 888 5666
 Email: sxpapercto@163.com,
 xinsui0374@163.com
 Web Address: www.papercto.com
Personnel:
 Sls. Mgr.: Haofei Wang
 Phone: (86) 374 888 5333
Total Employees at this Location: 380
Type of Operation: Paper mill
Paper/Paperboard Grades and Capacities:
 Total paper and paperboard capacity: 30,000 mt/y
 Tissue: 30,000 mt/y
Paper and Paperboard Mill Data:
 Paper Machines: 20
 PM 1-10, cylinder, total capacity 1,500 mt/y, Trim width 2.1 m, Tissue
 PM 11-20, total capacity 15,000 mt/y, Trim width 2.1 m, Tissue

⑩Henan Zhengzhou Dongsheng Paper Co., Ltd.
Ownership: 100% by private owners
East Qingnian Rd.
Zhengzhou, Henan, 451450
China
 Phone: (86) 371 6218 4772
 Fax: (86) 371 6218 4772
Mill Locations:
 Henan Zhengzhou Dongsheng Paper Co., Ltd., Zhengzhou Mill, East Qingnian Rd., Zhengzhou 451450, China, Capacity: 16,800 mt/y, (Paperboard mill)
 Phone: (86) 371 6218 4772
 Fax: (86) 371 6218 4772

⑩Henan Zhengzhou Dongsheng Paper Co., Ltd.
Zhengzhou Mill
East Qingnian Rd.
Zhengzhou, Henan, 451450
China
 Phone: (86) 371 6218 4772
 Fax: (86) 371 6218 4772
Personnel:
 Gen. Mgr.: Yunlai Zhu
 Phone: (86) 371 6218 4772
Total Employees at this Location: 340
Type of Operation: Paperboard mill
Pulp Grades and Capacities:
 Total pulp capacity: 15,000 mt/y
 Recycled Pulping: 15,000 mt/y
Pulp Mill Data:
 Pulp Lines: 2
 Recycled Fiber Treatment Lines:
 Flotation deinking lines: 2 at 15,000 admt/y
Paper/Paperboard Grades and Capacities:
 Total paper and paperboard capacity: 16,800 mt/y
 Tissue: 16,800 mt/y
Paper and Paperboard Mill Data:
 Paper Machines: 8
 PM 1-4, cylinder, total capacity 1,800 mt/y, Trim width 1.58 m, Tissue
 PM 5-8, cylinder, total capacity 2,400 mt/y, Trim width 2.1 m, Tissue
 Finishing Equipment:
 Winders: 8 at 20,000 mt/y
Energy Data:
 Power boilers: 1

China

ⓂHenan Zhumadian City Baiyun Paper Co., Ltd.
Zhumadian (Zhumadian Baiyun) Mill
Ownership: Henan Dahe Paper Co., Ltd.
North Worker Rd., Suiping County
Zhumadian, Henan, 463100
China
  Phone: (86) 396 490 2206/2211/2218
  Fax: (86) 396 491 4805/490 2299/2211/2251
  Email: byzy@dahepaper.com
  Web Address: www.baiyunpaper.com
Personnel:
  Chmn.: Haiquan Guo
  Phone: (86) 396 490 2206/2211/2218
  Gen. Mgr.: Gen Wang
  Phone: (86) 183 3961 9999
  CFO: Yingwei Qiao
  Phone: (86) 396 490 2206/2211/2218
  Asst. Mill Mgr.: Xiangtai Wang
  Phone: (86) 396 490 2206/2211/2218
  Sls. Mgr.: Haixiang Zhu
  Phone: (86) 396 490 2206/2211/2218
  Purch. Agent: Huaiwei Li
  Phone: (86) 396 490 2206/2211/2218
  Tech. Dir./Chief Eng.: Haiquan Guo
  Phone: (86) 396 490 2206/2211/2218
  Prod. Mgr.: Jianlun Yu
Total Employees at this Location: 1,000
Type of Operation: Pulp mill, Paper mill
Pulp Grades and Capacities:
  Total pulp capacity: 49,883 mt/y
  Other Pulp: 49,883 mt/y
Pulp Mill Data:
  Chemical Pulping Systems:
  Continuous digesters: 1
  Not Given: 1
Pulp Lines: 2
  Bleach Plant Systems: 2
  No. 1, Sequence: CEpH, Capacity 100,000 admt/y
  Chemical Recovery Equipment:
  Evaporator lines
  Recovery boilers: 1
  Recovery boilers: 1
Paper/Paperboard Grades and Capacities:
  Total paper and paperboard capacity: 294,000 mt/y
  Uncoated woodfree/freesheet: 294,000 mt/y
Paper and Paperboard Mill Data:
  Stock Preparation:
  Refiners: 5
Paper Machines: 6
  No. 1, fourdrinier, total capacity 35,000 mt/y, Trim width 2.64 m, Uncoated woodfree/freesheet
  No. 5, total capacity 13,500 mt/y, Trim width 2.64 m, Uncoated woodfree/freesheet
  No. 6, total capacity 13,500 mt/y, Trim width 2.64 m, Uncoated woodfree/freesheet
  No. 7, total capacity 13,500 mt/y, Trim width 2.64 m, Uncoated woodfree/freesheet
  No. 8, DuoFormer D, total capacity 13,500 mt/y, Trim width 2.64 m, Uncoated woodfree/freesheet
  No. 9, DuoFormer D, total capacity 205,000 mt/y, Trim width 5.28 m, Uncoated woodfree/freesheet
Finishing Equipment:
  Rewinders: 1
  Sheeters: 1
Energy Data:
  Power boilers: 3
  Steam turbines: 3 at 20, 3 MW
  Electrical demand for mill: 652 MWh/D

HUBEI

ⓂC&S Paper Co., Ltd.
Xiaogan Mill
No. 8 Xiaowu Ave., Xiaonan Economic Development Zone
Xiaogan, Hubei, 431200
China
  Phone: (86) 712 2515 512/507
  Fax: (86) 712 2515 508
  Web Address: www.zhongshungroup.com
Personnel:
  Gen. Mgr.: Ruiwen Zhen
  Phone: (86) 712 2515 512/507
Total Employees at this Location: 140
Type of Operation: Paper mill
Paper/Paperboard Grades and Capacities:
  Total paper and paperboard capacity: 22,500 mt/y
  Tissue: 22,500 mt/y
Paper and Paperboard Mill Data:
Paper Machines: 2
  No. 1, BF-10, Yankee dryer, total capacity 10,000 mt/y, Trim width 2.66 m, Tissue, Uncoated woodfree/freesheet
  No. 2, BF-10 EX, Yankee dryer, total capacity 12,500 mt/y, Trim width 2.66 m, Tissue, Uncoated woodfree/freesheet
Energy Data:
  Power boilers: 1
  Electrical demand for mill: 32 MWh/D

ⓂGold Hongye Paper (Hubei)
Xiaogan (Gold Hongye Paper) Mill
Ownership: Asia Pulp & Paper (APP)
No. 468 Xiaowu Ave., Xiaonan Economic Development Zone
Xiaogan, Hubei
China
Total Employees at this Location: 275
Type of Operation: Paper mill
Paper/Paperboard Grades and Capacities:
  Total paper and paperboard capacity: 120,095 mt/y
  Tissue: 120,095 mt/y
Paper and Paperboard Mill Data:
Paper Machines: 2
  No. 1, crescent former, total capacity 59,976 mt/y, Trim width 5.6 m, Tissue
  No. 2, crescent former, total capacity 60,119 mt/y, Trim width 5.6 m, Tissue, Uncoated woodfree/freesheet
Energy Data:
  Power boilers
  Steam turbines: 1
  Electrical demand for mill: 398 MWh/D

ⓗHubei Baoli Paper Co., Ltd.
Donghai Village, Maochen Town, Xiaonan District
Xiaogan, Hubei, 432100
China
Mill Locations:
  Hubei Baoli Paper Co., Ltd., Xiaogan Mill, Donghai Village, Maochen Town, Xiaonan District, Xiaogan 432100, China, Capacity: 120,000 mt/y, (Paper mill)

ⓂHubei Baoli Paper Co., Ltd.
Xiaogan Mill
Donghai Village, Maochen Town, Xiaonan District
Xiaogan, Hubei, 432100
China
Total Employees at this Location: 300
Type of Operation: Paper mill
Pulp Grades and Capacities:
  Total pulp capacity: 116,518 mt/y
  Recycled Pulping: 116,518 mt/y
Paper/Paperboard Grades and Capacities:
  Total paper and paperboard capacity: 120,000 mt/y
  Corrugating medium/fluting: 120,000 mt/y
Paper and Paperboard Mill Data:
Paper Machines: 1
  No. 1, twin-wire, total capacity 120,000 mt/y, Trim width 4.6 m, Corrugating medium/fluting
Energy Data:
  Power boilers: 1
  Steam turbines: 1 at 3 MW
  Electrical demand for mill: 147 MWh/D

ⓂHubei Chibi Chenli Paper Co., Ltd.
Chibi Mill
Ownership: 49% by Profit Pool Holdings, 51% by Guangdong Huashen Investment
No. 228 Chunchuan Av.
Chibi, Hubei, 437300
China
  Phone: (86) 715 526 9618
  Fax: (86) 715 526 9604
Total Employees at this Location: 1,000
Type of Operation: Paper mill
Pulp Grades and Capacities:
  Total pulp capacity: 61,181 mt/y
  Mechanical Pulp: 10,614 mt/y
  Other Pulp: 50,567 mt/y
Pulp Mill Data:
Pulp Lines: 2
  Bleach Plant Lines:
  No. 1, Sequence: CEH
  Chemical Recovery Equipment:
  Recovery boilers: 1
Paper/Paperboard Grades and Capacities:
  Total paper and paperboard capacity: 100,710 mt/y
  Uncoated woodfree/freesheet: 90,000 mt/y
  Uncoated mechanical/groundwood: 10,710 mt/y
Paper and Paperboard Mill Data:
Paper Machines: 4
  No. 1, SymFormer MB, total capacity 6,000 mt/y, Trim width 1.58 m, Uncoated woodfree/freesheet
  No. 2, fourdrinier, total capacity 40,000 mt/y, Trim width 2.4 m, Uncoated woodfree/freesheet
  No. 3, hybrid former, total capacity 44,000 mt/y, Trim width 2.64 m, Uncoated woodfree/freesheet
  No. 4, fourdrinier, total capacity 10,710 mt/y, Trim width 1.76 m, Uncoated mechanical/groundwood
Finishing Equipment:
  Rewinders: 2
  Sheeters: 2
Energy Data:
  Power boilers: 3
  Steam turbines: 2 at 3, 6 MW
  Electrical demand for mill: 302 MWh/D

ⓗHubei Enshi Jinhua Group
No. 30, Chengxiang Rd.
Enshi, Hubei, 445000
China
  Phone: (86) 718 820 0569/0925
  Fax: (86) 718 820 0924
  Email: jhzy@cntmi.com
Personnel:
  Chmn.: Ximing Jiang
  Phone: (86) 718 820 0569/0925
  Fax: (86) 718 820 0924
Mill Locations:
  Hubei Enshi Jinhua Group, Enshi Mill, No. 30, Bagong Rd., Enshi 445000, China, Capacity: 5,000 mt/y, (Paper mill)
  Phone: (86) 718 820 0569
  Fax: (86) 718 820 0924
  Email: 4554541182@qq.com

ⓂHubei Enshi Jinhua Group
Enshi Mill
No. 30, Bagong Rd.
Enshi, Hubei, 445000
China
  Phone: (86) 718 820 0569
  Fax: (86) 718 820 0924
  Email: 4554541182@qq.com
  Web Address: www.esjinhua.com
Personnel:
  Chmn.: Ximing Jiang
  Phone: (86) 718 820 0925
  Gen. Mgr.: Jing Yue
  Phone: (86) 718 820 0925
Total Employees at this Location: 178
Type of Operation: Paper mill
Paper/Paperboard Grades and Capacities:

China

Total paper and paperboard capacity: 5,000 mt/y
Tissue: 3,000 mt/y
Specialty and industrial: 2,000 mt/y
Paper and Paperboard Mill Data:
Paper Machines: 3
PM 1, fourdrinier, total capacity 2,000 mt/y, Trim width 1.88 m, Specialty and industrial
PM 2, cylinder, total capacity 900 mt/y, Trim width 1.09 m, Tissue
PM 3, fourdrinier, total capacity 2,100 mt/y, Trim width 2.7 m, Tissue
Energy Data:
Power boilers: 1

ⓜHubei Hengfeng Paper Co., Ltd.
Xianning Mill
Ownership: 65.32% by Heilongjiang Mudanjiang Hengfeng Paper Group Co., Ltd.
Mabai Rd., Xian'an District
Xianning, Hubei
China
Type of Operation: Paper mill
Paper/Paperboard Grades and Capacities:
Total paper and paperboard capacity: 6,000 mt/y
Specialty and industrial: 6,000 mt/y
Paper and Paperboard Mill Data:
Paper Machines: 2
PM 1, fourdrinier, total capacity 4,500 mt/y, Trim width 2.16 m, Specialty and industrial
PM 2, fourdrinier, total capacity 1,500 mt/y, Trim width 1.88 m, Specialty and industrial

ⓗⓜHubei Hongfa Renewable Resources Technology Development
Yichang Mill
Zhoujiahe Village, Honghuatao Town, Yidu
Yichang, Hubei
China
Phone: (86) 717 4803 339/329
Total Employees at this Location: 250
Type of Operation: Paper mill
Pulp Grades and Capacities:
Total pulp capacity: 208,142 mt/y
Recycled Pulping: 208,142 mt/y
Pulp Mill Data:
Recycled Fiber Treatment Lines:
Recycled packaging pulping lines: 1
Paper/Paperboard Grades and Capacities:
Total paper and paperboard capacity: 205,632 mt/y
Linerboard: 205,632 mt/y
Paper and Paperboard Mill Data:
Paper Machines: 1
No. 1, (started up November 2011), Multi-wire (4), total capacity 205,632 mt/y, Trim width 5.6 m, Linerboard
Energy Data:
Electrical demand for mill: 356 MWh/D

ⓜHubei Jianli Maxleaf Paper Co., Ltd.
Jingzhou Mill
Ownership: 100% by Hubei Maxleaf Paper Co., Ltd.
No. 45, Yanjiang Road, Rongcheng Village, Jianli County
Jingzhou, Hubei, 433300
China
Phone: (86) 716 338 0328/327 1387/1148
Fax: (86) 716 327 5119
Web Address: www.maxleaf.com.cn
Personnel:
Pres.: Qinghua Hu
Phone: (86) 716 327 1387/1148
Gen. Mgr.: PingAn Zhang
Phone: (86) 716 327 1387/1148
Chief Eng.: Caotang Zhu
Phone: (86) 716 327 1387/1148
Total Employees at this Location: 950
Type of Operation: Pulp mill, Paper mill
Pulp Mill Data:
Chemical Pulping Systems:
Batch digesters: 12
Pulp Lines: 1
Bleach Plant Systems: 1
No. 1
Chemical Recovery Equipment:
Evaporator lines
Recovery boilers: 1
Paper and Paperboard Mill Data:
Paper Machines: 4
No. 1, fourdrinier, total capacity 17,850 mt/y, Trim width 2.64 m, Uncoated woodfree/freesheet
No. 2, fourdrinier, total capacity 13,923 mt/y, Trim width 1.76 m, Uncoated woodfree/freesheet
No. 3, fourdrinier, total capacity 9,996 mt/y, Trim width 1.76 m, Uncoated woodfree/freesheet
No. 4, fourdrinier, total capacity 39,984 mt/y, Trim width 2.64 m, Uncoated woodfree/freesheet
Finishing Equipment:
Rewinders: 1
Energy Data:
Power boilers: 1

ⓗHubei Jingzhou Zhiyin Paper
No. 77 Yangtz River, Douhudi town, Gong'an county
Jingzhou, Hubei, 434300
China
Phone: (86) 716 8416859 5151199
Fax: (86) 716 8416259
Mill Locations:
Hubei Jingzhou Zhiyin Paper, Jingzhou Mill, No. 77 Yangtz River, Douhudi town, Gong'an county, Jingzhou 434300, China, Capacity: 12,000 mt/y, (Paper mill)
Phone: (86) 716 8416 859/5151 199
Fax: (86) 716 8416 259

ⓜHubei Jingzhou Zhiyin Paper
Jingzhou Mill
No. 77 Yangtz River, Douhudi town, Gong'an county
Jingzhou, Hubei, 434300
China
Phone: (86) 716 8416 859/5151 199
Fax: (86) 716 8416 259
Web Address: www.jzzyzy.com
Total Employees at this Location: 130
Type of Operation: Paper mill
Pulp Mill Data:
Bleach Plant Systems: 1
DIP
Recycled Fiber Treatment Lines:
Flotation deinking lines: 1
Paper/Paperboard Grades and Capacities:
Total paper and paperboard capacity: 12,000 mt/y
Tissue: 12,000 mt/y
Paper and Paperboard Mill Data:
Paper Machines: 4
No. 2, total capacity 500 mt/y, Trim width 1.58 m, Tissue
No. 3, total capacity 500 mt/y, Trim width 1.58 m, Tissue
No. 4, total capacity 500 mt/y, Trim width 1.58 m, Tissue
No. 5, BF-10 EX, total capacity 12,000 mt/y, Trim width 2.76 m, Tissue, Uncoated woodfree/freesheet
Energy Data:
Power boilers: 1
Electrical demand for mill: 22 MWh/D

ⓜHubei Junma Paper Co. Ltd
Jingzhou Mill
Ownership: Hubei Paima Paper Co., Ltd.
Paima Industry Park, Jinan Town
Jingzhou, Hubei, 430034
China
Phone: (86) 716 841 6007
Fax: (86) 716 841 6028
Personnel:
Chmn.: Xianlong Yang
Phone: (86) 716 841 6007
Total Employees at this Location: 500
Type of Operation: Paperboard mill
Paper/Paperboard Grades and Capacities:
Total paper and paperboard capacity: 100,000 mt/y
Boxboard/cartonboard: 100,000 mt/y
Paper and Paperboard Mill Data:
Paper Machines: 1
No. 1, fourdrinier (3), total capacity 100,000 mt/y, Trim width 2.76 m, Boxboard/cartonboard
Energy Data:
Power boilers: 3
Electrical demand for mill: 144 MWh/D

ⓗHubei Maxleaf Paper Co., Ltd.
Wujiashan EconomicZone
Wuhan, Hubei, 430040
China
Phone: (86) 27 8322 6272
Fax: (86) 27 8322 3133
Email: sales@maxleaf.com.cn
Web Address: www.maxleaf.com.cn
Personnel:
Chmn.: Jiayuan Hu
Phone: (86) 27 8322 6272
Fax: (86) 27 8322 3133
Sls. Mgr.: Mr. Wu
Phone: (86) 27 8325 9909
Total Employees of Company: 3,000
Mill Locations:
Hubei Jianli Maxleaf Paper Co., Ltd., Jingzhou Mill, No. 45, Yanjiang Road, Rongcheng Village, Jianli County, Jingzhou 433300, China, (Pulp mill, Paper mill)
Phone: (86) 716 338 0328/327 1387/1148
Fax: (86) 716 327 5119

ⓗHubei Paima Paper Co., Ltd.
Ownership: 100% by shareholders
Paima Industry Park
Jinan Town, Jinzhou, Hubei, 430034
China
Phone: (86) 716 841 6780
Fax: (86) 716 841 6231
Personnel:
Chmn.: Xianlong Yang
Phone: (86) 716 841 6780
Fax: (86) 716 841 6231
Total Employees of Company: 1,200
Total Employees at this Location: 300
Mill Locations:
Hubei Junma Paper Co. Ltd, Jingzhou Mill, Paima Industry Park, Jinan Town, Jingzhou 430034, China, Capacity: 100,000 mt/y, (Paperboard mill)
Phone: (86) 716 841 6007
Fax: (86) 716 841 6028
Hubei Paima Paper Co., Ltd., Jingzhou Mill, Paima Industry Park, Jinan Town, Jingzhou 430034, China, Capacity: 102,000 mt/y, (Paperboard mill)
Phone: (86) 716 841 6256
Fax: (86) 716 841 6231

ⓜHubei Paima Paper Co., Ltd.
Jingzhou Mill
Paima Industry Park, Jinan Town
Jingzhou, Hubei, 430034
China
Phone: (86) 716 841 6256
Fax: (86) 716 841 6231
Personnel:
Sls. Mgr.: Mr. Deng
Phone: (86) 716 841 6256
Total Employees at this Location: 100
Type of Operation: Paperboard mill
Pulp Grades and Capacities:
Total pulp capacity: 57,700 mt/y
Recycled Pulping: 57,700 mt/y
Paper/Paperboard Grades and Capacities:
Total paper and paperboard capacity: 102,000 mt/y
Boxboard/cartonboard: 102,000 mt/y
Paper and Paperboard Mill Data:
Paper Machines: 1
No. 1, fourdrinier, total capacity 102,000 mt/y, Trim width 2.76 m, Boxboard/cartonboard

Energy Data:
Electrical demand for mill: 161 MWh/D

ⓂⓂHubei Shuailun Paper Co. Ltd.
Wuhan Mill

Ownership: Hubei Shuailun Paper Co. Ltd.
No. 1, Chengjiangji Riverside, Jianghan District
Wuhan, Hubei, 430011
China
  Phone: (86) 27 8231 9169
  Fax: (86) 27 8235 3164
Personnel:
  Chmn. & Pres.: Jialong Gong
  Phone: (86) 27 8231 9169
Total Employees at this Location: 100
Type of Operation: Paper mill
Paper/Paperboard Grades and Capacities:
  Total paper and paperboard capacity: 12,000 mt/y
  Containerboard: 12,000 mt/y
  Linerboard
  Corrugating medium/fluting
Paper and Paperboard Mill Data:
Paper Machines: 1
PM 6, multi-wire, total capacity 12,000 mt/y, Trim width 2.1 m, Linerboard, Corrugating medium/fluting

ⓂⓂHubei Shulin Paper Co., Ltd
Yichang Mill

Baihe Village, Yiling District
Yichang, Hubei
China
Total Employees at this Location: 355
Type of Operation: Paperboard mill
Pulp Grades and Capacities:
  Total pulp capacity: 134,659 mt/y
  Recycled Pulping: 134,659 mt/y
Pulp Mill Data:
  Recycled Fiber Treatment Lines:
  Recycled packaging pulping lines: 1
Paper/Paperboard Grades and Capacities:
  Total paper and paperboard capacity: 136,374 mt/y
  Corrugating medium/fluting: 136,374 mt/y
Paper and Paperboard Mill Data:
Paper Machines: 4
No. 1, Multi-wire (3), total capacity 59,619 mt/y, Trim width 3.8 m, Corrugating medium/fluting
No. 2, fourdrinier, total capacity 19,635 mt/y, Trim width 2.2 m, Corrugating medium/fluting
No. 3, fourdrinier, total capacity 24,990 mt/y, Trim width 2.8 m, Corrugating medium/fluting
No. 4, fourdrinier, total capacity 32,130 mt/y, Trim width 3.2 m, Corrugating medium/fluting
Energy Data:
Power boilers
Electrical demand for mill: 216 MWh/D

ⓂHubei Shuyun Paper Co., Ltd.

No.438, Xiaoting Rd., Xiaoting District
Yichang, Hubei, 443007
China
  Phone: (86) 717 6536 742
  Fax: (86) 717 6536 099
Total Employees at this Location: 300
Mill Locations:
Hubei Shuyun Paper Co., Ltd., Yichang Mill, No.438, Xiaoting Rd., Xiaoting District, Yichang 443007, China, Capacity: 10,000 mt/y, (Paper mill)
  Phone: (86) 717 6536 742
  Fax: (86) 717 6536 099

ⓂHubei Shuyun Paper Co., Ltd.
Yichang Mill

No.438, Xiaoting Rd., Xiaoting District
Yichang, Hubei, 443007
China
  Phone: (86) 717 6536 742
  Fax: (86) 717 6536 099
  Web Address: www.shuyunpaper.com

Total Employees at this Location: 300
Type of Operation: Paper mill
Paper/Paperboard Grades and Capacities:
  Total paper and paperboard capacity: 10,000 mt/y
  Tissue: 10,000 mt/y
Paper and Paperboard Mill Data:
Paper Machines: 4
PM 1-4, total capacity 2,500 mt/y, Trim width 1.58 m, Tissue

ⓂHubei Vinda Paper (Hubei) Co., Ltd.
Xiaogan Mill

Ownership: Vinda International Holdings Limited.
Nanda Industry & Development Zone, Xiaonan District
Xiaogan, Hubei, 432100
China
  Phone: (86) 712 2519 099/ 007
  Fax: (86) 712 2519 089
  Web Address: www.vindapaper.com
Personnel:
  Chmn.: Zhaowang Li
  Tech.Dir: Yiping Dong
Total Employees at this Location: 500
Type of Operation: Paper mill
Paper/Paperboard Grades and Capacities:
  Total paper and paperboard capacity: 180,000 mt/y
  Tissue: 180,000 mt/y
Paper and Paperboard Mill Data:
Paper Machines: 13
No. 1, BF-10, Yankee dryer, total capacity 10,000 mt/y, Trim width 2.66 m, Tissue
No. 2, BF-10, Yankee dryer, total capacity 10,000 mt/y, Trim width 2.66 m, Tissue
No. 3, BF-10, Yankee dryer, total capacity 10,000 mt/y, Trim width 2.66 m, Tissue, Uncoated woodfree/freesheet
No. 4, BF-10, Yankee dryer, total capacity 10,000 mt/y, Trim width 2.66 m, Tissue, Uncoated woodfree/freesheet
No. 5, BF-10, Yankee dryer, total capacity 10,000 mt/y, Trim width 2.66 m, Tissue, Uncoated woodfree/freesheet
No. 6, BF-10 EX, Yankee dryer, total capacity 12,500 mt/y, Trim width 2.76 m, Tissue, Uncoated woodfree/freesheet
No. 7, BF-10 EX, Yankee dryer, total capacity 12,500 mt/y, Trim width 2.76 m, Tissue, Uncoated woodfree/freesheet
No. 8, BF-10 EX, Yankee dryer, total capacity 12,500 mt/y, Trim width 2.76 m, Tissue, Uncoated woodfree/freesheet
No. 9, BF-10 EX, Yankee dryer, total capacity 12,500 mt/y, Trim width 2.76 m, Tissue, Uncoated woodfree/freesheet
No. 10, crescent former, Yankee dryer, total capacity 20,000 mt/y, Trim width 2.7 m, Tissue, Uncoated woodfree/freesheet
No. 11, crescent former, Yankee dryer, total capacity 20,000 mt/y, Trim width 2.7 m, Tissue, Uncoated woodfree/freesheet
No. 12, crescent former, Yankee dryer, total capacity 20,000 mt/y, Trim width 2.7 m, Tissue, Uncoated woodfree/freesheet
No. 13, crescent former, Yankee dryer, total capacity 20,000 mt/y, Trim width 2.7 m, Tissue, Uncoated woodfree/freesheet
Finishing Equipment:
  Rewinders: 5
Energy Data:
Power boilers: 3
Electrical demand for mill: 277 MWh/D

ⓂHubei Wuhan Chenming Paper Co. Ltd.
Wuhan (Wuhan Chenming Hanyang Paper No. 2 Mill) Mill

Ownership: 50.93% by Chenming Paper Holdings Ltd., 49.07% by shareholders
Wuhan Economic & Technology Development Zone
Wuhan, Hubei, 430057
China
  Phone: (86) 27 84897382/ 4969
  Fax: (86) 27 8489 4713
  Email: whcom@whcmhy.com.cn
  Web Address: www.chenmingpaper.com
Personnel:
  Chmn.: Hongguo Chen
  Phone: (86) 27 84897382/ 4969
Total Employees at this Location: 270
Type of Operation: Pulp mill, Paper mill
Pulp Mill Data:
  Recycled Fiber Treatment Lines:
  Washing deinking lines: 1 at 150,000 admt/y
Paper/Paperboard Grades and Capacities:
  Total paper and paperboard capacity: 220,000 mt/y
  Uncoated woodfree/freesheet: 160,000 mt/y
  Tissue: 60,000 mt/y
Paper and Paperboard Mill Data:
Paper Machines: 2
No. 1, hybrid former, total capacity 160,000 mt/y, Trim width 4.8 m, Uncoated woodfree/freesheet
No. 2, total capacity 60,000 mt/y, Trim width 5.6 m, Tissue
Energy Data:
Power boilers: 1
Steam turbines: 3 at 11, 23, 25 MW
Electrical demand for mill: 309 MWh/D

ⓂHubei Wuhan Mulan Paper Co., Ltd.

Ownership: 100% by private owners
Shekou Industry Park, Huangpi District
Wuhan, Hubei, 430311
China
  Phone: (86) 27 6186 4818/ 4815
  Fax: (86) 27 6186 4815
  Email: whmlpaper@163.com
  Web Address: www.whmlpaper.com
Personnel:
  Gen. Mgr.: Wansheng Nie
  Phone: (86) 27 6186 4818/ 4815
Mill Locations:
Hubei Wuhan Mulan Paper Co., Ltd., Wuhan Mill, Shekou Industry Park, Huangpi District, Wuhan 430311, China, Capacity: 92,106 mt/y, (Paperboard mill)
  Phone: (86) 27 6186 4818/ 4815
  Fax: (86) 27 6186 4815
  Email: whmlpaper@163.com

ⓂHubei Wuhan Mulan Paper Co., Ltd.
Wuhan Mill

Shekou Industry Park, Huangpi District
Wuhan, Hubei, 430311
China
  Phone: (86) 27 6186 4818/ 4815
  Fax: (86) 27 6186 4815
  Email: whmlpaper@163.com
  Web Address: www.whmlpaper.com
Personnel:
  Gen. Mgr.: Wansheng Nie
  Phone: (86) 27 6186 4818/ 4815
Total Employees at this Location: 400
Type of Operation: Paperboard mill
Pulp Grades and Capacities:
  Total pulp capacity: 89,574 mt/y
  Recycled Pulping: 89,574 mt/y
Pulp Mill Data:
Pulp Lines: 1
  Recycled Fiber Treatment Lines:
  Recycled packaging pulping lines: 1 at 40,000 admt/y
Paper/Paperboard Grades and Capacities:
  Total paper and paperboard capacity: 92,106 mt/y
  Corrugating medium/fluting: 92,106 mt/y
Paper and Paperboard Mill Data:
Paper Machines: 3
No. 1, cylinder, total capacity 13,566 mt/y, Trim width 1.76 m, Corrugating medium/fluting
No. 3, cylinder, total capacity 18,921 mt/y, Trim width 2.1 m, Corrugating medium/fluting

China

No. 4, fourdrinier, total capacity 59,619 mt/y, Trim width 3.2 m, Corrugating medium/fluting
Energy Data:
Electrical demand for mill: 125 MWh/D

ⓗ Hubei Yadu Hengxing Paper Co., Ltd
Guangshui Industry Park
Guangshui, Hubei, 432700
China
 Phone: (86) 722 6494 721
 Fax: (86) 722 6494 721
Mill Locations:
Hubei Yadu Hengxing Paper Co., Ltd, Guangshui Mill, Guangshui Industry Park, Guangshui 432700, China, Capacity: 160,650 mt/y, (Paperboard mill)
 Phone: (86) 722 6494 882
 Fax: (86) 722 6494 721

ⓜ Hubei Yadu Hengxing Paper Co., Ltd
Guangshui Mill
Guangshui Industry Park
Guangshui, Hubei, 432700
China
 Phone: (86) 722 6494 882
 Fax: (86) 722 6494 721
Total Employees at this Location: 480
Type of Operation: Paperboard mill
Pulp Grades and Capacities:
 Total pulp capacity: 156,084 mt/y
 Recycled Pulping: 156,084 mt/y
Pulp Mill Data:
 Recycled Fiber Treatment Lines:
 Recycled packaging pulping lines: 1 at 200,000 admt/y
Paper/Paperboard Grades and Capacities:
 Total paper and paperboard capacity: 160,650 mt/y
 Corrugating medium/fluting: 160,650 mt/y
Paper and Paperboard Mill Data:
Paper Machines: 2
 No. 1, Multi-wire (2), total capacity 60,333 mt/y, Trim width 3.6 m, Corrugating medium/fluting
 No. 2, Multi-wire (2), total capacity 100,317 mt/y, Trim width 4.2 m, Corrugating medium/fluting
Energy Data:
Power boilers: 1
Steam turbines: 1 at 6 MW
Electrical demand for mill: 256 MWh/D

ⓗⓜ Hubei Yichang Baota Paper Co., Ltd
Yichang Mill
Ownership: 100% by State
No. 6 Changjiang Rd., Xiaoting District
Yichang, Hubei, 443000
China
 Phone: (86) 717 6917 286/ 284
 Fax: (86) 717 6917 298
 Email: zwd.1968@yahoo.com.cn
 Web Address: www.baota-paper.com
Personnel:
 Chmn.: Hong Xi
 Phone: (86) 717 6917 286/ 284
 Vice Chmn.: Xiang Xi
 Phone: (86) 717 6917 286/ 284
 Gen. Mgr.: Weidong Zhou
 Phone: (86) 717 6917 286/ 284
 VP-Technology: Deyao Pei
 Phone: (86) 717 6917 286/ 284
 Sls. Mgr.: Yiqun Chen
 Phone: (86) 717 6917 286/ 284
Total Employees at this Location: 340
Type of Operation: Paper mill
Pulp Grades and Capacities:
 Total pulp capacity: 22,500 mt/y
 Recycled Pulping: 10,000 mt/y
Pulp Mill Data:
Pulp Lines: 2
Paper/Paperboard Grades and Capacities:
 Total paper and paperboard capacity: 50,000 mt/y

Newsprint: 30,000 mt/y
Uncoated woodfree/freesheet: 20,000 mt/y
Paper and Paperboard Mill Data:
Paper Machines: 3
 No. 1, total capacity 15,000 mt/y, Trim width 1.76 m, Newsprint
 No. 2, fourdrinier, total capacity 15,000 mt/y, Trim width 1.76 m, Newsprint
 No. 3, fourdrinier, total capacity 20,000 mt/y, Trim width 1.76 m, Uncoated woodfree/freesheet
Finishing Equipment:
 Supercalenders: 1
 Rewinders: 3
 Sheeters: 1

ⓗⓜ Hubei Yingqiang Paper Co., Ltd
Zhongxiang Mill
Jianshe Street, Guanzhuanghu Farm
Zhongxiang, Hubei
China
Total Employees at this Location: 130
Type of Operation: Paperboard mill
Pulp Grades and Capacities:
 Total pulp capacity: 63,378 mt/y
 Recycled Pulping: 63,378 mt/y
Paper/Paperboard Grades and Capacities:
 Total paper and paperboard capacity: 66,000 mt/y
 Corrugating medium/fluting: 66,000 mt/y
Paper and Paperboard Mill Data:
Paper Machines: 1
 No. 1, fourdrinier, total capacity 66,000 mt/y, Trim width 4 m, Corrugating medium/fluting
Energy Data:
Power boilers: 1
Electrical demand for mill: 65 MWh/D

ⓜ Hubei Zhencheng Paper Co., Ltd.
Jingzhou Mill
Qingji Industrial Park, Gongan County
Jingzhou, Hubei
China
 Phone: (86) 716 5704 144/5101 778
Type of Operation: Paper mill
Paper/Paperboard Grades and Capacities:
 Total paper and paperboard capacity: 10,000 mt/y
 Tissue: 10,000 mt/y
Paper and Paperboard Mill Data:
Paper Machines: 1
 PM 1, total capacity 10,000 mt/y, Trim width 2.9 m, Tissue

ⓜ Wuhan Golden Phoenix Paper Co., Ltd.
Wuhan Mill
Jinkou Technology & Industrial Park, Jiangxiia District
Wuhan, Hubei, 430209
China
 Phone: (86) 27 8798 8111/8222/8333
 Fax: (86) 27 8798 7779
 Email: whgpp123@126.com
 Web Address: www.whgpp.com
Total Employees at this Location: 600
Type of Operation: Paper mill
Pulp Grades and Capacities:
 Total pulp capacity: 272,002 mt/y
 Recycled Pulping: 272,002 mt/y
Pulp Mill Data:
Pulp Lines: 2
Paper/Paperboard Grades and Capacities:
 Total paper and paperboard capacity: 280,000 mt/y
 Corrugating medium/fluting: 280,000 mt/y
Paper and Paperboard Mill Data:
Paper Machines: 2
 No. 1, twin-wire, total capacity 80,000 mt/y, Trim width 4 m, Corrugating medium/fluting
 No. 2, fourdrinier, total capacity 200,000 mt/y, Trim width 4.8 m, Corrugating medium/fluting
Energy Data:

Power boilers: 2
Steam turbines: 1 at 7 MW
Electrical demand for mill: 318 MWh/D

ⓗ Wuhan Shenlong Paper Co., Ltd.
No.23, Siwu Rd., Zhuankou Street, Caidian District
Hubei, Hubei, 430100
China
 Phone: (86) 27 8423 4319
Mill Locations:
Wuhan Shenlong Paper Co., Ltd., Wuhan Mill, No.23, Siwu Rd., Zhuankou Street, Caidian District, Hubei 430100, China, Capacity: 15,000 mt/y, (Paper mill)
 Phone: (86) 27 8423 4319

ⓜ Wuhan Shenlong Paper Co., Ltd.
Wuhan Mill
No.23, Siwu Rd., Zhuankou Street, Caidian District
Hubei, Hubei, 430100
China
 Phone: (86) 27 8423 4319
Type of Operation: Paper mill
Paper/Paperboard Grades and Capacities:
 Total paper and paperboard capacity: 15,000 mt/y
 Tissue: 15,000 mt/y
Paper and Paperboard Mill Data:
Paper Machines: 9
 PM 1-9, total capacity 1,700 mt/y, Trim width 2.4 m, Tissue

HUNAN

ⓜ Chenzhou Yunong Paper Co. Ltd
Chenzhou Mill
Yashi Ping, Bailu Tang, Suxian District
Chenzhou, Hunan, 423000
China
 Phone: (86) 735 7660 888
 Fax: (86) 735 7667 288
 Web Address: www.gdyn.com.cn
Type of Operation: Pulp mill
Pulp Grades and Capacities:
 Total pulp capacity: 170,000 mt/y
 Pulp available for market: 170,000 mt/y
Pulp Mill Data:
 Mechanical Pulping Systems:
 BCTMP systems: 1
Pulp Lines: 1

ⓗⓜ Hunan Baoqing Group Union Paper Co., Ltd
Suining Mill
No. 98, Gongye Rd
Suining, Hunan, 422600
China
 Phone: (86) 739 761 1234
 Fax: (86) 739 761 2578
Personnel:
 Chmn.: Ruifeng Jiang
 Phone: (86) 739 761 1234
Total Employees at this Location: 800
Type of Operation: Pulp mill
Pulp Grades and Capacities:
 Total pulp capacity: 110,000 mt/y
 Chemical Pulp: 110,000 mt/y
Pulp Mill Data:
 Chemical Pulping Systems:
 Continuous digesters: 2
Pulp Lines: 2
 Chemical Recovery Equipment:
 Recovery boilers: 2
Paper/Paperboard Grades and Capacities:
 Total paper and paperboard capacity: 152,000 mt/y
 Packaging papers: 140,000 mt/y
 Specialty and industrial: 12,000 mt/y
Paper and Paperboard Mill Data:

Paper Machines: 5
PM 1, total capacity 40,000 mt/y, Trim width 2.26 m, Packaging papers
PM 2, total capacity 50,000 mt/y, Trim width 2.1 m, Packaging papers
PM 3, total capacity 50,000 mt/y, Packaging papers
PM 4-5, total capacity 6,000 mt/y, Trim width 1.22 m, Specialty and industrial
Energy Data:
TMP Reboiler: 1

ⓜHunan Changde HengAn Paper Co., Ltd.
Changde Mill
Ownership: 100% by Fujian Hengan International Group
Tao Lin Road, Laishan Industrial Zone
Changde, Hunan, 415100
China
Phone: (86) 736 731 8489
Fax: (86) 736 730 0322
Email: ceha@hengan.com
Web Address: www.hengan.com
Personnel:
Chmn.: Wenbo Shi
Phone: (86) 736 731 8489
Pres.: Lianmin Xu
Phone: (86) 736 731 8489
VP/Asst. Mill Mgr.: You Liu
Phone: (86) 736 731 8489
Gen. Mgr.: Lianjie Xu
Phone: (86) 736 731 8489
Total Employees at this Location: 600
Type of Operation: Paper mill
Paper/Paperboard Grades and Capacities:
Total paper and paperboard capacity: 280,000 mt/y
Tissue: 280,000 mt/y
Paper and Paperboard Mill Data:
Paper Machines: 6
No. 1, crescent former, total capacity 35,000 mt/y, Trim width 3.65 m, Tissue, Uncoated woodfree/freesheet
No. 2, crescent former, total capacity 35,000 mt/y, Trim width 3.65 m, Tissue, Uncoated woodfree/freesheet
No. 7, crescent former, total capacity 60,000 mt/y, Trim width 5.55 m, Tissue, Uncoated woodfree/freesheet
No. 8, Advantage DCT 200 TS, total capacity 60,000 mt/y, Trim width 5.6 m, Tissue, Uncoated woodfree/freesheet
No. 17, crescent former, total capacity 60,000 mt/y, Trim width 5.6 m, Tissue, Uncoated woodfree/freesheet
No. 18, crescent former, total capacity 60,000 mt/y, Trim width 5.6 m, Tissue, Uncoated woodfree/freesheet
Finishing Equipment:
Rewinders: 3
Energy Data:
Power boilers: 4
Electrical demand for mill: 541 MWh/D

ⓜⓜHunan Dongshun Paper Co., Ltd
Xiangxi Mill
Mill is under construction, due to start up in Q2, 2015.
Xiangxi (Guangzhou) industrial park
Xiangxi autonomous prefecture, Hunan
China
Phone: (86) 743 8528 272
Web Address: www.dongshunpaper.com
Type of Operation: Paper mill
Paper/Paperboard Grades and Capacities:
Total paper and paperboard capacity: 12,000 mt/y
Tissue: 12,000 mt/y
Paper and Paperboard Mill Data:
Paper Machines: 1
PM 1, (due to start up in Q2, 2015), total capacity 12,000 mt/y, Trim width 2.76 m, Tissue

ⓜHunan Huayao Pulp & Paper Co., Ltd.
Changde Mill
Deshan Economic & Technological Development Aera
Changde, Hunan
China
Type of Operation: Pulp mill, Paper mill
Pulp Mill Data:
Pulp Lines: 1

ⓘHunan Jianhongda Group
No. 479 Furong Middle Rd.
Changsha, Hunan, 410005
China
Personnel:
Chmn.: Guojiang Yang
Mill Locations:
Hunan Xiangfeng Specialty Paper Co., Ltd., No. 1 Branch Mill, Shaoyang Mill, No. 77 Shizi Street, Wenduzhai Town, Longhui County, Shaoyang 422204, China, Capacity: 10,000 mt/y, (Paper mill)
Phone: (86) 739 875 5323
Fax: (86) 739 875 5762
Hunan Xiangfeng Specialty Paper Co., Ltd. No. 2 Branch Mill, Shaoyang Mill, Longhui County Industry Park, Longhui County, Shaoyang 422200, China, Capacity: 8,000 mt/y, (Paper mill)
Phone: (86) 739 818 7998/ 7800/ 7988
Fax: (86) 739 892 9555/ 824 7998

ⓘHunan Jingtianren Paper Co., Ltd.
Ownership: 100% by private owners
No. 1 Baihua Ave., Qianlianghu Town, Junshan District
Yueyang, Hunan, 414018
China
Phone: (86) 730 8925 111
Fax: (86) 730 8925 999
Email: hnjtr@sohu.com
Web Address: www.hnjtr.com
Mill Locations:
Hunan Jingtianren Paper Co., Ltd., Yueyang Mill, No. 1 Baihua Ave., Qianlianghu Town, Junshan District, Yueyang 414018, China, Capacity: 14,000 mt/y, (Paper mill)
Phone: (86) 730 8925 111
Fax: (86) 730 8925 999
Email: hnjtr@sohu.com

ⓜHunan Jingtianren Paper Co., Ltd.
Yueyang Mill
No. 1 Baihua Ave., Qianlianghu Town, Junshan District
Yueyang, Hunan, 414018
China
Phone: (86) 730 8925 111
Fax: (86) 730 8925 999
Email: hnjtr@sohu.com
Web Address: www.hnjtr.com
Personnel:
Gen. Mgr.: Xinmin Zhou
Phone: (86) 730 8925 111
Sls. Mgr.: Xiaomei Su
Phone: (86) 730 8925 111
Total Employees at this Location: 120
Type of Operation: Paper mill
Paper/Paperboard Grades and Capacities:
Total paper and paperboard capacity: 14,000 mt/y
Tissue: 10,000 mt/y
Paper and Paperboard Mill Data:
Paper Machines: 10
PM 1, total capacity 2,000 mt/y, Trim width 1.09 m
PM 2, total capacity 2,000 mt/y, Trim width 1.09 m
PM 3-10, total capacity 1,250 mt/y, Trim width 1.76 m, Tissue
Energy Data:
Power boilers: 3

ⓘHunan Jintaiyang Paper Co., Ltd.
Yubai New Village, Nanzui Town, Yuanjiang
Yiyang, Hunan, 413104
China
Phone: (86) 737 2296 712
Fax: (86) 737 2297 399
Email: jty2297399@163.com
Web Address: www.jty-paper.com
Personnel:
Chmn.: Yongxiang Xue
Phone: (86) 737 2296 712
Fax: (86) 737 2297 399
Mill Locations:
Hunan Jintaiyang Paper Co., Ltd., Yuanjiang Mill, Yubai New Village, Nanzui Town, Yuanjiang, Yiyang 413104, China, Capacity: 80,000 mt/y, (Pulp mill, Paper mill)
Phone: (86) 737 2296 712/2297 339
Fax: (86) 737 2297 399
Email: jty2297399@163.com

ⓜHunan Jintaiyang Paper Co., Ltd.
Yuanjiang Mill
Yubai New Village, Nanzui Town, Yuanjiang
Yiyang, Hunan, 413104
China
Phone: (86) 737 2296 712/2297 339
Fax: (86) 737 2297 399
Email: jty2297399@163.com
Web Address: www.jty-paper.com
Type of Operation: Pulp mill, Paper mill
Pulp Grades and Capacities:
Total pulp capacity: 60,000 mt/y
Pulp available for market: 7,579 mt/y
Other Pulp: 60,000 mt/y
Pulp Mill Data:
Pulp Lines: 1
Chemical Recovery Equipment:
Recovery boilers: 1
Paper/Paperboard Grades and Capacities:
Total paper and paperboard capacity: 80,000 mt/y
Uncoated woodfree/freesheet: 76,000 mt/y
Specialty and industrial: 4,000 mt/y
Paper and Paperboard Mill Data:
Paper Machines: 9
No. 1, fourdrinier, total capacity 6,000 mt/y, Trim width 1.58 m, Uncoated woodfree/freesheet
No. 2, fourdrinier, total capacity 6,000 mt/y, Trim width 1.58 m, Uncoated woodfree/freesheet
No. 3, fourdrinier, total capacity 6,000 mt/y, Trim width 1.58 m, Uncoated woodfree/freesheet
No. 4, fourdrinier, total capacity 4,000 mt/y, Trim width 1.58 m, Specialty and industrial
No. 5, fourdrinier, total capacity 8,000 mt/y, Trim width 1.76 m, Uncoated woodfree/freesheet
No. 6, fourdrinier, total capacity 8,000 mt/y, Trim width 1.76 m, Uncoated woodfree/freesheet
No. 7, fourdrinier, total capacity 14,000 mt/y, Trim width 2.64 m, Uncoated woodfree/freesheet
No. 8, fourdrinier, total capacity 14,000 mt/y, Trim width 2.64 m, Uncoated woodfree/freesheet
No. 9, fourdrinier, total capacity 14,000 mt/y, Trim width 2.64 m, Uncoated woodfree/freesheet
Energy Data:
Power boilers: 2
Steam turbines: 2 at 6, 6 MW
Electrical demand for mill: 240 MWh/D

ⓜⓜHunan Linyuan Paper Co., Ltd
Yiyang Mill
Luweichang, Shuangfeng Rural, Yuanjiang City
Yuanjiang, Hunan
China
Web Address: www.linyuanzc.com
Total Employees at this Location: 340
Type of Operation: Paper mill
Pulp Grades and Capacities:
Total pulp capacity: 35,561 mt/y
Other Pulp: 35,561 mt/y
Pulp Mill Data:
Chemical Pulping Systems:
Batch digesters: 1
Pulp Lines: 1
Bleach Plant Systems: 1
Chemical Recovery Equipment:
Evaporator lines
Recovery boilers

China

Paper/Paperboard Grades and Capacities:
Total paper and paperboard capacity: 64,974 mt/y
Uncoated woodfree/freesheet: 64,974 mt/y
Paper and Paperboard Mill Data:
Paper Machines: 3
No. 1, fourdrinier, total capacity 14,994 mt/y, Trim width 1.76 m, Uncoated woodfree/freesheet
No. 2, fourdrinier, total capacity 14,994 mt/y, Trim width 1.76 m, Uncoated woodfree/freesheet
No. 3, fourdrinier, total capacity 34,986 mt/y, Trim width 2.64 m, Uncoated woodfree/freesheet
Energy Data:
Power boilers
Steam turbines
Electrical demand for mill: 173 MWh/D

ⓜHunan No. 1 Paperboard Co., Ltd.
Ownership: 100% by private owners
Yangxi Bridge, Shuangqing District
Shaoyang, Hunan, 422001
China
 Phone: (86) 739 527 6093/ 6763/ 6777
 Fax: (86) 739 527 6725
 Email: root@yizhiban.com
Mill Locations:
Hunan No. 1 Paperboard Co., Ltd., Shaoyang Mill, Yangxi Bridge, Shuangqing District, Shaoyang 422001, China, Capacity: 30,000 mt/y, (Paper mill, Paperboard mill)
 Phone: (86) 739 527 6093/ 6763/ 6777
 Fax: (86) 739 527 6725
 Email: root@yizhiban.com

ⓜHunan No. 1 Paperboard Co., Ltd.
Shaoyang Mill
Yangxi Bridge, Shuangqing District
Shaoyang, Hunan, 422001
China
 Phone: (86) 739 527 6093/ 6763/ 6777
 Fax: (86) 739 527 6725
 Email: root@yizhiban.com
Personnel:
 Chmn.: Shaozi Jue Liu
 Phone: (86) 739 527 6093/ 6763/ 6777
 Gen. Mgr.: Wen Liao
 Phone: (86) 739 527 6093/ 6763/ 6777
Total Employees at this Location: 600
Type of Operation: Paper mill, Paperboard mill
Pulp Grades and Capacities:
 Total pulp capacity: 30,000 mt/y
Pulp Mill Data:
 Chemical Pulping Systems:
 Batch digesters: 3
Pulp Lines: 2
Paper/Paperboard Grades and Capacities:
 Total paper and paperboard capacity: 30,000 mt/y
 Boxboard/cartonboard: 30,000 mt/y
Paper and Paperboard Mill Data:
Paper Machines: 6
PM 3, (idle since May 2005), cylinder, Trim width 1.58 m, Boxboard/cartonboard
PM 4-5, cylinder, Trim width 1.58 m, Boxboard/cartonboard
PM 6-8, fourdrinier, Trim width 2.36 m, Boxboard/cartonboard

ⓜHunan Shuanghua Paper Co., Ltd.
Ownership: 100% by private owners
The Second Ring East Road, Jinzhou Ave., Economic & Industrial Development Park, Ningxiang County
Changsha, Hunan, 410600
China
 Phone: (86) 731 7808 159/ 749 1295/87809158
 Fax: (86) 731 7809 158/ 749 0578/87809159
 Email: shuanghua6999@163.com
 Web Address: www.shzye.com
Mill Locations:
Hunan Shuanghua Paper Co., Ltd., Changsha Mill, The Second Ring East Road, Jinzhou Ave., Economic & Industrial Development Park, Ningxiang County, Changsha 410600, China, Capacity: 76,398 mt/y, (Paperboard mill)
 Phone: (86) 731 7808 159/ 749 1295/87809158
 Fax: (86) 731 7809 158/ 749 0578/87809159
 Email: shuanghua6999@163.com

ⓜHunan Shuanghua Paper Co., Ltd.
Changsha Mill
The Second Ring East Road, Jinzhou Ave., Economic & Industrial Development Park, Ningxiang County
Changsha, Hunan, 410600
China
 Phone: (86) 731 7808 159/ 749 1295/87809158
 Fax: (86) 731 7809 158/ 749 0578/87809159
 Email: shuanghua6999@163.com
 Web Address: www.shzye.com
Personnel:
 Gen. Mgr.: Guihua Yan
 Phone: (86) 731 7808 159/ 749 1295
Total Employees at this Location: 428
Type of Operation: Paperboard mill
Pulp Grades and Capacities:
 Total pulp capacity: 74,256 mt/y
 Recycled Pulping: 74,256 mt/y
Pulp Mill Data:
Pulp Lines: 3
 Recycled Fiber Treatment Lines:
 Recycled packaging pulping lines: 3 at 120,000 admt/y
Paper/Paperboard Grades and Capacities:
 Total paper and paperboard capacity: 76,398 mt/y
 Corrugating medium/fluting: 76,398 mt/y
Paper and Paperboard Mill Data:
Paper Machines: 2
No. 1, Multi-wire (2), total capacity 52,479 mt/y, Trim width 3.8 m, Corrugating medium/fluting
No. 2, Multi-wire (2), total capacity 23,919 mt/y, Trim width 3.8 m, Corrugating medium/fluting
Energy Data:
Electrical demand for mill: 121 MWh/D

ⓜHunan Tiger Forest & Paper Group Co., Ltd
Ownership: 55.92% by China Chengtong Holding Group Ltd.
48 Dongsheng Road, Economic and Technology Development District
Changsha, Hunan, 410100
China
 Phone: (86) 731 4025555
 Fax: (86) 731 4025566
 Email: tigerfp@tigerfp.com
 Web Address: www.tigerfp.com
Personnel:
 Chmn.: Laiming Tong
 Phone: (86) 731 4025555
 Fax: (86) 731 4025566
 Gen. Mgr.: Liya Jiang
 Phone: (86) 731 4025555
 Fax: (86) 731 4025566
 CFO: Shouquan Li
 Phone: (86) 731 4025555
 Fax: (86) 731 4025566
 Vice Gen. Mgr.: Yuanmei Xu
 Phone: (86) 731 4025555
 Fax: (86) 731 4025566
 Vice Gen. Mgr.: Zuojun Tang
 Phone: (86) 731 4025555
 Fax: (86) 731 4025566
 Vice Gen. Mgr.: Chao Yin
 Phone: (86) 731 4025555
 Fax: (86) 731 4025566
 Vice Gen. Mgr.: Zhengguo Li
 Phone: (86) 731 4025555
 Fax: (86) 731 4025566
 Vice Gen. Mgr.: Shuguang Liu
 Phone: (86) 731 4025555
 Fax: (86) 731 4025566
Total Employees of Company: 4,371
Mill Locations:
Hunan Tiger Forest & Paper Group Yueyang Paper Co., Ltd., Yueyang Mill, Chenglingji, Yueyang 414002, China, Capacity: 834,996 mt/y, (Pulp mill, Paper mill, Paperboard mill)
 Phone: (86) 730 859 0241/ 856 6443/ 856 3139/ 856 1622/ 859 0456
 Fax: (86) 730 856 1262
 Email: office@yypaper.com, yzmzhxxx@sina.com
Hunan Tiger Forest & Paper Group Hongjiang Paper Co., Ltd, Hongjiang Mill, 45 Luobowan, Hebin Rd., Hongjiang District, Huaihua 418201, China, Capacity: 35,700 mt/y, (Paper mill)
 Phone: (86) 745 769 1750
 Fax: (86) 745 769 1858
Hunan Juntai Pulp & Paper Co., Ltd, Huaihua Mill, Industry Park, Zhongfang Town, Huaihua 418005, China, (Pulp mill)
 Phone: (86) 745 2837 009
 Fax: (86) 745 2837 009
 Email: lqh1005@126.com
Hunan Tiger Forest & Paper Group Yuanjiang Paper Co., Ltd., Yuanjiang Mill, 358 Shuyuan Rd., Yuanjiang 413100, China, Capacity: 159,641 mt/y, (Pulp mill, Paper mill)
 Phone: (86) 737 285 0000/0254
 Fax: (86) 737 285 0258
 Email: dzb@yj-paper.com
Hunan Tiger Forest & Paper Group Co., Ltd, Yongzhou Mill, No. 105, Xiahexian Rd., Lengshuitan District, Yongzhou 425000, China, Capacity: 202,062 mt/y, (Pulp mill, Paper mill)
 Phone: (86) 746 847 0536/ 1448/ 0529
 Fax: (86) 746 847 1569/ 0498
 Email: webmaster@xjpaper.com

ⓞⓜHunan Tiger Forest & Paper Group Yueyang Paper Co., Ltd.
Yueyang Mill
Ownership: Hunan Tiger Forest & Paper Group Co., Ltd
Chenglingji
Yueyang, Hunan, 414002
China
 Phone: (86) 730 859 0241/ 856 6443/ 856 3139/ 856 1622/ 859 0456
 Fax: (86) 730 856 1262
 Email: office@yypaper.com, yzmzhxxx@sina.com
 Web Address: www.yypaper.com
Personnel:
 Chmn. & Pres.: Laiming Tong
 Phone: (86) 730 859 0241/ 856 6443/ 856 3139/ 856 1622/ 859 0456
 Vice Chmn.: Jialin Wu
 Phone: (86) 730 859 0241/ 856 6443/ 856 3139/ 856 1622/ 859 0456
 Gen. Mgr.: Liya Jiang
 Phone: (86) 730 8590 869
 CFO: Shouquan Li
 Phone: (86) 730 859 0241/ 856 6443/ 856 3139/ 856 1622/ 859 0456
 Dpty. Mgr.: Shuguang Liu
 Phone: (86) 730 859 0241/ 856 6443/ 856 3139/ 856 1622/ 859 0456
 Dpty. Mgr.: Bo Hou
 Phone: (86) 730 859 0363
 Dpty. Mgr.: Zuojun Tang
 Phone: (86) 730 859 0241/ 856 6443/ 856 3139/ 856 1622/ 859 0456
Type of Operation: Pulp mill, Paper mill, Paperboard mill
Pulp Grades and Capacities:
 Total pulp capacity: 389,368 mt/y
 Chemical Pulp: 40,223 mt/y
 Mechanical Pulp: 88,224 mt/y
 Recycled Pulping: 166,627 mt/y
 Other Pulp: 94,294 mt/y
Pulp Mill Data:
 Chemical Pulping Systems:
 Batch digesters: 2
 Continuous digesters: 1
 Mechanical Pulping Systems:
 APMP Systems: 2

Pulp Lines: 7
Bleach Plant Systems: 3
Chemical Pulping System, Type: Reed/Softwood
Mechanical Pulping System, Type: Hardwood
Recycled Pulping System
Chemical Recovery Equipment:
Evaporator lines
Recovery boilers: 3
Recycled Fiber Treatment Lines:
Flotation deinking lines: 1 at 300,000 admt/y
Paper/Paperboard Grades and Capacities:
Total paper and paperboard capacity: 834,996 mt/y
Uncoated woodfree/freesheet: 513,100 mt/y
Uncoated mechanical/groundwood: 14,000 mt/y
Coated woodfree/freesheet: 10,000 mt/y
Coated mechanical/groundwood: 175,000 mt/y
Specialty and industrial: 112,900 mt/y
Corrugating medium/fluting: 9,996 mt/y
Paper and Paperboard Mill Data:
Paper Machines: 9
No. 1, Bel-Bond, total capacity 73,100 mt/y, Trim width 3.94 m, Uncoated woodfree/freesheet
No. 2, fourdrinier, total capacity 14,000 mt/y, Trim width 1.76 m, Uncoated mechanical/groundwood
No. 3, DuoFormer D, total capacity 85,000 mt/y, Trim width 3.75 m, Specialty and industrial
No. 4, fourdrinier, total capacity 14,400 mt/y, Trim width 2.36 m, Specialty and industrial
No. 5, fourdrinier, total capacity 13,500 mt/y, Trim width 2.36 m, Specialty and industrial
No. 6, cylinder, total capacity 9,996 mt/y, Trim width 1.6 m, Corrugating medium/fluting
No. 8, OptiFormer, total capacity 225,000 mt/y, Trim width 6.3 m, Coated mechanical/groundwood, Coated woodfree/freesheet, Uncoated woodfree/freesheet
No. 9, DuoFormer D, total capacity 200,000 mt/y, Trim width 5.28 m, Uncoated woodfree/freesheet
No. 10, DuoFormer D, total capacity 200,000 mt/y, Trim width 5.28 m, Uncoated woodfree/freesheet
Coating Machines: 2
No. 1, total capacity 50,000 mt/y.
PM 8, total capacity 250,000 mt/y., on machine
Finishing Equipment:
Rewinders: 20
Sheeters: 1
Energy Data:
Power boilers
Steam turbines: 6 at 137 MW
Electrical demand for mill: 2,229 MWh/D

ⓜHunan Tiger Forest & Paper Group Hongjiang Paper Co., Ltd
Hongjiang Mill
Ownership: 100% by Hunan Tiger Forest & Paper Group Co., Ltd
45 Luobowan, Hebin Rd., Hongjiang District
Huaihua, Hunan, 418201
China
 Phone: (86) 745 769 1750
 Fax: (86) 745 769 1858
Personnel:
 Gen. Mgr.: Shuihan Yang
 Phone: (86) 139 0745 9495
 Vice Gen. Mgr.: Jinming Li
 Phone: (86) 135 7458 7189
Total Employees at this Location: 520
Type of Operation: Paper mill
Pulp Grades and Capacities:
Total pulp capacity: 36,688 mt/y
Chemical Pulp: 36,688 mt/y
Pulp Mill Data:
Chemical Pulping Systems:
Batch digesters
Pulp Lines: 1
Chemical Recovery Equipment:
Evaporator lines
Recovery boilers
Lime Kiln
Pulp Dryers:
Fourdriniers 1
Paper/Paperboard Grades and Capacities:
Total paper and paperboard capacity: 35,700 mt/y
Packaging papers: 35,700 mt/y
Paper and Paperboard Mill Data:
Paper Machines: 4
No. 1, cylinder, total capacity 4,284 mt/y, Trim width 1.58 m, Packaging papers
No. 2, fourdrinier, total capacity 9,282 mt/y, Trim width 1.58 m, Packaging papers
No. 4, fourdrinier, total capacity 12,852 mt/y, Trim width 2.04 m, Packaging papers
No. 5, fourdrinier, total capacity 9,282 mt/y, Trim width 1.76 m, Packaging papers
Energy Data:
Power boilers: 1
Steam turbines: 2, total 6 MW
Electrical demand for mill: 103 MWh/D

ⓜHunan Juntai Pulp & Paper Co., Ltd
Huaihua Mill
Ownership: 100% by Hunan Tiger Forest & Paper Group Co., Ltd
Industry Park, Zhongfang Town
Huaihua, Hunan, 418005
China
 Phone: (86) 745 2837 009
 Fax: (86) 745 2837 009
 Email: lqh1005@126.com
Personnel:
 Vice Chief Eng. & Project Vice Commander: Ganghui He
 Phone: (86) 745 2837 009
 Email: aiker123@vip.163.com
Total Employees at this Location: 485
Type of Operation: Pulp mill
Pulp Grades and Capacities:
Total pulp capacity: 303,521 mt/y
Pulp available for market: 300,000 mt/y
Chemical Pulp: 303,521 mt/y
Pulp Mill Data:
Chemical Pulping Systems:
Batch digesters: 8
Continuous digesters: 1
Pulp Lines: 1
Bleach Plant Systems: 1
Chemical Pulping System, Type: Softwood/hardwood, Sequence: O₂ DoEopDPO
Chemical Recovery Equipment:
Evaporator lines: 1
Recovery boilers: 1
Lime Kiln
Pulp Dryers:
Air Float dryers 1, Twin Wire 1
Energy Data:
Power boilers: 2
Steam turbines: 1 at 70 MW
Electrical demand for mill: 773 MWh/D

ⓜHunan Tiger Forest & Paper Group Yuanjiang Paper Co., Ltd.
Yuanjiang Mill
Ownership: Hunan Tiger Forest & Paper Group Co., Ltd
358 Shuyuan Rd.
Yuanjiang, Hunan, 413100
China
 Phone: (86) 737 285 0000/0254
 Fax: (86) 737 285 0258
 Email: dzb@yj-paper.com
Personnel:
 Gen. Mgr.: Guoxin Mao
 Phone: (86) 737 285 0000/0254
Total Employees at this Location: 1,045
Type of Operation: Pulp mill, Paper mill
Pulp Grades and Capacities:
Total pulp capacity: 87,461 mt/y
Chemical Pulp: 34,248 mt/y
Other Pulp: 53,212 mt/y
Pulp Mill Data:
Chemical Pulping Systems:
Batch digesters: 2
Pulp Lines: 2
Bleach Plant Systems: 1
Chemical Recovery Equipment:
Evaporator lines
Recovery boilers: 1
Recovery boilers: 1
Paper/Paperboard Grades and Capacities:
Total paper and paperboard capacity: 159,641 mt/y
Uncoated woodfree/freesheet: 101,641 mt/y
Packaging papers: 52,000 mt/y
Specialty and industrial: 6,000 mt/y
Paper and Paperboard Mill Data:
Paper Machines: 10
No. 6, top former, total capacity 60,000 mt/y, Trim width 3.52 m, Packaging papers, Uncoated woodfree/freesheet
No. 7, fourdrinier, total capacity 12,000 mt/y, Trim width 2.36 m, Uncoated woodfree/freesheet
No. 8, fourdrinier, total capacity 12,000 mt/y, Trim width 2.36 m, Uncoated woodfree/freesheet
No. 9, fourdrinier, total capacity 12,500 mt/y, Trim width 1.76 m, Uncoated woodfree/freesheet
No. 10, fourdrinier, total capacity 12,500 mt/y, Trim width 1.76 m, Uncoated woodfree/freesheet
No. 13, cylinder, total capacity 3,000 mt/y, Trim width 1.58 m, Specialty and industrial
No. 14, cylinder, total capacity 4,641 mt/y, Trim width 1.58 m, Uncoated woodfree/freesheet
No. 14, cylinder, total capacity 3,000 mt/y, Trim width 1.58 m, Specialty and industrial
No. 17, fourdrinier, total capacity 20,000 mt/y, Trim width 2.64 m, Uncoated woodfree/freesheet
No. 18, fourdrinier, total capacity 20,000 mt/y, Trim width 2.64 m, Uncoated woodfree/freesheet
Energy Data:
Power boilers: 4
Steam turbines: 4 at 3, 3, 6, 15 MW
Electrical demand for mill: 372 MWh/D

ⓜHunan Tuopu Bamboo and Flax Industry Development Co., Ltd.
Yiyang Mill
Ownership: Jilin Chemical Fiber Group Co., Ltd.
No.42, Yinhe Rd., Maocaojie Town, Nan County
Yiyang, Hunan
China
 Web Address: www.jlhxjt.com
Type of Operation: Pulp mill
Pulp Grades and Capacities:
Total pulp capacity: 31,500 mt/y
Pulp available for market: 31,500 mt/y

ⓜHunan Xiangfeng Specialty Paper Co., Ltd., No. 1 Branch Mill
Shaoyang Mill
Ownership: 100% by Hunan Jianhongda Group
No. 77 Shizi Street, Wenduzhai Town, Longhui County
Shaoyang, Hunan, 422204
China
 Phone: (86) 739 875 5323
 Fax: (86) 739 875 5762
Personnel:
 Chmn.: Guojiang Yang
 Phone: (86) 739 875 5323
 Gen. Mgr.: Jianting Oyang
 Phone: (86) 739 875 5323
Total Employees at this Location: 400
Type of Operation: Paper mill
Paper/Paperboard Grades and Capacities:
Total paper and paperboard capacity: 10,000 mt/y
Specialty and industrial: 8,000 mt/y
Paper and Paperboard Mill Data:
Paper Machines: 4
PM 1-2, Trim width 1.58 m, Specialty and industrial

China

PM 3-4, cylinder, Trim width 1.88 m, Specialty and industrial

ⓜHunan Xiangfeng Specialty Paper Co., Ltd. No. 2 Branch Mill
Shaoyang Mill
Ownership: 100% by Hunan Jianhongda Group
Longhui County Industry Park, Longhui County
Shaoyang, Hunan, 422200
China
  Phone: (86) 739 818 7998/ 7800/ 7988
  Fax: (86) 739 892 9555/ 824 7998
Personnel:
  Chmn.: Guojiang Yang
  Phone: (86) 739 818 7998/ 7800/ 7988
  Sls. Mgr.: Jianting Oyang
  Phone: (86) 739 818 7998/ 7800/ 7988
Type of Operation: Paper mill
Paper/Paperboard Grades and Capacities:
  Total paper and paperboard capacity: 8,000 mt/y
  Specialty and industrial: 8,000 mt/y
Paper and Paperboard Mill Data:
Paper Machines: 1
  PM 1, fourdrinier, total capacity 8,000 mt/y, Trim width 2.55 m, Specialty and industrial
Energy Data:
  Power boilers: 1

ⓜHunan Tiger Forest & Paper Group Co., Ltd
Yongzhou Mill
Ownership: 55.92% by China Chengtong Holding Group Ltd.
No. 105, Xiahexian Rd., Lengshuitan District
Yongzhou, Hunan, 425000
China
  Phone: (86) 746 847 0536/ 1448/ 0529
  Fax: (86) 746 847 1569/ 0498
  Email: webmaster@xjpaper.com
Personnel:
  Mill Mgr.: Zhang Tian Liang
  Phone: (86) 746 847 0536/ 1448/ 0529
  Tech. Mgr.: Yue Luxiang
  Phone: (86) 746 847 0536/ 1448/ 0529
  Purch. Agent: Xiong Yunxin
  Phone: (86) 746 847 0536/ 1448/ 0529
Total Employees at this Location: 1,400
Type of Operation: Pulp mill, Paper mill
Pulp Grades and Capacities:
  Total pulp capacity: 205,841 mt/y
  Chemical Pulp: 205,841 mt/y
Pulp Mill Data:
  Chemical Pulping Systems:
  Batch digesters: 2
Pulp Lines: 3
  Bleach Plant Systems: 1
  Chemical Recovery Equipment:
  Evaporator lines
  Recovery boilers: 2
  Lime Kiln
Paper/Paperboard Grades and Capacities:
  Total paper and paperboard capacity: 202,062 mt/y
  Packaging papers: 202,062 mt/y
Paper and Paperboard Mill Data:
Paper Machines: 5
  No. 1, fourdrinier, total capacity 59,976 mt/y, Trim width 3.3 m, Packaging papers
  No. 2, fourdrinier, total capacity 59,976 mt/y, Trim width 3.3 m, Packaging papers
  No. 3, fourdrinier, total capacity 24,990 mt/y, Trim width 2.4 m, Packaging papers
  No. 4, fourdrinier, total capacity 42,126 mt/y, Trim width 3.4 m, Packaging papers
  No. 6, fourdrinier, total capacity 14,994 mt/y, Trim width 1.76 m, Packaging papers
Coating Machines: 1
  CM 7, total capacity 10,000 mt/y., off machine
Energy Data:

Power boilers: 2
Steam turbines: 2 at 33 MW
Electrical demand for mill: 606 MWh/D

ⓜHunan Yueyang Fengli Pulp & Paper Co. Ltd.
Ownership: 100% by Castle Peak Pulp & Paper (CPPP) Group
Lujiao Town
Yueyang, Hunan, 414107
China
  Phone: (86) 730 786 0030/7861 188
  Fax: (86) 730 786 0343
  Email: info@fengli.com.cn
  Web Address: www.fengli.com.cn
Personnel:
  Chmn.: Kaichen Yan
  VP: Zhiwu Xue
  Phone: (86) 730 7860 030
  Sls Mgr.: Zhenghui Zhang
Total Employees at this Location: 600
Mill Locations:
Hunan Yueyang Fengli Pulp & Paper Co. Ltd., Yueyang Mill, Lujiao Town, Yueyang 414107, China, (Pulp mill, Paper mill)
  Phone: (86) 730 786 0030/786 1188
  Fax: (86) 730 786 0343

ⓜHunan Yueyang Fengli Pulp & Paper Co. Ltd.
Yueyang Mill
Mill is for sale
Lujiao Town
Yueyang, Hunan, 414107
China
  Phone: (86) 730 786 0030/786 1188
  Fax: (86) 730 786 0343
Personnel:
  Chmn.: Kaichen Yan
  Phone: (86) 730 786 0030/7861 188
  VP: Zhiwu Xue
  Phone: (86) 730 7860 030
  Sls Mgr.: Zhenghui Zhang
  Phone: (86) 730 786 0030/7861 188
Total Employees at this Location: 600
Type of Operation: Pulp mill, Paper mill
Pulp Mill Data:
  Chemical Pulping Systems:
  Batch digesters: 1
  Continuous digesters: 1
Pulp Lines: 2
  Bleach Plant Systems: 2
  1, Type: Nonwood, Sequence: CEH, Capacity 60,000 admt/y
  1, Type: wood, Sequence: CEH, Capacity 30,000 admt/y
  Chemical Recovery Equipment:
  Recovery boilers: 1
Paper and Paperboard Mill Data:
Paper Machines: 11
  No. 1, cylinder, total capacity 12,500 mt/y, Trim width 1.6 m, Specialty and industrial
  No. 2, fourdrinier, total capacity 10,000 mt/y, Trim width 1.76 m, Uncoated woodfree/freesheet, Packaging papers
  No. 3, fourdrinier, total capacity 42,850 mt/y, Trim width 2.64 m
  T1-6, fourdrinier, total capacity 12,852 mt/y, Trim width 1.8 m, Tissue
  T7-8, fourdrinier, total capacity 2,100 mt/y, Trim width 1.58 m, Tissue
Energy Data:
  Power boilers: 1
  Steam turbines: 1 at 7.5 MW

ⓜHengshan Zhongkong International Paper Co., Ltd.
Hengyang Mill
Jinlong Industry Park, Hengshan County
Hengyang, Hunan, 421300
China

  Phone: (86) 734 285 6668/7778
Personnel:
  Chmn.: Guohua Ye
Total Employees at this Location: 300
Type of Operation: Paperboard mill
Pulp Grades and Capacities:
  Total pulp capacity: 48,589 mt/y
  Recycled Pulping: 48,589 mt/y
Pulp Mill Data:
Pulp Lines: 1
  Recycled Fiber Treatment Lines:
  Recycled packaging pulping lines: 1 at 150,000 admt/y
Paper/Paperboard Grades and Capacities:
  Total paper and paperboard capacity: 50,000 mt/y
  Corrugating medium/fluting: 50,000 mt/y
Paper and Paperboard Mill Data:
Paper Machines: 1
  No. 1, Multi-wire (3), total capacity 50,000 mt/y, Trim width 4.6 m, Corrugating medium/fluting
Energy Data:
  Power boilers: 2
  Steam turbines: 1 at 7.5 MW
  Electrical demand for mill: 61 MWh/D

INNER MONGOLIA

ⓜNine Dragons XingAn Paper Co., Ltd. (Inner Mongolia)
Zhalantun Mill
Ownership: 55% by Guangdong Dongguan Nine Dragons Paper Industries Co., Ltd., 45% by Inner Mongolia Forestry Industrial Co., Ltd.
No. 33, Zhijiang Street
Zhalantun, Inner Mongolia, 162650
China
  Phone: (86) 470 330 2447
  Fax: (86) 470 330 3820
Personnel:
  Chmn.: Yin Zhang
  CEO: Mingzhong Liu
  Phone: (86) 470 330 2447
Total Employees at this Location: 550
Type of Operation: Pulp mill, Paper mill
Pulp Grades and Capacities:
  Total pulp capacity: 94,945 mt/y
  Pulp available for market: 80,325 mt/y
  Chemical Pulp: 94,945 mt/y
Pulp Mill Data:
Pulp Lines: 1
  Chemical Recovery Equipment:
  Recovery boilers: 3
  Pulp Dryers:
  Twin Wire 1
Paper/Paperboard Grades and Capacities:
  Total paper and paperboard capacity: 14,994 mt/y
  Packaging papers: 14,994 mt/y
Paper and Paperboard Mill Data:
Paper Machines: 1
  No. 4, cylinder, total capacity 14,994 mt/y, Trim width 2.04 m, Packaging papers
Energy Data:
  Power boilers: 3
  Steam turbines: 2 at 12, 6 MW
  Electrical demand for mill: 182 MWh/D

JIANGSU

ⓜGold East Paper (Jiangsu) Co., Ltd.
Zhenjiang (Gold East Paper) Mill
Ownership: 100% by Asia Pulp & Paper (APP)
No. 8, Xinggang East Road, Dagang Economic Development Zone
Zhenjiang, Jiangsu, 212132
China
  Phone: (86) 511 8899 8888/6725

Fax: (86) 511 8899 7000/6669
Email: customer_service@goldeastpaper.com.cn
Web Address: www.goldeastpaper.com
Personnel:
Pres.: Zhiming Ma
Phone: (86) 511 8899 8888/6725
Vice Dir., Env. Prot. & Eng. Div.: Weyrehm Wang
Phone: (86) 511 8899 7305
Fax: (86) 511 8899 8998
Email: wangweyrehm@goldeastpaper.com.cn
Total Employees at this Location: 4,400
Type of Operation: Paper mill
Pulp Grades and Capacities:
Total pulp capacity: 199,570 mt/y
Mechanical Pulp: 199,570 mt/y
Pulp Mill Data:
Mechanical Pulping Systems:
APMP Systems: 1
Pulp Lines: 1
Paper/Paperboard Grades and Capacities:
Total paper and paperboard capacity: 2,255,000 mt/y
Coated woodfree/freesheet: 2,105,000 mt/y
Specialty and industrial: 150,000 mt/y
Paper and Paperboard Mill Data:
Paper Machines: 3
No. 1, DuoFormerTQv, total capacity 750,000 mt/y, Trim width 9.77 m, Specialty and industrial, Coated woodfree/freesheet
No. 2, DuoFormerTQv, total capacity 825,000 mt/y, Trim width 9.77 m, Coated woodfree/freesheet
No. 3, DuoFormerTQv, total capacity 680,000 mt/y, Trim width 9.77 m, Coated woodfree/freesheet
Coating Machines: 3
No. 1, total capacity 700,000 mt/y, off machine
No. 2, total capacity 700,000 mt/y, off machine
No. 3, total capacity 850,000 mt/y, on machine
Finishing Equipment:
Winders: 11
Supercalenders: 6
Sheeters: 26 at 1,500,000 mt/y
Energy Data:
Power boilers: 4
Combustion turbines: 4 at 80, 80, 80, 50 MW
Electrical demand for mill: 5,407 MWh/D

ⓂGold Hongye Paper (Suzhou Industrial Park) Co., Ltd.
Suzhou (Gold Hongye Paper) Mill
Ownership: 100% by Asia Pulp & Paper (APP)
No.1, Jinsheng Road, Shengpu Town, Industrial Zone
Suzhou, Jiangsu, 215126
China
Phone: (86) 512 6281 0228 Ext. 2150
Fax: (86) 512 6281 8276/6282 2101
Email: market@ghy.com.cn
Web Address: www.ghy.com.cn
Personnel:
Chmn. & Pres.: Zhiyuan Huang
Phone: (86) 512 6281 0228 Ext. 2150
VP & Gen. Mgr.: Tsungliang Lo
Phone: (86) 512 6281 0228 Ext. 2150
Exec. Vice Gen. Mgr.: Huihe Chen
Phone: (86) 512 6281 0228 Ext. 2150
Total Employees at this Location: 720
Type of Operation: Paper mill
Paper/Paperboard Grades and Capacities:
Total paper and paperboard capacity: 304,164 mt/y
Tissue: 304,164 mt/y
Paper and Paperboard Mill Data:
Paper Machines: 10
No. 1, crescent former, total capacity 59,976 mt/y, Trim width 5.6 m, Tissue
No. 2, crescent former, total capacity 59,976 mt/y, Trim width 5.6 m, Tissue
No. 3, fourdrinier, total capacity 9,996 mt/y, Trim width 2.8 m, Tissue, Uncoated woodfree/freesheet
No. 4, fourdrinier, total capacity 9,996 mt/y, Trim width 2.8 m, Tissue, Uncoated woodfree/freesheet
No. 5, fourdrinier, total capacity 9,996 mt/y, Trim width 2.8 m, Tissue, Uncoated woodfree/freesheet
No. 6, fourdrinier, total capacity 9,996 mt/y, Trim width 2.8 m, Tissue, Uncoated woodfree/freesheet
No. 7, fourdrinier, total capacity 12,138 mt/y, Trim width 3.5 m, Uncoated woodfree/freesheet, Tissue
No. 8, fourdrinier, total capacity 12,138 mt/y, Trim width 3.5 m, Uncoated woodfree/freesheet, Tissue
No. 9, crescent former, total capacity 59,976 mt/y, Trim width 5.6 m, Tissue
No. 10, crescent former, total capacity 59,976 mt/y, Trim width 5.6 m, Tissue
Energy Data:
Power boilers: 2
Steam turbines: 2 at 50, 50 MW
Electrical demand for mill: 972 MWh/D

ⓂGold Huasheng Paper (Suzhou Industrial Park) Co., Ltd.
Suzhou (Gold Huasheng Paper) Mill
Ownership: 100% by Asia Pulp & Paper (APP)
2, Jinsheng Road, Shengpu Town, Suzhou Industrial Park
Suzhou, Jiangsu, 215126
China
Phone: (86) 512 6283 6666/ 2070/ 2289
Fax: (86) 512 6281 5491
Email: webmaster@goldhs.com.cn
Web Address: www.goldhs.com.cn
Personnel:
VP & Gen. Mgr.: Junyan Huang
Phone: (86) 512 6283 6666/ 2070/ 2289
Purch. Mgr.: Junhui Xu
Phone: (86) 512 6283 6666/ 2070/ 2289
Sls. Mgr.: Wenxin Fu
Phone: (86) 512 6283 6666/ 2070/ 2289
Strat. Bus. Mgr.: Ze Huang
Phone: (86) 512 6283 6666/ 2070/ 2289
Technology Mgr.: Junwei Huang
Phone: (86) 512 6283 6666/ 2070/ 2289
Total Employees at this Location: 1,400
Type of Operation: Paper mill
Paper/Paperboard Grades and Capacities:
Total paper and paperboard capacity: 600,000 mt/y
Uncoated woodfree/freesheet: 455,000 mt/y
Coated woodfree/freesheet: 145,000 mt/y
Paper and Paperboard Mill Data:
Paper Machines: 4
No. 1, GapFormer, total capacity 300,000 mt/y, Trim width 7.36 m, Uncoated woodfree/freesheet
No. 2, fourdrinier, total capacity 82,500 mt/y, Trim width 3.25 m, Uncoated woodfree/freesheet
No. 3, hybrid former, total capacity 145,000 mt/y, Trim width 3.3 m, Coated woodfree/freesheet
No. 4, hybrid former, total capacity 72,500 mt/y, Trim width 3.7 m, Uncoated woodfree/freesheet
Coating Machines: 4
No. 3, total capacity 120,000 mt/y, off machine
No. 4, off machine
Ncr 1, total capacity 120,000 mt/y, off machine
Ncr 2, total capacity 120,000 mt/y, off machine
Energy Data:
Power boilers: 3
Steam turbines: 3 at 50, 50, 80 MW
Electrical demand for mill: 1,170 MWh/D

ⓂJiangsu Bohui Paper Industry Co., Ltd.
Dafeng Mill
Ownership: Shandong Bohui Paper Industry Co., Ltd.
Dafeng Port Economic Zone
Yancheng, Jiangsu
China
Phone: (86) 515 8328 7878/7880
Web Address: www.bohui.net
Total Employees at this Location: 645
Type of Operation: Paper mill
Pulp Grades and Capacities:
Total pulp capacity: 336,700 mt/y
Mechanical Pulp: 506,307 mt/y
Pulp Mill Data:
Chemical Pulping Systems:
Batch digesters: 1
Mechanical Pulping Systems:
BCTMP systems: 1
BCTMP systems: 1
Pulp Lines: 2
Bleach Plant Systems: 2
Chemical Pulping System, Type: Hardwood
Mechanical Pulping System, Type: Hardwood
Chemical Recovery Equipment:
Evaporator lines: 1
Recovery boilers: 1
Paper/Paperboard Grades and Capacities:
Total paper and paperboard capacity: 720,000 mt/y
Boxboard/cartonboard: 720,000 mt/y
Paper and Paperboard Mill Data:
Paper Machines: 1
No. 3, fourdrinier (3), total capacity 720,000 mt/y, Trim width 8.1 m, Boxboard/cartonboard
Coating Machines: 1
PM#3, on machine
Energy Data:
Power boilers: 1
Steam turbines: 1 at 300 MW
Electrical demand for mill: 2,843 MWh/D

ⓂJiangsu Chamfor Paper Industry Co. Ltd.
Ownership: 100% by private owners
Binjiang Industry Zone, HouXiang Town
Danyang, Jiangsu, 212312
China
Phone: (86) 511 8632 6666/6379
Fax: (86) 511 8632 0006
Email: ygz@cfpaper.com
Web Address: www.cfpaper.com
Mill Locations:
Jiangsu Chamfor Paper Industry Co. Ltd., Danyang Mill, Binjiang Industry Zone, HouXiang Town, Danyang 212312, China, Capacity: 450,000 mt/y, (Paper mill)
Phone: (86) 511 8632 6666/6379
Fax: (86) 511 8632 6006/6600
Email: ygz@cfpaper.com

ⓂJiangsu Chamfor Paper Industry Co. Ltd.
Danyang Mill
Binjiang Industry Zone, HouXiang Town
Danyang, Jiangsu, 212312
China
Phone: (86) 511 8632 6666/6379
Fax: (86) 511 8632 6006/6600
Email: ygz@cfpaper.com
Web Address: www.cfpaper.com
Personnel:
Chmn.: Jiannong Zhu
Phone: (86) 511 8632 6666/6379
VP: Guoping Zhu
Phone: (86) 139 0529 1203
VP of Tech.: Zhi Xu
Phone: (86) 511 8632 6666/6379
Gen. Mgr. - Fiber supply dept.: Xiufeng Cao
Phone: (86) 13775366612
Total Employees at this Location: 360
Type of Operation: Paper mill
Pulp Grades and Capacities:
Total pulp capacity: 442,565 mt/y
Recycled Pulping: 442,565 mt/y
Pulp Mill Data:
Pulp Lines: 2
Paper/Paperboard Grades and Capacities:
Total paper and paperboard capacity: 450,000 mt/y
Linerboard: 200,000 mt/y
Corrugating medium/fluting: 250,000 mt/y
Paper and Paperboard Mill Data:
Paper Machines: 3

China

No. 1, fourdrinier (2), total capacity 100,000 mt/y, Trim width 3.8 m, Corrugating medium/fluting
No. 2, fourdrinier (2), total capacity 150,000 mt/y, Trim width 4.6 m, Corrugating medium/fluting
No. 3, Multi-wire (3), total capacity 200,000 mt/y, Trim width 4.8 m, Linerboard
Energy Data:
Power boilers: 2
Steam turbines: 1 at 12 MW
Electrical demand for mill: 538 MWh/D

ⓂJiangsu Changshun Paper Co., Ltd.
Taicang Mill
Liunan Village, Liuhe Town, Taicang
Suzhou, Jiangsu, 215431
China
Phone: (86) 512 5360 0793
Type of Operation: Paper mill
Paper/Paperboard Grades and Capacities:
Total paper and paperboard capacity: 12,000 mt/y
Tissue: 12,000 mt/y
Paper and Paperboard Mill Data:
Paper Machines: 6
PM 1, total capacity 2,000 mt/y, Trim width 1.58 m, Tissue
PM 2, total capacity 2,000 mt/y, Trim width 1.58 m, Tissue
PM 3, total capacity 2,000 mt/y, Trim width 1.58 m, Tissue
PM 4, total capacity 2,000 mt/y, Trim width 1.58 m, Tissue
PM 5, total capacity 2,000 mt/y, Trim width 1.58 m, Tissue
PM 6, total capacity 2,000 mt/y, Trim width 1.58 m, Tissue

ⓊⓂJiangsu Feixiang Paper Co., Ltd
Huaian Mill
South West Chang Street
Huaian, Jiangsu
China
Total Employees at this Location: 460
Type of Operation: Paperboard mill
Pulp Grades and Capacities:
Total pulp capacity: 110,787 mt/y
Recycled Pulping: 110,787 mt/y
Pulp Mill Data:
Recycled Fiber Treatment Lines:
Recycled packaging pulping lines: 1
Paper/Paperboard Grades and Capacities:
Total paper and paperboard capacity: 112,812 mt/y
Corrugating medium/fluting: 112,812 mt/y
Paper and Paperboard Mill Data:
Paper Machines: 3
No. 1, fourdrinier, total capacity 60,333 mt/y, Trim width 4.2 m, Corrugating medium/fluting
No. 2, fourdrinier, total capacity 28,917 mt/y, Trim width 3.2 m, Corrugating medium/fluting
No. 3, fourdrinier, total capacity 23,562 mt/y, Trim width 3.2 m, Corrugating medium/fluting
Energy Data:
Power boilers
Electrical demand for mill: 168 MWh/D

ⓂJiangsu Fuxing Paper
Yancheng Mill
Fuyang Village, Yangzhai Town
Yancheng, Jiangsu
China
Phone: (86) 515 7867688
Type of Operation: Paperboard mill
Pulp Grades and Capacities:
Total pulp capacity: 218,147 mt/y
Recycled Pulping: 218,147 mt/y
Pulp Mill Data:
Recycled Fiber Treatment Lines:
Recycled packaging pulping lines: 1
Paper/Paperboard Grades and Capacities:
Total paper and paperboard capacity: 250,000 mt/y
Boxboard/cartonboard: 250,000 mt/y
Paper and Paperboard Mill Data:
Paper Machines: 1
No. 1, Fourdrinier (4), total capacity 250,000 mt/y, Trim width 4.6 m, Boxboard/cartonboard

Energy Data:
Electrical demand for mill: 336 MWh/D

ⓊJiangsu Huaji Zhangjiagang Huaxing Papermaking Co. Ltd.
Ownership: 100% by Jiangsu Huaji Machinery Group
EDZ (east), Jinfeng Town
Zhangjiagang, Jiangsu, 215625
China
Phone: (86) 512 5895 5818/1518
Fax: (86) 512 5895 1555/9366
Email: hslsh@tom.com
Web Address: www.jshuaji.com
Mill Locations:
Chongqing Wei Er Mei Paper, Chongqing Mill, Industrial Park, Tongnan County, Chongqing, China, Capacity: 54,000 mt/y, (Paper mill)
Phone: (86) 23 6789 9888
Jiangsu Huaji Zhangjiagang Huaxing Papermaking Co. Ltd., Zhangjiagang Mill, EDZ (east), Jinfeng Town, Zhangjiagang 215625, China, Capacity: 279,888 mt/y, (Pulp mill, Paperboard mill)
Phone: (86) 512 5895 5818/1518
Fax: (86) 512 5895 1555/9366
Email: hslsh@tom.com

ⓊJiangsu Huaji Zhangjiagang Huaxing Papermaking Co. Ltd.
Zhangjiagang Mill
EDZ (east), Jinfeng Town
Zhangjiagang, Jiangsu, 215625
China
Phone: (86) 512 5895 5818/1518
Fax: (86) 512 5895 1555/9366
Email: hslsh@tom.com
Web Address: www.jshuaji.com
Personnel:
CEO: Bin Shen
Phone: (86) 139 0624 4168
VP Sls. & Mktg. Mgr.: Liu Qiping
Phone: (86) 133 0624 8882
Total Employees at this Location: 450
Type of Operation: Pulp mill, Paperboard mill
Pulp Grades and Capacities:
Total pulp capacity: 281,633 mt/y
Recycled Pulping: 281,633 mt/y
Pulp Mill Data:
Pulp Lines: 4
Recycled Fiber Treatment Lines:
Recycled packaging pulping lines: 4 at 330,000 admt/y
Paper/Paperboard Grades and Capacities:
Total paper and paperboard capacity: 279,888 mt/y
Corrugating medium/fluting: 279,888 mt/y
Paper and Paperboard Mill Data:
Paper Machines: 2
No. 1, (Supplier: Jiangsu Huaji Group.), fourdrinier, total capacity 99,960 mt/y, Trim width 3.4 m, Corrugating medium/fluting
No. 2, (Supplier: Leshan Chengfa Paper Machinery.), fourdrinier, total capacity 179,928 mt/y, Trim width 5.2 m, Corrugating medium/fluting
Energy Data:
Power boilers: 3
Steam turbines: 2 at 3, 15 MW
Electrical demand for mill: 422 MWh/D

ⓊJiangsu Huangli Paper Industry Co., Ltd.
Ownership: 100% by shareholders
Nanqiu Rd., Chengchang Industry, Huangtu Town
Jiangyin, Jiangsu, 214445
China
Phone: (86) 510 8665 2218
Fax: (86) 510 8665 2208
Personnel:
Pres.: Xiaoping Xu

Phone: (86) 510 8665 2218
Mill Locations:
Jiangsu Huangli Paper Industry Co., Ltd., Jiangyin Mill, Nanqiu Rd., Chengchang Industry, Huangtu Town, Jiangyin 214445, China, Capacity: 108,885 mt/y, (Paperboard mill)
Phone: (86) 510 8665 2218
Fax: (86) 510 8665 2208

ⓂJiangsu Huangli Paper Industry Co., Ltd.
Jiangyin Mill
Nanqiu Rd., Chengchang Industry, Huangtu Town
Jiangyin, Jiangsu, 214445
China
Phone: (86) 510 8665 2218
Fax: (86) 510 8665 2208
Web Address: www.hlpaper.cn
Personnel:
Pres.: Xiaoping Xu
Phone: (86) 510 8665 2218
Total Employees at this Location: 800
Type of Operation: Paperboard mill
Pulp Grades and Capacities:
Total pulp capacity: 110,563 mt/y
Recycled Pulping: 110,563 mt/y
Pulp Mill Data:
Pulp Lines: 1
Paper/Paperboard Grades and Capacities:
Total paper and paperboard capacity: 108,885 mt/y
Linerboard: 78,540 mt/y
Boxboard/cartonboard: 30,345 mt/y
Paper and Paperboard Mill Data:
Paper Machines: 2
No. 1, Multi-wire (3), total capacity 78,540 mt/y, Trim width 3.6 m, Linerboard
No. 2, cylinder (6), total capacity 30,345 mt/y, Trim width 2.9 m, Boxboard/cartonboard
Energy Data:
Power boilers: 3
Steam turbines: 2 at 12, 12 MW
Electrical demand for mill: 188 MWh/D

ⓊJiangsu Jiangyin BESTO Special Paper Board Co., Ltd.
Ownership: 100% by shareholders
No. 2 Xinglong Rd., Changjiang Town
Jiangyin City, Jiangsu, 214411
China
Phone: (86) 510 8630 0005/ 1263
Fax: (86) 510 8630 1263
Email: xuyulian@chinabesto.com, jybesto@chinabesto.com
Web Address: www.chinabesto.com
Mill Locations:
Jiangsu Jiangyin BESTO Special Paper Board Co., Ltd., Jiangyin Mill, No. 2 Xinglong Rd., Changliang Town, Jiangyin 214411, China, Capacity: 32,000 mt/y, (Paperboard mill)
Phone: (86) 510 8630 0005/ 1263
Fax: (86) 510 8630 1263
Email: xuyulian@chinabesto.com, jybesto@chinabesto.com

ⓂJiangsu Jiangyin BESTO Special Paper Board Co., Ltd.
Jiangyin Mill
No. 2 Xinglong Rd., ChangJiang Town
Jiangyin, Jiangsu, 214411
China
Phone: (86) 510 8630 0005/ 1263
Fax: (86) 510 8630 1263
Email: xuyulian@chinabesto.com, jybesto@chinabesto.com
Web Address: www.chinabesto.com
Personnel:
Chmn. & Gen. Mgr.: Zhengwu Yang
Phone: (86) 510 8630 0005/ 1263
Vice. Gen. Mgr.: Ms. Yulian Xu

Phone: (86) 510 8630 0005/ 1263
Sls. Mgr.: Yajun Zhang
Phone: (86) 510 8630 0005/ 1263
Total Employees at this Location: 300
Type of Operation: Paperboard mill
Pulp Grades and Capacities:
Total pulp capacity: 35,000 mt/y
Pulp Mill Data:
Pulp Lines: 2
Paper/Paperboard Grades and Capacities:
Total paper and paperboard capacity: 32,000 mt/y
Boxboard/cartonboard: 32,000 mt/y
Paper and Paperboard Mill Data:
Paper Machines: 6
PM 1-2, fourdrinier, Trim width 1.58 m, Boxboard/cartonboard
PM 3-6, fourdrinier, Trim width 1.6 m, Boxboard/cartonboard

ⓘJiangsu Jiangyin Gushan Dongfang Paper Co., Ltd.
Ownership: 100% by shareholders
Yong An Bridge, Gushan Town
Jiangyin City, Jiangsu, 214413
China
Phone: (86) 510 8632 3688/ 3217
Fax: (86) 510 8632 3688
Email: web@jseastpaper.com,
zhouhuan@public1.wx.js.cn
Mill Locations:
Jiangsu Jiangyin Gushan Dongfang Paper Co., Ltd., Jiangyin Mill, Yong An Bridge, Gushan Town, Jiangyin 214413, China, Capacity: 25,000 mt/y, (Paperboard mill)
Phone: (86) 510 8632 3688/ 3217
Fax: (86) 510 8632 3688
Email: web@jseastpaper.com, zhouhuan@public1.wx.js.cn

ⓜJiangsu Jiangyin Gushan Dongfang Paper Co., Ltd.
Jiangyin Mill
Yong An Bridge, Gushan Town
Jiangyin, Jiangsu, 214413
China
Phone: (86) 510 8632 3688/ 3217
Fax: (86) 510 8632 3688
Email: web@jseastpaper.com,
zhouhuan@public1.wx.js.cn
Personnel:
Chmn.: Songliang Wang
Phone: (86) 510 8632 3688/ 3217
VP-Technology: Maokang Wu
Phone: (86) 510 8632 3688/ 3217
VP- Operations: Dajiang Wang
Phone: (86) 510 8632 3688/ 3217
Total Employees at this Location: 300
Type of Operation: Paperboard mill
Pulp Grades and Capacities:
Total pulp capacity: 25,000 mt/y
Recycled Pulping: 25,000 mt/y
Pulp Mill Data:
Pulp Lines: 2
Paper/Paperboard Grades and Capacities:
Total paper and paperboard capacity: 25,000 mt/y
Linerboard: 10,000 mt/y
Boxboard/cartonboard: 15,000 mt/y
Paper and Paperboard Mill Data:
Paper Machines: 2
PM 1, multi-fourdrinier, total capacity 15,000 mt/y, Trim width 1.09 m, Boxboard/cartonboard
PM 2, multi-fourdrinier, total capacity 10,000 mt/y, Trim width 1.6 m, Linerboard
Finishing Equipment:
Rewinders: 26

ⓜJiangsu Jiangyin YFY Mfg. Co, Ltd.
Jiangyin Mill
Mill is closed (in sometime of 2014)
Ownership: 100% by Yuen Foong Yu Inc.

258, Tongjiang South Road
Jiangyin, Jiangsu, 214433
China
Phone: (86) 510 8611 0141/0143
Fax: (86) 510 8611 8748
Personnel:
Gen. Mgr./Purch. Agent: Junlang Huang
Phone: (86) 510 8611 0141/0143
Tech. Mgr./Maint. Mgr.: Qingshui Gao
Phone: (86) 510 8611 0141/0143
Prod. Mgr.: Jilv Zhan
Phone: (86) 510 8611 0141/0143
Sls. Mgr.: Mingxian Chen
Phone: (86) 510 8611 0141/0143
Total Employees at this Location: 120
Type of Operation: Paperboard mill
Paper/Paperboard Grades and Capacities:
Total paper and paperboard capacity: 45,000 mt/y
Paper and Paperboard Mill Data:
Paper Machines: 1
PM 1, cylinder, total capacity 45,000 mt/y, Trim width 2.5 m, Boxboard/cartonboard

ⓜJiangsu Jinhuang Paper Co., Ltd.
Changzhou Mill
Jintan Enconomic Development Zone
Changzhou, Jiangsu
China
Phone: (86) 519 8268 3828
Web Address: www.hlpaper.cn
Total Employees at this Location: 410
Type of Operation: Paper mill
Pulp Grades and Capacities:
Total pulp capacity: 301,914 mt/y
Recycled Pulping: 301,914 mt/y
Pulp Mill Data:
Recycled Fiber Treatment Lines:
Recycled packaging pulping lines: 1
Paper/Paperboard Grades and Capacities:
Total paper and paperboard capacity: 300,000 mt/y
Linerboard: 160,000 mt/y
Boxboard/cartonboard: 140,000 mt/y
Paper and Paperboard Mill Data:
Paper Machines: 3
No. 1, Multi-wire (2), total capacity 80,000 mt/y, Trim width 4.4 m, Linerboard
No. 2, Multi-wire (2), total capacity 80,000 mt/y, Trim width 4.4 m, Linerboard
No. 3, Multi-wire (3), total capacity 140,000 mt/y, Trim width 3.2 m, Boxboard/cartonboard
Energy Data:
Electrical demand for mill: 357 MWh/D

ⓘJiangsu Jinlian Paper Co.
Ownership: 100% by private owners
89, East Jianshe Rd., Jinhu County
HuaiAn, Jiangsu, 211600
China
Phone: (86) 517 8688 2961/ 2515
Fax: (86) 517 8688 2875
Web Address: www.jlian.com
Mill Locations:
Jiangsu Jinlian Paper Co., HuaiAn Mill, 89, East Jianshe Rd., Jinhu County, HuaiAn 211600, China, Capacity: 36,000 mt/y, (Paper mill)
Phone: (86) 517 8688 2961/ 2515
Fax: (86) 517 8688 2875

ⓜJiangsu Jinlian Paper Co.
HuaiAn Mill
89, East Jianshe Rd., Jinhu County
HuaiAn, Jiangsu, 211600
China
Phone: (86) 517 8688 2961/ 2515
Fax: (86) 517 8688 2875
Web Address: www.jlian.com
Personnel:
Pres.: Suli Yu
Phone: (86) 517 8688 2961/ 2515

Chief Eng.: Chengjun Yong
Phone: (86) 517 8688 2961/ 2515
VP- Sls.: Yunqiang Gao
Phone: (86) 517 8688 2961/ 2515
Total Employees at this Location: 780
Type of Operation: Paper mill
Paper/Paperboard Grades and Capacities:
Total paper and paperboard capacity: 36,000 mt/y
Tissue: 36,000 mt/y
Paper and Paperboard Mill Data:
Paper Machines: 18
PM 1-18, cylinder, total capacity 2,000 mt/y, Trim width 1.58 m, Tissue

ⓜJiangsu Jiuxing Paper Co., Ltd.
Ownership: 100% by shareholders
No. 18 Dongmen Rd., Dongtai
Yancheng, Jiangsu, 224200
China
Phone: (86) 515 526 0943
Fax: (86) 515 522 5513
Email: jiangsujiuxing@126.com
Mill Locations:
Jiangsu Jiuxing Paper Co., Ltd., Yancheng Mill, No. 18 Dongmen Rd., Dongtai, Yancheng 224200, China, Capacity: 120,000 mt/y, (Paperboard mill)
Phone: (86) 515 526 0943
Fax: (86) 515 522 5513
Email: jiangsujiuxing@126.com

ⓜJiangsu Jiuxing Paper Co., Ltd.
Yancheng Mill
No. 18 Dongmen Rd., Dongtai
Yancheng, Jiangsu, 224200
China
Phone: (86) 515 526 0943
Fax: (86) 515 522 5513
Email: jiangsujiuxing@126.com
Personnel:
Chmn. & Pres.: Ze Wang
Phone: (86) 515 526 0943
Dir.: Fenghua Liu
Phone: (86) 515 526 0943
Sls. Mgr.: Fusen Yi
Phone: (86) 515 526 0943
Total Employees at this Location: 548
Type of Operation: Paperboard mill
Paper/Paperboard Grades and Capacities:
Total paper and paperboard capacity: 120,000 mt/y
Boxboard/cartonboard: 120,000 mt/y
Paper and Paperboard Mill Data:
Paper Machines: 2
PM 1, total capacity 50,000 mt/y, Trim width 1.76 m, Boxboard/cartonboard
PM 2, fourdrinier, total capacity 70,000 mt/y, Trim width 2.2 m, Boxboard/cartonboard

ⓜJiangsu Lee & Man Paper Manufacturing Co. Ltd.
Changshu Mill
Ownership: 100% by Lee & Man Paper Manufacturing Ltd.
Liwen Road, Yanjiang Industrial Park, Economic Development
Changshu, Jiangsu, 215536
China
Phone: (86) 512 5265 3333
Fax: (86) 512 5229 7118
Email: info@leemanpaper.com
Web Address: www.leemanpaper.com
Personnel:
Chmn.: Wenjun Li
CFO: Guoqiang Zhang
Sls. Mgr.: Xiuping Lan
Purch. Mgr.: Baigang Xie
Total Employees at this Location: 1,000
Type of Operation: Pulp mill, Paperboard mill
Pulp Grades and Capacities:

China

Total pulp capacity: 1,261,934 mt/y
Recycled Pulping: 1,261,934 mt/y
Pulp Mill Data:
Pulp Lines: 4
 Bleach Plant Systems: 2
  Recycled Pulping System
  Recycled Pulping System
 Recycled Fiber Treatment Lines:
  Flotation deinking lines: 2
  Recycled packaging pulping lines: 1
 Pulp Dryers:
  Air Float dryers 1
Paper/Paperboard Grades and Capacities:
 Total paper and paperboard capacity: 1,350,600 mt/y
 Linerboard: 1,025,600 mt/y
 Corrugating medium/fluting: 325,000 mt/y
Paper and Paperboard Mill Data:
Paper Machines: 4
 No. 5, twin-wire, total capacity 285,600 mt/y, Trim width 4.5 m, Linerboard
 No. 6, fourdrinier, total capacity 325,000 mt/y, Trim width 6.65 m, Corrugating medium/fluting
 No. 8, fourdrinier, total capacity 400,000 mt/y, Trim width 6.65 m, Linerboard
 No. 10, three-ply, total capacity 340,000 mt/y, Trim width 5.5 m, Linerboard
Energy Data:
 Power boilers: 2
 Steam turbines: 5 at 30, 30, 30, 25, 25 MW
 Electrical demand for mill: 1,802 MWh/D

ⓜJiangsu Longheng Paper Co. Ltd
Yancheng Mill
Jiangsu Xiangshui Coastal Economic Open Zone,
Xiangshui County
Yancheng, Jiangsu, 224631
China
 Phone: (86) 515 82076358
 Fax: (86) 515 82076356
Type of Operation: Paperboard mill
Pulp Grades and Capacities:
 Total pulp capacity: 261,776 mt/y
 Recycled Pulping: 261,776 mt/y
Paper/Paperboard Grades and Capacities:
 Total paper and paperboard capacity: 300,000 mt/y
 Boxboard/cartonboard: 300,000 mt/y
Paper and Paperboard Mill Data:
Paper Machines: 1
 No. 1, Fourdrinier (4), total capacity 300,000 mt/y, Trim width 4.55 m, Boxboard/cartonboard
Energy Data:
 Electrical demand for mill: 397 MWh/D

ⓞⓜJiangsu Nantong Xianglong Paper Co., Ltd
Nantong Mill
Gangzha District
Nantong, Jiangsu
China
Total Employees at this Location: 212
Type of Operation: Paperboard mill
Pulp Grades and Capacities:
 Total pulp capacity: 108,547 mt/y
 Recycled Pulping: 108,547 mt/y
Pulp Mill Data:
 Recycled Fiber Treatment Lines:
  Recycled packaging pulping lines: 1
Paper/Paperboard Grades and Capacities:
 Total paper and paperboard capacity: 111,741 mt/y
 Corrugating medium/fluting: 111,741 mt/y
Paper and Paperboard Mill Data:
Paper Machines: 2
 No. 1, fourdrinier, total capacity 61,404 mt/y, Trim width 3.9 m, Corrugating medium/fluting
 No. 2, fourdrinier, total capacity 50,337 mt/y, Trim width 3.2 m, Corrugating medium/fluting
Energy Data:
 Electrical demand for mill: 174 MWh/D

ⓜJiangsu Nine Dragons Paper Industries
Taicang Mill
Ownership: Guangdong Dongguan Nine Dragons Paper Industries Co., Ltd.
JiuLong Road, Taicang Port Development Area
Taicang, Jiangsu
China
 Phone: (86) 512 5370 3399
 Fax: (86) 512 5370 3800/ 3751
 Email: ndpaper@ndpaper.com.cn
 Web Address: www.ndpaper.com
Personnel:
 Chmn.: Yin Zhang
 CEO : Mingzhong Liu
 CFO: Yuanfu Zhang
Total Employees at this Location: 2,000
Type of Operation: Paperboard mill
Pulp Grades and Capacities:
 Total pulp capacity: 2,792,688 mt/y
 Recycled Pulping: 2,789,953 mt/y
Pulp Mill Data:
 Bleach Plant Systems: 1
 Recycled Fiber Treatment Lines:
  Flotation deinking lines
  Recycled packaging pulping lines: 5 at 2,000,000 admt/y
Paper/Paperboard Grades and Capacities:
 Total paper and paperboard capacity: 3,021,291 mt/y
 Uncoated woodfree/freesheet: 199,920 mt/y
 Linerboard: 1,736,091 mt/y
 Corrugating medium/fluting: 1,085,280 mt/y
Paper and Paperboard Mill Data:
Paper Machines: 8
 No. 5, fourdrinier (3), total capacity 454,104 mt/y, Trim width 6.65 m, Linerboard
 No. 8, fourdrinier (3), total capacity 452,319 mt/y, Trim width 6.8 m, Linerboard
 No. 16, fourdrinier (2), total capacity 392,700 mt/y, Trim width 7.2 m, Corrugating medium/fluting
 No. 17, fourdrinier (2), total capacity 392,700 mt/y, Trim width 7.2 m, Corrugating medium/fluting
 No. 20, fourdrinier (3), total capacity 429,828 mt/y, Trim width 6.66 m, Linerboard
 No. 21, (converted to printing and writing paper July 2011), fourdrinier, total capacity 199,920 mt/y, Trim width 7.25 m, Uncoated woodfree/freesheet
 No. 29, (started up January 2011), fourdrinier (3), total capacity 399,840 mt/y, Trim width 7.25 m, Linerboard
 No. 30, (started up January 2011), fourdrinier, total capacity 299,880 mt/y, Trim width 7.25 m, Corrugating medium/fluting
Energy Data:
 Power boilers
 Steam turbines at 420 MW
 Electrical demand for mill: 5,107 MWh/D

ⓞⓜJiangsu Oji Paper Nantong Co., Ltd.
Nantong Mill
Ownership: 90% by Oji Holdings Corporation, 10% by Nantong Economic and Technological Dev. Zone Corp.
Nantong Economic & Technological Development Zone
Nantong, Jiangsu, 226000
China
 Phone: (86) 21 6219 5555
 Fax: (86) 21 3223 1101
 Web Address: www.ojiholdings.co.jp/english
Personnel:
 CEO: Watanabe Tadashi
 Phone: (86) 21 6219 5555
 Gen. Mgr.: Muraji Nishi
 Phone: (86) 21 6219 5555
 Dep. Gen. Mgr.: Hiroyasu Hayano
 Phone: (86) 21 6219 5555
Total Employees at this Location: 800
Type of Operation: Paper mill
Pulp Mill Data:

Pulp Lines: 1
Paper/Paperboard Grades and Capacities:
 Total paper and paperboard capacity: 339,864 mt/y
 Uncoated woodfree/freesheet: 84,966 mt/y
 Coated woodfree/freesheet: 254,898 mt/y
Paper and Paperboard Mill Data:
Paper Machines: 1
 No. 1, DuoFormer TQv, total capacity 339,864 mt/y, Trim width 7.5 m, Coated woodfree/freesheet, Uncoated woodfree/freesheet
Coating Machines: 1
 PM 1, total capacity 255,000 mt/y., off machine
Finishing Equipment:
 Winders: 2
 Supercalenders: 2
Energy Data:
 Power boilers: 2
 Steam turbines: 2 at 80 MW
 Electrical demand for mill: 653 MWh/D

ⓜJiangsu Oji Paper Nepia (Suzhou) Co., Ltd.
Suzhou Mill
Ownership: 100% by Oji Holdings Corporation
No. 98 Jinshan Road, New District
Suzhou, Jiangsu, 215011
China
 Phone: (86) 512 6825 8526
 Fax: (86) 512 6825 9395
 Email: danny@nepia.com.cn
 Web Address: www.nepia.com
Personnel:
 Chmn.: Kamura Kikuo
 Phone: (86) 512 6825 8526
 Gen. Mgr.: Michihiro Yamashita
 Phone: (86) 512 6825 8526
Total Employees at this Location: 85
Type of Operation: Paper mill
Paper/Paperboard Grades and Capacities:
 Total paper and paperboard capacity: 20,000 mt/y
 Tissue: 20,000 mt/y
Paper and Paperboard Mill Data:
Paper Machines: 1
 No. 1, crescent former, Yankee dryer, total capacity 20,000 mt/y, Trim width 2.66 m, Tissue, Uncoated woodfree/freesheet
Finishing Equipment:
 Rewinders: 2
Energy Data:
 Electrical demand for mill: 57 MWh/D

ⓜJiangsu Peibo Paper Co., Ltd.
Taicang Mill
Yongle Development Zone, Taicang
Suzhou, Jiangsu, 215400
China
 Phone: (86) 512 5381 7208
 Fax: (86) 512 5381 7805
 Web Address: www.peibo.com.cn
Type of Operation: Paper mill
Paper/Paperboard Grades and Capacities:
 Total paper and paperboard capacity: 20,000 mt/y
 Tissue: 20,000 mt/y
Paper and Paperboard Mill Data:
Paper Machines: 12
 PM 1, total capacity 1,700 mt/y, Trim width 1.58 m, Tissue
 PM 2, total capacity 1,700 mt/y, Trim width 1.58 m, Tissue
 PM 3, total capacity 1,700 mt/y, Trim width 1.58 m, Tissue
 PM 4, total capacity 1,700 mt/y, Trim width 1.58 m, Tissue
 PM 5, total capacity 1,700 mt/y, Trim width 1.58 m, Tissue
 PM 6, total capacity 1,700 mt/y, Trim width 1.58 m, Tissue
 PM 7, total capacity 1,700 mt/y, Trim width 1.58 m, Tissue
 PM 8, total capacity 1,700 mt/y, Trim width 1.58 m, Tissue
 PM 9, total capacity 1,700 mt/y, Trim width 1.58 m, Tissue
 PM 10, total capacity 1,700 mt/y, Trim width 1.58 m, Tissue
 PM 11, total capacity 1,700 mt/y, Trim width 1.58 m, Tissue
 PM 12, total capacity 1,700 mt/y, Trim width 1.58 m, Tissue

China

ⓂJiangsu Stora Enso Suzhou Paper Co. Ltd.
Suzhou Mill
Ownership: 96.48% by Shanghai Stora Enso Asia Pacific, 3.52% by Suzhou New Zone Economy Development General Company
600, Binhe Rd.
Suzhou, Jiangsu, 215011
China
  Phone: (86) 512 6825 1060
  Fax: (86) 512 6825 1711
  Email: papyrus@public1.sz.js.cn
  Web Address: www.storaenso.com
Personnel:
  Man. Dir.: Jukka Kantola
  Phone: (86) 512 6825 1060
  Asst. Mill Mgr.: Jianwei Guo
  Phone: (86) 512 6825 1060
  Dir., Sls. & Mktg: Wangqiu Song
  Phone: (86) 512 6825 1060
Total Employees at this Location: 580
Type of Operation: Paper mill
Paper/Paperboard Grades and Capacities:
  Total paper and paperboard capacity: 245,000 mt/y
  Coated woodfree/freesheet: 245,000 mt/y
Paper and Paperboard Mill Data:
  Stock Preparation:
    Pulpers: 3
    Refiners: 6
  Paper Machines: 1
    No. 1, ValFormer, total capacity 245,000 mt/y, Trim width 3.8 m, Coated woodfree/freesheet
  Coating Machines: 1
    CM1, total capacity 245,000 mt/y., off machine
  Finishing Equipment:
    Supercalenders: 2
    Rewinders: 2
    Sheeters at 4 mt/y
  Energy Data:
    Power boilers: 3
    Steam turbines: 1 at 6 MW
    Electrical demand for mill: 455 MWh/D

ⒽⓂJiangsu Suqian Tiancheng Paper Co., Ltd
Suqian Mill
Yangzi Rd., Suqian Development Zone
Suqian, Jiangsu
China
  Phone: (86) 527 8483 9800
Total Employees at this Location: 300
Type of Operation: Paper mill
Pulp Grades and Capacities:
  Total pulp capacity: 97,232 mt/y
  Recycled Pulping: 97,232 mt/y
Pulp Mill Data:
  Recycled Fiber Treatment Lines:
    Recycled packaging pulping lines: 1
Paper/Paperboard Grades and Capacities:
  Total paper and paperboard capacity: 100,000 mt/y
  Corrugating medium/fluting: 100,000 mt/y
Paper and Paperboard Mill Data:
  Paper Machines: 3
    No. 1, fourdrinier, total capacity 40,000 mt/y, Trim width 3.6 m, Corrugating medium/fluting
    No. 2, cylinder, total capacity 25,000 mt/y, Trim width 2.85 m, Corrugating medium/fluting
    No. 3, fourdrinier, total capacity 35,000 mt/y, Trim width 3.2 m, Corrugating medium/fluting
  Energy Data:
    Power boilers: 2
    Electrical demand for mill: 121 MWh/D

ⒽJiangsu Taizhou Jinsong Paper Co., Ltd.
Ownership: 100% by private owners
No. 52 Haiyang Rd.
Taizhou, Jiangsu, 225300
China
  Phone: (86) 523 865 59075/56059/828 48114
  Fax: (86) 523 865 56059
Personnel:
  Gen. Mgr.: Jingrong Cai
  Phone: (86) 523 865 59075/56059/828 48114
  Sls. Mgr.: Chunxi Chang
  Phone: (86) 523 865 59075/56059/828 48114
Mill Locations:
Jiangsu Taizhou Jinsong Paper Co., Ltd., Taizhou Mill, No. 52 Haiyang Rd., Taizhou 225300, China, Capacity: 17,000 mt/y, (Paper mill)
  Phone: (86) 523 865 59075/56059/828 48114
  Fax: (86) 523 865 56059

ⒽJiangsu Taizhou Jinsong Paper Co., Ltd.
Taizhou Mill
No. 52 Haiyang Rd.
Taizhou, Jiangsu, 225300
China
  Phone: (86) 523 865 59075/56059/828 48114
  Fax: (86) 523 865 56059
Personnel:
  Gen. Mgr.: Jingrong Cai
  Phone: (86) 523 865 59075/56059/828 48114
  Sls. Mgr.: Chunxi Chang
  Phone: (86) 523 865 59075/56059/828 48114
Total Employees at this Location: 250
Type of Operation: Paper mill
Pulp Grades and Capacities:
  Total pulp capacity: 35,700 mt/y
  Recycled Pulping: 35,700 mt/y
Pulp Mill Data:
  Pulp Lines: 1
    Recycled Fiber Treatment Lines:
    Flotation deinking lines: 1 at 35,700 admt/y
Paper/Paperboard Grades and Capacities:
  Total paper and paperboard capacity: 17,000 mt/y
  Specialty and industrial: 17,000 mt/y
Paper and Paperboard Mill Data:
  Paper Machines: 2
    PM 1, fourdrinier, total capacity 7,000 mt/y, Trim width 1.58 m, Specialty and industrial
    PM 2, fourdrinier, total capacity 10,000 mt/y, Trim width 2.64 m, Specialty and industrial

ⒽJiangsu Taizhou Weidmann High Voltage Insulation Co. Ltd
Taizhou Mill
Ownership: 50% by Wicor Group, 50% by Taizhou Hope Investment Co., Ltd.
No.40 Haiyang Rd.
Taizhou, Jiangsu, 225300
China
  Phone: (86) 523 8656 6972/8655 9379/8284 8691
  Fax: (86) 523 8656 0610
  Email: michael.xu@weidmann.com.hk, xuluping@weidmann.com.cn
  Web Address: www.weidmann.com.cn
Personnel:
  Pres.: Jianning Zhang
  Phone: (86) 523 8655 9075/ 4018
  Gen. Mgr./ Mill Mgr.: Jinjun Wu
  Phone: (86) 523 8655 9075/ 4018
Type of Operation: Paper mill
Pulp Mill Data:
Paper/Paperboard Grades and Capacities:
  Total paper and paperboard capacity: 7,500 mt/y
  Boxboard/cartonboard: 7,500 mt/y

ⒽJiangsu UPM, Changshu Paper Industry Co., Ltd.
Changshu Mill
Ownership: 100% by UPM-Kymmene Corporation
Wushi, Xingang Town
Changshu, Jiangsu, 215536
China
  Phone: (86) 512 5265 1818
  Fax: (86) 512 5265 2300/2173
  Web Address: www.upm-kymmene.com.cn
Personnel:
  Gen. Mgr.: Pentti Putkinen
  Phone: (86) 512 5265 1818
  Fax: (86) 512 5265 2300
  Email: pentti.putkinen@upm.com
  Exec. VP, UPM Paper Asia: Kim Poulsen
  Phone: (86) 512 5265 1818
  Fax: (86) 512 5265 2300
  Production Dir: Yunfeng Xiao
  Phone: (86) 512 5265 1818 ext.3908
  Fax: (86) 512 5265 1334
  Email: xiao.yunfeng@upm.com
  PM1 Prod. Mgr.: Zhiyun Zhu
  Phone: (86) 512 5265 1818 ext.5602
  Fax: (86) 512 5229 6697
  Email: zhu.zhijian@upm.com
  PM2 Prod. Mgr.: Yun Chen
  Phone: (86) 5125 2651818 ext. 3240
  Email: chen.yun@upm.com
  Energy & Power Dir: Yong Xu
  Phone: (86) 512 5265 1818 ext. 5009
  Email: david.xu@upm.com
  R&D Mgr: Yan Zhang
  Phone: (86) 512 5265 1818 ext. 6708
  Fax: (86) 512 5229 9710
  Email: zhang.yan@upm.com
  HR Mgr: Hua Zhu
  Phone: (86) 512 5265 1818 ext.300
  Fax: (86) 512 5265 2301
  Email: zhu.hua@upm.com
  Marketing Dir: Ali Malassu
  Phone: (86) 21 6288 1919
  Fax: (86) 21 5292 8912
  Email: Ali.Malassu@upm.com
  Logistics Mgr: Xiang Huang
  Phone: (86) 512 1818 ext. 3691
  Fax: (86) 512 5265 2130
  Email: huang.xiang@upm.com
Total Employees at this Location: 600
Type of Operation: Paper mill
Paper/Paperboard Grades and Capacities:
  Total paper and paperboard capacity: 870,000 mt/y
  Uncoated woodfree/freesheet: 620,000 mt/y
  Coated woodfree/freesheet: 250,000 mt/y
Paper and Paperboard Mill Data:
  Stock Preparation:
    Pulpers: 2
  Paper Machines: 2
    No. 1, OptiFormer, total capacity 490,000 mt/y, Trim width 9.73 m, Uncoated woodfree/freesheet
    No. 2, SpeedFormer HHS, total capacity 380,000 mt/y, Trim width 8.66 m, Uncoated woodfree/freesheet, Coated woodfree/freesheet
  Coating Machines: 1
    PM 2, total capacity 240,000 mt/y., on machine
  Finishing Equipment:
    Winders: 2
    Supercalenders: 1
    Sheeters: 10
  Energy Data:
    Power boilers: 4
    Steam turbines: 2 at 50, 50 MW
    Electrical demand for mill: 1,719 MWh/D

ⒽJiangsu Wanda Paper Co., Ltd.
Ownership: 100% by Tung TAT Paper and Invest (China) Limited
Wanda Industrial Park, Yutang Town, Xinbei District
Changzhou, Jiangsu, 213033
China
  Phone: (86) 519 8506 6888/ 6838
  Fax: (86) 519 8506 6989/ 6860
  Email: zouji1101@126.cn
  Web Address: www.wandapaper.com
Total Employees at this Location: 800
Mill Locations:
Jiangsu Wanda Paper Co., Ltd., Changzhou Mill, Wanda

China

Industrial Park, Yutang Town, Xinbei District, Changzhou 213033, China, Capacity: 200,000 mt/y, (Paperboard mill)
Phone: (86) 519 8506 6888/ 6838
Fax: (86) 519 8506 6989/ 6860
Email: zouji1101@126.cm

(M)Jiangsu Wanda Paper Co., Ltd.
Changzhou Mill
Wanda Industrial Park, Yutang Town, Xinbei District
Changzhou, Jiangsu, 213033
China
Phone: (86) 519 8506 6888/ 6838
Fax: (86) 519 8506 6989/ 6860
Email: zouji1101@126.cm
Web Address: www.wandapaper.com
Personnel:
Dir. & Gen. Mgr.: Lin Bing Shi
Phone: (86) 519 8506 6888/ 6838
Total Employees at this Location: 800
Type of Operation: Paperboard mill
Pulp Grades and Capacities:
Total pulp capacity: 170,602 mt/y
Recycled Pulping: 170,602 mt/y
Pulp Mill Data:
Recycled Fiber Treatment Lines:
Recycled packaging pulping lines: 1
Paper/Paperboard Grades and Capacities:
Total paper and paperboard capacity: 200,000 mt/y
Linerboard: 200,000 mt/y
Paper and Paperboard Mill Data:
Paper Machines: 1
No. 1, Multi-wire (3), total capacity 200,000 mt/y, Trim width 4.4 m, Linerboard
Energy Data:
Electrical demand for mill: 260 MWh/D

(O)(M)Jiangsu Wanxing Paper Co., Ltd
Suqian Mill
East Zhongxing Rd
Suqian, Jiangsu
China
Type of Operation: Paperboard mill
Paper/Paperboard Grades and Capacities:
Total paper and paperboard capacity: 70,000 mt/y
Corrugating medium/fluting: 70,000 mt/y
Paper and Paperboard Mill Data:
Paper Machines: 1
PM 1, total capacity 70,000 mt/y, Trim width 4.4 m, Corrugating medium/fluting

(M)Jiangsu Wuxi Long Chen Paper Co., Ltd.
Wuxi Mill
Ownership: 94% by Long Chen Paper Co. Ltd., 6% by Wuxi Longda Industry Corporation
No. 43, Zhongxing West Road, Luoshe Town, Huishan District
Wuxi, Jiangsu, 214187
China
Phone: (86) 510 8331 1540/6666
Fax: (86) 510 8331 1826/2701
Email: wang@lcpc.biz,
w1997088@lcpc.biz
Web Address: www.lcpc.biz
Personnel:
Chmn. & Gen. Mgr.: Yingbin Zheng
Phone: (86) 510 8331 1540/6666
VP: Wenqing Lin
Phone: (86) 510 8331 1540/6666
Mill Mgr.: Guozhen Wu
Phone: (86) 510 8331 1540/6666
Total Employees at this Location: 890
Type of Operation: Paperboard mill
Pulp Grades and Capacities:
Total pulp capacity: 789,430 mt/y
Recycled Pulping: 789,430 mt/y
Pulp Mill Data:

Pulp Lines: 3
Bleach Plant Lines:
Recycled Pulping System
Recycled Fiber Treatment Lines:
Flotation deinking lines
Recycled packaging pulping lines
Paper/Paperboard Grades and Capacities:
Total paper and paperboard capacity: 800,000 mt/y
Linerboard: 350,000 mt/y
Corrugating medium/fluting: 450,000 mt/y
Paper and Paperboard Mill Data:
Paper Machines: 4
No. 1, Multi-wire (3), total capacity 100,000 mt/y, Trim width 3.25 m, Linerboard
No. 2, fourdrinier, total capacity 180,000 mt/y, Trim width 5 m, Corrugating medium/fluting
No. 3, fourdrinier, total capacity 270,000 mt/y, Trim width 6.66 m, Corrugating medium/fluting
No. 3B, Multi-wire (3), total capacity 250,000 mt/y, Trim width 6.66 m, Linerboard
Finishing Equipment:
Rewinders: 1
Energy Data:
Power boilers: 2
Combustion turbines: 1 at 40 MW
Electrical demand for mill: 975 MWh/D

(M)Jiangsu Xinda Paper Co. Ltd.
Ownership: shareholders
No.4, Xinhua Road
Xinyi, Jiangsu, 221400
China
Phone: (86) 516 8892 2622/8889 9932
Fax: (86) 516 8892 4247
Email: xdzy@xindapaper.com,
chenhm@public.xz.js.cn
Web Address: www.xindapaper.com
Personnel:
Chmn. & Pres.: Pei Wang
Gen. Mgr.: Jianzhong Liu
VP: Huaming Chen
VP, Technol. Mgr.: Xianjin Wei
Sls. Mgr.: Kaifeng Wang
Asst. Mill Mgr., VP: Shahua Zhang
Chief Eng.: Qingkun An
Total Employees at this Location: 1,700
Mill Locations:
Jiangsu Xinda Paper Co. Ltd., Xinyi Mill, No.4, Xinhua Road, Xinyi 221400, China, (Paper mill)
Phone: (86) 516 8861 0108/0268/6375/0210
Fax: (86) 516 8861 9296
Email: xdzy@xindapaper.com, chenhm@public.xz.js.cn

(M)Jiangsu Xinda Paper Co. Ltd.
Xinyi Mill
Mill is under bankruptcy protection (since 2013.11)
No.4, Xinhua Road
Xinyi, Jiangsu, 221400
China
Phone: (86) 516 8861 0108/0268/6375/0210
Fax: (86) 516 8861 9296
Email: xdzy@xindapaper.com,
chenhm@public.xz.js.cn
Web Address: www.xindapaper.com
Personnel:
Chmn. & Pres.: Pei Wang
Phone: (86) 516 8892 2622/8889 9932
Gen. Mgr.: Jianzhong Liu
Phone: (86) 516 8892 2622/8889 9932
VP: Huaming Chen
Phone: (86) 516 8892 2622/8889 9932
VP, Technol. Mgr.: Xianjin Wei
Phone: (86) 516 8892 2622/8889 9932
Sls. Mgr.: Kaifeng Wang
Phone: (86) 516 8892 2622/8889 9932
Asst. Mill Mgr.: Shahua Zhang
Phone: (86) 516 8892 2622/8889 9932
Chief Eng.: Qingkun An
Phone: (86) 516 8892 2622/8889 9932
Total Employees at this Location: 1,700

Type of Operation: Paper mill
Pulp Mill Data:
Chemical Pulping Systems:
Continuous digesters
Pulp Lines: 1
Bleach Plant Systems: 1
No. 1, Sequence: CEpH
Chemical Recovery Equipment:
Evaporator lines
Recovery boilers: 1
Paper and Paperboard Mill Data:
Stock Preparation:
Pulpers: 5
Paper Machines: 12
No. 1, fourdrinier, total capacity 10,000 mt/y, Trim width 1.76 m, Uncoated woodfree/freesheet
No. 2, fourdrinier, total capacity 15,000 mt/y, Trim width 2.64 m, Uncoated woodfree/freesheet
No. 3, total capacity 1,428 mt/y, Trim width 1.58 m, Tissue
No. 4, total capacity 1,428 mt/y, Trim width 1.58 m, Tissue
No. 5, total capacity 2,142 mt/y, Trim width 1.88 m, Tissue
No. 6, total capacity 2,142 mt/y, Trim width 1.88 m, Tissue
No. 7, total capacity 2,142 mt/y, Trim width 1.88 m, Tissue
No. 8, total capacity 2,142 mt/y, Trim width 1.88 m, Tissue
No. 9, total capacity 2,142 mt/y, Trim width 1.88 m, Tissue
No. 10, total capacity 1,428 mt/y, Trim width 1.88 m, Tissue
No. 11, total capacity 1,428 mt/y, Trim width 1.88 m, Tissue
No. 12, total capacity 1,428 mt/y, Trim width 1.88 m, Uncoated woodfree/freesheet
Energy Data:
Power boilers: 1

(M)Jiangsu Xuzhou Xinyuan Paper Co.,Ltd
Xuzhou Mill
Sunzhuang Village, Liuxing Town, Tongshan County
Xuzhou, Jiangsu
China
Phone: (86) 516 8268 8694
Fax: (86) 516 8508 5998
Email: 124791000@qq.com
Personnel:
Zhang
Total Employees at this Location: 260
Type of Operation: Paper mill
Pulp Grades and Capacities:
Total pulp capacity: 97,021 mt/y
Recycled Pulping: 97,021 mt/y
Paper/Paperboard Grades and Capacities:
Total paper and paperboard capacity: 99,960 mt/y
Corrugating medium/fluting: 99,960 mt/y
Paper and Paperboard Mill Data:
Paper Machines: 1
No. 1, fourdrinier, total capacity 99,960 mt/y, Trim width 4 m, Corrugating medium/fluting
Energy Data:
Electrical demand for mill: 158 MWh/D

(M)Jiangsu Yixing Zhangzhu Paper Mill
Ownership: 100% by private owners
No. 18, Zhugang Rd., Chating Village, Zhangzhu Town
Yixing, Jiangsu, 214213
China
Phone: (86) 510 8730 1374/ 1375
Fax: (86) 510 8730 1375
Mill Locations:
Jiangsu Yixing Zhangzhu Paper Mill, Yixing Mill, No. 18, Zhugang Rd., Chating Village, Zhangzhu Town, Yixing 214213, China, Capacity: 25,000 mt/y, (Paper mill)
Phone: (86) 510 8730 1374/ 1375
Fax: (86) 510 8730 1375

(M)Jiangsu Yixing Zhangzhu Paper Mill
Yixing Mill
No. 18, Zhugang Rd., Chating Village, Zhangzhu Town
Yixing, Jiangsu, 214213
China
Phone: (86) 510 8730 1374/ 1375
Fax: (86) 510 8730 1375

China

Personnel:
Chmn.: Jinshun Liu
Phone: (86) 510 8730 1374/ 1375
Mill Mgr.: Linming Chen
Phone: (86) 510 8730 1374/ 1375
Prod. Mgr.: Guoqiang Shen
Phone: (86) 510 8730 1374/ 1375
Total Employees at this Location: 500
Type of Operation: Paper mill
Pulp Grades and Capacities:
Total pulp capacity: 25,000 mt/y
Recycled Pulping: 25,000 mt/y

Pulp Mill Data:
Pulp Lines: 1
Paper/Paperboard Grades and Capacities:
Total paper and paperboard capacity: 25,000 mt/y
Corrugating medium/fluting: 25,000 mt/y
Paper and Paperboard Mill Data:
Paper Machines: 3
PM 1, cylinder, total capacity 2,000 mt/y, Trim width 1.6 m, Corrugating medium/fluting
PM 2, cylinder, total capacity 8,000 mt/y, Trim width 2.7 m, Corrugating medium/fluting
PM 3, multi-wire, total capacity 15,000 mt/y, Trim width 3.6 m, Corrugating medium/fluting
Energy Data:
Power boilers: 1

ⓂJiangsu Yuen Foong Yu Paper (Kunshan) Co. Ltd.
Kunshan Mill
Ownership: 100% by Yuen Foong Yu Inc.
No. 999, Yuen Foong Yu Rd., Yushan Town
Kunshan, Jiangsu, 215316
China
Phone: (86) 512 5779 2888
Fax: (86) 512 5779 2168
Email: yfywyh@public1.sz.js.cn
Web Address: www.yfy.com
Personnel:
Chmn.: Jinhong Wu
Phone: (86) 512 5779 2888
Gen. Mgr.: Tianyi Zhang
Phone: (86) 512 5779 2888
Total Employees at this Location: 224
Type of Operation: Paper mill
Paper/Paperboard Grades and Capacities:
Total paper and paperboard capacity: 41,000 mt/y
Tissue: 41,000 mt/y
Paper and Paperboard Mill Data:
Paper Machines: 2
No. 1, crescent former, total capacity 17,000 mt/y, Trim width 2.18 m, Tissue, Uncoated woodfree/freesheet
No. 2, crescent former, total capacity 24,000 mt/y, Trim width 2.4 m, Tissue, Uncoated woodfree/freesheet
Finishing Equipment:
Rewinders: 2
Energy Data:
Power boilers: 1
Electrical demand for mill: 106 MWh/D

ⓂJiangsu Yuen Foong Yu Paper (Yangzhou) Co., Ltd.
Yangzhou Mill
Ownership: 100% by YFY Cayman
No. 168, Chunjiang Road, Economy & Development Zone
Yangzhou, Jiangsu, 225000
China
Phone: (86) 514 8752 9888
Fax: (86) 514 8752 9889
Web Address: www.yfy.com/tw
Total Employees at this Location: 930
Type of Operation: Paper mill, Paperboard mill
Pulp Grades and Capacities:
Total pulp capacity: 848,964 mt/y
Recycled Pulping: 770,874 mt/y
Other Pulp: 78,090 mt/y

Pulp Mill Data:
Chemical Pulping Systems:
Continuous digesters: 1
Pulp Lines: 2
Recycled Fiber Treatment Lines:
Recycled packaging pulping lines: 1 at 390,000
Paper/Paperboard Grades and Capacities:
Total paper and paperboard capacity: 914,500 mt/y
Tissue: 64,500 mt/y
Linerboard: 680,000 mt/y
Corrugating medium/fluting: 170,000 mt/y
Paper and Paperboard Mill Data:
Paper Machines: 5
No. 1, fourdrinier, total capacity 170,000 mt/y, Trim width 3.96 m, Corrugating medium/fluting
No. 2, fourdrinier (3), total capacity 280,000 mt/y, Trim width 4.76 m, Linerboard
No. 3, fourdrinier (3), total capacity 400,000 mt/y, Trim width 6.66 m, Linerboard
No. 5, crescent former, Yankee dryer, total capacity 34,500 mt/y, Trim width 2.8 m, Tissue
No. 6, crescent former, Yankee dryer, total capacity 30,000 mt/y, Trim width 2.8 m, Tissue
Energy Data:
Power boilers: 1
Steam turbines: 1 at 4 MW
Electrical demand for mill: 1,247 MWh/D

ⓂJiangsu Yujie Paper Co., Ltd.
Xuzhou Mill
Chenlou Industrial Park, Pizhou
Xuzhou, Jiangsu, 221300
China
Phone: (86) 516 8691 9118
Fax: (86) 516 8691 9358
Web Address: www.shyjpaper.cn
Type of Operation: Paper mill
Paper/Paperboard Grades and Capacities:
Total paper and paperboard capacity: 16,000 mt/y
Tissue: 16,000 mt/y
Paper and Paperboard Mill Data:
Paper Machines: 8
PM 1, total capacity 2,000 mt/y, Trim width 1.58 m, Tissue
PM 2, total capacity 2,000 mt/y, Trim width 1.58 m, Tissue
PM 3, total capacity 2,000 mt/y, Trim width 1.58 m, Tissue
PM 4, total capacity 2,000 mt/y, Trim width 1.58 m, Tissue
PM 5, total capacity 2,000 mt/y, Trim width 1.58 m, Tissue
PM 6, total capacity 2,000 mt/y, Trim width 1.58 m, Tissue
PM 7, total capacity 2,000 mt/y, Trim width 1.58 m, Tissue
PM 8, total capacity 2,000 mt/y, Trim width 1.58 m, Tissue

ⓘJiangsu Zhangjiagang Mingxing Paper Co., Ltd.
Ownership: 100% by private owners
Miaoqiao Village
Zhangjiagang, Jiangsu, 215615
China
Phone: (86) 512 5846 1332/ 1313
Fax: (86) 512 5846 1332
Mill Locations:
Jiangsu Zhangjiagang Mingxing Paper Co., Ltd., Zhangjiagang Mill, Miaoqiao Village, Zhangjiagang 215615, China, Capacity: 25,000 mt/y, (Paperboard mill)
Phone: (86) 512 5846 1332/ 1313
Fax: (86) 512 5846 1332

ⓂJiangsu Zhangjiagang Mingxing Paper Co., Ltd.
Zhangjiagang Mill
Miaoqiao Village
Zhangjiagang, Jiangsu, 215615
China
Phone: (86) 512 5846 1332/ 1313
Fax: (86) 512 5846 1332
Personnel:
Pres.: Jianping Zhang
Phone: (86) 512 5846 1332/ 1313

Total Employees at this Location: 150
Type of Operation: Paperboard mill
Pulp Grades and Capacities:
Total pulp capacity: 25,000 mt/y
Recycled Pulping: 25,000 mt/y
Pulp Mill Data:
Pulp Lines: 1
Paper/Paperboard Grades and Capacities:
Total paper and paperboard capacity: 25,000 mt/y
Boxboard/cartonboard: 25,000 mt/y
Paper and Paperboard Mill Data:
Paper Machines: 1
PM 2, multi-wire, total capacity 25,000 mt/y, Trim width 2.36 m, Boxboard/cartonboard

ⓘJiangyin Xinhao Recycling Paper Co., Ltd.
665 South Outer Ring Road
Jiangyin, Jiangsu
China
Phone: (86) 0510-86108288
Fax: (86) 0510-86108867
Email: lbx008@xinhaopaper.com
Web Address: www.xinhaopaper.com
Mill Locations:
Jiangyin Xinhao Recycling Paper Co., Ltd., Jiangyin Mill, No 665 South Waihuan Road, Jiangyin 214433, China, Capacity: 187,425 mt/y, (Paper mill, Paperboard mill)
Phone: (86) 510 8610 8288
Fax: (86) 510 8610 8867
Email: john_xu0602@sina.com/lbx008@xinhaopaper.com

ⓂJiangyin Xinhao Recycling Paper Co., Ltd.
Jiangyin Mill
No 665 South Waihuan Road
Jiangyin, Jiangsu, 214433
China
Phone: (86) 510 8610 8288
Fax: (86) 510 8610 8867
Email: john_xu0602@sina.com/lbx008@xinhaopaper.com
Web Address: www.xinhaopaper.com
Personnel:
Chmn.: Haorong Zhang
Phone: (86) 510 8611 8800
Pres.: Junhua Li
Phone: (86) 510 8611 8800
VP: Xinhua Zhang
Phone: (86) 510 8611 8800
Total Employees at this Location: 440
Type of Operation: Paper mill, Paperboard mill
Pulp Grades and Capacities:
Total pulp capacity: 142,007 mt/y
Recycled Pulping: 142,007 mt/y

Pulp Mill Data:
Pulp Lines: 2
Recycled Fiber Treatment Lines:
Flotation deinking lines at 150,000 admt/y
Paper/Paperboard Grades and Capacities:
Total paper and paperboard capacity: 187,425 mt/y
Boxboard/cartonboard: 187,425 mt/y
Paper and Paperboard Mill Data:
Paper Machines: 2
No. 1, cylinder (7), total capacity 69,615 mt/y, Trim width 2.4 m, Boxboard/cartonboard
No. 2, fourdrinier, total capacity 117,810 mt/y, Trim width 2.64 m, Boxboard/cartonboard
Coating Machines: 2
PM 1, total capacity 70,000 mt/y., on machine
PM 2, total capacity 118,000 mt/y., on machine
Finishing Equipment:
Rewinders: 1
Sheeters: 6
Energy Data:
Electrical demand for mill: 241 MWh/D

China

ⓂKabool(Lianyungang) Rayon Co., Ltd.
Lianyungang Mill
No.1 Linhong Rd., Economic and Technological Development Zone
Lianyungang, Jiangsu, 222000
China
  Phone: (86) 518 8515 0851
  Fax: (86) 518 8515 0014
  Email: lyg@kaboollyg.com
  Web Address: www.kaboollyg.com
Total Employees at this Location: 413
Type of Operation: Pulp mill
Pulp Grades and Capacities:
  Total pulp capacity: 55,000 mt/y

ⓂKookil Paper (Zhangjiagang) Mfg. Co., Ltd.
Jifu Rd., Fenghuang Town
Zhangjiagang, Jiangsu, 215614
China
  Phone: (86) 512 5842 3721
  Fax: (86) 512 5842 1207
  Web Address: www.kookilpaper.com
Personnel:
  Gen. Mgr.: Fuzhen Li
  Phone: (86) 512 5842 3721
  Fax: (86) 512 5842 1207
Mill Locations:
Kookil Paper (Zhangjiagang) Mfg. Co., Ltd., Zhangjiagang Mill, Jifu Rd., Fenghuang Town, Zhangjiagang 215614, China, Capacity: 140,000 mt/y, (Paper mill)
  Phone: (86) 512 5842 3721
  Fax: (86) 512 5842 1207

ⓂKookil Paper (Zhangjiagang) Mfg. Co., Ltd.
Zhangjiagang Mill
Jifu Rd., Fenghuang Town
Zhangjiagang, Jiangsu, 215614
China
  Phone: (86) 512 5842 3721
  Fax: (86) 512 5842 1207
  Web Address: www.kookilpaper.com
Type of Operation: Paper mill
Paper/Paperboard Grades and Capacities:
  Total paper and paperboard capacity: 140,000 mt/y
  Specialty and industrial: 140,000 mt/y
Paper and Paperboard Mill Data:
Paper Machines: 2
  PM 1, total capacity 30,000 mt/y, Trim width 2.57 m, Specialty and industrial
  PM 2, total capacity 110,000 mt/y, Trim width 2.65 m, Specialty and industrial

ⓂShengda Group Jiangsu Shuangdeng Paper Co., Ltd.
Yancheng Mill
Ownership: Zhejiang Shengda Group
No. 28 Haigang Rd., Shuangdeng Industry Park, Huangshagang Town, Sheyang County
Yancheng, Jiangsu, 224341
China
  Phone: (86) 515 8226 3888/ 3907
  Fax: (86) 515 8226 3999
  Web Address: www.chinasund.com
Personnel:
  Chmn.: Lin Fang
  Phone: (86) 515 8226 3888/ 3907
  Gen. Mgr.: Lin Zhao
  Phone: (86) 515 8226 3888/ 3907
Total Employees at this Location: 415
Type of Operation: Pulp mill, Paper mill
Pulp Grades and Capacities:
  Total pulp capacity: 14,574 mt/y
  Recycled Pulping: 12,978 mt/y
  Other Pulp: 1,596 mt/y
Pulp Mill Data:
  Chemical Pulping Systems:
  Continuous digesters
  Pulp Lines: 2
  Bleach Plant Systems: 2
  Chemical Pulping System
  DIP
  Chemical Recovery Equipment:
  Recovery boilers: 1
  Recycled Fiber Treatment Lines:
  Flotation deinking lines: 1 at 60,000 admt/y
Paper/Paperboard Grades and Capacities:
  Total paper and paperboard capacity: 20,000 mt/y
  Tissue: 20,000 mt/y
Paper and Paperboard Mill Data:
Paper Machines: 14
  No. 1, cylinder, total capacity 3,356 mt/y, Trim width 1.88 m, Tissue
  No. 2, cylinder, total capacity 3,356 mt/y, Trim width 1.88 m, Tissue
  No. 3, cylinder, total capacity 3,356 mt/y, Trim width 1.88 m, Tissue
  No. 4, cylinder, total capacity 3,356 mt/y, Trim width 1.88 m, Tissue
  No. 5, cylinder, total capacity 3,356 mt/y, Trim width 1.88 m, Tissue
  No. 6, cylinder, total capacity 3,356 mt/y, Trim width 1.88 m, Tissue
  No. 7, cylinder, total capacity 3,356 mt/y, Trim width 1.88 m, Tissue
  No. 8, cylinder, total capacity 3,356 mt/y, Trim width 1.88 m, Tissue
  No. 9, cylinder, total capacity 3,356 mt/y, Trim width 1.88 m, Tissue
  No. 10, cylinder, total capacity 3,356 mt/y, Trim width 1.88 m, Tissue
  No. 11, cylinder, total capacity 3,356 mt/y, Trim width 1.88 m, Tissue
  No. 12, cylinder, total capacity 3,356 mt/y, Trim width 1.88 m, Tissue
  TM1, (Supplier: Hangzhou Dalu.), cylinder, total capacity 10,000 mt/y, Trim width 2.68 m, Tissue
  TM2, (Supplier: Hangzhou Dalu.), cylinder, total capacity 10,000 mt/y, Trim width 2.8 m, Tissue
Energy Data:
Power boilers: 2
Steam turbines: 1 at 3 MW
Electrical demand for mill: 161 MWh/D

ⓄⓂJiangsu Shuangsheng Paper Technology Development Co. Ltd.
Yancheng Mill
Ownership: Zhejiang Shengda Group
No.28, Haigang Rd., Huangshagang Town
Sheyang, Yancheng City, Jiangsu, 22434-4341
China
  Phone: (86) 515-82263888
  Web Address: www.sdgroup.cn
Total Employees at this Location: 150
Type of Operation: Paper mill
Pulp Grades and Capacities:
  Total pulp capacity: 148,687 mt/y
  Recycled Pulping: 148,687 mt/y
Pulp Mill Data:
  Recycled Fiber Treatment Lines:
  Recycled packaging pulping lines: 1
Paper/Paperboard Grades and Capacities:
  Total paper and paperboard capacity: 150,000 mt/y
  Corrugating medium/fluting: 150,000 mt/y
Paper and Paperboard Mill Data:
Paper Machines: 1
  No. 1, twin-wire, total capacity 150,000 mt/y, Trim width 4.4 m, Corrugating medium/fluting
Energy Data:
Power boilers
Electrical demand for mill: 171 MWh/D

ⓄZhenjiang Dadong Pulp & Paper Co. Ltd.
Ownership: state
61 Dong Wu Rd.
Zhenjiang, Jiangsu, 212001
China
  Phone: (86) 511 88820202
  Fax: (86) 511 88820201
  Email: ddppic@public.zj.js.cn
Personnel:
  Chmn./Pres.: Yifang Huang
  Phone: (86) 511 88820202
  Paper Mill Mgr.: Feng Zhao
  Phone: (86) 511 88820202
  Asst. Mill Mgr.: Ching-Yi hang
  Phone: (86) 511 88820202
  Sls. & Mktg. Mgr.: Ruiyan Su
  Phone: (86) 511 88820202
  Tech. Dir.: Jin-Cai Miao
  Phone: (86) 511 88820202
  Chief Eng.: Nan-Tai Miao
  Phone: (86) 511 88820202
  Maint. Mgr.: Jin-Hua Shen
  Phone: (86) 511 88820202
Mill Locations:
Zhenjiang Dadong Pulp & Paper Co. Ltd., Zhenjiang Mill, No. 8 Dongfang Rd., Zhenjiang New Aera, Zhenjiang 212001, China, Capacity: 90,860 mt/y, (Paper mill)
  Phone: (86) 511 88820202-7000/2412/4000/3000/2200
  Fax: (86) 511 88820201
  Email: dadong@zjddzy.com

ⓂZhenjiang Dadong Pulp & Paper Co. Ltd.
Zhenjiang Mill
No. 8 Dongfang Rd., Zhenjiang New Aera
Zhenjiang, Jiangsu, 212001
China
  Phone: (86) 511 88820202-7000/2412/4000/3000/2200
  Fax: (86) 511 88820201
  Email: dadong@zjddzy.com
  Web Address: www.zjddzy.com
Personnel:
  Chmn./Pres.: Yifang Huang
  Phone: (86) 511 88820202
  Paper Mill Mgr.: Feng Zhao
  Phone: (86) 511 88820202
  Asst. Mill Mgr.: Ching-Yi Chang
  Phone: (86) 511 88820202
  Sls. & Mktg. Mgr.: Ruiyan Su
  Phone: (86) 511 88820202
  Tech. Dir.: Jin-Cai Zhu
  Phone: (86) 511 88820202
  Chief Eng.: Nan-Tai Miao
  Phone: (86) 511 88820202
  Maint. Mgr.: Jin-Hua Shen
  Phone: (86) 511 88820202
Total Employees at this Location: 1,400
Type of Operation: Paper mill
Paper/Paperboard Grades and Capacities:
  Total paper and paperboard capacity: 90,860 mt/y
  Uncoated woodfree/freesheet: 58,000 mt/y
  Specialty and industrial: 2,860 mt/y
  Boxboard/cartonboard: 30,000 mt/y
Paper and Paperboard Mill Data:
  Stock Preparation:
  Pulpers: 10
  Refiners: 20
Paper Machines: 6
  No. 1, multi-fourdrinier, total capacity 30,000 mt/y, Trim width 1.88 m, Boxboard/cartonboard
  No. 2, fourdrinier, total capacity 5,000 mt/y, Trim width 1.88 m, Uncoated woodfree/freesheet
  No. 3, fourdrinier, total capacity 4,500 mt/y, Trim width 1.88 m, Uncoated woodfree/freesheet
  No. 4, fourdrinier, total capacity 2,860 mt/y, Trim width 1.88 m, Specialty and industrial
  No. 5, fourdrinier, total capacity 12,500 mt/y, Trim width 1.88 m, Uncoated woodfree/freesheet
  No. 8, fourdrinier, total capacity 36,000 mt/y, Trim width 1.88 m, Uncoated woodfree/freesheet
Coating Machines: 1

No. 1, total capacity 50,000 mt/y, off machine
Finishing Equipment:
  Supercalenders: 2
  Rewinders: 6
Energy Data:
Power boilers: 2
Steam turbines: 3 at 4 MW
Electrical demand for mill: 152 MWh/D

ⓂZhenjiang Wanfa Chemical Fiber Co., Ltd.
Zhenjiang Mill
Ownership: Henan Haiyang Chemical Fiber Group Co., Ltd.
Gaoqiao Town, Dantu District
Zhejiang, Jiangsu
China
  Phone: (86) 511 85572828
  Web Address: www.hyfiber.com
Type of Operation: Pulp mill
Pulp Grades and Capacities:
  Total pulp capacity: 10,000 mt/y

JIANGXI

ⓂJiangxi Chenming Paper Co., Ltd.
Nanchang (Jiangxi Chenming Paper) Mill
Ownership: 100% by Chenming Paper Holdings Ltd.
Changbei Economy and Technology District, Baishuihu Industry Park
Nanchang, Jiangxi, 330013
China
  Phone: (86) 791 3951 968/982
  Fax: (86) 791 388 7599
  Web Address: www.chenmingpaper.com
Personnel:
  Chmn.: Shaohua Zhou
  Phone: (86) 791 3951 968/982
Total Employees at this Location: 800
Type of Operation: Pulp mill, Paper mill
Pulp Grades and Capacities:
  Total pulp capacity: 223,767 mt/y
  Pulp available for market: 25,000 mt/y
  Mechanical Pulp: 126,970 mt/y
  Recycled Pulping: 96,797 mt/y
Pulp Mill Data:
  Mechanical Pulping Systems:
  BCTMP systems: 1
Pulp Lines: 2
  Recycled Fiber Treatment Lines:
  Flotation deinking lines: 1 at 400
  Pulp Dryers:
  Pulp Dryers 1
Paper/Paperboard Grades and Capacities:
  Total paper and paperboard capacity: 350,000 mt/y
  Uncoated mechanical/groundwood: 116,667 mt/y
  Coated mechanical/groundwood: 233,333 mt/y
Paper and Paperboard Mill Data:
Paper Machines: 1
No. 1, OptiFormer, total capacity 350,000 mt/y, Trim width 7.8 m, Coated mechanical/groundwood, Uncoated mechanical/groundwood
Coating Machines: 1
PM 1, total capacity 250,000 mt/y, on machine
Finishing Equipment:
  Winders: 2
  Supercalenders: 1
  Sheeters: 3
Energy Data:
Power boilers: 3
Steam turbines: 2 at 100 MW
Electrical demand for mill: 1,470 MWh/D

ⓂJiangxi Dexing City Hengsheng Paper Co., Ltd.
Ownership: 100% by private owners
Gujingtuo Longtoushan Village
Dexing City, Jiangxi, 334218
China
  Phone: (86) 793 7755 776/ 777
  Fax: (86) 793 7755 777
Mill Locations:
Jiangxi Dexing City Hengsheng Paper Co., Ltd., Dexing Mill, Gujingtuo Longtoushan Village, Dexing 334218, China, Capacity: 20,000 mt/y, (Paper mill)
  Phone: (86) 793 7755777
  Fax: (86) 793 7755 777

ⓂJiangxi Dexing City Hengsheng Paper Co., Ltd.
Dexing Mill
Gujingtuo Longtoushan Village
Dexing, Jiangxi, 334218
China
  Phone: (86) 793 7755777
  Fax: (86) 793 7755 777
Personnel:
  Gen. Mgr.: Ming Zhou
  Phone: (86) 793 7755 776/ 777
Total Employees at this Location: 300
Type of Operation: Paper mill
Pulp Grades and Capacities:
  Total pulp capacity: 20,000 mt/y
  Recycled Pulping: 20,000 mt/y
Pulp Mill Data:
Pulp Lines: 1
Paper/Paperboard Grades and Capacities:
  Total paper and paperboard capacity: 20,000 mt/y
  Uncoated woodfree/freesheet: 20,000 mt/y
Paper and Paperboard Mill Data:
Paper Machines: 2
No. 1, cylinder, total capacity 10,000 mt/y, Trim width 1.58 m, Uncoated woodfree/freesheet
No. 2, cylinder, total capacity 10,000 mt/y, Trim width 1.58 m, Uncoated woodfree/freesheet

ⓂJiangxi Fuzhou Sihai Paper Co., Ltd.
Fuzhou Mill
Fubei Industrial Park, Linchuan District
Fuzhou, Jiangxi, 344000
China
  Phone: (86) 794 8457 336/339
  Fax: (86) 794 8457 333
  Web Address: www.sihaipaper.com
Type of Operation: Paper mill
Pulp Grades and Capacities:
  Total pulp capacity: 39,284 mt/y
  Recycled Pulping: 39,284 mt/y
Paper/Paperboard Grades and Capacities:
  Total paper and paperboard capacity: 50,000 mt/y
  Tissue: 10,000 mt/y
  Corrugating medium/fluting: 40,000 mt/y
Paper and Paperboard Mill Data:
Paper Machines: 9
No. 1, cylinder, total capacity 1,429 mt/y, Trim width 1.58 m, Tissue
No. 2, cylinder, total capacity 1,429 mt/y, Trim width 1.58 m, Tissue
No. 3, cylinder, total capacity 1,429 mt/y, Trim width 1.58 m, Tissue
No. 4, cylinder, total capacity 1,429 mt/y, Trim width 1.58 m, Tissue
No. 5, cylinder, total capacity 1,429 mt/y, Trim width 1.58 m, Tissue
No. 6, cylinder, total capacity 1,429 mt/y, Trim width 1.58 m, Tissue
No. 7, cylinder, total capacity 1,429 mt/y, Trim width 1.58 m, Tissue
No. 8, twin-wire, total capacity 26,667 mt/y, Trim width 3.8 m, Corrugating medium/fluting
No. 9, fourdrinier, total capacity 13,333 mt/y, Trim width 3.2 m, Corrugating medium/fluting
Energy Data:
Electrical demand for mill: 69 MWh/D

ⓂJiangxi Ganzhou Hwagain Paper Co., Ltd
Ganzhou Mill
Ownership: Guangxi Hwagain Group
No. 168, Sangyanxia, Shuixi Town
Ganzhou, Jiangxi, 341000
China
  Phone: (86) 797 8251 388/ 771 5568 819
  Fax: (86) 797 8253 018/ 8257 111
  Email: jxnz@hwagain.com
  Web Address: www.hwagain.com
Personnel:
  Gen. Mgr.: Peihe Yan
  Phone: (86) 797 8251 388/ 771 5568 819
  Prod. Mgr.: Hanlin Liu
  Phone: (86) 797 8251 388/ 771 5568 819
Total Employees at this Location: 1,350
Type of Operation: Paper mill
Pulp Grades and Capacities:
  Total pulp capacity: 170,000 mt/y
Pulp Mill Data:
  Chemical Pulping Systems:
  Not Given: 1
Pulp Lines: 1
Paper/Paperboard Grades and Capacities:
  Total paper and paperboard capacity: 205,000 mt/y
  Uncoated woodfree/freesheet: 50,000 mt/y
  Tissue: 155,000 mt/y
Paper and Paperboard Mill Data:
Paper Machines: 14
PM 5, cylinder, total capacity 15,000 mt/y, Trim width 1.76 m, Uncoated woodfree/freesheet
PM 1-2, fourdrinier, total capacity 10,000 mt/y, Trim width 2.36 m, Uncoated woodfree/freesheet
PM 3-4, cylinder, total capacity 7,500 mt/y, Trim width 1.58 m, Uncoated mechanical/groundwood
TM 1, (started up September 2013), total capacity 60,000 mt/y, Trim width 5.6 m, Tissue
TM 2, (started June 2014), total capacity 60,000 mt/y, Trim width 5.6 m, Tissue
TM 3-4, cylinder, total capacity 3,900 mt/y, Trim width 1.58 m, Tissue
TM 5-9, cylinder, total capacity 1,000 mt/y, Trim width 1.58 m, Tissue
Coating Machines: 1
No. 1
Energy Data:
Power boilers: 2

ⓂJiangxi Jinggangshan Paper Co., Ltd.
Ownership: 100% by shareholders
Shishikou
Jinggangshan, Jiangxi, 343602
China
  Phone: (86) 796 661 0117/ 0048
  Fax: (86) 796 661 0720/ 0049
  Email: lvss0510@163.com
Mill Locations:
Jiangxi Jinggangshan Paper Co., Ltd., Jinggangshan Mill, Shishikou, Jinggangshan 343602, China, Capacity: 8,000 mt/y, (Paper mill)
  Phone: (86) 796 661 0117/ 0048
  Fax: (86) 796 661 0720/ 0049
  Email: lvss0510@163.com

ⓂJiangxi Jinggangshan Paper Co., Ltd.
Jinggangshan Mill
Shishikou
Jinggangshan, Jiangxi, 343602
China
  Phone: (86) 796 661 0117/ 0048
  Fax: (86) 796 661 0720/ 0049
  Email: lvss0510@163.com
Personnel:
  Pres.: Muning Zhou
  Phone: (86) 796 661 0117/ 0048
  Sls. Mgr.: Shusheng Lv
  Phone: (86) 796 661 0117/ 0048

China

Total Employees at this Location: 400
Type of Operation: Paper mill
Paper/Paperboard Grades and Capacities:
  Total paper and paperboard capacity: 8,000 mt/y
  Specialty and industrial: 8,000 mt/y
Paper and Paperboard Mill Data:
Paper Machines: 4
PM 1, cylinder, Trim width 1.09 m, Specialty and industrial
PM 2, cylinder, Trim width 1.58 m, Specialty and industrial
PM 3-4, fourdrinier, Trim width 1.88 m, Specialty and industrial

ⓜJiangxi Lee & Man Paper Co., Ltd.
Ruichang Mill
Ownership: Lee & Man Paper Manufacturing Ltd.
Matou Town
Ruichang, Jiangxi
China
  Web Address: www.leemanpaper.com
Total Employees at this Location: 300
Type of Operation: Paper mill
Pulp Grades and Capacities:
  Total pulp capacity: 315,594 mt/y
  Recycled Pulping: 315,594 mt/y
Pulp Mill Data:
  Recycled Fiber Treatment Lines:
  Recycled packaging pulping lines: 1
Paper/Paperboard Grades and Capacities:
  Total paper and paperboard capacity: 320,000 mt/y
  Linerboard: 320,000 mt/y
Paper and Paperboard Mill Data:
Paper Machines: 1
No. 18, fourdrinier (3), total capacity 320,000 mt/y, Trim width 6.65 m, Linerboard
Energy Data:
Power boilers: 1
Steam turbines at 75 MW
Electrical demand for mill: 404 MWh/D

ⓜJiujiang Hengsheng Chemical Fiber Co., Ltd.
Jiujiang Mill
Ownership: Henan Haiyang Chemical Fiber Group Co., Ltd.
Gutang Town, Lushan District
Jiujiang, Jiangxi, 332011
China
  Phone: (86) 792 8316 891
  Web Address: www.hyfiber.com
Type of Operation: Pulp mill
Pulp Grades and Capacities:
  Total pulp capacity: 18,000 mt/y

JILIN

ⓜJilin Baishan Qixiang Paper Co., Ltd.
Baishan Mill
No.49, Changbai Rd., Badaojiang District
Baishan, Jilin, 134300
China
  Phone: (86) 439 3389 008/017
Type of Operation: Paper mill
Paper/Paperboard Grades and Capacities:
  Total paper and paperboard capacity: 400,000 mt/y
  Linerboard: 100,000 mt/y
  Corrugating medium/fluting: 300,000 mt/y
Paper and Paperboard Mill Data:
Paper Machines: 4
No. 1, total capacity 100,000 mt/y, Corrugating medium/fluting
No. 2, total capacity 100,000 mt/y, Trim width 3.8 m, Corrugating medium/fluting
No. 3, fourdrinier, total capacity 100,000 mt/y, Trim width 4.4 m, Corrugating medium/fluting
No. 4, total capacity 100,000 mt/y, Trim width 4.4 m, Linerboard

Energy Data:
Power boilers: 3
Steam turbines: 1 at 12 MW

ⓞⓜJilin Chenming Paper Co. Ltd.
Jilin (Jilin Chenming Paper) Mill
Ownership: 70% by Chenming Paper Holdings Ltd.
Jinzhu Industrial Park, Longtan District
Jilin, Jilin
China
Type of Operation: Paper mill
Pulp Mill Data:
  Mechanical Pulping Systems:
  APMP Systems: 1
Pulp Lines: 2
  Recycled Fiber Treatment Lines:
  Flotation deinking lines: 1 at 142,800
Paper/Paperboard Grades and Capacities:
  Total paper and paperboard capacity: 250,000 mt/y
  Uncoated woodfree/freesheet: 250,000 mt/y
Paper and Paperboard Mill Data:
Paper Machines: 1
PM 12, (relocated from the down town area of the city, started in December 2013), OptiConcept, total capacity 250,000 mt/y, Trim width 6.95 m, Uncoated woodfree/freesheet
Energy Data:
Power boilers: 3
Steam turbines: 2 at 25 MW

ⓞⓜJilin Meihekou City Chuangda Paper Co., Ltd.
Meihekou Mill
Central Rizhao Street
Meihekou, Jilin, 135000
China
Personnel:
  Pres./Mill Mgr.: Qingjie Hu
Total Employees at this Location: 500
Type of Operation: Paper mill, Paperboard mill
Paper/Paperboard Grades and Capacities:
  Total paper and paperboard capacity: 20,000 mt/y
  Boxboard/cartonboard: 20,000 mt/y
Paper and Paperboard Mill Data:
Paper Machines: 2
No. 1-2, cylinder, Trim width 1.6 m, Boxboard/cartonboard
Coating Machines: 2
No. 1-2

ⓜJilin Meihekou Haishan Paper Mill
Meihekou Mill
No. 214, West Street, Shancheng Town
Meihekou, Jilin, 135022
China
  Phone: (86) 435 4800 504
  Fax: (86) 435 4800 504
Personnel:
  Mill Mgr.: Runtang Wang
  Phone: (86) 435 4800 504
  Tech. Mgr.: Min Xin Wei
  Phone: (86) 435 4800 504
  Purch. Agent: Baolin Lang
  Phone: (86) 435 4800 504
Total Employees at this Location: 648
Type of Operation: Paperboard mill
Paper/Paperboard Grades and Capacities:
  Total paper and paperboard capacity: 42,500 mt/y
  Boxboard/cartonboard: 42,500 mt/y
Paper and Paperboard Mill Data:
Paper Machines: 3
PM 2, total capacity 10,000 mt/y, Trim width 1.6 m, Boxboard/cartonboard
PM 3, total capacity 17,500 mt/y, Trim width 2.1 m, Boxboard/cartonboard
PM 4, total capacity 15,000 mt/y, Trim width 2.1 m, Boxboard/cartonboard

ⓜYanbian Shuanglu Chemical Fiber Co., Ltd.
Yanbian Mill
Ownership: 49% by Yanbian Shixian Bailu Paper Co., Ltd., 51% by Yanbian State-owned Assets Management Co., Ltd.
Kaishantun Town
Longjing, Jilin, 133400
China
  Phone: (86) 433 340 4567
  Fax: (86) 433 341 9200
  Email: ljwhxbl@public.yj.jl.cn
Personnel:
  Chmn.: Chunlin Zhang
  Phone: (86) 433 340 4567
  Gen. Mgr.: Qinjun Xu
  Phone: (86) 433 340 4567
  Mill Mgr.: Chen Wu
  Phone: (86) 433 340 4567
  Mill Mgr.: Zhiqiang Xu
  Phone: (86) 433 340 4325
  Purch. Mgr.: Jiamin Jin
  Phone: (86) 433 340 4567
Total Employees at this Location: 912
Type of Operation: Pulp mill, Paper mill
Pulp Grades and Capacities:
  Total pulp capacity: 41,650 mt/y
  Pulp available for market: 39,984 mt/y
  Chemical Pulp: 41,650 mt/y
Pulp Mill Data:
  Chemical Pulping Systems:
  Batch digesters: 6
Pulp Lines: 1
  Bleach Plant Systems: 1
  No. 1, Sequence: CEHH
  Pulp Dryers:
  Fourdriniers 1
Energy Data:
Power boilers: 4
Steam turbines: 2 at 12, 6 MW
Electrical demand for mill: 109 MWh/D

ⓜJilin Zhenlai Xinsheng Paper Co., Ltd.
Ownership: 100% by private owners
North Xinxing Street, Zhenlai Town, Zhenlai County
Baicheng, Jilin, 137300
China
  Phone: (86) 436 725 2466/ 722 2218
  Fax: (86) 436 723 7209/ 0699
Mill Locations:
Jilin Zhenlai Xinsheng Paper Co., Ltd., Baicheng Mill, North Xinxing Street, Zhenlai Town, Zhenlai County, Baicheng 137300, China, Capacity: 33,000 mt/y, (Paper mill)
  Phone: (86) 436 722 2218/723 0699
  Fax: (86) 436 723 7209/ 0699

ⓜJilin Zhenlai Xinsheng Paper Co., Ltd.
Baicheng Mill
North Xinxing Street, Zhenlai Town, Zhenlai County
Baicheng, Jilin, 137300
China
  Phone: (86) 436 722 2218/723 0699
  Fax: (86) 436 723 7209/ 0699
  Web Address: www.zlxszy.com/index1.html
Personnel:
  Chmn. & Gen. Mgr.: Maode Shao
  Phone: (86) 436 725 2466/ 722 2218
  Sls. Mgr.: Xiuwu Song
  Phone: (86) 436 725 2466/ 722 2218
Total Employees at this Location: 560
Type of Operation: Paper mill
Pulp Grades and Capacities:
  Total pulp capacity: 70,000 mt/y
  Chemical Pulp: 55,000 mt/y
Pulp Mill Data:
Pulp Lines: 2
Paper/Paperboard Grades and Capacities:

Total paper and paperboard capacity: 33,000 mt/y
Tissue: 33,000 mt/y
Paper and Paperboard Mill Data:
Paper Machines: 23
TM 1, fourdrinier, total capacity 1,400 mt/y, Trim width 2.4 m, Tissue
TM 10, fourdrinier, total capacity 1,450 mt/y, Trim width 2.4 m, Tissue
TM 11, fourdrinier, total capacity 1,450 mt/y, Trim width 2.4 m, Tissue
TM 12, fourdrinier, total capacity 1,450 mt/y, Trim width 2.4 m, Tissue
TM 13, fourdrinier, total capacity 1,450 mt/y, Trim width 2.4 m, Tissue
TM 14, fourdrinier, total capacity 1,450 mt/y, Trim width 2.4 m, Tissue
TM 15, fourdrinier, total capacity 1,450 mt/y, Trim width 2.4 m, Tissue
TM 16, fourdrinier, total capacity 1,450 mt/y, Trim width 2.4 m, Tissue
TM 17, fourdrinier, total capacity 1,450 mt/y, Trim width 2.4 m, Tissue
TM 18, fourdrinier, total capacity 1,450 mt/y, Trim width 2.4 m, Tissue
TM 19, fourdrinier, total capacity 1,450 mt/y, Trim width 2.4 m, Tissue
TM 2, fourdrinier, total capacity 1,400 mt/y, Trim width 2.4 m, Tissue
TM 20, fourdrinier, total capacity 1,450 mt/y, Trim width 2.4 m, Tissue
TM 21, total capacity 1,450 mt/y, Trim width 2.4 m, Tissue
TM 22, fourdrinier, total capacity 1,450 mt/y, Trim width 2.4 m, Tissue
TM 23, fourdrinier, total capacity 1,450 mt/y, Trim width 2.4 m, Tissue
TM 3, fourdrinier, total capacity 1,400 mt/y, Trim width 2.4 m, Tissue
TM 4, fourdrinier, total capacity 1,400 mt/y, Trim width 2.4 m, Tissue
TM 5, fourdrinier, total capacity 1,400 mt/y, Trim width 2.4 m, Tissue
TM 6, fourdrinier, total capacity 1,400 mt/y, Trim width 2.4 m, Tissue
TM 7, fourdrinier, total capacity 1,400 mt/y, Trim width 2.4 m, Tissue
TM 8, fourdrinier, total capacity 1,400 mt/y, Trim width 2.4 m, Tissue
TM 9, fourdrinier, total capacity 1,450 mt/y, Trim width 2.4 m, Tissue
Energy Data:
Power boilers: 3
Steam turbines: 1 at 9 MW

ⓜYanbian Hanji Paper Co., Ltd.
Tumen Mill
No.224, Tuhui Rd.
Tumen, Jilin, 133100
China
  Phone: (86) 433 3636 769
Type of Operation: Paper mill
Paper/Paperboard Grades and Capacities:
Total paper and paperboard capacity: 1,000 mt/y
Tissue: 1,000 mt/y
Paper and Paperboard Mill Data:
Paper Machines: 1
PM 1, total capacity 1,000 mt/y, Trim width 2.42 m, Tissue

ⓜYanbian Shixian Bailu Paper Co., Ltd.
Ownership: 7.30% by China Construction Bank Jilin Branch, 4% by China East Assets Management Co., Ltd., 6.60% by China Huarong Assets Management Co., Ltd., 18.50% by Jilin Shixian Paper Co., Ltd.
Shixian Village
Tumen City, Jilin, 133101
China
  Phone: (86) 433 386 9002/8139/381 0015/386 9125
  Fax: (86) 433 386 8143/8254/381 0019
  Email: shixian@shixianpaper.com, blzyzqb@vip.sina.com, cwg0048@vip.sina.com
  Web Address: www.shixianpaper.com
Personnel:
  Chmn. & Gen. Mgr.: Ming Yu
  CFO, Adm. Mgr., Dir.: Wengen Cui
  Gen. Mgr., Dpty. Mgr., Dir.: Dong Wei
  Dpty. Gen. Mgr.: Wensheng Sun
  Gen. Mgr.: Yanming Zheng
  Dir.: Pingsheng Sun
  Dir.: Xiaofeng Dong
  Tech. Dir.: Wei Li
  Indep. Dir.: Zhaoxiang Qiu
  Indep Dir.: Yaren An
  Indep Dir.: Jiejun Zhang
  Chief Eng.: Changshou Jin
  Dir.: Yuanfa Zhang
Total Employees at this Location: 1,980
Mill Locations:
Yanbian Shuanglu Chemical Fiber Co., Ltd., Yanbian Mill (49% owned), Kaishantun Town, Longjing 133400, China, (Pulp mill, Paper mill)
  Phone: (86) 433 340 4567
  Fax: (86) 433 341 9200
  Email: ljwhxbl@public.yj.jl.cn
Yanbian Shixian Bailu Paper Co., Ltd., Tumen Mill, Shixian Village, Tumen 133101, China, (Pulp mill, Paper mill)
  Phone: (86) 433 386 9002/8139/381 0015/386 9125
  Fax: (86) 433 386 8143/8254/381 0019
  Email: shixian@shixianpaper.com, blzyzqb@vip.sina.com, cwg0048@vip.sina.com

ⓜYanbian Shixian Bailu Paper Co., Ltd.
Tumen Mill
Shixian Village
Tumen, Jilin, 133101
China
  Phone: (86) 433 386 9002/8139/381 0015/386 9125
  Fax: (86) 433 386 8143/8254/381 0019
  Email: shixian@shixianpaper.com, blzyzqb@vip.sina.com, cwg0048@vip.sina.com
  Web Address: www.shixianpaper.com
Personnel:
  Chmn. & Gen. Mgr.: Ming Yu
  Phone: (86) 433 386 9002/8139/381 0015/386 9125
  CFO, Adm. Mgr., Dir.: Wengen Cui
  Phone: (86) 433 386 9002/8139/381 0015/386 9125
  Gen. Mgr., Dpty. Mgr., Dir.: Dong Wei
  Phone: (86) 433 386 9002/8139/381 0015/386 9125
  Dpty. Gen. Mgr.: Wensheng Sun
  Phone: (86) 433 386 9002/8139/381 0015/386 9125
  Gen. Mgr.: Yanming Zheng
  Phone: (86) 433 386 9002/8139/381 0015/386 9125
  Dir.: Pingsheng Sun
  Phone: (86) 433 386 9002/8139/381 0015/386 9125
  Dir.: Xiaofeng Dong
  Phone: (86) 433 386 9002/8139/381 0015/386 9125
  Tech. Dir.: Wei Li
  Phone: (86) 433 386 9002/8139/381 0015/386 9125
  Indep. Dir.: Zhaoxiang Qiu
  Phone: (86) 433 386 9002/8139/381 0015/386 9125
  Indep. Dir.: Yaren An
  Phone: (86) 433 386 9002/8139/381 0015/386 9125
  Indep. Dir.: Jiejun Zhang
  Phone: (86) 433 386 9002/8139/381 0015/386 9125
  Chief Eng.: Changshou Jin
  Phone: (86) 433 386 9002/8139/381 0015/386 9125
  Dir.: Yuanfa Zhang
  Phone: (86) 433 386 9002/8139/381 0015/386 9125
Total Employees at this Location: 1,980
Type of Operation: Pulp mill, Paper mill
Pulp Grades and Capacities:
Total pulp capacity: 60,241 mt/y
Pulp available for market: 60,000 mt/y
Chemical Pulp: 60,241 mt/y
Pulp Mill Data:
Pulp Lines: 3
Pulp Dryers:
Fourdriniers 1
Finishing Equipment:
Rewinders: 3
Sheeters: 2
Energy Data:
Power boilers: 4
Steam turbines: 2 at 12, 12 MW
Electrical demand for mill: 79 MWh/D

LIAONING

ⓜFushun Huasheng Paper Products Co., Ltd.
No.5, Qinghe Rd., Tukouzi Town, Qingyuan County
Fushun, Liaoning, 113304
China
  Phone: (86) 24 5314 1555
Mill Locations:
Fushun Huasheng Paper Products Co., Ltd., Fushun Mill, No.5, Qinghe Rd., Tukouzi Town, Qingyuan County, Fushun 113304, China, Capacity: 25,000 mt/y, (Paper mill)
  Phone: (86) 24 5314 1555

ⓜFushun Huasheng Paper Products Co., Ltd.
Fushun Mill
No.5, Qinghe Rd., Tukouzi Town, Qingyuan County
Fushun, Liaoning, 113304
China
  Phone: (86) 24 5314 1555
Type of Operation: Paper mill
Paper/Paperboard Grades and Capacities:
Total paper and paperboard capacity: 25,000 mt/y
Tissue: 25,000 mt/y
Paper and Paperboard Mill Data:
Paper Machines: 5
PM 1, total capacity 5,000 mt/y, Trim width 2.4 m, Tissue
PM 2, total capacity 5,000 mt/y, Trim width 2.4 m, Tissue
PM 3, total capacity 5,000 mt/y, Trim width 2.4 m, Tissue
PM 4, total capacity 5,000 mt/y, Trim width 2.4 m, Tissue
PM 5, total capacity 5,000 mt/y, Trim width 2.4 m, Tissue

ⓜLiaoning Dandong Fengcheng Dongfeng Paper Co., Ltd.
Fengcheng Mill
No. 5-8 Zhenxing Street
Fengcheng, Liaoning, 118100
China
  Phone: (86) 415 812 5977
  Fax: (86) 415 866 0099
Personnel:
  Chmn.: Dongfeng Wang
  Phone: (86) 415 812 5977
Type of Operation: Paper mill
Paper/Paperboard Grades and Capacities:
Total paper and paperboard capacity: 4,800 mt/y
Tissue: 4,800 mt/y
Paper and Paperboard Mill Data:
Paper Machines: 4
No. 1, (toilet seat cover paper), fourdrinier, total capacity 1,200 mt/y, Trim width 1.58 m, Tissue
No. 2, (toilet seat cover paper), fourdrinier, total capacity 1,200 mt/y, Trim width 1.58 m, Tissue
No. 3, (toilet seat cover paper), fourdrinier, total capacity 1,200 mt/y, Trim width 1.58 m, Tissue
No. 4, fourdrinier, total capacity 1,200 mt/y, Trim width 1.58 m, Tissue
Energy Data:
Power boilers: 2

ⓜLiaoning Dandong Hengyao Paper Co., Ltd.
Fengcheng Mill
No. 224 Shiqiao Rd.
Fengcheng, Liaoning, 118100
China

China

Phone: (86) 415 864 6111
Fax: (86) 415 8646 222
Personnel:
Chmn.: Tao Yu
Phone: (86) 415 823 5487/ 2201
Type of Operation: Paper mill
Paper/Paperboard Grades and Capacities:
Total paper and paperboard capacity: 6,000 mt/y
Tissue: 6,000 mt/y
Paper and Paperboard Mill Data:
Paper Machines: 5
No. 1, fourdrinier, total capacity 1,000 mt/y, Trim width 1.58 m, Tissue
No. 2, fourdrinier, total capacity 1,000 mt/y, Trim width 1.58 m, Tissue
No. 3, fourdrinier, total capacity 1,000 mt/y, Trim width 1.58 m, Tissue
No. 4, fourdrinier, total capacity 1,000 mt/y, Trim width 1.58 m, Tissue
No. 5, fourdrinier, total capacity 2,000 mt/y, Trim width 1.58 m, Tissue
Energy Data:
Power boilers: 1

ⓂLiaoning Hupo Paper
Fushun Mill
Ownership: 100% by Fushun Mining Group
No.4, Guchengzi Rd., Wanghuayuan District
Fushun, Liaoning, 113001
China
Phone: (86) 24 5254 8136
Fax: (86) 24 5259 5858
Web Address: www.hpzy.com.cn
Total Employees at this Location: 375
Type of Operation: Paper mill
Pulp Grades and Capacities:
Total pulp capacity: 279,057 mt/y
Recycled Pulping: 279,057 mt/y
Pulp Mill Data:
Recycled Fiber Treatment Lines:
Recycled packaging pulping lines: 1
Paper/Paperboard Grades and Capacities:
Total paper and paperboard capacity: 300,000 mt/y
Tissue: 20,000 mt/y
Linerboard: 280,000 mt/y
Paper and Paperboard Mill Data:
Paper Machines: 2
No. 1, crescent former, Yankee dryer, total capacity 20,000 mt/y, Trim width 5.6 m, Tissue
No. 2, fourdrinier (3), total capacity 280,000 mt/y, Trim width 6.66 m, Linerboard
Energy Data:
Electrical demand for mill: 397 MWh/D

ⓂⓂLiaoning Jincheng Paper Co., Ltd.
Linghai Mill
Ownership: 31.05% by Jinzhou Xintian Paper, 68.95% by shareholders
Jincheng Street
Linghai, Liaoning, 121203
China
Phone: (86) 416 835 0013
Fax: (86) 416 835 0004
Email: jzjincheng@online.ln.cn
Personnel:
Chmn., Gen. Mgr.: Jianbin Lu
Phone: (86) 416 835 0013
Vice Chmn.: Bingkun Zhang
Phone: (86) 416 835 0013
CFO: Quan Jiang
Phone: (86) 416 835 0013
Dpty. Gen. Mgr., Board Sec.: Ms. Li Lv
Phone: (86) 416 835 0006
Fax: (86) 416 835 0004
Email: Mli0416@sina.com
Dpty. Gen. Mgr.: Deliang Yin
Phone: (86) 416 835 0013
Total Employees at this Location: 2,750

Type of Operation: Pulp mill, Paper mill
Mill Locations:
Liaoning Jincheng Paper Jinbao Paper Co., Ltd., Linghai Mill, Jincheng Street, Linghai 121203, China, Capacity: 9,000 mt/y, (Paper mill)
Phone: (86) 416 828 5818
Fax: (86) 416 828 2643
Pulp Grades and Capacities:
Total pulp capacity: 43,777 mt/y
Other Pulp: 43,777 mt/y
Pulp Mill Data:
Chemical Pulping Systems:
Batch digesters: 7
Bleach Plant Systems: 1
No. 1
Paper/Paperboard Grades and Capacities:
Total paper and paperboard capacity: 50,000 mt/y
Uncoated woodfree/freesheet: 50,000 mt/y
Paper and Paperboard Mill Data:
Paper Machines: 2
No. 5, fourdrinier, total capacity 18,000 mt/y, Trim width 3.15 m, Uncoated woodfree/freesheet
No. 6, fourdrinier, total capacity 32,000 mt/y, Trim width 3.15 m, Uncoated woodfree/freesheet
Energy Data:
Power boilers: 5
Steam turbines: 2 at 12, 12 MW
Electrical demand for mill: 176 MWh/D

ⓂLiaoning Jincheng Paper Jinbao Paper Co., Ltd.
Linghai Mill
Ownership: 100% by Liaoning Jincheng Paper Co., Ltd.
Jincheng Street
Linghai, Liaoning, 121203
China
Phone: (86) 416 828 5818
Fax: (86) 416 828 2643
Total Employees at this Location: 2,300
Type of Operation: Paper mill
Paper/Paperboard Grades and Capacities:
Total paper and paperboard capacity: 9,000 mt/y
Tissue: 9,000 mt/y
Paper and Paperboard Mill Data:
Paper Machines: 10
PM 1, Trim width 2.18 m, Tissue
PM 2, Trim width 1.76 m, Tissue
PM 3-4, Trim width 1.58 m, Tissue
PM 5-10, Trim width 1.09 m, Tissue

ⓂLiaoning Jinzhou Jinri Paper Co., Ltd.
Linhai Mill
Jincheng Street
Linhai, Liaoning, 121203
China
Phone: (86) 416 835 1015/ 1066/ 1043
Fax: (86) 416 835 1000/ 1067/ 1044
Email: gaochengjun66@163.com, jrzy@jzjrzy.com
Web Address: www.jzjrzy.com
Personnel:
Chmn.: Chengjun Gao
Phone: (86) 416 835 1015/ 1066/ 1043
Sls. Mgr.: Dongmei Lu
Phone: (86) 416 835 1015/ 1066/ 1043
Total Employees at this Location: 1,000
Type of Operation: Paper mill
Pulp Grades and Capacities:
Total pulp capacity: 5,000 mt/y
Pulp Mill Data:
Pulp Lines: 1
Paper/Paperboard Grades and Capacities:
Total paper and paperboard capacity: 30,000 mt/y
Tissue: 30,000 mt/y
Paper and Paperboard Mill Data:
Paper Machines: 15

PM 1-4, cylinder, total capacity 800 mt/y, Trim width 1.58 m, Tissue
PM 10-15, fourdrinier, total capacity 2,700 mt/y, Trim width 1.88 m, Tissue
PM 5-9, fourdrinier, total capacity 1,600 mt/y, Trim width 1.76 m, Tissue

ⓂLiaoning Jinzhou Nuerhe Paper Co., Ltd.
Jinzhou Mill
No. 69 Xinxingli, Taihe District
Jinzhou, Liaoning, 121005
China
Phone: (86) 416 513 9211/ 266 0620/ 513 0904
Fax: (86) 416 513 9211/ 266 0620
Personnel:
Chmn.: Yanhua Liu
Phone: (86) 416 513 9211/ 266 0620/ 513 0904
Gen. Mgr.: Yanming Liu
Phone: (86) 416 513 9211/ 266 0620/ 513 0904
Sls. Mgr.: Jianlin Chen
Phone: (86) 416 513 9211/ 266 0620/ 513 0904
Type of Operation: Paper mill
Paper/Paperboard Grades and Capacities:
Total paper and paperboard capacity: 12,000 mt/y
Tissue: 12,000 mt/y
Paper and Paperboard Mill Data:
Paper Machines: 12
PM 1-6, cylinder, total capacity 700 mt/y, Trim width 1.58 m, Tissue
PM 7-12, fourdrinier, total capacity 1,300 mt/y, Trim width 1.58 m, Tissue
Energy Data:
Power boilers: 2

ⓂLiaoning Nine Dragons Paper Industries
Shenyang Mill
Dongying Bei Yi Road, Industry Zone of Dongcheng Xinmin, Shenyang, Liaoning, 110300
China
Phone: (86) 24-31782611
Fax: (86) 24-31782630
Email: nfo_sy@ndpaper.com
Web Address: www.ndpaper.com
Type of Operation: Paper mill
Paper/Paperboard Grades and Capacities:
Total paper and paperboard capacity: 350,000 mt/y
Linerboard: 175,000 mt/y
Corrugating medium/fluting: 175,000 mt/y
Paper and Paperboard Mill Data:
Paper Machines: 1
PM 37, (started September 2014), total capacity 350,000 mt/y, Linerboard

ⓂLiaoning Panjin Dongsheng Paper Co., Ltd.
Panjin Mill
Mill is under construction (provisional start up date of July 2014 delayed, no fixed date given)
Liaohekou Ecology Economic Zone
Panjin, Liaoning
China
Type of Operation: Paper mill
Paper/Paperboard Grades and Capacities:
Total paper and paperboard capacity: 48,000 mt/y
Tissue: 48,000 mt/y
Paper and Paperboard Mill Data:
Paper Machines: 3
PM 1, crescent former, total capacity 16,000 mt/y, Trim width 2.85 m, Tissue
PM 2, crescent former, total capacity 16,000 mt/y, Trim width 2.85 m, Tissue
PM 3, crescent former, total capacity 16,000 mt/y, Trim width 2.85 m, Tissue

ⓘⓜLiaoning Panjin Zhenxing Ecology Paper Co., Ltd
Panjin Mill
Dongguo Paper Making Industry Park, Panshan County,
Panjin City
Panjin, Liaoning, 124112
China
Phone: (86) 427 6577 888/777
Fax: (86) 427 6577 088
Email: zxstjt@163.com
Web Address: www.lnzxzz.com
Total Employees at this Location: 850
Type of Operation: Paper mill
Pulp Grades and Capacities:
 Total pulp capacity: 130,199 mt/y
 Pulp available for market: 70,000 mt/y
 Other Pulp: 130,199 mt/y
Pulp Mill Data:
 Chemical Pulping Systems:
  Continuous digesters: 1
 Pulp Lines: 1
  Bleach Plant Systems: 1
   No. 1, Type: ECF Capacity 150,000 admt/y
  Chemical Recovery Equipment:
   Evaporator lines
   Recovery boilers
  Pulp Dryers:
   Pulp Dryers 1
Paper/Paperboard Grades and Capacities:
 Total paper and paperboard capacity: 75,000 mt/y
 Uncoated woodfree/freesheet: 75,000 mt/y
Paper and Paperboard Mill Data:
Paper Machines: 2
 No. 1, fourdrinier, total capacity 37,500 mt/y, Trim width 2.73 m, Uncoated woodfree/freesheet
 No. 2, fourdrinier, total capacity 37,500 mt/y, Trim width 2.73 m, Uncoated woodfree/freesheet
Energy Data:
 Power boilers: 2
 Electrical demand for mill: 386 MWh/D

ⓜLiaoning Shangyang Paper Co., Ltd.
Tieling Mill
Qinghe Industry Park
Tieling, Liaoning, 112003
China
Phone: (86) 24 3181 0270
Personnel:
 Gen. Mgr.: Guoqiang Chen
 Phone: (86) 410 213 2211
Total Employees at this Location: 150
Type of Operation: Paper mill
Paper/Paperboard Grades and Capacities:
 Total paper and paperboard capacity: 12,142 mt/y
 Tissue: 12,142 mt/y
Paper and Paperboard Mill Data:
Paper Machines: 4
 No. 2, cylinder, total capacity 1,250 mt/y, Trim width 1.58 m, Tissue
 No. 3, cylinder, total capacity 1,250 mt/y, Trim width 1.58 m, Tissue, Uncoated woodfree/freesheet
 No. 4, cylinder, total capacity 1,250 mt/y, Trim width 1.58 m, Tissue
 No. 5, fourdrinier, total capacity 10,000 mt/y, Trim width 1.88 m, Tissue, Uncoated woodfree/freesheet
Energy Data:
 Power boilers: 1
 Electrical demand for mill: 28 MWh/D

ⓜLiaoning Tieling Qinghe Gangxing Paper Co., Ltd.
Tieling Mill
No. 730, Houma Village Industry Park, Qinghe District
Tieling, Liaoning, 112003
China
Phone: (86) 410 218 4600
Fax: (86) 410 218 1300
Personnel:
 Chmn.: Baiji Ren
 Phone: (86) 410 218 4600
 Gen. Mgr.: Jingyan Wu
 Phone: (86) 410 218 4600
Type of Operation: Paper mill
Paper/Paperboard Grades and Capacities:
 Total paper and paperboard capacity: 3,600 mt/y
 Tissue: 3,600 mt/y
Paper and Paperboard Mill Data:
Paper Machines: 3
 PM 1, cylinder, total capacity 700 mt/y, Trim width 1.09 m, Tissue
 PM 2-3, fourdrinier, total capacity 1,450 mt/y, Trim width 1.58 m, Tissue

ⓜLiaoning Tongsheng Paper Co., Ltd.
Liaoyang Mill
No.21, Jianshe Rd., Baita District
Liaoyang, Liaoning, 111000
China
Phone: (86) 419 3305319
Web Address: www.ts-paper.com
Type of Operation: Paper mill
Paper/Paperboard Grades and Capacities:
 Total paper and paperboard capacity: 50,000 mt/y
 Boxboard/cartonboard: 50,000 mt/y
Paper and Paperboard Mill Data:
Paper Machines: 1
 PM 1, total capacity 50,000 mt/y, Trim width 2.4 m, Boxboard/cartonboard

ⓜLiaoning Xingqi Paper Co., Ltd.
Liaoyang Mill
Xizhuang Village, Wangshuitai Street
Liaoyang, Liaoning, 111000
China
Phone: (86) 419 330 6357
Fax: (86) 419 330 1108
Email: xqzy-xqyz@163.com
Web Address: www.xqzy.com
Personnel:
 Chmn.: Guirong Zhang
 Phone: (86) 419 330 6357
 Gen. Mgr.: Xiaowen Li
 Phone: (86) 419 330 6357
 Dir.: Xuancheng Li
 Phone: (86) 419 330 6357
Type of Operation: Paper mill
Paper/Paperboard Grades and Capacities:
 Total paper and paperboard capacity: 8,400 mt/y
 Tissue: 8,400 mt/y
Paper and Paperboard Mill Data:
Paper Machines: 6
 PM 1-6, fourdrinier, total capacity 1,400 mt/y, Trim width 1.58 m, Tissue
Energy Data:
 Power boilers: 1

ⓜLiaoning Yingkou Paper Mill
Yingkou Mill
1 Hewan North St., Zhanqian District
Yingkou, Liaoning, 115001
China
Phone: (86) 417 213 5860/5765
Fax: (86) 417 363 1195
Email: lnykzzc@163.com
Personnel:
 Mill Mgr.: Guoqing Zhao
 Phone: (86) 417 2135 777
 Mill Mgr./ Dpty. Man. Dir.: Xiaowei Wu
 Phone: (86) 417 213 5876
 Fax: (86) 417 363 1195
 Asst. Mgr.: Shoubao Guo
 Phone: (86) 417 213 5401
 Fax: (86) 417 363 1195
 Office Dir./ Asst. Mill Mgr.: Decheng Wang
 Phone: (86) 417 213 5876
 Fax: (86) 417 363 1195
 Chief Eng.: Zhang Shao
 Phone: (86) 417 213 5536
 Fax: (86) 417 363 1195
Total Employees at this Location: 2,221
Type of Operation: Pulp mill, Paper mill
Pulp Grades and Capacities:
 Total pulp capacity: 60,000 mt/y
 Pulp available for market: 40,000 mt/y
Pulp Mill Data:
 Chemical Pulping Systems:
  Batch digesters: 7
 Pulp Lines: 1
  Pulp Dryers:
   Twin Wire 1, Twin Wire 1
Paper/Paperboard Grades and Capacities:
 Total paper and paperboard capacity: 15,000 mt/y
 Uncoated woodfree/freesheet: 15,000 mt/y
Paper and Paperboard Mill Data:
 Stock Preparation:
  Pulpers: 15
  Refiners: 3
Paper Machines: 7
 PM 1-2, cylinder, total capacity 2,000 mt/y, Trim width 1.76 m, Uncoated woodfree/freesheet, Uncoated mechanical/groundwood
 PM 3-7, cylinder, total capacity 2,200 mt/y, Trim width 2.24 m, Uncoated woodfree/freesheet, Uncoated mechanical/groundwood
Energy Data:
 Power boilers: 2
 Steam turbines: 1 at 30 MW

ⓜLiaoning Yingkou Paper Mill
Ownership: 100% by shareholders
1 Hewan North St., Zhanqian District
Yingkou, Liaoning, 115001
China
Phone: (86) 417 213 5860, 417 2135765
Fax: (86) 417 363 1195
Email: lnykzzc@163.com
Total Employees of Company: 2,221
Mill Locations:
 Liaoning Yingkou Paper Mill, Yingkou Mill, 1 Hewan North St., Zhanqian District, Yingkou 115001, China, Capacity: 15,000 mt/y, (Pulp mill, Paper mill)
 Phone: (86) 417 213 5860/5765
 Fax: (86) 417 363 1195
 Email: lnykzzc@163.com

ⓜShenyang Jinxin Pulp & Paper Co., Ltd
Xinmin (Shenyang Jinxin Pulp & Paper) Mill
Ownership: Asia Pulp & Paper (APP), Xinmin Paper Mills
No.3, Shi Fu Road
Xinmin, Liaoning, 110300
China
Phone: (86) 24-87516619-506
Fax: (86) 24-87516605
Total Employees at this Location: 210
Type of Operation: Paper mill
Paper/Paperboard Grades and Capacities:
 Total paper and paperboard capacity: 60,000 mt/y
 Tissue: 60,000 mt/y
Paper and Paperboard Mill Data:
Paper Machines: 1
 No. 1, crescent former, Yankee dryer, total capacity 60,000 mt/y, Trim width 5.6 m, Tissue, Uncoated woodfree/freesheet
Energy Data:
 Power boilers: 2
 Steam turbines: 1 at 25 MW
 Electrical demand for mill: 174 MWh/D

ⓜShenyang Stainless Paper Industry Co., Ltd.
Shenyang Mill
No.13 Rd., Economic&Technology Development Zone, Tiexi District
Shenyang, Liaoning
China

China

Phone: (86) 24 8930 3888
Web Address: www.stls.cn
Type of Operation: Paper mill
Paper/Paperboard Grades and Capacities:
Total paper and paperboard capacity: 20,000 mt/y
Specialty and industrial: 20,000 mt/y
Paper and Paperboard Mill Data:
Paper Machines: 2
No. 1, total capacity 6,000 mt/y, Trim width 1.09 m, Specialty and industrial
No. 2, total capacity 14,000 mt/y, Trim width 2.64 m, Specialty and industrial

ⓜVinda Paper (Liaoning) Co., Ltd.
Anshan Mill
Ownership: Vinda International Holdings Limited.
Anshan Dadaowan Industry & Development Park
Anshan, Liaoning, 114013
China
Web Address: www.vindapaper.com
Total Employees at this Location: 280
Type of Operation: Paper mill
Paper/Paperboard Grades and Capacities:
Total paper and paperboard capacity: 54,000 mt/y
Tissue: 54,000 mt/y
Paper and Paperboard Mill Data:
Paper Machines: 4
No. 1, BF-10 EX, Yankee dryer, total capacity 12,000 mt/y, Trim width 2.76 m, Tissue, Uncoated woodfree/freesheet
No. 2, BF-10 EX, Yankee dryer, total capacity 12,000 mt/y, Trim width 2.76 m, Tissue, Uncoated woodfree/freesheet
No. 3, total capacity 15,000 mt/y, Trim width 2.66 m, Tissue, Uncoated woodfree/freesheet
No. 4, total capacity 15,000 mt/y, Trim width 2.65 m, Tissue, Uncoated woodfree/freesheet
Energy Data:
Electrical demand for mill: 96 MWh/D

NINGXIA

ⓗⓜMCC Meili Paper Industry Co., Ltd.
Zhongwei Mill
Ownership: 26.91% by MCC Paper Group Co., Ltd.
Rouyuan District
Zhongwei, Ningxia, 755000
China
 Phone: (86) 955 767 9339
 Fax: (86) 955 767 9438
 Email: mlzy@china-meili.com
 Web Address: www.china-meili.com
Personnel:
 Chmn.: Su Yan
 Phone: (86) 955 767 9339
 CFO: Guoqiang Ding
 Phone: (86) 955 767 9339
 Chief Eng.: Xianghong Zhou
 Phone: (86) 955 767 9339
 Dpty. Gen. Mrg.: Dongxu Wu
 Phone: (86) 955 767 9339
 Gen. Mgr.: Qiang Zhang
 Dpty. Gen. Mgr., Board Sec.: Jinhua Shao
 Phone: (86) 955 707 8069
 Fax: (86) 955 767 9216
 Email: SHJW1971@126.com
 Dpty. Gen. Mgr.: Yun Yang
 Phone: (86) 955 767 9339
 Dpty. Gen. Mgr.: Jianxiang Wang
 Phone: (86) 955 767 9339
 Dpty. Gen. Mgr.: Wei Xia
 Phone: (86) 955 767 9339
Total Employees at this Location: 4,010
Type of Operation: Pulp mill, Paper mill, Paperboard mill
Pulp Grades and Capacities:
Total pulp capacity: 108,290 mt/y
Other Pulp: 108,290 mt/y
Pulp Mill Data:
Chemical Pulping Systems:
Continuous digesters: 3
Pulp Lines: 3
Bleach Plant Systems: 1
No. 1, Type: Nonwood
Chemical Recovery Equipment:
Evaporator lines
Recovery boilers: 2
Recycled Fiber Treatment Lines:
Recycled packaging pulping lines: 1 at 20,000 admt/y
Paper/Paperboard Grades and Capacities:
Total paper and paperboard capacity: 257,040 mt/y
Uncoated woodfree/freesheet: 194,922 mt/y
Coated woodfree/freesheet: 39,984 mt/y
Linerboard: 22,134 mt/y
Paper and Paperboard Mill Data:
Paper Machines: 20
No. 1, DuoFormer D, total capacity 2,499 mt/y, Trim width 1.58 m, Uncoated woodfree/freesheet
No. 2, fourdrinier, total capacity 7,497 mt/y, Trim width 1.76 m, Uncoated woodfree/freesheet
No. 3, fourdrinier, total capacity 7,497 mt/y, Trim width 1.76 m, Uncoated woodfree/freesheet
No. 4, fourdrinier, total capacity 7,497 mt/y, Trim width 1.76 m, Uncoated woodfree/freesheet
No. 5, fourdrinier, total capacity 7,497 mt/y, Trim width 1.76 m, Uncoated woodfree/freesheet
No. 6, fourdrinier, total capacity 7,497 mt/y, Trim width 1.76 m, Uncoated woodfree/freesheet
No. 7, fourdrinier, total capacity 9,996 mt/y, Trim width 1.76 m, Uncoated woodfree/freesheet
No. 8, cylinder, total capacity 6,069 mt/y, Trim width 1.76 m, Linerboard
No. 9, fourdrinier, total capacity 2,499 mt/y, Trim width 1.58 m, Uncoated woodfree/freesheet
No. 10, fourdrinier, total capacity 7,497 mt/y, Trim width 1.76 m, Uncoated woodfree/freesheet
No. 11, fourdrinier, total capacity 21,420 mt/y, Trim width 1.76 m, Uncoated woodfree/freesheet
No. 12, cylinder, total capacity 16,065 mt/y, Trim width 2.5 m, Linerboard
No. 13, fourdrinier, total capacity 9,996 mt/y, Trim width 1.88 m, Uncoated woodfree/freesheet
No. 14, fourdrinier, total capacity 9,996 mt/y, Trim width 1.76 m, Uncoated woodfree/freesheet
No. 15, fourdrinier, total capacity 19,992 mt/y, Trim width 1.76 m, Coated woodfree/freesheet, Uncoated woodfree/freesheet
No. 16, fourdrinier, total capacity 19,992 mt/y, Trim width 1.76 m, Coated woodfree/freesheet
No. 17, fourdrinier, total capacity 28,560 mt/y, Trim width 2.64 m, Uncoated woodfree/freesheet
No. 18, fourdrinier, total capacity 24,990 mt/y, Trim width 2.64 m, Uncoated woodfree/freesheet
No. 19, fourdrinier, total capacity 19,992 mt/y, Trim width 2.64 m, Uncoated woodfree/freesheet
No. 20, fourdrinier, total capacity 19,992 mt/y, Trim width 1.76 m, Uncoated woodfree/freesheet
Coating Machines: 2
PM 15, total capacity 20,000 mt/y., off machine
PM 16, total capacity 20,000 mt/y., off machine
Energy Data:
Power boilers: 4
Steam turbines: 3 at 15, 15, 12 MW
Electrical demand for mill: 620 MWh/D

ⓗⓜNingxia Kejin Xiaguang Paper Co., Ltd.
Qingtongxia Mill
Qingtongxia Town
Qingtongxia, Ningxia, 751601
China
 Phone: (86) 953 3012 107/005
 Fax: (86) 953 3012 061
Personnel:
 Chmn.: Mijin Zhang
 Phone: (86) 953 3012 004/107/005
Total Employees at this Location: 1,000
Type of Operation: Pulp mill, Paper mill, Paperboard mill
Pulp Grades and Capacities:
Total pulp capacity: 46,168 mt/y
Recycled Pulping: 31,220 mt/y
Other Pulp: 14,947 mt/y
Paper/Paperboard Grades and Capacities:
Total paper and paperboard capacity: 55,000 mt/y
Uncoated woodfree/freesheet: 25,000 mt/y
Tissue
Linerboard: 30,000 mt/y
Paper and Paperboard Mill Data:
Paper Machines: 27
No. 1, cylinder, total capacity 1,000 mt/y, Trim width 1.88 m, Uncoated woodfree/freesheet
No. 2, cylinder, total capacity 1,000 mt/y, Trim width 1.88 m, Uncoated woodfree/freesheet
No. 3, cylinder, total capacity 1,000 mt/y, Trim width 1.88 m, Uncoated woodfree/freesheet
No. 4, cylinder, total capacity 1,000 mt/y, Trim width 1.88 m, Uncoated woodfree/freesheet
No. 5, cylinder, total capacity 1,000 mt/y, Trim width 1.88 m, Uncoated woodfree/freesheet
No. 6, cylinder, total capacity 1,000 mt/y, Trim width 1.88 m, Uncoated woodfree/freesheet
No. 7, cylinder, total capacity 1,000 mt/y, Trim width 1.88 m, Uncoated woodfree/freesheet
No. 8, cylinder, total capacity 1,000 mt/y, Trim width 1.88 m, Uncoated woodfree/freesheet
No. 9, cylinder, total capacity 1,000 mt/y, Trim width 1.88 m, Uncoated woodfree/freesheet
No. 10, cylinder, total capacity 1,000 mt/y, Trim width 1.88 m, Uncoated woodfree/freesheet
No. 11, cylinder, total capacity 1,071 mt/y, Trim width 1.76 m, Tissue
No. 12, cylinder, total capacity 1,071 mt/y, Trim width 1.76 m, Tissue
No. 13, cylinder, total capacity 1,071 mt/y, Trim width 1.76 m, Tissue
No. 14, cylinder, total capacity 1,071 mt/y, Trim width 1.76 m, Tissue
No. 15, cylinder, total capacity 1,071 mt/y, Trim width 1.76 m, Tissue
No. 16, cylinder, total capacity 1,071 mt/y, Trim width 1.76 m, Tissue
No. 17, cylinder, total capacity 1,071 mt/y, Trim width 1.76 m, Tissue
No. 18, cylinder, total capacity 1,071 mt/y, Trim width 1.76 m, Tissue
No. 19, cylinder, total capacity 1,071 mt/y, Trim width 1.76 m, Tissue
No. 20, cylinder, total capacity 1,071 mt/y, Trim width 1.76 m, Tissue
No. 21, cylinder, total capacity 1,071 mt/y, Trim width 1.76 m, Tissue
No. 22, cylinder, total capacity 1,071 mt/y, Trim width 1.76 m, Tissue
No. 23, cylinder, total capacity 1,071 mt/y, Trim width 1.76 m, Tissue
No. 24, fourdrinier, total capacity 10,000 mt/y, Trim width 1.88 m, Uncoated woodfree/freesheet
No. 25, fourdrinier, total capacity 10,000 mt/y, Trim width 1.88 m, Uncoated woodfree/freesheet
No. 26, fourdrinier, total capacity 5,000 mt/y, Trim width 1.58 m, Uncoated woodfree/freesheet
No. 27, cylinder, total capacity 30,000 mt/y, Trim width 3.2 m, Linerboard
Energy Data:
Power boilers: 2
Electrical demand for mill: 97 MWh/D

ⓜNingxia Zijinghua Paper Industry Co. Ltd.
Yinchuan Mill
Yanghe Industry, Yongning County
Yinchuan, Ningxia, 750100
China
 Phone: (86) 951 801 1426/7666/7546/1586/3178/3808
 Fax: (86) 951 801 4871/3355/802 0888
 Web Address: www.zijinhua.com.cn
Personnel:

Chmn.: Jubo Na
Phone: (86) 951 801 1421/7666/7546/1586
Pres.: Lijun Ma
Phone: (86) 951 801 1421/7666/7546/1586
VP: Zhengqiang Yu
Phone: (86) 951 801 1421/7666/7546/1586
Chief Eng.: Yong Wang
Phone: (86) 951 801 1421/7666/7546/1586
Technology Mgr.: Qilin Wang
Phone: (86) 951 801 1421/7666/7546/1586
CFO: Ms. Shuxian Feng
Phone: (86) 951 801 1421/7666/7546/1586
Materials Mgr.: Qingfeng Na
Phone: (86) 951 801 1421/7666/7546/1586
Pulp Mill Mgr.: Feng Li
Phone: (86) 951 801 1421/7666/7546/1586
Total Employees at this Location: 710
Type of Operation: Paper mill
Pulp Grades and Capacities:
Total pulp capacity: 10,622 mt/y
Other Pulp: 10,622 mt/y
Pulp Mill Data:
 Chemical Pulping Systems:
Continuous digesters: 1
Pulp Lines: 1
 Bleach Plant Systems: 1
Chemical Pulping System, Type: 1 Capacity 75,000 admt/y
 Chemical Recovery Equipment:
Recovery boilers: 1
Paper/Paperboard Grades and Capacities:
Total paper and paperboard capacity: 97,600 mt/y
Tissue: 97,600 mt/y
Paper and Paperboard Mill Data:
Paper Machines: 20
No. 1, cylinder, total capacity 2,800 mt/y, Trim width 2.7 m, Tissue, Uncoated woodfree/freesheet
No. 2, cylinder, total capacity 2,800 mt/y, Trim width 2.7 m, Tissue, Uncoated woodfree/freesheet
No. 3, cylinder, total capacity 2,800 mt/y, Trim width 2.7 m, Tissue, Uncoated woodfree/freesheet
No. 4, cylinder, total capacity 2,800 mt/y, Trim width 2.7 m, Tissue, Uncoated woodfree/freesheet
No. 5, cylinder, total capacity 2,800 mt/y, Trim width 2.7 m, Tissue, Uncoated woodfree/freesheet
No. 6, cylinder, total capacity 2,800 mt/y, Trim width 2.7 m, Tissue, Uncoated woodfree/freesheet
No. 7, cylinder, total capacity 2,800 mt/y, Trim width 2.7 m, Tissue, Uncoated woodfree/freesheet
No. 8, cylinder, total capacity 2,800 mt/y, Trim width 2.7 m, Tissue, Uncoated woodfree/freesheet
No. 9, cylinder, total capacity 2,800 mt/y, Trim width 2.7 m, Tissue, Uncoated woodfree/freesheet
No. 10, cylinder, total capacity 2,800 mt/y, Trim width 2.7 m, Tissue, Uncoated woodfree/freesheet
No. 11, cylinder, total capacity 2,800 mt/y, Trim width 2.7 m, Tissue, Uncoated woodfree/freesheet
No. 12, cylinder, total capacity 2,800 mt/y, Trim width 2.7 m, Tissue, Uncoated woodfree/freesheet
No. 13, cylinder, total capacity 2,800 mt/y, Trim width 2.7 m, Tissue, Uncoated woodfree/freesheet
No. 14, cylinder, total capacity 2,800 mt/y, Trim width 2.7 m, Tissue, Uncoated woodfree/freesheet
No. 15, cylinder, total capacity 2,800 mt/y, Trim width 2.7 m, Tissue, Uncoated woodfree/freesheet
No. 16, cylinder, total capacity 2,800 mt/y, Trim width 2.7 m, Tissue, Uncoated woodfree/freesheet
No. 17, cylinder, total capacity 2,800 mt/y, Trim width 2.7 m, Tissue, Uncoated woodfree/freesheet
No. 18, crescent former, total capacity 15,000 mt/y, Trim width 2.7 m, Tissue, Uncoated woodfree/freesheet
No. 19, cylinder, total capacity 10,000 mt/y, Trim width 2.85 m, Tissue, Uncoated woodfree/freesheet
No. 20, crescent former, total capacity 25,000 mt/y, Trim width 3.45 m, Tissue, Uncoated woodfree/freesheet
Energy Data:
Power boilers: 3
Steam turbines: 2 at 12 MW
Electrical demand for mill: 248 MWh/D

SHAANXI

ⓜShaanxi Pucheng Wuyang Paper Co., Ltd.
Weinan Mill
Qianer Street, Longyang Town, Pucheng County
Weinan, Shaanxi, 715509
China
Phone: (86) 913 7121768
Fax: (86) 913 7121768
Personnel:
Pres. & Gen. Mgr.: Yujiang Feng
Phone: (86) 913 7121768
Total Employees at this Location: 287
Type of Operation: Paperboard mill
Pulp Grades and Capacities:
Total pulp capacity: 34,026 mt/y
Recycled Pulping: 34,026 mt/y
Pulp Mill Data:
Pulp Lines: 1
Paper/Paperboard Grades and Capacities:
Total paper and paperboard capacity: 34,986 mt/y
Corrugating medium/fluting: 34,986 mt/y
Paper and Paperboard Mill Data:
Paper Machines: 1
No. 1, fourdrinier, total capacity 34,986 mt/y, Trim width 2.8 m, Corrugating medium/fluting
Energy Data:
Power boilers: 1
Electrical demand for mill: 55 MWh/D

ⓜShaanxi Shenglong Paper Co., Ltd.
Baoji Mill
Gongliu Industry District, Qishan County
Baoji, Shaanxi, 722405
China
Phone: (86) 917 858 0881/0888
Fax: (86) 917 858 0666/0884
Email: ceo@shenglong.cc
Web Address: www.shenglong.cc/index.php
Personnel:
Chmn.: Nailiang Qu
Phone: (86) 917 858 0881/0888
Pres. & Mill Mgr.: Xinquan Wang
Phone: (86) 917 858 0881/0888
VP - Sls. & Mktg.: Binke Yang
Phone: (86) 917 858 0881/0888
Tech. Mgr.: Junhao Yang
Phone: (86) 917 858 0881/0888
Total Employees at this Location: 1,000
Type of Operation: Paperboard mill
Pulp Grades and Capacities:
Total pulp capacity: 140,107 mt/y
Recycled Pulping: 140,107 mt/y
Pulp Mill Data:
Pulp Lines: 3
Paper/Paperboard Grades and Capacities:
Total paper and paperboard capacity: 142,443 mt/y
Corrugating medium/fluting: 112,455 mt/y
Boxboard/cartonboard: 29,988 mt/y
Paper and Paperboard Mill Data:
Paper Machines: 3
No. 4, cylinder (8), total capacity 29,988 mt/y, Trim width 2.4 m, Boxboard/cartonboard
No. 5, Multi-wire (4), total capacity 52,479 mt/y, Trim width 2.82 m, Corrugating medium/fluting
No. 6, fourdrinier, total capacity 59,976 mt/y, Trim width 4.2 m, Corrugating medium/fluting
Energy Data:
Power boilers: 1
Steam turbines: 2 at 1.5, 3 MW
Electrical demand for mill: 196 MWh/D

ⓘShaanxi Xi-An Lintong District Hanxing Co., Ltd.
Ownership: 100% by shareholders
Haoxing Village, Xinshi Town, Lintong District
Xi-An, Shaanxi, 710605
China
Phone: (86) 29 8384 6573/6574
Fax: (86) 29 8384 6575
Web Address: www.xahanxing.cn
Personnel:
Chmn. & Pres.: Jiuzhou Hao
Phone: (86) 29 8384 6573
Fax: (86) 29 8384 6575
Total Employees of Company: 3,000
Mill Locations:
Shaanxi Xi-An Lintong District Hanxing Co., Ltd., Xi-An Mill, Haoxing Village, Xinshi Town, Lintong District, Xi-An 710605, China, Capacity: 60,000 mt/y, (Paper mill)
Phone: (86) 29 8384 6573/6574
Fax: (86) 29 8384 6575

ⓜShaanxi Xi-An Lintong District Hanxing Co., Ltd.
Xi-An Mill
Haoxing Village, Xinshi Town, Lintong District
Xi-An, Shaanxi, 710605
China
Phone: (86) 29 8384 6573/6574
Fax: (86) 29 8384 6575
Web Address: www.xahanxing.cn
Personnel:
Chmn. & Pres.: Jiuzhou Hao
Phone: (86) 29 8384 6573/6574
Total Employees at this Location: 3,000
Type of Operation: Paper mill
Pulp Grades and Capacities:
Total pulp capacity: 50,000 mt/y
Pulp Mill Data:
Pulp Lines: 2
 Chemical Recovery Equipment:
Recovery boilers: 1
Paper/Paperboard Grades and Capacities:
Total paper and paperboard capacity: 60,000 mt/y
Tissue: 60,000 mt/y
Paper and Paperboard Mill Data:
Paper Machines: 43
PM 1760 (12 PMs), cylinder, total capacity 400 mt/y, Trim width 1.76 m, Tissue
PM 1880 (10 PMs), fourdrinier, total capacity 1,250 mt/y, Trim width 1.88 m, Tissue
PM 2100 (2 PMs), fourdrinier, total capacity 1,800 mt/y, Trim width 2.1 m, Tissue
PM 2400 (12 PMs), fourdrinier, total capacity 1,800 mt/y, Trim width 2.44 m, Tissue
PM 2800 (7 PMs), fourdrinier, total capacity 2,500 mt/y, Trim width 2.8 m, Tissue
Energy Data:
Power boilers: 2
Steam turbines: 2 at 30, 30 MW
Electrical demand for mill: 1,440 MWh/D

ⓜShaanxi Xi-An Weiyangqu Efang Paperboard Co., Ltd.
Xi-An Mill
No. 33 First Rd., Sanqiao Street
Xi-An, Shaanxi, 710083
China
Phone: (86) 29 8452 1248/8451 7887
Fax: (86) 29 8452 1248
Personnel:
Chmn.: Hongde Xu
Phone: (86) 29 8452 1248/8451 7887
Sls. Mgr.: Yaru Wang
Phone: (86) 29 8452 1248/8451 7887
Total Employees at this Location: 200
Type of Operation: Paperboard mill
Paper/Paperboard Grades and Capacities:
Total paper and paperboard capacity: 35,000 mt/y
Linerboard: 15,000 mt/y
Boxboard/cartonboard: 20,000 mt/y
Paper and Paperboard Mill Data:
Paper Machines: 3

China

PM 1, total capacity 5,000 mt/y, Trim width 1.58 m, Boxboard/cartonboard
PM 2, fourdrinier, total capacity 15,000 mt/y, Trim width 2.85 m, Linerboard
PM 3, fourdrinier, total capacity 15,000 mt/y, Trim width 2.85 m, Boxboard/cartonboard
Coating Machines: 2
CM 1, total capacity 5,000 mt/y, off machine
CM 2, total capacity 15,000 mt/y, on machine

ⓂShaanxi Xingbao Group Co., Ltd
Ownership: 100% by Shaanxi Xingbao Group Co., Ltd
Fengyi Industry Zone
Xingping, Shaanxi, 713100
China
Phone: (86) 29 3826 6112
Fax: (86) 29 3826 6112
Email: xsb@sxxingbao.com
Web Address: www.sxxingbao.com
Personnel:
Chmn.: Xiaohong Peng
Phone: (86) 29 3826 6112
Fax: (86) 29 3826 6112
Total Employees at this Location: 2,600
Mill Locations:
Shaanxi Xingbao Group Co., Ltd, Xingping Mill, Fengyi Industry Zone, Xingping 713100, China, Capacity: 52,000 mt/y, (Paper mill)
Phone: (86) 29 3826 6112
Fax: (86) 29 3826 6112
Email: xsb@sxxingbao.com

ⓂShaanxi Xingbao Group Co., Ltd
Xingping Mill
Ownership: 100% by Shaanxi Xingbao Group Co., Ltd
Fengyi Industry Zone
Xingping, Shaanxi, 713100
China
Phone: (86) 29 3826 6112
Fax: (86) 29 3826 6112
Email: xsb@sxxingbao.com
Web Address: www.sxxingbao.com
Personnel:
Chmn.: Xiaohong Peng
Phone: (86) 29 3826 6112
Total Employees at this Location: 2,600
Type of Operation: Paper mill
Pulp Grades and Capacities:
Total pulp capacity: 40,000 mt/y
Paper/Paperboard Grades and Capacities:
Total paper and paperboard capacity: 52,000 mt/y
Tissue: 52,000 mt/y
Paper and Paperboard Mill Data:
Paper Machines: 40
PM 1-14, total capacity 1,000 mt/y, Trim width 1.76 m, Tissue
PM 15-38, total capacity 1,100 mt/y, Trim width 2.4 m, Tissue
PM 39, BF-10 EX, total capacity 12,000 mt/y, Trim width 2.76 m, Tissue
PM 40, BF-10 EX, total capacity 12,000 mt/y, Trim width 2.76 m, Tissue

ⓂShaanxi Xiongdi Paper Co., Ltd.
Xi-An Mill
Haojing Industry Park, Wangsi Town, Chang-an District
Xi-An, Shaanxi, 710116
China
Phone: (86) 29 8590 2333
Fax: (86) 29 8580 0003
Email: brotherpaper@sohu.com
Web Address: brotherpaper.com
Personnel:
Chmn. & Gen. Mgr.: Zhimao Guan
Phone: (86) 29 8590 2333
Sls. Mgr.: Hao Wang
Phone: (86) 29 8590 2333
Total Employees at this Location: 500

Type of Operation: Paper mill, Paperboard mill
Pulp Grades and Capacities:
Total pulp capacity: 78,405 mt/y
Recycled Pulping: 78,405 mt/y
Pulp Mill Data:
Pulp Lines: 1
Recycled Fiber Treatment Lines:
Recycled packaging pulping lines: 1 at 150,000 admt/y
Paper/Paperboard Grades and Capacities:
Total paper and paperboard capacity: 80,682 mt/y
Corrugating medium/fluting: 80,682 mt/y
Paper and Paperboard Mill Data:
Paper Machines: 1
No. 1, fourdrinier, total capacity 80,682 mt/y, Trim width 4.1 m, Corrugating medium/fluting
Energy Data:
Electrical demand for mill: 130 MWh/D

ⓂXian Dubang Paper Co., Ltd.
No.12, Beiguanzheng Street, Lianhu District
XiAn, Shaanxi, 710015
China
Phone: (86) 29 8625 2755
Mill Locations:
Xian Dubang Paper Co., Ltd., XiAn Mill, No.12, Beiguanzheng Street, Lianhu District, XiAn 710015, China, Capacity: 3,600 mt/y, (Paper mill)
Phone: (86) 29 8625 2755

ⓂXian Dubang Paper Co., Ltd.
XiAn Mill
No.12, Beiguanzheng Street, Lianhu District
XiAn, Shaanxi, 710015
China
Phone: (86) 29 8625 2755
Type of Operation: Paper mill
Paper/Paperboard Grades and Capacities:
Total paper and paperboard capacity: 3,600 mt/y
Tissue: 3,600 mt/y
Paper and Paperboard Mill Data:
Paper Machines: 3
PM 1, total capacity 1,200 mt/y, Trim width 1.88 m, Tissue
PM 2, total capacity 1,200 mt/y, Trim width 1.88 m, Tissue
PM 3, total capacity 1,200 mt/y, Trim width 1.88 m, Tissue

ⓄⓂXingping Jinlong Chemical Fiber Co., Ltd.
Xingping Mill
Ownership: Henan Haiyang Chemical Fiber Group Co., Ltd.
Donghuan Rd., Xingping City
Xianyang, Shaanxi
China
Phone: (86) 29 3882 2014
Web Address: www.hyfiber.com
Type of Operation: Pulp mill
Pulp Grades and Capacities:
Total pulp capacity: 12,000 mt/y
Pulp Mill Data:
Pulp Lines: 3

SHANDONG

ⓂAhlstrom Binzhou
Binzhou Mill
Ownership: 100% by Ahlstrom Corporation Oy
No. 209 Huanghe Wu Rd.
Binzhou, Shandong, 256651
China
Phone: (86) 543-340-9777
Fax: (86) 543 340 2216
Email: sales@puri-filter.com, filter-shi@163.com

Web Address: www.ahlstrom.com
Personnel:
Gen. Mgr.: Zhonghua Liu
Phone: (86) 543 340 2209/ 2207
Senior Mgr. Prod & Tech. Develop.: Noël
Phone: (86) 543-340-9777
HR Mgr.: Mark Sun
Phone: (86) 543-340-9777
Email: mark.sun@ahlstrom.com
Prod. Develop. Mgr.: Shawn
Phone: (86) 543-340-9777
Prod. Develop. Engineer: Felicia
Phone: (86) 543-340-9777
Total Employees at this Location: 200
Type of Operation: Paper mill
Paper/Paperboard Grades and Capacities:
Total paper and paperboard capacity: 10,000 mt/y
Specialty and industrial: 10,000 mt/y
Paper and Paperboard Mill Data:
Paper Machines: 2
PM 2, inclined, total capacity 3,000 mt/y, Trim width 2.15 m, Specialty and industrial
PM 1, inclined, total capacity 3,000 mt/y, Trim width 2.15 m, Specialty and industrial

ⓂAhlstrom Yulong Specialty Paper Company Ltd.
Longkou Mill
Ownership: 60% by Ahlstrom Corporation Oy, 40% by Longkou Yulong Paper Co. Ltd.
Zhu You Guan Industrial Park
Longkou, Shandong, 265700
China
Phone: (86) 535 8589 778
Email: investor@ahlstrom.com, corporate.communications@ahlstrom.com
Web Address: www.ahlstrom.com
Personnel:
Gen. Mgr.: Vesa Yliherne
Phone: (86) 535 8589 778
Sls. Dir.: Michael Huan
Phone: (86) 535 8589 778
HR Mgr. of China: Mark Sun
Phone: (86) 535 8589 778
Email: mark.sun@ahlstrom.com
HR. Mgr., Sls. China Region & Admin. Mgr. : Flora Zhang
Phone: (86) 535 8589 778
Email: jingyi_Chang@163.com
Type of Operation: Paper mill
Paper/Paperboard Grades and Capacities:
Total paper and paperboard capacity: 28,000 mt/y
Specialty and industrial: 28,000 mt/y
Paper and Paperboard Mill Data:
Paper Machines: 1
No. 1, (started November 2012), total capacity 28,000 mt/y, Trim width 3.6 m, Specialty and industrial

ⓄChina Sunshine Paper Holdings Company Limited
Ownership: 100% by shareholders
Changle Economic Developed Zone, Changle County
Weifang, Shandong, 262400
China
Phone: (86) 536 218 1001
Fax: (86) 536 218 6006
Email: info@sunshinepaper.com.cn
Web Address: www.sunshinepaper.com.cn
Personnel:
Chmn. & Pres.: Dongxing Wang
Phone: (86) 536 2181001
Fax: (86) 536 2186006
Vice Chmn.: Weixi Shi
Phone: (86) 536 2181001
Fax: (86) 536 2186006
Gen. Mgr.: Xiaolei Ci
Phone: (86) 536 2181001
Fax: (86) 536 2186006
Dpty. Gen. Mgr.: Zengguo Zhang
Phone: (86) 536 2181001

Fax: (86) 536 2186006
Total Employees of Company: 2,560
Mill Locations:
China Sunshine Paper Holdings Company Limited, Weifang Mill, Changle Economic Developed Zone, Changle County, Weifang 262400, China, Capacity: 1,060,000 mt/y, (Paperboard mill)
Phone: (86) 536 218 1001/1006/1007
Fax: (86) 536 218 6006/1099
Email: info@sunshinepaper.com.cn

ⓂChina Sunshine Paper Holdings Company Limited
Weifang Mill
Changle Economic Developed Zone, Changle County
Weifang, Shandong, 262400
China
Phone: (86) 536 218 1001/1006/1007
Fax: (86) 536 218 6006/1099
Email: info@sunshinepaper.com.cn
Web Address: www.sunshinepaper.com.cn
Personnel:
Chmn. & Pres.: Dongxing Wang
Phone: (86) 536 218 1001/1006/1007
Vic. Chmn.: Weixin Shi
Phone: (86) 536 218 1001/1006/1007
VP: Zhenguo Zhang
Phone: (86) 536 218 1001/1006/1007
Grop. Fin. Cont. & Joint Com. Sec., Qual. Acco.: Kai Fung Cheung
Phone: (86) 536 218 1001/1006/1007
Spec. Assis. of CEO: Jie Jiao
Phone: (86) 536 218 1001/1006/1007
Exec. Dir.: Yilong Wang
Phone: (86) 536 218 1001/1006/1007
Dpty Gen. Mgr.- Dome. Sls.: Gang Hu
Phone: (86) 536 218 1001/1006/1007
Dpty Gen. Mgr.- Fina.: Gang Hu
Phone: (86) 536 218 1001/1006/1007
Dpty General Mgr.: Ziqian Sang
Phone: (86) 536 218 1001/1006/1007
Dpty General Mgr.- Infrastructure Proj.: Gaoting Ruan
Phone: (86) 536 218 1001/1006/1007
Dpty Gen. Mgr.- Int.: Xiaohui Zhang
Phone: (86) 536 218 1001/1006/1007
Total Employees at this Location: 800
Type of Operation: Paperboard mill
Pulp Grades and Capacities:
Total pulp capacity: 960,470 mt/y
Recycled Pulping: 960,470 mt/y
Pulp Mill Data:
Pulp Lines: 1
Bleach Plant Systems: 1
DIP
Recycled Fiber Treatment Lines:
Flotation deinking lines: 1 at 200,000 admt/y
Recycled packaging pulping lines
Paper/Paperboard Grades and Capacities:
Total paper and paperboard capacity: 1,060,000 mt/y
Linerboard: 810,000 mt/y
Corrugating medium/fluting: 50,000 mt/y
Boxboard/cartonboard: 200,000 mt/y
Paper and Paperboard Mill Data:
Paper Machines: 5
No. 1, fourdrinier (3), total capacity 110,000 mt/y, Trim width 3.4 m, Linerboard
No. 2, fourdrinier (3), total capacity 200,000 mt/y, Trim width 4.5 m, Linerboard
No. 3, fourdrinier, total capacity 50,000 mt/y, Trim width 3.2 m, Corrugating medium/fluting
No. 4, fourdrinier (3), total capacity 200,000 mt/y, Trim width 3.2 m, Boxboard/cartonboard
N1, ValFormer, total capacity 500,000 mt/y, Trim width 6.66 m, Linerboard
Coating Machines: 1
N1, on machine
Energy Data:
Power boilers: 5
Steam turbines: 2 at 12, 12 MW
Electrical demand for mill: 1,551 MWh/D

ⓂDezhou Huisheng Pingyuan Paper Co., Ltd.
Dezhou Mill
Ownership: 100% by Shandong Weifang Huisheng Group
Longmen Economy Zone, Pingyuan County
Dezhou, Shandong, 253100
China
Phone: (86) 534 2169 177
Fax: (86) 534 2169 107
Personnel:
Chmn.: Maosheng Ge
Phone: (86) 534 2169 177
Type of Operation: Paper mill
Pulp Grades and Capacities:
Total pulp capacity: 175,922 mt/y
Recycled Pulping: 175,922 mt/y
Paper/Paperboard Grades and Capacities:
Total paper and paperboard capacity: 180,000 mt/y
Linerboard: 54,000 mt/y
Boxboard/cartonboard: 126,000 mt/y
Paper and Paperboard Mill Data:
Paper Machines: 1
No. 9, fourdrinier (3), total capacity 180,000 mt/y, Trim width 4.4 m, Linerboard, Boxboard/cartonboard
Energy Data:
Electrical demand for mill: 198 MWh/D

ⓂInternational Paper & Sun Paper Cartonboard Co., Ltd.
Yanzhou Mill
Ownership: 55% by International Paper Co., 45% by Shandong Sun Paper Industry Joint Stock Co., Ltd.
1# Youyi Road
Yanzhou, Shandong, 272100
China
Phone: (86) 537 389 8588
Fax: (86) 537 389 8502
Web Address: www.ipapersun.com
Personnel:
Pres.: Cecilia Ho
Phone: (86) 537 389 8588
Gen. Mgr.: Wern-Lirn Paul Wang
Phone: (86) 537 389 8588
Email: paul.wang1@ipaper.com
Total Employees at this Location: 1,200
Type of Operation: Paperboard mill
Paper/Paperboard Grades and Capacities:
Total paper and paperboard capacity: 1,350,000 mt/y
Boxboard/cartonboard: 1,350,000 mt/y
Paper and Paperboard Mill Data:
Paper Machines: 4
No. 17, fourdrinier (3), total capacity 200,000 mt/y, Trim width 3.3 m, Boxboard/cartonboard
No. 18, Fourdrinier (4), total capacity 225,000 mt/y, Trim width 3.3 m, Boxboard/cartonboard
No. 22, fourdrinier (3), total capacity 375,000 mt/y, Trim width 4.58 m, Boxboard/cartonboard
No. 26, fourdrinier (3), total capacity 550,000 mt/y, Trim width 6.1 m, Boxboard/cartonboard
Coating Machines: 3
PM 17, total capacity 200,000 mt/y., on machine
PM 18, total capacity 234,000 mt/y, on machine
PM 22, total capacity 400,000 mt/y., on machine
Energy Data:
Electrical demand for mill: 2,049 MWh/D

ⓂJinan Haoyuan Paper Co., Ltd.
No.30 South of Xizhou Rd., Licheng District
Jinan, Shandong, 250100
China
Phone: (86) 531 8802 3115/3102
Fax: (86) 531 8801 2000
Mill Locations:
Jinan Haoyuan Paper Co., Ltd., Jinan Mill, No.30 South of Xizhou Rd., Licheng District, Jinan 250100, China, Capacity: 10,000 mt/y, (Paper mill)
Phone: (86) 531 8802 3115/3102
Fax: (86) 531 8801 2000

ⓂJinan Haoyuan Paper Co., Ltd.
Jinan Mill
No.30 South of Xizhou Rd., Licheng District
Jinan, Shandong, 250100
China
Phone: (86) 531 8802 3115/3102
Fax: (86) 531 8801 2000
Type of Operation: Paper mill
Paper/Paperboard Grades and Capacities:
Total paper and paperboard capacity: 10,000 mt/y
Uncoated woodfree/freesheet: 10,000 mt/y
Paper and Paperboard Mill Data:
Paper Machines: 2
PM 1, total capacity 5,000 mt/y, Trim width 1.76 m, Uncoated woodfree/freesheet
PM 2, total capacity 5,000 mt/y, Trim width 1.76 m, Uncoated woodfree/freesheet

ⓂMCC Paper Yinhe Co., Ltd.
Linqing Mill
Ownership: 100% by MCC Paper Group Co., Ltd.
No. 297, Ximenli Street
Linqing, Shandong, 252600
China
Phone: (86) 635 243 3886/3348/7949
Fax: (86) 635 243 7251/3346/6952
Email: yinhe@yinhepaper.com, info@yinhepaper.com
Web Address: www.mccyinhe.com
Personnel:
Chmn.: Jingchun Gao
Phone: (86) 635 243 4652/7949/2529/289 1102
CEO & Pres.: Shujian Li
Phone: (86) 635 243 4652/7949/2529/289 1102
VP & Exec. Gen. Mgr.: Zhonghua Wan
Phone: (86) 635 243 4652/7949/2529/289 1102
VP - Domestic Bus.: Yuzhen Xia
Phone: (86) 635 243 3858/ 6888
Fax: (86) 635 243 6952
Imp. & Exp. Dir.: Susan Huang
Phone: (86) 635 243 3818/ 7949/ 2529
Fax: (86) 635 243 7254
Email: susanhuang@yinhepaper.com
Tech. Dir.: Jesse Jiang
Phone: (86) 635 243 7949
Email: support@yinhepaper.com
Total Employees at this Location: 6,000
Type of Operation: Pulp mill, Paper mill, Paperboard mill
Pulp Grades and Capacities:
Total pulp capacity: 477,369 mt/y
Mechanical Pulp: 77,275 mt/y
Recycled Pulping: 271,767 mt/y
Other Pulp: 128,327 mt/y
Pulp Mill Data:
Chemical Pulping Systems:
Continuous digesters: 3
Mechanical Pulping Systems:
APMP Systems: 1
Pulp Lines: 6
Bleach Plant Systems: 2
No. 1, Type: Peroxide
No. 2
Chemical Recovery Equipment:
Evaporator lines
Recovery boilers: 4
Recycled Fiber Treatment Lines:
Recycled packaging pulping lines: 2 at 100,000 admt/y
Paper/Paperboard Grades and Capacities:
Total paper and paperboard capacity: 817,000 mt/y
Uncoated woodfree/freesheet: 355,500 mt/y
Uncoated mechanical/groundwood: 181,500 mt/y
Corrugating medium/fluting: 280,000 mt/y
Paper and Paperboard Mill Data:
Paper Machines: 30
No. 1, cylinder, total capacity 6,000 mt/y, Trim width 1.58 m, Uncoated woodfree/freesheet

China

No. 6, ValFormer, total capacity 12,000 mt/y, Trim width 1.76 m, Uncoated mechanical/groundwood
No. 8, ValFormer, total capacity 12,000 mt/y, Trim width 1.76 m, Uncoated mechanical/groundwood
No. 9, cylinder, total capacity 6,000 mt/y, Trim width 1.58 m, Uncoated woodfree/freesheet
No. 11, fourdrinier, total capacity 6,500 mt/y, Trim width 1.76 m, Uncoated mechanical/groundwood
No. 12, fourdrinier, total capacity 6,500 mt/y, Trim width 1.76 m, Uncoated mechanical/groundwood
No. 13, ValFormer, total capacity 12,000 mt/y, Trim width 1.76 m, Uncoated mechanical/groundwood
No. 14, ValFormer, total capacity 12,000 mt/y, Trim width 1.76 m, Uncoated mechanical/groundwood
No. 15, total capacity 12,000 mt/y, Trim width 1.76 m, Uncoated mechanical/groundwood
No. 16, fourdrinier, total capacity 20,000 mt/y, Trim width 1.76 m, Uncoated woodfree/freesheet
No. 17, fourdrinier, total capacity 6,500 mt/y, Trim width 1.76 m, Uncoated mechanical/groundwood
No. 18, fourdrinier, total capacity 6,500 mt/y, Trim width 1.76 m, Uncoated mechanical/groundwood
No. 19, total capacity 8,500 mt/y, Trim width 1.88 m, Uncoated woodfree/freesheet
No. 20, total capacity 8,500 mt/y, Trim width 1.88 m, Uncoated woodfree/freesheet
No. 21, fourdrinier, total capacity 6,500 mt/y, Trim width 1.76 m, Uncoated mechanical/groundwood
No. 22, fourdrinier, total capacity 6,500 mt/y, Trim width 1.76 m, Uncoated mechanical/groundwood
No. 23, multi-wire, total capacity 145,000 mt/y, Trim width 4.4 m, Corrugating medium/fluting
No. 24, multi-wire, total capacity 135,000 mt/y, Trim width 4.4 m, Corrugating medium/fluting
No. 25, fourdrinier, total capacity 40,000 mt/y, Trim width 2.64 m, Uncoated woodfree/freesheet
No. 26, fourdrinier, total capacity 13,300 mt/y, Trim width 2.64 m, Uncoated woodfree/freesheet
No. 27, fourdrinier, total capacity 12,000 mt/y, Trim width 2.36 m, Uncoated mechanical/groundwood
No. 28, fourdrinier, total capacity 12,000 mt/y, Trim width 2.36 m, Uncoated mechanical/groundwood
No. 29, fourdrinier, total capacity 13,300 mt/y, Trim width 2.64 m, Uncoated woodfree/freesheet
No. 30, fourdrinier, total capacity 13,300 mt/y, Trim width 2.64 m, Uncoated woodfree/freesheet
No. 31, fourdrinier, total capacity 13,300 mt/y, Trim width 2.64 m, Uncoated woodfree/freesheet
No. 32, fourdrinier, total capacity 13,300 mt/y, Trim width 2.64 m, Uncoated woodfree/freesheet
No. 33, fourdrinier, total capacity 20,000 mt/y, Trim width 3.6 m, Uncoated mechanical/groundwood
No. 34, fourdrinier, total capacity 18,500 mt/y, Trim width 3.3 m, Uncoated mechanical/groundwood
No. 35, fourdrinier, total capacity 20,000 mt/y, Trim width 3.6 m, Uncoated mechanical/groundwood
N-1, ValFormer, total capacity 200,000 mt/y, Trim width 5.8 m, Uncoated woodfree/freesheet
Energy Data:
Power boilers: 8
Steam turbines: 8 at 0.5, 15, 15, 15, 12, 12, 0.5, 0.5 MW
Electrical demand for mill: 1,632 MWh/D

ⓜAsia Symbol (Shandong) Pulp & Paper Co., Ltd.
Rizhao Mill
Ownership: 90% by Asia Pacific Resources International - APRIL, 5% by Rizhao First Light Industry Company, 5% by Shandong International Trust & Investment Company
No. 369 Beijing Rd., Donggang District
Rizhao, Shandong, 276826
China
Phone: (86) 633 336 1000/1168/1258/1209/1093/1179
Fax: (86) 633 336 1218/1111/1203/8359931/8360366
Email: thomas_leung@aprilchina.com
Web Address: asiasymbol.com, www.rgei.com.cn

Personnel:
Gen. Mgr.: Wenhai Huang
Phone: (86) 633 336 1006
Fax: (86) 633 336 9200
Email: huangwenhai@aprilchina.com
Dir.: Futai Qiu
Phone: (86) 633 336 1000/1168/1258/1209/1093/1179
Pres.: Allan Yang
Phone: (86) 633 336 1000/1168/1258/1209/1093/1179
Sls. Mgr.: Jin Lin
Phone: (86) 633 336 1000/1168/1258/1209/1093/1179
Exp. Dir.: Thomas Leung
Phone: (86) 633 336 1093
Fax: (86) 633 836 0366
Email: thomas_leung@aprilchina.com
Chief Eng.: Ruijin Qiu
Phone: (86) 633 336 1000/1168/1258/1209/1093/1179
Sls. Mgr.: Hongquan Zhao
Phone: (86) 138 6330 1828
Total Employees at this Location: 900
Type of Operation: Pulp mill, Paperboard mill
Pulp Grades and Capacities:
Total pulp capacity: 1,719,539 mt/y
Pulp available for market: 1,631,490 mt/y
Chemical Pulp: 1,798,761 mt/y
Pulp Mill Data:
Chemical Pulping Systems:
Continuous digesters: 2
Pulp Lines: 2
Bleach Plant Systems: 2
No. 1, Sequence: O_2 DEopDD, Capacity 300,000 admt/y
No. 2, Sequence: O_2 DEopDP, Capacity 1,400,000 admt/y
Chemical Recovery Equipment:
Recovery boilers: 2
Lime Kiln
Pulp Dryers:
Twin Wire 1, Twin Wire 1
Paper/Paperboard Grades and Capacities:
Total paper and paperboard capacity: 480,165 mt/y
Boxboard/cartonboard: 480,165 mt/y
Paper and Paperboard Mill Data:
Stock Preparation:
Pulpers: 10
Refiners: 8
Paper Machines: 2
No. 1, DuoFormer D, total capacity 180,285 mt/y, Trim width 3.62 m, Boxboard/cartonboard
BM 12, total capacity 299,880 mt/y, Trim width 4.6 m, Boxboard/cartonboard
Coating Machines: 1
CM 1, total capacity 180,000 mt/y., on machine
Finishing Equipment:
Supercalenders: 2
Rewinders: 1
Sheeters: 3
Energy Data:
Power boilers: 3
Steam turbines: 3 at 40, 92, 97 MW
Electrical demand for mill: 3,323 MWh/D

ⓜⓜShandong Baron Paper Co., Ltd.
Laiwu Mill
Ownership: 100% by shareholders
Fangxia Town, Laicheng County
Laiwu, Shandong, 271125
China
Phone: (86) 634 867 5566/5588/5666
Fax: (86) 634 867 5666
Web Address: www.baronpaper.cn
Personnel:
Chrmn. & Pres./Mill Mgr.: Gengxin Lu
Phone: (86) 634 661 1308/1306/3520
Exec. VP/Asst. Mill Mgr.: Zhongpin Qi
Phone: (86) 634 661 1308/1306/3520
VP: Shiru Liang
Phone: (86) 634 661 1308/1306/3520
VP: Hanmeng Di
Phone: (86) 634 661 1308/1306/3520
Sls. Mgr.: Ximing Xu
Phone: (86) 634 661 1308/1306/3520
Tech. Mgr.: Xiaoyong Liu
Phone: (86) 634 661 1308/1306/3520
Chief Eng.: Huale Yi
Phone: (86) 634 661 1308/1306/3520
Maint. Mgr.: Xinjiang Wang
Phone: (86) 634 661 1308/1306/3520
Env. Dir.: Fuchang Liu
Phone: (86) 634 661 1308/1306/3520
Purch. Agent: Jingjie Qi
Phone: (86) 634 661 1308/1306/3520
Total Employees at this Location: 1,800
Type of Operation: Paper mill
Pulp Grades and Capacities:
Total pulp capacity: 21,720 mt/y
Chemical Pulp: 21,720 mt/y
Pulp Mill Data:
Recycled Fiber Treatment Lines:
Flotation deinking lines: 1 at 71,400 admt/y
Paper/Paperboard Grades and Capacities:
Total paper and paperboard capacity: 147,750 mt/y
Uncoated woodfree/freesheet: 88,636 mt/y
Uncoated mechanical/groundwood: 8,400 mt/y
Coated woodfree/freesheet: 50,000 mt/y
Tissue: 714 mt/y
Paper and Paperboard Mill Data:
Stock Preparation:
Pulpers: 45
Paper Machines: 10
No. 1, Yankee dryer, total capacity 714 mt/y, Trim width 1.09 m, Tissue
No. 3, fourdrinier, total capacity 4,284 mt/y, Trim width 1.76 m, Uncoated woodfree/freesheet
No. 4, fourdrinier, total capacity 4,998 mt/y, Trim width 1.76 m, Uncoated woodfree/freesheet
No. 6, fourdrinier, total capacity 3,570 mt/y, Trim width 1.76 m, Uncoated woodfree/freesheet
No. 7, fourdrinier, total capacity 4,284 mt/y, Trim width 1.76 m, Uncoated woodfree/freesheet
No. 8, fourdrinier, total capacity 4,800 mt/y, Trim width 1.76 m, Uncoated woodfree/freesheet
No. 9, fourdrinier, total capacity 4,200 mt/y, Trim width 1.76 m, Uncoated woodfree/freesheet
No. 10, fourdrinier, total capacity 12,500 mt/y, Trim width 1.76 m, Uncoated woodfree/freesheet
No. 13, fourdrinier, total capacity 8,400 mt/y, Trim width 1.76 m, Uncoated mechanical/groundwood
No. 15, hybrid former, total capacity 100,000 mt/y, Trim width 4.58 m, Coated woodfree/freesheet, Uncoated woodfree/freesheet
Coating Machines: 2
CM 14, total capacity 25,000 mt/y., off machine
CM 15, total capacity 100,000 mt/y., on machine
Finishing Equipment:
Supercalenders: 2
Rewinders: 9
Sheeters: 15
Energy Data:
Power boilers: 6
Steam turbines: 4 at 1.5, 3, 6, 15 MW
Electrical demand for mill: 312 MWh/D

ⓜShandong Bohui Paper Industry Co., Ltd.
Ownership: 36.39% by Shandong Bohui Paper Holding
Maqiao Town, Huantai County
Zibo, Shandong, 256405
China
Phone: (86) 533 853 9966 / 853 0387
Fax: (86) 533 853 0372
Email: zqb@bohui.com, 05338866@163.com
Web Address: www.bohui.net

China

Personnel:
Chmn.: Yanliang Yang
Phone: (86) 533 853 8020/0389
Fax: (86) 533 853 0372/8686
Chmn of Bd. & Dir.: Jin Liangzong
Phone: (86) 533 853 8020/0389
Fax: (86) 533 853 0372/8686
Vice Chmn.: Wei Zhao
Phone: (86) 533 853 8020/0389
Fax: (86) 533 853 0372/8686
CFO: Xiao Shi
Phone: (86) 533 853 8020/0389
Fax: (86) 533 853 0372/8686
Gen. Mgr.: Zhengxing Yang
Phone: (86) 533 853 8020/0389
Fax: (86) 533 853 0372/8686
Dir. Supply: Shubing Jing
Phone: (86) 533 853 8020/0389
Fax: (86) 533 853 0372/8686
Board Sec.: Guodong Yang
Phone: (86) 533 853 9966
Fax: (86) 533 853 9966
Email: zqb@bohui.com
Exec. Dpty. Gen.Mgr.: Yougui Wang
Phone: (86) 533 853 8020/0389
Fax: (86) 533 853 0372/8686
Total Employees of Company: 5,338
Mill Locations:
Jiangsu Bohui Paper Industry Co., Ltd., Dafeng Mill, Dafeng Port EconomicZone, Yancheng, China, Capacity: 720,000 mt/y, (Paper mill)
Phone: (86) 515 8328 7878/7880
Shandong Bohui Paper Industry Co., Ltd., Zibo Mill, Maqiao Town, Huantai County, Zibo 256405, China, Capacity: 1,256,394 mt/y, (Pulp mill, Paper mill, Paperboard mill)
Phone: (86) 533 853 0389/0387/0366/853 9966/3397/4520
Fax: (86) 533 853 0372/8686
Email: zqb@bohui.com; 05338866@163.com

ⓜShandong Bohui Paper Industry Co., Ltd.
Zibo Mill
Maqiao Town, Huantai County
Zibo, Shandong, 256405
China
Phone: (86) 533 853 0389/0387/0366/853 9966/3397/4520
Fax: (86) 533 853 0372/8686
Email: zqb@bohui.com, 05338866@163.com
Web Address: www.bohui.net
Personnel:
Chmn.: Yanzhi Yang
Phone: (86) 533 853 8020/0389/9638/3827
CFO: Ms. Xiao Shi
Phone: (86) 533 853 8020/0389/9638/3827
Board Sec.: Guodong Yang
Phone: (86) 533 853 9966
Fax: (86) 533 853 9966
Email: zqb@bohui.com
Dpty. Gen.Mgr.: Yougui Wang
Phone: (86) 533 853 8020/0389/9638/3827
Dpty. Gen. Mgr.: Kejun Zhou
Phone: (86) 533 853 8020/0389/9638/3827
Mgr./Dir.: Shubing Jing
Phone: (86) 533 853 8020/0389/9638/3827
Total Employees at this Location: 3,435
Type of Operation: Pulp mill, Paper mill, Paperboard mill
Pulp Grades and Capacities:
Total pulp capacity: 880,908 mt/y
Chemical Pulp: 118,591 mt/y
Mechanical Pulp: 284,353 mt/y
Recycled Pulping: 154,226 mt/y
Pulp Mill Data:
Chemical Pulping Systems:
Batch digesters: 3
Mechanical Pulping Systems:
BCTMP systems: 1
BCTMP systems: 1
Pulp Lines: 6
Bleach Plant Systems: 6
Chemical Recovery Equipment:
Evaporator lines
Recovery boilers: 2
Recycled Fiber Treatment Lines:
Recycled packaging pulping lines at 305,000
Paper/Paperboard Grades and Capacities:
Total paper and paperboard capacity: 1,256,394 mt/y
Uncoated woodfree/freesheet: 106,394 mt/y
Uncoated mechanical/groundwood: 150,000 mt/y
Linerboard: 150,000 mt/y
Boxboard/cartonboard: 850,000 mt/y
Paper and Paperboard Mill Data:
Stock Preparation:
Pulpers:
Paper Machines: 30
No. 1, DuoFormer D, total capacity 7,854 mt/y, Trim width 1.76 m, Uncoated woodfree/freesheet
No. 2, fourdrinier, total capacity 7,854 mt/y, Trim width 1.76 m, Uncoated woodfree/freesheet
No. 3, fourdrinier, total capacity 7,854 mt/y, Trim width 1.76 m, Uncoated woodfree/freesheet
No. 4, fourdrinier, total capacity 7,854 mt/y, Trim width 1.76 m, Uncoated woodfree/freesheet
No. 5, fourdrinier, total capacity 10,000 mt/y, Trim width 1.76 m, Uncoated woodfree/freesheet
No. 6, fourdrinier, total capacity 10,000 mt/y, Trim width 1.76 m, Uncoated woodfree/freesheet
No. 7, fourdrinier, total capacity 7,854 mt/y, Trim width 1.76 m, Uncoated woodfree/freesheet
No. 8, fourdrinier, total capacity 7,854 mt/y, Trim width 1.76 m, Uncoated woodfree/freesheet
No. 9, fourdrinier, total capacity 7,854 mt/y, Trim width 1.76 m, Uncoated woodfree/freesheet
No. 10, fourdrinier, total capacity 7,854 mt/y, Trim width 1.76 m, Uncoated woodfree/freesheet
No. 11, fourdrinier, total capacity 7,854 mt/y, Trim width 1.76 m, Uncoated woodfree/freesheet
No. 12, fourdrinier, total capacity 7,854 mt/y, Trim width 1.76 m, Uncoated woodfree/freesheet
No. 13, fourdrinier, total capacity 7,854 mt/y, Trim width 1.76 m, Uncoated woodfree/freesheet
No. 14, fourdrinier, total capacity 7,500 mt/y, Trim width 1.76 m, Uncoated mechanical/groundwood
No. 15, fourdrinier, total capacity 13,750 mt/y, Trim width 1.76 m, Uncoated mechanical/groundwood
No. 16, fourdrinier, total capacity 13,750 mt/y, Trim width 1.76 m, Uncoated mechanical/groundwood
No. 17, fourdrinier, total capacity 11,500 mt/y, Trim width 2.64 m, Uncoated mechanical/groundwood
No. 18, fourdrinier, total capacity 11,500 mt/y, Trim width 2.64 m, Uncoated mechanical/groundwood
No. 19, fourdrinier, total capacity 11,500 mt/y, Trim width 2.64 m, Uncoated mechanical/groundwood
No. 20, fourdrinier, total capacity 11,500 mt/y, Trim width 2.64 m, Uncoated mechanical/groundwood
No. 21, fourdrinier, total capacity 11,500 mt/y, Trim width 2.64 m, Uncoated mechanical/groundwood
No. 22, fourdrinier, total capacity 11,500 mt/y, Trim width 2.64 m, Uncoated mechanical/groundwood
No. 23, fourdrinier, total capacity 11,500 mt/y, Trim width 2.64 m, Uncoated mechanical/groundwood
No. 24, fourdrinier, total capacity 11,500 mt/y, Trim width 2.64 m, Uncoated mechanical/groundwood
No. 25, fourdrinier, total capacity 11,500 mt/y, Trim width 2.64 m, Uncoated mechanical/groundwood
No. 26, fourdrinier, total capacity 11,500 mt/y, Trim width 2.64 m, Uncoated mechanical/groundwood
BM 1, Fourdrinier (4), total capacity 300,000 mt/y, Trim width 5.65 m, Boxboard/cartonboard
BM 2, Fourdrinier (3), total capacity 400,000 mt/y, Trim width 5.3 m, Boxboard/cartonboard
PM 3800, hybrid former, total capacity 150,000 mt/y, Trim width 3.8 m, Boxboard/cartonboard
PM 4400, hybrid former, total capacity 150,000 mt/y, Trim width 4.4 m, Linerboard
Coating Machines: 2
BM 1, total capacity 300,000 mt/y, on machine
BM 2, total capacity 400,000 mt/y, on machine
Energy Data:
Power boilers: 15
TMP Reboiler: 1
Steam turbines: 3 at 300 MW

ⓜShandong Bowen Paper Co., Ltd
Fangjia village, Jining
Qufu, Shandong
China
Phone: (86) 537-2222142
Fax: (86) 537-2222142
Email: sales@bowenpaper.com
Web Address: www.bowenpaper.com
Mill Locations:
Shandong Bowen Paper Co., Ltd, Qufu Mill, Fangjia village, Jining, Qufu, China, Capacity: 2,000 mt/y, (Paper mill)
Phone: (86) 537-2222142
Fax: (86) 537-2222142
Email: sales@bowenpaper.com

ⓜShandong Bowen Paper Co., Ltd
Qufu Mill
Fangjia village, Jining
Qufu, Shandong
China
Phone: (86) 537-2222142
Fax: (86) 537-2222142
Email: sales@bowenpaper.com
Web Address: www.bowenpaper.com
Type of Operation: Paper mill
Paper/Paperboard Grades and Capacities:
Total paper and paperboard capacity: 2,000 mt/y
Uncoated woodfree/freesheet: 2,000 mt/y
Paper and Paperboard Mill Data:
Paper Machines: 1
No. 1, total capacity 2,000 mt/y, Trim width 1.68 m, Uncoated woodfree/freesheet

ⓜⓜShandong Chenlong Paper Co., Ltd.
Zibo Mill
Ownership: 100% by shareholders
Tianzhuang Town, Huantai County
Zibo, Shandong, 256402
China
Phone: (86) 533 858 0035
Fax: (86) 533 858 0108
Web Address: www.sdcljt.com
Personnel:
Chmn. & Pres.: Shuzhi Huang
Phone: (86) 533 858 0035
Total Employees at this Location: 2,000
Type of Operation: Paper mill, Paperboard mill
Pulp Grades and Capacities:
Total pulp capacity: 192,132 mt/y
Recycled Pulping: 192,132 mt/y
Pulp Mill Data:
Recycled Fiber Treatment Lines:
Recycled packaging pulping lines
Paper/Paperboard Grades and Capacities:
Total paper and paperboard capacity: 210,000 mt/y
Newsprint: 210,000 mt/y
Paper and Paperboard Mill Data:
Paper Machines: 3
No. 1, fourdrinier, total capacity 100,000 mt/y, Trim width 4.2 m, Newsprint
No. 2, fourdrinier, total capacity 100,000 mt/y, Trim width 4.2 m, Newsprint
No. 3, fourdrinier, total capacity 10,000 mt/y, Trim width 2.4 m, Newsprint
Energy Data:
Electrical demand for mill: 582 MWh/D

ⓜChenming Paper Holdings Ltd.
Ownership: Public
No. 595 Shengcheng Rd., Chenming Industrial Park

China

Shouguang City, Shandong, 262700
China
  Phone: (86) 536 215 8000
  Fax: (86) 536 215 6111
  Email: gsb@chenming.com.cn
  Web Address: www.chenmingpaper.com
Personnel:
  Chmn.: Hongguo Chen
  Phone: (86) 536 215 8000
  Fax: (86) 536 215 6111
  Email: chenhongguo@chenming.com.cn
  Vice Chmn.: Tongyuan Yin
  Phone: (86) 536 215 8000
  Fax: (86) 536 215 6111
  Email: tintongyuan@chenming.com.cn
  Exec. Dir., Dpty. Gen. Mgr.: Feng Li
  Phone: (86) 536 215 8000
  Fax: (86) 536 215 6111
  Email: lifeng@chenming.com.cn
  Exec. Dir. & Dpty. Gen. Mgr. & Prod. Contrl.: Guanglin Geng
  Phone: (86) 536 215 8000
  Fax: (86) 536 215 6111
  Email: gengguanglin@chenming.com.cn
  Exec. Dir., Dpty. Gen. Mgr.: Shaohua Zhou
  Phone: (86) 536 215 8000
  Fax: (86) 536 215 6111
  Email: zhoushaohua@chenming.com.cn
  Dpty. Gen. Mgr., Sec. of the Board (Since 2014): Chunfang Wang
  Phone: (86) 536 215 8000
  Fax: (86) 536 215 6111
  Email: wangchunfang@chenming.com.cn
  Dir. & Dpty. Gen. Mgr.: Ms. Xueqin Li
  Phone: (86) 536 215 8000
  Fax: (86) 536 215 6111
  Email: lixueqin@chenming.com.cn
  Depy. Gen. Mgr. Zhanjiang Chenming Paper Pulp project: Changqing Hu
  Phone: (86) 536 215 8000
  Fax: (86) 536 215 6111
  Email: huchangqing@chenming.com.cn
Total Employees of Company: 12,954
Mill Locations:
  Heilongjiang Fuyu Chenming Paper Co., Ltd., Qiqihar (Heilongjiang Fuyu Chenming Paper) Mill, Fuyu County, Qiqihar 161021, China, Capacity: 69,972 mt/y, (Paper mill)
  Phone: (86) 452 3102 256/ 401/ 267
  Email: www.chenmingpaper.com
  Hubei Wuhan Chenming Paper Co. Ltd., Wuhan (Wuhan Chenming Hanyang Paper No. 2 Mill) Mill (50.93% owned), Wuhan Economic & Technology Development Zone, Wuhan 430057, China, Capacity: 220,000 mt/y, (Pulp mill, Paper mill)
  Phone: (86) 27 84897382/ 4969
  Fax: (86) 27 8489 4713
  Email: whcom@whcmhy.com.cn
  Jiangxi Chenming Paper Co., Ltd., Nanchang (Jiangxi Chenming Paper) Mill, Changbei Economy and Technology District, Baishuihu Industry Park, Nanchang 330013, China, Capacity: 350,000 mt/y, (Pulp mill, Paper mill)
  Phone: (86) 791 3951 968/982
  Fax: (86) 791 388 7599
  Jilin Chenming Paper Co. Ltd., Jilin (Jilin Chenming Paper) Mill (70% owned), Jinzhu Industrial Park, Longtan District, Jilin, China, Capacity: 250,000 mt/y, (Paper mill)
  Chenming Paper Holdings Ltd., Shouguang (Shouguang Chenming Specialty Paper No. 1) Mill, No. 595 Shengcheng Rd., Chenming Industrial Park, Shouguang 262700, China, Capacity: 143,800 mt/y, (Paper mill)
  Phone: (86) 536 215 6676/ 8000/ 8454/ 8073/ 6480
  Fax: (86) 536 215 6676/ 8225/ 8494/ 6482/ 8010
  Chenming Paper Holdings Ltd., Shouguang (Shouguang Chenming Lightweight Coated Paper No. 2) Mill, No. 595 Shengcheng Rd., Chenming Industrial Park, Shouguang 262700, China, Capacity: 170,000 mt/y, (Paper mill)
  Phone: (86) 536 215 6676/ 8000/ 8454/ 8073/ 6480
  Fax: (86) 536 215 6676/ 6111/ 8494/ 8010/ 6482
  Chenming Paper Holdings Ltd., Shouguang (Shouguang Chenming Coated Woodfree Paper No. 3) Mill, No. 595 Shengcheng Rd., Chenming Industrial Park, Shouguang 262700, China, Capacity: 380,000 mt/y, (Paper mill)
  Phone: (86) 536 215 8977/ 8000/ 6480
  Fax: (86) 536 215 8640/ 6111/ 6482
  Email: gsb@chenming.com.cn, ckkcm@chenming.com.cn
  Chenming Paper Holdings Ltd., Shouguang (Shouguang Chenming No. 4) Mill, No. 595, Shengcheng Rd., Chenming Industry Park, Shouguang 262700, China, Capacity: 460,000 mt/y, (Paper mill, Paperboard mill)
  Phone: (86) 536 215 6426/6901
  Fax: (86) 536 215 6426/6902
  Chenming Paper Holdings Ltd., Shouguang (Shouguang Chenming Newsprint No. 5) Mill, No. 595 Shengcheng Rd., Chenming Industrial Park, Shouguang 262700, China, Capacity: 450,000 mt/y, (Pulp mill, Paper mill)
  Phone: (86) 536 215 8000/6480/8073
  Fax: (86) 536 215 6111/8010/ 6482
  Chenming Paper Holdings Ltd., Shouguang (Shouguang Chenming Art Paper No. 6) Mill, No. 595 Shengcheng Rd., Chenming Industrial Park, Shouguang 262700, China, Capacity: 140,000 mt/y, (Paper mill)
  Phone: (86) 536 215 8073/ 215 6480
  Email: jeson@chenming.com.cn
  Shandong Shouguang Liben Papermaking, Shouguang (Shandong Shouguang Liben Papermaking) Mill, No. 595 Shengcheng Rd., Shouguang 262700, China, Capacity: 13,000 mt/y, (Paper mill)
  Phone: (86) 536 522 2151/528 0033
  Fax: (86) 536 522 1843/523 4234
  Email: staff2@public.wfptt.sd.cn
  Shouguang Meilun Paper, Shouguang (Shouguang Meilun Paper) Mill (70% owned), Xihuan Rd., Shouguang 262700, China, Capacity: 1,660,000 mt/y, (Pulp mill, Paper mill, Paperboard mill)
  Phone: (86) 536 215 6735/6744/6814
  Zhanjiang Chenming Paper Pulp Co., Ltd., Zhanjiang (Zhanjiang Chenming Pulp & Paper) Mill, Zhanjiang, China, Capacity: 649,820 mt/y, (Pulp mill, Paper mill)
  Phone: (86) 759 8216 086/087

ⓂChenming Paper Holdings Ltd. Shouguang (Shouguang Chenming Specialty Paper No. 1) Mill

No. 595 Shengcheng Rd., Chenming Industrial Park
Shouguang, Shandong, 262700
China
  Phone: (86) 536 215 6676/ 8000/ 8454/ 8073/ 6480
  Fax: (86) 536 215 6676/ 8225/ 8494/ 6482/ 8010
  Web Address: www.chenmingpaper.com
Personnel:
  Chmn.: Hongguo Chen
  Phone: (86) 536 215 6676/ 8000/ 8454/ 8073/ 6480
Total Employees at this Location: 768
Type of Operation: Paper mill
Pulp Grades and Capacities:
  Total pulp capacity: 54,082 mt/y
  Chemical Pulp: 54,082 mt/y
Pulp Mill Data:
  Chemical Pulping Systems:
  Continuous digesters
  Bleach Plant Systems: 1
  Chemical Pulping System, Type: Hardwood
  Chemical Recovery Equipment:
  Evaporator lines
  Recovery boilers: 2
Paper/Paperboard Grades and Capacities:
  Total paper and paperboard capacity: 143,800 mt/y
  Uncoated woodfree/freesheet: 143,800 mt/y
Paper and Paperboard Mill Data:
Paper Machines: 7
  No. 1, fourdrinier, total capacity 26,000 mt/y, Trim width 2.4 m, Uncoated woodfree/freesheet
  No. 2, fourdrinier, total capacity 4,500 mt/y, Trim width 1.76 m, Uncoated woodfree/freesheet
  No. 4, fourdrinier, total capacity 26,000 mt/y, Trim width 2.4 m, Uncoated woodfree/freesheet
  No. 5, fourdrinier, total capacity 5,800 mt/y, Trim width 1.76 m, Uncoated woodfree/freesheet
  No. 6, fourdrinier, total capacity 16,500 mt/y, Trim width 1.76 m, Uncoated woodfree/freesheet
  No. 8, fourdrinier, total capacity 20,000 mt/y, Trim width 1.76 m, Uncoated woodfree/freesheet
  No. 10, fourdrinier, total capacity 45,000 mt/y, Trim width 2.64 m, Uncoated woodfree/freesheet
Finishing Equipment:
  Supercalenders: 2
  Sheeters: 1
Energy Data:
  Power boilers
  Steam turbines: 4 at 43 MW
  Electrical demand for mill: 344 MWh/D

ⓂChenming Paper Holdings Ltd. Shouguang (Shouguang Chenming Lightweight Coated Paper No. 2) Mill

No. 595 Shengcheng Rd., Chenming Industrial Park
Shouguang, Shandong, 262700
China
  Phone: (86) 536 215 6676/ 8000/ 8454/ 8073/ 6480
  Fax: (86) 536 215 6676/ 6111/ 8494/ 8010/ 6482
  Web Address: www.chenmingpaper.com
Personnel:
  Chmn.: Hongguo Chen
  Phone: (86) 536 215 6676/ 8000/ 8454/ 8073/ 6480
Total Employees at this Location: 200
Type of Operation: Paper mill
Paper/Paperboard Grades and Capacities:
  Total paper and paperboard capacity: 170,000 mt/y
  Uncoated woodfree/freesheet: 34,000 mt/y
  Coated mechanical/groundwood: 136,000 mt/y
Paper and Paperboard Mill Data:
Paper Machines: 1
  No. 2, SymFormer MB, total capacity 170,000 mt/y, Trim width 4.62 m, Coated mechanical/groundwood, Uncoated woodfree/freesheet
Coating Machines: 1
  CM 2, total capacity 170,000 mt/y., on machine
Finishing Equipment:
  Winders: 1
Energy Data:
  Power boilers
  Steam turbines: 6 at 124 MW
  Electrical demand for mill: 319 MWh/D

ⓂChenming Paper Holdings Ltd. Shouguang (Shouguang Chenming Coated Woodfree Paper No. 3) Mill

No. 595 Shengcheng Rd., Chenming Industrial Park
Shouguang, Shandong, 262700
China
  Phone: (86) 536 215 8977/ 8000/ 6480
  Fax: (86) 536 215 8640/ 6111/ 6482
  Email: gsb@chenming.com.cn, ckkcm@chenming.com.cn
  Web Address: www.chenmingpaper.com
Personnel:
  Chmn.: Hongguo Chen
  Phone: (86) 536 215 8977/ 8000/ 6480
Total Employees at this Location: 300
Type of Operation: Paper mill
Paper/Paperboard Grades and Capacities:
  Total paper and paperboard capacity: 380,000 mt/y
  Coated woodfree/freesheet: 380,000 mt/y
Paper and Paperboard Mill Data:
Paper Machines: 1
  No. 3, SymFormer MB, total capacity 380,000 mt/y, Trim width 4.68 m, Coated woodfree/freesheet
Coating Machines: 1
  CM 3, total capacity 380,000 mt/y., off machine
Finishing Equipment:
  Winders: 2
  Supercalenders: 1
Energy Data:
  Power boilers
  Steam turbines: 6 at 124 MW
  Electrical demand for mill: 728 MWh/D

China

ⓜChenming Paper Holdings Ltd.
Shouguang (Shouguang Chenming No. 4) Mill
No. 595, Shengcheng Rd., Chenming Industry Park
Shouguang, Shandong, 262700
China
Phone: (86) 536 215 6426/6901
Fax: (86) 536 215 6426/6902
Web Address: www.chenmingpaper.com
Personnel:
Chmn.: Hongguo Chen
Phone: (86) 536 215 6426/6901
Total Employees at this Location: 525
Type of Operation: Paper mill, Paperboard mill
Pulp Grades and Capacities:
Total pulp capacity: 189,831 mt/y
Mechanical Pulp: 189,831 mt/y
Pulp Mill Data:
Mechanical Pulping Systems:
BCTMP systems: 1
Pulp Lines: 1
Bleach Plant Systems: 1
Mechanical Pulping System, Type: Hardwood
Paper/Paperboard Grades and Capacities:
Total paper and paperboard capacity: 460,000 mt/y
Boxboard/cartonboard: 460,000 mt/y
Paper and Paperboard Mill Data:
Stock Preparation:
Pulpers: 4
Paper Machines: 1
No. 3, fourdrinier (3), total capacity 460,000 mt/y, Trim width 5.65 m, Boxboard/cartonboard
Coating Machines: 1
PM#3, on machine
Energy Data:
Power boilers
TMP Reboiler: 1
Steam turbines at 155 MW
Electrical demand for mill: 1,770 MWh/D

ⓜChenming Paper Holdings Ltd.
Shouguang (Shouguang Chenming Newsprint No. 5) Mill
No. 595 Shengcheng Rd., Chenming Industrial Park
Shouguang, Shandong, 262700
China
Phone: (86) 536 215 8000/6480/8073
Fax: (86) 536 215 6111/8010/ 6482
Web Address: www.chenmingpaper.com
Personnel:
Chmn.: Hongguo Chen
Phone: (86) 536 215 8000/6480/8073
Vice Chmn.: Tongyuan Yin
Phone: (86) 536 215 8000/6480/8073
Total Employees at this Location: 286
Type of Operation: Pulp mill, Paper mill
Pulp Grades and Capacities:
Total pulp capacity: 425,433 mt/y
Recycled Pulping: 425,433 mt/y
Pulp Mill Data:
Pulp Lines: 1
Bleach Plant Systems: 1
Recycled Pulping System, Type: Deinked
Recycled Fiber Treatment Lines:
Washing deinking lines: 1 at 512,000 admt/y
Paper/Paperboard Grades and Capacities:
Total paper and paperboard capacity: 450,000 mt/y
Newsprint: 450,000 mt/y
Paper and Paperboard Mill Data:
Paper Machines: 1
No. 4, OptiConcept, total capacity 450,000 mt/y, Trim width 10.55 m, Newsprint
Energy Data:
Power boilers: 2
Steam turbines: 1 at 155 MW
Electrical demand for mill: 1,157 MWh/D

ⓜChenming Paper Holdings Ltd.
Shouguang (Shouguang Chenming Art Paper No. 6) Mill
No. 595 Shengcheng Rd., Chenming Industrial Park
Shouguang, Shandong, 262700
China
Phone: (86) 536 215 8073/ 215 6480
Email: jeson@chenming.com.cn
Web Address: www.chenmingpaper.com
Personnel:
Chmn.: Hongguo Chen
Phone: (86) 536 215 8073/ 215 6480
Vice Chmn.: Tongyuan Yin
Phone: (86) 536 215 8073/ 215 6480
CFO: Chunfang Wang
Phone: (86) 536 215 8073/ 215 6480
Total Employees at this Location: 220
Type of Operation: Paper mill
Paper/Paperboard Grades and Capacities:
Total paper and paperboard capacity: 140,000 mt/y
Uncoated woodfree/freesheet: 120,000 mt/y
Specialty and industrial: 20,000 mt/y
Paper and Paperboard Mill Data:
Paper Machines: 1
No. 5, top former, total capacity 140,000 mt/y, Trim width 4.1 m, Specialty and industrial, Uncoated woodfree/freesheet
Coating Machines: 1
PM 5, total capacity 159,000 mt/y., off machine
Energy Data:
Power boilers
Steam turbines at 155 MW
Electrical demand for mill: 269 MWh/D

ⓜShandong Jianghe Paper Co., Ltd.
Qihe Mill
Ownership: 100% by Henan Jianghe Paper Co., Ltd.
No.1 Chenming Road, Qihe County
Dezhou, Shandong, 251100
China
Phone: (86) 534 5028 600/5028 501
Email: 5qhcmbz@dz-public.sd.cninfo.net, qhbzc@163.net
Web Address: www.jianghe.com/main.aspx
Total Employees at this Location: 2,600
Type of Operation: Pulp mill, Paper mill, Paperboard mill
Pulp Grades and Capacities:
Total pulp capacity: 372,696 mt/y
Pulp available for market: 54,444 mt/y
Chemical Pulp: 100,000 mt/y
Mechanical Pulp: 61,242 mt/y
Recycled Pulping: 211,454 mt/y
Pulp Mill Data:
Chemical Pulping Systems:
Not Given: 2
Mechanical Pulping Systems:
BCTMP systems: 1
Pulp Lines: 3
Bleach Plant Lines:
No. 1
Chemical Recovery Equipment:
Recovery boilers: 1
Paper/Paperboard Grades and Capacities:
Total paper and paperboard capacity: 349,800 mt/y
Uncoated woodfree/freesheet: 36,200 mt/y
Linerboard: 200,000 mt/y
Corrugating medium/fluting: 13,600 mt/y
Boxboard/cartonboard: 100,000 mt/y
Paper and Paperboard Mill Data:
Stock Preparation:
Pulpers: 30
Paper Machines: 4
No. 2, Fourdrinier (4), total capacity 100,000 mt/y, Trim width 3.2 m, Boxboard/cartonboard
No. 3, fourdrinier, total capacity 36,200 mt/y, Trim width 2.85 m, Uncoated woodfree/freesheet
No. 4, fourdrinier, total capacity 13,600 mt/y, Trim width 1.76 m, Corrugating medium/fluting
No. 5, Fourdrinier (4), total capacity 200,000 mt/y, Trim width 4.4 m, Linerboard
Coating Machines: 1
No. 5, total capacity 300,000 mt/y.
Finishing Equipment:
Rewinders: 4
Energy Data:
Power boilers: 6
Steam turbines: 4 at 1.8 MW
Electrical demand for mill: 939 MWh/D

ⓜShandong Dadi Paper Co., Ltd.
Taian Mill
North Mengguan Rd., Ningyang County
Taian, Shandong, 271400
China
Phone: (86) 538 568 1288/0788/6188
Fax: (86) 538 568 0618
Email: sdddzy@163.com
Personnel:
Gen. Mgr.: Guoxin Zou
Phone: (86) 538 568 1288
Total Employees at this Location: 500
Type of Operation: Paperboard mill
Paper/Paperboard Grades and Capacities:
Total paper and paperboard capacity: 60,000 mt/y
Boxboard/cartonboard: 60,000 mt/y
Paper and Paperboard Mill Data:
Paper Machines: 1
No. 1, fourdrinier (3), total capacity 60,000 mt/y, Trim width 2.7 m, Boxboard/cartonboard
Energy Data:
Electrical demand for mill: 87 MWh/D

ⓜShandong Deguang Gongmao Co., Ltd.
Jieshan Industrial Park, Dongping County
Taian , Shandong, 271500
China
Phone: (86) 538 2315 788
Fax: (86) 538 2315 766
Web Address: www.sddggm.cn
Mill Locations:
Shandong Deguang Gongmao Co., Ltd., Taian Mill, Jieshan Industrial Park, Dongping County, Taian 271500, China, Capacity: 10,000 mt/y, (Paper mill)
Phone: (86) 538 2315 788
Fax: (86) 538 2315 766

ⓜShandong Deguang Gongmao Co., Ltd.
Taian Mill
Jieshan Industrial Park, Dongping County
Taian , Shandong, 271500
China
Phone: (86) 538 2315 788
Fax: (86) 538 2315 766
Web Address: www.sddggm.cn
Type of Operation: Paper mill
Paper/Paperboard Grades and Capacities:
Total paper and paperboard capacity: 10,000 mt/y
Tissue: 10,000 mt/y
Paper and Paperboard Mill Data:
Paper Machines: 4
PM 1-4, total capacity 2,500 mt/y, Trim width 1.58 m, Tissue

ⓜShandong Derong Paper Co., Ltd.
Zaozhuang Mill
Xinxing Rd., Zhangfan Town, Xuecheng District
Zaozhuang, Shandong, 277021
China
Phone: (86) 632 462 2577
Fax: (86) 632 461 9333
Web Address: www.derongpaper.com/index.asp
Personnel:

China

Gen. Mgr.: Mr. Yuan
Phone: (86) 632 462 2577
Total Employees at this Location: 230
Type of Operation: Paperboard mill
Pulp Grades and Capacities:
 Total pulp capacity: 51,680 mt/y
 Recycled Pulping: 51,680 mt/y
Pulp Mill Data:
 Recycled Fiber Treatment Lines:
 Recycled packaging pulping lines: 1 at 50,000 admt/y
Paper/Paperboard Grades and Capacities:
 Total paper and paperboard capacity: 50,694 mt/y
 Linerboard: 50,694 mt/y
Paper and Paperboard Mill Data:
Paper Machines: 1
No. 1, fourdrinier (3), total capacity 50,694 mt/y, Trim width 3.8 m, Linerboard
Energy Data:
Power boilers: 1
Electrical demand for mill: 92 MWh/D

ⓘ Shandong Dezhou Huabei Paper (Group) Co., Ltd.
Ownership: 100% by private owners
Ertun Town, Decheng District
Dezhou, Shandong, 253035
China
 Phone: (86) 534 274 3519/ 3068/ 3688
 Fax: (86) 534 274 2729/ 3688
 Email: hbzy@dzhbzy.com
 Web Address: www.dzhbzy.com
Personnel:
 Pres. & Gen. Mgr.: Xinghua Xie
Mill Locations:
Shandong Dezhou Huabei Paper (Group) Co., Ltd., Dezhou Mill, Ertun Town, Decheng District, Dezhou 253035, China, Capacity: 124,000 mt/y, (Paper mill)
 Phone: (86) 534 218 9079/7399/3299/2388/8791/8796
 Fax: (86) 534 218 9079/2388/7566
 Email: dzhbzy@163.com

ⓜ Shandong Dezhou Huabei Paper (Group) Co., Ltd.
Dezhou Mill
Ertun Town, Decheng District
Dezhou, Shandong, 253035
China
 Phone: (86) 534 218 9079/7399/3299/2388/8791/8796
 Fax: (86) 534 218 9079/2388/7566
 Email: dzhbzy@163.com
 Web Address: www.dzhbzy.net
Personnel:
 Pres. & Gen. Mgr.: Xinghua Xie
 Phone: (86) 534 274 3519/ 3068/ 3688
Total Employees at this Location: 730
Type of Operation: Paper mill
Pulp Mill Data:
 Chemical Pulping Systems:
 Batch digesters: 1
Pulp Lines: 1
 Bleach Plant Systems: 1
 Chemical Pulping System, Type: Straw
 Chemical Recovery Equipment:
 Evaporator lines
 Recovery boilers: 1
 Lime Kiln
Paper/Paperboard Grades and Capacities:
 Total paper and paperboard capacity: 124,000 mt/y
 Uncoated woodfree/freesheet: 29,000 mt/y
 Uncoated mechanical/groundwood: 45,000 mt/y
 Specialty and industrial: 50,000 mt/y
Paper and Paperboard Mill Data:
Paper Machines: 9
No. 1, fourdrinier, total capacity 7,500 mt/y, Trim width 1.76 m, Specialty and industrial
No. 2, fourdrinier, total capacity 15,000 mt/y, Trim width 1.76 m, Specialty and industrial
No. 3, fourdrinier, total capacity 7,250 mt/y, Trim width 1.76 m, Uncoated mechanical/groundwood
No. 4, fourdrinier, total capacity 7,250 mt/y, Trim width 1.76 m, Uncoated mechanical/groundwood
No. 5, fourdrinier, total capacity 9,500 mt/y, Trim width 1.88 m, Uncoated mechanical/groundwood
No. 6, fourdrinier, total capacity 9,500 mt/y, Trim width 1.88 m, Uncoated mechanical/groundwood
No. 7, fourdrinier, total capacity 11,500 mt/y, Trim width 1.88 m, Uncoated mechanical/groundwood
No. 8, fourdrinier, total capacity 29,000 mt/y, Trim width 2.73 m, Uncoated woodfree/freesheet
No. 9, (Supplier: Liaocheng Huasen
), fourdrinier, total capacity 27,500 mt/y, Trim width 2.88 m, Specialty and industrial
Energy Data:
Power boilers: 2
Steam turbines: 2 at 1.5, 6 MW
Electrical demand for mill: 480 MWh/D

ⓘⓜ Shandong Dezhou Huadong Paper Group
Dezhou Mill
Zhaodongfang Industry Zone, Wangfenglou Town, Pingyuan
Dezhou, Shandong, 253109
China
 Phone: (86) 534 2168 068/4752 006
 Fax: (86) 534 4752 369
Personnel:
 Chmn. & Gen. Mgr.: Dongyu Wang
 Phone: (86) 534 4752 006
 Sls. Mgr.: Baoyou Wang
 Phone: (86) 534 4752 006
Total Employees at this Location: 2,000
Type of Operation: Paper mill
Paper/Paperboard Grades and Capacities:
 Total paper and paperboard capacity: 100,000 mt/y
 Uncoated woodfree/freesheet: 100,000 mt/y
 Uncoated mechanical/groundwood
Paper and Paperboard Mill Data:
Paper Machines: 16
No. 1, fourdrinier, total capacity 4,000 mt/y, Trim width 1.76 m, Uncoated woodfree/freesheet
No. 2, fourdrinier, total capacity 4,000 mt/y, Trim width 1.76 m, Uncoated woodfree/freesheet
No. 3, fourdrinier, total capacity 6,700 mt/y, Trim width 1.88 m, Uncoated woodfree/freesheet
No. 4, fourdrinier, total capacity 6,700 mt/y, Trim width 1.88 m, Uncoated woodfree/freesheet
No. 4, fourdrinier, total capacity 6,700 mt/y, Trim width 1.88 m, Uncoated woodfree/freesheet
No. 5, fourdrinier, total capacity 6,700 mt/y, Trim width 1.88 m, Uncoated woodfree/freesheet
No. 6, fourdrinier, total capacity 6,700 mt/y, Trim width 1.88 m, Uncoated woodfree/freesheet
No. 7, fourdrinier, total capacity 6,700 mt/y, Trim width 1.88 m, Uncoated woodfree/freesheet
No. 8, fourdrinier, total capacity 6,700 mt/y, Trim width 1.88 m, Uncoated woodfree/freesheet
No. 9, fourdrinier, total capacity 6,700 mt/y, Trim width 1.88 m, Uncoated woodfree/freesheet
No. 10, fourdrinier, total capacity 6,700 mt/y, Trim width 1.88 m, Uncoated woodfree/freesheet
No. 11, fourdrinier, total capacity 6,700 mt/y, Trim width 1.88 m, Uncoated woodfree/freesheet
No. 12, fourdrinier, total capacity 8,000 mt/y, Trim width 2.73 m, Uncoated woodfree/freesheet
No. 13, fourdrinier, total capacity 8,000 mt/y, Trim width 2.73 m, Uncoated woodfree/freesheet
No. 14, fourdrinier, total capacity 8,000 mt/y, Trim width 2.73 m, Uncoated woodfree/freesheet
No. 15, fourdrinier, total capacity 8,000 mt/y, Trim width 2.73 m, Uncoated woodfree/freesheet
Energy Data:
Power boilers: 1
Steam turbines: 2 at 3, 10 MW

ⓘⓜ Shandong Dongming County Yongyue Paper Co., Ltd.
Heze Mill
170 Wu Si Shandong., Dongming County
Heze, Shandong, 274500
China
 Phone: (86) 133 9540 5208, 158 0679 5998
 Fax: (86) 530 625 3708
 Web Address: www.dmyyzy.com
Personnel:
 Chmn.: Yong Zhang
 Phone: (86) 133 9540 5208, 158 0679 5998
 Fax: (86) 530 625 3708
Total Employees at this Location: 150
Type of Operation: Paperboard mill
Pulp Grades and Capacities:
 Total pulp capacity: 69,443 mt/y
 Recycled Pulping: 69,443 mt/y
Pulp Mill Data:
 Recycled Fiber Treatment Lines:
 Recycled packaging pulping lines: 3 at 40,000 admt/y
Paper/Paperboard Grades and Capacities:
 Total paper and paperboard capacity: 70,000 mt/y
 Corrugating medium/fluting: 70,000 mt/y
Paper and Paperboard Mill Data:
Paper Machines: 1
No. 1, fourdrinier, total capacity 70,000 mt/y, Trim width 4.2 m, Corrugating medium/fluting
Energy Data:
Electrical demand for mill: 84 MWh/D

ⓘⓜ Shandong Dongshun Paper Group
Taian Mill
Dongshun Industrial Park, Dongping County
Taian, Shandong, 271500
China
 Phone: (86) 538 282 0378/5077/1614
 Fax: (86) 538 2820378
 Web Address: www.dongshunpaper.com
Personnel:
 Pres.: Shuming Chen
 Phone: (86) 538 282 1614/ 0378
Total Employees at this Location: 520
Type of Operation: Paper mill
Paper/Paperboard Grades and Capacities:
 Total paper and paperboard capacity: 187,000 mt/y
 Tissue: 187,000 mt/y
Paper and Paperboard Mill Data:
Paper Machines: 14
No. 1, BF-10, Yankee dryer, total capacity 10,000 mt/y, Trim width 2.66 m, Tissue, Uncoated woodfree/freesheet
No. 2, BF-10, Yankee dryer, total capacity 11,000 mt/y, Trim width 2.66 m, Tissue, Uncoated woodfree/freesheet
No. 3, BF-10 EX, Yankee dryer, total capacity 12,000 mt/y, Trim width 2.76 m, Tissue, Uncoated woodfree/freesheet
No. 4, BF-10 EX, Yankee dryer, total capacity 12,000 mt/y, Trim width 2.76 m, Tissue, Uncoated woodfree/freesheet
No. 5, BF-10 EX, Yankee dryer, total capacity 12,000 mt/y, Trim width 2.76 m, Tissue, Uncoated woodfree/freesheet
No. 6, BF-10 EX, Yankee dryer, total capacity 12,000 mt/y, Trim width 2.76 m, Tissue, Uncoated woodfree/freesheet
No. 7, BF-10 EX, Yankee dryer, total capacity 12,000 mt/y, Trim width 2.76 m, Tissue, Uncoated woodfree/freesheet
No. 8, BF-10 EX, Yankee dryer, total capacity 12,000 mt/y, Trim width 2.76 m, Tissue, Uncoated woodfree/freesheet
No. 9, total capacity 14,994 mt/y, Trim width 2.76 m, Tissue, Uncoated woodfree/freesheet
No. 10, total capacity 14,994 mt/y, Trim width 2.76 m, Tissue, Uncoated woodfree/freesheet
No. 11, total capacity 15,994 mt/y, Trim width 2.76 m, Tissue, Uncoated woodfree/freesheet

No. 12, total capacity 15,994 mt/y, Trim width 2.76 m, Tissue, Uncoated woodfree/freesheet
No. 13, total capacity 15,994 mt/y, Trim width 2.76 m, Tissue, Uncoated woodfree/freesheet
No. 14, total capacity 15,994 mt/y, Trim width 2.76 m, Tissue, Uncoated woodfree/freesheet
Energy Data:
Power boilers: 3
Electrical demand for mill: 198 MWh/D

ⓂShandong Dongyue Energy Co., Ltd.
Feicheng Mill
Yangzhuang Coal Mine, Laochen Town
Feicheng, Shandong, 271601
China
Phone: (86) 538 315 2145/ 314 3867
Fax: (86) 538 314 3999
Email: ykozy_xs@163.com
Personnel:
Gen. Mgr.: Qin Kong
Phone: (86) 538 315 2145/ 314 3867
Sls. Mgr.: Changsheng Liu
Phone: (86) 538 315 2145/ 314 3867
Total Employees at this Location: 400
Type of Operation: Paper mill
Pulp Grades and Capacities:
Total pulp capacity: 50,000 mt/y
Recycled Pulping: 50,000 mt/y
Pulp Mill Data:
Pulp Lines: 1
Paper/Paperboard Grades and Capacities:
Total paper and paperboard capacity: 20,000 mt/y
Tissue: 20,000 mt/y
Paper and Paperboard Mill Data:
Paper Machines: 8
No. 1, cylinder, total capacity 2,500 mt/y, Trim width 1.58 m, Tissue
No. 2, cylinder, total capacity 2,500 mt/y, Trim width 1.58 m, Tissue
No. 3, cylinder, total capacity 2,500 mt/y, Trim width 1.58 m, Tissue
No. 4, cylinder, total capacity 2,500 mt/y, Trim width 1.58 m, Tissue
No. 5, cylinder, total capacity 2,500 mt/y, Trim width 1.58 m, Tissue
No. 6, cylinder, total capacity 2,500 mt/y, Trim width 1.58 m, Tissue
No. 7, cylinder, total capacity 2,500 mt/y, Trim width 1.58 m, Tissue
No. 8, cylinder, total capacity 2,500 mt/y, Trim width 1.58 m, Tissue

ⓂShandong Feicheng Dongsheng Paper Co., Ltd.
Feicheng Mill
Shiheng Town
Feicheng, Shandong, 271600
China
Phone: (86) 538 366 0746
Fax: (86) 538 366 1347
Web Address: www.fcdszy.cn
Personnel:
Gen. Mgr.: Junheng Li
Phone: (86) 538 366 0746
Sls. Mgr.: Guang Wang
Phone: (86) 538 366 0746
Total Employees at this Location: 800
Type of Operation: Paper mill
Paper/Paperboard Grades and Capacities:
Total paper and paperboard capacity: 44,982 mt/y
Uncoated woodfree/freesheet: 44,982 mt/y
Paper and Paperboard Mill Data:
Paper Machines: 3
No. 1, fourdrinier, total capacity 8,568 mt/y, Trim width 1.76 m, Uncoated woodfree/freesheet
No. 2, fourdrinier, total capacity 18,207 mt/y, Trim width 1.76 m, Uncoated woodfree/freesheet
No. 3, fourdrinier, total capacity 18,207 mt/y, Trim width 1.76 m, Uncoated woodfree/freesheet

Finishing Equipment:
Rewinders: 8
Energy Data:
Power boilers: 4
Steam turbines: 1 at 9.4 MW
Electrical demand for mill: 83 MWh/D

ⓂShandong Fengyuan Zhongke Biology Technology Co., Ltd.
Zaozhuang Mill
No. 1 Zhongke Rd., Yicheng District, Wangzhuang Town
Zaozhuang, Shandong, 277300
China
Phone: (86) 632 3032 601
Fax: (86) 632 3032 596
Web Address: www.sdfyzk.com
Personnel:
Gen. Mgr.: Jian Liu
Phone: (86) 632 3032 601
Total Employees at this Location: 600
Type of Operation: Paperboard mill
Pulp Grades and Capacities:
Total pulp capacity: 205,253 mt/y
Recycled Pulping: 205,253 mt/y
Pulp Mill Data:
Pulp Lines: 2
Recycled Fiber Treatment Lines:
Recycled packaging pulping lines: 2 at 150,000 admt/y
Paper/Paperboard Grades and Capacities:
Total paper and paperboard capacity: 203,490 mt/y
Corrugating medium/fluting: 203,490 mt/y
Paper and Paperboard Mill Data:
Paper Machines: 2
No. 1, fourdrinier, total capacity 49,980 mt/y, Trim width 3.4 m, Corrugating medium/fluting
No. 2, fourdrinier, total capacity 153,510 mt/y, Trim width 4.8 m, Corrugating medium/fluting
Energy Data:
Electrical demand for mill: 318 MWh/D

ⓂShandong Gaomi Silver Hawk Chemical Fibre Group Co., Ltd.
Gaomi Mill
Ownership: Shandong Gaomi Silver Hawk Group Co., Ltd.
No. 1219 Renmin Rd.
Gaomi, Shandong, 261500
China
Phone: (86) 536 2916 666/2323 121
Fax: (86) 536 2323 187
Web Address: www.yying.cn
Personnel:
Chmn.: Yong Li
Total Employees at this Location: 1,000
Type of Operation: Pulp mill
Pulp Grades and Capacities:
Total pulp capacity: 90,744 mt/y
Pulp available for market: 90,000 mt/y
Chemical Pulp: 90,744 mt/y
Pulp Mill Data:
Chemical Pulping Systems:
Batch digesters
Pulp Lines: 3
Bleach Plant Systems: 3
Chemical Pulping System, Type: Cotton Linter
Chemical Pulping System, Type: Cotton Linter
Chemical Pulping System, Type: Cotton Linter
Pulp Dryers:
Fourdriniers 1, Fourdriniers 1, Fourdriniers 1
Energy Data:
Power boilers: 5
Steam turbines: 2 at 18 MW
Electrical demand for mill: 142 MWh/D

ⓂShandong Gaoqing Qingyuan Paper Co. Ltd.
Ownership: 100% by shareholders
No. 43 Qidong Rd., Gaoqing County
Zibo, Shandong, 236500
China
Phone: (86) 533 696 1745/7513
Fax: (86) 533 696 1745/1492
Web Address: www.qingyuan.com
Personnel:
Chmn. & Pres.: Bangli Sheng
Total Employees at this Location: 1,560
Mill Locations:
Shandong Gaoqing Qingyuan Paper Co. Ltd., Zibo Mill, No. 43 Qidong Rd., Gaoqing County, Zibo 236500, China, Capacity: 149,940 mt/y, (Pulp mill, Paper mill, Paperboard mill)
Phone: (86) 533 696 1745/7513
Fax: (86) 533 696 1745/1492

ⓂShandong Gaoqing Qingyuan Paper Co. Ltd.
Zibo Mill
No. 43 Qidong Rd., Gaoqing County
Zibo, Shandong, 236500
China
Phone: (86) 533 696 1745/7513
Fax: (86) 533 696 1745/1492
Web Address: www.qingyuan.com
Personnel:
Chmn. & Pres.: Bangli Sheng
Phone: (86) 533 696 1745/7513
Total Employees at this Location: 1,560
Type of Operation: Pulp mill, Paper mill, Paperboard mill
Pulp Mill Data:
Chemical Pulping Systems:
Batch digesters: 2
Pulp Lines: 2
Bleach Plant Systems: 1
Chemical Recovery Equipment:
Evaporator lines
Recovery boilers: 2
Recycled Fiber Treatment Lines:
Recycled packaging pulping lines
Paper/Paperboard Grades and Capacities:
Total paper and paperboard capacity: 149,940 mt/y
Uncoated woodfree/freesheet: 99,960 mt/y
Linerboard: 49,980 mt/y
Paper and Paperboard Mill Data:
Paper Machines: 11
No. 1, cylinder, total capacity 5,355 mt/y, Trim width 1.76 m, Uncoated woodfree/freesheet
No. 2, total capacity 8,211 mt/y, Trim width 1.76 m, Uncoated woodfree/freesheet
No. 3, total capacity 8,211 mt/y, Trim width 1.76 m, Uncoated woodfree/freesheet
No. 4, total capacity 8,211 mt/y, Trim width 1.76 m, Uncoated woodfree/freesheet
No. 5, total capacity 8,211 mt/y, Trim width 1.76 m, Uncoated woodfree/freesheet
No. 6, total capacity 8,211 mt/y, Trim width 1.76 m, Uncoated woodfree/freesheet
No. 7, total capacity 12,495 mt/y, Trim width 1.76 m, Uncoated woodfree/freesheet
No. 8, total capacity 12,495 mt/y, Trim width 1.76 m, Uncoated woodfree/freesheet
No. 10, total capacity 49,980 mt/y, Trim width 2.82 m, Linerboard
No. 11, total capacity 14,280 mt/y, Trim width 2.73 m, Uncoated woodfree/freesheet
No. 12, total capacity 14,280 mt/y, Trim width 2.73 m, Uncoated woodfree/freesheet

ⓂShandong Gaotang No. 2 Paper Mill
Liaocheng Mill
Ownership: Shandong Tranlin Paper Co. Ltd.
Beixin Village, Gaotang County

China

Liaocheng, Shandong, 252800
China
  Phone: (86) 635 397 3592
  Fax: (86) 635 397 3592
  Web Address: www.tralin.com
Total Employees at this Location: 110
Type of Operation: Paper mill
Paper/Paperboard Grades and Capacities:
  Total paper and paperboard capacity: 5,000 mt/y
  Uncoated woodfree/freesheet: 5,000 mt/y
Paper and Paperboard Mill Data:
Paper Machines: 1
  PM 1, cylinder, total capacity 5,000 mt/y, Trim width 1.58 m, Uncoated woodfree/freesheet

ⓜShandong Gaotang Quanjie Paper Co., Ltd.
Liaocheng Mill
Yijizhen Industry Park, Gaotang County
Liaocheng, Shandong, 252867
China
  Phone: (86) 635 367 9888
  Fax: (86) 635 367 9666
  Email: qjzy@zjzy.com.cn
  Web Address: www.qjzy.com.cn
Personnel:
  Chmn.: Hongfa Li
  Phone: (86) 635 367 9888
  Gen. Mgr.: Xinghe Hua
  Phone: (86) 635 367 9888
  Sls. Mgr.: Zhanzhong Ma
  Phone: (86) 635 367 9888
Total Employees at this Location: 300
Type of Operation: Paper mill
Paper/Paperboard Grades and Capacities:
  Total paper and paperboard capacity: 50,000 mt/y
  Tissue: 50,000 mt/y
Paper and Paperboard Mill Data:
Paper Machines: 8
  PM 1-5, Trim width 3.5 m, Tissue
  PM 6-8, Trim width 2.9 m, Tissue
Energy Data:
Power boilers: 1

ⓘShandong Gold Shankou Paper Co., Ltd.
Ownership: 100% by private
Shankou Town, Daishan Zone
TaiAn City, Shandong, 271038
China
  Phone: (86) 538 861 4266
  Fax: (86) 538 861 1737
  Web Address: www.tralin.com
Personnel:
  Mill Mgr., Pres: Chuanliang Zheng
  VP, Chief Eng.: Zhaoqin Sun
  VP, COO: Honglian Song
Mill Locations:
Shandong Gold Shankou Paper Co., Ltd., Taian Mill, Shankou Town, Daishan Zone, Taian 271038, China, Capacity: 45,000 mt/y, (Paper mill)

ⓜShandong Gold Shankou Paper Co., Ltd.
Taian Mill
Shankou Town, Daishan Zone
Taian, Shandong, 271038
China
Personnel:
  Mill Mgr., Pres: Chuanliang Zheng
  Phone: (86) 538 861 4266
  VP, Chief Eng.: Zhaoqin Sun
  Phone: (86) 538 861 4266
  VP, COO: Honglian Song
  Phone: (86) 538 861 4266
Total Employees at this Location: 1,200
Type of Operation: Paper mill
Paper/Paperboard Grades and Capacities:
  Total paper and paperboard capacity: 45,000 mt/y
  Uncoated woodfree/freesheet: 45,000 mt/y
Paper and Paperboard Mill Data:
Paper Machines: 7
  PM 1-4, cylinder, total capacity 4,500 mt/y, Trim width 1.09 m, Uncoated woodfree/freesheet
  PM 5-7, fourdrinier, total capacity 9,000 mt/y, Trim width 1.76 m, Uncoated woodfree/freesheet

ⓘShandong Golden Cailun Paper Co., Ltd.
Ownership: 100% by private owners
No. 2 Waihuan Rd., Yanggu County
Liaocheng, Shandong, 252300
China
  Phone: (86) 635 2958 869/104/682/860/616
  Fax: (86) 635 632 4766
  Web Address: www.gclpaper.com
Personnel:
  Pres. & Gen. Mgr.: Liren Chen
  Phone: (86) 635 632 2803
  Fax: (86) 635 632 4766
  Sls. Mgr.: Lingzhou Wang
  Phone: (86) 635 632 2803
  Fax: (86) 635 632 4766
Total Employees of Company: 1,000
Mill Locations:
Shandong Golden Cailun Paper Co., Ltd., Liaocheng Mill, No. 2 Waihuan Rd., Yanggu County, Liaocheng 252300, China, Capacity: 120,100 mt/y, (Paper mill)
  Phone: (86) 635 2958 869/104/682/860/616
  Fax: (86) 635 632 4766

ⓜShandong Golden Cailun Paper Co., Ltd.
Liaocheng Mill
No. 2 Waihuan Rd., Yanggu County
Liaocheng, Shandong, 252300
China
  Phone: (86) 635 2958 869/104/682/860/616
  Fax: (86) 635 632 4766
  Web Address: www.gclpaper.com
Personnel:
  Pres. & Gen. Mgr.: Liren Chen
  Phone: (86) 635 632 2803
  Vice Gen. Mgr.: Yupu Gao
  Phone: (86) 137 0635 6429
Total Employees at this Location: 1,000
Type of Operation: Paper mill
Paper/Paperboard Grades and Capacities:
  Total paper and paperboard capacity: 120,100 mt/y
  Uncoated mechanical/groundwood: 120,100 mt/y
Paper and Paperboard Mill Data:
Paper Machines: 8
  No. 2, fourdrinier, total capacity 6,700 mt/y, Trim width 1.76 m, Uncoated mechanical/groundwood
  No. 3, fourdrinier, total capacity 6,700 mt/y, Trim width 1.76 m, Uncoated mechanical/groundwood
  No. 4, fourdrinier, total capacity 10,000 mt/y, Trim width 1.88 m, Uncoated mechanical/groundwood
  No. 5, fourdrinier, total capacity 10,000 mt/y, Trim width 1.88 m, Uncoated mechanical/groundwood
  No. 6, fourdrinier, total capacity 10,000 mt/y, Trim width 1.88 m, Uncoated mechanical/groundwood
  No. 7, fourdrinier, total capacity 10,000 mt/y, Trim width 2.64 m, Uncoated mechanical/groundwood
  No. 8, fourdrinier, total capacity 30,000 mt/y, Trim width 3.15 m, Uncoated mechanical/groundwood
  No. 9, fourdrinier, total capacity 30,000 mt/y, Trim width 3.15 m, Uncoated mechanical/groundwood

ⓘShandong Guanghua Paper Group
Buhou Village, Shangye Town, Fei County
Linyi, Shandong, 273401
China
  Phone: (86) 539 5811 102/617/602
Mill Locations:
Shandong Guanghua Paper Group, Linyi Mill, Buhou Village, Shangye Town, Fei County, Linyi 273401, China, Capacity: 72,000 mt/y, (Paper mill)
  Phone: (86) 539 5811 102/617/602

ⓜShandong Guanghua Paper Group
Linyi Mill
Buhou Village, Shangye Town, Fei County
Linyi, Shandong, 273401
China
  Phone: (86) 539 5811 102/617/602
  Web Address: www.sdhlgh.com
Type of Operation: Paper mill
Paper/Paperboard Grades and Capacities:
  Total paper and paperboard capacity: 72,000 mt/y
  Uncoated woodfree/freesheet: 72,000 mt/y
Paper and Paperboard Mill Data:
Paper Machines: 2
  PM 1, Trim width 1.76 m, Uncoated woodfree/freesheet
  PM 2, Trim width 2.64 m, Uncoated woodfree/freesheet

ⓜShandong Guanjun Paper Co., Ltd.
Dezhou Mill
Pandian Town Industry Park, Qihe County
Dezhou, Shandong, 251125
China
  Phone: (86) 534 597 2888/ 5888
  Fax: (86) 534 597 5888
  Web Address: www.guanjunzhiye.com
Personnel:
  Chmn. & Gen. Mgr.: Xun Zhang
  Phone: (86) 534 597 2888/ 5888
  Sls. Mgr.: Maochang Yang
  Phone: (86) 534 597 2888/ 5888
  Purchasing Mgr.: Zheng Li
  Phone: (86) 534 597 2888/ 5888
Total Employees at this Location: 1,200
Type of Operation: Paper mill
Pulp Grades and Capacities:
  Total pulp capacity: 27,052 mt/y
  Recycled Pulping: 27,052 mt/y
Pulp Mill Data:
Pulp Lines: 3
  Recycled Fiber Treatment Lines:
  Flotation deinking lines: 3 at 100,000 admt/y
Paper/Paperboard Grades and Capacities:
  Total paper and paperboard capacity: 100,000 mt/y
  Uncoated woodfree/freesheet: 52,000 mt/y
  Uncoated mechanical/groundwood: 48,000 mt/y
Paper and Paperboard Mill Data:
Paper Machines: 6
  No. 5, fourdrinier, total capacity 8,000 mt/y, Trim width 1.76 m, Uncoated mechanical/groundwood
  No. 6, fourdrinier, total capacity 10,000 mt/y, Trim width 1.88 m, Uncoated woodfree/freesheet
  No. 7, fourdrinier, total capacity 10,000 mt/y, Trim width 1.88 m, Uncoated woodfree/freesheet
  No. 8, fourdrinier, total capacity 10,000 mt/y, Trim width 1.88 m, Uncoated woodfree/freesheet
  No. 9, fourdrinier, total capacity 40,000 mt/y, Trim width 2.64 m, Uncoated mechanical/groundwood
  No. 10, fourdrinier, total capacity 22,000 mt/y, Trim width 1.88 m, Uncoated woodfree/freesheet
Coating Machines: 1
  CM 1, total capacity 20,000 mt/y.
Energy Data:
Power boilers: 3
Electrical demand for mill: 216 MWh/D

ⓘShandong Guihe Paper Group Co., Ltd.
Ownership: 100% by shareholders
Xingjia Industry, Huantai County
Zibo, Shandong, 256408
China
  Phone: (86) 533 808 6977/1476
  Fax: (86) 533 808 1479
  Email: webmaster@sdguihe.com, kww_wd@126.com
Personnel:

China

Chmn.: Shudong Xu
Phone: (86) 533 808 6977/1476
Fax: (86) 533 808 1479
Pres.: Yong Wang
Phone: (86) 533 808 6977/1476
Fax: (86) 533 808 1479
VP: Hua Pan
Phone: (86) 533 808 6977/1476
Fax: (86) 533 808 1479
Dir.: Dong Wang
Phone: (86) 533 808 6977
Fax: (86) 533 808 6977
Email: kww_wd@126.com
Total Employees of Company: 1,500
Mill Locations:
Shandong Guihe Xianxing Paper Holding Pte. Ltd., Zibo Mill, Xingjia Industry, Huantai County, Zibo 256408, China, Capacity: 505,000 mt/y, (Paperboard mill)
Phone: (86) 533 808 6977/1476
Fax: (86) 533 808 1479
Email: kww_wd@126.com

ⓜShandong Guihe Xianxing Paper Holding Pte. Ltd.
Zibo Mill
Ownership: 100% by Shandong Guihe Paper Group Co., Ltd.
Xingjia Industry, Huantai County
Zibo, Shandong, 256408
China
Phone: (86) 533 808 6977/1476
Fax: (86) 533 808 1479
Email: kww_wd@126.com
Personnel:
Chmn.: Shudong Xu
Phone: (86) 533 808 6977/1476
Pres.: Yong Wang
Phone: (86) 533 808 6977/1476
VP: Hua Pan
Phone: (86) 533 808 6977/1476
Dir.: Dong Wang
Phone: (86) 533 808 6977
Fax: (86) 533 808 6977
Email: kww_wd@126.com
Total Employees at this Location: 730
Type of Operation: Paperboard mill
Pulp Grades and Capacities:
 Total pulp capacity: 486,304 mt/y
 Recycled Pulping: 440,553 mt/y
 Other Pulp: 45,751 mt/y
Pulp Mill Data:
Pulp Lines: 3
 Recycled Fiber Treatment Lines:
 Recycled packaging pulping lines: 2 at 240,000 admt/y
Paper/Paperboard Grades and Capacities:
 Total paper and paperboard capacity: 505,000 mt/y
 Specialty and industrial: 15,000 mt/y
 Linerboard: 240,000 mt/y
 Corrugating medium/fluting: 250,000 mt/y
Paper and Paperboard Mill Data:
Paper Machines: 5
 No. 1, fourdrinier, total capacity 100,000 mt/y, Trim width 4.4 m, Corrugating medium/fluting
 No. 2, fourdrinier, total capacity 30,000 mt/y, Trim width 2.64 m, Corrugating medium/fluting
 No. 3, fourdrinier, total capacity 120,000 mt/y, Trim width 4.4 m, Corrugating medium/fluting
 No. 4, fourdrinier, total capacity 15,000 mt/y, Trim width 2.64 m, Specialty and industrial
 No. 5, fourdrinier, total capacity 240,000 mt/y, Trim width 5.6 m, Linerboard
Energy Data:
 Power boilers: 2
 Steam turbines: 2 at 28, 28 MW
 Electrical demand for mill: 636 MWh/D

ⓜShandong Haiyang Yongping Paper Co., Ltd.
Haiyang Mill
Ownership: 100% by Shandong Yantai Jinhong Paper Co. Ltd.
No. 105, Dongfang Rd., Haiyang Economic & Technological Development Area
Haiyang, Shandong, 265100
China
Phone: (86) 535 310 5988/5997
Fax: (86) 535 310 5966/5959
Email: sales@yongpingpaper.com
Web Address: www.yongpingpaper.com
Personnel:
Gen. Mgr.: Chunping Li
Phone: (86) 535 320 5358
Sls. Mgr.: Hai Xin
Phone: (86) 535 320 5358
Chief Eng.: Xiaowei Yang
Phone: (86) 535 320 5358
Total Employees at this Location: 500
Type of Operation: Paper mill
Paper/Paperboard Grades and Capacities:
 Total paper and paperboard capacity: 12,000 mt/y
 Tissue: 12,000 mt/y
Paper and Paperboard Mill Data:
Paper Machines: 4
 PM 3-4, fourdrinier, total capacity 4,000 mt/y, Trim width 2.64 m, Tissue
 PM 5-6, total capacity 2,000 mt/y, Trim width 1.58 m, Tissue

ⓜShandong Helon Co., Ltd.
Weifang Mill
No.555, Hailong Rd., Hanting District
Weifang, Shandong, 261100
China
Phone: (86) 536 2275 216/167/245
Fax: (86) 536 2270 677/2275 086/245
Web Address: www.helon.cn
Type of Operation: Pulp mill
Pulp Grades and Capacities:
 Total pulp capacity: 90,000 mt/y
 Pulp available for market: 90,000 mt/y

①Shandong Henglian Paper Group C., Ltd.
Ownership: 100% by shareholders
High Technology Development District
Weifang City, Shandong, 261031
China
Phone: (86) 536 867 1522
Fax: (86) 536 866 5348
Web Address: www.henglianpaper.com
Personnel:
Chmn. & Pres.: Jian Xu
Phone: (86) 536 867 1522
Fax: (86) 536 866 5348
Total Employees of Company: 4,000
Mill Locations:
Shandong Weifang Henglian Art Paper Co., Ltd., Weifang Mill, No. 409, East Wolong Rd., Kuiwen Industry, Weifang 261031, China, Capacity: 100,000 mt/y, (Paper mill)
Phone: (86) 536 867 1625/866 9308/866 4564
Fax: (86) 536 866 8708
Shandong Weifang Henglian Cellophane Co., Ltd., Weifang Mill, No. 409, Wolong East Street, Kuiwen Dist., Weifang 201031, China, Capacity: 6,200 mt/y, (Paper mill)
Phone: (86) 536 728 8338
Fax: (86) 536 728 8333
Shandong Weifang Henglian Meilin Life-Uses Paper Limited Co., Weifang Mill (70% owned), 601 Longhai Road, Hanting District, Weifang 261041, China, Capacity: 40,000 mt/y, (Paper mill)
Phone: (86) 536 7283228
Fax: (86) 536 7283229
Shandong Weifang Henglian Pulp & Paper Co., Ltd., Weifang Mill, No. 601 Hailong Rd., Hanting District, Weifang 261000, China, (Pulp mill)
Phone: (86) 536 728 3106/728 3131
Fax: (86) 536 725 1647/728 3228
Shandong Weifang Yongxin Paper Co., Ltd., Changle Mill, Hetou Industry Zone, Changle 262416, China, Capacity: 19,992 mt/y, (Paper mill)
Phone: (86) 536 691 1126
Fax: (86) 536 691 1033

①Shandong Heze Luchen Paper Co., Ltd.
South Mudan Rd
Heze, Shandong
China
Phone: (86) 530 5188 750
Mill Locations:
Shandong Heze Luchen Paper Co., Ltd., Heze Mill, South Mudan Rd, Heze, China, Capacity: 12,000 mt/y, (Paper mill)
Phone: (86) 530 5188 750

ⓜShandong Heze Luchen Paper Co., Ltd.
Heze Mill
South Mudan Rd
Heze, Shandong
China
Phone: (86) 530 5188 750
Type of Operation: Paper mill
Paper/Paperboard Grades and Capacities:
 Total paper and paperboard capacity: 12,000 mt/y
 Tissue: 12,000 mt/y
Paper and Paperboard Mill Data:
Paper Machines: 6
 PM 1-6, total capacity 2,000 mt/y, Trim width 1.76 m, Tissue

①Shandong Heze Mudan Paper Co., Ltd.
Huanggang Industrial Park, Mudan District
Heze, Shandong, 274000
China
Phone: (86) 530 5669 669
Mill Locations:
Shandong Heze Mudan Paper Co., Ltd., Heze Mill, Huanggang Industrial Park, Mudan District, Heze 274000, China, Capacity: 30,000 mt/y, (Paper mill)
Phone: (86) 530 5669 669

ⓜShandong Heze Mudan Paper Co., Ltd.
Heze Mill
Huanggang Industrial Park, Mudan District
Heze, Shandong, 274000
China
Phone: (86) 530 5669 669
Type of Operation: Paper mill
Paper/Paperboard Grades and Capacities:
 Total paper and paperboard capacity: 30,000 mt/y
 Tissue: 30,000 mt/y
Paper and Paperboard Mill Data:
Paper Machines: 2
 PM 1, total capacity 15,000 mt/y, Trim width 2.8 m, Tissue
 PM 2, total capacity 15,000 mt/y, Trim width 2.8 m, Tissue

ⓜShandong Honghe Group Zoucheng Hengxiang Paper Co., Ltd.
Zoucheng Mill
No. 52, Yingxi Rd.
Zoucheng, Shandong, 273500
China
Phone: (86) 537 5300318
Fax: (86) 537 5312183
Web Address: www.sdhhjt.com
Personnel:
Chmn.: Yigang Ma
Phone: (86) 537 5300318

China

Pres.: Yufeng Liu
Phone: (86) 537 5300318
Total Employees at this Location: 635
Type of Operation: Paper mill
Pulp Grades and Capacities:
Total pulp capacity: 94,586 mt/y
Recycled Pulping: 94,586 mt/y
Pulp Mill Data:
Bleach Plant Systems: 1
Recycled Pulping System, Type: Deinked
Recycled Fiber Treatment Lines:
Flotation deinking lines: 1
Paper/Paperboard Grades and Capacities:
Total paper and paperboard capacity: 100,000 mt/y
Newsprint: 100,000 mt/y
Paper and Paperboard Mill Data:
Paper Machines: 7
No. 1, fourdrinier, total capacity 7,500 mt/y, Trim width 1.76 m, Newsprint
No. 2, fourdrinier, total capacity 7,500 mt/y, Trim width 1.76 m, Newsprint
No. 3, fourdrinier, total capacity 7,500 mt/y, Trim width 1.76 m, Newsprint
No. 4, fourdrinier, total capacity 7,500 mt/y, Trim width 1.76 m, Newsprint
No. 5, fourdrinier, total capacity 12,500 mt/y, Trim width 2.4 m, Newsprint
No. 6, fourdrinier, total capacity 12,500 mt/y, Trim width 2.4 m, Newsprint
No. 7, fourdrinier, total capacity 45,000 mt/y, Trim width 3.95 m, Newsprint
Energy Data:
Power boilers
Steam turbines
Electrical demand for mill: 263 MWh/D

ⓗⓜShandong Huajin Paper Group
Jining Mill
No.818, Jinzhuang Town, Sishui County
Jining, Shandong, 273201
China
Phone: (86) 537 403 6821/6860/1393/6894/ 21 6640 3141
Fax: (86) 537 403 1210/1393/1689/ 21 6640 3242
Email: xm1313@163169.net,
zmzwy@163.com,
huajinlbz@126.com,
huajinrzb@126.com
Personnel:
Chmn. & Pres./Mill Mgr.: Dongshang Xing
Phone: (86) 537 403 6821/6860/1393/6894/ 21 6640 3241
Sales Mgr.: Maozhi Zhang
Phone: (86) 21 6640 3241
Fax: (86) 21 66403242
Email: zmzwy@163.com
Total Employees of Company: 5,800
Total Employees at this Location: 2,000
Type of Operation: Pulp mill, Paper mill, Paperboard mill
Mill Locations:
Anhui Chaohu Jinhe Paper Co. Ltd, Chaohu Mill, East Tianmen Rd., Xiliangshan District, Baiqiao Town, He County, Chaohu 238267, China, Capacity: 165,000 mt/y, (Paperboard mill)
Phone: (86) 565 589 6888
Fax: (86) 565 589 6999
Email: daynow@163.com
Pulp Grades and Capacities:
Total pulp capacity: 22,383 mt/y
Chemical Pulp: 57,642 mt/y
Recycled Pulping: 13,401 mt/y
Other Pulp: 8,187 mt/y
Pulp Mill Data:
Chemical Pulping Systems:
Batch digesters
Pulp Lines: 1
Bleach Plant Systems: 2
No. 1, Type: Nonwood Pulp

Recycled Pulping System, Type: Deinked
Chemical Recovery Equipment:
Evaporator lines
Recovery boilers: 3
Recycled Fiber Treatment Lines:
Flotation deinking lines
Paper/Paperboard Grades and Capacities:
Total paper and paperboard capacity: 450,971 mt/y
Uncoated woodfree/freesheet: 151,011 mt/y
Boxboard/cartonboard: 299,960 mt/y
Paper and Paperboard Mill Data:
Paper Machines: 14
No. 1, fourdrinier, total capacity 2,856 mt/y, Trim width 1.54 m, Uncoated woodfree/freesheet
No. 2, fourdrinier, total capacity 7,497 mt/y, Trim width 1.76 m, Uncoated woodfree/freesheet
No. 8, fourdrinier, total capacity 9,996 mt/y, Trim width 1.76 m, Uncoated woodfree/freesheet
No. 9, fourdrinier, total capacity 7,497 mt/y, Trim width 1.76 m, Uncoated woodfree/freesheet
No. 10, fourdrinier, total capacity 9,996 mt/y, Trim width 1.76 m, Uncoated woodfree/freesheet
No. 11, fourdrinier, total capacity 16,065 mt/y, Trim width 1.88 m, Uncoated woodfree/freesheet
No. 15, fourdrinier, total capacity 14,994 mt/y, Trim width 2.36 m, Uncoated woodfree/freesheet
No. 16, fourdrinier, total capacity 14,994 mt/y, Trim width 2.36 m, Uncoated woodfree/freesheet
No. 17, fourdrinier, total capacity 7,497 mt/y, Trim width 1.88 m, Uncoated woodfree/freesheet
No. 18, fourdrinier, total capacity 7,497 mt/y, Trim width 1.88 m, Uncoated woodfree/freesheet
No. 19-20, fourdrinier, total capacity 32,130 mt/y, Trim width 2.64 m, Uncoated woodfree/freesheet
No. 22, Fourdrinier (5), total capacity 99,960 mt/y, Trim width 2.74 m, Boxboard/cartonboard
No. 23, fourdrinier, total capacity 19,992 mt/y, Trim width 3.6 m, Uncoated woodfree/freesheet
No. 24, fourdrinier (3), total capacity 200,000 mt/y, Trim width 3.4 m, Boxboard/cartonboard
Coating Machines: 2
PM 22, total capacity 100,000 mt/y., on machine
PM 24, total capacity 200,000 mt/y., on machine
Energy Data:
Power boilers: 5
Steam turbines: 2 at 15, 15 MW
Electrical demand for mill: 662 MWh/D

ⓗShandong Huapeng Paper Co. Ltd.
Mid Changguo Dong Rd.
Zibo, Shandong, 255071
China
Phone: (86) 533 211 5666
Fax: (86) 533 211 5388
Web Address: www.huapengzhiye.com
Mill Locations:
Shandong Huapeng Paper Co. Ltd., Zibo Mill, Mid Changguo Dong Rd., Zibo 255071, China, Capacity: 107,100 mt/y, (Paperboard mill)
Phone: (86) 533 211 5666
Fax: (86) 533 211 5388

ⓜShandong Huapeng Paper Co. Ltd.
Zibo Mill
Mid Changguo Dong Rd.
Zibo, Shandong, 255071
China
Phone: (86) 533 211 5666
Fax: (86) 533 211 5388
Personnel:
Gen. Mgr.: Mr. Qinghai Gao
Phone: (86) 533 211 5666
Total Employees at this Location: 310
Type of Operation: Paperboard mill
Pulp Grades and Capacities:
Total pulp capacity: 108,803 mt/y
Recycled Pulping: 108,803 mt/y
Pulp Mill Data:
Pulp Lines: 1

Recycled Fiber Treatment Lines:
Recycled packaging pulping lines: 1 at 120,000 admt/y
Paper/Paperboard Grades and Capacities:
Total paper and paperboard capacity: 107,100 mt/y
Linerboard: 107,100 mt/y
Paper and Paperboard Mill Data:
Paper Machines: 2
No. 1, cylinder (2), total capacity 35,700 mt/y, Trim width 2.8 m, Linerboard
No. 2, fourdrinier (2), total capacity 71,400 mt/y, Trim width 3.7 m, Linerboard
Energy Data:
Power boilers
Electrical demand for mill: 177 MWh/D

ⓗⓜShandong Huatai Paper Co., Ltd.
Dongying Mill
Ownership: 100% by Shandong Huatai Group Co., Ltd.
Huatai Industrial Park, Dawang Town, Guangrao County
Dongying, Shandong, 257335
China
Phone: (86) 546 6888 808 / 6888 818
Fax: (86) 546 6888 018
Email: htwm@huatai.com
Web Address: www.huataipaper.com
Personnel:
Chmn.: Jianhua Li
Phone: (86) 546 6888 692/ 423/ 818/ 808/ 219
Vice. Chmn.: Wanliang Zhu
Phone: (86) 546 6888 692/ 423/ 818/ 808/ 219
Gen. Mgr.: Gang Li
Phone: (86) 546 6888 692/ 423/ 818/ 808/ 219
Dpty Gen. Mgr.: Julong Tian
Phone: (86) 546 6888 692/ 423/ 818/ 808/ 219
Dpty Gen. Mgr.: Zhiding Tian
Phone: (86) 546 6888 692/ 423/ 818/ 808/ 219
Dpty. Gen. Mgr.: XiaoLiang Li
Phone: (86) 546 6888 692/ 423/ 818/ 808/ 219
Dpty. Gen. Mgr.: Jianhua Liu
Phone: (86) 546 6888 692/ 423/ 818/ 808/ 219
Dpty. Gen. Mgr.: Wenguang Wei
Phone: (86) 546 6888 692/ 423/ 818/ 808/ 219
Dpty. Gen. Mgr.: Yuxiang Chi
Phone: (86) 546 6888 692/ 423/ 818/ 808/ 219
CFO: Haibin Zhang
Phone: (86) 546 6888 692/ 423/ 818/ 808/ 219
Board Sec.: Huacun Xu
Phone: (86) 546 779 8848
Fax: (86) 546 687 1957
Email: xuhuacun@sina.com
Chief Eng.: Fenshan Zhang
Phone: (86) 546 6888 692/ 423/ 818/ 808/ 219
Total Employees of Company: 9,428
Total Employees at this Location: 6,000
Type of Operation: Pulp mill, Paper mill
Mill Locations:
Anhui Huatai Forest Pulp & Paper Co., Ltd., Anqing (Anhui Huatai) Mill (85% owned), Xihu, Laofeng town, Yingjiang dist., Anqing 246003, China, Capacity: 140,000 mt/y, (Pulp mill, Paper mill)
Phone: (86) 86-556-597 9326
Fax: (86) 86-556-597 9279
Shandong Huatai Group Co., Ltd., Jiangmen Mill, Lingtou Industrial Park, Shuangshui Town, Xinhui District, Jiangmen 529153 , China, Capacity: 200,000 mt/y, (Paper mill)
Phone: (86) 750 3411 768/728
Hebei Huatai Paper Co., Ltd., Shijiazhuang Mill, No.164, First Industry St., West Shita Rd., Zhao County, Shijiazhuang 051530, China, Capacity: 300,000 mt/y, (Paper mill)
Phone: (86) 311 84955555/7899300/4911710
Fax: (86) 311 8495 5520/4911710/4945663/7897051
Shandong Huatai Qinghe Industrial Co., Ltd, Dongying (Huatai Qinghe) Mill (83.67% owned), Huatai Industrial Park, Dawang Township, Dongying 257300, China, Capacity: 89,964 mt/y, (Paper mill)

Phone: (86) 546 7722 388
Fax: (86) 546 7729 899
Shandong Rizhao Huatai Paper Co. Ltd., Rizhao Mill (96% owned), No. 199 Juzhou Rd., Ju County, Rizhao 276500, China, Capacity: 53,570 mt/y, (Pulp mill, Paper mill)
Phone: (86) 633 688 2076
Fax: (86) 633 688 2881
Pulp Grades and Capacities:
Total pulp capacity: 1,010,745 mt/y
Mechanical Pulp: 194,420 mt/y
Recycled Pulping: 816,324 mt/y
Pulp Mill Data:
Mechanical Pulping Systems:
BCTMP systems
Pulp Lines: 5
Bleach Plant Systems: 2
Mechanical Pulping System, Type: BCTMP, Sequence: P
Recycled Pulping System
Recycled Fiber Treatment Lines:
Flotation deinking lines
Paper/Paperboard Grades and Capacities:
Total paper and paperboard capacity: 1,770,000 mt/y
Newsprint: 830,000 mt/y
Uncoated woodfree/freesheet: 515,000 mt/y
Coated woodfree/freesheet: 425,000 mt/y
Paper and Paperboard Mill Data:
Stock Preparation:
Pulpers: 17
Refiners: 27
Paper Machines: 7
No. 9, DuoFormer D, total capacity 180,000 mt/y, Trim width 6.06 m, Uncoated woodfree/freesheet
No. 10, DuoFormer TQv, total capacity 220,000 mt/y, Trim width 6.24 m, Newsprint, Uncoated woodfree/freesheet
No. 11, DuoFormer TQv, total capacity 400,000 mt/y, Trim width 10.2 m, Newsprint
No. 12, DuoFormer TQv, total capacity 400,000 mt/y, Trim width 10.2 m, Newsprint
No. 19, fourdrinier, total capacity 35,000 mt/y, Trim width 2.64 m, Uncoated woodfree/freesheet
No. 21, fourdrinier, total capacity 35,000 mt/y, Trim width 2.64 m, Uncoated woodfree/freesheet
PM 8, OptiFormer, total capacity 500,000 mt/y, Trim width 7.3 m, Coated woodfree/freesheet, Uncoated woodfree/freesheet
Coating Machines: 3
No. 8, total capacity 650,000 mt/y., on machine
No. 1-2
No. 10, off machine
Finishing Equipment:
Supercalenders: 2
Rewinders: 17
Sheeters: 17
Energy Data:
Power boilers: 2
HRSG boiler: 1
Steam turbines: 4 at 150, 150, 25, 25 MW
Electrical demand for mill: 5,219 MWh/D

ⓗⓜShandong Huatai Qinghe Industrial Co., Ltd
Dongying (Huatai Qinghe) Mill
Ownership: 83.67% by Shandong Huatai Group Co., Ltd.
Huatai Industrial Park, Dawang Township
Dongying, Shandong, 257300
China
Phone: (86) 546 7722 388
Fax: (86) 546 7729 899
Web Address: www.huatai.com
Total Employees of Company: 650
Total Employees at this Location: 650
Type of Operation: Paper mill
Pulp Grades and Capacities:
Total pulp capacity: 50,979 mt/y
Other Pulp: 50,979 mt/y
Pulp Mill Data:
Paper/Paperboard Grades and Capacities:
Total paper and paperboard capacity: 89,964 mt/y
Uncoated woodfree/freesheet: 89,964 mt/y
Paper and Paperboard Mill Data:
Paper Machines: 3
No. 1, fourdrinier, total capacity 9,996 mt/y, Trim width 1.76 m, Uncoated woodfree/freesheet
No. 2, fourdrinier, total capacity 39,984 mt/y, Trim width 2.64 m, Uncoated woodfree/freesheet
No. 3, fourdrinier, total capacity 39,984 mt/y, Trim width 2.64 m, Uncoated woodfree/freesheet
Energy Data:
Power boilers: 1
Steam turbines: 1 at 25 MW
Electrical demand for mill: 238 MWh/D

ⓗShandong Jining Jinsheng Paper Co., Ltd.
Ownership: 100% by private owners
Jinxiang Industry Park, Jiaxiang County
Jining, Shandong, 272400
China
Phone: (86) 537 685 4788
Fax: (86) 537 686 2516
Personnel:
Gen. Mgr.: Hongliang Liu
Mill Locations:
Shandong Jining Jinsheng Paper Co., Ltd., Jining Mill, Jinxiang Industry Park, Jiaxiang County, Jining 272400, China, Capacity: 20,000 mt/y, (Paper mill)
Phone: (86) 537 685 4788
Fax: (86) 537 686 2516

ⓜShandong Jining Jinsheng Paper Co., Ltd.
Jining Mill
Jinxiang Industry Park, Jiaxiang County
Jining, Shandong, 272400
China
Phone: (86) 537 685 4788
Fax: (86) 537 686 2516
Personnel:
Gen. Mgr.: Hongliang Liu
Phone: (86) 537 685 4788
Total Employees at this Location: 500
Type of Operation: Paper mill
Paper/Paperboard Grades and Capacities:
Total paper and paperboard capacity: 20,000 mt/y
Uncoated woodfree/freesheet: 20,000 mt/y
Paper and Paperboard Mill Data:
Paper Machines: 2
No. 1, fourdrinier, total capacity 10,000 mt/y, Trim width 1.76 m, Uncoated woodfree/freesheet
No. 2, fourdrinier, total capacity 10,000 mt/y, Trim width 1.76 m, Uncoated woodfree/freesheet
Energy Data:
Power boilers: 3
Electrical demand for mill: 37 MWh/D

ⓗⓜShandong Jining Lianhe Paper Co., Ltd
Jining Mill
Tangkou Industrial Park
Jining, Shandong
China
Personnel:
CEO: Lianhe Yang
Total Employees at this Location: 270
Type of Operation: Paperboard mill
Pulp Grades and Capacities:
Total pulp capacity: 101,256 mt/y
Recycled Pulping: 101,256 mt/y
Paper/Paperboard Grades and Capacities:
Total paper and paperboard capacity: 99,960 mt/y
Linerboard: 99,960 mt/y
Paper and Paperboard Mill Data:
Paper Machines: 2
No. 1, Multi-wire (3), total capacity 71,400 mt/y, Trim width 4.4 m, Linerboard
No. 2, fourdrinier (3), total capacity 28,560 mt/y, Trim width 2.8 m, Linerboard
Energy Data:
Power boilers: 1
Electrical demand for mill: 176 MWh/D

ⓜShandong Kaili Paper Co. Ltd.
Rongcheng Mill
No. 198 East Heyang Rd.
Rongcheng, Shandong, 264300
China
Phone: (86) 631 757 2758/2759/ 751 0288
Fax: (86) 631 757 1946
Email: kaili@kailipaper.cn
Web Address: www.kailipaper.cn
Personnel:
Chmn. & Pres.: Benchang Wang
Phone: (86) 631 757 2758/2759/ 751 0288
VP: Yongning Cong
Phone: (86) 631 757 2758/2759/ 751 0288
Purch. Agent: Dongliang Bi
Phone: (86) 631 757 2758/2759/ 751 0288
Total Employees at this Location: 700
Type of Operation: Paper mill
Paper/Paperboard Grades and Capacities:
Total paper and paperboard capacity: 35,000 mt/y
Specialty and industrial: 35,000 mt/y
Paper and Paperboard Mill Data:
Stock Preparation:
Refiners: 18
Paper Machines: 3
PM 1, total capacity 8,000 mt/y, Trim width 1.58 m, Specialty and industrial
PM 2, fourdrinier, total capacity 12,000 mt/y, Trim width 1.76 m, Specialty and industrial
PM 3, fourdrinier, total capacity 15,000 mt/y, Trim width 1.88 m, Specialty and industrial
Coating Machines: 1
PM 1, total capacity 10,000 mt/y., off machine
Finishing Equipment:
Supercalenders: 1

ⓗⓜShandong Laiwu Hengli Paper Co., Ltd.
Laiwu Mill
South of Daqiaogou Village, Yangzhuang Town, Laicheng District
Laiwu, Shandong, 271123
China
Phone: (86) 634 6632 079
Type of Operation: Paper mill
Paper/Paperboard Grades and Capacities:
Total paper and paperboard capacity: 1,200 mt/y
Tissue: 1,200 mt/y
Paper and Paperboard Mill Data:
Paper Machines: 2
PM 1, total capacity 600 mt/y, Trim width 1.09 m, Tissue
PM 2, total capacity 600 mt/y, Trim width 1.09 m, Tissue

ⓗShandong Laiwu Ronghe Paper Co., Ltd.
Yifeng Village, Yangli Town
Laiwu, Shandong
China
Mill Locations:
Shandong Laiwu Ronghe Paper Co., Ltd., Laiwu Mill, Yifeng Village, Yangli Town, Laiwu, China, Capacity: 4,000 mt/y, (Paper mill)

ⓜShandong Laiwu Ronghe Paper Co., Ltd.
Laiwu Mill
Yifeng Village, Yangli Town
Laiwu, Shandong
China
Type of Operation: Paper mill

China

Paper/Paperboard Grades and Capacities:
Total paper and paperboard capacity: 4,000 mt/y
Tissue: 4,000 mt/y

ⓜShandong Laizhou Lutong Speciality Paper Co., Ltd.
Laizhou Mill
No. 238 East Haimiao Rd.
Laizhou, Shandong, 261408
China
 Phone: (86) 535 248 3050/ 0641
 Fax: (86) 535 248 3050
Personnel:
 Chmn. & Pres.: Xiuyi Sun
 Phone: (86) 535 248 3050/ 0641
Total Employees at this Location: 500
Type of Operation: Paper mill
Paper/Paperboard Grades and Capacities:
 Total paper and paperboard capacity: 30,000 mt/y
 Specialty and industrial: 30,000 mt/y
Paper and Paperboard Mill Data:
Paper Machines: 8
PM 13, total capacity 4,000 mt/y, Trim width 2.4 m, Specialty and industrial
PM 14-17, total capacity 2,000 mt/y, Trim width 1.6 m, Specialty and industrial
PM 18-20, total capacity 4,000 mt/y, Trim width 2.4 m, Specialty and industrial

ⓜShandong Laizhou Yintong Paper Co., Ltd.
Laiyang Mill
No. 129 Danya Rd.
Laiyang, Shandong, 265202
China
 Phone: (86) 535 7318 208/715 8581
 Fax: (86) 535 7318 208
 Email: lcz@yintongpaper.cn
 Web Address: www.yinhaipaper.com
Personnel:
 Gen. Mgr.: Changzheng Li
 Phone: (86) 535 715 8581
 Sls. Mgr.: Hongwei Sun
 Phone: (86) 535 715 8581
Total Employees at this Location: 780
Type of Operation: Paper mill
Paper/Paperboard Grades and Capacities:
 Total paper and paperboard capacity: 50,000 mt/y
 Specialty and industrial: 50,000 mt/y
Paper and Paperboard Mill Data:
Paper Machines: 10
PM 1, cylinder, total capacity 2,500 mt/y, Trim width 1.09 m, Specialty and industrial
PM 2, cylinder, total capacity 3,500 mt/y, Trim width 1.58 m, Specialty and industrial
PM 3-6, fourdrinier, total capacity 5,000 mt/y, Trim width 1.58 m, Specialty and industrial
PM 7-10, fourdrinier, total capacity 6,000 mt/y, Trim width 1.76 m, Specialty and industrial

ⓜShandong Lianxi Paper Co. Ltd.
Rizhao Mill
173 Jiefang Rd., Hongning Town, Wulian County
Rizhao, Shandong, 262300
China
 Phone: (86) 633 532 1731
 Fax: (86) 633 532 1731
Personnel:
 Pres./Mill Mgr.: Xibin Wang
 Phone: (86) 633 532 1731
 VP - Technology/Chief Eng.: Zhenhua Liu
 Phone: (86) 633 532 1731
 VP - Operations: Lianxue Xu
 Phone: (86) 633 532 1731
Total Employees at this Location: 500
Type of Operation: Paper mill
Paper/Paperboard Grades and Capacities:
 Total paper and paperboard capacity: 13,000 mt/y
 Uncoated mechanical/groundwood: 10,000 mt/y
 Tissue: 3,000 mt/y
 Packaging papers
Paper and Paperboard Mill Data:
Paper Machines: 6
PM 1, fourdrinier, total capacity 5,000 mt/y, Trim width 1.88 m, Uncoated mechanical/groundwood
PM 2, (due to start in Q1 2013), fourdrinier, Trim width 1.76 m
PM 3, fourdrinier, total capacity 1,000 mt/y, Trim width 1.58 m, Tissue
PM 4, fourdrinier, total capacity 1,000 mt/y, Trim width 1.58 m, Tissue
PM 5, fourdrinier, total capacity 1,000 mt/y, Trim width 1.58 m, Tissue
PM 6, total capacity 5,000 mt/y, Trim width 1.88 m, Uncoated mechanical/groundwood

ⓜShandong Linqu Yulong Paper Co., Ltd.
Weifang Mill
Ownership: 51.50% by Shandong Wanhao Paper Group Co., Ltd.
Linqu Economy & Development District, Linqu
Weifang, Shandong, 262600
China
 Phone: (86) 536 315 8797/ 8862/ 8872
 Fax: (86) 536 315 8568
 Email: yulong@wanhao.com
 Web Address: www.wanhao.com
Personnel:
 Gen. Mgr.: Peinong Yin
 Phone: (86) 536 315 8797/ 8862/ 8872
Total Employees at this Location: 500
Type of Operation: Paper mill
Pulp Mill Data:
Paper/Paperboard Grades and Capacities:
 Total paper and paperboard capacity: 71,700 mt/y
 Uncoated woodfree/freesheet: 21,700 mt/y
 Coated woodfree/freesheet: 50,000 mt/y
Paper and Paperboard Mill Data:
Paper Machines: 5
No. 1, total capacity 16,636 mt/y, Trim width 1.76 m, Coated woodfree/freesheet
No. 2, total capacity 16,636 mt/y, Trim width 1.76 m, Coated woodfree/freesheet
No. 3, total capacity 16,728 mt/y, Trim width 1.76 m, Coated woodfree/freesheet
No. 4, total capacity 10,850 mt/y, Trim width 1.88 m, Uncoated woodfree/freesheet
No. 5, total capacity 10,850 mt/y, Trim width 1.88 m, Uncoated woodfree/freesheet
Coating Machines: 1
PM 9, total capacity 50,000 mt/y., off machine
Energy Data:
Electrical demand for mill: 141 MWh/D

ⓜShandong Linyi Sensen Paper Co. Ltd.
Linyi Mill
Zhengwang Town, Hedong District
Linyi, Shandong, 276000
China
 Phone: (86) 539 8813 599
 Fax: (86) 539 8813 277
 Web Address: www.shandongsensen.cn
Personnel:
 Pres.: Mr. You
 Phone: (86) 539 8813 599
 Sls. Mgr.: Guowu Zhang
 Phone: (86) 539 8813 599
Type of Operation: Paper mill
Paper/Paperboard Grades and Capacities:
 Total paper and paperboard capacity: 7,200 mt/y
 Tissue: 7,200 mt/y
Paper and Paperboard Mill Data:
Paper Machines: 4
PM 1-4, fourdrinier, total capacity 1,800 mt/y, Trim width 1.88 m, Tissue
Energy Data:
Power boilers: 1

ⓜShandong Liying Paper Co., Ltd.
Jining Mill
Liying Town, Rencheng District
Jining, Shandong, 272175
China
 Phone: (86) 537 203 7945/ 7718
 Fax: (86) 537 203 7005/ 7409
Personnel:
 Chmn.: Bing Tang
 Phone: (86) 537 203 7945/ 7718
 Pres./Mill Mgr.: Wei Gao
 Phone: (86) 537 203 7945/ 7718
Total Employees at this Location: 500
Type of Operation: Paper mill
Paper/Paperboard Grades and Capacities:
 Total paper and paperboard capacity: 5,000 mt/y
Paper and Paperboard Mill Data:
Paper Machines: 2
PM 3, (Joss paper), fourdrinier, total capacity 2,500 mt/y, Trim width 1.76 m
PM 4, (Joss paper), fourdrinier, total capacity 2,500 mt/y, Trim width 1.76 m

ⓜShandong Longkou Yulong Paper Co., Ltd.
Yantai Mill
North of Huangheying Village, Zhuyouguan Town, Longkou
Yantai, Shandong, 265712
China
 Phone: (86) 535 8589 536/501
 Fax: (86) 535 8589 555
 Web Address: www.yulongpaper.com
Total Employees at this Location: 1,200
Type of Operation: Paper mill
Pulp Grades and Capacities:
 Total pulp capacity: 30,000 mt/y
 Chemical Pulp: 30,000 mt/y
Pulp Mill Data:
Pulp Lines: 1
Paper/Paperboard Grades and Capacities:
 Total paper and paperboard capacity: 80,000 mt/y
 Uncoated woodfree/freesheet
 Uncoated mechanical/groundwood
Paper and Paperboard Mill Data:
Paper Machines: 4
PM 6, total capacity 20,000 mt/y, Trim width 1.88 m, Uncoated mechanical/groundwood, Uncoated woodfree/freesheet
PM 3-5, total capacity 20,000 mt/y, Trim width 1.76 m, Uncoated woodfree/freesheet
Energy Data:
Power boilers

ⓜShandong Lu An Paper Co., Ltd.
Anqiu Mill
Mill is under bankruptcy protection (in 2010)
No. 2, Xing An Rd.
Anqiu, Shandong, 262100
China
 Phone: (86) 536 422 1181/1836
 Fax: (86) 536 421 2920
Personnel:
 Pres./Mill Mgr.: Guotai Dong
 Phone: (86) 536 422 1181/ 1836
 Tech. Mgr.: Xuejin Xu
 Phone: (86) 536 422 1181/ 1836
 VP - Operation: Xinjun Zhang
 Phone: (86) 536 422 1181/ 1836
 Sls. Mgr.: Mr. Chu
 Phone: (86) 536 422 1181/ 1836
Total Employees at this Location: 2,000
Type of Operation: Pulp mill, Paper mill
Pulp Mill Data:
 Chemical Pulping Systems:
 Batch digesters: 8
Paper/Paperboard Grades and Capacities:
 Total paper and paperboard capacity: 120,000 mt/y

Uncoated woodfree/freesheet: 40,000 mt/y
Coated woodfree/freesheet: 80,000 mt/y
Paper and Paperboard Mill Data:
Paper Machines: 4
No. 1, fourdrinier, total capacity 15,000 mt/y, Trim width 1.76 m, Coated woodfree/freesheet
No. 2, fourdrinier, total capacity 15,000 mt/y, Trim width 1.76 m, Coated woodfree/freesheet
No. 3, fourdrinier, total capacity 15,000 mt/y, Trim width 1.76 m, Coated woodfree/freesheet
No. 4, fourdrinier, total capacity 15,000 mt/y, Trim width 1.76 m, Tissue

ⓜShandong Lunan Paper Industry Group
Linyi Mill
No. 276 Renmin Rd., Tancheng County
Linyi, Shandong, 276100
China
Phone: (86) 539 622 1670/ 613 0908/ 0893/ 0721
Fax: (86) 539 612 8003/ 622 1674/ 613 0893
Email: pbhou@hotmail.com
Web Address: www.lunanpaper.com
Personnel:
Chmn. & Pres.: Wenchang Chen
Phone: (86) 539 622 1670/ 613 0908/ 0893/ 0721
Sls. Mgr.: Wei Zhang
Phone: (86) 539 622 1670/ 613 0908/ 0893/ 0721
Exp. Dir.: Peibo Hou
Phone: (86) 539 612 8003
Fax: (86) 539 613 0893
Email: pbhou@hotmail.com
Total Employees at this Location: 5,000
Type of Operation: Paper mill
Paper/Paperboard Grades and Capacities:
Total paper and paperboard capacity: 300,000 mt/y
Specialty and industrial
Paper and Paperboard Mill Data:
Paper Machines: 17
PM 10, fourdrinier, total capacity 15,000 mt/y, Trim width 2.64 m, Specialty and industrial
PM 11-14, fourdrinier, total capacity 10,000 mt/y, Trim width 2.4 m, Specialty and industrial
PM 15-20, fourdrinier, total capacity 22,000 mt/y, Trim width 2.64 m, Specialty and industrial
PM 4-7, fourdrinier, total capacity 9,000 mt/y, Trim width 1.76 m, Specialty and industrial
PM 8-9, fourdrinier, total capacity 8,000 mt/y, Trim width 1.88 m, Specialty and industrial

ⓞⓜShandong Qifeng New Material Co., Ltd.
Zibo Mill
22, Zhutai Rd., Zhutai Town, Linzi
Zibo, Shandong, 255432
China
Phone: (86) 533 778 0161/0179
Fax: (86) 533 778 8998
Email: qifeng@qifeng.cn
Web Address: www.qifeng.cn
Personnel:
Pres.: Xuefeng Li
Total Employees of Company: 1,200
Type of Operation: Paper mill
Paper/Paperboard Grades and Capacities:
Total paper and paperboard capacity: 270,000 mt/y
Specialty and industrial: 270,000 mt/y
Paper and Paperboard Mill Data:
Paper Machines: 15
No. 1, total capacity 8,000 mt/y, Trim width 1.26 m, Specialty and industrial
No. 2, total capacity 8,000 mt/y, Trim width 1.26 m, Specialty and industrial
No. 3, total capacity 8,000 mt/y, Trim width 1.26 m, Specialty and industrial
No. 4, total capacity 8,000 mt/y, Trim width 1.36 m, Specialty and industrial
No. 5, total capacity 8,000 mt/y, Trim width 1.58 m
No. 6, total capacity 8,000 mt/y, Trim width 1.76 m, Specialty and industrial
No. 7, total capacity 8,000 mt/y, Trim width 1.76 m, Specialty and industrial
No. 8, total capacity 8,000 mt/y, Trim width 1.76 m, Specialty and industrial
No. 9, total capacity 20,000 mt/y, Trim width 2.64 m, Specialty and industrial
No. 10, total capacity 20,000 mt/y, Trim width 2.64 m, Specialty and industrial
No. 11, total capacity 20,000 mt/y, Trim width 2.64 m, Specialty and industrial
No. 12, total capacity 20,000 mt/y, Specialty and industrial
No. 13, total capacity 11,000 mt/y, Trim width 2.83 m, Specialty and industrial
No. 14, total capacity 15,000 mt/y, Trim width 3.75 m, Specialty and industrial
No. 15, total capacity 50,000 mt/y, Trim width 2.64 m, Specialty and industrial
Energy Data:
Power boilers: 2

ⓜShandong Qingdao Haiwang Paper Property Share Co., Ltd.
Ownership: 100% by state
No. 342, Haiwang Rd., Jiaonan District
Qingdao City, Shandong, 266400
China
Phone: (86) 532 8611 8663/8806 3075/8806 3050
Fax: (86) 532 8611 8509/ 7100/ 8585
Email: haiwangxs@haiwangpaper.com, haiwang@public.qd.sd.cn, haiwang@haiwangpaper.com
Web Address: www.haiwangpaper.com
Personnel:
Chmn.: Yuxi Leng
Pres./Mill Mgr.: Baohong Chen
VP, Sls. & Mktg. Mgr.: Kexiang Xu
Tech. Dir., /Chief Eng.: Guilan Zhang
Purch. Mgr.: Zengkui Yue
Total Employees of Company: 1,600
Mill Locations:
Shandong Qingdao Haiwang Paper Property Share Co., Ltd., Qingdao Mill, No. 342, Haiwang Rd., Jiaonan District, Qingdao 266400, China, Capacity: 152,725 mt/y, (Pulp mill, Paper mill, Paperboard mill)
Phone: (86) 532 8617 1652/8611 8663/7470/8597
Fax: (86) 532 8611 8509/7100/8585/5522
Email: haiwangxs@haiwangpaper.com, haiwang@public.qd.sd.cn, haiwang@haiwangpaper.com

ⓜShandong Qingdao Haiwang Paper Property Share Co., Ltd.
Qingdao Mill
No. 342, Haiwang Rd., Jiaonan District
Qingdao, Shandong, 266400
China
Phone: (86) 532 8617 1652/8611 8663/7470/8597
Fax: (86) 532 8611 8509/7100/8585/5522
Email: haiwangxs@haiwangpaper.com, haiwang@public.qd.sd.cn, haiwang@haiwangpaper.com
Web Address: www.haiwangpaper.com
Personnel:
Chmn.: Yuxi Leng
Phone: (86) 532 8611 8663/8806 3075/8806 3050
Pres./Mill Mgr.: Baohong Chen
Phone: (86) 532 8611 8663/8806 3075/8806 3050
VP, Sls. & Mktg. Mgr.: Kexiang Xu
Phone: (86) 532 8611 8663/8806 3075/8806 3050
Tech. Dir., /Chief Eng.: Guilan Zhang
Phone: (86) 532 8611 8663/8806 3075/8806 3050
Purch. Mgr.: Zengkui Yue
Phone: (86) 532 8611 8663/8806 3075/8806 3050
Total Employees at this Location: 1,600
Type of Operation: Pulp mill, Paper mill, Paperboard mill
Pulp Grades and Capacities:
Total pulp capacity: 139,441 mt/y
Recycled Pulping: 139,441 mt/y
Pulp Mill Data:
Pulp Lines: 2
Paper/Paperboard Grades and Capacities:
Total paper and paperboard capacity: 152,725 mt/y
Uncoated woodfree/freesheet: 4,284 mt/y
Packaging papers: 23,491 mt/y
Specialty and industrial: 1,071 mt/y
Linerboard: 103,887 mt/y
Boxboard/cartonboard: 19,992 mt/y
Paper and Paperboard Mill Data:
Paper Machines: 7
No. 1, fourdrinier, total capacity 3,499 mt/y, Trim width 1.58 m, Packaging papers
No. 2, cylinder, total capacity 1,071 mt/y, Trim width 1.6 m, Specialty and industrial
No. 3, fourdrinier, total capacity 19,992 mt/y, Trim width 1.76 m, Boxboard/cartonboard
No. 4, fourdrinier, total capacity 2,856 mt/y, Trim width 1.88 m, Uncoated woodfree/freesheet
No. 5, fourdrinier, total capacity 1,428 mt/y, Trim width 1.88 m, Uncoated woodfree/freesheet
No. 6, fourdrinier (3), total capacity 103,887 mt/y, Trim width 3.2 m, Linerboard
No. 7, fourdrinier, total capacity 19,992 mt/y, Trim width 3.6 m, Packaging papers
Energy Data:
Power boilers: 4
Steam turbines: 2 at 12, 6 MW
Electrical demand for mill: 255 MWh/D

ⓜShandong Qingdao Paper Mill
Qingdao Mill
No. 245 Siliu South Rd.
Qingdao, Shandong, 266042
China
Phone: (86) 532 8486 3637
Fax: (86) 532 8485 0745
Personnel:
Gen. Mgr.: Minhang Wang
Phone: (86) 532 8486 3637
Dpty. Mgr.: Shihuan Liu
Phone: (86) 532 8486 3637
Dpty. Mgr.: Sihui Yi
Phone: (86) 532 8486 3637
Dpty. Mgr.: Gende Sun
Phone: (86) 532 8486 3637
Chief Accountant: Hanlin Zhu
Phone: (86) 532 8486 3637
Maint. Mgr.: Jianting Du
Phone: (86) 532 8486 3637
Env. Dir.: Yue Wang
Phone: (86) 532 8486 3637
Conv. Plant Mgr.: Xinguang Han
Phone: (86) 532 8486 3637
Total Employees at this Location: 767
Type of Operation: Paper mill
Paper/Paperboard Grades and Capacities:
Total paper and paperboard capacity: 20,000 mt/y
Specialty and industrial: 20,000 mt/y
Paper and Paperboard Mill Data:
Stock Preparation:
Pulpers: 4
Refiners: 12
Paper Machines: 4
PM 1, fourdrinier, total capacity 3,000 mt/y, Trim width 1.76 m, Specialty and industrial
PM 2, fourdrinier, total capacity 2,000 mt/y, Trim width 1.88 m, Specialty and industrial
PM 3, fourdrinier, total capacity 12,000 mt/y, Trim width 2.63 m, Specialty and industrial
PM 4, fourdrinier, total capacity 3,000 mt/y, Trim width 1.88 m, Specialty and industrial
Finishing Equipment:
Rewinders: 2
Sheeters: 6
Energy Data:
Power boilers: 2

China

ⓂShandong Qingzhou Dongxin Paper Co., Ltd.
Qingzhou Mill
No. 2229, North Qingzhou Road
Qingzhou, Shandong, 262500
China
Phone: (86) 536 3283895/536 328 3868/4026
Fax: (86) 536 328 3869/3867
Total Employees at this Location: 400
Type of Operation: Paper mill
Paper/Paperboard Grades and Capacities:
Total paper and paperboard capacity: 100,000 mt/y
Specialty and industrial: 100,000 mt/y
Paper and Paperboard Mill Data:
Paper Machines: 10
PM 6, (second-hand), fourdrinier, total capacity 25,000 mt/y, Trim width 4.3 m, Specialty and industrial
PM 1-5, fourdrinier, total capacity 8,333 mt/y, Trim width 1.88 m, Specialty and industrial
PM 7-10, fourdrinier, total capacity 8,333 mt/y, Trim width 1.88 m, Specialty and industrial

ⓂShandong Qingzhou Dongyang Paper Co., Ltd.
Dongyanghe Industrial Park, Dongba Town, Qingzhou
Weifang, Shandong, 262517
China
Phone: (86) 536 3538 128
Mill Locations:
Shandong Qingzhou Dongyang Paper Co., Ltd., Weifang Mill, Dongyanghe Industrial Park, Dongba Town, Qingzhou, Weifang 262517, China, Capacity: 3,600 mt/y, (Paper mill)
Phone: (86) 536 3538 128

ⓂShandong Qingzhou Dongyang Paper Co., Ltd.
Weifang Mill
Dongyanghe Industrial Park, Dongba Town, Qingzhou
Weifang, Shandong, 262517
China
Phone: (86) 536 3538 128
Type of Operation: Paper mill
Paper/Paperboard Grades and Capacities:
Total paper and paperboard capacity: 3,600 mt/y
Tissue: 3,600 mt/y
Paper and Paperboard Mill Data:
Paper Machines: 3
PM 1-3, total capacity 1,200 mt/y, Trim width 1.88 m, Tissue

ⓂShandong Qinshi Group
Ownership: 100% by shareholders
Changjie Rd., TaiErzhuang District
Zaozhuang, Shandong, 277400
China
Phone: (86) 632 6688 111/ 000
Fax: (86) 632 6699 666/ 999
Email: qsjt@qsjt.com.cn
Web Address: www.qsjt.com.cn
Personnel:
Chmn.: Qiwen Dong
Phone: (86) 632 6688 111/ 000
Fax: (86) 632 6699 666/ 999
Total Employees of Company: 3,000
Mill Locations:
Shandong Qinshi Group Co., Ltd., Zaozhuang Mill, No. 1 Wantong Rd., TaiErzhuang District, Zaozhuang 277400, China, Capacity: 30,000 mt/y, (Paperboard mill)
Phone: (86) 632 6699 888/ 6688 111
Fax: (86) 632 6699 666

ⓂShandong Qinshi Group Co., Ltd.
Zaozhuang Mill
Ownership: Shandong Qinshi Group
No. 1 Wantong Rd., TaiErzhuang District
Zaozhuang, Shandong, 277400
China
Phone: (86) 632 6699 888/ 6688 111
Fax: (86) 632 6699 666
Web Address: www.qsjt.com.cn
Personnel:
Chmn.: Qinwen Dong
Phone: (86) 632 6699 888/ 6688 111
Total Employees at this Location: 328
Type of Operation: Paperboard mill
Paper/Paperboard Grades and Capacities:
Total paper and paperboard capacity: 30,000 mt/y
Specialty and industrial: 30,000 mt/y
Paper and Paperboard Mill Data:
Paper Machines: 4
PM 1, fourdrinier, total capacity 11,000 mt/y, Trim width 2.64 m, Specialty and industrial
PM 2, fourdrinier, total capacity 11,000 mt/y, Trim width 2.64 m, Specialty and industrial
PM 3, fourdrinier, total capacity 4,000 mt/y, Trim width 1.58 m, Specialty and industrial
PM 4, fourdrinier, total capacity 4,000 mt/y, Trim width 1.58 m, Specialty and industrial

ⓂShandong Qunxing Paper Holdings Co., Ltd.
Binzhou Mill
Sanlihe, Changsan Town, Zhouping County
Binzhou, Shandong, 256206
China
Phone: (86) 543 485 3668/ 2225
Fax: (86) 543 485 3668
Web Address: www.qxpaper.com
Personnel:
Chmn.: YuGuo Zhu
Phone: (86) 543 485 3668/ 2225
Vice. Chmn.: Moqun Zhu
Phone: (86) 543 485 3668/ 2225
Exec. Dir.: ZhenShui Sun
Phone: (86) 543 485 3668/ 2225
Non-Exec. Dir: RuiFang Sun
Phone: (86) 543 485 3668/ 2225
Non-Exec. Indep. Dir.: WeiZhao
Phone: (86) 543 485 3668/ 2225
Inde. Non-Exec. Dir.: Lu Wang
Phone: (86) 543 485 3668/ 2225
Total Employees at this Location: 2,000
Type of Operation: Paper mill
Paper/Paperboard Grades and Capacities:
Total paper and paperboard capacity: 379,848 mt/y
Uncoated woodfree/freesheet: 49,980 mt/y
Specialty and industrial: 329,868 mt/y
Paper and Paperboard Mill Data:
Paper Machines: 13
No. 1, cylinder, total capacity 9,996 mt/y, Trim width 1.58 m, Specialty and industrial
No. 2, fourdrinier, total capacity 19,992 mt/y, Trim width 2.64 m, Specialty and industrial
No. 3, fourdrinier, total capacity 29,988 mt/y, Trim width 2.64 m, Specialty and industrial
No. 4, fourdrinier, total capacity 49,980 mt/y, Trim width 2.64 m, Uncoated woodfree/freesheet
No. 5, cylinder, total capacity 29,988 mt/y, Trim width 1.58 m, Specialty and industrial
No. 6, cylinder, total capacity 29,988 mt/y, Trim width 1.58 m, Specialty and industrial
No. 7, fourdrinier, total capacity 29,988 mt/y, Trim width 2.64 m, Specialty and industrial
No. 8, cylinder, total capacity 29,988 mt/y, Trim width 1.58 m, Specialty and industrial
No. 9, cylinder, total capacity 29,988 mt/y, Trim width 1.58 m, Specialty and industrial
No. 10, fourdrinier, total capacity 29,988 mt/y, Specialty and industrial
No. 11, fourdrinier, total capacity 29,988 mt/y, Specialty and industrial
No. 12, fourdrinier, total capacity 29,988 mt/y, Trim width 2.64 m, Specialty and industrial
No. 13, fourdrinier, total capacity 29,988 mt/y, Trim width 2.64 m, Specialty and industrial
Energy Data:
Electrical demand for mill: 665 MWh/D

ⓂⓂShandong Renfeng Special Materials Co., Ltd.
Zibo Mill
No.1 Renfeng Rd., Qifeng Town, Huantai County
Zibo, Shandong
China
Phone: (86) 533 869 7688/8158
Fax: (86) 533 869 8159
Web Address: sdrenfeng.com
Total Employees at this Location: 400
Type of Operation: Paperboard mill
Pulp Grades and Capacities:
Total pulp capacity: 161,795 mt/y
Recycled Pulping: 161,795 mt/y
Pulp Mill Data:
Recycled Fiber Treatment Lines:
Recycled packaging pulping lines: 1
Paper/Paperboard Grades and Capacities:
Total paper and paperboard capacity: 167,433 mt/y
Corrugating medium/fluting: 167,433 mt/y
Paper and Paperboard Mill Data:
Paper Machines: 2
No. 1, fourdrinier (2), total capacity 96,033 mt/y, Trim width 3.8 m, Corrugating medium/fluting
No. 2, (started May 2011), fourdrinier, total capacity 71,400 mt/y, Trim width 4.4 m, Corrugating medium/fluting
Energy Data:
Power boilers: 2
Electrical demand for mill: 266 MWh/D

ⓂShandong Rizhao Huatai Paper Co. Ltd.
Rizhao Mill
Ownership: 96% by Shandong Huatai Group Co., Ltd., 4% by Shandong Dawang Fuli Tissue Paper Co., Ltd.
No. 199 Juzhou Rd., Ju County
Rizhao, Shandong, 276500
China
Phone: (86) 633 688 2076
Fax: (86) 633 688 2881
Web Address: www.huatai.com
Personnel:
Chmn. & Pres.: Xiangsheng Piao
Phone: (86) 633 688 2076
Total Employees at this Location: 400
Type of Operation: Pulp mill, Paper mill
Pulp Grades and Capacities:
Total pulp capacity: 50,874 mt/y
Chemical Pulp: 40,700 mt/y
Recycled Pulping: 10,175 mt/y
Pulp Mill Data:
Chemical Pulping Systems:
Batch digesters: 4
Pulp Lines: 1
Bleach Plant Systems: 1
No. 1, Sequence: CEH, Capacity 70,000 admt/y
Chemical Recovery Equipment:
Recovery boilers: 1
Paper/Paperboard Grades and Capacities:
Total paper and paperboard capacity: 53,570 mt/y
Tissue: 3,570 mt/y
Packaging papers: 50,000 mt/y
Paper and Paperboard Mill Data:
Stock Preparation:
Pulpers: 30
Refiners: 10
Paper Machines: 3
No. 1, fourdrinier, total capacity 15,000 mt/y, Trim width 1.76 m, Packaging papers
No. 2, fourdrinier, total capacity 35,000 mt/y, Trim width 2.64 m, Packaging papers
No. 6, cylinder, total capacity 3,570 mt/y, Trim width 1.58 m, Tissue
Coating Machines: 1
No. 1-2, total capacity 20,000 mt/y., off machine
Finishing Equipment:

Supercalenders: 4
Rewinders: 5
Sheeters: 8
Energy Data:
Power boilers: 2
Steam turbines: 2 at 15, 6 MW
Electrical demand for mill: 144 MWh/D

Ⓜ Shandong Rongcheng Haisheng Paper Co., Ltd.
Haodangjia Industrial Park, Rongcheng
Weihai, Shandong, 264305
China
  Phone: (86) 631 7438 223/232
  Web Address: www.homely.com.cn/cn/Newshow.asp?id=1324
Total Employees at this Location: 450
Mill Locations:
  Shandong Rongcheng Haisheng Paper Co., Ltd., Weihai Mill, Haodangjia Industrial Park, Rongcheng, Weihai 264305, China, Capacity: 210,000 mt/y, (Paper mill)
  Phone: (86) 631 7438 223/232

Ⓜ Shandong Rongcheng Haisheng Paper Co., Ltd.
Weihai Mill
Haodangjia Industrial Park, Rongcheng
Weihai, Shandong, 264305
China
  Phone: (86) 631 7438 223/232
  Web Address: www.homely.com.cn/cn/Newshow.asp?id=1324
Total Employees at this Location: 450
Type of Operation: Paper mill
Pulp Grades and Capacities:
  Total pulp capacity: 202,085 mt/y
  Recycled Pulping: 202,085 mt/y
Paper/Paperboard Grades and Capacities:
  Total paper and paperboard capacity: 210,000 mt/y
  Linerboard: 180,000 mt/y
  Corrugating medium/fluting: 30,000 mt/y
Paper and Paperboard Mill Data:
Paper Machines: 2
No. 1, Multi-wire (4), total capacity 180,000 mt/y, Trim width 4.45 m, Linerboard
No. 2, fourdrinier, total capacity 30,000 mt/y, Trim width 3.2 m, Corrugating medium/fluting
Energy Data:
Electrical demand for mill: 264 MWh/D

Ⓜ Shandong Ronghua Paper Co., Ltd.
Zaozhuang Mill
East of Changan Rd., Taierzhuang District
Zaozhuang, Shandong, 277400
China
  Phone: (86) 632 5130 106
  Fax: (86) 632 5130 972/982/973
  Web Address: ronghuapaper.com
Type of Operation: Paper mill
Pulp Grades and Capacities:
  Total pulp capacity: 173,427 mt/y
  Recycled Pulping: 173,427 mt/y
Paper/Paperboard Grades and Capacities:
  Total paper and paperboard capacity: 200,000 mt/y
  Boxboard/cartonboard: 200,000 mt/y
Paper and Paperboard Mill Data:
Paper Machines: 1
No. 1, Fourdrinier (5), total capacity 200,000 mt/y, Trim width 3.6 m, Boxboard/cartonboard
Energy Data:
Electrical demand for mill: 266 MWh/D

Ⓜ Shandong Shengquan Paper Co., Ltd.
Zibo Mill
North of Xiaodong Village, Zhaili Town, Zichuan District
Zibo, Shandong, 255150
China
  Phone: (86) 533 5615 399

Total Employees at this Location: 60
Type of Operation: Paper mill
Paper/Paperboard Grades and Capacities:
  Total paper and paperboard capacity: 30,000 mt/y
  Specialty and industrial: 30,000 mt/y
Paper and Paperboard Mill Data:
Paper Machines: 5
PM 1, fourdrinier, total capacity 800 mt/y, Trim width 1.6 m, Specialty and industrial
PM 2, fourdrinier, total capacity 800 mt/y, Trim width 1.76 m, Specialty and industrial
PM 3, fourdrinier, total capacity 700 mt/y, Trim width 1.88 m, Specialty and industrial
PM 4, fourdrinier, total capacity 700 mt/y, Trim width 1.88 m, Specialty and industrial
PM 5, total capacity 27,000 mt/y, Trim width 3.2 m, Specialty and industrial
Energy Data:
Power boilers: 1

Ⓜ Shandong Shouguang Liben Papermaking
Shouguang (Shandong Shouguang Liben Papermaking) Mill
Mill is for sale (from September 2011. Shandong Chenming to sell its stake)
Ownership: 100% by Chenming Paper Holdings Ltd.
No. 595 Shengcheng Rd.
Shouguang, Shandong, 262700
China
  Phone: (86) 536 522 2151/528 0033
  Fax: (86) 536 522 1843/523 4234
  Email: staff2@public.wfptt.sd.cn
Personnel:
  Gen. Mgr.: Ying Tong Yuan
  Phone: (86) 536 522 2151/528 0033
Total Employees at this Location: 200
Type of Operation: Paper mill
Paper/Paperboard Grades and Capacities:
  Total paper and paperboard capacity: 13,000 mt/y
  Uncoated woodfree/freesheet: 13,000 mt/y
Paper and Paperboard Mill Data:
Paper Machines: 4
No. 1, fourdrinier, Uncoated woodfree/freesheet
No. 9, fourdrinier, Uncoated woodfree/freesheet
No. 3, Uncoated woodfree/freesheet
No. 4, cylinder, Uncoated woodfree/freesheet

Ⓜ Shandong Stora Enso Huatai Paper
Dawang Mill
Ownership: 60% by Shanghai Stora Enso Asia Pacific, 40% by Shandong Huatai Group Co., Ltd.
Weigao Rd., Huatai Industrial Park, Dawang Township, Guangrao County
Dongying, Shandong, 257335
China
  Phone: (86) 546 7797 200/243
  Fax: (86) 546 7797 220
  Web Address: www.storaenso.com, www.huatai.com
Personnel:
  Dir. & Gen. Mgr.: Tao Gang
  Phone: (86) 546 7797 200/243
  Winder Supervisor: Bin Li
  Phone: (86) 546 7797 200/243
Total Employees at this Location: 245
Type of Operation: Pulp mill, Paper mill
Pulp Grades and Capacities:
  Total pulp capacity: 132,626 mt/y
  Recycled Pulping: 132,626 mt/y
Pulp Mill Data:
Pulp Lines: 1
Bleach Plant Systems: 1
DIP, Sequence: P, Capacity 178,000 admt/y
Recycled Fiber Treatment Lines:
Flotation deinking lines: 1 at 178,000 admt/y
Paper/Paperboard Grades and Capacities:
  Total paper and paperboard capacity: 170,000 mt/y

Uncoated mechanical/groundwood: 170,000 mt/y
Paper and Paperboard Mill Data:
Paper Machines: 1
No. 1, hybrid former, total capacity 170,000 mt/y, Trim width 6.84 m, Uncoated mechanical/groundwood
Finishing Equipment:
Supercalenders: 1 at 170,000 mt/y
Energy Data:
Electrical demand for mill: 429 MWh/D

Ⓜ Shandong Sun Paper Industry Joint Stock Co., Ltd.
Yanzhou Mill
No. 1 Youyi Road
Yanzhou, Shandong, 272100
China
  Phone: (86) 537 792 5888 / 792 8711 / 792 8710 / 792 8713
  Fax: (86) 537 792 8489
  Email: taiyangzhiye@163.com, taiyang@sunpapergroup.com
  Web Address: www.sunpapergroup.com
Personnel:
  Chmn., Pres. & CEO: Hongxin Li
  Phone: (86) 537 365 1888/8711/3369/8598/8911
  Fax: (86) 537 365 1777/8600/8386/3633489
  Vice Chmn., Dpty. Gen. Mgr.: Maolin Bai
  Phone: (86) 537 365 1888/8711/3369/8598/8911
  Fax: (86) 537 365 1777/8600/8386/3633489
  CFO: Ms. Yimei Niu
  Phone: (86) 537 365 1888/8711/3369/8598/8911
  Fax: (86) 537 365 1777/8600/8386/3633489
  Gen. Mgr.: Kevin Liu
  Phone: (86) 537 365 1888/8711/3369/8598/8911
  Fax: (86) 537 365 1777/8600/8386/3633489
  Dpty. Gen. Mgr., Chief Eng.: Guangdong Ying
  Phone: (86) 139 0537 5808
  Dety. Gen. Mgr., Board Sec.: Zhaojun Chen
  Phone: (86) 537 365 8715
  Fax: (86) 537 365 8762
  Email: sunpaperhzg@163.com
  Dpty. Gen. Mgr.: Zehua Liu
  Phone: (86) 537 365 1888/8711/3369/8598/8911
  Fax: (86) 537 365 1777/8600/8386/3633489
  Dpty. Gen. Mgr.: Jifei Li
  Phone: (86) 537 365 1888/8711/3369/8598/8911
  Fax: (86) 537 365 1777/8600/8386/3633489
  Dpty. Gen. Mgr.: Bingfen Su
  Phone: (86) 537 365 1888/8711/3369/8598/8911
  Fax: (86) 537 365 1777/8600/8386/3633489
  Dpty. Gen. Mgr.: Wenjun Chen
  Phone: (86) 537 365 1888/8711/3369/8598/8911
  Fax: (86) 537 365 1777/8600/8386/3633489
  Chief Economist: Zongliang Wang
  Phone: (86) 537 365 1888/8711/3369/8598/8911
  Fax: (86) 537 365 1777/8600/8386/3633489
  Export Mgr.: David Sun
  Phone: (86) 537 7925538
  Email: david@sunpaper.cn
Total Employees of Company: 6,105
Type of Operation: Pulp mill, Paper mill, Paperboard mill
Pulp Grades and Capacities:
  Total pulp capacity: 683,566 mt/y
  Pulp available for market: 50,000 mt/y
  Chemical Pulp: 348,391 mt/y
  Mechanical Pulp: 335,176 mt/y
Pulp Mill Data:
Chemical Pulping Systems:
Batch digesters: 1
Continuous digesters: 1
Mechanical Pulping Systems:
APMP Systems: 1
APMP Systems: 1
APMP Systems: 1
Pulp Lines: 7
Bleach Plant Systems: 2
No. 1, Sequence: DEopD, Capacity 200,000 admt/y
No. 2, Sequence: HP, Capacity 50,000 admt/y

China

Chemical Recovery Equipment:
Recovery boilers: 3
Recycled Fiber Treatment Lines:
Flotation deinking lines: 1
Recycled packaging pulping lines: 1
Pulp Dryers:
Twin Wire
Paper/Paperboard Grades and Capacities:
Total paper and paperboard capacity: 1,729,000 mt/y
Uncoated woodfree/freesheet: 669,000 mt/y
Coated woodfree/freesheet: 700,000 mt/y
Tissue: 60,000 mt/y
Boxboard/cartonboard: 300,000 mt/y
Paper and Paperboard Mill Data:
Stock Preparation:
Pulpers: 11
Refiners: 85
Paper Machines: 15
No. 2, fourdrinier, total capacity 10,000 mt/y, Trim width 1.76 m, Uncoated woodfree/freesheet
No. 3, fourdrinier, total capacity 15,000 mt/y, Trim width 1.88 m, Uncoated woodfree/freesheet
No. 6, fourdrinier, total capacity 9,000 mt/y, Trim width 1.76 m, Uncoated woodfree/freesheet
No. 7, fourdrinier, total capacity 8,000 mt/y, Trim width 1.76 m, Uncoated woodfree/freesheet
No. 8, fourdrinier, total capacity 15,000 mt/y, Trim width 1.88 m, Uncoated woodfree/freesheet
No. 9, fourdrinier, total capacity 7,000 mt/y, Trim width 1.58 m, Uncoated woodfree/freesheet
No. 11, fourdrinier, total capacity 6,000 mt/y, Trim width 2.36 m, Uncoated woodfree/freesheet
No. 12, fourdrinier, total capacity 9,000 mt/y, Trim width 2.8 m, Uncoated woodfree/freesheet
No. 15, Fourdrinier (4), total capacity 150,000 mt/y, Trim width 3.4 m, Boxboard/cartonboard
No. 16, fourdrinier (3), total capacity 150,000 mt/y, Trim width 3.52 m, Boxboard/cartonboard
No. 19, SymFormer MB, total capacity 300,000 mt/y, Trim width 4.95 m, Coated woodfree/freesheet
No. 21, GapFormer, total capacity 240,000 mt/y, Trim width 4.98 m, Uncoated woodfree/freesheet, Coated woodfree/freesheet
No. 23, GapFormer, total capacity 350,000 mt/y, Trim width 7.25 m, Uncoated woodfree/freesheet
No. 24, GapFormer, total capacity 400,000 mt/y, Trim width 7.28 m, Uncoated woodfree/freesheet, Coated woodfree/freesheet
No. 27, crescent former, total capacity 60,000 mt/y, Trim width 5.62 m, Tissue, Uncoated woodfree/freesheet
Coating Machines: 5
CM 1, total capacity 75,000 mt/y., on machine
CM 2, total capacity 40,000 mt/y., on machine
CM 3, total capacity 75,000 mt/y., off machine
CM 4, total capacity 60,000 mt/y., off machine
CM 20, total capacity 320,000 mt/y., off machine
Finishing Equipment:
Calenders: 1
Supercalenders: 20
Rewinders: 27
Sheeters: 21
Energy Data:
Power boilers: 10
Steam turbines: 9 at 12, 12, 12, 30, 30, 30, 135, 6, 15 MW
Electrical demand for mill: 5,196 MWh/D

ⓜShandong Taian Baichuan Paper Co., Ltd.
Taian Mill
Xiaoxie Town Industry
Taian, Shandong, 271221
China
Phone: (86) 538 786 6450/ 6147/ 6419
Fax: (86) 538 783 4952
Web Address: www.tabczy.com
Personnel:
Chmn.: Qingyuan Lang
Phone: (86) 538 786 6450/ 6147/ 6419
Gen. Mgr.: Qiming Dong

Phone: (86) 538 786 6450/ 6147/ 6419
Total Employees at this Location: 600
Type of Operation: Paper mill
Pulp Grades and Capacities:
Total pulp capacity: 70,379 mt/y
Recycled Pulping: 70,379 mt/y
Paper/Paperboard Grades and Capacities:
Total paper and paperboard capacity: 120,000 mt/y
Uncoated mechanical/groundwood: 36,000 mt/y
Specialty and industrial: 14,000 mt/y
Linerboard: 10,000 mt/y
Boxboard/cartonboard: 60,000 mt/y
Paper and Paperboard Mill Data:
Paper Machines: 7
No. 1, fourdrinier, total capacity 10,000 mt/y, Trim width 1.76 m, Linerboard
No. 2, fourdrinier, total capacity 10,000 mt/y, Trim width 1.88 m, Specialty and industrial, Uncoated mechanical/groundwood
No. 3, fourdrinier, total capacity 10,000 mt/y, Trim width 2.4 m, Specialty and industrial, Uncoated mechanical/groundwood
No. 4, fourdrinier, total capacity 30,000 mt/y, Trim width 2.64 m, Uncoated mechanical/groundwood
No. 5, fourdrinier, total capacity 20,000 mt/y, Trim width 1.88 m, Boxboard/cartonboard
No. 6, fourdrinier, total capacity 20,000 mt/y, Trim width 1.88 m, Boxboard/cartonboard
No. 7, fourdrinier, total capacity 20,000 mt/y, Trim width 1.88 m, Boxboard/cartonboard
Energy Data:
Electrical demand for mill: 194 MWh/D

ⓜShandong Taiding Material Technology Co., Ltd.
Zhengda Industrial Zone, Wanggaopu Town, Pingyuan County
Dezhou, Shandong, 253105
China
Phone: (86) 534 2162 333/456 2766/2044
Fax: (86) 534 2168 968/4561 258/2162 333
Email: zd4562766@163.com
Web Address: www.tdxcl.com
Personnel:
Chmn. & Pres./Mill Mgr.: Lianshui Wang
Phone: (86) 534 456 2766/2044
Fax: (86) 534 456 2044/1258
Total Employees of Company: 1,200
Mill Locations:
Shandong Taiding Material Technology Co., Ltd., Dezhou Mill, Zhengda Industrial Zone, Wanggaopu Town, Pingyuan County, Dezhou 253105, China, Capacity: 124,000 mt/y, (Pulp mill, Paper mill)
Phone: (86) 534 456 2766/2044/2162 333
Fax: (86) 534 456 2044/1258/2168 968
Email: zd4562766@163.com

ⓜShandong Taiding Material Technology Co., Ltd.
Dezhou Mill
Zhengda Industrial Zone, Wanggaopu Town, Pingyuan County
Dezhou, Shandong, 253105
China
Phone: (86) 534 456 2766/2044/2162 333
Fax: (86) 534 456 2044/1258/2168 968
Email: zd4562766@163.com
Web Address: www.tdxcl.com
Personnel:
Chmn. & Pres./Mill Mgr.: Lianshui Wang
Phone: (86) 534 456 2044/ 2766/ 2042
Total Employees at this Location: 800
Type of Operation: Pulp mill, Paper mill
Pulp Grades and Capacities:
Total pulp capacity: 75,138 mt/y
Mechanical Pulp: 20,030 mt/y
Recycled Pulping: 55,108 mt/y
Pulp Mill Data:
Mechanical Pulping Systems:

BCTMP systems: 1
Pulp Lines: 2
Bleach Plant Systems: 2
DIP
Mechanical Pulping System, Type: BCTMP, Sequence: P
Recycled Fiber Treatment Lines:
Flotation deinking lines: 1 at 80,000 admt/y
Paper/Paperboard Grades and Capacities:
Total paper and paperboard capacity: 124,000 mt/y
Newsprint: 35,000 mt/y
Uncoated mechanical/groundwood: 48,000 mt/y
Packaging papers: 25,000 mt/y
Specialty and industrial: 16,000 mt/y
Paper and Paperboard Mill Data:
Paper Machines: 8
No. 1, fourdrinier, total capacity 35,000 mt/y, Trim width 3.3 m, Newsprint
No. 2, fourdrinier, total capacity 25,000 mt/y, Trim width 2.4 m, Packaging papers
No. 3, fourdrinier, total capacity 15,000 mt/y, Trim width 1.76 m, Uncoated mechanical/groundwood
No. 4, fourdrinier, total capacity 8,000 mt/y, Trim width 1.88 m, Uncoated mechanical/groundwood
No. 5, fourdrinier, total capacity 6,000 mt/y, Trim width 1.88 m, Specialty and industrial
No. 6, fourdrinier, total capacity 5,000 mt/y, Trim width 1.76 m, Specialty and industrial
No. 7, fourdrinier, total capacity 5,000 mt/y, Trim width 1.76 m, Specialty and industrial
No. 8, fourdrinier, total capacity 25,000 mt/y, Trim width 2.64 m, Uncoated mechanical/groundwood
Energy Data:
Power boilers
Steam turbines: 1 at 9 MW
Electrical demand for mill: 379 MWh/D

ⓜShandong Texpack Paper Co., Ltd.
Dezhou Mill
Wangfenglou Town, Pingyuan County
Dezhou, Shandong, 253109
China
Phone: (86) 534 7881 888/ 135 8345 2616
Fax: (86) 534 7881 699
Web Address: www.papertech.com
Personnel:
Gen. Mgr.: Yong Zhong
Phone: (86) 534 7881 888/ 135 8345 2616
Total Employees at this Location: 200
Type of Operation: Paper mill
Pulp Grades and Capacities:
Total pulp capacity: 102,359 mt/y
Recycled Pulping: 102,359 mt/y
Pulp Mill Data:
Pulp Lines: 1
Paper/Paperboard Grades and Capacities:
Total paper and paperboard capacity: 100,317 mt/y
Boxboard/cartonboard: 100,317 mt/y
Paper and Paperboard Mill Data:
Paper Machines: 1
No. 1, Multi-wire (4), total capacity 100,317 mt/y, Trim width 3.6 m, Boxboard/cartonboard
Energy Data:
Power boilers: 2
Electrical demand for mill: 153 MWh/D

ⓜShandong Tiandiyuan Industry Co., Ltd.
Weiqiao Industrial Park, Zoucheng
Binzhou, Shandong
China
Phone: (86) 543 4737 999
Fax: (86) 543 4732 777
Email: tiandiyuanshiye@163.com
Web Address: www.tiandiyuanshiye.com
Total Employees at this Location: 680
Mill Locations:
Shandong Tiandiyuan Industry Co., Ltd., Binzhou Mill, Weiqiao Industrial Park, Zoucheng, Binzhou, China, Capacity: 215,000 mt/y, (Paper mill)

China

Phone: (86) 543 4737 999
Fax: (86) 543 4732 777
Email: tiandiyuanshiye@163.com

ⓜShandong Tiandiyuan Industry Co., Ltd.
Binzhou Mill
Weiqiao Industrial Park, Zoucheng
Binzhou, Shandong
China
Phone: (86) 543 4737 999
Fax: (86) 543 4732 777
Email: tiandiyuanshiye@163.com
Web Address: www.tiandiyuanshiye.com
Total Employees at this Location: 680
Type of Operation: Paper mill
Pulp Grades and Capacities:
Total pulp capacity: 216,105 mt/y
Recycled Pulping: 216,105 mt/y
Pulp Mill Data:
Recycled Fiber Treatment Lines:
Recycled packaging pulping lines: 1 at 216,100
Paper/Paperboard Grades and Capacities:
Total paper and paperboard capacity: 215,000 mt/y
Tissue
Corrugating medium/fluting: 215,000 mt/y
Paper and Paperboard Mill Data:
Paper Machines: 8
No. 1, fourdrinier, total capacity 50,000 mt/y, Trim width 3.6 m, Corrugating medium/fluting
No. 2, fourdrinier, total capacity 40,000 mt/y, Trim width 3.1 m, Corrugating medium/fluting
No. 3, fourdrinier, total capacity 25,000 mt/y, Trim width 2.88 m, Corrugating medium/fluting
No. 4, fourdrinier, total capacity 100,000 mt/y, Trim width 4.8 m, Corrugating medium/fluting
No. 5, cylinder, total capacity 2,499 mt/y, Trim width 2.9 m, Tissue, Uncoated woodfree/freesheet
No. 6, cylinder, total capacity 2,499 mt/y, Trim width 2.9 m, Tissue, Uncoated woodfree/freesheet
No. 7, cylinder, total capacity 2,499 mt/y, Trim width 2.9 m, Tissue, Uncoated woodfree/freesheet
No. 8, cylinder, total capacity 2,499 mt/y, Trim width 2.9 m, Tissue, Uncoated woodfree/freesheet
Energy Data:
Power boilers: 2
Hydro turbines: 1 at 25 MW
Electrical demand for mill: 262 MWh/D

ⓜShandong Tianhe Paper Co., Ltd.
Ownership: 100% by private owners
West Wenhua Rd., Ningyang County
Taian, Shandong, 271400
China
Phone: (86) 538 562 1942/1781/9671
Fax: (86) 538 562 0235
Email: nylnz@163.com
Web Address: www.sdtianhe.com
Personnel:
Chmn.: Zhenli Xu
Pres.: Zongwei Li
Total Employees at this Location: 1,000
Mill Locations:
Shandong Tianhe Paper Co., Ltd., Taian Mill, West Wenhua Rd., Ningyang County, Taian 271400, China, Capacity: 173,213 mt/y, (Paper mill)
Phone: (86) 538 562 1942/1781/9671
Fax: (86) 538 562 0235
Email: nylnz@163.com

ⓜShandong Tianhe Paper Co., Ltd.
Taian Mill
West Wenhua Rd., Ningyang County
Taian, Shandong, 271400
China
Phone: (86) 538 562 1942/1781/9671
Fax: (86) 538 562 0235
Email: nylnz@163.com
Web Address: www.sdtianhe.com.cn
Personnel:
Chmn.: Zhenli Xu
Phone: (86) 538 562 1942
Gen. Mgr.: Zongwei Li
Phone: (86) 538 562 1781
Total Employees at this Location: 1,000
Type of Operation: Paper mill
Pulp Grades and Capacities:
Total pulp capacity: 31,496 mt/y
Mechanical Pulp: 12,577 mt/y
Recycled Pulping: 18,919 mt/y
Pulp Mill Data:
Mechanical Pulping Systems:
APMP Systems: 1
Pulp Lines: 2
Recycled Fiber Treatment Lines:
Flotation deinking lines: 1 at 50,000
Paper/Paperboard Grades and Capacities:
Total paper and paperboard capacity: 173,213 mt/y
Uncoated woodfree/freesheet: 170,000 mt/y
Tissue: 1,071 mt/y
Specialty and industrial: 2,142 mt/y
Paper and Paperboard Mill Data:
Paper Machines: 7
No. 1, cylinder, total capacity 2,142 mt/y, Trim width 1.09 m, Specialty and industrial
No. 4, cylinder, total capacity 1,071 mt/y, Trim width 1.09 m, Tissue
No. 5, fourdrinier, total capacity 9,000 mt/y, Trim width 1.76 m, Uncoated woodfree/freesheet
No. 6, fourdrinier, total capacity 22,000 mt/y, Trim width 1.76 m, Uncoated woodfree/freesheet
No. 7, fourdrinier, total capacity 29,000 mt/y, Trim width 2.36 m, Uncoated woodfree/freesheet
No. 8, fourdrinier, total capacity 40,000 mt/y, Trim width 2.64 m, Uncoated woodfree/freesheet
No. 9, fourdrinier, total capacity 70,000 mt/y, Trim width 2.64 m, Uncoated woodfree/freesheet
Energy Data:
Power boilers: 4
Electrical demand for mill: 398 MWh/D

ⓜShandong Tianjian Paper Co., Ltd
Zibo Mill
Zhangfu Rd., Zichuan District
Zibo, Shandong, 255100
China
Phone: (86) 533 5183 783
Total Employees at this Location: 300
Type of Operation: Paper mill
Pulp Grades and Capacities:
Total pulp capacity: 81,424 mt/y
Recycled Pulping: 81,424 mt/y
Paper/Paperboard Grades and Capacities:
Total paper and paperboard capacity: 100,500 mt/y
Uncoated mechanical/groundwood: 19,500 mt/y
Linerboard: 6,000 mt/y
Corrugating medium/fluting: 75,000 mt/y
Paper and Paperboard Mill Data:
Paper Machines: 5
No. 1, multi-wire, total capacity 6,000 mt/y, Trim width 1.09 m, Linerboard
No. 2, fourdrinier, total capacity 6,500 mt/y, Trim width 1.76 m, Uncoated mechanical/groundwood
No. 3, fourdrinier, total capacity 6,500 mt/y, Trim width 1.76 m, Uncoated mechanical/groundwood
No. 4, fourdrinier, total capacity 6,500 mt/y, Trim width 1.88 m, Uncoated mechanical/groundwood
No. 5, fourdrinier, total capacity 75,000 mt/y, Trim width 3.52 m, Corrugating medium/fluting
Energy Data:
Power boilers
Electrical demand for mill: 154 MWh/D

ⓞⓜShandong Tranlin Paper Co. Ltd.
Gaotang Mill
Ownership: 100% by shareholders
Beijiao, Guandao Street North Rd., Gaotang County
Liaocheng, Shandong, 252800
China
Phone: (86) 635 396 1106/1873/1055/2214/1711
Fax: (86) 635 396 1597/1501
Email: dinglixing@sohu.com
Web Address: en.tralin.com
Personnel:
Chmn. & Pres./Mill Mgr.: Hongfa Li
Phone: (86) 635 396 1106/1873/1055/2214/1711
VP, Sls.: Fujun Sun
Phone: (86) 635 396 1106/1873/1055/2214/1711
Chief Mktg. Mgr.: Zhongfeng Ma
Phone: (86) 635 396 1106/1873/1055/2214/1711
Paper Mill Mgr.: Jihui Yang
Phone: (86) 635 396 1106/1873/1055/2214/1711
Purch. Agent: Hongxing Huang
Phone: (86) 635 396 1106/1873/1055/2214/1711
Office Dir.: Hua Dong
Phone: (86) 635 396 1106/1873/1055/2214/1711
Total Employees of Company: 12,000
Total Employees at this Location: 2,469
Type of Operation: Pulp mill, Paper mill
Mill Locations:
Shandong Gaotang No. 2 Paper Mill, Liaocheng Mill, Beixin Village, Gaotang County, Liaocheng 252800, China, Capacity: 5,000 mt/y, (Paper mill)
Phone: (86) 635 397 3592
Fax: (86) 635 397 3592
Shandong Tranlin Paper Chiping Co., Ltd., Liaocheng Mill, No. 187, Shunhe Street, Chiping County, Liaocheng 252100, China, Capacity: 45,000 mt/y, (Paper mill)
Phone: (86) 635 425 2171
Fax: (86) 635 425 1996
Shandong Tranlin Paper Xiajin Co., Ltd., Xiajin Mill, No. 45 Jianshe Street, Xiajin County, Dezhou 253200, China, Capacity: 85,323 mt/y, (Paper mill)
Phone: (86) 534 331 2199/ 3381
Fax: (86) 534 331 2139
Pulp Grades and Capacities:
Total pulp capacity: 220,908 mt/y
Other Pulp: 220,908 mt/y
Pulp Mill Data:
Chemical Pulping Systems:
Batch digesters: 1
Mechanical Pulping Systems:
APMP Systems: 1
Pulp Lines: 2
Bleach Plant Lines:
No. 1
Chemical Recovery Equipment:
Evaporator lines
Recovery boilers: 1
Lime Kiln
Paper/Paperboard Grades and Capacities:
Total paper and paperboard capacity: 627,780 mt/y
Uncoated woodfree/freesheet: 435,000 mt/y
Uncoated mechanical/groundwood: 52,800 mt/y
Coated woodfree/freesheet: 80,000 mt/y
Tissue: 59,980 mt/y
Paper and Paperboard Mill Data:
Paper Machines: 33
No. 6, fourdrinier, total capacity 6,000 mt/y, Trim width 1.76 m, Uncoated mechanical/groundwood
No. 7, fourdrinier, total capacity 7,800 mt/y, Trim width 1.76 m, Uncoated mechanical/groundwood
No. 8, fourdrinier, total capacity 7,800 mt/y, Trim width 1.76 m, Uncoated mechanical/groundwood
No. 9, fourdrinier, total capacity 7,800 mt/y, Trim width 1.76 m, Uncoated mechanical/groundwood
No. 10, fourdrinier, total capacity 7,800 mt/y, Trim width 1.76 m, Uncoated mechanical/groundwood
No. 11, fourdrinier, total capacity 7,800 mt/y, Trim width 1.76 m, Uncoated mechanical/groundwood
No. 12, fourdrinier, total capacity 7,800 mt/y, Trim width 1.76 m, Uncoated mechanical/groundwood
No. 20, fourdrinier, total capacity 80,000 mt/y, Trim width 3.8 m, Coated woodfree/freesheet
No. 21, fourdrinier, total capacity 35,000 mt/y, Trim width 2.73 m, Uncoated woodfree/freesheet
No. 22, fourdrinier, total capacity 100,000 mt/y, Trim width 3.7 m, Uncoated woodfree/freesheet

China

No. 23, fourdrinier, total capacity 100,000 mt/y, Trim width 3.75 m, Uncoated woodfree/freesheet
No. 24, fourdrinier, total capacity 200,000 mt/y, Trim width 6.1 m, Uncoated woodfree/freesheet
T1-20, fourdrinier, total capacity 49,980 mt/y, Trim width 2.9 m, Tissue
TM21, total capacity 10,000 mt/y, Trim width 2.8 m, Tissue
Coating Machines: 1
No. 1, total capacity 81,000 mt/y., off machine
Finishing Equipment:
Supercalenders: 6
Rewinders: 18
Sheeters: 22
Energy Data:
Power boilers: 3
Steam turbines: 2 at 24, 24 MW
Electrical demand for mill: 1,504 MWh/D

ⓂShandong Tranlin Paper Chiping Co., Ltd.
Liaocheng Mill
Ownership: 100% by Shandong Tranlin Paper Co. Ltd.
No. 187, Shunhe Street, Chiping County
Liaocheng, Shandong, 252100
China
Phone: (86) 635 425 2171
Fax: (86) 635 425 1996
Web Address: en.tralin.com
Personnel:
Chmn.: Hongfa Li
Phone: (86) 635 425 2171
Total Employees at this Location: 1,000
Type of Operation: Paper mill
Paper/Paperboard Grades and Capacities:
Total paper and paperboard capacity: 45,000 mt/y
Uncoated woodfree/freesheet: 45,000 mt/y
Paper and Paperboard Mill Data:
Paper Machines: 6
No. 1, cylinder, total capacity 7,500 mt/y, Trim width 1.76 m, Uncoated woodfree/freesheet
No. 2, cylinder, total capacity 7,500 mt/y, Trim width 1.76 m, Uncoated woodfree/freesheet
No. 3, cylinder, total capacity 7,500 mt/y, Trim width 1.76 m, Uncoated woodfree/freesheet
No. 4, cylinder, total capacity 7,500 mt/y, Trim width 1.76 m, Uncoated woodfree/freesheet
No. 5, cylinder, total capacity 7,500 mt/y, Trim width 1.76 m, Uncoated woodfree/freesheet
No. 6, cylinder, total capacity 7,500 mt/y, Trim width 1.76 m, Uncoated woodfree/freesheet

ⓂShandong Tranlin Paper Xiajin Co., Ltd.
Xiajin Mill
Ownership: 100% by Shandong Tranlin Paper Co. Ltd.
No. 45 Jianshe Street, Xiajin County
Dezhou, Shandong, 253200
China
Phone: (86) 534 331 2199/ 3381
Fax: (86) 534 331 2139
Web Address: en.tralin.com
Personnel:
Chmn. & Gen. Mgr.: Shanchang Dong
Phone: (86) 534 331 2199/ 3381
Total Employees at this Location: 1,200
Type of Operation: Paper mill
Paper/Paperboard Grades and Capacities:
Total paper and paperboard capacity: 85,323 mt/y
Uncoated woodfree/freesheet: 85,323 mt/y
Paper and Paperboard Mill Data:
Paper Machines: 5
No. 1, fourdrinier, total capacity 7,140 mt/y, Trim width 1.76 m, Uncoated woodfree/freesheet
No. 2, fourdrinier, total capacity 7,140 mt/y, Trim width 1.76 m, Uncoated woodfree/freesheet
No. 3, fourdrinier, total capacity 15,351 mt/y, Trim width 1.76 m, Uncoated woodfree/freesheet
No. 4, fourdrinier, total capacity 15,351 mt/y, Trim width 1.76 m, Uncoated woodfree/freesheet
No. 5, fourdrinier, total capacity 40,341 mt/y, Trim width 2.73 m, Uncoated woodfree/freesheet
Energy Data:
Power boilers: 1
Electrical demand for mill: 167 MWh/D

ⓂShandong Wanhao Paper Group Co., Ltd.
Ownership: 100% by shareholders
32 Industry Street, Linqu County
Weifang, Shandong, 262600
China
Phone: (86) 536 316 3364/ 315 8797
Fax: (86) 536 316 5340/ 315 8568
Email: wanhao@china.com
Web Address: www.wanhao.com
Personnel:
Chmn. & Gen. Mgr.: Jie Chu
Phone: (86) 536 316 3364/ 315 8797
Fax: (86) 536 316 5340/ 315 8568
Total Employees at this Location: 200
Mill Locations:
Shandong Linqu Yulong Paper Co., Ltd., Weifang Mill (51.50% owned), Linqu Economy & Development District, Linqu, Weifang 262600, China, Capacity: 71,700 mt/y, (Paper mill)
Phone: (86) 536 315 8797/ 8862/ 8872
Fax: (86) 536 315 8568
Email: yulong@wanhao.com

ⓂShandong Weifang HengAn Paper Co. Ltd.
Weifang Mill
Ownership: Fujian Hengan International Group
Beihai Rd., Fangzi District
Weifang, Shandong, 261200
China
Phone: (86) 536 776 1889/ 766 6888
Fax: (86) 536 776 1889/ 751 5603
Web Address: www.hengan.com
Personnel:
Chmn.: Wenbo Shi
Phone: (86) 536 776 1889/ 766 6888
Vice Chmn., CEO: Lianjie Xu
Phone: (86) 536 776 1889/ 766 6888
Total Employees at this Location: 600
Type of Operation: Paper mill
Paper/Paperboard Grades and Capacities:
Total paper and paperboard capacity: 189,996 mt/y
Tissue: 189,996 mt/y
Paper and Paperboard Mill Data:
Paper Machines: 5
No. 3, crescent former, total capacity 60,000 mt/y, Trim width 5.55 m, Tissue, Uncoated woodfree/freesheet
No. 5, crescent former, total capacity 60,000 mt/y, Trim width 5.55 m, Tissue, Uncoated woodfree/freesheet
No. 10, Advantage DCT 200 TS, Yankee dryer, total capacity 60,000 mt/y, Trim width 5.6 m, Tissue
T1, total capacity 4,998 mt/y, Trim width 2.8 m, Tissue
T2, total capacity 4,998 mt/y, Trim width 2.8 m, Tissue
Finishing Equipment:
Rewinders: 4
Energy Data:
Power boilers: 2
Steam turbines: 1 at 24 MW
Electrical demand for mill: 504 MWh/D

ⓂShandong Weifang Henglian Art Paper Co., Ltd.
Weifang Mill
Ownership: 100% by Shandong Henglian Paper Group C., Ltd.
No. 409, East Wolong Rd., Kuiwen Industry
Weifang, Shandong, 261031
China
Phone: (86) 536 867 1625/866 9308/866 4564
Fax: (86) 536 866 8708
Web Address: www.henglianpaper.com
Personnel:
Chmn.: Jian Xu
Phone: (86) 536 867 1625/866 9308/866 4564
Total Employees at this Location: 1,000
Type of Operation: Paper mill
Pulp Grades and Capacities:
Total pulp capacity: 32,094 mt/y
Chemical Pulp: 32,094 mt/y
Pulp Mill Data:
Pulp Lines: 2
Chemical Recovery Equipment:
Recovery boilers: 1
Paper/Paperboard Grades and Capacities:
Total paper and paperboard capacity: 100,000 mt/y
Uncoated woodfree/freesheet: 66,000 mt/y
Coated woodfree/freesheet: 7,000 mt/y
Specialty and industrial: 27,000 mt/y
Paper and Paperboard Mill Data:
Paper Machines: 6
No. 1, fourdrinier, total capacity 19,000 mt/y, Trim width 1.8 m, Uncoated woodfree/freesheet
No. 2, fourdrinier, total capacity 20,000 mt/y, Trim width 1.8 m, Uncoated woodfree/freesheet
No. 3, fourdrinier, total capacity 16,000 mt/y, Trim width 1.8 m, Uncoated woodfree/freesheet, Coated woodfree/freesheet, Specialty and industrial
No. 4, fourdrinier, total capacity 25,000 mt/y, Trim width 1.8 m, Uncoated woodfree/freesheet, Coated woodfree/freesheet, Specialty and industrial
No. 5, fourdrinier, total capacity 10,000 mt/y, Trim width 1.76 m, Uncoated woodfree/freesheet
No. 6, fourdrinier, total capacity 10,000 mt/y, Trim width 1.76 m, Uncoated woodfree/freesheet
Coating Machines: 2
CM 1, total capacity 50,000 mt/y., off machine
CM 2, total capacity 50,000 mt/y., off machine
Energy Data:
Power boilers: 2
Steam turbines: 3 at 3 x 7 MW
Electrical demand for mill: 233 MWh/D

ⓂShandong Weifang Henglian Cellophane Co., Ltd.
Weifang Mill
Ownership: Shandong Henglian Paper Group C., Ltd.
No. 409, Wolong East Street, Kuiwen Dist.
Weifang, Shandong, 201031
China
Phone: (86) 536 728 8338
Fax: (86) 536 728 8333
Web Address: www.hlblz.com
Personnel:
Chmn. & Gen. Mgr.: Ruifeng Li
Phone: (86) 536 867 1706
Total Employees at this Location: 600
Type of Operation: Paper mill
Paper/Paperboard Grades and Capacities:
Total paper and paperboard capacity: 6,200 mt/y
Specialty and industrial: 6,200 mt/y
Paper and Paperboard Mill Data:
Paper Machines: 4
PM 1, cylinder, total capacity 1,200 mt/y, Trim width 1.6 m, Specialty and industrial
PM 4, cylinder, total capacity 2,000 mt/y, Trim width 1.8 m, Specialty and industrial
PM 2-3, cylinder, total capacity 1,500 mt/y, Trim width 1.8 m, Specialty and industrial
Coating Machines: 1
CM 1, total capacity 3,000 mt/y., off machine
Energy Data:
Power boilers: 3
Steam turbines: 3 at 3, 6, 12 MW

ⓂShandong Weifang Henglian Meilin Life-Uses Paper Limited Co.
Weifang Mill
Ownership: 70% by Shandong Henglian Paper Group C., Ltd., 30% by Accel Products Limited, Hong Kong

China

601 Longhai Road, Hanting District
Weifang, Shandong, 261041
China
  Phone: (86) 536 7283228
  Fax: (86) 536 7283229
  Web Address: www.lancelhp.com
Personnel:
  Chmn.: Ruifeng Li
  Phone: (86) 536 7283228
  Gen. Mgr.: Jun Chen
  Phone: (86) 536 7283228
Total Employees at this Location: 210
Type of Operation: Paper mill
Paper/Paperboard Grades and Capacities:
  Total paper and paperboard capacity: 40,000 mt/y
  Tissue: 40,000 mt/y
Paper and Paperboard Mill Data:
Paper Machines: 3
No. 1, BF-10, total capacity 10,000 mt/y, Trim width 2.38 m, Tissue, Uncoated woodfree/freesheet
No. 2, total capacity 12,000 mt/y, Trim width 2.1 m, Tissue, Uncoated woodfree/freesheet
No. 3, total capacity 18,000 mt/y, Trim width 3.34 m, Tissue, Uncoated woodfree/freesheet
Energy Data:
Power boilers
Electrical demand for mill: 71 MWh/D

ⓂShandong Weifang Henglian Pulp & Paper Co., Ltd.
Weifang Mill
Ownership: Shandong Henglian Paper Group C., Ltd.
No. 601 Hailong Rd., Hanting District
Weifang, Shandong, 261000
China
  Phone: (86) 536 728 3106/ 728 3131
  Fax: (86) 536 725 1647/ 728 3228
  Web Address: www.henglianpaper.com
Personnel:
  Chmn. & Pres.: Jian Xu
  Phone: (86) 536 725 1647
Total Employees at this Location: 700
Type of Operation: Pulp mill
Pulp Grades and Capacities:
  Total pulp capacity: 80,050 mt/y
  Pulp available for market: 80,000 mt/y
  Chemical Pulp: 80,050 mt/y
Pulp Mill Data:
  Chemical Pulping Systems:
  Batch digesters: 2
  Continuous digesters: 1
Pulp Lines: 3
  Chemical Recovery Equipment:
  Recovery boilers: 1
  Pulp Dryers:
  Fourdriniers 1, Fourdriniers 1
Energy Data:
Power boilers: 1
Steam turbines: 1 at 3 MW
Electrical demand for mill: 112 MWh/D

ⓂShandong Weifang Huisheng Group
Ownership: 100% by shareholders
No.999, Weijiao Rd., New&High Technology Industry Development Zone
Weifang, Shandong, 261201
China
  Phone: (86) 536 866 9008/ 4708/ 1106/ 2439
  Fax: (86) 536 866 9008/ 1189
  Email: huisheng@cnpaper.cn
  Web Address: www.cnpaper.cn
Personnel:
  Chmn.: Maosheng Ge
  Phone: (86) 536 866 9008/ 4708/ 1106
  Fax: (86) 536 866 9008/ 1189
  Vice Chmn.: Xiliang Song
  Phone: (86) 536 866 9008/ 4708/ 1106
  Fax: (86) 536 866 9008/ 1189
  Vice Chmn.: Jinling Gong
  Phone: (86) 536 866 9008/ 4708/ 1106
  Fax: (86) 536 866 9008/ 1189
Total Employees of Company: 1,000
Mill Locations:
Dezhou Huisheng Pingyuan Paper Co., Ltd., Dezhou Mill, Longmen Economy Zone, Pingyuan County, Dezhou 253100, China, Capacity: 180,000 mt/y, (Paper mill)
  Phone: (86) 534 2169 177
  Fax: (86) 534 2169 107
Shandong Weifang Huisheng Group, Weifang Mill, No.999, Weijiao Rd., New&High Technology Industry Development Zone, Weifang 261201, China, Capacity: 217,000 mt/y, (Paper mill)
  Phone: (86) 536 866 9008/ 4708/ 1106/ 2439
  Fax: (86) 536 866 9008/ 1189
  Email: huisheng@cnpaper.cn

ⓂShandong Weifang Huisheng Group
Weifang Mill
No.999, Weijiao Rd., New&High Technology Industry Development Zone
Weifang, Shandong, 261201
China
  Phone: (86) 536 866 9008/ 4708/ 1106/ 2439
  Fax: (86) 536 866 9008/ 1189
  Email: huisheng@cnpaper.cn
  Web Address: www.cnpaper.cn
Personnel:
  Chmn.: Maosheng Ge
  Phone: (86) 536 866 9008/ 4708/ 1106/ 2439
Total Employees at this Location: 1,000
Type of Operation: Paper mill
Paper/Paperboard Grades and Capacities:
  Total paper and paperboard capacity: 217,000 mt/y
  Specialty and industrial: 17,000 mt/y
  Boxboard/cartonboard: 200,000 mt/y
Paper and Paperboard Mill Data:
Paper Machines: 4
PM 1, three-ply, total capacity 100,000 mt/y, Trim width 2.64 m, Boxboard/cartonboard
PM 4, three-ply, total capacity 100,000 mt/y, Trim width 2.2 m, Boxboard/cartonboard
PM 5, total capacity 5,000 mt/y, Trim width 2.2 m, Specialty and industrial
PM 6, total capacity 12,000 mt/y, Trim width 3.2 m, Specialty and industrial
Energy Data:
Power boilers: 2

ⓂShandong Weifang Yongxin Paper Co., Ltd.
Changle Mill
Ownership: 100% by Shandong Henglian Paper Group C., Ltd.
Hetou Industry Zone
Changle, Shandong, 262416
China
  Phone: (86) 536 691 1126
  Fax: (86) 536 691 1033
Personnel:
  Chmn. & Pres.: Ruifeng Li
  Phone: (86) 536 691 1126
Total Employees at this Location: 125
Type of Operation: Paper mill
Paper/Paperboard Grades and Capacities:
  Total paper and paperboard capacity: 19,992 mt/y
  Specialty and industrial: 19,992 mt/y
Paper and Paperboard Mill Data:
Paper Machines: 4
No. 1, Yankee dryer, total capacity 3,927 mt/y, Trim width 1.09 m, Specialty and industrial
No. 2, Yankee dryer, total capacity 3,927 mt/y, Trim width 1.09 m, Specialty and industrial
No. 3, Yankee dryer, total capacity 4,641 mt/y, Trim width 1.58 m, Specialty and industrial
No. 4, Yankee dryer, total capacity 7,497 mt/y, Trim width 1.76 m, Specialty and industrial
Energy Data:
Power boilers: 1
Electrical demand for mill: 50 MWh/D

ⓂShandong Xincheng Paper Co., Ltd.
Liaocheng Mill
H-Tech Industrial Park, Western Rd., Chiping County
Liaocheng, Shandong, 252100
China
  Phone: (86) 635 428 5466/ 3298
  Fax: (86) 635 428 3218
  Email: xcgroup@xcgroup.cn
  Web Address: www.xcgroup.com.cn, www.xcgroup.cn
Personnel:
  Gen. Mgr.: Zeqian Li
  Phone: (86) 635 428 5466/ 3298
  Mill Mgr.: Shouquan Hu
  Phone: (86) 635 428 5466/ 3298
Total Employees at this Location: 216
Type of Operation: Paper mill
Paper/Paperboard Grades and Capacities:
  Total paper and paperboard capacity: 5,000 mt/y
  Specialty and industrial: 5,000 mt/y
Paper and Paperboard Mill Data:
Paper Machines: 1
PM 1, total capacity 5,000 mt/y, Trim width 1.65 m, Specialty and industrial

ⓂShandong Xinma Paper Co., Ltd.
Huayuan Industrial Park, Suo Village, Huantai County
Zibo, Shandong, 256400
China
  Phone: (86) 533 8226 910
Total Employees at this Location: 300
Mill Locations:
Shandong Xinma Paper Co., Ltd., Zibo Mill, Huayuan Industrial Park, Suo Village, Huantai County, Zibo 256400, China, Capacity: 113,000 mt/y, (Paper mill)
  Phone: (86) 533 8226 910

ⓂShandong Xinma Paper Co., Ltd.
Zibo Mill
Huayuan Industrial Park, Suo Village, Huantai County
Zibo, Shandong, 256400
China
  Phone: (86) 533 8226 910
Total Employees at this Location: 300
Type of Operation: Paper mill
Pulp Grades and Capacities:
  Total pulp capacity: 114,904 mt/y
  Recycled Pulping: 114,904 mt/y
Paper/Paperboard Grades and Capacities:
  Total paper and paperboard capacity: 113,000 mt/y
  Linerboard: 50,000 mt/y
  Boxboard/cartonboard: 63,000 mt/y
Paper and Paperboard Mill Data:
Paper Machines: 5
No. 1, cylinder, total capacity 10,000 mt/y, Trim width 1.2 m, Boxboard/cartonboard
No. 2, cylinder, total capacity 25,000 mt/y, Trim width 2.8 m, Boxboard/cartonboard
No. 3, cylinder, total capacity 14,000 mt/y, Trim width 1.6 m, Boxboard/cartonboard
No. 4, cylinder, total capacity 14,000 mt/y, Trim width 1.6 m, Boxboard/cartonboard
No. 5, Multi-wire (3), total capacity 50,000 mt/y, Trim width 3.6 m, Linerboard
Energy Data:
Power boilers: 1
Electrical demand for mill: 126 MWh/D

ⓂⓂShandong Yantai Jinhong Paper Co. Ltd.
Yantai Mill
Ownership: 100% by sino-foreign JV

China

No. 105 Dongfang Road, Haiyang Economic & Tech. Development Zone
Yantai, Shandong, 265100
China
  Phone: (86) 535 320 2331 / 0503 / 0714 / 0322
  Fax: (86) 535 320 0266 / 2656
  Email: ytjinhong@sohu.com
Personnel:
  Chmn. & Pres./Mill Mgr.: Chunping Li
  Phone: (86) 535 320 2331 / 0503 / 0714 / 0322
  Vice Chmn.: Yulong Li
  Phone: (86) 535 320 2331 / 0503 / 0714 / 0322
  VP/Chief Eng.: Quanxin Liang
  Phone: (86) 535 320 2331 / 0503 / 0714 / 0322
  Dir. & VP: Jianghuai Xu
  Phone: (86) 535 320 2331 / 0503 / 0714 / 0322
  Dir./Asst. VP: Ling Wang
  Phone: (86) 535 320 2331 / 0503 / 0714 / 0322
Total Employees at this Location: 1,300
Type of Operation: Paper mill
Mill Locations:
  Shandong Haiyang Yongping Paper Co., Ltd., Haiyang Mill, No. 105, Dongfang Rd., Haiyang Economic & Technological Development Area, Haiyang 265100, China, Capacity: 12,000 mt/y, (Paper mill)
  Phone: (86) 535 310 5988/5997
  Fax: (86) 535 310 5966/5959
  Email: sales@yongpingpaper.com
Pulp Mill Data:
Pulp Lines: 1
  Chemical Recovery Equipment:
    Recovery boilers: 1
  Recycled Fiber Treatment Lines:
    Pulpers: 10 at 30,000 admt/y
Paper/Paperboard Grades and Capacities:
  Total paper and paperboard capacity: 54,978 mt/y
  Uncoated woodfree/freesheet: 49,266 mt/y
  Tissue: 5,712 mt/y
Paper and Paperboard Mill Data:
Paper Machines: 9
  No. 1, fourdrinier, total capacity 5,355 mt/y, Trim width 1.58 m, Uncoated woodfree/freesheet
  No. 2, fourdrinier, total capacity 5,712 mt/y, Trim width 1.76 m, Uncoated woodfree/freesheet
  No. 3, fourdrinier, total capacity 5,712 mt/y, Trim width 1.76 m, Uncoated woodfree/freesheet
  No. 4, fourdrinier, total capacity 6,426 mt/y, Trim width 1.76 m, Uncoated woodfree/freesheet
  No. 5, fourdrinier, total capacity 6,426 mt/y, Trim width 1.76 m, Uncoated woodfree/freesheet
  No. 6, fourdrinier, total capacity 9,639 mt/y, Trim width 1.76 m, Uncoated woodfree/freesheet
  No. 7, fourdrinier, total capacity 9,996 mt/y, Trim width 1.76 m, Uncoated woodfree/freesheet
  No. 10-11, total capacity 4,284 mt/y, Trim width 2.64 m, Tissue
  No. 8-9, total capacity 1,428 mt/y, Trim width 1.09 m, Tissue
Finishing Equipment:
  Supercalenders: 1
  Rewinders: 2
  Sheeters: 2
Energy Data:
  Power boilers: 2
  Steam turbines: 3 at 1.5, 1.5, 1.5 MW
  Electrical demand for mill: 120 MWh/D

ⓘShandong Yiren Paper Co., Ltd.
Jingbo Industrial Park, Boxing County
Binzhou, Shandong, 256505
China
  Phone: (86) 543 2874 888/999
  Fax: (86) 543 2874 666-887
  Web Address: www.yirenzhiye.com
Mill Locations:
  Shandong Yiren Paper Co., Ltd., Binzhou Mill, Jingbo Industrial Park, Boxing County, Binzhou 256505, China, Capacity: 108,000 mt/y, (Paper mill)
  Phone: (86) 543 2874 888/999
  Fax: (86) 543 2874 666-887

ⓜShandong Yiren Paper Co., Ltd.
Binzhou Mill
Company is temporarily closed, idle (since January 2014, may restart but no dates given)
Jingbo Industrial Park, Boxing County
Binzhou, Shandong, 256505
China
  Phone: (86) 543 2874 888/999
  Fax: (86) 543 2874 666-887
Type of Operation: Paper mill
Paper/Paperboard Grades and Capacities:
  Total paper and paperboard capacity: 108,000 mt/y
  Uncoated woodfree/freesheet: 24,000 mt/y
  Boxboard/cartonboard: 84,000 mt/y
Paper and Paperboard Mill Data:
Paper Machines: 2
  PM 1, Multi-wire (4), total capacity 84,000 mt/y, Trim width 2.73 m, Boxboard/cartonboard
  PM 2, total capacity 24,000 mt/y, Trim width 2.73 m, Uncoated woodfree/freesheet

ⓘⓜShandong Yongtai Paper Co., Ltd
Linyi Mill
Lunan Industrial Park
Linyi, Shandong
China
  Phone: (86) 539 731 1052
Total Employees at this Location: 160
Type of Operation: Paperboard mill
Pulp Grades and Capacities:
  Total pulp capacity: 64,529 mt/y
  Recycled Pulping: 64,529 mt/y
Pulp Mill Data:
  Recycled Fiber Treatment Lines:
    Pulpers
Paper/Paperboard Grades and Capacities:
  Total paper and paperboard capacity: 66,759 mt/y
  Corrugating medium/fluting: 66,759 mt/y
Paper and Paperboard Mill Data:
Paper Machines: 1
  No. 1, fourdrinier, total capacity 66,759 mt/y, Trim width 4 m, Corrugating medium/fluting
Energy Data:
  Electrical demand for mill: 105 MWh/D

ⓜShandong Zaozhuang Huarun Paper Co., Ltd.
Zaozhuang Mill
No. 93, Fuchuan Rd., Xincheng Industry Park, Shanting District
Zaozhuang, Shandong, 277200
China
  Phone: (86) 632 886 1956 / 1958 / 881 3851
  Fax: (86) 632 881 8558 / 886 1958
  Email: huarun@huarunpaper.com, marketing@huarunpaper.com
  Web Address: www.huarunpaper.com
Personnel:
  Chmn. & Gen. Mgr.: Hui Zhang
  Phone: (86) 632 886 1956 / 1958 / 881 3851
  Gen. Mgr.: Jinxiang Sun
  Phone: (86) 632 886 1956 / 1958 / 881 3851
  Tech Mgr.: Chuanjing Sun
  Phone: (86) 632 886 1956 / 1958 / 881 3851
  Chief Eng.: Minli Yao
  Phone: (86) 632 886 1956 / 1958 / 881 3851
Total Employees at this Location: 1,500
Type of Operation: Paper mill, Paperboard mill
Pulp Grades and Capacities:
  Total pulp capacity: 351,479 mt/y
  Recycled Pulping: 351,479 mt/y
Pulp Mill Data:
Pulp Lines: 3
  Recycled Fiber Treatment Lines:
    Recycled packaging pulping lines: 3 at 200,000 admt/y
Paper/Paperboard Grades and Capacities:
  Total paper and paperboard capacity: 350,000 mt/y
  Boxboard/cartonboard: 350,000 mt/y
Paper and Paperboard Mill Data:
Paper Machines: 2
  No. 3, fourdrinier (3), total capacity 150,000 mt/y, Trim width 3.8 m, Boxboard/cartonboard
  No. 4, Fourdrinier (4), total capacity 200,000 mt/y, Trim width 3.8 m, Boxboard/cartonboard
Energy Data:
  Power boilers: 3
  Turbines at 24 MW
  Electrical demand for mill: 461 MWh/D

ⓘⓜShandong Zhangqiu Huashi Paper Co., Ltd
Zhangqiu Mill
Hehua Road, Mingshui district, Zhangqiu
Zhangqiu, Shandong, 250200
China
  Phone: (86) 531 8325 3305
  Fax: (86) 531 8325 2988
  Email: jituanban@sdmingquan.com
  Web Address: www.sdmingquan.com
Total Employees at this Location: 2,000
Type of Operation: Paper mill
Paper/Paperboard Grades and Capacities:
  Total paper and paperboard capacity: 29,996 mt/y
  Uncoated mechanical/groundwood: 20,000 mt/y
  Specialty and industrial: 9,996 mt/y
Paper and Paperboard Mill Data:
Paper Machines: 4
  No. 1, fourdrinier, total capacity 10,000 mt/y, Trim width 1.88 m, Uncoated mechanical/groundwood
  No. 2, fourdrinier, total capacity 4,998 mt/y, Trim width 1.76 m, Specialty and industrial
  No. 5, fourdrinier, total capacity 4,998 mt/y, Trim width 1.76 m, Specialty and industrial
  No. 7, fourdrinier, total capacity 10,000 mt/y, Trim width 1.88 m, Uncoated mechanical/groundwood
Energy Data:
  Electrical demand for mill: 53 MWh/D

ⓘShandong Zhongmao Shengyuan Pulp Co., Ltd.
Ownership: 100% by Zhejiang Fuchunjiang Group
Linxian Economy Zone, Ling County
Dezhou, Shandong, 253500
China
  Phone: (86) 534 213 3500, 534 2138899
  Fax: (86) 534 213 3508
Personnel:
  Chmn. & Gen. Mgr.: Jun Li
  Phone: (86) 534 213 3500
  Fax: (86) 534 213 3508
  Dpty. Gen. Mgr.: Guoqing Hu
  Phone: (86) 534 213 3500
  Fax: (86) 534 213 3508
  Sls. Dir.: Zhejie Zu
  Phone: (86) 534 213 3500
  Fax: (86) 534 213 3508
Total Employees of Company: 750
Mill Locations:
  Shandong Zhongmao Shengyuan Pulp Co., Ltd., Dezhou Mill, Linxian Economy Zone, Ling County, Dezhou 253500, China, (Pulp mill)
  Phone: (86) 534 213 3500/8899
  Fax: (86) 534 213 3508

ⓜShandong Zhongmao Shengyuan Pulp Co., Ltd.
Dezhou Mill
Linxian Economy Zone, Ling County
Dezhou, Shandong, 253500
China
  Phone: (86) 534 213 3500/8899
  Fax: (86) 534 213 3508
Personnel:
  Chmn. & Gen. Mgr.: Jun Li
  Phone: (86) 534 213 3500/8899

Dpty. Gen. Mgr.: Guoqing Hu
Phone: (86) 534 213 3500/8899
Sls. Dir.: Zhejie Zu
Phone: (86) 534 213 3500/8899
Total Employees at this Location: 750
Type of Operation: Pulp mill
Pulp Grades and Capacities:
Total pulp capacity: 101,174 mt/y
Pulp available for market: 99,960 mt/y
Mechanical Pulp: 101,174 mt/y
Pulp Mill Data:
Mechanical Pulping Systems:
APMP Systems: 1
Pulp Lines: 1
Pulp Dryers:
Twin Wire 1, Twin Wire 1
Energy Data:
Power boilers: 2
Steam turbines: 1 at 15 MW
Electrical demand for mill: 538 MWh/D

ⓜShandong Zhucheng Xinxing Paper Co. Ltd.
Zhucheng Mill
Wulipu Beijiao
Zhucheng, Shandong, 262200
China
Phone: (86) 536 606 3867/ 3492
Fax: (86) 536 606 3867
Email: xinxing@xinxingpaper.cn, xxzygs@sohu.com
Personnel:
Chmn. & Gen. Mgr.: Dedong Sun
Phone: (86) 536 606 3867/ 3492
Asst. Mgr.: Ruiqiang Ji
Phone: (86) 536 606 3867/ 3492
Total Employees at this Location: 561
Type of Operation: Paper mill
Pulp Grades and Capacities:
Total pulp capacity: 71,400 mt/y
Recycled Pulping: 71,400 mt/y
Paper/Paperboard Grades and Capacities:
Total paper and paperboard capacity: 40,000 mt/y
Newsprint: 40,000 mt/y
Paper and Paperboard Mill Data:
Paper Machines: 8
PM 8, fourdrinier, total capacity 8,000 mt/y, Trim width 1.76 m, Newsprint
PM 1-4, cylinder, total capacity 4,300 mt/y, Trim width 1.58 m, Newsprint
PM 5-7, fourdrinier, total capacity 5,000 mt/y, Trim width 1.76 m, Newsprint

ⓜShandong Zhucheng City Qixianzi Products Co., Ltd.
Weifang Mill
Xiaowazi Village, Mizhou Rd., Zhucheng
Weifang, Shandong, 262218
China
Phone: (86) 536 6529 777/6189 977/977
Fax: (86) 536 6529 777/6069 858
Email: sdqxzzy@126.com/qixianzizhiye@126.com
Web Address: www.qxzzy.com
Personnel:
Chmn.: Qingbo Liang
Total Employees at this Location: 200
Type of Operation: Paper mill
Paper/Paperboard Grades and Capacities:
Total paper and paperboard capacity: 20,000 mt/y
Tissue: 20,000 mt/y
Paper and Paperboard Mill Data:
Paper Machines: 19
PM 1-19, cylinder, total capacity 1,052 mt/y, Trim width 1.58 m, Tissue
Energy Data:
Power boilers: 3
Steam turbines: 1 at 10 MW

ⓞⓜShandong Zhucheng Haoyang Paper Co., Ltd.
Weifang Mill
Wulipu Industrial Park, Mizhou Street, Zhucheng
Weifang, Shandong, 262200
China
Phone: (86) 86 137 9266 9663
Type of Operation: Paper mill
Paper/Paperboard Grades and Capacities:
Total paper and paperboard capacity: 12,000 mt/y
Tissue: 12,000 mt/y

ⓜShandong Zibo Guotai Paper Co., Ltd.
Zibo Mill
No. 36 Mingbo Rd., Gaoxin District
Zibo, Shandong, 255086
China
Phone: (86) 533 358 0813/1320
Fax: (86) 533 358 0813/3626
Email: bzlb@sdzbbz.com
Personnel:
Chmn. & Gen. Mgr.: Weizhi Cao
Phone: (86) 533 358 0813/1320
Total Employees at this Location: 200
Type of Operation: Paper mill, Paperboard mill
Pulp Grades and Capacities:
Total pulp capacity: 25,000 mt/y
Recycled Pulping: 25,000 mt/y
Pulp Mill Data:
Pulp Lines: 1
Paper/Paperboard Grades and Capacities:
Total paper and paperboard capacity: 25,000 mt/y
Uncoated woodfree/freesheet: 25,000 mt/y
Paper and Paperboard Mill Data:
Paper Machines: 1
No. 2, three-ply, total capacity 25,000 mt/y, Trim width 2.82 m, Uncoated woodfree/freesheet
Finishing Equipment:
Supercalenders: 2
Rewinders: 4
Sheeters: 4

ⓜShandong Zibo Paperboard Co., Ltd.
Zibo Mill
No. 36 Mingbo Rd., Gaoxin District
Zibo, Shandong, 255086
China
Phone: (86) 533 358 0813/ 1320
Fax: (86) 533 358 0813/ 3626
Web Address: www.sdzbbz.com
Personnel:
Pres. & Gen. Mgr.: Weizhi Cao
Phone: (86) 533 358 0813/ 1320
Purch. Agent: Weilong Li
Phone: (86) 533 358 0813/ 1320
Dir.: Hongqi Wang
Phone: (86) 533 358 0813/ 1320
Total Employees at this Location: 260
Type of Operation: Paper mill
Pulp Grades and Capacities:
Total pulp capacity: 30,000 mt/y
Recycled Pulping: 30,000 mt/y
Paper/Paperboard Grades and Capacities:
Total paper and paperboard capacity: 30,000 mt/y
Uncoated woodfree/freesheet: 30,000 mt/y
Paper and Paperboard Mill Data:
Stock Preparation:
Pulpers: 3
Refiners: 18
Paper Machines: 3
No. 1, cylinder, total capacity 4,000 mt/y, Trim width 1.76 m, Uncoated woodfree/freesheet
No. 2, fourdrinier, total capacity 20,000 mt/y, Trim width 2.88 m, Uncoated woodfree/freesheet
No. 3, cylinder, total capacity 6,000 mt/y, Trim width 1.76 m, Uncoated woodfree/freesheet
Finishing Equipment:
Supercalenders: 4
Rewinders: 4
Sheeters: 4

ⓜShandong Heze City Hongtai Paper Co., Ltd.
Heze Mill
Huang Gang Hou Ji Industrial Park, Mudan District
Heze, Shandong, 274000
China
Phone: (86) 530 566 0486
Fax: (86) 530 566 3262
Email: htzy566@126.com
Personnel:
Chmn. & Gen. Mgr.: Huaqiang Li
Phone: (86) 530 566 0486
Total Employees at this Location: 560
Type of Operation: Paper mill
Paper/Paperboard Grades and Capacities:
Total paper and paperboard capacity: 35,000 mt/y
Uncoated woodfree/freesheet: 31,000 mt/y
Specialty and industrial: 4,000 mt/y
Paper and Paperboard Mill Data:
Paper Machines: 6
No. 1, twin-wire, total capacity 5,000 mt/y, Trim width 1.58 m, Uncoated woodfree/freesheet
No. 2, fourdrinier, total capacity 6,000 mt/y, Trim width 1.76 m, Uncoated woodfree/freesheet
No. 3, twin-wire, total capacity 4,000 mt/y, Trim width 1.58 m, Specialty and industrial
No. 4, fourdrinier, total capacity 6,000 mt/y, Trim width 1.76 m, Uncoated woodfree/freesheet
No. 5, fourdrinier, total capacity 7,000 mt/y, Trim width 2.36 m, Uncoated woodfree/freesheet
No. 6, fourdrinier, total capacity 7,000 mt/y, Trim width 2.36 m, Uncoated woodfree/freesheet

ⓜShouguang Meilun Paper
Shouguang (Shouguang Meilun Paper) Mill
Ownership: 70% by Chenming Paper Holdings Ltd., 30% by CVC Asia Pacific
Xihuan Rd.
Shouguang, Shandong, 262700
China
Phone: (86) 536 215 6735/6744/6814
Web Address: www.chenmingpaper.com
Total Employees at this Location: 1,000
Type of Operation: Pulp mill, Paper mill, Paperboard mill
Pulp Grades and Capacities:
Total pulp capacity: 806,123 mt/y
Mechanical Pulp: 114,757 mt/y
Recycled Pulping: 691,366 mt/y
Pulp Mill Data:
Mechanical Pulping Systems:
BCTMP systems: 1
Pulp Lines: 2
Bleach Plant Systems: 2
Mechanical Pulping System, Type: BTMP
Recycled Pulping System, Type: DIP
Recycled Fiber Treatment Lines:
Flotation deinking lines: 1
Recycled packaging pulping lines: 1 at 857,500
Paper/Paperboard Grades and Capacities:
Total paper and paperboard capacity: 1,660,000 mt/y
Coated woodfree/freesheet: 800,000 mt/y
Tissue: 60,000 mt/y
Linerboard: 800,000 mt/y
Paper and Paperboard Mill Data:
Paper Machines: 3
No. 1, fourdrinier, Yankee dryer, total capacity 60,000 mt/y, Trim width 5.6 m, Tissue, Uncoated woodfree/freesheet
No. 6, fourdrinier, total capacity 800,000 mt/y, Trim width 10.4 m, Coated woodfree/freesheet
No. 7, fourdrinier, total capacity 800,000 mt/y, Trim width 9.66 m, Linerboard
Coating Machines: 2

China

PM 2, total capacity 600,000 mt/y., on machine
PM 6, total capacity 800,000 mt/y., on machine
Energy Data:
Electrical demand for mill: 2,821 MWh/D

ⓘⓜSunshine Oji (Shouguang) Specialty Paper Ltd.
Shouguang Mill
Ownership: 60% by Oji Holdings Corporation, 40% by Century Sunshine Paper
No. 69 Wenchang Rd., Shouguang
Weifang, Shandong, 262700
China
  Phone: (86) 536-218 1001
  Fax: (86) 536-218 6006
  Web Address: www.ojiholdings.co.jp, www.sunshinepaper.com.cn
Total Employees at this Location: 200
Type of Operation: Paper mill
Paper/Paperboard Grades and Capacities:
  Total paper and paperboard capacity: 35,000 mt/y
  Specialty and industrial: 35,000 mt/y
Paper and Paperboard Mill Data:
Paper Machines: 1
PM 1, fourdrinier, total capacity 35,000 mt/y, Trim width 2.71 m, Specialty and industrial

ⓘTaishan Gypsum Co., Ltd.
Dewenkou, Daiyue District
Taian, Shandong, 271026
China
  Phone: (86) 538 881 1449
  Fax: (86) 538 881 1323
  Email: taihe@public.taptt.sd.cn
  Web Address: www.taihegroup.com
Personnel:
  Chmn.: Tongchun Jia
  Phone: (86) 538 881 1449
  Fax: (86) 538 881 1323
Total Employees of Company: 3,000
Mill Locations:
Taishan Gypsum Co., Ltd., Taian Mill, Dawenkou, Daiyue Distric, Taian 271026, China, Capacity: 270,000 mt/y, (Paperboard mill)
  Phone: (86) 538 881 2017/ 1077/ 2002
  Fax: (86) 538 881 1323/ 1250/ 1348
  Email: taihe@public.taptt.sd.cn

ⓜTaishan Gypsum Co., Ltd.
Taian Mill
Dawenkou, Daiyue Distric
Taian, Shandong, 271026
China
  Phone: (86) 538 881 2017/ 1077/ 2002
  Fax: (86) 538 881 1323/ 1250/ 1348
  Email: taihe@public.taptt.sd.cn
  Web Address: www.taihegroup.com
Personnel:
  Chmn.: Tongchun Jia
  Phone: (86) 538 881 1499/ 2017/ 1077/ 2002
  Sls. Mgr.: Yanhuan Fu
  Phone: (86) 538 881 1499/ 2017/ 1077/ 2002
Total Employees at this Location: 1,000
Type of Operation: Paperboard mill
Pulp Grades and Capacities:
  Total pulp capacity: 270,882 mt/y
  Recycled Pulping: 270,882 mt/y
Pulp Mill Data:
  Recycled Fiber Treatment Lines:
  Recycled packaging pulping lines: 1 at 71,400 admt/y
  Washing deinking lines: 1 at 28,560 admt/y
Paper/Paperboard Grades and Capacities:
  Total paper and paperboard capacity: 270,000 mt/y
  Boxboard/cartonboard: 270,000 mt/y
Paper and Paperboard Mill Data:
Paper Machines: 2
No. 1, Multi-wire (3), total capacity 70,000 mt/y, Trim width 2.64 m, Boxboard/cartonboard

No. 2, Multi-wire (4), total capacity 200,000 mt/y, Trim width 3.8 m, Boxboard/cartonboard
Energy Data:
Electrical demand for mill: 350 MWh/D

ⓜVinda Paper (Shandong) Co., Ltd.
Laiwu Mill
Ownership: 100% by Vinda International Holdings Limited.
Laiwu Wenyang Industrial Park
Laiwu, Shandong
China
  Phone: (86) 634 5628 881
  Web Address: www.vindapaper.com
Type of Operation: Paper mill
Paper/Paperboard Grades and Capacities:
  Total paper and paperboard capacity: 50,000 mt/y
  Tissue: 50,000 mt/y
Paper and Paperboard Mill Data:
Paper Machines: 2
PM 1, (started September 2013), crescent former, total capacity 25,000 mt/y, Trim width 2.7 m, Tissue
PM 2, (started September 2013), total capacity 25,000 mt/y, Trim width 2.7 m, Tissue

ⓘWeifang Huagang Packing Material Co. Ltd
Ownership: 100% by Sino-foreign JV (with Hualu Light Industry Co. Ltd., Hong Kong)
No. 162 East Bao Tong Street, Qui Wen District
Weifang, Shandong, 261041
China
  Phone: (86) 536 882 3918, 536 882 3899
  Fax: (86) 536 882 3919, 536 882 3869
  Email: hgbzgs@public.wfptt.sd.cn, master@wfhgbz.com
  Web Address: www.wfhgbz.com
Personnel:
  Chmn.: Lizai Gao
  Phone: (86) 536 882 3918
  Fax: (86) 536 882 3919
  Pres.: Lifeng Gao
  Phone: (86) 536 882 3918
  Fax: (86) 536 882 3919
  VP.: Shibao Wang
  Phone: (86) 536 882 3918
  Fax: (86) 536 882 3919
Total Employees of Company: 600
Mill Locations:
Weifang Huagang Packing Material Co. Ltd, Weifang Mill, No. 162 East Bao Tong Street, Qui Wen District, Weifang 261041, China, Capacity: 28,000 mt/y, (Paper mill)
  Phone: (86) 536 882 3918/3899
  Fax: (86) 536 882 3919/3869
  Email: hgbzgs@public.wfptt.sd.cn, master@wfhgbz.com

ⓜWeifang Huagang Packing Material Co. Ltd
Weifang Mill
No. 162 East Bao Tong Street, Qui Wen District
Weifang, Shandong, 261041
China
  Phone: (86) 536 882 3918/3899
  Fax: (86) 536 882 3919/3869
  Email: hgbzgs@public.wfptt.sd.cn, master@wfhgbz.com
  Web Address: www.wfhgbz.com
Personnel:
  Chmn.: Lizai Gao
  Phone: (86) 536 882 3918/3899
  Pres.: Lifeng Gao
  Phone: (86) 536 882 3918/3899
  VP: Shibao Wang
  Phone: (86) 536 882 3918/3899
  VP: Shiyuan Liu
  Phone: (86) 536 882 3918/3899
Total Employees at this Location: 600
Type of Operation: Paper mill

Paper/Paperboard Grades and Capacities:
  Total paper and paperboard capacity: 28,000 mt/y
  Specialty and industrial: 28,000 mt/y
Paper and Paperboard Mill Data:
  Stock Preparation:
  Pulpers: 3
  Refiners: 2
Paper Machines: 5
PM 1, fourdrinier, total capacity 8,000 mt/y, Trim width 1.88 m, Specialty and industrial
PM 2, fourdrinier, total capacity 4,200 mt/y, Trim width 1.88 m, Specialty and industrial
PM 3, fourdrinier, total capacity 3,800 mt/y, Trim width 1.76 m, Specialty and industrial
PM 4, fourdrinier, total capacity 2,000 mt/y, Trim width 1.09 m, Specialty and industrial
PM 5, fourdrinier, total capacity 10,000 mt/y, Trim width 2.8 m, Specialty and industrial
Coating Machines: 1
CM 1, total capacity 10,000 mt/y., off machine
Finishing Equipment:
  Supercalenders: 1
  Rewinders: 3
  Sheeters: 1

ⓘWeihai Longgang Paper Co., Ltd.
Ownership: 100% by private owners
Yangting Town, Huancui District
Weihai, Shandong, 264204
China
  Phone: (86) 631 576 9888
  Fax: (86) 631 576 4806
Personnel:
  Gen. Mgr.: Ping Lin
  Phone: (86) 631 576 9888
  Fax: (86) 631 576 4806
Total Employees of Company: 180
Mill Locations:
Weihai Longgang Paper Co., Ltd., Weihai Mill, Yangting Town, Huancui District, Weihai 264204, China, Capacity: 60,333 mt/y, (Paperboard mill)
  Phone: (86) 631 576 9888
  Fax: (86) 631 576 4806

ⓜWeihai Longgang Paper Co., Ltd.
Weihai Mill
Yangting Town, Huancui District
Weihai, Shandong, 264204
China
  Phone: (86) 631 576 9888
  Fax: (86) 631 576 4806
  Web Address: www.lgzhiye.com/cn
Personnel:
  Gen. Mgr.: Ping Lin
  Phone: (86) 631 576 9888
Total Employees at this Location: 180
Type of Operation: Paperboard mill
Pulp Grades and Capacities:
  Total pulp capacity: 59,998 mt/y
  Recycled Pulping: 59,998 mt/y
Pulp Mill Data:
Pulp Lines: 3
  Recycled Fiber Treatment Lines:
  Recycled packaging pulping lines: 3 at 50,000 admt/y
Paper/Paperboard Grades and Capacities:
  Total paper and paperboard capacity: 60,333 mt/y
  Linerboard: 29,631 mt/y
  Corrugating medium/fluting: 30,702 mt/y
Paper and Paperboard Mill Data:
Paper Machines: 2
No. 1, fourdrinier, total capacity 29,631 mt/y, Trim width 2.85 m, Linerboard
No. 2, fourdrinier, total capacity 30,702 mt/y, Trim width 2.9 m, Corrugating medium/fluting
Energy Data:
Power boilers: 1
Electrical demand for mill: 86 MWh/D

ⓂYantai Longxiang Paper Co., Ltd.
Yantai Mill
Ownership: 100% by China Agro-Technology Holdings Ltd.
Yisongzhou Village, Dayao Town, Muping Disctrict
Yantai, Shandong, 264117
China
 Phone: (86) 535 465 2032/ 9898/ 412 2098
 Fax: (86) 535 465 2032/ 421 2098
 Web Address: www.ytlongxiang.cn
Personnel:
 Chmn. & CEO: Yuxiang Tang
 Phone: (86) 535 465 2032/ 9898/ 412 2098
 CFO: Shuzhi Qu
 Phone: (86) 535 465 2032/ 9898/ 412 2098
 VP & Gen. Mgr.: Shouping Yu
 Phone: (86) 535 465 2032/ 9898/ 412 2098
 VP, Purch. Mgr., Materials Mgr.: Xuezhou Qiao
 Phone: (86) 535 465 2032/ 9898/ 412 2098
 Chief Eng.: Min Jiang
 Phone: (86) 535 465 2032/ 9898/ 412 2098
 Admin. Mgr.: Dongqing Qu
 Phone: (86) 535 465 2032/ 9898/ 412 2098
Total Employees at this Location: 1,180
Type of Operation: Paper mill
Pulp Mill Data:
Paper/Paperboard Grades and Capacities:
 Total paper and paperboard capacity: 64,617 mt/y
 Uncoated woodfree/freesheet: 64,617 mt/y
Paper and Paperboard Mill Data:
Paper Machines: 7
 No. 1, fourdrinier, total capacity 8,925 mt/y, Trim width 1.76 m, Uncoated woodfree/freesheet
 No. 2, fourdrinier, total capacity 8,925 mt/y, Trim width 1.76 m, Uncoated woodfree/freesheet
 No. 3, fourdrinier, total capacity 8,925 mt/y, Trim width 1.76 m, Uncoated woodfree/freesheet
 No. 4, fourdrinier, total capacity 8,925 mt/y, Trim width 1.76 m, Uncoated woodfree/freesheet
 No. 5, fourdrinier, total capacity 8,925 mt/y, Trim width 1.76 m, Uncoated woodfree/freesheet
 No. 6, fourdrinier, total capacity 8,925 mt/y, Trim width 1.76 m, Uncoated woodfree/freesheet
 No. 9, fourdrinier, total capacity 11,067 mt/y, Trim width 2.4 m, Uncoated woodfree/freesheet
Coating Machines: 1
 PM 1, off machine
Energy Data:
 Power boilers: 2
 Steam turbines: 2 at 3, 6 MW
 Electrical demand for mill: 137 MWh/D

ⓂYuantong Paper (Shandong) Co., Ltd.
Zaozhuang Mill
No.3388 Caozao Rd., Xuecheng Dist.
Zaozhuang, Shandong, 277014
China
 Phone: (86) 632 440 1818/ 1836/ 1860
 Fax: (86) 632 440 1818
 Email: sales@upp-yt.com
 Web Address: www.upp-yt.com/www.samsonpaper.com
Personnel:
 Chmn.: Jieying Cen
 CEO: Chengren Li
 COO: Yongyuan Zhou
 CFO: Rugang Li
 Sls. Mgr.: Dianan Xu
Total Employees at this Location: 1,800
Type of Operation: Paperboard mill
Pulp Grades and Capacities:
 Total pulp capacity: 319,421 mt/y
 Recycled Pulping: 319,421 mt/y
Paper/Paperboard Grades and Capacities:
 Total paper and paperboard capacity: 371,637 mt/y
 Linerboard: 200,634 mt/y
 Boxboard/cartonboard: 171,003 mt/y
Paper and Paperboard Mill Data:
Paper Machines: 3
 No. 2, multi-wire, total capacity 66,045 mt/y, Trim width 2.4 m, Boxboard/cartonboard
 No. 3, Multi-wire (4), total capacity 104,958 mt/y, Trim width 3.2 m, Boxboard/cartonboard
 No. 5, Multi-wire (5), total capacity 200,634 mt/y, Trim width 5.5 m, Linerboard
Coating Machines: 2
 PM 2, total capacity 66,000 mt/y., on machine
 PM 3, total capacity 105,000 mt/y., on machine
Finishing Equipment:
 Rewinders: 5
 Sheeters: 2
Energy Data:
 Power boilers: 5
 Steam turbines: 1 at 48 MW
 Electrical demand for mill: 672 MWh/D

ⓂZhucheng East-Honor Industry & Trade Co., Ltd.
Zhucheng Mill
No.21 Industrial Park Rd., Xinxing Town, Zhucheng
Weifang, Shandong
China
 Phone: (86) 536 6527 888/ 6522 888
 Fax: (86) 536 6525 999
 Email: easthonor@163.com
 Web Address: www.cleanpaper.cn
Type of Operation: Paper mill
Paper/Paperboard Grades and Capacities:
 Total paper and paperboard capacity: 30,000 mt/y
 Tissue: 30,000 mt/y
Paper and Paperboard Mill Data:
Paper Machines: 6
 PM 1, total capacity 3,000 mt/y, Trim width 1.88 m, Tissue
 PM 2, total capacity 3,000 mt/y, Trim width 1.88 m, Tissue
 PM 3, total capacity 3,000 mt/y, Trim width 1.88 m, Tissue
 PM 4, total capacity 3,000 mt/y, Trim width 1.88 m, Tissue
 PM 5, total capacity 9,000 mt/y, Trim width 3.5 m, Tissue
 PM 6, total capacity 9,000 mt/y, Trim width 3.5 m, Tissue

SHANGHAI

ⓂShanghai Chung Loong Paper Co., Ltd.
Shanghai Mill
Ownership: 69.47% by Cheng Loong Corporation, Mitshubishi Paper Mills Ltd., Tokushu Tokai Paper Co., Ltd.
No. 489 Xiupu Road, Kang Qiao Industrial Zone, Pudong District
Shanghai, Shanghai, 201315
China
 Phone: (86) 21 58129798
 Fax: (86) 21 58128986
 Email: clp@mail.clc.com.tw
 Web Address: www.clc.com.tw, www.shclc.com.cn
Personnel:
 Gen. Mgr.: L.W. Cheng
 Phone: (86) 21 5812 9798/ 151/ 152/ 153/ 154/ 155
 Email: lwcheng@clc-china.com
 VP: M. S. Peng
 Phone: (86) 21 5812 9798/ 151/ 152/ 153/ 154/ 155
 Email: mspeng@mail.clc.com.tw
Total Employees at this Location: 300
Type of Operation: Paperboard mill
Pulp Grades and Capacities:
 Total pulp capacity: 407,274 mt/y
 Recycled Pulping: 407,274 mt/y
Pulp Mill Data:
 Recycled Fiber Treatment Lines:
 Recycled packaging pulping lines
Paper/Paperboard Grades and Capacities:
 Total paper and paperboard capacity: 420,118 mt/y
 Linerboard: 420,118 mt/y
Paper and Paperboard Mill Data:
Paper Machines: 1
 No. 1, DuoFormerTop, total capacity 420,118 mt/y, Trim width 6.4 m, Linerboard

Energy Data:
 Power boilers: 1
 Steam turbines: 2 at 24 MW
 Electrical demand for mill: 711 MWh/D

ⓂShanghai Fumin Paper Mill
Ownership: 100% by private owners
Gangyan Town
Chongming, Shanghai, 202158
China
 Phone: (86) 21 5946 5421
 Fax: (86) 21 5946 5421
Personnel:
 Mill Mgr.: Shiping Ma
 Phone: (86) 21 5946 5421
 Fax: (86) 21 5946 5421
 Sls. Mgr.: Chunxiang Ma
 Phone: (86) 21 5946 5421
 Fax: (86) 21 5946 5421
Total Employees of Company: 150
Mill Locations:
Shanghai Fumin Paper Mill, Chongming Mill, Gangyan Town, Chongming 202158, China, Capacity: 35,000 mt/y, (Paperboard mill)
 Phone: (86) 21 5946 5421
 Fax: (86) 21 5946 5421

ⓂShanghai Fumin Paper Mill
Chongming Mill
Gangyan Town
Chongming, Shanghai, 202158
China
 Phone: (86) 21 5946 5421
 Fax: (86) 21 5946 5421
Personnel:
 Mill Mgr.: Shiping Ma
 Phone: (86) 21 5946 5421
 Sls. Mgr.: Chunxiang Ma
 Phone: (86) 21 5946 5421
Total Employees at this Location: 150
Type of Operation: Paperboard mill
Pulp Grades and Capacities:
 Total pulp capacity: 34,738 mt/y
 Recycled Pulping: 34,738 mt/y
Pulp Mill Data:
Pulp Lines: 1
Paper/Paperboard Grades and Capacities:
 Total paper and paperboard capacity: 35,000 mt/y
 Corrugating medium/fluting: 35,000 mt/y
Paper and Paperboard Mill Data:
Paper Machines: 1
 No. 1, fourdrinier, total capacity 35,000 mt/y, Trim width 3.85 m, Corrugating medium/fluting
Energy Data:
 Power boilers: 3
 Electrical demand for mill: 42 MWh/D

ⓂShanghai Jinfengyuan Paper (Shanghai) Co., Ltd.
Shanghai (Shanghai Jinfengyuan Paper) Mill
Ownership: 80% by Asia Pulp & Paper (APP), 20% by Shanghai Kailun Papermaking & Printing Group Co., Ltd.
Liantang Rd. No. 251, Xinghuo Development Zone, Fengxian district
Shanghai, Shanghai, 201419
China
 Phone: (86) 21 5750 5588
 Fax: (86) 21 5750 1100
 Web Address: www.jfy-paper.com
Personnel:
 Chmn.: Zhiyuan Huang
 Phone: (86) 21 5750 5588
 Gen. Mgr.: Shuhua Bai
 Phone: (86) 21 5750 5588
 VP Sls.: Huirong Lin
 Phone: (86) 21 5750 5588
Total Employees at this Location: 400
Type of Operation: Paperboard mill

China

Paper/Paperboard Grades and Capacities:
Total paper and paperboard capacity: 100,000 mt/y
Boxboard/cartonboard: 100,000 mt/y
Paper and Paperboard Mill Data:
Paper Machines: 1
No. 8, fourdrinier, total capacity 100,000 mt/y, Trim width 3.2 m, Boxboard/cartonboard
Coating Machines: 1
PM 8, on machine
Energy Data:
Electrical demand for mill: 146 MWh/D

(M)Shanghai Kimberly-Clark (China) Paper Co. Ltd.
Shanghai Mill
Ownership: 80% by Kimberly-Clark Corp., 20% by Shanghai Jiangnan Paper Co.
139 Jinshatan, Songjiang District
Shanghai, Shanghai, 201600
China
 Phone: (86) 21 5782 2671
 Fax: (86) 21 5782 0386
 Email: wesen.zha@kcc.com
 Web Address: www.kimberly-clark.com/cn
Personnel:
 Chmn.: Stephen Shao
 Phone: (86) 21 5782 2671
 Gen. Mgr.: Naifang Wu
 Phone: (86) 21 5782 2671
Total Employees at this Location: 130
Type of Operation: Paper mill
Pulp Mill Data:
 Recycled Fiber Treatment Lines:
 Pulpers: 1
Paper/Paperboard Grades and Capacities:
Total paper and paperboard capacity: 24,000 mt/y
Tissue: 24,000 mt/y
Paper and Paperboard Mill Data:
 Stock Preparation:
 Pulpers: 1
 Refiners: 4
Paper Machines: 1
No. 1, crescent former, Yankee dryer, total capacity 24,000 mt/y, Trim width 2.4 m, Tissue, Uncoated woodfree/freesheet
Finishing Equipment:
 Rewinders: 2
 Sheeters: 3
Energy Data:
Power boilers: 1
Electrical demand for mill: 63 MWh/D

(M)Shanghai Orient Champion Huajie Paper Co., Ltd.
Shanghai Plaza, Zhongshan South Road 893, West Building on the third floor
Luwan, Shanghai
China
Mailing Address: Luwan, China
 Phone: (86) 021-58636607
 Fax: (86) 53026782/53019591
 Email: service@socp.com.cn
 Web Address: www.jieyun.cn
Mill Locations:
Shanghai Orient Champion Huajie Paper Co., Ltd., Jinshan Mill, No.1000, Linhui Rd, Jinshan District, Shanghai 201209, China, Capacity: 140,000 mt/y, (Paper mill)
 Phone: (86) 21 5863 6607/5727 7100/7153
 Fax: (86) 21 5302 6782/5301 9591

(M)Shanghai Orient Champion Huajie Paper Co., Ltd.
Jinshan Mill
No.1000, Linhui Rd, Jinshan District
Shanghai, Shanghai, 201209
China
 Phone: (86) 21 5863 6607/5727 7100/7153
 Fax: (86) 21 5302 6782/5301 9591
 Web Address: www.jieyun.cn
Personnel:
 Chmn.: Cixiong Li
 Phone: (86) 21 5863 6606
Total Employees at this Location: 400
Type of Operation: Paper mill
Paper/Paperboard Grades and Capacities:
Total paper and paperboard capacity: 140,000 mt/y
Tissue: 140,000 mt/y
Paper and Paperboard Mill Data:
Paper Machines: 8
No. 1, inclined, total capacity 10,000 mt/y, Trim width 2.78 m, Tissue, Uncoated woodfree/freesheet
No. 2, BF-12, Yankee dryer, total capacity 20,000 mt/y, Trim width 3.42 m, Tissue, Uncoated woodfree/freesheet
No. 3, BF-10, Yankee dryer, total capacity 10,000 mt/y, Trim width 2.68 m, Tissue, Uncoated woodfree/freesheet
No. 4, BF-10, Yankee dryer, total capacity 10,000 mt/y, Trim width 2.68 m, Tissue, Uncoated woodfree/freesheet
No. 5, BF-10, Yankee dryer, total capacity 10,000 mt/y, Trim width 2.68 m, Tissue, Uncoated woodfree/freesheet
No. 6, BF-10, Yankee dryer, total capacity 10,000 mt/y, Trim width 2.68 m, Tissue, Uncoated woodfree/freesheet
No. 7, Advantage DCT 100+, Yankee dryer, total capacity 30,000 mt/y, Trim width 2.85 m, Tissue, Uncoated woodfree/freesheet
No. 8, Advantage DCT 135+, Yankee dryer, total capacity 40,000 mt/y, Trim width 3.8 m, Tissue, Uncoated woodfree/freesheet
Energy Data:
Power boilers: 3
Electrical demand for mill: 313 MWh/D

(M)Shanghai Prosperous Paper Co., Ltd.
88, Lianqi Rd., Shengqiao Industry Park, Baoshan District
Shanghai, Shanghai, 200942
China
 Phone: (86) 21 5664 9708/ 9707
 Fax: (86) 21 5664 6488/ 6487
 Email: shpmenk@online.sh.cn
 Web Address: www.sppshanghai.com
Personnel:
 Chmn. & Pres.: Jun Kil Suh
 Phone: (86) 21 5664 9708/ 9707
 Fax: (86) 21 5664 6488/ 6487
 Gen. Mill Mgr.: Min Yong Sung
 Phone: (86) 21 5664 9708/ 9707
 Fax: (86) 21 5664 6488/ 6487
 Env. Dir.: Chenli Chang
 Phone: (86) 21 5664 9708/ 9707
 Fax: (86) 21 5664 6488/ 6487
Total Employees at this Location: 325
Mill Locations:
Shanghai Prosperous Paper Co., Ltd., Shanghai Mill, 88, Lianqi Rd., Shengqiao Industry Park, Baoshan District, Shanghai 200942, China, Capacity: 140,000 mt/y, (Paper mill)
 Phone: (86) 21 5664 9708/ 9707
 Fax: (86) 21 5664 6488/ 6487
 Email: shpmenk@online.sh.cn

(M)Shanghai Prosperous Paper Co., Ltd.
Shanghai Mill
88, Lianqi Rd., Shengqiao Industry Park, Baoshan District
Shanghai, Shanghai, 200942
China
 Phone: (86) 21 5664 9708/ 9707
 Fax: (86) 21 5664 6488/ 6487
 Email: shpmenk@online.sh.cn
 Web Address: www.sppshanghai.com
Personnel:
 Vice Chmn. & Pres.: Jun Kil Suh
 Phone: (86) 21 5664 9708/ 9707
 Gen. Mill Mgr.: Min Yong Sung
 Phone: (86) 21 5664 9708/ 9707
 Env. Dir.: Chenli Chang
 Phone: (86) 21 5664 9708/ 9707
Total Employees at this Location: 325
Type of Operation: Paper mill
Pulp Grades and Capacities:
Total pulp capacity: 128,594 mt/y
Recycled Pulping: 128,594 mt/y
Paper/Paperboard Grades and Capacities:
Total paper and paperboard capacity: 140,000 mt/y
Newsprint: 140,000 mt/y
Paper and Paperboard Mill Data:
Paper Machines: 1
No. 1, Bel-Baie III, total capacity 140,000 mt/y, Trim width 4.8 m, Newsprint
Energy Data:
Power boilers: 1
Electrical demand for mill: 370 MWh/D

(M)Shanghai Stora Enso Asia Pacific
Ownership: 100% by Stora Enso Oyj
Room 2201, Hong Kong New World Tower, 300 Huai Hai Zhong Road
Shanghai, Shanghai, 200 021
China
 Phone: (86) 21 6335 3050
 Fax: (86) 21 6335 3055
 Web Address: www.storaenso.com
Personnel:
 Exec. VP, Stora Enso Asia Pacific: Markku Pentikäinen
 Phone: (86) 21 6335 3050
 Fax: (86) 21 6335 3055
Mill Locations:
Jiangsu Stora Enso Suzhou Paper Co. Ltd., Suzhou Mill (96.48% owned), 600, Binhe Rd., Suzhou 215011, China, Capacity: 245,000 mt/y, (Paper mill)
 Phone: (86) 512 6825 1060
 Fax: (86) 512 6825 1711
 Email: papyrus@public1.sz.js.cn
Shandong Stora Enso Huatai Paper, Dawang Mill (60% owned), Weigao Rd., Huatai Industrial Park, Dawang Township, Guangrao County, Dongying 257335, China, Capacity: 170,000 mt/y, (Pulp mill, Paper mill)
 Phone: (86) 546 7797 200/243
 Fax: (86) 546 7797 220

(M)Shanghai Welfare Group Co., Ltd.
Ownership: 50% by Shanghai Shenda Eiderdown Production Co., Ltd., 50% by Singapore Mitron Managerment PTE. Ltd.
No. 88, Lane 3029, Xuhua Highway
Qingpu, Shanghai, Shanghai, 201705
China
 Phone: (86) 21 3987 3700
 Fax: (86) 21 3987 3188
 Email: welfare@public.sta.net.cn
 Web Address: www.welfare-group.cn
Personnel:
 Chmn.: Shengzhang Li
 Phone: (86) 21 3987 3700
 Fax: (86) 21 3987 3188
 Gen. Mgr.: Youcheng He
 Phone: (86) 21 3987 3700
 Fax: (86) 21 3987 3188
Total Employees at this Location: 500
Mill Locations:
Zhejiang Welfare Paper Co., Ltd., Shaoxing Mill, No. 17 East Yangjiang Rd., Shaoxing 312001, China, Capacity: 48,000 mt/y, (Paper mill)
 Phone: (86) 575 8820 7373
 Fax: (86) 575 8820 7375

SHANXI

(M)Shanxi Linyi Lida Paper Co., Ltd.
Yuncheng Mill
Huangdoujing Village, Yishi Town, Linyi County

China

Yuncheng, Shanxi, 044100
China
  Phone: (86) 359 406 8499
  Fax: (86) 359 406 8499
Personnel:
  Chmn.: Congrong Feng
  Phone: (86) 359 406 8499
  Gen. Mgr.: Sijiu Du
  Phone: (86) 359 406 8499
  Sls. Mgr.: Lei Du
  Phone: (86) 1375 3985 752
Type of Operation: Paper mill
Pulp Mill Data:
Paper/Paperboard Grades and Capacities:
  Total paper and paperboard capacity: 21,000 mt/y
  Tissue: 21,000 mt/y
Paper and Paperboard Mill Data:
Paper Machines: 8
  PM 3-4, fourdrinier, total capacity 1,500 mt/y, Trim width 1.88 m, Tissue
  PM 5-6, (Supplier: Hebei Mancheng Changda Paper Machinery), cylinder, total capacity 1,500 mt/y, Trim width 1.88 m, Tissue
  PM 7-10, (Supplier: Hebei Changda Paper Machinery), cylinder, total capacity 3,500 mt/y, Trim width 2.8 m, Tissue
Energy Data:
Power boilers: 3
Steam turbines

ⓂShanxi QiangWei Paper Co., Ltd.
Jinzhong Mill
Shouyang County Industrial Park
Jinzhong, Shanxi
China
  Phone: (86) 354 3909 788
  Email: info@qwpaper.com
  Web Address: www.qwpaper.com
Type of Operation: Paperboard mill
Pulp Grades and Capacities:
  Total pulp capacity: 360,946 mt/y
  Recycled Pulping: 360,946 mt/y
Paper/Paperboard Grades and Capacities:
  Total paper and paperboard capacity: 360,000 mt/y
  Boxboard/cartonboard: 360,000 mt/y
Paper and Paperboard Mill Data:
Paper Machines: 2
No. 4, Multi-wire (3), total capacity 180,000 mt/y, Trim width 3.6 m, Boxboard/cartonboard
No. 5, fourdrinier (3), total capacity 180,000 mt/y, Trim width 3.8 m, Boxboard/cartonboard
Energy Data:
Electrical demand for mill: 482 MWh/D

ⒽⓂShanxi Taiyuan Jiasheng Paper Co., Ltd
Taiyuan Mill
Wangguo Village
Taiyuan, Shanxi
China
Total Employees at this Location: 160
Type of Operation: Paperboard mill
Pulp Grades and Capacities:
  Total pulp capacity: 29,367 mt/y
  Recycled Pulping: 29,367 mt/y
Pulp Mill Data:
  Recycled Fiber Treatment Lines:
  Recycled packaging pulping lines: 1
Paper/Paperboard Grades and Capacities:
  Total paper and paperboard capacity: 30,345 mt/y
  Corrugating medium/fluting: 30,345 mt/y
Paper and Paperboard Mill Data:
Paper Machines: 1
No. 1, fourdrinier, total capacity 30,345 mt/y, Trim width 3.4 m, Corrugating medium/fluting
Energy Data:
Power boilers: 1
Electrical demand for mill: 48 MWh/D

SICHUAN

ⓂSichuan Zhongshun Tiantian Paper Co., Ltd.
Chengdu Mill
Ownership: 100% by C&S Paper Co., Ltd.
Mudan Avenue Industry Park
Pengzhou, Chengdu, Sichuan, 611930
China
  Phone: (86) 28 8373 5698/5266
  Fax: (86) 28 8380 6666
  Web Address: www.zhongshungroup.com
Personnel:
  Gen. Mgr.: Yong Yue
  Phone: (86) 28 8373 5698
  Sls. Mgr.: Binxian Li
  Phone: (86) 28 8373 5698
Total Employees at this Location: 280
Type of Operation: Paper mill
Paper/Paperboard Grades and Capacities:
  Total paper and paperboard capacity: 47,996 mt/y
  Tissue: 47,996 mt/y
Paper and Paperboard Mill Data:
Paper Machines: 10
No. 1, cylinder, total capacity 714 mt/y, Trim width 1.58 m, Tissue
No. 2, cylinder, total capacity 714 mt/y, Trim width 1.58 m, Tissue
No. 3, cylinder, total capacity 714 mt/y, Trim width 1.58 m, Tissue
No. 4, cylinder, total capacity 714 mt/y, Trim width 1.58 m, Tissue
No. 5, cylinder, total capacity 714 mt/y, Trim width 1.58 m, Tissue
No. 6, cylinder, total capacity 714 mt/y, Trim width 1.58 m, Tissue
No. 15, cylinder, total capacity 4,284 mt/y, Trim width 1.58 m, Tissue
No. 16, BF-10, Yankee dryer, total capacity 5,712 mt/y, Trim width 2.66 m, Tissue, Uncoated woodfree/freesheet
No. 17, BF-12, Yankee dryer, total capacity 10,000 mt/y, Trim width 2.66 m, Tissue, Uncoated woodfree/freesheet
No. 18, crescent former, Yankee dryer, total capacity 28,000 mt/y, Trim width 3.6 m, Tissue, Uncoated woodfree/freesheet
Energy Data:
Power boilers: 4
Electrical demand for mill: 158 MWh/D

ⒽChengdu Jujia Family Life Paper Making Co., Ltd.
No.45, Xinglong Rd., Longxing Town, Chongzhou
Chengdu, Sichuan, 611247
China
  Phone: (86) 28 8222 1258
  Fax: (86) 28 8222 2258
  Email: hulin321@126.com
  Web Address: www.scjujia.com
Total Employees at this Location: 300
Mill Locations:
Chengdu Jujia Family Life Paper Making Co., Ltd., Chengdu Mill, No.45, Xinglong Rd., Longxing Town, Chongzhou, Chengdu 611247, China, Capacity: 30,000 mt/y, (Paper mill)
  Phone: (86) 28 8222 1258
  Fax: (86) 28 8222 2258
  Email: hulin321@126.com

ⓂChengdu Jujia Family Life Paper Making Co., Ltd.
Chengdu Mill
No.45, Xinglong Rd., Longxing Town, Chongzhou
Chengdu, Sichuan, 611247
China
  Phone: (86) 28 8222 1258
  Fax: (86) 28 8222 2258
  Email: hulin321@126.com
  Web Address: www.scjujia.com
Total Employees at this Location: 300
Type of Operation: Paper mill
Paper/Paperboard Grades and Capacities:
  Total paper and paperboard capacity: 30,000 mt/y
  Tissue: 30,000 mt/y
Paper and Paperboard Mill Data:
Paper Machines: 18
No. 1, total capacity 1,400 mt/y, Tissue
No. 2, total capacity 1,400 mt/y, Tissue
No. 3, total capacity 1,400 mt/y, Tissue
No. 4, total capacity 1,400 mt/y, Tissue
No. 5, total capacity 1,400 mt/y, Tissue
No. 6, total capacity 1,400 mt/y, Tissue
No. 7, total capacity 1,400 mt/y, Tissue
No. 8, total capacity 1,400 mt/y, Tissue
No. 9, total capacity 1,400 mt/y, Tissue
No. 10, total capacity 1,400 mt/y, Tissue
No. 11, total capacity 1,400 mt/y, Tissue
No. 12, total capacity 1,400 mt/y, Tissue
No. 13, total capacity 1,400 mt/y, Tissue
No. 14, total capacity 1,400 mt/y, Tissue
No. 15, total capacity 1,400 mt/y, Tissue
No. 16, total capacity 1,400 mt/y, Tissue
No. 17, total capacity 3,800 mt/y, Trim width 3.88 m, Tissue
No. 18, total capacity 3,800 mt/y, Trim width 3.88 m, Tissue

ⒽChengdu R Paper Co., Ltd.
No.13 West of Junping Street, Pengzhou City
Chengdu, Sichuan, 611937
China
  Phone: (86) 28 8377 9118
  Fax: (86) 28 8377 9358
  Web Address: www.rpaper.net
Mill Locations:
Chengdu R Paper Co., Ltd., Chengdu Mill, No.13 West of Junping Street, Pengzhou City, Chengdu 611937, China, Capacity: 10,000 mt/y, (Paper mill)
  Phone: (86) 28 8377 9118
  Fax: (86) 28 8377 9358

ⓂChengdu R Paper Co., Ltd.
Chengdu Mill
No.13 West of Junping Street, Pengzhou City
Chengdu, Sichuan, 611937
China
  Phone: (86) 28 8377 9118
  Fax: (86) 28 8377 9358
  Web Address: www.rpaper.net
Type of Operation: Paper mill
Paper/Paperboard Grades and Capacities:
  Total paper and paperboard capacity: 10,000 mt/y
  Tissue: 10,000 mt/y

ⒽⓂChengdu Yatai Paper Industry Co., Ltd.
Chengdu Mill
Company is idle (since the end of 2013)
Ownership: 100% by Chengdu Yatai Paper Industry Co., Ltd
Jiaolong Industry Park
Chengdu, Sichuan, 610200
China
  Phone: (86) 28 85730478
  Fax: (86) 28 85730478
Total Employees at this Location: 200
Type of Operation: Paperboard mill
Paper and Paperboard Mill Data:
Paper Machines: 1
No. 1, fourdrinier, total capacity 60,333 mt/y, Trim width 2.9 m
Coating Machines: 1
PM1, on machine
Energy Data:
Power boilers: 1

China

⓪Chengdu Zhihao Paper Co., Ltd.
Eighth Xingye Rd., Dayi County
Chengdu, Sichuan, 611300
China
Mill Locations:
Chengdu Zhihao Paper Co., Ltd., Chengdu Mill, Eighth Xingye Rd., Dayi County, Chengdu 611300, China, Capacity: 20,000 mt/y, (Paper mill)

Ⓜ Chengdu Zhihao Paper Co., Ltd.
Chengdu Mill
Eighth Xingye Rd., Dayi County
Chengdu, Sichuan, 611300
China
Type of Operation: Paper mill
Paper/Paperboard Grades and Capacities:
Total paper and paperboard capacity: 20,000 mt/y
Tissue: 20,000 mt/y
Paper and Paperboard Mill Data:
Paper Machines: 6
PM 1, total capacity 3,300 mt/y, Trim width 1.88 m, Tissue
PM 2, total capacity 3,300 mt/y, Trim width 1.88 m, Tissue
PM 3, total capacity 3,300 mt/y, Trim width 1.88 m, Tissue
PM 4, total capacity 3,300 mt/y, Trim width 1.88 m, Tissue
PM 5, total capacity 3,300 mt/y, Trim width 1.88 m, Tissue
PM 6, total capacity 3,300 mt/y, Trim width 1.88 m, Tissue

⓪Guangan Anqi Paper Co., Ltd.
Guangan District
Guangan, Sichuan, 638000
China
  Phone: (86) 826 273 1093/235 1510/233 8879
  Fax: (86) 826 233 8876
  Web Address: www.gagsl.com/shql/anqi/anqi1.htm
Total Employees at this Location: 350
Mill Locations:
Guangan Anqi Paper Co., Ltd., Guangan Mill, Guangan District, Guangan 638000, China, Capacity: 12,000 mt/y, (Paper mill)
  Phone: (86) 826 273 1093/235 1510/233 8879
  Fax: (86) 826 233 8876

Ⓜ Guangan Anqi Paper Co., Ltd.
Guangan Mill
Guangan District
Guangan, Sichuan, 638000
China
  Phone: (86) 826 273 1093/235 1510/233 8879
  Fax: (86) 826 233 8876
  Web Address: www.gagsl.com/shql/anqi/anqi1.htm
Total Employees at this Location: 350
Type of Operation: Paper mill
Paper/Paperboard Grades and Capacities:
Total paper and paperboard capacity: 12,000 mt/y
Tissue: 12,000 mt/y
Paper and Paperboard Mill Data:
Paper Machines: 10
No. 1, total capacity 1,200 mt/y, Trim width 1.58 m, Tissue
No. 2, total capacity 1,200 mt/y, Trim width 1.58 m, Tissue
No. 3, total capacity 1,200 mt/y, Trim width 1.58 m, Tissue
No. 4, total capacity 1,200 mt/y, Trim width 1.58 m, Tissue
No. 5, total capacity 1,200 mt/y, Trim width 1.58 m, Tissue
No. 6, total capacity 1,200 mt/y, Trim width 1.58 m, Tissue
No. 7, total capacity 1,200 mt/y, Trim width 1.58 m, Tissue
No. 8, total capacity 1,200 mt/y, Trim width 1.58 m, Tissue
No. 9, total capacity 1,200 mt/y, Trim width 1.58 m, Tissue
No. 10, total capacity 1,200 mt/y, Trim width 1.58 m, Tissue

⓪Luzhou Shengfeng Paper Co., Ltd.
Huguo Town, Naxi District
Luzhou, Sichuan
China
  Phone: (86) 158 8478 0720
Mill Locations:
Luzhou Shengfeng Paper Co., Ltd., Luzhou Mill, Huguo Town, Naxi District, Luzhou, China, Capacity: 8,000 mt/y, (Paper mill)
  Phone: (86) 158 8478 0720

Ⓜ Luzhou Shengfeng Paper Co., Ltd.
Luzhou Mill
Huguo Town, Naxi District
Luzhou, Sichuan
China
  Phone: (86) 158 8478 0720
Type of Operation: Paper mill
Paper/Paperboard Grades and Capacities:
Total paper and paperboard capacity: 8,000 mt/y
Tissue: 8,000 mt/y
Paper and Paperboard Mill Data:
Paper Machines: 8
PM 1-8, total capacity 1,000 mt/y, Trim width 1.68 m, Tissue

Ⓜ MCC Meili Paper (Laishan) Co., Ltd.
Qionglai Mill
Ownership: MCC Paper Group Co., Ltd.
YangAn Town
Qionglai, Sichuan, 611543
China
  Phone: (86) 28 8875 8559/8330/8895
  Web Address: www.china-meili.com
Total Employees at this Location: 750
Type of Operation: Pulp mill
Pulp Grades and Capacities:
Total pulp capacity: 100,000 mt/y
Pulp available for market: 100,000 mt/y
Pulp Mill Data:
Chemical Pulping Systems:
Continuous digesters: 1
Pulp Lines: 1
Bleach Plant Systems: 1
No. 1, Sequence: O_2 DEopDD, Capacity 100,000 admt/y

Ⓜ Nine Dragons Pulp & Paper (Leshan) Co., Ltd.
Leshan Mill
Ownership: 100% by Guangdong Dongguan Nine Dragons Paper Industries Co., Ltd.
Yanzhi Village, Qingxi Town, Qianwei County
Leshan, Sichuan, 614005
China
  Phone: (86) 833 2299 999
  Fax: (86) 833 2299 666
  Web Address: www.ndpaper.com
Personnel:
  Chmn.: Yin Zhang
  CEO: Mingzhong Liu
  CFO: Yuanfu Zhang
Total Employees at this Location: 490
Type of Operation: Paper mill
Pulp Grades and Capacities:
Total pulp capacity: 257,982 mt/y
Recycled Pulping: 257,982 mt/y
Pulp Mill Data:
Recycled Fiber Treatment Lines:
Recycled packaging pulping lines: 1
Paper/Paperboard Grades and Capacities:
Total paper and paperboard capacity: 311,700 mt/y
Packaging papers: 10,000 mt/y
Specialty and industrial: 38,700 mt/y
Corrugating medium/fluting: 263,000 mt/y
Paper and Paperboard Mill Data:
Paper Machines: 6
No. 1, fourdrinier, total capacity 850 mt/y, Trim width 1.88 m, Specialty and industrial
No. 2, fourdrinier, total capacity 850 mt/y, Trim width 1.88 m, Specialty and industrial
No. 3, fourdrinier, total capacity 20,000 mt/y, Trim width 1.88 m, Specialty and industrial
No. 4, fourdrinier, total capacity 17,000 mt/y, Trim width 2.55 m, Specialty and industrial
No. 5, fourdrinier, total capacity 10,000 mt/y, Trim width 2.55 m, Packaging papers
No. 38, fourdrinier, total capacity 263,000 mt/y, Trim width 5.6 m, Corrugating medium/fluting
Energy Data:
Power boilers: 2

Ⓜ Sichuan Anxian Paper Co., Ltd.
Chengdu Mill
Suishui Town, An County
Chengdu, Sichuan, 622656
China
  Phone: (86) 816 467 1342/1355
  Fax: (86) 816 467 1287
  Email: yaazwj@yeah.net
Personnel:
  Chmn. & Pres.: Lin Kang
  Phone: (86) 816 467 1342/1355
Total Employees at this Location: 600
Type of Operation: Pulp mill, Paper mill
Pulp Grades and Capacities:
Total pulp capacity: 44,970 mt/y
Pulp available for market: 30,499 mt/y
Other Pulp: 44,970 mt/y
Pulp Mill Data:
Chemical Pulping Systems:
Not Given: 1
Pulp Lines: 1
Pulp Dryers:
Pulp Dryers 1
Paper/Paperboard Grades and Capacities:
Total paper and paperboard capacity: 32,000 mt/y
Uncoated woodfree/freesheet: 9,000 mt/y
Tissue: 20,000 mt/y
Specialty and industrial: 3,000 mt/y
Paper and Paperboard Mill Data:
Paper Machines: 4
No. 1, cylinder, total capacity 3,000 mt/y, Trim width 1.58 m, Specialty and industrial
No. 2, fourdrinier, total capacity 9,000 mt/y, Trim width 1.88 m, Uncoated woodfree/freesheet
T1, BF-10 EX, total capacity 10,000 mt/y, Trim width 2.76 m, Tissue, Uncoated woodfree/freesheet
T2, BF-10 EX, total capacity 10,000 mt/y, Trim width 2.76 m, Tissue, Uncoated woodfree/freesheet
Energy Data:
Electrical demand for mill: 151 MWh/D

⓪Sichuan Beiaijia Paper Co., Ltd.
Fengheba Village, Hongya County
Meishan, Sichuan
China
  Phone: (86) 28 3749 0990
  Fax: (86) 28 3749 0156
Mill Locations:
Sichuan Beiaijia Paper Co., Ltd., Meishan Mill, Fengheba Village, Hongya County, Meishan, China, Capacity: 10,000 mt/y, (Paper mill)
  Phone: (86) 28 3749 0990
  Fax: (86) 28 3749 0156

Ⓜ Sichuan Beiaijia Paper Co., Ltd.
Meishan Mill
Fengheba Village, Hongya County
Meishan, Sichuan
China
  Phone: (86) 28 3749 0990
  Fax: (86) 28 3749 0156
Type of Operation: Paper mill
Paper/Paperboard Grades and Capacities:
Total paper and paperboard capacity: 10,000 mt/y
Tissue: 10,000 mt/y
Paper and Paperboard Mill Data:
Paper Machines: 7
PM 1-7, total capacity 1,400 mt/y, Trim width 1.88 m, Tissue

Ⓜ Sichuan Changning Zhuhai Paper Co., Ltd.
Yibin Mill
No. 169, Zhiye Rd., Changning Town

Yibin, Sichuan, 644300
China
 Phone: (86) 831 4690 284/ 166
 Fax: (86) 831 4690 165/ 166
 Web Address: www.cn-grace.com
Personnel:
 Chmn. & Gen. Mgr.: Yongping Zou
 Phone: (86) 831 4690 284/ 166
 Tech. Dir.: Mr. Tang
 Phone: (86) 831 4690 588/136 0829 2110
Type of Operation: Pulp mill
Pulp Grades and Capacities:
 Total pulp capacity: 35,000 mt/y
 Pulp available for market: 35,000 mt/y
Pulp Mill Data:
Pulp Lines: 5

ⓂSichuan Chaolan Paper Co., Ltd.
Zitong Economic Development Zone
Mianyang, Sichuan, 622150
China
 Phone: (86) 816 8323 333/777
 Fax: (86) 816 8323 792
 Email: chaolanziye@163.com
 Web Address: www.chaolan.cn
Mill Locations:
Sichuan Chaolan Paper Co., Ltd., Mianyang Mill, Zitong Economic Development Zone, Mianyang 622150, China, Capacity: 30,000 mt/y, (Paper mill)
 Phone: (86) 816 8323 333/777
 Fax: (86) 816 8323 792
 Email: chaolanziye@163.com

ⓂSichuan Chaolan Paper Co., Ltd.
Mianyang Mill
Zitong Economic Development Zone
Mianyang, Sichuan, 622150
China
 Phone: (86) 816 8323 333/777
 Fax: (86) 816 8323 792
 Email: chaolanziye@163.com
 Web Address: www.chaolan.cn
Type of Operation: Paper mill
Paper/Paperboard Grades and Capacities:
 Total paper and paperboard capacity: 30,000 mt/y
 Tissue: 30,000 mt/y
Paper and Paperboard Mill Data:
Paper Machines: 4
TM 10, total capacity 10,000 mt/y, Trim width 2.6 m, Tissue
TM 11, (started October 2013), total capacity 10,000 mt/y, Trim width 2.82 m, Tissue
TM 12, (scheduled to start August 2014), total capacity 10,000 mt/y, Trim width 2.6 m, Tissue
TM 9, total capacity 10,000 mt/y, Trim width 2.6 m, Tissue

ⓂSichuan Chengdu Jiexin Paper Co., Ltd.
Chengdu Mill
No. 101 North 2 Rd., Xiandai Industry Harbor
Chengdu, Sichuan, 611743
China
 Phone: (86) 28 6611 8731
 Fax: (86) 28 6611 8731
 Web Address: www.cdjiexin.cn
Personnel:
 Chmn. & Gen. Mgr.: Dafu Ye
 Phone: (86) 28 6611 8731
 HR. Mgr.: Xuli Pang
 Phone: (86) 28 6611 8731
Type of Operation: Paper mill
Paper/Paperboard Grades and Capacities:
 Total paper and paperboard capacity: 4,000 mt/y
 Tissue: 4,000 mt/y
Paper and Paperboard Mill Data:
Paper Machines: 4
No. 1, fourdrinier, total capacity 1,000 mt/y, Trim width 1.88 m, Tissue
No. 2, fourdrinier, total capacity 1,000 mt/y, Trim width 1.88 m, Tissue
No. 3, fourdrinier, total capacity 1,000 mt/y, Trim width 1.88 m, Tissue
No. 4, fourdrinier, total capacity 1,000 mt/y, Trim width 1.88 m, Tissue

ⓂSichuan Chengdu Jinghua Paper Co., Ltd.
Chengdu Mill
Qianfu Village Tangyuan Town, Bi County
Chengdu, Sichuan, 611732
China
 Phone: (86) 28 8799 0998
 Fax: (86) 28 8799 0998
 Email: office@cd-jinghua.com
 Web Address: www.cd-jinghua.com
Personnel:
 Chmn. & Gen. Mgr.: Sanping Wang
 Phone: (86) 28 8799 0998
 Sls. Mgr.: Mr. Xu
 Phone: (86) 28 8799 0998
Total Employees at this Location: 350
Type of Operation: Paper mill
Paper/Paperboard Grades and Capacities:
 Total paper and paperboard capacity: 10,000 mt/y
 Tissue: 10,000 mt/y
Paper and Paperboard Mill Data:
Paper Machines: 10
No. 1, cylinder, total capacity 850 mt/y, Trim width 1.58 m, Tissue
No. 2, cylinder, total capacity 850 mt/y, Trim width 1.58 m, Tissue
No. 3, cylinder, total capacity 850 mt/y, Trim width 1.58 m, Tissue
No. 4, cylinder, total capacity 850 mt/y, Trim width 1.58 m, Tissue
No. 5, cylinder, total capacity 850 mt/y, Trim width 1.58 m, Tissue
No. 6, cylinder, total capacity 850 mt/y, Trim width 1.58 m, Tissue
No. 7, cylinder, total capacity 850 mt/y, Trim width 1.58 m, Tissue
No. 8, cylinder, total capacity 1,350 mt/y, Trim width 1.88 m, Tissue
No. 9, cylinder, total capacity 1,350 mt/y, Trim width 1.88 m, Tissue
No. 10, cylinder, total capacity 1,350 mt/y, Trim width 1.88 m, Tissue
Energy Data:
Power boilers: 1

ⓄⓂSichuan Chengdu Lianda Paper Co., Ltd
Chengdu Mill
Chongzhou Industry Development Zone
Chengdu, Sichuan
China
Total Employees at this Location: 148
Type of Operation: Paperboard mill
Pulp Grades and Capacities:
 Total pulp capacity: 61,079 mt/y
 Recycled Pulping: 61,079 mt/y
Pulp Mill Data:
 Recycled Fiber Treatment Lines:
 Recycled packaging pulping lines: 1
Paper/Paperboard Grades and Capacities:
 Total paper and paperboard capacity: 63,189 mt/y
 Corrugating medium/fluting: 63,189 mt/y
Paper and Paperboard Mill Data:
Paper Machines: 1
No. 1, fourdrinier, total capacity 63,189 mt/y, Trim width 3.8 m, Corrugating medium/fluting
Energy Data:
Power boilers: 2
Electrical demand for mill: 100 MWh/D

ⓂSichuan Chengdu Xiling Packaging Co., Ltd.
Chengdu Mill
North Binjiang East Rd., Jinyuan Town, Dayi County
Chengdu, Sichuan, 611330
China
 Phone: (86) 28 8829 4176
 Fax: (86) 28 8829 4176
 Email: xlpc@mail.sc.cninfo.net
Personnel:
 Chmn. /Pres./Mill Mgr.: Jirong Gao
 Phone: (86) 28 8829 4176
 Sls. Mgr.: Hong Zhang
 Phone: (86) 28 8829 4176
Total Employees at this Location: 250
Type of Operation: Paperboard mill
Pulp Grades and Capacities:
 Total pulp capacity: 188,257 mt/y
 Recycled Pulping: 188,257 mt/y
Pulp Mill Data:
Pulp Lines: 1
 Recycled Fiber Treatment Lines:
 Recycled packaging pulping lines: 1
Paper/Paperboard Grades and Capacities:
 Total paper and paperboard capacity: 190,000 mt/y
 Corrugating medium/fluting: 190,000 mt/y
Paper and Paperboard Mill Data:
Paper Machines: 3
No. 1, fourdrinier, total capacity 25,000 mt/y, Trim width 2.36 m, Corrugating medium/fluting
No. 2, fourdrinier, total capacity 15,000 mt/y, Trim width 1.88 m, Corrugating medium/fluting
No. 3, fourdrinier, total capacity 150,000 mt/y, Trim width 4.8 m, Corrugating medium/fluting
Energy Data:
Power boilers
Electrical demand for mill: 239 MWh/D

ⓂSichuan Chengdu Yuanzhou Industrial Co., Ltd.
Shifang Mill
Ownership: Sichuan Ruilong Group Co., Ltd.
Jiuligeng
Shifang, Sichuan, 618408
China
 Phone: (86) 838 860 3389
 Fax: (86) 838 860 3300
 Email: ruilong@scrl.cn
 Web Address: www.scrl.cn
Personnel:
 Chmn. & Gen. Mgr.: Ligong Hu
 Phone: (86) 838 860 3389
 Sls. Mgr.: Ms. Chunyan Hu
 Phone: (86) 838 860 3389
Type of Operation: Paper mill
Paper/Paperboard Grades and Capacities:
 Total paper and paperboard capacity: 30,000 mt/y
 Tissue: 30,000 mt/y
Paper and Paperboard Mill Data:
Paper Machines: 10
PM 1-6, fourdrinier, total capacity 2,650 mt/y, Trim width 1.88 m, Tissue
PM 7-10, fourdrinier, total capacity 3,500 mt/y, Trim width 2.4 m, Tissue
Energy Data:
Power boilers: 2

ⓄSichuan Eupon(youbang) Paper Co., Ltd.
South Zone of Guanghan Economic Development Zone, Guanghan
Deyang, Sichuan, 618300
China
 Phone: (86) 838 540 0028/2799/1933
 Fax: (86) 838 540 0158
 Email: sale@eupon.com
 Web Address: www.eupon.com
Total Employees at this Location: 200

China

Mill Locations:
Sichuan Eupon(youbang) Paper Co., Ltd., Deyang Mill, South Zone of Guanghan Economic Development Zone, Guanghan, Deyang 618300, China, Capacity: 8,000 mt/y, (Paper mill)
Phone: (86) 838 540 0028/2799/1933
Fax: (86) 838 540 0158
Email: sale@eupon.com

ⓂSichuan Eupon(youbang) Paper Co., Ltd.
Deyang Mill
South Zone of Guanghan Economic Development Zone, Guanghan
Deyang, Sichuan, 618300
China
Phone: (86) 838 540 0028/2799/1933
Fax: (86) 838 540 0158
Email: sale@eupon.com
Web Address: www.eupon.com
Total Employees at this Location: 200
Type of Operation: Paper mill
Paper/Paperboard Grades and Capacities:
Total paper and paperboard capacity: 8,000 mt/y
Tissue: 8,000 mt/y
Paper and Paperboard Mill Data:
Paper Machines: 1
PM 1, total capacity 8,000 mt/y, Trim width 2.88 m, Tissue

ⓘⓂSichuan F. Source Paper
Chengdu Mill
No.299, 7th Xingye Rd., Dayi Economic Development Zone
Chengdu, Sichuan, 611330
China
Phone: (86) 28 6926 8361/6890 1745/6926 8363
Email: chenping@scrszy.com
Web Address: www.f-sourcepaper.com
Type of Operation: Paper mill
Pulp Grades and Capacities:
Total pulp capacity: 147,846 mt/y
Recycled Pulping: 147,846 mt/y
Pulp Mill Data:
Pulp Lines: 1
Recycled Fiber Treatment Lines:
Recycled packaging pulping lines: 1 at 220,000
Paper/Paperboard Grades and Capacities:
Total paper and paperboard capacity: 150,000 mt/y
Linerboard: 75,000 mt/y
Corrugating medium/fluting: 75,000 mt/y
Paper and Paperboard Mill Data:
Paper Machines: 1
No. 1, twin-wire, total capacity 150,000 mt/y, Trim width 4.8 m, Corrugating medium/fluting, Linerboard
Energy Data:
Electrical demand for mill: 182 MWh/D

ⓂSichuan Gold Hongye Paper Co., Ltd.
Yaan (Gold Hongye Paper) Mill
Mill is under construction (civil engineering work started early January 2013. Mill due to start sometime in 2014)
Ownership: Asia Pulp & Paper (APP)
Caoba Industrial Park, Yucheng District
Yaan, Sichuan
China
Type of Operation: Paper mill
Paper and Paperboard Mill Data:
Paper Machines: 4
PM 1, fourdrinier, total capacity 27,000 mt/y, Trim width 2.8 m, Tissue
PM 2, total capacity 27,000 mt/y, Trim width 2.8 m, Tissue
PM 3, total capacity 27,000 mt/y, Trim width 2.8 m, Tissue
PM 4, fourdrinier, total capacity 27,000 mt/y, Trim width 2.8 m, Tissue

ⓘSichuan Guanghan City Shunfa Co., Ltd.
Ownership: 100% by private owners
Chunhui Village, Lianshan Town, Guanghan
Deyang, Sichuan, 618303
China
Phone: (86) 838 580 2196
Fax: (86) 838 510 0398
Personnel:
Pres.: Dafu Qian
Phone: (86) 838 580 2196
Fax: (86) 838 510 0398
Total Employees at this Location: 560
Mill Locations:
Sichuan Guanghan City Shunfa Co., Ltd., Deyang Mill, Chunhui Village, Lianshan Town, Guanghan, Deyang 618303, China, Capacity: 120,000 mt/y, (Paper mill)
Phone: (86) 838 580 2196
Fax: (86) 838 510 0398

ⓘⓂSichuan Guanghan City Shunfa Co., Ltd.
Deyang Mill
Chunhui Village, Lianshan Town, Guanghan
Deyang, Sichuan, 618303
China
Phone: (86) 838 580 2196
Fax: (86) 838 510 0398
Personnel:
Pres.: Dafu Qian
Phone: (86) 838 580 2196
Total Employees at this Location: 560
Type of Operation: Paper mill
Pulp Grades and Capacities:
Total pulp capacity: 140,000 mt/y
Recycled Pulping: 140,000 mt/y
Pulp Mill Data:
Pulp Lines: 1
Chemical Recovery Equipment:
Recovery boilers: 1
Paper/Paperboard Grades and Capacities:
Total paper and paperboard capacity: 120,000 mt/y
Linerboard
Corrugating medium/fluting: 120,000 mt/y
Paper and Paperboard Mill Data:
Paper Machines: 1
PM 1, three-ply, total capacity 120,000 mt/y, Trim width 3.6 m, Linerboard, Corrugating medium/fluting
Energy Data:
Power boilers: 2

ⓘⓂSichuan Haiteng Paper Co., Ltd.
Dujiangyan Mill
Xujia Town
Dujiangyan, Sichuan
China
Phone: (86) 28 8710 7808
Fax: (86) 28 8710 7808
Web Address: longspaper.com.cn
Type of Operation: Paper mill
Paper/Paperboard Grades and Capacities:
Tissue

ⓂSichuan Hefeng Paper Co., Ltd.
Leshan Mill
Ownership: 100% by Sichuan Yongfeng Paper-Making Joint-Stock Co., Ltd.
No.1981, Muyuan Rd., Muxi Town, Muchuan County
Leshan, Sichuan, 614500
China
Phone: (86) 833 4612 292
Web Address: www.yfzy.com
Type of Operation: Paper mill
Paper/Paperboard Grades and Capacities:
Total paper and paperboard capacity: 50,000 mt/y
Tissue: 50,000 mt/y
Paper and Paperboard Mill Data:

Paper Machines: 32
PM 1-30, total capacity 1,000 mt/y, Trim width 1.88 m, Tissue
PM 31, cylinder, total capacity 10,000 mt/y, Trim width 2.82 m, Tissue
PM 32, total capacity 10,000 mt/y, Trim width 2.82 m, Tissue

ⓂSichuan Huaqiao Fenghuang Paper Co., Ltd.
Deyang Mill
No.8, Dongguan Rd., Xiangyang Town, Guanghan City
Deyang, Sichuan, 618300
China
Phone: (86) 838 6098 666/088
Fax: (86) 838 6098 066
Email: fhzyzpchaoshi@163.com
Web Address: www.hqfhzy.com
Type of Operation: Paper mill
Pulp Grades and Capacities:
Total pulp capacity: 269,834 mt/y
Recycled Pulping: 269,834 mt/y
Paper/Paperboard Grades and Capacities:
Total paper and paperboard capacity: 300,000 mt/y
Boxboard/cartonboard: 300,000 mt/y
Paper and Paperboard Mill Data:
Paper Machines: 3
No. 1, cylinder (6), total capacity 20,000 mt/y, Trim width 1.76 m, Boxboard/cartonboard
No. 2, cylinder (5), total capacity 30,000 mt/y, Trim width 2.4 m, Boxboard/cartonboard
No. 3, Fourdrinier (5), total capacity 250,000 mt/y, Trim width 3.6 m, Boxboard/cartonboard
Energy Data:
Power boilers: 2
Steam turbines: 1 at 15 MW
Electrical demand for mill: 376 MWh/D

ⓘⓂSichuan Jiajiang Huarun Paper Co., Ltd.
Leshan Mill
Macun Town, Jiajiang County
Leshan, Sichuan, 614000
China
Phone: (86) 833 5660 228
Type of Operation: Paper mill
Paper/Paperboard Grades and Capacities:
Tissue

ⓂSichuan Jiajiang Huifeng Paper Co., Ltd.
Leshan Mill
Zhouba Village, Jiepai County, Jiajiang County
Leshan, Sichuan, 614100
China
Phone: (86) 833 582 9111/9617/9999/9966
Fax: (86) 833 582 9698
Email: jjhf5829111@sina.com
Web Address: www.jjhfpaper.com
Type of Operation: Pulp mill, Paper mill
Pulp Mill Data:
Pulp Lines: 1
Paper/Paperboard Grades and Capacities:
Total paper and paperboard capacity: 28,000 mt/y
Tissue: 28,000 mt/y
Paper and Paperboard Mill Data:
Paper Machines: 15
PM 1, total capacity 2,800 mt/y, Trim width 1.88 m, Tissue
PM 2, total capacity 2,800 mt/y, Trim width 1.88 m, Tissue
PM 3, total capacity 2,800 mt/y, Trim width 1.88 m, Tissue
PM 4, total capacity 2,800 mt/y, Trim width 1.88 m, Tissue
PM 5, total capacity 2,800 mt/y, Trim width 1.88 m, Tissue
PM 6, total capacity 2,800 mt/y, Trim width 1.88 m, Tissue
PM 7, total capacity 2,800 mt/y, Trim width 1.88 m, Tissue
PM 8, total capacity 2,800 mt/y, Trim width 1.88 m, Tissue
PM 9, total capacity 2,800 mt/y, Trim width 1.88 m, Tissue
PM 10, total capacity 2,800 mt/y, Trim width 1.88 m, Tissue

China

PM 11, (due to start up in 2014.10), total capacity 7,500 mt/y, Trim width 3.9 m, Tissue
PM 12, (due to start up in 2014.10), total capacity 7,500 mt/y, Trim width 3.9 m, Tissue
PM 13, (due to start up in 2014.10), total capacity 5,000 mt/y, Trim width 2.8 m, Tissue
PM 14, (due to start up in 2014.10), total capacity 5,000 mt/y, Trim width 2.8 m, Tissue
PM 15, (was due to start Oct. 2014, delayed), total capacity 5,000 mt/y, Trim width 2.8 m, Tissue

ⓜSichuan Jiajiang Ruijie Paper Co., Ltd.
No.447 East Yingchun Rd., Jiajiang County
Leshan, Sichuan
China
Phone: (86) 833 5659 392/13508146235
Mill Locations:
Sichuan Jiajiang Ruijie Paper Co., Ltd., Leshan Mill, No.447 East Yingchun Rd., Jiajiang County, Leshan, China, Capacity: 8,400 mt/y, (Paper mill)
Phone: (86) 833 5659 392/13508146235

ⓜSichuan Jiajiang Ruijie Paper Co., Ltd.
Leshan Mill
No.447 East Yingchun Rd., Jiajiang County
Leshan, Sichuan
China
Phone: (86) 833 5659 392/13508146235
Type of Operation: Paper mill
Paper/Paperboard Grades and Capacities:
Total paper and paperboard capacity: 8,400 mt/y
Tissue: 8,400 mt/y
Paper and Paperboard Mill Data:
Paper Machines: 7
PM 1-7, total capacity 1,200 mt/y, Trim width 1.58 m, Tissue

ⓜSichuan Jianwei Fengsheng Paper Co. Ltd.
Leshan Mill
Yongping Village, Xiaogu Town, Jianwei County
Leshan, Sichuan, 614400
China
Phone: (86) 833 425 1386/ 1716/ 1544
Fax: (86) 833 425 4579
Web Address: www.fengshenggroup.com.cn
Personnel:
Chmn.: Bigang Shui
Phone: (86) 833 425 1386/ 1716/ 1544
Gen. Mgr.: Dian Shui
Phone: (86) 833 425 1386/ 1716/ 1544
Vice Gen. Mgr.: Yincheng Wang
Phone: (86) 833 425 1386/ 1716/ 1544
VP & Chief Eng.: Sichang Wang
Phone: (86) 833 425 1386/ 1716/ 1544
Total Employees at this Location: 435
Type of Operation: Pulp mill
Pulp Grades and Capacities:
Total pulp capacity: 100,543 mt/y
Pulp available for market: 100,000 mt/y
Other Pulp: 100,543 mt/y
Pulp Mill Data:
Chemical Pulping Systems:
Batch digesters: 1
Pulp Lines: 1
Bleach Plant Systems: 1
Chemical Pulping System, Type: ECF
Chemical Recovery Equipment:
Evaporator lines: 1
Recovery boilers: 1
Pulp Dryers:
Pulp Dryers
Energy Data:
Electrical demand for mill: 214 MWh/D

ⓜSichuan Jiayi Paper Co., Ltd.
Meishan Mill
Shishou Industrial Park, Renshou County
Meishan, Sichuan, 620564
China
Phone: (86) 28 3605 1080/8568 6337
Fax: (86) 28 3605 1078
Email: jiayi2001@foxmail.com, 2275797155@qq.com
Web Address: www.scjyzy.com
Total Employees at this Location: 300
Type of Operation: Paper mill
Paper/Paperboard Grades and Capacities:
Tissue

ⓜSichuan Jin'an Pulp Co. Ltd.
Yaan (Sichuan Jin'an Pulp) Mill
Mill is closed (relocated to Sichuan Suining)
Ownership: 100% by Asia Pulp & Paper (APP)
No. 2 Ai Guo Road, Yucheng District
Yaan, Sichuan, 625000
China
Phone: (86) 835 2850 801/806/834
Fax: (86) 835 2850 092
Web Address: www.appjap.com.cn
Personnel:
Chmn.: Minggang Li
Phone: (86) 835 2850 816/801/806/834
VPTech.: Anqing Yang
Phone: (86) 835 2850 816/801/806/834
Gen. Mgr.: Yaolong Tian
Phone: (86) 835 2850 816/801/806/834
Total Employees at this Location: 850
Type of Operation: Paper mill
Pulp Grades and Capacities:
Total pulp capacity: 80,000 mt/y
Pulp available for market: 80,000 mt/y
Pulp Mill Data:
Pulp Lines: 1
Bleach Plant Lines:
No. 1, Sequence: C/DEoD
Chemical Recovery Equipment:
Recovery boilers: 1
Lime Kiln
Paper and Paperboard Mill Data:
Stock Preparation:
Pulpers: 1
Refiners: 1
Paper Machines: 1
No. 1, (idle), cylinder, total capacity 25,500 mt/y, Trim width 2.6 m, Uncoated woodfree/freesheet
Finishing Equipment:
Rewinders: 1
Sheeters: 1
Energy Data:
Power boilers: 2
Steam turbines: 2 at 6, 6 MW

ⓟⓜSichuan Jinfeng Paper Holdings Co. Ltd.
Chengdu Mill
Company is under bankruptcy protection
Ownership: Cheung Fung Technology, Hong Kong (majority share), China Tabacco Materials Corporation, Giant Target Investment Ltd. (Hong Kong), Raymond Industrial, Sichuan Chengdu Rongguang Enterprise Ltd.
Jinfeng Street, Chengdu Science Development Park for Taiwan and Foreign Investors
Chengdu, Sichuan, 611137
China
Phone: (86) 28 8263 3530/ 0751
Fax: (86) 28 8263 0174
Email: office@jfpaper.com
Personnel:
Chmn.: Yinghao Huang
Phone: (86) 28 8263 3530/ 0751
CEO: Shangyan Ye
Phone: (86) 28 8263 3530/ 0751
VP - Operation: Luyu Yu
Phone: (86) 28 8263 3530/ 0751
VP - Technology: Yongde Zhang
Phone: (86) 28 8263 3530/ 0751
Total Employees at this Location: 750
Type of Operation: Paper mill
Paper/Paperboard Grades and Capacities:
Total paper and paperboard capacity: 25,000 mt/y
Specialty and industrial: 25,000 mt/y
Paper and Paperboard Mill Data:
Paper Machines: 4
PM 1, fourdrinier, total capacity 3,000 mt/y, Trim width 1.88 m, Specialty and industrial
PM 2, fourdrinier, total capacity 8,000 mt/y, Trim width 3.3 m, Specialty and industrial
PM 3, inclined, total capacity 8,000 mt/y, Trim width 1.88 m, Specialty and industrial
PM 4, fourdrinier, total capacity 6,000 mt/y, Trim width 2.36 m, Specialty and industrial

ⓜSichuan Longchang Yuhong Paper Co., Ltd.
Neijiang Mill
Huangjiazhen, Longchang
Neijiang, Sichuan, 642153
China
Phone: (86) 832 365 0041
Fax: (86) 832 365 0041
Personnel:
Chmn. & Gen. Mgr.: Zeyong Xiang
Phone: (86) 832 365 0041
VP-Technology/Chief Eng.: Minglu Xiang
Phone: (86) 832 365 0041
Total Employees at this Location: 150
Type of Operation: Paperboard mill
Paper/Paperboard Grades and Capacities:
Total paper and paperboard capacity: 20,000 mt/y
Containerboard: 20,000 mt/y
Linerboard
Corrugating medium/fluting
Boxboard/cartonboard
Paper and Paperboard Mill Data:
Paper Machines: 2
No. 1, multi-wire, Trim width 1.6 m
No. 2, multi-wire, Trim width 1.58 m

ⓜSichuan Meishan City Hongyuan Paper Co., Ltd.
Meishan Mill
Meitang Rd., Nanmen, Dongpo District
Meishan, Sichuan, 620010
China
Phone: (86) 833 822 3496
Fax: (86) 833 822 3439
Personnel:
Chmn. & Pres.: Guomin Shen
Phone: (86) 833 822 3496
Gen. Mgr.: Ms. Manrong Jian
Phone: (86) 833 822 3496
Total Employees at this Location: 580
Type of Operation: Pulp mill, Paper mill
Pulp Grades and Capacities:
Total pulp capacity: 100,000 mt/y
Pulp available for market: 80,000 mt/y
Pulp Mill Data:
Pulp Lines: 2
Bleach Plant Lines:
No. 1
Chemical Recovery Equipment:
Recovery boilers: 1
Pulp Dryers:
Twin Wire 1
Paper/Paperboard Grades and Capacities:
Total paper and paperboard capacity: 28,000 mt/y
Tissue: 28,000 mt/y
Paper and Paperboard Mill Data:
Paper Machines: 20
PM 1-6, cylinder, total capacity 1,400 mt/y, Trim width 1.88 m, Tissue

China

PM 7 - 20, total capacity 1,400 mt/y, Trim width 1.88 m, Tissue
Energy Data:
Power boilers: 4

ⓜSichuan Meishan Fenghua Paper Co., Ltd.
Meishan Mill
Songjiang Economy & Industry Park, Dongcheng District
Meishan, Sichuan, 620010
China
  Phone: (86) 833 8010 182
  Fax: (86) 833 8010 068
  Email: office@fhpaper.cn
  Web Address: www.fhpaper.cn
Personnel:
  Chmn. & Pres.: Jinsong Liu
  Phone: (86) 833 8010 182
Total Employees at this Location: 780
Type of Operation: Pulp mill, Paper mill
Pulp Grades and Capacities:
  Total pulp capacity: 35,801 mt/y
  Other Pulp: 35,801 mt/y
Pulp Mill Data:
Pulp Lines: 2
  Chemical Recovery Equipment:
  Recovery boilers: 1
Paper/Paperboard Grades and Capacities:
  Total paper and paperboard capacity: 48,552 mt/y
  Uncoated woodfree/freesheet: 48,552 mt/y
Paper and Paperboard Mill Data:
Paper Machines: 8
No. 5, fourdrinier, total capacity 9,996 mt/y, Trim width 1.76 m, Uncoated woodfree/freesheet
No. 6, fourdrinier, total capacity 9,996 mt/y, Trim width 1.88 m, Uncoated woodfree/freesheet
No. 7, fourdrinier, total capacity 9,996 mt/y, Trim width 1.88 m, Uncoated woodfree/freesheet
No. 8, fourdrinier, total capacity 9,996 mt/y, Trim width 1.88 m, Uncoated woodfree/freesheet
No. 1-2, cylinder, total capacity 2,856 mt/y, Trim width 1.09 m, Uncoated woodfree/freesheet
No. 3-4, cylinder, total capacity 5,712 mt/y, Trim width 1.58 m, Uncoated woodfree/freesheet
Energy Data:
Power boilers: 13
Steam turbines: 1 at 7 MW
Electrical demand for mill: 130 MWh/D

ⓜSichuan Meishan Jieai Paper Co., Ltd.
Songjiang Industrial Park, Dongpo District
Meishan, Sichuan, 620030
China
  Phone: (86) 28 3801 2889
  Fax: (86) 28 3801 2899
  Email: 770185035@qq.com
  Web Address: www.jieaizhiye.com
Mill Locations:
Sichuan Meishan Jieai Paper Co., Ltd., Meishan Mill, Songjiang Industrial Park, Dongpo District, Meishan 620030, China, (Paper mill)
  Phone: (86) 28 3801 2889
  Fax: (86) 28 3801 2899
  Email: 770185035@qq.com

ⓜSichuan Meishan Jieai Paper Co., Ltd.
Meishan Mill
Songjiang Industrial Park, Dongpo District
Meishan, Sichuan, 620030
China
  Phone: (86) 28 3801 2889
  Fax: (86) 28 3801 2899
  Email: 770185035@qq.com
  Web Address: www.jieaizhiye.com
Type of Operation: Paper mill

ⓜSichuan Mingshan County Yunxiang Paper Co., Ltd.
Yaan Mill
No.53, Huxiaoqiao Rd., Mingshan County
Yaan, Sichuan, 625100
China
  Phone: (86) 835 322 8719/5605
  Fax: (86) 835 322 5605
  Email: yunxiang5605@sina.com
  Web Address: www.yunxiangzhiye.com
Personnel:
  Chmn.: Zhizhang Hu
  Phone: (86) 835 322 5605
  Email: yunxiang5605@sina.com, yunxianghzz@163.com
Type of Operation: Paper mill
Pulp Grades and Capacities:
  Total pulp capacity: 30,000 mt/y
Pulp Mill Data:
Pulp Lines: 1
  Recycled Fiber Treatment Lines:
  Flotation deinking lines: 1 at 10,000 admt/y
Paper/Paperboard Grades and Capacities:
  Total paper and paperboard capacity: 30,500 mt/y
  Uncoated woodfree/freesheet: 15,500 mt/y
  Tissue: 15,000 mt/y
Paper and Paperboard Mill Data:
Paper Machines: 14
PM 1, fourdrinier, total capacity 7,000 mt/y, Trim width 1.76 m, Uncoated woodfree/freesheet
PM 2, fourdrinier, total capacity 8,500 mt/y, Trim width 1.76 m, Uncoated woodfree/freesheet
TM 1-8, fourdrinier, Trim width 1.76 m, Tissue
TM 9-12, (started up in Aug. 2009), Trim width 1.88 m, Tissue
Energy Data:
Power boilers: 2

ⓞⓜSichuan Pengzhou Daliang Paper
Pengzhou Mill
North Junping
Pengzhou, Sichuan, 611937
China
  Phone: (86) 28 8377 8269 / 8266
  Fax: (86) 28 8377 8111
  Web Address: www.vipoon.net
Personnel:
  Sihong Du
  Phone: (86) 28 8377 8269 / 8266
Type of Operation: Paper mill
Paper/Paperboard Grades and Capacities:
  Total paper and paperboard capacity: 15,000 mt/y
  Tissue: 15,000 mt/y
Paper and Paperboard Mill Data:
Paper Machines: 19
PM 1-8, Trim width 1.09 m, Tissue
PM 9-19, Trim width 1.76 m, Tissue

ⓞSichuan Ruilong Group Co., Ltd.
Ownership: 100% by private owners
Xinan Industry Park, Xindu District
Chengdu, Sichuan, 610502
China
  Phone: (86) 28 8308 4998
  Fax: (86) 28 8308 7776
  Web Address: www.scrl.cn
Personnel:
  Chmn.: Ligong Hu
  Phone: (86) 28 8308 4998
  Fax: (86) 28 8308 7776
Total Employees at this Location: 100
Mill Locations:
Sichuan Chengdu Yuanzhou Industrial Co., Ltd., Shifang Mill, Jiuligeng, Shifang 618408, China, Capacity: 30,000 mt/y, (Paper mill)
  Phone: (86) 838 860 3389
  Fax: (86) 838 860 3300
  Email: ruilong@scrl.cn

ⓜSichuan Santai Sanjiao Living Paper Manufacture Co., Ltd.
Mianyang Mill
Nanhe Rd., Tongchuan Town, Santai County
Mianyang, Sichuan, 621100
China
  Phone: (86) 816 522 8978/ 8979
  Fax: (86) 816 522 1277
Personnel:
  Pres. & Mill Mgr.: Fukun Yang
  Phone: (86) 816 522 8978/ 8979
Total Employees at this Location: 450
Type of Operation: Paper mill
Paper/Paperboard Grades and Capacities:
  Total paper and paperboard capacity: 17,000 mt/y
  Tissue: 17,000 mt/y
Paper and Paperboard Mill Data:
Paper Machines: 1
PM 1, (was due to start in the second half of 2014, delayed), crescent former, total capacity 17,000 mt/y, Trim width 2.85 m, Tissue

ⓜSichuan Tianzhu Development of Bamboo Resource Co., Ltd.
Yibin Mill
Yangchun Industrial Park, JiangAn County
Yibin, Sichuan, 644004
China
  Phone: (86) 831 360 5519/5517/1113/5512
  Fax: (86) 831 360 5519
Personnel:
  Chmn.: Jinjun Wang
  Gen. Mgr.: Shengyong Wang
Type of Operation: Pulp mill
Pulp Grades and Capacities:
  Total pulp capacity: 95,000 mt/y
  Pulp available for market: 95,000 mt/y
Pulp Mill Data:
  Chemical Pulping Systems:
  Batch digesters: 1
Pulp Lines: 1
  Bleach Plant Systems: 1
  No. 1, Sequence: CEH
  Chemical Recovery Equipment:
  Recovery boilers: 1
  Pulp Dryers:
  Fourdriniers 1

ⓜSichuan WanAn Paper Co., Ltd.
Leshan Mill
Ownership: Guangdong Shantou City WanAn Paper Co., Ltd.
Xinmin Industry Park, Ganjiang Town, Jiajiang County
Leshan, Sichuan, 614102
China
  Phone: (86) 833 577 0878/2516
  Fax: (86) 833 577 0878
  Email: sc-wananzhiye@263.net
  Web Address: www.wananpaper.com
Personnel:
  Chmn.: Kangju Zhen
  Phone: (86) 833 577 2466
Total Employees at this Location: 230
Type of Operation: Paper mill
Paper/Paperboard Grades and Capacities:
  Total paper and paperboard capacity: 15,000 mt/y
  Tissue: 15,000 mt/y
Paper and Paperboard Mill Data:
Paper Machines: 10
PM 1-6, total capacity 1,200 mt/y, Trim width 1.88 m, Tissue
PM 7-10, fourdrinier, total capacity 2,000 mt/y, Trim width 2.4 m, Tissue

ⓜSichuan Xicheng Paper Co., Ltd.
Leshan
Mill is idle (for poor market demand)
Xiwan Village, Ganjiang Town, Jiajiang County

Leshan, Sichuan, 614100
China
  Phone: (86) 833 577 0806
Type of Operation: Paper mill
Pulp Mill Data:
  Chemical Pulping Systems:
  Batch digesters: 5
Paper/Paperboard Grades and Capacities:
  Total paper and paperboard capacity: 1,500 mt/y
  Specialty and industrial: 1,500 mt/y
Paper and Paperboard Mill Data:
Paper Machines: 2
No. 3, fourdrinier, total capacity 750 mt/y, Trim width 1.88 m, Specialty and industrial
No. 4, fourdrinier, total capacity 750 mt/y, Trim width 1.88 m, Specialty and industrial
Energy Data:
Power boilers: 1

ⓂSichuan Xilong Paper Co., Ltd.
Meishan Mill
Xilong Town, Qingshen County
Meishan, Sichuan, 620460
China
  Phone: (86) 028 3894 0033
  Web Address: www.hl-cd.cn
Personnel:
  Gen. Mgr.: Jun Zhou
  Phone: (86) 833 894 0033
  Vice. Gen. Mgr.: Yunhong Shuai
  Phone: (86) 833 894 0033
  Chief. Eng.: Jianhua Xue
  Phone: (86) 833 894 0033
Total Employees at this Location: 100
Type of Operation: Pulp mill, Paper mill
Pulp Grades and Capacities:
  Total pulp capacity: 135,000 mt/y
  Pulp available for market: 140,000 mt/y
Pulp Mill Data:
  Chemical Pulping Systems:
  Not Given: 2
Pulp Lines: 2
  Chemical Recovery Equipment:
  Recovery boilers: 1
  Pulp Dryers:
  Fourdriniers 1
Paper/Paperboard Grades and Capacities:
  Total paper and paperboard capacity: 10,000 mt/y
  Tissue: 10,000 mt/y
Paper and Paperboard Mill Data:
Paper Machines: 6
PM 5-10, cylinder, total capacity 1,800 mt/y, Trim width 1.88 m, Tissue
Energy Data:
Steam turbines: 2 at 3, 20 MW

ⓇSichuan Xinjihong Paper Co., Ltd.
Pingle Village, Fengming Town, Pengshan County
Meishan, Sichuan
China
  Phone: (86) 28 3764 1156
  Fax: (86) 28 3764 1109
  Email: wl671222@126.com
  Web Address: www.scxjhzy.com
Total Employees at this Location: 600
Mill Locations:
Sichuan Xinjihong Paper Co., Ltd., Meishan Mill, Pingle Village, Fengming Town, Pengshan County, Meishan, China, Capacity: 34,000 mt/y, (Pulp mill, Paper mill)
  Phone: (86) 28 3764 1156
  Fax: (86) 28 3764 1109
  Email: wl671222@126.com

ⓇSichuan Xinjihong Paper Co., Ltd.
Meishan Mill
Pingle Village, Fengming Town, Pengshan County
Meishan, Sichuan
China

  Phone: (86) 28 3764 1156
  Fax: (86) 28 3764 1109
  Email: wl671222@126.com
Total Employees at this Location: 600
Type of Operation: Pulp mill, Paper mill
Paper/Paperboard Grades and Capacities:
  Total paper and paperboard capacity: 34,000 mt/y
  Uncoated woodfree/freesheet: 4,000 mt/y
  Tissue: 30,000 mt/y

ⓇSichuan Xinjin Chenlong Paper Co., Ltd.
Xinjin Industrial Park
Chengdu, Sichuan, 611400
China
  Phone: (86) 28 8259 1878/2087
  Email: scxjclzy@163.com
  Web Address: www.xjclzy.com
Mill Locations:
Sichuan Xinjin Chenlong Paper Co., Ltd., Chengdu Mill, Xinjin Industrial Park, Xinjin County, Chengdu 611400, China, Capacity: 240,000 mt/y, (Paper mill)
  Phone: (86) 28 8259 1878/2087
  Email: scxjclzy@163.com

ⓇSichuan Xinjin Chenlong Paper Co., Ltd.
Chengdu Mill
Xinjin Industrial Park, Xinjin County
Chengdu, Sichuan, 611400
China
  Phone: (86) 28 8259 1878/2087
  Email: scxjclzy@163.com
  Web Address: www.scclzy.net
Total Employees at this Location: 365
Type of Operation: Paper mill
Pulp Grades and Capacities:
  Total pulp capacity: 237,580 mt/y
  Recycled Pulping: 237,580 mt/y
Pulp Mill Data:
  Recycled Fiber Treatment Lines:
  Recycled packaging pulping lines: 1
Paper/Paperboard Grades and Capacities:
  Total paper and paperboard capacity: 240,000 mt/y
  Linerboard: 80,000 mt/y
  Corrugating medium/fluting: 160,000 mt/y
Paper and Paperboard Mill Data:
Paper Machines: 2
No. 2, fourdrinier, total capacity 40,000 mt/y, Trim width 4.6 m, Corrugating medium/fluting
No. 3, fourdrinier (3), total capacity 200,000 mt/y, Trim width 5 m, Corrugating medium/fluting, Linerboard
Energy Data:
Power boilers: 1
Steam turbines: 2 at 6, 7.5 MW
Electrical demand for mill: 294 MWh/D

ⓇSichuan Yajie Paper Co., Ltd.
Yancheng Town, Jiajiang County
Leshan, Sichuan, 614100
China
Mill Locations:
Sichuan Yajie Paper Co., Ltd., Leshan Mill, Yancheng Town, Jiajiang County, Leshan 614100, China, Capacity: 24,000 mt/y, (Paper mill)

ⓇSichuan Yajie Paper Co., Ltd.
Leshan Mill
Yancheng Town, Jiajiang County
Leshan, Sichuan, 614100
China
Type of Operation: Paper mill
Paper/Paperboard Grades and Capacities:
  Total paper and paperboard capacity: 24,000 mt/y
  Tissue: 12,000 mt/y
Paper and Paperboard Mill Data:
Paper Machines: 9
PM 1-9, total capacity 1,400 mt/y, Trim width 1.88 m, Tissue

ⓇSichuan Yibin Paper Industry Co., Ltd.
Ownership: 42.37% by shareholders, 41.57% by Sichuan Yibin State Company, 16.06% by Sichuan Yibin Wuliangye Group Co., Ltd.
No. 54 West Minjiang Rd.
Yibin, Sichuan, 644007
China
  Phone: (86) 831 356 0128
  Fax: (86) 831 356 1965
  Email: dsh@ybzy.com.cn
  Web Address: www.yb-zy.com
Personnel:
  Chmn.: Cong Yi
  Vice Chmn., Pres.: Xiaohua Wang
  CFO: Qiang Wang
  Vice Pres.: Hao Liang
  Vice Pres.: Zhikai Ming
  Vice Pres.: Xuelin Zhou
  Vice Pres.: Bucheng Wang
  Adm. Mgr: Biao Lu
  Mgr./Dir.: Yun Luo
Total Employees at this Location: 2,332
Mill Locations:
Sichuan Yibin Paper Industry Co., Ltd., Yibin Mill, Light Industry Zone, Peishi Town, Nanxi District, Yibin, China, Capacity: 350,000 mt/y, (Paper mill)
  Phone: (86) 831 3560 376
  Fax: (86) 831 3561 965

ⓇSichuan Yibin Paper Industry Co., Ltd.
Yibin Mill
Mill is under construction (was expected to start September 2014, delayed)
Light Industry Zone, Peishi Town, Nanxi District
Yibin, Sichuan
China
  Phone: (86) 831 3560 376
  Fax: (86) 831 3561 965
  Web Address: www.yb-zy.com
Type of Operation: Paper mill
Paper/Paperboard Grades and Capacities:
  Total paper and paperboard capacity: 350,000 mt/y
Paper and Paperboard Mill Data:
Paper Machines: 1
PM 1, (due to start up in sep. 2014), total capacity 350,000 mt/y, Trim width 4.38 m, Boxboard/cartonboard

ⒶⓂSichuan Yinge Bamboo Pulp & Paper Co., Ltd.
Luzhou (Sichuan Yinge) Mill
Ownership: 40% by Henan Yinge Industrial Investment Co. Ltd., 30% by Guangdong Dongguan Longxing Paper Co., Ltd., 30% by Sichuan Luzhou Jusen Paper Co., Ltd.
Shuangqiao, Quba Town, Naxi District
Luzhou, Sichuan, 646300
China
  Phone: (86) 830 439 0999/0192/0555
  Fax: (86) 830 439 0777
Personnel:
  Chmn.: Lianggang Jia
  Phone: (86) 830 439 0999/0192/0555
  Gen. Mgr.: Zaifu Li
  Phone: (86) 830 439 0999/0192/0555
  Sales Mgr.: Zhuren Zhu
  Phone: (86) 830 439 0999/0192/0555
Total Employees at this Location: 1,000
Type of Operation: Paper mill
Pulp Grades and Capacities:
  Total pulp capacity: 75,735 mt/y
  Pulp available for market: 12,000 mt/y
  Other Pulp: 75,735 mt/y
Pulp Mill Data:
Pulp Lines: 1

China

Paper/Paperboard Grades and Capacities:
Total paper and paperboard capacity: 66,000 mt/y
Uncoated woodfree/freesheet: 26,500 mt/y
Packaging papers: 39,500 mt/y
Paper and Paperboard Mill Data:
Paper Machines: 9
No. 1, fourdrinier, total capacity 10,000 mt/y, Trim width 2.36 m, Packaging papers
No. 2, fourdrinier, total capacity 10,000 mt/y, Trim width 2.36 m, Packaging papers
No. 3, fourdrinier, total capacity 6,500 mt/y, Trim width 1.76 m, Packaging papers
No. 4, fourdrinier, total capacity 6,500 mt/y, Trim width 1.76 m, Packaging papers
No. 5, fourdrinier, total capacity 6,500 mt/y, Trim width 1.76 m, Packaging papers
No. 8, fourdrinier, total capacity 8,250 mt/y, Trim width 1.76 m, Uncoated woodfree/freesheet
No. 9, fourdrinier, total capacity 8,250 mt/y, Trim width 1.76 m, Uncoated woodfree/freesheet
No. 10, fourdrinier, total capacity 5,000 mt/y, Trim width 1.58 m, Uncoated woodfree/freesheet
No. 11, fourdrinier, total capacity 5,000 mt/y, Trim width 1.58 m, Uncoated woodfree/freesheet
Energy Data:
Power boilers: 1
Steam turbines: 2 at 2, 4 MW
Electrical demand for mill: 215 MWh/D

ⓂSichuan Yibin Lantian Paper
Yibin Mill
Luolong Industrial Zone, Nanxi County
Yibin, Sichuan
China
 Phone: (86) 83 330 2356/ 339 5222
 Web Address: www.ybltzy.com
Total Employees at this Location: 500
Type of Operation: Paperboard mill
Pulp Grades and Capacities:
Total pulp capacity: 146,404 mt/y
Recycled Pulping: 146,404 mt/y

Pulp Mill Data:
Bleach Plant Systems: 1
Recycled Pulping System, Type: Deinked
Recycled Fiber Treatment Lines:
Flotation deinking lines: 1
Recycled packaging pulping lines: 1
Paper/Paperboard Grades and Capacities:
Total paper and paperboard capacity: 179,928 mt/y
Boxboard/cartonboard: 179,928 mt/y
Paper and Paperboard Mill Data:
Paper Machines: 1
No. 1, Fourdrinier (4), total capacity 179,928 mt/y, Trim width 3.6 m, Boxboard/cartonboard
Coating Machines: 1
PM1, on machine
Energy Data:
Power boilers
Electrical demand for mill: 260 MWh/D

ⒽⓂSichuan Yongfeng Paper-Making Joint-Stock Co., Ltd.
Leshan Mill
Ownership: 100% by shareholders, 60% by Sichuan Yongfeng Paper-Making Joint-Stock Co., Ltd.
Yongfu Town, Muchuan County
Leshan, Sichuan, 614500
China
 Phone: (86) 833 465 1066/ 1020
 Fax: (86) 833 465 1066/ 1003
 Web Address: www.yfzy.com
Personnel:
Chmn.: Hejun Wu
Phone: (86) 833 465 1066/ 1020
Gen. Mgr.: Wenzhou Huang
Phone: (86) 833 465 1066/ 1020
Total Employees at this Location: 1,150
Type of Operation: Pulp mill, Paper mill

Mill Locations:
Sichuan Hefeng Paper Co., Ltd., Leshan Mill, No.1981, Muyuan Rd., Muxi Town, Muchuan County, Leshan 614500, China, Capacity: 50,000 mt/y, (Paper mill)
Phone: (86) 833 4612 292
Pulp Grades and Capacities:
Total pulp capacity: 130,000 mt/y
Pulp available for market: 58,767 mt/y
Other Pulp: 130,000 mt/y
Pulp Mill Data:
Chemical Pulping Systems:
Batch digesters: 2
Pulp Lines: 2
Bleach Plant Systems: 2
No. 1, Type: Bamboo, Sequence: O_2 DEopD
Chemical Pulping System, Type: Bamboo, Sequence: O_2 DEopD
Chemical Recovery Equipment:
Evaporator lines: 1
Recovery boilers: 2
Pulp Dryers:
Air Float dryers 1, Twin Wire 1
Paper/Paperboard Grades and Capacities:
Total paper and paperboard capacity: 80,000 mt/y
Uncoated woodfree/freesheet: 70,000 mt/y
Packaging papers: 10,000 mt/y
Paper and Paperboard Mill Data:
Paper Machines: 5
No. 3, fourdrinier, total capacity 5,000 mt/y, Trim width 1.76 m, Packaging papers
No. 4, fourdrinier, total capacity 5,000 mt/y, Trim width 1.76 m, Packaging papers
No. 5, fourdrinier, total capacity 15,000 mt/y, Trim width 1.76 m, Uncoated woodfree/freesheet
No. 6, fourdrinier, total capacity 15,000 mt/y, Trim width 1.76 m, Uncoated woodfree/freesheet
No. 7, fourdrinier, total capacity 40,000 mt/y, Trim width 2.64 m, Uncoated woodfree/freesheet
Energy Data:
Power boilers: 2
Steam turbines: 3 at 3, 3, 6 MW
Electrical demand for mill: 371 MWh/D

ⓂSichuan Zigong Tissue Paper Mill
Zigong Mill
Hujia Bridge, Caishi Village, Weiping Town, Yantan District
Zigong, Sichuan, 643031
China
 Phone: (86) 813 3860169
 Fax: (86) 813 3860169
Personnel:
Mill Mgr.: Guifang Shu
Phone: (86) 813 3860169
Total Employees at this Location: 330
Type of Operation: Paper mill
Paper/Paperboard Grades and Capacities:
Total paper and paperboard capacity: 10,000 mt/y
Tissue: 10,000 mt/y
Paper and Paperboard Mill Data:
Paper Machines: 10
PM 1-10, cylinder, total capacity 1,000 mt/y, Trim width 1.09 m, Tissue

ⓂVinda Paper (Sichuan) Co. Ltd.
Deyang Mill
Ownership: Vinda International Holdings Limited.
No. 19, three District, South Longquan Rd.
Deyang, Sichuan, 618000
China
 Phone: (86) 838 290 6199
 Fax: (86) 838 290 6311
 Web Address: www.vindapaper.com
Personnel:
Chmn.: Chaowang Li
Phone: (86) 838 290 6199
Total Employees at this Location: 230
Type of Operation: Paper mill

Paper/Paperboard Grades and Capacities:
Total paper and paperboard capacity: 45,000 mt/y
Tissue: 45,000 mt/y
Paper and Paperboard Mill Data:
Paper Machines: 4
No. 1, BF-10, Yankee dryer, total capacity 10,000 mt/y, Trim width 2.66 m, Tissue, Uncoated woodfree/freesheet
No. 2, BF-10, Yankee dryer, total capacity 10,000 mt/y, Trim width 2.66 m, Tissue, Uncoated woodfree/freesheet
No. 3, BF-10 EX, Yankee dryer, total capacity 12,500 mt/y, Trim width 2.76 m, Tissue, Uncoated woodfree/freesheet
No. 4, BF-10 EX, Yankee dryer, total capacity 12,500 mt/y, Trim width 2.76 m, Tissue, Uncoated woodfree/freesheet
Energy Data:
Power boilers: 1
Electrical demand for mill: 81 MWh/D

ⒽⓂYibin Changyi Pulp Co., Ltd.
Yibin Mill
Company is idle (Idled since December 2012)
Ownership: 50.40% by Yibin Xinya Stock Ltd. Corporation, 49.60% by The Taiwan Jingying Trade Corporation
Yanpingba, Nanguang Town, Cuiping District
Yibin, Sichuan, 644000
China
 Phone: (86) 831 2331 502/2360 496/318
 Email: sales@cn-grace.com
 Web Address: www.cn-grace.com
Total Employees at this Location: 500
Type of Operation: Pulp mill
Pulp Mill Data:
Chemical Pulping Systems:
Not Given: 2
Pulp Lines: 2
Bleach Plant Systems: 2
No. 1, Sequence: CEH
No. 2, Sequence: CEH
Chemical Recovery Equipment:
Evaporator lines
Recovery boilers
Pulp Dryers:
Fourdriniers 1, Fourdriniers 1
Energy Data:
Power boilers: 1

TIANJIN

ⓂNine Dragons Paper (Tianjin) Co., Ltd.
Tianjin Mill
Ownership: Guangdong Dongguan Nine Dragons Paper Industries Co., Ltd.
Jiulong Rd., Economy & Development Zone, Ninghe County
Tianjin, Tianjin, 301500
China
 Phone: (86) 22 6955 8585
 Fax: (86) 22 6922 2139
 Email: info@ndpaper.com, sales@ndpaper.com
 Web Address: www.ndpaper.com
Personnel:
Chmn.: Mrs. Yin Zhang
Vice Chmn., CEO: Mingzhong Liu
CFO: Yuanfu Zhang
Total Employees at this Location: 1,600
Type of Operation: Paperboard mill
Pulp Grades and Capacities:
Total pulp capacity: 1,817,783 mt/y
Recycled Pulping: 1,817,783 mt/y

Pulp Mill Data:
Bleach Plant Systems: 1
Recycled Pulping System

Recycled Fiber Treatment Lines:
Flotation deinking lines: 1
Recycled packaging pulping lines: 2
Paper/Paperboard Grades and Capacities:
Total paper and paperboard capacity: 1,976,352 mt/y
Linerboard: 953,190 mt/y
Corrugating medium/fluting: 473,025 mt/y
Boxboard/cartonboard: 550,137 mt/y
Paper and Paperboard Mill Data:
Paper Machines: 5
No. 25, fourdrinier, total capacity 428,400 mt/y, Trim width 6.66 m, Linerboard
No. 26, DuoFormer D, total capacity 285,600 mt/y, Trim width 6.66 m, Corrugating medium/fluting
No. 27, Multi-wire (3), total capacity 399,840 mt/y, Trim width 6.66 m, Linerboard
No. 31, Multi-wire (3), total capacity 312,375 mt/y, Trim width 6.66 m, Corrugating medium/fluting, Linerboard
No. 34, (started in June 2012.), Multi-wire (4), total capacity 550,137 mt/y, Trim width 6.6 m, Boxboard/cartonboard
Energy Data:
Power boilers
Steam turbines at 159 MW
Electrical demand for mill: 2,979 MWh/D

ⓜTianjin Golden Camel Group
Tianjin Mill
Wangqingtuo Town, Wuqing District
Tianjin, Tianjin, 301713
China
  Phone: (86) 22 2951 8320/ 8545/ 8313
  Fax: (86) 22 2951 8119
  Web Address: www.jintuojt.com
Personnel:
Chmn.: Linming Hu
Phone: (86) 22 2951 8320/ 8545/ 8313
Total Employees at this Location: 1,224
Type of Operation: Paper mill
Paper/Paperboard Grades and Capacities:
Total paper and paperboard capacity: 3,000 mt/y
Tissue: 3,000 mt/y
Paper and Paperboard Mill Data:
Paper Machines: 4
PM 1-4, cylinder, total capacity 750 mt/y, Trim width 1.09 m, Tissue
Energy Data:
Power boilers: 1

ⓘⓜTianjin Guangjuyuan Paper Co., Ltd
Tianjin Mill
  No. 25, Jingu Rd., Xianshuigu Town
Tianjin, Tianjin
China
  Phone: (86) 22 8851 0978/0919/0936
  Fax: (86)
Total Employees at this Location: 445
Type of Operation: Paperboard mill
Pulp Grades and Capacities:
Total pulp capacity: 125,827 mt/y
Recycled Pulping: 78,013 mt/y
Other Pulp: 47,814 mt/y
Pulp Mill Data:
Chemical Pulping Systems:
Batch digesters
Recycled Fiber Treatment Lines:
Recycled packaging pulping lines: 1
Paper/Paperboard Grades and Capacities:
Total paper and paperboard capacity: 129,591 mt/y
Corrugating medium/fluting: 129,591 mt/y
Paper and Paperboard Mill Data:
Paper Machines: 2
No. 1, fourdrinier, total capacity 39,627 mt/y, Trim width 3.8 m, Corrugating medium/fluting
No. 2, Multi-wire (2), total capacity 89,964 mt/y, Trim width 4.8 m, Corrugating medium/fluting
Energy Data:
Power boilers

Steam turbines
Electrical demand for mill: 225 MWh/D

ⓘⓜTianjin Wanli Natural Fiber Co., Ltd
Tianjin Mill
Shigezhuang Town, Wuqing District
Tianjin, Tianjin
China
  Phone: (86) 22 2215 9449
Personnel:
Vice Mgr.: Changhua Jia
Total Employees at this Location: 180
Type of Operation: Paperboard mill
Pulp Grades and Capacities:
Total pulp capacity: 79,476 mt/y
Recycled Pulping: 79,476 mt/y
Pulp Mill Data:
Recycled Fiber Treatment Lines:
Recycled packaging pulping lines: 1
Paper/Paperboard Grades and Capacities:
Total paper and paperboard capacity: 80,000 mt/y
Corrugating medium/fluting: 80,000 mt/y
Paper and Paperboard Mill Data:
Paper Machines: 2
No. 3, cylinder, total capacity 15,000 mt/y, Trim width 3.4 m, Corrugating medium/fluting
No. 5, fourdrinier, total capacity 65,000 mt/y, Trim width 3.8 m, Corrugating medium/fluting
Energy Data:
Power boilers: 4
Electrical demand for mill: 94 MWh/D

ⓜTianjin Zhongchao Paper Co. Ltd.
Tianjin Mill
Ownership: 24.93% by Guangdong Guanhao High-Tech Co., LTD., 24.48% by Tianjin Global Magnetic Card Co., Ltd., 25.94% by Zhongchao Enterprise
No. 38 Xinghua Ave., Xiqing Economy & Development District
Tianjin, Tianjin, 300381
China
  Phone: (86) 22 6037 0931/ 2396 0572
  Fax: (86) 22 2396 1457
  Email: zhagnchaoliushulin@163.com
  Web Address: www.tjzczy.com.cn
Personnel:
Gen. Mgr.: Shulin Liu
Phone: (86) 22 6037 0931/ 2396 0572
Total Employees at this Location: 280
Type of Operation: Paper mill
Paper/Paperboard Grades and Capacities:
Total paper and paperboard capacity: 6,100 mt/y
Tissue: 100 mt/y
Specialty and industrial: 6,000 mt/y
Paper and Paperboard Mill Data:
Paper Machines: 3
PM 1, fourdrinier, total capacity 3,000 mt/y, Trim width 1.76 m, Specialty and industrial
PM 2, cylinder, total capacity 3,000 mt/y, Trim width 1.58 m, Specialty and industrial
PM 3, cylinder, total capacity 100 mt/y, Trim width 1.58 m, Tissue

XINJIANG

ⓘXinjiang Bazhou Mingxing Paper Co., Ltd.
Tashidian Town, Kuerle
Bazhou, Xinjiang, 841012
China
  Phone: (86) 996 2187 247
  Fax: (86) 996 2188 148
Mill Locations:
Xinjiang Bazhou Mingxing Paper Co., Ltd., Bazhou, Tashidian Town, Kuerle , Bazhou 841012, China, Capacity: 12,500 mt/y, (Paper mill)

Phone: (86) 996 2187 247
Fax: (86) 996 2188 148

ⓜXinjiang Bazhou Mingxing Paper Co., Ltd.
Bazhou
Tashidian Town, Kuerle
Bazhou, Xinjiang, 841012
China
  Phone: (86) 996 2187 247
  Fax: (86) 996 2188 148
Personnel:
Gen. Mgr.: Zhongtao Yang
Type of Operation: Paper mill
Paper/Paperboard Grades and Capacities:
Total paper and paperboard capacity: 12,500 mt/y
Tissue: 12,500 mt/y
Paper and Paperboard Mill Data:
Paper Machines: 1
PM 1, (started October 10, 2013), BF-10 EX, total capacity 12,500 mt/y, Trim width 2.76 m, Tissue

ⓘXinjiang Bohu Reed Industry Stock Co., Ltd.
Ownership: 100% by shareholders
Loulan Rd., Xincheng district
Kuerle, Xinjiang, 841001
China
  Phone: (86) 996 215 1000/9775/ 216 0775/ 0000
  Fax: (86) 996 215 2070/ 3164
  Email: bohureed@163.com
  Web Address: www.bohureed.com
Personnel:
Chmn. & Pres.: Hong Lei
Gen. Mgr.: Zhiming Sun
Pulp Sls. Mgr.: Ms. Mei Yang
Phone: (86) 996 216 0000
Fax: (86) 996 215 3164
Paper Sls. Mgr.: Baozhen Wang
Phone: (86) 996 215 9999
Fax: (86) 996 215 3164
Total Employees of Company: 1,396
Mill Locations:
Xinjiang Bohu Reed Industry Stock Co., Ltd., Kuerle (No.1) Mill, Loulan Rd., Xincheng district, Kuerle 841001, China, Capacity: 50,500 mt/y, (Pulp mill, Paper mill)
Phone: (86) 996 215 1000/216 0000/216 1717
Fax: (86) 996 215 2070/ 3164
Email: bohureed@163.com
Xinjiang Bohu Reed Industry Stock Co., Ltd., Kuerle (No.2) Mill, Economic & Technology Development Area, Kuerle, China, (Pulp mill)
Phone: (86) 996 215 9728
Fax: (86) 996 215 2070/ 3164
Email: bohureed@163.com

ⓜXinjiang Bohu Reed Industry Stock Co., Ltd.
Kuerle (No.1) Mill
Loulan Rd., Xincheng district
Kuerle, Xinjiang, 841001
China
  Phone: (86) 996 215 1000/216 0000/216 1717
  Fax: (86) 996 215 2070/ 3164
  Email: bohureed@163.com
  Web Address: www.bohureed.com
Personnel:
Chmn. & Pres.: Hong Lei
Phone: (86) 996 215 1000/9775/ 216 0775/ 0000
Gen. Mgr.: Zhiming Sun
Phone: (86) 996 215 1000/9775/ 216 0775/ 0000
Pulp Sls. Mgr.: Ms. Mei Yang
Phone: (86) 996 216 0000
Fax: (86) 996 215 3164
Paper Sls. Mgr.: Baozhen Wang
Phone: (86) 996 215 9999
Fax: (86) 996 215 3164
Type of Operation: Pulp mill, Paper mill

China

Pulp Grades and Capacities:
Total pulp capacity: 31,522 mt/y
Other Pulp: 31,522 mt/y
Pulp Mill Data:
Chemical Pulping Systems:
Batch digesters: 2
Pulp Lines: 2
Bleach Plant Systems: 1
No. 1
Chemical Recovery Equipment:
Evaporator lines
Recovery boilers: 3
Paper/Paperboard Grades and Capacities:
Total paper and paperboard capacity: 50,500 mt/y
Uncoated woodfree/freesheet: 50,500 mt/y
Paper and Paperboard Mill Data:
Paper Machines: 5
No. 2, fourdrinier, total capacity 15,000 mt/y, Trim width 1.88 m, Uncoated woodfree/freesheet
No. 3, fourdrinier, total capacity 5,000 mt/y, Trim width 1.58 m, Uncoated woodfree/freesheet
No. 4, fourdrinier, total capacity 15,000 mt/y, Trim width 1.88 m, Uncoated woodfree/freesheet
No. 10, fourdrinier, total capacity 8,500 mt/y, Trim width 1.76 m, Uncoated woodfree/freesheet
No. 11, fourdrinier, total capacity 7,000 mt/y, Trim width 1.76 m, Uncoated woodfree/freesheet
Energy Data:
Power boilers: 4
Steam turbines: 4
Electrical demand for mill: 142 MWh/D

ⓂXinjiang Bohu Reed Industry Stock Co., Ltd.
Kuerle (No.2) Mill
Economic & Technology Development Area
Kuerle, Xinjiang
China
Phone: (86) 996 215 9728
Fax: (86) 996 215 2070/ 3164
Email: bohureed@163.com
Web Address: www.bohureed.com
Type of Operation: Pulp mill
Pulp Grades and Capacities:
Total pulp capacity: 100,345 mt/y
Pulp available for market: 100,000 mt/y
Other Pulp: 100,345 mt/y
Pulp Mill Data:
Pulp Lines: 1
Bleach Plant Systems: 1
No. 1, Sequence: O₂ DEopD, Capacity 100,000 admt/y
Chemical Recovery Equipment:
Recovery boilers: 1
Pulp Dryers:
Cylinder Dryer 1
Energy Data:
Power boilers: 1
Steam turbines: 1 at 15 MW
Electrical demand for mill: 183 MWh/D

ⓄXinjiang Helon Co., Ltd.
No.2 Industrial Park
Alaer, Xinjiang, 843300
China
Web Address: www.helon.cn
Mill Locations:
Xinjiang Helon Co., Ltd., Alaer Mill, No.2 Industrial Park, Alaer 843300, China, (Pulp mill)

ⓂXinjiang Helon Co., Ltd.
Alaer Mill
No.2 Industrial Park
Alaer, Xinjiang, 843300
China
Web Address: www.helon.cn
Type of Operation: Pulp mill
Pulp Grades and Capacities:
Total pulp capacity: 100,000 mt/y
Pulp available for market: 100,000 mt/y
Pulp Mill Data:
Chemical Pulping Systems:
Batch digesters
Pulp Lines: 2

ⓂXinjiang Manasi Aoyang Technology Co., Ltd.
Manasi Mill
Ownership: Jiangsu Aoyang Technology Co., Ltd.
The West Industrial Park, Manasi County
Changji, Xinjiang, 832200
China
Phone: (86) 994 6620 858
Fax: (86) 994 6620 858
Email: hollyandlucky@yahoo.com.cn
Web Address: www.aykj.cn
Type of Operation: Pulp mill
Pulp Grades and Capacities:
Total pulp capacity: 80,000 mt/y
Pulp available for market: 80,000 mt/y
Pulp Mill Data:
Chemical Pulping Systems:
Not Given: 1
Pulp Lines: 1

ⓂXinjiang Silver Hawk Gongmao Co., Ltd.
Tacheng Mill
Ownership: Shandong Gaomi Silver Hawk Group Co., Ltd.
Liumaowan Town, Shawan County
Tacheng, Xinjiang, 832100
China
Phone: (86) 993 6613 666
Fax: (86) 993 6613 111
Web Address: www.yying.cn
Total Employees at this Location: 1,000
Type of Operation: Pulp mill
Pulp Grades and Capacities:
Total pulp capacity: 120,126 mt/y
Pulp available for market: 120,000 mt/y
Chemical Pulp: 120,126 mt/y
Pulp Mill Data:
Chemical Pulping Systems:
Batch digesters: 3
Pulp Lines: 3
Bleach Plant Systems: 3
Chemical Pulping System, Type: Cotton Linter
Chemical Pulping System, Type: Cotton Linter
Chemical Pulping System, Type: Cotton Linter
Pulp Dryers:
Fourdriniers 1, Fourdriniers 1, Fourdriniers 1, Fourdriniers 1
Energy Data:
Power boilers: 3
Steam turbines
Electrical demand for mill: 179 MWh/D

ⓄXinjiang Taichang Industry Co., Ltd.
Xinier Industrial Park, Kuerler
Bazhou, Xinjiang
China
Phone: (86) 996 2100 010
Fax: (86) 996 2100 001
Email: xjtcsyyxzrgs@163.com
Web Address: www.taichang.ec.cn/chinese/F/03/default.asp
Total Employees at this Location: 478
Mill Locations:
Xinjiang Taichang Industry Co., Ltd., BazhouMill, Xinier Industrial Park, Kuerler, Bazhou, China, (Pulp mill)
Phone: (86) 996 2100 010
Fax: (86) 996 2100 001
Email: xjtcsyyxzrgs@163.com

ⓂXinjiang Taichang Industry Co., Ltd.
BazhouMill
Xinier Industrial Park, Kuerler
Bazhou, Xinjiang
China
Phone: (86) 996 2100 010
Fax: (86) 996 2100 001
Email: xjtcsyyxzrgs@163.com
Web Address: www.taichang.ec.cn/chinese/F/03/default.asp
Total Employees at this Location: 1,000
Type of Operation: Pulp mill
Pulp Grades and Capacities:
Total pulp capacity: 140,190 mt/y
Pulp available for market: 140,000 mt/y
Chemical Pulp: 140,190 mt/y
Pulp Mill Data:
Chemical Pulping Systems:
Batch digesters: 3
Pulp Lines: 3
Bleach Plant Lines:
Chemical Pulping System, Type: Catton Linter
Pulp Dryers:
Fourdriniers 1, Fourdriniers 1, Fourdriniers 1
Energy Data:
Power boilers
Steam turbines
Electrical demand for mill: 218 MWh/D

ⓄXinjiang Tianhong Paper Co., Ltd.
Ownership: 58.10% by shareholders, 41.90% by Xinjiang Shihezi Paper Mill
No. 17, Xisan Rd.
Shihezi, Xinjiang, 832009
China
Phone: (86) 993 251 5661/ 752 6027
Fax: (86) 993 251 1714/7749/7773/ 752 6088
Email: zcjzcz@jbip.com,
fzg63@263.net,
webmaster@thpaper.com
Web Address: www.xjth.cn
Personnel:
Chmn. & Pres.: Xia Li
Phone: (86) 993 251 5661
Fax: (86) 993 251 1714
VP/Mill Mgr.: Yuzhu Wang
Phone: (86) 993 251 5661
Fax: (86) 993 251 1714
CFO, Dpty. Gen. Mgr.: Qing Wang
Phone: (86) 993 251 5661
Fax: (86) 993 251 1714
Total Employees of Company: 1,200
Mill Locations:
Almaty Maolin Paper, Almaty Mill, Karasai District, Kazakhstan, Capacity: 5,000 mt/y, (Paper mill)
Xinjiang Tianhong Paper Co., Ltd., Shihezi Mill, No. 17, Xisan Rd., Shihezi 832009, China, Capacity: 24,000 mt/y, (Paper mill)
Phone: (86) 993 251 5661/ 752 6027
Fax: (86) 993 251 1714/7749/7773/ 752 6088
Email: zcjzcz@jbip.com, fzg63@263.net, webmaster@thpaper.com

ⓂXinjiang Tianhong Paper Co., Ltd.
Shihezi Mill
No. 17, Xisan Rd.
Shihezi, Xinjiang, 832009
China
Phone: (86) 993 251 5661/ 752 6027
Fax: (86) 993 251 1714/7749/7773/ 752 6088
Email: zcjzcz@jbip.com,
fzg63@263.net,
webmaster@thpaper.com
Web Address: www.xjth.cn
Personnel:
Chmn. & Pres.: Xia Li
VP/Mill Mgr.: Yuzhu Wang
CFO, Dpty. Gen. Mgr.: Qing Wang
Dpty. Gen. Mgr., Board Secretary, Dir.: Qiaoling Wang

Dpty. Gen. Mgr.: Bo Wang
Dpty. Gen. Mgr.: Jiang Yin
Dpty. Gen. Mgr.: Weidong Lou
Dpty. Gen. Mgr.: Junying Zhou
Total Employees at this Location: 1,200
Type of Operation: Paper mill
Pulp Grades and Capacities:
Total pulp capacity: 50,000 mt/y
Pulp Mill Data:
Pulp Lines: 2
Paper/Paperboard Grades and Capacities:
Total paper and paperboard capacity: 24,000 mt/y
Uncoated woodfree/freesheet: 20,000 mt/y
Tissue: 4,000 mt/y
Paper and Paperboard Mill Data:
Paper Machines: 9
PM 7, fourdrinier, total capacity 12,000 mt/y, Trim width 1.76 m, Uncoated woodfree/freesheet
PM 8, fourdrinier, total capacity 8,000 mt/y, Trim width 1.76 m, Uncoated woodfree/freesheet
PM 9, fourdrinier, total capacity 9,000 mt/y, Trim width 1.76 m, Uncoated woodfree/freesheet
PM 14, cylinder, total capacity 10,000 mt/y, Trim width 1.76 m, Uncoated woodfree/freesheet
PM 15, cylinder, total capacity 5,000 mt/y, Trim width 1.76 m, Uncoated woodfree/freesheet
TM 1, (leased to private owners), cylinder, total capacity 1,000 mt/y, Trim width 1.76 m, Tissue
TM 2, (leased to private owners), cylinder, total capacity 1,000 mt/y, Trim width 1.76 m, Tissue
TM 3, (leased to private owners), cylinder, total capacity 1,000 mt/y, Trim width 1.76 m, Tissue
TM 4, (leased to private owners), cylinder, total capacity 2,500 mt/y, Trim width 1.76 m, Tissue
Coating Machines: 1
No. 1, total capacity 9,000 mt/y.

ⓘXinjiang Tianli Paper Co., Ltd.
Tashidian Town, Kuerle
Bazhou, Xinjiang, 841012
China
Phone: (86) 996 2187 247
Fax: (86) 996 2188 148
Total Employees at this Location: 200
Mill Locations:
Xinjiang Tianli Paper Co., Ltd., Bazhou Mill, Tashidian Town, Kuerle, Bazhou 841012, China, (Paper mill)
Phone: (86) 996 2187 247
Fax: (86) 996 2188 148

ⓜXinjiang Tianli Paper Co., Ltd.
Bazhou Mill
Tashidian Town, Kuerle
Bazhou, Xinjiang, 841012
China
Phone: (86) 996 2187 247
Fax: (86) 996 2188 148
Total Employees at this Location: 200
Type of Operation: Paper mill
Paper and Paperboard Mill Data:
Paper Machines: 2
PM 1, total capacity 8,000 mt/y, Trim width 1.76 m, Newsprint
PM 8, total capacity 12,000 mt/y, Trim width 1.88 m, Newsprint
Energy Data:
Power boilers

YUNNAN

ⓘYunnan Luliang Yinhe Paper Co., Ltd.
No.51 Xinglong Rd, Luliang County
Qujing, Yunnan, 655600
China
Phone: (86) 874 6869 566/522/090/046
Mill Locations:
Yunnan Luliang Yinhe Paper Co., Ltd., Qujing Mill, No.51 Xinglong Rd, Luliang County, Qujing 655600, China,
Capacity: 50,000 mt/y, (Pulp mill, Paper mill)
Phone: (86) 874 6869 566/522/090/046

ⓜYunnan Luliang Yinhe Paper Co., Ltd.
Qujing Mill
No.51 Xinglong Rd, Luliang County
Qujing, Yunnan, 655600
China
Phone: (86) 874 6869 566/522/090/046
Type of Operation: Pulp mill, Paper mill
Pulp Grades and Capacities:
Total pulp capacity: 50,000 mt/y
Pulp Mill Data:
Pulp Lines: 1
Paper/Paperboard Grades and Capacities:
Total paper and paperboard capacity: 50,000 mt/y
Uncoated woodfree/freesheet: 50,000 mt/y
Paper and Paperboard Mill Data:
Paper Machines: 5
PM 5, total capacity 18,000 mt/y, Trim width 2.36 m, Uncoated woodfree/freesheet
PM 1-4, total capacity 8,000 mt/y, Trim width 1.88 m, Uncoated woodfree/freesheet

ⓜYunnan Changning Jianxing Paper Co., Ltd.
Baoshan Mill
Gongyu Village, Mangshui Town, Changning County
Baoshan, Yunnan, 678111
China
Phone: (86) 871 459 4513
Fax: (86) 871 459 4513
Personnel:
Chmn. & Pres.: Jainqiao Zhan
Phone: (86) 871 459 4513
Total Employees at this Location: 470
Type of Operation: Paper mill
Pulp Grades and Capacities:
Total pulp capacity: 20,000 mt/y
Pulp Mill Data:
Pulp Lines: 2
Paper/Paperboard Grades and Capacities:
Total paper and paperboard capacity: 30,000 mt/y
Uncoated woodfree/freesheet: 30,000 mt/y
Uncoated mechanical/groundwood
Paper and Paperboard Mill Data:
Paper Machines: 3
No. 1, cylinder, total capacity 6,000 mt/y, Trim width 1.58 m, Uncoated woodfree/freesheet, Uncoated mechanical/groundwood
No. 2, cylinder, total capacity 6,000 mt/y, Trim width 1.58 m, Uncoated mechanical/groundwood, Uncoated woodfree/freesheet
No. 3, fourdrinier, total capacity 18,000 mt/y, Trim width 1.76 m, Uncoated woodfree/freesheet, Uncoated mechanical/groundwood
Energy Data:
Power boilers: 3

ⓜYunnan Dali Huacheng Paper Co., Ltd.
Dali Mill
Xiaguan Town
Dali, Yunnan, 671000
China
Phone: (86) 872 212 4214/5555/5662/ 228 2858
Fax: (86) 872 212 3645/5964/ 222 3645
Email: dlxgw@163.net, lliu-xgll@163.com
Personnel:
Chmn. & Pres.: Xiang Shi
Phone: (86) 872 212 4214/5555/5662/ 228 2858
Total Employees at this Location: 430
Type of Operation: Paperboard mill, Paperboard mill
Pulp Grades and Capacities:
Total pulp capacity: 42,005 mt/y
Recycled Pulping: 42,005 mt/y
Pulp Mill Data:
Pulp Lines: 1
Chemical Recovery Equipment:
Recovery boilers: 1
Recycled Fiber Treatment Lines:
Recycled packaging pulping lines: 1 at 71,000 admt/y
Paper/Paperboard Grades and Capacities:
Total paper and paperboard capacity: 43,197 mt/y
Corrugating medium/fluting: 43,197 mt/y
Paper and Paperboard Mill Data:
Paper Machines: 1
No. 4, multi-wire, total capacity 43,197 mt/y, Trim width 2.8 m, Corrugating medium/fluting
Energy Data:
Electrical demand for mill: 59 MWh/D

ⓜYunnan Hanguang Paper Co., Ltd.
Yuxi Mill
Shuizhakou Qixiang Rd., Gaoda Village, Tonghai County
Yuxi, Yunnan, 652700
China
Phone: (86) 877 3031 789/807/517
Fax: (86) 877 3031 739
Web Address: thhg.china.b2b.cn
Personnel:
Chmn.: Hanguang Jun
Phone: (86) 877 3031 789/807
Sls. Mgr.: Yi Zhang
Phone: (86) 877 3031 789/807
Oper. Mgr.: Youxiong Guo
Phone: (86) 877 3031 789/807
Total Employees at this Location: 287
Type of Operation: Paper mill
Paper/Paperboard Grades and Capacities:
Total paper and paperboard capacity: 50,000 mt/y
Tissue: 50,000 mt/y
Paper and Paperboard Mill Data:
Paper Machines: 13
PM 1-4, cylinder, total capacity 3,850 mt/y, Trim width 2.04 m, Tissue
PM 5-13, cylinder, total capacity 3,850 mt/y, Trim width 2.04 m, Tissue
Energy Data:
Power boilers: 2

ⓜYunnan Hongta Blue Eagle Paper Co., Ltd.
Honghe Mill
Ownership: Julius Glatz GmbH Papierfabriken, Hongta Group
Zhuangzihe Village, Dongba Town, Jianshui County
Honghe District, Yunnan, 654300
China
Phone: (86) 873 765 2061/ 2341
Fax: (86) 873 765 2496/ 2061
Email: zoubaogang@ynhtbe.com, pengxingzhu@ynhtbe.com, yangfukang@ynhtbe.com
Web Address: www.ynhtbe.com
Personnel:
CEO: Fajia Yang
Phone: (86) 873 765 2061/ 2341
Gen. Mgr.: Deming Jia
Phone: (86) 873 765 2061/ 2341
VP-Technology/Chief: Fukang Yang
Phone: (86) 873 765 3573
Email: yangfukang@ynhtbe.com
Sls. Mgr.: Baogang Zhou
Phone: (86) 873 765 3556/ 7912
Email: zhoubaogang@ynhtbe.com
Total Employees at this Location: 860
Type of Operation: Paper mill
Paper/Paperboard Grades and Capacities:
Total paper and paperboard capacity: 24,000 mt/y
Specialty and industrial: 24,000 mt/y
Paper and Paperboard Mill Data:
Paper Machines: 2
PM 1, fourdrinier, total capacity 12,000 mt/y, Trim width 3.25 m, Specialty and industrial
PM 3, fourdrinier, total capacity 12,000 mt/y, Trim width 3.25 m, Specialty and industrial

China

Finishing Equipment:
Rewinders: 3
Sheeters: 1

ⓜYunnan Jiangchuan Cuifeng Paper Co., Ltd.
Yuxi Mill
Jiangchuan Cuifeng Industry Park, Jiangcheng Town
Yuxi, Yunnan, 652601
China
  Phone: (86) 877 8095 188/268/156
  Fax: (86) 877 8095 268
  Email: jccfzy@126.com
  Web Address: www.jccfzy.com
Personnel:
  Chmn. & Gen. Mgr.: Jihua Li
  Phone: (86) 877 8095 188/268/156
Total Employees at this Location: 800
Type of Operation: Paper mill
Paper/Paperboard Grades and Capacities:
  Total paper and paperboard capacity: 50,000 mt/y
  Tissue: 50,000 mt/y
Paper and Paperboard Mill Data:
Paper Machines: 36
PM 1-14, cylinder, total capacity 750 mt/y, Trim width 1.58 m, Tissue
PM 15-20, cylinder, total capacity 1,200 mt/y, Trim width 1.88 m, Tissue
PM 21-27, cylinder, total capacity 1,200 mt/y, Trim width 1.88 m, Tissue
PM 28-35, cylinder, total capacity 1,500 mt/y, Trim width 1.88 m, Tissue
PM 36, total capacity 12,000 mt/y, Trim width 2.7 m, Tissue
Energy Data:
Power boilers: 4

ⓜYunnan Kunming Zhenlong Paper Mill
Kunming Mill
Gou Street, Yiliang County
Kunming, Yunnan, 652100
China
  Phone: (86) 871 7611 218
  Fax: (86) 871 7611 218
Personnel:
  Gen. Mgr.: Dongrong Wu
  Phone: (86) 871 7611 218
Total Employees at this Location: 180
Type of Operation: Paper mill
Paper/Paperboard Grades and Capacities:
  Total paper and paperboard capacity: 10,000 mt/y
  Tissue: 10,000 mt/y
Paper and Paperboard Mill Data:
Paper Machines: 12
PM 1-12, cylinder, total capacity 835 mt/y, Trim width 1.58 m, Tissue

ⓜYunnan Lincang Nanhua Paper Co., Ltd.
Lincang Mill
Mill is idle (being rebuilt, due to start up early 2015)
Ownership: 100% by Guangxi Yangpu Nanhua Sugar Industry Group Co., Ltd.
Shifodong Village, Sipaishan Town, Gengma County
Lincang, Yunnan
China
  Phone: (86) 871 6354 1217
  Web Address: www.gxypnh.com
Type of Operation: Pulp mill, Paper mill
Pulp Grades and Capacities:
  Total pulp capacity: 95,000 mt/y
  Pulp available for market: 95,000 mt/y
Pulp Mill Data:
  Chemical Pulping Systems:
  Batch digesters: 1
Pulp Lines: 1
Bleach Plant Systems: 1
No. 1, Sequence: CEpH
Chemical Recovery Equipment:
Recovery boilers: 1
Paper/Paperboard Grades and Capacities:
  Total paper and paperboard capacity: 50,000 mt/y
Paper and Paperboard Mill Data:
Paper Machines: 2
PM 1, total capacity 25,000 mt/y, Trim width 2.64 m
PM 2, total capacity 25,000 mt/y, Trim width 2.64 m
Energy Data:
Power boilers: 2

ⓜYunnan Lujiang Paper Co., Ltd.
Kaiyuan Mill
Lebaidao Dongcheng District
Kaiyuan, Yunnan, 661600
China
  Phone: (86) 873 722 3561
  Fax: (86) 873 722 3348
Personnel:
  Chmn.: Chenghua He
  Phone: (86) 873 722 3561
Total Employees at this Location: 100
Type of Operation: Paper mill
Pulp Grades and Capacities:
  Total pulp capacity: 3,000 mt/y
  Recycled Pulping: 3,000 mt/y
Pulp Mill Data:
Pulp Lines: 1
Paper/Paperboard Grades and Capacities:
  Total paper and paperboard capacity: 2,940 mt/y
  Tissue: 2,940 mt/y
Paper and Paperboard Mill Data:
Paper Machines: 3
PM 6, cylinder, total capacity 1,500 mt/y, Trim width 1.58 m, Tissue
PM 4-5, cylinder, total capacity 720 mt/y, Trim width 1.09 m, Tissue

ⓜYunnan Wenshan Yunhe Paper Industry Co., Ltd.
Wenshan Mill
North Kaihua Rd., Wenshan County
Wenshan, Yunnan, 663000
China
  Phone: (86) 876 2623 803/ 705
  Fax: (86) 876 2623 688
Personnel:
  Chmn., Gen. Mgr.: Yunchuan Zheng
  Phone: (86) 876 2623 803/ 705
  Sls. Mgr.: Kuijun Song
  Phone: (86) 876 2623 803/ 705
Total Employees at this Location: 180
Type of Operation: Paper mill
Paper/Paperboard Grades and Capacities:
  Total paper and paperboard capacity: 7,000 mt/y
  Tissue: 7,000 mt/y
Paper and Paperboard Mill Data:
Paper Machines: 4
PM 1-2, cylinder, total capacity 1,250 mt/y, Trim width 1.09 m, Tissue
PM 3-4, cylinder, total capacity 2,250 mt/y, Trim width 1.58 m, Tissue

ⓜYunnan Xinping Nanen Sugar and Paper Co., Ltd.
No.16, Gasa Rd., Gasa Town, Xinping County
Yuxi, Yunnan, 653405
China
  Phone: (86) 877 7391 061
Mill Locations:
Yunnan Xinping Nanen Sugar and Paper Co., Ltd., Yuxi Mill, No.16, Gasa Rd., Gasa Town, Xinping County, Yuxi 653405 , China, Capacity: 20,000 mt/y, (Pulp mill, Paper mill)
Phone: (86) 877 7391 061

ⓜYunnan Xinping Nanen Sugar and Paper Co., Ltd.
Yuxi Mill
No.16, Gasa Rd., Gasa Town, Xinping County
Yuxi, Yunnan, 653405
China
  Phone: (86) 877 7391 061
Type of Operation: Pulp mill, Paper mill
Pulp Grades and Capacities:
  Total pulp capacity: 20,000 mt/y
Paper/Paperboard Grades and Capacities:
  Total paper and paperboard capacity: 20,000 mt/y
  Tissue: 20,000 mt/y
Paper and Paperboard Mill Data:
Paper Machines: 15
PM 1, total capacity 1,800 mt/y, Trim width 1.76 m, Tissue
PM 2, total capacity 1,300 mt/y, Trim width 1.58 m, Tissue
PM 3, total capacity 1,300 mt/y, Trim width 1.58 m, Tissue
PM 4, total capacity 1,300 mt/y, Trim width 1.58 m, Tissue
PM 5, total capacity 1,300 mt/y, Trim width 1.58 m, Tissue
PM 6, total capacity 1,300 mt/y, Trim width 1.58 m, Tissue
PM 7, total capacity 1,300 mt/y, Trim width 1.58 m, Tissue
PM 8, total capacity 1,300 mt/y, Trim width 1.58 m, Tissue
PM 9, total capacity 1,300 mt/y, Trim width 1.58 m, Tissue
PM 10, total capacity 1,300 mt/y, Trim width 1.58 m, Tissue
PM 11, total capacity 1,300 mt/y, Trim width 1.58 m, Tissue
PM 12, total capacity 1,300 mt/y, Trim width 1.58 m, Tissue
PM 13, total capacity 1,300 mt/y, Trim width 1.58 m, Tissue
PM 14, total capacity 1,300 mt/y, Trim width 1.58 m, Tissue
PM 15, total capacity 1,300 mt/y, Trim width 1.58 m, Tissue

ⓘYunnan Yun-Jing Forestry & Paper Mill Co., Ltd.
Ownership: 100% by Yunnan Development & Investment Corp.
No. 300, Linzhi Rd., Weiyuan Town
Jinggu County, Puer City, Yunnan, 666400
China
  Phone: (86) 879 5410 199/522 4275/4004
  Fax: (86) 879 5410 193
  Email: yunyinggongsi@sina.com
  Web Address: www.yjlzh.com
Personnel:
  Chmn. & Pres.: Haijian Liu
  Gen. Mgr.: Zhaowu You
  Vice Gen. Mgr.: Xinghong Chen
  Vice Gen. Mgr.: Shiyong Li
  Pulp Mill Mgr.: Mingfeng Liu
  Tech. Dir.: Yahui Yang
  Chief Eng.: Jianguo Zhou
  Environ. Dir.: Xuehong Li
Total Employees at this Location: 1,300
Mill Locations:
Yunnan Yun-Jing Forestry & Paper Mill Co., Ltd., Jinggu Mill, No. 300, Linzhi Rd., Weiyuan Town, Jinggu County, Puer 666400, China, (Pulp mill)
Phone: (86) 879 5410 199/522 4275/4004
Fax: (86) 879 5410 193
Email: yunyinggongsi@sina.com

ⓜYunnan Yun-Jing Forestry & Paper Mill Co., Ltd.
Jinggu Mill
No. 300, Linzhi Rd., Weiyuan Town, Jinggu County
Puer, Yunnan, 666400
China
  Phone: (86) 879 5410 199/522 4275/4004
  Fax: (86) 879 5410 193
  Email: yunyinggongsi@sina.com
Personnel:
  Chmn. & Pres.: Haijian Liu
  Phone: (86) 879 5410 199/522 4275/4004
  Gen. Mgr.: Zhaowu You
  Phone: (86) 879 5410 199/522 4275/4004
  Vice Gen. Mgr.: Xinghong Chen
  Phone: (86) 879 5410 199/522 4275/4004
  Vice Gen. Mgr.: Shiyong Li
  Phone: (86) 879 5410 199/522 4275/4004
  Pulp Mill Mgr.: Mingfeng Liu

China

Phone: (86) 879 5410 199/522 4275/4004
Tech. Dir.: Yahui Yang
Phone: (86) 879 5410 199/522 4275/4004
Chief Eng.: Jianguo Zhou
Phone: (86) 879 5410 199/522 4275/4004
Environ. Dir.: Xuehong Li
Phone: (86) 879 5410 199/522 4275/4004
Total Employees at this Location: 900
Type of Operation: Pulp mill
Pulp Grades and Capacities:
Total pulp capacity: 202,552 mt/y
Pulp available for market: 200,000 mt/y
Chemical Pulp: 202,552 mt/y
Pulp Mill Data:
Chemical Pulping Systems:
Batch digesters: 1
Continuous digesters: 1
Pulp Lines: 2
Bleach Plant Systems: 2
Chemical Pulping System, Type: Softwood/Euca/Hardwood - ECF, Sequence: O_2 DEopD, Capacity 110,000 admt/y
Chemical Pulping System, Type: Softwood/Euca -ECF, Sequence: O_2 DEopD, Capacity 90,000 admt/y
Chemical Recovery Equipment:
Evaporator lines
Recovery boilers: 1
Recovery boilers: 1
Recovery boilers: 1
Lime Kiln
Pulp Dryers:
Fourdriniers 1, Fourdriniers 1, Pulp Dryers 1, Pulp Dryers 1
Energy Data:
Power boilers: 1
Steam turbines: 4 at 43 MW
Electrical demand for mill: 450 MWh/D

ⓂYunnan Yuxi Dongsheng Paper Co., Ltd.
Yuxi Mill
Near Dongfeng Reservoir
Yuxi, Yunnan, 653100
China
Phone: (86) 877 205 0312/205 0670
Fax: (86) 877 205 6036
Personnel:
Deputy Gen. Mgr.: Baolin He
Phone: (86) 877 205 0312/205 0670
Total Employees at this Location: 80
Type of Operation: Paperboard mill
Pulp Grades and Capacities:
Total pulp capacity: 30,000 mt/y
Recycled Pulping: 30,000 mt/y
Pulp Mill Data:
Chemical Pulping Systems:
Batch digesters: 2
Pulp Lines: 4
Recycled Fiber Treatment Lines:
Recycled packaging pulping lines: 4 at 30,000 admt/y
Paper/Paperboard Grades and Capacities:
Total paper and paperboard capacity: 10,000 mt/y
Corrugating medium/fluting: 10,000 mt/y
Paper and Paperboard Mill Data:
Paper Machines: 4
No. 1, multi-wire, total capacity 10,000 mt/y, Trim width 1.6 m, Corrugating medium/fluting
No. 2, (idled since June 2008), multi-wire, total capacity 6,000 mt/y, Trim width 1.09 m, Corrugating medium/fluting
No. 3, (idled since June 2008), multi-wire, total capacity 6,000 mt/y, Trim width 1.09 m, Corrugating medium/fluting
No. 4, (idled since June 2008), multi-wire, total capacity 8,000 mt/y, Trim width 1.76 m, Corrugating medium/fluting
Energy Data:
Power boilers: 1

ZHEJIANG

ⓄAnji Huayingtai Paper Co., Ltd.
Anji County
Huzhou, Zhejiang, 311200
China
Phone: (86) 572 5218 696
Mill Locations:
Anji Huayingtai Paper Co., Ltd., Huzhou Mill, Anji County, Huzhou 311200, China, Capacity: 9,600 mt/y, (Paper mill)
Phone: (86) 572 5218 696

ⓂAnji Huayingtai Paper Co., Ltd.
Huzhou Mill
Anji County
Huzhou, Zhejiang, 311200
China
Phone: (86) 572 5218 696
Type of Operation: Paper mill
Paper/Paperboard Grades and Capacities:
Total paper and paperboard capacity: 9,600 mt/y
Tissue: 9,600 mt/y
Paper and Paperboard Mill Data:
Paper Machines: 4
PM 1, total capacity 1,500 mt/y, Trim width 1.88 m, Tissue
PM 2, total capacity 1,500 mt/y, Trim width 1.88 m, Tissue
PM 3, total capacity 3,300 mt/y, Trim width 2.4 m, Tissue
PM 4, total capacity 3,300 mt/y, Trim width 2.4 m, Tissue

ⓂC&S Paper Co., Ltd.
Jiaxing Mill
No. 222 Weisan Rd., Zhapu Town
Jiaxing, Zhejiang, 313301
China
Phone: (86) 573 8558 1109/1101/6005/3180
Fax: (86) 573 8558 1101
Web Address: www.zhongshungroup.com
Personnel:
Gen. Mgr.: Yuwu Liu
Phone: (86) 573 5583 798/ 8558 1109
Total Employees at this Location: 125
Type of Operation: Paper mill
Paper/Paperboard Grades and Capacities:
Total paper and paperboard capacity: 22,500 mt/y
Tissue: 22,500 mt/y
Paper and Paperboard Mill Data:
Paper Machines: 2
No. 1, BF-10, total capacity 10,000 mt/y, Trim width 2.66 m, Tissue, Uncoated woodfree/freesheet
No. 2, BF-10 EX, total capacity 12,500 mt/y, Trim width 2.76 m, Tissue, Uncoated woodfree/freesheet
Energy Data:
Electrical demand for mill: 32 MWh/D

ⓄFulida Group Holding Co., Ltd
Farm 2, Xinwan
Xiaoshan, Hanggzhou, Zhejiang, 311228
China
Phone: (86) 571 82125120
Fax: (86) 571 82127258
Email: fld@fulida.cn
Web Address: www.fulida.cn
Mill Locations:
Neucel Specialty Cellulose Ltd., Port Alice Mill, 300 Marine Drive, Port Alice, BC, Canada V0N 2N0, (Pulp mill)
Phone: (1) 250-284-3331
Fax: (1) 250-284-7715
Email: info@neucel.com

ⓄFuyang Jinfeng Paper Co., Ltd.
Fuyuan Village, Fuyang
Hangzhou, Zhejiang, 311421
China
Phone: (86) 571 2321 4888
Mill Locations:
Fuyang Jinfeng Paper Co., Ltd., Fuyang Mill, Fuyuan Village, Fuyang, Hangzhou 311421, China, Capacity: 9,000 mt/y, (Paper mill)
Phone: (86) 571 2321 4888

ⓂFuyang Jinfeng Paper Co., Ltd.
Fuyang Mill
Fuyuan Village, Fuyang
Hangzhou, Zhejiang, 311421
China
Phone: (86) 571 2321 4888
Type of Operation: Paper mill
Paper/Paperboard Grades and Capacities:
Total paper and paperboard capacity: 9,000 mt/y
Tissue: 9,000 mt/y
Paper and Paperboard Mill Data:
Paper Machines: 5
PM 1, total capacity 1,800 mt/y, Trim width 2.4 m, Tissue
PM 2, total capacity 1,800 mt/y, Trim width 2.4 m, Tissue
PM 3, total capacity 1,800 mt/y, Trim width 2.4 m, Tissue
PM 4, total capacity 1,800 mt/y, Trim width 2.4 m, Tissue
PM 5, total capacity 1,800 mt/y, Trim width 2.4 m, Tissue

ⓄFuyang Maohong Paper Co., Ltd.
Chunjiang Paper-making Industry Park, Chunjiang Street
Fuyang, Zhejiang, 311421
China
Phone: (86) 571 2328 8378
Fax: (86) 571 2322 4777
Mill Locations:
Fuyang Maohong Paper Co., Ltd., Fuyang Mill, Chunjiang Paper-making Industry Park, Chunjiang Street, Fuyang 311421, China, Capacity: 60,000 mt/y, (Paperboard mill)
Phone: (86) 571 2328 8378
Fax: (86) 571 2322 4777

ⓂFuyang Maohong Paper Co., Ltd.
Fuyang Mill
Chunjiang Paper-making Industry Park, Chunjiang Street
Fuyang, Zhejiang, 311421
China
Phone: (86) 571 2328 8378
Fax: (86) 571 2322 4777
Personnel:
Gen. Mgr.: Shenggen Jiang
Phone: (86) 571 2328 8378
Total Employees at this Location: 200
Type of Operation: Paperboard mill
Pulp Grades and Capacities:
Total pulp capacity: 53,596 mt/y
Recycled Pulping: 53,596 mt/y
Pulp Mill Data:
Pulp Lines: 2
Recycled Fiber Treatment Lines:
Recycled packaging pulping lines: 1
Paper/Paperboard Grades and Capacities:
Total paper and paperboard capacity: 60,000 mt/y
Linerboard: 60,000 mt/y
Paper and Paperboard Mill Data:
Paper Machines: 1
No. 1, Multi-wire (4), total capacity 60,000 mt/y, Trim width 3.6 m, Linerboard
Energy Data:
Electrical demand for mill: 105 MWh/D

ⓄHangzhou Dahua Paper Co., Ltd.
Jiangfeng Village, Lingqiao Town, Fuyang
Hangzhou, Zhejiang
China
Phone: (86) 571 6315 8998
Mill Locations:
Hangzhou Dahua Paper Co., Ltd., Fuyang Mill, Jiangfeng Village, Lingqiao Town, Fuyang, Hangzhou, China, Capacity: 16,000 mt/y, (Paper mill)
Phone: (86) 571 6315 8998

China

ⓂHangzhou Dahua Paper Co., Ltd.
Fuyang Mill
Jiangfeng Village, Lingqiao Town, Fuyang
Hangzhou, Zhejiang
China
  Phone: (86) 571 6315 8998
Type of Operation: Paper mill
Paper/Paperboard Grades and Capacities:
  Total paper and paperboard capacity: 16,000 mt/y
  Tissue: 16,000 mt/y
Paper and Paperboard Mill Data:
Paper Machines: 5
PM 1, total capacity 1,000 mt/y, Trim width 1.58 m, Tissue
PM 2, total capacity 1,000 mt/y, Trim width 1.58 m, Tissue
PM 3, total capacity 1,000 mt/y, Trim width 1.58 m, Tissue
PM 4, total capacity 6,500 mt/y, Trim width 3.6 m, Tissue
PM 5, total capacity 6,500 mt/y, Trim width 3.6 m, Tissue

ⓄⓂHangzhou Fulton Industry Co., Ltd
Hangzhou Mill
6F, No.45, TianMuShan Road
Hangzhou, Zhejiang, 310007
China
  Phone: (86) 571 85121801
  Fax: (86) 571 85121801
  Email: fulton@chinafulton.com
  Web Address: www.chinafulton.com
Total Employees at this Location: 80
Type of Operation: Paper mill
Paper/Paperboard Grades and Capacities:
  Total paper and paperboard capacity: 12,495 mt/y
  Specialty and industrial: 12,495 mt/y
Paper and Paperboard Mill Data:
Paper Machines: 1
No. 1, fourdrinier, total capacity 12,495 mt/y, Trim width 1.88 m, Specialty and industrial
Coating Machines: 1
PM# 1, off machine
Finishing Equipment:
  Sheeters
Energy Data:
Power boilers
Electrical demand for mill: 35 MWh/D

ⓂHangzhou Huajin Specialty Paper Co., Ltd.
Hangzhou Mill
Mill is idle (since Aug.2014)
Ownership: Hangzhou Huawang Group
No.18 North Binhe Rd., Qingshan Economic
Development Zone, Linan
Hangzhou, Zhejiang, 311305
China
  Phone: (86) 571 6375 7936
  Email: hw@hwpaper.cn
  Web Address: www.hwpaper.cn
Personnel:
  Chmn.: Zhengliang Dou
  Phone: (86) 571 2800 5225
Total Employees at this Location: 300
Type of Operation: Paper mill
Pulp Grades and Capacities:
  Total pulp capacity: 109,737 mt/y
  Recycled Pulping: 109,737 mt/y
Pulp Mill Data:
  Bleach Plant Systems: 1
  Recycled Fiber Treatment Lines:
  Flotation deinking lines
Paper/Paperboard Grades and Capacities:
  Total paper and paperboard capacity: 120,000 mt/y
  Newsprint: 120,000 mt/y
Paper and Paperboard Mill Data:
Paper Machines: 1
No. 1, total capacity 120,000 mt/y, Trim width 4.85 m, Newsprint
Energy Data:
Power boilers: 2
Electrical demand for mill: 341 MWh/D

ⓂHangzhou Huatian Paper Co., Ltd.
Linan Mill
Ownership: Hangzhou Huawang Group
No. 16, South Zhaoxi Rd. Jincheng Village
Linan, Zhejiang, 311300
China
  Phone: (86) 571 6375 6073
  Fax: (86) 571 6375 8086
Personnel:
  Chmn.: Zhengliang Dou
  Phone: (86) 571 6375 6073
Total Employees at this Location: 300
Type of Operation: Paper mill
Paper/Paperboard Grades and Capacities:
  Total paper and paperboard capacity: 30,000 mt/y
  Specialty and industrial: 30,000 mt/y
Paper and Paperboard Mill Data:
Paper Machines: 3
PM 1-3, fourdrinier, total capacity 10,000 mt/y, Trim width 1.76 m, Specialty and industrial

ⓄHangzhou Huawang Group
Ownership: 100% by Shareholders
No.18 North Binhe Rd, Qingshan Economic
Development Aera, LinAn
Hangzhou, Zhejiang, 311300
China
  Phone: (86) 571 6375 7936
  Fax: (86) 571 6375 7936
  Email: hw@hwpaper.cn
  Web Address: www.hwpaper.cn
Total Employees of Company: 1,200
Mill Locations:
Hangzhou Huajin Specialty Paper Co., Ltd., Hangzhou Mill, No.18 North Binhe Rd., Qingshan Economic Development Zone, Linan, Hangzhou 311305, China, Capacity: 120,000 mt/y, (Paper mill)
Phone: (86) 571 6375 7936
Email: hw@hwpaper.cn
Hangzhou Huatian Paper Co., Ltd., Linan Mill, No. 16, South Zhaoxi Rd. Jincheng Village, Linan 311300, China, Capacity: 30,000 mt/y, (Paper mill)
Phone: (86) 571 6375 6073
Fax: (86) 571 6375 8086
Hangzhou Huawang New Material Co., Ltd., Hangzhou Mill, No.18, North Binhe Rd., Qingshan Economic Development Zone, LinAn, Hangzhou 311305, China, Capacity: 20,000 mt/y, (Paper mill)
Phone: (86) 571 6375 2399/7936/6073/8496
Fax: (86) 571 61077680
Email: hw@hwpaper.cn
Hangzhou Jinjiang Paper Co., Ltd., Linan Mill, No. 16, South Zhaoxi Rd. Jincheng Village, Linan 311300, China, Capacity: 49,980 mt/y, (Paper mill)
Phone: (86) 571 6375 7081/ 3803
Fax: (86) 571 6375 7385/ 3803

ⓂHangzhou Huawang New Material Co., Ltd.
Hangzhou Mill
Ownership: Hangzhou Huawang Group
No.18, North Binhe Rd., Qingshan Economic
Development Zone, LinAn
Hangzhou, Zhejiang, 311305
China
  Phone: (86) 571 6375 2399/7936/6073/8496
  Fax: (86) 571 61077680
  Email: hw@hwpaper.cn
  Web Address: www.hwpaper.cn
Type of Operation: Paper mill
Paper/Paperboard Grades and Capacities:
  Total paper and paperboard capacity: 20,000 mt/y
  Specialty and industrial: 20,000 mt/y
Paper and Paperboard Mill Data:
Paper Machines: 2
PM 1-2, fourdrinier, total capacity 10,000 mt/y, Trim width 1.35 m, Specialty and industrial

ⓂHangzhou Jinjiang Paper Co., Ltd.
Linan Mill
Ownership: Hangzhou Huawang Group
No. 16, South Zhaoxi Rd. Jincheng Village
Linan, Zhejiang, 311300
China
  Phone: (86) 571 6375 7081/ 3803
  Fax: (86) 571 6375 7385/ 3803
Personnel:
  Chmn.: Zhengliang Dou
  Phone: (86) 571 6375 7081/ 3803
  VP: Zhengliang Chen
  Phone: (86) 571 6375 7081/ 3803
  VP: Zhongxin Lu
  Phone: (86) 571 6375 7081/ 3803
  Tech. Mgr.: Guozhao Jun
  Phone: (86) 571 6375 7081/ 3803
  Purch. Agent: Xiaoming Fang
  Phone: (86) 571 6375 7081/ 3803
  Env. Dir.: Yonglin Wu
  Phone: (86) 571 6375 7081/ 3803
Total Employees at this Location: 300
Type of Operation: Paper mill
Pulp Grades and Capacities:
  Total pulp capacity: 49,583 mt/y
  Recycled Pulping: 49,583 mt/y
Pulp Mill Data:
Pulp Lines: 1
  Bleach Plant Systems: 1
  Recycled Fiber Treatment Lines:
  Flotation deinking lines: 1 at 54,000
Paper/Paperboard Grades and Capacities:
  Total paper and paperboard capacity: 49,980 mt/y
  Newsprint: 49,980 mt/y
Paper and Paperboard Mill Data:
  Stock Preparation:
  Pulpers: 3
  Refiners: 2
Paper Machines: 1
No. 1, total capacity 49,980 mt/y, Trim width 3.95 m, Newsprint
Finishing Equipment:
  Rewinders: 1
  Sheeters: 1
Energy Data:
Electrical demand for mill: 129 MWh/D

ⓂKingdecor (Zhejiang) Co., Ltd.
Quzhou Mill
Ownership: 50% by Zhejiang Xianhe Specialty Paper, 50% by Schattdecor AG
No. 158 Tongjiang Rd., Qujiang District
Quzhou, Zhejiang, 324022
China
  Phone: (86) 570 8507 888/ 8575 739/ 8575 738
  Fax: (86) 570 8575 729
  Email: info@kingdecor.cn
  Web Address: www.schattdecor.com, www.xianhepaper.com
Personnel:
  Gen. Mgr.: Mingliang Wang
  Phone: (86) 570 8507 888/ 8575 739/ 8575 738
  Sls. Mgr.: Jin Wang
  Phone: (86) 570 8507 888/ 8575 739/ 8575 738
  Project Mgr.: Zhijian Luo
  Phone: (86) 570 8507 888/ 8575 739/ 8575 738
Total Employees at this Location: 200
Type of Operation: Paper mill
Paper/Paperboard Grades and Capacities:
  Total paper and paperboard capacity: 90,000 mt/y
  Specialty and industrial: 90,000 mt/y
Paper and Paperboard Mill Data:
Paper Machines: 4
PM 1, fourdrinier, total capacity 30,000 mt/y, Trim width 2.86 m, Specialty and industrial
PM 2, fourdrinier, total capacity 30,000 mt/y, Trim width 2.86 m, Specialty and industrial

PM 3, (start up planned for the spring of 2014.), total capacity 30,000 mt/y, Trim width 4.5 m, Specialty and industrial
PM 13, total capacity 30,000 mt/y, Trim width 2.8 m, Specialty and industrial

ⓂNingbo Muniu Paper Co. Ltd.
Ningbo Mill
Zhouhan Village, Jiangshan Town, Yinzhou District
Ningbo, Zhejiang, 315195
China
Phone: (86) 574 8846 4807/4815/ 8846 4811/ 4477
Fax: (86) 574 8846 70605016/ 8846 3725/ 4477
Email: muniu@pack.net.cn
Web Address: www.muniupaper.net
Personnel:
Pres./Mill Mgr.: Xiangfu He
Phone: (86) 574 8846 4807/4815/ 8846 4811/ 4477
Chief Eng.: Kaizhong Xu
Phone: (86) 574 8846 4807/4815/ 8846 4811/ 4477
VP - Sls. & Mktg.: Fangyu Gu
Phone: (86) 574 8846 4807/4815/ 8846 4811/ 4477
Total Employees at this Location: 935
Type of Operation: Paper mill
Pulp Grades and Capacities:
Total pulp capacity: 185,838 mt/y
Recycled Pulping: 185,838 mt/y
Pulp Mill Data:
Bleach Plant Systems: 3
Paper/Paperboard Grades and Capacities:
Total paper and paperboard capacity: 200,277 mt/y
Corrugating medium/fluting: 96,747 mt/y
Boxboard/cartonboard: 103,530 mt/y
Paper and Paperboard Mill Data:
Paper Machines: 5
No. 3, multi-wire, total capacity 21,777 mt/y, Trim width 1.76 m, Boxboard/cartonboard
No. 4, multi-wire, total capacity 21,777 mt/y, Trim width 1.76 m, Boxboard/cartonboard
No. 9, multi-wire, total capacity 41,769 mt/y, Trim width 3.2 m, Corrugating medium/fluting
No. 10, Fourdrinier (4), total capacity 59,976 mt/y, Trim width 2.7 m, Boxboard/cartonboard
No. 11, Multi-wire (2), total capacity 54,978 mt/y, Trim width 4.2 m, Corrugating medium/fluting
Coating Machines: 3
PM 10, total capacity 60,000 mt/y., on machine
PM 3, total capacity 22,000 mt/y., on machine
PM 4, total capacity 22,000 mt/y., on machine
Finishing Equipment:
Supercalenders: 1
Rewinders: 8
Sheeters: 6
Energy Data:
Power boilers: 1
Combustion turbines: 1 at 3.5 MW
Electrical demand for mill: 376 MWh/D

ⓂNingbo Stainless Paper Industry Co., Ltd.
Ningbo Mill
Ningchuan Rd., Beilun District
Ningbo, Zhejiang
China
Web Address: www.stls.cn
Type of Operation: Paper mill
Paper/Paperboard Grades and Capacities:
Total paper and paperboard capacity: 18,000 mt/y
Specialty and industrial: 18,000 mt/y
Paper and Paperboard Mill Data:
Paper Machines: 1
No. 1, total capacity 18,000 mt/y, Trim width 2.44 m, Specialty and industrial

ⒽPurico Group (China)
70 Luli Street
Jiaxing City, Zhejiang, 314000
China
Phone: (86) 573 282 0799/0700
Fax: (86) 573 282 0799/3361
Email: info@purico.cn
Web Address: www.purico.com, www.puricopaper.com.cn
Personnel:
CEO: Edward Holt
Phone: (86) 573 282 0799/0700
Fax: (86) 573 282 0799/3361
Gen. Mgr.: Jeremy Bazley
Phone: (86) 573 282 0799/0700
Fax: (86) 573 282 0799/3361
Mktg. Mgr.: Julia Wu
Phone: (86) 573 282 0799/0700
Fax: (86) 573 282 0799/3361
Total Employees of Company: 345
Mill Locations:
Zhejiang Minfeng Robert Special Paper Co., Ltd., Jiaxing Mill (51% owned), 70, Luli Street, Jiaxing 314001, China, Capacity: 12,000 mt/y, (Paper mill)
Phone: (86) 573 283 9600/9057
Fax: (86) 573 281 9766/2821027
Email: jb@minfengrobert.com
Zhejiang Purico Speciality Paper Company Limited, Jiaxing Mill, 70 Luli Street, Jiaxing 314000, China, Capacity: 10,000 mt/y, (Paper mill)
Phone: (86) 573 8283 9600/ 8282 0799
Fax: (86) 573 8282 0700/ 8281 7677
Email: jb@minfengrobert.com, info@purico.cn

ⓂShenghua Group
Huzhou Mill
Zhongguan Town Developing Zone, Deqing County
Huzhou, Zhejiang, 313220
China
Phone: (86) 572 840 3888
Fax: (86) 572 840 3189
Personnel:
Gen. Mgr.: Yueming Huang
Phone: (86) 572 840 3888
Total Employees at this Location: 180
Type of Operation: Paper mill
Pulp Grades and Capacities:
Total pulp capacity: 19,600 mt/y
Recycled Pulping: 19,600 mt/y
Pulp Mill Data:
Pulp Lines: 2
Paper/Paperboard Grades and Capacities:
Total paper and paperboard capacity: 15,000 mt/y
Newsprint: 15,000 mt/y
Paper and Paperboard Mill Data:
Paper Machines: 1
No. 1, fourdrinier, total capacity 15,000 mt/y, Trim width 2.36 m, Newsprint
Finishing Equipment:
Rewinders: 5
Sheeters: 3
Energy Data:
Power boilers: 1
Steam turbines: 1 at 7.5 MW

ⓂVinda Paper (Zhejiang) Co., Ltd.
Quzhou Mill
Ownership: Vinda International Holdings Limited.
No.9, Fengkun Rd., Longyou Industry Park, Longyou County
Quzhou, Zhejiang, 324000
China
Phone: (86) 570 7788 888/808
Fax: (86) 570 7608 202
Web Address: www.vindapaper.com
Personnel:
Chmn.: Zhaowang Li
Total Employees at this Location: 390
Type of Operation: Paper mill
Paper/Paperboard Grades and Capacities:
Total paper and paperboard capacity: 90,000 mt/y
Tissue: 90,000 mt/y
Paper and Paperboard Mill Data:
Paper Machines: 6
No. 1, BF-12, Yankee dryer, total capacity 20,000 mt/y, Trim width 3.4 m, Tissue, Uncoated woodfree/freesheet
No. 2, BF-12, Yankee dryer, total capacity 20,000 mt/y, Trim width 3.4 m, Tissue, Uncoated woodfree/freesheet
No. 3, BF-10 EX, Yankee dryer, total capacity 12,500 mt/y, Trim width 2.76 m, Tissue, Uncoated woodfree/freesheet
No. 4, BF-10 EX, Yankee dryer, total capacity 12,500 mt/y, Trim width 2.76 m, Tissue, Uncoated woodfree/freesheet
No. 5, BF-10 EX, Yankee dryer, total capacity 12,500 mt/y, Trim width 2.76 m, Tissue, Uncoated woodfree/freesheet
No. 6, BF-10 EX, Yankee dryer, total capacity 12,500 mt/y, Trim width 2.76 m, Tissue, Uncoated woodfree/freesheet
Energy Data:
Electrical demand for mill: 161 MWh/D

ⒽZhejiang Anji Yatong Paper Co., Ltd.
Xiatang Industrial Park, Xiaofeng Town, Anji County
Huzhou, Zhejiang
China
Phone: (86) 572 5500 226
Email: yatong@yatongpaper.com
Web Address: www.ajytzy.com
Mill Locations:
Zhejiang Anji Yatong Paper Co., Ltd., Huzhou Mill, Xiatang Industrial Park, Xiaofeng Town, Anji County, Huzhou, China, Capacity: 9,900 mt/y, (Paper mill)
Phone: (86) 572 5500 226
Email: yatong@yatongpaper.com

ⓂZhejiang Anji Yatong Paper Co., Ltd.
Huzhou Mill
Xiatang Industrial Park, Xiaofeng Town, Anji County
Huzhou, Zhejiang
China
Phone: (86) 572 5500 226
Email: yatong@yatongpaper.com
Web Address: www.ajytzy.com
Type of Operation: Paper mill
Paper/Paperboard Grades and Capacities:
Total paper and paperboard capacity: 9,900 mt/y
Tissue: 9,900 mt/y
Paper and Paperboard Mill Data:
Paper Machines: 3
PM 1, total capacity 3,300 mt/y, Trim width 2.3 m, Tissue
PM 2, total capacity 3,300 mt/y, Trim width 2.3 m, Tissue
PM 3, total capacity 3,300 mt/y, Trim width 2.3 m, Tissue

ⒽZhejiang Cixi Longfeng Paper Co., Ltd.
Ownership: 100% by private owners
Cidong Industry Zone, LongshanTown
Cixi City, Zhejiang, 315317
China
Phone: (86) 574 6397 2001/ 2018/2005
Fax: (86) 574 6397 2111/2000
Email: nblfzy@126.com, naochaner1@126.com
Web Address: www.nblongfeng.com
Personnel:
Gen. Mgr.: Guojun Mao
Phone: (86) 574 6397 2001/ 2018/2005
Sls. Mgr.: Wenda Mao
Phone: (86) 574 6397 2001/ 2018/2005
Dir.: Qimei Huang
Phone: (86) 574 6397 2001/ 2018/2005
Mill Locations:
Zhejiang Cixi Longfeng Paper Co., Ltd., Cixi Mill, Cidong Industry Zone, LongshanTown, Cixi 315317, China, Capacity: 52,836 mt/y, (Paperboard mill)
Phone: (86) 574 6397 2001/ 2018/2005
Fax: (86) 574 6397 2111/2000
Email: nblfzy@126.com, naochaner1@126.com

China

ⓜZhejiang Cixi Longfeng Paper Co., Ltd.
Cixi Mill
Cidong Industry Zone, LongshanTown
Cixi, Zhejiang, 315317
China
  Phone: (86) 574 6397 2001/ 2018/2005
  Fax: (86) 574 6397 2111/2000
  Email: nblfzy@126.com,
  naochaner1@126.com
  Web Address: www.nblongfeng.com
Personnel:
  Gen. Mgr.: Guojun Mao
  Phone: (86) 574 6397 2001/ 2018/2005
  Sls. Mgr.: Wenda Mao
  Phone: (86) 574 6397 2001/ 2018/2005
  Dir.: Qimei Huang
  Phone: (86) 574 6397 2001/ 2018/2005
Total Employees at this Location: 400
Type of Operation: Paperboard mill
Pulp Grades and Capacities:
  Total pulp capacity: 51,428 mt/y
  Recycled Pulping: 51,428 mt/y
Paper/Paperboard Grades and Capacities:
  Total paper and paperboard capacity: 52,836 mt/y
  Corrugating medium/fluting: 52,836 mt/y
Paper and Paperboard Mill Data:
Paper Machines: 2
No. 6, fourdrinier, total capacity 26,418 mt/y, Trim width 3.4 m, Corrugating medium/fluting
No. 7, fourdrinier, total capacity 26,418 mt/y, Trim width 3.4 m, Corrugating medium/fluting
Energy Data:
Power boilers: 3
Steam turbines: 1 at 1 MW
Electrical demand for mill: 75 MWh/D

ⓜZhejiang Dingxing Paper Co., Ltd.
Pinghu Mill
Ownership: 100% by Zhejiang Jingxing Paper Joint Stock Co., Ltd.
Jingxing Industry Park, Caoqiao Town
Pinghu, Zhejiang, 314214
China
  Phone: (86) 573 8597 8111/ 8199
  Fax: (86) 573 8597 8079
  Email: zyxfj0439@yahoo.com.cn
  Web Address: www.zjjxjt.com/index
Personnel:
  Pres.: Mitsuo Nagoshi
  Phone: (86) 573 8597 8111/ 8199
Total Employees at this Location: 220
Type of Operation: Pulp mill, Paperboard mill
Pulp Grades and Capacities:
  Total pulp capacity: 150,163 mt/y
  Recycled Pulping: 150,163 mt/y
Pulp Mill Data:
Pulp Lines: 1
Paper/Paperboard Grades and Capacities:
  Total paper and paperboard capacity: 150,000 mt/y
  Linerboard: 100,000 mt/y
  Corrugating medium/fluting: 50,000 mt/y
Paper and Paperboard Mill Data:
Paper Machines: 1
No. 13, combination, total capacity 150,000 mt/y, Trim width 4.85 m, Linerboard, Corrugating medium/fluting
Energy Data:
Electrical demand for mill: 199 MWh/D

ⓜZhejiang Fuyang Chenggong Paper Co., Ltd.
Fuyang Mill
Chunjiang Industry Park, Chunjiang Street
Fuyang, Zhejiang, 311421
China
  Phone: (86) 571 6358 3983
  Fax: (86) 571 6358 3983
Total Employees at this Location: 150
Type of Operation: Paperboard mill
Pulp Grades and Capacities:
  Total pulp capacity: 99,269 mt/y
  Recycled Pulping: 99,269 mt/y
Pulp Mill Data:
  Recycled Fiber Treatment Lines:
  Recycled packaging pulping lines: 1
Paper/Paperboard Grades and Capacities:
  Total paper and paperboard capacity: 100,000 mt/y
  Corrugating medium/fluting: 100,000 mt/y
Paper and Paperboard Mill Data:
Paper Machines: 1
No. 1, fourdrinier, total capacity 100,000 mt/y, Trim width 4.6 m, Corrugating medium/fluting
Energy Data:
Electrical demand for mill: 114 MWh/D

ⓘZhejiang Fuyang Chunsheng Paper Co., Ltd.
Ownership: 100% by private owners
Zhitang Industry Park, Chunjiang Street
Fuyang, Zhejiang, 311421
China
  Phone: (86) 571 6315 1326
  Fax: (86) 571 6358 2288
  Email: sguocan@126.com
  Web Address: www.fychunsheng.cn
Mill Locations:
Zhejiang Fuyang Chunsheng Paper Co., Ltd., Fuyang Mill, Zhitang Industry Park, Chunjiang Street, Fuyang 311421, China, Capacity: 138,159 mt/y, (Pulp mill, Paperboard mill)
  Phone: (86) 571 6315 1326
  Fax: (86) 571 6358 2288
  Email: sguocan@126.com

ⓜZhejiang Fuyang Chunsheng Paper Co., Ltd.
Fuyang Mill
Zhitang Industry Park, Chunjiang Street
Fuyang, Zhejiang, 311421
China
  Phone: (86) 571 6315 1326
  Fax: (86) 571 6358 2288
  Email: sguocan@126.com
  Web Address: www.fychunsheng.cn
Personnel:
  Pres. & Gen. Mgr.: Chengsheng Yu
  Phone: (86) 571 6315 1326
  Sls. Mgr.: Guocan Sun
  Phone: (86) 571 6315 1326
Total Employees at this Location: 450
Type of Operation: Pulp mill, Paperboard mill
Pulp Grades and Capacities:
  Total pulp capacity: 115,683 mt/y
  Recycled Pulping: 115,683 mt/y
Pulp Mill Data:
Pulp Lines: 4
  Recycled Fiber Treatment Lines:
  Recycled packaging pulping lines: 4 at 150,000 admt/y
Paper/Paperboard Grades and Capacities:
  Total paper and paperboard capacity: 138,159 mt/y
  Boxboard/cartonboard: 138,159 mt/y
Paper and Paperboard Mill Data:
Paper Machines: 2
No. 4, Fourdrinier (5), total capacity 27,489 mt/y, Trim width 1.76 m, Boxboard/cartonboard
No. 5, Fourdrinier (5), total capacity 110,670 mt/y, Trim width 3.6 m, Boxboard/cartonboard
Energy Data:
Electrical demand for mill: 198 MWh/D

ⓘZhejiang Fuyang City Huawei Paper Co., Ltd.
Ownership: 100% by private owners
Tingshandong Rd., Dayuan Town
Fuyang, Zhejiang, 311413
China
  Phone: (86) 571 6359 3166
  Fax: (86) 571 6355 3555
  Web Address: www.huaweizhiye.cn.alibaba.com
Mill Locations:
Zhejiang Fuyang City Huawei Paper Co., Ltd., Fuyang Mill, Tingshandong Rd., Dayuan Town, Fuyang 311413, China, Capacity: 13,200 mt/y, (Paper mill)
  Phone: (86) 571 6359 3166
  Fax: (86) 571 6355 3555

ⓜZhejiang Fuyang City Huawei Paper Co., Ltd.
Fuyang Mill
Tingshandong Rd., Dayuan Town
Fuyang, Zhejiang, 311413
China
  Phone: (86) 571 6359 3166
  Fax: (86) 571 6355 3555
  Web Address: www.huaweizhiye.cn.alibaba.com
Personnel:
  Pres. & Gen. Mgr.: Ting Hua
  Phone: (86) 571 6359 3166
  Sls. Mgr.: Cheng Hua
  Phone: (86) 571 6359 3166
Total Employees at this Location: 400
Type of Operation: Paper mill
Pulp Grades and Capacities:
  Total pulp capacity: 10,000 mt/y
  Recycled Pulping
Pulp Mill Data:
Pulp Lines: 3
  Recycled Fiber Treatment Lines:
  Flotation deinking lines: 1
  Recycled packaging pulping lines: 2
Paper/Paperboard Grades and Capacities:
  Total paper and paperboard capacity: 13,200 mt/y
  Tissue: 13,200 mt/y
Paper and Paperboard Mill Data:
Paper Machines: 9
PM 1-4, cylinder, total capacity 1,000 mt/y, Trim width 1.76 m, Tissue
PM 5-7, cylinder, total capacity 1,200 mt/y, Trim width 1.76 m, Tissue
PM 8-9, cylinder, total capacity 1,400 mt/y, Trim width 1.76 m, Tissue

ⓘⓜZhejiang Fuyang City Huitai Paper Co., Ltd.
Fuyang Mill
Ownership: 100% by private owners
Huagong Village, Chunjiang Industry Park
Fuyang, Zhejiang, 311401
China
  Phone: (86) 571 6358 0973
  Fax: (86) 571 6358 0972
  Web Address: www.huifengpaper.com
Personnel:
  Gen. Mgr.: Ms. Songqin Yu
  Phone: (86) 571 6358 0973
  Asst. Gen. Mgr.: Ms. Xinqin Ding
  Phone: (86) 571 6358 0973
Total Employees at this Location: 110
Type of Operation: Paperboard mill
Mill Locations:
Zhejiang Fuyang City Huitai Paper Co., Ltd., Fuyang Mill, Bayi Industry Park, Fuyang 311401, China, Capacity: 15,000 mt/y, (Paperboard mill)
  Phone: (86) 571 6358 1878
  Fax: (86) 571 6358 5578
Pulp Grades and Capacities:
  Total pulp capacity: 42,603 mt/y
  Recycled Pulping: 42,603 mt/y
Pulp Mill Data:
Pulp Lines: 1
  Recycled Fiber Treatment Lines:
  Recycled packaging pulping lines: 1 at 50,000 admt/y
Paper/Paperboard Grades and Capacities:
  Total paper and paperboard capacity: 49,980 mt/y

Boxboard/cartonboard: 49,980 mt/y
Paper and Paperboard Mill Data:
Paper Machines: 1
No. 1, Fourdrinier (4), total capacity 49,980 mt/y, Trim width 2.64 m, Boxboard/cartonboard
Energy Data:
Electrical demand for mill: 75 MWh/D

ⓜZhejiang Fuyang City Huitai Paper Co., Ltd.
Fuyang Mill
Bayi Industry Park
Fuyang, Zhejiang, 311401
China
  Phone: (86) 571 6358 1878
  Fax: (86) 571 6358 5578
  Web Address: www.huifengpaper.com
Personnel:
  Gen. Mgr.: Yanhong Tang
  Phone: (86) 571 6358 1878
Total Employees at this Location: 80
Type of Operation: Paperboard mill
Pulp Grades and Capacities:
  Total pulp capacity: 15,000 mt/y
  Recycled Pulping: 15,000 mt/y
Pulp Mill Data:
Pulp Lines: 1
  Recycled Fiber Treatment Lines:
  Recycled packaging pulping lines: 1 at 15,000 admt/y
Paper/Paperboard Grades and Capacities:
  Total paper and paperboard capacity: 15,000 mt/y
  Boxboard/cartonboard: 15,000 mt/y
Paper and Paperboard Mill Data:
Paper Machines: 1
PM 1, multi-cylinder, total capacity 15,000 mt/y, Trim width 1.76 m, Boxboard/cartonboard

ⓗZhejiang Fuyang Dingdian Paper Co., Ltd.
Ownership: 100% by private owners
Linjiang Village, Chunjiang Industry Park
Fuyang, Zhejiang, 311421
China
  Phone: (86) 571 2328 7338/ 7339
  Fax: (86) 571 2328 7338
  Email: toppot2007@126.com
Mill Locations:
Zhejiang Fuyang Dingdian Paper Co., Ltd., Fuyang Mill, Linjiang Village, Chunjiang Industry Park, Fuyang 311421, China, Capacity: 13,000 mt/y, (Paper mill)
  Phone: (86) 571 2328 7338/ 7339
  Fax: (86) 571 2328 7338
  Email: toppot2007@126.com

ⓜZhejiang Fuyang Dingdian Paper Co., Ltd.
Fuyang Mill
Linjiang Village, Chunjiang Industry Park
Fuyang, Zhejiang, 311421
China
  Phone: (86) 571 2328 7338/ 7339
  Fax: (86) 571 2328 7338
  Email: toppot2007@126.com
Personnel:
  Gen. Mgr.: Ms. Xiaojuan Sun
  Phone: (86) 571 2328 7338/ 7339
  Sls. Mgr.: Jinming Liu
  Phone: (86) 571 2328 7338/ 7339
Total Employees at this Location: 100
Type of Operation: Paper mill
Pulp Grades and Capacities:
  Total pulp capacity: 7,000 mt/y
  Recycled Pulping: 7,000 mt/y
Pulp Mill Data:
Pulp Lines: 1
  Recycled Fiber Treatment Lines:
  Flotation deinking lines: 1 at 7,000 admt/y

Paper/Paperboard Grades and Capacities:
  Total paper and paperboard capacity: 13,000 mt/y
  Tissue: 13,000 mt/y
Paper and Paperboard Mill Data:
Paper Machines: 9
No. 1, fourdrinier, total capacity 1,600 mt/y, Trim width 1.88 m, Tissue
No. 2, fourdrinier, total capacity 1,600 mt/y, Trim width 1.88 m, Tissue
No. 3, fourdrinier, total capacity 1,600 mt/y, Trim width 1.88 m, Tissue
No. 4, fourdrinier, total capacity 1,600 mt/y, Trim width 1.88 m, Tissue
No. 5, fourdrinier, total capacity 1,600 mt/y, Trim width 1.88 m, Tissue
No. 6, fourdrinier, total capacity 1,600 mt/y, Trim width 1.88 m, Tissue
No. 7, fourdrinier, total capacity 1,150 mt/y, Trim width 1.88 m, Tissue
No. 8, fourdrinier, total capacity 1,150 mt/y, Trim width 1.88 m, Tissue
No. 9, fourdrinier, total capacity 1,150 mt/y, Trim width 1.88 m, Tissue

ⓗZhejiang Fuyang Dongcheng Paper Co., Ltd.
Ownership: 100% by shareholders
Fuyuan Industrial Zone
Fuyang, Hangzhou, Zhejiang, 311400
China
  Phone: (86) 571 6358 2658 /2488
  Fax: (86) 571 6358 0687
  Email: info@dongchengpaper.com
Mill Locations:
Zhejiang Fuyang Dongcheng Paper Co., Ltd., Fuyang Mill, Fuyuan Industrial Zone, Fuyang 311400, China, Capacity: 150,000 mt/y, (Paper mill)
  Phone: (86) 571 6358 2658 /2488
  Fax: (86) 571 6358 0687
  Email: info@dongchengpaper.com

ⓜZhejiang Fuyang Dongcheng Paper Co., Ltd.
Fuyang Mill
Fuyuan Industrial Zone
Fuyang, Zhejiang, 311400
China
  Phone: (86) 571 6358 2658 /2488
  Fax: (86) 571 6358 0687
  Email: info@dongchengpaper.com
Personnel:
  Chmn. & Pres./Mill Mgr.: Zhengguo Qiu
  Phone: (86) 571 6358 2658 /2488
Total Employees at this Location: 600
Type of Operation: Paper mill
Paper/Paperboard Grades and Capacities:
  Total paper and paperboard capacity: 150,000 mt/y
  Boxboard/cartonboard: 150,000 mt/y
Paper and Paperboard Mill Data:
Paper Machines: 2
No. 1, total capacity 50,000 mt/y, Boxboard/cartonboard
No. 2, total capacity 100,000 mt/y, Boxboard/cartonboard

ⓗZhejiang Fuyang Feima Paper Co., Ltd.
Ownership: 100% by private owners
Linjiang Village, Paper Making Industry Zone
Fuyang City, Zhejiang, 311421
China
  Phone: (86) 571 6358 3788
  Fax: (86) 571 6358 5399
  Email: webmaster@feimapaper.com
  Web Address: www.feimapaper.com
Mill Locations:
Zhejiang Fuyang Feima Paper Co., Ltd., Fuyang Mill, Linjiang Village, Paper Making Industry Zone, Fuyang 311421, China, Capacity: 139,944 mt/y, (Paperboard mill)

  Phone: (86) 571 6358 3788
  Fax: (86) 571 6358 5399
  Email: webmaster@feimapaper.com

ⓜZhejiang Fuyang Feima Paper Co., Ltd.
Fuyang Mill
Linjiang Village, Paper Making Industry Zone
Fuyang, Zhejiang, 311421
China
  Phone: (86) 571 6358 3788
  Fax: (86) 571 6358 5399
  Email: webmaster@feimapaper.com
  Web Address: www.feimapaper.com
Personnel:
  Pres.: Jinwen Liu
  Phone: (86) 571 6358 3788
  Gen. Mgr.: Longfei Wang
  Phone: (86) 571 6358 3788
  Sls. Mgr.: Yuefei Wang
  Phone: (86) 571 6358 3788
Total Employees at this Location: 500
Type of Operation: Paperboard mill
Pulp Grades and Capacities:
  Total pulp capacity: 115,132 mt/y
  Recycled Pulping: 115,132 mt/y
Pulp Mill Data:
Pulp Lines: 3
  Recycled Fiber Treatment Lines:
  Recycled packaging pulping lines: 3 at 150,000 admt/y
Paper/Paperboard Grades and Capacities:
  Total paper and paperboard capacity: 139,944 mt/y
  Boxboard/cartonboard: 139,944 mt/y
Paper and Paperboard Mill Data:
Paper Machines: 2
No. 2, Fourdrinier (5), total capacity 99,960 mt/y, Trim width 2.88 m, Boxboard/cartonboard
No. 3, Fourdrinier (4), total capacity 39,984 mt/y, Trim width 1.95 m, Boxboard/cartonboard
Energy Data:
Electrical demand for mill: 197 MWh/D

ⓗZhejiang Fuyang Fuchunwan Paper Co., Ltd.
Mingzhu Industry Park, Chunjiang Street
Fuyang, Zhejiang, 311421
China
  Phone: (86) 571 6358 6888
  Fax: (86) 571 6358 2688
  Email: lyh@fuchunwan.com, fuchunwan@alibaba.com.cn
  Web Address: www.fuchunwan.com
Mill Locations:
Zhejiang Fuyang Fuchunwan Paper Co., Ltd., Fuyang Mill, Mingzhu Industry Park, Chunjiang Street, Fuyang 311421, China, Capacity: 8,000 mt/y, (Paper mill)
  Phone: (86) 571 6358 6888
  Fax: (86) 571 6358 2688
  Email: lyh@fuchunwan.com, fuchunwan@alibaba.com.cn

ⓜZhejiang Fuyang Fuchunwan Paper Co., Ltd.
Fuyang Mill
Mingzhu Industry Park, Chunjiang Street
Fuyang, Zhejiang, 311421
China
  Phone: (86) 571 6358 6888
  Fax: (86) 571 6358 2688
  Email: lyh@fuchunwan.com, fuchunwan@alibaba.com.cn
  Web Address: www.fuchunwan.com
Personnel:
  Pres. & Gen. Mgr.: Yihong Liu
  Phone: (86) 571 6358 6888
Total Employees at this Location: 180
Type of Operation: Paper mill

China

Paper/Paperboard Grades and Capacities:
  Total paper and paperboard capacity: 8,000 mt/y
  Specialty and industrial: 8,000 mt/y
Paper and Paperboard Mill Data:
Paper Machines: 2
  PM 1, fourdrinier, total capacity 3,000 mt/y, Trim width 1.76 m, Specialty and industrial
  PM 2, fourdrinier, total capacity 5,000 mt/y, Trim width 1.88 m, Specialty and industrial

ⓗⓜZhejiang Fuyang Fulong Paper Co., Ltd

Fuyang Mill
Chunjiang Street Industry Park
Fuyang, Zhejiang
China
Total Employees at this Location: 140
Type of Operation: Paperboard mill
Pulp Grades and Capacities:
  Total pulp capacity: 39,533 mt/y
  Recycled Pulping: 39,533 mt/y
Pulp Mill Data:
  Recycled Fiber Treatment Lines:
  Recycled packaging pulping lines: 1
Paper/Paperboard Grades and Capacities:
  Total paper and paperboard capacity: 40,698 mt/y
  Corrugating medium/fluting: 40,698 mt/y
Paper and Paperboard Mill Data:
Paper Machines: 1
  No. 1, fourdrinier, total capacity 40,698 mt/y, Trim width 3.9 m, Corrugating medium/fluting
Energy Data:
Electrical demand for mill: 62 MWh/D

ⓗZhejiang Fuyang Fuming Paper Co., Ltd.

Ownership: 100% by private owners
Chunjiang Papermaking Industry Park, Chunjiang Street
Fuyang, Zhejiang, 311421
China
  Phone: (86) 571 2328 1777/ 1188
  Fax: (86) 571 2328 1000
Mill Locations:
  Zhejiang Fuyang Fuming Paper Co., Ltd., Fuyang Mill, Chunjiang Papermaking Industry Park, Chunjiang Street, Fuyang 311421, China, Capacity: 34,986 mt/y, (Paperboard mill)
  Phone: (86) 571 2328 1777/ 1188
  Fax: (86) 571 2328 1000

ⓜZhejiang Fuyang Fuming Paper Co., Ltd.

Fuyang Mill
Chunjiang Papermaking Industry Park, Chunjiang Street
Fuyang, Zhejiang, 311421
China
  Phone: (86) 571 2328 1777/ 1188
  Fax: (86) 571 2328 1000
Personnel:
  Gen. Mgr.: Xujie Yu
  Phone: (86) 571 2328 1777/ 1188
Total Employees at this Location: 150
Type of Operation: Paperboard mill
Pulp Grades and Capacities:
  Total pulp capacity: 34,225 mt/y
  Recycled Pulping: 34,225 mt/y
Pulp Mill Data:
Pulp Lines: 1
  Recycled Fiber Treatment Lines:
  Recycled packaging pulping lines: 1 at 50,000 admt/y
Paper/Paperboard Grades and Capacities:
  Total paper and paperboard capacity: 34,986 mt/y
  Corrugating medium/fluting: 34,986 mt/y
Paper and Paperboard Mill Data:
Paper Machines: 1
  No. 1, fourdrinier, total capacity 34,986 mt/y, Trim width 3.8 m, Corrugating medium/fluting

Energy Data:
Electrical demand for mill: 54 MWh/D

ⓗⓜZhejiang Fuyang Futai Feifeng Paper Co., Ltd.

Fuyang Mill
Ownership: 100% by shareholders
Chunjiang Industry Park, Chunjiang Street
Fuyang, Zhejiang, 311421
China
  Phone: (86) 571 6315 9890
  Fax: (86) 571 6315 9858
Personnel:
  Sls. Mgr.: Jinjun Sun
  Phone: (86) 571 6315 9890
Total Employees at this Location: 240
Type of Operation: Paperboard mill
Pulp Grades and Capacities:
  Total pulp capacity: 85,137 mt/y
  Recycled Pulping: 85,137 mt/y
Pulp Mill Data:
  Bleach Plant Systems: 1
  Recycled Pulping System, Type: Deinked
  Recycled Fiber Treatment Lines:
  Flotation deinking lines: 1
  Recycled packaging pulping lines: 1
Paper/Paperboard Grades and Capacities:
  Total paper and paperboard capacity: 99,960 mt/y
  Boxboard/cartonboard: 99,960 mt/y
Paper and Paperboard Mill Data:
Paper Machines: 1
  No. 1, Fourdrinier (4), total capacity 99,960 mt/y, Trim width 2.64 m, Boxboard/cartonboard
Energy Data:
Electrical demand for mill: 140 MWh/D

ⓜZhejiang Fuyang Gaoyang Paper Co., Ltd.

Fuyang Mill
Ownership: Zhejiang Gaoyang Paper Co., Ltd.
Chunjiang Street Industry Park
Fuyang, Zhejiang, 311421
China
  Phone: (86) 571 6358 5999
  Fax: (86) 571 6358 9999
Personnel:
  Sls. Mgr.: Caiya Dong
  Phone: (86) 571 6358 5999
Type of Operation: Paperboard mill
Paper/Paperboard Grades and Capacities:
  Total paper and paperboard capacity: 20,000 mt/y
  Boxboard/cartonboard: 20,000 mt/y
Paper and Paperboard Mill Data:
Paper Machines: 2
  PM 1, cylinder, total capacity 8,000 mt/y, Trim width 1.09 m, Boxboard/cartonboard
  PM 2, cylinder, total capacity 12,000 mt/y, Trim width 1.76 m, Boxboard/cartonboard

ⓗZhejiang Fuyang Huali Paper Co., Ltd.

Ownership: 100% by private owners
Chunlian Village, Chunjiang Industrial Zone
Fuyang, Zhejiang, 311421
China
  Phone: (86) 571 6358 3048/2881
  Fax: (86) 571 6358 2881
  Email: webmaster@cnhuali.net
Mill Locations:
  Zhejiang Fuyang Huali Paper Co., Ltd., Fuyang Mill, Chunlian Village, Chunjiang Industrial Zone, Fuyang 311421, China, Capacity: 15,000 mt/y, (Paper mill)
  Phone: (86) 571 6358 3048/2881
  Fax: (86) 571 6358 2881
  Email: webmaster@cnhuali.net

ⓜZhejiang Fuyang Huali Paper Co., Ltd.

Fuyang Mill
Chunlian Village, Chunjiang Industrial Zone
Fuyang, Zhejiang, 311421
China
  Phone: (86) 571 6358 3048/2881
  Fax: (86) 571 6358 2881
  Email: webmaster@cnhuali.net
Personnel:
  Pres./Mill Mgr.: Zheng Hua Yang
  Phone: (86) 571 6358 3048/2881
  Sls. Mgr. & Purch. Mgr.: Xiaoming Yang
  Phone: (86) 571 6358 3048/2881
Total Employees at this Location: 100
Type of Operation: Paper mill
Paper/Paperboard Grades and Capacities:
  Total paper and paperboard capacity: 15,000 mt/y
  Boxboard/cartonboard: 15,000 mt/y
Paper and Paperboard Mill Data:
Paper Machines: 1
  PM 3, three-ply, total capacity 15,000 mt/y, Trim width 1.88 m, Boxboard/cartonboard

ⓗZhejiang Fuyang Hualong Paper Co., Ltd.

Ownership: 100% by private owners
Huagong Village, Chunjiang Industry Park
Fuyang, Zhejiang, 311421
China
  Phone: (86) 571 8723 8493
  Fax: (86) 571 8723 8493
Mill Locations:
  Zhejiang Fuyang Hualong Paper Co., Ltd., Fuyang Mill, Huagong Village, Chunjiang Industry Park, Fuyang 311421, China, Capacity: 100,000 mt/y, (Paperboard mill)
  Phone: (86) 571 8723 8493
  Fax: (86) 571 8723 8493

ⓜZhejiang Fuyang Hualong Paper Co., Ltd.

Fuyang Mill
Huagong Village, Chunjiang Industry Park
Fuyang, Zhejiang, 311421
China
  Phone: (86) 571 8723 8493
  Fax: (86) 571 8723 8493
Personnel:
  Pres. & Gen. Mgr.: Yeping Liu
  Phone: (86) 571 8723 8493
Total Employees at this Location: 150
Type of Operation: Paperboard mill
Pulp Grades and Capacities:
  Total pulp capacity: 90,161 mt/y
  Recycled Pulping: 90,161 mt/y
Pulp Mill Data:
Pulp Lines: 2
  Recycled Fiber Treatment Lines:
  Recycled packaging pulping lines: 2 at 100,000 admt/y
Paper/Paperboard Grades and Capacities:
  Total paper and paperboard capacity: 100,000 mt/y
  Boxboard/cartonboard: 100,000 mt/y
Paper and Paperboard Mill Data:
Paper Machines: 1
  No. 1, Multi-wire (5), total capacity 100,000 mt/y, Trim width 2.88 m, Boxboard/cartonboard
Energy Data:
Electrical demand for mill: 142 MWh/D

ⓗZhejiang Fuyang Huamao Paper Co., Ltd.

Ownership: 100% by private owners
Shanjian Village
Fuyang, Hangzhou, Zhejiang, 311421
China
  Phone: (86) 571 6358 3142/ 9188
  Fax: (86) 571 6358 5128
Mill Locations:
  Zhejiang Fuyang Huamao Paper Co., Ltd., Fuyang Mill, Shanjian Village, Fuyang 311421, China, Capacity:

59,976 mt/y, (Paperboard mill)
Phone: (86) 571 6358 3142/ 9188
Fax: (86) 571 6358 5128

ⓜZhejiang Fuyang Huamao Paper Co., Ltd.
Fuyang Mill
Shanjian Village
Fuyang, Zhejiang, 311421
China
Phone: (86) 571 6358 3142/ 9188
Fax: (86) 571 6358 5128
Personnel:
Gen. Mgr.: Zhirong Wang
Phone: (86) 571 6358 3142/ 9188
Sls. Mgr.: Xiaohua Lv
Phone: (86) 571 6358 3142/ 9188
Total Employees at this Location: 180
Type of Operation: Paperboard mill
Pulp Grades and Capacities:
Total pulp capacity: 59,233 mt/y
Recycled Pulping: 59,233 mt/y
Pulp Mill Data:
Pulp Lines: 1
Recycled Fiber Treatment Lines:
Recycled packaging pulping lines: 1 at 65,000 admt/y
Paper/Paperboard Grades and Capacities:
Total paper and paperboard capacity: 59,976 mt/y
Corrugating medium/fluting: 59,976 mt/y
Paper and Paperboard Mill Data:
Paper Machines: 1
No. 1, fourdrinier, total capacity 59,976 mt/y, Trim width 4.4 m, Corrugating medium/fluting
Energy Data:
Electrical demand for mill: 90 MWh/D

ⓜZhejiang Fuyang Huatian Paper Co., Ltd.
Zhitang Industry Park, Chuanjiang Street
Fuyang, Zhejiang, 311400
China
Phone: (86) 571 6358 4818
Fax: (86) 571 6315 0123
Mill Locations:
Zhejiang Fuyang Huatian Paper Co., Ltd., Fuyang Mill, Zhitang Industry Park, Chuanjiang Street, Fuyang 311400, China, Capacity: 144,228 mt/y, (Paperboard mill)
Phone: (86) 571 6358 4818
Fax: (86) 571 6315 0123

ⓜZhejiang Fuyang Huatian Paper Co., Ltd.
Fuyang Mill
Zhitang Industry Park, Chuanjiang Street
Fuyang, Zhejiang, 311400
China
Phone: (86) 571 6358 4818
Fax: (86) 571 6315 0123
Personnel:
Gen. Mgr.: Liqun Niu
Phone: (86) 571 6358 4818
Sls. Mgr.: Weiping Xu
Phone: (86) 571 6358 4818
Total Employees at this Location: 250
Type of Operation: Paperboard mill
Pulp Grades and Capacities:
Total pulp capacity: 127,439 mt/y
Recycled Pulping: 127,439 mt/y
Pulp Mill Data:
Pulp Lines: 1
Recycled Fiber Treatment Lines:
Recycled packaging pulping lines: 1 at 81,515 admt/y
Paper/Paperboard Grades and Capacities:
Total paper and paperboard capacity: 144,228 mt/y
Boxboard/cartonboard: 144,228 mt/y
Paper and Paperboard Mill Data:
Paper Machines: 1
No. 1, Multi-wire (3), total capacity 144,228 mt/y, Trim width 3.8 m, Boxboard/cartonboard
Coating Machines: 1
PM 1, total capacity 144,000 mt/y., on machine
Energy Data:
Electrical demand for mill: 256 MWh/D

ⓜZhejiang Fuyang Jin Xin Paper Co., Ltd.
Ownership: 100% by private owners
Huagong Village, Chunjiang Industry Park
Fuyang, Zhejiang, 311421
China
Phone: (86) 571 6358 5281
Fax: (86) 571 6358 5380
Email: hz_fyjxzy@163.com
Web Address: www.fyjxpaper.com
Mill Locations:
Zhejiang Fuyang Jin Xin Paper Co., Ltd., Fuyang Mill, Huagong Village, Chunjiang Industry Park, Fuyang 311421, China, Capacity: 20,000 mt/y, (Paperboard mill)
Phone: (86) 571 6358 5281
Fax: (86) 571 6358 5380
Email: hz_fyjxzy@163.com

ⓜZhejiang Fuyang Jin Xin Paper Co., Ltd.
Fuyang Mill
Huagong Village, Chunjiang Industry Park
Fuyang, Zhejiang, 311421
China
Phone: (86) 571 6358 5281
Fax: (86) 571 6358 5380
Email: hz_fyjxzy@163.com
Web Address: www.fyjxpaper.com
Personnel:
Gen. Mgr.: Yongming Hu
Phone: (86) 138 0576 5626
Sls. Mgr.: Haihong Liu
Phone: (86) 138 0651 5769
Total Employees at this Location: 125
Type of Operation: Paperboard mill
Pulp Grades and Capacities:
Total pulp capacity: 18,616 mt/y
Recycled Pulping: 18,616 mt/y
Pulp Mill Data:
Pulp Lines: 1
Bleach Plant Systems: 1
Recycled Pulping System, Type: DIP
Recycled Fiber Treatment Lines:
Flotation deinking lines: 1
Recycled packaging pulping lines: 1 at 15,000 admt/y
Paper/Paperboard Grades and Capacities:
Total paper and paperboard capacity: 20,000 mt/y
Boxboard/cartonboard: 20,000 mt/y
Paper and Paperboard Mill Data:
Paper Machines: 1
No. 1, cylinder (6), total capacity 20,000 mt/y, Trim width 1.76 m, Boxboard/cartonboard
Coating Machines: 1
PM #1, on machine
Energy Data:
Electrical demand for mill: 33 MWh/D

ⓜZhejiang Fuyang Jinchang Paper Co., Ltd.
Ownership: 100% by private owners
Zhitang Village, Chunjiang Street
Fuyang, Hangzhou, Zhejiang, 311421
China
Phone: (86) 571 6315 1796/ 1795/ 1797
Fax: (86) 571 6315 1797
Personnel:
Pres. & Gen. Mgr.: Xuejun Wang
Phone: (86) 571 6315 1796/ 1795/ 1797
Sls. Mgr.: Chaojun Yu
Phone: (86) 571 6315 1796/ 1795/ 1797
Mill Locations:
Zhejiang Fuyang Jinchang Paper Co., Ltd., Fuyang Mill, Zhitang Village, Chunjiang Street, Fuyang 311421, China, Capacity: 92,820 mt/y, (Paperboard mill)
Phone: (86) 571 6315 1796/ 1795/ 1797
Fax: (86) 571 6315 1797

ⓜZhejiang Fuyang Jinchang Paper Co., Ltd.
Fuyang Mill
Zhitang Village, Chunjiang Street
Fuyang, Zhejiang, 311421
China
Phone: (86) 571 6315 1796/ 1795/ 1797
Fax: (86) 571 6315 1797
Personnel:
Pres. & Gen. Mgr.: Xuejun Wang
Phone: (86) 571 6315 1796/ 1795/ 1797
Sls. Mgr.: Chaojun Yu
Phone: (86) 571 6315 1796/ 1795/ 1797
Total Employees at this Location: 150
Type of Operation: Paperboard mill
Pulp Grades and Capacities:
Total pulp capacity: 91,282 mt/y
Recycled Pulping: 91,282 mt/y
Pulp Mill Data:
Pulp Lines: 1
Recycled Fiber Treatment Lines:
Recycled packaging pulping lines: 1 at 70,000 admt/y
Paper/Paperboard Grades and Capacities:
Total paper and paperboard capacity: 92,820 mt/y
Linerboard: 92,820 mt/y
Paper and Paperboard Mill Data:
Paper Machines: 2
No. 1, twin-wire, total capacity 46,410 mt/y, Trim width 3.8 m, Linerboard
No. 2, fourdrinier, total capacity 46,410 mt/y, Trim width 3.8 m, Linerboard
Finishing Equipment:
Winders: 1 at 70,000 mt/y
Rewinders: 1 at 150,000 mt/y
Energy Data:
Electrical demand for mill: 139 MWh/D

ⓜZhejiang Fuyang Kangnan Paper Co., Ltd.
Ownership: 100% by private owners
Jianhua Village, Chunjiang Street
Fuyang, Zhejiang, 311421
China
Phone: (86) 571 2320 2268
Fax: (86) 571 2320 2268
Mill Locations:
Zhejiang Fuyang Kangnan Paper Co., Ltd., Fuyang Mill, Jianhua Village, Chunjiang Street, Fuyang 311421, China, Capacity: 99,960 mt/y, (Paperboard mill)
Phone: (86) 571 2320 2268
Fax: (86) 571 2320 2268

ⓜZhejiang Fuyang Kangnan Paper Co., Ltd.
Fuyang Mill
Jianhua Village, Chunjiang Street
Fuyang, Zhejiang, 311421
China
Phone: (86) 571 2320 2268
Fax: (86) 571 2320 2268
Total Employees at this Location: 200
Type of Operation: Paperboard mill
Pulp Grades and Capacities:
Total pulp capacity: 80,088 mt/y
Recycled Pulping: 80,088 mt/y
Paper/Paperboard Grades and Capacities:
Total paper and paperboard capacity: 99,960 mt/y
Boxboard/cartonboard: 99,960 mt/y
Paper and Paperboard Mill Data:
Paper Machines: 1
No. 1, Fourdrinier (5), total capacity 99,960 mt/y, Trim width 3.6 m, Boxboard/cartonboard

China

Energy Data:
Electrical demand for mill: 143 MWh/D

ⓘZhejiang Fuyang Kraft Paper Mill
Ownership: 100% by private owners
Linqiao Industry Park
Fuyang, Zhejiang, 311418
China
  Phone: (86) 571 6355 1828
  Fax: (86) 571 6355 0331
Mill Locations:
Zhejiang Fuyang Kraft Paper Mill, Fuyang Mill, Linqiao Industry Park, Fuyang 311418, China, Capacity: 12,000 mt/y, (Paper mill)
  Phone: (86) 571 6355 1828
  Fax: (86) 571 6355 0331

ⓜZhejiang Fuyang Kraft Paper Mill
Fuyang Mill
Linqiao Industry Park
Fuyang, Zhejiang, 311418
China
  Phone: (86) 571 6355 1828
  Fax: (86) 571 6355 0331
Personnel:
  Gen. Mgr.: Ming Lv
  Phone: (86) 571 6355 1828
Total Employees at this Location: 120
Type of Operation: Paper mill
Pulp Grades and Capacities:
  Total pulp capacity: 6,000 mt/y
  Recycled Pulping: 6,000 mt/y
Pulp Mill Data:
Pulp Lines: 1
  Recycled Fiber Treatment Lines:
  Recycled packaging pulping lines: 1 at 6,000 admt/y
Paper/Paperboard Grades and Capacities:
  Total paper and paperboard capacity: 12,000 mt/y
  Packaging papers: 12,000 mt/y
Paper and Paperboard Mill Data:
Paper Machines: 1
  PM 1, twin-wire, total capacity 12,000 mt/y, Trim width 2.88 m, Packaging papers

ⓘZhejiang Fuyang Lingtai Paper Co., Ltd.
Ownership: 100% by private owners
Lingqiao Industry Park, Shengli Village
Fuyang, Zhejiang, 311418
China
  Phone: (86) 571 6355 1661
  Fax: (86) 571 6355 8918
  Web Address: www.hzfy-lingtai.com.cn
Personnel:
  Gen. Mgr.: Shansheng Li
  Phone: (86) 571 6355 1661
  Sls. Mgr.: Peng Lu
  Phone: (86) 571 6355 1661
Mill Locations:
Zhejiang Fuyang Lingtai Paper Co., Ltd., Fuyang Mill, Lingqiao Industry Park, Shengli Village, Fuyang 311418, China, Capacity: 71,400 mt/y, (Paperboard mill)
  Phone: (86) 571 6355 1661
  Fax: (86) 571 6355 8918

ⓜZhejiang Fuyang Lingtai Paper Co., Ltd.
Fuyang Mill
Lingqiao Industry Park, Shengli Village
Fuyang, Zhejiang, 311418
China
  Phone: (86) 571 6355 1661
  Fax: (86) 571 6355 8918
Personnel:
  Gen. Mgr.: Shansheng Li
  Phone: (86) 571 6355 1661
  Sls. Mgr.: Peng Lu
  Phone: (86) 571 6355 1661
Total Employees at this Location: 220
Type of Operation: Paperboard mill
Pulp Grades and Capacities:
  Total pulp capacity: 62,603 mt/y
  Recycled Pulping: 62,603 mt/y
Pulp Mill Data:
Pulp Lines: 2
  Recycled Fiber Treatment Lines:
  Recycled packaging pulping lines: 2 at 60,000 admt/y
Paper/Paperboard Grades and Capacities:
  Total paper and paperboard capacity: 71,400 mt/y
  Boxboard/cartonboard: 71,400 mt/y
Paper and Paperboard Mill Data:
Paper Machines: 1
  No. 2, multi-wire, total capacity 71,400 mt/y, Trim width 3.6 m, Boxboard/cartonboard
Energy Data:
Electrical demand for mill: 150 MWh/D

ⓘZhejiang Fuyang Maoyuan Paper Co., Ltd.
Ownership: 100% by private owners
Zhenlong Village, Dayuan Town Industry Park
Fuyang, Zhejiang, 311413
China
  Phone: (86) 571 6359 4955
  Fax: (86) 571 6359 4956
Mill Locations:
Zhejiang Fuyang Maoyuan Paper Co., Ltd., Fuyang Mill, Zhenlong Village, Dayuan Town Industry Park, Fuyang 311413, China, Capacity: 45,000 mt/y, (Paperboard mill)
  Phone: (86) 571 6359 4955
  Fax: (86) 571 6359 4956

ⓜZhejiang Fuyang Maoyuan Paper Co., Ltd.
Fuyang Mill
Zhenlong Village, Dayuan Town Industry Park
Fuyang, Zhejiang, 311413
China
  Phone: (86) 571 6359 4955
  Fax: (86) 571 6359 4956
Personnel:
  Pres. & Gen. Mgr.: Zeyi Li
  Phone: (86) 571 6359 4955
Total Employees at this Location: 400
Type of Operation: Paperboard mill
Pulp Grades and Capacities:
  Total pulp capacity: 45,000 mt/y
  Recycled Pulping: 45,000 mt/y
Pulp Mill Data:
Pulp Lines: 3
  Recycled Fiber Treatment Lines:
  Flotation deinking lines: 1
  Recycled packaging pulping lines: 2
Paper/Paperboard Grades and Capacities:
  Total paper and paperboard capacity: 45,000 mt/y
  Boxboard/cartonboard: 45,000 mt/y
Paper and Paperboard Mill Data:
Paper Machines: 1
  PM 1, multi-ply, total capacity 45,000 mt/y, Trim width 1.88 m, Boxboard/cartonboard

ⓘZhejiang Fuyang Nanfa Paper Co., Ltd.
Ownership: 100% by private owners
Bayi Industry Park, Chunjiang Street
Fuyang, Zhejiang, 311241
China
  Phone: (86) 571 6352 5677
  Fax: (86) 571 6358 5638
  Web Address: www.nanfazhiye.cn
Mill Locations:
Zhejiang Fuyang Nanfa Paper Co., Ltd., Fuyang Mill, Bayi Industry Park, Chunjiang Street, Fuyang 311241, China, Capacity: 50,337 mt/y, (Paperboard mill)
  Phone: (86) 571 6352 5677
  Fax: (86) 571 6358 5638

ⓜZhejiang Fuyang Nanfa Paper Co., Ltd.
Fuyang Mill
Bayi Industry Park, Chunjiang Street
Fuyang, Zhejiang, 311241
China
  Phone: (86) 571 6352 5677
  Fax: (86) 571 6358 5638
  Web Address: www.nanfazhiye.cn
Personnel:
  Pres. & Gen. Mgr.: Nanfa Dong
  Phone: (86) 571 6352 5677
  Sls. Mgr.: Yinjun Dong
  Phone: (86) 571 6352 5677
Total Employees at this Location: 300
Type of Operation: Paperboard mill
Pulp Grades and Capacities:
  Total pulp capacity: 43,831 mt/y
  Recycled Pulping: 43,831 mt/y
Pulp Mill Data:
Pulp Lines: 2
  Recycled Fiber Treatment Lines:
  Recycled packaging pulping lines: 2 at 50,000 admt/y
Paper/Paperboard Grades and Capacities:
  Total paper and paperboard capacity: 50,337 mt/y
  Boxboard/cartonboard: 50,337 mt/y
Paper and Paperboard Mill Data:
Paper Machines: 2
  No. 1, cylinder, total capacity 15,351 mt/y, Trim width 1.58 m, Boxboard/cartonboard
  No. 2, Fourdrinier (5), total capacity 34,986 mt/y, Trim width 1.88 m, Boxboard/cartonboard
Energy Data:
Electrical demand for mill: 74 MWh/D

ⓘZhejiang Fuyang Runtong Paper Co., Ltd.
Ownership: 100% by private owners
Zhitang Village, Chunjiang Street
Fuyang, Zhejiang, 311400
China
  Phone: (86) 571 6352 9277
  Fax: (86) 571 6352 9271
Mill Locations:
Zhejiang Fuyang Runtong Paper Co., Ltd., Fuyang Mill, Zhitang Village, Chunjiang Street, Fuyang 311400, China, Capacity: 29,000 mt/y, (Paperboard mill)
  Phone: (86) 571 6352 9277
  Fax: (86) 571 6352 9271

ⓜZhejiang Fuyang Runtong Paper Co., Ltd.
Fuyang Mill
Mill is closed (in early 2014)
Zhitang Village, Chunjiang Street
Fuyang, Zhejiang, 311400
China
  Phone: (86) 571 6352 9277
  Fax: (86) 571 6352 9271
Personnel:
  Sls. Mgr.: Yuxiang Zhen
  Phone: (86) 571 6352 9277
Total Employees at this Location: 130
Type of Operation: Paperboard mill
Pulp Grades and Capacities:
  Total pulp capacity: 30,000 mt/y
  Recycled Pulping: 30,000 mt/y
Pulp Mill Data:
Pulp Lines: 2
  Recycled Fiber Treatment Lines:
  Recycled packaging pulping lines: 1 at 30,000 admt/y
Paper/Paperboard Grades and Capacities:
  Total paper and paperboard capacity: 29,000 mt/y

Boxboard/cartonboard: 29,000 mt/y
Paper and Paperboard Mill Data:
Paper Machines: 1
PM 1, multi-ply, total capacity 29,000 mt/y, Trim width 2.8 m, Boxboard/cartonboard

ⓘZhejiang Fuyang Senyuan Paper Co., Ltd.
Ownership: 100% by private owners
Dayuan Industry Park
Fuyang, Zhejiang, 311413
China
 Phone: (86) 571 6359 7008/ 7009
 Fax: (86) 571 6359 7009
Mill Locations:
Zhejiang Fuyang Senyuan Paper Co., Ltd., Fuyang Mill, Dayuan Industry Park, Fuyang 311413, China, Capacity: 7,000 mt/y, (Paper mill)
 Phone: (86) 571 6359 7008/ 7009
 Fax: (86) 571 6359 7009

ⓜZhejiang Fuyang Senyuan Paper Co., Ltd.
Fuyang Mill
Dayuan Industry Park
Fuyang, Zhejiang, 311413
China
 Phone: (86) 571 6359 7008/ 7009
 Fax: (86) 571 6359 7009
Personnel:
 Gen. Mgr.: Zhiguang Jiang
 Phone: (86) 571 6359 7008/ 7009
Total Employees at this Location: 130
Type of Operation: Paper mill
Paper/Paperboard Grades and Capacities:
 Total paper and paperboard capacity: 7,000 mt/y
 Specialty and industrial: 7,000 mt/y
Paper and Paperboard Mill Data:
Paper Machines: 1
PM 1, fourdrinier, total capacity 7,000 mt/y, Trim width 1.88 m, Specialty and industrial

ⓘZhejiang Fuyang Shangyou Paper Industry Co., Ltd.
No. 8, Chunlian Industry Zone, Chunjiang Street
Fuyang City, Zhejiang, 311421
China
 Phone: (86) 571 6315 3118/3137
 Fax: (86) 571 6358 3111/6313 1431
 Email: webmaster@cnnanhe.com
Personnel:
 Chmn. & Gen. Mgr.: Fumin Yang
 Sls. Mgr.: Xueming Liu
Total Employees at this Location: 200
Mill Locations:
Zhejiang Fuyang Shangyou Paper Industry Co., Ltd., Fuyang Mill, No. 8, Chunlian Industry Zone, Chunjiang Street, Fuyang 311421, China, Capacity: 99,960 mt/y, (Paperboard mill)
 Phone: (86) 571 6315 3118/3137
 Fax: (86) 571 6358 3111/6313 1431
 Email: webmaster@cnnanhe.com

ⓜZhejiang Fuyang Shangyou Paper Industry Co., Ltd.
Fuyang Mill
No. 8, Chunlian Industry Zone, Chunjiang Street
Fuyang, Zhejiang, 311421
China
 Phone: (86) 571 6315 3118/3137
 Fax: (86) 571 6358 3111/6313 1431
 Email: webmaster@cnnanhe.com
 Web Address: www.zjshangyou.com
Personnel:
 Chmn. & Gen. Mgr.: Fumin Yang
 Phone: (86) 571 6315 3118/3137
 Sls. Mgr.: Xueming Liu
 Phone: (86) 571 6315 3118/3137

Total Employees at this Location: 450
Type of Operation: Paperboard mill
Pulp Grades and Capacities:
 Total pulp capacity: 93,613 mt/y
 Recycled Pulping: 93,613 mt/y
Pulp Mill Data:
Pulp Lines: 1
 Recycled Fiber Treatment Lines:
 Flotation deinking lines
 Recycled packaging pulping lines
Paper/Paperboard Grades and Capacities:
 Total paper and paperboard capacity: 99,960 mt/y
 Corrugating medium/fluting: 9,996 mt/y
 Boxboard/cartonboard: 89,964 mt/y
Paper and Paperboard Mill Data:
Paper Machines: 2
No. 1, total capacity 9,996 mt/y, Trim width 1.76 m, Corrugating medium/fluting
No. 2, multi-former (5), total capacity 89,964 mt/y, Trim width 2.8 m, Boxboard/cartonboard
Coating Machines: 1
CM 1, total capacity 90,000 mt/y, on machine
Finishing Equipment:
 Winders: 3
 Sheeters: 3
Energy Data:
Electrical demand for mill: 158 MWh/D

ⓘZhejiang Fuyang Sunshi Paper Co., Ltd.
Ownership: Zhejiang Sunshi Paper Group Co., Ltd.
Xinjian Village, Chunjiang Street
Fuyang, Zhejiang, 311402
China
 Phone: (86) 571 6358 1171
 Fax: (86) 571 6358 1171
 Web Address: www.sunshipaper.com
Personnel:
 Gen. Mgr.: Jianjun Sun
 Phone: (86) 571 6358 1171
 Sls. Mgr.: Yanping Zhao
 Phone: (86) 571 6358 1171
Mill Locations:
Zhejiang Fuyang Sunshi Paper Co., Ltd., Fuyang Mill, Xinjian Village, Chunjiang Street, Fuyang 311402, China, Capacity: 30,000 mt/y, (Paperboard mill)
 Phone: (86) 571 6358 1171
 Fax: (86) 571 6358 1171

ⓜZhejiang Fuyang Sunshi Paper Co., Ltd.
Fuyang Mill
Ownership: Zhejiang Sunshi Paper Group Co., Ltd.
Xinjian Village, Chunjiang Street
Fuyang, Zhejiang, 311402
China
 Phone: (86) 571 6358 1171
 Fax: (86) 571 6358 1171
Personnel:
 Gen. Mgr.: Jianjun Sun
 Phone: (86) 571 6358 1171
 Sls. Mgr.: Yanping Zhao
 Phone: (86) 571 6358 1171
Total Employees at this Location: 320
Type of Operation: Paperboard mill
Pulp Grades and Capacities:
 Total pulp capacity: 30,000 mt/y
 Recycled Pulping: 30,000 mt/y
Pulp Mill Data:
Pulp Lines: 2
 Recycled Fiber Treatment Lines:
 Recycled packaging pulping lines: 2 at 30,000 admt/y
Paper/Paperboard Grades and Capacities:
 Total paper and paperboard capacity: 30,000 mt/y
 Boxboard/cartonboard: 30,000 mt/y
Paper and Paperboard Mill Data:
Paper Machines: 2

PM 1, cylinder, total capacity 12,000 mt/y, Trim width 1.09 m, Boxboard/cartonboard
PM 2, cylinder, total capacity 18,000 mt/y, Trim width 1.58 m, Boxboard/cartonboard

ⓘZhejiang Fuyang Wanfang Paper Co., Ltd.
Ownership: 100% by private owners
Yongfeng Village, Lingqiao Town
Fuyang, Zhejiang, 311418
China
 Phone: (86) 571 6355 2658
 Fax: (86) 571 6355 2668
 Web Address: www.wanfangzy.com
Mill Locations:
Zhejiang Fuyang Wanfang Paper Co., Ltd., Fuyang Mill, Yongfeng Village, Lingqiao Town, Fuyang 311418, China, Capacity: 12,000 mt/y, (Paper mill)
 Phone: (86) 571 6355 2658
 Fax: (86) 571 6355 2668

ⓜZhejiang Fuyang Wanfang Paper Co., Ltd.
Fuyang Mill
Yongfeng Village, Lingqiao Town
Fuyang, Zhejiang, 311418
China
 Phone: (86) 571 6355 2658
 Fax: (86) 571 6355 2668
 Web Address: www.wanfangzy.com
Personnel:
 Pres. & Gen. Mgr.: Jianzhong Xu
 Phone: (86) 571 6355 2658
Type of Operation: Paper mill
Paper/Paperboard Grades and Capacities:
 Total paper and paperboard capacity: 12,000 mt/y
 Packaging papers: 12,000 mt/y
Paper and Paperboard Mill Data:
Paper Machines: 1
PM 1, fourdrinier, total capacity 12,000 mt/y, Trim width 2.64 m, Packaging papers

ⓘZhejiang Fuyang Wansheng Paper Co., Ltd.
Ownership: 100% by private owners
No. 2 Industry Rd., Linqiao Industry Park
Fuyang, Zhejiang, 311418
China
 Phone: (86) 571 6355 8677
 Fax: (86) 571 6355 8679
Mill Locations:
Zhejiang Fuyang Wansheng Paper Co., Ltd., Fuyang Mill, No. 2 Industry Rd., Linqiao Industry Park, Fuyang 311418, China, Capacity: 20,000 mt/y, (Paperboard mill)
 Phone: (86) 571 6355 8679
 Fax: (86) 571 6355 8679

ⓜZhejiang Fuyang Wansheng Paper Co., Ltd.
Fuyang Mill
No. 2 Industry Rd., Linqiao Industry Park
Fuyang, Zhejiang, 311418
China
 Phone: (86) 571 6355 8679
 Fax: (86) 571 6355 8679
Personnel:
 Gen. Mgr.: Yaqing Zhuang
 Phone: (86) 571 6355 8677
Total Employees at this Location: 350
Type of Operation: Paperboard mill
Pulp Grades and Capacities:
 Total pulp capacity: 20,310 mt/y
 Recycled Pulping: 20,310 mt/y
Pulp Mill Data:
Pulp Lines: 2
 Recycled Fiber Treatment Lines:

China

Recycled packaging pulping lines: 2 at 28,000 admt/y
Paper/Paperboard Grades and Capacities:
Total paper and paperboard capacity: 20,000 mt/y
Linerboard: 20,000 mt/y
Paper and Paperboard Mill Data:
Paper Machines: 1
No. 1, multi-wire, total capacity 20,000 mt/y, Trim width 2.95 m, Linerboard
Energy Data:
Electrical demand for mill: 25 MWh/D

ⓗZhejiang Fuyang Xinyuan Paper Co., Ltd.
Ownership: 100% by private owners
Lingqiao Paper-making Industry Park
Fuyang, Zhejiang, 311418
China
  Phone: (86) 571 6355 8833
  Fax: (86) 571 6355 0568
  Email: xinyuanpaper@xinyuanpaper.com
  Web Address: www.xinyuanpaper.com
Personnel:
  Chmn.: Ms. Suying Wang
  Phone: (86) 571 6355 8833
Mill Locations:
Zhejiang Fuyang Xinyuan Paper Co., Ltd., Fuyang Mill, Lingqiao Paper-making Industry Park, Fuyang 311418, China, Capacity: 35,000 mt/y, (Paperboard mill)
  Phone: (86) 571 6355 8833
  Fax: (86) 571 6355 0568
  Email: xinyuanpaper@xinyuanpaper.com

ⓜZhejiang Fuyang Xinyuan Paper Co., Ltd.
Fuyang Mill
Lingqiao Paper-making Industry Park
Fuyang, Zhejiang, 311418
China
  Phone: (86) 571 6355 8833
  Fax: (86) 571 6355 0568
  Email: xinyuanpaper@xinyuanpaper.com
  Web Address: www.xinyuanpaper.com
Personnel:
  Chmn.: Ms. Suying Wang
  Phone: (86) 571 6355 8833
Total Employees at this Location: 150
Type of Operation: Paperboard mill
Pulp Grades and Capacities:
Total pulp capacity: 31,861 mt/y
Recycled Pulping: 31,861 mt/y
Pulp Mill Data:
Pulp Lines: 2
  Bleach Plant Systems: 1
    Recycled Pulping System, Type: DIP
  Recycled Fiber Treatment Lines:
    Flotation deinking lines: 1
    Recycled packaging pulping lines: 1
Paper/Paperboard Grades and Capacities:
Total paper and paperboard capacity: 35,000 mt/y
Boxboard/cartonboard: 35,000 mt/y
Paper and Paperboard Mill Data:
Paper Machines: 1
No. 1, cylinder (8), total capacity 35,000 mt/y, Trim width 2.64 m, Boxboard/cartonboard
Coating Machines: 1
PM#1, on machine
Energy Data:
Electrical demand for mill: 54 MWh/D

ⓗZhejiang Fuyang Zhenghua Paper Co., Ltd.
Ownership: 100% by private owners
Zhenglong Village, Dayuan Town Industry Park
Fuyang, Zhejiang, 311413
China
  Phone: (86) 571 6359 7299
  Fax: (86) 571 6359 7277
Mill Locations:
Zhejiang Fuyang Zhenghua Paper Co., Ltd., Fuyang Mill, Zhenglong Village, Dayuan Town Industry Park, Fuyang 311413, China, Capacity: 60,000 mt/y, (Paperboard mill)
  Phone: (86) 571 6359 7299
  Fax: (86) 571 6359 7277

ⓜZhejiang Fuyang Zhenghua Paper Co., Ltd.
Fuyang Mill
Zhenglong Village, Dayuan Town Industry Park
Fuyang, Zhejiang, 311413
China
  Phone: (86) 571 6359 7299
  Fax: (86) 571 6359 7277
Personnel:
  Gen. Mgr.: Peijin Wang
  Phone: (86) 571 6359 7299
Total Employees at this Location: 150
Type of Operation: Paperboard mill
Pulp Grades and Capacities:
Total pulp capacity: 58,354 mt/y
Recycled Pulping: 58,354 mt/y
Pulp Mill Data:
Pulp Lines: 1
  Recycled Fiber Treatment Lines:
    Recycled packaging pulping lines: 1 at 35,000 admt/y
Paper/Paperboard Grades and Capacities:
Total paper and paperboard capacity: 60,000 mt/y
Corrugating medium/fluting: 60,000 mt/y
Paper and Paperboard Mill Data:
Paper Machines: 1
No. 1, fourdrinier, total capacity 60,000 mt/y, Trim width 3.6 m, Corrugating medium/fluting
Energy Data:
Electrical demand for mill: 75 MWh/D

ⓗⓜZhejiang Gaoyang Paper Co., Ltd.
Fuyang Mill
Ownership: 100% by private owners
Chunjiang Street Industry Park
Fuyang, Zhejiang, 311421
China
  Phone: (86) 571 6315 3808/ 0588
  Fax: (86) 571 6358 5888
  Email: zjgyzy@zjgyzy.com
  Web Address: www.zjgyzy.com
Personnel:
  Chmn.: Renfa Dong
  Phone: (86) 571 6315 3808/ 0588
Total Employees at this Location: 375
Type of Operation: Paperboard mill
Mill Locations:
Zhejiang Fuyang Gaoyang Paper Co., Ltd., Fuyang Mill, Chunjiang Street Industry Park, Fuyang 311421, China, Capacity: 20,000 mt/y, (Paperboard mill)
  Phone: (86) 571 6358 5999
  Fax: (86) 571 6358 9999
Pulp Grades and Capacities:
Total pulp capacity: 129,576 mt/y
Recycled Pulping: 129,576 mt/y
Pulp Mill Data:
Pulp Lines: 1
  Recycled Fiber Treatment Lines:
    Flotation deinking lines: 1
    Recycled packaging pulping lines: 1 at 80,000 admt/y
    Recycled packaging pulping lines: 1
Paper/Paperboard Grades and Capacities:
Total paper and paperboard capacity: 149,583 mt/y
Boxboard/cartonboard: 149,583 mt/y
Paper and Paperboard Mill Data:
Paper Machines: 1
No. 1, Multi-wire (5), total capacity 149,583 mt/y, Trim width 3.8 m, Boxboard/cartonboard
Coating Machines: 1
PM 1, total capacity 150,000 mt/y., on machine
Energy Data:
Electrical demand for mill: 269 MWh/D

ⓜZhejiang Haijing Paper Co., Ltd.
Quzhou Mill
No.32, Jinxing Rd., Longyou Economic Development Zone
Quzhou, Zhejiang, 324400
China
  Phone: (86) 570 7858 899/871
  Fax: (86) 570 7858 111/871
  Email: zj@zjhjzy.com
  Web Address: www.zjhjzy.com
Total Employees at this Location: 200
Type of Operation: Paper mill
Paper/Paperboard Grades and Capacities:
Total paper and paperboard capacity: 21,000 mt/y
Specialty and industrial: 21,000 mt/y
Paper and Paperboard Mill Data:
Paper Machines: 1
PM 1, total capacity 21,000 mt/y, Trim width 2.64 m, Specialty and industrial

ⓜZhejiang Haining Bangda Paper Co., Ltd.
Haining Mill
Ownership: Zhejiang Hangzhou Xinhua Paper Industry Co., Ltd.
Jingshan Village, Zhouwang Temple Town
Haining, Zhejiang, 314411
China
  Phone: (86) 573 8793 3158
  Fax: (86) 573 8762 8181
Personnel:
  Gen. Mgr.: Jianliang Mao
  Phone: (86) 573 8793 3158
Type of Operation: Pulp mill, Paper mill
Pulp Grades and Capacities:
Total pulp capacity: 10,000 mt/y
Recycled Pulping: 10,000 mt/y
Pulp Mill Data:
Paper/Paperboard Grades and Capacities:
Total paper and paperboard capacity: 10,000 mt/y
Tissue: 10,000 mt/y
Paper and Paperboard Mill Data:
Paper Machines: 6
PM 1, Trim width 1.76 m, Tissue
PM 2, cylinder, Trim width 1.76 m, Tissue
PM 3, cylinder, Trim width 1.76 m, Tissue
PM 4, Trim width 1.76 m, Tissue
PM 5-6, Trim width 1.58 m, Tissue
Energy Data:
Power boilers: 2

ⓜZhejiang Halberd Paper Co., Ltd.
Quzhou Mill
Mill is bankrupt
Ownership: 51% by Arjowiggins SAS, 49% by Zhejiang Kan Specialty Material Co., Ltd.
No. 9 Donggang 4th Road, Donggang Industrial Zone
Quzhou, Zhejiang, 324000
China
  Phone: (86) 570 888 6836/6800/ 383 2662
  Fax: (86) 570 888 6831
Personnel:
  Chmn.: Bailang Wang
  Phone: (86) 570 888 6836/6800/ 383 2662
Type of Operation: Paper mill
Paper/Paperboard Grades and Capacities:
Total paper and paperboard capacity: 5,000 mt/y
Uncoated woodfree/freesheet: 5,000 mt/y
Specialty and industrial
Paper and Paperboard Mill Data:
Paper Machines: 1
No. 1 PM, fourdrinier, total capacity 5,000 mt/y, Trim width 1.88 m, Specialty and industrial

ⓗZhejiang Hangzhou Banqiao Paper Co., Ltd.
Bayi Industry Zone, Chunjiang Street
Fuyang, Zhejiang, 311421
China

Phone: (86) 571 6358 5686/2056
Fax: (86) 571 6358 5988
Mill Locations:
Zhejiang Hangzhou Banqiao Paper Co., Ltd., Fuyang Mill, Bayi Industry Zone, Chunjiang Street, Fuyang 311421, China, Capacity: 155,652 mt/y, (Paperboard mill)
Phone: (86) 571 6358 5686/2056
Fax: (86) 571 6358 5988

ⓂZhejiang Hangzhou Banqiao Paper Co., Ltd.
Fuyang Mill
Bayi Industry Zone, Chunjiang Street
Fuyang, Zhejiang, 311421
China
Phone: (86) 571 6358 5686/2056
Fax: (86) 571 6358 5988
Personnel:
Chmn.: Zhengqi Yu
Phone: (86) 571 6358 5686/2056
Chief Eng.: Jianhua Tong
Phone: (86) 571 6358 5686/2056
Total Employees at this Location: 600
Type of Operation: Paperboard mill
Pulp Grades and Capacities:
Total pulp capacity: 133,567 mt/y
Recycled Pulping: 133,567 mt/y
Paper/Paperboard Grades and Capacities:
Total paper and paperboard capacity: 155,652 mt/y
Uncoated woodfree/freesheet: 29,988 mt/y
Boxboard/cartonboard: 125,664 mt/y
Paper and Paperboard Mill Data:
Paper Machines: 3
No. 2, Fourdrinier (5), total capacity 90,678 mt/y, Trim width 2.8 m, Boxboard/cartonboard
No. 3, Fourdrinier (5), total capacity 34,986 mt/y, Trim width 2.64 m, Boxboard/cartonboard
No. 4, fourdrinier, total capacity 29,988 mt/y, Trim width 2.8 m, Uncoated woodfree/freesheet
Energy Data:
Electrical demand for mill: 256 MWh/D

ⒽZhejiang Hangzhou Dazhong Paper Co., Ltd.
Ownership: 100% by private owners
Shanjian Industry Park, Chunjiang Street
Fuyang, Hangzhou, Zhejiang, 311421
China
Phone: (86) 571 6358 3150/ 5088
Fax: (86) 571 6358 2110
Email: hzdzykf@126.com
Web Address: www.hzdz-paper.com
Mill Locations:
Zhejiang Hangzhou Dazhong Paper Co., Ltd., Fuyang Mill, Shanjian Industry Park, Chunjiang Street, Fuyang 311421, China, Capacity: 189,924 mt/y, (Paperboard mill)
Phone: (86) 571 6358 3150/ 5088
Fax: (86) 571 6358 2110
Email: hzdzykf@126.com

ⓂZhejiang Hangzhou Dazhong Paper Co., Ltd.
Fuyang Mill
Shanjian Industry Park, Chunjiang Street
Fuyang, Zhejiang, 311421
China
Phone: (86) 571 6358 3150/ 5088
Fax: (86) 571 6358 2110
Email: hzdzykf@126.com
Web Address: www.hzdz-paper.com
Personnel:
Pres. & Gen. Mgr.: Songpei Tang
Phone: (86) 571 6358 3150/ 5088
Total Employees at this Location: 218
Type of Operation: Paperboard mill
Pulp Grades and Capacities:
Total pulp capacity: 149,768 mt/y
Recycled Pulping: 149,768 mt/y
Pulp Mill Data:
Pulp Lines: 3
Recycled Fiber Treatment Lines:
Flotation deinking lines
Recycled packaging pulping lines
Paper/Paperboard Grades and Capacities:
Total paper and paperboard capacity: 189,924 mt/y
Boxboard/cartonboard: 189,924 mt/y
Paper and Paperboard Mill Data:
Paper Machines: 2
No. 1, cylinder (5), total capacity 39,984 mt/y, Trim width 1.76 m, Boxboard/cartonboard
No. 2, Fourdrinier (4), total capacity 149,940 mt/y, Trim width 4.3 m, Boxboard/cartonboard
Energy Data:
Electrical demand for mill: 272 MWh/D

ⒽZhejiang Hangzhou Dongda Paper Co., Ltd.
Ownership: 100% by private owners
Shangyang Industry Park, Chunjiang Street
Fuyang, Zhejiang, 311421
China
Phone: (86) 571 6315 1008/ 6358 1388
Fax: (86) 571 6358 5555
Email: ddzy@hzddzy.net
Web Address: www.hzddzy.net
Mill Locations:
Zhejiang Hangzhou Dongda Paper Co., Ltd., Fuyang Mill, Shangyang Industry Park, Chunjiang Street, Fuyang 311421, China, Capacity: 99,960 mt/y, (Paperboard mill)
Phone: (86) 571 6315 1008/ 6358 1388
Fax: (86) 571 6358 5555
Email: ddzy@hzddzy.net

ⓂZhejiang Hangzhou Dongda Paper Co., Ltd.
Fuyang Mill
Shangyang Industry Park, Chunjiang Street
Fuyang, Zhejiang, 311421
China
Phone: (86) 571 6315 1008/ 6358 1388
Fax: (86) 571 6358 5555
Email: ddzy@hzddzy.net
Web Address: www.hzddzy.net
Personnel:
Chmn. & Pres.: Jianglin Liu
Phone: (86) 571 6315 1008/ 6358 1388
Sls. Mgr.: Yanghuo Liu
Phone: (86) 571 6315 1008/ 6358 1388
Asst. Mgr., Vice Prod. Mgr.: Guanfa Sun
Phone: (86) 571 6315 1008/ 6358 1388
Manuf. Dir.: Weilong Wang
Phone: (86) 571 6315 1008/ 6358 1388
Total Employees at this Location: 650
Type of Operation: Paperboard mill
Pulp Grades and Capacities:
Total pulp capacity: 82,766 mt/y
Recycled Pulping: 82,766 mt/y
Pulp Mill Data:
Pulp Lines: 4
Recycled Fiber Treatment Lines:
Recycled packaging pulping lines: 4 at 120,000 admt/y
Paper/Paperboard Grades and Capacities:
Total paper and paperboard capacity: 99,960 mt/y
Boxboard/cartonboard: 99,960 mt/y
Paper and Paperboard Mill Data:
Paper Machines: 1
No. 2, Fourdrinier (5), total capacity 99,960 mt/y, Trim width 2.8 m, Boxboard/cartonboard
Energy Data:
Electrical demand for mill: 163 MWh/D

ⒽZhejiang Hangzhou Fulun Paper Co., Ltd.
Ownership: 100% by private owners
Linqiao Industry Park
Fuyang, Zhejiang, 311418
China
Phone: (86) 571 6355 1944
Fax: (86) 571 6355 0944
Email: fulun@fulunpaper.com
Web Address: www.fulunpaper.com
Mill Locations:
Zhejiang Hangzhou Fulun Paper Co., Ltd., Fuyang Mill, Linqiao Industry Park, Fuyang 311418, China, Capacity: 15,000 mt/y, (Paper mill)
Phone: (86) 571 6355 1944
Fax: (86) 571 6355 0944
Email: fulun@fulunpaper.com

ⓂZhejiang Hangzhou Fulun Paper Co., Ltd.
Fuyang Mill
Linqiao Industry Park
Fuyang, Zhejiang, 311418
China
Phone: (86) 571 6355 1944
Fax: (86) 571 6355 0944
Email: fulun@fulunpaper.com
Web Address: www.fulunpaper.com
Personnel:
Gen. Mgr.: Jun Yang
Phone: (86) 571 6355 1944
Total Employees at this Location: 100
Type of Operation: Paper mill
Pulp Grades and Capacities:
Total pulp capacity: 15,000 mt/y
Pulp Mill Data:
Recycled Fiber Treatment Lines:
Recycled packaging pulping lines: 1 at 15,000 admt/y
Paper/Paperboard Grades and Capacities:
Total paper and paperboard capacity: 15,000 mt/y
Packaging papers: 15,000 mt/y
Paper and Paperboard Mill Data:
Paper Machines: 1
PM 1, multi-ply, total capacity 15,000 mt/y, Trim width 3.6 m, Packaging papers

ⒽZhejiang Hangzhou Fuyang Jinying Industry Co., Ltd.
Ownership: 100% by private owners
Linqiao Industry Park
Fuyang, Hangzhou, Zhejiang, 311418
China
Phone: (86) 571 6355 0551/ 0552
Fax: (86) 571 6355 0718
Mill Locations:
Zhejiang Hangzhou Fuyang Jinying Industry Co., Ltd., Fuyang Mill, Linqiao Industry Park, Fuyang 311418, China, Capacity: 30,000 mt/y, (Paperboard mill)
Phone: (86) 571 6355 0551/ 0552
Fax: (86) 571 6355 0718

ⓂZhejiang Hangzhou Fuyang Jinying Industry Co., Ltd.
Fuyang Mill
Linqiao Industry Park
Fuyang, Zhejiang, 311418
China
Phone: (86) 571 6355 0551/ 0552
Fax: (86) 571 6355 0718
Personnel:
Gen. Mgr.: Ming Wang
Phone: (86) 571 6355 0551/ 0552
Total Employees at this Location: 200
Type of Operation: Paperboard mill
Pulp Grades and Capacities:
Total pulp capacity: 30,000 mt/y
Recycled Pulping: 30,000 mt/y

China

Pulp Mill Data:
Pulp Lines: 2
 Recycled Fiber Treatment Lines:
  Recycled packaging pulping lines: 2 at 30,000 admt/y
Paper/Paperboard Grades and Capacities:
 Total paper and paperboard capacity: 30,000 mt/y
 Boxboard/cartonboard: 30,000 mt/y
Paper and Paperboard Mill Data:
Paper Machines: 1
 PM 1, multi-layer, total capacity 30,000 mt/y, Trim width 1.88 m, Boxboard/cartonboard

ⓟZhejiang Hangzhou Guofeng Paper Co., Ltd.

Ownership: 100% by private owners
Zhitang Village, Chunjiang Street
Fuyang, Zhejiang, 311421
China
 Phone: (86) 571 6315 0071/ 6358 7395
 Fax: (86) 571 6315 3166/ 6358 7090
 Email: ymh@fyguofeng.com
 Web Address: www.fyguofeng.com
Mill Locations:
 Zhejiang Hangzhou Guofeng Paper Co., Ltd., Fuyang Mill, Zhitang Village, Chunjiang Street, Fuyang 311421, China, Capacity: 40,000 mt/y, (Paperboard mill)
 Phone: (86) 571 6315 0071/ 6358 7395
 Fax: (86) 571 6315 3166/ 6358 7090
 Email: ymh@fyguofeng.com

ⓜZhejiang Hangzhou Guofeng Paper Co., Ltd.
Fuyang Mill

Zhitang Village, Chunjiang Street
Fuyang, Zhejiang, 311421
China
 Phone: (86) 571 6315 0071/ 6358 7395
 Fax: (86) 571 6315 3166/ 6358 7090
 Email: ymh@fyguofeng.com
 Web Address: www.fyguofeng.com
Personnel:
 Gen. Mgr.: Minghua Xu
 Phone: (86) 571 6315 0071/ 6358 7395
Total Employees at this Location: 150
Type of Operation: Paperboard mill
Pulp Grades and Capacities:
 Total pulp capacity: 35,284 mt/y
 Recycled Pulping: 35,284 mt/y
Pulp Mill Data:
 Bleach Plant Systems: 1
  Recycled Pulping System, Type: DIP
 Recycled Fiber Treatment Lines:
  Recycled packaging pulping lines: 2 at 40,000 admt/y
Paper/Paperboard Grades and Capacities:
 Total paper and paperboard capacity: 40,000 mt/y
 Boxboard/cartonboard: 40,000 mt/y
Paper and Paperboard Mill Data:
Paper Machines: 2
 No. 1, Fourdrinier (4), total capacity 18,000 mt/y, Trim width 1.76 m, Boxboard/cartonboard
 No. 2, Fourdrinier (4), total capacity 22,000 mt/y, Trim width 1.88 m, Boxboard/cartonboard
Coating Machines: 2
 PM#1, on machine
 PM#2, on machine
Energy Data:
 Electrical demand for mill: 68 MWh/D

ⓜZhejiang Hangzhou Haichen Paper Co., Ltd.
Fuyang Mill

Ownership: Zhejiang Sunshi Paper Group Co., Ltd.
Zhaofangdun Village, Linqiao Town
Fuyang, Zhejiang, 311418
China
 Phone: (86) 571 6352 9873
 Fax: (86) 571 6352 9898
 Web Address: www.sunshipaper.com
Personnel:
 Gen. Mgr.: Jianjun Sun
 Phone: (86) 571 6352 9873
Total Employees at this Location: 310
Type of Operation: Paperboard mill
Pulp Grades and Capacities:
 Total pulp capacity: 68,920 mt/y
 Recycled Pulping: 68,920 mt/y
Pulp Mill Data:
Pulp Lines: 3
 Recycled Fiber Treatment Lines:
  Recycled packaging pulping lines: 3 at 80,000 admt/y
Paper/Paperboard Grades and Capacities:
 Total paper and paperboard capacity: 80,000 mt/y
 Boxboard/cartonboard: 80,000 mt/y
Paper and Paperboard Mill Data:
Paper Machines: 1
 No. 1, Fourdrinier (5), total capacity 80,000 mt/y, Trim width 2.64 m, Boxboard/cartonboard
Energy Data:
 Electrical demand for mill: 114 MWh/D

ⓟⓜZhejiang Hangzhou Huafeng Paper Co., Ltd.
Hangzhou Mill

Ownership: 56% by China Tobacco Co. Ltd., 30% by Overseas Dev. Co. (Singapore) Ltd., 14% by Zhejiang Hangzhou Xinfeng Paper Mill
No. 555 Hemu Rd., Gongye District
Hangzhou, Zhejiang, 310011
China
 Phone: (86) 571 8809 1424
 Fax: (86) 571 8809 1536
 Email: sales@hfpaper.com
 Web Address: www.hfpaper.com
Personnel:
 Chmn.: Shengli Huang
 Phone: (86) 571 8809 1424
 Pres.: Xiaoping Zhao
 Phone: (86) 571 8809 1424
 Vice Pres.: Peicheng Lu
 Phone: (86) 571 8809 1424
 Tech. Mgr.: Juxian Mao
 Phone: (86) 571 8809 1424
 Sls. & Mktg. Mgr.: Chunchao Wang
 Phone: (86) 571 8809 1424
 Export Sls. Mgr.: Huiqun Jin
 Phone: (86) 571 8809 1424
Total Employees at this Location: 2,000
Type of Operation: Paper mill
Paper/Paperboard Grades and Capacities:
 Total paper and paperboard capacity: 40,000 mt/y
 Specialty and industrial: 40,000 mt/y
Paper and Paperboard Mill Data:
 Stock Preparation:
  Refiners:
Paper Machines: 3
 PM 7, fourdrinier, total capacity 8,000 mt/y, Trim width 2.36 m, Specialty and industrial
 PM 8, fourdrinier, total capacity 10,000 mt/y, Trim width 3.2 m, Specialty and industrial
 PM 9, fourdrinier, total capacity 22,000 mt/y, Trim width 3.6 m, Specialty and industrial
Finishing Equipment:
 Rewinders: 10
 Sheeters: 5
Energy Data:
 Power boilers: 3

ⓟZhejiang Hangzhou Huasheng Paper Co., Ltd.

Ownership: 100% by shareholders
Zhitang Village, Chunjiang Papermaking Industry Park
Fuyang, Zhejiang, 311421
China
 Phone: (86) 571 6358 3157/ 7832
 Fax: (86) 571 6358 1717/ 7588
 Email: huashe@public.fy.hz.zj.cn
 Web Address: www.fyhuasheng.com
Total Employees at this Location: 280
Mill Locations:
 Zhejiang Hangzhou Huasheng Paper Co., Ltd., Fuyang Mill, Zhitang Village, Chunjiang Papermaking Industry Park, Fuyang 311421, China, Capacity: 119,952 mt/y, (Paperboard mill)
 Phone: (86) 571 6358 3157/ 7832
 Fax: (86) 571 6358 1717/ 7588
 Email: huashe@public.fy.hz.zj.cn

ⓜZhejiang Hangzhou Huasheng Paper Co., Ltd.
Fuyang Mill

Zhitang Village, Chunjiang Papermaking Industry Park
Fuyang, Zhejiang, 311421
China
 Phone: (86) 571 6358 3157/ 7832
 Fax: (86) 571 6358 1717/ 7588
 Email: huashe@public.fy.hz.zj.cn
 Web Address: www.fyhuasheng.com
Personnel:
 Pres.: Wensheng Yu
 Phone: (86) 571 6358 3157/ 7832
 Sls. Mgr.: Rujun Yu
 Phone: (86) 571 6358 3157/ 7832
Total Employees at this Location: 280
Type of Operation: Paperboard mill
Pulp Grades and Capacities:
 Total pulp capacity: 99,697 mt/y
 Recycled Pulping: 99,697 mt/y
Pulp Mill Data:
Pulp Lines: 3
 Recycled Fiber Treatment Lines:
  Flotation deinking lines: 1 at 40,000 admt/y
  Pulpers
Paper/Paperboard Grades and Capacities:
 Total paper and paperboard capacity: 119,952 mt/y
 Boxboard/cartonboard: 119,952 mt/y
Paper and Paperboard Mill Data:
Paper Machines: 2
 No. 2, cylinder, total capacity 19,992 mt/y, Trim width 1.88 m, Boxboard/cartonboard
 No. 3, Multi-wire (5), total capacity 99,960 mt/y, Trim width 2.88 m, Boxboard/cartonboard
Coating Machines: 2
 CM 2, total capacity 20,000 mt/y., on machine
 CM 3, total capacity 100,000 mt/y., on machine
Energy Data:
 Power boilers: 2
 Steam turbines: 1 at 6 MW
 Electrical demand for mill: 172 MWh/D

ⓟZhejiang Hangzhou Jintai Paper Co., Ltd.

Ownership: 100% by private owners
Jianshe Village, Chunjiang Paper-making Industry Park
Fuyang, Zhejiang, 311421
China
 Phone: (86) 571 6358 5668
 Fax: (86) 571 6358 5885
 Email: webmaster@jtpaper.com
 Web Address: www.jtpaper.com
Mill Locations:
 Zhejiang Hangzhou Jintai Paper Co., Ltd., Fuyang Mill, Jianshe Village, Chunjiang Paper-making Industry Park, Fuyang 311421, China, Capacity: 79,968 mt/y, (Pulp mill, Paperboard mill)
 Phone: (86) 571 6358 5668
 Fax: (86) 571 6358 5885
 Email: webmaster@jtpaper.com

ⓜZhejiang Hangzhou Jintai Paper Co., Ltd.
Fuyang Mill

Jianshe Village, Chunjiang Paper-making Industry Park
Fuyang, Zhejiang, 311421
China

Phone: (86) 571 6358 5668
Fax: (86) 571 6358 5885
Email: webmaster@jtpaper.com
Web Address: www.jtpaper.com
Personnel:
 Gen. Mgr.: Songyin Yu
 Phone: (86) 571 6358 5668
 Sls. Mgr.: Junshui Yu
 Phone: (86) 571 6358 5668
Total Employees at this Location: 200
Type of Operation: Pulp mill, Paperboard mill
Pulp Grades and Capacities:
 Total pulp capacity: 63,829 mt/y
 Recycled Pulping: 63,829 mt/y
Pulp Mill Data:
Pulp Lines: 4
 Recycled Fiber Treatment Lines:
 Recycled packaging pulping lines: 4 at 80,000 admt/y
Paper/Paperboard Grades and Capacities:
 Total paper and paperboard capacity: 79,968 mt/y
 Boxboard/cartonboard: 79,968 mt/y
Paper and Paperboard Mill Data:
Paper Machines: 1
 No. 1, Fourdrinier (5), total capacity 79,968 mt/y, Trim width 2.76 m, Boxboard/cartonboard
Finishing Equipment:
 Rewinders: 1 at 90,000 mt/y
Energy Data:
 Electrical demand for mill: 110 MWh/D

ⓗZhejiang Hangzhou Ruixing Paper Co., Ltd.
Ownership: Zhejiang Sunshi Paper Group Co., Ltd.
Linqiao Industry Park
Fuyang, Zhejiang, 311418
China
 Phone: (86) 571 6355 8182/ 8803
 Fax: (86) 571 6355 8805
Personnel:
 Sls. Mgr.: Xinxia Li
 Phone: (86) 571 6355 8182/ 8803
Mill Locations:
Zhejiang Hangzhou Ruixing Paper Co., Ltd., Fuyang Mill, Linqiao Industry Park, Fuyang 311418, China, Capacity: 119,952 mt/y, (Paperboard mill)
 Phone: (86) 571 6355 8182/ 8803
 Fax: (86) 571 6355 8805

ⓜZhejiang Hangzhou Ruixing Paper Co., Ltd.
Fuyang Mill
Ownership: Zhejiang Sunshi Paper Group Co., Ltd.
Linqiao Industry Park
Fuyang, Zhejiang, 311418
China
 Phone: (86) 571 6355 8182/ 8803
 Fax: (86) 571 6355 8805
 Web Address: www.sunshipaper.com
Personnel:
 Chmn.: Jianjun Sun
 Phone: (86) 571 6355 8182/ 8803
Total Employees at this Location: 400
Type of Operation: Paperboard mill
Pulp Grades and Capacities:
 Total pulp capacity: 101,383 mt/y
 Recycled Pulping: 101,383 mt/y
Pulp Mill Data:
Pulp Lines: 3
 Recycled Fiber Treatment Lines:
 Recycled packaging pulping lines: 3 at 90,000 admt/y
Paper/Paperboard Grades and Capacities:
 Total paper and paperboard capacity: 119,952 mt/y
 Boxboard/cartonboard: 119,952 mt/y
Paper and Paperboard Mill Data:
Paper Machines: 1
 No. 1, Fourdrinier (5), total capacity 119,952 mt/y, Trim width 3.6 m, Boxboard/cartonboard
Energy Data:

Power boilers: 2
Steam turbines: 2 at 3, 6 MW
Electrical demand for mill: 172 MWh/D

ⓗⓜZhejiang Hangzhou Tongda Paper Co., Ltd
Fuyang Mill
Chunlian Industry Zone, Chunjiang Street
Fuyang, Zhejiang
China
 Phone: (86) 571 6358 1558
Total Employees at this Location: 520
Type of Operation: Paper mill
Pulp Grades and Capacities:
 Total pulp capacity: 135,471 mt/y
 Recycled Pulping: 135,471 mt/y
Paper/Paperboard Grades and Capacities:
 Total paper and paperboard capacity: 169,932 mt/y
 Boxboard/cartonboard: 169,932 mt/y
Paper and Paperboard Mill Data:
Paper Machines: 2
 No. 2, cylinder, total capacity 44,268 mt/y, Trim width 2.4 m, Boxboard/cartonboard
 No. 3, Fourdrinier (4), total capacity 125,664 mt/y, Trim width 3.4 m, Boxboard/cartonboard
Coating Machines: 2
 PM#2, on machine
 PM#3, on machine
Energy Data:
Power boilers
Steam turbines
Electrical demand for mill: 241 MWh/D

ⓗZhejiang Hangzhou Xinfeng Paper Co., Ltd.
Ownership: 100% by JV
No. 555 Hemu Rd., Gongye District
Hangzhou, Zhejiang, 310011
China
 Phone: (86) 571 8809 1424
 Fax: (86) 571 8809 1536
 Email: sales@hfpaper.com
 Web Address: www.hfpaper.com
Mill Locations:
Zhejiang Hangzhou Xinfeng Paper Co., Ltd., Hangzhou Mill, No. 555 Hemu Rd., Gongye District, Hangzhou 310011, China, Capacity: 10,000 mt/y, (Paper mill)
 Phone: (86) 571 8809 1424
 Fax: (86) 571 8809 1536
 Email: sales@hfpaper.com

ⓜZhejiang Hangzhou Xinfeng Paper Co., Ltd.
Hangzhou Mill
No. 555 Hemu Rd., Gongye District
Hangzhou, Zhejiang, 310011
China
 Phone: (86) 571 8809 1424
 Fax: (86) 571 8809 1536
 Email: sales@hfpaper.com
 Web Address: www.hfpaper.com
Personnel:
 Pres.: Guangzhong Lin
 Phone: (86) 571 8809 1424
Total Employees at this Location: 400
Type of Operation: Paper mill
Paper/Paperboard Grades and Capacities:
 Total paper and paperboard capacity: 10,000 mt/y
 Specialty and industrial: 10,000 mt/y
Paper and Paperboard Mill Data:
Paper Machines: 11
 PM 1-6, fourdrinier, total capacity 1,000 mt/y, Trim width 2.2 m, Specialty and industrial
 PM 10-11, fourdrinier, total capacity 2,000 mt/y, Trim width 2.6 m, Specialty and industrial

ⓗZhejiang Hangzhou Xinhua Paper Industry Co., Ltd.
Ownership: 100% by shareholders
No. 186, Hushu South Road
Hangzhou, Zhejiang, 310005
China
 Phone: (86) 571 8807 5514/3319
 Fax: (86) 571 8807 4838
 Email: webmaster@xinhuapaper.com
 Web Address: www.xinhuapaper.com
Mill Locations:
Zhejiang Haining Bangda Paper Co., Ltd., Haining Mill, Jingshan Village, Zhouwang Temple Town, Haining 314411, China, Capacity: 10,000 mt/y, (Pulp mill, Paper mill)
 Phone: (86) 573 8793 3158
 Fax: (86) 573 8762 8181
Zhejiang Hangzhou Xinhua Paper Industry Co., Ltd., Hangzhou Mill, No. 186, Hushu South Road, Hangzhou 310005, China, Capacity: 10,000 mt/y, (Pulp mill, Paper mill)
 Phone: (86) 571 8807 5514/3319
 Fax: (86) 571 8807 4838
 Email: webmaster@xinhuapaper.com

ⓜZhejiang Hangzhou Xinhua Paper Industry Co., Ltd.
Hangzhou Mill
No. 186, Hushu South Road
Hangzhou, Zhejiang, 310005
China
 Phone: (86) 571 8807 5514/3319
 Fax: (86) 571 8807 4838
 Email: webmaster@xinhuapaper.com
 Web Address: www.xinhuapaper.com
Personnel:
 CEO: Li Qun
 Phone: (86) 571 8807 5514/3319
Total Employees at this Location: 1,100
Type of Operation: Pulp mill, Paper mill
Paper/Paperboard Grades and Capacities:
 Total paper and paperboard capacity: 10,000 mt/y
 Specialty and industrial: 10,000 mt/y

ⓗZhejiang Hangzhou Xushi Paper Co., Ltd.
Ownership: 100% by private owners
Linqiao Industry Park, Linqiao Town
Fuyang, Hangzhou, Zhejiang, 311418
China
 Phone: (86) 571 6352 9823/ 9813/ 9817
 Fax: (86) 571 6352 9815/ 9820
Mill Locations:
Zhejiang Hangzhou Xushi Paper Co., Ltd., Fuyang Mill, Linqiao Industry Park, Linqiao Town, Fuyang 311418, China, Capacity: 70,000 mt/y, (Paperboard mill)
 Phone: (86) 571 6352 9823/ 9813/ 9817
 Fax: (86) 571 6352 9815/ 9820

ⓜZhejiang Hangzhou Xushi Paper Co., Ltd.
Fuyang Mill
Linqiao Industry Park, Linqiao Town
Fuyang, Zhejiang, 311418
China
 Phone: (86) 571 6352 9823/ 9813/ 9817
 Fax: (86) 571 6352 9815/ 9820
Personnel:
 Pres. & Gen. Mgr.: Fageng Xu
 Phone: (86) 571 6352 9823/ 9813/ 9817
 Sls. Mgr.: Huagang Ji
 Phone: (86) 571 6352 9823/ 9813/ 9817
Total Employees at this Location: 280
Type of Operation: Paperboard mill
Pulp Grades and Capacities:
 Total pulp capacity: 62,166 mt/y
 Recycled Pulping: 62,166 mt/y

China

Pulp Mill Data:
Pulp Lines: 2
Recycled Fiber Treatment Lines:
Recycled packaging pulping lines: 2 at 50,000 admt/y
Paper/Paperboard Grades and Capacities:
Total paper and paperboard capacity: 70,000 mt/y
Boxboard/cartonboard: 70,000 mt/y
Paper and Paperboard Mill Data:
Paper Machines: 2
No. 1, cylinder, total capacity 35,000 mt/y, Trim width 2.64 m, Boxboard/cartonboard
No. 2, multi-wire, total capacity 35,000 mt/y, Trim width 2.64 m, Boxboard/cartonboard
Energy Data:
Electrical demand for mill: 105 MWh/D

ⒽZhejiang Hangzhou Yinfa Paper Co., Ltd.
Ownership: 100% by private owners
Linqiao Industry Park
Fuyang, Hangzhou, Zhejiang, 311418
China
Phone: (86) 571 6355 0885/ 8938/ 0889
Fax: (86) 571 6355 0883
Mill Locations:
Zhejiang Hangzhou Yinfa Paper Co., Ltd., Fuyang Mill, Linqiao Industry Park, Fuyang 311418, China, Capacity: 123,879 mt/y, (Paperboard mill)
Phone: (86) 571 6355 0885/ 8938/ 0889
Fax: (86) 571 6355 0883

ⓂZhejiang Hangzhou Yinfa Paper Co., Ltd.
Fuyang Mill
Linqiao Industry Park
Fuyang, Zhejiang, 311418
China
Phone: (86) 571 6355 0885/ 8938/ 0889
Fax: (86) 571 6355 0883
Personnel:
Pres. & Gen. Mgr.: Zhonglin Wang
Phone: (86) 571 6355 0885/ 8938/ 0889
Sls. Mgr.: Jianrong Dong
Phone: (86) 571 6355 0885/ 8938/ 0889
Total Employees at this Location: 450
Type of Operation: Paperboard mill
Pulp Grades and Capacities:
Total pulp capacity: 103,035 mt/y
Recycled Pulping: 103,035 mt/y
Pulp Mill Data:
Pulp Lines: 4
Recycled Fiber Treatment Lines:
Recycled packaging pulping lines: 4 at 140,000 admt/y
Paper/Paperboard Grades and Capacities:
Total paper and paperboard capacity: 123,879 mt/y
Boxboard/cartonboard: 123,879 mt/y
Paper and Paperboard Mill Data:
Paper Machines: 2
No. 1, cylinder (5), total capacity 34,986 mt/y, Trim width 1.88 m, Boxboard/cartonboard
No. 2, Fourdrinier (5), total capacity 88,893 mt/y, Trim width 2.88 m, Boxboard/cartonboard
Energy Data:
Electrical demand for mill: 178 MWh/D

ⒽZhejiang Hangzhou Yuanda Paper Co., Ltd.
Ownership: 100% by private owners
Linjiang Village, Chunjiang Paper-making Industry Park
Fuyang, Zhejiang, 311421
China
Phone: (86) 571 6358 6997/ 6988/ 6918
Fax: (86) 571 6358 6969
Email: yuandapaper_china@126.com
Web Address: www.ydpaper.com
Mill Locations:
Zhejiang Hangzhou Yuanda Paper Co., Ltd., Fuyang Mill, Linjiang Village, Chunjiang Paper-making Industry Park, Fuyang 311421, China, Capacity: 109,956 mt/y, (Paperboard mill)
Phone: (86) 571 6358 6997/ 6988/ 6918
Fax: (86) 571 6358 6969
Email: yuandapaper_china@126.com

ⓂZhejiang Hangzhou Yuanda Paper Co., Ltd.
Fuyang Mill
Linjiang Village, Chunjiang Paper-making Industry Park
Fuyang, Zhejiang, 311421
China
Phone: (86) 571 6358 6997/ 6988/ 6918
Fax: (86) 571 6358 6969
Email: yuandapaper_china@126.com
Web Address: www.ydpaper.com
Personnel:
Pres. & Gen. Mgr.: Zhenglai Xu
Phone: (86) 571 6358 6997/ 6988/ 6918
Total Employees at this Location: 600
Type of Operation: Paperboard mill
Pulp Grades and Capacities:
Total pulp capacity: 90,637 mt/y
Recycled Pulping: 90,637 mt/y
Pulp Mill Data:
Pulp Lines: 2
Recycled Fiber Treatment Lines:
Recycled packaging pulping lines: 2 at 120,000 admt/y
Paper/Paperboard Grades and Capacities:
Total paper and paperboard capacity: 109,956 mt/y
Boxboard/cartonboard: 109,956 mt/y
Paper and Paperboard Mill Data:
Paper Machines: 2
No. 1, Fourdrinier (5), total capacity 29,631 mt/y, Trim width 1.88 m, Boxboard/cartonboard
No. 2, Fourdrinier (5), total capacity 80,325 mt/y, Trim width 2.88 m, Boxboard/cartonboard
Energy Data:
Electrical demand for mill: 168 MWh/D

ⒽZhejiang Hangzhou Zhongyi Paper Co., Ltd.
Ownership: 100% by private owners
Chunjiang Papermaking Industry Park, Chunjiang Street
Fuyang, Hangzhou, Zhejiang, 311421
China
Phone: (86) 571 6358 7696
Fax: (86) 571 6358 7696
Web Address: www.zjzypaper.cn
Mill Locations:
Zhejiang Hangzhou Zhongyi Paper Co., Ltd., Fuyang Mill, Chunjiang Papermaking Industry Park, Chunjiang Street, Fuyang 311421, China, Capacity: 199,920 mt/y, (Paperboard mill)
Phone: (86) 571 6358 7696
Fax: (86) 571 6358 7696

ⓂZhejiang Hangzhou Zhongyi Paper Co., Ltd.
Fuyang Mill
Chunjiang Papermaking Industry Park, Chunjiang Street
Fuyang, Zhejiang, 311421
China
Phone: (86) 571 6358 7696
Fax: (86) 571 6358 7696
Web Address: www.zjzypaper.cn
Personnel:
Pres. & Gen. Mgr.: Desheng Xia
Phone: (86) 571 6358 7696
Sls. Mgr.: Jian Yu
Phone: (86) 571 6358 7696
Total Employees at this Location: 380
Type of Operation: Paperboard mill
Pulp Grades and Capacities:
Total pulp capacity: 159,966 mt/y
Recycled Pulping: 159,966 mt/y
Pulp Mill Data:
Pulp Lines: 4
Recycled Fiber Treatment Lines:
Recycled packaging pulping lines: 4 at 200,000 admt/y
Paper/Paperboard Grades and Capacities:
Total paper and paperboard capacity: 199,920 mt/y
Boxboard/cartonboard: 199,920 mt/y
Paper and Paperboard Mill Data:
Paper Machines: 2
No. 1, Fourdrinier (4), total capacity 99,960 mt/y, Trim width 3.2 m, Boxboard/cartonboard
No. 2, Fourdrinier (4), total capacity 99,960 mt/y, Trim width 3.2 m, Boxboard/cartonboard
Energy Data:
Electrical demand for mill: 284 MWh/D

ⓂZhejiang Hengda Paper Co., Ltd.
Quzhou Mill
Lake Town Industrial Park, Longyou County
Quzhou, Zhejiang, 324401
China
Phone: (86) 570 706 1686/1111/1199
Fax: (86) 570 706 1234
Web Address: www.hengdapaper.com
Type of Operation: Paper mill
Paper/Paperboard Grades and Capacities:
Total paper and paperboard capacity: 28,000 mt/y
Specialty and industrial: 28,000 mt/y
Paper and Paperboard Mill Data:
Paper Machines: 3
No. 1, fourdrinier, total capacity 5,000 mt/y, Trim width 1.88 m, Specialty and industrial
No. 2, fourdrinier, total capacity 18,000 mt/y, Trim width 2.64 m, Specialty and industrial
No. 3, fourdrinier, total capacity 5,000 mt/y, Trim width 1.88 m, Specialty and industrial

ⓂZhejiang Hongan Paper Co., Ltd.
Jiaxing Mill
Ownership: Zhejiang Zhenghua Paper Co., Ltd.
No.529, Dongfang Rd., Yanzhuang Town, Jiashan County
Jiaxing, Zhejiang, 314103
China
Phone: (86) 573 8484 6866
Fax: (86) 573 8484 6853
Web Address: zjhongan.com.cn
Type of Operation: Paper mill
Pulp Grades and Capacities:
Total pulp capacity: 39,428 mt/y
Recycled Pulping: 39,428 mt/y
Paper/Paperboard Grades and Capacities:
Total paper and paperboard capacity: 100,000 mt/y
Tissue: 60,000 mt/y
Corrugating medium/fluting: 40,000 mt/y
Paper and Paperboard Mill Data:
Paper Machines: 17
No. 1, cylinder, total capacity 5,000 mt/y, Trim width 3.8 m, Tissue, Uncoated woodfree/freesheet
No. 2, cylinder, total capacity 5,000 mt/y, Trim width 3.8 m, Tissue, Uncoated woodfree/freesheet
No. 3, cylinder, total capacity 5,000 mt/y, Trim width 3.8 m, Tissue, Uncoated woodfree/freesheet
No. 4, cylinder, total capacity 5,000 mt/y, Trim width 3.8 m, Tissue, Uncoated woodfree/freesheet
No. 5, cylinder, total capacity 5,000 mt/y, Trim width 3.8 m, Tissue, Uncoated woodfree/freesheet
No. 6, cylinder, total capacity 5,000 mt/y, Trim width 3.8 m, Tissue, Uncoated woodfree/freesheet
No. 7, cylinder, total capacity 3,000 mt/y, Trim width 2.95 m, Tissue, Uncoated woodfree/freesheet
No. 8, cylinder, total capacity 3,000 mt/y, Trim width 2.95 m, Tissue, Uncoated woodfree/freesheet
No. 9, cylinder, total capacity 3,000 mt/y, Trim width 2.95 m, Tissue, Uncoated woodfree/freesheet
No. 10, cylinder, total capacity 3,000 mt/y, Trim width 2.95 m, Tissue, Uncoated woodfree/freesheet
No. 11, cylinder, total capacity 3,000 mt/y, Trim width 2.95 m, Tissue, Uncoated woodfree/freesheet

China

No. 12, cylinder, total capacity 3,000 mt/y, Trim width 2.95 m, Tissue, Uncoated woodfree/freesheet
No. 13, cylinder, total capacity 3,000 mt/y, Trim width 2.95 m, Tissue, Uncoated woodfree/freesheet
No. 14, cylinder, total capacity 3,000 mt/y, Trim width 2.95 m, Tissue, Uncoated woodfree/freesheet
No. 15, cylinder, total capacity 3,000 mt/y, Trim width 2.95 m, Tissue, Uncoated woodfree/freesheet
No. 16, cylinder, total capacity 3,000 mt/y, Trim width 2.95 m, Tissue, Uncoated woodfree/freesheet
No. 17, fourdrinier, total capacity 40,000 mt/y, Trim width 3.6 m, Corrugating medium/fluting
Energy Data:
Electrical demand for mill: 161 MWh/D

Zhejiang Hongsheng Paper Co., Ltd.
Fuyang (Zhejiang Hongsheng Paper) Mill
Ownership: Zhejiang Zhengda Holding Group Co., Ltd.
Chunjiang Industry Zone
Fuyang, Zhejiang, 311421
China
Phone: (86) 571 6315 0969
Fax: (86) 571 6358 7578
Personnel:
Pres.: Linfa Sun
Phone: (86) 571 6315 0969
Total Employees at this Location: 300
Type of Operation: Paperboard mill
Pulp Grades and Capacities:
Total pulp capacity: 74,432 mt/y
Recycled Pulping: 74,432 mt/y
Pulp Mill Data:
Bleach Plant Systems: 1
Recycled Pulping System, Type: DIP
Recycled Fiber Treatment Lines:
Flotation deinking lines: 1
Recycled packaging pulping lines: 4
Paper/Paperboard Grades and Capacities:
Total paper and paperboard capacity: 85,000 mt/y
Boxboard/cartonboard: 85,000 mt/y
Paper and Paperboard Mill Data:
Paper Machines: 1
No. 2, Multi-wire (5), total capacity 85,000 mt/y, Trim width 2.56 m, Boxboard/cartonboard
Coating Machines: 2
PM#1, on machine
PM#2, on machine
Energy Data:
Electrical demand for mill: 154 MWh/D

Zhejiang Huachuan Industrial Group
Ownership: 100% by shareholders
No. 72 South Huachuan Rd.
ChiAn Town, Yiwu, Zhejiang, 322003
China
Phone: (86) 579 577 5142
Fax: (86) 579 577 5032
Email: hc@huachuangroup.com.cn
Web Address: www.huachuangroup.net
Personnel:
Chrmn. & Pres.: Chaoxing Feng
Phone: (86) 579 577 5142
Fax: (86) 579 577 5032
Total Employees of Company: 2,500
Total Employees at this Location: 1,350
Mill Locations:
Zhejiang Yiwu City Huachuan Paper Co., Ltd., Yiwu Mill, No. 72 South Huachuan Rd., Chian Town, Yiwu 322003, China, Capacity: 199,265 mt/y, (Paper mill, Paperboard mill)
Phone: (86) 579 577 5156/ 5458
Fax: (86) 579 577 5625
Zhejiang Yiwu City YiNan Paper Co., Ltd., Yiwu Mill, ChiAn No. 4 Village, Yiwu 322003, China, Capacity: 275,000 mt/y, (Paper mill, Paperboard mill)
Phone: (86) 579 577 7399/ 6518/ 6512
Fax: (86) 579 577 5068

Zhejiang Huakang Paper Co., Ltd.
Ownership: 100% by private owners
Feiyun New District
RuiAn, Zhejiang, 325207
China
Phone: (86) 577 6557 1333/ 6556 7777
Fax: (86) 577 6556 4600
Web Address: www.chinahuakang.com
Personnel:
Pres. & Gen. Mgr.: Qihui Xu
Phone: (86) 577 6557 1333/ 6556 7777
Mill Locations:
Zhejiang Huakang Paper Co., Ltd., Ruian Mill, Feiyun New District, Ruian 325207, China, Capacity: 96,390 mt/y, (Paperboard mill)
Phone: (86) 577 6557 1333/ 6556 7777
Fax: (86) 577 6556 4600

Zhejiang Huakang Paper Co., Ltd.
Ruian Mill
Feiyun New District
Ruian, Zhejiang, 325207
China
Phone: (86) 577 6557 1333/ 6556 7777
Fax: (86) 577 6556 4600
Web Address: www.chinahuakang.com
Personnel:
Pres. & Gen. Mgr.: Qihui Xu
Phone: (86) 577 6557 1333/ 6556 7777
Total Employees at this Location: 420
Type of Operation: Paperboard mill
Pulp Grades and Capacities:
Total pulp capacity: 95,428 mt/y
Recycled Pulping: 95,428 mt/y
Pulp Mill Data:
Pulp Lines: 4
Recycled Fiber Treatment Lines:
Recycled packaging pulping lines: 4 at 90,000 admt/y
Paper/Paperboard Grades and Capacities:
Total paper and paperboard capacity: 96,390 mt/y
Linerboard: 60,690 mt/y
Corrugating medium/fluting: 35,700 mt/y
Paper and Paperboard Mill Data:
Paper Machines: 3
No. 1, cylinder, total capacity 17,850 mt/y, Trim width 3 m, Linerboard
No. 2, multi-wire, total capacity 35,700 mt/y, Trim width 3.6 m, Corrugating medium/fluting
No. 3, multi-wire, total capacity 42,840 mt/y, Trim width 3.4 m, Linerboard
Energy Data:
Power boilers: 3
Electrical demand for mill: 133 MWh/D

Zhejiang Huaxin Paper Co., Ltd.
Ownership: 100% by private owners
Xindeng Industrial Park
Fuyang, Zhejiang, 311421
China
Phone: (86) 571 2328 3582/ 6358 8938
Fax: (86) 571 6358 4618
Email: xgl000@hotmail.com
Mill Locations:
Zhejiang Huaxin Paper Co., Ltd., Fuyang Mill, Xindeng Industrial Park, Fuyang 311421, China, Capacity: 99,960 mt/y, (Paperboard mill)
Phone: (86) 571 2328 3582/ 6358 8938
Fax: (86) 571 6358 4618
Email: xgl000@hotmail.com

Zhejiang Huaxin Paper Co., Ltd.
Fuyang Mill
Xindeng Industrial Park
Fuyang, Zhejiang, 311421
China
Phone: (86) 571 2328 3582/ 6358 8938
Fax: (86) 571 6358 4618
Email: xgl000@hotmail.com
Personnel:
Sls. Mgr.: Deqing Hu
Phone: (86) 571 2328 3582/ 6358 8938
Total Employees at this Location: 247
Type of Operation: Paperboard mill
Pulp Grades and Capacities:
Total pulp capacity: 82,772 mt/y
Recycled Pulping: 82,772 mt/y
Pulp Mill Data:
Pulp Lines: 2
Paper/Paperboard Grades and Capacities:
Total paper and paperboard capacity: 99,960 mt/y
Boxboard/cartonboard: 99,960 mt/y
Paper and Paperboard Mill Data:
Paper Machines: 1
No. 1, Fourdrinier (5), total capacity 99,960 mt/y, Trim width 2.64 m, Boxboard/cartonboard
Finishing Equipment:
Winders: 1
Rewinders: 1
Energy Data:
Electrical demand for mill: 147 MWh/D

Zhejiang Huayu Paper Co., Ltd.
Ownership: Hong Kong Yitai Group, Zhejiang Shaoxing Huayu Textile Printing-Dyeing Co., Ltd.
Binghai Industry Park
Shaoxing, Zhejiang, 312075
China
Phone: (86) 575 8552 9228/ 8562 1922/ 8488 1507
Fax: (86) 575 8488 3933
Mill Locations:
Zhejiang Huayu Paper Co., Ltd., Shaoxing Mill, Binghai Industry Park, Shaoxing 312075, China, Capacity: 339,507 mt/y, (Paperboard mill)
Phone: (86) 575 8552 9228/ 8562 1922/ 8488 1507
Fax: (86) 575 8488 3933

Zhejiang Huayu Paper Co., Ltd.
Shaoxing Mill
Binghai Industry Park
Shaoxing, Zhejiang, 312075
China
Phone: (86) 575 8552 9228/ 8562 1922/ 8488 1507
Fax: (86) 575 8488 3933
Personnel:
HR Mgr.: Guobao Wang
Phone: (86) 575 8552 9228/ 8562 1922/ 8488 1507
Total Employees at this Location: 500
Type of Operation: Paperboard mill
Pulp Grades and Capacities:
Total pulp capacity: 340,729 mt/y
Recycled Pulping: 340,729 mt/y
Paper/Paperboard Grades and Capacities:
Total paper and paperboard capacity: 339,507 mt/y
Linerboard: 184,926 mt/y
Corrugating medium/fluting: 154,581 mt/y
Paper and Paperboard Mill Data:
Paper Machines: 3
No. 1, fourdrinier (3), total capacity 184,926 mt/y, Trim width 4.8 m, Linerboard
No. 2, fourdrinier, total capacity 110,670 mt/y, Trim width 4.4 m, Corrugating medium/fluting
No. 3, multi-fourdrinier, total capacity 43,911 mt/y, Trim width 2.8 m, Corrugating medium/fluting
Energy Data:
Power boilers: 2
Electrical demand for mill: 553 MWh/D

Zhejiang Huayuan Paper Co., Ltd.
Ownership: 100% by private owners
Cailun Rd., Paper-making Industry District, Chunjiang Street
Fuyang, Zhejiang, 311421
China
Phone: (86) 571 6315 9938/ 9935
Fax: (86) 571 6315 9911
Web Address: www.zjhympaper.com.cn

China

Mill Locations:
Zhejiang Huayuan Paper Co., Ltd., Fuyang Mill, Cailun Rd., Paper-making Industry District, Chunjiang Street, Fuyang 311421, China, Capacity: 100,317 mt/y, (Paperboard mill)
Phone: (86) 571 6315 9938/ 9935
Fax: (86) 571 6315 9911

ⓂZhejiang Huayuan Paper Co., Ltd.
Fuyang Mill
Cailun Rd., Paper-making Industry District, Chunjiang Street
Fuyang, Zhejiang, 311421
China
Phone: (86) 571 6315 9938/ 9935
Fax: (86) 571 6315 9911
Web Address: www.zjhympaper.com.cn
Personnel:
Gen. Mgr.: Yeming Sun
Phone: (86) 571 6315 9938/ 9935
Total Employees at this Location: 350
Type of Operation: Paperboard mill
Pulp Grades and Capacities:
Total pulp capacity: 77,123 mt/y
Recycled Pulping: 77,123 mt/y
Pulp Mill Data:
Pulp Lines: 3
Recycled Fiber Treatment Lines:
Recycled packaging pulping lines: 3 at 100,000 admt/y
Paper/Paperboard Grades and Capacities:
Total paper and paperboard capacity: 100,317 mt/y
Boxboard/cartonboard: 100,317 mt/y
Paper and Paperboard Mill Data:
Paper Machines: 1
No. 1, Fourdrinier (5), total capacity 100,317 mt/y, Trim width 2.8 m, Boxboard/cartonboard
Finishing Equipment:
Rewinders: 1 at 130,000 mt/y
Energy Data:
Power boilers: 3
Electrical demand for mill: 133 MWh/D

ⓗZhejiang JiAn Paper Package Co., Ltd.
Ownership: 99.85% by Anhui Shanying Paper Industry Co., Ltd., 0.15% by private owners
No. A 5 Rd., Economy Develoment District
Haiyan County, Jiaxing city, Zhejiang, 314300
China
Personnel:
Chmn.: Mingwu Wu
Gen. Mgr.: Wenhuang Ke
Mill Locations:
Zhejiang JiAn Paper Package Co., Ltd., Jiaxing Mill, No. A 5 Rd., Economy Develoment District, Haiyan County, Jiaxing 314300, China, Capacity: 1,650,000 mt/y, (Paperboard mill)
Phone: (86) 573 8696 6188/ 686 1265
Fax: (86) 573 8686 1333
Email: man@zjjian.com

ⓂZhejiang JiAn Paper Package Co., Ltd.
Jiaxing Mill
Ownership: 99.85% by Anhui Shanying Paper Industry Co., Ltd.
No. A 5 Rd., Economy Develoment District, Haiyan County
Jiaxing, Zhejiang, 314300
China
Phone: (86) 573 8696 6188/ 686 1265
Fax: (86) 573 8686 1333
Email: man@zjjian.com
Personnel:
Chmn.: Mingwu Wu
Phone: (86) 573 8696 6188/ 686 1265
Gen. Mgr.: Wenhuang Ke
Phone: (86) 573 8696 6188/ 686 1265
Total Employees at this Location: 750

Type of Operation: Paperboard mill
Pulp Grades and Capacities:
Total pulp capacity: 1,566,316 mt/y
Recycled Pulping: 1,566,316 mt/y
Pulp Mill Data:
Pulp Lines: 2
Recycled Fiber Treatment Lines:
Recycled packaging pulping lines
Paper/Paperboard Grades and Capacities:
Total paper and paperboard capacity: 1,650,000 mt/y
Linerboard: 1,400,000 mt/y
Corrugating medium/fluting: 250,000 mt/y
Paper and Paperboard Mill Data:
Stock Preparation:
Refiners: 1
Paper Machines: 4
No. 1, fourdrinier, total capacity 450,000 mt/y, Trim width 6.65 m, Linerboard
No. 2, fourdrinier, total capacity 300,000 mt/y, Trim width 5.54 m, Linerboard
No. 3, ValFormer, total capacity 650,000 mt/y, Trim width 6.5 m, Linerboard
No. 5, hybrid former, total capacity 250,000 mt/y, Trim width 5.5 m, Corrugating medium/fluting
Energy Data:
Power boilers: 3
Steam turbines: 2 at 21, 21 MW
Electrical demand for mill: 2,214 MWh/D

ⓗZhejiang Jiashan Yongquan Paper Co., Ltd.
Xinkaihe, Weitang Town, Jiashan County
Jiaxing, Zhejiang, 314100
China
Phone: (86) 573 8416 1945/ 1944
Fax: (86) 573 8416 1522
Total Employees at this Location: 60
Mill Locations:
Zhejiang Jiashan Yongquan Paper Co., Ltd., Jiaxing Mill, Xinkaihe, Weitang Town, Jiashan County, Jiaxing 314100, China, Capacity: 4,000 mt/y, (Paper mill)
Phone: (86) 573 8416 1945/ 1944
Fax: (86) 573 8416 1522

ⓂZhejiang Jiashan Yongquan Paper Co., Ltd.
Jiaxing Mill
Xinkaihe, Weitang Town, Jiashan County
Jiaxing, Zhejiang, 314100
China
Phone: (86) 573 8416 1945/ 1944
Fax: (86) 573 8416 1522
Total Employees at this Location: 60
Type of Operation: Paper mill
Paper/Paperboard Grades and Capacities:
Total paper and paperboard capacity: 4,000 mt/y
Tissue: 4,000 mt/y
Paper and Paperboard Mill Data:
Paper Machines: 2
PM 1-2, total capacity 2,000 mt/y, Trim width 1.76 m, Tissue

ⓗZhejiang Jindong Paper Co., Ltd.
Ownership: 100% by private owners
Linqiao Industry Park
Fuyang, Zhejiang, 311418
China
Phone: (86) 571 6355 8799/ 8733/ 2899
Fax: (86) 571 6355 2789/ 8969
Email: jindongpaper@163.com
Web Address: www.zjjdpaper.com
Mill Locations:
Zhejiang Jindong Paper Co., Ltd., Fuyang Mill, Linqiao Industry Park, Fuyang 311418, China, Capacity: 125,307 mt/y, (Paperboard mill)
Phone: (86) 571 6355 8799/ 8733/ 2899
Fax: (86) 571 6355 2789/ 8969
Email: jindongpaper@163.com

ⓂZhejiang Jindong Paper Co., Ltd.
Fuyang Mill
Linqiao Industry Park
Fuyang, Zhejiang, 311418
China
Phone: (86) 571 6355 8799/ 8733/ 2899
Fax: (86) 571 6355 2789/ 8969
Email: jindongpaper@163.com
Web Address: www.zjjdpaper.com
Personnel:
Pres. & Gen. Mgr.: Faquan Jin
Phone: (86) 571 6355 8799/ 8733/ 2899
Total Employees at this Location: 460
Type of Operation: Paperboard mill
Pulp Grades and Capacities:
Total pulp capacity: 113,752 mt/y
Recycled Pulping: 113,752 mt/y
Pulp Mill Data:
Pulp Lines: 3
Recycled Fiber Treatment Lines:
Flotation deinking lines: 1
Recycled packaging pulping lines: 2
Paper/Paperboard Grades and Capacities:
Total paper and paperboard capacity: 125,307 mt/y
Boxboard/cartonboard: 125,307 mt/y
Paper and Paperboard Mill Data:
Paper Machines: 2
No. 1, cylinder, total capacity 25,347 mt/y, Trim width 3.2 m, Boxboard/cartonboard
No. 2, Fourdrinier (5), total capacity 99,960 mt/y, Trim width 2.8 m, Boxboard/cartonboard
Energy Data:
Electrical demand for mill: 168 MWh/D

ⓗⓂZhejiang Jingxing Paper Joint Stock Co., Ltd.
Pinghu Mill
Jingxing Industry Park, Caoqiao
Pinghu, Zhejiang, 314214
China
Phone: (86) 573 8596 6256/ 0666/ 6228/ 0111/ 1717
Fax: (86) 573 8596 0888/ 6983/ 6075
Email: jingxing@jxpaper.com.cn
Web Address: www.jxpaper.com.cn
Personnel:
Chmn.: Zailong Zhu
Phone: (86) 573 8596 0111
Fax: (86) 573 8596 6983
Vice Chmn.: Weimin Wang
Phone: (86) 573 8596 0111
Fax: (86) 573 8596 6983
Vice Chmn.: Haihua Ge
Phone: (86) 573 8596 0111
Fax: (86) 573 8596 0888/ 6983/ 6075
Board Sec.: Ms. Jieqing Yao
Phone: (86) 573 8596 9328
Fax: (86) 573 8596 3320
Email: yaojp0518@126.com
CFO, Dpty Gen. Mgr.: Xiaoying Sheng
Phone: (86) 573 8596 0111
Fax: (86) 573 8596 6983
Dpty. Gen. Mgr.: Zhiming Wang
Phone: (86) 573 8596 0111
Fax: (86) 573 8596 6983
Chief Eng.: Keliang Xu
Phone: (86) 573 8596 0111
Fax: (86) 573 8596 6983
Total Employees of Company: 2,254
Total Employees at this Location: 1,419
Type of Operation: Paper mill, Paperboard mill
Mill Locations:
Anhui Jingfeng Paper Co., Ltd., Huainan Mill (70% owned), West Zhenxing Rd., Huainan Economy & Technology Park, Huainan 232008, China, Capacity: 10,000 mt/y, (Paper mill)
Phone: (86) 554 3312 663
Fax: (86) 554 3312 663
Zhejiang Dingxing Paper Co., Ltd., Pinghu Mill, Jingxing

China

Industry Park, Caoqiao Town, Pinghu 314214, China,
Capacity: 150,000 mt/y, (Pulp mill, Paperboard mill)
Phone: (86) 573 8597 8111/ 8199
Fax: (86) 573 8597 8079
Email: zyxfj0439@yahoo.com.cn
Pulp Grades and Capacities:
Total pulp capacity: 756,333 mt/y
Recycled Pulping: 756,333 mt/y
Pulp Mill Data:
Chemical Recovery Equipment:
Recovery boilers
Recycled Fiber Treatment Lines:
Pulpers
Recycled packaging pulping lines
Paper/Paperboard Grades and Capacities:
Total paper and paperboard capacity: 775,000 mt/y
Linerboard: 730,000 mt/y
Boxboard/cartonboard: 45,000 mt/y
Paper and Paperboard Mill Data:
Paper Machines: 4
No. 5, cylinder, total capacity 45,000 mt/y, Trim width 2.4 m, Boxboard/cartonboard
No. 10, Fourdrinier (4), total capacity 200,000 mt/y, Trim width 4.85 m, Linerboard
No. 12, fourdrinier, total capacity 350,000 mt/y, Trim width 5.65 m, Linerboard
No. 15, Fourdrinier (4), total capacity 180,000 mt/y, Trim width 4.88 m, Linerboard
Finishing Equipment:
Supercalenders
Rewinders: 9
Energy Data:
Power boilers: 4
Steam turbines: 5 at 6, 6, 6, 6, 12 MW
Electrical demand for mill: 1,045 MWh/D

⓪Zhejiang Jintong Paper Co., Ltd.
Ownership: 100% by private owners
Jintong Industry Park, Luobu Town
Jinhua, Zhejiang, 321081
China
Phone: (86) 579 8261 0639
Fax: (86) 579 8261 0539
Email: xt838@sina.com
Mill Locations:
Zhejiang Jintong Paper Co., Ltd., Jinhua Mill, Jintong Industry Park, Luobu Town, Jinhua 321081, China, Capacity: 6,000 mt/y, (Paper mill)
Phone: (86) 579 8261 0639
Fax: (86) 579 8261 0539
Email: xt838@sina.com

ⓜZhejiang Jintong Paper Co., Ltd.
Jinhua Mill
Jintong Industry Park, Luobu Town
Jinhua, Zhejiang, 321081
China
Phone: (86) 579 8261 0639
Fax: (86) 579 8261 0539
Email: xt838@sina.com
Personnel:
Gen. Mgr.: Zhicun Ye
Phone: (86) 579 8261 0639
Sls. Mgr.: Ming Cheng
Phone: (86) 579 8261 0639
Total Employees at this Location: 130
Type of Operation: Paper mill
Paper/Paperboard Grades and Capacities:
Total paper and paperboard capacity: 6,000 mt/y
Tissue: 6,000 mt/y
Paper and Paperboard Mill Data:
Paper Machines: 4
PM 1-4, fourdrinier, total capacity 1,500 mt/y, Trim width 1.88 m, Tissue
Energy Data:
Power boilers: 1

ⓜZhejiang Kaifeng Paper Co., Ltd.
Quzhou Mill
Ownership: 60% by Zhejiang Kan Specialty Material Co., Ltd., 40% by Jihao
Economy & Development Park, Longyou Town
Quzhou, Zhejiang, 324400
China
Phone: (86) 570 7055 868/ 881
Fax: (86) 570 7055 868/ 796
Email: admin@kaifengpaper.com
Web Address: www.kaifengpaper.com
Personnel:
Chmn.: Hao Ji
Phone: (86) 570 7055 868/ 881
Total Employees at this Location: 130
Type of Operation: Paper mill
Paper/Paperboard Grades and Capacities:
Total paper and paperboard capacity: 24,000 mt/y
Specialty and industrial: 24,000 mt/y
Paper and Paperboard Mill Data:
Paper Machines: 2
PM 1, fourdrinier, total capacity 12,000 mt/y, Trim width 2.64 m, Specialty and industrial
PM 2, fourdrinier, total capacity 12,000 mt/y, Trim width 2.76 m, Specialty and industrial

ⓞⓜZhejiang Kan Specialty Material Co., Ltd.
Lishui Mill
Ownership: 100% by shareholders
No.108, Kann Road, Suichang County
Lishui, Zhejiang, 323300
China
Phone: (86) 578 812 3563/3536/3029
Fax: (86) 578 813 1224/4400
Email: postmaster@zjkan.com
Web Address: www.kangroup.com, www.zjkan.com
Personnel:
Chmn., Gen. Mgr.: Hao Ji
Phone: (86) 578 812 3563/3536/3029
CFO: Ms. Meizhen Xie
Phone: (86) 578 812 3563/3536/3029
Board Sec., Dpty. Gen. Mgr.: Zhiqiang Tian
Phone: (86) 578 812 3563/3536/3029
Dpty. Gen. Mgr.: Yiming Hua
Phone: (86) 578 812 8682
Fax: (86) 578 812 3717
Email: kantzq@263.com
Dpty. Gen. Mgr.: Jianping Chen
Phone: (86) 578 812 3563/3536/3029
Chief Eng.: Wanping Chen
Phone: (86) 578 812 3563/3536/3029
Dpty. Chief Eng.: Rong Lei
Phone: (86) 578 812 3563/3536/3029
Total Employees at this Location: 644
Type of Operation: Paper mill
Mill Locations:
Zhejiang Kaifeng Paper Co., Ltd., Quzhou Mill (60% owned), Economy & Development Park, Longyou Town, Quzhou 324400, China, Capacity: 24,000 mt/y, (Paper mill)
Phone: (86) 570 7055 868/ 881
Fax: (86) 570 7055 868/ 796
Email: admin@kaifengpaper.com
Paper/Paperboard Grades and Capacities:
Total paper and paperboard capacity: 11,000 mt/y
Specialty and industrial: 11,000 mt/y
Paper and Paperboard Mill Data:
Paper Machines: 11
No. 1-4, fourdrinier, Trim width 1.5 m, Specialty and industrial
No. 5-7, fourdrinier, Trim width 1.7 m, Specialty and industrial
No. 8-10, fourdrinier, Trim width 1.8 m, Specialty and industrial
PM 19, fourdrinier, total capacity 1,000 mt/y, Trim width 1.09 m, Specialty and industrial

ⓞZhejiang Lanniao Paper Co., Ltd.
Ownership: 100% by private owners
Fengtian Village, Chunjiang Street
Fuyang, Zhejiang, 311421
China
Phone: (86) 571 6358 0901
Fax: (86) 571 6358 2928
Mill Locations:
Zhejiang Lanniao Paper Co., Ltd., Fuyang Mill, Fengtian Village, Chunjiang Street, Fuyang 311421, China, Capacity: 85,323 mt/y, (Paperboard mill)
Phone: (86) 571 6358 0901
Fax: (86) 571 6358 2928

ⓜZhejiang Lanniao Paper Co., Ltd.
Fuyang Mill
Fengtian Village, Chunjiang Street
Fuyang, Zhejiang, 311421
China
Phone: (86) 571 6358 0901
Fax: (86) 571 6358 2928
Personnel:
Gen. Mgr.: Xiuwei Lv
Phone: (86) 571 6358 0901
Total Employees at this Location: 300
Type of Operation: Paperboard mill
Pulp Grades and Capacities:
Total pulp capacity: 73,890 mt/y
Recycled Pulping: 73,890 mt/y
Pulp Mill Data:
Pulp Lines: 2
Recycled Fiber Treatment Lines:
Recycled packaging pulping lines: 2 at 80,000 admt/y
Paper/Paperboard Grades and Capacities:
Total paper and paperboard capacity: 85,323 mt/y
Boxboard/cartonboard: 85,323 mt/y
Paper and Paperboard Mill Data:
Paper Machines: 1
No. 1, Fourdrinier (4), total capacity 85,323 mt/y, Trim width 2.8 m, Boxboard/cartonboard
Energy Data:
Electrical demand for mill: 115 MWh/D

ⓞZhejiang Linan Ma An Qianshi Paper Co., Ltd.
Ownership: 100% by shareholders
Shangtian Village, Banqiao Town, Chengdong
Linan City, Zhejiang, 311301
China
Phone: (86) 571 6376 9014
Fax: (86) 571 6376 9388
Mill Locations:
Zhejiang Linan Ma An Qianshi Paper Co., Ltd., Linan Mill, Shangtian Village, Banqiao Town, Chengdong, Linan 311301, China, Capacity: 8,500 mt/y, (Paper mill)
Phone: (86) 571 6376 9014
Fax: (86) 571 6376 9388

ⓜZhejiang Linan Ma An Qianshi Paper Co., Ltd.
Linan Mill
Shangtian Village, Banqiao Town, Chengdong
Linan, Zhejiang, 311301
China
Phone: (86) 571 6376 9014
Fax: (86) 571 6376 9388
Personnel:
Chmn.: Bingfa Qian
Phone: (86) 138 0570 6698
Pres.: Kangtao Qian
Phone: (86) 571 6376 9014
Total Employees at this Location: 1,000
Type of Operation: Paper mill
Pulp Grades and Capacities:
Total pulp capacity: 5,000 mt/y
Recycled Pulping: 5,000 mt/y
Paper/Paperboard Grades and Capacities:

China

Total paper and paperboard capacity: 8,500 mt/y
Newsprint: 8,500 mt/y
Specialty and industrial
Paper and Paperboard Mill Data:
Paper Machines: 2
No. 1, Trim width 3.9 m, Newsprint
No. 2, Trim width 2.3 m, Newsprint
Finishing Equipment:
Rewinders: 3
Sheeters: 3
Energy Data:
Power boilers: 1

Ⓟ Zhejiang Linglong Paper Group Co. Ltd.

Ownership: 100% by private owners
Linglong Industry Park
LinAn, Zhejiang, 311301
China
Phone: (86) 571 6376 2763/ 2271/ 4117/ 1028
Fax: (86) 571 6376 2763/ 2271
Email: linglong@linglongpaper.com
Web Address: www.linglongpaper.com
Mill Locations:
Zhejiang Linglong Paper Group Co. Ltd., Linan Mill, Linglong Industry Park, Linan 311301, China, Capacity: 8,000 mt/y, (Paper mill)
Phone: (86) 571 6376 2763/ 2271/ 4117/ 1028
Fax: (86) 571 6376 2763/ 2271

Ⓜ Zhejiang Linglong Paper Group Co. Ltd.
Linan Mill

Linglong Industry Park
Linan, Zhejiang, 311301
China
Phone: (86) 571 6376 2763/ 2271/ 4117/ 1028
Fax: (86) 571 6376 2763/ 2271
Personnel:
Chmn. & Pres.: Qingxiang Ren
Phone: (86) 571 6376 3868
VP - Technology/Chief Eng.: Bingfu Cai
Phone: (86) 571 6376 2763/ 2271/ 4117/ 1028
COO: Shengliang Ge
Phone: (86) 571 6376 2763/ 2271/ 4117/ 1028
Sls. Mgr.: Xinjun Wang
Phone: (86) 571 6376 2763/ 2271/ 4117/ 1028
Total Employees at this Location: 360
Type of Operation: Paper mill
Paper/Paperboard Grades and Capacities:
Total paper and paperboard capacity: 8,000 mt/y
Specialty and industrial: 8,000 mt/y
Paper and Paperboard Mill Data:
Paper Machines: 1
PM 1, cylinder, total capacity 8,000 mt/y, Trim width 1.58 m, Specialty and industrial

Ⓜ Zhejiang Long Chen Paper Co., Ltd.
Pinghu Mill

Ownership: 100% by Long Chen Paper Co. Ltd.
East Binghai Rod., Dushan port zone
Pinghu, Zhejiang, 314204
China
Phone: (86) 573 8581 0999
Fax: (86) 573 8581 1111
Email: g5287@lcpc.biz
Web Address: www.lcpc.biz
Personnel:
Chmn.: Yingbin Zhang
Phone: (86) 573 8581 0999
Gen. Mgr.: Fuyuan Li
Phone: (86) 573 8581 0999
Total Employees at this Location: 600
Type of Operation: Pulp mill, Paperboard mill
Pulp Grades and Capacities:
Total pulp capacity: 616,620 mt/y
Recycled Pulping: 616,620 mt/y
Pulp Mill Data:
Pulp Lines: 2
Recycled Fiber Treatment Lines:
Recycled packaging pulping lines at 648,000
Paper/Paperboard Grades and Capacities:
Total paper and paperboard capacity: 620,000 mt/y
Linerboard: 340,000 mt/y
Corrugating medium/fluting: 280,000 mt/y
Paper and Paperboard Mill Data:
Stock Preparation:
Pulpers:
Paper Machines: 2
No. 5, fourdrinier (3), total capacity 340,000 mt/y, Trim width 6.66 m, Linerboard
No. 6, fourdrinier, total capacity 280,000 mt/y, Trim width 6.66 m, Corrugating medium/fluting
Energy Data:
Power boilers: 3
Steam turbines: 1 at 50 MW
Electrical demand for mill: 779 MWh/D

Ⓜ Zhejiang Minfeng Benkete Paper Co., Ltd.
Jiaxing Mill

Ownership: 74% by Zhejiang Minfeng Special Paper Co., Ltd., 26% by German Benkete Holding Co.
No. 70 Ruli Rd.
Jiaxing, Zhejiang, 314000
China
Phone: (86) 573 8206 1951
Fax: (86) 573 8208 2630
Web Address: www.minfenggroup.com
Personnel:
Chmn. & Pres.: Qinyong Sun
Phone: (86) 573 8206 1951
Type of Operation: Paper mill
Paper/Paperboard Grades and Capacities:
Total paper and paperboard capacity: 15,000 mt/y
Specialty and industrial: 15,000 mt/y
Paper and Paperboard Mill Data:
Paper Machines: 1
PM 19, fourdrinier, total capacity 15,000 mt/y, Trim width 2 m, Specialty and industrial

Ⓜ Zhejiang Minfeng Robert Special Paper Co., Ltd.
Jiaxing Mill

Ownership: 51% by Purico Group (China), 10% by China National Tobacco Company, 39% by Zhejiang Minfeng Special Paper Co., Ltd.
70, Luli Street
Jiaxing, Zhejiang, 314001
China
Phone: (86) 573 283 9600/9057
Fax: (86) 573 281 9766/2821027
Email: jb@minfengrobert.com
Web Address: www.minfenggroup.com, www.puricopaper.com.cn
Personnel:
Chmn.: Jun Sheng
Phone: (86) 573 283 9600/9057
Gen. Mgr.: Jeremy Bazley
Phone: (86) 573 283 9600/9057
Depty. Gen. Man.: Yogesh Wagh
Phone: (86) 573 283 9600/9057
Purch. Mgr.: Sun Ze Zhu
Phone: (86) 573 283 9600/9057
Email: szz@minfengrobert.com
Dpty. Chmn.: Edward Holt
Phone: (44) 1204 526241
Fax: (44) 1204 521958
Email: eholt@blugilt.co.uk
Dpty. Gen. Man./Head of Sales: Jiang Min
Phone: (86) 573 283 9600/9057
Tech. Mgr.: Xie Li Nong
Phone: (86) 573 283 9600/9057
Total Employees at this Location: 209
Type of Operation: Paper mill
Paper/Paperboard Grades and Capacities:
Total paper and paperboard capacity: 12,000 mt/y
Specialty and industrial: 12,000 mt/y
Paper and Paperboard Mill Data:
Paper Machines: 2
PM 13, fourdrinier, total capacity 6,000 mt/y, Trim width 2.4 m, Specialty and industrial
PM 14, fourdrinier, total capacity 6,000 mt/y, Trim width 2.4 m, Specialty and industrial
Finishing Equipment:
Winders: 1
Sheeters: 4 at 12,000 mt/y

Ⓜ Zhejiang Minfeng Zanders Special Paper Co., Ltd
Jiaxing Mill

Ownership: 75% by Zhejiang Minfeng Special Paper Co., Ltd., 25% by Metsä Board
No. 70 Ruli Rd.
Jiaxing, Zhejiang, 314000
China
Phone: (86) 573 8281 2382
Fax: (86) 573 8281 2382
Web Address: www.minfenggroup.com
Type of Operation: Paper mill
Paper/Paperboard Grades and Capacities:
Total paper and paperboard capacity: 7,000 mt/y
Specialty and industrial: 7,000 mt/y
Paper and Paperboard Mill Data:
Paper Machines: 3
PM 9, (2nd hand PM from Minfeng Special Paper), Specialty and industrial
PM 12, (2nd hand PM from Minfeng Special Paper), total capacity 1,800 mt/y, Trim width 1.76 m, Specialty and industrial
PM 19, Specialty and industrial

Ⓟ Ⓜ Zhejiang Minfeng Special Paper Co., Ltd.
Jiaxing Mill

Ownership: 54.21% by Jiaxin Minfeng Group Co., Ltd.
No. 70 Ruli Rd.
Jiaxing, Zhejiang, 314000
China
Phone: (86) 573 8283 9114/ 9087/ 9051
Fax: (86) 573 8282 1135/ 8208 2630
Email: wuliangen@mfspchina.com
Web Address: www.minfenggroup.com
Personnel:
Chmn.: Lidong Wu
Phone: (86) 573 8283 9114/ 9087/ 9051
Vice Chmn., Gen. Mgr.: Weiwei Lu
Phone: (86) 573 8283 9114/ 9087/ 9051
CFO: Ms. Yan Fang
Phone: (86) 573 8283 9114/ 9087/ 9051
Vice Gen. Mgr.: Zhirong Shen
Phone: (86) 573 8283 9114/ 9087/ 9051
Dpty. Gen. Mgr.: Weiqiang Tao
Phone: (86) 573 8283 9114/ 9087/ 9051
Total Employees at this Location: 2,525
Type of Operation: Paper mill
Mill Locations:
Zhejiang Minfeng Benkete Paper Co., Ltd., Jiaxing Mill (74% owned), No. 70 Ruli Rd., Jiaxing 314000, China, Capacity: 15,000 mt/y, (Paper mill)
Phone: (86) 573 8206 1951
Fax: (86) 573 8208 2630
Zhejiang Minfeng Zanders Special Paper Co., Ltd, Jiaxing Mill (75% owned), No. 70 Ruli Rd., Jiaxing 314000, China, Capacity: 7,000 mt/y, (Paper mill)
Phone: (86) 573 8281 2382
Fax: (86) 573 8281 2382
Pulp Mill Data:
Chemical Pulping Systems:
Batch digesters: 11
Paper/Paperboard Grades and Capacities:
Total paper and paperboard capacity: 124,807 mt/y
Specialty and industrial: 124,807 mt/y

Paper and Paperboard Mill Data:
Paper Machines: 8
No. 10-11, fourdrinier, total capacity 3,927 mt/y, Trim width 1.76 m, Specialty and industrial
No. 13-14, total capacity 3,927 mt/y, Trim width 1.76 m, Specialty and industrial
No. 17, fourdrinier, total capacity 29,988 mt/y, Trim width 1.88 m, Specialty and industrial
No. 18, fourdrinier, total capacity 11,995 mt/y, Trim width 3.15 m, Specialty and industrial
No. 20, fourdrinier, total capacity 14,994 mt/y, Trim width 1.76 m, Specialty and industrial
No. 21, DuoFormer D, total capacity 59,976 mt/y, Trim width 3.5 m, Specialty and industrial
Finishing Equipment:
Supercalenders at 40,000 mt/y
Energy Data:
Power boilers
Steam turbines
Electrical demand for mill: 350 MWh/D

ⓂZhejiang Ningbo Asia Pulp and Paper Co., Ltd.
Beilun (Zhejiang Ningbo Asia Pulp and Paper) Mill
Ownership: 25% by Asia Pulp & Paper (APP), 75% by Ningbo City Government
Qingshi Industry Zone, Ningbo Economic and Technology Development Zone
Xiaogang, Ningbo, Zhejiang, 315803
China
 Phone: (86) 574 8698 9999/ 9087
 Fax: (86) 574 8698 9898/ 9086
 Web Address: www.app.com.cn
Personnel:
 CEO/Pres.: Chunfu Chen
 Phone: (86) 574 8698 9999/ 9087
 Dpty. Chief Pres. Office, Ningbo Zhonghua: Anton Hui
 Phone: (86) 574 8698 9999/ 9087
 VP, Prod.: Hsing Liang Chen
 Phone: (86) 574 8698 9999/ 9087
 Tech. Dir.: Anil Kaul
 Phone: (86) 574 8698 9999
 Fax: (86) 574 8698 9898
 Email: anilkaul@mail.zhonghua-paper.com
 PR Mgr.: Xincun Zhou
 Phone: (86) 574 8746 4811 Ext. 3006
 Fax: (86) 574 8749 3450
 Email: zhouxincun@mail.zhonghua-paper.com
Total Employees at this Location: 1,200
Type of Operation: Paperboard mill
Pulp Grades and Capacities:
 Total pulp capacity: 631,744 mt/y
 Recycled Pulping: 631,744 mt/y
Pulp Mill Data:
Pulp Lines: 5
 Recycled Fiber Treatment Lines:
 Flotation deinking lines: 5 at 714,000 admt/y
 Pulpers
Paper/Paperboard Grades and Capacities:
 Total paper and paperboard capacity: 2,010,000 mt/y
 Boxboard/cartonboard: 2,010,000 mt/y
Paper and Paperboard Mill Data:
 Stock Preparation:
 Refiners: 3
Paper Machines: 2
No. 4, fourdrinier (3), total capacity 1,000,000 mt/y, Trim width 7.3 m, Boxboard/cartonboard
No. 6, Fourdrinier (5), total capacity 1,010,000 mt/y, Trim width 8.1 m, Boxboard/cartonboard
Coating Machines: 1
CM, total capacity 1,000,000 mt/y., on machine
Finishing Equipment:
Winders: 2 at 642,600 mt/y
Energy Data:
Power boilers: 2
Steam turbines: 2 at 62.4, 62.4 MW
Electrical demand for mill: 3,133 MWh/D

ⒽZhejiang Ningbo Dongteng Paper Co., Ltd.
Ownership: 100% by private owners
Chayuan Village, Ninghai County
Ningbo, Zhejiang, 315602
China
 Phone: (86) 574 6512 5999/ 6600
 Fax: (86) 574 6512 4892
Personnel:
 Gen. Mgr.: Bidui Zhou
 Phone: (86) 574 6512 5999/ 6600
Mill Locations:
Zhejiang Ningbo Dongteng Paper Co., Ltd., Ningbo Mill, Chayuan Village, Ninghai County, Ningbo 315602, China, Capacity: 99,960 mt/y, (Paperboard mill)
 Phone: (86) 574 6512 5999/ 6600
 Fax: (86) 574 6512 4892

ⓂZhejiang Ningbo Dongteng Paper Co., Ltd.
Ningbo Mill
Chayuan Village, Ninghai County
Ningbo, Zhejiang, 315602
China
 Phone: (86) 574 6512 5999/ 6600
 Fax: (86) 574 6512 4892
Personnel:
 Gen. Mgr.: Bidui Zhou
 Phone: (86) 574 6512 5999/ 6600
Total Employees at this Location: 130
Type of Operation: Paperboard mill
Pulp Grades and Capacities:
 Total pulp capacity: 94,632 mt/y
 Recycled Pulping: 94,632 mt/y
Pulp Mill Data:
Pulp Lines: 2
 Recycled Fiber Treatment Lines:
 Recycled packaging pulping lines: 2 at 60,000 admt/y
Paper/Paperboard Grades and Capacities:
 Total paper and paperboard capacity: 99,960 mt/y
 Corrugating medium/fluting: 99,960 mt/y
Paper and Paperboard Mill Data:
Paper Machines: 2
No. 1, fourdrinier, total capacity 49,623 mt/y, Trim width 3.6 m, Corrugating medium/fluting
No. 2, multi-fourdrinier, total capacity 50,337 mt/y, Trim width 3.75 m, Corrugating medium/fluting
Energy Data:
Power boilers: 1
Electrical demand for mill: 133 MWh/D

ⒽZhejiang Ningbo Haishan Paper Co.
Ownership: 100% by shareholders
Haishan Road, Juexibeitang Industry Park
Xiangshan Town, Ningbo, Zhejiang, 315708
China
 Phone: (86) 574 6560 8800/ 9666
 Fax: (86) 574 6560 2777
 Email: yuhuajie410@sohu.com
 Web Address: www.chinahaishan.com
Mill Locations:
Zhejiang Ningbo Haishan Paper Co., Ningbo Mill, Haishan Road, Juexibeitang Industry Park, Xiangshan Town, Ningbo 315708, China, Capacity: 50,337 mt/y, (Paperboard mill)
 Phone: (86) 574 6560 8800/ 9666
 Fax: (86) 574 6560 2777
 Email: yuhuajie410@sohu.com

ⓂZhejiang Ningbo Haishan Paper Co.
Ningbo Mill
Haishan Road, Juexibeitang Industry Park, Xiangshan Town
Ningbo, Zhejiang, 315708
China
 Phone: (86) 574 6560 8800/ 9666
 Fax: (86) 574 6560 2777
 Email: yuhuajie410@sohu.com
 Web Address: www.chinahaishan.com
Personnel:
 Chmn. & Gen. Mgr.: Hailin Chen
 Phone: (86) 574 6560 8800/ 9666
 Sls. Mgr.: Li Zhen
 Phone: (86) 574 6560 8800/ 9666
Total Employees at this Location: 230
Type of Operation: Paperboard mill
Pulp Grades and Capacities:
 Total pulp capacity: 48,956 mt/y
 Recycled Pulping: 48,956 mt/y
Pulp Mill Data:
Pulp Lines: 1
Paper/Paperboard Grades and Capacities:
 Total paper and paperboard capacity: 50,337 mt/y
 Corrugating medium/fluting: 50,337 mt/y
Paper and Paperboard Mill Data:
Paper Machines: 1
No. 1, fourdrinier, total capacity 50,337 mt/y, Trim width 3.9 m, Corrugating medium/fluting
Energy Data:
Electrical demand for mill: 78 MWh/D

ⒽZhejiang Ningbo Ningxing Paper Co., Ltd.
Ownership: 100% by private owners
Keshi Rd., Ninghai Economy & Development District
Ninghai, Zhejiang, 315600
China
 Phone: (86) 574 6535 9990
 Fax: (86) 574 6535 9990
Mill Locations:
Zhejiang Ningbo Ningxing Paper Co., Ltd., Ninghai Mill, Keshi Rd., Ninghai Economy & Development District, Ninghai 315600, China, Capacity: 50,694 mt/y, (Paperboard mill)
 Phone: (86) 574 6535 9990
 Fax: (86) 574 6535 9990

ⓂZhejiang Ningbo Ningxing Paper Co., Ltd.
Ninghai Mill
Keshi Rd., Ninghai Economy & Development District
Ninghai, Zhejiang, 315600
China
 Phone: (86) 574 6535 9990
 Fax: (86) 574 6535 9990
Total Employees at this Location: 120
Type of Operation: Paperboard mill
Pulp Grades and Capacities:
 Total pulp capacity: 48,981 mt/y
 Recycled Pulping: 48,981 mt/y
Pulp Mill Data:
 Recycled Fiber Treatment Lines:
 Recycled packaging pulping lines: 1 at 70,000 admt/y
Paper/Paperboard Grades and Capacities:
 Total paper and paperboard capacity: 50,694 mt/y
 Corrugating medium/fluting: 50,694 mt/y
Paper and Paperboard Mill Data:
Paper Machines: 1
No. 1, fourdrinier, total capacity 50,694 mt/y, Trim width 3.8 m, Corrugating medium/fluting
Energy Data:
Power boilers: 1
Electrical demand for mill: 79 MWh/D

ⓂZhejiang Ningbo Zhonghua Paper
Ningbo (Zhejiang Ningbo Zhonghua Paper) Mill
Ownership: 100% by Asia Pulp & Paper (APP)
Qingshi Ind. Zone, Ningbo E &T Deve. Zone
Ningbo, Zhejiang, 315012
China
 Phone: (86) 574 87464811/ 86231466
 Fax: (86) 574 87493450/ 7535/ 86228207
 Email: sales@mail.zhonghua-paper.com, chenchusheng@mail.zhonghua-paper.com
 Web Address: www.zhonghua-paper.com, www.asiapulppaper.com

China

Personnel:
Chmn.: Oei Tjie Goan
Phone: (86) 574 87464811/86231466
CEO/ Gen. Mgr.: Chunfu Chen
Phone: (86) 574 87464811/86231466
Asst. Mgr.: Fengxi Huang
Phone: (86) 574 87464811/86231466
Chief Eng.: Shengde Wang
Phone: (86) 574 87464811/86231466
PR Mgr.: Xincun Zhou
Phone: (86) 574 8746 4811 ext. 3006
Fax: (86) 574 8749 3450
Email: zhouxincun@mail.zhonghua-paper.com
Total Employees at this Location: 1,700
Type of Operation: Paperboard mill
Pulp Grades and Capacities:
Total pulp capacity: 199,110 mt/y
Recycled Pulping: 199,110 mt/y
Pulp Mill Data:
Pulp Lines: 2
Recycled Fiber Treatment Lines:
Flotation deinking lines: 1 at 54,000 admt/y
Recycled packaging pulping lines: 1 at 45,000
Paper/Paperboard Grades and Capacities:
Total paper and paperboard capacity: 600,000 mt/y
Boxboard/cartonboard: 600,000 mt/y
Paper and Paperboard Mill Data:
Paper Machines: 3
No. 1, cylinder (8), total capacity 70,000 mt/y, Trim width 2.4 m, Boxboard/cartonboard
No. 2, Fourdrinier (4), total capacity 260,000 mt/y, Trim width 4.27 m, Boxboard/cartonboard
No. 3, Fourdrinier (4), total capacity 270,000 mt/y, Trim width 4.27 m, Boxboard/cartonboard
Coating Machines: 3
PM 1, total capacity 70,000 mt/y., on machine
PM 2, total capacity 250,000 mt/y., on machine
PM 3, total capacity 250,000 mt/y., on machine
Energy Data:
Power boilers: 3
Steam turbines: 2 at 38.3, 38.3 MW
Electrical demand for mill: 1,107 MWh/D

ⒽZhejiang Pinghu Fengli Paper Stock Co. Ltd.

Ownership: 100% by shareholders
Chenjiang Village, Lindi Town
Pinghu, Zhejiang, 314202
China
Phone: (86) 573 592 2295/2069
Fax: (86) 573 592 2192/2133
Personnel:
Chmn.: Jingchu Xu
Phone: (86) 573 592 2295/2069
Gen. Mgr./Mill Mgr.: Shanbo Xu
Phone: (86) 573 592 2295/2069
Sales Mgr.: Jinliang Xu
Phone: (86) 573 592 2295/2069
Mill Locations:
Zhejiang Pinghu Fengli Paper Stock Co. Ltd., Pinghu Mill, Chenjiang Village, Lindi Town, Pinghu 314202, China, Capacity: 42,840 mt/y, (Paperboard mill)
Phone: (86) 573 592 2295/2069
Fax: (86) 573 592 2192/2133

ⓂZhejiang Pinghu Fengli Paper Stock Co. Ltd.
Pinghu Mill

Chenjiang Village, Lindi Town
Pinghu, Zhejiang, 314202
China
Phone: (86) 573 592 2295/2069
Fax: (86) 573 592 2192/2133
Personnel:
Chmn.: Jingchu Xu
Phone: (86) 573 592 2295/2069
Gen. Mgr./Mill Mgr.: Shanbo Xu
Phone: (86) 573 592 2295/2069
Sales Mgr.: Jinliang Xu
Phone: (86) 573 592 2295/2069
Total Employees at this Location: 140
Type of Operation: Paperboard mill
Pulp Grades and Capacities:
Total pulp capacity: 41,663 mt/y
Recycled Pulping: 41,663 mt/y
Paper/Paperboard Grades and Capacities:
Total paper and paperboard capacity: 42,840 mt/y
Corrugating medium/fluting: 42,840 mt/y
Paper and Paperboard Mill Data:
Paper Machines: 2
No. 1, fourdrinier, total capacity 19,992 mt/y, Trim width 3 m, Corrugating medium/fluting
No. 2, fourdrinier, total capacity 22,848 mt/y, Trim width 3.4 m, Corrugating medium/fluting
Energy Data:
Power boilers: 3
Electrical demand for mill: 59 MWh/D

ⓂZhejiang Purico Speciality Paper Company Limited
Jiaxing Mill

Ownership: 100% by Purico Group (China)
70 Luli Street
Jiaxing, Zhejiang, 314000
China
Phone: (86) 573 8283 9600/ 8282 0799
Fax: (86) 573 8282 0700/ 8281 7677
Email: jb@minfengrobert.com,
info@purico.cn
Web Address: www.puricopaper.com.cn
Personnel:
Chmn.: Lu Shi Lin
Phone: (86) 573 8283 9600/ 8282 0799
Gen. Mgr.: Jeremy Bazley
Phone: (86) 573 8283 9600/ 8282 0799
Prod. Mgr.: Bert Waring
Phone: (86) 573 8283 9600/ 8282 0799
Dpty. Chmn.: Edward Holt
Phone: (86) 573 8283 9600/ 8282 0799
Email: eholt@blugilt.co.uk
Dpty. Gen. Mgr.: Lian Fu Shou
Phone: (86) 573 8283 9600/ 8282 0799
Mktg. Dir.: Julia Wu
Phone: (86) 573 8283 9600/ 8282 0799
Finan. Mgr.: Mao Jian Ming
Phone: (86) 573 8283 9600/ 8282 0799
Purch. Mgr.: Sun Ze Zhu
Phone: (86) 573 8283 9600/ 8282 0799
Total Employees at this Location: 136
Type of Operation: Paper mill
Paper/Paperboard Grades and Capacities:
Total paper and paperboard capacity: 10,000 mt/y
Specialty and industrial: 10,000 mt/y
Paper and Paperboard Mill Data:
Paper Machines: 1
PM 1, triple-wire, inclined, total capacity 10,000 mt/y, Trim width 3.4 m, Specialty and industrial

ⒽZhejiang Quzhou Shuangxiongmao Paper General Corp.

Ownership: 100% by private owners
Huangtankou, Qujiang District
Quzhou, Zhejiang, 324005
China
Phone: (86) 570 362 1986/ 1938/ 1088
Fax: (86) 570 362 1938
Mill Locations:
Zhejiang Quzhou Shuangxiongmao Paper General Corp., Quzhou Mill, Huangtankou, Qujiang District, Quzhou 324005, China, Capacity: 12,000 mt/y, (Paper mill)
Phone: (86) 570 362 1986/ 1938/ 1088
Fax: (86) 570 362 1938

ⓂZhejiang Quzhou Shuangxiongmao Paper General Corp.
Quzhou Mill

Huangtankou, Qujiang District
Quzhou, Zhejiang, 324005
China
Phone: (86) 570 362 1986/ 1938/ 1088
Fax: (86) 570 362 1938
Personnel:
Chmn. & Gen. Mgr.: Yuexiong Wang
Phone: (86) 570 362 1986/ 1938/ 1088
Total Employees at this Location: 173
Type of Operation: Paper mill
Pulp Grades and Capacities:
Total pulp capacity: 6,000 mt/y
Recycled Pulping: 6,000 mt/y
Pulp Mill Data:
Pulp Lines: 1
Recycled Fiber Treatment Lines:
Recycled packaging pulping lines: 127
Paper/Paperboard Grades and Capacities:
Total paper and paperboard capacity: 12,000 mt/y
Tissue: 12,000 mt/y
Paper and Paperboard Mill Data:
Paper Machines: 9
PM 1-7, cylinder, total capacity 1,285 mt/y, Trim width 1.58 m, Tissue
PM 8-9, cylinder, total capacity 1,500 mt/y, Trim width 1.76 m, Tissue

ⓂZhejiang Rongchang Paper Co., Ltd.
Quzhou Mill

Ownership: 100% by Zhejiang Tianting Yalun Paper Group Co., Ltd.
No. 151 Longlan Rd., Longyou County
Quzhou, Zhejiang, 324400
China
Phone: (86) 570 7090 058
Fax: (86) 570 7090 098
Personnel:
Gen. Mgr.: Chuanlin Xiang
Phone: (86) 570 7090 058
Sls. Mgr.: Jianxing Ye
Phone: (86) 570 7090 058
Total Employees at this Location: 500
Type of Operation: Paper mill
Paper/Paperboard Grades and Capacities:
Total paper and paperboard capacity: 15,000 mt/y
Specialty and industrial: 15,000 mt/y
Paper and Paperboard Mill Data:
Paper Machines: 1
PM 10, fourdrinier, total capacity 15,000 mt/y, Trim width 2.64 m, Specialty and industrial

ⒽZhejiang Rongfeng Paper

Ownership: 100% by China Tobacco Industry Corp.
Jiashan Exit of Shanghai-Hangzhou Expressway, Dagang Town
Jiashan County, Jiaxing, Zhejiang, 314113
China
Phone: (86) 573 8466 6127/ 6666/ 6113
Fax: (86) 573 8466 6099
Web Address: www.zjrf.cn
Mill Locations:
Zhejiang Rongfeng Paper, Jiaxing Mill, Jiashan Exit of Shanghai-Hangzhou Expressway, Dagang Town, Jiashan County, Jiaxing 314113, China, Capacity: 11,000 mt/y, (Paper mill)
Phone: (86) 573 8466 6127/ 6666/ 6113
Fax: (86) 573 8466 6099

ⓂZhejiang Rongfeng Paper
Jiaxing Mill

Jiashan Exit of Shanghai-Hangzhou Expressway, Dagang Town, Jiashan County
Jiaxing, Zhejiang, 314113
China
Phone: (86) 573 8466 6127/ 6666/ 6113
Fax: (86) 573 8466 6099
Web Address: www.zjrf.cn
Personnel:
Pres. & Gen. Mgr.: Songquan Wen

China

Phone: (86) 573 8466 6127/ 6666/ 6113
Sls. Mgr.: Hongwei Gou
Phone: (86) 573 8466 6127/ 6666/ 6113
Total Employees at this Location: 233
Type of Operation: Paper mill
Paper/Paperboard Grades and Capacities:
Total paper and paperboard capacity: 11,000 mt/y
Specialty and industrial: 11,000 mt/y
Paper and Paperboard Mill Data:
Paper Machines: 2
PM 1-2, fourdrinier, total capacity 5,500 mt/y, Trim width 1.88 m, Specialty and industrial

⊕Zhejiang Rongsheng Paper Co., Ltd.
Ownership: 100% by shareholders
Pinghu Economy & Development Park
Pinghu, Zhejiang, 314213
China
Phone: (86) 573 8598 8080/ 9555
Fax: (86) 573 8598 8880/ 6598
Email: rs@rszy.com
Web Address: www.rszy.com
Mill Locations:
Zhejiang Rongsheng Paper Co., Ltd., Pinghu Mill, Pinghu Economy & Development Park, Pinghu 314213, China, Capacity: 206,346 mt/y, (Paper mill, Paperboard mill)
Phone: (86) 573 8598 8080/ 9555
Fax: (86) 573 8598 8880/ 6598
Email: rs@rszy.com

⊕⊛Zhejiang Rongsheng Paper Co., Ltd.
Pinghu Mill
Pinghu Economy & Development Park
Pinghu, Zhejiang, 314213
China
Phone: (86) 573 8598 8080/ 9555
Fax: (86) 573 8598 8880/ 6598
Email: rs@rszy.com
Web Address: www.rszy.com
Personnel:
Gen. Mgr.: Ronghua Feng
Phone: (86) 573 8598 8080/ 9555
Total Employees at this Location: 600
Type of Operation: Paper mill, Paperboard mill
Pulp Grades and Capacities:
Total pulp capacity: 198,333 mt/y
Recycled Pulping: 198,333 mt/y
Pulp Mill Data:
Pulp Lines: 4
Recycled Fiber Treatment Lines:
Recycled packaging pulping lines: 4 at 300,000 admt/y
Paper/Paperboard Grades and Capacities:
Total paper and paperboard capacity: 206,346 mt/y
Linerboard: 102,816 mt/y
Corrugating medium/fluting: 103,530 mt/y
Paper and Paperboard Mill Data:
Paper Machines: 2
No. 6, multi-ply, total capacity 102,816 mt/y, Trim width 4.6 m, Linerboard
No. 8, multi-ply, total capacity 103,530 mt/y, Trim width 4.6 m, Corrugating medium/fluting
Energy Data:
Power boilers: 4
Steam turbines: 3 at 6, 6, 1.2 MW
Electrical demand for mill: 337 MWh/D

⊕Zhejiang Sanxing Paper Co., Ltd.
Ownership: 100% by shareholders
Shanjian Industry Park, Chunjiang Street
Fuyang, Zhejiang, 311421
China
Phone: (86) 571 6358 1003/ 5203/ 5189
Fax: (86) 571 6358 5189
Email: zjsxpaper@fy.hz.zj.cn
Web Address: www.zjsxpaper.com
Mill Locations:
Zhejiang Sanxing Paper Co., Ltd., Fuyang Mill, Shanjian Industry Park, Chunjiang Street, Fuyang 311421, China, Capacity: 181,178 mt/y, (Paperboard mill)
Phone: (86) 571 6358 1003/ 5203/ 5189
Fax: (86) 571 6358 5189
Email: zjsxpaper@fy.hz.zj.cn

⊛Zhejiang Sanxing Paper Co., Ltd.
Fuyang Mill
Shanjian Industry Park, Chunjiang Street
Fuyang, Zhejiang, 311421
China
Phone: (86) 571 6358 1003/ 5203/ 5189
Fax: (86) 571 6358 5189
Email: zjsxpaper@fy.hz.zj.cn
Web Address: www.zjsxpaper.com
Personnel:
Chmn. & Gen. Mgr.: Peigeng Tang
Phone: (86) 571 6358 1003/ 5203/ 5189
Total Employees at this Location: 1,000
Type of Operation: Paperboard mill
Pulp Grades and Capacities:
Total pulp capacity: 134,389 mt/y
Recycled Pulping: 134,389 mt/y
Pulp Mill Data:
Pulp Lines: 6
Paper/Paperboard Grades and Capacities:
Total paper and paperboard capacity: 181,178 mt/y
Boxboard/cartonboard: 181,178 mt/y
Paper and Paperboard Mill Data:
Paper Machines: 2
No. 2, Fourdrinier (4), total capacity 94,784 mt/y, Trim width 3.4 m, Boxboard/cartonboard
No. 3, Fourdrinier (4), total capacity 86,394 mt/y, Trim width 2.76 m, Boxboard/cartonboard
Energy Data:
Power boilers: 3
Steam turbines: 2 at 24.6, 24.6 MW
Electrical demand for mill: 247 MWh/D

⊕⊛Zhejiang Shangyu Blue Star Paper Co., Ltd
Shangyu Mill
Shangyu Industrial Park
Shangyu, Zhejiang
China
Phone: (86) 575 8215 5332/2001/5305
Fax: (86) 575 8215 2181
Email: mail@zjbluestar.com.cn
Web Address: www.zjbluestar.com.cn
Total Employees at this Location: 480
Type of Operation: Paperboard mill
Pulp Grades and Capacities:
Total pulp capacity: 38,997 mt/y
Recycled Pulping: 38,997 mt/y
Paper/Paperboard Grades and Capacities:
Total paper and paperboard capacity: 40,000 mt/y
Corrugating medium/fluting: 40,000 mt/y
Paper and Paperboard Mill Data:
Paper Machines: 1
No. 1, fourdrinier, total capacity 40,000 mt/y, Trim width 3.2 m, Corrugating medium/fluting
Energy Data:
Electrical demand for mill: 42 MWh/D

⊕⊛Zhejiang Shengda Group
Hangzhou Mill
Ownership: 100% by private owners
No. 2 Beitang Rd., Xiaoshan Economy & Technology District
Hangzhou, Zhejiang, 311215
China
Phone: (86) 571 8283 1019/ 5444
Fax: (86) 571 8283 2578
Email: office@sdgroup.cn, hr@sdgroup.cn
Web Address: www.sdgroup.cn
Personnel:
CEO: Daliang Teng
Phone: (86) 571 8283 1019/ 5444
Fax: (86) 571 8283 2578
Chmn.: Wuxiao Fang
Phone: (86) 571 8283 1019/ 5444
Fax: (86) 571 8283 2578
Total Employees of Company: 4,000
Total Employees at this Location: 200
Type of Operation: Paperboard mill
Mill Locations:
Shengda Group Jiangsu Shuangdeng Paper Co., Ltd., Yancheng Mill, No. 28 Haigang Rd., Shuangdeng Industry Park, Huangshagang Town, Sheyang County, Yancheng 224341, China, Capacity: 20,000 mt/y, (Pulp mill, Paper mill)
Phone: (86) 515 8226 3888/ 3907
Fax: (86) 515 8226 3999
Jiangsu Shuangsheng Paper Technology Development Co. Ltd., Yancheng Mill, No.28, Haigang Rd, Huangshagang Town, Sheyang, Yancheng City 22434-4341, China, Capacity: 150,000 mt/y, (Paper mill)
Phone: (86) 515-82263888
Pulp Grades and Capacities:
Total pulp capacity: 69,217 mt/y
Recycled Pulping: 69,217 mt/y
Pulp Mill Data:
Recycled Fiber Treatment Lines:
Recycled packaging pulping lines: 1
Paper/Paperboard Grades and Capacities:
Total paper and paperboard capacity: 70,000 mt/y
Linerboard: 35,000 mt/y
Corrugating medium/fluting: 35,000 mt/y
Paper and Paperboard Mill Data:
Paper Machines: 2
No. 1, Multi-wire (3), total capacity 35,000 mt/y, Trim width 3.2 m, Linerboard
No. 2, fourdrinier, total capacity 35,000 mt/y, Trim width 3.2 m, Corrugating medium/fluting
Energy Data:
Electrical demand for mill: 89 MWh/D

⊛Zhejiang Shunpu Paper Co., Ltd.
Quzhou Mill
No.22, Jinxing Rd., Longyou County
Quzhou, Zhejiang, 324400
China
Phone: (86) 570 739 0008
Fax: (86) 570 739 0018
Web Address: www.zjshunpu.com
Total Employees at this Location: 150
Type of Operation: Paper mill
Paper/Paperboard Grades and Capacities:
Total paper and paperboard capacity: 20,000 mt/y
Specialty and industrial: 20,000 mt/y
Paper and Paperboard Mill Data:
Paper Machines: 5
No. 1, cylinder (1), total capacity 2,000 mt/y, Trim width 1.09 m, Specialty and industrial
No. 2, cylinder (1), total capacity 4,500 mt/y, Trim width 1.88 m, Specialty and industrial
No. 3, cylinder (1), total capacity 4,500 mt/y, Trim width 1.88 m, Specialty and industrial
No. 4, cylinder (2), total capacity 4,500 mt/y, Trim width 1.88 m, Specialty and industrial
No. 5, multi-cylinder, total capacity 4,500 mt/y, Trim width 1.88 m, Specialty and industrial

⊕Zhejiang Tann Longyou Paper Industry Co., Ltd.
Ownership: 4% by Chinese Tobacco Monopoly, Tannpapers (China), 96% by Tann-Papier
No. 151-A Longlan Rd.
Longyou, Zhejiang, 324400
China
Phone: (86) 570 783 5064/5538
Fax: (86) 570 782 5211
Email: tannlongyou@tanngroup.com
Mill Locations:
Zhejiang Tann Longyou Paper Industry Co., Ltd., Longyou Mill, No. 151-A Longlan Rd., Longyou 324400, China,

China

Capacity: 10,000 mt/y, (Paper mill)
Phone: (86) 570 783 5064/5538
Fax: (86) 570 782 5211
Email: tannlongyou@tanngroup.com

ⓜZhejiang Tann Longyou Paper Industry Co., Ltd.
Longyou Mill
No. 151-A Longlan Rd.
Longyou, Zhejiang, 324400
China
Phone: (86) 570 783 5064/5538
Fax: (86) 570 782 5211
Email: tannlongyou@tanngroup.com
Personnel:
Pres.: Christian Trierenberg
Phone: (86) 570 783 5064/5538
Gen. Mgr.: Kunfu Ye
Phone: (86) 570 783 5064/5538
Mgr.: Bin Chen
Phone: (86) 570 783 5064/5538
Mgr.: Yimin Lin
Phone: (86) 570 783 5064/5538
Total Employees at this Location: 337
Type of Operation: Paper mill
Paper/Paperboard Grades and Capacities:
Total paper and paperboard capacity: 10,000 mt/y
Specialty and industrial: 10,000 mt/y
Paper and Paperboard Mill Data:
Paper Machines: 1
No. 1, fourdrinier, total capacity 10,000 mt/y, Trim width 2.36 m, Specialty and industrial
Finishing Equipment:
Supercalenders: 1
Rewinders: 1
Sheeters: 1

ⓜZhejiang Tiantianhong Paper Co., Ltd.
Chengbei Industry, Longyou County
Quzhou, Zhejiang, 324200
China
Phone: (86) 570 7035 465
Email: wxw@wztth.com
Web Address: www.wztth.com
Mill Locations:
Zhejiang Tiantianhong Paper Co., Ltd., Quzhou Mill, No.33, Jinxing Rd., Chengbei Industry, Longyou County, Quzhou 324200, China, Capacity: 38,000 mt/y, (Paper mill)
Phone: (86) 570 7258 386
Fax: (86) 570 7258 892/909

ⓜZhejiang Tiantianhong Paper Co., Ltd.
Quzhou Mill
No.33, Jinxing Rd., Chengbei Industry, Longyou County
Quzhou, Zhejiang, 324200
China
Phone: (86) 570 7258 386
Fax: (86) 570 7258 892/909
Web Address: www.tthpaper.com, www.tthpaper.com/en_l/
Personnel:
Mill Mgr.: Zhaoxiang Huang
Phone: (86) 570 7035 465
Sales Mgr.: Jianbin Zou
Phone: (86) 570 7035 465
Total Employees at this Location: 210
Type of Operation: Paper mill
Paper/Paperboard Grades and Capacities:
Total paper and paperboard capacity: 38,000 mt/y
Uncoated woodfree/freesheet: 38,000 mt/y
Paper and Paperboard Mill Data:
Paper Machines: 4
PM 1, total capacity 8,000 mt/y, Trim width 1.58 m, Uncoated woodfree/freesheet
PM 2, total capacity 10,000 mt/y, Trim width 1.88 m, Uncoated woodfree/freesheet
PM 3, total capacity 10,000 mt/y, Trim width 1.88 m, Uncoated woodfree/freesheet
PM 4, total capacity 10,000 mt/y, Trim width 1.88 m, Uncoated woodfree/freesheet

ⓞⓜZhejiang Tianting Paper Co., Ltd.
Jinhua Mill
Ownership: 100% by Shareholders
No.1, Banban Ave., Pujiang County
Jinhua, Zhejiang, 322200
China
Phone: (86) 579 8420 0200/0208/0202
Fax: (86) 579 8420 0812/0248
Email: ctp@ctpctp.com
Web Address: www.ctpctp.com
Personnel:
Chmn. & Pres.: Jianxiong Zhao
Phone: (86) 579 8420 0200/0208/0202
Pres.: Chuanlin Xiang
Phone: (86) 579 8420 0200/0208/0202
VP: Jiangguang Lou
Phone: (86) 579 8420 0200/0208/0202
Sls. Mgr.: Jianbao Xu
Phone: (86) 579 8420 0200/0208/0202
Chief Eng.: Zhenyuan Ye
Phone: (86) 579 8420 0200/0208/0202
Purch. Agent: Housheng Dai
Phone: (86) 579 8420 0200/0208/0202
Total Employees at this Location: 1,100
Type of Operation: Paperboard mill
Mill Locations:
Zhejiang Rongchang Paper Co., Ltd., Quzhou Mill, No. 151 Longlan Rd., Longyou County, Quzhou 324400, China, Capacity: 15,000 mt/y, (Paper mill)
Phone: (86) 570 7090 058
Fax: (86) 570 7090 098
Zhejiang Tianting Yalun Paper Group Co., Ltd., Quzhou Mill, No. 151 Longlan Rd., Longyou County, Quzhou 324400, China, Capacity: 60,000 mt/y, (Paper mill)
Phone: (86) 570 7090 102
Fax: (86) 570 7090 126
Pulp Grades and Capacities:
Total pulp capacity: 64,635 mt/y
Recycled Pulping: 64,635 mt/y
Paper/Paperboard Grades and Capacities:
Total paper and paperboard capacity: 74,970 mt/y
Boxboard/cartonboard: 74,970 mt/y
Paper and Paperboard Mill Data:
Stock Preparation:
Refiners: 12
Paper Machines: 1
No. 1, Fourdrinier (4), total capacity 74,970 mt/y, Trim width 2.76 m, Boxboard/cartonboard
Coating Machines: 2
CM 1, total capacity 15,000 mt/y., on machine
CM 2, total capacity 75,000 mt/y., on machine
Finishing Equipment:
Rewinders: 2
Sheeters: 7
Energy Data:
Power boilers: 3
Steam turbines: 2 at 1.5, 1.5 MW
Electrical demand for mill: 105 MWh/D

ⓞⓜZhejiang Tianting Yalun Paper Group Co., Ltd.
Quzhou Mill
Ownership: 100% by Zhejiang Tianting Paper Co., Ltd.
No. 151 Longlan Rd., Longyou County
Quzhou, Zhejiang, 324400
China
Phone: (86) 570 7090 102
Fax: (86) 570 7090 126
Personnel:
Pres./Mill Mgr.: Long Chen
Phone: (86) 570 7090 102
Tech. Mgr./Chief Eng.: Jinfu Huang
Phone: (86) 570 7090 102
VP - Operation: Chunzhong Xu
Phone: (86) 570 7090 102
Sls. Mgr.: Yousu Ding
Phone: (86) 570 7090 102
Total Employees at this Location: 1,000
Type of Operation: Paper mill
Mill Locations:
Zhejiang Rongchang Paper Co., Ltd., Quzhou Mill, No. 151 Longlan Rd., Longyou County, Quzhou 324400, China, Capacity: 15,000 mt/y, (Paper mill)
Phone: (86) 570 7090 058
Fax: (86) 570 7090 098
Pulp Mill Data:
Paper/Paperboard Grades and Capacities:
Total paper and paperboard capacity: 60,000 mt/y
Specialty and industrial: 60,000 mt/y
Paper and Paperboard Mill Data:
Paper Machines: 4
PM 1, multi-wire, total capacity 10,000 mt/y, Trim width 1.88 m, Specialty and industrial
PM 2, fourdrinier, total capacity 10,000 mt/y, Trim width 1.88 m, Specialty and industrial
PM 4, fourdrinier, total capacity 10,000 mt/y, Trim width 1.88 m, Specialty and industrial
PM 11, fourdrinier, total capacity 30,000 mt/y, Trim width 3.2 m, Specialty and industrial
Energy Data:
Power boilers: 3
Steam turbines: 2 at 12, 6 MW

ⓞⓜZhejiang Tongxiang Fuli Paper Co., Ltd
Tongxiang Mill
Wuzhen Town
Tongxiang, Zhejiang
China
Phone: (86) 573 8871 1411
Total Employees at this Location: 465
Type of Operation: Paperboard mill
Pulp Grades and Capacities:
Total pulp capacity: 86,959 mt/y
Recycled Pulping: 86,959 mt/y
Pulp Mill Data:
Bleach Plant Systems: 1
Recycled Pulping System, Type: Deinked
Recycled Fiber Treatment Lines:
Flotation deinking lines: 1
Recycled packaging pulping lines: 2
Paper/Paperboard Grades and Capacities:
Total paper and paperboard capacity: 97,818 mt/y
Boxboard/cartonboard: 97,818 mt/y
Paper and Paperboard Mill Data:
Paper Machines: 3
No. 2, cylinder, total capacity 13,209 mt/y, Trim width 1.6 m, Boxboard/cartonboard
No. 3, cylinder, total capacity 15,708 mt/y, Trim width 1.6 m, Boxboard/cartonboard
No. 4, Fourdrinier (4), total capacity 68,901 mt/y, Trim width 2.8 m, Boxboard/cartonboard
Coating Machines: 2
PM3, on machine
PM4, on machine
Energy Data:
Electrical demand for mill: 149 MWh/D

ⓞZhejiang Wanxin Paper Co., Ltd.
Ownership: 100% by private owners
Chunjiang Papermaking Industry Park
Fuyang, Zhejiang, 311421
China
Phone: (86) 571 6358 7561/ 7838/ 7828
Fax: (86) 571 6358 7870
Email: xmq@wxpaper.com
Web Address: www.wxpaper.com
Mill Locations:
Zhejiang Wanxin Paper Co., Ltd., Fuyang Mill, Chunjiang Papermaking Industry Park, Fuyang 311421, China, Capacity: 74,970 mt/y, (Paperboard mill)
Phone: (86) 571 6358 7561/ 7838/ 7828
Fax: (86) 571 6358 7870
Email: xmq@wxpaper.com

China

ⓜZhejiang Wanxin Paper Co., Ltd.
Fuyang Mill
Chunjiang Papermaking Industry Park
Fuyang, Zhejiang, 311421
China
  Phone: (86) 571 6358 7561/ 7838/ 7828
  Fax: (86) 571 6358 7870
  Email: xmq@wxpaper.com
  Web Address: www.wxpaper.com
Personnel:
  Gen. Mgr.: Mengqi Xia
  Phone: (86) 571 6358 7561/ 7838/ 7828
  Sls. Mgr.: Helin Tong
  Phone: (86) 571 6358 7561/ 7838/ 7828
Total Employees at this Location: 320
Type of Operation: Paperboard mill
Pulp Grades and Capacities:
  Total pulp capacity: 61,230 mt/y
  Recycled Pulping: 61,230 mt/y
Pulp Mill Data:
Pulp Lines: 1
Paper/Paperboard Grades and Capacities:
  Total paper and paperboard capacity: 74,970 mt/y
  Boxboard/cartonboard: 74,970 mt/y
Paper and Paperboard Mill Data:
Paper Machines: 1
No. 1, Fourdrinier (5), total capacity 74,970 mt/y, Trim width 2.88 m, Boxboard/cartonboard
Energy Data:
Electrical demand for mill: 106 MWh/D

ⓜZhejiang Wanzhong Paper Co., Ltd.
Fuyang Mill
Chunjiang Rd
Fuyang, Zhejiang, 311400
China
Total Employees at this Location: 463
Type of Operation: Paperboard mill
Pulp Grades and Capacities:
  Total pulp capacity: 101,800 mt/y
  Recycled Pulping: 101,800 mt/y
Paper/Paperboard Grades and Capacities:
  Total paper and paperboard capacity: 119,952 mt/y
  Boxboard/cartonboard: 119,952 mt/y
Paper and Paperboard Mill Data:
  Stock Preparation:
  Pulpers:
Paper Machines: 2
No. 1, Fourdrinier (5), total capacity 39,984 mt/y, Trim width 1.76 m, Boxboard/cartonboard
No. 2, Fourdrinier (5), total capacity 79,968 mt/y, Trim width 3.6 m, Boxboard/cartonboard
Coating Machines: 2
PM#1, on machine
PM#2, on machine
Energy Data:
Electrical demand for mill: 172 MWh/D

ⓜZhejiang Welbon Pulp & Paper Group
Ownership: 100% by private owners
21 Floor, Kaixuanmen Business Center, No. 11 Qingchun Rd.
Hangzhou, Zhejiang, 310009
China
  Phone: (86) 571 8721 8800
  Email: welb@mail.hz.zj.cn
  Web Address: www.welbon.com
Personnel:
  Chmn.: Shunhu Xu
  Phone: (86) 571 8721 8800
Total Employees of Company: 1,000
Mill Locations:
Anhui Winbon Gaosen Paper Manufacture Co., Ltd., Anqing Mill, No. 36 Gaobu Rd., Gaohe Town, Huaining County, Anqing 246121, China, Capacity: 12,000 mt/y, (Paper mill)
  Phone: (86) 556 4616 019/040/080
  Fax: (86) 556 461 7888
  Email: vivienne@welbon.com
Anhui Huabon Specialty Paper Co. Ltd., Huangshan Mill, North Xu Village, She County, Huangshan 245200, China, Capacity: 25,000 mt/y, (Paper mill)
  Phone: (86) 559 652 3166/ 3131
  Fax: (86) 559 652 3588
  Email: vivienne@welbon.com
Zhejiang Winbon Special Paper Co. Ltd., Quzhou Mill, No. 1 Jinxing Rd., Longyou County Economy & Industry District, Quzhou 324400, China, Capacity: 91,260 mt/y, (Paper mill)
  Phone: (86) 570 7055 822
  Fax: (86) 570 7055 818
  Email: zjhuabang@vip.163.com

ⓜZhejiang Welfare Paper Co., Ltd.
Shaoxing Mill
Ownership: 100% by Shanghai Welfare Group Co., Ltd.
No. 17 East Yangjiang Rd.
Shaoxing, Zhejiang, 312001
China
  Phone: (86) 575 8820 7373
  Fax: (86) 575 8820 7375
  Web Address: www.wef2008.com
Personnel:
  Chmn.: Shengzhang Li
  Phone: (86) 575 8820 7373
  Gen. Mgr.: Youcheng He
  Phone: (86) 575 8820 7373
  Sls. Mgr.: Xiaoli Fan
  Phone: (86) 575 8820 7373
Total Employees at this Location: 360
Type of Operation: Paper mill
Paper/Paperboard Grades and Capacities:
  Total paper and paperboard capacity: 48,000 mt/y
  Tissue: 48,000 mt/y
Paper and Paperboard Mill Data:
Paper Machines: 14
No. 1, (Supplier: Zhejiang Tonglu.), fourdrinier, total capacity 1,000 mt/y, Trim width 1.58 m, Tissue
No. 2, (Supplier: Zhejiang Tonglu.), fourdrinier, total capacity 1,000 mt/y, Trim width 1.58 m, Tissue
No. 3, (Supplier: Zhejiang Tonglu.), fourdrinier, total capacity 1,500 mt/y, Trim width 1.58 m, Tissue
No. 4, (Supplier: Zhejiang Tonglu.), fourdrinier, total capacity 1,500 mt/y, Trim width 1.58 m, Tissue
No. 5, (Supplier: Zhejiang Tonglu.), fourdrinier, total capacity 1,500 mt/y, Trim width 1.58 m, Tissue
No. 6, (Supplier: Zhejiang Tonglu.), fourdrinier, total capacity 1,500 mt/y, Trim width 1.58 m, Tissue
No. 7, (Supplier: Zhejiang Tonglu.), fourdrinier, total capacity 1,000 mt/y, Trim width 1.58 m, Tissue
No. 8, (Supplier: Zhejiang Tonglu.), fourdrinier, total capacity 1,000 mt/y, Trim width 1.58 m, Tissue
No. 9, (Supplier: Zhejiang Tonglu.), fourdrinier, total capacity 2,500 mt/y, Trim width 1.58 m, Tissue
No. 10, (Supplier: Zhejiang Tonglu.), fourdrinier, total capacity 2,500 mt/y, Trim width 1.58 m, Tissue
No. 11, BF-10 EX, total capacity 12,000 mt/y, Trim width 2.76 m, Tissue, Uncoated woodfree/freesheet
No. 12, BF-10 EX, total capacity 12,000 mt/y, Trim width 2.76 m, Tissue, Uncoated woodfree/freesheet
No. 13, BF-10 EX, total capacity 12,000 mt/y, Trim width 2.76 m, Tissue, Uncoated woodfree/freesheet
No. 14, BF-10 EX, total capacity 12,000 mt/y, Trim width 2.76 m, Tissue, Uncoated woodfree/freesheet
Energy Data:
Electrical demand for mill: 60 MWh/D

ⓜZhejiang Wenbo Paper Co., Ltd.
Fuyang (Zhejiang Wenbo Paper) Mill
Ownership: Zhejiang Zhengda Holding Group Co., Ltd.
Chunjiang Industry Zone
Fuyang, Zhejiang, 311421
China
  Phone: (86) 571 6358 7986
  Fax: (86) 571 6358 7717
Personnel:
  Pres.: Wenjun Dong
  Phone: (86) 571 6358 7986
  Gen. Mgr.: Cheng Ye
  Phone: (86) 571 6358 7986
Total Employees at this Location: 220
Type of Operation: Paperboard mill
Pulp Grades and Capacities:
  Total pulp capacity: 77,600 mt/y
  Recycled Pulping: 77,600 mt/y
Pulp Mill Data:
Pulp Lines: 2
  Bleach Plant Systems: 1
  Recycled Pulping System, Type: DIP
  Recycled Fiber Treatment Lines:
  Flotation deinking lines: 1
  Recycled packaging pulping lines: 1
Paper/Paperboard Grades and Capacities:
  Total paper and paperboard capacity: 90,000 mt/y
  Boxboard/cartonboard: 90,000 mt/y
Paper and Paperboard Mill Data:
Paper Machines: 1
No. 1, Multi-wire (5), total capacity 90,000 mt/y, Trim width 2.88 m, Boxboard/cartonboard
Coating Machines: 1
PM#1, on machine
Finishing Equipment:
  Winders: 2
  Rewinders: 1
Energy Data:
Power boilers: 1
Electrical demand for mill: 133 MWh/D

ⓞⓜZhejiang Wenfeng Paper Co., Ltd.
Fuyang Mill
Ownership: 100% by private owners
Fengtian Village, Chunjiang Street
Fuyang, Zhejiang, 311421
China
  Phone: (86) 571 6358 0922/ 2328 7799
  Fax: (86) 571 6358 2928/ 0933
  Email: pgjwyeaps@vip.163.com
  Web Address: www.wfpaper.com
Personnel:
  Pres. & Gen. Mgr.: Guanyu Dong
  Phone: (86) 571 6358 0922/ 2328 7799
Total Employees at this Location: 580
Type of Operation: Paperboard mill
Pulp Grades and Capacities:
  Total pulp capacity: 69,612 mt/y
  Recycled Pulping: 69,612 mt/y
Pulp Mill Data:
Pulp Lines: 3
  Recycled Fiber Treatment Lines:
  Recycled packaging pulping lines: 3 at 75,000 admt/y
Paper/Paperboard Grades and Capacities:
  Total paper and paperboard capacity: 75,000 mt/y
  Boxboard/cartonboard: 75,000 mt/y
Paper and Paperboard Mill Data:
Paper Machines: 1
No. 1, Multi-wire (5), total capacity 75,000 mt/y, Trim width 2.8 m, Boxboard/cartonboard

ⓜZhejiang Winbon Special Paper Co. Ltd.
Quzhou Mill
Ownership: Zhejiang Welbon Pulp & Paper Group
No. 1 Jinxing Rd., Longyou County Economy & Industry District
Quzhou, Zhejiang, 324400
China
  Phone: (86) 570 7055 822
  Fax: (86) 570 7055 818
  Email: zjhuabang@vip.163.com
  Web Address: www.winbonpaper.com/index.asp
Personnel:
  Chmn.: Shunhu Xu

China

Phone: (86) 571 8721 8800
Vice Chmn.: Xiaoyan Hu
Phone: (86) 571 8721 8800
Vice Gen. Mgr.: Min Li
Phone: (86) 571 8721 8800
Total Employees at this Location: 250
Type of Operation: Paper mill
Paper/Paperboard Grades and Capacities:
  Total paper and paperboard capacity: 91,260 mt/y
  Uncoated woodfree/freesheet: 3,927 mt/y
  Packaging papers: 2,856 mt/y
  Specialty and industrial: 84,477 mt/y
Paper and Paperboard Mill Data:
Paper Machines: 5
  No. 1, fourdrinier, total capacity 12,852 mt/y, Trim width 2.4 m, Specialty and industrial, Uncoated woodfree/freesheet
  No. 2, fourdrinier, total capacity 7,140 mt/y, Trim width 1.76 m, Specialty and industrial, Packaging papers
  No. 3, fourdrinier, total capacity 32,130 mt/y, Trim width 2.4 m, Specialty and industrial
  No. 4, fourdrinier, total capacity 12,138 mt/y, Trim width 1.88 m, Specialty and industrial
  No. 5, fourdrinier, total capacity 27,000 mt/y, Trim width 3.2 m, Specialty and industrial
Energy Data:
  Power boilers
  Electrical demand for mill: 159 MWh/D

⊕Zhejiang Wuxing Paper Co., Ltd

No.1, Donggang No.4 Rd, Shangmiao Village, Kecheng District
Quzhou City, Zhejiang, 324000
China
  Phone: (86) 570 858 8033/ 856 6100/ 6044
  Fax: (86) 570 383 1071
  Email: wx@zjwxzy.com
  Web Address: www.zjwxzy.com
Personnel:
  Chmn.: Yunfu Zhao
Mill Locations:
  Zhejiang Wuxing Paper Co., Ltd, Quzhou Mill, No.1, Donggang No.4 Rd, Shangmiao Village, Kecheng District, Quzhou 324000, China, Capacity: 150,000 mt/y, (Paper mill)
  Phone: (86) 570 858 8033/ 856 6100/ 6044
  Fax: (86) 570 383 1071
  Email: wx@zjwxzy.com
  Zhejiang Wuzhou Specialty Paper Co., Ltd., Quzhou (Zhejiang Wuzhou Specialty Paper) Mill, No.2, Tongbo North Rd., Quzhou, China, Capacity: 180,000 mt/y, (Paper mill)
  Phone: (86) 570 8566 022/8877 300
  Email: fivestarpaper@fivestarpaper.com

ⓂZhejiang Wuxing Paper Co., Ltd
Quzhou Mill

No.1, Donggang No.4 Rd, Shangmiao Village, Kecheng District
Quzhou, Zhejiang, 324000
China
  Phone: (86) 570 858 8033/ 856 6100/ 6044
  Fax: (86) 570 383 1071
  Email: wx@zjwxzy.com
  Web Address: www.zjwxzy.com
Personnel:
  Chmn.: Yunfu Zhao
Total Employees at this Location: 200
Type of Operation: Paper mill
Paper/Paperboard Grades and Capacities:
  Total paper and paperboard capacity: 150,000 mt/y
  Boxboard/cartonboard: 150,000 mt/y
Paper and Paperboard Mill Data:
Paper Machines: 1
  No. 3, fourdrinier (3), total capacity 150,000 mt/y, Trim width 3.4 m, Boxboard/cartonboard
Energy Data:
  Electrical demand for mill: 222 MWh/D

⊕ⓂZhejiang Wuzhou Specialty Paper Co., Ltd.
Quzhou (Zhejiang Wuzhou Specialty Paper) Mill

Ownership: 100% by Zhejiang Wuxing Paper Co., Ltd
No.2, Tongbo North Rd.
Quzhou, Zhejiang
China
  Phone: (86) 570 8566 022/8877 300
  Email: fivestarpaper@fivestarpaper.com
  Web Address: www.fivestarpaper.com
Type of Operation: Paper mill
Paper/Paperboard Grades and Capacities:
  Total paper and paperboard capacity: 180,000 mt/y
  Specialty and industrial: 80,000 mt/y
  Boxboard/cartonboard: 100,000 mt/y
Paper and Paperboard Mill Data:
Paper Machines: 4
  No. 1, fourdrinier, total capacity 25,000 mt/y, Trim width 2.4 m, Specialty and industrial
  No. 2, fourdrinier, total capacity 5,000 mt/y, Trim width 1.8 m, Specialty and industrial
  No. 3, fourdrinier, total capacity 50,000 mt/y, Trim width 3.4 m, Specialty and industrial
  No. 4, fourdrinier (3), total capacity 100,000 mt/y, Trim width 2.8 m, Boxboard/cartonboard
Finishing Equipment:
  Calenders
  Supercalenders
Energy Data:
  Electrical demand for mill: 241 MWh/D

⊕Zhejiang Xianglong Paper Co., Ltd.

Ownership: 100% by private owners
Chunjiang Street, Huagong Village
Fuyang, Zhejiang, 311421
China
  Phone: (86) 571 6315 3862
  Fax: (86) 571 6358 3863
Personnel:
  Pres. & Gen. Mgr.: Wenfu Zhao
  Phone: (86) 571 6358 7626/ 7917/ 7931
  Sls. Mgr.: Shiming Chen
  Phone: (86) 571 6358 7626/ 7917/ 7931
Mill Locations:
  Zhejiang Xianglong Paper Co., Ltd., Fuyang (Zhejiang Xianglong) Mill, Chunjiang Street, Huagong Village, Fuyang 311421, China, Capacity: 60,000 mt/y, (Paperboard mill)
  Phone: (86) 571 6315 3862
  Fax: (86) 571 6358 3863

ⓂZhejiang Xianglong Paper Co., Ltd.
Fuyang (Zhejiang Xianglong) Mill

Chunjiang Street, Huagong Village
Fuyang, Zhejiang, 311421
China
  Phone: (86) 571 6315 3862
  Fax: (86) 571 6358 3863
  Web Address: www.zjytpaper.net
Personnel:
  Pres. & Gen. Mgr.: Wenfu Zhao
  Phone: (86) 571 6358 7626/ 7917/ 7931
  Sls. Mgr.: Shiming Chen
  Phone: (86) 571 6358 7626/ 7917/ 7931
Total Employees at this Location: 230
Type of Operation: Paperboard mill
Pulp Grades and Capacities:
  Total pulp capacity: 54,390 mt/y
  Recycled Pulping: 54,390 mt/y
Pulp Mill Data:
Pulp Lines: 3
  Recycled Fiber Treatment Lines:
  Recycled packaging pulping lines: 3 at 60,000 admt/y
Paper/Paperboard Grades and Capacities:
  Total paper and paperboard capacity: 60,000 mt/y
  Boxboard/cartonboard: 60,000 mt/y
Paper and Paperboard Mill Data:
Paper Machines: 1
  No. 1, Multi-wire (5), total capacity 60,000 mt/y, Trim width 2.76 m, Boxboard/cartonboard
Energy Data:
  Electrical demand for mill: 89 MWh/D

⊕ⓂZhejiang Xianhe Specialty Paper
Quzhou Mill

Ownership: 100% by shareholders
81 Tongjiang Rd., Shenjia Development Zone
Quzhou, Zhejiang, 324022
China
  Phone: (86) 570 293 3109/ 1266
  Fax: (86) 570 293 1631/ 1266
  Web Address: www.xianhepaper.com
Personnel:
  Pres.: Minliang Wang
  Phone: (86) 570 293 1266
Total Employees of Company: 800
Type of Operation: Paper mill
Mill Locations:
  Henan Neixiang Xianhe Special Paper & Pulp Co., Ltd., Nanyang Mill, Neixiang County Industry District, Neixiang County, Nanyang 473000, China, Capacity: 99,960 mt/y, (Pulp mill, Paper mill)
  Phone: (86) 377 6532 7302/ 6531 3171
  Fax: (86) 377 6531 5570
  Kingdecor (Zhejiang) Co., Ltd., Quzhou Mill (50% owned), No. 158 Tongjiang Rd., Qujiang District, Quzhou 324022, China, Capacity: 90,000 mt/y, (Paper mill)
  Phone: (86) 570 8507 888/8575 739/8575 738
  Fax: (86) 570 8575 729
  Email: info@kingdecor.cn
Paper/Paperboard Grades and Capacities:
  Total paper and paperboard capacity: 180,000 mt/y
  Specialty and industrial: 180,000 mt/y
Paper and Paperboard Mill Data:
Paper Machines: 15
  No. 1, fourdrinier, Trim width 1.88 m, Specialty and industrial
  No. 2, fourdrinier, Trim width 1.88 m, Specialty and industrial
  No. 3, Trim width 1.6 m, Specialty and industrial
  No. 5, fourdrinier, Trim width 1.8 m, Specialty and industrial
  No. 6, fourdrinier, Trim width 1.73 m, Specialty and industrial
  No. 7, Trim width 1.76 m, Specialty and industrial
  No. 8, Trim width 2.1 m, Specialty and industrial
  No. 9, Trim width 2.64 m, Specialty and industrial
  No. 10, Trim width 2.64 m, Specialty and industrial
  No. 11, Trim width 2.75 m, Specialty and industrial
  No. 12, Trim width 2.8 m, Specialty and industrial
  No. 15, Trim width 2.8 m, Specialty and industrial
  No. 16, total capacity 30,000 mt/y, Trim width 4.15 m, Specialty and industrial
  No. 17, total capacity 30,000 mt/y, Trim width 4.4 m, Specialty and industrial
  No. 18, total capacity 30,000 mt/y, Trim width 4.4 m, Specialty and industrial
Coating Machines: 3
  No. 1
  No. 2
  No. 3
Energy Data:
  Power boilers: 2
  Steam turbines: 2 at 3, 7.5 MW

ⓂZhejiang Yiwu City Huachuan Paper Co., Ltd.
Yiwu Mill

Ownership: 100% by Zhejiang Huachuan Industrial Group
No. 72 South Huachuan Rd., Chian Town
Yiwu, Zhejiang, 322003
China
  Phone: (86) 579 577 5156/ 5458

China

Fax: (86) 579 577 5625
Web Address: www.huachuangroup.net
Personnel:
Chmn.: Chaoxing Feng
Gen. Mgr.: Xiaoyi Feng
Total Employees at this Location: 750
Type of Operation: Paper mill, Paperboard mill
Pulp Grades and Capacities:
Total pulp capacity: 126,432 mt/y
Recycled Pulping: 126,432 mt/y
Paper/Paperboard Grades and Capacities:
Total paper and paperboard capacity: 199,265 mt/y
Specialty and industrial: 64,265 mt/y
Corrugating medium/fluting: 100,000 mt/y
Boxboard/cartonboard: 35,000 mt/y
Paper and Paperboard Mill Data:
Paper Machines: 8
No. 9, fourdrinier, total capacity 12,000 mt/y, Trim width 2.36 m, Specialty and industrial
No. 10, fourdrinier, total capacity 14,280 mt/y, Trim width 2.36 m, Specialty and industrial
No. 11, cylinder (6), total capacity 35,000 mt/y, Trim width 2.4 m, Boxboard/cartonboard
No. 13, fourdrinier, total capacity 50,000 mt/y, Trim width 3.2 m, Corrugating medium/fluting
No. 14, fourdrinier, total capacity 7,997 mt/y, Trim width 1.88 m, Specialty and industrial
No. 15, fourdrinier, total capacity 50,000 mt/y, Trim width 3.2 m, Corrugating medium/fluting
No. 16, fourdrinier, total capacity 9,996 mt/y, Trim width 2.36 m, Specialty and industrial
No. 21, multi-wire, total capacity 19,992 mt/y, Trim width 2.4 m, Specialty and industrial
Energy Data:
Power boilers: 1
Steam turbines: 1 at 12 MW
Electrical demand for mill: 176 MWh/D

Ⓜ Zhejiang Yiwu City YiNan Paper Co., Ltd.
Yiwu Mill
Ownership: 100% by Zhejiang Huachuan Industrial Group
ChiAn No. 4 Village
Yiwu, Zhejiang, 322003
China
Phone: (86) 579 577 7399/ 6518/ 6512
Fax: (86) 579 577 5068
Web Address: www.huachuangroup.net
Personnel:
Chmn. & Pres.: Chaoxing Feng
Phone: (86) 579 577 7399/ 6518/ 6512
Gen. Mgr.: Tong Zhu
Phone: (86) 579 577 7399/ 6518/ 6512
Sls. Mgr.: Pinghong Zhu
Phone: (86) 579 577 7399/ 6518/ 6512
Finan. Mgr.: Xianwen Cheng
Phone: (86) 579 577 7399/ 6518/ 6512
Total Employees at this Location: 400
Type of Operation: Paper mill, Paperboard mill
Pulp Grades and Capacities:
Total pulp capacity: 235,682 mt/y
Recycled Pulping: 235,682 mt/y
Pulp Mill Data:
Pulp Lines: 2
Paper/Paperboard Grades and Capacities:
Total paper and paperboard capacity: 275,000 mt/y
Uncoated woodfree/freesheet: 35,000 mt/y
Linerboard: 60,000 mt/y
Corrugating medium/fluting: 150,000 mt/y
Boxboard/cartonboard: 30,000 mt/y
Paper and Paperboard Mill Data:
Paper Machines: 4
No. 17, Fourdrinier (4), total capacity 60,000 mt/y, Trim width 3.2 m, Linerboard
No. 18, fourdrinier, total capacity 35,000 mt/y, Trim width 3.6 m, Uncoated woodfree/freesheet
No. 19, fourdrinier (2), total capacity 150,000 mt/y, Trim width 4.8 m, Corrugating medium/fluting

No. 20, cylinder, total capacity 30,000 mt/y, Trim width 2.4 m, Boxboard/cartonboard
Energy Data:
Electrical demand for mill: 401 MWh/D

Ⓜ Zhejiang Yongjin Paper Co., Ltd.
Ownership: 100% by JV
Linjiang Village, Chunjiang Street
Fuyang, Zhejiang, 311421
China
Phone: (86) 571 6315 1236
Fax: (86) 571 6315 1222
Web Address: www.zjyjpaper.cn
Mill Locations:
Zhejiang Yongjin Paper Co., Ltd., Fuyang Mill, Linjiang Village, Chunjiang Street, Fuyang 311421, China, Capacity: 99,960 mt/y, (Paperboard mill)
Phone: (86) 571 6315 1236
Fax: (86) 571 6315 1222

Ⓜ Zhejiang Yongjin Paper Co., Ltd.
Fuyang Mill
Linjiang Village, Chunjiang Street
Fuyang, Zhejiang, 311421
China
Phone: (86) 571 6315 1236
Fax: (86) 571 6315 1222
Web Address: www.zjyjpaper.cn
Personnel:
Pres.: Yihong Yu
Phone: (86) 571 6315 1236
Sls. Mgr.: Jianxing Lu
Phone: (86) 571 6315 1236
Total Employees at this Location: 270
Type of Operation: Paperboard mill
Pulp Grades and Capacities:
Total pulp capacity: 86,256 mt/y
Recycled Pulping: 86,256 mt/y
Pulp Mill Data:
Bleach Plant Systems: 1
DIP
Recycled Fiber Treatment Lines:
Flotation deinking lines: 1
Paper/Paperboard Grades and Capacities:
Total paper and paperboard capacity: 99,960 mt/y
Boxboard/cartonboard: 99,960 mt/y
Paper and Paperboard Mill Data:
Paper Machines: 1
No. 1, Fourdrinier (5), total capacity 99,960 mt/y, Trim width 2.8 m, Boxboard/cartonboard
Coating Machines: 1
PM1, on machine
Energy Data:
Electrical demand for mill: 139 MWh/D

ⓄⓂ Zhejiang Yongtai Paper Group Co., Ltd.
Fuyang Mill
Ownership: 100% by shareholders
Fuyang Street, Xinjian Village
Fuyang, Zhejiang, 311421
China
Phone: (86) 571 6358 1001/ 7919/ 3521/ 3522
Fax: (86) 571 6358 3055/ 1426
Email: yttrans@vip.sohu.com
Personnel:
Chmn. & Pres./Mill Mgr.: Baigui Sun
Phone: (86) 571 6358 1001/ 7919/ 3521/ 3522
Vice Chmn. /VP: Xueqing Su
Phone: (86) 571 6358 1001/ 7919/ 3521/ 3522
Dir. & VP/Asst. Mill Mgr.: Yunan Zhao
Phone: (86) 571 6358 1001/ 7919/ 3521/ 3522
Dir. & VP/Operation: Jinlai Zhang
Phone: (86) 571 6358 1001/ 7919/ 3521/ 3522
VP-Tech: Xianzhong Chen
Phone: (86) 571 6358 1001/ 7919/ 3521/ 3522
VP: Weimin Zhang
Phone: (86) 571 6358 1001/ 7919/ 3521/ 3522

Total Employees at this Location: 1,235
Type of Operation: Paperboard mill
Pulp Grades and Capacities:
Total pulp capacity: 405,450 mt/y
Recycled Pulping: 405,450 mt/y
Pulp Mill Data:
Pulp Lines: 5
Recycled Fiber Treatment Lines:
Flotation deinking lines: 2 at 80,000 admt/y
Recycled packaging pulping lines: 3 at 180,000 admt/y
Paper/Paperboard Grades and Capacities:
Total paper and paperboard capacity: 491,232 mt/y
Specialty and industrial: 1,428 mt/y
Boxboard/cartonboard: 489,804 mt/y
Paper and Paperboard Mill Data:
Stock Preparation:
Refiners: 8
Paper Machines: 8
No. 1, pressure former, total capacity 14,994 mt/y, Trim width 1.58 m, Boxboard/cartonboard
No. 2, cylinder, total capacity 19,992 mt/y, Trim width 1.58 m, Boxboard/cartonboard
No. 3, Multi-wire (5), total capacity 69,972 mt/y, Trim width 2.88 m, Boxboard/cartonboard
No. 6, Multi-wire (5), total capacity 14,994 mt/y, Trim width 1.58 m, Boxboard/cartonboard
No. 7, (Owned by Zhejiang Yongli Paper), Multi-wire (5), total capacity 69,972 mt/y, Trim width 2.4 m, Boxboard/cartonboard
No. 8, (owned by Zhejiang Yonghong Paper), fourdrinier, total capacity 99,960 mt/y, Trim width 3.4 m, Boxboard/cartonboard
No. 9, DuoFormer D, total capacity 1,428 mt/y, Trim width 1.4 m, Specialty and industrial
No. 10, Multi-wire (4), total capacity 199,920 mt/y, Trim width 4.8 m, Boxboard/cartonboard
Finishing Equipment:
Rewinders: 3
Sheeters: 4
Energy Data:
Power boilers: 6
Steam turbines: 5 at 12, 24, 24 MW
Electrical demand for mill: 731 MWh/D

ⓄⓂ Zhejiang Zhengda Holding Group Co., Ltd.
Fuyang Mill
Ownership: 100% by private owners
No. 1 Chunlian Industry Zone, Chunjiang Street
Fuyang, Zhejiang, 311421
China
Phone: (86) 571 6358 7199/7222
Fax: (86) 571 6358 7799
Email: info@zhengda-paper.com
Web Address: www.zhengda-paper.com
Personnel:
Chmn.: Shaojian Yang
Phone: (86) 571 6358 7199/7222
Pres.: Wenzhong Wang
Phone: (86) 571 6358 7199/7222
VP & Sls. Mgr.: Linfa Sun
Phone: (86) 571 6358 7199/7222
Total Employees of Company: 2,000
Total Employees at this Location: 1,200
Type of Operation: Paperboard mill
Mill Locations:
Zhejiang Hongsheng Paper Co., Ltd., Fuyang (Zhejiang Hongsheng Paper) Mill, Chunjiang Industry Zone, Fuyang 311421, China, Capacity: 85,000 mt/y, (Paperboard mill)
Phone: (86) 571 6315 0969
Fax: (86) 571 6358 7578
Zhejiang Wenbo Paper Co., Ltd., Fuyang (Zhejiang Wenbo Paper) Mill, Chunjiang Industry Zone, Fuyang 311421, China, Capacity: 90,000 mt/y, (Paperboard mill)
Phone: (86) 571 6358 7986
Fax: (86) 571 6358 7717
Pulp Grades and Capacities:

Fiji

Total pulp capacity: 490,754 mt/y
Recycled Pulping: 490,754 mt/y
Pulp Mill Data:
Recycled Fiber Treatment Lines:
Recycled packaging pulping lines: 3 at 120,000 admt/y
Paper/Paperboard Grades and Capacities:
Total paper and paperboard capacity: 600,117 mt/y
Corrugating medium/fluting: 25,347 mt/y
Boxboard/cartonboard: 574,770 mt/y
Paper and Paperboard Mill Data:
Paper Machines: 8
No. 1, multi-wire, total capacity 91,035 mt/y, Trim width 2.88 m, Boxboard/cartonboard
No. 2, cylinder, total capacity 14,637 mt/y, Trim width 1.58 m, Boxboard/cartonboard
No. 3, multi-wire, total capacity 14,280 mt/y, Trim width 1.76 m, Boxboard/cartonboard
No. 4, multi-wire, total capacity 14,637 mt/y, Trim width 1.88 m, Boxboard/cartonboard
No. 5, multi-wire, total capacity 49,980 mt/y, Trim width 2 m, Boxboard/cartonboard
No. 6, multi-wire, total capacity 25,347 mt/y, Trim width 2.7 m, Corrugating medium/fluting
No. 7, multi-wire, total capacity 89,964 mt/y, Trim width 2.57 m, Boxboard/cartonboard
No. 8, Multi-wire (4), total capacity 300,237 mt/y, Trim width 4.4 m, Boxboard/cartonboard
Energy Data:
Electrical demand for mill: 958 MWh/D

ⓗZhejiang Zhenghua Paper Co., Ltd.
No.689, Dongfang Rd., Yaozhuang Town, Jiashan County
Jiaxing, Zhejiang, 314100
China
 Phone: (86) 573 8910 3888
 Fax: (86) 573 8910 3699
 Email: info@zhenghuazy.com
 Web Address: www.zjzhenghua.com
Mill Locations:
Zhejiang Hongan Paper Co., Ltd., Jiaxing Mill, No.529, Dongfang Rd., Yanzhuang Town, Jiashan County, Jiaxing 314103, China, Capacity: 100,000 mt/y, (Paper mill)
 Phone: (86) 573 8484 6866
 Fax: (86) 573 8484 6853
Zhejiang Zhenghua Paper Co., Ltd., Jiaxing Mill, No.689, Dongfang Rd., Yaozhuang Town, Jiashan County, Jiaxing 314100, China, Capacity: 30,500 mt/y, (Paper mill)
 Phone: (86) 573 8910 3888
 Fax: (86) 573 8910 3699
 Email: info@zhenghuazy.com

ⓜZhejiang Zhenghua Paper Co., Ltd.
Jiaxing Mill
No.689, Dongfang Rd., Yaozhuang Town, Jiashan County
Jiaxing, Zhejiang, 314100
China
 Phone: (86) 573 8910 3888
 Fax: (86) 573 8910 3699
 Email: info@zhenghuazy.com
 Web Address: www.zhenghuazy.com
Type of Operation: Paper mill
Paper/Paperboard Grades and Capacities:
Total paper and paperboard capacity: 30,500 mt/y
Tissue: 30,500 mt/y
Paper and Paperboard Mill Data:
Paper Machines: 20
PM 1, total capacity 1,400 mt/y, Trim width 1.76 m, Tissue
PM 2, total capacity 1,400 mt/y, Trim width 1.76 m, Tissue
PM 3, total capacity 1,400 mt/y, Trim width 1.76 m, Tissue
PM 4, total capacity 1,400 mt/y, Trim width 1.76 m, Tissue
PM 5, total capacity 1,400 mt/y, Trim width 1.76 m, Tissue
PM 6, total capacity 1,400 mt/y, Trim width 1.76 m, Tissue
PM 7, total capacity 1,400 mt/y, Trim width 1.76 m, Tissue
PM 8, total capacity 1,400 mt/y, Trim width 1.76 m, Tissue
PM 9, total capacity 1,400 mt/y, Trim width 1.76 m, Tissue
PM 10, total capacity 1,400 mt/y, Trim width 1.76 m
PM 11, total capacity 1,650 mt/y, Trim width 1.88 m, Tissue
PM 12, total capacity 1,650 mt/y, Trim width 1.88 m, Tissue
PM 13, total capacity 1,650 mt/y, Trim width 1.88 m, Tissue
PM 14, total capacity 1,650 mt/y, Trim width 1.88 m, Tissue
PM 15, total capacity 1,650 mt/y, Trim width 1.88 m, Tissue
PM 16, total capacity 1,650 mt/y, Trim width 1.88 m, Tissue
PM 17, total capacity 1,650 mt/y, Trim width 1.88 m, Tissue
PM 18, total capacity 1,650 mt/y, Trim width 1.88 m, Tissue
PM 19, total capacity 1,650 mt/y, Trim width 1.88 m, Tissue
PM 20, total capacity 1,650 mt/y, Trim width 1.88 m, Tissue

FIJI

ⓗSouth Pacific Waste Recyclers
5 Bulei Road, Laucala Beach Estate
Nabua, Suva
Fiji
 Phone: (679) 361 055, 334 1115
 Fax: (679) 361 480
 Email: spwr@cjsgroup.com.fj
 Web Address: www.cjsgroup.com.fj/spwr/index.html
Personnel:
Chrmn & MD: Charan Jeath Singh
 Phone: (679) 361 055
 Fax: (679) 361 480
Mill Locations:
South Pacific Waste Recyclers, Nabua Mill, 5 Bulei Road, Laucala Beach Estate, Nabua, Suva, Fiji, Capacity: 700 mt/y, (Paper mill)
 Phone: (679) 361 055
 Fax: (679) 361 480

ⓜSouth Pacific Waste Recyclers
Nabua Mill
5 Bulei Road, Laucala Beach Estate
Nabua, Suva
Fiji
 Phone: (679) 361 055
 Fax: (679) 361 480
Personnel:
Chrmn & MD: Charan Jeath Singh
Type of Operation: Paper mill
Paper/Paperboard Grades and Capacities:
Total paper and paperboard capacity: 700 mt/y
Tissue: 700 mt/y

GEORGIA

ⓗNeo-Print
Tserovani
380036 Tbilisi
Georgia
 Phone: (995) 995 32 528692 / 529022 / 725845
 Fax: (995) 995 32 528692
 Email: neoprint@caucasus.net
Personnel:
Dir.: Archil Faradze
 Phone: (995) 995 32 528692 / 529022 / 725845
 Fax: (995) 995 32 528692
Chief Acc.: Khatuna
 Phone: (995) 995 32 528692 / 529022 / 725845
 Fax: (995) 995 32 528692
Total Employees at this Location: 75
Mill Locations:
Neo-Print, Tbilisi Mill, Tserovani, 380036 Tbilisi, Georgia, Capacity: 3,500 mt/y, (Paper mill)
 Phone: (995) 995 32 528692 / 529022 / 725845
 Fax: (995) 995 32 528692
 Email: neoprint@caucasus.net

ⓜNeo-Print
Tbilisi Mill
Tserovani
380036 Tbilisi
Georgia
 Phone: (995) 995 32 528692 / 529022 / 725845
 Fax: (995) 995 32 528692
 Email: neoprint@caucasus.net
Personnel:
Dir.: Archil Faradze
 Phone: (995) 3272 5845
Total Employees at this Location: 75
Type of Operation: Paper mill
Paper/Paperboard Grades and Capacities:
Total paper and paperboard capacity: 3,500 mt/y
Uncoated woodfree/freesheet: 3,500 mt/y
Coated woodfree/freesheet
Specialty and industrial
Paper and Paperboard Mill Data:
Paper Machines: 1
No. 1, (started up September 2009), total capacity 3,500 mt/y, Trim width 1.2 m, Uncoated woodfree/freesheet, Coated woodfree/freesheet, Specialty and industrial
Energy Data:
Power boilers: 1
Steam turbines: 1
Electrical demand for mill: 7 MWh/D

ⓗRuloni
Chachava Str. 2-12
0159 Tbilisi
Georgia
 Phone: (995) 3251 7194
 Email: ruloni@live.com
 Web Address: ruloni.wordpress.com
Personnel:
Gen. Dir.: Teimuraz Janjalia
 Phone: (995) 3251 7194
Total Employees at this Location: 30
Mill Locations:
Ruloni, Tbilisi Mill, Chachava Str. 2-12, 0159 Tbilisi, Georgia, Capacity: 2,000 mt/y, (Paperboard mill)
 Phone: (995) 3251 7194
 Email: ruloni@live.com

ⓜRuloni
Tbilisi Mill
Chachava Str. 2-12
0159 Tbilisi
Georgia
 Phone: (995) 3251 7194
 Email: ruloni@live.com
 Web Address: ruloni.wordpress.com
Personnel:
Gen. Dir.: Teimuraz Janjalia
 Phone: (995) 99574140
Total Employees at this Location: 30
Type of Operation: Paperboard mill
Paper/Paperboard Grades and Capacities:
Total paper and paperboard capacity: 2,000 mt/y
Linerboard: 2,000 mt/y
Corrugating medium/fluting
Paper and Paperboard Mill Data:
Paper Machines: 1
No. 1, total capacity 2,000 mt/y, Trim width 1.52 m, Linerboard, Corrugating medium/fluting
Energy Data:
Electrical demand for mill: 3 MWh/D

HONG KONG

ⓗFook Woo Group
Ownership: 100% by private owners
Fook Woo Group Building, 3 Kui Sik Street, On Lok Tsuen
Fanling
Hong Kong
 Phone: (852) 2676 8700 / 8800
 Fax: (852) 2796 7158 / 2798 0954
 Email: info@fookwoo.com,

Hong Kong

cs@cmds.com.hk
Web Address: www.fookwoo.com
Mill Locations:
Guangdong Huizhou Fook Woo Paper Co., Ltd., Huizhou Mill, Liangwu District, Boluo County, Yuanzhou Town, Huizhou 516123, China, Capacity: 55,000 mt/y, (Paper mill)
Phone: (86) 752 681 2888
Fax: (86) 752 681 2628

⊕Hop Fung Group Holdings Limited
Block 22 E, F & H, Phase 2, Superluck Industry Centre, 57 Sha Tsui Rd.
Tsuen Wan
Hong Kong
Phone: (852) 2416 8100
Fax: (852) 2414 5508/ 2402 4140
Email: hopfung@hupfunggroup.com
Web Address: www.hopfunggroup.com
Personnel:
Chmn.: Sum Kwok Hui
Phone: (852) 2416 8100
Fax: (852) 2414 5508/ 2402 4140
Vice Chmn.: Sum Ping Hui
Phone: (852) 2416 8100
Fax: (852) 2414 5508/ 2402 4140
CEO, Exec. Dir.: Sum Tai Hui
Phone: (852) 2416 8100
Fax: (852) 2414 5508/ 2402 4140
Comp. Sec., Exec. Dir.: Yuen Li Hui
Phone: (852) 2416 8100
Fax: (852) 2414 5508/ 2402 4140
Exec. Dir.: Wing Por Wong
Phone: (852) 2416 8100
Fax: (852) 2414 5508/ 2402 4140
Dpty. Gen. Mgr.: Mui Wong
Phone: (852) 2416 8100
Fax: (852) 2414 5508/ 2402 4140
Project Mgr.: Fu Keung Yuen
Phone: (852) 2416 8100
Fax: (852) 2414 5508/ 2402 4140
Acco. Mgr.: Yuk Kwan Wong
Phone: (852) 2416 8100
Fax: (852) 2414 5508/ 2402 4140
Indep. Non-Exec. Dir.: Kwok Fai Liu
Phone: (852) 2416 8100
Fax: (852) 2414 5508/ 2402 4140
Indep. Non-Exec. Dir.: Man Sang Chee
Phone: (852) 2416 8100
Fax: (852) 2414 5508/ 2402 4140
Mill Locations:
Guangdong Green Forest (QingXin) Paper Industrial Limited, Qingyuan Mill, Green Forest Industrial Town, Taihe Industrial District, Qingxin County, Qingyuan 511850, China, Capacity: 349,860 mt/y, (Paperboard mill)
Phone: (86) 763 538 3348/ 3999
Fax: (86) 763 538 3358
Email: fkhf@hopfunggroup.com, gfgx@hopfunggroup.com.cn

⊕Lee & Man Paper Manufacturing Ltd.
Ownership: 53.92% by Gold Best Holdings Ltd., 12% by Nippon Paper Industries Co., Ltd.
5/F, Liven House, 61-63 King Yip Street, Kwun Tong
Kowloon
Hong Kong
Phone: (852) 23199889
Fax: (852) 23199393
Web Address: www.leemanpaper.com
Personnel:
CEO & Man. Dir.: Raymond Man Chun Lee
Phone: (852) 23199889
Fax: (852) 23199393
Exec. Dir. & Gen. Mgr. (Production, Sls, Oper, R&D, Maint): Edmond Man Bun Lee
Phone: (852) 23199889
Fax: (852) 23199393
Exec. Dir.: Kunihiko Kashima
Phone: (852) 23199889
Fax: (852) 23199393
Exec. Dir. (July 1, 2013): Ross King Wai Li
Phone: (852) 23199889
Fax: (852) 23199393
CFO & Company Sec.: Kwok Keung Cheung
Phone: (852) 23199889
Fax: (852) 23199393
Snr. Finan. Mgr.: Yuen Ling Li
Phone: (852) 23199889
Fax: (852) 23199393
Snr. Mgr. Global Procurement of Recovered Paper Bus.: Tse Pak Kong
Phone: (852) 23199889
Fax: (852) 23199393
Sls. & MKtg. Mgr.: Sau Ping Ping Lam
Phone: (852) 23199889
Fax: (852) 23199393
Snr. Prod. Mgr.: Chi Ho Chan
Phone: (852) 23199889
Fax: (852) 23199393
Total Employees of Company: 6,500
Mill Locations:
Chongqing Lee & Man Paper Co., Ltd., Chongqing Mill, Zhutuo Town, Yongchuan, Chongqing 402191, China, Capacity: 920,000 mt/y, (Pulp mill, Paper mill, Paperboard mill)
Phone: (86) 23 4960 3333
Fax: (86) 23 4960 3188
Chongqing Lee & Man Tissue Manufacturing Ltd., Chongqing Mill, Gangqiao Industrial Park, Zhutuo Town, Yongchuan, Chongqing 404100, China, Capacity: 30,000 mt/y, (Paper mill)
Phone: (86) 23 4960 3333
Guangdong Dongguan Hongmei Lee & Man Paper Co., Ltd., Dongguan (Hongmei) Mill, He Xi Industrial Park, Hongmei Town, Dongguan 523160, China, Capacity: 2,175,000 mt/y, (Paperboard mill)
Phone: (86) 769 8843 2168
Fax: (86) 769 8843 2188
Guangdong Dongguan Lee & Man Paper Co., Ltd., Dongguan (Huangyong) Mill, Huangyong Dist., Zhongtang Town, Dongguan 523221, China, Capacity: 670,000 mt/y, (Paperboard mill)
Phone: (86) 769 8888 8168
Fax: (86) 769 8889 9101/8888 5188
Email: info@leeman.com.hk
Jiangsu Lee & Man Paper Manufacturing Co. Ltd., Changshu Mill, Liwen Road, Yanjiang Industrial Park, Economic Development, Changshu 215536, China, Capacity: 1,350,600 mt/y, (Pulp mill, Paperboard mill)
Phone: (86) 512 5265 3333
Fax: (86) 512 5229 7118
Email: info@leemanpaper.com
Jiangxi Lee & Man Paper Co., Ltd., Ruichang Mill, Matou Town, Ruichang, China, Capacity: 320,000 mt/y, (Paper mill)
Vietnam Lee & Man Paper Manufacturing Ltd, Hau Giang Mill (75% owned), Chau Thanh district, Vietnam, Capacity: 400,000 mt/y, (Paper mill, Paperboard mill)

⊕Most China International Ltd.
Ownership: sino-foreign JV
Room 1602, 16/F Emperor Group Center 288, Hennessy Road
Hong Kong
Hong Kong
Phone: (852) 2545 5400
Fax: (852) 2543 5665
Email: npchk@netvigator.com
Personnel:
Man. Dir.: Wang Lei
Phone: (852) 2545 5400
Fax: (852) 2543 5665
Chief Accountant: Ms. Iris So
Phone: (852) 2545 5400
Fax: (852) 2543 5665
Total Employees of Company: 350
Total Employees at this Location: 10

⊕New Toyo Pulppy (Hong Kong) Limited
Ownership: 100% by Benline Investment Ltd. (Hong Kong)
Room 2804b, 28/F., Wu Chung House, 213 Queen's Road East
Wanchai, Hong Kong
Hong Kong
Phone: (852) 246 7 2173
Fax: (852) 245 4 0875
Email: info_hk@pulppy.com
Web Address: www.pulppy.com
Mill Locations:
New Toyo Pulppy (Vietnam) Co., Ltd., Thuan An District Mill, 8-VSIP, Str. 6, Vietnam-Singapore Industrial Park, Thuan An District, Vietnam, Capacity: 35,000 mt/y, (Paper mill)
Phone: (84) 650 374 3750
Fax: (84) 650 374 3754
Email: customerservice@pulppy.com
Pulppy Corelex (Vietnam), Hung Yen Mill, Pho Noi A Industrial Zone, Hung Yen, Vietnam, Capacity: 30,000 mt/y, (Paper mill)
Phone: (84) 4 3512 2601
Fax: (84) 4 3512 2602

⊕Nine Dragons Paper (Holdings) Ltd.
Ownership: 100% by private owners
Room 3129, 31/F., Sun Hung Kai Centre, 30 Harbour Road
Hong Kong
Hong Kong
Phone: (852) 3929 3800
Fax: (852) 3929 3890
Email: info_hk@ndpaper.com
Web Address: www.ndpaper.com
Personnel:
Chairlady: Yan Cheung
Phone: (852) 3929 3800
Fax: (852) 3929 3890
Depty. Chmn. & CEO: Ming Chung Liu
Phone: (852) 3929 3800
Fax: (852) 3929 3890
Exec. Dir. & Deputy CEO: Cheng Fei Zhang
Phone: (852) 3929 3800
Fax: (852) 3929 3890
Exec. Dir.: Chun Shun Lau
Phone: (852) 3929 3800
Fax: (852) 3929 3890
CFO & Exec. Dir.: Yuanfu Zhang
Phone: (852) 3929 3800
Fax: (852) 3929 3890
Total Employees of Company: 17,800
Mill Locations:
Cheng Yang Paper Mill Co., Ltd., Ben Cat Dist. (Cheng Yang Paper) Mill, D 15, My Phuoc Industrial Park, Ben Cat Dist, Vietnam, Capacity: 108,000 mt/y, (Paperboard mill)
Phone: (84) 650 3558006-8
Fax: (84) 650 3558009
Guangdong Dongguan Nine Dragons Paper Industries Co., Ltd., Dongguan Mill, Xinsha Port Industrial Zone, Mayong Town, Dongguan 523147, China, Capacity: 5,474,406 mt/y, (Paperboard mill)
Phone: (86) 769 8823 4888
Fax: (86) 769 8882 8111/4198
Email: info@ndpaper.com, sales@ndpaper.com
Hebei Yongxin Paper Co., Ltd., Tangshan (Hebei Yongxin) Mill (78.13% owned), No. 88 Guanxin Rd., Luannan County, Tangshan 063500, China, Capacity: 499,800 mt/y, (Paperboard mill)
Phone: (86) 315 411 0424
Fax: (86) 315 412 3486
Jiangsu Nine Dragons Paper Industries, Taicang Mill, JiuLong Road, Taicang Port Development Area, Taicang, China, Capacity: 3,021,291 mt/y, (Paperboard mill)
Phone: (86) 512 5370 3399
Fax: (86) 512 5370 3800/ 3751
Email: ndpaper@ndpaper.com.cn
Nine Dragons Pulp & Paper (Leshan) Co., Ltd., Leshan

India

Mill, Yanzhi Village, Qingxi Town, Qianwei County, Leshan 614005, China, Capacity: 311,700 mt/y, (Paper mill)
Phone: (86) 833 2299 999
Fax: (86) 833 2299 666

Nine Dragons Paper Industries (Chongqing) Co., Ltd., Chongqing Mill, Luohuang Industrial Park, Jiangjin Industry Park, Chongqing 402279, China, Capacity: 1,350,000 mt/y, (Paperboard mill)
Phone: (86) 23 6555 8888
Fax: (86) 23 6555 8999
Email: info_cq@ndpaper.com

Nine Dragons Paper Industries (Quanzhou) Co., Ltd., Quanzhou Mill, Quanzhou, China, Capacity: 650,000 mt/y, (Paperboard mill)
Email: info_group@ndpaper.com

Nine Dragons Paper (Tianjin) Co., Ltd., Tianjin Mill, Jiulong Rd., Economy & Development Zone, Ninghe County, Tianjin 301500, China, Capacity: 1,976,352 mt/y, (Paperboard mill)
Phone: (86) 22 6955 8585
Fax: (86) 22 6922 2139
Email: info@ndpaper.com, sales@ndpaper.com

Nine Dragons XingAn Paper Co., Ltd. (Inner Mongolia), Zhalantun Mill, No. 33, Zhijiang Street, Zhalantun 162650, China, Capacity: 14,994 mt/y, (Pulp mill, Paper mill)
Phone: (86) 470 330 2447
Fax: (86) 470 330 3820

ⓜSamson Paper Holdings Limited
Ownership: 90% by Universal Pulp & Paper Investments Ltd., 10% by Shenzhen Jialin Trading Company Limited
3rd Floor, Seapower Industrial Centre, 177 Hoi Bun Rd.,
Kwun Tong
Kowloon
Hong Kong
Phone: (852) 852 2342 7181
Fax: (852) 852 8147 0238
Email: info@samsonpaper.com, cs@samsonpaper.com
Web Address: www.samsonpaper.com

Personnel:
Chmn.: Kit Ying Sham
Phone: (852) 852 2342 7181
Fax: (852) 852 8147 0238
Deputy Chmn.: Seng Jin Lee
Phone: (852) 852 2342 7181
Fax: (852) 852 8147 0238
Exec. Dir.: Wing Kin, Patrick Pang
Phone: (852) 852 2342 7181
Fax: (852) 852 8147 0238

Total Employees of Company: 210
Mill Locations:
UPP Pulp & Paper (M) Sdn Bhd, Batang Berjuntai Mill, PO Box 225, Lot 225, Jalan Kuala Selangor, 45620 Ijok, Batang Berjuntai, Malaysia, Capacity: 85,000 mt/y, (Paper mill, Paperboard mill)
Phone: (60) 3 6038 6388
Fax: (60) 3 6038 5966
Email: sales.upb@upp-group.com

ⓜSateri Holdings Limited
Ownership: 98.39% by RGE International Group
21/F, China Building, 29 Queen's Road Central
Hong Kong
Hong Kong
Phone: (852) 2864 6638
Fax: (852) 2865 5499
Web Address: www.sateri.com

Personnel:
Chmn.: John Jeffrey Ying
Phone: (852) 2864 6638
Fax: (852) 2865 5499
CEO: Tey Wei Lin
Phone: (852) 2864 6638
Fax: (852) 2865 5499

Total Employees of Company: 2,425
Mill Locations:

Bahia Specialty Cellulose S.A. ("BSC"), Camaçari Mill, Rua Alfa 1033, AIN, COPEC, 42810-290 Camaçari, BA, Brazil, (Pulp mill)
Phone: (55) 71 3634 0401
Fax: (55) 71 3634 5462
Email: faleconosco@bahiaspeccell.com

ⓜVinda International Holdings Limited.
Company is for sale
Ownership: 51.40% by SCA - Svenska Cellulosa Aktiebolaget, 23.77% by FuAn International, 0.36% by others, 15.92% by the public
No. 506, 1 Nanyang Center, No. 75, Dongbumo Ave., Jianshazhui
529100 Kowloon
Hong Kong
Phone: (852) 2366 9853
Fax: (852) 2366 5805
Email: ir@vinda.com
Web Address: www.vindapaper.com

Personnel:
Exec. Chmn. of the board: Chao Wang Li
Phone: (852) 2366 9853
Fax: (852) 2782 5560
CEO, Exec. Dir.: Fang Zhang Dong
Phone: (852) 2366 9853
Fax: (852) 2782 5560
Exec. Vice Chmn. of the board: Fang Yu Yi
Phone: (852) 2366 9853
Fax: (852) 2782 5560
Chief Tech. Officer, Exec. Dir.: Ping Dong Yi
Phone: (852) 2366 9853
Fax: (852) 2782 5560
COO: Zhang Jian
Phone: (852) 2366 9853
Fax: (852) 2782 5560
acting CFO, Company Secretary: Ms. Tan Yi Yi
Phone: (852) 2366 9853
Fax: (852) 2782 5560
VP. Sales and Marketing: Xian He Hui
Phone: (852) 2366 9853
Fax: (852) 2782 5560
VP. Sales and Marketing: Jin Hu Yong
Phone: (852) 2366 9853
Fax: (852) 2782 5560
VP. Sales and Marketing: Tang Tang Hai

Total Employees of Company: 8,242
Mill Locations:
Beijing Vinda Paper (Beijing) Co., Ltd., Beijing Mill, No. 16, Hangyu Street, Binhe Industrial Park, Pinggu, Beijing 100023, China, Capacity: 30,000 mt/y, (Paper mill)
Phone: (86) 10 5822 0818
Fax: (86) 10 5822 0802

Guangdong Vinda Paper Co., Ltd., Sanjiang Mill, Bairniao Industrial Park, Sanjiang County, Xinhui District, Jiangmen 529100, China, Capacity: 107,250 mt/y, (Paper mill)

Guangdong Vinda Paper (Guangdong) Co., Ltd., Xinhui Mill, Donghou Industrial Zone, Huicheng Town, Xinhui 529100, China, Capacity: 57,000 mt/y, (Paper mill)
Phone: (86) 750 6122 846/6168 333
Fax: (86) 750 6120 239
Email: vd-computer@chinavinda.com

Guangdong Vinda Paper (Jiangmen) Co., Ltd., Jiangmen Mill, Yingbin Ave., Shuangshui Town, Xinhui Zone, Jiangmen 529100, China, Capacity: 120,000 mt/y, (Paper mill)
Phone: (86) 86 750 641 3111
Fax: (86) 86 750 641 3068

Hubei Vinda Paper (Hubei) Co., Ltd., Xiaogan Mill, Nanda Industry & Development Zone, Xiaonan District, Xiaogan 432100, China, Capacity: 180,000 mt/y, (Paper mill)
Phone: (86) 712 2519 099/ 007
Fax: (86) 712 2519 089

Vinda Paper (Sichuan) Co. Ltd., Deyang Mill, No. 19, three District, South Longquan Rd., Deyang 618000, China, Capacity: 45,000 mt/y, (Paper mill)
Phone: (86) 838 290 6199

Fax: (86) 838 290 6311

Vinda Paper (Shandong) Co., Ltd., Laiwu Mill, Laiwu Wenyang Industrial Park, Laiwu, China, Capacity: 50,000 mt/y, (Paper mill)
Phone: (86) 634 5628 881

Vinda Paper (Liaoning) Co., Ltd., Anshan Mill, Anshan Dadaowan Industry & Development Park, Anshan 114013, China, Capacity: 54,000 mt/y, (Paper mill)

Vinda Paper (Zhejiang) Co., Ltd., Quzhou Mill, No.9, Fengkun Rd., Longyou Industry Park, Longyou County, Quzhou 324000, China, Capacity: 90,000 mt/y, (Paper mill)
Phone: (86) 570 7788 888/808
Fax: (86) 570 7608 202

INDIA

ⓜAbhishek Industries Ltd.
Ownership: 100% by Public Limited Company
E-212, Kitchlu Nagar
141001 Dist. Ludhiana, Punjab
India
Phone: (91) 161 5038888/9999/2303333/11 23326666
Fax: (91) 161 5039900/11 23326667
Email: corp@tridentindia.com, paper@tridentindia.com
Web Address: www.tridentindia.com

Personnel:
CEO: Mr. Rajinder Gupta
Phone: (91) 161 2304444, 98 78999999
Fax: (91) 161 5038800
Email: rg@tridentindia.com
CFO: Arun Goyal
Phone: (91) 987 899 9991
Fax: (91) 161 5038800
Email: arungoyal@tridentindia.com
Bus. Head, Abhishek Paper: Rajeev Gupta
Phone: (91) 161 5038888/2303333/11 23326666
Fax: (91) 161 5038800
Email: rajeevgupta@tridentindia.com
Oper. Head: R. C. Johari
Phone: (91) 987 899 8376
Fax: (91) 161 503 8800
Email: rcjohari@tridentindia.com
Marketing Head: Naveet Jindal
Phone: (91) 987 899 8134
Fax: (91) 161 503 8800
Email: naveetjindal@tridentindia.com

Mill Locations:
Abhishek Industries Ltd., Barnala Mill, Trident Complex, Mansa Road, 148107 Dhaula, District Barnala, India, Capacity: 151,725 mt/y, (Pulp mill, Paper mill)
Phone: (91) 161 5038888/9999
Fax: (91) 161 5038800
Email: paperenquiry@tridentindia.com, corp@tridentindia.com

ⓜAbhishek Industries Ltd.
Barnala Mill
Trident Complex, Mansa Road
148107 Dhaula, District Barnala, Punjab
India
Phone: (91) 161 5038888/9999
Fax: (91) 161 5038800
Email: paperenquiry@tridentindia.com, corp@tridentindia.com
Web Address: www.tridentindia.com

Personnel:
Chief Executive (Paper Business): Ravij Mediratta
Phone: (91) 987 8997908
Fax: (91) 167 9885262
Head Engineering: Rajinder Shaunak
Phone: (91) 987 89997837
Email: rajindershaunak@tridentindia.com
HR & IR: Partha Bagachi
Phone: (91) 987 89997938

Email: parthabagchi@tridentindia.com
Head Pulp Mill: KP Reddy
Phone: (91) 987 8997898
Safety, Health & Environment: Niranjan Lal
Phone: (91) 987 8999137
Email: niranjanlal@tridentindia.com
Total Employees at this Location: 1,485
Type of Operation: Pulp mill, Paper mill
Pulp Grades and Capacities:
Total pulp capacity: 25,387 mt/y
Chemical Pulp: 25,387 mt/y

Pulp Mill Data:
Chemical Pulping Systems:
Batch digesters: 2
Continuous digesters: 2
Pulp Lines: 2
Bleach Plant Systems: 2
Straw Street, Wood Street, Sequence: O_2 DoEopD, Capacity 128,560 admt/y
Chemical Recovery Equipment:
Evaporator lines: 13
Recovery boilers: 2
Lime Kiln
Paper/Paperboard Grades and Capacities:
Total paper and paperboard capacity: 151,725 mt/y
Uncoated woodfree/freesheet: 151,725 mt/y
Paper and Paperboard Mill Data:
Stock Preparation:
Pulpers: 7
Refiners: 6
Paper Machines: 2
No. 1, fourdrinier, total capacity 44,625 mt/y, Trim width 3.31 m, Uncoated woodfree/freesheet
No. 2, twin-wire, total capacity 107,100 mt/y, Trim width 4.45 m, Uncoated woodfree/freesheet
Finishing Equipment:
Winders: 3 at 151,475 mt/y
Calenders: 2
Energy Data:
Power boilers: 3
Steam turbines: 3 at 9.4, 20, 20 MW
Electrical demand for mill: 428 MWh/D

ⓘAditya Birla Group
Ownership: shareholders
S. K. Ahire Marg
400 025 Worli, Mumbai
India
Phone: (91) 5652 5000/2499 5000
Fax: (91) 5652 5750
Email: investorrelations@adityabirla.com, pragnyaram@adityabirla.com
Web Address: www.adityabirla.com
Personnel:
Chmn.: Kumar Mangalam Birla
Phone: (91) 5652 5000
Fax: (91) 5652 5750
Chmn. Bus. Review Council, Manuf. Bus.: Shailendra K. Jain
Phone: (91) 5652 5000
Fax: (91) 5652 5750
Dir., HR & CEO Carbon Black: Dr. Santrupt B. Mirsra
Phone: (91) 5652 5000
Fax: (91) 5652 5750
CFO: Ajay Srinivasan
Phone: (91) 5652 5000
Fax: (91) 5652 5750
Mill Locations:
AV Cell Inc., Atholville Mill (95% owned), 175 Mill Rd, Atholville, NB, Canada E3N 4S7, (Pulp mill)
Phone: (1) 506-575-3294
Fax: (1) 506-575-3300
Email: pschriver@avcell.com
AV Nackawic Inc., Nackawic Mill (95% owned), 103 Pinder Rd, Nackawic, NB, Canada E6G 1W4, (Pulp mill)
Phone: (1) 506-575-3314
Fax: (1) 506-575-3300
Email: pat.bourgoin@avg.adityabirla.com
Domsjö Fabriker, Örnsköldsvik Mill, SE-891 86 Örnsköldsvik, Sweden, (Pulp mill)
Phone: (46) 660 75600
Fax: (46) 660 75990
Email: info@domsjoe.com
Grasim Industries Ltd, Harihar Polyfibers & Grasilene Division, Harihar, Dist Haveri, 581 123 Kumarpatanam, India, (Pulp mill)
Phone: (91) 08373 242171/75
Fax: (91) 08373 242875
Email: msamuel@adityabirla.com
AV Terrace Bay Pulp Inc., Terrace Bay Mill, 21 Mill Rd, Terrace Bay, ON, Canada P0T 2W0, (Pulp mill)
Phone: (1) 807-825-3211
Fax: (1) 807-825-3522

ⓘAfsons Industrial Corporation Ltd.
Wasrang Khopoli, Raigad, Maharashtra, 410203
Raigad, Maharashtra
India
Phone: (91) 22 22409977
Email: afsonsmumbai@yahoo.in
Personnel:
Man. Dir.: Taher Bhai Kagalwala
Phone: (91) 91 22 22418192
Sls. Mgr.: Mahendra Mehta
Phone: (91) 91 22 22418192
Mill Locations:
Afsons Industrial Corporation Ltd., Raigad Mill, Wasrang Khopoli, 410203 Raigad, India, Capacity: 5,400 mt/y, (Paper mill, Paperboard mill)
Phone: (91) 22 22409977
Email: afsonsmumbai@yahoo.in

ⓜAfsons Industrial Corporation Ltd.
Raigad Mill
Wasrang Khopoli
410203 Raigad, Maharashtra
India
Phone: (91) 22 22409977
Email: afsonsmumbai@yahoo.in
Personnel:
Man. Dir.: Mr. Taher Bhai Kagalwala
Phone: (91) 22 22418192
Sls. Mgr.: Mahendra Mehta
Phone: (91) 98 21226560
Type of Operation: Paper mill, Paperboard mill
Paper/Paperboard Grades and Capacities:
Total paper and paperboard capacity: 5,400 mt/y
Packaging papers
Boxboard/cartonboard

ⓜAgarwal Duplex Board Mills Ltd.
Muzzaffarnagar Mill
Ownership: 100% by Bindal Papers Limited
4th Km Stone, Bhopa Road
Muzzaffarnagar, Uttar Pradesh
India
Phone: (91) 131 2614623
Fax: (91) 131 2614881
Email: info@bindalpapers.com, edbml2008@rediffmail.com
Web Address: bindalpapers.com
Personnel:
Man. Dir.: Abhishek Agarwal
Phone: (91) 93 59421000
Email: abhi_iips@rediffmail.com
Sls. Exec.: Nand Gopal Agarwal
Phone: (91) 98 37046622
Mktg. Officer: Pankaj
Phone: (91) 93 13434612
Type of Operation: Paper mill, Paperboard mill
Paper/Paperboard Grades and Capacities:
Total paper and paperboard capacity: 50,000 mt/y
Specialty and industrial
Boxboard/cartonboard: 50,000 mt/y
Paper and Paperboard Mill Data:
Paper Machines: 2
No. 1, fourdrinier
No. 2, fourdrinier

ⓘAjanta Paper & General Products Ltd.
704, "Crystal Plaza" A.G. Link Road, Chakala, Andheri (E)
400099 Mumbai, Maharashtra
India
Personnel:
Man. Dir.: Rajesh Kedia
Phone: (91) 93 20361880
Exec. Dir.: Arun Kedia
Phone: (91) 93 33138476
Sls. Mgr.: S. N. Pandey
Phone: (91) 93 24507361
Total Employees of Company: 350
Total Employees at this Location: 25
Mill Locations:
Ajanta Paper & General Products Ltd., Jhagadia Mill, Plot No. 778, GIDC, 393 110 Jhagadia, India, Capacity: 24,000 mt/y, (Paper mill)
Phone: (91) 2645 226134/136
Fax: (91) 2645 226135
Email: ajantapm22@bsnl.in
Ajanta Paper & General Products Ltd., Kalyan Mill, Village Vadavali, Kalyan, 421301 Dist. Thane, India, Capacity: 12,000 mt/y, (Pulp mill, Paper mill)
Phone: (91) 22 28395416/59
Fax: (91) 251 2271484
Email: ajantapaper_gen@vsnl.com

ⓜAjanta Paper & General Products Ltd.
Jhagadia Mill
Plot No. 778, GIDC
393 110 Jhagadia, Gujarat
India
Phone: (91) 2645 226134/136
Fax: (91) 2645 226135
Email: ajantapm22@bsnl.in
Personnel:
Man. Dir.: Rajesh Keria
Phone: (91) 2645 226134/136
Type of Operation: Paper mill
Paper/Paperboard Grades and Capacities:
Total paper and paperboard capacity: 24,000 mt/y
Newsprint: 24,000 mt/y
Paper and Paperboard Mill Data:
Paper Machines: 1
PM 3, fourdrinier, total capacity 24,000 mt/y, Trim width 3.3 m, Newsprint

ⓜAjanta Paper & General Products Ltd.
Kalyan Mill
Village Vadavali, Kalyan
421301 Dist. Thane, Maharashtra
India
Phone: (91) 22 28395416/59
Fax: (91) 251 2271484
Email: ajantapaper_gen@vsnl.com
Personnel:
Pres./Man. Dir.: Rajesh Kedia
Phone: (91) 251 2271481/82
Email: ajantapaper@ol24.net
Tech. Mgr.: V. N. Khaitan
Phone: (91) 251 2271481/82
Gen. Mgr. Comm.: J. P. Lilha
Phone: (91) 251 2271481/82
Total Employees at this Location: 250
Type of Operation: Pulp mill, Paper mill
Pulp Mill Data:
Chemical Pulping Systems:
Batch digesters: 2
Paper/Paperboard Grades and Capacities:
Total paper and paperboard capacity: 12,000 mt/y
Newsprint: 10,000 mt/y
Uncoated woodfree/freesheet: 2,000 mt/y
Paper and Paperboard Mill Data:
Stock Preparation:
Pulpers: 4
Refiners: 8
Paper Machines: 2
PM 1, Trim width 1.2 m, Newsprint

India

PM 2, fourdrinier, total capacity 2,000 mt/y, Trim width 1.2 m, Uncoated woodfree/freesheet
Finishing Equipment:
 Rewinders: 3
 Sheeters: 2
Energy Data:
 Power boilers: 2

(I)Akshat Papers Ltd.
Block No 23, Village Tarsadi, Ta- Mahuya
394 350 Surat, Gujarat
India
Mill Locations:
 Akshat Papers Ltd., Surat Mill, Block No 23, Village Tarsadi, Ta- Mahuya, 394 350 Surat, India, Capacity: 25,000 mt/y, (Paper mill)

(M)Akshat Papers Ltd.
Surat Mill
Block No 23, Village Tarsadi, Ta- Mahuya
394 350 Surat, Gujarat
India
Personnel:
 Man. Dir.: Mr. Suresh Chandra Singhal
 Dir.: Akshat Singal
 Phone: (91) 98 98000211
 Mktg. Mgr.: Mahavir Bansal
 Phone: (91) 98 98016309
Total Employees at this Location: 80
Type of Operation: Paper mill
Paper/Paperboard Grades and Capacities:
 Total paper and paperboard capacity: 25,000 mt/y
 Packaging papers

(I)Amaravathi Sri Venkatesa Paper Mills Ltd.
"Nitya-Nilayam", Sri Venkatesa Mills Post Udumalpet
642 128 Coimbatore, Tamil Nadu
India
 Phone: (91) 4252 252286
 Fax: (91) 4252 252288/253700
 Email: cbt_asvpm@sanchamet.in
 Web Address: www.svg.in
Personnel:
 CEO: Mr. G. R. Vishnuvardan
 Phone: (91) 4252 252286
 Fax: (91) 4252 252288/253700
 Email: ce@svg.in
 Gen. Mgr. - Oper.: Mr. A. Srinivasan
 Phone: (91) 4252 252286
 Fax: (91) 4252 252288/253700
 Email: gmo@asvpm.com
 A.G.M. Finance: Mr. K. Chanrasekaran
 Phone: (91) 4252 252286
 Fax: (91) 4252 252288/253700
 Email: m_accs@asvpm.com
 Mktg. Mgr.: Mr. J. D. Johnson
 Phone: (91) 4252 252286
 Fax: (91) 4252 252288/253700
 Email: mm@asvpm.com
Mill Locations:
 Amaravathi Sri Venkatesa Paper Mills Ltd., Madathukulam Mill, Palani Rd., 642 113 Madathukulam, Coimbatore Dist., India, Capacity: 300,000 mt/y, (Pulp mill, Paper mill)
 Phone: (91) 4252 223099/4210/252286/2287/2 386/2344
 Fax: (91) 4252 52288
 Email: sales@asvpm.com
 V.G. Paper & Boards Ltd., Unit 1 Swaminathapuram, Palani Road, Madathukalam, 642 113 Swaminathapuram, India, Capacity: 13,000 mt/y, (Paper mill)
 Phone: (91) 4252 252288
 Fax: (91) 4252 253700

(M)Amaravathi Sri Venkatesa Paper Mills Ltd.
Madathukulam Mill
Palani Rd.
642 113 Madathukulam, Coimbatore Dist., Tamil Nadu
India
Mailing Address: "Nitya-Nilayam", Sri Venkatesa Mills Post, 642 128 Udumalpet, Coimbatore, Tamil Nadu, India
 Phone: (91) 4252 223099/4210/252286/2287/2 386/2344
 Fax: (91) 4252 52288
 Email: sales@asvpm.com
 Web Address: www.svg.in
Personnel:
 CEO: G. R. Vishnuvardan
 Phone: (91) 4252 223099/4210/252286/2287/2 386/2344
 Email: wtd@svg.in
 Chmn.: Dr. V. Gengusamy Naidu
 Phone: (91) 4252 223099/4210/252286/2287/2 386/2344
 Man. Dir.: Mr. Raveendran
 Phone: (91) 4252 223099/4210/252286/2287/2 386/2344
 Exec. Dir. : Mr. G. R. Harshavardhan
 Phone: (91) 4252 223099/4210/252286/2287/2 386/2344
 Email: ed@svg.in
 Gen. Mgr. (Operations): Mr. A. Srinivasan
 Phone: (91) 4252 223099/4210/252286/2287/2 386/2344
 Gen. Mgr. (Materials): Mr. M. Mounagurusamy
 Phone: (91) 4252 223099/4210/252286/2287/2 386/2344
 Gen. Mgr. (Technical): Mr. R. Raghupathy
 Phone: (91) 4252 223099/4210/252286/2287/2 386/2344
 Mktg. Mgr.: Mr. J. D. Johnson
 Phone: (91) 4252 223099/4210/252286/2287/2 386/2344
 Mgr. - Accounts: K. Chanrasekaran
 Phone: (91) 4252 223099/4210/252286/2287/2 386/2344
 Asst. Gen. Mgr.: J. D. Johnson
 Phone: (91) 4252 223099/4210/252286/2287/2 386/2344
Total Employees at this Location: 725
Type of Operation: Pulp mill, Paper mill
Pulp Grades and Capacities:
 Total pulp capacity: 215,581 mt/y
 Recycled Pulping: 215,581 mt/y
Pulp Mill Data:
 Bleach Plant Systems: 2
 Recycled Pulping System
 Recycled Pulping System
 Recycled Fiber Treatment Lines:
 Flotation deinking lines: 2
 Recycled packaging pulping lines: 1
Paper/Paperboard Grades and Capacities:
 Total paper and paperboard capacity: 300,000 mt/y
 Newsprint: 70,000 mt/y
 Uncoated woodfree/freesheet: 118,500 mt/y
 Packaging papers: 68,500 mt/y
 Boxboard/cartonboard: 43,000 mt/y
Paper and Paperboard Mill Data:
Paper Machines: 9
No. 1, fourdrinier, total capacity 20,000 mt/y, Trim width 2.5 m, Newsprint
No. 2, fourdrinier, total capacity 10,000 mt/y, Trim width 1.8 m, Uncoated woodfree/freesheet
No. 3, Vertiformer, total capacity 73,500 mt/y, Trim width 3.2 m, Uncoated woodfree/freesheet
No. 4, fourdrinier, total capacity 10,000 mt/y, Trim width 1.8 m, Packaging papers
No. 5, fourdrinier, total capacity 8,500 mt/y, Trim width 2.6 m, Packaging papers
No. 6, fourdrinier, total capacity 35,000 mt/y, Trim width 3.6 m, Uncoated woodfree/freesheet
No. 7, combination, total capacity 50,000 mt/y, Trim width 3.5 m, Packaging papers
No. 8, combination, total capacity 43,000 mt/y, Trim width 2.6 m, Boxboard/cartonboard
No. 9, hybrid former, total capacity 50,000 mt/y, Trim width 4.2 m, Newsprint
Coating Machines: 1
PM#8, on machine
Finishing Equipment:
 Rewinders: 6
 Sheeters: 7
Energy Data:
 Power boilers: 1
 Steam turbines: 1 at 1.2 MW
 Electrical demand for mill: 668 MWh/D

(M)Amol Paper Mills (P) Ltd
Raigad Mill
Vill. Ajiwali, AT & P.O.: Donwat, Tal. Khalapur
410 203 Raigad, Maharashtra
India
 Phone: (91) 2192 278 171/172
 Fax: (91) 2192 278 049
 Email: amolpapr@bom3.vsnl.net.in
Personnel:
 Man. Dir.: Amol Chandulal Shah
 Phone: (91) 22 24932196/24932780
 Email: shahaac@vsnl.net
Type of Operation: Paper mill, Paperboard mill
Paper/Paperboard Grades and Capacities:
 Total paper and paperboard capacity: 7,200 mt/y
 Packaging papers

(I)Amritsar Pulp & Board Mills (P) Ltd.
Jagdev Kalan Road, Vill. P.O. Gumtala Amritsar, Punjab,
Punjab
India
 Phone: (91) 183 250 3666/0565
 Fax: (91) 183 222 8546
Personnel:
 Man. Dir.: Satnam Singh Dhaliwal
 Phone: (91) 91 183 250 3666/0565
 Mgr.: Radesh Radesh
 Phone: (91) 91 183 250 3666/0565
Mill Locations:
 Amritsar Pulp & Board Mills (P) Ltd., Amritsar Mill, Jagdev Kalan Road, Vill. P.O. Gumtala, Amritsar, India, Capacity: 6,600 mt/y, (Paper mill, Paperboard mill)
 Phone: (91) 183 250 3666/0565
 Fax: (91) 183 222 8546

(M)Amritsar Pulp & Board Mills (P) Ltd.
Amritsar Mill
Jagdev Kalan Road, Vill. P.O. Gumtala
Amritsar, Punjab
India
 Phone: (91) 183 250 3666/0565
 Fax: (91) 183 222 8546
Personnel:
 Mgr.: Mr. Radesh
 Phone: (91) 9872411173
Type of Operation: Paper mill, Paperboard mill
Paper/Paperboard Grades and Capacities:
 Total paper and paperboard capacity: 6,600 mt/y
 Packaging papers

(I)Anand Duplex/Triplex Board Limited
9th km, Mawana Road, Vill. Saini
25006 Meerut District, Uttar Pradesh
India
 Phone: (91) 121 262 0985/86/87
 Fax: (91) 121 262 0988
 Email: anandduplex@gmail.com, anandpaper@gmail.com
Mill Locations:
 Anand Duplex/Triplex Board Limited, Meerut Mill, 9th km, Mawana Road, Vill. Saini, 25006 Meerut District, India, Capacity: 155,000 mt/y, (Paper mill, Paperboard mill)
 Phone: (91) 121 262 0985/88/2641 944
 Fax: (91) 121 262 0988
 Email: anandduplex@gmail.com, anandpaper@gmail.com

Anand Duplex/Triplex Board Limited
Meerut Mill
9th km, Mawana Road, Vill. Saini
25006 Meerut District, Uttar Pradesh
India
Phone: (91) 121 262 0985/88/2641 944
Fax: (91) 121 262 0988
Email: anandduplex@gmail.com, anandpaper@gmail.com
Web Address: www.anandduplex.com, www.anandtriplex.com
Personnel:
Exec. Dir.: Daman Vats
Phone: (91) 98 37045585
Gen. Mgr.: Vishal Vishnoi
Phone: (91) 99 99696777
Total Employees at this Location: 620
Type of Operation: Paper mill, Paperboard mill
Pulp Grades and Capacities:
Total pulp capacity: 151,599 mt/y
Recycled Pulping: 151,599 mt/y
Pulp Mill Data:
Bleach Plant Systems: 1
Recycled Pulping System, Type: DIP
Recycled Fiber Treatment Lines:
Flotation deinking lines: 1
Recycled packaging pulping lines: 1
Paper/Paperboard Grades and Capacities:
Total paper and paperboard capacity: 155,000 mt/y
Newsprint: 66,000 mt/y
Boxboard/cartonboard: 89,000 mt/y
Paper and Paperboard Mill Data:
Paper Machines: 3
No. 1, multi-wire, total capacity 25,000 mt/y, Trim width 2.75 m, Boxboard/cartonboard
No. 2, multi-wire, total capacity 64,000 mt/y, Trim width 2.75 m, Boxboard/cartonboard
No. 3, fourdrinier, total capacity 66,000 mt/y, Trim width 5 m, Newsprint
Coating Machines: 2
PM1, on machine
PM2, on machine
Finishing Equipment:
Calenders
Rewinders
Sheeters
Energy Data:
Power boilers: 1
Steam turbines: 1 at 10 MW
Electrical demand for mill: 261 MWh/D

Anand Tissues Ltd.
16 KM, Fitkari, Mawana Road
250401 Meerut, Uttar Pradesh
India
Phone: (91) 121 2887482/3
Fax: (91) 121 2887484
Email: info@anandtissues.com
Web Address: www.anandtissues.com
Mill Locations:
Anand Tissues Ltd., Meerut Mill, 16 KM, Fitkari, Mawana Road, 250401 Meerut, India, Capacity: 18,000 mt/y, (Paper mill)
Phone: (91) 121 2887482/3
Fax: (91) 121 2887484
Email: info@anandtissues.com

Anand Tissues Ltd.
Meerut Mill
16 KM, Fitkari, Mawana Road
250401 Meerut, Uttar Pradesh
India
Phone: (91) 121 2887482/3
Fax: (91) 121 2887484
Email: info@anandtissues.com
Web Address: www.anandtissues.com
Personnel:
Gen. Mgr. (Tech.): S. K. Sadhu
Phone: (91) 99 27066116
Dir.: Uday Sharma
Phone: (91) 121 2887482/3
Dir.: Sharad Sharma
Phone: (91) 121 2645725
Commer. Mgr.: Desh Bandhu Goel
Phone: (91) 99 27066117
Type of Operation: Paper mill
Paper/Paperboard Grades and Capacities:
Total paper and paperboard capacity: 18,000 mt/y
Packaging papers: 18,000 mt/y
Paper and Paperboard Mill Data:
Paper Machines: 1
No. 1, Trim width 2.5 m, Packaging papers
Energy Data:
Turbines at 2.5 MW

A.P. Paper Mills Ltd
245 industrial area, Phase 1
Chandigarh, Punjab
India
Phone: (91) 172 263 8032/33
Fax: (91) 172 263 8021
Personnel:
Man. Dir.: Sandeep Goyal
Phone: (91) 172 263 8032/33
Fax: (91) 172 263 8021
Mill Locations:
A.P. Paper Mills Ltd, Patiala Mill, Vill. Bhagwanpura, Barwala Road, Derabassi, 140 507 Dist. Mohali, India, Capacity: 21,600 mt/y, (Paper mill)
Phone: (91) 1762 280750/281 150
Fax: (91) 1762 281250
Email: appapermill@satyam.net.in, appapermills@yahoo.co.in

A.P. Paper Mills Ltd
Patiala Mill
Vill. Bhagwanpura, Barwala Road, Derabassi
140 507 Dist. Mohali, Punjab
India
Phone: (91) 1762 280750/281 150
Fax: (91) 1762 281250
Email: appapermill@satyam.net.in, appapermills@yahoo.co.in
Personnel:
Mill Mgr.: D D. Garg
Phone: (91) 1762 280 750/281 150
Sls. Mgr.: J. S. Walia
Phone: (91) 98 14066018
Total Employees at this Location: 500
Type of Operation: Paper mill
Paper/Paperboard Grades and Capacities:
Total paper and paperboard capacity: 21,600 mt/y
Uncoated woodfree/freesheet
Packaging papers
Paper and Paperboard Mill Data:
Paper Machines: 2
PM 1, Trim width 2.3 m
PM 2, Trim width 2 m

Apex Paper Mills
Opp. Patwardhan High School, Sitabuldi
440012 Nagpur, Maharashtra
India
Phone: (91) 712 2524038/2541387
Fax: (91) 712 2523556
Email: bppml1@yahoo.com
Personnel:
Owner/Dir./Partner: Suraj Agarwal
Phone: (91) 712 2524038/2541387
Fax: (91) 712 2523556
Owner/Dir./Partner: Jaiprakash Agarwal
Phone: (91) 712 2524038/2541387
Fax: (91) 712 2523556
Owner/Dir., Partner: Ritesh Agarwal
Phone: (91) 712 2524038/2541387
Fax: (91) 712 2523556
Total Employees of Company: 700
Total Employees at this Location: 10

Mill Locations:
Apex Paper Mills, Nagpur Mill, 22/1 Mouza Panchnoori, Bazargaon Amaravati Rd., Nagpur, India, Capacity: 4,000 mt/y, (Pulp mill, Paper mill)
Phone: (91) 7118 256523/252040/277142
Fax: (91) 712 523556
Email: bppml1@yahoo.com, bppml@yahoo.com
Bazargaon Paper & Pulp Mills Pvt. Ltd., Bazargaon Mill, Survey No. 32/34, Mouza Panchnavari, 440012 Bazargaon, Nagpur, India, Capacity: 30,000 mt/y, (Pulp mill, Paper mill, Paperboard mill)
Phone: (91) 712 2523040/2524038/2541387
Fax: (91) 712 523556, 7122 523556
Email: bppml@yahoo.com, bppml1@yahoo.com
Decor Paper Mills Ltd., Punjagutta, Hyderabad Mill, 413, 4th Flour, Topaz Building, Punjagutta, Hyderabad, A.P., India, Capacity: 40,000 mt/y, (Paper mill, Paperboard mill)
Phone: (91) 40 234 00194
Fax: (91) 40 664 64384
Email: dpml_hyd@yahoo.com
New Bombay Paper Mills Pvt Ltd., Bombay Mill, Village Ajivali, Post Donwat, Tehsil Khalapur, 410203 Dist. Raigarh, India, Capacity: 9,120 mt/y, (Paper mill)
Phone: (91) 2192 278416
Fax: (91) 2192 278416

Apex Paper Mills
Nagpur Mill
22/1 Mouza Panchnoori, Bazaragaon Amaravati Rd.
Nagpur, Maharashtra
India
Phone: (91) 7118 256523/252040/277142
Fax: (91) 712 523556
Email: bppml1@yahoo.com, bppml@yahoo.com
Personnel:
Owner/Dir.: Suraj Agarwal
Phone: (91) 7118 256523/252040/277142
Owner/Dir.: Jaiprakash Agarwal
Phone: (91) 7118 256523/252040/277142
Owner/Dir.: Ripesh Agarwal
Phone: (91) 7118 256523/252040/277142
Total Employees at this Location: 50
Type of Operation: Pulp mill, Paper mill
Pulp Mill Data:
Mechanical Pulping Systems:
Conventional grinders: 2
Recycled Fiber Treatment Lines:
Pulpers: 2
Pulp Dryers:
Flash dryers 1
Paper/Paperboard Grades and Capacities:
Total paper and paperboard capacity: 4,000 mt/y
Uncoated woodfree/freesheet: 4,000 mt/y
Paper and Paperboard Mill Data:
Stock Preparation:
Pulpers: 2
Refiners: 2
Paper Machines: 1
No. 1, fourdrinier, total capacity 4,000 mt/y, Trim width 1.5 m, Uncoated woodfree/freesheet
Finishing Equipment:
Winders: 2 at 7,200 mt/y
Rewinders: 2 at 7,200 mt/y
Energy Data:
Power boilers: 2
Electrical demand for mill: 9 MWh/D

Arjun Pulp And Paper (india) Private Limited
Ownership: 100% by Arjun Technologies India Limited (ATIL)
Robert V Chandran Tower, II Floor No.149, Velachery Tambaram High Road
600100 Pallikaranai, Chinnai
India
Phone: (91) 44 30453045
Fax: (91) 44 30453000

India

Email: ravishankar@arjuntech.com,
atil.marketing@arjuntech.com
Web Address: www.arjuntech.com
Personnel:
CEO: S Regupathy
Phone: (91) 44 30453045
Fax: (91) 44 30453000
Email: reghu@arjuntech.com
Group VP., Mktg & Bus. Dev.: Raphael Jose
Phone: (91) 44 30453045
Fax: (91) 44 30453000
Email: raphael@arjungroup.com
Chief Gen. Mgr., Projects & Operations: S Soundararajan
Phone: (91) 44 30453045
Fax: (91) 44 30453000
Email: soundar@arjuntech.com
Chief Gen. Mgr., Marketing: S Ravishankar
Phone: (91) 44 30453045
Fax: (91) 44 30453000
Email: ravishankar@arjuntech.com
Mill Locations:
Arjun Pulp And Paper (india) Private Limited, Thuvarasi Mill, Thuvarasi Village, Tirunelveli, India, (Paper mill)

ⓂArjun Pulp And Paper (india) Private Limited
Thuvarasi Mill
Mill is under construction (proposed new tissue mill scheduled for end of 2015 start)
Thuvarasi Village
Tirunelveli, Tamil Nadu
India
Type of Operation: Paper mill

ⓘAryan Paper Mills Pvt. Ltd.
Plot No. 177-178, Phase II, G.I.D.C.
396195 Vapi, Gujarat
India
Phone: (91) 260 2430110/0646/2423647
Fax: (91) 260 243 1008
Mill Locations:
Aryan Paper Mills Pvt. Ltd., Vapi Mill, Plot No. 177-178, Phase II, G.I.D.C., 396195 Vapi, India, Capacity: 50,000 mt/y, (Paper mill)
Phone: (91) 260 2430110/0646/2423647
Fax: (91) 260 243 1008

ⓂAryan Paper Mills Pvt. Ltd.
Vapi Mill
Plot No. 177-178, Phase II, G.I.D.C.
396195 Vapi, Gujarat
India
Phone: (91) 260 2430110/0646/2423647
Fax: (91) 260 243 1008
Web Address: aryanpaper.com
Personnel:
VP: K. N. Choudhary
Phone: (91) 2602 43 0110/0646/2423647
Man. Dir.: Sunil Shah
Phone: (91) 260 2401546
Dir.: Mihir Shah
Phone: (91) 2602 43 0110/0646/2423647
Works Mgr.: H. K. Mathur
Phone: (91) 2602 43 0110/0646/2423647
Mgr. (P&A): K. C. Varghese
Phone: (91) 2602 43 0110/0646/2423647
Chief Eng. (Elct.): Shyam Narayan
Phone: (91) 2602 43 0110/0646/2423647
Tech. Dir.: J. S. More
Phone: (91) 2602 43 0110/0646/2423647
Total Employees at this Location: 110
Type of Operation: Paper mill
Pulp Grades and Capacities:
Total pulp capacity: 49,773 mt/y
Recycled Pulping: 49,773 mt/y
Pulp Mill Data:
Recycled Fiber Treatment Lines:
Recycled packaging pulping lines: 1
Paper/Paperboard Grades and Capacities:
Total paper and paperboard capacity: 50,000 mt/y
Linerboard: 30,000 mt/y
Corrugating medium/fluting: 20,000 mt/y
Paper and Paperboard Mill Data:
Paper Machines: 1
No. 1, fourdrinier, total capacity 50,000 mt/y, Trim width 2.45 m, Linerboard, Corrugating medium/fluting
Energy Data:
Power boilers
Steam turbines
Electrical demand for mill: 63 MWh/D

ⓘⓂAshi Dipi Paper Mills Pvt. Ltd.
Ujjain Mill
53A, Industrial Area, Maxi Rd.
456 010 Ujjain, M.P
India
Phone: (91) 734 2516885/7966
Fax: (91) 734 2517966
Email: ashidipipapesr@gmail.com
Personnel:
Man. Dir.: Govind Khemani
Phone: (91) 734 2516885/7966
Email: govindkhemani@yahoo.com
VP: Ashish Khemeni
Total Employees at this Location: 26
Type of Operation: Pulp mill, Paper mill
Paper/Paperboard Grades and Capacities:
Total paper and paperboard capacity: 35,000 mt/y
Packaging papers: 35,000 mt/y
Paper and Paperboard Mill Data:
Stock Preparation:
Pulpers: 1
Refiners: 1
Paper Machines: 1
PM 1, total capacity 5,000 mt/y, Trim width 1.2 m, Packaging papers

ⓘAshmita Paper Pvt. Ltd.
Ahmedabad, Gujarat
India
Mill Locations:
Ashmita Paper Pvt. Ltd., Ahmedabad Mill, No. 303, Shikhar Complex, Near Navrangpura Railway Crossing, 380006 Navrangpura, Ahmedabad, India, Capacity: 60,000 mt/y, (Paper mill)
Phone: (91) (79)-65434745
Fax: (91) (79)-22885779
Ashmita Paper Pvt. Ltd., Navrangpura Mill, No. 303, Shikhar Complex, Near Navrangpura Railway Crossing, 380006 Navrangpura, Ahmedabad, India, Capacity: 42,900 mt/y, (Paper mill)
Phone: (91) 79 6543 4745

ⓂAshmita Paper Pvt. Ltd.
Ahmedabad Mill
No. 303, Shikhar Complex, Near Navrangpura Railway Crossing
380006 Navrangpura, Ahmedabad, Gujarat
India
Phone: (91) (79)-65434745
Fax: (91) (79)-22885779
Web Address: www.indiamart.com/ashmita-papers/
Personnel:
Owner: Mr. Tarun Jain
Phone: (91) 9099970904
Email: tarun@ashmitapapers.com
Total Employees at this Location: 145
Type of Operation: Paper mill
Pulp Grades and Capacities:
Total pulp capacity: 59,523 mt/y
Recycled Pulping: 59,523 mt/y
Pulp Mill Data:
Recycled Fiber Treatment Lines:
Recycled packaging pulping lines: 1
Paper/Paperboard Grades and Capacities:
Total paper and paperboard capacity: 60,000 mt/y
Specialty and industrial: 60,000 mt/y
Paper and Paperboard Mill Data:
Paper Machines: 1
No. 1, fourdrinier, total capacity 60,000 mt/y, Trim width 3.81 m, Specialty and industrial
Energy Data:
Power boilers
Electrical demand for mill: 74 MWh/D

ⓂAshmita Paper Pvt. Ltd.
Navrangpura Mill
No. 303, Shikhar Complex, Near Navrangpura Railway Crossing
380006 Navrangpura, Ahmedabad, Gujarat
India
Phone: (91) 79 6543 4745
Web Address: www.indiamart.com/ashmita-papers/
Personnel:
Owner, Dir.: Tarun Jain
Type of Operation: Paper mill
Paper/Paperboard Grades and Capacities:
Total paper and paperboard capacity: 42,900 mt/y
Packaging papers: 42,900 mt/y
Paper and Paperboard Mill Data:
Paper Machines: 1
No. 1, (started late 2013), total capacity 42,900 mt/y

ⓘAstron Paper & Board Ltd
Ganesh Meridian, D-702,7th Floor, Opposite High Court, S-G Highway
308 060 Ahmedabad, Gujarat
India
Phone: (91) 79-40081221
Fax: (91) 79-40081220
Email: info@astronpaper.com
Web Address: www.astronpaper.com
Personnel:
Man. Dir.: Kanu Patel
Man. Dir.: Kirit Patel
Man. Dir.: Ramakant Patel
Mill Locations:
Astron Paper & Board Ltd, Halvad Mill, Near Sukhpar Village, Dist:- Surendranagar, 363330 Halvad, India, Capacity: 77,000 mt/y, (Paper mill, Paperboard mill)
Phone: (91) 79 40081221
Email: info@astronpaper.com

ⓘⓂAstron Paper & Board Ltd
Halvad Mill
Near Sukhpar Village, Dist:- Surendranagar
363330 Halvad, Gujarat
India
Phone: (91) 79 40081221
Email: info@astronpaper.com
Web Address: www.astronpaper.com
Personnel:
Snr. Mgr.: Narendra Hothi
Type of Operation: Paper mill, Paperboard mill
Pulp Grades and Capacities:
Total pulp capacity: 87,500 mt/y
Recycled Pulping: 87,500 mt/y
Pulp Mill Data:
Pulp Lines: 1
Paper/Paperboard Grades and Capacities:
Total paper and paperboard capacity: 77,000 mt/y
Packaging papers: 77,000 mt/y
Paper and Paperboard Mill Data:
Paper Machines: 1
No. 1, triple-wire, total capacity 77,000 mt/y, Trim width 3.8 m
Energy Data:
Steam turbines: 1 at 3 MW

ⓘAurangabad Paper Mills Ltd.
Ownership: 42% by Mittal Group
171/B Mittal Tower, Nariman Pt.
400021 Mumbai, Maharashtra
India
Phone: (91) 22 22852247

India

Fax: (91) 22 22856834
Email: apm@bom3.vsnl.net.in,
sales@mittal.com
Personnel:
Exec. Dir.: Badal M. Mittal
Phone: (91) 22 22871929
Email: badalmittal@hotmail.com
Man. Dir.: P. G. Mittal
Phone: (91) 22 22852247
Fax: (91) 22 22856834
Total Employees of Company: 650
Mill Locations:
Aurangabad Paper Mills Ltd., Aurangabad Mill, Opposite Municipal School, MIDC industrial area, Bansilal Nagar, 431005 Aurangabad, India, Capacity: 32,000 mt/y, (Pulp mill, Paper mill)
Phone: (91) 240 233 3803

ⓂAurangabad Paper Mills Ltd.
Aurangabad Mill
Mill is for sale (Aurangabad Paper Mills is considering sale of its Plant, Machineries and Land subject to approval of the members and to conduct Postal Ballot for the same)
Opposite Municipal School, MIDC industrial area,
Bansilal Nagar
431005 Aurangabad, Maharashtra
India
Phone: (91) 240 233 3803
Personnel:
Man. Dir.: Parmeshwar G. Mittal
Total Employees at this Location: 650
Type of Operation: Pulp mill, Paper mill
Pulp Grades and Capacities:
Total pulp capacity: 36,500 mt/y
Chemical Pulp
Mechanical Pulp
Pulp Mill Data:
Chemical Pulping Systems:
Batch digesters: 8
Mechanical Pulping Systems:
CTMP systems
Bleach Plant Systems: 1
Paper/Paperboard Grades and Capacities:
Total paper and paperboard capacity: 32,000 mt/y
Newsprint: 18,000 mt/y
Packaging papers: 14,000 mt/y
Paper and Paperboard Mill Data:
Stock Preparation:
Pulpers: 5
Refiners: 14
Paper Machines: 2
No. 1, combination, total capacity 14,000 mt/y, Trim width 3.1 m, Packaging papers
No. 2, total capacity 18,000 mt/y, Trim width 2.6 m, Newsprint
Finishing Equipment:
Rewinders: 2
Sheeters: 1
Energy Data:
Power boilers: 3

ⒽAwade Pulp and Paper Mills Pvt. Ltd.
Awade Mala, Opp. Indira Gandhi Mahila
416143 Sahakari Soot Girani, Abdul-La, Maharashtra
India
Phone: (91) 230 329 0313/4660
Fax: (91) 2322 251 299/399
Email: awadepaper@rediffmail.com,
klp_awademil@sancharnet.in
Total Employees of Company: 146
Mill Locations:
Awade Pulp and Paper Mills Pvt. Ltd., Abdul-Lat Mill, Awade Mala, Opp. Indira Gandhi Mahila, 416143 Sahakari Soot Girani, Abdul-Lat, India, Capacity: 17,000 mt/y, (Paper mill)
Phone: (91) 230 329 0313/4660
Fax: (91) 2322 251 299/399
Email: awadepaper@rediffmail.com, klp_awademil@sancharnet.in

ⓂAwade Pulp and Paper Mills Pvt. Ltd.
Abdul-Lat Mill
Awade Mala, Opp. Indira Gandhi Mahila
416143 Sahakari Soot Girani, Abdul-Lat, Maharashtra
India
Phone: (91) 230 329 0313/4660
Fax: (91) 2322 251 299/399
Email: awadepaper@rediffmail.com,
klp_awademil@sancharnet.in
Personnel:
Man. Dir.: Swapnil Prakash Awade
Phone: (91) 230 2421306/2431666
Gen. Mgr.: M. T. Ganbawale
Phone: (91) 230 2421306/2431666
Prod. Mgr.: Jagdish Ballal
Phone: (91) 230 2421306/2431666
Mktg. Mgr.: Sudharm Shetti
Phone: (91) 230 2421306/2431666
Chief Eng.: Sanjay Kadge
Phone: (91) 230 2421306/2431666
Admin. Mgr.: R. K. Chougule
Phone: (91) 230 2421306/2431666
Total Employees at this Location: 146
Type of Operation: Paper mill
Paper/Paperboard Grades and Capacities:
Total paper and paperboard capacity: 17,000 mt/y
Packaging papers: 17,000 mt/y
Paper and Paperboard Mill Data:
Paper Machines: 2
No. 1, total capacity 12,000 mt/y, Trim width 2.38 m, Packaging papers
No. 2, total capacity 5,000 mt/y, Trim width 1.98 m, Packaging papers

ⒽⓂBalaji Cellulose Products Ltd.
Muzaffarnagar Mill
9 Km Stone Bhopa Rd.
251 001 Muzaffarnagar, Uttar Pradesh
India
Personnel:
Man. Dir.: A. Aggarwal
Type of Operation: Paper mill
Paper/Paperboard Grades and Capacities:
Total paper and paperboard capacity: 7,000 mt/y
Boxboard/cartonboard
Paper and Paperboard Mill Data:
Paper Machines: 1
No. 1, Trim width 3.2 m, Boxboard/cartonboard

ⒽⓂBalaji Paper Mills
Dist. Periyar Mill
380/1 Pudupeerkadavu Vill., Sathiyamangalam Taluk
632451 Dist. Periyar, Tamil Nadu
India
Phone: (91) 4295 243214
Fax: (91) 4295 222680
Type of Operation: Paper mill
Paper/Paperboard Grades and Capacities:
Total paper and paperboard capacity: 15,000 mt/y
Uncoated woodfree/freesheet

ⒽBalkrishna Industries Ltd.
418 Creative Ind. Estate, 72 NM Joshi, Marg
40001 Mumbai, Maharashtra
India
Phone: (91) 22 23071734 / 5441
Fax: (91) 22 23080830
Email: bpmho@bkt-tires.com
Personnel:
Man. Dir.: Mr. K. L. K. Jangir
Phone: (91) 22 23071734 / 5441
Fax: (91) 22 23080830
Email: klj@bkt-tires.com
Total Employees of Company: 300
Total Employees at this Location: 20
Mill Locations:
Balkrishna Paper Mills Ltd., Ambivli Mill, Vill. Ambivli, P.O. Atali, 421102 Taluka Kalyan, Dist. Thane, India, Capacity: 60,000 mt/y, (Paper mill, Paperboard mill)
Phone: (91) 251 2270701/2/3
Fax: (91) 251 2270705
Email: bpmfy@bpml.in, bpmfy@satyam.net.in

ⓂBalkrishna Paper Mills Ltd.
Ambivli Mill
Ownership: Balkrishna Industries Ltd.
Vill. Ambivli, P.O. Atali
421102 Taluka Kalyan, Dist. Thane, Maharashtra
India
Phone: (91) 251 2270701/2/3
Fax: (91) 251 2270705
Email: bpmfy@bpml.in,
bpmfy@satyam.net.in
Personnel:
Dir.: Mr. K. L. Jangir
Phone: (91) 22 23075441
Fax: (91) 22 23071828
Email: bpmho@bpml.in
VP (Tech.): M. L. Bhartia
Phone: (91) 251 2270701/2/3
Gen. Mgr. (Prod.): Manoj Rathi
Phone: (91) 251 2270701/2/3
Mktg. Mgr.: Ravindra K. Thanvi
Phone: (91) 22 23075441
Total Employees at this Location: 210
Type of Operation: Paper mill, Paperboard mill
Pulp Grades and Capacities:
Total pulp capacity: 56,137 mt/y
Recycled Pulping: 56,137 mt/y
Pulp Mill Data:
Recycled Fiber Treatment Lines:
Recycled packaging pulping lines: 2
Paper/Paperboard Grades and Capacities:
Total paper and paperboard capacity: 60,000 mt/y
Linerboard: 6,000 mt/y
Boxboard/cartonboard: 54,000 mt/y
Paper and Paperboard Mill Data:
Paper Machines: 1
No. 1, cylinder (8), total capacity 60,000 mt/y, Trim width 2.4 m, Boxboard/cartonboard, Linerboard
Coating Machines: 1
No. 1, total capacity 60,000 mt/y., on machine
Finishing Equipment:
Winders: 1
Sheeters: 3
Energy Data:
Power boilers: 3
Electrical demand for mill: 77 MWh/D

ⒽBallarpur Industries Ltd. (BILT)
Ownership: 49.42% by Avantha Group
First India Place, Tower 'C', Mehrauli-Gurgaon Rd.
122 002 Gurgaon, New Delhi, Haryana
India
Phone: (91) 124 280 4242/43/ 4099 484
Fax: (91) 124 280 4260/61
Email: corpcom@bilt.com
Web Address: www.bilt.com
Personnel:
Chmn.: Gautam Thapar
Phone: (91) 124 4099 506
Fax: (91) 124 2804 266
Email: gthapar@bilt.com
Man. Dir. & CEO: Yogesh Agarwal
Phone: (91) 124 2804 242
Fax: (91) 124 2804 260
Man. Dir.: Rajeev R. Vederah
Phone: (91) 124 4099 509
Fax: (91) 124 2804 260
Email: rrvedera@bilt.com
CFO: Vivek Kumar Goyal
Phone: (91) 124 4099 417
Fax: (91) 124 2804 261
Email: vgoyal@bilt.com
Key Management Personnel: Anup Kansal
Phone: (91) 124 280 4242
Fax: (91) 124 2804 260
Group. Dir. (Finan.): Bhuthalingam Hariharan

India

Phone: (91) 124 4099 217
Fax: (91) 124 2560 019
Email: bhariharan@bilt.com
Company Sec.: Akhil Mahajan
Phone: (91) 124 2804 242
Fax: (91) 124 2389 495
Total Employees of Company: 6,000
Mill Locations:
Ballarpur Industries Ltd. (BILT), Ashti Unit, Unit Ashti, Pal: Chamorshi, 442 707 Ashti, India, Capacity: 54,978 mt/y, (Paper mill)
Phone: (91) 7135 244143
Fax: (91) 7135 244147
Ballarpur Industries Ltd. (BILT), Pune Mill, 105 Milestone, Pune - Sholapur Highway, Bhadalwadi, Tal. Indapur, 413 105 Bhigwan, Dist. Pune, India, Capacity: 327,012 mt/y, (Paper mill)
Phone: (91) 2118 248201-12 / 1242 560025 / 1244 099325
Fax: (91) 2118 248225/26
Email: naggarwal@bilt.com, corpcom@bilt.com
Ballarpur Industries Ltd. (BILT), Ballarshah (Unit Ballarpur), District Chandrapur, 442 901 Ballarshah, India, Capacity: 290,241 mt/y, (Paper mill)
Phone: (91) 7172 240 282/270
Fax: (91) 7172 240548
Email: corpcom@bilt.com
Ballarpur Industries Ltd. (BILT), Kamalapuram Mill, P.O. Kamalapuram, 506172 Mangapet, Warangal, A.P., India, (Pulp mill)
Phone: (91) 8717 243228/243222
Fax: (91) 8717 243209
Email: corpcom@bilt.com
Ballarpur Industries Ltd. (BILT), Sewa Mill, Gaganapur, P.O. Jeypore, 764 002 Jeypore, Dist. Koratpur, India, Capacity: 39,270 mt/y, (Pulp mill, Paper mill)
Phone: (91) 6854 230220/206
Fax: (91) 6854 232931
Email: vinay.dwivedi@bilt.com
Ballarpur Industries Ltd. (BILT), Shree Gopal Mill, Unit Shree Gopal, 135 001 Yamunanagar, India, Capacity: 82,110 mt/y, (Pulp mill, Paper mill)
Phone: (91) 1732 292100
Email: naggarwal@bilt.com, corpcom@bilt.com
Premier Tissues India Ltd., Mysore Mill, Bannur, Mysore, India, Capacity: 8,400 mt/y, (Paper mill)
Sabah Forest Industries Sdn. Bhd., Sipitang Mill (97.78% owned), Komplek SFI, No 10 Jalan Jeti W.D.T. 31, 89859 Sipitang, Malaysia, Capacity: 144,228 mt/y, (Pulp mill, Paper mill)
Phone: (60) 87 801 018/026
Fax: (60) 87 802 087/463
Email: andrewchong@sfisb.com.my

ⓜBallarpur Industries Ltd. (BILT)
Ashti Unit
Unit Ashti, Pal: Chamorshi
442 707 Ashti, Maharashtra
India
Phone: (91) 7135 244143
Fax: (91) 7135 244147
Web Address: www.bilt.com
Personnel:
Gen. Mgr. (Works): Mr. V K Banth
Phone: (91) 7135 244151
Gen Mgr. (Paper Mill): Mr. K. P. Singh
Phone: (91) 7135 244143
Email: msingh@bilt.com
Gen Mgr. (Sack Plant): Mr. S. K. Panda
Phone: (91) 7135 244143
DM Commercial: Mr. M. Srivinas
Phone: (91) 7135 244143
DM Accounts: Mr. Manas Bash
Phone: (91) 7135 244143
Total Employees at this Location: 750
Type of Operation: Paper mill
Paper/Paperboard Grades and Capacities:
Total paper and paperboard capacity: 54,978 mt/y
Uncoated woodfree/freesheet: 54,978 mt/y
Paper and Paperboard Mill Data:
Stock Preparation:
Refiners: 4
Paper Machines: 1
No. 1, fourdrinier, total capacity 54,978 mt/y, Trim width 3.2 m, Uncoated woodfree/freesheet
Finishing Equipment:
Rewinders: 1 at 50,000 mt/y
Sheeters
Energy Data:
Power boilers: 1
Electrical demand for mill: 103 MWh/D

ⓜBallarpur Industries Ltd. (BILT)
Pune Mill
105 Milestone, Pune - Sholapur Highway, Bhadalwadi, Tal. Indapur
413 105 Bhigwan, Dist. Pune, Maharashtra
India
Phone: (91) 2118 248201-12 / 1242 560025 / 1244 099325
Fax: (91) 2118 248225/26
Email: naggarwal@bilt.com, corpcom@bilt.com
Web Address: www.bilt.com
Personnel:
VP, Operations: Nehar Aggarwal
Phone: (91) 2118 248201 Ext.100
Fax: (91) 2118 248225
Email: naggarwal@bilt.com
Gen. Mgr., Mill Mgr.: Dilip Keshavarao Wadodkar
Phone: (91) 2118 248201 Ext.152
Email: dilip.wadodkar@bilt.com
Total Employees at this Location: 745
Type of Operation: Paper mill
Paper/Paperboard Grades and Capacities:
Total paper and paperboard capacity: 327,012 mt/y
Coated woodfree/freesheet: 327,012 mt/y
Paper and Paperboard Mill Data:
Stock Preparation:
Refiners: 7
Paper Machines: 2
No. 1, hybrid former, total capacity 149,940 mt/y, Trim width 3.12 m, Coated woodfree/freesheet
No. 2, DuoFormer D, total capacity 177,072 mt/y, Trim width 4.81 m, Coated woodfree/freesheet
Coating Machines: 2
No. 1, total capacity 150,000 mt/y., off machine
PM 2, total capacity 177,000 mt/y., on machine
Finishing Equipment:
Calenders: 1
Rewinders: 2
Sheeters: 4
Energy Data:
Power boilers: 3
Steam turbines: 2 at 30.0, 30 MW
Electrical demand for mill: 800 MWh/D

ⓜBallarpur Industries Ltd. (BILT)
Ballarshah (Unit Ballarpur)
District Chandrapur
442 901 Ballarshah, Maharashtra
India
Phone: (91) 7172 240 282/270
Fax: (91) 7172 240548
Email: corpcom@bilt.com
Web Address: www.bilt.com
Personnel:
Ass. VP: Mr. S. S. Arora
Phone: (91) 7172 240 542
Total Employees at this Location: 1,500
Type of Operation: Paper mill
Pulp Grades and Capacities:
Total pulp capacity: 110,003 mt/y
Chemical Pulp: 75,796 mt/y
Other Pulp: 34,207 mt/y
Pulp Mill Data:
Chemical Pulping Systems:
Batch digesters: 10
Pulp Lines: 1
Bleach Plant Systems: 1
No. 1, Sequence: C/DEopHEpD, Capacity 125,000 admt/y
Chemical Recovery Equipment:
Evaporator lines: 4
Recovery boilers: 2
Lime Kiln
Paper/Paperboard Grades and Capacities:
Total paper and paperboard capacity: 290,241 mt/y
Uncoated woodfree/freesheet: 266,322 mt/y
Packaging papers: 23,919 mt/y
Paper and Paperboard Mill Data:
Paper Machines: 7
No. 1, fourdrinier, total capacity 18,207 mt/y, Trim width 3.12 m, Uncoated woodfree/freesheet, Packaging papers
No. 2, fourdrinier, total capacity 8,925 mt/y, Trim width 3.48 m, Packaging papers
No. 3, fourdrinier, total capacity 51,765 mt/y, Trim width 3.41 m, Uncoated woodfree/freesheet
No. 4, fourdrinier, total capacity 14,994 mt/y, Trim width 2.83 m, Uncoated woodfree/freesheet
No. 5, fourdrinier, total capacity 9,996 mt/y, Trim width 3.5 m, Packaging papers
No. 6, fourdrinier, total capacity 21,420 mt/y, Trim width 2.9 m, Uncoated woodfree/freesheet
No. 7, hybrid former, total capacity 164,934 mt/y, Trim width 5.46 m, Uncoated woodfree/freesheet
Finishing Equipment:
Rewinders: 6
Energy Data:
Power boilers: 4
Steam turbines: 3 at 7.5, 6.5, 12.5 MW
Electrical demand for mill: 709 MWh/D

ⓜBallarpur Industries Ltd. (BILT)
Kamalapuram Mill
Mill is temporarily closed (temporary shutdown from mid-May 2014 for an unspecified period)
P.O. Kamalapuram
506172 Mangapet, Warangal, A.P.
India
Phone: (91) 8717 243228/243222
Fax: (91) 8717 243209
Email: corpcom@bilt.com
Personnel:
Dpt. Gen. Mgr. Accounts: V.V.M. Gupta
Phone: (91) 8717 243228/243222
Total Employees at this Location: 1,200
Type of Operation: Pulp mill
Pulp Grades and Capacities:
Total pulp capacity: 103,299 mt/y
Pulp available for market: 98,715 mt/y
Chemical Pulp: 103,299 mt/y
Pulp Mill Data:
Chemical Pulping Systems:
Batch digesters: 9
Pulp Lines: 2
Bleach Plant Systems: 1
No. 1, Sequence: O_2 C/DEopHD
Chemical Recovery Equipment:
Evaporator lines: 1
Recovery boilers: 1
Energy Data:
Power boilers: 2
Combustion turbines: 2 at 12 MW
Electrical demand for mill: 301 MWh/D

ⓜBallarpur Industries Ltd. (BILT)
Sewa Mill
Gaganapur, P.O. Jeypore
764 002 Jeypore, Dist. Koratpur, Odisha
India
Phone: (91) 6854 230220/206
Fax: (91) 6854 232931
Email: vinay.dwivedi@bilt.com
Web Address: www.bilt.com
Personnel:
Unit Head: Vinay Dwivedi

India

Phone: (91) 6854 230220/206
Email: vinay.dwivedi@bilt.com
Gen. Mgr. (Eng.): Hirender Goyal
Phone: (91) 6854 230220/206
Email: ghirender@bilt.com
Dpty. Gen. Mgr. (Prod.): LVThapliyal
Phone: (91) 6854 230220/206
Email: lthapliyal@bilt.com
Dpty. Gen. Mgr. (Finance): R N Panda
Phone: (91) 6854 230220/206
Deputy Gen. Mgr. (R&D/QAS): P. Sridhar
Phone: (91) 9777 469211
Fax: (91) 6854232931
Dpty. Gen. Mgr. (HR): R P Srivastava
Phone: (91) 6854 230220/206
Deputy Gen. Mgr. (E&I): Ajay Rajvanshi
Phone: (91) 6854 230220/206
Dpty. Gen. Mgr. (Mech.): Gupteswar Mishra
Phone: (91) 6854 230220/206
Email: gupteswar.mishra@bilt.com
Gen. Mgr. (HR): Deepak Chaudhri
Phone: (91) 6854 230220/206
Email: chaudhri@bilt.com
Total Employees at this Location: 925
Type of Operation: Pulp mill, Paper mill
Pulp Grades and Capacities:
Total pulp capacity: 50,773 mt/y
Chemical Pulp: 50,773 mt/y

Pulp Mill Data:
Chemical Pulping Systems:
Batch digesters: 5
Pulp Lines: 1
Bleach Plant Systems: 1
No. 1, Sequence: CEpHHD, Capacity 60,000 admt/y
Chemical Recovery Equipment:
Evaporator lines: 1
Recovery boilers: 1
Lime Kiln
Paper/Paperboard Grades and Capacities:
Total paper and paperboard capacity: 39,270 mt/y
Uncoated woodfree/freesheet: 39,270 mt/y
Paper and Paperboard Mill Data:
Stock Preparation:
Pulpers: 1
Refiners: 4
Paper Machines: 1
No. 1, fourdrinier, total capacity 39,270 mt/y, Trim width 3.5 m, Uncoated woodfree/freesheet
Coating Machines: 1
No. 1, on machine
Finishing Equipment:
Rewinders: 2 at 53,000 mt/y, 40,000 mt/y
Sheeters: 3 at 15,000 mt/y, 15,000 mt/y
Energy Data:
Power boilers: 3
Steam turbines: 2 at 15 MW
Electrical demand for mill: 221 MWh/D

ⓂBallarpur Industries Ltd. (BILT)
Shree Gopal Mill
Unit Shree Gopal
135 001 Yamunanagar, Haryana
India
Phone: (91) 1732 292100
Email: naggarwal@bilt.com, corpcom@bilt.com
Web Address: www.bilt.com
Personnel:
Gen. Mgr. (Eng.): Mr. T. P. Dhiman
Phone: (91) 1732 292543/9812 302526 (mobil
Total Employees at this Location: 1,900
Type of Operation: Pulp mill, Paper mill
Pulp Grades and Capacities:
Total pulp capacity: 60,690 mt/y
Chemical Pulp: 60,690 mt/y

Pulp Mill Data:
Chemical Pulping Systems:
Batch digesters: 3
Bleach Plant Systems: 1
No. 1, Sequence: C/DEopDD, Capacity 60,000 admt/y
Chemical Recovery Equipment:
Evaporator lines: 2
Recovery boilers: 2
Lime Kiln
Paper/Paperboard Grades and Capacities:
Total paper and paperboard capacity: 82,110 mt/y
Uncoated woodfree/freesheet: 62,832 mt/y
Boxboard/cartonboard: 19,278 mt/y
Paper and Paperboard Mill Data:
Stock Preparation:
Pulpers: 13
Refiners: 28
Paper Machines: 5
No. 1, fourdrinier, total capacity 13,209 mt/y, Trim width 3.14 m, Uncoated woodfree/freesheet
No. 2, fourdrinier, total capacity 13,209 mt/y, Trim width 3.14 m, Uncoated woodfree/freesheet
No. 4, fourdrinier, total capacity 25,347 mt/y, Trim width 3.15 m, Uncoated woodfree/freesheet
No. 5, fourdrinier, total capacity 19,278 mt/y, Trim width 2.2 m, Boxboard/cartonboard
No. 7, fourdrinier, total capacity 11,067 mt/y, Trim width 2.8 m, Uncoated woodfree/freesheet
Coating Machines: 3
No. 1, total capacity 9,000 mt/y.
No. 2, total capacity 13,800 mt/y., off machine
No. 3, total capacity 20,000 mt/y.
Finishing Equipment:
Supercalenders: 2
Rewinders: 7
Sheeters: 8
Energy Data:
Power boilers: 5
Combustion turbines: 2 at 24.25 MW
Electrical demand for mill: 307 MWh/D

ⓂBallavpur Paper Mfg. Ltd.
Ownership: 100% by Emta Group
801, Central Plaza, 2/6, Sarat Bose Road
700020 Kolkata, West Bengal
India
Email: ballavpurpaper@gmail.com
Mill Locations:
Ballavpur Paper Mfg. Ltd., Ballavpur Mill, P.O. Ballavpur, Ballavpur, Raniganj, Dist. Bardhaman, India, Capacity: 50,000 mt/y, (Paper mill)

ⓂBallavpur Paper Mfg. Ltd.
Ballavpur Mill
P.O. Ballavpur
Ballavpur, Raniganj, Dist. Bardhaman, West Bengal
India
Total Employees at this Location: 145
Type of Operation: Paper mill
Pulp Grades and Capacities:
Total pulp capacity: 49,912 mt/y
Recycled Pulping: 49,912 mt/y

Pulp Mill Data:
Recycled Fiber Treatment Lines:
Recycled packaging pulping lines: 1
Paper/Paperboard Grades and Capacities:
Total paper and paperboard capacity: 50,000 mt/y
Linerboard: 50,000 mt/y
Paper and Paperboard Mill Data:
Paper Machines: 1
No. 1, fourdrinier, total capacity 50,000 mt/y, Linerboard
Energy Data:
Power boilers
Steam turbines at 3.5 MW
Electrical demand for mill: 57 MWh/D

ⓂBank Note Paper Mill India Private Limited
First Floor at SR Complex, #2, Thavarekere Main Road, SG Palya
560029 Bagalore, Karnataka
India
Phone: (91) 80 2254 0000
Fax: (91) 80 2254 0222
Email: info@bnpmindia.com
Web Address: www.bnpmindia.com
Personnel:
Man. Dir.: Shri S. C. Agrawal
Gen. Mgr (accounts): Shri A.K. Mandal
Gen. Mgr (civil): Shri C. Selvarajan
Gen. Mgr. (Technical): Shri K.G. Viswanathan
Mill Locations:
Bank Note Paper Mill India Private Limited, Mysore Mill, Note Mudran Nagar, 570 003 Mysore, India, Capacity: 12,000 mt/y, (Paper mill)
Phone: (91) 0821-2581905
Fax: (91) 0821-2581905
Email: info@bnpmindia.com

ⓂBank Note Paper Mill India Private Limited
Mysore Mill
Mill is under construction (first machine, due to start January 2015)
Note Mudran Nagar
570 003 Mysore, Karnataka
India
Phone: (91) 0821-2581905
Fax: (91) 0821-2581905
Email: info@bnpmindia.com
Web Address: www.bnpmindia.com
Type of Operation: Paper mill
Paper/Paperboard Grades and Capacities:
Total paper and paperboard capacity: 12,000 mt/y
Paper and Paperboard Mill Data:
Paper Machines: 2
PM 1, (due to start January 2015), total capacity 6,000 mt/y, Trim width 2.8 m
PM 2, (due to start up April 2015), total capacity 6,000 mt/y, Trim width 2.8 m

ⓂBansi Pulp & Paper Mills Pvt. Ltd.
S. No. 655/657, AT Post Kasbe Diraj, Samdoli Road, Tal. Miraj
416305 Dist. Sangli, Maharashtra
India
Phone: (91) 233 2437297/306/722
Fax: (91) 233 2437768
Email: bansipapers@gmail.com
Web Address: www.bppm.in/
Total Employees of Company: 150
Mill Locations:
Bansi Pulp & Paper Mills Pvt. Ltd., Miraj, Sangli District Mill, S. No. 655/657, AT Post Kasbe Diraj, Samdoli Road, Tal. Miraj, 416305 Dist. Sangli, India, Capacity: 14,400 mt/y, (Pulp mill, Paper mill)
Phone: (91) 233 2437 722/297/306/
Fax: (91) 233 2437768
Email: bansipapers@gmail.com

ⓂBansi Pulp & Paper Mills Pvt. Ltd.
Miraj, Sangli District Mill
S. No. 655/657, AT Post Kasbe Diraj, Samdoli Road, Tal. Miraj
416305 Dist. Sangli, Maharashtra
India
Phone: (91) 233 2437 722/297/306/
Fax: (91) 233 2437768
Email: bansipapers@gmail.com
Web Address: www.bppm.in
Personnel:
Exec. Dir.: Gobind Bansilal Biyani
Phone: (91) 233 2437297/306/722
Exec. Dir.: Mahesh Ramesh Biyani
Phone: (91) 98 22935555
Email: mahesh_biyani@yahoo.com
Exec. Dir.: Dilip Ghanshyam Biyani
Phone: (91) 233 2437297/306/722
Exec. Dir.: Pawan Ramesh Biyani
Phone: (91) 98 22130702
Gen. Mgr.: Suresh Dwarkadas Loheya

India

Phone: (91) 233 2437297/306/722
Total Employees at this Location: 150
Type of Operation: Pulp mill, Paper mill
Paper/Paperboard Grades and Capacities:
Total paper and paperboard capacity: 14,400 mt/y
Packaging papers: 14,400 mt/y
Paper and Paperboard Mill Data:
Paper Machines: 2
PM 1, Trim width 2.45 m, Packaging papers
PM 2, Trim width 3.1 m, Packaging papers

ⓂBanwari Paper Mills Ltd.
Kashipur Mill
Ownership: 100% by J.S. Goraya
4th Km Stone, Ram Nagar Rd., Udham Singh Nagar
244 713 Kashipur, Uttarakhand
India
Phone: (91) 5947 275740/840/274880
Fax: (91) 5947 275840/41
Personnel:
Owner/Man. Dir.: Jasbir Singh Goraya
Phone: (91) 98 37077886
Dir. Tech: Arvind Gupta
Phone: (91) 5947 275740
Gen. Mgr. (Sls): Arvinder Singh
Phone: (91) 98 39020710
Total Employees at this Location: 150
Type of Operation: Paper mill
Mill Locations:
Fiber Marx Papers Ltd., Kashipur Mill, 7 Km Jaspur Road, 244 713 Kashipur, India, Capacity: 45,000 mt/y, (Paper mill)
Phone: (91) 98370 37883
Fax: (91) 59472 29011
Paper/Paperboard Grades and Capacities:
Total paper and paperboard capacity: 12,000 mt/y
Uncoated woodfree/freesheet: 12,000 mt/y
Paper and Paperboard Mill Data:
Stock Preparation:
Pulpers: 1
Paper Machines: 1
PM 1, fourdrinier, total capacity 12,000 mt/y, Trim width 2.15 m, Uncoated woodfree/freesheet
Energy Data:
Power boilers: 1

ⓂBazargaon Paper & Pulp Mills Pvt. Ltd.
Bazargaon Mill
Ownership: Apex Paper Mills
Survey No. 32/34, Mouza Panchnavari
440012 Bazargaon, Nagpur, Maharashtra
India
Phone: (91) 712 2523040/2524038/2541387
Fax: (91) 712 523556, 7122 523556
Email: bppml@yahoo.com, bppml1@yahoo.com
Personnel:
Owner/Dir.: Suraj R. Agarwal
Phone: (91) 40 23400194
Owner/Dir.: Jaiprakash N. Agarwal
Phone: (91) 95 7118 56523/2523040/2524038/2541387
Owner/Dir.: Ripesh Agarwal
Phone: (91) 95 7118 56523/2523040/2524038/2541387
Total Employees at this Location: 125
Type of Operation: Pulp mill, Paper mill, Paperboard mill
Pulp Grades and Capacities:
Total pulp capacity: 29,415 mt/y
Recycled Pulping: 29,415 mt/y
Pulp Mill Data:
Recycled Fiber Treatment Lines:
Recycled packaging pulping lines: 1
Paper/Paperboard Grades and Capacities:
Total paper and paperboard capacity: 30,000 mt/y
Corrugating medium/fluting: 30,000 mt/y

Paper and Paperboard Mill Data:
Paper Machines: 1
No. 1, cylinder, total capacity 30,000 mt/y, Corrugating medium/fluting
Energy Data:
Power boilers: 2
Electrical demand for mill: 37 MWh/D

ⓂBedse Pulp Conversion Industries (P) Ltd.
F-30-32, M.I.D.C., Chikalkhana
431210 Aurangabad, Maharashtra
India
Phone: (91) 240 248 3333/6969/7117/8118
Fax: (91) 240 248 3131
Mill Locations:
Bedse Pulp Conversion Industries (P) Ltd., Aurangabad Mill, F-30-32, M.I.D.C., Chikalkhana, 431210 Aurangabad, India, Capacity: 14,400 mt/y, (Paper mill)
Phone: (91) 240 248 3333/6969/7117/8118
Fax: (91) 240 248 3131

ⓂBedse Pulp Conversion Industries (P) Ltd.
Aurangabad Mill
F-30-32, M.I.D.C., Chikalkhana
431210 Aurangabad, Maharashtra
India
Phone: (91) 240 248 3333/6969/7117/8118
Fax: (91) 240 248 3131
Personnel:
Man. Dir.: Mr. Mahesh Yadav Rao Patil
Phone: (91) 240 248 3333/6969/7117
Purch. Mgr.: Mr. Ashok Y. Patil
Phone: (91) 240 248 3333/6969/7117
Type of Operation: Paper mill
Paper/Paperboard Grades and Capacities:
Total paper and paperboard capacity: 14,400 mt/y
Packaging papers: 14,400 mt/y

ⓂBest Paper Mills Pvt. Ltd.
57-GH, 1st phase, GIDC
396195 Vapi, Gujarat
India
Phone: (91) 260 2432991/2427266/2431318
Fax: (91) 260 2428155
Personnel:
Man. Dir.: Ramesh K. Shah
Phone: (91) 98 241494376
Dir.: Ketan K. Shah
Phone: (91) 98 24199919
Mill Locations:
Best Paper Mills Pvt. Ltd., Vapi Mill, 57-GH, 1st phase, GIDC, 396195 Vapi, India, Capacity: 90,000 mt/y, (Paper mill)
Phone: (91) 260 2432991/2427266/2431318
Fax: (91) 260 2428155

ⓂBest Paper Mills Pvt. Ltd.
Vapi Mill
57-GH, 1st phase, GIDC
396195 Vapi, Gujarat
India
Phone: (91) 260 2432991/2427266/2431318
Fax: (91) 260 2428155
Personnel:
Man. Dir.: Ramesh K. Shah
Phone: (91) 98 241494376
Dir.: Ketan K. Shah
Phone: (91) 98 24199919
Total Employees at this Location: 145
Type of Operation: Paper mill
Pulp Grades and Capacities:
Total pulp capacity: 93,656 mt/y
Recycled Pulping: 93,656 mt/y
Pulp Mill Data:
Recycled Fiber Treatment Lines:
Recycled packaging pulping lines: 1

Paper/Paperboard Grades and Capacities:
Total paper and paperboard capacity: 90,000 mt/y
Packaging papers: 90,000 mt/y
Paper and Paperboard Mill Data:
Paper Machines: 2
No. 1, fourdrinier, total capacity 30,000 mt/y, Trim width 2.8 m, Packaging papers
No. 2, fourdrinier, total capacity 60,000 mt/y, Trim width 3.2 m, Packaging papers
Energy Data:
Power boilers: 2
Electrical demand for mill: 138 MWh/D

ⓂBhandari Deepak Industries Ltd
36, Industrial Area, Baddi
173 205 Solan, Himachal Pradesh
India
Fax: (91) 1795 246 228
Email: mail@bhandarideepakindustries.com, bdilbaddi@gmail.com
Total Employees of Company: 180
Mill Locations:
Bhandari Deepak Industries Ltd, Solan Mill, 36, Industrial Area, Baddi, 173 205 Solan, India, Capacity: 9,000 mt/y, (Paper mill)
Fax: (91) 1795 246 228
Email: mail@bhandarideepakindustries.com, bdilbaddi@gmail.com

ⓂBhandari Deepak Industries Ltd
Solan Mill
36, Industrial Area, Baddi
173 205 Solan, Himachal Pradesh
India
Fax: (91) 1795 246 228
Email: mail@bhandarideepakindustries.com, bdilbaddi@gmail.com
Personnel:
Man. Dir.: Mr. Deepak Bhandari
Email: bhandari.bdil@gmail.com
Dir.: Anita Bhandari
Total Employees at this Location: 180
Type of Operation: Paper mill
Paper/Paperboard Grades and Capacities:
Total paper and paperboard capacity: 9,000 mt/y
Packaging papers: 9,000 mt/y

ⓂBharat Papers Ltd.
P.B. 181, Beantpura, Chandigarh Road
141 008 Ludhiana
India
Phone: (91) 161 2824562-65
Fax: (91) 161 2824596
Email: jain.bpl@gmail.com
Web Address: www.bbfgroup.com
Mill Locations:
Bharat Papers Ltd., Kathua Mill, Logate Village, Kathua, India, Capacity: 87,500 mt/y, (Paperboard mill)

ⓂBharat Papers Ltd.
Kathua Mill
Logate Village
Kathua, Jammu and Kashmir
India
Web Address: www.bbfgroup.com
Personnel:
Man. Dir.: Rajinder Aggarwal
Email: procurement.bpl@gmail.com
Dir.: Anil Kashyap
Purch. Mgr.: R. N. Sharma
Phone: (91) 94 170 13284
Email: rnsharma.bpl@gmail.com
Total Employees at this Location: 100
Type of Operation: Paperboard mill
Pulp Grades and Capacities:
Total pulp capacity: 82,038 mt/y
Recycled Pulping: 82,038 mt/y
Pulp Mill Data:
Recycled Fiber Treatment Lines:

India

Recycled packaging pulping lines
Paper/Paperboard Grades and Capacities:
Total paper and paperboard capacity: 87,500 mt/y
Linerboard: 50,000 mt/y
Corrugating medium/fluting: 10,000 mt/y
Boxboard/cartonboard: 27,500 mt/y
Paper and Paperboard Mill Data:
Paper Machines: 1
No. 1, multi-fourdrinier, total capacity 87,500 mt/y, Trim width 3.5 m, Linerboard, Corrugating medium/fluting, Boxboard/cartonboard
Energy Data:
Power boilers
Electrical demand for mill: 115 MWh/D

ⓘBhikusa Papers Pvt. Ltd.
178, Hirawadi Road
420003 Panchwati, Maharashtra
India
Phone: (91) 253 2517689/2427
Fax: (91) 253 2515439
Email: bhikusapapers@yahoo.co.in
Mill Locations:
Bhikusa Papers Pvt. Ltd., Nasik Mill, 178, Hirawadi Road, 420003 Panchwati, India, Capacity: 9,000 mt/y, (Paper mill)
Phone: (91) 253 2517689/2427
Fax: (91) 253 2515439
Email: bhikusapapers@yahoo.co.in

ⓜBhikusa Papers Pvt. Ltd.
Nasik Mill
178, Hirawadi Road
420003 Panchwati, Maharashtra
India
Phone: (91) 253 2517689/2427
Fax: (91) 253 2515439
Email: bhikusapapers@yahoo.co.in
Personnel:
Dir.: Parashram Kshatriya
Phone: (91) 94 22254292
Dir.: Balram Kshatriya
Phone: (91) 94 22254294
Dir.: Mahendra V. Kshatriya
Phone: (91) 9422254290
Mill Mgr.: Mr. Jundre
Phone: (91) 253 2517689/2427
Type of Operation: Paper mill
Paper/Paperboard Grades and Capacities:
Total paper and paperboard capacity: 9,000 mt/y
Packaging papers: 9,000 mt/y
Paper and Paperboard Mill Data:
Paper Machines: 1
No. 1, Trim width 1.98 m, Packaging papers

ⓘBindal Papers Limited
NP-151B, Maurya Enclave, PitamPura
110088 Delhi
India
Phone: (91) 11 27323105/06/07/08
Fax: (91) 11 27323104
Email: info@bindalpapers.com
Web Address: bindalpapers.com
Personnel:
Chmn. & Man. Dir.: Rakesh Kumar Bindal
Phone: (91) 11 27323105/06/07/08
Fax: (91) 11 27323104
Mill Locations:
Agarwal Duplex Board Mills Ltd., Muzzaffarnagar Mill, 4th Km Stone, Bhopa Road, Muzzaffarnagar, India, Capacity: 50,000 mt/y, (Paper mill, Paperboard mill)
Phone: (91) 131 2614623
Fax: (91) 131 2614881
Email: info@bindalpapers.com, edbml2008@reddifmail.com
Bindal Papers Limited, Muzzaffarnagar Mill, 8th Km, Bhopa Road, 251001 Muzzaffarnagar, India, Capacity: 89,964 mt/y, (Paper mill)
Phone: (91) 131 2468446/8381
Email: info@bindalpapers.com
Bindals Duplex Ltd., Muzaffarnagar Mill, 10.6 Km., Bhopa Rd. Village Jatmunjhera, 251 003 Muzaffarnagar, India, Capacity: 53,000 mt/y, (Paper mill)
Phone: (91) 131 2468589
Fax: (91) 131 2468588
Tehri Pulp & Paper Ltd., Muzaffarnagar Mill, 9th Km Stone, Bhopa Rd., 251002 Muzaffarnagar, India, Capacity: 87,500 mt/y, (Paper mill)
Phone: (91) 0131 2468383, 84, 85, 86
Email: info@tehripaper.com

ⓜBindal Papers Limited
Muzzaffarnagar Mill
8th Km, Bhopa Road
251001 Muzzaffarnagar, Uttar Pradesh
India
Phone: (91) 131 2468446/8381
Email: info@bindalpapers.com
Web Address: www.bindalpapers.com
Personnel:
Man. Dir.: Mayank Bindal
Phone: (91) 9837027405
Email: mayank@bindalpapers.com
Gen. Mgr. (Mktg.): Vijay Kumar Agarwal
Phone: (91) 97 11797944
Total Employees at this Location: 550
Type of Operation: Paper mill
Pulp Grades and Capacities:
Total pulp capacity: 71,003 mt/y
Chemical Pulp: 71,003 mt/y
Pulp Mill Data:
Chemical Pulping Systems:
Continuous digesters: 1
Pulp Lines: 1
Bleach Plant Systems: 1
No. 1, Sequence: O_2 DoEopD
Chemical Recovery Equipment:
Evaporator lines
Recovery boilers
Paper/Paperboard Grades and Capacities:
Total paper and paperboard capacity: 89,964 mt/y
Uncoated woodfree/freesheet: 89,964 mt/y
Paper and Paperboard Mill Data:
Paper Machines: 1
No. 1, top-wire, total capacity 89,964 mt/y, Trim width 5 m, Uncoated woodfree/freesheet
Finishing Equipment:
Winders: 1
Energy Data:
Power boilers: 1
Steam turbines: 1 at 15 MW
Electrical demand for mill: 283 MWh/D

ⓜBindals Duplex Ltd.
Muzaffarnagar Mill
Ownership: Bindal Papers Limited
10.6 Km., Bhopa Rd. Village Jatmunjhera
251 003 Muzaffarnagar, Uttar Pradesh
India
Phone: (91) 131 2468589
Fax: (91) 131 2468588
Web Address: www.bindalpapers.com
Personnel:
Director: Padam Vanfal
Man. Dir.: Shrawan Kumar
Phone: (91) 98 37022374
Chief Exec. Dir.: Pankaj Aggarwal
Total Employees at this Location: 200
Type of Operation: Paper mill
Paper/Paperboard Grades and Capacities:
Total paper and paperboard capacity: 53,000 mt/y
Packaging papers
Boxboard/cartonboard: 53,000 mt/y
Paper and Paperboard Mill Data:
Paper Machines: 2
PM 1, Trim width 2.5 m
PM 2, fourdrinier, Trim width 2.7 m
Energy Data:
Power boilers: 1

ⓘⓜBiodeal Laboratories Pvt. Ltd. (Paper Mill Div.)
Vapi Mill
Ownership: 100% by Biodeal Laboratories PVT. Ltd (Paper Division)
Plot No. 105, Morai, Vapi
396191 Dist. Valsad, Gujarat
India
Phone: (91) 260 2437084/85/99
Fax: (91) 260 2437051
Email: dharm02@radiffmail.com, biodeal_ad1@sancharnet.in
Personnel:
Man. Dir.: Jayantilal B. Patel
Phone: (91) 98 98115616
Chmn. & Man. Dir.: Mr. T. K. Patel
Phone: (91) 260 2437084/85/99
Finan. Dir.: Devang Patel
Phone: (91) 98 25224446
Mill Mgr.: B. D. Patel
Phone: (91) 260 2437084/85/99
Maint. Mgr.: Rajesh Bhavsar
Phone: (91) 260 2437084/85/99
Total Employees of Company: 160
Total Employees at this Location: 110
Type of Operation: Pulp mill, Paper mill
Pulp Grades and Capacities:
Total pulp capacity: 27,084 mt/y
Recycled Pulping: 27,084 mt/y
Pulp Mill Data:
Recycled Fiber Treatment Lines:
Recycled packaging pulping lines: 1
Paper/Paperboard Grades and Capacities:
Total paper and paperboard capacity: 27,000 mt/y
Linerboard: 27,000 mt/y
Paper and Paperboard Mill Data:
Stock Preparation:
Pulpers: 1
Refiners: 2
Paper Machines: 1
No. 1, fourdrinier, total capacity 27,000 mt/y, Trim width 2.6 m, Linerboard
Finishing Equipment:
Rewinders: 2 at 40,000 mt/y
Energy Data:
Power boilers: 1
Electrical demand for mill: 34 MWh/D

ⓘBrahmaputra Paper Pvt. Ltd.
Dolabari NO. 2, Tinmile, P.O Kaliabhomra
Tezpur, Assam
India
Phone: (91) 3712 287177
Mill Locations:
Brahmaputra Paper Pvt. Ltd., Tezpur Mill, Dolabari NO. 2, Tinimile, P.O Kaliabhomra, Tezpur, India, Capacity: 17,500 mt/y, (Paper mill)
Phone: (91) 3712 287177

ⓜBrahmaputra Paper Pvt. Ltd.
Tezpur Mill
Dolabari NO. 2, Tinimile, P.O Kaliabhomra
Tezpur, Assam
India
Phone: (91) 3712 287177
Personnel:
Man. Dir.: Manas Tiberwal
Phone: (91) 94 35080472
Dir.: Ritesh Kumar Tiberwal
Phone: (91) 94 35081179
Type of Operation: Paper mill
Paper/Paperboard Grades and Capacities:
Total paper and paperboard capacity: 17,500 mt/y
Packaging papers: 17,500 mt/y
Paper and Paperboard Mill Data:
Paper Machines: 1
No. 1, total capacity 17,500 mt/y, Trim width 2.3 m, Packaging papers

India

Energy Data:
Steam turbines: 1 at 4 MW

ⓘCentury Pulp & Paper
Ownership: 100% by B.K. Birla Group Company
Industry House, 11th Floor, 10 Camac St.
700017 Kolkata
India
Phone: (91) 33 22827927/33 39573942/33 39590114
Fax: (91) 33 22821999
Email: cppcal@centurypaper.org.in
Web Address: www.centurypaperindia.com
Personnel:
Chmn.: B. K. Birla
Phone: (91) 33 22827927/33 39573942/33 39590114
Fax: (91) 33 22821999
Exec. Pres. & Sec. (Corp. Finan.): D. K. Agarwal
Phone: (91) 33 22827927/33 39573942/33 39590114
Fax: (91) 33 22821999
Pres. (Works): R. L. Lakhotia
Phone: (91) 33 22827927/33 39573942/33 39590114
Fax: (91) 33 22821999
Email: rll@centurypaper.org.in
Deputy Gen. Mgr. (Mktg.): K. K. Bagla
Phone: (91) 98 13218500
Total Employees at this Location: 4
Mill Locations:
Century Pulp & Paper, Lalkua Mill, Ghanshyamdham, PO-Lalkua, 262 402 Nainital, India, Capacity: 447,321 mt/y, (Pulp mill, Paper mill)
Phone: (91) 5945 268044/46/70/86
Fax: (91) 5945 268047
Email: adm@centurypaper.org.in

ⓜCentury Pulp & Paper
Lalkua Mill
Ghanshyamdham, PO-Lalkua
262 402 Nainital, Uttarakhand
India
Phone: (91) 5945 268044/46/70/86
Fax: (91) 5945 268047
Email: adm@centurypaper.org.in
Web Address: www.centurypaperindia.com
Personnel:
Senior Pres.: R. L. Lakhotia
Phone: (91) 93 13188222
Email: rll@centurypaper.org.in
VP: D. P. Chandarana
Phone: (91) 5945 268044/46/70/86
Email: sales@centurypaper.org.in
SrVP, Tech.: A C Mittal
Phone: (91) 5945 268044/46/70/86
Total Employees at this Location: 2,500
Type of Operation: Pulp mill, Paper mill
Pulp Grades and Capacities:
Total pulp capacity: 161,840 mt/y
Chemical Pulp: 91,233 mt/y
Recycled Pulping: 70,607 mt/y
Pulp Mill Data:
Chemical Pulping Systems:
Batch digesters: 7
Continuous digesters: 1
Pulp Lines: 3
Bleach Plant Systems: 2
Hardwood pulp line, Sequence: EPHHDS
Hardwood pulp line
Nonwood pulp line, Sequence: D/CE/O D
Recycled pulp line
Chemical Recovery Equipment:
Recovery boilers: 2
Pulp Dryers:
Air Float dryers 1
Paper/Paperboard Grades and Capacities:
Total paper and paperboard capacity: 447,321 mt/y
Uncoated woodfree/freesheet: 210,273 mt/y
Tissue: 42,126 mt/y
Boxboard/cartonboard: 194,922 mt/y
Paper and Paperboard Mill Data:
Stock Preparation:
Pulpers: 4
Paper Machines: 6
No. 1, fourdrinier, total capacity 17,850 mt/y, Trim width 2.69 m, Uncoated woodfree/freesheet
No. 2, fourdrinier, total capacity 17,850 mt/y, Trim width 2.69 m, Uncoated woodfree/freesheet
No. 3, top former, total capacity 84,609 mt/y, Trim width 5.2 m, Uncoated woodfree/freesheet
No. 4, fourdrinier, total capacity 89,964 mt/y, Trim width 5.2 m, Uncoated woodfree/freesheet
No. 5, crescent former, total capacity 42,126 mt/y, Trim width 2.85 m, Tissue
No. 6, fourdrinier, total capacity 194,922 mt/y, Trim width 4.3 m, Boxboard/cartonboard
Finishing Equipment:
Rewinders: 2 at 45,000 mt/y, 88,500 mt/y
Sheeters: 2 at 21,000 mt/y, 45,000 mt/y
Energy Data:
Power boilers: 3
Steam turbines: 3 at 6.8, 21, 43 MW
Electrical demand for mill: 900 MWh/D

ⓘChadha Papers Ltd
A-129, New Friends Colony
110065 New Delhi
India
Email: cpltd@vsnl.com
Personnel:
Gen. Mgr. (Mktg.): Asif Khan
Phone: (91) 99 90059936
Joint Man. Dir.: Rajinder Singh Chadha
Mill Locations:
Chadha Papers Ltd, Bilaspur, Dist. Rampur Mill, Compound Chadha Palace Prince Rd., Chadha Estate, Nainital Rd., Dist. Rampur, India, Capacity: 78,500 mt/y, (Paper mill)
Phone: (91) 595 242679/241267/2412224
Fax: (91) 595 2413335

ⓜChadha Papers Ltd
Bilaspur, Dist. Rampur Mill
Compound Chadha Palace Prince Rd., Chadha Estate, Nainital Rd.
Dist. Rampur, Uttar Pradesh
India
Mailing Address: Chadha Estate Nainital Road, Post Office Bilaspur, Moradabad, India
Phone: (91) 595 242679/241267/2412224
Fax: (91) 595 2413335
Personnel:
Man. Dir.: Hardeep Singh Chadha
Phone: (91) 120 4232476
Type of Operation: Paper mill
Paper/Paperboard Grades and Capacities:
Total paper and paperboard capacity: 78,500 mt/y
Packaging papers: 78,500 mt/y
Paper and Paperboard Mill Data:
Stock Preparation:
Pulpers: 2
Paper Machines: 2
No. 2, Trim width 2.8 m, Packaging papers
PM 1, Yankee dryer, Trim width 2.5 m, Packaging papers
Energy Data:
Power boilers: 1

ⓘChandpur Enterprises Ltd.
2nd Km Stone Noorpur Road, Chandpur Dist. Bijnor, Uttar Pradesh, 246725
Uttar Pradesh
India
Phone: (91) 1345 220140
Fax: (91) 1345 222330/224140
Web Address: www.chandpurpapers.com
Personnel:
Man. Dir.: Amit Kumar Mittal
Phone: (91) 1345 220140
Fax: (91) 1345 222330
Mill Locations:
Chandpur Enterprises Ltd., Dist. Bijnor Mill, 2nd Km Stone Noorpur Road, Chandpur, 246725 Dist. Bijnor, India, Capacity: 8,250 mt/y, (Paper mill)
Phone: (91) 1345 220140
Fax: (91) 1345 222330/224140

ⓜChandpur Enterprises Ltd.
Dist. Bijnor Mill
2nd Km Stone Noorpur Road, Chandpur
246725 Dist. Bijnor, Uttar Pradesh
India
Phone: (91) 1345 220140
Fax: (91) 1345 222330/224140
Web Address: www.chandpurpapers.com
Personnel:
Man. Dir.: Amit Kumar Mittal
Phone: (91) 94 12217165
Gen. Mgr. (Works): Mr. Devesh K. Singhal
Phone: (91) 9412713426
Email: deveshksinghal@gmail.com
Type of Operation: Paper mill
Paper/Paperboard Grades and Capacities:
Total paper and paperboard capacity: 8,250 mt/y
Newsprint
Packaging papers
Paper and Paperboard Mill Data:
Paper Machines: 1
No. 1, Trim width 3.1 m, Newsprint, Packaging papers

ⓘⓜCheema Paper Mills Pvt. Ltd.
Nainital Mill
Ram Raj Road, Post Office Bazpur
262401 Dist. Udham Singh Nagar, Uttarakhand
India
Phone: (91) 5949 281305
Fax: (91) 05947 75272sh
Personnel:
Chmn.: Amarjeet Singh Cheema
Phone: (91) 5949 88304/5/6
Fax: (91) 5947 75272
Man. Dir.: G. S. Cheema
Phone: (91) 99 27026094
Gen. Mgr. (Sls.) : Gurmeet Singh
Phone: (91) 99 27026092
Gen. Mgr.: R. K. Chauhan
Phone: (91) 99 27026095
Total Employees at this Location: 215
Type of Operation: Paper mill, Paperboard mill
Pulp Grades and Capacities:
Total pulp capacity: 51,181 mt/y
Recycled Pulping: 51,181 mt/y
Pulp Mill Data:
Chemical Pulping Systems:
Batch digesters: 6
Bleach Plant Systems: 1
Recycled Pulping System
Recycled Fiber Treatment Lines:
Flotation deinking lines: 1
Recycled packaging pulping lines: 1
Paper/Paperboard Grades and Capacities:
Total paper and paperboard capacity: 54,000 mt/y
Linerboard: 18,000 mt/y
Boxboard/cartonboard: 36,000 mt/y
Paper and Paperboard Mill Data:
Stock Preparation:
Refiners: 7
Paper Machines: 1
No. 1, Multi-wire (3), total capacity 54,000 mt/y, Trim width 2.4 m, Boxboard/cartonboard, Linerboard
Coating Machines: 1
PM 1, on machine
Energy Data:
Power boilers: 2
Steam turbines at 3 MW

India

ⓘChhattisgarh Industries Ltd.
Village Chaple Tehsil Kharsia Dist. Raigarh
496661 Raigarh, Chattisgarh
India
 Phone: (91) 22877333
 Fax: (91) 22803101
 Email: investorgcil@gmail.com
Mill Locations:
Chhattisgarh Industries Ltd., Raigarh Mill, Village Chaple Tehsil Kharsia Dist. Raigarh , 496661 Raigarh, India, Capacity: 8,250 mt/y, (Paper mill)
 Phone: (91) 22877333
 Fax: (91) 22803101
 Email: investorgcil@gmail.com

ⓂChhattisgarh Industries Ltd.
Raigarh Mill
Village Chaple Tehsil Kharsia Dist. Raigarh
496661 Raigarh, Chattisgarh
India
 Phone: (91) 22877333
 Fax: (91) 22803101
 Email: investorgcil@gmail.com
Personnel:
 Chmn.: Sri M. K. Ganguly
 Phone: (91) 22877333
 Dir.: Smt Rama Garg
 Phone: (91) 22877333
Type of Operation: Paper mill
Paper/Paperboard Grades and Capacities:
 Total paper and paperboard capacity: 8,250 mt/y

ⓘCholan Paper & Board Mills Ltd.
7/A, New-23, Krishnaswamy Avenue, Mylapore
600004 Chennai, Tamil Nadu
India
 Phone: (91) 44 2466 0075
Personnel:
 Man. Dir.: A. R. M. Govindarajan
 Gen. Mgr.: D. Ulaganathan
Mill Locations:
Cholan Paper & Board Mills Ltd., Kanchepuram Mill, Bukkathurai, Maduranthagam Taluk, 603 116 Kanchepuram, India, Capacity: 6,000 mt/y, (Paper mill)
 Phone: (91) 44 27565269
 Fax: (91) 44 27565268

ⓂCholan Paper & Board Mills Ltd.
Kanchepuram Mill
Bukkathurai, Maduranthagam Taluk
603 116 Kanchepuram, Tamil Nadu
India
 Phone: (91) 44 27565269
 Fax: (91) 44 27565268
Total Employees at this Location: 100
Type of Operation: Paper mill
Paper/Paperboard Grades and Capacities:
 Total paper and paperboard capacity: 6,000 mt/y
 Uncoated woodfree/freesheet
Paper and Paperboard Mill Data:
Paper Machines: 1
No. 1, Trim width 2.1 m, Uncoated woodfree/freesheet

ⓘCircar Paper Mills Ltd.
3/491, Lakshmipuram, Village Gudipallipadu
524 002 Nellore, A.P.
India
 Phone: (91) 861 27446/417
 Fax: (91) 861 231987
Mill Locations:
Circar Paper Mills Ltd., Nellore Mill, 3/491, Lakshmipuram, Village Gudipallipadu, 524 002 Nellore, A.P., India, Capacity: 12,000 mt/y, (Pulp mill, Paper mill)
 Phone: (91) 861 27446/417
 Fax: (91) 861 231987

ⓂCircar Paper Mills Ltd.
Nellore Mill
3/491, Lakshmipuram, Village Gudipallipadu
524 002 Nellore, A.P.
India
 Phone: (91) 861 27446/417
 Fax: (91) 861 231987
Personnel:
 Mgr.: A. Radha Mohan
 Phone: (91) 926.817745803357
 Prod. Mgr.: B. Surya Narayaha
 Phone: (91) 926.817745803357
Total Employees at this Location: 335
Type of Operation: Pulp mill, Paper mill
Pulp Grades and Capacities:
 Total pulp capacity: 5,840 mt/y
Pulp Mill Data:
 Chemical Pulping Systems:
 Batch digesters: 5
 Bleach Plant Systems: 1
 No. 1, Sequence: CEH
 Recycled Fiber Treatment Lines:
 Pulpers: 2
Paper/Paperboard Grades and Capacities:
 Total paper and paperboard capacity: 12,000 mt/y
 Uncoated woodfree/freesheet
 Packaging papers
 Boxboard/cartonboard
Paper and Paperboard Mill Data:
 Stock Preparation:
 Refiners: 2
Paper Machines: 2
No. 1, fourdrinier, Trim width 2.5 m
No. 2, Yankee dryer, Trim width 2.3 m
Finishing Equipment:
 Rewinders: 1
 Sheeters: 1
Energy Data:
Power boilers: 3

ⓘCoastal Agro Industries Ltd
K. Savaram Village
534 211 West Godavari, Tanuku, A.P.
India
Mailing Address: Post Box No. 27, West Godavari, Tanuku, A.P., India
 Phone: (91) 8819 224 982/222 4927
 Fax: (91) 8819 224 927
Mill Locations:
Coastal Agro Industries Ltd, West Godavari Mill, K. Savaram Village, 534 211 West Godavari, Tanuku, A.P., India, Capacity: 28,500 mt/y, (Paper mill)
 Phone: (91) 8819 224 982/222 4927
 Fax: (91) 8819 224 927

ⓂCoastal Agro Industries Ltd
West Godavari Mill
K. Savaram Village
534 211 West Godavari, Tanuku, A.P.
India
Mailing Address: Post Box No. 27, West Godavari, Tanuku, A.P., India
 Phone: (91) 8819 224 982/222 4927
 Fax: (91) 8819 224 927
Personnel:
 Man. Dir.: Mr. K. Visweswara Rao
 Phone: (91) 8819 224 982/222 4927
 Exec. Dir.: Mr. Ramakrishna
 Phone: (91) 8819 224 982/222 4927
Total Employees at this Location: 250
Type of Operation: Paper mill
Paper/Paperboard Grades and Capacities:
 Total paper and paperboard capacity: 28,500 mt/y
 Packaging papers
 Boxboard/cartonboard: 10,000 mt/y
Paper and Paperboard Mill Data:
Paper Machines: 2
No. 1
No. 3, fourdrinier

ⓘCochin Kagaz Ltd.
Ownership: KGS Nelsun Paper Mill Ltd.
2nd Floor, K Towers
683106 Ernakulam, Kerala
India
 Phone: (91) 91 48 4263 3042
 Email: cochinkagaz@satyam.net.in, cochinkagazlimited@gmail.com, cochinkagas@sify.com
Mill Locations:
Cochin Kagaz Ltd., Ernakulam Mill, Karakutty, Angamaly Via District, 680756 Ernakulam, India, Capacity: 9,000 mt/y, (Paper mill)
 Phone: (91) 484 2451417/1117
 Fax: (91) 484 2451317
 Email: cochinkagaz@satyam.net.in, cochinkagazlimited@gmail.com, cochinkagas@sify.com

ⓂCochin Kagaz Ltd.
Ernakulam Mill
Karakutty, Angamaly Via District
680756 Ernakulam, Kerala
India
 Phone: (91) 484 2451417/1117
 Fax: (91) 484 2451317
 Email: cochinkagaz@satyam.net.in, cochinkagazlimited@gmail.com, cochinkagas@sify.com
Personnel:
 Man. Dir.: Joy Kurian
 Phone: (91) 484 2451417/1117
 Sls. Mgr.: Manoharan
 Phone: (91) 484 2451417/1117
Total Employees at this Location: 150
Type of Operation: Paper mill
Paper/Paperboard Grades and Capacities:
 Total paper and paperboard capacity: 9,000 mt/y
 Packaging papers: 9,000 mt/y
Paper and Paperboard Mill Data:
Paper Machines: 2
No. 1, Packaging papers
No. 2, Packaging papers

ⓘCoral Newsprints Limited
4th Km. Stone, Delhi Road, Gajraula Jia Phule Nagar, Uttar Pradesh, 244 235
Uttar Pradesh
India
 Phone: (91) 05924-253313, 011-22010998
 Fax: (91) 011-22429586
 Email: info@coralnewsprintslimited.com
 Web Address: www.coralnewsprintslimited.com
Personnel:
 Chmn. of Bd.: Shri Chetandra Pratap Singh Chauhan
 Phone: (91) 05924-253313, 011-22010998
 Fax: (91) 011-22429586
 Dir.: Shri Puspendra Pratap Singh Chauhan
 Phone: (91) 05924-253313, 011-22010998
 Fax: (91) 011-22429586
 CFO: Shri Shailendra Singh
 Phone: (91) 05924-253313, 011-22010998
 Fax: (91) 011-22429586
Mill Locations:
Coral Newsprints Limited, Jyotibaphulenagar Mill, 4th Km. Stone, Delhi Road, Garaula, 244 235 Jia Phule Nagar, India, Capacity: 15,000 mt/y, (Paper mill)

ⓂCoral Newsprints Limited
Jyotibaphulenagar Mill
4th Km. Stone, Delhi Road, Garaula
244 235 Jia Phule Nagar, Uttar Pradesh
India
Personnel:
 Man. Dir.: Pushpendra Chauhan
 Phone: (91) 93 11208775
 Mktg. Head: Rajesh Jain
Type of Operation: Paper mill
Paper/Paperboard Grades and Capacities:

India

Total paper and paperboard capacity: 15,000 mt/y
Newsprint
Packaging papers
Paper and Paperboard Mill Data:
Paper Machines: 1
No. 1, Trim width 2.54 m, Newsprint, Packaging papers

ⒽCoromandel Papers
G-8 Industrial Estate, Dindigul, Tamil Nadu, 624003
Tamil Nadu
India
Phone: (91) 91 451 2470149
Fax: (91) 91 451-2430685
Personnel:
Owner, CEO: Sankar Palanisamy
Phone: (91) 91-451-2470149
Fax: (91) 91-451-2430685
Total Employees of Company: 40
Mill Locations:
Coromandel Papers, Dindigul Mill, G-8 Industrial Estate, 624003 Dindigul, India, Capacity: 9,900 mt/y, (Paperboard mill)
Phone: (91) 91 451 2470149
Fax: (91) 91 451 2430685

ⓂCoromandel Papers
Dindigul Mill
G-8 Industrial Estate
624003 Dindigul, Tamil Nadu
India
Phone: (91) 91 451 2470149
Fax: (91) 91 451 2430685
Personnel:
Man. Dir.: Shankar Palanisamy
Phone: (91) 91-451-2470149
Fax: (91) 91-451-2430685
Total Employees at this Location: 40
Type of Operation: Paperboard mill
Paper/Paperboard Grades and Capacities:
Total paper and paperboard capacity: 9,900 mt/y
Linerboard: 9,900 mt/y

ⒽCosboard Industries Ltd.
16-10-1/5/345/1&2, Sai Krupa Market
500036 Malakpet, Hyderabad, A.P.
India
Phone: (91) 040 64515015
Fax: (91) 040 24555528
Mill Locations:
Cosboard Industries Ltd., Jagatpur Mill, New Industrial Area, Phase II, Jagatpur, 754 021 Dist. Cuttack, India, Capacity: 19,800 mt/y, (Pulp mill, Paper mill, Paperboard mill)
Phone: (91) 671 2491966/495/295
Fax: (91) 671 2490944
Email: info@cosboard.com , cosboardind@yahoo.co.in

ⓂCosboard Industries Ltd.
Jagatpur Mill
New Industrial Area, Phase II, Jagatpur
754 021 Dist. Cuttack, Odisha
India
Phone: (91) 671 2491966/495/295
Fax: (91) 671 2490944
Email: info@cosboard.com, cosboardind@yahoo.co.in
Web Address: www.cosboard.com
Personnel:
Chmn., Man. Dir.: Ratan Kumar Gilra
Phone: (91) 94 37025334
Dir.: Anil Kumar Gilra
Phone: (91) 94 37049129
Mktg. Mgr.: Pawan Kumar Sharma
Phone: (91) 94 37061885
Total Employees at this Location: 500
Type of Operation: Pulp mill, Paper mill, Paperboard mill
Paper/Paperboard Grades and Capacities:
Total paper and paperboard capacity: 19,800 mt/y
Newsprint: 10,000 mt/y
Packaging papers: 5,000 mt/y
Boxboard/cartonboard: 4,800 mt/y
Paper and Paperboard Mill Data:
Stock Preparation:
Pulpers: 3
Refiners: 2
Paper Machines: 3
No. 1, cylinder (5), total capacity 4,800 mt/y, Trim width 1.7 m, Boxboard/cartonboard
No. 2, total capacity 5,000 mt/y, Trim width 2.4 m, Packaging papers
No. 3, total capacity 10,000 mt/y, Trim width 2.5 m, Newsprint

ⒽCraft Corner Paper Mills Pvt. Ltd.
Anant Niwas, Road No. 4 Rajawadi, Ghatkopar (E)
400077 Mumbai, Maharashtra
India
Phone: (91) 22 25162273
Fax: (91) 22 25110380
Personnel:
Chmn. & Man. Dir.: Prabodh Bhavanji Dedhia
Phone: (91) 22 25162273
Fax: (91) 22 25110380
Dir.: Jayanti Jethalal Dedhia
Phone: (91) 22 25162273
Fax: (91) 22 25110380
Dir.: Rajesh Bhavanji Dedhia
Phone: (91) 22 25162273
Fax: (91) 22 25110380
Dir.: Vijay Bapu Madnaik
Phone: (91) 982 5115549
Total Employees at this Location: 95
Mill Locations:
Craft Corner Paper Mills Pvt. Ltd., Vapi Dist., Valsad Mill, Plot No. 1703/A, 3rd Phase G.I.D.C. Ind. Est., Vapi, 396195 Dist. Valsad, India, Capacity: 21,500 mt/y, (Paper mill)
Phone: (91) 260 2424292/2430292
Fax: (91) 260 2425384
Email: val_craft@sancharnet.in, ccpm_vapi@yahoo.co.in

ⓂCraft Corner Paper Mills Pvt. Ltd.
Vapi Dist., Valsad Mill
Plot No. 1703/A, 3rd Phase G.I.D.C. Ind. Est., Vapi
396195 Dist. Valsad, Gujarat
India
Phone: (91) 260 2424292/2430292
Fax: (91) 260 2425384
Email: val_craft@sancharnet.in, ccpm_vapi@yahoo.co.in
Personnel:
Dir.: Prabodh Bhavanji Dedhia
Phone: (91) 98 20351788
Dir.: Rajesh Bhavanji Dedhia
Phone: (91) 98 20351790
Dir.: Vijay Bapu Madnaik
Phone: (91) 98 25115549
Sr. Exec.: B. N. Shah
Phone: (91) 260 2424292/2430292
Total Employees at this Location: 80
Type of Operation: Paper mill
Pulp Grades and Capacities:
Total pulp capacity: 21,055 mt/y
Recycled Pulping: 21,055 mt/y
Pulp Mill Data:
Recycled Fiber Treatment Lines:
Recycled packaging pulping lines: 1
Paper/Paperboard Grades and Capacities:
Total paper and paperboard capacity: 21,500 mt/y
Corrugating medium/fluting: 21,500 mt/y
Paper and Paperboard Mill Data:
Paper Machines: 1
No. 1, fourdrinier, total capacity 21,500 mt/y, Trim width 2.4 m, Corrugating medium/fluting
Energy Data:
Power boilers: 1
Electrical demand for mill: 24 MWh/D

ⒽⓂDaman Ganga Papers Mills (P) Ltd.
Vapi Mill
Ownership: Daman-Ganga Group
256, Selvas Rd., G.I.D.C.
396195 Vapi, Dist. Valsad, Gujarat
India
Mailing Address: P.O.Box 65, 396195 Vapi, Gujarat, India
Phone: (91) 260 2422522/2523
Fax: (91) 260 2430522/0239
Email: info@damanganga.com, damanganga@damanganga.com
Web Address: www.damanganga.com
Personnel:
Man. Dir.: Ashok Shah
Phone: (91) 260 2422522/2523
Man. Dir.: Mr. T. M. Shah
Phone: (91) 260 2422522/2523
Converting Plant Mgr.: Ashwin Shah
Phone: (91) 260 2422522/2523
Total Employees at this Location: 150
Type of Operation: Paper mill, Paperboard mill
Paper/Paperboard Grades and Capacities:
Total paper and paperboard capacity: 21,000 mt/y
Boxboard/cartonboard: 21,000 mt/y
Paper and Paperboard Mill Data:
Stock Preparation:
Pulpers: 2
Refiners: 2
Paper Machines: 1
PM 2, fourdrinier, Trim width 1.7 m, Boxboard/cartonboard
Finishing Equipment:
Rewinders: 1
Energy Data:
Power boilers: 1

ⒽDanalakshmi Paper Mills Pvt. Ltd.
Ownership: Serval Industries Ltd.
10-Z, Bharathi Park VII Cross
641 011 Coimbatore, Tamil Nadu
India
Phone: (91) 422 4333344
Fax: (91) 422 4333355
Email: ho@danalakshmi.in
Web Address: www.servalakshmi.in
Personnel:
Chmn.: R. Ramaswamy
Phone: (91) 422 4333344
Fax: (91) 422 4333355
Dir.: Mr. D. Muthusamy
Phone: (91) 422 4333344
Fax: (91) 422 4333355
Email: mills@danalakshmi.in
Gen. Mgr. (Commercial): Mr. S. P. Guptha
Phone: (91) 422 4333344
Fax: (91) 422 4333355
Mill Locations:
Danalakshmi Paper Mills Pvt. Ltd., Dindigul Mill, Vilampatti, 624 219 Nilakottai Taluk, Dindigul, India, Capacity: 21,500 mt/y, (Pulp mill, Paper mill)
Phone: (91) 4543 236433 to 35, 236443
Fax: (91) 4543 236402
Email: mills@danalakshmi.in

ⓂDanalakshmi Paper Mills Pvt. Ltd.
Dindigul Mill
Ownership: Serval Industries Ltd.
Vilampatti
624 219 Nilakottai Taluk, Dindigul, Tamil Nadu
India
Phone: (91) 4543 236433 to 35, 236443
Fax: (91) 4543 236402
Email: mills@danalakshmi.in

Personnel:
Dir.: D. Muthusamy
Phone: (91) 4543 236433 to 35, 236443
Email: mills@danalakshmi.in
Head of Operation: Mr. S. Manivannan
Phone: (91) 4543 236433 to 35, 236443
Email: manivannan@danalakshmi.in
Senior Gen. Mgr. Commer.: Mr. S.P. Guptha
Phone: (91) 4543 236433 to 35, 236443
Total Employees at this Location: 138
Type of Operation: Pulp mill, Paper mill
Pulp Grades and Capacities:
Total pulp capacity: 40,000 mt/y
Recycled Pulping: 40,000 mt/y
Paper/Paperboard Grades and Capacities:
Total paper and paperboard capacity: 21,500 mt/y
Newsprint: 10,750 mt/y
Uncoated woodfree/freesheet: 10,750 mt/y
Paper and Paperboard Mill Data:
Stock Preparation:
Pulpers: 2
Refiners: 2
Paper Machines: 2
No. 1, fourdrinier, total capacity 10,750 mt/y, Trim width 1.68 m, Newsprint
No. 2, fourdrinier, total capacity 10,750 mt/y, Trim width 2.1 m, Uncoated woodfree/freesheet
Finishing Equipment:
Rewinders: 2
Sheeters: 1
Energy Data:
Power boilers: 1

ⓗⓜDecor Paper Mills Ltd.
Punjagutta, Hyderabad Mill
Ownership: Apex Paper Mills
413, 4th Flour, Topaz Building
Punjagutta, Hyderabad, A.P.
India
 Phone: (91) 40 234 00194
 Fax: (91) 40 664 64384
 Email: dpml_hyd@yahoo.com
Personnel:
Owner/Dir.: Jaiprakash Agrawal
Phone: (91) 94 22146032
Owner/Dir.: Suraj Agarwal
Phone: (91) 40 234 00194
Owner/Dir.: Ritesh Agarwal
Phone: (91) 40 234 00194
Dir.: Shelly Agrawal
Phone: (91) 40 234 00194
Mgr.: Mr. Sharma
Phone: (91) 40 234 00194
Total Employees at this Location: 150
Type of Operation: Paper mill, Paperboard mill
Pulp Grades and Capacities:
Total pulp capacity: 40,935 mt/y
Recycled Pulping: 40,935 mt/y
Pulp Mill Data:
Recycled Fiber Treatment Lines:
Recycled packaging pulping lines
Paper/Paperboard Grades and Capacities:
Total paper and paperboard capacity: 40,000 mt/y
Packaging papers: 20,000 mt/y
Linerboard: 20,000 mt/y
Paper and Paperboard Mill Data:
Stock Preparation:
Pulpers: 1
Refiners: 1
Paper Machines: 1
No. 1, fourdrinier (3), total capacity 40,000 mt/y, Trim width 2.5 m, Packaging papers, Linerboard
Finishing Equipment:
Winders: 1 at 107,100 mt/y
Calenders: 2
Energy Data:
Electrical demand for mill: 54 MWh/D

ⓗⓜDelta Paper Mills Ltd.
Vendra Mill
Ownership: 100% by Laila Group of Companies
Palakoderu Mandal
534 210 Vendra, West Godavari Dist, A.P.
India
 Phone: (91) 8816 248881-4
 Fax: (91) 8816 24885/248208
 Email: elr_deltpap@sancharnet.in,
 elr_deltmill@sancharnet.in
 Web Address: www.deltapapermills.com
Personnel:
Chmn.: Dr. G. Ganga Raju
Phone: (91) 8816 248881-4
Fax: (91) 866 247 5278
Exec. Dir.: G. Rama Raju
Phone: (91) 8816 248881-4
Man. Dir.: G.V. K. Ranga Raju
Phone: (91) 8816 248881-84
Fax: (91) 8816 248885
CEO: G. Panduranga Raju
Phone: (91) 8816 248881-84
Fax: (91) 8816 248885
Mgr. Exec.: G. Rama Krishnam Raju
Phone: (91) 8816 248881-84
Fax: (91) 8816 248885
VP: D.S. Raju
Phone: (91) 8816 248208
Fax: (91) 8816 248208
Technical Adviser: M. Subrahmanyam
Email: elr_deltmill@sancharnet.in
Sr. DGM (Prod.): V. Vijaya Rama Raju
Phone: (91) 8816 248335/37
DGM (Chemical Recovery & Pulp Mill): N. Ranganadham
Phone: (91) 8816 248335/37
Mgr.: M.R.K. Mohan Roy
Phone: (91) 8816 248881-4
Total Employees of Company: 736
Total Employees at this Location: 734
Type of Operation: Pulp mill, Paper mill
Pulp Grades and Capacities:
Total pulp capacity: 43,237 mt/y
Chemical Pulp: 33,320 mt/y
Recycled Pulping: 9,917 mt/y
Pulp Mill Data:
Chemical Pulping Systems:
Batch digesters: 5
Continuous digesters: 1
Pulp Lines: 3
Bleach Plant Systems: 1
No. 1, Sequence: CEpHH, Capacity 31,000 admt/y
Chemical Recovery Equipment:
Evaporator lines: 1
Recovery boilers: 1
Recycled Fiber Treatment Lines:
Flotation deinking lines: 2 at 15,000 admt/y
Pulpers: 1 at 13,600 admt/y
Pulpers: 1 at 17,000
Washing deinking lines: 2 at 15,000 admt/y
Paper/Paperboard Grades and Capacities:
Total paper and paperboard capacity: 51,765 mt/y
Uncoated woodfree/freesheet: 51,765 mt/y
Paper and Paperboard Mill Data:
Stock Preparation:
Pulpers: 2
Refiners: 3
Paper Machines: 3
No. 1, fourdrinier, total capacity 14,994 mt/y, Trim width 2.74 m, Uncoated woodfree/freesheet
No. 2, fourdrinier, total capacity 21,777 mt/y, Trim width 2.74 m, Uncoated woodfree/freesheet
No. 3, fourdrinier, total capacity 14,994 mt/y, Trim width 2.94 m, Uncoated woodfree/freesheet
Finishing Equipment:
Winders: 1 at 18,000 mt/y
Rewinders: 3 at 18,000 mt/y, 24,000 mt/y, 15,000 mt/y
Sheeters: 6 at 20,000 mt/y
Energy Data:
Power boilers: 3
HRSG boiler: 1
Steam turbines: 3 at 12.9 MW
Electrical demand for mill: 162 MWh/D

ⓗⓜDelux Kraft Board Ltd.
Vapi Mill
Plot no. 289/1, GIDC Area, Dist. Valsad
396195 Vapi, Gujarat
India
 Phone: (91) 260 231975/230575
 Fax: (91) 260 230090
Personnel:
Man. Dir.: Rameshbhai V. Shah
Phone: (91) 260 231975/230575
Dir.: Kishorebhai V. Shah
Phone: (91) 260 231975/230575
Partner: H. V. Shah
Phone: (91) 260 231975/230575
Total Employees at this Location: 80
Type of Operation: Pulp mill, Paper mill
Paper/Paperboard Grades and Capacities:
Total paper and paperboard capacity: 21,600 mt/y
Packaging papers: 21,600 mt/y
Paper and Paperboard Mill Data:
Stock Preparation:
Pulpers: 4
Refiners: 2
Paper Machines: 1
No. 1, fourdrinier, Trim width 1.9 m, Packaging papers
Finishing Equipment:
Rewinders: 1
Energy Data:
Power boilers: 1

ⓗDeoria Paper Mills Ltd.
Hata road off Gorakhpur Rd, Narayanpu
274001 Deoria, Uttar Pradesh
India
Total Employees of Company: 26
Mill Locations:
Deoria Paper Mills Ltd., Deoria Mill, Hata road off Gorakhpur Rd, 274001 Deoria, India, Capacity: 18,000 mt/y, (Paper mill)
Phone: (91) 5562-222036
Fax: (91) 5562-223317

ⓜDeoria Paper Mills Ltd.
Deoria Mill
Hata road off Gorakhpur Rd
274001 Deoria, Uttar Pradesh
India
 Phone: (91) 5562-222036
 Fax: (91) 5562-223317
Personnel:
Dir.: Mr. Mahatam Singh
Type of Operation: Paper mill
Paper/Paperboard Grades and Capacities:
Total paper and paperboard capacity: 18,000 mt/y
Packaging papers: 18,000 mt/y
Paper and Paperboard Mill Data:
Paper Machines: 1
No. 1, total capacity 18,000 mt/y, Packaging papers

ⓗⓜDev Kiran Paper Mills (P) Ltd.
Bangalore Mill
nº 24 Gudimavu. Kumbalgodu post
560 074 Bangalore, Karnataka
India
 Phone: (91) 80 28437288
 Fax: (91) 80 28437527
 Email: contact@devkiranpaper.com,
 devkiranpaper@rediffmail.com
 Web Address: www.devkiranpaper.com
Personnel:
Man. Dir.: R. H. Ramanuja Setty
Phone: (91) 80 28437288
Email: devkiran@tatanova.com
Mill Mgr.: Mr. Rajashekhar

India

Phone: (91) 80 28437288
Tech. Dir.: R. H. Sreenivasa Setty
Phone: (91) 80 28437288
Total Employees at this Location: 90
Type of Operation: Paper mill
Pulp Grades and Capacities:
Total pulp capacity: 35,212 mt/y
Recycled Pulping: 35,212 mt/y
Pulp Mill Data:
Recycled Fiber Treatment Lines:
Recycled packaging pulping lines: 1
Paper/Paperboard Grades and Capacities:
Total paper and paperboard capacity: 35,700 mt/y
Specialty and industrial: 7,140 mt/y
Linerboard: 14,280 mt/y
Corrugating medium/fluting: 14,280 mt/y
Paper and Paperboard Mill Data:
Stock Preparation:
Pulpers: 1
Refiners: 7
Paper Machines: 1
No. 1, fourdrinier, total capacity 35,700 mt/y, Trim width 2.5 m, Corrugating medium/fluting, Linerboard, Specialty and industrial
Finishing Equipment:
Rewinders: 1
Sheeters: 1
Energy Data:
Power boilers: 2
Electrical demand for mill: 44 MWh/D

ⓘDev Priya Product Ltd.
44 123 Shankarvihar, 2nd Floor Vikas Marg
110092 Delhi
India
Phone: (91) 11 22013159
Fax: (91) 11 22013156
Email: sales@devproduct.com
Personnel:
Man. Dir.: Sanjeev Gupta
Phone: (91) 11 2283980
Asst. Man. Dir.: Rajeev Gupta
Phone: (91) 11 2283980
Mill Locations:
Dev Priya Papers Pvt. Ltd., Meerut Mill, 8th Km, Village Saini, Mawana Rd., 250002 Meerut, India, Capacity: 17,000 mt/y, (Paper mill)
Phone: (91) 121 2620784/343-4
Fax: (91) 121 2620884
Email: info@devpriyagroup.com

ⓘDev Priya Fibres Pvt. Ltd.
Village Panchli, 10th Km., Baghpat Road
Meerut, Uttar Pradesh
India
Phone: (91) 121 2439029/10
Fax: (91) 121 2439026
Email: amul_net@yahoo.com,
info@devfibres.com
Web Address: www.devfibres.com
Mill Locations:
Dev Priya Fibres Pvt. Ltd., Meerut Mill, Village Panchli, 10th Km., Baghpat Road, Meerut, India, Capacity: 84,000 mt/y, (Paper mill)
Phone: (91) 121 2439029/10
Fax: (91) 121 2439026
Email: amul_net@yahoo.com, info@devfibres.com

ⓜDev Priya Fibres Pvt. Ltd.
Meerut Mill
Village Panchli, 10th Km., Baghpat Road
Meerut, Uttar Pradesh
India
Phone: (91) 121 2439029/10
Fax: (91) 121 2439026
Email: amul_net@yahoo.com,
info@devfibres.com
Web Address: www.devfibres.com
Personnel:

Dir.: Sunny Gupta
Phone: (91) 9837022317, 9359722317
Total Employees at this Location: 150
Type of Operation: Paper mill
Pulp Grades and Capacities:
Total pulp capacity: 84,143 mt/y
Recycled Pulping: 84,143 mt/y
Pulp Mill Data:
Recycled Fiber Treatment Lines:
Recycled packaging pulping lines: 1
Paper/Paperboard Grades and Capacities:
Total paper and paperboard capacity: 84,000 mt/y
Linerboard: 84,000 mt/y
Paper and Paperboard Mill Data:
Paper Machines: 2
No. 1, fourdrinier, total capacity 42,000 mt/y, Trim width 2.54 m, Linerboard
No. 2, fourdrinier, total capacity 42,000 mt/y, Trim width 2.8 m, Linerboard
Energy Data:
Power boilers
Electrical demand for mill: 96 MWh/D

ⓘⓜDev Priya Industries Limited
Meerut Mill
8th Km, Village Saini, Mawana Rd.
250002 Meerut District, Uttar Pradesh
India
Phone: (91) 121 2620343
Fax: (91) 121 2620344
Personnel:
Dir: Ashok Kumar Gupta
Phone: (91) 121 2620343
Total Employees at this Location: 300
Type of Operation: Paperboard mill
Pulp Grades and Capacities:
Total pulp capacity: 138,701 mt/y
Recycled Pulping: 138,701 mt/y
Pulp Mill Data:
Recycled Fiber Treatment Lines:
Recycled packaging pulping lines: 1
Paper/Paperboard Grades and Capacities:
Total paper and paperboard capacity: 140,000 mt/y
Linerboard: 104,000 mt/y
Corrugating medium/fluting: 36,000 mt/y
Paper and Paperboard Mill Data:
Paper Machines: 2
No. 1, fourdrinier (3), total capacity 50,000 mt/y, Trim width 2.55 m, Linerboard
No. 2, fourdrinier (3), total capacity 90,000 mt/y, Trim width 4.1 m, Linerboard, Corrugating medium/fluting
Energy Data:
Power boilers

ⓜDev Priya Papers Pvt. Ltd.
Meerut Mill
Ownership: Dev Priya Product Ltd.
8th Km, Village Saini, Mawana Rd.
250002 Meerut, Uttar Pradesh
India
Phone: (91) 121 2620784/343-4
Fax: (91) 121 2620884
Email: info@devpriyagroup.com
Personnel:
Man. Dir.: Suresh Chand Gupta
Phone: (91) 98 37022150
Dir.: Sumit Gupta
Phone: (91) 98 37070560
Works Mgr.: S. K. Sadhu
Phone: (91) 121 2620343/2620344
Sls. Mgr.: Manoj Pant
Phone: (91) 98 18669770
Email: mp2004123@rediffmail.com
Type of Operation: Paper mill
Paper/Paperboard Grades and Capacities:
Total paper and paperboard capacity: 17,000 mt/y
Boxboard/cartonboard: 17,000 mt/y
Paper and Paperboard Mill Data:

Stock Preparation:
Pulpers: 2
Paper Machines: 1
PM 1, Trim width 2.2 m, Boxboard/cartonboard
Finishing Equipment:
Rewinders: 1
Sheeters: 1
Energy Data:
Power boilers: 1

ⓘDhanlaxmi Paper Mills Pvt Ltd
31,Bharati Park, 7th Cross, Sibaba Colony Coimbatore,
Tamil Nadu, 641011
Tamil Nadu
India
Phone: (91) 422 4333344
Fax: (91) 422 4333355
Mill Locations:
Dhanlaxmi Paper Mills Pvt Ltd, Coimbatore Mill, 31,Bharati Park, 7th Cross, Sibaba Colony, 641011 Coimbatore, India, Capacity: 7,200 mt/y, (Paperboard mill)
Phone: (91) 422 4333344
Fax: (91) 422 4333355

ⓜDhanlaxmi Paper Mills Pvt Ltd
Coimbatore Mill
31,Bharati Park, 7th Cross, Sibaba Colony
641011 Coimbatore, Tamil Nadu
India
Phone: (91) 422 4333344
Fax: (91) 422 4333355
Type of Operation: Paperboard mill
Paper/Paperboard Grades and Capacities:
Total paper and paperboard capacity: 7,200 mt/y
Linerboard: 7,200 mt/y

ⓜDhruv Craft Mill Private Limited (DCMPL)
Morbi Mill
Ownership: 100% by Dhruv Packaging Pvt. Ltd.
Lakhdhirpur Road, National Highway
363642 Morbi, Gujarat
India
Phone: (91) 265 288 6332
Personnel:
Dir.: Maganbhai Gami
Total Employees at this Location: 105
Type of Operation: Paper mill
Pulp Grades and Capacities:
Total pulp capacity: 33,985 mt/y
Recycled Pulping: 33,985 mt/y
Pulp Mill Data:
Recycled Fiber Treatment Lines:
Recycled packaging pulping lines: 1
Paper/Paperboard Grades and Capacities:
Total paper and paperboard capacity: 35,000 mt/y
Corrugating medium/fluting: 35,000 mt/y
Paper and Paperboard Mill Data:
Paper Machines: 1
No. 1, fourdrinier, total capacity 35,000 mt/y, Corrugating medium/fluting
Energy Data:
Power boilers
Electrical demand for mill: 40 MWh/D

ⓘDurga Duplex Mill Private Limited
907/101 Maharaja Agrasen, Mark
110006 Delhi
India
Phone: (91) 11 23243133
Personnel:
Dir.: Vijay Goel
Mill Locations:
Durga Duplex Mill Private Limited, Malerkotla Mill, Dhuri Road, 148023 Malerkotla, India, Capacity: 3,000 mt/y, (Paperboard mill)
Phone: (91) 1675 259337

India

ⓜDurga Duplex Mill Private Limited
Malerkotla Mill
Dhuri Road
148023 Malerkotla, Punjab
India
Phone: (91) 1675 259337
Personnel:
Man. Dir.: Ajay Goel
Phone: (91) 98 11315353
Dir.: Vijay Goel
Phone: (91) 98 10048307
Type of Operation: Paperboard mill
Paper/Paperboard Grades and Capacities:
Total paper and paperboard capacity: 3,000 mt/y
Boxboard/cartonboard: 3,000 mt/y
Paper and Paperboard Mill Data:
Paper Machines: 1
No. 1, total capacity 3,000 mt/y, Boxboard/cartonboard

ⓗDurga Paper Mills
IID Industrial Area
Kathua, Jammu and Kashmir
India
Phone: (91) 1922 238691, 92 16841102
Fax: (91) 1922 238691
Mill Locations:
Durga Paper Mills, Kathua Mill, IID Industrial Area, Kathua, India, Capacity: 10,500 mt/y, (Paper mill)
Phone: (91) 1922 238691, 92 16841102
Fax: (91) 1922 238691

ⓜDurga Paper Mills
Kathua Mill
IID Industrial Area
Kathua, Jammu and Kashmir
India
Phone: (91) 1922 238691, 92 16841102
Fax: (91) 1922 238691
Personnel:
Man. Dir.: Gopal Goel
Phone: (91) 98 10157736
Email: gopalgoel_dmc@yahoo.com
Dir.: Vijay Aggarwal
Phone: (91) 92 16841101, 94 19150820
Type of Operation: Paper mill
Paper/Paperboard Grades and Capacities:
Total paper and paperboard capacity: 10,500 mt/y
Tissue: 10,500 mt/y
Paper and Paperboard Mill Data:
Paper Machines: 1
PM 1, (second hand, started in October 2009), total capacity 10,500 mt/y, Tissue

ⓗEast India Paper & Board Mills
95, Park Street,
700 016. Kolkata, West Bengal
India
Phone: (91) 33 2226 6167/6168/5408
Fax: (91) 33 2226 2128
Email: recycle@cal.vsnl.net.in
Web Address: www.eastindiapaperboard.com
Personnel:
Dir.: Mr. Pranav Agarwal
Phone: (91) 33 2226 6167/6168/5408
Fax: (91) 33 2226 2128
Email: pranagarwal@gmail.com
Mill Locations:
East India Paper & Board Mills, Howeah Mill, 8, Belur Road, Liluah, 711204 Howeah, India, Capacity: 10,700 mt/y, (Paperboard mill)
Phone: (91) 33 2655 6368/5648
Fax: (91) 33 2655 0251
Email: eastindiapaper@vsnl.com
GRD Paper Industries PVT. Ltd, Howrah Mill, NH 6, Mouja, Chamrail. Liluah, 711323 Howrah, India, Capacity: 35,000 mt/y, (Paper mill)

ⓜEast India Paper & Board Mills
Howeah Mill
8, Belur Road, Liluah
711204 Howeah, West Bengal
India
Phone: (91) 33 2655 6368/5648
Fax: (91) 33 2655 0251
Email: eastindiapaper@vsnl.com
Web Address: www.eastindiapaperboard.com
Personnel:
Dir.: Dayanand N. Agarwal
Phone: (91) 33 22266167-8
Email: dayanandagarwal@hotmail.com
Dir.: D. N. Agarwal
Phone: (91) 33 22266167
Exec.: Rajesh Agarwal
Phone: (91) 33 2655 6368/5648
Type of Operation: Paperboard mill
Paper/Paperboard Grades and Capacities:
Total paper and paperboard capacity: 10,700 mt/y
Linerboard
Boxboard/cartonboard: 10,700 mt/y
Paper and Paperboard Mill Data:
Paper Machines: 1
No. 1, total capacity 10,700 mt/y, Linerboard, Boxboard/cartonboard

ⓗEllora Paper Mills Ltd.
Ownership: 30% by institutions/public, 70% by promoters
M.I.D.C Area, B-Cross Road
400 093 Andheri (East), Mumbai, Maharashtra
India
Phone: (91) 22 283 83967-282 19180/15901
Fax: (91) 22 258 38229-283 69948
Email: epml@vsnl.net.
Personnel:
Exec. Dir.: Sudhir Goenka
Phone: (91) 22 258 00 318/319
Fax: (91) 712 255 04 98
Email: ellora_ngp@sancharnet.in
Dir.: Sandeep Goenka
Phone: (91) 22 258 00 318/319
Fax: (91) 22 304 04 500
Email: scgoenka@yahoo.com
Total Employees of Company: 300
Total Employees at this Location: 15
Mill Locations:
Ellora Paper Mills Ltd., Tumsar, Dist. Bhandara Mill, Dewada-Khurd, 441 912 Tumsar, Dist. Bhandara, India, Capacity: 15,000 mt/y, (Paper mill)
Email: ellora_ngp@sancharnet.in

ⓜEllora Paper Mills Ltd.
Tumsar, Dist. Bhandara Mill
Dewada-Khurd
441 912 Tumsar, Dist. Bhandara, Maharashtra
India
Email: ellora_ngp@sancharnet.in
Web Address: www.ellorapaper.com
Personnel:
Exec. Dir.: Sudhir Goenka
Phone: (91) 712 255 0496/97
Man. Dir: C. P. Goenka
Type of Operation: Paper mill
Pulp Grades and Capacities:
Paper/Paperboard Grades and Capacities:
Total paper and paperboard capacity: 15,000 mt/y
Newsprint
Uncoated woodfree/freesheet
Uncoated mechanical/groundwood
Paper and Paperboard Mill Data:
Stock Preparation:
Refiners: 2
Paper Machines: 1
No. 1, fourdrinier, Trim width 2.44 m, Newsprint, Uncoated woodfree/freesheet
Energy Data:
Power boilers: 1
Steam turbines: 1 at 1.4 MW
Electrical demand for mill: 42 MWh/D

ⓗEmami Paper Mills Ltd.
Ownership: 98% by Emami Group of Companies
687, Anandapur, 4th Floor, E.M. Byepass
700 107 Kolkata, West Bengal
India
Phone: (91) 33 6613 6264
Fax: (91) 33 6613 6400
Email: emamipaper@emamipaper.in
Web Address: www.emamipaper.in
Personnel:
Exec. Chmn.: R. S. Goenka
Phone: (91) 33 2248 8592/8654
Fax: (91) 33 2248 9288
Pres.: M. B. Nair
Phone: (91) 33 2248 8592/8654
Fax: (91) 33 2248 9288
Man. Dir.: A. C. Gupta
Phone: (91) 33 2248 8592/8654
Fax: (91) 33 2248 9288
Exec. Dir.: P. S. Patwari
Phone: (91) 33 2248 8592/8654
Fax: (91) 33 2248 9288
VP: Ashish A. Gupta
Phone: (91) 33 2248 8592/8654
Fax: (91) 33 2248 9288
VP (Technical): K. S. Maheswari
Phone: (91) 33 2248 8592/8654
Fax: (91) 33 2248 9288
VP (Finan. & Sec.): G. Saraf
Phone: (91) 33 2248 8592/8654
Fax: (91) 33 2248 9288
VP (Works): M. K. Ganguly
Phone: (91) 33 2248 8592/8654
Fax: (91) 33 2248 9288
VP (Finance): S. K. Khetan
Phone: (91) 33 2248 8592/8654
Fax: (91) 33 2248 9288
Sr. Mktg. Mgr.: V. K. Chandalia
Phone: (91) 33 2248 8592/8654
Fax: (91) 33 2248 9288
Mill Locations:
Emami Paper Mills Ltd., Orissa Mill, Dist. Balasore, India, (Paper mill)
Emami Paper Mills Ltd., Balasore Mill, Balgopalpur, P.O. Rasulpur, 756 020 Dist. Balasore, India, Capacity: 128,520 mt/y, (Pulp mill, Paper mill)
Phone: (91) 6782 275723/26/79
Fax: (91) 6782 275778
Email: balasore@emamipaper.in
Emami Paper Mills Ltd., Kolkata Mill, R.N. Tagore Road, Alambazar, Dakshinewar, 700 035 Kolkata, India, Capacity: 16,500 mt/y, (Paper mill)
Phone: (91) 33 6540 9611
Fax: (91) 33 564 8926

ⓜEmami Paper Mills Ltd.
Orissa Mill
Mill is under construction (new high-end packaging paper mill due to start March 2015)
Dist. Balasore, Odisha
India
Type of Operation: Paper mill

ⓜEmami Paper Mills Ltd.
Balasore Mill
Balgopalpur, P.O. Rasulpur
756 020 Dist. Balasore, Odisha
India
Phone: (91) 6782 275723/26/79
Fax: (91) 6782 275778
Email: balasore@emamipaper.in
Web Address: www.emamipaper.in
Personnel:
Finan. Pres., CFO: S. K. Khetan
Phone: (91) 94 3706 2386
Email: skkhetan@emamipaper.in
VP, (Tech.): B. Chandhiery
Phone: (91) 94 3756 3381
Exec. Dir.: P. S. Patwari
Phone: (91) 98 3003 0067

India

Fax: (91) 33 6613 6400
Email: patwari@emamipaper.in
Oper. Dir.: M. B. S. Nair
Phone: (91) 94 3706 6745
Email: mbsnair@emamipaper.in
Gen. Mgr. (Mktg.): V. K. Chandalia
Phone: (91) 33 6613 6405
Fax: (91) 33 6613 6400
Email: vkc@emamipaper.in
Gen. Mgr. (Works): K. R. Chowdhary
Phone: (91) 6782 275723/55/79
Email: krc@emamipaper.in
Sr. Gen. Mgr. (Prod.): S. Acharya
Phone: (91) 94 3708 2044
Email: achrys@emamipaper.in
Sr. Gen. Mgr. (Power Plant): B. R.D. Agarwal
Phone: (91) 94 3757 7732
Email: affarwal@emamipaper.in
Asst. VP (HR & IR): A. K. Upadhyay
Phone: (91) 94 3708 7630
Email: akupadhyay@emanipaper.in
Sr. Dpty. Gen. Mgr. (Inst.): Basant Srivastava
Phone: (91) 94 3702 1019
Email: srib@emanipaper.in
Total Employees at this Location: 700
Type of Operation: Pulp mill, Paper mill
Pulp Grades and Capacities:
Total pulp capacity: 129,313 mt/y
Recycled Pulping: 129,313 mt/y
Pulp Mill Data:
Bleach Plant Systems: 2
DIP
DIP, Sequence: O_2 CEHHH
Recycled Fiber Treatment Lines:
Flotation deinking lines: 2 at 50,000 admt/y
Pulpers: 3 at 55,000 admt/y
Paper/Paperboard Grades and Capacities:
Total paper and paperboard capacity: 128,520 mt/y
Newsprint: 113,526 mt/y
Uncoated woodfree/freesheet: 14,994 mt/y
Paper and Paperboard Mill Data:
Stock Preparation:
Refiners: 3
Paper Machines: 3
No. 1, fourdrinier, total capacity 14,994 mt/y, Trim width 2.1 m, Uncoated woodfree/freesheet
No. 2, fourdrinier, total capacity 28,203 mt/y, Trim width 2.9 m, Newsprint
No. 3, (second hand), Bel-Baie IV, total capacity 85,323 mt/y, Trim width 3.5 m, Newsprint
Finishing Equipment:
Winders: 3
Energy Data:
Power boilers: 2
Steam turbines: 2 at 5, 15 MW
Electrical demand for mill: 366 MWh/D

ⓜEmami Paper Mills Ltd.
Kolkata Mill
R.N. Tagore Road, Alambazar, Dakshineswar
700 035 Kolkata, West Bengal
India
Phone: (91) 33 6540 9611
Fax: (91) 33 564 8926
Web Address: www.emamipaper.in
Personnel:
Prod. Mgr.: H. K. Mohanty
Phone: (91) 33 6540 9611
Total Employees at this Location: 400
Type of Operation: Paper mill
Paper/Paperboard Grades and Capacities:
Total paper and paperboard capacity: 16,500 mt/y
Newsprint: 16,500 mt/y
Paper and Paperboard Mill Data:
Stock Preparation:
Pulpers: 3
Refiners: 5
Paper Machines: 1
No. 1, fourdrinier, Yankee dryer, total capacity 16,500 mt/y, Trim width 2.5 m, Newsprint

Finishing Equipment:
Rewinders: 1
Sheeters: 1
Energy Data:
Power boilers: 1

ⓜEverest Paper Mills (P) Ltd.
67 Park St.
700 016 Kolkata, West Bengal
India
Phone: (91) 33 2246 3336/229 0614
Fax: (91) 33 2229 1346
Email: everestpapermill@gmail.com
Personnel:
Dir.: Amit Kumar Chhajer
Phone: (91) 33 2246 3336/229 0614
Fax: (91) 33 2229 1346
Chartered Accountant: S. K. Thakur
Phone: (91) 33 2246 3336/229 0614
Fax: (91) 33 2229 1346
Total Employees at this Location: 148
Mill Locations:
Everest Paper Mills (P) Ltd., Ganganagar Mill, Ganganagar, 24-Pargannas (N), Kolkata, India, Capacity: 6,600 mt/y, (Paperboard mill)
Phone: (91) 33 253 83731/87085
Everest Paper Mills (P) Ltd., Janakpurdham Mill, P.O. Box No. 8, Mahendranagar, Janakpurdham, Nepal, Capacity: 10,000 mt/y, (Paper mill)
Phone: (977) 41 20512/20093/22259
Fax: (977) 41 20317/21021
Email: epm@ntc.net.np, everest@ntc.net.np, info@everestgroup.com.np

ⓜEverest Paper Mills (P) Ltd.
Ganganagar Mill
Ganganagar, 24-Pargannas (N)
Kolkata, West Bengal
India
Phone: (91) 33 253 83731/87085
Personnel:
Dir.: Amit Kumar Chhajer
Phone: (91) 33 25387085
Total Employees at this Location: 236
Type of Operation: Paperboard mill
Paper/Paperboard Grades and Capacities:
Total paper and paperboard capacity: 6,600 mt/y
Boxboard/cartonboard: 6,600 mt/y
Paper and Paperboard Mill Data:
Paper Machines: 1
No. 1, total capacity 6,600 mt/y, Trim width 1.9 m, Boxboard/cartonboard

ⓜFiber Marx Papers Ltd.
Kashipur Mill
Ownership: Banwari Paper Mills Ltd.
7Km Jaspur Road
244 713 Kashipur, Uttarakhand
India
Phone: (91) 98370 37883
Fax: (91) 59472 29011
Personnel:
Man. Dir.: K.K. Patel
Phone: (91) 98370 37883
Mill Mgr.: Jasdeep Goraya
Phone: (91) 98370 37883
Total Employees at this Location: 185
Type of Operation: Paper mill
Pulp Grades and Capacities:
Total pulp capacity: 39,771 mt/y
Recycled Pulping: 39,771 mt/y
Pulp Mill Data:
Bleach Plant Systems: 1
Recycled Pulping System
Recycled Fiber Treatment Lines:
Flotation deinking lines: 1
Paper/Paperboard Grades and Capacities:
Total paper and paperboard capacity: 45,000 mt/y
Uncoated woodfree/freesheet: 45,000 mt/y

Paper and Paperboard Mill Data:
Paper Machines: 1
No. 1, fourdrinier, total capacity 45,000 mt/y, Trim width 3.25 m, Uncoated woodfree/freesheet
Energy Data:
Power boilers
Electrical demand for mill: 115 MWh/D

ⓒFibre Foils Ltd.
A/6, M.I.D.C., Road No. 5
400093 Andheri, Mumbai, Maharashtra
India
Phone: (91) 22 2832 6228
Fax: (91) 22 2837 2145
Email: praveen@shetrongroup.com, shetron@vsnl.com
Web Address: www.shetrongroup.com
Personnel:
Chmn.: D. S. Shetti
Phone: (91) 22 2832 6228
Fax: (91) 22 2837 2145
Dir.: Praveen Nally
Phone: (91) 22 2832 6228
Fax: (91) 22 2837 2145
Mill Locations:
Fibre Foils Ltd., Khalapur Mill, Village Dheku, Off Khopoli-Pen Road, 410203 Khalapur, Raigad, India, Capacity: 10,000 mt/y, (Paper mill, Paperboard mill)
Phone: (91) 952192 263408/263410/268930
Fax: (91) 952192 268619

ⓜFibre Foils Ltd.
Khalapur Mill
Village Dheku, Off Khopoli-Pen Road
410203 Khalapur, Raigad, Maharashtra
India
Phone: (91) 952192 263408/263410/268930
Fax: (91) 952192 268619
Web Address: www.shetrongroup.com
Personnel:
Pres.: A. N. Kuklarni
Phone: (91) 952192 263408/263410/268930
Plant Mgr.: A. N. Dirwat
Phone: (91) 952192 263408/263410/268930
Total Employees at this Location: 100
Type of Operation: Paper mill, Paperboard mill
Paper/Paperboard Grades and Capacities:
Total paper and paperboard capacity: 10,000 mt/y
Linerboard
Boxboard/cartonboard: 10,000 mt/y
Paper and Paperboard Mill Data:
Stock Preparation:
Pulpers: 3
Paper Machines: 1
No. 1, cylinder, total capacity 10,000 mt/y, Trim width 1.6 m, Linerboard, Boxboard/cartonboard
Finishing Equipment:
Sheeters: 1

ⓒFortune Paper Mills
8A, National Highway, Opp. Dariyalal Resorts
Morbi, Gujarat
India
Phone: (91) 2822240152
Email: fortunepapers@gmail.com
Mill Locations:
Fortune Paper Mills, Morbi Mill, 8A, National Highway, Opp. Dariyalal Resorts, Morbi, India, Capacity: 50,000 mt/y, (Paper mill)
Phone: (91) 2822240152
Email: fortunepapers@gmail.com

ⓜFortune Paper Mills
Morbi Mill
8A, National Highway, Opp. Dariyalal Resorts
Morbi, Gujarat
India
Phone: (91) 2822240152
Email: fortunepapers@gmail.com

Personnel:
Owner, Dir.: Bhavik Ubhadia
Phone: (91) 98 23289289
Email: fortunepapers@gmail.com
Type of Operation: Paper mill
Pulp Mill Data:
Recycled Fiber Treatment Lines:
Recycled packaging pulping lines: 1
Paper/Paperboard Grades and Capacities:
Total paper and paperboard capacity: 50,000 mt/y
Paper and Paperboard Mill Data:
Paper Machines: 1
No. 1, total capacity 50,000 mt/y, Trim width 4 m, Linerboard

ⓘGahir Paper Mills Ltd.
Tungan Kularan Road, Vill. Akalagarh, Sunam
148028 Sangrur, Punjab
India
Phone: (91) 1676 221380/280
Fax: (91) 1676 220480
Email: gahirindia@gmail.com
Web Address: www.gahirindia.com
Mill Locations:
Gahir Paper Mills Ltd., Sangrur Mill, Tungan Kularan Road, Vill. Akalagarh, Sunam, 148028 Sangrur, India, Capacity: 7,500 mt/y, (Paper mill, Paperboard mill)
Phone: (91) 1676 221380/280
Fax: (91) 1676 220480
Email: gahirindia@gmail.com

ⓜGahir Paper Mills Ltd.
Sangrur Mill
Tungan Kularan Road, Vill. Akalagarh, Sunam
148028 Sangrur, Punjab
India
Phone: (91) 1676 221380/280
Fax: (91) 1676 220480
Email: gahirindia@gmail.com
Web Address: www.gahirindia.com
Personnel:
Chmn.: Nihal Singh Gahir
Phone: (91) 1676 221380/280
Man. Dir.: Gurmail Singh Gahir
Phone: (91) 1676 221380/280
98 76677680.: Jasmail Singh Gahir
Phone: (91) 98 76677680
Email: jasgahir@hotmail.com
Man. Dir.: Jagroop Singh Gahir
Phone: (91) 1676 221380/280
Man. Dir.: Surjit Singh
Phone: (91) 9876611580
Total Employees at this Location: 150
Type of Operation: Paper mill, Paperboard mill
Paper/Paperboard Grades and Capacities:
Total paper and paperboard capacity: 7,500 mt/y
Uncoated woodfree/freesheet
Boxboard/cartonboard: 7,500 mt/y
Paper and Paperboard Mill Data:
Stock Preparation:
Refiners: 4
Paper Machines: 2
PM 1, Yankee dryer
No. 2, cylinder mould, Trim width 1.6 m
Finishing Equipment:
Rewinders: 1
Sheeters: 2
Energy Data:
Power boilers: 1

ⓘGajanan Paper Mill (P) Ltd
Plot No. B-10, 11&12 M.I.D.C., Malkapur Buldana,
Maharashtra, 443 101
Maharashtra
India
Phone: (91) 7267 252 351/338
Fax: (91) 7267 252 338
Personnel:
Man. Dir.: Prabhakar Narayan Patil
Phone: (91) 7267 252 351/338
Fax: (91) 7267 252 338
Finan. Mgr.: Rupesh Sharma
Phone: (91) 7267 252 351/338
Fax: (91) 7267 252 338
Mill Locations:
Gajanan Paper Mill (P) Ltd, Buldana Mill, Plot No. B-10, 11&12 M.I.D.C., Malkapur, 443 101 Buldana, India, Capacity: 9,000 mt/y, (Paper mill, Paperboard mill)
Phone: (91) 7267 252 351/338
Fax: (91) 7267 252 338

ⓜGajanan Paper Mill (P) Ltd
Buldana Mill
Plot No. B-10, 11&12 M.I.D.C., Malkapur
443 101 Buldana, Maharashtra
India
Phone: (91) 7267 252 351/338
Fax: (91) 7267 252 338
Personnel:
Finan. Mgr.: Rupesh Sharma
Phone: (91) 94 03198722
Type of Operation: Paper mill, Paperboard mill
Paper/Paperboard Grades and Capacities:
Total paper and paperboard capacity: 9,000 mt/y
Packaging papers

ⓘGanga Papers India
D-8, Sanskriti Prangan, Baner, Balewadi Road
411 005 Pune, Maharashtra
India
Phone: (91) 20 2325685/677/25533490/66206581
Fax: (91) 20 25533230/66206582
Personnel:
Man. Dir.: Sandeep Kanoria
Phone: (91) 93 26917586
Mill Locations:
Ganga Papers India, Pune Mill, G-80, Gate No. 241, Village Bebedhoal, Taluka Maval, Dist. Pune, India, Capacity: 43,200 mt/y, (Paper mill)
Phone: (91) 2114 22242/622/281729
Fax: (91) 2114 222642

ⓜGanga Papers India
Pune Mill
G-80, Gate No. 241, Village Bebedhoal
Taluka Maval, Dist. Pune, Maharashtra
India
Phone: (91) 2114 22242/622/281729
Fax: (91) 2114 222642
Personnel:
Man. Dir: Sandeep Kanoria
Phone: (91) 93 26917586
Gen. Mgr. (Mktg): O. G. Shukla
Phone: (91) 96 71911712
Prod. Mgr.: K. K. Datta
Phone: (91) 2149.75884244373
Mill Mgr.: S. K. Poddar
Phone: (91) 2149.75884244373
Total Employees at this Location: 170
Type of Operation: Paper mill
Paper/Paperboard Grades and Capacities:
Total paper and paperboard capacity: 43,200 mt/y
Newsprint
Uncoated woodfree/freesheet: 31,000 mt/y
Packaging papers
Paper and Paperboard Mill Data:
Stock Preparation:
Refiners: 0
Paper Machines: 2
No. 1, Trim width 2.8 m
No. 2, Trim width 2 m
Energy Data:
Power boilers

ⓘⓜGangotri Paper Mills Pvt Ltd.
Muzaffarnagar Mill
Muzaffarnagar, Uttar Pradesh
India

Personnel:
Pres, Contr.: Vinod Mattal
Total Employees at this Location: 170
Type of Operation: Paper mill
Pulp Grades and Capacities:
Total pulp capacity: 69,821 mt/y
Recycled Pulping: 69,821 mt/y
Pulp Mill Data:
Recycled Fiber Treatment Lines:
Recycled packaging pulping lines: 1
Paper/Paperboard Grades and Capacities:
Total paper and paperboard capacity: 70,000 mt/y
Linerboard: 70,000 mt/y
Paper and Paperboard Mill Data:
Paper Machines: 1
No. 1, fourdrinier, total capacity 70,000 mt/y, Trim width 4.11 m, Linerboard
Energy Data:
Power boilers
Electrical demand for mill: 80 MWh/D

ⓘGarg Duplex & Paper Mills Pvt. Ltd.
8.5 km, Bhopa Road Muzaffarnagar, Uttar Pradesh, 251001
Uttar Pradesh
India
Phone: (91) 31 2468600/01, 31 413878/413860
Personnel:
Dir.: Rajesh Jain
Phone: (91) 31 413878/413860
Dir.: Rajeev Jain
Phone: (91) 31 413878/413860
Gen. Mgr.: Devesh Garg
Phone: (91) 31 413878/413860
Mill Locations:
Garg Duplex & Paper Mills Pvt. Ltd., Muzaffarnagar Mill, 8.5 km, Bhopa Road, 251001 Muzaffarnagar, India, Capacity: 15,000 mt/y, (Paper mill)
Phone: (91) 131 246 8600/01, 131 413878/413860

ⓜGarg Duplex & Paper Mills Pvt. Ltd.
Muzaffarnagar Mill
8.5 km, Bhopa Road
251001 Muzaffarnagar, Uttar Pradesh
India
Phone: (91) 131 246 8600/01, 131 413878/413860
Personnel:
Dir.: Rajesh Jain
Phone: (91) 93 59797071
Gen. Mgr.: Devesh Garg
Phone: (91) 98 37027552
Type of Operation: Paper mill
Paper/Paperboard Grades and Capacities:
Total paper and paperboard capacity: 15,000 mt/y
Packaging papers: 15,000 mt/y
Paper and Paperboard Mill Data:
Paper Machines: 2
No. 1, Packaging papers
No. 2, Packaging papers

ⓘGaurav Paper Mills
Ownership: 100% by Ravindra Steel Ltd.
F-201, Jagat Plaza, Opp. Law College Sq., Amravati rd
440 010 Nagpur, Maharashtra
India
Phone: (91) 712 2542790/2542791
Fax: (91) 712 2554563
Email: admin@gpml.in
Personnel:
Exec. Dir.: Abhay Agarwala
Phone: (91) 712 2542790/2542791
Fax: (91) 712 2554563
Chmn./Man. Dir.: Surendra Agarwala
Phone: (91) 712 2542790/2542791
Fax: (91) 712 2554563
Chief Accounts Officer: B.V. Saoji
Phone: (91) 712 2542790/2542791
Fax: (91) 712 2554563
Total Employees of Company: 125

India

Mill Locations:
Gaurav Paper Mills, Chandrapur Mill, Hardoli, Tehsil Bramhapuri, 441206 Chandrapur, India, Capacity: 10,000 mt/y, (Pulp mill, Paper mill)
Phone: (91) 7177 272154-5
Fax: (91) 7177 272155
Email: admin@gpml.in, gpm1010_ngp@sanchamet.com

ⓂGaurav Paper Mills
Chandrapur Mill
Hardoli, Tehsil Bramhapuri
441206 Chandrapur, Maharashtra
India
Phone: (91) 7177 272154-5
Fax: (91) 7177 272155
Email: admin@gpml.in,
gpm1010_ngp@sanchamet.com
Personnel:
Man. Dir.: Surendra Agarwal
Phone: (91) 98 23075366
Exec. Dir.: Abhay Agarwal
Phone: (91) 712 25420790
Fax: (91) 712 2554563
Gen. Mgr.: S. B. Purohit
Phone: (91) 94 23100961
Prod. Mgr.: M. G. Rao
Phone: (91) 7177 272154/155
Type of Operation: Pulp mill, Paper mill
Pulp Grades and Capacities:
Total pulp capacity: 18,000 mt/y
Pulp Mill Data:
Chemical Pulping Systems:
Batch digesters: 2
Continuous digesters: 1
Paper/Paperboard Grades and Capacities:
Total paper and paperboard capacity: 10,000 mt/y
Newsprint: 10,000 mt/y
Paper and Paperboard Mill Data:
Stock Preparation:
Refiners: 4
Paper Machines: 1
No. 1, fourdrinier, Trim width 2.8 m, Newsprint
Energy Data:
Power boilers: 2

ⓄGayatri Paper Mills Pvt. Ltd.
Ownership: 100% by Gayatri Investment Company, South Africa
12/18, C.P. Tank, V.P. Road, 10th Floor, Opp. Union Bank of India
400004 Mumbai, Maharashtra
India
Phone: (91) 22 22420715/62
Fax: (91) 22 22420697
Personnel:
Man. Dir.: P. D. Choudhary
Phone: (91) 22 22420715/62
Fax: (91) 22 22420697
Mill Locations:
Gayatri Paper Mill, Germiston Mill, 1 Power Street Industries West, Germiston 1400, South Africa, Capacity: 90,000 mt/y, (Paper mill, Paperboard mill)
Phone: (27) 11 821 8600
Fax: (27) 11 872 1884
Email: sales@gayatripaper.co.za
Gayatri Paper Mills Pvt. Ltd., Raigarh Mill, A-32 MIDC, PatalGanga, Tehsil Khopoli, 410 220 Raigarh, India, Capacity: 8,000 mt/y, (Paper mill)
Phone: (91) 02528 250322
Fax: (91) 02528 254739

ⓂGayatri Paper Mills Pvt. Ltd.
Raigarh Mill
A-32 MIDC, PatalGanga, Tehsil Khopoli
410 220 Raigarh, Maharashtra
India
Phone: (91) 02528 250322
Fax: (91) 02528 254739

Personnel:
Man. Dir.: P. B. Choudhary
Phone: (91) 22094232/260
Dir. Works: Sanjeev K. Choudhary
Phone: (91) 22094232/260
Comm. Mgr./ Factory Mgr.: T. V. Bhaskaran
Phone: (91) 22094232/260
Prod. Mgr.: Tapan Kr. Ganguly
Phone: (91) 22094232/260
Total Employees at this Location: 125
Type of Operation: Paper mill
Paper/Paperboard Grades and Capacities:
Total paper and paperboard capacity: 8,000 mt/y
Packaging papers: 8,000 mt/y
Paper and Paperboard Mill Data:
Paper Machines: 1
No. 1, Trim width 1.9 m, Packaging papers

ⓄGayatrishakti Paper & Boards Ltd.
Raheja Universal Pvt. Ltd.
400 053 Andheri (West), Mumbai, Maharashtra
India
Phone: (91) (022) 42380000
Fax: (91) (022) 42380011
Email: gayatrishakti@vsnl.net, info@gspbl.com
Web Address: www.gspbl.com
Personnel:
Chmn.: Shri N.R. Agarwal
CEO: Shri R.N Agarwal
Man. Dir.: Shri G.N. Agarwal
Mill Locations:
Gayatrishakti Paper & Boards Ltd., Vapi Mill, Plot No. 799/1, 3rd Phase, 396195 Vapi, India, Capacity: 60,000 mt/y, (Paperboard mill)
Phone: (91) 260 2400451/2401588/2424560
Email: gspbl_vapi@sify.com, info@gspbl.com

ⓂGayatrishakti Paper & Boards Ltd.
Vapi Mill
Plot No. 799/1, 3rd Phase
396195 Vapi, Gujarat
India
Phone: (91) 260 2400451/2401588/2424560
Email: gspbl_vapi@sify.com, info@gspbl.com
Web Address: www.gspbl.com
Personnel:
Gen. Mgr. (Production): B. Drison
Phone: (91) 260 2400451/2401588/2424560
Tech. Dir.: A. K. Bansal
Phone: (91) 99 09300555/96 99956622
Email: akbansal@gspbl.com
Total Employees at this Location: 250
Type of Operation: Paperboard mill
Pulp Grades and Capacities:
Total pulp capacity: 55,690 mt/y
Recycled Pulping: 55,690 mt/y
Pulp Mill Data:
Bleach Plant Systems: 1
DIP
Recycled Fiber Treatment Lines:
Flotation deinking lines: 1
Recycled packaging pulping lines: 1
Paper/Paperboard Grades and Capacities:
Total paper and paperboard capacity: 60,000 mt/y
Boxboard/cartonboard: 60,000 mt/y
Paper and Paperboard Mill Data:
Paper Machines: 1
No. 1, fourdrinier, total capacity 60,000 mt/y, Trim width 2.92 m, Boxboard/cartonboard
Coating Machines: 1
No. 1, total capacity 60,000 mt/y., on machine
Energy Data:
Power boilers: 1
Steam turbines: 1 at 5 MW
Electrical demand for mill: 79 MWh/D

ⓄGenus Paper Products Limited
Ownership: 100% by Kailash Group of Companies
D-116, Okhla Industrial Area, Phase-I
110020 New Delhi, Delhi
India
Phone: (91) 911126371882 / 83 / 84 / 85
Fax: (91) 911126371881
Mill Locations:
Genus Paper Products Limited, Moradabad Mill, Village Aghwanpur, 10 km Stone, Kanth Road, 244001 Moradabad, India, Capacity: 90,000 mt/y, (Paper mill)
Phone: (91) 915912511171 / 2511531 / 2511532 / 2511060
Fax: (91) 915912511242
Email: info@genuspaper.com

ⓂGenus Paper Products Limited
Moradabad Mill
Village Aghwanpur, 10 km Stone, Kanth Road
244001 Moradabad, Uttar Pradesh
India
Phone: (91) 915912511171 / 2511531 / 2511532 / 2511060
Fax: (91) 915912511242
Email: info@genuspaper.com
Web Address: www.genuspaper.com
Personnel:
Chmn.: Ishwar Chand Agarwal
Phone: (91) 591 2511171/5533844/5533899
Man. Dir.: Kailash Chandra Agarwal
Phone: (91) 591 2511171/5533844/5533899
Dir.: Himanshu Agarawal
Phone: (91) 591 2511171/5533844/5533899
Dir.: Rameshwar Pareek
Phone: (91) 591 2511171/5533844/5533899
Dir.: Surendra Agarwal
Phone: (91) 591 2511171/5533844/5533899
Total Employees at this Location: 270
Type of Operation: Paper mill
Pulp Grades and Capacities:
Total pulp capacity: 89,982 mt/y
Recycled Pulping: 89,982 mt/y
Pulp Mill Data:
Recycled Fiber Treatment Lines:
Recycled packaging pulping lines: 1
Paper/Paperboard Grades and Capacities:
Total paper and paperboard capacity: 90,000 mt/y
Linerboard: 90,000 mt/y
Paper and Paperboard Mill Data:
Paper Machines: 2
No. 1, fourdrinier, total capacity 40,000 mt/y, Trim width 2.24 m, Linerboard
No. 2, multi-fourdrinier, total capacity 50,000 mt/y, Trim width 3.8 m, Linerboard
Energy Data:
Power boilers
Steam turbines at 6 MW
Electrical demand for mill: 131 MWh/D

ⓄⓂGit-Vijay Paper Mills (P) Ltd.
Mehsana Mill
Near Sobhasan Railway Crossing
384 002 Mehsana, Gujarat
India
Phone: (91) 2762 252 556/257 311
Personnel:
Man. Dir.: Mahendra Sinh Vaghela
Phone: (91) 2762 252 556/257 311
Type of Operation: Paper mill
Paper/Paperboard Grades and Capacities:
Total paper and paperboard capacity: 7,200 mt/y
Packaging papers: 7,200 mt/y
Paper and Paperboard Mill Data:
Paper Machines: 1
No. 1, total capacity 7,200 mt/y, Packaging papers

ⓘGodavari Pulp and Papers Mills (P) Ltd

Ownership: 100% by Promoter Group
Gut No. 405, Village - Lakhmapur, Taluka - Dindori
422 202 Nasik, Maharashtra
India
 Phone: (91) 2557 250517/518/519
 Fax: (91) 2557 250325
 Email: godavari@mansingkaenterprises.com
Mill Locations:
Godavari Pulp and Papers Mills (P) Ltd, Nasik Mill, Gut No. 405, Village - Lakhmapur, Taluka - Dindori, 422 202 Nasik, India, Capacity: 50,000 mt/y, (Paper mill)
Phone: (91) 2557 250517/518/519
Fax: (91) 2557 250325
Email: godavari@mansingkaenterprises.com

ⓂGodavari Pulp and Papers Mills (P) Ltd
Nasik Mill

Gut No. 405, Village - Lakhmapur, Taluka - Dindori
422 202 Nasik, Maharashtra
India
 Phone: (91) 2557 250517/518/519
 Fax: (91) 2557 250325
 Email: godavari@mansingkaenterprises.com
Personnel:
 Man. Dir.: Pankaj Mann Singh
 Phone: (91) 98 22458623
 Mill Mgr.: Madaiya Omprakash Jaggaram
 Phone: (91) 2557 250517/518/519
Total Employees at this Location: 100
Type of Operation: Paper mill
Pulp Grades and Capacities:
 Total pulp capacity: 48,794 mt/y
 Recycled Pulping: 48,794 mt/y
Pulp Mill Data:
 Mechanical Pulping Systems:
 Conventional grinders: 2
 Pulp Lines: 1
 Recycled Fiber Treatment Lines:
 Pulpers: 3 at 25,000 admt/y
Paper/Paperboard Grades and Capacities:
 Total paper and paperboard capacity: 50,000 mt/y
 Corrugating medium/fluting: 50,000 mt/y
Paper and Paperboard Mill Data:
 Stock Preparation:
 Pulpers: 3
 Refiners: 3
 Paper Machines: 1
 No. 1, multi-wire, total capacity 50,000 mt/y, Trim width 2.18 m, Corrugating medium/fluting
 Finishing Equipment:
 Winders: 1 at 84,000 mt/y
Energy Data:
 Power boilers: 1
 Electrical demand for mill: 62 MWh/D

ⓘGoodwill Team Papers Ltd

Team Garden, Uthappanaickanur
Usilampatti, Madurai, Tamil Nadu
India
 Phone: (91) 4543 227 329
 Fax: (91) 4543 227 459
 Email: gtpl@sancharnet.in
Mill Locations:
Goodwill Team Papers Ltd, Usilampatti Mill, Team Garden, Uthappanaickanur, Usilampatti, Madurai, India, Capacity: 8,500 mt/y, (Paper mill)
Phone: (91) 4543 227 329
Fax: (91) 4543 227 459
Email: gtpl@sancharnet.in

ⓂGoodwill Team Papers Ltd
Usilampatti Mill

Team Garden, Uthappanaickanur
Usilampatti, Madurai, Tamil Nadu
India
 Phone: (91) 4543 227 329
 Fax: (91) 4543 227 459
 Email: gtpl@sancharnet.in
Personnel:
 Man. Dir.: Mr. P. Rajendran
 Phone: (91) 98 42930011
 Sls. Mgr.: S. Raghunath
 Phone: (91) 98 42127329
Type of Operation: Paper mill
Paper/Paperboard Grades and Capacities:
 Total paper and paperboard capacity: 8,500 mt/y
 Packaging papers: 8,500 mt/y
Paper and Paperboard Mill Data:
Paper Machines: 1
No. 1, Trim width 2.3 m, Packaging papers

ⓘⓂGoraya Straw Board Mills (P) Ltd
Udham Singh Nagar Mill

2kM Mile Stone, Bazpur Road, Kashiûr
244 713 Kashipur, Uttarakhand
India
 Phone: (91) 5947277026
 Fax: (91) 5947277026
Personnel:
 VP, Oper. Mgr.: Parul Kohli
 Phone: (91) 98 37088454
 Man. Dir.: Sukhwinder Singh Goraya
 Phone: (91) 98 37048821
 Gen. Mgr., Commer. Dir.: Sudhir Chandra Karnatic
 Phone: (91) 98 97444825
Type of Operation: Paper mill, Paperboard mill
Paper/Paperboard Grades and Capacities:
 Total paper and paperboard capacity: 8,250 mt/y
 Packaging papers
 Boxboard/cartonboard: 8,250 mt/y

ⓂGramox Paper & Boards Ltd.
Ernakulam Mill

Puthuppady P.O. Muvattupuza
686673 Ernakulam, Kerala
India
 Phone: (91) 485 2815592/6192
 Fax: (91) 485 2815810
 Email: gramox@eth.net,
 gramox08@bsnl.in
Personnel:
 Office Mgr.: Manoj Kumar
 Phone: (91) 485 2815592/6192
 Man. Dir.: George C. Moolayil
 Phone: (91) 485 2815592/6192
 Dir.: M. C. Joseph
 Phone: (91) 94 47034592
Type of Operation: Paper mill, Paperboard mill
Paper/Paperboard Grades and Capacities:
 Total paper and paperboard capacity: 12,000 mt/y
 Boxboard/cartonboard: 12,000 mt/y
Paper and Paperboard Mill Data:
Paper Machines: 1
No. 1, total capacity 12,000 mt/y, Trim width 2 m, Boxboard/cartonboard

ⓘGrasim Industries Ltd

Ownership: Aditya Birla Group
PO Birlagram
456 331 Nagda, M.P
India
 Phone: (91) 7366 46760/62/64/66
 Fax: (91) 7366 44114/46024
 Web Address: www.adityabirla.com,
 www.grasim.com,
 www.birlaviscose.com
Personnel:
 Chmn.: Kumar Mangalam Birla
 Phone: (91) 7366 46760/62/64/66
 Fax: (91) 7366 44114/46024
 Pulp & Fibre Bus. Dir.: Shailendra KumarJain
 Phone: (91) 7366 46760/62/64/66
 Fax: (91) 7366 44114/46024
Mill Locations:
Grasim Industries Ltd, Harihar Polyfibers & Grasilene Division, Harihar, Dist Haveri, 581 123 Kumarpatanam, India, (Pulp mill)
Phone: (91) 08373 242171/75
Fax: (91) 08373 242875
Email: msamuel@adityabirla.com

ⓂGrasim Industries Ltd
Harihar Polyfibers & Grasilene Division

Ownership: Aditya Birla Group
Harihar, Dist Haveri
581 123 Kumarpatanam, Karnataka
India
 Phone: (91) 08373 242171/75
 Fax: (91) 08373 242875
 Email: msamuel@adityabirla.com
 Web Address: www.grasim.com
Personnel:
 Sr. Exec. Pres.: Thomas S. Varghese
 Phone: (91) 08373 242171/75
 Email: varghese@adityabirla.com
 Sr. VP: B.N. Agarwal
 Phone: (91) 08373 242171/75
 Email: bnagarwal@adityabirla.com
 VP: Mr. Manjunath
 Phone: (91) 08373 242171/75
 Email: manjunath@adityabirla.com
Total Employees at this Location: 500
Type of Operation: Pulp mill
Pulp Grades and Capacities:
 Total pulp capacity: 80,127 mt/y
 Pulp available for market: 74,970 mt/y
 Chemical Pulp: 80,127 mt/y
Pulp Mill Data:
 Chemical Pulping Systems:
 Batch digesters: 9
 Pulp Lines: 1
 Bleach Plant Systems: 1
 No. 1, Sequence: CEoHED/SO$_2$, Capacity 81,600 admt/y
 Chemical Recovery Equipment:
 Evaporator lines: 2
 Recovery boilers: 2
 Pulp Dryers:
 Flash dryers 1
Energy Data:
 Power boilers: 2
 Steam turbines: 1 at 10.0 MW
 Electrical demand for mill: 214 MWh/D

ⓂGRD Paper Industries PVT. Ltd
Howrah Mill

Ownership: East India Paper & Board Mills
NH 6, Mouja, Chamrail. Liluah
711323 Howrah, West Bengal
India
 Web Address: www.eastindiapaperboard.com
Type of Operation: Paper mill
Paper/Paperboard Grades and Capacities:
 Total paper and paperboard capacity: 35,000 mt/y
 Newsprint
 Uncoated woodfree/freesheet
Paper and Paperboard Mill Data:
Paper Machines: 1
No. 1, fourdrinier, Newsprint, Uncoated woodfree/freesheet

ⓘGreenland Paper Mill Ltd

AP 1/34 A, Kummalloor Adichanalloor
691 573 Kollam
India
 Phone: (91) 474 259 4174/2520, 470 262 9846
Personnel:
 Chair & Man. Dir.: A. M. Ashraf
 Phone: (91) 470 2624496/3202699
 Sls. Dir.: Rajendran Pillai
 Phone: (91) 94 47460954
Total Employees at this Location: 150

India

Mill Locations:
Greenland Paper Mill Ltd, Kollam Mill, AP 1/34 A, Kummalloor Adichanalloor, 691 573 Kollam, India, Capacity: 9,000 mt/y, (Paper mill)
Phone: (91) 474 259 4174/2520, 470 262 9846

ⓂGreenland Paper Mill Ltd
Kollam Mill
AP 1/34 A, Kummalloor Adichanalloor
691 573 Kollam, Kerala
India
Phone: (91) 474 259 4174/2520, 470 262 9846
Personnel:
Chair & Man. Dir.: Mr. A. M. Ashraf
Phone: (91) 470 2624496/3202699
Sls. Dir.: Rajendran Pillai
Phone: (91) 94 47460954
Total Employees at this Location: 150
Type of Operation: Paper mill
Paper/Paperboard Grades and Capacities:
Total paper and paperboard capacity: 9,000 mt/y
Packaging papers: 9,000 mt/y

ⓂGugan Paper Mills Pvt Ltd
Gugan Paper Mills Pvt Ltd
#9/45, P.M.P. Vasantham, V.K.L Nagar Main Road, Thudiyalur Post,
641034 Coimbatore, Tamil Nadu
India
Phone: (91) 9047277000
Fax: (91) 9443033315
Personnel:
Dir.: Mr. Gunaseelam
Type of Operation: Paper mill
Pulp Grades and Capacities:
Total pulp capacity: 49,317 mt/y
Recycled Pulping: 49,317 mt/y
Paper/Paperboard Grades and Capacities:
Total paper and paperboard capacity: 50,000 mt/y
Linerboard: 30,000 mt/y
Corrugating medium/fluting: 20,000 mt/y
Paper and Paperboard Mill Data:
Paper Machines: 1
No. 1, multi-wire, total capacity 50,000 mt/y, Trim width 2.55 m, Corrugating medium/fluting, Linerboard
Energy Data:
Electrical demand for mill: 61 MWh/D

ⓂGVG Paper Mills Ltd.
Ownership: 100% by private
168/2, Sikandhar Batcha St., Gandhi Nagar
642154 Udumalpet, Dist. Tirupur, Tamil Nadu
India
Phone: (91) 4252 224113/513/943
Fax: (91) 4252 225425
Email: gvgpaper@md4.vsnl.net.in
Web Address: www.gvgpaper.com
Personnel:
Group Gen. Mgr.: R. Duraiswamy
Phone: (91) 94433 74513
Fax: (91) 4252 225425
Total Employees of Company: 245
Mill Locations:
GVG Paper Mills Ltd., Palani Taluk Mill, Nallur, Pushpathur, 424618 Palani Taluk, Dist. Dindigul, India, Capacity: 103,000 mt/y, (Paper mill)
Phone: (91) 4252 252327/536
Fax: (91) 4252 225425
Email: gvgpaper@md4.vsnl.net.in
Shri Harikrishna Papers PVT. Ltd., Palani Taluk Mill, Nallur, PushpathurVillage, 624 618 Palani Taluk, India, Capacity: 36,500 mt/y, (Paper mill)
Phone: (91) 4252 252541/542
Email: gvgpaper@md4.vsnl.net.in

ⓂGVG Paper Mills Ltd.
Palani Taluk Mill
Nallur, Pushpathur
424618 Palani Taluk, Dist. Dindigul, Tamil Nadu
India
Phone: (91) 4252 252327/536
Fax: (91) 4252 225425
Email: gvgpaper@md4.vsnl.net.in
Web Address: www.gvgpaper.com
Personnel:
Man. Dir.: Mr. M. Amarnath
Phone: (91) 98 43072212
Gen. Mgr. (Finan.): Mr. N. P. Madhavan
Phone: (91) 98 43024113
Gen. Mgr.: S. Sukumar
Phone: (91) 98 43024113
Total Employees at this Location: 400
Type of Operation: Paper mill
Pulp Grades and Capacities:
Total pulp capacity: 96,118 mt/y
Recycled Pulping: 96,118 mt/y
Pulp Mill Data:
Bleach Plant Systems: 1
Recycled Pulping System
Recycled Fiber Treatment Lines:
Flotation deinking lines: 1
Recycled packaging pulping lines: 1
Paper/Paperboard Grades and Capacities:
Total paper and paperboard capacity: 103,000 mt/y
Newsprint: 15,000 mt/y
Uncoated woodfree/freesheet: 20,000 mt/y
Corrugating medium/fluting: 14,000 mt/y
Boxboard/cartonboard: 54,000 mt/y
Paper and Paperboard Mill Data:
Stock Preparation:
Refiners: 7
Paper Machines: 4
No. 1, fourdrinier, total capacity 15,000 mt/y, Trim width 2.75 m, Newsprint
No. 2, fourdrinier, total capacity 20,000 mt/y, Trim width 2.65 m, Uncoated woodfree/freesheet
No. 3, fourdrinier, total capacity 14,000 mt/y, Trim width 2.8 m, Corrugating medium/fluting
No. 4, cylinder (7), total capacity 54,000 mt/y, Trim width 2.9 m, Boxboard/cartonboard
Coating Machines: 1
PM4, on machine
Finishing Equipment:
Rewinders: 1
Energy Data:
Power boilers: 2
Steam turbines at 3 MW
Wind turbines at 1.5 MW
Electrical demand for mill: 164 MWh/D

ⓂHanuman Agro Industries Ltd.
Paragaon, Nawapara, Rajim
493885 Raipur, Chattisgarh
India
Phone: (91) 7701 233922/219
Fax: (91) 7701 233689
Email: hail@sancharnet.in
Web Address: www.hanumangroup.com
Mill Locations:
Hanuman Agro Industries Ltd., Raipur Mill, Paragaon, Nawapara, Rajim, 493885 Raipur, India, Capacity: 12,500 mt/y, (Pulp mill, Paper mill)
Phone: (91) 7701 233922/219
Fax: (91) 7701 233689
Email: hail@sancharnet.in

ⓂHanuman Agro Industries Ltd.
Raipur Mill
Paragaon, Nawapara, Rajim
493885 Raipur, Chattisgarh
India
Phone: (91) 7701 233922/219
Fax: (91) 7701 233689
Email: hail@sancharnet.in
Web Address: www.hanumangroup.com
Personnel:
Technol. Mgr.: Anjan Kanori
Phone: (91) 7701 233922/219
Prod. Mgr., Mktg. Mgr.: Anil Kanoria
Phone: (91) 7701 233922/219
Gen. Mgr.: Avijit Roy Choudhury
Phone: (91) 94 25206510
Email: royc_avijit@yahoo.com
Commer. Dir.: R. K. Thakur
Phone: (91) 7701 233922/219
Total Employees at this Location: 150
Type of Operation: Pulp mill, Paper mill
Pulp Mill Data:
Bleach Plant Lines:
No. 1, Sequence: CEH
Paper/Paperboard Grades and Capacities:
Total paper and paperboard capacity: 12,500 mt/y
Uncoated woodfree/freesheet: 12,500 mt/y
Paper and Paperboard Mill Data:
Stock Preparation:
Refiners: 1
Paper Machines: 1
No. 1, fourdrinier, total capacity 12,500 mt/y, Trim width 1.9 m, Uncoated woodfree/freesheet
Finishing Equipment:
Sheeters: 1 at 13,000 mt/y
Energy Data:
Power boilers: 1

ⓂHanuman Chromocoates Ltd.
Nicco House, Block "C", 5th Flr., 2, Hare St
700001 Kolkata, West Bengal
India
Email: hanuman@cal.vsnl.net.in
Mill Locations:
Hanuman Chromocoates Ltd., Chhindwara Mill, Borgoan Industrial Area, Tehsil Sansar, 480 106 Chhindwara, M.P., India, Capacity: 6,600 mt/y, (Paper mill, Paperboard mill)
Email: hanuman@cal.vsnl.net.in

ⓂHanuman Chromocoates Ltd.
Chhindwara Mill
Borgoan Industrial Area, Tehsil Sansar
480 106 Chhindwara, M.P
India
Email: hanuman@cal.vsnl.net.in
Personnel:
Man. Dir.: Anand Kanoria
Phone: (91) 98 30040797
Type of Operation: Paper mill, Paperboard mill
Paper/Paperboard Grades and Capacities:
Total paper and paperboard capacity: 6,600 mt/y
Specialty and industrial

ⓂHardoli Paper Mills Ltd.
42, km. Stone, Nagpur Amravati Road, Vill. Hardoli
Nagpur, Maharashtra
India
Phone: (91) 712 2770968
Email: hardolipaper@gmail.com, hardoli.ndp@sancharnet.in
Mill Locations:
Hardoli Paper Mills Ltd., Nagpur Mill, 42, km. Stone, Nagpur Amravati Road, Vill. Hardoli, Nagpur, India, Capacity: 20,000 mt/y, (Paper mill)
Phone: (91) 712 2770968
Email: hardolipaper@gmail.com, hardoli.ndp@sancharnet.in

ⓂHardoli Paper Mills Ltd.
Nagpur Mill
42, km. Stone, Nagpur Amravati Road, Vill. Hardoli
Nagpur, Maharashtra
India
Phone: (91) 712 2770968
Email: hardolipaper@gmail.com, hardoli.ndp@sancharnet.in
Personnel:
Man. Dir.: Kailashchandra Agrawal
Phone: (91) 712 2770968

India

Dir.: Anilkumar Lakhotiya
Phone: (91) 98 23020315
Total Employees at this Location: 234
Type of Operation: Paper mill
Paper/Paperboard Grades and Capacities:
Total paper and paperboard capacity: 20,000 mt/y
Packaging papers: 20,000 mt/y
Paper and Paperboard Mill Data:
Paper Machines: 1
No. 1, Trim width 2.78 m, Packaging papers

ⓂⓂHari Ohm Paper Mills (P) Ltd.
Surat Mill
Ownership: 100% by Private Shareholders
Post Gangadhara
394 310 Surat, Gujarat
India
Phone: (91) 2622 263229/203
Fax: (91) 2622 263229
Personnel:
Chmn.: Ramanbhai H. Patel
Phone: (91) 2622 263229/203
Man. Dir.: Amruth J. Pandya
Phone: (91) 98 24193430
Total Employees at this Location: 120
Type of Operation: Paper mill
Paper/Paperboard Grades and Capacities:
Total paper and paperboard capacity: 5,600 mt/y
Packaging papers: 5,600 mt/y
Paper and Paperboard Mill Data:
Paper Machines: 1
No. 1, Trim width 1.7 m, Packaging papers

ⓂⓂHariom Industries Limited
Kanpur Mill
74\276 Halsy Road
Kanpur, Uttar Pradesh
India
Phone: (91) 9369910814
Personnel:
Dir.: Surendra Gupda
Phone: (91) 9369910814
Dir.: Virendra Gupta
Phone: (91) 9369910814
Total Employees at this Location: 145
Type of Operation: Paper mill
Pulp Grades and Capacities:
Total pulp capacity: 33,998 mt/y
Recycled Pulping: 33,998 mt/y
Pulp Mill Data:
Recycled Fiber Treatment Lines:
Recycled packaging pulping lines: 1
Paper/Paperboard Grades and Capacities:
Total paper and paperboard capacity: 35,000 mt/y
Corrugating medium/fluting: 35,000 mt/y
Paper and Paperboard Mill Data:
Paper Machines: 1
No. 1, fourdrinier, total capacity 35,000 mt/y, Trim width 4.3 m, Corrugating medium/fluting
Energy Data:
Power boilers
Electrical demand for mill: 42 MWh/D

ⓂHarisar Papers Ltd
V.P.O.Dhanansu, Tajpur Road
Ludhiana, Punjab
India
Phone: (91) 161 284 3001/283 0002
Fax: (91) 161 283 0002
Email: harisarpapers@yahoo.com
Mill Locations:
Harisar Papers Ltd, Ludhiana Mill, V.P.O.Dhanansu, Tajpur Road, Ludhiana, India, Capacity: 7,200 mt/y, (Paper mill, Paperboard mill)
Phone: (91) 161 284 3001/283 0002
Fax: (91) 161 283 0002
Email: harisarpapers@yahoo.com

ⓂHarisar Papers Ltd
Ludhiana Mill
V.P.O.Dhanansu, Tajpur Road
Ludhiana, Punjab
India
Phone: (91) 161 284 3001/283 0002
Fax: (91) 161 283 0002
Email: harisarpapers@yahoo.com
Personnel:
Man. Dir.: Tek Singh
Phone: (91) 94 17034083
Dir.: Sukhuvir Sing
Phone: (91) 98 76002449
Dir.: Rajbir Singh
Phone: (91) 98 15500578
Email: fadehjassar@yahoo.co.in
Type of Operation: Paper mill, Paperboard mill
Paper/Paperboard Grades and Capacities:
Total paper and paperboard capacity: 7,200 mt/y
Packaging papers

ⓂⓂHemkunt Paper Mills Ltd
Ludhiana Mill
Vill. Ladhowal
141002 Ludhiana, Punjab
India
Phone: (91) 1613946002/ 6450919
Fax: (91) 1612871348
Email: hemkuntpaper@gmail.com, gurbirs4@gmail.com
Web Address: www.hemkuntpaper.com/
Personnel:
Man. Dir.: Jatinder Pal Singh
Phone: (91) 98 72641515
Sls. Mgr.: Gurbir Singh
Phone: (91) 98 15598154
Total Employees at this Location: 44
Type of Operation: Paper mill
Paper/Paperboard Grades and Capacities:
Total paper and paperboard capacity: 9,000 mt/y
Packaging papers
Linerboard
Boxboard/cartonboard

ⓂHindustan Paper Corp. Ltd.
Ownership: 100% by Government of India
Ruby Building, 75 C, Park Street, 5th Floor
700 016 Kolkata, West Bengal
India
Phone: (91) 33 22496931/32/34/35
Fax: (91) 33 22494996/22497335
Email: chqmain@gems.vsnl.net.in
Web Address: www.hindpaper.in
Personnel:
Chmn. & Man. Dir.: MV Narasimha Rao
Phone: (91) 33 22267806
Fax: (91) 33 2249 4996
Email: mvnrao@mail.hpc.co.in
Dir. Oper.: Shri. Subhendra K. Bhattacharyya
Phone: (91) 33 22656357
Fax: (91) 33 22494996/454932
Email: do.hpc@mail.hpc.co.in
Dir. Mktng. : Shri. Sashi Kanth Jain
Phone: (91) 33 22177970
Email: skjain@mail.hpc.co.in
Total Employees of Company: 4,000
Mill Locations:
Hindustan Paper Corp. Ltd., CPM, Cachar Paper Mill, Panchgram, Dist. Hailakandi, 788 802 Cachar, India, Capacity: 83,181 mt/y, (Pulp mill, Paper mill)
Phone: (91) 3845 273086/80
Fax: (91) 3845 268266
Email: lvenkat-rao@yahoo.com
Hindustan Paper Corp. Ltd., NPM, Nagaon Paper Mill, Kagajnagar, Jagiroad, 782 413 Morigaon, India, Capacity: 104,958 mt/y, (Pulp mill, Paper mill)
Phone: (91) 3678 244516/245900
Fax: (91) 3678 242244/245911
Hindustan Newsprint Ltd., Kottayam Dist. Mill, PO Newsprint Nagar, Mavellor, 686616 Kottayam Dist., India, Capacity: 114,240 mt/y, (Pulp mill, Paper mill)
Phone: (91) 4829 256211 to 256221
Fax: (91) 4829 256777/256705
Email: hnl@hnlonline.com

ⓂHindustan Paper Corp. Ltd., CPM
Cachar Paper Mill
Ownership: Hindustan Paper Corp. Ltd.
Panchgram, Dist. Hailakandi
788 802 Cachar, Assam
India
Phone: (91) 3845 273086/80
Fax: (91) 3845 268266
Email: lvenkat-rao@yahoo.com
Web Address: www.hindpaper.in
Personnel:
CEO: A. K. Bhatia
Phone: (91) 3845 273086/80
Mill Mgr.: D. Kishnamurthy
Phone: (91) 3845 273086/80
Mgr. Utilities: A. Mannan
Phone: (91) 3845 273086/80
Dpty. Mgr. Eng.: K. Acharjee
Phone: (91) 3845 273086/80
Total Employees at this Location: 1,285
Type of Operation: Pulp mill, Paper mill
Pulp Grades and Capacities:
Total pulp capacity: 92,423 mt/y
Chemical Pulp: 92,423 mt/y
Pulp Mill Data:
Chemical Pulping Systems:
Continuous digesters: 1
Bleach Plant Systems: 1
No. 1, Sequence: CEHED
Chemical Recovery Equipment:
Recovery boilers: 1
Paper/Paperboard Grades and Capacities:
Total paper and paperboard capacity: 83,181 mt/y
Uncoated woodfree/freesheet: 83,181 mt/y
Paper and Paperboard Mill Data:
Stock Preparation:
Pulpers: 4
Refiners: 5
Paper Machines: 2
No. 1, Tri Nip press, total capacity 51,765 mt/y, Trim width 4.87 m, Uncoated woodfree/freesheet
No. 2, Tri Nip press, total capacity 51,765 mt/y, Trim width 4.87 m, Uncoated woodfree/freesheet
Finishing Equipment:
Rewinders: 2
Sheeters: 5
Energy Data:
Power boilers: 3
Steam turbines: 2 at 30.0 MW
Electrical demand for mill: 306 MWh/D

ⓂHindustan Paper Corp. Ltd., NPM
Nagaon Paper Mill
Ownership: Hindustan Paper Corp. Ltd.
Kagajnagar, Jagiroad
782 413 Morigaon, Assam
India
Phone: (91) 3678 244516/245900
Fax: (91) 3678 242244/245911
Web Address: www.hindpaper.in
Personnel:
CEO: Shri D. D. Adhikary
Phone: (91) 03678 242331
Dpty. Gen. Mgr. (E&I): Mr. M. Jha
Phone: (91) 3678 244516/245900
Dpty. Gen. Mgr. (Env.): Mr. N.D. Rajkhowa
Phone: (91) 3678 244516/245900
Dpty. Gen. Mgr. (P&A): Mr. A.K. Tripathy
Phone: (91) 3678 244516/245900
Dpty. Gen. Mgr. (Utility): Mr. P.K. Bhuyan
Phone: (91) 3678 244516/245900
Dpty. Gen. Mgr. (Forestry): Mr. H.N. Baruah
Phone: (91) 3678 244516/245900

India

Dpty. Gen. Mgr. (Eng.): Mr. S.N. Pandey
Phone: (91) 3678 244516/245900
Total Employees at this Location: 1,464
Type of Operation: Pulp mill, Paper mill
Pulp Grades and Capacities:
Total pulp capacity: 115,430 mt/y
Chemical Pulp: 115,430 mt/y
Pulp Mill Data:
Chemical Pulping Systems:
Continuous digesters: 1
Bleach Plant Systems: 2
No. 1, Sequence: CEHED, Capacity 118,000 admt/y
Chemical Recovery Equipment:
Evaporator lines: 1
Recovery boilers: 1
Lime Kiln
Paper/Paperboard Grades and Capacities:
Total paper and paperboard capacity: 104,958 mt/y
Uncoated woodfree/freesheet: 104,958 mt/y
Paper and Paperboard Mill Data:
Stock Preparation:
Pulpers: 4
Refiners: 5
Paper Machines: 2
No. 1, (Supplier: Larsen & Toubro.), fourdrinier, total capacity 64,974 mt/y, Trim width 4.87 m, Uncoated woodfree/freesheet
No. 2, fourdrinier, total capacity 64,974 mt/y, Trim width 4.87 m, Uncoated woodfree/freesheet
Finishing Equipment:
Winders: 2
Rewinders: 2
Sheeters: 5
Energy Data:
Power boilers: 3
Combustion turbines: 2 at 30 MW
Electrical demand for mill: 436 MWh/D

ⓜHindustan Newsprint Ltd.
Kottayam Dist. Mill
Ownership: Hindustan Paper Corp. Ltd.
PO Newsprint Nagar, Mavellor
686616 Kottayam Dist., Kerala
India
Phone: (91) 4829 256211 to 256221
Fax: (91) 4829 256777/256705
Email: hnl@hnlonline.com
Web Address: www.hnlonline.com
Personnel:
Man. Dir.: M. V. Narasimha Rao
Phone: (91) 4829 256701
Fax: (91) 4829 256777
Email: mvnrao@hnlonline.com
Dpty. Gen. Mgr. (O & M): Ek Shajahan
Phone: (91) 4829 257805
Email: shajahan@hnlonline.com
Total Employees at this Location: 932
Type of Operation: Pulp mill, Paper mill
Pulp Grades and Capacities:
Total pulp capacity: 115,827 mt/y
Chemical Pulp: 23,007 mt/y
Mechanical Pulp: 57,913 mt/y
Recycled Pulping: 34,907 mt/y
Pulp Mill Data:
Chemical Pulping Systems:
Batch digesters: 5
Mechanical Pulping Systems:
CTMP systems: 1
Pulp Lines: 3
Bleach Plant Systems: 1
No. 1, Sequence: CP, Capacity 30,000 admt/y
Chemical Recovery Equipment:
Evaporator lines: 3
Recovery boilers: 1
Lime Kiln
Recycled Fiber Treatment Lines:
Flotation deinking lines: 1 at 33,000 admt/y
Pulpers: 1 at 33,000 admt/y
Paper/Paperboard Grades and Capacities:
Total paper and paperboard capacity: 114,240 mt/y
Newsprint: 114,240 mt/y
Paper and Paperboard Mill Data:
Stock Preparation:
Pulpers: 2
Refiners: 6
Paper Machines: 1
No. 1, DuoFormer C, total capacity 114,240 mt/y, Trim width 6.8 m, Newsprint
Finishing Equipment:
Rewinders: 1 at 120,000 mt/y
Energy Data:
Power boilers: 3
Steam turbines: 2 at 22 MW
Electrical demand for mill: 620 MWh/D

ⓜHRA Papers Pvt Ltd
Kangra Mill
Village Tibbi, Kangra, Himachal Pradesh
India
Total Employees at this Location: 160
Type of Operation: Paper mill
Pulp Grades and Capacities:
Total pulp capacity: 23,232 mt/y
Recycled Pulping: 23,232 mt/y
Pulp Mill Data:
Bleach Plant Systems: 1
Recycled Pulping System
Recycled Fiber Treatment Lines:
Flotation deinking lines: 1
Paper/Paperboard Grades and Capacities:
Total paper and paperboard capacity: 25,000 mt/y
Newsprint: 12,500 mt/y
Uncoated woodfree/freesheet: 12,500 mt/y
Paper and Paperboard Mill Data:
Paper Machines: 1
No. 1, fourdrinier, total capacity 25,000 mt/y, Trim width 3.3 m, Uncoated woodfree/freesheet, Newsprint
Energy Data:
Power boilers

ⓜIndo Afrique Paper Mills Ltd.
Aditi Commerce Centre, IV Fl. 2406, East St.
411001 Pune, Maharashtra
India
Phone: (91) 20 2634 5283
Fax: (91) 20 26347403/51068
Email: iapaper@pn2.vsnl.net.in,
indoafrique@vsnl.com
Personnel:
Man. Dir.: Jitu A. Patel
Phone: (91) 99 23 40 57 90
Gen. Mgr.: C. K. Poovaiah
Phone: (91) 20 2634 5283
Fax: (91) 20 26347403/51068
Gen. Mgr. (Tech.): S. Pal
Phone: (91) 20 2634 5283
Fax: (91) 20 26347403/51068
Total Employees at this Location: 130
Mill Locations:
Indo Afrique Paper Mill, Pune Mill, Vill. Pande, Pune-Satara Road, Tal. Bhor, P.O. Sarole, 412205 Pune, India, Capacity: 36,500 mt/y, (Pulp mill, Paper mill)
Phone: (91) 2113 282342/343
Fax: (91) 2113 282653
Email: info@indoafrique.com, info.indoafrique@gmail.com, indoafrique@vsnl.com

ⓜIndo Afrique Paper Mill
Pune Mill
Ownership: Indo Afrique Paper Mills Ltd.
Vill. Pande, Pune-Satara Road, Tal. Bhor, P.O. Sarole
412205 Pune, Maharashtra
India
Phone: (91) 2113 282342/343
Fax: (91) 2113 282653
Email: info@indoafrique.com,
info.indoafrique@gmail.com,
indoafrique@vsnl.com
Personnel:
Man. Dir.: Jitu Patel
Phone: (91) 99 23 40 57 90
Gen. Mgr. (Tech.): S. Pal
Phone: (91) 2113 282342/343
Sr. Mgr. (Prod.): A. K. Patni
Phone: (91) 2113 282342/343
Mgr. (Admin.): H. G. Desai
Phone: (91) 2113 282342/343
Asst. Mgr. (Sls.): S. Patra
Phone: (91) 20 26345364
Mgr. (Finan.): A. L. Jain
Phone: (91) 2113 282342/343
Total Employees at this Location: 130
Type of Operation: Pulp mill, Paper mill
Paper/Paperboard Grades and Capacities:
Total paper and paperboard capacity: 36,500 mt/y
Newsprint
Uncoated woodfree/freesheet
Paper and Paperboard Mill Data:
Stock Preparation:
Refiners: 2
Paper Machines: 2
No. 1, fourdrinier, combination, total capacity 10,000 mt/y, Trim width 2.6 m
No. 2, fourdrinier, total capacity 26,500 mt/y
Finishing Equipment:
Rewinders: 3
Sheeters: 1
Energy Data:
Power boilers: 2

ⓜInternational Paper APPM Ltd.
Ownership: 96.50% by International Paper Co., 3.50% by Public
Krishe Sapphire Building, 8th Floor 1-89/3/B/40 to 42/KS/801 Hitech City Main Road, Madhapur
500 081 Hyderabad, A.P.
India
Phone: (91) 40 3312 1000, 1111
Fax: (91) 40 3312 1010
Email: appmcorp@andhrapaper.com
Web Address: www.andhrapaper.com
Personnel:
Man. Dir & CEO, Pres. IP India (effective November 1, 2014): Rampraveen Swaminathan
Phone: (91) 40 3312 1000
Fax: (91) 40 3312 1010
Email: swaminathan@andhrapaper.com
CFO: Jayashree Satagopan
Phone: (91) 40 3312 1000
Fax: (91) 40 3312 1010
Sr. VP (Corp. Affrs) & Company Sec.: C. Prabhakar
Phone: (91) 40 2789 7019
Fax: (91) 40 3312 1010
Email: prabhakarc@andhrapaper.com
VP, Sls. & Mktg.: Jaspal Singh
Phone: (91) 40 3048 2666
Fax: (91) 40 2784 1812
Email: jaspal@andhrapaper.com
VP, Oper.: Vasantharao Veera
Phone: (91) 40 3312 1000
Fax: (91) 40 3312 1010
CIO: Sreenivas Parnidimukkala
Phone: (91) 40 3312 1000
Fax: (91) 40 3312 1010
Total Employees of Company: 2,632
Total Employees at this Location: 91
Mill Locations:
International Paper APPM Ltd., Kadiam Mill, Industrial Dev Area, Kadiyam Mandal, 533 126 Madhavarayudu Palem, East Godavari District, A.P., India, Capacity: 69,000 mt/y, (Pulp mill, Paper mill, Paperboard mill)
Phone: (91) 883 2424651/52/53/54/55
Fax: (91) 883 2453538
Email: appmcp@andhapaper.com
International Paper APPM Ltd., Rajahmundry Mill, Shriramnagar, 533 105 Rajahmundry, East Godavari, A.P., India, Capacity: 195,993 mt/y, (Pulp mill, Paper mill)

Phone: (91) 883 2471831 to 37
Fax: (91) 883 2461764/2471383
Email: appmrjy@andhrapaper.com

⊕International Paper APPM Ltd.
Kadiam Mill
Ownership: 96.50% by International Paper Co.
Industrial Dev Area, Kadiyam Mandal
533 126 Madhavarayudu Palem, East Godavari District, A.P.
India
Phone: (91) 883 2424651/52/53/54/55
Fax: (91) 883 2453538
Email: appmcp@andhapaper.com
Web Address: www.andhrapaper.com

Personnel:
Dir. (Operations): P.K. Suri
Phone: (91) 98480 29404
Email: pksuri@andhrapaper.com
Assoc. VP: R. G. Mandhani
Phone: (91) 883 2454651 to 55
Fax: (91) 883 2453538
Email: mandhaniarg@andhrapaper.com
DGM (Production): E. V.G.K. Sharma
Phone: (91) 883 2454651
Email: sharmaevgk@andhrapaper.com

Total Employees at this Location: 661
Type of Operation: Pulp mill, Paper mill, Paperboard mill

Pulp Grades and Capacities:
Total pulp capacity: 53,946 mt/y
Recycled Pulping: 53,946 mt/y

Pulp Mill Data:
Chemical Pulping Systems:
Batch digesters: 4
Pulp Lines: 4
Bleach Plant Systems: 2
No. 1, Sequence: CHH, Capacity 8,250 admt/y
No. 2, Sequence: P, Capacity 36,300 admt/y
Chemical Recovery Equipment:
Evaporator lines: 1
Recycled Fiber Treatment Lines:
Flotation deinking lines: 27 at 36,300 admt/y
Pulpers: 1 at 36,300 admt/y
Recycled packaging pulping lines: 1 at 19,800 admt/y
Washing deinking lines: 1 at 36,300 admt/y

Paper/Paperboard Grades and Capacities:
Total paper and paperboard capacity: 69,000 mt/y
Uncoated woodfree/freesheet: 69,000 mt/y

Paper and Paperboard Mill Data:
Stock Preparation:
Pulpers: 4
Refiners: 4
Paper Machines: 3
No. 1, fourdrinier, total capacity 5,000 mt/y, Trim width 1.3 m, Uncoated woodfree/freesheet
No. 2, fourdrinier, total capacity 10,000 mt/y, Trim width 2.35 m, Uncoated woodfree/freesheet
No. 3, fourdrinier, total capacity 54,000 mt/y, Trim width 3.6 m, Uncoated woodfree/freesheet
Finishing Equipment:
Rewinders: 3 at 4,000 mt/y, 18,000 mt/y, 40,000 mt/y
Sheeters: 7 at 6,000 mt/y, 2 mt/y, 10,000 mt/y, 2 mt/y
Energy Data:
Power boilers: 4
Steam turbines: 1 at 5.74 MW
Electrical demand for mill: 156 MWh/D

⊕International Paper APPM Ltd.
Rajahmundry Mill
Ownership: 96.50% by International Paper Co.
Shriramnagar
533 105 Rajahmundry, East Godavari, A.P.
India
Phone: (91) 883 2471831 to 37
Fax: (91) 883 2461764/2471383
Email: appmrjy@andhrapaper.com
Web Address: www.andhrapaper.com

Personnel:
Dir. (Operations): P.K. Suri
Phone: (91) 98480 29404
Email: pksuri@andhrapaper.com
Chief Mentor: U.V. Satyanarayana
Phone: (91) 883 2471831 to 38
Email: uvs@andhapaper.com

Total Employees at this Location: 1,880
Type of Operation: Pulp mill, Paper mill

Pulp Grades and Capacities:
Total pulp capacity: 200,317 mt/y
Chemical Pulp: 170,567 mt/y
Other Pulp: 29,750 mt/y

Pulp Mill Data:
Chemical Pulping Systems:
Continuous digesters: 1
Pulp Lines: 1
Bleach Plant Systems: 1
No. 1, Sequence: O_2 DoEopD, Capacity 201,600 admt/y
Chemical Recovery Equipment:
Evaporator lines: 1
Recovery boilers: 1
Lime Kiln
Recycled Fiber Treatment Lines:
Pulpers: 1 at 14,280 admt/y
Pulpers: 1 at 53,550
Pulp Dryers:
Wet Lap machine 3

Paper/Paperboard Grades and Capacities:
Total paper and paperboard capacity: 195,993 mt/y
Uncoated woodfree/freesheet: 163,149 mt/y
Specialty and industrial: 32,844 mt/y

Paper and Paperboard Mill Data:
Paper Machines: 6
No. 1, cylinder, total capacity 7,140 mt/y, Trim width 2 m, Specialty and industrial
No. 2, cylinder, total capacity 22,848 mt/y, Trim width 3.25 m, Specialty and industrial
No. 3, DuoFormer, total capacity 40,341 mt/y, Trim width 3.15 m, Uncoated woodfree/freesheet
No. 4, cylinder, total capacity 2,856 mt/y, Trim width 2 m, Specialty and industrial
No. 5, fourdrinier, total capacity 35,343 mt/y, Trim width 3.15 m, Uncoated woodfree/freesheet
No. 6, (2nd hand), twin former, total capacity 87,465 mt/y, Trim width 3.36 m, Uncoated woodfree/freesheet

Finishing Equipment:
Rewinders: 4 at 132,000 mt/y
Sheeters: 6 at 70,000 mt/y

Energy Data:
Power boilers: 6
Steam turbines: 4 at 56 MW
Electrical demand for mill: 789 MWh/D

⊕ITC Limited
Ownership: 16.18% by FIIs, 39.53% by Others, 32.42% by Promoter, 11.87% by Public
Virginia House, 37 Jawaharlal Nehru Road
700 071 Kolkata, West Bengal
India
Phone: (91) 33 22889371
Fax: (91) 33 22882358
Email: webmaster@itc.in
Web Address: www.itcportal.com

Personnel:
Chmn.: Yogesh Chander Deveshwar
Phone: (91) 33 22889371
Fax: (91) 33 22882358
CFO: Rajiv Tandon
Phone: (91) 33 22889371
Fax: (91) 33 22882358
Exc. VP & Gen. Sec.: Biswa Behari Chatterjee
Phone: (91) 33 22889371
Fax: (91) 33 22882358
General Council.: Kannadiputhur Sundararaman Suresh
Phone: (91) 33 22889371
Fax: (91) 33 22882358

Total Employees of Company: 25,959
Mill Locations:
ITC Limited, Paperboards & Specialty Papers Division, Kovai Mill, Thekkampatty Village, Vivekanandapuram Post, Mettupalayam Taluk, 641 113 Coimbatore, India, Capacity: 100,000 mt/y, (Paperboard mill)
Phone: (91) 4254 284301/302/303/305
Fax: (91) 4254 284304
ITC Limited, Paperboards & Specialty Papers Division, Bhadrachalam Mill, P.B. No 4, Sarapaka Village, 507 128 Khammam, Bhadrachalam, A.P., India, Capacity: 406,623 mt/y, (Pulp mill, Paper mill, Paperboard mill)
Phone: (91) 8746 242331/ 333-337/8743 232594
Fax: (91) 8746 242460/8743 242460
ITC Limited, Paperboards & Specialty Papers Division, Tribeni Mill, P.O. Chandrahati, 712 504 Chandrahati, Hooghly, India, Capacity: 35,000 mt/y, (Pulp mill, Paper mill)
Phone: (91) 33 30917361/62/08
Fax: (91) 33 30937130
Email: gautam.sen@itc.in

⊕ITC Limited, Paperboards & Specialty Papers Division
Ownership: ITC Limited
106 Sardar Patel Rd.
500 003 Secunderabad, A.P.
India
Phone: (91) 40 2784 6566/73
Fax: (91) 40 2781 0034
Email: webmaster@itcpspd.com, sn.venky@itc.in
Web Address: www.itcpspd.com

Personnel:
CEO: Pradeep Dhobale
Phone: (91) 40 27846561/2
Fax: (91) 40 27811954
Email: pradeep.dhobale@itc.co.in
Exec. VP - Manuf.: Sanjay Singh
Phone: (91) 40 27840581
Email: sanjay.singh@itc.co.in
Head of Mktg.: K. I. Vishwanathan
Phone: (91) 40 27810408
Email: k.vishy@itc.co.in
Gen. Mgr., Exports: S.N. Venkataraman
Phone: (91) 40 278 46563
Email: sn.venky@itc.in
Chief Plan. Mgr.: J. Ponthiagaraj
Phone: (91) 40 2784 6566/73
Fax: (91) 40 2781 0034
Email: j.ponthiagaraj@itc.in

Total Employees of Company: 4,030
Total Employees at this Location: 200
Mill Locations:
ITC Limited, Paperboards & Specialty Papers Division, Kovai Mill, Thekkampatty Village, Vivekanandapuram Post, Mettupalayam Taluk, 641 113 Coimbatore, India, Capacity: 100,000 mt/y, (Paperboard mill)
Phone: (91) 4254 284301/302/303/305
Fax: (91) 4254 284304
ITC Limited, Paperboards & Specialty Papers Division, Bhadrachalam Mill, P.B. No 4, Sarapaka Village, 507 128 Khammam, Bhadrachalam, A.P., India, Capacity: 406,623 mt/y, (Pulp mill, Paper mill, Paperboard mill)
Phone: (91) 8746 242331/ 333-337/8743 232594
Fax: (91) 8746 242460/8743 242460
ITC Limited, Paperboards & Specialty Papers Division, Tribeni Mill, P.O. Chandrahati, 712 504 Chandrahati, Hooghly, India, Capacity: 35,000 mt/y, (Pulp mill, Paper mill)
Phone: (91) 33 30917361/62/08
Fax: (91) 33 30937130
Email: gautam.sen@itc.in

⊕ITC Limited, Paperboards & Specialty Papers Division
Kovai Mill
Ownership: ITC Limited

India

Thekkampatty Village, Vivekanandapuram Post, Mettupalayam Taluk
641 113 Coimbatore, Tamil Nadu
India
Phone: (91) 4254 284301/302/303/305
Fax: (91) 4254 284304
Web Address: www.itcpspd.com
Personnel:
VP (Oper.): A.V. Rao
Email: av.rao@itc.in
Total Employees at this Location: 337
Type of Operation: Paperboard mill
Pulp Grades and Capacities:
Total pulp capacity: 93,116 mt/y
Recycled Pulping: 93,116 mt/y
Pulp Mill Data:
Pulp Lines: 2
Recycled Fiber Treatment Lines:
Recycled packaging pulping lines
Washing deinking lines
Paper/Paperboard Grades and Capacities:
Total paper and paperboard capacity: 100,000 mt/y
Boxboard/cartonboard: 100,000 mt/y
Paper and Paperboard Mill Data:
Stock Preparation:
Pulpers: 3
Refiners: 5
Paper Machines: 1
No. 2, fourdrinier, total capacity 100,000 mt/y, Trim width 3.12 m, Boxboard/cartonboard
Coating Machines: 1
PM 2, total capacity 100,000 mt/y., on machine
Energy Data:
Power boilers: 1
Steam turbines: 1 at 8 MW
Electrical demand for mill: 186 MWh/D

ⓜITC Limited, Paperboards & Specialty Papers Division
Bhadrachalam Mill
Ownership: ITC Limited
P.B. No 4, Sarapaka Village
507 128 Khammam, Bhadrachalam, A.P.
India
Mailing Address: P.B. No. 4, Sarapaka village, 507 128 Bhadrachalam, A.P., India
Phone: (91) 8746 242331/333-337/8743 232594
Fax: (91) 8746 242460/8743 242460
Web Address: www.itcpspd.com
Personnel:
VP (Oper.): A.V. Rao
Phone: (91) 8746 242583
Email: av.rao@itc.in
Gen. Mgr., Production: Kanna Babu
Phone: (91) 8746 242357/9849496031
Dpty. Gen. Mgr. (Paper): Rakesh Gupta
Phone: (91) 8746 242331/333-337/8743 232594
Email: rakesh.gupta@itc.in
Dpty. Gen. Mgr. (Proj.) Pulp Mill Mgr.: T.R. Dhar
Phone: (91) 8746 242331/333-337/8743 232594
Gen. Mgr. (Tech.): A. Das
Phone: (91) 8746 242331/333-337/8743 232594
Email: a.das@itc.in
Maint. Mgr.: N B Srinivasa Rao
Phone: (91) 8746 242331/333-337/8743 232594
Email: nb.srinivasarao@itc.in
Env. Mgr.: DR. Raghuveer
Phone: (91) 8746 242331/333-337/8743 232594
Email: s.raghuveer@itc.in
VP (Commer.): BVS Joga Rao
Phone: (91) 4027 815962
Fax: (91) 4027 842997
Email: jogarao.b@itc.in
Total Employees at this Location: 2,500
Type of Operation: Pulp mill, Paper mill, Paperboard mill
Pulp Grades and Capacities:
Total pulp capacity: 255,477 mt/y
Chemical Pulp: 177,979 mt/y
Recycled Pulping: 77,498 mt/y
Pulp Mill Data:
Chemical Pulping Systems:
Batch digesters: 8
Pulp Lines: 2
Bleach Plant Systems: 2
No. 1, Type: Ze-D-Eop-D, Sequence: O_2 DEpD, Capacity 110,000 admt/y
No. 2, Type: D-Ze-DP, Sequence: O_2 ZD1 EopD2, Capacity 180,000 admt/y
Chemical Recovery Equipment:
Evaporator lines: 1
Recovery boilers: 1
Lime Kiln
Recycled Fiber Treatment Lines:
Pulpers: 4 at 200,000 admt/y
Paper/Paperboard Grades and Capacities:
Total paper and paperboard capacity: 406,623 mt/y
Uncoated woodfree/freesheet: 84,966 mt/y
Coated woodfree/freesheet: 59,976 mt/y
Specialty and industrial: 6,069 mt/y
Boxboard/cartonboard: 255,612 mt/y
Paper and Paperboard Mill Data:
Stock Preparation:
Pulpers: 3
Refiners: 34
Paper Machines: 6
No. 1, Multi-wire (5), total capacity 44,982 mt/y, Trim width 3.76 m, Boxboard/cartonboard
No. 2, (second hand), fourdrinier, total capacity 24,990 mt/y, Trim width 3.12 m, Uncoated woodfree/freesheet
No. 3, Yankee dryer, total capacity 6,069 mt/y, Trim width 3.1 m, Specialty and industrial
No. 4, SymFormer MB, total capacity 130,662 mt/y, Trim width 3.76 m, Boxboard/cartonboard
No. 5, (second hand), fourdrinier, total capacity 79,968 mt/y, Trim width 3.3 m, Boxboard/cartonboard
No. 6, (second hand), DuoFormer D, total capacity 119,952 mt/y, Trim width 4.75 m, Uncoated woodfree/freesheet, Coated woodfree/freesheet
Coating Machines: 4
PM 1, total capacity 65,000 mt/y., on machine
PM 4, total capacity 131,000 mt/y., on machine
PM 5, total capacity 80,000 mt/y., on machine
PM 6, total capacity 60,000 mt/y., on machine
Finishing Equipment:
Rewinders: 4
Sheeters: 10
Energy Data:
Power boilers: 6
Steam turbines: 4 at 40 MW
Electrical demand for mill: 974 MWh/D

ⓜITC Limited, Paperboards & Specialty Papers Division
Tribeni Mill
Ownership: ITC Limited
P.O. Chandrahati
712 504 Chandrahati, Hooghly, West Bengal
India
Phone: (91) 33 30917361/62/08
Fax: (91) 33 30937130
Email: gautam.sen@itc.in
Web Address: www.itcpspd.com
Personnel:
Mill Mgr.: Mr. Niret
Phone: (91) 33 2684 6028/29/20/21/22/99/6737
Tech. Mgr.: Dr. N.C. Behera
Phone: (91) 33 2684 6028/29/20/21/22/99/6737
Chief Eng.: Susanta Kumar Sarkar
Phone: (91) 33 2684 6028/29/20/21/22/99/6737
VP Purch.: BVS Joga Rao
Phone: (91) 33 2684 6028/29/20/21/22/99/6737
Process Unit Head: Basab Ghosh
Phone: (91) 33 2684 6028/29/20/21/22/99/6737
Total Employees at this Location: 993
Type of Operation: Pulp mill, Paper mill
Pulp Mill Data:
Paper/Paperboard Grades and Capacities:
Total paper and paperboard capacity: 35,000 mt/y
Uncoated woodfree/freesheet
Tissue
Specialty and industrial
Paper and Paperboard Mill Data:
Stock Preparation:
Pulpers: 4
Refiners: 34
Paper Machines: 3
No. 1, fourdrinier, Trim width 3.2 m, Specialty and industrial
No. 2, fourdrinier, Trim width 2.7 m
No. 3, fourdrinier, Trim width 2.7 m
Finishing Equipment:
Supercalenders: 1
Rewinders: 5
Sheeters: 1
Energy Data:
Power boilers: 5
Steam turbines: 3 at 33 MW

ⓜJ B Daruka Paper Ltd
A-1 Industrial Area, Advania Grant, Sahjahanpur Road
Sitapur, Uttar Pradesh
India
Fax: (91) 2862 223301/244 060
Mill Locations:
J B Daruka Paper Ltd, Sitapur Mill, A-1 Industrial Area, Advania Grant, Sahjahanpur Road, Sitapur, India, Capacity: 14,400 mt/y, (Paper mill)
Fax: (91) 2862 223301/244 060

ⓜJ B Daruka Paper Ltd
Sitapur Mill
A-1 Industrial Area, Advania Grant, Sahjahanpur Road
Sitapur, Uttar Pradesh
India
Fax: (91) 2862 223301/244 060
Personnel:
Man. Dir: Suresh Kumar Agrawal
Phone: (91) 94 15047448
Dir.: Sanjay Agrawal
Phone: (91) 94 15047094
Dir.: Umesh Agrawal
Phone: (91) 94 15047462
Type of Operation: Paper mill
Paper/Paperboard Grades and Capacities:
Total paper and paperboard capacity: 14,400 mt/y
Packaging papers
Paper and Paperboard Mill Data:
Paper Machines: 1
No. 1, Packaging papers

ⓞⓜJammu Paper (P) Ltd.
Jammu Tawi Mill
Ownership: 100% by Private
Sidco Commercial Complex, Phase II, Bari Brahmana
181133 Jammu, Jammu and Kashmir
India
Phone: (91) 1923 221491/220316
Fax: (91) 1923 221491
Email: jammu_paper@yahoo.co.in
Personnel:
Man. Dir.: S. C. Dogra
Phone: (91) 1923 221491
Sls. Officer: Vivekanand
Phone: (91) 94 19199189
Total Employees at this Location: 200
Type of Operation: Paperboard mill
Paper/Paperboard Grades and Capacities:
Total paper and paperboard capacity: 12,000 mt/y
Boxboard/cartonboard: 12,000 mt/y
Paper and Paperboard Mill Data:
Paper Machines: 1
No. 1, total capacity 12,000 mt/y, Trim width 2.1 m, Boxboard/cartonboard

India

ⓄJayanti Board Mills Ltd.
Mandapaka Village Tanuku
534 218 West Godavari, A.P.
India
  Phone: (91) 8819 222 201/223 811
  Fax: (91) 8819 225 411
  Email: jayantiboards@rediffmail.com
Mill Locations:
  Jayanti Board Mills Ltd., West Godavari Mill, Mandapaka Village Tanuku, 534 218 West Godavari, A.P., India, Capacity: 7,000 mt/y, (Paper mill, Paperboard mill)
  Phone: (91) 8819 222 201/223 811
  Fax: (91) 8819 225 411
  Email: jayantiboards@rediffmail.com

ⓄJayanti Board Mills Ltd.
West Godavari Mill
Mandapaka Village Tanuku
534 218 West Godavari, A.P.
India
  Phone: (91) 8819 222 201/223 811
  Fax: (91) 8819 225 411
  Email: jayantiboards@rediffmail.com
Personnel:
  Man. Dir.: Ashok Kumar Jain
  Phone: (91) 8819 222 201/223 811
  Gen. Mgr.: Manoj Jain
  Phone: (91) 94 40033000
  Sls. Mgr. : Nair
  Phone: (91) 93 20237093
Type of Operation: Paper mill, Paperboard mill
Paper/Paperboard Grades and Capacities:
  Total paper and paperboard capacity: 7,000 mt/y

ⓄJeet Enterprises PVT. Ltd. (Sister Concern of Miglani Paper Mills)
Tarantaran Road, Outside Chattiwind Gate
Amritsar, Punjab
India
  Phone: (91) 183 248 28 47
  Fax: (91) 183 248 28 48
Mill Locations:
  Jeet Enterprises PVT. Ltd. (Sister Concern of Miglani Paper Mills), Amritsar Mill, Tarantaran Road, Outside Chattiwind Gate, Amritsar, India, Capacity: 10,800 mt/y, (Paper mill)
  Phone: (91) 183 248 28 47
  Fax: (91) 183 248 28 48

ⓄJeet Enterprises PVT. Ltd. (Sister Concern of Miglani Paper Mills)
Amritsar Mill
Tarantaran Road, Outside Chattiwind Gate
Amritsar, Punjab
India
  Phone: (91) 183 248 28 47
  Fax: (91) 183 248 28 48
Personnel:
  Man. Dir.: Sukhvindar Singh
  Phone: (91) 98 55282847
Type of Operation: Paper mill
Paper/Paperboard Grades and Capacities:
  Total paper and paperboard capacity: 10,800 mt/y
  Newsprint
  Uncoated woodfree/freesheet

ⓄⓄJejani Pulp and Paper Mills Pvt. Ltd.
Gadchiroli Mill
Desaiganj Wadsa
Gadchiroli, M.S.
India
  Phone: (91) 7137 272901/902
  Fax: (91) 7137 272900
  Email: jejani@dataone.in
Personnel:
  Man. Dir.: Sharad Jejani
  Phone: (91) 94 22145200
  Exec. Dir.: Sushil Jejani
  Phone: (91) 94 22145201
Type of Operation: Paper mill
Paper/Paperboard Grades and Capacities:
  Total paper and paperboard capacity: 9,000 mt/y
  Uncoated woodfree/freesheet: 9,000 mt/y
Paper and Paperboard Mill Data:
Paper Machines: 1
  No. 1, fourdrinier, total capacity 9,000 mt/y, Uncoated woodfree/freesheet

ⓄJK Paper Ltd.
Ownership: 100% by JK Singhania Group
Nehru House, 4 Bahadur Shah Zafar Marg.
110 002 New Delhi, Delhi
India
  Phone: (91) 11 33001112/32/30179446
  Fax: (91) 11 233 53708/237 12680
  Email: marketing@jkmail.com
  Web Address: www.jkpaper.com
Personnel:
  Man. Dir.: Harsh Pati Singhania
  Phone: (91) 11 30179414
  Email: hps@jkmail.com
  COO: P. Ramnath
  Phone: (91) 11 30179503
  Email: p.ramnath@jkmail.com
  CFO: V. Kumaraswamy
  Phone: (91) 11 30179510
  Email: vkmr@jkmail.com
  CEO (New Projects): Ashish De
  Phone: (91) 11 30179595
  Email: ashishde@jkmail.com
  Whole Time Dir.: Om Prakash Goyal
  Phone: (91) 11 30179501
  Email: opg@jkmail.com
  VP Sales and Marketing: Santosh Wakhloo
  Phone: (91) 11 30179570
  VP (Materials): Amit Datta
  Phone: (91) 11 30179570
  Email: amitdatta@jkmail.com
Total Employees of Company: 2,661
Total Employees at this Location: 148
Mill Locations:
  JK Paper Ltd., Central Pulp Mills-CPM, Songadh Mill, 394 660 Fort Songadh, Dist. Tapi, India, Capacity: 133,980 mt/y, (Pulp mill, Paper mill, Paperboard mill)
  Phone: (91) 2624 220 228/220 278-80
  Fax: (91) 2624 220 138
  Email: cpm@cpmjk.jkmail.com
  JK Paper Ltd., JK Paper Mills - JKPM, 765 017 Jaykaypur, Rayagada Dist., India, Capacity: 296,000 mt/y, (Pulp mill, Paper mill)
  Phone: (91) 6856 222 070/050
  Fax: (91) 6856 222238/242652
  Email: jkpaper@jkpm.jkmail.com

ⓄJK Paper Ltd.
Central Pulp Mills-CPM, Songadh Mill
394 660 Fort Songadh, Dist. Tapi, Gujarat
India
Mailing Address: 394 660, Fort Songadh, India
  Phone: (91) 2624 220 228/220 278-80
  Fax: (91) 2624 220 138
  Email: cpm@cpmjk.jkmail.com
  Web Address: www.jkpaper.com
Personnel:
  ExecVP (Works): N. K. Agarwal
  Phone: (91) 2624 220 228/220 278-80
  Email: nka@cpmjk.jkmail.com
  VP (Tech. - Paper): N. K. Khanna
  Phone: (91) 2624 220 228/220 278-80
  Email: nkkhanna@cpmjk.jkmail.com
  Whole Time Dir.: O. P. Goyal
  Phone: (91) 2624 220 228/220 278-80
  Email: opg@cpmijk.jkmail
Total Employees at this Location: 1,150
Type of Operation: Pulp mill, Paper mill, Paperboard mill
Pulp Grades and Capacities:
  Total pulp capacity: 98,206 mt/y
  Chemical Pulp: 34,351 mt/y
  Recycled Pulping: 46,888 mt/y
  Other Pulp: 16,967 mt/y
Pulp Mill Data:
  Chemical Pulping Systems:
  Batch digesters: 5
Pulp Lines: 1
  Bleach Plant Systems: 1
  No. 1, Sequence: O_2 CEopHD, Capacity 55,000 admt/y
  Chemical Recovery Equipment:
  Evaporator lines: 1
  Recovery boilers: 1
  Lime Kiln
  Recycled Fiber Treatment Lines:
  Recycled packaging pulping lines
Paper/Paperboard Grades and Capacities:
  Total paper and paperboard capacity: 133,980 mt/y
  Uncoated woodfree/freesheet: 49,980 mt/y
  Boxboard/cartonboard: 84,000 mt/y
Paper and Paperboard Mill Data:
  Stock Preparation:
  Pulpers: 2
  Refiners: 5
Paper Machines: 3
  No. 1, fourdrinier, total capacity 21,420 mt/y, Trim width 2.5 m, Uncoated woodfree/freesheet
  No. 2, fourdrinier, total capacity 28,560 mt/y, Trim width 3.15 m, Uncoated woodfree/freesheet
  No. 3, (second hand), DuoFormer D, total capacity 84,000 mt/y, Trim width 2.6 m, Boxboard/cartonboard
Coating Machines: 1
  BM 3, total capacity 64,000 mt/y., on machine
Finishing Equipment:
  Rewinders: 3
  Sheeters: 1
Energy Data:
  Power boilers: 4
  Steam turbines: 4 at 30 MW
  Electrical demand for mill: 276 MWh/D

ⓄJK Paper Ltd.
JK Paper Mills - JKPM
765 017 Jaykaypur, Rayagada Dist., Odisha
India
  Phone: (91) 6856 222 070/050
  Fax: (91) 6856 222238/242652
  Email: jkpaper@jkpm.jkmail.com
  Web Address: www.jkpaper.com
Personnel:
  Exec. VP (Works): M. C. Goel
  Phone: (91) 6856 222 070/050
  Email: mcgoel@jkpm.jkmail.com
  Whole Time Dir.: O. P. Goyal
  Phone: (91) 6856 222 070/050
Total Employees at this Location: 1,200
Type of Operation: Pulp mill, Paper mill
Pulp Grades and Capacities:
  Total pulp capacity: 202,876 mt/y
  Chemical Pulp: 202,876 mt/y
Pulp Mill Data:
  Chemical Pulping Systems:
  Continuous digesters: 1
Pulp Lines: 1
  Bleach Plant Systems: 1
  No. 1, Sequence: O_2 C/DEopD
  Chemical Recovery Equipment:
  Evaporator lines: 1
  Recovery boilers: 1
  Lime Kiln
  Pulp Dryers:
  Fourdriniers 1, Fourdriniers 1
Paper/Paperboard Grades and Capacities:
  Total paper and paperboard capacity: 296,000 mt/y
  Uncoated woodfree/freesheet: 224,500 mt/y
  Coated woodfree/freesheet: 71,500 mt/y
Paper and Paperboard Mill Data:
  Stock Preparation:
  Pulpers: 4
  Refiners: 11

India

Paper Machines: 5
No. 1, fourdrinier, total capacity 55,000 mt/y, Trim width 3.3 m, Coated woodfree/freesheet
No. 3, fourdrinier, total capacity 36,000 mt/y, Trim width 3.7 m, Uncoated woodfree/freesheet
No. 4, fourdrinier, total capacity 15,000 mt/y, Trim width 2.5 m, Uncoated woodfree/freesheet
No. 5, fourdrinier, total capacity 25,000 mt/y, Trim width 2.6 m, Uncoated woodfree/freesheet
No. 6, fourdrinier, total capacity 165,000 mt/y, Trim width 5.85 m, Uncoated woodfree/freesheet, Coated woodfree/freesheet
Coating Machines: 1
No. 1, total capacity 55,000 mt/y., off machine
Finishing Equipment:
 Rewinders: 6
 Sheeters: 11
Energy Data:
Power boilers: 1
Steam turbines: 2 at 25, 30 MW
Electrical demand for mill: 848 MWh/D

ⓘJ&K Pulp & Paper Pvt. Ltd.
Sidco Industrial Area, Phase II, Lane No. 6
Bari Brahmana, Dist. Jammu, Jammu and Kashmir
India
 Phone: (91) 1923 222334/221930
 Fax: (91) 1926 221930
Mill Locations:
J&K Pulp & Paper Pvt. Ltd., Jammu Mill, Sidco Industrial Area, Phase II, Lane No. 6, Bari Brahmana, Dist. Jammu, India, Capacity: 10,000 mt/y, (Paper mill)
 Phone: (91) 1923 222334/221930
 Fax: (91) 1926 221930

ⓜJ&K Pulp & Paper Pvt. Ltd.
Jammu Mill
Sidco Industrial Area, Phase II, Lane No. 6
Bari Brahmana, Dist. Jammu, Jammu and Kashmir
India
 Phone: (91) 1923 222334/221930
 Fax: (91) 1926 221930
Personnel:
 Man. Dir.: Pawan Dubey
 Phone: (91) 1923 222334/221930
 Exec. Dir: K. D. Sharma
 Phone: (91) 1923 222334/221930
 Gen. Mgr.: H. K. Khanna
 Phone: (91) 1923 222334/221930
Type of Operation: Paper mill
Paper/Paperboard Grades and Capacities:
 Total paper and paperboard capacity: 10,000 mt/y
 Uncoated woodfree/freesheet: 10,000 mt/y
Paper and Paperboard Mill Data:
Paper Machines: 1
No. 1, total capacity 10,000 mt/y, Uncoated woodfree/freesheet

ⓘJollyboard Limited
501 Rewa Chambers, 31, Sir Vithaldas Thackersey Marg
400020 Mumbai, Maharashtra
India
 Phone: (91) 22 25781348/22078531/ 22089233
 Fax: (91) 22 25784559/22069533
 Web Address: www.jollyboard.com
Mill Locations:
Jollyboard Limited, Mumbai Mill, 501 Rewa Chambers, 31, Sir Vithaldas Thackersey Marg, 400020 Mumbai, India, Capacity: 52,000 mt/y, (Paperboard mill)
 Phone: (91) 22 25781348/22078531/ 22089233
 Fax: (91) 22 25784559/22069533

ⓜJollyboard Limited
Mumbai Mill
501 Rewa Chambers, 31, Sir Vithaldas Thackersey Marg
400020 Mumbai, Maharashtra
India
 Phone: (91) 22 25781348/22078531/ 22089233
 Fax: (91) 22 25784559/22069533
 Web Address: www.jollyboard.com
Personnel:
 Chmn. & Man. Dir: Arjun Jolly
 Phone: (91) 22 25781348/22078531/ 22089233
 Email: arjun@jollyboard.com
 Dir.: P. K. Dasgupta
 Phone: (91) 98 21220399
Total Employees at this Location: 367
Type of Operation: Paperboard mill
Paper/Paperboard Grades and Capacities:
 Total paper and paperboard capacity: 52,000 mt/y
 Boxboard/cartonboard: 52,000 mt/y

ⓘJR Group
4th Floor, JR Plaza, Tank Stre
635109 Hosur, Tamil Nadu
India
 Phone: (91) 4344 244166
 Fax: (91) 4344 244266
 Email: jrp@jrgroup.in
 Web Address: www.jrgroup.in
Personnel:
 Man. Dir.: Subash Chandru Ramamurthy
 Phone: (91) 9443330555
 Email: subash@jrgroup.in
Mill Locations:
Venkraft Paper Mills Private Ltd., Hosur Mill, 10th km of Kelalmangalam Road, 635110 Hosur, India, Capacity: 119,238 mt/y, (Paper mill)
 Phone: (91) 4344-652152/ 4344-645355
 Fax: (91) 4344-244266
 Email: venkraft@jrgroup.in

ⓘKalptaru Papers Ltd.
701, Avdhesh, Opp. Gurudwara, Thaltej, S. G. Highway
380 054 Ahmedabad, Gujarat
India
 Phone: (91) 79-26858510, 79- 40230230
 Fax: (91) 79-30171202
 Email: contact@kalptaru.co.in
 Web Address: www.kalptaru.co.in
Mill Locations:
Kalptaru Papers Ltd., Gandhinagar, Ahmadabad Mill, 116, Village Karoli Khatraj Chokri, Near Vadsar Air Base Taluka Kalol, Gandhinagar,Ahmadabad, India, Capacity: 39,270 mt/y, (Paper mill)
 Phone: (91) 2764 281040/301
 Fax: (91) 2764 281302
 Email: paper@kalptaru.co.in

ⓜKalptaru Papers Ltd.
Gandhinagar, Ahmadabad Mill
116, Village Karoli Khatraj Chokri, Near Vadsar Air Base Taluka Kalol
Gandhinagar,Ahmadabad, Gujarat
India
 Phone: (91) 2764 281040/301
 Fax: (91) 2764 281302
 Email: paper@kalptaru.co.in
 Web Address: www.kalptaru.co.in/kalptaru_papers_ltd.html
Personnel:
 Chmn.:J. K. Gupta
 Phone: (91) 79 30171200
 Email: jkgupta@kalptaru.co.in
 Man. Dir.: Naveen Gupta
 Phone: (91) 2764 281040/301
 Email: naveen@kalptaru.co.in
Type of Operation: Paper mill
Paper/Paperboard Grades and Capacities:
 Total paper and paperboard capacity: 39,270 mt/y
 Newsprint
 Packaging papers
Paper and Paperboard Mill Data:
Paper Machines: 2
No. 1, total capacity 17,850 mt/y, Trim width 1.32 m
No. 2, total capacity 21,420 mt/y, Trim width 2.57 m

ⓘKamakshi Papers Pvt. Ltd.
No.68, (Old No.40), 2nd Main Road, Ambattur Indl Estate
600 058 Chennai , Tamil Nadu
India
 Phone: (91) (44)-26248316/ 26257696
 Fax: (91) (44)-26258944
 Web Address: www.kamakshilamipack.com
Mill Locations:
Kamakshi Papers Pvt. Ltd., JP Nagar Mill, Industrial Estate, Delhi Road Gajraula, 244 223 JP Nagar, India, Capacity: 7,200 mt/y, (Paper mill)
 Phone: (91) 5924 252035/2435/2835
 Fax: (91) 5924 252844/2444/2623

ⓜKamakshi Papers Pvt. Ltd.
JP Nagar Mill
Industrial Estate, Delhi Road Gajraula
244 223 JP Nagar, Uttar Pradesh
India
 Phone: (91) 5924 252035/2435/2835
 Fax: (91) 5924 252844/2444/2623
Personnel:
 Pres.: Anil Kr. Agarawal
 Phone: (91) 5924 252035/2435/2835
 Pres.: Krishna Kr. Aggarwal
 Phone: (91) 5924 252035/2435/2835
 Man. Dir.: Garg Ayush
 Phone: (91) 98 18738520
 Email: gargayush87@yahoo.com
 Mkg.Mgr.: Mr. N. Soundararajan
 Phone: (91) (44)-26248316/ 26257696
Type of Operation: Paper mill
Paper/Paperboard Grades and Capacities:
 Total paper and paperboard capacity: 7,200 mt/y
 Newsprint

ⓘKaranja Industries (P) Ltd., Paper Division
Akkamahadevi Colony
585 401 Bidar, Karnataka
India
 Phone: (91) 8482 228147/228262
 Fax: (91) 8482 228203
Personnel:
 Chmn.:Jagannath Lachuriye
 Phone: (91) 8482 228147/228262
 Fax: (91) 8482 228203
 Man. Dir.:V. K. Patil
 Phone: (91) 8482 228147/228262
 Fax: (91) 8482 228203
 Dir.: Madhav Raonitturkar
 Phone: (91) 8482 228147/228262
 Fax: (91) 8482 228203
 Sls. Mgr.: Krishna Joshi
 Phone: (91) 8482 228147/228262
 Fax: (91) 8482 228203
Mill Locations:
Karanja Industries (P) Ltd., Paper Division, Bidar Mill, Village Sindpadagi, Tal. Humnabad, Bidar, India, Capacity: 6,000 mt/y, (Paper mill, Paperboard mill)
 Phone: (91) 8483 274292
 Fax: (91) 8483 274019
 Email: karanjabidar@yahoo.com

ⓜKaranja Industries (P) Ltd., Paper Division
Bidar Mill
Village Sindpadagi, Tal. Humnabad
Bidar, Karnataka
India
 Phone: (91) 8483 274292
 Fax: (91) 8483 274019
 Email: karanjabidar@yahoo.com
Personnel:
 Man. Dir.: H. S. Biradar
 Phone: (91) 94 49625888
 Factory Mgr.: Rajendra Patil
 Phone: (91) 8483 274292

Prod. Mgr.: C. H. Devidas
Phone: (91) 8483 274292
Total Employees at this Location: 185
Type of Operation: Paper mill, Paperboard mill
Pulp Mill Data:
 Bleach Plant Systems: 1
 No. 1, Sequence: CEH
Paper/Paperboard Grades and Capacities:
 Total paper and paperboard capacity: 6,000 mt/y
 Packaging papers
 Boxboard/cartonboard: 6,000 mt/y
Paper and Paperboard Mill Data:
 Stock Preparation:
 Pulpers: 3
 Refiners: 3
Paper Machines: 2
 No. 1, cylinder, Trim width 1.7 m, Boxboard/cartonboard
 No. 2, Packaging papers
Finishing Equipment:
 Rewinders: 1
Energy Data:
 Power boilers: 1

ⓘKarnal Card Board Industries
Mann Industrial Estate, Chirao, Kaithal Road
Karnal, Haryana
India
 Phone: (91) 184 2291793/3111222/2221540
 Fax: (91) 184 2272485/4788
 Email: agrotracs@hotmail.com,
  agrotracs@rediffmail.com
Mill Locations:
 Karnal Card Board Industries, Karnal Mill, Mann
 Industrial Estate, Chirao, Kaithal Road, Karnal, India,
 Capacity: 5,000 mt/y, (Paperboard mill)
 Phone: (91) 184 2291793/3111222/2221540
 Fax: (91) 184 2272485/4788
 Email: agrotracs@hotmail.com, agrotracs@rediffmail.
 com

ⓘKarnal Card Board Industries
Karnal Mill
Mann Industrial Estate, Chirao, Kaithal Road
Karnal, Haryana
India
 Phone: (91) 184 2291793/3111222/2221540
 Fax: (91) 184 2272485/4788
 Email: agrotracs@hotmail.com,
  agrotracs@rediffmail.com
Personnel:
 Chmn & Man. Dir.: Ranvir Singh Mann
 Phone: (91) 184 229 1793/311 1222
Total Employees at this Location: 60
Type of Operation: Paperboard mill
Paper/Paperboard Grades and Capacities:
 Total paper and paperboard capacity: 5,000 mt/y
 Linerboard
 Boxboard/cartonboard

ⓘKarthikeya Paper & Board Ltd.
No 14, Kalingarayan Street, Ram Nagar, Ram Nagar
641009 Coimbatore, Tamil Nadu
India
 Phone: (91) +91 422 223 8524
Mill Locations:
 Karthikeya Paper & Board Ltd., Erode District Mill, 797/1,
 Rajan Nagar, Baguthampalayam Sathyamangalam,
 Erode District, India, Capacity: 9,000 mt/y, (Paper mill)

ⓘKarthikeya Paper & Board Ltd.
Erode District Mill
797/1, Rajan Nagar, Baguthampalayam
Sathyamangalam
Erode District, Tamil Nadu
India
Personnel:
 Man. Dir.: Priya K. Vasant
 Phone: (91) 98 42228420
 Email: kpblcbe@yahoo.co.in

Mktg. Mgr.: Paneer Selvam
Phone: (91) 98 42239840
Type of Operation: Paper mill
Paper/Paperboard Grades and Capacities:
 Total paper and paperboard capacity: 9,000 mt/y
 Uncoated woodfree/freesheet

ⓘKarur KCP Packagings Ltd.
330/1, Chinna Andan Kovil Road
639001 Karur, Tamil Nadu
India
 Phone: (91) 4324 260363/264363/240663
 /240163
 Fax: (91) 4324 263963/240963
 Email: kkpl@eth.net
 Web Address: www.karurkcp.in
Personnel:
 Chmn. & Man. Dir.: Mr. K. C. Palanisamy
 Phone: (91) 4324 260363/264363/240663
 /240163
 Fax: (91) 4324 263963/240963
 Joint Man. Dir.: Mr. K. C.P. Sivaraman
 Phone: (91) 4324 260363/264363/240663
 /240163
 Fax: (91) 4324 263963/240963
 Depty. Gen.Mgr. - Commercial: Mr. V. Sudharson
 Phone: (91) 4324 260363/264363/240663
 /240163
 Fax: (91) 4324 263963/240963
 Gen. Mgr.: Mr. C. Karunanithi
 Phone: (91) 4324 260363/264363/240663
 /240163
 Fax: (91) 4324 263963/240963
Mill Locations:
 Karur KCP Packagings Ltd., Pondicherry Mill, R.S. No.
 112 Thiruvandarkoil (PO), Mannadipet Commune,
 605102 Pondicherry, India, Capacity: 25,000 mt/y,
 (Paper mill)
 Phone: (91) 413 2640559/560/561
 Fax: (91) 413 2641009
 Email: karurkcp@satyam.net.in

ⓘKarur KCP Packagings Ltd.
Pondicherry Mill
R.S. No. 112 Thiruvandarkoil (PO), Mannadipet
Commune
605102 Pondicherry, Pondicherry
India
 Phone: (91) 413 2640559/560/561
 Fax: (91) 413 2641009
 Email: karurkcp@satyam.net.in
 Web Address: www.karurkcp.in
Personnel:
 Chmn. & Man. Dir.: Mr. K. C. Palanisamy
 Phone: (91) 413 2640559/560/561
 Joint Man. Dir.: Mr. K. C.P. Sivaraman
 Phone: (91) 413 2640559/560/561
 Gen. Mgr.: Mr. C. Karunanithi
 Phone: (91) 413 2640559/560/561
 Email: karunanithi@karurkcp.in
Type of Operation: Paper mill
Paper/Paperboard Grades and Capacities:
 Total paper and paperboard capacity: 25,000 mt/y
 Packaging papers: 25,000 mt/y

ⓘKay Power & Paper Limited
B-54, M.I.D.C.
415004 Satara, Maharashtra
India
 Phone: (91) 2162 246153-56
 Fax: (91) 2162 246133
 Email: kaybouvet@hotmail.com
Personnel:
 Man. Dir.: Neeraj Chandra
 Phone: (91) 2162 246153-56
 Fax: (91) 2162 246133
Mill Locations:
 Kay Power & Paper Limited, Satara Mill, Gat No.
 454/457, Borgaon, 415519 Satara, India, Capacity:
 23,100 mt/y, (Paper mill)

Phone: (91) 2162 265329/65292/260
Fax: (91) 2162 265052
Email: kaypower@sancharnet.in

ⓘKay Power & Paper Limited
Satara Mill
Gat No. 454/457, Borgaon
415519 Satara, Maharashtra
India
 Phone: (91) 2162 265329/65292/260
 Fax: (91) 2162 265052
 Email: kaypower@sancharnet.in
Personnel:
 Man. Dir.: Mr. Neeraj Chandra
 Phone: (91) 2162 246153
 Factory Mgr.: Mr. V. J. Patel
 Phone: (91) 2162 246153
Type of Operation: Paper mill
Paper/Paperboard Grades and Capacities:
 Total paper and paperboard capacity: 23,100 mt/y
 Packaging papers

ⓘKaygaon Paper Mills Ltd.
131/133 Old Hanuman Lane, 1st Flr: No.11-b,
Kalbadevi Rd
400002 Mumbai, Maharashtra
India
 Phone: (91) 240-334696, 334731, 341157
 Fax: (91) 240 321855
Personnel:
 Man. Dir.: Om Prakash Damodar Rathi
 Phone: (91) 240 2334696/4731
 Fax: (91) 240 2321855
 Gen. Mgr.: Mr. P. K. Poddar
 Phone: (91) 240 2334696/4731
 Fax: (91) 240 2321855
Mill Locations:
 Kaygaon Paper Mills Ltd., Tq. Gangapur, Aurangabad
 Mill, Gat. No. 184, Kaygaon, 431005 Tq. Gangapur,
 Aurangabad, India, Capacity: 30,000 mt/y, (Paper mill)

ⓘKaygaon Paper Mills Ltd.
Tq. Gangapur, Aurangabad Mill
Gat. No. 184, Kaygaon
431005 Tq. Gangapur, Aurangabad, Maharashtra
India
Personnel:
 Comm. Officer: L. K. Digraskar
 Gen. Mgr.: Mr. P. K. Poddar
Total Employees at this Location: 40
Type of Operation: Paper mill
Paper/Paperboard Grades and Capacities:
 Total paper and paperboard capacity: 30,000 mt/y
 Newsprint
 Packaging papers
Paper and Paperboard Mill Data:
Paper Machines: 1
 No. 1, fourdrinier, Trim width 2.4 m, Newsprint,
 Packaging papers

ⓘⓘKhanna Paper Mills Pvt. Ltd.
Amritsar Mill
Fatehgarh Road
143001 Amritsar, Punjab
India
 Phone: (91) 183 5067 100/109
 Fax: (91) 183 5067 110/111
 Email: info@khannapaper.com
 Web Address: www.khannapaper.com
Personnel:
 Chmn. : Shri Mohan Khanna
 Phone: (91) 183 5067 100/109
 Man. Dir.: Suneet Kochhar
 Phone: (91) 183 5067 100/109
 Mktg. Mgr.: Vinay Verma
 Phone: (91) 98 76014690
 Email: vinay.verma@khannapaper.com
Total Employees of Company: 1,500
Total Employees at this Location: 300

India

Type of Operation: Paper mill, Paperboard mill
Pulp Grades and Capacities:
  Total pulp capacity: 324,077 mt/y
  Recycled Pulping: 324,077 mt/y
Pulp Mill Data:
Pulp Lines: 2
  Bleach Plant Systems: 2
  Recycled Fiber Treatment Lines:
  Flotation deinking lines
  Pulpers: 2
Paper/Paperboard Grades and Capacities:
  Total paper and paperboard capacity: 338,079 mt/y
  Newsprint: 107,100 mt/y
  Uncoated woodfree/freesheet: 125,307 mt/y
  Boxboard/cartonboard: 105,672 mt/y
Paper and Paperboard Mill Data:
Paper Machines: 4
  No. 1, fourdrinier, total capacity 69,972 mt/y, Trim width 2.9 m, Boxboard/cartonboard
  No. 2, total capacity 35,700 mt/y, Trim width 2.13 m, Boxboard/cartonboard
  No. 4, (second hand), total capacity 125,307 mt/y, Trim width 4.35 m, Uncoated woodfree/freesheet
  No. 5, (second hand), total capacity 107,100 mt/y, Trim width 7 m, Newsprint
Coating Machines: 2
  No. 1, total capacity 70,000 mt/y., on machine
  No. 2, total capacity 35,700 mt/y., on machine
Finishing Equipment:
  Rewinders: 1
  Sheeters: 1
Energy Data:
  Power boilers: 2
  Steam turbines: 1 at 15 MW
  Electrical demand for mill: 876 MWh/D

ⓘKhatema Fibres Ltd.
404-405. Vikas Deep Building, Laxmi Nagar
110 092 Dist. Centre, Delhi
India
  Phone: (91) 11 22422471/8
  Fax: (91) 11 22422480/22526933
  Email: info@khatemafibres.com
  Web Address: www.khatemafibres.com
Personnel:
  CEO: Rakesh Chandra Rastogi
  Phone: (91) 99271 04000
Total Employees of Company: 493
Total Employees at this Location: 50
Mill Locations:
  Khatema Fibres Ltd., Khatema Dist., Udham Singh Nagar Mill, UPSIDC Industrial Area, Lohia Head Road, 262 308 Khatema Dist., Udham Singh Nagar, India, Capacity: 64,974 mt/y, (Pulp mill, Paper mill, Paperboard mill)
  Phone: (91) 5943 251001-8/250180
  Fax: (91) 5943 250474
  Email: info@khatemafibres.com

ⓂKhatema Fibres Ltd.
Khatema Dist., Udham Singh Nagar Mill
UPSIDC Industrial Area, Lohia Head Road
262 308 Khatema Dist., Udham Singh Nagar, Uttar Pradesh
India
  Phone: (91) 5943 251001-8/250180
  Fax: (91) 5943 250474
  Email: info@khatemafibres.com
  Web Address: www.khatemafibres.com
Personnel:
  CEO: Rakesh Chandra Rastogi
  Phone: (91) 98 11333198
  Fax: (91) 5943 250474
  Email: rastogi@khatemafibres.com
  VP (Technical): Achal Sharma
  Phone: (91) 9837788471
  Fax: (91) 5943 250474
  Email: achalsharma@khatemafibres.com
  Mgr. (Finance): Jagpal Sharma
  Phone: (91) 11 22422471-08
  Fax: (91) 11 22422480
  Email: accounts@khatemafibres.com
  Prod. Mgr.: Arunn Kumar
  Phone: (91) 5943 251001-8/250180
  Comm. Dir.: Nirpun Rastogi
  Phone: (91) 11 22422471-08
  Fax: (91) 11 22422480
  Email: infoworks@khatemafibres.com
  Mgr. (Pulp): S. N. Misra
  Phone: (91) 5943 251001-8/250180
  Mgr. (Mechanical): Sugreev Sharma
  Phone: (91) 5943 251001-8/250180
  Mgr. (Electrical): S. K. Goel
  Phone: (91) 5943 251001-8/250180
  Mgr. (Quality Ctrl.): Dr. Y. P. Singh
  Phone: (91) 5943 251001-8/250180
Total Employees at this Location: 250
Type of Operation: Pulp mill, Paper mill, Paperboard mill
Pulp Grades and Capacities:
  Total pulp capacity: 55,533 mt/y
  Recycled Pulping: 55,533 mt/y
Pulp Mill Data:
Pulp Lines: 3
  Bleach Plant Systems: 2
  Recycled Fiber Treatment Lines:
  Pulpers: 8 at 70,000 admt/y
  Washing deinking lines: 3 at 18,000 admt/y
Paper/Paperboard Grades and Capacities:
  Total paper and paperboard capacity: 64,974 mt/y
  Specialty and industrial: 22,134 mt/y
  Linerboard: 42,840 mt/y
Paper and Paperboard Mill Data:
  Stock Preparation:
  Pulpers: 10
  Refiners: 10
Paper Machines: 3
  No. 1, multi-layer, total capacity 42,840 mt/y, Trim width 2.35 m, Linerboard
  No. 2, Yankee dryer, total capacity 9,996 mt/y, Trim width 3.3 m, Specialty and industrial
  No. 3, Yankee dryer, total capacity 12,138 mt/y, Trim width 3.3 m, Specialty and industrial
Finishing Equipment:
  Winders: 3 at 72,000 mt/y
  Calenders: 5
  Rewinders: 2 at 2 mt/y
  Sheeters: 3 at 3,200 mt/y, 6,400 mt/y, 9,600 mt/y
Energy Data:
  Power boilers: 3
  Electrical demand for mill: 69 MWh/D

ⓘⓂKherani Paper Mills Ltd.
Valsad Mill
808/C, Phase III, G.I.D.C. Vapi
396195 Dist. Valsad, Gujarat
India
Personnel:
  Man. Dir.: Gajendra Aggarwal
  Phone: (91) 22 26796889
  Sls. Mgr.: Tonny Pereira
  Phone: (91) 22 26795281, 98 33056613
  Email: tonny@gspbl.com
Type of Operation: Paperboard mill
Paper/Paperboard Grades and Capacities:
  Total paper and paperboard capacity: 18,000 mt/y
  Boxboard/cartonboard: 18,000 mt/y
Paper and Paperboard Mill Data:
Paper Machines: 1
  No. 1, total capacity 18,000 mt/y, Trim width 1.68 m, Boxboard/cartonboard

ⓘKingston Paptech Pvt Ltd
Village Sonia Taluka
Sabarkantha district
India
  Phone: (91) 079 2929 7702
Personnel:
  Dir.: Monohar Patel
  Phone: (91) 079 2929 7702
Mill Locations:
  Kingston Paptech Pvt Ltd, Sabarkantha Mill, Village Sonia Taluka, Sabarkantha district , India, Capacity: 42,000 mt/y, (Paper mill)

ⓂKingston Paptech Pvt Ltd
Sabarkantha Mill
Village Sonia Taluka
Sabarkantha district , Gujarat
India
Personnel:
  Dir. : Monohar Patel
Total Employees at this Location: 100
Type of Operation: Paper mill
Pulp Grades and Capacities:
  Total pulp capacity: 41,909 mt/y
  Recycled Pulping: 41,909 mt/y
Pulp Mill Data:
  Recycled Fiber Treatment Lines:
  Recycled packaging pulping lines: 1
Paper/Paperboard Grades and Capacities:
  Total paper and paperboard capacity: 42,000 mt/y
  Linerboard: 42,000 mt/y
Paper and Paperboard Mill Data:
Paper Machines: 1
  No. 1, multi-wire, total capacity 42,000 mt/y, Trim width 3 m, Linerboard
Energy Data:
  Power boilers
  Electrical demand for mill: 52 MWh/D

ⓘKohinoor Paper & Newsprint (P) Ltd
16A Everest House, 46CJ.L. Nehru Road, Kolkata 700071
700071 Kolkata
India
  Phone: (91) 91 33 22883104
  Fax: (91) 91 33 22883105
  Email: admin@kohinoorindia.in
  Web Address: www.kohinoorindia.in
Personnel:
  Dir.: Rajesh
  Phone: (91) 33 40036693
  Mill Mgr.: Saehi
  Phone: (91) 990 390 4564
Mill Locations:
  Kohinoor Pulp & Paper Pvt Ltd, Matia Mill, Plot Block C, Village Momoi, Industrial Growth Centre , Matia, Dist. Goalpara, India, (Paper mill, Paperboard mill)
  Kohinoor Paper & Newsprint (P) Ltd, Parganas Mill, 19, Falta Industrial Growth Centre, Phase II, Sector- V, Dist. 24, Parganas, India, Capacity: 70,000 mt/y, (Paper mill)
  Phone: (91) 990 390 4564/33 4003 6692/93
  Email: nilanjana@kohinoorpaper.in

ⓂKohinoor Pulp & Paper Pvt. Ltd
Matia Mill
Mill is under construction (scheduled to start operations in April 2015)
Ownership: Kohinoor Paper & Newsprint (P) Ltd
Plot Block C, Village Momoi, Industrial Growth Centre
Matia, Dist. Goalpara, Assam
India
Type of Operation: Paper mill, Paperboard mill

ⓂKohinoor Paper & Newsprint (P) Ltd
Parganas Mill
19, Falta Industrial Growth Centre, Phase II, Sector- V, Dist. 24
Parganas, West Bengal
India
  Phone: (91) 990 390 4564/33 4003 6692/93
  Email: nilanjana@kohinoorpaper.in
  Web Address: www.kohinoorindia.in/paper.html
Personnel:
  Dir.: Mr. Rajesh
  Phone: (91) 33 40036693

Mill Mgr.: Mr. Saehi
Phone: (91) 990 390 4564
Total Employees at this Location: 225
Type of Operation: Paper mill
Pulp Grades and Capacities:
Total pulp capacity: 61,648 mt/y
Recycled Pulping: 61,648 mt/y
Pulp Mill Data:
Bleach Plant Systems: 1
Recycled Pulping System
Recycled Fiber Treatment Lines:
Flotation deinking lines: 1 at 43,750
Paper/Paperboard Grades and Capacities:
Total paper and paperboard capacity: 70,000 mt/y
Uncoated woodfree/freesheet: 70,000 mt/y
Paper and Paperboard Mill Data:
Paper Machines: 1
No. 1, fourdrinier, total capacity 70,000 mt/y, Trim width 4.3 m, Uncoated woodfree/freesheet
Energy Data:
Power boilers: 1
Steam turbines: 1 at 6 MW
Electrical demand for mill: 169 MWh/D

⊕⊕Komal Straw Board & Mill Board Industries
Gurdaspur Mill
Ownership: 100% by Private ownership
Dera Baba Nanak Rd. Village & Post. Hayat Nagar
143521 Gurdaspur, Punjab
India
Phone: (91) 98 76200714
Personnel:
Man. Dir.: Sarovar Kumar Aggrawal
Man. Patr.: Chander Mohan Aggrawal
Total Employees at this Location: 100
Type of Operation: Paper mill
Paper/Paperboard Grades and Capacities:
Total paper and paperboard capacity: 9,000 mt/y
Packaging papers
Paper and Paperboard Mill Data:
Stock Preparation:
Pulpers: 2
Paper Machines: 2
PM 1, Yankee dryer, Trim width 1.8 m, Packaging papers
PM 2, fourdrinier, Trim width 1.8 m, Packaging papers
Finishing Equipment:
Rewinders: 2
Sheeters: 1
Energy Data:
Power boilers: 1

⊕⊕Kovai Maruthi Papers & Boards (P) Ltd.
Salem Mill
S.F. 524/1, Irukkur Kabilaramalai, Tramathyuelur
637208 Salem, Tamil Nadu
India
Phone: (91) 4268 254712/715
Fax: (91) 4268 254718
Personnel:
Man. Dir.: Mr. Rajagopalan
Phone: (91) 94 43327175
Proj. Dir.: K. Soundararajan
Phone: (91) 4268 254712/715
Total Employees at this Location: 250
Type of Operation: Paper mill
Paper/Paperboard Grades and Capacities:
Total paper and paperboard capacity: 28,800 mt/y
Packaging papers: 28,800 mt/y
Paper and Paperboard Mill Data:
Paper Machines: 2
No. 1, Trim width 2.14 m, Packaging papers
No. 2, Trim width 2.14 m, Packaging papers

⊕⊕KR Pulp & Papers Ltd.
Shahjahanpur Mill
Ownership: 100% by Private
Jalalabad Road
242001 Shahjahanpur, Uttar Pradesh
India
Phone: (91) 5842 240135/6/7/320999
Fax: (91) 5842 240250/1
Email: info@krpapers.com,
kr@krpapers.com
Web Address: www.krpapers.com
Personnel:
Owner/Mill Dir.: M. G. Agarwal
Phone: (91) 5842 240135/6/7/320999
Email: info@krpapers.com
Owner/Mill Dir.: S. G. Agarwal
Phone: (91) 5842 240250/240251
Total Employees of Company: 500
Total Employees at this Location: 500
Type of Operation: Pulp mill, Paper mill
Pulp Grades and Capacities:
Total pulp capacity: 61,087 mt/y
Other Pulp: 61,087 mt/y
Pulp Mill Data:
Chemical Pulping Systems:
Batch digesters
Continuous digesters
Bleach Plant Systems: 1
Chemical Pulping System, Type: Bagasse
Chemical Recovery Equipment:
Evaporator lines: 1
Recovery boilers: 1
Recycled Fiber Treatment Lines:
Recycled packaging pulping lines: 1
Paper/Paperboard Grades and Capacities:
Total paper and paperboard capacity: 104,958 mt/y
Uncoated woodfree/freesheet: 67,473 mt/y
Packaging papers: 37,485 mt/y
Paper and Paperboard Mill Data:
Paper Machines: 2
No. 1, total capacity 37,485 mt/y, Trim width 3.2 m, Packaging papers
No. 2, fourdrinier, total capacity 67,473 mt/y, Trim width 5 m, Uncoated woodfree/freesheet
Energy Data:
Power boilers
Steam turbines: 1 at 14.5 MW
Electrical demand for mill: 289 MWh/D

⊕Kuantum Papers Ltd
SCO 18-19, 1st Floor, Sector 8-C Madhya Marg.
160009 Chandigarh
India
Phone: (91) 172 2781631
Fax: (91) 172 2770208
Personnel:
Chmn, MD: J.K Khaitan
Fax: (91) 1884 30244
Dir.: Yashovardhan Saboo
Man. Dir.: Pavan Khaitan
Mill Locations:
Kuantum Papers Ltd, Hoshiarpur Mill, Saila Khurd, 144529 Dist. Hoshiarpur, India, Capacity: 122,094 mt/y, (Paper mill)
Phone: (91) 1884-230241/230242
Fax: (91) 1884-230244
Email: kuantummill@kuantumpapers.com

⊕Kuantum Papers Ltd
Hoshiarpur Mill
Saila Khurd
144529 Dist. Hoshiarpur, Punjab
India
Mailing Address: PO Sailakhurd, 144 529 Dist. Hoshiarpur, Punjab, India
Phone: (91) 1884-230241/230242
Fax: (91) 1884-230244
Email: kuantummill@kuantumpapers.com
Web Address: kuantumpapers.com/
Personnel:
Pres. (Works): A. K. Chatterjee
Phone: (91) 1884 230267
VP (HR & Admin.): Shriban Kishen
Phone: (91) 1884 230267
Man. Dir.: Mr. Pavan Khaitan
Phone: (91) 172 2548566
Email: pavankhaitan@abcpaper.in
Gen. Mgr. (Tech.): V. K. Jethi
Phone: (91) 1884 230241/42
Dpty. Gen. Mgr., Tech.: S. N. Ray
Phone: (91) 1884 230241/42/66
Total Employees at this Location: 1,250
Type of Operation: Paper mill
Pulp Grades and Capacities:
Total pulp capacity: 40,063 mt/y
Chemical Pulp: 40,063 mt/y
Pulp Mill Data:
Chemical Pulping Systems:
Batch digesters: 1
Bleach Plant Systems: 1
Chemical Pulping System, Sequence: CEHH
Paper/Paperboard Grades and Capacities:
Total paper and paperboard capacity: 122,094 mt/y
Uncoated woodfree/freesheet: 122,094 mt/y
Paper and Paperboard Mill Data:
Paper Machines: 4
No. 1, fourdrinier, total capacity 7,854 mt/y, Trim width 1.88 m, Uncoated woodfree/freesheet
No. 2, fourdrinier, total capacity 7,854 mt/y, Trim width 1.88 m, Uncoated woodfree/freesheet
No. 3, fourdrinier, total capacity 34,986 mt/y, Trim width 3.33 m, Uncoated woodfree/freesheet
No. 4, fourdrinier, total capacity 71,400 mt/y, Trim width 3.9 m, Uncoated woodfree/freesheet
Energy Data:
Electrical demand for mill: 145 MWh/D

⊕Kulik Paper Industries (P) Ltd.
Raiganj Mill
Chottoparua, P.O. Karnajora Raiganj
Uttar Dinajpur, West Bengal
India
Type of Operation: Paper mill
Pulp Grades and Capacities:
Paper/Paperboard Grades and Capacities:
Total paper and paperboard capacity: 6,000 mt/y
Packaging papers: 6,000 mt/y
Paper and Paperboard Mill Data:
Paper Machines: 2
No. 1, Trim width 1.6 m, Packaging papers
No. 2, Trim width 2.2 m, Packaging papers

⊕⊕Kwality Pulp & Paper Mills
Valsad Mill
Plot No. 183, II Phase G.I.D.C., Vapi
396195 Valsad, Gujarat
India
Mailing Address: P.O.Box.: 47, 396195 Valsad, Gujarat, India
Phone: (91) 260 243 2149/1049/2149
Fax: (91) 260 2432049
Email: val_kwality@yahoo.co.in
Personnel:
Partner: Prabodh Bhavanji Dedhia
Phone: (91) 98 20351788
Partner: Vijay Bapu Madnaik
Phone: (91) 98 25115549
Partner: Rajesh Bhavanji Dedhia
Phone: (91) 98 20351790
Partner: Jayanti Jethalal Dedhia
Phone: (91) 98 20080300
Type of Operation: Paper mill
Paper/Paperboard Grades and Capacities:
Total paper and paperboard capacity: 20,000 mt/y
Packaging papers: 20,000 mt/y
Paper and Paperboard Mill Data:
Paper Machines: 2
PM 1, Yankee dryer, Trim width 1 m, Packaging papers
PM 2, Yankee dryer, Trim width 2.13 m, Packaging papers
Finishing Equipment:
Rewinders: 2

India

Energy Data:
Power boilers: 1

ⓘLadhar Paper Mill
Ownership: NRI Group
Village Ladhran, Malsian Road, Nakodar
144004 Dist. Jalandhar, Punjab
India
Phone: (91) 1821 224588
Mill Locations:
Ladhar Paper Mill, Jalandhar Mill, Village Ladhran, Malsian Road, Nakodar, 144004 Dist. Jalandhar, India, Capacity: 24,000 mt/y, (Paper mill)
Phone: (91) 1821 224588

ⓜLadhar Paper Mill
Jalandhar Mill
Village Ladhran, Malsian Road, Nakodar
144004 Dist. Jalandhar, Punjab
India
Phone: (91) 1821 224588
Personnel:
COO: Ashwani Kant Aggarwal
Phone: (91) 92 16156700, 98 76856700
Email: ashwani66@rediffmail.com
Man. Dir.: Abhay Sharma
Phone: (91) 1821 224588
Total Employees at this Location: 150
Type of Operation: Paper mill
Pulp Grades and Capacities:
Total pulp capacity: 21,283 mt/y
Recycled Pulping: 21,283 mt/y
Pulp Mill Data:
Bleach Plant Systems: 1
Recycled Pulping System
Recycled Fiber Treatment Lines:
Flotation deinking lines: 1
Paper/Paperboard Grades and Capacities:
Total paper and paperboard capacity: 24,000 mt/y
Uncoated woodfree/freesheet: 24,000 mt/y
Paper and Paperboard Mill Data:
Paper Machines: 1
No. 1, fourdrinier, total capacity 24,000 mt/y, Trim width 2.85 m, Uncoated woodfree/freesheet
Energy Data:
Power boilers
Electrical demand for mill: 57 MWh/D

ⓘLalji Board Industries (P) Ltd.
396, St. No. 14, Arya Ngr.
283203 Firozabad, Uttar Pradesh
India
Phone: (91) 5612-242349
Mill Locations:
Lalji Board Industries (P) Ltd., Firozabad Mill, A-34, Industrial Estate, 283203 Firozabad, India, Capacity: 7,200 mt/y, (Paper mill)
Fax: (91) 5612 245251

ⓜLalji Board Industries (P) Ltd.
Firozabad Mill
A-34, Industrial Estate
283203 Firozabad, Uttar Pradesh
India
Fax: (91) 5612 245251
Personnel:
Man. Dir: Bal Krishan Vij
Phone: (91) 98 37035017
Exec. Dir.: Surendra Kumar Vij
Phone: (91) 98 37819901
Dir: Omkar Nath Vij
Phone: (91) 98 37005014
Type of Operation: Paper mill
Paper/Paperboard Grades and Capacities:
Total paper and paperboard capacity: 7,200 mt/y
Coated woodfree/freesheet
Packaging papers

ⓘⓜLaxmi Board & Paper Mills Ltd.
Thane Mill
Plot No. 2, M.I.D.C. Kalyan Bhiwandi Road, Saravali
421311 Dist. Thane, Maharashtra
India
Phone: (91) 2522 280641/708/371
Fax: (91) 2522 280643
Email: lbpm@vsnl.net
Personnel:
Dir.: Mr. Patel
Phone: (91) 2522 280641/708/371
Email: ajax_patel@yahoo.com
Gen. Mgr. (Works): Mr. G. N. Bhat
Phone: (91) 2522 280641/708/371
Joint Man. Dir.: Rajesh Modi
Phone: (91) 2522 280641/708/371
Sls. Mgr.: S. Lobo
Phone: (91) 2522 280641/708/371
Type of Operation: Paper mill
Paper/Paperboard Grades and Capacities:
Total paper and paperboard capacity: 120,000 mt/y
Paper and Paperboard Mill Data:
Paper Machines: 3
No. 1, total capacity 35,000 mt/y, Trim width 2.6 m
No. 2, total capacity 45,000 mt/y, Trim width 3.3 m
No. 3, total capacity 40,000 mt/y, Trim width 2.65 m

ⓘLaxmi Paper Mills
A/P Kolhar, Tal. Rahata
421301 Dist. Ahmednagar
India
Personnel:
Man. Dir.: Nikhil Kharde
Phone: (91) 98 90091989
Man. Dir.: Raj Kumar Kharde
Phone: (91) 98 22650540
Mill Locations:
Laxmi Paper Mills, Thane Mill, A/P Kolhar, Tal. Rahata, 421301 Dist. Ahmednagar, India, Capacity: 14,400 mt/y, (Paper mill)

ⓜLaxmi Paper Mills
Thane Mill
A/P Kolhar, Tal. Rahata
421301 Dist. Ahmednagar, Maharashtra
India
Personnel:
Man. Dir.: Nikhil Kharde
Phone: (91) 98 90091989
Man. Dir.: Raj Kumar Kharde
Phone: (91) 98 22650540
Type of Operation: Paper mill
Paper/Paperboard Grades and Capacities:
Total paper and paperboard capacity: 14,400 mt/y
Packaging papers

ⓘM.P. Boards & Paper Mills (P) Ltd.
Udaigiri Rd.
462011 Dist. Vidisha, M.P
India
Phone: (91) 7592 232610
Fax: (91) 7592 232610
Email: mpboardbpl@hotmail.com
Personnel:
Dir.: Hemanshu Kothari
Phone: (91) 94 25009875
Fax: (91) 7592 232610
Man. Dir.: Deepak Kothari
Phone: (91) 94 25304007
Fax: (91) 7592 232610
Mill Locations:
M.P. Boards & Paper Mills (P) Ltd., Dist. Vidisha Mill, Udaigiri Rd., 462011 Dist. Vidisha, M.P, India, Capacity: 8,500 mt/y, (Paper mill)
Phone: (91) 7592 232610
Fax: (91) 7592 232610
Email: mpboardbpl@hotmail.com

ⓜM.P. Boards & Paper Mills (P) Ltd.
Dist. Vidisha Mill
Udaigiri Rd.
462011 Dist. Vidisha, M.P
India
Phone: (91) 7592 232610
Fax: (91) 7592 232610
Email: mpboardbpl@hotmail.com
Personnel:
Man. Dir.: Mr. Deepak Kothari
Phone: (91) 94 25304007
Dir.: Mr. Hemanshu Kothari
Phone: (91) 94 25009875
Email: hemanshu.kothari@rediffmail.com
Type of Operation: Paper mill
Paper/Paperboard Grades and Capacities:
Total paper and paperboard capacity: 8,500 mt/y
Packaging papers
Specialty and industrial

ⓘMaa Chandi Papers Pvt. Ltd.
Kanjilal Avenue, Durgapur - 10
Burdwan
India
Phone: (91) 3432 554449
Fax: (91) 3432 554450
Email: maachandipapers@yahoo.com
Mill Locations:
Maa Chandi Papers Pvt. Ltd., Burdwan Mill, Kanjilal Avenue, Durgapur - 10, Burdwan, India, Capacity: 24,000 mt/y, (Paper mill)
Phone: (91) 3432 554449
Fax: (91) 3432 554450
Email: maachandipapers@yahoo.com

ⓜMaa Chandi Papers Pvt. Ltd.
Burdwan Mill
Kanjilal Avenue, Durgapur - 10
Burdwan, West Bengal
India
Phone: (91) 3432 554449
Fax: (91) 3432 554450
Email: maachandipapers@yahoo.com
Type of Operation: Paper mill
Paper/Paperboard Grades and Capacities:
Total paper and paperboard capacity: 24,000 mt/y
Newsprint
Uncoated woodfree/freesheet
Paper and Paperboard Mill Data:
Paper Machines: 2
No. 1, total capacity 15,000 mt/y
No. 2, (started late 2010), total capacity 9,000 mt/y

ⓘMadhya Bharat Papers Ltd.
Ownership: 36.83% by Financial institutions, 56.60% by Indian promoters, 2.40% by Other, 4.17% by Private owners
113, Park Street, North Block 4th Floor
700016 Kolkata, West Bengal
India
Phone: (91) 3322 46 2274/2280
Fax: (91) 3322 49 3675
Email: mbpcph@rediffmail.com
Personnel:
Pres.: Mr. V. K. Khanna
Phone: (91) 3322 652274
Fax: (91) 3322 493675
Email: vkkhanna@sardaplywood.com
Man. Dir.: Mr. J. Chitlangia
Phone: (91) 3322 652274
Email: jaydeep@sardaplywood.com
Mgr. Finan.: A. K. Agarwal
Phone: (91) 3322 46 2274/2280
Fax: (91) 3322 49 3675
Total Employees of Company: 332
Mill Locations:
Madhya Bharat Papers Ltd., Dist. Janjgir-Champa Mill, Birgahni, Champa, 495 671 Dist. Janjgir-Champa, India, Capacity: 16,500 mt/y, (Paper mill)

India

Phone: (91) 7819 245050/52/55
Fax: (91) 7819 245051
Email: mbpcph@rediffmail.com, info@mbpl.in

ⓂMadhya Bharat Papers Ltd.
Dist. Janjgir-Champa Mill
Birgahni, Champa
495 671 Dist. Janjgir-Champa, Chattisgarh
India
Phone: (91) 7819 245050/52/55
Fax: (91) 7819 245051
Email: mbpcph@rediffmail.com, info@mbpl.in
Web Address: www.mbpl.in
Personnel:
Pres.: Mr. V.K. Khanna
Phone: (91) 3322 652274
Fax: (91) 3322 493675
Email: vkkhanna@sardaplywood.com
AGM (Com.): Mr. L. K. Jakhar
Phone: (91) 7819 245050/52/55
Email: mbpcph@rediffmail.com
Total Employees at this Location: 332
Type of Operation: Paper mill
Pulp Grades and Capacities:
Total pulp capacity: 16,500 mt/y
Pulp Mill Data:
Chemical Pulping Systems:
Batch digesters: 6
Bleach Plant Systems: 1
No. 1, Sequence: CEH
Paper/Paperboard Grades and Capacities:
Total paper and paperboard capacity: 16,500 mt/y
Newsprint
Uncoated woodfree/freesheet
Packaging papers
Paper and Paperboard Mill Data:
Stock Preparation:
Pulpers: 2
Refiners: 4
Paper Machines: 1
No. 1, fourdrinier, total capacity 16,500 mt/y, Trim width 2.8 m, Newsprint, Uncoated woodfree/freesheet, Packaging papers
Finishing Equipment:
Rewinders: 1
Sheeters: 1
Energy Data:
Power boilers: 1
Steam turbines: 1 at 3.1 MW
Electrical demand for mill: 65 MWh/D

ⓗⓂMaghan Paper Mills (P) Ltd.
Sangrur Mill
Sunam Road
148001 Sangrur, Punjab
India
Phone: (91) 1672-223680
Fax: (91) 1672 223684
Email: maghang@sify.com
Personnel:
Man. Dir.: Mr. V. P. Maghan
Dir.: Gaurav Maghan
Phone: (91) 98 76029102
Total Employees at this Location: 135
Type of Operation: Paperboard mill
Paper/Paperboard Grades and Capacities:
Total paper and paperboard capacity: 18,000 mt/y
Boxboard/cartonboard: 18,000 mt/y
Paper and Paperboard Mill Data:
Paper Machines: 2
No. 1
No. 2

ⓗMagnum Ventures Ltd.
Magnum House, 3/4326, Ansari Road
110 002 Darya Ganj, Delhi
India
Phone: (91) 11 23262983

Fax: (91) 11 23260623
Email: info@magnumventures.com
Web Address: www.magnumventures.in
Personnel:
Dep. Dir.: Satyendra Prasad Singh
Phone: (91) 11 23262983
Mill Locations:
Magnum Ventures Ltd., Ghaziabad Mill, 18/41, Site No. 4, Sahibabad, Dist. Ghaziabad, India, Capacity: 64,000 mt/y, (Paper mill)
Phone: (91) 120 4199200
Fax: (91) 120 4199234
Email: magnumventures@gmail.com

ⓗMagnum Ventures Ltd.
Ghaziabad Mill
18/41, Site No. 4
Sahibabad, Dist. Ghaziabad, Uttar Pradesh
India
Phone: (91) 120 4199200
Fax: (91) 120 4199234
Email: magnumventures@gmail.com
Web Address: www.magnumventures.in
Personnel:
Man. Dir. & Exec. Chmn.: Praveen Kumar Jain
Phone: (91) 120 2895200/04
Man. Dir.: Pradeep Kumar Jain
Phone: (91) 120 2895200/04
Gen. Mgr. (Admin): B. K. Ina
Phone: (91) 120 2895200/04
Dep. Dir.: Satyendra Prasad Singh
Phone: (91) 120 2895200/04
Total Employees at this Location: 255
Type of Operation: Paper mill
Pulp Grades and Capacities:
Total pulp capacity: 62,266 mt/y
Recycled Pulping: 62,266 mt/y
Pulp Mill Data:
Pulp Lines: 1
Bleach Plant Systems: 1
Recycled Pulping System
Recycled Fiber Treatment Lines:
Flotation deinking lines
Recycled packaging pulping lines at 40,000
Paper/Paperboard Grades and Capacities:
Total paper and paperboard capacity: 64,000 mt/y
Newsprint: 26,400 mt/y
Boxboard/cartonboard: 37,600 mt/y
Paper and Paperboard Mill Data:
Stock Preparation:
Pulpers: 3
Refiners: 3
Paper Machines: 3
No. 1, fourdrinier, total capacity 13,268 mt/y, Trim width 1.1 m, Newsprint
No. 2, cylinder, total capacity 37,600 mt/y, Trim width 2.2 m, Boxboard/cartonboard
No. 3, fourdrinier, total capacity 13,132 mt/y, Newsprint
Coating Machines: 1
PM2, on machine
Finishing Equipment:
Rewinders: 2
Energy Data:
Power boilers: 1
Steam turbines: 1 at 4.5 MW
Electrical demand for mill: 123 MWh/D

ⓗMaheshwari Paper Limited
Palanpur, Deesa Highway, Opp. Hotel, Green Wood, Badarpura
Tal Palanpur
India
Phone: (91) 2742 280601/2
Fax: (91) 2742 280603
Personnel:
Man. Dir.: Lalit B. Maheshwari
Phone: (91) 2742 280601/2
Fax: (91) 2742 280603
Dir.: M. R. Maheshwari

Phone: (91) 2742 280601/2
Fax: (91) 2742 280603
Mill Locations:
Maheshwari Paper Limited, Tal Palanpur Mill, Palanpur, Deesa Highway, Opp. Hotel, Green Wood, Badarpura, Tal Palanpur, India, Capacity: 6,000 mt/y, (Paper mill)
Phone: (91) 2742 280601/2
Fax: (91) 2742 280603

ⓗMaheshwari Paper Limited
Tal Palanpur Mill
Palanpur, Deesa Highway, Opp. Hotel, Green Wood, Badarpura
Tal Palanpur, Gujarat
India
Phone: (91) 2742 280601/2
Fax: (91) 2742 280603
Personnel:
Man. Dir.: Lalit B. Maheshwari
Phone: (91) 98 25084918
Dir.: Mr. M. R. Maheshwari
Phone: (91) 2742 280601
Type of Operation: Paper mill
Paper/Paperboard Grades and Capacities:
Total paper and paperboard capacity: 6,000 mt/y
Packaging papers
Paper and Paperboard Mill Data:
Paper Machines: 1
No. 1, Trim width 3.2 m, Packaging papers

ⓗMalu Paper Mills Ltd.
Ownership: Malu Group
Heera Plaza, 4th Fl., Near Telephone Exchange, Central Avenue
440 002 Nagpur, Maharashtra
India
Phone: (91) 712 2760308/2778506/2733100
Fax: (91) 712 2760310
Email: info@malupaper.com
Web Address: www.malupaper.com
Personnel:
VP: Venu Malu
Phone: (91) 712 2760308/2778506/2733100
Fax: (91) 712 2760310
Email: venumalu@malupaper.com
VP: Narayan Malu
Phone: (91) 712 2760308/2778506/2733100
Fax: (91) 712 2760310
Email: narayanmalu@malupaper.com
CFO: Girish Malpani
Phone: (91) 712 2760308
Email: gmalpani@malupaper.com
Man. Dir.: Punamchand Malu
Phone: (91) 712 2760308/2778506/2733100
Fax: (91) 712 2760310
Joint Man. Dir.: Banwarilal Malu
Phone: (91) 712 2760308/2778506/2733100
Fax: (91) 712 2760310
Mill Locations:
Malu Paper Mills Ltd., Nagpur 1 & 2 Mill, Village Borujwada, Taluka-Saoner, 31 Km Stone, Nagpur Saoner Road, Dist. Nagpur, India, Capacity: 47,000 mt/y, (Paper mill)
Phone: (91) 712 2733 100
Email: info@malupaper.com, contact@malupaper.com
Malu Paper Mills Ltd., Nagpur 3 Mill, Village Heti (Surla), Saoner MIDC Industrial Area, Dist. Nagpur, India, Capacity: 50,000 mt/y, (Paper mill)
Phone: (91) 712 2733 100
Email: info@malupaper.com, contact@malupaper.com

ⓗMalu Paper Mills Ltd.
Nagpur 1 & 2 Mill
Village Borujwada, Taluka-Saoner, 31 Km Stone, Nagpur Saoner Road
Dist. Nagpur, Maharashtra
India

India

Phone: (91) 712 2733 100
Email: info@malupaper.com,
contact@malupaper.com
Web Address: www.malupaper.com
Total Employees at this Location: 180
Type of Operation: Paper mill
Pulp Grades and Capacities:
 Total pulp capacity: 46,150 mt/y
 Recycled Pulping: 46,150 mt/y
Pulp Mill Data:
 Recycled Fiber Treatment Lines:
 Recycled packaging pulping lines: 1
Paper/Paperboard Grades and Capacities:
 Total paper and paperboard capacity: 47,000 mt/y
 Linerboard: 15,000 mt/y
 Corrugating medium/fluting: 32,000 mt/y
Paper and Paperboard Mill Data:
Paper Machines: 2
 No. 1, fourdrinier, total capacity 15,000 mt/y, Trim width 2.1 m, Linerboard
 No. 2, fourdrinier, total capacity 32,000 mt/y, Trim width 3.2 m, Corrugating medium/fluting
Energy Data:
 Power boilers
 Electrical demand for mill: 54 MWh/D

ⓂMalu Paper Mills Ltd.
Nagpur 3 Mill
Village Heti (Surla), Saoner MIDC Industrial Area
Dist. Nagpur, Maharashtra
India
 Phone: (91) 712 2733 100
 Email: info@malupaper.com,
 contact@malupaper.com
 Web Address: www.malupaper.com
Total Employees at this Location: 255
Type of Operation: Paper mill
Pulp Grades and Capacities:
 Total pulp capacity: 48,177 mt/y
 Recycled Pulping: 48,177 mt/y
Pulp Mill Data:
Pulp Lines: 1
 Bleach Plant Systems: 1
 Recycled Pulping System
 Recycled Fiber Treatment Lines:
 Flotation deinking lines: 1 at 52,500
Paper/Paperboard Grades and Capacities:
 Total paper and paperboard capacity: 50,000 mt/y
 Newsprint: 50,000 mt/y
Paper and Paperboard Mill Data:
Paper Machines: 1
 No. 1, fourdrinier, total capacity 50,000 mt/y, Trim width 3.5 m, Newsprint
Energy Data:
 Power boilers: 1
 Steam turbines: 1 at 6 MW
 Electrical demand for mill: 124 MWh/D

ⓄⓂMamta Papers Pvt Ltd
Jagatpur Mill
Jagatpur Industrial Estate, Cuttack district
754021 Jagatpur, Odisha
India
 Phone: (91) 0671 2491607
 Fax: (91) 0671 2491384
 Email: mamtapapers@yahoo.in
Personnel:
 Man. Dir.: Indramani Mulia
 Phone: (91) 09438161818
Type of Operation: Paperboard mill
Paper/Paperboard Grades and Capacities:
 Total paper and paperboard capacity: 7,000 mt/y
 Linerboard: 7,000 mt/y
Paper and Paperboard Mill Data:
Paper Machines: 1
 No. 1, total capacity 7,000 mt/y, Linerboard

ⓂManaylux Papers & Boards (P) Ltd.
Yediyur Taluk Tumkur Mill
Ownership: Manaylux Papers & Boards (P) Ltd.
Yediyur Kunigal
572 142 Taluk Tumkur, Karnataka
India
Personnel:
 Mgr. (Admin.): P. S. Bist
Total Employees at this Location: 200
Type of Operation: Paper mill
Paper/Paperboard Grades and Capacities:
 Total paper and paperboard capacity: 7,300 mt/y
 Uncoated woodfree/freesheet
 Packaging papers
Paper and Paperboard Mill Data:
 Stock Preparation:
 Refiners: 3
Paper Machines: 1
 No. 1, (switch machine UWF or Kraft paper with 7,300 tonnes/yr capacity), total capacity 7,300 mt/y, Trim width 2.2 m, Uncoated woodfree/freesheet, Packaging papers
 Finishing Equipment:
 Rewinders: 1
 Sheeters: 1
Energy Data:
 Power boilers: 1

ⓄⓂMandya National Paper Mills Ltd.
Belagola Mill
K.R.S. Rd.
570606 Belagola, Karnataka
India
Personnel:
 Man. Dir.: Mr. S. K. Sen Gupta
Type of Operation: Paper mill
Paper/Paperboard Grades and Capacities:
 Total paper and paperboard capacity: 19,800 mt/y
 Uncoated woodfree/freesheet
 Packaging papers
 Linerboard

ⓂMBD Group
Gagret town, Una district
India
 Phone: (91) 11 2331 7931/8301, 41509091-94
 Email: mbdgroup@vsnl.net
 Web Address: www.mbdgroup.com
Personnel:
 Chmn. & Man. Dir.: A.K. Malhotra
 Phone: (91) 11 2331 7931/8301
Mill Locations:
 MBD Group, Gagret town, Una district Mill, Gagret town, Una district, India, Capacity: 37,500 mt/y, (Paper mill)

ⓂMBD Group
Gagret town, Una district Mill
Gagret town, Una district, Himachal Pradesh
India
 Web Address: www.mbdgroup.com
Total Employees at this Location: 200
Type of Operation: Paper mill
Pulp Grades and Capacities:
 Total pulp capacity: 29,814 mt/y
 Recycled Pulping: 29,814 mt/y
Pulp Mill Data:
 Bleach Plant Systems: 1
 Recycled Pulping System
 Recycled Fiber Treatment Lines:
 Flotation deinking lines: 1
Paper/Paperboard Grades and Capacities:
 Total paper and paperboard capacity: 37,500 mt/y
 Uncoated woodfree/freesheet: 37,500 mt/y
Paper and Paperboard Mill Data:
Paper Machines: 1
 No. 1, fourdrinier, total capacity 37,500 mt/y, Trim width 3.8 m, Uncoated woodfree/freesheet

Energy Data:
 Power boilers
 Electrical demand for mill: 86 MWh/D

ⓄⓂMeenu Paper Mills (P) Ltd.
Muzaffarnagar Mill
9.5 Km Stone, Bhopa Road
251001 Muzaffarnagar, Uttar Pradesh
India
 Phone: (91) 131 2468542
 Fax: (91) 131 2468544
Personnel:
 Chmn.: Mr. J. K. Kapoor
 Phone: (91) 99 97419000
 Dir.: Ajay Kapoor
 Phone: (91) 99 97480000
Type of Operation: Paper mill
Paper/Paperboard Grades and Capacities:
 Total paper and paperboard capacity: 9,000 mt/y
 Packaging papers
Paper and Paperboard Mill Data:
Paper Machines: 1
 No. 1, Trim width 2.5 m, Packaging papers

ⓂMilano Papers Pvt. Ltd.
Survey No. 153, Opposite Sartanpar Village, Sartanpar Road
363 621 Rajkot, Morbi, Gujarat
India
 Phone: (91) 9724999999
 Email: harsh@milanopapers.com
 Web Address: www.indiamart.com/milano-papers/query.html
Mill Locations:
 Milano Papers Pvt. Ltd., Rajkot Mill, Survey No. 153, Opposite Sartanpar Village, Sartanpar Road, 363 621 Rajkot, Morbi, India, Capacity: 68,000 mt/y, (Paperboard mill)
 Phone: (91) 02828 304011 / 12 / 13 / 14
 Fax: (91) 02828 304010
 Email: info@milanopapers.com

ⓄⓂMilano Papers Pvt. Ltd.
Rajkot Mill
Survey No. 153, Opposite Sartanpar Village, Sartanpar Road
363 621 Rajkot, Morbi, Gujarat
India
 Phone: (91) 02828 304011 / 12 / 13 / 14
 Fax: (91) 02828 304010
 Email: info@milanopapers.com
 Web Address: milanopapers.com
Personnel:
 Owner: Harsh Patel
 Phone: (91) 9724999999
 Email: harsh@milanopapers.com
 Dir.: Nikunj Patel
 Phone: (91) 7878513135
Total Employees at this Location: 155
Type of Operation: Paperboard mill
Pulp Grades and Capacities:
 Total pulp capacity: 57,929 mt/y
 Recycled Pulping: 57,929 mt/y
Pulp Mill Data:
 Bleach Plant Systems: 1
 Recycled Pulping System
 Recycled Fiber Treatment Lines:
 Flotation deinking lines: 1
 Recycled packaging pulping lines: 1
Paper/Paperboard Grades and Capacities:
 Total paper and paperboard capacity: 68,000 mt/y
 Boxboard/cartonboard: 68,000 mt/y
Paper and Paperboard Mill Data:
Paper Machines: 1
 No. 1, cylinder (8), total capacity 68,000 mt/y, Trim width 3.2 m, Boxboard/cartonboard
Coating Machines: 1
 PM1, on machine
Energy Data:

Power boilers: 1
Electrical demand for mill: 88 MWh/D

ⓗMillenium Papers Pvt. Ltd.
Old Rafaleshwar, B/h Delta Ceramics, Lalpar
363642 Morbi, Gujarat
India
  Phone: (91) 2822 302121 / 2 / 3 / 4 GSM:
  9724023444, 9725819444, 9725818444
  Fax: (91) 2822 302120
  Email: info@milleniumpapers.com,
  support@milleniumpapers.com
  Web Address: milleniumpapers.co.in
Mill Locations:
Millenium Papers Pvt. Ltd., Morbi Mill, Old Rafaleshwar,
B/h Delta Ceramics, Lalpar, 363642 Morbi, India,
Capacity: 70,000 mt/y, (Paperboard mill)
Phone: (91) 2822 302121 / 2 / 3 / 4
Fax: (91) 2822 302120
Email: info@milleniumpapers.com; support@
milleniumpapers.com

ⓗMillenium Papers Pvt. Ltd.
Morbi Mill
Old Rafaleshwar, B/h Delta Ceramics, Lalpar
363642 Morbi, Gujarat
India
  Phone: (91) 2822 302121 / 2 / 3 / 4
  Fax: (91) 2822 302120
  Email: info@milleniumpapers.com,
  support@milleniumpapers.com
  Web Address: milleniumpapers.co.in
Total Employees at this Location: 260
Type of Operation: Paperboard mill
Pulp Grades and Capacities:
  Total pulp capacity: 66,538 mt/y
  Recycled Pulping: 66,538 mt/y
Pulp Mill Data:
  Bleach Plant Systems: 1
  Recycled Pulping System
  Recycled Fiber Treatment Lines:
  Flotation deinking lines: 1
  Recycled packaging pulping lines: 1
Paper/Paperboard Grades and Capacities:
  Total paper and paperboard capacity: 70,000 mt/y
  Boxboard/cartonboard: 70,000 mt/y
Paper and Paperboard Mill Data:
Paper Machines: 1
No. 1, cylinder (7), total capacity 70,000 mt/y, Trim
  width 3.25 m, Boxboard/cartonboard
Coating Machines: 1
PM1, on machine
Energy Data:
Power boilers
Electrical demand for mill: 91 MWh/D

ⓗⓜModinagar Paper Mills Ltd.
Modinagar Mill
Major Asha Ram Tyagi Rd. Sikri Kalan
201 204 Modinagar, Uttar Pradesh
India
  Phone: (91) 1232 242586
  Fax: (91) 8066 885627
  Email: admin@mpml.co.in
Personnel:
  Exec. Dir.: B. K. Agarwal
  Phone: (91) 9897 466 166
  Email: bka@mpml.co.in
  Tech. Dir.: Anubhav Gupta
  Phone: (91) 9760 046 620
  Email: anubhav@mpml.co.in
Total Employees of Company: 250
Total Employees at this Location: 120
Type of Operation: Pulp mill, Paper mill
Pulp Grades and Capacities:
  Total pulp capacity: 34,109 mt/y
  Recycled Pulping: 34,109 mt/y
Pulp Mill Data:
  Recycled Fiber Treatment Lines:
  Recycled packaging pulping lines: 1
Paper/Paperboard Grades and Capacities:
  Total paper and paperboard capacity: 35,000 mt/y
  Corrugating medium/fluting: 35,000 mt/y
Paper and Paperboard Mill Data:
  Stock Preparation:
  Pulpers: 2
Paper Machines: 1
No. 1, fourdrinier, total capacity 35,000 mt/y, Trim width
  3 m, Corrugating medium/fluting
Energy Data:
Power boilers
Electrical demand for mill: 42 MWh/D

ⓗMohit Paper Mills Ltd.
9 Km Stone, Gandhi Market, Nagina Road
246701 Bijnor
India
  Phone: (91) 11 25886797
  Email: mohitpaper9@bsnl.in
Personnel:
  Chmn./Man. Dir.: Sandeep Jain
  Phone: (91) 11 25886797, 1342 262406/596
  Dir.: Sushil Kumar Patidar
  Phone: (91) 11 25886797, 1342 262406/596
  Promoter Dir.: Anju Jain
  Phone: (91) 11 25886797, 1342 262406/596
Total Employees at this Location: 160
Mill Locations:
Mohit Paper Mills Ltd., Bijnor Mill, 9 Km Stone, Gandhi
  Market, Nagina Road, 246701 Bijnor, India, Capacity:
  25,000 mt/y, (Paper mill)
Phone: (91) 11 25886797
Email: mohitpaper9@bsnl.in

ⓗMohit Paper Mills Ltd.
Bijnor Mill
9 Km Stone, Gandhi Market, Nagina Road
246701 Bijnor, Uttar Pradesh
India
  Phone: (91) 11 25886797
  Email: mohitpaper9@bsnl.in
Personnel:
  Chmn./Man. Dir.: Mr. Sandeep Jain
  Phone: (91) 98 37067240
  Dir.: Sushil Kumar Patidar
  Phone: (91) 1342 262406/596
  Promoter Dir.: Mrs. Anju Jain
  Phone: (91) 1342 262406/596
Total Employees at this Location: 160
Type of Operation: Paper mill
Paper/Paperboard Grades and Capacities:
  Total paper and paperboard capacity: 25,000 mt/y
  Uncoated woodfree/freesheet
Paper and Paperboard Mill Data:
Paper Machines: 1
No. 1, total capacity 25,000 mt/y, Trim width 2.7 m,
  Uncoated woodfree/freesheet
Energy Data:
Turbines at 4, 5 MW

ⓗMultiwal Pulp & Board Mills Ltd.
9th Kilometer Stone, Bajpur Road, Kashipur
244713 Dist. Udham Singh Nagar
India
  Phone: (91) 91 5912492695
Personnel:
  Man. Dir.: Waseem Ahmad Khan
  Phone: (91) 91 5912492695
  Tech. Dir.: Pres. N. C. Joshi
  Phone: (91) 91 5912492695
  Gen. Mgr. (Prod.): R. B. Singh
  Phone: (91) 91 5912492695
Mill Locations:
Multiwal Pulp & Board Mills Ltd., Dist. Udham Singh
  Nagar Mill, 9th Kilometer Stone, Bajpur Road, Kashipur,
  244713 Dist. Udham Singh Nagar, India, Capacity:
  150,000 mt/y, (Paper mill)

ⓗMultiwal Pulp & Board Mills Ltd.
Dist. Udham Singh Nagar Mill
9th Kilometer Stone, Bajpur Road, Kashipur
244713 Dist. Udham Singh Nagar, Uttarakhand
India
Personnel:
  Man. Dir.: Waseem Ahmad Khan
  Phone: (91) 98 37036763
  Pres. (Tech.): Mr. Pres. N. C. Joshi
  Gen. Mgr. (Pur.): Ajay Kumar Singh
  Phone: (91) 98370 95833
  Email: multiwal@gmail.com
Total Employees at this Location: 600
Type of Operation: Paper mill
Pulp Grades and Capacities:
  Total pulp capacity: 139,218 mt/y
  Recycled Pulping: 139,218 mt/y
Pulp Mill Data:
  Bleach Plant Systems: 2
  Recycled Pulping System
  Recycled Pulping System
  Recycled Fiber Treatment Lines:
  Flotation deinking lines: 2
  Recycled packaging pulping lines: 1
Paper/Paperboard Grades and Capacities:
  Total paper and paperboard capacity: 150,000 mt/y
  Uncoated woodfree/freesheet: 24,000 mt/y
  Packaging papers: 24,000 mt/y
  Boxboard/cartonboard: 102,000 mt/y
Paper and Paperboard Mill Data:
Paper Machines: 5
No. 1, fourdrinier, total capacity 24,000 mt/y, Uncoated
  woodfree/freesheet
No. 2, fourdrinier, total capacity 24,000 mt/y, Packaging
  papers
No. 3, fourdrinier, total capacity 50,000 mt/y, Boxboard/
  cartonboard
No. 4, fourdrinier, total capacity 26,000 mt/y, Boxboard/
  cartonboard
No. 5, fourdrinier, total capacity 26,000 mt/y, Boxboard/
  cartonboard
Coating Machines: 3
PM3, on machine
PM4, on machine
PM5, on machine
Energy Data:
Power boilers
Electrical demand for mill: 300 MWh/D

ⓗMurli Industries Ltd.
101, Jai Bhawani Society, Central Avenue
440 008 Wardhman Nagar, Nagpur, Maharashtra
India
  Phone: (91) 712 3050200
  Fax: (91) 712 2761145/2684422
  Web Address: www.murliindustries.com
Mill Locations:
Murli Industries Ltd., Nagpur Mill, 27th Km Stone,
  Nagpur-Bhandara Road, Nagpur, India, Capacity:
  204,500 mt/y, (Pulp mill, Paper mill, Paperboard mill)
Phone: (91) 7109 268261-5
Fax: (91) 7109 268146
Email: info@murliindustries.com, snmaloo@nagpur.
  net.in

ⓗMurli Industries Ltd.
Nagpur Mill
27th Km Stone, Nagpur-Bhandara Road
Nagpur, Maharashtra
India
  Phone: (91) 7109 268261-5
  Fax: (91) 7109 268146
  Email: info@murliindustries.com,
  snmaloo@nagpur.net.in
  Web Address: www.murliindustries.com
Personnel:
  Man. Dir.: Nandlal Malco
  Phone: (91) 9370986162/3
Total Employees at this Location: 640

India

Type of Operation: Pulp mill, Paper mill, Paperboard mill
Pulp Grades and Capacities:
Total pulp capacity: 56,149 mt/y
Recycled Pulping: 56,149 mt/y
Pulp Mill Data:
Pulp Lines: 1
Bleach Plant Systems: 1
Recycled Pulping System
Recycled Fiber Treatment Lines:
Flotation deinking lines: 1
Recycled packaging pulping lines: 1
Paper/Paperboard Grades and Capacities:
Total paper and paperboard capacity: 204,500 mt/y
Newsprint: 32,000 mt/y
Uncoated woodfree/freesheet: 65,000 mt/y
Boxboard/cartonboard: 107,500 mt/y
Paper and Paperboard Mill Data:
Paper Machines: 4
No. 1, multi-wire, total capacity 27,500 mt/y, Trim width 2.5 m, Boxboard/cartonboard
No. 2, fourdrinier, total capacity 32,000 mt/y, Trim width 4.1 m, Newsprint
No. 3, fourdrinier, total capacity 65,000 mt/y, Trim width 4.5 m, Uncoated woodfree/freesheet
No. 4, fourdrinier (3), total capacity 80,000 mt/y, Trim width 2.4 m, Boxboard/cartonboard
Coating Machines: 2
PM1, on machine
PM4, on machine
Energy Data:
Power boilers
Steam turbines: 2 at 3, 15 MW
Electrical demand for mill: 393 MWh/D

ⓂMysore Paper Mills Ltd.
16/4 Ali Asker Rd., PB No. 112
560 052 Bangalore, Karnataka
India
Phone: (91) 80 22255459
Fax: (91) 80 22253478
Email: info@mpm.co.in,
mpmbl@blr.vsnl.net.in,
cmdmpm@vsnl.net
Web Address: www.mpm.co.in
Personnel:
Chmn.: Sri. Araga Jnanendra
Phone: (91) 80 22255459
Fax: (91) 80 22253478
Man. Dir.: Sri. B H Anil Kumar
Phone: (91) 80 22255459
Fax: (91) 80 22253478
Email: cmd@mpm.co.in
Gen. Mgr. (Finan) : Sri. Shamraj H. Tankasali
Phone: (91) 80 22256881
Email: dirfin@mpm.co.in
Gen. Mgr. (Mktng): M. R. Lokesh
Phone: (91) 984 509 9566 (GSM)
Email: gmmktg@mpm.co.in
Company Sec.: H.S. Nrao
Phone: (91) 80 222 66979
Email: cs@mpm.co.in
Total Employees of Company: 5,000
Mill Locations:
Mysore Paper Mills Ltd., Shimoga Mill, P.O. PaperTown, 577 302 Bhadravati, Shimoga, India, Capacity: 116,025 mt/y, (Pulp mill, Paper mill)
Phone: (91) 8282 270201/0208/8182/0941
Fax: (91) 8282 270937/8182/0473
Email: info@mpm.co.in

ⓂMysore Paper Mills Ltd.
Shimoga Mill
P.O. PaperTown
577 302 Bhadravati, Shimoga, Karnataka
India
Phone: (91) 8282 270201/0208/8182/0941
Fax: (91) 8282 270937/8182/0473
Email: info@mpm.co.in

Web Address: www.mpm.co.in
Personnel:
Director (Operations & Mktg.): Sri. N.P. Prabhu
Phone: (91) 8282 270780/9741925063
Email: dirops@mpm.co.in
General Manager (HRD&A): B.N. Srinivas
Phone: (91) 8282 270743/99725 81024
Email: gmhrda@mpm.co.in
Dir. Gen. Mgr. (Projects): B. P. Ravindranath
Phone: (91) 8282 270830/270984/99451 76693
Email: dgmprojects@mpm.co.in
Asst.Gen. Mgr (Sugar & Pulp Mill (Maint): K. Suresh Kumar
Phone: (91) 8282 270936/99805 55469
Email: agmsugar@mpm.co.in
Asst. Gen. Mgr. (Fin): Viswanath S Malghan
Phone: (91) 8282 270832/99725 81037
Email: agmfin@mpm.co.in
Total Employees at this Location: 1,550
Type of Operation: Pulp mill, Paper mill
Pulp Grades and Capacities:
Total pulp capacity: 117,612 mt/y
Chemical Pulp: 21,817 mt/y
Mechanical Pulp: 86,473 mt/y
Other Pulp: 9,322 mt/y
Pulp Mill Data:
Chemical Pulping Systems:
Batch digesters: 1
Continuous digesters: 1
Mechanical Pulping Systems:
CTMP systems: 1
Pulp Lines: 3
Bleach Plant Systems: 2
No. 1, Type: wood, Sequence: CEpHH
No. 2, Type: bagasse, Sequence: CEpH
Chemical Recovery Equipment:
Evaporator lines: 1
Recovery boilers: 1
Lime Kiln
Paper/Paperboard Grades and Capacities:
Total paper and paperboard capacity: 116,025 mt/y
Newsprint: 85,680 mt/y
Uncoated woodfree/freesheet: 21,420 mt/y
Specialty and industrial: 8,925 mt/y
Paper and Paperboard Mill Data:
Stock Preparation:
Pulpers: 8
Refiners: 20
Paper Machines: 4
No. 1, fourdrinier, total capacity 8,925 mt/y, Trim width 2.4 m, Specialty and industrial
No. 2, fourdrinier, total capacity 8,925 mt/y, Trim width 2.4 m, Uncoated woodfree/freesheet
No. 3, fourdrinier, total capacity 12,495 mt/y, Trim width 3.2 m, Uncoated woodfree/freesheet
No. 4, twin-wire, total capacity 85,680 mt/y, Trim width 6.65 m, Newsprint
Finishing Equipment:
Rewinders: 2
Sheeters: 4
Energy Data:
Power boilers: 3
Combustion turbines: 2 at 25.0 MW
Electrical demand for mill: 685 MWh/D

ⓂNaachiar Paper Boards Private Ltd.
123-A, P.K.N. Road
626189 Sivakasi, Tamil Nadu
India
Personnel:
Man. Dir.: V. Ragavan Alagarsamy
Phone: (91) 9442622265
Joint Man. Dir.: S. Ravi Durai
Phone: (91) 9443160295
Sls. Mgr.: N. Babu Sankar
Phone: (91) 9442622235
Mill Locations:
Naachiar Paper Boards Private Ltd., Sivakasi Mill, SF No. 352-353, Sevalpatti, 626140 Sivakasi, India, Capacity: 39,000 mt/y, (Paperboard mill)

Phone: (91) 4562-239242, 4562-239352
Fax: (91) 4562-239132
Email: naachiarmills@yahoo.co.in

ⓂNaachiar Paper Boards Private Ltd.
Sivakasi Mill
SF No. 352-353, Sevalpatti
626140 Sivakasi, Tamil Nadu
India
Phone: (91) 4562-239242, 4562-239352
Fax: (91) 4562-239132
Email: naachiarmills@yahoo.co.in
Web Address: www.naachiar.com
Personnel:
Man. Dir.: V. Ragavan Alagarsamy
Phone: (91) 94 42622265
Joint Man. Dir.: S. Ravi Durai
Phone: (91) 94 43160295
Prod. Mgr.: V.S. Ragunath
Phone: (91) 9442622245
Sls. Mgr.: N. Babu Sankar
Phone: (91) 94 42622235
Total Employees at this Location: 160
Type of Operation: Paperboard mill
Pulp Grades and Capacities:
Total pulp capacity: 36,719 mt/y
Recycled Pulping: 36,719 mt/y
Pulp Mill Data:
Recycled Fiber Treatment Lines:
Flotation deinking lines: 1
Recycled packaging pulping lines: 1
Paper/Paperboard Grades and Capacities:
Total paper and paperboard capacity: 39,000 mt/y
Boxboard/cartonboard: 39,000 mt/y
Paper and Paperboard Mill Data:
Paper Machines: 1
No. 1, cylinder (7), total capacity 39,000 mt/y, Boxboard/cartonboard
Coating Machines: 1
No. 3 bar coaters
Energy Data:
Power boilers
Electrical demand for mill: 51 MWh/D

ⓂⓂNabha Paper Mills Ltd.
Malerkotla Mill
Dhuri Rd.
148023 Malerkotla, Punjab
India
Phone: (91) 1675 253662
Fax: (91) 1675 254228
Personnel:
Man. Dir.: Mr. B. R. Jindal
Phone: (91) 93560 55751
Prod. Mgr.: Puran C. Bansal
Phone: (91) 93560 55712
Gen. Mgr.: Arun Sharma
Phone: (91) 93 56055753
Type of Operation: Paperboard mill
Mill Locations:
Nabha Paper Mills Ltd., Nabha Mill, Village Dhingi, Malekotla Road, Nabha, 147207 Dist. Patiala, India, Capacity: 14,000 mt/y, (Paperboard mill)
Phone: (91) 1675 253662 / 325228
Fax: (91) 1675 254228
Paper/Paperboard Grades and Capacities:
Total paper and paperboard capacity: 7,500 mt/y
Boxboard/cartonboard: 7,500 mt/y
Paper and Paperboard Mill Data:
Paper Machines: 3
No. 1
No. 2
No. 3

ⓂNabha Paper Mills Ltd.
Nabha Mill
Village Dhingi, Malekotla Road, Nabha
147207 Dist. Patiala, Punjab
India

India

Phone: (91) 1675 253662 / 325228
Fax: (91) 1675 254228
Personnel:
Man. Dir.: Rakesh Garg
Phone: (91) 92 16122298
Gen. Mgr.: Mukesh Sharma
Dir.: Virendra Gupta
Type of Operation: Paperboard mill
Paper/Paperboard Grades and Capacities:
Total paper and paperboard capacity: 14,000 mt/y
Boxboard/cartonboard: 14,000 mt/y
Paper and Paperboard Mill Data:
Paper Machines: 2
No. 1, Trim width 2 m, Boxboard/cartonboard
No. 2, Trim width 2 m, Boxboard/cartonboard

ⓘNachiketa Papers Ltd.
Village Mubarakpur, Derabassi, Ramgarh Road
Dist. Mohali
India
Phone: (91) 1762 280250/364
Fax: (91) 1762 280889
Email: npgroup@rediffmail.com
Personnel:
Man. Dir.: Ashok Kumar Garg
Phone: (91) 1762 280250/364
Fax: (91) 1762 280889
Mill Locations:
Nachiketa Papers Ltd., Dist. Patiala Mill, Village
Mubarakpur, Derabassi, Ramgarh Road, Dist. Mohali,
India, Capacity: 12,000 mt/y, (Paper mill)
Phone: (91) 1762 280250/364
Fax: (91) 1762 280889
Email: npgroup@rediffmail.com

ⓜNachiketa Papers Ltd.
Dist. Patiala Mill
Village Mubarakpur, Derabassi, Ramgarh Road
Dist. Mohali, Punjab
India
Phone: (91) 1762 280250/364
Fax: (91) 1762 280889
Email: npgroup@rediffmail.com
Personnel:
Man. Dir.: Ashok Kumar Garg
Phone: (91) 1762 280250/364
Type of Operation: Paper mill
Paper/Paperboard Grades and Capacities:
Total paper and paperboard capacity: 12,000 mt/y
Uncoated woodfree/freesheet
Paper and Paperboard Mill Data:
Paper Machines: 1
No. 1, Trim width 2.75 m

ⓘNaini Papers Ltd.
7.5th Km Stone, Moradabad Rd.
244713 Kashipur
India
Phone: (91) 5947 275913/14/15
Fax: (91) 5947 260831
Email: info@nainigroup.com
Web Address: www.nainigroup.com
Personnel:
Chrm., Man. Dir.: Pramod Kumar Agarwal
Phone: (91) 5947 275913/14/15
Fax: (91) 5947 260831
Jnt. Mgr. Dir.: Pawan Agarwal
Phone: (91) 5947 275913/14/15
Fax: (91) 5947 260831
Mill Locations:
Naini Papers Ltd., Kashipur Mill, 7.5th Km Stone,
Moradabad Rd., 244713 Kashipur, India, Capacity:
82,000 mt/y, (Paper mill)
Phone: (91) 5947 275913/14/15
Fax: (91) 5947 260831
Email: info@nainigroup.com

ⓜNaini Papers Ltd.
Kashipur Mill
7.5th Km Stone, Moradabad Rd.
244713 Kashipur, Uttarakhand
India
Phone: (91) 5947 275913/14/15
Fax: (91) 5947 260831
Email: info@nainigroup.com
Web Address: www.nainigroup.com
Personnel:
Chrm., Man. Dir.: Mr. Pramod Kumar Agarwal
Phone: (91) 5947 275913/14/15
Jnt. Mgr. Dir.: Pawan Agarwal
Phone: (91) 5947 275913/14/15
Total Employees at this Location: 530
Type of Operation: Paper mill
Pulp Grades and Capacities:
Total pulp capacity: 65,013 mt/y
Other Pulp: 65,013 mt/y
Pulp Mill Data:
Chemical Pulping Systems:
Batch digesters
Pulp Lines: 2
Bleach Plant Systems: 1
Chemical Pulping System, Type: Bagasse/Straw,
Sequence: CEpHH
Chemical Recovery Equipment:
Evaporator lines: 1
Recovery boilers: 1
Paper/Paperboard Grades and Capacities:
Total paper and paperboard capacity: 82,000 mt/y
Uncoated woodfree/freesheet: 82,000 mt/y
Paper and Paperboard Mill Data:
Paper Machines: 2
No. 1, fourdrinier, total capacity 32,000 mt/y, Trim width
2.96 m, Uncoated woodfree/freesheet
No. 2, fourdrinier, total capacity 50,000 mt/y, Trim width
2.85 m, Uncoated woodfree/freesheet
Energy Data:
Power boilers
Steam turbines: 1 at 2 MW
Electrical demand for mill: 257 MWh/D

ⓘNath Pulp & Paper Mills Ltd.
Ownership: 17% by financial institutions, 34% by promoters, 49% by public
Nath House, Nath Rd.
431 005 Aurangabad, Maharashtra
India
Phone: (91) 240 2376314-15-17
Fax: (91) 240 2376188
Email: admin@nathpaper.com,
sales@nathpaper.com
Web Address: www.nathpaper.com
Personnel:
Chmn.: Nandkishore Kagliwal
Phone: (91) 240 2376315
Fax: (91) 240 2376188
Email: nk@nathgroup.com
VP (Works): S. K. Chopra
Phone: (91) 2431 232091
Fax: (91) 2431 232092
Exec. Dir.: D. K. Datta
Phone: (91) 240 2376315, 932 5220936 (gsm)
Fax: (91) 240 2376188
Email: dkdutt@nathpaper.com
Mill Dir.: Akash Kagliwal
Phone: (91) 932 5015055 (gsm)
Fax: (91) 240 2376188
Email: akagliwal@nathpaper.com
Total Employees of Company: 500
Total Employees at this Location: 70
Mill Locations:
Nath Pulp & Paper Mills Ltd., Aurangabad Mill, Nathnagar,
T.Q. Paithan, 431 106 Aurangabad, India, Capacity:
50,000 mt/y, (Paperboard mill)
Phone: (91) 2402376315
Fax: (91) 2402376188
Email: akagliwal@nathgroup.com

ⓜNath Pulp & Paper Mills Ltd.
Aurangabad Mill
Nathnagar, T.Q. Paithan
431 106 Aurangabad, Maharashtra
India
Phone: (91) 2402376315
Fax: (91) 2402376188
Email: akagliwal@nathgroup.com
Web Address: www.nathpaper.com
Personnel:
Chairman: Nandkishor Kagliwal
Phone: (91) 2431 232091/181
Fax: (91) 2402376188
Email: nk@nathgroup.com
Director: Akash Kagliwal
Phone: (91) 2402376315
Fax: (91) 2402376188
Email: akagliwal@nathgroup.com
Total Employees at this Location: 350
Type of Operation: Paperboard mill
Pulp Grades and Capacities:
Paper/Paperboard Grades and Capacities:
Total paper and paperboard capacity: 50,000 mt/y
Coated woodfree/freesheet
Packaging papers
Specialty and industrial
Linerboard
Boxboard/cartonboard
Paper and Paperboard Mill Data:
Paper Machines: 2
No. 1, fourdrinier, Trim width 1.8 m
No. 2, fourdrinier, Trim width 1.8 m

ⓘNav Bharat Duplex Ltd.
Village Badnouli, Hapur, Modinagar Rd
245101 Hapur
India
Phone: (91) 122 2316328/2301531
Fax: (91) 122 2301531
Personnel:
Dir.: A. Agarwal
Phone: (91) 122 2316328/2301531
Fax: (91) 122 2301531
Total Employees at this Location: 70
Mill Locations:
Nav Bharat Duplex Ltd., Hapur Mill, Village Badnouli,
Hapur, Modinagar Rd, 245101 Hapur, India, Capacity:
7,500 mt/y, (Paper mill)
Phone: (91) 122 2316328/2301531
Fax: (91) 122 2301531

ⓜNav Bharat Duplex Ltd.
Hapur Mill
Village Badnouli, Hapur, Modinagar Rd
245101 Hapur, Uttar Pradesh
India
Phone: (91) 122 2316328/2301531
Fax: (91) 122 2301531
Personnel:
Dir.: A. Agarwal
Phone: (91) 221 230 1531
Total Employees at this Location: 70
Type of Operation: Paper mill
Paper/Paperboard Grades and Capacities:
Total paper and paperboard capacity: 7,500 mt/y
Newsprint
Uncoated woodfree/freesheet
Paper and Paperboard Mill Data:
Stock Preparation:
Pulpers: 3
Paper Machines: 1
PM 1, Trim width 2.15 m, Uncoated woodfree/freesheet
Finishing Equipment:
Rewinders: 1
Sheeters: 1
Energy Data:
Power boilers: 1

ⓘNelsun Paper Mills Ltd.
Solagampatti, Thogur Maya
613 102 Thanjavur
India
Phone: (91) 44 24364366/98 43056328

India

Fax: (91) 44 24364365/43 62 286422
Mill Locations:
Nelsun Paper Mills Ltd., Chennai Mill, Solagampatti, Thogur Maya, 613 102 Thanjavur, India, Capacity: 12,500 mt/y, (Paper mill)
Phone: (91) 44 24364366/98 43056328
Fax: (91) 44 24364365/43 62 286422

ⓂNelsun Paper Mills Ltd.
Chennai Mill
Solagampatti, Thogur Maya
613 102 Thanjavur, Tamil Nadu
India
Phone: (91) 44 24364366/98 43056328
Fax: (91) 44 24364365/43 62 286422
Personnel:
Man. Dir: Mr. K. P. Kumaran
Phone: (91) 9843056328
Type of Operation: Paper mill
Paper/Paperboard Grades and Capacities:
Total paper and paperboard capacity: 12,500 mt/y
Packaging papers: 12,500 mt/y

ⓂNEPA Ltd.
Ownership: PSU
P.O. Nepanagar
450 221 Nepanagar, Burhanpur District, M.P
India
Phone: (91) 7325 222 133/134/158
Fax: (91) 7325 222 162/174/165
Email: nepaltd@nepamills.nic.in
Web Address: www.nepamills.nic.in
Personnel:
Chmn. & Man. Dir.: V.J.M. Reddy
Phone: (91) 7325 222 133/134/158
Fax: (91) 7325 222 162/174/165
Email: vjr@nepamills.nic.in
Mgr. (Works): A.V.N.S. Rao
Phone: (91) 7325 222 133/134/158
Fax: (91) 7325 222 162/174/165
Email: tech@nepamills.nic.in
Dpty. Mktg. Mgr.: A. Chatterjee
Phone: (91) 7325 222 178
Email: nepalimited@nepamills.nic.in
Gen. Mgr. (Comm.): R. K. Jain
Phone: (91) 7325 222 242
Email: skjain@nepamills.nic.in
Tech. Mgr.: Niazi R.A. Khan
Phone: (91) 7325 222 133/134/158
Fax: (91) 7325 222 162/174/165
Email: technical@nepamills.nic.in
Qlty. & Envir. Mgr.: R.M. Ghonge
Phone: (91) 7325 222 133/134/158
Fax: (91) 7325 222 162/174/165
Finan. Mgr.: A.N. Deshmukia
Phone: (91) 7325 222 262
Fax: (91) 7325 222 176
Co. Sec.: Swati Gangrade
Phone: (91) 7325 222 133/134/158
Fax: (91) 7325 222 162/174/165
Email: nepalimited@nepamills.nic.in
Total Employees of Company: 1,377
Total Employees at this Location: 1,363
Mill Locations:
NEPA Ltd., Nepanagar Mill, P.O. Nepanagar, 450221 Nepanagar, Burhanpur District, M.P, India, Capacity: 62,475 mt/y, (Pulp mill, Paper mill)
Phone: (91) 7325 222133
Fax: (91) 7325 222176
Email: nepaltd@nepamills.nic.in

ⓂNEPA Ltd.
Nepanagar Mill
P.O. Nepanagar
450221 Nepanagar, Burhanpur District, M.P
India
Phone: (91) 7325 222133
Fax: (91) 7325 222176
Email: nepaltd@nepamills.nic.in
Web Address: www.nepamills.nic.in
Personnel:
Chmn., Man. Dir.: Brigadier SK Mutreja
Phone: (91) 07325 - 222134
Gen. Mgr. (Works): Mr. A.V.N.S. Rao
Phone: (91) 9425952012
Fax: (91) 7325 222162
Email: tech@nepamills.nic.in
Mgr (Projects & Tech.): Niazi R.A. Khan
Phone: (91) 7325 222131
Fax: (91) 7325 222162
Email: tech@nepamills.nic.in
Mgr. (PM): S. S. Kothallcar
Phone: (91) 7325 222131
Fax: (91) 7325 222162
Email: tech@nepamills.nic.in
Commer. Mgr.: R. K. Jain
Phone: (91) 7325 222242
Fax: (91) 7325 222744
Email: rkjain@nepamills.nic.in
Qlty. & Envir. Mgr.: R. M. Ghonge
Phone: (91) 7325 222131
Fax: (91) 7325 222162
Email: tech@nepamills.nic.in
Mechan. Mgr.: B. D. Sohni
Phone: (91) 7325 222133
Total Employees at this Location: 1,180
Type of Operation: Pulp mill, Paper mill
Pulp Grades and Capacities:
Total pulp capacity: 59,500 mt/y
Recycled Pulping: 59,500 mt/y
Pulp Mill Data:
Bleach Plant Systems: 1
No. 1, Sequence: CEH
Recycled Fiber Treatment Lines:
Pulpers: 4 at 68,000 admt/y
Paper/Paperboard Grades and Capacities:
Total paper and paperboard capacity: 62,475 mt/y
Newsprint: 62,475 mt/y
Paper and Paperboard Mill Data:
Stock Preparation:
Pulpers: 4
Refiners: 2
Paper Machines: 2
No. 1, Bel-Form, total capacity 41,055 mt/y, Trim width 5.3 m, Newsprint
No. 2, total capacity 21,420 mt/y, Trim width 5.3 m, Newsprint
Finishing Equipment:
Winders: 2 at 88,000 mt/y
Calenders: 4
Energy Data:
Power boilers: 4
Steam turbines: 5 at 12.27 MW
Electrical demand for mill: 148 MWh/D

ⓂNew Bombay Paper Mills Pvt Ltd.
Bombay Mill
Ownership: Apex Paper Mills
Village Ajivali, Post Donwat, Tehsil Khalapur
410203 Dist. Raigarh, Maharashtra
India
Phone: (91) 2192 278416
Fax: (91) 2192 278416
Personnel:
Owner/Dir.: Jaiprakash Agarwal
Phone: (91) 22 2852 5731
Owner/Dir.: Suraj Agarwal
Phone: (91) 22 2852 5731
Owner/Dir.: Ripesh Agarwal
Phone: (91) 22 2852 5731
Total Employees at this Location: 30
Type of Operation: Paper mill
Paper/Paperboard Grades and Capacities:
Total paper and paperboard capacity: 9,120 mt/y
Packaging papers
Paper and Paperboard Mill Data:
Paper Machines: 1
PM 1, total capacity 9,120 mt/y, Packaging papers

ⓂNice Papers Ltd.
Plot No. 138, Village Ghoghali, Tah. Kamleshwar
441501 Dist. Nagpur
India
Personnel:
Dir.: Aditya Saraf
Phone: (91) 0712 2521349
Dir.: Rajendra Saraf
Phone: (91) 0712 2521349
Mill Locations:
Nice Papers Ltd., Kamleshwar, Dist. Nagpur Mill, Plot No. 138, Village Ghoghali, Tah. Kamleshwar, 441501 Dist. Nagpur, India, Capacity: 14,400 mt/y, (Paper mill)

ⓂNice Papers Ltd.
Kamleshwar, Dist. Nagpur Mill
Plot No. 138, Village Ghoghali, Tah. Kamleshwar
441501 Dist. Nagpur, Maharashtra
India
Personnel:
Dir.: Aditya Saraf
Phone: (91) 93 71421349
Dir.: Rajendra Saraf
Type of Operation: Paper mill
Paper/Paperboard Grades and Capacities:
Total paper and paperboard capacity: 14,400 mt/y
Packaging papers: 14,400 mt/y
Paper and Paperboard Mill Data:
Paper Machines: 1
No. 1, total capacity 14,400 mt/y, Trim width 2.3 m, Packaging papers

ⓂNikita Paper (P) Ltd.
C-10, Industrial Estate, Panipat Rd., Shamli
247776 Dist. Muzzaffarnagar
India
Phone: (91) 1398 252189/253189/254189
Fax: (91) 1398 251189
Email: nikitapaper@hotmail.com
Personnel:
Man. Dir.: Naresh Chandra Bansal
Phone: (91) 1398 252189/253189
Fax: (91) 1398 251189
Mill Locations:
Nikita Paper (P) Ltd., Shamli Mill, C-10, Industrial Estate, Panipat Rd., Shamli, 247776 Dist. Muzzaffarnagar, India, Capacity: 10,000 mt/y, (Paper mill)
Phone: (91) 1398 252189/253189/254189
Fax: (91) 1398 251189
Email: nikitapaper@hotmail.com

ⓂNikita Paper (P) Ltd.
Shamli Mill
C-10, Industrial Estate, Panipat Rd., Shamli
247776 Dist. Muzzaffarnagar, Uttar Pradesh
India
Phone: (91) 1398 252189/253189/254189
Fax: (91) 1398 251189
Email: nikitapaper@hotmail.com
Web Address: www.nikitapapers.com
Personnel:
Man. Dir.: Naresh Chandra Bansal
Phone: (91) 1398 252189/253189/254189
Type of Operation: Paper mill
Paper/Paperboard Grades and Capacities:
Total paper and paperboard capacity: 10,000 mt/y
Packaging papers
Linerboard: 10,000 mt/y

ⓂNR Agarwal Industries Ltd.
415-418, Janki Centre, 29, Shah Industrial Estate, Off. Veera Desai Road, Andheri (West)
400 053 Mumbai, Maharashtra
India
Phone: (91) 22 26730913/14/ 17/26730570/6731 7500
Fax: (91) 22 2673 0227
Email: admin@nrail.com
Web Address: www.nrail.com

Personnel:
Exec. Chmn.: N.R. Agarwal
Phone: (91) 22 26730913/14/ 17/26730570/6731 7500
Fax: (91) 22 2673 0227
Man. Dir. & CEO: R. N. Agarwal
Phone: (91) 22 26730913/14/ 17/26730570/6731 7500
Fax: (91) 22 2673 0227
Mill Locations:
NR Agarwal Industries Ltd., Vapi, Valsad (Unit I) Mill, 169, GIDC, Phase II, 396 195 Vapi, Valsad, India, Capacity: 70,000 mt/y, (Paper mill)
Phone: (91) 260 2431634
Fax: (91) 260 2431706
Email: admin@nrail.com
NR Agarwal Industries Ltd., Unit II, Plot No. 1, Phase 1, GIDC, 396 195 Vapi, Dist. Valsad, India, Capacity: 40,000 mt/y, (Paper mill)
Phone: (91) 260 2431942
Fax: (91) 260 2426979/2428320
Email: admin@nrail.com
NR Agarwal Industries Ltd., Unit III and Unit IV, Plot No. 901. 3rd Phase, GIDC, 396 195 Vapi, Dist. Valsad, India, Capacity: 56,000 mt/y, (Paperboard mill)
Phone: (91) 260 240 0052/242 1124
Fax: (91) 260 240 1836
Email: admin@nrail.com

ⓜNR Agarwal Industries Ltd.
Unit-V (Sarigam)
Govanvadi Road, Sarigam, Taluka Umbergaon
396115 Sarigam, Valsad, Gujarat
India
Web Address: www.nrail.com
Type of Operation: Paper mill
Pulp Mill Data:
Recycled Fiber Treatment Lines:
Flotation deinking lines: 1 at 100,000
Paper/Paperboard Grades and Capacities:
Total paper and paperboard capacity: 100,000 mt/y
Uncoated woodfree/freesheet: 100,000 mt/y
Paper and Paperboard Mill Data:
Paper Machines: 1
No. 1, total capacity 90,000 mt/y, Newsprint, Uncoated woodfree/freesheet
Energy Data:
Power boilers: 1
Steam turbines: 1 at 15 MW

ⓜNR Agarwal Industries Ltd.
Vapi, Valsad (Unit I) Mill
169, GIDC, Phase II
396195 Vapi, Valsad, Gujarat
India
Phone: (91) 260 2431634
Fax: (91) 260 2431706
Email: admin@nrail.com
Web Address: www.nrail.com
Personnel:
Gen. Mgr. Tech.: A. K. Bansal
Phone: (91) 260 2431634
Gen. Mgr. Op.: A. K. Bhattacharya
Phone: (91) 260 2431634
Type of Operation: Paper mill
Paper/Paperboard Grades and Capacities:
Total paper and paperboard capacity: 70,000 mt/y
Boxboard/cartonboard: 70,000 mt/y
Paper and Paperboard Mill Data:
Paper Machines: 3
No. 1, Trim width 2 m, Boxboard/cartonboard
No. 2, Trim width 2 m, Boxboard/cartonboard
No. 3, Trim width 2 m, Boxboard/cartonboard
Coating Machines: 1
No. 1, off machine

ⓜNR Agarwal Industries Ltd.
Unit II
Plot No. 1, Phase 1, GIDC
396 195 Vapi, Dist. Valsad, Gujarat
India
Phone: (91) 260 2431942
Fax: (91) 260 2426979/2428320
Email: admin@nrail.com
Web Address: www.nrail.com
Type of Operation: Paper mill
Paper/Paperboard Grades and Capacities:
Total paper and paperboard capacity: 40,000 mt/y
Newsprint: 40,000 mt/y
Paper and Paperboard Mill Data:
Paper Machines: 3
No. 1, Trim width 1.9 m, Newsprint
No. 2, Trim width 2.1 m, Newsprint
No. 3, Trim width 1.7 m, Newsprint

ⓜNR Agarwal Industries Ltd.
Unit III and Unit IV
Plot No. 901.3rd Phase, GIDC
396 195 Vapi, Dist. Valsad, Gujarat
India
Phone: (91) 260 240 0052/242 1124
Fax: (91) 260 240 1836
Email: admin@nrail.com
Web Address: www.nrail.com
Personnel:
CEO: V. Prabhakaran
Phone: (91) 260 240 0052/242 1124
Type of Operation: Paperboard mill
Paper/Paperboard Grades and Capacities:
Total paper and paperboard capacity: 56,000 mt/y
Boxboard/cartonboard: 56,000 mt/y

ⓜOm Srinivasa Paper Boards Pvt. Ltd.
183 – C Thillai Nagar, Bypass Road
626203 Sattur, Tamil Nadu
India
Phone: (91) 4562 260875
Email: info@ohmsrinivasa.com.
Web Address: www.ohmsrinivasa.com
Mill Locations:
Om Srinivasa Paper Boards Pvt. Ltd., Sattur Mill, Sindhapally Village, Venkatachalapuram Post, 626203 Sattur, India, Capacity: 28,000 mt/y, (Paper mill)
Phone: (91) 99524 11111
Email: info@ohmsrinivasa.com.

ⓜOm Srinivasa Paper Boards Pvt. Ltd.
Sattur Mill
Sindhapally Village, Venkatachalapuram Post
626203 Sattur, Tamil Nadu
India
Phone: (91) 99524 11111
Email: info@ohmsrinivasa.com.
Web Address: www.ohmsrinivasa.com.
Total Employees at this Location: 150
Type of Operation: Paper mill
Pulp Grades and Capacities:
Total pulp capacity: 26,135 mt/y
Recycled Pulping: 26,135 mt/y
Pulp Mill Data:
Bleach Plant Systems: 1
Recycled Pulping System
Recycled Fiber Treatment Lines:
Flotation deinking lines: 1
Recycled packaging pulping lines: 1
Paper/Paperboard Grades and Capacities:
Total paper and paperboard capacity: 28,000 mt/y
Boxboard/cartonboard: 28,000 mt/y
Paper and Paperboard Mill Data:
Paper Machines: 1
No. 1, multi-fourdrinier, total capacity 28,000 mt/y, Trim width 2.65 m, Boxboard/cartonboard
Coating Machines: 1
PM 1, on machine
Energy Data:
Power boilers

ⓜOpel Paper Mill Ltd.
Vapi Mill
Ownership: Speciality Papers Ltd.
Vapi, Gujarat
India
Phone: (91) opel@reliablepaperindia.com
Email: opel@reliablepaperindia.com
Type of Operation: Paper mill
Paper/Paperboard Grades and Capacities:
Total paper and paperboard capacity: 17,500 mt/y
Coated woodfree/freesheet
Specialty and industrial
Paper and Paperboard Mill Data:
Paper Machines: 2
PM 2, total capacity 6,000 mt/y, Trim width 1.25 m, Coated woodfree/freesheet
PM 3, Trim width 1.25 m, Coated woodfree/freesheet
Coating Machines: 1
PM 1, total capacity 3,600 mt/y.

ⓜOrient Paper & Industries Ltd.
Ownership: Birla Group
Birla Building, 9/I, R.N. Mukherjee Rd.
700 001 Kolkata, West Bengal
India
Phone: (91) 33 2248 0135/2213 1680/2213 0741/2242 3533
Fax: (91) 33 2243 0490/42 0933/2230 7726
Email: pachisia@orientpaperindia.com, info@orientpaperindia.com
Web Address: www.orientpaperindia.com
Personnel:
Chmn.: C. K. Birla
Phone: (91) 33 2248 0135/2213 1680/2213 0741/2242 3533
Fax: (91) 33 2243 0490/42 0933/2230 7726
Man. Dir.: M. L. Pachisia
Phone: (91) 33 2248 5629
Fax: (91) 33 2242 0933
Email: pachisia@orientpaperindia.com
Exec. VP Finan.: P. K. Sonthalia
Phone: (91) 33 2248 3406
Fax: (91) 33 2248 5141
Email: pks@orientpaperindia.com
VP Sls.: Gautam Mullick
Phone: (91) 33 2213 0741
Fax: (91) 33 2220 7726
Email: gautam@orientpaperindia.com
VP Projects: N. K. Saha
Phone: (91) 33 2210 3782
Fax: (91) 33 2243 0490
Email: nks@orientpaperindia.com
Mill Locations:
Orient Paper Mills, Amlai mill, Amlai, 484 117 Shahdol, M.P, India, Capacity: 108,171 mt/y, (Pulp mill, Paper mill)
Phone: (91) 7652 286275/76/77
Fax: (91) 7652 286274
Email: unit_amlai@orientpaperindia.com

ⓜOrient Paper Mills
Amlai mill
Ownership: Orient Paper & Industries Ltd.
Amlai
484 117 Shahdol, M.P
India
Phone: (91) 7652 286275/76/77
Fax: (91) 7652 286274
Email: unit_amlai@orientpaperindia.com
Web Address: www.orientpaperindia.com
Personnel:
Sr. Pres.: N. K. Thusu
Phone: (91) 7652 286275
Fax: (91) 7652 286274
Email: nkthusu@orientpaperindia.com
Sr. VP (Operations): P. K. Sarka
Phone: (91) 7652 286275/76/77
Email: pksarkar@orientpaperindia.com
VP (HR): D. N. Swain

India

Phone: (91) 7652 286275/76/77
Email: dnswain@orientpaperindia.com
AVP (Com): Kamal Thapar
Phone: (91) 7652 286275/76/77
Deputy Gen. Mgr. (Projects): M. S. Maheshwari
Phone: (91) 7652 286275/76/77
Email: projects_amlai@orientpaperindia.com
Total Employees at this Location: 1,955
Type of Operation: Pulp mill, Paper mill
Pulp Grades and Capacities:
Total pulp capacity: 79,730 mt/y
Chemical Pulp: 29,750 mt/y
Other Pulp: 49,980 mt/y
Pulp Mill Data:
Chemical Pulping Systems:
Batch digesters: 7
Bleach Plant Systems: 1
No. 1, Sequence: CEopHP, Capacity 75,000 admt/y
Chemical Recovery Equipment:
Evaporator lines: 1
Recovery boilers: 1
Paper/Paperboard Grades and Capacities:
Total paper and paperboard capacity: 108,171 mt/y
Uncoated woodfree/freesheet: 79,968 mt/y
Tissue: 28,203 mt/y
Paper and Paperboard Mill Data:
Stock Preparation:
Pulpers: 4
Refiners: 15
Paper Machines: 4
No. 1, fourdrinier, total capacity 69,972 mt/y, Trim width 5.6 m, Uncoated woodfree/freesheet
No. 2, fourdrinier, total capacity 9,996 mt/y, Trim width 1.27 m, Uncoated woodfree/freesheet
No. 3, total capacity 9,996 mt/y, Trim width 2.75 m, Tissue, Uncoated woodfree/freesheet
No. 4, (trial runs May 2009, commercial production September 2009), total capacity 18,207 mt/y, Trim width 2.75 m, Tissue, Uncoated woodfree/freesheet
Finishing Equipment:
Rewinders: 3 at 85,000 mt/y
Sheeters: 6
Energy Data:
Power boilers: 3
Steam turbines: 2 at 16.0, 6.0 MW
Electrical demand for mill: 343 MWh/D

ⓘPaalson Paper & Board
4050, South 4th Street
Puddukottai
India
Phone: (91) 4322 221965
Personnel:
Man. Dir.: M. Kasi
Phone: (91) 4322 221965
Dir.: P. L. Muthupalan
Phone: (91) 4322 221965
Mill Locations:
Paalson Paper & Board, Puddukottai Mill, 4050, South 4th Street, Puddukottai, India, Capacity: 9,900 mt/y, (Paper mill)
Phone: (91) 4322 221965

ⓘPaalson Paper & Board
Puddukottai Mill
4050, South 4th Street
Puddukottai, Tamil Nadu
India
Phone: (91) 4322 221965
Personnel:
Man. Dir.: M. Kasi
Phone: (91) 94 43161008
Dir.: Mr. P. L. Muthupalan
Phone: (91) 94 43161008
Type of Operation: Paper mill
Paper/Paperboard Grades and Capacities:
Total paper and paperboard capacity: 9,900 mt/y
Packaging papers

ⓘPalode Paper Mills Ltd.
Cheaiakuzhy Buildings, Peroorkada
695005 Trivendrum
India
Phone: (91) 0471 2434142
Personnel:
Man. Dir.: Joseph Thomas
Phone: (91) 0471 2434142, 94 47130142
Mktg. Exec.: Mathews M. Vechoor
Phone: (91) 0471 2434142, 94 47130142
Mill Locations:
Palode Paper Mills Ltd., Thiruvananthapuram Dist. Mill, Cheaiakuzhy Buildings, Peroorkada, 695005 Trivendrum, India, Capacity: 7,200 mt/y, (Paper mill)

ⓜPalode Paper Mills Ltd.
Thiruvananthapuram Dist. Mill
Cheaiakuzhy Buildings, Peroorkada
695005 Trivendrum, Kerala
India
Personnel:
Man. Dir.: Joseph Thomas
Phone: (91) 98 47066142
Mktg. Exec.: Mathews M. Vechoor
Phone: (91) 94 47130142
Type of Operation: Paper mill
Paper/Paperboard Grades and Capacities:
Total paper and paperboard capacity: 7,200 mt/y
Packaging papers
Specialty and industrial

ⓘPaper Packaging Pvt. Ltd. Corp.
Ownership: 100% by Karnataka State Industrial and Infrastructure Development Corporation (KSIIDC)
PO Box 124, KIADB Industrial Estate
577201 Mandli, Shimoga Dist., Karnataka
India
Phone: (91) 08182-220584, 223765
Fax: (91) 08182-278438
Email: paperpkg@dataone.in
Personnel:
CEO: S. Naik
Phone: (91) 08182-220584
Fax: (91) 08182-278438
Total Employees of Company: 25
Mill Locations:
Paper Packaging Pvt. Ltd. Corp., Mandli Mill, PO Box 124, KIADB Industrial Estate, 577 201 Mandli, Shimoga Dist., India, Capacity: 50,000 mt/y, (Paper mill)
Phone: (91) 08182-220584, 223765
Fax: (91) 08182-278438
Email: paperpkg@dataone.in

ⓜPaper Packaging Pvt. Ltd. Corp.
Mandli Mill
PO Box 124, KIADB Industrial Estate
577 201 Mandli, Shimoga Dist., Karnataka
India
Phone: (91) 08182-220584, 223765
Fax: (91) 08182-278438
Email: paperpkg@dataone.in
Personnel:
CEO: Mr. S. S. Naik
Phone: (91) 08182-220584, 223765
Total Employees at this Location: 145
Type of Operation: Paper mill
Pulp Grades and Capacities:
Total pulp capacity: 49,482 mt/y
Recycled Pulping: 49,482 mt/y
Pulp Mill Data:
Recycled Fiber Treatment Lines:
Recycled packaging pulping lines: 1
Paper/Paperboard Grades and Capacities:
Total paper and paperboard capacity: 50,000 mt/y
Linerboard: 20,000 mt/y
Corrugating medium/fluting: 30,000 mt/y
Paper and Paperboard Mill Data:
Paper Machines: 2
No. 1, fourdrinier, total capacity 20,000 mt/y, Trim width 2 m, Linerboard
No. 2, fourdrinier, total capacity 30,000 mt/y, Trim width 2.6 m, Corrugating medium/fluting
Energy Data:
Power boilers
Electrical demand for mill: 61 MWh/D

ⓘParamount Paper Mills
316-317, Industrial Area, Phase - I
134109 Panchkula
India
Phone: (91) 172 2560542/443
Fax: (91) 172 2560542/442
Personnel:
Man. Dir.: R. K. Bhasin
Phone: (91) 172 2560542/443
Fax: (91) 172 2560542/442
Dir.: Yogesh Bhasin
Phone: (91) 172 2560542/443
Fax: (91) 172 2560542/442
Email: yb_1975@rediffmail.com
Mill Locations:
Paramount Paper Mills, Panchkula Mill, 316-317, Industrial Area, Phase - I, 134109 Panchkula, India, Capacity: 5,400 mt/y, (Paper mill)
Phone: (91) 172 2560542/443
Fax: (91) 172 2560542/442

ⓜParamount Paper Mills
Panchkula Mill
316-317, Industrial Area, Phase - I
134109 Panchkula, Haryana
India
Phone: (91) 172 2560542/443
Fax: (91) 172 2560542/442
Personnel:
Man. Dir.: Mr. R. K. Bhasin
Phone: (91) 93 12601874
Type of Operation: Paper mill
Paper/Paperboard Grades and Capacities:
Total paper and paperboard capacity: 5,400 mt/y
Uncoated woodfree/freesheet

ⓘⓜParijat Paper Mills Ltd.
Muzaffarnagar Mill
10.6 Km Stone, Bhopa Rd.
251001 Muzaffarnagar, Uttar Pradesh
India
Phone: (91) 131 2468591/92
Fax: (91) 131 2468595
Email: paper_ppml@rediffmail.com
Web Address: www.parijatpapermills.tradeindia.com
Personnel:
Man. Dir.: Mr. N. C. Mittal
Phone: (91) 131 2468591/92
Type of Operation: Paper mill
Paper/Paperboard Grades and Capacities:
Total paper and paperboard capacity: 8,250 mt/y
Packaging papers
Paper and Paperboard Mill Data:
Paper Machines: 2
No. 1, Packaging papers
No. 2, Packaging papers

ⓘPaswara Paper Mill Limited
Paswara House, Baghpat Road
Meerut, Uttar Pradesh
India
Phone: (91) 121 2511692/4005107
Fax: (91) 121 4003257
Email: info@paswara.com
Web Address: www.paswara.com
Mill Locations:
Paswara Paper Mill Limited, Meerut Mill, N.H. – 58, Village – Mohiuddinpur, Delhi Road, Meerut, India, Capacity: 15,000 mt/y, (Paper mill)
Phone: (91) 121 2410502/5
Fax: (91) 121 2410505
Email: paswara@ndf.vsnl.net.in

India

ⓂPaswara Paper Mill Limited
Meerut Mill
N.H. – 58, Village – Mohiuddinpur, Delhi Road
Meerut, Uttar Pradesh
India
  Phone: (91) 121 2410502/5
  Fax: (91) 121 2410505
  Email: paswara@ndf.vsnl.net.in
  Web Address: www.paswara.com
Personnel:
  Gen. Mgr.: Vinod Kumar
  Dir.: Arvind Agarwal
Total Employees at this Location: 200
Type of Operation: Paper mill
Paper/Paperboard Grades and Capacities:
  Total paper and paperboard capacity: 15,000 mt/y
  Packaging papers
Paper and Paperboard Mill Data:
  Stock Preparation:
  Pulpers: 2
  Refiners: 6
Paper Machines: 2
No. 1, fourdrinier, Trim width 2.1 m, Linerboard
No. 2, Trim width 2.1 m, Containerboard
Finishing Equipment:
  Rewinders: 2
Energy Data:
  Power boilers: 1

ⓗPitambar Coated Papers Ltd.
A-912, Phase III, RIICO Industrial Area
301019 Bhiwadi
India
  Phone: (91) 1493 220158/222424/423
  Fax: (91) 1493 220158
  Email: sgsunilgupta4@gmail.com
Personnel:
  Chmn. & Man. Dir.: Ved Bhushan Aggarwal
  Phone: (91) 1493 220158/222424/423
  Fax: (91) 1493 220158
Mill Locations:
Pitambar Coated Papers Ltd., Bhiwadi Mill, A-912,
Phase III, RIICO Industrial Area, 301019 Bhiwadi, India,
Capacity: 18,000 mt/y, (Paper mill)
  Phone: (91) 1493 220158/222424/423
  Fax: (91) 1493 220158
  Email: sgsunilgupta4@gmail.com

ⓂPitambar Coated Papers Ltd.
Bhiwadi Mill
A-912, Phase III, RIICO Industrial Area
301019 Bhiwadi, Rajasthan
India
  Phone: (91) 1493 220158/222424/423
  Fax: (91) 1493 220158
  Email: sgsunilgupta4@gmail.com
Personnel:
  Chmn. & Man. Dir.: Ved Bhushan Aggarwal
  Phone: (91) 1493 220158/222424/423
  Dir.: Ashish Aggarwal
  Phone: (91) 1493 220158/222424/423
Type of Operation: Paper mill
Paper/Paperboard Grades and Capacities:
  Total paper and paperboard capacity: 18,000 mt/y
  Uncoated woodfree/freesheet
  Coated woodfree/freesheet
  Specialty and industrial
Paper and Paperboard Mill Data:
Paper Machines: 1
No. 1
Coating Machines: 1
No. 1, off machine

ⓗPragati Paper Industries Ltd.
10/5, East Patel Nagar
110 008 New Delhi
India
  Phone: (91) 11 25764511/512/25767489/1847
  Fax: (91) 11 25765940
  Email: pragati@vsnl.net

Personnel:
  Man. Dir.: Mr. R. K. Aggarwal
  Phone: (91) 11 25764511/512/25767489/1847
  Fax: (91) 11 25765940
Mill Locations:
Pragati Paper Mills Ltd., Dist. Ghaziabad Mill, A-21/2, Site - 4,
Sahibabad Industrial Area, 201010 Dist. Ghaziabad, India,
Capacity: 15,000 mt/y, (Paper mill, Paperboard mill)
  Phone: (91) 120 2771316/0213
Pragati Paper Industries Ltd., Patiala Mill, Vill. Handesra,
Derabassi Dist., Patiala, India, Capacity: 75,000 mt/y,
(Paper mill)
  Phone: (91) 171 2775780/81/82/83
  Email: pragati@vsnl.net
Pragati Paper Industries Ltd., Sirmaur Mill, Kala-Amb, Dist.
Sirmaur, India, Capacity: 12,000 mt/y, (Paper mill)
  Email: pragati@vsnl.net

ⓂPragati Paper Mills Ltd.
Dist. Ghaziabad Mill
Ownership: Pragati Paper Industries Ltd.
A-21/2, Site - 4, Sahibabad Industrial Area
201010 Dist. Ghaziabad, Uttar Pradesh
India
  Phone: (91) 120 2771316/0213
Personnel:
  Man. Dir.: Mr. R. K. Aggarwal
  Phone: (91) 120 2771316/0213
Type of Operation: Paper mill, Paperboard mill
Paper/Paperboard Grades and Capacities:
  Total paper and paperboard capacity: 15,000 mt/y
  Uncoated woodfree/freesheet
  Boxboard/cartonboard
Paper and Paperboard Mill Data:
Paper Machines: 1
PM 1, fourdrinier, Uncoated woodfree/freesheet,
Boxboard/cartonboard

ⓂPragati Paper Industries Ltd.
Patiala Mill
Vill. Handesra
Derabassi Dist., Patiala, Punjab
India
  Phone: (91) 171 2775780/81/82/83
  Email: pragati@vsnl.net
Personnel:
  Man. Dir.: Mr. R. K. Aggarwal
  Phone: (91) 25 886711/883512
Total Employees at this Location: 200
Type of Operation: Paper mill
Paper/Paperboard Grades and Capacities:
  Total paper and paperboard capacity: 75,000 mt/y
  Newsprint
  Uncoated woodfree/freesheet
Paper and Paperboard Mill Data:
Paper Machines: 1
No. 1, fourdrinier, total capacity 75,000 mt/y

ⓂPragati Paper Industries Ltd.
Sirmaur Mill
Kala-Amb
Dist. Sirmaur, Himachal Pradesh
India
  Email: pragati@vsnl.net
  Web Address: www.pragatipapers.com
Personnel:
  Man. Dir.: Mr. R. K. Aggarwal
Total Employees at this Location: 200
Type of Operation: Paper mill
Paper/Paperboard Grades and Capacities:
  Total paper and paperboard capacity: 12,000 mt/y
  Newsprint
  Uncoated woodfree/freesheet

ⓗPranavraj Paper Mills Pvt. Ltd.
188-190, GIDC
396195 Vapi, Dist. Valsad
India

  Phone: (91) 260 2428506, 260 6541226
Mill Locations:
Pranavraj Paper Mills Pvt. Ltd., Vapi, Dist. Valsad Mill, 188-
190, GIDC, 396195 Vapi, Dist. Valsad, India, Capacity:
5,400 mt/y, (Paperboard mill)
  Phone: (91) 260 2428506

ⓂPranavraj Paper Mills Pvt. Ltd.
Vapi, Dist. Valsad Mill
188-190, GIDC
396195 Vapi, Dist. Valsad, Gujarat
India
  Phone: (91) 260 2428506
Type of Operation: Paperboard mill
Paper/Paperboard Grades and Capacities:
  Total paper and paperboard capacity: 5,400 mt/y
  Boxboard/cartonboard

ⓗPrayas Papers (P) Ltd.
34, Behari Lal Ghosh Road
700 057 Kolkata, West Bengal
India
  Phone: (91) 33 2553 1625/5491
  Fax: (91) 33 2553 2295
  Email: pearlex@vsnl.net.in
Personnel:
  Dir.: Sajal Kumar Bose
  Phone: (91) 33 25633053
  Dir.: P. K. Sadhu
  Phone: (91) 98 30049784
Total Employees of Company: 75
Total Employees at this Location: 8
Mill Locations:
Prayas Papers (P) Ltd., Parganas Mill, 7 Ekford Rd.,
Khardah, PO Sukchar, 343 179 North 24-Parganas,
India, Capacity: 4,000 mt/y, (Paperboard mill)
  Phone: (91) 33 25533948/25633053

ⓂPrayas Papers (P) Ltd.
Parganas Mill
7 Ekford Rd., Khardah, PO Sukchar
343 179 North 24-Parganas, West Bengal
India
  Phone: (91) 33 25533948/25633053
Personnel:
  Factory Mgr.: N. Das Gupta
  Phone: (91) 33 25533948/25633053
Total Employees at this Location: 70
Type of Operation: Paperboard mill
Paper/Paperboard Grades and Capacities:
  Total paper and paperboard capacity: 4,000 mt/y
  Boxboard/cartonboard: 4,000 mt/y
Paper and Paperboard Mill Data:
  Stock Preparation:
  Pulpers: 2
Paper Machines: 1
No. 1, total capacity 4,000 mt/y, Trim width 1.6 m,
Boxboard/cartonboard
Finishing Equipment:
  Rewinders: 1
Energy Data:
  Power boilers: 1

ⓗPremier Paper Mills Ltd.
23 Ahmed Block
New Garden Town, Punjab
India
  Phone: (91) 42 3588 5717-9
  Fax: (91) 42 35866084
  Email: headoffice@premiergroup.pk
  Web Address: www.premiergroup.pk
Total Employees of Company: 250
Mill Locations:
Premier Paper Mills Ltd., Sheikhupura Mill, Km. 8, Lahore
Road, P.O. Kot Saleem, 39350 Sheikhupura, Pakistan,
Capacity: 36,000 mt/y, (Pulp mill, Paper mill)
  Phone: (92) (563) 406 611/2
  Fax: (92) (563) 406 613
  Email: ppmltd@skp.wol.net.pk

India

ⓂPremier Tissues India Ltd.
Ownership: 100% by Ballarpur Industries Ltd. (BILT)
No.230, 2nd Floor, 15th Cross, Sampige Road
560003 Malleswaram, Bangalore, Karnataka
India
Phone: (91) 80 23445191/23449298-99
Fax: (91) 80 23445192
Email: sales@premiertissues.com
Web Address: www.premiertissues.com
Personnel:
Chair & MD.: G. G. Shenoy
Phone: (91) 80 23445191/23449298-99
Fax: (91) 80 23445192
Mill Locations:
Premier Tissues India Ltd., Mysore Mill, Bannur, Mysore, India, Capacity: 8,400 mt/y, (Paper mill)

ⓂPremier Tissues India Ltd.
Mysore Mill
Ownership: 100% by Ballarpur Industries Ltd. (BILT)
Bannur, Mysore, Karnataka
India
Web Address: www.premiertissues.com
Type of Operation: Paper mill
Paper/Paperboard Grades and Capacities:
Total paper and paperboard capacity: 8,400 mt/y
Tissue: 8,400 mt/y
Paper and Paperboard Mill Data:
Paper Machines: 2
No. 1, total capacity 2,800 mt/y, Tissue
No. 2, total capacity 5,600 mt/y, Tissue

ⓂPremium Paper & Boards Ind. Ltd.
S.R. 460, Anaval Village, Mahuva Taluka
396510 Surat
India
Phone: (91) 2625 252711/252068
Fax: (91) 2625 252069
Email: info@premiumpaper.in, service@premiumpaper.in
Web Address: www.premiumpaper.in
Personnel:
Man. Dir.: Praful Gandhi
Phone: (91) 2625 252711/252068
Fax: (91) 2625 252069
Email: praful@premiumpaper.in
Exec. Dir.: Avinash Gandhi
Phone: (91) 2625 252711/252068
Fax: (91) 2625 252069
Export Dir.: Mitesh Gandhi
Phone: (91) 2625 252711/252068
Fax: (91) 2625 252069
Email: mitesh@premiumpaper.in
VP (Tech.): R. K. Saxena
Phone: (91) 2625 252711/252068
Fax: (91) 2625 252069
Email: saxena@premiumpaper.in
Total Employees at this Location: 79
Mill Locations:
Premium Paper & Boards Ind. Ltd., Surat Mill, S.R. 460, Anaval Village, Mahuva Taluka, 396510 Surat, India, Capacity: 67,200 mt/y, (Paper mill, Paperboard mill)
Phone: (91) 2625 252711/252068
Fax: (91) 2625 252069
Email: info@premiumpaper.in, service@premiumpaper.in

ⓂPremium Paper & Boards Ind. Ltd.
Surat Mill
S.R. 460, Anaval Village, Mahuva Taluka
396510 Surat, Gujarat
India
Phone: (91) 2625 252711/252068
Fax: (91) 2625 252069
Email: info@premiumpaper.in, service@premiumpaper.in
Web Address: www.premiumpaper.in
Personnel:
Man. Dir.: Praful Gandhi
Phone: (91) 992 522 3954
Email: praful@preniumpaper.in
Exec. Dir.: Avinash Gandhi
Phone: (91) 932 349 6496
Export Dir.: Mitesh Gandhi
Phone: (91) 996 777 0465
Email: mitesh@premiumpaper.in
VP (Tech.): R. K. Saxena
Phone: (91) 992 522 3881
Email: saxena@premiumpaper.in
VP (Oper.): V. K. Sharma
Phone: (91) 992 522 3679
Email: vksharma@premiumpaper.in
Type of Operation: Paper mill, Paperboard mill
Pulp Grades and Capacities:
Total pulp capacity: 60,000 mt/y
Paper/Paperboard Grades and Capacities:
Total paper and paperboard capacity: 67,200 mt/y
Packaging papers: 38,400 mt/y
Linerboard: 7,200 mt/y
Boxboard/cartonboard: 21,600 mt/y
Paper and Paperboard Mill Data:
Stock Preparation:
Pulpers: 4
Refiners: 6
Paper Machines: 2
No. 1, Performer, Trim width 2.13 m, Linerboard, Packaging papers, Boxboard/cartonboard
No. 2, fourdrinier, Trim width 2.5 m, Linerboard, Packaging papers
Finishing Equipment:
Winders: 2 at 50,000 mt/y
Calenders: 2
Energy Data:
Power boilers: 2
Electrical demand for mill: 60 MWh/D

ⓂProgressive Paper Mills (P) Ltd.
34/1 Bhirilal Ghosh Rd.
700057 Kolkata, West Bengal
India
Phone: (91) 33 25531625/35491
Fax: (91) 33 25532295
Email: pearlex@vsnl.com
Mill Locations:
Progressive Paper Mills (P) Ltd., Kolkata Mill, 34/1 Bhirilal Ghosh Rd., 700057 Kolkata, India, Capacity: 1,800 mt/y, (Paper mill)
Phone: (91) 33 25531625/35491
Fax: (91) 33 25532295
Email: pearlex@vsnl.com

ⓂProgressive Paper Mills (P) Ltd.
Kolkata Mill
34/1 Bhirilal Ghosh Rd.
700057 Kolkata, West Bengal
India
Phone: (91) 33 25531625/35491
Fax: (91) 33 25532295
Email: pearlex@vsnl.com
Personnel:
Mill Mgr.: S. Bagh
Phone: (91) 33 25531625/35491
Total Employees at this Location: 54
Type of Operation: Paper mill
Pulp Mill Data:
Recycled Fiber Treatment Lines:
Pulpers: 2
Paper/Paperboard Grades and Capacities:
Total paper and paperboard capacity: 1,800 mt/y
Packaging papers: 1,800 mt/y
Paper and Paperboard Mill Data:
Paper Machines: 1
No. 1, Trim width 1.5 m, Packaging papers
Finishing Equipment:
Rewinders: 1

ⓂProlific Papers Pvt. Ltd.
Village Girdhai, Aliganj Road
244713 Kashipur, Udham Singh Nagar
India
Phone: (91) 5947 260838
Fax: (91) 5947 272022
Email: info@prolificpapers.com
Web Address: prolificpapers.com
Personnel:
Chmn., Man. Dir.: Hemant Kumar Jodhani
Phone: (91) 5947 260838
Fax: (91) 5947 272022
Exec. Dir.: Shyam lal Tayal
Phone: (91) 5947 260838
Fax: (91) 5947 272022
Exec. Dir.: Abhishek Kumar Agarwal
Phone: (91) 5947 260838
Fax: (91) 5947 272022
Mill Locations:
Prolific Papers Pvt. Ltd., Kashipur, Udham Singh Nagar Mill, Village Girdhai, Aliganj Road, 244713 Kashipur, Udham Singh Nagar, India, Capacity: 36,300 mt/y, (Paper mill)
Phone: (91) 5947 260838/ 11 2328 4468
Fax: (91) 5947 272022
Email: info@prolificpapers.com

ⓂProlific Papers Pvt. Ltd.
Kashipur, Udham Singh Nagar Mill
Village Girdhai, Aliganj Road
244713 Kashipur, Udham Singh Nagar, Uttarakhand
India
Phone: (91) 5947 260838/ 11 2328 4468
Fax: (91) 5947 272022
Email: info@prolificpapers.com
Web Address: www.prolificpapers.com
Personnel:
Chmn, Man. Dir.: Hemant Kumar Jodhani
Phone: (91) 5947 260838
Exec. Dir.: Shyam lal Tayal
Phone: (91) 5947 260838
Exec. Dir.: Abhishek Kumar Agarwal
Phone: (91) 5947 260838
Total Employees at this Location: 215
Type of Operation: Paper mill
Pulp Grades and Capacities:
Total pulp capacity: 34,489 mt/y
Recycled Pulping: 34,489 mt/y
Pulp Mill Data:
Bleach Plant Systems: 1
Recycled Pulping System
Recycled Fiber Treatment Lines:
Flotation deinking lines: 1
Recycled packaging pulping lines: 1
Paper/Paperboard Grades and Capacities:
Total paper and paperboard capacity: 36,300 mt/y
Uncoated woodfree/freesheet: 19,800 mt/y
Packaging papers: 16,500 mt/y
Paper and Paperboard Mill Data:
Paper Machines: 2
No. 1, fourdrinier, total capacity 19,800 mt/y, Trim width 3.32 m, Uncoated woodfree/freesheet
No. 2, fourdrinier, total capacity 16,500 mt/y, Trim width 3.3 m, Packaging papers
Energy Data:
Power boilers: 1
Electrical demand for mill: 68 MWh/D

ⓂPudumjee Industries Ltd. (PIL)
Pune Mill
Ownership: Pudumjee Pulp & Paper Mills Ltd.
Thergaon, Chinchwad
411033 Pune, Maharashtra
India
Phone: (91) 20 30613333/27275381
Fax: (91) 20 72723294
Email: sk@pune.pudumjee.com
Web Address: www.pudumjee.com
Personnel:

India

Man. Dir.: Mr. S. M. Jatia
Phone: (91) 20 30613333/27275381
Snr. Gen. Mgr. (Oper.): Dr. N. V. Gune
Phone: (91) 20 30613333/27275381
Total Employees at this Location: 500
Type of Operation: Paper mill
Paper/Paperboard Grades and Capacities:
Total paper and paperboard capacity: 27,500 mt/y
Tissue
Specialty and industrial
Paper and Paperboard Mill Data:
Paper Machines: 2
PM 6, cylinder, Yankee dryer, total capacity 15,000 mt/y, Trim width 2.6 m, Tissue, Packaging papers, Specialty and industrial
PM 7, cylinder, Yankee dryer, total capacity 12,500 mt/y, Trim width 2.6 m, Tissue, Packaging papers, Specialty and industrial

ⓂPudumjee Pulp & Paper Mills Ltd.
Ownership: 60.87% by M. P. Jatia Group Companies
Jatia Chambers, 60, Drive VB Gandhi Marg, Fort
400 023 Mumbai, Maharashtra
India
  Phone: (91) 22 30213333
  Fax: (91) 22 22658316
  Email: pudumjee@pudumjee.com
  Web Address: www.pudumjee.com
Personnel:
  Chmn./Man. Dir.: M. P. Jatia
  Phone: (91) 22 22674485/529/22 30213333
  Fax: (91) 22 22658316
  Email: jatia.mp@pudumjee.com
  Constitute Attorney: S. M. Jatia
  Phone: (91) 22 22674485/529/22 30213333
  Fax: (91) 22 22658316
  Email: jatia.shyam@pudumjee.com
  Dir.: A. K. Jatia
  Phone: (91) 22 22674485/529/22 30213333
  Fax: (91) 22 22658316
  Email: jatia.arun@pudumjee.com
  Finan. Mgr.: Surendrakumar Bansal
  Phone: (91) 22 22674485/529/22 30213333
  Fax: (91) 20 30613388
  Email: skb@pune.pudumjee.com
  Dir.: Ved. P. Leekha
  Phone: (91) 22 22674485/529/22 30213333
  Fax: (91) 20 30613388
  Email: vpl@pune.pudumjee.com
Total Employees of Company: 650
Total Employees at this Location: 21
Mill Locations:
Pudumjee Industries Ltd. (PIL), Pune Mill, Thergaon, Chinchwad, 411033 Pune, India, Capacity: 27,500 mt/y, (Paper mill)
  Phone: (91) 20 30613333/27275381
  Fax: (91) 20 72723294
  Email: sk@pune.pudumjee.com
Pudumjee Pulp & Paper Mills Ltd., Pune Mill, Thergaon, 411 033 Chinchwad, Pune, India, Capacity: 42,483 mt/y, (Pulp mill, Paper mill)
  Phone: (91) 20 30613333/27275381/88
  Fax: (91) 20 27273294
  Email: sk@pune.pudumjee.com

ⓂPudumjee Pulp & Paper Mills Ltd.
Pune Mill
Thergaon
411 033 Chinchwad, Pune, Maharashtra
India
  Phone: (91) 20 30613333/27275381/88
  Fax: (91) 20 27273294
  Email: sk@pune.pudumjee.com
  Web Address: www.pudumjee.com
Personnel:
  Chmn. & Man. Dir.: M. P. Jatia
  Phone: (91) 22 30213333
  Fax: (91) 22 22658316
  Email: jatia.mp@pudumjee.com

Constituted Attorney: S. M. Jatia
Phone: (91) 22 30213333
Fax: (91) 22 22658316
Email: jatia.shyam@pudumjee.com
Tech. Dir.: Ved P. Leekha
Phone: (91) 20 30613402
Fax: (91) 20 27273294
Email: vpl@pune.pudumjee.com
Dir.: S. K. Bansal
Phone: (91) 20 30613401
Sen. Gen. Mgr. Operations: Dr. N. V. Gune
Phone: (91) 20 30613406
Email: nvg@pune.pudumjee.pune
Total Employees at this Location: 185
Type of Operation: Pulp mill, Paper mill
Pulp Grades and Capacities:
Total pulp capacity: 19,178 mt/y
Recycled Pulping: 19,178 mt/y
Pulp Mill Data:
Bleach Plant Systems: 1
No. 1, Sequence: CEH
Recycled Fiber Treatment Lines:
Flotation deinking lines: 1 at 20,000 admt/y
Pulpers: 1 at 20,000 admt/y
Paper/Paperboard Grades and Capacities:
Total paper and paperboard capacity: 42,483 mt/y
Uncoated woodfree/freesheet: 18,921 mt/y
Specialty and industrial: 23,562 mt/y
Paper and Paperboard Mill Data:
Stock Preparation:
Pulpers: 3
Paper Machines: 2
No. 1, fourdrinier, total capacity 18,921 mt/y, Trim width 3.2 m, Specialty and industrial
No. 2, fourdrinier, total capacity 23,562 mt/y, Trim width 3.25 m, Specialty and industrial, Uncoated woodfree/freesheet
Energy Data:
Power boilers: 3
Electrical demand for mill: 134 MWh/D

ⓂPurvi Bharat Paper & Power Ltd.
Cuttack Mill
Mill is under construction (due to start at the end of 2013)
Ownership: 100% by Kandoi Transport Ltd
At-Chhatisa-2 & Indranipatna,
753003 Cuttack, Odisha
India
  Phone: (91) 0671-2442222/2445366
  Fax: (91) 0671-2445377
  Email: nk@ktlgroup.in,
  navinkandoi@hotmail.com
  Web Address: www.ktlgroup.in/group_companies.php
Personnel:
  Tech. Dir. : Mr. G. Panda
Type of Operation: Paper mill
Paper/Paperboard Grades and Capacities:
Total paper and paperboard capacity: 51,100 mt/y
Newsprint
Uncoated woodfree/freesheet
Paper and Paperboard Mill Data:
Paper Machines: 1
No. 1, (expected to be completed by end of 2013.), fourdrinier, total capacity 51,100 mt/y, Trim width 3.6 m

ⓄR A Shaikh Paper Mills Pvt. Ltd.
185, II Phase G.I.D.C.
396195 Vapi
India
Personnel:
  Man. Dir.: A. N. Shaikh
  Phone: (91) 260 2432686
  Dir.: Saifan K. Shaikh
  Phone: (91) 98 25111986
Total Employees at this Location: 64
Mill Locations:
R A Shaikh Paper Mills Pvt. Ltd., Valsad Mill, 185, II Phase G.I.D.C., 396195 Vapi, India, Capacity: 18,000 mt/y, (Paper mill)

ⓄR A Shaikh Paper Mills Pvt. Ltd.
Valsad Mill
185, II Phase G.I.D.C.
396195 Vapi, Gujarat
India
Personnel:
  Man. Dir.: Mr. A. N. Shaikh
  Phone: (91) 260 2432686
  Dir.: Saifan K. Shaikh
  Phone: (91) 98 25111986
Total Employees at this Location: 64
Type of Operation: Paper mill
Paper/Paperboard Grades and Capacities:
Total paper and paperboard capacity: 18,000 mt/y
Packaging papers

ⓄⓂThe Rahuri Pulp & Paper Mills
Ahmednagar Mill
Shri Shivajinagar, Tal. Rahuri
413 706 Ahmednagar, Maharashtra
India
  Phone: (91) 2426 251447/451
  Fax: (91) 2426 251436
Personnel:
  Man. Dir.: P. B. Tanpure
  Phone: (91) 2426 251447/451
  Mill Mgr.: B. P. Jundre
  Phone: (91) 2426 251447/451
  Man. Dir.: N. M. Chavan
  Phone: (91) 2426 251447/451
Total Employees at this Location: 100
Type of Operation: Paper mill
Pulp Mill Data:
Chemical Pulping Systems:
Batch digesters: 4
Paper/Paperboard Grades and Capacities:
Total paper and paperboard capacity: 9,000 mt/y
Packaging papers: 9,000 mt/y
Paper and Paperboard Mill Data:
Stock Preparation:
Refiners: 2
Paper Machines: 1
No. 1, fourdrinier, Trim width 2.4 m, Packaging papers

ⓄRainbow Papers Ltd.
801, Avdhesh House, Opp. Shri Govind Gurudwara,
S.G. Highway
380054 Ahmedabad, Gujarat
India
  Phone: (91) 79 2685 5714/5716
  Fax: (91) 79 26855712
  Email: info@rainbowpapers.com
  Web Address: www.rainbowpapers.com
Personnel:
  Man. Dir.: Mr. Ajay Goenka
  Phone: (91) 79 2685 5714/5716
  Fax: (91) 79 26855712
  Email: ajaygoenka7@hotmail.com
  Exec. Dir., VP Commercial : Mr. Rahul Maheshveri
  Phone: (91) 79 2685 5714/5716
  Fax: (91) 79 26855712
  Chmn of Board: Mr. Rajendra Patawari
  Phone: (91) 98250 31951
  Chmn Audit committee : Mr. Shashikant Thakar
  Independent Director: Mr. Kantibhai Patel
Total Employees of Company: 330
Total Employees at this Location: 30
Mill Locations:
Rainbow Papers Ltd., Mehsana Mill, 1453, Vill. Rajpur, Taluka Kadi, Kalol-Mehsana Highway, 382715 Mehsana, India, Capacity: 291,562 mt/y, (Paper mill)
  Phone: (91) 2764 278492/3
  Fax: (91) 2764 278492
  Email: info@rainbowpapers.com

India

ⓂRainbow Papers Ltd.
Mehsana Mill
1453, Vill. Rajpur, Taluka Kadi, Kalol-Mehsana Highway
382715 Mehsana, Gujarat
India
  Phone: (91) 2764 278492/3
  Fax: (91) 2764 278492
  Email: info@rainbowpapers.com
  Web Address: www.rainbowpapers.com
Personnel:
  Exec. Dir.: Mr. Rahul Maheshwari
  Snr. VP Finance: Mrs. Niyati Agarwal
  VP Production: Mr. P. C. Jain
  VP Product & Developement: Mr. K. C. Majumdar
  VP Power: Mr. J. B. Suhag
Total Employees at this Location: 300
Type of Operation: Paper mill
Pulp Grades and Capacities:
  Total pulp capacity: 164,194 mt/y
  Recycled Pulping: 164,194 mt/y
Pulp Mill Data:
Pulp Lines: 2
  Bleach Plant Systems: 1
  No. 1, Type: recycled pulp
Paper/Paperboard Grades and Capacities:
  Total paper and paperboard capacity: 291,562 mt/y
  Newsprint: 35,700 mt/y
  Uncoated woodfree/freesheet: 165,898 mt/y
  Boxboard/cartonboard: 89,964 mt/y
Paper and Paperboard Mill Data:
Paper Machines: 5
  No. 2, cylinder, total capacity 21,420 mt/y, Trim width 2.14 m, Boxboard/cartonboard
  No. 4, cylinder, total capacity 17,850 mt/y, Trim width 2.14 m, Boxboard/cartonboard
  No. 6, cylinder, total capacity 50,694 mt/y, Trim width 2.24 m, Boxboard/cartonboard
  No. 7, (second hand, started up August 2009), fourdrinier, total capacity 79,611 mt/y, Trim width 4.5 m, Newsprint, Uncoated woodfree/freesheet
  No. 8, fourdrinier, total capacity 121,987 mt/y, Trim width 4.5 m, Uncoated woodfree/freesheet
Coating Machines: 3
  PM 2, total capacity 21,000 mt/y., on machine
  PM 4, total capacity 18,000 mt/y., on machine
  PM 6, total capacity 51,000 mt/y., on machine
Energy Data:
  Power boilers
  Steam turbines: 2 at 5, 10 MW
  Electrical demand for mill: 410 MWh/D

①ⓂRajesh Paper Mills Ltd.
Shikohabad Mill
Bara Pech, Village Asua
205 135 Shikohabad, Uttar Pradesh
India
  Phone: (91) 5676 234343/4543
  Fax: (91) 5676 234340
Personnel:
  Dir. Gen.: Vishrut K. Vora
  Phone: (91) 5676 234343/4543
Total Employees at this Location: 100
Type of Operation: Paper mill
Paper/Paperboard Grades and Capacities:
  Total paper and paperboard capacity: 6,000 mt/y
  Packaging papers
Paper and Paperboard Mill Data:
  Stock Preparation:
  Refiners: 3
Paper Machines: 2
  No. 1, fourdrinier, Trim width 1.66 m, Packaging papers
  No. 2, fourdrinier, Trim width 2.34 m, Packaging papers
Finishing Equipment:
  Rewinders: 2
  Sheeters: 2
Energy Data:
  Power boilers: 1

ⓂShree Rama Newsprint Ltd.
Barbhodan Mill
Ownership: 59.79% by The West Coast Paper Mills Ltd.
Taluka Olpad
395 005 Barbhodan, Surat District, Gujarat
India
  Phone: (91) 2621 224 203/204/205
  Fax: (91) 2621 224 206
  Email: ramanpl_ad1@sanchamet.in, ramasurat@ramanewsprint.com
  Web Address: www.ramanewsprint.com
Personnel:
  Pres. (Works): Shri B. S. Mundra
  Phone: (91) 2621 224 211
  Email: bsmundra@ramanewsprint.com
  Chmn.: Shri Shree Kumar Bangur
  Phone: (91) 2621 224 203/204/205
  Exec. Dir.: Shri Vaishnav Das Bajaj
  Phone: (91) 2621 224 203/204/205
  Joint Pres. (Works): Shri A. K. Bhatia
  Phone: (91) 2621 224215
  Senior VP: Shri B. K. Surana
  Phone: (91) 2621 224 223
  Email: bksurana@ramanewsprint.com
  VP (Purch. & Mat.): Shri C.L. Gupta
  Phone: (91) 2621 224 203/204/205
  VP (Utility): Shri K. D. Mantri
  Phone: (91) 2621 224 216
  Email: kdmantri@ramanewsprint.com
Total Employees at this Location: 500
Type of Operation: Paper mill
Pulp Grades and Capacities:
  Total pulp capacity: 62,277 mt/y
  Recycled Pulping: 62,277 mt/y
Pulp Mill Data:
  Bleach Plant Systems: 1
  DIP, Sequence: P
  Recycled Fiber Treatment Lines:
  Flotation deinking lines: 2 at 138,000 admt/y
  Pulpers: 2 at 138,000 admt/y
Paper/Paperboard Grades and Capacities:
  Total paper and paperboard capacity: 132,090 mt/y
  Newsprint: 60,690 mt/y
  Uncoated woodfree/freesheet: 71,400 mt/y
Paper and Paperboard Mill Data:
Paper Machines: 2
  No. 1, fourdrinier, total capacity 60,690 mt/y, Trim width 5.35 m, Newsprint
  No. 2, fourdrinier, total capacity 71,400 mt/y, Trim width 6.32 m, Uncoated woodfree/freesheet
Finishing Equipment:
  Rewinders: 2 at 150,000 mt/y
  Sheeters: 3 at 20,000 mt/y
Energy Data:
  Power boilers: 3
  Steam turbines: 3 at 8, 8.5, 23 MW
  Electrical demand for mill: 304 MWh/D

①Rama Paper Mills Ltd.
12/22, 2nd floor, East Patel Nagar
110 008 New Delhi
India
  Phone: (91) 11 2585 0503/1785
  Fax: (91) 11 25762624
  Email: delhi@ramapaper.com, mpl@nda.vsnl.net.in
  Web Address: www.ramapaper.com
Personnel:
  Chmn./Man. Dir.: Pramod Kumar
  Phone: (91) 11 2585 0503/1785
  Fax: (91) 11 25762624
  Email: cmd@ramapaper.com
  Exec. Dir.: Arun Goel
  Phone: (91) 11 2585 0503/1785
  Fax: (91) 11 25762624
  Sr. Tech. Mgr.: Dr. Y. P. Singh
  Phone: (91) 11 2585 0503/1785
  Fax: (91) 11 25762624
  Prod. Mgr.: R. K. Bhatia
  Phone: (91) 11 2585 0503/1785
  Fax: (91) 11 25762624
  Mktg. Mgr.: Anurag Garg
  Phone: (91) 11 2585 0503/1785
  Fax: (91) 11 25762624
Mill Locations:
  Rama Paper Mills Ltd., Bijnor Mill, 4th Km Stone, Najibabad Rd., 746 731 Kiratpur, Bijnor, India, Capacity: 57,500 mt/y, (Paper mill)
  Phone: (91) 1341 240300/301
  Fax: (91) 1341 225302
  Email: works@ramapaper.com

①Rama Paper Mills Ltd.
Bijnor Mill
4th Km Stone, Najibabad Rd.
746 731 Kiratpur, Bijnor, Uttar Pradesh
India
  Phone: (91) 1341 240300/301
  Fax: (91) 1341 225302
  Email: works@ramapaper.com
  Web Address: www.ramapaper.com
Personnel:
  Chmn./Man. Dir.: Pramod Kumar Agarwal
  Phone: (91) 1341 240300/301
  Email: cmd@ramapaper.com
Total Employees at this Location: 400
Type of Operation: Paper mill
Pulp Grades and Capacities:
  Total pulp capacity: 55,945 mt/y
  Recycled Pulping: 55,945 mt/y
Pulp Mill Data:
  Bleach Plant Systems: 2
  Recycled Pulping System
  Recycled Pulping System
  Recycled Fiber Treatment Lines:
  Flotation deinking lines: 2
  Recycled packaging pulping lines: 1
Paper/Paperboard Grades and Capacities:
  Total paper and paperboard capacity: 57,500 mt/y
  Newsprint: 23,000 mt/y
  Uncoated woodfree/freesheet: 13,250 mt/y
  Tissue: 8,750 mt/y
  Boxboard/cartonboard: 12,500 mt/y
Paper and Paperboard Mill Data:
Paper Machines: 4
  No. 1, multi-wire, total capacity 12,500 mt/y, Trim width 1.75 m, Boxboard/cartonboard
  No. 2, fourdrinier, total capacity 12,500 mt/y, Trim width 2.2 m, Newsprint, Uncoated woodfree/freesheet
  No. 3, fourdrinier, total capacity 20,000 mt/y, Trim width 2.7 m, Newsprint
  No. 4, fourdrinier, total capacity 12,500 mt/y, Trim width 4.2 m, Uncoated woodfree/freesheet, Tissue
Coating Machines: 1
  PM 1, on machine
Energy Data:
  Power boilers
  Steam turbines: 1 at 6 MW
  Electrical demand for mill: 159 MWh/D

ⓂRama Pulp & Papers Ltd.
Vapi, Dist. Valsad Mill
Ownership: The West Coast Paper Mills Ltd.
292-294 GIDC
396 195 Vapi, Dist. Valsad, Gujarat
India
  Phone: (91) 260 2992 115 / 3296 710
  Fax: (91) 260 2430 880
  Email: paper@nathgroup.com, val_ramavapi@sanchamet.in
  Web Address: www.ramapulp.com
Personnel:
  Mill Dir.: Akhilesh Kumar Sharma
  Phone: (91) 9374 986 674
  Email: ak_sharma05@yahoo.co.in
Total Employees at this Location: 250
Type of Operation: Paper mill

India

Pulp Grades and Capacities:
Total pulp capacity: 9,900 mt/y
Pulp Mill Data:
Chemical Pulping Systems:
Batch digesters: 6
Paper/Paperboard Grades and Capacities:
Total paper and paperboard capacity: 15,000 mt/y
Uncoated woodfree/freesheet: 10,000 mt/y
Tissue: 5,000 mt/y
Paper and Paperboard Mill Data:
Stock Preparation:
Pulpers: 1
Refiners: 2
Paper Machines: 2
No. 1, combination, total capacity 10,000 mt/y, Trim width 2.55 m, Uncoated woodfree/freesheet
No. 2, Yankee dryer, total capacity 5,000 mt/y, Trim width 2.3 m, Tissue
Finishing Equipment:
Rewinders: 1 at 20,000 mt/y
Sheeters: 1 at 5,000 mt/y
Energy Data:
Power boilers: 1
Electrical demand for mill: 3 MWh/D

ⓄⓂRama Shyma Papers Ltd.
Bareilly Mill
Rajau Paraspur, 12th Km Faridpur Rd.
234001 Bareilly, Uttar Pradesh
India
  Phone: (91) 581 274034/874
  Fax: (91) 581 2572516
  Email: ramashyma@rediffmail.com
  Web Address: www.eindiabusiness.com/ramashymapapers
Personnel:
  Man. Dir.: Punit Kumar Agrawal
  Phone: (91) 581 274034/874
Type of Operation: Paper mill
Paper/Paperboard Grades and Capacities:
Total paper and paperboard capacity: 10,800 mt/y
Packaging papers

ⓄⓂRaman Boards Ltd.
Mysore Mill
Ownership: 100% by ABB Limited
Mysore Ooty Road, Thandava Pura
571325 Mysore, Karnataka
India
  Phone: (91) 821 – 2536100
  Fax: (91) 8221 – 228608
  Email: balaji.bs@in.abb.com
  Web Address: www.ramanboards.com
Personnel:
  Chmn.: T. A. Subba Rao
  Phone: (91) 8221 228609/10/11
  Man. Dir.: Aroon Raman
  Phone: (91) 8221 228609/10/11
  Email: aroonraman@ramanboards.com
  Group Adviser (Corp.): T. A. Subba Rao
  Phone: (91) 8221 228609/10/11
  Gen. Mgr. (Operations): Dr. M. S. Chandrashekhar
  Phone: (91) 8221 228609/10/11
  Gen. Mgr. Finan. & Co. Secr.: V. S. Kumar
  Phone: (91) 8221 228609/10/11
  Gen. Mgr. Mktg.: Ravishankar Raju
  Phone: (91) 8221 228609/10/11
  Prod. Mgr.: P. S. Tilak
  Phone: (91) 8221 228609/10/11
  Dpty. Gen. Mgr. (Sls.&Mktg.): S. Ravikumar
  Phone: (91) 8221 228609/10/11
  Email: sravikumar@ramanboards.com
  Mgr. Proj. & Liasion: K. S. Shankar Prasad
  Phone: (91) 8221 228609/10/11
Total Employees at this Location: 160
Type of Operation: Paperboard mill
Paper/Paperboard Grades and Capacities:
Total paper and paperboard capacity: 6,000 mt/y
Packaging papers: 3,000 mt/y
Boxboard/cartonboard: 3,000 mt/y

Paper and Paperboard Mill Data:
Stock Preparation:
Refiners: 8
Paper Machines: 4
No. 1, total capacity 2,000 mt/y, Trim width 3.2 m, Boxboard/cartonboard
No. 2, total capacity 2,000 mt/y, Trim width 3.2 m, Boxboard/cartonboard
No. 3, Trim width 4 m, Packaging papers
No. 4, Trim width 4 m, Packaging papers
Energy Data:
Power boilers: 2

ⓄRampal Paper Mills
Jadupur Vill. & P.O. Dhumadhigi
732101 Dist. Malda
India
  Email: pinkajr@dte.vsnl.net.in
Mill Locations:
Rampal Paper Mills, Dist. Malda Mill, Jadupur Vill. & P.O. Dhumadhigi, 732101 Dist. Malda, India, Capacity: 6,600 mt/y, (Paper mill, Paperboard mill)
  Email: pinkajr@dte.vsnl.net.in

ⓄRampal Paper Mills
Dist. Malda Mill
Jadupur Vill. & P.O. Dhumadhigi
732101 Dist. Malda, West Bengal
India
  Email: pinkajr@dte.vsnl.net.in
Type of Operation: Paper mill, Paperboard mill
Paper/Paperboard Grades and Capacities:
Total paper and paperboard capacity: 6,600 mt/y
Specialty and industrial
Linerboard
Boxboard/cartonboard

ⓄRana Papers Ltd.
8 Km Jansath Rd.
251001 Muzaffarnagar
India
  Phone: (91) 131 2661612/1712
  Fax: (91) 131 2661104
  Email: info@ranapapers.com
  Web Address: www.ranapapers.com
Personnel:
  Man. Dir.: Noor Salim Rana
  Phone: (91) 131 2661612/1712
  Fax: (91) 131 2661104
Mill Locations:
Rana Papers Ltd., Muzaffarnagar Mill, 8 Km Jansath Rd., 251001 Muzaffarnagar, India, Capacity: 50,000 mt/y, (Paper mill)
  Phone: (91) 131 2661612/1712
  Fax: (91) 131 2661104
  Email: info@ranapapers.com

ⓂRana Papers Ltd.
Muzaffarnagar Mill
8 Km Jansath Rd.
251001 Muzaffarnagar, Uttar Pradesh
India
  Phone: (91) 131 2661612/1712
  Fax: (91) 131 2661104
  Email: info@ranapapers.com
  Web Address: www.ranapapers.com
Personnel:
  Man. Dir.: Noor Salim Rana
  Phone: (91) 9837062912
Type of Operation: Paper mill
Paper/Paperboard Grades and Capacities:
Total paper and paperboard capacity: 50,000 mt/y
Packaging papers
Linerboard: 50,000 mt/y
Paper and Paperboard Mill Data:
Paper Machines: 2
PM 1
PM 2, Linerboard
Energy Data:
Turbines at 6 MW

ⓄRavindra Paper Mills (P) Ltd.
Mann Industrial Estate, Chiao, Kaithal Rd.
Karnal
India
Personnel:
  Man. Dir.: Ravir Singh Mann
Mill Locations:
Ravindra Paper Mills (P) Ltd., Karnal Mill, Mann Industrial Estate, Chiao, Kaithal Rd., Karnal, India, Capacity: 14,400 mt/y, (Paper mill)

ⓂRavindra Paper Mills (P) Ltd.
Karnal Mill
Mann Industrial Estate, Chiao, Kaithal Rd.
Karnal, Haryana
India
Personnel:
  Man. Dir.: Ravir Singh Mann
Type of Operation: Paper mill
Paper/Paperboard Grades and Capacities:
Total paper and paperboard capacity: 14,400 mt/y
Packaging papers

ⓄRayana Paper & Board Industries Ltd.
Rayana Regency, Rustampur West
273005 Gorakhpur, Uttar Pradesh
India
  Phone: (91) 551 2320977
  Fax: (91) 551 2320791
  Email: rayanapaper@gmail.com
Mill Locations:
Rayana Paper & Board Industries Ltd., Basti Mill, Village Dhaurahara, Deegha, Khalilabad, Basti, India, Capacity: 14,850 mt/y, (Pulp mill, Paper mill)

ⓂRayana Paper & Board Industries Ltd.
Basti Mill
Village Dhaurahara, Deegha, Khalilabad
Basti, Uttar Pradesh
India
Personnel:
  Man. Dir.: Lal Ji Singh
  Fax: (91) 5547 222959
  Prod. Mgr.: S. Murliyadar
  Finan. Mgr.: Titendra Gupta
  Phone: (91) 551 3097522
  Fax: (91) 5547 22959
  Dir.: Ramji Singh
  Fax: (91) 5547 222959
Total Employees at this Location: 77
Type of Operation: Pulp mill, Paper mill
Pulp Mill Data:
Chemical Pulping Systems:
Continuous digesters: 10
Paper/Paperboard Grades and Capacities:
Total paper and paperboard capacity: 14,850 mt/y
Packaging papers: 14,850 mt/y
Paper and Paperboard Mill Data:
Stock Preparation:
Pulpers: 2
Refiners: 5
Paper Machines: 1
PM 1, total capacity 14,850 mt/y, Trim width 2 m, Packaging papers
Finishing Equipment:
Rewinders: 1 at 14,850 mt/y
Sheeters: 1
Energy Data:
Power boilers: 1

ⓂReliable Paper (India) Pvt. Ltd.
Surat Mill
Ownership: Speciality Papers Ltd.
Village Tarsadi, Bardoli, Mahuva Road
394601 Bardoli, Taluka - Mahuva, Surat, Gujarat
India
  Phone: (91) 2625 254085
  Email: reliable@reliablepaperindia.com

India

Web Address: www.reliablepaperindia.com
Total Employees at this Location: 270
Type of Operation: Paper mill
Pulp Grades and Capacities:
 Total pulp capacity: 59,441 mt/y
 Recycled Pulping: 59,441 mt/y
Pulp Mill Data:
 Bleach Plant Systems: 1
 Recycled Pulping System
 Recycled Fiber Treatment Lines:
 Flotation deinking lines: 1
 Recycled packaging pulping lines: 1
Paper/Paperboard Grades and Capacities:
 Total paper and paperboard capacity: 65,000 mt/y
 Tissue: 6,000 mt/y
 Specialty and industrial: 9,000 mt/y
 Boxboard/cartonboard: 50,000 mt/y
Paper and Paperboard Mill Data:
Paper Machines: 2
 No. 1, fourdrinier, total capacity 15,000 mt/y, Trim width 2.35 m, Uncoated woodfree/freesheet, Specialty and industrial
 No. 2, Fourdrinier (4), total capacity 50,000 mt/y, Trim width 1.75 m, Boxboard/cartonboard
Coating Machines: 1
 PM2
Energy Data:
 Power boilers
 Electrical demand for mill: 94 MWh/D

ⓜ Remco Paper & Board Industries Pvt. Ltd.
Shop no. S5, Vijayshree Apartment, Tatya Gharpure Path, Opposite Mangal wadi, Mumbad lane, Girgaun
400004 Mumbai, Maharashtra
India
 Phone: (91) 22 2380 4555/5565
 Fax: (91) 22 23804544
 Email: info@remcopapers.com
 Web Address: www.remcopapers.com
Personnel:
 Man. Dir.: Paresh Mangaldas Dharia
 Phone: (91) 22 2380 4555/5565
 Fax: (91) 22 23804544
 Dir.: Mrs. Rekha Dharia
 Phone: (91) 22 2380 4555/5565
 Fax: (91) 22 23804544
 Dir.: Kunal Dharia
 Phone: (91) 22 2380 4555/5565
 Fax: (91) 22 23804544
Mill Locations:
Remco Paper & Board Industries Pvt. Ltd., Valsad Mill, 205-206 G.I.D.C. Vapi Pardi, 396195 Valsad, India, Capacity: 22,000 mt/y, (Paper mill, Paperboard mill)
 Phone: (91) 260 2401585/2432390
 Fax: (91) 260 2431993

ⓜ Remco Paper & Board Industries Pvt. Ltd.
Valsad Mill
205-206 G.I.D.C. Vapi Pardi
396195 Valsad, Gujarat
India
 Phone: (91) 260 2401585/2432390
 Fax: (91) 260 2431993
 Web Address: www.remcopapers.com
Personnel:
 Prod. Dir.: Sunny Dharia
 Phone: (91) 260 2401585/2432390
Total Employees at this Location: 250
Type of Operation: Paper mill, Paperboard mill
Paper/Paperboard Grades and Capacities:
 Total paper and paperboard capacity: 22,000 mt/y
 Packaging papers
 Specialty and industrial
 Boxboard/cartonboard: 22,000 mt/y
Paper and Paperboard Mill Data:
Paper Machines: 2
 No. 1
 No. 2

ⓜ Rolex Paper Mills Ltd.
Vill. Chinta Parru Mill
4-96, Palakol Mandal
534 250 Vill. Chinta Parru, A.P.
India
 Phone: (91) 8816 228997/228998
 Fax: (91) 8814 228627
 Email: rolex_paper@yahoo.co.in
Personnel:
 Man. Dir.: Mr. P.V. Narasimha Raju
 Phone: (91) 8816 228997/228998
 Dir.: Mr. Rao
 Phone: (91) 8816 228997/228998
Type of Operation: Paper mill
Paper/Paperboard Grades and Capacities:
 Total paper and paperboard capacity: 20,000 mt/y
 Newsprint
 Uncoated woodfree/freesheet
 Packaging papers

ⓜ Roshan Lal Paper Mills Pvt Ltd
Mansa Road
151001 Bhatinda
India
 Phone: (91) 164 2212153
 Fax: (91) 164 2213217
Personnel:
 Dir.: Jander
 Phone: (91) 164 2212153
 Fax: (91) 164 2213217
Mill Locations:
Roshan Lal Paper Mills Pvt Ltd, Bhatinda Mill, Mansa Road, 151001 Bhatinda, India, Capacity: 6,600 mt/y, (Paper mill)
 Phone: (91) 164 2212153
 Fax: (91) 164 2213217

ⓜ Roshan Lal Paper Mills Pvt Ltd
Bhatinda Mill
Mansa Road
151001 Bhatinda, Punjab
India
 Phone: (91) 164 2212153
 Fax: (91) 164 2213217
Personnel:
 Dir.: Mr Jander
 Phone: (91) 164 2212153
Type of Operation: Paper mill
Paper/Paperboard Grades and Capacities:
 Total paper and paperboard capacity: 6,600 mt/y
 Packaging papers: 6,600 mt/y

ⓜ Ruby Macons Ltd.
Ownership: 100% by MeadWestvaco Corporation
A-203/204, Angelina Apartments, Sarojini Road, Vile Parle (W)
400056 Mumbai, Maharashtra
India
 Phone: (91) 22 26186771/772
 Fax: (91) 22 26186773
 Email: bombay@rubymacons.com
 Web Address: rubymacons.com
Personnel:
 Man. Dir.: Ashraf Nathani
 Phone: (91) 22 26186771/772
 Fax: (91) 22 26186773
 Exec. Dir.: Arshad Nathani
 Phone: (91) 22 26186771/772
 Fax: (91) 22 26186773
Total Employees of Company: 500
Total Employees at this Location: 3
Mill Locations:
Ruby Macons Ltd., Morai Mill, Survey No.56/1, Morai, India, Capacity: 92,820 mt/y, (Paperboard mill)
 Email: mail@rubymacons.com
Ruby Macons Ltd., Vapi Mill, 789/4, 3rd Phase Road G.I.D.C., 396 195 Vapi, India, Capacity: 64,260 mt/y, (Paperboard mill)
 Phone: (91) 260 3050000
 Fax: (91) 260 2410910
 Email: mail@rubymacons.com

ⓞⓜ Ruby Macons Ltd.
Morai Mill
Ownership: 100% by MeadWestvaco Corporation
Survey No.56/1
Morai, Gujarat
India
 Email: mail@rubymacons.com
 Web Address: rubymacons.com
Total Employees of Company: 500
Total Employees at this Location: 250
Type of Operation: Paperboard mill
Mill Locations:
Ruby Macons Ltd., Vapi Mill, 789/4, 3rd Phase Road G.I.D.C., 396 195 Vapi, India, Capacity: 64,260 mt/y, (Paperboard mill)
 Phone: (91) 260 3050000
 Fax: (91) 260 2410910
 Email: mail@rubymacons.com
Pulp Grades and Capacities:
 Total pulp capacity: 92,067 mt/y
 Recycled Pulping: 92,067 mt/y
Pulp Mill Data:
 Recycled Fiber Treatment Lines:
 Recycled packaging pulping lines
Paper/Paperboard Grades and Capacities:
 Total paper and paperboard capacity: 92,820 mt/y
 Linerboard: 69,615 mt/y
 Corrugating medium/fluting: 23,205 mt/y
Paper and Paperboard Mill Data:
Paper Machines: 1
 RM 3, fourdrinier (3), total capacity 92,820 mt/y, Trim width 4.4 m, Linerboard, Corrugating medium/fluting
Energy Data:
 Power boilers: 2
 Steam turbines: 2 at 4.95, 1.2 MW
 Electrical demand for mill: 118 MWh/D

ⓜ Ruby Macons Ltd.
Vapi Mill
Ownership: 100% by MeadWestvaco Corporation
789/4, 3rd Phase Road G.I.D.C.
396 195 Vapi, Gujarat
India
 Phone: (91) 260 3050000
 Fax: (91) 260 2410910
 Email: mail@rubymacons.com
 Web Address: www.rubymacons.com
Personnel:
 Man. Dir.: Ashraf Nathani
 Phone: (91) 260 3050000
 Exec. Dir.: Arshad Nathani
 Phone: (91) 260 3050000
Total Employees at this Location: 250
Type of Operation: Paperboard mill
Pulp Grades and Capacities:
 Total pulp capacity: 63,980 mt/y
 Recycled Pulping: 63,980 mt/y
Pulp Mill Data:
 Recycled Fiber Treatment Lines:
 Recycled packaging pulping lines: 2
Paper/Paperboard Grades and Capacities:
 Total paper and paperboard capacity: 64,260 mt/y
 Linerboard: 28,560 mt/y
 Corrugating medium/fluting: 10,710 mt/y
 Boxboard/cartonboard: 24,990 mt/y
Paper and Paperboard Mill Data:
Paper Machines: 2
 RM 1, fourdrinier, total capacity 24,990 mt/y, Trim width 2.1 m, Boxboard/cartonboard
 RM 2, fourdrinier, total capacity 39,270 mt/y, Trim width 3.2 m, Linerboard, Corrugating medium/fluting
Energy Data:
 Power boilers: 1
 Steam turbines: 1 at 2 MW
 Electrical demand for mill: 82 MWh/D

India

ⓜRuchira Papers Ltd.
Kala-Amb Mill
Trilokpur Rd.
173 030 Kala-Amb, Himachal Pradesh
India
Email: info@ruchirapapers.com
Web Address: www.ruchirapapers.com
Total Employees at this Location: 490
Type of Operation: Paper mill, Paperboard mill
Pulp Grades and Capacities:
Total pulp capacity: 101,627 mt/y
Recycled Pulping: 54,449 mt/y
Other Pulp: 47,178 mt/y
Pulp Mill Data:
Chemical Pulping Systems:
Batch digesters
Pulp Lines: 2
Bleach Plant Systems: 2
Chemical Pulping System, Type: Bagasse/Straw,
Sequence: C/DEoD
Recycled Pulping System
Chemical Recovery Equipment:
Recovery boilers: 1
Recycled Fiber Treatment Lines:
Flotation deinking lines: 1
Recycled packaging pulping lines: 1
Paper/Paperboard Grades and Capacities:
Total paper and paperboard capacity: 105,600 mt/y
Uncoated woodfree/freesheet: 52,800 mt/y
Linerboard: 39,680 mt/y
Boxboard/cartonboard: 13,120 mt/y
Paper and Paperboard Mill Data:
Paper Machines: 3
No. 1, fourdrinier (3), total capacity 20,000 mt/y, Trim width 2.1 m, Linerboard
No. 2, fourdrinier (3), total capacity 32,800 mt/y, Trim width 2.33 m, Linerboard, Boxboard/cartonboard
No. 3, fourdrinier, total capacity 52,800 mt/y, Trim width 3.25 m, Uncoated woodfree/freesheet
Energy Data:
Power boilers
Steam turbines: 1 at 7.2 MW
Electrical demand for mill: 253 MWh/D

ⓞⓜS.N. Paper Mills (P) Ltd.
Dist. Ludhiana Mill
Vill. Mannewal, P.O. Ladhowal
141008 Dist. Ludhiana, Punjab
India
Phone: (91) 161 5040680/1, 92 1614 1683
Email: snpaper@sify.com
Web Address: www.snpapermills.com
Personnel:
Dir.: Gurtej Singh Gill
Phone: (91) 98 15041681
Sls. & Mktg. Mgr.: Amrinder Singh Gill
Phone: (91) 92 16241683
Total Employees at this Location: 100
Type of Operation: Paper mill, Paperboard mill
Paper/Paperboard Grades and Capacities:
Total paper and paperboard capacity: 10,800 mt/y
Packaging papers
Linerboard: 10,800 mt/y
Boxboard/cartonboard
Paper and Paperboard Mill Data:
Paper Machines: 1
No. 1, total capacity 10,800 mt/y, Boxboard/cartonboard, Packaging papers, Linerboard

ⓞSabarmati Papers Pvt Limited
Ownership: 100% by private owners
604, Aditya, Opp. Sardar Patel Seva Samaj, Mithakhali Six Roads
380 006 Ellisbridge, Ahmedabad, Gujarat
India
Phone: (91) 79 2640 2858/26463544
Fax: (91) 79 2640 6137
Email: sabarmatipapers@email.com
Web Address: www.sabarmatipapers.com
Personnel:
Chmn. & Man. Dir.: Mahendra G. Patel
Phone: (91) 79 2640 2858/26463544
Fax: (91) 79 2640 6137
Total Employees of Company: 250
Total Employees at this Location: 10
Mill Locations:
Sabarmati Papers Limited, Aglo Mill, Village Aglod, Taluka Vijapur, 382805 Dist. Mehsana, India, Capacity: 26,250 mt/y, (Paperboard mill)
Phone: (91) 2763 283723 /759
Fax: (91) 2763 283318
Email: info@sabarmatipapers.com

ⓜSabarmati Papers Limited
Aglo Mill
Ownership: 100% by Sabarmati Papers Pvt Limited
Village Aglod, Taluka Vijapur
382805 Dist. Mehsana, Gujarat
India
Phone: (91) 2763 283723 /759
Fax: (91) 2763 283318
Email: info@sabarmatipapers.com
Web Address: www.sabarmatipapers.com
Personnel:
Chmn. & Man. Dir.: Mahendra G. Patel M
Phone: (91) 26406138
Fax: (91) 26406134
Total Employees at this Location: 240
Type of Operation: Paperboard mill
Pulp Grades and Capacities:
Total pulp capacity: 18,139 mt/y
Recycled Pulping: 18,139 mt/y
Pulp Mill Data:
Recycled Fiber Treatment Lines:
Recycled packaging pulping lines: 1
Paper/Paperboard Grades and Capacities:
Total paper and paperboard capacity: 26,250 mt/y
Boxboard/cartonboard: 26,250 mt/y
Paper and Paperboard Mill Data:
Stock Preparation:
Pulpers: 4
Refiners: 3
Paper Machines: 1
No. 1, cylinder (7), total capacity 26,250 mt/y, Trim width 1.6 m, Boxboard/cartonboard
Coating Machines: 1
PM1, on machine
Finishing Equipment:
Rewinders: 1
Sheeters: 2
Energy Data:
Power boilers
Steam turbines
Electrical demand for mill: 47 MWh/D

ⓞSaber Group
A - 301, 3rd Floor, Statesman
110001 New Delhi
India
Phone: (91) 11-23354551
Web Address: saber.asia/index.html
Personnel:
Man. Dir.: Dinesh Soin
Phone: (91) 11-23354551
Joint Man. Dir.: Abhishek Soin
Phone: (91) 11-23354551
Dir.: Nitin Khanna
Phone: (91) 11-23354551
Dir.: Ulrich Nyffeler
Phone: (91) 11-23354551
Mill Locations:
Saber Swiss Quality Paper AG, Balsthal Mill, Tiergartenstr. 1, CH-4710 Balsthal, Switzerland, Capacity: 37,000 mt/y, (Paper mill)
Phone: (41) 62 386 4111
Fax: (41) 62 386 4123
Email: info@swissqualitypaper.com

ⓞSaffron Industries Ltd.
Manegaon, Taluka Saoner
440025 Nagpur, Maharashtra
India
Email: mplpaper@nagpur.net.in, madhyadesh@rediffmail.com
Web Address: www.saffronindustries.in
Personnel:
Pres: K. Jain
Phone: (91) 712 2284013
Fax: (91) 7113 232400
Man. Dir.: Nimish Maheshwari
Phone: (91) 712 2284013
Fax: (91) 7113 232400
Total Employees of Company: 135
Mill Locations:
Saffron Industries Ltd., Nagpur Mill, Manegaon, Saoner, 440025 Nagpur, India, Capacity: 21,780 mt/y, (Paper mill)
Phone: (91) 94 2310 4919/2310 5176
Fax: (91) 7113 232400/712 2284015
Email: mplpaper@nagpur.net.in, madhyadesh@rediffmail.com

ⓜSaffron Industries Ltd.
Nagpur Mill
Manegaon, Saoner
440025 Nagpur, Maharashtra
India
Phone: (91) 94 2310 4919/2310 5176
Fax: (91) 7113 232400/712 2284015
Email: mplpaper@nagpur.net.in, madhyadesh@rediffmail.com
Web Address: www.saffronindustries.in
Personnel:
Pres.: Mr. K. C. Jain
Man. Dir.: Mr. Nimish V. Maheshwari
Phone: (91) 712 2284013/17
Mktg. Mgr.: Rajesh Gadge
Phone: (91) 94 23104919
Asst. Mktg. Mgr.: P. S. Thakur
Phone: (91) 94 23105176
Total Employees at this Location: 170
Type of Operation: Paper mill
Pulp Grades and Capacities:
Total pulp capacity: 21,637 mt/y
Recycled Pulping: 21,637 mt/y
Pulp Mill Data:
Bleach Plant Systems: 1
Recycled Pulping System, Type: DIP
Recycled Fiber Treatment Lines:
Flotation deinking lines: 1
Paper/Paperboard Grades and Capacities:
Total paper and paperboard capacity: 21,780 mt/y
Newsprint: 21,780 mt/y
Paper and Paperboard Mill Data:
Paper Machines: 1
No. 1, fourdrinier, total capacity 21,780 mt/y, Trim width 2.72 m, Newsprint
Energy Data:
Power boilers
Steam turbines: 1 at 3.5 MW
Electrical demand for mill: 66 MWh/D

ⓞSai Rayalaseema Paper Mills Ltd. (SRPML)
Ownership: B.V. Satya Sai Prasad & Associates (BVSSPA)
Plot No. 6, H. No. 6-3-569/1/4, 2nd Floor, Rockdale Compound, Opp: RTA Office, Somajiguda
500 082 Hyderabad, A.P.
India
Phone: (91) 40 233 25183
Fax: (91) 40 233 25184
Email: mktg@srpml.com
Web Address: www.srpml.com
Personnel:
Chmn. & Man. Dir.: Shri B. V. Sathya Sai Prasad
Phone: (91) 40 233 25183

India

Fax: (91) 40 233 25184
Email: cmd@srpml.com
VP: B. S. Kanda
Phone: (91) 99 63333360
Email: planning@srpm.com
Total Employees of Company: 675
Total Employees at this Location: 25
Mill Locations:
Sai Rayalaseema Paper Mills Ltd. (SRPML), Kurnool Mill, Vasant Nagar, Gondiparla, 518 004 Kurnool, A.P., India, Capacity: 49,980 mt/y, (Pulp mill, Paper mill)
Phone: (91) 8518 280312/13
Fax: (91) 8518 280130
Email: works@srpml.com, mktg@srpml.com

ⓂSai Rayalaseema Paper Mills Ltd. (SRPML)
Kurnool Mill
Vasant Nagar, Gondiparla
518 004 Kurnool, A.P.
India
Phone: (91) 8518 280312/13
Fax: (91) 8518 280130
Email: works@srpml.com, mktg@srpml.com
Web Address: www.srpml.com
Personnel:
Dir. Works: Shri P. Vaikunta Rao
Phone: (91) 8518 280312/13
Total Employees at this Location: 650
Type of Operation: Pulp mill, Paper mill
Pulp Mill Data:
 Chemical Pulping Systems:
 Batch digesters: 4
Pulp Lines: 1
 Bleach Plant Systems: 1
 Chemical Pulping System, Sequence: CEHH
 Chemical Recovery Equipment:
 Evaporator lines: 1
 Recovery boilers: 1
Paper/Paperboard Grades and Capacities:
 Total paper and paperboard capacity: 49,980 mt/y
 Uncoated woodfree/freesheet: 49,980 mt/y
Paper and Paperboard Mill Data:
 Stock Preparation:
 Pulpers: 2
 Refiners: 13
Paper Machines: 1
No. 1, fourdrinier, total capacity 49,980 mt/y, Trim width 3.47 m, Uncoated woodfree/freesheet
Coating Machines: 1
No. 1, off machine
Finishing Equipment:
 Supercalenders: 1
 Rewinders: 3
 Sheeters: 6
Energy Data:
Power boilers: 4
Combustion turbines: 2 at 15.0 MW
Electrical demand for mill: 125 MWh/D

ⓘⓂSainath Paper Mills
Dist. Valsad Mill
AT. & Post Dungri
396 375 Dist. Valsad, Gujarat
India
Phone: (91) 2632 285226/526
Fax: (91) 2632 285531
Personnel:
Owner: Shashikant Bhai G. Patel
Phone: (91) 94 26482401
Exec. (Sales): A. K. Patel
Phone: (91) 2632 285226/526
Type of Operation: Paper mill, Paperboard mill
Paper/Paperboard Grades and Capacities:
Total paper and paperboard capacity: 10,800 mt/y
Packaging papers
Linerboard: 10,800 mt/y

ⓘSainsons Paper Industries Ltd.
506, 3rd Fl., Sharp Bhawan, Comercial Complex, Azadpur
110033 Delhi
India
Phone: (91) 11 27677608
Fax: (91) 11 27672925
Email: sainsons@indiatimes.com
Web Address: www.sainsons.net
Personnel:
Senior VP: Sushil Kumar Sadana
Phone: (91) 9417 109988
Man. Dir.: Pradeep Saini
Phone: (91) 11 27677608
Fax: (91) 11 27672925
Dir.: Hari Krishan Saini
Phone: (91) 11 27677608
Fax: (91) 11 27672925
Dir.: Sadhu Ram Saini
Phone: (91) 11 27677608
Fax: (91) 11 27672925
Dir.: Bal Krishan Saini
Phone: (91) 11 27677608
Fax: (91) 11 27672925
Mill Locations:
Sainsons Paper Industries Ltd., Kurukshetra Mill, Plot No. 5, Village Bhakli, Pehowa, 136128 Dist. Kurukshetra, India, Capacity: 80,000 mt/y, (Paper mill)
Phone: (91) 1741 220919/220986/221615
Fax: (91) 1741 221086
Email: sainsons@indiatimes.com

ⓜSainsons Paper Industries Ltd.
Kurukshetra Mill
Plot No. 5, Village Bhakli, Pehowa
136128 Dist. Kurukshetra, Haryana
India
Phone: (91) 1741 220919/220986/221615
Fax: (91) 1741 221086
Email: sainsons@indiatimes.com
Web Address: www.sainsons.net
Total Employees at this Location: 185
Type of Operation: Paper mill
Pulp Grades and Capacities:
 Total pulp capacity: 79,099 mt/y
 Recycled Pulping: 35,056 mt/y
 Other Pulp: 44,044 mt/y
Pulp Mill Data:
 Chemical Pulping Systems:
 Batch digesters
 Chemical Recovery Equipment:
 Evaporator lines: 1
 Recovery boilers: 1
 Recycled Fiber Treatment Lines:
 Recycled packaging pulping lines: 1
Paper/Paperboard Grades and Capacities:
Total paper and paperboard capacity: 80,000 mt/y
Linerboard: 34,000 mt/y
Corrugating medium/fluting: 46,000 mt/y
Paper and Paperboard Mill Data:
Paper Machines: 2
No. 1, fourdrinier, total capacity 34,000 mt/y, Trim width 2.28 m, Linerboard
No. 2, fourdrinier, total capacity 46,000 mt/y, Trim width 3.05 m, Corrugating medium/fluting
Energy Data:
Power boilers
Steam turbines at 3 MW
Electrical demand for mill: 140 MWh/D

ⓘⓂSaiyed Paper Mills Ltd.
Vapi Mill
Plot No. 162, II Phase, G.I.D.C., LIC Sector, G. Rd.
396195 Vapi, Gujarat
India
Personnel:
Man. Dir.: Ayoob Y. Saiyed
Phone: (91) 98 24001230
Type of Operation: Paper mill, Paperboard mill

Paper/Paperboard Grades and Capacities:
Total paper and paperboard capacity: 10,000 mt/y
Packaging papers
Linerboard: 10,000 mt/y
Paper and Paperboard Mill Data:
Paper Machines: 1
No. 1, Trim width 2.54 m, Packaging papers, Linerboard

ⓘSandeep Paper Mills Pvt. Ltd.
A-20, Sector IV, Noida, Gautam Budh
201301 Nagar
India
Phone: (91) 91-11-23642750, 91-0120-4208803, 4208804
Fax: (91) 91-11-23653429
Email: sandeeppapernoida@rediff.com
Web Address: www.sandeeppapermills.com
Personnel:
Man. Dir.: J. N. Arora
Phone: (91) 91-11-23642750, 91-0120-4208803, 4208804
Fax: (91) 91-11-23653429
Dir.: Sandeep Arora
Phone: (91) 91-11-23642750, 91-0120-4208803, 4208804
Fax: (91) 91-11-23653429
Email: sandeeparora052@gmail.com
Sls. Mgr.: Sushil Verma
Phone: (91) 91-11-23642750, 91-0120-4208803, 4208804
Fax: (91) 91-11-23653429
Mill Locations:
Sandeep Paper Mills Pvt. Ltd., Noida, Ghaziabad Mill, A-20, Sector IV, Noida, Gautam Budh, 201301 Nagar, India, Capacity: 16,200 mt/y, (Paper mill)
Phone: (91) 91-11-23642750, 91-0120-4208803, 4208804
Fax: (91) 91-11-23653429
Email: sandeeppapernoida@rediff.com

ⓜSandeep Paper Mills Pvt. Ltd.
Noida, Ghaziabad Mill
A-20, Sector IV, Noida, Gautam Budh
201301 Nagar, Uttar Pradesh
India
Phone: (91) 91-11-23642750, 91-0120-4208803, 4208804
Fax: (91) 91-11-23653429
Email: sandeeppapernoida@rediff.com
Personnel:
Man. Dir.: J. N. Arora
Phone: (91) 98 10002970
Dir.: Sandeep Arora
Phone: (91) 98 10367467
Email: sandeeparora052@gmail.com
Type of Operation: Paper mill
Paper/Paperboard Grades and Capacities:
Total paper and paperboard capacity: 16,200 mt/y

ⓘSangal Papers Ltd.
Apsara Cinema Bldg., Mawana Rd
250 002 Meerut, Uttar Pradesh
India
Phone: (91) 1233 271134, 271464, 271515
Fax: (91) 1233 272051
Email: info@sangalpapers.com, sangalpapers@hotmail.com
Web Address: www.sangalpapers.com
Personnel:
Man. Dir.: Himanshi Sangal
Phone: (91) 98370 95263
Email: himanshisangal@hotmail.com
Gen. Mgr. (Plant): S. K. Sadhu
Phone: (91) 98370 99174
Dir.: Amit Sangal
Phone: (91) 98370 43287
Total Employees of Company: 114
Total Employees at this Location: 114
Mill Locations:
Sangal Papers Ltd., Meerut Mill, 22 Km Stone, Bhansa,

India

Mawana Road, 250002 Meerut, India, Capacity: 35,000 mt/y, (Paper mill)
Phone: (91) 1233 271 137/464/515
Fax: (91) 1233 272051
Email: admin@sangalpapers.com

ⓂSangal Papers Ltd.
Meerut Mill
22 Km Stone, Bhansa, Mawana Road
250002 Meerut, Uttar Pradesh
India
Phone: (91) 1233 271 137/464/515
Fax: (91) 1233 272051
Email: admin@sangalpapers.com
Web Address: www.sangalpapers.com
Total Employees at this Location: 70
Type of Operation: Paper mill
Pulp Grades and Capacities:
 Total pulp capacity: 6,000 mt/y
Paper/Paperboard Grades and Capacities:
 Total paper and paperboard capacity: 35,000 mt/y
 Newsprint
 Uncoated mechanical/groundwood
 Packaging papers
Paper and Paperboard Mill Data:
 Stock Preparation:
 Pulpers: 3
 Refiners: 3
Paper Machines: 3
 No. 1, Newsprint
 No. 2, fourdrinier, Trim width 2.4 m, Newsprint
 No. 3, Packaging papers
Finishing Equipment:
 Rewinders: 1
 Sheeters: 6
Energy Data:
 Power boilers: 1
 Steam turbines: 1 at 3 MW
 Electrical demand for mill: 65 MWh/D

ⓁSaraogi Paper Mills (P) Ltd.
Dinajpur Rd.
855107 Kishanganj
India
Phone: (91) 6456 222653/709
Fax: (91) 6456 222553
Mill Locations:
Saraogi Paper Mills (P) Ltd., Kishanganj Mill, Dinajpur Rd., 855107 Kishanganj, India, Capacity: 10,000 mt/y, (Paper mill)
Phone: (91) 6456 222653/709
Fax: (91) 6456 222553

ⓂSaraogi Paper Mills (P) Ltd.
Kishanganj Mill
Dinajpur Rd.
855107 Kishanganj, Bihar
India
Phone: (91) 6456 222653/709
Fax: (91) 6456 222553
Personnel:
 Man. Dir.: Anil Saraogi
 Phone: (91) 94 31232653
 Email: anil_spm@rediffmail.com
 Dir.: Mr. Vikash
 Phone: (91) 6456 222653/709
 Email: vikash.saraogi@email.com
 Dir.: Akash Saraogi
 Phone: (91) 98 00017000
 Email: akash_spm@rediffmail.com
Type of Operation: Paper mill
Paper/Paperboard Grades and Capacities:
 Total paper and paperboard capacity: 10,000 mt/y
 Packaging papers: 10,000 mt/y
Paper and Paperboard Mill Data:
Paper Machines: 1
 PM 1, total capacity 10,000 mt/y, Trim width 2 m, Packaging papers

ⓁSaraswati Udyog India Ltd.
Thidurnal Rd., Kabilarmalai
637204 Namakkal Dist.
India
Phone: (91) 4268 254811/822
Fax: (91) 4268 254822
Email: suil@eth.net
Personnel:
 Chmn.: M. Balusamy
 Phone: (91) 4268 254811/822
 Fax: (91) 4268 254822
 Man. Dir.: B. Mohan
 Phone: (91) 4268 254811/822
 Fax: (91) 4268 254822
 Exec. Dir.: B. Anandhan
 Phone: (91) 4268 254811/822
 Fax: (91) 4268 254822
 Depty. Gen. Mgr.: S. Sathiakeerthi
 Phone: (91) 4268 254811/822
 Fax: (91) 4268 254822
Total Employees at this Location: 500
Mill Locations:
Saraswati Udyog India Ltd., Namakkal Dist. Mill, Thidurnal Rd., Kabilarmalai, 637204 Namakkal Dist., India, Capacity: 65,000 mt/y, (Paperboard mill)
Phone: (91) 4268 254811/822
Fax: (91) 4268 254822
Email: suil@eth.net

ⓂSaraswati Udyog India Ltd.
Namakkal Dist. Mill
Thidurnal Rd., Kabilarmalai
637204 Namakkal Dist., Tamil Nadu
India
Phone: (91) 4268 254811/822
Fax: (91) 4268 254822
Email: suil@eth.net
Personnel:
 Chmn.: Mr. M. Balusamy
 Phone: (91) 4268 254811/822
 Exec. Dir.: Mr. B. Anandhan
 Phone: (91) 4268 254811/822
 Man. Dir.: Mr. B. Mohan
 Phone: (91) 4268 254811/822
 Depty. Gen. Mgr.: Mr. S. Sathiakeerthi
 Phone: (91) 4268 254811/822
 Head of Eng. & Develpt.: Mr. K. Rajiah
 Phone: (91) 4268 254811/822
Total Employees at this Location: 270
Type of Operation: Paperboard mill
Pulp Grades and Capacities:
 Total pulp capacity: 59,876 mt/y
 Recycled Pulping: 59,876 mt/y
Pulp Mill Data:
 Recycled Fiber Treatment Lines:
 Flotation deinking lines: 1
 Pulpers: 4 at 60,000 admt/y
 Recycled packaging pulping lines: 1
Paper/Paperboard Grades and Capacities:
 Total paper and paperboard capacity: 65,000 mt/y
 Boxboard/cartonboard: 65,000 mt/y
Paper and Paperboard Mill Data:
 Stock Preparation:
 Pulpers: 4
 Refiners: 3
Paper Machines: 1
 No. 1, cylinder (8), total capacity 65,000 mt/y, Trim width 2.85 m, Boxboard/cartonboard
Coating Machines: 1
 No. 1, on machine
Finishing Equipment:
 Calenders: 2
 Rewinders: 1 at 22,000 mt/y
 Sheeters: 2 at 48,000 mt/y
Energy Data:
 Power boilers: 1
 Steam turbines: 1 at 5 MW
 Electrical demand for mill: 83 MWh/D

ⓁSardhana Papers (P) Ltd.
Opp. Power Sub. Station, Meerut Rd.
250342 Sardhana
India
Phone: (91) 1237 236226/826
Fax: (91) 1237 236825
Personnel:
 Man. Dir.: Neeraj Gupta
 Phone: (91) 1237 236226/826
 Fax: (91) 1237 236825
 Dir.: Saurabh Gupta
 Phone: (91) 1237 236226/826
 Fax: (91) 1237 236825
Mill Locations:
Sardhana Papers (P) Ltd., Sardhana Mill, Opp. Power Sub. Station, Meerut Rd., 250342 Sardhana, India, Capacity: 16,500 mt/y, (Paper mill)
Phone: (91) 1237 236226/826
Fax: (91) 1237 236825

ⓂSardhana Papers (P) Ltd.
Sardhana Mill
Opp. Power Sub. Station, Meerut Rd.
250342 Sardhana, Uttar Pradesh
India
Phone: (91) 1237 236226/826
Fax: (91) 1237 236825
Personnel:
 Man. Dir.: Neeraj Gupta
 Phone: (91) 1237 236226/826
Type of Operation: Paper mill
Paper/Paperboard Grades and Capacities:
 Total paper and paperboard capacity: 16,500 mt/y
 Packaging papers: 16,500 mt/y
Paper and Paperboard Mill Data:
Paper Machines: 2
 PM 1, Trim width 0.82 m, Packaging papers
 PM 2, Trim width 0.92 m, Packaging papers

ⓁSastha Paper Mills
No.15, Ulagalandhar Mada Street
631502 Kanchipuram
India
Phone: (91) 411 2235840, 044 27294228
Email: sasthapaper@gmail.com
Web Address: www.sasthapaper.com
Personnel:
 Gen. Mgr.: Sanjay Archarya
 Phone: (91) 411 2235840, 044 27294228
Mill Locations:
Sastha Paper Mills, Kanchipuram Mill, No.15, Ulagalandhar Mada Street, 631502 Kanchipuram, India, Capacity: 84,000 mt/y, (Paper mill)
Phone: (91) 411 2235840, 044 27294228
Email: sasthapaper@gmail.com

ⓂSastha Paper Mills
Kanchipuram Mill
No.15, Ulagalandhar Mada Street
631502 Kanchipuram, Tamil Nadu
India
Phone: (91) 411 2235840, 044 27294228
Email: sasthapaper@gmail.com
Web Address: www.sasthapaper.com
Personnel:
 Gen. Mgr.: Sanjay Archarya
 Phone: (91) 411 2235840
Total Employees at this Location: 180
Type of Operation: Paper mill
Pulp Grades and Capacities:
 Total pulp capacity: 83,516 mt/y
 Recycled Pulping: 83,516 mt/y
Pulp Mill Data:
 Recycled Fiber Treatment Lines:
 Recycled packaging pulping lines: 1
Paper/Paperboard Grades and Capacities:
 Total paper and paperboard capacity: 84,000 mt/y
 Linerboard: 70,000 mt/y
 Corrugating medium/fluting: 14,000 mt/y

India

Paper and Paperboard Mill Data:
Paper Machines: 2
No. 1, fourdrinier, total capacity 14,000 mt/y, Trim width 2 m, Corrugating medium/fluting
No. 2, fourdrinier, total capacity 70,000 mt/y, Trim width 4.5 m, Linerboard
Energy Data:
Power boilers
Electrical demand for mill: 97 MWh/D

ⒽⓂSatia Paper Mills Ltd.
Muktsar Mill
Village Rupana, Muktsar Malout Rd.
153032 Dist. Muktsar, Punjab
India
Phone: (91) 1633 262215/2001/3585/62001/63585
Fax: (91) 1633 263499
Email: satiah@jla.vsnl.net.in, satiaho@jla.vsnl.net.in, satiapml@vsnl.com
Personnel:
Chmn. / Man. Dir.: Dr. Ajay Satia
Phone: (91) 1633 262215/2001/3585/62001/63585
Dir.: R. K. Bhandari
Phone: (91) 1633 262215/2001/3585/62001/63585
Email: satiapaper@gmail.com
Pres. (Comm.): Sarv Mittar Wadhwa
Phone: (91) 98 10047567
Email: paper@sarvmittar.com
Pres. (Works): H. K. Gupta
Phone: (91) 1633 262215/2001/3585/62001/63585
Factory Mgr.: Mr. J.R. Sharma
Phone: (91) 1633 262215/2001/3585/62001/63585
Total Employees at this Location: 680
Type of Operation: Paper mill
Pulp Grades and Capacities:
Total pulp capacity: 17,453 mt/y
Chemical Pulp: 17,453 mt/y
Pulp Mill Data:
Chemical Pulping Systems:
Batch digesters: 8
Bleach Plant Systems: 1
No. 1, Sequence: CEHH, Capacity 20,000 admt/y
Paper/Paperboard Grades and Capacities:
Total paper and paperboard capacity: 75,684 mt/y
Uncoated woodfree/freesheet: 75,684 mt/y
Paper and Paperboard Mill Data:
Paper Machines: 4
No. 1, fourdrinier, total capacity 8,211 mt/y, Trim width 2.2 m, Uncoated woodfree/freesheet
No. 2, fourdrinier, total capacity 8,211 mt/y, Trim width 2.2 m, Uncoated woodfree/freesheet
No. 3, (second hand), fourdrinier, total capacity 29,631 mt/y, Trim width 2.8 m, Uncoated woodfree/freesheet
No. 4, fourdrinier, total capacity 29,631 mt/y, Trim width 2.8 m, Uncoated woodfree/freesheet
Finishing Equipment:
Rewinders: 3
Sheeters: 3
Energy Data:
Power boilers: 2
Steam turbines: 1 at 5 MW
Electrical demand for mill: 112 MWh/D

ⒽSatyam Industries Private Ltd.
37, Sector 11, Huda
Panipat, Haryana
India
Phone: (91) 0180 2690140
Personnel:
Man. Dir.: Adesh Aggarwal
Sls. Dir.: Subhash Mittal
Exec. Dir.: Sumit Aggarwal
Phone: (91) 09896711722

Mill Locations:
Satyam Industries Private Ltd., Panipat Mill, Village Pardhana, Tehsil Isran, 132103 Panipat, India, Capacity: 71,000 mt/y, (Paper mill)
Phone: (91) 09996 106922
Fax: (91) 0180 4002722

ⓂSatyam Industries Private Ltd.
Panipat Mill
Mill is for sale
Village Pardhana, Tehsil Isran
132103 Panipat, Haryana
India
Phone: (91) 09996 106922
Fax: (91) 0180 4002722
Personnel:
Man. Dir.: Adesh Aggarwal
Type of Operation: Paper mill
Paper/Paperboard Grades and Capacities:
Total paper and paperboard capacity: 71,000 mt/y
Packaging papers: 71,000 mt/y
Paper and Paperboard Mill Data:
Paper Machines: 1
PM 1, (started up March 2009), twin-wire, total capacity 71,000 mt/y, Trim width 4.7 m, Packaging papers

ⒽSaurashtra Paper & Board Mills Ltd.
204, Pattani Bldg., Mahatma Gandhi Road
360001 Rajkot, Gujarat
India
Phone: (91) 281 2 222331/2233368
Fax: (91) 281 2 223636
Email: spbml@rediffmail.com, spbmltd@gmail.com
Personnel:
Man. Dir.: Deepak S. Mehta
Phone: (91) 281 2222331
Sr. Mgr. (Legal & Admin.): S. S. Tiwari
Phone: (91) 281 2 222331/2233368
Fax: (91) 281 2 223636
Total Employees at this Location: 20
Mill Locations:
Saurashtra Paper & Board Mills Ltd., Navagam Mill, N.H., 8-B, Navagam, Rajkot, India, Capacity: 6,000 mt/y, (Pulp mill, Paper mill)
Phone: (91) 281 2701755/56
Fax: (91) 281 2457759
Email: spbml@rediffmail.com, spbmltd@gmail.com
Saurashtra Paper & Board Mills Ltd., Shapar Mill, (Opposite Empire Flour Mill), N.H. 8-B, Shapar-Verval, Dist., Rajkot, India, Capacity: 15,000 mt/y, (Pulp mill, Paper mill)
Phone: (91) 281 2 222331
Fax: (91) 281 2 223636
Email: spbml@rediffmail.com, spbmltd@gmail.com

ⓂSaurashtra Paper & Board Mills Ltd.
Navagam Mill
N.H., 8-B, Navagam
Rajkot, Gujarat
India
Phone: (91) 281 2701755/56
Fax: (91) 281 2457759
Email: spbml@rediffmail.com, spbmltd@gmail.com
Personnel:
Gen. Mgr.: Mr. Akchakravorby
Phone: (91) 281 2701755/56
Man. Dir.: Deepak S. Mehta
Phone: (91) 281 2222331
Total Employees at this Location: 80
Type of Operation: Pulp mill, Paper mill
Pulp Grades and Capacities:
Total pulp capacity: 7,000 mt/y
Pulp Mill Data:
Recycled Fiber Treatment Lines:
Pulpers: 1 at 7,200 admt/y
Paper/Paperboard Grades and Capacities:
Total paper and paperboard capacity: 6,000 mt/y
Packaging papers: 6,000 mt/y
Paper and Paperboard Mill Data:
Stock Preparation:
Pulpers: 1
Refiners: 1
Paper Machines: 1
PM 1, fourdrinier, total capacity 6,000 mt/y, Trim width 1.29 m, Packaging papers
Finishing Equipment:
Rewinders: 1 at 7,500 mt/y
Energy Data:
Electrical demand for mill: 6 MWh/D

ⓂSaurashtra Paper & Board Mills Ltd.
Shapar Mill
(Opposite Empire Flour Mill), N.H. 8-B, Shapar-Verval, Dist. Rajkot, Gujarat
India
Phone: (91) 281 2 222331
Fax: (91) 281 2 223636
Email: spbml@rediffmail.com, spbmltd@gmail.com
Personnel:
Man. Dir.: Deepak S. Mehta
Phone: (91) 281 2233368
Gen. Mgr. (Works): A. K. Chakravorty
Phone: (91) 281 2 222331
Email: akchakravorty@rediffmail.com
Total Employees at this Location: 290
Type of Operation: Pulp mill, Paper mill
Pulp Grades and Capacities:
Total pulp capacity: 20,000 mt/y
Paper/Paperboard Grades and Capacities:
Total paper and paperboard capacity: 15,000 mt/y
Uncoated woodfree/freesheet
Paper and Paperboard Mill Data:
Stock Preparation:
Pulpers: 1
Refiners: 1
Paper Machines: 1
PM 2, fourdrinier, total capacity 15,000 mt/y, Trim width 1.8 m, Uncoated woodfree/freesheet
Finishing Equipment:
Rewinders: 1 at 14,000 mt/y
Sheeters: 1 at 12,000 mt/y
Energy Data:
Power boilers: 1

ⒽⓂSecurity Printing and Minting Corporation Of India Limited (SPMCIL)
Hoshangabad Mill
461005 Hoshangabad, M.P
India
Phone: (91) 7574 255259
Fax: (91) 7574 255170
Email: info@spmcil.com
Web Address: spmhoshangabad.spmcil.com/SPMCIL/Interface/Home.aspx
Personnel:
Gen. Mgr.: Ashwini Kumar
Phone: (91) 7574 255259
Mill Mgr: Rahj Kumar
Phone: (91) 7574 279847
Total Employees at this Location: 1,800
Type of Operation: Paper mill
Paper/Paperboard Grades and Capacities:
Total paper and paperboard capacity: 2,900 mt/y
Uncoated woodfree/freesheet: 2,900 mt/y

ⒽSenapathy-Whiteley (P) Ltd.
Ownership: private limited
No. 5 Primrose Road, Off MG Road
560 025 Bangalore, Karnataka
India
Phone: (91) 80 25564512/93307/145/277 559 3145/3291/3307
Fax: (91) 80 25593392
Email: info@senapathy.com
Web Address: www.senapathy.com

Mill Locations:
Senapathy-Whiteley (P) Ltd., Ramangram Mill, Achalu Village, Ramangram, India, Capacity: 8,000 mt/y, (Paper mill, Paperboard mill)
Phone: (91) 0 80 255 93145/93307/272 72428
Fax: (91) 0 80 255 93145/93392/97778
Email: info@senapathy.com

ⓜSenapathy-Whiteley (P) Ltd.
Ramangram Mill
Achalu Village
Ramangram, Karnataka
India
Phone: (91) 0 80 255 93145/93307/272 72428
Fax: (91) 0 80 255 93145/93392/97778
Email: info@senapathy.com
Web Address: www.senapathy.com
Personnel:
Gen. Mgr: Tushar Udgata
Phone: (91) 934 189 5860
Fax: (91) 080 272 71989
Email: tushar@senapathy.com
Purch. Mgr.: M. G. Srinivasan
Phone: (91) 0 80 255 93145/93307/272 72428
Sen. Mktg. Mgr.: Mr. Nandan
Phone: (91) 934 386 4757
Email: nandan@senapathy.com
Type of Operation: Paper mill, Paperboard mill
Paper/Paperboard Grades and Capacities:
Total paper and paperboard capacity: 8,000 mt/y
Specialty and industrial: 4,800 mt/y
Boxboard/cartonboard: 3,200 mt/y

ⓜServalakshmi Paper Ltd.
Servall Mill
Ownership: Serval Industries Ltd.
Kodangallur Villagee, Vaduganpatti Post
627 010 Tirunelveli, Tamil Nadu
India
Phone: (91) 4634 292724, 462 2568500
Email: servalakshmi@gmail.com, officeadmin@servalakshmi.in
Web Address: www.servalakshmi.in
Total Employees at this Location: 300
Type of Operation: Paper mill
Pulp Grades and Capacities:
Total pulp capacity: 85,504 mt/y
Recycled Pulping: 85,504 mt/y
Pulp Mill Data:
Pulp Lines: 1
Recycled Fiber Treatment Lines:
Flotation deinking lines: 1 at 100,000
Paper/Paperboard Grades and Capacities:
Total paper and paperboard capacity: 90,000 mt/y
Newsprint: 40,000 mt/y
Uncoated woodfree/freesheet: 50,000 mt/y
Paper and Paperboard Mill Data:
Paper Machines: 1
No. 1, fourdrinier, total capacity 90,000 mt/y, Trim width 4.45 m, Uncoated woodfree/freesheet, Newsprint
Energy Data:
Power boilers: 1
Steam turbines: 1 at 15 MW
Electrical demand for mill: 229 MWh/D

ⓜServalakshmi Paper & Boards Ltd. (SLPB)
Ownership: Serval Industries Ltd.
31 Bharathi Park, 7th Cross, Saibaba Colony
641 011 Coimbatore, Tamil Nadu
India
Phone: (91) 422 4333344/4320010
Fax: (91) 422 4333355
Email: sppl@servalakshmi.in, ho@servalakshmi.in
Web Address: www.servalakshmi.in
Personnel:
Chrmn & Man. Dir.: R. Ramswamy
Phone: (91) 422 4333344/4320010
Fax: (91) 422 4333355
Man. Dir.: Mr. Y. Shivram Prasad
Phone: (91) 422 4333344/4320010
Fax: (91) 422 4333355
Dir.: Mr. B. Sriram
Phone: (91) 422 4333344/4320010
Fax: (91) 422 4333355
Gen. Mgr. (Oper.): Mr. M. Raveendranathan
Phone: (91) 422 4333344/4320010
Fax: (91) 422 4333355
Total Employees of Company: 120
Mill Locations:
Servalakshmi Paper & Boards Ltd. (SLPB), Nilakottai Talu Mill, Vilampatti, 624 219 Nilakottai Talu, Dindigul Dist., India, Capacity: 18,000 mt/y, (Paper mill)
Phone: (91) 4543 236433 to 35/236443, 236443
Fax: (91) 4543 236402
Email: sppl@servalakshmi.in, ho@servalakshmi.in, mills@danalakshmi.in

ⓜServalakshmi Paper & Boards Ltd. (SLPB)
Nilakottai Talu Mill
Ownership: Serval Industries Ltd.
Vilampatti
624 219 Nilakottai Talu, Dindigul Dist., Tamil Nadu
India
Phone: (91) 4543 236433 to 35/236443, 236443
Fax: (91) 4543 236402
Email: sppl@servalakshmi.in, ho@servalakshmi.in, mills@danalakshmi.in
Web Address: www.servalakshmi.in
Personnel:
Head of Operation: Mr. Mamivannan
Phone: (91) 4543 236433
Email: manivannan@danalakshmi.in
Dir.: D. Muthusamy
Phone: (91) 4543 236433 to 35/236443, 236443
Senior Gen. Mgr. Commer.: S.P. Guptha
Phone: (91) 4543 236433 to 35/236443, 236443
Total Employees at this Location: 146
Type of Operation: Paper mill
Paper/Paperboard Grades and Capacities:
Total paper and paperboard capacity: 18,000 mt/y
Newsprint
Uncoated woodfree/freesheet
Paper and Paperboard Mill Data:
Stock Preparation:
Refiners: 1
Paper Machines: 1
No. 1, fourdrinier, Trim width 2.1 m, Newsprint
Finishing Equipment:
Rewinders: 1
Energy Data:
Power boilers: 1
Steam turbines at 5.5 MW

ⓜSeshasayee Paper & Boards Ltd.
Tirunelveli Mill
Elaindakulam Village, Singamparai
627 601 Mukkudal, Tirunelveli, Tamil Nadu
India
Phone: (91) 463 4325544
Fax: (91) 463 4275200
Personnel:
Dir. & CEO: Arun K Subbiah
Phone: (91) 463 4325544
Dir. & COO: Badrinath Atmaram
Phone: (91) 463 4325544
VP Op's: B. Chalapathi Rao
Phone: (91) 463 3293633/944 2274000
Gen. Mgr, R & D: Mr. M. K. Rao
Phone: (91) 463 4325544
Gen. Mgr., Eng.: Mr. R. Chakraborthy
Phone: (91) 463 4325544
Email: dgmengg.paper@subburaj.com
Gen. Mgr., Paper: Mr. S. Manivannan
Phone: (91) 463 4325544
Sr. Mgr. Paper: Mr. R. K. Rao
Phone: (91) 463 4325544
Mgr. Pulp: Mr. Kesavan
Phone: (91) 463 4325544
Senior Mgr.: Mr. Manthosh Karmakar
Phone: (91) 463 4325544
Total Employees at this Location: 200
Type of Operation: Pulp mill, Paper mill
Pulp Grades and Capacities:
Total pulp capacity: 76,160 mt/y
Recycled Pulping: 76,160 mt/y
Pulp Mill Data:
Recycled Fiber Treatment Lines:
Flotation deinking lines: 1 at 110,000 admt/y
Pulpers: 1 at 150,000 admt/y
Paper/Paperboard Grades and Capacities:
Total paper and paperboard capacity: 107,100 mt/y
Uncoated woodfree/freesheet: 107,100 mt/y
Paper and Paperboard Mill Data:
Stock Preparation:
Pulpers: 1
Refiners: 3
Paper Machines: 1
No. 1, (second-hand), fourdrinier, total capacity 107,100 mt/y, Trim width 4.35 m, Uncoated woodfree/freesheet
Finishing Equipment:
Winders: 1 at 90,000 mt/y
Sheeters: 2 at 50,000 mt/y
Energy Data:
Power boilers: 1
Steam turbines: 1 at 6 MW
Electrical demand for mill: 324 MWh/D

ⓘSeshasayee Paper & Boards Ltd.
Ownership: 100% by Esvin Group
Pallipalayam, Namakkal Dist.
638 007 Erode, Tamil Nadu
India
Phone: (91) 4288 240221/228
Fax: (91) 4288 240229
Email: edoff@spbltd.com
Web Address: www.spbltd.com
Personnel:
Chrmn. & Man. Dir.: N. Gopala Ratnam
Phone: (91) 4288 240480
Email: gopal@spbltd.com
Dpty. Man.: K. S. Kasi Viswanathan
Phone: (91) 4288 241705
Email: kasi@spbltd.com
Finan. Mgr., Admin. Mgr.: V. Pichai
Phone: (91) 4288 240322
Email: pichai@spbltd.com
Pres., Commer. Dir.: Mr. S. Kannan
Phone: (91) 44 24984571
Email: kannan@spbltd.com
Process Mgr.: Mr. A. Susharsan Srinivasan
Phone: (91) 4288 240220240220
Email: srinivasanas@spbltd.com
Environ. Dir.: Mr. K Shanmugam
Phone: (91) 4288 240220240220
Email: kshanmugam@spbltd.com
Indus. Mgr.: Mr. M. Balaraman
Phone: (91) 4288 240220240220
Email: balaraman@spbltd.com
Machine Supt.: Mr. K. Balakrishnan
Phone: (91) 4288 240220
Email: kbalakrishnan@spbltd.com
Machine Supt.: Mr. P. Subramaniam
Phone: (91) 4288 240220
Email: mf3@spbltd.com
Pulp Mill Mgr.: Mr. R. Sridhar
Phone: (91) 4288 240220
Email: rdhprocess@spbltd.com
Total Employees at this Location: 1,330
Mill Locations:
Seshasayee Paper & Boards Ltd., Tirunelveli Mill, Elaindakulam Village, Singamparai, 627 601 Mukkudal, Tirunelveli, India, Capacity: 107,100 mt/y, (Pulp mill, Paper mill)

India

Phone: (91) 463 4325544
Fax: (91) 463 4275200
Seshasayee Paper & Boards Ltd., Erode Mill, Pallipalayam, Namakkal Dist., 638 007 Erode, India, Capacity: 106,743 mt/y, (Pulp mill, Paper mill, Paperboard mill)
Phone: (91) 4288 240221/228
Fax: (91) 4288 240229
Email: edoff@spbltd.com

ⓂSeshasayee Paper & Boards Ltd.
Erode Mill
Pallipalayam, Namakkal Dist.
638 007 Erode, Tamil Nadu
India
Phone: (91) 4288 240221/228
Fax: (91) 4288 240229
Email: edoff@spbltd.com
Web Address: www.spbltd.com
Personnel:
Chmn. & Man. Dir.: N. Gopala Ratnam
Phone: (91) 4288 240480
Email: gopal@spbltd.com
Dpty. Man.: K. S. Kasi Viswanathan
Phone: (91) 4288 241705
Email: kasi@spbltd.com
Finan. Mgr., Admin. Mgr.: V. Pichai
Phone: (91) 4288 240322
Email: pichai@spbltd.com
Pres., Commer. Dir.: Mr. S. Kannan
Phone: (91) 44 24984571
Email: kannan@spbltd.com
Process Mgr.: Mr. A. Susharsan Srinivasan
Phone: (91) 4288 240220
Email: srinivasanas@spbltd.com
Environ. Dir.: Mr. K. Shanmugam
Phone: (91) 4288 240220
Email: kshanmugam@spbltd.com
Indus. Mgr.: Mr. M. Balaraman
Phone: (91) 4288 240220
Email: balaraman@spbltd.com
Machine Supt.: Mr. K. Balakrishnan
Phone: (91) 4288 240220
Email: kbalakrishnan@spbltd.com
Machine Supt.: Mr. P. Subramaniam
Phone: (91) 4288 240220
Email: mf3@spbltd.com
Pulp Mill Mgr.: Mr. R. Sridhar
Phone: (91) 4288 240220
Email: rdhprocess@spbltd.com
Total Employees at this Location: 1,330
Type of Operation: Pulp mill, Paper mill, Paperboard mill
Pulp Grades and Capacities:
Total pulp capacity: 107,100 mt/y
Chemical Pulp: 49,583 mt/y
Other Pulp: 57,517 mt/y
Pulp Mill Data:
Chemical Pulping Systems:
Batch digesters: 4
Continuous digesters: 2
Pulp Lines: 2
Bleach Plant Systems: 2
No. 1, Type: hardwood, Sequence: O_2 DEopD, Capacity 140,000 admt/y
No. 2, Type: bagasse, Sequence: DEopD, Capacity 50,000 admt/y
Chemical Recovery Equipment:
Evaporator lines: 1
Recovery boilers: 1
Lime Kiln
Pulp Dryers:
Wet Lap machine 1
Paper/Paperboard Grades and Capacities:
Total paper and paperboard capacity: 106,743 mt/y
Uncoated woodfree/freesheet: 67,116 mt/y
Specialty and industrial: 29,631 mt/y
Boxboard/cartonboard: 9,996 mt/y
Paper and Paperboard Mill Data:
Stock Preparation:
Pulpers: 1
Refiners: 19
Paper Machines: 5
No. 1, fourdrinier, total capacity 17,850 mt/y, Trim width 3.05 m, Uncoated woodfree/freesheet
No. 2, fourdrinier, total capacity 19,992 mt/y, Trim width 3.1 m, Boxboard/cartonboard, Specialty and industrial
No. 3, fourdrinier, total capacity 19,635 mt/y, Trim width 3.1 m, Specialty and industrial
No. 4, fourdrinier, total capacity 9,996 mt/y, Trim width 2.34 m, Uncoated woodfree/freesheet
No. 5, fourdrinier, total capacity 60,690 mt/y, Trim width 2.8 m, Uncoated woodfree/freesheet
Coating Machines: 1
PM 5, total capacity 55,000 mt/y., on machine
Finishing Equipment:
Rewinders: 6 at 124,250 mt/y
Sheeters: 8 at 124,250 mt/y
Energy Data:
Power boilers: 4
Combustion turbines: 4 at 2.5, 3, 21, 16 MW

ⓂSevenhills Papers (P) Ltd.
G. Ragampeta (via), Samalkot
533440 East Godavari Dist.
India
Phone: (91) 884 2327762, 2327742
Fax: (91) 884 2327643
Email: info@sevenhillspapers.com, 7hillspapers@gmail.com
Web Address: www.sevenhillspapers.com
Personnel:
Mgr.: Kiran
Phone: (91) 884 2327762, 2327742
Fax: (91) 884 2327643
Mill Locations:
Sevenhills Papers (P) Ltd., East Godavari Dist. Mill, G. Ragampeta (via), Samalkot, 533440 East Godavari Dist., A.P., India, Capacity: 7,000 mt/y, (Paper mill, Paperboard mill)
Phone: (91) 884 2327762, 2327742
Fax: (91) 884 2327643
Email: info@sevenhillspapers.com, 7hillspapers@gmail.com

ⓂSevenhills Papers (P) Ltd.
East Godavari Dist. Mill
G. Ragampeta (via), Samalkot
533440 East Godavari Dist., A.P.
India
Phone: (91) 884 2327762, 2327742
Fax: (91) 884 2327643
Email: info@sevenhillspapers.com, 7hillspapers@gmail.com
Web Address: www.sevenhillspapers.com
Personnel:
Mgr.: Mr. Kiran
Phone: (91) 990 8812345
Type of Operation: Paper mill, Paperboard mill
Paper/Paperboard Grades and Capacities:
Total paper and paperboard capacity: 7,000 mt/y
Boxboard/cartonboard
Paper and Paperboard Mill Data:
Paper Machines: 2
PM 1
PM 2

ⓂShah Paper Mills Ltd.
202, B-Wing, Anjeline Apartments, 2nd Floor, Vile Parle (W)
400056 Mumbai, Maharashtra
India
Phone: (91) 22 26161932
Email: info@shahpaper.com
Mill Locations:
Shah Paper Mills Ltd., Valsad Mill, Unit I, 5202, III Phase G.I.D.C. Vapi, Unit II, 1004/2B, III Phase G.I.D.C. Vapi Pardi, 396195 Valsad, India, Capacity: 50,000 mt/y, (Paper mill)
Phone: (91) 260 2432388/0248/0670
Fax: (91) 260 2430995
Email: info@shahpaper.com

ⓂShah Paper Mills Ltd.
Valsad Mill
Unit I, 5202, III Phase G.I.D.C. Vapi, Unit II, 1004/2B, III Phase G.I.D.C. Vapi Pardi
396195 Valsad, Gujarat
India
Phone: (91) 260 2432388/0248/0670
Fax: (91) 260 2430995
Email: info@shahpaper.com
Type of Operation: Paper mill
Paper/Paperboard Grades and Capacities:
Total paper and paperboard capacity: 50,000 mt/y
Packaging papers
Paper and Paperboard Mill Data:
Paper Machines: 2
No. 1, fourdrinier
No. 2, fourdrinier

ⓂShah Pulp & Paper Mills Ltd.
Angelina Apart., B-202, 2nd Floor, Sarojni Road
400 056 Vile Parle, Mumbai, Maharashtra
India
Phone: (91) 22 26161932/74619
Fax: (91) 22 26173673
Email: info@shapaper.com
Personnel:
Chmn.: Amrutlal K. Shah
Phone: (91) 22 26161932/74619
Fax: (91) 22 26173673
Mill Locations:
Shah Pulp & Paper Mills Ltd., Valsad Mill, 97, Silvasa Road, G.I.D.C., 396 195 Vapi Pardi, Valsad, India, Capacity: 36,000 mt/y, (Paper mill)
Phone: (91) 260 2400031/2 2400133/2425858
Fax: (91) 260 2431749
Email: shahpulp@gmail.com

ⓂShah Pulp & Paper Mills Ltd.
Valsad Mill
97, Silvasa Road, G.I.D.C.
396 195 Vapi Pardi, Valsad, Gujarat
India
Phone: (91) 260 2400031/2 2400133/2425858
Fax: (91) 260 2431749
Email: shahpulp@gmail.com
Personnel:
Man. Dir.: M. H. Shah
Phone: (91) 260 2400031/2 2400133/2425858
Dir.: Deepen Gosrani
Phone: (91) 260 2400031/2 2400133/2425858
Prod. Mgr.: H. Modi
Phone: (91) 260 2400031/2 2400133/2425858
Total Employees at this Location: 143
Type of Operation: Paper mill
Pulp Grades and Capacities:
Total pulp capacity: 35,589 mt/y
Recycled Pulping: 35,589 mt/y
Pulp Mill Data:
Bleach Plant Systems: 1
Recycled Pulping System
Recycled Fiber Treatment Lines:
Flotation deinking lines: 1
Paper/Paperboard Grades and Capacities:
Total paper and paperboard capacity: 36,000 mt/y
Newsprint: 36,000 mt/y
Paper and Paperboard Mill Data:
Paper Machines: 1
No. 1, fourdrinier, total capacity 36,000 mt/y, Trim width 3.65 m, Newsprint
Energy Data:
Power boilers: 3
Electrical demand for mill: 108 MWh/D

ⓂShakumbhri Pulp & Paper Mills Ltd.
4.5 Km, Bhopa Road
251002 Muzaffarnagar
India

India

Phone: (91) 131 3291882, 3201882
Personnel:
Chmn.: Paeven Gupta
Phone: (91) 131 3291882, 3201882
Man. Dir.: Vinod Mittal
Phone: (91) 131 3291882, 3201882
Mill Locations:
Shakumbhri Pulp & Paper Mills Ltd., Muzaffarnagar Mill, 4.5 Km, Bhopa Road, 251002 Muzaffarnagar, India, Capacity: 10,000 mt/y, (Paper mill)
Phone: (91) 131 3291882, 3201882

ⓂShakumbhri Pulp & Paper Mills Ltd.
Muzaffarnagar Mill
4.5 Km, Bhopa Road
251002 Muzaffarnagar, Uttar Pradesh
India
Phone: (91) 131 3291882, 3201882
Personnel:
Chmn.: Paeven Gupta
Man. Dir.: Vinod Mittal
Type of Operation: Paper mill
Paper/Paperboard Grades and Capacities:
Total paper and paperboard capacity: 10,000 mt/y
Packaging papers: 10,000 mt/y
Paper and Paperboard Mill Data:
Paper Machines: 1
No. 4, total capacity 10,000 mt/y, Packaging papers

ⓘShakumbhri Straw Products Ltd.
B-92, Gandhi Nagar
244001 Moradabad, Uttar Pradesh
India
Phone: (91) 591 249 0440/3365
Fax: (91) 591 249 3064
Email: s_spl@usa.net, info@shakumbhri.co.in
Web Address: shakumbhri.co.in
Personnel:
Chmn.: Sunil Kr. Rastogi
Phone: (91) 591 249 0440/3365
Fax: (91) 591 249 3064
Man. Dir.: Kapil Rastogi
Phone: (91) 591 249 0440/3365
Fax: (91) 591 249 3064
VP: Manoj Ranjan
Phone: (91) 591 249 0440/3365
Fax: (91) 591 249 3064
Mill Locations:
Shakumbhri Straw Products Ltd., Moradabad Mill, Vill. Devri, Moradabad - 32 Km, Chandausi Rd., Tehsil Bilari, Moradabad, India, Capacity: 97,000 mt/y, (Paper mill, Paperboard mill)
Phone: (91) 5921 270 905/791/515/366
Fax: (91) 5921 270 904

ⓂShakumbhri Straw Products Ltd.
Moradabad Mill
Vill. Devri, Moradabad - 32 Km, Chandausi Rd.
Tehsil Bilari, Moradabad, Uttar Pradesh
India
Phone: (91) 5921 270 905/791/515/366
Fax: (91) 5921 270 904
Personnel:
Man. Dir.: Kapil Rastogi
Phone: (91) 5921 270 905/791/515/366
Total Employees at this Location: 362
Type of Operation: Paper mill, Paperboard mill
Pulp Grades and Capacities:
Total pulp capacity: 95,884 mt/y
Recycled Pulping: 95,884 mt/y
Paper/Paperboard Grades and Capacities:
Total paper and paperboard capacity: 97,000 mt/y
Newsprint: 31,500 mt/y
Uncoated woodfree/freesheet: 13,500 mt/y
Linerboard: 35,000 mt/y
Corrugating medium/fluting: 17,000 mt/y
Paper and Paperboard Mill Data:
Paper Machines: 3

No. 1, fourdrinier, total capacity 17,000 mt/y, Trim width 2.54 m, Corrugating medium/fluting
No. 2, twin-wire, total capacity 35,000 mt/y, Trim width 3 m, Linerboard
No. 3, fourdrinier, total capacity 45,000 mt/y, Trim width 3.7 m, Uncoated woodfree/freesheet, Newsprint
Energy Data:
Steam turbines: 1 at 12 MW
Electrical demand for mill: 199 MWh/D

ⓘⓂShalimar Krafts and Tissue (P) Ltd.
Muzaffarnagar Mill
8.5th Km Stone, Jansath Rd., Nirana, P.O. Bhikki
251001 Muzaffarnagar, Uttar Pradesh
India
Phone: (91) 131 2660904/1191
Personnel:
Man. Dir.: Sanjay Agarawal
Phone: (91) 99 27032598
Total Employees at this Location: 100
Type of Operation: Paper mill
Paper/Paperboard Grades and Capacities:
Total paper and paperboard capacity: 6,000 mt/y
Packaging papers: 6,000 mt/y
Paper and Paperboard Mill Data:
Paper Machines: 1
No. 1, Packaging papers

ⓘShalimar Paper Mills (P) Ltd.
8th Km Stone, Jansath Rd. Nirana
251001 Muzaffarnagar
India
Phone: (91) 131 2661422/0941
Fax: (91) 131 2402289/7206
Email: sukam@nde.vsnl.net.in, info@sukamindustries.com
Personnel:
Man. Dir.: Alok Swarup
Phone: (91) 131 2661422/0941
Fax: (91) 131 2402289/7206
Email: sukam333@yahoo.com
Mill Locations:
Shalimar Paper Mills (P) Ltd., Muzaffarnagar Mill, 8th Km Stone, Jansath Rd. Nirana, 251001 Muzaffarnagar, India, Capacity: 10,000 mt/y, (Paper mill)
Phone: (91) 131 2661422/0941
Fax: (91) 131 2402289/7206
Email: sukam@nde.vsnl.net.in, info@sukamindustries.com

ⓂShalimar Paper Mills (P) Ltd.
Muzaffarnagar Mill
8th Km Stone, Jansath Rd. Nirana
251001 Muzaffarnagar, Uttar Pradesh
India
Phone: (91) 131 2661422/0941
Fax: (91) 131 2402289/7206
Email: sukam@nde.vsnl.net.in, info@sukamindustries.com
Personnel:
Man. Dir.: Alok Swarup
Phone: (91) 131 2661422/0941
Email: sukam333@yahoo.com
Type of Operation: Paper mill
Paper/Paperboard Grades and Capacities:
Total paper and paperboard capacity: 10,000 mt/y
Packaging papers
Linerboard

ⓘShamli Paper Mills Ltd.
8 Km Delhi-Saharanpur Highway
Vill. Sikka Shamli
India
Phone: (91) 1398 252500/250801/740
Fax: (91) 1398 250800
Email: spml50093@yahoo.com
Personnel:
Man. Dir.: Rajeshwar Bansal
Phone: (91) 1398 252500/250801

Fax: (91) 1398 250800
Mill Locations:
Shamli Paper Mills Ltd., Vill. Sikka Shamli Mill, 8 Km Delhi-Saharanpur Highway, Vill. Sikka Shamli, India, Capacity: 5,400 mt/y, (Paper mill)
Phone: (91) 1398 252500/250801/740
Fax: (91) 1398 250800
Email: spml50093@yahoo.com

ⓂShamli Paper Mills Ltd.
Vill. Sikka Shamli Mill
8 Km Delhi-Saharanpur Highway
Vill. Sikka Shamli, Uttar Pradesh
India
Phone: (91) 1398 252500/250801/740
Fax: (91) 1398 250800
Email: spml50093@yahoo.com
Personnel:
Man. Dir.: Rajeshwar Bansal
Phone: (91) 1398 252500/250801/740
Type of Operation: Paper mill
Paper/Paperboard Grades and Capacities:
Total paper and paperboard capacity: 5,400 mt/y
Packaging papers
Linerboard
Paper and Paperboard Mill Data:
Paper Machines: 1
No. 1, fourdrinier, Packaging papers, Linerboard

ⓘⓂShayona Pulp Conversion Mills Pvt. Ltd.
Aurangabad Mill
D-8 MIDC, Waluj
Aurangabad, Maharashtra
India
Phone: (91) 0240 6611178, 6611179
Fax: (91) 0240 2555379
Email: shayonapaper@gmail.com, shayonapaper@hotmail.com
Personnel:
Man. Dir.: Pinal Raman Patel
Phone: (91) 240 6511453
Total Employees at this Location: 50
Type of Operation: Paper mill
Paper/Paperboard Grades and Capacities:
Total paper and paperboard capacity: 18,000 mt/y
Packaging papers: 18,000 mt/y
Paper and Paperboard Mill Data:
Paper Machines: 1
No. 1, fourdrinier

ⓘShelavi Pulp & Paper Mills (P) Ltd.
Blok No. 926, Kadi Rd., Near GEB Sub. Station
Chhatral, Dist. Mehsana
India
Phone: (91) 2764 233995
Fax: (91) 2764 233903
Email: shelaviad1@sancharnet.in
Personnel:
Man. Dir.: Mihir V. Patel
Phone: (91) 2764 233995
Fax: (91) 2764 233903
Mill Locations:
Shelavi Pulp & Paper Mills (P) Ltd., Mehsana Mill, Blok No. 926, Kadi Rd., Near GEB Sub. Station, Chhatral, Dist. Mehsana, India, Capacity: 6,000 mt/y, (Paper mill)
Phone: (91) 2764 233995
Fax: (91) 2764 233903
Email: shelaviad1@sancharnet.in

ⓂShelavi Pulp & Paper Mills (P) Ltd.
Mehsana Mill
Blok No. 926, Kadi Rd., Near GEB Sub. Station
Chhatral, Dist. Mehsana, Gujarat
India
Phone: (91) 2764 233995
Fax: (91) 2764 233903
Email: shelaviad1@sancharnet.in

India

Personnel:
Man. Dir.: Mihir V. Patel
Phone: (91) 98 250 17271
Type of Operation: Paper mill
Paper/Paperboard Grades and Capacities:
Total paper and paperboard capacity: 6,000 mt/y
Packaging papers
Specialty and industrial

ⓂShiv Shakti Kraft Board Mills (P) Ltd.
Gut. No. 322, Dhakhepal Rd., At Post Dhovkin
431001 Dist. Aurangabad
India
Phone: (91) 240-2343027, 240 3129815
Fax: (91) 240-2343027, 240 3120091
Email: shivshaktikraft@rediffmail.com
Personnel:
Man. Dir.: Mahesh Gandhi
Phone: (91) 240-2343027
Fax: (91) 240-2343027
Dir.: Himanshu Doshi
Phone: (91) 240-2343027
Fax: (91) 240-2343027
Mill Locations:
Shiv Shakti Kraft Board Mills (P) Ltd., Dist. Aurangabad Mill, Gut. No. 322, Dhakhepal Rd., At Post Dhovkin, 431001 Dist. Aurangabad, India, Capacity: 7,500 mt/y, (Paper mill, Paperboard mill)
Phone: (91) 240-2343027, 240 3129815
Fax: (91) 240-2343027, 240 3120091
Email: shivshaktikraft@rediffmail.com

ⓂShiv Shakti Kraft Board Mills (P) Ltd.
Dist. Aurangabad Mill
Gut. No. 322, Dhakhepal Rd., At Post Dhovkin
431001 Dist. Aurangabad, Maharashtra
India
Phone: (91) 240-2343027, 240 3129815
Fax: (91) 240-2343027, 240 3120091
Email: shivshaktikraft@rediffmail.com
Personnel:
Man. Dir.: Mahesh Gandhi
Phone: (91) 240-2343027
Fax: (91) 240-2343027
Dir.: Himanshu Doshi
Phone: (91) 240-2343027
Fax: (91) 240-2343027
Type of Operation: Paper mill, Paperboard mill
Paper/Paperboard Grades and Capacities:
Total paper and paperboard capacity: 7,500 mt/y
Packaging papers
Linerboard

ⓄⓂShiva Shakti Paper Mills Ltd.
Vidisha Mill
Jatrapura
464 001 Vidisha, M.P
India
Phone: (91) 7592 233105/235530
Fax: (91) 7592 232605
Personnel:
Man. Dir.: R. K. Agrawal
Phone: (91) 7592 234749
Email: rksspm@rediffmail.com
Gen. Mgr. Prod.: C. L. Goyal
Phone: (91) 7592 233105
Mgr.: S. K. Verma
Phone: (91) 7592 233105
Total Employees at this Location: 150
Type of Operation: Paper mill
Paper/Paperboard Grades and Capacities:
Total paper and paperboard capacity: 7,500 mt/y
Packaging papers: 7,500 mt/y
Paper and Paperboard Mill Data:
Stock Preparation:
Pulpers: 2
Refiners: 2
Paper Machines: 2
No. 1, Trim width 2.1 m, Packaging papers

No. 2, Trim width 2.1 m, Packaging papers
Energy Data:
Power boilers: 1

ⓄShree Ajit Pulp and Paper Ltd.
Survey No. 239, Near Morai, Railway Crossing, Vill.
Salvav, Via-Vapi
396191 Dist. Valsad
India
Phone: (91) 260 2437090/7059/7113/14
Fax: (91) 260 437114
Email: shreeajit@shreeajit.com
Web Address: www.shreeajit.com
Personnel:
Dir.: Dhansukhlal G. Shah
Phone: (91) 260 2437090/7059
Fax: (91) 260 437114
Tech. Dir.: P. M. Kanyadi
Phone: (91) 260 2437090/7059
Fax: (91) 260 437114
Mill Locations:
Shree Ajit Pulp and Paper Ltd., Dist. Valsad Mill, Survey No. 239, Near Morai, Railway Crossing, Vill. Salvav, Via-Vapi, 396191 Dist. Valsad, India, Capacity: 16,500 mt/y, (Paper mill)
Phone: (91) 260 2437090/7059/7113/14
Fax: (91) 260 437114
Email: shreeajit@shreeajit.com

ⓂShree Ajit Pulp and Paper Ltd.
Dist. Valsad Mill
Survey No. 239, Near Morai, Railway Crossing, Vill.
Salvav, Via-Vapi
396191 Dist. Valsad, Gujarat
India
Phone: (91) 260 2437090/7059/7113/14
Fax: (91) 260 437114
Email: shreeajit@shreeajit.com
Web Address: www.shreeajit.com
Personnel:
Man. Dir.: Gautam D. Shah
Phone: (91) 260 2437090/7059/7113/14
Dir.: Dhansukhlal G. Shah
Phone: (91) 260 2437090/7059/7113/14
Tech. Dir.: Shri P. M. Kanyadi
Phone: (91) 260 2437090/7059/7113/14
Type of Operation: Paper mill
Paper/Paperboard Grades and Capacities:
Total paper and paperboard capacity: 16,500 mt/y
Packaging papers

ⓂShree Ambeshwar Paper Mills Ltd.
Ankleshwar Mill
140/3, GIDC Industrial Estate, Bharuch
393 002 Ankleshwar, Gujarat
India
Email: davemanoj@hotmail.com, sapml@satyam.net.in
Personnel:
Chmn.: Shantilal B. Dave
Phone: (91) 2646 220467/223109/115
Man. Dir.: M. B. Dave
Phone: (91) 2646 220467/223109/115
Mgr. (Operations): S. P. Panchal
Phone: (91) 2646 220467/223109/115
Gen. Mgr.: R. M. Shah
Phone: (91) 2646 220467/223109/115
Total Employees at this Location: 250
Type of Operation: Pulp mill, Paper mill
Pulp Grades and Capacities:
Total pulp capacity: 9,500 mt/y
Paper/Paperboard Grades and Capacities:
Total paper and paperboard capacity: 22,500 mt/y
Packaging papers: 22,500 mt/y
Paper and Paperboard Mill Data:
Stock Preparation:
Pulpers: 2
Refiners: 5
Paper Machines: 2

No. 1, Yankee dryer, fourdrinier, total capacity 14,300 mt/y, Trim width 2.1 m, Packaging papers
No. 2, fourdrinier, Yankee dryer, total capacity 8,200 mt/y, Trim width 2.2 m, Packaging papers
Finishing Equipment:
Rewinders: 2
Energy Data:
Power boilers: 2

ⓄShree Ambeshwar Paper Mills Ltd.
S. Deepak Kumar & Co., Shop No. 82, 4th Ln.,
Mangaldas Market
400 002 Mumbai, Maharashtra
India
Personnel:
Jr. Man. Dir.: Y. C. Oza
Man. Dir.: D. A. Dave
Mill Locations:
Shree Ambeshwar Paper Mills Ltd., Ankleshwar Mill, 140/3, GIDC Industrial Estate, Bharuch, 393 002 Ankleshwar, India, Capacity: 22,500 mt/y, (Pulp mill, Paper mill)
Email: davemanoj@hotmail.com, sapml@satyam.net.in

ⓄShree Badri Kedar Papers (P) Ltd.
5 Km Nagina Rd., Vill. Sikandarpur Basi
246763 Najibabad
India
Phone: (91) 1341 231316, 230275
Fax: (91) 1341 230276
Personnel:
Pres.: Dinesh Kumar Goel
Phone: (91) 1341 231316, 230275
Fax: (91) 1341 230276
Man. Dir.: Arvind Kumar Aggrawal
Phone: (91) 1341 231316, 230275
Fax: (91) 1341 230276
Total Employees of Company: 82
Mill Locations:
Shree Badri Kedar Papers (P) Ltd., Najibabad Mill, 5 Km Nagina Rd., Vill. Sikandarpur Basi, 246763 Najibabad, India, Capacity: 9,000 mt/y, (Paper mill)
Phone: (91) 1341 231316, 230275
Fax: (91) 1341 230276

ⓂShree Badri Kedar Papers (P) Ltd.
Najibabad Mill
5 Km Nagina Rd., Vill. Sikandarpur Basi
246763 Najibabad, Uttar Pradesh
India
Phone: (91) 1341 231316, 230275
Fax: (91) 1341 230276
Personnel:
Pres.: Dinesh Kumar Goel
Phone: (91) 1341 231316, 230275
Fax: (91) 1341 230276
Man. Dir.: Arvind Kumar Aggrawal
Phone: (91) 1341 231316, 230275
Fax: (91) 1341 230276
Total Employees at this Location: 82
Type of Operation: Paper mill
Paper/Paperboard Grades and Capacities:
Total paper and paperboard capacity: 9,000 mt/y
Packaging papers: 9,000 mt/y
Paper and Paperboard Mill Data:
Paper Machines: 1
No. 1, Packaging papers

ⓂShree Bhageshwari Papers Ltd
Muzaffarnagar Mill
Ownership: *Sidharth Papers Ltd.*
9th Km stone, Bhopa Road
251 001 Muzaffarnagar, Uttar Pradesh
India
Phone: (91) 131-2468388 / 89
Fax: (91) 131-2468391
Email: bppl_mzn@yahoo.co.in
Web Address: www.sidharthpapers.com
Personnel:

Man. Dir.: Mr. Divesh Bansal
Phone: (91) 131-2468388 / 89
Total Employees at this Location: 185
Type of Operation: Paper mill
Pulp Grades and Capacities:
Total pulp capacity: 33,935 mt/y
Recycled Pulping: 24,162 mt/y
Other Pulp: 9,773 mt/y

Pulp Mill Data:
Chemical Pulping Systems:
Batch digesters: 1
Bleach Plant Systems: 1
Recycled Pulping System, Type: DIP
Chemical Recovery Equipment:
Evaporator lines: 1
Recovery boilers: 1
Recycled Fiber Treatment Lines:
Flotation deinking lines: 1
Paper/Paperboard Grades and Capacities:
Total paper and paperboard capacity: 33,100 mt/y
Tissue: 13,860 mt/y
Packaging papers: 9,240 mt/y
Corrugating medium/fluting: 10,000 mt/y
Paper and Paperboard Mill Data:
Paper Machines: 2
No. 1, fourdrinier, total capacity 10,000 mt/y, Trim width 2.03 m, Corrugating medium/fluting
No. 2, fourdrinier, total capacity 23,100 mt/y, Trim width 4.72 m, Packaging papers, Tissue
Energy Data:
Power boilers
Steam turbines at 6 MW
Electrical demand for mill: 77 MWh/D

ⓜShree Bhawani Paper Mills Ltd.
33 Dayanand Marg
211 002 Allahabad, Uttar Pradesh
India
Phone: (91) 532 254 8401/04/06
Fax: (91) 532 254 8425
Email: sbpmills1@sancharnet.in,
sbpmills1@gmail.com
Web Address: www.shbhawani.com
Personnel:
Chmn.: Shri Badri Vishal Tandon
Phone: (91) 532 254 8407
Man. Dir.: Shri Girish Tandon
Phone: (91) 532 254 8404
Email: girishtandon@shbhawani.com
VP (Sls): Shri Ajay Gupta
Phone: (91) 532 254 8401/04/06
Fax: (91) 532 254 8425
Email: ajaygupta@shbhawani.com
Sec.: Babita Jain
Phone: (91) 532 325 9427
Email: babitajain@shbhawani.com
Total Employees of Company: 600
Total Employees at this Location: 25
Mill Locations:
Shree Bhawani Paper Mills Ltd., Rae Bareli Mill, Industrial Area I, Sultanpur Rd., 229010 Rae Bareli, India, Capacity: 65,000 mt/y, (Pulp mill, Paper mill)
Phone: (91) 535 2702155/6
Fax: (91) 535 2702159
Email: sbpml@lw1.vsnl.net.in, spadmanabhan@shbhawani.com, sbpml@sify.com

ⓜShree Bhawani Paper Mills Ltd.
Rae Bareli Mill
Industrial Area I, Sultanpur Rd.
229010 Rae Bareli, Uttar Pradesh
India
Phone: (91) 535 2702155/6
Fax: (91) 535 2702159
Email: sbpml@lw1.vsnl.net.in,
spadmanabhan@shbhawani.com,
sbpml@sify.com
Web Address: www.shbhawani.com
Personnel:
Man. Dir.: Shri Girish Tandon
Phone: (91) 535 2702155/6
Email: girishtandon@shbhawani.com
Gen. Mgr. (Prod.): Shri S. Padmanabham
Phone: (91) 535 2702155/6
Email: spadmanabhan@shbhawani.com
Gen. Mgr. (Sls.): Shri Ajay Gupta
Phone: (91) 535 2702155/6
Finan. Mgr.: Shri Kamal Srivastava
Phone: (91) 535 2702155/6
Total Employees at this Location: 387
Type of Operation: Pulp mill, Paper mill
Pulp Grades and Capacities:
Total pulp capacity: 62,635 mt/y
Recycled Pulping: 51,184 mt/y
Other Pulp: 11,451 mt/y

Pulp Mill Data:
Chemical Pulping Systems:
Batch digesters: 10
Pulp Lines: 2
Bleach Plant Systems: 1
No. 1, Sequence: CEH
Chemical Recovery Equipment:
Recovery boilers: 1
Recycled Fiber Treatment Lines:
Not Given at 54,000
Paper/Paperboard Grades and Capacities:
Total paper and paperboard capacity: 65,000 mt/y
Newsprint: 51,800 mt/y
Uncoated woodfree/freesheet: 13,200 mt/y
Paper and Paperboard Mill Data:
Stock Preparation:
Refiners: 4
Paper Machines: 3
No. 1, fourdrinier, total capacity 10,500 mt/y, Trim width 1.9 m, Newsprint
No. 2, fourdrinier, total capacity 10,500 mt/y, Trim width 1.96 m, Newsprint
No. 3, fourdrinier, total capacity 44,000 mt/y, Trim width 4.2 m, Newsprint, Uncoated woodfree/freesheet
Finishing Equipment:
Rewinders: 2
Sheeters: 3
Energy Data:
Power boilers: 4
Steam turbines: 1 at 3 MW
Electrical demand for mill: 196 MWh/D

ⓜShree Gajanan Papers & Boards (P) Ltd.
781/1-40, Shed Area, G.I.D.C.
396195 Vapi, Dist. Valsad
India
Phone: (91) 260 2425953/2435492/2400571/3091376
Fax: (91) 260 2431228/2401328
Email: sgpbvapi@rediffmail.com
Web Address: www.shreegajananpaper.com
Personnel:
Man. Dir.: Sunil M. Agarwal
Phone: (91) 260 2425953/2435492
Fax: (91) 260 2431228/2401328
Prod. Dir.: Sanjay M. Agarwal
Phone: (91) 260 2425953/2435492
Fax: (91) 260 2431228/2401328
Mill Locations:
Shree Gajanan Papers & Boards (P) Ltd., Vapi, Dist. Valsad Mill, 781/1-40, Shed Area, G.I.D.C., 396195 Vapi, Dist. Valsad, India, Capacity: 36,000 mt/y, (Paper mill)
Phone: (91) 260 2425953/2435492/2400571/3091376
Fax: (91) 260 2431228/2401328
Email: sgpbvapi@rediffmail.com

ⓜShree Gajanan Papers & Boards (P) Ltd.
Vapi, Dist. Valsad Mill
781/1-40, Shed Area, G.I.D.C.
396195 Vapi, Dist. Valsad, Gujarat
India
Phone: (91) 260 2425953/2435492/2400571/3091376
Fax: (91) 260 2431228/2401328
Email: sgpbvapi@rediffmail.com
Web Address: www.shreegajananpaper.com
Personnel:
Man. Dir.: Sunil M. Agarwal
Phone: (91) 260 2425953/2435492/2400571/3091376
Prod. Dir.: Sanjay M. Agarwal
Phone: (91) 260 2425953/2435492/2400571/3091376
Type of Operation: Paper mill
Paper/Paperboard Grades and Capacities:
Total paper and paperboard capacity: 36,000 mt/y
Packaging papers: 36,000 mt/y

ⓜⓜShree Ganesh Agroils (Paper Division)
Ludhiana Mill
Vill. Gaunspur, Near Humbran
141008 Ludhiana, Punjab
India
Phone: (91) 161 2871013
Personnel:
Man. Dir.: Satish Mehra
Phone: (91) 161 2871013
Type of Operation: Paper mill
Paper/Paperboard Grades and Capacities:
Total paper and paperboard capacity: 7,200 mt/y
Packaging papers

ⓜShree Gopinath Paper Mills Pvt. Ltd
Surendranagar Mill
Surendranagar-Rajkot Highway, Near Lokvidyalaya, Khareli
363 020 Surendranagar, Gujarat
India
Phone: (91) 2752 229901
Fax: (91) 2752 229901
Email: info@gopinathpaper.com
Web Address: www.gopinathpaper.com
Total Employees at this Location: 100
Type of Operation: Paper mill
Pulp Grades and Capacities:
Total pulp capacity: 34,012 mt/y
Recycled Pulping: 34,012 mt/y

Pulp Mill Data:
Recycled Fiber Treatment Lines:
Recycled packaging pulping lines: 1
Paper/Paperboard Grades and Capacities:
Total paper and paperboard capacity: 35,000 mt/y
Corrugating medium/fluting: 35,000 mt/y
Paper and Paperboard Mill Data:
Paper Machines: 1
No. 1, twin-wire, total capacity 35,000 mt/y, Trim width 3.2 m, Corrugating medium/fluting
Energy Data:
Power boilers
Electrical demand for mill: 41 MWh/D

ⓜShree Gopinath Paper Mills Pvt. Ltd
3, Silver Mention, Opp. Dr. Dinesh Jani's Hospital, Tramway Road
363 002 Surendranagar, Gujarat
India
Phone: (91) 2752 229901
Fax: (91) 2752 229901
Email: info@gopinathpaper.com,
gopipaper@yahoo.com
Web Address: www.gopinathpaper.com
Personnel:
Dir.: Sumit Patel
Phone: (91) 99250 10345
Dir.: Kalpesh Patel
Phone: (91) 99250 10734
Dir.: Tarun Patel
Phone: (91) 99789 31426
Total Employees of Company: 106

India

Mill Locations:
Shree Gopinath Paper Mills Pvt. Ltd, Surendranagar Mill, Surendranagar-Rajkot Highway, Near Lokvidyalaya, Khareli, 363 020 Surendranagar, India, Capacity: 35,000 mt/y, (Paper mill)
Phone: (91) 2752 229901
Fax: (91) 2752 229901
Email: info@gopinathpaper.com

ⓘⓜShree Jagdambe Paper Mills Ltd.
Sirsa Mill
Begu Road
125055 Sirsa, Haryana
India
Phone: (91) 1666 245270/271
Fax: (91) 1666 245459
Personnel:
Chmn., Man. Dir.: Surinder Goyal
Phone: (91) 1666 245270/271
Total Employees at this Location: 64
Type of Operation: Paper mill
Paper/Paperboard Grades and Capacities:
Total paper and paperboard capacity: 10,000 mt/y
Packaging papers

ⓘShree Jee Paper Industries
Vill. Makla, Ingoria Rd.
456335 Nagda
India
Phone: (91) 7366 244260/245260
Fax: (91) 751 2332077
Personnel:
Man. Dir.: Mohan Panchal
Phone: (91) 7366 244260/245260
Fax: (91) 751 2332077
Mill Locations:
Shree Jee Paper Industries, Nagda Mill, Vill. Makla, Ingoria Rd., 456335 Nagda, M.P, India, Capacity: 9,900 mt/y, (Paperboard mill)
Phone: (91) 7366 244260/245260
Fax: (91) 751 2332077

ⓜShree Jee Paper Industries
Nagda Mill
Vill. Makla, Ingoria Rd.
456335 Nagda, M.P
India
Phone: (91) 7366 244260/245260
Fax: (91) 751 2332077
Personnel:
Man. Dir.: Mohan Panchal
Phone: (91) 99 07536760
Type of Operation: Paperboard mill
Paper/Paperboard Grades and Capacities:
Total paper and paperboard capacity: 9,900 mt/y
Boxboard/cartonboard
Paper and Paperboard Mill Data:
Paper Machines: 1
No. 1, Boxboard/cartonboard

ⓘⓜShree Kaiwal Paper Mill
Dist. Panchmahal Mill
At. & PO Timbagam, Ta-Godhra
388711 Dist. Panchmahal, Gujarat
India
Personnel:
Man. Dir.: Mr. Manharbhai M. Patel
Phone: (91) 98 25048146
Total Employees at this Location: 90
Type of Operation: Paper mill
Paper/Paperboard Grades and Capacities:
Total paper and paperboard capacity: 10,800 mt/y
Packaging papers
Paper and Paperboard Mill Data:
Paper Machines: 1
No. 1, Packaging papers

ⓘShree Karthik Papers Ltd.
Puliyangandi, Aliyar Nagar, Kottur Village, Pollachi T.K. Dist. Coimbatore
India
Phone: (91) 91-0422-2313551/2313552
Fax: (91) 91-0422-2313558
Email: akshayasri23@hotmail.com
Personnel:
Chmn. & Man. Dir.: M. S. Velu
Phone: (91) 91-0422-2313551/2313552
Fax: (91) 91-0422-2313558
Dir.: S. S. Velu
Phone: (91) 91-0422-2313551/2313552
Fax: (91) 91-0422-2313558
Dir.: K. Arumugam
Phone: (91) 91-0422-2313551/2313552
Fax: (91) 91-0422-2313558
Dir.: P. Kanagavadivelu
Phone: (91) 91-0422-2313551/2313552
Fax: (91) 91-0422-2313558
Total Employees at this Location: 90
Mill Locations:
Shree Karthik Papers Ltd., Dist. Coimbatore Mill, Puliyangandi, Aliyar Nagar, Kottur Village, Pollachi T.K., Dist. Coimbatore, India, Capacity: 13,200 mt/y, (Paper mill)
Phone: (91) 91-0422-2313551/2313552
Fax: (91) 91-0422-2313558
Email: akshayasri23@hotmail.com

ⓜShree Karthik Papers Ltd.
Dist. Coimbatore Mill
Puliyangandi, Aliyar Nagar, Kottur Village, Pollachi T.K. Dist. Coimbatore, Tamil Nadu
India
Phone: (91) 91-0422-2313551/2313552
Fax: (91) 91-0422-2313558
Email: akshayasri23@hotmail.com
Personnel:
Chmn. & Man. Dir.: M. S. Velu
Phone: (91) 91-0422-2313551/2313552
Fax: (91) 91-0422-2313558
Dir.: S. S. Velu
Phone: (91) 91-0422-2313551/2313552
Fax: (91) 91-0422-2313558
Dir.: K. Arumugam
Phone: (91) 91-0422-2313551/2313552
Fax: (91) 91-0422-2313558
Dir.: P. Kanagavadivelu
Phone: (91) 91-0422-2313551/2313552
Fax: (91) 91-0422-2313558
Total Employees at this Location: 90
Type of Operation: Paper mill
Paper/Paperboard Grades and Capacities:
Total paper and paperboard capacity: 13,200 mt/y
Uncoated woodfree/freesheet
Specialty and industrial

ⓘShree Krishna Paper Mills & Ind Ltd
4830/24, Ansari Road Darya Ganj
110002 New Delhi, Delhi
India
Phone: (91) 11 23261728/23267253/30180200
Fax: (91) 11 23266708
Email: info@skpmil.com
Web Address: www.skpmil.com
Personnel:
Pres.: Dev Kishan Chanda
Phone: (91) 11 30180201
Email: devkishan.chanda@skpmil.com
Man. Dir.: Narendra Kumar Pasari
Phone: (91) 11 23261728/23267253/30180200
Fax: (91) 11 23266708
Total Employees of Company: 650
Total Employees at this Location: 300
Mill Locations:
Shree Krishna Paper Mills & Ind Ltd, Jaipur Mill, Plot No. SPL-A, RIICO Industrial Area, Vill. Keshwana, Teh. Kotputli, 303108 Jaipur, India, Capacity: 40,000 mt/y, (Paper mill)
Phone: (91) 11 3095 3200/3201
Fax: (91) 11 2326 6708
Email: info@skpmil.com
Shree Krishna Paper Mills & Ind Ltd, Haryana Coating Division, T-4, Old Industrial Area, 124507 Bahadurgarh, India, Capacity: 18,000 mt/y, (Paper mill)
Phone: (91) 11 3095 3200/3201
Fax: (91) 11 2326 6708
Email: info@skpmil.com

ⓜShree Krishna Paper Mills & Ind Ltd
Jaipur Mill
Plot No. SPL-A, RIICO Industrial Area, Vill. Keshwana, Teh. Kotputli
303108 Jaipur, Rajasthan
India
Phone: (91) 11 3095 3200/3201
Fax: (91) 11 2326 6708
Email: info@skpmil.com
Web Address: www.skpmil.com
Personnel:
Man. Dir.: N. K. Pasari
Phone: (91) 1494 513571, 320907
Chief Prod. Mgr.: J. Nagarajan
Phone: (91) 1494 513571, 320907
Total Employees at this Location: 215
Type of Operation: Paper mill
Pulp Grades and Capacities:
Total pulp capacity: 40,228 mt/y
Recycled Pulping: 40,228 mt/y
Pulp Mill Data:
Bleach Plant Systems: 1
Chemical Pulping System
Recycled Fiber Treatment Lines:
Flotation deinking lines: 1
Paper/Paperboard Grades and Capacities:
Total paper and paperboard capacity: 40,000 mt/y
Newsprint: 40,000 mt/y
Paper and Paperboard Mill Data:
Paper Machines: 1
No. 1, fourdrinier, total capacity 40,000 mt/y, Trim width 3.74 m, Newsprint
Coating Machines: 2
No. 3
No. 1 & 2
Energy Data:
Power boilers
Combustion turbines
Electrical demand for mill: 107 MWh/D

ⓘⓜShree Krishna Paper Mills & Ind Ltd
Haryana Coating Division
T-4, Old Industrial Area
124507 Bahadurgarh, Haryana
India
Phone: (91) 11 3095 3200/3201
Fax: (91) 11 2326 6708
Email: info@skpmil.com
Web Address: www.skpmil.com
Total Employees of Company: 650
Total Employees at this Location: 250
Type of Operation: Paper mill
Mill Locations:
Shree Krishna Paper Mills & Ind Ltd, Jaipur Mill, Plot No. SPL-A, RIICO Industrial Area, Vill. Keshwana, Teh. Kotputli, 303108 Jaipur, India, Capacity: 40,000 mt/y, (Paper mill)
Phone: (91) 11 3095 3200/3201
Fax: (91) 11 2326 6708
Email: info@skpmil.com
Paper/Paperboard Grades and Capacities:
Total paper and paperboard capacity: 18,000 mt/y
Coated woodfree/freesheet: 18,000 mt/y
Coating Machines: 3
No. 1, total capacity 6,000 mt/y., off machine
No. 2, total capacity 6,000 mt/y., off machine
No. 3, total capacity 6,000 mt/y., off machine

India

⑪Shree Marathawada Paper Mills (P) Ltd.
Ownership: 50% by Ashoake J. Patil, 50% by Pratap J. Patil
Vill. Rohital, Tehsil Georai
431127 Dist. Beed
India
  Phone: (91) 2447 250601/602
  Fax: (91) 2447 250601/602
Personnel:
  Man. Dir.: Pratap J. Patil
  Phone: (91) 2447 250601/602
  Fax: (91) 2447 250601/602
  Maint. Mgr.: V. R. Patil
  Phone: (91) 2447 250601/602
  Fax: (91) 2447 250601/602
  Purch. Mgr.: P. V. Musale
  Phone: (91) 2447 250601/602
  Fax: (91) 2447 250601/602
Total Employees at this Location: 150
Mill Locations:
Shree Marathawada Paper Mills (P) Ltd., Dist. Beed Mill, Vill. Rohital, Tehsil Georai, 431127 Dist. Beed, India, Capacity: 9,000 mt/y, (Paper mill)
  Phone: (91) 2447 250601/602
  Fax: (91) 2447 250601/602

⑪Shree Marathawada Paper Mills (P) Ltd.
Dist. Beed Mill
Vill. Rohital, Tehsil Georai
431127 Dist. Beed, Maharashtra
India
  Phone: (91) 2447 250601/602
  Fax: (91) 2447 250601/602
Personnel:
  Man. Dir.: Pratap J. Patil
  Phone: (91) 240 2485423/26
  Fax: (91) 240 2485423/26
  Maint. Mgr.: V. R. Patil
  Phone: (91) 2447 250601/602
  Purch. Mgr.: P. V. Musale
  Phone: (91) 2447 250601/602
  Shift in charge: N. A. Admane
  Phone: (91) 2447 250601/602
  Shift in charge: V. S. Chopade
  Phone: (91) 2447 250601/602
Total Employees at this Location: 150
Type of Operation: Paper mill
Paper/Paperboard Grades and Capacities:
  Total paper and paperboard capacity: 9,000 mt/y
  Packaging papers: 9,000 mt/y
Paper and Paperboard Mill Data:
  Stock Preparation:
  Pulpers: 1
  Refiners: 1
Paper Machines: 1
No. 1, fourdrinier, total capacity 9,000 mt/y, Trim width 1.8 m, Packaging papers
Finishing Equipment:
  Rewinders: 1 at 10,000 mt/y
Energy Data:
Power boilers: 1
Electrical demand for mill: 1 MWh/D

⑪Shree Papers Ltd.
Ownership: 100% by Mr. P. Kaleswara Rao & Associates
G. Ragampeta, Vial Samalkot
533440 East Godavari
India
  Mailing Address: G. Ragameta, P.O. Box No. 6, 533440 Samalkot, East Godavari
  Phone: (91) 883 276999/264266
  Fax: (91) 883 276324
  Email: shreepapers@yahoo.com
Personnel:
  Man. Dir.: P. Kaleswara Rao
  Phone: (91) 883 276999/264266
  Fax: (91) 883 276324
  Email: parvatanenikarao@yahoo.com
  Exec. Dir.: P. Sreedhar Chowdary
  Phone: (91) 883 276999/264266
  Fax: (91) 883 276324
  Gen. Mgr. (Technical): Ghandrashekar Hedge
  Phone: (91) 883 276999/264266
  Fax: (91) 883 276324
Total Employees at this Location: 200
Mill Locations:
Shree Papers Ltd., East Godavari Mill, G. Ragampeta, Vial Samalkot, 533 440 East Godavari, A.P., India, Capacity: 4,500 mt/y, (Paperboard mill)
  Phone: (91) 883 276999/264266
  Fax: (91) 883 276324
  Email: shreepapers@yahoo.com

⑪Shree Papers Ltd.
East Godavari Mill
G. Ragampeta, Vial Samalkot
533 440 East Godavari, A.P.
India
  Mailing Address: G. Ragameta, P.O. Box No. 6, 533 440 Samalkot, East Godavari, India
  Phone: (91) 883 276999/264266
  Fax: (91) 883 276324
  Email: shreepapers@yahoo.com
Personnel:
  Man. Dir.: P. Kaleswara Rao
  Phone: (91) 883 24769999
  Email: parvatanenikarao@yahoo.com
  Exec. Dir.: P. Sreedhar Chowdary
  Phone: (91) 884 2327262/2327324
  Fax: (91) 884 2327525
  Gen. Mgr. (Technical): Ghandrashekar Hedge
  Phone: (91) 884 2327262/2327324
  Fax: (91) 884 2327525
Total Employees at this Location: 200
Type of Operation: Paperboard mill
Pulp Mill Data:
  Recycled Fiber Treatment Lines:
  Pulpers: 3 at 13,000 admt/y
Paper/Paperboard Grades and Capacities:
  Total paper and paperboard capacity: 4,500 mt/y
  Linerboard
  Boxboard/cartonboard
Paper and Paperboard Mill Data:
  Stock Preparation:
  Refiners: 3
Paper Machines: 1
No. 1, cylinder, total capacity 7,500 mt/y, Trim width 1.7 m, Linerboard, Boxboard/cartonboard
Energy Data:
Power boilers: 1

⑪Shree Raj- Rajeshwari Pap-Chem Industries (P) Ltd.
Nasik Mill
G - 5, Malegaon, MIDC, Sinner
422103 Dist. Nasik, Maharashtra
India
  Phone: (91) 2551 230391, 230078, 230849.
  Fax: (91) 2551 230798
Personnel:
  Dir.: Parag D. Shah
  Phone: (91) 98 20293643
  Email: srrppc@sify.com
Total Employees at this Location: 200
Type of Operation: Paper mill
Paper/Paperboard Grades and Capacities:
  Total paper and paperboard capacity: 27,500 mt/y
  Packaging papers: 27,500 mt/y
Paper and Paperboard Mill Data:
Paper Machines: 1
No. 1, fourdrinier, Packaging papers

⑪Shree Raj- Rajeshwari Pap-Chem Industries (P) Ltd.
G - 5, Malegaon, MIDC, Sinner
422103 Dist. Nasik
India
Personnel:
  Dir.: Parag D. Shah
  Phone: (91) 2551 230391, 230078, 230849.
  Fax: (91) 2551 230798
  Email: srrppc@sify.com
Total Employees at this Location: 200
Mill Locations:
Shree Raj- Rajeshwari Pap-Chem Industries (P) Ltd., Nasik Mill, G - 5, Malegaon, MIDC, Sinner, 422103 Dist. Nasik, India, Capacity: 27,500 mt/y, (Paper mill)
  Phone: (91) 2551 230391, 230078, 230849.
  Fax: (91) 2551 230798

⑪⑪Shree Rajeshwaranand Paper Mills Ltd.
Dist. Bharuch Mill
Bharuch-Jhagadia Rd., Vill.: Govali Tq. Jhagadia
Dist. Bharuch, Gujarat
India
  Phone: (91) 2645-27705/6/7/8
  Fax: (91) 2645-27709
  Email: srpmlad1@sancharnet.in
Personnel:
  Chrmn.: Amrish R Pate
  Phone: (91) 2646 284103/4/5/6/7/8
  Fax: (91) 2646 284109
  Man. Dir: Prakash R. Vora
  Phone: (91) 2646 284103/4/5/6/7/8
  Fax: (91) 2646 284109
Total Employees at this Location: 125
Type of Operation: Paper mill
Pulp Mill Data:
  Bleach Plant Lines:
  No. 1, Sequence: HH
Paper/Paperboard Grades and Capacities:
  Total paper and paperboard capacity: 39,000 mt/y
  Newsprint: 21,000 mt/y
  Uncoated woodfree/freesheet: 18,000 mt/y
Paper and Paperboard Mill Data:
Paper Machines: 1
No. 1, Trim width 2.44 m, Uncoated woodfree/freesheet
Finishing Equipment:
  Rewinders: 1
Energy Data:
Power boilers: 1

⑪Shree Ram Krupa Paper Mill
Surendranagar Mill
Krushna nagar Rd
363510 Surendranagar, Gujarat
India
Type of Operation: Paperboard mill
Paper/Paperboard Grades and Capacities:
  Total paper and paperboard capacity: 18,000 mt/y
  Containerboard: 18,000 mt/y
Paper and Paperboard Mill Data:
Paper Machines: 1
No. 1, total capacity 18,000 mt/y, Trim width 3.2 m, Containerboard

⑪Shree Rama Newsprint Ltd.
Ownership: 59.79% by The West Coast Paper Mills Ltd.
Nariman Bhawan, 12th Floor, 227, Vinay K. Shah Marg, Nariman Point
400 021 Mumbai, Maharashtra
India
  Phone: (91) 22 2202 0511
  Fax: (91) 22 22821430
  Email: ramanewsprint@ramanewsprint.com
  Web Address: www.ramanewsprint.com
Personnel:
  Chrmn.: V. D. Bajaj

India

Phone: (91) 22 22020511
Fax: (91) 22 22821430
Email: vdbajaj@ramanewsprint.com
Corp. Dev. Dir.: S. S. Mande
Phone: (91) 22 22020511
Fax: (91) 22 22821430
Mills Ops. Dir.: S. C. Bhargova
Phone: (91) 22 22020511
Fax: (91) 22 22821430
Total Employees of Company: 530
Total Employees at this Location: 60
Mill Locations:
Shree Rama Newsprint Ltd., Barbhodan Mill, Taluka Olpad, 395 005 Barbhodan, Surat District, India, Capacity: 132,090 mt/y, (Paper mill)
Phone: (91) 2621 224 203/204/205
Fax: (91) 2621 224 206
Email: ramanpl_ad1@sancharnet.in, ramasurat@ramanewsprint.com

ⓂShree Rishabh Papers
Nawanshaher Mill
Ownership: 100% by Shreyans Industries Ltd.
144522 Banah, Dist. Nawanshahar, Punjab
India
Phone: (91) 1881 273627, 273628, 273629
Fax: (91) 1881 273645
Email: srp@shreyansgroup.com
Web Address: www.shreyansgroup.com
Personnel:
Pres.: Vijay K. Arora
Phone: (91) 1881 273627
Fax: (91) 1881 273645
Email: srp@shreyansgroup.com
Total Employees at this Location: 325
Type of Operation: Pulp mill, Paper mill
Pulp Grades and Capacities:
Total pulp capacity: 21,666 mt/y
Other Pulp: 21,666 mt/y
Pulp Mill Data:
Chemical Pulping Systems:
Batch digesters: 6
Continuous digesters: 1
Pulp Lines: 2
Bleach Plant Systems: 1
MSRP, Sequence: O_2 CEopHH, Capacity 27,000 admt/y
Chemical Recovery Equipment:
Evaporator lines: 7
Recycled Fiber Treatment Lines:
Pulpers: 1 at 600 admt/y
Paper/Paperboard Grades and Capacities:
Total paper and paperboard capacity: 29,000 mt/y
Uncoated woodfree/freesheet: 29,000 mt/y
Paper and Paperboard Mill Data:
Stock Preparation:
Refiners: 1
Paper Machines: 1
No. 1, fourdrinier, total capacity 29,000 mt/y, Trim width 2.48 m, Uncoated woodfree/freesheet
Finishing Equipment:
Winders: 2 at 39,000 mt/y
Calenders: 2
Rewinders: 2 at 39,000 mt/y
Sheeters: 2 at 16,000 mt/y
Energy Data:
Power boilers: 1
Steam turbines at 4.8 MW
Electrical demand for mill: 91 MWh/D

ⓄⓂShree Saptashringi Board & Paper Mill (P) Ltd.
Dist. Aurangabad Mill
Kesapuri, Nasik Rd., Aurangabad
431002 Dist. Aurangabad, Maharashtra
India
Phone: (91) 240 2615602
Personnel:
Man. Dir.: Chander Gidwani

Phone: (91) 98 22442288
Gen. Mgr.: Deepak Chabra
Phone: (91) 93 71187855
Type of Operation: Paperboard mill
Paper/Paperboard Grades and Capacities:
Total paper and paperboard capacity: 5,400 mt/y
Boxboard/cartonboard

ⓄShree Satpura Tapi Parisar Sahkari Sakhar Karkhanal Ltd.
Mittal Court C-Wing, Room No. 105, 10th Fl. Nariman Point
Mumbai, Maharashtra
India
Phone: (91) 22 22028528/851772
Fax: (91) 22 22028528
Email: mdssksd@bom6.vsnl.net.in
Mill Locations:
Shree Satpura Tapi Parisar Sahkari Sakhar Karkhanal Ltd., Dist. Nandurban Mill, Purushottam Nagar, Tal. Shahada, Dist. Nandurban, India, Capacity: 20,000 mt/y, (Paper mill)

ⓄShree Satpura Tapi Parisar Sahkari Sakhar Karkhanal Ltd.
Dist. Nandurban Mill
Purushottam Nagar, Tal. Shahada
Dist. Nandurban, Maharashtra
India
Type of Operation: Paper mill
Paper/Paperboard Grades and Capacities:
Total paper and paperboard capacity: 20,000 mt/y
Uncoated woodfree/freesheet

ⓄShree Shyam Pulp & Board Mills Ltd.
A-257, Road No. 6, National Highway No. 8, Mahipalpur
110 058 New Delhi
India
Phone: (91) 11 43271000, 11 26783068/69
Fax: (91) 11 26781864
Email: service@ogromen.com, shreeshyam@shyampapers.com
Web Address: ogromen.com, sspbml.in
Personnel:
Man. Dir.: Naresh Kumar Gupta
Phone: (91) 98 11106653
Fax: (91) 11 26781864
Dir.: Amit Gupta
Phone: (91) 98 10025575
Fax: (91) 11 26781864
Total Employees of Company: 1,200
Mill Locations:
Shree Shyam Pulp & Board Mills Ltd., Kashipur Mill, 5th K.M. Moradabad Road, Kashipur, 244713 Udham Singh Nagar, Uttakhand, India, Capacity: 125,000 mt/y, (Paper mill)
Phone: (91) 5947 274909 / 274910 / 274911
Fax: (91) 11 26781864
Email: shreeshyam@shyampapers.com

ⓄShree Shyam Pulp & Board Mills Ltd.
Kashipur Mill
5th K.M. Moradabad Road, Kashipur
244713 Udham Singh Nagar, Uttakhand, Uttarakhand
India
Phone: (91) 5947 274909 / 274910 / 274911
Fax: (91) 11 26781864
Email: shreeshyam@shyampapers.com
Web Address: ogromen.com, sspbml.in
Personnel:
Pres. Oper.: Jasvinder Singh Rana
Phone: (91) 5947 274909
Gen. Mgr. Sls.: Kuldeep Pandey
Phone: (91) 5947 274909
Gen. Mgr. Purch.: Ramesh Butani
Phone: (91) 5947 274909

Type of Operation: Paper mill
Paper/Paperboard Grades and Capacities:
Total paper and paperboard capacity: 125,000 mt/y
Uncoated woodfree/freesheet
Paper and Paperboard Mill Data:
Paper Machines: 4
PM 1, Trim width 2.92 m, Uncoated woodfree/freesheet, Coated woodfree/freesheet
PM 2, Trim width 2.94 m, Uncoated woodfree/freesheet, Coated woodfree/freesheet, Packaging papers
PM 3
PM 4

ⓄⓂShree Sitaram Paper Mills Ltd.
Dist. Kohlapur Mill
At & Post Warananagar, Tal. Panhaiha
416113 Dist. Kohlapur, Maharashtra
India
Phone: (91) 2328 224081/089
Fax: (91) 2328 224090
Personnel:
Man. Dir.: Mr. V. S. Chavan
Phone: (91) 2328 224081/089
Type of Operation: Paper mill
Mill Locations:
Shree Sitaram Paper Mills Ltd., Bharuch Mill, Govali Rd., Village Nanasanjha, Taluka Jhagadia, Dist. Bharuch, India, Capacity: 24,000 mt/y, (Paper mill)
Phone: (91) 2645 220162/761/866/7723
Fax: (91) 2645 220262, 11 27450352
Paper/Paperboard Grades and Capacities:
Total paper and paperboard capacity: 6,600 mt/y
Uncoated woodfree/freesheet

ⓄShree Sitaram Paper Mills Ltd.
25, Pritam Soc. No. 1
392002 Bharuch, Gujarat
India
Phone: (91) 2642 249948/245348
Fax: (91) 2648 249657
Personnel:
Man. Dir.: Praveen Kumar Goyal
Phone: (91) 2642 249948/245348
Fax: (91) 2648 249657
Mktg. Exec.: Rajesh Goyal
Phone: (91) 2642 249948/245348
Fax: (91) 2648 249657
Mill Locations:
Shree Sitaram Paper Mills Ltd., Dist. Kohlapur Mill, At & Post Warananagar, Tal. Panhaiha, 416113 Dist. Kohlapur, India, Capacity: 6,600 mt/y, (Paper mill)
Phone: (91) 2328 224081/089
Fax: (91) 2328 224090
Shree Sitaram Paper Mills Ltd., Bharuch Mill, Govali Rd., Village Nanasanjha, Taluka Jhagadia, Dist. Bharuch, India, Capacity: 24,000 mt/y, (Paper mill)
Phone: (91) 2645 220162/761/866/7723
Fax: (91) 2645 220262, 11 27450352

ⓂShree Sitaram Paper Mills Ltd.
Bharuch Mill
Govali Rd., Village Nanasanjha, Taluka Jhagadia
Dist. Bharuch, Gujarat
India
Phone: (91) 2645 220162/761/866/7723
Fax: (91) 2645 220262, 11 27450352
Personnel:
Gen. Mgr.: Vinod Agarwal
Phone: (91) 2645 220162/761/866/7723
Type of Operation: Paper mill
Paper/Paperboard Grades and Capacities:
Total paper and paperboard capacity: 24,000 mt/y
Packaging papers: 24,000 mt/y

ⓄShree Sudarshan Paper Mills Ltd.
Muthatalapalyam, Sirmugai Rd.
641302 Mettupalamam
India
Phone: (91) 4254 252413/14

India

Fax: (91) 4254 252412
Mill Locations:
Shree Sudarshan Paper Mills Ltd., Mettupalamam Mill, Muthatalapalyam, Sirmugai Rd., 641302 Mettupalamam, India, Capacity: 5,000 mt/y, (Paper mill)
Phone: (91) 4254 252413/14
Fax: (91) 4254 252412

ⓂShree Sudarshan Paper Mills Ltd.
Mettupalamam Mill
Muthatalapalyam, Sirmugai Rd.
641302 Mettupalamam, Tamil Nadu
India
Phone: (91) 4254 252413/14
Fax: (91) 4254 252412
Type of Operation: Paper mill
Paper/Paperboard Grades and Capacities:
Total paper and paperboard capacity: 5,000 mt/y
Uncoated woodfree/freesheet
Specialty and industrial

ⓄⓂShree Swami Harigiri Paper Mills Ltd.
Bharuch Mill
Plot 621/P GIDC, Pamoli
394116 Dist. Bharuch, Gujarat
India
Phone: (91) 2646 272282/96/97
Fax: (91) 2646 272291
Personnel:
Chmn.: Shantilal B. Dave
Phone: (91) 2646 272282/296/297
Partner: Mr. Kaplesh
Phone: (91) 93 74315411
Partner: Ishan Dave
Phone: (91) 98 25139556
Man. Dir.: Mr. M.B. Oza
Phone: (91) 93 74345726
Works Man.: S. K. Shasrabudhe
Phone: (91) 2646 272282/296/297
Total Employees at this Location: 220
Type of Operation: Paper mill, Paperboard mill
Paper/Paperboard Grades and Capacities:
Total paper and paperboard capacity: 15,000 mt/y
Boxboard/cartonboard: 15,000 mt/y
Paper and Paperboard Mill Data:
Stock Preparation:
Pulpers: 2
Refiners: 3
Paper Machines: 1
PM 1, total capacity 15,000 mt/y, Trim width 1.85 m, Boxboard/cartonboard

ⓄShree Vindhya Paper Mills Ltd.
Ownership: 11.11% by Financial Institutions, 8.98% by Private cooperative banks & others, 45.98% by Promoters, 33.93% by Public
Indian Mercantile Chambers, 3rd Floor 14 Kamani Marg Ballard Estate
400 001 Fort Mumbai, Maharashtra
India
Phone: (91) 22 66314181/182
Fax: (91) 22 66314186
Email: vindhyapaper@yahoo.co.in
Personnel:
Chmn. & Man. Dir.: N. K. Somani
Phone: (91) 22 66314181/182
Fax: (91) 22 66314186
Exec. Dir.: Shekhar Somani
Phone: (91) 22 66314181/182
Fax: (91) 22 66314186
Tech. Dir.: R.K. Mishra
Phone: (91) 22 66314181/182
Fax: (91) 22 66314186
Finan. Dir.: L. R. Daga
Phone: (91) 22 66314181/182
Fax: (91) 22 66314186
Total Employees of Company: 200

Total Employees at this Location: 12
Mill Locations:
Shree Vindhya Paper Mills Ltd., Jalgaon Mill, Somani Nagar, Duskheda, Bhusaval, Jalgaon, India, Capacity: 33,000 mt/y, (Pulp mill, Paper mill)
Phone: (91) 22 22612557/ 22612449
Fax: (91) 22 22617288
Email: svpm_bsl@indiatimes.com

ⓂShree Vindhya Paper Mills Ltd.
Jalgaon Mill
Somani Nagar, Duskheda
Bhusaval, Jalgaon, Maharashtra
India
Phone: (91) 22 22612557/ 22612449
Fax: (91) 22 22617288
Email: svpm_bsl@indiatimes.com
Type of Operation: Pulp mill, Paper mill
Paper/Paperboard Grades and Capacities:
Total paper and paperboard capacity: 33,000 mt/y
Uncoated woodfree/freesheet

ⓄShreyans Industries Ltd.
Village Bholapur, Post Office Sahabana, Chandigarh Road
141123 Ludhiana, Punjab
India
Phone: (91) 161 2685271 / 2685272 / 6574125
Fax: (91) 161 2685270
Email: atl@shreyansgroup.com
Web Address: www.shreyansgroup.com
Personnel:
Chmn. & Man. Dir.: Rajneesh Oswal
Phone: (91) 161 2685271
Fax: (91) 161 2685270
Exec. Dir. & CEO: Anil Kumar
Phone: (91) 161 2685271
Fax: (91) 161 2685270
Dir.: Kunal Oswal
Phone: (91) 161 2685271
Fax: (91) 161 2685270
Total Employees of Company: 1,100
Mill Locations:
Shree Rishabh Papers, Nawanshaher Mill, 144522 Banah, Dist. Nawanshahar, India, Capacity: 29,000 mt/y, (Pulp mill, Paper mill)
Phone: (91) 1881 273627, 273628, 273629
Fax: (91) 1881 273645
Email: srp@shreyansgroup.com
Shreyans Papers, Ahmedgarh Mill, Malikpur, 148 021 Ahmedgarh, Dist. Sangrur, India, Capacity: 39,984 mt/y, (Pulp mill, Paper mill)
Phone: (91) 1675 240347, 240348, 240349, 661300
Fax: (91) 1675 240512
Email: spm@shreyansgroup.com, shreyans.ahmd@smx.sril.in

ⓂShreyans Papers
Ahmedgarh Mill
Ownership: 100% by Shreyans Industries Ltd.
Malikpur
148 021 Ahmedgarh, Dist. Sangrur, Punjab
India
Phone: (91) 1675 240347, 240348, 240349, 661300
Fax: (91) 1675 240512
Email: spm@shreyansgroup.com, shreyans.ahmd@smx.sril.in
Web Address: www.shreyansgroup.com
Personnel:
Exec. Dir. & CEO: Anil Kumar
Total Employees at this Location: 745
Type of Operation: Pulp mill, Paper mill
Pulp Grades and Capacities:
Total pulp capacity: 32,130 mt/y
Other Pulp: 32,130 mt/y
Pulp Mill Data:
Chemical Pulping Systems:
Continuous digesters: 1
Bleach Plant Systems: 1

Chemical Recovery Equipment:
Recovery boilers: 1
Paper/Paperboard Grades and Capacities:
Total paper and paperboard capacity: 39,984 mt/y
Uncoated woodfree/freesheet: 39,984 mt/y
Paper and Paperboard Mill Data:
Paper Machines: 1
No. 1, fourdrinier, total capacity 39,984 mt/y, Trim width 2.83 m, Uncoated woodfree/freesheet
Energy Data:
Power boilers: 3
Steam turbines: 2 at 3.5, 2.5 MW
Electrical demand for mill: 100 MWh/D

ⓄShreyas Papers Pvt. Ltd.
Plot No. 11, Kerwad Vill.
581325 Dandeli
India
Phone: (91) 836 2355296/0653
Email: shreyasp@sanchamet.in
Personnel:
Chmn. & Man. Dir.: Ramnath R. Nayak
Phone: (91) 836 2355296/0653
Email: md@shreyaspaper.com
Sls. Officer: Jagadish S. K
Phone: (91) 836 2355296/0653
Total Employees of Company: 99
Mill Locations:
Shreyas Papers Pvt. Ltd., Dandeli Mill, Plot No. 11, Kerwad Vill., 581325 Dandeli, India, Capacity: 9,000 mt/y, (Paperboard mill)
Phone: (91) 836 2355296/0653
Email: shreyasp@sanchamet.in

ⓂShreyas Papers Pvt. Ltd.
Dandeli Mill
Plot No. 11, Kerwad Vill.
581325 Dandeli, Karnataka
India
Phone: (91) 836 2355296/0653
Email: shreyasp@sanchamet.in
Personnel:
Chmn. & Man. Dir.: Mr. Ramnath R. Nayak
Phone: (91) 8284 230346/231346
Email: md@shreyaspaper.com
Sls. Officer: Jagadish S. K.
Phone: (91) 94 48288157
Total Employees at this Location: 99
Type of Operation: Paperboard mill
Paper/Paperboard Grades and Capacities:
Total paper and paperboard capacity: 9,000 mt/y
Boxboard/cartonboard: 9,000 mt/y
Paper and Paperboard Mill Data:
Paper Machines: 1
No. 1, total capacity 9,000 mt/y, Trim width 1.68 m, Boxboard/cartonboard

ⓄⓂShri Bankey Bihari Lal Board Mills
Ghaziabad Mill
C-33/2 Industrial Area, Meerut Rd.
Ghaziabad, Uttar Pradesh
India
Phone: (91) 575 27292683/120 3291303
Fax: (91) 120 2702653
Email: sbblbm@yahoo.com, info@sbblbm.com
Web Address: www.sbblbm.com
Type of Operation: Paper mill
Paper/Paperboard Grades and Capacities:
Total paper and paperboard capacity: 40,400 mt/y
Packaging papers: 40,400 mt/y

ⓂShri Harikrishna Papers PVT. Ltd.
Palani Taluk Mill
Ownership: GVG Paper Mills Ltd.
Nallur, Pushpathur Village
624 618 Palani Taluk, Tamil Nadu
India
Phone: (91) 4252 252541/542

India

Email: gvgpaper@md4.vsnl.net.in
Personnel:
Gen. Mgr. Tech.: Mr. Regunath
Phone: (91) 4252 252541/542
Sls. Adviser: S. Sukumar
Phone: (91) 4252 252541/542
Type of Operation: Paper mill
Paper/Paperboard Grades and Capacities:
Total paper and paperboard capacity: 36,500 mt/y
Newsprint: 4,800 mt/y
Uncoated woodfree/freesheet: 19,700 mt/y
Specialty and industrial: 12,000 mt/y
Paper and Paperboard Mill Data:
Paper Machines: 3
PM 1, total capacity 10,500 mt/y, Trim width 1.8 m, Newsprint, Uncoated woodfree/freesheet
PM 2, total capacity 14,000 mt/y, Trim width 2.14 m, Uncoated woodfree/freesheet
PM 3, (second hand), total capacity 12,000 mt/y, Trim width 2.83 m, Specialty and industrial

ⓗⓜShri Krishna Fire Works
Sivakasi Mill
Paernayakkanpatti Village
Sivakasi, Tamil Nadu
India
Type of Operation: Paper mill
Paper/Paperboard Grades and Capacities:
Total paper and paperboard capacity: 14,000 mt/y
Specialty and industrial: 14,000 mt/y
Paper and Paperboard Mill Data:
Paper Machines: 1
No. 1, total capacity 14,000 mt/y

ⓗⓜShri Krishna Paper & Board Mills
Dombivli Mill
Plot No. B-42, Phase No. 1, M.I.D.C.
Dombivli, Maharashtra
India
Phone: (91) 251 2471395 /2434285
Fax: (91) 251 2470374
Email: krishna_kraft@rediffmail.com
Personnel:
Man. Dir.: Dilip Kumar M. Suchak
Phone: (91) 98 20547096
Mgr.: Pradish K. Shah
Phone: (91) 93 22251318
Total Employees at this Location: 90
Type of Operation: Paper mill, Paperboard mill
Paper/Paperboard Grades and Capacities:
Total paper and paperboard capacity: 9,000 mt/y
Packaging papers: 9,000 mt/y

ⓗⓜShri Ramchander Straw Products Ltd.
Dist. Moradabad Mill
Vill. Vijaypur, Tehsil Biari
244001 Dist. Moradabad, Uttar Pradesh
India
Phone: (91) 591 2490171/8843
Fax: (91) 591 2490375
Email: singhalr@nde.vsnl.net.in
Personnel:
Mktg. Mgr.: L. P. Tyagi
Phone: (91) 591 2498843
Man. Dir.: Ravi Kumar Singhal
Phone: (91) 98 37023385
Type of Operation: Paper mill
Paper/Paperboard Grades and Capacities:
Total paper and paperboard capacity: 15,000 mt/y
Packaging papers
Paper and Paperboard Mill Data:
Paper Machines: 1
No. 1, Packaging papers

ⓜSiddheshwari Industries Ltd.
Muzaffarnagar Mill
Ownership: Sidharth Papers Ltd.
8.6th Km, Jansath Road
Muzaffarnagar, Uttar Pradesh
India
Phone: (91) 131-2660191 / 92
Fax: (91) 131 2660193
Email: sil_mzn@sidharthpapers.com
Web Address: www.sidharthpapers.com
Total Employees at this Location: 125
Type of Operation: Paper mill
Pulp Grades and Capacities:
Total pulp capacity: 35,195 mt/y
Recycled Pulping: 35,195 mt/y
Pulp Mill Data:
Recycled Fiber Treatment Lines:
Recycled packaging pulping lines: 1
Paper/Paperboard Grades and Capacities:
Total paper and paperboard capacity: 35,000 mt/y
Linerboard: 35,000 mt/y
Paper and Paperboard Mill Data:
Paper Machines: 1
No. 1, multi-wire, total capacity 35,000 mt/y, Linerboard
Energy Data:
Power boilers
Electrical demand for mill: 42 MWh/D

ⓜSiddheshwari Paper Udhyog Ltd.
Kashipur Mill
Ownership: Sidharth Papers Ltd.
7 Km Stone, Moradabad Rd.
244713 Kashipur, Uttarakhand
India
Phone: (91) 5947 273992, 275289
Fax: (91) 5947 275802, 275286
Email: spul@sidharthpapers.com
Personnel:
Man. Dir.: Jitendra Kumar
Phone: (91) 5947 273992, 275289
Total Employees at this Location: 170
Type of Operation: Paper mill
Pulp Grades and Capacities:
Total pulp capacity: 38,868 mt/y
Other Pulp: 38,868 mt/y
Pulp Mill Data:
Chemical Pulping Systems:
Batch digesters
Chemical Recovery Equipment:
Evaporator lines: 1
Recovery boilers: 1
Paper/Paperboard Grades and Capacities:
Total paper and paperboard capacity: 40,000 mt/y
Corrugating medium/fluting: 40,000 mt/y
Paper and Paperboard Mill Data:
Paper Machines: 1
No. 1, fourdrinier, total capacity 40,000 mt/y, Corrugating medium/fluting
Energy Data:
Power boilers
Steam turbines at 6 MW
Electrical demand for mill: 90 MWh/D

ⓗⓜSidharth Papers Ltd.
Kashipur Mill
7th Km. Moradabad Rd. Dist. Udhamsingh Nagar
244713 Kashipur, Uttarakhand
India
Mailing Address: PO Kashipur, 244713 Dist. Nainital, Uttaranchal, India
Phone: (91) 5947 275804, 275287,
Fax: (91) 5947 275286
Email: spl@sidharthpapers.com
Web Address: www.sidharthpapers.com
Personnel:
Man. Dir.: Jitendra Kumar
Phone: (91) 5947 275804, 275287,
Email: jitendra_kumar@sidharthpapers.com
Whole Time Dir.: Sushil Kumar Bansal
Phone: (91) 5947 275804, 275287
Total Employees at this Location: 145

Type of Operation: Paper mill
Mill Locations:
Shree Bhageshwari Papers Ltd, Muzaffarnagar Mill, 9th Km stone, Bhopa Road, 251 001 Muzaffarnagar, India, Capacity: 33,100 mt/y, (Paper mill)
Phone: (91) 131-2468388 / 89
Fax: (91) 131-2468391
Email: bppl_mzn@yahoo.co.in
Siddheshwari Industries Ltd., Muzaffarnagar Mill, 8.6th Km, Jansath Road, Muzaffarnagar, India, Capacity: 35,000 mt/y, (Paper mill)
Phone: (91) 131-2660191 / 92
Fax: (91) 2660193
Email: sil_mzn@sidharthpapers.com
Siddheshwari Paper Udhyog Ltd., Kashipur Mill, 7 Km Stone, Moradabad Rd., 244713 Kashipur, India, Capacity: 40,000 mt/y, (Paper mill)
Phone: (91) 5947 273992, 275289
Fax: (91) 5947 275802, 275286
Email: spul@sidharthpapers.com
Sidharth Papers Ltd., Kashipur Mill (Unit 2), 7th Km. Moradabad Rd. Dist. Udhamsingh Nagar, Kashipur, India, Capacity: 79,968 mt/y, (Paper mill)
Phone: (91) 5947 270875, 275287
Fax: (91) 5947 270873, 275286
Email: spl@sidharthpapers.com
Sidharth Papers Ltd., MuzzafarNagar Mill, 8.6th Km Stone, Jansath Road, 251001 MuzzafarNagar, India, Capacity: 18,000 mt/y, (Paper mill)
Phone: (91) 131 2660191
Fax: (91) 131 2660192
Email: spl@sidharthpapers.com
Pulp Grades and Capacities:
Total pulp capacity: 33,162 mt/y
Recycled Pulping: 3,316 mt/y
Other Pulp: 29,846 mt/y
Pulp Mill Data:
Chemical Pulping Systems:
Batch digesters
Chemical Recovery Equipment:
Evaporator lines: 1
Recovery boilers: 1
Recycled Fiber Treatment Lines:
Recycled packaging pulping lines: 1
Paper/Paperboard Grades and Capacities:
Total paper and paperboard capacity: 33,000 mt/y
Linerboard: 33,000 mt/y
Paper and Paperboard Mill Data:
Paper Machines: 1
No. 1, twin-wire, total capacity 33,000 mt/y, Trim width 2.2 m, Linerboard
Finishing Equipment:
Rewinders: 1
Sheeters: 1
Energy Data:
Power boilers: 1
Electrical demand for mill: 72 MWh/D

ⓜSidharth Papers Ltd.
Kashipur Mill (Unit 2)
7th Km. Moradabad Rd. Dist. Udhamsingh Nagar
Kashipur, Uttarakhand
India
Phone: (91) 5947 270875, 275287
Fax: (91) 5947 270873, 275286
Email: spl@sidharthpapers.com
Web Address: www.sidharthpapers.com
Total Employees at this Location: 200
Type of Operation: Paper mill
Pulp Grades and Capacities:
Total pulp capacity: 75,856 mt/y
Recycled Pulping: 75,856 mt/y
Pulp Mill Data:
Recycled Fiber Treatment Lines:
Flotation deinking lines
Flotation deinking lines
Paper/Paperboard Grades and Capacities:
Total paper and paperboard capacity: 79,968 mt/y
Boxboard/cartonboard: 79,968 mt/y

Paper and Paperboard Mill Data:
Paper Machines: 1
No. 1, (second-hand), twin-wire, total capacity 79,968 mt/y, Trim width 3 m, Boxboard/cartonboard
Coating Machines: 1
PM 1, total capacity 80,000 mt/y., on machine
Energy Data:
Power boilers
Steam turbines: 1 at 6 MW
Electrical demand for mill: 134 MWh/D

ⓜSidharth Papers Ltd.
MuzzafarNagar Mill
8.6th Km Stone, Jansath Road
251001 MuzzafarNagar, Uttar Pradesh
India
 Phone: (91) 131 2660191
 Fax: (91) 131 2660192
 Email: spl@sidharthpapers.com
 Web Address: www.sidharthpapers.com
Type of Operation: Paper mill
Paper/Paperboard Grades and Capacities:
 Total paper and paperboard capacity: 18,000 mt/y
Paper and Paperboard Mill Data:
Paper Machines: 1
No. 1, (started up end June 2010), total capacity 18,000 mt/y, Trim width 4.7 m

ⓞⓜSilvertoan Papers Ltd.
Muzaffarnagar Mill
Ownership: 100% by Naveen Aggarwal, Amit Garg
9th km, Bhopa Road
251 003 Muzaffarnagar, Uttar Pradesh
India
 Phone: (91) 131 2468783/3205656/3297080/3297272
 Fax: (91) 131 2468784/2600644
 Email: silvertoanpapers@rediffmail.com
 Web Address: www.silvertoanpapers.com
Personnel:
CEO: Ashkay Jain
 Phone: (91) 131 2468783/3205656/3297080/3297272
Man. Dir.: Deepak Goel
 Phone: (91) 131 2468783/3205656/3297080/3297272
Type of Operation: Paper mill
Pulp Grades and Capacities:
 Total pulp capacity: 50,000 mt/y
Pulp Mill Data:
 Chemical Pulping Systems:
 Not Given: 1
Pulp Lines: 1
Paper/Paperboard Grades and Capacities:
 Total paper and paperboard capacity: 50,000 mt/y
 Linerboard: 50,000 mt/y
Paper and Paperboard Mill Data:
Paper Machines: 1
PM 1, total capacity 50,000 mt/y, Trim width 2.5 m, Linerboard
Finishing Equipment:
 Rewinders: 1
 Sheeters: 1
Energy Data:
Power boilers: 1
Steam turbines: 1 at 4 MW

ⓞThe Sirpur Paper Mills Ltd.
Ownership: 13.18% by Aravali Securities
3rd Floor, UCO Bank Building, Parliament Street
110 001 New Delhi, Delhi
India
 Phone: (91) 11 23722200/23717329
 Fax: (91) 11 23718447
 Email: sirpurpaper@vsnl.com
 Web Address: www.sirpurpaper.com
Personnel:
Exec. Dir.: Mr. S. K. Khare
 Phone: (91) 8738 238044/5
 Fax: (91) 8738 238642
 Email: spmled@sancharnet.in
Sr. VP (Mills Mgt): Mir M.P. Dokania
 Phone: (91) 11 23722200/23717329
 Fax: (91) 11 23718447
COO: Devashish Poddar
 Phone: (91) 11 23722200/23717329
 Fax: (91) 11 23718447
VP Mktg.: S. C. Gupta
 Phone: (91) 11 23717013
 Fax: (91) 11 23718447
VP (Corp. Plan.): Mr. Mahesh Kumar Birla
 Phone: (91) 11 23722200/23717329
 Fax: (91) 11 23718447
Gen. Mgr. (Tech.): Mr. C.T. Dathathreya
 Phone: (91) 11 23722200/23717329
 Fax: (91) 11 23718447
Gen. Mgr. (Paper): Mr. A. Venkateswara Rao
 Phone: (91) 11 23722200/23717329
 Fax: (91) 11 23718447
Gen. Mgr. (Raw Mat.): Mr. R.V.P. Murthy
 Phone: (91) 11 23722200/23717329
 Fax: (91) 11 23718447
Gen. Mgr. (Finan.): Mr. S.K. Modani
 Phone: (91) 11 23722200/23717329
 Fax: (91) 11 23718447
Dpty. Gen. Mgr. (Services): Mr. A. Raji Reddy
 Phone: (91) 11 23722200/23717329
 Fax: (91) 11 23718447
Dpty. Gen. Mgr. (Eng.): Mr. V.R. Moghe
 Phone: (91) 11 23722200/23717329
 Fax: (91) 11 23718447
Total Employees of Company: 3,115
Total Employees at this Location: 20
Mill Locations:
Sirpur Paper Mills Ltd., Adilabad Mill, 504 296 Sirpur-Kaghaznagar, Dist. Adilabad, A.P., India, Capacity: 129,948 mt/y, (Pulp mill, Paper mill, Paperboard mill)
 Phone: (91) 8738 238044/45
 Fax: (91) 8738 238642/323
 Email: spmled@sancharnet.in, edoffice@sirpurpaper.com

ⓜSirpur Paper Mills Ltd.
Adilabad Mill
Mill is temporarily closed (idled from the end of September 2014, due to a shortfall in its furnish)
Ownership: The Sirpur Paper Mills Ltd.
504 296 Sirpur-Kaghaznagar, Dist. Adilabad, A.P.
India
 Phone: (91) 8738 238044/45
 Fax: (91) 8738 238642/323
 Email: spmled@sancharnet.in, edoffice@sirpurpaper.com
 Web Address: www.sirpurpaper.com
Personnel:
Exec. Dir.: R. L. Lakhotia
 Phone: (91) 8738 239 314
 Fax: (91) 8738 238 323
 Email: rllakhotia@sirpurpaper.com
VP (Prod.): D. C Agarwal
 Phone: (91) 8738 235 405
 Fax: (91) 8738 238 323
 Email: dcagrawal@sirpurpaper.com
VP (F&C): S. K. Modani
 Phone: (91) 40 2323 5575
 Fax: (91) 40 2323 2470
 Email: skmodani@sirpurpaper.com
VP (Commercial): Vimal Arora
 Phone: (91) 99 6302 8478
 Fax: (91) 8738 238 642
 Email: vimarlarora@sirpurpaper.com
VP (HR & Admin.): B. C. Sharma
 Phone: (91) 8738 236 615
 Fax: (91) 8738 235 148
 Email: bcsharma@sirpurpaper.com
Sr. Gen. Mgr. (Ele. & Instrument): S. L. Goyal
 Phone: (91) 98 6634 6109
 Fax: (91) 8738 238 323
 Email: slgoyal@sirpurpaper.com
Gen. Mgr. (Env. & Central Lab): K. Radha Mohan
 Phone: (91) 89 7808 8004
 Fax: (91) 8738 238 323
 Email: kradhamohan@sirpurpaper.com
Gen. Mgr. (Maint.): P. K. Agarwal
 Phone: (91) 98 6650 0515
 Fax: (91) 8738 238 323
 Email: pkagarwal@sirpurpaper.com
Gen. Mgr. (Mat.): G. C. Kothari
 Phone: (91) 8738 239 806
 Fax: (91) 8738 238 642
 Email: gckothari@sirpurpaper.com
Dpty. Gen. Mgr. (Paper): R. K. Birla
 Phone: (91) 89 7870 0097
 Fax: (91) 8738 238 323
 Email: rkbirla@sirpurpaper.com
Dpty. Gen. Mgr. (Power & Boiler): K. Bhaskar Rao
 Phone: (91) 96 7649 8123
 Email: kbhaskarrao@sirpurpaper.com
Total Employees at this Location: 2,350
Type of Operation: Pulp mill, Paper mill, Paperboard mill
Pulp Grades and Capacities:
 Total pulp capacity: 116,223 mt/y
 Chemical Pulp: 116,223 mt/y
Pulp Mill Data:
 Chemical Pulping Systems:
 Batch digesters: 7
Pulp Lines: 1
 Bleach Plant Systems: 1
 ECF, Sequence: O_2 DoEopD
 Chemical Recovery Equipment:
 Evaporator lines: 1
 Recovery boilers: 1
 Lime Kiln
Paper/Paperboard Grades and Capacities:
 Total paper and paperboard capacity: 129,948 mt/y
 Uncoated woodfree/freesheet: 112,812 mt/y
 Boxboard/cartonboard: 17,136 mt/y
Paper and Paperboard Mill Data:
 Stock Preparation:
 Pulpers: 2
 Refiners: 38
Paper Machines: 8
No. 1, fourdrinier, total capacity 11,067 mt/y, Trim width 3.05 m, Uncoated woodfree/freesheet
No. 2, fourdrinier, total capacity 11,067 mt/y, Trim width 3.05 m, Uncoated woodfree/freesheet
No. 3, fourdrinier, total capacity 13,923 mt/y, Trim width 3.25 m, Uncoated woodfree/freesheet
No. 4, fourdrinier, total capacity 3,213 mt/y, Trim width 1.88 m, Uncoated woodfree/freesheet
No. 5, fourdrinier, total capacity 4,284 mt/y, Trim width 1.88 m, Uncoated woodfree/freesheet
No. 6, cylinder, total capacity 17,136 mt/y, Trim width 2.69 m, Boxboard/cartonboard
No. 7, fourdrinier, total capacity 21,420 mt/y, Trim width 2.6 m, Uncoated woodfree/freesheet
No. 8, (second hand), fourdrinier, total capacity 53,550 mt/y, Trim width 3.63 m, Uncoated woodfree/freesheet
Finishing Equipment:
 Winders: 6 at 164,250 mt/y
 Supercalenders
 Rewinders: 5 at 28,100 mt/y
 Sheeters: 10 at 25 mt/y, 25 mt/y, 50 mt/y, 15 mt/y, 15 mt/y, 60 mt/y, 25 mt/y, 10 mt/y, 15 mt/y, 50 mt/y
Energy Data:
Power boilers: 2
Steam turbines: 4 at 27 MW
Electrical demand for mill: 419 MWh/D

ⓞSKG Pulp & Paper
90/28, Tallygunge Circular Road
700 053 New Alipore, Kolkata
India
 Phone: (91) 033-24988479
 Fax: (91) 033-24988480

India

Email: skgpulp@rediffmail.com
Personnel:
Gen. Dir.: Avijit Ghosh
Phone: (91) 033-24988479
Fax: (91) 033-24988480
Mill Locations:
SKG Pulp & Paper, New Alipore, Kolkata Mill, 90/28, Tallygunge Circular Road, 700 053 New Alipore, Kolkata, India, Capacity: 25,000 mt/y, (Paper mill)
Phone: (91) 033-24988479
Fax: (91) 033-24988480
Email: skgpulp@rediffmail.com

ⓂSKG Pulp & Paper
New Alipore, Kolkata Mill
90/28, Tallygunge Circular Road
700 053 New Alipore, Kolkata, West Bengal
India
Phone: (91) 033-24988479
Fax: (91) 033-24988480
Email: skgpulp@rediffmail.com
Personnel:
Gen. Dir.: Avijit Ghosh
Phone: (91) 033-24988479
Total Employees at this Location: 100
Type of Operation: Paper mill
Pulp Grades and Capacities:
Total pulp capacity: 24,555 mt/y
Recycled Pulping: 24,555 mt/y
Pulp Mill Data:
Recycled Fiber Treatment Lines:
Recycled packaging pulping lines: 1
Paper/Paperboard Grades and Capacities:
Total paper and paperboard capacity: 25,000 mt/y
Linerboard: 10,000 mt/y
Corrugating medium/fluting: 15,000 mt/y
Paper and Paperboard Mill Data:
Paper Machines: 1
No. 1, twin-wire, total capacity 25,000 mt/y, Trim width 2.67 m, Linerboard, Corrugating medium/fluting
Energy Data:
Power boilers
Steam turbines at 6 MW
Electrical demand for mill: 32 MWh/D

ⓘSolid Containers Ltd.
Tiecicon House, Dr. E. Moses Rd.
400011 Mumbai, Maharashtra
India
Phone: (91) 22 24923158/159
Fax: (91) 22 22048688
Personnel:
Man. Dir.: Cyrus Bagwadia
Phone: (91) 22 24923158/159
Fax: (91) 22 22048688
Finan. Mgr.: Sunil Darda
Phone: (91) 22 24923158/159
Fax: (91) 22 22048688
Sec.: Sanjay Basantani
Phone: (91) 22 24923158/159
Fax: (91) 22 22048688
Mill Locations:
Solid Containers Ltd., Thane Mill, Vadavali., P.O. Mohone, 421102 Thane, India, Capacity: 27,000 mt/y, (Paper mill, Paperboard mill)

ⓂSolid Containers Ltd.
Thane Mill
Vadavali, P.O. Mohone
421102 Thane, Maharashtra
India
Type of Operation: Paper mill, Paperboard mill
Paper/Paperboard Grades and Capacities:
Total paper and paperboard capacity: 27,000 mt/y
Packaging papers: 13,500 mt/y
Boxboard/cartonboard: 13,500 mt/y

ⓘSona Paper & Boards Ltd.
Vill. Kurawala, Barwala Rd., Dera Bassi
Dist. Mohali
India
Phone: (91) 2430564, 2431069
Personnel:
Man. Dir.: Shanti Lal Sethia
Phone: (91) 94 17211506, 93 17611506
Dir.: Vinod Sethia
Phone: (91) 93 17611508
Mill Locations:
Sona Paper & Boards Ltd., Patiala Mill, Vill. Kurawala, Barwala Rd., Dera Bassi, Dist. Mohali, India, Capacity: 10,800 mt/y, (Paper mill)
Phone: (91) 2430564, 2431069

ⓂSona Paper & Boards Ltd.
Patiala Mill
Vill. Kurawala, Barwala Rd., Dera Bassi
Dist. Mohali, Punjab
India
Phone: (91) 2430564, 2431069
Personnel:
Man. Dir.: Mr. Shanti Lal Sethia
Phone: (91) 94 17211506, 93 17611506
Type of Operation: Paper mill
Paper/Paperboard Grades and Capacities:
Total paper and paperboard capacity: 10,800 mt/y
Packaging papers
Linerboard

ⓘⓂSouth India Paper Mills Ltd.
Nanjangud Mill
Chikkayana Chatra
571 301 Nanjangud, Karnataka
India
Phone: (91) 8221 228264 / 228265 / 228266 / 228267
Fax: (91) 8221 228270
Email: marketing@sipaper.com
Web Address: www.sipaper.com
Personnel:
Man. Dir.: Mahendra A. Patel
Phone: (91) 8221 228264
Fax: (91) 8221 228270
Jt. Man. Dir.: Manish M. Patel
Phone: (91) 8221 228264
Fax: (91) 8221 228270
Gen. Mgr., Commercial: K. R. Ramaprasad
Phone: (91) 8221 228264
Fax: (91) 8221 228270
Gen. Mgr.: K. Chandran
Phone: (91) 8221 228264
Fax: (91) 8221 228270
Total Employees at this Location: 365
Type of Operation: Pulp mill, Paper mill
Pulp Grades and Capacities:
Total pulp capacity: 25,000 mt/y
Chemical Pulp
Pulp Mill Data:
Chemical Pulping Systems:
Batch digesters: 5
Bleach Plant Systems: 1
Paper/Paperboard Grades and Capacities:
Total paper and paperboard capacity: 46,200 mt/y
Newsprint: 7,000 mt/y
Uncoated woodfree/freesheet: 17,000 mt/y
Packaging papers
Paper and Paperboard Mill Data:
Stock Preparation:
Pulpers: 2
Refiners: 7
Paper Machines: 3
PM 1, fourdrinier, Trim width 2.6 m
PM 2, fourdrinier, Trim width 1.8 m
PM 3, fourdrinier, Trim width 1.3 m
Finishing Equipment:
Rewinders: 3
Sheeters: 3
Energy Data:
Power boilers: 2
Steam turbines: 1 at 8.0 MW

ⓘSpaa Straw Board Ind. Pvt. Ltd.
Chormara, P.O. Bijepur
Bolangir
India
Phone: (91) 6655 220609/20895/222387
Fax: (91) 6655 220603/271164
Email: spaastraw@hotmail.com, spaastraw@bsnl.in
Personnel:
Man. Dir.: P. K. Meher
Phone: (91) 6655 220609/20895
Fax: (91) 6655 220603/271164
Email: pkmeher@sancharnet.in
Dir.: Kalyani Meher
Phone: (91) 6655 220609/20895
Fax: (91) 6655 220603/271164
Dir.: S. C. Patel
Phone: (91) 6655 220609/20895
Fax: (91) 6655 220603/271164
Mgr. (Finan. & Accounts): Nitai Bhattacharya
Phone: (91) 6655 220609/20895
Fax: (91) 6655 220603/271164
Email: nitai_bhattacharya@yahoo.co.in
Total Employees at this Location: 206
Mill Locations:
Spaa Straw Board Ind. Pvt. Ltd., Bolangir Mill, Chormara, P.O. Bijepur, Bolangir, India, Capacity: 9,900 mt/y, (Pulp mill, Paper mill)
Phone: (91) 6655 220609/20895/222387
Fax: (91) 6655 220603/271164
Email: spaastraw@hotmail.com, spaastraw@bsnl.in

ⓂSpaa Straw Board Ind. Pvt. Ltd.
Bolangir Mill
Chormara, P.O. Bijepur
Bolangir, Odisha
India
Phone: (91) 6655 220609/20895/222387
Fax: (91) 6655 220603/271164
Email: spaastraw@hotmail.com, spaastraw@bsnl.in
Personnel:
Man. Dir.: P. K. Meher
Phone: (91) 6655 222387/220148
Email: pkmeher@sancharnet.in
Dir.: Kalyani Meher
Phone: (91) 6655 220736
Dir.: S. C. Patel
Phone: (91) 6655 271166
Pulp Mill Mgr.: N. Nagar
Phone: (91) 6655 271164
Mgr. (Finan. & Accounts): Nitai Bhattacharya
Phone: (91) 6655 222387
Email: nitai_bhattacharya@yahoo.co.in
Mgr. (Stores & Commercials): P. K. Chand
Phone: (91) 6655 271164
Paper Maker: B. N. Bhol
Phone: (91) 6655 271164
Laboratory In Charge: P. K. Mahanty
Phone: (91) 6655 220609/20895/222387
Maint. Mgr.: Padhi Kumar Basanta
Phone: (91) 6655 220609/20895/222387
Env. Eng.: Panda Priyabrata
Phone: (91) 6655 220609/20895/222387
Total Employees at this Location: 206
Type of Operation: Pulp mill, Paper mill
Pulp Grades and Capacities:
Total pulp capacity: 9,900 mt/y
Paper/Paperboard Grades and Capacities:
Total paper and paperboard capacity: 9,900 mt/y
Newsprint
Uncoated woodfree/freesheet
Packaging papers
Paper and Paperboard Mill Data:
Stock Preparation:
Pulpers: 1
Refiners: 2
Paper Machines: 1

India

No. 1, fourdrinier, total capacity 9,900 mt/y, Trim width 2.1 m, Newsprint, Uncoated woodfree/freesheet, Packaging papers
Finishing Equipment:
Winders: 1 at 9,900 mt/y
Calenders: 1
Rewinders: 1 at 9,900 mt/y
Sheeters: 1 at 9,900 mt/y
Energy Data:
Power boilers: 1
Electrical demand for mill: 1 MWh/D

ⓘⓜSpeciality Papers Ltd.
Ownership: The Reliable Group
27, Kermani Bldg., 3rd Floor, Opp.Citi Bank, P. M. Road
400 001 Fort, Mumbai, Maharashtra
India
Phone: (91) 22 6631 0058/2282 8225
Fax: (91) 22 2282 1999
Email: splpaper@hathway.com
Web Address: www.reliablepaperindia.com
Personnel:
CEO: Vipul Desai
Phone: (91) 22 6631 0058/2282 8225
Fax: (91) 22 2282 1999
Man. Dir.: Mekan Gala
Phone: (91) 22 6631 0058/2282 8225
Fax: (91) 22 2282 1999
Total Employees at this Location: 10
Mill Locations:
Opel Paper Mill Ltd., Vapi Mill, Vapi, India, Capacity: 17,500 mt/y, (Paper mill)
Phone: (91) opel@reliablepaperindia.com
Email: opel@reliablepaperindia.com
Reliable Paper (India) Pvt. Ltd., Surat Mill, Village Tarsadi, Bardoli, Mahuva Road, 394601 Bardoli, Taluka - Mahuva, Surat, India, Capacity: 65,000 mt/y, (Paper mill)
Phone: (91) 2625 254085
Email: reliable@reliablepaperindia.com
Speciality Papers Ltd., Valsad Mill, Morai Village, National Highway No.8, 396 191 Vapi, Dist. Valsad, India, Capacity: 50,000 mt/y, (Paper mill)
Phone: (91) 260 2437160/7414
Fax: (91) 260 2437159
Email: speciality@reliablepaperindia.com

ⓜSpeciality Papers Ltd.
Valsad Mill
Morai Village, National Highway No.8
396 191 Vapi, Dist. Valsad, Gujarat
India
Phone: (91) 260 2437160/7414
Fax: (91) 260 2437159
Email: speciality@reliablepaperindia.com
Web Address: www.reliablepaperindia.com
Personnel:
CEO: Vipul Desai
Phone: (91) 22 5631 0058/59/60
Total Employees at this Location: 100
Type of Operation: Paper mill
Paper/Paperboard Grades and Capacities:
Total paper and paperboard capacity: 50,000 mt/y
Uncoated woodfree/freesheet
Tissue: 8,000 mt/y
Packaging papers
Specialty and industrial
Paper and Paperboard Mill Data:
Paper Machines: 3
No. 1, Yankee dryer, Trim width 2.3 m, Tissue
No. 2, Yankee dryer, Trim width 2.54 m, Tissue, Specialty and industrial
No. 3, multi-former, Trim width 2.5 m, Uncoated woodfree/freesheet, Packaging papers, Specialty and industrial
Finishing Equipment:
Rewinders: 3
Sheeters: 2
Energy Data:
Power boilers: 1

ⓘⓜSree Raja Rajeswari Paper Mills Ltd
Bapulapadu Branch
Opp. Nazvid RS, Bapulapadu, Hanuman Junction (Post)
521 105 Krishna, A.P.
India
Phone: (91) (8657) 42038, 42686
Fax: (91) (8657) 42159
Personnel:
Man. Dir.: Dr. A. K. Prasad
Phone: (91) 8657 242038/686
Total Employees at this Location: 300
Type of Operation: Pulp mill, Paper mill
Pulp Grades and Capacities:
Total pulp capacity: 4,950 mt/y
Paper/Paperboard Grades and Capacities:
Total paper and paperboard capacity: 6,600 mt/y
Boxboard/cartonboard
Paper and Paperboard Mill Data:
Stock Preparation:
Refiners: 3
Paper Machines: 1
No. 1, cylinder, Trim width 1.6 m, Boxboard/cartonboard
Finishing Equipment:
Rewinders: 1
Sheeters: 1
Energy Data:
Power boilers: 1

ⓘSree Sakthi Paper Mills Ltd.
"Sree Kailash", 57/2993 Paliam Rd.
682 016 Ernakulam, Kochi, Kerala
India
Phone: (91) 484 2373230 / 4092999 / 2371085
Fax: (91) 484 2370395
Email: sreesakthi@sreekailas.com
Web Address: www.sreekailas.com
Personnel:
Vice Chmn. & Man. Dir.: S. Rajkumar
Phone: (91) 984 6079089
Fax: (91) 484 2370395
Email: s.rajkumar@sreekailas.com
Exec. Dir.: Mr. A. Padmanabhan
Phone: (91) 484 2373230
Fax: (91) 484 2370395
Dir. Oper. (from February 1st, 2013): N. Rajagopal Pai
Phone: (91) 484 2373230
Fax: (91) 484 2370395
Company Sec.: Mr. Binu Alex V
Phone: (91) 944 7796956
Fax: (91) 484 2370395
Email: v.binualex@sreekailas.com
Total Employees of Company: 1,100
Total Employees at this Location: 150
Mill Locations:
Sree Sakthi Paper Mills Ltd., Chalakkudy Mill, Pariyaram, Trichur Dist., 680 721 Kanjirappilly, Chalakkudy, India, Capacity: 28,560 mt/y, (Paperboard mill)
Phone: (91) 480 2746129, 480 2747529
Fax: (91) 480 2746410
Email: sreesakthi@eth.net
Sree Sakthi Paper Mills Ltd., Edayar Mill, Industrial Development Area, Edayar, Muppathadam, 683102 Aluva, India, Capacity: 80,000 mt/y, (Paper mill)
Phone: (91) 484 2540622 / 2555451
Fax: (91) 484 2555835
Email: info@sreekailas.com

ⓜSree Sakthi Paper Mills Ltd.
Chalakkudy Mill
Pariyaram, Trichur Dist.
680 721 Kanjirappilly, Chalakkudy, Kerala
India
Phone: (91) 480 2746129, 480 2747529
Fax: (91) 480 2746410
Email: sreesakthi@eth.net
Web Address: www.sreekailas.com
Personnel:
Man. Dir.: Mr. S. Rajkumar
Phone: (91) 984 6079089
Email: s.rajkumar@sreekailas.com
Total Employees at this Location: 120
Type of Operation: Paperboard mill
Pulp Grades and Capacities:
Total pulp capacity: 27,186 mt/y
Recycled Pulping: 27,186 mt/y
Pulp Mill Data:
Bleach Plant Systems: 1
Recycled Pulping System
Recycled Fiber Treatment Lines:
Flotation deinking lines: 1
Recycled packaging pulping lines: 1
Paper/Paperboard Grades and Capacities:
Total paper and paperboard capacity: 28,560 mt/y
Boxboard/cartonboard: 28,560 mt/y
Paper and Paperboard Mill Data:
Paper Machines: 1
No. 1, multi-fourdrinier, total capacity 28,560 mt/y, Trim width 2.55 m, Boxboard/cartonboard
Coating Machines: 1
PM1, on machine
Energy Data:
Power boilers
Electrical demand for mill: 39 MWh/D

ⓜSree Sakthi Paper Mills Ltd.
Edayar Mill
Industrial Development Area, Edayar, Muppathadam
683102 Aluva, Kerala
India
Phone: (91) 484 2540622 / 2555451
Fax: (91) 484 2555835
Email: info@sreekailas.com
Web Address: www.sreekailas.com
Personnel:
V. Chmn. & Man. Dir.: Mr. S. Rajkumar
Phone: (91) 9846079089, 484373230
Email: s.rajkumar@sreekailas.com
Total Employees at this Location: 200
Type of Operation: Paper mill
Pulp Grades and Capacities:
Total pulp capacity: 79,349 mt/y
Recycled Pulping: 79,349 mt/y
Pulp Mill Data:
Recycled Fiber Treatment Lines:
Recycled packaging pulping lines: 1
Paper/Paperboard Grades and Capacities:
Total paper and paperboard capacity: 80,000 mt/y
Linerboard: 52,000 mt/y
Corrugating medium/fluting: 28,000 mt/y
Paper and Paperboard Mill Data:
Paper Machines: 2
No. 1, fourdrinier, total capacity 28,000 mt/y, Trim width 2.35 m, Corrugating medium/fluting
No. 2, multi-fourdrinier, total capacity 52,000 mt/y, Trim width 3.37 m, Linerboard
Finishing Equipment:
Rewinders: 1 at 15,000 mt/y
Energy Data:
Power boilers: 1
Steam turbines at 2 MW
Electrical demand for mill: 94 MWh/D

ⓘⓜSri Luxmi Tulasi Agro Paper Pvt Ltd.
Rajahmundry Mill
D.No. 25-2-20, Jayakrishnapuram
533015 Rajahmundry, A.P.
India
Mailing Address: Main Road, 501307 Aswaraopeta, Khammam District, A.P., India
Phone: (91) 883 2476877
Fax: (91) 883 2441577
Email: contact@sriluxmitulasi.com
Web Address: sriluxmitulasi.com
Personnel:
Chmn. & Man. Dir.: P. Satyanarayana Reddy
Phone: (91) 883 2476877
Fax: (91) 883 2441577
Joint Man. Dir.: V. Manohar Reddy

India

Phone: (91) 883 2476877
Fax: (91) 883 2441577
Mktg. Dir.: T. Satyanarayana Reddy
Phone: (91) 883 2476877
Fax: (91) 883 2441577
Total Employees at this Location: 93
Type of Operation: Paper mill
Paper/Paperboard Grades and Capacities:
 Total paper and paperboard capacity: 40,000 mt/y
 Newsprint
 Uncoated woodfree/freesheet
 Packaging papers
Paper and Paperboard Mill Data:
Paper Machines: 2
 PM 1, Trim width 2.2 m, Packaging papers
 PM 2, Trim width 3.15 m, Packaging papers
Energy Data:
 Power boilers: 1
 Steam turbines: 1 at 4 MW

ⓘⓜSri Ramalingeswara Paper Products (P) Ltd.
East Godavari Dist. Mill
RS-172/2, Vemulapalli, Dwarapudi
533341 East Godavari Dist., A.P.
India
 Phone: (91) 8857 227563/686
 Fax: (91) 8857 227813
 Email: srlppl@gmail.com
Personnel:
 Man. Dir.: Medapati Ramalinga Reddy
 Phone: (91) 8857 226202
 Email: medapati_reddy@rediffmail.com
 Exec. Dir.: Sudhakar Medapati Reddy
 Phone: (91) 98 49215387
 Dir.: Suresh Kumar
 Phone: (91) 98 49703636
Total Employees of Company: 215
Total Employees at this Location: 215
Type of Operation: Paper mill
Paper/Paperboard Grades and Capacities:
 Total paper and paperboard capacity: 7,500 mt/y
 Newsprint
 Uncoated woodfree/freesheet
Paper and Paperboard Mill Data:
 Stock Preparation:
 Pulpers: 1
 Refiners: 1
Paper Machines: 1
 PM 1, total capacity 7,500 mt/y, Trim width 2 m, Newsprint
Finishing Equipment:
 Winders: 1 at 9,000 mt/y
 Calenders: 1
 Sheeters: 2 at 3,000 mt/y
Energy Data:
 Power boilers: 1

ⓘSri Vinayaka Paper Boards (P) Ltd.
404 A, 4th Floor, Concourse, 7-1-58, Greenland Road, Ameerpet
500016 Hyderabad, Andhra Pradesh
India
 Phone: (91) 40 23743596
 Fax: (91) 40 23743597
 Email: info@srivinayakapaper.com
 Web Address: www.srivinayakapaper.com
Personnel:
 Man. Dir.: Sri. Debabrata Kantha
 Phone: (91) 40 23743596
 Fax: (91) 40 23743597
 Gen. Mgr. & Mktg. Mgr.: Sri. C. Bramha Reddy
 Phone: (91) 40 23743596
 Fax: (91) 40 23743597
Total Employees of Company: 223
Mill Locations:
 Sri Vinayaka Paper Boards (P) Ltd., Rajanagaram Mandal Mill, Kanavaram Village, 2 Medapadu Road, 533294 Rajanagaram Mandal, A.P., India, Capacity: 14,000 mt/y, (Paper mill)
 Phone: (91) 883 2489459/60, 2462093
 Fax: (91) 883 2489460, 2465767
 Email: info@srivinayakapaper.com

ⓘⓜSri Vinayaka Paper Boards (P) Ltd.
Rajanagaram Mandal Mill
Kanavaram Village, 2 Medapadu Road
533294 Rajanagaram Mandal, A.P.
India
 Phone: (91) 883 2489459/60, 2462093
 Fax: (91) 883 2489460, 2465767
 Email: info@srivinayakapaper.com
 Web Address: www.srivinayakapaper.com
Personnel:
 Man. Dir.: Sri. K. Siva Shankara Reddy
 Phone: (91) 98 49793117
Total Employees at this Location: 223
Type of Operation: Paper mill
Paper/Paperboard Grades and Capacities:
 Total paper and paperboard capacity: 14,000 mt/y
 Packaging papers: 14,000 mt/y
Paper and Paperboard Mill Data:
Paper Machines: 1
 No. 1, Trim width 2.28 m, Packaging papers

ⓘSripathi Paper & Boards Pvt.Ltd
994, 2nd Floor, Trichy Road
641 045 Coimbatore, Tamilnadu
India
 Phone: (91) 422 4300445
 Email: admin@sripathi.net
 Web Address: sripathi.net
Personnel:
 Chmn & Man. Dir.: R. Krishna Swamy
 Phone: (91) 422 4300445
 Email: krk@sripathipaperboards.com
 Dir. Mktg.: A. Raghupathi
 Phone: (91) 422 4300445
 Email: sales@sripathipaperboards.com
Mill Locations:
 Sripathi Paper & Boards Pvt.Ltd, Sivakasi Mill, Sukkiravarpatti, 626 130 Sivakasi, India, Capacity: 135,000 mt/y, (Paper mill, Paperboard mill)
 Phone: (91) 4562 238171, 238117, 238014, 238049
 Fax: (91) 4562 238147
 Email: sales@sripathi.net
 Sudirman Paper Private Ltd., Sathyamangalam Mill, SF No.297/2, 308/1, Rajan Nagar, 638401 Puduvadavalli, Sathyamangalam, India, Capacity: 14,000 mt/y, (Paper mill)
 Phone: (91) 4295 243463
 Fax: (91) 4295 243473
 Email: admin@sripathi.net

ⓘⓜSripathi Paper & Boards Pvt.Ltd
Sivakasi Mill
Sukkiravarpatti
626 130 Sivakasi, Tamil Nadu
India
 Phone: (91) 4562 238171, 238117, 238014, 238049
 Fax: (91) 4562 238147
 Email: sales@sripathi.net
 Web Address: sripathi.net
Personnel:
 Man. Dir.: K. Ravichandran
 Phone: (91) 4562 238171
 Fax: (91) 4562 238147
Total Employees at this Location: 450
Type of Operation: Paper mill, Paperboard mill
Pulp Grades and Capacities:
 Total pulp capacity: 129,900 mt/y
 Recycled Pulping: 129,900 mt/y
Pulp Mill Data:
 Bleach Plant Systems: 1
 Recycled Pulping System
 Recycled Fiber Treatment Lines:
 Flotation deinking lines: 1
 Recycled packaging pulping lines: 1
Paper/Paperboard Grades and Capacities:
 Total paper and paperboard capacity: 135,000 mt/y
 Linerboard: 35,000 mt/y
 Corrugating medium/fluting: 20,000 mt/y
 Boxboard/cartonboard: 80,000 mt/y
Paper and Paperboard Mill Data:
Paper Machines: 3
 No. 1, Multi-wire (3), total capacity 35,000 mt/y, Trim width 2.5 m, Linerboard
 No. 2, Fourdrinier (4), total capacity 80,000 mt/y, Trim width 2.8 m, Boxboard/cartonboard
 No. 3, fourdrinier, total capacity 20,000 mt/y, Corrugating medium/fluting
Coating Machines: 1
 PM2, on machine
Energy Data:
 Power boilers
 Combustion turbines: 1 at 6 MW
 Electrical demand for mill: 168 MWh/D

ⓘStadfast Paper Mills Pvt. Ltd.
3rd Floor, Meadows House, 39, Nagindas Master Rd., Fort
400023 Mumbai, Maharashtra
India
 Phone: (91) 22 30286071
 Fax: (91) 22 22654154
Personnel:
 Dir., Sls., Purch., Mktg.: Ashok Nandlal Patwari
 Phone: (91) 22 22656783
 Dir., Sls., Purch., Mktg.: Rakesh Mahendra Patwari
 Phone: (91) 260 3291533
 Email: rakeshpatwari@hotmail.com
Total Employees at this Location: 31
Mill Locations:
 Stadfast Paper Mills Pvt. Ltd., Valsad Mill, Village Dungra, Via Vapi, 395191 Dist. Bulsar, India, Capacity: 7,500 mt/y, (Paper mill)
 Phone: (91) 260 2452564/3091533/2451533
 Fax: (91) 260 2451533
 Email: dungra@vsnl.com, dungrachemicals@hotmail.com

ⓘⓜStadfast Paper Mills Pvt. Ltd.
Valsad Mill
Village Dungra, Via Vapi
395191 Dist. Bulsar, Gujarat
India
 Phone: (91) 260 2452564/3091533/2451533
 Fax: (91) 260 2451533
 Email: dungra@vsnl.com, dungrachemicals@hotmail.com
Personnel:
 Man. Dir.: Mahendra Nandlal Patwari
 Phone: (91) 260 5543399
 Fax: (91) 260 2451533
 Prod. Mgr.: Sahebrao V. Jadhav
 Phone: (91) 260 2452564/3091533
Total Employees at this Location: 60
Type of Operation: Paper mill
Pulp Grades and Capacities:
 Total pulp capacity: 12,000 mt/y
 Recycled Pulping: 12,000 mt/y
Paper/Paperboard Grades and Capacities:
 Total paper and paperboard capacity: 7,500 mt/y
 Packaging papers: 7,500 mt/y
Paper and Paperboard Mill Data:
 Stock Preparation:
 Pulpers: 2
Paper Machines: 1
 PM 1, total capacity 7,500 mt/y, Trim width 1.5 m, Packaging papers
Finishing Equipment:
 Rewinders: 1 at 12,000 mt/y
 Sheeters: 1
Energy Data:
 Power boilers: 1
 Electrical demand for mill: 6 MWh/D

India

ⓘStallion Duplex (P) Ltd.
Mann Industrial Estate, Aithal Rd., Chirao
132001 Karnal
India
 Phone: (91) 184 2291793
 Fax: (91) 184 2272458/4788
 Email: mannco@vsnl.net
Personnel:
 Man. Dir.: Ranvir Singh Mann
 Phone: (91) 184 2291793
 Fax: (91) 184 2272458/4788
Mill Locations:
Stallion Duplex (P) Ltd., Karnal Mill, Mann Industrial Estate, Aithal Rd., Chirao, 132001 Karnal, India, Capacity: 14,400 mt/y, (Paper mill, Paperboard mill)
 Phone: (91) 184 2291793
 Fax: (91) 184 2272458/4788
 Email: mannco@vsnl.net

ⓜStallion Duplex (P) Ltd.
Karnal Mill
Mann Industrial Estate, Aithal Rd., Chirao
132001 Karnal, Haryana
India
 Phone: (91) 184 2291793
 Fax: (91) 184 2272458/4788
 Email: mannco@vsnl.net
Personnel:
 Man. Dir.: Ranvir Singh Mann
 Phone: (91) 184 2291793
Type of Operation: Paper mill, Paperboard mill
Paper/Paperboard Grades and Capacities:
 Total paper and paperboard capacity: 14,400 mt/y
 Linerboard: 5,000 mt/y
 Boxboard/cartonboard: 5,000 mt/y

ⓘⓜStar Paper Mills Ltd.
Saharanpur Mill
Ownership: Duncan Goenka Group
B. D. Bajoria Road
247 001 Saharanpur, Uttar Pradesh
India
 Phone: (91) 132 2714 101 (ten lines)
 Fax: (91) 132 2714 121
 Email: star.sre@starpapers.com
 Web Address: www.starpapers.com
Personnel:
 Chmn.: G. P. Goenka
 Phone: (91) 132 2714 101 (ten lines)
 Man. Dir.: Madhukar Mishra
 Phone: (91) 11 23701300
 Email: mktg.del@starpapers.com
 Snr. Gen. Mgr. (Eng.): I.J. Singh
 Phone: (91) 132 2714 101 (ten lines)
 Gen. Mgr. (Proj. & Dev.): Anil Tarkroo
 Phone: (91) 9927 052729
Total Employees of Company: 1,500
Total Employees at this Location: 1,500
Type of Operation: Pulp mill, Paper mill
Pulp Grades and Capacities:
 Total pulp capacity: 74,970 mt/y
 Chemical Pulp: 74,970 mt/y
Pulp Mill Data:
 Chemical Pulping Systems:
 Batch digesters: 6
Pulp Lines: 1
 Bleach Plant Systems: 2
 No. 1, Sequence: CEpHH, Capacity 28,600 admt/y
 Chemical Recovery Equipment:
 Evaporator lines: 1
 Recovery boilers: 1
Paper/Paperboard Grades and Capacities:
 Total paper and paperboard capacity: 34,986 mt/y
 Uncoated woodfree/freesheet: 34,986 mt/y
Paper and Paperboard Mill Data:
 Stock Preparation:
 Pulpers: 7
 Refiners: 11
Paper Machines: 4

No. 1, fourdrinier, total capacity 15,708 mt/y, Trim width 2.6 m, Uncoated woodfree/freesheet
No. 2, fourdrinier, total capacity 32,487 mt/y, Trim width 3.8 m, Uncoated woodfree/freesheet
No. 3, fourdrinier, total capacity 18,207 mt/y, Trim width 3.8 m, Uncoated woodfree/freesheet
No. 4, fourdrinier, total capacity 10,710 mt/y, Trim width 3.8 m, Uncoated woodfree/freesheet
Finishing Equipment:
 Rewinders: 4
Energy Data:
Electrical demand for mill: 265 MWh/D

ⓘⓜSuchak Paper Manufacturing Co. (P) Ltd.
Dist. Thane Mill
Plot No. C-8/1, M.I.D.C., Dombivli
Dist. Thane, Maharashtra
India
 Phone: (91) 251 2471651
 Fax: (91) 251 2471957
Personnel:
 Dir.: Venkat Dvkatte
 Phone: (91) 251 2471651
 Man. Dir.: Mr. Ravindra M. Suchak
 Phone: (91) 251 2471651
Type of Operation: Paper mill
Paper/Paperboard Grades and Capacities:
 Total paper and paperboard capacity: 6,000 mt/y
 Packaging papers
Paper and Paperboard Mill Data:
Paper Machines: 1
No. 1, Packaging papers

ⓘSudhir Papers Ltd.
Ownership: Narsingh Dass Group
47, Jigani Industrial Area, Jigani, Anekal, Taluk
562106 Bangalore
India
 Phone: (91) 80 27825348
 Fax: (91) 80 27826349/80 22258500
 Email: info@indiapaper.com,
 info@artica.in
 Web Address: www.indiapaper.com
Personnel:
 Man. Dir.: Rajiv Gupta
 Phone: (91) 80 27825348
 Fax: (91) 80 27826349/80 22258500
 Email: spl@indiapaper.com
Total Employees at this Location: 150
Mill Locations:
Sudhir Papers Ltd., Bangalore Mill, 47, Jigani Industrial Area, Jigani, Anekal, Taluk, 562106 Bangalore, India, Capacity: 7,500 mt/y, (Paper mill)
 Phone: (91) 80 27825348
 Fax: (91) 80 27826349/80 22258500
 Email: info@indiapaper.com, info@artica.in

ⓜSudhir Papers Ltd.
Bangalore Mill
47, Jigani Industrial Area, Jigani, Anekal, Taluk
562106 Bangalore, Karnataka
India
 Phone: (91) 80 27825348
 Fax: (91) 80 27826349/80 22258500
 Email: info@indiapaper.com,
 info@artica.in
 Web Address: www.indiapaper.com
Personnel:
 Man. Dir.: Rajiv Gupta
 Phone: (91) 80 22262819
 Fax: (91) 80 22258500
 Email: spl@indiapaper.com
Total Employees at this Location: 150
Type of Operation: Paper mill
Paper/Paperboard Grades and Capacities:
 Total paper and paperboard capacity: 7,500 mt/y
 Coated woodfree/freesheet
 Specialty and industrial

Paper and Paperboard Mill Data:
Paper Machines: 1
PM 1, total capacity 7,500 mt/y, Trim width 1.6 m, Coated woodfree/freesheet, Specialty and industrial
Finishing Equipment:
 Winders: 1 at 2,500 mt/y
 Calenders: 2
 Sheeters: 2 at 5,000 mt/y

ⓘⓜSudirman Paper Private Ltd.
Sathyamangalam Mill
Ownership: 100% by Sripathi Paper & Boards Pvt. Ltd
SF No.297/2, 308/1, Rajan Nagar
638401 Puduvadavalli, Sathyamangalam, Tamil Nadu
India
Mailing Address: 11b, 4th Cross street, Kalaimagal Nagar, Chennai, Tamil Nadu, India
 Phone: (91) 4295 243463
 Fax: (91) 4295 243473
 Email: admin@sripathi.net
 Web Address: sripathi.net
Personnel:
 Gen. Dir.: Mr. R. Ramasamy
Type of Operation: Paper mill
Paper/Paperboard Grades and Capacities:
 Total paper and paperboard capacity: 14,000 mt/y
 Uncoated woodfree/freesheet: 14,000 mt/y
Paper and Paperboard Mill Data:
Paper Machines: 1
No. 1, total capacity 14,000 mt/y, Trim width 1.85 m, Uncoated woodfree/freesheet

ⓘⓜSukhraj Agro Papers Ltd.
Dist. Sangrur Mill
Dhilwan Rd., Tapa Mandi
148108 Dist. Sangrur, Punjab
India
 Phone: (91) 1679 272972/3073
 Fax: (91) 1679 272972
Personnel:
 Man. Dir.: Mr. G. S. Kattra
 Phone: (91) 92 16100825
Type of Operation: Paper mill
Paper/Paperboard Grades and Capacities:
 Total paper and paperboard capacity: 10,800 mt/y
 Coated woodfree/freesheet
 Packaging papers
Paper and Paperboard Mill Data:
Paper Machines: 1
No. 1, Packaging papers

ⓘSumit Agro Products Ltd.
Baghpat Road, Village Panchli
Meerut
India
 Phone: (91) 121 2439028
 Fax: (91) 121 2439041
Personnel:
 Man.Dir.: Sumit Kumar
 Phone: (91) 121 2439028
 Fax: (91) 121 2439041
Mill Locations:
Sumit Agro Products Ltd., Meerut Mill, Baghpat Road, Village Panchli, Meerut, India, Capacity: 8,000 mt/y, (Paper mill)
 Phone: (91) 121 2439028
 Fax: (91) 121 2439041

ⓜSumit Agro Products Ltd.
Meerut Mill
Baghpat Road, Village Panchli
Meerut, Uttar Pradesh
India
 Phone: (91) 121 2439028
 Fax: (91) 121 2439041
Personnel:
 Man.Dir.: Sumit Kumar

India

Phone: (91) 121 2439028
Type of Operation: Paper mill
Paper/Paperboard Grades and Capacities:
Total paper and paperboard capacity: 8,000 mt/y
Newsprint
Uncoated woodfree/freesheet
Paper and Paperboard Mill Data:
Paper Machines: 1
No. 1, fourdrinier

ⓗⓜSun Paper Mills Co. Ltd.
Dist. Tirunelveli Mill
Cheranmahedevi
627414 Dist. Trunelveli, Tamil Nadu
India
Mailing Address: PB 2, 627414 Nellai Kottabomman, Tamil Nadu, India
Phone: (91) 4634 261229-260156/336/261227/229/236
Fax: (91) 4634 260166
Email: sunpaper@sancharnet.in
Personnel:
Chmn., Man. Dir.: Dr. B. Sivanthi Adityan
Phone: (91) 4634 260156/336/261227/229/236
Finan. Mgr. & Sec.: Mr. G. Viswanathan
Phone: (91) 4634 260156/336/261227/229/236
Gen. Mgr. (T&O): Mr. T.R. Balakrishna
Phone: (91) 4634 260156/336/261227/229/236
Admin. Mgr.: Mr. V. Ramaswamy
Phone: (91) 44 26618503
Total Employees at this Location: 817
Type of Operation: Paper mill
Pulp Mill Data:
Bleach Plant Systems: 1
Paper/Paperboard Grades and Capacities:
Total paper and paperboard capacity: 22,000 mt/y
Newsprint
Uncoated woodfree/freesheet
Paper and Paperboard Mill Data:
Paper Machines: 2
PM 2, Trim width 2.65 m, Newsprint, Uncoated woodfree/freesheet
No. 2, Trim width 1.85 m, Newsprint, Uncoated woodfree/freesheet

ⓗSundaram Multi Pap Ltd.
903, Dev Plaza, Opp Andheri Fire Station, S.V. Road, Andheri (W)
400 058 Mumbai
India
Phone: (91) 22 6760 2200
Fax: (91) 22 6760 2244
Email: info@sundaramgroups.in
Web Address: www.sundaramgroups.in
Personnel:
Chmn. & Man. Dir, CEO: Amrut P. Shah
Phone: (91) 22 67602200
Fax: (91) 22 67602244
CFO: Hasmukh Gada
Phone: (91) 22 67602200
Fax: (91) 22 67602244
Dir.: Shantilal P. Shah
Phone: (91) 22 67602200
Fax: (91) 22 67602244
Mill Locations:
Sundaram Multi Pap Ltd., Nagpur Mill, Village Sihora, P.O. Khandelwal Nagar, Tah. Parseoni, 441401 Kanhan, Dist. Nagpur, India, Capacity: 17,500 mt/y, (Paper mill)
Phone: (91) 7102 236 144/145
Fax: (91) 7102 236 236/240
Email: info@sundaramgroups.in, sundarampaperunit@gmail.com

ⓜSundaram Multi Pap Ltd.
Nagpur Mill
Village Sihora, P.O. Khandelwal Nagar, Tah. Parseoni
441401 Kanhan, Dist. Nagpur, Maharashtra
India
Phone: (91) 7102 236 144/145
Fax: (91) 7102 236 236/240
Email: info@sundaramgroups.in, sundarampaperunit@gmail.com
Web Address: www.sundaramgroups.in
Personnel:
Dir.: Shantilal P. Shah
Phone: (91) 22 6760 2200
Fax: (91) 22 6760 2244
Email: sundarampap@vsnl.com
Total Employees at this Location: 82
Type of Operation: Paper mill
Pulp Mill Data:
Recycled Fiber Treatment Lines:
Pulpers: 2 at 20,000 admt/y
Paper/Paperboard Grades and Capacities:
Total paper and paperboard capacity: 17,500 mt/y
Packaging papers: 17,500 mt/y
Paper and Paperboard Mill Data:
Stock Preparation:
Pulpers: 2
Refiners: 2
Paper Machines: 1
No. 1, (2nd hand), fourdrinier, Trim width 1.95 m, Packaging papers
Finishing Equipment:
Calenders: 2
Sheeters: 2
Energy Data:
Power boilers: 1
Electrical demand for mill: 22 MWh/D

ⓗⓜSunshine Paper India Ltd
Kakinada Mill
D.NO:70-15-42/5, Suresh nagar., NFCL Road
Kakinada , A.P.
India
Phone: (91) 884-2375655
Fax: (91) 986-6535555
Email: satyaprasad_t@yahoo.com
Type of Operation: Paper mill
Paper/Paperboard Grades and Capacities:
Total paper and paperboard capacity: 28,500 mt/y
Tissue: 28,500 mt/y
Paper and Paperboard Mill Data:
Paper Machines: 1
No. 1, Yankee dryer, total capacity 28,500 mt/y, Trim width 3.2 m, Tissue

ⓗⓜSuper Deluxe Paper Mills Pvt. Ltd.
Vapi, Dist. Valsad Mill
322/5, 6-A Shed Area, GIDC, Vapi
396195 Dist. Valsad, Gujarat
India
Phone: (91) 260 2431446, 2400547
Fax: (91) 260 2424875
Email: sdpm@sify.com
Personnel:
Man. Dir.: Shanti Lal R. Chheda
Phone: (91) 260 2431446
Dir.: Mr. Kalpesh N. Hira
Phone: (91) 9825145694
Dir.: Hiten K. Shah
Phone: (91) 260 2431446
Type of Operation: Paper mill
Paper/Paperboard Grades and Capacities:
Total paper and paperboard capacity: 25,000 mt/y
Packaging papers: 25,000 mt/y
Paper and Paperboard Mill Data:
Paper Machines: 1
No. 1, Trim width 2.39 m, Packaging papers

ⓗSupreme Coated Board Mills Pvt. Ltd.
Ownership: Supreme Group of Industries (private)
2/2203 Supreme Nagar
626123 Sivakasi, Tamil Nadu
India
Phone: (91) 4562 284022, 4562 284155
Fax: (91) 4562 284011
Email: sales@scbmpl.com, sales@supremegroups.org
Web Address: www.scbmpl.com
Personnel:
CEO: K. Mariappan
Phone: (91) 4562 284022
Fax: (91) 4562 284011
Total Employees of Company: 200
Mill Locations:
Supreme Coated Board Mills Pvt. Ltd., Vembakottai Mill, 2/2203 Supreme Nagar, 626123 Sivakasi, India, Capacity: 50,000 mt/y, (Paperboard mill)
Phone: (91) 4562 284022, 4562 284155
Fax: (91) 4562 284011
Email: sales@scbmpl.com, sales@supremegroups.org

ⓜSupreme Coated Board Mills Pvt. Ltd.
Vembakottai Mill
Previously Supreme Duplex Board Mill
2/2203 Supreme Nagar
626123 Sivakasi, Tamil Nadu
India
Phone: (91) 4562 284022, 4562 284155
Fax: (91) 4562 284011
Email: sales@scbmpl.com, sales@supremegroups.org
Web Address: www.scbmpl.com
Personnel:
CEO: K. Mariappan
Phone: (91) 4562 284022
Fax: (91) 4562 284011
Total Employees at this Location: 200
Type of Operation: Paperboard mill
Pulp Grades and Capacities:
Total pulp capacity: 45,613 mt/y
Recycled Pulping: 45,613 mt/y
Pulp Mill Data:
Bleach Plant Systems: 1
Recycled Pulping System
Recycled Fiber Treatment Lines:
Flotation deinking lines: 1
Recycled packaging pulping lines: 1
Paper/Paperboard Grades and Capacities:
Total paper and paperboard capacity: 50,000 mt/y
Boxboard/cartonboard: 50,000 mt/y
Paper and Paperboard Mill Data:
Paper Machines: 1
No. 1, Fourdrinier (4), total capacity 50,000 mt/y, Trim width 2.9 m, Boxboard/cartonboard
Coating Machines: 1
PM 1, on machine
Energy Data:
Power boilers
Steam turbines
Wind turbines at 1.5 MW
Electrical demand for mill: 68 MWh/D

ⓗSupreme Paper Mills Ltd.
Ownership: Vistarr Group (Todi Family - private)
12 Darga Rd., Ground Floor
700017 Kolkata, West Bengal
India
Phone: (91) 33 40141313
Fax: (91) 33 40141346
Email: info@supremepaper.com
Web Address: supremepaper.com
Personnel:
Chmn. & Man Dir. : Raj Kumar Todi
Phone: (91) 33 40141313
Fax: (91) 33 40141346
Dir. & CFO: Dhruv Todi
Phone: (91) 33 40141313
Fax: (91) 33 40141346
Dir. & Head Power Plan Proj.: Sanat Kumar Mondal
Phone: (91) 33 40141313
Fax: (91) 33 40141346
Mill Locations:
Supreme Paper Mills Ltd., Chakdaha Mill, Vill. Raninagar,

Chakdaha, 741222 Nadia, India, Capacity: 15,000 mt/y, (Paper mill)
Phone: (91) 3473 246679/751/242032
Email: info@supremepaper.com

ⓘⓜSupreme Paper Mills Ltd.
Chakdaha Mill
Vill. Raninagar, Chakdaha
741222 Nadia, West Bengal
India
Phone: (91) 3473 246679/751/242032
Email: info@supremepaper.com
Web Address: supremepaper.com
Personnel:
Tech. Mgr.: Dr. P. Karori
Phone: (91) 3322 803010
Email: p.karori@supremepapers.com
Sls. Mgr.: Tapan Ghosal
Phone: (91) 98 31129871
Total Employees at this Location: 600
Type of Operation: Paper mill
Paper/Paperboard Grades and Capacities:
Total paper and paperboard capacity: 15,000 mt/y
Uncoated woodfree/freesheet
Paper and Paperboard Mill Data:
Stock Preparation:
Pulpers: 3
Refiners: 4
Paper Machines: 1
No. 1, fourdrinier, total capacity 15,000 mt/y, Trim width 2.1 m, Uncoated woodfree/freesheet
Finishing Equipment:
Rewinders: 1
Sheeters: 2
Energy Data:
Power boilers: 4

ⓘⓜSurat Board & Paper Mills Pvt. Ltd.
Surat Mill
Ownership: 100% by family
37-A Main Rd., Udhna
394 210 Surat, Gujarat
India
Phone: (91) 261 677 117, 677 861
Fax: (91) 261 677 861
Personnel:
Man. Dir.: M. Khalid Maniar
Phone: (91) 261 267 7117/6187
Total Employees at this Location: 101
Type of Operation: Paperboard mill
Paper/Paperboard Grades and Capacities:
Total paper and paperboard capacity: 3,600 mt/y
Boxboard/cartonboard: 3,600 mt/y
Paper and Paperboard Mill Data:
Paper Machines: 1
No. 1, multi-layer, Trim width 2.13 m, Boxboard/cartonboard

ⓘⓜSurya Chandra Paper Mills Ltd.
East Godavari Dist. Mill
Maredubaka, near Mandapeta
533 308 East Godavari Dist., A.P.
India
Phone: (91) 8855 232755/66/777
Fax: (91) 8855 232483
Email: scpaper@rediffmail.com
Personnel:
Chmn. & Man. Dir.: Mutyala Rama Rao
Phone: (91) 8855 232755/66/777
Exec.: Mr. M. V.V.J. Jagen Mohan Chowdary
Phone: (91) 8855 232755/66/777
Total Employees at this Location: 200
Type of Operation: Pulp mill, Paper mill
Pulp Grades and Capacities:
Total pulp capacity: 7,200 mt/y
Chemical Pulp
Pulp Mill Data:
Chemical Pulping Systems:
Batch digesters: 3
Bleach Plant Systems: 1
No. 1, Sequence: CEH
Paper/Paperboard Grades and Capacities:
Total paper and paperboard capacity: 16,000 mt/y
Newsprint: 8,000 mt/y
Uncoated woodfree/freesheet: 8,000 mt/y
Paper and Paperboard Mill Data:
Stock Preparation:
Refiners: 2
Paper Machines: 2
No. 1, Yankee dryer, Trim width 1.35 m, Newsprint, Uncoated woodfree/freesheet
No. 2, fourdrinier, Trim width 1.62 m, Newsprint, Uncoated woodfree/freesheet
Finishing Equipment:
Rewinders: 1
Sheeters: 2
Energy Data:
Power boilers: 2
Steam turbines: 2

ⓘSurya Paper Mills
G-7, Block D, Om Complex, Fafa
492009 Raipur, Chattisgarh
India
Phone: (91) 771 5059525/3113111
Fax: (91) 771 2524111
Email: suryapaper@rediffmail.com
Web Address: www.spm.itgo.com
Personnel:
Partner: Manoj Patel
Mill Locations:
Surya Paper Mills, Raipur Mill, Village Dhaneli, P.O. Girad, B, 493111 Raipur, India, Capacity: 7,000 mt/y, (Paper mill)
Phone: (91) 771 5059525/5037386/3100907/3100924
Fax: (91) 771 2524111
Email: suryapaper@rediffmail.com

ⓜSurya Paper Mills
Raipur Mill
Village Dhaneli, P.O. Girad, B
493111 Raipur, Chattisgarh
India
Phone: (91) 771 5059525/5037386/3100907/3100924
Fax: (91) 771 2524111
Email: suryapaper@rediffmail.com
Web Address: www.spm.itgo.com
Type of Operation: Paper mill
Paper/Paperboard Grades and Capacities:
Total paper and paperboard capacity: 7,000 mt/y
Packaging papers: 7,000 mt/y
Paper and Paperboard Mill Data:
Paper Machines: 1
No. 1, total capacity 7,000 mt/y, Packaging papers

ⓘSushila Pulp & Paper Limited
Plot No. E-18, 19 & C-27, 28, UPSIDC Industrial Estate, Superpur
210301 Hamirpur
India
Mill Locations:
Sushila Pulp & Paper Limited, Hamirpur Mill, Plot No. E-18, 19 & C-27, 28, UPSIDC Industrial Estate, Superpur, 210301 Hamirpur, India, Capacity: 9,000 mt/y, (Pulp mill, Paper mill)

ⓜSushila Pulp & Paper Limited
Hamirpur Mill
Plot No. E-18, 19 & C-27, 28, UPSIDC Industrial Estate, Superpur
210301 Hamirpur, Uttar Pradesh
India
Type of Operation: Pulp mill, Paper mill
Paper/Paperboard Grades and Capacities:
Total paper and paperboard capacity: 9,000 mt/y

ⓘSuyash Paper Mills
Ganeshpur Road, Basti, Uttar Pradesh
272001 Basti district, Uttar Pradesh
India
Phone: (91) 91-5542-208909, 91-9336784205/9161551100
Fax: (91) 91-5542-241029
Email: suyashpaper_ramji@rediffmail.com, customercare@suyashpaper.com
Web Address: www.suyashpaper.com
Personnel:
Chmn.: Ramji Jaiswal
Phone: (91) 91-5542-208909
Fax: (91) 91-5542-241029
Man. Dir.: Manish Jaiswal
Phone: (91) 91-5542-208909
Fax: (91) 91-5542-241029
Mill Locations:
Suyash Paper Mills, Basti district Mill, Ganeshpur Road, Basti, Uttar Pradesh, 272001 Basti district, Uttar Pradesh, India, Capacity: 45,500 mt/y, (Paper mill)
Phone: (91) 91-5542-208909, 91-9336784205/9161551100
Fax: (91) 91-5542-241029
Email: suyashpaper_ramji@rediffmail.com, customercare@suyashpaper.com

ⓜSuyash Paper Mills
Basti district Mill
Ganeshpur Road, Basti, Uttar Pradesh
272001 Basti district, Uttar Pradesh, Uttar Pradesh
India
Phone: (91) 91-5542-208909, 91-9336784205/9161551100
Fax: (91) 91-5542-241029
Email: suyashpaper_ramji@rediffmail.com, customercare@suyashpaper.com
Web Address: www.suyashpaper.com
Personnel:
Chmn.: Ramji Jaiswal
Phone: (91) 91-5542-208909
Fax: (91) 91-5542-241029
Man. Dir.: Manish Jaiswal
Phone: (91) 91-5542-208909
Fax: (91) 91-5542-241029
Total Employees at this Location: 125
Type of Operation: Paper mill
Pulp Grades and Capacities:
Total pulp capacity: 44,918 mt/y
Recycled Pulping: 44,918 mt/y
Pulp Mill Data:
Recycled Fiber Treatment Lines:
Pulpers
Paper/Paperboard Grades and Capacities:
Total paper and paperboard capacity: 45,500 mt/y
Tissue: 3,500 mt/y
Linerboard: 42,000 mt/y
Paper and Paperboard Mill Data:
Paper Machines: 2
No. 1, twin-wire, total capacity 42,000 mt/y, Trim width 3.84 m, Linerboard
No. 2, fourdrinier, total capacity 3,500 mt/y, Trim width 2.84 m, Tissue, Uncoated woodfree/freesheet
Energy Data:
Power boilers
Steam turbines at 3 MW
Electrical demand for mill: 58 MWh/D

ⓘT.T.K. Pharma Ltd. (Paper division)
Pungal Bhavani Sagar
638451 Dist. Erode
India
Personnel:
Man. Dir.: M.V. Kumar
Gen. Mgr.: Srinivasan
Mill Locations:
T.T.K. Pharma Ltd. (Paper division), Dist. Erode Mill, Pungal Bhavani Sagar, 638451 Dist. Erode, India, Capacity: 9,360 mt/y, (Paper mill, Paperboard mill)

India

ⓜTamil Nadu Newsprint and Papers Limited (TNPL)

Ownership: 3.23% by HDFC Trustee Company Ltd - HDFC MF Monthly Income Plan Long Term Plan, 35.32% by Governor Of Tamilnadu., 3.96% by Warburg Value Fund, 3.05% by General Insurance Corporation Of India, 9.96% by Life Insurance Corporation Of India, 5.75% by HDFC Trustee Company Limited - HDFC Prudence Fund, 2.48% by Reliance Capital Trustee Company Limited, A/C Reliance Growth Fund, 1.03% by Finquest Securities Pvt. Limited, 1.44% by ICICI Prudential Discovery Fund, 1.94% by Bajaj Allianz Life Insurance Co. Ltd.

67, Mount Road, Guindy
600 032 Chennai, Tamil Nadu
India
Phone: (91) 44 2235 4415 to 4418/22301094 to 22301097
Fax: (91) 44 2235 0834/4614/0827
Email: response@tnpl.co.in, export@tnpl.co.in
Web Address: www.tnpl.co.in
Personnel:
Chairman & Managing Director: N. S. Palaniappan
Phone: (91) 44 22300532
Email: palaniappan.n@tnpl.co.in
Depty. Man. Dir. & Sec.: A. Velliangiri
Phone: (91) 44 22350811
Fax: (91) 44 22350827
Email: velliangiri.a@tnpl.co.in
Dir. (Oper.): R. Mani
Phone: (91) 4324 277001-010
Fax: (91) 4324 277285
Email: mani.r@tnpl.co.in
Dir.: V. Narayanan
Phone: (91) 44 2235 4415
Dir.: N. Kumaravelu
Phone: (91) 44 2235 4415
Dir.: M. R. Kumar
Phone: (91) 44 2235 4415
Dir.: V. Nagappan
Phone: (91) 44 2235 4415
Dir.: Sarada Jagan
Phone: (91) 44 2235 4415
Total Employees of Company: 1,925
Total Employees at this Location: 129
Mill Locations:
Tamil Nadu Newsprint and Papers Limited (TNPL), Srirangam Mill, Manapparai-Kulithalai highway, Mondipatti village, Srirangam, India, (Paperboard mill)
Tamil Nadu Newsprint and Papers Limited (TNPL), Kagithapuram Mill, 639 136 Karur Dist., Kagithapuram, India, Capacity: 400,000 mt/y, (Pulp mill, Paper mill)
Phone: (91) 4324 277 001 to 4324 277 017
Fax: (91) 4324 277 025 to 4324 277 029
Email: it.fo@tnpl.co.in, mktg.fo@tnpl.co.in

ⓜTamil Nadu Newsprint and Papers Limited (TNPL)
Srirangam Mill

Mill is under construction (expected to be completed by December 2015)
Manapparai-Kulithalai highway
Mondipatti village, Srirangam, Tiruchirappalli
India
Type of Operation: Paperboard mill

ⓜTamil Nadu Newsprint and Papers Limited (TNPL)
Kagithapuram Mill

639 136 Karur Dist., Kagithapuram, Tamil Nadu
India
Phone: (91) 4324 277 001 to 4324 277 017
Fax: (91) 4324 277 025 to 4324 277 029
Email: it.fo@tnpl.co.in, mktg.fo@tnpl.co.in
Web Address: www.tnpl.com
Personnel:
Chief Gen. Mgr. (Oper.): Mr. R. Mani
Phone: (91) 4324 277 295
Email: mani.r@tnpl.co.in
Gen. Mgr. (R&D and Qlty. Ctrl.): S. V. Subrahmanyam
Phone: (91) 432432375480, 4324 277001-10 Ext. 2203
Email: subrahmanyam@tnpl.co.in
Gen. Mgr. (Proj.): S. Udayasankar
Phone: (91) 4324 275 331
Fax: (91) 4324 275 027
Email: udayasankar.s@tnpl.co.in
Gen. Mgr. (Paper): M. Subramanian
Phone: (91) 432432375480, 4324 277001-10
Email: subramanian.m@tnpl.co.in
Gen. Mgr. (Pulp & Recovery Boiler): K. Kuppusamy
Phone: (91) 432432375480, 4324 277001-10 Ext. 2332
Email: kuppusamy.k@tnpl.co.in
Gen. Mgr. (Ele. & Instrument): A. Balasubramanian
Phone: (91) 4324 276 200
Email: balasubramanian.a@tnpl.co.in
Gen. Mgr. (Mat. & Logist.): C. Rajagopalan
Phone: (91) 4324 275 334
Fax: (91) 4324 277 026
Email: rajagopalan.c@tnpl.co.in
Gen. Mgr. (Finance): P. Giridharan
Phone: (91) 432432375480, 4324 277001-10 Ext. 2673
Email: giridharan.p@tnpl.co.in
Dpty. Gen. Mgr. (HR): P. Pattabiraman
Phone: Ext. 2602
Fax: (91) 4324 277 273
Email: pattabiraman.p@tnpl.co.in
Asst. Gen. Mgr. (Tech.): P. Rajakumar
Phone: (91) 432432375480, 4324 277001-10 Ext. 2407
Email: rajakumar.p@tnpl.co.in
Total Employees at this Location: 1,821
Type of Operation: Pulp mill, Paper mill
Pulp Grades and Capacities:
Total pulp capacity: 272,047 mt/y
Chemical Pulp: 148,074 mt/y
Other Pulp: 123,974 mt/y
Pulp Mill Data:
Chemical Pulping Systems:
Batch digesters: 4
Continuous digesters: 6
Pulp Lines: 3
Bleach Plant Systems: 3
bagasse, Type: ECF, Sequence: O_2 DEopD, Capacity 196,400 admt/y
wood, Type: ECF, Sequence: O_2 DEopD, Capacity 42,900 admt/y
wood, Type: ECF, Sequence: O_2 C, Capacity 107,100 admt/y
Chemical Recovery Equipment:
Evaporator lines: 2
Recovery boilers: 2
Lime Kiln
Recycled Fiber Treatment Lines:
Flotation deinking lines: 1 at 105,000
Pulp Dryers:
Wet Lap machine 2
Paper/Paperboard Grades and Capacities:
Total paper and paperboard capacity: 400,000 mt/y
Uncoated woodfree/freesheet: 345,000 mt/y
Coated woodfree/freesheet: 55,000 mt/y
Paper and Paperboard Mill Data:
Stock Preparation:
Pulpers: 2
Refiners: 8
Paper Machines: 3
No. 1, twin-wire, total capacity 115,000 mt/y, Trim width 6.8 m, Uncoated woodfree/freesheet
No. 2, DuoFormer, total capacity 130,000 mt/y, Trim width 6.6 m, Uncoated woodfree/freesheet
No. 3, hybrid former, total capacity 155,000 mt/y, Trim width 6.1 m, Uncoated woodfree/freesheet, Coated woodfree/freesheet
Finishing Equipment:
Winders: 3 at 400,000 mt/y
Rewinders: 4 at 35,000 mt/y
Sheeters: 3 at 7,000 mt/y, 3,000 mt/y, 50,000 mt/y
Energy Data:
Power boilers: 4
Steam turbines: 4 at 18, 24.6, 20,41 MW
Wind turbines: 3 at 35.5 MW
Electrical demand for mill: 1,187 MWh/D

ⓞⓜTehri Pulp & Paper Ltd.
Muzaffarnagar Mill

Ownership: Bindal Papers Limited
9th Km Stone, Bhopa Rd.
251002 Muzaffarnagar, Uttar Pradesh
India
Phone: (91) 0131 2468383, 84, 85, 86
Email: info@tehripaper.com
Web Address: www.tehripaper.com
Personnel:
Man. Dir.: Rakesh Kumar
Type of Operation: Paper mill
Paper/Paperboard Grades and Capacities:
Total paper and paperboard capacity: 87,500 mt/y
Packaging papers: 87,500 mt/y
Paper and Paperboard Mill Data:
Paper Machines: 2
No. 1, total capacity 17,500 mt/y, Packaging papers
No. 2, total capacity 70,000 mt/y, Packaging papers

ⓞⓜTej Card Board & Paper Industries (P) Ltd.
Dist. Amritsar Mill

Loharaka Rd., P.O. Gumtala
Dist. Amritsar, Punjab
India
Phone: (91) 183 2500573
Fax: (91) 183 2500004
Email: tejcard@yahoo.com
Personnel:
Man. Dir.: Jas Pal Singh
Phone: (91) 950 1022323
Type of Operation: Paper mill
Paper/Paperboard Grades and Capacities:
Total paper and paperboard capacity: 5,000 mt/y
Packaging papers: 5,000 mt/y

ⓜTejal Paper Mills Pvt. Ltd.

Ownership: 100% by private limited company
A-1/40 GIDC Ind. Estate, Kalol
382721 Mehsana
India
Phone: (91) 2764 220691/214166
Personnel:
Man. Dir., Prod. Mgr.: Lalitkumar C. Patel
Phone: (91) 2764 220691/214166
Total Employees at this Location: 125
Mill Locations:
Tejal Paper Mills Pvt. Ltd., Mehsana Mill, A-1/40 GIDC Ind. Estate, Kalol, 382721 Mehsana, India, Capacity: 5,000 mt/y, (Paper mill)
Phone: (91) 2764 220691/214166

ⓜTejal Paper Mills Pvt. Ltd.
Mehsana Mill

A-1/40 GIDC Ind. Estate, Kalol
382721 Mehsana, Gujarat
India
Phone: (91) 2764 220691/214166
Personnel:
Man. Dir.: Lalitkumar C. Patel
Phone: (91) 79 7471372/7472889
Total Employees at this Location: 125
Type of Operation: Paper mill
Paper/Paperboard Grades and Capacities:
Total paper and paperboard capacity: 5,000 mt/y
Packaging papers: 5,000 mt/y
Paper and Paperboard Mill Data:
Stock Preparation:
Pulpers: 1
Refiners: 1
Paper Machines: 1
PM 1, Trim width 1.83 m, Packaging papers

Finishing Equipment:
Rewinders: 1 at 10,000 mt/y
Sheeters: 1
Energy Data:
Power boilers: 2

ⓘTelangana Paper Mills Ltd.
D-3, MIDC, T.T. Creeck Industrial Area, Trubhe
Navi Mumbai
India
Mill Locations:
Telangana Paper Mills Ltd., Navi Mumbai Mill, D-3, MIDC, T.T. Creeck Industrial Area, Trubhe, Navi Mumbai, India, Capacity: 10,000 mt/y, (Paper mill)

ⓜTelangana Paper Mills Ltd.
Navi Mumbai Mill
D-3, MIDC, T.T. Creeck Industrial Area, Trubhe
Navi Mumbai, Maharashtra
India
Type of Operation: Paper mill
Paper/Paperboard Grades and Capacities:
Total paper and paperboard capacity: 10,000 mt/y

ⓜThree M Paper Mfg. Co. Pvt. Ltd.
Ratnagiri Mill
F-I, M.I.D.C Kherdi, Chiplun
415 604 Ratnagiri, Maharashtra
India
Phone: (91) 2355 256882
Fax: (91) 2355 256003
Email: threem@bol.net.in
Web Address: threempaper.com
Personnel:
Gen. Mgr.: Narendra M. Shah
Phone: (91) 2355 256882/003
Dir.: Suresh T. Gogri
Phone: (91) 2355 256882/003
Dir.: Hiten D. Shah
Phone: (91) 2355 256882/003
Mgr.: Ravi D. Palaye
Phone: (91) 2355 256882/003
Total Employees at this Location: 200
Type of Operation: Paperboard mill
Pulp Grades and Capacities:
Total pulp capacity: 46,545 mt/y
Recycled Pulping: 46,545 mt/y
Pulp Mill Data:
Bleach Plant Systems: 1
Recycled Pulping System
Recycled Fiber Treatment Lines:
Flotation deinking lines: 1
Recycled packaging pulping lines: 1
Paper/Paperboard Grades and Capacities:
Total paper and paperboard capacity: 50,000 mt/y
Boxboard/cartonboard: 50,000 mt/y
Paper and Paperboard Mill Data:
Paper Machines: 1
No. 1, cylinder (9), total capacity 50,000 mt/y, Trim width 2.48 m, Boxboard/cartonboard
Coating Machines: 1
PM1, on machine
Energy Data:
Power boilers
Electrical demand for mill: 63 MWh/D

ⓘThree M Paper Mfg. Co. Pvt. Ltd.
E-2, 1st Floor, Ranjit Studio, Dada Saheb Phalke Road
400 014 Dadar (East) Mumbai
India
Phone: (91) 22 40175971
Email: threem@bol.net.in
Web Address: threempaper.com
Mill Locations:
Three M Paper Mfg. Co. Pvt. Ltd., Ratnagiri Mill, F-I, M.I.D.C Kherdi, Chiplun, 415 604 Ratnagiri, India, Capacity: 50,000 mt/y, (Paperboard mill)
Phone: (91) 2355 256882

Fax: (91) 2355 256003
Email: threem@bol.net.in

ⓘThree Star Paper Mills (P) Ltd.
913/17 Mela Ram Market, Chawri Bazar
110 006 Delhi
India
Phone: (91) 11 23263002/79559
Fax: (91) 11 23279559/120 2663142
Email: threestarpaper@rediffmail.com
Personnel:
CEO: Madan Mohan Chawla
Phone: (91) 11 23263002/79559
Fax: (91) 11 23279559/120 2663142
Email: mmchawla@rediffmail.com
Mill Locations:
Three Star Paper Mills (P) Ltd., Dist. Gautam Budh Nagar Mill, Village Chathera, Tehsil Dadri, Dist. Gautam Budh Nagar, India, Capacity: 7,500 mt/y, (Paper mill)

ⓜThree Star Paper Mills (P) Ltd.
Dist. Gautam Budh Nagar Mill
Village Chathera, Tehsil Dadri
Dist. Gautam Budh Nagar, Uttar Pradesh
India
Personnel:
Man. Dir.: Jag Mohan Chawla
Total Employees at this Location: 100
Type of Operation: Paper mill
Paper/Paperboard Grades and Capacities:
Total paper and paperboard capacity: 7,500 mt/y
Newsprint
Uncoated woodfree/freesheet
Packaging papers
Finishing Equipment:
Rewinders: 2

ⓘTirthak Paper Mill Pvt. Ltd.
S.no.14, Lalpar Road, Lalpar
363641 Morbi
India
Phone: (91) 2822-220277
Fax: (91) 2822-220377
Email: tirthak_papermill@rediffmail.com
Web Address: www.tirthakpapermill.hpage.com
Personnel:
Man. Dir.: Kiritbhai Patel
Phone: (91) 2822 220277
Fax: (91) 2822 220377
Total Employees of Company: 200
Mill Locations:
Tirthak Paper Mill Pvt. Ltd., Morbi Mill, S.no. 14, Lalpar Road, Lalpar, 363641 Morbi, India, Capacity: 110,000 mt/y, (Paperboard mill)
Phone: (91) 2822-220277
Fax: (91) 2822-220377
Email: tirthak_papermill@rediffmail.com

ⓜTirthak Paper Mill Pvt. Ltd.
Morbi Mill
S.no. 14, Lalpar Road, Lalpar
363641 Morbi, Gujarat
India
Phone: (91) 2822-220277
Fax: (91) 2822-220377
Email: tirthak_papermill@rediffmail.com
Web Address: www.tirthakpapermill.hpage.com
Personnel:
Man. Dir.: Kiritbhai Patel
Phone: (91) 2822 220277
Fax: (91) 2822 220377
Total Employees at this Location: 300
Type of Operation: Paperboard mill
Pulp Grades and Capacities:
Total pulp capacity: 102,924 mt/y
Recycled Pulping: 102,924 mt/y
Pulp Mill Data:
Bleach Plant Systems: 1
Recycled Pulping System
Recycled Fiber Treatment Lines:
Flotation deinking lines: 1
Recycled packaging pulping lines: 1
Paper/Paperboard Grades and Capacities:
Total paper and paperboard capacity: 110,000 mt/y
Boxboard/cartonboard: 110,000 mt/y
Paper and Paperboard Mill Data:
Paper Machines: 2
No. 1, multi-wire, total capacity 60,000 mt/y, Trim width 2.96 m, Boxboard/cartonboard
No. 2, multi-wire, total capacity 50,000 mt/y, Trim width 2.88 m, Boxboard/cartonboard
Coating Machines: 2
PM1, on machine
PM2, on machine
Energy Data:
Power boilers
Steam turbines
Electrical demand for mill: 147 MWh/D

ⓘTitagarh Paper Mills Co. Ltd.
113 Park St.
700 016 Kolkata, West Bengal
India
Fax: (91) 33 22260437
Email: titagarh.corpcal@gems.vsnl.net.in
Web Address: www.titagarhindustries.com/paper_mills.htm
Personnel:
Chmn. & Man. Dir.: J. P. Chowdhury
Fax: (91) 33 22260437
VP: P. Nath
Fax: (91) 33 22260437
Dpty. Gen. Mgr.: S. K. Sarangi
Fax: (91) 33 22260437
Mill Locations:
Titagarh Paper Mills Co. Ltd., No. 1 Mill, 24 Parganas, 743 188 Titagarh, India, Capacity: 66,000 mt/y, (Pulp mill, Paper mill)
Email: titagarh.corpcal@gems.vsnl.net.in
Titagarh Paper Mills Co. Ltd., No. 2, Kankinara Mill, Kankinara, India, (Paper mill)

ⓜTitagarh Paper Mills Co. Ltd.
No. 1 Mill
24 Parganas
743 188 Titagarh, West Bengal
India
Email: titagarh.corpcal@gems.vsnl.net.in
Web Address: www.titagarhindustries.com
Personnel:
Chief Tech. Advisor: Samir Banerjee
Total Employees at this Location: 245
Type of Operation: Pulp mill, Paper mill
Pulp Mill Data:
Chemical Pulping Systems:
Batch digesters: 20
Chemical Recovery Equipment:
Recovery boilers: 1
Paper/Paperboard Grades and Capacities:
Total paper and paperboard capacity: 66,000 mt/y
Boxboard/cartonboard
Paper and Paperboard Mill Data:
Paper Machines: 5
No. 1, Yankee dryer, Trim width 1.8 m, Boxboard/cartonboard
No. 2, fourdrinier, Trim width 2.1 m, Boxboard/cartonboard
No. 3, fourdrinier, Trim width 2.7 m, Boxboard/cartonboard
No. 4, fourdrinier, Trim width 3 m, Boxboard/cartonboard
No. 5, fourdrinier, Trim width 1.7 m, Boxboard/cartonboard
Finishing Equipment:
Rewinders: 3
Sheeters: 5
Energy Data:
Power boilers: 4
Combustion turbines: 2

India

ⓂTitagarh Paper Mills Co. Ltd.
No. 2, Kankinara Mill
Kankinara, West Bengal
India
Web Address: www.titagarhindustries.com/paper_mills.htm
Type of Operation: Paper mill

ⓂTravancore Paper Mills (P) Ltd.
Alappuzha Dist. Mill
Kaduvinal P.O., Vallikunam
Alappuzha Dist, Karnataka
India
Phone: (91) 479 2335454
Fax: (91) 479 2335443
Personnel:
Man. Dir.: Mr. K. S. Harilal
Phone: (91) 479 2335454
Type of Operation: Paper mill
Paper/Paperboard Grades and Capacities:
Total paper and paperboard capacity: 7,500 mt/y
Packaging papers

ⓂT.T.K. Pharma Ltd. (Paper division)
Dist. Erode Mill
Pungal Bhavani Sagar
638451 Dist. Erode, Tamil Nadu
India
Personnel:
Man. Dir.: Mr. M. V. Kumar
Gen. Mgr.: Mr. Srinivasan
Type of Operation: Paper mill, Paperboard mill
Paper/Paperboard Grades and Capacities:
Total paper and paperboard capacity: 9,360 mt/y
Coated woodfree/freesheet
Packaging papers
Linerboard

ⓂTulsi Paper Mills Pvt. Ltd.
Bardoli Mill
D-1411, Raghukul Textile Marke
395001 Bardoli, Surat, Gujarat
India
Total Employees at this Location: 155
Type of Operation: Paperboard mill
Pulp Grades and Capacities:
Total pulp capacity: 50,242 mt/y
Recycled Pulping: 50,242 mt/y

Pulp Mill Data:
Bleach Plant Systems: 1
Recycled Pulping System
Recycled Fiber Treatment Lines:
Flotation deinking lines: 1
Recycled packaging pulping lines: 1
Paper/Paperboard Grades and Capacities:
Total paper and paperboard capacity: 54,000 mt/y
Boxboard/cartonboard: 54,000 mt/y
Paper and Paperboard Mill Data:
Paper Machines: 1
No. 1, cylinder, total capacity 54,000 mt/y, Trim width 3.2 m, Boxboard/cartonboard
Coating Machines: 1
PM 1, on machine
Energy Data:
Power boilers
Steam turbines at 3 MW
Electrical demand for mill: 75 MWh/D

ⓂTulsi Paper Mills Pvt. Ltd.
D-1411, Raghukul Textile Marke
395001 Bardoli, Surat, Gujarat
India
Mill Locations:
Tulsi Paper Mills Pvt. Ltd., Bardoli Mill, D-1411, Raghukul Textile Marke, 395001 Bardoli, Surat, India, Capacity: 54,000 mt/y, (Paperboard mill)

ⓂUmesh Board & Paper Mills (P) Ltd.
Tq. & Dist. Aurangabad Mill
Gate No. 125, 27 Km Stone Beed Highway Pandhari Pimalgaon
Tq. & Dist. Aurangabad, Maharashtra
India
Personnel:
Man. Dir.: Mohan Lal Agrawal
Type of Operation: Paper mill, Paperboard mill
Paper/Paperboard Grades and Capacities:
Total paper and paperboard capacity: 5,400 mt/y
Packaging papers
Linerboard

ⓂUmesh Board & Paper Mills (P) Ltd.
7, Samarat Apartments, Seven Hills, Gajanan Maharaj Mandir Road, Chetan Nagar
431005 Aurangabad-Maharashtra
India
Phone: (91) 240 2452340, 240 3090822
Fax: (91) 240 2452678
Personnel:
Dir.: Nitin Agrawal
Phone: (91) 240 2452340
Fax: (91) 240 2452678
Mill Locations:
Umesh Board & Paper Mills (P) Ltd., Tq. & Dist. Aurangabad Mill, Gate No. 125, 27 Km Stone Beed Highway Pandhari Pimalgaon, Tq. & Dist. Aurangabad, India, Capacity: 5,400 mt/y, (Paper mill, Paperboard mill)

ⓂUmiya Board & Paper Mills
Village Sadduvidhan Sabha Road, Raipur
492007 Raipur
India
Phone: (91) 91 771 2282371
Fax: (91) 91 771 4040467
Mill Locations:
Umiya Board & Paper Mills, Dist. Raipur Mill, Vill. Sadhu, Dist. Raipur, India, Capacity: 5,100 mt/y, (Paper mill, Paperboard mill)

ⓂUmiya Board & Paper Mills
Dist. Raipur Mill
Vill. Sadhu
Dist. Raipur, Chattisgarh
India
Type of Operation: Paper mill, Paperboard mill
Paper/Paperboard Grades and Capacities:
Total paper and paperboard capacity: 5,100 mt/y

ⓂUnitech Paper & Board Industries (P) Ltd.
Dist. West Midnapore Mill
Mouza Ganzasimul, P.O. Rajabasa
721513 Dist. West Midnapore, West Bengal
India
Personnel:
Man. Dir.: Ravi Jalan
Type of Operation: Paper mill
Paper/Paperboard Grades and Capacities:
Total paper and paperboard capacity: 5,000 mt/y
Packaging papers

ⓂUnitech Paper Mills (P) Ltd.
53 A, Rafi Ahmed Kidwai Road, 3rd fl.
700 016 Kolkata, West Bengal
India
Phone: (91) 33 2229 7162/7812
Fax: (91) 33 22458089/22172089
Email: unitech@cal3.vsnl.net.in
Personnel:
Man. Dir.: D. K. Jalan
Phone: (91) 33 2229 7162/7812
Fax: (91) 33 22458089/22172089
Sls. Mgr.: Sudip Ghosh
Phone: (91) 33 2229 7162/7812
Fax: (91) 33 22458089/22172089
Mill Locations:
Unitech Paper Mills (P) Ltd., Midnapore Mill, Vill. Paschim Beguni, P.S. Dhera, Balichak, Midnapore, India, Capacity: 10,800 mt/y, (Paper mill)
Phone: (91) 3222 244294

ⓂUnitech Paper Mills (P) Ltd.
Midnapore Mill
Vill. Paschim Beguni, P.S. Dhera, Balichak
Midnapore, West Bengal
India
Phone: (91) 3222 244294
Personnel:
Gen. Mgr.: A. K. Banerjee
Phone: (91) 3222 244294
Total Employees at this Location: 220
Type of Operation: Paper mill
Paper/Paperboard Grades and Capacities:
Total paper and paperboard capacity: 10,800 mt/y
Packaging papers: 10,800 mt/y
Paper and Paperboard Mill Data:
Stock Preparation:
Refiners: 1
Paper Machines: 2
No. 1, Yankee dryer, Trim width 1.9 m, Packaging papers
No. 2, Uncoated woodfree/freesheet
Finishing Equipment:
Rewinders: 2

ⓂUnited Paper Boards Limited
Near Patliputra Industrial Area
800013 Patna
India
Phone: (91) 612 2262639/2764/6898
Personnel:
Dir.: Dhanpat Singh Pagaria
Phone: (91) 612 2262639/2764/6898
Mill Locations:
United Paper Boards Limited, Patna Mill, Near Patliputra Industrial Area, 800013 Patna, India, Capacity: 12,000 mt/y, (Paper mill, Paperboard mill)
Phone: (91) 612 2262639/2764/6898

ⓂUnited Paper Boards Limited
Patna Mill
Near Patliputra Industrial Area
800013 Patna, Bihar
India
Phone: (91) 612 2262639/2764/6898
Personnel:
Dir.: Dhanpat Singh Pagaria
Phone: (91) 612 2262639/2764/6898
Type of Operation: Paper mill, Paperboard mill
Paper/Paperboard Grades and Capacities:
Total paper and paperboard capacity: 12,000 mt/y
Uncoated woodfree/freesheet
Packaging papers
Boxboard/cartonboard: 9,000 mt/y

ⓂUrvashi Pulp & Paper Mills Pvt. Ltd.
P.O. Box 7, 315-316/1 GIDC Estate
393 002 Ankleshwar, Dist. Bharuch
India
Phone: (91) 22 26231340/2646 252093
Fax: (91) 2646 220096
Personnel:
Man. Dir.: Sundeep Shah
Phone: (91) 22 26231340/2646 252093
Fax: (91) 2646 220096
Mill Locations:
Urvashi Pulp & Paper Mills Pvt. Ltd., Bharuch Mill, P.O. Box 7, 315-316/1 GIDC Estate, 393 002 Ankleshwar, Dist. Bharuch, India, Capacity: 35,000 mt/y, (Paper mill)
Phone: (91) 22 26231340/2646 252093
Fax: (91) 2646 220096

ⓂUrvashi Pulp & Paper Mills Pvt. Ltd.
Bharuch Mill
P.O. Box 7, 315-316/1 GIDC Estate

393 002 Ankleshwar, Dist. Bharuch, Gujarat
India
  Phone: (91) 22 26231340/2646 252093
  Fax: (91) 2646 220096
Personnel:
  Man. Dir.: Sundeep Shah
  Phone: (91) 22 26231340/2646 252093
Total Employees at this Location: 100
Type of Operation: Paper mill
Pulp Grades and Capacities:
  Total pulp capacity: 34,026 mt/y
  Recycled Pulping: 34,026 mt/y
Pulp Mill Data:
  Recycled Fiber Treatment Lines:
  Recycled packaging pulping lines: 1
Paper/Paperboard Grades and Capacities:
  Total paper and paperboard capacity: 35,000 mt/y
  Corrugating medium/fluting: 35,000 mt/y
Paper and Paperboard Mill Data:
  Stock Preparation:
  Pulpers: 2
Paper Machines: 1
  No. 1, fourdrinier, total capacity 35,000 mt/y, Trim width 2 m, Corrugating medium/fluting
Energy Data:
  Power boilers: 1
  Electrical demand for mill: 40 MWh/D

ⓂVadbhag Paper & Board Mills (P) Ltd.
Hooghly Mill
N.H. 2, Mouza Kusaigarh, Opp. Mother dairy Dankunj
Hooghly, West Bengal
India
  Phone: (91) 659 23498/99
Personnel:
  Man. Dir.: Makhan Singh
Type of Operation: Paperboard mill
Paper/Paperboard Grades and Capacities:
  Total paper and paperboard capacity: 7,500 mt/y
  Boxboard/cartonboard

ⓄVadbhag Paper & Board Mills (P) Ltd.
N.H. 2, Mouza Kusaigarh, Opp. Mother dairy Dankunj
Hooghly
India
  Phone: (91) 659 23498/99
Personnel:
  Man. Dir.: Makhan Singh
  Phone: (91) 659 23498/99
Mill Locations:
Vadbhag Paper & Board Mills (P) Ltd., Hooghly Mill, N.H. 2, Mouza Kusaigarh, Opp. Mother dairy Dankunj, Hooghly, India, Capacity: 7,500 mt/y, (Paperboard mill)
Phone: (91) 659 23498/99

ⓄVaibhav Paper Boards (P)Ltd.
Ownership: 100% by Private Owner
Gala No 3, Ground Fl., Shiley Ind. Estate, Udyognagar,
S.V. Road, Goregaon (W)
400 062 Mumbai, Maharashtra
India
  Phone: (91) 260 2401720
  Fax: (91) 260 2427232
  Email: info@vaibhavpaper.in, kraftpaper@bsnl.in
Personnel:
  CEO: Nimish J. Shah
  Phone: (91) 260 2401720
  Fax: (91) 260 2427232
  Tech. Man.: Suresh C. Desai
  Phone: (91) 260 2401720
  Fax: (91) 260 2427232
  SEO: Munjal S. Nagda
  Phone: (91) 260 2401720
  Fax: (91) 260 2427232
Total Employees of Company: 150
Mill Locations:
Vaibhav Paper Boards (P)Ltd., Vapi, Dist. Valsad Mill, Plot 1810-1811, 3rd Phase, GIDC Ind. Estate, 396 195 Vapi, Dist. Valsad, India, Capacity: 18,000 mt/y, (Paper mill)
  Phone: (91) 260 2401720
  Fax: (91) 260 2427232
  Email: info@vaibhavpaper.in, kraftpaper@bsnl.in

ⓂVaibhav Paper Boards (P)Ltd.
Vapi, Dist. Valsad Mill
Plot 1810-1811, 3rd Phase, GIDC Ind. Estate
396 195 Vapi, Dist. Valsad, Gujarat
India
  Phone: (91) 260 2401720
  Fax: (91) 260 2427232
  Email: info@vaibhavpaper.in, kraftpaper@bsnl.in
Personnel:
  Chmn.: Jinesh F. Shah
  Phone: (91) 260 2401720
  Dir.: Chandulal R. Dodhia
  Phone: (91) 260 2401720
  Dir.: Ramniklal K. Shah
  Phone: (91) 260 2401720
Total Employees at this Location: 140
Type of Operation: Paper mill
Paper/Paperboard Grades and Capacities:
  Total paper and paperboard capacity: 18,000 mt/y
  Packaging papers: 18,000 mt/y
Paper and Paperboard Mill Data:
  Stock Preparation:
  Pulpers: 2
  Refiners: 3
Paper Machines: 1
  No. 1, fourdrinier, total capacity 18,000 mt/y, Trim width 2.75 m, Packaging papers
Finishing Equipment:
  Winders: 2 at 20,000 mt/y
Energy Data:
  Power boilers: 1

ⓄVaishnav Fibers Ltd.
30-31 B, Industrial Area, Pilukhedi
465667 Rajgarh
India
  Phone: (91) 7375 244266/356
  Fax: (91) 7375 244216
Mill Locations:
Vaishnav Fibers Ltd., Rajgarh Mill, 30-31 B, Industrial Area, Pilukhedi, 465667 Rajgarh, M.P, India, Capacity: 15,000 mt/y, (Paper mill)
  Phone: (91) 7375 244266/356
  Fax: (91) 7375 244216

ⓂVaishnav Fibers Ltd.
Rajgarh Mill
30-31 B, Industrial Area, Pilukhedi
465667 Rajgarh, M.P
India
  Phone: (91) 7375 244266/356
  Fax: (91) 7375 244216
Type of Operation: Paper mill
Paper/Paperboard Grades and Capacities:
  Total paper and paperboard capacity: 15,000 mt/y
  Packaging papers

ⓄⓂVamsadhara Paper Mills Ltd.
Dist. Srikakulam Mill
Vill. & Post Madapam, Narasannapeta Mandalam
532 422 Dist. Srikakulam, A.P.
India
  Phone: (91) 8942 232132/282132/138/151
  Fax: (91) 8942 232151/282151
Personnel:
  Man. Dir.: Mr. S R Rabindar
  Phone: (91) 8942 232132/282132/138/151
  Jt. Man. Dir.: Mr. Rajendran
  Phone: (91) 8942 232132/282132/138/151
  Email: rajendransennar@yahoo.com
  Gen. Mgr.(Project): Mr. D Sudhakar
  Phone: (91) 8942 232132/282132/138/151
  Gen. Mgr: Mr. T. V. Bhaskara Rao
  Phone: (91) 8942 232132/282132/138/151
Type of Operation: Pulp mill, Paper mill
Pulp Grades and Capacities:
  Total pulp capacity: 11,600 mt/y
  Chemical Pulp
Pulp Mill Data:
  Chemical Pulping Systems:
  Batch digesters: 4
  Bleach Plant Systems: 1
Paper/Paperboard Grades and Capacities:
  Total paper and paperboard capacity: 16,500 mt/y
  Packaging papers: 16,500 mt/y
Paper and Paperboard Mill Data:
  Stock Preparation:
  Refiners: 2
Paper Machines: 1
  No. 1, Trim width 2.5 m, Packaging papers
Finishing Equipment:
  Rewinders: 1
Energy Data:
  Power boilers: 2

ⓄVapi Paper Mills Ltd.
213 Udyog Mandir No.1, 7/C Pitamber Ln., Mahim
400 016 Mumbai, Maharashtra
India
  Phone: (91) 22 2444 9826/9753
  Fax: (91) 22 2444 9752
Personnel:
  Chmn.: J. R. Patel
  Phone: (91) 22 2444 9826/9753
  Fax: (91) 22 2444 9752
  Sls. Dir.: A. K. Sachdeva
  Phone: (91) 22 2444 9826/9753
  Fax: (91) 22 2444 9752
  Purch. Dir.: R. R. Patel
  Phone: (91) 22 2444 9826/9753
  Fax: (91) 22 2444 9752
  Gen. Mgr. (Admin): Mr. M. C. Mistry
  Phone: (91) 22 2444 9826/9753
  Fax: (91) 22 2444 9752
Mill Locations:
Vapi Paper Mills Ltd., Vapi, Dist. Valsad Mill, 298-301 2 nd Phase GIDC Vapi, Pardi, 396 195 Vapi, Dist. Valsad, India, Capacity: 15,000 mt/y, (Pulp mill, Paper mill)
  Phone: (91) 260 3290969/3090969/6541750/24 30125/20124
  Fax: (91) 260 2423857
  Email: vapipaper@gmail.com, vpml@egujarat.net

ⓂVapi Paper Mills Ltd.
Vapi, Dist. Valsad Mill
298-301 2 nd Phase GIDC Vapi, Pardi
396 195 Vapi, Dist. Valsad, Gujarat
India
  Phone: (91) 260 3290969/3090969/6541750/24 30125/20124
  Fax: (91) 260 2423857
  Email: vapipaper@gmail.com, vpml@egujarat.net
Personnel:
  Man. Dir.: Manoj Patel
  Phone: (91) 22 2445 7528
  Fax: (91) 22 2444 9752
Total Employees at this Location: 120
Type of Operation: Pulp mill, Paper mill
Pulp Mill Data:
  Chemical Pulping Systems:
  Batch digesters: 4
  Recycled Fiber Treatment Lines:
  Pulpers: 3 at 15,000 admt/y
Paper/Paperboard Grades and Capacities:
  Total paper and paperboard capacity: 15,000 mt/y
  Packaging papers: 15,000 mt/y
Paper and Paperboard Mill Data:
Paper Machines: 1

India

No. 2, cylinder mould, total capacity 15,000 mt/y, Trim width 2.4 m, Packaging papers

Ⓗ ⓜ Ved Cellulose Limited
Ghaziabad Mill
16 Km Stone, P.O. Galand, Vill. Lakhan, Hapur Rd.
Ghaziabad, Uttar Pradesh
India
Phone: (91) 120 2677478
Fax: (91) 122 2320931
Web Address: www.vedcellulose.com
Personnel:
Gen. Mgr. Tech.: Dharmendra Verma
Phone: (91) 120 2677478
Fax: (91) 122 2320931
Email: dvproduction@vedcellulose.com
Total Employees at this Location: 150
Type of Operation: Paper mill
Paper/Paperboard Grades and Capacities:
Total paper and paperboard capacity: 45,000 mt/y
Packaging papers
Specialty and industrial
Paper and Paperboard Mill Data:
Paper Machines: 2
No. 1, combination, Yankee dryer, Packaging papers
No. 2, fourdrinier, Yankee dryer, Specialty and industrial

ⓜ Vedadri Paper Mill PVT. Ltd.
Kodad Mill
Nalgonda district
520 008 Chimiryala village, Kodad (M), A.P.
India
Phone: (91) 866 6456499/9848125856
Fax: (91) 866 2497997
Email: Vedadripapermills@yahoo.co.in
Web Address: www.vedadri.in
Personnel:
Exec. Dir.: Krishna K Murali
Phone: (91) 866 6456499/9848125856
Tech. Dir.: Rao K. S. Krishna
Phone: (91) 866 6456499/9848125856
Type of Operation: Paper mill
Paper/Paperboard Grades and Capacities:
Total paper and paperboard capacity: 17,500 mt/y
Newsprint
Uncoated woodfree/freesheet
Paper and Paperboard Mill Data:
Paper Machines: 1
No. 1, total capacity 17,500 mt/y, Newsprint, Uncoated woodfree/freesheet

Ⓗ Vedadri Paper Mill PVT. Ltd.
59-11-7a, Ghantasalavari Street, Gayatri Nagar
520008 Vijayawada, A.P.
India
Phone: (91) 866-2497996
Fax: (91) 866-2497997
Email: Vedadripapermills@yahoo.co.in
Web Address: www.vedadri.in
Personnel:
Man. Dir.: K. Subrahmanyeswara Rao
Phone: (91) 866-2497996
Fax: (91) 866-2497997
Total Employees of Company: 220
Mill Locations:
Vedadri Paper Mill PVT. Ltd., Kodad Mill, Nalgonda district, 520 008 Chimiryala village, Kodad (M), A.P., India, Capacity: 17,500 mt/y, (Paper mill)
Phone: (91) 866 6456499/9848125856
Fax: (91) 866 2497997
Email: Vedadripapermills@yahoo.co.in

Ⓗ Veer Industries Limited
Tranja Vill., Matar Taluka
Dist. Kheda
India
Mill Locations:
Veer Industries Limited, Dist. Kheda Mill, Tranja Vill., Matar Taluka, Dist. Kheda, India, Capacity: 10,000 mt/y, (Paper mill)

ⓜ Veer Industries Limited
Dist. Kheda Mill
Tranja Vill., Matar Taluka
Dist. Kheda, Gujarat
India
Type of Operation: Paper mill
Paper/Paperboard Grades and Capacities:
Total paper and paperboard capacity: 10,000 mt/y

Ⓗ ⓜ Veerachola Papers
Veerachola Papers
5, Kombai Thottam, Nanjappa Gounder Street
641 604 Tirupur, Tamil Nadu
India
Type of Operation: Paperboard mill
Paper/Paperboard Grades and Capacities:
Total paper and paperboard capacity: 16,000 mt/y
Linerboard
Corrugating medium/fluting
Paper and Paperboard Mill Data:
Paper Machines: 1
No. 1, (started up Q1 210), total capacity 16,000 mt/y

ⓜ Venkraft Paper Mills Private Ltd.
Hosur Mill
Ownership: JR Group
10th km of Kelalmangalam Road
635110 Hosur, Tamil Nadu
India
Phone: (91) 4344-652152/ 4344-645355
Fax: (91) 4344-244266
Email: venkraft@jrgroup.in
Web Address: www.jrgroup.biz
Personnel:
Man. Dir.: Subash Chandru Ramamurthry
Phone: (91) 9443330555
Email: subash@jrgroup.in
Total Employees at this Location: 500
Type of Operation: Paper mill
Pulp Grades and Capacities:
Total pulp capacity: 122,112 mt/y
Recycled Pulping: 122,112 mt/y
Pulp Mill Data:
Recycled Fiber Treatment Lines:
Flotation deinking lines at 32,000
Recycled packaging pulping lines at 63,000
Paper/Paperboard Grades and Capacities:
Total paper and paperboard capacity: 119,238 mt/y
Linerboard: 14,994 mt/y
Corrugating medium/fluting: 14,994 mt/y
Boxboard/cartonboard: 89,250 mt/y
Paper and Paperboard Mill Data:
Paper Machines: 2
No. 1, cylinder, total capacity 29,988 mt/y, Trim width 2.85 m, Linerboard, Corrugating medium/fluting
No. 2, (started up December 2010), cylinder, total capacity 89,250 mt/y, Trim width 3.25 m, Boxboard/cartonboard
Coating Machines: 1
PM 2, total capacity 89,000 mt/y., on machine
Energy Data:
Power boilers: 2
Electrical demand for mill: 176 MWh/D

Ⓗ V.G. Paper & Boards Ltd.
Ownership: Amaravathi Sri Venkatesa Paper Mills Ltd., Public Limited Company
Venkata Nilayam, Venkatesa Mills Port
642 128 Udamalpet, Tamil Nadu
India
Phone: (91) 4252 252 344/286/287
Fax: (91) 4252 252288
Email: cbt_asvpm@sancharnet.in
Web Address: www.vgpb.com
Personnel:
Depty. Gen. Mgr.: Mr. P. R. Arunachalam
Phone: (91) 4252 252 344/286/287
Fax: (91) 4252 252288

Dir.: G. Raveendran
Phone: (91) 4252 252 344/286/287
Fax: (91) 4252 252288
Mill Locations:
V.G. Paper & Boards Ltd., Unit 1 Swaminathapuram, Palani Road, Madathukalam, 642 113 Swaminathapuram, India, Capacity: 13,000 mt/y, (Paper mill)
Phone: (91) 4252 252288
Fax: (91) 4252 253700

ⓜ V.G. Paper & Boards Ltd.
Unit 1 Swaminathapuram
Ownership: Amaravathi Sri Venkatesa Paper Mills Ltd.
Palani Road, Madathukalam
642 113 Swaminathapuram, Tamil Nadu
India
Phone: (91) 4252 252288
Fax: (91) 4252 253700
Web Address: www.vgpb.com
Personnel:
Prod. Mgr.: R. Udayakumer
Phone: (91) 4252 252288
Total Employees at this Location: 150
Type of Operation: Paper mill
Paper/Paperboard Grades and Capacities:
Total paper and paperboard capacity: 13,000 mt/y
Newsprint
Uncoated woodfree/freesheet
Paper and Paperboard Mill Data:
Stock Preparation:
Refiners: 4
Paper Machines: 1
No. 1, Trim width 2.4 m, Uncoated woodfree/freesheet

ⓜ Victory Paper & Boards (India) Ltd.
Pallakad Mill
IV / 120-A, Mannukkade, P.O. Vengodi
678 611 Pallakad, Kerala
India
Phone: (91) 491 863 409
Fax: (91) 491 863 285
Type of Operation: Paper mill, Paperboard mill
Paper/Paperboard Grades and Capacities:
Total paper and paperboard capacity: 16,500 mt/y
Newsprint: 15,000 mt/y

Ⓗ ⓜ Victory Paper & Boards (India) Ltd.
Thrissur Mill
1/281-G, Victory Press Buildings, Kunnamkulum
680 503 Thrissur, Kerala
India
Fax: (91) 4885 222494
Email: victory@vsnl.com
Personnel:
Chmn.: Mr K. T. Puvanny
Man. Dir.: Mr. K. P. Davis
Joint Man. Dir.: Mr. K. P. Saxon
Type of Operation: Paper mill, Paperboard mill
Mill Locations:
Victory Paper & Boards (India) Ltd., Pallakad Mill, IV/ 120-A, Mannukkade, P.O. Vengodi, 678 611 Pallakad, India, Capacity: 16,500 mt/y, (Paper mill, Paperboard mill)
Phone: (91) 491 863 409
Fax: (91) 491 863 285

Ⓗ Vijayalakshmi Paper Mills
Ownership: Serval Industries Ltd.
Vilampatti
624 219 Nilakottai Taluk, Dindigul
India
Phone: (91) 4543 236433-35, 236443
Fax: (91) 4543 236402
Email: mills@danalakshmi.in
Personnel:
Dir.: D. Muthusamy

India

Phone: (91) 4543 236433-35
Fax: (91) 4543 236402
Senior Gen. Mgr. Commer.: S.P. Guptha
Phone: (91) 4543 236433-35
Fax: (91) 4543 236402
Head of Operation: S. Manivannan
Phone: (91) 4543 236433-35
Fax: (91) 4543 236402
Email: manivannan@danalakshmi.in
Total Employees at this Location: 78
Mill Locations:
Vijayalakshmi Paper Mills, Dindigul Mill, Vilampatti, Nilakottai Taluk, 624 219 Dindigul, India, Capacity: 7,800 mt/y, (Paper mill)
Phone: (91) 4543 2364 33/34/35/43
Fax: (91) 4543 236402
Email: mills@danalakshmi.in

ⓜVijayalakshmi Paper Mills
Dindigul Mill
Ownership: Serval Industries Ltd.
Vilampatti, Nilakottai Taluk
624 219 Dindigul, Tamil Nadu
India
Phone: (91) 4543 2364 33/34/35/43
Fax: (91) 4543 236402
Email: mills@danalakshmi.in
Personnel:
Dir.: Mr. D. Muthusamy
Phone: (91) 4543 2364 33/34/35/43
Head of Operation: S. Manivannan
Phone: (91) 4543 2364 33/34/35/43
Senior Gen. Mgr. Commer.: S.P. Guptha
Phone: (91) 4543 2364 33/34/35/43
Total Employees at this Location: 78
Type of Operation: Paper mill
Paper/Paperboard Grades and Capacities:
Total paper and paperboard capacity: 7,800 mt/y
Packaging papers: 7,800 mt/y
Paper and Paperboard Mill Data:
Stock Preparation:
Pulpers: 1
Refiners: 2
Paper Machines: 1
No. 1, Trim width 2.4 m, Packaging papers
Finishing Equipment:
Rewinders: 1
Energy Data:
Power boilers: 1

ⓘⓜVishal Coaters Ltd.
Patiala Mill
Vill. Khusaropur, Mainroad
147001 Patiala, Punjab
India
Phone: (91) 175 5030370
Fax: (91) 175 5030372
Web Address: vishalpapers.com
Personnel:
Chmn.: Vidya Sagar
Phone: (91) 175 5030370
Fax: (91) 175 5030372
Dir.: Sanjeev Kumar
Phone: (91) 175 5030370
Fax: (91) 175 5030372
Dir.: Mohan Parkash
Phone: (91) 175 5030370
Fax: (91) 175 5030372
Type of Operation: Paper mill
Paper/Paperboard Grades and Capacities:
Total paper and paperboard capacity: 6,600 mt/y
Uncoated woodfree/freesheet

ⓘVishal Paper Mills Ltd.
Sangpur Rd
148023 Malerkotla
India
Phone: (91) 1675 253841/251283
Fax: (91) 1675 255249
Personnel:
Man. Dir.: Krishan Mohan Gupta
Phone: (91) 1675 253841/251283
Fax: (91) 1675 255249
Mill Locations:
Vishal Paper Mills Ltd., Malerkotla Mill, Sangpur Rd., 148023 Malerkotla, India, Capacity: 6,000 mt/y, (Paper mill, Paperboard mill)
Phone: (91) 1675 253841/251283
Fax: (91) 1675 255249

ⓜVishal Paper Mills Ltd.
Malerkotla Mill
Sangpur Rd.
148023 Malerkotla, Punjab
India
Phone: (91) 1675 253841/251283
Fax: (91) 1675 255249
Personnel:
Man. Dir.: Krishan Mohan Gupta
Phone: (91) 1675 253841/251283
Type of Operation: Paper mill, Paperboard mill
Paper/Paperboard Grades and Capacities:
Total paper and paperboard capacity: 6,000 mt/y
Packaging papers
Boxboard/cartonboard: 6,000 mt/y

ⓘVishnupriya Paper Mill Private Ltd.
Jagannathapuram, Ponneri Taluk
600 067 Thiruvallur Dist., Chennai
India
Phone: (91) 4119 284276/4350
Personnel:
Man. Dir.: M. S. Sampath
Phone: (91) 4119 284276/4350
Mill Locations:
Vishnupriya Paper Mill Private Ltd., Chennai Mill, Jagannathapuram, Ponneri Taluk, 600 067 Thiruvallur Dist., Chennai, India, Capacity: 10,000 mt/y, (Paper mill)
Phone: (91) 4119 284276/4350

ⓜVishnupriya Paper Mill Private Ltd.
Chennai Mill
Jagannathapuram, Ponneri Taluk
600 067 Thiruvallur Dist., Chennai, Tamil Nadu
India
Phone: (91) 4119 284276/4350
Personnel:
Man. Dir.: Mr. M. S. Sampath
Phone: (91) 4119 284276/4350
Type of Operation: Paper mill
Paper/Paperboard Grades and Capacities:
Total paper and paperboard capacity: 10,000 mt/y
Newsprint
Packaging papers

ⓘVishwa Paper Mills
Gate No. 85, Vill. Farola Tehsil, Paithan
431105 Dist. Aurangabad
India
Phone: (91) 2431 251676/677/678
Email: info@yogroup.com
Personnel:
Man. Dir.: Narandra V. Jhadav
Phone: (91) 2431 251676/677/678
Mill Locations:
Vishwa Paper Mills, Aurangabad Mill, No. 10, Shriniketan Colony, Jalna Road, 431105 Dist. Aurangabad, India, Capacity: 54,000 mt/y, (Paper mill)
Phone: (91) 0240-2344127, 2344135, 2324996, 2332191
Fax: (91) 0240-2333397
Email: info@yogroup.com

ⓜVishwa Paper Mills
Aurangabad Mill
No. 10, Shriniketan Colony, Jalna Road
431105 Dist. Aurangabad, Maharashtra
India
Phone: (91) 0240-2344127, 2344135, 2324996, 2332191
Fax: (91) 0240-2333397
Email: info@yogroup.com
Web Address: www.yoggroup.com/vishwa_paper.htm
Personnel:
Man. Dir.: Mr. S. G. Pawar
Phone: (91) 0240-2333396
Total Employees at this Location: 42
Type of Operation: Paper mill
Paper/Paperboard Grades and Capacities:
Total paper and paperboard capacity: 54,000 mt/y
Packaging papers: 27,000 mt/y
Paper and Paperboard Mill Data:
Paper Machines: 1
No. 1, total capacity 27,000 mt/y, Packaging papers

ⓜWell Pack Papers & Containers Ltd.
Mehsana Mill
Block No. 2023, 6th K.M. Stone, Kalol-Varnaj Road
382 734 Vamaj, Kadi, Mehsana, Gujarat
India
Mailing Address: 313, GIDC Estate, Chhatral-382 729 Kalol (N.G.), Dist. Gandhinagar, Gujarat State, India
Phone: (91) 2764 285589/645
Fax: (91) 2764 285644
Email: wellpack@satyam.net.in
Personnel:
Chmn. & Man. Dir.: Mr. V. M. Patel
Phone: (91) 2764 285589/645
Prod. Mgr.: Mr. V. M. Bahuguna
Phone: (91) 2764 285589/645
Man. Dir., Purch. & Sls.: Mr. A. M. Patel
Phone: (91) 2764 33666-67
Fax: (91) 2764 85644/32367
Chief. Eng.: Mr. Ramanbhai M. Patel
Phone: (91) 2764 285589/645
Qlty. Contr. Mgr.: Mr. Naeem A. Kadri
Phone: (91) 2764 85589
Fax: (91) 2764 85644/32367
Dir.: Mr. R. M. Patel
Phone: (91) 2764 285589/645
Total Employees at this Location: 89
Type of Operation: Paper mill
Paper/Paperboard Grades and Capacities:
Total paper and paperboard capacity: 16,500 mt/y
Packaging papers: 16,500 mt/y
Paper and Paperboard Mill Data:
Stock Preparation:
Pulpers: 2
Refiners: 2
Paper Machines: 1
No. 1, fourdrinier, total capacity 16,500 mt/y, Trim width 2.54 m, Packaging papers
Finishing Equipment:
Rewinders: 1 at 13,200 mt/y

ⓘWell Pack Papers & Containers Ltd.
Ownership: 100% by public
Block No. 2023, 6th K.M. Stone, Kalol-Varnaj Road
382 734 Vamaj, Kadi, Mehsana
India
Mailing Address: 313, GIDC Estate, Chhatral-382 729 Kalol (N.G.), Dist. Gandhinaga
Phone: (91) 2764 285589/645
Fax: (91) 2764 285644
Email: wellpack@satyam.net.in
Personnel:
Chmn. & Man. Dir.: V. M. Patel
Phone: (91) 2764 285589/645
Fax: (91) 2764 285644
Dir.: R. M. Patel
Phone: (91) 2764 285589/645
Fax: (91) 2764 285644
Chief. Eng.: Ramanbhai M. Patel
Phone: (91) 2764 285589/645
Fax: (91) 2764 285644
Total Employees at this Location: 89
Mill Locations:

India

Well Pack Papers & Containers Ltd., Mehsana Mill, Block No. 2023, 6th K.M. Stone, Kalol-Vamaj Road, 382 734 Vamaj, Kadi, Mehsana, India, Capacity: 16,500 mt/y, (Paper mill)
Phone: (91) 2764 285589/645
Fax: (91) 2764 285644
Email: wellpack@satyam.net.in

ⓂThe West Coast Paper Mills Ltd.
Ownership: 100% by S.K. Bangur Group
Chandrakiran, 4th Floor, 10/A, Kasturba Road
560 001 Bangalore, Karnataka
India
Phone: (91) 80 22231828 to 2231837/8487 331391/395
Fax: (91) 80 22231838/8487 331225/330443/332150/148
Email: wcpm@westcoastpaper.com, wcpm.tech@westcoastpaper.com
Web Address: www.westcoastpaper.com
Personnel:
Chmn. & Man. Dir.: S. K. Bangur
Phone: (91) 80 22231828 to 2231837/8487 331391/395
Fax: (91) 80 22231838/8487 331225/330443/332150/148
Email: skbangur@westcoastpaper.com
Exec. Dir.: K. L. Chandak
Phone: (91) 80 22231828 to 2231837/8487 331391/395
Fax: (91) 80 22231838/8487 331225/330443/332150/148
Email: klchandak@westcoastpaper.com
Pres. Corp.: Mr. J. K. Mandelia
Phone: (91) 80 22231828 to 2231837/8487 331391/395
Fax: (91) 80 22231838/8487 331225/330443/332150/148
Email: jkmandelia@westcoastpaper.com
Pres. Tech.: S. S. Pal
Phone: (91) 80 22231828 to 2231837/8487 331391/395
Fax: (91) 80 22231838/8487 331225/330443/332150/148
Email: sspal@westcoastpaper.com
Snr. VP, Mktg.: Mr. V. Subbiah
Phone: (91) 80 222301828
Email: vsubbiah@westcoastpaper.com
VP, Finan. & Corp. Sec.: Mr. P. K. Mundra
Phone: (91) 80 22231828 to 2231837/8487 331391/395
Fax: (91) 80 22231838/8487 331225/330443/332150/148
Email: pkmundra@westcoastpaper.com
Total Employees of Company: 2,500
Total Employees at this Location: 45
Mill Locations:
Shree Rama Newsprint Ltd., Barbhodan Mill (59.79% owned), Taluka Olpad, 395 005 Barbhodan, Surat District, India, Capacity: 132,090 mt/y, (Paper mill)
Phone: (91) 2621 224 203/204/205
Fax: (91) 2621 224 206
Email: ramanpl_ad1@sancharnet.in, ramasurat@ramanewsprint.com
Rama Pulp & Papers Ltd., Vapi, Dist. Valsad Mill, 292-294 GIDC, 396 195 Vapi, Dist. Valsad, India, Capacity: 15,000 mt/y, (Paper mill)
Phone: (91) 260 2992 115 / 3296 710
Fax: (91) 260 2430 880
Email: paper@nathgroup.com, val_ramavapi@sancharnet.in
The West Coast Paper Mills Ltd., Dandeli Mill, P.B. No. 5, Bangur Nagar, 581 325 Dandeli, Uttara Kannada, India, Capacity: 282,030 mt/y, (Pulp mill, Paper mill, Paperboard mill)
Phone: (91) 8383 31391-395
Fax: (91) 8383 31225 /330 443 /332 148
Email: wcpm@bgl.vsnl.net.in, costing.dandeli@westcoastpaper.com

ⓂThe West Coast Paper Mills Ltd.
Dandeli Mill
P.B. No. 5, Bangur Nagar
581 325 Dandeli, Uttara Kannada, Karnataka
India
Mailing Address: Bangur Nagar, P. Box No.5, 581 325 Dandeli, Karnataka, India
Phone: (91) 8383 31391-395
Fax: (91) 8383 31225 /330 443 /332 148
Email: wcpm@bgl.vsnl.net.in, costing.dandeli@westcoastpaper.com
Web Address: www.westcoastpaper.com
Personnel:
Exec. Dir.: K. L. Chandak
Phone: (91) 8383 31391-395
Fax: (91) 8383 31225
Email: klchandak@westcoastpaper.com
Total Employees at this Location: 2,400
Type of Operation: Pulp mill, Paper mill, Paperboard mill
Pulp Grades and Capacities:
Total pulp capacity: 232,447 mt/y
Chemical Pulp: 178,897 mt/y
Recycled Pulping: 53,550 mt/y
Pulp Mill Data:
Chemical Pulping Systems:
Batch digesters: 12
Pulp Lines: 1
Bleach Plant Systems: 1
No. 1, Sequence: CEpHH, Capacity 260,000 admt/y
Chemical Recovery Equipment:
Evaporator lines: 4
Recovery boilers: 1
Paper/Paperboard Grades and Capacities:
Total paper and paperboard capacity: 282,030 mt/y
Uncoated woodfree/freesheet: 187,068 mt/y
Specialty and industrial: 35,700 mt/y
Boxboard/cartonboard: 59,262 mt/y
Paper and Paperboard Mill Data:
Stock Preparation:
Refiners: 20
Paper Machines: 6
No. 1, fourdrinier, total capacity 34,272 mt/y, Trim width 3.1 m, Uncoated woodfree/freesheet
No. 2, fourdrinier, total capacity 35,700 mt/y, Trim width 3.15 m, Specialty and industrial
No. 3, Papriformer, total capacity 44,982 mt/y, Trim width 3.1 m, Uncoated woodfree/freesheet
No. 4, cylinder, total capacity 34,272 mt/y, Trim width 2.56 m, Boxboard/cartonboard
No. 5, total capacity 24,990 mt/y, Trim width 2.5 m, Boxboard/cartonboard
No. 6, (started April 2010), top former, total capacity 107,814 mt/y, Trim width 5.2 m, Uncoated woodfree/freesheet
Coating Machines: 3
No. 1, on machine
No. 4, total capacity 33,000 mt/y., on machine
No. 5, total capacity 24,750 mt/y., on machine
Finishing Equipment:
Rewinders: 4 at 82,500 mt/y
Sheeters: 10 at 115,000 mt/y
Energy Data:
Power boilers: 7
Steam turbines: 5 at 70.3 MW
Electrical demand for mill: 873 MWh/D

ⓂWood Papers Ltd.
Antalia
396 325 Bilimora
India
Phone: (91) 2634 284026
Fax: (91) 2634 284026
Personnel:
Man. Dir.: K. Patel
Phone: (91) 2634 284026
Fax: (91) 2634 284026
Total Employees at this Location: 100
Mill Locations:
Wood Papers Ltd., Bilimora Mill, Antalia, 396 325 Bilimora, India, Capacity: 18,000 mt/y, (Pulp mill, Paper mill)
Phone: (91) 2634 284026
Fax: (91) 2634 284026

ⓂWood Papers Ltd.
Bilimora Mill
Antalia
396 325 Bilimora, Gujarat
India
Phone: (91) 2634 284026
Fax: (91) 2634 284026
Personnel:
Man. Dir.: K. Patel
Phone: (91) 2634 284026
Total Employees at this Location: 100
Type of Operation: Pulp mill, Paper mill
Pulp Mill Data:
Chemical Pulping Systems:
Batch digesters: 4
Paper/Paperboard Grades and Capacities:
Total paper and paperboard capacity: 18,000 mt/y
Packaging papers: 18,000 mt/y
Paper and Paperboard Mill Data:
Stock Preparation:
Pulpers: 3
Paper Machines: 1
No. 1, cylinder, Yankee dryer, Trim width 2.3 m, Packaging papers
Finishing Equipment:
Rewinders: 1

ⓂⓂYash Papers Ltd.
Faizabad Mill
Yash Nagar
224 135 Faizabad, Uttar Pradesh
India
Phone: (91) 5278 326611-14
Fax: (91) 5278 258062
Email: info@yash-papers.com
Web Address: www.yash-papers.com
Personnel:
Man. Dir.: Ved Krishna
Phone: (91) 5278 326611-14
Email: ved@yash-papers.com
Total Employees of Company: 400
Total Employees at this Location: 275
Type of Operation: Pulp mill, Paper mill
Pulp Grades and Capacities:
Total pulp capacity: 45,191 mt/y
Pulp available for market: 14,280 mt/y
Other Pulp: 45,191 mt/y
Pulp Mill Data:
Chemical Pulping Systems:
Continuous digesters: 1
Pulp Lines: 2
Bleach Plant Systems: 1
No. 1, Sequence: CEH, Capacity 25,000 admt/y
Chemical Recovery Equipment:
Evaporator lines: 1
Recovery boilers: 1
Recycled Fiber Treatment Lines:
Pulpers: 2
Pulp Dryers:
Fourdriniers 1, Fourdriniers 1, Fourdriniers 1
Paper/Paperboard Grades and Capacities:
Total paper and paperboard capacity: 38,913 mt/y
Packaging papers: 8,211 mt/y
Specialty and industrial: 30,702 mt/y
Paper and Paperboard Mill Data:
Stock Preparation:
Pulpers: 1
Refiners: 8
Paper Machines: 3
No. 1, Yankee dryer, total capacity 6,426 mt/y, Trim width 2.1 m, Specialty and industrial, Packaging papers

No. 2, Yankee dryer, total capacity 9,282 mt/y, Trim width 2.1 m, Specialty and industrial, Packaging papers
No. 3, Yankee dryer, total capacity 23,205 mt/y, Trim width 4 m, Specialty and industrial, Packaging papers
Finishing Equipment:
Winders: 2 at 12,500 mt/y, 27,000 mt/y
Sheeters: 3 at 9,000 mt/y, 3,000 mt/y, 9,000 mt/y
Energy Data:
Power boilers: 3
Steam turbines: 2 at 2.5, 6 MW
Electrical demand for mill: 150 MWh/D

ⓘⓜ Zaveri Paper & Board Mills
Dist. Dohad Mill
Vill. Palli, Teh. Limkheda
389140 Dist. Dohad, Gujarat
India
  Phone: (91) 2677 222628/666
  Fax: (91) 2677 222628
Personnel:
  Man. Dir.: Arun Bhai Zaveri
  Phone: (91) 2677 222628/666
Type of Operation: Paper mill
Paper/Paperboard Grades and Capacities:
  Total paper and paperboard capacity: 5,250 mt/y
  Packaging papers: 5,250 mt/y

INDONESIA

ⓘ PT Adiprima Suraprinta
Ownership: 100% by Jawa Pos
Gedung Graha Pena, Jln. Achmad Yani 88
60234 Surabaya, East Java
Indonesia
  Phone: (62) 31 8202078/79/90
  Fax: (62) 31 825 00 02
  Email: marketing@adiprima.com, adiprima@adiprima.com
  Web Address: www.adiprima.com
Personnel:
  Pres. Dir.: Misbahul Huda
  Phone: (62) 31 820 20 83/85
  Fax: (62) 31 825 00 02
  Email: huda@temprina.com
  Commer. Dir.: Dwi Permata Sari Surya
  Phone: (62) 31 820 20 83/85
  Fax: (62) 31 825 00 02
  Email: sari@adiprima.com
  Mktg. Dir.: Eny Soenardi
  Phone: (62) 31 8202078
  Email: eny@adiprima.com
Total Employees of Company: 690
Mill Locations:
PT Adiprima Suraprinta, Gresik Mill, Desa Sumengko, Kecamatan Wringinanom, 61176 Gresik, Indonesia, Capacity: 143,000 mt/y, (Paper mill)
  Phone: (62) 31 897 5475
  Fax: (62) 31 897 1562
  Email: marketing@adiprima.com, adiprima@adiprima.com

ⓘ PT Adiprima Suraprinta
Gresik Mill
Desa Sumengko, Kecamatan Wringinanom
61176 Gresik, East Java
Indonesia
  Phone: (62) 31 897 5475
  Fax: (62) 31 897 1562
  Email: marketing@adiprima.com, adiprima@adiprima.com
  Web Address: www.adiprima.com
Personnel:
  Pres./Dir.: Misbahul Huda
  Phone: (62) 31 897 5475
  Fax: (62) 31 897 1562
  Email: huda@temprina.com

  Prod. Mgr.: Dwi Sugianto
  Phone: (62) 31 897 5475
  Fax: (62) 31 897 1562
  Email: dwi.sugianto@adiprima.com
  PM 1 Prod. Mgr.: Andri Warsito
  Phone: (62) 31 897 5475
  Fax: (62) 31 897 1562
  PM 2 Prod. Mgr.: Budi Haryono
  Phone: (62) 31 897 5475
  Fax: (62) 31 897 1562
  Email: budi.haryono@adiprima.com
  R & D Mgr.: Muhaimin Muhaimin
  Phone: (62) 31 897 5475
  Fax: (62) 31 897 1562
Total Employees at this Location: 500
Type of Operation: Paper mill
Pulp Grades and Capacities:
  Total pulp capacity: 135,480 mt/y
  Recycled Pulping: 135,480 mt/y
Pulp Mill Data:
  Bleach Plant Systems: 2
  DIP, Sequence: P
  DIP, Sequence: P
  Recycled Fiber Treatment Lines:
  Flotation deinking lines: 1
  Flotation deinking lines: 1
Paper/Paperboard Grades and Capacities:
  Total paper and paperboard capacity: 143,000 mt/y
  Newsprint: 143,000 mt/y
Paper and Paperboard Mill Data:
Paper Machines: 2
No. 1, fourdrinier, total capacity 53,000 mt/y, Trim width 3.45 m, Newsprint
No. 2, fourdrinier, total capacity 90,000 mt/y, Trim width 3.9 m, Newsprint
Energy Data:
Power boilers: 1
Electrical demand for mill: 400 MWh/D

ⓘⓜ PT Asia Paper Mills
Tangerang Mill
Jalan Arya Kemuning, Kp.Pengasinan RT. 003, RW. 03, Kel.Periuk Jaya, Kec. Periuk, Jatiuwung
Tangerang, West Java
Indonesia
  Phone: (62) 21 55764833, 21 55764844, 21 55764839, 21 5576442 ext. 122
  Fax: (62) 21 55764832, 21 55764835
  Email: marketing@asiapapermills.com, headoffice@asiapapermills.com
  Web Address: www.asiapapermills.com
Personnel:
  Pres. Dir.: Herman Rusli
  Phone: (62) 21-55764833/4/5/9
  Dir.: Hengky Wantah
  Phone: (62) 21-55764833/4/5/9
  Dir.: Achmad Ridwan
  Phone: (62) 21-55764833/4/5/9
Total Employees at this Location: 280
Type of Operation: Paperboard mill
Pulp Grades and Capacities:
  Total pulp capacity: 97,354 mt/y
  Recycled Pulping: 97,354 mt/y
Pulp Mill Data:
  Recycled Fiber Treatment Lines:
  Recycled packaging pulping lines: 1
Paper/Paperboard Grades and Capacities:
  Total paper and paperboard capacity: 96,000 mt/y
  Linerboard: 48,000 mt/y
  Corrugating medium/fluting: 48,000 mt/y
Paper and Paperboard Mill Data:
Paper Machines: 1
No. 1, fourdrinier, total capacity 96,000 mt/y, Trim width 3.1 m, Linerboard, Corrugating medium/fluting
Energy Data:
Power boilers: 3
Electrical demand for mill: 124 MWh/D

ⓘ Asia Pulp & Paper (APP)
Ownership: 100% by Sinar Mas Group
BII Plaza, Tower II, 15th Floor, Jl. M.H. Thamrin No. 51
10350 Jakarta
Indonesia
  Phone: (62) 21 3929266-69
  Fax: (62) 21 3162617
  Email: customer_talk@app.co.id, app_investors@app.co.id
  Web Address: www.asiapulppaper.com
Personnel:
  CEO & Chmn.: Teguh Ganda Wijaya
  Man. Dir., Sustainability: Ms. Aida Greenbury
  Phone: (62) 21 3929266
  Fax: (62) 21 3162617
  Email: aida_greenbury@app.co.id
  Director of Sustainability: Ian Lifshitz
  Phone: (62) 21 3929266-69
  Fax: (62) 21 3162617
  Global Head of Commun.: Darragh Ooi
  Phone: (62) 21 29650800
  Email: darragh_ooi@app.co.id
Total Employees of Company: 62,000
Mill Locations:
PT Ekamas Fortuna, Malang (PT Ekamas Fortuna) Mill, Desa Gampingan, Kecamatan Pagak, PO Box 259, 65101 Malang, Indonesia, Capacity: 166,005 mt/y, (Paperboard mill)
  Phone: (62) 341 - 311901 up to 311905
  Fax: (62) 341-311900
Gold East Paper (Jiangsu) Co., Ltd., Zhenjiang (Gold East Paper) Mill, No. 8, Xinggang East Road, Dagang Economic Development Zone, Zhenjiang 212132, China, Capacity: 2,255,000 mt/y, (Paper mill)
  Phone: (86) 511 8899 8888/6725
  Fax: (86) 511 8899 7000/6669
  Email: customer_service@goldeastpaper.com.cn
Gold Hongye Paper (Hubei), Xiaogan (Gold Hongye Paper) Mill, No. 468 Xiaowu Ave., Xiaonan Economic Development Zone, Xiaogan, China, Capacity: 120,095 mt/y, (Paper mill)
Gold Hongye Paper (Suzhou Industrial Park) Co., Ltd., Suzhou (Gold Hongye Paper) Mill, No.1, Jinsheng Road, Shengpu Town, Industrial Zone, Suzhou 215126, China, Capacity: 304,164 mt/y, (Paper mill)
  Phone: (86) 512 6281 0228 Ext. 2150
  Fax: (86) 512 6281 8276/6282 2101
  Email: market@ghy.com.cn
Gold Huasheng Paper (Suzhou Industrial Park) Co., Ltd., Suzhou (Gold Huasheng Paper) Mill, 2, Jinsheng Road, Shengpu Town, Suzhou Industrial Park, Suzhou 215126, China, Capacity: 600,000 mt/y, (Paper mill)
  Phone: (86) 512 6283 6666/ 2070/ 2289
  Fax: (86) 512 6281 5491
  Email: webmaster@goldhs.com.cn
Guangxi Guofa Forest & Paper Co. Ltd., Liuzhou (Guangxi Guofa Forest & Paper) Mill, No.2 Miyuan Rd. Luorong Town, Yufeng District, Liuzhou 545616, China, Capacity: 120,000 mt/y, (Pulp mill, Pulp mill, Paper mill)
  Phone: (86) 772 8255 676/697
  Fax: (86) 772 8255 668/6511 006
  Email: gxgflz@appjg.com.cn
Guangxi Jingui Pulp & Paper Co., Ltd., Qinzhou (Guangxi Jingui Pulp & Paper) Mill, Dalanping Industry Park, Linhai Industry District, Qinzhou 535000, China, Capacity: 1,000,000 mt/y, (Pulp mill, Paperboard mill)
  Phone: (86) 777 3698 606/022/012/3696 205
Hainan Gold Hongye Paper Co., Ltd., Yangpu (Gold Hongye Paper) Mill, D12, Yangpu Eco. Deve. Zone, Haikou 578101, China, Capacity: 409,218 mt/y, (Paper mill)
  Phone: (86) 898 28822288
  Fax: (86) 898 28821260
Hainan Gold Shengpu Paper Co., Ltd., Haikou (Gold Shengpu Paper) Mill, D12, Yangpu Eco. Deve. Zone, Haikou 578101, China, Capacity: 202,062 mt/y, (Paper mill)
  Phone: (86) 898 28822288
  Fax: (86) 898 28821260
Hainan Jinhai Pulp & Paper Industry Co., Ltd., Yangpu

Indonesia

(Hainan Jinhai Pulp & Paper Industry) Mill, D12, Yangpu Eco. Deve. Zone, Haikou 578101, China, Capacity: 1,035,300 mt/y, (Pulp mill, Paper mill)
Phone: (86) 898 28822288/28821513
Fax: (86) 898 28821260

PT Indah Kiat Pulp & Paper Corp., Perawang (PT Indah Kiat Pulp & Paper) Mill, Jl. Raya Minas - Perawang Km. 26, 12780 Siak, Bengkalis, Indonesia, Capacity: 1,455,000 mt/y, (Pulp mill, Paper mill)
Phone: (62) 761 91088, 91373/91030
Fax: (62) 761 91373/76
Email: info@ikperawang.com

PT Indah Kiat Pulp & Paper Corp., Serang (PT Indah Kiat Pulp & Paper) Mill, Jln. Raya Serang Km. 76, Desa Kragilan, Jawa Barat, 42184 Serang, Indonesia, Capacity: 1,470,000 mt/y, (Paperboard mill)
Phone: (62) 254 281988
Fax: (62) 254 280918/2809136

PT Indah Kiat Pulp & Paper Corp., Tangerang (PT Indah Kiat Pulp & Paper) Mill, Gedung B, Jl. Raya Serpong Km. 8, 15310 Serpong, Tangerang, Indonesia, Capacity: 103,000 mt/y, (Paper mill)
Phone: (62) 21 539 8891/92
Fax: (62) 21 539 8890/5380009

PT Lontar Papyrus Pulp & Paper Industry, Jambi (PT Lontar Papyrus Pulp & Paper) Mill, Ds. Tebing Tinggi, Kec. Tungkal Ulu, Jambi, Indonesia, Capacity: 178,548 mt/y, (Pulp mill, Paper mill)
Phone: (62) 741 62645/51051
Fax: (62) 741 62621
Email: lp3i-adm_ttg@app.co.id

PT Pindo Deli Pulp & Paper Mills, Karawang No. 1 (PT Pindo Deli Pulp & Paper Mills) Mill, Jln. Prof. Dr. Ir. H. Soetami No. 88, Teluk Jambe, Karawang, Indonesia, Capacity: 235,000 mt/y, (Paper mill)
Phone: (62) 267 402355/553
Fax: (62) 267 405250
Email: customer_talk@app.co.id

PT Pindo Deli Pulp & Paper Mills, Karawang No. 2 (PT Pindo Deli Pulp & Paper Mills) Mill, Ds. Kuta Mekar BTB 6/9, Kec. Teluk Jambe, Karawang, Indonesia, Capacity: 540,000 mt/y, (Paper mill)
Phone: (62) 267 440111
Fax: (62) 267 440839
Email: customer_talk@app.co.id

PT Pindo Deli Pulp & Paper Mills Hive, Perawang (Pindo Deli Pulp & Paper Mills Hive) Mill, Jl. Raya Minas - Perawang Km. 26, 12780 Siak, Bengkalis, Indonesia, Capacity: 391,200 mt/y, (Paper mill)
Phone: (62) 761 91373/91030
Fax: (62) 761 91373/76

Shanghai Jinfengyuan Paper (Shanghai) Co., Ltd., Shanghai (Shanghai Jinfengyuan Paper) Mill (80% owned), Liantang Rd. No. 251, Xinghuo Development Zone, Fengxian district, Shanghai 201419, China, Capacity: 100,000 mt/y, (Paperboard mill)
Phone: (86) 21 5750 5588
Fax: (86) 21 5750 1100

Shenyang Jinxin Pulp & Paper Co., Ltd, Xinmin (Shenyang Jinxin Pulp & Paper) Mill, No.3, Shi Fu Road, Xinmin 110300, China, Capacity: 60,000 mt/y, (Paper mill)
Phone: (86) 24-87516619-506
Fax: (86) 24-87516605

Sichuan Gold Hongye Paper Co., Ltd., Yaan (Gold Hongye Paper) Mill, Caoba Industrial Park, Yucheng District, Yaan, China, (Paper mill)

Sichuan Jin'an Pulp Co. Ltd., Yaan (Sichuan Jin'an Pulp) Mill, No. 2 Ai Guo Road, Yucheng District, Yaan 625000, China, (Paper mill)
Phone: (86) 835 2850 801/806/834
Fax: (86) 835 2850 092

PT Pabrik Kertas Tjiwi Kimia Tbk, Mojokerto (PT Pabrik Kertas Tjiwi Kimia) Mill, Tarik Jl. Raya Surabaya, Mojokerto Km. 44, Mojokerto, Indonesia, Capacity: 1,380,000 mt/y, (Paper mill, Paperboard mill)
Phone: (62) 321 361552
Fax: (62) 321 361615

PT The Univenus Co. Ltd., Perawang (PT The Univenus) Mill, Jl Raya Minas, Perawang Km 26, Tualang Kab Siak, Perawang, Indonesia, Capacity: 20,000 mt/y, (Paper mill)

Phone: (62) 761 91030, 3950, 3951
Fax: (62) 761 91030

Zhejiang Ningbo Asia Pulp and Paper Co., Ltd., Beilun (Zhejiang Ningbo Asia Pulp and Paper) Mill (25% owned), Qingshi Industry Zone, Ningbo Economic and Technology Development Zone, Xiaogang, Ningbo 315803, China, Capacity: 2,010,000 mt/y, (Paperboard mill)
Phone: (86) 574 8698 9999/ 9087
Fax: (86) 574 8698 9898/ 9086

Zhejiang Ningbo Zhonghua Paper, Ningbo (Zhejiang Ningbo Zhonghua Paper) Mill, Qingshi Ind. Zone, Ningbo E &T Deve. Zone, Ningbo 315012, China, Capacity: 600,000 mt/y, (Paperboard mill)
Phone: (86) 574 87464811/86231466
Fax: (86) 574 87493450/7535/86228207
Email: sales@mail.zhonghua-paper.com, chenchusheng@mail.zhonghua-paper.com

ⓘ PT Aspex Kumbong

Ownership: Korindo Group

Wisma Korindo 11th Floor, Jln. M.T. Haryono Kav. 62
12780 Jakarta
Indonesia

Mailing Address: PO Box 3646, 12780 Jakarta, Indonesia
Phone: (62) 21 797 5959
Fax: (62) 21 797 6402
Email: aspex@korindo.co.id
Web Address: www.korindo.co.id

Personnel:
CEO: Eun Ho Seung
Phone: (62) 21 797 5959
Fax: (62) 21 797 6402
Vice Chmn.: Dong-Hwan Kim
Phone: (62) 21 797 5959
Fax: (62) 21 797 6402
Man. Dir.: In Yong Sung
Phone: (62) 21 797 5959
Fax: (62) 21 797 6402
Dir.: Lee Byung Ki
Phone: (62) 21 797 5959
Fax: (62) 21 797 6402
Dir.: Rein Silvester Ranti
Phone: (62) 21 797 5959
Fax: (62) 21 797 6402
Dir.: Kim Ki Seoak
Phone: (62) 21 797 5959
Fax: (62) 21 797 6402

Total Employees of Company: 1,535
Mill Locations:
PT Aspex Kumbong, Bogor Mill, Jln. Raya Narogong Km 26, Desa Dayeuh, Kec. Cileungsi, 16967 Bogor, Indonesia, Capacity: 420,189 mt/y, (Paper mill)
Phone: (62) 21 8230681/7975959/6142
Fax: (62) 21 8230682/7976402
Email: aspex@korindo.co.id

ⓘ PT Aspex Kumbong
Bogor Mill

Ownership: Korindo Group

Jln. Raya Narogong Km 26, Desa Dayeuh, Kec. Cileungsi
16967 Bogor, West Java
Indonesia
Phone: (62) 21 8230681/7975959/6142
Fax: (62) 21 8230682/7976402
Email: aspex@korindo.co.id
Web Address: www.korindo.co.id

Personnel:
VP: Lee Won Je
Phone: (62) 21 8230681/7975959/6142
Mill Dir.: Ko Jai Woong
Phone: (62) 21 8230681/7975959/6142
DIP Mgr.: Chang Su Park
Phone: (62) 21 8230681/7975959/6142
Production Manager for PM 1 & 2: Sung Gu Kang
Phone: (62) 21 8230681/7975959/6142

Total Employees at this Location: 1,535
Type of Operation: Paper mill

Pulp Grades and Capacities:
Total pulp capacity: 418,976 mt/y
Recycled Pulping: 418,976 mt/y

Pulp Mill Data:
Recycled Fiber Treatment Lines:
Flotation deinking lines: 3 at 420,000 admt/y

Paper/Paperboard Grades and Capacities:
Total paper and paperboard capacity: 420,189 mt/y
Newsprint: 366,282 mt/y
Uncoated woodfree/freesheet: 53,907 mt/y

Paper and Paperboard Mill Data:
Stock Preparation:
Pulpers: 4
Refiners: 2

Paper Machines: 3
No. 1, Bel-Baie II, total capacity 90,321 mt/y, Trim width 4.5 m, Newsprint
No. 2, Bel-Baie II, total capacity 107,814 mt/y, Trim width 4.5 m, Newsprint, Uncoated woodfree/freesheet
No. 3, Bel-Baie IV, total capacity 222,054 mt/y, Trim width 6.5 m, Newsprint

Finishing Equipment:
Supercalenders: 3
Rewinders: 3
Sheeters: 2

Energy Data:
Power boilers: 1
Combustion turbines: 1 at 22.0 MW
Electrical demand for mill: 1,239 MWh/D

ⓘⓜ PT Kertas Basuki Rachmat
Banyuwangi Mill

Ownership: 10% by Government of Indonesia, 90% by PT Indhasana

Jalan Jenderal Basuki Rachmat, PO Box 6
68414 Banyuwangi, East Java
Indonesia
Phone: (62) 333 421025/422453
Fax: (62) 333 422532
Email: info@kbri.co.id, bpriyadi@kbri.co.id
Web Address: www.kbri.co.id

Personnel:
Chmn.: Anton Hudyana
Phone: (62) 333 421025
Fax: (62) 333 422532
CEO: Yusuf Ardhi
Phone: (62) 333 421025
Fax: (62) 333 422532
Mill Mgr.: Ir. Suwardi AR
Phone: (62) 333 421025
Fax: (62) 333 422532
Email: suwardi_kbr@yahoo.com
Finan. & Account Mgr.: Dwi Setiawan
Phone: (62) 333 421025
Fax: (62) 333 422532
HR Dir.: Syaifur Lukman
Phone: (62) 333 421025
Fax: (62) 333 422532
Maint. Mgr.: Ir. Erianto Hadi
Phone: (62) 333 421025
Fax: (62) 333 422532
Email: erianto.h_kbr@yahoo.com
Prod. Mgr.: Ir. Sumitro Handoko
Phone: (62) 333 421025
Fax: (62) 333 422532
Email: sumitro.h_kbr@yahoo.com

Total Employees at this Location: 350
Type of Operation: Paper mill

Paper/Paperboard Grades and Capacities:
Total paper and paperboard capacity: 12,000 mt/y
Uncoated woodfree/freesheet: 12,000 mt/y

Paper and Paperboard Mill Data:
Stock Preparation:
Pulpers: 1
Refiners: 7

Paper Machines: 1
PM 1, fourdrinier, total capacity 12,000 mt/y, Trim width 2.85 m, Uncoated woodfree/freesheet

Finishing Equipment:
Winders: 1 at 7,000 mt/y
Calenders: 1
Rewinders: 1
Sheeters: 1
Energy Data:
Power boilers: 1
Electrical demand for mill: 43 MWh/D

ⓗⓜPT Kertas Blabak Megelang
Magelang Mill
Ownership: Private investors from Singapore
Mungkid, Blabak, PO Box 109
56101 Magelang, Central Java
Indonesia
Phone: (62) 293 782 642/484
Fax: (62) 293 782 355
Email: kertasblabak@gmail.com
Personnel:
Finan. Dir.: BSc. Sudjadi
Phone: (62) 293 782 642
Fax: (62) 293 782 355
Prod. Mgr.: ST. Agoes Suharyanto
Phone: (62) 293 782 642
Fax: (62) 293 782 355
Tech. Mgr.: Ir. Sugiyanto Sugiyanto
Phone: (62) 293 782 642
Fax: (62) 293 782 355
Commer. Mgr.: Mr. Ismaryanto Ismaryanto
Phone: (62) 293 782 642
Fax: (62) 293 782 355
HR Mgr.: Ihtiyarti Mahatmi
Phone: (62) 293 782 642
Fax: (62) 293 782 355
Purch. Mgr.: Didik Khumeidi
Phone: (62) 293 782 642
Fax: (62) 293 782 355
Total Employees at this Location: 250
Type of Operation: Paper mill, Paperboard mill
Pulp Grades and Capacities:
Total pulp capacity: 36,416 mt/y
Recycled Pulping: 36,416 mt/y
Pulp Mill Data:
Bleach Plant Systems: 1
No. 1, Sequence: HH, Capacity 5,000 admt/y
Recycled Fiber Treatment Lines:
Recycled packaging pulping lines: 1
Paper/Paperboard Grades and Capacities:
Total paper and paperboard capacity: 36,000 mt/y
Packaging papers: 7,500 mt/y
Corrugating medium/fluting: 20,500 mt/y
Boxboard/cartonboard: 8,000 mt/y
Paper and Paperboard Mill Data:
Stock Preparation:
Pulpers: 2
Refiners: 4
Paper Machines: 2
No. 1, fourdrinier, total capacity 11,500 mt/y, Trim width 2.34 m, Packaging papers, Corrugating medium/fluting
No. 2, (second hand.), multi-wire, total capacity 24,500 mt/y, Trim width 2.65 m, Corrugating medium/fluting, Boxboard/cartonboard
Coating Machines: 1
No. 1, on machine
Finishing Equipment:
Winders: 2
Supercalenders: 2
Rewinders: 1 at 45,000 mt/y
Sheeters: 1 at 55,000 mt/y
Energy Data:
Power boilers: 1
Electrical demand for mill: 45 MWh/D

ⓜPT Buana Megah
Pasuruan Mill
Pasuruan, East Java
Indonesia
Type of Operation: Paperboard mill
Paper/Paperboard Grades and Capacities:
Total paper and paperboard capacity: 24,000 mt/y
Containerboard: 24,000 mt/y

ⓗⓜPT Bukit Muria Jaya
Karawang Mill
Jl. Karawang Spoor Kec. Teluk Jambe, PO Box 54 KW 41300 Karawang, West Java
Indonesia
Phone: (62) 267 601030, 600168-170
Fax: (62) 267 601968, 600700
Email: info@bmj-indonesia.com
Web Address: www.bmj-indonesia.com
Personnel:
CEO & Pres.: George I. Hendrata
Phone: (62) 267 601030
Fax: (62) 267 601968
Gen. Mgr.: Ahmad Gozali
Phone: (62) 267 601030
Fax: (62) 267 601968
Utility Mgr.: Ervan Effendi
Phone: (62) 267 601030
Fax: (62) 267 601968
Prod. Develop. & Serv. Mgr.: Rizal Herdian
Phone: (62) 267 601030
Fax: (62) 267 601968
Snr. Account Mgr & Bus. Develop.: Agustian Tjahjadi
Phone: (62) 267 601030
Fax: (62) 267 601968
Eng. Mgr.: Alimuddin Hamsan
Phone: (62) 267 601030
Fax: (62) 267 601968
HR Mgr.: Deny Rozalia
Phone: (62) 267 601030
Fax: (62) 267 601968
Dir.: Harris C. A. Titus
Phone: (62) 267 600168
Fax: (62) 267 601968
Email: RINA.DARMAWIRYA@BMJ-INDONESIA.COM
Tech. Serv. Mgr.: Andri Gunawan
Phone: (62) 267 601030
Fax: (62) 267 601968
Email: andri.gunawan07@gmail.com
Total Employees of Company: 1,100
Total Employees at this Location: 1,100
Type of Operation: Paper mill
Paper/Paperboard Grades and Capacities:
Total paper and paperboard capacity: 15,000 mt/y
Specialty and industrial
Paper and Paperboard Mill Data:
Paper Machines: 1
PM 1, fourdrinier, total capacity 15,000 mt/y, Trim width 2.34 m, Specialty and industrial

ⓜPT Chiral Filindo Utama
Sucaco Bldg, 5th Fl., Jl. Kebon Sirih No. 71
Jakarta, Sukabumi, Sumatra
Indonesia
Phone: (62) 21 3100249
Fax: (62) 21 6393835
Personnel:
Pres.: Soeharjo Soedarjo
Man. Dir.: Ms. Marie Bernadette
Man. Dir.: Marco Soedarjo
Mill Locations:
PT Chiral Filindo Utama, Jakarta, Sukabumi Mill, Sucaco Bldg, 5th Fl., Jl. Kebon Sirih No. 71, Jakarta, Sukabumi, Indonesia, Capacity: 1,440 mt/y, (Paper mill)
Phone: (62) 21 3100249
Fax: (62) 21 6393835

ⓜPT Chiral Filindo Utama
Jakarta, Sukabumi Mill
Sucaco Bldg, 5th Fl., Jl. Kebon Sirih No. 71
Jakarta, Sukabumi, West Java
Indonesia
Phone: (62) 21 3100249
Fax: (62) 21 6393835
Personnel:
Pres.: Soeharjo Soedarjo
Phone: (62) 21 3100249
Man. Dir.: Ms. Marie Bernadette
Phone: (62) 21 3100249
Man. Dir.: Marco Soedarjo
Phone: (62) 21 3100249
Total Employees at this Location: 154
Type of Operation: Paper mill
Paper/Paperboard Grades and Capacities:
Total paper and paperboard capacity: 1,440 mt/y
Specialty and industrial: 1,440 mt/y

ⓗⓜPT Cipta Paperia
Serang, Banten Mill
Jalan Raya Serang Km 76, Desa Kragilan
42112 Serang, Banten, West Java
Indonesia
Phone: (62) 254 401368, 254 401968, 254 401298, 254 401668
Fax: (62) 254 401 768/404119
Email: swidjaja@ciptapaperia.com
Web Address: www.ciptapaperia.com
Personnel:
Pres. Dir.: Jasin Widjaya
Phone: (62) 254 401968/298/668
Dir.: Rudy Sutomo
Phone: (62) 254 401968/298/668
Total Employees at this Location: 200
Type of Operation: Paper mill
Pulp Grades and Capacities:
Total pulp capacity: 73,163 mt/y
Recycled Pulping: 73,163 mt/y
Pulp Mill Data:
Recycled Fiber Treatment Lines:
Recycled packaging pulping lines: 1
Paper/Paperboard Grades and Capacities:
Total paper and paperboard capacity: 74,970 mt/y
Corrugating medium/fluting: 74,970 mt/y
Paper and Paperboard Mill Data:
Paper Machines: 2
No. 1, fourdrinier, total capacity 42,840 mt/y, Trim width 3.2 m, Corrugating medium/fluting
No. 2, fourdrinier, total capacity 32,130 mt/y, Trim width 2.3 m, Corrugating medium/fluting
Energy Data:
Power boilers: 2
Electrical demand for mill: 91 MWh/D

ⓗⓜPT Ekamas Fortuna
Malang (PT Ekamas Fortuna) Mill
Ownership: Asia Pulp & Paper (APP)
Desa Gampingan, Kecamatan Pagak, PO Box 259
65101 Malang, Jawa Timur
Indonesia
Mailing Address: Jl. Bromo 62, 65101 Pagak, Malang, East Java, Indonesia
Phone: (62) 341 - 311901 up to 311905
Fax: (62) 341-311900
Web Address: ekamasfortuna.com
Personnel:
Pres. Dir.: Teguh Ganda Wijaya
Phone: (62) 341 311901/359501
Fax: (62) 341 311900
Mill Mgr.: Mr. Tatkli
Phone: (62) 341 311901/359501
Fax: (62) 341 311900
Dir.: Yudi Setiawan Lin
Phone: (62) 341 311901/359501
Fax: (62) 341 311900
Dir.: Suresh Kilam
Phone: (62) 341 311901/359501
Fax: (62) 341 311900
Dir.: Hendra Jaya Kosasih
Phone: (62) 341 311901/359501
Fax: (62) 341 311900
Maint. Mgr.: Heru Yuwono
Phone: (62) 341 311901/359501
Fax: (62) 341 311900
HR. Mgr.: Dominggus Ariza Mardanam
Phone: (62) 341 311901/359501

Indonesia

Fax: (62) 341 311900
Instrument Mgr.: Wahyudi Wahyudi
Phone: (62) 341 311901/359501
Fax: (62) 341 311900
Total Employees of Company: 480
Total Employees at this Location: 480
Type of Operation: Paperboard mill
Pulp Grades and Capacities:
  Total pulp capacity: 161,229 mt/y
  Recycled Pulping: 161,229 mt/y
Pulp Mill Data:
  Recycled Fiber Treatment Lines:
  Recycled packaging pulping lines: 1
Paper/Paperboard Grades and Capacities:
  Total paper and paperboard capacity: 166,005 mt/y
  Linerboard: 53,550 mt/y
  Corrugating medium/fluting: 53,550 mt/y
  Boxboard/cartonboard: 58,905 mt/y
Paper and Paperboard Mill Data:
Paper Machines: 2
No. 1, multi-wire, total capacity 58,905 mt/y, Trim width 2.5 m, Boxboard/cartonboard
No. 2, twin-wire, total capacity 107,100 mt/y, Trim width 3.9 m, Corrugating medium/fluting, Linerboard
Finishing Equipment:
  Rewinders: 2
Energy Data:
  Power boilers: 3
  Electrical demand for mill: 218 MWh/D

ⓜPT Enggal Subur Kertas
Pati Mill
Previously PT Enggal Mumbul Kertas
Jalan Raya Kudus – Pati Km. 12
Pati, Central Java
Indonesia
  Phone: (62) 0291 424 6119
Total Employees at this Location: 200
Type of Operation: Paperboard mill
Pulp Grades and Capacities:
  Total pulp capacity: 105,222 mt/y
  Recycled Pulping: 105,222 mt/y
Pulp Mill Data:
  Recycled Fiber Treatment Lines:
  Recycled packaging pulping lines: 1 at 105,500
Paper/Paperboard Grades and Capacities:
  Total paper and paperboard capacity: 107,100 mt/y
  Linerboard: 35,700 mt/y
  Corrugating medium/fluting: 71,400 mt/y
Paper and Paperboard Mill Data:
Paper Machines: 2
No. 1, fourdrinier (2), total capacity 35,700 mt/y, Trim width 3.6 m, Linerboard
No. 2, fourdrinier, total capacity 71,400 mt/y, Trim width 4.2 m, Corrugating medium/fluting
Energy Data:
  Power boilers: 2
  Electrical demand for mill: 127 MWh/D

ⓞPT Esa Kertas Nusantara
Jl. Tanah Abang II No. 15
10160 Jakarta Pusat
Indonesia
  Phone: (62) 21 350 3215
  Fax: (62) 21 350 3218
  Web Address: www.esakertas.co.id
Personnel:
  Pres. Dir.: Ali Alimsah
  Phone: (62) 21 350 3215
  Fax: (62) 21 350 3218
  Mgr.: A Andrian
  Phone: (62) 21 350 3215
  Fax: (62) 21 350 3218
  Email: andrian@esakertas.co.id
  Mktg. Mgr.: Suhardi Karko
  Phone: (62) 21 350 3215
  Fax: (62) 21 350 3218
  Email: suhardi.k@esakertas.co.id
Total Employees of Company: 429
Mill Locations:
PT Esa Kertas Nusantara, Karawang Mill, Jl. Raya Pangkalan RT. 022 RW. 001, Desa Tanah Mekar, Pangkalan, Karawang, Indonesia, Capacity: 156,000 mt/y, (Paper mill)

ⓜPT Esa Kertas Nusantara
Karawang Mill
Jl. Raya Pangkalan RT. 022 RW. 001, Desa Tanah Mekar, Pangkalan
Karawang, West Java
Indonesia
  Web Address: www.esakertas.co.id
Total Employees at this Location: 340
Type of Operation: Paper mill
Paper/Paperboard Grades and Capacities:
  Total paper and paperboard capacity: 156,000 mt/y
  Uncoated woodfree/freesheet: 96,000 mt/y
  Coated woodfree/freesheet: 60,000 mt/y
Paper and Paperboard Mill Data:
Paper Machines: 1
No. 1, fourdrinier, total capacity 156,000 mt/y, Uncoated woodfree/freesheet, Coated woodfree/freesheet
Coating Machines: 1
No. 1, off machine
Energy Data:
  Power boilers
  Steam turbines
  Electrical demand for mill: 284 MWh/D

ⓞⓜPT Eureka Aba
Mojosari Mill
Ownership: 100% by private owner
Jln. Erlangga 57, Mojosari
61382 Mojokerto, East Java
Indonesia
  Phone: (62) 321 91453/92263
  Fax: (62) 321 91451
Personnel:
  Pres. Dir.: Hendro Widjaya
  Phone: (62) 321 91453/92263
  Gen. Mgr.: Ir. Koritian Tanizar
  Phone: (62) 321 91453/92263
Total Employees at this Location: 850
Type of Operation: Pulp mill, Paper mill
Pulp Grades and Capacities:
  Total pulp capacity: 30,500 mt/y
Pulp Mill Data:
  Chemical Pulping Systems:
  Batch digesters: 1
Paper/Paperboard Grades and Capacities:
  Total paper and paperboard capacity: 40,000 mt/y
  Specialty and industrial: 30,000 mt/y
  Containerboard: 10,000 mt/y
  Linerboard
  Corrugating medium/fluting
Paper and Paperboard Mill Data:
Paper Machines: 2
PM 1, cylinder, total capacity 9,000 mt/y, Trim width 2.3 m, Packaging papers, Linerboard, Corrugating medium/fluting
PM 2, cylinder, total capacity 4,500 mt/y, Trim width 1.57 m, Corrugating medium/fluting
Finishing Equipment:
  Rewinders: 2

ⓜPT Evergreen International Paper
Medan Mill
Jln Utama Desa Dalu X A & B, Tanjung Morawa Km 16
20360 Deli Serdang, Medan, Sumatra
Indonesia
  Phone: (62) 61 794 7333 Ext. 105, 61 794 2836
  Fax: (62) 61 794 2688
  Email: hrd_department@eip.co.id
  Web Address: www.evergreen.co.id
Personnel:
  Energy Mgr.: Ronal Mangatur Siregar
  Phone: (62) 061-7942688

Total Employees at this Location: 200
Type of Operation: Paperboard mill
Pulp Grades and Capacities:
  Total pulp capacity: 74,649 mt/y
  Recycled Pulping: 74,649 mt/y
Pulp Mill Data:
  Recycled Fiber Treatment Lines:
  Recycled packaging pulping lines: 1
Paper/Paperboard Grades and Capacities:
  Total paper and paperboard capacity: 75,600 mt/y
  Linerboard: 45,360 mt/y
  Corrugating medium/fluting: 30,240 mt/y
Paper and Paperboard Mill Data:
Paper Machines: 1
No. 1, fourdrinier (2), total capacity 75,600 mt/y, Linerboard, Corrugating medium/fluting
Energy Data:
  Power boilers
  Steam turbines: 2 at 7.5 MW
  Electrical demand for mill: 92 MWh/D

ⓞPT Fajar Surya Wisesa Tbk.
Ownership: 100% by shareholders
Jln. Abdul Muis No. 30
10160 Jakarta
Indonesia
  Phone: (62) 21 344 1316-344/8887
  Fax: (62) 21 345 7643-344/8889
  Email: contact@fajarpaper.com
  Web Address: www.fajarpaper.com
Personnel:
  Pres. Dir.: Winarko Sulistyo
  Phone: (62) 21 3441316
  Dir.: Roy Teguh
  Phone: (62) 21 344 1316-344/8887
  Fax: (62) 21 345 7643-344/8889
  Dir., Finan.: Hadi Rebowo Ongkowidjojo
  Phone: (62) 21 344 1316-344/8887
  Fax: (62) 21 345 7643-344/8889
  Mktg Dir.: Yustinus Yusuf Kusumah
  Phone: (62) 21 89 00 330
  Email: yustinus@fajarpaper.com
  Pres. Commissioner: Airlangga Hartarto
  Phone: (62) 21 344 1316-344/8887
  Fax: (62) 21 345 7643-344/8889
  Commissioner: Lila Notoprandono
  Phone: (62) 21 344 1316-344/8887
  Fax: (62) 21 345 7643-344/8889
  Indep. Commissioner: Tony Tjandra
  Phone: (62) 21 344 1316-344/8887
  Fax: (62) 21 345 7643-344/8889
Total Employees of Company: 2,544
Mill Locations:
PT Fajar Surya Wisesa Tbk, Bekasi Mill, Jalan Kampung Gardu Sawah, RT.001/1-1, Desa Kalijaya, 17520 Cikarang Barat, Bekasi, Indonesia, Capacity: 1,200,000 mt/y, (Paper mill, Paperboard mill)
  Phone: (62) 21 890 0030/0330/0331
  Fax: (62) 21 890 2775/1126
  Email: fswmis@fasw.co.id

ⓜPT Fajar Surya Wisesa Tbk.
Bekasi Mill
Jalan Kampung Gardu Sawah, RT.001/1-1, Desa Kalijaya
17520 Cikarang Barat, Bekasi, West Java
Indonesia
  Phone: (62) 21 890 0030/0330/0331
  Fax: (62) 21 890 2775/1126
  Email: fswmis@fasw.co.id
  Web Address: www.fajarpaper.com
Personnel:
  Pres. Dir.: Winarko Sulistyo
  Phone: (62) 21 890 0030/0330/0331
  Fax: (62) 21 890 2775/1126
  Finan. Dir.: Hadirebowo Ongkowidjojo
  Phone: (62) 21 890 0030/0330/0331
  Fax: (62) 21 890 2775/1126
  Mill Mgr.: C. T. Pedder

Phone: (62) 21 890 0030/0330/0331
Fax: (62) 21 890 2775/1126
Mktg. Dir.: Yustinus Yusuf Kusumah
Phone: (62) 21 89 00 330
Fax: (62) 21 890 2775/1126
Email: yustinus@fajarpaper.com
Gen. Mgr. Prod.: Karlheinz Schimmel
Phone: (62) 21 890 0030/0330/0331
Fax: (62) 21 890 2775/1126
Dir.: Roy Teguh
Phone: (62) 21 890 0030/0330/0331
Fax: (62) 21 890 2775/1126
Total Employees at this Location: 2,314
Type of Operation: Paper mill, Paperboard mill
Pulp Grades and Capacities:
Total pulp capacity: 1,198,085 mt/y
Recycled Pulping: 1,198,085 mt/y

Pulp Mill Data:
Recycled Fiber Treatment Lines:
Flotation deinking lines: 1 at 30,000 admt/y
Recycled packaging pulping lines: 3
Paper/Paperboard Grades and Capacities:
Total paper and paperboard capacity: 1,200,000 mt/y
Linerboard: 550,000 mt/y
Corrugating medium/fluting: 500,000 mt/y
Boxboard/cartonboard: 150,000 mt/y
Paper and Paperboard Mill Data:
Stock Preparation:
Pulpers:
Paper Machines: 5
No. 1, Ultraformer (5), total capacity 150,000 mt/y, Trim width 3.6 m, Boxboard/cartonboard
No. 2, fourdrinier (3), total capacity 200,000 mt/y, Trim width 4.35 m, Linerboard
No. 3, fourdrinier, total capacity 200,000 mt/y, Trim width 5 m, Corrugating medium/fluting
No. 5, fourdrinier, total capacity 300,000 mt/y, Trim width 6.7 m, Corrugating medium/fluting
No. 7, fourdrinier, total capacity 350,000 mt/y, Trim width 6.65 m, Linerboard
Coating Machines: 2
No. 1, total capacity 150,000 mt/y., on machine
No. 2, total capacity 25,000 mt/y., off machine
Finishing Equipment:
Supercalenders: 2
Rewinders: 3
Sheeters: 4
Energy Data:
Power boilers: 4
Combustion turbines: 2 at 32.5, 35 MW
Electrical demand for mill: 1,569 MWh/D

⊕⊚Gaya Baru Paper CV
Malang Mill
Ownership: 100% by private owners
Jln. Kol. Sugiono X A No.8
Malang, East Java
Indonesia
Phone: (62) 341 801162/412
Fax: (62) 341 801875
Email: jps388@yahoo.com
Personnel:
Dir.: Jonson Puspo Judodihardjo
Phone: (62) 341 801162/412
Email: ericadjonny@yahoo.com
Finan. Dir.: Jonny Puspo Judodihardjo
Phone: (62) 341 801162/412
Total Employees of Company: 250
Type of Operation: Paper mill
Pulp Grades and Capacities:
Total pulp capacity: 19,366 mt/y
Recycled Pulping: 19,366 mt/y
Paper/Paperboard Grades and Capacities:
Total paper and paperboard capacity: 20,000 mt/y
Boxboard/cartonboard: 20,000 mt/y
Paper and Paperboard Mill Data:
Stock Preparation:
Pulpers: 3
Refiners: 3

Paper Machines: 1
No. 1, multi-wire, total capacity 20,000 mt/y, Trim width 2.4 m, Boxboard/cartonboard
Finishing Equipment:
Rewinders: 1 at 40,000 mt/y
Sheeters: 2
Energy Data:
Power boilers: 1
TMP Reboiler: 1

⊕PT Graha Cemerlang Paper Utama (Grace Paper)
Ownership: Kompas Gramedia Group
Jl. Jend. A. Yani No. 39, KIKC Kav II A-1
41373 Cikampek, Karawang, Jawa Barat
Indonesia
Phone: (62) 264 301567
Fax: (62) 264 301559
Email: gracepaper@pcpu.co.id
Web Address: www.tessatissue.com
Personnel:
Pres.: Harris F. Sitorus
Pres.: Tan Kwang Hwa
Mill Mgr.: Bambang Dwi Setiawan
Finan. Mgr.: Jordan Tarigans
Email: jordan@gcpu.co.id
Mill Locations:
PT Graha Cemerlang Paper Utama (Grace Paper), Cikampek, Karawang Mill, Jl. Jend. A. Yani No. 39, KIKC Kav II A-1, 41373 Cikampek, Karawang, Indonesia, Capacity: 72,000 mt/y, (Paper mill)
Phone: (62) 264 301567
Fax: (62) 264 301559
Email: gracepaper@pcpu.co.id

⊕PT Graha Cemerlang Paper Utama (Grace Paper)
Cikampek, Karawang Mill
Jl. Jend. A. Yani No. 39, KIKC Kav II A-1
41373 Cikampek, Karawang, Jawa Barat
Indonesia
Phone: (62) 264 301567
Fax: (62) 264 301559
Email: gracepaper@pcpu.co.id
Web Address: www.tessatissue.com
Personnel:
Pres.: Harris F. Sitorus
Phone: (62) 264 301567
Pres.: Tan Kwang Hwa
Phone: (62) 264 301567
Mill Mgr.: Bambang Dwi Setiawan
Phone: (62) 264 301567
Finan. Mgr.: Jordan Tarigans
Phone: (62) 264 301567
Total Employees at this Location: 255
Type of Operation: Paper mill
Paper/Paperboard Grades and Capacities:
Total paper and paperboard capacity: 72,000 mt/y
Tissue: 72,000 mt/y
Paper and Paperboard Mill Data:
Paper Machines: 2
No. 1, crescent former, total capacity 35,000 mt/y, Trim width 3.65 m, Tissue, Uncoated woodfree/freesheet
No. 2, crescent former, total capacity 37,000 mt/y, Trim width 3.65 m, Tissue
Energy Data:
Power boilers: 1
Electrical demand for mill: 218 MWh/D

⊕⊚PT Gunung Jaya Agung
Karawaci Mill
Jln. Imam Bonjol Km. 3 No. 265
Karawaci, Tangerang, Jawa Barat
Indonesia
Phone: (62) 21 5523607/09
Fax: (62) 21 5525594
Personnel:
Pres. Dir.: Mr. Suwondo
Phone: (62) 21 5523607/09

Total Employees of Company: 389
Type of Operation: Paper mill
Paper/Paperboard Grades and Capacities:
Total paper and paperboard capacity: 41,000 mt/y
Uncoated woodfree/freesheet: 24,000 mt/y
Tissue: 5,000 mt/y
Packaging papers: 12,000 mt/y
Linerboard

⊕PT Indah Kiat Pulp & Paper Corp.
Ownership: Asia Pulp & Paper (APP)
Plaza BII Menara II, 32nd Floor, Jl. M.H. Thamrin No. 51
10350 Jakarta
Indonesia
Phone: (62) 21 392 9001/2/3
Fax: (62) 21 392 6203/8875
Web Address: www.ikserang.com
Personnel:
Pres. Dir.: Teguh Ganda Wijaya
Phone: (62) 21 392 9001/2/3
Fax: (62) 21 392 6203/8875
VP Dir.: Muktar Widjaya
Phone: (62) 21 392 9001/2/3
Fax: (62) 21 392 6203/8875
VP Dir.: Hendra Jaya Kosasih
Phone: (62) 21 392 9001/2/3
Fax: (62) 21 392 6203/8875
VP Dir.: Chen Wang Chi
Phone: (62) 21 392 9001/2/3
Fax: (62) 21 392 6203/8875
Pres., Dir.: Yudi Setiawan Lin
Phone: (62) 21 392 9001/2/3
Fax: (62) 21 392 6203/8875
VP, Dir.: Suresh Kiarn
Phone: (62) 21 392 9001/2/3
Fax: (62) 21 392 6203/8875
Dir.: Didi Harsa
Phone: (62) 21 392 9001/2/3
Fax: (62) 21 392 6203/8875
Dir.: Agustian Rachmansjah Partawidjaja
Phone: (62) 21 392 9001/2/3
Fax: (62) 21 392 6203/8875
Dir.: Yan Partawijaya
Phone: (62) 21 392 9001/2/3
Fax: (62) 21 392 6203/8875
VP, Dir.: ShunKeng Lin
Phone: (62) 21 392 9001/2/3
Fax: (62) 21 392 6203/8875
VP, Dir.: Linda Suryasari Wijaya Limantara
Phone: (62) 21 392 9001/2/3
Fax: (62) 21 392 6203/8875
Dir.: Raymond Liu Ph. D.
Phone: (62) 21 392 9001/2/3
Fax: (62) 21 392 6203/8875
Dir.: Buyung Wahab
Phone: (62) 21 392 9001/2/3
Fax: (62) 21 392 6203/8875
Mill Locations:
PT Indah Kiat Pulp & Paper Corp., Perawang (PT Indah Kiat Pulp & Paper) Mill, Jl. Raya Minas - Perawang Km. 26, 12780 Siak, Bengkalis, Indonesia, Capacity: 1,455,000 mt/y, (Pulp mill, Paper mill)
Phone: (62) 761 91088, 91373/91030
Fax: (62) 761 91373/76
Email: info@ikperawang.com
PT Indah Kiat Pulp & Paper Corp., Serang (PT Indah Kiat Pulp & Paper) Mill, Jln. Raya Serang Km. 76, Desa Kragilan, Jawa Barat, 42184 Serang, Indonesia, Capacity: 1,470,000 mt/y, (Paperboard mill)
Phone: (62) 254 281988
Fax: (62) 254 280918/2809136
PT Indah Kiat Pulp & Paper Corp., Tangerang (PT Indah Kiat Pulp & Paper) Mill, Gedung B, Jl. Raya Serpong Km. 8, 15310 Serpong, Tangerang, Indonesia, Capacity: 103,000 mt/y, (Paper mill)
Phone: (62) 21 539 8891/92
Fax: (62) 21 539 8890/5380009

Indonesia

ⓜPT Indah Kiat Pulp & Paper Corp.
Perawang (PT Indah Kiat Pulp & Paper) Mill
Ownership: Asia Pulp & Paper (APP)
Jl. Raya Minas - Perawang Km. 26
12780 Siak, Bengkalis, Riau, Sumatra
Indonesia
  Phone: (62) 761 91088, 91373/91030
  Fax: (62) 761 91373/76
  Email: info@ikperawang.com
  Web Address: ikperawang.com
Personnel:
  Mill Mgr.: Shyr Chaur Hann
  Phone: (62) 761 91373/91030
  Fax: (62) 761 91376
  Paper Mill Mgr.: Hsu Huei Li
  Phone: (62) 761 91373/91030
  Fax: (62) 761 91376
  Chief Eng.: Chiu Chun Ter
  Phone: (62) 761 91373/91030
  Fax: (62) 761 91376
  Pulp Mill Mgr.: Chen Feng Wen
  Phone: (62) 761 91373/91030
  Fax: (62) 761 91376
  Gen. Affairs: Margareta Cheng
  Phone: (62) 761 91373
  Fax: (62) 761 91376
  Coordinator Bus. Unit#1 & Instrument Mgr.: Muralikrishna Prathipati Leela
  Phone: (62) 761 91373
  Fax: (62) 761 91376
  Recovery Boiler Group Ldr.: Boy Lesmana
  Phone: (62) 761 91373
  Fax: (62) 761 91376
Total Employees at this Location: 3,100
Type of Operation: Pulp mill, Paper mill
Pulp Grades and Capacities:
  Total pulp capacity: 2,477,379 mt/y
  Pulp available for market: 1,342,221 mt/y
  Chemical Pulp: 2,300,000 mt/y
  Recycled Pulping: 29,600 mt/y
Pulp Mill Data:
  Chemical Pulping Systems:
  Batch digesters: 25
  Continuous digesters: 2
  Pulp Lines: 5
  Bleach Plant Systems: 5
  No. 1, Sequence: O_2 DEopDED, Capacity 200,000 admt/y
  No. 2, Sequence: O_2 C/DEoDED, Capacity 130,000 admt/y
  No. 3, Sequence: O_2 C/DEoDD, Capacity 560,000 admt/y
  No. 4, Sequence: C/DEoDD, Capacity 480,000 admt/y
  No. 5, Sequence: C/DEoDD, Capacity 240,000 admt/y
  Chemical Recovery Equipment:
  Evaporator lines: 3
  Recovery boilers: 5
  Lime Kiln
  Pulp Dryers:
  Flash dryers 1, Twin Wire 1, Twin Wire 1, Twin Wire 1, Twin Wire 1, Twin Wire 1
Paper/Paperboard Grades and Capacities:
  Total paper and paperboard capacity: 1,455,000 mt/y
  Uncoated woodfree/freesheet: 1,425,000 mt/y
  Linerboard: 30,000 mt/y
Paper and Paperboard Mill Data:
  Stock Preparation:
  Pulpers: 10
  Refiners: 16
Paper Machines: 8
  No. 1, fourdrinier, total capacity 65,000 mt/y, Trim width 3.35 m, Uncoated woodfree/freesheet
  No. 2, Bel-Form, total capacity 200,000 mt/y, Trim width 6.65 m, Uncoated woodfree/freesheet
  No. 3, Bel-Baie IV, total capacity 370,000 mt/y, Trim width 8.95 m, Uncoated woodfree/freesheet
  No. 5, fourdrinier, total capacity 45,000 mt/y, Trim width 2.6 m, Uncoated woodfree/freesheet
  No. 6, fourdrinier, total capacity 500,000 mt/y, Trim width 9.7 m, Uncoated woodfree/freesheet
  No. 7, twin-wire, total capacity 175,000 mt/y, Trim width 5.35 m, Uncoated woodfree/freesheet
  No. 8, fourdrinier, total capacity 70,000 mt/y, Trim width 4 m, Uncoated woodfree/freesheet
  No. 9, fourdrinier, total capacity 30,000 mt/y, Trim width 2.4 m, Linerboard
Coating Machines: 1
  No. 1, total capacity 50,000 mt/y, off machine
Finishing Equipment:
  Winders: 3
  Supercalenders: 6
  Rewinders: 8
  Sheeters: 12
Energy Data:
  Power boilers: 9
  Steam turbines: 13 at 380.0 MW

ⓜPT Indah Kiat Pulp & Paper Corp.
Serang (PT Indah Kiat Pulp & Paper) Mill
Ownership: Asia Pulp & Paper (APP)
Jln. Raya Serang Km. 76, Desa Kragilan, Jawa Barat
42184 Serang, West Java
Indonesia
  Phone: (62) 254 281988
  Fax: (62) 254 280918/2809136
  Web Address: www.ikserang.com, www.asiapulppaper.com
Personnel:
  Paper Mill Mgr.: Stan Wang
  Phone: (62) 254 281988
  Asst. Mill Mgr.: Wu Tien Wang
  Phone: (62) 254 281988
  Asst. Mill Mgr.: Lin Po Shi
  Phone: (62) 254 281988
  Gen. Affairs: Margareta Cheng
  Phone: (62) 254 281988
  Fax: (62) 254 280918/2809136
  HR. Mgr.: Chandra Wijaya
  Phone: (62) 254 281988
  Fax: (62) 254 280918/2809136
  Assist. Mgr. Maint. Utility: Satrio Agung Wijonarko
  Phone: (62) 254 281988
  Fax: (62) 254 280918/2809136
  Converting Plant Mgr.: Chou Shou Jeng
  Phone: (62) 254 281988
  Maint. Mgr.: Lee Chun Yi
  Phone: (62) 254 281988
Total Employees at this Location: 5,000
Type of Operation: Paperboard mill
Pulp Grades and Capacities:
  Total pulp capacity: 1,182,559 mt/y
  Recycled Pulping: 1,182,559 mt/y
Pulp Mill Data:
  Bleach Plant Systems: 1
  Recycled Fiber Treatment Lines:
  Pulpers: 4 at 1,000,000 admt/y
Paper/Paperboard Grades and Capacities:
  Total paper and paperboard capacity: 1,470,000 mt/y
  Linerboard: 710,000 mt/y
  Corrugating medium/fluting: 350,000 mt/y
  Boxboard/cartonboard: 410,000 mt/y
Paper and Paperboard Mill Data:
  Stock Preparation:
  Pulpers: 4
  Refiners: 9
Paper Machines: 6
  No. 1, fourdrinier (3), total capacity 350,000 mt/y, Trim width 6.5 m, Linerboard
  No. 2, twin-wire, total capacity 350,000 mt/y, Trim width 6.55 m, Corrugating medium/fluting
  No. 3, Fourdrinier (4), total capacity 210,000 mt/y, Trim width 4.2 m, Boxboard/cartonboard
  No. 4, fourdrinier (3), total capacity 200,000 mt/y, Trim width 4.5 m, Linerboard
  No. 5, fourdrinier (3), total capacity 160,000 mt/y, Trim width 4.5 m, Linerboard
  No. 6, Fourdrinier (4), total capacity 200,000 mt/y, Trim width 4.2 m, Boxboard/cartonboard
Coating Machines: 3
  No. 1, total capacity 175,000 mt/y., on machine
  No. 2, total capacity 260,000 mt/y., on machine
  No. 3, total capacity 175,000 mt/y., on machine
Finishing Equipment:
  Rewinders: 2
  Sheeters: 12
Energy Data:
  Power boilers: 4
  Steam turbines: 4 at 175.0 MW
  Electrical demand for mill: 2,177 MWh/D

ⓜPT Indah Kiat Pulp & Paper Corp.
Tangerang (PT Indah Kiat Pulp & Paper) Mill
Ownership: Asia Pulp & Paper (APP)
Gedung B, Jl. Raya Serpong Km. 8
15310 Serpong, Tangerang, West Java
Indonesia
  Phone: (62) 21 539 8891/92
  Fax: (62) 21 539 8890/5380009
  Web Address: www.iktangerang.com
Personnel:
  Mill Mgr.: Hsu Cha Ming
  Phone: (62) 21 539 8891/92
  Asst. Mill Mgr.: Chen Shi Yu
  Phone: (62) 21 539 8891/92
  PPIC Mgr. (Matl. Mgr.): Julius Chandra
  Phone: (62) 21 539 8891
  Fax: (62) 21 539 8890
  Finishing Mgr.: Wiza Bachtiar
  Phone: (62) 21 539 8891
  Fax: (62) 21 539 8890
  Bus. Unit Mgr.: Sylvia Rasmono
  Phone: (62) 21 539 8891
  Fax: (62) 21 539 8890
  HR Mgr.: Chandra Wijaya
  Phone: (62) 21 539 8891
  Fax: (62) 21 539 8890
Total Employees at this Location: 475
Type of Operation: Paper mill
Paper/Paperboard Grades and Capacities:
  Total paper and paperboard capacity: 103,000 mt/y
  Uncoated woodfree/freesheet: 103,000 mt/y
Paper and Paperboard Mill Data:
Paper Machines: 3
  No. 1, fourdrinier, total capacity 33,000 mt/y, Trim width 3 m, Uncoated woodfree/freesheet
  No. 2, fourdrinier, total capacity 35,000 mt/y, Trim width 3 m, Uncoated woodfree/freesheet
  No. 3, fourdrinier, total capacity 35,000 mt/y, Trim width 3 m, Uncoated woodfree/freesheet
Finishing Equipment:
  Rewinders: 1
  Sheeters: 5
Energy Data:
  Power boilers
  Steam turbines: 1 at 5.1 MW
  Electrical demand for mill: 216 MWh/D

ⓜPT Indo Paper Primajaya
Jl. Karang Bolong Raya 10
14430 Ancol Barat
Indonesia
  Phone: (62) 21 6909440/141
  Fax: (62) 21 6904837/1764
  Email: pramarko@centrin.net.id
Personnel:
  Man. Dir.: Roy Prasetya
  Phone: (62) 21 6909440/141
  Fax: (62) 21 6904837/1764
  Finan. Dir.: Lenny Hendra
  Phone: (62) 21 6909440/141
  Fax: (62) 21 6904837/1764
  Plant Mgr.: Ono Dudung
  Phone: (62) 21 6909440/141
  Fax: (62) 21 6904837/1764

Indonesia

Mktg. Mgr.: Daniel Solihin
Phone: (62) 21 6909440/141
Fax: (62) 21 6904837/1764
R&D Mgr.: Mia Prasetya
Phone: (62) 21 6909440/141
Fax: (62) 21 6904837/1764
Email: pramarko@centrin.net.id
Total Employees of Company: 400
Mill Locations:
PT Indo Paper Primajaya, Tangerang Mill, Jalan Raya Mauk Km. 5.6 Ds. Periok, Tangerang, Indonesia, Capacity: 15,000 mt/y, (Paper mill)
Phone: (62) 21 5520636
Fax: (62) 21 6904837
Email: pramarko@centrin.net.id

ⓜPT Indo Paper Primajaya
Tangerang Mill
Jalan Raya Mauk Km. 5.6 Ds. Periok
Tangerang, Jawa Barat
Indonesia
Phone: (62) 21 5520636
Fax: (62) 21 6904837
Email: pramarko@centrin.net.id
Personnel:
Mill Mgr.: Roy Prasetya
Phone: (62) 21 5520636
Converting Plant Mgr.: Mia Prasetya
Phone: (62) 21 5520636
Purch. Agent: Lenny Prasetya
Phone: (62) 21 5520636
Dir.: Daniel Solihin
Phone: (62) 21 5520636
Total Employees at this Location: 400
Type of Operation: Paper mill
Paper/Paperboard Grades and Capacities:
Total paper and paperboard capacity: 15,000 mt/y
Tissue: 15,000 mt/y
Paper and Paperboard Mill Data:
Stock Preparation:
Pulpers: 3
Refiners: 3
Paper Machines: 3
No. 1, cylinder, Trim width 1.2 m, Tissue
No. 2, cylinder, Trim width 1.2 m, Tissue
No. 3, (second hand), cylinder, Trim width 3.4 m, Tissue
Finishing Equipment:
Rewinders: 3
Energy Data:
Power boilers: 2

ⓜPT Integra Lestari (Surabaya)
Kec. Ngoro Mill
Jalan Mojokerto - Gempol, Kembangsri No.1
Kec. Ngoro, Mojokerto, East Java
Indonesia
Phone: (62) 321 6816261, 321 6816263, 321 681624, 321 6816265
Personnel:
Purch. Mgr.: Evi Retnowati
Phone: (62) 321 6816261
Total Employees at this Location: 180
Type of Operation: Paperboard mill
Pulp Grades and Capacities:
Total pulp capacity: 58,734 mt/y
Recycled Pulping: 58,734 mt/y
Pulp Mill Data:
Recycled Fiber Treatment Lines:
Recycled packaging pulping lines: 1
Paper/Paperboard Grades and Capacities:
Total paper and paperboard capacity: 60,000 mt/y
Linerboard: 24,000 mt/y
Corrugating medium/fluting: 36,000 mt/y
Paper and Paperboard Mill Data:
Paper Machines: 1
No. 1, multi-fourdrinier, total capacity 60,000 mt/y, Trim width 3.2 m, Linerboard, Corrugating medium/fluting
Energy Data:
Power boilers
Electrical demand for mill: 80 MWh/D

ⓜPT Java Paperindo Utama Industries
Jl. Kertopaten No. 2
60145 Surabaya, East Java
Indonesia
Phone: (62) 31 3718173
Fax: (62) 31 3717223
Email: marketing@javapaperindo.com
Web Address: www.javapaperindo.com
Personnel:
Dir.: Steven Tirtowidjojo
Phone: (62) 31 3716173/376662691
Fax: (62) 31 3714345/3717223/3762689
Total Employees of Company: 200
Mill Locations:
PT Java Paperindo Utama Industries, Mojokerto Mill, Desa Ngimbangan, Kecamatan Mojosari, 61382 Mojokerto, Indonesia, Capacity: 53,784 mt/y, (Paper mill)
Phone: (62) 321 591377/376/660
Fax: (62) 321 591776
Email: marketing@javapaperindo.com

ⓜPT Java Paperindo Utama Industries
Mojokerto Mill
Desa Ngimbangan, Kecamatan Mojosari
61382 Mojokerto, East Java
Indonesia
Phone: (62) 321 591377/376/660
Fax: (62) 321 591776
Email: marketing@javapaperindo.com
Web Address: www.javapaperindo.com
Personnel:
Pres. Dir.: Henry S. Widjojo
Phone: (62) 321 591377/376/660
Dir.: Steven Tirtowidjojo
Phone: (62) 321 591377/376/660
Total Employees at this Location: 200
Type of Operation: Paper mill
Paper/Paperboard Grades and Capacities:
Total paper and paperboard capacity: 53,784 mt/y
Tissue: 4,284 mt/y
Specialty and industrial: 49,500 mt/y
Paper and Paperboard Mill Data:
Paper Machines: 1
No. 1, fourdrinier, total capacity 82,503 mt/y, Trim width 3.2 m, Specialty and industrial, Tissue
Energy Data:
Power boilers
Electrical demand for mill: 126 MWh/D

ⓜPT Jaya Kertas
Semut Megah Plaza, Jalan Stasiun Kota No. 26 Q/Blok E-15
60161 Surabaya, Jawa Timur
Indonesia
Phone: (62) 31 3520820
Fax: (62) 31 3530503/6675
Personnel:
Chmn.: Ongko Prawiro
Phone: (62) 31 3520820
Fax: (62) 31 3530503/6675
Pres. Dir.: Mrs. Kinarti Suwito
Phone: (62) 31 3520820
Fax: (62) 31 3530503/6675
Export Sls. Mgr.: Catharina Loekito
Phone: (62) 31 3520820
Fax: (62) 31 3530503/6675
Dir.: Mardi Hartono
Phone: (62) 31 3520820
Fax: (62) 31 3530503/6675
Total Employees of Company: 1,002
Mill Locations:
PT Jaya Kertas, Nganjuk Mill, Desa Kepuh, Kec. Kertosono, Nganjuk, Indonesia, Capacity: 218,500 mt/y, (Paper mill, Paperboard mill)
Phone: (62) 358 551161
Fax: (62) 358 552521

ⓜPT Jaya Kertas
Nganjuk Mill
Desa Kepuh, Kec. Kertosono
Nganjuk, East Java
Indonesia
Phone: (62) 358 551161
Fax: (62) 358 552521
Personnel:
Chmn.: Ongko Prawiro
Phone: (62) 358 551161
Fax: (62) 358 552521
Pres. Dir.: Mrs. Kinarti Suwito
Phone: (62) 358 551161
Fax: (62) 358 552521
Logist. Mgr.: Rahmad Mulyadi
Phone: (62) 358 551161
Fax: (62) 358 552521
Total Employees at this Location: 1,002
Type of Operation: Paper mill, Paperboard mill
Paper/Paperboard Grades and Capacities:
Total paper and paperboard capacity: 218,500 mt/y
Uncoated woodfree/freesheet: 31,000 mt/y
Coated woodfree/freesheet: 5,000 mt/y
Tissue: 13,200 mt/y
Packaging papers
Containerboard: 112,000 mt/y
Linerboard
Corrugating medium/fluting
Boxboard/cartonboard

ⓜPT Juara Prayasa Jawa
Jln. Simpang Dukuh No. 38-40
60275 Genteng, Surabaya
Indonesia
Phone: (62) 31 5923679
Fax: (62) 31 5927263
Personnel:
Pres./Dir.: Rosally Orwis
Phone: (62) 31 5923679
Fax: (62) 31 5927263
Dir.: Tarianto
Phone: (62) 31 5923679
Fax: (62) 31 5927263
Total Employees at this Location: 50
Mill Locations:
PT Juara Prayasa Jawa, Genteng, Surabaya Mill, Jln. Simpang Dukuh No. 38-40, 60275 Genteng, Surabaya, Indonesia, Capacity: 1,000 mt/y, (Paper mill)
Phone: (62) 31 5923679
Fax: (62) 31 5927263

ⓜPT Juara Prayasa Jawa
Genteng, Surabaya Mill
Jln. Simpang Dukuh No. 38-40
60275 Genteng, Surabaya, East Java
Indonesia
Phone: (62) 31 5923679
Fax: (62) 31 5927263
Personnel:
Pres./Dir.: Rosally Orwis
Phone: (62) 31 5923679
Dir.: Mr. Tarianto
Phone: (62) 31 5923679
Total Employees at this Location: 50
Type of Operation: Paper mill
Paper/Paperboard Grades and Capacities:
Total paper and paperboard capacity: 1,000 mt/y
Specialty and industrial: 1,000 mt/y

ⓞⓜPT Karya Tulada
Karawaci Mill
Ownership: 100% by Private owner
Jln. Raya Karawaci Km 2
15115 Tangerang, Banten, West Java
Indonesia
Phone: (62) 21 552 2315/4984/4985
Fax: (62) 21 5524119
Personnel:
Pres. Dir.: Anton Kusnadi

Indonesia

Phone: (62) 21 552 2315/4984/4985
Dir.: Rudy R.
Phone: (62) 21 552 2315/4984/4985
Total Employees at this Location: 170
Type of Operation: Paper mill
Paper/Paperboard Grades and Capacities:
Total paper and paperboard capacity: 8,600 mt/y
Packaging papers: 4,600 mt/y
Boxboard/cartonboard: 4,000 mt/y
Paper and Paperboard Mill Data:
Paper Machines: 2
No. 1, Yankee dryer, Trim width 1.6 m, Specialty and industrial
No. 2, Yankee dryer, Trim width 2.35 m
Finishing Equipment:
Rewinders: 2
Sheeters: 2

⊕⊚PT Kertas Leces (Persero) Probolinggo Mill
Ownership: 100% by Indonesian Government
Jl. Raya Leces
67202 Probolinggo, East Java
Indonesia
Phone: (62) 335 680993
Fax: (62) 335 680954
Email: leces@kertasleces.co.id, marketing@kertasleces.co.id
Web Address: www.kertasleces.co.id
Personnel:
Chmn.: Singgih Riphat
Phone: (62) 335 680993
Fax: (62) 335 680954
Email: marketing@kertasleces.com
Pres. Dir.: Robert Simanjuntak
Phone: (62) 335 680993
Fax: (62) 335 680954
Email: marketing@kertasleces.com
Dir., Prod. & Dvlpt.: Syarif Hidayat
Phone: (62) 335 680993
Fax: (62) 335 680954
Email: plant_mgr@kertasleces.co.id
Dir. Finan, HR & Gen. Affair: Zainal Arifin
Phone: (62) 335 680993
Fax: (62) 335 680954
Qlty. Mgr.: Harry Susianto
Phone: (62) 335 680993
Fax: (62) 335 680954
Qlty., Assur. and Env. Mgr.: Ir. Nugroho Basuki
Phone: (62) 335 680993
Fax: (62) 335 680954
Email: basuki.nugroho@gmail.com
Plt. Mgr.: Slamet Riyanto
Phone: (62) 335 680993
Fax: (62) 335 680954
R&D Mgr.: Heri Sucahyo
Phone: (62) 335 680993
Fax: (62) 335 680954
Email: heri_sucahyo@yahoo.co.id
Dir.: zainal Arifin
Phone: (62) 335 680993
Fax: (62) 335 680954
Email: inyakoe.diyah@gmail.com
Total Employees at this Location: 2,129
Type of Operation: Pulp mill, Paper mill, Paperboard mill
Pulp Grades and Capacities:
Total pulp capacity: 10,135 mt/y
Recycled Pulping: 10,135 mt/y
Pulp Mill Data:
Chemical Pulping Systems:
Continuous digesters: 2
Pulp Lines: 1
Bleach Plant Lines:
No. 1, Sequence: H, Capacity 10,000 admt/y
No. 2, Sequence: O_2 CEH, Capacity 170,000 admt/y
Chemical Recovery Equipment:
Evaporator lines: 1
Recovery boilers: 1
Lime Kiln

Recycled Fiber Treatment Lines:
Flotation deinking lines: 5 at 95,000 admt/y
Pulpers: 1
Washing deinking lines: 4 at 95,000 admt/y
Pulp Dryers:
Wet Lap machine 1
Paper/Paperboard Grades and Capacities:
Total paper and paperboard capacity: 200,000 mt/y
Uncoated woodfree/freesheet: 180,000 mt/y
Tissue: 10,000 mt/y
Corrugating medium/fluting: 10,000 mt/y
Paper and Paperboard Mill Data:
Paper Machines: 5
No. 1, fourdrinier, total capacity 10,000 mt/y, Trim width 2.4 m, Corrugating medium/fluting
No. 2, hybrid former, total capacity 20,000 mt/y, Trim width 2.36 m, Uncoated woodfree/freesheet
No. 3, fourdrinier, total capacity 70,000 mt/y, Trim width 5.35 m, Uncoated woodfree/freesheet
No. 4, fourdrinier, Yankee dryer, total capacity 10,000 mt/y, Trim width 2.2 m, Tissue, Uncoated woodfree/freesheet
No. 5, DuoFormer F, total capacity 90,000 mt/y, Trim width 6.35 m, Uncoated woodfree/freesheet
Finishing Equipment:
Winders: 5
Calenders: 5
Supercalenders: 2
Rewinders: 5
Sheeters: 3
Energy Data:
Power boilers: 5
Steam turbines: 3 at 65 MW
Electrical demand for mill: 419 MWh/D

⊕PT Kertas Nusantara
Ownership: 100% by Anugera Cipta Investama, United Fiber Systems (UFS)
Bidakara Building, 9-10th floor Jln Gatot Subrota Kav. 71-73
12780 Jakarta
Indonesia
Phone: (62) 21 8379 3211
Fax: (62) 21 8379 3215
Email: marketing@corp.kertas-nusantara.com
Web Address: www.kiani.com
Personnel:
Pres. Dir.: Prabowo Subianto
Phone: (62) 21 8379 3211
Fax: (62) 21 8379 3215
Dir.: Iwan Wahyu Bharata
Phone: (62) 21 8379 3211
Fax: (62) 21 8379 3215
Dir.: Andy Rayes
Phone: (62) 21 8379 3211
Fax: (62) 21 8379 3215
Dir.: Agus Suprayogi
Phone: (62) 21 8379 3211
Fax: (62) 21 8379 3215
Dir.: Rianggono Prawiroardjo
Phone: (62) 21 8379 3211
Fax: (62) 21 8379 3215
Oper. Dir.: Yossy Haryoso
Phone: (62) 21 8379 3211
Fax: (62) 21 8379 3215
Total Employees of Company: 1,400
Mill Locations:
PT Kertas Nusantara, Tanjung Redep Mill, Desa Mangkajang, 77371 Sambaliung, Berau, Indonesia, (Pulp mill)
Phone: (62) 21 797 5172

⊕PT Kertas Nusantara Tanjung Redep Mill
Mill is temporarily closed (Company stopped production on November 23, 2013 because of supply and debt management problems.)
Desa Mangkajang
77371 Sambaliung, Berau, East Kalimantan
Indonesia
Phone: (62) 21 797 5172
Web Address: www.kiani.com
Personnel:
Pulp Mgr.: Ery Irwansyah
Email: eirwansyah@kertas-nusantara.com
Total Employees at this Location: 1,400
Type of Operation: Pulp mill
Pulp Mill Data:
Chemical Pulping Systems:
Batch digesters: 10
Pulp Lines: 1
Bleach Plant Systems: 1
No. 1
Chemical Recovery Equipment:
Evaporator lines: 1
Recovery boilers: 1
Lime Kiln
Pulp Dryers:
Air Float dryers 1
Energy Data:
Power boilers: 1
Steam turbines: 2 at 63.3 MW

⊕PT Klambir Jaya
Jln. Brigjen. Katamso No.43 RST
20151 Medan, North Sumatra
Indonesia
Phone: (62) 61 551333
Fax: (62) 61 321 731/37
Personnel:
Pres. Dir.: Jauhari Chandra
Phone: (62) 61 551333
Fax: (62) 61 321 731/37
Dir.: William F. Chandra
Phone: (62) 61 551333
Fax: (62) 61 321 731/37
Dir.: Michael M. Chandra
Phone: (62) 61 551333
Fax: (62) 61 321 731/37
Total Employees of Company: 450
Mill Locations:
PT Klambir Jaya, Deli Serdang Mill, Klambir Lima, Ds. Tj. Gurita, Kec. Sunggal, Deli Serdang, Indonesia, Capacity: 8,000 mt/y, (Paper mill)
Phone: (62) 61 551333
Fax: (62) 61 321731

⊕PT Klambir Jaya Deli Serdang Mill
Klambir Lima, Ds. Tj. Gurita, Kec. Sunggal
Deli Serdang, North Sumatera
Indonesia
Phone: (62) 61 551333
Fax: (62) 61 321731
Type of Operation: Paper mill
Paper/Paperboard Grades and Capacities:
Total paper and paperboard capacity: 8,000 mt/y
Specialty and industrial: 8,000 mt/y

⊕Korindo Group
Ownership: 80% by Panwell Industrial Ltd., 20% by PT Aspex
Kalimantan
Indonesia
Phone: (62) 0771 24775
Email: aspex@korindo.co.id
Web Address: www.korindo.co.id
Mill Locations:
PT Aspex Kumbong, Bogor Mill, Jln. Raya Narogong Km 26, Desa Dayeuh, Kec. Cileungsi, 16967 Bogor, Indonesia, Capacity: 420,189 mt/y, (Paper mill)
Phone: (62) 21 8230681/7975959/6142
Fax: (62) 21 8230682/7976402
Email: aspex@korindo.co.id

⊕PT Lispap Rayasentosa
Ownership: 50% by Dennish Lesmana, 50% by Firman Rusli

Indonesia

Jl. Tomang Utara No. 32 PO Box 1588 JAK
11440 Jakarta
Indonesia
  Phone: (62) 21 5683835/00823/824
  Fax: (62) 21 5600671
  Email: lispapys@yahoo.com
Personnel:
  Chmn./Man. Dir.: Firman Rusli
  Phone: (62) 21 5683835/00823/824
  Fax: (62) 21 5600671
  Pres.: Dennish Lesmana
  Phone: (62) 21 5683835/00823/824
  Fax: (62) 21 5600671
  Owner: David Rusli
  Phone: (62) 21 5683835/00823/824
  Fax: (62) 21 5600671
  Email: ruslid@gmail.com
  Mktg. Dir.: Ms. Endang
  Phone: (62) 21 5683835/00823/824
  Fax: (62) 21 5600671
Total Employees at this Location: 25
Mill Locations:
  PT Lispap Rayasentosa, Tangerang, Banten Mill, Jln. Raya Mauk Km 6, Tangerang, Banten, Indonesia, Capacity: 7,200 mt/y, (Paper mill)
  Phone: (62) 21 568 3835/0823/0824 (HQ)
  Fax: (62) 21 560 0671 (HQ)

ⓜPT Lispap Rayasentosa
Tangerang, Banten Mill
Jln. Raya Mauk Km 6
Tangerang, Banten, Jawa Barat
Indonesia
  Phone: (62) 21 568 3835/0823/0824 (HQ)
  Fax: (62) 21 560 0671 (HQ)
Personnel:
  Pres. Dir.: Dr. Med. Dennish Lesmana
  Phone: (62) 21 568 3835/0823/0824 (HQ)
  Dir.: Firman Rusli
  Phone: (62) 21 568 3835/0823/0824 (HQ)
  Owner: David Rusli
  Phone: (62) 21 568 3835/0823/0824 (HQ)
Total Employees at this Location: 200
Type of Operation: Paper mill
Pulp Grades and Capacities:
  Total pulp capacity: 10,000 mt/y
Paper/Paperboard Grades and Capacities:
  Total paper and paperboard capacity: 7,200 mt/y
  Tissue: 7,200 mt/y
Paper and Paperboard Mill Data:
Paper Machines: 4
  No. 1, total capacity 1,800 mt/y, Trim width 2 m, Tissue
  No. 2, total capacity 1,800 mt/y, Trim width 2 m, Tissue
  No. 3, total capacity 1,800 mt/y, Trim width 2 m, Tissue
  No. 4, total capacity 1,800 mt/y, Trim width 2 m, Tissue

ⓜⓜPT Lontar Papyrus Pulp & Paper Industry
Jambi (PT Lontar Papyrus Pulp & Paper) Mill
Ownership: Asia Pulp & Paper (APP)
Ds. Tebing Tinggi, Kec. Tungkal Ulu
Jambi, South Sumatra
Indonesia
  Phone: (62) 741 62645/51051
  Fax: (62) 741 62621
  Email: lp3i-adm_ttg@app.co.id
  Web Address: www.asiapulppaper.com
Personnel:
  Vice Section Chief: Ajay Goel
  Phone: (62) 741 62645/51051
  Fax: (62) 741 62621
  Cust. Serv.: Donny Idonk
  Phone: (62) 741 62645/51051
  Fax: (62) 741 62621
  IT Mgr.: Amin Chen
  Phone: (62) 741 62645/51051
  Fax: (62) 741 62621
Total Employees of Company: 1,500
Total Employees at this Location: 1,500
Type of Operation: Pulp mill, Paper mill
Pulp Grades and Capacities:
  Total pulp capacity: 998,485 mt/y
  Pulp available for market: 813,011 mt/y
  Chemical Pulp: 998,485 mt/y
Pulp Mill Data:
  Chemical Pulping Systems:
  Continuous digesters: 1
Pulp Lines: 2
  Bleach Plant Systems: 2
  Chemical Pulping System - Hardwood, Sequence: O_2 C/DEopD
  Chemical Pulping System - Hardwood, Sequence: O_2 DEopD
  Chemical Recovery Equipment:
  Evaporator lines: 1
  Recovery boilers: 1
  Lime Kiln
  Pulp Dryers:
  Flakt dryer 1, Flakt dryer 1
Paper/Paperboard Grades and Capacities:
  Total paper and paperboard capacity: 178,548 mt/y
  Tissue: 178,548 mt/y
Paper and Paperboard Mill Data:
Paper Machines: 7
  No. 1, crescent former, Yankee dryer, total capacity 58,548 mt/y, Trim width 5.5 m, Tissue, Uncoated woodfree/freesheet
  No. 2, fourdrinier, total capacity 20,000 mt/y, Trim width 2.8 m, Tissue
  No. 3, fourdrinier, total capacity 20,000 mt/y, Trim width 2.8 m, Tissue
  No. 4, fourdrinier, total capacity 20,000 mt/y, Trim width 2.8 m, Tissue
  No. 5, fourdrinier, total capacity 20,000 mt/y, Trim width 2.8 m, Tissue
  No. 6, fourdrinier, total capacity 20,000 mt/y, Trim width 2.8 m, Tissue
  No. 7, fourdrinier, total capacity 20,000 mt/y, Trim width 2.8 m, Tissue
Energy Data:
  Power boilers: 2
  Steam turbines: 5 at 130 MW
  Electrical demand for mill: 2,524 MWh/D

ⓜPT Niki Tunggal
Jalan Raya Sumber Suko, Sukodono
67352 Lumajang
Indonesia
  Phone: (62) 334 882116/1986
Personnel:
  Pres. Dir.: Hengki Matios
  Phone: (62) 334 882116/1986
Total Employees at this Location: 190
Mill Locations:
  PT Niki Tunggal, Lumajang Mill, Jalan Raya Sumber Suko, Sukodono, 67352 Lumajang, Indonesia, Capacity: 3,600 mt/y, (Paper mill)
  Phone: (62) 334 882116/1986

ⓜPT Niki Tunggal
Lumajang Mill
Jalan Raya Sumber Suko, Sukodono
67352 Lumajang, East Java
Indonesia
  Phone: (62) 334 882116/1986
Personnel:
  Pres. Dir.: Hengki Matios
  Phone: (62) 334 882116/1986
Total Employees at this Location: 190
Type of Operation: Paper mill
Paper/Paperboard Grades and Capacities:
  Total paper and paperboard capacity: 3,600 mt/y
  Specialty and industrial
Paper and Paperboard Mill Data:
Paper Machines: 1
  No. 1, total capacity 3,600 mt/y, Specialty and industrial

ⓜPT Pabrik Kertas Noree Indonesia
Ownership: 100% by private owner
Jln. Hayam Wuruk 5 B/5
10120 Jakarta
Indonesia
  Phone: (62) 21 3811959/3860308
  Fax: (62) 21 3809788/3842903
  Email: marketing@noreepaper.com
  Web Address: www.noreepaper.com
Personnel:
  Pres. Dir.: Dauddy Bahar
  Phone: (62) 21 3811959/3860308
  Fax: (62) 21 3809788/3842903
  Email: dauddyba@indo.net.id
  Dir.: Dadang K. Wikara
  Phone: (62) 21 3811959/3860308
  Fax: (62) 21 3809788/3842903
Total Employees of Company: 385
Total Employees at this Location: 385
Mill Locations:
  PT Pabrik Kertas Noree Indonesia, Bekasi Mill, Jalan Raya Babelan Km 7-8, 17610 Bekasi, Indonesia, Capacity: 55,000 mt/y, (Paperboard mill)
  Phone: (62) 21 8921155/8921243
  Fax: (62) 21 892 1244
  Email: marketing@noreepaper.com

ⓜPT Pabrik Kertas Noree Indonesia
Bekasi Mill
Ownership: PT Pabrik Kertas Noree Indonesia
Jalan Raya Babelan Km 7-8
17610 Bekasi, West Java
Indonesia
  Phone: (62) 21 8921155/8921243
  Fax: (62) 21 892 1244
  Email: marketing@noreepaper.com
  Web Address: www.noreepaper.com
Personnel:
  Pres. Commissioner: Lukman Wikara
  Phone: (62) 21 8921155/8921243
  Pres. Dir.: Dauddy Bahar
  Phone: (62) 21 8921155/8921243
  Dir.: Dadang K. Wikara
  Phone: (62) 21 8921155/8921243
  Qlty. Mgr.: Ichwan Nurdin
  Phone: (62) 21 892 1155
  Fax: (62) 21 892 1244
Total Employees at this Location: 315
Type of Operation: Paperboard mill
Pulp Grades and Capacities:
  Total pulp capacity: 54,936 mt/y
  Recycled Pulping: 54,936 mt/y
Pulp Mill Data:
  Recycled Fiber Treatment Lines:
  Recycled packaging pulping lines: 2
Paper/Paperboard Grades and Capacities:
  Total paper and paperboard capacity: 55,000 mt/y
  Boxboard/cartonboard: 55,000 mt/y
Paper and Paperboard Mill Data:
Paper Machines: 2
  No. 1, cylinder, total capacity 20,000 mt/y, Trim width 1.8 m, Boxboard/cartonboard
  No. 2, fourdrinier, total capacity 35,000 mt/y, Trim width 2.4 m, Boxboard/cartonboard
Coating Machines: 2
  PM1, total capacity 12,500 mt/y., off machine
  PM2, off machine
Finishing Equipment:
  Calenders: 2
  Rewinders: 2 at 50,000 mt/y
  Sheeters: 2 at 50,000 mt/y
Energy Data:
  Power boilers
  Electrical demand for mill: 98 MWh/D

ⓜPT Pabrik Kertas Indonesia (Pakerin)
Ownership: 100% by Private Owner
Jln. Kertopaten No. 3
60145 Surabaya, Jawa Timur
Indonesia
  Phone: (62) 31 371 6173
  Fax: (62) 31 371 7223/4345

Indonesia

Email: contact@pakerin.co.id
Web Address: www.pakerin.co.id
Personnel:
Pres. Dir.: David Siemens Kurniawan
Phone: (62) 31 371 6173
Fax: (62) 31 371 7223/4345
VP/Dir./ Finan. Mgr.: Henry Susilowidjojo
Phone: (62) 31 371 6173
Fax: (62) 31 371 7223/4345
Dir./ Prod. Mgr.: Steven Tirtowidjojo
Phone: (62) 31 371 6173
Fax: (62) 31 371 7223/4345
Total Employees of Company: 2,500
Mill Locations:
PT Pabrik Kertas Indonesia (Pakerin), Mojokerto Mill, Desa Bangun, Kec. Pungging, 61384 Mojokerto, Indonesia, Capacity: 468,025 mt/y, (Pulp mill, Paperboard mill)
Phone: (62) 321 361552
Fax: (62) 321 361615
Email: contact@pakerin.co.id

ⓗⓜPT Pabrik Kertas Indonesia (Pakerin)
Mojokerto Mill
Desa Bangun, Kec. Pungging
61384 Mojokerto, East Java
Indonesia
Phone: (62) 321 361552
Fax: (62) 321 361615
Email: contact@pakerin.co.id
Web Address: www.pakerin.co.id
Personnel:
Mill Mgr.: Wu Tien Wang
Phone: (62) 321 361552
Fax: (62) 321 361615
Dir.: Steven Tirtowidjojo
Phone: (62) 321 361552
Fax: (62) 321 361615
VP/Dir.: Henry Susilowidjojo
Phone: (62) 321 361552
Fax: (62) 321 361615
Snr. Mgr.: Gilbert Porras
Phone: (62) 321 361552
Fax: (62) 321 361615
Maint. Mgr.: Surya Dinata
Phone: (62) 321 361552
Fax: (62) 321 361615
Quality Mgr.: Liliana Dewi
Phone: (62) 321 361552
Fax: (62) 321 361615
Sec.: Feny S. Tjipto
Phone: (62) 321 361552
Fax: (62) 321 361615
Total Employees at this Location: 1,250
Type of Operation: Pulp mill, Paperboard mill
Pulp Grades and Capacities:
Total pulp capacity: 460,964 mt/y
Recycled Pulping: 460,964 mt/y
Pulp Mill Data:
Recycled Fiber Treatment Lines:
Flotation deinking lines: 1 at 425,000 admt/y
Recycled packaging pulping lines: 3
Paper/Paperboard Grades and Capacities:
Total paper and paperboard capacity: 468,025 mt/y
Linerboard: 178,400 mt/y
Corrugating medium/fluting: 160,000 mt/y
Boxboard/cartonboard: 129,625 mt/y
Paper and Paperboard Mill Data:
Paper Machines: 6
No. 1, cylinder (7), total capacity 32,000 mt/y, Trim width 2.4 m, Boxboard/cartonboard
No. 2, cylinder (6), total capacity 53,000 mt/y, Trim width 2.4 m, Boxboard/cartonboard
No. 3, fourdrinier, total capacity 71,400 mt/y, Trim width 3.7 m, Linerboard
No. 5, fourdrinier, total capacity 107,000 mt/y, Trim width 4.35 m, Linerboard
No. 6, fourdrinier, total capacity 160,000 mt/y, Trim width 6 m, Corrugating medium/fluting
No. 7, cylinder (7), total capacity 44,625 mt/y, Trim width 2.1 m, Boxboard/cartonboard
Coating Machines: 3
No. 1, total capacity 21,000 mt/y, on machine
No. 2, total capacity 40,000 mt/y, on machine
No. 3, total capacity 240,000 mt/y, on machine
Energy Data:
Power boilers: 1
Steam turbines: 2 at 50.2 MW
Electrical demand for mill: 616 MWh/D

ⓗⓜPT Kertas Padalarang
Padalarang Mill
Ownership: 13% by government company, 41% by Indonesian government, 46% by public company
Jln. Cihaliwung No.181
40553 Padalarang, Bandung, West Java
Indonesia
Phone: (62) 22 6809315/93
Fax: (62) 22 6809284
Email: ptkp@indosat.net.id, office@kertas-padalarang.co.id
Web Address: www.kertas-padalarang.co.id
Personnel:
Pres. Dir.: Atje Mohamad Daryan
Phone: (62) 22 6809315
Fax: (62) 22 6809284
Finan. Dir.: Agustaman
Phone: (62) 22 6809315
Fax: (62) 22 6809284
Prod. Mgr.: DJuli Suwardi
Phone: (62) 22 6809315
Fax: (62) 22 6809284
Mktg. Dir.: Bambang Prayitno
Phone: (62) 22 6809315
Fax: (62) 22 6809284
Total Employees at this Location: 473
Type of Operation: Pulp mill, Paper mill
Pulp Grades and Capacities:
Total pulp capacity: 3,000 mt/y
Pulp Mill Data:
Chemical Pulping Systems:
Batch digesters: 5
Continuous digesters: 1
Bleach Plant Systems: 3
Paper/Paperboard Grades and Capacities:
Total paper and paperboard capacity: 7,900 mt/y
Uncoated woodfree/freesheet
Specialty and industrial
Paper and Paperboard Mill Data:
Stock Preparation:
Pulpers: 2
Refiners: 3
Paper Machines: 3
No. 1, fourdrinier, fourdrinier, total capacity 2,800 mt/y, Trim width 2.7 m, Uncoated woodfree/freesheet
No. 2, fourdrinier, fourdrinier, total capacity 2,500 mt/y, Trim width 2.45 m, Uncoated woodfree/freesheet
No. 3, fourdrinier, total capacity 2,600 mt/y, Trim width 2.7 m, Specialty and industrial
Finishing Equipment:
Supercalenders: 2
Energy Data:
Power boilers: 4

ⓗPT Panca Usaha Paramita
Ownership: 100% by Private Owner
Jl. Tomang Raya 2F
11430 Jakarta
Indonesia
Phone: (62) 21 5667050/00102
Fax: (62) 21 5600100
Email: pupjkt@indosat.net.id
Personnel:
Pres. Dir.: Minanto Wiyono
Phone: (62) 21 5667050/00102
Fax: (62) 21 5600100
Dir.: Ng Ming Hwie
Phone: (62) 21 5667050/00102
Fax: (62) 21 5600100
Total Employees of Company: 320
Mill Locations:
PT Panca Usaha Paramita, Banten Mill, Jln. Raya Serpong Km 7, Tangerang, Banten, Indonesia, Capacity: 12,000 mt/y, (Paper mill)
Phone: (62) 21 5600102/67050
Fax: (62) 21 5600100
Email: pupjkt@indosat.net.id

ⓗⓜPT Panca Usaha Paramita
Banten Mill
Jln. Raya Serpong Km 7
Tangerang, Banten, Jawa Barat
Indonesia
Phone: (62) 21 5600102/67050
Fax: (62) 21 5600100
Email: pupjkt@indosat.net.id
Personnel:
Pres. Dir.: Minanto Wiyono
Phone: (62) 21 5600102/67050
Dir.: Ming Hwie Ng
Phone: (62) 21 5600102/67050
Total Employees at this Location: 321
Type of Operation: Paper mill
Paper/Paperboard Grades and Capacities:
Total paper and paperboard capacity: 12,000 mt/y
Tissue: 12,000 mt/y
Paper and Paperboard Mill Data:
Paper Machines: 4
No. 1, total capacity 7,000 mt/y, Tissue
No. 2, Tissue
No. 3, total capacity 2,400 mt/y, Tissue
No. 4, Tissue
Energy Data:
Power boilers: 3

ⓗⓜPT Papertech Indonesia
Subang Mill
Ownership: 100% by Papertech S.L.
Jln. Raya Cipeundeuy Km 1, Desa Cipeundeuy
41272 Subang, Jawa Barat
Indonesia
Phone: (62) 260 710645
Fax: (62) 260 710644
Email: pti@id.papertech.com
Web Address: www.papertech.com
Personnel:
Pres. Dir.: Yao Jie Ping
Phone: (62) 260 710645
Fax: (62) 260 710644
Gen. Mgr.: Erfan P. Santoso
Phone: (62) 260 710645
Fax: (62) 260 710644
Email: esantoso@id.papertech.com
Man. Dir., Texpack Group: Jeff Jie Ping Yao
Phone: (62) 260 710645
Fax: (62) 260 710644
Deputy Gen. Mgr.: Kwee Ie Hung
Phone: (62) 260 710645
Fax: (62) 260 710644
Email: kweeih@id.papertech.com
Dir.: Fernando Martinez
Phone: (62) 260 710645
Fax: (62) 260 710644
Email: fmartinez@papertech.com
Dir.: Michel Joseph Schmidlin
Phone: (62) 260 710645
Fax: (62) 260 710644
Total Employees at this Location: 103
Type of Operation: Paper mill
Mill Locations:
PT Papertech Indonesia, Blabak Mill, Jalan Sanggrahan Gatak No.23, 56511 Blabak, Mungkid, Indonesia, Capacity: 26,000 mt/y, (Paperboard mill)
PT Papertech Indonesia, Unit II, Kabupaten Magelang, Jl. Sanggrahan Gatak No. 23, Desa Mungkid, 56511 Kecamatan Mungkid, Kabupaten Magelang, Indonesia, Capacity: 17,500 mt/y, (Paperboard mill)
Phone: (62) 293 327231

Fax: (62) 293 327230
Email: pti@id.papertech.com
Pulp Grades and Capacities:
Total pulp capacity: 61,422 mt/y
Recycled Pulping: 61,422 mt/y
Pulp Mill Data:
Recycled Fiber Treatment Lines:
Recycled packaging pulping lines: 1
Paper/Paperboard Grades and Capacities:
Total paper and paperboard capacity: 60,000 mt/y
Boxboard/cartonboard: 60,000 mt/y
Paper and Paperboard Mill Data:
Paper Machines: 1
No. 1, multi-fourdrinier, total capacity 60,000 mt/y, Trim width 2.3 m, Boxboard/cartonboard
Energy Data:
Electrical demand for mill: 96 MWh/D

PT Papertech Indonesia
Blabak Mill
Ownership: 100% by Papertech S.L.
Jalan Sanggrahan Gatak No.23
56511 Blabak, Mungkid, Central Java
Indonesia
Web Address: www.papertech.com
Total Employees at this Location: 80
Type of Operation: Paperboard mill
Pulp Grades and Capacities:
Total pulp capacity: 26,620 mt/y
Recycled Pulping: 26,620 mt/y
Pulp Mill Data:
Recycled Fiber Treatment Lines:
Recycled packaging pulping lines: 1
Paper/Paperboard Grades and Capacities:
Total paper and paperboard capacity: 26,000 mt/y
Boxboard/cartonboard: 26,000 mt/y
Paper and Paperboard Mill Data:
Paper Machines: 1
No. 1, fourdrinier, total capacity 26,000 mt/y, Trim width 1.5 m, Boxboard/cartonboard
Energy Data:
Electrical demand for mill: 42 MWh/D

PT Papertech Indonesia
Unit II, Kabupaten Magelang
Ownership: 100% by Papertech S.L.
Jl. Sanggrahan Gatak No. 23, Desa Mungkid
56511 Kecamatan Mungkid, Kabupaten Magelang,
Jawa Tengah
Indonesia
Phone: (62) 293 327231
Fax: (62) 293 327230
Email: pti@id.papertech.com
Web Address: www.papertech.com
Personnel:
Gen. Mgr.: Erfan P. Santoso
Phone: (62) 293 327231
Email: esantoso@id.papertech.com
Sls. Mgr.: Kwee Le Hung
Phone: (62) 293 327231
Email: kweeih@id.papertech.com
Type of Operation: Paperboard mill
Paper/Paperboard Grades and Capacities:
Total paper and paperboard capacity: 17,500 mt/y
Boxboard/cartonboard
Paper and Paperboard Mill Data:
Paper Machines: 1
No. 1, fourdrinier, total capacity 17,500 mt/y, Trim width 1.5 m

PT Papyrus Sakti
Graha Sukandamulia Bldg. 5th floor, Jln. Tomang Raya Terusan Kav. 71-73
11440 Jakarta Barat
Indonesia
Phone: (62) 21 5636208/12
Fax: (62) 21 5636213/17
Email: contact@pspm.com

Web Address: www.pspm.com
Personnel:
Pres.: Albert Cahyadi Sukandadinat
Phone: (62) 21 5636208/12
Fax: (62) 21 5636213/17
Dir.: Kurniawan Mulyadi
Phone: (62) 21 5636208/12
Fax: (62) 21 5636213/17
Mill Locations:
PT Papyrus Sakti, Bandung Mill, Jln. Raya Banjaran Km 16.2, Banjaran, Bandung, Indonesia, Capacity: 77,500 mt/y, (Paper mill, Paperboard mill)
Phone: (62) 22 594 0140
Fax: (62) 22 594 0039
Email: contact@pspm.com, sales@pspm.com

PT Papyrus Sakti
Bandung Mill
Jln. Raya Banjaran Km 16.2
Banjaran, Bandung, West Java
Indonesia
Phone: (62) 22 594 0140
Fax: (62) 22 594 0039
Email: contact@pspm.com, sales@pspm.com
Web Address: www.pspm.com
Personnel:
Pres. Dir.: Albert Cahyadi S.
Phone: (62) 22 594 0140
VP/Dir.: Rudy Cahyadi S.
Phone: (62) 22 594 0140
Dir.: Kurniawan Mulyadi
Phone: (62) 22 594 0140
Total Employees at this Location: 540
Type of Operation: Paper mill, Paperboard mill
Pulp Grades and Capacities:
Total pulp capacity: 60,896 mt/y
Recycled Pulping: 60,896 mt/y
Pulp Mill Data:
Recycled Fiber Treatment Lines:
Recycled packaging pulping lines: 1
Paper/Paperboard Grades and Capacities:
Total paper and paperboard capacity: 77,500 mt/y
Uncoated woodfree/freesheet: 5,500 mt/y
Boxboard/cartonboard: 72,000 mt/y
Paper and Paperboard Mill Data:
Paper Machines: 3
No. 1, cylinder, total capacity 5,500 mt/y, Trim width 2 m, Uncoated woodfree/freesheet
No. 2, cylinder (7), total capacity 32,000 mt/y, Trim width 2.5 m, Boxboard/cartonboard
No. 3, cylinder (8), total capacity 40,000 mt/y, Trim width 2.5 m, Boxboard/cartonboard
Coating Machines: 2
No. 1, total capacity 32,000 mt/y., on machine
No. 2, total capacity 43,000 mt/y.
Finishing Equipment:
Winders: 1
Sheeters: 1
Energy Data:
Power boilers: 2
Electrical demand for mill: 113 MWh/D

PT Parisindo Pratama
Ownership: 75% by Prospect Motor, 25% by Warga Djaja
Imora Building 3rd Fl., Jln. P. Jayakarta No. 50
10730 Jakarta
Indonesia
Phone: (62) 21 6010812/8672059/6010813/6010815
Fax: (62) 21 6260727/8671236/6393361
Email: mail@parisindopratama.com, info@parisindopratama.com
Web Address: home.indo.net.id/~pratama
Personnel:
Pres.: Suhardi Budiman
Phone: (62) 21 639 3376
Fax: (62) 21 639 3361

Gen. Mgr.: Haryanto W. Angundjaja
Phone: (62) 21 8672059
Fax: (62) 21 8671236
Email: mail@parisindopratama.com
Overseas Mktg. Mgr.: Eric Iskandar
Phone: (62) 21 6010812/8672059/6010813/6010815
Fax: (62) 21 6260727/8671236/6393361
Email: eric_iskandar@parisindopratama.com
Ass. Mgr.: Lina Suteja
Phone: (62) 21 6010812/8672059/6010813/6010815
Fax: (62) 21 6260727/8671236/6393361
Email: lina@parisindopratama.com
Dir.: Herman Iskandar
Phone: (62) 21 639 3376
Fax: (62) 21 639 3361
Factory Mgr.: Atmadja Diredja
Phone: (62) 21 6010812/8672059/6010813/6010815
Fax: (62) 21 6260727/8671236/6393361
Tech. Advisor: Bernard Georges Giroux
Phone: (62) 21 6010812/8672059/6010813/6010815
Fax: (62) 21 6260727/8671236/6393361
Mill Locations:
PT Parisindo Pratama, Bogor Mill, Gunung Putri, Citeureup, Cibinong, PO Box 8, Bogor, Indonesia, Capacity: 24,000 mt/y, (Paper mill)
Phone: (62) 21 8672059
Fax: (62) 21 8671236
Email: pratama@indo.net.id, mail@parisindopratama.com

PT Parisindo Pratama
Bogor Mill
Gunung Putri, Citeureup, Cibinong, PO Box 8
Bogor, West Java
Indonesia
Phone: (62) 21 8672059
Fax: (62) 21 8671236
Email: pratama@indo.net.id, mail@parisindopratama.com
Web Address: home.indo.net.id/~pratama/
Personnel:
Pres. Dir.: Suhardi Budiman
Phone: (62) 21 8672059
Dir.: Herman Iskandar
Phone: (62) 21 8672059
Gen. Mgr.: Haryanto Angundjaja
Phone: (62) 21 8672059
Email: mail@parisindopratama.com
Mill Mgr.: Atmadja Diredja
Phone: (62) 21 8672059
Tech. Advisor: Bernard Georges Giroux
Phone: (62) 21 8672059
Overseas Mktg. Mgr.: Mr. Sandhy Johan
Phone: (62) 21 8672059
Total Employees at this Location: 185
Type of Operation: Paper mill
Paper/Paperboard Grades and Capacities:
Total paper and paperboard capacity: 24,000 mt/y
Uncoated woodfree/freesheet: 21,600 mt/y
Packaging papers: 2,400 mt/y
Paper and Paperboard Mill Data:
Stock Preparation:
Pulpers: 2
Refiners: 4
Paper Machines: 1
No. 1, fourdrinier, total capacity 24,000 mt/y, Trim width 3.6 m, Uncoated woodfree/freesheet, Packaging papers
Coating Machines: 1
No. 1, total capacity 2,000 mt/y., off machine
Finishing Equipment:
Supercalenders: 1
Rewinders: 1
Sheeters: 4
Energy Data:
Power boilers: 1

Indonesia

Combustion turbines: 2 at 5.2 MW
Electrical demand for mill: 47 MWh/D

ⓘⓜSchweitzer-Mauduit International Inc.
Medan Mill
Company is Schweitzer-Mauduit (SWM) have reached an agreement to sell the mill pending Indonesian government approval and expect to close on the sale during the first quarter of 2013.
Jln. Brigjend. Zein Hamid Km 6.9, Titi Kuning
20146 Medan, Sumatra
Indonesia
 Phone: (62) 61 7867 648/ 973
 Fax: (62) 61 7863 004
 Web Address: www.swmintl.com
Personnel:
 Gen. Mgr.: Djoni Tjandra
 Phone: (62) 61 7867 648-105/973
 Email: dtjandra@swmintl.com
 Mill Mgr.: Mr. Quanny
 Phone: (62) 61 7867 648-105/973
 Email: quanny@swmintl.com
 Finan. Mgr.: Marcus Hartanto
 Phone: (62) 61 7867 648-105/973
 Email: mhartanto@swmintl.com
Total Employees at this Location: 208
Type of Operation: Paper mill
Paper/Paperboard Grades and Capacities:
 Total paper and paperboard capacity: 3,200 mt/y
 Specialty and industrial: 3,200 mt/y
Paper and Paperboard Mill Data:
Paper Machines: 1
 No. 1, fourdrinier, total capacity 3,200 mt/y, Trim width 2 m, Specialty and industrial

ⓜPT Pelita Cengkareng Paper
Subang Mill
Jl. Raya Pabuaran Km 1.8
Subang, West Java
Indonesia
 Phone: (62) 62-260 7613598, 7613599
 Fax: (62) 62-260 7613599
 Email: info@pcp.co.id, pcp@centrin.net.id
 Web Address: www.pcp.co.id
Personnel:
 Project Mgr.: Adi Widianto
Total Employees at this Location: 400
Type of Operation: Paperboard mill
Pulp Grades and Capacities:
 Total pulp capacity: 346,610 mt/y
 Recycled Pulping: 346,610 mt/y
Pulp Mill Data:
 Recycled Fiber Treatment Lines:
 Recycled packaging pulping lines: 1
Paper/Paperboard Grades and Capacities:
 Total paper and paperboard capacity: 350,000 mt/y
 Linerboard: 210,000 mt/y
 Corrugating medium/fluting: 140,000 mt/y
Paper and Paperboard Mill Data:
Paper Machines: 1
 No. 7, fourdrinier (3), total capacity 350,000 mt/y, Trim width 6.66 m, Corrugating medium/fluting, Linerboard
Energy Data:
 Power boilers
 HRSG boiler: 2
 Combustion turbines: 2 at 24 MW
 Electrical demand for mill: 434 MWh/D

ⓘPT Pelita Cengkareng Paper
Ownership: 36% by Sarirasa Sejahtera Best, 33% by Wijayaraya Sejahtera
Jln. Raya Daan Mogot Km. 18
15122 Cengkareng, Tangerang, Jawa Barat
Indonesia
Mailing Address: PO Box 4649/JAK, 11046 Jakarta, Indonesia
 Phone: (62) 21 61970 12/13/14/20, 5522592, 5523969
 Fax: (62) 21 5408028, 6197021
 Email: info@pcp.co.id, pcp@centrin.net.id
 Web Address: www.pcp.co.id
Personnel:
 Pres.: Jotje Wantah
 Phone: (62) 21 61970 12/13/14/20, 5522592, 5523969
 Fax: (62) 21 5408028, 6197021
 Chief Comissioner: Herman Rusli
 Phone: (62) 21 61970 12/13/14/20, 5522592, 5523969
 Fax: (62) 21 5408028, 6197021
 Mill Mgr.: Tommy Sumendap
 Phone: (62) 21 61970 12/13/14/20, 5522592, 5523969
 Fax: (62) 21 5408028, 6197021
 Email: pcp@centrin.net.id
 Finan. Mgr.: Lie Sie Giem
 Phone: (62) 21 61970 12/13/14/20, 5522592, 5523969
 Fax: (62) 21 5408028, 6197021
 Tech. Mgr.: Redy Bintoro
 Phone: (62) 21 61970 12/13/14/20, 5522592, 5523969
 Fax: (62) 21 5408028, 6197021
Mill Locations:
PT Pelita Cengkareng Paper, Subang Mill, Jl. Raya Pabuaran Km 1.8, Subang, Indonesia, Capacity: 350,000 mt/y, (Paperboard mill)
 Phone: (62) 62-260 7613598, 7613599
 Fax: (62) 62-260 7613599
 Email: info@pcp.co.id, pcp@centrin.net.id
PT Pelita Cengkareng Paper, Tangerang Mill, Jln. Raya Daan Mogot Km. 18, 15122 Cengkareng, Tangerang, Indonesia, Capacity: 195,000 mt/y, (Paperboard mill)
 Phone: (62) 21 61970 12/13/14/20, 5522592, 5523969
 Fax: (62) 21 5408028, 6197021
 Email: info@pcp.co.id, pcp@centrin.net.id

ⓜPT Pelita Cengkareng Paper
Tangerang Mill
Jln. Raya Daan Mogot Km. 18
15122 Cengkareng, Tangerang, West Java
Indonesia
Mailing Address: PO Box 4649/JAK, 11046 Jakarta, Indonesia
 Phone: (62) 21 61970 12/13/14/20, 5522592, 5523969
 Fax: (62) 21 5408028, 6197021
 Email: info@pcp.co.id, pcp@centrin.net.id
 Web Address: www.pcp.co.id
Personnel:
 Pres.: Jotje Wantah
 Phone: (62) 21 61970 12/13/14/20, 5522592, 5523969
 Fax: (62) 21 5408028, 6197021
 Chief Comissioner: Herman Rusli
 Phone: (62) 21 61970 12/13/14/20, 5522592, 5523969
 Fax: (62) 21 5408028, 6197021
 Mill. Mgr.: Tommy Sumendap
 Phone: (62) 21 61970 12/13/14/20, 5522592, 5523969
 Fax: (62) 21 5408028, 6197021
 Email: pcp@centrin.net.id
 Prod. Mgr.: Herry Hendriansyah
 Phone: (62) 21 61970 12/13/14/20, 5522592, 5523969
 Fax: (62) 21 5408028, 6197021
 Finan. Mgr.: Lie Sie Giem
 Phone: (62) 21 61970 12/13/14/20, 5522592, 5523969
 Fax: (62) 21 5408028, 6197021
 Tech. Mgr.: Redy Bintoro
 Phone: (62) 21 61970 12/13/14/20, 5522592, 5523969
 Fax: (62) 21 5408028, 6197021
Total Employees at this Location: 500
Type of Operation: Paperboard mill
Pulp Grades and Capacities:
 Total pulp capacity: 193,237 mt/y
 Recycled Pulping: 193,237 mt/y
Pulp Mill Data:
 Recycled Fiber Treatment Lines:
 Flotation deinking lines: 1
 Recycled packaging pulping lines: 2
Paper/Paperboard Grades and Capacities:
 Total paper and paperboard capacity: 195,000 mt/y
 Linerboard: 89,000 mt/y
 Corrugating medium/fluting: 85,000 mt/y
 Boxboard/cartonboard: 21,000 mt/y
Paper and Paperboard Mill Data:
 Stock Preparation:
 Pulpers: 5
 Refiners: 12
Paper Machines: 4
 No. 1, cylinder, total capacity 10,000 mt/y, Trim width 1.8 m, Corrugating medium/fluting
 No. 2, cylinder, total capacity 35,000 mt/y, Trim width 2.4 m, Boxboard/cartonboard, Linerboard
 No. 3, fourdrinier, total capacity 50,000 mt/y, Trim width 2.9 m, Corrugating medium/fluting, Linerboard
 No. 5, multi-wire, total capacity 100,000 mt/y, Trim width 3.6 m, Linerboard, Corrugating medium/fluting
Coating Machines: 1
 No. 1, total capacity 36,000 mt/y., on machine
Finishing Equipment:
 Supercalenders: 1
 Rewinders: 4
 Sheeters: 2
Energy Data:
 Power boilers: 6
 Combustion turbines: 2 at 11 MW
 Electrical demand for mill: 270 MWh/D

ⓘPT Pindo Deli Pulp & Paper Mills
Ownership: Asia Pulp & Paper (APP)
Plaza BII Menara II, 17th Fl, Jln. M.H. Thamrin No 51
10350 Jakarta
Indonesia
Mailing Address: PO Box 4070 JKTF, 11040 Jakarta, Indonesia
 Phone: (62) 21 3929266/69
 Fax: (62) 21 3929461-63
 Email: customer_talk@app.co.id
 Web Address: www.asiapulppaper.com
Personnel:
 Pres. Dir.: Teguh Ganda Wijaya
 Phone: (62) 21 3929266/69
 Fax: (62) 21 3929461-63
 VP/Dir.: Hendra Jaya Kosasih
 Phone: (62) 21 3929266/69
 Fax: (62) 21 3929461-63
 VP/Dir.: Muktar Widjaja
 Phone: (62) 21 3929266/69
 Fax: (62) 21 3929461-63
 Dir.: Suresh Kilam
 Phone: (62) 21 3929266/69
 Fax: (62) 21 3929461-63
 Pres. Comm.: Indra Widjaja
 Phone: (62) 21 3929266/69
 Fax: (62) 21 3929461-63
 Comm.: Yudi Setiawan Lin
 Phone: (62) 21 3929266/69
 Fax: (62) 21 3929461-63
 Comm.: Arthur Tahya
 Phone: (62) 21 3929266/69
 Fax: (62) 21 3929461-63
Total Employees of Company: 9,556
Mill Locations:
PT Pindo Deli Pulp & Paper Mills, Karawang No. 1 (PT Pindo Deli Pulp & Paper Mills) Mill, Jln. Prof. Dr. Ir. H. Soetami No. 88, Teluk Jambe, Karawang, Indonesia, Capacity: 235,000 mt/y, (Paper mill)
 Phone: (62) 267 402355/553
 Fax: (62) 267 405250

Indonesia

Email: customer_talk@app.co.id
PT Pindo Deli Pulp & Paper Mills, Karawang No. 2 (PT Pindo Deli Pulp & Paper Mills) Mill, Ds. Kuta Mekar BTB 6/9, Kec. Teluk Jambe, Karawang, Indonesia, Capacity: 540,000 mt/y, (Paper mill)
Phone: (62) 267 440111
Fax: (62) 267 440839
Email: customer_talk@app.co.id

ⓜPT Pindo Deli Pulp & Paper Mills
Karawang No. 1 (PT Pindo Deli Pulp & Paper Mills) Mill
Ownership: Asia Pulp & Paper (APP)
Jln. Prof. Dr. Ir. H. Soetami No. 88, Teluk Jambe
Karawang, West Java
Indonesia
Phone: (62) 267 402355/553
Fax: (62) 267 405250
Email: customer_talk@app.co.id
Web Address: www.asiapulppaper.com
Personnel:
Pres./Dir.: Teguh Ganda Wijaya
Phone: (62) 267 402355/553
VP/Dir.: Hendra Jaya Kosasih
Phone: (62) 267 402355/553
VP/Dir.: Muktar Widjaja
Phone: (62) 267 402355/553
Dir.: Suresh Kilam
Phone: (62) 267 402355/553
Mill Mgr.: Mr. Bismak
Phone: (62) 881 5805838
Total Employees at this Location: 14,042
Type of Operation: Paper mill
Paper/Paperboard Grades and Capacities:
Total paper and paperboard capacity: 235,000 mt/y
Uncoated woodfree/freesheet: 67,000 mt/y
Coated woodfree/freesheet: 72,000 mt/y
Tissue: 12,000 mt/y
Boxboard/cartonboard: 84,000 mt/y
Paper and Paperboard Mill Data:
Paper Machines: 7
No. 1, fourdrinier, total capacity 10,000 mt/y, Trim width 1.9 m, Uncoated woodfree/freesheet
No. 2, fourdrinier, total capacity 9,000 mt/y, Trim width 1.9 m, Uncoated woodfree/freesheet
No. 3, fourdrinier, total capacity 18,000 mt/y, Trim width 2.7 m, Uncoated woodfree/freesheet
No. 4, fourdrinier (2), total capacity 30,000 mt/y, Trim width 2.7 m, Uncoated woodfree/freesheet
No. 5, fourdrinier, total capacity 12,000 mt/y, Trim width 2.9 m, Tissue
No. 6, fourdrinier, total capacity 72,000 mt/y, Trim width 2.7 m, Coated woodfree/freesheet
No. 7, Multi-wire (3), total capacity 84,000 mt/y, Trim width 2.7 m, Boxboard/cartonboard
Coating Machines: 6
No. 1, off machine
No. 2, total capacity 10,000 mt/y., off machine
No. 3, off machine
No. 4, total capacity 15,000 mt/y., on machine
No. 5, total capacity 66,000 mt/y., off machine
No. 6, total capacity 70,000 mt/y., on machine
Finishing Equipment:
Supercalenders: 3
Rewinders: 5
Sheeters: 1
Energy Data:
Power boilers: 4
Electrical demand for mill: 419 MWh/D

ⓜPT Pindo Deli Pulp & Paper Mills
Karawang No. 2 (PT Pindo Deli Pulp & Paper Mills) Mill
Ownership: Asia Pulp & Paper (APP)
Ds. Kuta Mekar BTB 6/9, Kec. Teluk Jambe
Karawang, West Java
Indonesia
Phone: (62) 267 440111
Fax: (62) 267 440839
Email: customer_talk@app.co.id
Web Address: www.asiapulppaper.com
Personnel:
Pres./Dir.: Teguh Ganda
Phone: (62) 267 440111
Total Employees at this Location: 670
Type of Operation: Paper mill
Paper/Paperboard Grades and Capacities:
Total paper and paperboard capacity: 540,000 mt/y
Uncoated woodfree/freesheet: 480,000 mt/y
Tissue: 60,000 mt/y
Paper and Paperboard Mill Data:
Paper Machines: 3
No. 8, Bel-Baie IV, total capacity 240,000 mt/y, Trim width 6.77 m, Uncoated woodfree/freesheet
No. 9, Bel-Baie IV, total capacity 240,000 mt/y, Trim width 6.77 m, Uncoated woodfree/freesheet
No. 11, crescent former, total capacity 60,000 mt/y, Trim width 5.6 m, Tissue, Uncoated woodfree/freesheet
Coating Machines: 6
No. 1, total capacity 220,000 mt/y., on machine
No. 2, total capacity 15,000 mt/y., off machine
No. 3, off machine
No. 4, total capacity 15,000 mt/y., off machine
No. 5, total capacity 15,000 mt/y., off machine
No. 6, total capacity 200,000 mt/y., on machine
Finishing Equipment:
Rewinders: 4
Sheeters: 6
Energy Data:
Power boilers: 1
Combustion turbines: 1 at 32 MW
Steam turbines: 1 at 30 MW
Electrical demand for mill: 1,150 MWh/D

ⓜPT Pindo Deli Pulp & Paper Mills Hive
Perawang (Pindo Deli Pulp & Paper Mills Hive) Mill
Ownership: Asia Pulp & Paper (APP)
Jl. Raya Minas - Perawang Km. 26
12780 Siak, Bengkalis, Riau, Sumatra
Indonesia
Phone: (62) 761 91373/91030
Fax: (62) 761 91373/76
Web Address: www.asiapulppaper.com
Total Employees at this Location: 725
Type of Operation: Paper mill
Paper/Paperboard Grades and Capacities:
Total paper and paperboard capacity: 391,200 mt/y
Tissue: 367,200 mt/y
Specialty and industrial: 24,000 mt/y
Paper and Paperboard Mill Data:
Paper Machines: 17
No. 1, crescent former, total capacity 28,000 mt/y, Trim width 2.63 m, Tissue, Uncoated woodfree/freesheet
No. 2, crescent former, total capacity 28,000 mt/y, Trim width 2.63 m, Tissue, Uncoated woodfree/freesheet
No. 3, crescent former, total capacity 28,000 mt/y, Trim width 2.63 m, Tissue, Uncoated woodfree/freesheet
No. 4, crescent former, total capacity 28,000 mt/y, Trim width 2.63 m, Tissue, Uncoated woodfree/freesheet
No. 5, crescent former, total capacity 20,000 mt/y, Trim width 2.8 m, Tissue, Uncoated woodfree/freesheet
No. 6, crescent former, total capacity 20,000 mt/y, Trim width 2.8 m, Tissue, Uncoated woodfree/freesheet
No. 7, crescent former, total capacity 20,000 mt/y, Trim width 2.8 m, Tissue, Uncoated woodfree/freesheet
No. 8, crescent former, total capacity 20,000 mt/y, Trim width 2.8 m, Tissue, Uncoated woodfree/freesheet
No. 9, crescent former, total capacity 20,000 mt/y, Trim width 2.8 m, Tissue, Uncoated woodfree/freesheet
No. 10, crescent former, total capacity 20,000 mt/y, Trim width 2.8 m, Tissue, Uncoated woodfree/freesheet
No. 11, crescent former, total capacity 20,000 mt/y, Trim width 2.8 m, Tissue, Uncoated woodfree/freesheet
No. 12, crescent former, total capacity 20,000 mt/y, Trim width 2.8 m, Tissue, Uncoated woodfree/freesheet
No. 13, crescent former, total capacity 20,000 mt/y, Trim width 2.8 m, Tissue, Uncoated woodfree/freesheet
No. 14, crescent former, total capacity 20,000 mt/y, Trim width 2.8 m, Tissue, Uncoated woodfree/freesheet
No. 15, Yankee dryer, total capacity 12,000 mt/y, Trim width 2.8 m, Specialty and industrial
No. 16, Yankee dryer, total capacity 12,000 mt/y, Trim width 2.8 m, Specialty and industrial
No. 17, Yankee dryer, total capacity 60,000 mt/y, Trim width 5.6 m, Tissue, Uncoated woodfree/freesheet
Energy Data:
Electrical demand for mill: 872 MWh/D

ⓜPT Pola Pulpindo Mantap
Jln. Yos Sudarso No. 77 E-F
Lampung
Indonesia
Phone: (62) 721 484303/5587/8084
Fax: (62) 721 481275
Personnel:
Pres. Dir.: Sunaryo Mustopo
Phone: (62) 721 484303/5587/8084
Fax: (62) 721 481275
Man. Dir.: H. T. Djaman Suryasantana
Phone: (62) 721 484303/5587/8084
Fax: (62) 721 481275
Mill Locations:
PT Pola Pulpindo Mantap, Lampung Mill, Jalan Yos Sudarso No. 77, Desa Sukadana Udik, Kecamatan Sungkai Selatan, Lampung, Indonesia, Capacity: 32,000 mt/y, (Pulp mill, Paper mill)

ⓜPT Pola Pulpindo Mantap
Lampung Mill
Jalan Yos Sudarso No. 77, Desa Sukadana Udik, Kecamatan Sungkai Selatan
Lampung, Sumatra
Indonesia
Personnel:
Gen. Mgr.: Sukijan Sukijan
Man. Dir.: H. T. Djaman Suryasantana
Total Employees at this Location: 225
Type of Operation: Pulp mill, Paper mill
Pulp Grades and Capacities:
Total pulp capacity: 42,000 mt/y
Paper/Paperboard Grades and Capacities:
Total paper and paperboard capacity: 32,000 mt/y
Corrugating medium/fluting: 16,000 mt/y
Boxboard/cartonboard: 16,000 mt/y
Paper and Paperboard Mill Data:
Paper Machines: 1
No. 1, total capacity 32,000 mt/y, Corrugating medium/fluting, Boxboard/cartonboard

ⓜPT Evergreen International Paper
Jln Utama Desa Dalu X A & B, Tanjung Morawa Km 16
20362 Deli Serdang, Medan
Indonesia
Phone: (62) 61 794 7333 Ext. 105, 61 794 2836
Fax: (62) 61 794 2688
Email: hrd_department@eip.co.id
Web Address: www.evergreen.co.id
Personnel:
Energy Mgr.: Ronal Mangatur Siregar
Phone: (62) 061-7942688, 061-7942836
Mill Locations:
PT Evergreen International Paper, Medan Mill, Jln Utama Desa Dalu X A & B, Tanjung Morawa Km 16, 20362 Deli Serdang, Medan, Indonesia, Capacity: 75,600 mt/y, (Paperboard mill)
Phone: (62) 61 794 7333 Ext. 105, 61 794 2836
Fax: (62) 61 794 2688
Email: hrd_department@eip.co.id

ⓜPT Integra Lestari (Surabaya)
Jalan Mojokerto - Gempol, Kembangsri No.1
Kec. Ngoro, Mojokerto
Indonesia
Phone: (62) 321 6816261, 321 6816263, 321 681624, 321 6816265

Indonesia

Personnel:
Purch. Mgr.: Evi Retnowati
Phone: (62) 321 6816261
Mill Locations:
PT Integra Lestari (Surabaya), Kec. Ngoro Mill, Jalan Mojokerto - Gempol, Kembangsri No.1, Kec. Ngoro, Mojokerto, Indonesia, Capacity: 60,000 mt/y, (Paperboard mill)
Phone: (62) 321 6816261, 321 6816263, 321 681624, 321 6816265

⊕PT Simanda
Jl. Medan-Morawa Km. 18.5
Serdang, Medan
Indonesia
Phone: (62) 61 7941604
Personnel:
Pres. Dir.: Erik Zahara Batubara
Phone: (62) 61 7941604
Dir.: Achmad Nasution
Phone: (62) 61 7941604
Total Employees at this Location: 180
Mill Locations:
PT Simanda, Serdang, Medan Mill, Jl. Medan-Morawa Km. 18.5, Serdang, Medan, Indonesia, Capacity: 7,200 mt/y, (Paper mill)
Phone: (62) 61 7941604

⊕◉PT Surya Zig Zag
Kediri Mill
Jalan Raya Kediri Kertosono KM 7, Ds. Ngebrak, Gampengrejo
64182 Kediri, East Java
Indonesia
Phone: (62) 354 684 661
Fax: (62) 354 681 926
Email: info@suryazigzag.com
Web Address: www.suryazigzag.com
Personnel:
Pres. Dir.: Bodhi Suwarna Tanumulya
Phone: (62) 354 684 661
Email: bsuwarna@suryazigzag.com
Dir.: Wahyudi SH
Phone: (62) 354 684 661
Email: wahyudi@suryazigzag.com
Total Employees of Company: 434
Type of Operation: Paper mill
Paper/Paperboard Grades and Capacities:
Total paper and paperboard capacity: 24,000 mt/y
Specialty and industrial: 24,000 mt/y
Paper and Paperboard Mill Data:
Paper Machines: 2
PM 1, fourdrinier, total capacity 10,000 mt/y, Trim width 3.7 m, Specialty and industrial
PM 2, fourdrinier, total capacity 14,000 mt/y, Trim width 3.6 m, Specialty and industrial

⊕◉PT Tri Daya Kreasi
Purwakarta Mill
Jln. Raya Cempaka, Cipinang
11140 Purwakarta, West Java
Indonesia
Phone: (62) 264 210127/210128/202392
Fax: (62) 264 202393
Web Address: www.tridayakreasi.co.id
Personnel:
Pres. Commissioner: dr. Ratnawati Tanu Tanto
Phone: (62) 264 210127
Fax: (62) 264 202393
Pres. Dir.: dr Edi Hambal
Phone: (62) 264 210127
Fax: (62) 264 202393
Man. Dir.: Drs. Sartono
Phone: (62) 264 210127
Fax: (62) 264 202393
CFO: Johanes SE
Phone: (62) 264 210127
Fax: (62) 264 202393
Oper. Dir.: Kenny Widjaja S.Sos. MM
Phone: (62) 264 210127

Fax: (62) 264 202393
Total Employees of Company: 305
Total Employees at this Location: 250
Type of Operation: Paper mill
Pulp Grades and Capacities:
Total pulp capacity: 135,157 mt/y
Chemical Pulp: 29,416 mt/y
Recycled Pulping: 105,741 mt/y
Pulp Mill Data:
Chemical Pulping Systems:
Continuous digesters: 1
Recycled Fiber Treatment Lines:
Recycled packaging pulping lines: 1
Paper/Paperboard Grades and Capacities:
Total paper and paperboard capacity: 142,800 mt/y
Linerboard: 49,980 mt/y
Corrugating medium/fluting: 49,980 mt/y
Boxboard/cartonboard: 42,840 mt/y
Paper and Paperboard Mill Data:
Paper Machines: 2
No. 1, cylinder, total capacity 71,400 mt/y, Trim width 3.2 m, Corrugating medium/fluting, Boxboard/cartonboard
No. 2, cylinder, total capacity 71,400 mt/y, Trim width 3.2 m, Linerboard, Boxboard/cartonboard
Energy Data:
Power boilers
Electrical demand for mill: 190 MWh/D

⊕PT Wirajaya Packindo
Jl. Raya Mauk Km. 7 Desa Pabuaran
15112 Tangerang
Indonesia
Phone: (62) 021 5537891, 5537890
Fax: (62) 021 5520043
Email: hrdwirapaper@gmail.com, wirajaya@gmail.com
Web Address: www.wirajaya.co.id
Personnel:
Owner: Wira Rahardja
Phone: (62) 021 5537891, 5537890
Fax: (62) 021 5520043
Commissioner: Hadi Rahardja
Phone: (62) 021 5537891, 5537890
Fax: (62) 021 5520043
Coating Mgr.: Ari Liberto
Phone: (62) 021 5537891, 5537890
Fax: (62) 021 5520043
Prod. Mgr.: Lim Giok Lim
Phone: (62) 021 5537891, 5537890
Fax: (62) 021 5520043
Mill Locations:
PT Wirajaya Packindo, Tangerang Mill, Jl. Raya Mauk Km. 7 Desa Pabuaran, 15112 Tangerang, Indonesia, Capacity: 185,640 mt/y, (Paperboard mill)
Phone: (62) 021 5537891, 5537890
Fax: (62) 021 5520043
Email: hrdwirapaper@gmail.com, wirajaya@gmail.com

⊕PT Buana Megah
Jl. Raya Bangil KM. 4 Beji, Bangil, Pasuruan
Pasuruan
Indonesia
Mill Locations:
PT Buana Megah, Pasuruan Mill, Pasuruan, Indonesia, Capacity: 24,000 mt/y, (Paperboard mill)

⊕PT Enggal Subur Kertas
Jalan Raya Kudus – Pati Km. 12
Pati, Central Java
Indonesia
Phone: (62) 0291 424 6119
Total Employees of Company: 200
Mill Locations:
PT Enggal Subur Kertas, Pati Mill, Jalan Raya Kudus – Pati Km. 12, Pati, Indonesia, Capacity: 107,100 mt/y, (Paperboard mill)
Phone: (62) 0291 424 6119

⊕◉PT Mount Dreams
Gresik Mill
Jl. Pertamina 77, Kec. Wringinanom
61176 Gresik, Jawa Timur
Indonesia
Phone: (62) 31 8990077
Fax: (62) 31 8990088
Web Address: www.mountdreams.com
Personnel:
Owner: Johan Darsono
Phone: (62) 31 8990077
Fax: (62) 31 8990088
HR Recruitment & T Training: Dewi Iswari Kartikawati
Phone: (62) 31 8990077
Fax: (62) 31 8990088
Total Employees at this Location: 480
Type of Operation: Paper mill
Pulp Grades and Capacities:
Total pulp capacity: 211,230 mt/y
Recycled Pulping: 211,230 mt/y
Pulp Mill Data:
Recycled Fiber Treatment Lines:
Flotation deinking lines: 1 at 66,000
Paper/Paperboard Grades and Capacities:
Total paper and paperboard capacity: 265,000 mt/y
Uncoated woodfree/freesheet: 65,000 mt/y
Linerboard: 39,000 mt/y
Corrugating medium/fluting: 161,000 mt/y
Paper and Paperboard Mill Data:
Paper Machines: 3
No. 1, Multi-wire (3), total capacity 60,000 mt/y, Trim width 4 m, Linerboard, Corrugating medium/fluting
No. 2, fourdrinier, total capacity 65,000 mt/y, Trim width 4.7 m, Uncoated woodfree/freesheet
No. 3, fourdrinier, total capacity 140,000 mt/y, Trim width 7.2 m, Corrugating medium/fluting
Energy Data:
Power boilers: 1
Electrical demand for mill: 409 MWh/D

⊕PT Sinar Indah Kertas
Jl. Raya Pati – Kudus Km. 4
Desa Pegandan Kec. Margorejo
Indonesia
Phone: (62) 295 385 762
Fax: (62) 295 385 762
Mill Locations:
PT Sinar Indah Kertas, Desa Pegandan Kecamatan Margorajo, Pati Mill, Jl. Raya Pati – Kudus Km. 4, Desa Pegandan Kecamatan Margorejo, Pati, Indonesia, Capacity: 20,000 mt/y, (Paper mill, Paperboard mill)
Phone: (62) 295 385 762
Fax: (62) 295 385 762

⊕◉PT Pura Barutama
Kudus Mill
Ownership: Pura Group
Jln. AKBP Agil Kusumadya Km 4, No. 203, PO Box 29
59347 Kudus, Central Java
Indonesia
Phone: (62) 291 444361/432203
Fax: (62) 291 432586
Email: marketing@puragroup.com
Web Address: www.puragroup.com
Personnel:
Pres./Dir.: Jacobus Busono
Phone: (62) 291 444361
Fax: (62) 291 432586
Dir.: Purnama Setiawan
Phone: (62) 291 444361
Fax: (62) 291 432586
Email: saonah@kudus.puragroup.com
Mill Mgr.: Yansri Budi
Phone: (62) 291 444361
Fax: (62) 291 432586
Email: yan90mb@yahoo.com
Asst. Mill Mgr.: Bambang Widayanto
Phone: (62) 291 444361
Fax: (62) 291 432586

Tech. Mgr.: Aris Wicaksono
Phone: (62) 291 444361
Fax: (62) 291 432586
Chief Eng.: Kristanto Adji
Phone: (62) 291 444361
Fax: (62) 291 432586
Purch. Mgr.: Iin Kristyawati
Phone: (62) 291 444361
Fax: (62) 291 432586
Mktg. Mgr.: Johan Hartono
Phone: (62) 291 444361
Fax: (62) 291 432586
Converting Plant Mgr.: Joko Suprayogi
Phone: (62) 291 444361
Fax: (62) 291 432586
Env. Dir.: Eddy Soesanto Soewandi
Phone: (62) 291 444361
Fax: (62) 291 432586
Sls. Exec.: Didi Prastyo
Phone: (62) 291 444361
Fax: (62) 291 432586
Exporter: Adrianus Hadisoebroto
Phone: (62) 291 444361, M: 813 2589 1039
Fax: (62) 291 432586
Email: adrian@kudus.puragroup.com
Total Employees of Company: 615
Total Employees at this Location: 615
Type of Operation: Paper mill, Paperboard mill
Pulp Grades and Capacities:
Total pulp capacity: 98,583 mt/y
Recycled Pulping: 98,583 mt/y

Pulp Mill Data:
Recycled Fiber Treatment Lines:
Recycled packaging pulping lines: 1
Paper/Paperboard Grades and Capacities:
Total paper and paperboard capacity: 123,000 mt/y
Uncoated woodfree/freesheet: 4,000 mt/y
Packaging papers: 20,000 mt/y
Specialty and industrial: 14,000 mt/y
Linerboard: 65,000 mt/y
Corrugating medium/fluting: 20,000 mt/y
Paper and Paperboard Mill Data:
Stock Preparation:
Pulpers: 9
Refiners: 25
Paper Machines: 7
No. 1, cylinder, total capacity 6,000 mt/y, Trim width 1.85 m, Uncoated woodfree/freesheet, Specialty and industrial
No. 3, fourdrinier, total capacity 9,000 mt/y, Trim width 2 m, Specialty and industrial
No. 5, multi-wire, total capacity 35,000 mt/y, Trim width 3 m, Linerboard, Corrugating medium/fluting
No. 6, multi-wire, total capacity 15,000 mt/y, Trim width 2.5 m, Linerboard, Corrugating medium/fluting
No. 7, multi-wire, total capacity 35,000 mt/y, Trim width 2.9 m, Linerboard
No. 9, multi-wire, total capacity 20,000 mt/y, Trim width 3.6 m, Packaging papers
No. 10, total capacity 3,000 mt/y, Trim width 1.52 m, Specialty and industrial
Coating Machines: 1
No. 1, total capacity 7,000 mt/y., off machine
Finishing Equipment:
Supercalenders: 2
Rewinders: 7
Sheeters: 10
Energy Data:
Power boilers: 3
Steam turbines: 2 at 7.5, 7.5 MW
Electrical demand for mill: 195 MWh/D

ⓘ Pura Group
Ownership: 11% by Jacobus Busono, 76% by Pt. Purawidya Graha, 11% by Albertus Busono
JL. AKBP. Agil Kusumadya 203
59346 Kudus, Central Java
Indonesia
 Phone: (62) 62 291 444 361
 Fax: (62) 62 291 444 403
Email: marketing@puragroup.com
Web Address: en.puragroup.com
Personnel:
Pres./Dir.: Jacobus Busono
Phone: (62) 291 444 361
Fax: (62) 291 444 403
Dir.: Purnama Setiawan
Phone: (62) 291 444 361
Fax: (62) 291 444 403
Email: saonah@kudus.puragroup.com
Mill Locations:
PT Pura Barutama, Kudus Mill, Jln. AKBP Agil Kusumadya Km 4, No. 203, PO Box 29, 59347 Kudus, Indonesia, Capacity: 123,000 mt/y, (Paper mill, Paperboard mill)
Phone: (62) 291 444361/432203
Fax: (62) 291 432586
Email: marketing@puragroup.com
PT Pura Nusapersada, Terban, Kudus Mill, Jln. Raya Kudus-Pati Km 12, 59382 Terban, Kudus, Indonesia, Capacity: 62,050 mt/y, (Paper mill)
Phone: (62) 291 431312/439285
Fax: (62) 291 431452
Email: marketing@puragroup.com, purapnp@yahoo.com

ⓘⓜ PT Pura Nusapersada
Terban, Kudus Mill
Ownership: Pura Group
Jln. Raya Kudus-Pati Km 12
59382 Terban, Kudus, Central Java
Indonesia
 Phone: (62) 291 431312/439285
 Fax: (62) 291 431452
 Email: marketing@puragroup.com, purapnp@yahoo.com
 Web Address: www.puragroup.com
Personnel:
Pres./Dir.: Y. Moelyono Soebijanto
Phone: (62) 291 431312/439285
Dir.: Yoyok Soebagyo
Phone: (62) 291 431312/439285
Mktg. Mgr.: Gunawan
Phone: (62) 291 431312/439285
Account. Mgr.: Ilham Pratama
Phone: (62) 291 431312
Fax: (62) 291 431452
Total Employees of Company: 230
Total Employees at this Location: 230
Type of Operation: Paper mill
Pulp Grades and Capacities:
Total pulp capacity: 49,311 mt/y
Recycled Pulping: 49,311 mt/y

Pulp Mill Data:
Recycled Fiber Treatment Lines:
Flotation deinking lines: 1
Recycled packaging pulping lines: 1
Paper/Paperboard Grades and Capacities:
Total paper and paperboard capacity: 62,050 mt/y
Packaging papers: 16,897 mt/y
Linerboard: 9,800 mt/y
Corrugating medium/fluting: 20,652 mt/y
Boxboard/cartonboard: 14,700 mt/y
Paper and Paperboard Mill Data:
Stock Preparation:
Pulpers: 4
Refiners: 7
Paper Machines: 2
No. 7, cylinder (3), total capacity 24,500 mt/y, Trim width 2.2 m, Boxboard/cartonboard, Linerboard
No. 8, fourdrinier, total capacity 37,550 mt/y, Trim width 3.2 m, Corrugating medium/fluting, Packaging papers
Finishing Equipment:
Rewinders: 2 at 24,500 mt/y, 37,550 mt/y
Sheeters: 3 at 48,000 mt/y
Energy Data:
Power boilers: 2
Electrical demand for mill: 82 MWh/D

ⓘⓜ PT Riau Andalan Pulp & Paper (RAPP)
Ownership: 98.50% by Asia Pacific Resources International - APRIL
Jalan Teluk Betung No. 31, Kebon Metali, Tanah Abang
10230 Jakarta
Indonesia
 Phone: (62) 21 5482003
 Fax: (62) 21 5482039
 Email: info@aprilasia.com
 Web Address: www.aprilasia.com
Personnel:
Pres./CEO: A. J. Devansen
Phone: (62) 21 319 30134
Fax: (62) 21 314 4604
Pres./Dir.: Rudi Fajar
Phone: (62) 21 319 30134
Fax: (62) 21 314 4604
Man. Dir.: Mr. Funadi Wongso
Phone: (62) 21 319 30134
Fax: (62) 21 314 4604
Email: funadi_wongso@aprilasia.com
Mill Locations:
PT Riau Andalan Pulp & Paper (RAPP), Riaupulp and Riaupaper Mill Kerinci, Desa Pangkalan Kerinci, Kecamatan Langgam, Kab. Pelalawan, 28300 Pekanbaru - Riau, Indonesia, Capacity: 840,000 mt/y, (Pulp mill, Paper mill)
Phone: (62) 761 95529 (Pulp) 491000 (Paper)
Fax: (62) 761 95681 (Pulp) 95456 (Paper)
Email: info@aprilasia.com

ⓘⓜ PT Riau Andalan Pulp & Paper (RAPP)
Riaupulp and Riaupaper Mill Kerinci
Ownership: 98.50% by Asia Pacific Resources International - APRIL
Desa Pangkalan Kerinci, Kecamatan Langgam, Kab. Pelalawan
28300 Pekanbaru - Riau, Riau, Sumatra
Indonesia
Mailing Address: PO Box 1080, 28300 Pekanbaru, Riau, Sumatra, Indonesia
 Phone: (62) 761 95529 (Pulp) 491000 (Paper)
 Fax: (62) 761 95681 (Pulp) 95456 (Paper)
 Email: info@aprilasia.com
 Web Address: www.aprilasia.com
Personnel:
Pres. & COO: A.J. Devanesan
Phone: (62) 761 95529 (Pulp) 491000 (Paper)
Fax: (62) 761 95681 (Pulp) 95456 (Paper)
Pres., Global Fiber: Jouko Virta
Phone: (62) 761 95529 (Pulp) 491000 (Paper)
Fax: (62) 761 95681 (Pulp) 95456 (Paper)
Pres. Dir.: Kusnan Rahmin
Phone: (62) 761 95529 (Pulp) 491000 (Paper)
Fax: (62) 761 95681 (Pulp) 95456 (Paper)
Global Fiber Dir.: Ben J. Mitai
Phone: (62) 761 95529 (Pulp) 491000 (Paper)
Fax: (62) 761 95681 (Pulp) 95456 (Paper)
Gen. Affairs: Jasrial Effendy
Phone: (62) 761 95529 (Pulp) 491000 (Paper)
Fax: (62) 761 95681 (Pulp) 95456 (Paper)
Head of Real Fiber: Vinod Kesavan
Phone: (62) 761 95529 (Pulp) 491000 (Paper)
Fax: (62) 761 95681 (Pulp) 95456 (Paper)
Automation Specialist Dept. Head: Afrizal Sy
Phone: (62) 761 95529 (Pulp) 491000 (Paper)
Fax: (62) 761 95681 (Pulp) 95456 (Paper)
Sls. Admin. Head: Frisca Halim
Phone: (62) 761 95529 (Pulp) 491000 (Paper)
Fax: (62) 761 95681 (Pulp) 95456 (Paper)
Eng. Mgr.: Tukirin Tukirin
Phone: (62) 761 95529 (Pulp) 491000 (Paper)
Fax: (62) 761 95681 (Pulp) 95456 (Paper)
Total Employees at this Location: 1,960
Type of Operation: Pulp mill, Paper mill
Pulp Grades and Capacities:
Total pulp capacity: 2,859,139 mt/y

Indonesia

Pulp available for market: 2,220,000 mt/y
Chemical Pulp: 2,859,139 mt/y
Pulp Mill Data:
Chemical Pulping Systems:
Batch digesters: 28
Continuous digesters: 1
Pulp Lines: 3
Bleach Plant Systems: 3
Chemical Pulping System - Hardwood (ECF), Sequence: O_2 DEopDD
Chemical Pulping System - Hardwood (ECF), Sequence: O_2 DEopDD, Capacity 675,000 admt/y
Chemical Pulping System - Hardwood (ECF), Sequence: O_2 DEopDD, Capacity 1,000,000 admt/y
Chemical Recovery Equipment:
Evaporator lines: 3
Recovery boilers: 3
Lime Kiln
Pulp Dryers:
Flakt dryer 1, Flakt dryer 1, Fourdriniers 1, Fourdriniers 1, Twin Wire 1
Paper/Paperboard Grades and Capacities:
Total paper and paperboard capacity: 840,000 mt/y
Uncoated woodfree/freesheet: 840,000 mt/y
Paper and Paperboard Mill Data:
Stock Preparation:
Pulpers: 2
Refiners: 8
Paper Machines: 2
No. 1, SpeedFormer HHS, total capacity 420,000 mt/y, Trim width 8.65 m, Uncoated woodfree/freesheet
No. 2, OptiFormer, total capacity 420,000 mt/y, Trim width 8.65 m, Uncoated woodfree/freesheet
Finishing Equipment:
Winders: 2 at 360,000 mt/y
Calenders: 2
Rewinders: 1 at 1,500 mt/y
Sheeters: 4 at 250,000 mt/y
Energy Data:
Power boilers: 3
Combustion turbines: 3 at 4.5, 4.5, 4.5 MW
Steam turbines: 6 at 27.5, 53.8, 53.8, 100, 100, 100 MW
Electrical demand for mill: 7,467 MWh/D

ⓘⓜPT Sekarindo Inti Serasi
Bogor Mill
Desa Palasasi, Kec. Jeruk
Bogor, West Java
Indonesia
Personnel:
Pres./Dir.: Ir. Sam Nanurung
Total Employees at this Location: 25
Type of Operation: Paper mill
Paper/Paperboard Grades and Capacities:
Total paper and paperboard capacity: 3,000 mt/y
Specialty and industrial: 3,000 mt/y

ⓘⓜPT Setia Kawan
Tulungagung Mill
Ownership: 100% by private owners
Jalan Jayengkusumo VII 12
66251 Tulungagung, East Java
Indonesia
Phone: (62) 355 323190
Fax: (62) 355 323187
Personnel:
Pres. Dir.: Mr. Basuki
Phone: (62) 355 323190
Dir.: Mr. Soehadi
Phone: (62) 355 323190
Dir.: Fendy Gunawan
Phone: (62) 355 323190
Dir.: Mr. Sasongko
Phone: (62) 355 323190
Total Employees at this Location: 200
Type of Operation: Paper mill
Pulp Grades and Capacities:
Total pulp capacity: 30,787 mt/y
Recycled Pulping: 30,787 mt/y
Pulp Mill Data:
Bleach Plant Systems: 1
Recycled Pulping System, Type: DIP
Recycled Fiber Treatment Lines:
Flotation deinking lines: 1
Recycled packaging pulping lines: 1
Paper/Paperboard Grades and Capacities:
Total paper and paperboard capacity: 31,000 mt/y
Newsprint: 25,000 mt/y
Corrugating medium/fluting: 6,000 mt/y
Paper and Paperboard Mill Data:
Paper Machines: 1
No. 1, fourdrinier, total capacity 31,000 mt/y, Trim width 3.2 m, Newsprint, Corrugating medium/fluting
Energy Data:
Power boilers: 1
Electrical demand for mill: 78 MWh/D

ⓜPT Simanda
Serdang, Medan Mill
Jl. Medan-Morawa Km. 18.5
Serdang, Medan, North Sumatera
Indonesia
Phone: (62) 61 7941604
Personnel:
Pres. Dir.: Erik Zahara Batubara
Phone: (62) 61 7941604
Dir.: Achmad Nasution
Phone: (62) 61 7941604
Total Employees at this Location: 180
Type of Operation: Paper mill
Paper/Paperboard Grades and Capacities:
Total paper and paperboard capacity: 7,200 mt/y
Specialty and industrial: 7,200 mt/y

ⓘPT Sinar Hoperindo
Jl. Pangeran Jayakarta 139 D-E
10730 Jakarta
Indonesia
Phone: (62) 21 6291096
Fax: (62) 21 6290258/6012403
Email: info@sinar-hoperindo.com
Web Address: sinar-hoperindo.com
Personnel:
Chmn.: Lily Chandradinata
Phone: (62) 21 6291096 /6495035
Fax: (62) 21 6495035
Email: lilyadiwidjaja@sinar-hoperindo.com
Pres. Dir.: Linda Chandradinata
Phone: (62) 21 6291096 /6495035
Fax: (62) 21 6495035
Gen. Mgr.: Emad El-Ghandour
Phone: (62) 21 6291096 /6495035
Fax: (62) 21 6495035
Email: emad-elghandour@sinar-hoperindo.com
Prod. Mgr.: Yulius Indrawan
Phone: (62) 21 6495035
Email: purchasing@sinar-hoperindo.com
Mktg.: Ricky Wijaya
Phone: (62) 21 6291096 /6495035
Fax: (62) 21 6290258/6012403
Total Employees of Company: 750
Total Employees at this Location: 408
Mill Locations:
PT Sinar Hoperindo, Bogor Mill, Jln. Raya Narogong Km. 17.5, Desa Cikreuwis, Limusnunggal, Cileungsi, 10820 Bogor, Indonesia, Capacity: 18,000 mt/y, (Paper mill)
Phone: (62) 21 8231511-13
Fax: (62) 21 8231512
Email: info@sinar-hoperindo.com

ⓜPT Sinar Hoperindo
Bogor Mill
Jln. Raya Narogong Km. 17.5, Desa Cikreuwis, Limusnunggal, Cileungsi
10820 Bogor, West Java
Indonesia
Phone: (62) 21 8231511-13
Fax: (62) 21 8231512
Email: info@sinar-hoperindo.com
Web Address: www.sinar-hoperindo.com
Personnel:
Pres. Dir.: Linda Chandradinata
Phone: (62) 21 8231513
Prod. Mgr.: Ma Lan Qing
Phone: (62) 21 8231513
Purch. Mgr.: Hengki Irawan
Phone: (62) 21 8231513
Total Employees at this Location: 255
Type of Operation: Paper mill
Paper/Paperboard Grades and Capacities:
Total paper and paperboard capacity: 18,000 mt/y
Packaging papers
Paper and Paperboard Mill Data:
Paper Machines: 1
No. 1, fourdrinier, total capacity 18,000 mt/y, Trim width 3.5 m, Packaging papers
Energy Data:
Power boilers

ⓜPT Sinar Indah Kertas
Desa Pegandan Kecamatan Margorajo, Pati Mill
Jl. Raya Pati – Kudus Km. 4
Desa Pegandan Kecamatan Margorejo, Pati, Central Java
Indonesia
Phone: (62) 295 385 762
Fax: (62) 295 385 762
Type of Operation: Paper mill, Paperboard mill
Pulp Grades and Capacities:
Total pulp capacity: 19,667 mt/y
Recycled Pulping: 19,667 mt/y
Paper/Paperboard Grades and Capacities:
Total paper and paperboard capacity: 20,000 mt/y
Linerboard: 10,000 mt/y
Corrugating medium/fluting: 10,000 mt/y
Paper and Paperboard Mill Data:
Paper Machines: 1
No. 1, fourdrinier, total capacity 20,000 mt/y, Trim width 2.4 m, Linerboard, Corrugating medium/fluting
Energy Data:
Electrical demand for mill: 25 MWh/D

ⓘⓜPT Sopanusa Tissue
Mojokerto Mill
Ownership: Private
Jl. Raya Ngoro 100, Ds. Manduromanggunggajah, Kec. Ngoro
61385 Mojokerto, East Java
Indonesia
Phone: (62) 31 3726904, 321 6819081
Fax: (62) 31 3727431, 321 6819079
Email: sales_nas@sopanusa.co.id, scoord@sopanusa.co.id
Web Address: www.sopanusa.co.id
Personnel:
Pres./Dir.: Mr. Dermawan
Phone: (62) 321 619 089/080/081/289/290/291
COO: Mr. Charu Joglekar
Phone: (62) 321 619 089/080/081/289/290/291
Email: charu@surabaya.wasantara.net.id
VP: Mr. Mintono
Phone: (62) 321 619 089/080/081/289/290/291
Email: mintono_sps@yanoo.com
Gen. Mgr. Mktg.: Mr. Danny Kristono
Phone: (62) 321 619 089/080/081/289/290/291
Total Employees at this Location: 269
Type of Operation: Paper mill
Mill Locations:
PT Sun Paper Source, Mojokerto Mill (PT Sun Paper Source), Jl. Raya Ngoro 100, Ds. Manduromanggunggajah, Kec. Ngoro, 61385 Mojokerto, Indonesia, Capacity: 25,000 mt/y, (Paper mill)
Phone: (62) 31 3726904, 321 6819081
Fax: (62) 321 6819079, 31 3727431
Email: sales_nas@sopanusa.co.id, scoord@sopanusa.co.id

Indonesia

Paper/Paperboard Grades and Capacities:
Total paper and paperboard capacity: 53,500 mt/y
Tissue: 51,000 mt/y
Specialty and industrial: 2,500 mt/y
Paper and Paperboard Mill Data:
Stock Preparation:
Pulpers: 10
Paper Machines: 3
No. 1, fourdrinier, total capacity 15,000 mt/y, Trim width 3.5 m, Tissue, Uncoated woodfree/freesheet
No. 2, fourdrinier, total capacity 2,500 mt/y, Trim width 2.7 m, Specialty and industrial
No. 3, crescent former, total capacity 36,000 mt/y, Trim width 2.85 m, Tissue
Finishing Equipment:
Rewinders: 3
Energy Data:
Power boilers: 3
Combustion turbines: 1 at 4.2 MW
Electrical demand for mill: 151 MWh/D

ⓜPT Sun Paper Source
Mojokerto Mill (PT Sun Paper Source)
Ownership: PT Sopanusa Tissue
Jl. Raya Ngoro 100, Ds. Manduromanggunggajah, Kec. Ngoro
61385 Mojokerto, East Java
Indonesia
Phone: (62) 31 3726904, 321 6819081
Fax: (62) 321 6819079, 31 3727431
Email: sales_nas@sopanusa.co.id, scoord@sopanusa.co.id
Web Address: www.sopanusa.co.id
Type of Operation: Paper mill
Paper/Paperboard Grades and Capacities:
Total paper and paperboard capacity: 25,000 mt/y
Tissue: 25,000 mt/y
Paper and Paperboard Mill Data:
Paper Machines: 1
TM 1, (started December 19, 2013), Yankee dryer, total capacity 25,000 mt/y, Trim width 2.75 m, Tissue

ⓜPT Suparma, TBK
Jl. Sulung Sekolahan No. 6A
60174 Surabaya, Jawa Timur
Indonesia
Mailing Address: PO Box 1448, 60174 Surabaya, East Java, Indonesia
Phone: (62) 31 3539888/3776
Fax: (62) 31 3533827/3522165
Email: purchasing@ptsuparmatbk.com, commercial@ptsuparmatbk.com
Web Address: www.ptsuparmatbk.com
Personnel:
Pres. Dir.: Mr. Welly
Phone: (62) 31 3539888
Fax: (62) 31 3533827
Dir.: M. B. Lanniwati
Phone: (62) 31 3539888
Fax: (62) 31 3533827
Dir.: Hendro Luhur
Phone: (62) 31 3539888
Fax: (62) 31 3533827
Dir.: Edward Sopanan
Phone: (62) 31 3539888
Fax: (62) 31 3533827
Purch. Mgr.: Ms Trilianty
Phone: (62) 31 3531336
Fax: (62) 31 3533827
Email: commercial@ptsuparmatbk.com
Total Employees at this Location: 1,203
Mill Locations:
PT Suparma, Tbk., Surabaya Mill, Jl. Mastrip No.856 Kec. Karang Pilang, 60221 Surabaya, Indonesia, Capacity: 166,000 mt/y, (Paper mill, Paperboard mill)
Phone: (62) 31 766 6666, 31 766 2490, 31 7662492, 31 7662493
Fax: (62) 31 7663287
Email: customerservice@ptsuparmatbk.com, marketing@ptsuparmatbk.com

ⓜPT Suparma, Tbk.
Surabaya Mill
Ownership: PT Suparma, TBK
Jl. Mastrip No.856 Kec. Karang Pilang
60221 Surabaya, East Java
Indonesia
Phone: (62) 31 766 6666, 31 766 2490, 31 7662492, 31 7662493
Fax: (62) 31 7663287
Email: customerservice@ptsuparmatbk.com, marketing@ptsuparmatbk.com
Web Address: www.ptsuparmatbk.com
Personnel:
Gen. Mgr.: Richard Ong
Phone: (62) 31 3533776
Fax: (62) 31 3533827
Email: richardong@ptsuparmatbk.com
Dir.: Hendro Luhur
Phone: (62) 31 3533776
Fax: (62) 31 3533827
Tech. Support.: Candra Cipta Waluyojati
Phone: (62) 31 3533776
Fax: (62) 31 3533827
Assist. Mgr.: Elnath Yonatan
Phone: (62) 31 3533776
Fax: (62) 31 3533827
Purch. Mgr.: Trilianty Judijanto
Phone: (62) 31 3533776
Fax: (62) 31 3533827
Email: purchasing@ptsuparmatbk.com
Purch. Mgr.: Agnes Theng
Phone: (62) 31 3533776
Fax: (62) 31 3533827
Email: purchasing@ptsuparmatbk.com
Total Employees at this Location: 1,500
Type of Operation: Paper mill, Paperboard mill
Pulp Grades and Capacities:
Total pulp capacity: 159,836 mt/y
Recycled Pulping: 159,836 mt/y
Pulp Mill Data:
Recycled Fiber Treatment Lines:
Flotation deinking lines: 1 at 40,800 admt/y
Recycled packaging pulping lines: 1 at 115,500 admt/y
Paper/Paperboard Grades and Capacities:
Total paper and paperboard capacity: 166,000 mt/y
Tissue: 15,000 mt/y
Packaging papers: 86,500 mt/y
Boxboard/cartonboard: 64,500 mt/y
Paper and Paperboard Mill Data:
Stock Preparation:
Pulpers: 14
Refiners: 1
Paper Machines: 7
No. 1, fourdrinier, total capacity 7,000 mt/y, Trim width 1.9 m, Packaging papers
No. 2, fourdrinier, total capacity 15,000 mt/y, Trim width 2.3 m, Packaging papers
No. 3, fourdrinier, total capacity 15,000 mt/y, Trim width 2.3 m, Packaging papers
No. 5, multi-cylinder, total capacity 15,000 mt/y, Trim width 2.67 m, Boxboard/cartonboard
No. 6, fourdrinier, total capacity 49,500 mt/y, Trim width 3.2 m, Packaging papers
No. 7, multi-cylinder, total capacity 49,500 mt/y, Trim width 1.9 m, Boxboard/cartonboard
No. 8, cylinder, total capacity 15,000 mt/y, Trim width 2.56 m, Tissue, Uncoated woodfree/freesheet
Coating Machines: 1
No. 6, total capacity 27,000 mt/y., on machine
Finishing Equipment:
Supercalenders: 4
Rewinders: 5
Sheeters: 4
Energy Data:
Power boilers: 1
Steam turbines: 1 at 27.0 MW
Electrical demand for mill: 277 MWh/D

ⓜPT Surabaya Agung Industri Pulp & Kertas
Jl. Kedungdoro No. 60, 8-10th floor
60251 Surabaya, East Java
Indonesia
Phone: (62) 31 5482003
Fax: (62) 31 5482039/40
Email: ird@suryakertas.com
Web Address: www.suryakertas.com
Personnel:
Pres. Dir.: Tirtomulyadi Sulistyo
Phone: (62) 31 5482003
Fax: (62) 31 5482039/40
Dir.: Rasmachahjana Sulistyo
Phone: (62) 31 5482003
Fax: (62) 31 5482039/40
Dir.: Sinduchayana Sulistyo
Phone: (62) 31 5482003
Fax: (62) 31 5482039/40
Dir.: Any Indrawati
Phone: (62) 31 5482003
Fax: (62) 31 5482039/40
Pres. Commissioner: Yogyo Pranoto
Phone: (62) 31 5482003
Fax: (62) 31 5482039/40
Commissioner: Imanuel Robert Najoan
Phone: (62) 31 5482003
Fax: (62) 31 5482039/40
Commissioner: Y. M. Kenny Wailanduw
Phone: (62) 31 5482003
Fax: (62) 31 5482039/40
Indep. Commissioner: Hariyadi Welim
Phone: (62) 31 5482003
Fax: (62) 31 5482039/40
Mill Locations:
PT Surabaya Agung Industri Pulp & Kertas, Driyorejo Mill, Jalan Raya Driyorejo, Kecamatan Driyorejo, 61177 Gresik, Indonesia, Capacity: 329,600 mt/y, (Paper mill, Paperboard mill)
Phone: (62) 31 7507129-30
Fax: (62) 31 7507363
Email: ird@suryakertas.com

ⓜPT Surabaya Agung Industri Pulp & Kertas
Driyorejo Mill
Jalan Raya Driyorejo, Kecamatan Driyorejo
61177 Gresik, East Java
Indonesia
Phone: (62) 31 7507129-30
Fax: (62) 31 7507363
Email: ird@suryakertas.com
Web Address: www.suryakertas.com
Personnel:
Pres. Dir.: Tirtomulyadi Sulistyo
Phone: (62) 31 7507129-30
Fax: (62) 31 7507363
Dir.: Rasmachayana Sulistyo
Phone: (62) 31 7507129-30
Fax: (62) 31 7507363
Dir.: Any Indrawati
Phone: (62) 31 7507129-30
Fax: (62) 31 7507363
Dir.: John Simon Widjaja
Phone: (62) 31 7507129-30
Fax: (62) 31 7507363
Total Employees at this Location: 850
Type of Operation: Paper mill, Paperboard mill
Pulp Grades and Capacities:
Total pulp capacity: 114,356 mt/y
Recycled Pulping: 114,356 mt/y
Pulp Mill Data:
Recycled Fiber Treatment Lines:
Flotation deinking lines: 2 at 40,000 admt/y
Recycled packaging pulping lines: 1
Paper/Paperboard Grades and Capacities:
Total paper and paperboard capacity: 329,600 mt/y
Newsprint: 32,000 mt/y
Uncoated woodfree/freesheet: 124,000 mt/y

Indonesia

Specialty and industrial: 26,000 mt/y
Boxboard/cartonboard: 147,600 mt/y
Paper and Paperboard Mill Data:
Paper Machines: 7
No. 1, fourdrinier, total capacity 14,000 mt/y, Trim width 1.7 m, Uncoated woodfree/freesheet
No. 3, fourdrinier, total capacity 16,000 mt/y, Trim width 3.08 m, Uncoated woodfree/freesheet, Specialty and industrial
No. 5, fourdrinier, total capacity 18,000 mt/y, Trim width 4.68 m, Specialty and industrial
No. 6, Ultraformer (3), total capacity 52,200 mt/y, Trim width 3.22 m, Boxboard/cartonboard
No. 7, Ultraformer (6), total capacity 54,000 mt/y, Trim width 3.16 m, Boxboard/cartonboard
No. 8, Ultraformer (8), total capacity 41,400 mt/y, Trim width 2.8 m, Boxboard/cartonboard
No. 9, SymFormer MB, total capacity 134,000 mt/y, Trim width 4.95 m, Uncoated woodfree/freesheet, Newsprint
Coating Machines: 7
No. 1, total capacity 13,000 mt/y., off machine
No. 2, total capacity 29,000 mt/y., on machine
No. 3, off machine
No. 4, total capacity 65,000 mt/y., on machine
No. 5, total capacity 36,000 mt/y., on machine
No. 6, total capacity 180,000 mt/y., on machine
No. 7, total capacity 180,000 mt/y., on machine
Finishing Equipment:
Supercalenders: 1
Rewinders: 4
Energy Data:
Power boilers: 1
Combustion turbines: 1 at 36 MW
Electrical demand for mill: 762 MWh/D

PT Surabaya Mekabox
Ownership: 100% by private owner
Jl. Bongkaran No. 64-66
60010 Surabaya, Jawa Timur
Indonesia
Mailing Address: P.O. Box 1061, Surabaya
Phone: (62) 31 3523274/4041
Fax: (62) 31 3532582
Email: info@sbymekabox.com
Web Address: www.sbymekabox.com
Personnel:
Pres. Dir.: Mr. Soeparsono
Phone: (62) 31 3523274/4041
Fax: (62) 31 3532582
Dir.: Rudy Soetarso
Phone: (62) 31 3523274/4041
Fax: (62) 31 3532582
Mktg. Dir.: Reynold Soetarso
Phone: (62) 31 3523274/4041
Fax: (62) 31 3532582
Purch. Mgr.: Iwan Gondowahyudi
Phone: (62) 31 3523274/4041
Fax: (62) 31 3532582
Total Employees of Company: 1,000
Mill Locations:
PT Surabaya Mekabox, Driyorejo Mill, Jl. Bongkaran No.66, 60161 Surabaya, Indonesia, Capacity: 82,000 mt/y, (Paper mill, Paperboard mill)
Phone: (62) 31 3523274
Fax: (62) 31 3532582
Email: info@sbymekabox.com

PT Surabaya Mekabox
Driyorejo Mill
Jl. Bongkaran No.66
60161 Surabaya, East Java
Indonesia
Mailing Address: P.O. Box 1061 SBY, Surabaya
Phone: (62) 31 3523274
Fax: (62) 31 3532582
Email: info@sbymekabox.com
Web Address: www.sbymekabox.com
Personnel:
Paper Mill Mgr.: Hengky Hartadi

Phone: (62) 31 7507266/8059
Fax: (62) 31 3532582
Gen. Mgr.: Djoko Andono
Phone: (62) 31 7507266/8059
Fax: (62) 31 3532582
Export Import Mgr.: Yohanes Hartadi
Phone: (62) 31 3523274/4041
Fax: (62) 31 3532582
Procurement Mgr.: Bambang Nurawan
Phone: (62) 31 7507266/8059
Fax: (62) 31 3532582
Total Employees at this Location: 180
Type of Operation: Paper mill, Paperboard mill
Pulp Grades and Capacities:
Total pulp capacity: 81,138 mt/y
Recycled Pulping: 81,138 mt/y
Pulp Mill Data:
Recycled Fiber Treatment Lines:
Recycled packaging pulping lines: 1
Paper/Paperboard Grades and Capacities:
Total paper and paperboard capacity: 82,000 mt/y
Linerboard: 30,000 mt/y
Corrugating medium/fluting: 52,000 mt/y
Paper and Paperboard Mill Data:
Paper Machines: 3
No. 1, fourdrinier (2), total capacity 30,000 mt/y, Trim width 2.5 m, Linerboard
No. 2, fourdrinier, total capacity 22,000 mt/y, Trim width 2.8 m, Corrugating medium/fluting
No. 3, fourdrinier, total capacity 30,000 mt/y, Trim width 3.2 m, Corrugating medium/fluting
Finishing Equipment:
Rewinders: 4 at 82,000 mt/y
Energy Data:
Power boilers: 4
Electrical demand for mill: 105 MWh/D

PT Surya Mas Aditama
Jl. Raya Cikande Km 4.5, Rangkas Bitung
Banten
Indonesia
Phone: (62) 0252 201800, 0252 206788
Total Employees at this Location: 110
Mill Locations:
PT Surya Mas Aditama, Banten Mill, Jl. Raya Cikande Km 4.5, Rangkas Bitung, Banten, Indonesia, Capacity: 4,800 mt/y, (Paper mill)
Phone: (62) 0252 201800, 0252 206788

PT Surya Mas Aditama
Banten Mill
Jl. Raya Cikande Km 4.5, Rangkas Bitung
Banten, West Java
Indonesia
Phone: (62) 0252 201800, 0252 206788
Total Employees at this Location: 110
Type of Operation: Paper mill
Paper/Paperboard Grades and Capacities:
Total paper and paperboard capacity: 4,800 mt/y
Specialty and industrial: 4,800 mt/y
Paper and Paperboard Mill Data:
Paper Machines: 1
PM 1, total capacity 5,000 mt/y, Uncoated mechanical/groundwood

PT Surya Pamenang
Kediri Mill
Ownership: PT Gudang Garam
Jln. Raya Kediri Kertosono Km 7
64182 Kediri, East Java
Indonesia
Mailing Address: PO BOX 154, Kediri, Indonesia
Phone: (62) 354 681360, 354 681361
Fax: (62) 354 681591
Email: hq@suryapamenang.com, marketing@suryapamenang.com
Web Address: www.suryapamenang.com
Personnel:
Pres. Dir.: Djajusman Surjowijono
Phone: (62) 354 6813 60

Fax: (62) 354 6815 91
Email: d.surjowijono@suryapamenang.com
Pres. Dir.: Juni Setiawati Wonowidjojo
Phone: (62) 354 6813 60
Fax: (62) 354 6815 91
Email: j.wonowidjojo@suryapamenang.com
VP. Dir.: Susilo Wonowidjojo
Phone: (62) 354 6813 60
Fax: (62) 354 6815 91
Dir. Prod.: Hendra Hudiono
Phone: (62) 354 6813 60
Fax: (62) 354 6815 91
Email: hq@suryapamenang.com
Dir.: Ernawati Hyanchu
Phone: (62) 354 6813 60
Fax: (62) 354 6815 91
Email: e.hyanchu@gudanggaramtbk.com
Dir.: Anita Muktiwidjojo
Phone: (62) 354 6813 60
Fax: (62) 354 6815 91
Email: a.muktiwidjojo@suryapamenang.com
Dir.: Buntoro Turutan
Phone: (62) 354 6813 60
Fax: (62) 354 6815 91
Email: b.turutan@suryapamenang.com
Sls. Mgr.: Berlianto Y. Abdi
Phone: (62) 354 6813 60
Fax: (62) 354 6815 91
Email: marketing@spamenang.com
Total Employees of Company: 1,012
Total Employees at this Location: 500
Type of Operation: Paper mill, Paperboard mill
Pulp Mill Data:
Bleach Plant Systems: 1
Paper/Paperboard Grades and Capacities:
Total paper and paperboard capacity: 150,000 mt/y
Boxboard/cartonboard: 150,000 mt/y
Paper and Paperboard Mill Data:
Stock Preparation:
Pulpers: 4
Refiners: 6
Paper Machines: 1
No. 1, fourdrinier (3), total capacity 150,000 mt/y, Trim width 4.25 m, Boxboard/cartonboard
Coating Machines: 2
No. 1, total capacity 150,000 mt/y., on machine
No. 2, total capacity 150,000 mt/y., on machine
Finishing Equipment:
Rewinders: 1 at 150,000 mt/y
Sheeters: 3 at 60,000 mt/y
Energy Data:
Power boilers: 5
Combustion turbines: 1 at 23 MW
Electrical demand for mill: 242 MWh/D

PT Tanjung Enim Lestari Pulp & Paper
Ownership: 85% by Marubeni Corporation, 15% by Sumatera Pulp Corporation (JICA, Nippon Paper, Marubeni)
Menara Jamsostek, North 18th Floor, Suite TA-1802 Jl. Jend. Gatot Subroto No.38
12710 Jakarta
Indonesia
Phone: (62) 21 52902088
Fax: (62) 21 52902099
Web Address: www.telpp.com
Personnel:
Pres. Dir.: Kyo Oshima
Phone: (62) 713 324150
Fax: (62) 713 324195
Vice Pres. Dir.: Tomoyuki Iida
Phone: (62) 21 52902088
Fax: (62) 21 52902099
VP: Yoshiharu Kanbe
Phone: (62) 21 52902088
Fax: (62) 21 52902099
Total Employees of Company: 1,000
Mill Locations:
PT Tanjung Enim Lestari Pulp & Paper, Musi Pulp Mill, Desa Niru, Tebang Agung, Kec. Rambang Dangku,

31172 Kab. Muara Enim, Indonesia, (Pulp mill)
Phone: (62) 713 324 150/160
Fax: (62) 713 324 182/190

ⓜPT Tanjung Enim Lestari Pulp & Paper
Musi Pulp Mill
Ownership: 85% by Marubeni Corporation
Desa Niru, Tebang Agung, Kec. Rambang Dangku
31172 Kab. Muara Enim, South Sumatra
Indonesia
 Phone: (62) 713 324 150/160
 Fax: (62) 713 324 182/190
 Web Address: www.telpp.com
Personnel:
 Purch. Mgr.: Yudi Wijaya
 Phone: (62) 713 324 150/160
 Prod. Mgr.: Damianus Pinem
 Phone: (62) 713 324 150/160
 Tech. Dir.: Subhash Maheshwari
 Phone: (62) 713 324 150/160
 Instrument & Automation Contrl. Supervisor: Junaidi Asmar
 Phone: (62) 713 324 150/160
 Finan. Dir.: Yoshihiro Ishihara
 Phone: (62) 713 324 150/160
 HR Dir.: Rudi Fajar
 Phone: (62) 713 324 150/160
 Fax: (62) 713 324 182/190
 Environ. Mgr.: Pipit Andi
 Phone: (62) 713 324 150/160
 Sls. & Mktg. Mgr.: Yunita Rahmayani
 Phone: (62) 713 324 150/160
Total Employees at this Location: 820
Type of Operation: Pulp mill
Pulp Grades and Capacities:
 Total pulp capacity: 486,108 mt/y
 Pulp available for market: 485,000 mt/y
 Chemical Pulp: 486,108 mt/y
Pulp Mill Data:
 Pulp Lines: 1
 Bleach Plant Systems: 1
  Chemical Pulping System - Hardwood, Sequence: O₂ DEopDED
 Chemical Recovery Equipment:
  Evaporator lines: 1
  Recovery boilers: 1
  Lime Kiln
 Pulp Dryers:
  Flakt dryer 1
 Energy Data:
  Power boilers: 1
  Steam turbines: 1 at 75 MW
  Electrical demand for mill: 1,138 MWh/D

ⓜPT Pabrik Kertas Tjiwi Kimia Tbk
Mojokerto (PT Pabrik Kertas Tjiwi Kimia) Mill
Ownership: Asia Pulp & Paper (APP)
Tarik Jl. Raya Surabaya, Mojokerto Km. 44
Mojokerto, East Java
Indonesia
Mailing Address: PO Box 115, Mojokerto, East Java, Indonesia
 Phone: (62) 321 361552
 Fax: (62) 321 361615
 Web Address: www.tjiwi.co.id, www.asiapulppaper.com
Personnel:
 Pres./Dir.: Yudi Setiawan Lin
 Phone: (62) 321 361552
 Paper Factory I Mgr.: Chen Chun Chang
 Phone: (62) 321 361552
 Paper Factory II Mgr.: Lu Ho Chang
 Phone: (62) 321 361552
 Paper Factory III Mgr.: Udin S.
 Phone: (62) 321 361552
 Tech. Mgr.: George Prasetya
 Phone: (62) 321 361552
 Chief Eng.: Budi Sutanto
 Phone: (62) 321 361552
 Purch. Agent: Kris Lay
 Phone: (62) 321 361552
 Com. Pres.: Teguh Ganda Wijaya
 Phone: (62) 321 361552
 Maint. Mgr.: G. T. Prasetya
 Phone: (62) 321 361552
 R&D Mgr.: Hanafi Pratomo
 Phone: (62) 321 361552
 Dir.: Hendra Jaya Kosasih
 Phone: (62) 321 361552
 Dir.: Muktar Wijaya
 Phone: (62) 321 361552
 Dir.: Suresh Kilam
 Phone: (62) 321 361552
Total Employees at this Location: 14,000
Type of Operation: Paper mill, Paperboard mill
Pulp Grades and Capacities:
 Total pulp capacity: 43,265 mt/y
 Recycled Pulping: 43,265 mt/y
Pulp Mill Data:
 Chemical Pulping Systems:
  Batch digesters: 14
  Bleach Plant Lines:
  No. 1, Sequence: CH
 Recycled Fiber Treatment Lines:
  Flotation deinking lines: 2
  Pulpers: 4
  Washing deinking lines: 1
Paper/Paperboard Grades and Capacities:
 Total paper and paperboard capacity: 1,380,000 mt/y
 Uncoated woodfree/freesheet: 829,000 mt/y
 Coated woodfree/freesheet: 370,000 mt/y
 Packaging papers: 8,200 mt/y
 Specialty and industrial: 132,800 mt/y
 Boxboard/cartonboard: 40,000 mt/y
Paper and Paperboard Mill Data:
 Stock Preparation:
  Refiners: 60
 Paper Machines: 13
  No. 1, fourdrinier, total capacity 9,000 mt/y, Trim width 1.84 m, Uncoated woodfree/freesheet
  No. 2, fourdrinier, total capacity 10,000 mt/y, Trim width 1.84 m, Specialty and industrial
  No. 3, fourdrinier, total capacity 15,000 mt/y, Trim width 2.36 m, Uncoated woodfree/freesheet
  No. 4, fourdrinier, total capacity 15,000 mt/y, Trim width 2.36 m, Uncoated woodfree/freesheet
  No. 5, SymFormer MB, total capacity 50,000 mt/y, Trim width 3.08 m, Uncoated woodfree/freesheet
  No. 6, cylinder (8), total capacity 40,000 mt/y, Trim width 2.2 m, Boxboard/cartonboard
  No. 7, fourdrinier, total capacity 11,000 mt/y, Trim width 2.3 m, Packaging papers, Specialty and industrial
  No. 8, fourdrinier, total capacity 80,000 mt/y, Trim width 3.7 m, Uncoated woodfree/freesheet
  No. 9, Bel-Form, total capacity 230,000 mt/y, Trim width 6.65 m, Uncoated woodfree/freesheet
  No. 10, fourdrinier, total capacity 280,000 mt/y, Trim width 6.75 m, Uncoated woodfree/freesheet, Coated woodfree/freesheet
  No. 11, Bel-Baie IV, total capacity 400,000 mt/y, Trim width 8.95 m, Uncoated woodfree/freesheet
  No. 12, fourdrinier, total capacity 120,000 mt/y, Trim width 3.45 m, Coated woodfree/freesheet
  No. 13, fourdrinier, total capacity 120,000 mt/y, Trim width 6 m, Specialty and industrial
 Coating Machines: 10
  No. 1, total capacity 46,000 mt/y., off machine
  No. 2, total capacity 4,000 mt/y., off machine
  No. 3, total capacity 35,000 mt/y., on machine
  No. 4, total capacity 20,000 mt/y., off machine
  No. 5, total capacity 220,000 mt/y., on machine
  No. 6, total capacity 250,000 mt/y., on machine
  No. 7, total capacity 230,000 mt/y., off machine
  No. 8, total capacity 370,000 mt/y., on machine
  No. 9, total capacity 50,000 mt/y., off machine
  No. 10, off machine
 Finishing Equipment:
  Supercalenders: 4
  Rewinders: 13
  Sheeters: 5
 Energy Data:
  Power boilers: 3
  Steam turbines: 2 at 140 MW
  Electrical demand for mill: 2,610 MWh/D

ⓜPT Toba Pulp Lestari Tbk.
Ownership: 9.40% by public, 90.60% by Pinnacle Company Limited
Uniplaza, East Tower 7th Fl., Jln. Jend. Haryono M.T., A-1
20231 Medan
Indonesia
 Phone: (62) 61 4532088
 Fax: (62) 61 4530967
 Email: (firstname_lastname@tobapulp.com), investor_relation@tobapulp.com
 Web Address: www.tobapulp.com
Personnel:
 Pres. Dir.: Subhash Chander Paruthi
 Phone: (62) 61 4532155
 Fax: (62) 61 4573428
 Dir.: Min Sin Tshi
 Phone: (62) 61 4532155
 Fax: (62) 61 4573428
 Dir.: Anwar Lawden
 Phone: (62) 61 4532155
 Fax: (62) 61 4573428
Total Employees of Company: 1,052
Mill Locations:
PT Toba Pulp Lestari Tbk. - TPL, Kec. Porsea, Kab. Toba Samosir Mill, Desa Sosor Ladang, Kec. Porsea, Kab. Toba Samosir, Indonesia, (Pulp mill)
 Phone: (62) 632 7346000/46001
 Fax: (62) 632 7346006
 Email: investor_relation@tobapulp.com

ⓜPT Toba Pulp Lestari Tbk. - TPL
Kec. Porsea, Kab. Toba Samosir Mill
Ownership: PT Toba Pulp Lestari Tbk.
Desa Sosor Ladang
Kec. Porsea, Kab. Toba Samosir, North Sumatera
Indonesia
 Phone: (62) 632 7346000/46001
 Fax: (62) 632 7346006
 Email: investor_relation@tobapulp.com
 Web Address: www.tobapulp.com
Personnel:
 Managing Director: Roli Arifin
 Phone: (62) 632 7346000/46001
 Dir.: Juanda Panjaitan
 Phone: (62) 632 7346000/46001
 Dir.: Firman Purba SH
 Phone: (62) 632 7346000/46001
 Dir.: Mulia Nauli
 Phone: (62) 632 7346000/46001
 SH. Dir.: Dedy Sutanto
 Phone: (62) 632 7346000/46001
 Chief Eng.: Trevor Shields
 Phone: (62) 632 7346000/46001
 Tech. Mgr.: Dr. Murray St. John
 Phone: (62) 632 7346000/46001
 Tech. Mgr.: Thomas Handoko
 Phone: (62) 632 7346000/46001
 Prod. Mgr.: B. K. Gupta
 Phone: (62) 632 7346000/46001
Total Employees at this Location: 800
Type of Operation: Pulp mill
Pulp Grades and Capacities:
 Total pulp capacity: 208,649 mt/y
 Pulp available for market: 200,000 mt/y
 Chemical Pulp: 208,649 mt/y
Pulp Mill Data:
 Chemical Pulping Systems:
  Batch digesters: 8
 Bleach Plant Systems: 1
  No. 1, Sequence: DEopDD, Capacity 240,000 admt/y

Iran

Chemical Recovery Equipment:
Evaporator lines: 1
Recovery boilers: 1
Pulp Dryers:
Air Float dryers 1
Energy Data:
Power boilers: 2
Steam turbines: 2 at 120 MW
Electrical demand for mill: 677 MWh/D

⊕ⓂPT Triguna Pratama
Karawang Mill
Ds. Gintungkerta, Kec. Klari
41371 Karawang, West Java
Indonesia
 Phone: (62) 267 431366/367
Personnel:
 Pres. Dir.: Ir. Satria Rifai
 Phone: (62) 267 431366/367
 Dir.: Ir. Ade Priadi
 Phone: (62) 267 431366/367
Total Employees at this Location: 500
Type of Operation: Paper mill
Paper/Paperboard Grades and Capacities:
 Total paper and paperboard capacity: 3,600 mt/y
 Specialty and industrial: 3,600 mt/y

⊕ⓂPT Uninga Bima Sakti
Sukabumi Mill
Ownership: 40% by Asianto Sunjono, 60% by Edi Dion J.
Jln. Cimandiri No. 25
Sukabumi, West Java
Indonesia
 Phone: (62) 266 227700
Personnel:
 Pres./Dir.: Asianto Sunjono
 Phone: (62) 266 227700
 Mill Mgr.: Heri Samsudin J.
 Phone: (62) 266 227700
 Paper Mill/Maint./Tech. Mgr.: Mr. Sumitro
 Phone: (62) 266 227700
 Asst. Mill Mgr.: Mr. Lim
 Phone: (62) 266 227700
 Maint. Mgr./Chief Eng.: Mr. Sakimin
 Phone: (62) 266 227700
 Maint. Mgr.: Mr. Sugeng
 Phone: (62) 266 227700
 Dir.: Edi Djon
 Phone: (62) 266 227700
 Dir.: Herry S.
 Phone: (62) 266 227700
Total Employees at this Location: 51
Type of Operation: Pulp mill, Paper mill
Pulp Grades and Capacities:
 Total pulp capacity: 500 mt/y
Pulp Mill Data:
 Recycled Fiber Treatment Lines:
 Flotation deinking lines: 2 at 10 admt/y
 Pulpers: 3 at 20 admt/y
 Washing deinking lines: 3 at 20 admt/y
Paper/Paperboard Grades and Capacities:
 Total paper and paperboard capacity: 6,500 mt/y
 Specialty and industrial: 6,500 mt/y
Paper and Paperboard Mill Data:
 Stock Preparation:
 Pulpers: 3
 Refiners: 3
Paper Machines: 2
 No. 1, Yankee dryer, total capacity 3,000 mt/y, Trim width 1.6 m, Specialty and industrial
 No. 2, multi-cylinder, total capacity 3,500 mt/y, Trim width 1.6 m, Specialty and industrial
Finishing Equipment:
 Rewinders: 1
 Sheeters: 2

⊕ⓂPT Unipa Daya
Tangerang Mill
Jl. Imam Bonjol Km 3.5
Karawaci, Tangerang, Jawa Barat
Indonesia
Mailing Address: PO Box 63, Tangerang, West Java, Indonesia
 Phone: (62) 21 5523975-76
 Fax: (62) 21 5523977
Personnel:
 Pres. Dir.: Hasan Basuki
 Phone: (62) 21 5523975-76
 Dir.: Winston Basuki
 Phone: (62) 21 5523975-76
Total Employees at this Location: 394
Type of Operation: Paper mill
Paper/Paperboard Grades and Capacities:
 Total paper and paperboard capacity: 15,000 mt/y
 Uncoated woodfree/freesheet
 Packaging papers
Paper and Paperboard Mill Data:
Paper Machines: 2
 PM 1, fourdrinier, Trim width 2.56 m, Packaging papers, Specialty and industrial
 PM 2, fourdrinier, Trim width 2.56 m, Packaging papers, Specialty and industrial

ⓂPT The Univenus Co. Ltd.
Perawang (PT The Univenus) Mill
Ownership: Asia Pulp & Paper (APP)
Jl Raya Minas, Perawang Km 26, Tualang Kab Siak
Perawang , Riau, Sumatra
Indonesia
Mailing Address: P.O. Box 4295, 10001 Jakarta, West Java, Indonesia
 Phone: (62) 761 91030, 3950, 3951
 Fax: (62) 761 91030
 Web Address: www.asiapulppaper.com
Personnel:
 Pres./Dir.: Teguh Ganda Wijaya
 Phone: (62) 761 91030, 3950, 3951
 Dir.: Franky Oesman Widjaya
 Phone: (62) 761 91030, 3950, 3951
 Dir.: Hendra Jaya Kosasih
 Phone: (62) 761 91030, 3950, 3951
 Dir.: Muktar Widjaya
 Phone: (62) 761 91030, 3950, 3951
 Dir.: John Pandelaki
 Phone: (62) 761 91030, 3950, 3951
 Dir.: Njauw Kwet Meen
 Phone: (62) 761 91030, 3950, 3951
Total Employees at this Location: 92
Type of Operation: Paper mill
Paper/Paperboard Grades and Capacities:
 Total paper and paperboard capacity: 20,000 mt/y
 Tissue: 20,000 mt/y
Paper and Paperboard Mill Data:
Paper Machines: 1
 No. 1, fourdrinier, total capacity 20,000 mt/y, Trim width 3.6 m, Tissue, Uncoated woodfree/freesheet
Finishing Equipment:
 Rewinders: 2
Energy Data:
Power boilers: 1
Electrical demand for mill: 46 MWh/D

ⓂPT Wirajaya Packindo
Tangerang Mill
Jl. Raya Mauk Km. 7 Desa Pabuaran
15112 Tangerang, West Java
Indonesia
 Phone: (62) 021 5537891, 5537890
 Fax: (62) 021 5520043
 Email: hrdwirapaper@gmail.com, wirajaya@gmail.com
 Web Address: www.wirajaya.co.id
Personnel:
 Owner: Wira Rahardja
 Phone: (62) 021 5537891, 5537890
 Fax: (62) 021 5520043
 Commissioner: Hadi Rahardja
 Phone: (62) 021 5537890
 Fax: (62) 021 5520043
 Coating Mgr.: Ari Liberto
 Phone: (62) 021 5537890
 Fax: (62) 021 5520043
 Prod. Mgr.: Lim Giok Lim
 Phone: (62) 021 5537890
 Fax: (62) 021 5520043
Total Employees at this Location: 540
Type of Operation: Paperboard mill
Pulp Grades and Capacities:
 Total pulp capacity: 180,917 mt/y
 Recycled Pulping: 180,917 mt/y
Pulp Mill Data:
 Bleach Plant Systems: 1
 DIP
 Recycled Fiber Treatment Lines:
 Flotation deinking lines: 1
 Recycled packaging pulping lines: 1
Paper/Paperboard Grades and Capacities:
 Total paper and paperboard capacity: 185,640 mt/y
 Linerboard: 85,680 mt/y
 Corrugating medium/fluting: 57,120 mt/y
 Boxboard/cartonboard: 42,840 mt/y
Paper and Paperboard Mill Data:
Paper Machines: 2
 No. 1, twin-wire, total capacity 142,800 mt/y, Trim width 4.4 m, Linerboard, Corrugating medium/fluting
 No. 2, cylinder (4), total capacity 42,840 mt/y, Trim width 2.4 m, Boxboard/cartonboard
Coating Machines: 1
 PM#2, on machine
Energy Data:
Power boilers: 2
Electrical demand for mill: 236 MWh/D

IRAN

⊕ Atrak Pulp & Paper Industry Company
No.1, Reza Building, Koohenoor St., Ostad Motahari Ave.
Teheran
Iran
 Phone: (98) 21 88500382/4 - 88731326
 Fax: (98) 21 88735500
 Email: hosseinzadeh@atrak-p-p.com
 Web Address: www.atrak-p-p.com/raw.html
Personnel:
 Owner: Mahmoud Khosrowshahi
 Phone: (98) 21 88500382/4 - 88731326
 Fax: (98) 21 88735500
Mill Locations:
Atrak Pulp & Paper Industry Company, Foulad Mill, Baba Shaikh Ali Zone, Km 55 Isfehan-Shahrekord Road, Foulad Industrial City, Esfahan, Iran, Capacity: 100,000 mt/y, (Paperboard mill)
 Phone: (98) 334 6352788-90/311 661 8383
 Fax: (98) 334 6352773/311 6611701
 Email: info@atrak-p-p.com

Ⓜ Atrak Pulp & Paper Industry Company
Foulad Mill
Baba Shaikh Ali Zone, Km 55 Isfehan-Shahrekord Road
Foulad Industrial City, Esfahan
Iran
 Phone: (98) 334 6352788-90/311 661 8383
 Fax: (98) 334 6352773/311 6611701
 Email: info@atrak-p-p.com
 Web Address: www.atrak-p-p.com/raw.html
Personnel:
 Mahmoud Khosrowshahi
 Phone: (98) 334 6352788-90/311 661 8383
Total Employees at this Location: 200

Type of Operation: Paperboard mill
Pulp Grades and Capacities:
Total pulp capacity: 77,641 mt/y
Recycled Pulping: 77,641 mt/y
Pulp Mill Data:
Recycled Fiber Treatment Lines:
Recycled packaging pulping lines: 1
Paper/Paperboard Grades and Capacities:
Total paper and paperboard capacity: 100,000 mt/y
Boxboard/cartonboard: 100,000 mt/y
Paper and Paperboard Mill Data:
Paper Machines: 1
No. 1, cylinder (6), Yankee dryer, total capacity 100,000 mt/y, Trim width 2.6 m, Boxboard/cartonboard
Coating Machines: 1
PM1, on machine
Energy Data:
Power boilers
Electrical demand for mill: 137 MWh/D

ⓂChouka Pulp & Paper Mill
Rezvanshahr Mill
Ownership: Iran Wood-Paper Industries
Anzaly Astara Road km 35
43841 Rezvanshahr
Iran
Mailing Address: PO Box 17, Bandar Anzaly, Iran
Phone: (98) 182465 3000-7
Fax: (98) 182465 3033
Email: info@chouka.com
Web Address: www.chouka.com
Personnel:
Man. Dir.: N. Sadeghi
Phone: (98) 182465 3000-7
Mill Mgr.: A. Amjadi
Phone: (98) 182465 3000-7
Sls. Mgr.: A. S. Marashi
Phone: (98) 182465 3000-7
Total Employees at this Location: 1,800
Type of Operation: Pulp mill, Paper mill, Paperboard mill
Pulp Grades and Capacities:
Total pulp capacity: 135,393 mt/y
Chemical Pulp: 130,053 mt/y
Recycled Pulping: 5,340 mt/y
Pulp Mill Data:
Chemical Pulping Systems:
Continuous digesters: 1
Chemical Recovery Equipment:
Evaporator lines: 1
Recovery boilers: 1
Lime Kiln
Recycled Fiber Treatment Lines:
Recycled packaging pulping lines: 1
Paper/Paperboard Grades and Capacities:
Total paper and paperboard capacity: 130,000 mt/y
Packaging papers: 30,000 mt/y
Linerboard: 60,000 mt/y
Corrugating medium/fluting: 40,000 mt/y
Paper and Paperboard Mill Data:
Stock Preparation:
Pulpers: 1
Refiners: 6
Paper Machines: 1
No. 1, fourdrinier (2), total capacity 130,000 mt/y, Trim width 6.7 m, Linerboard, Corrugating medium/fluting, Packaging papers
Finishing Equipment:
Rewinders: 2
Energy Data:
Power boilers: 1
Combustion turbines: 1 at 15.8 MW
Electrical demand for mill: 336 MWh/D

ⓁⓂGharb Paper Ind. Co.
Tehran Mill
Daftere Aement Abieg, Blv. Behare
15156 Tehran
Iran
Mailing Address: PO Box 11385-3913, 15156 Tehran, Iran
Phone: (98) 21 88733203-5/ 88736988
Fax: (98) 21 88736732
Email: gpic@srtnet.net
Personnel:
Man. Dir.: Shahrokh Khakpour
Phone: (98) 21 88733203-5/ 88736988
Mgr.: Eng. Abdolreza Behmanesh
Phone: (98) 21 88733203-5/ 88736988
Type of Operation: Pulp mill, Paper mill
Pulp Grades and Capacities:
Total pulp capacity: 50,000 mt/y
Pulp Mill Data:
Mechanical Pulping Systems:
Conventional grinders: 1
Paper/Paperboard Grades and Capacities:
Uncoated woodfree/freesheet

ⓂHarir Khuzestan Tissue Co.
Haft-Tappeh, Shoosh Mill
Ownership: Latif Paper Co.
Haft-Tappeh, Shoosh, Khuzestan
Iran
Phone: (98) 642234 3331/2
Fax: (98) 642234 3330
Email: info@harirpaperco.com
Web Address: www.harirpaperco.com
Personnel:
Chmn.: Afshin Pirjani
Phone: (98) 642234 3331
Fax: (98) 642234 3330
Bd. Mbr.: Omid Ameri
Phone: (98) 642234 3331
Fax: (98) 642234 3330
Bd. Mbr.: Tatar Mirjalali
Phone: (98) 642234 3331
Fax: (98) 642234 3330
Man. Dir.: Ahmad Mazarei
Phone: (98) 642234 3331
Fax: (98) 642234 3330
Mgr.: Fahimeh Tabar
Phone: (98) 642234 3331
Fax: (98) 642234 3330
Email: Fahimeh.Tabar@harirpaperco.com
Prod. Mgr.: Hadi Torfi
Phone: (98) 642234 3331
Fax: (98) 642234 3330
Total Employees at this Location: 74
Type of Operation: Pulp mill, Paper mill
Paper/Paperboard Grades and Capacities:
Total paper and paperboard capacity: 10,000 mt/y
Tissue: 10,000 mt/y
Paper and Paperboard Mill Data:
Paper Machines: 1
No. 1, crescent former, Yankee dryer, total capacity 10,000 mt/y, Trim width 2.7 m, Tissue, Uncoated woodfree/freesheet
Finishing Equipment:
Rewinders: 2
Energy Data:
Power boilers
Electrical demand for mill: 27 MWh/D

ⓂHayat Kimya A.S.
Zencan Mill
Ownership: Hayat Kagit ve Enerji A.S.
Zencan
Iran
Total Employees at this Location: 250
Type of Operation: Paper mill
Paper/Paperboard Grades and Capacities:
Total paper and paperboard capacity: 65,000 mt/y
Tissue: 65,000 mt/y
Paper and Paperboard Mill Data:
Paper Machines: 1
No. 1, Advantage DCT 200 TS, Yankee dryer, total capacity 65,000 mt/y, Trim width 5.6 m, Tissue, Uncoated woodfree/freesheet
Energy Data:
Power boilers
Electrical demand for mill: 166 MWh/D

ⓂIran Papyrus Co. Ltd.
Ownership: 79% by Ali Asghar Mohammadi, 21% by Other Partners
No. 11 Shenasa Ale. Vali Asr Ave.
1967743481 Tehran
Iran
Phone: (98) 21 220 105 41/42/43
Fax: (98) 21 220 121 47
Email: info@iranpapyrus.com
Web Address: www.iranpapyrus.com
Personnel:
Chmn./Man. Dir.: Ali Asghar Mohammadi
Phone: (98) 21 220 105 41/42/43
Fax: (98) 21 220 121 47
Email: ali@iranpapyrus.com
Sls./Mktg. Dir.: Shahin Mohammadi
Phone: (98) 912 120 69 04
Email: shahin@iranpapyrus.com
Prod. Mgr.: Shahram Mohammadi
Phone: (98) 912 119 27 77
Email: shahram@iranpapyrus.com
Total Employees of Company: 200
Total Employees at this Location: 20
Mill Locations:
Iran Papyrus Co. Ltd., Saveh Mill, 11th St. Kaveh Ind. City, Saveh, Iran, Capacity: 16,000 mt/y, (Paperboard mill)
Phone: (98) 256234 2282/2836
Fax: (98) 256234 2799
Email: info@iranpapyrus.com

ⓂIran Papyrus Co. Ltd.
Saveh Mill
11th St. Kaveh Ind. City
Saveh, Markazi
Iran
Phone: (98) 256234 2282/2836
Fax: (98) 256234 2799
Email: info@iranpapyrus.com
Web Address: www.iranpapyrus.com
Personnel:
Mill Mgr./Prod. Mgr.: Shahram Mohammadi
Phone: (98) 912 119 2777
Email: shahram@iranpapirus.com
Chief Eng.: Soheil Golkar Sistani
Phone: (98) 256234.804654443
Purch. Agt.: Parvin Aghazadeh
Phone: (98) 256234.804654443
Mgr.: Eng. Ali Asghar Mohammadi
Phone: (98) 256234.804654443
Total Employees at this Location: 131
Type of Operation: Paperboard mill
Pulp Grades and Capacities:
Total pulp capacity: 16,301 mt/y
Recycled Pulping: 16,301 mt/y
Pulp Mill Data:
Recycled Fiber Treatment Lines:
Pulpers: 2 at 25,000 admt/y
Paper/Paperboard Grades and Capacities:
Total paper and paperboard capacity: 16,000 mt/y
Linerboard: 11,000 mt/y
Boxboard/cartonboard: 5,000 mt/y
Paper and Paperboard Mill Data:
Stock Preparation:
Pulpers: 2
Refiners: 2
Paper Machines: 1
No. 1, cylinder (3), total capacity 16,000 mt/y, Trim width 2.5 m, Linerboard, Boxboard/cartonboard
Finishing Equipment:
Rewinders: 1
Energy Data:
Power boilers
Electrical demand for mill: 23 MWh/D

Iran

⊕Iran Wood-Paper Industries
Ownership: 100% by NIIO
No. 12, Esfandyar St., Vali Asr Ave.
19677 Tehran
Iran
Mailing Address: P.O. Box 19395, 4361 Tehran, Iran
Phone: (98) 21 88780304-6/4-88694273 21 98
Fax: (98) 21 88878580
Email: manager@chouka.com
Web Address: www.chouka.com
Personnel:
Chmn.: Ehsan Khatami
Phone: (98) 21 88780304-6
Fax: (98) 21 88878580
Man. Dir.: M. Akhoundzadeh
Phone: (98) 21 88780304-6
Fax: (98) 21 88878580
Prod. Mgr.: Akbar Amjadi
Phone: (98) 21 88780304-6
Fax: (98) 21 88878580
Sls./Mktg. Dir.: M. Eghdam Talab
Phone: (98) 21 88780304-6
Fax: (98) 21 88878580
Purch. Dir.: Mohammad Naimi
Phone: (98) 21 88780304-6
Fax: (98) 21 88878580
Ind. Dir.: Akbar Amjadi
Phone: (98) 21 88780304-6
Fax: (98) 21 88878580
Total Employees at this Location: 1,800
Mill Locations:
Chouka Pulp & Paper Mill, Rezvanshahr Mill, Anzaly Astara Road km 35, 43841 Rezvanshahr, Iran, Capacity: 130,000 mt/y, (Pulp mill, Paper mill, Paperboard mill)
Phone: (98) 182465 3000-7
Fax: (98) 182465 3033
Email: info@chouka.com

⊕⊛Kahrizak Paper Mill
Tehran Mill
Ownership: 92% by Gemayel family, 8% by Sarmaye Sozari Melli Iran
Avenue Azadi Avenue Rudaki Shomali 3
1457894653 Tehran
Iran
Mailing Address: PO Box 11155-444, 14578 94653 Tehran, Iran
Phone: (98) 21 66923161/0307
Fax: (98) 21 66932671
Email: info@kpmpaper.com
Web Address: www.kpmpaper.com
Personnel:
Pres. of the Board: Faramarz Chaigan
Phone: (98) 21 66923161/0307
CEO & Pres.: Louis Gemayel
Phone: (98) 21 66923161/0307
Mill Mgr.: M. R. Nazar Begi
Phone: (98) 21 66923161/0307
Admin. Dir.: Mr. Rahemi
Phone: (98) 21 66923161/0307
Prod. & Proj. Dir.: Patrick Gemayel
Phone: (98) 21 66923161/0307
Commercial Dir.: Paul Gemayel
Phone: (98) 21 66923161/0307
Total Employees at this Location: 320
Type of Operation: Paperboard mill
Pulp Grades and Capacities:
Total pulp capacity: 58,080 mt/y
Recycled Pulping: 58,080 mt/y
Pulp Mill Data:
Recycled Fiber Treatment Lines:
Recycled packaging pulping lines: 1
Paper/Paperboard Grades and Capacities:
Total paper and paperboard capacity: 60,000 mt/y
Linerboard: 40,000 mt/y
Corrugating medium/fluting: 20,000 mt/y
Paper and Paperboard Mill Data:
Stock Preparation:
Pulpers: 5

Refiners: 8
Paper Machines: 3
No. 2, fourdrinier, total capacity 5,000 mt/y, Trim width 1.8 m, Linerboard
No. 3, fourdrinier, total capacity 25,000 mt/y, Trim width 2.4 m, Corrugating medium/fluting, Linerboard
No. 4, fourdrinier (2), total capacity 30,000 mt/y, Trim width 2.2 m, Linerboard
Finishing Equipment:
Supercalenders: 1
Rewinders: 3
Sheeters: 1
Energy Data:
Power boilers: 5
Electrical demand for mill: 86 MWh/D

⊕Kaveh Paper Industries Co.
No 5, N. Lotfi Street - 6th Fl., 7th Tir Square
15898 Tehran
Iran
Mailing Address: PO Box 15875-5195, Tehran, Iran
Fax: (98) 21 88824174
Email: kavehpaperi.co@neda.net
Web Address: www.kavehpaper.co.ir
Personnel:
Export Dep.: Mrs. Mina Shahneshin
Phone: (98) 21 88300570
Fax: (98) 21 88824174
Sales Dep.: Mr. Ghaffari
Phone: (98) 21 88822552
Fax: (98) 21 88824174
Mill Locations:
Kaveh Paper Industries Co., Saveh Mill, 7th St., Kaveh Industrial City, 39131 Saveh, Iran, Capacity: 25,000 mt/y, (Paper mill, Paperboard mill)
Phone: (98) 21 8823477/30585/34266/23477
Fax: (98) 21 8824174
Email: kavehpaper@neda.net

⊛Kaveh Paper Industries Co.
Saveh Mill
7th St., Kaveh Industrial City
39131 Saveh, Markazi
Iran
Phone: (98) 21 8823477/30585/34266/23477
Fax: (98) 21 8824174
Email: kavehpaper@neda.net
Web Address: www.kavehpaper.co.ir
Personnel:
Mill Mgr.: Mohammad hossein Saffar
Phone: (98) 21 8823477/30585/34266/23477
Mgr.: Zangene Nejad
Phone: (98) 2188841532
Fax: (98) 255 2343008
Total Employees at this Location: 100
Type of Operation: Paper mill, Paperboard mill
Pulp Grades and Capacities:
Total pulp capacity: 25,491 mt/y
Recycled Pulping: 25,491 mt/y
Pulp Mill Data:
Recycled Fiber Treatment Lines:
Recycled packaging pulping lines: 1
Paper/Paperboard Grades and Capacities:
Total paper and paperboard capacity: 25,000 mt/y
Linerboard: 15,000 mt/y
Boxboard/cartonboard: 10,000 mt/y
Paper and Paperboard Mill Data:
Paper Machines: 2
No. 1, fourdrinier, total capacity 10,000 mt/y, Trim width 2 m, Boxboard/cartonboard
No. 2, fourdrinier, total capacity 15,000 mt/y, Trim width 2 m, Linerboard
Energy Data:
Power boilers
Electrical demand for mill: 36 MWh/D

⊕Latif Paper Co.
Ownership: 100% by Social Security Service Organization
No 11-15th (Shahid Ahmadian) St.- Bokharest , (Ahmad ghasir) Ave.-Argentina Sq
1513814311 Tehran
Iran
Phone: (98) 21 8855 2088/3066/3077
Fax: (98) 21 88552077
Web Address: www.latifpaper.com
Mill Locations:
Harir Khuzestan Tissue Co., Haft-Tappeh, Shoosh Mill, Haft-Tappeh, Shoosh, Iran, Capacity: 10,000 mt/y, (Pulp mill, Paper mill)
Phone: (98) 642234 3331/2
Fax: (98) 642234 3330
Email: info@harirpaperco.com
Latif Paper Products Co., Hashtgerd Mill, Km. 70th of Tehran-Qazvin Rd., Hashtgerd, Iran, Capacity: 21,000 mt/y, (Paper mill)
Phone: (98) 2697 6761
Fax: (98) 2697 2006

⊛Latif Paper Products Co.
Hashtgerd Mill
Ownership: Latif Paper Co.
Km. 70th of Tehran-Qazvin Rd.
Hashtgerd, Markazi
Iran
Phone: (98) 2697 6761
Fax: (98) 2697 2006
Personnel:
Chmn.: Mr. H. Azizi
Phone: (98) 2697 6761
Man. Dir.: S. A. Mirmohammadsadeghi
Phone: (98) 2697 6761
VP/Dpty. Man. Dir.: M. Moazenchi
Phone: (98) 2697 6761
Finan. Mgr.: M.J. Moetamedimehr
Phone: (98) 2697 6761
Prod. Mgr.: J. Pishvaei
Phone: (98) 2697 6761
Mgr.: Morteza Dadashi
Phone: (98) 2697 6761
Tech. Advisor: J. Pishaie
Phone: (98) 2697 6761
Total Employees at this Location: 80
Type of Operation: Paper mill
Pulp Grades and Capacities:
Total pulp capacity: 6,731 mt/y
Recycled Pulping: 6,731 mt/y
Pulp Mill Data:
Recycled Fiber Treatment Lines:
Flotation deinking lines: 1
Paper/Paperboard Grades and Capacities:
Total paper and paperboard capacity: 21,000 mt/y
Tissue: 21,000 mt/y
Paper and Paperboard Mill Data:
Paper Machines: 1
No. 1, crescent former, Yankee dryer, total capacity 21,000 mt/y, Trim width 2.74 m, Tissue, Uncoated woodfree/freesheet
Energy Data:
Power boilers: 2
Electrical demand for mill: 63 MWh/D

⊕Maragheh Paper Industries Company (M.P.I.C)
No.1, Mir Emad 10, Motahari St.
Tehran
Iran
Mailing Address: P.O. Box 15875-5956, Tehran, Iran
Phone: (98) 21 88750756
Fax: (98) 21 88750758
Email: info@mpic.ir
Personnel:
R&D Mgr.: Omid Ramezani
Phone: (98) 21 88750756
Fax: (98) 21 88750758
Mill Locations:
Maragheh Paper Industries Company (M.P.I.C), Maragheh Mill, No 1, 10th Street, Miremad Avenue,

Maragheh, Iran, Capacity: 60,000 mt/y, (Pulp mill, Paper mill)
Phone: (98) 21 88754528/0756
Fax: (98) 21 88750758
Email: info@mpic.ir

ⓜMaragheh Paper Industries Company (M.P.I.C)
Maragheh Mill
No 1, 10th Street, Miremad Avenue
Maragheh, East Azerbaijan
Iran
Phone: (98) 21 88754528/0756
Fax: (98) 21 88750758
Email: info@mpic.ir
Web Address: www.mpic.ir
Personnel:
Pres. & Dir.: Shapour Kouhzadi
Phone: (98) 88503707
Comm. Dir.: A. F. Jahromi
Phone: (98) 21 88754528/0756
Total Employees at this Location: 352
Type of Operation: Pulp mill, Paper mill
Pulp Grades and Capacities:
Total pulp capacity: 37,125 mt/y
Mechanical Pulp: 37,125 mt/y

Pulp Mill Data:
Mechanical Pulping Systems:
BCTMP systems: 1
Pulp Lines: 1
Bleach Plant Systems: 1
Mechanical Pulping System, Sequence: P
Paper/Paperboard Grades and Capacities:
Total paper and paperboard capacity: 60,000 mt/y
Uncoated mechanical/groundwood: 30,000 mt/y
Coated mechanical/groundwood: 30,000 mt/y
Paper and Paperboard Mill Data:
Paper Machines: 1
No. 1, fourdrinier, total capacity 60,000 mt/y, Trim width 3.5 m, Uncoated mechanical/groundwood, Coated mechanical/groundwood
Coating Machines: 2
PM 1, off machine
PM 1, off machine
Finishing Equipment:
Sheeters
Energy Data:
Electrical demand for mill: 260 MWh/D

ⓜMashad Carton
Mashhad Mill
18th Km of Ghoochan Rd
Mashhad, Khorsan
Iran
Mailing Address: P.O.Box 91375/4361, Mashhad, Khorsan, Iran
Phone: (98) 51 620262-5
Fax: (98) 51 620267
Email: Info@cartonmashhadco.com
Web Address: www.cartonmashhadco.com
Personnel:
Man. Dir.: Hossein Matin Rad
Phone: (98) 51 620262-5
Total Employees at this Location: 40
Type of Operation: Paperboard mill
Pulp Grades and Capacities:
Total pulp capacity: 10,179 mt/y
Recycled Pulping: 10,179 mt/y

Pulp Mill Data:
Recycled Fiber Treatment Lines:
Recycled packaging pulping lines: 1
Paper/Paperboard Grades and Capacities:
Total paper and paperboard capacity: 10,000 mt/y
Linerboard: 10,000 mt/y
Paper and Paperboard Mill Data:
Paper Machines: 1
No. 1, fourdrinier, total capacity 10,000 mt/y, Trim width 2 m, Linerboard

Energy Data:
Power boilers
Electrical demand for mill: 14 MWh/D

ⓜMashad Carton
18th Km of Ghoochan Rd
Mashhad
Iran
Mailing Address: P.O.Box 91375/4361, Mashhad
Phone: (98) 51 620262-5
Fax: (98) 51 620267
Email: Info@cartonmashhadco.com
Web Address: www.cartonmashhadco.com
Personnel:
Man. Dir.: Hossein Matin Rad
Phone: (98) 51 620262-5
Fax: (98) 51 620267
Mill Locations:
Mashad Carton, Mashhad Mill, 18th Km of Ghoochan Rd, Mashhad, Iran, Capacity: 10,000 mt/y, (Paperboard mill)
Phone: (98) 51 620262-5
Fax: (98) 51 620267
Email: Info@cartonmashhadco.com

ⓜMazandaran Wood & Industries (MWPI)
Ownership: 58.06% by Bank Melli, Iran, 41.94% by Civil Retirement ORG, Social Security ORG
No. 32 Shahid Ghanbari St. Syyed Jamaledin Asad Abadi Ave.
14337 Tehran
Iran
Phone: (98) 21 88727009
Fax: (98) 21 88712378
Email: mwpi@mazpaper.com
Web Address: www.mazpaper.com
Personnel:
Chmn.: A. Kazazi
Phone: (98) 21 88727009
Fax: (98) 21 88712378
Advisor: P. Arjmand
Phone: (98) 21 88727009
Fax: (98) 21 88712378
Man. Dir.: M. Mahdi Aslani
Phone: (98) 151 3882001 2019
Email: m.d@mazpaper.com
Finan. Dir.: H. H. Zarei
Phone: (98) 21 88727009
Fax: (98) 21 88712378
PR Mgr.: A. H. Pourzand
Phone: (98) 21 88727009
Fax: (98) 21 88712378
Commer. Mgr.: D. A. Sadjadi
Phone: (98) 21 88727009
Fax: (98) 21 88712378
Total Employees of Company: 1,807
Total Employees at this Location: 57
Mill Locations:
Mazandaran Wood & Paper Industries Co., Sari Mill, Km. 12th of Semnan-Sari Rd., PO Box 311, Sari, Iran, Capacity: 175,000 mt/y, (Pulp mill, Paper mill, Paperboard mill)
Phone: (98) 151 388 2202
Fax: (98) 151 388 2020
Email: mwpi@mazpaper.com

ⓜMazandaran Wood & Paper Industries Co.
Sari Mill
Ownership: Mazandaran Wood & Industries (MWPI)
Km. 12th of Semnan-Sari Rd., PO Box 311
Sari, Mazandaran
Iran
Phone: (98) 151 388 2202
Fax: (98) 151 388 2020
Email: mwpi@mazpaper.com
Web Address: www.mazpaper.com

Personnel:
Man. Dir.: Eng. M. Mahdi Aslani
Phone: (98) 151 3882001 2019
Pulp Mill Supt.: Mr. V. Mehdipour
Phone: (98) 152 388 2138
Fax: (98) 152 388 2020
Email: mwpi@mazpaper.com
Paper Mill Supt.: Mr. A. Barzan
Phone: (98) 151 388 2632
Fax: (98) 151 388 2020
Email: mwpi_alibarzan@yahoo.com
Mill Mgr.: H. Khajevand
Phone: (98) 151 388 2202
PR Mgr.: A. H. Pourzand
Phone: (98) 151 388 2202
Total Employees at this Location: 1,750
Type of Operation: Pulp mill, Paper mill, Paperboard mill
Pulp Grades and Capacities:
Total pulp capacity: 172,265 mt/y
Chemical Pulp: 81,870 mt/y
Mechanical Pulp: 85,302 mt/y
Recycled Pulping: 5,093 mt/y

Pulp Mill Data:
Chemical Pulping Systems:
Continuous digesters: 2
Mechanical Pulping Systems:
Conventional grinders: 8
Pulp Lines: 2
Bleach Plant Systems: 1
No. 1, Sequence: C, Capacity 102,300 admt/y
Chemical Recovery Equipment:
Evaporator lines: 6
Recovery boilers: 1
Recycled Fiber Treatment Lines:
Pulpers: 3
Paper/Paperboard Grades and Capacities:
Total paper and paperboard capacity: 175,000 mt/y
Newsprint: 54,000 mt/y
Uncoated mechanical/groundwood: 31,000 mt/y
Coated mechanical/groundwood: 5,000 mt/y
Linerboard: 10,000 mt/y
Corrugating medium/fluting: 75,000 mt/y
Paper and Paperboard Mill Data:
Stock Preparation:
Pulpers: 8
Refiners: 8
Paper Machines: 2
No. 1, DuoFormer, total capacity 90,000 mt/y, Trim width 6 m, Newsprint, Uncoated mechanical/groundwood, Coated mechanical/groundwood
No. 2, fourdrinier, total capacity 85,000 mt/y, Trim width 4 m, Corrugating medium/fluting, Linerboard
Finishing Equipment:
Winders: 2 at 175,000 mt/y
Calenders: 1
Rewinders: 1 at 5,500 mt/y
Sheeters: 1
Energy Data:
Power boilers: 1
Electrical demand for mill: 576 MWh/D

ⓞⓜNovzohour Co. Ltd.
Tehran Mill
Abad Karaj old road, 17th Shahrivar Street
13786 Tehran
Iran
Mailing Address: PO Box 13185-587, Tehran, Iran
Phone: (98) 21 6802081-3
Fax: (98) 21 6802085
Email: info@novzohour.com
Web Address: www.novzohour.com
Personnel:
Chmn.: M. Daneshbodi
Phone: (98) 21 6802081-3
Man. Dir.: Sadegh Mohamadi
Phone: (98) 21 6802081-3
Man. Dir.: Mr. Soltan-Zadeh
Phone: (98) 21 6802081-3

Israel

Mill Mgr.: R. Ferdowsi
Phone: (98) 21 6802081-3
Chief Eng.: A. Haidari
Phone: (98) 21 6802081-3
Purch. Agent: Gh. Kia
Phone: (98) 21 6802081-3
Converting Plant Mgr.: I. Golrokh
Phone: (98) 21 6802081-3
Asst. Mill Mgr.: A. Maleki
Phone: (98) 21 6802081-3
Tech. Mgr.: A. Mahboubi
Phone: (98) 21 6802081-3
Type of Operation: Paper mill
Paper/Paperboard Grades and Capacities:
Total paper and paperboard capacity: 5,000 mt/y
Tissue: 5,000 mt/y
Paper and Paperboard Mill Data:
Stock Preparation:
Pulpers: 1
Refiners: 2
Paper Machines: 1
No. 1, fourdrinier, total capacity 5,000 mt/y, Tissue
Finishing Equipment:
Rewinders: 1

ⓘPars Paper Industrial Group
No. 7, 2nd Alley, Ahmad Ghassir St., Dr. Beheshti Ave
15146 Tehran
Iran
Mailing Address: P.O. Box 13145 – 538, Tehran, Iran
Phone: (98) 21 88735434/5605/7284
Fax: (98) 21 88738106
Email: parspaper@neda.net
Personnel:
Man. Dir.: J. M. Jazayeri
Phone: (98) 21 88735434/5605/7284
Fax: (98) 21 88738106
Dpty. Man. Dir.: A. H. Mohammadi
Phone: (98) 21 88735434/5605/7284
Fax: (98) 21 88738106
Finan. Mgr.: S. Shojaei
Phone: (98) 21 88735434/5605/7284
Fax: (98) 21 88738106
Commer. Dir.: Abdulhamid Adibi
Phone: (98) 21 88738106
Total Employees of Company: 1,700
Mill Locations:
Pars Paper Industrial Group, Ahwaz Mill, Haft Tappeh, Shoush Danial, Ahwaz, Iran, Capacity: 115,000 mt/y, (Pulp mill, Paper mill)
Phone: (98) 64 22 34 3340/4262
Fax: (98) 64 22 34 23 11
Email: parspaper@neda.net

ⓜPars Paper Industrial Group
Ahwaz Mill
Haft Tappeh, Shoush Danial
Ahwaz, Khuzestan
Iran
Phone: (98) 64 22 34 3340/4262
Fax: (98) 64 22 34 23 11
Email: parspaper@neda.net
Personnel:
Mill Mgr.: Abdullah Mohammadi
Phone: (98) 64 22 34 23 10
Fax: (98) 64 22 34 23 11
Eng. Mgr.: R. Motaghirad
Phone: (98) 64 22 34 3340/4262
Qlty Mgr.: Mr. Safizade
Phone: (98) 64 22 34 42 47
Commer. Dir.: Abdulhamid Adibi
Phone: (98) 64 22 34 3340/4262
Fax: (98) 21 88738106
Total Employees at this Location: 400
Type of Operation: Pulp mill, Paper mill
Pulp Grades and Capacities:
Total pulp capacity: 70,029 mt/y
Other Pulp: 70,029 mt/y
Pulp Mill Data:
Chemical Pulping Systems:
Continuous digesters: 2
Bleach Plant Systems: 2
No. 1, Sequence: CEH, Capacity 23,000 admt/y
Chemical Recovery Equipment:
Evaporator lines: 1
Recovery boilers: 1
Paper/Paperboard Grades and Capacities:
Total paper and paperboard capacity: 115,000 mt/y
Uncoated woodfree/freesheet: 115,000 mt/y
Paper and Paperboard Mill Data:
Stock Preparation:
Pulpers: 2
Refiners: 12
Paper Machines: 3
No. 1, fourdrinier, total capacity 35,000 mt/y, Trim width 3.8 m, Uncoated woodfree/freesheet
No. 2, fourdrinier, total capacity 40,000 mt/y, Trim width 3.7 m, Uncoated woodfree/freesheet
No. 3, fourdrinier, total capacity 40,000 mt/y, Trim width 3.7 m, Uncoated woodfree/freesheet
Finishing Equipment:
Rewinders: 2
Sheeters: 7
Energy Data:
Power boilers: 6
Steam turbines: 1
Electrical demand for mill: 338 MWh/D

ⓘSagheh Cellulose Iran Industrial Company (P.J.S.)
Heydarieh Industrial Zone, 18th KM of Takestan, Zanjan Rd.
Takestan
Iran
Phone: (98) 21 55682203/4/5
Fax: (98) 21 55682203/4/5
Email: daftar.sagheh@yahoo.com
Web Address: sci-paper.com
Mill Locations:
Sagheh Cellulose Iran Industrial Company (P.J.S.), Takestan Mill, Heydarieh Industrial Zone, 18th KM of Takestan, Zanjan Rd., Takestan, Iran, Capacity: 10,000 mt/y, (Paperboard mill)
Phone: (98) 21 55682203/4/5
Fax: (98) 21 55682203/4/5
Email: daftar.sagheh@yahoo.com

ⓜSagheh Cellulose Iran Industrial Company (P.J.S.)
Takestan Mill
Heydarieh Industrial Zone, 18th KM of Takestan, Zanjan Rd.
Takestan, Qazvin
Iran
Phone: (98) 21 55682203/4/5
Fax: (98) 21 55682203/4/5
Email: daftar.sagheh@yahoo.com
Web Address: sci-paper.com
Total Employees at this Location: 40
Type of Operation: Paperboard mill
Pulp Grades and Capacities:
Total pulp capacity: 10,026 mt/y
Recycled Pulping: 10,026 mt/y
Pulp Mill Data:
Recycled Fiber Treatment Lines:
Recycled packaging pulping lines: 1
Paper/Paperboard Grades and Capacities:
Total paper and paperboard capacity: 10,000 mt/y
Corrugating medium/fluting: 10,000 mt/y
Paper and Paperboard Mill Data:
Paper Machines: 1
No. 1, fourdrinier, total capacity 10,000 mt/y, Trim width 2.2 m, Corrugating medium/fluting
Energy Data:
Power boilers
Electrical demand for mill: 14 MWh/D

ISRAEL

ⓘⓜHadera Paper Industries Ltd.
Hadera Mill
Ownership: 100% by Hadera Paper Ltd
Meizer St., P.O. Box 142, Industrial Zone
IL - 38101 Hadera
Israel
Mailing Address: PO Box 142, 38101 Hadera, Israel
Phone: (972) 4 6349 349
Fax: (972) 4 6339 740
Email: hq@aipm.co.il
Web Address: www.hadera-paper.co.il
Personnel:
Group CEO: Ofer Bloch
Phone: (972) 4 6349 333
Fax: (972) 4 6336 798
Chmn. of Board: Johanan Locker
Phone: (972) 4 6349 333
Fax: (972) 4 6336 798
CFO & Bus. Dev. Off.: Shaul Gliksberg
Phone: (972) 4 6349 333
Fax: (972) 4 6336 798
COO, Gen. Mgr. of Hadera Paper - Development & Infrastructure: Gideon Lieberman
Phone: (972) 4 6349 333
Fax: (972) 4 6336 798
CEO of Hadera Paper Packaging & Recycling and Gen. Mgr of Hadera Paper Packaging & Recycling: Gur Ben-David
Phone: (972) 4 6349 333
Fax: (972) 4 6336 798
Total Employees of Company: 3,300
Total Employees at this Location: 800
Type of Operation: Paper mill, Paperboard mill
Mill Locations:
Hadera Paper-Printing & Writing Paper Ltd, Hadera Mill, Meizerstreet, Industrial Zone, PO Box 142, 38101 Hadera, Israel, Capacity: 145,000 mt/y, (Paper mill)
Phone: (972) 4 6349551
Fax: (972) 4 6346602
Pulp Grades and Capacities:
Total pulp capacity: 329,340 mt/y
Recycled Pulping: 329,340 mt/y
Pulp Mill Data:
Bleach Plant Systems: 1
Recycled Pulping System
Recycled Fiber Treatment Lines:
Flotation deinking lines: 1
Recycled packaging pulping lines: 1
Paper/Paperboard Grades and Capacities:
Total paper and paperboard capacity: 330,000 mt/y
Linerboard: 180,000 mt/y
Corrugating medium/fluting: 140,000 mt/y
Boxboard/cartonboard: 10,000 mt/y
Paper and Paperboard Mill Data:
Stock Preparation:
Pulpers: 7
Refiners: 10
Paper Machines: 2
No. 6, fourdrinier (2), total capacity 100,000 mt/y, Trim width 3.3 m, Boxboard/cartonboard, Corrugating medium/fluting, Linerboard
No. 8, DuoFormer Base, total capacity 230,000 mt/y, Trim width 6.05 m, Corrugating medium/fluting, Linerboard
Coating Machines: 1
No. 1, total capacity 10,000 mt/y., off machine
Finishing Equipment:
Supercalenders: 1
Rewinders: 3
Sheeters: 6 at 25,000 mt/y
Energy Data:
Power boilers: 2
Steam turbines: 1 at 26 MW
Electrical demand for mill: 462 MWh/D

Israel

ⓘHogla-Kimberly Ltd.
Ownership: 50.10% by Kimberly-Clark Corp., 49.90% by Hadera Paper Ltd.
TLV Ramle Rd, Zrifin
72101 Ramle
Israel
Mailing Address: PO Box 231, 72101 Ramle, Israel
  Phone: (972) 8 9772707
  Fax: (972) 8 9772895
  Email: HQ@aipm.co.il
  Web Address: www.aipm.co.il
Personnel:
  Gen. Mgr.: Arik Schor
  Phone: (972) 8 9772707
  Fax: (972) 8 9772895
  Naharya Paper Mill Mgr.: Ofer Lux
  Phone: (972) 8 9772707
  Fax: (972) 8 9772895
Total Employees of Company: 1,000
Total Employees at this Location: 400
Mill Locations:
  Hogla-Kimberly Ltd., Hadera Mill, 4 Myzer Street, Industrial Zone Hadera, 38101 Hadera, Israel, Capacity: 31,000 mt/y, (Paper mill)
  Phone: (972) 4 634 9232
  Fax: (972) 4 632 6761
  Hogla-Kimberly Ltd., Naharya Mill, Industrial Zone PO Box 313, 46101 Naharya, Israel, Capacity: 26,000 mt/y, (Paper mill)
  Phone: (972) 4 9106100
  Fax: (972) 4 9823255

ⓜHogla-Kimberly Ltd.
Hadera Mill
Ownership: 50.10% by Kimberly-Clark Corp.
4 Myzer Street, Industrial Zone Hadera
38101 Hadera
Israel
Mailing Address: PO Box 142, 38101 Hadera, Israel
  Phone: (972) 4 634 9232
  Fax: (972) 4 632 6761
  Web Address: www.aipm.co.il
Personnel:
  Mill Mgr.: Guy Shubinsky
  Phone: (972) 4 634 9566
  Email: guy.shubinsky@hogla-kimberly.co.il
Total Employees at this Location: 800
Type of Operation: Paper mill
Pulp Grades and Capacities:
  Total pulp capacity: 25,200 mt/y
  Recycled Pulping: 25,200 mt/y
Pulp Mill Data:
  Recycled Fiber Treatment Lines:
  Flotation deinking lines: 1
Paper/Paperboard Grades and Capacities:
  Total paper and paperboard capacity: 31,000 mt/y
  Tissue: 31,000 mt/y
Paper and Paperboard Mill Data:
Paper Machines: 1
  No. 3, crescent former, Yankee dryer, total capacity 31,000 mt/y, Trim width 3.3 m, Tissue
Energy Data:
  Power boilers
  Combustion turbines
  Steam turbines
  Electrical demand for mill: 103 MWh/D

ⓜHogla-Kimberly Ltd.
Naharya Mill
Ownership: 50.10% by Kimberly-Clark Corp.
Industrial Zone PO Box 313
46101 Naharya
Israel
  Phone: (972) 4 9106100
  Fax: (972) 4 9823255
  Web Address: www.aipm.co.il
Personnel:
  Mill Mgr.: Mr Goldman
  Phone: (972) 4 9106106
Total Employees at this Location: 100
Type of Operation: Paper mill
Pulp Grades and Capacities:
  Total pulp capacity: 27,637 mt/y
  Recycled Pulping: 27,637 mt/y
Pulp Mill Data:
  Recycled Fiber Treatment Lines:
  Flotation deinking lines: 1
Paper/Paperboard Grades and Capacities:
  Total paper and paperboard capacity: 26,000 mt/y
  Tissue: 26,000 mt/y
Paper and Paperboard Mill Data:
  Stock Preparation:
  Pulpers: 1
  Refiners: 2
Paper Machines: 1
  No. 1, crescent former, total capacity 26,000 mt/y, Trim width 2.66 m, Tissue
Finishing Equipment:
  Rewinders: 1
Energy Data:
  Power boilers: 1
  Electrical demand for mill: 84 MWh/D

ⓘⓜIsraPaper Paper Industries Ltd.
Netanya Mill
Ownership: 100% by private owner
Industrial Zone Kiriat Nordau PO Box 8121
42293 Netanya
Israel
  Phone: (972) 9 8651122
  Fax: (972) 9 8652255
  Email: yoel@israpaper.co.il
Personnel:
  Man. Dir.: Yoel Lichtman
  Phone: (972) 9 8651122
  Email: yoel@israpaper.co.il
  Sls./Mktg. Dir.: Yoel Lichtman
  Phone: (972) 9 8651122
  Tech. Mgr.: Gregory Rabinovitch
  Phone: (972) 9 8651122
Total Employees at this Location: 100
Type of Operation: Paper mill
Pulp Grades and Capacities:
  Total pulp capacity: 1,200 mt/y
  Chemical Pulp: 1,200 mt/y
Paper/Paperboard Grades and Capacities:
  Total paper and paperboard capacity: 10,000 mt/y
  Tissue: 10,000 mt/y
Paper and Paperboard Mill Data:
  Stock Preparation:
  Pulpers: 1
  Refiners: 2
Paper Machines: 1
  No. 1, fourdrinier, Yankee dryer, total capacity 10,000 mt/y, Trim width 2.6 m, Tissue
Energy Data:
  Power boilers: 1

ⓘⓜJerusalem White Paper & Neeman (2000) Ltd
Kiryat Gat Mill
Ownership: 100% by private owner
35/1 Israel Pollak Street
82025 Kiryat Gat
Israel
Mailing Address: POB 6, 82000 Kiryat Gat, Israel
  Phone: (972) 8 6811 263
  Fax: (972) 8 6811 677
Total Employees at this Location: 40
Type of Operation: Paper mill
Paper/Paperboard Grades and Capacities:
  Total paper and paperboard capacity: 4,000 mt/y
  Tissue: 3,000 mt/y
Paper and Paperboard Mill Data:
  Stock Preparation:
  Pulpers: 2
Paper Machines: 1
  No. 1, Trim width 2.2 m, Tissue
Energy Data:
  Power boilers: 1

ⓜHadera Paper-Printing & Writing Paper Ltd
Hadera Mill
Ownership: 100% by Hadera Paper Ltd
Meizerstreet, Industrial Zone, PO Box 142
38101 Hadera
Israel
  Phone: (972) 4 6349551
  Fax: (972) 4 6346602
  Web Address: www.hadera-paper.co.il/en/mondi-hadera-paper
Personnel:
  CEO: Avner Solel
  Phone: (972) 4 6349 554
  Fax: (972) 73 245 3144
  Email: avner.solel@haderapaper.co.il
  CFO: David Muhlgay
  Phone: (972) 4 6349 201
  Fax: (972) 4 6346 608
  Email: david.muhlgay@haderapaper.co.il
  Paper Mill Mgr.: Yehonathan Roash
  Phone: (972) 4 6369 412
  Fax: (972) 4 6349 253
  Email: yehonathan.roash@haderapaper.co.il
  Prod. Mgr.: Doron Benizri
  Phone: (972) 4 6349 477
  Fax: (972) 4 6349 253
  Email: doron.benizri@haderapaper.co.il
  Tech. Eng.: Stalina Dzubu
  Phone: (972) 4 6349 481
  Fax: (972) 4 6349 253
  Email: stalina.dzubu@haderapaper.co.il
  Export & Procurement Dir.: Micky Pinkas
  Phone: (972) 4 6349496
  Fax: (972) 4 6346602
  Email: micky.pinkas@haderapaper.co.il
Total Employees at this Location: 310
Type of Operation: Paper mill
Paper/Paperboard Grades and Capacities:
  Total paper and paperboard capacity: 145,000 mt/y
  Uncoated woodfree/freesheet: 145,000 mt/y
Paper and Paperboard Mill Data:
  Stock Preparation:
  Pulpers: 3
  Refiners: 7
Paper Machines: 1
  No. 7, hybrid former, total capacity 145,000 mt/y, Trim width 5.2 m, Uncoated woodfree/freesheet
Finishing Equipment:
  Supercalenders: 1 at 12,000 mt/y
  Rewinders: 2 at 15,000 mt/y
  Sheeters: 4 at 96,000 mt/y
Energy Data:
  Power boilers: 2
  Steam turbines: 2 at 8, 18 MW
  Electrical demand for mill: 285 MWh/D

ⓘShaniv Paper Industries Ltd.
11 Odem St.
49517 Petach Tikva
Israel
  Phone: (972) 3 89908230
  Email: info@shaniv.com
  Web Address: www.shaniv.com
Personnel:
  Chmn. of the Board: Abraham Bernat
  Phone: (972) 3 5750893
  CEO: Pesach Bernat
  Phone: (972) 3 89908230
  COO: Avi Hayun
  Phone: (972) 3 89908230
  Email: avi.h@shaniv.com
  Sls. Mgr.: Yeuda Ass
  Phone: (972) 3 89908230

Japan

Total Employees of Company: 166
Total Employees at this Location: 5
Mill Locations:
Shaniv Paper Industries Ltd., Ofakim Paper Mill, Bezalel 7 St, Industrial Zone, 80300 Ofakim, Israel, Capacity: 42,080 mt/y, (Paper mill)
Phone: (972) 899 22 555/3 5244596
Fax: (972) 899 22 577/3 5246486
Email: info@Shaniv.com

ⓜShaniv Paper Industries Ltd.
Ofakim Paper Mill
Bezalel 7 St, Industrial Zone
80300 Ofakim
Israel
Phone: (972) 899 22 555/3 5244596
Fax: (972) 899 22 577/3 5246486
Email: info@Shaniv.com
Web Address: www.shaniv.com
Personnel:
CEO: Pesach Bernat
Phone: (972) 899 22 555/3 5244596
Mill Mgr.: Avi Hayun
Phone: (972) 899 22 555/3 5244596
Man. Dir.: Israel Cafri
Phone: (972) 899 22 555/3 5244596
Plant Eng.: Shmuel Factorowitz
Phone: (972) 899 22 573/555
Total Employees at this Location: 130
Type of Operation: Paper mill
Pulp Grades and Capacities:
Total pulp capacity: 30,187 mt/y
Recycled Pulping: 30,187 mt/y
Pulp Mill Data:
Recycled Fiber Treatment Lines:
Flotation deinking lines: 1
Paper/Paperboard Grades and Capacities:
Total paper and paperboard capacity: 42,080 mt/y
Tissue: 42,080 mt/y
Paper and Paperboard Mill Data:
Stock Preparation:
Pulpers: 2
Refiners: 4
Paper Machines: 2
No. 1, crescent former, Yankee dryer, total capacity 19,004 mt/y, Trim width 2.7 m, Tissue
No. 2, crescent former, Yankee dryer, total capacity 23,076 mt/y, Trim width 2.8 m, Tissue, Uncoated woodfree/freesheet
Finishing Equipment:
Rewinders: 1
Energy Data:
Power boilers: 2
Electrical demand for mill: 157 MWh/D

JAPAN

ⓕⓜKoryo Seishi K.K.
Fuji Mill
Ownership: Omiya Seishi Co., Ltd.
329 Nonaka-cho
Fuji, Shizuoka Pref.
Japan
Phone: (81) 544 234-521
Fax: (81) 544 234-637
Web Address: www.omiyaseishi.co.jp
Total Employees at this Location: 40
Type of Operation: Paper mill
Pulp Grades and Capacities:
Total pulp capacity: 14,052 mt/y
Recycled Pulping: 14,052 mt/y
Pulp Mill Data:
Recycled Fiber Treatment Lines:
Flotation deinking lines
Paper/Paperboard Grades and Capacities:
Total paper and paperboard capacity: 13,000 mt/y
Tissue: 13,000 mt/y
Paper and Paperboard Mill Data:
Paper Machines: 4
No. 1, Yankee dryer, total capacity 3,000 mt/y, Trim width 1.78 m, Tissue
No. 2, Yankee dryer, total capacity 3,000 mt/y, Trim width 1.78 m, Tissue
No. 3, Yankee dryer, total capacity 3,000 mt/y, Trim width 1.78 m, Tissue
No. 4, Yankee dryer, total capacity 4,000 mt/y, Trim width 2.59 m, Tissue
Energy Data:
Power boilers
Electrical demand for mill: 44 MWh/D

ⓕⓜAthena Paper Manufacturing Co., Ltd.
Okayama Mill
Minami-ku Ofuku 721
Okayama-shi, Okayama Pref., 701-0204
Japan
Phone: (81) 862 82 0251
Fax: (81) 862 82 1859
Email: info@athenapaper.com
Web Address: www.athenapaper.com
Personnel:
Pres.: Tomio Hatta
Phone: (81) 862 82 0251
Total Employees of Company: 39
Total Employees at this Location: 39
Type of Operation: Paperboard mill
Pulp Grades and Capacities:
Total pulp capacity: 38,327 mt/y
Recycled Pulping: 38,327 mt/y
Pulp Mill Data:
Recycled Fiber Treatment Lines:
Recycled packaging pulping lines: 1 at 19,800 admt/y
Paper/Paperboard Grades and Capacities:
Total paper and paperboard capacity: 40,000 mt/y
Boxboard/cartonboard: 40,000 mt/y
Paper and Paperboard Mill Data:
Stock Preparation:
Pulpers: 3
Refiners: 6
Paper Machines: 2
No. 1, cylinder, total capacity 15,000 mt/y, Trim width 1.73 m, Boxboard/cartonboard
No. 2, cylinder, total capacity 25,000 mt/y, Trim width 1.73 m, Boxboard/cartonboard
Coating Machines: 1
No. 1, total capacity 25,884 mt/y., on machine
Finishing Equipment:
Sheeters: 2
Energy Data:
Power boilers: 1
Electrical demand for mill: 62 MWh/D

ⓕAwa Paper Manufacturing Co., Ltd.
3-10-18, Minami-yaso-cho
Tokushima-shi, Tokushima Pref., 770-0005
Japan
Phone: (81) 88 631 8100
Fax: (81) 88 632 5951
Email: info@awapaper.co.jp
Web Address: www.awapaper.co.jp
Personnel:
Pres.: Yasuhiro Miki
Phone: (81) 88 631 8108
Fax: (81) 88 632 2076
Man. Dir./Gen. Prod. Mgr.: Seiichi Yoshioka
Phone: (81) 88 631 8108
Fax: (81) 88 632 2076
Dir./ GM Affairs: Takeyoshi Sano
Phone: (81) 88 631 8108
Fax: (81) 88 632 2076
Dir./Gen. Mgr. Techn. Div.: Fujihiko Miki
Phone: (81) 88 631 8108
Fax: (81) 88 632 2076
Total Employees of Company: 415
Mill Locations:
Awa Paper Manufacturing Co., Ltd., Anan Mill, 72-3 Shinhama, Tsunomine-cho, Anan-shi 774-0021, Japan, Capacity: 3,000 mt/y, (Paper mill)
Phone: (81) 884 27 3132
Fax: (81) 884 27 3134
Email: info@awapaper.co.jp
Awa Paper Manufacturing Co., Ltd., Tokushima Mill, 3-10-18 Minami-yaso-cho, Tokushima 770-0005, Japan, Capacity: 10,000 mt/y, (Paper mill)
Phone: (81) 88 631 8108
Fax: (81) 88 632 2076
Email: info@awapaper.co.jp

ⓜAwa Paper Manufacturing Co., Ltd.
Anan Mill
72-3 Shinhama, Tsunomine-cho
Anan-shi, Tokushima Pref., 774-0021
Japan
Phone: (81) 884 27 3132
Fax: (81) 884 27 3134
Email: info@awapaper.co.jp
Web Address: www.awapaper.co.jp
Personnel:
Mill Mgr.: Nobuo Matsumura
Phone: (81) 884 27 3132
Type of Operation: Paper mill
Paper/Paperboard Grades and Capacities:
Total paper and paperboard capacity: 3,000 mt/y
Specialty and industrial
Paper and Paperboard Mill Data:
Paper Machines: 2
PM 6, combination, Trim width 2.4 m, Specialty and industrial
PM 7, combination, Trim width 2.4 m, Specialty and industrial

ⓜAwa Paper Manufacturing Co., Ltd.
Tokushima Mill
3-10-18 Minami-yaso-cho
Tokushima, Tokushima Pref., 770-0005
Japan
Phone: (81) 88 631 8108
Fax: (81) 88 632 2076
Email: info@awapaper.co.jp
Web Address: www.awapaper.co.jp
Personnel:
Mill Mgr./Prod. Mgr.: Keiji Yamanaka
Phone: (81) 88 631 8108
Tech. Dev. Dir.: Takeyoshi Sano
Phone: (81) 88 631 8108
Type of Operation: Paper mill
Paper/Paperboard Grades and Capacities:
Total paper and paperboard capacity: 10,000 mt/y
Specialty and industrial
Paper and Paperboard Mill Data:
Paper Machines: 4
No. 2, fourdrinier, cylinder, Trim width 1.35 m, Specialty and industrial
No. 3, fourdrinier, Trim width 2 m, Specialty and industrial
No. 4, Tanmo, Trim width 1.65 m, Specialty and industrial
No. 5, fourdrinier, cylinder, Trim width 1.25 m, Specialty and industrial

ⓕⓜAzumi Filter Paper Co., Ltd.
Honsha Mill
4-2-15 Komatsu, Higashiyodogawa-ku
Osaka-shi, Osaka Pref., 533-0004
Japan
Phone: (81) 6 6327 5145
Fax: (81) 6 6328 0490
Email: gaikoku@azumi-filter.co.jp
Web Address: www.azumi-filter.co.jp
Personnel:
Chmn.: Jiro Azumi
Phone: (81) 6 6327 5145
Fax: (81) 6 6328 0490
Pres. & CEO: Satoro Azumi

Japan

Phone: (81) 6 6327 5145
Fax: (81) 6 6328 0490
Dir. / Advisor: Misao Azumi
Phone: (81) 6 6327 5145
Fax: (81) 6 6328 0492
Man. Dir.: Osamu Nakazawa
Phone: (81) 6 6327 5145
Fax: (81) 6 6328 0492
Total Employees of Company: 180
Total Employees at this Location: 180
Type of Operation: Paper mill
Paper/Paperboard Grades and Capacities:
Total paper and paperboard capacity: 4,200 mt/y
Specialty and industrial: 4,200 mt/y
Paper and Paperboard Mill Data:
Paper Machines: 2
No. 1, cylinder, Trim width 1.3 m, Specialty and industrial
No. 2, Tanmo, Trim width 1.3 m, Specialty and industrial
Coating Machines: 1
No. 1, total capacity 2,400 mt/y., off machine
Finishing Equipment:
Rewinders: 3

ⓞⓜBiwa Paper Mfg. Co., Ltd.
Nagahama-shi Mill
1636 Ochi-cho
Nagahama-shi, Shiga Pref., 526-0243
Japan
Phone: (81) 749 74 0353
Fax: (81) 749 74 0355
Personnel:
Pres.: Yasutoshi Inoguchi
Phone: (81) 749 74 0353
Total Employees at this Location: 29
Type of Operation: Paperboard mill
Paper/Paperboard Grades and Capacities:
Total paper and paperboard capacity: 7,800 mt/y
Boxboard/cartonboard: 7,800 mt/y
Paper and Paperboard Mill Data:
Paper Machines: 1
No. 3, cylinder, total capacity 7,800 mt/y, Trim width 2.2 m, Boxboard/cartonboard

ⓗChuetsu Pulp & Paper Co., Ltd.
10-6, Ginza 2-chome, Chuo-ku
Tokyo, 104-8124
Japan
Phone: (81) 3 3544 1524
Fax: (81) 3 5550 6201
Web Address: www.chuetsu-pulp.co.jp
Personnel:
Pres. & CEO (From 2014): Akiyoshi Kato
Phone: (81) 3 3544 1524/1522
Fax: (81) 3 5550 6201
Dir., Exec. Officer: Masafumi Harada
Phone: (81) 3 3544 1524/1522
Fax: (81) 3 5550 6201
Dir. Admin.: Hideharu Araya
Phone: (81) 3 3544 1524
Fax: (81) 3 5550 6201
Total Employees of Company: 828
Total Employees at this Location: 48
Mill Locations:
Chuetsu Pulp & Paper Co., Ltd., Takaoka (Futatsuka) Mill, 3288 Futatsuka, Takaoka-shi 933-8526, Japan, Capacity: 183,855 mt/y, (Pulp mill, Paper mill)
Phone: (81) 766 28 6600
Fax: (81) 766 28 6623
Chuetsu Pulp & Paper Co., Ltd., Takaoka (Nohmachi) Mill, 282, Yonejima, Takaoka-shi 933-8533, Japan, Capacity: 445,536 mt/y, (Pulp mill, Paper mill, Paperboard mill)
Phone: (81) 766 26 2401
Fax: (81) 766 27 0020
Chuetsu Pulp & Paper Co., Ltd., Sendai Mill, 1-26, Miyauchi-machi, Satsumasendai-shi 895-8540, Japan, Capacity: 324,513 mt/y, (Pulp mill, Paper mill)
Phone: (81) 99 622 2211
Fax: (81) 99 621 1157

ⓜChuetsu Pulp & Paper Co., Ltd.
Takaoka (Futatsuka) Mill
3288 Futatsuka
Takaoka-shi, Toyama Pref., 933-8526
Japan
Phone: (81) 766 28 6600
Fax: (81) 766 28 6623
Web Address: www.chuetsu-pulp.co.jp
Personnel:
Mill Mgr.: Shigezane Miyawaki
Phone: (81) 766 28 6600
Asst. Mill Mgr.: Takashi Kobayashi
Phone: (81) 766 28 6600
Asst. Mill Mgr.: Yutaka Haruyama
Phone: (81) 766 28 6600
Total Employees at this Location: 205
Type of Operation: Pulp mill, Paper mill
Pulp Grades and Capacities:
Total pulp capacity: 228,480 mt/y
Mechanical Pulp: 92,423 mt/y
Recycled Pulping: 136,057 mt/y
Pulp Mill Data:
Mechanical Pulping Systems:
Conventional grinders: 2
RMP systems: 2
TMP systems: 1
Bleach Plant Systems: 1
Recycled Pulping System, Type: Deinked
Recycled Fiber Treatment Lines:
Flotation deinking lines: 1
Paper/Paperboard Grades and Capacities:
Total paper and paperboard capacity: 183,855 mt/y
Newsprint: 183,855 mt/y
Paper and Paperboard Mill Data:
Stock Preparation:
Pulpers: 3
Refiners: 10
Paper Machines: 2
No. 2, twin-wire, total capacity 64,260 mt/y, Trim width 3.25 m, Newsprint
No. 3, Bel-Baie II, total capacity 169,575 mt/y, Trim width 6.5 m, Newsprint
Finishing Equipment:
Winders: 2
Rewinders: 3
Energy Data:
Power boilers: 2
TMP Reboiler
Steam turbines: 2 at 51.9 MW
Electrical demand for mill: 1,063 MWh/D

ⓜChuetsu Pulp & Paper Co., Ltd.
Takaoka (Nohmachi) Mill
282, Yonejima
Takaoka-shi, Toyama Pref., 933-8533
Japan
Phone: (81) 766 26 2401
Fax: (81) 766 27 0020
Web Address: www.chuetsu-pulp.co.jp
Personnel:
Dir./Mill Mgr.: Shigezane Miyawaki
Phone: (81) 766 26 2401
Man. Dir.: Takashi Kobayashi
Phone: (81) 766 26 2401
Man. Dir.: Yutaka Haruyama
Phone: (81) 766 26 2401
Total Employees at this Location: 403
Type of Operation: Pulp mill, Paper mill, Paperboard mill
Pulp Grades and Capacities:
Total pulp capacity: 445,457 mt/y
Pulp available for market: 149,226 mt/y
Chemical Pulp: 445,457 mt/y
Pulp Mill Data:
Chemical Pulping Systems:
Continuous digesters: 2
Pulp Lines: 2
Bleach Plant Systems: 2
No. 1, Sequence: CEDHD, Capacity 162,000 admt/y
No. 2, Sequence: C/DEoHD, Capacity 288,000 admt/y
Chemical Recovery Equipment:
Evaporator lines: 1
Recovery boilers: 3
Lime Kiln
Pulp Dryers:
Pulp Dryers 1
Paper/Paperboard Grades and Capacities:
Total paper and paperboard capacity: 445,536 mt/y
Uncoated woodfree/freesheet: 128,163 mt/y
Coated woodfree/freesheet: 172,074 mt/y
Packaging papers: 79,968 mt/y
Specialty and industrial: 20,349 mt/y
Boxboard/cartonboard: 44,982 mt/y
Paper and Paperboard Mill Data:
Paper Machines: 5
No. 1, total capacity 15,351 mt/y, Trim width 3.27 m, Specialty and industrial
No. 3, fourdrinier, total capacity 84,966 mt/y, Trim width 3.23 m, Packaging papers, Specialty and industrial
No. 5, Ultraformer, total capacity 44,982 mt/y, Trim width 1.68 m, Boxboard/cartonboard
No. 6, top former, total capacity 85,323 mt/y, Trim width 3.27 m, Uncoated woodfree/freesheet
N1, SymFormer, total capacity 214,914 mt/y, Trim width 5.6 m, Uncoated woodfree/freesheet, Coated woodfree/freesheet
Coating Machines: 1
No. 1, total capacity 252,700 mt/y, off machine
Finishing Equipment:
Winders: 5
Supercalenders: 2
Sheeters: 1
Energy Data:
Power boilers: 3
TMP Reboiler: 3
Steam turbines: 4 at 2.8, 7.8, 14, 46.1 MW
Electrical demand for mill: 1,675 MWh/D

ⓜChuetsu Pulp & Paper Co., Ltd.
Sendai Mill
1-26, Miyauchi-machi
Satsumasendai-shi, Kagoshima Pref., 895-8540
Japan
Phone: (81) 99 622 2211
Fax: (81) 99 621 1157
Web Address: www.chuetsu-pulp.co.jp
Personnel:
Mill Mgr., Dpty. sls. Mgr.: Toshiro Senhaku
Phone: (81) 99 622 2211
Fax: (81) 99 621 1157
Total Employees at this Location: 290
Type of Operation: Pulp mill, Paper mill
Pulp Grades and Capacities:
Total pulp capacity: 256,643 mt/y
Pulp available for market: 49,980 mt/y
Chemical Pulp: 226,893 mt/y
Recycled Pulping: 29,750 mt/y
Pulp Mill Data:
Chemical Pulping Systems:
Batch digesters: 7
Continuous digesters: 1
Pulp Lines: 2
Bleach Plant Systems: 2
Chemical Pulping System - Hardwood/Softwood, Type: ECF
Recycled Pulping System
Chemical Recovery Equipment:
Evaporator lines: 1
Recovery boilers: 2
Recovery boilers: 1
Lime Kiln
Recycled Fiber Treatment Lines:
Pulpers: 1 at 33,000
Pulp Dryers:
Pulp Dryers 1
Paper/Paperboard Grades and Capacities:
Total paper and paperboard capacity: 324,513 mt/y
Uncoated woodfree/freesheet: 119,952 mt/y

Japan

Coated mechanical/groundwood: 99,603 mt/y
Packaging papers: 104,958 mt/y
Paper and Paperboard Mill Data:
Paper Machines: 6
No. 1, fourdrinier, total capacity 24,276 mt/y, Trim width 2.1 m, Packaging papers
No. 2, fourdrinier, total capacity 25,347 mt/y, Trim width 1.97 m, Packaging papers
No. 3, fourdrinier, total capacity 55,335 mt/y, Trim width 3.06 m, Packaging papers
No. 4, DuoFormer D, total capacity 89,964 mt/y, Trim width 3.27 m, Uncoated woodfree/freesheet
No. 6, DuoFormer D, total capacity 99,603 mt/y, Trim width 3.29 m, Coated mechanical/groundwood
No. 8, fourdrinier, total capacity 29,988 mt/y, Trim width 1.6 m, Uncoated woodfree/freesheet
Coating Machines: 1
PM 6, total capacity 100,000 mt/y., on machine
Finishing Equipment:
Winders: 7
Supercalenders: 1
Rewinders: 5
Energy Data:
Power boilers: 9
Steam turbines: 3 at 9, 12, 45.9 MW
Electrical demand for mill: 1,058 MWh/D

Corelex Co., Ltd.
2-15-15, Nihonbashi-ningyocho, Chuo-ku
Tokyo, 103-0013
Japan
Phone: (81) 3 3666 1221
Fax: (81) 3 3669 6567
Web Address: www.corelex.jp
Personnel:
Pres.: Noboru Kurosaki
Phone: (81) 3 3666 1221
Fax: (81) 3 3669 6567
Total Employees of Company: 10
Mill Locations:
Doh-Ei Paper Mfg. Co., Ltd., Hokkaido Mill, 283 Aza Hirafu, Kutuchan-cho, Abuta-gun 044-0077, Japan, Capacity: 20,000 mt/y, (Paper mill)
Phone: (81) 136 23 2323
Fax: (81) 136 23 2545
Email: dohei@corelex.co.jp
Doh-Ei Paper Mfg. Co., Ltd., Fuji Mill, 1280 Hina, Fuji-shi 417-0847, Japan, Capacity: 12,000 mt/y, (Paper mill)
Phone: (81) 545 34 1096
Fax: (81) 545 34 2016
Kyoku-Ei Paper Mfg. Co., Fuji Mill, 1450 Nakanogo, Fuji 421-3306, Japan, Capacity: 9,000 mt/y, (Paper mill)
Phone: (81) 0545-81-0323
Fax: (81) 0545-81-3122
Kyoku-Ei Paper Mfg. Co., Ltd., Fuji-shi Mill, 575 Nakanogo, Fuji-shi 421-3306, Japan, Capacity: 11,200 mt/y, (Paper mill)
Phone: (81) 545 81 0323
Fax: (81) 545 81 3122
Nishinihon Eizai Co., Ltd., Tatsuno-shi Mill, 566 Tatsunocho-daido, Tatsuno-shi 679-4169, Japan, Capacity: 45,000 mt/y, (Paper mill)
Phone: (81) 791 63 1181
Fax: (81) 791 63 3617
Oita Seishi Corporation, Honsha Mill, 2-15-27, Nishiki-cho, Oita-shi 870-8691, Japan, Capacity: 27,000 mt/y, (Paper mill)
Phone: (81) 97 534 7777
Fax: (81) 97 537 2101
Email: info@oita-seishi.com
Oita Seishi Corporation, Buzen Mill, 312 Kutsukawa, Buzen-shi 828-0023, Japan, Capacity: 70,000 mt/y, (Paper mill)
Phone: (81) 979 83 2101
Fax: (81) 979 82 5500
Email: info@oita-seishi.com
Pulppy Corelex (Vietnam), Hung Yen Mill, Pho Noi A Industrial Zone, Hung Yen, Vietnam, Capacity: 30,000 mt/y, (Paper mill)
Phone: (84) 4 3512 2601
Fax: (84) 4 3512 2602

San-Ei Regulator Co., Ltd., Fujinomiya Mill, 775-1, Agoyama, Fujinomiya-Shi 418-0037, Japan, Capacity: 113,000 mt/y, (Paper mill)
Phone: (81) 544 23 0303
Fax: (81) 544 26 2760
San-Ei Regulator Co., Ltd., Tokyo Mill, 6-10 Mizue-cho, Kawasaki-ku, Kawasaki-shi 210-0086, Japan, Capacity: 50,000 mt/y, (Paper mill)
Phone: (81) 44 281 1100
Fax: (81) 44 281 1101
San-Paper Co., Ltd., Nishiyatsushiro-gun Mill, 1469-3, Ichikawa-daimon-cho, Nishiyatsushiro-gun 409-3601, Japan, Capacity: 8,400 mt/y, (Paper mill)
Phone: (81) 55 272 1331
Fax: (81) 55 272 0717
Email: sanpaper@corelex.co.jp
Shin-Ei Paper Mfg. Co., Ltd., Fujinomiya-Shi Mill, 31-6 Nishi-machi, Fujinomiya-Shi 418-0056, Japan, Capacity: 18,000 mt/y, (Paper mill)
Phone: (81) 544 27 2513
Fax: (81) 544 23 3300
Email: shinei@corelex.co.jp

Daini Seishi Co., Ltd.
Fuji-shi Mill
2-10-2 Imaizumi
Fuji-shi, Shizuoka Pref., 417-0001
Japan
Phone: (81) 545 524142
Fax: (81) 545 514624
Personnel:
Pres.: Yoko Takiguchi
Phone: (81) 545 524142
Chmn.: Kazuhiko Takiguchi
Phone: (81) 545 524142
Total Employees at this Location: 37
Type of Operation: Paper mill
Pulp Mill Data:
Recycled Fiber Treatment Lines:
Pulpers: 2
Paper/Paperboard Grades and Capacities:
Total paper and paperboard capacity: 36,000 mt/y
Uncoated mechanical/groundwood: 24,000 mt/y
Packaging papers: 12,000 mt/y
Paper and Paperboard Mill Data:
Paper Machines: 2
No. 2, fourdrinier, total capacity 24,000 mt/y, Trim width 2.78 m, Uncoated mechanical/groundwood
No. 3, fourdrinier, total capacity 12,000 mt/y, Trim width 2.23 m, Packaging papers
Finishing Equipment:
Rewinders: 2
Energy Data:
Power boilers: 2

Daio Paper Corp.
Ownership: 78.76% by various Public, 21.24% by Hokuetsu Kishu Paper Co. Ltd.
2-60, Mishima-Kamiya-cho
Shikokuchuo-shi, Ehime Pref., 799-0492
Japan
Phone: (81) 896 23 9001, 896 23 3300
Fax: (81) 896 23 5694
Web Address: www.daio-paper.co.jp
Personnel:
Pres. & CEO: Masayoshi Sako
Phone: (81) 896 23 9001
Fax: (81) 896 23 5694
Snr. Man. Dir. (Prod. Management & Gen. Mgr. Planning): Hidetaka Ikawa
Phone: (81) 896 23 9001
Fax: (81) 896 23 5694
Snr. Mang. Dir. (Management Gen. Mgr.): Toshihiro Adachi
Phone: (81) 896 23 9001
Fax: (81) 896 23 5694
Exec. Dir. (Resources & Mat'l Div.): Keiji Miyazaki
Phone: (81) 896 23 9001
Fax: (81) 896 23 5694

Exec. Dir. (Prod. Gen. Mgr.): Kenichi Mori
Phone: (81) 896 23 9001
Fax: (81) 896 23 5694
Exec. Dir. (Paper Bus. Mgr. & Bus. Develop. Gen. Mgr.): Kunihiro Okazaki
Phone: (81) 896 23 9001
Fax: (81) 896 23 5694
Dir. Eng. Dept.: Nobuo Yamamoto
Phone: (81) 896 23 9001
Fax: (81) 896 23 5694
Corp. Officer (Gen. Affairs Div.): Kenjiro Hayashi
Phone: (81) 896 23 9001
Fax: (81) 896 23 5694
Corp. Officer (Personnel & Rel. Bus. Div.): Tetsuya Watanabe
Phone: (81) 896 23 9001
Fax: (81) 896 23 5694
Total Employees of Company: 7,348
Mill Locations:
Koryo Seishi K.K., Fuji Mill, 329 Nonaka-cho, Fuji, Japan, Capacity: 13,000 mt/y, (Paper mill)
Phone: (81) 544 234-521
Fax: (81) 544 234-637
Akabira Paper Corporation K.K., Akabira Mill, 199-5 Kyowacho, Akabira, Japan, Capacity: 16,000 mt/y, (Paper mill)
Phone: (81) 125 322250
Fax: (81) 125 320118
Daio Paper Corp., Kani Mill, 500, Tsuchida, Kani-shi 509-0295, Japan, Capacity: 354,858 mt/y, (Pulp mill, Paper mill)
Phone: (81) 574 28 7111
Fax: (81) 574 28 7100
Daio Paper Corp., Mishima Mill, 5-1 Mishima-Kamiya-cho, Shikokuchuo-shi 799-0402, Japan, Capacity: 2,155,535 mt/y, (Pulp mill, Paper mill, Paperboard mill)
Phone: (81) 896 23 9022
Fax: (81) 896 24 5253
Iwaki Daio Paper Corp., Iwaki Mill (1.79% owned), 4-3-6 Minamidai, Iwaki-shi 974-8242, Japan, Capacity: 414,120 mt/y, (Paper mill, Paperboard mill)
Phone: (81) 246 62 1111
Fax: (81) 246 62 8600
Honen Seishi K.K., Fuji Mill, 329 Nonaka-cho, Fuji, Japan, Capacity: 27,000 mt/y, (Paper mill)
Phone: (81) 544 234-521
Fax: (81) 544 234-637
Omiya Seishi Co., Ltd., Fujinomiya Mill, 329 Naka-cho, Fujinomiya-Shi 418-0038, Japan, Capacity: 104,000 mt/y, (Paper mill)
Phone: (81) 544 23 4521
Fax: (81) 544 23 4637
Omiya Seishi Co., Ltd., Fuji Takaoka Mill, 261-1 Kuzawa, Fuji-shi 419-0202, Japan, Capacity: 29,000 mt/y, (Paper mill)
Phone: (81) 545 71 1026
Fax: (81) 545 71 1164
Sanyo Paper Co., Ltd., Sennan-shi Mill, 6-4-25 Onosato, Sennan-shi 590-0526, Japan, Capacity: 7,200 mt/y, (Paper mill)
Phone: (81) 724 82 7201
Fax: (81) 724 82 7204
Email: crepe@sanyo-paper.co.jp
Sanyo Paper Manufacturing Co., Ltd., Tottori Mill, 185 Fruichi, Tottori-shi 680-0865, Japan, Capacity: 251,685 mt/y, (Paperboard mill)
Phone: (81) 857 23 7131
Fax: (81) 857 27 6320

Akabira Paper Corporation K.K.
Akabira Mill
Ownership: 100% by Daio Paper Corp.
199-5 Kyowacho
Akabira, Hokkaido Pref.
Japan
Phone: (81) 125 322250
Fax: (81) 125 320118
Web Address: www.elleair-akabira.com
Personnel:
Chmn.: Tai Matsumoto

Japan

Total Employees at this Location: 84
Type of Operation: Paper mill
Paper/Paperboard Grades and Capacities:
Total paper and paperboard capacity: 16,000 mt/y
Tissue: 16,000 mt/y
Paper and Paperboard Mill Data:
Paper Machines: 1
No. 1, twin-wire, Yankee dryer, total capacity 16,000 mt/y, Trim width 2.37 m, Tissue
Energy Data:
Power boilers
Electrical demand for mill: 43 MWh/D

ⓂDaio Paper Corp.
Kani Mill
500, Tsuchida
Kani-shi, Gifu Pref., 509-0295
Japan
Phone: (81) 574 28 7111
Fax: (81) 574 28 7100
Web Address: www.daio-paper.co.jp
Personnel:
Mill Mgr.: Keiji Fujita
Phone: (81) 574 28 7111
Total Employees at this Location: 500
Type of Operation: Pulp mill, Paper mill
Pulp Grades and Capacities:
Total pulp capacity: 333,137 mt/y
Chemical Pulp: 294,001 mt/y
Recycled Pulping: 39,136 mt/y
Pulp Mill Data:
Chemical Pulping Systems:
Batch digesters: 3
Continuous digesters: 1
Bleach Plant Systems: 2
Chemical Pulping System, Type: HW/SW - WCL DIP
Chemical Recovery Equipment:
Evaporator lines: 1
Recovery boilers: 3
Lime Kiln
Recycled Fiber Treatment Lines:
Flotation deinking lines: 1 at 36,000 admt/y
Paper/Paperboard Grades and Capacities:
Total paper and paperboard capacity: 354,858 mt/y
Uncoated woodfree/freesheet: 192,780 mt/y
Tissue: 100,317 mt/y
Packaging papers: 4,998 mt/y
Specialty and industrial: 56,763 mt/y
Paper and Paperboard Mill Data:
Paper Machines: 9
No. 1, Yankee dryer, total capacity 12,495 mt/y, Trim width 2.91 m, Specialty and industrial, Packaging papers
No. 2, Yankee dryer, total capacity 13,209 mt/y, Trim width 2.91 m, Specialty and industrial, Packaging papers
N1, Yankee dryer, total capacity 11,424 mt/y, Trim width 1.97 m, Tissue
N2, Yankee dryer, total capacity 36,057 mt/y, Trim width 2.91 m, Specialty and industrial
N3, fourdrinier, total capacity 89,250 mt/y, Trim width 3.39 m, Uncoated woodfree/freesheet
N4, fourdrinier, total capacity 103,530 mt/y, Trim width 3.45 m, Uncoated woodfree/freesheet
N5, Yankee dryer, total capacity 23,919 mt/y, Trim width 3.94 m, Tissue
N6, Yankee dryer, total capacity 32,487 mt/y, Trim width 3.88 m, Tissue
N7, Yankee dryer, total capacity 32,487 mt/y, Trim width 3.88 m, Tissue
Coating Machines: 1
No. 1, total capacity 26,207 mt/y.
Finishing Equipment:
Winders: 5
Supercalenders: 1
Sheeters: 4
Energy Data:
Power boilers: 4
Steam turbines: 5 at 700 MW
Electrical demand for mill: 1,150 MWh/D

ⓂDaio Paper Corp.
Mishima Mill
5-1 Mishima-Kamiya-cho
Shikokuchuo-shi, Ehime Pref., 799-0402
Japan
Phone: (81) 896 23 9022
Fax: (81) 896 24 5253
Web Address: www.daio-paper.co.jp
Personnel:
Mill Mgr./Dir.: Takashi Ono
Phone: (81) 896 23 9022
Total Employees at this Location: 3,000
Type of Operation: Pulp mill, Paper mill, Paperboard mill
Pulp Grades and Capacities:
Total pulp capacity: 2,063,002 mt/y
Pulp available for market: 254,327 mt/y
Chemical Pulp: 1,178,070 mt/y
Mechanical Pulp: 335,482 mt/y
Recycled Pulping: 549,450 mt/y
Pulp Mill Data:
Chemical Pulping Systems:
Continuous digesters: 5
Mechanical Pulping Systems:
Conventional grinders: 13
Pressurized grinders: 6
TMP systems: 4
Bleach Plant Systems: 4
Chemical Pulping System, Type: Hardwood - A-ZePP
Chemical Pulping System, Type: Softwood, Sequence: DEopD
Mechanical Pulping System, Type: Softwood (TMP), Sequence: P/Y
Mechanical Pulping System, Type: Softwood (PGW), Sequence: P/Y
Chemical Recovery Equipment:
Evaporator lines: 1
Recovery boilers: 5
Lime Kiln
Recycled Fiber Treatment Lines:
Recycled packaging pulping lines: 1
Pulp Dryers:
Air Float dryers 1
Paper/Paperboard Grades and Capacities:
Total paper and paperboard capacity: 2,155,535 mt/y
Newsprint: 528,000 mt/y
Uncoated woodfree/freesheet: 68,000 mt/y
Uncoated mechanical/groundwood: 37,000 mt/y
Coated woodfree/freesheet: 550,000 mt/y
Coated mechanical/groundwood: 407,000 mt/y
Tissue: 30,000 mt/y
Packaging papers: 209,535 mt/y
Linerboard: 326,000 mt/y
Paper and Paperboard Mill Data:
Paper Machines: 18
No. 1, fourdrinier, Yankee dryer, total capacity 18,500 mt/y, Trim width 2.33 m, Packaging papers
No. 3, Yankee dryer, total capacity 11,000 mt/y, Trim width 2.5 m, Tissue
No. 4, Yankee dryer, total capacity 8,000 mt/y, Trim width 2.8 m, Tissue
No. 10, DuoFormer D, total capacity 91,000 mt/y, Trim width 3.29 m, Uncoated woodfree/freesheet, Coated woodfree/freesheet
No. 11, SymFormer MB, total capacity 70,000 mt/y, Trim width 3.25 m, Coated woodfree/freesheet
No. 12, Yankee dryer, total capacity 11,000 mt/y, Trim width 2.8 m, Tissue
No. 15, twin-wire, total capacity 72,000 mt/y, Trim width 3.3 m, Uncoated mechanical/groundwood, Coated mechanical/groundwood
No. 16, twin-wire, total capacity 84,000 mt/y, Trim width 3.3 m, Coated mechanical/groundwood
N1, twin-wire, total capacity 126,000 mt/y, Trim width 4.25 m, Packaging papers, Linerboard
N1, Bel-Bond, total capacity 91,035 mt/y, Trim width 3.7 m, Packaging papers
N10, DuoFormer TQv, total capacity 288,000 mt/y, Trim width 8.1 m, Coated mechanical/groundwood
N2, Bel-Bond, total capacity 300,000 mt/y, Trim width 4.1 m, Linerboard
N3, Bel-Baie, total capacity 180,000 mt/y, Trim width 8.13 m, Newsprint
N4, Bel-Baie, total capacity 211,000 mt/y, Trim width 8.13 m, Newsprint
N5, DuoFormer, total capacity 137,000 mt/y, Trim width 5.12 m, Newsprint
N6, DuoFormer, total capacity 157,000 mt/y, Trim width 5.12 m, Uncoated woodfree/freesheet, Coated woodfree/freesheet
N7, DuoFormer F, total capacity 150,000 mt/y, Trim width 5.12 m, Coated woodfree/freesheet
N8, twin-wire, total capacity 150,000 mt/y, Trim width 5.12 m, Coated woodfree/freesheet
Coating Machines: 5
No. 1, total capacity 144,000 mt/y.
No. 2, total capacity 126,000 mt/y.
No. 3
No. 4, total capacity 5,400 mt/y.
No. 5, total capacity 5,400 mt/y., on machine
Finishing Equipment:
Supercalenders: 9
Energy Data:
Power boilers: 17
Steam turbines: 14 at 549 MW
Electrical demand for mill: 7,040 MWh/D

ⒽⓂDaiwa Itagami Co., Ltd.
Daiwa Mill
5-32, Kawara-cho
Kashiwabara-shi, Osaka Pref., 582-0004
Japan
Phone: (81) 729 71 1445
Fax: (81) 729 71 1449
Web Address: www.ecopaper.gr.jp
Personnel:
Chmn.: Mitsuo Kitamura
Phone: (81) 729 71 1445
Fax: (81) 729 71 1449
Pres.: Takanori Kitamura
Phone: (81) 729 71 1445
Sls. Mgr.: Makoto Sato
Phone: (81) 729 71 1445
Fax: (81) 729 71 1449
Total Employees of Company: 91
Total Employees at this Location: 91
Type of Operation: Paperboard mill
Pulp Grades and Capacities:
Total pulp capacity: 57,891 mt/y
Recycled Pulping: 57,891 mt/y
Paper/Paperboard Grades and Capacities:
Total paper and paperboard capacity: 57,000 mt/y
Boxboard/cartonboard: 57,000 mt/y
Paper and Paperboard Mill Data:
Stock Preparation:
Pulpers: 8
Refiners: 14
Paper Machines: 2
No. 1, cylinder, total capacity 27,000 mt/y, Trim width 1.71 m, Boxboard/cartonboard
No. 2, cylinder, Yankee dryer, total capacity 30,000 mt/y, Trim width 1.71 m, Boxboard/cartonboard
Finishing Equipment:
Rewinders: 1
Energy Data:
Power boilers: 2
Electrical demand for mill: 68 MWh/D

ⒽⓂDoh-Ei Paper Mfg. Co., Ltd.
Hokkaido Mill
Ownership: Corelex Co., Ltd.
283 Aza Hirafu, Kutuchan-cho
Abuta-gun, Hokkaido Pref., 044-0077
Japan
Phone: (81) 136 23 2323
Fax: (81) 136 23 2545

Japan

Email: dohei@corelex.co.jp
Web Address: www.corelex.co.jp
Personnel:
Pres.: Noboru Kurosaki
Phone: (81) 136 23 2323
VP: Masashi Kobayashi
Phone: (81) 136 23 2323
Dir./Mill Mgr.: Hiroharu Yamamoto
Phone: (81) 136 23 2323
Total Employees at this Location: 30
Type of Operation: Paper mill
Mill Locations:
Doh-Ei Paper Mfg. Co., Ltd., Fuji Mill, 1280 Hina, Fuji-shi 417-0847, Japan, Capacity: 12,000 mt/y, (Paper mill)
Phone: (81) 545 34 1096
Fax: (81) 545 34 2016
Pulp Grades and Capacities:
Total pulp capacity: 20,949 mt/y
Recycled Pulping: 20,949 mt/y
Pulp Mill Data:
Recycled Fiber Treatment Lines:
Flotation deinking lines
Paper/Paperboard Grades and Capacities:
Total paper and paperboard capacity: 20,000 mt/y
Tissue: 20,000 mt/y
Paper and Paperboard Mill Data:
Paper Machines: 1
No. 1, Yankee dryer, total capacity 20,000 mt/y, Trim width 4.2 m, Tissue
Finishing Equipment:
Rewinders: 9
Energy Data:
Power boilers
Electrical demand for mill: 60 MWh/D

ⓂDoh-Ei Paper Mfg. Co., Ltd.
Fuji Mill
Ownership: Corelex Co., Ltd.
1280 Hina
Fuji-shi, Shizuoka Pref., 417-0847
Japan
Phone: (81) 545 34 1096
Fax: (81) 545 34 2016
Web Address: www.corelex.jp
Total Employees at this Location: 30
Type of Operation: Paper mill
Pulp Grades and Capacities:
Total pulp capacity: 12,810 mt/y
Recycled Pulping: 12,810 mt/y
Pulp Mill Data:
Recycled Fiber Treatment Lines:
Flotation deinking lines
Paper/Paperboard Grades and Capacities:
Total paper and paperboard capacity: 12,000 mt/y
Tissue: 12,000 mt/y
Paper and Paperboard Mill Data:
Paper Machines: 2
No. 1, Yankee dryer, total capacity 2,500 mt/y, Trim width 1.65 m, Tissue
No. 2, Yankee dryer, total capacity 9,500 mt/y, Trim width 2.65 m, Tissue
Energy Data:
Power boilers
Electrical demand for mill: 40 MWh/D

ⓘDynic Corporation
1-3-4 Shiba-daimon, Minato-ku
Tokyo, 105-0012
Japan
Phone: (81) 3 5402 1811
Fax: (81) 3 5402 3146
Web Address: www.dynic.co.jp
Personnel:
Pres.: Toshio Hosoda
Phone: (81) 3 5402 1811
Fax: (81) 3 5402 3146
Vice Pres., Dir.: Yoshio Ohishi
Phone: (81) 3 5402 1811
Fax: (81) 3 5402 3146

Senior Man. Dir.: Takaaki Amano
Phone: (81) 3 5402 1811
Fax: (81) 3 5402 3146
Man. Dir., Mgr. of Tokyo Office Sls.: Tetsuji Saito
Phone: (81) 3 5402 1811
Fax: (81) 3 5402 3146
Man. Dir., Mgr. of Main Office Planning: Masaharu Minato
Phone: (81) 3 5402 1811
Fax: (81) 3 5402 3146
Man. Dir.: Akira Uno
Phone: (81) 3 5402 1811
Fax: (81) 3 5402 3146
Exec. Dir.: Shigeru Kosugi
Phone: (81) 3 5402 1811
Fax: (81) 3 5402 3146
Total Employees of Company: 628
Mill Locations:
Dynic Corporation, Fuji Mill, Udogawanishi-machi 1-2, Fuji-shi 417-0854, Japan, Capacity: 7,000 mt/y, (Paper mill)
Phone: (81) 545 52 3885
Fax: (81) 545 52 3519

ⓂDynic Corporation
Fuji Mill
Udogawanishi-machi 1-2
Fuji-shi, Shizuoka Pref., 417-0854
Japan
Phone: (81) 545 52 3885
Fax: (81) 545 52 3519
Personnel:
Mill Mgr.: Toyoharu Ikura
Phone: (81) 545 52 3885
Total Employees at this Location: 12
Type of Operation: Paper mill
Paper/Paperboard Grades and Capacities:
Total paper and paperboard capacity: 7,000 mt/y
Specialty and industrial: 7,000 mt/y
Paper and Paperboard Mill Data:
Paper Machines: 1
No. 1, fourdrinier, Trim width 2.3 m, Specialty and industrial

ⓘEcopaper JP Co. Ltd
Ownership: Japan Pulp & Paper Co.
82-1 Higashi, Haruoka-cho
Owariasahi-Shi, Aichi Pref., 488-0031
Japan
Phone: (81) 561 53 3315
Fax: (81) 561 53 3362
Email: info@ecopaper.jp
Web Address: www.ecopaper.jp
Personnel:
Pres. & CEO: Katsuhiro Tsukuma
Phone: (81) 52 745 1300
Fax: (81) 52 745 1331
Man. Dir.: Yamada Yoshimi
Phone: (81) 52 745 1300
Fax: (81) 52 745 1331
Total Employees of Company: 754
Total Employees at this Location: 431
Mill Locations:
Ecopaper JP Co. Ltd, Owariasahi Mill, 82-1 Higashi, Haruoka-cho, Owariasahi-Shi 488-0031, Japan, Capacity: 135,000 mt/y, (Paper mill, Paperboard mill)
Phone: (81) 561 53 3315
Fax: (81) 561 53 3362
Email: info@ecopaper.jp

ⓂEcopaper JP Co. Ltd
Owariasahi Mill
82-1 Higashi, Haruoka-cho
Owariasahi-Shi, Aichi Pref., 488-0031
Japan
Phone: (81) 561 53 3315
Fax: (81) 561 53 3362
Email: info@ecopaper.jp
Web Address: www.ecopaper.jp

Personnel:
Dir.: Kasai Koji
Phone: (81) 561 53 3315
Fax: (81) 561 53 3362
Dir.: Uemura Ken
Phone: (81) 561 53 3315
Fax: (81) 561 53 3362
Total Employees at this Location: 116
Type of Operation: Paper mill, Paperboard mill
Pulp Grades and Capacities:
Total pulp capacity: 130,185 mt/y
Recycled Pulping: 130,185 mt/y
Pulp Mill Data:
Pulp Lines: 1
Paper/Paperboard Grades and Capacities:
Total paper and paperboard capacity: 135,000 mt/y
Uncoated woodfree/freesheet: 35,000 mt/y
Corrugating medium/fluting: 100,000 mt/y
Paper and Paperboard Mill Data:
Stock Preparation:
Pulpers: 6
Refiners: 10
Paper Machines: 2
No. 1, fourdrinier, total capacity 35,000 mt/y, Trim width 2.71 m, Uncoated woodfree/freesheet
No. 3, fourdrinier, total capacity 100,000 mt/y, Trim width 3.2 m, Corrugating medium/fluting
Coating Machines: 1
No. 1, total capacity 52,800 mt/y., on machine
Finishing Equipment:
Rewinders: 3 at 165,600 mt/y
Energy Data:
Power boilers: 6
Steam turbines: 1 at 3.15 MW
Electrical demand for mill: 184 MWh/D

ⓘⓂEhime Paper Mfg. Co., Ltd.
Shikokuchuo-shi Mill
370 Muramatsu-cho
Shikokuchuo-shi, Ehime Pref., 799-0401
Japan
Phone: (81) 896 24 3330
Fax: (81) 896 28 1030
Email: info@ehimepaper.co.jp.
Web Address: www.ehimepaper.co.jp.
Personnel:
Pres.: Katsumasa Ikawa
Phone: (81) 896 24 3330
Mill Mgr.: Koichi Shinohara
Phone: (81) 896 24 3330
Total Employees of Company: 208
Total Employees at this Location: 208
Type of Operation: Paper mill, Paperboard mill
Pulp Grades and Capacities:
Total pulp capacity: 227,341 mt/y
Recycled Pulping: 227,341 mt/y
Pulp Mill Data:
Recycled Fiber Treatment Lines:
Pulpers: 1 at 281,000
Paper/Paperboard Grades and Capacities:
Total paper and paperboard capacity: 400,000 mt/y
Tissue: 130,000 mt/y
Linerboard: 110,000 mt/y
Corrugating medium/fluting: 160,000 mt/y
Paper and Paperboard Mill Data:
Stock Preparation:
Pulpers:
Paper Machines: 8
No. 1, fourdrinier (2), total capacity 110,000 mt/y, Trim width 2.7 m, Linerboard
No. 2, fourdrinier, total capacity 160,000 mt/y, Trim width 3.8 m, Corrugating medium/fluting
No. 5, twin-wire, Yankee dryer, total capacity 12,000 mt/y, Trim width 2.2 m, Tissue
No. 6, twin-wire, Yankee dryer, total capacity 15,000 mt/y, Trim width 2.8 m, Tissue
No. 7, twin-wire, Yankee dryer, total capacity 16,000 mt/y, Trim width 2.8 m, Tissue

No. 8, twin-wire, Yankee dryer, total capacity 22,000 mt/y, Trim width 2.8 m, Tissue
No. 10, crescent former, Yankee dryer, total capacity 30,000 mt/y, Trim width 3.6 m, Tissue
No. 11, crescent former, Yankee dryer, total capacity 35,000 mt/y, Trim width 4.24 m, Tissue
Finishing Equipment:
Winders: 2
Energy Data:
Power boilers: 5
Combustion turbines: 1 at 3.5 MW
Steam turbines: 3 at 2.25, 12.3, 12.8 MW
Electrical demand for mill: 737 MWh/D

ⓘⓜFuji Paper Mill Cooperatives
Awagami Mill
136 Aza-Kawahigashi, Yamakawa-cho
Oe-gun, Tokushima Pref., 799-3401
Japan
Phone: (81) 883 42 2035
Fax: (81) 883 42 6085
Email: info@awagami.or.jp
Web Address: www.awagami.or.jp
Personnel:
CEO: Yoichi Fujimori
Phone: (81) 883 42 2035
Fax: (81) 883 42 6085
Total Employees of Company: 41
Total Employees at this Location: 41
Type of Operation: Paper mill
Paper/Paperboard Grades and Capacities:
Uncoated woodfree/freesheet

ⓘⓜFuji Satowa Paper Co., LTD.
Fuji Mill
4-19, TAKAOKAHONCHO
Fuji, Shizuoka Pref., 419-0203
Japan
Phone: (81) 545 71 3005
Fax: (81) 545 71 6858
Personnel:
Owner, Pres.: Yoshimasa Satowa
Total Employees at this Location: 48
Type of Operation: Paper mill
Pulp Grades and Capacities:
Total pulp capacity: 12,948 mt/y
Recycled Pulping: 12,948 mt/y
Paper/Paperboard Grades and Capacities:
Total paper and paperboard capacity: 12,000 mt/y
Tissue: 12,000 mt/y
Paper and Paperboard Mill Data:
Paper Machines: 2
No. 1, Yankee dryer, total capacity 6,000 mt/y, Trim width 1.75 m, Tissue
No. 2, Yankee dryer, total capacity 6,000 mt/y, Trim width 1.75 m, Tissue
Energy Data:
Power boilers
Electrical demand for mill: 40 MWh/D

ⓘⓜFujieda Seishi Co. Ltd.
Fujieda-shi Mill
Ownership: 100% by Goto Kazuo
1-18-21 Maejima
Fujieda-shi, Shizuoka Pref., 426-8631
Japan
Phone: (81) 54 635 2015
Fax: (81) 54 636 0980
Personnel:
Pres.: Kazuki Goto
Phone: (81) 54 635 2015
Total Employees at this Location: 86
Type of Operation: Paper mill
Pulp Grades and Capacities:
Total pulp capacity: 25,931 mt/y
Recycled Pulping: 25,931 mt/y
Pulp Mill Data:
Recycled Fiber Treatment Lines:
Flotation deinking lines
Paper/Paperboard Grades and Capacities:
Total paper and paperboard capacity: 24,000 mt/y
Tissue: 24,000 mt/y
Paper and Paperboard Mill Data:
Paper Machines: 2
No. 1, Yankee dryer, total capacity 12,000 mt/y, Trim width 2.9 m, Tissue
No. 2, Yankee dryer, total capacity 12,000 mt/y, Trim width 3.26 m, Tissue
Energy Data:
Power boilers: 2
Electrical demand for mill: 81 MWh/D

ⓘFujifilm Corp.
7-3, Akasaka 9-chome, Minato-ku
Tokyo, 107-0052
Japan
Phone: (81) 3 6271 3111
Web Address: www.fujifilm.co.jp
Personnel:
Chmn. & CEO: Shigetaka Komori
Phone: (81) 3 6271 3111
Pres. & COO: Shigehiro Nakajima
Phone: (81) 3 6271 3111
Total Employees of Company: 7,284
Mill Locations:
Fujifilm Corp., Fujinomiya Mill, 200 Oonakazato, Fujinomiya-Shi 418-8666, Japan, Capacity: 90,400 mt/y, (Paper mill)
Phone: (81) 544 26 7111
Fax: (81) 544 26 7104

ⓜFujifilm Corp.
Fujinomiya Mill
200 Oonakazato
Fujinomiya-Shi, Shizuoka Pref., 418-8666
Japan
Phone: (81) 544 26 7111
Fax: (81) 544 26 7104
Web Address: www.fujifilm.co.jp
Personnel:
Mill Mgr.: Tomoyoshi Ueno
Phone: (81) 544 26 7111
Total Employees at this Location: 966
Type of Operation: Paper mill
Paper/Paperboard Grades and Capacities:
Total paper and paperboard capacity: 90,400 mt/y
Uncoated woodfree/freesheet
Coated woodfree/freesheet
Paper and Paperboard Mill Data:
Paper Machines: 2
No. 1, fourdrinier, Trim width 1.4 m, Uncoated woodfree/freesheet
No. 4, fourdrinier, Trim width 3.3 m, Uncoated woodfree/freesheet
Energy Data:
Combustion turbines: 2 at 16, 16 MW

ⓘFujikyowa Paper Mfg. Co., Ltd.
1-1-2 Kuzawa
Fuji-Shi, Shizuoka Pref., 419-0202
Japan
Phone: (81) 545 71 1400
Fax: (81) 545 71 0561
Web Address: www.fujikyowa.co.jp
Total Employees of Company: 140
Mill Locations:
Fujikyowa Paper Mfg. Co., Ltd., Fuji Mill, 1-1-2 Kuzawa, Fuji-Shi 419-0202, Japan, Capacity: 12,000 mt/y, (Paper mill)
Phone: (81) 545 71 1400
Fax: (81) 545 71 0561

ⓜFujikyowa Paper Mfg. Co., Ltd.
Fuji Mill
1-1-2 Kuzawa
Fuji-Shi, Shizuoka Pref., 419-0202
Japan
Phone: (81) 545 71 1400
Fax: (81) 545 71 0561
Total Employees at this Location: 119
Type of Operation: Paper mill
Paper/Paperboard Grades and Capacities:
Total paper and paperboard capacity: 12,000 mt/y
Specialty and industrial: 12,000 mt/y
Paper and Paperboard Mill Data:
Paper Machines: 4
PM 1, cylinder, total capacity 3,000 mt/y, Trim width 1.3 m, Specialty and industrial
PM 2, cylinder, total capacity 4,000 mt/y, Trim width 1.4 m, Specialty and industrial
PM 3, cylinder, total capacity 3,000 mt/y, Trim width 1.04 m, Specialty and industrial
PM 5, cylinder, total capacity 2,000 mt/y, Trim width 0.94 m, Specialty and industrial
Coating Machines: 1
No. 1, total capacity 1,000 mt/y.

ⓘⓜFukuda Paper Manufacturing Co., Ltd.
Iyomishima Mill
2384 Sangawa-cho
Shikokuchuo-shi, Ehime Pref., 799-0431
Japan
Phone: (81) 896 25 1465
Fax: (81) 896 25 1468
Personnel:
Chmn.: Masahiko Fukuda
Phone: (81) 896 25 1465
Pres.: Yasutoshi Kadokura
Phone: (81) 896 25 1465
Total Employees at this Location: 57
Type of Operation: Paper mill
Pulp Grades and Capacities:
Total pulp capacity: 5,863 mt/y
Recycled Pulping: 5,863 mt/y
Pulp Mill Data:
Recycled Fiber Treatment Lines:
Flotation deinking lines: 1
Paper/Paperboard Grades and Capacities:
Total paper and paperboard capacity: 10,000 mt/y
Tissue: 10,000 mt/y
Paper and Paperboard Mill Data:
Stock Preparation:
Pulpers: 2
Refiners: 1
Paper Machines: 2
No. 1, Yankee dryer, total capacity 4,000 mt/y, Trim width 1.4 m, Tissue
No. 6, Yankee dryer, total capacity 6,000 mt/y, Trim width 1.9 m, Tissue
Energy Data:
Power boilers: 3
Electrical demand for mill: 31 MWh/D

ⓘⓜFukuyama Paper Co., Ltd.
Osaka Mill
2-2-1, Kashima, Yodogawa-ku
Osaka, Osaka Pref., 532-0031
Japan
Phone: (81) 6 6301 2131
Fax: (81) 6 6301 2919
Email: fukuyama-paper@osaka.email.ne.jp
Web Address: www.fukuyama-paper.jp
Personnel:
Pres.: Yasuhiro Ogiwara
Phone: (81) 6 6301 2131
Mill Mgr.: Satoshi Tanaka
Phone: (81) 6 6301 2131
Total Employees at this Location: 128
Type of Operation: Paperboard mill
Paper/Paperboard Grades and Capacities:
Total paper and paperboard capacity: 279,200 mt/y
Corrugating medium/fluting: 227,600 mt/y
Boxboard/cartonboard: 51,600 mt/y
Paper and Paperboard Mill Data:
Stock Preparation:

Japan

Pulpers: 2
Refiners: 3
Paper Machines: 3
No. 5, Dynaformer, total capacity 180,000 mt/y, Trim width 4.2 m, Corrugating medium/fluting
N2, top former, total capacity 47,600 mt/y, Trim width 4 m, Corrugating medium/fluting
NN, fourdrinier, total capacity 51,600 mt/y, Trim width 3.8 m, Boxboard/cartonboard
Finishing Equipment:
Rewinders: 3
Energy Data:
Power boilers: 2
Combustion turbines: 4

ⓘⓜGojo Paper Mfg. Co., Ltd.
Fuji Mill
451-1 Harada
Fuji-shi, Shizuoka Pref., 417-8555
Japan
Phone: (81) 545 57 1111
Fax: (81) 545 57 1130
Web Address: www.gojo.co.jp
Personnel:
Chmn., CEO: Isokazu Kawaguchi
Phone: (81) 545 57 1111
Pres., COO: Koichiro Kawaguchi
Total Employees of Company: 160
Total Employees at this Location: 160
Type of Operation: Paper mill, Paperboard mill
Paper/Paperboard Grades and Capacities:
Total paper and paperboard capacity: 42,000 mt/y
Boxboard/cartonboard: 42,000 mt/y
Paper and Paperboard Mill Data:
Paper Machines: 1
No. 4, fourdrinier, total capacity 42,000 mt/y, Trim width 1.76 m, Boxboard/cartonboard
Coating Machines: 5
No. 6, on machine
No. 7
No. 8, off machine
No. 10, on machine
No. 5, off machine

ⓘⓜGoshika Seishi Co. Ltd.
Shikokuchuo Mill
2523, Sangawacho
Shikokuchuo, Ehime Pref., 799-0431
Japan
Phone: (81) 896252323
Total Employees at this Location: 25
Type of Operation: Paper mill
Paper/Paperboard Grades and Capacities:
Total paper and paperboard capacity: 5,500 mt/y
Tissue: 5,500 mt/y
Paper and Paperboard Mill Data:
Paper Machines: 3
No. 1, Yankee dryer, total capacity 1,500 mt/y, Trim width 1.2 m, Tissue
No. 2, Yankee dryer, total capacity 2,000 mt/y, Trim width 1.45 m, Tissue
No. 3, Yankee dryer, total capacity 2,000 mt/y, Trim width 1.45 m, Tissue
Energy Data:
Power boilers
Electrical demand for mill: 17 MWh/D

ⓘⓜHattori Seishi K.K.
Shinmachi Mill
Ownership: Hattori Paper Mfg. Co., Ltd
682 Kamibun-cho
Shikokuchuo, Ehime Pref., 799-0121
Japan
Phone: (81) 896-58-3005
Fax: (81) 896-58-3306
Web Address: www.hattoripaper.co.jp
Personnel:
Pres & CEO: Masakazu Hattori
Phone: (81) 896-58-3005
Fax: (81) 896-58-3306
Total Employees of Company: 120
Total Employees at this Location: 20
Type of Operation: Paper mill
Pulp Grades and Capacities:
Total pulp capacity: 6,424 mt/y
Recycled Pulping: 6,424 mt/y
Pulp Mill Data:
Recycled Fiber Treatment Lines:
Flotation deinking lines
Paper/Paperboard Grades and Capacities:
Total paper and paperboard capacity: 6,000 mt/y
Tissue: 6,000 mt/y
Paper and Paperboard Mill Data:
Paper Machines: 1
No. 1, Yankee dryer, total capacity 6,000 mt/y, Trim width 2.2 m, Tissue
Energy Data:
Power boilers
Electrical demand for mill: 20 MWh/D

ⓘHavix Corporation Ltd.
3-5-7 Fukumitsu-Higashi
Gifu, Gifu Pref., 502-0813
Japan
Phone: (81) 58 296 3911
Fax: (81) 58 296 3921
Web Address: www.havix.co.jp
Personnel:
Exec. Chmn.: Sakai Shogo
Phone: (81) 58 296 3911
Fax: (81) 58 296 3921
Pres. & CEO: Toshiyuki Kimura
Phone: (81) 58 296 3911
Fax: (81) 58 296 3921
Snr. Man. Dir.: Kojima Yasuhiko
Phone: (81) 58 296 3911
Fax: (81) 58 296 3921
Exec. Dir.: Hiroaki Kubota
Phone: (81) 58 296 3911
Fax: (81) 58 296 3921
Total Employees of Company: 162
Mill Locations:
Havix Corporation Ltd., Hozumi Mill, Hozumi, Gifu City, Sobuecho Sobue, Gifu, Japan, Capacity: 33,000 mt/y, (Paper mill)
Phone: (81) 58 327 5057
Fax: (81) 58 327 5072
Email: soumu@havix.co.jp

ⓘHavix Corporation Ltd.
Hozumi Mill
Hozumi, Gifu City, Sobuecho Sobue
Gifu, Gifu Pref.
Japan
Phone: (81) 58 327 5057
Fax: (81) 58 327 5072
Email: soumu@havix.co.jp
Web Address: www.havix.co.jp
Personnel:
Chmn.: Seigo Sakei
Pres.: Toshiyuki Kimura
Total Employees at this Location: 60
Type of Operation: Paper mill
Paper/Paperboard Grades and Capacities:
Total paper and paperboard capacity: 33,000 mt/y
Tissue: 33,000 mt/y
Paper and Paperboard Mill Data:
Paper Machines: 3
No. 1, BF-10, Yankee dryer, total capacity 10,000 mt/y, Trim width 2.49 m, Tissue
No. 2, BF-10, Yankee dryer, total capacity 11,000 mt/y, Trim width 2.86 m, Tissue
No. 3, BF-12, Yankee dryer, total capacity 12,000 mt/y, Trim width 3.2 m, Tissue
Energy Data:
Power boilers
Electrical demand for mill: 89 MWh/D

ⓘHokuetsu Kishu Paper Co. Ltd.
Ownership: Public, 24.72% by Mitsubishi Paper Mills Ltd.
3-2-2, Hongoku-cho, Nihonbashi, Chuo-ku
Tokyo, 103-0021
Japan
Phone: (81) 3 3245 4500/4578
Fax: (81) 3 3245 4511
Email: info@hpaper-na.co.jp
Web Address: www.hokuetsu-kishu.jp
Personnel:
Pres. & CEO: Sekio Kishimoto
Phone: (81) 3 3245 4500
Fax: (81) 3 3245 4511
Man. Dir., Chied Fir. Western Paper. Bus.: Takayuki Sasaki
Phone: (81) 3 3245 4500
Fax: (81) 3 3245 4511
Man. Dir., Niigata Plt. Mgr. White Board Bus.: Michio Tsuchida
Phone: (81) 3 3245 4500
Fax: (81) 3 3245 4511
Exec. Officer, Dir. Coated Paper Sls.: Shigeharu Tachibana
Phone: (81) 3 3245 4500
Fax: (81) 3 3245 4511
Total Employees of Company: 4,124
Total Employees at this Location: 179
Mill Locations:
Bernard Dumas SAS, Creysse Mill, 2 Rue de la Papeterie, F-24100 Creysse, France, Capacity: 10,000 mt/y, (Paper mill)
Phone: (33) 5 53 23 21 05
Fax: (33) 5 53 23 37 13
Email: bdumas@bernard-dumas.fr; tec@bernrad-dumas.com
Hokuetsu Kishu Paper Co. Ltd., Kanto Ichikawa Mill, 3-21-1 Osu, Ichikawa-shi 272-0032, Japan, Capacity: 144,228 mt/y, (Paper mill, Paperboard mill)
Phone: (81) 47 378 0101
Fax: (81) 47 378 0180
Hokuetsu Kishu Paper Co. Ltd., Kanto Katsuta Mill, 1760 Takaba, Hitachinaka-shi 312-0062, Japan, Capacity: 101,745 mt/y, (Paperboard mill)
Phone: (81) 29 275 5500
Fax: (81) 29 275 5548
Hokuetsu Kishu Paper Co. Ltd., Nagaoka Mill, 3-2-1, Zao, Nagaoka-shi 940-0028, Japan, Capacity: 22,300 mt/y, (Paper mill)
Phone: (81) 258 24 0630
Fax: (81) 258 24 5468
Email: info@hpaper-na.co.jp
Hokuetsu Kishu Paper Co. Ltd., Niigata Mill, 57 Enoki-cho, Higashi-ku, Niigata-shi 950-0881, Japan, Capacity: 1,320,543 mt/y, (Pulp mill, Paper mill, Paperboard mill)
Phone: (81) 25 273 1141
Fax: (81) 25 271 1537
Email: info@hpaper-na.co.jp
Hokuetsu Kishu Paper Co. Ltd., Kishu Mill, 182 Udono-mura, Minamimuro-gun 519-5701, Japan, Capacity: 322,371 mt/y, (Pulp mill, Paper mill)
Phone: (81) 735 32 1111
Fax: (81) 735 32 2327
Email: contact@kishu.co.jp
Jiangmen Xinghui Paper Mill Co., Ltd, Jiangmen Mill (60% owned), Yinzhouhu Paper Making Park, Shuangshui Town, Xinhui District, Jiangmen, China, Capacity: 240,000 mt/y, (Paper mill)

ⓜHokuetsu Kishu Paper Co. Ltd.
Kanto Ichikawa Mill
3-21-1 Osu
Ichikawa-shi, Chiba Pref., 272-0032
Japan
Phone: (81) 47 378 0101
Fax: (81) 47 378 0180
Web Address: www.hokuetsu-kishu.jp
Personnel:
Dir. / Mill Mgr.: Shohei Onoda
Phone: (81) 47 378 0101

Assist. Mill Mgr.: Akihiro Aoki
Phone: (81) 47 378 0101
Total Employees at this Location: 117
Type of Operation: Paper mill, Paperboard mill
Pulp Grades and Capacities:
Total pulp capacity: 142,007 mt/y
Recycled Pulping: 142,007 mt/y
Paper/Paperboard Grades and Capacities:
Total paper and paperboard capacity: 144,228 mt/y
Boxboard/cartonboard: 144,228 mt/y
Paper and Paperboard Mill Data:
Paper Machines: 2
No. 4, combination, total capacity 75,684 mt/y, Trim width 2.56 m, Boxboard/cartonboard
No. 5, Ultraformer, total capacity 68,544 mt/y, Trim width 2.58 m, Boxboard/cartonboard
Coating Machines: 2
PM 4, total capacity 78,000 mt/y., on machine
PM 5, total capacity 54,100 mt/y., on machine
Finishing Equipment:
Rewinders: 2
Energy Data:
Power boilers: 1
Combustion turbines: 1 at 17 MW
Steam turbines: 1 at 6 MW
Electrical demand for mill: 292 MWh/D

⑩Hokuetsu Kishu Paper Co. Ltd.
Kanto Katsuta Mill
1760 Takaba
Hitachinaka-shi, Ibaraki Pref., 312-0062
Japan
Phone: (81) 29 275 5500
Fax: (81) 29 275 5548
Web Address: www.hokuetsu-kishu.jp
Personnel:
Mill Mgr.: Shohei Onoda
Phone: (81) 29 275 5500
Asst. Mill Mgr.: Akihiro Aoki
Phone: (81) 29 275 5500
Total Employees at this Location: 112
Type of Operation: Paperboard mill
Pulp Grades and Capacities:
Total pulp capacity: 93,217 mt/y
Recycled Pulping: 93,217 mt/y
Pulp Mill Data:
Recycled Fiber Treatment Lines:
Flotation deinking lines: 1
Recycled packaging pulping lines: 1
Paper/Paperboard Grades and Capacities:
Total paper and paperboard capacity: 101,745 mt/y
Boxboard/cartonboard: 101,745 mt/y
Paper and Paperboard Mill Data:
Stock Preparation:
Pulpers: 4
Refiners: 6
Paper Machines: 1
No. 1, Ultraformer, total capacity 101,745 mt/y, Trim width 3.3 m, Boxboard/cartonboard
Coating Machines: 2
No. 4
No. 5
Finishing Equipment:
Winders: 1
Rewinders: 1
Sheeters: 2
Energy Data:
Power boilers: 1
Combustion turbines: 1 at 7.1 MW
Steam turbines: 1 at 41 MW
Electrical demand for mill: 159 MWh/D

⑩Hokuetsu Kishu Paper Co. Ltd.
Nagaoka Mill
3-2-1, Zao
Nagaoka-shi, Niigata Pref., 940-0028
Japan
Phone: (81) 258 24 0630
Fax: (81) 258 24 5468
Email: info@hpaper-na.co.jp
Web Address: www.hokuetsu-kishu.jp
Personnel:
Mill Mgr.: Minoru Hotta
Phone: (81) 258 24 0630
Total Employees at this Location: 243
Type of Operation: Paper mill
Paper/Paperboard Grades and Capacities:
Total paper and paperboard capacity: 22,300 mt/y
Specialty and industrial: 22,300 mt/y
Paper and Paperboard Mill Data:
Paper Machines: 4
No. 2, Yankee dryer, cylinder, total capacity 1,600 mt/y, Trim width 1.73 m, Specialty and industrial
No. 3, fourdrinier, cylinder, total capacity 10,400 mt/y, Trim width 1.68 m, Specialty and industrial
No. 4, cylinder, total capacity 3,000 mt/y, Trim width 1.2 m, Specialty and industrial
No. 6, cylinder, total capacity 7,300 mt/y, Trim width 2.45 m, Specialty and industrial
Coating Machines: 2
No. 1, total capacity 3,600 mt/y.
No. 2, total capacity 3,600 mt/y.
Finishing Equipment:
Supercalenders: 1
Rewinders: 5
Sheeters: 2
Energy Data:
Power boilers: 2
Steam turbines: 2 at 12.1 MW

⑩Hokuetsu Kishu Paper Co. Ltd.
Niigata Mill
57 Enoki-cho, Higashi-ku
Niigata-shi, Niigata Pref., 950-0881
Japan
Phone: (81) 25 273 1141
Fax: (81) 25 271 1537
Email: info@hpaper-na.co.jp
Web Address: www.hokuetsu-kishu.jp
Personnel:
Man. Dir, Mill Mgr.: Hiroshi Sugawara
Phone: (81) 25 273 1141
Prod. Mgr.: Hideo Yazawa
Phone: (81) 25 273 1141
Total Employees at this Location: 579
Type of Operation: Pulp mill, Paper mill, Paperboard mill
Pulp Grades and Capacities:
Total pulp capacity: 912,333 mt/y
Pulp available for market: 160,650 mt/y
Chemical Pulp: 851,247 mt/y
Recycled Pulping: 61,087 mt/y
Pulp Mill Data:
Chemical Pulping Systems:
Continuous digesters: 2
Bleach Plant Systems: 2
Chemical Pulping System, Type: HW - ECF
DIP
Chemical Recovery Equipment:
Evaporator lines: 4
Recovery boilers: 1
Recovery boilers: 1
Recovery boilers: 1
Lime Kiln
Recycled Fiber Treatment Lines:
Flotation deinking lines: 1
Paper/Paperboard Grades and Capacities:
Total paper and paperboard capacity: 1,320,543 mt/y
Uncoated woodfree/freesheet: 182,784 mt/y
Coated woodfree/freesheet: 905,352 mt/y
Coated mechanical/groundwood: 177,072 mt/y
Boxboard/cartonboard: 55,335 mt/y
Paper and Paperboard Mill Data:
Stock Preparation:
Pulpers: 12
Refiners: 25
Paper Machines: 8
No. 2, SymFormer MB, total capacity 42,840 mt/y, Trim width 3.27 m, Uncoated woodfree/freesheet
No. 3, SymFormer MB, total capacity 72,114 mt/y, Trim width 3.27 m, Coated mechanical/groundwood
No. 4, fourdrinier, total capacity 55,335 mt/y, Trim width 2.56 m, Boxboard/cartonboard
No. 5, DuoFormer D, total capacity 169,932 mt/y, Trim width 5.6 m, Uncoated woodfree/freesheet
No. 6, SymFormer MB, total capacity 160,650 mt/y, Trim width 5.26 m, Coated woodfree/freesheet
No. 7, Sym-Press, total capacity 199,920 mt/y, Trim width 5.1 m, Coated woodfree/freesheet
No. 8, DuoFormer D, total capacity 299,880 mt/y, Trim width 7.6 m, Coated woodfree/freesheet
No. 9, OptiFormer, total capacity 349,860 mt/y, Trim width 9.8 m, Coated mechanical/groundwood, Coated woodfree/freesheet
Coating Machines: 5
No. 4, total capacity 46,000 mt/y., on machine
No. 6, total capacity 130,300 mt/y., on machine
No. 7, total capacity 163,000 mt/y.
No. 8, total capacity 255,500 mt/y.
No. 9, total capacity 380,000 mt/y., on machine
Finishing Equipment:
Winders: 4
Supercalenders: 6
Rewinders: 5
Sheeters: 8
Energy Data:
Power boilers: 3
Combustion turbines: 1 at 17 MW
Steam turbines: 6 at 237.2 MW
Electrical demand for mill: 3,809 MWh/D

⑩Hokuetsu Kishu Paper Co. Ltd.
Kishu Mill
182 Udono-mura
Minamimuro-gun, Mie Pref., 519-5701
Japan
Phone: (81) 735 32 1111
Fax: (81) 735 32 2327
Email: contact@kishu.co.jp
Web Address: www.kishu.co.jp
Personnel:
Man. Dir. & Mill Mgr.: Yoichi Haruki
Phone: (81) 735 32 1111
Total Employees at this Location: 370
Type of Operation: Pulp mill, Paper mill
Pulp Grades and Capacities:
Total pulp capacity: 212,207 mt/y
Chemical Pulp: 187,006 mt/y
Recycled Pulping: 25,201 mt/y
Pulp Mill Data:
Chemical Pulping Systems:
Continuous digesters: 1
Bleach Plant Systems: 1
Chemical Pulping System, Type: ECF, Sequence: O_2 C/DEHD, Capacity 200,000 admt/y
Chemical Recovery Equipment:
Evaporator lines: 6
Recovery boilers: 1
Lime Kiln
Recycled Fiber Treatment Lines:
Flotation deinking lines: 1
Pulpers: 1
Paper/Paperboard Grades and Capacities:
Total paper and paperboard capacity: 322,371 mt/y
Uncoated woodfree/freesheet: 298,452 mt/y
Specialty and industrial: 23,919 mt/y
Paper and Paperboard Mill Data:
Stock Preparation:
Pulpers: 2
Refiners: 21
Paper Machines: 4
No. 5, fourdrinier, total capacity 23,919 mt/y, Trim width 2.7 m, Specialty and industrial
No. 6, Bel-Form, total capacity 83,895 mt/y, Trim width 3.25 m, Uncoated woodfree/freesheet
No. 7, DuoFormer D, total capacity 120,666 mt/y, Trim width 4.8 m, Uncoated woodfree/freesheet

Japan

No. 8, Bel-Form, total capacity 93,891 mt/y, Trim width 3.25 m, Uncoated woodfree/freesheet
Finishing Equipment:
Rewinders: 6
Sheeters: 10
Energy Data:
Power boilers: 1
Steam turbines: 2 at 53 MW
Electrical demand for mill: 918 MWh/D

ⒽⓂHyogo Paper Mfg. Co., Ltd.
Himeji Mill
2288, Toyotomi, Toyotomi-cho
Himeji-shi, Hyogo Pref., 679-2123
Japan
Phone: (81) 792 64 1221
Fax: (81) 792 64 1401
Personnel:
Pres.: Yusuke Igawa
Phone: (81) 792 64 1221
Chmn.: Naotake Igawa
Total Employees of Company: 310
Total Employees at this Location: 307
Type of Operation: Paper mill, Paperboard mill
Pulp Grades and Capacities:
Total pulp capacity: 162,237 mt/y
Recycled Pulping: 162,237 mt/y
Pulp Mill Data:
Recycled Fiber Treatment Lines:
Recycled packaging pulping lines: 1
Paper/Paperboard Grades and Capacities:
Total paper and paperboard capacity: 224,196 mt/y
Newsprint: 42,126 mt/y
Linerboard: 182,070 mt/y
Paper and Paperboard Mill Data:
Paper Machines: 3
No. 2, Bel-Bond, total capacity 24,276 mt/y, Trim width 2.03 m, Newsprint
No. 3, top former, total capacity 17,850 mt/y, Trim width 2.03 m, Newsprint
n1, Ultraformer, total capacity 182,070 mt/y, Trim width 4.5 m, Linerboard
Energy Data:
Power boilers
Steam turbines: 2
Electrical demand for mill: 422 MWh/D

ⒽⓂHyogo Pulp Industries, Ltd.
Tanigawa Mill
Ownership: 100% by Taikawa Shoji KK
858 Tanigawa, Sannan-cho
Tanba-shi, Hyogo Pref., 669-3131
Japan
Phone: (81) 795 77 1081
Fax: (81) 795 77 2591
Web Address: www.hyogopulp.co.jp
Personnel:
Pres.: Yuji Ikawa
Phone: (81) 795 77 1081
Fax: (81) 795 77 2591
Mill Mgr.: Itsuo Yokotani
Phone: (81) 795 77 1081
Fax: (81) 795 77 2591
Total Employees of Company: 141
Total Employees at this Location: 134
Type of Operation: Pulp mill
Pulp Grades and Capacities:
Total pulp capacity: 202,635 mt/y
Pulp available for market: 199,920 mt/y
Chemical Pulp: 202,635 mt/y
Pulp Mill Data:
Chemical Pulping Systems:
Continuous digesters: 1
Pulp Lines: 1
Chemical Recovery Equipment:
Evaporator lines: 2
Recovery boilers: 1
Pulp Dryers:
Wet Lap machine 1, Wet Lap machine 1, Wet Lap machine 1
Energy Data:
Power boilers: 1
Steam turbines: 4 at 6.7, 7.3, 40, 18 MW
Electrical demand for mill: 289 MWh/D

ⒽⓂIchikawa Seishi K.K.
Fuji Mill
Ownership: Marutomi Paper Mfg. Co., Ltd.
650-1, Hina
Fuji, Shizuoka Pref., 417-0847
Japan
Phone: (81) 545 34 0840
Fax: (81) 545 34 0806
Total Employees at this Location: 70
Type of Operation: Paper mill
Pulp Grades and Capacities:
Total pulp capacity: 16,186 mt/y
Recycled Pulping: 16,186 mt/y
Pulp Mill Data:
Recycled Fiber Treatment Lines:
Flotation deinking lines: 1
Paper/Paperboard Grades and Capacities:
Total paper and paperboard capacity: 15,000 mt/y
Tissue: 15,000 mt/y
Paper and Paperboard Mill Data:
Paper Machines: 3
No. 1, Yankee dryer, total capacity 4,000 mt/y, Trim width 1.85 m, Tissue
No. 2, Yankee dryer, total capacity 5,000 mt/y, Trim width 2.46 m, Tissue
No. 3, Yankee dryer, total capacity 6,000 mt/y, Trim width 2.98 m, Tissue
Energy Data:
Power boilers
Electrical demand for mill: 50 MWh/D

ⓂIde Shigyo K.K.
Fuji Shimadacho Mill
2-198, Shimadacho
Fuji, Shizuoka Pref., 417-0033
Japan
Phone: (81) 545511003
Type of Operation: Paper mill
Paper/Paperboard Grades and Capacities:
Total paper and paperboard capacity: 38,000 mt/y
Tissue: 38,000 mt/y

ⓂIzumi Seishi K.K.
Kawanoe Mill
Ownership: Ide Shigyo K.K.
1523, Kawanoe-cho
Shikokuchuo, Ehime Pref., 799-0101
Japan
Phone: (81) 896 582427
Fax: (81) 896 586589
Total Employees at this Location: 25
Type of Operation: Paper mill
Pulp Grades and Capacities:
Total pulp capacity: 12,910 mt/y
Recycled Pulping: 12,910 mt/y
Pulp Mill Data:
Recycled Fiber Treatment Lines:
Flotation deinking lines
Paper/Paperboard Grades and Capacities:
Total paper and paperboard capacity: 12,000 mt/y
Tissue: 12,000 mt/y
Paper and Paperboard Mill Data:
Paper Machines: 1
No. 1, Yankee dryer, total capacity 12,000 mt/y, Trim width 2.75 m, Tissue
Energy Data:
Power boilers
Electrical demand for mill: 38 MWh/D

ⓂIzumi Seishi K.K.
Fuji Mill
Ownership: Ide Shigyo K.K.
111-1, Harada
Fuji, Shizuoka Pref., 417-0801
Japan
Total Employees at this Location: 25
Type of Operation: Paper mill
Pulp Grades and Capacities:
Total pulp capacity: 10,771 mt/y
Recycled Pulping: 10,771 mt/y
Pulp Mill Data:
Recycled Fiber Treatment Lines:
Flotation deinking lines
Paper/Paperboard Grades and Capacities:
Total paper and paperboard capacity: 10,000 mt/y
Tissue: 10,000 mt/y
Paper and Paperboard Mill Data:
Paper Machines: 1
No. 1, Yankee dryer, total capacity 10,000 mt/y, Trim width 2.75 m, Tissue
Energy Data:
Power boilers
Electrical demand for mill: 32 MWh/D

ⓂSanko Seishi K.K.
Fuji Matsuoka Mill
Ownership: Ide Shigyo K.K.
1597-1, Matsuoka
Fuji, Shizuoka Pref., 416-0909
Japan
Phone: (81) 545610015
Total Employees at this Location: 20
Type of Operation: Paper mill
Pulp Grades and Capacities:
Total pulp capacity: 5,408 mt/y
Recycled Pulping: 5,408 mt/y
Pulp Mill Data:
Recycled Fiber Treatment Lines:
Flotation deinking lines
Paper/Paperboard Grades and Capacities:
Total paper and paperboard capacity: 5,000 mt/y
Tissue: 5,000 mt/y
Paper and Paperboard Mill Data:
Paper Machines: 2
No. 1, Yankee dryer, total capacity 2,500 mt/y, Trim width 1.4 m, Tissue
No. 2, Yankee dryer, total capacity 2,500 mt/y, Trim width 1.4 m, Tissue
Energy Data:
Power boilers
Electrical demand for mill: 17 MWh/D

ⓂItoman Co., Ltd.
681 Shimobun Kinsei-cho
Shikokuchuo-shi, Ehime Pref., 799-0111
Japan
Phone: (81) 896 58 1010
Fax: (81) 896 58 1014
Email: itoman@us.ehime-iinet.or.jp
Web Address: www.e-itoman.jp/index.html
Mill Locations:
Itoman Co., Ltd., Kawanoe Mill, 681 Shimobun Kinsei-cho, Shikokuchuo-shi 799-0111, Japan, Capacity: 34,000 mt/y, (Paper mill)
Phone: (81) 896 58 1010
Fax: (81) 896 58 1014
Email: itoman@us.ehime-iinet.or.jp

ⓂItoman Co., Ltd.
Kawanoe Mill
681 Shimobun Kinsei-cho
Shikokuchuo-shi, Ehime Pref., 799-0111
Japan
Phone: (81) 896 58 1010
Fax: (81) 896 58 1014
Email: itoman@us.ehime-iinet.or.jp

Japan

Web Address: www.e-itoman.jp/index.html
Personnel:
Pres.: Shunichiro Ito
Phone: (81) 896 58 1010
Man. Dir.: Mitsunobu Hoshikawa
Phone: (81) 896 58 1010
Man. Dir.: Michiko Ito
Phone: (81) 896 58 1010
Total Employees at this Location: 145
Type of Operation: Paper mill
Pulp Grades and Capacities:
Total pulp capacity: 36,463 mt/y
Recycled Pulping: 36,463 mt/y
Pulp Mill Data:
Recycled Fiber Treatment Lines:
Flotation deinking lines: 1
Paper/Paperboard Grades and Capacities:
Total paper and paperboard capacity: 34,000 mt/y
Tissue: 34,000 mt/y
Paper and Paperboard Mill Data:
Paper Machines: 5
No. 5, Yankee dryer, total capacity 3,500 mt/y, Trim width 2.2 m, Tissue
No. 6, Yankee dryer, total capacity 3,500 mt/y, Trim width 2.2 m, Tissue
N2, BF-10, Yankee dryer, total capacity 9,000 mt/y, Trim width 2.35 m, Tissue
N3, BF-10, Yankee dryer, total capacity 9,000 mt/y, Trim width 2.35 m, Tissue
N7, BF-10, Yankee dryer, total capacity 9,000 mt/y, Trim width 2.4 m, Tissue
Energy Data:
Power boilers: 1
Combustion turbines: 1 at 1.5 MW
Electrical demand for mill: 106 MWh/D

ⓘⓜIwaki Daio Paper Corp.
Iwaki Mill
Ownership: 1.79% by Daio Paper Corp.
4-3-6 Minamidai
Iwaki-shi, Fukushima Pref., 974-8242
Japan
Phone: (81) 246 62 1111
Fax: (81) 246 62 8600
Web Address: www.iwaki-daio.co.jp
Personnel:
Pres.: Isao Hoshikawa
Phone: (81) 246 62 1111
Mill Mgr. / Dir.: Hideki Ohara
Phone: (81) 246 62 1111
Total Employees at this Location: 210
Type of Operation: Paper mill, Paperboard mill
Pulp Grades and Capacities:
Total pulp capacity: 428,400 mt/y
Recycled Pulping: 428,400 mt/y
Pulp Mill Data:
Bleach Plant Systems: 1
DIP
Recycled Fiber Treatment Lines:
Pulpers: 6
Paper/Paperboard Grades and Capacities:
Total paper and paperboard capacity: 414,120 mt/y
Newsprint: 114,240 mt/y
Linerboard: 299,880 mt/y
Paper and Paperboard Mill Data:
Stock Preparation:
Pulpers: 6
Paper Machines: 2
No. 1, multi-fourdrinier, total capacity 299,880 mt/y, Trim width 4.5 m, Linerboard
No. 2, multi-former, total capacity 114,240 mt/y, Trim width 3.43 m, Newsprint
Finishing Equipment:
Winders: 4
Energy Data:
Power boilers: 4
Steam turbines: 2 at 39.76 MW
Electrical demand for mill: 855 MWh/D

ⓘⓜKaga Paper Mfg. Co., Ltd.
Kaga Paper Mill
1-111, Nishi-kanazawa
Kanazawa-shi, Ishikawa Pref., 921-8054
Japan
Phone: (81) 76 241 1151
Fax: (81) 76 241 0239
Email: webmaster@kaga.co.jp
Web Address: www.kaga.co.jp
Personnel:
Pres.: Hideo Nakajima
Phone: (81) 76 241 1151
Fax: (81) 76 241 0239
Man. Dir.: Sanada Chisato
Phone: (81) 76 241 1151
Fax: (81) 76 241 0239
Mill Mgr.: Masaki Shimizu
Phone: (81) 76 241 1151
Fax: (81) 76 241 0239
Total Employees of Company: 120
Total Employees at this Location: 120
Type of Operation: Paperboard mill
Pulp Grades and Capacities:
Total pulp capacity: 61,799 mt/y
Recycled Pulping: 61,799 mt/y
Paper/Paperboard Grades and Capacities:
Total paper and paperboard capacity: 60,000 mt/y
Boxboard/cartonboard: 60,000 mt/y
Paper and Paperboard Mill Data:
Stock Preparation:
Pulpers: 8
Paper Machines: 2
No. 2, cylinder (10), total capacity 30,000 mt/y, Trim width 1.76 m, Boxboard/cartonboard
No. 3, cylinder (9), total capacity 30,000 mt/y, Trim width 1.73 m, Boxboard/cartonboard
Finishing Equipment:
Rewinders: 1
Energy Data:
Power boilers: 1
Steam turbines: 1 at 2.1 MW
Electrical demand for mill: 80 MWh/D

ⓘⓜKasuga Seishi Kogyo Co., Ltd.
Fuji-shi Mill
760-1 Hina
Fuji-shi, Shizuoka Pref., 417-0847
Japan
Phone: (81) 545 34 1003
Fax: (81) 545 34 3751
Email: mail@kasuga.co.jp
Web Address: www.kasuga.co.jp
Personnel:
Pres.: Kanichiro Hara
Phone: (81) 545 34 1003
Chmn.: Ryuzo Kubota
Total Employees of Company: 140
Total Employees at this Location: 140
Type of Operation: Paper mill
Pulp Grades and Capacities:
Total pulp capacity: 63,842 mt/y
Recycled Pulping: 63,842 mt/y
Pulp Mill Data:
Recycled Fiber Treatment Lines:
Flotation deinking lines: 1
Paper/Paperboard Grades and Capacities:
Total paper and paperboard capacity: 62,000 mt/y
Uncoated woodfree/freesheet: 5,000 mt/y
Uncoated mechanical/groundwood: 20,000 mt/y
Tissue: 33,000 mt/y
Packaging papers: 4,000 mt/y
Paper and Paperboard Mill Data:
Paper Machines: 4
No. 8, BF-10, Yankee dryer, total capacity 5,000 mt/y, Trim width 1.6 m, Tissue
N1, fourdrinier, total capacity 29,000 mt/y, Trim width 2.35 m, Uncoated mechanical/groundwood, Uncoated woodfree/freesheet, Packaging papers
N6, crescent former, Yankee dryer, total capacity 20,000 mt/y, Trim width 2.56 m, Tissue
N7, BF-10, Yankee dryer, total capacity 8,000 mt/y, Trim width 2.11 m, Tissue
Finishing Equipment:
Supercalenders: 1
Rewinders: 1
Energy Data:
Power boilers: 1
Combustion turbines: 1 at 5.8 MW
Electrical demand for mill: 151 MWh/D

ⓘⓜKawamura Seishi K.K.
Akanabe Mill
3-258, Akanabeshinsho
Gifu, Gifu Pref., 500-8263
Japan
Phone: (81) 58 274 2221
Fax: (81) 58 274 2222
Email: p-brunet@aioros.ocn.ne.jp
Web Address: www.s-adia.com/kawamura
Personnel:
Pres.: Mayumi Kawamura
Phone: (81) 58 274 2221
Fax: (81) 58 274 2222
Snr. Man. Dir.: Michiharu Kawamura
Phone: (81) 58 274 2221
Fax: (81) 58 274 2222
Man. Dir.: Yoshiro Kawamura
Phone: (81) 58 274 2221
Fax: (81) 58 274 2222
Dir.: Kenji Kawamura
Phone: (81) 58 274 2221
Fax: (81) 58 274 2222
Total Employees at this Location: 46
Type of Operation: Paper mill
Pulp Grades and Capacities:
Total pulp capacity: 8,653 mt/y
Recycled Pulping: 8,653 mt/y
Pulp Mill Data:
Recycled Fiber Treatment Lines:
Flotation deinking lines
Paper/Paperboard Grades and Capacities:
Total paper and paperboard capacity: 8,000 mt/y
Tissue: 8,000 mt/y
Paper and Paperboard Mill Data:
Paper Machines: 2
No. 1, Yankee dryer, total capacity 4,000 mt/y, Trim width 1.65 m, Tissue
No. 2, Yankee dryer, total capacity 4,000 mt/y, Trim width 1.65 m, Tissue
Energy Data:
Power boilers: 1
Electrical demand for mill: 27 MWh/D

ⓘⓜKawano Seishi K.K.
Kochi Mill
71, Shimojimacho
Kochi, Kochi Pref., 780-0934
Japan
Phone: (81) 888223107
Personnel:
Pres.: Norihisa Kawano
Phone: (81) 888223107
Gen. Mgr. R&D: Kenji Taniguchi
Phone: (81) 888223107
Total Employees at this Location: 25
Type of Operation: Paper mill
Pulp Grades and Capacities:
Total pulp capacity: 5,408 mt/y
Recycled Pulping: 5,408 mt/y
Pulp Mill Data:
Recycled Fiber Treatment Lines:
Flotation deinking lines
Paper/Paperboard Grades and Capacities:
Total paper and paperboard capacity: 5,000 mt/y
Tissue: 5,000 mt/y
Paper and Paperboard Mill Data:
Paper Machines: 5

Japan

No. 1, Yankee dryer, total capacity 1,000 mt/y, Trim width 1.21 m, Tissue
No. 2, Yankee dryer, total capacity 1,000 mt/y, Trim width 1.21 m, Tissue
No. 3, Yankee dryer, total capacity 1,000 mt/y, Trim width 1.21 m, Tissue
No. 4, Yankee dryer, total capacity 1,000 mt/y, Trim width 1.21 m, Tissue
No. 5, Yankee dryer, total capacity 1,000 mt/y, Trim width 1.21 m, Tissue
Energy Data:
Power boilers
Electrical demand for mill: 17 MWh/D

Keio Paper Mfg. Co., Ltd.
Fuji-shi Mill
4-4 Minami-cho
Fuji-shi, Shizuoka Pref., 417-0026
Japan
 Phone: (81) 545 52 0351
 Fax: (81) 545 53 6133
 Email: master@keiopaper.co.jp
 Web Address: www.keiopaper.co.jp
Personnel:
 Pres.: Yukihide Saito
 Phone: (81) 545 52 0351
Total Employees at this Location: 100
Type of Operation: Pulp mill, Paper mill, Paperboard mill
Paper/Paperboard Grades and Capacities:
 Total paper and paperboard capacity: 24,000 mt/y
 Specialty and industrial: 11,000 mt/y
Paper and Paperboard Mill Data:
Paper Machines: 2
No. 1, cylinder, total capacity 6,000 mt/y, Trim width 1.3 m
No. 2, Yankee dryer, cylinder, total capacity 18,000 mt/y, Trim width 1.76 m, Specialty and industrial

Kinsei Seishi Co. Ltd.
Iguchi Mill
63 Iguchi-cho, Kochi-sh
Kochi-ken, Kochi Pref., 780-0921
Japan
 Phone: (81) 88-822-8105
 Fax: (81) 88-822-8108
 Web Address: www.kinseiseishi.co.jp
Personnel:
 Pres.: Wataru Takenouchi
 Phone: (81) 88 822 8105
 Fax: (81) 88 822 8108
Total Employees of Company: 120
Total Employees at this Location: 20
Type of Operation: Paper mill
Pulp Grades and Capacities:
 Total pulp capacity: 10,771 mt/y
 Recycled Pulping: 10,771 mt/y
Pulp Mill Data:
 Recycled Fiber Treatment Lines:
 Flotation deinking lines
Paper/Paperboard Grades and Capacities:
 Total paper and paperboard capacity: 10,000 mt/y
 Tissue: 10,000 mt/y
Paper and Paperboard Mill Data:
Paper Machines: 1
No. 1, Yankee dryer, total capacity 10,000 mt/y, Trim width 2.1 m, Tissue
Energy Data:
Power boilers
Electrical demand for mill: 33 MWh/D

Kitakami Paper Co., Ltd.
Ichinoseki Mill
Ownership: Nippon Paper Industries Co., Ltd.
10-1, Asahi-machi
Ichinoseki-shi, Iwate Pref., 021-0864
Japan
 Phone: (81) 191 23 3366
 Fax: (81) 191 23 6192
 Email: psoumu@kitakami-p.jp
 Web Address: www.kitakami-p.jp
Personnel:
 Pres.: Kouro Fukudome
 Phone: (81) 191 23 3366
 Mill Mgr. / Dir.: Sachitaka Murada
 Phone: (81) 191 23 3366
Total Employees at this Location: 86
Type of Operation: Paper mill, Paperboard mill
Pulp Grades and Capacities:
 Total pulp capacity: 135,109 mt/y
 Recycled Pulping: 135,109 mt/y
Pulp Mill Data:
 Mechanical Pulping Systems:
 Conventional grinders: 1
 Recycled Fiber Treatment Lines:
 Flotation deinking lines: 1 at 12,000 admt/y
 Pulpers: 1 at 12,000 admt/y
Paper/Paperboard Grades and Capacities:
 Total paper and paperboard capacity: 135,000 mt/y
 Newsprint: 15,000 mt/y
 Linerboard: 120,000 mt/y
Paper and Paperboard Mill Data:
 Stock Preparation:
 Pulpers: 6
 Refiners: 6
Paper Machines: 2
No. 2, cylinder (5), total capacity 120,000 mt/y, Trim width 3.6 m, Linerboard
No. 3, DuoFormer D, total capacity 15,000 mt/y, Trim width 2.05 m, Newsprint
Finishing Equipment:
 Winders: 2
 Sheeters: 1
Energy Data:
Power boilers: 3
Steam turbines: 1 at 3.1 MW
Electrical demand for mill: 178 MWh/D

Kitakami Hitec Paper Corp.
Kitakami-shi Mill
Ownership: Mitsubishi Paper Mills Ltd.
35 Sasanagane, Aisari-cho
Kitakami-shi, Iwate Pref., 024-0051
Japan
 Phone: (81) 197 67 3211
 Fax: (81) 197 67 2365
 Web Address: www.kitakami-hitec.co.jp
Personnel:
 Gen. Mgr.: Naoya Tashiro
 Phone: (81) 197 67 3211
 Fax: (81) 197 67 2365
 Technology & Environ. Mgr.: Kazuhisa Taguchi
 Phone: (81) 197 67 3211
 Fax: (81) 197 67 2365
Total Employees at this Location: 254
Type of Operation: Pulp mill, Paper mill
Pulp Grades and Capacities:
 Total pulp capacity: 165,109 mt/y
 Pulp available for market: 79,968 mt/y
 Chemical Pulp: 165,109 mt/y
Pulp Mill Data:
 Chemical Pulping Systems:
 Continuous digesters: 1
 Pulp Lines: 1
 Bleach Plant Systems: 1
 Chemical Pulping System - Hardwood, Sequence: O_2 DEoDED, Capacity 130,000 admt/y
 Chemical Recovery Equipment:
 Evaporator lines: 1
 Recovery boilers: 1
 Lime Kiln
 Pulp Dryers:
 Flakt dryer 1
Paper/Paperboard Grades and Capacities:
 Total paper and paperboard capacity: 118,881 mt/y
 Uncoated woodfree/freesheet: 108,171 mt/y
 Tissue: 10,710 mt/y
Paper and Paperboard Mill Data:
Paper Machines: 2
No. 2, SymFormer MB, total capacity 108,171 mt/y, Trim width 5.2 m, Uncoated woodfree/freesheet
K1, Yankee dryer, total capacity 10,710 mt/y, Trim width 2.8 m, Tissue
Energy Data:
Power boilers: 1
Steam turbines: 3 at 11.1 MW
Electrical demand for mill: 502 MWh/D

KJ Specialty Paper Co., Ltd.
Ownership: 100% by Mitsubishi Corporation
4-1-21, Nihombashi-muro-cho, Chuo-ku
Tokyo, 103-0022
Japan
 Phone: (81) 3 3242 3018/3011
 Fax: (81) 3 3242 3054
 Web Address: www.kohjin.co.jp
Personnel:
 Pres.: Kazuya Mizuno
 Phone: (81) 3 3242 3018/3011
 Fax: (81) 3 3242 3054
Total Employees of Company: 665
Mill Locations:
KJ Specialty Paper Co., Ltd., Fuji Mill, 7-1 Shinbashi-machi, Fuji-shi 417-0004, Japan, Capacity: 48,000 mt/y, (Paper mill)
 Phone: (81) 545 52 4075
 Fax: (81) 545 52 3824

KJ Specialty Paper Co., Ltd.
Fuji Mill
7-1 Shinbashi-machi
Fuji-shi, Shizuoka Pref., 417-0004
Japan
 Phone: (81) 545 52 4075
 Fax: (81) 545 52 3824
 Web Address: www.kohjin.co.jp
Personnel:
 Mill Mgr.: Masayuki Murata
 Phone: (81) 545 52 4075
Total Employees at this Location: 183
Type of Operation: Paper mill
Paper/Paperboard Grades and Capacities:
 Total paper and paperboard capacity: 48,000 mt/y
 Specialty and industrial: 48,000 mt/y
Paper and Paperboard Mill Data:
 Stock Preparation:
 Pulpers: 9
 Refiners: 10
Paper Machines: 6
No. 1, fourdrinier, total capacity 12,000 mt/y, Trim width 2.1 m, Specialty and industrial
No. 2, fourdrinier, Yankee dryer, total capacity 7,300 mt/y, Trim width 1.6 m, Specialty and industrial
No. 3, fourdrinier, Yankee dryer, total capacity 8,100 mt/y, Trim width 1.42 m, Specialty and industrial
No. 4, fourdrinier, cylinder, total capacity 2,900 mt/y, Trim width 1.3 m, Specialty and industrial
No. 5, fourdrinier, Yankee dryer, total capacity 3,700 mt/y, Trim width 1.6 m, Specialty and industrial
N1, fourdrinier, total capacity 14,000 mt/y, Trim width 2.1 m, Specialty and industrial
Coating Machines: 2
No. 1, total capacity 1,000 mt/y., off machine
No. 3, total capacity 4,700 mt/y., off machine
Finishing Equipment:
 Supercalenders: 1
 Rewinders: 8
 Sheeters: 2
Energy Data:
Power boilers: 1

Koa Kogyo Co., Ltd.
Fuji-shi Mill
Ownership: 79.29% by Marubeni Corporation
1286-2, Hina
Fuji-shi, Shizuoka Pref., 417-0847
Japan

Phone: (81) 545 38 0123
Fax: (81) 545 38 1167/1174
Email: info@koa-kogyo.co.jp
Web Address: www.koa-kogyo.co.jp
Personnel:
Pres.: Hatta Kenichi
Phone: (81) 545 38 0123
Fax: (81) 545 38 1167
Snr. Man. Dir.: Arai Minoru
Phone: (81) 545 38 0123
Fax: (81) 545 38 1167
Man. Dir.: Okubo Kenji
Phone: (81) 545 38 0123
Fax: (81) 545 38 1167
Total Employees at this Location: 269
Type of Operation: Pulp mill, Paper mill, Paperboard mill
Pulp Grades and Capacities:
Total pulp capacity: 581,117 mt/y
Recycled Pulping: 574,692 mt/y
Pulp Mill Data:
Chemical Pulping Systems:
Batch digesters: 16
Chemical Recovery Equipment:
Recovery boilers: 2
Recycled Fiber Treatment Lines:
Recycled packaging pulping lines: 3
Paper/Paperboard Grades and Capacities:
Total paper and paperboard capacity: 581,910 mt/y
Packaging papers: 53,550 mt/y
Linerboard: 187,425 mt/y
Corrugating medium/fluting: 290,955 mt/y
Boxboard/cartonboard: 49,980 mt/y
Paper and Paperboard Mill Data:
Stock Preparation:
Pulpers: 12
Refiners: 20
Paper Machines: 6
No. 1, DuoFormer D, total capacity 149,940 mt/y, Trim width 3.85 m, Corrugating medium/fluting
No. 2, DuoFormer D, total capacity 141,015 mt/y, Trim width 3.85 m, Corrugating medium/fluting
No. 4, CombiPress, total capacity 23,205 mt/y, Trim width 1.7 m, Boxboard/cartonboard
No. 5, CombiPress, total capacity 26,775 mt/y, Trim width 1.7 m, Boxboard/cartonboard
No. 6, fourdrinier, total capacity 187,425 mt/y, Trim width 3.8 m, Linerboard
No. 8, fourdrinier, total capacity 53,550 mt/y, Trim width 3.25 m, Packaging papers
Coating Machines: 2
No. 1, on machine
No. 2, on machine
Finishing Equipment:
Rewinders: 4
Energy Data:
Power boilers: 3
Steam turbines: 3 at 84.8 MW
Electrical demand for mill: 1,007 MWh/D

ⓘKotobuki Paper Co. Ltd.
Fukuoka Konoike bldg. 1-14-45 Daimyo-cho
Chuo-ku, Fukuoka Pref., 810-0041
Japan
Phone: (81) 92 717 1070
Fax: (81) 92 717 1071
Personnel:
Pres.: Taisuke Muto
Phone: (81) 92 717 1070
Fax: (81) 92 717 1071
Total Employees of Company: 110
Mill Locations:
Kotobuki Paper Co. Ltd., Saga Mill, 1318 Oaza Katsu, Ushizu-cho, Ogi-shi 849-0306, Japan, Capacity: 38,500 mt/y, (Paper mill)
Phone: (81) 952 66 1511
Fax: (81) 952 66 4948

ⓜKotobuki Paper Co. Ltd.
Saga Mill
1318 Oaza Katsu, Ushizu-cho
Ogi-shi, Saga Pref., 849-0306
Japan
Phone: (81) 952 66 1511
Fax: (81) 952 66 4948
Web Address: www.kotobukiseishi.com
Personnel:
Chmn.: Chiichiro Saito
Pres.: Yasusuke Butou
Total Employees at this Location: 110
Type of Operation: Paper mill
Pulp Grades and Capacities:
Total pulp capacity: 41,156 mt/y
Recycled Pulping: 41,156 mt/y
Pulp Mill Data:
Bleach Plant Systems: 1
Recycled Pulping System, Type: Deinked
Recycled Fiber Treatment Lines:
Flotation deinking lines: 1
Paper/Paperboard Grades and Capacities:
Total paper and paperboard capacity: 38,500 mt/y
Tissue: 38,500 mt/y
Paper and Paperboard Mill Data:
Paper Machines: 6
No. 1, BF-10, Yankee dryer, total capacity 9,000 mt/y, Trim width 2.23 m, Tissue
No. 2, Yankee dryer, total capacity 9,000 mt/y, Trim width 2.23 m, Tissue
No. 3, Yankee dryer, total capacity 3,000 mt/y, Trim width 1.2 m, Tissue
No. 5, Yankee dryer, total capacity 5,000 mt/y, Trim width 2.23 m, Tissue
No. 6, BF-10, Yankee dryer, total capacity 3,500 mt/y, Trim width 1.2 m, Tissue
No. 7, BF-12, Yankee dryer, total capacity 9,000 mt/y, Trim width 2.23 m, Tissue
Finishing Equipment:
Rewinders: 7
Energy Data:
Power boilers: 2
Electrical demand for mill: 118 MWh/D

ⓘⓜKoyo Paper Mfg. Co., Ltd.
Honsha Mill
Ownership: 89.71% by Nippon Paper Industries Co., Ltd.
450 Hina
Fuji-shi, Shizuoka Pref., 417-0847
Japan
Phone: (81) 545 34 0820
Fax: (81) 545 38 2138
Email: info@koyopaper.co.jp
Web Address: www.koyopaper.co.jp
Personnel:
Pres.: Ken Hamaoki
Phone: (81) 545 34 0820
Snr. Man. Dir. / Mill Mgr.: Hiroaki Kobe
Phone: (81) 545 34 0820
Gen. Affairs Mgr.: Atsushi Kunichika
Phone: (81) 545 34 0820
Email: somubu@koyopaper.co
Total Employees of Company: 185
Total Employees at this Location: 185
Type of Operation: Pulp mill, Paper mill
Pulp Grades and Capacities:
Total pulp capacity: 9,723 mt/y
Recycled Pulping: 9,723 mt/y
Paper/Paperboard Grades and Capacities:
Total paper and paperboard capacity: 62,000 mt/y
Tissue: 26,000 mt/y
Boxboard/cartonboard: 36,000 mt/y
Paper and Paperboard Mill Data:
Stock Preparation:
Pulpers: 7
Refiners: 10
Paper Machines: 3
No. 1, cylinder (7), Yankee dryer, total capacity 14,000 mt/y, Trim width 1.81 m, Boxboard/cartonboard
No. 2, cylinder (6), Yankee dryer, total capacity 22,000 mt/y, Trim width 1.65 m, Boxboard/cartonboard
No. 3, crescent former, Yankee dryer, total capacity 26,000 mt/y, Trim width 3.28 m, Tissue
Coating Machines: 2
No. 1, total capacity 7,200 mt/y., on machine
No. 2, on machine
Finishing Equipment:
Rewinders: 4 at 32,400 mt/y
Sheeters: 5 at 32,400 mt/y
Energy Data:
Power boilers: 10
Combustion turbines: 2 at 3.3 MW
Electrical demand for mill: 117 MWh/D

ⓘⓜKyoku-Ei Paper Mfg. Co.
Fuji Mill
Ownership: Corelex Co., Ltd.
1450 Nakanogo
Fuji, Shizuoka Pref., 421-3306
Japan
Phone: (81) 0545-81-0323
Fax: (81) 0545-81-3122
Web Address: www.corelex.jp/kyokuei/company/company.html
Total Employees at this Location: 30
Type of Operation: Paper mill
Pulp Grades and Capacities:
Total pulp capacity: 9,721 mt/y
Recycled Pulping: 9,721 mt/y
Pulp Mill Data:
Recycled Fiber Treatment Lines:
Flotation deinking lines
Paper/Paperboard Grades and Capacities:
Total paper and paperboard capacity: 9,000 mt/y
Tissue: 9,000 mt/y
Paper and Paperboard Mill Data:
Paper Machines: 2
No. 1, Yankee dryer, total capacity 3,000 mt/y, Trim width 1.65 m, Tissue
No. 2, Yankee dryer, total capacity 6,000 mt/y, Trim width 2.56 m, Tissue
Energy Data:
Power boilers
Electrical demand for mill: 30 MWh/D

ⓘⓜKyoku-Ei Paper Mfg. Co., Ltd.
Fuji-shi Mill
Ownership: Corelex Co., Ltd.
575 Nakanogo
Fuji-shi, Shizuoka Pref., 421-3306
Japan
Phone: (81) 545 81 0323
Fax: (81) 545 81 3122
Web Address: www.corelex.jp
Personnel:
Pres.: Noboru Kurosaki
Phone: (81) 545 81 0323
Total Employees at this Location: 80
Type of Operation: Paper mill
Paper/Paperboard Grades and Capacities:
Total paper and paperboard capacity: 11,200 mt/y
Specialty and industrial: 11,200 mt/y
Paper and Paperboard Mill Data:
Paper Machines: 2
No. 5, fourdrinier, Trim width 2.41 m, Specialty and industrial
No. 7, cylinder, Yankee dryer, Trim width 1.8 m, Specialty and industrial

ⓘLintec Corp.
Ownership: 28.70% by Nippon Paper Industries Co., Ltd.
23-23 Hon-machi, Itabashi-ku
Tokyo, 173-0001
Japan

Japan

Phone: (81) 3 5248 7711
Fax: (81) 3 5248 7760
Web Address: www.lintec.co.jp
Personnel:
Pres. (From April 1, 2014): Hiroyuki Nishio
Phone: (81) 3 5248 7711
Fax: (81) 3 5248 7760
Exec. VP. & Dir.: Hitoshi Asai
Phone: (81) 3 5248 7711
Fax: (81) 3 5248 7760
Exec. VP. & Dir.: Shigeru Kawasaki
Phone: (81) 3 5248 7711
Fax: (81) 3 5248 7760
Snr. Man. Exec. Officer.: Koji Ichisashi
Phone: (81) 3 5248 7711
Fax: (81) 3 5248 7760
Total Employees of Company: 2,552
Mill Locations:
Lintec Corp., Kumagaya Mill, 3478 Mankichi, Kumagaya-shi 360-0161, Japan, Capacity: 69,495 mt/y, (Paper mill)
Phone: (81) 48 539 1212
Fax: (81) 48 539 1291
Lintec Corp., Mishima Mill, 2-46 Mishima-Kamiya-cho, Shikokuchuo-shi 799-0402, Japan, Capacity: 78,132 mt/y, (Paper mill)
Phone: (81) 896 23 4400
Fax: (81) 896 24 4400

ⓂLintec Corp.
Kumagaya Mill
Ownership: 28.70% by Nippon Paper Industries Co., Ltd.
3478 Mankichi
Kumagaya-shi, Saitama Pref., 360-0161
Japan
Phone: (81) 48 539 1212
Fax: (81) 48 539 1291
Web Address: www.lintec.co.jp
Personnel:
Mill Mgr.: Koichi Ohiwa
Phone: (81) 48 539 1212
Total Employees at this Location: 325
Type of Operation: Paper mill
Paper/Paperboard Grades and Capacities:
Total paper and paperboard capacity: 69,495 mt/y
Packaging papers: 28,000 mt/y
Specialty and industrial: 41,495 mt/y
Paper and Paperboard Mill Data:
Paper Machines: 3
No. 1, fourdrinier, total capacity 29,000 mt/y, Trim width 2.7 m, Specialty and industrial, Packaging papers
No. 2, fourdrinier, total capacity 12,495 mt/y, Trim width 1.65 m, Specialty and industrial
No. 3, DuoFormer D, total capacity 28,000 mt/y, Trim width 2.7 m, Specialty and industrial, Packaging papers
Finishing Equipment:
Supercalenders: 2
Rewinders: 3
Sheeters: 2
Energy Data:
Power boilers: 12
Combustion turbines: 4 at 9.4, 0.93, 2.3 MW
Electrical demand for mill: 184 MWh/D

ⓂLintec Corp.
Mishima Mill
Ownership: 28.70% by Nippon Paper Industries Co., Ltd.
2-46 Mishima-Kamiya-cho
Shikokuchuo-shi, Ehime Pref., 799-0402
Japan
Phone: (81) 896 23 4400
Fax: (81) 896 24 4400
Web Address: www.lintec.co.jp
Personnel:
Mill Mgr.: Seiji Takemura
Phone: (81) 896 23 4400
Total Employees at this Location: 309
Type of Operation: Paper mill
Paper/Paperboard Grades and Capacities:
Total paper and paperboard capacity: 78,132 mt/y
Packaging papers: 29,000 mt/y
Specialty and industrial: 49,132 mt/y
Paper and Paperboard Mill Data:
Paper Machines: 3
No. 1, fourdrinier, total capacity 27,132 mt/y, Trim width 2.5 m, Specialty and industrial
No. 2, fourdrinier, total capacity 28,000 mt/y, Trim width 1.95 m, Specialty and industrial, Packaging papers
No. 3, fourdrinier, total capacity 23,000 mt/y, Trim width 2.28 m, Specialty and industrial, Packaging papers
Finishing Equipment:
Supercalenders: 2
Rewinders: 3
Sheeters: 4
Energy Data:
Power boilers: 10
Combustion turbines: 2 at 5.8 MW
Electrical demand for mill: 184 MWh/D

ⓄⓂMaki Seishi K.K.
Mino Mill
43-1, Kamino
Mino, Gifu Pref., 501-3787
Japan
Phone: (81) 575 37 2311
Fax: (81) 575 37 2312
Email: maki-s@bird.ocn.ne.jp
Web Address: www.maki-seishi.com
Personnel:
Chmn., Pres.: Toshio Oda
Phone: (81) 575 37 2311
Fax: (81) 575 37 2312
Snr. Man. Dir.: Tsuyoshi Usui
Phone: (81) 575 37 2311
Fax: (81) 575 37 2312
Man. Dir.: Katsue Oda
Phone: (81) 575 37 2311
Fax: (81) 575 37 2312
Total Employees at this Location: 34
Type of Operation: Paper mill
Pulp Grades and Capacities:
Total pulp capacity: 5,408 mt/y
Recycled Pulping: 5,408 mt/y
Pulp Mill Data:
Recycled Fiber Treatment Lines:
Flotation deinking lines
Paper/Paperboard Grades and Capacities:
Total paper and paperboard capacity: 5,000 mt/y
Tissue: 5,000 mt/y
Paper and Paperboard Mill Data:
Paper Machines: 2
No. 1, Yankee dryer, total capacity 2,500 mt/y, Trim width 1.75 m, Tissue
No. 2, Yankee dryer, total capacity 2,500 mt/y, Trim width 1.75 m, Tissue
Energy Data:
Power boilers
Electrical demand for mill: 17 MWh/D

ⓄMarubeni Corporation
Ownership: Public
4-2, Ohtemachi 1-chome, Chiyoda-ku
Tokyo, 100-8088
Japan
Phone: (81) 3 3282 2111
Fax: (81) 3 3282 4241
Email: tokb191@marubenicorp.com
Web Address: www.marubeni.com
Personnel:
Chmn. & Board Member: Teruo Asada
Phone: (81) 3 3282 2111
Fax: (81) 3 3282 4241
Pres. & CEO: Fumiya Kokubu
Phone: (81) 3 3282 2111
Fax: (81) 3 3282 4241
CIO, COO, & Gen. Affairs: Yutaka Nomura
Phone: (81) 3 3282 2111
Fax: (81) 3 3282 4241
CFO: Yukihiko Matsumura
Phone: (81) 3 3282 2111
Fax: (81) 3 3282 4241
Total Employees of Company: 4,166
Mill Locations:
Koa Kogyo Co., Ltd., Fuji-shi Mill (79.29% owned), 1286-2, Hina, Fuji-shi 417-0847, Japan, Capacity: 581,910 mt/y, (Pulp mill, Paper mill, Paperboard mill)
Phone: (81) 545 38 0123
Fax: (81) 545 38 1167/1174
Email: info@koa-kogyo.co.jp
PT Tanjung Enim Lestari Pulp & Paper, Musi Pulp Mill (85% owned), Desa Niru, Tebang Agung, Kec. Rambang Dangku, 31172 Kab. Muara Enim, Indonesia, (Pulp mill)
Phone: (62) 713 324 150/160
Fax: (62) 713 324 182/190

ⓄⓂMarui Paper Industry Co., Ltd.
Kuzawa
37 Kuzawa
Fuji-shi, Shizuoka Pref., 419-0293
Japan
Phone: (81) 545 71 2320
Fax: (81) 545 71 7874
Email: maruinfo@maruipaper.com/, marui@plum.ocn.ne.jp
Web Address: www.maruipaper.com
Personnel:
Chmn.: Kiyoaki Ide
Phone: (81) 545 71 2320
Fax: (81) 545 71 7874
Pres.: Hiroyuki Ide
Phone: (81) 545 71 2320
Fax: (81) 545 71 7874
Paperboard Mill Mgr.: Yoshio Ito
Phone: (81) 545 71 2320
Total Employees of Company: 120
Total Employees at this Location: 120
Type of Operation: Paperboard mill
Pulp Grades and Capacities:
Total pulp capacity: 40,968 mt/y
Recycled Pulping: 40,968 mt/y
Paper/Paperboard Grades and Capacities:
Total paper and paperboard capacity: 44,000 mt/y
Boxboard/cartonboard: 44,000 mt/y
Paper and Paperboard Mill Data:
Paper Machines: 2
No. 1, cylinder (7), total capacity 18,000 mt/y, Trim width 1.7 m, Boxboard/cartonboard
No. 2, cylinder (8), total capacity 26,000 mt/y, Trim width 1.7 m, Boxboard/cartonboard
Energy Data:
Power boilers: 2
Electrical demand for mill: 67 MWh/D

ⓄⓂMarukin Seishi K.K.
Fuji Mill
4-1, Takaokahoncho
Fuji, Shizuoka Pref., 419-0203
Japan
Phone: (81) 545712100
Personnel:
Pres.: Tomoyuki Suzuki
Phone: (81) 244 22 3111
Fax: (81) 244 22 0650
Man. Dir.: Masaru Suzuki
Phone: (81) 244 22 3111
Fax: (81) 244 22 0650
Dir. & Mill Mgr.: Touru Sugatani
Phone: (81) 244 22 3111
Fax: (81) 244 22 0650
Total Employees at this Location: 20
Type of Operation: Paper mill
Pulp Grades and Capacities:
Total pulp capacity: 5,408 mt/y
Recycled Pulping: 5,408 mt/y
Pulp Mill Data:

Japan

Recycled Fiber Treatment Lines:
Flotation deinking lines
Paper/Paperboard Grades and Capacities:
Total paper and paperboard capacity: 5,000 mt/y
Tissue: 5,000 mt/y
Paper and Paperboard Mill Data:
Paper Machines: 2
No. 1, Yankee dryer, total capacity 2,000 mt/y, Trim width 1.65 m, Tissue
No. 2, Yankee dryer, total capacity 3,000 mt/y, Trim width 1.95 m, Tissue
Energy Data:
Power boilers
Electrical demand for mill: 17 MWh/D

ⓄⓂMarusan Paper Mfg. Co., Ltd.
Honsha Mill
Ownership: 94.86% by Rengo Co., Ltd.
1-12-1, Aoba-cho
Haramachi-ku, Minami-soma-shi, Fukushima Pref., 975-0039
Japan
 Phone: (81) 244 22 3111
 Fax: (81) 244 22 0650
 Email: soumu@marusan-paper.co.jp
 Web Address: www.marusan-paper.co.jp, www.rengo.co.jp
Personnel:
Pres. (From June, 2013): Hakaru Mita
 Phone: (81) 244 22 3111
 Fax: (81) 244 22 0650
Man. Dir.: Atsushi Kamiyama
 Phone: (81) 244 22 3111
 Fax: (81) 244 22 0650
Man. Dir.: Hiroshi Watanabe
 Phone: (81) 244 22 3111
 Fax: (81) 244 22 0650
Total Employees at this Location: 205
Type of Operation: Paper mill, Paperboard mill
Pulp Grades and Capacities:
Total pulp capacity: 303,450 mt/y
Recycled Pulping: 303,450 mt/y
Pulp Mill Data:
Recycled Fiber Treatment Lines:
Recycled packaging pulping lines: 1
Paper/Paperboard Grades and Capacities:
Total paper and paperboard capacity: 313,446 mt/y
Specialty and industrial: 6,426 mt/y
Linerboard: 114,240 mt/y
Corrugating medium/fluting: 192,780 mt/y
Paper and Paperboard Mill Data:
Paper Machines: 3
No. 2, cylinder, total capacity 6,426 mt/y, Trim width 2.05 m, Specialty and industrial
No. 6, (restarted July 6, 2011, after the March 11 quake and tsunami), cylinder, total capacity 114,240 mt/y, Trim width 4.55 m, Linerboard
No. 7, (restarted July 3, 2011, after the March 11 quake and tsunami), top former, total capacity 192,780 mt/y, Trim width 3.85 m, Corrugating medium/fluting
Energy Data:
Power boilers: 2
Steam turbines: 1 at 5.1 MW
Electrical demand for mill: 510 MWh/D

ⓂMarusan Paper Corparation
Shikokuchuo-shi Mill
Ownership: Rengo Co., Ltd.
742 Shimobun, Kinsei-cho
Shikokuchuo-shi, Ehime Pref., 799-0111
Japan
 Phone: (81) 896 58 3450
 Fax: (81) 896 58 3502
Personnel:
Pres.: Seiji Setsuda
 Phone: (81) 896 58 3450
Man. Dir.: Yoshiaki Kato
 Phone: (81) 896 58 3450

Total Employees at this Location: 20
Type of Operation: Paper mill
Paper/Paperboard Grades and Capacities:
Total paper and paperboard capacity: 2,700 mt/y
Tissue
Packaging papers
Specialty and industrial
Paper and Paperboard Mill Data:
Paper Machines: 3
No. 1, Yankee dryer, cylinder, Trim width 1.1 m, Specialty and industrial
No. 2, combination, Trim width 1.1 m, Specialty and industrial
No. 3, Yankee dryer, cylinder, Trim width 2.2 m, Specialty and industrial

ⓂMarusumi Paper Co., Ltd.
826, Kawanoe-cho
Shikokuchuo-shi, Ehime Pref., 799-0196
Japan
 Phone: (81) 896 57 2222
 Fax: (81) 896 59 1001
 Email: soumuka@marusumi.co.jp
 Web Address: www.marusumi.co.jp
Personnel:
Pres.: Kazuya Hoshikawa
 Phone: (81) 896 57 2222
 Fax: (81) 896 59 1001
Gen. Mgr. Facility & Construction: Toshikazu Ichihara
 Phone: (81) 896 57 2222
 Fax: (81) 896 59 1001
Total Employees of Company: 690
Mill Locations:
Marusumi Paper Co., Ltd., Kawanoe Mill, 826 Kawanoe-cho, Shikokuchuo-shi 799-0196, Japan, Capacity: 219,200 mt/y, (Paper mill)
 Phone: (81) 896 57 2250
 Fax: (81) 896 57 2266
 Email: soumuka@marusumi.co.jp
Marusumi Paper Co., Ltd., Ohe Mill, 4085 Kawanoe-cho, Shikokuchuo-shi 799-0196, Japan, Capacity: 535,500 mt/y, (Pulp mill, Paper mill)
 Phone: (81) 896 57 2270
 Email: soumuka@marusumi.co.jp

ⓂMarusumi Paper Co., Ltd.
Kawanoe Mill
826 Kawanoe-cho
Shikokuchuo-shi, Ehime Pref., 799-0196
Japan
 Phone: (81) 896 57 2250
 Fax: (81) 896 57 2266
 Email: soumuka@marusumi.co.jp
 Web Address: www.marusumi.co.jp
Personnel:
Mill Mgr.: Minoru Niwa
 Phone: (81) 896 57 2250
Total Employees at this Location: 267
Type of Operation: Paper mill
Pulp Grades and Capacities:
Total pulp capacity: 381,600 mt/y
Chemical Pulp
Mechanical Pulp: 147,600 mt/y
Recycled Pulping: 135,000 mt/y
Pulp Mill Data:
Chemical Pulping Systems:
Continuous digesters: 1
Mechanical Pulping Systems:
Conventional grinders: 5
RMP systems: 1
TMP systems: 1
Bleach Plant Systems: **2**
No. 1 Capacity 90,000 admt/y
No. 2 Capacity 60,000 admt/y
Chemical Recovery Equipment:
Evaporator lines: 1
Recovery boilers: 2
Recycled Fiber Treatment Lines:
Flotation deinking lines: 2

Pulpers: 2
Washing deinking lines: 2
Paper/Paperboard Grades and Capacities:
Total paper and paperboard capacity: 219,200 mt/y
Newsprint: 36,000 mt/y
Uncoated mechanical/groundwood: 151,200 mt/y
Packaging papers: 32,000 mt/y
Paper and Paperboard Mill Data:
Stock Preparation:
Pulpers: 3
Refiners: 15
Paper Machines: 4
No. 2, Bel-Form, total capacity 43,200 mt/y, Trim width 3.27 m, Uncoated mechanical/groundwood
No. 3, Yankee dryer, fourdrinier, total capacity 32,000 mt/y, Trim width 3.35 m, Packaging papers
No. 4, SymFormer MB, total capacity 72,000 mt/y, Trim width 3.27 m, Uncoated mechanical/groundwood
No. 5, Bel-Baie II, total capacity 72,000 mt/y, Trim width 3.27 m, Uncoated mechanical/groundwood, Newsprint
Coating Machines: 2
No. 1, total capacity 42,000 mt/y.
No. 2, total capacity 67,000 mt/y.
Finishing Equipment:
Supercalenders: 12
Rewinders: 5
Sheeters: 1
Energy Data:
Power boilers: 6
Steam turbines: 4 at 16.4, 70, 8, 40 MW

ⓂMarusumi Paper Co., Ltd.
Ohe Mill
4085 Kawanoe-cho
Shikokuchuo-shi, Ehime Pref., 799-0196
Japan
 Phone: (81) 896 57 2270
 Email: soumuka@marusumi.co.jp
 Web Address: www.marusumi.co.jp
Personnel:
Mill Mgr.: Minoru Niwa
 Phone: (81) 896 57 2270
Total Employees at this Location: 309
Type of Operation: Pulp mill, Paper mill
Pulp Grades and Capacities:
Total pulp capacity: 423,243 mt/y
Mechanical Pulp: 115,033 mt/y
Recycled Pulping: 308,210 mt/y
Pulp Mill Data:
Chemical Pulping Systems:
Continuous digesters: 1
Mechanical Pulping Systems:
CTMP systems: 1
TMP systems: 1
Pulp Lines: **3**
Bleach Plant Lines:
Recycled pulp system bleaching, Sequence: P/HS
Chemical Recovery Equipment:
Recovery boilers: 1
Recycled Fiber Treatment Lines:
Flotation deinking lines: 2 at 250,000 admt/y
Paper/Paperboard Grades and Capacities:
Total paper and paperboard capacity: 535,500 mt/y
Newsprint: 360,570 mt/y
Coated woodfree/freesheet: 84,966 mt/y
Coated mechanical/groundwood: 89,964 mt/y
Paper and Paperboard Mill Data:
Paper Machines: 3
No. 1, Bel-Baie II, total capacity 174,930 mt/y, Trim width 8.8 m, Newsprint
No. 2, twin-wire, total capacity 214,200 mt/y, Trim width 9 m, Newsprint
No. 3, top former, total capacity 174,930 mt/y, Trim width 5.65 m, Coated mechanical/groundwood, Coated woodfree/freesheet
Coating Machines: 1
PM 3, total capacity 175,000 mt/y., on machine
Finishing Equipment:

Japan

Rewinders: 5
Energy Data:
Power boilers: 7
Steam turbines: 4 at 110.5 MW
Electrical demand for mill: 2,057 MWh/D

ⓗⓜMarutomi Paper Mfg. Co., Ltd.
Fujine Mill
686 Tenma
Fuji-shi, Shizuoka Pref., 419-0295
Japan
 Phone: (81) 545 71 0816/0103
 Fax: (81) 545 71 6350
 Email: info@marutomo-seishi.co.jp
 Web Address: www.marutomi-seishi.co.jp
Personnel:
 Pres.: Takeo Sano
 Phone: (81) 545 71 0816
Total Employees of Company: 290
Total Employees at this Location: 72
Type of Operation: Paper mill
Mill Locations:
Ichikawa Seishi K.K., Fuji Mill, 650-1, Hina, Fuji 417-0847, Japan, Capacity: 15,000 mt/y, (Paper mill)
 Phone: (81) 545 34 0840
 Fax: (81) 545 34 0806
Marutomi Paper Mfg. Co., Ltd., Imaizumi Mill, 7-8-25 Imaizumi, Fuji-shi 417-0001, Japan, Capacity: 15,000 mt/y, (Paper mill)
 Phone: (81) 545 52 3055
 Fax: (81) 545 52 3056
 Email: info@marutomo-seishi.co.jp
Marutomi Paper Mfg. Co., Ltd., Numazu Mill, 35 Ohoka, Numazu-shi 410-0022, Japan, Capacity: 25,000 mt/y, (Paper mill)
 Phone: (81) 559 63 5380
 Fax: (81) 559 63 5385
 Email: info@marutomo-seishi.co.jp
Mifuji Seishi K.K., Fuji Mill, 2-3-41, Imaizumi, Fuji 417-0001, Japan, Capacity: 8,000 mt/y, (Paper mill)
Ono Seishi K.K., Fuji Mill, 344, Harada, Fuji 417 0852, Japan, Capacity: 12,000 mt/y, (Paper mill)
 Phone: (81) 545520282
Pulp Grades and Capacities:
 Total pulp capacity: 34,343 mt/y
 Recycled Pulping: 34,343 mt/y
Pulp Mill Data:
 Bleach Plant Systems: 1
 Recycled Pulping System, Type: Deinked
 Recycled Fiber Treatment Lines:
 Flotation deinking lines: 1
Paper/Paperboard Grades and Capacities:
 Total paper and paperboard capacity: 33,000 mt/y
 Tissue: 33,000 mt/y
Paper and Paperboard Mill Data:
Paper Machines: 1
 No. 1, crescent former, Yankee dryer, total capacity 33,000 mt/y, Trim width 3.15 m, Tissue
Energy Data:
Power boilers: 5
Combustion turbines
Electrical demand for mill: 96 MWh/D

ⓜMarutomi Paper Mfg. Co., Ltd.
Imaizumi Mill
7-8-25 Imaizumi
Fuji-shi, Shizuoka Pref., 417-0001
Japan
 Phone: (81) 545 52 3055
 Fax: (81) 545 52 3056
 Email: info@marutomo-seishi.co.jp
 Web Address: www.marutomi-seishi.co.jp
Personnel:
 Mill Mgr.: Ikuyuki Ohkawa
 Phone: (81) 545 52 3055
Total Employees at this Location: 36
Type of Operation: Paper mill
Pulp Grades and Capacities:
 Total pulp capacity: 16,224 mt/y
 Recycled Pulping: 16,224 mt/y
Pulp Mill Data:
 Recycled Fiber Treatment Lines:
 Flotation deinking lines: 1
Paper/Paperboard Grades and Capacities:
 Total paper and paperboard capacity: 15,000 mt/y
 Tissue: 15,000 mt/y
Paper and Paperboard Mill Data:
Paper Machines: 2
 No. 2, Yankee dryer, total capacity 6,000 mt/y, Trim width 1.78 m, Tissue
 No. 3, Yankee dryer, total capacity 9,000 mt/y, Trim width 2.8 m, Tissue
Finishing Equipment:
 Rewinders: 10
Energy Data:
Power boilers: 3
Electrical demand for mill: 51 MWh/D

ⓜMarutomi Paper Mfg. Co., Ltd.
Numazu Mill
35 Ohoka
Numazu-shi, Shizuoka Pref., 410-0022
Japan
 Phone: (81) 559 63 5380
 Fax: (81) 559 63 5385
 Email: info@marutomo-seishi.co.jp
 Web Address: www.marutomi-seishi.co.jp
Personnel:
 Mill Mgr.: Koji Kiuchi
 Phone: (81) 559 63 5380
Total Employees at this Location: 40
Type of Operation: Paper mill
Pulp Grades and Capacities:
 Total pulp capacity: 26,770 mt/y
 Recycled Pulping: 26,770 mt/y
Pulp Mill Data:
 Recycled Fiber Treatment Lines:
 Flotation deinking lines: 1
Paper/Paperboard Grades and Capacities:
 Total paper and paperboard capacity: 25,000 mt/y
 Tissue: 25,000 mt/y
Paper and Paperboard Mill Data:
 Stock Preparation:
 Pulpers: 1
Paper Machines: 2
 No. 2, crescent former, Yankee dryer, total capacity 12,500 mt/y, Trim width 2.65 m, Tissue
 No. 3, crescent former, Yankee dryer, total capacity 12,500 mt/y, Trim width 2.65 m, Tissue
Finishing Equipment:
 Rewinders: 6
 Sheeters: 2
Energy Data:
Power boilers: 4
Electrical demand for mill: 77 MWh/D

ⓗⓜMasuko Seishi K.K.
Fujinomiya Mill
14-12, Asamacho
Fuji, Shizuoka Pref., 418-0032
Japan
 Phone: (81) 544 27 0251
 Fax: (81) 544 23 4557
 Web Address: www.masukoo.co.jp
Personnel:
 Pres.: Akihiko Masuda
 Phone: (81) 544 27 0251
 Fax: (81) 544 23 4557
 Snr. Man. Dir.: Hirokazu Masuda
 Phone: (81) 544 27 0251
 Fax: (81) 544 23 4557
 Man. Dir.: Hidefumi Yura
 Phone: (81) 544 27 0251
 Fax: (81) 544 23 4557
Total Employees at this Location: 30
Type of Operation: Paper mill
Pulp Grades and Capacities:
 Total pulp capacity: 17,309 mt/y
 Recycled Pulping: 17,309 mt/y
Paper/Paperboard Grades and Capacities:
 Total paper and paperboard capacity: 16,000 mt/y
 Tissue: 16,000 mt/y
Paper and Paperboard Mill Data:
Paper Machines: 2
 No. 1, Yankee dryer, total capacity 5,000 mt/y, Trim width 1.45 m, Tissue
 No. 2, Yankee dryer, total capacity 11,000 mt/y, Trim width 2.18 m, Tissue
Energy Data:
Power boilers
Electrical demand for mill: 55 MWh/D

ⓗⓜMatsuoka Seishi K.K
Fuji Mill
1788 Funaba, Matsuoka
Fuji, Shizuoka Pref., 416-0909
Japan
 Phone: (81) 545 61 0254
 Fax: (81) 545 62 1008
 Email: matsuoka-gyomu@tuba.ocn.ne.jp
Personnel:
 Chmn.: Shigeru Kobayashi
 Pres.: Hisatoshi Kobayashi
Total Employees at this Location: 18
Type of Operation: Paper mill
Paper/Paperboard Grades and Capacities:
 Total paper and paperboard capacity: 8,000 mt/y
 Tissue: 8,000 mt/y
Paper and Paperboard Mill Data:
Paper Machines: 4
 No. 1, Yankee dryer, total capacity 2,000 mt/y, Trim width 1.37 m, Tissue
 No. 2, Yankee dryer, total capacity 2,000 mt/y, Trim width 1.37 m, Tissue
 No. 3, Yankee dryer, total capacity 2,000 mt/y, Trim width 1.4 m, Tissue
 No. 4, Yankee dryer, total capacity 2,000 mt/y, Trim width 1.56 m, Tissue
Energy Data:
Power boilers
Electrical demand for mill: 24 MWh/D

ⓗⓜMeiji Seishi Co., Ltd.
Takaoka Mill
Ownership: 88.10% by Tokushu Tokai Paper Co., Ltd., 11.70% by Mitsubishi Corporation, 0.20% by Tokai-Kakoshi Co., Ltd.
167-1 Aza Nakase Atsuhara
Fuji-shi, Shizuoka Pref., 419-0201
Japan
 Phone: (81) 545 71 1122
 Fax: (81) 545 71 1181
 Web Address: www.meijiseishi.co.jp
Personnel:
 Pres.: Hiroshi Watabe
 Phone: (81) 545 71 1122
 Fax: (81) 545 71 1181
 Mill Mgr.: Tsuyoshi Mochizuki
 Phone: (81) 545 71 1122
 Fax: (81) 545 71 1181
Total Employees of Company: 60
Total Employees at this Location: 60
Type of Operation: Paper mill
Pulp Grades and Capacities:
 Total pulp capacity: 39,674 mt/y
 Recycled Pulping: 39,674 mt/y
Pulp Mill Data:
 Bleach Plant Systems: 1
 Recycled Pulping System, Type: Deinked
 Recycled Fiber Treatment Lines:
 Flotation deinking lines: 1
Paper/Paperboard Grades and Capacities:
 Total paper and paperboard capacity: 37,000 mt/y
 Tissue: 37,000 mt/y
Paper and Paperboard Mill Data:
Paper Machines: 3

Japan

No. 1, Yankee dryer, total capacity 13,000 mt/y, Trim width 2.74 m, Tissue
No. 2, Yankee dryer, total capacity 12,000 mt/y, Trim width 2.74 m, Tissue
No. 3, Yankee dryer, total capacity 12,000 mt/y, Trim width 2.74 m, Tissue
Energy Data:
Power boilers: 3
Electrical demand for mill: 116 MWh/D

ⓞⓜMifuji Seishi K.K.
Fuji Mill
Ownership: Marutomi Paper Mfg. Co., Ltd.
2-3-41, Imaizumi
Fuji, Shizuoka Pref., 417-0001
Japan
Total Employees at this Location: 30
Type of Operation: Paper mill
Pulp Grades and Capacities:
Total pulp capacity: 8,653 mt/y
Recycled Pulping: 8,653 mt/y
Paper/Paperboard Grades and Capacities:
Total paper and paperboard capacity: 8,000 mt/y
Tissue: 8,000 mt/y
Paper and Paperboard Mill Data:
Paper Machines: 2
No. 1, Yankee dryer, total capacity 3,000 mt/y, Trim width 1.46 m, Tissue
No. 2, Yankee dryer, total capacity 5,000 mt/y, Trim width 2.1 m, Tissue
Energy Data:
Power boilers
Electrical demand for mill: 27 MWh/D

ⓞⓜMiki Tokushu Paper Mfg. Co., Ltd.
Kawanoe Mill
156 Kawanoe-cho
Shikokuchuo-shi, Ehime Pref., 799-0101
Japan
  Phone: (81) 896 58 3373
  Fax: (81) 896 58 2105
  Email: info@mikitoku.co.jp
  Web Address: www.mikitoku.co.jp
Personnel:
Chmn.: Teruhisa Miki
  Phone: (81) 896 58 3373
  Fax: (81) 896 58 2105
Pres.: Masato Miki
  Phone: (81) 896 58 3373
  Fax: (81) 896 58 2105
Man. Dir.: Yoshinori Miki
  Phone: (81) 896 58 3373
  Fax: (81) 896 58 2105
Total Employees of Company: 163
Total Employees at this Location: 163
Type of Operation: Paper mill
Mill Locations:
Anhui Mikitoku Paper Co., Ltd, Anqing Mill (65% owned), No. 36, Gaobu Road, Gaohe Town, Anqing, China, Capacity: 2,856 mt/y, (Paper mill)
  Phone: (86) 556 485 6888/461 6888
  Fax: (86) 556 461 6288
Paper/Paperboard Grades and Capacities:
Total paper and paperboard capacity: 50,000 mt/y
Specialty and industrial
Paper and Paperboard Mill Data:
Paper Machines: 6
No. 6, combination, multi-cylinder, Trim width 1.35 m
No. 7, cylinder, Yankee dryer, Trim width 1.35 m
No. 8, Yankee dryer, cylinder, Trim width 2 m
N1, cylinder, Yankee dryer, Trim width 0.66 m
N3, combination, multi-cylinder, Trim width 2.9 m
N5, cylinder, total capacity 15,600 mt/y, Trim width 1.25 m

ⓜMitsubishi Paper Mills Ltd.
Ownership: Public
2-10-14 Ryogoku, Sumida-ku
Tokyo, 130-0026
Japan
  Phone: (81) 3 5600 1488
  Fax: (81) 3 5600 1489
  Email: webmaster@mpm.co.jp
  Web Address: www.mpm.co.jp
Personnel:
Pres. & CEO: Kunio Suzuki
  Phone: (81) 3 3213 3751
  Fax: (81) 3 3214 2338
Snr. Man. Exec. Officers (Raw Materials & Purch.): Masami Mizuno
  Phone: (81) 3 3213 3751
  Fax: (81) 3 3214 2338
Snr. Man. Exec. Officer Paper Div. & German Oper.: Mitsuo Ushijima
  Phone: (81) 3 3213 3751
  Fax: (81) 3 3214 2338
Snr. Man. Exec. Officers (Finan. & Accounting Dept.): Kanji Itakura
  Phone: (81) 3 3213 3751
  Fax: (81) 3 3214 2338
Man. Exec. Officers (Gen. Affairs & Personnel. Dept.): Hiroshi Nozawa
  Phone: (81) 3 3213 3751
  Fax: (81) 3 3214 2338
Man. Exec. Officers (Technology & Environ. Dept.): Fukumi Kanehama
  Phone: (81) 3 3213 3751
  Fax: (81) 3 3214 2338
Total Employees of Company: 4,133
Mill Locations:
Kitakami Hitec Paper Corp., Kitakami-shi Mill, 35 Sasanagane, Aisari-cho, Kitakami-shi 024-0051, Japan, Capacity: 118,881 mt/y, (Pulp mill, Paper mill)
  Phone: (81) 197 67 3211
  Fax: (81) 197 67 2365
Mitsubishi HiTec Paper Europe GmbH, Bielefeld Mill, Niedernholz 23, D-33699 Bielefeld, Germany, Capacity: 150,000 mt/y, (Paper mill)
  Phone: (49) 521 20910
  Fax: (49) 521 2091411
  Email: info.mpe@mitsubishi-paper.com
Mitsubishi HiTec Paper Europe GmbH, Flensburg Mill, Husumer Str. 12, D-24941 Flensburg, Germany, Capacity: 35,000 mt/y, (Paper mill)
  Phone: (49) 461 8695 0
  Fax: (49) 461 8695500
  Email: info.mpe@mitsubishi-paper.com
Mitsubishi Paper Mills Ltd., Hachinohe Mill, Kawaragi-Aomoriyachi, Hachinohe-shi 031-1197, Japan, Capacity: 907,494 mt/y, (Pulp mill, Paper mill, Paperboard mill)
  Phone: (81) 178 29 2111
  Fax: (81) 178 29 2750
Mitsubishi Paper Mills Ltd., Kyoto Mill, 6-6, Kaiden 1-chome, Nagaokakyo-shi 617-8666, Japan, Capacity: 32,000 mt/y, (Paper mill)
  Phone: (81) 75 951 1181
  Fax: (81) 75 951 1081
Mitsubishi Paper Mills Ltd., Shirakawa Mill, 3, Aza Maeyamanishi, Nishigo-mura, Nishi-Shirakawa-gun 961-8054, Japan, Capacity: 6,000 mt/y, (Pulp mill)
  Phone: (81) 248 22 8111
  Fax: (81) 248 23 3427
Mitsubishi Paper Mills Ltd., Takasago Mill, 105 Sakae-machi, Takasago-cho, Takasago-shi 676-8677, Japan, Capacity: 107,814 mt/y, (Paper mill)
  Phone: (81) 794 42 3101
  Fax: (81) 794 43 6012

ⓜMitsubishi Paper Mills Ltd.
Hachinohe Mill
Kawaragi-Aomoriyachi
Hachinohe-shi, Aomori, 031-1197
Japan
  Phone: (81) 178 29 2111
  Fax: (81) 178 29 2750
  Web Address: www.mpm.co.jp
Personnel:
Mill Mgr.: Yoshihiko Hibino
  Phone: (81) 178 29 2111
  Fax: (81) 178 29 2750
Deputy Gen. Mgr. (Equipment Planning Office): Akira Takeuchi
  Phone: (81) 178 29 2111
  Fax: (81) 178 29 2750
Total Employees at this Location: 491
Type of Operation: Pulp mill, Paper mill, Paperboard mill
Pulp Grades and Capacities:
Total pulp capacity: 627,923 mt/y
Chemical Pulp: 557,713 mt/y
Mechanical Pulp: 21,420 mt/y
Recycled Pulping: 48,790 mt/y
Pulp Mill Data:
Chemical Pulping Systems:
Batch digesters: 4
Continuous digesters: 1
Mechanical Pulping Systems:
CTMP systems: 1
Pulp Lines: 4
Bleach Plant Lines:
Chemical pulping system bleaching
Mechanical pulping system bleaching
Recycled pulping bleaching
Chemical Recovery Equipment:
Recovery boilers: 1
Recycled Fiber Treatment Lines:
Flotation deinking lines: 1 at 5,000
Paper/Paperboard Grades and Capacities:
Total paper and paperboard capacity: 907,494 mt/y
Uncoated woodfree/freesheet: 286,314 mt/y
Coated woodfree/freesheet: 562,275 mt/y
Boxboard/cartonboard: 58,905 mt/y
Paper and Paperboard Mill Data:
Stock Preparation:
Refiners: 7
Paper Machines: 7
No. 1, fourdrinier, total capacity 58,905 mt/y, Trim width 3.3 m, Boxboard/cartonboard
No. 2, fourdrinier, total capacity 72,828 mt/y, Trim width 3.34 m, Coated woodfree/freesheet
No. 3, DuoFormer D, total capacity 146,013 mt/y, Trim width 4.87 m, Coated woodfree/freesheet
No. 4, DuoFormer D, total capacity 154,938 mt/y, Trim width 5.11 m, Uncoated woodfree/freesheet, Coated woodfree/freesheet
No. 5, Bel-Form, total capacity 154,938 mt/y, Trim width 5.08 m, Coated woodfree/freesheet
No. 6, Bel-Form, total capacity 169,932 mt/y, Trim width 5.15 m, Uncoated woodfree/freesheet
No. 7, DuoFormer D, total capacity 149,940 mt/y, Trim width 5.15 m, Uncoated woodfree/freesheet, Coated woodfree/freesheet
Coating Machines: 4
Off 2, total capacity 68,400 mt/y., off machine
Off 3, total capacity 250,200 mt/y., off machine
Off 5, total capacity 195,100 mt/y., off machine
On 4, total capacity 155,000 mt/y., on machine
Finishing Equipment:
Supercalenders: 9 at 595,200 mt/y
Rewinders: 11 at 678,000 mt/y
Sheeters: 10 at 341,400 mt/y
Energy Data:
Power boilers: 4
Steam turbines: 7 at 8.6, 11, 9, 10.8, 36.7, 57.5, 18.8 MW
Electrical demand for mill: 2,622 MWh/D

ⓜMitsubishi Paper Mills Ltd.
Kyoto Mill
6-6, Kaiden 1-chome
Nagaokakyo-shi, Kyoto Pref., 617-8666
Japan
  Phone: (81) 75 951 1181
  Fax: (81) 75 951 1081
  Web Address: www.mpm.co.jp
Personnel:
Mill Mgr.: Motoshige Yamada
  Phone: (81) 75 951 1181
  Fax: (81) 75 951 1081

Japan

Total Employees at this Location: 159
Type of Operation: Paper mill
Paper/Paperboard Grades and Capacities:
 Total paper and paperboard capacity: 32,000 mt/y
 Uncoated woodfree/freesheet: 32,000 mt/y
Coating Machines: 3
 No. 1, off machine
 No. 2, off machine
 No. 3, off machine

ⓜMitsubishi Paper Mills Ltd.
Shirakawa Mill
3, Aza Maeyamanishi, Nishigo-mura
Nishi-Shirakawa-gun, Fukushima Pref., 961-8054
Japan
 Phone: (81) 248 22 8111
 Fax: (81) 248 23 3427
 Web Address: www.mpm.co.jp
Personnel:
 Mill Mgr.: Shinichi Inoue
 Phone: (81) 248 22 8111
Total Employees at this Location: 3
Type of Operation: Pulp mill
Pulp Grades and Capacities:
 Total pulp capacity: 15,000 mt/y
 Chemical Pulp: 15,000 mt/y
Paper/Paperboard Grades and Capacities:
 Total paper and paperboard capacity: 6,000 mt/y
 Specialty and industrial: 6,000 mt/y
Paper and Paperboard Mill Data:
Paper Machines: 2
 No. 1, cylinder, total capacity 5,900 mt/y, Trim width 2.2 m, Specialty and industrial
 No. 2, cylinder, total capacity 36 mt/y, Trim width 1.7 m, Specialty and industrial
Energy Data:
 Combustion turbines: 2 at 7.5 MW

ⓜMitsubishi Paper Mills Ltd.
Takasago Mill
105 Sakae-machi, Takasago-cho
Takasago-shi, Hyogo Pref., 676-8677
Japan
 Phone: (81) 794 42 3101
 Fax: (81) 794 43 6012
 Web Address: www.mpm.co.jp
Personnel:
 Mill Mgr.: Shinichi Suzuki
 Phone: (81) 794 42 3101
 Fax: (81) 794 43 6012
Total Employees at this Location: 301
Type of Operation: Paper mill
Paper/Paperboard Grades and Capacities:
 Total paper and paperboard capacity: 107,814 mt/y
 Uncoated woodfree/freesheet: 99,246 mt/y
 Specialty and industrial: 8,568 mt/y
Paper and Paperboard Mill Data:
 Stock Preparation:
 Pulpers: 8
 Refiners: 44
Paper Machines: 5
 No. 1, fourdrinier, total capacity 4,284 mt/y, Trim width 2.15 m, Specialty and industrial
 No. 3, fourdrinier, total capacity 18,207 mt/y, Trim width 2.36 m, Uncoated woodfree/freesheet
 No. 4, fourdrinier, total capacity 11,424 mt/y, Trim width 1.85 m, Uncoated woodfree/freesheet
 No. 11, fourdrinier, total capacity 4,284 mt/y, Trim width 2.05 m, Specialty and industrial
 No. 12, (closed September 2010), fourdrinier, total capacity 69,615 mt/y, Trim width 4.95 m, Uncoated woodfree/freesheet
Coating Machines: 6
 No. 7, total capacity 5,700 mt/y., off machine
 No. 8, total capacity 14,600 mt/y., off machine
 No. 10, total capacity 18,300 mt/y., off machine
 No. 11, total capacity 24,500 mt/y., off machine
 No. 12, total capacity 62,100 mt/y., off machine
 LK, total capacity 3,500 mt/y., off machine

Finishing Equipment:
 Winders: 11
 Supercalenders: 2
 Rewinders: 12 at 96 mt/y
 Sheeters: 6
Energy Data:
 Power boilers: 7
 Combustion turbines: 4 at 5.5 MW
 Steam turbines: 1 at 13.54 MW
 Electrical demand for mill: 232 MWh/D

ⓜMolza Corp.
Muge Mill
983 Hachiman, Mugegawa-cho
Seki-shi, Gifu Pref., 501-2603
Japan
 Phone: (81) 575 46 2168
 Fax: (81) 575 46 3928
 Web Address: www.molza.co.jp
Personnel:
 Pres.: Atsuya Sawamura
 Phone: (81) 575 46 2168
Total Employees at this Location: 75
Type of Operation: Paper mill
Paper/Paperboard Grades and Capacities:
 Total paper and paperboard capacity: 10,320 mt/y
 Uncoated woodfree/freesheet
 Specialty and industrial
Paper and Paperboard Mill Data:
Paper Machines: 5
 No. 1, cylinder, total capacity 1,440 mt/y
 No. 2, cylinder, total capacity 1,320 mt/y
 No. 3, cylinder, total capacity 1,560 mt/y
 No. 4, cylinder, total capacity 2,400 mt/y
 No. 5, cylinder, total capacity 3,600 mt/y

ⓜNakagawa Seishi KK
718 Sogo-Shinmachi
Hakusan-shi, 924-0028
Japan
 Phone: (81) 76 276 5551
 Fax: (81) 76 276 7135
Personnel:
 Man. Dir., Mill Mgr.: Toshiyuki Hirose
 Phone: (81) 76 276 5551
 Fax: (81) 76 276 7135
Total Employees at this Location: 70
Mill Locations:
 Nakagawa Seishi KK, Mattsuto Mill, 718 Sogo-Shinmachi, Hakusan-shi 924-0028, Japan, Capacity: 54,800 mt/y, (Paperboard mill)
 Phone: (81) 76 276 5551
 Fax: (81) 76 276 7135

ⓜNakagawa Seishi KK
Mattsuto Mill
718 Sogo-Shinmachi
Hakusan-shi, Ishikawa Pref., 924-0028
Japan
 Phone: (81) 76 276 5551
 Fax: (81) 76 276 7135
 Web Address: www.nakagawa-paper.co.jp
Personnel:
 President: Akihiko Shibada
 Man. Dir/Mill Mgr.: Toshiyuki Hirose
 Phone: (81) 76 276 5551
Total Employees at this Location: 70
Type of Operation: Paperboard mill
Pulp Grades and Capacities:
 Total pulp capacity: 53,423 mt/y
 Recycled Pulping: 53,423 mt/y
Paper/Paperboard Grades and Capacities:
 Total paper and paperboard capacity: 54,800 mt/y
 Packaging papers: 6,680 mt/y
 Specialty and industrial: 23,400 mt/y
 Linerboard: 24,720 mt/y
Paper and Paperboard Mill Data:
 Stock Preparation:
 Pulpers: 6
 Refiners: 8

Paper Machines: 3
 No. 5, cylinder (6), total capacity 16,700 mt/y, Trim width 2.05 m, Packaging papers, Linerboard
 No. 6, cylinder (5), total capacity 14,700 mt/y, Trim width 1.8 m, Linerboard
 No. 7, cylinder (5), total capacity 23,400 mt/y, Trim width 2.8 m, Specialty and industrial
Coating Machines: 1
 No. 1, off machine
Finishing Equipment:
 Rewinders: 3
Energy Data:
 Power boilers: 7
 Electrical demand for mill: 73 MWh/D

ⓜNiko Seishi Co., Ltd.
Honsha Mill
2329 Minami Matsuno, Fujikawa-cho
Ihara-gun, Shizuoka Pref., 421-3303
Japan
 Phone: (81) 545 85 2630
 Fax: (81) 545 85 2611
Personnel:
 Pres.: Hikotaro Kawaguchi
 Phone: (81) 545 85 2630
Total Employees at this Location: 25
Type of Operation: Paper mill
Paper/Paperboard Grades and Capacities:
 Total paper and paperboard capacity: 5,000 mt/y
 Tissue: 5,000 mt/y
Paper and Paperboard Mill Data:
Paper Machines: 1
 No. 1, (second hand Paper machine.), Yankee dryer, total capacity 5,000 mt/y, Trim width 2.8 m, Tissue
Energy Data:
 Power boilers
 Steam turbines: 3 at 0.87 MW
 Electrical demand for mill: 13 MWh/D

ⓜNiko Seishi Co., Ltd.
Ownership: Kao Co.
2329 Minami Matsuno, Fujikawa-cho
Ihara-gun, 421-3303
Japan
 Phone: (81) 545 85 2630
 Fax: (81) 545 85 2611
Personnel:
 Pres.: Hikotaro Kawaguchi
 Phone: (81) 545 85 2630
 Fax: (81) 545 85 2611
Total Employees at this Location: 25
Mill Locations:
 Niko Seishi Co., Ltd., Honsha Mill, 2329 Minami Matsuno, Fujikawa-cho, Ihara-gun 421-3303, Japan, Capacity: 5,000 mt/y, (Paper mill)
 Phone: (81) 545 85 2630
 Fax: (81) 545 85 2611

ⓜNippon Paper Industries Co., Ltd.
Ohtake Mill
Ownership: 100% by Nippon Paper Industries Co., Ltd.
1-16-1, Higashi-Sakae
Ohtake-shi, Hiroshima Pref., 739-0601
Japan
 Phone: (81) 827 52 4111
 Fax: (81) 827 53 5700
 Web Address: www.nipponpapergroup.com/e/index.html
Personnel:
 Mill Mgr.: Kunio Osada
 Phone: (81) 827 52 4111
Total Employees at this Location: 303
Type of Operation: Pulp mill, Paper mill
Pulp Mill Data:
 Chemical Pulping Systems:
 Continuous digesters: 1
 Bleach Plant Systems: 1

Japan

Chemical Recovery Equipment:
Evaporator lines: 5
Recovery boilers: 1
Paper/Paperboard Grades and Capacities:
Total paper and paperboard capacity: 109,242 mt/y
Uncoated woodfree/freesheet: 109,242 mt/y
Paper and Paperboard Mill Data:
Stock Preparation:
Pulpers: 6
Refiners: 25
Paper Machines: 4
No. 1, fourdrinier, total capacity 21,420 mt/y, Trim width 3.34 m, Uncoated woodfree/freesheet
No. 2, fourdrinier, total capacity 11,781 mt/y, Trim width 3.33 m, Uncoated woodfree/freesheet
No. 3, fourdrinier, total capacity 4,641 mt/y, Trim width 1.92 m, Uncoated woodfree/freesheet
No. 6, SymFormer, total capacity 71,400 mt/y, Trim width 3.3 m, Uncoated woodfree/freesheet
Coating Machines: 1
No. 1 C/R, total capacity 70,000 mt/y., off machine
Finishing Equipment:
Supercalenders: 2
Rewinders: 5
Sheeters: 9
Energy Data:
Power boilers: 2
Steam turbines: 3 at 24.9 MW
Electrical demand for mill: 310 MWh/D

ⓂNippon Paper Industries Co., Ltd.
Akita Mill

Ownership: 100% by Nippon Paper Industries Co., Ltd.
2-1-1 Mukaihama
Akita-shi, Akita Pref., 010-1601
Japan
Phone: (81) 18 896 7700
Fax: (81) 18 896 7690
Web Address: www.nipponpapergroup.com/e/index.html
Personnel:
Mill Mgr.: Kenichi Hanabuchi
Phone: (81) 18 896 7700
Total Employees at this Location: 400
Type of Operation: Pulp mill, Paper mill, Paperboard mill
Pulp Grades and Capacities:
Total pulp capacity: 706,711 mt/y
Pulp available for market: 149,940 mt/y
Chemical Pulp: 538,323 mt/y
Recycled Pulping: 168,388 mt/y
Pulp Mill Data:
Chemical Pulping Systems:
Continuous digesters: 2
Pulp Lines: 3
Chemical Recovery Equipment:
Recovery boilers: 2
Recycled Fiber Treatment Lines:
Recycled packaging pulping lines: 1 at 357,000 admt/y
Pulp Dryers:
Pulp Dryers 1, Twin Wire 1, Wet Lap machine 1
Paper/Paperboard Grades and Capacities:
Total paper and paperboard capacity: 574,770 mt/y
Uncoated woodfree/freesheet: 19,635 mt/y
Coated woodfree/freesheet: 119,595 mt/y
Specialty and industrial: 35,700 mt/y
Linerboard: 399,840 mt/y
Paper and Paperboard Mill Data:
Stock Preparation:
Pulpers: 3
Refiners: 9
Paper Machines: 2
L1, Inverformer, total capacity 399,840 mt/y, Trim width 6.3 m, Linerboard
N1, Bel-Form, total capacity 174,930 mt/y, Trim width 5.3 m, Coated woodfree/freesheet, Uncoated woodfree/freesheet, Specialty and industrial
Coating Machines: 1
No. 1, total capacity 178,500 mt/y., off machine
Finishing Equipment:
Rewinders: 2 at 13,000 mt/y
Energy Data:
Power boilers: 5
Steam turbines: 4 at 77 MW
Electrical demand for mill: 1,741 MWh/D

ⓂNippon Paper Industries Co., Ltd.
Ashikaga Mill

Ownership: 100% by Nippon Paper Industries Co., Ltd.
12-7 Miyakita-machi
Ashikaga-shi, Tochigi Pref., 326-0027
Japan
Phone: (81) 284 41 5151
Fax: (81) 284 41 8372
Web Address: www.nipponpapergroup.com/e/index.html
Personnel:
Mill Mgr.: Koji Shinoda
Phone: (81) 284 41 5151
Asst. Mill Mgr.: Kazuyuki Misawa
Phone: (81) 284 41 5151
Total Employees at this Location: 82
Type of Operation: Paperboard mill
Pulp Grades and Capacities:
Total pulp capacity: 206,618 mt/y
Recycled Pulping: 206,618 mt/y
Pulp Mill Data:
Recycled Fiber Treatment Lines:
Pulpers: 4 at 224,000 admt/y
Paper/Paperboard Grades and Capacities:
Total paper and paperboard capacity: 205,000 mt/y
Corrugating medium/fluting: 155,000 mt/y
Boxboard/cartonboard: 50,000 mt/y
Paper and Paperboard Mill Data:
Stock Preparation:
Pulpers: 4
Refiners: 9
Paper Machines: 2
No. 1, cylinder (7), total capacity 50,000 mt/y, Trim width 2.82 m, Boxboard/cartonboard
No. 3, DuoFormer D, total capacity 155,000 mt/y, Trim width 3.85 m, Corrugating medium/fluting
Finishing Equipment:
Rewinders: 2 at 180,000 mt/y
Energy Data:
Power boilers: 1
Steam turbines: 1 at 9.9 MW
Electrical demand for mill: 287 MWh/D

ⓂNippon Paper Industries Co., Ltd.
Otake Mill

Ownership: 100% by Nippon Paper Industries Co., Ltd.
2-1-18 Higashi-Sakae
Otake-shi, Hiroshima Pref., 739-0601
Japan
Phone: (81) 8275 2 4131/4111
Fax: (81) 8275 3 0025/5700
Web Address: www.nipponpapergroup.com/e/index.html
Personnel:
Mill Mgr.: Shunichi Karube
Phone: (81) 8275 2 4131/4111
Total Employees at this Location: 277
Type of Operation: Pulp mill, Paperboard mill
Pulp Grades and Capacities:
Total pulp capacity: 239,190 mt/y
Chemical Pulp: 87,267 mt/y
Recycled Pulping: 151,923 mt/y
Pulp Mill Data:
Chemical Pulping Systems:
Batch digesters: 5
Pulp Lines: 1
Bleach Plant Systems: 1
No. 1, Sequence: O_2 CEopHD
Chemical Recovery Equipment:
Evaporator lines: 6
Recovery boilers: 2
Recycled Fiber Treatment Lines:
Pulpers: 4
Paper/Paperboard Grades and Capacities:
Total paper and paperboard capacity: 239,190 mt/y
Specialty and industrial: 53,550 mt/y
Linerboard: 185,640 mt/y
Paper and Paperboard Mill Data:
Stock Preparation:
Pulpers: 11
Refiners: 27
Paper Machines: 2
No. 8, fourdrinier, total capacity 53,550 mt/y, Trim width 2.6 m, Specialty and industrial
No. 9, DuoFormer D, total capacity 185,640 mt/y, Trim width 4.5 m, Linerboard
Coating Machines: 1
On 8, total capacity 50,000 mt/y., on machine
Finishing Equipment:
Supercalenders: 3
Rewinders: 10
Sheeters: 13
Energy Data:
Power boilers: 5
Steam turbines: 6 at 59.5 MW
Electrical demand for mill: 639 MWh/D

ⓂNippon Paper Industries Co., Ltd.
Soka Mill

Ownership: 100% by Nippon Paper Industries Co., Ltd.
4-3-39 Matsue
Soka-shi, Saitama Pref., 340-0013
Japan
Phone: (81) 48 931 9571
Fax: (81) 48 931 8405
Web Address: www.nipponpapergroup.com/e/index.html
Personnel:
Man. Dir./Mill Mgr.: Takehisa Watanabe
Phone: (81) 48 932 7562
Fax: (81) 48 9321 8405
Total Employees at this Location: 128
Type of Operation: Pulp mill, Paperboard mill
Pulp Grades and Capacities:
Total pulp capacity: 555,730 mt/y
Recycled Pulping: 413,016 mt/y
Pulp Mill Data:
Recycled Fiber Treatment Lines:
Pulpers: 12
Paper/Paperboard Grades and Capacities:
Total paper and paperboard capacity: 546,210 mt/y
Linerboard: 173,145 mt/y
Corrugating medium/fluting: 348,075 mt/y
Boxboard/cartonboard: 24,990 mt/y
Paper and Paperboard Mill Data:
Stock Preparation:
Refiners: 26
Paper Machines: 4
No. 1, Bel-Bond, total capacity 133,875 mt/y, Trim width 3.8 m, Corrugating medium/fluting
No. 2, Ultraformer, total capacity 173,145 mt/y, Trim width 4.35 m, Linerboard
No. 3, cylinder, total capacity 24,990 mt/y, Trim width 1.9 m, Boxboard/cartonboard
No. 4, Ultraformer, total capacity 214,200 mt/y, Trim width 5.6 m, Corrugating medium/fluting
Finishing Equipment:
Rewinders: 3 at 16,900 mt/y
Sheeters: 1 at 1,800 mt/y
Energy Data:
Power boilers: 6
Combustion turbines: 2 at 17 MW
Steam turbines: 7 at 41 MW
Electrical demand for mill: 910 MWh/D

Japan

ⓂNippon Paper Industries Co., Ltd.
Yoshinaga Mill
Ownership: 100% by Nippon Paper Industries Co., Ltd.
798 Hina
Fuji-shi, Shizuoka Pref., 417-8520
Japan
  Phone: (81) 545 57 3212
  Fax: (81) 545 57 3441
  Web Address: www.nipponpapergroup.com/e/index.html
Personnel:
  Mill Mgr.: Hidetsugu Yamada
  Phone: (81) 545 57 3212
Total Employees at this Location: 176
Type of Operation: Pulp mill, Paper mill, Paperboard mill
Pulp Mill Data:
  Chemical Pulping Systems:
  Continuous digesters: 1
  Bleach Plant Lines:
  No. 1, Sequence: O_2 C/DEDED, Capacity 134,000 admt/y
  Chemical Recovery Equipment:
  Recovery boilers
  Pulp Dryers:
  Air Float dryers 1
Paper/Paperboard Grades and Capacities:
  Total paper and paperboard capacity: 533,715 mt/y
  Linerboard: 303,450 mt/y
  Boxboard/cartonboard: 230,265 mt/y
Paper and Paperboard Mill Data:
  Stock Preparation:
  Pulpers: 3
  Refiners: 40
Paper Machines: 3
  No. 14, multi-fourdrinier, total capacity 303,450 mt/y, Trim width 5.75 m, Linerboard
  No. 50, Ultraformer (7), total capacity 99,960 mt/y, Trim width 3.28 m, Boxboard/cartonboard
  No. 51, Ultraformer, total capacity 130,305 mt/y, Trim width 3.38 m, Boxboard/cartonboard
Coating Machines: 2
  PM 50, total capacity 100,000 mt/y., on machine
  PM 51, total capacity 130,000 mt/y., on machine
Finishing Equipment:
  Winders: 6
  Sheeters: 6
Energy Data:
  Power boilers: 6
  Steam turbines: 5 at 25, 29.3, 70, 27, 10.3 MW
  Electrical demand for mill: 1,265 MWh/D

ⓂNippon Paper Chemicals Co., Ltd.
Ownership: 100% by Nippon Paper Industries Co., Ltd.
1-2-2 Hitotsubashi, Chiyoda-ku
Tokyo, 100-0003
Japan
  Phone: (81) 3 6665 5900
  Fax: (81) 3 3217 3280
  Email: info@npchem.co.jp
  Web Address: www.npchem.co.jp
Personnel:
  Pres. CEO: Masami Yamaki
  Phone: (81) 3 6665 5900
  Fax: (81) 3 3217 3280
  Man. Dir.: Shinji Kumakiri
  Phone: (81) 3 6665 5900
  Fax: (81) 3 3217 3280
  Man. Dir. / Gen. Mgr. Tech. Div.: Nobuaki Fujioka
  Phone: (81) 3 6665 5900
  Fax: (81) 3 3217 3280
  Man. Dir.: Yusuke Makita
  Phone: (81) 3 6665 5900
  Fax: (81) 3 3217 3280
Total Employees of Company: 386
Mill Locations:
Nippon Paper Chemicals Co., Ltd., Gotsu Mill, 1280 Gotsu-cho, Gotsu-shi 695-0011, Japan, (Pulp mill)
  Phone: (81) 855 52 6000
  Fax: (81) 855 52 6029

ⓂNippon Paper Chemicals Co., Ltd.
Gotsu Mill
Ownership: 100% by Nippon Paper Industries Co., Ltd.
1280 Gotsu-cho
Gotsu-shi, Shimane Pref., 695-0011
Japan
  Phone: (81) 855 52 6000
  Fax: (81) 855 52 6029
  Web Address: www.nipponpapergroup.com/e/index.html
Personnel:
  Mill Mgr.: Kuniaki Monden
  Phone: (81) 855 52 6000
Total Employees at this Location: 111
Type of Operation: Pulp mill
Pulp Grades and Capacities:
  Total pulp capacity: 106,703 mt/y
  Pulp available for market: 99,960 mt/y
  Chemical Pulp: 106,703 mt/y
Pulp Mill Data:
  Chemical Pulping Systems:
  Batch digesters: 6
Pulp Lines: 2
  Bleach Plant Systems: 2
  No. 1, Sequence: CEH, Capacity 178,500 admt/y
  Chemical Recovery Equipment:
  Evaporator lines: 2
  Recovery boilers: 1
  Pulp Dryers:
  Air Float dryers 2
Energy Data:
  Power boilers: 1
  Steam turbines: 4 at 10, 6, 2.5, 0.72 MW
  Electrical demand for mill: 742 MWh/D

ⓂNippon Paper Crecia Co., Ltd.
Ownership: 100% by Nippon Paper Industries Co., Ltd.
2-2 Hitotsubashi 1-chome, Chiyoda-ku
Tokyo, 100-8156
Japan
  Phone: (81) 3 6665 5300
  Fax: (81) 3 3212 6000
  Web Address: www.crecia.co.jp
Personnel:
  Pres.: Kazuhiro Sakai
  Phone: (81) 3 6665 5300
  Fax: (81) 3 3212 6000
  Sen. Man. Dir. /Gen. Mgr.: Hideto Shikano
  Phone: (81) 3 6665 5300
  Fax: (81) 3 3212 6000
  Kyoto Mill Mgr.: Masatoshi Motegi
  Phone: (81) 3 6665 5300
  Fax: (81) 3 3212 6000
Total Employees of Company: 648
Mill Locations:
Nippon Paper Crecia Co., Ltd., Kaisei Mill, 500 Yoshidajima, Kaisei-machi, Ashigarakami-gun 258-0021, Japan, Capacity: 55,000 mt/y, (Paper mill)
  Phone: (81) 465 83 2311
  Fax: (81) 465 83 0766
Nippon Paper Crecia Co., Ltd., Kyoto Mill, 1-54 Osadano-cho, Fukuchiyama-shi 620-0853, Japan, Capacity: 70,000 mt/y, (Paper mill)
  Phone: (81) 773 27 6311
  Fax: (81) 773 27 3123
Nippon Paper Crecia Co., Ltd., Tokyo Mill, 4-2-16 Matsue, Soka-shi 340-0013, Japan, Capacity: 86,000 mt/y, (Paper mill)
  Phone: (81) 48 931 1151
  Fax: (81) 48 936 0247

ⓂNippon Paper Crecia Co., Ltd.
Kaisei Mill
Ownership: 100% by Nippon Paper Industries Co., Ltd.
500 Yoshidajima, Kaisei-machi
Ashigarakami-gun, Kanagawa Pref., 258-0021
Japan
  Phone: (81) 465 83 2311
  Fax: (81) 465 83 0766
  Web Address: www.nipponpapergroup.com/e/index.html
Personnel:
  Man. Dir. / Mill Mgr.: Kazuo Ohmura
  Phone: (81) 465 83 2311
Total Employees at this Location: 53
Type of Operation: Paper mill
Paper/Paperboard Grades and Capacities:
  Total paper and paperboard capacity: 55,000 mt/y
  Tissue: 55,000 mt/y
Paper and Paperboard Mill Data:
Paper Machines: 2
  No. 3, fourdrinier, Yankee dryer, total capacity 25,000 mt/y, Trim width 3.34 m, Tissue
  No. 4, twin-wire, Yankee dryer, total capacity 30,000 mt/y, Trim width 3.34 m, Tissue
Energy Data:
  Power boilers: 1
  Combustion turbines: 1 at 5.1 MW
  Electrical demand for mill: 156 MWh/D

ⓂNippon Paper Crecia Co., Ltd.
Kyoto Mill
Ownership: 100% by Nippon Paper Industries Co., Ltd.
1-54 Osadano-cho
Fukuchiyama-shi, Kyoto Pref., 620-0853
Japan
  Phone: (81) 773 27 6311
  Fax: (81) 773 27 3123
  Web Address: www.crecia.co.jp
Personnel:
  Dir. / Mill Mgr.: Masatoshi Motegi
  Phone: (81) 773 27 6311
Total Employees at this Location: 65
Type of Operation: Paper mill
Paper/Paperboard Grades and Capacities:
  Total paper and paperboard capacity: 70,000 mt/y
  Tissue: 70,000 mt/y
Paper and Paperboard Mill Data:
  Stock Preparation:
  Pulpers: 3
Paper Machines: 2
  No. 1, crescent former, Yankee dryer, total capacity 30,000 mt/y, Trim width 3.96 m, Tissue
  No. 2, crescent former, Yankee dryer, total capacity 40,000 mt/y, Trim width 4.99 m, Tissue
Energy Data:
  Power boilers: 1
  Electrical demand for mill: 189 MWh/D

ⓂNippon Paper Crecia Co., Ltd.
Tokyo Mill
Ownership: 100% by Nippon Paper Industries Co., Ltd.
4-2-16 Matsue
Soka-shi, Saitama Pref., 340-0013
Japan
  Phone: (81) 48 931 1151
  Fax: (81) 48 936 0247
  Web Address: www.crecia.co.jp
Personnel:
  Man. Dir./Mill Mgr.: Yutaka Atami
  Phone: (81) 48 931 1151
  Gen. Affairs Div. Mgr.: Takao Mori
  Phone: (81) 48 931 1151
  Mfg. Affair Div. Mgr.: Takashi Yamaguchi
  Phone: (81) 48 931 1151
Total Employees at this Location: 89
Type of Operation: Paper mill

Japan

Pulp Grades and Capacities:
Total pulp capacity: 22,666 mt/y
Recycled Pulping: 22,666 mt/y

Pulp Mill Data:
Recycled Fiber Treatment Lines:
Flotation deinking lines: 1

Paper/Paperboard Grades and Capacities:
Total paper and paperboard capacity: 86,000 mt/y
Tissue: 86,000 mt/y

Paper and Paperboard Mill Data:
Stock Preparation:
Pulpers: 7
Refiners: 7

Paper Machines: 3
No. 2, fourdrinier, Yankee dryer, total capacity 21,000 mt/y, Trim width 3.15 m, Tissue
No. 3, fourdrinier, Yankee dryer, total capacity 27,000 mt/y, Trim width 3.35 m, Tissue
N 1, crescent former, Yankee dryer, total capacity 38,000 mt/y, Trim width 4.93 m, Tissue

Finishing Equipment:
Supercalenders: 7
Rewinders: 3

Energy Data:
Power boilers: 1
Combustion turbines: 2 at 3.8, 3.8 MW
Electrical demand for mill: 249 MWh/D

ⓘNippon Paper Industries Co., Ltd.
Ownership: Public
4-6, Kanda-Surugadai, Chiyoda-ku
Tokyo, 101-0062
Japan
Phone: (81) 3 6665 1111
Fax: (81) 3 3217 3001
Email: pub@npaper.co.jp
Web Address: www.nipponpapergroup.com/e/index.html

Personnel:
Chmn & Rep. Dir.: Yoshio Haga
Phone: (81) 3 6665 1111
Fax: (81) 3 3217 3001
Pres & CEO: Fumio Manoshiro
Phone: (81) 3 6665 1111
Fax: (81) 3 3217 3001
Exec. VP & Rep. Dir. (Gen. Mgr. Finan. Div. & CSR Div.): Masaru Motomura
Phone: (81) 3 6665 1111
Fax: (81) 3 3217 3001
Exec. VP & Rep. Dir. (Gen. Mgr. Paperboard Div.): Hironori Iwase
Phone: (81) 3 6665 1111
Fax: (81) 3 3217 3001
Dir. (Gen. Mgr. Personnel & Gen. Affairs Div.): Shuhei Marukawa
Phone: (81) 3 6665 1111
Fax: (81) 3 3217 3001
Dir. (Gen. Mgr. Tech. & Eng. Div. & Energy Bus. Div.): Kazufumi Yamasaki
Phone: (81) 3 6665 1111
Fax: (81) 3 3217 3001
Dir. (Gen. Mgr. Raw Mat'l & Purch. Div.): Haruo Fujisawa
Phone: (81) 3 6665 1111
Fax: (81) 3 3217 3001

Total Employees of Company: 13,052

Mill Locations:
Australian Paper, Maryvale Mill, Maryvale Road, Morwell, VIC 3840, Australia, Capacity: 605,000 mt/y, (Pulp mill, Paper mill, Paperboard mill)
Phone: (61) 3 5136 0360
Fax: (61) 3 5134 6127
Email: (firstname.surname@australianpaper.com.au)
Australian Paper, Shoalhaven Mill, 340 Bolong Road, Bomaderry, NSW 2541, Australia, Capacity: 16,000 mt/y, (Pulp mill, Paper mill, Paperboard mill)
Phone: (61) 2 4428 6444
Fax: (61) 2 4423 1066
Email: (firstname.lastname@australianpaper.com.au)
Daishowa-Marubeni International Ltd., Peace River Pulp Division (50% owned), Peace River, AB, Canada T8S 1V7, (Pulp mill)
Phone: (1) 780-624-7000
Fax: (1) 780-624-7329
Email: webmaster@dmi.ca
Jujo Thermal Ltd., Kauttua Mill, Paperitehtaantie 15, FI-27500 Kauttua, Finland, Capacity: 80,000 mt/y, (Paper mill)
Phone: (358) 10 303 200
Fax: (358) 10 303 2419, 2418
Email: jujo.thermal@jujothermal.com, jujosales@jujothermal.com
Kitakami Paper Co., Ltd., Ichinoseki Mill, 10-1, Asahi-machi, Ichinoseki-shi 021-0864, Japan, Capacity: 135,000 mt/y, (Paper mill, Paperboard mill)
Phone: (81) 191 23 3366
Fax: (81) 191 23 6192
Email: psoumu@kitakami-p.jp
Koyo Paper Mfg. Co., Ltd., Honsha Mill (89.71% owned), 450 Hina, Fuji-shi 417-0847, Japan, Capacity: 62,000 mt/y, (Pulp mill, Paper mill)
Phone: (81) 545 34 0820
Fax: (81) 545 38 2138
Email: info@koyopaper.co.jp
Lintec Corp., Kumagaya Mill (28.70% owned), 3478 Mankichi, Kumagaya-shi 360-0161, Japan, Capacity: 69,495 mt/y, (Paper mill)
Phone: (81) 48 539 1212
Fax: (81) 48 539 1291
Lintec Corp., Mishima Mill (28.70% owned), 2-46 Mishima-Kamiya-cho, Shikokuchuo-shi 799-0402, Japan, Capacity: 78,132 mt/y, (Paper mill)
Phone: (81) 896 23 4400
Fax: (81) 896 24 4400
Nippon Paper Industries Co., Ltd., Ohtake Mill, 1-16-1, Higashi-Sakae, Ohtake-shi 739-0601, Japan, Capacity: 109,242 mt/y, (Pulp mill, Paper mill)
Phone: (81) 827 5 2 4111
Fax: (81) 827 5 3 5700
Nippon Paper Industries Co., Ltd., Akita Mill, 2-1-1 Mukaihama, Akita-shi 010-1601, Japan, Capacity: 574,770 mt/y, (Pulp mill, Paper mill, Paperboard mill)
Phone: (81) 18 896 7700
Fax: (81) 18 896 7690
Nippon Paper Industries Co., Ltd., Ashikaga Mill, 12-7 Miyakita-machi, Ashikaga-shi 326-0027, Japan, Capacity: 205,000 mt/y, (Paperboard mill)
Phone: (81) 284 41 5151
Fax: (81) 284 41 8372
Nippon Paper Industries Co., Ltd., Otake Mill, 2-1-18 Higashi-Sakae, Otake-shi 739-0601, Japan, Capacity: 239,190 mt/y, (Pulp mill, Paperboard mill)
Phone: (81) 8275 2 4131/4111
Fax: (81) 8275 3 0025/5700
Nippon Paper Industries Co., Ltd., Soka Mill, 4-3-39 Matsue, Soka-shi 340-0013, Japan, Capacity: 546,210 mt/y, (Pulp mill, Paperboard mill)
Phone: (81) 48 931 9571
Fax: (81) 48 931 8405
Nippon Paper Industries Co., Ltd., Yoshinaga Mill, 798 Hina, Fuji-shi 417-8520, Japan, Capacity: 533,715 mt/y, (Pulp mill, Paper mill, Paperboard mill)
Phone: (81) 545 57 3212
Fax: (81) 545 57 3441
Nippon Paper Chemicals Co., Ltd., Gotsu Mill, 1280 Gotsu-cho, Gotsu-shi 695-0011, Japan, (Pulp mill)
Phone: (81) 855 52 6000
Fax: (81) 855 52 6029
Nippon Paper Crecia Co., Ltd., Kaisei Mill, 500 Yoshidajima, Kaisei-machi, Ashigarakami-gun 258-0021, Japan, Capacity: 55,000 mt/y, (Paper mill)
Phone: (81) 465 83 2311
Fax: (81) 465 83 0766
Nippon Paper Crecia Co., Ltd., Kyoto Mill, 1-54 Osadano-cho, Fukuchiyama-shi 620-0853, Japan, Capacity: 70,000 mt/y, (Paper mill)
Phone: (81) 773 27 6311
Fax: (81) 773 27 3123
Nippon Paper Crecia Co., Ltd., Tokyo Mill, 4-2-16 Matsue, Soka-shi 340-0013, Japan, Capacity: 86,000 mt/y, (Paper mill)
Phone: (81) 48 931 1151
Fax: (81) 48 936 0247
Nippon Paper Industries Co., Ltd., Fuji Mill, 4-1-1, Imai, Fuji-shi 417-8610, Japan, Capacity: 368,067 mt/y, (Paper mill)
Phone: (81) 545 30 3589
Fax: (81) 545 30 3050
Nippon Paper Industries Co., Ltd., Hokkaido Mill - Asahikawa, 505-1 Pulp-cho, Asahikawa-shi 070-8611, Japan, Capacity: 293,811 mt/y, (Pulp mill, Paper mill, Paperboard mill)
Phone: (81) 166 259 730
Fax: (81) 166 259 775
Nippon Paper Industries Co., Ltd., Hokkaido Mill - Shiraoi, 181 Kita-Yoshiwara, Shiraoi 059-0993, Japan, Capacity: 433,755 mt/y, (Pulp mill, Paper mill)
Phone: (81) 144 83 2711
Fax: (81) 144 83 1400
Nippon Paper Industries Co., Ltd., Hokkaido Mill - Yufutsu, 143 Yufutsu, Tomakomai-shi 059-1395, Japan, Capacity: 275,604 mt/y, (Pulp mill, Paper mill)
Phone: (81) 144 56 0111
Fax: (81) 144 56 0485
Nippon Paper Industries Co., Ltd., Ishinomaki Mill, 2-2-1 Nanko-cho, Ishinomaki-shi 986-0836, Japan, Capacity: 856,000 mt/y, (Pulp mill, Paper mill)
Phone: (81) 225 95 0111
Fax: (81) 225 93 6060
Nippon Paper Industries Co., Ltd., Iwakuni Mill, 2-8-1 Iida-machi, Iwakuni-shi 740-0003, Japan, Capacity: 665,000 mt/y, (Pulp mill, Paper mill)
Phone: (81) 827 24 6222
Fax: (81) 827 24 6390
Nippon Paper Industries Co., Ltd., Iwanuma Mill, 1-1 Daishowa, Iwanuma-shi 989-2492, Japan, Capacity: 601,545 mt/y, (Pulp mill, Paper mill)
Phone: (81) 223 22 6111
Fax: (81) 223 29 2250
Nippon Paper Industries Co., Ltd., Kushiro Mill, 2-1-47 Tottori-Minami, Kushiro-shi 084-0905, Japan, Capacity: 385,560 mt/y, (Pulp mill, Paper mill)
Phone: (81) 154 52 7605
Fax: (81) 154 51 3525
Nippon Paper Industries USA Co., Ltd., Port Angeles Mill, 1902 Marine Dr, Port Angeles, WA 98362, USA, Capacity: 148,155 mt/y, (Pulp mill, Paper mill)
Phone: (1) 360-457-4474
Fax: (1) 360-452-6576
Email: questions@npiusa.com
Nippon Paper Industries Co., Ltd., Yatsushiro Mill, 1-1, Jujo-machi, Yatsushiro-shi 866-8602, Japan, Capacity: 529,000 mt/y, (Pulp mill, Paper mill)
Phone: (81) 965 33 2111
Fax: (81) 965 35 1227
Nippon Paper Papylia Co., Ltd., Harada Mill, 506 Harada, Fuji-shi 417-0852, Japan, Capacity: 51,051 mt/y, (Paper mill)
Phone: (81) 545 52 4060
Fax: (81) 545 53 7175
Nippon Paper Papylia Co., Ltd., Harada Mill (Yodahashi), 37-1 Yodahashi, Fuji-shi, Japan, Capacity: 4,800 mt/y, (Paper mill)
Phone: (81) 545 32 2218
Fax: (81) 545 32 2287
Nippon Paper Papylia Co., Ltd., Kochi Mill, 3380 Ino-cho, Agawa-Gun 781-2110, Japan, Capacity: 758,625 mt/y, (Pulp mill, Paper mill)
Phone: (81) 88 8 92 1122
Fax: (81) 88 8 93 4469
Nippon Paper Papylia Co., Ltd., Suita Mill, 11-46, Higashi Otabi, Suita-shi 564-0033, Japan, Capacity: 11,500 mt/y, (Paper mill)
Phone: (81) 6 6381 2255
Fax: (81) 6 6382 2661
North Pacific Paper Corp. (Norpac), Longview Mill (50% owned), 3000 Industrial Way, Longview, WA 98632, USA, Capacity: 758,625 mt/y, (Paper mill)
Phone: (1) 360-636-6400
Fax: (1) 360-636-6881
Siam Nippon Industrial Paper Co., BanPong Mill (55% owned), 19 Saeng Xuto Road, Tha Pha, BanPong

Japan

70110, Thailand, Capacity: 43,000 mt/y, (Paper mill)
Phone: (66) 32 200 746-60/211 386-90/221
Fax: (66) 32 211 699/371 407

ⓜNippon Paper Industries Co., Ltd.
Ownership: 100% by Nippon Paper Industries Co., Ltd.
4-6, Kanda-Surugadai, Chiyoda-ku
Tokyo, 101-0062
Japan
  Phone: (81) 3 6665 1111
  Web Address: www.nipponpapergroup.com/e/index.html
Personnel:
  Pres.: Hironori Iwase
  Phone: (81) 3 6665 5000
  Fax: (81) 3 3217 3200
Total Employees of Company: 1,020
Mill Locations:
Nippon Paper Industries Co., Ltd., Ohtake Mill, 1-16-1, Higashi-Sakae, Ohtake-shi 739-0601, Japan, Capacity: 109,242 mt/y, (Pulp mill, Paper mill)
  Phone: (81) 827 5 2 4111
  Fax: (81) 827 5 3 5700
Nippon Paper Industries Co., Ltd., Akita Mill, 2-1-1 Mukaihama, Akita-shi 010-1601, Japan, Capacity: 574,770 mt/y, (Pulp mill, Paper mill, Paperboard mill)
  Phone: (81) 18 896 7700
  Fax: (81) 18 896 7690
Nippon Paper Industries Co., Ltd., Ashikaga Mill, 12-7 Miyakita-machi, Ashikaga-shi 326-0027, Japan, Capacity: 205,000 mt/y, (Paperboard mill)
  Phone: (81) 284 41 5151
  Fax: (81) 284 41 8272
Nippon Paper Industries Co., Ltd., Otake Mill, 2-1-18 Higashi-Sakae, Otake-shi 739-0601, Japan, Capacity: 239,190 mt/y, (Pulp mill, Paperboard mill)
  Phone: (81) 8275 2 4131/4111
  Fax: (81) 8275 3 0025/5700
Nippon Paper Industries Co., Ltd., Soka Mill, 4-3-39 Matsue, Soka-shi 340-0013, Japan, Capacity: 546,210 mt/y, (Pulp mill, Paperboard mill)
  Phone: (81) 48 931 9571
  Fax: (81) 48 931 8405
Nippon Paper Industries Co., Ltd., Yoshinaga Mill, 798 Hina, Fuji-shi 417-8520, Japan, Capacity: 533,715 mt/y, (Pulp mill, Paper mill, Paperboard mill)
  Phone: (81) 545 57 3212
  Fax: (81) 545 57 3441

ⓜNippon Paper Industries Co., Ltd.
Fuji Mill
4-1-1, Imai
Fuji-shi, Shizuoka Pref., 417-8610
Japan
  Phone: (81) 545 30 3589
  Fax: (81) 545 30 3050
  Web Address: www.nipponpapergroup.com/e/index.html
Personnel:
  Dir. / Mill Mgr.: Hidetsugu Yamada
  Phone: (81) 545 30 3589
Total Employees at this Location: 414
Type of Operation: Paper mill
Pulp Grades and Capacities:
  Total pulp capacity: 310,628 mt/y
  Chemical Pulp: 167,160 mt/y
  Mechanical Pulp: 47,093 mt/y
  Recycled Pulping: 96,375 mt/y
Pulp Mill Data:
  Chemical Pulping Systems:
  Batch digesters: 4
  Continuous digesters: 2
  Mechanical Pulping Systems:
  RMP systems
  Bleach Plant Systems: 3
  Chemical Pulping system, Sequence: O_2 ADoEopD
  Mechanical Pulping system
  Recycled fiber treatmen

Chemical Recovery Equipment:
  Recovery boilers: 1
  Lime Kiln
  Recycled Fiber Treatment Lines:
  Flotation deinking lines
  Pulpers: 3 at 257,000 admt/y
Paper/Paperboard Grades and Capacities:
  Total paper and paperboard capacity: 368,067 mt/y
  Newsprint: 71,400 mt/y
  Uncoated woodfree/freesheet: 101,031 mt/y
  Uncoated mechanical/groundwood: 41,412 mt/y
  Coated woodfree/freesheet: 74,970 mt/y
  Coated mechanical/groundwood: 70,329 mt/y
  Specialty and industrial: 8,925 mt/y
Paper and Paperboard Mill Data:
  Stock Preparation:
  Pulpers: 2
  Refiners: 35
  Paper Machines: 5
  No. 1, fourdrinier, total capacity 8,925 mt/y, Trim width 2.83 m, Specialty and industrial
  No. 2, fourdrinier, total capacity 30,345 mt/y, Trim width 2.85 m, Uncoated woodfree/freesheet
  No. 11, SymFormer R, total capacity 70,686 mt/y, Trim width 3.77 m, Uncoated woodfree/freesheet
  No. 12, DuoFormer D, total capacity 112,812 mt/y, Trim width 5.75 m, Newsprint, Uncoated mechanical/groundwood
  No. 13, DuoFormer, total capacity 145,299 mt/y, Trim width 5.9 m, Coated woodfree/freesheet, Coated mechanical/groundwood
  Finishing Equipment:
  Winders: 7
  Supercalenders: 6
  Rewinders: 9
  Energy Data:
  Power boilers: 6
  Steam turbines: 6 at 151.2 MW
  Electrical demand for mill: 1,227 MWh/D

ⓜNippon Paper Industries Co., Ltd.
Hokkaido Mill - Asahikawa
505-1 Pulp-cho
Asahikawa-shi, Hokkaido Pref., 070-8611
Japan
  Phone: (81) 166 259 730
  Fax: (81) 166 259 775
  Web Address: www.nipponpapergroup.com/e/index.html
Personnel:
  Mill Mgr.: Masahiko Ohta
  Phone: (81) 166 259 730
Total Employees at this Location: 400
Type of Operation: Pulp mill, Paper mill, Paperboard mill
Pulp Grades and Capacities:
  Total pulp capacity: 322,076 mt/y
  Pulp available for market: 60,690 mt/y
  Chemical Pulp: 266,670 mt/y
  Mechanical Pulp: 34,616 mt/y
  Recycled Pulping: 20,790 mt/y
Pulp Mill Data:
  Chemical Pulping Systems:
  Batch digesters: 7
  Continuous digesters: 1
  Mechanical Pulping Systems:
  Conventional grinders: 5
  Pulp Lines: 6
  Bleach Plant Systems: 4
  Chemical Pulping System - Hardwood, Type: Hardwood - DE/PHD
  Chemical Pulping System - Softwood, Type: Softwood - DE/PHD
  Mechanical Pulping System - Softwood
  Recycled Pulping System
  Chemical Recovery Equipment:
  Evaporator lines
  Recovery boilers: 1
  Lime Kiln

Recycled Fiber Treatment Lines:
  Flotation deinking lines: 1 at 36,000
  Pulp Dryers:
  Pulp Dryers 1
Paper/Paperboard Grades and Capacities:
  Total paper and paperboard capacity: 293,811 mt/y
  Uncoated woodfree/freesheet: 116,382 mt/y
  Coated mechanical/groundwood: 125,664 mt/y
  Packaging papers: 21,420 mt/y
  Specialty and industrial: 21,420 mt/y
  Boxboard/cartonboard: 8,925 mt/y
Paper and Paperboard Mill Data:
  Paper Machines: 5
  No. 1, DuoFormer D, total capacity 125,664 mt/y, Trim width 6.51 m, Coated mechanical/groundwood
  No. 2, fourdrinier, total capacity 42,840 mt/y, Trim width 6.5 m, Packaging papers, Specialty and industrial
  No. 4, SymFormer MB, total capacity 69,615 mt/y, Trim width 3.25 m, Uncoated woodfree/freesheet
  No. 5, fourdrinier, total capacity 46,767 mt/y, Trim width 3.25 m, Uncoated woodfree/freesheet
  B, cylinder, total capacity 8,925 mt/y, Trim width 1.85 m, Boxboard/cartonboard
  Coating Machines: 1
  PM 1, total capacity 120,000 mt/y., on machine
  Finishing Equipment:
  Winders: 9
  Sheeters: 4
  Energy Data:
  Power boilers: 5
  Steam turbines: 4 at 5, 17.5, 14.7, 14.7 MW
  Electrical demand for mill: 1,296 MWh/D

ⓜNippon Paper Industries Co., Ltd.
Hokkaido Mill - Shiraoi
181 Kita-Yoshiwara
Shiraoi, Hokkaido Pref., 059-0993
Japan
  Phone: (81) 144 83 2711
  Fax: (81) 144 83 1400
  Web Address: www.nipponpapergroup.com/e/index.html
Personnel:
  Mill Mgr.: Masahiko Ohta
  Phone: (81) 144 83 2711
Total Employees at this Location: 244
Type of Operation: Pulp mill, Paper mill
Pulp Grades and Capacities:
  Total pulp capacity: 369,693 mt/y
  Chemical Pulp: 369,693 mt/y
Pulp Mill Data:
  Chemical Pulping Systems:
  Continuous digesters: 2
  Pulp Lines: 1
  Bleach Plant Systems: 1
  No. 1, Type: ECF, Sequence: O_2 DEoHDD, Capacity 363,000 admt/y
  Chemical Recovery Equipment:
  Evaporator lines: 2
  Recovery boilers: 4
  Lime Kiln
  Pulp Dryers:
  Air Float dryers 1
Paper/Paperboard Grades and Capacities:
  Total paper and paperboard capacity: 433,755 mt/y
  Uncoated woodfree/freesheet: 233,835 mt/y
  Coated woodfree/freesheet: 199,920 mt/y
Paper and Paperboard Mill Data:
  Stock Preparation:
  Pulpers: 6
  Refiners: 29
  Paper Machines: 3
  No. 8, fourdrinier, total capacity 83,895 mt/y, Trim width 5.18 m, Uncoated woodfree/freesheet
  No. 9, DuoFormer D, total capacity 199,920 mt/y, Trim width 6.48 m, Coated woodfree/freesheet
  No. 10, fourdrinier, total capacity 149,940 mt/y, Trim width 6.48 m, Uncoated woodfree/freesheet
  Coating Machines: 1

No. 3, total capacity 200,000 mt/y., off machine
Finishing Equipment:
  Supercalenders: 2
  Sheeters: 9
Energy Data:
  Power boilers: 10
  Combustion turbines: 5 at 119.5 MW
  Electrical demand for mill: 1,324 MWh/D

ⓜNippon Paper Industries Co., Ltd.
Hokkaido Mill - Yufutsu
143 Yufutsu
Tomakomai-shi, Hokkaido Pref., 059-1395
Japan
  Phone: (81) 144 56 0111
  Fax: (81) 144 56 0485
  Web Address: www.nipponpapergroup.com/e/index.html
Personnel:
  Man. Dir.: Masahiko Ohta
  Phone: (81) 144 56 0111
Total Employees at this Location: 274
Type of Operation: Pulp mill, Paper mill
Pulp Grades and Capacities:
  Total pulp capacity: 293,930 mt/y
  Pulp available for market: 49,980 mt/y
  Chemical Pulp: 165,807 mt/y
  Mechanical Pulp: 20,230 mt/y
  Recycled Pulping: 107,893 mt/y
Pulp Mill Data:
  Chemical Pulping Systems:
  Continuous digesters: 1
  Mechanical Pulping Systems:
  TMP systems
  Bleach Plant Systems: 3
  Chemical pulping system bleaching, Type: Hardwood, Ozone process: MC, Sequence: O_2 Z/DEpO, Capacity 190,000 admt/y
  Mechanical pulping system bleaching
  Recycled treatment bleaching
  Chemical Recovery Equipment:
  Evaporator lines: 1
  Recovery boilers: 1
  Lime Kiln
  Recycled Fiber Treatment Lines:
  Flotation deinking lines
  Pulp Dryers:
  Air Float dryers 1
Paper/Paperboard Grades and Capacities:
  Total paper and paperboard capacity: 275,604 mt/y
  Newsprint: 132,090 mt/y
  Uncoated woodfree/freesheet: 143,514 mt/y
Paper and Paperboard Mill Data:
  Stock Preparation:
  Pulpers: 4
  Refiners: 3
Paper Machines: 4
  No. 2, fourdrinier, total capacity 14,994 mt/y, Trim width 2.12 m, Uncoated woodfree/freesheet
  No. 4, fourdrinier, total capacity 30,345 mt/y, Trim width 2.54 m, Uncoated woodfree/freesheet
  No. 5, DuoFormer D, total capacity 105,315 mt/y, Trim width 4.85 m, Uncoated woodfree/freesheet
  No. 7, Bel-Baie II, total capacity 132,090 mt/y, Trim width 4.88 m, Newsprint
Finishing Equipment:
  Winders: 5
  Sheeters: 7
Energy Data:
  Power boilers: 2
  Steam turbines: 5 at 31.4, 6, 15, 9.3, 2.8 MW
  Electrical demand for mill: 1,060 MWh/D

ⓜNippon Paper Industries Co., Ltd.
Ishinomaki Mill
2-2-1 Nanko-cho
Ishinomaki-shi, Miyagi Pref., 986-0836
Japan
  Phone: (81) 225 95 0111
  Fax: (81) 225 93 6060
  Web Address: www.nipponpapergroup.com/e/index.html
Personnel:
  Exec. Man. & Dir, Ishimaki Mill Mgr.: Hirobi Kurada
  Phone: (81) 225 95 0111
  Dir. Safety & Environment: Kazumori Fukushima
  Phone: (81) 225 95 0111
  Dir. Tech. Dept.: Sho Kanemori
  Phone: (81) 225 95 0111
  Dir. Paper Making: Yoshiaki Uchida
  Phone: (81) 225 95 0111
  Dir. Power Dept.: Fumisaka Sato
  Phone: (81) 225 95 0111
Total Employees at this Location: 518
Type of Operation: Pulp mill, Paper mill
Pulp Grades and Capacities:
  Total pulp capacity: 622,463 mt/y
  Chemical Pulp: 316,575 mt/y
  Mechanical Pulp: 85,882 mt/y
  Recycled Pulping: 220,007 mt/y
Pulp Mill Data:
  Chemical Pulping Systems:
  Continuous digesters: 2
  Mechanical Pulping Systems:
  Conventional grinders: 16
  TMP systems: 2
Pulp Lines: 7
  Bleach Plant Systems: 4
  DIP, Type: 2 lines, Sequence: P, Capacity 214,200 admt/y
  HW kraft line, Sequence: O_2 DEPD, Capacity 270,000 admt/y
  SW kraft line, Sequence: O_2 DEPD, Capacity 110,000 admt/y
  TMP, Sequence: P, Capacity 97,000 admt/y
  Chemical Recovery Equipment:
  Evaporator lines: 1
  Recovery boilers: 1
  Recovery boilers: 1
  Lime Kiln
  Recycled Fiber Treatment Lines:
  Flotation deinking lines: 2 at 214,000 admt/y
Paper/Paperboard Grades and Capacities:
  Total paper and paperboard capacity: 856,000 mt/y
  Uncoated woodfree/freesheet: 54,000 mt/y
  Coated woodfree/freesheet: 268,000 mt/y
  Coated mechanical/groundwood: 534,000 mt/y
Paper and Paperboard Mill Data:
Paper Machines: 6
  No. 7, OptiFormer, total capacity 108,000 mt/y, Trim width 4.8 m, Coated woodfree/freesheet, Uncoated woodfree/freesheet
  No. 8, OptiFormer, total capacity 112,000 mt/y, Trim width 5.49 m, Coated mechanical/groundwood
  N-2, DuoFormer D, total capacity 89,000 mt/y, Trim width 3.38 m, Coated woodfree/freesheet
  N-4, DuoFormer D, total capacity 125,000 mt/y, Trim width 5.07 m, Coated woodfree/freesheet
  N-5, DuoFormer D, total capacity 150,000 mt/y, Trim width 6.51 m, Coated mechanical/groundwood
  N-6, OptiFormer, total capacity 272,000 mt/y, Trim width 8.5 m, Coated mechanical/groundwood
Coating Machines: 2
  Off 2, total capacity 89,000 mt/y., off machine
  Off 4, total capacity 125,000 mt/y., off machine
Finishing Equipment:
  Winders: 11
  Supercalenders: 6
  Sheeters: 8
Energy Data:
  Power boilers: 5
  Steam turbines: 7 at 229.3 MW
  Electrical demand for mill: 2,660 MWh/D

ⓜNippon Paper Industries Co., Ltd.
Iwakuni Mill
2-8-1 Iida-machi
Iwakuni-shi, Yamaguchi Pref., 740-0003
Japan
  Phone: (81) 827 24 6222
  Fax: (81) 827 24 6390
  Web Address: www.nipponpapergroup.com/e/index.html
Personnel:
  Mill Mgr. / Dir.: Tetsumi Ohko
  Phone: (81) 827 24 6222
Total Employees at this Location: 398
Type of Operation: Pulp mill, Paper mill
Pulp Grades and Capacities:
  Total pulp capacity: 648,347 mt/y
  Pulp available for market: 148,023 mt/y
  Chemical Pulp: 648,347 mt/y
Pulp Mill Data:
  Chemical Pulping Systems:
  Continuous digesters: 2
Pulp Lines: 2
  Bleach Plant Systems: 2
  HW Kraft, Type: ECF, Sequence: O_2 Z/DEopD, Capacity 558,000 admt/y
  SW Kraft, Type: ECF, Sequence: O_2 DEpD, Capacity 90,000 admt/y
  Chemical Recovery Equipment:
  Evaporator lines: 1
  Recovery boilers: 1
  Lime Kiln
  Pulp Dryers:
  Air Float dryers 5
Paper/Paperboard Grades and Capacities:
  Total paper and paperboard capacity: 665,000 mt/y
  Uncoated woodfree/freesheet: 140,000 mt/y
  Coated woodfree/freesheet: 525,000 mt/y
Paper and Paperboard Mill Data:
  Stock Preparation:
  Refiners: 24
Paper Machines: 4
  No. 6, DuoFormer D, total capacity 98,000 mt/y, Trim width 3.27 m, Coated woodfree/freesheet
  No. 7, SymFormer MB, total capacity 177,000 mt/y, Trim width 4.73 m, Coated woodfree/freesheet
  No. 8, SymFormer MB, total capacity 140,000 mt/y, Trim width 4.9 m, Uncoated woodfree/freesheet
  No. 9, DuoFormer D, total capacity 250,000 mt/y, Trim width 7.04 m, Coated woodfree/freesheet
Coating Machines: 3
  No. 2, total capacity 8,030 mt/y., off machine
  No. 4, total capacity 91,250 mt/y., off machine
  No. 5, total capacity 178,900 mt/y., off machine
Finishing Equipment:
  Winders: 4
  Supercalenders: 6
  Rewinders: 12
  Sheeters: 14
Energy Data:
  Power boilers: 3
  Steam turbines: 3 at 30, 70, 35 MW
  Electrical demand for mill: 2,259 MWh/D

ⓜNippon Paper Industries Co., Ltd.
Iwanuma Mill
1-1 Daishowa
Iwanuma-shi, Miyagi Pref., 989-2492
Japan
  Phone: (81) 223 22 6111
  Fax: (81) 223 29 2250
  Web Address: www.nipponpapergroup.com/e/index.html
Personnel:
  Dir. / Mill Mgr.: Masahiro Hirakawa
  Phone: (81) 223 22 6111
Total Employees at this Location: 272
Type of Operation: Pulp mill, Paper mill
Pulp Grades and Capacities:
  Total pulp capacity: 591,033 mt/y
  Chemical Pulp: 86,473 mt/y
  Mechanical Pulp: 104,720 mt/y
  Recycled Pulping: 399,840 mt/y
Pulp Mill Data:
  Chemical Pulping Systems:

Japan

Continuous digesters: 1
Mechanical Pulping Systems:
TMP systems: 1
Pulp Lines: 5
Bleach Plant Systems: 2
Chemical Pulping System, Type: SW/HW, Sequence: O_2 CEopHD, Capacity 146,000 admt/y
DIP
Chemical Recovery Equipment:
Evaporator lines: 1
Recovery boilers: 2
Lime Kiln
Recycled Fiber Treatment Lines:
Flotation deinking lines: 1 at 175,000
Flotation deinking lines: 1 at 135,000
Flotation deinking lines: 1 at 95,000
Flotation deinking lines: 1 at 72,000
Paper/Paperboard Grades and Capacities:
Total paper and paperboard capacity: 601,545 mt/y
Newsprint: 460,530 mt/y
Coated woodfree/freesheet: 107,100 mt/y
Coated mechanical/groundwood: 33,915 mt/y
Paper and Paperboard Mill Data:
Stock Preparation:
Pulpers: 3
Refiners: 18
Paper Machines: 4
No. 1, DuoFormer F, total capacity 178,500 mt/y, Trim width 8.1 m, Newsprint
No. 2, (due to be closed by late February 2012), DuoFormer D, total capacity 141,015 mt/y, Trim width 5.73 m, Coated woodfree/freesheet, Coated mechanical/groundwood
No. 3, Bel-Baie III, total capacity 160,650 mt/y, Trim width 8.1 m, Newsprint
No. 4, Bel-Baie III, total capacity 149,940 mt/y, Trim width 8.1 m, Newsprint
Coating Machines: 1
No. 30, total capacity 141,000 mt/y, off machine
Finishing Equipment:
Winders: 1
Supercalenders: 2
Rewinders: 5
Sheeters: 4
Energy Data:
Power boilers: 5
Steam turbines: 5 at 12.9, 55, 65.8, 3.25, 46 MW
Electrical demand for mill: 2,310 MWh/D

ⓂNippon Paper Industries Co., Ltd.
Kushiro Mill
2-1-47 Tottori-Minami
Kushiro-shi, Hokkaido Pref., 084-0905
Japan
Phone: (81) 154 52 7605
Fax: (81) 154 51 3525
Web Address: www.nipponpapergroup.com/e/index.html
Personnel:
Mill Mgr.: Tsutomu Naito
Phone: (81) 154 52 7605
Paper Prod. Mgr: Naohiro Ohyama
Phone: (81) 154 52 7605
Total Employees at this Location: 241
Type of Operation: Pulp mill, Paper mill
Pulp Grades and Capacities:
Total pulp capacity: 518,840 mt/y
Chemical Pulp: 104,323 mt/y
Mechanical Pulp: 108,687 mt/y
Recycled Pulping: 305,830 mt/y
Pulp Mill Data:
Chemical Pulping Systems:
Continuous digesters: 1
Mechanical Pulping Systems:
TMP systems: 1
Pulp Lines: 2
Bleach Plant Systems: 1
No. 1, Sequence: O_2 H, Capacity 126,400 admt/y
Chemical Recovery Equipment:
Evaporator lines: 12
Recovery boilers: 1
Pulp Dryers:
Air Float dryers 2
Paper/Paperboard Grades and Capacities:
Total paper and paperboard capacity: 385,560 mt/y
Newsprint: 385,560 mt/y
Paper and Paperboard Mill Data:
Stock Preparation:
Pulpers: 7
Refiners: 8
Paper Machines: 3
No. 6, Bel-Baie II, total capacity 133,875 mt/y, Trim width 6.5 m, Newsprint
No. 7, Bel-Baie II, total capacity 139,230 mt/y, Trim width 6.5 m, Newsprint
No. 8, Bel-Baie II, total capacity 157,080 mt/y, Trim width 6.5 m, Newsprint
Finishing Equipment:
Rewinders: 4
Energy Data:
Power boilers: 6
Steam turbines: 7 at 132.5 MW
Electrical demand for mill: 1,995 MWh/D

ⓂNippon Paper Industries Co., Ltd.
Yatsushiro Mill
1-1, Jujo-machi
Yatsushiro-shi, Kumamoto Pref., 866-8602
Japan
Phone: (81) 965 33 2111
Fax: (81) 965 35 1227
Web Address: www.nipponpapergroup.com/e/index.html
Personnel:
Dir./Gen. Mgr.: Isamu Harada
Phone: (81) 965 33 2111
Total Employees at this Location: 330
Type of Operation: Pulp mill, Paper mill
Pulp Grades and Capacities:
Total pulp capacity: 589,638 mt/y
Pulp available for market: 80,595 mt/y
Chemical Pulp: 288,000 mt/y
Mechanical Pulp: 65,498 mt/y
Recycled Pulping: 236,140 mt/y
Pulp Mill Data:
Chemical Pulping Systems:
Continuous digesters: 2
Mechanical Pulping Systems:
TMP systems: 1
TMP systems: 1
Pulp Lines: 6
Bleach Plant Systems: 4
DIP, Sequence: P, Capacity 214,200 admt/y
HW Kraft, Type: ECF, Sequence: O_2 DEpD, Capacity 45,700 admt/y
SW Kraft, Type: ECF, Sequence: O_2 Z/DEopD, Capacity 185,700 admt/y
TMP, Sequence: P, Capacity 142,800 admt/y
Chemical Recovery Equipment:
Evaporator lines: 12
Recovery boilers: 2
Recovery boilers: 1
Lime Kiln
Recycled Fiber Treatment Lines:
Flotation deinking lines: 2 at 214,000
Pulp Dryers:
Air Float dryers 1, Twin Wire 1
Paper/Paperboard Grades and Capacities:
Total paper and paperboard capacity: 529,000 mt/y
Newsprint: 270,000 mt/y
Uncoated woodfree/freesheet: 234,000 mt/y
Uncoated mechanical/groundwood: 25,000 mt/y
Paper and Paperboard Mill Data:
Paper Machines: 4
No. 4, fourdrinier, total capacity 39,000 mt/y, Trim width 2.36 m, Uncoated woodfree/freesheet
No. 6, DuoFormer D, total capacity 75,000 mt/y, Trim width 3.36 m, Uncoated woodfree/freesheet
N1, Bel-Form, total capacity 145,000 mt/y, Trim width 5 m, Uncoated woodfree/freesheet, Uncoated mechanical/groundwood
N2, DuoFormer CFD, total capacity 270,000 mt/y, Trim width 8.29 m, Newsprint
Finishing Equipment:
Rewinders: 4
Sheeters: 4
Energy Data:
Power boilers: 7
Steam turbines: 5 at 145.5 MW
Electrical demand for mill: 2,034 MWh/D

ⓂNippon Paper Papylia Co., Ltd.
Ownership: 100% by Nippon Paper Industries Co., Ltd.
1-2-2 Hitotsubashi, Chiyoda-ku
Tokyo, 100-0003
Japan
Phone: (81) 3 6665 5800
Fax: (81) 3 3212 0550
Web Address: www.papylia.com
Personnel:
Pres.: Masahiro Hiragawa
Senior VP, Fukida Mill Mng.: Koichiro Nakayama
Exec. VP, Paper Business: Shinsuke Sugiyama
Exec. VP, Research & Engineering: Hiroshi Hara
Exec. VP, Kochi Mill Mng.: Senkei Inefuku
Total Employees of Company: 420
Mill Locations:
Nippon Paper Papylia Co., Ltd., Harada Mill, 506 Harada, Fuji-shi 417-0852, Japan, Capacity: 51,051 mt/y, (Paper mill)
Phone: (81) 545 52 4060
Fax: (81) 545 53 7175
Nippon Paper Papylia Co., Ltd., Harada Mill (Yodahashi), 37-1 Yodahashi, Fuji-shi, Japan, Capacity: 4,800 mt/y, (Paper mill)
Phone: (81) 545 32 2218
Fax: (81) 545 32 2287
Nippon Paper Papylia Co., Ltd., Kochi Mill, 3380 Ino-cho, Agawa-Gun 781-2110, Japan, Capacity: 15,620 mt/y, (Pulp mill, Paper mill)
Phone: (81) 88 8 92 1122
Fax: (81) 88 8 93 4469
Nippon Paper Papylia Co., Ltd., Suita Mill, 11-46, Higashi Otabi, Suita-shi 564-0033, Japan, Capacity: 11,500 mt/y, (Paper mill)
Phone: (81) 6 6381 2255
Fax: (81) 6 6382 2661

ⓂNippon Paper Papylia Co., Ltd.
Harada Mill
Ownership: 100% by Nippon Paper Industries Co., Ltd.
506 Harada
Fuji-shi, Shizuoka Pref., 417-0852
Japan
Phone: (81) 545 52 4060
Fax: (81) 545 53 7175
Web Address: www.papylia.com
Personnel:
Mill Mgr.: Koichiro Nakayama
Phone: (81) 545 52 4060
Total Employees at this Location: 150
Type of Operation: Paper mill
Pulp Mill Data:
Chemical Pulping Systems:
Batch digesters: 4
Pulp Lines: 1
Paper/Paperboard Grades and Capacities:
Total paper and paperboard capacity: 51,051 mt/y
Uncoated woodfree/freesheet: 21,777 mt/y
Coated woodfree/freesheet: 8,568 mt/y
Specialty and industrial: 20,706 mt/y
Paper and Paperboard Mill Data:
Stock Preparation:
Pulpers: 5
Refiners: 15

Japan

Paper Machines: 5
No. 1, fourdrinier, total capacity 8,925 mt/y, Trim width 1.68 m, Uncoated woodfree/freesheet
No. 2, fourdrinier, total capacity 4,998 mt/y, Trim width 2.14 m, Specialty and industrial
No. 3, fourdrinier, total capacity 12,852 mt/y, Trim width 2.15 m, Uncoated woodfree/freesheet
No. 4, fourdrinier, total capacity 15,708 mt/y, Trim width 2.61 m, Specialty and industrial
No. 5, fourdrinier, total capacity 8,568 mt/y, Trim width 1.68 m, Coated woodfree/freesheet
Coating Machines: 1
No. 5, on machine
Finishing Equipment:
Winders: 4
Supercalenders: 4
Sheeters: 2
Energy Data:
Power boilers: 1
Steam turbines: 1 at 10.7 MW
Electrical demand for mill: 136 MWh/D

ⓜNippon Paper Papylia Co., Ltd.
Harada Mill (Yodahashi)
Ownership: 100% by Nippon Paper Industries Co., Ltd.
37-1 Yodahashi
Fuji-shi, Shizuoka Pref.
Japan
Phone: (81) 545 32 2218
Fax: (81) 545 32 2287
Web Address: www.papylia.com
Personnel:
Mill Mgr.: Koichiro Nakayama
Phone: (81) 545 32 2218
Type of Operation: Paper mill
Paper/Paperboard Grades and Capacities:
Total paper and paperboard capacity: 4,800 mt/y
Specialty and industrial: 4,800 mt/y
Paper and Paperboard Mill Data:
Paper Machines: 1
No. 6, Tanmo, cylinder, combination, total capacity 4,800 mt/y, Trim width 2.58 m, Specialty and industrial
Coating Machines: 1
No. 1
Finishing Equipment:
Winders: 2
Energy Data:
Power boilers: 1

ⓜNippon Paper Papylia Co., Ltd.
Kochi Mill
Ownership: 100% by Nippon Paper Industries Co., Ltd.
3380 Ino-cho
Agawa-Gun, Kochi Pref., 781-2110
Japan
Phone: (81) 88 8 92 1122
Fax: (81) 88 8 93 4469
Web Address: www.papylia.com
Personnel:
Dir./Mill Mgr.: Chikei Inafuku
Phone: (81) 88 8 92 1122
Total Employees at this Location: 100
Type of Operation: Pulp mill, Paper mill
Pulp Grades and Capacities:
Total pulp capacity: 9,000 mt/y
Pulp Mill Data:
Chemical Pulping Systems:
Batch digesters: 4
Paper/Paperboard Grades and Capacities:
Total paper and paperboard capacity: 15,620 mt/y
Specialty and industrial: 15,620 mt/y
Paper and Paperboard Mill Data:
Stock Preparation:
Pulpers: 5
Refiners: 6
Paper Machines: 10
K4, Yankee dryer, cylinder, total capacity 1,260 mt/y, Trim width 0.99 m, Specialty and industrial
K5, Yankee dryer, Tanmo, combination, cylinder, total capacity 360 mt/y, Trim width 1.01 m, Specialty and industrial
N1, Yankee dryer, cylinder, total capacity 2,340 mt/y, Trim width 1.42 m, Specialty and industrial
N2, Tanmo, combination, cylinder, Yankee dryer, total capacity 1,620 mt/y, Trim width 1.42 m, Specialty and industrial
N3, Tanmo, combination, cylinder, Yankee dryer, total capacity 1,620 mt/y, Trim width 1.52 m, Specialty and industrial
N6, Yankee dryer, Tanmo, combination, cylinder, total capacity 3,780 mt/y, Trim width 2.23 m, Specialty and industrial
N7, Yankee dryer, Tanmo, combination, cylinder, total capacity 1,800 mt/y, Trim width 1.5 m, Specialty and industrial
S1, combination, total capacity 1,260 mt/y, Trim width 1.85 m, Specialty and industrial
S2, combination, total capacity 720 mt/y, Trim width 1.47 m, Specialty and industrial
S3, Yankee dryer, cylinder, total capacity 860 mt/y, Trim width 1.47 m, Specialty and industrial
Finishing Equipment:
Winders: 15
Supercalenders: 1
Sheeters: 1
Energy Data:
Power boilers: 2

ⓜNippon Paper Papylia Co., Ltd.
Suita Mill
Ownership: 100% by Nippon Paper Industries Co., Ltd.
11-46, Higashi Otabi
Suita-shi, Osaka Pref., 564-0033
Japan
Phone: (81) 6 6381 2255
Fax: (81) 6 6382 2661
Web Address: www.papylia.com
Personnel:
Mill Mgr.: Yuji Kimura
Phone: (81) 6 6381 2255
Total Employees at this Location: 100
Type of Operation: Paper mill
Paper/Paperboard Grades and Capacities:
Total paper and paperboard capacity: 11,500 mt/y
Specialty and industrial: 11,500 mt/y
Paper and Paperboard Mill Data:
Stock Preparation:
Pulpers: 1
Refiners: 3
Paper Machines: 2
No. 2, fourdrinier, total capacity 4,300 mt/y, Trim width 2.11 m, Specialty and industrial
No. 3, fourdrinier, total capacity 7,200 mt/y, Trim width 2.14 m, Specialty and industrial
Finishing Equipment:
Supercalenders: 1
Rewinders: 1
Sheeters: 1
Energy Data:
Power boilers: 1

ⓜNishinihon Eizai Co., Ltd.
Tatsuno-shi Mill
Ownership: Corelex Co., Ltd.
566 Tatsunocho-daido
Tatsuno-shi, Hyogo Pref., 679-4169
Japan
Phone: (81) 791 63 1181
Fax: (81) 791 63 3617
Web Address: www.nne.co.jp
Personnel:
Pres.: Takenobu Gouda
Phone: (81) 791 63 1181
Fax: (81) 791 63 3617
Snr. Man. Dir.: Yasuto Gouda
Phone: (81) 791 63 1181
Fax: (81) 791 63 3617
Total Employees at this Location: 130
Type of Operation: Paper mill
Pulp Grades and Capacities:
Total pulp capacity: 48,266 mt/y
Recycled Pulping: 48,266 mt/y
Pulp Mill Data:
Recycled Fiber Treatment Lines:
Flotation deinking lines: 1 at 53,550
Paper/Paperboard Grades and Capacities:
Total paper and paperboard capacity: 45,000 mt/y
Tissue: 45,000 mt/y
Paper and Paperboard Mill Data:
Paper Machines: 5
No. 1, Yankee dryer, total capacity 4,000 mt/y, Trim width 1.68 m, Tissue
No. 2, Yankee dryer, total capacity 9,000 mt/y, Trim width 2.61 m, Tissue
No. 3, Yankee dryer, total capacity 9,000 mt/y, Trim width 2.61 m, Tissue
No. 5, Yankee dryer, total capacity 15,000 mt/y, Trim width 2.58 m, Tissue
No. 6, Yankee dryer, total capacity 8,000 mt/y, Trim width 3.47 m, Tissue
Finishing Equipment:
Winders: 11
Sheeters: 4
Energy Data:
Power boilers: 2
Electrical demand for mill: 145 MWh/D

ⓜNisshinbo Paper Products, Inc.
Ownership: Nisshinbo Holdings Inc.
2-31-11 Ningyo-cho, Nihombashi, Chuo-ku
Tokyo, 103-8650
Japan
Phone: (81) 3 5695 8915
Fax: (81) 3 5695 8982
Web Address: www.nisshinbo-paper-products.co.jp, www.nishinbo.co.jp
Personnel:
Pres.: Akihiro Yoshino
Phone: (81) 3 5695 8915
Fax: (81) 3 5695 8982
Total Employees of Company: 411
Mill Locations:
Nisshinbo Paper Products, Inc., Fuji Mill, 7-34 Yodabashi-cho, Fuji-shi 417-0003, Japan, Capacity: 7,600 mt/y, (Paper mill)
Phone: (81) 545 52 3132
Fax: (81) 545 52 2162
Nisshinbo Paper Products, Inc., Shimada Mill, 8-1 Horai-cho, Shimada-shi 427-8581, Japan, Capacity: 36,000 mt/y, (Paper mill)
Phone: (81) 547 37 2131
Fax: (81) 547 35 2729
Nisshinbo Paper Products, Inc., Tokushima Mill, 635 Nakajama, Kawauchi-cho, Tokushima-shi 771-0187, Japan, Capacity: 14,400 mt/y, (Paper mill)
Phone: (81) 88 6 52 9171
Fax: (81) 88 6 65 5317
Tokai Seishi Kougyou Co., Ltd., Fuji Mill, 60-1, Harada, Fuji, Japan, Capacity: 25,000 mt/y, (Paper mill)

ⓜNisshinbo Paper Products, Inc.
Fuji Mill
7-34 Yodabashi-cho
Fuji-shi, Shizuoka Pref., 417-0003
Japan
Phone: (81) 545 52 3132
Fax: (81) 545 52 2162
Web Address: www.nisshinbo.co.jp
Personnel:
Mill Mgr.: Manabu Miyoshi
Phone: (81) 545 52 3132
Total Employees at this Location: 117
Type of Operation: Paper mill

Japan

Paper/Paperboard Grades and Capacities:
Total paper and paperboard capacity: 7,600 mt/y
Specialty and industrial: 7,600 mt/y
Paper and Paperboard Mill Data:
Paper Machines: 3
No. 2, cylinder, total capacity 3,000 mt/y, Trim width 2.36 m, Specialty and industrial
No. 3, cylinder, total capacity 2,300 mt/y, Trim width 2.36 m, Specialty and industrial
No. 4, fourdrinier, total capacity 2,300 mt/y, Trim width 1.3 m, Specialty and industrial
Coating Machines: 1
No. 1, on machine
Finishing Equipment:
Supercalenders: 1
Sheeters: 2
Energy Data:
Power boilers: 8

ⓂNisshinbo Paper Products, Inc.
Shimada Mill
8-1 Horai-cho
Shimada-shi, Shizuoka Pref., 427-8581
Japan
  Phone: (81) 547 37 2131
  Fax: (81) 547 35 2729
  Web Address: www.nisshinbo.co.jp
  Personnel:
    Mill Mgr.: Tetsuji Takeuchi
    Phone: (81) 547 37 2131
Total Employees at this Location: 117
Type of Operation: Paper mill
Pulp Grades and Capacities:
Total pulp capacity: 9,580 mt/y
Recycled Pulping: 9,580 mt/y
Pulp Mill Data:
Recycled Fiber Treatment Lines:
Flotation deinking lines: 1
Paper/Paperboard Grades and Capacities:
Total paper and paperboard capacity: 36,000 mt/y
Tissue: 36,000 mt/y
Paper and Paperboard Mill Data:
Paper Machines: 3
No. 1, Yankee dryer, total capacity 9,000 mt/y, Trim width 2.83 m, Tissue
No. 2, twin-wire, Yankee dryer, total capacity 9,000 mt/y, Trim width 2.38 m, Tissue
No. 3, twin-wire, Yankee dryer, total capacity 18,000 mt/y, Trim width 2.38 m, Tissue
Finishing Equipment:
Winders: 2
Energy Data:
Power boilers
Electrical demand for mill: 99 MWh/D

ⓂNisshinbo Paper Products, Inc.
Tokushima Mill
635 Nakajama, Kawauchi-cho
Tokushima-shi, Tokushima Pref., 771-0187
Japan
  Phone: (81) 88 6 52 9171
  Fax: (81) 88 6 65 5317
  Web Address: www.nisshinbo.co.jp
  Personnel:
    Mill Mgr.: Kenji Uno
    Phone: (81) 88 6 52 9171
Total Employees at this Location: 71
Type of Operation: Paper mill
Paper/Paperboard Grades and Capacities:
Total paper and paperboard capacity: 14,400 mt/y
Uncoated woodfree/freesheet: 14,400 mt/y
Paper and Paperboard Mill Data:
Paper Machines: 2
No. 1, fourdrinier, total capacity 7,200 mt/y, Trim width 2.36 m, Uncoated woodfree/freesheet
No. 2, fourdrinier, total capacity 7,200 mt/y, Trim width 2.36 m, Uncoated woodfree/freesheet

ⓂNisshinkogyo Co., Ltd.
2-23-4, Senju-higashi, Adachi-ku
Tokyo, 120-0025
Japan
  Phone: (81) 3 3882 2424
  Fax: (81) 3 3881 2450
  Email: info@nisshinkogyo.co.jp
  Web Address: www.nisshinkogyo.co.jp
  Personnel:
    Pres.: Kimitaka Sodai
    Phone: (81) 3 3882 2424
    Fax: (81) 3 3881 2450
Total Employees of Company: 295
Mill Locations:
Nisshinkogyo Co., Ltd., Yamagata Mill, Nakagawara 438, Minamidate, Yamagata-shi 990-2461, Japan, Capacity: 55,200 mt/y, (Paperboard mill)
  Phone: (81) 236 43 0437
  Fax: (81) 236 43 0436
  Email: info@nisshinkogyo.co.jp

ⓂNisshinkogyo Co., Ltd.
Yamagata Mill
Nakagawara 438, Minamidate
Yamagata-shi, Yamagata Pref., 990-2461
Japan
  Phone: (81) 236 43 0437
  Fax: (81) 236 43 0436
  Email: info@nisshinkogyo.co.jp
  Web Address: www.nisshinkogyo.co.jp
  Personnel:
    Mill Mgr.: Isao Takase
    Phone: (81) 236 43 0437
Total Employees at this Location: 129
Type of Operation: Paperboard mill
Pulp Grades and Capacities:
Total pulp capacity: 57,616 mt/y
Recycled Pulping: 57,616 mt/y
Paper/Paperboard Grades and Capacities:
Total paper and paperboard capacity: 55,200 mt/y
Specialty and industrial: 55,200 mt/y
Paper and Paperboard Mill Data:
Paper Machines: 3
No. 1, cylinder, total capacity 19,200 mt/y, Trim width 2.4 m, Specialty and industrial
No. 2, cylinder, total capacity 3,600 mt/y, Trim width 1.3 m, Specialty and industrial
No. 5, cylinder, total capacity 32,400 mt/y, Trim width 3.2 m, Specialty and industrial
Energy Data:
Electrical demand for mill: 70 MWh/D

ⓄⓂNittoku Co., Ltd.
Fuji-shi Mill
514-1 Imaizumi
Fuji-shi, Shizuoka Pref., 417-0001
Japan
  Phone: (81) 545 52 4123
  Fax: (81) 545 53 1977
  Personnel:
    Pres.: Junichi Ide
    Phone: (81) 545 52 4123
Total Employees at this Location: 110
Type of Operation: Paper mill
Paper/Paperboard Grades and Capacities:
Total paper and paperboard capacity: 11,000 mt/y
Tissue: 11,000 mt/y
Paper and Paperboard Mill Data:
Paper Machines: 3
No. 1, Yankee dryer, total capacity 4,000 mt/y, Trim width 2.8 m, Tissue
No. 2, Yankee dryer, total capacity 3,000 mt/y, Trim width 2 m, Tissue
No. 3, Yankee dryer, total capacity 4,000 mt/y, Trim width 2.95 m, Tissue
Energy Data:
Power boilers
Electrical demand for mill: 30 MWh/D

ⓄⓂOhtaka Seishi K.K.
Iyomishima Mill
2437 Sangawacho
Shikokuchuo, Ehime Pref., 799 0431
Japan
Total Employees at this Location: 25
Type of Operation: Paper mill
Pulp Grades and Capacities:
Total pulp capacity: 6,489 mt/y
Recycled Pulping: 6,489 mt/y
Pulp Mill Data:
Recycled Fiber Treatment Lines:
Flotation deinking lines
Paper/Paperboard Grades and Capacities:
Total paper and paperboard capacity: 6,000 mt/y
Tissue: 6,000 mt/y
Paper and Paperboard Mill Data:
Paper Machines: 3
No. 1, Yankee dryer, total capacity 2,000 mt/y, Trim width 1.25 m, Tissue
No. 2, Yankee dryer, total capacity 2,000 mt/y, Trim width 1.4 m, Tissue
No. 3, Yankee dryer, total capacity 2,000 mt/y, Trim width 1.8 m, Tissue
Energy Data:
Power boilers
Electrical demand for mill: 20 MWh/D

ⓄⓂOi Seishi Co., Ltd.
Ena Paper Mill
920 Shoge, Osashima-cho
Ena-shi, Gifu Pref., 509-7203
Japan
  Phone: (81) 573 25 5331
  Fax: (81) 573 26 0034
  Personnel:
    Pres.: Kuniaki Katsutani
    Phone: (81) 573 25 5331
    Fax: (81) 573 26 0034
    Dir.: Akikatsu Taoka
    Phone: (81) 573 25 5331
    Fax: (81) 573 26 0034
    Dir.: Kiyoshi Hiyama
    Phone: (81) 573 25 5331
    Fax: (81) 573 26 0034
Total Employees of Company: 44
Total Employees at this Location: 44
Type of Operation: Paperboard mill
Pulp Grades and Capacities:
Total pulp capacity: 38,420 mt/y
Recycled Pulping: 38,420 mt/y
Paper/Paperboard Grades and Capacities:
Total paper and paperboard capacity: 38,000 mt/y
Linerboard: 38,000 mt/y
Paper and Paperboard Mill Data:
Stock Preparation:
Pulpers: 3
Refiners: 1
Paper Machines: 1
No. 1, multi-cylinder, total capacity 38,000 mt/y, Trim width 2.7 m, Linerboard
Energy Data:
Power boilers: 1
Electrical demand for mill: 48 MWh/D

ⓄⓂOita Seishi Corporation
Honsha Mill
Ownership: Corelex Co., Ltd.
2-15-27, Nishiki-cho
Oita-shi, Oita Pref., 870-8691
Japan
  Phone: (81) 97 534 7777
  Fax: (81) 97 537 2101
  Email: info@oita-seishi.com
  Web Address: www.oita-seishi.com
  Personnel:
    Pres.: Hiroyuki Takita
    Phone: (81) 97 534 7777

Fax: (81) 97 537 2101
VP. & Honsha Mill Mgr.: Youichi Takita
Phone: (81) 97 534 7777
Fax: (81) 97 537 2101
Snr. Man. Dir. Sls.: Minoru Sakamotu
Phone: (81) 97 534 7777
Fax: (81) 97 537 2101
Total Employees of Company: 230
Total Employees at this Location: 30
Type of Operation: Paper mill
Mill Locations:
Oita Seishi Corporation, Buzen Mill, 312 Kutsukawa, Buzen-shi 828-0023, Japan, Capacity: 70,000 mt/y, (Paper mill)
Phone: (81) 979 83 2101
Fax: (81) 979 82 5500
Email: info@oita-seishi.com
Pulp Grades and Capacities:
Total pulp capacity: 28,718 mt/y
Recycled Pulping: 28,718 mt/y
Pulp Mill Data:
Recycled Fiber Treatment Lines:
Flotation deinking lines: 1
Paper/Paperboard Grades and Capacities:
Total paper and paperboard capacity: 27,000 mt/y
Tissue: 27,000 mt/y
Paper and Paperboard Mill Data:
Paper Machines: 1
No. 9, crescent former, Yankee dryer, total capacity 27,000 mt/y, Trim width 2.8 m, Tissue
Energy Data:
TMP Reboiler: 1
Electrical demand for mill: 82 MWh/D

ⓜOita Seishi Corporation
Buzen Mill
Ownership: Corelex Co., Ltd.
312 Kutsukawa
Buzen-shi, Fukuoka Pref., 828-0023
Japan
Phone: (81) 979 83 2101
Fax: (81) 979 82 5500
Email: info@oita-seishi.com
Web Address: www.oita-seishi.com
Personnel:
Mill Mgr.: Nobuyuki Takita
Phone: (81) 979 83 2101
Fax: (81) 979 82 5500
Total Employees at this Location: 120
Type of Operation: Paper mill
Pulp Grades and Capacities:
Total pulp capacity: 54,739 mt/y
Recycled Pulping: 54,739 mt/y
Pulp Mill Data:
Recycled Fiber Treatment Lines:
Flotation deinking lines: 1
Paper/Paperboard Grades and Capacities:
Total paper and paperboard capacity: 70,000 mt/y
Tissue: 70,000 mt/y
Paper and Paperboard Mill Data:
Paper Machines: 7
No. 1, Yankee dryer, total capacity 7,500 mt/y, Trim width 1.8 m, Tissue
No. 2, Yankee dryer, total capacity 7,500 mt/y, Trim width 1.8 m, Tissue
No. 5, Yankee dryer, total capacity 7,000 mt/y, Trim width 1.65 m, Tissue
No. 6, BF-12, total capacity 12,000 mt/y, Trim width 2.36 m, Tissue
No. 7, BF-10, total capacity 10,000 mt/y, Trim width 2.36 m, Tissue
No. 8, BF-10, total capacity 10,000 mt/y, Trim width 2.36 m, Tissue
No. 10, Yankee dryer, total capacity 16,000 mt/y, Trim width 2.36 m, Tissue
Energy Data:
Power boilers
Electrical demand for mill: 213 MWh/D

ⓜOji F-Tex Co., Ltd.
Dai-ichi Mill
Previously Oji Specialty Paper Co., Ltd.
Ownership: 100% by Oji Holdings Corporation
1-1-1 Iriyamase
Fuji-shi, Shizuoka Pref., 419-0204
Japan
Phone: (81) 545 72 1111
Fax: (81) 545 72 1031
Web Address: www.ojif-tex.co.jp
Personnel:
Mill Mgr.: Hirohisa Ishikawa
Phone: (81) 545 72 1111
Total Employees at this Location: 35
Type of Operation: Paper mill
Paper/Paperboard Grades and Capacities:
Total paper and paperboard capacity: 7,500 mt/y
Specialty and industrial: 7,500 mt/y
Paper and Paperboard Mill Data:
Stock Preparation:
Pulpers: 5
Paper Machines: 1
No. 1, top former, multi-cylinder, total capacity 7,500 mt/y, Trim width 1.3 m, Specialty and industrial
Finishing Equipment:
Sheeters: 1
Energy Data:
Power boilers: 3

ⓜOji F-Tex Co., Ltd.
Ebetsu Mill
Previously Oji Specialty paper Ltd.
Ownership: 100% by Oji Holdings Corporation
1 Oji
Ebetsu-shi, Hokkaido Pref., 067-0001
Japan
Phone: (81) 11 384 7311
Fax: (81) 11 384 3516
Web Address: www.ojif-tex.co.jp
Personnel:
Mill Mgr.: Sakujiro Oka
Phone: (81) 11 384 7311
Fax: (81) 11 384 3516
Total Employees at this Location: 250
Type of Operation: Pulp mill, Paper mill
Pulp Grades and Capacities:
Total pulp capacity: 135,147 mt/y
Chemical Pulp: 135,147 mt/y
Pulp Mill Data:
Chemical Pulping Systems:
Continuous digesters: 1
Bleach Plant Systems: 1
No. 1, Type: ECF Capacity 200,000 admt/y
Chemical Recovery Equipment:
Evaporator lines: 2
Recovery boilers: 3
Paper/Paperboard Grades and Capacities:
Total paper and paperboard capacity: 215,985 mt/y
Uncoated woodfree/freesheet: 113,883 mt/y
Specialty and industrial: 102,102 mt/y
Paper and Paperboard Mill Data:
Stock Preparation:
Pulpers: 5
Refiners: 45
Paper Machines: 7
No. 1, SymFormer, total capacity 75,327 mt/y, Trim width 3.3 m, Uncoated woodfree/freesheet
No. 2, fourdrinier, total capacity 27,846 mt/y, Trim width 2.62 m, Uncoated woodfree/freesheet, Specialty and industrial
No. 4, fourdrinier, total capacity 19,635 mt/y, Trim width 2.18 m, Uncoated woodfree/freesheet, Specialty and industrial
No. 5, Yankee dryer, total capacity 2,142 mt/y, Trim width 2 m, Specialty and industrial
No. 6, MB former, total capacity 71,400 mt/y, Trim width 3.3 m, Specialty and industrial
No. 7, Yankee dryer, total capacity 5,355 mt/y, Trim width 2.1 m, Specialty and industrial

No. 10, fourdrinier, total capacity 14,280 mt/y, Trim width 3.25 m, Specialty and industrial
Coating Machines: 1
PM6, on machine
Finishing Equipment:
Supercalenders: 1
Rewinders: 9
Sheeters: 8
Energy Data:
Power boilers: 2
Steam turbines: 4 at 35.5 MW
Electrical demand for mill: 716 MWh/D

ⓜOji F-Tex Co., Ltd.
Fuji Mill
Previously Oji Specialty Paper Co., Ltd.
Ownership: 100% by Oji Holdings Corporation
14-1 Maeda
Fuji-shi, Shizuoka Pref., 419-0937
Japan
Phone: (81) 545 62 8888
Fax: (81) 545 62 8855
Web Address: www.ojif-tex.co.jp
Personnel:
Mill Mgr. & Man.Dir.: Katsuhiko Shimazaki
Phone: (81) 545 62 8888
Fax: (81) 545 62 8855
Total Employees at this Location: 87
Type of Operation: Paper mill
Paper/Paperboard Grades and Capacities:
Total paper and paperboard capacity: 20,200 mt/y
Specialty and industrial: 20,200 mt/y
Paper and Paperboard Mill Data:
Paper Machines: 3
No. 3, fourdrinier, total capacity 5,800 mt/y, Trim width 1.4 m, Specialty and industrial
No. 5, fourdrinier, total capacity 6,100 mt/y, Trim width 1.25 m, Specialty and industrial
No. 7, cylinder, total capacity 8,300 mt/y, Trim width 2.88 m, Specialty and industrial
Finishing Equipment:
Supercalenders: 1
Rewinders: 2
Sheeters: 1
Energy Data:
Power boilers: 1

ⓜOji F-Tex Co., Ltd.
Fujinomiya Mill
Mill is mill will cease production in September 2014
Ownership: 100% by Oji Holdings Corporation
326-1 Koizumi
Fujinomiya-shi, Shizuoka Pref., 418-002
Japan
Phone: (81) 544 25 3171
Fax: (81) 544 25 3174
Web Address: www.ojif-tex.co.jp
Personnel:
Mill Mgr.: Keiji Mochitsuki
Phone: (81) 544 25 3171
Fax: (81) 544 25 3174
Total Employees at this Location: 72
Type of Operation: Paper mill, Paperboard mill
Pulp Grades and Capacities:
Total pulp capacity: 83,853 mt/y
Recycled Pulping: 83,853 mt/y
Paper/Paperboard Grades and Capacities:
Total paper and paperboard capacity: 83,000 mt/y
Boxboard/cartonboard: 83,000 mt/y
Paper and Paperboard Mill Data:
Paper Machines: 2
No. 1, cylinder, total capacity 47,000 mt/y, Trim width 2.9 m, Boxboard/cartonboard
No. 2, cylinder, total capacity 36,000 mt/y, Trim width 3 m, Boxboard/cartonboard
Energy Data:
Power boilers: 13
Electrical demand for mill: 123 MWh/D

Japan

ⓜOji F-Tex Co., Ltd.
Iwabuchi Mill
Mill is was Oji Specialty Paper Co., Ltd.
Ownership: 100% by Oji Holdings Corporation
1157-1 Nakanogo
Fujikawa-cho, Ihara-gun, Shizuoka Pref., 421-3306
Japan
  Phone: (81) 545 81 0075
  Fax: (81) 545 81 1303
  Web Address: www.ojif-tex.co.jp
Personnel:
  Mill Mgr.: Shogo Fushimi
  Phone: (81) 545 81 0075
  Fax: (81) 545 81 1303
Total Employees at this Location: 100
Type of Operation: Paper mill
Paper/Paperboard Grades and Capacities:
  Total paper and paperboard capacity: 46,410 mt/y
  Specialty and industrial: 46,410 mt/y
Paper and Paperboard Mill Data:
Paper Machines: 2
  No. 3, fourdrinier, total capacity 32,130 mt/y, Trim width 3.3 m, Specialty and industrial
  No. 4, fourdrinier, total capacity 14,280 mt/y, Trim width 2.64 m, Specialty and industrial
Coating Machines: 3
  N1, total capacity 12,000 mt/y.
  N2
  N3
Finishing Equipment:
  Winders: 4
  Supercalenders: 1
  Sheeters: 3
Energy Data:
  Power boilers: 3
  Combustion turbines: 1 at 6.9 MW
  Electrical demand for mill: 125 MWh/D

ⓜOji F-Tex Co., Ltd.
Nakatsu Mill
Previously Oji Specialty Paper Co., Ltd.
Ownership: 100% by Oji Holdings Corporation
3465-1 Nakatsugawa
Nakatsugawa-shi, Gifu Pref., 508-8686
Japan
  Phone: (81) 573 66 1152
  Fax: (81) 573 66 2412
  Web Address: www.ojif-tex.co.jp
Personnel:
  Mill Mgr.: Fumio Takehisa
  Phone: (81) 573 66 1152
  Fax: (81) 573 66 2412
  Dir. Prod.: Kouhei Michikawa
  Phone: (81) 573 66 1152
  Fax: (81) 573 66 2412
  Dir. Oper.: Masao Kato
  Phone: (81) 573 66 1152
  Fax: (81) 573 66 2412
Total Employees at this Location: 240
Type of Operation: Paper mill
Pulp Grades and Capacities:
  Total pulp capacity: 452 mt/y
  Recycled Pulping: 452 mt/y
Paper/Paperboard Grades and Capacities:
  Total paper and paperboard capacity: 49,980 mt/y
  Specialty and industrial: 49,980 mt/y
Paper and Paperboard Mill Data:
Paper Machines: 4
  No. 1, fourdrinier, total capacity 13,209 mt/y, Trim width 2.5 m, Specialty and industrial
  No. 6, fourdrinier, total capacity 28,560 mt/y, Trim width 3.5 m, Specialty and industrial
  G2, fourdrinier, total capacity 2,142 mt/y, Trim width 2.55 m, Specialty and industrial
  TB, hybrid former, total capacity 6,069 mt/y, Trim width 3.2 m, Specialty and industrial
Finishing Equipment:
  Winders: 8
  Supercalenders: 4
  Sheeters: 1
Energy Data:
  Power boilers: 2
  Steam turbines: 1 at 10.5 MW
  Electrical demand for mill: 123 MWh/D

ⓜOji F-Tex Co., Ltd.
Shibakawa Mill
Previously Oji Specialty Paper Co., Ltd
Ownership: 100% by Oji Holdings Corporation
1231-2 Habuna, Shibakawa-cho
Fuji-gun, Shizuoka Pref., 419-0316
Japan
  Phone: (81) 544 65 1211
  Fax: (81) 544 65 1923
  Web Address: www.ojispecialtypaper.co.jp
Personnel:
  Mill Mgr.: Hiroyuki Ide
  Phone: (81) 544 65 1211
  Fax: (81) 544 65 1923
Total Employees at this Location: 93
Type of Operation: Paper mill, Paperboard mill
Paper/Paperboard Grades and Capacities:
  Total paper and paperboard capacity: 41,200 mt/y
  Boxboard/cartonboard: 41,200 mt/y
Paper and Paperboard Mill Data:
Paper Machines: 2
  No. 1, cylinder, total capacity 20,000 mt/y, Trim width 1.98 m, Boxboard/cartonboard
  No. 2, Tanmo, total capacity 21,200 mt/y, Trim width 1.68 m, Boxboard/cartonboard
Coating Machines: 3
  No. 2, total capacity 5,475 mt/y., off machine
  No. 3, total capacity 5,475 mt/y., off machine
  No. 4, total capacity 5,200 mt/y., off machine
Finishing Equipment:
  Rewinders: 4
  Sheeters: 4
Energy Data:
  Power boilers: 8
  Hydro turbines: 1 at 1.5 MW
  Electrical demand for mill: 58 MWh/D

ⓜOji F-Tex Co., Ltd.
Shiga Mill
Previously Oji Specialty Paper Co. Ltd.
Ownership: 100% by Oji Holdings Corporation
66 Asakuni
Konan-shi, Shiga Pref., 520-3251
Japan
  Phone: (81) 748 72 2691
  Fax: (81) 748 72 2838
  Web Address: www.ojif-tex.co.jp
Personnel:
  Mill Mgr.: Taisuke Ito
  Phone: (81) 748 72 2691
  Fax: (81) 748 72 2838
  Dir., Oper.: Masa Abe
  Phone: (81) 748 72 2691
  Fax: (81) 748 72 2838
Total Employees at this Location: 129
Type of Operation: Paper mill
Energy Data:
  Power boilers: 2

ⓜOji Materia Co., Ltd.
Edogawa Mill
Previously Oji Paperboard Co., Ltd.
Ownership: Oji Holdings Corporation
3-2 Higashi Shinozaki 2-chome
Edogawa-ku, Tokyo, 133-8511
Japan
  Phone: (81) 3 3679 1111
  Fax: (81) 3 3677 1122
  Web Address: www.ojimateria.co.jp, www.ojiholdings.co.jp/english
Personnel:
  Mill Mgr.: Masahiro Haramura
  Phone: (81) 3 3679 1111
  Operations Mgr.: Takumi Matuoka
Total Employees at this Location: 88
Type of Operation: Paper mill, Paperboard mill
Pulp Grades and Capacities:
  Total pulp capacity: 124,152 mt/y
  Recycled Pulping: 124,152 mt/y
Pulp Mill Data:
  Recycled Fiber Treatment Lines:
  Flotation deinking lines: 1
  Pulpers: 4
  Pulpers: 1
Paper/Paperboard Grades and Capacities:
  Total paper and paperboard capacity: 144,000 mt/y
  Boxboard/cartonboard: 144,000 mt/y
Paper and Paperboard Mill Data:
  Stock Preparation:
  Pulpers: 1
  Refiners: 0
Paper Machines: 1
  No. 5, cylinder (7), total capacity 144,000 mt/y, Trim width 3.3 m, Boxboard/cartonboard
Coating Machines: 1
  PM 5, total capacity 144,000 mt/y., on machine
Finishing Equipment:
  Rewinders: 1
  Sheeters: 1
Energy Data:
  Power boilers: 4
  Steam turbines: 1 at 7.0 MW
  Electrical demand for mill: 235 MWh/D

ⓜOji Materia Co., Ltd.
Gifu (Ena) Mill
Previously Oji Paperboard Co., Ltd.
Ownership: Oji Holdings Corporation
696 Oi-cho
Ena-shi, Gifu Pref., 509-7201
Japan
  Phone: (81) 573 26 1611
  Fax: (81) 573 26 1656
  Web Address: www.ojimateria.co.jp, www.ojiholdings.co.jp/english
Personnel:
  Mill Mgr.: Kazuhisa Okamoto
  Phone: (81) 573 26 1611
  Fax: (81) 573 26 1656
  Dir. Eng.: Hayashi Giten
  Phone: (81) 573 26 1611
  Fax: (81) 573 26 1656
Total Employees at this Location: 83
Type of Operation: Paperboard mill
Pulp Grades and Capacities:
  Total pulp capacity: 250,611 mt/y
  Recycled Pulping: 250,611 mt/y
Pulp Mill Data:
  Recycled Fiber Treatment Lines:
  Recycled packaging pulping lines: 1
Paper/Paperboard Grades and Capacities:
  Total paper and paperboard capacity: 256,000 mt/y
  Linerboard: 170,667 mt/y
  Corrugating medium/fluting: 85,333 mt/y
Paper and Paperboard Mill Data:
Paper Machines: 1
  No. 3, DuoFormer, total capacity 256,000 mt/y, Trim width 4.85 m, Linerboard, Corrugating medium/fluting
Energy Data:
  Power boilers
  Steam turbines
  Electrical demand for mill: 371 MWh/D

ⓜOji Materia Co., Ltd.
Kushiro Mill
Previously Oji Paperboard Co., Ltd.
Ownership: Oji Holdings Corporation
3-2-5 Otanoshike
Kushiro-shi, Hokkaido Pref., 084-0917
Japan

Phone: (81) 154 57 3305
Fax: (81) 154 57 8277
Web Address: www.ojimateria.co.jp, www.ojiholdings.co.jp/english
Personnel:
Mill. Mgr.: Tetsuji Fujimura
Phone: (81) 154 57 3305
Total Employees at this Location: 45
Type of Operation: Paperboard mill
Pulp Grades and Capacities:
Total pulp capacity: 508,983 mt/y
Chemical Pulp: 305,390 mt/y
Recycled Pulping: 203,593 mt/y
Paper/Paperboard Grades and Capacities:
Total paper and paperboard capacity: 490,875 mt/y
Linerboard: 490,875 mt/y
Paper and Paperboard Mill Data:
Paper Machines: 1
L-1, Bel-Bond, total capacity 490,875 mt/y, Trim width 6.5 m, Linerboard
Finishing Equipment:
Winders: 1
Energy Data:
Electrical demand for mill: 1,151 MWh/D

ⓜOji Materia Co., Ltd.
Matsumoto Mill
Previously Oji Paperboard Co., Ltd.
Ownership: Oji Holdings Corporation
5200-1 Sasaga
Matsumoto-shi, Nagano Pref., 399-0033
Japan
Phone: (81) 263 25 5432
Fax: (81) 263 25 6595
Web Address: www.ojimateria.co.jp, www.ojiholdings.co.jp/english
Personnel:
Mill Mgr.: Naoyuki Takei
Phone: (81) 263 25 5432
Fax: (81) 263 25 6595
Oper. Dir.: Ryoichi Hoshina
Phone: (81) 263 25 5432
Fax: (81) 263 25 6595
Eng. Dir.: Yoichi Sato
Phone: (81) 263 25 5432
Fax: (81) 263 25 6595
Total Employees at this Location: 84
Type of Operation: Paperboard mill
Pulp Grades and Capacities:
Total pulp capacity: 94,736 mt/y
Recycled Pulping: 94,736 mt/y
Pulp Mill Data:
Recycled Fiber Treatment Lines:
Recycled packaging pulping lines: 1
Paper/Paperboard Grades and Capacities:
Total paper and paperboard capacity: 122,000 mt/y
Linerboard: 122,000 mt/y
Paper and Paperboard Mill Data:
Stock Preparation:
Pulpers: 7
Refiners: 12
Paper Machines: 1
No. 5, cylinder (5), total capacity 122,000 mt/y, Trim width 4 m, Linerboard
Finishing Equipment:
Winders: 1
Energy Data:
Power boilers: 7
Electrical demand for mill: 179 MWh/D

ⓜOji Materia Co., Ltd.
Gifu (Nakatsugawa) Mill
Previously Oji Paperboard Co. Ltd.
Ownership: Oji Holdings Corporation
2-3 Ogawa-cho
Nakatsugawa-shi, Gifu Pref., 508-8585
Japan
Phone: (81) 573 66 1511
Fax: (81) 573 66 6220
Web Address: www.ojiholdings.co.jp/english
Personnel:
Man. Dir./Mill Mgr.: Kazuhiro Okamoto
Phone: (81) 573 66 1511
Total Employees at this Location: 55
Type of Operation: Paperboard mill
Pulp Grades and Capacities:
Total pulp capacity: 154,398 mt/y
Recycled Pulping: 154,398 mt/y
Paper/Paperboard Grades and Capacities:
Total paper and paperboard capacity: 150,000 mt/y
Corrugating medium/fluting: 150,000 mt/y
Paper and Paperboard Mill Data:
Paper Machines: 1
No. 1, DuoFormer, total capacity 150,000 mt/y, Trim width 3.65 m, Corrugating medium/fluting
Energy Data:
Electrical demand for mill: 235 MWh/D

ⓜOji Materia Co., Ltd.
Nayoro Mill
Previously Oji Paperboard Co., Ltd.
Ownership: Oji Holdings Corporation
20-6 Tokuda
Nayoro-shi, Hokkaido Pref., 096-8555
Japan
Phone: (81) 1654 3 3111
Fax: (81) 1654 2 2832
Web Address: www.ojimateria.co.jp, www.ojiholdings.co.jp/english
Personnel:
Mill Mgr.: Mitsuru Murata
Phone: (81) 1654 3 3111
Fax: (81) 1654 2 2832
Dpty. Mgr.: Hikoyasu Ikeda
Phone: (81) 1654 3 3111
Fax: (81) 1654 2 2832
Tech. Dir: Etsujiro Koga
Phone: (81) 1654 3 3111
Fax: (81) 1654 2 2832
Total Employees at this Location: 110
Type of Operation: Pulp mill, Paperboard mill
Pulp Grades and Capacities:
Total pulp capacity: 245,829 mt/y
Chemical Pulp: 41,832 mt/y
Recycled Pulping: 203,997 mt/y
Pulp Mill Data:
Chemical Pulping Systems:
Continuous digesters: 2
Pulp Lines: 2
Chemical Recovery Equipment:
Evaporator lines: 1
Recovery boilers: 1
Recycled Fiber Treatment Lines:
Recycled packaging pulping lines: 6
Paper/Paperboard Grades and Capacities:
Total paper and paperboard capacity: 253,000 mt/y
Linerboard: 60,000 mt/y
Corrugating medium/fluting: 188,000 mt/y
Boxboard/cartonboard: 5,000 mt/y
Paper and Paperboard Mill Data:
Paper Machines: 2
No. 2, fourdrinier (2), total capacity 65,000 mt/y, Trim width 3.4 m, Linerboard, Boxboard/cartonboard
No. 3, fourdrinier, total capacity 188,000 mt/y, Trim width 4.4 m, Corrugating medium/fluting
Energy Data:
Power boilers: 1
Combustion turbines: 3 at 0.5 MW
Steam turbines: 2 at 9, 3.5 MW
Electrical demand for mill: 407 MWh/D

ⓜOji Materia Co., Ltd.
Nikko Mill
Previously Oji Paperboard Co., Ltd.
Ownership: Oji Holdings Corporation
592 Shirasawa
Utsunomiya-shi, Tochigi Pref., 329-1102
Japan
Phone: (81) 28 661 1011
Fax: (81) 28 661 1013
Web Address: www.ojimateria.co.jp, www.ojiholdings.co.jp/english
Personnel:
Mill Mgr.: Hajime Fujio
Phone: (81) 28 661 1011
Fax: (81) 28 661 1013
Total Employees at this Location: 107
Type of Operation: Pulp mill, Paperboard mill
Pulp Grades and Capacities:
Total pulp capacity: 246,686 mt/y
Chemical Pulp: 36,289 mt/y
Recycled Pulping: 210,397 mt/y
Pulp Mill Data:
Chemical Pulping Systems:
Batch digesters: 2
Bleach Plant Systems: 1
No. 1, Sequence: O_2 HP, Capacity 36,000 admt/y
Chemical Recovery Equipment:
Evaporator lines: 1
Recovery boilers: 1
Recycled Fiber Treatment Lines:
Recycled packaging pulping lines: 1
Paper/Paperboard Grades and Capacities:
Total paper and paperboard capacity: 244,000 mt/y
Linerboard: 180,000 mt/y
Corrugating medium/fluting: 32,000 mt/y
Boxboard/cartonboard: 32,000 mt/y
Paper and Paperboard Mill Data:
Paper Machines: 3
No. 1, cylinder, total capacity 32,000 mt/y, Trim width 2.45 m, Corrugating medium/fluting
No. 2, cylinder, total capacity 32,000 mt/y, Trim width 2.45 m, Boxboard/cartonboard
No. 3, Ultraformer, total capacity 180,000 mt/y, Trim width 3.7 m, Linerboard
Finishing Equipment:
Rewinders: 2
Sheeters: 6
Energy Data:
Power boilers: 3
Combustion turbines: 1 at 6.3 MW
Steam turbines: 1 at 11.6 MW
Electrical demand for mill: 412 MWh/D

ⓜOji Materia Co., Ltd.
Oita Mill
Previously Oji Paperboard Co., Ltd.
Ownership: Oji Holdings Corporation
872-1 Enomichi Onakajima
Oita-shi, Oita Pref., 870-0195
Japan
Phone: (81) 97 521 1112
Fax: (81) 97 522 1631
Web Address: www.ojimateria.co.jp, www.ojiholdings.co.jp/english
Personnel:
Mill Mgr.: Masaaki Okada
Phone: (81) 97 521 1112
Fax: (81) 97 522 1631
Eng. Dir.: Mitsuaki Fujimoto
Phone: (81) 97 521 1112
Fax: (81) 97 522 1631
Oper. Dir.: Masaaki Shinohara
Phone: (81) 97 521 1112
Fax: (81) 97 522 1631
Total Employees at this Location: 157
Type of Operation: Pulp mill, Paperboard mill
Pulp Grades and Capacities:
Total pulp capacity: 357,430 mt/y
Recycled Pulping: 357,430 mt/y
Pulp Mill Data:
Recycled Fiber Treatment Lines:
Recycled packaging pulping lines: 6
Paper/Paperboard Grades and Capacities:
Total paper and paperboard capacity: 356,000 mt/y

Japan

Linerboard: 296,000 mt/y
Boxboard/cartonboard: 60,000 mt/y
Paper and Paperboard Mill Data:
Paper Machines: 3
No. 1, hybrid former, total capacity 216,000 mt/y, Trim width 3.75 m, Linerboard
No. 3, Tanmo, total capacity 90,000 mt/y, Trim width 3 m, Linerboard, Boxboard/cartonboard
No. 5, cylinder, total capacity 50,000 mt/y, Trim width 1.95 m, Boxboard/cartonboard
Coating Machines: 1
No. 1, total capacity 50,000 mt/y., on machine
Finishing Equipment:
Winders: 3
Sheeters: 2
Energy Data:
Power boilers: 2
Steam turbines: 2 at 25, 17.8 MW
Electrical demand for mill: 522 MWh/D

ⓂOji Materia Co., Ltd.
Osaka Mill
Previously Oji Paperboard Co., Ltd.
Ownership: Oji Holdings Corporation
3-15-58 Minamieguchi, Higashiyodogawa-ku
Osaka-shi, Osaka Pref., 533-0003
Japan
Phone: (81) 6 6329 6871
Fax: (81) 6 6329 6877
Web Address: www.ojimateria.co.jp, www.ojiholdings.co.jp/english
Personnel:
Mill Mgr.: Masaaki Okada
Phone: (81) 6 6329 6871
Fax: (81) 6 6329 6877
Dpty. Mgr.: Shuichi Numazaki
Phone: (81) 6 6329 6871
Fax: (81) 6 6329 6877
Oper. Mgr.: Takebu Komura
Phone: (81) 6 6329 6871
Fax: (81) 6 6329 6877
Total Employees at this Location: 86
Type of Operation: Paperboard mill
Pulp Grades and Capacities:
Total pulp capacity: 225,961 mt/y
Recycled Pulping: 225,961 mt/y
Pulp Mill Data:
Recycled Fiber Treatment Lines:
Recycled packaging pulping lines: 1
Paper/Paperboard Grades and Capacities:
Total paper and paperboard capacity: 240,000 mt/y
Linerboard: 240,000 mt/y
Paper and Paperboard Mill Data:
Paper Machines: 1
No. 2, fourdrinier (2), total capacity 240,000 mt/y, Trim width 4.55 m, Linerboard
Finishing Equipment:
Rewinders: 1
Energy Data:
Power boilers
Combustion turbines: 3 at 4.2, 7.87 MW
Steam turbines: 1 at 11 MW
Electrical demand for mill: 345 MWh/D

ⓂOji Materia Co., Ltd.
Saga Mill
Previously Oji Paperboard Co., Ltd.
Ownership: Oji Holdings Corporation
1 Kubota, Kubota-cho
Saga-shi, Saga Pref., 849-0204
Japan
Phone: (81) 952 68 3111
Fax: (81) 952 68 4259
Web Address: www.ojimateria.co.jp, www.ojiholdings.co.jp/english
Personnel:
Mill Mgr.: Seiichi Saishita
Phone: (81) 952 68 3111

Fax: (81) 952 68 4259
Total Employees at this Location: 157
Type of Operation: Paperboard mill
Pulp Grades and Capacities:
Total pulp capacity: 320,955 mt/y
Recycled Pulping: 320,955 mt/y
Pulp Mill Data:
Chemical Recovery Equipment:
Recovery boilers: 1
Recycled Fiber Treatment Lines:
Recycled packaging pulping lines: 3
Paper/Paperboard Grades and Capacities:
Total paper and paperboard capacity: 325,000 mt/y
Linerboard: 160,000 mt/y
Corrugating medium/fluting: 152,000 mt/y
Boxboard/cartonboard: 13,000 mt/y
Paper and Paperboard Mill Data:
Stock Preparation:
Pulpers: 8
Paper Machines: 3
No. 1, fourdrinier, total capacity 80,000 mt/y, Trim width 3.3 m, Corrugating medium/fluting
No. 4, fourdrinier, total capacity 72,000 mt/y, Trim width 3.1 m, Corrugating medium/fluting
No. 5, Multi-wire (5), total capacity 173,000 mt/y, Trim width 3.6 m, Boxboard/cartonboard, Linerboard
Finishing Equipment:
Winders: 5
Energy Data:
Power boilers: 3
Combustion turbines: 1 at 9 MW
Steam turbines: 2 at 14.7, 10.5 MW
Electrical demand for mill: 468 MWh/D

ⓂOji Materia Co., Ltd.
Sobue Mill
Previously Oji Paperboard Co., Ltd
Ownership: Oji Holdings Corporation
150, Sobue Sotohira, Sobue-cho
Inazawa-shi, Aichi Pref., 495-8601
Japan
Phone: (81) 587 97 2111
Fax: (81) 587 97 2118
Web Address: www.ojimateria.co.jp, www.ojiholdings.co.jp/english
Personnel:
Man. Dir.: Kazumitsu Takahashi
Phone: (81) 587 97 2111
Fax: (81) 587 97 2118
Oper. Dir.: Makoto Sugasawa
Phone: (81) 587 97 2111
Fax: (81) 587 97 2118
Total Employees at this Location: 165
Type of Operation: Paperboard mill
Pulp Grades and Capacities:
Total pulp capacity: 339,857 mt/y
Recycled Pulping: 339,857 mt/y
Pulp Mill Data:
Recycled Fiber Treatment Lines:
Pulpers: 10
Paper/Paperboard Grades and Capacities:
Total paper and paperboard capacity: 367,000 mt/y
Linerboard: 205,000 mt/y
Boxboard/cartonboard: 162,000 mt/y
Paper and Paperboard Mill Data:
Stock Preparation:
Pulpers: 12
Refiners: 26
Paper Machines: 3
No. 5, combination, total capacity 75,600 mt/y, Trim width 2.55 m, Boxboard/cartonboard
No. 6, combination, total capacity 86,400 mt/y, Trim width 2.55 m, Boxboard/cartonboard
No. 7, multi-wire, total capacity 205,000 mt/y, Trim width 3.8 m, Linerboard
Coating Machines: 2
PM 5, total capacity 75,000 mt/y., on machine
PM 6, total capacity 86,000 mt/y., on machine
Finishing Equipment:

Supercalenders: 12
Rewinders: 4
Sheeters: 7
Energy Data:
Power boilers: 2
Steam turbines: 1 at 23.3 MW
Electrical demand for mill: 628 MWh/D

ⓂOji Nepia Co., Ltd.
Ownership: 100% by Oji Holdings Corporation
5-12-8, Ginza, Chuo-Ku
Tokyo, 104-8319
Japan
Phone: (81) 3 3248 3111
Fax: (81) 3 3248 2860
Web Address: www.nepia.co.jp
Personnel:
Pres.: Shuichi Sada
Phone: (81) 3 3248 3111
Fax: (81) 3 3248 2860
Total Employees of Company: 1,100
Mill Locations:
Oji Nepia Co., Ltd., Nagoya Mill, 1, Oji-cho, Kasugai-shi Aichi Pref. 486-0834, Japan, Capacity: 165,000 mt/y, (Paper mill)
Phone: (81) 568 85 2185
Fax: (81) 568 85 2475
Oji Nepia Co., Ltd., Tokushima Mill, 1-2 Tatsumi-cho, Anan-shi Pref. 774-0001, Japan, Capacity: 50,000 mt/y, (Paper mill)
Phone: (81) 884 23 7511
Fax: (81) 884 23 1499
Oji Nepia Co., Ltd., Tomakomai Mill, 143 Yufutsu, Tomakomai-shi 059-1372, Japan, Capacity: 72,000 mt/y, (Paper mill)
Phone: (81) 144 56 0244
Fax: (81) 144 56 0247

ⓂOji Nepia Co., Ltd.
Nagoya Mill
Ownership: 100% by Oji Holdings Corporation
1, Oji-cho
Kasugai-shi, Aichi Pref., Aichi Pref. 486-0834
Japan
Phone: (81) 568 85 2185
Fax: (81) 568 85 2475
Web Address: www.nepia.co.jp, www.ojiholdings.co.jp/english
Personnel:
Mill. Mgr.: Masachi Kogawa
Phone: (81) 568 85 2185
Total Employees at this Location: 89
Type of Operation: Paper mill
Paper/Paperboard Grades and Capacities:
Total paper and paperboard capacity: 165,000 mt/y
Tissue: 165,000 mt/y
Paper and Paperboard Mill Data:
Paper Machines: 4
T1, fourdrinier, Yankee dryer, total capacity 34,000 mt/y, Trim width 5.2 m, Tissue
T2, twin-wire, Yankee dryer, total capacity 45,000 mt/y, Trim width 5.2 m, Tissue
T3, twin-wire, Yankee dryer, total capacity 43,000 mt/y, Trim width 5.45 m, Tissue
T4, twin-wire, Yankee dryer, total capacity 43,000 mt/y, Trim width 5.45 m, Tissue
Energy Data:
Electrical demand for mill: 453 MWh/D

ⓂOji Nepia Co., Ltd.
Tokushima Mill
Ownership: 100% by Oji Holdings Corporation
1-2 Tatsumi-cho
Anan-shi, Tokushima Pref., Pref. 774-0001
Japan
Phone: (81) 884 23 7511
Fax: (81) 884 23 1499
Web Address: www.nepia.co.jp

Japan

Personnel:
Mill Mgr.: Tomoji Miyoshi
Phone: (81) 884 23 7511
Total Employees at this Location: 29
Type of Operation: Paper mill
Paper/Paperboard Grades and Capacities:
Total paper and paperboard capacity: 50,000 mt/y
Tissue: 50,000 mt/y
Paper and Paperboard Mill Data:
Paper Machines: 1
T1, (Supplier: Kawanoe Zoki / Metso), Periformer, Yankee dryer, total capacity 50,000 mt/y, Trim width 6.03 m, Tissue
Energy Data:
Power boilers: 1
Electrical demand for mill: 128 MWh/D

ⓜ Oji Nepia Co., Ltd.
Tomakomai Mill
Ownership: 100% by Oji Holdings Corporation
143 Yufutsu
Tomakomai-shi, Hokkaido Pref., 059-1372
Japan
Phone: (81) 144 56 0244
Fax: (81) 144 56 0247
Web Address: www.nepia.co.jp
Personnel:
Mill Mgr.: Moyu Taida
Phone: (81) 144 56 0244
Total Employees at this Location: 64
Type of Operation: Paper mill
Pulp Grades and Capacities:
Total pulp capacity: 23,705 mt/y
Recycled Pulping: 23,705 mt/y
Pulp Mill Data:
Recycled Fiber Treatment Lines:
Flotation deinking lines: 1
Paper/Paperboard Grades and Capacities:
Total paper and paperboard capacity: 72,000 mt/y
Tissue: 72,000 mt/y
Paper and Paperboard Mill Data:
Paper Machines: 2
No. 1, fourdrinier, Yankee dryer, total capacity 38,000 mt/y, Trim width 5 m, Tissue
No. 2, fourdrinier, Yankee dryer, total capacity 34,000 mt/y, Trim width 5 m, Tissue
Finishing Equipment:
Supercalenders: 2
Rewinders: 4
Energy Data:
Power boilers: 2
Steam turbines: 2 at 9 MW
Electrical demand for mill: 216 MWh/D

ⓞ Oji Holdings Corporation
Ownership: Public
Ginza 4-7-5, Chuo-ku
Tokyo, 104-0061
Japan
Phone: (81) 3 3563 1111
Fax: (81) 3 3563 1135
Web Address: www.ojiholdings.co.jp/english
Personnel:
Chmn.: Kazuhisa Shinoda
Phone: (81) 3 3563 1111
Fax: (81) 3 3563 1135
Pres. & CEO: Kiyotaka Shindo
Phone: (81) 3 3563 1111
Fax: (81) 3 3563 1135
Pres., Forest Resources & Environ. Mktg. Company (From april 1, 2014): Susumu Yajima
Phone: (81) 3 3563 1111
Fax: (81) 3 3563 1135
Total Employees of Company: 27,360
Mill Locations:
GS Paper & Packaging Group ("GSPP"), Banting Mill, Lot 7090, Mukim Tanjung 12 Karung Berkunci No. 206, 42700 Daerah Kuala Langat, Banting, Malaysia, Capacity: 295,000 mt/y, (Paperboard mill)
Phone: (60) 3 3149 1393/31825000
Fax: (60) 3 3149 1315/31825100
Email: gsip@pc.jaring.my, ley@gspp.com.my
Jiangsu Oji Paper Nantong Co., Ltd., Nantong Mill (90% owned), Nantong Economic & Technological Development Zone, Nantong 226000, China, Capacity: 339,864 mt/y, (Paper mill)
Phone: (86) 21 6219 5555
Fax: (86) 21 3223 1101
Jiangsu Oji Paper Nepia (Suzhou) Co., Ltd., Suzhou Mill, No. 98 Jinshan Road, New District, Suzhou 215011, China, Capacity: 20,000 mt/y, (Paper mill)
Phone: (86) 512 6825 8526
Fax: (86) 512 6825 9395
Email: danny@nepia.com.cn
Kanzan Spezialpapiere GmbH, Neumühl Mill (95.20% owned), Nippesstr. 5, D-52349 Düren, Germany, Capacity: 60,000 mt/y, (Paper mill)
Phone: (49) 2421 5924 0
Fax: (49) 2421 5924 19
Email: sales@kanzan.de, info@kanzan.de
Oji F-Tex Co., Ltd., Dai-ichi Mill, 1-1-1 Iriyamase, Fuji-shi 419-0204, Japan, Capacity: 7,500 mt/y, (Paper mill)
Phone: (81) 545 72 1111
Fax: (81) 545 72 1031
Oji F-Tex Co., Ltd., Ebetsu Mill, 1 Oji, Ebetsu-shi 067-0001, Japan, Capacity: 215,985 mt/y, (Pulp mill, Paper mill)
Phone: (81) 11 384 7311
Fax: (81) 11 384 3516
Oji F-Tex Co., Ltd., Fuji Mill, 14-1 Maeda, Fuji-shi 419-0937, Japan, Capacity: 20,200 mt/y, (Paper mill)
Phone: (81) 545 62 8888
Fax: (81) 545 62 8855
Oji F-Tex Co., Ltd., Fujinomiya Mill, 326-1 Koizumi, Fujinomiya-shi 418-002, Japan, Capacity: 83,000 mt/y, (Paper mill, Paperboard mill)
Phone: (81) 544 25 3171
Fax: (81) 544 25 3174
Oji F-Tex Co., Ltd., Iwabuchi Mill, 1157-1 Nakanogo, Fujikawa-cho, Ihara-gun 421-3306, Japan, Capacity: 46,410 mt/y, (Paper mill)
Phone: (81) 545 81 0075
Fax: (81) 545 81 1303
Oji F-Tex Co., Ltd., Nakatsu Mill, 3465-1 Nakatsugawa, Nakatsugawa-shi 508-8686, Japan, Capacity: 49,980 mt/y, (Paper mill)
Phone: (81) 573 66 1152
Fax: (81) 573 66 2412
Oji F-Tex Co., Ltd., Shibakawa Mill, 1231-2 Habuna, Shibakawa-cho, Fuji-gun 419-0316, Japan, Capacity: 41,200 mt/y, (Paper mill, Paperboard mill)
Phone: (81) 544 65 1211
Fax: (81) 544 65 1923
Oji F-Tex Co., Ltd., Shiga Mill, 66 Asakuni, Konan-shi 520-3251, Japan, (Paper mill)
Phone: (81) 748 72 2691
Fax: (81) 748 72 2838
Oji Materia Co., Ltd., Edogawa Mill, 3-2 Higashi Shinozaki 2-chome, Edogawa-ku, Tokyo 133-8511, Japan, Capacity: 144,000 mt/y, (Paper mill, Paperboard mill)
Phone: (81) 3 3679 1111
Fax: (81) 3 3677 1122
Oji Materia Co., Ltd., Gifu (Ena) Mill, 696 Oi-cho, Ena-shi 509-7201, Japan, Capacity: 256,000 mt/y, (Paperboard mill)
Phone: (81) 573 26 1611
Fax: (81) 573 26 1656
Oji Materia Co., Ltd., Kushiro Mill, 3-2-5 Otanoshike, Kushiro-shi 084-0917, Japan, Capacity: 490,875 mt/y, (Paperboard mill)
Phone: (81) 154 57 3305
Fax: (81) 154 57 8277
Oji Materia Co., Ltd., Matsumoto Mill, 5200-1 Sasaga, Matsumoto-shi 399-0033, Japan, Capacity: 122,000 mt/y, (Paperboard mill)
Phone: (81) 263 25 5432
Fax: (81) 263 25 6595
Oji Materia Co., Ltd., Gifu (Nakatsugawa) Mill, 2-3 Ogawa-cho, Nakatsugawa-shi 508-8585, Japan, Capacity: 150,000 mt/y, (Paperboard mill)
Phone: (81) 573 66 1511
Fax: (81) 573 66 6220
Oji Materia Co., Ltd., Nayoro Mill, 20-6 Tokuda, Nayoro-shi 096-8555, Japan, Capacity: 253,000 mt/y, (Pulp mill, Paperboard mill)
Phone: (81) 1654 3 3111
Fax: (81) 1654 2 2832
Oji Materia Co., Ltd., Nikko Mill, 592 Shirasawa, Utsunomiya-shi 329-1102, Japan, Capacity: 244,000 mt/y, (Pulp mill, Paperboard mill)
Phone: (81) 28 661 1011
Fax: (81) 28 661 1013
Oji Materia Co., Ltd., Oita Mill, 872-1 Enomichi Onakajima, Oita-shi 870-0195, Japan, Capacity: 356,000 mt/y, (Pulp mill, Paperboard mill)
Phone: (81) 97 521 1112
Fax: (81) 97 522 1631
Oji Materia Co., Ltd., Osaka Mill, 3-15-58 Minamieguchi, Higashiyodogawa-ku, Osaka-shi 533-0003, Japan, Capacity: 240,000 mt/y, (Paperboard mill)
Phone: (81) 6 6329 6871
Fax: (81) 6 6329 6877
Oji Materia Co., Ltd., Saga Mill, 1 Kubota, Kubota-cho, Saga-shi 849-0204, Japan, Capacity: 325,000 mt/y, (Paperboard mill)
Phone: (81) 952 68 3111
Fax: (81) 952 68 4259
Oji Materia Co., Ltd., Sobue Mill, 150, Sobue Sotohira, Sobue-cho, Inazawa-shi 495-8601, Japan, Capacity: 367,000 mt/y, (Paperboard mill)
Phone: (81) 587 97 2111
Fax: (81) 587 97 2118
Oji Nepia Co., Ltd., Nagoya Mill, 1, Oji-cho, Kasugai-shi Aichi Pref. 486-0834, Japan, Capacity: 165,000 mt/y, (Paper mill)
Phone: (81) 568 85 2185
Fax: (81) 568 85 2475
Oji Nepia Co., Ltd., Tokushima Mill, 1-2 Tatsumi-cho, Anan-shi Pref. 774-0001, Japan, Capacity: 50,000 mt/y, (Paper mill)
Phone: (81) 884 23 7511
Fax: (81) 884 23 1499
Oji Nepia Co., Ltd., Tomakomai Mill, 143 Yufutsu, Tomakomai-shi 059-1372, Japan, Capacity: 72,000 mt/y, (Paper mill)
Phone: (81) 144 56 0244
Fax: (81) 144 56 0247
Oji Paper Co., Ltd., Fuji Mill, 300 Heigaki, Fuji-shi 416-8656, Japan, Capacity: 250,000 mt/y, (Pulp mill, Paper mill, Paperboard mill)
Phone: (81) 545 60 2200
Fax: (81) 545 60 2201
Oji Paper Co., Ltd., Kasugai Mill, 1 Oji-cho, Kasugai-shi 486-0834, Japan, Capacity: 676,158 mt/y, (Pulp mill, Paper mill)
Phone: (81) 568 81 1111
Fax: (81) 568 85 2056
Oji Materia Co., Ltd., Kure Mill, 2-1-1 Hirosuehiro, Kure-shi 737-0133, Japan, Capacity: 270,000 mt/y, (Pulp mill, Paper mill)
Phone: (81) 823 74 8700
Fax: (81) 823 71 3294
Oji Paper Co., Ltd., Kushiro Mill, 3-2-5 Otanoshike, Kushiro-shi 084-0917, Japan, (Paper mill)
Phone: (81) 154 57 3305
Fax: (81) 154 57 8277
Oji Paper Co., Ltd., Nichinan Mill, 1850 Oaza-todaka, Nichinan-shi 887-0031, Japan, Capacity: 279,000 mt/y, (Pulp mill, Paper mill)
Phone: (81) 987 23 2181
Fax: (81) 987 23 8192
Oji Paper Co., Ltd., Tomakomai Mill, 2-1-1 Oji-cho, Tomakomai-shi 058-8711, Japan, Capacity: 1,409,000 mt/y, (Pulp mill, Paper mill)
Phone: (81) 144 32 0111
Fax: (81) 144 32 0114
Oji Paper Co., Ltd., Tomioka Mill, 1 Yoshida, Toyomasu-cho, Anan-shi 774-0002, Japan, Capacity: 525,000 mt/y, (Paper mill, Paperboard mill)
Phone: (81) 884 22 2211
Fax: (81) 884 23 5340

Japan

Oji Paper Co., Ltd., Yonago Mill, 373 Yoshioka, Yonago-shi 689-3592, Japan, Capacity: 567,000 mt/y, (Pulp mill, Paper mill, Paperboard mill)
Phone: (81) 859 27 3112
Fax: (81) 859 27 3434

Oji Materia Co., Ltd., Fuji Mill, 1180-1 Dempo, Fuji-shi 417-8535, Japan, Capacity: 200,000 mt/y, (Pulp mill, Paper mill, Paperboard mill)
Phone: (81) 545 52 4070
Fax: (81) 545 52 8230

Oji Papéis Especiais Ltda, Piracicaba Mill, Via Comendador Pedro Morganti, 3393 Bairro Monte Alegre, 13415-900 Piracicaba, SP, Brazil, Capacity: 114,988 mt/y, (Paper mill)
Phone: (55) 19 2106 9200, 19 2106 9609
Fax: (55) 19 2106 9619
Email: lucimara.didone@ojipapeis.com.br

Pan Pac Forest Products Ltd., Whirinaki Mill (87% owned), 1161, SH2, Wairoa Rd., 4142 Napier, New Zealand, (Pulp mill)
Phone: (64) 6 831 0100
Fax: (64) 6 831 0102/836 6443
Email: (firstname.surname@panpac.com)

Sunshine Oji (Shouguang) Specialty Paper Ltd., Shouguang Mill (60% owned), No. 69 Wenchang Rd., Shouguang, Weifang 262700, China, Capacity: 35,000 mt/y, (Paper mill)
Phone: (86) 536-218 1001
Fax: (86) 536-218 6006

ⓜOji Paper Co., Ltd.
Fuji Mill

Ownership: Oji Holdings Corporation
300 Heigaki
Fuji-shi, Shizuoka Pref., 416-8656
Japan
Phone: (81) 545 60 2200
Fax: (81) 545 60 2201
Web Address: www.ojiholdings.co.jp/english
Personnel:
Man. Dir./Mill Mgr.: Masahiro Todome
Phone: (81) 545 60 2200
Total Employees at this Location: 350
Type of Operation: Pulp mill, Paper mill, Paperboard mill
Pulp Grades and Capacities:
Total pulp capacity: 228,203 mt/y
Recycled Pulping: 228,203 mt/y
Pulp Mill Data:
Pulp Lines: 4
Bleach Plant Systems: 2
Recycled Pulping System, Type: Deinked
Recycled Fiber Treatment Lines:
Flotation deinking lines: 3 at 240,000
Recycled packaging pulping lines: 1 at 120,000
Paper/Paperboard Grades and Capacities:
Total paper and paperboard capacity: 250,000 mt/y
Boxboard/cartonboard: 250,000 mt/y
Paper and Paperboard Mill Data:
Stock Preparation:
Pulpers: 3
Paper Machines: 1
N2, Fourdrinier (5), total capacity 250,000 mt/y, Trim width 4 m, Boxboard/cartonboard
Coating Machines: 1
PM N2, total capacity 289,000 mt/y., on machine
Finishing Equipment:
Winders: 3
Supercalenders: 4
Sheeters: 8
Energy Data:
Power boilers: 5
Steam turbines: 3 at 100 MW
Electrical demand for mill: 1,440 MWh/D

ⓜOji Paper Co., Ltd.
Kasugai Mill

Ownership: Oji Holdings Corporation
1 Oji-cho
Kasugai-shi, Aichi Pref., 486-0834
Japan
Phone: (81) 568 81 1111
Fax: (81) 568 85 2056
Web Address: www.ojiholdings.co.jp/english
Personnel:
Mill Mgr.: Hiroshi Kizuka
Phone: (81) 568 81 1111
Total Employees at this Location: 540
Type of Operation: Pulp mill, Paper mill
Pulp Grades and Capacities:
Total pulp capacity: 545,307 mt/y
Chemical Pulp: 497,159 mt/y
Recycled Pulping: 48,148 mt/y
Pulp Mill Data:
Chemical Pulping Systems:
Continuous digesters: 2
Pulp Lines: 4
Bleach Plant Systems: 3
No. 1, Sequence: CEoHD, Capacity 330,000 admt/y
No. 2, Sequence: C/OE/OHD, Capacity 200,000 admt/y
Recycled Pulping Process, Type: Deinked
Chemical Recovery Equipment:
Evaporator lines: 2
Recovery boilers: 5
Recovery boilers: 1
Lime Kiln
Recycled Fiber Treatment Lines:
Flotation deinking lines: 1 at 120,000 admt/y
Pulpers: 2 at 200,000 admt/y
Washing deinking lines: 1 at 120,000 admt/y
Paper/Paperboard Grades and Capacities:
Total paper and paperboard capacity: 676,158 mt/y
Uncoated woodfree/freesheet: 112,455 mt/y
Coated woodfree/freesheet: 396,984 mt/y
Packaging papers: 84,609 mt/y
Specialty and industrial: 82,110 mt/y
Paper and Paperboard Mill Data:
Stock Preparation:
Pulpers: 1
Refiners:
Paper Machines: 6
No. 4, Bel-Form, total capacity 51,408 mt/y, Trim width 3.27 m, Uncoated woodfree/freesheet, Coated woodfree/freesheet
No. 6, Bel-Bond, total capacity 121,380 mt/y, Trim width 5.1 m, Coated woodfree/freesheet
No. 7, DuoFormer D, total capacity 122,451 mt/y, Trim width 5.1 m, Uncoated woodfree/freesheet, Coated woodfree/freesheet
No. 8, fourdrinier, total capacity 120,309 mt/y, Trim width 5.1 m, Packaging papers, Specialty and industrial
No. 9, fourdrinier, total capacity 46,410 mt/y, Trim width 5.15 m, Specialty and industrial
No. 10, SymFormer F, total capacity 214,200 mt/y, Trim width 5.66 m, Coated woodfree/freesheet
Coating Machines: 3
No. 1, total capacity 146,000 mt/y., off machine
No. 3, total capacity 250,000 mt/y., off machine
No. 2 (closed 3/2010), total capacity 80,000 mt/y., off machine
Finishing Equipment:
Supercalenders: 6
Rewinders: 9
Sheeters: 11
Energy Data:
Power boilers: 4
Steam turbines: 5 at 68.5, 23.65, 16.5, 26, 17 MW
Electrical demand for mill: 2,156 MWh/D

ⓜOji Materia Co., Ltd.
Kure Mill

Ownership: Oji Holdings Corporation
2-1-1 Hirosuehiro
Kure-shi, Hiroshima Pref., 737-0133
Japan
Phone: (81) 823 74 8700
Fax: (81) 823 71 3294
Web Address: www.ojimateria.co.jp, www.ojiholdings.co.jp/english
Personnel:
Mill Mgr.: Masaki Yoshino
Phone: (81) 823 74 8700
Fax: (81) 823 71 3294
Total Employees at this Location: 200
Type of Operation: Pulp mill, Paper mill
Pulp Grades and Capacities:
Total pulp capacity: 418,494 mt/y
Pulp available for market: 137,000 mt/y
Chemical Pulp: 372,633 mt/y
Recycled Pulping: 45,861 mt/y
Pulp Mill Data:
Chemical Pulping Systems:
Batch digesters: 7
Continuous digesters: 1
Bleach Plant Systems: 1
Chemical Pulping System, Type: Softwood - DEO(P)D
Chemical Recovery Equipment:
Evaporator lines: 3
Recovery boilers: 1
Lime Kiln
Recycled Fiber Treatment Lines:
Recycled packaging pulping lines: 1
Pulp Dryers:
Air Float dryers 1
Paper/Paperboard Grades and Capacities:
Total paper and paperboard capacity: 270,000 mt/y
Packaging papers: 270,000 mt/y
Paper and Paperboard Mill Data:
Paper Machines: 2
No. 1, twin-wire, total capacity 90,000 mt/y, Trim width 4.1 m, Packaging papers
No. 5, twin-wire, total capacity 180,000 mt/y, Trim width 5.12 m, Packaging papers
Finishing Equipment:
Sheeters: 4
Energy Data:
Power boilers: 3
Steam turbines: 5 at 93 MW
Electrical demand for mill: 997 MWh/D

ⓜOji Paper Co., Ltd.
Nichinan Mill

Ownership: Oji Holdings Corporation
1850 Oaza-todaka
Nichinan-shi, Miyazaki Pref., 887-0031
Japan
Phone: (81) 987 23 2181
Fax: (81) 987 23 8192
Web Address: www.ojiholdings.co.jp/english
Personnel:
Mill Mgr.: Toshihiro Tokudome
Phone: (81) 987 23 2181
Total Employees at this Location: 303
Type of Operation: Pulp mill, Paper mill
Pulp Grades and Capacities:
Total pulp capacity: 392,662 mt/y
Pulp available for market: 50,000 mt/y
Chemical Pulp: 321,230 mt/y
Recycled Pulping: 71,432 mt/y
Pulp Mill Data:
Chemical Pulping Systems:
Continuous digesters: 1
Pulp Lines: 1
Bleach Plant Systems: 2
Chemical Pulping System - Hardwood, Type: ZEPD Capacity 224,000 admt/y
Recycled Pulping System, Sequence: P/Y, Capacity 105,000 admt/y
Chemical Recovery Equipment:
Evaporator lines: 2
Recovery boilers: 1
Recovery boilers: 1
Lime Kiln
Pulp Dryers:
Air Float dryers 1

Japan

Paper/Paperboard Grades and Capacities:
Total paper and paperboard capacity: 279,000 mt/y
Uncoated woodfree/freesheet: 279,000 mt/y
Paper and Paperboard Mill Data:
Stock Preparation:
Pulpers: 3
Paper Machines: 4
No. 2, fourdrinier, total capacity 45,000 mt/y, Trim width 3.28 m, Uncoated woodfree/freesheet
No. 3, SymFormer MB, total capacity 91,000 mt/y, Trim width 3.3 m, Uncoated woodfree/freesheet
No. 5, fourdrinier, total capacity 50,000 mt/y, Trim width 3.27 m, Uncoated woodfree/freesheet
No. 8, SymFormer MB, total capacity 93,000 mt/y, Trim width 3.27 m, Uncoated woodfree/freesheet
Coating Machines: 4
No. 1, off machine
No. 2, off machine
No. 3, off machine
No. 4, off machine
Finishing Equipment:
Supercalenders: 1
Rewinders: 5
Sheeters: 10
Energy Data:
Power boilers: 1
Steam turbines: 6 at 60.8 MW
Electrical demand for mill: 918 MWh/D

ⓂOji Paper Co., Ltd.
Tomakomai Mill
Ownership: Oji Holdings Corporation
2-1-1 Oji-cho
Tomakomai-shi, Hokkaido Pref., 058-8711
Japan
  Phone: (81) 144 32 0111
  Fax: (81) 144 32 0114
  Web Address: www.ojiholdings.co.jp/english
Personnel:
Mill Mgr.: Yoshiki Koseki
  Phone: (81) 144 32 0111
Asst. Mill Mgr.: Akihiko Uemura
  Phone: (81) 144 32 0111
Total Employees at this Location: 606
Type of Operation: Pulp mill, Paper mill
Pulp Grades and Capacities:
Total pulp capacity: 1,497,296 mt/y
Pulp available for market: 70,000 mt/y
Chemical Pulp: 218,907 mt/y
Mechanical Pulp: 542,638 mt/y
Recycled Pulping: 735,752 mt/y
Pulp Mill Data:
Chemical Pulping Systems:
Continuous digesters: 1
Mechanical Pulping Systems:
Conventional grinders: 8
Pressurized grinders: 3
RMP systems: 1
TMP systems: 2
Pulp Lines: 11
Bleach Plant Systems: 11
BSKP, Sequence: O_2 DoEopD, Capacity 210,000 admt/y
Mechanical pulp, Sequence: P/HS, Capacity 539,000 admt/y
RCP, Sequence: P/Y, Capacity 773,500 admt/y
Chemical Recovery Equipment:
Evaporator lines: 1
Recovery boilers: 1
Lime Kiln
Recycled Fiber Treatment Lines:
Flotation deinking lines: 5 at 773,500 admt/y
Pulp Dryers:
Air Float dryers 1
Paper/Paperboard Grades and Capacities:
Total paper and paperboard capacity: 1,409,000 mt/y
Newsprint: 1,174,000 mt/y
Uncoated mechanical/groundwood: 120,000 mt/y
Coated mechanical/groundwood: 115,000 mt/y
Paper and Paperboard Mill Data:
Stock Preparation:
Pulpers: 5
Paper Machines: 9
No. 2, twin-wire, total capacity 73,000 mt/y, Trim width 3.25 m, Newsprint
No. 9, DuoFormer D, total capacity 115,000 mt/y, Trim width 4.63 m, Coated mechanical/groundwood
No. 11, Bel-Baie III, total capacity 120,000 mt/y, Trim width 4.88 m, Uncoated mechanical/groundwood
N1, twin-wire, total capacity 140,000 mt/y, Trim width 6.5 m, Newsprint
N2, Bel-Baie II, total capacity 115,000 mt/y, Trim width 6.5 m, Newsprint
N3, twin-wire, total capacity 180,000 mt/y, Trim width 8.13 m, Newsprint
N4, Bel-Baie, total capacity 196,000 mt/y, Trim width 8.13 m, Newsprint
N5, twin-wire, total capacity 210,000 mt/y, Trim width 8.13 m, Newsprint
N6, twin-wire, total capacity 260,000 mt/y, Trim width 8.13 m, Newsprint
Coating Machines: 1
No. 9, total capacity 115,000 mt/y, on machine
Finishing Equipment:
Supercalenders: 3
Sheeters: 2
Energy Data:
Power boilers: 7
Steam turbines: 13 at 268.0 MW
Electrical demand for mill: 6,708 MWh/D

ⓂⓂOji Paper Co., Ltd.
Tomioka Mill
Ownership: Oji Holdings Corporation
1 Yoshida, Toyomasu-cho
Anan-shi, Tokushima Pref., 774-0002
Japan
  Phone: (81) 884 22 2211
  Fax: (81) 884 23 5340
  Web Address: www.ojiholdings.co.jp/english
Personnel:
Mill Mgr.: Masaki Yoshino
Hitoshi Watanabe
Katsuaki Onishi
Masahiro Nishida
Tetsuro Imai
Yoshihiro Konishi
Total Employees at this Location: 336
Type of Operation: Paper mill, Paperboard mill
Mill Locations:
Oji Paper Co., Ltd., Fuji Mill, 300 Heigaki, Fuji-shi 416-8656, Japan, Capacity: 250,000 mt/y, (Pulp mill, Paper mill, Paperboard mill)
  Phone: (81) 545 60 2200
  Fax: (81) 545 60 2201
Oji Paper Co., Ltd., Kasugai Mill, 1 Oji-cho, Kasugai-shi 486-0834, Japan, Capacity: 676,158 mt/y, (Pulp mill, Paper mill)
  Phone: (81) 568 81 1111
  Fax: (81) 568 85 2056
Oji Paper Co., Ltd., Kushiro Mill, 3-2-5 Otanoshike, Kushiro-shi 084-0917, Japan, (Paper mill)
  Phone: (81) 154 57 3305
  Fax: (81) 154 57 8277
Oji Paper Co., Ltd., Nichinan Mill, 1850 Oaza-todaka, Nichinan-shi 887-0031, Japan, Capacity: 279,000 mt/y, (Pulp mill, Paper mill)
  Phone: (81) 987 23 2181
  Fax: (81) 987 23 8192
Oji Paper Co., Ltd., Tomakomai Mill, 2-1-1 Oji-cho, Tomakomai-shi 058-8711, Japan, Capacity: 1,409,000 mt/y, (Pulp mill, Paper mill)
  Phone: (81) 144 32 0111
  Fax: (81) 144 32 0114
Oji Paper Co., Ltd., Yonago Mill, 373 Yoshioka, Yonago-shi 689-3592, Japan, Capacity: 567,000 mt/y, (Pulp mill, Paper mill, Paperboard mill)
  Phone: (81) 859 27 3112
  Fax: (81) 859 27 3434

Pulp Grades and Capacities:
Total pulp capacity: 391,742 mt/y
Chemical Pulp: 274,308 mt/y
Recycled Pulping: 117,433 mt/y
Pulp Mill Data:
Chemical Pulping Systems:
Continuous digesters: 2
Pulp Lines: 3
Bleach Plant Systems: 3
BHKP, Sequence: Z/DEopD, Capacity 335,000 admt/y
BHKP/BSKP, Sequence: Z/DEopD, Capacity 300,000 admt/y
DIP, Sequence: P, Capacity 110,000 admt/y
Chemical Recovery Equipment:
Evaporator lines: 2
Recovery boilers: 1
Recovery boilers: 1
Lime Kiln
Recycled Fiber Treatment Lines:
Flotation deinking lines: 1 at 110,000
Paper/Paperboard Grades and Capacities:
Total paper and paperboard capacity: 525,000 mt/y
Coated woodfree/freesheet: 175,000 mt/y
Coated mechanical/groundwood: 350,000 mt/y
Paper and Paperboard Mill Data:
Paper Machines: 2
No. 9, SymFormer F, total capacity 175,000 mt/y, Trim width 5.38 m, Coated woodfree/freesheet
N-1, OptiFormer, total capacity 350,000 mt/y, Trim width 9.18 m, Coated mechanical/groundwood
Coating Machines: 2
N-1, total capacity 350,000 mt/y., on machine
OFF9, total capacity 175,000 mt/y., off machine
Finishing Equipment:
Winders: 2 at 350,000 mt/y
Supercalenders: 4 at 175,000 mt/y, 350,000 mt/y
Sheeters: 8
Energy Data:
Power boilers: 1
Steam turbines: 5 at 18, 18, 20, 38, 32 MW
Electrical demand for mill: 1,441 MWh/D

ⓂOji Paper Co., Ltd.
Yonago Mill
Ownership: Oji Holdings Corporation
373 Yoshioka
Yonago-shi, Tottori Pref., 689-3592
Japan
  Phone: (81) 859 27 3112
  Fax: (81) 859 27 3434
  Web Address: www.ojiholdings.co.jp/english
Personnel:
Man. Dir.: Hideyuki Ohba
  Phone: (81) 859 27 3112
Total Employees at this Location: 382
Type of Operation: Pulp mill, Paper mill, Paperboard mill
Pulp Grades and Capacities:
Total pulp capacity: 163,127 mt/y
Pulp available for market: 110,000 mt/y
Chemical Pulp: 163,127 mt/y
Pulp Mill Data:
Chemical Pulping Systems:
Continuous digesters: 2
Pulp Lines: 2
Bleach Plant Systems: 2
BHKP, Type: ECF, Sequence: O_2 DED
BSKP, Type: ECF, Sequence: O_2 DEopD
Chemical Recovery Equipment:
Evaporator lines: 2
Recovery boilers: 1
Recovery boilers: 1
Lime Kiln
Pulp Dryers:
Twin Wire 1
Paper/Paperboard Grades and Capacities:
Total paper and paperboard capacity: 567,000 mt/y
Uncoated woodfree/freesheet: 15,000 mt/y

Japan

Coated woodfree/freesheet: 472,000 mt/y
Boxboard/cartonboard: 80,000 mt/y
Paper and Paperboard Mill Data:
Paper Machines: 4
No. 1, fourdrinier, total capacity 115,000 mt/y, Trim width 3.3 m, Coated woodfree/freesheet
No. 2, fourdrinier, total capacity 95,000 mt/y, Trim width 3.3 m, Uncoated woodfree/freesheet, Coated woodfree/freesheet
No. 3, fourdrinier, total capacity 107,000 mt/y, Trim width 3.3 m, Boxboard/cartonboard, Coated woodfree/freesheet
N-1, GapFormer, total capacity 250,000 mt/y, Trim width 7.4 m, Coated woodfree/freesheet
Coating Machines: 5
N1, total capacity 252,000 mt/y., off machine
N5, total capacity 15,000 mt/y., off machine
Off 1, total capacity 115,000 mt/y., off machine
Off 2, total capacity 110,000 mt/y., off machine
On 3, total capacity 100,000 mt/y., on machine
Finishing Equipment:
Supercalenders: 4
Rewinders: 3
Sheeters: 10
Energy Data:
Power boilers: 1
Steam turbines: 4 at 68, 14, 17, 10 MW
Electrical demand for mill: 1,420 MWh/D

Oji Materia Co., Ltd.
Ownership: Oji Holdings Corporation
5-12-18, Ginza, Chuo-ku
Tokyo, 104-0061
Japan
Phone: (81) 3 3543 1111
Fax: (81) 3 3543 1220
Web Address: www.ojimateria.co.jp, www.ojiholdings.co.jp/english
Personnel:
Pres.: Yoshiki Koseki
Phone: (81) 3 3543 1111
Fax: (81) 3 3543 1220
Total Employees of Company: 1,850
Mill Locations:
Oji Materia Co., Ltd., Edogawa Mill, 3-2 Higashi Shinozaki 2-chome, Edogawa-ku, Tokyo 133-8511, Japan, Capacity: 144,000 mt/y, (Paper mill, Paperboard mill)
Phone: (81) 3 3679 1111
Fax: (81) 3 3677 1122
Oji Materia Co., Ltd., Gifu (Ena) Mill, 696 Oi-cho, Ena-shi 509-7201, Japan, Capacity: 256,000 mt/y, (Paperboard mill)
Phone: (81) 573 26 1611
Fax: (81) 573 26 1656
Oji Materia Co., Ltd., Kushiro Mill, 3-2-5 Otanoshike, Kushiro-shi 084-0917, Japan, Capacity: 490,875 mt/y, (Paperboard mill)
Phone: (81) 154 57 3305
Fax: (81) 154 57 8277
Oji Materia Co., Ltd., Matsumoto Mill, 5200-1 Sasaga, Matsumoto-shi 399-0033, Japan, Capacity: 122,000 mt/y, (Paperboard mill)
Phone: (81) 263 25 5432
Fax: (81) 263 25 6595
Oji Materia Co., Ltd., Gifu (Nakatsugawa) Mill, 2-3 Ogawa-cho, Nakatsugawa-shi 508-8585, Japan, Capacity: 150,000 mt/y, (Paperboard mill)
Phone: (81) 573 66 1511
Fax: (81) 573 66 6220
Oji Materia Co., Ltd., Nayoro Mill, 20-6 Tokuda, Nayoro-shi 096-8555, Japan, Capacity: 253,000 mt/y, (Pulp mill, Paperboard mill)
Phone: (81) 1654 3 3111
Fax: (81) 1654 2 2832
Oji Materia Co., Ltd., Nikko Mill, 592 Shirasawa, Utsunomiya-shi 329-1102, Japan, Capacity: 244,000 mt/y, (Pulp mill, Paperboard mill)
Phone: (81) 28 661 1011
Fax: (81) 28 661 1013
Oji Materia Co., Ltd., Oita Mill, 872-1 Enomichi Onakajima, Oita-shi 870-0195, Japan, Capacity: 356,000 mt/y, (Pulp mill, Paperboard mill)
Phone: (81) 97 521 1112
Fax: (81) 97 522 1631
Oji Materia Co., Ltd., Osaka Mill, 3-15-58 Minamieguchi, Higashiyodogawa-ku, Osaka-shi 533-0003, Japan, Capacity: 240,000 mt/y, (Paperboard mill)
Phone: (81) 6 6329 6871
Fax: (81) 6 6329 6877
Oji Materia Co., Ltd., Saga Mill, 1 Kubota, Kubota-cho, Saga-shi 849-0204, Japan, Capacity: 325,000 mt/y, (Paperboard mill)
Phone: (81) 952 68 3111
Fax: (81) 952 68 4259
Oji Materia Co., Ltd., Sobue Mill, 150, Sobue Sotohira, Sobue-cho, Inazawa-shi 495-8601, Japan, Capacity: 367,000 mt/y, (Paperboard mill)
Phone: (81) 587 97 2111
Fax: (81) 587 97 2118
Oji Materia Co., Ltd., Kure Mill, 2-1-1 Hirosuehiro, Kure-shi 737-0133, Japan, Capacity: 270,000 mt/y, (Pulp mill, Paper mill)
Phone: (81) 823 74 8700
Fax: (81) 823 71 3294
Oji Materia Co., Ltd., Fuji Mill, 1180-1 Dempo, Fuji-shi 417-8535, Japan, Capacity: 200,000 mt/y, (Pulp mill, Paper mill, Paperboard mill)
Phone: (81) 545 52 4070
Fax: (81) 545 52 8230

Oji Materia Co., Ltd.
Fuji Mill
Ownership: Oji Holdings Corporation
1180-1 Dempo
Fuji-shi, Shizuoka Pref., 417-8535
Japan
Phone: (81) 545 52 4070
Fax: (81) 545 52 8230
Web Address: www.ojimateria.co.jp, www.ojiholdings.co.jp/english
Personnel:
Mill Mgr.: Kagenobu Urushihata
Phone: (81) 545 52 4070
Total Employees at this Location: 87
Type of Operation: Pulp mill, Paper mill, Paperboard mill
Pulp Grades and Capacities:
Total pulp capacity: 196,823 mt/y
Recycled Pulping: 196,823 mt/y
Pulp Mill Data:
Chemical Pulping Systems:
Batch digesters: 3
Continuous digesters: 1
Chemical Recovery Equipment:
Recovery boilers: 1
Recycled Fiber Treatment Lines:
Recycled packaging pulping lines: 1
Paper/Paperboard Grades and Capacities:
Total paper and paperboard capacity: 200,000 mt/y
Corrugating medium/fluting: 200,000 mt/y
Paper and Paperboard Mill Data:
Paper Machines: 1
No. 10, DuoFormer D, total capacity 200,000 mt/y, Trim width 4.75 m, Corrugating medium/fluting
Energy Data:
Power boilers: 1
Steam turbines: 1 at 17.7 MW
Electrical demand for mill: 259 MWh/D

Okayama Paper Industries Co., Ltd.
Okayama-shi Mill
Ownership: 32.40% by Oji Holdings Corporation
1- 4- 34, Hamano
Okayama-shi, Okayama Pref., 700-0845
Japan
Phone: (81) 86 262 8750/1101
Fax: (81) 86 264 4943
Web Address: www.okayamaseishi.co.jp
Personnel:
Chm.: Yasuhiro Hirose
Phone: (81) 86 262 8750/1101
Total Employees at this Location: 172
Type of Operation: Paperboard mill
Pulp Grades and Capacities:
Total pulp capacity: 161,963 mt/y
Recycled Pulping: 161,963 mt/y
Pulp Mill Data:
Paper/Paperboard Grades and Capacities:
Total paper and paperboard capacity: 160,000 mt/y
Corrugating medium/fluting: 108,000 mt/y
Boxboard/cartonboard: 52,000 mt/y
Paper and Paperboard Mill Data:
Paper Machines: 3
No. 1, cylinder (7), total capacity 30,000 mt/y, Trim width 2.1 m, Boxboard/cartonboard
No. 2, cylinder (8), total capacity 22,000 mt/y, Trim width 2.1 m, Boxboard/cartonboard
No. 3, fourdrinier, total capacity 108,000 mt/y, Trim width 3.45 m, Corrugating medium/fluting
Energy Data:
Power boilers: 7
Combustion turbines: 1 at 4.78 MW
Steam turbines: 1 at 4.2 MW
Electrical demand for mill: 187 MWh/D

Okitsugawa Seishi Co., Ltd.
Shizuoka-shi Mill
1-530 Yatsu-cho, Shimizu-ku
Shizuoka-shi, Shizuoka Pref., 424-0211
Japan
Phone: (81) 54 369 0131
Fax: (81) 54 255 1750
Personnel:
Pres.: Yoshihide Nishimae
Phone: (81) 54 369 0131
Total Employees at this Location: 63
Type of Operation: Paperboard mill
Paper/Paperboard Grades and Capacities:
Total paper and paperboard capacity: 10,800 mt/y
Boxboard/cartonboard: 10,800 mt/y
Paper and Paperboard Mill Data:
Paper Machines: 2
No. 2, Yankee dryer, cylinder, total capacity 5,300 mt/y, Trim width 1.32 m, Boxboard/cartonboard
No. 3, Yankee dryer, cylinder, total capacity 5,500 mt/y, Trim width 1.12 m, Boxboard/cartonboard

Honen Seishi K.K.
Fuji Mill
Ownership: Omiya Seishi Co., Ltd.
329 Nonaka-cho
Fuji, Shizuoka Pref.
Japan
Phone: (81) 544 234-521
Fax: (81) 544 234-637
Web Address: www.omiyaseishi.co.jp
Total Employees at this Location: 117
Type of Operation: Paper mill
Pulp Grades and Capacities:
Total pulp capacity: 5,364 mt/y
Recycled Pulping: 5,364 mt/y
Pulp Mill Data:
Recycled Fiber Treatment Lines:
Flotation deinking lines
Paper/Paperboard Grades and Capacities:
Total paper and paperboard capacity: 27,000 mt/y
Tissue: 27,000 mt/y
Paper and Paperboard Mill Data:
Paper Machines: 3
No. 1, Yankee dryer, total capacity 7,000 mt/y, Trim width 1.8 m, Tissue
No. 2, BF-10, Yankee dryer, total capacity 10,000 mt/y, Trim width 2.38 m, Tissue
No. 3, BF-10, Yankee dryer, total capacity 10,000 mt/y, Trim width 2.38 m, Tissue
Energy Data:
Power boilers

Electrical demand for mill: 76 MWh/D

ⓂOmiya Seishi Co., Ltd.
Ownership: Daio Paper Corp.
329 Naka-cho
Fujinomiya-Shi, 418-0038
Japan
  Phone: (81) 544 23 4521
  Fax: (81) 544 23 4637
  Web Address: www.omiyaseishi.co.jp
Personnel:
  Exec. Mgr.: Hideji Ozaki
  Phone: (81) 544 23 4521
  Fax: (81) 544 23 4637
Total Employees of company: 425
Mill Locations:
  Koryo Seishi K.K., Fuji Mill, 329 Nonaka-cho, Fuji, Japan, Capacity: 13,000 mt/y, (Paper mill)
  Phone: (81) 544 234-521
  Fax: (81) 544 234-637
  Honen Seishi K.K., Fuji Mill, 329 Nonaka-cho, Fuji, Japan, Capacity: 27,000 mt/y, (Paper mill)
  Phone: (81) 544 234-521
  Fax: (81) 544 234-637
  Omiya Seishi Co., Ltd., Fujinomiya Mill, 329 Naka-cho, Fujinomiya-Shi 418-0038, Japan, Capacity: 104,000 mt/y, (Paper mill)
  Phone: (81) 544 23 4521
  Fax: (81) 544 23 4637
  Omiya Seishi Co., Ltd., Fuji Takaoka Mill, 261-1 Kuzawa, Fuji-shi 419-0202, Japan, Capacity: 29,000 mt/y, (Paper mill)
  Phone: (81) 545 71 1026
  Fax: (81) 545 71 1164

ⓂOmiya Seishi Co., Ltd.
Fujinomiya Mill
Ownership: Daio Paper Corp.
329 Naka-cho
Fujinomiya-Shi, Shizuoka Pref., 418-0038
Japan
  Phone: (81) 544 23 4521
  Fax: (81) 544 23 4637
  Web Address: www.omiyaseishi.co.jp
Personnel:
  Exec. Mgr.: Hideji Ozaki
  Phone: (81) 544 23 4521
Total Employees at this Location: 380
Type of Operation: Paper mill
Pulp Grades and Capacities:
  Total pulp capacity: 53,712 mt/y
  Recycled Pulping: 53,712 mt/y
Pulp Mill Data:
  Recycled Fiber Treatment Lines:
  Flotation deinking lines
Paper/Paperboard Grades and Capacities:
  Total paper and paperboard capacity: 104,000 mt/y
  Tissue: 104,000 mt/y
Paper and Paperboard Mill Data:
Paper Machines: 7
  No. 1, twin-wire, Yankee dryer, total capacity 35,000 mt/y, Trim width 4 m, Tissue
  No. 2, crescent former, Yankee dryer, total capacity 36,000 mt/y, Trim width 4 m, Tissue
  D1, twin-wire, Yankee dryer, total capacity 18,000 mt/y, Trim width 3.59 m, Tissue
  K1, Yankee dryer, total capacity 4,500 mt/y, Trim width 2.45 m, Tissue
  K2, Yankee dryer, total capacity 3,500 mt/y, Trim width 1.65 m, Tissue
  K3, Yankee dryer, total capacity 3,500 mt/y, Trim width 1.65 m, Tissue
  K4, Yankee dryer, total capacity 3,500 mt/y, Trim width 1.65 m, Tissue
Energy Data:
Power boilers
Electrical demand for mill: 300 MWh/D

ⓂOmiya Seishi Co., Ltd.
Fuji Takaoka Mill
Ownership: Daio Paper Corp.
261-1 Kuzawa
Fuji-shi, Shizuoka Pref., 419-0202
Japan
  Phone: (81) 545 71 1026
  Fax: (81) 545 71 1164
  Web Address: www.omiyaseishi.co.jp
Total Employees at this Location: 40
Type of Operation: Paper mill
Pulp Grades and Capacities:
  Total pulp capacity: 15,599 mt/y
  Recycled Pulping: 15,599 mt/y
Pulp Mill Data:
  Recycled Fiber Treatment Lines:
  Flotation deinking lines
Paper/Paperboard Grades and Capacities:
  Total paper and paperboard capacity: 29,000 mt/y
  Tissue: 29,000 mt/y
Paper and Paperboard Mill Data:
Paper Machines: 1
  No. 1, twin-wire, Yankee dryer, total capacity 29,000 mt/y, Trim width 4 m, Tissue
Energy Data:
Power boilers
Electrical demand for mill: 87 MWh/D

ⓄⓂOno Seishi K.K.
Fuji Mill
Ownership: Marutomi Paper Mfg. Co., Ltd.
344, Harada
Fuji, Shizuoka Pref., 417 0852
Japan
  Phone: (81) 545520282
Total Employees at this Location: 30
Type of Operation: Paper mill
Pulp Grades and Capacities:
  Total pulp capacity: 12,963 mt/y
  Recycled Pulping: 12,963 mt/y
Paper/Paperboard Grades and Capacities:
  Total paper and paperboard capacity: 12,000 mt/y
  Tissue: 12,000 mt/y
Paper and Paperboard Mill Data:
Paper Machines: 2
  No. 1, Yankee dryer, total capacity 5,000 mt/y, Trim width 1.9 m, Tissue
  No. 2, Yankee dryer, total capacity 7,000 mt/y, Trim width 2.4 m, Tissue
Energy Data:
Power boilers
Electrical demand for mill: 40 MWh/D

ⓄⓂOsaka Paper Co., Ltd.
Osaka-shi Mill
Ownership: 77.70% by Rengo Co., Ltd.
7-1-60, Tukuda, Nishiyodogawa-ku
Osaka-shi, Osaka Pref., 555-0001
Japan
  Phone: (81) 6 6472 6331
  Fax: (81) 6 6474 6431
  Web Address: www.osaka-paper.co.jp
Personnel:
  Pres.: Hisaharu Yashino
  Phone: (81) 6 6472 6331
Total Employees at this Location: 110
Type of Operation: Paper mill, Paperboard mill
Pulp Grades and Capacities:
  Total pulp capacity: 96,762 mt/y
  Recycled Pulping: 96,762 mt/y
Pulp Mill Data:
  Bleach Plant Lines:
  No. 1
  Recycled Fiber Treatment Lines:
  Flotation deinking lines
Paper/Paperboard Grades and Capacities:
  Total paper and paperboard capacity: 100,000 mt/y
  Newsprint: 46,000 mt/y
  Boxboard/cartonboard: 54,000 mt/y
Paper and Paperboard Mill Data:
Paper Machines: 2
  M1, SymFormer R, total capacity 46,000 mt/y, Trim width 3.25 m, Newsprint
  M2, cylinder, total capacity 54,000 mt/y, Trim width 2.6 m, Boxboard/cartonboard
Finishing Equipment:
  Winders: 2
  Sheeters: 2
Energy Data:
Power boilers: 2
Combustion turbines: 2 at 12.6 MW
Electrical demand for mill: 189 MWh/D

ⓄⓂOtsu-Paperboard Co., Ltd.
Otsu-shi Mill
1-15-15 Baba
Otsu-shi, Shiga Pref., 520-0802
Japan
  Phone: (81) 77 522 4171
  Fax: (81) 77 522 5687
  Email: soumu@otsu-itagami.co.jp.
  Web Address: www.otsu-itagami.co.jp/
Personnel:
  Pres.: Takeshi Miyazaki
  Phone: (81) 77 522 4171
Total Employees at this Location: 155
Type of Operation: Paperboard mill
Pulp Grades and Capacities:
  Total pulp capacity: 21,023 mt/y
  Recycled Pulping: 21,023 mt/y
Pulp Mill Data:
  Recycled Fiber Treatment Lines:
  Recycled packaging pulping lines: 1
Paper/Paperboard Grades and Capacities:
  Total paper and paperboard capacity: 215,985 mt/y
  Linerboard: 215,985 mt/y
Paper and Paperboard Mill Data:
  Stock Preparation:
  Pulpers: 4
  Refiners: 10
Paper Machines: 2
  No. 2, twin-wire, total capacity 116,025 mt/y, Trim width 2.75 m, Linerboard
  No. 4, twin-wire, total capacity 99,960 mt/y, Trim width 3.05 m, Linerboard
Finishing Equipment:
  Rewinders: 2
Energy Data:
Power boilers: 1
Combustion turbines: 1 at 8.3 MW
Electrical demand for mill: 331 MWh/D

ⓄRengo Co., Ltd.
Ownership: Public
Nakanoshima Central Tower, 2-2-7, Nakanoshima
Kita-ku, Osaka, 530-0005
Japan
  Phone: (81) 6 6223 2371
  Fax: (81) 6 4706 9909
  Web Address: www.rengo.co.jp
Personnel:
  Pres. & Chmn.: Kiyoshi Otsubo
  Phone: (81) 6 6223 2371
  Fax: (81) 6 4706 9909
  Exec. Officer, Chief Dir. Finan. & Accounting: Yukio Okano
  Phone: (81) 6 6223 2371
  Fax: (81) 6 4706 9909
  Exec. Officer, Chief Dir., Prod. & Manuf.: Ryuzo Shinano
  Phone: (81) 6 6223 2371
  Fax: (81) 6 4706 9909
  Exec. Officer, Chief Dir., Packaging Technology Develop.: Toshihiro Yoneda
  Phone: (81) 6 6223 2371
  Fax: (81) 6 4706 9909
  Chief Dir. Sls.: Koichi Hirano

Japan

Phone: (81) 6 6223 2371
Fax: (81) 6 4706 9909
Total Employees of Company: 13,082
Mill Locations:
Marusan Paper Mfg. Co., Ltd., Honsha Mill (94.86% owned), 1-12-1, Aoba-cho, Haramachi-ku, Minamisoma-shi 975-0039, Japan, Capacity: 313,446 mt/y, (Paper mill, Paperboard mill)
Phone: (81) 244 22 3111
Fax: (81) 244 22 0650
Email: soumu@marusan-paper.co.jp
Marusan Paper Corparation, Shikokuchuo-shi Mill, 742 Shimobun, Kinsei-cho, Shikokuchuo-shi 799-0111, Japan, Capacity: 2,700 mt/y, (Paper mill)
Phone: (81) 896 58 3450
Fax: (81) 896 58 3502
Osaka Paper Co., Ltd., Osaka-shi Mill (77.70% owned), 7-1-60, Tukuda, Nishiyodogawa-ku, Osaka-shi 555-0001, Japan, Capacity: 100,000 mt/y, (Paper mill, Paperboard mill)
Phone: (81) 6 6472 6331
Fax: (81) 6 6474 6431
Rengo Co., Ltd., Amagasaki Mill, 1-4-1, Minamishin-machi, Kuise, Amagasaki-shi 660-0822, Japan, Capacity: 400,000 mt/y, (Paperboard mill)
Phone: (81) 6 6488 2566
Fax: (81) 6 6489 1119
Rengo Co., Ltd., Kanazu Mill, 1-8-10 Jiyuugaoka, Awara-shi 919-0698, Japan, Capacity: 210,000 mt/y, (Paperboard mill)
Phone: (81) 776 73 1234
Fax: (81) 776 73 7038
Rengo Co., Ltd., Tonegawa Mill, 5269 Iwai, Bando-shi 306-0631, Japan, Capacity: 372,351 mt/y, (Paperboard mill)
Phone: (81) 297 35 2302
Fax: (81) 297 35 2594
Rengo Co., Ltd., Yashio Mill, 330 Nishibukuro, Yashio-shi 340-0833, Japan, Capacity: 980,000 mt/y, (Pulp mill, Paperboard mill)
Phone: (81) 48 922 1131
Fax: (81) 48 922 1138
Rengo Co., Ltd., Yodogawa Mill, 4-1-186, Ohhiraki, Fukushima-ku, Osaka-shi 553-0007, Japan, Capacity: 126,735 mt/y, (Paperboard mill)
Phone: (81) 6 6462 1231
Fax: (81) 6 6462 8659

ⓂRengo Co., Ltd.
Amagasaki Mill
1-4-1, Minamishin-machi
Kuise, Amagasaki-shi, Hyogo Pref., 660-0822
Japan
Phone: (81) 6 6488 2566
Fax: (81) 6 6489 1119
Web Address: www.rengo.co.jp
Personnel:
Mill Mgr.: Yukihiko Sakurai
Phone: (81) 6 6488 2566
Total Employees at this Location: 150
Type of Operation: Paperboard mill
Pulp Grades and Capacities:
Total pulp capacity: 389,680 mt/y
Recycled Pulping: 389,680 mt/y
Pulp Mill Data:
Recycled Fiber Treatment Lines:
Recycled packaging pulping lines
Paper/Paperboard Grades and Capacities:
Total paper and paperboard capacity: 400,000 mt/y
Linerboard: 100,000 mt/y
Corrugating medium/fluting: 250,000 mt/y
Boxboard/cartonboard: 50,000 mt/y
Paper and Paperboard Mill Data:
Stock Preparation:
Pulpers: 6
Refiners: 9
Paper Machines: 3
No. 6, fourdrinier (3), total capacity 100,000 mt/y, Trim width 3.4 m, Linerboard
No. 7, multi-cylinder, total capacity 50,000 mt/y, Trim width 2.95 m, Boxboard/cartonboard
No. 8, DuoFormer F, total capacity 250,000 mt/y, Trim width 4.85 m, Corrugating medium/fluting
Finishing Equipment:
Rewinders: 3 at 360,000 mt/y
Energy Data:
Power boilers: 1
Combustion turbines: 2 at 6, 5.5 MW
Steam turbines: 1 at 9 MW
Electrical demand for mill: 489 MWh/D

ⓂRengo Co., Ltd.
Kanazu Mill
1-8-10 Jiyuugaoka
Awara-shi, Fukui Pref., 919-0698
Japan
Mailing Address: 1-8-10 Jiyuugaoka, Awara-shi, Fukui Pref., 919-0698, Japan
Phone: (81) 776 73 1234
Fax: (81) 776 73 7038
Web Address: www.rengo.co.jp
Personnel:
Mill Mgr.: Yoshitaka
Phone: (81) 776 73 1234
Total Employees at this Location: 225
Type of Operation: Paperboard mill
Pulp Grades and Capacities:
Total pulp capacity: 206,478 mt/y
Recycled Pulping: 206,478 mt/y
Pulp Mill Data:
Recycled Fiber Treatment Lines:
Recycled packaging pulping lines: 1
Paper/Paperboard Grades and Capacities:
Total paper and paperboard capacity: 210,000 mt/y
Corrugating medium/fluting: 210,000 mt/y
Paper and Paperboard Mill Data:
Paper Machines: 1
No. 2, DuoFormer, total capacity 210,000 mt/y, Trim width 4.4 m, Corrugating medium/fluting
Finishing Equipment:
Rewinders: 1
Energy Data:
Power boilers: 2
Steam turbines: 3 at 12.7, 2.7, 24.8 MW
Electrical demand for mill: 281 MWh/D

ⓂRengo Co., Ltd.
Tonegawa Mill
5269 Iwai
Bando-shi, Ibaraki Pref., 306-0631
Japan
Phone: (81) 297 35 2302
Fax: (81) 297 35 2594
Web Address: www.rengo.co.jp
Personnel:
Mill Mgr.: Yoichi Tsuno
Phone: (81) 297 35 2302
Total Employees at this Location: 238
Type of Operation: Paperboard mill
Pulp Grades and Capacities:
Total pulp capacity: 325,663 mt/y
Recycled Pulping: 325,663 mt/y
Pulp Mill Data:
Recycled Fiber Treatment Lines:
Recycled packaging pulping lines: 2
Paper/Paperboard Grades and Capacities:
Total paper and paperboard capacity: 372,351 mt/y
Linerboard: 243,831 mt/y
Boxboard/cartonboard: 128,520 mt/y
Paper and Paperboard Mill Data:
Stock Preparation:
Pulpers: 8
Refiners: 12
Paper Machines: 2
No. 1, Ultraformer (7), total capacity 128,520 mt/y, Trim width 3.4 m, Boxboard/cartonboard
No. 4, Ultraformer, total capacity 243,831 mt/y, Trim width 4.05 m, Linerboard
Coating Machines: 1
No. 1, total capacity 120,000 mt/y., on machine
Finishing Equipment:
Rewinders: 2 at 340,000 mt/y
Sheeters: 4 at 83,300 mt/y
Energy Data:
Power boilers: 1
Steam turbines: 2 at 12.6, 5.3 MW
Electrical demand for mill: 654 MWh/D

ⓂRengo Co., Ltd.
Yashio Mill
330 Nishibukuro
Yashio-shi, Saitama Pref., 340-0833
Japan
Phone: (81) 48 922 1131
Fax: (81) 48 922 1138
Web Address: www.rengo.co.jp
Personnel:
Mill Mgr.: Osamu Nishimura
Phone: (81) 48 922 1131
Total Employees at this Location: 219
Type of Operation: Pulp mill, Paperboard mill
Pulp Grades and Capacities:
Total pulp capacity: 940,979 mt/y
Recycled Pulping: 940,979 mt/y
Pulp Mill Data:
Recycled Fiber Treatment Lines:
Recycled packaging pulping lines: 1
Paper/Paperboard Grades and Capacities:
Total paper and paperboard capacity: 980,000 mt/y
Linerboard: 300,000 mt/y
Corrugating medium/fluting: 630,000 mt/y
Boxboard/cartonboard: 50,000 mt/y
Paper and Paperboard Mill Data:
Paper Machines: 5
No. 1, twin-wire, total capacity 280,000 mt/y, Trim width 6.05 m, Corrugating medium/fluting
No. 2, cylinder (7), total capacity 27,000 mt/y, Trim width 2.2 m, Boxboard/cartonboard
No. 3, cylinder (8), total capacity 23,000 mt/y, Trim width 1.69 m, Boxboard/cartonboard
No. 5, fourdrinier (3), total capacity 300,000 mt/y, Trim width 4.85 m, Linerboard
No. 7, twin-wire, total capacity 350,000 mt/y, Trim width 7.25 m, Corrugating medium/fluting
Energy Data:
Power boilers: 2
Steam turbines: 4 at 9, 3.5, 30.4, 3.5 MW
Electrical demand for mill: 1,132 MWh/D

ⓂRengo Co., Ltd.
Yodogawa Mill
4-1-186, Ohhiraki, Fukushima-ku
Osaka-shi, Osaka Pref., 553-0007
Japan
Phone: (81) 6 6462 1231
Fax: (81) 6 6462 8659
Web Address: www.rengo.co.jp
Personnel:
Mill Mgr.: Jiro Kitamura
Phone: (81) 6 6462 1231
Total Employees at this Location: 90
Type of Operation: Paperboard mill
Pulp Grades and Capacities:
Total pulp capacity: 117,810 mt/y
Recycled Pulping: 117,810 mt/y
Pulp Mill Data:
Recycled Fiber Treatment Lines:
Recycled packaging pulping lines: 1
Paper/Paperboard Grades and Capacities:
Total paper and paperboard capacity: 126,735 mt/y
Linerboard: 126,735 mt/y
Paper and Paperboard Mill Data:
Paper Machines: 1
No. 1, Ultraformer, total capacity 126,735 mt/y, Trim width 4.05 m, Linerboard
Energy Data:
Power boilers: 2

Combustion turbines: 1 at 5.3 MW
Electrical demand for mill: 189 MWh/D

ⓂRicoh Co., Ltd.
8-13-1 Ginza, Chuo-ku
Tokyo, 104-8222
Japan
Phone: (81) 3 6278 2111
Personnel:
Pres.: Zenji Miura
Phone: (81) 3 6278 2111
Chmn.: Shiro Kondo
Phone: (81) 3 6278 2111
Exec. VP.: Shiro Sasaki
Phone: (81) 3 6278 2111
Snr. VP.: Soichi Nagamatsu
Phone: (81) 3 6278 2111
VP.: Masahiro Nakamura
Phone: (81) 3 6278 2111
Total Employees of Company: 108,500
Mill Locations:
Ricoh Co., Ltd., Fukui mill, 64-1 Sakaicho Oaji, Sakai-gun 919-0547, Japan, (Paper mill)
Phone: (81) 776 72 2700

ⓂRicoh Co., Ltd.
Fukui mill
64-1 Sakaicho Oaji
Sakai-gun, Fukui Pref., 919-0547
Japan
Phone: (81) 776 72 2700
Total Employees at this Location: 332
Type of Operation: Paper mill

ⓄⓂSan-Ei Regulator Co., Ltd.
Fujinomiya Mill
Ownership: Corelex Co., Ltd.
775-1, Agoyama
Fujinomiya-Shi, Shizuoka Pref., 418-0037
Japan
Phone: (81) 544 23 0303
Fax: (81) 544 26 2760
Web Address: www.corelex.jp
Personnel:
Pres.: Noboru Kurosaki
Phone: (81) 544 23 0303
Total Employees at this Location: 25
Type of Operation: Paper mill
Mill Locations:
San-Ei Regulator Co., Ltd., Tokyo Mill, 6-10 Mizue-cho, Kawasaki-ku, Kawasaki-shi 210-0086, Japan, Capacity: 50,000 mt/y, (Paper mill)
Phone: (81) 44 281 1100
Fax: (81) 44 281 1101
Paper/Paperboard Grades and Capacities:
Total paper and paperboard capacity: 113,000 mt/y
Tissue: 113,000 mt/y

ⓂSan-Ei Regulator Co., Ltd.
Tokyo Mill
Ownership: Corelex Co., Ltd.
6-10 Mizue-cho, Kawasaki-ku
Kawasaki-shi, Kanagawa Pref., 210-0086
Japan
Phone: (81) 44 281 1100
Fax: (81) 44 281 1101
Web Address: www.corelex.jp
Total Employees at this Location: 40
Type of Operation: Paper mill
Pulp Grades and Capacities:
Total pulp capacity: 53,267 mt/y
Recycled Pulping: 53,267 mt/y
Pulp Mill Data:
Bleach Plant Systems: 1
No. 1, Sequence: P
Recycled Fiber Treatment Lines:
Flotation deinking lines: 1
Paper/Paperboard Grades and Capacities:
Total paper and paperboard capacity: 50,000 mt/y
Tissue: 50,000 mt/y
Paper and Paperboard Mill Data:
Paper Machines: 1
No. 1, crescent former, Yankee dryer, total capacity 50,000 mt/y, Trim width 5.6 m, Tissue
Energy Data:
Power boilers
Electrical demand for mill: 149 MWh/D

ⓂSan-Paper Co., Ltd.
Nishiyatsushiro-gun Mill
Ownership: Corelex Co., Ltd.
1469-3, Ichikawa-daimon-cho
Nishiyatsushiro-gun, Yamanashi Pref., 409-3601
Japan
Phone: (81) 55 272 1331
Fax: (81) 55 272 0717
Email: sanpaper@corelex.co.jp
Web Address: www.corelex.jp/sanpaper/
Personnel:
Chmn.: Noboru Kurosaki
Phone: (81) 55 272 1331
Pre.: Asatsuki Kurozaki
Total Employees at this Location: 45
Type of Operation: Paper mill
Pulp Grades and Capacities:
Total pulp capacity: 9,085 mt/y
Recycled Pulping: 9,085 mt/y
Pulp Mill Data:
Recycled Fiber Treatment Lines:
Flotation deinking lines: 1
Paper/Paperboard Grades and Capacities:
Total paper and paperboard capacity: 8,400 mt/y
Tissue: 8,400 mt/y
Paper and Paperboard Mill Data:
Paper Machines: 1
No. 1, Yankee dryer, total capacity 8,400 mt/y, Trim width 1.93 m, Tissue
Finishing Equipment:
Rewinders: 2
Energy Data:
Power boilers
Electrical demand for mill: 28 MWh/D

ⓄⓂSanko Seishi Kogyo KK
Fuji-shi Mill
1597-1 Matsuoka
Fuji-shi, Shizuoka Pref., 416-0909
Japan
Phone: (81) 545 61 0015
Fax: (81) 545 63 3090
Personnel:
Pres.: Akio Suzuki
Phone: (81) 545 61 0015
Total Employees at this Location: 27
Type of Operation: Paper mill
Paper/Paperboard Grades and Capacities:
Total paper and paperboard capacity: 32,000 mt/y
Uncoated mechanical/groundwood: 32,000 mt/y
Paper and Paperboard Mill Data:
Paper Machines: 2
No. 1, fourdrinier, multi-cylinder, total capacity 16,000 mt/y, Trim width 1.52 m, Uncoated mechanical/groundwood
No. 2, fourdrinier, multi-cylinder, total capacity 15,600 mt/y, Trim width 1.52 m, Uncoated woodfree/freesheet

ⓄⓂSanwa Seishi K.K.
Fuji Mill
170, Kuzawa
Fuji, Shizuoka Pref., 419-0202
Japan
Phone: (81) 545 71 3139
Fax: (81) 545 71 3259
Email: Sanwatp@wonder.ocn.ne.jp
Personnel:
Pres.: Akihiro Furutani
Tech. Dir.: Takashi Takeda
Total Employees at this Location: 17
Type of Operation: Paper mill
Pulp Grades and Capacities:
Total pulp capacity: 5,408 mt/y
Recycled Pulping: 5,408 mt/y
Pulp Mill Data:
Recycled Fiber Treatment Lines:
Flotation deinking lines
Paper/Paperboard Grades and Capacities:
Total paper and paperboard capacity: 5,000 mt/y
Tissue: 5,000 mt/y
Paper and Paperboard Mill Data:
Paper Machines: 1
No. 1, Yankee dryer, total capacity 5,000 mt/y, Trim width 2 m, Tissue
Energy Data:
Power boilers: 1
Electrical demand for mill: 17 MWh/D

ⓄⓂSanyo Itagami Kogyo KK
Okayama-shi Mill
1-2-55, Saioji-higashi
Okayama-shi, Okayama Pref., 704-8114
Japan
Phone: (81) 86 943 6111
Fax: (81) 86 943 5277
Personnel:
Pres.: Tokunori Ihara
Phone: (81) 86 943 6111
Total Employees at this Location: 77
Type of Operation: Paperboard mill
Paper/Paperboard Grades and Capacities:
Total paper and paperboard capacity: 98,000 mt/y
Boxboard/cartonboard: 98,000 mt/y
Paper and Paperboard Mill Data:
Stock Preparation:
Pulpers: 4
Refiners: 4
Paper Machines: 3
No. 1, multi-cylinder, total capacity 14,600 mt/y, Trim width 1.68 m, Boxboard/cartonboard
No. 2, multi-cylinder, total capacity 58,400 mt/y, Trim width 2.97 m, Boxboard/cartonboard
No. 3, multi-cylinder, total capacity 25,000 mt/y, Trim width 2.55 m, Boxboard/cartonboard
Energy Data:
Power boilers: 2

ⓄⓂSanyo Paper Co., Ltd.
Sennan-shi Mill
Ownership: Daio Paper Corp.
6-4-25 Onosato
Sennan-shi, Osaka Pref., 590-0526
Japan
Phone: (81) 724 82 7201
Fax: (81) 724 82 7204
Email: crepe@sanyo-paper.co.jp
Web Address: www.sanyo-paper.co.jp
Personnel:
Pres.: Rokujiro Harada
Phone: (81) 724 82 7201
Total Employees at this Location: 49
Type of Operation: Paper mill
Paper/Paperboard Grades and Capacities:
Total paper and paperboard capacity: 7,200 mt/y
Packaging papers: 7,200 mt/y
Paper and Paperboard Mill Data:
Paper Machines: 2
No. 1, fourdrinier, total capacity 3,000 mt/y, Trim width 0.97 m, Packaging papers
No. 2, fourdrinier, total capacity 4,200 mt/y, Trim width 1.3 m, Packaging papers

ⓄⓂSanyo Paper Manufacturing Co., Ltd.
Tottori Mill
Ownership: Daio Paper Corp.

Japan

185 Fruichi
Tottori-shi, Tottori Pref., 680-0865
Japan
 Phone: (81) 857 23 7131
 Fax: (81) 857 27 6320
Personnel:
 Pres.: Kazunaga Ikawa
 Phone: (81) 857 23 7131
Total Employees at this Location: 130
Type of Operation: Paperboard mill
Pulp Grades and Capacities:
 Total pulp capacity: 258,230 mt/y
 Chemical Pulp: 92,423 mt/y
 Recycled Pulping: 165,807 mt/y
Pulp Mill Data:
 Chemical Pulping Systems:
 Continuous digesters: 1
 Chemical Recovery Equipment:
 Recovery boilers: 1
 Recycled Fiber Treatment Lines:
 Recycled packaging pulping lines: 1
Paper/Paperboard Grades and Capacities:
 Total paper and paperboard capacity: 251,685 mt/y
 Corrugating medium/fluting: 251,685 mt/y
Paper and Paperboard Mill Data:
Paper Machines: 2
No. 1, fourdrinier, total capacity 59,976 mt/y, Trim width 2.75 m, Corrugating medium/fluting
No. 2, fourdrinier, total capacity 191,709 mt/y, Trim width 4.21 m, Corrugating medium/fluting
Energy Data:
 Power boilers: 1
 Steam turbines at 9.6 MW
 Electrical demand for mill: 435 MWh/D

ⒽⓂSanzen Paper Mfg. Co., Ltd.
Kanazawa Mill
3-1-1, Kanaishi-kita
Kanazawa-shi, Ishikawa Pref., 920-0338
Japan
 Phone: (81) 76 267 1151
 Fax: (81) 76 268 4215
 Email: sanzen@sanzenseishi.co.jp
 Web Address: www.sanzenseishi.co.jp
Personnel:
 Pres.: Mitsuo Haida
 Phone: (81) 76 267 1151
 Sls. Mgr.: Masamitsu Otani
 Phone: (81) 76 267 1151
 Deputy Sls. Mgr.: Tsuyoshi Sato
Total Employees at this Location: 52
Type of Operation: Paper mill
Paper/Paperboard Grades and Capacities:
 Total paper and paperboard capacity: 12,200 mt/y
 Uncoated mechanical/groundwood
 Specialty and industrial
Paper and Paperboard Mill Data:
Paper Machines: 2
No. 1, fourdrinier, total capacity 5,000 mt/y, Trim width 1.4 m, Uncoated mechanical/groundwood, Specialty and industrial
No. 2, fourdrinier, total capacity 7,200 mt/y, Trim width 1.6 m, Uncoated mechanical/groundwood, Specialty and industrial
Finishing Equipment:
 Winders: 1
 Supercalenders: 2
 Rewinders: 1
 Sheeters: 1
Energy Data:
 Power boilers: 5

ⓂShin-Ei Paper Mfg. Co., Ltd.
Fujinomiya-Shi Mill
Ownership: Corelex Co., Ltd.
31-6 Nishi-machi
Fujinomiya-Shi, Shizuoka Pref., 418-0056
Japan
 Phone: (81) 544 27 2513
 Fax: (81) 544 23 3300
 Email: shinei@corelex.co.jp
 Web Address: www.corelex.jp/shinei/
Personnel:
 Pres.: Akatsuki Kurosaki
 Phone: (81) 544 27 2513
 Chrmn. of the Board: Noburo Kurosaki
 Phone: (81) 544 27 2513
Total Employees at this Location: 50
Type of Operation: Paper mill
Pulp Grades and Capacities:
 Total pulp capacity: 19,278 mt/y
 Recycled Pulping: 19,278 mt/y
Paper/Paperboard Grades and Capacities:
 Total paper and paperboard capacity: 18,000 mt/y
 Tissue: 18,000 mt/y
Paper and Paperboard Mill Data:
Paper Machines: 1
No. 1, Yankee dryer, total capacity 18,000 mt/y, Trim width 2.9 m, Tissue
Finishing Equipment:
 Winders: 5
 Sheeters: 4
Energy Data:
 Electrical demand for mill: 54 MWh/D

ⒽⓂShinbashi Seishi K.K
Fuji Mill
1-5, Yobadashicho
Fuji, Shizuoka Pref., 417-0003
Japan
 Phone: (81) 545-52-2003
 Fax: (81) 545-52-2989
Total Employees at this Location: 24
Type of Operation: Paper mill
Pulp Grades and Capacities:
 Total pulp capacity: 5,401 mt/y
 Recycled Pulping: 5,401 mt/y
Pulp Mill Data:
 Recycled Fiber Treatment Lines:
 Flotation deinking lines
Paper/Paperboard Grades and Capacities:
 Total paper and paperboard capacity: 5,000 mt/y
 Tissue: 5,000 mt/y
Paper and Paperboard Mill Data:
Paper Machines: 3
No. 1, Yankee dryer, total capacity 1,000 mt/y, Trim width 1.27 m, Tissue
No. 2, Yankee dryer, total capacity 1,000 mt/y, Trim width 1.27 m, Tissue
No. 3, Yankee dryer, total capacity 3,000 mt/y, Trim width 2.6 m, Tissue
Energy Data:
 Power boilers
 Electrical demand for mill: 17 MWh/D

ⒽⓂShiroyama Paper Mfg. Co., Ltd.
Shikokuchuo-shi Mill
Ownership: Itoc
301-1 Kamibun-cho
Shikokuchuo-shi, Ehime Pref., 799-0121
Japan
 Phone: (81) 896 58 2220
 Fax: (81) 896 58 3143/3141
Personnel:
 Pres.: Takemasa Kaneko
 Phone: (81) 896 58 2220
Total Employees at this Location: 38
Type of Operation: Paper mill
Paper/Paperboard Grades and Capacities:
 Total paper and paperboard capacity: 8,400 mt/y
 Packaging papers: 8,400 mt/y
Paper and Paperboard Mill Data:
Paper Machines: 2
No. 1, fourdrinier, Yankee dryer, total capacity 3,600 mt/y, Trim width 1.3 m, Packaging papers
No. 2, fourdrinier, Yankee dryer, total capacity 4,800 mt/y, Trim width 1.55 m, Packaging papers

ⒽⓂShowa Seishi K.K.
Gushikawa Mill
708-1, Taba
Uruma, Okinawa Pref., 904-2213
Japan
 Phone: (81) 989734125
Total Employees at this Location: 30
Type of Operation: Paper mill
Pulp Grades and Capacities:
 Total pulp capacity: 9,717 mt/y
 Recycled Pulping: 9,717 mt/y
Pulp Mill Data:
 Recycled Fiber Treatment Lines:
 Flotation deinking lines: 1
Paper/Paperboard Grades and Capacities:
 Total paper and paperboard capacity: 9,000 mt/y
 Tissue: 9,000 mt/y
Paper and Paperboard Mill Data:
Paper Machines: 3
No. 1, Yankee dryer, total capacity 3,000 mt/y, Trim width 1.4 m, Tissue
No. 2, Yankee dryer, total capacity 3,000 mt/y, Trim width 1.6 m, Tissue
No. 3, Yankee dryer, total capacity 3,000 mt/y, Trim width 1.7 m, Tissue
Energy Data:
 Power boilers
 Electrical demand for mill: 30 MWh/D

ⒽⓂSunko Seishi Co., Ltd.
Shizuoka-shi Mill
Okitsunaka-machi 992-1
Shimizu-ku, Shizuoka-shi, Shizuoka Pref., 424-0204
Japan
 Phone: (81) 543 69 1138
 Fax: (81) 543 69 4706
Personnel:
 Pres.: Hiroaki Kaneko
 Phone: (81) 543 69 1138
Total Employees of Company: 30
Type of Operation: Paperboard mill
Pulp Grades and Capacities:
 Total pulp capacity: 36,474 mt/y
 Recycled Pulping: 36,474 mt/y
Paper/Paperboard Grades and Capacities:
 Total paper and paperboard capacity: 36,000 mt/y
 Linerboard: 36,000 mt/y
Paper and Paperboard Mill Data:
Paper Machines: 1
No. 2, cylinder, total capacity 36,000 mt/y, Trim width 3.05 m, Linerboard
Energy Data:
 Electrical demand for mill: 45 MWh/D

ⒽⓂTagonoura Pulp K.K.
Fuji Mill
8-24, Aratajimacho
Fuji, 417-0043
Japan
 Phone: (81) 545520286
Total Employees at this Location: 20
Type of Operation: Paper mill
Paper/Paperboard Grades and Capacities:
 Total paper and paperboard capacity: 7,000 mt/y
 Tissue: 7,000 mt/y
Paper and Paperboard Mill Data:
Paper Machines: 1
No. 1, Yankee dryer, total capacity 7,000 mt/y, Trim width 2.3 m, Tissue
Energy Data:
 Power boilers
 Electrical demand for mill: 21 MWh/D

ⒽⓂTaiho Paper Co., Ltd.
Kamo-gun Mill
252-1 Kamikawabe, Kawabe-cho
Kamo-gun, Gifu Pref., 509-0302
Japan

Phone: (81) 574 53 2626
Fax: (81) 574 53 2629
Email: soumu@taihoseishi.co.jp
Web Address: www.taihoseishi.co.jp
Personnel:
Pres.: Takeyoshi Wada
Phone: (81) 574 53 2626
Total Employees at this Location: 85
Type of Operation: Paperboard mill
Pulp Grades and Capacities:
Total pulp capacity: 130,381 mt/y
Recycled Pulping: 130,381 mt/y
Paper/Paperboard Grades and Capacities:
Total paper and paperboard capacity: 130,000 mt/y
Linerboard: 24,000 mt/y
Corrugating medium/fluting: 106,000 mt/y
Paper and Paperboard Mill Data:
Stock Preparation:
Pulpers: 3
Refiners: 5
Paper Machines: 2
No. 1, Ultraformer, total capacity 80,000 mt/y, Trim width 3.85 m, Linerboard, Corrugating medium/fluting
No. 2, cylinder (4), total capacity 50,000 mt/y, Trim width 3.2 m, Corrugating medium/fluting
Finishing Equipment:
Supercalenders: 2
Rewinders: 2
Energy Data:
Power boilers: 1
Steam turbines: 1 at 4.3 MW
Electrical demand for mill: 153 MWh/D

Taiko Paper Mfg. Co., Ltd.
Fuji-shi Mill
10, Kamiyokowari
Fuji-shi, Shizuoka Pref., 416-8660
Japan
Phone: (81) 545 61 2500/2501/2502
Fax: (81) 545 61 5971
Web Address: tk-paper.co.jp
Personnel:
Pres.: Shiro Nagaki
Phone: (81) 545 61 2500
Total Employees at this Location: 213
Type of Operation: Pulp mill, Paper mill
Pulp Grades and Capacities:
Total pulp capacity: 120,319 mt/y
Pulp available for market: 17,850 mt/y
Chemical Pulp: 120,319 mt/y
Pulp Mill Data:
Chemical Pulping Systems:
Batch digesters: 2
Continuous digesters: 1
Chemical Recovery Equipment:
Evaporator lines: 1
Recovery boilers: 1
Recycled Fiber Treatment Lines:
Flotation deinking lines: 1 at 4,000 admt/y
Pulpers: 3 at 20,000 admt/y
Pulp Dryers:
Pulp Dryers 1
Paper/Paperboard Grades and Capacities:
Total paper and paperboard capacity: 97,461 mt/y
Packaging papers: 32,130 mt/y
Specialty and industrial: 65,331 mt/y
Paper and Paperboard Mill Data:
Stock Preparation:
Pulpers: 7
Refiners: 20
Paper Machines: 4
No. 1, fourdrinier, total capacity 14,637 mt/y, Trim width 2.02 m, Specialty and industrial, Packaging papers
No. 2, fourdrinier, total capacity 25,704 mt/y, Trim width 2.06 m, Specialty and industrial, Packaging papers
No. 5, fourdrinier, total capacity 47,124 mt/y, Trim width 3.26 m, Specialty and industrial, Packaging papers
No. 6, fourdrinier, total capacity 9,996 mt/y, Trim width 2.54 m, Specialty and industrial

Coating Machines: 1
No. 3, total capacity 27,375 mt/y., on machine
Energy Data:
Power boilers: 2
Combustion turbines: 1 at 2.6 MW
Steam turbines: 1 at 35.0 MW
Electrical demand for mill: 349 MWh/D

Taisei Paper Industries Co., Ltd.
Tsuyama-shi Mill
200-1 Kawasaki
Tsuyama-shi, Okayama Pref.
Japan
Phone: (81) 868 26 1114
Fax: (81) 868 26 5567
Personnel:
Pres.: Takahiro Igawa
Phone: (81) 868 26 1114
Total Employees at this Location: 90
Type of Operation: Paperboard mill
Pulp Grades and Capacities:
Total pulp capacity: 78,926 mt/y
Recycled Pulping: 78,926 mt/y
Pulp Mill Data:
Recycled Fiber Treatment Lines:
Recycled packaging pulping lines: 1
Paper/Paperboard Grades and Capacities:
Total paper and paperboard capacity: 85,000 mt/y
Linerboard: 85,000 mt/y
Paper and Paperboard Mill Data:
Paper Machines: 2
No. 1, Ultraformer, total capacity 45,000 mt/y, Trim width 3.4 m, Linerboard
No. 2, Multi-wire (5), total capacity 40,000 mt/y, Trim width 3.6 m, Linerboard
Energy Data:
Power boilers
Electrical demand for mill: 110 MWh/D

Taisei Paper Industries Co., Ltd.
200-1 Kawasaki
Tsuyama-shi
Japan
Phone: (81) 868 26 1114
Fax: (81) 868 26 5567
Personnel:
Pres.: Takahiro Igawa
Phone: (81) 868 26 1114
Fax: (81) 868 26 5567
Total Employees at this Location: 160
Mill Locations:
Taisei Paper Industries Co., Ltd., Tsuyama-shi Mill, 200-1 Kawasaki, Tsuyama-shi, Japan, Capacity: 85,000 mt/y, (Paperboard mill)
Phone: (81) 868 26 1114
Fax: (81) 868 26 5567

Takano Paper Co., Ltd.
Fuji-shi Mill
10-4 Aza-kawagishiba, Yayoishinden
Fuji-shi, Shizuoka Pref., 417-0065
Japan
Phone: (81) 545 51 0567
Fax: (81) 545 53 5400
Email: tskk@cf6.so-net.ne.jp
Personnel:
Pres.: Katsumi Takano
Phone: (81) 545 51 0567
Total Employees at this Location: 45
Type of Operation: Paper mill
Pulp Grades and Capacities:
Total pulp capacity: 6,489 mt/y
Recycled Pulping: 6,489 mt/y
Pulp Mill Data:
Recycled Fiber Treatment Lines:
Flotation deinking lines: 1
Paper/Paperboard Grades and Capacities:
Total paper and paperboard capacity: 6,000 mt/y

Tissue: 6,000 mt/y
Paper and Paperboard Mill Data:
Paper Machines: 1
No. 1, Yankee dryer, total capacity 6,000 mt/y, Trim width 2.2 m, Tissue
Energy Data:
Power boilers
Electrical demand for mill: 20 MWh/D

Takasago Paper Co., Ltd.
Mitsukaido-shi Mill
60, Ko, Toyooka-cho
Mitsukaido-shi, Ibaraki Pref., 303-0041
Japan
Phone: (81) 297 24 0611
Fax: (81) 297 24 0617
Personnel:
Pres.: Eiichiro Sudo
Phone: (81) 297 24 0611
Total Employees at this Location: 75
Type of Operation: Paperboard mill
Pulp Grades and Capacities:
Total pulp capacity: 122,186 mt/y
Recycled Pulping: 122,186 mt/y
Paper/Paperboard Grades and Capacities:
Total paper and paperboard capacity: 120,000 mt/y
Boxboard/cartonboard: 120,000 mt/y
Paper and Paperboard Mill Data:
Paper Machines: 1
No. 1, multi-wire, total capacity 120,000 mt/y, Trim width 4.4 m, Boxboard/cartonboard
Energy Data:
Electrical demand for mill: 151 MWh/D

Takizawa Seishi K.K.
Fuji Mill
775-1, Agoyama
Fuji, Shizuoka Pref., 418-0037
Japan
Phone: (81) 545711520
Web Address: www.corelex.jp/
Total Employees at this Location: 30
Type of Operation: Paper mill
Pulp Grades and Capacities:
Total pulp capacity: 8,653 mt/y
Recycled Pulping: 8,653 mt/y
Pulp Mill Data:
Recycled Fiber Treatment Lines:
Flotation deinking lines
Paper/Paperboard Grades and Capacities:
Total paper and paperboard capacity: 8,000 mt/y
Tissue: 8,000 mt/y
Paper and Paperboard Mill Data:
Paper Machines: 2
No. 1, Yankee dryer, total capacity 4,000 mt/y, Trim width 1.99 m, Tissue
No. 2, Yankee dryer, total capacity 4,000 mt/y, Trim width 2.3 m, Tissue
Energy Data:
Power boilers
Electrical demand for mill: 27 MWh/D

Tateyama Paper Mill Co., Ltd.
Nakashinkawa-gun Mill
141, Gohyakuseki, Tateyama-cho
Nakashinkawa-gun, Toyama Pref., 930-0214
Japan
Phone: (81) 76 463 1311
Fax: (81) 76 463 0590
Email: tateyama@tateyamaseishi.jp
Web Address: www.tateyamaseishi.jp
Personnel:
Pres.: Tsunehiko Ikeda
Phone: (81) 76 463 1311
Total Employees at this Location: 92
Type of Operation: Pulp mill, Paperboard mill
Paper/Paperboard Grades and Capacities:
Total paper and paperboard capacity: 3,000 mt/y

Japan

Paper and Paperboard Mill Data:
Paper Machines: 2
No. 1, cylinder, total capacity 1,200 mt/y, Trim width 1.5 m
No. 2, cylinder, total capacity 1,800 mt/y, Trim width 1.9 m
Energy Data:
Power boilers: 2

ⒽTenma Paper Mills & Co.
729 Tenma
Fuji-shi, 419-0205
Japan
 Phone: (81) 545 71 2115
 Fax: (81) 545 71 0694
Personnel:
 Mill Mgr.: Shizuo Ishikawa
 Phone: (81) 545 71 2115
 Asst. Mill Mgr.: M. Kawarazaki
 Phone: (81) 545 71 2115
Total Employees at this Location: 91
Mill Locations:
Tenma Paper Mills (Thailand) Co., Ltd., Pakkred Mill, 6/2 Sukaprachasarn 2 Road, Bangpood, Pakkred 11120, Thailand, Capacity: 35,000 mt/y, (Paperboard mill)
 Phone: (66) 2 582 8216/584 3596 7
 Fax: (66) 2 583 7846
 Email: thaitenma@hotmail.com

ⒽⓂTentok Paper Co., Ltd.
Fuji-shi Mill
264 Tenma
Fuji-shi, Shizuoka Pref., 419-0205
Japan
 Phone: (81) 545 71 2620
 Fax: (81) 545 72 1363
 Email: esales@tentok.co.jp
 Web Address: www.tentok.co.jp
Personnel:
 Pres.: Takemasa Kaneko
 Phone: (81) 545 71 2620
Total Employees at this Location: 140
Type of Operation: Paper mill
Paper/Paperboard Grades and Capacities:
Total paper and paperboard capacity: 22,000 mt/y
Specialty and industrial: 22,000 mt/y
Paper and Paperboard Mill Data:
 Stock Preparation:
 Pulpers: 4
 Refiners: 2
 Paper Machines: 3
No. 1, fourdrinier, Yankee dryer, total capacity 10,000 mt/y, Trim width 2.6 m, Specialty and industrial
No. 2, fourdrinier, Yankee dryer, total capacity 5,000 mt/y, Trim width 1.65 m, Specialty and industrial
No. 3, fourdrinier, Yankee dryer, total capacity 7,000 mt/y, Trim width 1.95 m, Specialty and industrial
 Finishing Equipment:
 Winders: 3
 Supercalenders: 1
Energy Data:
Power boilers: 7

ⒽToho Tokushu Pulp Co., Ltd.
Ohtemachi 21 Bldg. 5th Floor, 1-4-1, Uchikanda, Chiyoda-ku
Tokyo, 101-0047
Japan
 Phone: (81) 3 3295 7740
 Fax: (81) 3 3295 7760
Personnel:
 Pres.: Masaaki Iguchi
 Phone: (81) 3 3295 7740
 Fax: (81) 3 3295 7760
Total Employees at this Location: 47
Mill Locations:
Toho Tokushu Pulp Co., Ltd., Oyama Mill, 340 Mamada, Oyama-Shi 329-0205, Japan, (Pulp mill)
 Phone: (81) 285 45 1213
 Fax: (81) 285 45 1010

ⓂToho Tokushu Pulp Co., Ltd.
Oyama Mill
340 Mamada
Oyama-Shi, Tochigi Pref., 329-0205
Japan
 Phone: (81) 285 45 1213
 Fax: (81) 285 45 1010
Personnel:
 Mill Mgr.: Yoshinori Yazawa
 Phone: (81) 285 45 1213
Total Employees at this Location: 30
Type of Operation: Pulp mill
Pulp Grades and Capacities:
 Total pulp capacity: 2,800 mt/y

ⒽⓂTokai Seishi Kougyou Co., Ltd.
Fuji Mill
Ownership: Nisshinbo Paper Products, Inc.
60-1, Harada
Fuji
Japan
Total Employees at this Location: 50
Type of Operation: Paper mill
Pulp Grades and Capacities:
 Total pulp capacity: 27,024 mt/y
 Recycled Pulping: 27,024 mt/y
Paper/Paperboard Grades and Capacities:
 Total paper and paperboard capacity: 25,000 mt/y
 Tissue: 25,000 mt/y
Paper and Paperboard Mill Data:
 Paper Machines: 4
No. 1, Yankee dryer, total capacity 6,000 mt/y, Trim width 2 m, Tissue
No. 2, Yankee dryer, total capacity 6,000 mt/y, Trim width 2 m, Tissue
No. 3, Yankee dryer, total capacity 6,000 mt/y, Trim width 2 m, Tissue
No. 4, Yankee dryer, total capacity 7,000 mt/y, Trim width 2.3 m, Tissue
Energy Data:
Power boilers
Electrical demand for mill: 84 MWh/D

ⒽTokushu Tokai Paper Co., Ltd.
Ownership: 9.07% by Tokushu Tokai Paper Co., Ltd, 1.84% by Oji Holdings Corp., 3% by Daio Paper Corp., 1.60% by Takeo Co., Ltd. , 2.65% by Tokushu Tokai Paper Business Association , 3.08% by Shinsei Pulp & Paper Co., Ltd. , 2.27% by Mitsubishi UFJ Financial Group, Inc., 3.53% by The Shizuoka Bank, Ltd., 8.45% by Mitsubishi Corp., 3.37% by Chuo Building Co., Ltd.
Jyowayaesu Bldg. 4-1, Yaesu 2-chome, Chuo-ku
Tokyo, 104-0028
Japan
 Phone: (81) 3 3273 8281
 Fax: (81) 3 3281 4970
 Email: info@m.tt-paper.co.jp
 Web Address: www.tt-paper.co.jp
Personnel:
 Pres.: Kiyotoshi Misawa
 Phone: (81) 3 3273 8281
 Fax: (81) 3 3281 4970
Total Employees at this Location: 80
Mill Locations:
Meiji Seishi Co., Ltd., Takaoka Mill (88.10% owned), 167-1 Aza Nakase Atsuhara, Fuji-shi 419-0201, Japan, Capacity: 37,000 mt/y, (Paper mill)
 Phone: (81) 545 71 1122
 Fax: (81) 545 71 1181
Tokushu Tokai Paper Co., Ltd., Gifu Mill, 814 Kamikawate, Gifu-Shi 500-8245, Japan, Capacity: 6,700 mt/y, (Paper mill)
 Phone: (81) 58 246 9111
 Fax: (81) 58 246 9116
Tokushu Tokai Paper Co., Ltd., Mishima Mill, 501 Honjuku, Nagaizumi-cho, Sunto-Gun 411-8750, Japan, Capacity: 64,974 mt/y, (Paper mill)
 Phone: (81) 559 88 1120/1110
 Fax: (81) 559 88 1147
Tokushu Tokai Paper Co., Ltd., Shimada Mill, 4379 Mukaijima-cho, Shimada-shi 427-8510, Japan, Capacity: 743,988 mt/y, (Pulp mill, Paper mill, Paperboard mill)
 Phone: (81) 547 36 5151
 Fax: (81) 547 35 5818
Tokushu Tokai Paper Co., Ltd., Yokoi mill, Yokoi 4 Chome 18 - 1, Shimada-shi 427-0024, Japan, Capacity: 35,700 mt/y, (Paper mill)
 Phone: (81) 547 35 7111
 Fax: (81) 547 36 5120

ⓂTokushu Tokai Paper Co., Ltd.
Gifu Mill
814 Kamikawate
Gifu-Shi, Gifu Pref., 500-8245
Japan
 Phone: (81) 58 246 9111
 Fax: (81) 58 246 9116
 Web Address: www.tt-paper.co.jp
Personnel:
 Mill Mgr.: Yasuichi Watanabe
 Phone: (81) 58 246 9111
Total Employees at this Location: 90
Type of Operation: Paper mill
Paper/Paperboard Grades and Capacities:
 Total paper and paperboard capacity: 6,700 mt/y
 Uncoated woodfree/freesheet: 6,700 mt/y
Paper and Paperboard Mill Data:
 Paper Machines: 2
No. 5, cylinder, total capacity 2,500 mt/y, Trim width 1.15 m, Uncoated woodfree/freesheet
No. 6, fourdrinier, total capacity 4,200 mt/y, Trim width 1.35 m, Uncoated woodfree/freesheet

ⓂTokushu Tokai Paper Co., Ltd.
Mishima Mill
501 Honjuku, Nagaizumi-cho
Sunto-Gun, Shizuoka Pref., 411-8750
Japan
 Phone: (81) 559 88 1120/1110
 Fax: (81) 559 88 1147
 Web Address: www.tt-paper.co.jp
Personnel:
 Dir./ Mill Mgr.: Michiaki Sano
 Phone: (81) 559 88 1120
Total Employees at this Location: 200
Type of Operation: Paper mill
Paper/Paperboard Grades and Capacities:
 Total paper and paperboard capacity: 64,974 mt/y
 Uncoated woodfree/freesheet: 27,489 mt/y
 Specialty and industrial: 37,485 mt/y
Paper and Paperboard Mill Data:
 Paper Machines: 6
No. 3, cylinder, total capacity 1,785 mt/y, Trim width 1.14 m, Uncoated woodfree/freesheet
No. 11, fourdrinier, total capacity 3,927 mt/y, Trim width 1.35 m, Uncoated woodfree/freesheet
No. 12, fourdrinier, total capacity 3,927 mt/y, Trim width 1.4 m, Uncoated woodfree/freesheet
No. 13, fourdrinier, total capacity 24,990 mt/y, Trim width 2.65 m, Specialty and industrial
No. 14, fourdrinier, total capacity 17,850 mt/y, Trim width 2.64 m, Uncoated woodfree/freesheet
No. 15, fourdrinier, total capacity 12,495 mt/y, Trim width 1.48 m, Specialty and industrial
 Coating Machines: 4
No. 2, total capacity 5,700 mt/y., off machine
No. 7, total capacity 2,100 mt/y., off machine
No. 8, total capacity 16,000 mt/y., off machine
No. 10, total capacity 4,300 mt/y., off machine
Energy Data:
Power boilers
Combustion turbines: 1 at 0.4 MW
Electrical demand for mill: 164 MWh/D

ⓂTokushu Tokai Paper Co., Ltd.
Shimada Mill
4379 Mukaijima-cho

Japan

Shimada-shi, Shizuoka Pref., 427-8510
Japan
 Phone: (81) 547 36 5151
 Fax: (81) 547 35 5818
 Web Address: www.tt-paper.co.jp
Personnel:
 Dir./ Mill Mgr.: Katsuhiro Watanabe
 Phone: (81) 547 36 5151
Total Employees at this Location: 750
Type of Operation: Pulp mill, Paper mill, Paperboard mill
Pulp Grades and Capacities:
 Total pulp capacity: 842,662 mt/y
 Pulp available for market: 71,400 mt/y
 Chemical Pulp: 610,772 mt/y
 Recycled Pulping: 231,890 mt/y
Pulp Mill Data:
 Chemical Pulping Systems:
 Continuous digesters: 2
 Chemical Recovery Equipment:
 Evaporator lines: 1
 Recovery boilers: 1
 Recycled Fiber Treatment Lines:
 Recycled packaging pulping lines: 1
 Pulp Dryers:
 Pulp Dryers 1, Pulp Dryers 1
Paper/Paperboard Grades and Capacities:
 Total paper and paperboard capacity: 743,988 mt/y
 Specialty and industrial: 128,877 mt/y
 Linerboard: 484,806 mt/y
 Corrugating medium/fluting: 124,950 mt/y
 Boxboard/cartonboard: 5,355 mt/y
Paper and Paperboard Mill Data:
Paper Machines: 6
 No. 6, Bel-Form, total capacity 47,838 mt/y, Trim width 3.15 m, Specialty and industrial
 No. 7, Ultraformer, total capacity 184,926 mt/y, Trim width 3.8 m, Linerboard
 No. 8, fourdrinier, total capacity 81,039 mt/y, Trim width 4.1 m, Specialty and industrial
 No. 9, Bel-Bond, total capacity 299,880 mt/y, Trim width 5.1 m, Linerboard
 No. 10, cylinder, total capacity 5,355 mt/y, Trim width 1.65 m, Boxboard/cartonboard
 No. 12, fourdrinier, total capacity 124,950 mt/y, Trim width 1.52 m, Corrugating medium/fluting
Finishing Equipment:
 Supercalenders: 1
 Sheeters: 1
Energy Data:
 Power boilers: 12
 Combustion turbines: 1 at 5.5 MW
 Steam turbines: 5 at 8.1, 4, 24.85, 38.2, 16.3 MW
 Hydro turbines: 1 at 6 MW
 Electrical demand for mill: 1,677 MWh/D

ⓂTokushu Tokai Paper Co., Ltd.
Yokoi mill
Mill is due to be closed by December 2015
Yokoi 4 Chome 18 - 1
Shimada-shi, Shizuoka Pref., 427-0024
Japan
 Phone: (81) 547 35 7111
 Fax: (81) 547 36 5120
 Web Address: www.tt-paper.co.jp
Total Employees at this Location: 80
Type of Operation: Paper mill
Paper/Paperboard Grades and Capacities:
 Total paper and paperboard capacity: 35,700 mt/y
 Specialty and industrial: 35,700 mt/y
Paper and Paperboard Mill Data:
Paper Machines: 2
 No. 1, fourdrinier, total capacity 17,850 mt/y, Trim width 2.02 m, Specialty and industrial
 No. 2, fourdrinier, total capacity 17,850 mt/y, Trim width 2 m, Specialty and industrial
Energy Data:
 Power boilers
 Electrical demand for mill: 101 MWh/D

ⓄⓂTokyo Paper Mfg. Co., Ltd.
Fujinomiya-Shi Mill
866 Koizumi
Fujinomiya-Shi, Shizuoka Pref., 418-0022
Japan
 Phone: (81) 544 26 3121
 Fax: (81) 544 23 6678
Personnel:
 Pres.: Kenji Sano
 Phone: (81) 544 26 3121
Total Employees at this Location: 247
Type of Operation: Paper mill
Paper/Paperboard Grades and Capacities:
 Total paper and paperboard capacity: 21,000 mt/y
 Specialty and industrial: 21,000 mt/y
Paper and Paperboard Mill Data:
Paper Machines: 2
 No. 1, Yankee dryer, cylinder (5), total capacity 9,000 mt/y, Trim width 1.65 m, Specialty and industrial
 No. 2, Yankee dryer, cylinder (6), total capacity 12,000 mt/y, Trim width 1.65 m, Specialty and industrial
Coating Machines: 1
 No. 1, total capacity 29,200 mt/y., off machine
Finishing Equipment:
 Winders: 2
 Sheeters: 3
Energy Data:
 Power boilers: 2
 Steam turbines: 1 at 6 MW

ⓄⓂTomoegawa Paper Co., Ltd.
Shizuoka Mill
3-1, Mochimune Tomoe-cho, Suruga-ku
Shizuoka-Shi, Shizuoka Pref., 421-0192
Japan
 Phone: (81) 54 256 4120
 Fax: (81) 54 256 4284
 Web Address: www.tomoegawa.co.jp/english
Personnel:
 Pres.: Gantetsu Morita
 Phone: (81) 54 256 4120
Total Employees of Company: 72
Type of Operation: Paper mill
Paper/Paperboard Grades and Capacities:
 Total paper and paperboard capacity: 50,200 mt/y
 Specialty and industrial: 50,200 mt/y
Paper and Paperboard Mill Data:
 Stock Preparation:
 Refiners: 0
Paper Machines: 4
 No. 1, fourdrinier, total capacity 10,800 mt/y, Trim width 2.02 m, Specialty and industrial
 No. 2, cylinder, total capacity 9,000 mt/y, Trim width 2.04 m, Specialty and industrial
 No. 7, fourdrinier, total capacity 12,500 mt/y, Trim width 2.25 m, Specialty and industrial
 No. 9, fourdrinier, total capacity 17,900 mt/y, Trim width 2.91 m, Specialty and industrial
Finishing Equipment:
 Supercalenders: 4
 Sheeters: 2
Energy Data:
 Power boilers: 2
 Steam turbines at 2.0 MW

ⓄⓂToyama Seishi KK
Toyama Mill
3-14 Shimoshinnishi-machi
Toyama-shi, Toyama Pref., 930-0807
Japan
 Phone: (81) 76 432 1147
 Fax: (81) 76 431 4498
Personnel:
 Pres.: Toshiharu Terasaki
 Phone: (81) 76 432 1147
 Mill Mgr.: Michiya Ito
 Phone: (81) 76 432 1147
Total Employees of Company: 94
Total Employees at this Location: 80
Type of Operation: Paperboard mill
Pulp Grades and Capacities:
 Total pulp capacity: 118,523 mt/y
 Chemical Pulp: 94,818 mt/y
 Recycled Pulping: 23,705 mt/y
Pulp Mill Data:
 Chemical Pulping Systems:
 Continuous digesters: 1
 Chemical Recovery Equipment:
 Recovery boilers: 1
 Lime Kiln
 Recycled Fiber Treatment Lines:
 Recycled packaging pulping lines: 1
Paper/Paperboard Grades and Capacities:
 Total paper and paperboard capacity: 115,000 mt/y
 Corrugating medium/fluting: 115,000 mt/y
Paper and Paperboard Mill Data:
 Stock Preparation:
 Pulpers: 2
 Refiners: 3
Paper Machines: 2
 No. 3, Ultraformer, total capacity 43,000 mt/y, Trim width 3.3 m, Corrugating medium/fluting
 No. 5, fourdrinier, total capacity 72,000 mt/y, Trim width 3.3 m, Corrugating medium/fluting
Energy Data:
 Power boilers: 2
 Combustion turbines: 2 at 9.0 MW
 Electrical demand for mill: 243 MWh/D

ⓄⓂToyo Paper Mfg. Co., Ltd.
Shikokuchuo-shi Mill
1952-1 Shimowake Kinsei-cho
Shikokuchuo-shi, Ehime Pref., 799-0111
Japan
 Phone: (81) 896 58 3456
 Fax: (81) 896 58 0702
 Email: soumuka@toyo-paper.co.jp
 Web Address: www.toyo-paper.co.jp
Personnel:
 Pres.: Yuji Nagano
 Phone: (81) 896 58 3456
Total Employees at this Location: 188
Type of Operation: Paper mill
Pulp Grades and Capacities:
 Total pulp capacity: 25,840 mt/y
 Recycled Pulping: 25,840 mt/y
Pulp Mill Data:
 Recycled Fiber Treatment Lines:
 Flotation deinking lines: 1
Paper/Paperboard Grades and Capacities:
 Total paper and paperboard capacity: 36,000 mt/y
 Tissue: 30,000 mt/y
 Specialty and industrial: 6,000 mt/y
Paper and Paperboard Mill Data:
Paper Machines: 9
 No. 1, Yankee dryer, total capacity 1,000 mt/y, Trim width 1.8 m, Specialty and industrial
 No. 2, Yankee dryer, total capacity 1,000 mt/y, Trim width 1.8 m, Specialty and industrial
 No. 3, Yankee dryer, total capacity 1,000 mt/y, Trim width 1.8 m, Specialty and industrial
 No. 5, twin-wire, Yankee dryer, total capacity 6,000 mt/y, Trim width 1.8 m, Tissue
 No. 6, twin-wire, Yankee dryer, total capacity 6,000 mt/y, Trim width 1.8 m, Tissue
 No. 7, twin-wire, Yankee dryer, total capacity 18,000 mt/y, Trim width 2.7 m, Tissue
 H1, Yankee dryer, total capacity 1,000 mt/y, Trim width 1.3 m, Specialty and industrial
 H2, Yankee dryer, total capacity 1,000 mt/y, Trim width 1.3 m, Specialty and industrial
 T1, Yankee dryer, total capacity 1,000 mt/y, Trim width 1.3 m, Specialty and industrial
Energy Data:
 Power boilers
 Electrical demand for mill: 115 MWh/D

Jordan

ⓗⓜToyo Tokushi Seishi K.K
Kochi Mill
112-1, Saiwaicho, Inocho
Agawa-Gun, Kochi Pref., 781-2103
Japan
 Phone: (81) 88 892 0058
 Fax: (81) 88 893 4808
 Email: ga-ty@ninus.ocn.ne.jp
 Web Address: www.toyotokushi.jp
Total Employees at this Location: 55
Type of Operation: Paper mill
Paper/Paperboard Grades and Capacities:
 Total paper and paperboard capacity: 2,360 mt/y
 Tissue: 2,360 mt/y
Paper and Paperboard Mill Data:
Paper Machines: 2
 No. 1, total capacity 960 mt/y, Trim width 1.21 m, Tissue
 No. 2, total capacity 1,400 mt/y, Trim width 1.21 m, Tissue

ⓗⓜYamakyo Paper Mills Ltd.
Honsha Fuji Mill
Kawanarijima 213
Fuji-shi, Shizuoka Pref., 416-0939
Japan
 Phone: (81) 545 61 0221
 Fax: (81) 545 64 2054
Personnel:
 Pres.: Nobuhide Yamada
 Phone: (81) 545 61 0221
Total Employees at this Location: 65
Type of Operation: Paper mill
Paper/Paperboard Grades and Capacities:
 Total paper and paperboard capacity: 24,000 mt/y
Paper and Paperboard Mill Data:
Paper Machines: 2
 No. 2, cylinder, total capacity 12,000 mt/y, Trim width 1.7 m
 No. 3, cylinder, total capacity 12,000 mt/y, Trim width 1.8 m

ⓗⓜYame Seishisho Co., Ltd.
Yame-shi Mill
624 Oaza Tadami
Yame-shi, Fukuoka Pref., 834-0014
Japan
 Phone: (81) 943 22 4161
 Fax: (81) 943 24 5108
Personnel:
 Pres.: Yoshiaki Sasabuchi
 Phone: (81) 943 22 4161
Total Employees of Company: 50
Total Employees at this Location: 47
Type of Operation: Paper mill
Pulp Grades and Capacities:
 Total pulp capacity: 5,408 mt/y
 Recycled Pulping: 5,408 mt/y
Pulp Mill Data:
 Recycled Fiber Treatment Lines:
 Flotation deinking lines
Paper/Paperboard Grades and Capacities:
 Total paper and paperboard capacity: 5,000 mt/y
 Tissue: 5,000 mt/y
Paper and Paperboard Mill Data:
Paper Machines: 2
 No. 1, Yankee dryer, total capacity 2,500 mt/y, Trim width 1.17 m, Tissue
 No. 2, Yankee dryer, total capacity 2,500 mt/y, Trim width 1.17 m, Tissue
Energy Data:
 Power boilers: 1
 Electrical demand for mill: 17 MWh/D

ⓗⓜYawatahama Shigyo K.K
Yawatahama Mill
1280, Showa street
Yawatahama, Ehime Pref., 796-0033
Japan
 Phone: (81) 894 23 2121
 Fax: (81) 894 24 1331
Personnel:
 Chmn.: Toshikiyo Kikuchi
Total Employees at this Location: 27
Type of Operation: Paper mill
Paper/Paperboard Grades and Capacities:
 Total paper and paperboard capacity: 5,000 mt/y
 Tissue: 5,000 mt/y
Paper and Paperboard Mill Data:
Paper Machines: 2
 No. 1, cylinder, Yankee dryer, total capacity 2,500 mt/y, Trim width 1.8 m, Tissue
 No. 2, cylinder, Yankee dryer, total capacity 2,500 mt/y, Trim width 1.8 m, Tissue

JORDAN

ⓗⓜAl Alamiyya Paper Mill
Amman Mill
Amman
Jordan
Type of Operation: Paper mill
Paper/Paperboard Grades and Capacities:
 Total paper and paperboard capacity: 2,000 mt/y
 Tissue: 2,000 mt/y

ⓜAl Keena Hygienic Paper Mill Co. Ltd.
Amman Mill
Ownership: 100% by Nuqul Group
Queen Rania Airport Street
11118 Al-Jiza, Amman
Jordan
Mailing Address: PO Box 154, 11118 Amman, Jordan
 Phone: (962) 6440 3001
 Fax: (962) 6440 3003
 Email: alkeena@complex.nuqul.com.jo, nt@nuqulgroup.com
 Web Address: www.alkeena.com, www.nuqulgroup.com
Personnel:
 Man. Dir.: Hani Nuqul
 Phone: (962) 6 440 3001
 Email: hnuqul@nuqulgroup.com
 Mill Mgr.: Hisham Ahmad
 Phone: (962) 6 440 3001
 Email: hahmed@nuqulgroup.com
 Sls. Dir.: Osama Diab
 Phone: (962) 6 440 3001
 Email: odiab@nuqulgroup.com
 Prod. Mgr.: Khalid Banat
 Phone: (962) 6 440 3001
 Email: kbanat@nuqulgroup.com
 Head of Procurement Section: Linda Al Masri
 Phone: (962) 6 440 3001
 Email: masri@nuqulgroup.com
 R&D Mgr.: Nidal Zeidan
 Phone: (962) 6 440 3001
 Business Development & Marketing: Raed Abu-Laban
 Phone: (962) 6 440 3001
 Nuqul Tissue Oper. Dir.: Robert Walker
 Phone: (962) 6 440 3001
 Admin. Mgr.: Emad Alwak
 Phone: (962) 6 440 3001
Total Employees at this Location: 1,000
Type of Operation: Paper mill
Paper/Paperboard Grades and Capacities:
 Total paper and paperboard capacity: 30,000 mt/y
 Tissue: 30,000 mt/y
Paper and Paperboard Mill Data:
 Stock Preparation:
 Pulpers: 2
 Refiners: 2
Paper Machines: 1
 No. 2, twin-wire, Yankee dryer, total capacity 30,000 mt/y, Trim width 3.52 m, Tissue, Uncoated woodfree/freesheet
Finishing Equipment:
 Winders: 3 at 30,000 mt/y
 Calenders: 1
 Supercalenders: 1 at 30,000 mt/y
 Rewinders: 1 at 30,000 mt/y
Energy Data:
 Power boilers: 1
 Combustion turbines: 1
 Electrical demand for mill: 72 MWh/D

ⓜAl Snobar Hygienic Paper Mill
Amman Mill
Ownership: 100% by Nuqul Group
Queen Rania Airport Street
11118 Al-Jiza, Amman
Jordan
Mailing Address: P.O. Box 154, 11118 Amman, Jordan
 Phone: (962) 6440 3001
 Fax: (962) 6440 3003
 Email: alsnobar@nuqulgroup.com, nt@nuqulgroup.com
 Web Address: www.nuqultissue.com
Personnel:
 Site Oper. Mgr.: Waheed Al Qannas
 Phone: (962) 6440 3001
 Fax: (962) 6440 3003
 Mgr.: Mr. Adel Afar
 Phone: (962) 6 440 3001 Ext. 128
 Fax: (962) 6440 3003
Total Employees at this Location: 1,000
Type of Operation: Paper mill
Paper/Paperboard Grades and Capacities:
 Total paper and paperboard capacity: 54,000 mt/y
 Tissue: 54,000 mt/y
Paper and Paperboard Mill Data:
Paper Machines: 1
 No. 4, Advantage DCT 200 TS, Yankee dryer, total capacity 54,000 mt/y, Trim width 5.4 m, Tissue
Energy Data:
 Power boilers
 Combustion turbines: 1
 Electrical demand for mill: 137 MWh/D

ⓗArab Cardboard Mfg. Co.
Ownership: Atlas Paper Industries, Michel Abu-Aitah, Tamas Abu-Aitah, Tawfiq Abut-Aitah
P.O. Box 15, Abdulla II Bin Al-Hussein, Industrial Estate
Sahab
Jordan
 Phone: (962) 6-4022870/1
 Fax: (962) 6-4022869
Mill Locations:
Arab Cardboard Mfg. Co., Sahab Mill, P.O. Box 15, Abdulla II Bin Al-Hussein, Industrial Estate, Sahab, Jordan, Capacity: 15,000 mt/y, (Paper mill)
 Phone: (962) 6-4022870/1
 Fax: (962) 6-4022869

ⓜArab Cardboard Mfg. Co.
Sahab Mill
P.O. Box 15, Abdulla II Bin Al-Hussein, Industrial Estate
Sahab
Jordan
 Phone: (962) 6-4022870/1
 Fax: (962) 6-4022869
 Web Address: arabcardboard.abuaitah.com
Personnel:
 Chmn./Board of Dir.: Tawfiq G. Abut-Aitah
 Phone: (962) 6-4022870/1
 Member/Board of Dir.: Michel G. Abut-Aitah
 Phone: (962) 6-4022870/1
 Member/Board of Dir.: Tanas G. Abut-Aitah
 Phone: (962) 6-4022870/1
Total Employees at this Location: 135
Type of Operation: Paper mill

Kazakhstan

Pulp Grades and Capacities:
Total pulp capacity: 14,949 mt/y
Recycled Pulping: 14,949 mt/y
Paper/Paperboard Grades and Capacities:
Total paper and paperboard capacity: 15,000 mt/y
Corrugating medium/fluting: 15,000 mt/y
Paper and Paperboard Mill Data:
Stock Preparation:
Pulpers: 2
Refiners: 2
Paper Machines: 1
No. 1, fourdrinier, total capacity 15,000 mt/y, Trim width 2.2 m, Corrugating medium/fluting
Finishing Equipment:
Rewinders: 1
Energy Data:
Power boilers: 1
Electrical demand for mill: 22 MWh/D

ⓘⓜJordan Paper & Cardboard Factories Co. Ltd.
Zarka Mill
PO Box 1051
13110 Awajan, Zarka
Jordan
  Phone: (962) 5 3650411
  Fax: (962) 5 3650481
  Email: jopaper@nets.com.jo
Personnel:
  Chmn.: Rouf Abu Jaber
  Phone: (962) 5 3650411
  Gen. Mgr.: Usama Alami
  Phone: (962) 79 6151515
  Plant Mgr.: Sulaiman Naser
  Phone: (962) 777 514238
  Mktg. & Sls. Mgr.: Hani Sa'adeh
  Phone: (962) 79 5537796
  Purch. Dept.: Mohammad Assad
  Phone: (962) 79 6844366
Total Employees at this Location: 170
Type of Operation: Paperboard mill
Pulp Grades and Capacities:
Total pulp capacity: 75,836 mt/y
Recycled Pulping: 75,836 mt/y
Paper/Paperboard Grades and Capacities:
Total paper and paperboard capacity: 75,000 mt/y
Linerboard: 42,000 mt/y
Corrugating medium/fluting: 28,000 mt/y
Boxboard/cartonboard: 5,000 mt/y
Paper and Paperboard Mill Data:
Stock Preparation:
Pulpers: 1
Refiners: 1
Paper Machines: 2
No. 2, fourdrinier (2), total capacity 15,000 mt/y, Trim width 2.6 m, Corrugating medium/fluting, Linerboard
No. 3, fourdrinier (2), total capacity 60,000 mt/y, Trim width 2.5 m, Corrugating medium/fluting, Linerboard, Boxboard/cartonboard
Finishing Equipment:
Winders: 1 at 60 mt/y
Calenders: 1
Supercalenders: 1
Rewinders: 1 at 60 mt/y
Sheeters: 1
Energy Data:
Power boilers: 3
Electrical demand for mill: 110 MWh/D

ⓘⓜMillenium Paper Mill
Sokhna, Zarqa Mill
Company is planning to relocate its tissue machine from Al Zarka to Abu Dhabi, UAE during 2014.
Ownership: 100% by Emirates Co., UAE
PO Box 9190
13498 Sokhna, Zarqa
Jordan
  Phone: (962) 5 3811145
  Fax: (962) 5 3811361

Personnel:
  Gen. Mgr.: Mohammad Al-Zoubi
  Phone: (962) 5 3811145
  Dpty. Gen. Mgr., Tech. Affairs: Ibrahim Bsieso
  Phone: (962) 5 3811145
  Finan. Mgr.: Sameeh Mestarehi
  Phone: (962) 5 3811145
Total Employees at this Location: 140
Type of Operation: Paper mill
Pulp Grades and Capacities:
Total pulp capacity: 12,000 mt/y
Pulp Mill Data:
Recycled Fiber Treatment Lines:
Flotation deinking lines: 2
Pulpers: 1 at 5,000 admt/y
Washing deinking lines: 2
Paper/Paperboard Grades and Capacities:
Total paper and paperboard capacity: 10,000 mt/y
Tissue: 10,000 mt/y
Paper and Paperboard Mill Data:
Stock Preparation:
Pulpers: 1
Refiners: 1
Paper Machines: 1
No. 1, crescent former, total capacity 10,000 mt/y, Trim width 2.7 m, Tissue
Finishing Equipment:
Rewinders: 1 at 10,000 mt/y

ⓘNuqul Group
Ownership: 100% by Mr. Elia Nuqul & Sons
Mohammad Ali Aldeir str, Abound bldg # 84
11118 Amman
Jordan
Mailing Address: P.O. Box 154, 11118 Amman, Jordan
  Phone: (962) 6 4652688
  Fax: (962) 6 4645669
  Email: infocenter@nuqulgroup.com
  Web Address: www.nuqulgroup.com
Personnel:
  CEO: Eng. Salim Karadsheh
  Phone: (962) 6 4652688
  Fax: (962) 6 4645669
  Email: skaradsheh@nuqulgroup.com
  Corp. Purch. Mgr.: Hadi Sayess
  Phone: (962) 6 4652688
  Fax: (962) 6 4645669
  Email: hsayess@nuqulgroup.com
Total Employees of Company: 5,500
Total Employees at this Location: 270
Mill Locations:
Al Bardi Paper Mill Co. (S.A.E.), 6 October City Mill, 4th Industrial zone, 6 October City, Egypt, Capacity: 20,000 mt/y, (Paper mill)
  Phone: (20) 23 8330960/1922
  Fax: (20) 23 8330747
  Email: bpm@link.net, nt@nuqulgroup.com
Al Keena Hygienic Paper Mill Co. Ltd., Amman Mill, Queen Rania Airport Street, 11118 Al-Jiza, Amman, Jordan, Capacity: 30,000 mt/y, (Paper mill)
  Phone: (962) 6440 3001
  Fax: (962) 6440 3003
  Email: alkeena@complex.nuqul.com.jo, nt@nuqulgroup.com
Al Sindian Paper Mill Co. S.A.E., 6 October City Mill, Plot 49-51, 4th Industrial Zone, 6 October City, Egypt, Capacity: 54,000 mt/y, (Paper mill)
  Phone: (20) 2 38330960/1922/1923
  Fax: (20) 2 8330747
  Email: shabib@albardifine.com, nt@nuqulgroup.com
Al Snobar Hygienic Paper Mill, Amman Mill, Queen Rania Airport Street, 11118 Al-Jiza, Amman, Jordan, Capacity: 54,000 mt/y, (Paper mill)
  Phone: (962) 6440 3001
  Fax: (962) 6440 3003
  Email: alsnobar@nuqulgroup.com, nt@nuqulgroup.com

KAZAKHSTAN

ⓜAlmaty Maolin Paper
Almaty Mill
Ownership: Xinjiang Tianhong Paper Co., Ltd.
Karasai District, Almaty Obl.
Kazakhstan
Type of Operation: Paper mill
Paper/Paperboard Grades and Capacities:
Total paper and paperboard capacity: 5,000 mt/y
Tissue: 5,000 mt/y
Paper and Paperboard Mill Data:
Paper Machines: 2
No. 1, (leased from Maolin Paper), total capacity 2,500 mt/y, Trim width 1.09 m, Tissue
No. 2, (leased from Maolin Paper), total capacity 2,500 mt/y, Trim width 1.76 m, Tissue

ⓘKazakhstan Kagazy
Ownership: 27.50% by Phoenicia Capital LLC, 29.90% by Employee Benefit Trust
86, Khadzhy Mukan Str, Business Centre Alma Tau, Medeu district
050020 Almaty
Kazakhstan
  Phone: (7) 727 244 87 87
  Fax: (7) 727 244 87 82
  Email: kagazy@kagazy.kz
  Web Address: www.kazakhstankagazy.com
Personnel:
  CEO: Tomas Mateos Werner
  Phone: (7) 727 244 87 87
  Fax: (7) 727 244 87 82
  Deputy CEO, Gen. Dir.: Mrs. Taissiya Kogutyuk
  Phone: (7) 727 244 87 87
  Fax: (7) 727 244 87 82
  Chairman of the Group: Sir Tony Baldry
  Acting Group CFO: Vitaliy Podolskiy
  Phone: (7) 727 244 87 87
  Fax: (7) 727 244 87 82
  Group as advisor to the CEO: Aida Yelgeldiyeva
  Phone: (7) 727 244 87 87
  Fax: (7) 727 244 87 82
  Group Head Paper Business: Jos van Lent
  Phone: (7) 727 244 87 87
  Fax: (7) 727 244 87 82
  Corp. Finan. & Investor Relations Dir., COB: Alessandro Manghi
  Phone: (7) 727 244 87 97/71
  Fax: (7) 727 244 87 71
  Email: a.manghi@kagazy.kz
  Head of PR Department: Nelly Kim
  Phone: (7) 727 244 87 36
  Fax: (7) 727 244 87 87
  Email: pr@kagazy.kz
Total Employees of Company: 1,200
Mill Locations:
Kagazy Recycling LLP, Almaty Mill, Abai Village, 040905 Karasai district, Almaty, Kazakhstan, Capacity: 72,000 mt/y, (Paperboard mill)
  Phone: (7) 727 2 980 371 /727 3201200
  Fax: (7) 727 2 375272
  Email: kagazy@kagazy.kz; info@kagazy.kz

ⓜKagazy Recycling LLP
Almaty Mill
Ownership: 100% by Kazakhstan Kagazy
Abai Village
040905 Karasai district, Almaty, Almaty Obl.
Kazakhstan
  Phone: (7) 727 2 980 371 /727 3201200
  Fax: (7) 727 2 375272
  Email: kagazy@kagazy.kz, info@kagazy.kz
  Web Address: www.kazakhstankagazy.com
Personnel:
  Gen. Dir. (Eff. October 2014): Bolat Uternisov

Kuwait

Phone: (7) 727 2 980 370
Fax: (7) 727 2 375 272
Tech. Dir.: Yuriy Ermakov
Phone: (7) 727 2 980 370
Fax: (7) 727 2 375 272
Paper Technology Dir.: Olga Sitnikova
Phone: (7) 727 2 980 370
Fax: (7) 727 2 375 272
Mktg. Dept. Kseniya Shilina
Phone: (7) 727 2 448 802
Email: x.shilina@kagazy.kz
Mgr.: Oleg Sannikov
Phone: (7) 727 3 201 200
Fax: (7) 727 2 375 272
Email: o.sannikov@kagazy.kz
Waste paper collection Mgr.: Igor Savitskiy
Phone: (7) 727 3 201 200
Fax: (7) 727 2 375 272
Email: i.savitskiy@kagazy.kz
Total Employees at this Location: 706
Type of Operation: Paperboard mill
Paper/Paperboard Grades and Capacities:
Total paper and paperboard capacity: 72,000 mt/y
Linerboard: 28,800 mt/y
Corrugating medium/fluting: 43,200 mt/y
Paper and Paperboard Mill Data:
Stock Preparation:
Pulpers: 1
Paper Machines: 2
No. 1, (second hand), total capacity 36,000 mt/y, Corrugating medium/fluting, Linerboard
No. 2, (second hand), total capacity 36,000 mt/y, Linerboard, Corrugating medium/fluting
Energy Data:
Power boilers: 3

ⓘ Karina Trading PLC
264 Kazybayev Str.
05014 Almaty, Almaty Obl.
Kazakhstan
Phone: (7) 727 2 3841718/77/16
Fax: (7) 727 2 3841718/77
Email: info@karina.kz,
agasi@zavaryan.com
Web Address: www.karina.kz
Mill Locations:
Karina Trading PLC, Almaty Mill, 264 Kazybayev Str., 05014 Almaty, Kazakhstan, Capacity: 18,000 mt/y, (Paper mill)
Phone: (7) 727 2 3841718/77/16
Fax: (7) 727 2 3841718/77
Email: info@karina.kz; agasi@zavaryan.com

ⓘⓜ Karina Trading PLC
Almaty Mill
264 Kazybayev Str.
05014 Almaty, Almaty Obl.
Kazakhstan
Phone: (7) 727 2 3841718/77/16
Fax: (7) 727 2 3841718/77
Email: info@karina.kz,
agasi@zavaryan.com
Web Address: www.karina.kz
Personnel:
Man. Dir.: Airas Volodyevich Gevorkyan
Phone: (7) 727 2 3841718/77/16
Chief Eng.: Aleksandr Anatolyevich Yarin
Phone: (7) 7014294166
Prod.Dir.: Oganes Azatovich Navosordyan
Com.Dir. and Deputy Dir.: Khachatur Achaganovich Sarkhoshyan
Fin. Mgr.: Svetlana Valerievna Bobrova
Total Employees at this Location: 300
Type of Operation: Paper mill
Paper/Paperboard Grades and Capacities:
Total paper and paperboard capacity: 18,000 mt/y
Tissue: 18,000 mt/y
Paper and Paperboard Mill Data:
Paper Machines: 1
PM 1, (second hand), total capacity 18,000 mt/y, Trim width 2.4 m, Tissue
Energy Data:
Power boilers: 3

KUWAIT

ⓘⓜ Gulf Paper Mfg. Co. k.s.c.
Kuwait Mill
Ownership: 88% by Al-Moasherji & Al-Rashid Group
Plot 3, Block 43, West Shuaiba Industrial Area
West Mina Abdulla, Ahmadi Governorate
Kuwait
Mailing Address: PO Box 7506, 64006 Al-Fahaheel, Kuwait
Phone: (965) 3262072/69
Fax: (965) 3263778
Email: gpmc@gulfpaper.com.kw
Web Address: www.gulfpaper.com
Personnel:
Chmn.: Mohd Saqer Al-Mousherji
Phone: (965) 3262072/69
Dpty. Chrmn.: Ali Mohd Al-Rashid
Phone: (965) 3262072/69
Bd. Mbr.: Saqer Ahmed Al-Moasherji
Phone: (965) 3262072/69
Gen. Mgr.: Tareq Mohammed Al-Moasherji
Phone: (965) 3262072/69
Fax: (965) 3262058
Man. Dir./Prod. Mgr.: Ghaleb Al-Hadhrami
Phone: (965) 3262072/69
Email: gpmc@gulfpaper.com.kw
Qlty. Control Mgr.: Quaim Hussain Shah
Phone: (965) 3262072/69
Email: gpmc@gulfpaper.com.kw
Purch. Dir.: Basel Ahmed Al-Moasherji
Phone: (965) 3262072/69
Email: purchase@gulfpaper.com.kw
Sls./Mktg. Mgr.: Hussain Mohammed Ghaddar
Phone: (965) 3262072/69
Fax: (965) 3263926
Finan. & Admin. Mgr.: Wagih I. Masoud
Phone: (965) 3262072/69
Total Employees at this Location: 373
Type of Operation: Paper mill, Paperboard mill
Mill Locations:
Gulf Paper Manufacturing Free Zone Company, Dubai Mill, P.O. Box 18075 J.A., Jebel Ali Free Zone, Dubai, United Arab Emirates, Capacity: 55,000 mt/y, (Paperboard mill)
Phone: (971) 4 883 3885
Fax: (971) 4 883 34418
Email: gpmc@emirates.net.ae
Pulp Grades and Capacities:
Total pulp capacity: 49,536 mt/y
Recycled Pulping: 49,536 mt/y
Pulp Mill Data:
Recycled Fiber Treatment Lines:
Recycled packaging pulping lines: 1
Paper/Paperboard Grades and Capacities:
Total paper and paperboard capacity: 65,000 mt/y
Tissue: 15,000 mt/y
Linerboard: 20,000 mt/y
Corrugating medium/fluting: 25,000 mt/y
Boxboard/cartonboard: 5,000 mt/y
Paper and Paperboard Mill Data:
Stock Preparation:
Pulpers: 4
Refiners: 3
Paper Machines: 2
No. 1, fourdrinier (2), total capacity 50,000 mt/y, Trim width 2.3 m, Corrugating medium/fluting, Linerboard, Boxboard/cartonboard
No. 2, Periformer, Yankee dryer, total capacity 15,000 mt/y, Trim width 2.2 m, Tissue, Uncoated woodfree/freesheet

PM 1, (second hand), total capacity 18,000 mt/y, Trim width 2.4 m, Tissue
Energy Data:
Power boilers: 3

Finishing Equipment:
Rewinders: 3 at 60,000 mt/y
Sheeters: 1
Energy Data:
Power boilers: 2
Electrical demand for mill: 116 MWh/D

ⓘⓜ United Paper Industries
Shuaiba Mill
Shuaiba Industrial Area
13052 Kuwait City
Kuwait
Phone: (965) 23260501
Fax: (965) 23260508
Personnel:
Gen. Mgr.: Dikheel Al-Dikheel
Total Employees at this Location: 115
Type of Operation: Paper mill
Pulp Grades and Capacities:
Total pulp capacity: 55,017 mt/y
Recycled Pulping: 55,017 mt/y
Pulp Mill Data:
Recycled Fiber Treatment Lines:
Recycled packaging pulping lines: 1
Paper/Paperboard Grades and Capacities:
Total paper and paperboard capacity: 60,000 mt/y
Packaging papers: 20,000 mt/y
Linerboard: 20,000 mt/y
Corrugating medium/fluting: 15,000 mt/y
Boxboard/cartonboard: 5,000 mt/y
Paper and Paperboard Mill Data:
Paper Machines: 1
No. 1, fourdrinier, total capacity 60,000 mt/y, Trim width 2.6 m, Packaging papers, Linerboard, Corrugating medium/fluting, Boxboard/cartonboard
Energy Data:
Power boilers
Electrical demand for mill: 89 MWh/D

KYRGYZSTAN

ⓜ OOO Altyn Ajydaar
Bishkek Mill
ul. Isakeeva, 1a
720048 Bishkek
Kyrgyzstan
Phone: (996) 312 632086/53/67
Fax: (996) 312 632067
Email: admin@altynbox.kg,
otdel-kadrov@altynbox.kg,
altyn_adr@mail.ru
Web Address: www.altynbox.kg
Personnel:
Mill Mgr.: Pavel Terekhov
Phone: (996) 312 632086/53/67
Tech. Dir.: Vyacheslav Terekhov
Phone: (996) 312 632086/53/67
Sls. Mgr.: Alik Terekhov
Phone: (996) 312 632086/53/67
Sls. Mgr.: Evgeniy Borisovich Nisnevich
Phone: (996) 312 632147
Type of Operation: Paper mill
Paper/Paperboard Grades and Capacities:
Total paper and paperboard capacity: 9,000 mt/y
Corrugating medium/fluting: 9,000 mt/y
Paper and Paperboard Mill Data:
Paper Machines: 1
PM 1, cylinder, Yankee dryer, total capacity 9,000 mt/y, Trim width 1.6 m, Corrugating medium/fluting
Energy Data:
Power boilers: 2

ⓘ Amal
ul. Lermontova, 1A Bishkek, 720000
Bishkek
Kyrgyzstan

Phone: (996) 312 365826/679
Fax: (996) 312 365826
Email: spamal@mail.ru
Personnel:
Dir.: Akhmed Ibragimovich Uzhakhov
Phone: (996) 996 312 365826
Fax: (996) 996 312 365826
Prod. Mgr.: Aleksamdr Fedorovich Kolodyazhnyj
Phone: (996) 996 312 365826
Fax: (996) 996 312 365826
Sls. Mgr.: Vilen Tursunovich Gaparov
Phone: (996) 996 312 365826
Fax: (996) 996 312 365826
Total Employees of Company: 54
Mill Locations:
Amal, Bishkek Mill, ul. Lermontova, 1A, 720000 Bishkek, Kyrgyzstan, Capacity: 1,400 mt/y, (Paper mill)
Phone: (996) 312 365826/679
Fax: (996) 312 365826
Email: spamal@mail.ru

ⓜAmal
Bishkek Mill
ul. Lermontova, 1A
720000 Bishkek
Kyrgyzstan
Phone: (996) 312 365826/679
Fax: (996) 312 365826
Email: spamal@mail.ru
Personnel:
Dir.: Akhmed Ibragimovich Uzhakhov
Phone: (996) 312 365826/679
Prod. Mgr.: Aleksamdr Fedorovich Kolodyazhnyj
Phone: (996) 312 365826/679
Sls. Mgr.: Vilen Tursunovich Gaparov
Phone: (996) 312 365826/679
Total Employees at this Location: 54
Type of Operation: Paper mill
Paper/Paperboard Grades and Capacities:
Total paper and paperboard capacity: 1,400 mt/y
Tissue: 1,400 mt/y
Paper and Paperboard Mill Data:
Paper Machines: 2
No. 1, total capacity 700 mt/y, Trim width 1.4 m, Tissue
No. 2, total capacity 700 mt/y, Trim width 1.4 m, Tissue
Energy Data:
Electrical demand for mill: 4 MWh/D

ⓜKyrgyz-Chinese Paper Mill
Chuj-Tokmok Mill
Ownership: 72.50% by MCC Paper Group Co., Ltd., 27.50% by China National Complete Plant Import & Export Co. Ltd.
Promzona
724919 Chuj-Tokmok, Chujskaya Obl.
Kyrgyzstan
Phone: (996) 3138 55655
Fax: (996) 3138 55650
Personnel:
Mill Mgr.: Dujshobaj Omuralievich Omuraliev
Phone: (996) 3138 55655
Prod. Mgr.: Askarbek Kasenovich Tagaev
Phone: (996) 3138 55655
Sls. Mgr.: Talant Kuramaev
Phone: (996) 3138 55655
Type of Operation: Paper mill
Paper/Paperboard Grades and Capacities:
Total paper and paperboard capacity: 11,000 mt/y
Uncoated woodfree/freesheet: 10,000 mt/y
Tissue: 1,000 mt/y
Paper and Paperboard Mill Data:
Paper Machines: 2
PM 1, total capacity 10,000 mt/y, Trim width 0.8 m, Uncoated woodfree/freesheet
PM 2, total capacity 1,000 mt/y, Trim width 0.12 m, Tissue
Energy Data:
Electrical demand for mill: 3 MWh/D

ⓘOOO Altyn Ajydaar
Ownership: 68% by Pavel Terehov
ul. Isakeeva, 1a
720048 Bishkek
Kyrgyzstan
Phone: (996) 312 632086/53/67
Fax: (996) 312 632067
Email: admin@altynbox.kg, otdel-kadrov@altynbox.kg, altyn_adr@mail.ru
Web Address: www.altynbox.kg
Personnel:
Man. Dir.: Pavel Terekhov
Phone: (996) 312 632086/53/67
Fax: (996) 312 632067
Tech. Dir.: Vyacheslav Terekhov
Phone: (996) 312 632086/53/67
Fax: (996) 312 632067
Sls. Mgr.: Alik Terekhov
Phone: (996) 312 632086/53/67
Fax: (996) 312 632067
Mill Locations:
OOO Altyn Ajydaar, Bishkek Mill, ul. Isakeeva, 1a, 720048 Bishkek, Kyrgyzstan, Capacity: 9,000 mt/y, (Paper mill)
Phone: (996) 312 632086/53/67
Fax: (996) 312 632067
Email: admin@altynbox.kg; otdel-kadrov@altynbox.kg; altyn_adr@mail.ru

LAOS

ⓘLong Van
Huaphanh province
Laos
Mill Locations:
Long Van, Huaphanh province Mill, Huaphanh province, Laos, (Pulp mill)

ⓜLong Van
Huaphanh province Mill
Huaphanh province
Laos
Type of Operation: Pulp mill
Pulp Grades and Capacities:
Total pulp capacity: 36,000 mt/y

LEBANON

ⓘINDEVCO - Industrial Development Company sal
Tellet Al Assafir, Indevco Building
Ajaltoun, Kesrwan
Lebanon
Phone: (961) 9 230 130
Fax: (961) 9 235 541
Email: info@indevcogroup.com
Web Address: www.indevcogroup.com
Personnel:
Founder & Chairman: Georges Frem
Phone: (961) 9 230 130
Fax: (961) 9 235 541
CEO: Neemat Frem
Phone: (961) 9 230 130
Fax: (961) 9 235 541
Man. Dir.: Fayssal Frem
Phone: (961) 9 230 130
Fax: (961) 9 235 541
Email: fayssal.frem@indevcogroup.com
Total Employees of Company: 9,400
Mill Locations:
Interstate Paper Industries, Sadat City Mill, 85 km North of Cairo Desert Road, P.O. Box 165, Sadat City, Egypt, Capacity: 75,000 mt/y, (Paper mill)
Phone: (20) 4 8261 3080/77
Fax: (20) 4 8261 3076
Email: papermaking@indevcogroup.com , pcd@indevcogroup.com, info@ipitissue.com
Interstate Paper L.L.C., Riceboro Mill, 2366 Interstate Paper Rd, Riceboro, GA 31323, USA, Capacity: 317,717 mt/y, (Pulp mill, Paper mill, Paperboard mill)
Phone: (1) 912-884-3371
Fax: (1) 912-884-3426
Email: info@interstatepaper.com
Unipak Tissue Mill, Jbeil Mill, Old Seaside Road, Halat, Jbeil, Lebanon, Capacity: 18,000 mt/y, (Paper mill)
Phone: (961) 9 478911/2/3
Fax: (961) 9 478909
Email: exportsales@unipak-tissue-mill.com, customercare@utmlb.com
United Corrstack LLC, Reading Mill, 720 Laurel St, Reading, PA 19602, USA, Capacity: 156,753 mt/y, (Paperboard mill)
Phone: (1) 610-374-3000
Fax: (1) 610-376-8215
Email: info@InterstateResources.com

ⓘⓜMimosa Sanitary Paper
Kaa El Rim. Bekaa Mill
P.O. Box 38 Zahleh
Kaa El Rim. Bekaa
Lebanon
Phone: (961) 8 823 600
Fax: (961) 8 803 050
Email: info@mimosa.com.lb
Web Address: www.mimosa.com.lb
Personnel:
General Mgr.: Antoine Saliba
Phone: (961) 8 815 815
Prod. Mgr.: Mounir Saliba
Phone: (961) 8 823 600
Email: mimosa@mimosa.com.lb
HR Mgr.: George Saliba
Phone: (961) 8 823 600
Total Employees of Company: 550
Total Employees at this Location: 550
Type of Operation: Pulp mill, Paper mill, Paperboard mill
Pulp Grades and Capacities:
Total pulp capacity: 13,355 mt/y
Recycled Pulping: 13,355 mt/y
Pulp Mill Data:
Recycled Fiber Treatment Lines:
Pulpers
Paper/Paperboard Grades and Capacities:
Total paper and paperboard capacity: 29,000 mt/y
Tissue: 22,000 mt/y
Linerboard: 5,000 mt/y
Boxboard/cartonboard: 2,000 mt/y
Paper and Paperboard Mill Data:
Paper Machines: 4
No. 1, fourdrinier, Yankee dryer, total capacity 6,000 mt/y, Trim width 2.8 m, Tissue
No. 3, fourdrinier (2), total capacity 7,000 mt/y, Trim width 1.65 m, Linerboard, Boxboard/cartonboard
No. 4, crescent former, Yankee dryer, total capacity 7,000 mt/y, Trim width 2.3 m, Uncoated woodfree/freesheet, Tissue
No. 5, crescent former, Yankee dryer, total capacity 9,000 mt/y, Trim width 2.1 m, Tissue
Energy Data:
Power boilers: 1
Electrical demand for mill: 79 MWh/D

ⓘⓜNinex Paper
Beirut Mill
JAL EL DIB, METN
Beirut
Lebanon
Phone: (961) 961-04-718818
Personnel:
Dir: Mr. Marguerite Aboujaoudeh
Total Employees at this Location: 21
Type of Operation: Paper mill
Paper/Paperboard Grades and Capacities:

Malaysia

Total paper and paperboard capacity: 5,000 mt/y
Tissue: 5,000 mt/y

ⓘⓜSicomo S.A.L.
Kab-Elias, Bekaa Mill
Ownership: 100% by private owner
Kab-Elias, Bekaa
Lebanon
 Phone: (961) 8 500 550
 Fax: (961) 8 500 809
 Email: sicomo@sicomo.com.lb
 Web Address: www.sicomo.com.lb
Personnel:
 Mill Mgr.: Michel Ayoub
 Phone: (961) 8 500 550
 Email: gm@sicomo.com.lb
 Tech. Mgr. & Depty. Mill Mgr.: Karim Haddad
 Phone: (961) 8 500 550
 Email: technical@sicomo.com.lb
Total Employees of Company: 110
Total Employees at this Location: 110
Type of Operation: Paperboard mill
Pulp Grades and Capacities:
 Total pulp capacity: 23,823 mt/y
 Recycled Pulping: 23,823 mt/y
Paper/Paperboard Grades and Capacities:
 Total paper and paperboard capacity: 24,000 mt/y
 Boxboard/cartonboard: 24,000 mt/y
Paper and Paperboard Mill Data:
 Stock Preparation:
 Pulpers: 3
 Refiners: 4
Paper Machines: 1
No. 1, cylinder, blade, metering bar, total capacity 24,000 mt/y, Trim width 1.9 m, Boxboard/cartonboard
Finishing Equipment:
 Rewinders: 3 at 30,000 mt/y
 Sheeters: 2 at 30,000 mt/y
Energy Data:
 Power boilers: 3
 Electrical demand for mill: 32 MWh/D

ⓘⓜSIPCO-Soc. Ind. de Papier et de Carton Ondule SAL
Beirut Mill
Philimon Wehbe St.
Kfarchima, Beirut
Lebanon
Mailing Address: PO Box 11-4186, Kfarchima, Beirut, Lebanon
 Phone: (961) 5 433553/1048/0675
 Fax: (961) 5 433047
 Email: sipco@sipcolb.com
Personnel:
 Gen. Mgr./ Chmn.: Mohammad Gandour
 Phone: (961) 5 433553/1048/0675
 Admin. Asst. & Purch. Mgr.: Sara Hamoud
 Phone: (961) 5 433553/1048/0675
Total Employees at this Location: 80
Type of Operation: Paperboard mill
Paper/Paperboard Grades and Capacities:
 Total paper and paperboard capacity: 15,000 mt/y
 Containerboard
 Linerboard
 Corrugating medium/fluting
 Boxboard/cartonboard: 15,000 mt/y
Paper and Paperboard Mill Data:
 Stock Preparation:
 Pulpers: 5
 Refiners: 3
Paper Machines: 1
No. 1, cylinder, fourdrinier, total capacity 15,000 mt/y, Trim width 1.9 m
Coating Machines: 3
No. 1, on machine
No. 2, on machine
No. 3, on machine
Finishing Equipment:
 Supercalenders: 2
 Rewinders: 1
 Sheeters: 1
Energy Data:
 Power boilers: 3

ⓜSOLICAR-Société Libanaise de Carton
Beirut Mill
Sin-El-Fil, Wadi Chahrour
55017 Beirut
Lebanon
Mailing Address: P.O. Box 14, Wadi Chahrour, Lebanon
 Phone: (961) 5 940403
 Fax: (961) 5 940409
 Email: solicar@sodetel.net.lb, contact@solicar.com
 Web Address: www.solicar.com
Personnel:
 Chmn./Gen. Mgr.: Dr. Fady Gemayel
 Phone: (961) 5 940248
 Email: fjg@solicar.com
 Oper. Mgr.: Mr. Hady Kik
 Phone: (961) 594 0248
Total Employees at this Location: 200
Type of Operation: Paperboard mill
Pulp Grades and Capacities:
 Total pulp capacity: 56,014 mt/y
 Recycled Pulping: 56,014 mt/y
Paper/Paperboard Grades and Capacities:
 Total paper and paperboard capacity: 55,000 mt/y
 Linerboard: 35,000 mt/y
 Boxboard/cartonboard: 20,000 mt/y
Paper and Paperboard Mill Data:
 Stock Preparation:
 Pulpers: 3
 Refiners: 8
Paper Machines: 1
No. 1, fourdrinier (2), total capacity 55,000 mt/y, Trim width 2.6 m, Linerboard, Boxboard/cartonboard
Finishing Equipment:
 Rewinders: 1 at 50,000 mt/y
 Sheeters: 1
Energy Data:
 Power boilers: 2
 Electrical demand for mill: 79 MWh/D

ⓘSOLICAR-Société Libanaise de Carton
Ownership: 100% by S.A.L
Sin-El-Fil, Wadi Chahrour
55017 Beirut
Lebanon
Mailing Address: P.O. Box 14, Wadi Chahrour
 Phone: (961) 5 940403
 Fax: (961) 5 940409
 Email: solicar@sodetel.net.lb, contact@solicar.com
 Web Address: www.solicar.com
Personnel:
 Chmn. & Gen. Mgr.: Fady Gemayel
 Phone: (961) 5 940248
 Fax: (961) 5 940409
 Oper. Mgr.: Hady Kik
 Phone: (961) 5 940248
 Fax: (961) 5 940409
 Prod. Mgr.: Joe Varkat
 Phone: (961) 5 940403
 Fax: (961) 5 940409
Total Employees of Company: 200
Mill Locations:
SOLICAR-Société Libanaise de Carton, Beirut Mill, Sin-El-Fil, Wadi Chahrour, 55017 Beirut, Lebanon, Capacity: 55,000 mt/y, (Paperboard mill)
 Phone: (961) 5 940403
 Fax: (961) 5 940409
 Email: solicar@sodetel.net.lb, contact@solicar.com

ⓜUnipak Tissue Mill
Jbeil Mill
Ownership: Interstate Resources, Inc.
Old Seaside Road, Halat
Jbeil, Jounieh
Lebanon
Mailing Address: P.O.Box: 22, Jounieh, Lebanon
 Phone: (961) 9 478911/2/3
 Fax: (961) 9 478909
 Email: exportsales@unipak-tissue-mill.com, customercare@utmlb.com
 Web Address: www.unipak-tissue-mill.com
Personnel:
 Gen. Mgr.: Elie Farhat
 Phone: (961) 9 478911
 Fax: (961) 9 478909
 Email: elie.farhat@utmlb.com
 Mill. Mgr.: Elias Salim
 Phone: (961) 9 478911
 Fax: (961) 9 478909
 Email: elias.selim@utmlb.com
 Process Improv. Mgr.: Jihad Hasrouni
 Phone: (961) 9 478911
 Fax: (961) 9 478909
 Email: jihad.hasrouni@utmlb.com
 Maint. Mgr.: Christian Karam
 Phone: (961) 9 478911
 Fax: (961) 9 478909
 Qlty. Assur & Cust. Care Mgr.: Claudine Daccache
 Phone: (961) 9 478911
 Fax: (961) 9 478909
 Email: claudine.daccache@utmlb.com
 Tech. Mgr.: Marc Azzi
 Phone: (961) 9 478911
 Fax: (961) 9 478909
 Email: marc.azzi@utmlb.com
 Commer. Mgr.: Ibrahim Baz
 Phone: (961) 9 478911
 Fax: (961) 9 478909
 Email: ibrahim.baz@utmlb.com
 Export Sls. Mgr.: Georges Zouein
 Phone: (961) 9 478911
 Fax: (961) 9 478909
 Email: georges.zouein@utmlb.com
Total Employees at this Location: 60
Type of Operation: Paper mill
Pulp Grades and Capacities:
 Total pulp capacity: 10,037 mt/y
 Recycled Pulping: 10,037 mt/y
Pulp Mill Data:
 Recycled Fiber Treatment Lines:
 Pulpers: 1 at 20,000 admt/y
 Washing deinking lines: 1 at 15,000 admt/y
Paper/Paperboard Grades and Capacities:
 Total paper and paperboard capacity: 18,000 mt/y
 Tissue: 18,000 mt/y
Paper and Paperboard Mill Data:
 Stock Preparation:
 Pulpers: 2
 Refiners: 3
Paper Machines: 1
No. 1, twin-wire, Yankee dryer, total capacity 18,000 mt/y, Trim width 2.65 m, Tissue, Uncoated woodfree/freesheet
Finishing Equipment:
 Winders: 3 at 35,000 mt/y
 Calenders: 1
Energy Data:
 Power boilers
 Combustion turbines: 3 at 4 MW
 Electrical demand for mill: 57 MWh/D

MALAYSIA

ⓘCHH Pacific Paper Sdn Bhd (CHHPP)
36, Jln Anggerik Vanila Z 31/Z
40460 Kota Kemuning, Selangor Darul Ehsan
Malaysia
 Phone: (60) 3-51217972
 Fax: (60) 3-51227102

Malaysia

Personnel:
Mktng. Mgr.: Tian Ricky
Total Employees of Company: 200
Mill Locations:
CHH Pacific Paper Sdn Bhd (CHHPP), Bentong Mill, Lot 1, Bentong Industrial Park IIB, 28700 Mukim Sabai, Bentong, Malaysia, Capacity: 70,000 mt/y, (Paperboard mill)
Phone: (60) 09-2213333

ⓟⓜCHH Pacific Paper Sdn Bhd (CHHPP)
Bentong Mill
Lot 1, Bentong Industrial Park IIB
28700 Mukim Sabai, Bentong, Pahang Darul Makmur
Malaysia
Phone: (60) 09-2213333
Total Employees of Company: 200
Type of Operation: Paperboard mill
Paper/Paperboard Grades and Capacities:
Total paper and paperboard capacity: 70,000 mt/y
Boxboard/cartonboard
Paper and Paperboard Mill Data:
Paper Machines: 1
No. 1, total capacity 70,000 mt/y, Boxboard/cartonboard

ⓟⓜCita Peuchoon Paper Mills Sdn. Bhd.
Sungai Petani Mill
Lot 1385, Tikam Batu Industries Estate
08600 Sungai Petani, Kedah
Malaysia
Phone: (60) 4 4388206/8689
Fax: (60) 4 4388373
Email: citappm@streamyx.com
Personnel:
Mill Mgr.: W.K. Chen
Phone: (60) 4 4388206/8689
Man. Dir.: Loh Peng Hong
Phone: (60) 4 4388206/8689
Dir.: Loh Wan Tin
Phone: (60) 4 4388206/8689
Total Employees of Company: 250
Total Employees at this Location: 150
Type of Operation: Paper mill, Paperboard mill
Pulp Grades and Capacities:
Total pulp capacity: 15,000 mt/y
Paper/Paperboard Grades and Capacities:
Total paper and paperboard capacity: 30,000 mt/y
Packaging papers
Specialty and industrial
Linerboard: 13,000 mt/y
Boxboard/cartonboard: 13,000 mt/y
Paper and Paperboard Mill Data:
Stock Preparation:
Pulpers: 6
Refiners: 9
Paper Machines: 4
No. 1, cylinder, total capacity 250 mt/y, Trim width 1.4 m
No. 2, cylinder, total capacity 250 mt/y, Trim width 1.4 m
No. 3, cylinder, total capacity 1,700 mt/y, Trim width 1.8 m, Boxboard/cartonboard
No. 5, cylinder, total capacity 450 mt/y, Trim width 7.2 m
Finishing Equipment:
Winders: 2 at 40,000 mt/y
Calenders: 6
Rewinders: 2 at 40,000 mt/y
Sheeters: 2 at 26,000 mt/y
Energy Data:
Power boilers: 2

ⓟEko Pulp & Paper Sdn. Bhd.
Ownership: 100% by TSH Resources Bhd
KM 56, Jalan Tawau-Kunak Tawau, Sabah,
Sabah
Malaysia
Phone: (60) 6089 912 020
Fax: (60) 6089 913 000
Email: tsh@tsh.com.my
Web Address: www.ekopulpnpaper.com
Personnel:
Gen. Mgr., Bus. Develop. Mgr.: Tee Thean Wai
Phone: (60) 03 2084 0888
Fax: (60) 03 2084 0828
Mktg. Mgr.: Ng Swee Yin
Phone: (60) 03 2084 0888
Fax: (60) 03 2084 0828
Mill Locations:
Eko Pulp & Paper Sdn. Bhd., Tawau Mill, KM 56, Jalan Tawau-Kunak, Tawau, Malaysia, (Pulp mill, Paper mill)
Phone: (60) 6089 912 020
Fax: (60) 6089 913 000
Email: tsh@tsh.com.my

ⓜEko Pulp & Paper Sdn. Bhd.
Tawau Mill
KM 56, Jalan Tawau-Kunak
Tawau, Sabah
Malaysia
Phone: (60) 6089 912 020
Fax: (60) 6089 913 000
Email: tsh@tsh.com.my
Web Address: www.ekopulpnpaper.com
Personnel:
Gen. Mgr., Bus. Develop. Mgr.: Tee Thean Wai
Phone: (60) 03 2084 0888
Fax: (60) 03 2084 0828
Mktg. Mgr.: Ng Swee Yin
Phone: (60) 03 2084 0888
Fax: (60) 03 2084 0828
Type of Operation: Pulp mill, Paper mill
Pulp Grades and Capacities:
Total pulp capacity: 30,000 mt/y
Pulp available for market: 30,000 mt/y

ⓟⓜGS Paper & Packaging Group ("GSPP")
Banting Mill
Ownership: Oji Holdings Corporation
Lot 7090, Mukim Tanjung 12 Karung Berkunci No. 206
42700 Daerah Kuala Langat, Banting, Selangor Darul Ehsan
Malaysia
Phone: (60) 3 3149 1393/31825000
Fax: (60) 3 3149 1315/31825100
Email: gsip@pc.jaring.my,
ley@gspp.com.my
Web Address: www.gspp.com.my
Personnel:
CEO: T. S. Ong
Phone: (60) 3 3149 1393/31825000
Exec. VP Paper Div.: Sia Bong Soon
Phone: (60) 3 318 25 190
Fax: (60) 3 318 25 100
Email: bssia@gspp.com.my
Mktg. Mgr.: Yap Yuh Fah
Phone: (60) 3 3149 1393/31825000
Total Employees of Company: 36,000
Total Employees at this Location: 450
Type of Operation: Paperboard mill
Pulp Grades and Capacities:
Total pulp capacity: 283,379 mt/y
Recycled Pulping: 283,379 mt/y
Pulp Mill Data:
Recycled Fiber Treatment Lines:
Pulpers: 1 at 8,300
Pulpers: 1 at 314,000
Paper/Paperboard Grades and Capacities:
Total paper and paperboard capacity: 295,000 mt/y
Linerboard: 180,000 mt/y
Corrugating medium/fluting: 115,000 mt/y
Paper and Paperboard Mill Data:
Stock Preparation:
Pulpers: 4
Refiners: 11
Paper Machines: 2
No. 1, fourdrinier, total capacity 230,000 mt/y, Trim width 4.62 m, Linerboard, Corrugating medium/fluting
No. 2, fourdrinier, total capacity 65,000 mt/y, Trim width 3.3 m, Linerboard
Coating Machines: 1
PM2, off machine
Finishing Equipment:
Rewinders: 2
Sheeters: 1
Energy Data:
Power boilers: 1
Combustion turbines: 3 at 720 MW
Electrical demand for mill: 364 MWh/D

ⓟHai Ming Holdings Bhd.
Lot 765, Jalan Haji Sirat, Off Jalan Meru
42100 Klang, Selangor Darul Ehsan
Malaysia
Phone: (60) 32915566
Fax: (60) 32914489
Email: enquiry@haiming.com
Web Address: www.haiming.com
Mill Locations:
Hai Ming Paper Mills Sdn Bhd, Kota Samarahan Mill, Lot 292 & 294, ½Km Jalan Muara Tuang, 94300 Kota Samarahan, Malaysia, Capacity: 4,000 mt/y, (Paper mill)
Phone: (60) 82 610688
Fax: (60) 82 610788
Email: enquiry@haiming.com

ⓜHai Ming Paper Mills Sdn Bhd
Kota Samarahan Mill
Ownership: Hai Ming Holdings Bhd.
Lot 292 & 294, ½Km Jalan Muara Tuang
94300 Kota Samarahan, Sarawak, Borneo
Malaysia
Phone: (60) 82 610688
Fax: (60) 82 610788
Email: enquiry@haiming.com
Web Address: www.haiming.com
Personnel:
Oper. Mgr.: Lee Chen Hen
Phone: (60) 82 610688
Sls. & Mktg. Mgr.: Chu Kiong Cheong
Phone: (60) 82 610688
Total Employees at this Location: 50
Type of Operation: Paper mill
Paper/Paperboard Grades and Capacities:
Total paper and paperboard capacity: 4,000 mt/y
Tissue: 4,000 mt/y

ⓜJohmewah Maju Paper Mill Sdn. Bhd.
Yong Peng Mill
2 ¾ Mile, Jalan Air Hitam
83700 Yong Peng, Johor Darul Takzim
Malaysia
Mailing Address: P.O. Box 7, 83700 Yong Peng, Johor, Malaysia
Phone: (60) 7 4674888
Fax: (60) 7 4674488
Personnel:
Man. Dir.: C.P. Loh
Phone: (60) 7 4674888
Total Employees at this Location: 100
Type of Operation: Paperboard mill
Paper/Paperboard Grades and Capacities:
Total paper and paperboard capacity: 56,000 mt/y
Linerboard: 56,000 mt/y
Corrugating medium/fluting
Paper and Paperboard Mill Data:
Paper Machines: 2
PM 1, cylinder, total capacity 14,400 mt/y, Trim width 2.5 m, Linerboard
PM 2, fourdrinier, Trim width 2.5 m, Corrugating medium/fluting
Energy Data:
Power boilers: 2

Malaysia

①Johmewah Maju Paper Mill Sdn. Bhd.
2 ¾ Mile, Jalan Air Hitam
83700 Yong Peng, Johor Darul Takzim
Malaysia
Mailing Address: P.O. Box 7, 83700 Yong Peng, Johor, Malaysia
Phone: (60) 7 4674888
Fax: (60) 7 4674488
Mill Locations:
Johmewah Maju Paper Mill Sdn. Bhd., Yong Peng Mill, 2 ¾ Mile, Jalan Air Hitam, 83700 Yong Peng, Malaysia, Capacity: 56,000 mt/y, (Paperboard mill)
Phone: (60) 7 4674888
Fax: (60) 7 4674488

①⑩Kimberly-Clark Products (Malaysia) Sdn. Bhd.
Kluang Mill
Ownership: 100% by Kimberly-Clark Corp.
4-1/2 Mile Jalan Mersing
86007 Kluang, Johor Darul Takzim
Malaysia
Phone: (60) 7 787 9381
Fax: (60) 7 787 9234/170
Web Address: www.kcc.com
Personnel:
CEO: Naphan Kandapper
Phone: (60) 7 787 9381
Gen. Mgr.: Chen June Thiam
Phone: (60) 7 787 9381
Tissue Mill Mgr.: Lau Wen Pin
Phone: (60) 7 787 2000
Total Employees of Company: 58,000
Total Employees at this Location: 152
Type of Operation: Paper mill
Pulp Grades and Capacities:
 Total pulp capacity: 24,711 mt/y
 Recycled Pulping: 24,711 mt/y
Pulp Mill Data:
 Bleach Plant Systems: 1
 DIP
 Recycled Fiber Treatment Lines:
 Flotation deinking lines: 1
Paper/Paperboard Grades and Capacities:
 Total paper and paperboard capacity: 40,000 mt/y
 Tissue: 40,000 mt/y
Paper and Paperboard Mill Data:
Paper Machines: 2
 No. 1, twin-wire, total capacity 19,000 mt/y, Trim width 2.4 m, Tissue, Uncoated woodfree/freesheet
 No. 2, twin-wire, total capacity 21,000 mt/y, Trim width 2.45 m, Tissue, Uncoated woodfree/freesheet
Energy Data:
 Power boilers: 1
 Electrical demand for mill: 140 MWh/D

①⑩Lekok Paper Sdn Bhd
Melaka Mill
Ownership: Likok Paper Trading Pte Ltd
Lot 1-9, Jalan T.T.C. Satu, Kawasan Perindustrian Cheng
72520 Melaka
Malaysia
Phone: (60) 63372288
Fax: (60) 63372828
Email: lekoksb@streamyx.com, kokchoon@lekok.com
Web Address: www.likokpaper.com
Personnel:
Man. Dir.: Tan Tian Soon
Phone: (60) 63372288
Email: lekoksb@streamyx.com
Dir.: Tan Hook Wan
Phone: (60) 63372288
Email: lekoksb@streamyx.com
Director: Tan Kok Choon
Phone: (65) 179018080 (gsm)
Email: kokchoon@lekok.com
Mgr.: K. C. Tan
Phone: (60) 179018080
Fax: (60) 1 6 337 2828
Email: kokchoon@lekok.com
Total Employees at this Location: 250
Type of Operation: Paper mill
Pulp Grades and Capacities:
 Total pulp capacity: 116,684 mt/y
 Recycled Pulping: 116,684 mt/y
Pulp Mill Data:
 Recycled Fiber Treatment Lines:
 1
Paper/Paperboard Grades and Capacities:
 Total paper and paperboard capacity: 120,000 mt/y
 Corrugating medium/fluting: 120,000 mt/y
Paper and Paperboard Mill Data:
 Stock Preparation:
 Pulpers: 2
 Refiners: 2
Paper Machines: 2
 No. 1, fourdrinier, total capacity 30,000 mt/y, Trim width 3.15 m, Corrugating medium/fluting
 No. 2, fourdrinier, total capacity 90,000 mt/y, Trim width 4.1 m, Corrugating medium/fluting
Finishing Equipment:
 Rewinders: 2
 Sheeters: 4
Energy Data:
 Power boilers: 1
 Electrical demand for mill: 139 MWh/D

①Malaysian Newsprint Industries Sdn. Bhd.
Ownership: 34% by Norske Skog ASA, 34% by Hong Leong, 21% by News Straits Times, 11% by Rimbunan Hijau Group
Level 7, Wisma Hong Leong, 18 Jalan Perak
50450 Kuala Lumpur
Malaysia
Phone: (60) 3 77859988
Fax: (60) 3 77856888
Email: mnihq@mni.hongleong.com.my
Web Address: www.newsprint.com.my
Personnel:
CEO: Phang Kwok Keong
Phone: (60) 3 77859988
Fax: (60) 3 77856888
Email: kkphang@mnipaper.com
Gen. Mgr., RPD: Chu Chiu Loc
Phone: (60) 3 77859988
Fax: (60) 3 77856888
Email: ccl@mnipaper.com
Finan. Controller: Wong Pek Yee
Phone: (60) 3 77859988
Fax: (60) 3 77856888
Email: pywong@mnipaper.com
Sls. & Mktg. Mgr.: Teoh Chee Hiang
Phone: (60) 3 77859988
Fax: (60) 3 77856888
Email: chteoh@mnipaper.com
Product Serv. Mgr.: Jennifer Tang
Phone: (60) 3 77859988
Fax: (60) 3 77856888
Email: jt@mnipaper.com
Total Employees at this Location: 38
Mill Locations:
Malaysian Newsprint Industries Sdn. Bhd., Mentakab Mill, Lot 3771 Jalan Lencongan Mentakab-Temerloh, Temerloh Industrial Pahang, 28400 Mentakab, Malaysia, Capacity: 280,245 mt/y, (Paper mill)
Phone: (60) 6 09 2779898
Fax: (60) 6 092715115
Email: mni_mill@tm.net.my

①Malaysian Newsprint Industries Sdn. Bhd.
Mentakab Mill
Ownership: 34% by Norske Skog ASA
Lot 3771 Jalan Lencongan Mentakab-Temerloh, Temerloh Industrial Pahang
28400 Mentakab, Pahang Darul Makmur
Malaysia
Phone: (60) 6 09 2779898
Fax: (60) 6 092715115
Email: mni_mill@tm.net.my
Web Address: www.newsprint.com.my
Personnel:
CEO: Phang Kwok Keong
Phone: (60) 327159808
Fax: (60) 321636363
Email: kkphang@mni.hongleong.com.my
Gen. Mgr. (Mill): Anthony Tan Lee Ngie
Phone: (60) 92715103
Pulp Mill Mgr.: Mr. Selvam Suppiah
Phone: (60) 92715104
Email: selvam@mni.hongleong.com.my
Senior Paper Mill Mgr.: Wong Kam Choy
Phone: (60) 92715367
Fax: (60) 92715115
Email: kcwong@mni.hongleong.com.my
Utilities Mgr.: Khairul Anuar
Phone: (60) 92175361
Fax: (60) 92175115
Senior Mrg./Maint.: Lim Kian Guan
Phone: (60) 6092715331
Fax: (60) 6092779800
Email: limkianguan@mni.hongleong.com.my
Total Employees at this Location: 298
Type of Operation: Paper mill
Pulp Grades and Capacities:
 Total pulp capacity: 284,786 mt/y
 Recycled Pulping: 284,786 mt/y
Pulp Mill Data:
 Recycled Fiber Treatment Lines:
 Flotation deinking lines: 1 at 260,000 admt/y
 Pulpers: 2 at 130,000 admt/y
Paper/Paperboard Grades and Capacities:
 Total paper and paperboard capacity: 280,245 mt/y
 Newsprint: 280,245 mt/y
Paper and Paperboard Mill Data:
Paper Machines: 1
 No. 1, DuoFormer CFD, total capacity 280,245 mt/y, Trim width 7.99 m, Newsprint
Finishing Equipment:
 Winders: 2 at 1,200 mt/y
 Calenders: 1
Energy Data:
 Power boilers: 3
 Steam turbines: 3 at 25 MW
 Electrical demand for mill: 811 MWh/D

①Metro Knight (M) Sdn. Bhd.
Ownership: Ecofuture
Batu 10 Jalan Labis, PO Box 57
85007 Segamat
Malaysia
Phone: (60) 7 9451062, 7 9451063
Fax: (60) 7 94511309
Email: info@ecofibre.com, info@ecofuture.com.my
Web Address: www.ecofibre.com, www.ecofuture.com.my
Personnel:
Exec. Chmn./Man. Dir.: Yeo Kim Luang
Phone: (60) 7 9451062, 7 9451063
Fax: (60) 7 94511309
Dir.: Lim Si Pin
Phone: (60) 7 9451062, 7 9451063
Fax: (60) 7 94511309
Non-Exec. Dir.: Wye Pong (Brian) Wong
Phone: (60) 7 9451062, 7 9451063
Fax: (60) 7 94511309
Chief Eng.: Balachandran A/L Govindasamy
Phone: (60) 7 9451062, 7 9451063
Fax: (60) 7 94511309
Finan. Mgr: Saw Sui Hock
Phone: (60) 7 9451062, 7 9451063
Fax: (60) 7 94511309

Malaysia

Total Employees at this Location: 400
Mill Locations:
Metro Knight (M) Sdn. Bhd., Segamat Mill, Batu 10 Jalan Labis, PO Box 57, 85007 Segamat, Malaysia, (Pulp mill)
  Phone: (60) 7 9451062, 7 9451063
  Fax: (60) 7 94511309
  Email: info@ecofibre.com, info@ecofuture.com.my

ⓂMetro Knight (M) Sdn. Bhd.
Segamat Mill
Batu 10 Jalan Labis, PO Box 57
85007 Segamat, Johor Darul Takzim
Malaysia
  Phone: (60) 7 9451062, 7 9451063
  Fax: (60) 7 94511309
  Email: info@ecofibre.com, info@ecofuture.com.my
  Web Address: www.ecofibre.com, www.ecofuture.com.my
Personnel:
  Exec. Chmn./Man. Dir.: Yeo Kim Luang
  Phone: (60) 7 94511489
  Finan. Mgr.: Saw Sui Hock
  Phone: (60) 7 94511489
  Chief Eng.: Balachandran A/L Govindasamy
  Phone: (60) 7 94511489
  Non-Exec. Dir.: Wye Pong (Brian) Wong
  Phone: (60) 7 94511489
  Dir.: Lim Si Pin
  Phone: (60) 7 94511489
Type of Operation: Pulp mill
Pulp Grades and Capacities:
  Total pulp capacity: 7,000 mt/y
Pulp Mill Data:
Pulp Lines: 1

ⓂMuda Holdings Berhad
Lot no. 7, Jln. 51A/241
46100 Petaling Jaya, Selangor Darul Ehsan
Malaysia
  Phone: (60) 3 78759549
  Fax: (60) 3 78759519
  Email: mudahq@po.jaring.my
  Web Address: www.muda.com
Personnel:
  Chmn.: Tan Sri Dato Lim Guan Teik
  Phone: (60) 3 78759549
  Fax: (60) 3 78759519
  Independent Dir.: Datuk Yahya Yeop Ishak
  Phone: (60) 3 78759549
  Fax: (60) 3 78759519
  Man. Dir.: Azaman Bin Abu Bakar
  Phone: (60) 3 78759549
  Fax: (60) 3 78759519
  Exec. Dir.: Lim Wan Hoi
  Phone: (60) 3 78759549
  Fax: (60) 3 78759519
  Exec. Dir.: Dato' Lim Wan Peng
  Phone: (60) 3 78759549
  Fax: (60) 3 78759519
  Sr. Independent Dir.: Datuk Nik Hussain Bin Nik Ali
  Phone: (60) 3 78759549
  Fax: (60) 3 78759519
Mill Locations:
Muda Paper Mills Sdn. Bhd., Kajang Mill, 1.5 miles off Jalan Sungai Chua, 43000 Kajang, Malaysia, Capacity: 320,000 mt/y, (Paper mill, Paperboard mill)
  Phone: (60) 3 87361245
  Fax: (60) 3 87366869
  Email: mpmk@mpmsb.com
Muda Paper Mills Sdn. Bhd., Tasek Mill, 391 Jl. Tasek, Simpang Ampat, 14120 Seberang Prai Selatan, Malaysia, Capacity: 181,000 mt/y, (Paper mill, Paperboard mill)
  Phone: (60) 4 588 7335/36
  Fax: (60) 4 588 7646
  Email: mpmt@mpmsb.com

ⓂMuda Paper Mills Sdn. Bhd.
Kajang Mill
Ownership: 100% by Muda Holdings Berhad
1.5 miles off Jalan Sungai Chua
43000 Kajang, Selangor Darul Ehsan
Malaysia
  Phone: (60) 3 87361245
  Fax: (60) 3 87366869
  Email: mpmk@mpmsb.com
  Web Address: www.mpmsb.com
Personnel:
  Senior Gen. Mgr.: Cheong Weng Kok
  Phone: (60) 3 87361245
  Email: cwk@mpmsb.com
  Gen. Mgr. Tech.: Ang Lee Yang
  Phone: (60) 3 87361245
  Email: lyang@mpmsb.com
  Dpty. Gen. Mgr./Mktg.: Lim Siew Ling
  Phone: (60) 3 87361245
  Fax: (60) 3 87365455
  Email: siewling.lim@mpmsb.com
  Mgr.: Wong Peng Khoon
  Phone: (60) 3 87302205
  Email: pkwong@mpmkj.com
Total Employees at this Location: 400
Type of Operation: Paper mill, Paperboard mill
Pulp Grades and Capacities:
  Total pulp capacity: 315,895 mt/y
  Recycled Pulping: 315,895 mt/y
Pulp Mill Data:
  Recycled Fiber Treatment Lines:
  Recycled packaging pulping lines: 1
Paper/Paperboard Grades and Capacities:
  Total paper and paperboard capacity: 320,000 mt/y
  Linerboard: 136,000 mt/y
  Corrugating medium/fluting: 184,000 mt/y
Paper and Paperboard Mill Data:
  Stock Preparation:
  Pulpers: 4
  Refiners: 8
Paper Machines: 5
  No. 1, cylinder, total capacity 30,000 mt/y, Trim width 2.5 m, Linerboard
  No. 3, cylinder, total capacity 34,000 mt/y, Trim width 2.4 m, Corrugating medium/fluting
  No. 4, fourdrinier, total capacity 56,000 mt/y, Trim width 3.2 m, Linerboard
  No. 5, fourdrinier (2), total capacity 50,000 mt/y, Trim width 2.5 m, Linerboard
  No. 6, fourdrinier, total capacity 150,000 mt/y, Trim width 4.45 m, Corrugating medium/fluting
Finishing Equipment:
  Rewinders: 6 at 50,000 mt/y
  Sheeters: 3
Energy Data:
  Power boilers: 5
  Combustion turbines: 1 at 10 MW
  Electrical demand for mill: 375 MWh/D

ⓂMuda Paper Mills Sdn. Bhd.
Tasek Mill
Ownership: 100% by Muda Holdings Berhad
391 Jl. Tasek, Simpang Ampat
14120 Seberang Prai Selatan, Penang
Malaysia
  Phone: (60) 4 588 7335/36
  Fax: (60) 4 588 7646
  Email: mpmt@mpmsb.com
  Web Address: www.mpmsb.com
Personnel:
  Gen. Mgr.: Chaik Phoay Tan
  Phone: (60) 4 588 7335/36
  Email: cptan@mpmsb.com
  Dpty. Gen. Mgr.: Eddie Kok
  Phone: (60) 4 588 7335/36
  Email: eddie@mpmsb.com
  Mill Mgr.: Teoh Choo Wah
  Phone: (60) 4 588 7335/36
  Email: cwteoh@mpmsb.com
  Dpty. Tech. Gen. Mgr.: Chua Hwee Hooi
  Phone: (60) 4 588 7335/36
  Email: hhchua@mpmsb.com
  Dpty. Mills Mgr.: Chang Lim For
  Phone: (60) 4 588 7335/36
  Email: lfchang@mpmsb.com
  Asst. Facility Mgr.: Khaw Boon Tatt
  Phone: (60) 4 588 7335/36
  Email: electrical@mpmsb.com
Total Employees at this Location: 470
Type of Operation: Paper mill, Paperboard mill
Pulp Grades and Capacities:
  Total pulp capacity: 183,095 mt/y
  Recycled Pulping: 183,095 mt/y
Pulp Mill Data:
  Recycled Fiber Treatment Lines:
  Flotation deinking lines: 1
  Recycled packaging pulping lines: 1
Paper/Paperboard Grades and Capacities:
  Total paper and paperboard capacity: 181,000 mt/y
  Linerboard: 31,400 mt/y
  Corrugating medium/fluting: 29,600 mt/y
  Boxboard/cartonboard: 120,000 mt/y
Paper and Paperboard Mill Data:
  Stock Preparation:
  Pulpers: 6
  Refiners: 5
Paper Machines: 5
  No. 5, cylinder, total capacity 18,000 mt/y, Trim width 2.1 m, Linerboard
  No. 6, fourdrinier, total capacity 16,000 mt/y, Trim width 1.65 m, Linerboard, Corrugating medium/fluting
  No. 7, cylinder (4), total capacity 70,000 mt/y, Trim width 3.1 m, Boxboard/cartonboard
  No. 8, cylinder (4), total capacity 50,000 mt/y, Trim width 2.65 m, Boxboard/cartonboard
  No. 3A, fourdrinier, total capacity 27,000 mt/y, Trim width 2.15 m, Linerboard, Corrugating medium/fluting
Finishing Equipment:
  Rewinders: 6
  Sheeters: 6
Energy Data:
  Power boilers: 8
  Electrical demand for mill: 185 MWh/D

ⓄⓂNibong Tebal Paper Mills Sdn. Bhd. (NTPM)
Seberang Prai Sel Mill
Ownership: NTPM Holdings Berhad
886 Jalan Bandar Baru, Sungai Kecil
14300 Nibong Tebal, Seberang Prai Sel, Penang
Malaysia
  Phone: (60) 4 593 1296/5491326
  Fax: (60) 4 593 3373
  Email: hooifung@ntpm.com.my, lcchat@ntpm.com.my, gmteoh@ntpm.po.my
  Web Address: www.ntpm.com.my
Personnel:
  Gen. Man. Dir.: See Jin Lee
  Phone: (60) 4 593 1296
  Fax: (60) 4 593 3373
  Exec. Dir.: Chong Choon Lee
  Phone: (60) 4 593 1296
  Fax: (60) 4 593 3373
  Email: cclee@ntpm.com.my
Total Employees of Company: 1,000
Total Employees at this Location: 450
Type of Operation: Paper mill
Mill Locations:
Union Paper Industries Sdn. Bhd., Bentung Mill, Lot 65, Kawasan Perindustrian Bentong, 28700 Bentung, Malaysia, Capacity: 10,000 mt/y, (Paper mill)
  Phone: (60) 9 2226916
  Fax: (60) 9 2226915
  Email: upibtg@tm.net.my
Pulp Grades and Capacities:
  Total pulp capacity: 49,859 mt/y
  Recycled Pulping: 49,859 mt/y

Malaysia

Pulp Mill Data:
  Recycled Fiber Treatment Lines:
  Flotation deinking lines: 4 at 95,000 admt/y
  Pulpers: 15 at 100,000 admt/y
Paper/Paperboard Grades and Capacities:
  Total paper and paperboard capacity: 100,982 mt/y
  Tissue: 100,982 mt/y
Paper and Paperboard Mill Data:
  Stock Preparation:
  Pulpers: 12
  Refiners: 11
Paper Machines: 21
  No. 1, cylinder, total capacity 2,499 mt/y, Tissue
  No. 2, cylinder, total capacity 2,570 mt/y, Trim width 3.6 m, Tissue
  No. 3, cylinder, total capacity 2,570 mt/y, Trim width 3.6 m, Tissue
  No. 4, cylinder, total capacity 2,570 mt/y, Trim width 3.6 m, Tissue
  No. 5, cylinder, total capacity 2,570 mt/y, Trim width 3.6 m, Tissue
  No. 6, cylinder, total capacity 2,570 mt/y, Trim width 3.6 m, Tissue
  No. 7, cylinder, total capacity 2,570 mt/y, Trim width 3.6 m, Tissue
  No. 8, cylinder, total capacity 2,570 mt/y, Trim width 3.6 m, Tissue
  No. 9, cylinder, total capacity 2,570 mt/y, Trim width 3.6 m, Tissue
  No. 10, cylinder, total capacity 2,570 mt/y, Trim width 3.6 m, Tissue
  No. 11, cylinder, total capacity 2,570 mt/y, Trim width 3.6 m, Tissue
  No. 12, cylinder, total capacity 2,570 mt/y, Trim width 3.6 m, Tissue
  No. 13, cylinder, total capacity 2,570 mt/y, Trim width 3.6 m, Tissue
  No. 14, cylinder, total capacity 2,570 mt/y, Trim width 3.6 m, Tissue
  No. 15, total capacity 9,000 mt/y, Trim width 3.4 m, Tissue, Uncoated woodfree/freesheet
  No. 16, crescent former, total capacity 35,000 mt/y, Trim width 3.4 m, Tissue, Uncoated woodfree/freesheet
  No. 17, cylinder, total capacity 2,499 mt/y, Tissue
  No. 18, cylinder, total capacity 2,499 mt/y, Trim width 1.88 m, Tissue
  No. 19, cylinder, total capacity 2,499 mt/y, Trim width 1.88 m, Tissue
  No. 20, cylinder, total capacity 2,499 mt/y, Trim width 1.88 m, Tissue
  No. 21, cylinder, total capacity 11,000 mt/y, Trim width 2.82 m, Tissue, Uncoated woodfree/freesheet
  Finishing Equipment:
  Rewinders: 4 at 35,000 mt/y
Energy Data:
  Power boilers: 6
  Electrical demand for mill: 187 MWh/D

ⓘⓜ Pascorp Paper Industries Bhd.
Bentong Mill
Ownership: Perbadanan Kemajuan Negeri Pahang
Lot 1A, Kawasan Perindustrian Bentong
28700 Bentong, Pahang Darul Makmur
Malaysia
  Phone: (60) 9 222 3355
  Fax: (60) 9 222 2266
  Email: ppiphg92@tm.net.my
  Web Address: www.pascorppaper.en.ec21.com
Personnel:
  Man. Dir.: Mas'ut A. Samah
  Phone: (60) 9 222 3355
  Email: mas'ut@pascorp.com.my
Total Employees of Company: 280
Total Employees at this Location: 280
Type of Operation: Paper mill, Paperboard mill
Pulp Grades and Capacities:
  Total pulp capacity: 180,880 mt/y
  Recycled Pulping: 180,880 mt/y
Paper/Paperboard Grades and Capacities:
  Total paper and paperboard capacity: 180,285 mt/y
  Linerboard: 102,102 mt/y
  Corrugating medium/fluting: 78,183 mt/y
Paper and Paperboard Mill Data:
  Stock Preparation:
  Pulpers: 3
  Refiners: 4
Paper Machines: 2
  No. 1, fourdrinier, total capacity 60,690 mt/y, Trim width 3.1 m, Corrugating medium/fluting, Linerboard
  No. 2, fourdrinier, total capacity 119,595 mt/y, Trim width 3.5 m, Corrugating medium/fluting, Linerboard
  Finishing Equipment:
  Winders: 2 at 135,000 mt/y
  Calenders: 2
  Rewinders: 2 at 80,000 mt/y
Energy Data:
  Power boilers: 2

ⓘⓜ Sabah Forest Industries Sdn. Bhd.
Sipitang Mill
Ownership: 97.78% by Ballarpur Industries Ltd. (BILT), 2.22% by Sabah State Government
Kompleks SFI, No 10 Jalan Jeti W.D.T. 31
89859 Sipitang, Sabah
Malaysia
  Phone: (60) 87 801 018/026
  Fax: (60) 87 802 087/463
  Email: andrewchong@sfisb.com.my
  Web Address: www.bilt.com
Personnel:
  CEO: Abinash Daneja
  Phone: (60) 87 801 393
  Fax: (60) 87 801 068
  Dpty. CEO: K. L. Ho
  Phone: (60) 87 802 199
  Fax: (60) 87 802 263
Total Employees at this Location: 950
Type of Operation: Pulp mill, Paper mill
Pulp Grades and Capacities:
  Total pulp capacity: 354,637 mt/y
  Pulp available for market: 115,647 mt/y
  Chemical Pulp: 354,637 mt/y
Pulp Mill Data:
  Chemical Pulping Systems:
  Continuous digesters: 1
Pulp Lines: 1
  Bleach Plant Systems: 1
  No. 1, Sequence: C/DEoDD, Capacity 240,000 admt/y
  Chemical Recovery Equipment:
  Evaporator lines: 1
  Recovery boilers: 1
  Lime Kiln
  Pulp Dryers:
  Fourdriniers 1
Paper/Paperboard Grades and Capacities:
  Total paper and paperboard capacity: 144,228 mt/y
  Uncoated woodfree/freesheet: 144,228 mt/y
Paper and Paperboard Mill Data:
  Stock Preparation:
  Pulpers: 1
  Refiners: 6
Paper Machines: 2
  No. 1, fourdrinier, total capacity 74,256 mt/y, Trim width 4.8 m, Uncoated woodfree/freesheet
  No. 2, fourdrinier, total capacity 69,972 mt/y, Trim width 4.8 m, Uncoated woodfree/freesheet
  Finishing Equipment:
  Rewinders: 2 at 6,600 mt/y
  Sheeters: 4 at 92,400 mt/y
Energy Data:
  Power boilers: 2
  Steam turbines: 2 at 45 MW
  Electrical demand for mill: 660 MWh/D

ⓘⓜ Taiping Paper Mills Sdn. Bhd.
Taiping Mill
Ownership: Tropical Consolidated Corp SDN. BHD.
2.75 miles Taiping Rd., Simpang
34700 Taiping, Perak
Malaysia
  Phone: (60) 5 8472 6 30/36
  Fax: (60) 5 8472 714
  Email: costumer@taipingpaper.com, tpminfo@tm.net.my
  Web Address: www.taipingpaper.com
Personnel:
  Mill Mgr.: Ang Teow Soon
  Email: hcteh@tropical.grp.com
Total Employees at this Location: 50
Type of Operation: Paper mill
Paper/Paperboard Grades and Capacities:
  Total paper and paperboard capacity: 3,000 mt/y
  Tissue: 3,000 mt/y
Paper and Paperboard Mill Data:
Paper Machines: 1
  PM 3, cylinder, total capacity 3,000 mt/y, Trim width 3.05 m, Tissue
Energy Data:
  Power boilers: 2

ⓘⓜ Theen Seng Paper Manufacturing Sdn. Bhd.
Rasa Mill
32nd Miles, Jalan Ipoh
44200 Rasa, Hulu Selangor, Selangor Darul Ehsan
Malaysia
  Phone: (60) 3 60573101/102
  Fax: (60) 3 60573250
  Email: tspmsb@tm.net.my
  Web Address: www.theenseng.com
Personnel:
  CEO: Kevin Lai Tak Kuan
  Phone: (60) 3 60573101
  Fax: (60) 3 60573250
  Email: kevin@theeseng.com
  Purch. Officer: Kuan On Loon
  Phone: (60) 3 60573101
  Fax: (60) 3 60573250
  Qlty. Cont.: Thoo Swee Hock
  Phone: (60) 3 60573101
  Fax: (60) 3 60573250
  Tech. Mgr.: Muthamil Chelvan
  Phone: (60) 3 60573101
  Fax: (60) 3 60573250
  Finan. Dir.: Tan Choon Kwee
  Phone: (60) 3 60573101
  Fax: (60) 3 60573250
Total Employees at this Location: 153
Type of Operation: Paper mill
Pulp Grades and Capacities:
  Total pulp capacity: 12,000 mt/y
Paper/Paperboard Grades and Capacities:
  Total paper and paperboard capacity: 30,000 mt/y
  Packaging papers: 15,000 mt/y
  Specialty and industrial: 15,000 mt/y

ⓘⓜ Trio Paper Mills Sdn. Bhd.
Simpang Ampat Mill
Ownership: 96.06% by HPI Resources Bhd
No. 395 Jln. Tasek, Kampung Seberang Padang Lalang
14120 Simpang Ampat, Pulau Pinang
Malaysia
  Phone: (60) 4 588 9093
  Fax: (60) 4 588 7327
  Email: triopap@po.garing.my
Personnel:
  Senior Prod. Mgr.: Low Cheng Booen
  Phone: (60) 4 588 9093
Total Employees of Company: 150
Total Employees at this Location: 90
Type of Operation: Paper mill
Pulp Grades and Capacities:
  Total pulp capacity: 37,297 mt/y
  Recycled Pulping: 37,297 mt/y
Pulp Mill Data:
  Recycled Fiber Treatment Lines:

Recycled packaging pulping lines: 1
Paper/Paperboard Grades and Capacities:
Total paper and paperboard capacity: 42,141 mt/y
Specialty and industrial: 4,641 mt/y
Corrugating medium/fluting: 25,000 mt/y
Boxboard/cartonboard: 12,500 mt/y
Paper and Paperboard Mill Data:
Paper Machines: 6
No. 1, cylinder, total capacity 1,160 mt/y, Trim width 1.5 m, Specialty and industrial
No. 2, cylinder, total capacity 1,160 mt/y, Trim width 1.5 m, Specialty and industrial
No. 3, cylinder, total capacity 1,160 mt/y, Trim width 1.5 m, Specialty and industrial
No. 4, cylinder, total capacity 1,160 mt/y, Trim width 1.5 m, Specialty and industrial
No. 5, cylinder, total capacity 12,500 mt/y, Trim width 1.7 m, Boxboard/cartonboard
No. 6, cylinder, total capacity 25,000 mt/y, Trim width 2.9 m, Corrugating medium/fluting
Energy Data:
Power boilers: 2
Steam turbines: 1
Electrical demand for mill: 46 MWh/D

ⓘⓜ Union Paper Industries Sdn. Bhd.
Bentung Mill
Ownership: 100% by Nibong Tebal Paper Mills Sdn. Bhd. (NTPM)
Lot 65, Kawasan Perindustrian Bentong
28700 Bentung, Pahang Darul Makmur
Malaysia
 Phone: (60) 9 2226916
 Fax: (60) 9 2226915
 Email: upibtg@tm.net.my
Personnel:
 CEO: Mohd. Faizal
 Phone: (60) 9 2226916
 Mill Mgr.: C. M. Lee
 Phone: (60) 9 2226916
Total Employees of Company: 100
Type of Operation: Paper mill
Paper/Paperboard Grades and Capacities:
Total paper and paperboard capacity: 10,000 mt/y
Tissue: 10,000 mt/y
Paper and Paperboard Mill Data:
Paper Machines: 2
PM 1, total capacity 5,000 mt/y, Trim width 2.7 m, Tissue
PM 2, cylinder, total capacity 5,000 mt/y, Trim width 2.7 m, Tissue
Energy Data:
Power boilers: 2

ⓜ UPP Pulp & Paper (M) Sdn Bhd
Batang Berjuntai Mill
Previously United Paper Board (M) Sdn Bhd
Ownership: 87.50% by UPP Holdings Limited
PO Box 225, Lot 225, Jalan Kuala Selangor
45620 Ijok, Batang Berjuntai, Selangor Darul Ehsan
Malaysia
 Phone: (60) 3 6038 6388
 Fax: (60) 3 6038 5966
 Email: sales.upb@upp-group.com
 Web Address: www.upp-group.com
Personnel:
 Gen. Mgr.: Tong Kim Chai
 Phone: (60) 3 6038 6388
 Fax: (60) 3 6038 5832
Total Employees at this Location: 220
Type of Operation: Paper mill, Paperboard mill
Pulp Mill Data:
 Recycled Fiber Treatment Lines:
 Pulpers: 7 at 75,000 admt/y
Paper/Paperboard Grades and Capacities:
Total paper and paperboard capacity: 85,000 mt/y
Packaging papers
Specialty and industrial
Linerboard: 65,000 mt/y

Corrugating medium/fluting
Boxboard/cartonboard: 20,000 mt/y
Paper and Paperboard Mill Data:
 Stock Preparation:
 Pulpers: 4
 Refiners: 8
Paper Machines: 3
No. 2, cylinder, Trim width 2.5 m
No. 3, cylinder, Trim width 2.67 m
No. 4, cylinder, Trim width 2.5 m
 Finishing Equipment:
 Rewinders: 3
 Sheeters: 3
Energy Data:
Power boilers: 4

ⓜ Yeong Chaur Shing Paper Mill Sdn. Bhd.
Melaka Mill
Lot 736, Mukim Krubong
75250 Melaka
Malaysia
 Phone: (60) 3 40436691/24404
 Fax: (60) 3 40420962
 Email: wingseow@tm.net.my,
 ycsptan@pd.jaring.my,
 wingseow@streamyx.com
 Web Address: ycsi.asiaep.com
Personnel:
 Man. Dir., Export Dir.: Tan Seng Poo
 Phone: (60) 12 388 6252
Total Employees at this Location: 150
Type of Operation: Paper mill
Pulp Grades and Capacities:
Total pulp capacity: 5,753 mt/y
Recycled Pulping: 5,753 mt/y
Pulp Mill Data:
 Bleach Plant Systems: 1
 DIP
 Recycled Fiber Treatment Lines:
 Flotation deinking lines: 1
Paper/Paperboard Grades and Capacities:
Total paper and paperboard capacity: 10,000 mt/y
Tissue: 10,000 mt/y
Paper and Paperboard Mill Data:
Paper Machines: 1
No. 1, total capacity 10,000 mt/y, Trim width 3.1 m, Tissue, Uncoated woodfree/freesheet
Energy Data:
Power boilers: 1
Electrical demand for mill: 27 MWh/D

ⓘ Yeong Chaur Shing Paper Mill Sdn. Bhd.
Lot 736, Mukim Krubong
75250 Melaka
Malaysia
 Phone: (60) 3 40436691/24404
 Fax: (60) 3 40420962
 Email: wingseow@tm.net.my,
 ycsptan@pd.jaring.my,
 wingseow@streamyx.com
 Web Address: ycsi.asiaep.com
Personnel:
 Man. Dir., Export Dir.: Tan Seng Poo
 Phone: (60) 3 40436691/24404
 Fax: (60) 3 40420962
Total Employees at this Location: 150
Mill Locations:
Yeong Chaur Shing Paper Mill Sdn. Bhd., Melaka Mill, Lot 736, Mukim Krubong, 75250 Melaka, Malaysia, Capacity: 10,000 mt/y, (Paper mill)
Phone: (60) 3 40436691/24404
Fax: (60) 3 40420962
Email: wingseow@tm.net.my, ycsptan@pd.jaring.my, wingseow@streamyx.com

MYANMAR

ⓘ Myanma Paper and Chemical Industries (MPCI)
Ownership: 100% by State
No. 192, Kaba Aye Pagoda Road, Bahan P.O. 11201
Yangon
Myanmar
 Phone: (95) 1 565776
 Fax: (95) 1 577744
 Email: mpci@myanmar.com.mm
Personnel:
 Gen. Mgr.: U Thein Win
 Phone: (95) 1 565776
 Fax: (95) 1 577744
Mill Locations:
Myanma Paper and Chemical Industries (MPCI), Sittuong No. 1 Paper Mill, Kyaik Hto Township, Theinzayat, Myanmar, Capacity: 12,000 mt/y, (Pulp mill, Paper mill)
Email: mpci@industry1myanmar.com
Myanma Paper and Chemical Industries (MPCI), Thabaung Pulp & Paper Mill, Thabaung, Pathein, Myanmar, Capacity: 18,000 mt/y, (Pulp mill)
Myanma Paper and Chemical Industries (MPCI), Yeni Mill, Yangon-Mandalay Highway, Yedashe Township, Yeni, Myanmar, Capacity: 36,750 mt/y, (Paper mill)
Phone: (95) 67 2120

ⓜ Myanma Paper and Chemical Industries (MPCI)
Sittuong No. 1 Paper Mill
Kyaik Hto Township
Theinzayat, Mon State
Myanmar
 Email: mpci@industry1myanmar.com
Personnel:
 Mill Mgr.: U. Aung Soe
Total Employees at this Location: 1,626
Type of Operation: Pulp mill, Paper mill
Pulp Grades and Capacities:
Total pulp capacity: 12,000 mt/y
Chemical Pulp
Pulp Mill Data:
 Chemical Pulping Systems:
 Batch digesters: 4
 Chemical Recovery Equipment:
 Recovery boilers: 1
Paper/Paperboard Grades and Capacities:
Total paper and paperboard capacity: 12,000 mt/y
Uncoated woodfree/freesheet: 12,000 mt/y
Paper and Paperboard Mill Data:
Paper Machines: 3
No. 1, fourdrinier, Trim width 2.32 m, Uncoated woodfree/freesheet
No. 2, fourdrinier, Trim width 2.32 m, Uncoated woodfree/freesheet
No. 3, cylinder, Trim width 1.7 m, Uncoated woodfree/freesheet

ⓜ Myanma Paper and Chemical Industries (MPCI)
Thabaung Pulp & Paper Mill
Mill is for sale
Thabaung, Pathein, Ayeyewaddy
Myanmar
Type of Operation: Pulp mill
Pulp Grades and Capacities:
Total pulp capacity: 70,000 mt/y
Pulp Mill Data:
 Pulp Lines: 1
Paper/Paperboard Grades and Capacities:
Total paper and paperboard capacity: 18,000 mt/y
Uncoated woodfree/freesheet: 18,000 mt/y
Paper and Paperboard Mill Data:
Paper Machines: 1

Nepal

No. 1, total capacity 18,000 mt/y, Uncoated woodfree/freesheet

ⓜMyanma Paper and Chemical Industries (MPCI)
Yeni Mill
Yangon-Mandalay Highway
Yedashe Township, Yeni, Bago Division
Myanmar
Phone: (95) 67 2120
Personnel:
Mill Mgr.: U. Tin Htut
Phone: (95) 67 2120
Total Employees at this Location: 1,000
Type of Operation: Paper mill
Pulp Grades and Capacities:
Total pulp capacity: 17,500 mt/y
Chemical Pulp: 17,500 mt/y
Paper/Paperboard Grades and Capacities:
Total paper and paperboard capacity: 36,750 mt/y
Packaging papers: 36,750 mt/y
Paper and Paperboard Mill Data:
Paper Machines: 2
No. 1, fourdrinier, total capacity 8,750 mt/y, Packaging papers
No. 2, total capacity 28,000 mt/y, Packaging papers

ⓜMyanmar Jute Enterprise
Pantaput village, Maubin town Mill
Pantaput village, Maubin town
Myanmar
Type of Operation: Paper mill
Paper/Paperboard Grades and Capacities:
Total paper and paperboard capacity: 5,000 mt/y
Uncoated woodfree/freesheet: 5,000 mt/y
Paper and Paperboard Mill Data:
Paper Machines: 1
No. 1, total capacity 5,000 mt/y, Uncoated woodfree/freesheet

ⓗMyanmar Jute Enterprise
Pantaput village, Maubin town
Myanmar
Mill Locations:
Myanmar Jute Enterprise, Pantaput village, Maubin town Mill, Pantaput village, Maubin town, Myanmar, Capacity: 5,000 mt/y, (Paper mill)

NEPAL

ⓜEverest Paper Mills (P) Ltd.
Janakpurdham Mill
P.O. Box No. 8
Mahendranagar, Janakpurdham, Dhausha District
Nepal
Phone: (977) 41 20512/20093/22259
Fax: (977) 41 20317/21021
Email: epm@ntc.net.np, everest@ntc.net.np, info@everestgroup.com.np
Web Address: www.everestgroup.com.np
Personnel:
Chmn.: O. P. Saraff
Phone: (977) 41 20512/20093/22259
Man. Dir.: K. K. Saraff
Phone: (977) 41 20512/20093/22259
Purch. Mgr.: B. L. Karn
Phone: (977) 41 525941
Fax: (977) 41 520317
Total Employees at this Location: 313
Type of Operation: Paper mill
Pulp Grades and Capacities:
Total pulp capacity: 14,000 mt/y
Pulp Mill Data:
Pulp Lines: 1

Paper/Paperboard Grades and Capacities:
Total paper and paperboard capacity: 10,000 mt/y
Uncoated woodfree/freesheet: 10,000 mt/y

ⓗⓜReliance Paper Mills
Bhairahawa Mill
Semari, Bhairahawa, Post Box No. 32ox 10905
Bhairahawa
Nepal
Phone: (977) 1 4227237/4227831
Fax: (977) 1 4246788/4230360
Email: info@reliancegroupnepal.com
Web Address: www.reliancegroupnepal.com
Personnel:
Mgr.: Bharat Kumar Todi
Phone: (977) 1 422 7831
Fax: (977) 1 424 6788
Mgr.: Shyam Agrawal
Phone: (977) 1 422 7831
Fax: (977) 1 424 6788
Total Employees at this Location: 42
Type of Operation: Paper mill
Paper/Paperboard Grades and Capacities:
Total paper and paperboard capacity: 22,750 mt/y
Newsprint
Uncoated woodfree/freesheet
Packaging papers: 14,700 mt/y
Paper and Paperboard Mill Data:
Paper Machines: 2
No. 1, total capacity 14,700 mt/y, Trim width 2.74 m, Packaging papers
No. 2, total capacity 8,050 mt/y, Trim width 2.23 m

NEW ZEALAND

ⓗCarter Holt Harvey Pulp & Paper
Company is for sale (The Commission has given clearance for Oji Oceania Management (NZ) Limited (Oji) to acquire up to 100% of the shares in Carter Holt Harvey Pulp & Paper Limited from Carter Holt Harvey Limited.)
Ownership: 100% by The Rank Group
Head Office, State Highway 1
3444 Tokoroa
New Zealand
Mailing Address: Private Bag 6, Tokoroa, New Zealand
Phone: (64) 7 885 5999
Fax: (64) 7 885 5614
Email: pulpenquiries@chh.com
Web Address: www.chh.com, www.chhpulpandpaper.com
Personnel:
CEO: Jon Ryder
Phone: (64) 7 885 5805
Fax: (64) 7 885 5614
Email: jon.ryder@chh.co.nz
CIO: Jonathan Iles
Phone: (64) 7 885 5999
Fax: (64) 7 885 5614
CFO: Karl Klinge
Phone: (64) 7 885 5999
Fax: (64) 7 885 5614
Gen. Counsel: Denver Simpson
Phone: (64) 7 885 5999
Fax: (64) 7 885 5614
Total Employees of Company: 800
Mill Locations:
Carter Holt Harvey Pulp & Paper, Kinleith Mill, State Highway 1, 3444 Tokoroa, New Zealand, Capacity: 339,864 mt/y, (Pulp mill, Paper mill, Paperboard mill)
Phone: (64) 7 885 5999
Fax: (64) 7 885 5614
Email: (firstname.surname@chh.com)
Carter Holt Harvey Pulp & Paper, Penrose Mill, 33 Hugo Johnson Dr., 1642 Penrose, New Zealand, Capacity: 85,000 mt/y, (Paper mill, Paperboard mill)
Phone: (64) 9 525 4549
Fax: (64) 9 525 4548
Email: (firstname.surname@chh.com), fusion@chh.co.nz
Carter Holt Harvey Pulp & Paper, Tasman Mill, Fletcher Avenue, 3169 Kawerau, New Zealand, (Pulp mill)
Phone: (64) 7 306 9050
Fax: (64) 7 306 9051

ⓜCarter Holt Harvey Pulp & Paper
Kinleith Mill
State Highway 1
3444 Tokoroa
New Zealand
Mailing Address: Private Bag 6, Tokoroa, New Zealand
Phone: (64) 7 885 5999
Fax: (64) 7 885 5614
Email: (firstname.surname@chh.com)
Web Address: www.chh.com, www.chhpulpandpaper.com
Personnel:
Mill Mgr.: Ian Whyte
Phone: (64) 7 885 5999
Fax: (64) 7 885 5614
Email: ian.whyte@chh.co.nz
Paper Mill: Business Unit Leader: Simon Clark
Phone: (64) 7 885 5999
Fax: (64) 7 885 5614
Email: simon.clark@chh.co.nz
Pulp Mill: Business Unit Leader: Keith Haystead
Phone: (64) 7 885 5999
Fax: (64) 7 885 5614
Email: keith.haystead@chh.co.nz
Tech. Serv. Mgr.: Tom Clark
Phone: (64) 7 885 5999
Fax: (64) 7 885 5614
Email: tom.clark@@chh.co.nz
Total Employees at this Location: 540
Type of Operation: Pulp mill, Paper mill, Paperboard mill
Pulp Grades and Capacities:
Total pulp capacity: 638,640 mt/y
Pulp available for market: 279,888 mt/y
Chemical Pulp: 531,311 mt/y
Recycled Pulping: 107,329 mt/y
Pulp Mill Data:
Chemical Pulping Systems:
Batch digesters: 12
Continuous digesters: 2
Bleach Plant Systems: 1
No. 1, Sequence: O_2 DEoD
Chemical Recovery Equipment:
Evaporator lines: 2
Recovery boilers: 2
Lime Kiln
Recycled Fiber Treatment Lines:
Pulpers
Pulp Dryers:
Air Float dryers 1, Fourdriniers 1
Paper/Paperboard Grades and Capacities:
Total paper and paperboard capacity: 339,864 mt/y
Linerboard: 309,876 mt/y
Corrugating medium/fluting: 29,988 mt/y
Paper and Paperboard Mill Data:
Paper Machines: 1
No. 6, fourdrinier, total capacity 339,864 mt/y, Trim width 6.3 m, Linerboard, Corrugating medium/fluting
Energy Data:
Power boilers: 2
Steam turbines: 1 at 40 MW
Electrical demand for mill: 1,406 MWh/D

ⓜCarter Holt Harvey Pulp & Paper
Penrose Mill
33 Hugo Johnson Dr.
1642 Penrose, Auckland
New Zealand

New Zealand

Mailing Address: Private Bag 92808, Penrose, Auckland, New Zealand
Phone: (64) 9 525 4549
Fax: (64) 9 525 4548
Email: (firstname.surname@chh.com), fusion@chh.co.nz
Web Address: www.chh.com, www.chhpulpandpaper.com

Personnel:
Mill Mgr. (Mgr Fiber Processing): Mark Bendikson
Phone: (64) 9 525 4549
Fax: (64) 9 525 4548
Email: mark.bendikson@chh.co.nz
Eng. Mgr.: Craig Allan
Phone: (64) 9 525 4549
Fax: (64) 9 525 4548
Email: craig.allan@chh.co.nz

Total Employees at this Location: 73
Type of Operation: Paper mill, Paperboard mill

Pulp Grades and Capacities:
Total pulp capacity: 87,915 mt/y
Recycled Pulping: 87,915 mt/y

Pulp Mill Data:
Recycled Fiber Treatment Lines:
Pulpers: 1 at 80,000 admt/y

Paper/Paperboard Grades and Capacities:
Total paper and paperboard capacity: 85,000 mt/y
Corrugating medium/fluting: 85,000 mt/y

Paper and Paperboard Mill Data:
Stock Preparation:
Pulpers: 1
Refiners: 2

Paper Machines: 1
No. 1, fourdrinier, total capacity 85,000 mt/y, Trim width 2.26 m, Corrugating medium/fluting

Finishing Equipment:
Rewinders: 1

Energy Data:
Power boilers: 1
Electrical demand for mill: 101 MWh/D

ⓜ Carter Holt Harvey Pulp & Paper
Tasman Mill

Fletcher Avenue
3169 Kawerau, Bay of Plenty
New Zealand
Mailing Address: Private Bag 1005, Kawerau, New Zealand
Phone: (64) 7 306 9050
Fax: (64) 7 306 9051
Web Address: www.chh.com, www.chhpulpandpaper.com

Personnel:
Mill Mgr.: Murray Lucas
Phone: (64) 7 306 9286
Fax: (64) 7 306 9051
Email: murray.lucas@chh.co.nz
Tech. Mgr.: Steven Woollacott
Phone: (64) 7 306 9050
Fax: (64) 7 306 9051
Email: steven.woollacott@chh.co.nz

Total Employees at this Location: 282
Type of Operation: Pulp mill

Pulp Grades and Capacities:
Total pulp capacity: 303,307 mt/y
Pulp available for market: 300,000 mt/y
Chemical Pulp: 303,307 mt/y

Pulp Mill Data:
Chemical Pulping Systems:
Continuous digesters: 2
Bleach Plant Systems: 2
No. 1, Type: (idle), Sequence: HH, Capacity 125,000 admt/y
Chemical Pulping System - Hardwood/Softwood, Type: Hardwood/Softwood - D/Eop/P/D, Sequence: O_2 DEopD, Capacity 175,000 admt/y
Chemical Recovery Equipment:
Evaporator lines: 2
Recovery boilers: 1
Lime Kiln
Pulp Dryers:
Air Float dryers 1, Flakt dryer 1, Fourdriniers 1, Twin Wire 1

Energy Data:
Power boilers: 2
Hydro turbines: 3 at 8, 10, 15 MW
Electrical demand for mill: 616 MWh/D

ⓜ Norske Skog Tasman
Tasman Mill

Ownership: 100% by Norske Skog ASA
Private Bag, Fletcher Avenue
3169 Kawerau, Bay of Plenty
New Zealand
Phone: (64) 7 323 3999
Fax: (64) 7 323 3790
Email: (firstname.surname@norskeskog.com)
Web Address: www.norskeskog.com

Personnel:
Mill Mgr.: Peter McCarty
Phone: (64) 7 323 3999
Fax: (64) 7 323 3790
Email: peter.mccarty@norskeskog.com
Environ. Mgr.: Chris Bruns
Phone: (64) 7 323 3999
Fax: (64) 7 323 3790
Email: chris.bruns@norskeskog.com
Bus. Develop. Eng.: Keith Anderson
Phone: (64) 7 323 3999
Fax: (64) 7 323 3790
Tech. Mgr.: Steve Brine
Phone: (64) 7 323 3999
Fax: (64) 7 323 3790
Email: steve.brine@norskeskog.com

Total Employees at this Location: 183
Type of Operation: Paper mill

Pulp Grades and Capacities:
Total pulp capacity: 157,447 mt/y
Mechanical Pulp: 157,447 mt/y

Pulp Mill Data:
Mechanical Pulping Systems:
RMP systems: 2
TMP systems: 2
Bleach Plant Systems: 2
Mechanical Pulping System - Softwood RMP, Type: Softwood RMP, Sequence: H
Mechanical Pulping System - Softwood TMP, Type: Softwood TMP, Sequence: H

Paper/Paperboard Grades and Capacities:
Total paper and paperboard capacity: 154,938 mt/y
Newsprint: 149,940 mt/y
Uncoated mechanical/groundwood: 4,998 mt/y

Paper and Paperboard Mill Data:
Stock Preparation:
Pulpers: 1
Refiners: 4

Paper Machines: 1
No. 3, top former, total capacity 154,938 mt/y, Trim width 6.85 m, Newsprint, Uncoated mechanical/groundwood

Finishing Equipment:
Winders: 3
Rewinders: 1

Energy Data:
Power boilers
Steam turbines: 1 at 8 MW
Electrical demand for mill: 1,481 MWh/D

ⓞⓜ Pan Pac Forest Products Ltd.
Whirinaki Mill

Ownership: 87% by Oji Holdings Corporation, 13% by Nippon Paper Industries Co., Ltd.
1161, SH2, Wairoa Rd.
4142 Napier, Hawke's Bay
New Zealand
Mailing Address: Private Bag 6203, Napier, New Zealand
Phone: (64) 6 831 0100
Fax: (64) 6 831 0102/836 6443
Email: (firstname.surname@panpac.com)
Web Address: www.panpac.co.nz

Personnel:
Man. Dir.: Doug Ducker
Phone: (64) 6 831 0100
Fax: (64) 6 836 6443
Email: doug.ducker@panpac.co.nz
Mgr. Tech. & Environ.: Peter Allan
Phone: (64) 6 831 0100
Fax: (64) 6 836 6443
Email: peter.allan@panpac.com.nz
Gen. Mgr. Pulp: Tony Clifford
Phone: (64) 6 831 0100
Fax: (64) 6 836 6443
Email: tony.clifford@panpac.co.nz
Gen. Mgr. HR.: Olwen Hyslop
Phone: (64) 6 831 0100
Fax: (64) 6 836 6443
Email: olwen.hyslop@panpac.co.nz
Oper. Mgr.: Neil Weber
Phone: (64) 6 831 0100
Fax: (64) 6 836 6443
Email: neil.weber@panpac.co.nz

Total Employees of Company: 194
Total Employees at this Location: 194
Type of Operation: Pulp mill

Pulp Grades and Capacities:
Total pulp capacity: 291,272 mt/y
Pulp available for market: 283,815 mt/y
Mechanical Pulp: 291,272 mt/y

Pulp Mill Data:
Mechanical Pulping Systems:
TMP systems: 4
Pulp Lines: 1
Bleach Plant Systems: 2
Mechanical Pulping System - Softwood BCTMP, Type: Softwood BCTMP - Pretreatment, Sequence: P
Mechanical Pulping System - Softwood TMP, Type: Softwood TMP, Sequence: P
Pulp Dryers:
Flash dryers 1, Flash dryers 1

Energy Data:
Power boilers: 2
TMP Reboiler
Steam turbines: 1 at 13 MW
Electrical demand for mill: 1,675 MWh/D

ⓜ SCA Hygiene Products Australasia
Kawerau Mill

Ownership: 50% by SCA - Svenska Cellulosa Aktiebolaget
Fletcher Avenue
3169 Kawerau, Bay of Plenty
New Zealand
Phone: (64) 7 323 9899
Fax: (64) 7 323 6601
Email: (firstname.lastname@sca.com)
Web Address: www.sca.com

Personnel:
Gen. Mgr. Oper.: Mark Kennedy
Phone: (64) 7 323 9899
Email: mark.kennedy@sca-ha.com
RST Mgr. - Wide Winder: Lester Murfitt
Phone: (64) 7 323 9899
Email: lester.murfitt@sca-ha.com
Tech. Mgr.: Brian Fahey
Phone: (64) 7 323 9899
Email: brian.fahey@sca-ha.com

Total Employees at this Location: 130
Type of Operation: Paper mill

Pulp Mill Data:
Mechanical Pulping Systems:
CTMP systems: 1

Paper/Paperboard Grades and Capacities:
Total paper and paperboard capacity: 57,000 mt/y
Tissue: 57,000 mt/y

Paper and Paperboard Mill Data:

Oman

Paper Machines: 2
No. 2, Yankee dryer, total capacity 33,000 mt/y, Trim width 3.4 m, Tissue
No. 3, Yankee dryer, total capacity 24,000 mt/y, Trim width 3.4 m, Tissue
Finishing Equipment:
Rewinders: 1
Sheeters: 1
Energy Data:
Power boilers: 2
Electrical demand for mill: 171 MWh/D

ⓂWhakatane Mill Ltd.
Whakatane Mill
Mill Road
Whakatane, Bay of Plenty
New Zealand
Mailing Address: Private Bag 1000, 3080 Whakatane, Bay of Plenty, New Zealand
Phone: (64) 7 307 1899
Fax: (64) 7 307 1655
Email: firstname.lastname@whakatanemill.co.nz
Web Address: www.rankgroup.co.nz
Personnel:
CEO & Mill Mgr.: Graham Millar
Phone: (64) 7 307 1899
Email: graham.millar@whakatanemill.co.nz
Total Employees at this Location: 259
Type of Operation: Pulp mill, Paperboard mill
Pulp Grades and Capacities:
Total pulp capacity: 68,227 mt/y
Mechanical Pulp: 68,227 mt/y
Pulp Mill Data:
Mechanical Pulping Systems:
Conventional grinders: 5
Paper/Paperboard Grades and Capacities:
Total paper and paperboard capacity: 114,954 mt/y
Boxboard/cartonboard: 114,954 mt/y
Paper and Paperboard Mill Data:
Stock Preparation:
Pulpers: 2
Refiners: 12
Paper Machines: 1
No. 3, fourdrinier (3), total capacity 114,954 mt/y, Trim width 3.75 m, Boxboard/cartonboard
Coating Machines: 3
No. 1, on machine
No. 2, on machine
No. 3, on machine
Finishing Equipment:
Rewinders: 1
Sheeters: 2
Energy Data:
Power boilers: 3
Combustion turbines: 2 at 10 MW
Electrical demand for mill: 514 MWh/D

ⒽWhakatane Mill Ltd.
Ownership: Reynolds Group Holdings Ltd.
Mill Road
Whakatane, Bay of Plenty
New Zealand
Phone: (64) 7 307 1899
Fax: (64) 7 307 1655
Email: firstname.lastname@whakatanemill.co.nz
Web Address: www.rankgroup.co.nz
Personnel:
CEO & Mill Mgr.: Graham Millar
Phone: (64) 7 307 1899
Fax: (64) 7 307 1655
Email: graham.millar@whakatanemill.co.nz
Tech. Mgr.: Anna Schooler
Phone: (64) 7 307 1899
Fax: (64) 7 307 1655
Email: anna.schooler@whakatanemill.co.nz
Total Employees of Company: 259
Mill Locations:
Whakatane Mill Ltd., Whakatane Mill, Mill Road, Whakatane, New Zealand, Capacity: 114,954 mt/y, (Pulp mill, Paperboard mill)
Phone: (64) 7 307 1899
Fax: (64) 7 307 1655
Email: firstname.lastname@whakatanemill.co.nz

ⒽWinstone Pulp International Ltd.
Ownership: Ernslaw One
Level 22, Bdo Tower, 120 Albert St.
1010 Auckland
New Zealand
Mailing Address: PO Box 6268, Wellesley Street, 1141 Auckland, New Zealand
Phone: (64) 9 302 1187
Fax: (64) 9 302 1187
Email: communications@wpi-international.co.nz
Web Address: www.wpi-international.co.nz
Personnel:
Man. Dir.: David Anderson
Phone: (64) 9 302 1187
Fax: (64) 9 302 1182
Email: david.anderson@wpi-international.co.nz
Pulp Sls. & Mktg. Mgr.: Mike Ryan
Phone: (64) 9 302 1187
Fax: (64) 9 302 1182
Email: mike.ryan@wpi-international.co.nz
Group Mgr. Health & Safety: Terry Phillips
Phone: (64) 9 302 1187
Fax: (64) 9 302 1182
Email: terry.phillips@wpi-international.co.nz
Project Mgr.: Dennis Rowe
Phone: (64) 9 302 1187
Fax: (64) 9 302 1182
Email: dennis.rowe@wpi-international.co.nz
Tech. Sls. Mgr.: Danie Loots
Total Employees of Company: 300
Mill Locations:
Winstone Pulp International Ltd., Karioi Pulp Mill, State Highway 49, 4691 Karioi, Ohakune, New Zealand, (Pulp mill)
Phone: (64) 6 385 8545
Fax: (64) 6 385 8547
Email: (first name.surname@wpi-international.co.nz)

ⓂWinstone Pulp International Ltd.
Karioi Pulp Mill
State Highway 49
4691 Karioi, Ohakune
New Zealand
Mailing Address: PO Box 48, 4660 Ohakune, New Zealand
Phone: (64) 6 385 8545
Fax: (64) 6 385 8547
Email: (first, name.surname@wpi-international.co.nz)
Web Address: www.wpi-international.co.nz
Personnel:
Mill Mgr.: Paul Saunders
Phone: (64) 6 385 8545
Fax: (64) 6 385 8547
Email: paul.saunders@wpi-international.co.nz
Tech. Mgr.: Gustav Barn
Phone: (64) 6 385 8545
Fax: (64) 6 385 8547
Email: gustav.barn@wpi-international.co.nz
Total Employees at this Location: 145
Type of Operation: Pulp mill
Pulp Grades and Capacities:
Total pulp capacity: 196,628 mt/y
Pulp available for market: 192,066 mt/y
Mechanical Pulp: 196,628 mt/y
Pulp Mill Data:
Mechanical Pulping Systems:
BCTMP systems: 1
Bleach Plant Systems: 1
Mechanical Pulping System, Type: Softwood, Sequence: P
Pulp Dryers:
Flash dryers 1, Flash dryers 1
Energy Data:
Power boilers: 1
TMP Reboiler: 1
Electrical demand for mill: 1,107 MWh/D

OMAN

ⒽSuhar Paper Mill
Ownership: Atlas Paper Industries
Suhar
Oman
Mill Locations:
Suhar Paper Mill, Suhar Mill, Suhar, Oman, Capacity: 4,000 mt/y, (Paperboard mill)

ⓂSuhar Paper Mill
Suhar Mill
Suhar
Oman
Type of Operation: Paperboard mill
Paper/Paperboard Grades and Capacities:
Total paper and paperboard capacity: 4,000 mt/y
Linerboard: 2,000 mt/y
Corrugating medium/fluting: 2,000 mt/y
Paper and Paperboard Mill Data:
Paper Machines: 1
No. 1, total capacity 4,000 mt/y, Linerboard, Corrugating medium/fluting

PAKISTAN

ⒽASL Paper Mills
Plot No 17, 18, 19, Sector 21, Korangi Industrial Area
Karachi, Sindh
Pakistan
Phone: (92) 21 5020973/5022401/5011321
Fax: (92) 21 6313052/5022401
Email: aslpapermills@yahoo.com
Mill Locations:
ASL Paper Mills, Karachi Mill, Plot No 17, 18, 19, Sector 21, Korangi Industrial Area, Karachi, Pakistan, Capacity: 7,000 mt/y, (Pulp mill, Paper mill)
Phone: (92) 21 5020973/5022401/5011321
Fax: (92) 21 6313052/5022401
Email: aslpapermills@yahoo.com

ⓂASL Paper Mills
Karachi Mill
Plot No 17, 18, 19, Sector 21, Korangi Industrial Area
Karachi, Sindh
Pakistan
Phone: (92) 21 5020973/5022401/5011321
Fax: (92) 21 6313052/5022401
Email: aslpapermills@yahoo.com
Personnel:
Man. Dir.: Sajjad Ali Mehkeri
Phone: (92) 21 5020973/5022401/5011321
Mgr.: Anwar Ahmed Khan
Phone: (92) 21 5020973/5022401/5011321
Total Employees at this Location: 150
Type of Operation: Pulp mill, Paper mill
Pulp Grades and Capacities:
Total pulp capacity: 6,000 mt/y
Recycled Pulping: 6,000 mt/y
Paper/Paperboard Grades and Capacities:
Total paper and paperboard capacity: 7,000 mt/y
Uncoated woodfree/freesheet: 7,000 mt/y
Paper and Paperboard Mill Data:
Stock Preparation:
Refiners: 1
Paper Machines: 1
No. 1, cylinder, total capacity 7,000 mt/y, Trim width 2.2 m, Uncoated woodfree/freesheet

Pakistan

Finishing Equipment:
Rewinders: 1 at 4,500 mt/y

ⓘⓜ Atas Paper (Pvt) Ltd.
Sheikhupura Mill
Ownership: 100% by Syed Group of Companies
16th Km Lahore Sheikhupura Road
Sheikhupura, Punjab
Pakistan
  Phone: (92) 42 7970219
  Fax: (92) 42 7970319
Personnel:
  Chief Exec.: Gul Malik
  Phone: (92) 42 7970219
Total Employees of Company: 180
Total Employees at this Location: 80
Type of Operation: Pulp mill, Paper mill
Pulp Grades and Capacities:
  Total pulp capacity: 8,000 mt/y
  Recycled Pulping: 8,000 mt/y
Paper/Paperboard Grades and Capacities:
  Total paper and paperboard capacity: 6,000 mt/y
  Packaging papers
  Specialty and industrial
Paper and Paperboard Mill Data:
  Stock Preparation:
  Pulpers: 1
  Refiners: 3
Paper Machines: 1
  No. 1, Yankee dryer, cylinder, total capacity 6,000 mt/y, Trim width 2.2 m, Packaging papers, Specialty and industrial
Finishing Equipment:
  Rewinders: 1 at 4,000 mt/y
  Sheeters: 1 at 4,500 mt/y
Energy Data:
  Power boilers: 2

ⓘ Bulleh Shah Packaging (Private) Limited
Ownership: 35% by Stora Enso Oyj, 25% by the public, 25.40% by Packages Ltd., 14.60% by local financial institutions
Shahrah-e-Roomi PO Amer-sidhu
54760 Lahore
Pakistan
  Phone: (92) 42 358 11541-6, 358 11191-4
  Fax: (92) 42 358 11195, 358 20147
  Email: info@packages.com.pk
  Web Address: www.packages.com.pk, www.storaenso.com/
Personnel:
  Chmn.: Towfiq Habib Chinoy
  Phone: (92) 21 583 1618
  Fax: (92) 21 586 0251
  CEO & Man. Dir.: Syed Hyder Ali
  Phone: (92) 21 583 1618
  Fax: (92) 21 586 0251
  Dir. & Gen. Mgr.: Syed Aslam Mehdi
  Phone: (92) 21 583 1618
  Fax: (92) 21 586 0251
  Dir. & Finan. Mgr.: Khalid Yacob
  Phone: (92) 21 583 1618
  Fax: (92) 21 586 0251
Total Employees of Company: 1,891
Mill Locations:
Bulleh Shah Packaging (Private) Limited, Bulleh Shah Paper Mill, Kasur Factory 11 km Kasur-Kot Radha Kishan Road, Kasur, Pakistan, Capacity: 255,000 mt/y, (Pulp mill, Paper mill, Paperboard mill)
  Phone: (92) 344 413123/492 717335
Bulleh Shah Packaging (Private) Limited, Lahore Mill, Shahrah-E-Roomi PO Amer Sidhu, 54760 Lahore, Pakistan, Capacity: 33,000 mt/y, (Pulp mill, Paper mill, Paperboard mill)
  Phone: (92) 42 5811541-6/191-4
  Fax: (92) 42 5811195/5820147
  Email: info@packages.com.pk

ⓘ Century Paper & Board Mills Ltd.
Lakson Sq., Bldg. No. 2, Sarwar Shaheed Rd.
74200 Karachi, Sindh
Pakistan
  Phone: (92) 21 3569 8000
  Fax: (92) 21 3568 1163
  Email: info@centurypaper.com.pk
  Web Address: www.centurypaper.com.pk
Personnel:
  Chmn.: Iqbal Ali Lakhani
  Phone: (92) 21 3568 2425
  Fax: (92) 21 3568 1163
  CEO: Aftab Ahmad
  Phone: (92) 21 3569 8000
  Fax: (92) 21 3568 1163
  Email: aftab-ahmad@centurypaper.com.pk
  CFO: Syed Ahmad Ashraf
  Phone: (92) 21 3569 8000
  Fax: (92) 21 3568 1163
  Email: ahmad-ashraf@centurypaper.com.pk
  Gen. Mgr., Mktg.: Tanveer Ahmad Khalid
  Phone: (92) 21 3569 8034
  Fax: (92) 21 3568 1163
  Email: tanveer-ahmed@centurypaper.com.pk
  Gen. Mgr. Supply chain: Sabiar Imtiaz
  Phone: (92) 21 3568 5960
  Fax: (92) 21 3568 1163
  Email: sabirimtiaz@centurypaper.com.pk
  Company Sec.: Mansoor Ahmed
  Phone: (92) 21 3569 8000
  Fax: (92) 21 3568 1163
  Email: mansoor-ahmed@centurypaper.com.pk
Total Employees of Company: 1,643
Total Employees at this Location: 60
Mill Locations:
Century Paper & Board Mills Ltd., Kasur Mill, 62-Km, Lahore Multan Rd., N-5, Jamber Khurd, Bhai Pheru, Dist. Kasur, Pakistan, Capacity: 248,000 mt/y, (Pulp mill, Paper mill, Paperboard mill)
  Phone: (92) 49 451 0061/62
  Fax: (92) 49 451 0063
  Email: info@centurypaper.com.pk

ⓜ Century Paper & Board Mills Ltd.
Kasur Mill
62-Km, Lahore Multan Rd., N-5, Jamber Khurd
Bhai Pheru, Dist. Kasur
Pakistan
  Phone: (92) 49 451 0061/62
  Fax: (92) 49 451 0063
  Email: info@centurypaper.com.pk
  Web Address: www.centurypaper.com.pk
Personnel:
  Gen. Mgr. (Prod.): Jehanzeb Ali Akhtar
  Phone: (92) 49 451 0061
  Fax: (92) 49 451 0063
  Email: jahanzeb-ali@centurypaper.com.pk
  Gen. Mgr. Tech.: Nadeem Ullah Shaikh
  Phone: (92) 49 451 0061
  Fax: (92) 49 451 0063
  Email: nadeem-ullah@centurypaper.com.pk
Total Employees at this Location: 670
Type of Operation: Pulp mill, Paper mill, Paperboard mill
Pulp Grades and Capacities:
  Total pulp capacity: 225,351 mt/y
  Recycled Pulping: 202,073 mt/y
  Other Pulp: 23,278 mt/y
Pulp Mill Data:
  Chemical Pulping Systems:
  Batch digesters: 5
  Bleach Plant Systems: 2
  BL-1, Type: ECF, Sequence: HH, Capacity 30,000 admt/y
  BL-2, Type: ECF, Sequence: HH, Capacity 15,000 admt/y
  Chemical Recovery Equipment:
  Recovery boilers
  Recycled Fiber Treatment Lines:
  Flotation deinking lines: 2 at 30,000
  Pulpers: 6 at 200,000 admt/y
Paper/Paperboard Grades and Capacities:
  Total paper and paperboard capacity: 248,000 mt/y
  Uncoated woodfree/freesheet: 35,000 mt/y
  Specialty and industrial: 3,000 mt/y
  Boxboard/cartonboard: 210,000 mt/y
Paper and Paperboard Mill Data:
  Stock Preparation:
  Pulpers: 7
  Refiners: 7
Paper Machines: 7
  No. 1, fourdrinier, total capacity 22,000 mt/y, Trim width 2.4 m, Boxboard/cartonboard
  No. 2, fourdrinier, total capacity 17,000 mt/y, Trim width 2.4 m, Uncoated woodfree/freesheet
  No. 3, fourdrinier, total capacity 3,000 mt/y, Trim width 1.85 m, Specialty and industrial
  No. 4, fourdrinier (3), total capacity 33,000 mt/y, Trim width 2.4 m, Boxboard/cartonboard
  No. 5, fourdrinier (2), total capacity 25,000 mt/y, Trim width 2.4 m, Boxboard/cartonboard
  No. 6, fourdrinier, total capacity 18,000 mt/y, Trim width 2.4 m, Uncoated woodfree/freesheet
  No. 7, Fourdrinier (4), total capacity 130,000 mt/y, Trim width 3.1 m, Boxboard/cartonboard
Coating Machines: 2
  I, total capacity 14,000 mt/y., off machine
  II, total capacity 21,000 mt/y., off machine
Finishing Equipment:
  Rewinders: 7 at 300,000 mt/y
  Sheeters: 9 at 200,000 mt/y
Energy Data:
  Power boilers: 5
  HRSG boiler: 7
  Combustion turbines: 4 at 5 MW
  Electrical demand for mill: 397 MWh/D

ⓘ Chilya Corrugated Board Mills Ltd
Ownership: Private Ltd.
Near National Cement Stadium Road
Karachi, Sindh
Pakistan
  Phone: (92) 4987156-57
Personnel:
  Chmn.: Mr. Muhammad Ali
  Phone: (92) 5860678
  Fax: (92) 5864651
  Dir.: Mr. Abbas Ali
  Phone: (92) 5860678
  Fax: (92) 5864651
  Prod. Mgr.: Fazal Hussain
  Phone: (92) 4987156-57
Total Employees at this Location: 80
Mill Locations:
Chilya Corrugated Board Mills Ltd, Karachi Mill, Near National Cement Stadium Road, Karachi, Pakistan, Capacity: 6,500 mt/y, (Pulp mill, Paper mill, Paperboard mill)

ⓜ Chilya Corrugated Board Mills Ltd
Karachi Mill
Near National Cement Stadium Road
Karachi, Sindh
Pakistan
Personnel:
  Paper Mill Incharge: Mr. Tajuddin
  Pulp Mill Incharge: Abdul Ghafoor
Total Employees at this Location: 75
Type of Operation: Pulp mill, Paper mill, Paperboard mill
Pulp Grades and Capacities:
  Total pulp capacity: 6,000 mt/y
Pulp Mill Data:
  Chemical Pulping Systems:
  Batch digesters: 4
Paper/Paperboard Grades and Capacities:
  Total paper and paperboard capacity: 6,500 mt/y
  Corrugating medium/fluting: 6,500 mt/y
Paper and Paperboard Mill Data:

Pakistan

Stock Preparation:
  Pulpers: 2
  Refiners: 3
Paper Machines: 1
  No. 1, fourdrinier, total capacity 6,500 mt/y, Trim width 1.54 m, Corrugating medium/fluting
Finishing Equipment:
  Rewinders: 1 at 3,500 mt/y
Energy Data:
  Power boilers: 1

Faruki Pulp Mills Ltd.
Ownership: 52.31% by Public Ltd., 47.69% by JDW Sugar Mills Limited
Ground Floor RB1, Awami Complex, 1/4 Usman Block, New Garden Town
54000 Lahore, Punjab
Pakistan
  Phone: (92) 42 35869593
  Fax: (92) 42 3586 9592
  Email: mail@farukipulpmills.com
  Web Address: www.farukipulpmills.com, www.jdw-group.com/AboutJDW.html#FarukiPulp
Personnel:
  CEO: Salim A. Faruki
  Phone: (92) 42 35869593
  Fax: (92) 42 3586 9592
  Email: 300 8405768
  COO: Shahid Faruki
  Phone: (92) 42 35869593
  Fax: (92) 42 3586 9592
  CFO: Shahid Rana
  Phone: (92) 42 35869593
  Fax: (92) 42 3586 9592
  Mill Mgr.: Mohammad Nazir
  Phone: (92) 42 35869593
  Fax: (92) 42 3586 9592
  Proj. Dir.: Baljinder Singh
  Phone: (92) 42 35869593
  Fax: (92) 42 3586 9592
  Exec. Dir.: Waleed Faruki
  Phone: (92) 42 35869593
  Fax: (92) 42 3586 9592
Total Employees at this Location: 25
Mill Locations:
Faruki Pulp Mills Ltd., Mangowal, Gujrat Mill, 20KM Gujrat Sargodha Road, Mangowal, Gujrat, Pakistan, (Pulp mill)
  Phone: (92) 53 3545207-702
  Fax: (92) 53 354 6005
  Email: info@farukipulpmills.com

Faruki Pulp Mills Ltd.
Mangowal, Gujrat Mill
Mill is idle (idle since September 2012 because of problems with power supply, due to restart before the end of 2014)
20KM Gujrat Sargodha Road
Mangowal, Gujrat, Punjab
Pakistan
  Phone: (92) 53 3545207-702
  Fax: (92) 53 354 6005
  Email: info@farukipulpmills.com
  Web Address: www.farukipulpmills.com
Personnel:
  COO: Shahid A. Faruki
  Phone: (92) 53 354 5207/6006/5701
  Email: shahid@farukipulpmills.com
  Exec. Dir.: Waleed A. Faruki
  Phone: (92) 53 354 5207/6006/5701
  Email: wfaruki78@yahoo.com
  Mill Mgr.: Muhammad Nazir
  Phone: (92) 53 354 5207/6006/5701
  Asst. Mill Mgr.: Hamid Mehmood
  Phone: (92) 53 354 5207/6006/5701
  Chief Eng.: Haji Gulfraz Khan
  Phone: (92) 53 354 5207/6006/5701
Total Employees at this Location: 80
Type of Operation: Pulp mill
Pulp Mill Data:
  Chemical Pulping Systems:
    Batch digesters: 3
  Pulp Lines: 1
  Bleach Plant Systems: 1
    Chemical Pulping System, Type: HW
  Chemical Recovery Equipment:
    Evaporator lines: 5
    Recovery boilers: 1
    Lime Kiln
  Pulp Dryers:
    Air Float dryers
Energy Data:
  Power boilers: 1
  Steam turbines: 1 at 7.5 MW
  Electrical demand for mill: 161 MWh/D

Flying Group of Industries Ltd.
103 Fazil Road, Street John Park
Lahore, Punjab
Pakistan
  Phone: (92) 42 667 4301/5
  Fax: (92) 42 666 0693
  Email: info@flyinggroup.com.pk
Personnel:
  Chmn.: Momim Qamar
  Phone: (92) 42 6674301
  Fax: (92) 42 6660693
  Pres./Sls. Dir.: Imran Qamar
  Phone: (92) 42 667 4301/5
  Fax: (92) 42 666 0693
  Pres./R&D Dir.: Kamran Khan
  Phone: (92) 42 667 4301/5
  Fax: (92) 42 666 0693
  Mill Mgr.: Mohammad Israr
  Phone: (92) 42 667 4301/5
  Fax: (92) 42 666 0693
  Prod. Mgr.: Younas Khan
  Phone: (92) 42 667 4301/5
  Fax: (92) 42 666 0693
  Admin. Mgr.: Maj. Naeem Amjad
  Phone: (92) 42 667 4301/5
  Fax: (92) 42 666 0693
Mill Locations:
Flying Board and Paper Products Ltd., Sheikhupura Mill, 26 Km. Lahore - Sheikhupura Rd., Sheikhupura, Pakistan, Capacity: 30,000 mt/y, (Pulp mill, Paper mill)
  Phone: (92) 563 406 143
Flying Kraft Paper Mills Ltd., Charsadda Mill, Noshehra Road, Charsadda, Pakistan, Capacity: 30,000 mt/y, (Pulp mill, Paper mill)
  Phone: (92) 1 511272 / 511304-6
  Fax: (92) 42 6660693
  Email: info@flyingpaper.com.pk
Poly Paper & Board Mills (Pvt.) Ltd., Sheikhupura Mill, Km. 13, Sheikhupura-Faisalabad Road, Sheikhupura, Pakistan, Capacity: 4,000 mt/y, (Pulp mill, Paper mill)
  Phone: (92) (4948) 211 152
  Fax: (92) (42) 666 0693
  Email: info@flyingtissue.com
Zarnan Paper and Board Mills Ltd., Sheikhupura Mill, 10 km. Faisalabad Rd., Sheikhupura, Pakistan, Capacity: 20,000 mt/y, (Pulp mill, Paper mill, Paperboard mill)
  Phone: (92) 42 6674301-5
  Fax: (92) 42 6660693

Flying Board and Paper Products Ltd.
Sheikhupura Mill
Ownership: Flying Group of Industries Ltd.
26 Km. Lahore - Sheikhupura Rd.
Sheikhupura, Punjab
Pakistan
  Phone: (92) 563 406 143
Personnel:
  CEO: Kamran Khan
  Phone: (92) 563 406 143
  Exec. Dir.: Muhamman Durez
  Phone: (92) 563 406 143
Total Employees at this Location: 215
Type of Operation: Pulp mill, Paper mill
Pulp Grades and Capacities:
  Total pulp capacity: 17,040 mt/y
  Other Pulp: 17,040 mt/y
Pulp Mill Data:
  Chemical Pulping Systems:
    Batch digesters: 5
  Bleach Plant Systems: 1
    No. 1, Sequence: C, Capacity 10,000 admt/y
  Chemical Recovery Equipment:
    Evaporator lines: 1
    Recovery boilers: 1
Paper/Paperboard Grades and Capacities:
  Total paper and paperboard capacity: 30,000 mt/y
  Uncoated woodfree/freesheet: 30,000 mt/y
Paper and Paperboard Mill Data:
  Stock Preparation:
    Pulpers: 3
    Refiners: 8
  Paper Machines: 1
    No. 1, fourdrinier, total capacity 30,000 mt/y, Trim width 2.8 m, Uncoated woodfree/freesheet
  Finishing Equipment:
    Supercalenders: 1 at 4,000 mt/y
    Rewinders: 1 at 12,000 mt/y
    Sheeters: 2 at 3,500 mt/y
Energy Data:
  Power boilers: 2
  Electrical demand for mill: 84 MWh/D

Flying Kraft Paper Mills Ltd.
Charsadda Mill
Ownership: Flying Group of Industries Ltd.
Noshehra Road
Charsadda, Khyber Pakhtunkhwa
Pakistan
  Phone: (92) 1 511272 / 511304-6
  Fax: (92) 42 6660693
  Email: info@flyingpaper.com.pk
  Web Address: www.flyingpaper.com.pk
Personnel:
  CEO: Momin Qamar
  Phone: (92) 1 511272 / 511304-6
  Mill Mgr.: Younus Khan
  Phone: (92) 1 511272 / 511304-6
  Fax: (92) 42 6660693
Type of Operation: Pulp mill, Paper mill
Pulp Grades and Capacities:
  Total pulp capacity: 30,000 mt/y
  Recycled Pulping: 30,000 mt/y
Pulp Mill Data:
  Chemical Pulping Systems:
    Batch digesters: 4
    Continuous digesters: 1
  Bleach Plant Systems: 1
    No. 1, Sequence: CEH, Capacity 30,000 admt/y
  Chemical Recovery Equipment:
    Evaporator lines: 5
    Recovery boilers: 1
Paper/Paperboard Grades and Capacities:
  Total paper and paperboard capacity: 30,000 mt/y
  Packaging papers: 30,000 mt/y
Paper and Paperboard Mill Data:
  Stock Preparation:
    Pulpers: 2
    Refiners: 5
  Paper Machines: 2
    No. 1, fourdrinier, Trim width 3.2 m, Packaging papers
    No. 2, fourdrinier, Trim width 3.2 m, Packaging papers
  Finishing Equipment:
    Rewinders: 2 at 7,000 mt/y
    Sheeters: 3 at 10,000 mt/y
Energy Data:
  Power boilers: 3

Malik Board and Paper Industries
Ownership: 100% by Private Ltd.
119 / 1-D Block, Model Town
Lahore, Punjab
Pakistan
  Phone: (92) 42 5866637/39023

Pakistan

Fax: (92) 42 5861823
Email: mbi@wol.net.pk
Personnel:
CEO: Ahmed Muzzaffer Malik
Phone: (92) 42 5866637/39023
Fax: (92) 42 5861823
Total Employees of Company: 1,300
Total Employees at this Location: 60
Mill Locations:
Malik Board and Paper Industries, Lahore Mill, 21 K.M. Lahore Sheikhupura Rd., Lahore, Pakistan, Capacity: 40,000 mt/y, (Pulp mill, Paper mill)
Phone: (92) 42 7970014-15 /0394
Fax: (92) 42 7970394
Email: mbi@wol.net.pk

Malik Board Mills
Ownership: Public Ltd.
31 Km Lahore Sheikhupura Road
Sheikhupura, Punjab
Pakistan
Phone: (92) 42 5877384
Fax: (92) 42 5877385
Mill Locations:
Malik Board Mills, Sheikhupura Mill, 31 Km Lahore Sheikhupura Road, Sheikhupura, Pakistan, Capacity: 7,500 mt/y, (Pulp mill, Paper mill)
Phone: (92) 42 5877384
Fax: (92) 42 5877385

Malik Board Mills
Sheikhupura Mill
31 Km Lahore Sheikhupura Road
Sheikhupura, Punjab
Pakistan
Phone: (92) 42 5877384
Fax: (92) 42 5877385
Personnel:
Mill Mgr.: Mohammed Dean Mirva
Phone: (92) 42 5877384
Type of Operation: Pulp mill, Paper mill
Pulp Grades and Capacities:
Total pulp capacity: 6,000 mt/y
Pulp Mill Data:
Chemical Pulping Systems:
Batch digesters: 2
Bleach Plant Systems: 1
No. 1 Capacity 6,000 admt/y
Paper/Paperboard Grades and Capacities:
Total paper and paperboard capacity: 7,500 mt/y
Uncoated woodfree/freesheet: 4,000 mt/y
Boxboard/cartonboard: 3,500 mt/y
Paper and Paperboard Mill Data:
Paper Machines: 1
No. 1, fourdrinier, total capacity 7,500 mt/y, Trim width 3 m, Uncoated woodfree/freesheet, Boxboard/cartonboard

Malik Board and Paper Industries
Lahore Mill
21 K.M. Lahore Sheikhupura Rd.
Lahore, Punjab
Pakistan
Phone: (92) 42 7970014-15 /0394
Fax: (92) 42 7970394
Email: mbi@wol.net.pk
Personnel:
CEO: Muzzaffer Ahmed Malik
Phone: (92) 42 5866637/5839023
Fax: (92) 42 5861823
Total Employees at this Location: 800
Type of Operation: Pulp mill, Paper mill
Pulp Grades and Capacities:
Total pulp capacity: 35,919 mt/y
Recycled Pulping: 35,919 mt/y
Pulp Mill Data:
Pulp Lines: 10
Paper/Paperboard Grades and Capacities:
Total paper and paperboard capacity: 40,000 mt/y
Boxboard/cartonboard: 40,000 mt/y
Paper and Paperboard Mill Data:
Paper Machines: 1
No. 1, multi-cylinder, total capacity 40,000 mt/y, Trim width 2.1 m, Boxboard/cartonboard

Mandiali Paper Mill Ltd.
Sheikhupura Mill
Ownership: 100% by private limited company
Km. 21, Lahore-Sheikhupura Rd. PO Kot Abdul Malik
Sheikhupura, Punjab
Pakistan
Phone: (92) 42 7970251-52 / 111767767
Fax: (92) 42 797 1416
Email: mandiali@brain.net.pk, ali@mandiali.com, mail@mandiali.com
Personnel:
Chmn./Pres.: Sheikh Ali Manzoor
Phone: (92) 42 7970251-52 / 111767767
Dir.: Adil Manzoor
Phone: (92) 42 7970251-52 / 111767767
Total Employees of Company: 320
Total Employees at this Location: 320
Type of Operation: Pulp mill, Paper mill
Pulp Grades and Capacities:
Total pulp capacity: 22,031 mt/y
Other Pulp: 22,031 mt/y
Pulp Mill Data:
Chemical Pulping Systems:
Batch digesters: 5
Bleach Plant Systems: 1
No. 1
Chemical Recovery Equipment:
Evaporator lines: 1
Recovery boilers: 1
Paper/Paperboard Grades and Capacities:
Total paper and paperboard capacity: 36,000 mt/y
Uncoated woodfree/freesheet: 36,000 mt/y
Paper and Paperboard Mill Data:
Stock Preparation:
Pulpers: 5
Refiners: 3
Paper Machines: 2
No. 1, fourdrinier, total capacity 14,000 mt/y, Trim width 1.5 m, Uncoated woodfree/freesheet
No. 2, fourdrinier, total capacity 22,000 mt/y, Uncoated woodfree/freesheet
Finishing Equipment:
Rewinders: 1 at 3,000 mt/y
Energy Data:
Power boilers
Electrical demand for mill: 106 MWh/D

Master Papers (Pvt) Ltd
Karachi Mill
Ownership: 100% by private limited company
Plot No. 35, Sector 12-B North Industrial Area
75850 Karachi, Sindh
Pakistan
Phone: (92) 21 6909071/2/3
Fax: (92) 21 6909622
Personnel:
Chief Exec.: Muhammad Aziz
Phone: (92) 21 6909071/2/3
Dir.: Ahmed Tufail
Phone: (92) 21 6909072
Dir.: Ahmed Suhail
Phone: (92) 21 6909071/2/3
Total Employees at this Location: 325
Type of Operation: Pulp mill, Paper mill
Pulp Grades and Capacities:
Total pulp capacity: 6,000 mt/y
Pulp Mill Data:
Pulp Dryers:
Flash dryers 5
Paper/Paperboard Grades and Capacities:
Total paper and paperboard capacity: 6,000 mt/y
Corrugating medium/fluting: 6,000 mt/y
Paper and Paperboard Mill Data:
Paper Machines: 1
PM 1, cylinder mould, total capacity 6,000 mt/y, Trim width 1.7 m, Corrugating medium/fluting

Mohammadi Paper & Board Industries (Pvt.) Ltd.
Sheikhupura Lahore Unit 1
Ownership: Chawla Group
27 Km. Lahore-Sheikhupura Road
54000 Sheikhupura Lahore, Punjab
Pakistan
Phone: (92) 563 0311110/406312
Fax: (92) 425 393382
Email: mohammadiindustries@hotmail.com
Personnel:
Man. Dir.: Abbas Ali Chawla
Phone: (92) 563 0311110/406312
Total Employees at this Location: 25
Type of Operation: Paper mill
Mill Locations:
Mohammadi Paper & Board Industries (Pvt.) Ltd., Sheikhupura Lahore Unit 2, 31 Km. Lahore Sheikhupura Rd., 5400 Sheikhupura Lahore, Pakistan, Capacity: 15,000 mt/y, (Pulp mill, Paper mill, Paperboard mill)
Phone: (92) 563 406532
Shaheen Paper & Board Industries (pvt) Ltd, Raiwind Lahore Mill, 4 km Raiwind Manga Road, District Kasoor Raiwind, Raiwind Lahore, Pakistan, Capacity: 8,000 mt/y, (Paper mill)
Phone: (92) 42 5392382/5391030
Fax: (92) 42 5393382
Email: shaheenindustries@hotmail.com
Paper/Paperboard Grades and Capacities:
Total paper and paperboard capacity: 15,000 mt/y
Uncoated woodfree/freesheet: 15,000 mt/y

Mohammadi Paper & Board Industries (Pvt.) Ltd.
Sheikhupura Lahore Unit 2
31 Km. Lahore Sheikhupura Rd.
5400 Sheikhupura Lahore, Punjab
Pakistan
Phone: (92) 563 406532
Personnel:
Man. Dir.: Abbas Ali Chawla
Phone: (92) 563 406532
Total Employees at this Location: 200
Type of Operation: Pulp mill, Paper mill, Paperboard mill
Pulp Grades and Capacities:
Total pulp capacity: 12,000 mt/y
Pulp Mill Data:
Pulp Lines: 3
Bleach Plant Systems: 1
Pulp Dryers:
Flash dryers 1
Paper/Paperboard Grades and Capacities:
Total paper and paperboard capacity: 15,000 mt/y
Packaging papers
Linerboard
Corrugating medium/fluting
Boxboard/cartonboard
Paper and Paperboard Mill Data:
Stock Preparation:
Pulpers: 3
Refiners: 3
Paper Machines: 1
No. 1, fourdrinier, cylinder (2), total capacity 15,000 mt/y, Trim width 2.2 m, Packaging papers, Containerboard
Coating Machines: 1
No. 1, total capacity 3,500 mt/y.
Finishing Equipment:
Rewinders: 1 at 2,500 mt/y

Pakistan

Sheeters: 1
Energy Data:
Electrical demand for mill: 30 MWh/D

Olympia Paper & Board Mills (Pvt) Ltd
Peshawar Mill
Ownership: 100% by Private Shareholders, Shah Zaman (Pvt) Ltd.
Plot # 27-28, Industries Estate, Jamrud Road
Peshawar, Khyber Pakhtunkhwa
Pakistan
  Phone: (92) 91 813799/815729
  Fax: (92) 91 813799
Personnel:
  CEO: Brig.(Rtd) Abdul Samad Khan
  Phone: (92) 91 813799
  Gen. Mgr. Admin.: Dawood Khan
  Phone: (92) 91 813799
  Gen. Mgr. Prod.: Hamayoon Khan
  Phone: (92) 91 813799/815729
Total Employees of Company: 142
Total Employees at this Location: 65
Type of Operation: Pulp mill, Paper mill, Paperboard mill
Pulp Grades and Capacities:
  Total pulp capacity: 18,000 mt/y
Pulp Mill Data:
  Chemical Pulping Systems:
  Batch digesters: 3
Paper/Paperboard Grades and Capacities:
  Total paper and paperboard capacity: 16,000 mt/y
  Boxboard/cartonboard: 16,000 mt/y
Paper and Paperboard Mill Data:
  Stock Preparation:
  Pulpers: 2
  Refiners: 5
Paper Machines: 2
No. 1, fourdrinier, Yankee dryer, Trim width 2.6 m, Boxboard/cartonboard
No. 2, fourdrinier, Trim width 2.6 m, Boxboard/cartonboard
Finishing Equipment:
  Rewinders: 1 at 6,000 mt/y
  Sheeters: 2 at 4,500 mt/y

Omer Tissue Mills (Pvt) Ltd
Ownership: 100% by private limited company
16 Bank Square Model Town
Lahore, Punjab
Pakistan
  Email: omertiss@shoa.net
Personnel:
  CEO: Munawar Ahmed Malik
  Phone: (92) 42 5122481
  Email: omertiss@shoa.net
Total Employees of Company: 80
Total Employees at this Location: 40
Mill Locations:
Omer Tissue Mills (Pvt) Ltd, Lahore Mill, 132/5 Industrial Estate Kot Lakhpat, Lahore, Pakistan, Capacity: 6,000 mt/y, (Paper mill)
  Phone: (92) 42 5122481/50181
  Fax: (92) 42 5152572
  Email: omertiss@shoa.net

Omer Tissue Mills (Pvt) Ltd
Lahore Mill
132/5 Industrial Estate Kot Lakhpat
Lahore, Punjab
Pakistan
  Phone: (92) 42 5122481/50181
  Fax: (92) 42 5152572
  Email: omertiss@shoa.net
Personnel:
  Chief Exec.: Munawar Ahmed Malik
  Phone: (92) 42 5122481/50181
Total Employees at this Location: 300

Type of Operation: Paper mill
Pulp Grades and Capacities:
  Total pulp capacity: 4,000 mt/y
Paper/Paperboard Grades and Capacities:
  Total paper and paperboard capacity: 6,000 mt/y
  Tissue: 1,000 mt/y
  Packaging papers: 5,000 mt/y
Paper and Paperboard Mill Data:
Paper Machines: 1
PM 1, cylinder mould, total capacity 6,000 mt/y, Trim width 1.7 m

Bulleh Shah Packaging (Private) Limited
Bulleh Shah Paper Mill
Ownership: 35% by Stora Enso Oyj
Kasur Factory 11 km Kasur-Kot Radha Kishan Road
Kasur
Pakistan
  Phone: (92) 344 413123/492 717335
  Web Address: www.packages.com.pk
Total Employees at this Location: 770
Type of Operation: Pulp mill, Paper mill, Paperboard mill
Pulp Grades and Capacities:
  Total pulp capacity: 151,900 mt/y
  Recycled Pulping: 112,756 mt/y
  Other Pulp: 39,144 mt/y
Pulp Mill Data:
  Chemical Pulping Systems:
  Batch digesters: 1
  Mechanical Pulping Systems:
  CTMP systems: 1
  Bleach Plant Systems: 2
  Chemical Pulping System, Type: Straw
  DIP
  Chemical Recovery Equipment:
  Evaporator lines: 1
  Recovery boilers: 1
  Recycled Fiber Treatment Lines:
  Flotation deinking lines: 1
  Recycled packaging pulping lines: 1
Paper/Paperboard Grades and Capacities:
  Total paper and paperboard capacity: 255,000 mt/y
  Uncoated woodfree/freesheet: 92,000 mt/y
  Linerboard: 70,000 mt/y
  Corrugating medium/fluting: 23,000 mt/y
  Boxboard/cartonboard: 70,000 mt/y
Paper and Paperboard Mill Data:
Paper Machines: 2
No. 6, Multi-wire (3), total capacity 140,000 mt/y, Trim width 4.5 m, Boxboard/cartonboard, Linerboard
No. 7, fourdrinier, total capacity 115,000 mt/y, Trim width 4.4 m, Uncoated woodfree/freesheet, Corrugating medium/fluting
Coating Machines: 1
No. 6, total capacity 200,000 mt/y., on machine
Energy Data:
Power boilers
Combustion turbines: 1 at 11 MW
Steam turbines at 41 MW
Electrical demand for mill: 469 MWh/D

Bulleh Shah Packaging (Private) Limited
Lahore Mill
Ownership: 35% by Stora Enso Oyj
Shahrah-E-Roomi PO Amer Sidhu
54760 Lahore, Punjab
Pakistan
  Phone: (92) 42 5811541-6/191-4
  Fax: (92) 42 5811195/5820147
  Email: info@packages.com.pk
  Web Address: www.packages.com.pk
Personnel:
  Man. Dir.: Syed Hyder Ali
  Phone: (92) 42 5811541-6/191-4
  Fax: (92) 42 5811978

  Email: hydera@packages.com.pk
  Dir. & Gen. Mgr.: Rashid Mujeeb
  Phone: (92) 42 5811549
  Email: mujeeb@packages.com.pk
  Dir. & Finan. Mgr.: Khalid Yacob
  Phone: (92) 42 5810872
  Email: kyfrn@packages.com.pk
  Materials Mgr. (Fibrous): Tariq Ashfaq
  Phone: (92) 42 5810904
  Email: tashfaq@packages.com.pk
  Dpty. Gen. Mgr.: Syed Aslam Mehdi
  Phone: (92) 42 5810870
  Email: mehdi@packages.com.pk
  Mill Mgr.: Seppo Pakkanen
  Phone: (92) 42 5810908
  Email: seppo@packages.com.pk
  Prod. Mgr. (P&B): Sahirzada Rashid Hameed
  Phone: (92) 42 5811541-6/191-4
  Email: srashad@packages.com.pk
  Paper Mill Mgr.: Masood Abdullah
  Phone: (92) 42 5811541-6/191-4
  Email: masooda@packages.com.pk
  Tech. Mgr. (Mech.): Khalid Mahmood Butt
  Phone: (92) 42 5811541-6/191-4
  Email: khalid@packages.com.pk
  Tech. Mgr. (Power): Tariq M. Niaz
  Phone: (92) 42 5811482
  Email: tariqn@packages.com.pk
  R&D Mgr.: Dr. Asad Javed
  Phone: (92) 42 5811541-6/191-4
  Email: asadj@packages.com.pk
  Qlty. Assurance Mgr.: Muhammad Latif
  Phone: (92) 42 5811541-6/191-4
  Email: mlatif@packages.com.pk
  Dpty. Mktg. Mgr.: Nadeem Aslam
  Phone: (92) 42 5810878
  Email: nadeema@packages.com.pk
Type of Operation: Pulp mill, Paper mill, Paperboard mill
Pulp Grades and Capacities:
  Total pulp capacity: 3,033 mt/y
  Recycled Pulping: 3,033 mt/y
Pulp Mill Data:
  Chemical Pulping Systems:
  Continuous digesters: 3
  Bleach Plant Systems: 1
  No. 1, Sequence: H, Capacity 24,000 admt/y
  Chemical Recovery Equipment:
  Evaporator lines: 1
  Recovery boilers: 1
  Recycled Fiber Treatment Lines:
  Flotation deinking lines: 1 at 7,000 admt/y
  Pulpers: 3 at 108,000 admt/y
Paper/Paperboard Grades and Capacities:
  Total paper and paperboard capacity: 33,000 mt/y
  Tissue: 33,000 mt/y
Paper and Paperboard Mill Data:
  Stock Preparation:
  Pulpers: 4
  Refiners: 10
Paper Machines: 1
No. 9, crescent former, total capacity 33,000 mt/y, Trim width 2.85 m, Tissue, Uncoated woodfree/freesheet
Coating Machines: 1
No. 1, total capacity 22,000 mt/y., off machine
Finishing Equipment:
  Rewinders: 4
  Sheeters: 1
Energy Data:
Power boilers: 3
Steam turbines: 2 at 16.0 MW

Paramount Paper Board Mills (Pvt) Ltd.
Haripur Mill
Ownership: private limited company
Plot no. 99, Phase 5, Hattar Industrial Estate
Haripur
Pakistan

Pakistan

Phone: (92) 995 617037/637
Fax: (92) 51 2274904
Email: paramount-98@sat.et.pk
Personnel:
CEO: Alpaf Hassain Malik
Phone: (92) 995 617037/637
Ops. Dir.: Saisal Hussain Malik
Phone: (92) 321 850 1040
Total Employees of Company: 75
Total Employees at this Location: 240
Type of Operation: Paper mill
Pulp Grades and Capacities:
Total pulp capacity: 59,940 mt/y
Recycled Pulping: 59,940 mt/y

Pulp Mill Data:
Chemical Pulping Systems:
Batch digesters
Bleach Plant Systems: 1
DIP
Recycled Fiber Treatment Lines:
Flotation deinking lines: 1
Recycled packaging pulping lines: 1
Paper/Paperboard Grades and Capacities:
Total paper and paperboard capacity: 67,000 mt/y
Linerboard: 45,000 mt/y
Boxboard/cartonboard: 22,000 mt/y
Paper and Paperboard Mill Data:
Stock Preparation:
Pulpers: 3
Refiners: 4
Paper Machines: 2
No. 1, fourdrinier, total capacity 22,000 mt/y, Trim width 2.82 m, Boxboard/cartonboard
No. 2, fourdrinier, total capacity 45,000 mt/y, Trim width 3.1 m, Linerboard
Coating Machines: 1
PM#1, on machine
Finishing Equipment:
Rewinders: 1
Sheeters: 2
Energy Data:
Power boilers
Electrical demand for mill: 96 MWh/D

⊕⋒Pioneer Board Products (Pvt) Ltd.
Lahore Mill
Ownership: Private Limited
Qamar Chamber, 1/1 Turner Road
Lahore, Punjab
Pakistan
Phone: (92) 42 7323777/7354747
Fax: (92) 42 7120222
Email: fahimqmr@yahoo.com
Personnel:
Chmn.: Mian Fahim Qamar
Phone: (92) 300 8480 385
Pres.: Ahsan Saeed
Phone: (92) 42 7323777/7354747
Gen. Mgr. / Coordination: N. H. Mistry
Phone: (92) 42 7323777/7354747
Sr. Mgr.: M. M. Abdullah
Phone: (92) 42 7323777/7354747
Mgr., Corp. Affairs: M. Arshad Waheed
Phone: (92) 42 7323777/7354747
Admin. & Personnel Mgr.: Muhammad Munir
Phone: (92) 42 7323777/7354747
Total Employees at this Location: 130
Type of Operation: Pulp mill, Paper mill
Paper/Paperboard Grades and Capacities:
Total paper and paperboard capacity: 14,000 mt/y
Linerboard: 10,000 mt/y
Boxboard/cartonboard: 4,000 mt/y

⋒Poly Paper & Board Mills (Pvt.) Ltd.
Sheikhupura Mill
Ownership: Flying Group of Industries Ltd.
Km. 13, Sheikhupura-Faisalabad Road
Sheikhupura, Punjab
Pakistan

Phone: (92) (4948) 211 152
Fax: (92) (42) 666 0693
Email: info@flyingtissue.com
Web Address: www.flyingtissue.com
Personnel:
Dir.: Imran Qamar
Phone: (92) 342 6674301
Total Employees at this Location: 230
Type of Operation: Pulp mill, Paper mill
Pulp Grades and Capacities:
Total pulp capacity: 3,500 mt/y
Pulp Mill Data:
Pulp Lines: 1
Bleach Plant Systems: 2
No. 1
Paper/Paperboard Grades and Capacities:
Total paper and paperboard capacity: 4,000 mt/y
Tissue: 4,000 mt/y
Paper and Paperboard Mill Data:
Paper Machines: 1
No. 1, total capacity 4,000 mt/y, Tissue

⊕⋒Premier Paper Mills Ltd.
Sheikhupura Mill
Km. 8, Lahore Road, P.O. Kot Saleem
39350 Sheikhupura
Pakistan
Phone: (92) (563) 406 611/2
Fax: (92) (563) 406 613
Email: ppmltd@skp.wol.net.pk
Web Address: www.premiergroup.pk
Personnel:
Chmn.: Sheikh Zahoor Ali
Phone: (92) 4931 5885717-9/4931 6812
VP Purch./Sls.: Sheikh Manzoor Ali
Phone: (92) 4931 5885717-9/4931 6812
Mill Mgr./Prod. Mgr.: Mr. Razzak
Phone: (92) 4931 5885717-9/4931 6812
Email: ppmltd@skp.wol.net.pk
Tech. Mgr.: Muhammad Hanif Malik
Phone: (92) 4931 4055113
Fax: (92) 4931 612702
Email: ppmltd@skp.wol.net.pk
Sls. Dir.: Sheikh Saeed Zahoor Ali
Phone: (92) 4931 5885717-9/4931 6812
Dir.: Altaf Quereshi
Phone: (92) 4931 5885717-9/4931 6812
Total Employees of Company: 350
Total Employees at this Location: 250
Type of Operation: Pulp mill, Paper mill
Pulp Grades and Capacities:
Total pulp capacity: 33,000 mt/y
Pulp available for market: 4,000 mt/y

Pulp Mill Data:
Chemical Pulping Systems:
Batch digesters: 3
Bleach Plant Systems: 2
No. 1 Capacity 45,000 admt/y
Paper/Paperboard Grades and Capacities:
Total paper and paperboard capacity: 36,000 mt/y
Uncoated woodfree/freesheet: 36,000 mt/y
Paper and Paperboard Mill Data:
Stock Preparation:
Pulpers: 2
Refiners: 5
Paper Machines: 1
No. 1, fourdrinier, total capacity 36,000 mt/y, Trim width 3 m, Uncoated woodfree/freesheet
Coating Machines: 1
No. 1, total capacity 16,000 mt/y.
Finishing Equipment:
Supercalenders: 1
Rewinders: 2 at 3,000 mt/y
Sheeters: 2 at 6,000 mt/y

⊕⋒Qadria Board Mills
Sheikhupura Mill
Ownership: 100% by private limited company
37 Km. Lahore-Sheikhupura Rd.
Sheikhupura, Punjab
Pakistan
Phone: (92) 431 6614403
Fax: (92) 431 6614111
Personnel:
CEO: Hussain Saim
Phone: (92) 431 6614403
Total Employees at this Location: 50
Type of Operation: Pulp mill, Paperboard mill
Paper/Paperboard Grades and Capacities:
Total paper and paperboard capacity: 3,000 mt/y

⊕⋒Rehman Classic Pvt. Ltd
Gujranwala Mill
Ownership: 100% by private limited company
16 KM Chainwali Gujanwala to Lahore Road
Gujranwala, Punjab
Pakistan
Phone: (92) 55 326 3327/3784
Fax: (92) 55 326 3766
Email: rehmanclassics@gmail.com
Personnel:
CEO: Ch. Naveed-ur-Rehman
Phone: (92) 431 866363
Fax: (92) 425 118593
Total Employees at this Location: 90
Type of Operation: Pulp mill, Paper mill
Pulp Grades and Capacities:
Total pulp capacity: 3,000 mt/y
Paper/Paperboard Grades and Capacities:
Total paper and paperboard capacity: 4,000 mt/y
Uncoated woodfree/freesheet: 4,000 mt/y
Paper and Paperboard Mill Data:
Paper Machines: 1
PM 1, fourdrinier, total capacity 4,000 mt/y, Trim width 1.4 m, Uncoated woodfree/freesheet

⊕⋒Sayid Paper Mills
Lahore Mill
Ownership: 100% by Sayid Paper (Pvt) Ltd.
21st Km, Lahore-Sheikhupura Road
54000 Lahore, Punjab
Pakistan
Phone: (92) 42 7970721/0722/0246/0247
Fax: (92) 42 7970723
Email: info@sayid.net
Web Address: www.sayid.net
Personnel:
Chmn.: W. M. Sayid
Phone: (92) 42 7970721/0722/0246/0247
Email: wms@sayid.net
CEO: Aizad H. Sayid
Phone: (92) 42 7970721/0722/0246/0247
Fax: (92) 42 5833383
Email: aizad@sayid.net
CFO: Mahmood Chaudhry
Phone: (92) 42 7970721/0722/0246/0247
Email: mahmood@sayid.net
Mill Mgr.: Parvez Bhatti
Phone: (92) 42 797 0712
Tech. Dir.: Faisal M. Sayid
Phone: (92) 42 7970721/0722/0246/0247
Email: faisal@sayid.net
Supervisor of Stock Preparation: Parvez Bhatti
Phone: (92) 42 7970721/0722/0246/0247
Total Employees at this Location: 200
Type of Operation: Pulp mill, Paper mill
Pulp Grades and Capacities:
Total pulp capacity: 16,482 mt/y
Recycled Pulping: 16,482 mt/y
Pulp Mill Data:
Recycled Fiber Treatment Lines:
Flotation deinking lines: 1
Pulpers: 2
Washing deinking lines: 1
Paper/Paperboard Grades and Capacities:
Total paper and paperboard capacity: 20,000 mt/y
Uncoated woodfree/freesheet: 20,000 mt/y

Pakistan

Paper and Paperboard Mill Data:
Stock Preparation:
Pulpers: 3
Refiners: 8
Paper Machines: 1
No. 1, fourdrinier, total capacity 20,000 mt/y, Trim width 2.4 m, Uncoated woodfree/freesheet
Finishing Equipment:
Rewinders: 1
Sheeters: 1
Energy Data:
Electrical demand for mill: 51 MWh/D

ⓘSecurity Papers Ltd.
Ownership: 10% by Ind. Dev. & Renovation Org. of Iran, 40% by Pakistan Security Prtg. Corp., 10% by Turkeiy Seluloz ve Kagit Fabrikalari
Jinnah Avenue, Malir Halt
75100 Karachi, Sindh
Pakistan
  Phone: (92) 21 992 4 8285
  Fax: (92) 21 992 4 8286
  Email: splcs@cyber.net.pk
  Web Address: www.security-papers.com
Personnel:
  CEO: Mrs. Naiyer Muzafar Husain
  Phone: (92) 21 992 4 8285
  Fax: (92) 21 992 4 8286
  CFO: Rizwan Ul Haq Khan
  Phone: (92) 21 992 4 8285
  Fax: (92) 21 992 4 8286
  Gen. Mgr. HR: Nadeem Azhar
  Phone: (92) 21 992 4 8285
  Fax: (92) 21 992 4 8286
  Email: hr@security-papers.com
  Company Sec.: Muhmmad Abdul Aleem
  Phone: (92) 21 992 4 8285
  Fax: (92) 21 992 4 8286
  Email: comsec@security-papers.com
  Gen. Mgr. Eng: Khalil Ahmed
  Phone: (92) 21 992 4 8285
  Fax: (92) 21 992 4 8286
  Email: engineering@security-papers.com
Total Employees of Company: 408
Total Employees at this Location: 5
Mill Locations:
Security Papers Ltd., Karachi Mill, Jinnah Avenue, Malir Halt, 75100 Karachi, Pakistan, Capacity: 2,000 mt/y, (Pulp mill, Paper mill)
  Phone: (92) 21 992 4 8536 / 37
  Fax: (92) 21 992 4 8616
  Email: info@security-papers.com

ⓘSecurity Papers Ltd.
Karachi Mill
Jinnah Avenue, Malir Halt
75100 Karachi, Sindh
Pakistan
  Phone: (92) 21 992 4 8536 / 37
  Fax: (92) 21 992 4 8616
  Email: info@security-papers.com
  Web Address: www.security-papers.com
Personnel:
  Div. Gen. Mgr. Prod.: Muhammad Imran Awan
  Phone: (92) 21 992 4 8536
  Fax: (92) 21 992 4 8616
  Email: imran@security-papers.com
  Div. Gen. Mgr. Qlty/R&D: Saadat Ali
  Phone: (92) 21 992 4 8536
  Fax: (92) 21 992 4 8616
  Email: qc@security-papers.com
  Div. Gen. Mgr. Process System & IT: Imad Ahmed Khan
  Phone: (92) 21 992 4 8536
  Fax: (92) 21 992 4 8616
  Email: imad@security-papers.com
Total Employees at this Location: 558
Type of Operation: Pulp mill, Paper mill
Pulp Grades and Capacities:
  Total pulp capacity: 2,000 mt/y
Pulp Mill Data:
  Chemical Pulping Systems:
  Batch digesters: 2
  Bleach Plant Lines:
  No. 1, Sequence: H, Capacity 1,700 admt/y
  Recycled Fiber Treatment Lines:
  Pulpers: 1 at 225 admt/y
Paper/Paperboard Grades and Capacities:
  Total paper and paperboard capacity: 2,000 mt/y
  Uncoated woodfree/freesheet: 2,000 mt/y
Paper and Paperboard Mill Data:
  Stock Preparation:
  Pulpers: 1
  Refiners: 0
Paper Machines: 1
PM 2, total capacity 2,000 mt/y, Uncoated woodfree/freesheet
Finishing Equipment:
  Supercalenders: 1
  Sheeters: 1
Energy Data:
Power boilers: 2

ⓜShaheen Paper & Board Industries (pvt) Ltd
Raiwind Lahore Mill
Ownership: Mohammadi Paper & Board Industries (Pvt.) Ltd.
4 km Raiwind Manga Road, District Kasoor Raiwind
Raiwind Lahore
Pakistan
  Phone: (92) 42 5392382/5391030
  Fax: (92) 42 5393382
  Email: shaheenindustries@hotmail.com
Personnel:
  Dir.: Shei Khabbas
  Phone: (92) 42 5392382/5391030
Type of Operation: Paper mill
Paper/Paperboard Grades and Capacities:
  Total paper and paperboard capacity: 8,000 mt/y
  Uncoated woodfree/freesheet: 8,000 mt/y
Paper and Paperboard Mill Data:
Paper Machines: 1
PM 1, total capacity 8,000 mt/y, Uncoated woodfree/freesheet

ⓘⓜStar Paper Mills Pvt. Ltd.
Kotri Mill
Ownership: 100% by private limited company
G-4 Site
76010 Kotri, Sindh
Pakistan
  Phone: (92) 221 870006/235
  Fax: (92) 221 870813
Personnel:
  Chmn.: Haji Nawal Khan
  Phone: (92) 221 870006/235
  Man. Dir.: Harneed Adam Guaba
  Phone: (92) 221 870006/235
  Mill Mgr.: Nazir Ahmad
  Phone: (92) 221 870006/235
  Prod. Mgr.: Abdul Rashid Khan
  Phone: (92) 221 870006/235
  Sls. Dir.: Haji Jahandad Khan
  Phone: (92) 221 870006/235
  Purch. Dir.: Shah Ummer Khan
  Phone: (92) 221 870006/235
  Purch. Dir.: Ali Laiq
  Phone: (92) 221 870006/235
Total Employees of Company: 142
Total Employees at this Location: 140
Type of Operation: Pulp mill, Paper mill
Pulp Grades and Capacities:
  Total pulp capacity: 6,000 mt/y
Pulp Mill Data:
  Chemical Pulping Systems:
  Batch digesters: 2
  Continuous digesters: 1

Paper/Paperboard Grades and Capacities:
  Total paper and paperboard capacity: 6,000 mt/y
  Specialty and industrial: 6,000 mt/y
Paper and Paperboard Mill Data:
  Stock Preparation:
  Pulpers: 3
  Refiners: 2
Paper Machines: 1
No. 1, fourdrinier, total capacity 6,000 mt/y, Trim width 2.14 m, Specialty and industrial
Finishing Equipment:
  Rewinders: 1

ⓘⓜSultan Paper Board Mills Ltd.
Gujranwala Mill
Ownership: 100% by Chowdry Group of Companies
18-A, Small Industries Estate
Gujranwala, Punjab
Pakistan
  Phone: (92) 431 82199
  Fax: (92) 431 82107
Personnel:
  Mill Mgr.: Ch. Mohammad Rafique
  Phone: (92) 431 82199
  Fax: (92) 431 82107
Total Employees at this Location: 90
Type of Operation: Pulp mill, Paper mill, Paperboard mill
Pulp Grades and Capacities:
  Total pulp capacity: 10,000 mt/y
Pulp Mill Data:
  Chemical Pulping Systems:
  Batch digesters: 1
  Continuous digesters: 1
Paper/Paperboard Grades and Capacities:
  Total paper and paperboard capacity: 10,000 mt/y
Paper and Paperboard Mill Data:
Paper Machines: 1
No. 1, cylinder, total capacity 10,000 mt/y, Trim width 1 m

ⓘⓜZaman Paper and Board Mills Ltd.
Sheikhupura Mill
Ownership: Flying Group of Industries Ltd.
10 km. Faisalabad Rd.
Sheikhupura, Punjab
Pakistan
  Phone: (92) 42 6674301-5
  Fax: (92) 42 6660693
  Web Address: flyingpaper.com.pk/paper_industries.html#zaman_paper
Personnel:
  Dir.: Mr. Kamran Khan
  Phone: (92) 42 6674301-5
Total Employees of Company: 105
Total Employees at this Location: 105
Type of Operation: Pulp mill, Paper mill, Paperboard mill
Pulp Grades and Capacities:
  Total pulp capacity: 19,048 mt/y
  Recycled Pulping: 19,048 mt/y
Pulp Mill Data:
  Bleach Plant Systems: 1
  DIP
  Recycled Fiber Treatment Lines:
  Flotation deinking lines: 1
  Recycled packaging pulping lines: 1
Paper/Paperboard Grades and Capacities:
  Total paper and paperboard capacity: 20,000 mt/y
  Boxboard/cartonboard: 20,000 mt/y
Paper and Paperboard Mill Data:
Paper Machines: 1
No. 1, cylinder, total capacity 20,000 mt/y, Boxboard/cartonboard
Coating Machines: 1
PM 1, on machine
Energy Data:

Power boilers
Electrical demand for mill: 37 MWh/D

ⓄZamindara Paper & Board Mill Ltd.
Ownership: 100% by private limited company
241-N Model Town Extension
Lahore, Punjab
Pakistan
 Phone: (92) 42 5203062
 Fax: (92) 42 5202802
 Email: zpm@wol.net.pk
Personnel:
 Chmn.: Ahmed Malik Shamim
 Phone: (92) 42 5203062
 Fax: (92) 42 5202802
 Mill Mgr.: Syed Imran
 Phone: (92) 42 5203062
 Fax: (92) 42 5202802
Total Employees of Company: 194
Total Employees at this Location: 14
Mill Locations:
Zamindara Paper & Board Mill Ltd., Sheikhupura Mill, 10 Km. Faisalabad Road, Sheikhupura, Pakistan, Capacity: 18,000 mt/y, (Paperboard mill)
 Phone: (92) 56 388 2156/2177
 Email: zpm@wol.net.pk

ⓂZamindara Paper & Board Mill Ltd.
Sheikhupura Mill
10 Km. Faisalabad Road
Sheikhupura, Punjab
Pakistan
 Phone: (92) 56 388 2156/2177
 Email: zpm@wol.net.pk
Personnel:
 Mill. Mgr.: Imren Ali Saeed
 Phone: (92) 56 388 2156/2177
Total Employees at this Location: 180
Type of Operation: Paperboard mill
Paper/Paperboard Grades and Capacities:
 Total paper and paperboard capacity: 18,000 mt/y
 Boxboard/cartonboard: 18,000 mt/y
Paper and Paperboard Mill Data:
Paper Machines: 2
 No. 1, Boxboard/cartonboard
 No. 2, (second hand)
Coating Machines: 1
 No. 1, off machine

PHILIPPINES

ⓄAlbay Agro Industrial Development Corp. (Alindeco)
5/F Sagittarius Bldg., H.V. dela Costa St., Salcedo Village
1200 Makati, Metro Manila
Philippines
 Phone: (63) 2 816 3877 / 816 3878
 Fax: (63) 2 810 5987 / 752 5003
 Email: info@alindeco.com
 Web Address: www.alindeco.com
Personnel:
 Chmn.: Felix S. Imperial Jr.
 Phone: (63) 2 816 3877
 Fax: (63) 2 810 5987
 Pres. & CEO: Menardo R. Jimenez
 Phone: (63) 2 816 3877
 Fax: (63) 2 810 5987
 VP Management Services: Felix M. Imperial III
 Phone: (63) 2 816 3877
 Fax: (63) 2 810 5987
 Exec. VP: Orpha M. Noveno
 Phone: (63) 2 816 3877
 Fax: (63) 2 810 5987
 Asst. VP Mgmt. Services: Emelita N. Guerrero
 Phone: (63) 2 816 3877
 Fax: (63) 2 810 5987

Mill Locations:
Albay Agro Industrial Development Corp. (Alindeco), Malinao Mill, Barrio Balading, 4512 Malinao, Bicol Region, Philippines, (Pulp mill)
 Phone: (63) 52 488 4588
 Fax: (63) 52 488 4288
 Email: info@alindeco.com

ⓂAlbay Agro Industrial Development Corp. (Alindeco)
Malinao Mill
Barrio Balading
4512 Malinao, Bicol Region, Albay
Philippines
 Phone: (63) 52 488 4588
 Fax: (63) 52 488 4288
 Email: info@alindeco.com
 Web Address: www.alindeco.com
Personnel:
 Plt. Mgr.: Danilo D. Higwit
 Phone: (63) 52 488 4588
 Fax: (63) 52 488 4288
 Snr. Mgr. Tech. Serv.: Ing. Hugo F. Duran
 Phone: (63) 52 488 4588
 Fax: (63) 52 488 4288
 Email: qms@alindeco.com
Type of Operation: Pulp mill
Pulp Grades and Capacities:
 Total pulp capacity: 8,300 mt/y
Pulp Mill Data:
Pulp Lines: 2

ⓄAsia Paper Industrial Corp.
34 Narciso St.
East Canumay, Valenzuela City, Bulacan
Philippines
 Phone: (63) 2 9838000
 Fax: (63) 2 362 2888 / 2 444 1006
 Email: jimmysy@info.com.ph
Total Employees of Company: 120
Mill Locations:
Asia Paper Industrial Corp., Valenzuela City Mill, 34 Narciso St., East Canumay, Valenzuela City, Philippines, Capacity: 12,000 mt/y, (Paper mill)
 Phone: (63) 2 9838000
 Fax: (63) 2 362 2888 / 2 444 1006
 Email: jimmysy@info.com.ph

ⓂAsia Paper Industrial Corp.
Valenzuela City Mill
34 Narciso St.
East Canumay, Valenzuela City, Bulacan
Philippines
 Phone: (63) 2 9838000
 Fax: (63) 2 362 2888 / 2 444 1006
 Email: jimmysy@info.com.ph
Personnel:
 Gen. Mgr.: Tan Tiansiong
 Phone: (63) 2 9838000
Type of Operation: Paper mill
Paper/Paperboard Grades and Capacities:
 Total paper and paperboard capacity: 12,000 mt/y
 Uncoated woodfree/freesheet: 12,000 mt/y
Paper and Paperboard Mill Data:
Paper Machines: 1
 No. 1, total capacity 12,000 mt/y, Uncoated woodfree/freesheet
Energy Data:
Power boilers: 1

ⓄⓂBataan 2020
Baesa Mill
226 Quirino Highway
1106 Baesa, Quezon City
Philippines
 Phone: (63) 2 361 1601 / 361 0699 (Printing & Writing Paper) / 362 7834 (Tissue & Board)
 Fax: (63) 2 361 0701 / 361 0700

 Email: sales@bataan2020.net
 Web Address: www.bataan2020.net
Personnel:
 Pres.: Alfred Y. Huang
 Phone: (63) 2 3611601
 Gen. Mgr.: Larry Tan
 Phone: (63) 2 3611601
 Mill Mgr.: Emmanuel Y. Gaspar
 Phone: (63) 2 3611601
 Sls. & Mktg. Mgr.: Kirby T. Ong
 Phone: (63) 2 3611601
 Email: kirby.ong@bataan2020.net
Total Employees at this Location: 135
Type of Operation: Paper mill
Mill Locations:
Bataan 2020, Samal Mill, Roman Superhighway, Samal, Bataan, Philippines, Capacity: 60,000 mt/y, (Paper mill)
 Phone: (63) 47 791 4155 / 47 791 4157 / 47 791 4162
 Fax: (63) 2 711 7705 / 2 711 3658
Pulp Grades and Capacities:
 Total pulp capacity: 17,209 mt/y
 Recycled Pulping: 17,209 mt/y
Pulp Mill Data:
 Recycled Fiber Treatment Lines:
 Recycled packaging pulping lines: 1
Paper/Paperboard Grades and Capacities:
 Total paper and paperboard capacity: 30,000 mt/y
 Uncoated woodfree/freesheet: 12,500 mt/y
 Corrugating medium/fluting: 17,500 mt/y
Paper and Paperboard Mill Data:
Paper Machines: 1
No. 1, total capacity 30,000 mt/y, Uncoated woodfree/freesheet, Corrugating medium/fluting
Energy Data:
Electrical demand for mill: 47 MWh/D

ⓂBataan 2020
Samal Mill
Roman Superhighway
Samal, Bataan
Philippines
 Phone: (63) 47 791 4155 / 47 791 4157 / 47 791 4162
 Fax: (63) 2 711 7705 / 2 711 3658
 Web Address: www.bataan2020.net
Personnel:
 Pres.: Alfred Y. Huang
 Phone: (63) 47 791 4155/57
 Mill Mgr.: Vicente P. Banatao
 Phone: (63) 47 791 4155/57
Total Employees at this Location: 315
Type of Operation: Paper mill
Pulp Grades and Capacities:
 Total pulp capacity: 46,220 mt/y
 Recycled Pulping: 46,220 mt/y
Pulp Mill Data:
 Chemical Pulping Systems:
 Batch digesters: 3
 Bleach Plant Systems: 2
 DIP
 DIP
 Chemical Recovery Equipment:
 Recovery boilers: 1
 Recycled Fiber Treatment Lines:
 Flotation deinking lines: 2
Paper/Paperboard Grades and Capacities:
 Total paper and paperboard capacity: 60,000 mt/y
 Newsprint: 30,000 mt/y
 Uncoated woodfree/freesheet: 10,000 mt/y
 Tissue: 20,000 mt/y
Paper and Paperboard Mill Data:
Paper Machines: 3
No. 1, fourdrinier, total capacity 40,000 mt/y, Trim width 3.1 m, Newsprint, Uncoated woodfree/freesheet
No. 2, fourdrinier, total capacity 10,000 mt/y, Trim width 2.22 m, Tissue, Uncoated woodfree/freesheet
No. 3, fourdrinier, total capacity 10,000 mt/y, Trim width 2.22 m, Tissue, Uncoated woodfree/freesheet

Philippines

Energy Data:
Power boilers: 1
Steam turbines: 1 at 12.5 MW
Electrical demand for mill: 172 MWh/D

ⓘⓜCanlubang Pulp Mfg. Corp.
Makati Mill
Yulo Bldg., Don Bosco cor. Pasong Tamo
3117 Makati, Metro Manila
Philippines
 Phone: (63) 2 810 0116
 Fax: (63) 2 817 1559
Personnel:
 Pres./Gen. Mgr.: Jose Ramon A. Yulo
 Phone: (63) 2 810 0116
 VP/Oper. Dir.: Arturo P. Gorrez
 Phone: (63) 2 810 0116
 Mill Mgr.: Jorge M. Barairo
 Phone: (63) 49 5497471
 Fax: (63) 49 5497507
 Asst. Mill Mgr.: Leoncio D. Malicedem Jr.
 Phone: (63) 49 549 7471
 Fax: (63) 49 549 7507
 Chief Eng.: Bernard E. Sangel
 Phone: (63) 49 549 7471
 Fax: (63) 49 549 7507
 Chief Chemist: Bernardita G. Ordanell Jr.
 Phone: (63) 2 810 0116
 Prod. & Qlty. Control Head: Jeriel R. Calica
 Phone: (63) 2 810 0116
 Purch. Dir.: Jesus Miguel Yulo Jr.
 Phone: (63) 2 810 0116
Type of Operation: Pulp mill
Pulp Grades and Capacities:
 Total pulp capacity: 7,200 mt/y
 Pulp available for market: 7,200 mt/y
Pulp Mill Data:
 Chemical Pulping Systems:
 Batch digesters: 4
Pulp Lines: 1
Energy Data:
Combustion turbines at 10.0 MW

ⓘⓜContainer Corp. of the Philippines
Quezon City Mill
Ownership: 100% by private corporation
122 Joy Street, Grace Village, Balangasa
Quezon City
Philippines
 Phone: (63) 2 361 9801
 Fax: (63) 2 362 0370
Personnel:
 Pres.: Manuel Lychiaoco
 Phone: (63) 2 361 9801
 Chmn.: Benito C. Pascual
 Phone: (63) 2 361 9801
 VP Operations: Victor Pascual
 Phone: (63) 2 361 9801
 VP Finan.: Daniel Pascual
 Phone: (63) 2 361 9801
 Prod. Mgr.: Urbano H. Sedigo
 Phone: (63) 2 361 9801
 Purch. Supervisor: Fernando Martinez
 Phone: (63) 2 361 9801
 Tech. Mgr.: Marissa Ligay
 Phone: (63) 2 361 9801
Total Employees at this Location: 300
Type of Operation: Paper mill
Paper/Paperboard Grades and Capacities:
 Total paper and paperboard capacity: 72,000 mt/y
 Linerboard: 48,000 mt/y
 Corrugating medium/fluting
 Boxboard/cartonboard: 24,000 mt/y
Paper and Paperboard Mill Data:
 Stock Preparation:
 Pulpers: 5
 Refiners: 7
Paper Machines: 3
No. 1, cylinder, Trim width 2.1 m
No. 2, fourdrinier, Trim width 2.5 m
No. 3, fourdrinier, Trim width 3.2 m
Finishing Equipment:
 Supercalenders: 1
 Rewinders: 3
 Sheeters: 1
Energy Data:
Power boilers: 3

ⓘⓜFedco Paper Corp.
Calamba City Mill
Carmelray Industrial Park, Canlubang
Calamba City, Laguna
Philippines
 Phone: (63) 2 633 8085
 Fax: (63) 2 634 5311
Personnel:
 Dir.: Carlos Cheng
 Phone: (63) 2 8135589
Total Employees of Company: 165
Total Employees at this Location: 165
Type of Operation: Paper mill
Pulp Grades and Capacities:
 Total pulp capacity: 22,987 mt/y
 Recycled Pulping: 22,987 mt/y
Pulp Mill Data:
 Bleach Plant Systems: 1
 Recycled Pulping System
 Recycled Fiber Treatment Lines:
 Flotation deinking lines: 1
 Recycled packaging pulping lines: 1
Paper/Paperboard Grades and Capacities:
 Total paper and paperboard capacity: 24,000 mt/y
 Uncoated woodfree/freesheet: 12,000 mt/y
 Packaging papers: 12,000 mt/y
Paper and Paperboard Mill Data:
Paper Machines: 1
No. 1, fourdrinier, total capacity 24,000 mt/y, Trim width 3 m, Uncoated woodfree/freesheet, Packaging papers
Energy Data:
Electrical demand for mill: 51 MWh/D

ⓘGlobe Paper Mills
1000 Gov. E. Pascual Ave.
1470 Malabon, Metro Manila
Philippines
 Phone: (63) 2 361 2516/18
 Fax: (63) 2 3615096 /2420198
Mill Locations:
Globe Paper Mills, Keng Hua Mill, 1000 Gov. E. Pascual Ave., 1470 Malabon, Philippines, Capacity: 107,000 mt/y, (Paper mill)
 Phone: (63) 2 361 2516/18
 Fax: (63) 2 3615096 /2420198

ⓜGlobe Paper Mills
Keng Hua Mill
1000 Gov. E. Pascual Ave.
1470 Malabon, Metro Manila
Philippines
 Phone: (63) 2 361 2516/18
 Fax: (63) 2 3615096 /2420198
Personnel:
 Man. Dir.: Carlos Yu
 Phone: (63) 2 361 2516/18
Total Employees at this Location: 1,000
Type of Operation: Paper mill
Paper/Paperboard Grades and Capacities:
 Total paper and paperboard capacity: 107,000 mt/y
 Uncoated woodfree/freesheet
 Tissue
 Linerboard: 50,000 mt/y
Paper and Paperboard Mill Data:
Paper Machines: 5
No. 1
No. 2
No. 3
No. 4
No. 5

ⓘⓜHansson Paper Corp.
Pasig City Mill
RFM Compound, Bo. Manggahan
Pasig City, Metro Manila
Philippines
 Phone: (63) 2 646 21 60/64
 Fax: (63) 2 646 21 05
Personnel:
 Man. Dir.: George So
 Phone: (63) 2 646 21 60/64
Total Employees of Company: 120
Type of Operation: Paper mill
Paper/Paperboard Grades and Capacities:
 Total paper and paperboard capacity: 15,000 mt/y
 Newsprint: 5,000 mt/y
 Uncoated woodfree/freesheet: 10,000 mt/y
Paper and Paperboard Mill Data:
Paper Machines: 4
PM 1, Trim width 1.8 m
PM 2, fourdrinier, Trim width 1.8 m
PM 3, Trim width 1.8 m
PM 4, Trim width 1.8 m
Energy Data:
Power boilers: 1

ⓘⓜLiberty Paper Mill, Inc.
Malinta Mill
751 Paso del Blas
Valenzuela, Bulacan
Philippines
 Phone: (63) 936 2750
 Fax: (63) 939 5052/6657
Personnel:
 Pres.: Frank Chiongson
 Phone: (63) 936 2750
 Plant Mgr.: Anthony Chiongson
 Phone: (63) 936 2750
Type of Operation: Pulp mill
Pulp Grades and Capacities:
 Total pulp capacity: 5,000 mt/y
Paper/Paperboard Grades and Capacities:
 Total paper and paperboard capacity: 5,000 mt/y
 Tissue
Paper and Paperboard Mill Data:
Paper Machines: 1
No. 1, Trim width 1.42 m, Tissue
Energy Data:
Power boilers: 1

ⓜNewtech Pulp Inc.
Lanao del Norte Mill
Previously Glatfelter Lanao del Norte.
Ownership: Glatfelter
Bo. Maria Cristina, Balo-I
9217 Lanao del Norte
Philippines
 Phone: (63) 2 893 7640
 Fax: (63) 2 893 2819
 Email: info@glatfelter.com
 Web Address: www.glatfelter.com
Personnel:
 Pres. & CEO.: Alberto Jr Fenix
 Phone: (63) 2 893 7640
 Fax: (63) 2 893 2819
Type of Operation: Pulp mill
Pulp Grades and Capacities:
 Total pulp capacity: 18,000 mt/y

ⓜNoah's Paper Mills, Inc.
Calumpang, Marikina Mill
Southeast Marcos Bridge, Marcos Highway
1801 Calumpang, Marikina, Metro Manila
Philippines
 Phone: (63) 2 645 5678
 Fax: (63) 2 645 5684/843 9075
Personnel:
 Man. Dir.: David Hwang
 Phone: (63) 2 645 5678

Philippines

Email: davidh@mydestiny.net
Total Employees at this Location: 80
Type of Operation: Paper mill
Energy Data:
Power boilers: 1

ⓘNoah's Paper Mills, Inc.
Southeast Marcos Bridge, Marcos Highway
1801 Calumpang, Marikina
Philippines
Phone: (63) 2 645 5678
Fax: (63) 2 645 5684/843 9075
Personnel:
Man. Dir.: David Hwang
Phone: (63) 2 645 5678
Fax: (63) 2 645 5684/843 9075
Email: davidh@mydestiny.net
Total Employees at this Location: 80
Mill Locations:
Noah's Paper Mills, Inc., Calumpang, Marikina Mill, Southeast Marcos Bridge, Marcos Highway, 1801 Calumpang, Marikina, Philippines, (Paper mill)
Phone: (63) 2 645 5678
Fax: (63) 2 645 5684/843 9075

ⓘⓂPaperland, Inc.
Quezon City Mill
Lelland Drive, Balintawak
Quezon City
Philippines
Phone: (63) 2 361 8531
Fax: (63) 2 362 3607
Personnel:
Pres.: Kee Hing Gan
Phone: (63) 2 361 8531
Chmn. of the Bd.: Miguel Tan
Phone: (63) 2 361 8531
VP: She Ling Tan
Phone: (63) 2 361 8531
Gen. Mgr.: Jose Gan
Phone: (63) 2 361 8531
Purch. Mgr.: Francisco Gan
Phone: (63) 2 361 8531
Sls. Mgr.: Johnny Leh
Phone: (63) 2 361 8531
Type of Operation: Paper mill, Paperboard mill
Paper/Paperboard Grades and Capacities:
Total paper and paperboard capacity: 10,000 mt/y
Packaging papers: 5,000 mt/y
Corrugating medium/fluting: 5,000 mt/y
Paper and Paperboard Mill Data:
Paper Machines: 1
No. 1, fourdrinier, total capacity 10,000 mt/y, Packaging papers, Corrugating medium/fluting
Energy Data:
Power boilers: 2

ⓘPulp Specialties Philippines, Inc. (PSPI)
7th Floor Citibank Center, 8741 Paseo de Roxas
1200 Makati, Metro Manila
Philippines
Phone: (63) 2 841 0634/810 44 74/75/76/77
Fax: (63) 2 893 4844
Web Address: www.pulpspecialties.com
Personnel:
Pres.: Dennis Villareal
Phone: (63) 2 841 0634
Fax: (63) 2 893 4844
VP. Mktg.: Lorenzo D. Inocando
Phone: (63) 2 841 0634
Fax: (63) 2 893 4844
Email: ldipspi@yahoo.com
Total Employees of Company: 1,005
Mill Locations:
Pulp Specialties Philippines, Inc. (PSPI), Leyte Plant, Sitio Magbangon, Barangay Tinag-an, Albuera, Philippines, (Pulp mill)
Phone: (63) 53 562 9562
Fax: (63) 53 562 9372
Email: ldipspi@yahoo.com

ⓂPulp Specialties Philippines, Inc. (PSPI)
Leyte Plant
Sitio Magbangon, Barangay Tinag-an
Albuera, Leyte
Philippines
Phone: (63) 53 562 9562
Fax: (63) 53 562 9372
Email: ldipspi@yahoo.com
Web Address: www.pulpspecialties.com, pulpspecialties.weebly.com/index.html
Personnel:
VP., Dir. Mktg. Mgr.: Lorenzo Inocando
Email: ldipspi@yahoo.com
Type of Operation: Pulp mill
Pulp Grades and Capacities:
Total pulp capacity: 14,000 mt/y
Pulp Mill Data:
Pulp Lines: 2

ⓘQuanta Paper Corporation
49 Rev. G. Aglipay Street, Barangay Old Zaniga
1550 Mandaluyong City
Philippines
Phone: (63) 3 533 9250 / 533 9832 / 2 531 0160
Fax: (63) 3 533 7295
Email: customer.care@quantapaper.com
Web Address: www.quantapaper.com
Total Employees of Company: 1,000
Mill Locations:
Quanta Paper Corporation, Pampanga Mill, Ninoy Aquino Highway, Barangay Paralayunan, Mabalacat, Pampanga , Philippines, Capacity: 6,000 mt/y, (Paper mill)
Phone: (63) 2 533 9250 / 533 9832
Fax: (63) 2 533 7295
Email: customer.care@quantapaper.com

ⓂQuanta Paper Corporation
Pampanga Mill
Ninoy Aquino Highway, Barangay Paralayunan, Mabalacat
Pampanga , Pampanga
Philippines
Phone: (63) 2 533 9250 / 533 9832
Fax: (63) 2 533 7295
Email: customer.care@quantapaper.com
Web Address: www.quantapaper.com
Type of Operation: Paper mill
Paper/Paperboard Grades and Capacities:
Total paper and paperboard capacity: 6,000 mt/y
Tissue: 6,000 mt/y
Paper and Paperboard Mill Data:
Paper Machines: 1
PM 1-4, total capacity 6,000 mt/y, Tissue

ⓘⓂTransnational Paper Corp.
Cavite Mill
Governor's Drive, Tanza
Calvite City, Calabarzon, Laguna
Philippines
Phone: (63) 2 633 4213 to 18/125 100 1923
Fax: (63) 2 633 9492
Personnel:
Man. Dir.: Celestino Zulueta
Phone: (63) 2 633 4213 to 18/125 100 1923
Type of Operation: Pulp mill
Pulp Grades and Capacities:
Total pulp capacity: 23,000 mt/y
Paper/Paperboard Grades and Capacities:
Total paper and paperboard capacity: 73,500 mt/y
Uncoated woodfree/freesheet: 20,000 mt/y
Linerboard: 11,500 mt/y
Corrugating medium/fluting: 42,000 mt/y
Paper and Paperboard Mill Data:
Stock Preparation:
Pulpers:
Paper Machines: 3
No. 1, cylinder, Trim width 2 m
No. 2, cylinder, Trim width 3.6 m
No. 3, fourdrinier, Trim width 3.3 m

ⓘⓂTri-Asia Paper Mill, Inc.
Cabuyao Mill
Canlubang Industrial Estate, Barrio Pittland
Cabuyao City, Laguna
Philippines
Fax: (63) 2 895 1547, 890-9647
Type of Operation: Paperboard mill
Pulp Grades and Capacities:
Total pulp capacity: 20,000 mt/y
Paper/Paperboard Grades and Capacities:
Total paper and paperboard capacity: 15,000 mt/y
Linerboard: 15,000 mt/y
Corrugating medium/fluting

ⓘTrust International Paper Corp. (TIPCO)
6th Flr. ACE Bldg., 101 Rada cor., Dela Rosa St., Legaspi Village
Makati City, Metro Manila
Philippines
Phone: (63) 2 817 5723 / 819 0284
Fax: (63) 2 815 9460 / 894 0056
Email: sales@tipco.com.ph
Web Address: www.tipco.com.ph
Personnel:
Pres.: Tomas Apacible
Phone: (63) 2 817 5723
Fax: (63) 2 815 9460
Sen. VP: Alfredo Chan
Phone: (63) 2 817 5723
Fax: (63) 2 815 9460
Mill Locations:
Trust International Paper Corp. (TIPCO), Mabalacat Mill, Ninoy Aquino Highway, Bandagul, Mabalacat, Philippines, Capacity: 230,265 mt/y, (Paper mill)
Phone: (63) 45 893 0676
Fax: (63) 45 893 0682
Email: info@tipco.com.ph

ⓂTrust International Paper Corp. (TIPCO)
Mabalacat Mill
Ninoy Aquino Highway, Bandagul
Mabalacat, Pampanga
Philippines
Phone: (63) 45 893 0676
Fax: (63) 45 893 0682
Email: info@tipco.com.ph
Web Address: www.tipco.com.ph
Personnel:
VP Manufacturing: Jerry Miranda
Phone: (63) 45 893 0676
Total Employees at this Location: 600
Type of Operation: Paper mill
Pulp Grades and Capacities:
Total pulp capacity: 235,223 mt/y
Recycled Pulping: 235,223 mt/y
Pulp Mill Data:
Bleach Plant Systems: 2
Recycled Pulping System, Type: Deinked, Sequence: P
Recycled Pulping System, Type: Deinked, Sequence: H
Recycled Fiber Treatment Lines:
Flotation deinking lines: 2
Paper/Paperboard Grades and Capacities:
Total paper and paperboard capacity: 230,265 mt/y
Newsprint: 230,265 mt/y
Paper and Paperboard Mill Data:
Paper Machines: 2
No. 2, (second hand.), fourdrinier, total capacity 124,950 mt/y, Trim width 7.3 m, Newsprint

Saudi Arabia

No. 3, (second hand.), Vertiformer, total capacity 105,315 mt/y, Trim width 7 m, Newsprint
Energy Data:
Power boilers
Steam turbines at 52 MW
Electrical demand for mill: 655 MWh/D

ⓘ United Pulp & Paper Co., Inc.
Ownership: 98.60% by SCG Paper Public Co., Ltd.
5th Fl., Phinma Bldg., 39 Plaza Drive, Rockwell Center
1200 Makati, Metro Manila
Philippines
 Phone: (63) 2 8700 100/489/491/323
 Fax: (63) 2 8700 411/413
Personnel:
 Pres.: Chartchai Leukulwatanachai
 Phone: (63) 2 8700 348
 Fax: (63) 2 8700 392
 Email: chartchl@uppci.net
 VP Mktg.: Vipapat Cholsawad
 Phone: (63) 2 8700 323
 Fax: (63) 2 8700 411
 VP Finan. & Procurement: Danaidej Ketsuwan
 Phone: (63) 2 8700 340
 Purch. Mgr.: Imelda Pia Orendain
 Phone: (63) 28700316
 Fax: (63) 2 8700392
Total Employees at this Location: 50
Mill Locations:
United Pulp & Paper Co., Inc., Calumpit Mill, Km 48 Bo. Iba Estate, 3003 Calumpit, Philippines, Capacity: 230,000 mt/y, (Paper mill, Paperboard mill)
 Phone: (63) 44 202 4722/23/4301
 Fax: (63) 44 2024306
 Email: info@uppc.com.ph

ⓜ United Pulp & Paper Co., Inc.
Calumpit Mill
Ownership: 98.60% by SCG Paper Public Co., Ltd.
Km 48 Bo. Iba Estate
3003 Calumpit, Bulacan
Philippines
 Phone: (63) 44 202 4722/23/4301
 Fax: (63) 44 2024306
 Email: info@uppc.com.ph
 Web Address: www.scgpaper.com.ph
Personnel:
 VP: Luis Rolando Fadrigo
 Phone: (63) 44 2024300
 Fax: (63) 44 2024306
 Email: luisf@ppci.net
 VP, Mill Mgr.: Jesda Saeliang
 Phone: (63) 44 2024300
 Fax: (63) 44 2024306
 Prod. Mgr.: Thanate Pongapaiboon
 Phone: (63) 44 2024608
 Fax: (63) 44 2024606
 Maint. Mgr.: Manuel P. Macairap
 Phone: (63) 44 2024301 ext. 176
 Fax: (63) 44 2024306
 Email: manuelma@uppci.net
 Quality Ctrl. Mgr.: Ines D. Molina
 Phone: (63) 44 2024301 ext. 160
 Fax: (63) 44 2024306
 Email: inesm@uppci.net
 Mgr.: Pasuk Banatao
 Phone: (63) 44 2025624
 Fax: (63) 44 2024304
 Email: pasukb@uppci.net
 HR Mgr.: Gilbert D. Pimentel
 Phone: (63) 44 2024301
 Fax: (63) 44 2024306
 Email: gilbertp@uppci.net
 Gen. Mgr.: Anastacio C. Tanjuaquio
 Phone: (63) 44 202 4722/23/4301
 Prod. Mgr.: Victor S. Reyes
 Phone: (63) 44 202 4722/23/4301
 Chief Eng.: Ricardo M. Uychoco
 Phone: (63) 44 202 4722/23/4301
 Paper Mill Mgr.: Julio F. Cristales

 Phone: (63) 44 202 4722/23/4301
 Asst. Mgr., Mill Mgr.: Felizardo D. Domingo Jr.
 Phone: (63) 44 2024301 ext.186
 Fax: (63) 44 2024607
 Email: felizard@uppci.net
Total Employees at this Location: 400
Type of Operation: Paper mill, Paperboard mill
Pulp Grades and Capacities:
 Total pulp capacity: 228,694 mt/y
 Recycled Pulping: 228,694 mt/y
Pulp Mill Data:
 Recycled Fiber Treatment Lines:
 Recycled packaging pulping lines: 1
Paper/Paperboard Grades and Capacities:
 Total paper and paperboard capacity: 230,000 mt/y
 Linerboard: 153,000 mt/y
 Corrugating medium/fluting: 77,000 mt/y
Paper and Paperboard Mill Data:
 Stock Preparation:
 Pulpers: 1
 Refiners: 4
Paper Machines: 2
No. 1, fourdrinier, total capacity 60,000 mt/y, Trim width 3.05 m, Corrugating medium/fluting
No. 2, DuoFormer, total capacity 170,000 mt/y, Trim width 4.32 m, Corrugating medium/fluting, Linerboard
Finishing Equipment:
 Calenders: 4
 Rewinders: 1 at 150,000 mt/y
Energy Data:
 Power boilers: 3
 Steam turbines: 1 at 30 MW
 Electrical demand for mill: 286 MWh/D

ⓘⓜ Vanson Paper Industrial Corp.
Valenzuela Mill
150 Ramon Delfin Street
Marulas, Valenzuela, Metro Manila
Philippines
 Phone: (63) 2 291 6806, 2 293 4708
 Fax: (63) 2 291 6818
Personnel:
 Pres.: Cheng Su
 Phone: (63) 2 293 1397/4708
 Mill Mgr./Gen. Mgr.: Barretto Sy
 Phone: (63) 2 293 1397/4708
 VP/Dpty. Man. Dir.: Eddie C. Sy
 Phone: (63) 2 293 1397/4708
 Admin. Mgr.: Dionicio Go
 Phone: (63) 2 293 1397/4708
Total Employees at this Location: 100
Type of Operation: Paper mill, Paperboard mill
Pulp Grades and Capacities:
 Total pulp capacity: 12,000 mt/y
Paper/Paperboard Grades and Capacities:
 Total paper and paperboard capacity: 9,000 mt/y
 Boxboard/cartonboard: 9,000 mt/y
Paper and Paperboard Mill Data:
 Stock Preparation:
 Pulpers: 2
 Refiners: 7
Paper Machines: 2
No. 1, Yankee dryer, Trim width 1.6 m
No. 2, Yankee dryer, Trim width 1.7 m
Finishing Equipment:
 Rewinders: 2
 Sheeters: 1
Energy Data:
 Power boilers: 2

SAUDI ARABIA

ⓘⓜ Arab Paper Manufacturing Co. Ltd. (Waraq)
Dammam Mill
Ownership: 100% by Group of 50 Saudi Investors
2nd Industrial City - Makkah St. - Road 139
31423 Dammam
Saudi Arabia
Mailing Address: PO Box 9840, 31423 Dammam, Saudi Arabia
 Phone: (966) 3 8121255
 Fax: (966) 3 8121251
 Email: info@waraq.com
 Web Address: www.waraq.com
Personnel:
 CEO: Mohamed Alhashim
 Phone: (966) 3 8121255
 Email: alhashim@waraq.com
 Dir.: Atul Kaul
 Phone: (966) 3 8121255
 Finan. Mgr.: Ashraf Ali
 Phone: (966) 3 8121255
 Proj. and Dev. Mgr.: S. N. Jayakumar
 Phone: (966) 3 8121255
Total Employees of Company: 555
Type of Operation: Paper mill
Pulp Grades and Capacities:
 Total pulp capacity: 197,869 mt/y
 Recycled Pulping: 197,869 mt/y
Pulp Mill Data:
 Recycled Fiber Treatment Lines:
 Recycled packaging pulping lines: 1 at 70,000 admt/y
 Recycled packaging pulping lines: 1 at 200,000
Paper/Paperboard Grades and Capacities:
 Total paper and paperboard capacity: 200,000 mt/y
 Linerboard: 130,000 mt/y
 Corrugating medium/fluting: 45,000 mt/y
 Boxboard/cartonboard: 25,000 mt/y
Paper and Paperboard Mill Data:
Paper Machines: 2
No. 1, fourdrinier, total capacity 70,000 mt/y, Trim width 4.25 m, Corrugating medium/fluting, Boxboard/cartonboard
No. 2, fourdrinier (2), total capacity 130,000 mt/y, Trim width 5 m, Linerboard
Energy Data:
 Power boilers: 6
 Combustion turbines at 50 MW
 Electrical demand for mill: 280 MWh/D

ⓘ Gulf Paper Industries Factory
Ownership: 100% by Al Rajhi Group
Hunaya Al Kharj Street
Riyadh
Saudi Arabia
Mailing Address: PO Box 42185, 11541 Riyadh, Saudi Arabia
 Phone: (966) 1 5458660, 5458661
 Fax: (966) 1 5458665
 Email: paperinfo@alrajhigroup.com
 Web Address: www.alrajhigroup.com
Mill Locations:
Gulf Paper Industries Factory, Riyadh Mill, Hunaya Al Kharj Street, Riyadh, Saudi Arabia, Capacity: 70,000 mt/y, (Paper mill, Paperboard mill)
 Phone: (966) 1 5458660, 5458661
 Fax: (966) 1 5458665
 Email: paperinfo@alrajhigroup.com

ⓜ Gulf Paper Industries Factory
Riyadh Mill
Hunaya Al Kharj Street
Riyadh
Saudi Arabia
Mailing Address: PO Box 42185, 11541 Riyadh, Saudi Arabia
 Phone: (966) 1 5458660, 5458661
 Fax: (966) 1 5458665
 Email: paperinfo@alrajhigroup.com
 Web Address: www.alrajhigroup.com
Personnel:
 Man. Dir.: Khaled A Al-Rajhi
 Phone: (966) 1 5458660, 5458661
Total Employees at this Location: 120
Type of Operation: Paper mill, Paperboard mill

Saudi Arabia

Pulp Grades and Capacities:
Total pulp capacity: 34,405 mt/y
Recycled Pulping: 34,405 mt/y
Pulp Mill Data:
Recycled Fiber Treatment Lines:
Recycled packaging pulping lines: 1
Paper/Paperboard Grades and Capacities:
Total paper and paperboard capacity: 70,000 mt/y
Tissue: 35,000 mt/y
Linerboard: 20,000 mt/y
Corrugating medium/fluting: 10,000 mt/y
Boxboard/cartonboard: 5,000 mt/y
Paper and Paperboard Mill Data:
Paper Machines: 2
No. 1, fourdrinier (3), total capacity 35,000 mt/y, Trim width 2.2 m, Corrugating medium/fluting, Linerboard, Boxboard/cartonboard
No. 2, crescent former, Yankee dryer, total capacity 35,000 mt/y, Trim width 2.8 m, Tissue, Uncoated woodfree/freesheet
Energy Data:
Power boilers
Electrical demand for mill: 141 MWh/D

ⓂMiddle East Paper Company - (MEPCO)
Al Khumrah - Near water treatment plant: PO Box 32913
21438 Jeddah
Saudi Arabia
Phone: (966) 2 6380111
Fax: (966) 2 6389111
Email: shaikhfm@middleeastpaper.com, marketing@middleeastpaper.com
Web Address: www.middleeastpaper.com
Personnel:
CEO: Sami Al Safran
Man. Dir.: Abdullah Almoammor
Mktng. Mgr: Shaikh Faisal Mubin
Phone: (966) 2 6380111 (Ext. 106)
Fax: (966) 2 6389111
Mill Locations:
Middle East Paper Company - (MEPCO), Jeddah Mill, Al Khumrah, PO Box 32913, 21438 Jeddah, Saudi Arabia, Capacity: 615,000 mt/y, (Paper mill, Paperboard mill)
Phone: (966) 2 6380111
Fax: (966) 2 6389111
Email: shaikhfm@middleeastpaper.com
Middle East Paper Company - (MEPCO), Jeddah Mill, Al Khumrah, PO Box 32913, 21438 Jeddah, Saudi Arabia, Capacity: 615,000 mt/y, (Paper mill, Paperboard mill)
Phone: (966) 2 6380111
Fax: (966) 2 6389111
Email: shaikhfm@middleeastpaper.com

ⓂMiddle East Paper Company - (MEPCO)
Jeddah Mill
Ownership: 100% by Middle East Paper Company - (MEPCO)
Al Khumrah, PO Box 32913
21438 Jeddah
Saudi Arabia
Phone: (966) 2 6380111
Fax: (966) 2 6389111
Email: shaikhfm@middleeastpaper.com
Web Address: www.middleeastpaper.com
Personnel:
Man. Dir.: Abdullah A. Almoammar
Phone: (966) 2 6380111
Email: almoammar@mepco.biz
Reg. Mgr.: Rikthesh Ramakrishnan
Phone: (966) 2 6380111 ext. 126, 555 697479 (mobile)
Fax: (966) 2 6389111
Email: rikthesh@mepco.biz
Mktg. Mgr.: Shaikh Faisal Mubin
Phone: (966) 2 6380111 ext. 106, 505 642473 (mobile)
Fax: (966) 2 6389111
Email: shaikhfm@middleeastpaper.com
Reg. Sls. Mgr.: Faheem Usmani
Phone: (966) 2 6380111 ext. 106, 500 058509 (mobile)
Fax: (966) 2 6389111
Email: faheem@mepco.biz
Total Employees at this Location: 300
Type of Operation: Paper mill, Paperboard mill
Pulp Grades and Capacities:
Total pulp capacity: 614,019 mt/y
Recycled Pulping: 614,019 mt/y
Pulp Mill Data:
Recycled Fiber Treatment Lines:
Recycled packaging pulping lines: 1
Paper/Paperboard Grades and Capacities:
Total paper and paperboard capacity: 615,000 mt/y
Packaging papers: 20,000 mt/y
Linerboard: 285,000 mt/y
Corrugating medium/fluting: 270,000 mt/y
Boxboard/cartonboard: 40,000 mt/y
Paper and Paperboard Mill Data:
Paper Machines: 3
No. 1, fourdrinier, total capacity 120,000 mt/y, Trim width 2.5 m, Corrugating medium/fluting, Linerboard, Packaging papers
No. 2, Bel-Bond, total capacity 220,000 mt/y, Trim width 4.5 m, Corrugating medium/fluting, Linerboard, Boxboard/cartonboard
No. 3, fourdrinier (2), total capacity 275,000 mt/y, Trim width 5 m, Corrugating medium/fluting, Linerboard
Finishing Equipment:
Winders: 1
Energy Data:
Power boilers: 5
Electrical demand for mill: 827 MWh/D

ⓂObeikan Paper Industry
Riyadh Mill
PO Box 6672
11452 Riyadh
Saudi Arabia
Phone: (966) 1 265 1144
Fax: (966) 1 265 0272
Email: info@obeikan.com.sa
Web Address: www.obeikan.com.sa
Personnel:
Gen. Mgr.: Mohammed Al-Mowkley
Sls. & Mkt. Mgr.: Mr. Nizar Kouki
Phone: (966) 1 265 4328 / 1084 Ext. 103
Fax: (966) 1 294 1281
Total Employees at this Location: 3,000
Type of Operation: Paperboard mill
Pulp Grades and Capacities:
Total pulp capacity: 138,404 mt/y
Recycled Pulping: 138,404 mt/y
Paper/Paperboard Grades and Capacities:
Total paper and paperboard capacity: 180,000 mt/y
Boxboard/cartonboard: 180,000 mt/y
Paper and Paperboard Mill Data:
Stock Preparation:
Pulpers: 5
Refiners: 5
Paper Machines: 1
No. 1, Fourdrinier (5), total capacity 180,000 mt/y, Trim width 2.96 m, Boxboard/cartonboard
Coating Machines: 1
PM 1, total capacity 180,000 mt/y., on machine
Finishing Equipment:
Winders: 1
Sheeters: 4 at 200,000 mt/y
Energy Data:
Power boilers
Steam turbines
Electrical demand for mill: 382 MWh/D

ⓂObeikan Paper Industry
PO Box 6672
11452 Riyadh
Saudi Arabia
Phone: (966) 1 265 1144
Fax: (966) 1 265 0272
Email: info@obeikan.com.sa
Web Address: www.obeikan.com.sa
Personnel:
Gen. Mgr.: Mohammed Al-Mowkley
Phone: (966) 1 265 1144
Fax: (966) 1 265 0272
Sls. & Mkt. Mgr.: Nizar Kouki
Phone: (966) 1 265 4328 Ext. 103
Fax: (966) 1 294 1281
Total Employees of Company: 3,000
Mill Locations:
Obeikan Paper Industry, Riyadh Mill, PO Box 6672, 11452 Riyadh, Saudi Arabia, Capacity: 180,000 mt/y, (Paperboard mill)
Phone: (966) 1 265 1144
Fax: (966) 1 265 0272
Email: info@obeikan.com.sa

ⓄⓂSaudi Paper Manufacturing Co. (SPMC)
Dammam Mill
Ownership: 100% by Saudi Company
PO Box 8663, 2nd Industrial City
31492 Dammam
Saudi Arabia
Phone: (966) 3 812 1016
Fax: (966) 3 812 1060
Email: ceo@saudipaper.com
Web Address: www.saudipaper.com
Personnel:
Chmn.: HRH Abdullah Abdulaziz Al-Saud
Phone: (966) 1 472 8418
Fax: (966) 1 472 8414
Vice Chmn.: Raed Al-Mashal
Phone: (966) 1 472 8418
Fax: (966) 1 472 8414
Pres./CEO: Mubarak A. Al Khater
Phone: (966) 3 812 1016
Fax: (966) 3 812 3209
Email: mubarak.alkhater@saudipaper.com
Gen. Mgr.: Elie Wanna
Phone: (966) 3 812 1016
Email: elie@saudipaper.com
Sls. & Mktg. Mgr.: Ghannam Al Ghamdi
Phone: (966) 3 812 1016
Email: ghannam@saudipaper.com
Plant Mgr.: Ibrahim Saber
Phone: (966) 3 812 1016
Email: saber@saudipaper.com
Sr. Advisor: Riyadhs Aldakheel
Phone: (966) 3 812 1016
Fax: (966) 3 812 3205
Email: riyadh.aldakheel@saudipaper.com
Maint. Mgr.: James J. Pullat
Phone: (966) 3 812 1016
Email: pullat@saudipaper.com
Total Employees at this Location: 410
Type of Operation: Paper mill
Pulp Grades and Capacities:
Total pulp capacity: 65,545 mt/y
Recycled Pulping: 65,545 mt/y
Pulp Mill Data:
Recycled Fiber Treatment Lines:
Flotation deinking lines: 2 at 90,000 admt/y
Pulpers: 2 at 90,000 admt/y
Washing deinking lines: 2 at 90,000 admt/y
Paper/Paperboard Grades and Capacities:
Total paper and paperboard capacity: 138,000 mt/y
Tissue: 138,000 mt/y
Paper and Paperboard Mill Data:
Stock Preparation:
Pulpers: 5
Refiners: 8
Paper Machines: 4
No. 1, twin-wire, Yankee dryer, total capacity 20,000 mt/y, Trim width 2.66 m, Tissue, Uncoated woodfree/freesheet

Singapore

No. 2, twin-wire, Yankee dryer, total capacity 26,000 mt/y, Trim width 2.66 m, Tissue, Uncoated woodfree/freesheet
No. 3, crescent former, Yankee dryer, total capacity 32,000 mt/y, Trim width 3.6 m, Tissue
No. 4, Advantage DCT 200 TS, Yankee dryer, total capacity 60,000 mt/y, Trim width 5.5 m, Tissue
Finishing Equipment:
Winders: 11
Calenders: 3
Rewinders: 3 at 80,000 mt/y
Energy Data:
Power boilers: 5
Combustion turbines
Electrical demand for mill: 454 MWh/D

SINGAPORE

ⓘAsia Pacific Resources International - APRIL
Ownership: 100% by Blu Diamond Inc. (Private)
80 Raffles Place, # 50-01, UOB Plaza 1
048624 Singapore
Singapore
 Phone: (65) 6216 9318/9179
 Fax: (65) 6539 0020
 Email: sales@aprilasia.com
 Web Address: www.aprilasia.com
Personnel:
 CEO: Sukanto Tanoto
 Phone: (65) 6216 9318
 Fax: (65) 6538 0020
 Pres. & COO: A. J. Devanesan
 Phone: (65) 6216 9318
 Fax: (65) 6538 0020
 CFO: Praveen Singhavi
 Phone: (65) 6216 9318
 Fax: (65) 6538 0020
 Pres. Dir.: Kusnan Rahim
 Phone: (65) 6216 9318
 Fax: (65) 6538 0020
 Finan. Dir. & Group Bus. Contr.: Niap Juan Loh
 Phone: (65) 6216 9318
 Fax: (65) 6538 0020
 Sls. Mgr.: Ashay Bhise
 Phone: (65) 6216 9318
 Fax: (65) 6538 0020
 Email: ashay@aprilasia.com
 Commun. Mgr. (Sustainability & Corp. Affairs): Jamie Menon
 Phone: (65) 6216 9318
 Fax: (65) 6538 0020
 Bus. Contrl.: Sumit Rathor
 Phone: (65) 6216 9318
 Fax: (65) 6538 0020
Total Employees of Company: 4,500
Total Employees at this Location: 71
Mill Locations:
Asia Symbol (Guangdong) Paper Co., Ltd., Jiangmen Mill, No.1, Ruifeng Industrial Park, Shalu Village, Shuangshui Town, Xinhui district, Jiangmen 529153, China, Capacity: 450,000 mt/y, (Paper mill)
 Phone: (86) 750 650 3000/3150
 Fax: (86) 750 650 3166
PT Riau Andalan Pulp & Paper (RAPP), Riaupulp and Riaupaper Mill Kerinci (98.50% owned), Desa Pangkalan Kerinci, Kecamatan Langgam, Kab. Pelalawan, 28300 Pekanbaru - Riau, Indonesia, Capacity: 840,000 mt/y, (Pulp mill, Paper mill)
 Phone: (62) 761 95529 (Pulp) 491000 (Paper)
 Fax: (62) 761 95681 (Pulp) 95456 (Paper)
 Email: info@aprilasia.com
Asia Symbol (Shandong) Pulp & Paper Co., Ltd., Rizhao Mill (90% owned), No. 369 Beijing Rd., Donggang District, Rizhao 276826, China, Capacity: 480,165 mt/y, (Pulp mill, Paperboard mill)
 Phone: (86) 633 336
 1000/1168/1258/1209/1093/1179
 Fax: (86) 633 336 1218/1111/1203/8359931/8360366
 Email: thomas_leung@aprilchina.com

ⓘNorske Skog PanAsia
Ownership: 100% by Norske Skog ASA
4 Shenton Way, #29-02 SGX Centre 2
068807 Singapore
Singapore
 Phone: (65) 6327 4188
 Fax: (65) 6327 4264
 Web Address: www.norskeskog.com
Personnel:
 Gen. Mgr. Norske Skog PanAsia: Hannes Skisaker
 Phone: (65) 6327 4188
 Fax: (65) 6327 4264
Total Employees of Company: 2,000
Total Employees at this Location: 9

ⓘUPP Holdings Limited
Company is previously United Paper Industries Pte. Ltd.
Ownership: 99% by Samson Paper Holdings Limited
1 Kim Seng Promenade 14-01, Great Wall City, East Tower
237994 Singapore
Singapore
 Phone: (65) 6836 5522
 Fax: (65) 6836 5500
 Email: admin@upp-group.com
 Web Address: www.upp-group.com
Personnel:
 Exec. Chmn., CEO: Tong Kooi Ong
 Phone: (65) 6836 5522
 Fax: (65) 6836 5500
 Exec. Dir., Pres. & COO: (James) Koh Wan Kai
 Phone: (65) 6836 5522
 Fax: (65) 6836 5500
Mill Locations:
UPP Pulp & Paper (M) Sdn Bhd, Batang Berjuntai Mill (87.50% owned), PO Box 225, Lot 225, Jalan Kuala Selangor, 45620 Ijok, Batang Berjuntai, Malaysia, Capacity: 85,000 mt/y, (Paper mill, Paperboard mill)
 Phone: (60) 3 6038 6388
 Fax: (60) 3 6038 5966
 Email: sales.upb@upp-group.com

SOUTH KOREA

ⓜAhlstrom Korea Co., Ltd.
Hyunpoong Mill
Ownership: Ahlstrom Corporation Oy
7, Geum-ri, Yuga-myeon, Dalseong-gun
711-882 Daegu-si, Daegu-si
South Korea
 Phone: (82) 53 611-0491/92
 Fax: (82) 53 611-0493
 Email: investor@ahlstrom.com, corporate.communications@ahlstrom.com
 Web Address: www.ahlstrom.com
Personnel:
 Pres. & CEO: Howard Jin
 Phone: (82) 53 611-0491/92
 Fax: (82) 53 611-0493
 Sls, Develop & Transp. Asia Dir. : Biju John
 Phone: (82) 53 611-0491/92
 Fax: (82) 53 611-0493
 Mill Mgr.: Wikle Park
 Phone: (82) 53 611-0491/92
 Fax: (82) 53 611-0493
 Email: wikle.park@ahlstrom.com
 Commer. Mgr.: Dong-Yun Kim
 Phone: (82) 53 611-0491/92
 Fax: (82) 53 611-0493
 HR Mgr.: Sebastian Nam
 Phone: (82) 53 611-0491/92
 Fax: (82) 53 611-0493
 Email: sebastian.nam@ahlstrom.com
 Purch. Mgr.: Jeus Hwang
 Phone: (82) 53 611-0491/92
 Fax: (82) 53 611-0493
 R&D Mgr.: Henry Han
 Phone: (82) 53 611-0491/92
 Fax: (82) 53 611-0493
 Email: henry.han@ahlstrom.com
Total Employees at this Location: 110
Type of Operation: Paper mill
Paper/Paperboard Grades and Capacities:
 Total paper and paperboard capacity: 27,000 mt/y
 Specialty and industrial: 27,000 mt/y
Paper and Paperboard Mill Data:
Paper Machines: 2
No. 1, total capacity 12,000 mt/y, Specialty and industrial
No. 2, total capacity 15,000 mt/y, Specialty and industrial

ⓘⓜAjin Paper Mfg. Co. Ltd.
Hyunpoong Mill
92-1, Singi-ri, Hyeongpung-myeon
711-871 Dalseong-gun, Daegu-si, Daegu-si
South Korea
 Phone: (82) 53 611-1121
 Fax: (82) 53 614-274
 Email: ykap@ajinpaper.co.kr
Personnel:
 Pres.: Tae-Hwa Chung
 Phone: (82) 53 611-1121
 Fax: (82) 53 614-1274
 VP: In-Ki Baek
 Phone: (82) 53 611-1121
 Purch. Mgr.: Jum-Joon An
 Phone: (82) 53 611-1121
Total Employees of Company: 103
Total Employees at this Location: 100
Type of Operation: Paperboard mill
Pulp Grades and Capacities:
 Total pulp capacity: 246,116 mt/y
 Recycled Pulping: 246,116 mt/y
Pulp Mill Data:
 Recycled Fiber Treatment Lines:
 Recycled packaging pulping lines: 1
Paper/Paperboard Grades and Capacities:
 Total paper and paperboard capacity: 250,000 mt/y
 Linerboard: 90,000 mt/y
 Corrugating medium/fluting: 160,000 mt/y
Paper and Paperboard Mill Data:
Paper Machines: 2
No. 1, fourdrinier, total capacity 90,000 mt/y, Trim width 4.2 m, Linerboard
No. 2, fourdrinier, total capacity 160,000 mt/y, Trim width 5.45 m, Corrugating medium/fluting
Energy Data:
Power boilers
Electrical demand for mill: 304 MWh/D

ⓘAsia Paper Mfg. Co., Ltd.
Ownership: 37.87% by Asia Cement Mfg.Co.Ltd.
9th Fl, Asia Tower, 726, Yeoksam-dong, Gangnam-gu
135-719 Seoul
South Korea
 Phone: (82) 2 527-6882
 Fax: (82) 2 527-6859
 Email: webmaster@asiapaper.co.kr
 Web Address: www.asiapaper.co.kr
Personnel:
 Chmn.: Byung-Moo Lee
 Phone: (82) 2 527-6501
 Fax: (82) 2 563-0323
 Email: leebm@asiacement.co.kr
 V. Chmn: Yoon-Moo Lee
 Phone: (82) 2 527-6505
 Fax: (82) 2 568-0323

South Korea

Email: leeym@asiacement.co.kr
Pres.: Jae-Hong Lee
Phone: (82) 43 270-7700
Fax: (82) 43 270-7707
Email: webmaster@asiapaper.co.kr
Man. Dir.: In-Beom Lee
Phone: (82) 43 270-7800
Fax: (82) 43 275-5497
Man. Dir.: Geon-Je Hong
Phone: (82) 43 270-7800
Fax: (82) 43 275-5497
Total Employees of Company: 192
Total Employees at this Location: 42
Mill Locations:
Asia Paper Mfg. Co., Ltd., Cheongwon Mill, 501, Gumho-ri, Buyong-myeon, 363-942 Cheongwon-gun, South Korea, Capacity: 530,000 mt/y, (Paper mill, Paperboard mill)
Phone: (82) 43 270-7800
Fax: (82) 43 275-5497
Asia Papertec Inc., Shihwa Mill, 1706, Jeongwang-dong, 429-860 Siheung-si, South Korea, Capacity: 250,000 mt/y, (Paper mill, Paperboard mill)
Phone: (82) 31 499-6366
Fax: (82) 31 434-7411
Email: webmaster@asiapapertec.com
Kyongsan Paper Co., Ltd., Daegu-si Mill, 161, Geum-ri, Yuga-myeon, Dalseong-gun, 711-882 Daegu-si, South Korea, Capacity: 120,000 mt/y, (Paperboard mill)
Phone: (82) 53 615-6285
Fax: (82) 53 615-6292

ⓜAsia Paper Mfg. Co., Ltd.
Cheongwon Mill
501, Gumho-ri, Buyong-myeon
363-942 Cheongwon-gun, Chungcheongbuk-do
South Korea
Phone: (82) 43 270-7800
Fax: (82) 43 275-5497
Web Address: www.asiapaper.co.kr
Personnel:
Mill Mgr.: Dae-Hyun Han
Phone: (82) 43 2707600
Total Employees at this Location: 160
Type of Operation: Paper mill, Paperboard mill
Pulp Grades and Capacities:
Total pulp capacity: 476,245 mt/y
Recycled Pulping: 476,245 mt/y
Pulp Mill Data:
Recycled Fiber Treatment Lines:
Recycled packaging pulping lines: 1
Paper/Paperboard Grades and Capacities:
Total paper and paperboard capacity: 530,000 mt/y
Packaging papers: 52,000 mt/y
Linerboard: 437,500 mt/y
Boxboard/cartonboard: 40,500 mt/y
Paper and Paperboard Mill Data:
Stock Preparation:
Pulpers: 7
Refiners: 19
Paper Machines: 2
No. 1, fourdrinier, total capacity 270,000 mt/y, Trim width 4.1 m, Linerboard, Boxboard/cartonboard
No. 3, multi-wire, total capacity 260,000 mt/y, Trim width 4.4 m, Linerboard, Packaging papers
Energy Data:
Power boilers: 5
Electrical demand for mill: 695 MWh/D

ⓞⓜAsia Papertec Inc.
Shihwa Mill
Ownership: Asia Paper Mfg. Co., Ltd., 56.94% by Asia Cement & Asia Paper
1706, Jeongwang-dong
429-860 Siheung-si, Gyeonggi-do
South Korea
Phone: (82) 31 499-6366
Fax: (82) 31 434-7411
Email: webmaster@asiapapertec.com
Web Address: www.asiapaper.co.kr
Personnel:
Pres.: Won-Hee Park
Phone: (82) 31 499-6366
Fax: (82) 31 434-7411
Email: parkwh@asiapapertec.com
Exec. Dir.: Yeong-Yil Kim
Phone: (82) 31 499-6366
Fax: (82) 31 434-7411
Inter. Auditor, Non-Exec. Inde. Dir.: No-Wun Park
Phone: (82) 31 499-6366
Exec. Dir.: Seung-Hwan Yoo
Phone: (82) 31 499-6366
Total Employees of Company: 109
Total Employees at this Location: 109
Type of Operation: Paper mill, Paperboard mill
Mill Locations:
Kyongsan Paper Co., Ltd., Daegu-si Mill, 161, Geum-ri, Yuga-myeon, Dalseong-gun, 711-882 Daegu-si, South Korea, Capacity: 120,000 mt/y, (Paperboard mill)
Phone: (82) 53 615-6285
Fax: (82) 53 615-6292
Pulp Grades and Capacities:
Total pulp capacity: 247,437 mt/y
Recycled Pulping: 247,437 mt/y
Pulp Mill Data:
Recycled Fiber Treatment Lines:
Recycled packaging pulping lines: 1
Paper/Paperboard Grades and Capacities:
Total paper and paperboard capacity: 250,000 mt/y
Linerboard: 250,000 mt/y
Paper and Paperboard Mill Data:
Paper Machines: 1
No. 3, fourdrinier, total capacity 250,000 mt/y, Trim width 5.3 m, Linerboard
Energy Data:
Power boilers
Electrical demand for mill: 362 MWh/D

ⓜResolute Paper Korea Ltd.
Mokpo mill
Ownership: 100% by Resolute Forest Products Canada Inc.
1694-1, Nanjeon-ri, Samho-eup
526-892 Yeongam-gun, Jeollanam-do
South Korea
Phone: (82) 2-3453-7323
Fax: (82) 61 460-6158
Email: info@resolutefp.com
Web Address: www.resolutefp.com
Personnel:
VP: Terry Cook
Phone: (82) 2 2076-3320
Fax: (82) 2 725-9096
Email: terry.cook@resolutefp.com
Dir.: Sang Chun Lee
Phone: (82) 61 460-6800
Fax: (82) 61 460-6537
Email: leesc@resolutefp.com
Man. Dir.: Wang Don Yoo
Phone: (82) 61 460-6050
Fax: (82) 61 460-6220
Email: yoowd@resolutefp.com
Man. Dir.: Yong Woo Kim
Phone: (82) 2-3453-7323
Total Employees at this Location: 180
Type of Operation: Paper mill
Pulp Grades and Capacities:
Total pulp capacity: 197,840 mt/y
Recycled Pulping: 197,840 mt/y
Pulp Mill Data:
Bleach Plant Systems: 1
DIP
Recycled Fiber Treatment Lines:
Flotation deinking lines: 1
Paper/Paperboard Grades and Capacities:
Total paper and paperboard capacity: 200,000 mt/y
Newsprint: 200,000 mt/y
Paper and Paperboard Mill Data:
Paper Machines: 1
No. 1, DuoFormer CFD, total capacity 200,000 mt/y, Trim width 7.8 m, Newsprint
Finishing Equipment:
Rewinders: 2 at 250,000 mt/y
Energy Data:
Power boilers: 3
Electrical demand for mill: 551 MWh/D

ⓞⓜDae Wang Paper Co., Ltd.
Gunsan Mill
25-9, Soryong-dong
573-879 Gunsan-si, Jeollabuk-do
South Korea
Phone: (82) 63 467-8051
Fax: (82) 63 467-1591
Web Address: www.dwpaper.co.kr/
Personnel:
Pres.: Chang-gyu Kim
Phone: (82) 63 467-8051
Total Employees of Company: 70
Total Employees at this Location: 70
Type of Operation: Paper mill
Pulp Grades and Capacities:
Total pulp capacity: 9,933 mt/y
Recycled Pulping: 9,933 mt/y
Pulp Mill Data:
Bleach Plant Systems: 1
DIP
Recycled Fiber Treatment Lines:
Flotation deinking lines: 1
Paper/Paperboard Grades and Capacities:
Total paper and paperboard capacity: 17,300 mt/y
Tissue: 17,300 mt/y
Paper and Paperboard Mill Data:
Paper Machines: 1
No. 2, crescent former, total capacity 17,300 mt/y, Trim width 2.73 m, Tissue
Energy Data:
Power boilers: 1
Electrical demand for mill: 48 MWh/D

ⓜDaehan Paper Co., Ltd.
Ownership: 43% by Seung Hak Yang, 43% by Seung Ryoung Yang
445-5 Gwangjang-Dong
143-813 Gwangjin-Gu, Seoul
South Korea
Phone: (82) 2 2049-7000
Fax: (82) 2 2049-7788
Email: webmaster_daehan@daehanpaper.com
Web Address: www.daehanpaper.co.kr
Personnel:
VP: Sung-Hee Hong
Phone: (82) 2 2049-7000
Fax: (82) 2 2049-7788
Man. Dir.: Han-Je Cho
Phone: (82) 2 2049-7000
Fax: (82) 2 2049-7788
Headquarter Mgr.: Yong-Ho Jeong
Phone: (82) 2 2049-7000
Fax: (82) 2 2049-7788
Total Employees of Company: 332
Mill Locations:
Daehan Paper Co., Ltd., Cheongwon Mill, 131-1, Ssangcheong-ri, Gangoe-myeon, 363-952 Cheongwon-gun, South Korea, Capacity: 288,000 mt/y, (Pulp mill, Paper mill)
Phone: (82) 43 249-6000
Fax: (82) 43 238-3706
Email: webmaster_daehan@daehanpaper.com

ⓜDaehan Paper Co., Ltd.
Cheongwon Mill
131-1, Ssangcheong-ri, Gangoe-myeon
363-952 Cheongwon-gun, Chungcheongbuk-do
South Korea
Phone: (82) 43 249-6000
Fax: (82) 43 238-3706

South Korea

Email: webmaster_daehan@daehanpaper.com
Web Address: www.daehanpaper.com
Personnel:
Man. Dir.: Han-Je Cho
Phone: (82) 43 249-6013
Fax: (82) 43 238-3706
Dpty. Gen. Mgr.: Dae-Kyung Kang
Phone: (82) 43 249-6013
Fax: (82) 43 238-3706
Total Employees at this Location: 285
Type of Operation: Pulp mill, Paper mill
Pulp Grades and Capacities:
Total pulp capacity: 269,843 mt/y
Recycled Pulping: 269,843 mt/y
Pulp Mill Data:
Mechanical Pulping Systems:
Conventional grinders: 1
Pressurized grinders: 5
Bleach Plant Systems: 3
DIP
Paper/Paperboard Grades and Capacities:
Total paper and paperboard capacity: 288,000 mt/y
Newsprint: 227,000 mt/y
Uncoated mechanical/groundwood: 61,000 mt/y
Paper and Paperboard Mill Data:
Stock Preparation:
Pulpers: 6
Refiners: 11
Paper Machines: 2
No. 1, (with Gate Roll Size Press), fourdrinier, total capacity 61,000 mt/y, Trim width 2.4 m, Uncoated mechanical/groundwood
No. 3, (With Gate Roll Size Press), Bel-Baie III, total capacity 227,000 mt/y, Trim width 6.4 m, Newsprint
Coating Machines: 3
PM 1, total capacity 57,000 mt/y., on machine
PM 2, total capacity 61,000 mt/y., on machine
PM 3, total capacity 198,000 mt/y., on machine
Finishing Equipment:
Supercalenders: 2
Rewinders: 4
Sheeters: 2
Energy Data:
Power boilers: 4
Electrical demand for mill: 842 MWh/D

ⓘⓜDaehan Papertech Co., Ltd.
Danyang Mill
Ownership: Hansol Paper Co., Ltd., Doorim Construction
1063-2, Daechi-ri
517-923 Daejeon-myeon, Damyang-gun, Jeollanam-do
South Korea
Phone: (82) 61 380-0380
Fax: (82) 61 380-0398
Email: hl4cfb@hanmail.net
Web Address: hansol.com/english/hansol/current/papertec.html
Personnel:
Pres.: Byeong-Woon Jeong
Phone: (82) 61 380-0380
Email: hl4cfb@hanmail.net
Sls. Dir.: Dae-Young Kim
Phone: (82) 61 380-0380
Purch. Dpty. Mgr.: Byeong-Yeon Kim
Phone: (82) 61 380 0330
Total Employees of Company: 170
Total Employees at this Location: 170
Type of Operation: Paperboard mill
Pulp Grades and Capacities:
Total pulp capacity: 182,759 mt/y
Recycled Pulping: 182,759 mt/y
Pulp Mill Data:
Recycled Fiber Treatment Lines:
Recycled packaging pulping lines
Paper/Paperboard Grades and Capacities:
Total paper and paperboard capacity: 216,000 mt/y
Linerboard: 180,000 mt/y
Corrugating medium/fluting: 36,000 mt/y

Paper and Paperboard Mill Data:
Paper Machines: 2
No. 2, fourdrinier, total capacity 36,000 mt/y, Trim width 3.7 m, Corrugating medium/fluting
No. 3, fourdrinier, total capacity 180,000 mt/y, Trim width 4.3 m, Linerboard
Energy Data:
Power boilers: 1
Electrical demand for mill: 281 MWh/D

ⓘⓜDaejin Paper Mfg. Co., Ltd.
Daegu Mill
913-1, Chimsan-dong
702-872 Buk-gu, Daegu-si, Daegu-si
South Korea
Phone: (82) 53 355-0444
Fax: (82) 53 354-7948
Email: daejinpaper77@hanmail.net
Personnel:
Pres.: Won-Sil Choi
Phone: (82) 53 355 0444
Man. Dir.: Min-Young Choi
Phone: (82) 53 355 0444
Total Employees at this Location: 42
Type of Operation: Paper mill
Paper/Paperboard Grades and Capacities:
Total paper and paperboard capacity: 13,200 mt/y
Tissue: 13,200 mt/y
Paper and Paperboard Mill Data:
Paper Machines: 2
PM 1, cylinder, total capacity 5,000 mt/y, Trim width 2.5 m, Tissue
PM 2, cylinder, total capacity 8,200 mt/y, Trim width 2.5 m, Tissue
Energy Data:
Power boilers: 1

ⓘⓜDaelim Paper Co. Ltd.
Daelim Paper
Ownership: 15.35% by Jong-U Ryu, 22.36% by Chang-Seung Ryu
169, Nueup-dong, Hwangsae-ro
447-160 Osan-si, Gyeonggi-do
South Korea
Phone: (82) 31 373-7670
Fax: (82) 31 373-0662
Email: webmaster@daelimpaper.co.kr
Web Address: www.daelimpaper.co.kr
Personnel:
CEO (from 2009): Chang-seung Ryu
Phone: (82) 31 373-7670
Fax: (82) 31 3730662
Total Employees at this Location: 80
Type of Operation: Paper mill
Pulp Grades and Capacities:
Total pulp capacity: 157,120 mt/y
Recycled Pulping: 157,120 mt/y
Pulp Mill Data:
Recycled Fiber Treatment Lines:
Recycled packaging pulping lines
Paper/Paperboard Grades and Capacities:
Total paper and paperboard capacity: 160,650 mt/y
Corrugating medium/fluting: 160,650 mt/y
Paper and Paperboard Mill Data:
Stock Preparation:
Pulpers: 2
Paper Machines: 1
No. 2, fourdrinier (2), total capacity 160,650 mt/y, Trim width 4.1 m, Corrugating medium/fluting
Finishing Equipment:
Rewinders
Energy Data:
Turbines
Electrical demand for mill: 197 MWh/D

ⓘDaewang Paper Co. Ltd.
239-14 Dangjeong-dong
435-831 Gunpo-si, Gyeonggi-do
South Korea
Mill Locations:
Daewang Paper Co. Ltd., Gunpo Mill, 239-14 Dangjeong-dong, 435-831 Gunpo-si, South Korea, Capacity: 10,000 mt/y, (Paper mill)
Phone: (82) 31 452-3338

ⓘⓜDaewang Paper Co. Ltd.
Gunpo Mill
239-14 Dangjeong-dong
435-831 Gunpo-si, Gyeonggi-do
South Korea
Phone: (82) 31 452-3338
Personnel:
Man. Dir.: Seung-gyu Kim
Phone: (82) 31 452-8230
Type of Operation: Paper mill
Paper/Paperboard Grades and Capacities:
Total paper and paperboard capacity: 10,000 mt/y
Tissue: 10,000 mt/y
Paper and Paperboard Mill Data:
Paper Machines: 2
PM 1, total capacity 4,500 mt/y, Tissue
PM 2, total capacity 5,500 mt/y, Tissue

ⓘⓜDaewha Paper Board Mfg. Co., Ltd.
Gunpo Mill
#148-1 Geumjeong-dong
435-824 Gunpo-si, Gyeonggi-do
South Korea
Phone: (82) 31 452-3765
Fax: (82) 31 452-0182
Web Address: www.daewhapaper.com
Personnel:
CEO: Sang Hun Oh
Phone: (82) 31 452 3765
Fax: (82) 31 452 0182
Exec. Dir.: Jong Suk Kim
Phone: (82) 31 452 3765
Fax: (82) 31 452 0182
Dir.: Jong Ho Kim
Phone: (82) 31 452 3765
Fax: (82) 31 452 0182
Total Employees of Company: 100
Total Employees at this Location: 65
Type of Operation: Paperboard mill
Pulp Grades and Capacities:
Total pulp capacity: 56,788 mt/y
Recycled Pulping: 56,788 mt/y
Paper/Paperboard Grades and Capacities:
Total paper and paperboard capacity: 56,000 mt/y
Boxboard/cartonboard: 56,000 mt/y
Paper and Paperboard Mill Data:
Stock Preparation:
Pulpers: 2
Refiners: 1
Paper Machines: 2
No. 1, multi-fourdrinier, total capacity 36,000 mt/y, Trim width 2.4 m, Boxboard/cartonboard
No. 2, multi-fourdrinier, total capacity 20,000 mt/y, Trim width 1.25 m, Boxboard/cartonboard
Energy Data:
Power boilers: 2
Electrical demand for mill: 59 MWh/D

ⓘⓜDaeyang Paper Mfg. Co. Ltd.
Ansan Mill
Ownership: Shindaeyang Paper Co., Ltd., 20.17% by Hyeok-Yong Kwon, 10.36% by Yeong Kwon
1062-1 Singil-dong, Danwon-gu
425-839 Ansan-si, Gyeonggi-do
South Korea
Phone: (82) 31 432-5416
Fax: (82) 31 432-5410
Web Address: www.dygroup.co.kr
Personnel:
Chmn.: Hyuk-Yong Kwon

South Korea

Phone: (82) 2 3472 5915
V. Chmn.: Hyuk-Hong Kwon
Phone: (82) 2 3472 5915
Pres. CEO: Young Kwon
Phone: (82) 31 432-5416
Mill Mgr.: Sang-Yeop Han
Phone: (82) 31 491 1641
Fax: (82) 31 494 8936
Indep. Dir.: Chang-Hyeon Kim
Phone: (82) 31 432-5416
Total Employees of Company: 77
Total Employees at this Location: 77
Type of Operation: Paperboard mill
Pulp Grades and Capacities:
  Total pulp capacity: 439,107 mt/y
  Recycled Pulping: 439,107 mt/y
Pulp Mill Data:
  Recycled Fiber Treatment Lines:
  Recycled packaging pulping lines
Paper/Paperboard Grades and Capacities:
  Total paper and paperboard capacity: 438,000 mt/y
  Linerboard: 438,000 mt/y
Paper and Paperboard Mill Data:
  Stock Preparation:
  Pulpers: 3
  Refiners: 4
Paper Machines: 2
  No. 1, fourdrinier, total capacity 108,000 mt/y, Trim width 3.85 m, Linerboard
  No. 2, fourdrinier, total capacity 330,000 mt/y, Trim width 4.85 m, Linerboard
Finishing Equipment:
  Winders: 2 at 264,000 mt/y
  Calenders: 2
  Rewinders: 3
Energy Data:
  Power boilers: 1
  Electrical demand for mill: 533 MWh/D

ⓜⓜDongil Paper Mfg. Co., Ltd.
Ansan Mill
Ownership: 29.83% by Tailim Packaging industrial Co., 8.97% by Yeong-Seop Jeong, 11.93% by Dong-Seop Jeong
492-1, Banwol Industrial Complex, Mongnae-dong, Danwon-gu
425-100 Ansan-si, Gyeonggi-do
South Korea
  Phone: (82) 31 491-0010
  Fax: (82) 31 491-0023
  Email: jkpark@dongilpaper.co.kr
  Web Address: www.dongilpaper.co.kr
Personnel:
  Chmn., Co-CEO: Dong-Seop Jung
  Phone: (82) 31 491 0010
  Fax: (82) 31 491 0023
  Pres. & Co-CEO: Yeong-Seop Jung
  Phone: (82) 31 491 0010
  Fax: (82) 31 491 0023
  VP., Dir.: Jin Du Kim
  Phone: (82) 31 491 0010
  Fax: (82) 31 491 0023
  Man. Dir.: Chung Se Jung
  Phone: (82) 31 491 0010
  Fax: (82) 31 491 0023
  Dir.: Sam Gyu Goh
  Phone: (82) 31 491 0010
  Fax: (82) 31 491 0023
  Dir.: Yu Cheon Jung
  Phone: (82) 31 491 0010
  Fax: (82) 31 491 0023
Total Employees at this Location: 120
Type of Operation: Paper mill, Paperboard mill
Mill Locations:
  Dongil Packaging, Jinju-si Mill, 55-59 Sangpyeong-dong, 660-902 Jinju-si, South Korea, Capacity: 50,000 mt/y, (Paperboard mill)
  Phone: (82) 55 755-1211
  Fax: (82) 55 758-1025
  Dongil Paper Mfg. Co., Ltd., Uiryeong Mill, 1540-1, Dongdong-ri, Uiryeong-Eup, 636-803 Uiryeong-gun, South Korea, Capacity: 100,000 mt/y, (Paperboard mill)
  Phone: (82) 55 572-3020
  Fax: (82) 55 572-3025
  Email: jpark@dongilpaper.co.kr
  Dongwon Paper Mfg. Co., Ltd., Jeongup Mill, Yeongpa-dong, 580-080 Jeongeup-si, South Korea, Capacity: 180,000 mt/y, (Paperboard mill)
  Phone: (82) 63 536 8811
  Fax: (82) 63 536 8815
  Wolsan Paper Mfg. Co., Ltd., Haman Mill, Chilseo Industrial Complex 4B-7L, 637-940 Chilseo-myeon, Haman-gun, South Korea, Capacity: 320,000 mt/y, (Paperboard mill)
  Phone: (82) 55 586-6000
  Fax: (82) 55 587-7585/586-3999
  Email: choiss2085@yahoo.co.kr
Pulp Grades and Capacities:
  Total pulp capacity: 236,888 mt/y
  Recycled Pulping: 236,888 mt/y
Pulp Mill Data:
  Recycled Fiber Treatment Lines:
  Recycled packaging pulping lines
Paper/Paperboard Grades and Capacities:
  Total paper and paperboard capacity: 250,000 mt/y
  Linerboard: 200,000 mt/y
  Corrugating medium/fluting: 50,000 mt/y
Paper and Paperboard Mill Data:
  Stock Preparation:
  Pulpers: 3
  Refiners: 8
Paper Machines: 1
  No. 1, Bel-Bond, total capacity 250,000 mt/y, Trim width 4.1 m, Linerboard, Corrugating medium/fluting
Coating Machines: 1
  PM 1, on machine
Finishing Equipment:
  Calenders: 1
  Rewinders: 1
Energy Data:
  Power boilers: 1
  Steam turbines: 1
  Electrical demand for mill: 331 MWh/D

ⓜⓜDongil Packaging
Jinju-si Mill
Ownership: Dongil Paper Mfg. Co., Ltd.
55-59 Sangpyeong-dong
660-902 Jinju-si, Gyeongsangnam-do
South Korea
  Phone: (82) 55 755-1211
  Fax: (82) 55 758-1025
  Web Address: www.dongilpaper.co.kr
Personnel:
  Pres.: Sang-Mun Cheong
  Phone: (82) 55 755 1211
  Exec. Dir.: Ku-Bong Kim
  Phone: (82) 55 755 1211
  Prod. Dir.: Du-Ho Chung
  Phone: (82) 55 755 1211
Total Employees at this Location: 50
Type of Operation: Paperboard mill
Pulp Grades and Capacities:
  Total pulp capacity: 50,340 mt/y
  Recycled Pulping: 50,340 mt/y
Pulp Mill Data:
  Recycled Fiber Treatment Lines:
  Recycled packaging pulping lines
Paper/Paperboard Grades and Capacities:
  Total paper and paperboard capacity: 50,000 mt/y
  Linerboard: 50,000 mt/y
Paper and Paperboard Mill Data:
Paper Machines: 1
  No. 1, fourdrinier, total capacity 50,000 mt/y, Trim width 3.3 m, Linerboard
Energy Data:
  Electrical demand for mill: 65 MWh/D

ⓜDongil Paper Mfg. Co., Ltd.
Uiryeong Mill
1540-1, Dongdong-ri, Uiryeong-Eup
636-803 Uiryeong-gun, Gyeongsangnam-do
South Korea
  Phone: (82) 55 572-3020
  Fax: (82) 55 572-3025
  Email: jpark@dongilpaper.co.kr
  Web Address: www.dongilpaper.co.kr
Personnel:
  Mill Mgr.: Dong-Woo Lee
  Phone: (82) 55 572 3020
  Purch. Mgr.: Chi-Sun Baek
  Phone: (82) 55 572 3020
Total Employees at this Location: 58
Type of Operation: Paperboard mill
Pulp Grades and Capacities:
  Total pulp capacity: 97,351 mt/y
  Recycled Pulping: 97,351 mt/y
Pulp Mill Data:
  Recycled Fiber Treatment Lines:
  Recycled packaging pulping lines
Paper/Paperboard Grades and Capacities:
  Total paper and paperboard capacity: 100,000 mt/y
  Corrugating medium/fluting: 100,000 mt/y
Paper and Paperboard Mill Data:
  Stock Preparation:
  Pulpers: 2
Paper Machines: 1
  No. 1, SymFormer MB, total capacity 100,000 mt/y, Trim width 3.7 m, Corrugating medium/fluting
Finishing Equipment:
  Rewinders: 1
Energy Data:
  Power boilers
  Electrical demand for mill: 115 MWh/D

ⓜDongwon Paper Mfg. Co., Ltd.
Jeongup Mill
Ownership: 10.77% by Wolsan Paper Mfg. Co., Ltd., 21.97% by Young-Seop Jeon, 21.97% by Sang-Moon Jeon
Yeongpa-dong
580-080 Jeongeup-si, Jeollabuk-do
South Korea
  Phone: (82) 63 536 8811
  Fax: (82) 63 536 8815
Personnel:
  Pres.: Young-Seop Jeong
  Phone: (82) 63 536 8811
  Gen. Mgr.: Je Yul Kim
  Phone: (82) 63 536 8811
  Bus. Mgr.: Jung Hwan Joung
  Phone: (82) 63 536 8811
Total Employees at this Location: 150
Type of Operation: Paperboard mill
Pulp Grades and Capacities:
  Total pulp capacity: 181,026 mt/y
  Recycled Pulping: 181,026 mt/y
Pulp Mill Data:
  Recycled Fiber Treatment Lines:
  Recycled packaging pulping lines
Paper/Paperboard Grades and Capacities:
  Total paper and paperboard capacity: 180,000 mt/y
  Linerboard: 180,000 mt/y
Paper and Paperboard Mill Data:
Paper Machines: 2
  No. 1, cylinder, total capacity 85,000 mt/y, Trim width 3.9 m, Linerboard
  No. 2, cylinder, total capacity 95,000 mt/y, Trim width 3.6 m, Linerboard
Energy Data:
  Power boilers: 6
  Electrical demand for mill: 233 MWh/D

ⓜⓜDongyang Paper Mfg. Co., Ltd.
Asan Mill
265, Sirok-dong

South Korea

336-020 Ansan-si, Chungcheongnam-do
South Korea
  Phone: (82) 41 541-5970
  Fax: (82) 41 547-0150
  Web Address: www.dypaper.com
Personnel:
  Pres.: Eui Bum Lee
  Phone: (82) 41 541 5970
  Mill Mgr.: Won Sup Choi
  Phone: (82) 41 541 5970
Total Employees of Company: 99
Total Employees at this Location: 99
Type of Operation: Paper mill
Pulp Grades and Capacities:
  Total pulp capacity: 6,300 mt/y
  Chemical Pulp: 6,300 mt/y
Paper/Paperboard Grades and Capacities:
  Total paper and paperboard capacity: 11,550 mt/y
  Specialty and industrial: 11,550 mt/y
Paper and Paperboard Mill Data:
  Stock Preparation:
  Pulpers: 5
  Refiners: 5
Paper Machines: 3
  No. 1, cylinder, total capacity 7,000 mt/y, Trim width 2.85 m, Specialty and industrial
  No. 2, fourdrinier, total capacity 2,450 mt/y, Trim width 1.35 m, Specialty and industrial
  No. 3, cylinder, total capacity 2,100 mt/y, Trim width 1.4 m, Specialty and industrial
Finishing Equipment:
  Rewinders: 3
Energy Data:
  Power boilers: 2

ⒽE-papertech Co. Ltd.
4-8, Wonpyeong-ri, Oga-myeon
340-915 Yesan-gun, Chungcheongnam-do
South Korea
  Phone: (82) 41 333-2935
  Fax: (82) 41 333-2939
Mill Locations:
  E-papertech Co. Ltd., Yesan-gun Mill, 4-8, Wonpyeong-ri, Oga-myeon, 340-915 Yesan-gun, South Korea, Capacity: 14,100 mt/y, (Paper mill)
  Phone: (82) 41 333-2935
  Fax: (82) 41 333-2939

ⓂE-papertech Co. Ltd.
Yesan-gun Mill
4-8, Wonpyeong-ri, Oga-myeon
340-915 Yesan-gun, Chungcheongnam-do
South Korea
  Phone: (82) 41 333-2935
  Fax: (82) 41 333-2939
Type of Operation: Paper mill
Paper/Paperboard Grades and Capacities:
  Total paper and paperboard capacity: 14,100 mt/y
  Tissue: 14,100 mt/y
Paper and Paperboard Mill Data:
Paper Machines: 2
  PM 1, total capacity 5,400 mt/y, Tissue
  PM 2, total capacity 8,700 mt/y, Tissue

ⒽGreen Papertech
179-67, Doma 1-dong, Seo-gu
302-821 Daejeon-si
South Korea
  Phone: (82) 42 568-2710
  Fax: (82) 42 568-2713
Mill Locations:
  Green Papertech, Daejeon Mill, 179-67, Doma 1-dong, Seo-gu, 302-821 Daejeon-si, South Korea, Capacity: 5,300 mt/y, (Paper mill)
  Phone: (82) 42 568-2710
  Fax: (82) 42 568-2713

ⓂGreen Papertech
Daejeon Mill
179-67, Doma 1-dong, Seo-gu
302-821 Daejeon-si, Daejeon
South Korea
  Phone: (82) 42 568-2710
  Fax: (82) 42 568-2713
Type of Operation: Paper mill
Paper/Paperboard Grades and Capacities:
  Total paper and paperboard capacity: 5,300 mt/y
  Tissue: 5,300 mt/y
Paper and Paperboard Mill Data:
Paper Machines: 2
  PM 1, total capacity 3,000 mt/y, Tissue
  PM 1, total capacity 3,000 mt/y, Tissue

ⒽHana Paper Co., Ltd.
706-4, Yulseok-ri, Wabu-eup
472-904 Namyangju-si, Gyeonggi-do
South Korea
  Phone: (82) 31-555-1411, 31-521-6690
  Fax: (82) 31-563-0309
  Email: gushusky@hotmail.com
  Web Address: hanapaper.com/index-e.html
Personnel:
  Dir.: Jeonsang Lee
Mill Locations:
  Hana Paper Co., Ltd., Ulju-gun Mill, 522, Goyeon-ri, Ungchon-myeon, Ulju-gun, 689-871 Ulsan, South Korea, Capacity: 7,000 mt/y, (Paper mill)
  Phone: (82) 31 521 6690/555 1411
  Fax: (82) 31 563 0309
  Email: gushusky@hotmail.com

ⓂHana Paper Co., Ltd.
Ulju-gun Mill
522, Goyeon-ri, Ungchon-myeon, Ulju-gun
689-871 Ulsan
South Korea
  Phone: (82) 31 521 6690/555 1411
  Fax: (82) 31 563 0309
  Email: gushusky@hotmail.com
  Web Address: hanapaper.com/index-e.html
Type of Operation: Paper mill
Paper/Paperboard Grades and Capacities:
  Total paper and paperboard capacity: 7,000 mt/y
  Tissue
  Packaging papers

ⒽHanchang Paper Co., Ltd.
Ownership: 26.62% by Seung-Han Kim, 4.61% by Mr. Seung-Han Kim's family
11th Fl., Excon Venture Bldg. 15-24, Yeouido-dong
150-969 Yeongdeungpo-gu, Seoul
South Korea
  Phone: (82) 2 3774-5400
  Fax: (82) 2 3774-5489
  Email: webmaster@hanchangpaper.co.kr
  Web Address: www.hanchangpaper.co.kr
Personnel:
  Chmn.: Seung-Han Kim
  Phone: (82) 2 3774-5304
  CEO & V. Chmn.: Jong-Sun Kim
  Phone: (82) 2 3774 5330
  Purch. Gen. Mgr.: Jin-Hong Park
  Phone: (82) 2 3774 5410
Total Employees of Company: 279
Total Employees at this Location: 50
Mill Locations:
  Hanchang Paper Co., Ltd., Yangsan-si Mill, 270, Yongdang-ri, Ungsang-eup, 626-847 Yangsan-si, South Korea, Capacity: 124,950 mt/y, (Paperboard mill)
  Phone: (82) 55 370-2000
  Fax: (82) 55 370-2199
  Email: webmaster@hanchangpaper.co.kr

ⓂHanchang Paper Co., Ltd.
Yangsan-si Mill
270, Yongdang-ri, Ungsang-eup
626-847 Yangsan-si, Gyeongsangnam-do
South Korea
  Phone: (82) 55 370-2000
  Fax: (82) 55 370-2199
  Email: webmaster@hanchangpaper.co.kr
  Web Address: www.hanchangpaper.co.kr
Personnel:
  Pres.: Sang Hwang Han
  Phone: (82) 55 370 2000
  Mill Mgr.: Yoo Soon Kim
  Phone: (82) 55 370 2000
Total Employees at this Location: 229
Type of Operation: Paperboard mill
Pulp Grades and Capacities:
  Total pulp capacity: 99,563 mt/y
  Recycled Pulping: 99,563 mt/y
Paper/Paperboard Grades and Capacities:
  Total paper and paperboard capacity: 124,950 mt/y
  Boxboard/cartonboard: 124,950 mt/y
Paper and Paperboard Mill Data:
Paper Machines: 2
  No. 1, fourdrinier, total capacity 71,400 mt/y, Trim width 2.45 m, Boxboard/cartonboard
  No. 3, fourdrinier, total capacity 89,250 mt/y, Trim width 2.7 m, Boxboard/cartonboard
Coating Machines: 3
  No. 1, total capacity 66,600 mt/y, on machine
  No. 2, total capacity 44,640 mt/y, on machine
  No. 3, total capacity 61,560 mt/y, on machine
Energy Data:
  Power boilers: 3
  Electrical demand for mill: 400 MWh/D

ⒽHankuk Paper Mfg. Co., Ltd.
Ownership: 49.31% by Jea-Wan Dan & the persons concerned
Haesung Bldg, 942 Daechi-Dong
Kangnam-Ku, Seoul
South Korea
  Phone: (82) 2 3475-7200
  Fax: (82) 2 3473-2133/2123
  Email: heryu@hiper.com
  Web Address: www.hiper.com
Personnel:
  Chmn.: Jae-Wan Dan
  Phone: (82) 2 3475 7200
  Fax: (82) 2 3473 2133/2123
  Pres. & CEO: Kwang-Kwon Kim
  Phone: (82) 2 3475 7200
  Fax: (82) 2 3473 2133/2123
  VP.: Kwang-Kwon Kim
  Phone: (82) 2 3475-7240
  Fax: (82) 2 3473-2123
  Email: kkkim@hiper.com
  Sr. Man. Dir.: U-Yeong Dan
  Phone: (82) 2 3475-7208
  Fax: (82) 2 34732133
  Auditor: Dong-Hee Lee
  Phone: (82) 2 3475-7205
  Fax: (82) 2 3473-2133
  Email: dhnow@hiper.com
  Asst. Man. Dir.: Seung-Seok Seo
  Phone: (82) 2 3475 7200
  Fax: (82) 2 3473 2133/2123
Total Employees of Company: 502
Total Employees at this Location: 96
Mill Locations:
  Hankuk Paper Mfg. Co., Ltd., Onsan Mill, 350, Dangwol-ri, Onsan-eup, Ulju-gun, 689-892 Ulsan-si, South Korea, Capacity: 528,360 mt/y, (Paper mill)
  Phone: (82) 52 231-7700
  Fax: (82) 52 239-0048
  Email: kite@hiper.com

ⓂHankuk Paper Mfg. Co., Ltd.
Onsan Mill
350, Dangwol-ri, Onsan-eup, Ulju-gun
689-892 Ulsan-si, Gyeongsangnam-do
South Korea
  Phone: (82) 52 231-7700
  Fax: (82) 52 239-0048
  Email: kite@hiper.com
  Web Address: www.hiper.com

Personnel:
Mill Mgr.: Seung-Suck Seo
Phone: (82) 52 231-7701
Email: william@hiper.com
Vice Mill Mgr.: Cheong-Hwan Rha
Phone: (82) 52 231-7700
Prod. Mgr. PM 4: Mr. Kim
Phone: (82) 52 231-7700
Total Employees at this Location: 403
Type of Operation: Paper mill
Paper/Paperboard Grades and Capacities:
Total paper and paperboard capacity: 528,360 mt/y
Uncoated woodfree/freesheet: 314,160 mt/y
Coated woodfree/freesheet: 214,200 mt/y
Paper and Paperboard Mill Data:
Paper Machines: 4
No. 1, SymFormer MB, total capacity 107,100 mt/y, Trim width 3.37 m, Coated woodfree/freesheet
No. 2, OptiFormer, total capacity 114,240 mt/y, Trim width 3.46 m, Uncoated woodfree/freesheet
No. 3, DuoFormer D, total capacity 107,100 mt/y, Trim width 3.37 m, Coated woodfree/freesheet
No. 4, OptiFormer, total capacity 199,920 mt/y, Trim width 5.2 m, Uncoated woodfree/freesheet
Coating Machines: 2
CM 1, total capacity 107,000 mt/y., off machine
CM 3, total capacity 107,000 mt/y., on machine
Finishing Equipment:
Supercalenders: 5
Rewinders: 5
Sheeters: 5
Energy Data:
Power boilers: 5
Electrical demand for mill: 1,000 MWh/D

ⓜHansol Artone Paper Co., Ltd.
Ownership: 46.51% by Hansol Paper Co., Ltd., 6.63% by Shinan Group, 23.78% by Shinhan Bank
281-1, Seongsu 2-ga 3-dong
133-832 Seongdong-gu, Seoul
South Korea
 Phone: (82) 2 6209-6300
 Fax: (82) 2 6209-6392
 Web Address: www.hansolartonepaper.co.kr
Personnel:
Pres.: Kyo-Taik Kwon
Phone: (82) 2 6209-6300
Fax: (82) 2 6209-6351
Gen. Mgr. Sales: Jae-Woo Sur
Phone: (82) 2 6209 6300/6382
Fax: (82) 2 6209-6351
Gen. Mgr.: Jun-Mo Seoung
Phone: (82) 2 6209 6300/6382
Fax: (82) 2 6209-6351
Man. Dir.: Byeong-Yun Kang
Phone: (82) 2 6209 6300/6382
Fax: (82) 2 6209-6351
Total Employees of Company: 385
Total Employees at this Location: 88
Mill Locations:
Hansol Artone Paper Co., Ltd., Osan Mill, 150, Nueup-dong, 447-160 Ohsan-si, South Korea, Capacity: 89,250 mt/y, (Paper mill)
Phone: (82) 31 370-7700
Fax: (82) 31 370-7720
Hansol Artone Paper Co., Ltd., Sintanjin Mill, 13 Block, Complex 4, 1691, Sinil-dong, 306-230 Daedeok-gu, South Korea, Capacity: 297,024 mt/y, (Paper mill)
Phone: (82) 42 939-2000
Fax: (82) 42 939-2013

ⓜHansol Artone Paper Co., Ltd.
Osan Mill
Previously Artone Paper Mfg. Co. Ltd.
Ownership: 46.51% by Hansol Paper Co., Ltd.
150, Nueup-dong
447-160 Ohsan-si, Gyeonggi-do
South Korea
 Phone: (82) 31 370-7700
 Fax: (82) 31 370-7720
 Web Address: www.hansolartonepaper.co.kr
Personnel:
Mill Mgr.: Kyu-Ho Hang
Phone: (82) 31 370-7701
Total Employees at this Location: 155
Type of Operation: Paper mill
Paper/Paperboard Grades and Capacities:
Total paper and paperboard capacity: 89,250 mt/y
Coated woodfree/freesheet: 89,250 mt/y
Paper and Paperboard Mill Data:
Paper Machines: 1
No. 3, fourdrinier, total capacity 89,250 mt/y, Trim width 3.46 m, Coated woodfree/freesheet
Coating Machines: 1
CM#1, total capacity 100,000 mt/y., off machine
Finishing Equipment:
Supercalenders: 1
Rewinders: 3
Sheeters: 5
Energy Data:
Electrical demand for mill: 166 MWh/D

ⓜHansol Artone Paper Co., Ltd.
Sintanjin Mill
Previously Artone Paper Mfg. Co., Ltd.
Ownership: 46.51% by Hansol Paper Co., Ltd.
13 Block, Complex 4, 1691, Sinil-dong
306-230 Daedeok-gu, Daejeon
South Korea
 Phone: (82) 42 939-2000
 Fax: (82) 42 939-2013
 Web Address: www.hansolartonepaper.co.kr
Personnel:
Mill Mgr.: Chang-Ho Hwang
Phone: (82) 42 939-2001
Total Employees at this Location: 173
Type of Operation: Paper mill
Paper/Paperboard Grades and Capacities:
Total paper and paperboard capacity: 297,024 mt/y
Uncoated woodfree/freesheet: 66,045 mt/y
Coated woodfree/freesheet: 230,979 mt/y
Paper and Paperboard Mill Data:
Paper Machines: 1
No. 3, SpeedFormer HHS, total capacity 297,024 mt/y, Trim width 5.25 m, Uncoated woodfree/freesheet, Coated woodfree/freesheet
Coating Machines: 1
CM#1, total capacity 231,000 mt/y., off machine
Finishing Equipment:
Supercalenders: 1
Sheeters: 4
Energy Data:
Electrical demand for mill: 560 MWh/D

ⓜHansol Paper Co., Ltd.
23-24 FL, B-PINE AVENUE Bldg., Eulji Street 100 (Euljiro 2-ga)
100-192 Jung-gu, Seoul
South Korea
 Phone: (82) 2 3287 7114/6708/6442
 Fax: (82) 2 6031 0908
 Web Address: www.hansolpaper.co.kr
Personnel:
CEO: Sanghun Lee
Phone: (82) 2 3287 7114
Fax: (82) 2 6031 0908
Email: sanghun@hansol.com
VP.: Chang Man Son
Phone: (82) 2 3287 7114
Fax: (82) 2 6031 0908
VP.: Byeong Yin Yoon
Phone: (82) 2 3287 7114
Fax: (82) 2 6031 0908
International Sls. Mktg.: Jack Jang
Phone: (82) 2 3287 6442
Fax: (82) 2 3287 6014
Asia/Middle East Sls. Mktg.: Annie Min
Phone: (82) 2 3287 6867
Fax: (82) 2 6031 0908
Email: xuanji@hansol.com
Total Employees of Company: 903
Total Employees at this Location: 219
Mill Locations:
Daehan Papertech Co., Ltd., Danyang Mill, 1063-2, Daechi-ri, 517-923 Daejeon-myeon, Damyang-gun, South Korea, Capacity: 216,000 mt/y, (Paperboard mill)
Phone: (82) 61 380-0380
Fax: (82) 61 380-0398
Email: hl4cfb@hanmail.net
Hansol Artone Paper Co., Ltd., Osan Mill (46.51% owned), 150, Nueup-dong, 447-160 Ohsan-si, South Korea, Capacity: 89,250 mt/y, (Paper mill)
Phone: (82) 31 370-7700
Fax: (82) 31 370-7720
Hansol Artone Paper Co., Ltd., Sintanjin Mill (46.51% owned), 13 Block, Complex 4, 1691, Sinil-dong, 306-230 Daedeok-gu, South Korea, Capacity: 297,024 mt/y, (Paper mill)
Phone: (82) 42 939-2000
Fax: (82) 42 939-2013
Hansol Paper Co., Ltd., Changhang Mill, 481-8, Hwacheon-ri, Janghang-eup, 325-908 Seocheun-gun, South Korea, Capacity: 746,130 mt/y, (Paper mill)
Phone: (82) 41 955-1111
Fax: (82) 41 956-6488
Email: hskim@hansol.co.kr
Hansol Paper Co., Ltd., Chonan Mill, 40-1 Haengjeong-ri, Gwangdeok-myeon, 330-922 Cheonan-si, South Korea, Capacity: 89,964 mt/y, (Paper mill)
Phone: (82) 41 559-6202
Fax: (82) 41 559-6177
Hansol Paper Co. Ltd., Daejeon Mill, 1674-2, Sinil-dong, Daedeok-gu, 306-230 Daejeon, South Korea, Capacity: 570,000 mt/y, (Paperboard mill)
Phone: (82) 42 939-1114
Fax: (82) 42 939-1112
Email: eskim@hansol.co.kr

ⓜHansol Paper Co., Ltd.
Changhang Mill
481-8, Hwacheon-ri, Janghang-eup
325-908 Seocheun-gun, Chungcheongnam-do
South Korea
 Phone: (82) 41 955-1111
 Fax: (82) 41 956-6488
 Email: hskim@hansol.co.kr
 Web Address: www.hansolpaper.co.kr
Personnel:
Dir./ Mill Mgr.: Yang-Taek Chung
Phone: (82) 41 955-1533
Fax: (82) 42 939-1172
Email: jungyt@hansol.co.kr
Total Employees at this Location: 313
Type of Operation: Paper mill
Paper/Paperboard Grades and Capacities:
Total paper and paperboard capacity: 746,130 mt/y
Uncoated woodfree/freesheet: 119,595 mt/y
Coated woodfree/freesheet: 626,535 mt/y
Paper and Paperboard Mill Data:
Paper Machines: 3
No. 21, Bel-Form, total capacity 229,194 mt/y, Trim width 5.1 m, Uncoated woodfree/freesheet, Coated woodfree/freesheet
No. 22, Bel-Form, total capacity 252,756 mt/y, Trim width 5.1 m, Uncoated woodfree/freesheet, Coated woodfree/freesheet
No. 23, fourdrinier, total capacity 264,180 mt/y, Trim width 5.1 m, Coated woodfree/freesheet
Coating Machines: 2
PM 21, total capacity 290,000 mt/y., off machine
PM 23, total capacity 264,000 mt/y., off machine
Finishing Equipment:
Winders: 4
Sheeters: 8

ⓜHansol Paper Co., Ltd.
Chonan Mill
40-1 Haengjeong-ri, Gwangdeok-myeon

South Korea

330-922 Cheonan-si, Chungcheongnam-do
South Korea
  Phone: (82) 41 559-6202
  Fax: (82) 41 559-6177
  Web Address: www.hansolpaper.co.kr
Total Employees at this Location: 300
Type of Operation: Paper mill
Paper/Paperboard Grades and Capacities:
  Total paper and paperboard capacity: 89,964 mt/y
  Uncoated woodfree/freesheet: 89,964 mt/y
Paper and Paperboard Mill Data:
  Stock Preparation:
  Pulpers: 6
  Refiners: 14
Paper Machines: 3
No. 1, cylinder, total capacity 19,992 mt/y, Trim width 1.7 m, Uncoated woodfree/freesheet
No. 2, fourdrinier, total capacity 49,980 mt/y, Trim width 3.3 m, Uncoated woodfree/freesheet
No. 3, cylinder, total capacity 19,992 mt/y, Trim width 1.7 m, Uncoated woodfree/freesheet
Coating Machines: 2
CM 1, total capacity 15,000 mt/y., off machine
CM 2, total capacity 12,000 mt/y., off machine
Finishing Equipment:
  Rewinders: 3
  Sheeters: 3
Energy Data:
Electrical demand for mill: 189 MWh/D

(M)Hansol Paper Co. Ltd.
Daejeon Mill
Ownership: Hansol Paper Co., Ltd.
1674-2, Sinil-dong, Daedeok-gu
306-230 Daejeon, Daejeon
South Korea
  Phone: (82) 42 939-1114
  Fax: (82) 42 939-1112
  Email: eskim@hansol.co.kr
  Web Address: www.hansolpaper.co.kr
Personnel:
  Mill Mgr.: Eun-Sunk Kim
  Phone: (82) 42 939 1100
  Fax: (82) 42 939 1172
  Email: eskim@hansol.co.kr
Total Employees at this Location: 250
Type of Operation: Paperboard mill
Pulp Grades and Capacities:
  Total pulp capacity: 490,615 mt/y
  Recycled Pulping: 490,615 mt/y
Pulp Mill Data:
  Recycled Fiber Treatment Lines:
  Flotation deinking lines: 1
  Recycled packaging pulping lines: 1
Paper/Paperboard Grades and Capacities:
  Total paper and paperboard capacity: 570,000 mt/y
  Boxboard/cartonboard: 570,000 mt/y
Paper and Paperboard Mill Data:
Paper Machines: 2
No. 31, fourdrinier, total capacity 270,000 mt/y, Trim width 4.73 m, Boxboard/cartonboard
No. 32, fourdrinier, total capacity 300,000 mt/y, Trim width 4.73 m, Boxboard/cartonboard
Coating Machines: 2
PM 31, total capacity 270,000 mt/y., on machine
PM 32, total capacity 300,000 mt/y., on machine
Energy Data:
Power boilers
Electrical demand for mill: 774 MWh/D

(I)Hongwon Paper Mfg. Co., Ltd.
Ownership: 100% by Soon-Ho Hong & his family
14th Fl., Imgwang Bldg., 267, Migeun-dong
120-705 Seodaemun-gu, Seoul
South Korea
  Phone: (82) 2 360-6300
  Fax: (82) 2 360-6405
  Email: webmaster@hongwon.com
  Web Address: www.hongwon.com
Personnel:
  Chmn.: Chong-Hwa Hong
  Phone: (82) 2 360-6391
  Fax: (82) 2 360-6409
  Pres.: Soon-Ho Hong
  Phone: (82) 2 360-6392
  Fax: (82) 2 360-6409
  Exec. Dir.: Kyung-Sik Kang
  Phone: (82) 2 360-6383
  Fax: (82) 2 360-6405
Total Employees of Company: 406
Total Employees at this Location: 29
Mill Locations:
Hongwon Paper Mfg. Co., Ltd., Jinwi Mill, 37, Habuk-ri, Jinwi-myeon, 451-860 Pyeongtaek-si, South Korea, Capacity: 340,188 mt/y, (Paper mill)
  Phone: (82) 31 660-8001-2
  Fax: (82) 31 668-4148
  Email: webmaster@hongwon.com

(M)Hongwon Paper Mfg. Co., Ltd.
Jinwi Mill
37, Habuk-ri, Jinwi-myeon
451-860 Pyeongtaek-si, Gyeonggi-do
South Korea
  Phone: (82) 31 660-8001-2
  Fax: (82) 31 668-4148
  Email: webmaster@hongwon.com
  Web Address: www.hongwon.com
Personnel:
  Mill Mgr.: Hee Chun Kang
  Phone: (82) 31 660-8171
  Fax: (82) 31 668-4148
  Email: hck76@hongwon.com
Total Employees at this Location: 377
Type of Operation: Paper mill
Paper/Paperboard Grades and Capacities:
  Total paper and paperboard capacity: 340,188 mt/y
  Uncoated woodfree/freesheet: 196,317 mt/y
  Coated woodfree/freesheet: 143,871 mt/y
Paper and Paperboard Mill Data:
  Stock Preparation:
  Pulpers: 2
  Refiners: 8
Paper Machines: 2
No. 1, DuoFormer D, total capacity 100,317 mt/y, Trim width 3.22 m, Uncoated woodfree/freesheet
No. 2, Tamformer, total capacity 239,868 mt/y, Trim width 5.25 m, Uncoated woodfree/freesheet, Coated woodfree/freesheet
Coating Machines: 2
CM 2, total capacity 144,000 mt/y., off machine
CM 1 -idle, off machine
Finishing Equipment:
  Winders: 3
  Supercalenders: 1
  Sheeters: 8
Energy Data:
Power boilers: 4
Electrical demand for mill: 666 MWh/D

(I)Jeonju Paper Corporation, Ltd.
Ownership: 42% by Morgan Stanley Private Equity Asia, Private Equity Funds; PEF, 58% by Shinhan Private Equity
6th Floor, KCCL Building 45, Namdaemunno 4-ga
100-743 Jung-gu, Seoul
South Korea
  Phone: (82) 2 6050-2600
  Fax: (82) 2 6050-2659
  Web Address: www.jeonjupaper.com
Personnel:
  Pres. & CEO: In-Soo Han
  Phone: (82) 2 6050 2656
  Fax: (82) 2 6050 2656 9
  Email: ishan@jeonju.com
Total Employees of Company: 750
Total Employees at this Location: 53
Mill Locations:
Jeonju Paper Corporation, Ltd., Cheongju mill, 60-1, Hogye-ri, Gangoe-myeon, 363-951 Cheongwon-gun, South Korea, Capacity: 183,000 mt/y, (Pulp mill, Paper mill)
  Phone: (82) 43 249-3300
  Fax: (82) 43 249-3309
Jeonju Paper Corporation, Ltd., Jeonju Mill, 180, Palbok-dong 2-ga Deokjin-gu, 561-723 Jeonju-si, South Korea, Capacity: 840,000 mt/y, (Pulp mill, Paper mill)
  Phone: (82) 63 210-8114
  Fax: (82) 63 212-8513

(M)Jeonju Paper Corporation, Ltd.
Cheongju mill
60-1, Hogye-ri, Gangoe-myeon
363-951 Cheongwon-gun, Chungcheongbuk-do
South Korea
  Phone: (82) 43 249-3300
  Fax: (82) 43 249-3309
  Web Address: www.jeonjupaper.com
Personnel:
  Man. Dir./Mill Mgr.: Jae Woong Ko
  Phone: (82) 43 249-3400
  Fax: (82) 43 249-3309
  Email: jwko@panasiakorea.com
Total Employees at this Location: 132
Type of Operation: Pulp mill, Paper mill
Pulp Grades and Capacities:
  Total pulp capacity: 182,100 mt/y
  Recycled Pulping: 182,100 mt/y
Pulp Mill Data:
Pulp Lines: 1
  Bleach Plant Systems: 1
  DIP
  Recycled Fiber Treatment Lines:
  Flotation deinking lines: 1
Paper/Paperboard Grades and Capacities:
  Total paper and paperboard capacity: 183,000 mt/y
  Newsprint: 183,000 mt/y
Paper and Paperboard Mill Data:
  Stock Preparation:
  Pulpers: 1
Paper Machines: 1
No. 3, SpeedFormer HS, total capacity 183,000 mt/y, Trim width 6.38 m, Newsprint
Finishing Equipment:
  Winders: 1
  Calenders: 1
  Rewinders: 1
Energy Data:
Power boilers
Electrical demand for mill: 506 MWh/D

(M)Jeonju Paper Corporation, Ltd.
Jeonju Mill
180, Palbok-dong 2-ga Deokjin-gu
561-723 Jeonju-si, Jeollabuk-do
South Korea
  Phone: (82) 63 210-8114
  Fax: (82) 63 212-8513
  Web Address: www.jeonjupaper.com
Personnel:
  Dir. & Mill Mgr.: Young-Jae Kim
  Phone: (82) 63 210-8300
  Fax: (82) 63 212-8531
Total Employees at this Location: 550
Type of Operation: Pulp mill, Paper mill
Pulp Grades and Capacities:
  Total pulp capacity: 801,612 mt/y
  Mechanical Pulp: 136,849 mt/y
  Recycled Pulping: 664,763 mt/y
Pulp Mill Data:
  Mechanical Pulping Systems:
  TMP systems: 1
  Bleach Plant Lines:
  Recycled Pulping system bleaching
  TMP Mechanical Pulping system bleaching
  Recycled Fiber Treatment Lines:
  Flotation deinking lines: 5

Paper/Paperboard Grades and Capacities:
Total paper and paperboard capacity: 840,000 mt/y
Newsprint: 682,000 mt/y
Uncoated mechanical/groundwood: 158,000 mt/y
Paper and Paperboard Mill Data:
Paper Machines: 4
No. 3, hybrid former, total capacity 97,000 mt/y, Trim width 4.8 m, Uncoated mechanical/groundwood
No. 5, GapFormer, total capacity 186,000 mt/y, Trim width 7.88 m, Newsprint, Uncoated mechanical/groundwood
No. 6, GapFormer, total capacity 272,000 mt/y, Trim width 7.88 m, Newsprint
No. 7, GapFormer, total capacity 285,000 mt/y, Trim width 7.88 m, Newsprint
Energy Data:
Power boilers: 6
TMP Reboiler: 2
Steam turbines: 3 at 67.1 (2 idle) MW
Electrical demand for mill: 3,051 MWh/D

ⓞJin Young Paper Co., Ltd.
498-1, Gyo-ri, Yangmok-myeon
718-813 Chilgok-gun, Gyeongsangbuk-do
South Korea
Phone: (82) 54 974-6804
Fax: (82) 54 974-6800
Personnel:
Pres.: Soo-Il Park
Phone: (82) 54 974 6804
Pulp Mill Mgr.: Il-Sik Kim
Phone: (82) 54 974 6804
Purch. Agent (Chief): Jong-Gab Kim
Phone: (82) 54 974 6804
Mill Locations:
Jin Young Paper Co., Ltd., Chilgok-gun Mill, 498-1, Gyo-ri, Yangmok-myeon, 718-813 Chilgok-gun, South Korea, Capacity: 100,000 mt/y, (Paperboard mill)
Phone: (82) 54 974-6804
Fax: (82) 54 974-6800

ⓜJin Young Paper Co., Ltd.
Chilgok-gun Mill
498-1, Gyo-ri, Yangmok-myeon
718-813 Chilgok-gun, Gyeongsangbuk-do
South Korea
Phone: (82) 54 974-6804
Fax: (82) 54 974-6800
Personnel:
Pres.: Soo-Il Park
Phone: (82) 54 974 6804
Pulp Mill Mgr.: Il-Sik Kim
Phone: (82) 54 974 6804
Purch. Agent (Chief): Jong-Gab Kim
Phone: (82) 54 974 6804
Total Employees at this Location: 53
Type of Operation: Paperboard mill
Pulp Grades and Capacities:
Total pulp capacity: 97,273 mt/y
Recycled Pulping: 97,273 mt/y
Pulp Mill Data:
Recycled Fiber Treatment Lines:
Pulpers: 4 at 94,000 admt/y
Paper/Paperboard Grades and Capacities:
Total paper and paperboard capacity: 100,000 mt/y
Linerboard: 58,000 mt/y
Corrugating medium/fluting: 42,000 mt/y
Paper and Paperboard Mill Data:
Stock Preparation:
Pulpers: 4
Refiners: 5
Paper Machines: 2
No. 1, cylinder, total capacity 42,000 mt/y, Trim width 2.8 m, Corrugating medium/fluting
No. 2, cylinder, total capacity 58,000 mt/y, Trim width 3.3 m, Linerboard
Finishing Equipment:
Rewinders: 2
Energy Data:
Electrical demand for mill: 123 MWh/D

ⓞKleanNara Co., Ltd.
Ownership: 71.81% by Heesung Electronics Co., Ltd.
Shinjoyang B/D 49-17, Chungmuro 2-ga
100-012 Jung-gu, Seoul
South Korea
Phone: (82) 2 2270-9200
Fax: (82) 2 2275-7679
Email: khlim@dhpulp.co.kr
Web Address: www.kleannara.com
Personnel:
Pres.: Jong-Tae Yoon
Phone: (82) 2 2270-9201
Email: khlim@dhpulp.co.kr
Repr. Officer: Hur Won
Phone: (82) 2 2270-9205
Email: hwon@dhpulp.co.kr
Mill Mgr.: Dong-Soo Lim
Phone: (82) 43 230-7206
Email: dongsu@dhpulp.co.kr
Purch. Mgr.: James Jung
Phone: (82) 2 2270-9361
Email: ponder@dhpulp.co.kr
Prod. Mgr.: Jung-Tae Kim
Phone: (82) 43 230-7231
Email: jtkim@dhpulp.co.kr
Total Employees of Company: 498
Total Employees at this Location: 109
Mill Locations:
KleanNara Co., Ltd., Chongju Mill, 258, Hwangtan-ri, Gangnae-myeon, Cheongwon-gun, South Korea, Capacity: 379,491 mt/y, (Paper mill, Paperboard mill)
Phone: (82) 43 230-7200
Fax: (82) 43 231-1525

ⓜKleanNara Co., Ltd.
Chongju Mill
258, Hwangtan-ri, Gangnae-myeon
Cheongwon-gun, Chungcheongbuk-do
South Korea
Phone: (82) 43 230-7200
Fax: (82) 43 231-1525
Personnel:
Mill Mgr.: Dong-Soo Lim
Phone: (82) 43 230-7256
Prod. Mgr.: Jung-Tae Kim
Phone: (82) 43 230 7200
Environ. Mgr.: Tae-Woo Chea
Phone: (82) 43 230 7200
Mgr, Gen. Affairs: Shi-Woo Jun
Phone: (82) 43 230 7200
Total Employees at this Location: 450
Type of Operation: Paper mill, Paperboard mill
Pulp Grades and Capacities:
Total pulp capacity: 335,557 mt/y
Recycled Pulping: 335,557 mt/y
Pulp Mill Data:
Bleach Plant Systems: 2
Recycled Deinked Pulping System
Recycled DIP Pulping System
Recycled Fiber Treatment Lines:
Flotation deinking lines: 1 at 62,000
Flotation deinking lines: 1 at 55,200
Recycled packaging pulping lines: 1 at 218,200
Paper/Paperboard Grades and Capacities:
Total paper and paperboard capacity: 379,491 mt/y
Tissue: 63,546 mt/y
Boxboard/cartonboard: 315,945 mt/y
Paper and Paperboard Mill Data:
Stock Preparation:
Pulpers: 14
Refiners: 17
Paper Machines: 7
No. 1, Ultraformer, total capacity 57,120 mt/y, Trim width 2.5 m, Boxboard/cartonboard
No. 2, total capacity 60,690 mt/y, Trim width 2.5 m, Boxboard/cartonboard
No. 3, total capacity 198,135 mt/y, Trim width 3.1 m, Boxboard/cartonboard
TM 1, twin-wire, total capacity 14,994 mt/y, Trim width 2.9 m, Tissue
TM 2, suction former, total capacity 7,140 mt/y, Trim width 2.9 m, Tissue
TM 3, crescent former, total capacity 20,706 mt/y, Trim width 2.9 m, Tissue
TM 4, crescent former, total capacity 20,706 mt/y, Trim width 2.9 m, Tissue
Coating Machines: 3
No. 1, total capacity 57,120 mt/y., on machine
No. 2, total capacity 60,700 mt/y., on machine
No. 3, total capacity 198,135 mt/y., on machine
Finishing Equipment:
Rewinders: 3
Sheeters: 10
Energy Data:
Power boilers: 4
Electrical demand for mill: 713 MWh/D

ⓞKorea Export Packaging Ind. Co., Ltd.
Ownership: 40% by other, 30% by representatives, 30% by stockholders
4th Fl., Readers Bldg., 1599-11, Seocho-dong
137-912 Seocho-gu
South Korea
Phone: (82) 2 525-2981
Fax: (82) 2 522-3546
Email: kep@keppack.co.kr, cwk4br@keppack.co.kr
Web Address: www.keppack.co.kr
Personnel:
Chmn.: Suk Rak Huh
Phone: (82) 2 525 2981
Fax: (82) 2 522 3546
Pres.: Yong Sam Huh
Phone: (82) 2 525 2981
Fax: (82) 2 522 3546
VP: Jeong Hun Huh
Phone: (82) 2 525 2981
Fax: (82) 2 522 3546
Man. Dir.: Yong So An
Phone: (82) 2 525 2981
Fax: (82) 2 522 3546
Sls. Dir.: Young Ho Oh
Phone: (82) 2 525 2981
Fax: (82) 2 522 3546
Total Employees of Company: 91
Total Employees at this Location: 37
Mill Locations:
Korea Export Packing Ind. Co., Ltd., Osan Mill, 80-1, Nueup-dong, 447-160 Osan-si, South Korea, Capacity: 212,000 mt/y, (Paperboard mill)
Phone: (82) 31 373-2981
Fax: (82) 31 374-2645
Email: sdkim@keppack.co.kr

ⓜKorea Export Packing Ind. Co., Ltd.
Osan Mill
Ownership: Korea Export Packaging Ind. Co., Ltd.
80-1, Nueup-dong
447-160 Osan-si, Gyeonggi-do
South Korea
Phone: (82) 31 373-2981
Fax: (82) 31 374-2645
Email: sdkim@keppack.co.kr
Web Address: www.keppack.co.kr
Personnel:
Mill Mgr.: Sun Jae Lee
Phone: (82) 31 373 2981
Asst. Mill Mgr/Ppr./Tech./Eng.: Jeong-Sik Kim
Phone: (82) 31 373 2981
Total Employees at this Location: 80
Type of Operation: Paperboard mill
Pulp Grades and Capacities:
Total pulp capacity: 213,355 mt/y
Recycled Pulping: 213,355 mt/y

South Korea

Pulp Mill Data:
Recycled Fiber Treatment Lines:
Recycled packaging pulping lines: 1
Paper/Paperboard Grades and Capacities:
Total paper and paperboard capacity: 212,000 mt/y
Linerboard: 212,000 mt/y
Paper and Paperboard Mill Data:
Stock Preparation:
Pulpers: 4
Refiners: 8
Paper Machines: 1
No. 1, fourdrinier, total capacity 212,000 mt/y, Trim width 4.05 m, Linerboard
Finishing Equipment:
Rewinders: 1
Sheeters: 5
Energy Data:
Power boilers: 2
Electrical demand for mill: 273 MWh/D

ⓜKorea Green Paper Mfg., Co. Ltd. - KGP

Ownership: 49.35% by Kukil Paper Mfg. Co., Ltd.
Dawin Bldg., 180-14 Dogok-dong
135-504 Gangnam-gu, Seoul
South Korea
Phone: (82) 2 578-5920
Fax: (82) 2 6006-4381
Web Address: www.k-paper.kr/
Personnel:
CEO: Woo-Sik Choi
Phone: (82) 2 6006 4313
Fax: (82) 2 6006 4381
Total Employees of Company: 240
Total Employees at this Location: 25
Mill Locations:
Korea Green Paper Mfg., Co. Ltd. - KGP, Asan Mill, 941 Oncheon-dong, 336-010 Asan-si, South Korea, Capacity: 62,000 mt/y, (Paper mill)
Phone: (82) 41 549-0811
Fax: (82) 41 546-2235
Korea Green Paper Mfg., Co. Ltd. - KGP, Pyoengtaek Mill, 205-1, Habuk-ri, Jinwi-myeon, 451-864 Pyeongtaek-si, South Korea, Capacity: 7,345 mt/y, (Paper mill)
Phone: (82) 31 668-2201
Fax: (82) 31 668-6821

ⓜKorea Green Paper Mfg., Co. Ltd. - KGP
Asan Mill

Ownership: 49.35% by Kukil Paper Mfg. Co., Ltd.
941 Oncheon-dong
336-010 Asan-si, Chungcheongnam-do
South Korea
Phone: (82) 41 549-0811
Fax: (82) 41 546-2235
Web Address: www.k-paper.kr/
Personnel:
Mill Mgr.: Ho-Yong Lee
Phone: (82) 41 549-0811
Total Employees at this Location: 100
Type of Operation: Paper mill
Paper/Paperboard Grades and Capacities:
Total paper and paperboard capacity: 62,000 mt/y
Packaging papers: 18,600 mt/y
Specialty and industrial: 43,400 mt/y
Paper and Paperboard Mill Data:
Stock Preparation:
Pulpers: 6
Refiners: 9
Paper Machines: 1
No. 1, fourdrinier, total capacity 62,000 mt/y, Trim width 3.24 m, Packaging papers, Specialty and industrial
Finishing Equipment:
Rewinders: 2
Sheeters: 1
Energy Data:
Power boilers: 4
Electrical demand for mill: 85 MWh/D

ⓜKorea Green Paper Mfg., Co. Ltd. - KGP
Pyoengtaek Mill

Ownership: 49.35% by Kukil Paper Mfg. Co., Ltd.
205-1, Habuk-ri, Jinwi-myeon
451-864 Pyeongtaek-si, Gyeonggi-do
South Korea
Phone: (82) 31 668-2201
Fax: (82) 31 668-6821
Web Address: www.k-paper.kr/
Personnel:
CEO: Son Seon Yeong
Mill Mgr.: Kyung-Sang Yoon
Phone: (82) 31 668-2201
Total Employees at this Location: 64
Type of Operation: Paper mill
Paper/Paperboard Grades and Capacities:
Total paper and paperboard capacity: 7,345 mt/y
Specialty and industrial: 7,345 mt/y
Paper and Paperboard Mill Data:
Stock Preparation:
Pulpers: 6
Refiners: 13
Paper Machines: 2
No. 4, cylinder, total capacity 3,300 mt/y, Trim width 2.58 m, Specialty and industrial
No. 6, fourdrinier, total capacity 5,200 mt/y, Trim width 2 m, Specialty and industrial
Energy Data:
Power boilers: 2
Combustion turbines: 40 at 5.8 MW
Electrical demand for mill: 13 MWh/D

ⓜⓜKorea Paper Mfg. Co., Ltd.
Siheung-si Mill

Ownership: 60% by Sambo Corrugated Board Co. Ltd., 40% by Daelim Paper Co. Ltd.
1705 Jeongwang-dong
429-859 Siheung-si, Gyeonggi-do
South Korea
Phone: (82) 31 497-0322 / 496-7200
Fax: (82) 31 497-0320
Email: webmaster@koreapaper.co.kr
Web Address: www.koreapaper.co.kr
Personnel:
Pres.: Kyung-Ho Ryu
Phone: (82) 31 496-7200
Email: khryu@koreapaper.co.kr
Vice Chmn.: C. K. Ryu
Phone: (82) 31 496-7200
Email: ckryu@koreapaper.co.kr
Man. Dir.: K. S. Lee
Phone: (82) 31 496-7200
Email: kslee@koreapaper.co.kr
Mill Mgr.: D. Y. Lee
Phone: (82) 31 496-7200
Email: dylee@koreapaper.co.kr
Sls. Dir.: H. Kim
Phone: (82) 31 496-7200
Email: thkim@koreapaper.co.kr
Total Employees of Company: 114
Total Employees at this Location: 101
Type of Operation: Paperboard mill
Pulp Grades and Capacities:
Total pulp capacity: 386,940 mt/y
Recycled Pulping: 386,940 mt/y
Pulp Mill Data:
Recycled Fiber Treatment Lines:
Recycled packaging pulping lines: 1
Paper/Paperboard Grades and Capacities:
Total paper and paperboard capacity: 428,000 mt/y
Linerboard: 428,000 mt/y
Paper and Paperboard Mill Data:
Stock Preparation:
Pulpers: 4
Refiners: 6
Paper Machines: 1
No. 1, Fourdrinier (4), total capacity 428,000 mt/y, Trim width 5.65 m, Linerboard
Coating Machines: 1
No. 1, total capacity 115,200 mt/y.
Finishing Equipment:
Winders: 1 at 289,000 mt/y
Calenders: 1 at 428,400 mt/y
Rewinders: 1 at 438,000 mt/y
Energy Data:
Power boilers: 1
TMP Reboiler: 2
Steam turbines
Electrical demand for mill: 536 MWh/D

ⓜKukil Paper Mfg. Co., Ltd.

Ownership: 41% by Woo-Sik Choi, 12.13% by Yeong-Cheol Choi, 5% by Seong-Sik
2nd Fl., Dawin Bldg., 180-14, Dogok-dong
135-504 Gangnam-gu, Seoul
South Korea
Phone: (82) 2 574-9111
Fax: (82) 2 578-9151
Email: webmaster@kukilpaper.co.kr
Web Address: www.kukilpaper.co.kr
Personnel:
Chmn.: Young-Chul Choi
Phone: (82) 2 578-9110
Fax: (82) 2 578-9151
Pres. & CEO: Woo-Sik Choi
Phone: (82) 2 578-9110
Fax: (82) 2 578-9151
Pres.: Duk-Hwan Kim
Phone: (82) 2 578-9110
Fax: (82) 2 578-9151
Total Employees of Company: 109
Total Employees at this Location: 25
Mill Locations:
Korea Green Paper Mfg., Co. Ltd. - KGP, Asan Mill (49.35% owned), 941 Oncheon-dong, 336-010 Asan-si, South Korea, Capacity: 62,000 mt/y, (Paper mill)
Phone: (82) 41 549-0811
Fax: (82) 41 546-2235
Korea Green Paper Mfg., Co. Ltd. - KGP, Pyoengtaek Mill (49.35% owned), 205-1, Habuk-ri, Jinwi-myeon, 451-864 Pyeongtaek-si, South Korea, Capacity: 7,345 mt/y, (Paper mill)
Phone: (82) 31 668-2201
Fax: (82) 31 668-6821
Kukil Paper Mfg. Co., Ltd., Idong-myeon, Yongin-si Mill, 151-3, Chun-ri, 449-833 Idong-myeon, Yongin-si, South Korea, Capacity: 19,500 mt/y, (Paper mill)
Phone: (82) 31 339-9100
Fax: (82) 31 339-2725
Email: webmaster@kukilpaper.co.kr

ⓜKukil Paper Mfg. Co., Ltd.
Idong-myeon, Yongin-si Mill

151-3, Chun-ri
449-833 Idong-myeon, Yongin-si, Gyeonggi-do
South Korea
Phone: (82) 31 339-9100
Fax: (82) 31 339-2725
Email: webmaster@kukilpaper.co.kr
Web Address: www.kukilpaper.co.kr
Personnel:
Mill Mgr.: Tae-Young Chung
Phone: (82) 31 339-9100
Fax: (82) 31 339-2725
Total Employees at this Location: 84
Type of Operation: Paper mill
Paper/Paperboard Grades and Capacities:
Total paper and paperboard capacity: 19,500 mt/y
Specialty and industrial: 19,500 mt/y
Paper and Paperboard Mill Data:
Paper Machines: 4
No. 1, total capacity 2,000 mt/y, Trim width 2.15 m, Specialty and industrial
No. 2, total capacity 3,500 mt/y, Trim width 2 m, Specialty and industrial

South Korea

No. 3, total capacity 6,000 mt/y, Trim width 2.2 m, Specialty and industrial
No. 5, total capacity 8,000 mt/y, Trim width 2.6 m, Specialty and industrial
Energy Data:
Power boilers: 2

ⓂⓂKyongsan Paper Co., Ltd.
Daegu-si Mill
Ownership: Asia Papertec Inc.
161, Geum-ri, Yuga-myeon, Dalseong-gun
711-882 Daegu-si, Daegu-si
South Korea
Phone: (82) 53 615-6285
Fax: (82) 53 615-6292
Personnel:
Pres.: Yeong-Seok Kang
Phone: (82) 53 615 6285
Total Employees of Company: 90
Total Employees at this Location: 90
Type of Operation: Paperboard mill
Pulp Grades and Capacities:
Total pulp capacity: 117,325 mt/y
Recycled Pulping: 117,325 mt/y
Pulp Mill Data:
Recycled Fiber Treatment Lines:
Recycled packaging pulping lines: 1
Paper/Paperboard Grades and Capacities:
Total paper and paperboard capacity: 120,000 mt/y
Corrugating medium/fluting: 120,000 mt/y
Paper and Paperboard Mill Data:
Paper Machines: 1
No. 1, cylinder, total capacity 120,000 mt/y, Trim width 4.2 m, Corrugating medium/fluting
Energy Data:
Electrical demand for mill: 137 MWh/D

ⓂⓂMirae Paper Co., Ltd.
Jeonju Mill
403, Palbok-dong, Deokjin-gu
561-841 Jeonju-si, Jeollabuk-do
South Korea
Phone: (82) 63 214-2018
Fax: (82) 63 214-2002
Email: mirae-paper@hanmail.net
Personnel:
Pres.: Jae-rak Byun
Phone: (82) 63 214 2018
Fax: (82) 63 214 2002
Purch. Dpty. Mgr.: Young Hee Choi
Phone: (82) 63 214 2018
Fax: (82) 63 214 2002
Email: cyh0419@hanmail.net
Total Employees of Company: 74
Total Employees at this Location: 170
Type of Operation: Paper mill
Pulp Grades and Capacities:
Total pulp capacity: 70,370 mt/y
Recycled Pulping: 70,370 mt/y
Pulp Mill Data:
Bleach Plant Systems: 1
DIP
Recycled Fiber Treatment Lines:
Flotation deinking lines: 1
Paper/Paperboard Grades and Capacities:
Total paper and paperboard capacity: 66,000 mt/y
Tissue: 66,000 mt/y
Paper and Paperboard Mill Data:
Paper Machines: 3
No. 1, total capacity 19,000 mt/y, Trim width 2.65 m, Tissue, Uncoated woodfree/freesheet
No. 2, total capacity 20,000 mt/y, Trim width 2.74 m, Tissue, Uncoated woodfree/freesheet
No. 3, total capacity 27,000 mt/y, Trim width 3.13 m, Tissue, Uncoated woodfree/freesheet
Energy Data:
Power boilers
Electrical demand for mill: 219 MWh/D

ⓂMonalisa Co., Ltd.
395-70, Sindaebang-dong
156-849 Dongjak-gu, Seoul
South Korea
Phone: (82) 2 829-8800
Fax: (82) 2 829-8899
Email: main@monalisa.co.kr
Personnel:
Chmn.: Yoon-Soo Kim
Phone: (82) 2 829-8885
Email: kys@monarisa.co.kr
Dir.: Jong-Won Park
Phone: (82) 2 829-8840
Email: jwpark@monarisa.co.kr
Head of Sls., Dir.: Yeong-Hyun Yang
Phone: (82) 2 829-8870
Email: yuyang@monarisa.co.kr
Internal Auditor: GapSik Kim
Phone: (82) 2 829 8800
Fax: (82) 2 829 8899
Dir.: HuiSeong Noh
Phone: (82) 2 829 8800
Fax: (82) 2 829 8899
Non-Exec. Indep. Dir.: ChiDong Yeo
Phone: (82) 2 829 8800
Fax: (82) 2 829 8899
Total Employees of Company: 179
Total Employees at this Location: 68
Mill Locations:
Monalisa Co., Ltd., Jeonju Mill, 400-2, Palbok-dong 3-ga Deokjin-gu, 561-203 Jeonju-si, South Korea, Capacity: 54,000 mt/y, (Paper mill)
Phone: (82) 63 212-2221
Fax: (82) 63 212-2223
Ssangyong C&B, Chochiwon Mill, 9 Beonam-ri, 339-804 Jochiwon-eup, Yeongi-gun, South Korea, Capacity: 98,000 mt/y, (Paper mill)
Phone: (82) 41 861-5000
Fax: (82) 41 861-4819

ⓂMonalisa Co., Ltd.
Jeonju Mill
400-2, Palbok-dong 3-ga Deokjin-gu
561-203 Jeonju-si, Jeollabuk-do
South Korea
Phone: (82) 63 212-2221
Fax: (82) 63 212-2223
Web Address: www.monarisa.co.kr
Personnel:
Mill Mgr.: Young-Ki Kim
Phone: (82) 63 212-2221
Fax: (82) 63 212-2111
Total Employees at this Location: 160
Type of Operation: Paper mill
Pulp Grades and Capacities:
Total pulp capacity: 22,221 mt/y
Recycled Pulping: 22,221 mt/y
Pulp Mill Data:
Bleach Plant Systems: 1
DIP
Recycled Fiber Treatment Lines:
Flotation deinking lines: 1
Paper/Paperboard Grades and Capacities:
Total paper and paperboard capacity: 54,000 mt/y
Tissue: 54,000 mt/y
Paper and Paperboard Mill Data:
Paper Machines: 3
No. 1, crescent former, total capacity 18,000 mt/y, Trim width 2.71 m, Tissue, Uncoated woodfree/freesheet
No. 2, crescent former, total capacity 18,000 mt/y, Trim width 2.71 m, Tissue
No. 3, crescent former, total capacity 18,000 mt/y, Tissue
Energy Data:
Power boilers: 2
Electrical demand for mill: 126 MWh/D

ⓂMoorim Paper Co., Ltd.
Ownership: 19.65% by Moorim SP Co., Ltd., 34.37% by Dong-Uk Lee & related
505, Shinsa-dong, Gangnam-gu
135-887 Seoul
South Korea
Phone: (82) 2 3485-1500
Fax: (82) 2 3485-1690
Web Address: www.moorim.co.kr
Personnel:
Chmn.: Dong-Wook Lee
Phone: (82) 2 3485-1501
Fax: (82) 2 511-4040
Email: dwlee@moorim.co.kr
CEO (From December 2, 2013): Suk-man Kim
Phone: (82) 2 3485-1507
Fax: (82) 2 514-14040
VP Sls Div.: In-Kyu Park
Phone: (82) 2 3485-1508
Fax: (82) 2 514-13400
Email: ipark@moorim.co.kr
VP: Kenny Lee
Phone: (82) 2 3485-1510
Fax: (82) 2 548-3954
Email: kennylee@moorim.co.kr
Man. Dir. (Admin): Young-Sik Kim
Phone: (82) 2 3485-1518
Email: ysk@moorim.co.kr
Man. Dir. (DomesticSls.): Young-Sil Lee
Phone: (82) 2 3485-1500
Fax: (82) 2 3485 1690
Email: ddr@moorim.co.kr
Total Employees of Company: 600
Total Employees at this Location: 146
Mill Locations:
Moorim Paper Co., Ltd., Jinju Mill, 281-1, Sangpyeong-dong, 660-722 Jinju-si, South Korea, Capacity: 568,587 mt/y, (Paper mill)
Phone: (82) 55 751-1234
Fax: (82) 55 751-1235
Email: webmaster@moorim.co.kr
Moorim P&P Co. Ltd., Ulsan Mill (49.23% owned), 1 Dangwol-ri, Onsan-eup, Ulju-gun, 689 892 Ulsan-si, South Korea, Capacity: 450,000 mt/y, (Pulp mill, Paper mill)
Phone: (82) 52 231-7000
Fax: (82) 52 348-1822

ⓂMoorim Paper Co., Ltd.
Jinju Mill
Ownership: 19.65% by Moorim SP Co., Ltd.
281-1, Sangpyeong-dong
660-722 Jinju-si, Gyeongsangnam-do
South Korea
Phone: (82) 55 751-1234
Fax: (82) 55 751-1235
Email: webmaster@moorim.co.kr
Web Address: www.moorim.co.kr
Personnel:
Sen. Mill Mgr.: In-Sup Park
Phone: (82) 55 761-1483
Email: ispark@moorim.co.kr
Vice Mill Mgr.: Ki Yeon Hwang
Phone: (82) 55 751-1205
Email: hwang5172@moorim.co.kr
Total Employees at this Location: 600
Type of Operation: Paper mill
Paper/Paperboard Grades and Capacities:
Total paper and paperboard capacity: 568,587 mt/y
Uncoated woodfree/freesheet: 76,284 mt/y
Coated woodfree/freesheet: 492,303 mt/y
Paper and Paperboard Mill Data:
Stock Preparation:
Pulpers: 6
Refiners: 16
Paper Machines: 3
No. 1, fourdrinier, total capacity 172,431 mt/y, Trim width 3.36 m, Coated woodfree/freesheet

South Korea

No. 2, fourdrinier, total capacity 175,530 mt/y, Trim width 3.48 m, Uncoated woodfree/freesheet, Coated woodfree/freesheet
No. 3, SpeedFormer HHS, total capacity 220,626 mt/y, Trim width 3.68 m, Uncoated woodfree/freesheet, Coated woodfree/freesheet
Coating Machines: 2
CM#2, total capacity 235,000 mt/y., off machine
CM#3, total capacity 229,000 mt/y., off machine
Finishing Equipment:
 Supercalenders: 4
 Rewinders: 5 at 520,000 mt/y
 Sheeters: 11 at 460,000 mt/y
Energy Data:
 Electrical demand for mill: 1,078 MWh/D

Moorim P&P Co. Ltd.
Ulsan Mill
Ownership: 49.23% by Moorim Paper Co., Ltd., 22.51% by Merchant Bank and Daegu Bank
1 Dangwol-ri, Onsan-eup, Ulju-gun
689 892 Ulsan-si
South Korea
 Phone: (82) 52 231-7000
 Fax: (82) 52 348-1822
 Web Address: www.moorimpnp.co.kr
Personnel:
 CEO (From December 2, 2013): Mr. Suk-man Kim
 VP.: In-Sup Park
 Phone: (82) 55 751-1234
Total Employees at this Location: 465
Type of Operation: Pulp mill, Paper mill
Pulp Grades and Capacities:
 Total pulp capacity: 449,710 mt/y
 Pulp available for market: 262,085 mt/y
 Chemical Pulp: 449,710 mt/y

Pulp Mill Data:
 Chemical Pulping Systems:
  Batch digesters: 5
  Continuous digesters: 2
 Pulp Lines: 2
 Bleach Plant Systems: 2
  Chemical Pulping System - Hardwood, Type: Hardwood - O D-P/O-D Capacity 160,000 admt/y
  Chemical Pulping System - Hardwood, Sequence: C/D O/E DED, Capacity 240,000 admt/y
 Chemical Recovery Equipment:
  Evaporator lines: 2
  Recovery boilers: 2
  Lime Kiln
 Pulp Dryers:
  Flakt dryer 1, Other dryers 1, Twin Wire 1
Paper/Paperboard Grades and Capacities:
 Total paper and paperboard capacity: 450,000 mt/y
 Uncoated woodfree/freesheet: 45,000 mt/y
 Coated woodfree/freesheet: 405,000 mt/y
Paper and Paperboard Mill Data:
Paper Machines: 1
No. 1, (started in 2011.), hybrid former, total capacity 450,000 mt/y, Trim width 8.65 m, Coated woodfree/freesheet, Uncoated woodfree/freesheet
Coating Machines: 1
No. 1, total capacity 450,000 mt/y., off machine
Finishing Equipment:
 Winders: 1
 Supercalenders: 2
 Rewinders: 1
 Sheeters: 1
Energy Data:
 Power boilers: 1
 Steam turbines: 2 at 14.4, 22.7 MW
 Electrical demand for mill: 1,540 MWh/D

Moorim SP Co., Ltd.
Ownership: 54.02% by Dong Wook Lee and related parties
505, Sinsa-dong, Gangnam-gu
135-887 Seoul
South Korea
 Phone: (82) 2 3485 1500
 Fax: (82) 2 511 4040
 Email: webmaster@moorim.co.kr
 Web Address: www.moorim.co.kr
Personnel:
 Chmn.: Dong-Wook Lee
 Phone: (82) 2 3485-1501
 Fax: (82) 2 512-6479
 Email: dwlee@moorim.co.kr
 CEO (From December 2, 2013): Suk-man Kim
 VP, Admin. Div.: In-Kyu Park
 Phone: (82) 2 3485-1513
 Email: inpark@moorim.co.kr
 VP, Manuf. Admin.: Seok-Man Kim
 Phone: (82) 2 3485-1508
 Fax: (82) 2 3443-2297
 Sr. Man. (Admin. Div.): Kyu-Hyun Lee
 Phone: (82) 2 3485-1510
 Fax: (82) 2 548-3954
 Man. Dir., Purch. Div.: Hong-Seok An
 Phone: (82) 2 3485-1512
 Fax: (82) 2 3485-1737
 Email: hsan@moorim.co;kr
 Exec. Dir., Plan. Admin.: Young-Sik Kim
 Phone: (82) 2 3485-1518
 Fax: (82) 2 3485-1735
 Exec. Dir., CFO Admin.: Hyun-Chang Kim
 Phone: (82) 2 3485-1519
 Exec. Dir., Dom. Sls.: Young-Sil Lee
 Phone: (82) 2 3485-1520
 Fax: (82) 2 511-1340
 Email: yslee@moorim.co.kr
 Outside Dir.: Mok-Sang Lee
 Phone: (82) 2 3485 1500
 Fax: (82) 2 511 4040
Total Employees of Company: 224
Total Employees at this Location: 42
Mill Locations:
Moorim Paper Co., Ltd., Jinju Mill (19.65% owned), 281-1, Sangpyeong-dong, 660-722 Jinju-si, South Korea, Capacity: 568,587 mt/y, (Paper mill)
 Phone: (82) 55 751-1234
 Fax: (82) 55 751-1235
 Email: webmaster@moorim.co.kr
Moorim P&P Co. Ltd., Ulsan Mill, 1 Dangwol-ri, Onsan-eup, Ulju-gun, 689 892 Ulsan-si, South Korea, Capacity: 450,000 mt/y, (Pulp mill, Paper mill)
 Phone: (82) 52 231-7000
 Fax: (82) 52 348-1822
Moorim SP Co., Ltd., Daegu Mill, 550, Chimsan-dong, 702-858 Buk-gu, South Korea, Capacity: 89,200 mt/y, (Paper mill)
 Phone: (82) 53 351-8111
 Fax: (82) 53 351-8120

Moorim SP Co., Ltd.
Daegu Mill
550, Chimsan-dong
702-858 Buk-gu, Daegu-si
South Korea
 Phone: (82) 53 351-8111
 Fax: (82) 53 351-8120
 Web Address: www.moorim.co.kr
Personnel:
 Senior Mill Mgr.: Suk-Man Kim
 Phone: (82) 53 351-8111
 Fax: (82) 53 351-8120
 Man. Dir. Mfg.: Kyoung-Lae Kim
 Phone: (82) 53 351-8126
 Fax: (82) 53 351-8120
Total Employees at this Location: 182
Type of Operation: Paper mill
Paper/Paperboard Grades and Capacities:
 Total paper and paperboard capacity: 89,200 mt/y
 Uncoated woodfree/freesheet: 40,000 mt/y
 Coated woodfree/freesheet: 45,000 mt/y
 Specialty and industrial
Paper and Paperboard Mill Data:
Paper Machines: 2
No. 1, twin former, total capacity 74,800 mt/y, Trim width 2.4 m, Specialty and industrial
No. 2, fourdrinier, total capacity 20,400 mt/y, Trim width 1.3 m, Uncoated woodfree/freesheet
Coating Machines: 2
Cast Coater #1, total capacity 25,550 mt/y., off machine
CM#1, total capacity 37,400 mt/y., off machine
Energy Data:
 Power boilers: 3

Namgang Paper Co., Ltd.
Chinju Mill
Company is previously Busung Paper Mfg. Co., Ltd.
33-118, Sangdae-dong
660-802 Jinju-si, Gyeongsangnam-do
South Korea
 Phone: (82) 55 752-1717 / 752-1718
 Fax: (82) 55 755-7639
 Email: ngpaperha@naver.com
 Web Address: bspaper.koreasme.com
Personnel:
 Chmn.: Kae-Baek Ha
 Phone: (82) 55 7582054
 Fax: (82) 55 7557639
 Email: kaebaek@hanmir.com
 Exec. Man. Dir.: Seung-Geun Moon
 Phone: (82) 55 7521717
 Fax: (82) 55 7557639
 Email: sgm1220@paran.com
 Plant Man. Dir.: Jeong-Ho Kim
 Phone: (82) 55 7520777
 Fax: (82) 55 7557639
 Sls. Man. Dir.: Kae-Do Ha
 Phone: (82) 55 7521717
 Fax: (82) 55 7557639
Total Employees of Company: 51
Total Employees at this Location: 51
Type of Operation: Paper mill
Paper/Paperboard Grades and Capacities:
 Total paper and paperboard capacity: 7,500 mt/y
 Packaging papers: 7,500 mt/y
Paper and Paperboard Mill Data:
Paper Machines: 2
PM 1, Yankee dryer, total capacity 3,250 mt/y, Trim width 2.45 m, Packaging papers
PM 3, Yankee dryer, total capacity 4,250 mt/y, Trim width 3.1 m, Packaging papers

Paper Corea Inc.
2 Jochon-dong
573-883 Gunsan-si, Jeollabuk-do
South Korea
 Phone: (82) 63 440 5000
 Fax: (82) 63 440 5050
 Email: webmaster@papercorea.co.kr
 Web Address: www.papercorea.co.kr
Personnel:
 CEO (From March 22, 2013): Geon-Pyo Park
 Phone: (82) 2 3788 0300
 Fax: (82) 2 756 7070
 Prod. Mgr.: Joo-Bong Park
 Phone: (82) 2 3788 0300
 Fax: (82) 2 756 7070
 Sls. Dir.: Hwa-Joong Yoon
 Phone: (82) 2 3788 0300
 Fax: (82) 2 756 7070
 Man. Dir.: Yong-Ho Ko
 Phone: (82) 2 3788 0300
 Fax: (82) 2 756 7070
Total Employees of Company: 199
Mill Locations:
Paper Corea Inc., Gunsan Mill, 2, Jochon-dong, 573-883 Gunsan-si, South Korea, Capacity: 320,000 mt/y, (Pulp mill, Paper mill)
 Phone: (82) 63 440-5000
 Fax: (82) 63 440-5050
 Email: webmaster@papercorea.co.kr

Paper Corea Inc.
Gunsan Mill
2, Jochon-dong

573-883 Gunsan-si, Jeollabuk-do
South Korea
 Phone: (82) 63 440-5000
 Fax: (82) 63 440-5050
 Email: webmaster@papercorea.co.kr
 Web Address: www.papercorea.co.kr
Personnel:
 Man. Dir.: Joo-Bong Park
 Phone: (82) 63 440-5300
Total Employees at this Location: 199
Type of Operation: Pulp mill, Paper mill
Pulp Grades and Capacities:
 Total pulp capacity: 326,414 mt/y
 Recycled Pulping: 326,414 mt/y
Pulp Mill Data:
 Bleach Plant Systems: 1
 DIP
 Recycled Fiber Treatment Lines:
 Flotation deinking lines: 1 at 160,700 admt/y
 Flotation deinking lines: 1
 Pulpers: 7
 Recycled packaging pulping lines: 1
Paper/Paperboard Grades and Capacities:
 Total paper and paperboard capacity: 320,000 mt/y
 Newsprint: 248,000 mt/y
 Packaging papers: 72,000 mt/y
Paper and Paperboard Mill Data:
 Stock Preparation:
 Pulpers: 4
 Refiners: 15
Paper Machines: 3
 No. 1, twin-wire, total capacity 106,000 mt/y, Trim width 4.73 m, Newsprint
 No. 2, twin-wire, total capacity 142,000 mt/y, Trim width 4.73 m, Newsprint
 No. 3, fourdrinier, total capacity 72,000 mt/y, Trim width 4.73 m, Packaging papers
Energy Data:
 Power boilers: 7
 Steam turbines: 1 at 12.0 MW
 Electrical demand for mill: 892 MWh/D

⑪Samil Paper Co., Ltd.
656-282, Seongsu 1-ga, Seongdong-gu
133-111 Seoul
South Korea
 Phone: (82) 2 461-1911
 Fax: (82) 2 469-1664
 Web Address: www.samilpaper.co.kr
Personnel:
 Pres.: Sang Bum Kang
 Phone: (82) 2 461 1911/15
 Fax: (82) 2 469 1664
 VP: Jong Su Lee
 Phone: (82) 2 461 1911/15
 Fax: (82) 2 469 1664
 Sls. Mgr./Mktg. Mgr./Purch Dir.: Sang Jo Lee
 Phone: (82) 2 464-3104
 Fax: (82) 2 464-0544
Total Employees of Company: 185
Total Employees at this Location: 31
Mill Locations:
Samil Paper Co., Ltd., Hanam Mill, 50, Cheonhyeon-dong, 465-816 Hanam-si, South Korea, Capacity: 56,406 mt/y, (Paper mill)
 Phone: (82) 31 791 6846~8/794 3102~5
 Fax: (82) 31 791-6849
 Email: salep@samilpaper.co.kr

⑪Samil Paper Co., Ltd.
Hanam Mill
50, Cheonhyeon-dong
465-816 Hanam-si, Gyeonggi-do
South Korea
 Phone: (82) 31 791 6846~8/794 3102~5
 Fax: (82) 31 791-6849
 Email: salep@samilpaper.co.kr
 Web Address: www.samilpaper.co.kr
Personnel:
 Mill Mgr.: Joon-Sik Park
 Phone: (82) 31 791-6846
Total Employees at this Location: 89
Type of Operation: Paper mill
Paper/Paperboard Grades and Capacities:
 Total paper and paperboard capacity: 56,406 mt/y
 Uncoated woodfree/freesheet: 46,410 mt/y
 Specialty and industrial: 9,996 mt/y
Paper and Paperboard Mill Data:
Paper Machines: 3
 No. 1, fourdrinier, total capacity 8,925 mt/y, Trim width 1.29 m, Specialty and industrial
 No. 3, fourdrinier, total capacity 3,570 mt/y, Trim width 1.44 m, Specialty and industrial
 No. 4, fourdrinier, total capacity 46,410 mt/y, Trim width 2.58 m, Uncoated woodfree/freesheet
Finishing Equipment:
 Rewinders: 1
Energy Data:
 Power boilers: 1
 Electrical demand for mill: 145 MWh/D

⑪⑪Samjung Pulp Ind. Co., Ltd.
Pyeongtaek Mill
250, Haechang-ri
451-843 Godeok-myeon, Pyeongtaek-si, Gyeonggi-do
South Korea
 Phone: (82) 31 664-5377
 Fax: (82) 31 663-1676
Personnel:
 Chmn.: Chae-Joon Chun
 Phone: (82) 31 664 5377
 Pres.: Sung-Oh Chun
 Phone: (82) 31 664 5377
 Purch. Dir.: Dong-Bin Chi
 Phone: (82) 31 664 5377
 Asst. Mill Mgr.: Kyu-Ahn Chang
 Phone: (82) 31 664 5377
 Indep. Dir.: SungHee Park
 Phone: (82) 31 664 5377
 Inter. Auditor, Dir.: HyeSang Yoo
 Phone: (82) 31 664 5377
Total Employees of Company: 312
Total Employees at this Location: 187
Type of Operation: Paper mill
Mill Locations:
Samjung Pulp Ind. Co., Ltd., Cheonan Mill, 187, Namgwan-ri Pungse-myeon, 330-911 Cheonan-si, Dongnam-gu, South Korea, Capacity: 19,000 mt/y, (Paper mill)
 Phone: (82) 41 574-8083
 Fax: (82) 41-574-8086
Samjung Pulp Ind. Co., Ltd., Haman Mill, 759, Yegok-ri, Chilwon-myeon, 637-923 Haman-gun, South Korea, Capacity: 43,000 mt/y, (Paper mill)
 Phone: (82) 55 586-2581
 Fax: (82) 55-568-2585
Pulp Grades and Capacities:
 Total pulp capacity: 41,663 mt/y
 Recycled Pulping: 41,663 mt/y
Pulp Mill Data:
 Bleach Plant Systems: 1
 DIP
 Recycled Fiber Treatment Lines:
 Flotation deinking lines: 1
Paper/Paperboard Grades and Capacities:
 Total paper and paperboard capacity: 81,000 mt/y
 Tissue: 81,000 mt/y
Paper and Paperboard Mill Data:
 Stock Preparation:
 Pulpers: 6
 Refiners: 10
Paper Machines: 5
 No. 1, total capacity 14,000 mt/y, Trim width 2.6 m, Tissue
 No. 2, total capacity 14,000 mt/y, Trim width 2.6 m, Tissue
 No. 3, total capacity 10,000 mt/y, Trim width 2.56 m, Tissue
 No. 4, total capacity 18,000 mt/y, Trim width 2.9 m, Tissue, Uncoated woodfree/freesheet
 No. 5, crescent former, total capacity 25,000 mt/y, Trim width 2.62 m, Tissue, Uncoated woodfree/freesheet
Finishing Equipment:
 Rewinders: 3
 Sheeters: 3
Energy Data:
 Power boilers: 2

⑪Samjung Pulp Ind. Co., Ltd.
Cheonan Mill
187, Namgwan-ri Pungse-myeon
330-911 Cheonan-si, Dongnam-gu, Chungcheongnam-do
South Korea
 Phone: (82) 41 574-8083
 Fax: (82) 41-574-8086
Total Employees at this Location: 85
Type of Operation: Paper mill
Pulp Grades and Capacities:
 Total pulp capacity: 11,366 mt/y
 Recycled Pulping: 11,366 mt/y
Pulp Mill Data:
 Bleach Plant Systems: 1
 DIP
 Recycled Fiber Treatment Lines:
 Flotation deinking lines: 1
Paper/Paperboard Grades and Capacities:
 Total paper and paperboard capacity: 19,000 mt/y
 Tissue: 19,000 mt/y
Paper and Paperboard Mill Data:
Paper Machines: 2
 No. 1, total capacity 9,500 mt/y, Trim width 2.6 m, Tissue, Uncoated woodfree/freesheet
 No. 2, total capacity 9,500 mt/y, Trim width 2.6 m, Tissue, Uncoated woodfree/freesheet
Energy Data:
 Power boilers
 Electrical demand for mill: 53 MWh/D

⑪Samjung Pulp Ind. Co., Ltd.
Haman Mill
759, Yegok-ri, Chilwon-myeon
637-923 Haman-gun, Gyeongsangnam-do
South Korea
 Phone: (82) 55 586-2581
 Fax: (82) 55-568-2585
Total Employees at this Location: 127
Type of Operation: Paper mill
Pulp Grades and Capacities:
 Total pulp capacity: 26,184 mt/y
 Recycled Pulping: 26,184 mt/y
Pulp Mill Data:
 Bleach Plant Systems: 1
 DIP
 Recycled Fiber Treatment Lines:
 Flotation deinking lines: 1
Paper/Paperboard Grades and Capacities:
 Total paper and paperboard capacity: 43,000 mt/y
 Tissue: 43,000 mt/y
Paper and Paperboard Mill Data:
Paper Machines: 3
 No. 1, total capacity 16,750 mt/y, Trim width 2.6 m, Tissue, Uncoated woodfree/freesheet
 No. 2, total capacity 16,750 mt/y, Trim width 2.6 m, Tissue, Uncoated woodfree/freesheet
 No. 3, total capacity 9,500 mt/y, Trim width 2.41 m, Tissue
Energy Data:
 Power boilers
 Electrical demand for mill: 128 MWh/D

⑪Samwha Paper Co. Ltd.
10th Fl., Samwha Bldg., 112-44, Sogong-dong, Jung-gu
100-070 Seoul
South Korea
 Phone: (82) 2 753-1136
 Fax: (82) 2 773-7484
 Email: export@samwhapaper.com
 Web Address: www.samwhapaper.com
Personnel:

South Korea

Chmn. & CEO: Sung-Ho Kim
Phone: (82) 2 753 1136/39
Fax: (82) 2 773 7484
Chmn. & CEO: Yem-Ho Kim
Phone: (82) 2 753 1136/39
Fax: (82) 2 773 7484
Pres.: Tai-Ho Kim
Phone: (82) 2 753 1136/39
Fax: (82) 2 773 7484
Total Employees of Company: 250
Total Employees at this Location: 54
Mill Locations:
Samwha Paper Co., Ltd., Chongwon Mill, San 135, Hojuk-ri, Oksan-myeon, 363-912 Cheongwon-gun, South Korea, Capacity: 55,692 mt/y, (Paper mill)
Phone: (82) 43 230-7500
Fax: (82) 43 230-7666
Email: samwha@samwhapaper.com

ⓂSamwha Paper Co., Ltd.
Chongwon Mill
Ownership: Samwha Paper Co. Ltd.
San 135, Hojuk-ri, Oksan-myeon
363-912 Cheongwon-gun, Chungcheongbuk-do
South Korea
Phone: (82) 43 230-7500
Fax: (82) 43 230-7666
Email: samwha@samwhapaper.com
Web Address: www.samwhapaper.com
Personnel:
Mill Mgr.: Myung-Jin An
Phone: (82) 43 230-7510
Fax: (82) 43 230-7641
Total Employees at this Location: 151
Type of Operation: Paper mill
Paper/Paperboard Grades and Capacities:
Total paper and paperboard capacity: 55,692 mt/y
Uncoated woodfree/freesheet: 55,692 mt/y
Paper and Paperboard Mill Data:
Paper Machines: 2
No. 1, fourdrinier, total capacity 27,846 mt/y, Trim width 1.25 m, Uncoated woodfree/freesheet
No. 2, fourdrinier, Yankee dryer, total capacity 41,769 mt/y, Trim width 1.7 m, Uncoated woodfree/freesheet
Coating Machines: 2
Cast Coater # 1, total capacity 6,500 mt/y., off machine
Cast Coater #2, total capacity 18,000 mt/y., off machine
Finishing Equipment:
Supercalenders: 1
Energy Data:
Power boilers: 2
Electrical demand for mill: 143 MWh/D

ⓂSeha Corporation
505, Sinsa-dong, Gangnam-gu
135-887 Seoul
South Korea
Phone: (82) 2 2056-8800
Fax: (82) 2 2056-8995
Email: swsohn@serim.co.kr
Web Address: www.seha.co.kr
Personnel:
Chmn., CEO & Owner: Dong-Yoon Lee
Phone: (82) 2 2056 8801
Fax: (82) 2 2056 8900
Email: dylee@seha.co.kr
Co- CEO: Hong-Bin Ra
Phone: (82) 2 2056 800
Fax: (82) 2 2056 8995
Pres.: Moo-Woong Lee
Phone: (82) 2 2056 800
Fax: (82) 2 2056 8995
Asst. Man. Dir.: Bong-Jin Kim
Phone: (82) 2 2056 800
Fax: (82) 2 2056 8995
Asst. Man. Dir.: Jae-Won Lim
Phone: (82) 2 2056 8810
Fax: (82) 2 2056 8877
Email: jwlee@seha.co.kr
Inter. Auditor: Jung-Gwon Yoon
Phone: (82) 2 2056 800
Fax: (82) 2 2056 8995
Non-Exec. Indep. Dir.: Sang-Man Lee
Phone: (82) 2 2056 800
Fax: (82) 2 2056 8995
Exec. Dir.: Hyun-Joon Kim
Phone: (82) 2 2056 8805
Fax: (82) 2 2056 8902
Email: hjkim@seha.co.kr
Total Employees of Company: 252
Total Employees at this Location: 40
Mill Locations:
Seha Corporation, Hyunpoong Mill, 720, Sang-ri, Yuga-myeon, 711-883 Dalseong-gun, Daegu-si, South Korea, Capacity: 190,000 mt/y, (Paper mill, Paperboard mill)
Phone: (82) 53 603-0600
Fax: (82) 53 611-2230

ⓂSeha Corporation
Hyunpoong Mill
720, Sang-ri, Yuga-myeon
711-883 Dalseong-gun, Daegu-si, Daegu-si
South Korea
Phone: (82) 53 603-0600
Fax: (82) 53 611-2230
Web Address: www.seha.co.kr
Personnel:
Mill Mgr.: Ik-Mok Kwon
Phone: (82) 53 603 0701
Fax: (82) 53 611 2022
Email: imkwon@seha.co.kr
Prod. Dir.: Bong-Jin Kim
Phone: (82) 53 603 0602
Fax: (82) 53 611 0120
Email: bjkim@seha.co.kr
Total Employees at this Location: 200
Type of Operation: Paper mill, Paperboard mill
Pulp Grades and Capacities:
Total pulp capacity: 164,146 mt/y
Recycled Pulping: 164,146 mt/y
Pulp Mill Data:
Recycled Fiber Treatment Lines:
Flotation deinking lines: 3 at 105,000 admt/y
Recycled packaging pulping lines
Paper/Paperboard Grades and Capacities:
Total paper and paperboard capacity: 190,000 mt/y
Boxboard/cartonboard: 190,000 mt/y
Paper and Paperboard Mill Data:
Stock Preparation:
Pulpers: 8
Refiners: 7
Paper Machines: 2
No. 1, multi-wire, total capacity 115,000 mt/y, Trim width 2.44 m, Boxboard/cartonboard
No. 2, Ultraformer, total capacity 75,000 mt/y, Trim width 2.44 m, Boxboard/cartonboard
Coating Machines: 2
CM 1, total capacity 114,000 mt/y., on machine
CM 2, total capacity 75,000 mt/y., on machine
Finishing Equipment:
Winders: 2
Sheeters: 6
Energy Data:
Power boilers: 3
Electrical demand for mill: 259 MWh/D

ⓂShinchang Paper
100-1, Sirok-dong
336-020 Asan-si
South Korea
Phone: (82) 41 533-0290
Fax: (82) 41 533-0295
Web Address: www.scpaper.co.kr
Mill Locations:
Shinchang Paper, Asan Mill, 100-1, Sirok-dong, 336-020 Asan-si, South Korea, Capacity: 34,200 mt/y, (Paper mill)
Phone: (82) 41 533-0290-4
Fax: (82) 41 533-0295

ⓂShinchang Paper
Asan Mill
100-1, Sirok-dong
336-020 Asan-si, Chungcheongnam-do
South Korea
Phone: (82) 41 533-0290-4
Fax: (82) 41 533-0295
Web Address: www.scpaper.co.kr
Total Employees at this Location: 90
Type of Operation: Paper mill
Pulp Grades and Capacities:
Total pulp capacity: 24,081 mt/y
Recycled Pulping: 24,081 mt/y
Pulp Mill Data:
Recycled Fiber Treatment Lines:
Flotation deinking lines: 1
Recycled packaging pulping lines: 1
Paper/Paperboard Grades and Capacities:
Total paper and paperboard capacity: 34,200 mt/y
Tissue: 34,200 mt/y
Paper and Paperboard Mill Data:
Paper Machines: 2
No. 1, total capacity 17,100 mt/y, Trim width 3.45 m, Tissue
No. 2, total capacity 17,100 mt/y, Trim width 3.45 m, Tissue
Energy Data:
Power boilers
Electrical demand for mill: 94 MWh/D

ⓂShindaeyang Paper Co., Ltd.
Ownership: Dygroup, 61% by Hyuk-Hong Kwon
490-2, Moknae-Dong
425-100 Ansan-Si, Gyeonggi-do
South Korea
Phone: (82) 31 432-5814
Fax: (82) 31 499-0598
Email: kskim@dygroup.co.kr
Web Address: www.sdypaper.co.kr
Personnel:
Chmn. & Pres.: Hyeok Hong Kwon
Phone: (82) 31 432 5811
Co-CEO, Dir.: Yeong Gwoe
Phone: (82) 31 432 5814/16
Fax: (82) 31 499 0598
Non-Exec. Indep. Dir.: Won Gil Lee
Phone: (82) 31 432 5814/16
Fax: (82) 31 499 0598
Mill Locations:
Daeyang Paper Mfg. Co. Ltd., Ansan Mill, 1062-1 Singil-dong, Danwon-gu, 425-839 Ansan-si, South Korea, Capacity: 438,000 mt/y, (Paperboard mill)
Phone: (82) 31 432-5416
Fax: (82) 31 432-5410
Shindaeyang Paper Co., Ltd., Ansan Mill, 490-2, Mongnae-dong, 425-100 Ansan-si, South Korea, Capacity: 217,000 mt/y, (Paperboard mill)
Phone: (82) 31 494-7911
Fax: (82) 31 492-1510
Shindaeyang Paper Co., Ltd., Shihwa Mill, 674, Seonggok-dong, Danwon-gu, 425-836 Ansan-si, South Korea, Capacity: 429,000 mt/y, (Paperboard mill)
Phone: (82) 31 499-0880
Fax: (82) 31 499-1780
Email: kskim@dygroup.co.kr

ⓂShindaeyang Paper Co., Ltd.
Ansan Mill
490-2, Mongnae-dong
425-100 Ansan-si, Gyeonggi-do
South Korea
Phone: (82) 31 494-7911
Fax: (82) 31 492-1510
Web Address: www.sdypaper.co.kr
Personnel:
Mill Mgr.: Taek-Whan Kwon
Phone: (82) 31 494-7911
Total Employees at this Location: 78

Type of Operation: Paperboard mill
Pulp Grades and Capacities:
  Total pulp capacity: 212,984 mt/y
  Recycled Pulping: 212,984 mt/y
Pulp Mill Data:
  Recycled Fiber Treatment Lines:
  Recycled packaging pulping lines
Paper/Paperboard Grades and Capacities:
  Total paper and paperboard capacity: 217,000 mt/y
  Corrugating medium/fluting: 217,000 mt/y
Paper and Paperboard Mill Data:
  Stock Preparation:
  Pulpers: 2
  Refiners: 4
Paper Machines: 2
No. 1, fourdrinier, total capacity 93,000 mt/y, Trim width 3.25 m, Corrugating medium/fluting
No. 2, fourdrinier, total capacity 124,000 mt/y, Trim width 3.85 m, Corrugating medium/fluting
Finishing Equipment:
  Winders: 2 at 217,000 mt/y
  Supercalenders: 1
  Rewinders: 1
Energy Data:
Power boilers: 1
Electrical demand for mill: 251 MWh/D

ⓂShindaeyang Paper Co., Ltd.
Shihwa Mill
674, Seonggok-dong, Danwon-gu
425-836 Ansan-si, Gyeonggi-do
South Korea
  Phone: (82) 31 499-0880
  Fax: (82) 31 499-1780
  Email: kskim@dygroup.co.kr
  Web Address: www.sdypaper.co.kr
Personnel:
  Mill Mgr.: Sung Ho Won
  Phone: (82) 31 499-0880
Total Employees at this Location: 63
Type of Operation: Paperboard mill
Pulp Grades and Capacities:
  Total pulp capacity: 394,728 mt/y
  Recycled Pulping: 394,728 mt/y
Pulp Mill Data:
  Recycled Fiber Treatment Lines:
  Recycled packaging pulping lines: 1
Paper/Paperboard Grades and Capacities:
  Total paper and paperboard capacity: 429,000 mt/y
  Linerboard: 429,000 mt/y
Paper and Paperboard Mill Data:
  Stock Preparation:
  Pulpers: 4
  Refiners: 6
Paper Machines: 1
No. 3, fourdrinier, total capacity 429,000 mt/y, Trim width 5.6 m, Linerboard
Finishing Equipment:
  Winders: 2 at 500,000 mt/y
  Calenders: 1
Energy Data:
Power boilers: 2
Electrical demand for mill: 521 MWh/D

ⒹⓂShinpoong Paper Mfg. Co., Ltd.
Pyongtaek Mill
15 Haechang-ri Godeok-myeon
451-843 Pyeongtaek-si, Gyeonggi-do
South Korea
  Phone: (82) 31 669-8271
  Fax: (82) 31 669-8221
Personnel:
  Chmn.: Il Hong Chung
  Phone: (82) 31 669-8271
  Pres.: Mun-Heon Song
  Phone: (82) 31 669-8271
  Mill Mgr.: Jin-Ho Byun
  Phone: (82) 31 669-8271
  Co-CEO, Dir.: Mun-Heon Song
  Phone: (82) 31 669-8271
  Vice Chmn.: HakHun Jung
  Phone: (82) 31 669-8271
  Inter. Auditor, Dir.: ByeongDo Seo
  Phone: (82) 31 669-8271
Total Employees of Company: 182
Total Employees at this Location: 110
Type of Operation: Paperboard mill
Pulp Grades and Capacities:
  Total pulp capacity: 104,678 mt/y
  Recycled Pulping: 104,678 mt/y
Pulp Mill Data:
  Bleach Plant Systems: 1
  DIP
  Recycled Fiber Treatment Lines:
  Flotation deinking lines: 1
  Recycled packaging pulping lines: 1
Paper/Paperboard Grades and Capacities:
  Total paper and paperboard capacity: 120,000 mt/y
  Boxboard/cartonboard: 120,000 mt/y
Paper and Paperboard Mill Data:
  Stock Preparation:
  Pulpers: 7
  Refiners: 10
Paper Machines: 1
No. 6, Ultraformer, total capacity 120,000 mt/y, Trim width 3.23 m, Boxboard/cartonboard
Coating Machines: 1
No. 1, total capacity 155,000 mt/y., on machine
Finishing Equipment:
  Rewinders: 1
  Sheeters: 1
Energy Data:
Power boilers: 2
Steam turbines: 1 at 12.0 MW
Electrical demand for mill: 1,071 MWh/D

ⒹⓂSonghak Paper Co., Ltd.
Yangsan Mill
75-1, Junam-ri, Ungsang-eup
626-790 Yangsan-si, Gyeongsangnam-do
South Korea
  Phone: (82) 55 363-6300
  Fax: (82) 55 363-6305
Personnel:
  Pres.: MG Shim
  Phone: (82) 55 363 6300
  Man. Dir.: Jong-Duk Ahn
  Phone: (82) 11 9314-6301
  Mill Mgr.: Jin-Ha Kim
  Phone: (82) 55 363 6300
Total Employees at this Location: 70
Type of Operation: Paper mill
Pulp Grades and Capacities:
  Total pulp capacity: 56,079 mt/y
  Recycled Pulping: 56,079 mt/y
Pulp Mill Data:
  Recycled Fiber Treatment Lines:
  Recycled packaging pulping lines: 1
Paper/Paperboard Grades and Capacities:
  Total paper and paperboard capacity: 55,000 mt/y
  Packaging papers: 55,000 mt/y
Paper and Paperboard Mill Data:
  Stock Preparation:
  Pulpers: 3
  Refiners: 4
Paper Machines: 1
No. 1, fourdrinier, total capacity 55,000 mt/y, Trim width 3.2 m, Packaging papers
Finishing Equipment:
  Winders: 1
  Rewinders: 1
Energy Data:
Power boilers: 2
Electrical demand for mill: 94 MWh/D

ⒹⓂSsangyong Paper Co., Ltd.
Osan Mill
Company is closed (since April 2014)
Ownership: Softbank Korea
188, Cheonghak-dong
447-130 Osan-si, Gyeonggi-do
South Korea
  Phone: (82) 31 370-4651/4850
  Fax: (82) 31 370-4870/4667
  Web Address: www.sypaper.co.kr
Personnel:
  CEO & Chmn.: Jay Y. Lee
  Phone: (82) 31 370-4851
  Email: jaylee@sypaper.co.kr
  Pres.: Jan-Whan Kim
  Phone: (82) 31 370-4800
  Email: kim.jw@sypaper.co.kr
  Man. Dir.: Suk-Hyun Kwak
  Phone: (82) 31 370-4650
  Fax: (82) 31 372-2085
  Email: shkwak@sypaper.co.kr
  Plant Mgr.: Jong-Wha Park
  Phone: (82) 31 370-4601
  Fax: (82) 31 370-4784
  Email: park.jh@sypaper.co.kr
  Sls. Team Mgr.: Ju-Hak Kang
  Phone: (82) 31 370-4882
  Fax: (82) 31 370-4877
  Purch. Mgr.: Jae-Chun Ahn
  Phone: (82) 31 370-4651
  Fax: (82) 31 370-4870
Total Employees of Company: 153
Total Employees at this Location: 150
Type of Operation: Paper mill
Pulp Grades and Capacities:
  Total pulp capacity: 47,625 mt/y
  Recycled Pulping: 47,625 mt/y
Pulp Mill Data:
  Recycled Fiber Treatment Lines:
  Recycled packaging pulping lines: 1
Paper/Paperboard Grades and Capacities:
  Total paper and paperboard capacity: 119,952 mt/y
  Packaging papers: 86,394 mt/y
  Specialty and industrial: 33,558 mt/y
Paper and Paperboard Mill Data:
  Stock Preparation:
  Pulpers: 3
  Refiners: 2
Paper Machines: 2
No. 1, fourdrinier, total capacity 47,838 mt/y, Trim width 3.2 m, Specialty and industrial, Packaging papers
No. 2, fourdrinier, total capacity 72,114 mt/y, Trim width 3.2 m, Specialty and industrial, Packaging papers
Finishing Equipment:
  Calenders: 1
  Rewinders: 2
Energy Data:
Power boilers: 3
Electrical demand for mill: 249 MWh/D

ⓂSsangyong C&B
Chochiwon Mill
Ownership: 100% by Monalisa Co., Ltd.
9 Beonam-ri
339-804 Jochiwon-eup, Yeongi-gun,
Chungcheongnam-do
South Korea
  Phone: (82) 41 861-5000
  Fax: (82) 41 861-4819
  Web Address: www.ssycnb.co.kr
Personnel:
  Mill Mgr.: Jung Jae Lee
  Phone: (82) 41 861 5000
Total Employees at this Location: 255
Type of Operation: Paper mill
Pulp Grades and Capacities:
  Total pulp capacity: 22,882 mt/y
  Recycled Pulping: 22,882 mt/y
Pulp Mill Data:
  Bleach Plant Systems: 1
  DIP
  Recycled Fiber Treatment Lines:

South Korea

Flotation deinking lines: 1
Paper/Paperboard Grades and Capacities:
Total paper and paperboard capacity: 98,000 mt/y
Tissue: 98,000 mt/y
Paper and Paperboard Mill Data:
Paper Machines: 5
No. 1, total capacity 10,000 mt/y, Trim width 2.1 m, Tissue
No. 3, twin-wire, Yankee dryer, total capacity 18,000 mt/y, Trim width 2.2 m, Tissue, Uncoated woodfree/freesheet
No. 4, twin-wire, Yankee dryer, total capacity 20,000 mt/y, Trim width 2.2 m, Tissue, Uncoated woodfree/freesheet
No. 5, crescent former, Yankee dryer, total capacity 32,000 mt/y, Trim width 2.73 m, Tissue, Uncoated woodfree/freesheet
No. 6, total capacity 18,000 mt/y, Trim width 2.9 m, Tissue, Uncoated woodfree/freesheet
Energy Data:
Power boilers: 2
Electrical demand for mill: 275 MWh/D

ⓗSunglim Paper
774-2, Cheon-ri, Idong-myeon, Cheoin-gu
449-833 Yongin-si
South Korea
  Phone: (82) 31 333-7771
  Fax: (82) 31 333-7774
  Email: sunglim@sunglim.net
  Web Address: www.sunglim.net/
Mill Locations:
Sunglim Paper, Yongin Mill, 774-2, Cheon-ri, Idong-myeon, Cheoin-gu, 449-833 Yongin-si, South Korea, Capacity: 5,400 mt/y, (Paper mill)
  Phone: (82) 31 333-7771
  Fax: (82) 31 333-7774
  Email: sunglim@sunglim.net

ⓜSunglim Paper
Yongin Mill
774-2, Cheon-ri, Idong-myeon, Cheoin-gu
449-833 Yongin-si, Gyeonggi-do
South Korea
  Phone: (82) 31 333-7771
  Fax: (82) 31 333-7774
  Email: sunglim@sunglim.net
  Web Address: www.sunglim.net/
Type of Operation: Paper mill
Paper/Paperboard Grades and Capacities:
Total paper and paperboard capacity: 5,400 mt/y
Uncoated woodfree/freesheet
Tissue
Paper and Paperboard Mill Data:
Paper Machines: 2
PM 1, total capacity 3,200 mt/y
PM 3, total capacity 2,200 mt/y

ⓜWolsan Paper Mfg. Co., Ltd.
Haman Mill
Ownership: 100% by Dongil Paper Mfg. Co., Ltd.
Chilseo Industrial Complex 4B-7L
637-940 Chilseo-myeon, Haman-gun, Gyeongsangnam-do
South Korea
  Phone: (82) 55 586-6000
  Fax: (82) 55 587-7585/586-3999
  Email: choiss2085@yahoo.co.kr
  Web Address: www.wolsanpaper.co.kr
Personnel:
Chmn.: Dong-Sup Jung
  Phone: (82) 55 586-6000
Pres.: Young-Sup Jung
  Phone: (82) 55 586-6000
VP: Seong-Seop Son
  Phone: (82) 55 586-6000
Mill Mgr.: Won-Sup Jung
  Phone: (82) 55 586-6000
Purch. Mgr.: Do-Hyeung Kim
  Phone: (82) 55 586-6000
Total Employees at this Location: 99
Type of Operation: Paperboard mill
Pulp Grades and Capacities:
Total pulp capacity: 274,990 mt/y
Recycled Pulping: 274,990 mt/y
Pulp Mill Data:
Recycled Fiber Treatment Lines:
Recycled packaging pulping lines: 1
Paper/Paperboard Grades and Capacities:
Total paper and paperboard capacity: 320,000 mt/y
Specialty and industrial: 48,000 mt/y
Linerboard: 160,000 mt/y
Corrugating medium/fluting: 112,000 mt/y
Paper and Paperboard Mill Data:
Paper Machines: 1
No. 1, (3-ply with SymBelt Shoe Press,), SymFormer MB, total capacity 320,000 mt/y, Trim width 4.6 m, Corrugating medium/fluting, Linerboard, Specialty and industrial
Energy Data:
Power boilers
Electrical demand for mill: 382 MWh/D

ⓗⓜYoungpoong Paper Mfg. Co., Ltd.
Pyeongtaek-si Mill
571-6, Gyeongsan-ri, Jinwi-myeon
451-863 Pyeongtaek-si, Gyeonggi-do
South Korea
Mailing Address: 571-6 Kyungsan-ri, Jinwi-myon, Pyungtaek-Si
  Phone: (82) 31 660-8200
  Fax: (82) 31 668-2655
  Email: ycjeon@yp21.co.kr
  Web Address: www.yp21.co.kr
Personnel:
Chmn.: Moo-Jin Lee
  Phone: (82) 31 660 8200
Pres.: Taek-Sup Lee
  Phone: (82) 31 660 8200
Man. Dir.: Sang-Baek Han
  Phone: (82) 31 660 8200
Auditor: Il Jin Chung
  Phone: (82) 31 660 8200
Total Employees of Company: 115
Total Employees at this Location: 115
Type of Operation: Paper mill
Pulp Grades and Capacities:
Total pulp capacity: 274,386 mt/y
Recycled Pulping: 274,386 mt/y
Pulp Mill Data:
Recycled Fiber Treatment Lines:
Recycled packaging pulping lines: 1
Paper/Paperboard Grades and Capacities:
Total paper and paperboard capacity: 270,000 mt/y
Linerboard: 80,000 mt/y
Boxboard/cartonboard: 190,000 mt/y
Paper and Paperboard Mill Data:
Paper Machines: 2
No. 2, cylinder (6), total capacity 100,000 mt/y, Trim width 3.3 m, Boxboard/cartonboard
No. 3, multi-wire, total capacity 170,000 mt/y, Trim width 4.1 m, Boxboard/cartonboard, Linerboard
Energy Data:
Electrical demand for mill: 314 MWh/D

ⓗYuhan-Kimberly Ltd.
Ownership: 70% by Kimberly-Clark Corp., 30% by Yuhan Corp.
942, Daechi 3-dong, Gangnam-gu
135-725 Seoul
South Korea
  Phone: (82) 2 528-1001
  Fax: (82) 2 528-1086
  Email: webmaster.korea@y-k.co.kr
  Web Address: www.yuhan-kimberly.co.kr
Personnel:
CEO/Pres.: Joong-Kon Kim
  Phone: (82) 2 528 1001
  Fax: (82) 2 528 1086
Mktg. Dir.: Kyoo-Bok Choe
  Phone: (82) 2 528 1001
  Fax: (82) 2 528 1086
Purch. & Overseas Biz Dir.: Tae-Soo Choe
  Phone: (82) 2 528 1001
  Fax: (82) 2 528 1086
VP: Byeong-Seon Choe
  Phone: (82) 2 528 1001
  Fax: (82) 2 528 1086
HR Dir.: Deok-Jin Lee
  Phone: (82) 2 528 1001
  Fax: (82) 2 528 1086
VP, PR: Eun-Wook Lee
  Phone: (82) 2 528 1001
  Fax: (82) 2 528 1086
Total Employees of Company: 1,420
Total Employees at this Location: 435
Mill Locations:
Yuhan-Kimberly Ltd., Daejeon Mill, 41-1, Munpyeong-dong, Daedeok-gu, 306-220 Daejeon-si, South Korea, Capacity: 17,600 mt/y, (Paper mill)
  Phone: (82) 42 939-7100
  Fax: (82) 42 931-7105/06
  Email: webmaster.korea@y-k.co.kr
Yuhan-Kimberly Ltd., Kimcheon Mill, 746-1, Daegwang-dong, 740-170 Gimcheon-si, South Korea, Capacity: 107,000 mt/y, (Paper mill)
  Phone: (82) 54 420-5500
  Fax: (82) 54 420-5555
  Email: webmaster.korea@y-k.co.kr
Yuhan-Kimberly Ltd., Kunpo Mill, 27-4, Dangjeong-dong, 435-831 Gunpo-si, South Korea, Capacity: 23,000 mt/y, (Paper mill)
  Phone: (82) 31 450-8567
  Fax: (82) 31 455-9609
  Email: webmaster.korea@y-k.co.kr

ⓜYuhan-Kimberly Ltd.
Daejeon Mill
Ownership: 70% by Kimberly-Clark Corp.
41-1, Munpyeong-dong, Daedeok-gu
306-220 Daejeon-si, Daejeon
South Korea
  Phone: (82) 42 939-7100
  Fax: (82) 42 931-7105/06
  Email: webmaster.korea@y-k.co.kr
  Web Address: www.yuhan-kimberly.co.kr
Personnel:
Mill Mgr.: Kwang-Ho Kim
  Phone: (82) 42 939 7110
Total Employees at this Location: 250
Type of Operation: Paper mill
Paper/Paperboard Grades and Capacities:
Total paper and paperboard capacity: 17,600 mt/y
Tissue: 17,600 mt/y

ⓜYuhan-Kimberly Ltd.
Kimcheon Mill
Ownership: 70% by Kimberly-Clark Corp.
746-1, Daegwang-dong
740-170 Gimcheon-si, Gyeongsangbuk-do
South Korea
  Phone: (82) 54 420-5500
  Fax: (82) 54 420-5555
  Email: webmaster.korea@y-k.co.kr
  Web Address: www.yuhan-kimberly.co.kr
Personnel:
Mill Mgr.: Young Hwa Lim
  Phone: (82) 54 420-5508
Total Employees at this Location: 270
Type of Operation: Paper mill
Pulp Grades and Capacities:
Total pulp capacity: 52,608 mt/y
Recycled Pulping: 52,608 mt/y
Pulp Mill Data:
Bleach Plant Systems: 1
DIP
Recycled Fiber Treatment Lines:

Flotation deinking lines: 1
Paper/Paperboard Grades and Capacities:
Total paper and paperboard capacity: 107,000 mt/y
Tissue: 107,000 mt/y
Paper and Paperboard Mill Data:
Paper Machines: 5
TM4, total capacity 11,300 mt/y, Trim width 2.3 m, Tissue
TM6, total capacity 22,850 mt/y, Trim width 3.3 m, Tissue, Uncoated woodfree/freesheet
TM7, total capacity 22,850 mt/y, Trim width 3.3 m, Tissue
TM8, crescent former, total capacity 25,000 mt/y, Trim width 3.4 m, Tissue
TM9, crescent former, total capacity 25,000 mt/y, Trim width 3.4 m, Tissue
Energy Data:
Power boilers
Electrical demand for mill: 266 MWh/D

ⓂYuhan-Kimberly Ltd.
Kunpo Mill
Ownership: 70% by Kimberly-Clark Corp.
27-4, Dangjeong-dong
435-831 Gunpo-si, Gyeonggi-do
South Korea
  Phone: (82) 31 450-8567
  Fax: (82) 31 455-9609
  Email: webmaster.korea@y-k.co.kr
  Web Address: www.yuhan-kimberly.co.kr
Personnel:
  Mill Mgr.: Myoung Sik Song
  Phone: (82) 31 450 8567
  Qlty. Assurance: Kyung Hoon Wang
  Phone: (82) 31 450 8567
  Feminine Care Op.: In-Cho Jee
  Phone: (82) 31 450 8567
  Infant Care Op.: Bong-Cheol Shin
  Phone: (82) 31 450 8567
Total Employees at this Location: 92
Type of Operation: Paper mill
Paper/Paperboard Grades and Capacities:
Total paper and paperboard capacity: 23,000 mt/y
Tissue: 23,000 mt/y
Paper and Paperboard Mill Data:
  Stock Preparation:
  Pulpers: 4
  Refiners: 4
Paper Machines: 2
No. 2, total capacity 11,500 mt/y, Trim width 2.2 m, Tissue
No. 5, total capacity 11,500 mt/y, Trim width 2.2 m, Tissue
  Finishing Equipment:
  Supercalenders: 4
  Rewinders: 2 at 24,500 mt/y
Energy Data:
Power boilers: 2
Electrical demand for mill: 62 MWh/D

SRI LANKA

ⓘNational Paper Co. Ltd. (NPCL)
Ownership: 100% by Government
93 Jawatta Road
02 Colombo
Sri Lanka
Mailing Address: P.O.Box 1367, 356 Union Place, 2 Colombo, Sri Lanka
  Phone: (94) 11 2556470
  Email: natpaper@slt.lk
  Web Address: www.npc.lk
Personnel:
  Chmn./Man. Dir.: S. Amarasinghe
  Phone: (94) 1 2554191
  Fax: (94) 1 2556473
  Exec. Dir.: S. Leelarathne
  Phone: (94) 11 2556470
  Gen. Mgr.: V. Abeysinghe
  Phone: (94) 1 2556465
  Finan. Mgr.: C. Priyadarsika
  Phone: (94) 1 2554189
  Chief Risk Auditor: S. Kokulakumaran
  Phone: (94) 2554 188
  Supplies Mgr.: A. Ranaweers
  Phone: (94) 2556 472
  Email: nat_paper@slt.lk
Total Employees of Company: 550
Total Employees at this Location: 35
Mill Locations:
Valaichenai Paper Mills, Valaichenai Mill, Valaichenai, Sri Lanka, Capacity: 24,000 mt/y, (Pulp mill, Paper mill, Paperboard mill)
  Phone: (94) 65 57312/246/311
  Fax: (94) 65 57706
  Email: natpaper@slt.lk

ⓂValaichenai Paper Mills
Valaichenai Mill
Ownership: National Paper Co. Ltd. (NPCL)
Valaichenai
Sri Lanka
  Phone: (94) 65 57312/246/311
  Fax: (94) 65 57706
  Email: natpaper@slt.lk
Personnel:
  Competent Authority: Mangala Senarath
  Phone: (94) 65 57312/246/311
Total Employees at this Location: 175
Type of Operation: Pulp mill, Paper mill, Paperboard mill
Pulp Grades and Capacities:
Total pulp capacity: 24,500 mt/y
Pulp Mill Data:
  Chemical Pulping Systems:
  Batch digesters: 3
  Bleach Plant Lines:
  No. 1, Sequence: H
  Recycled Fiber Treatment Lines:
  Pulpers: 4 at 25,000 admt/y
Paper/Paperboard Grades and Capacities:
Total paper and paperboard capacity: 24,000 mt/y
Packaging papers
Specialty and industrial
Linerboard
Corrugating medium/fluting
Boxboard/cartonboard
Paper and Paperboard Mill Data:
  Stock Preparation:
  Pulpers: 4
  Refiners: 6
Paper Machines: 2
No. 1, fourdrinier, Trim width 2.5 m
No. 2, fourdrinier, Trim width 2.2 m
  Finishing Equipment:
  Rewinders: 2
  Sheeters: 2
Energy Data:
Power boilers: 1
Combustion turbines: 1 at 2.0 MW

SYRIA

ⓘⓂArab Company for Paper Product (Arapepco)
Aleppo Mill
Khan Al-Assel
Aleppo
Syria
Mailing Address: P.O. Box 1777, Aleppo, Syria
  Phone: (963) 21 511 0000
  Fax: (963) 21 512 3000
  Email: info@arapepco.com, arapepco@net.sy, production@arapepco.com
  Web Address: www.arapepco.com
Personnel:
  Chmn.: Hasan Mohammed Adeeb Badinjki
  Phone: (963) 21 511 0000
  Fax: (963) 21 512 3000
  Email: chairman@arapepco.com
  Plt. Mgr.: Ihsan Badinjki
  Phone: (963) 21 511 0000
  Fax: (963) 21 512 3000
  Email: Ihsanbadenjki@arapepco.com
Total Employees of Company: 110
Total Employees at this Location: 110
Type of Operation: Paperboard mill
Pulp Grades and Capacities:
Total pulp capacity: 52,760 mt/y
Recycled Pulping: 52,760 mt/y
Pulp Mill Data:
  Recycled Fiber Treatment Lines:
  Recycled packaging pulping lines: 1
Paper/Paperboard Grades and Capacities:
Total paper and paperboard capacity: 52,500 mt/y
Linerboard: 20,000 mt/y
Corrugating medium/fluting: 15,000 mt/y
Boxboard/cartonboard: 17,500 mt/y
Paper and Paperboard Mill Data:
Paper Machines: 1
No. 1, fourdrinier, total capacity 52,500 mt/y, Trim width 2.6 m, Corrugating medium/fluting, Linerboard, Boxboard/cartonboard
Energy Data:
Power boilers
Electrical demand for mill: 79 MWh/D

ⓘSyropaper
Ownership: 100% by Azzouz Group
Aleppo road
Al-Barkoum, Damascus
Syria
  Phone: (963) 21-6217200
  Email: nader@azzouzco.com
Personnel:
  Chairman of the Board: Hani Camille Azzouz
  Vice Chairman: Bassel Hani Azzouz
Total Employees of Company: 200
Mill Locations:
Syropaper, Al-Barkoum Mill, Aleppo road., Al-Barkoum, Damascus, Syria, Capacity: 75,000 mt/y, (Paperboard mill)

ⓂDinatex Ltd. Co.
Adra Mill
Ownership: Oriental Paper - Lanatex
Industry Zone
Adra
Syria
  Phone: (963) 11 5850868
  Fax: (963) 11 5850871
Personnel:
  Man. Dir.: Hassane Debs
  Phone: (963) 11 5850868
  Dir.: Dr. Jamal Kanbarieh
  Phone: (963) 11 5850868
  Tech. Mgr.: Mr. Amer
  Phone: (963) 11 5850868
Total Employees at this Location: 80
Type of Operation: Paper mill
Pulp Grades and Capacities:
Total pulp capacity: 8,951 mt/y
Recycled Pulping: 8,951 mt/y
Pulp Mill Data:
  Recycled Fiber Treatment Lines:
  Flotation deinking lines: 1
Paper/Paperboard Grades and Capacities:
Total paper and paperboard capacity: 28,000 mt/y
Tissue: 28,000 mt/y

Syria

Paper and Paperboard Mill Data:
Paper Machines: 1
No. 1, crescent former, Yankee dryer, total capacity 28,000 mt/y, Trim width 2.8 m, Tissue
Energy Data:
Power boilers
Electrical demand for mill: 81 MWh/D

ⓘGeneral Company for Paper Industry (GENCO)
Ownership: Vimpex Al Nemsawia
Almuhandessen Bldg., Floor 11, Salhia Gate
Damascus
Syria
 Phone: (963) 221202/051
 Fax: (963) 224006 /051
Personnel:
 Gen. Mgr. GENCO: Eng. Khalil Al Jameel
 Phone: (963) 51 214 729
 Fax: (963) 51 224 006
Total Employees of Company: 700
Mill Locations:
General Company for Paper Industry (GENCO), Deir Ez-Zor Mill, PO Box 19, PO Box 111, Deir Ez-Zor, Syria, Capacity: 60,000 mt/y, (Pulp mill, Paper mill)
 Phone: (963) 51 224397
 Fax: (963) 51 258026
 Email: rjbashir@scs-net.org

ⓜGeneral Company for Paper Industry (GENCO)
Deir Ez-Zor Mill
PO Box 19, PO Box 111
Deir Ez-Zor
Syria
Mailing Address: Salhia Gate Almuhandessen Bldg., Floor 11, Damascus, Syria
 Phone: (963) 51 224397
 Fax: (963) 51 258026
 Email: rjbashir@scs-net.org
Personnel:
 Mill Mgr.: Dr. Babar Ali
 Phone: (963) 51 224397
 Fax: (963) 51 258026
 Email: packgsdz@scs-net.org
 Tech. Mgr./ Assistant Mill Mgr.: Zuhair Al Naief
 Phone: (963) 51 224397
 Fax: (963) 51 258026
 Email: zu-naief@scs-net.org
 Chief Paper Maker: Khalid Mahmood
 Phone: (963) 51 224397
 Fax: (963) 51 258026
 Prod. Mgr.: Badri Al Abed
 Phone: (963) 51 221202
 Fax: (963) 51 224006
 Tech. Mgr.: Riadh Rajab
 Phone: (963) 51 221202
 Fax: (963) 51 224006
Total Employees at this Location: 650
Type of Operation: Pulp mill, Paper mill
Pulp Grades and Capacities:
 Total pulp capacity: 60,898 mt/y
 Recycled Pulping: 29,867 mt/y
 Other Pulp: 31,030 mt/y
Pulp Mill Data:
 Chemical Pulping Systems:
 Batch digesters: 1
 Bleach Plant Systems: 1
 Chemical Pulping System, Type: Straw, Sequence: PH
 Chemical Recovery Equipment:
 Evaporator lines: 1
 Recovery boilers: 1
 Recycled Fiber Treatment Lines:
 Pulpers: 3 at 120,000 admt/y
Paper/Paperboard Grades and Capacities:
 Total paper and paperboard capacity: 60,000 mt/y
 Packaging papers: 30,000 mt/y
 Corrugating medium/fluting: 30,000 mt/y
Paper and Paperboard Mill Data:
Stock Preparation:
 Pulpers: 3
 Refiners: 11
Paper Machines: 2
No. 1, fourdrinier, total capacity 30,000 mt/y, Trim width 4.5 m, Corrugating medium/fluting
No. 2, fourdrinier, total capacity 30,000 mt/y, Trim width 4.5 m, Packaging papers
Coating Machines: 1
No. 1, on machine
Finishing Equipment:
 Winders: 2 at 200,000 mt/y
 Sheeters: 3 at 3 mt/y
Energy Data:
Power boilers: 2
Electrical demand for mill: 125 MWh/D

ⓜMediterranean Paper Mills (MPM)
Lattakia Mill
Jableh, Lattakia
Syria
 Phone: (963) 41 814537
 Fax: (963) 41 814536
 Email: mpmjalol@scs-net.org
Personnel:
 Gen. Mgr.: Ali Maged Jalloul
 Phone: (963) 41 814537
 Asst. Gen. Mgr.: Mohammad Jalloul
 Phone: (963) 41 814537
Total Employees at this Location: 120
Type of Operation: Paper mill
Pulp Grades and Capacities:
 Total pulp capacity: 7,464 mt/y
 Recycled Pulping: 7,464 mt/y
Pulp Mill Data:
 Recycled Fiber Treatment Lines:
 Flotation deinking lines: 1
Paper/Paperboard Grades and Capacities:
 Total paper and paperboard capacity: 14,000 mt/y
 Tissue: 14,000 mt/y
Paper and Paperboard Mill Data:
Paper Machines: 1
No. 1, crescent former, Yankee dryer, total capacity 14,000 mt/y, Trim width 2.25 m, Tissue, Uncoated woodfree/freesheet
Energy Data:
Power boilers
Electrical demand for mill: 44 MWh/D

ⓘMediterranean Paper Mills (MPM)
Jableh, Lattakia
Syria
 Phone: (963) 41 814537
 Fax: (963) 41 814536
 Email: mpmjalol@scs-net.org
Personnel:
 Gen. Mgr.: Ali Maged Jalloul
 Phone: (963) 41 814537
 Fax: (963) 41 814536
 Asst. Gen. Mgr.: Mohammad Jalloul
 Phone: (963) 41 814537
 Fax: (963) 41 814536
Total Employees at this Location: 120
Mill Locations:
Mediterranean Paper Mills (MPM), Lattakia Mill, Jableh, Lattakia , Syria, Capacity: 14,000 mt/y, (Paper mill)
 Phone: (963) 41 814537
 Fax: (963) 41 814536
 Email: mpmjalol@scs-net.org

ⓘⓜOriental Paper - Lanatex
Damascus Mill
Airport Road - 4th Bridge
Damascus
Syria
Mailing Address: P.O. Box 12304, Damascus, Syria
 Phone: (963) 11 6470000
 Fax: (963) 11 6470001
 Email: orla@net.sy
Personnel:
 Man. Dir.: Hassane Debs
 Phone: (963) 11 6470000
 Dir.: Jamal Kanbarieh
 Phone: (963) 11 6470000
 Tech. Dir.: Mr. Amer
 Phone: (963) 11 6470000
Total Employees at this Location: 100
Type of Operation: Paper mill
Mill Locations:
Dinatex Ltd. Co., Adra Mill, Industry Zone, Adra, Syria, Capacity: 28,000 mt/y, (Paper mill)
 Phone: (963) 11 5850868
 Fax: (963) 11 5850871
Pulp Grades and Capacities:
 Total pulp capacity: 16,048 mt/y
 Recycled Pulping: 16,048 mt/y
Pulp Mill Data:
 Recycled Fiber Treatment Lines:
 Flotation deinking lines: 1
Paper/Paperboard Grades and Capacities:
 Total paper and paperboard capacity: 30,000 mt/y
 Tissue: 30,000 mt/y
Paper and Paperboard Mill Data:
Paper Machines: 2
No. 1, inclined, Yankee dryer, total capacity 10,000 mt/y, Trim width 2.7 m, Tissue
No. 2, crescent former, Yankee dryer, total capacity 20,000 mt/y, Trim width 2.7 m, Tissue
Energy Data:
Power boilers
Electrical demand for mill: 95 MWh/D

ⓜSaffouri Company for Tissue Manufacturing
Damascus Mill
Kherbat Al Wared, Hosh Blas
14141 Damascus
Syria
 Phone: (963) 11 6471002 / 93 211012
 Fax: (963) 11 6473140
 Email: info@saffoury.com
 Web Address: www.saffoury.com
Personnel:
 Gen. Mgr.: Mouhammad Soffory
 Phone: (963) 11 6471002
Type of Operation: Paper mill
Paper/Paperboard Grades and Capacities:
 Total paper and paperboard capacity: 4,000 mt/y
 Tissue: 4,000 mt/y
Paper and Paperboard Mill Data:
Paper Machines: 1
No. 1, (second hand), total capacity 4,000 mt/y, Trim width 2.2 m, Tissue

ⓘSaffouri Company for Tissue Manufacturing
Kherbat Al Wared, Hosh Blas
14141 Damascus
Syria
 Phone: (963) 11 6471002 / 93 211012
 Fax: (963) 11 6473140
 Email: info@saffoury.com
 Web Address: www.saffoury.com
Personnel:
 Gen. Mgr.: Mouhammad Soffory
 Phone: (963) 11 6471002 / 93 211012
 Fax: (963) 11 6473140
Mill Locations:
Saffouri Company for Tissue Manufacturing, Damascus Mill, Kherbat Al Wared, Hosh Blas, 14141 Damascus, Syria, Capacity: 4,000 mt/y, (Paper mill)
 Phone: (963) 11 6471002 / 93 211012
 Fax: (963) 11 6473140
 Email: info@saffoury.com

ⓜSyropaper
Al-Barkoum Mill
Aleppo road.
Al-Barkoum, Damascus
Syria

Personnel:
Managing Director: Nader Yaghmour Azzouz
General Manager: Abboud Bakestani
Total Employees at this Location: 200
Type of Operation: Paperboard mill
Pulp Grades and Capacities:
Total pulp capacity: 67,278 mt/y
Recycled Pulping: 67,278 mt/y
Pulp Mill Data:
Recycled Fiber Treatment Lines:
Recycled packaging pulping lines: 1
Paper/Paperboard Grades and Capacities:
Total paper and paperboard capacity: 75,000 mt/y
Packaging papers: 15,000 mt/y
Linerboard: 30,000 mt/y
Corrugating medium/fluting: 30,000 mt/y
Paper and Paperboard Mill Data:
Paper Machines: 1
No. 1, fourdrinier, total capacity 75,000 mt/y, Trim width 4.3 m, Linerboard, Corrugating medium/fluting, Packaging papers
Energy Data:
Power boilers
Electrical demand for mill: 102 MWh/D

ⓘUnited for Paper Industries (UNI PAPER)
P.O. Box 855
Jordanian-Syrian Free Zone
Syria
Phone: (963) 15 272500,272500,272502
Fax: (963) 15 272505
Email: info@unipaper-ind.com
Mill Locations:
United for Paper Industries (UNI PAPER), Free Zone Mill, P.O. Box 855, Jordanian-Syrian Free Zone, Syria, Capacity: 60,000 mt/y, (Paperboard mill)
Phone: (963) 15 272500,272500,272502
Fax: (963) 15 272505
Email: info@unipaper-ind.com

ⓘⓜUnited for Paper Industries (UNI PAPER)
Free Zone Mill
P.O. Box 855
Jordanian-Syrian Free Zone
Syria
Phone: (963) 15 272500,272500,272502
Fax: (963) 15 272505
Email: info@unipaper-ind.com
Total Employees at this Location: 140
Type of Operation: Paperboard mill
Pulp Grades and Capacities:
Total pulp capacity: 59,771 mt/y
Recycled Pulping: 59,771 mt/y
Pulp Mill Data:
Recycled Fiber Treatment Lines:
Recycled packaging pulping lines: 1
Paper/Paperboard Grades and Capacities:
Total paper and paperboard capacity: 60,000 mt/y
Linerboard: 35,000 mt/y
Corrugating medium/fluting: 25,000 mt/y
Paper and Paperboard Mill Data:
Paper Machines: 1
No. 1, fourdrinier, total capacity 60,000 mt/y, Trim width 2.5 m, Linerboard, Corrugating medium/fluting
Energy Data:
Power boilers
Electrical demand for mill: 83 MWh/D

TAIWAN

ⓘChang Chun Plastics Co., Ltd.
7F, 301, Song Kiang Rd.
Taipei, 10483
Taiwan
Phone: (886) 2 2500 1800
Fax: (886) 2 2501 8317/2518 7988
Email: paul@ccp.com.tw
Web Address: www.ccp.com.tw
Personnel:
Chmn.: S. H. Lin
Phone: (886) 2 25001800
Fax: (886) 2 25018317
Pres.: S. Y. Tseng
Phone: (886) 2 25001800
Fax: (886) 2 25018317
Total Employees of Company: 530
Total Employees at this Location: 125
Mill Locations:
Chang Chun Plastics Co., Ltd., Ta Liao Mill, 8, Hwa Syi Rd., Ta Fa Industrial Park, Ta Liao District 83167, Taiwan, Capacity: 60,000 mt/y, (Paper mill)
Phone: (886) 7 787 2654/ 788 1165
Fax: (886) 7 787 2408/ 787 1710
Email: tafa@ccp.com.tw, tfservice@ms.dcc.com.tw

ⓘⓜChang Chun Plastics Co., Ltd.
Ta Liao Mill
8, Hwa Syi Rd., Ta Fa Industrial Park
Ta Liao District, Kaohsiung City, 83167
Taiwan
Phone: (886) 7 787 2654/ 788 1165
Fax: (886) 7 787 2408/ 787 1710
Email: tafa@ccp.com.tw,
tfservice@ms.dcc.com.tw
Web Address: www.ccp.com.tw
Personnel:
Mill Mgr.: E.T. Lin
Phone: (886) 7 7872654
Email: etlin@ccp.com.tw
Total Employees at this Location: 300
Type of Operation: Paper mill
Paper/Paperboard Grades and Capacities:
Total paper and paperboard capacity: 60,000 mt/y
Specialty and industrial

ⓘⓜChang Shin Paper Mfg. Co., Ltd.
Dah Yuan Mill
Ownership: 100% by private owners
39-1 Gu Ting, Jiumm Tour Village
Dah Yuan, Taoyuan County, 33757
Taiwan
Phone: (886) 3 3865 111
Fax: (886) 3 3865 336
Email: cs.paper@msa.hinet.net
Web Address: www.cspaper.com.tw
Personnel:
Chmn.: S. S. Song
Phone: (886) 3 3865111
Pres.: Luo Long-Siong
Phone: (886) 3 3865111
Type of Operation: Paperboard mill
Paper/Paperboard Grades and Capacities:
Total paper and paperboard capacity: 23,000 mt/y
Linerboard: 23,000 mt/y
Paper and Paperboard Mill Data:
Paper Machines: 2
No. 1, cylinder, total capacity 11,500 mt/y, Trim width 1.25 m, Linerboard
No. 2, cylinder, total capacity 11,500 mt/y, Trim width 1.25 m, Linerboard

ⓘⓜChang Tang Industrial Co., Ltd.
Yuanlin Mill
100, Lane 389, Sec. 2, Yuan Chi Rd.
Yuanlin, Changhua County, 51063
Taiwan
Phone: (886) 4 8356135
Fax: (886) 4 8359474
Personnel:
Chmn.: S. Huang
Phone: (886) 4 8356135
Mgr.: J. T. Lin
Phone: (886) 4 8356135
Total Employees at this Location: 47
Type of Operation: Paper mill
Paper/Paperboard Grades and Capacities:
Total paper and paperboard capacity: 4,500 mt/y
Tissue: 4,500 mt/y

ⓘⓜChao Yang Paper Mfg. Co., Ltd.
Tsao Chiao Mill
Ownership: 100% by private owners
100, Chao Yang Rd., Chao Yang Village
Tsao Chiao, Miaoli County, 36144
Taiwan
Phone: (886) 37 562766
Fax: (886) 37 563966
Personnel:
Chmn.: Wan Shun Chang
Phone: (886) 37 562766
Pres.: C. Y. Chang
Phone: (886) 37 562766
Total Employees at this Location: 45
Type of Operation: Paperboard mill
Paper/Paperboard Grades and Capacities:
Total paper and paperboard capacity: 40,000 mt/y
Boxboard/cartonboard: 40,000 mt/y
Paper and Paperboard Mill Data:
Paper Machines: 1
PM 1, cylinder, total capacity 40,000 mt/y, Trim width 3.4 m, Boxboard/cartonboard

ⓘⓜCheeyee Enterprise Corp.
Ping Tung Mill
201, Ta Cheng Rd.
Pingtung, Pingtung County, 90088
Taiwan
Phone: (886) 8 7529717-9
Fax: (886) 8 7536781
Email: cheeyee201@yahoo.com.tw
Personnel:
Chmn.: H.C. Hou
Phone: (886) 8 7529717-9
Pres.: Y. C. Hou
Phone: (886) 8 7529717-9
Mill Mgr.: P.S. Lee
Phone: (886) 8 7529717-9
Total Employees at this Location: 94
Type of Operation: Pulp mill, Paperboard mill
Paper/Paperboard Grades and Capacities:
Total paper and paperboard capacity: 25,000 mt/y
Corrugating medium/fluting: 25,000 mt/y
Paper and Paperboard Mill Data:
Stock Preparation:
Pulpers: 5
Refiners: 6
Paper Machines: 2
No. 1, fourdrinier, Trim width 2.4 m, Corrugating medium/fluting
No. 2, fourdrinier, Trim width 2.4 m, Corrugating medium/fluting
Finishing Equipment:
Supercalenders: 3
Rewinders: 2

ⓘⓜChen Ho Paper Mfg. Co., Ltd.
Pu Li Mill
104-1, Lung-Sheng Rd.
Pu Li, Nantou County, 54548
Taiwan
Phone: (886) 49 2982680
Fax: (886) 49 2989788
Personnel:
Chmn.: Y. H. Chen Lee
Phone: (886) 49 2982680
Pres.: J. L. Chen
Phone: (886) 49 2982680
Total Employees of Company: 11
Type of Operation: Paper mill
Paper/Paperboard Grades and Capacities:
Total paper and paperboard capacity: 120 mt/y
Uncoated woodfree/freesheet

Taiwan

ⓐⓜ Chen Tjun Paper Mill Industrial Co., Ltd.
Chu Nan Mill
17, Kao Tai Rd.
Chu Nan, Miaoli County, 35057
Taiwan
Phone: (886) 37 467181
Fax: (886) 37 466567
Personnel:
Chmn.: C. W. Liu
Phone: (886) 37 467180
Dir.: S. H. Liu
Phone: (886) 37 467180
Total Employees at this Location: 40
Type of Operation: Paperboard mill
Paper/Paperboard Grades and Capacities:
Total paper and paperboard capacity: 35,000 mt/y
Corrugating medium/fluting: 35,000 mt/y

ⓐⓜ Cheng Dah Paper Co., Ltd
Pu Shin Mill
Ownership: 100% by private owners
271, Sec. 2, Yuan Lu Rd., Tung Men Tsun
Pu Shin, Changhua County, 51347
Taiwan
Phone: (886) 4 8296542
Fax: (886) 4 8292968
Email: paichi@ms12.hinet.net
Personnel:
Chmn. & Pres.: W. C. Wu
Phone: (886) 4 8296542
Special Asst.: J. H. Tsai
Phone: (886) 4 8296542
Total Employees at this Location: 105
Type of Operation: Paper mill
Paper/Paperboard Grades and Capacities:
Total paper and paperboard capacity: 8,500 mt/y
Tissue: 8,500 mt/y

ⓐⓜ Cheng Fung Paper Co., Ltd.
Feng Yuan Mill
Ownership: 100% by private owners
39, Lane 115, Shui Yuan Rd.
Feng Yuan District, Taichung City, 42078
Taiwan
Phone: (886) 4 2524 2141-3
Fax: (886) 4 2527 7270/ 2220
Email: chengcy8@ms54.hinet.net
Personnel:
Chmn./Pres.: J. S. Chuang
Phone: (886) 4 25242141-3
Mill Mgr.: B. C. Chuang
Phone: (886) 4 25242141-3
Total Employees at this Location: 70
Type of Operation: Paperboard mill
Pulp Grades and Capacities:
Total pulp capacity: 23,499 mt/y
Recycled Pulping: 23,499 mt/y
Pulp Mill Data:
Recycled Fiber Treatment Lines:
Recycled packaging pulping lines
Paper/Paperboard Grades and Capacities:
Total paper and paperboard capacity: 23,800 mt/y
Linerboard: 23,800 mt/y
Paper and Paperboard Mill Data:
Paper Machines: 1
No. 1, cylinder, total capacity 23,800 mt/y, Trim width 2.85 m, Linerboard
Energy Data:
Power boilers
Electrical demand for mill: 30 MWh/D

ⓐ Cheng Loong Corporation
1, Sec.1, Min Sheng Rd.
Panchiao District, New Taipei City, 22069
Taiwan
Phone: (886) 2 2222 5131
Fax: (886) 2 2222 6110
Email: clc@mail.clc.com.tw
Web Address: www.clc.com.tw, www.clc.com.tw/eng_index.asp
Personnel:
Chmn.: Suanne Cheng
Phone: (886) 2 2222 5131
Fax: (886) 2 2222 6110
Email: meiko@mail.clc.com.tw
Head of Finan.: Zhonglin Zhou
Phone: (886) 2 2222 5131
Fax: (886) 2 2222 6110
Independent Dir.: Yongji Wang
Phone: (886) 2 2222 5131
Fax: (886) 2 2222 6110
Independent Dir.: Yaoming Yang
Phone: (886) 2 2222 5131
Fax: (886) 2 2222 6110
IR Contact Officer: Maggie Chen
Phone: (886) 2 2222 5131 ext: 205
Fax: (886) 2 2959 9287
Email: jyichen@mail.clc.com.tw
Total Employees of Company: 9,680
Total Employees at this Location: 310
Mill Locations:
Cheng Loong Corporation, Chu Pei Mill, 300, Sec. 2, Chiang Ching Rd., Ta-I Li, Chu Pei 30282, Taiwan, Capacity: 90,000 mt/y, (Paper mill, Paperboard mill)
Phone: (886) 3 5561226/ 1227/ 1228
Fax: (886) 3 5561236/ 2280
Email: clc@mail.clc.com.tw
Cheng Loong Corporation, Hou Li Mill, 2, San-Fong Rd., Hou Li 42147, Taiwan, Capacity: 1,000,000 mt/y, (Paper mill, Paperboard mill)
Phone: (886) 4 2556 5160-9
Fax: (886) 4 2557 2303
Email: clc@mail.clc.com.tw
Cheng Loong Corporation, Hsinchu Mill, No. 308, Niu Pu Rd. 300, Chung Pu Li 30091, Taiwan, Capacity: 68,000 mt/y, (Paperboard mill)
Phone: (886) 3 5388193
Fax: (886) 3 5387548
Email: clc@mail.clc.com.tw
Cheng Loong Corporation Tayuan Mill, Ta Yuan Mill, 116 Ta-kung Rd., Lin 15, Beigang Tsuen, Ta Yuan 33759, Taiwan, Capacity: 500,000 mt/y, (Paperboard mill)
Phone: (886) 3 386 8311
Fax: (886) 3 386 6372/ 385 2420
Email: clc@mail.clc.com.tw
Shanghai Chung Loong Paper Co., Ltd., Shanghai Mill (69.47% owned), No. 489 Xiupu Road, Kang Qiao Industrial Zone, Pudong District, Shanghai 201315, China, Capacity: 420,118 mt/y, (Paperboard mill)
Phone: (86) 21 58129798
Fax: (86) 21 58128986
Email: clp@mail.clc.com.tw

ⓜ Cheng Loong Corporation
Chu Pei Mill
300, Sec. 2, Chiang Ching Rd., Ta-I Li
Chu Pei, Hsinchu County, 30282
Taiwan
Phone: (886) 3 5561226/ 1227/ 1228
Fax: (886) 3 5561236/ 2280
Email: clc@mail.clc.com.tw
Web Address: www.clc.com.tw
Personnel:
Mill Mgr.: Yin-Li Chen
Phone: (886) 3 5561226/ 1227/ 1228
Email: billychen@mail.clc.com.tw
Total Employees at this Location: 250
Type of Operation: Paper mill, Paperboard mill
Pulp Grades and Capacities:
Total pulp capacity: 40,264 mt/y
Recycled Pulping: 40,264 mt/y
Pulp Mill Data:
Bleach Plant Systems: 1
DIP
Recycled Fiber Treatment Lines:
Flotation deinking lines: 1 at 18,000 admt/y
Pulpers: 1 at 30,000 admt/y
Washing deinking lines: 1 at 18,000 admt/y
Paper/Paperboard Grades and Capacities:
Total paper and paperboard capacity: 90,000 mt/y
Tissue: 48,000 mt/y
Boxboard/cartonboard: 42,000 mt/y
Paper and Paperboard Mill Data:
Stock Preparation:
Pulpers: 9
Refiners: 15
Paper Machines: 3
No. 11, cylinder, Yankee dryer, total capacity 8,000 mt/y, Trim width 1.9 m, Tissue
No. 13, cylinder, total capacity 42,000 mt/y, Trim width 2.54 m, Boxboard/cartonboard
No. 15, crescent former, Yankee dryer, total capacity 40,000 mt/y, Trim width 3.65 m, Tissue, Uncoated woodfree/freesheet
Coating Machines: 1
No. 1, total capacity 35,000 mt/y., on machine
Finishing Equipment:
Winders: 4
Rewinders: 4
Sheeters: 4
Energy Data:
Power boilers: 3
Combustion turbines: 1 at 4.0 MW
Electrical demand for mill: 209 MWh/D

ⓜ Cheng Loong Corporation
Hou Li Mill
2, San-Fong Rd.
Hou Li, Taichung City, 42147
Taiwan
Phone: (886) 4 2556 5160-9
Fax: (886) 4 2557 2303
Email: clc@mail.clc.com.tw
Web Address: www.clc.com.tw
Personnel:
Mill Mgr.: Rong Yi Chang
Phone: (886) 4 2556 5160-9
Email: yon@mail.clc.com.tw
Purch. Agt.: H. L. Lu
Phone: (886) 4 2556 5160-9
Email: hlliu@mail.clc.com.tw
Asst. VP: C. T. Chen
Phone: (886) 4 2556 5160-9
Email: ctchen1@mail.clc.com.tw
Total Employees at this Location: 800
Type of Operation: Paper mill, Paperboard mill
Pulp Grades and Capacities:
Total pulp capacity: 880,339 mt/y
Recycled Pulping: 880,339 mt/y
Pulp Mill Data:
Recycled Fiber Treatment Lines:
Recycled packaging pulping lines
Paper/Paperboard Grades and Capacities:
Total paper and paperboard capacity: 1,000,000 mt/y
Uncoated woodfree/freesheet: 25,000 mt/y
Coated woodfree/freesheet: 60,000 mt/y
Linerboard: 600,000 mt/y
Corrugating medium/fluting: 240,000 mt/y
Boxboard/cartonboard: 75,000 mt/y
Paper and Paperboard Mill Data:
Stock Preparation:
Pulpers: 5
Refiners: 1
Paper Machines: 6
No. 5, (Supplier: Kobayashi/Metso.), fourdrinier, total capacity 40,000 mt/y, Trim width 2.7 m, Boxboard/cartonboard
No. 6, (Supplier: Kobayashi/Yueli.), cylinder, total capacity 35,000 mt/y, Trim width 2.5 m, Boxboard/cartonboard
No. 7, Gap former (2), total capacity 240,000 mt/y, Trim width 6.9 m, Corrugating medium/fluting
No. 8, Ultraformer, total capacity 180,000 mt/y, Trim width 4.2 m, Linerboard
No. 9, SymFormer, total capacity 85,000 mt/y, Trim width 3.4 m, Uncoated woodfree/freesheet, Coated woodfree/freesheet

No. 10, fourdrinier (3), total capacity 420,000 mt/y, Trim width 7.25 m, Linerboard
Coating Machines: 1
PM 9, total capacity 61,000 mt/y., off machine
Finishing Equipment:
Supercalenders: 1 at 78,000 mt/y
Rewinders: 2 at 108,000 mt/y
Sheeters: 3 at 108,000 mt/y
Energy Data:
Power boilers: 3
Steam turbines: 2 at 87 MW
Electrical demand for mill: 1,323 MWh/D

Ⓜ Cheng Loong Corporation
Hsinchu Mill
No. 308, Niu Pu Rd. 300
Chung Pu Li, Hsinchu County, 30091
Taiwan
Phone: (886) 3 5388193
Fax: (886) 3 5387548
Email: clc@mail.clc.com.tw
Web Address: www.clc.com.tw
Personnel:
Mill Mgr.: H. J. Lin
Phone: (886) 3 5388193
Total Employees at this Location: 100
Type of Operation: Paperboard mill
Pulp Grades and Capacities:
Total pulp capacity: 66,970 mt/y
Recycled Pulping: 66,970 mt/y
Pulp Mill Data:
Recycled Fiber Treatment Lines:
Recycled packaging pulping lines
Paper/Paperboard Grades and Capacities:
Total paper and paperboard capacity: 68,000 mt/y
Linerboard: 68,000 mt/y
Paper and Paperboard Mill Data:
Stock Preparation:
Pulpers: 3
Refiners: 6
Paper Machines: 1
No. 3, cylinder (6), total capacity 68,000 mt/y, Trim width 3.5 m, Linerboard
Finishing Equipment:
Rewinders: 1 at 57,000 mt/y
Energy Data:
Power boilers: 1
Electrical demand for mill: 89 MWh/D

Ⓜ Cheng Loong Corporation Tayuan Mill
Ta Yuan Mill
Ownership: 100% by Cheng Loong Corporation
116 Ta-kung Rd., Lin 15, Beigang Tsuen
Ta Yuan, Taoyuan County, 33759
Taiwan
Phone: (886) 3 386 8311
Fax: (886) 3 386 6372/ 385 2420
Email: clc@mail.clc.com.tw
Web Address: www.clc.com.tw
Personnel:
Mill Mgr.: Stoney Chung
Phone: (886) 3 386 8311
Email: stoney@mail.clc.com.tw
Chief. Eng.: Jeffrey Lee
Phone: (886) 3 386 8311
Email: jefflee@mail.clc.com.tw
Total Employees at this Location: 250
Type of Operation: Paperboard mill
Pulp Grades and Capacities:
Total pulp capacity: 482,047 mt/y
Recycled Pulping: 482,047 mt/y
Pulp Mill Data:
Recycled Fiber Treatment Lines:
Recycled packaging pulping lines
Paper/Paperboard Grades and Capacities:
Total paper and paperboard capacity: 500,000 mt/y
Linerboard: 280,000 mt/y
Corrugating medium/fluting: 220,000 mt/y
Paper and Paperboard Mill Data:
Stock Preparation:
Pulpers: 5
Refiners: 10
Paper Machines: 2
No. 1, fourdrinier (3), total capacity 280,000 mt/y, Trim width 4.6 m, Linerboard
No. 2, fourdrinier (3), total capacity 220,000 mt/y, Trim width 4.6 m, Corrugating medium/fluting
Finishing Equipment:
Rewinders: 2 at 450,000 mt/y
Energy Data:
Power boilers: 1
Steam turbines: 1 at 10.8 MW
Electrical demand for mill: 578 MWh/D

ⓄⓂ Chi Hsiang Paper Co., Ltd.
Tou Liu Mill
Ownership: 100% by private owners
39, Fu Hsing Rd.
Tou Liu, Yunlin County, 64069
Taiwan
Phone: (886) 5 5570958
Fax: (886) 5 5570314
Email: chi.hsiang@msa.hinet.net
Personnel:
Chmn.: M. J. Hsiao
Phone: (886) 5 5570958
Pres.: S. H. Hsu
Phone: (886) 5 5570958
Total Employees at this Location: 20
Type of Operation: Paper mill
Paper/Paperboard Grades and Capacities:
Total paper and paperboard capacity: 5,000 mt/y
Specialty and industrial: 5,000 mt/y

Ⓜ Chi Sheng Paper Product Co., Ltd.
Hua Tan Mill
Ownership: Juei Fong Paper Co., Ltd.
327, Sec.1, Yao Feng Rd.
Pu Hsin, Changhua County, 51344
Taiwan
Phone: (886) 4 8291856
Fax: (886) 4 8296164
Email: sunti@ms18.hinet.net
Personnel:
Chmn.: M. H. Kao Lin
Phone: (886) 4 8296161
Pres.: J. Y. Kao
Phone: (886) 4 8296161
Mill Mgr.: K. S. Hsyu
Phone: (886) 4 8296161
Total Employees at this Location: 37
Type of Operation: Paper mill
Paper/Paperboard Grades and Capacities:
Total paper and paperboard capacity: 2,000 mt/y
Tissue: 2,000 mt/y
Paper and Paperboard Mill Data:
Stock Preparation:
Pulpers: 2
Refiners: 3
Paper Machines: 1
No. 1, cylinder, Yankee dryer, Tissue
Coating Machines: 1
No. 1
Finishing Equipment:
Rewinders: 1
Energy Data:
Power boilers: 1

ⓄⓂ Chiao Feng Paper Co., Ltd.
Yuanlin Mill
37, Chung Yung Li
Yuanlin, Changhua County, 51064
Taiwan
Phone: (886) 4 8320968
Fax: (886) 4 8342068
Email: qoo59850105@yahoo.com.tw
Personnel:
Chmn.: Y. J. Wang
Phone: (886) 4 8335668/ 8320968
Pres.: C. T. Wang
Phone: (886) 4 8335668/ 8320968
Total Employees at this Location: 39
Type of Operation: Paper mill
Paper/Paperboard Grades and Capacities:
Total paper and paperboard capacity: 3,500 mt/y
Tissue: 3,500 mt/y

Ⓞ Ching Mei Paper Co., Ltd.
Ownership: 100% by private owners
8F, 50, Sec. 3 Roosevelt Rd.
Taipei, 10088
Taiwan
Phone: (886) 2 23622888
Fax: (886) 2 23659666
Email: tiffany@kpp.com.tw
Web Address: www.kpp.com.tw
Personnel:
Chmn.: Peter Chen
Phone: (886) 2 23622888
Fax: (886) 2 23659666
VP: Y C Huang
Phone: (886) 2 23622888
Fax: (886) 2 23659666
Total Employees of Company: 88
Total Employees at this Location: 8
Mill Locations:
Ching Mei Paper Co., Ltd., Kuan Yin Mill, 10, Rong Kung N. Rd., Kuan Yin Industry Park, Kuan Yin 32853, Taiwan, Capacity: 50,000 mt/y, (Paperboard mill)
Phone: (886) 3 4838666
Fax: (886) 3 4838686
Email: tiffany@kpp.com.tw
King Paper(Xiamen) Co., Ltd., Xiamen Mill, No. 66 Xiafei Rd., Xinyang Industrial Park, Haicang, Xiamen 361022, China, Capacity: 60,000 mt/y, (Paperboard mill)
Phone: (86) 592 651 2288
Fax: (86) 592 651 2277
Email: service@kpp.com.tw

Ⓜ Ching Mei Paper Co., Ltd.
Kuan Yin Mill
10, Rong Kung N. Rd., Kuan Yin Industry Park
Kuan Yin, Taoyuan County, 32853
Taiwan
Phone: (886) 3 4838666
Fax: (886) 3 4838686
Email: tiffany@kpp.com.tw
Personnel:
Mill Mgr.: S. L. Chen
Phone: (886) 3 4838666
Total Employees at this Location: 80
Type of Operation: Paperboard mill
Paper/Paperboard Grades and Capacities:
Total paper and paperboard capacity: 50,000 mt/y
Boxboard/cartonboard: 50,000 mt/y
Paper and Paperboard Mill Data:
Paper Machines: 2
No. 1, multi-cylinder, Trim width 1.6 m, Boxboard/cartonboard
No. 2, multi-cylinder, Trim width 2.2 m, Boxboard/cartonboard
Energy Data:
Power boilers

Ⓞ Chung Hwa Pulp Corporation
Ownership: 55% by Yuen Foong Yu Inc.
4F, 20, Sec. 3, Pateh Rd.
Taipei, 10559
Taiwan
Phone: (886) 2 25794001
Fax: (886) 2 25790175
Email: chp@mail.chp.com.tw
Web Address: www.chp.com.tw
Personnel:

Taiwan

Chmn.: Cheng-Shyong Kuo
Phone: (886) 2 25794001
Fax: (886) 2 25790175
Dpty. Gen. Mgr.: Gu-Feng Lin
Phone: (886) 2 25794001
Fax: (886) 2 25790175
Dpty. Gen. Mgr.: Sheng-Fei Yan
Phone: (886) 2 25794001
Fax: (886) 2 25790175
R&D Dir.: B Y Lo
Phone: (886) 2 25794001
Fax: (886) 2 25790175
Total Employees of Company: 747
Total Employees at this Location: 47
Mill Locations:
Chung Hwa Pulp Corporation, Hualien Mill, 100, Kuang Hwa, Chi An 97356, Taiwan, Capacity: 117,096 mt/y, (Pulp mill, Paper mill)
Phone: (886) 3 8421171
Fax: (886) 3 8422843
Email: shawmj@mail.chp.com.tw, chp@mail.chp.com.tw

ⓜChung Hwa Pulp Corporation
Chiutang Mill
Ownership: 55% by Yuen Foong Yu Inc.
112, Chiu Tang Rd.
Ta Shu District, Kaohsiung City, 84041
Taiwan
Phone: (886) 7 6512611-9
Fax: (886) 7 6512610
Email: yehpinghuang@yfy.com
Web Address: www.chp.com.tw
Personnel:
Mill Mgr.: C. C. Huang
Phone: (886) 7 6512611-9
Assistant Mill Mgr.: F.Y. Charm
Phone: (886) 7 6512611-9
Total Employees at this Location: 667
Type of Operation: Paper mill
Paper/Paperboard Grades and Capacities:
Total paper and paperboard capacity: 399,483 mt/y
Uncoated woodfree/freesheet: 108,171 mt/y
Coated woodfree/freesheet: 291,312 mt/y
Paper and Paperboard Mill Data:
Stock Preparation:
Pulpers: 10
Refiners: 19
Paper Machines: 4
No. 18, hybrid former, total capacity 44,982 mt/y, Trim width 3.32 m, Uncoated woodfree/freesheet
No. 19, fourdrinier, total capacity 63,189 mt/y, Trim width 3.32 m, Uncoated woodfree/freesheet
No. 20, SymFormer, total capacity 105,315 mt/y, Trim width 3.37 m, Coated woodfree/freesheet
No. 21, Bel-Bond, total capacity 185,997 mt/y, Trim width 5.1 m, Coated woodfree/freesheet
Coating Machines: 4
No. 2, total capacity 3,000 mt/y., off machine
No. 6, total capacity 35,000 mt/y., off machine
No. 1 for PM 21, total capacity 186,000 mt/y., off machine
No. 7 for PM 20, total capacity 105,000 mt/y., off machine
Finishing Equipment:
Supercalenders: 13
Rewinders: 11
Sheeters: 20
Energy Data:
Power boilers: 7
Electrical demand for mill: 769 MWh/D

ⓜChung Hwa Pulp Corporation
Taitung Mill
Ownership: 55% by Yuen Foong Yu Inc.
371, Sec. 4, Chung Hsin Rd.
Taitung, Taitung County, 95060
Taiwan
Phone: (886) 89 382250
Fax: (886) 89 382256
Email: tsaur@yfy.com
Web Address: www.yfy.com
Personnel:
Mill Mgr.: R. M. Lin
Phone: (886) 89 382250
Assistant Mill Mgr.: T. S. Tu
Phone: (886) 89 382250
Total Employees at this Location: 467
Type of Operation: Paper mill, Paperboard mill
Paper/Paperboard Grades and Capacities:
Total paper and paperboard capacity: 138,000 mt/y
Uncoated woodfree/freesheet: 40,000 mt/y
Boxboard/cartonboard: 98,000 mt/y
Paper and Paperboard Mill Data:
Stock Preparation:
Pulpers: 6
Refiners: 15
Paper Machines: 5
No. 1, multi-cylinder, Trim width 2.5 m
No. 7, multi-cylinder, Trim width 2.5 m
No. 10, fourdrinier, Trim width 2.5 m
No. 11, multi-cylinder, Trim width 2.5 m
No. 12, Trim width 1.6 m
Coating Machines: 5
No. 1, total capacity 54,000 mt/y., on machine
No. 7, total capacity 48,000 mt/y., on machine
No. 11, total capacity 18,000 mt/y., on machine
No. 4
No. 5, total capacity 21,600 mt/y., on machine
Finishing Equipment:
Rewinders: 3
Sheeters: 5
Energy Data:
Power boilers: 3
Combustion turbines: 2 at 5.8 MW

ⓜChung Hwa Pulp Corporation
Hualien Mill
Ownership: 55% by Yuen Foong Yu Inc.
100, Kuang Hwa
Chi An, Hualien County, 97356
Taiwan
Phone: (886) 3 8421171
Fax: (886) 3 8422843
Email: shawmj@mail.chp.com.tw, chp@mail.chp.com.tw
Web Address: www.chp.com.tw
Personnel:
Dpty. Gen. Mgr.: Sheng-Fei Yan
Phone: (886) 3 8421171
Dpty. Gen. Mgr.: Jhen-Kun Liou
Phone: (886) 3 8421171
Total Employees at this Location: 700
Type of Operation: Pulp mill, Paper mill
Pulp Grades and Capacities:
Total pulp capacity: 275,105 mt/y
Pulp available for market: 211,701 mt/y
Chemical Pulp: 275,105 mt/y
Pulp Mill Data:
Chemical Pulping Systems:
Batch digesters: 11
Pulp Lines: 1
Bleach Plant Systems: 4
No. 1, Sequence: D/CEoHD, Capacity 130,000 admt/y
Chemical Recovery Equipment:
Evaporator lines: 2
Recovery boilers: 2
Pulp Dryers:
Air Float dryers 1, Air Float dryers 1
Paper/Paperboard Grades and Capacities:
Total paper and paperboard capacity: 117,096 mt/y
Uncoated woodfree/freesheet: 97,104 mt/y
Coated woodfree/freesheet: 19,992 mt/y
Paper and Paperboard Mill Data:
Stock Preparation:
Pulpers: 4
Refiners: 7
Paper Machines: 2
No. 1, fourdrinier, total capacity 50,694 mt/y, Trim width 3.25 m, Uncoated woodfree/freesheet
No. 2, fourdrinier, total capacity 66,402 mt/y, Trim width 3.25 m, Uncoated woodfree/freesheet, Coated woodfree/freesheet
Coating Machines: 1
PM 2, total capacity 20,000 mt/y., on machine
Finishing Equipment:
Supercalenders: 1
Rewinders: 2
Sheeters: 2
Energy Data:
Power boilers: 2
Combustion turbines: 4 at 40.0 MW
Electrical demand for mill: 693 MWh/D

ⓜChung Rhy Special Paper Mfg. Co. Ltd.
5, Wu Chuan 2nd Rd. Wu Ku Industrial Park
Wu Ku District, New Taipei City, 24890
Taiwan
Phone: (886) 2 22990977
Fax: (886) 2 22995400
Email: Pateck@ms2.hinet.net
Web Address: www.paperworld.com.tw
Personnel:
Chmn.: Tao-Sheng Chen
Phone: (886) 2 22990977
Fax: (886) 2 22995400
VP: W. P. Tsai
Phone: (886) 2 22990977
Fax: (886) 2 22995400
Mgr. R & D: L. C. Wang
Phone: (886) 2 22990977
Fax: (886) 2 22995400
Mgr.: M. C. Huang
Phone: (886) 2 22990977
Fax: (886) 2 22995400
Total Employees of Company: 150
Total Employees at this Location: 24
Mill Locations:
Chung Rhy Special Paper Mfg. Co., Ltd., Pu Li Mill, 737, Sec. 3, Chung Shan Rd., Pu Li 54551, Taiwan, Capacity: 4,000 mt/y, (Paper mill)
Phone: (886) 49 2913025
Fax: (886) 49 2913367
Email: pateck@ms2.hinet.net

ⓜChung Rhy Special Paper Mfg. Co., Ltd.
Pu Li Mill
Ownership: Chung Rhy Special Paper Mfg. Co. Ltd.
737, Sec. 3, Chung Shan Rd.
Pu Li, Nantou County, 54551
Taiwan
Phone: (886) 49 2913025
Fax: (886) 49 2913367
Email: pateck@ms2.hinet.net
Personnel:
Chmn.: T. S. Chen
Phone: (886) 49 2913025
VP: C. J. Lin
Phone: (886) 49 2913025
Mgr.: M. C. Huang
Phone: (886) 49 2913025
Total Employees at this Location: 126
Type of Operation: Paper mill
Paper/Paperboard Grades and Capacities:
Total paper and paperboard capacity: 4,000 mt/y
Specialty and industrial: 4,000 mt/y
Paper and Paperboard Mill Data:
Paper Machines: 5
No. 1, Yankee dryer, Trim width 1 m
No. 2, Yankee dryer, Trim width 1.3 m
No. 3, Yankee dryer, Trim width 1.8 m
No. 5, Yankee dryer, Trim width 1.3 m
No. 6, Trim width 1.3 m

Taiwan

①⑩Der Lih Paper Co., Ltd.
Tou Liu Mill
7, Min Leh St., Liu Chung Li
Tou Liu, Yunlin County, 64069
Taiwan
  Phone: (886) 5 5571515
  Fax: (886) 5 5572630
Personnel:
  Chmn.: L. Y. Wu
  Phone: (886) 5 5571515
  Pres.: Jen-Jer Chen
  Phone: (886) 5 5571515
Total Employees at this Location: 13
Type of Operation: Paper mill
Paper/Paperboard Grades and Capacities:
  Total paper and paperboard capacity: 4,500 mt/y
  Specialty and industrial: 4,500 mt/y

①⑩Dong Da Paper Mfg. Co., Ltd.
Ming Chien Mill
10-1, Tien Liao Lane, Hsin Che Tsun
Ming Chien, Nantou County, 55148
Taiwan
  Phone: (886) 49 2223769
  Fax: (886) 49 2231113
  Email: abcd1234pound@yahoo.com.tw
Personnel:
  Mill Mgr.: T. S. Yang
  Phone: (886) 49 2223769
  Chmn.: L. F. Lo
  Phone: (886) 49 2223769
Total Employees at this Location: 22
Type of Operation: Paper mill
Paper/Paperboard Grades and Capacities:
  Total paper and paperboard capacity: 4,500 mt/y
  Specialty and industrial: 4,500 mt/y

①⑩Dong Fa Paper Mfg. Co., Ltd.
Puyen Mill
160, Sec.2, Chang Shue Rd.
Pu Yien, Changhua County, 51641
Taiwan
  Phone: (886) 4 8653111-2
  Fax: (886) 4 8653113
  Email: Dongfa@ms37.hinet.net
Personnel:
  Pres. & Chmn.: Y. C. Chen
  Phone: (886) 4 8653111
  Mill Mgr.: J. S. Chen
  Phone: (886) 4 8653111
Total Employees at this Location: 47
Type of Operation: Paper mill
Paper/Paperboard Grades and Capacities:
  Total paper and paperboard capacity: 3,600 mt/y
  Packaging papers
Paper and Paperboard Mill Data:
Paper Machines: 1
PM 1, cylinder, total capacity 3,600 mt/y, Trim width 1.6 m, Packaging papers

①Eng Fong Paper Co., Ltd.
28-6, Po Ya Tou Rd
Taisan District, New Taipei City, 24341
Taiwan
  Phone: (886) 2 29097071
  Fax: (886) 2 29097367
Personnel:
  Chmn.: Y. J. Wang
  Phone: (886) 2 29097071
  Fax: (886) 2 29097367
  Pres.: C. T. Wang
  Phone: (886) 2 29097071
  Fax: (886) 2 29097367
Total Employees of Company: 60
Mill Locations:
Eng Fong Paper Co., Ltd., Yuanlin Mill, 18-7, Chung Yung Li, Yuanlin 51064, Taiwan, Capacity: 1,800 mt/y, (Paper mill)
  Phone: (886) 4 8335668
  Fax: (886) 4 8342068
  Email: qoo59850105@yahoo.com.tw

①Eng Fong Paper Co., Ltd.
Yuanlin Mill
18-7, Chung Yung Li
Yuanlin, Changhua County, 51064
Taiwan
  Phone: (886) 4 8335668
  Fax: (886) 4 8342068
  Email: qoo59850105@yahoo.com.tw
Personnel:
  Mill Mgr.: C. M. Huang
  Phone: (886) 4 8335668
Total Employees at this Location: 60
Type of Operation: Paper mill
Paper/Paperboard Grades and Capacities:
  Total paper and paperboard capacity: 1,800 mt/y
  Tissue: 1,800 mt/y
Paper and Paperboard Mill Data:
Paper Machines: 1
PM 1, cylinder, total capacity 1,800 mt/y, Trim width 1.58 m, Tissue

①⑩Gai Chin Paper Co., Ltd.
Hou Lung Mill
27-1, Du Chuan Tou
Hou Lung, Miaoli County, 35657
Taiwan
  Phone: (886) 37 432803
  Fax: (886) 37 432703
  Email: j570924@ms89.url.com.tw
Personnel:
  Chmn.: C. S. Fan
  Phone: (886) 37 432803
  Pres.: J. H. Fan
  Phone: (886) 37 432803
  Mill Mgr.: J. J. Fan
  Phone: (886) 37 432803
Total Employees at this Location: 36
Type of Operation: Paper mill
Paper/Paperboard Grades and Capacities:
  Total paper and paperboard capacity: 3,700 mt/y
  Specialty and industrial

①⑩Gain Hwang Paper Mfg. Co., Ltd.
Shan Hua Mill
233, Hsing Nung Rd.
Shan Hua, Tainan City, 74160
Taiwan
  Phone: (886) 6 5817111-3
  Fax: (886) 6 5815953
  Email: gain-hwang@umail.hinet.net
Personnel:
  Chmn.: P. L. Liao
  Phone: (886) 6 5817111-3
  VP: Y. C. Lin
  Phone: (886) 6 5817111-3
Total Employees at this Location: 90
Type of Operation: Paper mill
Pulp Grades and Capacities:
  Total pulp capacity: 35,640 mt/y
  Recycled Pulping: 35,640 mt/y
Pulp Mill Data:
  Recycled Fiber Treatment Lines:
  Recycled packaging pulping lines: 1
Paper/Paperboard Grades and Capacities:
  Total paper and paperboard capacity: 35,000 mt/y
  Packaging papers: 35,000 mt/y
Paper and Paperboard Mill Data:
Paper Machines: 1
No. 1, fourdrinier, total capacity 35,000 mt/y, Packaging papers
Energy Data:
Electrical demand for mill: 80 MWh/D

①⑩Horng Ming Paper Co., Ltd.
Chu Nan Mill
15-1, Dah Buu Ding, Kong Goan Lii
Chu Nan, Miaoli County, 35057
Taiwan
  Phone: (886) 37 622777
  Fax: (886) 37 623046
  Email: hmpaper@ms46.hinet.net
Personnel:
  Chmn.: X. J. Liao
  Phone: (886) 37 624677
Total Employees of Company: 19
Type of Operation: Paper mill, Paperboard mill
Paper/Paperboard Grades and Capacities:
  Total paper and paperboard capacity: 24,000 mt/y
  Corrugating medium/fluting: 24,000 mt/y
Paper and Paperboard Mill Data:
Paper Machines: 2
No. 1, cylinder, Trim width 3.1 m, Corrugating medium/fluting
No. 2, cylinder, Trim width 2.2 m, Corrugating medium/fluting
Finishing Equipment:
  Rewinders: 1
Energy Data:
Power boilers: 2

①⑩Hsing Chung Paper Corp.
Wu Chieh Mill
Ownership: employees
7, Xihe Rd.
Wu Chieh, Ilan County, 26844
Taiwan
  Phone: (886) 3 9659000
  Fax: (886) 3 9651127
  Email: a2361@hcpaper.com.tw
  Web Address: www.hcpaper.com.tw
Personnel:
  Chmn.: Sing-Fong Wang
  Phone: (886) 3 9659000
  Pres.: Ming-Chih Lin
  Phone: (886) 3 9659000
  VP: M. J. Lin
  Phone: (886) 3 9659000
  Mgr.: J. C. Wang
  Phone: (886) 3 9659000
  Mill Mgr.: Chen-Gin Kuo
  Phone: (886) 3 9659000
Total Employees at this Location: 218
Type of Operation: Paper mill
Pulp Grades and Capacities:
  Total pulp capacity: 1,393 mt/y
  Recycled Pulping: 1,393 mt/y
Pulp Mill Data:
  Mechanical Pulping Systems:
  Conventional grinders
  RMP systems
Pulp Lines: 1
Paper/Paperboard Grades and Capacities:
  Total paper and paperboard capacity: 22,800 mt/y
  Uncoated woodfree/freesheet: 11,400 mt/y
  Packaging papers: 11,400 mt/y
Paper and Paperboard Mill Data:
  Stock Preparation:
  Pulpers: 6
  Refiners: 18
Paper Machines: 2
No. 5, fourdrinier, total capacity 7,800 mt/y, Trim width 1.88 m, Uncoated woodfree/freesheet, Packaging papers
No. 7, fourdrinier, total capacity 15,000 mt/y, Trim width 2.5 m, Uncoated woodfree/freesheet, Packaging papers
Coating Machines: 2
No. 1, total capacity 42,000 mt/y., on machine
No. 2, total capacity 10,000 mt/y., off machine
Finishing Equipment:
  Supercalenders: 1
  Rewinders: 5
  Sheeters: 3
Energy Data:

Taiwan

Power boilers: 4
Electrical demand for mill: 42 MWh/D

ⒸⓂHua Te Mei Paper Co., Ltd.
Pu Hsing mill
70, Shi-An S. Rd.
Pu Hsing, Changhua County, 51345
Taiwan
  Phone: (886) 4 8291106
  Fax: (886) 4 8296878
  Email: t8291106@ms32.hinet.net
Personnel:
  Chmn.: C. T. Cheng
  Phone: (886) 4 8291106
  Pres.: C. K. Hung
  Phone: (886) 4 8291106
Total Employees at this Location: 56
Type of Operation: Paperboard mill
Paper/Paperboard Grades and Capacities:
  Total paper and paperboard capacity: 23,000 mt/y
  Boxboard/cartonboard: 23,000 mt/y

ⒸⓂIexon Enterprises Co., Ltd.
Shen Kang Mill
885, Chung Shan Rd.
Shen Kang, Taichung City, 42941
Taiwan
  Phone: (886) 4 25623406
  Fax: (886) 4 25620917
Personnel:
  Pres. & Gen. Mgr.: W. H. Chen
  Phone: (886) 4 25623406
Type of Operation: Paperboard mill
Paper/Paperboard Grades and Capacities:
  Total paper and paperboard capacity: 960 mt/y

ⒸⓂJeng Chia Paper Product Co., Ltd.
Tai Pao Mill
19, Chung Shin Rd., Chia-Tai Ind. Park
Tai Pao, Chia-I County, 61252
Taiwan
  Phone: (886) 5 2379966
  Fax: (886) 5 2379969
Personnel:
  Chmn.: S. C. Lin
  Phone: (886) 5 2379966
  Pres.: Y. Y. Lin
  Phone: (886) 5 2379966
Total Employees at this Location: 29
Type of Operation: Paper mill
Paper/Paperboard Grades and Capacities:
  Total paper and paperboard capacity: 22,000 mt/y
  Specialty and industrial

ⓂJih Sun Paper Ind. Co., Ltd.
Kuanyin Hsiang Mill
5, Kuo Chien 3rd Road
Kuanyin Hsiang, Taoyuan County, 32844
Taiwan
  Phone: (886) 3 483 2877
  Fax: (886) 3 483 2399
  Email: jsp.paper@msa.hinet.net
Personnel:
  Chmn.: Ting-Shing Lin
  Phone: (886) 3 483 2877
  Pres.: Jhe-Huei Lin
  Phone: (886) 3 483 2877
  VP: Ching-Jhang Huang
  Phone: (886) 3 483 2877
  Man. Dir.: Shu-Fen Huang
  Phone: (886) 3 483 2877
Total Employees at this Location: 135
Type of Operation: Paper mill
Paper/Paperboard Grades and Capacities:
  Total paper and paperboard capacity: 50,000 mt/y
  Uncoated woodfree/freesheet: 50,000 mt/y
Paper and Paperboard Mill Data:
Paper Machines: 1
No. 1, fourdrinier, total capacity 50,000 mt/y, Trim width 2.6 m, Uncoated woodfree/freesheet
Energy Data:
Power boilers
Electrical demand for mill: 98 MWh/D

ⒸJih Sun Paper Ind. Co., Ltd.
5, Kuo Chien 3rd Road
Kuanyin Hsiang, Taoyuan County, 32844
Taiwan
  Phone: (886) 3 483 2877
  Fax: (886) 3 483 2399
  Email: jsp.paper@msa.hinet.net
Mill Locations:
Jih Sun Paper Ind. Co., Ltd., Kuanyin Hsiang Mill, 5, Kuo Chien 3rd Road, Kuanyin Hsiang 32844, Taiwan, Capacity: 50,000 mt/y, (Paper mill)
  Phone: (886) 3 483 2877
  Fax: (886) 3 483 2399
  Email: jsp.paper@msa.hinet.net

ⒸⓂJin Diing Co Ltd.
Hsin Ying Mill
14, Pa Teh Rd.
Hsinying District, Tainan City, 73054
Taiwan
  Phone: (886) 6 6529957
  Fax: (886) 6 6527621
  Email: jing.din@msa.hinet.net
Personnel:
  Chmn. & Pres.: H. S. Lin
  Phone: (886) 6 6529955-6
  VP: H. F. Chen
  Phone: (886) 6 6529955-6
Total Employees at this Location: 38
Type of Operation: Paper mill
Paper/Paperboard Grades and Capacities:
  Total paper and paperboard capacity: 2,600 mt/y
  Tissue: 2,600 mt/y
Paper and Paperboard Mill Data:
Paper Machines: 1
PM 1, cylinder, total capacity 2,600 mt/y, Trim width 2.36 m, Tissue

ⒸⓂJoung Yin Enterprise Co., Ltd.
Hsin Kang Mill
66, Yaio Tze Chu, Tsai Kong Village
Hsin Kang, Chia-I County, 61642
Taiwan
  Phone: (886) 5 3771211
  Fax: (886) 5 3770223
Personnel:
  Chmn.: W. H. Lin
  Phone: (886) 5 3771211
Total Employees at this Location: 25
Type of Operation: Paper mill
Paper/Paperboard Grades and Capacities:
  Total paper and paperboard capacity: 1,500 mt/y
  Uncoated woodfree/freesheet

ⒸJuei Fong Paper Co., Ltd.
345, Sec. 1, Yaofong Rd., Pu Hsin
Changhwa County, 51344
Taiwan
  Phone: (886) 4 829 6161
  Fax: (886) 4 829 6163
  Email: sunti@ms18.hinet.net
Personnel:
  Chmn.: M. H. Kao Lin
  Phone: (886) 4 829 6161
  Fax: (886) 4 829 6163
  Pres.: J. Y. Kao
  Phone: (886) 4 829 6161
  Fax: (886) 4 829 6163
Total Employees at this Location: 22
Mill Locations:
Chi Sheng Paper Product Co., Ltd., Hua Tan Mill, 327, Sec.1, Yao Feng Rd., Pu Hsin 51344, Taiwan, Capacity: 2,000 mt/y, (Paper mill)
  Phone: (886) 4 8291856
  Fax: (886) 4 8296164
  Email: sunti@ms18.hinet.net
Juei Fong Paper Co., Ltd., Pi Tou Mill, 32, Sec. 4, Chang Shui Rd., Be Tou 52341, Taiwan, Capacity: 6,000 mt/y, (Paper mill)
  Phone: (886) 4 8922126
  Fax: (886) 4 8927736
Juei Fong Paper Co., Ltd., Pu Shin Mill, 345, Sec.1, Yaofong Rd., Pu Hsin 51344, Taiwan, Capacity: 7,000 mt/y, (Paper mill)
  Phone: (886) 4 8296161
  Fax: (886) 4 8296163
  Email: sunti@ms18.hinet.net

ⓂJuei Fong Paper Co., Ltd.
Pi Tou Mill
32, Sec. 4, Chang Shui Rd.
Be Tou, Changhua County, 52341
Taiwan
  Phone: (886) 4 8922126
  Fax: (886) 4 8927736
Personnel:
  Mill Mgr.: J. Y. Huang
  Phone: (886) 4 8922126
Total Employees at this Location: 38
Type of Operation: Paper mill
Paper/Paperboard Grades and Capacities:
  Total paper and paperboard capacity: 6,000 mt/y
  Tissue: 6,000 mt/y

ⓂJuei Fong Paper Co., Ltd.
Pu Shin Mill
345, Sec.1, Yaofong Rd.
Pu Hsin, Changhua County, 51344
Taiwan
  Phone: (886) 4 8296161
  Fax: (886) 4 8296163
  Email: sunti@ms18.hinet.net
Personnel:
  Mill Mgr.: W. Y. Lai
  Phone: (886) 4 8296161
Total Employees at this Location: 42
Type of Operation: Paper mill
Paper/Paperboard Grades and Capacities:
  Total paper and paperboard capacity: 7,000 mt/y
  Tissue: 7,000 mt/y

ⒸⓂKao Nan Pulp & Paper Mfg. Co., Ltd.
Nan Tzyy Dist Mill
900-1, Kao Nan Rd.
Nan Tzyy District, Kaohsiung City, 81160
Taiwan
  Phone: (886) 7 3511762
  Fax: (886) 7 3526374
  Email: e410220@yahoo.com.tw
Personnel:
  Chmn./Pres.: R. C. Lee
  Phone: (886) 7 3511762
  Mgr.: M. T. Lee
  Phone: (886) 7 3511762
Total Employees at this Location: 40
Type of Operation: Paper mill
Paper/Paperboard Grades and Capacities:
  Total paper and paperboard capacity: 4,000 mt/y
  Packaging papers: 4,000 mt/y
  Specialty and industrial

ⒸKimberly-Clark Taiwan
Ownership: 100% by Kimberly-Clark Corp.
8F, 8, Sec. 5, Hsin Yi Rd.
Taipei, 11049
Taiwan
  Phone: (886) 2 23458388
  Fax: (886) 2 23458387
  Email: jenny.yeh@kcc.com
  Web Address: www.kcc.com
Personnel:
  Chmn.: Achal Agarwal

Taiwan

Phone: (886) 2 23458388
Fax: (886) 2 23458387
Pres.: Varaporn Dhamcharee
Phone: (886) 2 23458388
Fax: (886) 2 23458387
VP (Marketing & Research): K. D. Kim
Phone: (886) 2 23458388
Fax: (886) 2 23458387
Dir. (Family Care): C. M. Chen
Phone: (886) 2 23458388
Fax: (886) 2 23458387
Dir. (Finance): LiLi Chang
Phone: (886) 2 23458388
Fax: (886) 2 23458387
Dir. (Human Resources): Fiona Tsai
Phone: (886) 2 23458388
Fax: (886) 2 23458387
Dir. (Sales): Thomas Hsu
Phone: (886) 2 23458388
Fax: (886) 2 23458387
Dir. (Baby & Infant Care): Grace Hong
Phone: (886) 2 23458388
Fax: (886) 2 23458387
Dir. (Feminine Care): Angela Hsieh
Phone: (886) 2 23458388
Fax: (886) 2 23458387
Total Employees at this Location: 270
Mill Locations:
Kimberly-Clark Taiwan, Chungli Mill, 240, Chung Hsin Rd., Hsin Wu 32750, Taiwan, Capacity: 23,000 mt/y, (Paper mill)
Phone: (886) 3 4772772
Fax: (886) 3 4772777
Email: chungming.huang@kcc.com
Kimberly-Clark Taiwan, Hsinying Mill, 321, Tai Tze Rd., Hsinying 73044, Taiwan, Capacity: 40,000 mt/y, (Paper mill)
Phone: (886) 6 6563446
Fax: (886) 6 6561436
Email: chente.yang@kcc.com
Kimberly-Clark Taiwan, Tayuan Mill, 262 Chung Shan Rd., Tayuan 33759, Taiwan, Capacity: 39,992 mt/y, (Paper mill)
Phone: (886) 3 386 4935
Fax: (886) 3 386 4400
Email: Lance.Yang@kcc.com

Ⓜ Kimberly-Clark Taiwan
Chungli Mill
Ownership: 100% by Kimberly-Clark Corp.
240, Chung Hsin Rd.
Hsin Wu, Taoyuan County, 32750
Taiwan
Phone: (886) 3 4772772
Fax: (886) 3 4772777
Email: chungming.huang@kcc.com
Web Address: www.kcc.com
Personnel:
Mill Mgr. (FC): C. M. Huang
Phone: (886) 3 4772772
Mill Mgr. (PC): C. H. Hsieh
Phone: (886) 3 4772772
Total Employees at this Location: 95
Type of Operation: Paper mill
Paper/Paperboard Grades and Capacities:
Total paper and paperboard capacity: 23,000 mt/y
Tissue: 23,000 mt/y
Paper and Paperboard Mill Data:
Stock Preparation:
Pulpers: 2
Refiners: 2
Paper Machines: 2
No. 1, total capacity 11,500 mt/y, Trim width 2.2 m, Tissue
No. 2, total capacity 11,500 mt/y, Trim width 2.2 m, Tissue, Uncoated woodfree/freesheet
Finishing Equipment:
Supercalenders: 3
Rewinders: 2
Sheeters: 2

Energy Data:
Power boilers: 1
Electrical demand for mill: 46 MWh/D

Ⓜ Kimberly-Clark Taiwan
Hsinying Mill
Ownership: 100% by Kimberly-Clark Corp.
321, Tai Tze Rd.
Hsinying, Tainan City, 73044
Taiwan
Phone: (886) 6 6563446
Fax: (886) 6 6561436
Email: chente.yang@kcc.com
Web Address: www.kcc.com, www.sujay.com.tw/index.asp
Personnel:
Mill Mgr.: Y. F. Tu
Phone: (886) 6 6563446
Total Employees at this Location: 175
Type of Operation: Paper mill
Paper/Paperboard Grades and Capacities:
Total paper and paperboard capacity: 40,000 mt/y
Tissue: 40,000 mt/y
Paper and Paperboard Mill Data:
Stock Preparation:
Pulpers: 7
Refiners: 4
Paper Machines: 3
No. 1, fourdrinier, Yankee dryer, total capacity 13,500 mt/y, Trim width 2.1 m, Tissue, Uncoated woodfree/freesheet
No. 2, fourdrinier, Yankee dryer, total capacity 13,500 mt/y, Trim width 2.1 m, Tissue, Uncoated woodfree/freesheet
No. 3, fourdrinier, Yankee dryer, total capacity 13,000 mt/y, Trim width 2.1 m, Tissue, Uncoated woodfree/freesheet
Finishing Equipment:
Rewinders: 3
Energy Data:
Power boilers: 2
Electrical demand for mill: 120 MWh/D

Ⓜ Kimberly-Clark Taiwan
Tayuan Mill
Ownership: 100% by Kimberly-Clark Corp.
262 Chung Shan Rd.
Tayuan, Taoyuan County, 33759
Taiwan
Phone: (886) 3 386 4935
Fax: (886) 3 386 4400
Email: Lance.Yang@kcc.com
Web Address: www.kcc.com
Personnel:
Mill Mgr./Mfg. Dir. (Family Care): C. M. Huang
Phone: (886) 3 386 4935
Tissue Machine Mgr.: J. K. Lee
Phone: (886) 3 386 4935
Mgr. (Converting): M. H. Lin
Phone: (886) 3 386 4935
Total Employees at this Location: 165
Type of Operation: Paper mill
Paper/Paperboard Grades and Capacities:
Total paper and paperboard capacity: 39,992 mt/y
Tissue: 39,992 mt/y
Paper and Paperboard Mill Data:
Stock Preparation:
Pulpers: 2
Refiners: 2
Paper Machines: 2
No. 1, suction former, total capacity 19,992 mt/y, Trim width 2.9 m, Tissue
No. 2, suction former, total capacity 20,000 mt/y, Trim width 2.9 m, Tissue
Finishing Equipment:
Rewinders: 1
Energy Data:
Power boilers: 1
Electrical demand for mill: 57 MWh/D

ⓄⓂ Kuan Yuan Paper Mfg. Co., Ltd.
Chunan Mill
18, Chu Nan, Shan Jia Li
Chu Nan, Miaoli County, 35048
Taiwan
Phone: (886) 37 477715
Fax: (886) 37 476668
Email: kycm@kyp.com.tw
Web Address: www.kyp.com.tw
Personnel:
Chmn.: Kuan Yuan Hsieh
Phone: (886) 37 477715
Pres.: L. H. Hsieh
Phone: (886) 37 477715
VP: Dong Lung Hsieh
Phone: (886) 37 477715
VP: Chin Fong Hsieh
Phone: (886) 37 477715
Mgr.: Tong Pin Kuo
Phone: (886) 37 477715
Total Employees of Company: 320
Total Employees at this Location: 75
Type of Operation: Paperboard mill
Mill Locations:
Kuan Yuan Paper Mfg. Co. Ltd., Taichung Mill, 1, Gon 1st Rd., Dajia District 43767, Taiwan, Capacity: 216,000 mt/y, (Paperboard mill)
Phone: (886) 4 26414465
Fax: (886) 4 26812200
Email: kytm@ kyp.com.tw
Paper/Paperboard Grades and Capacities:
Total paper and paperboard capacity: 25,200 mt/y
Boxboard/cartonboard: 25,200 mt/y
Paper and Paperboard Mill Data:
Paper Machines: 2
No. 2, cylinder, Trim width 1.3 m, Boxboard/cartonboard
No. 3, cylinder, Trim width 1.9 m, Boxboard/cartonboard
Coating Machines: 1
No. 1, total capacity 18,000 mt/y., on machine
Finishing Equipment:
Rewinders: 1
Sheeters: 2

Ⓜ Kuan Yuan Paper Mfg. Co. Ltd.
Taichung Mill
Ownership: Kuan Yuan Paper Mfg. Co., Ltd.
1, Gon 1st Rd.
Dajia District, Taichung City, 43767
Taiwan
Phone: (886) 4 26414465
Fax: (886) 4 26812200
Email: kytm@, kyp.com.tw
Web Address: www.kyp.com.tw
Personnel:
Chmn.: Guangyuan Xie
Gen. Mgr.: Luhe Xie
V.P., Mill Mgr.: Dong Lung Hsieh
Phone: (886) 4 26814468
CFO: S. L. Chen
Phone: (886) 4 26814468
Total Employees at this Location: 210
Type of Operation: Paperboard mill
Pulp Grades and Capacities:
Total pulp capacity: 199,591 mt/y
Recycled Pulping: 199,591 mt/y
Pulp Mill Data:
Recycled Fiber Treatment Lines:
Flotation deinking lines: 2
Pulpers: 7
Paper/Paperboard Grades and Capacities:
Total paper and paperboard capacity: 216,000 mt/y
Boxboard/cartonboard: 216,000 mt/y
Paper and Paperboard Mill Data:
Stock Preparation:
Pulpers: 9
Refiners: 10
Paper Machines: 2

Taiwan

No. 1, cylinder (8), total capacity 90,000 mt/y, Trim width 2.8 m, Boxboard/cartonboard
No. 2, cylinder (10), total capacity 126,000 mt/y, Trim width 3.3 m, Boxboard/cartonboard
Coating Machines: 2
PM 1, total capacity 70,000 mt/y., on machine
PM 2, total capacity 130,000 mt/y., on machine
Finishing Equipment:
Rewinders: 2
Sheeters: 5
Energy Data:
Power boilers: 2
Steam turbines
Electrical demand for mill: 305 MWh/D

Kuo Zong Paper Mfg. Co., Ltd.
Kuan Tien Mill
77, Gong Yeh W. Rd., Erh Chen Tsun
Kuan Tien District, Tainan City, 72048
Taiwan
  Phone: (886) 6 6985665
  Fax: (886) 6 6987785
Personnel:
  Chmn.: M. C. Tseng
  Phone: (886) 6 6985665
  Pres.: K. S. Tseng
  Phone: (886) 6 6985665
Total Employees at this Location: 21
Type of Operation: Paper mill
Paper/Paperboard Grades and Capacities:
  Total paper and paperboard capacity: 8,000 mt/y
  Specialty and industrial
Paper and Paperboard Mill Data:
Paper Machines: 2
PM 1, cylinder, Trim width 2.5 m, Boxboard/cartonboard
PM 2, cylinder, Trim width 3 m, Boxboard/cartonboard

Lien Tai Paper Co., Ltd.
Tsao Chiao mill
107, Chao Yang Tsun, Chao Yang Rd.
Tsao Chiao, Miaoli County
Taiwan
  Phone: (886) 37 563257
  Fax: (886) 37 562799
  Email: shenyuan803@yahoo.com.tw
Personnel:
  Chmn.: Wan Kuey Lien
  Phone: (886) 37 563257
  Pres.: Wan-Long Lien
  Phone: (886) 37 563257
Total Employees at this Location: 33
Type of Operation: Paper mill
Pulp Grades and Capacities:
  Total pulp capacity: 8,000 mt/y
  Recycled Pulping: 8,000 mt/y
Pulp Mill Data:
Pulp Lines: 1
  Recycled Fiber Treatment Lines:
  Flotation deinking lines: 1 at 8,000 admt/y

Lih Tai Industrial Corp.
1st Floor, 42, Shing Chang Street
San Ming District, Kaohsiung City, 80767
Taiwan
  Phone: (886) 7 387 3780
  Fax: (886) 7 380 7856
  Email: lihtai@ms36.hinet.net
  Web Address: www.tungtay.com.tw/c_lihtai.htm
Total Employees of Company: 155
Total Employees at this Location: 28
Mill Locations:
Lih Tai Industrial Corp., Chu Tien Mill, 57, Ta Chen Rd., Ta Fu Tsun, Chu Tien 91141, Taiwan, Capacity: 10,000 mt/y, (Paper mill)
  Phone: (886) 8 7773367
  Fax: (886) 8 7773382
  Email: lihtai@ms36.hinet.net

Lih Tai Industrial Corp.
Chu Tien Mill
57, Ta Chen Rd., Ta Fu Tsun
Chu Tien, Pingtung County, 91141
Taiwan
  Mailing Address: Rm. 412, 10, Chung Ching S. Rd., Sec. 1, Taipei, Pingtung County, 100, Taiwan
  Phone: (886) 8 7773367
  Fax: (886) 8 7773382
  Email: lihtai@ms36.hinet.net
  Web Address: www.tungtay.com.tw/c_lihtai.htm
Personnel:
  Chmn.: C. S. Chen
  Phone: (886) 8 7773367
  Mill Mgr.: W. T. Lin
  Phone: (886) 8 7773367
Total Employees at this Location: 127
Type of Operation: Paper mill
Paper/Paperboard Grades and Capacities:
  Total paper and paperboard capacity: 10,000 mt/y
  Packaging papers: 10,000 mt/y
Paper and Paperboard Mill Data:
Paper Machines: 2
No. 1, fourdrinier, Trim width 1.3 m, Packaging papers
No. 2, fourdrinier, Trim width 2.5 m, Packaging papers
Finishing Equipment:
  Rewinders: 2

Long Chen Paper Co. Ltd.
10F, No. 337, Fuxing N. Rd.
Taipei, 10544
Taiwan
  Phone: (886) 2 5581 1777
  Fax: (886) 2 5581 1778
  Email: lcp@longchenpaper.com
  Web Address: www.longchenpaper.com
Personnel:
  Chmn. & CEO: Bengo Ying Pin Cheng
  Phone: (886) 2 5581 1777
  Fax: (886) 2 5581 1778
  Pres.: Ying Chi Cheng
  Phone: (886) 2 5581 1777
  Fax: (886) 2 5581 1778
  Deputy Gen. Mgr.: Chang Kun Yao
  Phone: (886) 2 5581 1777
  Fax: (886) 2 5581 1778
  Deputy Gen. Mgr.: Li Ling Lin
  Phone: (886) 2 5581 1777
  Fax: (886) 2 5581 1778
  Dir.: Xiao Bo Xu
  Phone: (886) 2 5581 1777
  Fax: (886) 2 5581 1778
Total Employees of Company: 3,504
Total Employees at this Location: 989
Mill Locations:
Jiangsu Wuxi Long Chen Paper Co., Ltd., Wuxi Mill (94% owned), No. 43, Zhongxing West Road, Luoshe Town, Huishan District, Wuxi 214187, China, Capacity: 800,000 mt/y, (Paperboard mill)
  Phone: (86) 510 8331 1540/6666
  Fax: (86) 510 8331 1826/2701
  Email: wang@lcpc.biz, w1997088@lcpc.biz
Long Chen Paper Co., Ltd., Erh-Lin Mill, No. 1-1, Guangxing-Lane, Guangxing, ErhLin 52652, Taiwan, Capacity: 390,000 mt/y, (Pulp mill, Paperboard mill)
  Phone: (886) 4 8962111
  Fax: (886) 4 8962119
  Email: k0019@longchenpaper.com
Zhejiang Long Chen Paper Co., Ltd., Pinghu Mill, East Binghai Rd., Dushan port zone, Pinghu 314204, China, Capacity: 620,000 mt/y, (Pulp mill, Paperboard mill)
  Phone: (86) 573 8581 0999
  Fax: (86) 573 8581 1111
  Email: g5287@lcpc.biz

Long Chen Paper Co. Ltd.
Erh-Lin Mill
No. 1-1, Guangxing-Lane, Guangxing
ErhLin, Changhua County, 52652
Taiwan
  Phone: (886) 4 8962111
  Fax: (886) 4 8962119
  Email: k0019@longchenpaper.com
  Web Address: www.longchenpaper.com
Personnel:
  Chmn.: Yingbin Zheng
  Gen. Mill Mgr.: Shi-Ping Chen
  Phone: (886) 4 8962111
  Vice Mill Mgr.: C. H. Cheng
  Phone: (886) 4 8962111
  Purch. Agent: D. C. Li
  Phone: (886) 4 8962111
  Tech. Mgr.: M. Y. Chou
  Phone: (886) 4 8962111
  Sls. Mgr.: X. E. Lv
  Phone: (886) 4 8962111
Total Employees at this Location: 300
Type of Operation: Pulp mill, Paperboard mill
Pulp Grades and Capacities:
  Total pulp capacity: 382,178 mt/y
  Recycled Pulping: 382,178 mt/y
Pulp Mill Data:
  Recycled Fiber Treatment Lines:
  Recycled packaging pulping lines
Paper/Paperboard Grades and Capacities:
  Total paper and paperboard capacity: 390,000 mt/y
  Linerboard: 210,000 mt/y
  Corrugating medium/fluting: 180,000 mt/y
Paper and Paperboard Mill Data:
  Stock Preparation:
  Pulpers: 6
  Refiners: 20
Paper Machines: 4
No. 2, fourdrinier, total capacity 50,000 mt/y, Trim width 2.3 m, Corrugating medium/fluting
No. 3, fourdrinier, total capacity 70,000 mt/y, Trim width 3.05 m, Corrugating medium/fluting
No. 5, fourdrinier, total capacity 100,000 mt/y, Trim width 3.7 m, Linerboard, Corrugating medium/fluting
No. 6, fourdrinier (3), total capacity 170,000 mt/y, Trim width 4.3 m, Linerboard
Finishing Equipment:
  Rewinders: 4
Energy Data:
Power boilers: 2
Steam turbines: 2 at 26 MW
Electrical demand for mill: 470 MWh/D

Mei Ho Paper Mfg. Co., Ltd.
Ho Mei Mill
92, Tong Min Rd., Kan Chin Li
Ho Mei, Changhua County, 50847
Taiwan
  Phone: (886) 4 7552670
  Fax: (886) 4 7564852
  Email: mcho12670@yahoo.com.tw
Personnel:
  Pres.: S. L. Lin
  Phone: (886) 4 7552670
Type of Operation: Paper mill
Paper/Paperboard Grades and Capacities:
  Total paper and paperboard capacity: 4,800 mt/y
  Tissue: 4,800 mt/y
Paper and Paperboard Mill Data:
Paper Machines: 2
PM 1, cylinder, total capacity 3,000 mt/y, Trim width 3.3 m, Tissue
PM 2, (idle since May 2007), cylinder, total capacity 1,800 mt/y, Trim width 1.7 m, Tissue

Pu Li Paper Mfg. Co., Ltd.
Pu Li Mill
22, Sec. 2, Lung Sheng Rd.
Pu Li, Nantou County, 54548
Taiwan
  Phone: (886) 49 2981228
  Fax: (886) 49 2993542
  Email: puli@ms5.hinet.net
Personnel:

Taiwan

Chmn.: Y.S.X. Chang
Phone: (886) 49 2981228
President: C. F. Chang
Phone: (886) 49 2981228
Total Employees at this Location: 48
Type of Operation: Paper mill
Paper/Paperboard Grades and Capacities:
Total paper and paperboard capacity: 1,800 mt/y
Specialty and industrial: 1,800 mt/y

⊕⋒Sam Bard Co., Ltd.
Min Hsiung Mill
42, 14 Jia, Ta Chi Tsun
Min Hsiung, Chia-I County, 62147
Taiwan
Phone: (886) 5 2212003
Fax: (886) 5 2212043
Email: sambunyen@yahoo.com.tw
Personnel:
Chmn.: K. S. Y. Yen
Phone: (886) 5 2212003
Pres.: J. T. Yen
Phone: (886) 5 2212003
Total Employees at this Location: 49
Type of Operation: Paper mill
Paper/Paperboard Grades and Capacities:
Total paper and paperboard capacity: 13,000 mt/y
Specialty and industrial

⊕⋒San Yang Paper Making Co., Ltd.
Pai Ho Mill
81-3, Ho Tung Li
Pai Ho District, Tainan City, 73252
Taiwan
Phone: (886) 6 6859945
Fax: (886) 6 6830435
Personnel:
Chmn.: K. P. Y. Chen
Phone: (886) 6 6859945
Pres.: H. H. Chen
Phone: (886) 6 6859945
Mill Mgr.: C. J. Chen
Phone: (886) 6 6859945
Total Employees at this Location: 19
Type of Operation: Paper mill
Paper/Paperboard Grades and Capacities:
Total paper and paperboard capacity: 13,000 mt/y
Specialty and industrial

⊕⋒San Yi Paper Industry Co., Ltd.
Chung Pu Mill
39-1, Shih Kung Pu, Ho Mei Tsun
Chung Pu, Chia-I County, 60646
Taiwan
Phone: (886) 5 2393596
Fax: (886) 5 2396598
Personnel:
Chmn.: T. S. Yen
Phone: (886) 5 2393596
Pres. & Mill Mgr.: J. C. Yen
Phone: (886) 5 2393596
Total Employees at this Location: 44
Type of Operation: Paper mill
Paper/Paperboard Grades and Capacities:
Total paper and paperboard capacity: 11,000 mt/y
Specialty and industrial

⊕Shihlin Paper Corp.
31, Fu Teh Rd., Shihlin
Taipei, 11163
Taiwan
Phone: (886) 2 28811111
Fax: (886) 2 28827099
Email: shc@shihlin.com.tw
Web Address: www.shihlin.com.tw
Personnel:
Chmn.: Chao-Chuan Chen
Phone: (886) 2 28811111
Fax: (886) 2 28827099
Dpty. Gen. Mgr.: Mei-Ru Chen
Phone: (886) 2 28811111
Fax: (886) 2 28827099
Gen. Mgr., Dir.: Jian-Kun Chen
Phone: (886) 2 28811111
Fax: (886) 2 28827099
Vice Chmn.: Bo-Ting Chen
Phone: (886) 2 28811111
Fax: (886) 2 28827099
Total Employees at this Location: 50
Mill Locations:
Shihlin Paper Corp., Yung An Mill, 35-1 Pen Kang Tsun, Hsin Wu 32748, Taiwan, Capacity: 99,960 mt/y, (Paper mill, Paperboard mill)
Phone: (886) 3 4768077-9
Fax: (886) 3 4769120

⋒Shihlin Paper Corp.
Yung An Mill
Mill is closed (Shihlin Paper permanently stopped paper and board production at the mill at end of June 2014, converting business is still in operation.)
35-1 Pen Kang Tsun
Hsin Wu, Taoyuan County, 32748
Taiwan
Phone: (886) 3 4768077-9
Fax: (886) 3 4769120
Web Address: www.shihlin.com.tw
Personnel:
Gen. Mgr., Dir.: Jian-Kun Chen
Phone: (886) 3 4768077-9
Depty. Gen. Mgr.: Mei-Ru Chen
Phone: (886) 3 4768077-9
Mill Mgr.: Te-Kuen Suen
Phone: (886) 3 4768077-9
Total Employees at this Location: 287
Type of Operation: Paper mill, Paperboard mill
Pulp Grades and Capacities:
Total pulp capacity: 63,070 mt/y
Recycled Pulping: 63,070 mt/y
Paper/Paperboard Grades and Capacities:
Total paper and paperboard capacity: 99,960 mt/y
Specialty and industrial: 10,710 mt/y
Boxboard/cartonboard: 89,250 mt/y
Paper and Paperboard Mill Data:
Stock Preparation:
Pulpers: 7
Refiners: 26
Paper Machines: 4
No. 1, cylinder, total capacity 20,706 mt/y, Trim width 2.5 m, Boxboard/cartonboard
No. 2, total capacity 57,834 mt/y, Trim width 2.5 m, Boxboard/cartonboard
No. 3, cylinder, total capacity 10,710 mt/y, Trim width 2.5 m, Boxboard/cartonboard
No. 4, cylinder, total capacity 10,710 mt/y, Trim width 2.3 m, Specialty and industrial
Coating Machines: 3
PM 2, total capacity 58,000 mt/y., on machine
PM 3, total capacity 11,000 mt/y., on machine
PM 4, total capacity 110,000 mt/y., on machine
Finishing Equipment:
Rewinders: 2
Sheeters: 5
Energy Data:
Power boilers: 1
Electrical demand for mill: 180 MWh/D

⊕⋒Shin Kwang Hwa Paper Mfg. Co., Ltd.
Pu Li Mill
Ownership: 100% by family
15-1, Shin Seng Rd.
Pu Li, Nantou County, 54548
Taiwan
Phone: (886) 49 2982011
Fax: (886) 49 2981104
Email: skh.paper@msa.hinet.net
Web Address: www.techpaper.com.tw
Personnel:
Chmn.: Tai-Cheng You
Phone: (886) 49 2982011
Pres.: Jung-San Chen
Phone: (886) 49 2982011
Mill Mgr.: Yu-Lung Chang
Phone: (886) 49 2982011
Total Employees at this Location: 64
Type of Operation: Paper mill
Paper/Paperboard Grades and Capacities:
Total paper and paperboard capacity: 2,500 mt/y
Specialty and industrial: 2,500 mt/y
Paper and Paperboard Mill Data:
Stock Preparation:
Pulpers: 2
Refiners: 4
Paper Machines: 3
PM 1, cylinder, Yankee dryer, total capacity 500 mt/y, Trim width 0.98 m, Specialty and industrial
PM 2, cylinder, Yankee dryer, total capacity 1,000 mt/y, Trim width 2.01 m, Specialty and industrial
PM 3, deltaformer, total capacity 1,000 mt/y, Trim width 2.01 m, Specialty and industrial
Finishing Equipment:
Rewinders: 5
Sheeters: 1
Energy Data:
Power boilers: 1

⊕⋒Shine Yan Paper Co., Ltd.
Fengyuan Mill
55, Lane 271, Chen Tsuen Rd.
Fengyuan District, Taichung City, 42071
Taiwan
Phone: (886) 4 25366475
Fax: (886) 4 25366476
Email: jud1111@yahoo.com.tw
Personnel:
Chmn.: A. S. Huang
Phone: (886) 4 25366475
Pres. & Mill Mgr.: J. H. Huang
Phone: (886) 4 25366475
Total Employees at this Location: 22
Type of Operation: Paper mill
Paper/Paperboard Grades and Capacities:
Total paper and paperboard capacity: 1,300 mt/y
Tissue: 1,300 mt/y
Paper and Paperboard Mill Data:
Paper Machines: 1
PM 1, total capacity 1,300 mt/y, Trim width 2.25 m, Tissue

⊕⋒Sun Thing Co., Ltd.
Houbi Mill
259, Jia Min Village
Houbi District, Tainan City, 73141
Taiwan
Phone: (886) 6 6881455
Fax: (886) 6 6882539
Personnel:
Chmn.: C. H. Yen
Phone: (886) 6 6881455
Pres.: J. Z. Yen
Phone: (886) 6 6881455
Total Employees at this Location: 29
Type of Operation: Paper mill
Paper/Paperboard Grades and Capacities:
Total paper and paperboard capacity: 29,000 mt/y
Specialty and industrial

⊕⋒Ta Chang Paper Mfg. Co., Ltd.
Lungchin Mill
238, Sec. 4, Sha Tien Rd.
Long Ching District, Taichung City, 43452
Taiwan
Phone: (886) 4 26352510
Fax: (886) 4 26352518
Email: tc.paper@msa.hinet.net
Personnel:

Taiwan

Chmn.: J. L. Tung
Phone: (886) 4 26352510
Pres.: T. W. Yang
Phone: (886) 4 26352510
Mgr.: S. W. Chen
Phone: (886) 4 26352510
Mill Mgr.: C. Y. Wu
Phone: (886) 4 26352510
Total Employees at this Location: 74
Type of Operation: Paperboard mill
Paper/Paperboard Grades and Capacities:
Total paper and paperboard capacity: 39,000 mt/y
Linerboard: 27,000 mt/y
Corrugating medium/fluting: 12,000 mt/y
Paper and Paperboard Mill Data:
Stock Preparation:
Pulpers: 6
Refiners: 11
Paper Machines: 3
No. 1, cylinder, Trim width 2.1 m, Containerboard
No. 2, cylinder, Trim width 2.3 m, Containerboard
No. 3, cylinder, Trim width 3.1 m, Containerboard
Finishing Equipment:
Rewinders: 2

ⓗⓜ Tai Kuang Paper Co., Ltd.
San Chung Mill
47, Lane 240, Chung Hsin N. Rd.
San Chung, New Taipei City, 24158
Taiwan
Phone: (886) 2 29952217
Fax: (886) 2 29953339
Email: tk.paper@msa.hinet.net
Personnel:
Chmn./Pres.: C. M. Chuang
Phone: (886) 2 29952217
Total Employees at this Location: 24
Type of Operation: Paper mill
Paper/Paperboard Grades and Capacities:
Total paper and paperboard capacity: 1,600 mt/y

ⓗⓜ Taiwan Chi Suen Enterprise Co., Ltd.
Pu Li Mill
6, Herng Jyi Lane, Ta Cherng Li
Pu Li, Nantou County, 54545
Taiwan
Phone: (886) 49 2915442
Fax: (886) 49 2915212
Personnel:
Chmn.: T. C. Lin
Phone: (886) 49 2915442
Total Employees at this Location: 13
Type of Operation: Paper mill
Paper/Paperboard Grades and Capacities:
Uncoated woodfree/freesheet

ⓗ Taiwan Pulp & Paper Corp.
10F, 96, Sec.1, Chen Kuo N. Rd.
Taipei, 10489
Taiwan
Phone: (886) 2 25153969
Fax: (886) 2 25153955-6
Email: u341@tppc.com.tw
Web Address: www.tppc.com.tw
Personnel:
Chmn.: Shu Mei Chang
Phone: (886) 2 25153969
Fax: (886) 2 25153955-6
Gen. Mgr., Man. Dir.: Bor Horng Chang
Phone: (886) 2 25153969
Fax: (886) 2 25153955-6
Man. Dir.: HengYi Du
Phone: (886) 2 25153969
Fax: (886) 2 25153955-6
Dpty. Gen. Mgr., Dir.: Congming Jian
Phone: (886) 2 25153969
Fax: (886) 2 25153955-6
Dpty. Gen. Mgr., Dir.: Tiaorong Yang
Phone: (886) 2 25153969
Fax: (886) 2 25153955-6
Dpty. Gen. Mgr.: Yongfu Su
Phone: (886) 2 25153969
Fax: (886) 2 25153955-6
Dir.: Zongzhen Chen
Phone: (886) 2 25153969
Fax: (886) 2 25153955-6
Dir.: Junzheng Lin
Phone: (886) 2 25153969
Fax: (886) 2 25153955-6
Dir.: Liren Zhu
Phone: (886) 2 25153969
Fax: (886) 2 25153955-6
Total Employees at this Location: 56
Mill Locations:
Taiwan Pulp & Paper Corp., Hsin Ying Mill, 94, Nan Tzu St., Hsinying District 73044, Taiwan, Capacity: 95,319 mt/y, (Pulp mill, Paper mill)
Phone: (886) 6 6563811
Fax: (886) 6 6567683
Email: tppc7683@ms27.hinet.net, u345@tppc.com.tw

ⓜ Taiwan Pulp & Paper Corp.
Hsin Ying Mill
94, Nan Tzu St.
Hsinying District, Tainan City, 73044
Taiwan
Phone: (886) 6 6563811
Fax: (886) 6 6567683
Email: tppc7683@ms27.hinet.net, u345@tppc.com.tw
Web Address: www.tppc.com.tw
Personnel:
VP: T. M. Chien
Phone: (886) 6 6563811
CEO: K. C. Tseng
Phone: (886) 6 6563811
Paper Mill Mgr.: M. C. Lee
Phone: (886) 6 6563811
Pulp Mill Mgr.: H. C. Huang
Phone: (886) 6 6563811
Eng. & Maintenance Mgr.: T. Y. Liou
Phone: (886) 6 6563811
Secial Assistant: M. D. Chang
Phone: (886) 6 6563811
Chem. Plant Mgr.: K. Y. Lin
Phone: (886) 6 6563811
Total Employees at this Location: 465
Type of Operation: Pulp mill, Paper mill
Pulp Grades and Capacities:
Total pulp capacity: 141,306 mt/y
Pulp available for market: 96,747 mt/y
Chemical Pulp: 141,306 mt/y
Pulp Mill Data:
Chemical Pulping Systems:
Batch digesters: 6
Bleach Plant Systems: 1
No. 1, Sequence: O_2 D/CEoD, Capacity 150,000 admt/y
Chemical Recovery Equipment:
Evaporator lines: 1
Recovery boilers: 1
Lime Kiln
Pulp Dryers:
Flakt dryer 1, Wet Lap machine 1
Paper/Paperboard Grades and Capacities:
Total paper and paperboard capacity: 95,319 mt/y
Uncoated woodfree/freesheet: 95,319 mt/y
Paper and Paperboard Mill Data:
Stock Preparation:
Pulpers: 3
Refiners: 8
Paper Machines: 3
No. 7, (Supplier: Sano.), fourdrinier, total capacity 65,331 mt/y, Trim width 3.46 m, Uncoated woodfree/freesheet
No. 8, (Supplier: Fuyo Iron Works.), fourdrinier, total capacity 19,992 mt/y, Trim width 1.9 m, Uncoated woodfree/freesheet
No. 9, twin-wire, total capacity 9,996 mt/y, Trim width 2.4 m, Uncoated woodfree/freesheet
Finishing Equipment:
Supercalenders: 2
Rewinders: 3
Sheeters: 4
Energy Data:
Power boilers: 1
Steam turbines: 2 at 20, 4.1 MW
Electrical demand for mill: 438 MWh/D

ⓗⓜ Tao Yuan Paper Mfg. Co., Ltd.
Lu Chu Mill
186-6, Hai Hu Tsuan
Lu Chu, Taoyuan County, 33856
Taiwan
Phone: (886) 3 3541836
Fax: (886) 3 3543105
Email: taoyuan.mfg@msa.hinet.net
Personnel:
Chmn., Pres.: P. K. Yung
Phone: (886) 3 3541836
Mgr.: H. H. Hsu
Phone: (886) 3 3541836
Mgr.: H. T. Hsu
Phone: (886) 3 3541836
Mill Mgr.: M. C. Wang
Phone: (886) 3 3541836
Total Employees at this Location: 80
Type of Operation: Paperboard mill
Pulp Grades and Capacities:
Total pulp capacity: 45,623 mt/y
Recycled Pulping: 45,623 mt/y
Pulp Mill Data:
Recycled Fiber Treatment Lines:
Recycled packaging pulping lines: 1
Paper/Paperboard Grades and Capacities:
Total paper and paperboard capacity: 45,000 mt/y
Linerboard: 45,000 mt/y
Paper and Paperboard Mill Data:
Paper Machines: 1
No. 1, cylinder (5), total capacity 45,000 mt/y, Trim width 3.1 m, Linerboard
Energy Data:
Power boilers
Electrical demand for mill: 59 MWh/D

ⓗⓜ Tong Long Paper Co., Ltd.
Ta Liao Mill
544, Feng Lin 1st Rd.
Ta Liao District, Kaohsiung City, 83166
Taiwan
Phone: (886) 7 6416152
Fax: (886) 7 6422000
Email: tonglong@seed.net.tw
Personnel:
Chmn.: C. H. Hsu
Phone: (886) 7 6416152
Total Employees at this Location: 50
Type of Operation: Paperboard mill
Paper/Paperboard Grades and Capacities:
Total paper and paperboard capacity: 16,000 mt/y
Linerboard: 16,000 mt/y
Paper and Paperboard Mill Data:
Paper Machines: 1
No. 1, cylinder, total capacity 16,000 mt/y, Trim width 2 m, Linerboard

ⓗⓜ Top-Comment Technology Enterprise Co. Ltd.
Chiayi Mill
10 Kung Ye 1st Rd., Shing Nan Tsun
Ming Hsiung, Chia-I County, 62149
Taiwan
Phone: (886) 5 2211526-8
Fax: (886) 5 2131560
Email: scha.ind@msa.hinet.net
Web Address: www.topcomm.com.tw

Taiwan

Personnel:
Chmn.: Hsueh-Ping Cheng
Phone: (886) 5 2211526-8
Pres.: Chien-Yuan Hung
Phone: (886) 5 2211526-8
Mgr.: J. C. Tsai
Phone: (886) 5 2211526-8
Mill Mgr.: L. C. Chao
Phone: (886) 5 2211526-8
Total Employees at this Location: 133
Type of Operation: Paperboard mill
Paper/Paperboard Grades and Capacities:
Total paper and paperboard capacity: 60,000 mt/y
Linerboard: 60,000 mt/y
Paper and Paperboard Mill Data:
Stock Preparation:
Pulpers: 7
Refiners: 17
Paper Machines: 3
No. 1, cylinder, Trim width 3.1 m, Containerboard
No. 2, cylinder, Trim width 2.6 m, Containerboard
No. 3, cylinder, Trim width 2.6 m, Containerboard
Finishing Equipment:
Supercalenders: 3
Rewinders: 3
Sheeters: 1
Energy Data:
Power boilers: 2

Tung Chi Paper Corp.
372, Sec. 2, Chung San Rd.
Chung Ho District, New Taipei City, 23557
Taiwan
Phone: (886) 2 22406622
Fax: (886) 2 22405522
Email: tcs99@tungchi.com.tw
Web Address: www.tungchi.com.tw
Personnel:
Chmn.: Y. K. Chen
Phone: (886) 2 22406622
Fax: (886) 2 22405522
Pres.: M. B. Chen
Phone: (886) 2 22406622
Fax: (886) 2 22405522
VP: J. L. Chen
Phone: (886) 2 22406622
Fax: (886) 2 22405522
Total Employees of Company: 274
Mill Locations:
Tung Chi Paper Corp., Lung Ching Mill, 342, Sec. 4, Sa Tien Rd., Lung Ching District 43452, Taiwan, Capacity: 114,570 mt/y, (Paper mill, Paperboard mill)
Phone: (886) 4 26353511
Fax: (886) 4 26359324
Email: tcs99@tungchi.com.tw

Tung Chi Paper Corp.
Lung Ching Mill
342, Sec. 4, Sa Tien Rd.
Lung Ching District, Taichung City, 43452
Taiwan
Phone: (886) 4 26353511
Fax: (886) 4 26359324
Email: tcs99@tungchi.com.tw
Web Address: www.tungchi.com.tw
Personnel:
VP: J. L. Chen
Phone: (886) 4 26353511
Mill Mgr.: M. C. Lin
Phone: (886) 4 26353511
Total Employees at this Location: 250
Type of Operation: Paper mill, Paperboard mill
Pulp Grades and Capacities:
Total pulp capacity: 95,268 mt/y
Recycled Pulping: 95,268 mt/y
Pulp Mill Data:
Recycled Fiber Treatment Lines:
Recycled packaging pulping lines: 1
Paper/Paperboard Grades and Capacities:
Total paper and paperboard capacity: 114,570 mt/y
Specialty and industrial: 3,570 mt/y
Boxboard/cartonboard: 111,000 mt/y
Paper and Paperboard Mill Data:
Stock Preparation:
Pulpers: 6
Refiners: 8
Paper Machines: 4
No. 2, cylinder, total capacity 3,570 mt/y, Trim width 1.3 m, Specialty and industrial
No. 3, cylinder (6), total capacity 26,000 mt/y, Trim width 1.9 m, Boxboard/cartonboard
No. 5, cylinder (8), total capacity 35,000 mt/y, Trim width 2.8 m, Boxboard/cartonboard
No. 6, cylinder (8), Yankee dryer, total capacity 50,000 mt/y, Trim width 3.6 m, Boxboard/cartonboard
Coating Machines: 3
PM 3, total capacity 27,000 mt/y., on machine
PM 5, total capacity 36,000 mt/y., on machine
PM 6, total capacity 50,000 mt/y., on machine
Finishing Equipment:
Rewinders: 3
Sheeters: 4
Energy Data:
Power boilers
Steam turbines
Electrical demand for mill: 165 MWh/D

Tung I Paper Corp.
Feng Yuan Mill
365, Pei Yang Rd.
Feng Yuan District, Taichung City, 42084
Taiwan
Phone: (886) 4 25272220
Fax: (886) 4 25247341
Personnel:
Chmn.: B. C. Chuan
Phone: (886) 4 25272220
Pres.: Y. Y. Chuan
Phone: (886) 4 25272220
Total Employees at this Location: 71
Type of Operation: Paper mill
Paper/Paperboard Grades and Capacities:
Total paper and paperboard capacity: 3,500 mt/y
Tissue: 3,500 mt/y
Paper and Paperboard Mill Data:
Paper Machines: 1
PM 1, cylinder, total capacity 3,500 mt/y, Trim width 3.45 m, Tissue

Tung Yuan Paper Mfg. Co., Ltd.
Chiao Tou Mill
24, Chia Hsin Rd.
Chiao Tou District, Kaohsiung City, 82547
Taiwan
Phone: (886) 7 693 8836
Fax: (886) 7 693 1178
Personnel:
Pres. & Chmn.: H. L. Kao
Phone: (886) 7 6938836
Type of Operation: Paperboard mill
Paper/Paperboard Grades and Capacities:
Linerboard
Corrugating medium/fluting

Union Paper Corp.
17F, 51, Sec.2, Chung Ching S. Rd
Taipei, 10075
Taiwan
Phone: (886) 2395 5168
Fax: (886) 2321 1033
Email: chuang@upcpaper.com
Web Address: www.upcpaper.com
Personnel:
Chmn. & Pres.: C. L. Tsai
Phone: (886) 2395 5168
Fax: (886) 2321 1033
Total Employees of Company: 400
Total Employees at this Location: 12
Mill Locations:
Union Paper Corp., Lin Nei Mill, 65, Jui Noun, Lin Chung Village, Lin Nei 64345, Taiwan, Capacity: 50,000 mt/y, (Paper mill)
Phone: (886) 5 5896666/ 2 23955168
Fax: (886) 5 5896222/ 2 23218818
Email: chuang@upcpaper.com

Union Paper Corp.
Lin Nei Mill
65, Jui Noun, Lin Chung Village
Lin Nei, Yunlin County, 64345
Taiwan
Phone: (886) 5 5896666/ 2 23955168
Fax: (886) 5 5896222/ 2 23218818
Email: chuang@upcpaper.com
Web Address: www.upcpaper.com
Personnel:
VP: W. M. Hong
Phone: (886) 5 5896666/ 2 23955168
Tech. Mgr.: M. C. Lin
Phone: (886) 5 5896666/ 2 23955168
VP: J. C. King
Phone: (886) 5 5896666/ 2 23955168
Total Employees at this Location: 388
Type of Operation: Paper mill
Paper/Paperboard Grades and Capacities:
Total paper and paperboard capacity: 50,000 mt/y
Specialty and industrial: 50,000 mt/y
Paper and Paperboard Mill Data:
Stock Preparation:
Pulpers: 8
Refiners: 14
Paper Machines: 7
PM 1, Yankee dryer, fourdrinier, Trim width 2 m
PM 2, Yankee dryer, fourdrinier, Trim width 2 m
PM 3, cylinder, Yankee dryer, Trim width 1 m
PM 4, cylinder, Yankee dryer, total capacity 5,000 mt/y, Trim width 1.75 m, Specialty and industrial
PM 5, cylinder, Yankee dryer, total capacity 5,000 mt/y, Trim width 1.75 m, Specialty and industrial
PM 6, Yankee dryer, fourdrinier, Trim width 3 m
PM 7, fourdrinier, Trim width 2 m
Coating Machines: 4
No. 1, total capacity 36,000 mt/y., off machine
No. 2, total capacity 9,000 mt/y., off machine
No. 3, total capacity 6,000 mt/y., off machine
No. 4, total capacity 5,400 mt/y., off machine
Finishing Equipment:
Supercalenders: 7
Rewinders: 11
Sheeters: 5
Energy Data:
Power boilers: 3

Yuen Foong Yu Inc.
Ownership: Public
51, Sec.2. Chung Ching South Rd.
Taipei, 10075
Taiwan
Phone: (886) 2 2396 1166
Fax: (886) 2 2396 6771
Email: pypeng@yfy.com
Web Address: www.yfy.com
Personnel:
Pres.: Melody Chiu
Phone: (886) 2 2396 1166
Fax: (886) 2 2396 6771
Chmn. & Gen. Mgr.: H. C. Chuang
Phone: (886) 2 2396 1166
Fax: (886) 2 2396 6771
VP, Eng. Dept.: C. C. Huang
Phone: (886) 2 2396 1166
Fax: (886) 2 2396 6771
Pres. Chung Hwa Pulp. Corp.: Carl S. Kuo
Phone: (886) 2 2396 1166
Fax: (886) 2 2396 6771
Dir., Investor Rel.: James Lin
Phone: (886) 2 2396 1166 Ext. 1728
Fax: (886) 2 2351 7021

Taiwan

Email: james.lin@yfy.com
Dir., HR: K. Y. Cheng
Phone: (886) 2 2396 1166 Ext. 1113
Fax: (886) 2 2322 7809
Dir., Public Rel.: Ms. Wen Peng
Phone: (886) 2 2396 1166 Ext. 1852
Fax: (886) 2 2391 9106
Email: wenpeng@yfy.com
Total Employees of Company: 4,756
Mill Locations:
Chung Hwa Pulp Corporation, Chiutang Mill (55% owned), 112, Chiu Tang Rd., Ta Shu District 84041, Taiwan, Capacity: 399,483 mt/y, (Paper mill)
Phone: (886) 7 6512611-9
Fax: (886) 7 6512610
Email: yehpinghuang@yfy.com
Chung Hwa Pulp Corporation, Taitung Mill (55% owned), 371, Sec. 4, Chung Hsin Rd., Taitung 95060, Taiwan, Capacity: 138,000 mt/y, (Paper mill, Paperboard mill)
Phone: (886) 89 382250
Fax: (886) 89 382256
Email: tsaur@yfy.com
Chung Hwa Pulp Corporation, Hualien Mill (55% owned), 100, Kuang Hwa, Chi An 97356, Taiwan, Capacity: 117,096 mt/y, (Pulp mill, Paper mill)
Phone: (886) 3 8421171
Fax: (886) 3 8422843
Email: shawmj@mail.chp.com.tw, chp@mail.chp.com.tw
Guangdong Dingfeng Paper Corporation, Zhaoqing Mill (73% owned), Shouyue, South Street, Guangning, Zhaoqing 526300, China, (Pulp mill)
Phone: (86) 758 865 6436/9000/6808
Fax: (86) 758 865 6450/9168
Email: dingfung@gddfpaper.com
Jiangsu Jiangyin YFY Mfg. Co., Ltd., Jiangyin Mill, 258, Tongjiang South Road, Jiangyin 214433, China, Capacity: 45,000 mt/y, (Paperboard mill)
Phone: (86) 510 8611 0141/0143
Fax: (86) 510 8611 8748
Jiangsu Yuen Foong Yu Paper (Kunshan) Co. Ltd., Kunshan Mill, No. 999, Yuen Foong Yu Rd., Yushan Town, Kunshan 215316, China, Capacity: 41,000 mt/y, (Paper mill)
Phone: (86) 512 5779 2888
Fax: (86) 512 5779 2168
Email: yfywyh@public1.sz.js.cn
Jiangsu Yuen Foong Yu Paper (Yangzhou) Co., Ltd., Yangzhou Mill, No. 168, Chunjiang Road, Economy & Development Zone, Yangzhou 225000, China, Capacity: 914,500 mt/y, (Paper mill, Paperboard mill)
Phone: (86) 514 8752 9888
Fax: (86) 514 8752 9889
Yuen Foong Yu Consumer Products Co., Ltd, Ching Shui Mill, 22-1, Jiow Juang Rd., Hai Feng Li, Ching Shui District 43641, Taiwan, Capacity: 31,000 mt/y, (Paper mill)
Phone: (886) 4 2620 1200
Fax: (886) 4 2620 0000
Email: bightwang@yfy.com
Yuen Foong Yu Consumer Products Co., Ltd., Yang-Mei Mill, 41-2, Bei Gau Shan Din, Gau Rong Li, Yang Mei 326661, Taiwan, Capacity: 43,000 mt/y, (Paper mill)
Phone: (886) 3 4902631
Fax: (886) 3 4905965
Email: jie@yfy.com
Yuen Foong Yu Packaging Inc., Chengkung Mill, No. 546, Sec. 3, Chung Shan Rd., Wu Jih District 41453, Taiwan, Capacity: 240,000 mt/y, (Paperboard mill)
Phone: (886) 4 23381126
Fax: (886) 4 23363154
Email: v0109@yfy.com, meg_wu@yfy.com
Yuen Foong Yu Packaging Inc., Hsin Wu Mill, 250, Hsia Chuangtsu, Tsu, Yuen An Tsun, Hsin Wu 32744, Taiwan, Capacity: 460,000 mt/y, (Paperboard mill)
Phone: (886) 3 4861701
Fax: (886) 3 4861078
Email: changjc@yfy.com
Yuen Foong Yu Inc., Beijing Mill, No.1, East Park of Mafang Industrial Park, Pinggu District, Beijing 101204, China, Capacity: 15,000 mt/y, (Paper mill)
Phone: (86) 10 6099 9688
Fax: (86) 10 6099 9611

ⓜ Yuen Foong Yu Consumer Products Co., Ltd.

Ownership: Yuen Foong Yu Inc.
16F. 51 Sec.2. Chung Ching South Rd.
Taipei City, New Taipei City, 10075
Taiwan
Phone: (886) 2 2356 7867
Fax: (886) 2 2356 7880
Email: bill@yfy.com
Web Address: www.yfycpg.com
Personnel:
Chmn. & Pres.: Felix Y. Ho
Mill Locations:
Yuen Foong Yu Consumer Products Co., Ltd., Yang-Mei Mill, 41-2, Bei Gau Shan Din, Gau Rong Li, Yang Mei 326661, Taiwan, Capacity: 43,000 mt/y, (Paper mill)
Phone: (886) 3 4902631
Fax: (886) 3 4905965
Email: jie@yfy.com

ⓜ Yuen Foong Yu Consumer Products Co., Ltd
Ching Shui Mill

Ownership: Yuen Foong Yu Inc.
22-1, Jiow Juang Rd., Hai Feng Li
Ching Shui District, Taichung City, 43641
Taiwan
Phone: (886) 4 2620 1200
Fax: (886) 4 2620 0000
Email: bightwang@yfy.com
Web Address: www.yfy.com
Personnel:
Mill Mgr.: H. L. Fu
Phone: (886) 4 2620 1200
Mgr.: S. C. Hong
Phone: (886) 4 2620 1200
Total Employees at this Location: 95
Type of Operation: Paper mill
Paper/Paperboard Grades and Capacities:
Total paper and paperboard capacity: 31,000 mt/y
Tissue: 31,000 mt/y
Paper and Paperboard Mill Data:
Paper Machines: 2
No. 1, cylinder, total capacity 13,000 mt/y, Trim width 2.4 m, Tissue
No. 2, crescent former, total capacity 18,000 mt/y, Trim width 2.4 m, Tissue
Energy Data:
Power boilers: 1
Electrical demand for mill: 87 MWh/D

ⓜ Yuen Foong Yu Consumer Products Co., Ltd.
Yang-Mei Mill

Ownership: Yuen Foong Yu Inc.
41-2, Bei Gau Shan Din, Gau Rong Li
Yang Mei, Taoyuan County, 326661
Taiwan
Phone: (886) 3 4902631
Fax: (886) 3 4905965
Email: jie@yfy.com
Web Address: www.yfy.com
Personnel:
Mill Mgr.: C. H. Chang
Phone: (886) 3 4902631
Dpty. Mill Mgr.: S. Y. Tseng
Phone: (886) 3 4902631
Total Employees at this Location: 100
Type of Operation: Paper mill
Paper/Paperboard Grades and Capacities:
Total paper and paperboard capacity: 43,000 mt/y
Tissue: 43,000 mt/y
Paper and Paperboard Mill Data:
Stock Preparation:
Pulpers: 2
Refiners: 6
Paper Machines: 2
No. 1, twin-wire, total capacity 20,000 mt/y, Trim width 2.3 m, Tissue, Uncoated woodfree/freesheet
No. 2, crescent former, total capacity 23,000 mt/y, Trim width 2.3 m, Tissue, Uncoated woodfree/freesheet
Finishing Equipment:
Rewinders: 2
Sheeters: 16
Energy Data:
Power boilers: 2
Electrical demand for mill: 122 MWh/D

ⓜ Yuen Foong Yu Packaging Inc.
Chengkung Mill

Ownership: YFY Cayman
No. 546, Sec. 3, Chung Shan Rd.
Wu Jih District, Taichung City, 41453
Taiwan
Phone: (886) 4 23381126
Fax: (886) 4 23363154
Email: v0109@yfy.com, meg_wu@yfy.com
Web Address: www.yfy.com
Personnel:
Mill Mgr.: C. K. Lin
Phone: (886) 4 23381126
Asst. Mill Mgr.: D. W. Chuang
Phone: (886) 4 23381126
Total Employees at this Location: 200
Type of Operation: Paperboard mill
Pulp Grades and Capacities:
Total pulp capacity: 235,638 mt/y
Recycled Pulping: 235,638 mt/y
Pulp Mill Data:
Recycled Fiber Treatment Lines:
Recycled packaging pulping lines: 1
Paper/Paperboard Grades and Capacities:
Total paper and paperboard capacity: 240,000 mt/y
Corrugating medium/fluting: 240,000 mt/y
Paper and Paperboard Mill Data:
Stock Preparation:
Pulpers: 2
Refiners: 3
Paper Machines: 3
No. 5, fourdrinier, total capacity 30,000 mt/y, Trim width 2.9 m, Corrugating medium/fluting
No. 7, fourdrinier, total capacity 70,000 mt/y, Trim width 3.6 m, Corrugating medium/fluting
No. 9, fourdrinier, total capacity 140,000 mt/y, Trim width 4.6 m, Corrugating medium/fluting
Finishing Equipment:
Rewinders: 3
Energy Data:
Power boilers: 2
Steam turbines
Electrical demand for mill: 286 MWh/D

ⓜ Yuen Foong Yu Packaging Inc.
Hsin Wu Mill

Ownership: YFY Cayman
250, Hsia Chuangtsu, Tsu, Yuen An Tsun
Hsin Wu, Taoyuan County, 32744
Taiwan
Phone: (886) 3 4861701
Fax: (886) 3 4861078
Email: changjc@yfy.com
Web Address: www.yfy.com
Personnel:
Pres., Eng. Dept.: C. C. Huang
Phone: (886) 3 4861701
Vice Mill Mgr.: Y. L. Chou
Phone: (886) 3 4861701
Total Employees at this Location: 315
Type of Operation: Paperboard mill
Pulp Grades and Capacities:
Total pulp capacity: 407,548 mt/y

Recycled Pulping: 407,548 mt/y
Pulp Mill Data:
Bleach Plant Systems: 1
DIP
Recycled Fiber Treatment Lines:
Flotation deinking lines: 1
Recycled packaging pulping lines: 2
Paper/Paperboard Grades and Capacities:
Total paper and paperboard capacity: 460,000 mt/y
Linerboard: 300,000 mt/y
Boxboard/cartonboard: 160,000 mt/y
Paper and Paperboard Mill Data:
Paper Machines: 2
No. 1, Multi-wire (3), total capacity 300,000 mt/y, Trim width 4.6 m, Linerboard
No. 2, Multi-wire (4), total capacity 160,000 mt/y, Trim width 3.5 m, Boxboard/cartonboard
Coating Machines: 1
PM 2, total capacity 120,000 mt/y., on machine
Finishing Equipment:
Rewinders: 2
Energy Data:
Power boilers: 1
Steam turbines: 2 at 26 MW
Electrical demand for mill: 641 MWh/D

ⓘⓜYuen Min Paper Product Co., Ltd.
Chu Nan Mill
6-1, Chung Mei Li
Chu Nan, Miaoli County, 35050
Taiwan
 Phone: (886) 37 462060
 Fax: (886) 37 468338
Personnel:
 Chmn.: K. C. Lin
 Phone: (886) 37 462060/ 468338
 Pres.: C. H. Lin
 Phone: (886) 37 462060/ 468338
 Mill Mgr.: W. H. Lo
 Phone: (886) 37 462060/ 468338
Total Employees at this Location: 20
Type of Operation: Paper mill
Paper/Paperboard Grades and Capacities:
Total paper and paperboard capacity: 7,500 mt/y
Specialty and industrial: 7,500 mt/y
Paper and Paperboard Mill Data:
Paper Machines: 1
PM 1-3, total capacity 2,500 mt/y, Trim width 2 m, Specialty and industrial

ⓘⓜYung Fang Paper Mfg., Co
Hsi Chou Mill
167, Wen Hwa Rd.
Hsi Chou, Changhua County, 52441
Taiwan
 Phone: (886) 4 8884658
 Fax: (886) 4 8889292
Personnel:
 Chmn.: C. H. Huang
 Phone: (886) 4 8884658
Total Employees at this Location: 31
Type of Operation: Paper mill
Pulp Grades and Capacities:
Total pulp capacity: 3,500 mt/y
Pulp Mill Data:
Pulp Lines: 1
Paper/Paperboard Grades and Capacities:
Total paper and paperboard capacity: 3,500 mt/y
Tissue: 3,500 mt/y
Paper and Paperboard Mill Data:
Paper Machines: 1
PM 1, cylinder, total capacity 3,500 mt/y, Trim width 3 m, Tissue

ⓘⓜYung-Seng Development Enterprise Co., Ltd.
Taoyuan Mill
27-2, 2 Lin, Tien Shin
Taoyuan, Taoyuan County, 33753
Taiwan
 Phone: (886) 3 3862819
 Fax: (886) 3 3869906
 Email: yung2819@ms35.hinet.net
Personnel:
 Chmn.: L. C. Chen
 Phone: (886) 3 3862819
 Pres., Mill Mgr.: L. Chao
 Phone: (886) 3 3862819
Total Employees at this Location: 35
Type of Operation: Paper mill
Paper/Paperboard Grades and Capacities:
Total paper and paperboard capacity: 32,000 mt/y
Packaging papers
Linerboard
Corrugating medium/fluting

THAILAND

ⓘⓜAsia Kraft Paper Co., Ltd.
Samut Sakhon Mill
99 Moo 5, Rama 2 Road, Thasai, Amphur Muang
Samut Sakhon, 74000
Thailand
 Phone: (66) 3442 3506 9
 Fax: (66) 3442 2599
 Email: asiakraft@asa.co.th
 Web Address: www.asa.co.th
Personnel:
 Man. Dir.: Somchai Mahasiri
 Phone: (66) 3442 3506 9
 Email: mahasiri@asa.co.th
Total Employees of Company: 267
Total Employees at this Location: 245
Type of Operation: Paper mill, Paperboard mill
Pulp Grades and Capacities:
Total pulp capacity: 191,266 mt/y
Recycled Pulping: 191,266 mt/y
Pulp Mill Data:
Recycled Fiber Treatment Lines:
Recycled packaging pulping lines: 1
Paper/Paperboard Grades and Capacities:
Total paper and paperboard capacity: 200,000 mt/y
Linerboard: 112,000 mt/y
Corrugating medium/fluting: 88,000 mt/y
Paper and Paperboard Mill Data:
Stock Preparation:
Pulpers: 2
Paper Machines: 2
No. 1, fourdrinier, total capacity 80,000 mt/y, Trim width 3.75 m, Corrugating medium/fluting, Linerboard
No. 2, (PM#2 also produces small amount of White Top Linerboard.), fourdrinier, total capacity 120,000 mt/y, Trim width 4.6 m, Corrugating medium/fluting, Linerboard
Energy Data:
Power boilers: 6
Electrical demand for mill: 257 MWh/D

ⓘBang Pa-In Paper Mill Industry Co., Ltd.
Ownership: 100% by private owner
129 Luang Rd., Pomprab
Bangkok, 10100
Thailand
 Phone: (66) 2 225 4191-9
 Fax: (66) 2 222 6178
 Email: bangpain@hotmail.com
Personnel:
 Man. Dir.: Wattana Uthokthum
 Phone: (66) 2 225 4191-9
 Fax: (66) 2 222 6178
 Email: bangpain@hotmail.com
 Mktg. Mgr.: Boonchana Charoenphol
 Phone: (66) 2 225 4191-9
 Fax: (66) 2 222 6178
 Gen. Mgr.: Uthai Thongsai
 Phone: (66) 35 261 4302
 Fax: (66) 35 261 4334
 Email: bangpain@hotmail.com
Total Employees of Company: 350
Mill Locations:
Bang Pa-In Paper Mill Industry Co., Ltd., Ayutthaya Mill, 48 Moo 7, Tumbon Bangkrasan, Amphur Bang Pa-in, Phra Nakhon Si Ayutthaya 13160, Thailand, Capacity: 24,000 mt/y, (Pulp mill, Paper mill)
 Phone: (66) 35 261 430-2
 Fax: (66) 35 261 433-4
 Email: bangpain@hotmail.com

ⓘBang Pa-In Paper Mill Industry Co., Ltd.
Ayutthaya Mill
48 Moo 7, Tumbon Bangkrasan, Amphur Bang Pa-in
Phra Nakhon Si Ayutthaya, 13160
Thailand
 Phone: (66) 35 261 430-2
 Fax: (66) 35 261 433-4
 Email: bangpain@hotmail.com
Personnel:
 Plant Mgr.: Wirote Samawattakul
 Phone: (66) 35 261 430-2
 Gen. Mgr.: Uthai Thongsai
 Phone: (66) 35 261 430-2
 Mktg. Mgr.: Boonchana Charoenphol
 Phone: (66) 35 261 430-2
 Dpty. Mktg. Dir.: Sirichai Nimitsrisawad
 Phone: (66) 35 261 430-2
 Email: sirichai_n@hotmail.com
Total Employees at this Location: 145
Type of Operation: Pulp mill, Paper mill
Pulp Mill Data:
Chemical Pulping Systems:
Batch digesters: 6
Bleach Plant Lines:
No. 1, Sequence: CEH, Capacity 10,000 admt/y
Paper/Paperboard Grades and Capacities:
Total paper and paperboard capacity: 24,000 mt/y
Uncoated woodfree/freesheet: 24,000 mt/y
Paper and Paperboard Mill Data:
Stock Preparation:
Pulpers: 2
Refiners: 6
Paper Machines: 1
No. 1, fourdrinier, total capacity 24,000 mt/y, Trim width 3.3 m, Uncoated woodfree/freesheet
Finishing Equipment:
Winders: 1
Sheeters: 1
Energy Data:
Power boilers: 2
Steam turbines: 2 at 4.5 MW
Electrical demand for mill: 47 MWh/D

ⓘⓜBanglane Paper Mill Co., Ltd.
Nakhon Pathom Mill
89 Moo 1, Suchart-patana Rd.
Banglane District, Nakhon Pathom, Nakhon Pathom, 73190
Thailand
 Phone: (66) 34 399 396
 Fax: (66) 34 399 398
Personnel:
 Man. Dir.: Walapa Tantisunthorn
 Phone: (66) 34 399 396
 Email: salesandservice@bpm.co.th
 Prod. Mgr.: Pornchai Punpipatpaiboon
 Phone: (66) 34 399 396
 Email: pornchai@bpm.co.th
 Purch. Mgr.: Rawee Kiengwarangkul
 Phone: (66) 34 399 396
 Email: rawee.bpm@gmail.com
Total Employees of Company: 180
Total Employees at this Location: 150

Thailand

Type of Operation: Paperboard mill
Pulp Grades and Capacities:
Total pulp capacity: 46,461 mt/y
Recycled Pulping: 46,461 mt/y
Pulp Mill Data:
Bleach Plant Systems: 1
DIP
Recycled Fiber Treatment Lines:
Flotation deinking lines: 1
Recycled packaging pulping lines: 1
Paper/Paperboard Grades and Capacities:
Total paper and paperboard capacity: 55,000 mt/y
Boxboard/cartonboard: 55,000 mt/y
Paper and Paperboard Mill Data:
Paper Machines: 1
No. 1, cylinder, total capacity 55,000 mt/y, Trim width 3.25 m, Boxboard/cartonboard
Coating Machines: 1
PM1, on machine
Energy Data:
Power boilers
Electrical demand for mill: 81 MWh/D

ⓗⓜBerli Jucker Cellox Ltd.
Bangplee Mill
330 Moo 9, Bangna Trad Rd. (Km. 19)
Bangchalong, Bangplee, Samut Prakarn, 10540
Thailand
  Phone: (66) 2 312 6115 30
  Fax: (66) 2 312 6173
  Web Address: www.bjc.co.th
Personnel:
  Gen. Mgr.: Rachpong Pruchyaphinan
  Phone: (66) 2 312 6115 30 Ext. 113
  Email: rachponp@bjc.co.th
  Mill Mgr. (Prachinburi Mill): Thirasak Kruthem
  Phone: (66) 2 312 6115 30
  Email: thirasak@bjc.co.th
  Mill Dir. (Bangplee mill): Lek Techapatikul
  Phone: (66) 2 312 6115 30 Ext. 110
  Email: lekt@bjc.co.th
  Mktg. Dir.: Thanate Chirasuk
  Phone: (66) 2 312 6115 30
  Finan. & Acctg. Dir.: Sureerat Silpsakulsuk
  Phone: (66) 2 312 6115 30
Total Employees of Company: 900
Total Employees at this Location: 100
Type of Operation: Paper mill
Mill Locations:
Berli Jucker Cellox Ltd., Prachinburi Mill, 598, Moo 10, Thathoom, Srimahapoth, Prachinburi 25140, Thailand, Capacity: 25,000 mt/y, (Paper mill)
Phone: (66) 3 7270 000
Fax: (66) 3 7270 099
Pulp Grades and Capacities:
Total pulp capacity: 4,482 mt/y
Recycled Pulping: 4,482 mt/y
Pulp Mill Data:
Bleach Plant Systems: 1
Recycled Pulping System, Type: Deinked
Recycled Fiber Treatment Lines:
Flotation deinking lines: 1
Paper/Paperboard Grades and Capacities:
Total paper and paperboard capacity: 24,000 mt/y
Tissue: 24,000 mt/y
Paper and Paperboard Mill Data:
Stock Preparation:
Pulpers: 3
Refiners: 4
Paper Machines: 2
No. 2, fourdrinier, total capacity 6,400 mt/y, Trim width 2.4 m, Tissue
No. 3, crescent former, total capacity 17,600 mt/y, Trim width 2.49 m, Tissue, Uncoated woodfree/freesheet
Finishing Equipment:
Winders: 2
Energy Data:
Power boilers: 3
Electrical demand for mill: 52 MWh/D

ⓜBerli Jucker Cellox Ltd.
Prachinburi Mill
598, Moo 10, Thathoom
Srimahapoth, Prachinburi, 25140
Thailand
  Phone: (66) 3 7270 000
  Fax: (66) 3 7270 099
Personnel:
  Mill Dir: Thirasak Kruthem
  Phone: (66) 3 7270 000
  Email: thirasak@bjc.co.th
Total Employees at this Location: 87
Type of Operation: Paper mill
Pulp Grades and Capacities:
Total pulp capacity: 13,223 mt/y
Recycled Pulping: 13,223 mt/y
Pulp Mill Data:
Bleach Plant Systems: 1
Recycled Pulping System, Type: Deinked
Recycled Fiber Treatment Lines:
Flotation deinking lines: 1
Paper/Paperboard Grades and Capacities:
Total paper and paperboard capacity: 25,000 mt/y
Tissue: 25,000 mt/y
Paper and Paperboard Mill Data:
Paper Machines: 1
No. 4, crescent former, total capacity 25,000 mt/y, Trim width 2.75 m, Tissue
Energy Data:
Power boilers
Electrical demand for mill: 71 MWh/D

ⓜCharoen Aksorn Holding Group Co. Ltd. (CAS Group)
1 Charoenrat Road, Thung Wat Don, Sathon
Bangkok, 10120
Thailand
  Phone: (66) 2210 8888
  Fax: (66) 2210 8811
  Email: webmaster_group@cas-group.com
  Web Address: www.cas-group.com
Personnel:
  Man. Dir.: Torpong Thongcharoen
  Phone: (66) 2 661 3486
  Fax: (66) 2 661 3012
  Sls. Mgr.: Phatchraphorn Auimlaorphakdee
  Phone: (66) 2 661 3486
  Fax: (66) 2 661 3012
  Snr. Mgr. Supply & Logistics Dept.: Ms. Arunee Suthimaskul
  Phone: (66) 2 661 3486
  Fax: (66) 2 661 3012
Total Employees at this Location: 29
Mill Locations:
Charoen Aksorn Holding Group Co. Ltd. (CAS Group), Singburi Mill (10% owned), 64/3 Moo 3, Asian Highway Phokruam, Route No. 32, Sec. Singburi-Chainart, Amphur Muang, Singburi 16000, Thailand, Capacity: 124,950 mt/y, (Paper mill)
Phone: (66) 36 531 111
Fax: (66) 36 531 100
Charoen Aksorn Holding Group Co. Ltd. (CAS Group), Singburi Mill (10% owned), 64/3 Moo 3, Asian Highway Phokruam, Route No. 32, Sec. Singburi-Chainart, Amphur Muang, Singburi 16000, Thailand, Capacity: 124,950 mt/y, (Paper mill)
Phone: (66) 36 531 111
Fax: (66) 36 531 100

ⓜCharoen Aksorn Holding Group Co. Ltd. (CAS Group)
Singburi Mill
Mill is Previously: Norske Skog (Thailand) Co., Ltd.
Ownership: 10% by Charoen Aksorn Holding Group Co. Ltd. (CAS Group)
64/3 Moo 3, Asian Highway Phokruam, Route No. 32, Sec. Singburi-Chainart
Amphur Muang, Singburi, 16000
Thailand
  Phone: (66) 36 531 111
  Fax: (66) 36 531 100
  Web Address: www.cas-group.com
Personnel:
  Man. Dir., Mill Mgr.: Torpong Thongcharoen
  Phone: (66) 2 661 3486-90
  Fax: (66) 2 661 3012
Total Employees at this Location: 239
Type of Operation: Paper mill
Pulp Grades and Capacities:
Total pulp capacity: 127,330 mt/y
Recycled Pulping: 127,330 mt/y
Pulp Mill Data:
Bleach Plant Systems: 1
DIP
Recycled Fiber Treatment Lines:
Flotation deinking lines: 1
Paper/Paperboard Grades and Capacities:
Total paper and paperboard capacity: 124,950 mt/y
Newsprint: 124,950 mt/y
Paper and Paperboard Mill Data:
Stock Preparation:
Pulpers: 2
Paper Machines: 1
No. 1, twin-wire, total capacity 124,950 mt/y, Trim width 4.8 m, Newsprint
Finishing Equipment:
Rewinders: 1 at 127,000 mt/y
Energy Data:
Power boilers: 2
Electrical demand for mill: 327 MWh/D

ⓗⓜCharoen Chai Co., Ltd.
Bangkok Mill
16, Soi Ekkachi 83/1, Bangbon
Bangkok, Bangkok, 10150
Thailand
  Phone: (66) 2 415 2042
  Fax: (66) 2 415 4695
Personnel:
  Man. Dir.: Wanchai Techavesnukul
  Phone: (66) 2 415 2042
Type of Operation: Paperboard mill
Paper/Paperboard Grades and Capacities:
Total paper and paperboard capacity: 4,800 mt/y
Linerboard
Corrugating medium/fluting

ⓗⓜDouble A (1991) Public Co., Ltd.
Prachinburi Mill
Ownership: 14.48% by Always Rich Holdings, 4.89% by Wiseley Managment Private, 1.99% by Other Private investors, 16.13% by Double A (1991) Public Co., Ltd., 62.51% by Double A Holdings Limited
1 Moo 2, Tha Toom District
Amphur Sri Maha Phote, Prachinburi, 25140
Thailand
  Phone: (66) 37 208800
  Fax: (66) 37 208850-1
  Web Address: www.doubleapaper.com
Personnel:
  Founder Chmn., Exec. Dir.: Kitti Dumnerncharnvanit
  Phone: (66) 37 208800
  Fax: (66) 37 208850-1
  Pres. Exec. Dir. Man. Dir.: Yothin Dumnernchanvanit
  Phone: (66) 37 208800
  Fax: (66) 37 208850-1
  Chmn Bd. Directors & Exec.: Narong Srisa-an
  Phone: (66) 37 208800
  Fax: (66) 37 208850-1
  Vice Chmn.: Sirin Nimmanhaerninda
  Phone: (66) 37 208800
  Fax: (66) 37 208850-1
  Chmn of Exec. Bd.: Dr. Virabongsa Ramangkrua
  Phone: (66) 37 208800
  Fax: (66) 37 208850-1
  Sen. Exec. VP: Khun Charnvit Jarusombathi

Thailand

Phone: (66) 37 208800
Fax: (66) 37 208850-1
Exec. Dir.: Pracha Charutrakulchai
Phone: (66) 37 208800
Fax: (66) 37 208850-1
Indep. Dir.: Narong Mahanonda
Phone: (66) 37 208800
Fax: (66) 37 208850-1
Invest. Relat. Section Mgr.: Parawee Sriviriyaporn
Phone: (66) 37 208800
Fax: (66) 37 208850-1
Email: parawee_s@advanceagro.com
Total Employees of Company: 923
Total Employees at this Location: 850
Type of Operation: Pulp mill, Paper mill
Mill Locations:
Double A (1991) Public Co., Ltd., Alizay Mill, Z.I. du Clos Pré, BP 1, F-27460 Alizay, France, Capacity: 300,000 mt/y, (Paper mill)
Phone: (33) 2 35 02 72 72
Fax: (33) 2 35 02 14 60
Pulp Grades and Capacities:
Total pulp capacity: 584,684 mt/y
Chemical Pulp: 584,684 mt/y
Pulp Mill Data:
Chemical Pulping Systems:
Batch digesters: 2
Pulp Lines: 2
Bleach Plant Systems: 2
No. 1, Sequence: O_2 DoEopD
No. 2, Sequence: O_2 DoEopD
Chemical Recovery Equipment:
Evaporator lines: 1
Recovery boilers: 2
Lime Kiln
Pulp Dryers:
Flakt dryer 1, Wet Lap machine 1
Paper/Paperboard Grades and Capacities:
Total paper and paperboard capacity: 712,295 mt/y
Uncoated woodfree/freesheet: 712,295 mt/y
Paper and Paperboard Mill Data:
Paper Machines: 3
No. 1, Bel-Form, total capacity 252,399 mt/y, Trim width 6.9 m, Uncoated woodfree/freesheet
No. 2, Bel-Form, total capacity 259,896 mt/y, Trim width 6.9 m, Uncoated woodfree/freesheet
No. 3, fourdrinier, total capacity 200,000 mt/y, Trim width 5.28 m, Uncoated woodfree/freesheet
Finishing Equipment:
Sheeters: 8
Energy Data:
Power boilers: 2
Combustion turbines: 2 at 150, 150 MW
Steam turbines: 3 at 37, 37, 33 MW
Electrical demand for mill: 1,566 MWh/D

ⓄⓂDouble A (1991) Public Co., Ltd.
Chachoengsao Mill
Ownership: 14.48% by Always Rich Holdings, 4.89% by Wiseley Managment Private, 1.99% by Other Private investors, 16.13% by Double A (1991) Public Co., Ltd., 62.51% by Double A Holdings Limited
99/1 Moo 3, Tumbon Kaohinzon
Amphur Phanomsarakarm, Chachoengsao, 24120
Thailand
Phone: (66) 38 855 055
Fax: (66) 38 855 055 ext. 5201
Personnel:
CEO: Somyoch Ketintra
Phone: (66) 38 855 055
Email: somyoch_k@doublea1991.com
Mill Mgr.: Marnus Srituntananon
Phone: (66) 38 855 055
Email: manus_s@doublea1991.com
Mktg. Mgr.: Pakwipa Kasemsrirat
Phone: (66) 38 855 055
Email: pakwipa_k@doublea1991.com
Purch. Mgr.: Prartana Peungcharoenkul

Phone: (66) 38 855 055
Email: prartana_p@doublea1991.com
Total Employees at this Location: 134
Type of Operation: Paper mill

ⓄThe Eastern Industrial Co., Ltd.
Ownership: 20% by Mr. Chuan Yipyintum, 20% by Mr. Monkol Yipyintum, 5% by Mr. Samlith Yipyintum, 20% by Mr. Samran Yipyintum, 5% by Mr. Suthipong Pipattanatikanant, 20% by Mrs. Malee Yipyintum
156 Moo 1, Vibhavadee-Rangsit Rd., Bangkhen
Laksi, Bangkok, 10210
Thailand
Phone: (66) 2 984 8901-6
Fax: (66) 2 984 8900
Email: easternpaper@hotmail.com
Personnel:
Man. Dir.: Vithaya Janviriyasopark
Phone: (66) 2 573 3976
Fax: (66) 2 984 8900
Email: easternpaper@hotmail.com
Total Employees of Company: 600
Mill Locations:
The Eastern Industrial Co., Ltd., Pathumthani Mill, 76/1 Moo 4, Tumbon Banklang, Amphur Muang, Pathumthani 10200, Thailand, Capacity: 95,000 mt/y, (Paper mill, Paperboard)
Phone: (66) 2 581 6527/5826616-7/5815142
Fax: (66) 2 581 6526

ⓂThe Eastern Industrial Co., Ltd.
Pathumthani Mill
76/1 Moo 4, Tumbon Banklang
Amphur Muang, Pathumthani, 10200
Thailand
Phone: (66) 2 581 6527/5826616-7/5815142
Fax: (66) 2 581 6526
Personnel:
Man. Dir.: Vithaya Janviriyasopark
Phone: (66) 2 984 8901-6
Fax: (66) 2 984 8900
Email: easternpaper@hotmail.com
Total Employees at this Location: 600
Type of Operation: Paper mill, Paperboard mill
Paper/Paperboard Grades and Capacities:
Total paper and paperboard capacity: 95,000 mt/y
Uncoated woodfree/freesheet: 55,000 mt/y
Boxboard/cartonboard: 40,000 mt/y
Paper and Paperboard Mill Data:
Paper Machines: 2
No. 5, fourdrinier
No. 10, fourdrinier

ⓄEnvironment Pulp and Paper Co., Ltd.
Ownership: King Wan Group, Thai Indentity Sugar Group
24 Aekphol Building, 2nd floor, Vibhavadee-Rangsit Rd
Din-Daeng, Bangkok, 10400
Thailand
Phone: (66) 2 247 0920-3
Fax: (66) 2 247 0925
Email: marketing@eppcopulp.com
Web Address: www.eppcopulp.com
Personnel:
Man. Dir.: Parpan Siriviriyakul
Phone: (66) 2 247 0920-23
Fax: (66) 2 247 0925
Email: hq_eppco@tis-sugar.com
Gen. Mgr.: Pornpiboon Petchaskol
Phone: (66) 2 247 0920-23
Fax: (66) 2 247 0925
Email: marketing@eppcopulp.com
Mill Mgr.: Warin Supakijpaisal
Phone: (66) 2 247 0920-23
Fax: (66) 2 247 0925
Email: hq_eppco@tis-sugar.com
Purch. Mgr.: Ratana Suvachitanont

Phone: (66) 2 247 0920-23
Fax: (66) 2 247 0925
Mktg. Mgr.: Thanee Pongyila
Phone: (66) 2 247 0667
Dep. Man. Dir.: Somchai Suwachittanont
Phone: (66) 2 247 0920-23
Fax: (66) 2 247 0925
Mktg. Mgr.: Chaiwat Kulteerapongtorn
Phone: (66) 2 247 0920-23
Fax: (66) 2 247 0925
Email: chaiwat@eppcopulp.com
Total Employees of Company: 500
Mill Locations:
Environment Pulp and Paper Co., Ltd., Nakhon Sawan Mill, 9/9 Moo 1, Nongpho District, Amphur Takli, Nakhon Sawan 60140, Thailand, (Pulp mill)
Phone: (66) 56 338 338
Fax: (66) 56 338 339
Email: marketing@eppcopulp.com

ⓂEnvironment Pulp and Paper Co., Ltd.
Nakhon Sawan Mill
9/9 Moo 1
Nongpho District, Amphur Takli, Nakhon Sawan, 60140
Thailand
Phone: (66) 56 338 338
Fax: (66) 56 338 339
Email: marketing@eppcopulp.com
Web Address: www.eppcopulp.com
Personnel:
Mill Mgr.: Warin Supakijpaisal
Phone: (66) 56 338 338
Email: hq_eppco@tis-sugar.com
Type of Operation: Pulp mill
Pulp Grades and Capacities:
Total pulp capacity: 100,000 mt/y
Pulp available for market: 100,000 mt/y
Pulp Mill Data:
Chemical Pulping Systems:
Continuous digesters: 2
Pulp Lines: 1
Bleach Plant Systems: 1
No. 1, Sequence: DEopD, Capacity 100,000 admt/y
Chemical Recovery Equipment:
Evaporator lines: 1
Recovery boilers: 1
Pulp Dryers:
Fourdriniers 2
Energy Data:
Power boilers: 2
Steam turbines: 2 at 32 MW

ⓄFiber Pattana Co., Ltd.
999/130 Moo 6, Teparak Road, Teparak
Amphur Muang, Samut Prakarn, 10270
Thailand
Phone: (66) 02 397 9453-5
Fax: (66) 02 397 9451
Total Employees of Company: 45
Mill Locations:
Fiber Pattana Co., Ltd., Samut Prankan Mill, 30/11 Moo 11, Soi Wat Bangsaotong, Bangna-Trad Road (Km.23), Bang Sao Thong 10540, Thailand, (Pulp mill)
Phone: (66) 086 321 3621
Fax: (66) 02 422 5055

ⓂFiber Pattana Co., Ltd.
Samut Prankan Mill
30/11 Moo 11, Soi Wat Bangsaotong, Bangna-Trad Road (Km.23)
Bang Sao Thong, Samut Prakarn, 10540
Thailand
Phone: (66) 086 321 3621
Fax: (66) 02 422 5055
Personnel:
Tech. Dir.: Paijit Sangchai
Email: paijits@flexoresearch.com
Type of Operation: Pulp mill

Thailand

Pulp Grades and Capacities:
Total pulp capacity: 18,000 mt/y
Pulp available for market: 18,000 mt/y

ⓂHiang Seng Fibre Container Co., Ltd.
Ownership: Dr. Supote Tejavibulya, Mr. Liang Tejavibulya, Mr. Prasert Tejavibulya, Mr. Surapong Tejavibulya, Mr. Suthas Tejavibulya, Mr. Suthi Tejavibulya
389 Rimtangrotfire-Chongnonsee Road, Klongtoey
Bangkok, 10110
Thailand
Phone: (66) 2 249 0251
Fax: (66) 2 249 5713
Personnel:
Pres.: Suthas Tejavibulya
Phone: (66) 2 249 0251
Fax: (66) 2 249 5713
Man. Dir.: Sarunyou Tejavibulya
Phone: (66) 2 249 0251-4
Fax: (66) 2 249 5714
Email: sarunyou@hsfc.co.th
Asst. Man. Dir.: Sombun Peratanakul
Phone: (66) 2 249 0251
Fax: (66) 2 249 5713
Email: sombun@hsfc.co.th
Total Employees of Company: 1,000
Mill Locations:
Hiang Seng Fibre Container Co., Ltd., Samut Sakohn Mill, 110/4 Moo 4, Sethakit 1 Road, Ban- Khow, Amphur Muang, Samut Sakohn 74000, Thailand, Capacity: 500,000 mt/y, (Paper mill, Paperboard mill)
Phone: (66) 34 423 019
Fax: (66) 34 424 680

ⓂHiang Seng Fibre Container Co., Ltd.
Samut Sakohn Mill
110/4 Moo 4, Sethakit 1 Road, Ban- Khow
Amphur Muang, Samut Sakohn, 74000
Thailand
Phone: (66) 34 423 019
Fax: (66) 34 424 680
Web Address: www.hsfc.co.th
Personnel:
Pres.: Mr. Suthas Tejavibulya
Phone: (66) 34 423 019
Fax: (66) 34 424 680
Exec. Dir.: Sutee Tejavibulya
Phone: (66) 34 423 019
Fax: (66) 34 424 680
Man. Dir.: Sarunyou Tejavibulya
Phone: (66) 34 423 019
Fax: (66) 34 424 680
Email: sarunyou@hsfc.co.th
Exec. Dir.: Chotinon Tejavibulya
Phone: (66) 34 423 019
Fax: (66) 34 424 680
Total Employees at this Location: 500
Type of Operation: Paper mill, Paperboard mill
Pulp Grades and Capacities:
Total pulp capacity: 466,786 mt/y
Recycled Pulping: 466,786 mt/y
Pulp Mill Data:
Chemical Recovery Equipment:
Evaporator lines
Recycled Fiber Treatment Lines:
Recycled packaging pulping lines: 1
Paper/Paperboard Grades and Capacities:
Total paper and paperboard capacity: 500,000 mt/y
Packaging papers: 52,500 mt/y
Linerboard: 245,500 mt/y
Corrugating medium/fluting: 202,000 mt/y
Paper and Paperboard Mill Data:
Stock Preparation:
Pulpers: 7
Refiners: 12
Paper Machines: 4
No. 1, multi-fourdrinier, total capacity 145,000 mt/y, Trim width 4.4 m, Corrugating medium/fluting, Linerboard
No. 2, fourdrinier, total capacity 70,000 mt/y, Trim width 4.2 m, Corrugating medium/fluting
No. 3, multi-fourdrinier, total capacity 180,000 mt/y, Trim width 4.3 m, Corrugating medium/fluting, Linerboard
No. 4, multi-fourdrinier, total capacity 105,000 mt/y, Trim width 4.3 m, Packaging papers, Corrugating medium/fluting
Finishing Equipment:
Supercalenders: 2
Rewinders: 3
Sheeters: 2
Energy Data:
Power boilers: 2
Steam turbines: 3 at 38.0 MW

ⓂThe Industrial Krungthai Co., Ltd.
6 Rongmuang Lane 2 St.
Patumwan, Bangkok, 10330
Thailand
Phone: (66) 2 214 4009/3881
Fax: (66) 2 215 5816
Personnel:
Man. Dir.: Mr. Thamanoon Trakulyuthachai
Phone: (66) 2 2144319/5262
Fax: (66) 2 9779522
Total Employees of Company: 250
Mill Locations:
The Industrial Krungthai Co., Ltd., Pathumthani Mill, 72/2 Moo 1 Tumbon Bangkrachang, Amphur Muang, Pathumthani 12000, Thailand, Capacity: 28,000 mt/y, (Paper mill)
Phone: (66) 2 979 6011-2
Fax: (66) 2 581 5381

ⓂThe Industrial Krungthai Co., Ltd.
Pathumthani Mill
72/2 Moo 1 Tumbon Bangkrachang
Amphur Muang, Pathumthani, 12000
Thailand
Phone: (66) 2 979 6011-2
Fax: (66) 2 581 5381
Personnel:
Man. Dir.: Mr. Thamanoon Trakulyuthachai
Phone: (66) 2 979 6011-2
Total Employees at this Location: 250
Type of Operation: Paper mill
Paper/Paperboard Grades and Capacities:
Total paper and paperboard capacity: 28,000 mt/y
Uncoated woodfree/freesheet: 28,000 mt/y

ⓂInter Pacific Paper Co., Ltd
99 Moo 4, Baan Sang-Klong Sarapee Road
Bangpluang, Prachin Buri, 25150
Thailand
Phone: (66) 37 213 333
Fax: (66) 37 214 999
Mill Locations:
Inter Pacific Paper Co., Ltd, Banpluang, Baansang Mill, 99 Moo 4 Baansang-Klong Sarapee Rd., Banpluang, Baansang, Prachinburi 25140, Thailand, Capacity: 90,000 mt/y, (Paper mill)
Phone: (66) 37 213 333
Fax: (66) 37 214 999

ⓂInter Pacific Paper Co., Ltd
Banpluang, Baansang Mill
99 Moo 4 Baansang-Klong Sarapee Rd.
Banpluang, Baansang, Prachinburi, 25140
Thailand
Phone: (66) 37 213 333
Fax: (66) 37 214 999
Web Address: www.ippth.com
Personnel:
Man. Dir: Mr. Somchai Rangnoktai
Phone: (66) 2 421 9999 ext. 230
Fax: (66) 2 454 3385
Email: somchai@ippth.com
VP Mktg.: Ms. Sukanya Rangnoktai
Phone: (66) 37 213 333
Mill Mgr.: Mr. Kamol Soponphan
Phone: (66) 37 213 333
Total Employees at this Location: 200
Type of Operation: Paper mill
Pulp Grades and Capacities:
Total pulp capacity: 87,886 mt/y
Recycled Pulping: 87,886 mt/y
Pulp Mill Data:
Recycled Fiber Treatment Lines:
Recycled packaging pulping lines
Paper/Paperboard Grades and Capacities:
Total paper and paperboard capacity: 90,000 mt/y
Linerboard: 15,000 mt/y
Corrugating medium/fluting: 75,000 mt/y
Paper and Paperboard Mill Data:
Paper Machines: 1
No. 1, fourdrinier, total capacity 90,000 mt/y, Linerboard, Corrugating medium/fluting
Energy Data:
Power boilers
Steam turbines: 2 at 9.5 MW
Electrical demand for mill: 104 MWh/D

ⓂKimberly-Clark Thailand Ltd.
Ownership: Kimberly-Clark Corp.
32nd-33rd Floor, United Center Bldg., 323 Silom Rd.
Bangrak, Bangkok, 10500
Thailand
Phone: (66) 2 230 3000
Fax: (66) 2 267 6093/6122
Web Address: www.kimberly-clark.com/Thailand/
Personnel:
Man. Dir.: Paul Patelis
Phone: (66) 2 230 3000
Fax: (66) 2 267 6093/6122
Email: paul.s.patelis@kcc.com
Mill Mgr.: Pakinai Tangtrakul
Phone: (66) 2 230 3000
Fax: (66) 2 267 6093/6122
Email: pakinai.tangtrakul@kcc.com
Sls. Dir.: Sathit Lertsukwibul
Phone: (66) 2 230 3000
Fax: (66) 2 267 6093/6122
Email: sathit.lertsukwibul@kcc.com
Logistic Mgr.: Nittaya Palittapongkanpim
Phone: (66) 2 230 3000
Fax: (66) 2 267 6093/6122
Email: nittaya.palittaponkanpim@kcc.com
Total Employees of Company: 601
Mill Locations:
Kimberly-Clark Thailand Ltd., Pathumthani Mill, 54 Moo 6 Tambon Bangkayang, Amphur Muang, Pathumthani 12000, Thailand, Capacity: 20,000 mt/y, (Paper mill)
Phone: (66) 2 598 2700-14
Fax: (66) 2 975 3099/5982711
Kimberly-Clark Thailand Ltd., Samut Prakan Mill, 58 Moo 2 Poochaosamingprai Road, Tambon Bangyapraek, Amphur Phrapradaeng 10130, Thailand, Capacity: 17,493 mt/y, (Paper mill)
Phone: (66) 2 755 9011-13
Fax: (66) 2 384 3594

ⓂKimberly-Clark Thailand Ltd.
Pathumthani Mill
Mill is
Ownership: Kimberly-Clark Corp.
54 Moo 6 Tambon Bangkayang
Amphur Muang, Pathumthani, 12000
Thailand
Phone: (66) 2 598 2700-14
Fax: (66) 2 975 3099/5982711
Web Address: www.kimberly-clark.com/thailand
Personnel:
Mill Mgr.: Pakinai Tangtrakul
Phone: (66) 2 598 2700-14 ext. 104
Fax: (66) 2 950 2318

Thailand

Email: pakinai.tangtrakul@kcc.com
Man. Dir.: Paul Patelis
Phone: (66) 2 598 2700-14
Email: paul.s.patelis@kcc.com
Total Employees at this Location: 601
Type of Operation: Paper mill
Pulp Grades and Capacities:
Total pulp capacity: 13,697 mt/y
Recycled Pulping: 13,697 mt/y
Pulp Mill Data:
Bleach Plant Systems: 1
DIP
Recycled Fiber Treatment Lines:
Flotation deinking lines: 1
Paper/Paperboard Grades and Capacities:
Total paper and paperboard capacity: 20,000 mt/y
Tissue: 20,000 mt/y
Paper and Paperboard Mill Data:
Paper Machines: 1
No. 2, crescent former, total capacity 20,000 mt/y, Trim width 2.45 m, Tissue, Uncoated woodfree/freesheet
Energy Data:
Power boilers: 2
Electrical demand for mill: 64 MWh/D

ⓜKimberly-Clark Thailand Ltd.
Samut Prakan Mill
Ownership: Kimberly-Clark Corp.
58 Moo 2 Poochaosamingprai Road, Tambon Bangyapraek
Amphur Phrapradaeng, Samut Prakam, 10130
Thailand
Phone: (66) 2 755 9011-13
Fax: (66) 2 384 3594
Web Address: www.kcc.com
Personnel:
Mill Mgr.: Sukanya Prakongwittaya
Phone: (66) 2 755 9011-13
Total Employees at this Location: 120
Type of Operation: Paper mill
Paper/Paperboard Grades and Capacities:
Total paper and paperboard capacity: 17,493 mt/y
Tissue: 17,493 mt/y
Paper and Paperboard Mill Data:
Paper Machines: 1
No. 1, twin-wire, total capacity 17,493 mt/y, Trim width 2.21 m, Tissue
Energy Data:
Power boilers: 1
Electrical demand for mill: 52 MWh/D

ⓟⓜKrishna Mongkol Co., Ltd.
Nakhon Pathom Mill
2/1 Moo 8/Kong-Thong Road, Tumbon Wangnamkhew
Amphur Kampangsan, Nakhon Pathom, Nakhon Pathom, 73140
Thailand
Phone: (66) 34 204 491-6
Fax: (66) 34 204 493/496
Personnel:
Man. Dir.: Wanchai Tachavejnukul
Phone: (66) 34 204 491-6
Total Employees of Company: 100
Total Employees at this Location: 90
Type of Operation: Paperboard mill
Pulp Grades and Capacities:
Total pulp capacity: 19,338 mt/y
Recycled Pulping: 19,338 mt/y
Pulp Mill Data:
Recycled Fiber Treatment Lines:
Recycled packaging pulping lines: 1
Paper/Paperboard Grades and Capacities:
Total paper and paperboard capacity: 20,000 mt/y
Corrugating medium/fluting: 20,000 mt/y
Paper and Paperboard Mill Data:
Paper Machines: 1

No. 1, (Supplier: Shandong Ludu.), cylinder, total capacity 20,000 mt/y, Trim width 1.88 m, Corrugating medium/fluting
Energy Data:
Electrical demand for mill: 24 MWh/D

ⓟⓜMahachai Kraft Paper Co., Ltd.
Samut Sakohn Mill
Ownership: 65% by Mr. Sangchai Sodtivarakul, 35% by Ms. Darat Sodtivarakul
93/9 G.4 Soi Watbangpla, Sethakit Rd., Tumbon Bankao
Amphur Muang, Samut Sakohn, 74000
Thailand
Phone: (66) 34 468 135-9
Fax: (66) 34 830 100/468 134
Email: mkpc@mahachaikraftpaper.com
Web Address: www.mahachaikraftpaper.com
Personnel:
Dir.: Dr. Sangchai Sodtivorakul
Phone: (66) 34 468 135-9
Man. Dir.: Nucharin Kovitkanit
Phone: (66) 34 468 135-9
Mill Mgr.: Paiboon Maungnoijarean
Phone: (66) 34 468 135-9
Email: factory@mahachaikraftpaper.com
Dpty. Man. Dir.: Daorin Sodtivarakul
Phone: (66) 34 468 135-9
Mill Mgr.: Veerawit Kaewkrong
Phone: (66) 34 468 135-9
Asst. to Dpty. Man. Dir.: Umpai Wongsueb
Phone: (66) 34 468 135-9
Email: sale@mahachaikraftpaper.com
Asst. to Man. Dir.: Sarin Sodtivarakul
Phone: (66) 34 468 135-9
Email: sarin@mahachaikraftpaper.com
Total Employees at this Location: 260
Type of Operation: Pulp mill, Paper mill, Paperboard mill
Pulp Grades and Capacities:
Total pulp capacity: 85,330 mt/y
Recycled Pulping: 85,330 mt/y
Pulp Mill Data:
Recycled Fiber Treatment Lines:
Recycled packaging pulping lines: 2
Paper/Paperboard Grades and Capacities:
Total paper and paperboard capacity: 90,713 mt/y
Specialty and industrial: 3,213 mt/y
Linerboard: 17,500 mt/y
Corrugating medium/fluting: 70,000 mt/y
Paper and Paperboard Mill Data:
Stock Preparation:
Pulpers: 6
Refiners: 5
Paper Machines: 3
No. 1, cylinder, total capacity 12,500 mt/y, Trim width 2.25 m, Corrugating medium/fluting, Linerboard
No. 2, fourdrinier, total capacity 75,000 mt/y, Trim width 4.5 m, Corrugating medium/fluting, Linerboard
No. 3, Yankee dryer, total capacity 3,213 mt/y, Trim width 1.54 m, Specialty and industrial
Finishing Equipment:
Supercalenders: 3
Rewinders: 4
Sheeters: 1
Energy Data:
Power boilers: 4
Electrical demand for mill: 108 MWh/D

ⓟPanjapol Paper Industry Company Limited and Panjapol Pulp Industry Public Co., Ltd.
Ownership: 5% by Others, 95% by Tejavibulya Family
323 United Center Building, 44th Floor Silom Road
Bangrak, Bangkok, 10500
Thailand
Phone: (66) 2 231 1100-10
Fax: (66) 2 231 1422

Personnel:
CFO: Ms. Pinsri Liyamapornsakul
Phone: (66) 2 231 1100-10
Fax: (66) 2 231 1422
Email: pinsri@ppi.co.th
Sls. Mgr.: Mr. Peeraphong Wongkulawat
Phone: (66) 2 231 1100-10
Fax: (66) 2 231 1422
Email: peeraphong@ppi.co.th
Mill Inspector: Mr. Sawat Pusanadilok
Phone: (66) 2 231 1100-10
Fax: (66) 2 231 1422
Email: sawat@ppi.co.th
Purch. Mgr.: Mrs. Phalakorn Ratawessanun
Phone: (66) 2 231 1100-10
Fax: (66) 2 231 1422
Email: phalakorn@ppi.co.th
Sls. Department: Ms. Benjarat Sanguanpong
Phone: (66) 2 231 1100-10
Fax: (66) 2 231 1422
Email: nongpooppi@hotmail.com
Total Employees of Company: 720

ⓜPanjapol Paper Industry Co. Ltd. and Panjapol Pulp Industry Public Co., Ltd.
Ayutthaya Mill
51 Moo 3, Pathum-Sena Road, T.Hormok
Bangsai District, Ayutthaya, 13190
Thailand
Phone: (66) 3520 1997-8
Fax: (66) 3520 1993
Email: missilom@ppi.co.th
Personnel:
Mill Mgr.: Mr. Sawat Pusanadilok
Phone: (66) 35 201 997-8
Fax: (66) 35 201 997
Email: sawat@ppi.co.th
CFO: Ms. Pinsri Liyamapornsakul
Phone: (66) 3520 1997-8
Email: pinsri@ppi.co.th
Sls. Mgr.: Mr. Peeraphong Wongkulawat
Phone: (66) 3520 1997-8
Email: peeraphong@ppi.co.th
Purch. Mgr.: Ms. Phalakorn Ratawessanun
Phone: (66) 3520 1997-8
Email: phalakorn@ppi.co.th
Total Employees at this Location: 670
Type of Operation: Pulp mill, Paperboard mill
Pulp Grades and Capacities:
Total pulp capacity: 319,469 mt/y
Chemical Pulp: 73,036 mt/y
Recycled Pulping: 246,433 mt/y
Pulp Mill Data:
Chemical Pulping Systems:
Continuous digesters: 1
Chemical Recovery Equipment:
Recovery boilers: 1
Lime Kiln
Recycled Fiber Treatment Lines:
Recycled packaging pulping lines: 1 at 220,000
Paper/Paperboard Grades and Capacities:
Total paper and paperboard capacity: 320,000 mt/y
Linerboard: 180,000 mt/y
Corrugating medium/fluting: 140,000 mt/y
Paper and Paperboard Mill Data:
Paper Machines: 1
No. 1, fourdrinier (3), total capacity 320,000 mt/y, Trim width 7.1 m, Linerboard, Corrugating medium/fluting
Finishing Equipment:
Winders: 1
Energy Data:
Power boilers: 2
Steam turbines at 20 MW
Electrical demand for mill: 453 MWh/D

ⓜPanjapol Paper Industry Co. Ltd. and Panjapol Pulp Industry Public Co., Ltd.
51 Moo 3, Pathum-Sena Road, T.Hormok
Bangsai District, Ayutthaya, 1
Thailand

Thailand

Mailing Address: Hormok, Thailand
Phone: (66) 3520 1997-8
Fax: (66) 3520 1993
Email: missilom@ppi.co.th
Personnel:
CFO: Pinsri Liyamapornsakul
Phone: (66) 66 35 201 997-8
Fax: (66) 66 35 201 997
Email: pinsri@ppi.co.th
Mill Mgr: Sawat Pusanadilok
Phone: (66) 66 35 201 997-8
Fax: (66) 66 35 201 997
Email: sawat@ppi.co.th
Sls. Mgr: Peeraphong Wongkulawat
Phone: (66) 66 35 201 997-8
Fax: (66) 66 35 201 997
Email: peeraphong@ppi.co.th
Total Employees of Company: 720
Mill Locations:
Panjapol Paper Industry Co. Ltd. and Panjapol Pulp Industry Public Co., Ltd., Ayutthaya Mill, 51 Moo 3, Pathum-Sena Road, T.Hormok, Bangsai District, Ayutthaya 13190, Thailand, Capacity: 320,000 mt/y, (Pulp mill, Paperboard mill)
Phone: (66) 3520 1997-8
Fax: (66) 3520 1993
Email: missilom@ppi.co.th

ⓜPatoom Dhanee Paper Factory Ltd. Part

Ownership: 60% by Mr. Boonma Payoongthanakorn, 40% by Other
30/2 Moo 1, Tiwanont Rd., Tambon Banmai Amphur Muang, Pathumthani, 12000
Thailand
Phone: (66) 2 501 2843-6
Fax: (66) 2 501 2847
Personnel:
Man. Dir., Mktg. Mgr.: Boonma Payoongthanakorn
Phone: (66) 2 501 2843-6
Fax: (66) 2 501 2847
Mill Mgr., Gen. Mgr.: Kriang Intamonkolsuk
Phone: (66) 2 501 2843-6
Fax: (66) 2 501 2847
Total Employees at this Location: 250
Mill Locations:
Patoom Dhanee Paper Factory Ltd. Part, Pathumthani Mill, 30/2 Moo 1, Tiwanont Rd., Tambon Banmai, Amphur Muang, Pathumthani 12000, Thailand, Capacity: 50,500 mt/y, (Paper mill)
Phone: (66) 2 501 2843-6
Fax: (66) 2 501 2847

ⓜPatoom Dhanee Paper Factory Ltd. Part
Pathumthani Mill

30/2 Moo 1, Tiwanont Rd., Tambon Banmai Amphur Muang, Pathumthani, 12000
Thailand
Phone: (66) 2 501 2843-6
Fax: (66) 2 501 2847
Personnel:
Man. Dir./Mktg. Mgr.: Mr. Boonma Payoongthanakorn
Phone: (66) 2 501 2843-6
Mill Mgr., Gen. Mgr.: Mr. Kriang Intamonkolsuk
Phone: (66) 2 501 2843-6
Total Employees at this Location: 185
Type of Operation: Paper mill
Pulp Grades and Capacities:
Total pulp capacity: 49,925 mt/y
Recycled Pulping: 49,925 mt/y
Pulp Mill Data:
Recycled Fiber Treatment Lines:
Recycled packaging pulping lines: 1
Paper/Paperboard Grades and Capacities:
Total paper and paperboard capacity: 50,500 mt/y
Linerboard: 5,500 mt/y
Corrugating medium/fluting: 45,000 mt/y
Paper and Paperboard Mill Data:
Paper Machines: 1
No. 1, fourdrinier, total capacity 50,500 mt/y, Trim width 3.6 m, Corrugating medium/fluting, Linerboard
Energy Data:
Power boilers
Electrical demand for mill: 60 MWh/D

ⓜPhoenix Pulp & Paper Public Company, Ltd.

Ownership: 98.37% by SCG Paper Public Co., Ltd.
1 Siam Cement Rd.
Bangsue, Bangkok, 10800
Thailand
Phone: (66) 2586 6260/6295/6296
Fax: (66) 2586 6771
Email: mailbox@phoenixpulp.com
Web Address: www.scg.co.th
Personnel:
President, SCG Paper: Roongrote Rangsiyopash
Man. Dir.: Amnuay Ponpued
Phone: (66) 2586 6399
Fax: (66) 2586 6928
Email: amnuayp@scg.co.th
Mill Dir.: Jesda Saeliang
Phone: (66) 43 433 104-6
Fax: (66) 43 433-101
Email: jesdas@scg.co.th
Mktg. Mgr.: Chutimon Wiriyaaumpaiwong
Phone: (66) 2586 1200
Fax: (66) 2586 2164
Email: chutimon@scg.co.th
Total Employees of Company: 1,044
Mill Locations:
Phoenix Pulp & Paper Public Company, Ltd., Nam Phong Mill, 99 Moo 3, Tambol Kudnamsai, Amphur Nampong, Khon Kaen 40310, Thailand, Capacity: 159,936 mt/y, (Pulp mill, Paper mill, Paperboard mill)
Phone: (66) 43 433 104-6/373 406-8
Fax: (66) 43 433 101
Email: mailbox@scg.co.th, mailbox@phoenixpulp.com

ⓜPhoenix Pulp & Paper Public Company, Ltd.
Nam Phong Mill

Ownership: 98.37% by SCG Paper Public Co., Ltd.
99 Moo 3, Tambol Kudnamsai
Amphur Nampong, Khon Kaen, 40310
Thailand
Phone: (66) 43 433 104-6/373 406-8
Fax: (66) 43 433 101
Email: mailbox@scg.co.th, mailbox@phoenixpulp.com
Web Address: www.scg.co.th
Personnel:
Man. Dir.: Mr. Amnuay Ponpued
Phone: (66) 2586 6399
Fax: (66) 2586 6928
Email: amnuayp@scg.co.th
Total Employees at this Location: 800
Type of Operation: Pulp mill, Paper mill, Paperboard mill
Pulp Grades and Capacities:
Total pulp capacity: 276,172 mt/y
Pulp available for market: 159,936 mt/y
Chemical Pulp: 276,172 mt/y
Pulp Mill Data:
Chemical Pulping Systems:
Batch digesters: 1
Continuous digesters: 1
Pulp Lines: 2
Bleach Plant Systems: 2
Chemical Pulping System - Hardwood, Sequence: O_2 DEDD
Chemical Pulping System - Hardwood, Sequence: O_2 C=DED
Chemical Recovery Equipment:
Evaporator lines: 1
Recovery boilers: 2
Lime Kiln
Pulp Dryers:
Pulp Dryers 1, Pulp Dryers 1
Paper/Paperboard Grades and Capacities:
Total paper and paperboard capacity: 159,936 mt/y
Uncoated woodfree/freesheet: 159,936 mt/y
Paper and Paperboard Mill Data:
Paper Machines: 1
No. 1, DuoFormer D, total capacity 159,936 mt/y, Trim width 5.28 m, Uncoated woodfree/freesheet
Energy Data:
Power boilers: 3
Steam turbines: 4 at 5.5, 23, 35, 31 MW
Electrical demand for mill: 799 MWh/D

ⓜRiverpro Group

48 Moo 3, Tepparak Rd., Tambon Tepparak Amphur Mung.
Samut Prakarn, 10270
Thailand
Phone: (66) 2 384 7378 80
Fax: (66) 2 384 2901
Web Address: www.riverpro.co.th
Personnel:
Man. Dir.: Sumrit Yipyintum
Phone: (66) 2 384 7378 80
Fax: (66) 2 384 2901
Email: sumrit@riverpro.co.th
Prod. Dir.: Somjate Pulpol
Phone: (66) 2 384 7378 80
Fax: (66) 2 384 2901
Email: somjate@riverpro.co.th
Mill Locations:
Riverpro Pulp & Paper Co., Ltd., Saraburi Mill, 59 Moo 4 SIL Industrial Estate, Nongprakadee Rd., Tumbon Bualoi, Amphur Nong Kae, Saraburi 18140, Thailand, Capacity: 43,000 mt/y, (Paper mill)
Phone: (66) 36 373 717
Fax: (66) 36 373 719
Thanatarn Paper Co., Ltd., Taparak Mill, 48 Moo 3, Teparak Rd., Taparak 10270, Thailand, Capacity: 14,500 mt/y, (Paper mill)
Phone: (66) 2 384 7378-80/5656-60
Fax: (66) 2 384 2901
Email: thana1@ksc.th.com

ⓜRiverpro Pulp & Paper Co., Ltd.
Saraburi Mill

Ownership: Riverpro Group
59 Moo 4 SIL Industrial Estate, Nongprakadee Rd., Tumbon Bualoi, Amphur Nong Kae
Saraburi, 18140
Thailand
Phone: (66) 36 373 717
Fax: (66) 36 373 719
Web Address: www.riverpro.co.th
Personnel:
Man. Dir.: Sumrit Yipyintum
Phone: (66) 36 373 717
Prod. Dir: Somjate Pulpol
Phone: (66) 36 373 717
Type of Operation: Paper mill
Paper/Paperboard Grades and Capacities:
Total paper and paperboard capacity: 43,000 mt/y
Tissue: 43,000 mt/y
Paper and Paperboard Mill Data:
Paper Machines: 2
No. 1, total capacity 18,000 mt/y, Tissue
No. 2, (2nd hand, started February 2014), total capacity 25,000 mt/y, Trim width 3.1 m, Tissue

ⓜSaraburi Paper Co., Ltd

123 Mu6, Thumbol Kampran, Wang Muang
Saraburi, Bangkok, 18220
Thailand
Phone: (66) 36 226445-6
Fax: (66) 36 226447
Web Address: www.daatspaper.com
Personnel:

Thailand

Man.Dir: Adisorn Trakuyuthachai
Phone: (66) 36 226445-6
Fax: (66) 36 226447
Email: adisorn@daatspaper.com
Mktg.Mgr: Sumalee Arkaradejdachachai
Phone: (66) 36 226445-6
Fax: (66) 36 226447
Email: sumalee@daatspaper.com
Mill Mgr.: kitti Arkaradejdachachai
Phone: (66) 36 226445-6
Fax: (66) 36 226447
Email: kitti@daatspaper.com
Purch.Mgr.: Threerames Khanaporgputimes
Phone: (66) 36 226445-6
Fax: (66) 36 226447
Email: threerames@daatspaper.com
Total Employees at this Location: 120
Mill Locations:
Saraburi Paper Co., Ltd, Saraburi Mill, 123 Mu6, Thumbol Kampran, Wang Muang, Saraburi 18220, Thailand, Capacity: 72,000 mt/y, (Paper mill)
Phone: (66) 36 226445-6
Fax: (66) 36 226447

ⓜSaraburi Paper Co., Ltd
Saraburi Mill
123 Mu6, Thumbol Kampran, Wang Muang
Saraburi , Bangkok, 18220
Thailand
Phone: (66) 36 226445-6
Fax: (66) 36 226447
Web Address: www.daatspaper.com
Personnel:
Man.Dir: Mr. Adisorn Trakuyuthachai
Email: adisorn@daatspaper.com
Mktg.Mgr: Ms. Sumalee Arkaradejdachachai
Email: sumalee@daatspaper.com
Mill Mgr.: Mr. kitti Arkaradejdachachai
Email: kitti@daatspaper.com
Purch.Mgr.: Mr. Threerames Khanaporgputimes
Email: threerames@daatspaper.com
Total Employees at this Location: 120
Type of Operation: Paper mill
Pulp Grades and Capacities:
Total pulp capacity: 69,797 mt/y
Recycled Pulping: 69,797 mt/y

Pulp Mill Data:
Bleach Plant Systems: 1
Recycled Pulping System, Type: DIP
Recycled Fiber Treatment Lines:
Flotation deinking lines: 1
Paper/Paperboard Grades and Capacities:
Total paper and paperboard capacity: 72,000 mt/y
Newsprint: 72,000 mt/y
Paper and Paperboard Mill Data:
Paper Machines: 1
No. 1, fourdrinier, total capacity 72,000 mt/y, Trim width 4.8 m, Newsprint
Energy Data:
Power boilers
Electrical demand for mill: 204 MWh/D

ⓜSCG Paper Public Co., Ltd.
Ownership: Public
1 Siam Cement Rd.
Bangsue, Bangkok, 10800
Thailand
Phone: (66) 2586 4444/3333
Fax: (66) 2586 2164, 5347
Web Address: www.scg.co.th/en, paper.scg.co.th/en
Personnel:
Chmn.: Chirayu Isarangkun Na Ayuthaya
Phone: (66) 2586 4444/3333
Fax: (66) 2586 2164, 5347
Pres & CEO: Kan Trakulhoon
Phone: (66) 2586 4444/3333
Fax: (66) 2586 2164, 5347
Email: kant@scg.co.th

Pres.: Roongrote Rangsiyopash
Phone: (66) 2586 4444/3333
Fax: (66) 2586 2164, 5347
Email: roongror@scg.co.th
VP & CFO: Chaovalit Ekabut
Phone: (66) 2586 4444/3333
Fax: (66) 2586 2164, 5347
Email: chaovalite@scg.co.th
VP Operation.: Somchai Wangwattanapanich
Phone: (66) 2586 4444/3333
Fax: (66) 2586 2164, 5347
Email: somchaiw@scg.co.th
Dir., Corp. Mkrg.: Marty Lin Mahaplerkpong
Phone: (66) 2586 6575/6577
Fax: (66) 2587 2207
Email: marty@scg.co.th
Total Employees of Company: 168
Mill Locations:
Phoenix Pulp & Paper Public Company, Ltd., Nam Phong Mill (98.37% owned), 99 Moo 3, Tambol Kudnamsai, Amphur Nampong, Khon Kaen 40310, Thailand, Capacity: 159,936 mt/y, (Pulp mill, Paper mill, Paperboard mill)
Phone: (66) 43 433 104-6/373 406-8
Fax: (66) 43 433 101
Email: mailbox@scg.co.th, mailbox@phoenixpulp.com
SCG Paper Public Co., Ltd., BanPong Mill, 19 Saeng Xuto Road, Tha Pha, BanPong 70110, Thailand, (Pulp mill)
Phone: (66) 32 200 746-60/211 386-90/221 976-85
Fax: (66) 32 211 699/371 407
Email: witsonj@scg.co.th
Siam Cellulose Co., Ltd., Kanchanaburi Mill, 99 Moo 6, Saeng Xuto Rd., Wangsala, Tha Muang Distr., Kanchanaburi 71130, Thailand, (Pulp mill)
Phone: (66) 34 615 000 20
Fax: (66) 34 615 081
Siam Kraft Industry Co., Ltd., BanPong Mill (99% owned), 19 Saeng Xuto Rd., Tha Pha, BanPong 70110, Thailand, Capacity: 360,600 mt/y, (Paperboard mill)
Phone: (66) 32 200 746-60/211 388-90
Fax: (66) 32 371 411/221 716
Email: info@siamkraft.com
Thai Cane Paper Public Co., Ltd., Kanchanaburi Mill #1 (85.24% owned), 222 Moo 1, Saeng Xuto Road, Wangkhanai, Amphur Tha Muang, Kanchanaburi 71110, Thailand, Capacity: 100,000 mt/y, (Paperboard mill)
Phone: (66) 34 611 959 61
Fax: (66) 34 611 956
Email: infotcp@thaicane.com
Thai Cane Paper Public Co., Ltd., Prachinburi Mill #2 (85.24% owned), 70 Moo 4, Nongsang-Wang Thakian Rd., Tumbon Bo-thong, Amphur Kabinburi, Prachinburi 25110, Thailand, Capacity: 175,000 mt/y, (Paperboard mill)
Phone: (66) 37 2981115
Fax: (66) 37 298116
Email: infotcp@thaicane.com
Thai Kraft Paper Industry Co., Ltd., Wangsala Mill, 99 Moo 6, Saeng Xuto Rd. Wangsala, Tha Muang Distr., Kanchanaburi 71130, Thailand, Capacity: 600,000 mt/y, (Paper mill, Paperboard mill)
Phone: (66) 34 615 000-20
Fax: (66) 34 561 199/615 070
Thai Paper Co., Ltd., BanPong Mill, 19 Saeng Xuto Rd., BanPong 70110, Thailand, Capacity: 307,020 mt/y, (Paper mill)
Phone: (66) 32 211 38690, 32 371 37197
Fax: (66) 32 371 411
Thai Union Paper Public Co., Ltd., Prapradaeng Mill, 131 Moo 2, Poochaosamingprai Rd., Samrong Klang, Prapradaeng 10130, Thailand, Capacity: 76,041 mt/y, (Paper mill, Paperboard mill)
Phone: (66) 2 754 2100
Fax: (66) 2 754 2118
Thai Union Paper Industry Co., Ltd., Wangsala Mill, 99 Moo 6, Saeng-Xuto Road Wangsala, Tha Muang Distr. 71110, Thailand, Capacity: 162,435 mt/y, (Paperboard mill)

Phone: (66) 34 615 000-20
Fax: (66) 34 615 076
United Pulp & Paper Co., Inc., Calumpit Mill (98.60% owned), Km 48 Bo. Iba Estate, 3003 Calumpit, Philippines, Capacity: 230,000 mt/y, (Paper mill, Paperboard mill)
Phone: (63) 44 202 4722/23/4301
Fax: (63) 44 2024306
Email: info@uppc.com.ph
Vina Kraft Paper, Ho Chi Minh City Mill (70% owned), My Phuoc 3 Industrial Park, Ho Chi Minh City, Vietnam, Capacity: 250,000 mt/y, (Paperboard mill)

ⓜSCG Paper Public Co., Ltd.
BanPong Mill
19 Saeng Xuto Road, Tha Pha
BanPong, Ratchaburi, 70110
Thailand
Phone: (66) 32 200 746-60/211 386-90/221 976-85
Fax: (66) 32 211 699/371 407
Email: witsonj@scg.co.th
Web Address: www.paper.scg.co.th
Personnel:
Mill Dir.: Mr. Witson Jeraratanasopa
Phone: (66) 32 200 746-60
Fax: (66) 32 221699
Prod. Mgr.: Suchai Pataputthipong
Phone: (66) 32 200 746-60/211 386-90/221 976-85
Fax: (66) 32 221699
Email: suchaip@scg.co.th
Dir. Product & Tech. Devel. Center: Dr. Thananan Akhadejdamrong
Phone: (66) 32 200 746-60/211 386-90/221 976-85
Fax: (66) 32 371407
Email: thananaa@scg.co.th
Total Employees at this Location: 117
Type of Operation: Pulp mill
Pulp Grades and Capacities:
Total pulp capacity: 44,000 mt/y
Pulp available for market: 44,000 mt/y
Chemical Pulp: 44,000 mt/y

Pulp Mill Data:
Chemical Pulping Systems:
Batch digesters: 1
Mechanical Pulping Systems:
CTMP systems: 1
Bleach Plant Systems: 1
No. 1, Sequence: CEH, Capacity 45,000 admt/y
Chemical Recovery Equipment:
Evaporator lines: 1
Recovery boilers: 1
Energy Data:
Power boilers
Steam turbines: 1 at 4.6 MW
Electrical demand for mill: 69 MWh/D

ⓜSiam Cellulose Co., Ltd.
Kanchanaburi Mill
Ownership: 100% by SCG Paper Public Co., Ltd.
99 Moo 6, Saeng Xuto Rd., Wangsala, Tha Muang Distr.
Kanchanaburi, Kanchanaburi, 71130
Thailand
Phone: (66) 34 615 000 20
Fax: (66) 34 615 081
Web Address: www.paper.scg.co.th
Personnel:
Man. Dir.: Phaskorn Buranawit
Phone: (66) 2586 4709
Fax: (66) 2587 0746
Email: phaskorb@scg.co.th
Mill Dir.: Mr. Witson Jeraratanasopa
Phone: (66) 346 15000-20
Fax: (66) 346 15081
Prod. Mgr.: Mr. Pornthep Kamalanon
Phone: (66) 34 615 000 20
Email: pornthka@scg.co.th
Mktg. Mgr.: Chutimon Wiriyaumpaiwong
Phone: (66) 2586 1200
Fax: (66) 2586 2164

Thailand

Email: chutimow@scg.co.th
Purch. Mgr.: Wichan Jitpukdee
Phone: (66) 2 586 4565 6
Fax: (66) 2 586 2378
Email: wichanj@scg.co.th
Total Employees at this Location: 300
Type of Operation: Pulp mill
Pulp Grades and Capacities:
Total pulp capacity: 120,480 mt/y
Pulp available for market: 120,000 mt/y
Chemical Pulp: 120,480 mt/y
Pulp Mill Data:
Chemical Pulping Systems:
Continuous digesters: 1
Bleach Plant Systems: 1
Chemical Pulping System, Type: HWRW
Chemical Recovery Equipment:
Evaporator lines: 1
Recovery boilers: 1
Lime Kiln
Pulp Dryers:
Pulp Dryers 1
Energy Data:
Power boilers
Steam turbines: 1 at 5.5 MW
Electrical demand for mill: 290 MWh/D

ⓂSiam Kraft Industry Co., Ltd.
BanPong Mill
Ownership: 99% by SCG Paper Public Co., Ltd.
19 Saeng Xuto Rd., Tha Pha
BanPong, Ratchaburi, 70110
Thailand
Phone: (66) 32 200 746-60/211 388-90
Fax: (66) 32 371 411/221 716
Email: info@siamkraft.com
Web Address: www.paper.scg.co.th
Personnel:
Man. Dir.: Chartchai Leukulwatanachai
Phone: (66) 2 586 5643-4
Fax: (66) 2 587 2207
Email: chartchl@scg.co.th
Mill Dir.: Mr. Sangchai Wiriyaampaiwong
Phone: (66) 32 211 388 90
Fax: (66) 32 371 411
Email: sangchai@scg.co.th
Mktg. Dir.: Pornchai Vittayakoonsakulchai
Phone: (66) 2586 4600
Fax: (66) 2587 2207
Email: pornchav@scg.co.th
Mktg. Plan. Mgr.: Boonchoo Panjarattanakorn
Phone: (66) 2 586 5153
Fax: (66) 2 586 2827
Email: boonchop@scg.co.th
Procurement Dir.: Wichan Jitpukdee
Phone: (66) 2 586 4565 6
Fax: (66) 2 586 2378
Email: wichanj@scg.co.th
Total Employees at this Location: 500
Type of Operation: Paperboard mill
Pulp Grades and Capacities:
Total pulp capacity: 315,991 mt/y
Recycled Pulping: 315,991 mt/y
Pulp Mill Data:
Chemical Pulping Systems:
Continuous digesters: 1
Chemical Recovery Equipment:
Recovery boilers: 1
Recycled Fiber Treatment Lines:
Recycled packaging pulping lines: 1
Paper/Paperboard Grades and Capacities:
Total paper and paperboard capacity: 360,600 mt/y
Linerboard: 210,860 mt/y
Corrugating medium/fluting: 149,740 mt/y
Paper and Paperboard Mill Data:
Stock Preparation:
Pulpers: 4
Refiners: 17
Paper Machines: 3

No. 1, fourdrinier, total capacity 185,000 mt/y, Trim width 5.2 m, Linerboard, Corrugating medium/fluting
No. 2, fourdrinier, total capacity 40,000 mt/y, Trim width 2.7 m, Corrugating medium/fluting
No. 3, fourdrinier, total capacity 135,600 mt/y, Trim width 4.3 m, Linerboard, Corrugating medium/fluting
Finishing Equipment:
Winders: 3
Energy Data:
Power boilers: 2
Steam turbines: 4 at 17.2 MW
Electrical demand for mill: 451 MWh/D

ⓘⓂSiam Nippon Industrial Paper Co.
BanPong Mill
Ownership: 55% by Nippon Paper Industries Co., Ltd., 45% by SKG Pulp & Paper
19 Saeng Xuto Road, Tha Pha
BanPong, Ratchaburi, 70110
Thailand
Phone: (66) 32 200 746-60/211 386-90/221
Fax: (66) 32 211 699/371 407
Web Address: www.scg.co.th
Type of Operation: Paper mill
Paper/Paperboard Grades and Capacities:
Total paper and paperboard capacity: 43,000 mt/y
Packaging papers: 43,000 mt/y
Paper and Paperboard Mill Data:
Paper Machines: 1
No. 1, (started July 2014), Yankee dryer, total capacity 43,000 mt/y, Trim width 5.1 m, Packaging papers
Finishing Equipment:
Calenders: 1 at 43,000 mt/y

ⓘSiam Paper J.N.K. Industrial Co., Ltd.
1369 Jan Rd., Tung Waddom, Yannawa
Bangkok
Thailand
Phone: (66) 2 287 1585-6
Fax: (66) 2 213 1566
Personnel:
Man. Dir.: Mr. Prakob Jarusuksawad
Phone: (66) 2 287 1585-6
Fax: (66) 2 436 7893-4
Total Employees of Company: 300
Mill Locations:
Siam Paper J.N.K. Industrial Co., Ltd., Bangkok Mill, 34 Moo 1 Soi Paper Factory, Rachaburana Roa, Bangkok 10140, Thailand, Capacity: 6,000 mt/y, (Paper mill)
Phone: (66) 2 463 7893-4
Fax: (66) 2 816 7231

ⓂSiam Paper J.N.K. Industrial Co., Ltd.
Bangkok Mill
34 Moo 1 Soi Paper Factory, Rachaburana Roa
Bangkok, Bangkok, 10140
Thailand
Phone: (66) 2 463 7893-4
Fax: (66) 2 816 7231
Personnel:
Man. Dir.: Mr. Prakob Jarusuksawad
Phone: (66) 2 287 1585-6
Fax: (66) 2 213 1566
Total Employees at this Location: 300
Type of Operation: Paper mill
Paper/Paperboard Grades and Capacities:
Total paper and paperboard capacity: 6,000 mt/y
Packaging papers: 6,000 mt/y

ⓘSirisak Paper Industries Co., Ltd.
Ownership: 27.23% by Mr. Chuphong Siriphotchanakul, 5% by Mr. Lin Yun Peng, 10% by Mr. Sutham Thammawitthayakul, 5% by Ms. Watthana Soemphornwiwat, 11.77% by Others, 41% by Success Real Estate Co., Ltd.
659/98 Satopradit Road
Yannawa, Bangkok, 10180
Thailand

Phone: (66) 2 682 4844
Fax: (66) 2 682 4845
Personnel:
Man. Dir.: Mr. Surasak Siripochanakul
Phone: (66) 2 682 4844
Fax: (66) 2 682 4845
Mktg. & Sls. Mgr.: Mr. Teerachai Siripochanakul
Phone: (66) 2 682 4844
Fax: (66) 2 682 4845
Mill Mgr.: Mr. Prapon Siripochanakul
Phone: (66) 2 682 4844
Fax: (66) 2 682 4845
Purch. Mgr.: Ms. Panida Udomlertsirikul
Phone: (66) 2 682 4844
Fax: (66) 2 682 4845
Sls. Mgr.: Mr. Teerachai Siripochanakul
Phone: (66) 2 682 4844
Fax: (66) 2 682 4845
Total Employees of Company: 100
Mill Locations:
Sirisak Paper Industries Co., Ltd., Kanchanaburi Mill, 2 Saeng-Xuto Rd., Tambon Ban-Nua, Amphur Muang, Kanchanaburi, Thailand, Capacity: 6,000 mt/y, (Paper mill)
Phone: (66) 34 511 156/513 596
Fax: (66) 34 513 597

ⓂSirisak Paper Industries Co., Ltd.
Kanchanaburi Mill
2 Saeng-Xuto Rd., Tambon Ban-Nua
Amphur Muang, Kanchanaburi, Kanchanaburi
Thailand
Phone: (66) 34 511 156/513 596
Fax: (66) 34 513 597
Personnel:
Mill Mgr.: Praphon Siripochanakun
Phone: (66) 34 511 156/513 596
Man. Dir.: Surasak Siripochanakul
Phone: (66) 34 511 156/513 596
Total Employees at this Location: 100
Type of Operation: Paper mill
Paper/Paperboard Grades and Capacities:
Total paper and paperboard capacity: 6,000 mt/y
Uncoated woodfree/freesheet: 6,000 mt/y

ⓘⓂSouth East Asia Paper Ltd.
Bankae Mill
118 Moo 1 Petchkasem Rd.
Bangkae Nua, Bankae, Bangkok, 10600
Thailand
Phone: (66) 2 455 3677/3884/413 1046
Fax: (66) 2 413 1046
Personnel:
Man. Dir.: Mr. Boontavee Uaphongsukkit
Phone: (66) 2 455 3677
Fax: (66) 2 413 1046
Plant Mgr.: Mr. Somsak Uaphongsukkit
Phone: (66) 2 455 3677/3884/413 1046
Total Employees of Company: 20
Type of Operation: Paperboard mill
Paper/Paperboard Grades and Capacities:
Total paper and paperboard capacity: 1,050 mt/y
Boxboard/cartonboard: 1,050 mt/y
Paper and Paperboard Mill Data:
Paper Machines: 1
No. 1, total capacity 1,050 mt/y, Boxboard/cartonboard

ⓘStar Kraft Co., Ltd.
44/60 Moo2, Vibhavadee Rangsit Road, Talad Bang Khen, Bang Khen
Laksi, Bangkok, Bangkok, 10210
Thailand
Phone: (66) 02 940 8575-8
Fax: (66) 02 561 1561
Email: info@starkraft.co.th
Web Address: www.starkraft.co.th
Total Employees of Company: 50
Mill Locations:
Star Kraft Co., Ltd., Tak Mill, 188/1 Moo 8, Takaok, Ban Tak, Tak 63120, Thailand, Capacity: 8,500 mt/y,

Thailand

(Paperboard mill)
Phone: (66) 055 591 999
Fax: (66) 055 591 379
Email: info@starkraft.co.th

ⓜStar Kraft Co., Ltd.
Tak Mill
188/1 Moo 8, Takaok, Ban Tak
Tak, 63120
Thailand
Phone: (66) 055 591 999
Fax: (66) 055 591 379
Email: info@starkraft.co.th
Web Address: www.starkraft.co.th
Personnel:
Man. Dir, Plant Mgr: Poj Panityanubarn
Phone: (66) 055 591 999
Fax: (66) 055 591 379
Email: info@starkraft.co.th
Type of Operation: Paperboard mill
Paper/Paperboard Grades and Capacities:
Total paper and paperboard capacity: 8,500 mt/y
Boxboard/cartonboard: 8,500 mt/y

ⓜSupatrtanagorn Paper Mill Co., Ltd.
75 Vorachak Road, Tapsiri, Pomprab
Bangkok, 10110
Thailand
Phone: (66) 2 225 3070-9
Fax: (66) 2 224 6962
Total Employees of Company: 500
Mill Locations:
Supatrtanagorn Paper Mill Co., Ltd., Angtong Mill, 58 Moo 1, Ayutaya - Ang Thong Road, Posa District, Ang Thong Province 14000, Thailand, Capacity: 60,000 mt/y, (Paperboard mill)
Phone: (66) 35 672 202
Fax: (66) 35 672 199

ⓜSupatrtanagorn Paper Mill Co., Ltd.
Angtong Mill
58 Moo 1, Ayutaya - Ang Thong Road
Posa District, Ang Thong Province, 14000
Thailand
Phone: (66) 35 672 202
Fax: (66) 35 672 199
Personnel:
Man. Dir.: Mr. Panachai Suveepattananont
Phone: (66) 2 225 3070-9
Fax: (66) 2 224 6962
Email: supatr@gmail.com
Type of Operation: Paperboard mill
Paper/Paperboard Grades and Capacities:
Total paper and paperboard capacity: 60,000 mt/y
Boxboard/cartonboard: 60,000 mt/y

ⓜTenma Paper Mills (Thailand) Co., Ltd.
Ownership: Tenma Paper Mills & Co., other Thai Partners
183 Regent House Building 8th Floor, Rajadamri Road, Lumpinee
Pathumwan, Bangkok, 10330
Thailand
Phone: (66) 2 252 8240/254 4369/253 6446
Fax: (66) 2 253 3842
Email: thaitenma@hotmail.com
Personnel:
Man. Dir., Mktg. Mgr.: Yong Ngamsirivat
Phone: (66) 2 252 8240
Fax: (66) 2 253 3842
Email: thaitenma@hotmail.com
Mill Mgr.: Ms. Pathamarat Sartsara
Phone: (66) 2 252 8240/254 4369/253 6446
Fax: (66) 2 253 3842
Email: phat_sst@yahoo.com
Purch. Mgr.: Mr. Pramual Tan-orn
Phone: (66) 2 252 8240/254 4369/253 6446
Fax: (66) 2 253 3842
Email: thaitenma@hotmail.com

Total Employees of Company: 280
Mill Locations:
Tenma Paper Mills (Thailand) Co., Ltd., Pakkred Mill, 6/2 Sukaprachasarn 2 Road, Bangpood, Pakkred 11120, Thailand, Capacity: 35,000 mt/y, (Paperboard mill)
Phone: (66) 2 582 8216/584 3596 7
Fax: (66) 2 583 7846
Email: thaitenma@hotmail.com

ⓜTenma Paper Mills (Thailand) Co., Ltd.
Pakkred Mill
Ownership: Tenma Paper Mills & Co.
6/2 Sukaprachasarn 2 Road, Bangpood
Pakkred, Nonthaburi, 11120
Thailand
Phone: (66) 2 582 8216/584 3596 7
Fax: (66) 2 583 7846
Email: thaitenma@hotmail.com
Personnel:
Man. Dir.: Mr. Yong Ngamsirivat
Phone: (66) 2 252 8240 / 253 6446
Fax: (66) 2 253 3842
Email: thaitenma@hotmail.com
Mill Mgr.: Mr. Pathamarat Sartsara
Phone: (66) 2 582 8216/584 3596 7
Email: phat_ssr@yahoo.com
Purch. Mgr.: Pramual Tan-rn
Phone: (66) 2 582 8216/584 3596 7
Total Employees at this Location: 150
Type of Operation: Paperboard mill
Pulp Grades and Capacities:
Total pulp capacity: 29,478 mt/y
Recycled Pulping: 29,478 mt/y
Pulp Mill Data:
Bleach Plant Systems: 1
DIP
Recycled Fiber Treatment Lines:
Flotation deinking lines: 1
Recycled packaging pulping lines: 1
Paper/Paperboard Grades and Capacities:
Total paper and paperboard capacity: 35,000 mt/y
Boxboard/cartonboard: 35,000 mt/y
Paper and Paperboard Mill Data:
Paper Machines: 1
No. 1, cylinder (7), total capacity 35,000 mt/y, Trim width 1.7 m, Boxboard/cartonboard
Coating Machines: 1
PM 1, on machine
Energy Data:
Power boilers
Electrical demand for mill: 53 MWh/D

ⓜⓜTeppatana Paper Mill Co., Ltd.
Amphur Muan Mill
Ownership: 11.54% by Mr. Tanes Phanichewa, 9.57% by Mr. Tarnin Phanichewa, 10% by Mr. Thamajuk Phanichewa, 10% by Mr. Thanakij Phanichewa, 6.96% by Ruamchewa Co. Ltd., 25.86% by Tepratarn Karnrae Co. Ltd., 17.75% by Tongerawan Co. Ltd.
220/1 Saiwatkoke Rd.
Amphur Muang, Phathum Thani, 12000
Thailand
Phone: (66) 2 581 8060 2
Fax: (66) 2 581 6141
Email: contact@teppatana.com
Web Address: www.teppatana.com
Personnel:
Chmn.: Sombath Phanichewa
Phone: (66) 2 581 8060 2
Man. Dir.: Narongrit Phanichewa
Phone: (66) 2 581 1211-3
Email: contact@teppatana.com
Mktg. Mgr.: Mr. Sirisak Arunratanothai
Phone: (66) 2 581 1211-3
Email: sirisak.a@teppatana.com
Oper. Mgr.: Pradit Chaengkom

Phone: (66) 2 581 8060 2
Email: pradit.c@teppatana.com
Total Employees at this Location: 210
Type of Operation: Paper mill, Paperboard mill
Paper/Paperboard Grades and Capacities:
Total paper and paperboard capacity: 15,500 mt/y
Uncoated woodfree/freesheet: 5,500 mt/y
Boxboard/cartonboard: 10,000 mt/y
Paper and Paperboard Mill Data:
Stock Preparation:
Pulpers: 7
Refiners: 12
Paper Machines: 3
No. 1, cylinder, Trim width 1.6 m
No. 2, fourdrinier, Trim width 1.8 m
No. 3, cylinder, Trim width 1.8 m
Finishing Equipment:
Rewinders: 1
Sheeters: 2
Energy Data:
Power boilers: 2

ⓜThai Cane Paper Public Co., Ltd.
Ownership: 85.24% by SCG Paper Public Co., Ltd.
26th Floor, Sinn Sathom Tower, 77/107-108, Krung Thonburi Road, Klongtonsai
Klongsan, Bangkok, 10600
Thailand
Phone: (66) 2 440 0707
Fax: (66) 2 440 0716-7
Email: infotcp@thaicane.com
Web Address: www.thaicane.com
Personnel:
Man. Dir.: Twatchai Wongpaisan
Phone: (66) 2 440 0707 Ext. 106
Fax: (66) 2 440 0716
Email: twatchaw@scg.co.th
EVP. Finan./Accounting & MIS: Ong-Ard Limprayulyong
Phone: (66) 2 440 0707 Ext. 250
Email: ong_ard@scg.co.th
EVP. Mktg.: Mrs. Naphaporn Kanjanatawewat
Phone: (66) 2 440 0707 Ext. 111
Email: napapork@scg.co.th
Mill Mgr. PM 1: Ekasit Kitisakchaikul
Phone: (66) 34 611 959-61
Fax: (66) 34 611 956
Email: ekasitk@scg.co.th
Mill Dir. PM 2: Saharath Pattanavibool
Phone: (66) 37 298 111-5
Fax: (66) 37 298 116
Email: saharutp@scg.co.th
Total Employees of Company: 412
Total Employees at this Location: 55
Mill Locations:
Thai Cane Paper Public Co., Ltd., Kanchanaburi Mill #1, 222 Moo 1, Saeng Xuto Road, Wangkhanai, Amphur Tha Muang, Kanchanaburi 71110, Thailand, Capacity: 100,000 mt/y, (Paperboard mill)
Phone: (66) 34 611 959 61
Fax: (66) 34 611 956
Email: infotcp@thaicane.com
Thai Cane Paper Public Co., Ltd., Prachinburi Mill #2, 70 Moo 4, Nongsang-Wang Thakian Rd., Tumbon Bo-thong, Amphur Kabinburi, Prachinburi 25110, Thailand, Capacity: 175,000 mt/y, (Paperboard mill)
Phone: (66) 37 2981115
Fax: (66) 37 298116
Email: infotcp@thaicane.com

ⓜThai Cane Paper Public Co., Ltd.
Kanchanaburi Mill #1
Ownership: 85.24% by SCG Paper Public Co., Ltd.
222 Moo 1, Saeng Xuto Road, Wangkhanai
Amphur Tha Muang, Kanchanaburi, Kanchanaburi, 71110
Thailand
Phone: (66) 34 611 959 61
Fax: (66) 34 611 956
Email: infotcp@thaicane.com

Thailand

Web Address: www.thaicane.com
Personnel:
Man. Dir.: Twatchai Wongpaisarn
Phone: (66) 2 440 0707 Ext. 106
Fax: (66) 2 440 0716
Email: twatchaw@scg.co.th
Total Employees at this Location: 165
Type of Operation: Paperboard mill
Pulp Grades and Capacities:
Total pulp capacity: 97,763 mt/y
Recycled Pulping: 97,763 mt/y
Pulp Mill Data:
Recycled Fiber Treatment Lines:
Recycled packaging pulping lines: 1
Paper/Paperboard Grades and Capacities:
Total paper and paperboard capacity: 100,000 mt/y
Corrugating medium/fluting: 100,000 mt/y
Paper and Paperboard Mill Data:
Paper Machines: 1
No. 1, fourdrinier, total capacity 100,000 mt/y, Corrugating medium/fluting
Energy Data:
Power boilers
Electrical demand for mill: 118 MWh/D

ⓜThai Cane Paper Public Co., Ltd.
Prachinburi Mill #2
Ownership: 85.24% by SCG Paper Public Co., Ltd.
70 Moo 4, Nongsang-Wang Thakian Rd., Tumbon Bo-thong
Amphur Kabinburi, Prachinburi, 25110
Thailand
Phone: (66) 37 2981115
Fax: (66) 37 298116
Email: infotcp@thaicane.com
Web Address: www.thaicane.com
Personnel:
Man. Dir.: Twatchai Wongpaisarn
Phone: (66) 2 440 0707 Ext. 106
Fax: (66) 2 440 0716
Email: twatchaw@scg.co.th
Mill Dir.: Saharath Pattanavibool
Phone: (66) 37 2981115
Email: saharutp@scg.co.th
Total Employees at this Location: 250
Type of Operation: Paperboard mill
Pulp Grades and Capacities:
Total pulp capacity: 164,179 mt/y
Recycled Pulping: 164,179 mt/y
Pulp Mill Data:
Recycled Fiber Treatment Lines:
Recycled packaging pulping lines: 1
Paper/Paperboard Grades and Capacities:
Total paper and paperboard capacity: 175,000 mt/y
Linerboard: 175,000 mt/y
Paper and Paperboard Mill Data:
Paper Machines: 1
No. 2, Fourdrinier (4), total capacity 175,000 mt/y, Trim width 4.3 m, Linerboard
Finishing Equipment:
Calenders: 1
Energy Data:
Power boilers: 1
Steam turbines at 26.07 MW

ⓞⓜThai Card Board Co Ltd.
Sampran Mill
1/22 Moo 2, Tumbon Raiking
Sampran, Nakhon Pathom, 73210
Thailand
Phone: (66) 34 321 210/311 554
Fax: (66) 34 311 005
Email: salesandservice@bpm.co.th
Personnel:
Man. Dir.: Mr. Suwit Tantisunthorn
Phone: (66) 34 321 210/311 554
Email: salesandservice@bpm.co.th
Sls. Mgr.: Walapa Tanisunthorn

Phone: (66) 34 321 210/311 554
Total Employees at this Location: 150
Type of Operation: Paperboard mill
Pulp Grades and Capacities:
Total pulp capacity: 25,791 mt/y
Recycled Pulping: 25,791 mt/y
Pulp Mill Data:
Bleach Plant Systems: 1
DIP
Recycled Fiber Treatment Lines:
Flotation deinking lines: 1
Recycled packaging pulping lines: 1
Paper/Paperboard Grades and Capacities:
Total paper and paperboard capacity: 30,000 mt/y
Boxboard/cartonboard: 30,000 mt/y
Paper and Paperboard Mill Data:
Paper Machines: 1
No. 1, cylinder, total capacity 30,000 mt/y, Trim width 3.25 m, Boxboard/cartonboard
Coating Machines: 1
PM1, on machine
Energy Data:
Power boilers
Electrical demand for mill: 51 MWh/D

ⓞⓜThai Development Paper Co., Ltd.
Samut Prakan Mill
247 Moo 2, Taiban Road, Tumbon Taiban
Amphur Muang, Samut Prakan, Samut Prakarn, 10280
Thailand
Phone: (66) 2 388 0137 44
Fax: (66) 2 387 1194
Personnel:
Man. Dir.: Mr. Surachai Cheevaphansri
Phone: (66) 2 388 0137 44
Email: surachai@tdp.co.th
VP: Piyapot Kunapis
Phone: (66) 2 388 0137 44
Total Employees at this Location: 230
Type of Operation: Paper mill
Pulp Grades and Capacities:
Total pulp capacity: 48,897 mt/y
Recycled Pulping: 48,897 mt/y
Paper/Paperboard Grades and Capacities:
Total paper and paperboard capacity: 47,600 mt/y
Boxboard/cartonboard: 47,600 mt/y
Paper and Paperboard Mill Data:
Stock Preparation:
Pulpers: 5
Refiners: 5
Paper Machines: 1
No. 1, cylinder, total capacity 47,600 mt/y, Trim width 2.1 m, Boxboard/cartonboard
Coating Machines: 3
No. 1, total capacity 36,000 mt/y., on machine
No. 2, total capacity 36,000 mt/y., on machine
No. 3, total capacity 36,000 mt/y., on machine
Finishing Equipment:
Winders: 1
Sheeters: 1
Energy Data:
Electrical demand for mill: 70 MWh/D

ⓜThai Gorilla Pulp Ltd. (TGP)
Rayong city Mill
66/2 Moo 3, Naongbue, Bankhai
Rayong city, 20110
Thailand
Phone: (66) 38 961 891
Fax: (66) 38 961 476
Email: pannakorn.k@tgpulp.com
Personnel:
CEO: Ryosuke Tanaka
Phone: (66) 38 961 891
Email: info@gorillapulp.com
Man. Dir.: Takuya Yakoo
Phone: (66) 38 961 891
Email: yakoo@tgpulp.com
Type of Operation: Pulp mill

Pulp Grades and Capacities:
Total pulp capacity: 16,425 mt/y
Pulp available for market: 16,425 mt/y

ⓜThai Gorilla Pulp Ltd. (TGP)
Ownership: 100% by Pulp GreenTech Holding AG in Liechtenstein.
66/2 Moo 3, Naongbue, Bankhai
Rayong city, 20110
Thailand
Phone: (66) 38 961 891
Fax: (66) 38 961 476
Email: pannakorn.k@tgpulp.com
Personnel:
CEO: Ryosuke Tanaka
Phone: (66) 38 961 891
Fax: (66) 38 961 476
Email: info@gorillapulp.com
Man. Dir.: Takuya Yakoo
Phone: (66) 38 961 891
Fax: (66) 38 961 476
Email: yakoo@tgpulp.com
Mill Locations:
Thai Gorilla Pulp Ltd. (TGP), Rayong city Mill, 66/2 Moo 3, Naongbue, Bankhai, Rayong city 20110, Thailand, (Pulp mill)
Phone: (66) 38 961 891
Fax: (66) 38 961 476
Email: pannakorn.k@tgpulp.com

ⓜThai Kraft Paper Industry Co., Ltd.
Ownership: 100% by SCG Paper Public Co., Ltd.
1 Siam Cement Rd., Bangsue
Bangkok, 10800
Thailand
Phone: (66) 2 586 4620/5137
Fax: (66) 2 586 2997/8
Web Address: www.scg.co.th/paper
Personnel:
Man. Dir.: Chartchai Leukulwatanachai
Phone: (66) 2 586 5643-4
Fax: (66) 2 587 2207
Email: chartchl@scg.co.th
Mill Dir.: Sangchai Wiriyaumpaiwong
Phone: (66) 34 615000/20
Fax: (66) 34 561199/615
Email: sangchaw@scg.co.th
Mktg. Dir.: Pornchai Vittayakoonsakulchai
Phone: (66) 2 586 4600 1
Fax: (66) 2 587 2207
Email: pornchav@scg.co.th
Mktg. Plan. Mgr.: Boonchoo Panjarattanakorn
Phone: (66) 2 586 4540
Fax: (66) 2 586 2827
Email: boonchop@scg.co.th
Procur. Dir.: Wicahn Jitpukdee
Phone: (66) 2 586 4565 6
Fax: (66) 2 586 2378
Email: wichanj@scg.co.th
Total Employees of Company: 694
Mill Locations:
Thai Kraft Paper Industry Co., Ltd., Wangsala Mill, 99 Moo 6, Saeng Xuto Rd. Wangsala, Tha Muang Distr., Kanchanaburi 71130, Thailand, Capacity: 600,000 mt/y, (Paper mill, Paperboard mill)
Phone: (66) 34 615 000-20
Fax: (66) 34 561 199/615 070

ⓜThai Kraft Paper Industry Co., Ltd.
Wangsala Mill
Ownership: 100% by SCG Paper Public Co., Ltd.
99 Moo 6, Saeng Xuto Rd. Wangsala
Tha Muang Distr., Kanchanaburi, Kanchanaburi, 71130
Thailand
Phone: (66) 34 615 000-20
Fax: (66) 34 561 199/615 070
Web Address: www.paper.scg.co.th
Personnel:
Man. Dir.: Chartchai Leukulwatanachai

Thailand

Phone: (66) 2 586 5643-4
Fax: (66) 2 587 2207
Email: chartchl@scg.co.th
Mill Dir.: Sangchai Wiriyaumpaiwong
Phone: (66) 3 461 2261-5
Email: sangchaw@scg.co.th
Mktg. Plann. Dir.: Boonchoo Panjarattanakorn
Phone: (66) 2 586 4540
Fax: (66) 2 586 2827
Email: boonchop@scg.co.th
Procur. Dir.: Wichan Jitpukdee
Phone: (66) 34 615 000-20
Email: wichanj@scg.co.th
Total Employees at this Location: 660
Type of Operation: Paper mill, Paperboard mill
Pulp Grades and Capacities:
Total pulp capacity: 560,309 mt/y
Recycled Pulping: 560,309 mt/y
Pulp Mill Data:
Recycled Fiber Treatment Lines:
Recycled packaging pulping lines: 1
Paper/Paperboard Grades and Capacities:
Total paper and paperboard capacity: 600,000 mt/y
Packaging papers: 39,600 mt/y
Linerboard: 468,000 mt/y
Corrugating medium/fluting: 92,400 mt/y
Paper and Paperboard Mill Data:
Paper Machines: 4
No. 4, fourdrinier, total capacity 132,000 mt/y, Trim width 4.08 m, Packaging papers, Corrugating medium/fluting
No. 5, fourdrinier (3), total capacity 140,000 mt/y, Trim width 4.3 m, Linerboard
No. 6, fourdrinier (3), total capacity 165,000 mt/y, Trim width 4.3 m, Linerboard
No. 7, fourdrinier (3), total capacity 163,000 mt/y, Trim width 4.3 m, Linerboard
Energy Data:
Power boilers: 1
Electrical demand for mill: 775 MWh/D

ⓜThai Paper Co., Ltd.
BanPong Mill
Ownership: 100% by SCG Paper Public Co., Ltd.
19 Saeng Xuto Rd.
BanPong, Ratchaburi, 70110
Thailand
  Phone: (66) 32 211 38690, 32 371 37197
  Fax: (66) 32 371 411
  Web Address: www.thaipaper.com
Personnel:
Man. Dir.: Phaskorn Buranawit
Phone: (66) 2 586 4709
Fax: (66) 2 587 0746
Email: phaskorb@scg.co.th
Mill Dir.: Wiwat Walaipacchara
Phone: (66) 32 211 38690, 32 371 37197
Email: viwatw@scg.co.th
Mktg. Mgr.: Vipapat Cholsawad
Phone: (66) 2 586 2411
Fax: (66) 2 586 2070
Procurement Dir.: Wichan Jitpukdee
Phone: (66) 2 586 4565 6
Email: wichanj@scg.co.th
Total Employees at this Location: 750
Type of Operation: Paper mill
Paper/Paperboard Grades and Capacities:
Total paper and paperboard capacity: 307,020 mt/y
Uncoated woodfree/freesheet: 158,865 mt/y
Coated woodfree/freesheet: 148,155 mt/y
Paper and Paperboard Mill Data:
Stock Preparation:
Pulpers: 13
Refiners: 8
Paper Machines: 5
No. 1, fourdrinier, total capacity 19,992 mt/y, Trim width 2.36 m, Uncoated woodfree/freesheet
No. 2, fourdrinier, total capacity 23,205 mt/y, Trim width 1.58 m, Coated woodfree/freesheet
No. 3, fourdrinier, total capacity 42,840 mt/y, Trim width 3.18 m, Uncoated woodfree/freesheet
No. 4, SymFormer, total capacity 96,033 mt/y, Trim width 3.4 m, Uncoated woodfree/freesheet
No. 5, SymFormer MB, total capacity 124,950 mt/y, Trim width 3.9 m, Coated woodfree/freesheet
Coating Machines: 2
OMCA, total capacity 26,500 mt/y., on machine
OMCB, total capacity 125,000 mt/y., no machine
Finishing Equipment:
Winders: 3
Supercalenders: 3
Sheeters: 6
Energy Data:
Power boilers: 3
Steam turbines at 80 MW
Electrical demand for mill: 596 MWh/D

ⓜThai Paper Mill Co., Ltd.
Ownership: 3.50% by Mr. Anuwat Trirattanavasai, 4% by Mr. Boonleart Samritvanicha, 15% by Mr. Chu Chun Hua, 3.50% by Mr. Kanis Trirattanavasia, 3.50% by Mr. Nut Trirattanavasai, 5% by Mr. Nutapol Peeganont, 3.33% by Mr. Pornsak Tamkongka
36.36/1 Puttamonthon II Road, Bangpai
Bangkae, Bangkok, 10160
Thailand
  Phone: (66) 2 413 4359/ 413 3014/ 455 8227/ 455 8232
  Fax: (66) 2 803 0359-70
Personnel:
Mill Mgr.: Mr. Chusak Hongyok
Phone: (66) 2 413 4359/ 413 3014/ 455 8227/ 455 8232
Fax: (66) 2 803 0370
Email: chusak@thaipapermill.com
Man Dir.: Mr. Thongchai Thirattanavasai
Phone: (66) 38 961 376 81
Fax: (66) 38 961 382 83
Email: thongchai@thaipapermill.com
Total Employees of Company: 350
Mill Locations:
Thai Paper Mill Co., Ltd., Rayong Mill, 66, 66/19 Moo 3 Tumbon Nongbua, Amphur Bankhai, Rayong 21120, Thailand, Capacity: 120,000 mt/y, (Paperboard mill)
Phone: (66) 38 961 376-81
Fax: (66) 38 961 382-83

ⓜThai Paper Mill Co., Ltd.
Rayong Mill
66, 66/19 Moo 3 Tumbon Nongbua
Amphur Bankhai, Rayong, 21120
Thailand
  Phone: (66) 38 961 376-81
  Fax: (66) 38 961 382-83
  Web Address: www.thaipapermill.com/Welcome_Eng/thaipapermill.htm
Personnel:
Man. Dir.: Mr. Thongchai Trirattanavasai
Phone: (66) 2 4134359/3014
Fax: (66) 2 8030370
Email: thongchai@thaipapermill.com
Mill Mgr.: Mr. Chusak Hongyok
Phone: (66) 38 961 376-81
Email: chusak@thaipapermill.com
Total Employees at this Location: 300
Type of Operation: Paperboard mill
Pulp Grades and Capacities:
Total pulp capacity: 115,218 mt/y
Recycled Pulping: 115,218 mt/y
Pulp Mill Data:
Recycled Fiber Treatment Lines:
Recycled packaging pulping lines: 1
Paper/Paperboard Grades and Capacities:
Total paper and paperboard capacity: 120,000 mt/y
Linerboard: 84,000 mt/y
Corrugating medium/fluting: 36,000 mt/y
Paper and Paperboard Mill Data:
Paper Machines: 3
No. 1, fourdrinier, total capacity 36,000 mt/y, Trim width 2.64 m, Corrugating medium/fluting
No. 2, fourdrinier, total capacity 26,000 mt/y, Trim width 2.64 m, Linerboard
No. 3, fourdrinier, total capacity 58,000 mt/y, Trim width 3 m, Linerboard
Energy Data:
Power boilers
Electrical demand for mill: 152 MWh/D

ⓜThai Product Paper Mill Co Ltd.
13 Soi Chokechai Jongjurnroen, Rama 3 Road
Yannawa, Bangpongpang, Bangkok, 10120
Thailand
  Phone: (66) 2 683 0570-8
  Fax: (66) 2 295 2057
  Email: thaiproductp@yahoo.com, rtb@clickta.com
Personnel:
Man. Dir.: Wira Sermpornwiwat
Phone: (66) 2 683 0570-8
Fax: (66) 2 295 2057
Email: thaiproductp@yahoo.com
Mill Mgr.: Kawee Sujipinyo
Phone: (66) 38 593 060
Fax: (66) 38 847 353
Email: thaiproductp@yahoo.com
Mill Locations:
Thai Product Paper Mill Co., Ltd., Chachoengsao Mill, 70/1 Moo 7, Suwintawrong Rd., Chlonnakornnoengkaed, Amphur Muang, Chachoengsao 24000, Thailand, Capacity: 20,000 mt/y, (Paperboard mill)
Phone: (66) 38 593 060/ 1 847 350-2
Fax: (66) 38 847 353
Email: thaiproductp@yahoo.com

ⓜThai Product Paper Mill Co., Ltd.
Chachoengsao Mill
Ownership: Thai Product Paper Mill Co Ltd.
70/1 Moo 7, Suwintawrong Rd.,
Chlonnakornnoengkaed
Amphur Muang, Chachoengsao, 24000
Thailand
  Phone: (66) 38 593 060/ 1 847 350-2
  Fax: (66) 38 847 353
  Email: thaiproductp@yahoo.com
Personnel:
Man. Dir.: Wira Sermpornwiwat
Phone: (66) 2 294 8270 8
Fax: (66) 2 295 2057
Email: thaiproductp@yahoo.com
Type of Operation: Paperboard mill
Paper/Paperboard Grades and Capacities:
Total paper and paperboard capacity: 20,000 mt/y
Boxboard/cartonboard: 20,000 mt/y

ⓒⓜThai Union Paper Public Co., Ltd.
Prapradaeng Mill
Ownership: Siam Paper Public Co., Ltd.
131 Moo 2, Poochaosamingprai Rd., Samrong Klang
Prapradaeng, Samut Prakarn, 10130
Thailand
  Phone: (66) 2 754 2100
  Fax: (66) 2 754 2118
  Web Address: www.paper.scg.co.th
Personnel:
Man. Dir.: Phaskorn Buranawit
Phone: (66) 2 586 4709-10
Fax: (66) 2 587 0746
Email: phaskorb@scg.co.th
Mill Mgr.: Kwanchai Wacharapairoj
Phone: (66) 2 754 2100
Fax: (66) 2 754 2118
Email: kwanchaw@scg.co.th
Mktg. Dir.: Vipapat Cholsawad
Phone: (66) 2 586 2411
Fax: (66) 2 586 2070

Thailand

Procurement Dir.: Wichan Jitpukdee
Phone: (66) 2 586 4565 6
Fax: (66) 2 586 2378
Email: wichanj@scg.co.th
Total Employees at this Location: 300
Type of Operation: Paper mill, Paperboard mill
Pulp Grades and Capacities:
Total pulp capacity: 22,525 mt/y
Recycled Pulping: 22,525 mt/y
Pulp Mill Data:
Recycled Fiber Treatment Lines:
Recycled packaging pulping lines: 1
Paper/Paperboard Grades and Capacities:
Total paper and paperboard capacity: 76,041 mt/y
Coated woodfree/freesheet: 29,274 mt/y
Specialty and industrial: 24,633 mt/y
Boxboard/cartonboard: 22,134 mt/y
Paper and Paperboard Mill Data:
Stock Preparation:
Pulpers: 20
Refiners: 29
Paper Machines: 7
No. 1, Yankee dryer, total capacity 4,641 mt/y, Trim width 2.1 m, Specialty and industrial
No. 2, Yankee dryer, total capacity 6,426 mt/y, Trim width 2.1 m, Specialty and industrial
No. 3, Yankee dryer, total capacity 6,426 mt/y, Trim width 2.1 m, Specialty and industrial
No. 4, Yankee dryer, total capacity 7,140 mt/y, Trim width 2.1 m, Specialty and industrial
No. 5, cylinder, total capacity 22,134 mt/y, Trim width 1.9 m, Boxboard/cartonboard
No. 6, fourdrinier, total capacity 10,710 mt/y, Trim width 2 m, Coated woodfree/freesheet
No. 7, fourdrinier, total capacity 18,564 mt/y, Trim width 2.9 m, Coated woodfree/freesheet
Coating Machines: 5
No. 1, total capacity 8,800 mt/y., off machine
No. 2, total capacity 17,000 mt/y., off machine
No. 3, total capacity 17,000 mt/y., off machine
No. 4, total capacity 20,000 mt/y., off machine
No. 5, total capacity 15,000 mt/y., on machine
Finishing Equipment:
Winders: 7
Supercalenders: 3
Sheeters: 8
Energy Data:
Power boilers: 4
Electrical demand for mill: 181 MWh/D

ⓂThai Union Paper Industry Co., Ltd.
Wangsala Mill
Ownership: 100% by SCG Paper Public Co., Ltd.
99 Moo 6, Saeng-Xuto Road Wangsala
Tha Muang Distr., Kanchanaburi, 71110
Thailand
Phone: (66) 34 615 000-20
Fax: (66) 34 615 076
Web Address: www.paper.scg.co.th, www.tupi.co.th
Personnel:
Man. Dir.: Wichan Charoenkitsupat
Phone: (66) 2 586 6695-6
Fax: (66) 2 586 6688
Prod. Mgr.: Kasem Chutirnataewin
Phone: (66) 3461 5000-20
Fax: (66) 3461 5076
Email: kasemc@scg.co.th
Sales & Mktg. Mgr.: Ms Orawan Iamsirikulmit
Phone: (66) 2 586 2412
Fax: (66) 2 586 2828
Email: orawani@scg.co.th
Procur. Dir.: Wichan Jitpukdee
Phone: (66) 2 586 4565
Fax: (66) 2 586 2378
Email: wichanj@scg.co.th
Total Employees at this Location: 199
Type of Operation: Paperboard mill
Pulp Grades and Capacities:
Total pulp capacity: 143,477 mt/y
Recycled Pulping: 143,477 mt/y
Paper/Paperboard Grades and Capacities:
Total paper and paperboard capacity: 162,435 mt/y
Boxboard/cartonboard: 162,435 mt/y
Paper and Paperboard Mill Data:
Paper Machines: 2
No. 8, SymFormer MB, total capacity 67,830 mt/y, Trim width 2.66 m, Boxboard/cartonboard
No. 9, Ultraformer (7), total capacity 94,605 mt/y, Trim width 2.66 m, Boxboard/cartonboard
Coating Machines: 1
PM 9, total capacity 110,000 mt/y., on machine
Energy Data:
Electrical demand for mill: 319 MWh/D

ⓃⓂThai Victory Paper Co., Ltd.
Bangkok Mill
95/5 Moo 7, Soi Watkumpaeng Rama II Rd.
Samaedam, Bangkhuntian, Bangkok, Bangkok, 10150
Thailand
Phone: (66) 2 899 5350
Fax: (66) 2 899 5351
Email: thaivic_paper@yahoo.com
Personnel:
Man. Dir.: Charnchai Hernvitistham
Phone: (66) 2 899 5350 ext. 16
Fax: (66) 2 899 5351
Mill Mgr.: Sakchai Sangjon
Phone: (66) 2 899 5350
Mktg. Mgr.: Atig Laprattanakon
Phone: (66) 2 899 5350
Total Employees of Company: 80
Type of Operation: Paper mill
Paper/Paperboard Grades and Capacities:
Total paper and paperboard capacity: 1,800 mt/y
Tissue: 1,800 mt/y
Paper and Paperboard Mill Data:
Paper Machines: 1
No. 1, Trim width 2.2 m, Tissue

ⓃⓂThanakorn Paper Industry Co., Ltd.
Amphur Muang, Pathumthani Mill
9/9 Moo 1, Soi Watdaodung, Tiwanont Rd., Tambon Bangkadee
Amphur Muang, Pathumthani, 12000
Thailand
Phone: (66) 2 963 7042
Fax: (66) 2 963 7044
Personnel:
Gen. Mgr.: Ms. Ruantip Phayongthanakorn
Phone: (66) 2 963 7042
Man. Dir.: Mr. Boonmee Phayongthanakorn
Phone: (66) 2 963 7042
Mill Mgr.: Mr. Thongchai Phayongthanakorn
Phone: (66) 2 963 7042
Email: thongchai@thanakornpaper.com
Mktg. Mgr.: Mr. Thaweewat Phayongthanakorn
Phone: (66) 2 963 7042
Type of Operation: Paperboard mill
Paper/Paperboard Grades and Capacities:
Total paper and paperboard capacity: 32,000 mt/y
Containerboard: 32,000 mt/y
Linerboard
Corrugating medium/fluting

ⓃⓂThanatarn Paper Co., Ltd.
Taparak Mill
Ownership: Riverpro Group
48 Moo 3, Teparak Rd.
Taparak, Samut Prakarn, 10270
Thailand
Phone: (66) 2 384 7378-80/5656-60
Fax: (66) 2 384 2901
Email: thana1@ksc.th.com
Web Address: www.riverpro.co.th
Personnel:
Man. Dir.: Sumit Yipyinturn
Phone: (66) 2 384 7378-80/5656-60
Purch. Mgr.: Ms. Jinda Duangmanee
Phone: (66) 2 384 7378-80/5656-60
Email: jinda@riverpro.co.th
Total Employees at this Location: 380
Type of Operation: Paper mill
Pulp Mill Data:
Recycled Fiber Treatment Lines:
Flotation deinking lines: 4
Pulpers: 3
Washing deinking lines: 2
Paper/Paperboard Grades and Capacities:
Total paper and paperboard capacity: 14,500 mt/y
Tissue: 14,500 mt/y
Paper and Paperboard Mill Data:
Stock Preparation:
Pulpers: 3
Refiners: 4
Paper Machines: 4
No. 1, cylinder, Trim width 0.8 m, Tissue
No. 2, cylinder, Trim width 0.9 m, Tissue
No. 3, cylinder, Trim width 2.2 m, Tissue
No. 4, fourdrinier, Trim width 2.3 m, Tissue
Finishing Equipment:
Rewinders: 3
Energy Data:
Power boilers: 1

ⓃUnited Paper Public Co., Ltd.
Ownership: 12.08% by Marketing Consultant Co., Ltd., 13.03% by Mr. Chin Chinsettawong, 13.53% by Mr. Mongkol Mangkornkanok, 12.61% by Mrs. Achara Chinsettawong, 13.74% by Union Paper Carton Co., Ltd.
113-115 Rimklong Pra-pa Rd.
Bangsue, Bangkok, 10800
Thailand
Phone: (66) 2 910 2700
Fax: (66) 2 910 2709
Web Address: www.unitedpaper.co.th
Personnel:
Chmn.: Prapha Viriyapraphaikit
Phone: (66) 2 910 2700
Fax: (66) 2 910 2709
Vice Chmn.: Chin Chinsettawong
Phone: (66) 2 910 2700
Fax: (66) 2 910 2709
Man. Dir.: Mr. Mongkol Mangkornkanok
Phone: (66) 2 910 2700
Fax: (66) 2 910 2709
Email: mongkol@unitedpaper.co.th
Dpty. Man. Dir.: Mr. Wachara Chinsettawong
Phone: (66) 2 910 2700-8
Fax: (66) 2 910 2709
Email: wachara@unitedpaper.co.th
Mgr. of Fina. and HR: Phensiri Chinsettawong
Phone: (66) 2 910 2700
Fax: (66) 2 910 2709
Mill Mgr.: Ruangchai Khiawad
Phone: (66) 2 910 2700
Fax: (66) 2 910 2709
Email: ruangchai@unitedpaper.co.th
Mkgt. Mgr.: Mr. Jirasak Denkriangkrai
Phone: (66) 2 910 2700
Fax: (66) 2 910 2709
Email: jirasak@unitedpaper.co.th
Total Employees of Company: 220
Total Employees at this Location: 22
Mill Locations:
United Paper Public Co. Ltd., Amphur Muang Mill, 61 Moo 8, Tumbon Watboth, Amphur Muang, Prachinburi, 25000, Thailand, Capacity: 115,000 mt/y, (Paperboard mill)
Phone: (66) 37 287 361-9
Fax: (66) 37 287 370

ⓂUnited Paper Public Co. Ltd.
Amphur Muang Mill
Ownership: United Paper Public Co., Ltd.
61 Moo 8, Tumbon Watboth

Amphur Muang, Prachinburi, 25000
Thailand
  Phone: (66) 37 287 361-9
  Fax: (66) 37 287 370
  Web Address: www.unitedpaper.co.th
  Personnel:
  Man. Dir.: Mr. Mongkol Mangkomkanok
  Phone: (66) 37 287 361-9
  Email: mongkol@unitedpaper.co.th
  Dpty. Man. Dir.: Mr. Wachara Chinsettawong
  Phone: (66) 2 910 2700
  Fax: (66) 2 910 2709
  Email: wachara@unitedpaper.co.th
  Mktg. Mgr.: Mr. Jirasak Denkriangkrai
  Phone: (66) 37 287 361-9
  Email: Jirasak@unitedpaper.co.th
  Mill Mgr.: Mr. Ruangchai Khiawad
  Phone: (66) 37 287 361-9
  Email: ruangchai@unitedpaper.co.th
  Purch. Mgr.: Ms. Surasie Petaibanlue
  Phone: (66) 37 287 361-9
  Email: surasie@unitedpaper.co.th
Total Employees at this Location: 210
Type of Operation: Paperboard mill
Pulp Grades and Capacities:
  Total pulp capacity: 111,308 mt/y
  Recycled Pulping: 111,308 mt/y
Pulp Mill Data:
  Recycled Fiber Treatment Lines:
  Recycled packaging pulping lines: 1
Paper/Paperboard Grades and Capacities:
  Total paper and paperboard capacity: 115,000 mt/y
  Linerboard: 34,500 mt/y
  Corrugating medium/fluting: 80,500 mt/y
Paper and Paperboard Mill Data:
Paper Machines: 1
  No. 1, fourdrinier, total capacity 115,000 mt/y, Trim width 2.4 m, Corrugating medium/fluting, Linerboard
Energy Data:
  Power boilers: 2
  Steam turbines: 2 at 7.5, 2 MW
  Electrical demand for mill: 133 MWh/D

ⓘWang N.T. Paper Co., Ltd.
Ownership: Mr. Aree Chunfung, Mr. Boonyarit Na Wangkanai, Mr. Kris Jungsiriwat, Mr. Rachan Taweewong, Mr. Sahaphob Meephasri, Mr. Teera Na Wangkanai, Others
889 Thai CC Tower, 27 Floor, South Sathorn Rd.
Yannawa Sathorn, Bangkok, 10120
Thailand
  Phone: (66) 2 675 8321
  Fax: (66) 2 675 8322
  Web Address: www.wangkanai.co.th
Total Employees of Company: 170
Mill Locations:
Wang N.T. Paper Co., Ltd., Lopburi Mill, 99 Moo 2 Kangpakgood Sub-District, Thaluang Distr., Lopburi 15230, Thailand, Capacity: 12,200 mt/y, (Paper mill)
  Phone: (66) 36 497 1068
  Fax: (66) 36 497 1068
  Email: wntpaper@cscoms.com

ⓜWang N.T. Paper Co., Ltd.
Lopburi Mill
99 Moo 2 Kangpakgood Sub-District
Thaluang Distr., Lopburi, 15230
Thailand
Mailing Address: 889 Thai CC Tower, 27th floor, South Sathorn Road, Bangkok, 10120, Thailand
  Phone: (66) 36 497 1068
  Fax: (66) 36 497 1068
  Email: wntpaper@cscoms.com
  Web Address: www.wangkanai.co.th
Personnel:
  Man. Dir.: Boonyarit Na Wangkanai
  Phone: (66) 36 497 1068
  Email: bnw_wnt@wangkanai.co.th
  Finan. Dir.: Nakorn Visalathaphant
  Phone: (66) 36 497 1068
  Email: nakorn_wnt@wangkanai.co.th
Total Employees at this Location: 170
Type of Operation: Paper mill
Paper/Paperboard Grades and Capacities:
  Total paper and paperboard capacity: 12,200 mt/y
  Tissue: 12,200 mt/y
Paper and Paperboard Mill Data:
Paper Machines: 1
  No. 1 & 2, fourdrinier, Tissue
Finishing Equipment:
  Rewinders: 2 at 5,000 mt/y
Energy Data:
  Power boilers: 1

TURKEY

ⓘⓜAk Gida San. ve Tic. A.Ş
Pamukova Mill
Gökgözü Köyü
Pamukova
Turkey
  Phone: (90) 264 554 00 00
  Fax: (90) 264 554 00 20
  Email: insankaynaklari@akgida.ulker.com.tr
  Web Address: www.akgida.com.tr/tr/
Personnel:
  Chair. of board: Murat Ülker
  Phone: (90) 0264 554 00 00
  Fax: (90) 0264 554 00 20
  Hon., Chair. : Sabri Ülker
  Phone: (90) 0264 554 00 00
  Fax: (90) 0264 554 00 20
  Gen. Mgr.: Hüseyin Avci
  Phone: (90) 0264 554 00 00
  Fax: (90) 0264 554 00 20
  Mill Mgr./Project: Erkan Timavali
  Phone: (90) 0264 554 00 00
  Fax: (90) 0264 554 00 20
  Email: erkan.timavali@tulkagit.com
Total Employees at this Location: 251
Type of Operation: Paper mill
Paper/Paperboard Grades and Capacities:
  Total paper and paperboard capacity: 70,000 mt/y
  Tissue: 70,000 mt/y
Paper and Paperboard Mill Data:
Paper Machines: 1
  No. 1, (started up in late August 2011), Advantage DCT 200 TS, Yankee dryer, total capacity 70,000 mt/y, Trim width 5.6 m, Tissue, Uncoated woodfree/freesheet
Finishing Equipment:
  Rewinders: 1 at 70,000 mt/y
Energy Data:
  Combustion turbines: 1 at 15 MW
  Electrical demand for mill: 166 MWh/D

ⓘⓜAkasan Adana Kagit San ve Tic. Ltd. Sti.
Adana Mill
Ownership: 100% by Mithat Topal Construction Co.
Adana Organize San. Bölgesi (AOSB) Yakapýnar
Adana
Turkey
Mailing Address: Haci Sabanci OSB Anafartalar Caddesi No: 1 Sariçam, Adana
  Phone: (90) 322 3943564
  Fax: (90) 322 3943564
  Email: akasan@akasan.com.tr
  Web Address: www.akasan.com.tr
Personnel:
  Owner/Gen. Mgr.: Mithat Topal
  Phone: (90) 322 3943564
  Commer. Oper. Mgr.: Esin Topal
  Phone: (90) 322 3943564
  Prod. Mgr.: Ali Çevik
  Phone: (90) 322 3943564
  Commercial Mgr.: Hüseyin Tekin
  Phone: (90) 322 3943564
  Qlty. Control Mgr.: Mutlu Canatar
  Phone: (90) 322 3943564
  Cust. Rel.: Fatma Cortancioglu
  Phone: (90) 322 3943564
Total Employees at this Location: 72
Type of Operation: Paper mill
Pulp Grades and Capacities:
  Total pulp capacity: 59,636 mt/y
  Recycled Pulping: 59,636 mt/y
Paper/Paperboard Grades and Capacities:
  Total paper and paperboard capacity: 60,000 mt/y
  Linerboard: 30,000 mt/y
  Corrugating medium/fluting: 30,000 mt/y
Paper and Paperboard Mill Data:
  Stock Preparation:
  Pulpers: 2
  Refiners: 2
Paper Machines: 1
  No. 1, fourdrinier, total capacity 60,000 mt/y, Trim width 2.9 m, Linerboard, Corrugating medium/fluting
Finishing Equipment:
  Winders: 1 at 35,000 mt/y
Energy Data:
  Power boilers: 1
  Electrical demand for mill: 79 MWh/D

ⓘAlbayrak Sirketler Grubu
Ownership: 100% by Albayrak Group
Cayhane Sok. No:1 Topkapi
TR-34020 Topkapi-Istanbul
Turkey
  Phone: (90) 212 544 3333 / 212 467 3636
  Fax: (90) 212 544 4748
  Email: info@albayrak.com.tr
  Web Address: www.albayrak.com.tr
Personnel:
  Exec. Chmn.: Mustafa Albayrak
  Phone: (90) 212 544 3333
  Fax: (90) 212 544 4748
Total Employees of Company: 6,000
Total Employees at this Location: 150
Mill Locations:
Balikesir Albayrak Kagit Fabrikasi, Balikesir Mill, Pasaköy, TR-10059 Balikesir, Turkey, Capacity: 120,000 mt/y, (Pulp mill, Paper mill)
  Phone: (90) 266 2672425
  Fax: (90) 266 2672425
  Email: info@albayrak.com.tr

ⓘⓜAlkim Kagit Sanayi ve Ticaret A.S
Izmir Mill
Ownership: Kora Family
Kirovasi Mevkii Kemalpasa
TR-35170 Izmir, Izmir
Turkey
  Phone: (90) 232 877 0606
  Fax: (90) 232 877 0605
  Email: info@alkimkagit.com.tr
  Web Address: www.alkimkagit.com.tr
Personnel:
  Chmn.: Mehmet Reha Kora
  Phone: (90) 232 877 0606
  Gen. Mgr.: Halil Sonmez
  Phone: (90) 232 877 0606
  Email: h.sonmez@alkimkagit.com.tr
  Dpty. Gen. Mgr.: T. Salt
  Phone: (90) 232 877 0606
  Email: t.salt@alkimkagit.com.tr
  Tech. Mgr.: T. Toplu
  Phone: (90) 232 877 0606
  Email: t.toplu@alkimkagit.com.tr
  Prod. Mgr.: O. Madran
  Phone: (90) 232 877 0606
  Email: o.madran@alkimkagit.com.tr
  PR Responsible: M. Uygun
  Phone: (90) 232 441 54 55

Turkey

Fax: (90) 232 445 00 39
Email: m.uygun@alkimkagit.com.tr
Planning Mgr.: F. Emekli
Phone: (90) 232 877 0606
Email: f.emekli@alkimkagit.com.tr
Paper Prod. Chief: G. Yuce
Phone: (90) 232 877 0606
Email: g.yuce@alkimkagit.com.tr
Purch. Mgr.: C. Capkin
Phone: (90) 232 877 0606
Email: c.capkin@alkimkagit.com.tr
Imp./Exp. Mgr.: S. Capkin
Phone: (90) 232 877 0606
Email: s.capkin@alkimkagit.com.tr
Total Employees of Company: 235
Total Employees at this Location: 185
Type of Operation: Paper mill
Pulp Grades and Capacities:
Total pulp capacity: 7,434 mt/y
Recycled Pulping: 7,434 mt/y
Paper/Paperboard Grades and Capacities:
Total paper and paperboard capacity: 90,000 mt/y
Uncoated woodfree/freesheet: 85,000 mt/y
Coated woodfree/freesheet: 5,000 mt/y
Paper and Paperboard Mill Data:
Stock Preparation:
Pulpers: 3
Refiners: 10
Paper Machines: 1
No. 1, hybrid former, total capacity 90,000 mt/y, Trim width 3.48 m, Uncoated woodfree/freesheet, Coated woodfree/freesheet
Coating Machines: 1
PM 1, total capacity 10,000 mt/y., on machine
Finishing Equipment:
Winders: 1
Calenders: 2
Sheeters: 4
Energy Data:
Power boilers: 2
Combustion turbines: 1 at 5.5 MW
Electrical demand for mill: 155 MWh/D

ⓜBalikesir Albayrak Kagit Fabrikasi
Balikesir Mill
Mill is idle
Ownership: 100% by Albayrak Sirketler Grubu
Pasaköy
TR-10059 Balikesir
Turkey
Phone: (90) 266 2672425
Fax: (90) 266 2672425
Email: info@albayrak.com.tr
Web Address: www.albayrak.com.tr
Type of Operation: Pulp mill, Paper mill
Pulp Grades and Capacities:
Total pulp capacity: 80,000 mt/y
Mechanical Pulp: 80,000 mt/y
Pulp Mill Data:
Mechanical Pulping Systems:
Conventional grinders: 6
CTMP systems: 3
Pressurized grinders: 3
Bleach Plant Systems: 1
No. 1 Capacity 108,000 admt/y
Paper/Paperboard Grades and Capacities:
Total paper and paperboard capacity: 120,000 mt/y
Newsprint: 120,000 mt/y
Paper and Paperboard Mill Data:
Stock Preparation:
Pulpers: 1
Refiners: 1
Paper Machines: 1
No. 1, twin-wire, total capacity 120,000 mt/y, Trim width 6.9 m, Newsprint
Energy Data:
Power boilers: 2
Steam turbines: 1 at 9.3 MW

ⓜCopikas Kagit ve Oluklu Mukavva Kutu A.S.
Olmuksa Copikas Mill
Ownership: 100% by Olmuksa International Paper-Sabanci Ambalaj Sanayi ve Ticaret A.S.
Ankara Yolu 4 km
Corum
Turkey
Phone: (90) 364 2350050
Fax: (90) 364 2350067
Email: sales.corum@ipaper.com
Web Address: www.olmuksan-ipaper.com
Personnel:
Mill Mgr.: Özay Özdemir
Phone: (90) 364 2350050
Fax: (90) 364 2350064
Prod. Mgr.: Haydar Keskin
Phone: (90) 364 2350050 Ext. 122
Fax: (90) 364 2350064
Total Employees at this Location: 35
Type of Operation: Paperboard mill
Pulp Grades and Capacities:
Total pulp capacity: 30,213 mt/y
Recycled Pulping: 30,213 mt/y
Pulp Mill Data:
Recycled Fiber Treatment Lines:
Pulpers: 2
Paper/Paperboard Grades and Capacities:
Total paper and paperboard capacity: 30,000 mt/y
Corrugating medium/fluting: 30,000 mt/y
Paper and Paperboard Mill Data:
Paper Machines: 1
No. 1, fourdrinier, total capacity 30,000 mt/y, Trim width 2.6 m, Corrugating medium/fluting
Energy Data:
Power boilers: 1
Electrical demand for mill: 40 MWh/D

ⓘⓜDentaş Ambalaj Ve Kagit San. A.S
Denizli Mill
Ownership: 100% by Prinzhorn Holding GmbH
Akhan Mah. 104 Sok. No:8
Denizli
Turkey
Phone: (90) 258 268 0580
Fax: (90) 258 268 1085
Email: info@dentas.com.tr,
dentas@dentas.com.tr
Web Address: www.dentas.com.tr, www.dentaskagit.com.tr
Personnel:
Chmn. of the Board: Ismet Abalioglu
Phone: (90) 258 268 0580
Vice Chair.: Mehmet Ali Abalioglu
Phone: (90) 258 268 0580
Gen. Mgr.: Idris Nebi Kayacan
Phone: (90) 258 268 0580
Export Mgr.: Özge Kemal Kaya
Phone: (90) 258 268 0580
Sales & Mrkt. Dir.: Ömer Egilmez
Phone: (90) 258 268 0580
Paper Mill Dir.: Ahmet Oguz Arpacioglu
Phone: (90) 258 268 1161
Total Employees of Company: 660
Total Employees at this Location: 90
Type of Operation: Paperboard mill
Mill Locations:
Dentaş Ambalaj Ve Kagit San. A.S, Vakıflar Köyü Mevkii E5 Karayolu Üzeri P.K:55 Ulaş Kasabası, Çorlu, Tekirdag, Turkey, Capacity: 80,000 mt/y, (Paperboard mill)
Phone: (90) 672 24 25
Fax: (90) 672 28 74
Email: dentas.corlu@dentas.com.tr
Pulp Grades and Capacities:
Total pulp capacity: 90,185 mt/y
Recycled Pulping: 90,185 mt/y
Pulp Mill Data:
Pulp Lines: 2
Recycled Fiber Treatment Lines:
Pulpers: 3 at 142,000 admt/y
Pulp Dryers:
Fourdriniers 2
Paper/Paperboard Grades and Capacities:
Total paper and paperboard capacity: 90,000 mt/y
Linerboard: 45,000 mt/y
Corrugating medium/fluting: 45,000 mt/y
Paper and Paperboard Mill Data:
Stock Preparation:
Pulpers: 4
Refiners: 5
Paper Machines: 2
No. 1, fourdrinier, total capacity 45,000 mt/y, Trim width 2.5 m, Corrugating medium/fluting
No. 2, fourdrinier (2), total capacity 45,000 mt/y, Trim width 2.5 m, Linerboard
Finishing Equipment:
Winders: 2 at 90,000 mt/y
Rewinders: 2 at 170,400 mt/y
Sheeters: 2 at 1,000 mt/y
Energy Data:
Power boilers: 2
Combustion turbines: 1 at 5.2 MW
Electrical demand for mill: 110 MWh/D

ⓜDentaş Ambalaj Ve Kagit San. A.S
Çorlu Mill
Ownership: 100% by Prinzhorn Holding GmbH
Vakıflar Köyü Mevkii E5 Karayolu Üzeri P.K:55 Ulaş Kasabası
Çorlu, Tekirdag,
Turkey
Phone: (90) 672 24 25
Fax: (90) 672 28 74
Email: dentas.corlu@dentas.com.tr
Web Address: www.dentas.com.tr
Total Employees at this Location: 160
Type of Operation: Paperboard mill
Pulp Grades and Capacities:
Total pulp capacity: 80,621 mt/y
Recycled Pulping: 80,621 mt/y
Pulp Mill Data:
Recycled Fiber Treatment Lines:
Recycled packaging pulping lines
Paper/Paperboard Grades and Capacities:
Total paper and paperboard capacity: 80,000 mt/y
Linerboard: 48,000 mt/y
Corrugating medium/fluting: 32,000 mt/y
Paper and Paperboard Mill Data:
Paper Machines: 1
No. 1, fourdrinier (2), total capacity 80,000 mt/y, Trim width 2.55 m, Corrugating medium/fluting, Linerboard
Energy Data:
Power boilers
Electrical demand for mill: 109 MWh/D

ⓜDoruk Kagit San. TIC. A.S
Kayseri Mill
Organize Sanayi Bolgesi 12. Cadde No:60
TR-38070 Kayseri
Turkey
Mailing Address: Organize Sanayi Bolgesi 12. Cadde No:33, TR-38070 Kayseri
Phone: (90) 352 321 17 15/12 24
Fax: (90) 352 321 17 45
Email: info@dorukpaper.com
Web Address: www.dorukkagit.com.tr, www.dorukpaper.com
Personnel:
Chmn. of the Board: Muzaffer Nalbantoglu
Phone: (90) 352 321 17 15/12 24
Assist. Chmn. of the Board: Emir Nalbantoglu
Phone: (90) 352 321 17 15/12 24
Mill Mgr.: Osman Kababiz
Phone: (90) 352 321 2330
Prod. Mgr.: Tacettin Oruç
Phone: (90) 352 321 17 15/12 24
Electrical Eng.: Azmi Nalbantoglu

Turkey

Phone: (90) 352 321 2330
Total Employees at this Location: 80
Type of Operation: Paperboard mill
Pulp Grades and Capacities:
Total pulp capacity: 76,793 mt/y
Recycled Pulping: 76,793 mt/y

Pulp Mill Data:
Recycled Fiber Treatment Lines:
Recycled packaging pulping lines: 1
Paper/Paperboard Grades and Capacities:
Total paper and paperboard capacity: 75,000 mt/y
Packaging papers: 35,000 mt/y
Corrugating medium/fluting: 40,000 mt/y
Paper and Paperboard Mill Data:
Stock Preparation:
Pulpers: 2
Refiners: 2
Paper Machines: 3
No. 1, fourdrinier, Yankee dryer, total capacity 15,000 mt/y, Trim width 2.2 m, Packaging papers
No. 2, fourdrinier, Yankee dryer, total capacity 20,000 mt/y, Trim width 3 m, Packaging papers
No. 3, fourdrinier, total capacity 40,000 mt/y, Trim width 3 m, Corrugating medium/fluting
Finishing Equipment:
Sheeters: 1 at 15,000 mt/y
Energy Data:
Power boilers: 2
Electrical demand for mill: 122 MWh/D

ⓜDoruk Kagit San. TIC. A.S

Ownership: 100% by Nalbantoglu family
Organize Sanayi Bolgesi 12. Cadde No:60 Kayseri,
TR-38070
Kayseri
Turkey
Phone: (90) 352 321 17 15/12 24
Fax: (90) 352 321 17 45
Email: info@dorukpaper.com
Web Address: www.dorukkagit.com.tr,
www.dorukpaper.com
Personnel:
Chmn. of Bd.: Muzaffer Nalbantoglu
Phone: (90) 352 321 17 15/12 24
Fax: (90) 352 321 17 45
Assist. Chmn. of Bd.: Emir Nalbantoglu
Phone: (90) 352 321 17 15/12 24
Fax: (90) 352 321 17 45
Prod. Mgr.: Tacettin Oruç
Phone: (90) 352 321 17 15/12 24
Fax: (90) 352 321 17 45
Total Employees of Company: 80
Mill Locations:
Doruk Kagit San. TIC. A.S, Kayseri Mill, Organize Sanayi Bolgesi 12. Cadde No:60, TR-38070 Kayseri, Turkey, Capacity: 75,000 mt/y, (Paperboard mill)
Phone: (90) 352 321 17 15/12 24
Fax: (90) 352 321 17 45
Email: info@dorukpaper.com

ⓜEKA Industrial Paper Production Limited
Izmit Mill

Ankara Cad. No : 138
41200 Kosekoy, Izmit, Kocaeli
Turkey
Phone: (90) 262 322 2588
Fax: (90) 262 322 7455
Email: nolgac@ekakagit.com
Web Address: www.ekakagit.com.tr
Personnel:
Owner & Pres.: Necmi Olgaç
Phone: (90) 262 322 2588
Email: nolgac@ekakagit.com
Mill Mgr.: Kadir Çobanoğlu
Phone: (90) 262 322 2588
Total Employees at this Location: 125
Type of Operation: Paper mill
Pulp Grades and Capacities:
Total pulp capacity: 12,446 mt/y
Recycled Pulping: 12,446 mt/y
Pulp Mill Data:
Recycled Fiber Treatment Lines:
Flotation deinking lines: 1
Paper/Paperboard Grades and Capacities:
Total paper and paperboard capacity: 48,000 mt/y
Tissue: 24,000 mt/y
Packaging papers: 24,000 mt/y
Paper and Paperboard Mill Data:
Paper Machines: 2
No. 1, crescent former, Yankee dryer, total capacity 24,000 mt/y, Trim width 2.85 m, Tissue, Uncoated woodfree/freesheet
No. 10, fourdrinier, Yankee dryer, total capacity 24,000 mt/y, Trim width 3.5 m, Packaging papers
Finishing Equipment:
Rewinders: 1
Sheeters: 1
Energy Data:
Power boilers
Electrical demand for mill: 107 MWh/D

ⓜEKA Industrial Paper Production Limited

Ownership: 100% by Mr. Necmi Olgac
Ankara Cad. No : 138 Kosekoy, Izmit, Kocaeli, 41200
Kocaeli
Turkey
Phone: (90) 262 322 2588
Fax: (90) 262 322 7455
Email: nolgac@ekakagit.com
Web Address: www.ekakagit.com.tr
Personnel:
Owner & Pres.: Necmi Olgaç
Phone: (90) 262 322 2588
Fax: (90) 262 322 7455
Email: nolgac@ekakagit.com
Mill Mgr.: Kadir Çobanoglu
Phone: (90) 262 322 2588
Fax: (90) 262 322 7455
Total Employees of Company: 125
Mill Locations:
EKA Industrial Paper Production Limited, Izmit Mill, Ankara Cad. No : 138, 41200 Kosekoy, Izmit, Turkey, Capacity: 48,000 mt/y, (Paper mill)
Phone: (90) 262 322 2588
Fax: (90) 262 322 7455
Email: nolgac@ekakagit.com

ⓜⓜErtok Oluklu Mukavva San.ve tic. ltd. Sti
Izmir Mill

Kosbi, Ankara Asfalti 13. Km
35730 Ulucak, Izmir
Turkey
Phone: (90) 0236 314 6561
Fax: (90) 0236 314 6571
Email: info@ertokgroup.com
Web Address: www.ertokgroup.com/
Type of Operation: Paperboard mill
Paper/Paperboard Grades and Capacities:
Total paper and paperboard capacity: 6,500 mt/y
Paper and Paperboard Mill Data:
Paper Machines: 1
PM 1, (2nd hand, started mid-2012), fourdrinier, total capacity 6,500 mt/y, Trim width 1.6 m

ⓜEssel Selüloz ve Kağıt Sanayi Ticaret A.Ş

Ownership: 100% by Essel Group
Merkez: Körfez Mah. Sanayi Cad. Berk Sk. Dolphin İş Merkezi Kat:5 No:516-518 İzmit. 41000 Kocaeli, Turkey
Phone: (90) 262 323 3365
Email: info@essel.com.tr
Web Address: www.essel.com.tr
Mill Locations:
Essel Selüloz ve Kâ??t Sanayi Tic. A.?, Caycuma Mill, Organize San. Bölgesi 8, Çaycuma , Turkey, Capacity: 24,000 mt/y, (Paper mill)
Phone: (90) 372 638 6490
Email: info@essel.com.tr

ⓜEssel Selüloz ve Kağıt Sanayi Ticaret A.Ş
Caycuma Mill

Organize San. Bölgesi 8
Çaycuma , Zonguldak
Turkey
Phone: (90) 372 638 6490
Email: info@essel.com.tr
Web Address: www.essel.com.tr
Total Employees at this Location: 50
Type of Operation: Paper mill
Paper/Paperboard Grades and Capacities:
Total paper and paperboard capacity: 24,000 mt/y
Tissue: 24,000 mt/y
Paper and Paperboard Mill Data:
Stock Preparation:
Pulpers: 2
Refiners: 4
Paper Machines: 1
No. 3, crescent former, Yankee dryer, total capacity 24,000 mt/y, Trim width 2.8 m, Tissue, Uncoated woodfree/freesheet
Finishing Equipment:
Rewinders: 1
Energy Data:
Electrical demand for mill: 60 MWh/D

ⓜⓜHalkali Kagit Karton San. ve Tic. A.S.
Istanbul Mill

Ownership: 100% by Saral Family
Halkali Merkez Mah, Dereboyu Caddesi No:72/1
TR-34303 Küçükçekmece, Istanbul
Turkey
Phone: (90) 212 6939334
Fax: (90) 212 5483221
Email: info@halkalikagit.com.tr
Web Address: www.halkalikagit.com
Personnel:
Chmn.: Mustafa Saral
Phone: (90) 212 6939334
Gen. Mgr.: Sevim Saral
Phone: (90) 212 6939334
Email: sskavruk@halkalikagit.com
Prod. Mgr., PM 1: Süleyman Saral
Phone: (90) 212 6939334
Prod. Mgr., PM 2: Turker Ciplakoglu
Phone: (90) 212 6939334
Email: turker@halkalikagit.com
Mill Mgr., Waste Paper: Bulent kaya
Phone: (90) 212 6939334
Maint. Mgr. & R&D Mgr.: Gurkan Yangoz
Phone: (90) 212 6939334
Sls. Mgr.: Fatma Saral
Phone: (90) 212 6939334
Email: arge@halkalikagit.com
Sales Exec.: Tolga Mentas
Email: tmentas@halkalikagit.com
Total Employees at this Location: 200
Type of Operation: Paper mill, Paperboard mill
Pulp Grades and Capacities:
Total pulp capacity: 134,942 mt/y
Recycled Pulping: 134,942 mt/y
Paper/Paperboard Grades and Capacities:
Total paper and paperboard capacity: 135,000 mt/y
Linerboard: 55,000 mt/y
Corrugating medium/fluting: 50,000 mt/y
Boxboard/cartonboard: 30,000 mt/y
Paper and Paperboard Mill Data:
Stock Preparation:
Pulpers: 3
Refiners: 4
Paper Machines: 2

Turkey

No. 1, cylinder, total capacity 30,000 mt/y, Trim width 2.2 m, Boxboard/cartonboard
No. 2, fourdrinier (2), total capacity 105,000 mt/y, Trim width 3.48 m, Corrugating medium/fluting, Linerboard
Finishing Equipment:
Winders: 2 at 150,000 mt/y
Sheeters: 2 at 30,000 mt/y
Energy Data:
Power boilers: 1
Combustion turbines: 2 at 10.4 MW
Electrical demand for mill: 165 MWh/D

ⒽⓂHayat Kagit ve Enerji A.S.
Corum Mill
Ownership: 100% by Yahya Kigli
Ankara Yolu Bulvari No.35
TR-19100 Corum
Turkey
Phone: (90) 364 235 03 30/31
Fax: (90) 364 235 03 34
Email: info@hayatkagit.com
Web Address: www.hayatkagit.com
Personnel:
Chmn.: Mehmet Salur
Phone: (90) 364 235 03 30/31
Gen. Mgr.: Aydin Armagan
Phone: (90) 364 235 03 30/31
Prod. Mgr.: Hüseyin Ates
Phone: (90) 364 235 03 30/31
Email: huseyinates@hayatkagit.com
Fin. Mgr.: Faruk Cakir
Phone: (90) 364 235 03 30/31
Total Employees of Company: 104
Total Employees at this Location: 110
Type of Operation: Pulp mill, Paperboard mill
Mill Locations:
Hayat Kimya A.S., Mersin Mill, Tarsus Organize Sanayi Bölgesi, 117 Ada 3 No'lu Parsel, Mersin, Turkey, Capacity: 70,000 mt/y, (Paper mill)
Hayat Kimya A.S., Zencan Mill, Zencan, Iran, Capacity: 65,000 mt/y, (Paper mill)
Hayat Kimya A.S., Yeniköy (Kocaeli) Mill, Sepetlipinar Mah. Hayat Cad. No 1, 41275 Yeniköy, Izmit, Turkey, Capacity: 135,000 mt/y, (Paper mill)
Phone: (90) 262 317 5400 / 341 24 80
Fax: (90) 262 341 4504 / 341 32 81
Email: hayat@hayat.com.tr
Natron-Hayat d.o.o., Maglaj Mill, Lijesnica bb, 74 250 Maglaj, Bosnia & Herzegovina, Capacity: 155,500 mt/y, (Pulp mill, Paper mill, Paperboard mill)
Phone: (387) 32 603 142
Fax: (387) 32 603 405
Email: natron-hayat@natron-hayat.ba
Pulp Grades and Capacities:
Total pulp capacity: 44,891 mt/y
Recycled Pulping: 44,891 mt/y
Pulp Mill Data:
Pulp Lines: 2
Paper/Paperboard Grades and Capacities:
Total paper and paperboard capacity: 45,000 mt/y
Linerboard: 20,000 mt/y
Corrugating medium/fluting: 25,000 mt/y
Paper and Paperboard Mill Data:
Paper Machines: 1
No. 1, fourdrinier (2), total capacity 45,000 mt/y, Trim width 2.5 m, Corrugating medium/fluting, Linerboard
Finishing Equipment:
Winders: 1 at 45,000 mt/y
Rewinders: 1 at 40,000 mt/y
Energy Data:
Power boilers: 1
Combustion turbines: 1 at 7.5 MW
Electrical demand for mill: 62 MWh/D

ⒽⓂHayat Kimya A.S.
Mersin Mill
Company is under construction (due to start up at the end of 2015)
Ownership: Hayat Kagit ve Enerji A.S.
Tarsus Organize Sanayi Bölgesi, 117 Ada 3 No'lu Parsel
Mersin
Turkey
Total Employees of Company: 5,000
Type of Operation: Paper mill
Mill Locations:
Hayat Kimya A.S., Zencan Mill, Zencan, Iran, Capacity: 65,000 mt/y, (Paper mill)
Hayat Kimya A.S., Yeniköy (Kocaeli) Mill, Sepetlipinar Mah. Hayat Cad. No 1, 41275 Yeniköy, Izmit, Turkey, Capacity: 135,000 mt/y, (Paper mill)
Phone: (90) 262 317 5400 / 341 24 80
Fax: (90) 262 341 4504 / 341 32 81
Email: hayat@hayat.com.tr
Natron-Hayat d.o.o., Maglaj Mill (90% owned), Lijesnica bb, 74 250 Maglaj, Bosnia & Herzegovina, Capacity: 155,500 mt/y, (Pulp mill, Paper mill, Paperboard mill)
Phone: (387) 32 603 142
Fax: (387) 32 603 405
Email: natron-hayat@natron-hayat.ba
Paper/Paperboard Grades and Capacities:
Total paper and paperboard capacity: 70,000 mt/y
Tissue: 70,000 mt/y
Paper and Paperboard Mill Data:
Paper Machines: 1
PM 1, (due to start up near the end of 2015), Advantage DCT 200 TS, total capacity 70,000 mt/y, Trim width 5.6 m, Tissue

ⒽHayat Kimya A.S.
Ownership: Hayat Kagit ve Enerji A.S.
Mahir Iz Caddesi No: 25 PK
TR-34662 Altunizade, Istanbul
Turkey
Phone: (90) 216 554 4000
Fax: (90) 216 474 0060
Email: hayat@hayat.com.tr, export@hayat.com.tr
Web Address: www.hayat.com.tr
Personnel:
Chmn.: Yahya Kigili
Phone: (90) 216 554 4000
Fax: (90) 216 474 0060
Gen. Mgr. (Hayat Group): Prof. Dr. Orhan Idil
Phone: (90) 216 554 4000
Fax: (90) 216 474 0060
Gen. Mgr.: Avni Kigli
Phone: (90) 216 554 4000
Fax: (90) 216 474 0060
Email: makigli@hayat.com.tr
Total Employees of Company: 5,000
Mill Locations:
Hayat Kimya A.S., Mersin Mill, Tarsus Organize Sanayi Bölgesi, 117 Ada 3 No'lu Parsel, Mersin, Turkey, Capacity: 70,000 mt/y, (Paper mill)
Hayat Kimya A.S., Zencan Mill, Zencan, Iran, Capacity: 65,000 mt/y, (Paper mill)
Hayat Kimya A.S., Yeniköy (Kocaeli) Mill, Sepetlipinar Mah. Hayat Cad. No 1, 41275 Yeniköy, Izmit, Turkey, Capacity: 135,000 mt/y, (Paper mill)
Phone: (90) 262 317 5400 / 341 24 80
Fax: (90) 262 341 4504 / 341 32 81
Email: hayat@hayat.com.tr
Natron-Hayat d.o.o., Maglaj Mill (90% owned), Lijesnica bb, 74 250 Maglaj, Bosnia & Herzegovina, Capacity: 155,500 mt/y, (Pulp mill, Paper mill, Paperboard mill)
Phone: (387) 32 603 142
Fax: (387) 32 603 405
Email: natron-hayat@natron-hayat.ba

ⓂHayat Kimya A.S.
Yeniköy (Kocaeli) Mill
Ownership: Hayat Kagit ve Enerji A.S.
Sepetlipinar Mah. Hayat Cad. No 1
41275 Yeniköy, Izmit, Kocaeli
Turkey
Phone: (90) 262 317 5400 / 341 24 80
Fax: (90) 262 341 4504 / 341 32 81
Email: hayat@hayat.com.tr
Web Address: www.hayat.com.tr
Personnel:
Mill Dir.: Lütfi Aydin
Phone: (90) 262 317 54 01
Email: laydin@hayat.com.tr
Prod. Mgr.: Hayrettin Kutluok
Phone: (90) 262 317 54 40
Email: hkutluok@hayat.com.tr
Convert. Plt. Mgr.: Cemal Özkök
Phone: (90) 262 317 54 50
Email: cozkok@hayat.com.tr
Maint. Mgr.: Levent Yavas
Phone: (90) 262 317 54 60
Email: lyavas@hayat.com.tr
Electric & Automation Mgr.: Kemal Tugay
Phone: (90) 262 317 54 70
Email: ktugay@hayat.com.tr
Power Plt. Mgr.: Fahri Altincekic
Phone: (90) 262 317 54 80
Email: faltincekic@hayat.com.tr
Proj. Mgr.: Kemal Arslan
Phone: (90) 262 317 54 41
Email: karslan@hayat.com.tr
Convert. Chief Eng.: Sahin Civelek
Phone: (90) 262 317 54 51
Email: scivelek@hayat.com.tr
R&D, Env. & Qlty. Control Chief Eng.: Fatma Bayar
Phone: (90) 262 317 54 30
Email: fbayar@hayat.com.tr
Total Employees at this Location: 700
Type of Operation: Paper mill
Paper/Paperboard Grades and Capacities:
Total paper and paperboard capacity: 135,000 mt/y
Tissue: 135,000 mt/y
Paper and Paperboard Mill Data:
Stock Preparation:
Pulpers: 3
Refiners: 4
Paper Machines: 2
No. 1, crescent former, Yankee dryer, total capacity 70,000 mt/y, Trim width 5.45 m, Tissue
No. 2, Advantage DCT 200 TS, Yankee dryer, total capacity 65,000 mt/y, Trim width 5.5 m, Tissue
Finishing Equipment:
Winders: 2 at 40,000 mt/y, 20,000 mt/y
Rewinders: 4 at 50,000 mt/y
Energy Data:
Power boilers: 2
Combustion turbines: 2 at 15 MW
Electrical demand for mill: 340 MWh/D

ⒽIpek Kagit San. ve Tic. A.S.
Ownership: 100% by Eczacibasi Holding
Kanyon Ofis. Büyükdere Caddesi No:185
TR-34394 Levent/Istanbul
Turkey
Phone: (90) 212 371 7000
Fax: (90) 212 353 1346
Email: info@ipekkagit.com.tr
Web Address: www.ipekkagit.com.tr
Personnel:
Gen. Mgr.: Fertac Nisli
Phone: (90) 212 371 7000
Fax: (90) 212 353 1346
Mill Dir.: Ertem Ulkumen
Phone: (90) 212 371 7000
Fax: (90) 212 353 1346
Finan. Dir.: Cem Aktinar
Phone: (90) 212 371 7000
Fax: (90) 212 353 1346
Export Mgr.: Erdinc Ayhan
Phone: (90) 212 371 7000
Fax: (90) 212 353 1346
Mrkt. Mgr.: Isin Er
Phone: (90) 212 371 7000
Fax: (90) 212 353 1346
Total Employees of Company: 405
Total Employees at this Location: 63
Mill Locations:
Ipek Kagit San. ve Tic. A.S., Manisa Mill, Manisa

Turkey

Organized Industrial Zone, Manisa, Turkey, (Paper mill)
Email: info@ipekkagit.com.tr
Ipek Kagit San. ve Tic. A.S., Karamürsel Mill, Tokmak Köyü Altýnova, TR-77700 Yalova, Turkey, Capacity: 100,000 mt/y, (Paper mill)
Phone: (90) 232 445 88 13, 226 462 85 23
Fax: (90) 216 470 90 55, 226 462 90 55
Email: info@ipekkagit.com.tr

Ipek Kagit San. ve Tic. A.S.
Manisa Mill
Mill is under construction (set to start up in mid-2015)
Manisa Organized Industrial Zone
Manisa
Turkey
Email: info@ipekkagit.com.tr
Web Address: www.ipekkagit.com.tr
Type of Operation: Paper mill
Paper and Paperboard Mill Data:
Paper Machines: 1
PM 1, (due to start mid-2015), Advantage DCT 200 TS, Yankee dryer, total capacity 60,000 mt/y, Trim width 5.6 m, Tissue

Ipek Kagit San. ve Tic. A.S.
Karamürsel Mill
Tokmak Köyü Altýnova
TR-77700 Yalova
Turkey
Phone: (90) 232 445 88 13, 226 462 85 23
Fax: (90) 216 470 90 55, 226 462 90 55
Email: info@ipekkagit.com.tr
Web Address: www.ipekkagit.com.tr
Personnel:
Mill Mgr.: Erdem Ulkumen
Phone: (90) 226 462 85 23
Fax: (90) 216 470 90 55
Email: erdem.ulkumen@ipekkagit.com.tr
Paper Prod. Mgr.: Recep Parlak
Phone: (90) 226 462 85 23
Fax: (90) 216 470 90 55
Email: recep.parlak@ipekkagit.com.tr
Quality Ass. & Environ. Mgr.: Bahar Marlali
Phone: (90) 226 462 85 23
Fax: (90) 216 470 90 55
Email: bahar.marlali@ipekkagit.com.tr
Sen. Qlty As. & Environ. Specialist: Hidir Ceylan
Phone: (90) 226 462 85 23
Fax: (90) 216 470 90 55
Email: hidir.ceylan@ipekkagit.com.tr
Prod. Develp. Mgr.: Meral Yurdakul
Phone: (90) 226 462 85 23
Fax: (90) 216 470 90 55
Email: meral.yurdakul@ipekkagit.com.tr
Total Employees at this Location: 369
Type of Operation: Paper mill
Pulp Mill Data:
Recycled Fiber Treatment Lines:
Pulpers: 1 at 4,000 admt/y
Paper/Paperboard Grades and Capacities:
Total paper and paperboard capacity: 100,000 mt/y
Tissue: 100,000 mt/y
Paper and Paperboard Mill Data:
Stock Preparation:
Pulpers: 5
Refiners: 7
Paper Machines: 3
No. 1, Periformer, Yankee dryer, total capacity 15,000 mt/y, Trim width 2.2 m, Tissue
No. 2, crescent former, Yankee dryer, total capacity 25,000 mt/y, Trim width 2.64 m, Uncoated woodfree/freesheet, Tissue
No. 3, crescent former, Yankee dryer, total capacity 60,000 mt/y, Trim width 5.3 m, Tissue
Finishing Equipment:
Rewinders: 3 at 100,000 mt/y
Energy Data:
Power boilers: 3
Combustion turbines: 1 at 8.7 MW
Electrical demand for mill: 273 MWh/D

Kahramanmaras Kagit San ve TIC A.S (KMK Paper)
Ownership: 100% by Ciger Family
Degirmenyolu Cad. Birman Is Merkezi No:11, Kat:4
TR-34752 Icerenkoy, Istanbul
Turkey
Phone: (90) 216 574 46 16
Fax: (90) 216 574 46 32
Email: info@kmppaper.com
Web Address: www.kmkpaper.com
Personnel:
Chmn.: Ahmet Ciger
Phone: (90) 216 574 46 16
Fax: (90) 216 574 46 32
Vice Chmn.: Mahmut Ciger
Phone: (90) 216 574 46 16
Fax: (90) 216 574 46 32
Bd. Mbr.: Siddik Ciger
Phone: (90) 216 574 46 16
Fax: (90) 216 574 46 32
Email: sciger@kmkpaper.com
Gen. Mgr.: Ahmet Tasci
Phone: (90) 216 574 46 16
Fax: (90) 216 574 46 32
Email: ahmettasci@kmkpaper.com
Purch. Mgr.: Bülent Eskalen
Phone: (90) 216 574 46 16
Fax: (90) 216 574 46 32
Email: beskalen@kmkpaper.com
Total Employees of Company: 210
Total Employees at this Location: 28
Mill Locations:
Kahramanmaras Kagit San ve TIC A.S (KMK Paper), Kahramanmaras Mill, Kahramanmaraş Paper Mill : Eyüp Sultan Mah. Recep Tayyip Erdoğan Bulvan No:136/A, Kahramanmaras, TR-46200, Turkey, Capacity: 150,000 mt/y, (Paper mill)
Phone: (90) 344 236 08 30
Fax: (90) 344 236 08 34
Email: info@kmkpaper.com
Kahramanmaras Kagit San ve TIC A.S (KMK Paper), Kütahya Mill, Kütahya 2. Org. Sanayi Bölgesi Çalca Mevkii (Eski Azot Fabrikasý Arkasý), TR-43000 Kütahya, Turkey, Capacity: 85,000 mt/y, (Paper mill)
Phone: (90) 274 220 0005
Fax: (90) 274 220 0009
Email: info@kmkpaper.com

Kahramanmaras Kagit San ve TIC A.S (KMK Paper)
Kahramanmaras Mill
Kahramanmaraş Paper Mill : Eyüp Sultan Mah. Recep Tayyip Erdoğan Bulvan No:136/A
Kahramanmaras, TR-46200
Turkey
Phone: (90) 344 236 08 30
Fax: (90) 344 236 08 34
Email: info@kmkpaper.com
Web Address: www.kmkpaper.com
Personnel:
Bd. Mbr.: Siddik Ciger
Phone: (90) 344 236 08 30
Email: sciger@kmkpaper.com
Gen. Mgr.: Ahmet Tasci
Phone: (90) 216 574 46 16
Prod. Mgr.: Bekir Yemsem
Phone: (90) 344 236 08 30
Chief Mech. Eng.: Ali Karagel
Total Employees at this Location: 177
Type of Operation: Paper mill
Pulp Grades and Capacities:
Total pulp capacity: 151,662 mt/y
Recycled Pulping: 151,662 mt/y
Pulp Mill Data:
Recycled Fiber Treatment Lines:
Pulpers: 3 at 115,000 admt/y
Paper/Paperboard Grades and Capacities:
Total paper and paperboard capacity: 150,000 mt/y
Linerboard: 60,000 mt/y
Corrugating medium/fluting: 80,000 mt/y
Boxboard/cartonboard: 10,000 mt/y
Paper and Paperboard Mill Data:
Stock Preparation:
Pulpers: 3
Refiners: 2
Paper Machines: 2
No. 1, fourdrinier (2), total capacity 100,000 mt/y, Trim width 3.62 m, Corrugating medium/fluting, Linerboard
No. 2, fourdrinier (2), total capacity 50,000 mt/y, Trim width 2.3 m, Corrugating medium/fluting, Linerboard, Boxboard/cartonboard
Finishing Equipment:
Calenders: 1
Rewinders: 2 at 100,000 mt/y
Energy Data:
Power boilers: 1
Steam turbines: 3 at 6, 6, 10 MW
Electrical demand for mill: 195 MWh/D

Kahramanmaras Kagit San ve TIC A.S (KMK Paper)
Kütahya Mill
Ownership: 100% by Ciger Family
Kütahya 2. Org. Sanayi Bölgesi Çalca Mevkii (Eski Azot Fabrikasý Arkasý)
TR-43000 Kütahya
Turkey
Phone: (90) 274 220 0005
Fax: (90) 274 220 0009
Email: info@kmkpaper.com
Web Address: www.kmkpaper.com
Total Employees at this Location: 98
Type of Operation: Paper mill
Pulp Grades and Capacities:
Total pulp capacity: 86,862 mt/y
Recycled Pulping: 86,862 mt/y
Pulp Mill Data:
Pulp Lines: 3
Bleach Plant Systems: 1
Recycled Pulping System, Type: DIP
Recycled Fiber Treatment Lines:
Flotation deinking lines: 1
Pulpers: 1
Recycled packaging pulping lines: 1
Paper/Paperboard Grades and Capacities:
Total paper and paperboard capacity: 85,000 mt/y
Newsprint: 60,000 mt/y
Uncoated mechanical/groundwood: 5,000 mt/y
Packaging papers: 5,000 mt/y
Linerboard: 10,000 mt/y
Corrugating medium/fluting: 5,000 mt/y
Paper and Paperboard Mill Data:
Paper Machines: 1
No. 3, fourdrinier, total capacity 85,000 mt/y, Trim width 3.1 m, Newsprint, Uncoated mechanical/groundwood, Linerboard, Corrugating medium/fluting, Packaging papers
Finishing Equipment:
Winders: 1 at 85,000 mt/y
Energy Data:
Power boilers: 1
Combustion turbines: 1 at 5 MW
Electrical demand for mill: 192 MWh/D

Kartonsan - Karton Sanayi ve Ticaret AS
Prof. Dr. Bülent Tarcan Sokak. No. 5 - Pak IS Merkezi, Kat 3
TR-34349 Gayrettepe-Istanbul
Turkey
Phone: (90) 212 273 20 00
Fax: (90) 212 273 21 60
Email: kartonsan@kartonsan.com.tr
Web Address: www.kartonsan.com.tr

Turkey

Personnel:
Gen. Mgr.: Mehmet Talu Uray
Phone: (90) 212 273 20 00
Fax: (90) 212 273 21 60
Mktg. Mgr.: Rasit Kemal Özkirim
Phone: (90) 212 273 20 00
Fax: (90) 212 273 2160
Purch. Mgr.: Atiye Poyrazoğlu
Phone: (90) 212 273 20 00
Fax: (90) 212 273 2163
Finan. Mgr.: Bülent Koru
Phone: (90) 212 273 20 00
Fax: (90) 212 273 21 60
Total Employees of Company: 420
Total Employees at this Location: 30
Mill Locations:
Kartonsan - Karton Sanayi ve Ticaret AS, Kullar Koyu Mill, Kullar Köyü, 41270 Izmit, Turkey, Capacity: 205,000 mt/y, (Paperboard mill)
Phone: (90) 262 349 61 50
Fax: (90) 262 349 33 00
Email: kartonsan@kartonsan.com.tr

ⓜKartonsan - Karton Sanayi ve Ticaret AS
Kullar Koyu Mill
Kullar Köyü
41270 Izmit, Kocaeli
Turkey
Phone: (90) 262 349 61 50
Fax: (90) 262 349 33 00
Email: kartonsan@kartonsan.com.tr
Web Address: www.kartonsan.com.tr
Personnel:
Asst. Gen. Mgr.: Haluk Iber
Phone: (90) 262 349 61 50
Prod. Serv & HR Mgr.: Yalçın Özel
Phone: (90) 262 349 61 50
Prod. Mgr.: Ümit Özkan
Phone: (90) 262 349 61 50
Tech. Serv. Mgr.: Ilker Bodur
Phone: (90) 262 349 61 50
Total Employees at this Location: 390
Type of Operation: Paperboard mill
Pulp Grades and Capacities:
Total pulp capacity: 186,027 mt/y
Recycled Pulping: 186,027 mt/y
Pulp Mill Data:
Recycled Fiber Treatment Lines:
Flotation deinking lines: 1
Recycled packaging pulping lines: 1
Paper/Paperboard Grades and Capacities:
Total paper and paperboard capacity: 205,000 mt/y
Boxboard/cartonboard: 205,000 mt/y
Paper and Paperboard Mill Data:
Stock Preparation:
Pulpers: 9
Refiners: 19
Paper Machines: 2
No. 1, cylinder (9), total capacity 80,000 mt/y, Trim width 2.16 m, Boxboard/cartonboard
No. 2, multi-wire, total capacity 125,000 mt/y, Trim width 3.6 m, Boxboard/cartonboard
Coating Machines: 2
No. 1, total capacity 75,000 mt/y., on machine
No. 2, total capacity 110,000 mt/y., on machine
Finishing Equipment:
Winders: 1
Rewinders: 2
Sheeters: 4
Energy Data:
Power boilers: 6
Combustion turbines: 4 at 19.2 MW
Electrical demand for mill: 303 MWh/D

ⓘKipas Kagit Sanayi Isletmeleri A.S
Ownership: 100% by Kipas Holding A.S
Adana Yolu Üzeri 21. Km Çakmak Mevkii Kibb/Türkoglu/Kahramanmaras
Kahramanmaras
Turkey
Phone: (90) 344 629 2520
Fax: (90) 344 629 2524
Email: kipas@kipas.com.tr
Web Address: www.kipas.com.tr
Personnel:
Pres.: M. Hanifi Oksuz
Phone: (90) 90 344 629 2520
Fax: (90) 90 344 629 2524
VP: H. Ibrahim Gumuser
Phone: (90) 90 344 629 2520
Fax: (90) 90 344 629 2524
Bd. Mbr.: Ahmet Oksuz
Phone: (90) 90 344 629 2520
Fax: (90) 90 344 629 2524
Mill Locations:
Kipas Kagit Sanayi Isletmeleri A.S, Kahramanmaras Mill, Adana Yolu Üzeri 21. Km Çakmak Mevkii Kibb/Türkoglu/Kahramanmaras, Kahramanmaras, Turkey, Capacity: 400,000 mt/y, (Paperboard mill)
Phone: (90) 344 629 2520
Fax: (90) 344 629 2524
Email: info@kipaskagit.com

ⓜKipas Kagit Sanayi Isletmeleri A.S
Kahramanmaras Mill
Adana Yolu Üzeri 21. Km Çakmak Mevkii Kibb/Türkoglu/Kahramanmaras
Kahramanmaras
Turkey
Phone: (90) 344 629 2520
Fax: (90) 344 629 2524
Email: info@kipaskagit.com
Web Address: www.kipas.com.tr, www.kipaskagit.com/en
Personnel:
Pres.: M. Hanifi Oksuz
Phone: (90) 90 344 629 2520
Fax: (90) 90 344 629 2524
VP: H. Ibrahim Gumuser
Phone: (90) 90 344 629 2520
Fax: (90) 90 344 629 2524
Bd. Mbr.: Ahmet Oksuz
Phone: (90) 90 344 629 2520
Fax: (90) 90 344 629 2524
Type of Operation: Paperboard mill
Paper/Paperboard Grades and Capacities:
Total paper and paperboard capacity: 400,000 mt/y
Containerboard: 400,000 mt/y
Linerboard
Corrugating medium/fluting
Paper and Paperboard Mill Data:
Paper Machines: 1
PM 1, (started February 2014), OptiFormer, total capacity 400,000 mt/y, Trim width 8.6 m, Linerboard, Corrugating medium/fluting

ⓘKöknar Kagit Karton San ve Tic A.S.
Ownership: 100% by Türkoglu family
Evrensekiz Beldesi Gündo?u Mah. Köyalt? Cad. No.2
PK:39790
Luleburgaz, Kirklareli
Turkey
Phone: (90) 288 443 8010
Fax: (90) 288 443 8019
Email: koknar@komar.com.tr
Web Address: www.koknar.com.tr
Personnel:
Owner & Gen. Mgr.: Yusuf Türkoglu
Phone: (90) 288 443 8010
Fax: (90) 288 443 8019
Sls. Mgr.: Fati Satih
Phone: (90) 288 443 8010
Fax: (90) 288 443 8019
Total Employees of Company: 82
Mill Locations:
Köknar Kagit Karton San ve Tic A.S., Kirklareli Mill, Evrensekiz Beldesi Gündoğu Mah. Köyaltı Cad. No:2 Luleburgaz, Kirklareli, Turkey 39790, Capacity: 153,000 mt/y, (Pulp mill, Paperboard mill)
Phone: (90) 288 443 8010
Fax: (90) 288 443 8019
Email: koknar@komar.com.tr

ⓜKöknar Kagit Karton San ve Tic A.S.
Kirklareli Mill
Evrensekiz Beldesi Gündoğu Mah. Köyaltı Cad. No:2
Luleburgaz, Kirklareli
Turkey 39790
Phone: (90) 288 443 8010
Fax: (90) 288 443 8019
Email: koknar@komar.com.tr
Web Address: www.koknar.com.tr
Personnel:
Owner & Gen. Mgr.: Yusuf Türkoglu
Phone: (90) 288 443 8010
Advisor: Nelio Stroppa
Phone: (90) 536 549 0863
Fax: (90) 212 662 6558
Total Employees at this Location: 82
Type of Operation: Pulp mill, Paperboard mill
Pulp Grades and Capacities:
Total pulp capacity: 156,633 mt/y
Recycled Pulping: 156,633 mt/y
Pulp Mill Data:
Recycled Fiber Treatment Lines:
Pulpers at 153,000 admt/y
Recycled packaging pulping lines at 153,000 admt/y
Paper/Paperboard Grades and Capacities:
Total paper and paperboard capacity: 153,000 mt/y
Boxboard/cartonboard: 153,000 mt/y
Paper and Paperboard Mill Data:
Stock Preparation:
Pulpers: 1
Paper Machines: 1
No. 1, fourdrinier (2), total capacity 153,000 mt/y, Trim width 3.25 m, Boxboard/cartonboard
Finishing Equipment:
Calenders: 1
Rewinders: 1 at 140,000 mt/y
Energy Data:
Power boilers: 1
Electrical demand for mill: 192 MWh/D

ⓘKombassan Holding
Nisantasi Mh. Sahinaga Sk. Kombassan Is Mrk. Selcuklu
TR-42060 Konya
Turkey
Phone: (90) 332 2212000
Fax: (90) 332 2212408
Email: kombassan@kombassan.com.tr
Web Address: www.kombassan.com.tr
Personnel:
Chmn. of the Board: Hasim Şahin
Phone: (90) 332 2212000
Fax: (90) 332 2212408
V. Chmn. of the Board: Ahmet Şan
Phone: (90) 332 2212000
Fax: (90) 332 2212408
Member of the Board: Ali Baloğlu
Phone: (90) 332 2212000
Fax: (90) 332 2212408
Member of the Board: Sami Selçuk Duran
Phone: (90) 332 2212000
Fax: (90) 332 2212408
Member of the Board: H. Rahman Bostan
Phone: (90) 332 2212000
Fax: (90) 332 2212408
International Rel. Mgr.: Adam Unoar
Phone: (90) 332 2212000
Fax: (90) 332 2212408
Total Employees of Company: 8,000
Total Employees at this Location: 225
Mill Locations:
Kombassan San. ve Tic. AS, Konya Mill, 2 Organize Sanayi, Bölgesi Vezirköy Sokak No: 1, TR-42300 Selcuklu, Konya, Turkey, Capacity: 60,000 mt/y, (Paper mill)
Phone: (90) 332 239 0054

Turkey

Fax: (90) 332 239 05 61 /68
Email: kagit_info@kombassan.com.tr; matbaa_info@kombassan.com.tr; kagit@kombassan.com.tr

ⓂKombassan San. ve Tic. AS
Konya Mill
Ownership: 100% by Kombassan Holding
2 Organize Sanayi, Bölgesi Vezirköy Sokak No: 1
TR-42300 Selcuklu, Konya
Turkey
Phone: (90) 332 239 0054
Fax: (90) 332 239 05 61 /68
Email: kagit_info@kombassan.com.tr,
matbaa_info@kombassan.com.tr,
kagit@kombassan.com.tr
Web Address: www.kagit.kombassan.com.tr
Personnel:
Gen. Mgr.: Mehmet Eray Nasöz
Phone: (90) 332 239 0054
Email: mnasoz@kombassan.com.tr
Maint. Mgr.: Erol Sagir
Phone: (90) 332 239 0054
Email: esagir@kombassan.com.tr
Process Mgr.: A. Kadir Özdemir
Phone: (90) 332 239 0054
Email: arozdemir@kombassan.com.tr
Electronics Control Eng.: Murat Secgin
Phone: (90) 332 239 0054
Elec. & Inst. Mgr.: Murat Akman
Phone: (90) 332 239 0054
Energy Mgr.: Fahretin Akça
Phone: (90) 332 239 0054
Main Engineer: Mesut Astilli
Phone: (90) 332 239 0054
Total Employees at this Location: 230
Type of Operation: Paper mill
Paper/Paperboard Grades and Capacities:
Total paper and paperboard capacity: 60,000 mt/y
Uncoated woodfree/freesheet: 60,000 mt/y
Paper and Paperboard Mill Data:
Stock Preparation:
Pulpers: 2
Refiners: 5
Paper Machines: 1
No. 2, fourdrinier, total capacity 60,000 mt/y, Trim width 3.25 m, Uncoated woodfree/freesheet
Finishing Equipment:
Winders: 1 at 60,000 mt/y
Calenders: 1
Rewinders: 1
Sheeters: 1 at 33,000 mt/y
Energy Data:
Power boilers: 2
Combustion turbines: 1 at 5.5 MW
Electrical demand for mill: 106 MWh/D

ⓄⓂLevent Kağit San. ve TIC. A.S
Izmir Mill
Ownership: Oran and Ürkmez families
Kemalpasa Asfalti 25. Km, Kemalpasa
TR-35170 Izmir, Izmir
Turkey
Mailing Address: Izmir-Ankara Karayolu 25. Km., No. 158, TR-35175 Kemalpasa, Izmir, Turkey
Phone: (90) 232 8770 416
Fax: (90) 232 8770 674
Email: leventkagit@leventkagit.com.tr
Web Address: www.leventkagit.com.tr
Personnel:
Chmn. of the Board: Bülent Ürkmez
Phone: (90) 232 8770 416
Member of Board: Firat Oran
Phone: (90) 232 8770 416
Gen. Mgr.: Bülent Özakdag
Phone: (90) 533 580 2239
Email: bulent.ozakdag@leventkagit.com.tr
Prod. Mgr.: Erhan Türkozan
Phone: (90) 232 8770 416
Maint. Chief: Resit Goren

Energy and Automation Mgr.: Hüseyin Özcan
Phone: (90) 532 335 1783
Purch. Mgr.: Ibrahim Demirciler
Phone: (90) 232 8770 416
Export Mgr.: Ali Faik Uzdil
Phone: (90) 533 632 5585
Imp. Chief: Suleunin Yildez
Phone: (90) 533 476 1272
BM 1 & BM 2 Chief: Necati Abis
Phone: (90) 232 8770 416
Total Employees at this Location: 150
Type of Operation: Paper mill
Pulp Grades and Capacities:
Total pulp capacity: 10,837 mt/y
Recycled Pulping: 10,837 mt/y
Paper/Paperboard Grades and Capacities:
Total paper and paperboard capacity: 20,000 mt/y
Tissue: 20,000 mt/y
Paper and Paperboard Mill Data:
Stock Preparation:
Pulpers: 5
Refiners: 3
Paper Machines: 1
No. 2, fourdrinier, Yankee dryer, total capacity 20,000 mt/y, Trim width 4.6 m, Tissue, Uncoated woodfree/freesheet
Energy Data:
Power boilers: 1
Electrical demand for mill: 60 MWh/D

ⓄLila Kagit San. ve Tic. A.S.
Ownership: 100% by Marmara Pamuklu Mensucat San.ve TiC. A.S. Group
Tekstilkent Koza Plaza A Blok Kat:23
TR-34235 Esenler - Istanbul
Turkey
Phone: (90) 212 4382919
Fax: (90) 212 4382928
Email: info@lilakagit.com
Web Address: www.lilakagit.com
Personnel:
Chmn.: Orhan Ögücü
Phone: (90) 212 4382919
Fax: (90) 212 4382928
Project Asst.: Alp Ögücü
Phone: (90) 212 4382919
Fax: (90) 212 4382928
Email: alp.ogucu@gmail.com
Finished Products Mgr.: Sule Demir
Phone: (90) 212 4382919
Fax: (90) 212 4382928
Email: sule.demir@lilakagit.com
Total Employees of Company: 500
Total Employees at this Location: 130
Mill Locations:
Lila Kagit San. ve Tic. A.S., Çorlu-Takrdad Mill, Edirne Karayolu 7th Km., Çorlu-Takrdad, Turkey, Capacity: 140,000 mt/y, (Paper mill)
Phone: (90) 282 686 2594
Fax: (90) 282 686 2597
Email: info@lilakagit.com

ⓄLila Kagit San. ve Tic. A.S.
Çorlu-Takrdad Mill
Edirne Karayolu 7th Km.
Çorlu-Takrdad, Tekirdag
Turkey
Phone: (90) 282 686 2594
Fax: (90) 282 686 2597
Email: info@lilakagit.com
Web Address: www.lilakagit.com
Personnel:
Mill Mgr.: Erkan Ternavalo
Phone: (90) 282 686 2594
Total Employees at this Location: 200
Type of Operation: Paper mill
Paper/Paperboard Grades and Capacities:
Total paper and paperboard capacity: 140,000 mt/y
Tissue: 140,000 mt/y
Paper and Paperboard Mill Data:

Paper Machines: 2
No. 1, Advantage DCT 200 TS, Yankee dryer, total capacity 70,000 mt/y, Trim width 5.65 m, Tissue, Uncoated woodfree/freesheet
No. 2, Advantage DCT 200 TS, Yankee dryer, total capacity 70,000 mt/y, Trim width 5.65 m, Tissue, Uncoated woodfree/freesheet
Energy Data:
Electrical demand for mill: 351 MWh/D

ⓂMarmara Kagit ve Ambalaj Sanayii ve Ticaret AS
Ownership: Özköseoglu Group
Büyükdere Cad. Bengün Han No: 107 Kat 3 Gayrettepe
TR-83000 Istanbul
Turkey
Phone: (90) 212 217 43 00/37 43
Fax: (90) 212 217 42 46
Email: marmara@marmarakagit.com
Web Address: www.marmarakagit.com
Personnel:
Chmn.: Ahmet Ozkoseoglu
Phone: (90) 212 217 43 00/37 43
Fax: (90) 212 217 42 46
VP: Ahmed Alp
Phone: (90) 212 217 43 00/37 43
Fax: (90) 212 217 42 46
Gen. Mgr.: Erdal Sukan
Phone: (90) 212 217 43 00/37 43
Fax: (90) 212 217 42 46
Asst. Gen. Mgr. (Techn.): Mustafa Demirbas
Phone: (90) 212 217 43 00/37 43
Fax: (90) 212 217 42 46
Asst. Gen. Mgr. (Admin. Fin.): Gunay Temel
Phone: (90) 212 217 43 00/37 43
Fax: (90) 212 217 42 46
Admin. Affairs Mgr.: Ibrahim Ocek
Phone: (90) 212 217 43 00/37 43
Fax: (90) 212 217 42 46
Acc.& Finan. Mgr.: Sukran Elcitorunu
Phone: (90) 212 217 43 00/37 43
Fax: (90) 212 217 42 46
Purch. Mgr.: Mehmet Ozden
Phone: (90) 212 217 43 00/37 43
Fax: (90) 212 217 42 46
Mktg./Sls. Mgr.: Cumhur Aksu
Phone: (90) 212 217 43 00/37 43
Fax: (90) 212 217 42 46
Total Employees of Company: 190
Total Employees at this Location: 20
Mill Locations:
Marmara Kagit ve Ambalaj Sanayii ve Ticaret AS, Vezirhan Mill, Yeni Mahalle Sanayii Bölgesi Atatürk Bulvari Vezirhan, TR-11130 Bilecik, Vezirhan, Turkey, Capacity: 50,000 mt/y, (Pulp mill, Paper mill, Paperboard mill)
Phone: (90) 228 233 10 11/10 12
Fax: (90) 228 233 10 65
Email: marmara@marmarakagit.com

ⓂMarmara Kagit ve Ambalaj Sanayii ve Ticaret AS
Vezirhan Mill
Yeni Mahalle Sanayii Bölgesi Atatürk Bulvari Vezirhan
TR-11130 Bilecik, Vezirhan, Bilecik
Turkey
Phone: (90) 228 233 10 11/10 12
Fax: (90) 228 233 10 65
Email: marmara@marmarakagit.com
Web Address: www.marmarakagit.com
Personnel:
Asst. Gen. Mgr. (Prod.): Murat Gumey
Phone: (90) 228 233 10 11/10 12
Pulp & Paper Mill Mgr.: Yusaf Cascan
Energy Chief: Yasar Ciftci
Phone: (90) 228 233 10 11/10 12
Utilities and Maint. Mgr.: Omaes Corapli
Total Employees at this Location: 240
Type of Operation: Pulp mill, Paper mill, Paperboard mill

Turkey

Pulp Grades and Capacities:
Total pulp capacity: 50,020 mt/y
Recycled Pulping: 34,775 mt/y
Other Pulp: 15,245 mt/y
Paper/Paperboard Grades and Capacities:
Total paper and paperboard capacity: 50,000 mt/y
Linerboard: 20,000 mt/y
Corrugating medium/fluting: 30,000 mt/y
Paper and Paperboard Mill Data:
Stock Preparation:
Pulpers: 2
Refiners: 7
Paper Machines: 1
No. 1, fourdrinier (2), total capacity 50,000 mt/y, Trim width 3.4 m, Corrugating medium/fluting, Linerboard
Finishing Equipment:
Rewinders: 1 at 80,000 mt/y
Energy Data:
Power boilers
Combustion turbines: 1 at 2.5 MW
Electrical demand for mill: 87 MWh/D

ⓜModern Karton Sanayi Ticaret AS

Ownership: 93% by Eren Holding, 7% by Others
Merkez Mah. Kavak Sokak No. 39
TR-34530 Bahcelievler, Istanbul
Turkey
Phone: (90) 212 639 89 00
Fax: (90) 212 639 89 26
Email: modernkarton@modernkarton.com.tr
Web Address: www.modernkarton.com.tr, www.erenholding.com.tr
Personnel:
Gen. Mgr.: Hamdullah Eren
Phone: (90) 212 639 89 00
Fax: (90) 212 639 89 26
Email: nagehan.tun@erenholding.com.tr
Mill Mgr.: Bulent Binat
Phone: (90) 212 639 89 00
Fax: (90) 212 639 89 26
Export Sls.Specialist: Murat Durmus
Phone: (90) 212 639 89 00
Fax: (90) 212 639 89 26
Email: murat.durmus@modernkarton.com.tr
Total Employees of Company: 600
Total Employees at this Location: 30
Mill Locations:
Modern Karton Sanayi Ticaret AS, Çorlu Mill, E-5 Karayolu 18 Üzeri 8.km Ulas Köyü Mevkii, TR-59860 Çorlu, Turkey, Capacity: 680,000 mt/y, (Paperboard mill)
Phone: (90) 282 655 5821
Fax: (90) 282 656 6448
Email: modernkarton@modernkarton.com.tr

ⓜModern Karton Sanayi Ticaret AS
Çorlu Mill

E-5 Karayolu 18 Üzeri 8.km Ulas Köyü Mevkii
TR-59860 Çorlu, Tekirdag
Turkey
Phone: (90) 282 655 5821
Fax: (90) 282 656 6448
Email: modernkarton@modernkarton.com.tr
Web Address: www.modernkarton.com.tr
Personnel:
Mill Mgr.: Bulent Binat
Phone: (90) 282 655 5821
Fax: (90) 282 656 6448
Email: bbinat@modernkarton.com.tr
Dpty. Gen. Mgr. (From 2013): Recep Agcı
Phone: (90) 282 655 5821
Fax: (90) 282 656 6448
PM 3 Mill Eng.: Selami Avci
Phone: (90) 282 655 5821
Fax: (90) 282 656 6448
Qlty. Syst. Mgr.: Emine Türkdemir
Phone: (90) 282 655 5821
Fax: (90) 282 656 6448
Email: emine.iscan@modernkarton.com.tr
Total Employees at this Location: 440
Type of Operation: Paperboard mill
Pulp Grades and Capacities:
Total pulp capacity: 667,449 mt/y
Recycled Pulping: 667,449 mt/y
Pulp Mill Data:
Pulp Lines: 3
Recycled Fiber Treatment Lines:
Flotation deinking lines: 1 at 142,800
Pulpers: 5 at 300,000 admt/y
Recycled packaging pulping lines: 1 at 400,000 admt/y
Recycled packaging pulping lines: 1 at 267,800
Paper/Paperboard Grades and Capacities:
Total paper and paperboard capacity: 680,000 mt/y
Linerboard: 420,000 mt/y
Corrugating medium/fluting: 260,000 mt/y
Paper and Paperboard Mill Data:
Stock Preparation:
Pulpers: 5
Refiners: 14
Paper Machines: 2
No. 3, DuoFormer DK, total capacity 280,000 mt/y, Trim width 5 m, Corrugating medium/fluting, Linerboard
No. 4, OptiFormer, total capacity 400,000 mt/y, Trim width 7.8 m, Corrugating medium/fluting, Linerboard
Finishing Equipment:
Winders: 1
Rewinders: 3 at 300,000 mt/y
Energy Data:
Power boilers: 2
Combustion turbines: 1 at 24 MW
Steam turbines: 1 at 6.7 MW
Electrical demand for mill: 830 MWh/D

ⓜⓜMondi Tire Kutsan Paper and Packaging Industry Inc.
Tire Mill

Ownership: 53.56% by Mondi Europe & International Division, 46.44% by the Public
Bekleme Mevkii
TR-35900 Tire, Izmir
Turkey
Phone: (90) 232 512 1156/1943
Fax: (90) 232 512 3871/1046
Email: info@tirekutsan.com.tr
Web Address: www.tirekutsan.com.tr
Personnel:
Member of Board of Dir.: Thomas Ott
Phone: (90) 232 512 1399
Fax: (90) 232 512 0530
CEO & Vice Chmn.: Selim Hakan Tifftik
Phone: (90) 232 512 1156
Fax: (90) 232 512 3871
Finan. Dir.: Özgür Do?an Ozdogru
Phone: (90) 232 512 1156
Fax: (90) 232 512 3871
Man. Dir. Tire Paper Plt.: Veli?ah ?ner
Phone: (90) 232 512 1156/1943
Fax: (90) 232 512 3871/1046
Plt. Contr.: Bora Firtiina
Phone: (90) 232 512 1156
Fax: (90) 232 512 3871
Qlty. Mgr.: Miray Senol
Phone: (90) 232 512 1156/194
Fax: (90) 232 512 3871/1046
Email: miray.senol@mondigroup.com
Total Employees of Company: 300
Total Employees at this Location: 300
Type of Operation: Paper mill, Paperboard mill
Pulp Grades and Capacities:
Total pulp capacity: 132,682 mt/y
Recycled Pulping: 132,682 mt/y
Pulp Mill Data:
Recycled Fiber Treatment Lines:
Pulpers: 2 at 150,000 admt/y
Paper/Paperboard Grades and Capacities:
Total paper and paperboard capacity: 135,000 mt/y
Linerboard: 70,000 mt/y
Corrugating medium/fluting: 65,000 mt/y
Paper and Paperboard Mill Data:
Stock Preparation:
Pulpers: 2
Refiners: 5
Paper Machines: 2
No. 1, fourdrinier, total capacity 65,000 mt/y, Trim width 2.4 m, Corrugating medium/fluting
No. 2, fourdrinier (2), total capacity 70,000 mt/y, Trim width 2.23 m, Linerboard
Finishing Equipment:
Rewinders: 2
Energy Data:
Power boilers: 3
Steam turbines: 2 at 0.65, 8 MW
Electrical demand for mill: 188 MWh/D

ⓜMopak Dalaman Pulp-Paper Cardboard Plant
Dalaman Mill

Ownership: 100% by Mopak Kagit Karton San. ve Tic. A.S.
Atakent Mah. Gazi Bulvari No: 189 Dalaman
TR-48770 Mugla
Turkey
Phone: (90) 252 6975600
Fax: (90) 252 6975473
Web Address: www.mopak.com.tr
Personnel:
Mill Mgr.: Günnaz Ertan
Phone: (90) 252 6975600
Purch. Mgr.: Haluk Durgun
Phone: (90) 252 6975600
Email: hdurgun@mopak.com.tr
Total Employees at this Location: 270
Type of Operation: Pulp mill, Paper mill, Paperboard mill
Pulp Grades and Capacities:
Total pulp capacity: 266,189 mt/y
Pulp available for market: 7,000 mt/y
Chemical Pulp: 86,227 mt/y
Recycled Pulping: 179,962 mt/y
Pulp Mill Data:
Chemical Pulping Systems:
Batch digesters: 4
Continuous digesters: 1
Pulp Lines: 2
Bleach Plant Systems: 2
Hardwood line, Sequence: CEHDED, Capacity 70,000 admt/y
Softwood line, Sequence: CEHH, Capacity 16,500 admt/y
Chemical Recovery Equipment:
Evaporator lines: 1
Recovery boilers: 1
Lime Kiln
Recycled Fiber Treatment Lines:
Flotation deinking lines: 1
Recycled packaging pulping lines: 1
Pulp Dryers:
Flash dryers 2
Paper/Paperboard Grades and Capacities:
Total paper and paperboard capacity: 270,000 mt/y
Newsprint: 92,000 mt/y
Uncoated woodfree/freesheet: 68,000 mt/y
Coated woodfree/freesheet: 10,000 mt/y
Linerboard: 50,000 mt/y
Boxboard/cartonboard: 50,000 mt/y
Paper and Paperboard Mill Data:
Stock Preparation:
Pulpers: 21
Refiners: 17
Paper Machines: 2
No. 1, fourdrinier, total capacity 175,000 mt/y, Trim width 4.35 m, Newsprint, Uncoated woodfree/freesheet, Coated woodfree/freesheet
No. 2, multi-wire, total capacity 100,000 mt/y, Trim width 4.35 m, Boxboard/cartonboard, Linerboard
Coating Machines: 1
No. 1, total capacity 45,000 mt/y., off machine

Finishing Equipment:
Supercalenders: 2
Rewinders: 3
Sheeters: 6
Energy Data:
Power boilers: 2
Steam turbines: 2 at 26.2 MW
Electrical demand for mill: 686 MWh/D

⊕Mopak Tasköprü Pulp and Cigarette Paper Plant
Kastamonu Mill
Ownership: 100% by Mopak Kagit Karton San. ve Tic. A.S.
Taskopru
TR-37400 Kastamonu
Turkey
Phone: (90) 366 482 8001
Fax: (90) 366 482 8017
Web Address: www.mopak.com.tr
Personnel:
Mill Mgr.: Hakan Dokald
Phone: (90) 366 482 8001
Total Employees at this Location: 120
Type of Operation: Pulp mill, Paper mill
Pulp Grades and Capacities:
Total pulp capacity: 4,493 mt/y
Other Pulp: 4,493 mt/y
Pulp Mill Data:
Chemical Pulping Systems:
Batch digesters: 3
Pulp Lines: 1
Bleach Plant Systems: 1
1, Sequence: CEH, Capacity 5,000 admt/y
Chemical Recovery Equipment:
Evaporator lines: 1
Paper/Paperboard Grades and Capacities:
Total paper and paperboard capacity: 15,000 mt/y
Uncoated woodfree/freesheet: 5,000 mt/y
Specialty and industrial: 10,000 mt/y
Paper and Paperboard Mill Data:
Stock Preparation:
Pulpers: 1
Refiners: 6
Paper Machines: 1
No. 1, fourdrinier, total capacity 15,000 mt/y, Trim width 3.7 m, Specialty and industrial, Uncoated woodfree/freesheet
Finishing Equipment:
Rewinders: 6
Energy Data:
Power boilers: 2
Electrical demand for mill: 41 MWh/D

⊕⊕Mopak Kagit Karton San. ve Tic. A.S.
Kemalpasa Mill
Ownership: 100% by Mehmet Ali Molay
Kirovasi Mevkii PK.10
TR-35170 Kemalpasa, Izmir
Turkey
Phone: (90) 232 8770235
Fax: (90) 232 8770230
Email: export@mopak.com.tr
Web Address: www.mopak.com.tr
Personnel:
Mktg. Dir.: Kursad Devecioglu
Phone: (90) 232 8770235
Email: hdevecioglu@mopak.com.tr
Owner/Pres.: Mehmet Ali Molay
Phone: (90) 232 8770235
Coor. for Sls. and Prod.: Ms. Buket Tezcan
Phone: (90) 232 8770235
Mill Mgr.: Ali Riza Iseri
Phone: (90) 232 8770235
Total Employees of Company: 800
Total Employees at this Location: 380
Type of Operation: Paper mill

Mill Locations:
Mopak Dalaman Pulp-Paper Cardboard Plant, Dalaman Mill, Atakent Mah. Gazi Bulvari No: 189 Dalaman, TR-48770 Mugla, Turkey, Capacity: 270,000 mt/y, (Pulp mill, Paper mill, Paperboard mill)
Phone: (90) 252 6975600
Fax: (90) 252 6975473
Mopak Tasköprü Pulp and Cigarette Paper Plant, Kastamonu Mill, Taskopru, TR-37400 Kastamonu, Turkey, Capacity: 15,000 mt/y, (Pulp mill, Paper mill)
Phone: (90) 366 482 8001
Fax: (90) 366 482 8017
Paper/Paperboard Grades and Capacities:
Total paper and paperboard capacity: 60,000 mt/y
Uncoated woodfree/freesheet: 60,000 mt/y
Paper and Paperboard Mill Data:
Paper Machines: 1
No. 1, fourdrinier, Yankee dryer, total capacity 60,000 mt/y, Trim width 2.42 m, Uncoated woodfree/freesheet
Finishing Equipment:
Calenders: 1
Rewinders: 2
Sheeters: 2
Energy Data:
Power boilers: 1
Combustion turbines: 1 at 4.8 MW
Electrical demand for mill: 115 MWh/D

⊕⊕Muratli Karton Fabrikasi
Tekirdag Mill
Ownership: 51% by Kozoglu, 49% by Kombassan Holding
Karistiran Yolu Üzeri PK. 42 - Muratli
TR-59700 Tekirdag, Tekirdag
Turkey
Phone: (90) 282 361 6229/6302
Fax: (90) 282 361 6266
Email: info@muratlikarton.com.tr
Web Address: www.muratlikarton.com.tr
Personnel:
Chmn.: Mehmet Sahbaz
Phone: (90) 282 361 6229/6302
Mill Mgr.: Nezati Akyildiz
Phone: (90) 282 361 6229/6302
Purch. Mgr.: Yasin Altintas
Phone: (90) 282 361 6229/6302
Email: yasin.altintas@muratlikarton.com.tr
Assis. Gen Mgr.: Adnan Sen
Phone: (90) 282 361 6229/6302
Total Employees at this Location: 185
Type of Operation: Pulp mill, Paperboard mill
Pulp Grades and Capacities:
Total pulp capacity: 82,149 mt/y
Recycled Pulping: 82,149 mt/y
Pulp Mill Data:
Pulp Lines: 1
Recycled Fiber Treatment Lines:
Flotation deinking lines at 28,000 admt/y
Washing deinking lines at 28,000 admt/y
Paper/Paperboard Grades and Capacities:
Total paper and paperboard capacity: 90,000 mt/y
Boxboard/cartonboard: 90,000 mt/y
Paper and Paperboard Mill Data:
Stock Preparation:
Pulpers: 3
Paper Machines: 1
No. 1, cylinder, Yankee dryer, total capacity 90,000 mt/y, Trim width 2.6 m, Boxboard/cartonboard
Coating Machines: 1
No. 1, total capacity 95,000 mt/y.
Finishing Equipment:
Rewinders: 1 at 87,500 mt/y
Sheeters: 1 at 17,000 mt/y
Energy Data:
Power boilers: 1
Combustion turbines: 1 at 5.2 MW
Electrical demand for mill: 125 MWh/D

⊕Olmuksa International Paper-Sabanci Ambalaj Sanayi ve Ticaret A.S.
Ownership: 87.50% by International Paper Co., 12.50% by Sabanci Holding
Sabanci Center
TR-34330 Levent, Istanbul
Turkey
Phone: (90) 212 385 8600
Fax: (90) 212 280 8971 / 281 3747 / 282 8096
Email: contact@olmuksa.com.tr
Web Address: www.olmuksan-ipaper.com
Personnel:
Chmn. (Eff. january 2013): Jonathan Edward Ernst
Phone: (90) 212 385 8600
Fax: (90) 212 280 8971
Gen. Mgr.: Ergun Hepvar
Phone: (90) 212 385 8600
Fax: (90) 212 280 8971
Finan. Dir.: Selda Ercantan Aksoy
Phone: (90) 212 385 8600
Fax: (90) 212 280 8971
Strat. & Paper Dir.: Serdar Çilo?lu
Phone: (90) 212 385 8600
Fax: (90) 212 280 8971
Total Employees of Company: 941
Total Employees at this Location: 20
Mill Locations:
Copikas Kagit ve Oluklu Mukavva Kutu A.S., Olmuksa Copikas Mill, Ankara Yolu 4 km, Corum, Turkey, Capacity: 30,000 mt/y, (Paperboard mill)
Phone: (90) 364 2350050
Fax: (90) 364 2350067
Email: sales.corum@ipaper.com
Olmuksa International Paper-Sabanci Ambalaj Sanayi ve Ticaret A.S., Olmuksa Edirne Mill, Sazlidere Mevkii, Pk. 110 Tayakadin Köyü, TR-22160 Edirne, Turkey, Capacity: 70,000 mt/y, (Pulp mill, Paper mill)
Phone: (90) 284 268 64 24
Fax: (90) 284 268 62 42
Email: contacttr@ipaper.com

⊕Olmuksa International Paper-Sabanci Ambalaj Sanayi ve Ticaret A.S.
Olmuksa Edirne Mill
Ownership: 87.50% by International Paper Co.
Sazlidere Mevkii, Pk. 110 Tayakadin Köyü
TR-22160 Edirne
Turkey
Phone: (90) 284 268 64 24
Fax: (90) 284 268 62 42
Email: contacttr@ipaper.com
Web Address: www.olmuksan-ipaper.com
Personnel:
Mill Mgr.: Necmi Türkoglu
Phone: (90) 284 268 64 24
Prod. Mgr.: Bülent Egeli
Phone: (90) 284 268 64 24
Prod. Eng.: Altan Bayram
Phone: (90) 284 268 64 24
Total Employees at this Location: 90
Type of Operation: Pulp mill, Paper mill
Pulp Grades and Capacities:
Total pulp capacity: 70,453 mt/y
Recycled Pulping: 70,453 mt/y
Pulp Mill Data:
Chemical Pulping Systems:
Batch digesters: 5
Paper/Paperboard Grades and Capacities:
Total paper and paperboard capacity: 70,000 mt/y
Linerboard: 25,000 mt/y
Corrugating medium/fluting: 45,000 mt/y
Paper and Paperboard Mill Data:
Stock Preparation:
Pulpers: 2
Refiners: 7
Paper Machines: 1
No. 1, fourdrinier, total capacity 70,000 mt/y, Trim width 2.5 m, Linerboard, Corrugating medium/fluting

Turkey

Finishing Equipment:
Rewinders: 1
Energy Data:
Electrical demand for mill: 96 MWh/D

ⓂOYKA Kagit Ve Ambalaj San Tic A.S.
Çaycuma Mill
Ystasyon Mah.Perpembe Yolu
67900 Çaycuma, Zonguldak
Turkey
Phone: (90) 372 615 11 82
Fax: (90) 372 615 11 81
Email: bilgi@oyka.com.tr,
Info@oyka.com.tr
Web Address: www.oyka.com.tr
Personnel:
Gen. Mgr.: Aytekin R. Kadioglu
Phone: (90) 372 615 11 82
Prod. Mgr.: Erdin Güler
Phone: (90) 372 615 11 82
Prod. Planning Eng.: Alev Büyükbayrau
Phone: (90) 372 615 11 82
Email: alev.buyukbayram@oyka.com.tr
Quality & Job Develpt. Mgr.: Mustafa Cayiroglu
Phone: (90) 372 615 11 82
Maint. Mgr.: Adil Gokhan Akkaya
Phone: (90) 372 615 11 82
Tech. Consultant: Ilhami Erdoðan
Phone: (90) 372 615 11 82
PM Eng.: Levent Durmaz
Phone: (90) 372 615 11 82
Assist. to Gen. Mgr. (Admin. Mgr.): Ali Yalcin
Phone: (90) 372 615 11 82
PM Chief: Kemal Özgur Dizer
Phone: (90) 372 615 11 82
Assist. to Gen. Mgr. (Sls. & Mktg. Mgr.): Kazim Sonmez
Phone: (90) 372 615 11 82
Assist. to Gen. Mgr. (Tech. Mgr.): Volkan Turt
Phone: (90) 372 615 11 82
Total Employees at this Location: 270
Type of Operation: Pulp mill, Paper mill
Pulp Grades and Capacities:
Total pulp capacity: 82,878 mt/y
Chemical Pulp: 66,000 mt/y
Recycled Pulping: 16,877 mt/y
Pulp Mill Data:
Chemical Pulping Systems:
Batch digesters: 5
Chemical Recovery Equipment:
Evaporator lines: 6
Recovery boilers: 1
Lime Kiln
Recycled Fiber Treatment Lines:
Recycled packaging pulping lines: 1 at 66,000 admt/y
Paper/Paperboard Grades and Capacities:
Total paper and paperboard capacity: 80,000 mt/y
Packaging papers: 70,000 mt/y
Linerboard: 10,000 mt/y
Paper and Paperboard Mill Data:
Stock Preparation:
Pulpers: 9
Refiners: 6
Paper Machines: 1
No. 1, fourdrinier, total capacity 80,000 mt/y, Trim width 5.2 m, Packaging papers, Linerboard
Finishing Equipment:
Winders: 1 at 80,000 mt/y
Calenders: 1
Supercalenders: 1
Rewinders: 1
Energy Data:
Power boilers: 2
Steam turbines: 1 at 9.5 MW
Electrical demand for mill: 205 MWh/D

ⓄOYKA Kagit Ve Ambalaj San Tic A.S.
Ownership: 100% by OYAK Cement Group
Ceyhan Yolu Üzeri 12 km
TR-01321 Adana
Turkey
Phone: (90) 322 332 92 40
Fax: (90) 322 332 94 26
Email: Info@oyka.com.tr
Web Address: www.oyka.com.tr/
Personnel:
Gen. Mgr.: Aytekin Kadioglu
Phone: (90) 322 332 92 40
Fax: (90) 322 332 94 26
Total Employees of Company: 347
Mill Locations:
OYKA Kagit Ve Ambalaj San Tic A.S., Çaycuma Mill, Ystasyon Mah.Perpembe Yolu, 67900 Çaycuma, Turkey, Capacity: 80,000 mt/y, (Pulp mill, Paper mill)
Phone: (90) 372 615 11 82
Fax: (90) 372 615 11 81
Email: bilgi@oyka.com.tr, Info@oyka.com.tr

ⓄⓂParteks Tekstil ve Kagit San Tic. Ltd. Sti.
Kayseri Mill
Ownership: 100% by Capar family
Organize Sanayi Bölgesi 39. Cad No:1
TR-59700 Kayseri
Turkey
Phone: (90) 352 322 00 80
Fax: (90) 352 322 00 84
Email: info@partekspaper.com
Web Address: www.partekspaper.com
Personnel:
Gen. Mgr.: Osman Çapar
Phone: (90) 352 322 00 80
Email: ocapar@partekspaper.com
Mill Mgr.: Turan Aksu
Phone: (90) 352 322 00 80
Email: turanaksu@hotmail.com
Purch. Mgr.: Rifat Çalik
Phone: (90) 352 322 00 80
Plan. Supervisor: Senol Bahar
Phone: (90) 352 322 00 80
Tissue Coordinator: Fati Çapar
Phone: (90) 533 435 9484
Total Employees of Company: 260
Total Employees at this Location: 300
Type of Operation: Paperboard mill
Pulp Grades and Capacities:
Total pulp capacity: 32,082 mt/y
Recycled Pulping: 32,082 mt/y
Paper/Paperboard Grades and Capacities:
Total paper and paperboard capacity: 65,000 mt/y
Tissue: 40,000 mt/y
Linerboard: 15,000 mt/y
Corrugating medium/fluting: 10,000 mt/y
Paper and Paperboard Mill Data:
Stock Preparation:
Pulpers: 2
Refiners: 3
Paper Machines: 3
No. 1, fourdrinier, total capacity 25,000 mt/y, Trim width 2.44 m, Corrugating medium/fluting, Linerboard
No. 2, fourdrinier, Yankee dryer, total capacity 15,000 mt/y, Trim width 2.75 m, Tissue, Uncoated woodfree/freesheet
No. 3, total capacity 25,000 mt/y, Trim width 2.85 m, Tissue, Uncoated woodfree/freesheet
Finishing Equipment:
Rewinders: 1 at 30,000 mt/y
Energy Data:
Power boilers: 1
Electrical demand for mill: 78 MWh/D

ⓄPehlivanoglu Kagit, Kagit Mamülleri ve Ambalaj San.Tic. A.S.
Organize San. Bölgesi, Fatih Bulvari No:33
Çerkezköy, Tekirdag
Turkey
Phone: (90) 282 758 1325/1545
Fax: (90) 282 758 1328
Email: info@pehlivanoglu.com.tr
Web Address: www.pehlivanoglukagit.com.tr
Personnel:
Technical Gen. Mgr./Coordinator: Emin Orsel
Phone: (90) 212 619 5996
Fax: (90) 212 594 1136
Prod. Mgr.: Orhan Kuscu
Phone: (90) 212 619 5996
Fax: (90) 212 594 1136
Total Employees of Company: 120
Total Employees at this Location: 20
Mill Locations:
Pehlivanoglu Kagit, Kagit Mamülleri ve Ambalaj San.Tic. A.S., Çerkezköy Mill, Organize San. Bölgesi, Fatih Bulvari No:33, Çerkezköy, Turkey, Capacity: 84,000 mt/y, (Paperboard mill)
Phone: (90) 282 758 1325/1545
Fax: (90) 282 758 1328
Email: info@pehlivanoglu.com.tr

ⓂPehlivanoglu Kagit, Kagit Mamülleri ve Ambalaj San.Tic. A.S.
Çerkezköy Mill
Organize San. Bölgesi, Fatih Bulvari No:33
Çerkezköy, Tekirdag
Turkey
Phone: (90) 282 758 1325/1545
Fax: (90) 282 758 1328
Email: info@pehlivanoglu.com.tr
Web Address: www.pehlivanoglukagit.com.tr
Personnel:
Prod. Mgr.: Orhan Kuscu
Phone: (90) 282 758 1325/1545
Technical Gen. Mgr.: Emin Orsel
Phone: (90) 282 758 1325/1545
Projects Chief: Cangiz Altunbas
Phone: (90) 282 758 1325/1545
Total Employees at this Location: 120
Type of Operation: Paperboard mill
Pulp Grades and Capacities:
Total pulp capacity: 84,068 mt/y
Recycled Pulping: 84,068 mt/y
Paper/Paperboard Grades and Capacities:
Total paper and paperboard capacity: 84,000 mt/y
Linerboard: 34,000 mt/y
Corrugating medium/fluting: 50,000 mt/y
Paper and Paperboard Mill Data:
Stock Preparation:
Pulpers: 2
Refiners: 3
Paper Machines: 1
No. 1, fourdrinier (2), total capacity 84,000 mt/y, Trim width 2.6 m, Corrugating medium/fluting, Linerboard
Finishing Equipment:
Winders: 1 at 40,000 mt/y
Energy Data:
Electrical demand for mill: 110 MWh/D

ⓄⓂSelkasan Kagit ve Paketleme Malzemeleri Imalati San. ve Tic. AS
Manisa Mill
Ownership: DS Smith Plc
Organize Sanayi Bölgesi, PK.199
45001 Manisa
Turkey
Phone: (90) 236 213 02 73-77
Fax: (90) 236 213 0278
Email: selkasan@superonline.com
Web Address: www.selkasan.com
Personnel:
Gen. Mgr.: Fikret Özveren
Phone: (90) 236 213 02 73 77
Fax: (90) 236 213 0278
Email: fikret.ozveren@selkasan.com
Man. Dir.: Engin Denizmen
Phone: (90) 236 213 02 73 77
Fax: (90) 236 213 0278
Email: e.denizmen@selkasan.com
Asst. Gen. Mgr. Finan.: Ali Bülent Atabey
Phone: (90) 236 213 02 73 77
Fax: (90) 236 213 0278

Turkey

Email: a.atabey@selkasan.com
Acct. Mgr.: Figen Basdogan
Phone: (90) 236 213 02 73 77
Fax: (90) 236 213 0278
Email: f.basdogan@selkosan.com
Imp/Exp. Mgr.: Füsün Tugrul
Phone: (90) 236 213 02 73 77
Fax: (90) 236 213 0278
Email: f.tugrul@selkasan.com
Prod. Coord.: Seyit Sahin
Phone: (90) 236 213 02 73 77
Fax: (90) 236 213 0278
Email: s.sahin@selkasan.com
Prod. Eng.: Recep Baci
Phone: (90) 236 213 02 73 77
Fax: (90) 236 213 0278
Email: recep.baci@selkasan.com
Tech. Asst. of Gen. Mgr.: Kamil Tokatli
Phone: (90) 236 213 02 73 77
Fax: (90) 236 213 0278
Email: k.tokatli@selkasan.com
Total Employees of Company: 130
Total Employees at this Location: 130
Type of Operation: Paper mill
Pulp Grades and Capacities:
  Total pulp capacity: 169,434 mt/y
  Recycled Pulping: 169,434 mt/y
Paper/Paperboard Grades and Capacities:
  Total paper and paperboard capacity: 170,000 mt/y
  Linerboard: 70,000 mt/y
  Corrugating medium/fluting: 100,000 mt/y
Paper and Paperboard Mill Data:
  Stock Preparation:
  Pulpers: 6
  Refiners: 4
Paper Machines: 2
  No. 1, fourdrinier (2), total capacity 70,000 mt/y, Trim width 2.5 m, Linerboard, Corrugating medium/fluting
  No. 2, GapFormer, total capacity 100,000 mt/y, Trim width 2.5 m, Corrugating medium/fluting, Linerboard
Finishing Equipment:
  Winders: 2 at 200,000 mt/y
Energy Data:
  Power boilers: 3
  Combustion turbines: 1 at 4.7 MW
  Steam turbines: 1 at 4.3 MW
  Electrical demand for mill: 200 MWh/D

⓪ⓂSimka Kagit San. Ve Tic A.S
Kayseri Mill
Ownership: 24% by Mehmet Karamercn, 10% by Mehmet Özsuveren, 10% by Oguzhan Karamercan, 40% by Osman Özsuveren, 16% by Sedat Aksoy
Organize Sanayi. Bol. 11, Cad. No. 21
TR-38070 Kayseri
Turkey
  Phone: (90) 352 3211213/1314
  Fax: (90) 352 3211212
  Email: info@simkakagit.com.tr
  Web Address: www.simkapaper.com.tr,
  www.simkakagit.com.tr
Personnel:
Chmn.: Osman Özsuveren
  Phone: (90) 352 3211213/1314
Gen. Mgr.: Ibrahim Kulajsizolu
  Phone: (90) 352 3211213/1314
  Email: ibrahimkulajsizolu@simkakagit.com.tr
Prod. Mgr.: Yucel Bincasla
  Phone: (90) 352 3211213/1314
Sls. Mgr.: Oguzhan Karamercan
  Phone: (90) 352 3211213/1314
Lab. & Qlty. Responsible: Selen Yildiz
  Phone: (90) 352 3211213/1314
Total Employees of Company: 50
Total Employees at this Location: 50
Type of Operation: Paper mill
Pulp Grades and Capacities:
  Total pulp capacity: 44,701 mt/y
  Recycled Pulping: 44,701 mt/y
Pulp Mill Data:
  Recycled Fiber Treatment Lines:
  Washing deinking lines: 1
Paper/Paperboard Grades and Capacities:
  Total paper and paperboard capacity: 45,000 mt/y
  Corrugating medium/fluting: 45,000 mt/y
Paper and Paperboard Mill Data:
  Stock Preparation:
  Pulpers: 2
  Refiners: 1
Paper Machines: 1
  No. 1, fourdrinier, total capacity 45,000 mt/y, Trim width 2 m, Corrugating medium/fluting
Finishing Equipment:
  Sheeters: 1
Energy Data:
  Power boilers: 2
  Electrical demand for mill: 61 MWh/D

⓪Sun-Ka Kagit ve Karton San. ve Tic. Ltd. sti
Corum Mill
Samsun Asfalt 3km, Sungurlu
Corum
Turkey
  Phone: (90) 364 311 0224
  Fax: (90) 364 311 0227
  Email: sunka@sunkapaper.com
  Web Address: www.sunkapaper.com
Personnel:
Gen. Mgr.: Salih Zeki Öztekin
  Phone: (90) 364 311 0224
  Email: salihzeki@sunkapaper.com
Gen. Mgr. Assist.: Levent Öztekin
  Phone: (90) 364 311 0224
  Email: leventoz@sunkapaper.com
Total Employees at this Location: 23
Type of Operation: Paperboard mill
Paper/Paperboard Grades and Capacities:
  Total paper and paperboard capacity: 12,000 mt/y
  Boxboard/cartonboard: 12,000 mt/y
Paper and Paperboard Mill Data:
Paper Machines: 1
  PM 1, fourdrinier, Yankee dryer, total capacity 12,000 mt/y, Trim width 1.85 m, Boxboard/cartonboard

⓪Sun-Ka Kagit ve Karton San. ve Tic. Ltd. sti
Ownership: 100% by Öztekin Family
Samsun Asfalt 3km, Sungurlu
Corum
Turkey
  Phone: (90) 364 311 0224
  Fax: (90) 364 311 0227
  Email: sunka@sunkapaper.com
  Web Address: www.sunkapaper.com
Personnel:
Gen. Mgr.: Salih Zeki Öztekin
  Phone: (90) 364 311 0224
  Fax: (90) 364 311 0227
  Email: salihzeki@sunkapaper.com
Gen. Mgr. Assist.: Levent Öztekin
  Phone: (90) 364 311 0224
  Fax: (90) 364 311 0227
  Email: leventoz@sunkapaper.com
Total Employees of Company: 23
Mill Locations:
Sun-Ka Kagit ve Karton San. ve Tic. Ltd. sti, Corum Mill, Samsun Asfalt 3km, Sungurlu, Corum, Turkey, Capacity: 12,000 mt/y, (Paperboard mill)
  Phone: (90) 364 311 0224
  Fax: (90) 364 311 0227
  Email: sunka@sunkapaper.com

⓪ⓂTezol Tütün ve Kagit San ve Tic A.S.
Izmir Mill
Ownership: 100% by Tezol Family
Philsa Cad. No:36
TR-35860 Torbali, Izmir, Izmir
Turkey
  Phone: (90) 232 8531144
  Fax: (90) 232 8531181
  Email: info@tezol.com.tr
  Web Address: www.tezol.com.tr
Personnel:
Chmn. of the Bd. & CEO: Ersin Tezol
  Phone: (90) 232 8531144
Bd. Mbr. & CFO: Erhan Tezol
  Phone: (90) 232 8531144
Purch. Mgr.: Gila Levi
  Phone: (90) 232 8531144
Prod. Mgr.: Kadir Tuna
  Phone: (90) 232 8531144
Sls. Mgr.: Alpay Ziker
  Phone: (90) 232 8531144
Env. Mgr.: Müge Inan
  Phone: (90) 232 8531144
Tech. Mgr.: Kemal Gezer
  Phone: (90) 232 8531144
Total Employees of Company: 290
Total Employees at this Location: 160
Type of Operation: Paper mill, Paper mill
Pulp Grades and Capacities:
  Total pulp capacity: 7,634 mt/y
  Recycled Pulping: 7,634 mt/y
Pulp Mill Data:
  Recycled Fiber Treatment Lines:
  Flotation deinking lines: 1
Paper/Paperboard Grades and Capacities:
  Total paper and paperboard capacity: 54,000 mt/y
  Tissue: 54,000 mt/y
Paper and Paperboard Mill Data:
  Stock Preparation:
  Pulpers: 1
  Refiners: 2
Paper Machines: 2
  No. 1, twin-wire, Yankee dryer, total capacity 18,000 mt/y, Trim width 2.73 m, Tissue
  No. 2, crescent former, Yankee dryer, total capacity 36,000 mt/y, Trim width 2.8 m, Tissue, Uncoated woodfree/freesheet
Finishing Equipment:
  Rewinders: 1
Energy Data:
  Power boilers: 2
  Electrical demand for mill: 144 MWh/D

⓪Toprak Temizlik Kagidi San. Tic. A.S.
Ownership: 100% by Halis Toprak Holding Co.
Merkez, Toprak Center-Ihlamur Yildiz Cad. No:10, Besiktas
TR- 34353 Istanbul
Turkey
  Phone: (90) 212 558 1919
  Fax: (90) 212 558 1919
  Email: paper@toprak.com.tr, temizlikkg@toprak.com.tr
  Web Address: www.toprak.com.tr
Personnel:
Purch. Mgr.: Meliha Güler
  Phone: (90) 212 558 1919
  Fax: (90) 212 558 1919
  Email: mguler@toprak.com.tr
Total Employees of Company: 462
Total Employees at this Location: 10
Mill Locations:
Toprak Temizlik Kagidi San. Tic. A.S., Bozuyuk Mill, Eskisehir Yolu, 7 Km, TR-11360 Bozuyuk, Turkey, Capacity: 67,116 mt/y, (Paper mill)
  Phone: (90) 228 314 4300
  Fax: (90) 228 314 4310
  Email: paper@toprak.com.tr

ⓜToprak Temizlik Kagidi San. Tic. A.S.
Bozuyuk Mill
Eskisehir Yolu, 7 Km
TR-11360 Bozuyuk, Bilecik
Turkey

Turkey

Phone: (90) 228 314 4300
Fax: (90) 228 314 4310
Email: paper@toprak.com.tr
Web Address: www.toprak.com.tr
Personnel:
Mill Mgr.: Necdet Basaran
Phone: (90) 228 314 4300
Email: nbasaran@toprak.com.tr
Sls. Mgr.: Vely Korgun
Phone: (90) 228 314 4300
Total Employees at this Location: 452
Type of Operation: Paper mill
Paper/Paperboard Grades and Capacities:
Total paper and paperboard capacity: 67,116 mt/y
Uncoated woodfree/freesheet: 39,984 mt/y
Tissue: 27,132 mt/y
Paper and Paperboard Mill Data:
Stock Preparation:
Pulpers: 3
Refiners: 7
Paper Machines: 2
No. 1, Periformer, Yankee dryer, total capacity 27,132 mt/y, Trim width 3.14 m, Tissue, Uncoated woodfree/freesheet
No. 2, fourdrinier, total capacity 39,984 mt/y, Trim width 2.9 m, Uncoated woodfree/freesheet
Coating Machines: 2
No. 1, total capacity 37,500 mt/y., on machine No. 2
Finishing Equipment:
Winders: 2 at 67,000 mt/y
Calenders: 1
Rewinders: 3 at 21,000 mt/y
Sheeters: 1 at 20,000 mt/y
Energy Data:
Power boilers: 3
Electrical demand for mill: 160 MWh/D

ⓞⓜTrakya Kagit San ve TIC. A.S.
Tekirdag Mill
Ownership: 10% by Gülay Uncuoglu, 75% by Halil Uncuoglu
Çorlu Deri Organize Sanayi Bölgesi, Istasyon Civari no: 35 Çorlu
TR-59860 Tekirdag, Tekirdag
Turkey
Phone: (90) 282 6862044/45
Fax: (90) 282 6861890
Email: trakyakagit@superonline.com, info@trakya-kagit.com
Personnel:
Owner & Chmn.: Halil Uncuoglu
Phone: (90) 282 6862044/45
Gen. Mgr.: Yavuz Uncuoglu
Phone: (90) 282 6862044/45
Prod. Mgr.: Hasan Eser
Phone: (90) 282 6862044/45
Sls. Mgr.: Kenan Sen
Phone: (90) 282 6862044/45
Total Employees at this Location: 48
Type of Operation: Paper mill, Paperboard mill
Pulp Grades and Capacities:
Total pulp capacity: 35,993 mt/y
Recycled Pulping: 35,993 mt/y
Paper/Paperboard Grades and Capacities:
Total paper and paperboard capacity: 35,000 mt/y
Tissue: 7,000 mt/y
Packaging papers: 4,000 mt/y
Boxboard/cartonboard: 24,000 mt/y
Paper and Paperboard Mill Data:
Stock Preparation:
Pulpers: 1
Paper Machines: 2
No. 1, cylinder, Yankee dryer, total capacity 24,000 mt/y, Trim width 2.16 m, Boxboard/cartonboard
No. 2, fourdrinier, Yankee dryer, total capacity 11,000 mt/y, Trim width 2.45 m, Tissue, Packaging papers
Energy Data:
Power boilers: 1
Electrical demand for mill: 56 MWh/D

ⓞTuranlar Group
Ownership: 100% by Turan family
Halkali Cad. No: 170, Sefaköy-Istanbul
TR-34306 Küçukcekmece-Istanbul
Turkey
Phone: (90) 212 698 8992
Fax: (90) 212 698 8995
Email: info@turanlargroup.com
Web Address: www.turanlargroup.com
Personnel:
Chmn.: Fuat Turan
Phone: (90) 212 698 8992
Fax: (90) 212 698 8995
Coordinator: Murat Turan
Phone: (90) 212 698 8992
Fax: (90) 212 698 8995
Asst. Coordinator: Meltem Turan
Phone: (90) 212 698 8992
Fax: (90) 212 698 8995
Total Employees of Company: 1,000
Mill Locations:
Vezirköprü Orman Ürünleri ve Gida Ticaret As., Samsun Mill, Esentepe Mahallesi Vezirköprü, TR-55900 Samsun, Turkey, Capacity: 4,000 mt/y, (Paper mill)
Phone: (90) 362 647 17 40
Fax: (90) 362 647 15 78
Email: veziragac@turanlargroup.com

ⓞUCAL Donusen Kagit San ve Tic A.S.
Ownership: 100% by Hakki Uçal
58 Bulvar Cad. No. 70, 35 Zeytinburnu
TR-11360 Istanbul
Turkey
Phone: (90) 212 582 5987
Fax: (90) 212 558 9313
Email: ucalkagit@ucalkagit.com.tr
Web Address: www.ucalkagit.com.tr
Personnel:
Owner & Chmn.: Hakki Oray Uçal
Phone: (90) 532 314 3641
Total Employees of Company: 150
Total Employees at this Location: 10
Mill Locations:
UCAL Donusen Kagit San ve Tic A.S., Sirapinar Mill, Beykoz Cad. No: 89, Sirapinar, Umraniye, Istanbul, Turkey, Capacity: 33,000 mt/y, (Paper mill, Paperboard mill)
Phone: (90) 216 435 7374/75
Fax: (90) 216 435 7379
Email: ucalkagit@ucalkagit.com.tr

ⓞUCAL Donusen Kagit San ve Tic A.S.
Sirapinar Mill
Beykoz Cad. No: 89
Sirapinar, Umraniye, Istanbul
Turkey
Phone: (90) 216 435 7374/75
Fax: (90) 216 435 7379
Email: ucalkagit@ucalkagit.com.tr
Web Address: www.ucalkagit.com.tr
Personnel:
Mill Mgr.: Nejat Olgun
Phone: (90) 216 435 7374/75
Chmn. & Owner: Hakki Oray Uçal
Phone: (90) 532 314 3641
Total Employees at this Location: 90
Type of Operation: Paper mill, Paperboard mill
Pulp Grades and Capacities:
Total pulp capacity: 33,559 mt/y
Recycled Pulping: 33,559 mt/y
Paper/Paperboard Grades and Capacities:
Total paper and paperboard capacity: 33,000 mt/y
Packaging papers: 10,000 mt/y
Corrugating medium/fluting: 3,000 mt/y
Boxboard/cartonboard: 20,000 mt/y
Paper and Paperboard Mill Data:
Paper Machines: 2
No. 1, fourdrinier, total capacity 13,000 mt/y, Trim width 2.28 m, Packaging papers, Corrugating medium/fluting
No. 2, cylinder, total capacity 20,000 mt/y, Trim width 1.8 m, Boxboard/cartonboard
Energy Data:
Electrical demand for mill: 48 MWh/D

ⓞⓜVe-Ge Hassas Kagit ve Yapistirici Bant San. ve Tic. A.S.
Kemalpasa Mill
Ulucak Beldesi Istiklal Mah. 5. sok No:8
35170 Kemalpasa, Izmir
Turkey
Phone: (90) 232 877 0356/0890
Fax: (90) 232 877 03659/0984
Email: kalgan@vege.com.tr
Web Address: www.ve-ge.com.tr
Personnel:
Paper Mill Mgr.: Cemgiz Gumul
Total Employees at this Location: 125
Type of Operation: Paper mill
Paper/Paperboard Grades and Capacities:
Total paper and paperboard capacity: 72,000 mt/y
Uncoated woodfree/freesheet: 72,000 mt/y
Paper and Paperboard Mill Data:
Paper Machines: 1
No. 1, fourdrinier, total capacity 72,000 mt/y, Trim width 3.2 m, Uncoated woodfree/freesheet
Energy Data:
Power boilers
Combustion turbines: 1
Electrical demand for mill: 143 MWh/D

ⓜVezirköprü Orman Ürünleri ve Gida Ticaret As.
Samsun Mill
Ownership: 100% by Turanlar Group
Esentepe Mahallesi Vezirköprü
TR-55900 Samsun
Turkey
Phone: (90) 362 647 17 40
Fax: (90) 362 647 15 78
Email: veziragac@turanlargroup.com
Web Address: www.turanlargroup.com
Personnel:
Mill Mgr.: Hanesi Canak
Phone: (90) 362 647 17 40
Email: h.canak@gmail.com
Total Employees at this Location: 300
Type of Operation: Paper mill
Paper/Paperboard Grades and Capacities:
Total paper and paperboard capacity: 4,000 mt/y
Specialty and industrial: 4,000 mt/y
Paper and Paperboard Mill Data:
Stock Preparation:
Pulpers: 2
Paper Machines: 1
No. 1, (second hand from 1985), fourdrinier, total capacity 4,000 mt/y, Specialty and industrial
Finishing Equipment:
Rewinders: 1 at 8,000 mt/y
Energy Data:
Power boilers: 1

ⓞⓜViking Kagit ve Seluloz A.S.
Viking Paper Mill
Ownership: 47.13% by Other, 52.87% by Yasar Holding
Hürriyet Cd. No:474
TR-35800 Aliaga, Izmir
Turkey
Phone: (90) 232 6160600
Fax: (90) 232 6160206
Email: info@viking.com.tr
Web Address: www.viking.com.tr
Personnel:
Chmn.: Idil Yigitbasi

Phone: (90) 232 616 0600
Fax: (90) 232 616 0206
Gen. Mgr.: Mesut Sezer
Phone: (90) 232 616 0600
Fax: (90) 232 616 0206
Email: mesut.sezer@viking.com.tr
Mill Mgr.: Ahmet Senyasa
Phone: (90) 232 616 0600 Ext. 202
Fax: (90) 232 616 0206
Email: ahmet.senyasa@viking.com.tr
Finan. Mgr.: Bayram Akyuz
Phone: (90) 232 616 0600
Fax: (90) 232 616 0206
Email: bayram.akyuz@viking.com.tr
Total Employees of Company: 323
Total Employees at this Location: 323
Type of Operation: Paper mill
Pulp Grades and Capacities:
Total pulp capacity: 20,675 mt/y
Recycled Pulping: 20,675 mt/y
Pulp Mill Data:
Recycled Fiber Treatment Lines:
Flotation deinking lines: 1 at 31,500 admt/y
Pulpers: 1
Paper/Paperboard Grades and Capacities:
Total paper and paperboard capacity: 45,000 mt/y
Tissue: 45,000 mt/y
Paper and Paperboard Mill Data:
Stock Preparation:
Pulpers: 2
Refiners: 7
Paper Machines: 2
No. 1, fourdrinier, Yankee dryer, total capacity 18,000 mt/y, Trim width 4.4 m, Tissue
No. 2, crescent former, Yankee dryer, total capacity 27,000 mt/y, Trim width 2.75 m, Tissue, Uncoated woodfree/freesheet
Finishing Equipment:
Rewinders: 2 at 20,000 mt/y, 25,000 mt/y
Sheeters: 1 at 2,500 mt/y
Energy Data:
Power boilers: 2
Electrical demand for mill: 137 MWh/D

ⓘYasar Ambalaj Kagit Bobin San. ve Tic. A.S.
Ownership: 7.16% by Yusuf Dytun Gilkiz, 15.47% by Didem Büyükbese, 66.37% by Yasar Gilkiz, 8.57% by Fahriye Ergisci, 0.21% by Melisa Gilkiz, 2.22% by Neval Gilkiz
Organize Sanayi Bolgesi Baspinar
TR-27120 Gaziantep
Turkey
Phone: (90) 342 337 9460
Fax: (90) 342 337 9465
Email: export@yasarcone.com
Web Address: www.yasarcone.com, www.yasarambalaj.com
Personnel:
Expt. Dept.: Dilge Kiskir
Phone: (90) 342 337 9460
Fax: (90) 342 337 9465
Mill Locations:
Yasar Ambalaj Kagit Bobin San. ve Tic. A.S., Malatya Mill, Kayseri Yolu Kotan Gölü Mevkii Akçadag, Malatya, Turkey, Capacity: 36,000 mt/y, (Paper mill)
Phone: (90) 422 426 22 43 / 342 518 21 00
Fax: (90) 422 417 22 35 / 342 518 21 00
Email: info@yasarcone.com/ info@yasarambalaj.com

ⓂYasar Ambalaj Kagit Bobin San. ve Tic. A.S.
Malatya Mill
Kayseri Yolu Kotan Gölü Mevkii Akçadag
Malatya
Turkey
Phone: (90) 422 426 22 43 / 342 518 21 00
Fax: (90) 422 417 22 35 / 342 518 21 00
Email: info@yasarcone.com/,

info@yasarambalaj.com
Web Address: www.yasarcone.com
Personnel:
Mill Mgr.: Erol Yildirim
Phone: (90) 422 426 22 43 / 342 518 21 00
Purch. Mgr.: Ibrahim Akdeniz
Phone: (90) 422 426 22 43 / 342 518 21 00
Mant. Mgr.: Bulent Dag
Phone: (90) 422 426 22 43, 342 518 21 00
Env. Mgr.: Duygu Batur
Phone: (90) 422 426 22 43, 342 518 21 00
Total Employees at this Location: 66
Type of Operation: Paper mill
Pulp Grades and Capacities:
Total pulp capacity: 36,159 mt/y
Recycled Pulping: 36,159 mt/y
Pulp Mill Data:
Chemical Recovery Equipment:
Evaporator lines
Recycled Fiber Treatment Lines:
Recycled packaging pulping lines: 1
Paper/Paperboard Grades and Capacities:
Total paper and paperboard capacity: 36,000 mt/y
Boxboard/cartonboard: 36,000 mt/y
Paper and Paperboard Mill Data:
Stock Preparation:
Pulpers: 1
Paper Machines: 1
No. 1, fourdrinier, total capacity 36,000 mt/y, Trim width 1.6 m, Boxboard/cartonboard
Energy Data:
Power boilers
Electrical demand for mill: 48 MWh/D

TURKMENISTAN

ⓘYashlyk Pulp & Paper Mill
Ownership: Calik Holding, Turkey
Yashlyk, Akbuldai etrat, Gyaurs district
Akbuldai etrat, Akhal velat
Turkmenistan
Phone: (993) 12 51 1491 / 0987 / 12 350936
Fax: (993) 12 350936 / 510987
Personnel:
Project Dir.: Vahit Gohan
Phone: (993) 12 51 1491
Fax: (993) 12 35 0936
Mill Locations:
Yashlyk Pulp & Paper Mill, Yashlyk, Akbuldai etrat Mill, Yashlyk, Akbuldai etrat, Gyaurs district, Turkmenistan, Capacity: 63,000 mt/y, (Pulp mill, Paper mill)
Phone: (993) 12 51 1491 / 0987 / 12 350936
Fax: (993) 12 350936 / 510987

ⓂYashlyk Pulp & Paper Mill
Yashlyk, Akbuldai etrat Mill
Yashlyk, Akbuldai etrat, Gyaurs district, Akhal velat
Turkmenistan
Phone: (993) 12 51 1491 / 0987 / 12 350936
Fax: (993) 12 350936 / 510987
Personnel:
Project Dir.: Vahit Gohan
Phone: (993) 12 51 1491 / 0987
Type of Operation: Pulp mill, Paper mill
Pulp Grades and Capacities:
Total pulp capacity: 64,000 mt/y
Pulp Mill Data:
Pulp Lines: 2
Paper/Paperboard Grades and Capacities:
Total paper and paperboard capacity: 63,000 mt/y
Uncoated woodfree/freesheet: 63,000 mt/y
Paper and Paperboard Mill Data:
Paper Machines: 1
No. 1, DuoFormer, fourdrinier, total capacity 63,000 mt/y, Uncoated woodfree/freesheet

UNITED ARAB EMIRATES

ⓘⓂAbu Dhabi National Paper Mill
Abu Dhabi Mill
Ownership: 94% by Abu Dhabi National Industrial Projects Company, 6% by Queenex Group
Mussafah Industrial Area
Abu Dhabi, Shaikhdom of Abu Dhabi
United Arab Emirates
Mailing Address: P.O. Box 27683, Abu Dhabi, United Arab Emirates
Phone: (971) 2 509 9200
Fax: (971) 2 550 1544
Email: info@adnpm.ae
Web Address: www.adnpm.ae
Personnel:
Gen. Mgr.: Helmut Berger
Phone: (971) 2 550 1886
Fax: (971) 2 550 1544
Prod. Mgr.: Jaber Abdul Hameed
Phone: (971) 2 550 1886
Email: gaber@adpaper.ae
Sls. & Mktg. Mgr.: Khalil Shamiah
Phone: (971) 2 550 1886
Fax: (971) 2 550 1544
Purch. Mgr.: Amwar Ulhaq
Phone: (971) 2 550 1886
Fax: (971) 2 550 1544
Total Employees at this Location: 190
Type of Operation: Pulp mill, Paper mill
Pulp Grades and Capacities:
Total pulp capacity: 8,976 mt/y
Recycled Pulping: 8,976 mt/y
Pulp Mill Data:
Pulp Lines: 1
Recycled Fiber Treatment Lines:
Flotation deinking lines: 1 at 30,000
Paper/Paperboard Grades and Capacities:
Total paper and paperboard capacity: 70,000 mt/y
Tissue: 70,000 mt/y
Paper and Paperboard Mill Data:
Paper Machines: 2
No. 1, OVER Former-CR, Yankee dryer, total capacity 28,000 mt/y, Trim width 2.75 m, Tissue, Uncoated woodfree/freesheet
No. 2, OVER Former-CR, Yankee dryer, total capacity 42,000 mt/y, Trim width 3.6 m, Tissue
Energy Data:
Power boilers
Electrical demand for mill: 204 MWh/D

ⓘCrown Paper Mill Ltd.
Ajman Free Zone
Ajman
United Arab Emirates
Mailing Address: P.O. Box 4192, Ajman, United Arab Emirates
Phone: (971) 6 7407754
Fax: (971) 6 7408868
Email: info@crownpapermill.com
Web Address: crownpapermill.com/
Mill Locations:
Crown Paper Mill Ltd., Abu Dhabi Branch, ICAD 3 – Industrial City Abu Dhabi, Abu Dhabi, United Arab Emirates, Capacity: 35,000 mt/y, (Paper mill)
Phone: (971) 6-7407754
Fax: (971) 6-7408868
Email: info@crownpapermill.com

ⓂCrown Paper Mill Ltd.
Abu Dhabi Branch
ICAD 3 – Industrial City Abu Dhabi
Abu Dhabi, Shaikhdom of Abu Dhabi
United Arab Emirates
Phone: (971) 6-7407754

Uzbekistan

Fax: (971) 6-7408868
Email: info@crownpapermill.com
Web Address: www.crownpapermill.com
Personnel:
Man. Dir.: Majid Rasheed
Phone: (971) 6-7407754
Total Employees at this Location: 170
Type of Operation: Paper mill
Pulp Grades and Capacities:
Total pulp capacity: 7,290 mt/y
Recycled Pulping: 7,290 mt/y
Pulp Mill Data:
Recycled Fiber Treatment Lines:
Flotation deinking lines: 1 at 26,000
Paper/Paperboard Grades and Capacities:
Total paper and paperboard capacity: 35,000 mt/y
Tissue: 35,000 mt/y
Paper and Paperboard Mill Data:
Paper Machines: 2
No. 1, fourdrinier, Yankee dryer, total capacity 11,000 mt/y, Trim width 1.85 m, Tissue, Uncoated woodfree/freesheet
No. 2, crescent former, Yankee dryer, total capacity 24,000 mt/y, Trim width 2.77 m, Tissue, Uncoated woodfree/freesheet
Energy Data:
Power boilers
Electrical demand for mill: 102 MWh/D

ⓜGulf Paper Manufacturing Free Zone Company
Dubai Mill
Ownership: Gulf Paper Mfg. Co. k.s.c.
P.O. Box 18075 J.A.
Jebel Ali Free Zone, Dubai
United Arab Emirates
Phone: (971) 4 883 3885
Fax: (971) 4 883 34418
Email: gpmc@emirates.net.ae
Web Address: www.gulfpaper.com
Personnel:
Man. Dir.: Ghaleb Al Hadhrami
Phone: (971) 4 883 3885
Email: ghaleb78@hotmail.com
Total Employees at this Location: 125
Type of Operation: Paperboard mill
Pulp Grades and Capacities:
Total pulp capacity: 55,136 mt/y
Recycled Pulping: 55,136 mt/y
Paper/Paperboard Grades and Capacities:
Total paper and paperboard capacity: 55,000 mt/y
Linerboard: 18,000 mt/y
Corrugating medium/fluting: 35,000 mt/y
Boxboard/cartonboard: 2,000 mt/y
Paper and Paperboard Mill Data:
Paper Machines: 1
No. 1, fourdrinier, total capacity 55,000 mt/y, Trim width 4.11 m, Corrugating medium/fluting, Linerboard, Boxboard/cartonboard
Energy Data:
Power boilers: 1
Electrical demand for mill: 77 MWh/D

ⓜQueenex Hygiene Paper Manufacturing L.L.C
Abu Dhabi Mill
Ownership: 100% by Queenex Group
Mussafah 16
2991 Abu Dhabi, Shaikhdom of Abu Dhabi
United Arab Emirates
Mailing Address: P.O. Box : 2991, Abu Dhabi, Shaikhdom of Abu Dhabi, United Arab Emirates
Phone: (971) 2-5554700
Fax: (971) 2-5553434
Email: export@queenex.ae
Web Address: www.queenex.ae
Personnel:
Chrmn.: Hamad Al Hajiri

Phone: (971) 2-5554700
Ops Dir: Mohammed Adel
Phone: (971) 2-5554700
Total Employees at this Location: 80
Type of Operation: Paper mill
Pulp Grades and Capacities:
Total pulp capacity: 35,101 mt/y
Recycled Pulping: 35,101 mt/y
Pulp Mill Data:
Pulp Lines: 1
Recycled Fiber Treatment Lines:
Flotation deinking lines: 1
Paper/Paperboard Grades and Capacities:
Total paper and paperboard capacity: 33,000 mt/y
Tissue: 33,000 mt/y
Paper and Paperboard Mill Data:
Paper Machines: 1
No. 1, OVER Former-CR, Yankee dryer, total capacity 33,000 mt/y, Trim width 2.85 m, Tissue, Uncoated woodfree/freesheet
Energy Data:
Power boilers
Electrical demand for mill: 113 MWh/D

ⓜUnion Paper Mills
Ownership: M.A.H.Y. Khoory & Co.
Al Quoz Industrial Area No. 3, Abu Dhabi Road
Dubai
United Arab Emirates
Mailing Address: P.O. Box 41, Dubai
Phone: (971) 4 339 3339
Fax: (971) 4 339 3931
Email: upm@emirates.net.ae, wm@upm.ae
Personnel:
Dpty. Gen. Mgr.: D. Gandhi
Phone: (971) 4 339 3339
Fax: (971) 4 339 3931
Email: gandhi@upm.ae
Gen. Mgr., Sls & Mktg.: K. Deva Rao
Phone: (971) 4 266 6300
Fax: (971) 4 266 7454
Email: gmsales@upm.ae
Procurement Mgr. (Raw Materials): J. Subramanyiam
Phone: (971) 4 339 3937
Fax: (971) 4 339 3963
Email: j.subramanyam@upm.ae
Mktg. & Contracts Mgr.: Huzaifa F. Rangwala
Phone: (971) 4 339 3937
Fax: (971) 4 339 3931
Email: huzaifa@upm.ae
Total Employees at this Location: 125
Mill Locations:
Union Paper Mills, Dubai Mill, Al Quoz Industrial Area No. 3, Abu Dhabi Road, Dubai, United Arab Emirates, Capacity: 178,000 mt/y, (Paperboard mill)
Phone: (971) 4 33 93 339
Fax: (971) 4 33 93 931
Email: upm@emirates.net.ae, wm@upm.ae

ⓜUnion Paper Mills
Dubai Mill
Al Quoz Industrial Area No. 3, Abu Dhabi Road
Dubai
United Arab Emirates
Mailing Address: P.O. Box 41, Dubai, United Arab Emirates
Phone: (971) 4 33 93 339
Fax: (971) 4 33 93 931
Email: upm@emirates.net.ae, wm@upm.ae
Web Address: www.upm.ae
Personnel:
Dpty. Gen. Mgr.: Mr. D. Gandhi
Phone: (971) 4 339 3339
Fax: (971) 4 339 3931
Email: gandhi@upm.ae
Gen. Mgr., Sls & Mktg.: K. Deva Rao

Phone: (971) 4 266 6300
Fax: (971) 4 266 7454
Email: gmsales@upm.ae
Procurement Mgr. (Raw Materials): Mr. J. Subramanyiam
Phone: (971) 4 339 3937
Fax: (971) 4 339 3963
Email: j.subramanyam@upm.ae
Mktg. & Contracts Mgr.: Huzaifa F. Rangwala
Phone: (971) 4 339 3937
Fax: (971) 4 339 3931
Email: huzaifa@upm.ae
Total Employees at this Location: 125
Type of Operation: Paperboard mill
Pulp Grades and Capacities:
Total pulp capacity: 176,818 mt/y
Recycled Pulping: 176,818 mt/y
Paper/Paperboard Grades and Capacities:
Total paper and paperboard capacity: 178,000 mt/y
Linerboard: 73,000 mt/y
Corrugating medium/fluting: 100,000 mt/y
Boxboard/cartonboard: 5,000 mt/y
Paper and Paperboard Mill Data:
Paper Machines: 2
No. 1, fourdrinier, total capacity 35,000 mt/y, Trim width 2.5 m, Corrugating medium/fluting, Linerboard, Boxboard/cartonboard
No. 2, fourdrinier (2), total capacity 143,000 mt/y, Trim width 3.7 m, Corrugating medium/fluting, Linerboard
Finishing Equipment:
Rewinders: 1 at 35,000 mt/y
Energy Data:
Power boilers: 1
Electrical demand for mill: 246 MWh/D

UZBEKISTAN

ⓡⓜAngren Pack
Bulbak Mill
Ownership: 47% by Angren Pack, 53% by Paper Mill Holding
101200 Angren, pos. Bulbak, Tashkentskaya obl.
Uzbekistan
Phone: (998) 95 142 4206
Fax: (998) 95 170 2420
Email: sales.angrenpack@gmail.com
Web Address: www.angrenpack.com
Personnel:
Chmn.: Bakhodir Marnatovich Tuykhiev
Phone: (998) 95 170 2420
Fax: (998) 95 170 2420
Head of Recycle Fiber (Waste Paper): Tatyana Aleksandrovna Abidova
Phone: (998) 371 268 1716
Fax: (998) 95 170 2420
Email: lara-bat@rambler.ru
Social Affairs Dir.: Gayrat ?bduvakhobovich ?bdurakhmanov
Phone: (998) 93 388 1100
Fax: (998) 95 170 2420
Email: gayrat.karton@yandex.ru
Office Mgr.: Czaros Alisherovna ??pilova
Phone: (998) 95 170 2420
Fax: (998) 95 170 2420
Email: charos-sqqs@yandex.ru
Total Employees of Company: 600
Total Employees at this Location: 550
Type of Operation: Paper mill
Pulp Grades and Capacities:
Recycled Pulping
Paper/Paperboard Grades and Capacities:
Total paper and paperboard capacity: 103,000 mt/y
Tissue: 3,000 mt/y
Linerboard: 50,000 mt/y
Corrugating medium/fluting: 50,000 mt/y
Paper and Paperboard Mill Data:
Paper Machines: 3

K-28, (2nd hand), total capacity 100,000 mt/y,
  Linerboard, Corrugating medium/fluting
PM 1, Trim width 1.76 m, Tissue
PM 2, Trim width 1.76 m, Tissue
Coating Machines: 1
K-28, total capacity 100,000 mt/y., off machine
Energy Data:
Power boilers: 7
Electrical demand for mill: 192 MWh/D

ⓂⓜOAO Toshkent Qogoze
Tashkent Mill
Ownership: 100% by National Bank
Fergana Str. 23, Khamza District
700005 Tashkent, Tashkentskaya obl.
Uzbekistan
  Phone: (998) 71 291 6588/6807/6425
  Fax: (998) 371 191 6588
  Email: uzbum@mail.ru
Personnel:
  Gen. Dir.: Zair Takhirovich Khadzhay
  Phone: (998) 71 291 6588/6807/6425
  Chief Eng./Chmn.: Vladimir Vladimirovich Vladimirov
  Phone: (998) 71 291 6588/6807/6425
Total Employees of Company: 350
Total Employees at this Location: 220
Type of Operation: Paper mill, Paperboard mill
Paper/Paperboard Grades and Capacities:
  Total paper and paperboard capacity: 43,100 mt/y
  Uncoated woodfree/freesheet: 30,000 mt/y
  Tissue: 2,000 mt/y
  Specialty and industrial
  Containerboard
Paper and Paperboard Mill Data:
Paper Machines: 7
No. 1, total capacity 8,000 mt/y, Trim width 1.5 m
No. 2, Trim width 1.7 m
No. 3, Trim width 1.7 m
No. 4, total capacity 10,000 mt/y, Trim width 2.1 m,
  Uncoated woodfree/freesheet
No. 5, (come on-line in Q1, 2012), total capacity 2,000
  mt/y, Tissue
No. 6, (started first half of 2012), total capacity 2,100
  mt/y
No. 7, (started first half of 2012), total capacity 9,000
  mt/y, Containerboard
Energy Data:
Power boilers: 3
Electrical demand for mill: 7 MWh/D

ⓂTashkent Paper Mill of GPO Davlat Belgisi
Darkhan Mill
111104 Vil. Darkhan, Tashkent Distr., Tashkentskaya obl.
Uzbekistan
  Phone: (998) 71 1403456/0
  Fax: (998) 71 1401576
  Email: paperuz@rol.uz,
  securitypaper@buzton.com
  Web Address: www.davlat-belgisi.uz
Personnel:
  Gen. Mgr.: Suleyman Khudaykulov
  Phone: (998) 71 140 3450
  Purch. Mgr. & Sls./Mktg. Mgr.: Mumindzhon Atilovich
  Khidoyatov
  Phone: (998) 71 140 2453
  Mill Mgr.: Abduazin Fatarovich Irgashev
  Phone: (998) 71 171 2058
  Chief Eng.: Evgeniy Vladimirovich Debre
  Phone: (998) 71 1403460
  Dpty. Prod. Dir.: Delfod Irisaevich Sedikov
  Phone: (998) 71 1403470
Type of Operation: Pulp mill
Pulp Grades and Capacities:
  Chemical Pulp
Paper/Paperboard Grades and Capacities:
  Total paper and paperboard capacity: 43,000 mt/y
  Specialty and industrial: 43,000 mt/y
Paper and Paperboard Mill Data:
Paper Machines: 1
No. 1, (second-hand), total capacity 43,000 mt/y, Trim
  width 1.8 m, Specialty and industrial
Energy Data:
Power boilers: 4

ⓂTashkent Paper Mill of GPO Davlat Belgisi
Ownership: 100% by state
Vil. Darkhan
111104 Tashkent Distr, Tashkentskaya obl.
Uzbekistan
  Phone: (998) 71 1403456
  Fax: (998) 71 1401576
  Email: paperuz@rol.uz,
  securitypaper@buzton.com
  Web Address: www.davlat-belgisi.uz
Mill Locations:
Tashkent Paper Mill of GPO Davlat Belgisi, Darkhan
  Mill, 111104 Vil. Darkhan, Tashkent Distr., Uzbekistan,
  Capacity: 43,000 mt/y, (Pulp mill)
  Phone: (998) 71 1403456/0
  Fax: (998) 71 1401576
  Email: paperuz@rol.uz, securitypaper@buzton.com

VIETNAM

ⓂAn Binh Paper Corporation-ABPAPER
Di An District Mill
27/5 Kha Vang Can St., An Binh Ward
Di An District, Binh Duong Province
Vietnam
  Phone: (84) 8 38960 155/38963 314
  Fax: (84) 8 38960 700
  Email: info@anbinhpaper.com
  Web Address: www.anbinhpaper.com
Personnel:
  Chmn./Gen. Mgr.: Han Vinh Quang
  Phone: (84) 90 9886868
  Paper Mill Mgr.: Han Manh Hung
  Phone: (84) 90 373 0383
  Prod. Mgr.: Asokan Arumugan
  Phone: (84) 8 38960 155/38963 314
  Project Mgr.: Dr. Prof. Nguyen Kien Loi
  Phone: (84) 3896 0155
  Gen. Mgr.: Mr. Han Vinh Quang
  Phone: (84) 90 9006868
  Email: trinhhanvinhquang@gmail.com
Total Employees at this Location: 150
Type of Operation: Paper mill, Paperboard mill
Pulp Grades and Capacities:
  Total pulp capacity: 60,000 mt/y
Pulp Mill Data:
  Recycled Fiber Treatment Lines:
  Pulpers: 2 at 20,000 admt/y
  Recycled packaging pulping lines: 1 at 60,000 admt/y
Paper/Paperboard Grades and Capacities:
  Total paper and paperboard capacity: 80,000 mt/y
  Linerboard: 54,000 mt/y
  Corrugating medium/fluting: 26,000 mt/y
Paper and Paperboard Mill Data:
Paper Machines: 5
1, cylinder, total capacity 18,000 mt/y, Trim width 2.7
  m, Linerboard
No. 2, cylinder, total capacity 18,000 mt/y, Trim width
  2.7 m, Linerboard
No. 3, cylinder, total capacity 12,000 mt/y, Trim width
  3.2 m, Corrugating medium/fluting
No. 4, cylinder, total capacity 18,000 mt/y, Trim width
  2.7 m, Linerboard
No. 5, cylinder, total capacity 14,000 mt/y, Trim width
  2.7 m, Corrugating medium/fluting
Finishing Equipment:
  Rewinders: 6 at 45,000 mt/y
  Sheeters: 2
Energy Data:
Power boilers: 3
Electrical demand for mill: 40 MWh/D

ⓂAn Binh Paper Corporation-ABPAPER
*Ownership: 8.60% by Mr. Han Manh Hung,
91.40% by Mr. Han Vinh Quang*
27/5 Kha Vang Can St., An Binh Ward Di An District
Binh Duong Province
Vietnam
  Phone: (84) 8 38960 155/38963 314
  Fax: (84) 8 38960 700
  Email: info@anbinhpaper.com
  Web Address: www.anbinhpaper.com
Personnel:
  Chmn./Gen. Mgr.: Han Vinh Quang
  Phone: (84) 90 9886868
  Paper Mill Mgr.: Han Manh Hung
  Phone: (84) 90 373 0383
  Prod. Mgr.: Asokan Arumugan
  Phone: (84) 90 373 0383
  Project Mgr.: Nguyen Kien Loi
  Phone: (84) 3896 0155
  Gen. Mgr.: Han Vinh Quang
  Phone: (84) 90 9006868
  Email: trinhhanvinhquang@gmail.com
Total Employees of Company: 150
Mill Locations:
An Binh Paper Corporation-ABPAPER, Di An District
  Mill, 27/5 Kha Vang Can St., An Binh Ward, Di An
  District, Vietnam, Capacity: 80,000 mt/y, (Paper mill,
  Paperboard mill)
  Phone: (84) 8 38960 155/38963 314
  Fax: (84) 8 38960 700
  Email: info@anbinhpaper.com

ⓂAn Hoa Paper and Pulp Factory
Ownership: GELEXIMCO
6th floor, Geleximco Building, 36, Hoang Cau Street, O
Cho Dua Ward, Dong Da District
Hanoi City
Vietnam
  Phone: (84) 35141199
  Fax: (84) 35143939
  Email: anhoapulp@gmail.com,
  info@anhoapulp.com
  Web Address: anhoapulp.com
Mill Locations:
An Hoa Paper and Pulp Factory, Vinh Loi Commune
  Mill, Son Duong district, Vinh Loi Commune, Vietnam,
  (Pulp mill)

ⓂAn Hoa Paper and Pulp Factory
Vinh Loi Commune Mill
Son Duong district
Vinh Loi Commune, Tuyen Quang
Vietnam
Total Employees at this Location: 400
Type of Operation: Pulp mill
Pulp Grades and Capacities:
  Total pulp capacity: 130,052 mt/y
  Pulp available for market: 130,000 mt/y
  Chemical Pulp: 130,052 mt/y
Pulp Mill Data:
  Chemical Pulping Systems:
  Continuous digesters: 4
Pulp Lines: 1
  Bleach Plant Systems: 1
  Hardwood Chemical Pulping System, Type: Hardwood
  Roundwood DEOP
  Chemical Recovery Equipment:
  Evaporator lines: 1
  Recovery boilers: 1
  Lime Kiln
  Pulp Dryers:
  Pulp Dryers 1
Energy Data:

Vietnam

Power boilers: 1
Steam turbines: 1
Electrical demand for mill: 285 MWh/D

ⓘⓜVietnam Paper Corporation (Vinapaco)-Bai Bang Paper
Bai Bang Paper
Ownership: Vietnam Paper Corporation (Vinapaco), DEVYT
Tam Vong Park, Phong Châu Town
Phu Ninh District, Phú Tho Province
Vietnam
  Phone: (84) 210 3829 755/3762 556
  Fax: (84) 210 3829 177/3827 052
  Email: bapacopn@hn.vnn.vn
  Web Address: vinapaco.com.vn
Personnel:
  Mat. Mgr.: Mr. Dao Van Hai
  Phone: (84) 210 3829755/5235
  Qlty. Mgr.: Mrs. Chu Thi Viet
  Phone: (84) 210 3829755/5252
  Dir. of Pulp Mill: Mr. Nguyen Tran Thuan
  Phone: (84) 210 3829755/5106
  Dir. of Power Plant: Mr. Nguyen Que Son
  Phone: (84) 210 3829755/5275
  Dir. of Chemical Plant: Mr. Nguyen Ngoc An
  Phone: (84) 210 3829755/5232
Total Employees at this Location: 1,957
Type of Operation: Pulp mill, Paper mill
Pulp Grades and Capacities:
  Total pulp capacity: 80,127 mt/y
  Chemical Pulp: 57,913 mt/y
  Other Pulp: 22,213 mt/y
Pulp Mill Data:
  Chemical Pulping Systems:
  Batch digesters: 4
  Pulp Lines: 1
  Bleach Plant Systems: 1
  No. 1 Capacity 71,000 admt/y
  Chemical Recovery Equipment:
  Evaporator lines: 1
  Recovery boilers: 1
Paper/Paperboard Grades and Capacities:
  Total paper and paperboard capacity: 149,940 mt/y
  Newsprint: 49,980 mt/y
  Uncoated woodfree/freesheet: 99,960 mt/y
Paper and Paperboard Mill Data:
  Stock Preparation:
  Pulpers: 3
  Refiners: 16
Paper Machines: 3
  No. 1, Periformer, total capacity 39,984 mt/y, Trim width 3.8 m, Uncoated woodfree/freesheet
  No. 2, top former, total capacity 59,976 mt/y, Trim width 3.8 m, Uncoated woodfree/freesheet
  No. 3, fourdrinier, total capacity 49,980 mt/y, Newsprint
Finishing Equipment:
  Winders: 1
  Calenders: 1
  Supercalenders: 2
  Rewinders: 2
  Sheeters: 2
Energy Data:
Power boilers: 1
Steam turbines: 2 at 28 MW
Electrical demand for mill: 305 MWh/D

ⓜBai Bang Paper Joint-stock Co., Ltd.
Ky Son Mill
Ownership: Vietnam Paper Corporation (Vinapaco)
Dan Ha Ward
Ky Son, Hoa Binh Province
Vietnam
  Phone: (84) 18 3842191
Personnel:
  Dir.: Mr. Tran Ngoc Que
  Phone: (84) 913 283145
Total Employees at this Location: 293

Type of Operation: Pulp mill
Pulp Grades and Capacities:
  Total pulp capacity: 19,099 mt/y
  Recycled Pulping: 10,751 mt/y
  Other Pulp: 8,348 mt/y
Pulp Mill Data:
  Chemical Pulping Systems:
  Batch digesters
  Bleach Plant Systems: 2
  Chemical Pulping System, Type: Straw
  Recycled Pulping System
  Chemical Recovery Equipment:
  Evaporator lines: 1
  Recovery boilers: 1
  Recycled Fiber Treatment Lines:
  Flotation deinking lines
Paper/Paperboard Grades and Capacities:
  Total paper and paperboard capacity: 50,000 mt/y
  Newsprint: 11,000 mt/y
  Uncoated woodfree/freesheet: 39,000 mt/y
Paper and Paperboard Mill Data:
Paper Machines: 1
  No. 1, fourdrinier, total capacity 50,000 mt/y, Trim width 3.8 m, Uncoated woodfree/freesheet, Newsprint
Energy Data:
Power boilers
Electrical demand for mill: 119 MWh/D

ⓘBinh Minh Paper Company
Ownership: private owner
Ha Giang Village, Phu Lam Ward
Tien Du, Bac Ninh Province
Vietnam
  Phone: (84) 241 3837917
  Fax: (84) 241 3838942
Mill Locations:
Binh Minh Paper Company, Tien Du Mill, Ha Giang Village, Phu Lam Ward, Tien Du, Vietnam, Capacity: 17,000 mt/y, (Pulp mill, Paper mill)
  Phone: (84) 241 3837917
  Fax: (84) 241 3838942

ⓜBinh Minh Paper Company
Tien Du Mill
Ha Giang Village, Phu Lam Ward
Tien Du, Bac Ninh Province
Vietnam
  Phone: (84) 241 3837917
  Fax: (84) 241 3838942
Personnel:
  Dir.: Mr. Dinh Binh Nguyen
  Phone: (84) 241 3837917
  Dpty. Mgr.: Mr. Dinh Tu Nguyen
  Phone: (84) 241 3837917
  Dpty. Mgr.: Trong Kieu Nguyen
  Phone: (84) 241 3837917
Total Employees at this Location: 80
Type of Operation: Pulp mill, Paper mill
Pulp Grades and Capacities:
  Total pulp capacity: 1,000 mt/y
Paper/Paperboard Grades and Capacities:
  Total paper and paperboard capacity: 17,000 mt/y
  Uncoated woodfree/freesheet: 7,000 mt/y
  Packaging papers: 10,000 mt/y

ⓜCheng Yang Paper Mill Co., Ltd.
Ben Cat Dist. (Cheng Yang Paper) Mill
Ownership: 60% by Guangdong Dongguan Nine Dragons Paper Industries Co., Ltd., 40% by Taiwan investors
D 15, My Phuoc Industrial Park
Ben Cat Dist., Binh Duong Province
Vietnam
  Phone: (84) 650 3558006-8
  Fax: (84) 650 3558009
Total Employees at this Location: 210
Type of Operation: Paperboard mill
Pulp Grades and Capacities:

Total pulp capacity: 107,162 mt/y
Recycled Pulping: 107,162 mt/y
Pulp Mill Data:
  Recycled Fiber Treatment Lines:
  Recycled packaging pulping lines at 100,000 admt/y
Paper/Paperboard Grades and Capacities:
  Total paper and paperboard capacity: 108,000 mt/y
  Linerboard: 75,600 mt/y
  Corrugating medium/fluting: 32,400 mt/y
Paper and Paperboard Mill Data:
Paper Machines: 1
  No. 1, fourdrinier (3), total capacity 108,000 mt/y, Trim width 3.3 m, Linerboard, Corrugating medium/fluting
Energy Data:
Power boilers: 3
Electrical demand for mill: 132 MWh/D

ⓘDiana Paper
Vinh Tuy Industrial Zone, Linh Nam Street
Hanoi
Vietnam
  Phone: (84) 4 3644 5758
  Fax: (84) 4 3644 5777
  Email: daina@hn.vnn.vn,
  infir@diana.com
  Web Address: www.diana.com.vn
Mill Locations:
Diana Paper, Tien Du Mill, Tan Chi Industrial zone, Tien Du, Vietnam, Capacity: 20,000 mt/y, (Paper mill)
  Phone: (84) 241 372 1666
  Fax: (84) 4 3644 5777

ⓜDiana Paper
Tien Du Mill
Tan Chi Industrial zone
Tien Du, Bac Ninh Province
Vietnam
  Phone: (84) 241 372 1666
  Fax: (84) 4 3644 5777
  Web Address: www.diana.com.vn
Total Employees at this Location: 124
Type of Operation: Paper mill
Pulp Mill Data:
  Bleach Plant Systems: 1
  DIP
  Recycled Fiber Treatment Lines:
  Flotation deinking lines: 1
Paper/Paperboard Grades and Capacities:
  Total paper and paperboard capacity: 20,000 mt/y
  Tissue: 20,000 mt/y
Paper and Paperboard Mill Data:
Paper Machines: 1
  No. 1, (started up July 2010), total capacity 20,000 mt/y, Tissue
Energy Data:
Power boilers

ⓜGlatz Finepaper Vietnam Co. Ltd.
Ho Chi Minh City Mill
Ownership: Julius Glatz GmbH Papierfabriken
No. 8 Dan Chu Street, V.S.I.P II, Hoa Phu
Thu Dau Mot, Binh Duong Province
Vietnam
  Phone: (84) 650 358 9558
  Web Address: www.glatz.de
Type of Operation: Paper mill
Paper/Paperboard Grades and Capacities:
  Total paper and paperboard capacity: 12,000 mt/y
  Specialty and industrial: 12,000 mt/y
Paper and Paperboard Mill Data:
Paper Machines: 1
  No. 1, (started March 2010), fourdrinier, total capacity 12,000 mt/y, Trim width 3.9 m, Specialty and industrial

ⓜHai Ha Pulp Mill
Bac Quang Dist. Mill
Ownership: 100% by Hai Phong Paper Joint-Stock Co. (Hapaco)

Vietnam

Vinh Tuy Ward
Bac Quang Dist., Ha Giang Province
Vietnam
  Phone: (84) 19 3824663
  Fax: (84) 19 3824663
  Web Address: www.hapaco.vn
Total Employees at this Location: 300
Type of Operation: Pulp mill
Pulp Grades and Capacities:
  Total pulp capacity: 32,000 mt/y
  Chemical Pulp: 32,000 mt/y
Pulp Mill Data:
Pulp Lines: 1

Hai Phong Paper Joint-Stock Co. (Hapaco)
Hai Phong City Mill
Ownership: joint stock
441A Ton Duc Thang Street
Hai Phong City
Vietnam
  Phone: (84) 31 3853369/3835538/397
  Fax: (84) 31 3835462/701014
  Email: hapaco@hn.vnn.vn
Personnel:
  Gen. Dir/Chmn. of BOM: Dr. Vu Duong Hien
  Phone: (84) 31 3853538
  Fax: (84) 31 3853462
  V. Chmn. of BOM: Mr. Vu Van Chung
  Phone: (84) 31 3853369/3835538/397
  V. Chmn. of BOM: Mr. Vu Xuan Thuy
  Phone: (84) 31 3853369/3835538/397
  Dpty. Gen. Dir.: Mr. Vu Xuan Thinh
  Phone: (84) 31 3853369/3835538/397
  Dpty. Gen. Dir.: Mr. Hoang Xuan Truyen
  Phone: (84) 31 3853369/3835538/397
  Dpty. Gen. Dir.: Mr. Van Buon Pham
  Phone: (84) 31 3853369/3835538/397
Total Employees at this Location: 700
Type of Operation: Pulp mill, Paper mill
Mill Locations:
Hai Ha Pulp Mill, Bac Quang Dist. Mill, Vinh Tuy Ward, Bac Quang Dist., Vietnam, (Pulp mill)
  Phone: (84) 19 3824663
  Fax: (84) 19 3824663
Hai Phong Paper Mill, Hai Phong City Mill, Road n° 5 Industrial Park, Dai Ban Ward, Hai Phong City, Vietnam, Capacity: 25,000 mt/y, (Paper mill)
Hapaco Joss Paper Mill, Tran Yen District Mill, Tran Yen District, Vietnam, Capacity: 2,000 mt/y, (Paper mill)
Hapaco Paper Mill, Van Ban District Mill, Van Ban District, Vietnam, Capacity: 4,000 mt/y, (Paper mill)
Hapaco Pulp Mill, Mai Chau District Mill, Van Mai Ward, Mai Chau District, Vietnam, Capacity: 9,000 mt/y, (Pulp mill, Paper mill)
Hoa Binh Pulp Mill, Ky Son Dist. Mill, Ky Son Dist., Vietnam, Capacity: 12,500 mt/y, (Pulp mill, Paper mill)
Yen Son Joint-Stock Co., Yen Bai Town Mill, 638 Dien Bien Road, Yen Bai Town, Vietnam, Capacity: 13,000 mt/y, (Pulp mill, Paper mill)
  Phone: (84) 29 3851982/4491/2026
  Fax: (84) 29 3855555
  Email: yensonco@hn.vnn.vn
Pulp Grades and Capacities:
  Total pulp capacity: 5,200 mt/y
Paper/Paperboard Grades and Capacities:
  Total paper and paperboard capacity: 5,000 mt/y
  Tissue: 5,000 mt/y
Paper and Paperboard Mill Data:
Paper Machines: 1
PM 1, total capacity 5,000 mt/y, Trim width 1.58 m, Tissue

Hai Phong Paper Mill
Hai Phong City Mill
Ownership: 100% by Hai Phong Paper Joint-Stock Co. (Hapaco)
Road n° 5 Industrial Park, Dai Ban Ward
Hai Phong City, Hong Bang District
Vietnam
Personnel:
  Dir.: Mr. Xuan Cuong Vu
Total Employees at this Location: 190
Type of Operation: Paper mill
Pulp Grades and Capacities:
  Total pulp capacity: 22,203 mt/y
  Recycled Pulping: 22,203 mt/y
Pulp Mill Data:
  Bleach Plant Lines:
  DIP
  Recycled Fiber Treatment Lines:
  Flotation deinking lines: 1
  Recycled packaging pulping lines: 1
Paper/Paperboard Grades and Capacities:
  Total paper and paperboard capacity: 25,000 mt/y
  Boxboard/cartonboard: 25,000 mt/y
Paper and Paperboard Mill Data:
Paper Machines: 1
No. 1, multi-cylinder, total capacity 25,000 mt/y, Trim width 2.85 m, Boxboard/cartonboard
Coating Machines: 1
PM 1, on machine
Energy Data:
Power boilers
Electrical demand for mill: 47 MWh/D

Halong Trading Company
Ownership: 100% by Government of Vietnam, People Committee of Quang Ninh Province
162 Le Thanh Tong Street
Ha Long City, Quang Ninh Province
Vietnam
  Phone: (84) 33 3828024/26
  Fax: (84) 33 3828025
Mill Locations:
Halong Trading Company, Tien Yen District Mill, Tien Yen District, Vietnam, Capacity: 5,200 mt/y, (Paper mill)
  Phone: (84) 33 3828024/26
  Fax: (84) 33 3828025

Halong Trading Company
Tien Yen District Mill
Ownership: Halong Trading Company
Tien Yen District, Quang Ninh Province
Vietnam
  Phone: (84) 33 3828024/26
  Fax: (84) 33 3828025
Personnel:
  Dir.: Mr. Pham Van Trinh
  Phone: (84) 33 3828024/26
  Dpty. Dir.: Mr. Pham Van Bay
  Phone: (84) 33 3876319
Total Employees at this Location: 230
Type of Operation: Paper mill
Pulp Grades and Capacities:
  Total pulp capacity: 12,000 mt/y
Pulp Mill Data:
Pulp Lines: 5
Paper/Paperboard Grades and Capacities:
  Total paper and paperboard capacity: 5,200 mt/y
  Specialty and industrial: 5,200 mt/y
Paper and Paperboard Mill Data:
Paper Machines: 5
PM 1, total capacity 1,000 mt/y, Specialty and industrial
PM 2, total capacity 1,000 mt/y, Specialty and industrial
PM 3, total capacity 200 mt/y, Specialty and industrial
PM 4, total capacity 1,500 mt/y, Specialty and industrial
PM 5, total capacity 1,500 mt/y, Specialty and industrial

Hapaco Joss Paper Mill
Tran Yen District Mill
Ownership: 100% by Hai Phong Paper Joint-Stock Co. (Hapaco)
Tran Yen District, Yen Bai Province
Vietnam
Total Employees at this Location: 55
Type of Operation: Paper mill
Paper/Paperboard Grades and Capacities:
  Total paper and paperboard capacity: 2,000 mt/y
  Specialty and industrial: 2,000 mt/y

Hapaco Paper Mill
Van Ban District Mill
Ownership: Hai Phong Paper Joint-Stock Co. (Hapaco)
Van Ban District, Lao Cai Province
Vietnam
Personnel:
  Dir.: Mr. Ba Lang Nguyen
Total Employees at this Location: 110
Type of Operation: Paper mill
Paper/Paperboard Grades and Capacities:
  Total paper and paperboard capacity: 4,000 mt/y
  Specialty and industrial: 4,000 mt/y

Hapaco Pulp Mill
Mai Chau District Mill
Ownership: 100% by Hai Phong Paper Joint-Stock Co. (Hapaco)
Van Mai Ward
Mai Chau District, Hoa Binh Province
Vietnam
Personnel:
  Dir.: Mr. Van Huong Nguyen
Total Employees at this Location: 150
Type of Operation: Pulp mill, Paper mill
Paper/Paperboard Grades and Capacities:
  Total paper and paperboard capacity: 9,000 mt/y
  Specialty and industrial: 9,000 mt/y

Hoa Binh Pulp Mill
Ky Son Dist. Mill
Ownership: 100% by Hai Phong Paper Joint-Stock Co. (Hapaco)
Ky Son Dist., Hoa Binh Province
Vietnam
  Phone: (84) 18 3867812
  Fax: (84) 18 3868350
Personnel:
  Dir.: Nguyen Van Huong
  Phone: (84) 18 3867812
Total Employees at this Location: 162
Type of Operation: Pulp mill, Paper mill
Pulp Grades and Capacities:
  Total pulp capacity: 12,500 mt/y
Paper/Paperboard Grades and Capacities:
  Total paper and paperboard capacity: 12,500 mt/y

Hoang Van Thu Paper Joint Stock Company
Thai Nguyen City Mill
Ownership: Vietnam Paper Corporation (Vinapaco)
Quan Trieu Ward
Thai Nguyen City, Thai Nguyen Province
Vietnam
  Phone: (84) 280 3844 652
  Fax: (84) 280 3844 548
Personnel:
  Chmn./Gen. Dir.: Mr. Chu Hien Du
  Phone: (84) 912 908757
  Dpty. Dir.: Mrs. Nguyen Viet Hong
  Phone: (84) 280 844170
  Dpty. Gen. Dir.: Mr. Ho Anh Tu
  Phone: (84) 280 3844 652
  Dpty. Gen. Dir.: Mr. Vu Thai Son
  Phone: (84) 280 3844 652
Total Employees at this Location: 280
Type of Operation: Paper mill
Paper/Paperboard Grades and Capacities:
  Total paper and paperboard capacity: 20,000 mt/y
  Packaging papers: 3,000 mt/y
  Linerboard: 15,000 mt/y

Vietnam

Corrugating medium/fluting: 2,000 mt/y
Paper and Paperboard Mill Data:
 Stock Preparation:
  Pulpers: 4
  Refiners: 12
Paper Machines: 4
 PM 1, cylinder, total capacity 1,500 mt/y, Packaging papers
 PM 2, cylinder, total capacity 1,500 mt/y, Packaging papers
 PM 3, cylinder, total capacity 2,000 mt/y, Corrugating medium/fluting
 PM 4, cylinder, total capacity 15,000 mt/y, Linerboard
Finishing Equipment:
 Supercalenders: 1 at 15,000 mt/y
 Rewinders: 1 at 15,000 mt/y
 Sheeters: 1
Energy Data:
 Power boilers: 3

ⓂLam Son Paper Joint-Stock Company
Nong Cong Mill
Van Thang Ward
Nong Cong District, Thanh Hoa Province
Vietnam
 Phone: (84) 37 3851461
 Fax: (84) 37 3854 323
Total Employees at this Location: 400
Type of Operation: Pulp mill, Paper mill
Pulp Grades and Capacities:
 Total pulp capacity: 4,000 mt/y
Pulp Mill Data:
 Chemical Pulping Systems:
 Batch digesters
Paper/Paperboard Grades and Capacities:
 Total paper and paperboard capacity: 17,000 mt/y
 Linerboard: 12,000 mt/y
 Corrugating medium/fluting: 5,000 mt/y

ⓘLam Son Paper Joint-Stock Company
Ownership: 30% by Govt. of Vietnam
Van Thang Ward
Nong Cong District, Thanh Hoa Province
Vietnam
 Phone: (84) 37 3851461
 Fax: (84) 37 3854 323
Mill Locations:
Lam Son Paper Joint-Stock Company, Nong Cong Mill, Van Thang Ward, Nong Cong District, Vietnam, Capacity: 17,000 mt/y, (Pulp mill, Paper mill)
 Phone: (84) 37 3851461
 Fax: (84) 37 3854 323

ⓘLinh Xuan Paper Joint-Stock Co.
Ho Chi Minh City Mill
34 Road No. 9, Quarter No. 5, Linh Xuan Ward
Thu Duc District, Ho Chi Minh City, Binh Duong Province
Vietnam
 Phone: (84) 8 372 40744
 Fax: (84) 8 372 40512
 Email: linhxuanpaper@vnn.vn
 Web Address: www.linhxuanpaper.com
Personnel:
 Chmn. of the Bd. & Gen. Dir.: Mrs. Thi Thuy Nguyen
 Phone: (84) 8 37240744/38889696
 Dir.: Mr. Van Ngoan Tong
 Phone: (84) 8 7241153
 Dpty. Dir.: Mr. Phuong Cao Minh
 Phone: (84) 8 37240744/38889696
Total Employees at this Location: 130
Type of Operation: Paper mill
Pulp Mill Data:
 Recycled Fiber Treatment Lines:
 Flotation deinking lines: 1 at 3,000 admt/y
 Recycled packaging pulping lines: 1 at 20,000 admt/y
Paper/Paperboard Grades and Capacities:
 Total paper and paperboard capacity: 18,000 mt/y
 Tissue: 3,000 mt/y
 Linerboard: 15,000 mt/y
Paper and Paperboard Mill Data:
Paper Machines:
 No. 1, cylinder, total capacity 600 mt/y, Tissue
 No. 2, cylinder, total capacity 600 mt/y, Tissue
 No. 3, cylinder, total capacity 15,000 mt/y, Trim width 2.6 m, Linerboard
 No. 4, cylinder, total capacity 1,800 mt/y, Tissue

ⓘLinh Xuan Paper Joint-Stock Co.
Ownership: 100% by Joint-Stock
34 Road No. 9, Quarter No. 5, Linh Xuan Ward
Thu Duc District, Ho Chi Minh
Vietnam
 Phone: (84) 8 372 40744
 Fax: (84) 8 372 40512
 Email: linhxuanpaper@vnn.vn
 Web Address: www.linhxuanpaper.com
Personnel:
 Chmn. of the Bd. & Gen. Dir.: Thi Thuy Nguyen
 Phone: (84) 8 37240744/38889696
 Fax: (84) 8 37240512
 Dir.: Van Ngoan Tong
 Phone: (84) 8 37240744/38889696
 Fax: (84) 8 37240512
 Dpty. Dir.: Phuong Cao Minh
 Phone: (84) 8 37240744/38889696
 Fax: (84) 8 37240512
Total Employees of Company: 130
Mill Locations:
Linh Xuan Paper Joint-Stock Co., Ho Chi Minh City Mill, 34 Road No. 9, Quarter No. 5, Linh Xuan Ward, Thu Duc District, Ho Chi Minh City, Vietnam, Capacity: 18,000 mt/y, (Paper mill)
 Phone: (84) 8 372 40744
 Fax: (84) 8 372 40512
 Email: linhxuanpaper@vnn.vn

ⓂLua Viet Paper Joint-Stock Co.
Ha Hoa District Mill
Ha Hoa Town
Ha Hoa District, Phú Tho Province
Vietnam
 Phone: (84) 210 3883117
 Fax: (84) 210 3833120
Personnel:
 Chmn.: Mr. Van Ly Nguyen
 Phone: (84) 210 3883969
 Dir.: Mr. Vu Nguyen Dat
 Phone: (84) 210 3883359
Total Employees at this Location: 250
Type of Operation: Pulp mill, Paper mill
Pulp Grades and Capacities:
 Total pulp capacity: 5,000 mt/y
Pulp Mill Data:
 Chemical Pulping Systems:
 Batch digesters: 6
Paper/Paperboard Grades and Capacities:
 Total paper and paperboard capacity: 5,000 mt/y
 Tissue: 1,000 mt/y
 Packaging papers: 4,000 mt/y
Paper and Paperboard Mill Data:
Paper Machines: 3
 PM 1, cylinder, total capacity 1,500 mt/y, Packaging papers
 PM 2, cylinder, total capacity 2,500 mt/y, Packaging papers
 PM 3, cylinder, total capacity 1,000 mt/y, Tissue

ⓘLua Viet Paper Joint-Stock Co.
Ha Hoa Town
Ha Hoa District
Vietnam
 Phone: (84) 210 3883117
 Fax: (84) 210 3833120
Personnel:
 Chmn.: Van Ly Nguyen
 Phone: (84) 210 3883117
 Fax: (84) 210 3833120
 Dir.: Vu Nguyen Dat
 Phone: (84) 210 3883117
 Fax: (84) 210 3833120
Total Employees at this Location: 250
Mill Locations:
Lua Viet Paper Joint-Stock Co., Ha Hoa District Mill, Ha Hoa Town, Ha Hoa District, Vietnam, Capacity: 5,000 mt/y, (Pulp mill, Paper mill)
 Phone: (84) 210 3883117
 Fax: (84) 210 3833120

ⓂMai Lan Paper Joint-Stock Company
Tan Binh Mill
129 Au Co Str., Ward 13
Tan Binh, Ho Chi Minh City
Vietnam
 Phone: (84) 8 38496102/5953
 Fax: (84) 8 38425594
 Email: mailanpaper@hcm.vnn.vn
Personnel:
 Dir.: Mr. Bui Quang Man
 Phone: (84) 8 38496102/5953
Total Employees at this Location: 120
Type of Operation: Paper mill
Paper/Paperboard Grades and Capacities:
 Total paper and paperboard capacity: 2,000 mt/y
 Tissue: 2,000 mt/y
Paper and Paperboard Mill Data:
Paper Machines: 1
 No. 1, Trim width 1.3 m, Tissue

ⓘMai Lan Paper Joint-Stock Company
129 Au Co Str., Ward 13
Tan Binh
Vietnam
 Phone: (84) 8 38496102/5953
 Fax: (84) 8 38425594
 Email: mailanpaper@hcm.vnn.vn
Personnel:
 Dir.: Bui Quang Man
 Phone: (84) 8 38496102/5953
 Fax: (84) 8 38425594
Total Employees at this Location: 120
Mill Locations:
Mai Lan Paper Joint-Stock Company, Tan Binh Mill, 129 Au Co Str., Ward 13, Tan Binh, Vietnam, Capacity: 2,000 mt/y, (Paper mill)
 Phone: (84) 8 38496102/5953
 Fax: (84) 8 38425594
 Email: mailanpaper@hcm.vnn.vn

ⓘMien Tay Packing Co. Ltd.
Ownership: private owner
84 Mau Than Street
Can Tho City
Vietnam
 Phone: (84) 71 3899299
 Fax: (84) 71 3894525
 Email: baobimientay-pvt@hcm.vnn.vn
Personnel:
 Dir.: Quang Thuan Phan
 Phone: (84) 71 3899299
 Fax: (84) 71 3894525
Total Employees at this Location: 150
Mill Locations:
Mien Tay Packing Co. Ltd., Can Tho City Mill, 84 Mau Than Street, Can Tho City, Vietnam, Capacity: 5,000 mt/y, (Paper mill)
 Phone: (84) 71 3899299
 Fax: (84) 71 3894525
 Email: baobimientay-pvt@hcm.vnn.vn

ⓂMien Tay Packing Co. Ltd.
Can Tho City Mill
84 Mau Than Street
Can Tho City
Vietnam

Phone: (84) 71 3899299
Fax: (84) 71 3894525
Email: baobimientay-pvt@hcm.vnn.vn
Personnel:
Dir.: Mr. Quang Thuan Phan
Phone: (84) 71 3899299
Total Employees at this Location: 150
Type of Operation: Paper mill
Paper/Paperboard Grades and Capacities:
Total paper and paperboard capacity: 5,000 mt/y
Packaging papers: 5,000 mt/y
Paper and Paperboard Mill Data:
Paper Machines: 2
PM 1, total capacity 2,000 mt/y, Trim width 1.58 m, Packaging papers
PM 2, total capacity 3,000 mt/y, Trim width 1.58 m, Packaging papers

ⓂMuc Son Paper Paper Joint-Stock Co.
Tho Xuan Mill
Muc Son Ward
Tho Xuan District, Thanh Hoa Province
Vietnam
Phone: (84) 37 3834074/69
Fax: (84) 37 3834099
Personnel:
Dir.: Trinh Ngoc Ha
Phone: (84) 903 21 9714
Total Employees at this Location: 310
Type of Operation: Pulp mill, Paper mill
Pulp Grades and Capacities:
Total pulp capacity: 16,000 mt/y
Paper/Paperboard Grades and Capacities:
Total paper and paperboard capacity: 15,000 mt/y
Linerboard: 15,000 mt/y
Paper and Paperboard Mill Data:
Paper Machines: 3
No. 1, Linerboard
No. 2, Linerboard
No. 3, Linerboard

ⓂMuc Son Paper Paper Joint-Stock Co.
Muc Son Ward
Tho Xuan District
Vietnam
Phone: (84) 37 3834074/69
Fax: (84) 37 3834099
Personnel:
Dir.: Trinh Ngoc Ha
Phone: (84) 37 3834074/69
Fax: (84) 37 3834099
Total Employees at this Location: 310
Mill Locations:
Muc Son Paper Paper Joint-Stock Co., Tho Xuan Mill, Muc Son Ward, Tho Xuan District, Vietnam, Capacity: 15,000 mt/y, (Pulp mill, Paper mill)
Phone: (84) 37 3834074/69
Fax: (84) 37 3834099

ⓂMy Huong Paper Joint-stock Co.
Hai Phong Mill
110 To Hieu Street, Le Chan Dist
Hai Phong City
Vietnam
Phone: (84) 31 3840056
Type of Operation: Paperboard mill
Paper/Paperboard Grades and Capacities:
Total paper and paperboard capacity: 45,000 mt/y
Containerboard: 45,000 mt/y
Linerboard
Corrugating medium/fluting
Paper and Paperboard Mill Data:
Paper Machines: 1
PM 1, (started up May 2010), total capacity 45,000 mt/y
Energy Data:
HRSG boiler: 2

ⓂNew Toyo Pulppy (Vietnam) Co., Ltd.
Thuan An District Mill
Ownership: New Toyo Pulppy (Hong Kong) Limited
8-VSIP, Str. 6, Vietnam-Singapore Industrial Park
Thuan An District, Binh Duong Province
Vietnam
Phone: (84) 650 374 3750
Fax: (84) 650 374 3754
Email: customerservice@pulppy.com
Web Address: www.pulppy.com
Total Employees at this Location: 195
Type of Operation: Paper mill
Pulp Grades and Capacities:
Total pulp capacity: 26,478 mt/y
Recycled Pulping: 26,478 mt/y
Pulp Mill Data:
Bleach Plant Systems: 1
DIP
Recycled Fiber Treatment Lines:
Flotation deinking lines: 1
Paper/Paperboard Grades and Capacities:
Total paper and paperboard capacity: 35,000 mt/y
Tissue: 35,000 mt/y
Paper and Paperboard Mill Data:
Paper Machines: 2
No. 1, (Supplier: San-Ei.), total capacity 17,500 mt/y, Trim width 3.3 m, Tissue, Uncoated woodfree/freesheet
No. 2, (Supplier: San-Ei.), total capacity 17,500 mt/y, Trim width 3.3 m, Tissue, Uncoated woodfree/freesheet
Energy Data:
Power boilers
Electrical demand for mill: 79 MWh/D

ⓂPham Thu Processing and Trading Co., Ltd
Ho Chi Minh City Mill
14/6 Thoi Tay Village, Tan Hiep Ward, Hoc Mon District
Ho Chi Minh City, Binh Duong Province
Vietnam
Phone: (84) 8 37100405/05044/45
Fax: (84) 8 37100406
Email: phamthuco-ltd@hcm.vnn.vn
Personnel:
Dir.: Mr. Pham Thu Nguyen
Phone: (84) 8 387105139
Fax: (84) 8 37100406
Dpty. Gen. Dir., Accounting & Finan.: Mrs. Suong Pham Thi Minh
Phone: (84) 8 37100405/05044/45
Man. Dir.: Son Lam Tuan Buu
Phone: (84) 8 37100405/05044/45
Eng. Mgr.: Khoa Huynh
Phone: (84) 8 37100405/05044/45
Mill Mgr.: De Ton Kinh
Phone: (84) 8 37100405/05044/45
Asst. Mill Mgr.: Phat Le Xuan
Phone: (84) 8 37100405/05044/45
Total Employees at this Location: 86
Type of Operation: Paper mill
Paper/Paperboard Grades and Capacities:
Total paper and paperboard capacity: 5,400 mt/y
Linerboard: 1,800 mt/y
Corrugating medium/fluting: 3,600 mt/y
Paper and Paperboard Mill Data:
Stock Preparation:
Pulpers: 2
Refiners: 4
Paper Machines: 2
PM 1, cylinder, total capacity 3,000 mt/y, Trim width 1.7 m, Linerboard, Corrugating medium/fluting
PM 2, cylinder, total capacity 2,400 mt/y, Trim width 1.4 m, Linerboard, Corrugating medium/fluting
Finishing Equipment:
Rewinders: 2 at 6,000 mt/y
Energy Data:
Power boilers: 2

ⓂPham Thu Processing and Trading Co., Ltd
Ownership: 100% by shareholding company
14/6 Thoi Tay Village, Tan Hiep Ward, Hoc Mon District
Ho Chi Minh City
Vietnam
Phone: (84) 8 37100405/05044/45
Fax: (84) 8 37100406
Email: phamthuco-ltd@hcm.vnn.vn
Personnel:
Dir.: Pham Thu Nguyen
Phone: (84) 8 37100405/05044/45
Fax: (84) 8 37100406
Man. Dir.: Son Lam Tuan Buu
Phone: (84) 8 37100405/05044/45
Fax: (84) 8 37100406
Dpty. Gen. Dir., Accounting & Finan.: Suong Pham Thi Minh
Phone: (84) 8 37100405/05044/45
Fax: (84) 8 37100406
Total Employees at this Location: 86
Mill Locations:
Pham Thu Processing and Trading Co., Ltd, Ho Chi Minh City Mill, 14/6 Thoi Tay Village, Tan Hiep Ward, Hoc Mon District, Ho Chi Minh City, Vietnam, Capacity: 5,400 mt/y, (Paper mill)
Phone: (84) 8 37100405/05044/45
Fax: (84) 8 37100406
Email: phamthuco-ltd@hcm.vnn.vn

ⓂPhu Giang Paper and Packaging Co., Ltd.
Tien Du Mill
Tam Tao, Phu Lam
Tien Du, Bac Ninh Province
Vietnam
Phone: (84) 241 3838 087 - 387 1999
Fax: (84) 241 387 1555 - 3838 270
Email: admin@phugiang.com.vn, phugiang-co@hn.vnn.vn
Web Address: phugiang.com.vn
Personnel:
Dir.: Mr. Nguyen Nhan Phuong
Phone: (84) 241 383 8087
Fax: (84) 241 387 1555
Total Employees at this Location: 400
Type of Operation: Paper mill
Paper/Paperboard Grades and Capacities:
Total paper and paperboard capacity: 32,500 mt/y
Linerboard: 8,500 mt/y
Corrugating medium/fluting: 24,000 mt/y
Paper and Paperboard Mill Data:
Paper Machines: 5
No. 1, cylinder, total capacity 4,000 mt/y, Corrugating medium/fluting
No. 2, cylinder, total capacity 2,500 mt/y, Linerboard
No. 3, cylinder, total capacity 3,000 mt/y, Linerboard
No. 4, cylinder, total capacity 4,000 mt/y, Corrugating medium/fluting
No. 5, total capacity 20,000 mt/y

ⓂPhu Giang Paper and Packaging Co., Ltd.
Tam Tao, Phu Lam
Tien Du
Vietnam
Phone: (84) 241 383 8087 - 387 1999
Fax: (84) 241 387 1555 - 383 7270
Email: admin@phugiang.com.vn, phugiang-co@hn.vnn.vn
Web Address: phugiang.com.vn
Personnel:
Dir., Mill Mgr.: Nguyen Nhan Phuong
Phone: (84) 241 383 8087
Fax: (84) 241 387 1555
Total Employees of Company: 400
Mill Locations:
Phu Giang Paper and Packaging Co., Ltd., Tien Du Mill, Tam Tao, Phu Lam, Tien Du, Vietnam, Capacity: 32,500 mt/y, (Paper mill)

Vietnam

Phone: (84) 241 3838 087 - 387 1999
Fax: (84) 241 387 1555 - 3838 270
Email: admin@phugiang.com.vn, phugiang-co@hn.vnn.vn

Phu Thinh Paper Co., Ltd.
1/166 A Nguyen Van Qua Road, Dong Hung Thuan Ward, District No. 12
Ho Chi Minh City
Vietnam
  Phone: (84) 8 37190584
  Fax: (84) 8 37190409
Personnel:
  Chmn. of Bd., Dir.: Huynh Van Duyen
  Phone: (84) 8 37190584
  Fax: (84) 8 37190409
  Dpty. Dir.: Lam PhuocThanh
  Phone: (84) 8 37190584
  Fax: (84) 8 37190409
Total Employees at this Location: 81
Mill Locations:
  Phu Thinh Paper Co., Ltd., Ho Chi Minh City Mill, 1/166 A Nguyen Van Qua Road, Dong Hung Thuan Ward, District No. 12, Ho Chi Minh City, Vietnam, Capacity: 13,600 mt/y, (Paperboard mill)
  Phone: (84) 8 37190584
  Fax: (84) 8 37190409

Phu Thinh Paper Co., Ltd.
Ho Chi Minh City Mill
1/166 A Nguyen Van Qua Road, Dong Hung Thuan Ward, District No. 12
Ho Chi Minh City, Binh Duong Province
Vietnam
  Phone: (84) 8 37190584
  Fax: (84) 8 37190409
Personnel:
  Chmn. of BOM, Dir.: Huynh Van Duyen
  Phone: (84) 8 37190584
  Dpty. Dir.: Lam PhuocThanh
  Phone: (84) 8 37190584
Total Employees at this Location: 81
Type of Operation: Paperboard mill
Paper/Paperboard Grades and Capacities:
  Total paper and paperboard capacity: 13,600 mt/y
  Corrugating medium/fluting: 13,600 mt/y
Paper and Paperboard Mill Data:
Paper Machines: 3
No. 1, fourdrinier, total capacity 3,000 mt/y, Trim width 1.25 m, Corrugating medium/fluting
No. 2, cylinder, total capacity 3,600 mt/y, Trim width 1.7 m, Corrugating medium/fluting
No. 3, cylinder, total capacity 7,000 mt/y, Trim width 2.45 m, Corrugating medium/fluting

Phuong Nam Kenaf Pulp Mill and Paper Company
Phuong Nam Mill
Mill is closed (operations were suspended in 2009, went back into service in 2012, closed again in mid-2013, closed permanently in May 2014)
Ownership: Vietnam Paper Corporation (Vinapaco)
Ba Luong hamlet, Thuan Nghia Hoa commune
Phuong Nam, Long An
Vietnam
  Web Address: phuongnampaper.com
Type of Operation: Pulp mill
Pulp Grades and Capacities:
  Total pulp capacity: 100,000 mt/y
  Pulp available for market: 100,000 mt/y
Pulp Mill Data:
Pulp Lines: 1

Pulppy Corelex (Vietnam)
Hung Yen Mill
Ownership: New Toyo Pulppy (Hong Kong) Limited, Corelex Co., Ltd.
Pho Noi A Industrial Zone
Hung Yen, Hung Yen Province
Vietnam
  Phone: (84) 4 3512 2601
  Fax: (84) 4 3512 2602
  Web Address: www.pulppy.com
Personnel:
  Gen. Dir.: Masahiro Takamatsu
  Phone: (84) 4 3512 2601
Total Employees at this Location: 125
Type of Operation: Paper mill
Pulp Grades and Capacities:
  Total pulp capacity: 20,949 mt/y
  Recycled Pulping: 20,949 mt/y
Pulp Mill Data:
  Bleach Plant Systems: 1
  Recycled Pulping System, Type: Deinked
  Recycled Fiber Treatment Lines:
  Flotation deinking lines: 1
Paper/Paperboard Grades and Capacities:
  Total paper and paperboard capacity: 30,000 mt/y
  Tissue: 30,000 mt/y
Paper and Paperboard Mill Data:
Paper Machines: 1
No. 1, crescent former, total capacity 30,000 mt/y, Trim width 2.8 m, Tissue, Uncoated woodfree/freesheet
Energy Data:
  Power boilers
  Electrical demand for mill: 103 MWh/D

Quang Phat Co., Ltd.
374 Le Hong Phong Street, Ward No. 1, District No. 10
Ho Chi Minh City
Vietnam
  Phone: (84) 8 9968007/6675
  Fax: (84) 8 9966676
Personnel:
  Dir.: Cam Nguyen
  Phone: (84) 8 9968007/6675
  Fax: (84) 8 9966676
  Dpty. Dir.: Nguyen Duc Quoc
  Phone: (84) 8 9968007/6675
  Fax: (84) 8 9966676
Total Employees at this Location: 160
Mill Locations:
  Quang Phat Co., Ltd., Ho Chi Minh City Mill, 374 Le Hong Phong Street, Ward No. 1, District No. 10, Ho Chi Minh City, Vietnam, Capacity: 8,400 mt/y, (Paperboard mill)
  Phone: (84) 8 9968007/6675
  Fax: (84) 8 9966676

Quang Phat Co., Ltd.
Ho Chi Minh City Mill
374 Le Hong Phong Street, Ward No. 1, District No. 10
Ho Chi Minh City, Binh Duong Province
Vietnam
  Phone: (84) 8 9968007/6675
  Fax: (84) 8 9966676
Personnel:
  Dir.: Mr. Cam Nguyen
  Phone: (84) 903 800897
  Fax: (84) 8 9875226
  Dpty. Dir.: Mr. Nguyen Duc Quoc
  Phone: (84) 903 759650
Total Employees at this Location: 120
Type of Operation: Paperboard mill
Paper/Paperboard Grades and Capacities:
  Total paper and paperboard capacity: 8,400 mt/y
  Containerboard: 8,400 mt/y
Paper and Paperboard Mill Data:
Paper Machines: 3
No. 1, cylinder, total capacity 3,500 mt/y, Trim width 2.15 m, Containerboard
No. 2, cylinder, total capacity 3,500 mt/y, Trim width 2.15 m, Containerboard
No. 3, cylinder, total capacity 1,400 mt/y, Trim width 1.3 m, Containerboard

Rang Dong Paper Joint-stock Co.
Dien Khanh District Mill
Dien Phuoc Ward
Dien Khanh District, Khanh Hoa Province
Vietnam
  Phone: (84) 58 3780914
  Fax: (84) 58 3780123
  Email: an-tom@hotmail.com
Personnel:
  Dir.: Mr. Dao Vu Lam
  Phone: (84) 58 3780914
  Fax: (84) 58 3780123
  Dpty. Dir.: Mr. Le Ba Quynh
  Phone: (84) 58 3780914
  Fax: (84) 58 3780123
Total Employees at this Location: 240
Type of Operation: Paper mill, Paperboard mill
Paper/Paperboard Grades and Capacities:
  Total paper and paperboard capacity: 12,000 mt/y
  Tissue: 200 mt/y
  Linerboard: 500 mt/y
  Corrugating medium/fluting: 8,800 mt/y
Paper and Paperboard Mill Data:
Paper Machines: 4
PM 1, cylinder, total capacity 2,500 mt/y, Trim width 1.75 m
PM 2, fourdrinier, total capacity 7,000 mt/y, Trim width 2.65 m
PM 3, fourdrinier, total capacity 1,000 mt/y, Trim width 1.4 m
PM 4, cylinder, total capacity 1,000 mt/y, Trim width 1.4 m

Rang Dong Paper Joint-stock Co.
Ownership: 100% by shareholders
Dien Phuoc Ward
Dien Khanh District
Vietnam
  Phone: (84) 58 3780914
  Fax: (84) 58 3780123
  Email: an-tom@hotmail.com
Personnel:
  Man. Dir.: Dao Vu Lam
  Phone: (84) 58 3780914
  Fax: (84) 58 3780123
  Dpty. Dir.: Le Ba Quynh
  Phone: (84) 58 3780914
  Fax: (84) 58 3780123
Total Employees of Company: 240
Mill Locations:
  Rang Dong Paper Joint-stock Co., Dien Khanh District Mill, Dien Phuoc Ward, Dien Khanh District, Vietnam, Capacity: 12,000 mt/y, (Paper mill, Paperboard mill)
  Phone: (84) 58 3780914
  Fax: (84) 58 3780123
  Email: an-tom@hotmail.com

Saigon Paper Joint Stock Company
Ownership: 47.50% by Mr. Tien Vi Cao, 14.50% by Bridgehead, 33.80% by Daio Paper Corp.
Suite 1.1-1.2, 1st Flr., ETown 1, 364 Cong Hoa Str., Ward 13
Tan Binh Dis, Ho Chi Minh City
Vietnam
  Phone: (84) 8 6288 4333
  Fax: (84) 8 6288 4335
  Email: contact@saigonpaper.com
  Web Address: www.saigonpaper.com
Personnel:
  Chmn. of the board: Mr. Huu Tin Mai
  Phone: (84) 8 6288 4333
  Fax: (84) 8 6288 4335
  Vice Chmn and CEO: Mr. Tien Vi Cao
  Phone: (84) 8 6288 4333
  Fax: (84) 8 6288 4335
  Mmbr of board, VP Finance: Mr. Xuan Nam Tran
  Phone: (84) 8 6288 4333
  Fax: (84) 8 6288 4335
  VP & COO: Mr. Denis Lafreniere
  Phone: (84) 8 6288 4333
  Fax: (84) 8 6288 4335
  VP R&D: Mrs. Thi Kieu Nguyet Dang
  Phone: (84) 8 6288 4333

Vietnam

Fax: (84) 8 6288 4335
VP: Mr. Van Trung Pham
Phone: (84) 8 6288 4333
Fax: (84) 8 6288 4335
Sls Dir. Tissue: Mr. Thanh Hiep Vu
Phone: (84) 8 6288 4333
Fax: (84) 8 6288 4335
Sls Dir. IP: Mr. Hoang Phuoc Le
Phone: (84) 8 6288 4333
Fax: (84) 8 6288 4335
Total Employees of Company: 1,300
Total Employees at this Location: 30
Mill Locations:
Saigon Paper, My Xuan I Mill, My Xuan A Industrial Zone, Phu My Ward, Tan Thanh Dist., Ba Ria - Vung Tau, Vietnam, Capacity: 70,800 mt/y, (Paper mill, Paperboard mill)
Phone: (84) 64 3899338
Fax: (84) 64 3899337
Email: contact@saigonpaper.com
Saigon Paper, My Xuan II Mill, My Xuan A Industrial Zone, Phu My Ward, Tan Thanh Dist., Ba Ria - Vung Tau, Vietnam, Capacity: 230,000 mt/y, (Paper mill)
Email: contact@saigonpaper.com

⑩Saigon Paper
My Xuan I Mill
Ownership: 100% by Saigon Paper Joint Stock Company
My Xuan A Industrial Zone, Phu My Ward
Tan Thanh Dist., Ba Ria - Vung Tau
Vietnam
Phone: (84) 64 3899338
Fax: (84) 64 3899337
Email: contact@saigonpaper.com
Web Address: www.saigonpaper.com
Personnel:
Mill Mgr.: Mr. Hoang Phong Pham
Phone: (84) 64 3899338
Dpty. Mill Mgr.: Mr. Thi Kieu Nguyet Dang
Phone: (84) 64 3899338
Total Employees at this Location: 275
Type of Operation: Paper mill, Paperboard mill
Pulp Grades and Capacities:
Total pulp capacity: 67,157 mt/y
Recycled Pulping: 67,157 mt/y
Pulp Mill Data:
Bleach Plant Systems: 1
DIP
Recycled Fiber Treatment Lines:
Flotation deinking lines: 1 at 23,400 admt/y
Recycled packaging pulping lines: 1 at 78,000 admt/y
Washing deinking lines: 1 at 23,400 admt/y
Paper/Paperboard Grades and Capacities:
Total paper and paperboard capacity: 70,800 mt/y
Tissue: 10,800 mt/y
Linerboard: 20,000 mt/y
Corrugating medium/fluting: 40,000 mt/y
Paper and Paperboard Mill Data:
Stock Preparation:
Pulpers: 3
Refiners: 13
Paper Machines: 4
No. 1, cylinder, total capacity 20,000 mt/y, Trim width 3.3 m, Linerboard
No. 2, cylinder, total capacity 20,000 mt/y, Trim width 3.3 m, Corrugating medium/fluting
No. 3, cylinder, total capacity 20,000 mt/y, Trim width 3.3 m, Corrugating medium/fluting
No. 10, cylinder, total capacity 10,800 mt/y, Trim width 2.4 m, Tissue, Uncoated woodfree/freesheet
Energy Data:
Power boilers
Electrical demand for mill: 100 MWh/D

⑩Saigon Paper
My Xuan II Mill
Ownership: 100% by Saigon Paper Joint Stock Company
My Xuan A Industrial Zone, Phu My Ward
Tan Thanh Dist., Ba Ria - Vung Tau, Dong Nam Bo
Vietnam
Email: contact@saigonpaper.com
Web Address: www.saigonpaper.com
Type of Operation: Paper mill
Pulp Grades and Capacities:
Total pulp capacity: 213,499 mt/y
Recycled Pulping: 213,499 mt/y
Paper/Paperboard Grades and Capacities:
Total paper and paperboard capacity: 230,000 mt/y
Tissue: 32,000 mt/y
Linerboard: 43,200 mt/y
Corrugating medium/fluting: 100,800 mt/y
Boxboard/cartonboard: 54,000 mt/y
Paper and Paperboard Mill Data:
Paper Machines: 3
No. 4, fourdrinier, total capacity 144,000 mt/y, Trim width 4.1 m, Corrugating medium/fluting, Linerboard
No. 5, Fourdrinier (4), total capacity 54,000 mt/y, Trim width 2.7 m, Boxboard/cartonboard
No. 6, fourdrinier, total capacity 32,000 mt/y, Trim width 2.85 m, Tissue, Uncoated woodfree/freesheet

⑩Song Duong Tissue Paper Company
Long Bien District, Hanoi City Mill
Ownership: Vietnam Paper Corporation (Vinapaco)
Duc Giang Ward
Long Bien District, Hanoi City
Vietnam
Phone: (84) 4 38271 440
Fax: (84) 4 38271 607
Email: tissue.sd@hn.vnn.vn, sales@tissuesd.com.vn
Web Address: www.tissuesd.com.vn
Personnel:
Dir.: Mr. Nguyen Viet Duc
Phone: (84) 4 3652 0423
Fax: (84) 4 3827 1407
Dpty Dir./Econ.: Mr. Hoang Anh Tuan
Phone: (84) 4 3877 1654
Dpty. Dir./Tech. & Prod.: Mr. Nguyen Van Quan
Phone: (84) 4 3877 4423
Admin. Mgr.: Mr. Ha Huy Luc
Phone: (84) 4 3827 1106
Mktg. Mgr.: Mr. Vu Xuan Thang
Phone: (84) 4 38770 157
Mgr. of Tech. Dept.: Mr. Vu Phuong
Phone: (84) 4 36520 424
Chief Account.: Mr. Tran Van Toan
Phone: (84) 4 38271 204
Mgr. of Material Dep.: Mr. Ta Quang Van
Phone: (84) 4 38271 104
Mgr. of Tissue Paper Workshop: Mr. Dinh Quoc Hung
Phone: (84) 4 38271 421
Mgr. of Convert. Workshop: Mr. Nguyen Van Bai
Phone: (84) 4 38271 414
Mgr. of Plywood Workshop: Mr. Doan Huu Thanh
Phone: (84) 4 38271 436
Mgr. of Mechan. Workshop: Mr. Nguyen Ngoc Le
Phone: (84) 4 38271 440
Total Employees at this Location: 84
Type of Operation: Paper mill
Pulp Grades and Capacities:
Total pulp capacity: 12,692 mt/y
Recycled Pulping: 12,692 mt/y
Pulp Mill Data:
Bleach Plant Systems: 1
DIP
Recycled Fiber Treatment Lines:
Flotation deinking lines: 1
Paper/Paperboard Grades and Capacities:
Total paper and paperboard capacity: 17,000 mt/y
Tissue: 17,000 mt/y
Paper and Paperboard Mill Data:
Stock Preparation:
Pulpers: 2
Refiners: 2
Paper Machines: 1
No. 1, crescent former, total capacity 17,000 mt/y, Trim width 3.71 m, Tissue, Uncoated woodfree/freesheet
Energy Data:
Power boilers: 1
Electrical demand for mill: 48 MWh/D

⑩Song Lam Paper Joint-Stock Co.
Hung Nguyen Dist. Mill
Hung Phu Ward
Hung Nguyen Dist.
Vietnam
Phone: (84) 383 3760128
Fax: (84) 383 3760158
Personnel:
Chmn. of BOM, Dir.: Hoang Phung
Phone: (84) 383 3760128
Dpty. Dir.: Le Ba Quynh
Phone: (84) 383 3760128
Total Employees at this Location: 200
Type of Operation: Pulp mill, Paperboard mill
Pulp Grades and Capacities:
Total pulp capacity: 10,000 mt/y
Paper/Paperboard Grades and Capacities:
Total paper and paperboard capacity: 18,000 mt/y
Linerboard: 6,000 mt/y
Corrugating medium/fluting: 8,000 mt/y
Boxboard/cartonboard: 4,000 mt/y
Paper and Paperboard Mill Data:
Paper Machines: 4
No. 1, cylinder, total capacity 4,000 mt/y, Trim width 1.76 m, Boxboard/cartonboard
No. 2, fourdrinier, total capacity 4,000 mt/y, Trim width 1.4 m
No. 3, fourdrinier, total capacity 4,000 mt/y, Trim width 1.4 m
No. 4, cylinder, total capacity 12,000 mt/y, Trim width 2.6 m

⑩Song Lam Paper Joint-Stock Co.
Ownership: 100% by shareholders
Hung Phu Ward
Hung Nguyen Dist.
Vietnam
Phone: (84) 383 3760128
Fax: (84) 383 3760158
Personnel:
Chmn. of BOM., Dir.: Hoang Phung
Phone: (84) 383 3760128
Fax: (84) 383 3760158
Dpty. Dir.: Le Ba Quynh
Phone: (84) 383 3760128
Fax: (84) 383 3760158
Total Employees at this Location: 200
Mill Locations:
Song Lam Paper Joint-Stock Co., Hung Nguyen Dist. Mill, Hung Phu Ward, Hung Nguyen Dist., Vietnam, Capacity: 18,000 mt/y, (Pulp mill, Paperboard mill)
Phone: (84) 383 3760128
Fax: (84) 383 3760158

⑩Tan Hong Export-Import Joint-stock Co.
A18 - BT3, My Dinh Urban II
Tu Liem, Hanoi
Vietnam
Phone: (84) 4 3787 0827
Fax: (84) 4 3787 0827
Email: info@tanhong.com.vn
Web Address: www.tanhong.com.vn
Total Employees of Company: 500
Mill Locations:
Tan Hong Pulp Mill, Con Cuong Mill, Chi Khe Ward, Con Cuong, Vietnam, (Pulp mill)
Phone: (84) 3787 0827 / 3787 0490
Fax: (84) 3787 0827
Email: info@tanhong.com.vn; tanhonggroup@hotmail.com

Vietnam

ⓂTan Hong Pulp Mill
Con Cuong Mill
Ownership: Tan Hong Export-Import Joint-stock Co.
Chi Khe Ward
Con Cuong
Vietnam
 Phone: (84) 3787 0827 / 3787 0490
 Fax: (84) 3787 0827
 Email: info@tanhong.com.vn,
 tanhonggroup@hotmail.com
 Web Address: www.tanhong.com.vn
Type of Operation: Pulp mill
Pulp Grades and Capacities:
 Total pulp capacity: 50,000 mt/y
 Chemical Pulp: 50,000 mt/y
Pulp Mill Data:
 Chemical Pulping Systems:
 Batch digesters: 15
Pulp Lines: 1

ⓅⓂTan Mai Group Joint Stock Co.
Tan Mai Mill
Mill idled October 2012 to move production line to the green field building in Long Thanh district.
Ownership: 25.92% by Vietnam Paper Corporation (Vinapaco)
Thong Nhat Ward
Bien Hoa City, Dong Nai Province
Vietnam
 Phone: (84) 61 3822257/271
 Fax: (84) 61 3824915
 Email: info@tanmaipaper.com
 Web Address: www.tanmaipaper.com
Personnel:
 Chmn. of the Board & Gen. Mgr.: Mr. Tran Duc Thinh
 Phone: (84) 61 3822257/271
 Eng. Mgr.: Mr. Nguyen Hung Dong
 Phone: (84) 61 3822257/271
 Email: donghung-ktcd@tanmaipaper.com.vn
 Dpty. Gen. Dir.: Mr. Phan Minh Nghia
 Phone: (84) 61 3822257/271
 Process Mgr.: Mrs. Tran Mai Loan
 Phone: (84) 61 3822257/271
 Email: mailoan-ktcn@tanmaipaper.com.vn
 Dpty. Gen. Dir.: Mr. Le Quang Huy
 Phone: (84) 61 3822257/271
 Purch. Mgr.: Mr. Pham Danh Than
 Phone: (84) 61 3822257/271
 Sls. Mgr.: Mrs. Lê Thi Ngoc Lan
 Phone: (84) 61 3822257/271
 Email: ngoclan-kd@tanmaipaper.com.vn
Total Employees of Company: 1,500
Type of Operation: Pulp mill, Paper mill
Mill Locations:
 Tan Mai Group Joint Stock Co., Binh An Mill, Binh An Ward, Di An District, Vietnam, Capacity: 30,345 mt/y, (Paper mill)
 Phone: (84) 650 3751635/437
 Fax: (84) 650 3750389
 Email: binhan@tanmaipaper.com
 Tan Mai Group Joint Stock Co., Dong Nai Mill, Road No. 11, Bien Hoa Industrial Zone No.1, Bien Hoa City, Vietnam, Capacity: 20,000 mt/y, (Paper mill, Paperboard mill)
 Phone: (84) 61 3836 201/190
 Fax: (84) 61 3836231
 Email: cogido@hcm.vnn.vn
 Tan Mai Group Joint Stock Co., Mien Dong Mill, Mien Dong, Vietnam, (Paper mill)
 Tan Mai Group Joint Stock Co., Quang Ngai Mill, Binh Son district, Vietnam, (Paper mill)
Pulp Mill Data:
 Mechanical Pulping Systems:
 CTMP systems: 2
 Recycled Fiber Treatment Lines:
 Flotation deinking lines: 1 at 20,000 admt/y
 Pulpers: 1 at 28,000 admt/y
 Recycled packaging pulping lines: 1
 Washing deinking lines: 1 at 20,000 admt/y

Pulp Dryers:
 Air Float dryers 1
Paper and Paperboard Mill Data:
 Stock Preparation:
 Pulpers: 7
 Refiners: 11
Paper Machines: 3
 PM 1, fourdrinier, total capacity 15,000 mt/y, Trim width 2.52 m
 PM 2, fourdrinier, total capacity 15,000 mt/y, Trim width 2.52 m
 PM 3, twin-wire, total capacity 45,000 mt/y, Trim width 4.2 m, Newsprint
Finishing Equipment:
 Winders: 1 at 45,000 mt/y
 Rewinders: 1 at 6,000 mt/y
 Sheeters: 1
Energy Data:
 Power boilers: 2

ⓂTan Mai Group Joint Stock Co.
Binh An Mill
Binh An Ward, Di An District, Binh Duong Province
Vietnam
 Phone: (84) 650 3751635/437
 Fax: (84) 650 3750389
 Email: binhan@tanmaipaper.com
 Web Address: www.tanmaipaper.com
Personnel:
 Dir.: Mr. Thai Van Thao
 Phone: (84) 913 95 0069
 Dpty. Dir.: Phan Quyet Tien
 Phone: (84) 913 68 4767
Total Employees at this Location: 340
Type of Operation: Paper mill
Paper/Paperboard Grades and Capacities:
 Total paper and paperboard capacity: 30,345 mt/y
 Uncoated woodfree/freesheet: 30,345 mt/y
Paper and Paperboard Mill Data:
Paper Machines: 1
 No. 4, (second hand), fourdrinier, total capacity 30,345 mt/y, Trim width 2.86 m, Uncoated woodfree/freesheet
Finishing Equipment:
 Winders: 1
Energy Data:
 Power boilers: 2
 Electrical demand for mill: 97 MWh/D

ⓂTan Mai Group Joint Stock Co.
Dong Nai Mill
Road No. 11, Bien Hoa Industrial Zone No.1
Bien Hoa City, Dong Nai Province
Vietnam
 Phone: (84) 61 3836 201/190
 Fax: (84) 61 3836231
 Email: cogido@hcm.vnn.vn
Personnel:
 Gen. Dir.: Mr. Nguyen Ngoc Minh
 Phone: (84) 61 3836 201/190
 Bd. Mbr.: Mr. Nguyen Phuc Lap
 Phone: (84) 61 3836 201/190
 Bd. Mbr.: Mr. Nguyen Thi Phi Yen
 Phone: (84) 61 3836 201/190
 Bd. Mbr.: Mr. Tran Duc Quang
 Phone: (84) 61 3836 201/190
 Dpty. Dir./Prod.: Mr. Le Quang Phuc
 Phone: (84) 61 3836 201/190
 Dpty. Dir./Tech.: Mr. Do Van Tap
 Phone: (84) 61 3836 201/190
 Dpty. Dir./Investment & Env.: Mr. Vu Trong Hung
 Phone: (84) 61 3836 201/190
 Dpty. Dir./Personnel: Mr. Nguyen Phuc Long
 Phone: (84) 61 3836 201/190
Total Employees at this Location: 340
Type of Operation: Paper mill, Paperboard mill
Pulp Mill Data:
 Bleach Plant Lines:
 No. 1

Paper/Paperboard Grades and Capacities:
 Total paper and paperboard capacity: 20,000 mt/y
 Uncoated woodfree/freesheet: 16,000 mt/y
 Packaging papers: 4,000 mt/y
Paper and Paperboard Mill Data:
Paper Machines: 3
 No. 1, fourdrinier, total capacity 7,000 mt/y, Trim width 2.3 m, Uncoated woodfree/freesheet
 No. 2, fourdrinier, total capacity 9,000 mt/y, Trim width 2.6 m, Uncoated woodfree/freesheet
 No. 3, cylinder, total capacity 4,000 mt/y, Trim width 1.7 m, Packaging papers

ⓂTan Mai Group Joint Stock Co.
Mien Dong Mill
Mill is under construction (was due to start before year end 2012, however it has been delayed with no official date for start-up)
Mien Dong, Dong Nai Province
Vietnam
 Web Address: www.tanmaipaper.com
Type of Operation: Paper mill
Paper and Paperboard Mill Data:
Paper Machines: 1
 PM 1, (was due to start before year end 2012, however has been delayed), total capacity 150,000 mt/y, Newsprint

ⓂTan Mai Group Joint Stock Co.
Quang Ngai Mill
Mill is under construction (was due to start before year end 2012, however it has been delayed with no official date for start-up)
Binh Son district, Binh Duong Province
Vietnam
Type of Operation: Paper mill

ⓂTruc Bach Paper Joint-Stock Co.
Hanoi City Mill
Thanh Liet Ward
Thanh Tri District, Hanoi City
Vietnam
 Phone: (84) 4 36889458
 Fax: (84) 4 36881393
 Email: trucbach@trucbachpaper.com,
 trucbach@hn.vnn.vn
Personnel:
 Chmn. & Dir.: Mr. Quang Hung Le
 Phone: (84) 4 36889458 (22)
 Dpty. Dir.: Mr. Nguyen Dau
 Phone: (84) 4 36889458 (16)
 Dpty. Dir.: Mr. Nguyen Xuyen Son
 Phone: (84) 4 36889458 (24)
Total Employees at this Location: 115
Type of Operation: Paper mill
Pulp Mill Data:
 Recycled Fiber Treatment Lines:
 Flotation deinking lines: 3 at 5,000 admt/y
Paper/Paperboard Grades and Capacities:
 Total paper and paperboard capacity: 3,000 mt/y
 Tissue: 3,000 mt/y
Paper and Paperboard Mill Data:
Paper Machines: 2
 PM 2, cylinder, total capacity 1,500 mt/y, Trim width 1.57 m, Tissue
 PM 4, cylinder, total capacity 1,500 mt/y, Trim width 2.6 m, Tissue

ⓂTruc Bach Paper Joint-Stock Co.
Ownership: 30% by Govt. of Vietnam, 65% by others
Thanh Liet Ward
Thanh Tri District, Hanoi City
Vietnam
 Phone: (84) 4 36889458
 Fax: (84) 4 36881393
 Email: trucbach@trucbachpaper.com,
 trucbach@hn.vnn.vn

Vietnam

Personnel:
Chmn. & Dir.: Quang Hung Le
Phone: (84) 4 36889458
Fax: (84) 4 36881393
Dpty. Dir.: Nguyen Dau
Phone: (84) 4 36889458
Fax: (84) 4 36881393
Dpty. Dir.: Nguyen Xuyen Son
Phone: (84) 4 36889458
Fax: (84) 4 36881393
Total Employees at this Location: 115
Mill Locations:
Truc Bach Paper Joint-Stock Co., Hanoi City Mill, Thanh Liet Ward, Thanh Tri District, Hanoi City, Vietnam, Capacity: 3,000 mt/y, (Paper mill)
Phone: (84) 4 36889458
Fax: (84) 4 36881393
Email: trucbach@trucbachpaper.com, trucbach@hn.vnn.vn

ⓂVan Diem Paper Joint-Stock Co.
Phu Minh Ward
Phu Xuyen District
Vietnam
Phone: (84) 34 3784251
Fax: (84) 34 3784210
Personnel:
Dir.: Nguyen Dinh Tuan
Phone: (84) 34 3784251
Fax: (84) 34 3784210
Dpty. Dir.: Pham Huy Van
Phone: (84) 34 3784251
Fax: (84) 34 3784210
Dpty. Dir.: Nguyen Quang Bien
Phone: (84) 34 3784251
Fax: (84) 34 3784210
Total Employees at this Location: 138
Mill Locations:
Van Diem Paper Joint-Stock Co., Phu Xuyen Mill, Phu Minh Ward, Phu Xuyen District, Vietnam, Capacity: 16,000 mt/y, (Paper mill)
Phone: (84) 34 3784251
Fax: (84) 34 3784210

ⓂVan Diem Paper Joint-Stock Co.
Phu Xuyen Mill
Phu Minh Ward
Phu Xuyen District, Ha Tay Province
Vietnam
Phone: (84) 34 3784251
Fax: (84) 34 3784210
Personnel:
Dir.: Mr. Nguyen Dinh Tuan
Phone: (84) 34 3784210
Fax: (84) 34 3784234
Dpty. Dir.: Mr. Pham Huy Van
Phone: (84) 34 3784211
Fax: (84) 34 3784229
Dpty. Dir.: Mr. Nguyen Quang Bien
Phone: (84) 34 3784251
Total Employees at this Location: 138
Type of Operation: Paper mill
Paper/Paperboard Grades and Capacities:
Total paper and paperboard capacity: 16,000 mt/y
Uncoated woodfree/freesheet: 12,000 mt/y
Linerboard: 4,000 mt/y
Paper and Paperboard Mill Data:
Paper Machines: 4
PM 1, cylinder, total capacity 2,000 mt/y, Trim width 1.58 m, Linerboard
PM 2, cylinder, total capacity 1,000 mt/y, Trim width 1.09 m, Linerboard
PM 3, cylinder, total capacity 1,000 mt/y, Trim width 1.09 m, Linerboard
PM 4, (second hand), total capacity 12,000 mt/y, Trim width 1.92 m, Uncoated woodfree/freesheet

ⓂVien Dong Paper Joint-Stock Company
Ho Chi Minh City Mill
129 Au Co Street, Ward No. 14, Tan Binh District
Ho Chi Minh City, Binh Duong Province
Vietnam
Phone: (84) 8 384 96056/6643/28633
Fax: (84) 8 384 2588
Email: vidon@vidon.com.vn
Web Address: www.vidon.com.vn
Personnel:
Dir.: Mr. Bui Quang Man
Phone: (84) 8 384 96056/6643/28633
Dpty. Dir.: Mrs. Nguyen Thi Viet Anh
Phone: (84) 8 384 96056/6643/28633
Type of Operation: Paper mill
Paper/Paperboard Grades and Capacities:
Total paper and paperboard capacity: 1,800 mt/y
Tissue: 1,800 mt/y
Paper and Paperboard Mill Data:
Paper Machines: 4
PM 1, total capacity 600 mt/y, Tissue
PM 2, total capacity 600 mt/y, Tissue
PM 3, total capacity 300 mt/y, Tissue
PM 4, total capacity 300 mt/y, Tissue

ⓂVien Dong Paper Joint-Stock Company
Ownership: 100% by Joint-Stock
129 Au Co Street, Ward No. 14, Tan Binh District
Ho Chi Minh City
Vietnam
Phone: (84) 8 384 96056/6643/28633
Fax: (84) 8 384 2588
Email: vidon@vidon.com.vn
Web Address: www.vidon.com.vn
Personnel:
Dir.: Bui Quang Man
Phone: (84) 8 384 96056/6643/28633
Fax: (84) 8 384 2588
Dpty. Dir.: Nguyen Thi Viet Anh
Phone: (84) 8 384 96056/6643/2863
Fax: (84) 8 384 2588
Mill Locations:
Vien Dong Paper Joint-Stock Company, Ho Chi Minh City Mill, 129 Au Co Street, Ward No. 14, Tan Binh District, Ho Chi Minh City, Vietnam, Capacity: 1,800 mt/y, (Paper mill)
Phone: (84) 8 384 96056/6643/28633
Fax: (84) 8 384 2588
Email: vidon@vidon.com.vn

ⓂViet Thang Paper & Packing Co., Ltd.
Thuong Tin Dist. Mill
Ha Binh Phuong Industrial Zone
Thuong Tin Dist., Ha Tay Province
Vietnam
Phone: (84) 34 3763451/52
Fax: (84) 34 3762573
Email: vietthangpaper@hn.vnn.vn
Personnel:
Dir.: Do Ba Thang
Phone: (84) 903 41 2082
Dpty. Dir.: Le Quang Hao
Phone: (84) 34 3763451/52
Total Employees at this Location: 240
Type of Operation: Paper mill
Paper/Paperboard Grades and Capacities:
Total paper and paperboard capacity: 70,000 mt/y
Uncoated woodfree/freesheet: 20,000 mt/y
Coated woodfree/freesheet: 50,000 mt/y
Paper and Paperboard Mill Data:
Stock Preparation:
Pulpers: 2
Refiners: 6
Paper Machines: 2
No. 1, fourdrinier, total capacity 20,000 mt/y, Trim width 2 m, Uncoated woodfree/freesheet
No. 2, fourdrinier, total capacity 50,000 mt/y, Trim width 3.5 m, Coated woodfree/freesheet
Coating Machines: 1
PM#2, off machine
Finishing Equipment:
Winders: 1 at 20,000 mt/y
Rewinders: 1 at 20,000 mt/y
Energy Data:
Power boilers: 2
Electrical demand for mill: 131 MWh/D

ⓂViet Thang Paper & Packing Co., Ltd.
Ownership: 33.34% by Mr. Do Ba Thang, 33.32% by Mr. Le Quang Hao, 33.34% by Mrs. Nguyen Thi Lan Phuong
Ha Binh Phuong Industrial Zone
Thuong Tin Dist.
Vietnam
Phone: (84) 34 3763451/52
Fax: (84) 34 3762573
Email: vietthangpaper@hn.vnn.vn
Personnel:
Dir.: Do Bang Thang
Phone: (84) 34 3763451/52
Fax: (84) 34 3762573
Dpty. Dir.: Le Quang Hao
Phone: (84) 34 3763451/52
Fax: (84) 34 3762573
Total Employees at this Location: 125
Mill Locations:
Viet Thang Paper & Packing Co., Ltd., Thuong Tin Dist. Mill, Ha Binh Phuong Industrial Zone, Thuong Tin Dist., Vietnam, Capacity: 70,000 mt/y, (Paper mill)
Phone: (84) 34 3763451/52
Fax: (84) 34 3762573
Email: vietthangpaper@hn.vnn.vn

ⓂViet Tri Paper Company
Viet Tri Mill
Ownership: 29% by Vietnam Paper Corporation (Vinapaco), 71% by shareholders
Ben Cat Ward
Viet Tri City, Phú Tho Province
Vietnam
Phone: (84) 210 3846702
Fax: (84) 210 3851109
Web Address: giayviettri.com.vn
Personnel:
Mill Mgr.: Mr. Nguyen Van Hien
Phone: (84) 210 3846702
Dpty. Dir.: Mr. Khong Minh Tri
Phone: (84) 210 3846702
Total Employees at this Location: 250
Type of Operation: Pulp mill, Paper mill
Pulp Grades and Capacities:
Total pulp capacity: 34,264 mt/y
Chemical Pulp: 10,734 mt/y
Recycled Pulping: 23,531 mt/y
Pulp Mill Data:
Chemical Pulping Systems:
Batch digesters
Bleach Plant Systems: 2
Chemical Pulping System, Type: Hardwood
Recycled Pulping System, Type: DIP
Chemical Recovery Equipment:
Recovery boilers: 1
Recycled Fiber Treatment Lines:
Flotation deinking lines: 1
Recycled packaging pulping lines: 1
Paper/Paperboard Grades and Capacities:
Total paper and paperboard capacity: 40,000 mt/y
Uncoated woodfree/freesheet: 12,000 mt/y
Tissue: 3,000 mt/y
Boxboard/cartonboard: 25,000 mt/y
Paper and Paperboard Mill Data:
Paper Machines: 3
No. 1, fourdrinier, total capacity 3,000 mt/y, Trim width 2.4 m, Tissue

Vietnam

No. 2, fourdrinier, total capacity 12,000 mt/y, Trim width 2.4 m, Uncoated woodfree/freesheet
No. 6, cylinder, total capacity 25,000 mt/y, Trim width 2.7 m, Boxboard/cartonboard
Coating Machines: 1
PM6, on machine
Energy Data:
Power boilers
Electrical demand for mill: 85 MWh/D

ⓂVietnam Lee & Man Paper Manufacturing Ltd
Hau Giang Mill
Mill is under construction (start up is scheduled at the end of 2014)
Ownership: 75% by Lee & Man Paper Manufacturing Ltd., 25% by Wise Sense Investments
Chau Thanh district, Ha Giang Province
Vietnam
Type of Operation: Paper mill, Paperboard mill
Paper/Paperboard Grades and Capacities:
Total paper and paperboard capacity: 400,000 mt/y
Linerboard: 200,000 mt/y
Corrugating medium/fluting: 200,000 mt/y
Paper and Paperboard Mill Data:
Paper Machines: 1
PM 19, (due to start late 2014), total capacity 400,000 mt/y, Containerboard

ⓂVietnam Paper Corporation (Vinapaco)
Ownership: 100% by Government of Vietnam
25A Ly Thuong Kiet Street, Hoan Kiem District
Hanoi City
Vietnam
Phone: (84) 4 38247773
Fax: (84) 4 38260381
Email: vinapimex-vp@hn.vnn.vn, vpl@vinapimex.com.vn, vp.hn@vinapaco.com.vn
Web Address: www.vinapaco.com.vn, www.vinapimex.com
Personnel:
Chmn. of Bd.: Mr. Do Xuan Tru
Phone: (84) 4 38247 793
Email: tru.dx@vinapaco.com.vn
Gen. Dir.: Mr. Vo Sy Dong
Phone: (84) 4 38247 792
Email: dong.vs@vinapaco.com.vn
Bd. Mbr.: Mr. Huynh Duc Nhan
Phone: (84) 4 39343 758
Fax: (84) 210 829275
Email: nhan.hd@vinapaco.com.vn
Bd. Mbr.: Mrs. Nguyen Thi Thu Ha
Phone: (84) 8 83214 330
Fax: (84) 8 8231011
Email: thuha@hcm.vnn.vn
Bd. Mbr.: Mr. Pham Van Tu
Phone: (84) 4 38260 146
Email: tu.pv@vinapaco.com.vn
Dpty. Gen. Dir.: Mr. Trinh Van Lam
Phone: (84) 8 38211 588/ 210 3762 565
Fax: (84) 8 8231 011/ 210 3829 177
Email: lam.tv@vinapaco.com.vn
Dpty. Gen. Dir.: Mr. Nguyen The Binh
Phone: (84) 4 38247 553
Email: binh.nt@vinapaco.com.vn
Dpty. Gen. Dir.: Mr. Hoang Van Vuong
Phone: (84) 210 3829 152
Fax: (84) 210 3829 177
Email: vuonghv@vinapaco.com.vn
Dpty. Gen. Dir.: Mr. Vu Thanh Binh
Phone: (84) 210 829259/ 210 3830 184
Fax: (84) 210 3829 177
Email: binh.vt@vinapaco.com.vn
Chief of Admin.: Mr. Dang The Dan
Phone: (84) 4 38260143
Email: dan.vp@vinapaco.com.vn

Personnel Mgr.: Mrs. Nguyen Van Hoa
Phone: (84) 210 3829 636
Fax: (84) 210 3829 177
Email: tcld.hn@vinapaco.com.vn
Mgr. of Finan. Depart.: Mr. Nong Van Quyet
Phone: (84) 210 3829 051
Fax: (84) 210 3829 177
Email: tckt.bb@vinapaco.com.vn
Investment Mgr.: Mr. Ho Dinh Yen
Phone: (84) 4 38210454
Fax: (84) 210 3829 177
Email: xdcb.bb@vinapaco.com.vn
Total Employees at this Location: 66
Mill Locations:
Vietnam Paper Corporation (Vinapaco)-Bai Bang Paper, Bai Bang Paper, Tam Vong Park, Phong Châu Town, Phu Ninh District, Vietnam, Capacity: 149,940 mt/y, (Pulp mill, Paper mill)
Phone: (84) 210 3829 755/3762 556
Fax: (84) 210 3829 177/3827 052
Email: bapacopn@hn.vnn.vn
Bai Bang Paper Joint-stock Co., Ltd., Ky Son Mill, Dan Ha Ward, Ky Son, Vietnam, Capacity: 50,000 mt/y, (Pulp mill)
Phone: (84) 18 3842191
Hoang Van Thu Paper Joint Stock Company, Thai Nguyen City Mill, Quan Trieu Ward, Thai Nguyen City, Vietnam, Capacity: 20,000 mt/y, (Paper mill)
Phone: (84) 280 3844 652
Fax: (84) 280 3844 548
Phuong Nam Kenaf Pulp Mill and Paper Company, Phuong Nam Mill, Ba Luong hamlet, Thuan Nghia Hoa commune, Phuong Nam, Vietnam, (Pulp mill)
Song Duong Tissue Paper Company, Long Bien District, Hanoi City Mill, Duc Giang Ward, Long Bien District, Hanoi City, Vietnam, Capacity: 17,000 mt/y, (Paper mill)
Phone: (84) 4 38271 440
Fax: (84) 4 38271 607
Email: tissue.sd@hn.vnn.vn, sales@tissuesd.com.vn
Viet Tri Paper Company, Viet Tri Mill (29% owned), Ben Cat Ward, Viet Tri City, Vietnam, Capacity: 40,000 mt/y, (Pulp mill, Paper mill)
Phone: (84) 210 3846702
Fax: (84) 210 3851109

ⓂVinh Hue Paper Joint-Stock Co. (Vihimex)
Ownership: 85% by others, 15% by state
66/5 Stata Road No.1, Linh Xuan Ward
Thu Duc District, Ho Chi Minh
Vietnam
Phone: (84) 8 37240870/3896092/38369916
Fax: (84) 8 37240530
Personnel:
Chmn. of Bd./Dir.: Nguyen Hoa
Phone: (84) 8 37240870/3896092
Fax: (84) 8 37240530
Dpty. Dir.: Le Thanh Liem
Phone: (84) 8 37240870/3896092
Fax: (84) 8 37240530
Dpty. Dir.: Tran Thanh Phuong
Phone: (84) 8 37240870/3896092
Fax: (84) 8 37240530
Total Employees at this Location: 600
Mill Locations:
Vinh Hue Paper Joint-Stock Co. (Vihimex), Ho Chi Minh City Mill, 66/5 Stata Road No.1, Linh Xuan Ward, Thu Duc District, Ho Chi Minh City, Vietnam, Capacity: 11,800 mt/y, (Pulp mill, Paper mill, Paperboard mill)
Phone: (84) 8 37240870/3896092/38369916
Fax: (84) 8 37240530

ⓂVina Kraft Paper
Ho Chi Minh City Mill
Ownership: 70% by SCG Paper Public Co., Ltd., 30% by Rengo Co., Ltd.
My Phuoc 3 Industrial Park
Ho Chi Minh City, Binh Duong Province
Vietnam
Web Address: www.scg.co.th

Personnel:
Gen. Dir.: Mr. Chalokeporn Phalajivin
Phone: (66) 2 586 5643-4
Fax: (66) 2 587-2207
Email: chaloke.p@vinakraft.com
Total Employees at this Location: 220
Type of Operation: Paperboard mill
Pulp Grades and Capacities:
Total pulp capacity: 239,137 mt/y
Recycled Pulping: 239,137 mt/y
Pulp Mill Data:
Recycled Fiber Treatment Lines:
Recycled packaging pulping lines: 1
Paper/Paperboard Grades and Capacities:
Total paper and paperboard capacity: 250,000 mt/y
Linerboard: 150,000 mt/y
Corrugating medium/fluting: 100,000 mt/y
Paper and Paperboard Mill Data:
Paper Machines: 1
No. 1, fourdrinier (3), total capacity 250,000 mt/y, Trim width 5.3 m, Linerboard, Corrugating medium/fluting
Energy Data:
Power boilers: 1
Steam turbines: 1 at 26 MW
Electrical demand for mill: 313 MWh/D

ⓂVinh Hue Paper Joint-Stock Co. (Vihimex)
Ho Chi Minh City Mill
66/5 Stata Road No.1, Linh Xuan Ward
Thu Duc District, Ho Chi Minh City, Binh Duong Province
Vietnam
Phone: (84) 8 37240870/3896092/38369916
Fax: (84) 8 37240530
Personnel:
Chmn. of Bd./Dir.: Mr. Nguyen Hoa
Phone: (84) 8 37241 458
Fax: (84) 8 37240 530
Dpty. Dir.: Mr. Le Thanh Liem
Phone: (84) 8 37240870/3896092/38369916
Dpty. Dir.: Mr. Tran Thanh Phuong
Phone: (84) 8 37240870/3896092/38369916
Total Employees at this Location: 600
Type of Operation: Pulp mill, Paper mill, Paperboard mill
Pulp Grades and Capacities:
Total pulp capacity: 12,000 mt/y
Pulp available for market: 1,545 mt/y
Paper/Paperboard Grades and Capacities:
Total paper and paperboard capacity: 11,800 mt/y
Tissue: 4,000 mt/y
Packaging papers
Specialty and industrial: 5,600 mt/y

ⓂXuan Duc Joint-Stock Paper Company
Ho Chi Minh City Mill
Ownership: 80% by shareholders, 20% by state
54B Nam Hoa Street, Phuoc Long A Ward, District No. 9
Ho Chi Minh City, Binh Duong Province
Vietnam
Phone: (84) 8 37313006/0012
Fax: (84) 8 37313238
Email: xuanducco@hcm.fpt.vn
Personnel:
Chmn./Dir.: Mr. Duong Van Cao
Phone: (84) 8 7310 012
Fax: (84) 8 7313 238
Email: xuanducco@hcm.vnn.vn
Dpty. Dir.: Mr. Huynh Ngoc Duc
Phone: (84) 8 37313006/0012
Total Employees at this Location: 220
Type of Operation: Paper mill, Paperboard mill
Pulp Grades and Capacities:
Total pulp capacity: 26,000 mt/y
Recycled Pulping: 26,000 mt/y

Pulp Mill Data:
  Recycled Fiber Treatment Lines:
  Flotation deinking lines: 1 at 6,000 admt/y
  Recycled packaging pulping lines: 2 at 20,000 admt/y
Paper/Paperboard Grades and Capacities:
  Total paper and paperboard capacity: 22,000 mt/y
  Uncoated woodfree/freesheet: 6,000 mt/y
  Linerboard: 16,000 mt/y
Paper and Paperboard Mill Data:
Paper Machines: 6
PM 1, cylinder, Linerboard
PM 2, cylinder, Linerboard
PM 3, cylinder, Uncoated woodfree/freesheet
PM 4, cylinder, Uncoated woodfree/freesheet
PM 5, cylinder, Linerboard
PM 6, cylinder, total capacity 10,000 mt/y, Trim width 2.6 m, Linerboard

YenBai Joint-Stock Forest Agricultural and Foodstuff Company
Yen Bai City Mill
Ownership: 100% by Government of Vietnam
Nguyen Phuc Ward
Yen Bai City, Yen Bai Province
Vietnam
  Phone: (84) 29 3862278/7310012
  Fax: (84) 29 3862804
  Email: yfaco@yahoo.com
Personnel:
  Dir.: Mr. Cong Binh Tran
  Phone: (84) 29 3863286
  Dpty. Dir.: Mr. Xo Hong Pham
  Phone: (84) 29 3863213
Total Employees of Company: 200
Total Employees at this Location: 50
Type of Operation: Pulp mill, Paper mill
Pulp Grades and Capacities:
  Total pulp capacity: 12,000 mt/y
Pulp Mill Data:
Pulp Lines: 2
Paper/Paperboard Grades and Capacities:
  Total paper and paperboard capacity: 12,000 mt/y
  Specialty and industrial: 12,000 mt/y
Paper and Paperboard Mill Data:
Paper Machines: 4
PM 1, total capacity 1,500 mt/y, Specialty and industrial
PM 2, total capacity 1,500 mt/y, Specialty and industrial
PM 3, total capacity 4,500 mt/y, Specialty and industrial
PM 4, total capacity 4,500 mt/y, Specialty and industrial

Yen Son Joint-Stock Co.
Yen Bai Town Mill
Ownership: 100% by Hai Phong Paper Joint-Stock Co. (Hapaco)
638 Dien Bien Road
Yen Bai Town, Yen Bai Province
Vietnam
  Phone: (84) 29 3851982/4491/2026
  Fax: (84) 29 3855555
  Email: yensonco@hn.vnn.vn
Personnel:
  Mill Mgr.: Nguyen Duc Hau
  Phone: (84) 29 3851982/4491/2026
  Dpty. Dir.: Bui Duc Thong
  Phone: (84) 29 825397
  Dpty. Dir.: Vu Van Mo
  Phone: (84) 29 857757
Total Employees at this Location: 276
Type of Operation: Pulp mill, Paper mill
Pulp Grades and Capacities:
  Total pulp capacity: 14,000 mt/y
Paper/Paperboard Grades and Capacities:
  Total paper and paperboard capacity: 13,000 mt/y
  Specialty and industrial: 13,000 mt/y
Paper and Paperboard Mill Data:
Paper Machines: 1
No. 1-6, cylinder, total capacity 13,000 mt/y, Trim width 0.87 m, Specialty and industrial

Do you want the *whole* story on global pulp and paper markets?

From pulp price movements in Brazil; to capacity expansions in Finland; to exports of recovered paper from the United States to China, PPI Global gives you a complete understanding of the market forces affecting your company's global sales.

PPI Global offers you:

- The industry's most trusted pulp and paper price reporting
- In-depth analysis on how significant events are shaping the global pulp & paper industry
- Coverage of prices and markets on 600 grades of fiber, recovered paper, wood pulp, graphic papers and packaging
- The most extensive team covering the pulp and paper industry worldwide.

Get access to all of PPI Global for just the additional price of one newsletter.

Sign up today for a free trial at www.risi.com/tryglobal

PULP and PAPER MILLS in Latin America

ARGENTINA

①Alto Paraná S.A.
Ownership: Celulosa Arauco y Constitución S.A.
Gobernador Valentín Vergara 403 - Piso 3
B1638AEC Vicente López, Buenos Aires
Argentina
 Phone: (54) 11 5556 6000
 Fax: (54) 11 5556 6017
 Email: info@altoparana.com
 Web Address: www.altoparana.com
Personnel:
 Gen. Mgr.: Pablo Mainardi
 Phone: (54) 11 5556 6000
 Fax: (54) 11 5556 6017
 Email: pmainardi@altoparana.com
 Mktg. Mgr: Martín Lavarello
 Phone: (54) 11 5556 6000
 Fax: (54) 11 5556 6017
 Email: mlavarello@altoparana.com
 Finan. Mgr: Marcelo Miceli
 Phone: (54) 11 5556 6000
 Fax: (54) 11 5556 6017
 Email: mmiceli@altoparana.com
 Admin. Mgr: Sergio Gantuz
 Phone: (54) 11 5556 6000
 Fax: (54) 11 5556 6017
 Email: sgantuz@altoparana.com
 Logist. Mgr.: Ignacio Mendez
 Phone: (54) 11 5556 6000
 Fax: (54) 11 5556 6017
 Email: imendez@altoparana.com
Total Employees at this Location: 179
Mill Locations:
 Alto Paraná S.A., Misiones Mill, Ruta Nacional 12 Km 1589, N3378WCA Puerto Esperanza, Argentina, (Pulp mill)
 Phone: (54) 3757 488000
 Fax: (54) 3757 488099
 Email: infocelulosa@altoparana.com

①Alto Paraná S.A.
Misiones Mill
Ownership: Celulosa Arauco y Constitución S.A.
Ruta Nacional 12 Km 1589
N3378WCA Puerto Esperanza, Misiones
Argentina
 Phone: (54) 3757 488000
 Fax: (54) 3757 488099
 Email: infocelulosa@altoparana.com
 Web Address: www.altoparana.com
Personnel:
 Mill Mgr.: John Cifuentes
 Phone: (54) 3757 488000
 Fax: (54) 3757 488099
 Email: jcifuentes@altoparana.com
 Pulp Oper. Mgr.: Gustavo M. Traini
 Phone: (54) 3757 488000 Ext. 225
 Fax: (54) 3757 488099
 Email: gtraini@altoparana.com
 Environ. & Safety Mgr.: Jorge Mastrocola
 Phone: (54) 3757 488000
 Fax: (54) 3757 488099
 Email: jmastrocola@altoparana.com
Total Employees at this Location: 380
Type of Operation: Pulp mill
Pulp Grades and Capacities:
 Total pulp capacity: 362,554 mt/y
 Pulp available for market: 349,860 mt/y
 Chemical Pulp: 362,554 mt/y
Pulp Mill Data:
 Chemical Pulping Systems:
 Continuous digesters: 1
Pulp Lines: 2
 Bleach Plant Systems: 1
 Chemical Pulping System, Type: Softwood, Sequence: O_2 DEOpDEpD, Capacity 350,000 admt/y
 Chemical Recovery Equipment:
 Evaporator lines: 1
 Recovery boilers: 1
 Lime Kiln
 Pulp Dryers:
 Air Float dryers 1, Flakt dryer 1, Fourdriniers 1, Fourdriniers 1
Energy Data:
 Power boilers: 1
 Combustion turbines: 1 at 2.7 MW
 Steam turbines: 1 at 40.0 MW
 Electrical demand for mill: 2,000 MWh/D

①⑩Papelera Andina S.A.
Papelera Andina
Ownership: 10% by Grupo Zucamor
Rodriguez Peña
3900-5511 Godoy Cruz, Maipu, Mendoza
Argentina
 Phone: (54) 261 4978 217
 Fax: (54) 261 4931 426
 Email: papeleraandina@papeleraandina.com
 Web Address: www.papelerandina.com
Personnel:
 Pres.: Oscar Esteban Fornes
 Phone: (54) 261 4978 217
 VP: Juan Carlos Veiga
 Phone: (54) 261 4978 217
 Prod. Mgr.: Guillermo Amulphi
 Phone: (54) 261 4978 217
Total Employees of Company: 148
Total Employees at this Location: 148
Type of Operation: Paper mill, Paperboard mill
Pulp Grades and Capacities:
 Total pulp capacity: 31,129 mt/y
 Recycled Pulping: 31,129 mt/y
Pulp Mill Data:
 Recycled Fiber Treatment Lines:
 Recycled packaging pulping lines: 1 at 33,700
Paper/Paperboard Grades and Capacities:
 Total paper and paperboard capacity: 30,702 mt/y
 Corrugating medium/fluting: 30,702 mt/y
Paper and Paperboard Mill Data:
 Stock Preparation:
 Pulpers: 2
 Refiners: 6
Paper Machines: 1
 No. 3, fourdrinier, total capacity 30,702 mt/y, Trim width 2 m, Corrugating medium/fluting
Finishing Equipment:
 Rewinders: 4
 Sheeters: 4
Energy Data:
 Power boilers: 3
 Electrical demand for mill: 46 MWh/D

①⑩Ansabo S.A.
Quilmes Mill
Av. Isidoro Iriarte 1257 Villa La Florida
1881 Quilmes, Buenos Aires
Argentina
 Phone: (54) 11 4250 2905
 Fax: (54) 11 4200 5462
 Email: administracion@ansabo.com.ar
Personnel:
 Chmn./Mill Mgr.: Ricardo M. Angeletti
 Phone: (54) 11 4250 2905
 Fax: (54) 11 4200 5462
 Email: rangeletti@ansabo.com.ar
 Quality Trl. Mgr., Assur. Mgr. & Sls. Mgr.: Susana A. Angeletti
 Phone: (54) 11 4250 2905
 Fax: (54) 11 4200 5462
 Email: sangeletti@ansabo.com.ar
 Maint. Mgr.: Pablo Giuliani
 Phone: (54) 11 4250 2905
 Fax: (54) 11 4200 5462
 Email: pgiuliani@ansabo.com.ar
Total Employees of Company: 100
Total Employees at this Location: 80
Type of Operation: Paperboard mill
Pulp Grades and Capacities:
 Total pulp capacity: 14,178 mt/y
 Recycled Pulping: 14,178 mt/y
Pulp Mill Data:
 Recycled Fiber Treatment Lines:
 Pulpers: 2
Paper/Paperboard Grades and Capacities:
 Total paper and paperboard capacity: 13,923 mt/y
 Linerboard: 6,069 mt/y
 Corrugating medium/fluting: 7,854 mt/y
Paper and Paperboard Mill Data:
 Stock Preparation:
 Pulpers: 1
 Refiners: 3
Paper Machines: 1
 No. 2, fourdrinier, total capacity 13,923 mt/y, Trim width 1.7 m, Linerboard, Corrugating medium/fluting
Finishing Equipment:
 Rewinders: 1
Energy Data:
 Power boilers: 1
 Electrical demand for mill: 25 MWh/D

①⑩Argencraft S.A.
Andino Mill
Ownership: 100% by Alberto Gazzoti
Juan Domingo Perón n° 2
2215 Andino, Santa Fé
Argentina
 Phone: (54) 3476 496092/3
 Fax: (54) 3476 496094
 Email: ventas@argencraft.com, info@argencraft.com
Personnel:
 Prod. Mgr. : Daniel Del Turco
 Phone: (54) 3476 496092/3
 Fax: (54) 3476 496094
 Mktg Mgr.: Pablo Chait
 Phone: (54) 3476 496092/3
 Fax: (54) 3476 496094
 Programmer.: Hugo Walter Quintana
 Phone: (54) 3476 496092/3
 Fax: (54) 3476 496094
 Commer. Representative: Ricardo Javier GIL
 Phone: (54) 3476 496092/3
 Fax: (54) 3476 496094
Total Employees of Company: 110
Total Employees at this Location: 106

Argentina

Type of Operation: Paper mill
Pulp Grades and Capacities:
Total pulp capacity: 19,969 mt/y
Recycled Pulping: 19,969 mt/y
Pulp Mill Data:
Recycled Fiber Treatment Lines:
Pulpers: 2 at 22,000
Paper/Paperboard Grades and Capacities:
Total paper and paperboard capacity: 19,635 mt/y
Linerboard: 3,570 mt/y
Corrugating medium/fluting: 16,065 mt/y
Paper and Paperboard Mill Data:
Stock Preparation:
Refiners: 4
Paper Machines: 2
No. 1, fourdrinier, total capacity 17,136 mt/y, Trim width 2.1 m, Corrugating medium/fluting, Linerboard
No. 4, fourdrinier, total capacity 2,499 mt/y, Trim width 2 m, Corrugating medium/fluting
Finishing Equipment:
Rewinders: 1
Energy Data:
Power boilers: 2
Electrical demand for mill: 31 MWh/D

ⓂⓄCelulosa Argentina S.A.
Capitán Bermúdez Mill
Ownership: Douglas Albrecht, José Urtubey
Av. Humberto Pornilio s/n
S2154FVS Capitán Bermúdez, Santa Fé
Argentina
Phone: (54) 341 4911402
Fax: (54) 341 4911401
Email: contacto.comercial@celulosaargentina.com.ar
Web Address: www.celulosaargentina.com.ar
Personnel:
Industrial Mgr.: Sergio Cuis
Phone: (54) 341 4911402
Fax: (54) 341 4911401
Email: sergio.cuis@celulosaargentina.com.ar
Finan. & Admin. Mgr.: Diego Tuttolomondo
Phone: (54) 341 4911402
Fax: (54) 341 4911401
Email: diego.tuttolomondo@celulosaargentina.com.ar
Mktg. Mgr.: Diego Dorado
Phone: (54) 11 4717 6077
Fax: (54) 341 4911401
Email: diego.dorado@celulosaargentina.com.ar
Asst. Mill Mgr.: Gabriel Morin
Phone: (54) 341 4911402
Fax: (54) 341 4911401
Email: gabriel.morin@celulosaargentina.com.ar
Total Employees of Company: 730
Total Employees at this Location: 460
Type of Operation: Pulp mill, Paper mill
Mill Locations:
Celulosa Argentina S.A., Zárate Mill, Aristóbulo del Valle 594, 2800 Zárate, Argentina, Capacity: 49,980 mt/y, (Paper mill)
Phone: (54) 3487 425800
Fax: (54) 3487 425800 Ext. 210
FANAPEL - Fábrica Nacional de Papel S.A., Juan Lacaze Mill (97.60% owned), Av. Rep. Argentina s/n 102, 70001 Juan Lacaze, Uruguay, Capacity: 62,118 mt/y, (Pulp mill, Paper mill)
Phone: (598) 4586 2022
Fax: (598) 4586 2912
Email: planta.industrial@fanapel.com.uy
Pulp Grades and Capacities:
Total pulp capacity: 174,963 mt/y
Pulp available for market: 90,321 mt/y
Chemical Pulp: 174,963 mt/y
Pulp Mill Data:
Chemical Pulping Systems:
Batch digesters: 4
Pulp Lines: 1
Bleach Plant Systems: 1
Chemical Pulping System, Type: ECF - Hardwood (planted eucalyptus), Sequence: O_2 DEopDPO,
Capacity 180,000 admt/y
Chemical Recovery Equipment:
Evaporator lines: 1
Recovery boilers: 1
Lime Kiln
Pulp Dryers:
Fourdriniers 1, Fourdriniers 1
Paper/Paperboard Grades and Capacities:
Total paper and paperboard capacity: 95,319 mt/y
Uncoated woodfree/freesheet: 77,112 mt/y
Packaging papers: 18,207 mt/y
Paper and Paperboard Mill Data:
Stock Preparation:
Pulpers: 7
Refiners: 6
Paper Machines: 2
No. 2, fourdrinier, total capacity 77,112 mt/y, Trim width 3.87 m, Uncoated woodfree/freesheet
No. 4, fourdrinier, total capacity 18,207 mt/y, Trim width 2.64 m, Packaging papers
Finishing Equipment:
Rewinders: 1
Sheeters: 4
Energy Data:
Power boilers: 1
Steam turbines: 2 at 29.0 MW
Electrical demand for mill: 488 MWh/D

ⓂCelulosa Argentina S.A.
Zárate Mill
Aristóbulo del Valle 594
2800 Zárate, Buenos Aires
Argentina
Phone: (54) 3487 425800
Fax: (54) 3487 425800 Ext. 210
Web Address: www.celulosaargentina.com.ar
Personnel:
Prod. Mgr.: Jose Luiz Fernandez
Phone: (54) 3487 425800
Email: jose.fernandez@celulosaargentina.com.ar
Total Employees at this Location: 110
Type of Operation: Paper mill
Paper/Paperboard Grades and Capacities:
Total paper and paperboard capacity: 49,980 mt/y
Uncoated woodfree/freesheet: 49,980 mt/y
Paper and Paperboard Mill Data:
Stock Preparation:
Pulpers: 5
Refiners: 4
Paper Machines: 1
No. 4, fourdrinier, total capacity 49,980 mt/y, Trim width 3.7 m, Uncoated woodfree/freesheet
Finishing Equipment:
Winders: 1
Supercalenders: 2
Rewinders: 1
Energy Data:
Power boilers: 3
Steam turbines: 2 at 26.9 (idle) MW
Electrical demand for mill: 103 MWh/D

ⓄCelulosa Baradero S.A.
M.T. Alvear 4025 (B1678CJB) Caseros
Buenos Aires, Buenos Aires
Argentina
Phone: (54) 11 4115 8614/33 29485020
Fax: (54) 11 4581 8614 108
Email: info@celulosabaraderosa.com.ar
Web Address: www.celulosabaraderosa.com.ar
Total Employees of Company: 60
Total Employees at this Location: 8
Mill Locations:
Celulosa Baradero S.A., Baradero Mill, Alte. Brown s/n (2942), Baradero, Argentina, Capacity: 6,000 mt/y, (Paper mill)
Phone: (54) 3329 48 5020/1950
Email: info@celulosabaradero.com.ar

ⓂCelulosa Baradero S.A.
Baradero Mill
Alte. Brown s/n (2942)
Baradero, Buenos Aires
Argentina
Phone: (54) 3329 48 5020/1950
Email: info@celulosabaraderosa.com.ar
Web Address: www.celulosabaraderosa.com.ar
Personnel:
Prod. Mgr.: Julián Perez
Phone: (54) 3329 48 5020
Sls. Mgr.: Carolina Perez
Phone: (54) 3329 48 5020
Email: info@celulosabaraderosa.com.ar
Total Employees at this Location: 24
Type of Operation: Paper mill
Paper/Paperboard Grades and Capacities:
Total paper and paperboard capacity: 6,000 mt/y
Tissue: 6,000 mt/y

ⓄPapelera Berazategui S.A.
Calle 7779
B1884BCO Berazategui, Buenos Aires
Argentina
Phone: (54) 11 4256 1139/2411/4216-1297
Email: info@papeleraberazategui.com
Web Address: www.papeleraberazategui.com
Personnel:
Pres.: Rubén Gonzav
Phone: (54) 11 4256 1139/2411/4216-1297
VP: Martín Muiña
Phone: (54) 11 4256 1139/2411/4216-1297
Mill Locations:
Papelera Berazategui S.A., Berazategui Mill, Av. Gaston Rigollau 2530, 1884 Berazategui, Argentina, Capacity: 38,913 mt/y, (Paper mill, Paperboard mill)
Phone: (54) 11 4275 8382
Fax: (54) 11 4275 8382
Email: compras@papeleraberazategui.com

ⓂPapelera Berazategui S.A.
Berazategui Mill
Av. Gaston Rigollau 2530
1884 Berazategui, Buenos Aires
Argentina
Phone: (54) 11 4275 8382
Fax: (54) 11 4275 8382
Email: compras@papeleraberazategui.com
Web Address: www.papeleraberazategui.com
Personnel:
Mgr.: Marcelo Souto
Phone: (54) 11 4275 8382
Fax: (54) 11 4275 8382
Email: marcelos@papeleraberazategui.com
Total Employees at this Location: 88
Type of Operation: Paper mill, Paperboard mill
Pulp Grades and Capacities:
Total pulp capacity: 39,697 mt/y
Recycled Pulping: 39,697 mt/y
Pulp Mill Data:
Recycled Fiber Treatment Lines:
Pulpers: 1 at 43,300
Paper/Paperboard Grades and Capacities:
Total paper and paperboard capacity: 38,913 mt/y
Linerboard: 19,992 mt/y
Corrugating medium/fluting: 18,921 mt/y
Paper and Paperboard Mill Data:
Paper Machines: 1
No. 1, cylinder, total capacity 38,913 mt/y, Trim width 3 m, Corrugating medium/fluting, Linerboard
Energy Data:
Power boilers: 1
Electrical demand for mill: 59 MWh/D

ⓄCartocor S.A.
Ownership: Arcor
Av. Fulvio S. Pagani 487
2434 Arroyito, Córdoba
Argentina
Phone: (54) 3576 425247/425218

Argentina

Fax: (54) 3576 425338
Email: jmonteporsi@arcor.com
Web Address: www.cartocor.com
Personnel:
mill Mgr., Contr.: Mario J. Valente
Phone: (54) 343 4206022
Fax: (54) 343 4206056
Email: mvalente@arcor.com
Bus. Mgr.: Guillermo Muller
Phone: (54) 343 4206022
Fax: (54) 343 4206056
Email: gmuller@arcor.com
Paper Mill Mgr.: Jorge Gabriel Monteporsi
Phone: (54) 3576 425247/425218
Fax: (54) 3576 4255515
Email: jmonteporsi@arcor.com
Prod. Mgr.: Guillermo Diamante
Phone: (54) 343 4206022
Fax: (54) 343 4206056
Email: gdiamante@arcor.com
Gen. Sec.: Nora Fernández
Phone: (54) 343 4206022
Fax: (54) 343 4206056
Email: nfernandez@arcor.com
Oper. Mgr.: Daniel Schroeder
Phone: (54) 343 4206090
Fax: (54) 343 4206009
Email: dschroeder@arcor.com
Total Employees of Company: 98
Mill Locations:
Cartocor S.A., Arroyito Mill, Av. Fulvio S. Pagani 487, 2434 Arroyito, Argentina, Capacity: 47,838 mt/y, (Paperboard mill)
Phone: (54) 3576 425247/425218
Fax: (54) 3576 425338
Email: jmonteporsi@arcor.com

ⓂCartocor S.A.
Arroyito Mill
Av. Fulvio S. Pagani 487
2434 Arroyito, Córdoba
Argentina
  Phone: (54) 3576 425247/425218
  Fax: (54) 3576 425338
  Email: jmonteporsi@arcor.com
  Web Address: www.cartocor.com
Personnel:
mill Mgr., Contr.: Mario J. Valente
Phone: (54) 343 4206022
Fax: (54) 343 4206056
Email: mvalente@arcor.com
Bus. Mgr.: Guillermo Muller
Phone: (54) 343 4206022
Fax: (54) 343 4206056
Email: gmuller@arcor.com
Paper Mill Mgr.: Jorge Gabriel Monteporsi
Phone: (54) 3576 425247/425218
Fax: (54) 3576 4255515
Email: jmonteporsi@arcor.com
Prod. Mgr.: Guillermo Diamante
Phone: (54) 343 4206022
Fax: (54) 343 4206056
Email: gdiamante@arcor.com
Gen. Sec.: Nora Fernández
Phone: (54) 343 4206022
Fax: (54) 343 4206056
Email: nfernandez@arcor.com
Oper. Mgr.: Daniel Schroeder
Phone: (54) 343 4206090
Fax: (54) 343 4206009
Email: dschroeder@arcor.com
Total Employees at this Location: 98
Type of Operation: Paperboard mill
Pulp Grades and Capacities:
Total pulp capacity: 48,838 mt/y
Recycled Pulping: 48,838 mt/y

Pulp Mill Data:
Recycled Fiber Treatment Lines:
Pulpers: 1 at 53,000
Paper/Paperboard Grades and Capacities:
Total paper and paperboard capacity: 47,838 mt/y
Linerboard: 44,625 mt/y
Corrugating medium/fluting: 3,213 mt/y
Paper and Paperboard Mill Data:
Stock Preparation:
Refiners: 3
Paper Machines: 1
No. 1, fourdrinier, total capacity 47,838 mt/y, Trim width 2.4 m, Linerboard, Corrugating medium/fluting
Energy Data:
Power boilers: 1
Electrical demand for mill: 60 MWh/D

ⒽⓂCelu Paper S.A.
San Pedro Mill
Av. Independencia s/n
B2930AEM San Pedro, Buenos Aires
Argentina
  Phone: (54) 3329 425 943/633
  Email: galcorta@redsp.com.ar
Personnel:
Dir.: Luis Zanuttini
Phone: (54) 3329 425 943
Total Employees at this Location: 150
Type of Operation: Paper mill
Pulp Grades and Capacities:
Total pulp capacity: 18,843 mt/y
Recycled Pulping: 18,843 mt/y

Pulp Mill Data:
Bleach Plant Systems: 1
Recycled Pulping System, Type: DIP
Recycled Fiber Treatment Lines:
Flotation deinking lines: 1
Paper/Paperboard Grades and Capacities:
Total paper and paperboard capacity: 24,990 mt/y
Tissue: 24,990 mt/y
Paper and Paperboard Mill Data:
Paper Machines: 3
No. 1, fourdrinier, total capacity 7,140 mt/y, Trim width 2.5 m, Tissue
No. 2, fourdrinier, total capacity 8,211 mt/y, Trim width 2.5 m, Tissue
No. 3, fourdrinier, total capacity 9,639 mt/y, Trim width 2.5 m, Tissue
Energy Data:
Power boilers
Electrical demand for mill: 113 MWh/D

ⒽCelulosa Campana S.A.
Darragueira 1261
1822 Valentín-Alsina, Buenos Aires
Argentina
  Phone: (54) 11 4208 1224
  Fax: (54) 11 4209 4746
  Email: info@celulosacampana.com.ar
  Web Address: www.celulosacampana.com.ar
Personnel:
Dir.: Oscar Muiña
Phone: (54) 11 4208 1224
Fax: (54) 11 4209 4746
Email: omuina@celulosacampana.com.ar
Mill Locations:
Celulosa Campana S.A., Lima Mill, Camino Central Atucha 1 km 6, 2806 Lima, Argentina, Capacity: 32,130 mt/y, (Paper mill)
Phone: (54) 3487 481874
Fax: (54) 3487 481874
Email: info@celulosacampana.com.ar

ⓂCelulosa Campana S.A.
Lima Mill
Camino Central Atucha 1 km 6
2806 Lima, Buenos Aires
Argentina
  Phone: (54) 3487 481874
  Fax: (54) 3487 481874
  Email: info@celulosacampana.com.ar
  Web Address: www.celulosacampana.com.ar/historia.html
Personnel:
Mill Mgr.: Eduardo Suárez
Phone: (54) 3487 481874
HR. Mgr.: Marina Marchetti
Phone: (54) 3487 481874
Email: mmarchetti@celulosacampana.com.ar
Total Employees at this Location: 120
Type of Operation: Paper mill
Pulp Grades and Capacities:
Total pulp capacity: 23,727 mt/y
Recycled Pulping: 23,727 mt/y

Pulp Mill Data:
Bleach Plant Systems: 1
Recycled Pulping System, Type: DIP
Recycled Fiber Treatment Lines:
Flotation deinking lines: 1
Paper/Paperboard Grades and Capacities:
Total paper and paperboard capacity: 32,130 mt/y
Tissue: 32,130 mt/y
Paper and Paperboard Mill Data:
Paper Machines: 2
No. 1, crescent former, total capacity 16,065 mt/y, Trim width 2.7 m, Tissue
No. 2, fourdrinier, total capacity 16,065 mt/y, Trim width 2.4 m, Tissue, Uncoated woodfree/freesheet
Energy Data:
Power boilers
Electrical demand for mill: 124 MWh/D

ⒽⓂCIFIVE S.A.I.C.
Recreo Sur Mill
Canonigo Rodriguez y Cno (v) a Esperanza
3001 Recreo Sur, Santa Fé
Argentina
Mailing Address: Casilla de Correo 331, 3000 Santa Fe, Argentina
  Phone: (54) 342 489 1866/1778
  Fax: (54) 342 489 1778
  Email: administracion@cifive.com, otecnica@cifive.com
  Web Address: www.cifive.com
Personnel:
VP.: Javier Ferrer
Phone: (54) 11 4381 7518
Fax: (54) 11 4382 3811
Email: jferrer@cifive.com
Man. Dir. & Mill Mgr.: Ignacio Ferraro
Phone: (54) 342 489 1866
Fax: (54) 342 489 1778
Email: iferraro@cifive.com
Dir.: Raul Fernandez
Phone: (54) 342 489 1866
Fax: (54) 342 489 1778
Email: rfernandez@cifive.com
Total Employees of Company: 105
Total Employees at this Location: 105
Type of Operation: Paperboard mill
Pulp Grades and Capacities:
Total pulp capacity: 12,800 mt/y

Pulp Mill Data:
Recycled Fiber Treatment Lines:
Pulpers: 2 at 15,000 admt/y
Paper/Paperboard Grades and Capacities:
Total paper and paperboard capacity: 12,000 mt/y
Boxboard/cartonboard: 12,000 mt/y
Paper and Paperboard Mill Data:
Stock Preparation:
Pulpers: 2
Refiners: 1
Paper Machines: 2
No. 1, cylinder (5), total capacity 8,700 mt/y, Trim width 2.1 m, Boxboard/cartonboard
No. 2, cylinder (5), total capacity 3,300 mt/y, Trim width 2.24 m, Boxboard/cartonboard
Finishing Equipment:
Rewinders: 1
Sheeters: 5
Energy Data:
Power boilers: 1
Electrical demand for mill: 19 MWh/D

Argentina

ⓘⓜCooperativa Pachi Lara
Ciudad Azul Mill
Laprida 250
7300 Ciudad Azul, Buenos Aires
Argentina
Personnel:
Pres.: Jorge Scabuzzo
Mill Mgr.: Abel Amaya
Adm. Mgr.: Margarita Lopez
Type of Operation: Paper mill
Paper/Paperboard Grades and Capacities:
Total paper and paperboard capacity: 5,000 mt/y
Corrugating medium/fluting: 5,000 mt/y
Paper and Paperboard Mill Data:
Paper Machines: 1
PM 1, total capacity 5,000 mt/y, Corrugating medium/fluting

ⓘⓜCOPSI Compañía Papelera Sinsacate S.R.L.
Sinsacate Mill
Ruta 9 km 755
402800 Sinsacate, Córdoba
Argentina
Mailing Address: C.P. X5221BBH, 402800-C.C. 28 Sinsacate, Córdoba, Argentina
Phone: (54) 3525 402800
Fax: (54) 3525 402800
Email: ventas@copsi.com.ar, hcresta@copsi.com.ar
Web Address: www.copsi.com.ar
Personnel:
Owner & Man. Dir.: Horacio Cresta
Phone: (54) 3525 402800
Fax: (54) 3525 402800
Email: hcresta@copsi.com.ar
Prod. Supervisor: Jorge Moron
Phone: (54) 3525 402800
Fax: (54) 3525 402800
Email: jmoron@copsi.com.ar
Total Employees of Company: 80
Type of Operation: Paper mill, Paperboard mill
Paper/Paperboard Grades and Capacities:
Total paper and paperboard capacity: 24,000 mt/y
Packaging papers: 12,000 mt/y
Boxboard/cartonboard: 12,000 mt/y
Paper and Paperboard Mill Data:
Paper Machines: 3
PM 1, total capacity 6,000 mt/y, Boxboard/cartonboard
PM 2, fourdrinier, total capacity 12,000 mt/y, Packaging papers
PM 3, total capacity 6,000 mt/y, Boxboard/cartonboard

ⓘPapelera Entre Ríos S.A.
Av. del Libertador 7820, 7th floor B
1429 Capital Federal, Buenos Aires
Argentina
Phone: (54) 11 47011617
Fax: (54) 11 47012202
Email: ventas@papentrerios.com.ar
Web Address: www.papentrerios.com.ar
Personnel:
Pres.: Isaac Abuaf
Phone: (54) 11 4701 1617
Fax: (54) 11 4701 2202
Email: iabuaf@papersa.com.ar
Gen. Mgr.: Edgardo Dario Abuaf
Phone: (54) 11 4701 1617
Fax: (54) 11 4701 2202
Adm. Mgr. Sec.: Silvia Donato
Phone: (54) 343 4331444
Email: adm@papersa.com.ar
Admin. Mgr.: Maria Ana Aranguren
Phone: (54) 11 4701 1617
Fax: (54) 11 4701 2202
Email: maranguren@papentrerios.com.ar
Accounting Mgr.: Cesar Pablo Vicentin
Phone: (54) 11 4701 1617
Fax: (54) 11 4701 2202
Email: pvicentin@papentrerios.com.ar
HR Mgr.: Carlos Cipriani
Phone: (54) 11 4701 1617
Fax: (54) 11 4701 2202
Total Employees of Company: 100
Mill Locations:
Papelera Entre Ríos S.A., Paraná Mill, Ayacucho, 3047 Paraná, Entre Ríos, Entre Ríos, Argentina
Phone: (54) 343 4331444
Fax: (54) 343 4242444
Email: ventas@papentrerios.com.ar
Web Address: www.papentrerios.com.ar

ⓜPapelera Entre Ríos S.A.
Paraná Mill
Ayacucho
3047 Paraná, Entre Ríos, Entre Ríos
Argentina
Mailing Address: CC 352, 3100 Paraná, Entre Ríos, Argentina
Phone: (54) 343 4331444
Fax: (54) 343 4242444
Email: ventas@papentrerios.com.ar
Web Address: www.papentrerios.com.ar
Personnel:
Pres.: Isaac Abuaf
Phone: (54) 343 4331444
Fax: (54) 343 4242444
Chief Eng.: Luis De Angeli
Phone: (54) 343 4331444
Fax: (54) 343 4242444
Email: mantenimiento@papentrerios.com.ar
Accounting Mgr.: Cesar Pablo Vicentin
Phone: (54) 343 4331444
Fax: (54) 343 4242444
Email: pvicentin@papentrerios.com.ar
Tech. Mgr.: Enrique Rebora
Phone: (54) 343 4331444
Fax: (54) 343 4242444
HR Mgr.: Carlos Cipriani
Phone: (54) 343 4331444
Fax: (54) 343 4242444
Total Employees of Company: 100
Total Employees at this Location: 95
Type of Operation: Paperboard mill
Pulp Grades and Capacities:
Total pulp capacity: 21,134 mt/y
Recycled Pulping: 21,134 mt/y
Pulp Mill Data:
Recycled Fiber Treatment Lines:
Pulpers: 1 at 21,400
Paper/Paperboard Grades and Capacities:
Total paper and paperboard capacity: 20,706 mt/y
Linerboard: 10,710 mt/y
Corrugating medium/fluting: 9,996 mt/y
Paper and Paperboard Mill Data:
Stock Preparation:
Pulpers:
Paper Machines: 1
No. 1, cylinder, total capacity 20,706 mt/y, Trim width 2.5 m, Linerboard, Corrugating medium/fluting
Finishing Equipment:
Rewinders: 3
Energy Data:
Power boilers: 1
Electrical demand for mill: 36 MWh/D

ⓘⓜPapelera La Helice S.A.I.C.
San Fernando Mill
Rivadavia 760
1646 San Fernando, Buenos Aires
Argentina
Phone: (54) 11 4744 7066
Fax: (54) 11 4744 7066
Personnel:
Pres.: Alejandro Salsa
Phone: (54) 11 4744 7066
Type of Operation: Paperboard mill
Paper/Paperboard Grades and Capacities:
Total paper and paperboard capacity: 6,000 mt/y
Specialty and industrial
Corrugating medium/fluting
Paper and Paperboard Mill Data:
Paper Machines: 1
PM 1, total capacity 6,000 mt/y, Specialty and industrial, Corrugating medium/fluting

ⓜKimberly-Clark S.A.
Bernal Mill
Ownership: 100% by Kimberly-Clark Corp.
Espora 50
1876 Bernal, Buenos Aires
Argentina
Phone: (54) 11 4365 7209
Fax: (54) 11 4365 7244
Email: gustavo.magnani@kcc.com
Web Address: www.kimberly-clark.com
Personnel:
Gen. Mgr.: Pablo Latrónico
Phone: (54) 11 4365 7209
Fax: (54) 11 4365 7244
Email: pablo.latronico@kcc.com
Finan. Dir.: Héctor Vidal Ponte
Phone: (54) 11 4365 7209
Fax: (54) 11 4365 7244
Email: hector.vidalponte@kcc.com
HR Mgr.: Martin Chavez
Phone: (54) 11 4365 7209
Fax: (54) 11 4365 7244
Email: martin.chavez@kcc.com
Mktg. Mgr.: Julieta Carman
Phone: (54) 11 4365 7209
Fax: (54) 11 4365 7244
Email: julieta.carman@kcc.com
Supply Chain: Walter Olha
Phone: (54) 11 4365 7209
Fax: (54) 11 4365 7244
Email: walter.olha@kcc.com
Oper. Mgr.: Daniel Masiero
Phone: (54) 11 4365 7209
Fax: (54) 11 4365 7244
Email: daniel.masiero@kcc.com
Total Employees at this Location: 189
Type of Operation: Paper mill
Paper/Paperboard Grades and Capacities:
Total paper and paperboard capacity: 34,986 mt/y
Tissue: 34,986 mt/y
Paper and Paperboard Mill Data:
Stock Preparation:
Pulpers: 2
Refiners: 3
Paper Machines: 1
No. 1, crescent former, total capacity 34,986 mt/y, Trim width 3.55 m, Tissue, Uncoated woodfree/freesheet
Finishing Equipment:
Rewinders: 2
Energy Data:
Power boilers
Electrical demand for mill: 103 MWh/D

ⓘLedesma S.A.A.I.
Corrientes 415
Buenos Aires, Buenos Aires
Argentina
Phone: (54) 11 4378 1620/1555/1661
Email: institucionales@ledesma.com.ar
Web Address: www.ledesma.com.ar
Personnel:
Man. Dir.: Miguel Ascárate
Phone: (54) 11 4378 1620/1555
Email: mascarate@ledesma.com.ar
Bus. Mgr.: Marcos Uribelarrea
Phone: (54) 11 4378 1620/1555
Email: muribelarrea@ledesma.com.ar
Purch. Mgr.: Juan Carlos do Pico
Phone: (54) 11 4378 1620/1555
Email: jdopico@ledesma.com.ar
Corp. Affairs: Vicente Amadeo
Phone: (54) 11 4378 1620/1555

Argentina

Email: vamadeo@ledesma.com.ar
Commer. Mgr. : Martin Franzini
Phone: (54) 11 4378 1578
Email: mfranzini@ledesma.com.ar
Total Employees of Company: 7,300
Mill Locations:
Ledesma S.A.A.I., Libertador General Mill, Salta s/n, Barrio Ledesma, 4512 Libertador General San Martín, Argentina, Capacity: 129,948 mt/y, (Pulp mill, Paper mill)
Phone: (54) 3886 429300
Fax: (54) 3886 429304
Email: institucionales@ledesma.com.ar

ⓂLedesma S.A.A.I.
Libertador General Mill
Salta s/n, Barrio Ledesma
4512 Libertador General San Martín, Jujuy
Argentina
Phone: (54) 3886 429300
Fax: (54) 3886 429304
Email: institucionales@ledesma.com.ar
Web Address: www.ledesma.com.ar
Personnel:
Tech. Mgr.: Ricardo Barros
Phone: (54) 3886 429300
Fax: (54) 3886 429304
Email: rbarros@ledesma.com.ar
Corp. Affairs: Vicente Amadeo
Phone: (54) 11 4378 1620
Fax: (54) 3886 429304
Email: vamadeo@ledesma.com.ar
Mgr.: Humberto Sola
Phone: (54) 3886 429300
Fax: (54) 3886 429304
Email: hsola@ledesma.com.ar
Total Employees at this Location: 403
Type of Operation: Pulp mill, Paper mill
Pulp Grades and Capacities:
Total pulp capacity: 79,161 mt/y
Other Pulp: 79,161 mt/y
Pulp Mill Data:
Chemical Pulping Systems:
Continuous digesters: 2
Pulp Lines: 1
Bleach Plant Systems: 1
Chemical Pulping System, Type: Bagasse
Chemical Recovery Equipment:
Evaporator lines: 2
Recovery boilers: 1
Lime Kiln
Paper/Paperboard Grades and Capacities:
Total paper and paperboard capacity: 129,948 mt/y
Uncoated woodfree/freesheet: 107,457 mt/y
Coated woodfree/freesheet: 22,491 mt/y
Paper and Paperboard Mill Data:
Stock Preparation:
Pulpers:
Refiners: 4
Paper Machines: 1
No. 1, fourdrinier, total capacity 129,948 mt/y, Trim width 3.8 m, Uncoated woodfree/freesheet, Coated woodfree/freesheet
Coating Machines: 1
No. 1, off machine
Finishing Equipment:
Winders: 2
Calenders: 2
Energy Data:
Power boilers: 1
Steam turbines: 1
Electrical demand for mill: 377 MWh/D

ⓂPapelera Mediterránea S.A.
Av. L.N. Alem 350
2500 Cañada de Gómez, Santa Fé
Argentina
Phone: (54) 3471 428183
Fax: (54) 3471 428188
Email: info@papelmediterranea.com.ar
Web Address: www.papelmediterranea.com.ar
Personnel:
Pres.: Álvaro Enrique Lucena
Phone: (54) 3471 428183
Fax: (54) 3471 428188
Prod. Mgr.: Edgardo Reale
Phone: (54) 3471 428183
Fax: (54) 3471 428188
Mill Locations:
Papelera Mediterránea S.A., Córdoba Mill, Calle Bv. Ascasubi, 1290, Bell Ville, 2550 Córdoba, Argentina, Capacity: 12,000 mt/y, (Paperboard mill)
Phone: (54) 3537 410881
Email: info@papelmediterranea.com.ar

ⓂPapelera Mediterránea S.A.
Córdoba Mill
Calle Bv. Ascasubi, 1290, Bell Ville
2550 Córdoba, Córdoba
Argentina
Phone: (54) 3537 410881
Email: info@papelmediterranea.com.ar
Web Address: www.papelmediterranea.com.ar
Personnel:
Prod. Mgr.: Ing. Wolfon
Phone: (54) 3534 425014/410881
Type of Operation: Paperboard mill
Paper/Paperboard Grades and Capacities:
Total paper and paperboard capacity: 12,000 mt/y
Linerboard
Corrugating medium/fluting: 12,000 mt/y
Paper and Paperboard Mill Data:
Paper Machines: 1
No. 1, Trim width 2 m, Corrugating medium/fluting, Linerboard

ⓂPapel Misionero S.A.I.F.C.
Ownership: 96% by Grupo Zucamor, 4% by others
Brasil 160
1063 Buenos Aires, Buenos Aires
Argentina
Phone: (54) 11 5169 5500
Fax: (54) 11 5169 5501
Email: ventas@grupozucamor.com.ar
Web Address: www.papel-misionero.com.ar
Personnel:
Pres.: Marcelo Campo
Phone: (54) 11 5169 5503
Fax: (54) 11 5169 5503
Email: marcelo.campo@grupozucamor.com.ar
Resident Mgr.: Eduardo Borge
Phone: (54) 11 5169 5503
Fax: (54) 11 5169 5503
Email: eduardo.borge@grupozucamor.com.ar
Admin./Finan. Dir.: Ricardo Rogers
Phone: (54) 11 5169 5500
Fax: (54) 11 5169 5501
Email: ricardo.rogers@grupozucamor.com.ar
Sls. Mgr.: Daniel Wanschelbaum
Phone: (54) 3743 493700
Fax: (54) 3743 493757
Email: daniel.wanhelsbaum@grupozucamor.com.ar
Total Employees of Company: 500
Total Employees at this Location: 10
Mill Locations:
Papel Misionero S.A.I.F.C., Puerto Mineral Mill, Puerto Mineral, Ruta 12 Km 1457, 3332 Capioví, Argentina, Capacity: 99,960 mt/y, (Pulp mill, Paper mill, Paperboard mill)
Phone: (54) 3743 493 700/444
Fax: (54) 3743 493 757/237
Email: info@grupozucamor.com.ar

ⓂPapel Misionero S.A.I.F.C.
Puerto Mineral Mill
Ownership: 96% by Grupo Zucamor
Puerto Mineral, Ruta 12 Km 1457
3332 Capioví, Misiones
Argentina
Phone: (54) 3743 493 700/444
Fax: (54) 3743 493 757/237
Email: info@grupozucamor.com.ar
Web Address: www.grupozucamor.com
Personnel:
Prod. & Ind. Mgr.: Camilo Paniego
Phone: (54) 3743 493700 Ext. 605
Fax: (54) 3743 493 757
Email: camilo.paniego@grupozucamor.com.ar
Finan. Mgr.: Ricardo Rogers
Phone: (54) 3743 493700
Fax: (54) 3743 493 757
Email: ricardo.rogers@grupozucamor.com.ar
Cell. Dept. Chief: Roberto Briñocoli
Phone: (54) 3743 493700 ext 645
Fax: (54) 3743 493 757
Email: roberto.brincoli@grupozucamor.com.ar
Purch. Asst. Chief: Rodolfo Kopp
Phone: (54) 3743 493700 ext 631
Fax: (54) 3743 493 757
Email: rodolfo.kopp@grupozucamor.com.ar
Forestry Area Chief: Martin Chiluk
Phone: (54) 3743 493700 ext 738
Fax: (54) 3743 493 757
Email: martin.chiluk@grupozucamor.com.ar
Total Employees at this Location: 275
Type of Operation: Pulp mill, Paper mill, Paperboard mill
Pulp Grades and Capacities:
Total pulp capacity: 102,601 mt/y
Chemical Pulp: 102,601 mt/y
Pulp Mill Data:
Chemical Pulping Systems:
Batch digesters: 4
Pulp Lines: 1
Chemical Recovery Equipment:
Evaporator lines: 1
Recovery boilers: 1
Lime Kiln
Pulp Dryers:
Air Float dryers 1
Paper/Paperboard Grades and Capacities:
Total paper and paperboard capacity: 99,960 mt/y
Packaging papers: 32,487 mt/y
Linerboard: 67,473 mt/y
Paper and Paperboard Mill Data:
Stock Preparation:
Refiners: 6
Paper Machines: 1
No. 1, fourdrinier, total capacity 99,960 mt/y, Trim width 3.4 m, Linerboard, Packaging papers
Finishing Equipment:
Rewinders: 1 at 100,000 mt/y
Sheeters: 1
Energy Data:
Power boilers: 2
Steam turbines: 2 at 9.5, 15 MW
Electrical demand for mill: 319 MWh/D

ⓂPapelera del NOA S.A.
Av. 25 Mayo N° 555, Piso 5
1002 Buenos Aires, Buenos Aires
Argentina
Phone: (54) 11 5555 1350
Fax: (54) 11 5555 1365
Personnel:
Owner & Pres.: Juan Cruz Adrogué
Phone: (54) 11 5555 1350
Fax: (54) 11 5555 1365
Pres. Asst.: Martina Oriarte
Phone: (54) 11 5555 1350
Fax: (54) 11 5555 1365
Mgr. : Ricardo Aguado
Phone: (54) 11 5555 1350
Fax: (54) 11 5555 1365
Admin. Dir. & Finan.: Mario Vales
Phone: (54) 11 5555 1350
Fax: (54) 11 5555 1365
Sls. Mgr.: Rubén Ochoa
Phone: (54) 388 4020403/0412

Argentina

Email: ventas@papelnoa.com.ar
Oper. Mgr.: Osvaldo Lopez
Phone: (54) 11 5555 1350
Fax: (54) 11 5555 1365
Prod. Mgr.: Hugo Mendez
Phone: (54) 11 5555 1350
Fax: (54) 11 5555 1365
Total Employees of Company: 170
Total Employees at this Location: 20
Mill Locations:
Papelera del NOA S.A., Rio Blanco Mill, Ruta 1, Km. 9, 4601 Río Blanco, Jujuy, Argentina, Capacity: 49,980 mt/y, (Paper mill, Paperboard mill)
Phone: (54) 388 402 0403
Fax: (54) 388 402 0412
Email: ventas@papelnoa.com.ar, administracion@papelnoa.com.ar
Papel Pampa. NOA, Quilmes Mill (50% owned), Camino Gral. Belgrano, Km. 14,500, 1878 Quilmes, Argentina, (Pulp mill, Paper mill, Paperboard mill)
Phone: (54) 11 4365 1000
Fax: (54) 11 4200 0464

ⓂPapelera del NOA S.A.
Rio Blanco Mill
Ruta 1, Km. 9
4601 Río Blanco, Jujuy, Jujuy
Argentina
Phone: (54) 388 402 0403
Fax: (54) 388 402 0412
Email: ventas@papelnoa.com.ar, administracion@papelnoa.com.ar
Personnel:
Paper Mill Mgr.: Hugo Mendez
Phone: (54) 388 402 0403
Fax: (54) 388 402 0412
Email: fabrica@papelnoa.com.ar
Oper. Mgr.: Oscar Zacur
Phone: (54) 388 402 0403
Fax: (54) 388 402 0412
Email: ozacur@papelnoa.com.ar
Tech. Mgr.: Luis Vera
Phone: (54) 388 402 0403
Fax: (54) 388 402 0412
Email: lvera@papelnoa.com.ar
Sls. Mgr. Assistant: Rubén Ochoa
Phone: (54) 388 402 0403
Fax: (54) 388 402 0412
Email: ventas@papelnoa.com.ar
Total Employees at this Location: 175
Type of Operation: Paper mill, Paperboard mill
Pulp Grades and Capacities:
Total pulp capacity: 51,423 mt/y
Chemical Pulp: 42,167 mt/y
Recycled Pulping: 9,256 mt/y
Pulp Mill Data:
Chemical Pulping Systems:
Batch digesters: 4
Pulp Lines: 2
Chemical Recovery Equipment:
Evaporator lines: 6
Recovery boilers: 1
Lime Kiln
Recycled Fiber Treatment Lines:
Pulpers: 2 at 20,000 admt/y
Pulp Dryers:
Air Float dryers 1, Fourdriniers 1
Paper/Paperboard Grades and Capacities:
Total paper and paperboard capacity: 49,980 mt/y
Corrugating medium/fluting: 49,980 mt/y
Paper and Paperboard Mill Data:
Stock Preparation:
Pulpers: 2
Refiners: 6
Paper Machines: 1
No. 2, fourdrinier, total capacity 49,980 mt/y, Trim width 3.8 m, Corrugating medium/fluting
Finishing Equipment:
Winders: 1 at 80,000 mt/y
Rewinders: 2

Energy Data:
Power boilers: 2
Steam turbines: 1 at 4.0 MW
Electrical demand for mill: 95 MWh/D

ⓂNorpapel S.A.I.C.
H. Yrigoyen 385, Piso °, Of. 1
1878 Quilmes, Buenos Aires
Argentina
Phone: (54) 11 4326 2646/4224 6162/6037
Fax: (54) 11 4224 6162/6037
Email: marcelopayer@norpapel.com.ar
Web Address: www.norpapel.com.ar
Mill Locations:
Norpapel S.A.I.C., Villa Ocampo Mill, 25 de Mayo y San Jorge, 3580 Villa Ocampo, Argentina, Capacity: 24,000 mt/y, (Paperboard mill)
Phone: (54) 34 8246 7578/7900
Fax: (54) 34 8246 7 900
Email: danielponisio@norpapel.com.ar

ⓂNorpapel S.A.I.C.
Villa Ocampo Mill
25 de Mayo y San Jorge
3580 Villa Ocampo, Santa Fé
Argentina
Phone: (54) 34 8246 7578/7900
Fax: (54) 34 8246 7 900
Email: danielponisio@norpapel.com.ar
Web Address: www.norpapel.com.ar
Personnel:
Dir: Ing Daniel Ponisio
Phone: (54) 11 5594 5813
Email: danielponisio@norpapel.com.ar
Total Employees at this Location: 160
Type of Operation: Paperboard mill
Paper/Paperboard Grades and Capacities:
Total paper and paperboard capacity: 24,000 mt/y
Packaging papers: 16,000 mt/y
Linerboard: 2,000 mt/y
Corrugating medium/fluting: 6,000 mt/y

ⓂPapel Pampa. NOA
Quilmes Mill
Mill is closed (closed since May 2010. Acquired by Papelera del NOA in July 2013 with the intention to reactivate the plant.)
Ownership: 50% by Papelera del NOA S.A., 50% by MW Gestora
Camino Gral. Belgrano, Km. 14,500
1878 Quilmes, Buenos Aires
Argentina
Phone: (54) 11 4365 1000
Fax: (54) 11 4200 0464
Personnel:
Exec. Dir.: Guillermo Moreno
Phone: (54) 11 4365 1000
Mill Mgr.: Mr. Llovera
Phone: (54) 11 4365 1000
Type of Operation: Pulp mill, Paper mill, Paperboard mill
Pulp Mill Data:
Chemical Pulping Systems:
Continuous digesters: 1
Bleach Plant Systems: 1
Paper and Paperboard Mill Data:
Stock Preparation:
Pulpers: 3
Refiners: 5
Paper Machines: 2
No. 1, fourdrinier, total capacity 29,988 mt/y, Trim width 2.24 m
No. 4, fourdrinier, total capacity 48,909 mt/y, Trim width 3.2 m
Finishing Equipment:
Rewinders: 3
Sheeters: 2

ⓂPapelera Rio Quequén
Calle 588 N° 1551
7631 Quequén, Partido de Necochea, Buenos Aires
Argentina
Phone: (54) 4 314 3469
Fax: (54) 4 314 3469
Email: info@cinfa.net
Web Address: www.papelerarioquequen.com.ar, www.papelquequen.com
Personnel:
Gen. Mgr.: Ing. Gerardo Barbieri
Phone: (54) 4 314 3469
Fax: (54) 4 314 3469
Mill Mgr.: Ing. Gerardo Barbieri
Phone: (54) 4 314 3469
Fax: (54) 4 314 3469
Commer. Mgr.: Pablo Barbieri
Phone: (54) 4 314 3469
Fax: (54) 4 314 3469
Total Employees of Company: 70
Total Employees at this Location: 70
Mill Locations:
Papelera Rio Quequén, Quequén Mill, Calle 588 N° 1551, 7631 Quequén, Partido de Necochea, Argentina, Capacity: 3,600 mt/y, (Paper mill)
Phone: (54) 011 4314-3469
Fax: (54) 011 4314-3469
Email: info@cinfa.net

ⓂPapelera Rio Quequén
Quequén Mill
Calle 588 N° 1551
7631 Quequén, Partido de Necochea, Buenos Aires
Argentina
Phone: (54) 011 4314-3469
Fax: (54) 011 4314-3469
Email: info@cinfa.net
Web Address: papelquequen.com/
Personnel:
Mill Mgr.: Gerardo Barbieri
Phone: (54) 4 314 3469
Fax: (54) 4 314 3469
Commer. Mgr: Pablo Barbieri
Phone: (54) 4 314 3469
Fax: (54) 4 314 3469
Total Employees at this Location: 56
Type of Operation: Paper mill
Pulp Mill Data:
Recycled Fiber Treatment Lines:
Pulpers: 1
Paper/Paperboard Grades and Capacities:
Total paper and paperboard capacity: 3,600 mt/y
Packaging papers
Linerboard
Corrugating medium/fluting
Paper and Paperboard Mill Data:
Stock Preparation:
Refiners: 3
Paper Machines: 1
No. 1, fourdrinier, Linerboard, Corrugating medium/fluting, Boxboard/cartonboard, Packaging papers

ⓄⓂPapeles PM S.A.I.C.
San Martín Mill
Moreno (ex 48) 4520
1650 San Martín, Buenos Aires
Argentina
Phone: (54) 11 4755 0496
Fax: (54) 11 4754 3050
Email: info@papelespm.com.ar
Web Address: www.papelespm.com
Personnel:
Gen. Mgr.: Eduardo Aceiro
Phone: (54) 11 4755 0496
Fax: (54) 11 4754 3050
Mill Mgr.: Osvaldo Barroso
Phone: (54) 11 4755 0496
Fax: (54) 11 4754 3050
Email: ventas@papelespm.com.ar

Argentina

Tech. Mgr.: Francisco Chiossone
Phone: (54) 11 4755 0496
Fax: (54) 11 4754 3050
Oper. Mgr.: Alejandro Simboli
Phone: (54) 11 4755 0496
Fax: (54) 11 4754 3050
Email: operaciones@papelespm.com.ar
Prod. Supt.: Julio Schuster
Phone: (54) 11 4755 0496
Fax: (54) 11 4754 3050
Email: produccion@papelespm.com.ar
Finan. Mgr.: Gerardo Sapia
Phone: (54) 11 4755 0496
Fax: (54) 11 4754 3050
Commer. Mgr.: Claudio Marcelo Tessari
Phone: (54) 11 4755 0496
Fax: (54) 11 4754 3050
HR Mgr.: Sergio Maestri
Phone: (54) 11 4755 0496
Fax: (54) 11 4754 3050
Total Employees of Company: 100
Type of Operation: Paper mill
Pulp Mill Data:
 Recycled Fiber Treatment Lines:
 Pulpers: 1 at 10,000 admt/y
Paper/Paperboard Grades and Capacities:
 Total paper and paperboard capacity: 13,225 mt/y
 Specialty and industrial
Paper and Paperboard Mill Data:
 Stock Preparation:
 Pulpers: 1
 Refiners: 2
Paper Machines: 1
No. 1, fourdrinier, total capacity 13,225 mt/y, Trim width 2.25 m, Specialty and industrial
Finishing Equipment:
 Rewinders: 1
 Sheeters: 3
Energy Data:
Power boilers: 1

ⓞⓜPapeltex Argentina S.A.I.C.
Lanus Oeste Mill
Bolivia 1960
1824 Lanus Oeste, Buenos Aires
Argentina
 Phone: (54) 11 4225 8020/4942/4357 0038
 Fax: (54) 11 4225 8020
 Email: ptx@ciudad.com.ar
Personnel:
 Mill Mgr.: Alejandro Molenberg
 Phone: (54) 11 4225 8020/4942/4357 0038
Total Employees of Company: 40
Total Employees at this Location: 40
Type of Operation: Paperboard mill
Paper/Paperboard Grades and Capacities:
 Total paper and paperboard capacity: 10,000 mt/y
 Corrugating medium/fluting: 6,000 mt/y
 Boxboard/cartonboard: 4,000 mt/y
Paper and Paperboard Mill Data:
Paper Machines: 2
PM 1, total capacity 6,000 mt/y, Corrugating medium/fluting
PM 2, total capacity 4,000 mt/y, Boxboard/cartonboard

ⓞⓜPapelera Paysandú S.A.I.C.
Wilde Mill
Col. Rondeau 466
1875 Wilde, Buenos Aires
Argentina
 Phone: (54) 11 4207 8858
 Fax: (54) 11 4206 5082
Personnel:
 Mill Mgr.: Agustin Vieira
 Phone: (54) 11 4207 8858
 Admin. Mgr.: Nicolás Ranea
 Phone: (54) 11 4207 8858
 Email: nicolasranea@yahoo.com.ar
Total Employees of Company: 67

Total Employees at this Location: 67
Type of Operation: Paper mill, Paperboard mill
Paper/Paperboard Grades and Capacities:
 Total paper and paperboard capacity: 15,000 mt/y
 Uncoated woodfree/freesheet
 Uncoated mechanical/groundwood: 1,000 mt/y
 Packaging papers
 Specialty and industrial
 Linerboard: 3,000 mt/y
 Corrugating medium/fluting: 3,000 mt/y
Paper and Paperboard Mill Data:
 Stock Preparation:
 Pulpers: 2
 Refiners: 2
Paper Machines: 1
No. 1, fourdrinier, total capacity 15,000 mt/y, Trim width 2 m, Uncoated woodfree/freesheet
Finishing Equipment:
 Rewinders: 2
 Sheeters: 1
Energy Data:
Power boilers: 1

ⓜPapelera del Plata
Ownership: 100% by Empresas CMPC S.A.
Otto Kraus 4950
1667 Malvinas Argentinas
Argentina
 Phone: (54) 11 4630 0100 / 4918 1535
 Fax: (54) 11 4630 0110
 Email: mcoronado@cmpc.com.ar,
 rrhhempleos@cmpc.com.ar
 Web Address: www.papeleradelplata.com.ar
Personnel:
 Gen. Mgr.: Juan La Selva
 Phone: (54) 11 4630 0100
 Fax: (54) 11 4918 1535
 Admin. Mgr.: Cristian K
 Phone: (54) 11 4630 0100
 Fax: (54) 11 4918 1535
 Commer. Dir.: María Wladimyra Villanueva
 Phone: (54) 11 4630 0100
 Fax: (54) 11 4918 1535
 HR. Dir.: Paula Jimena Cecchini
 Phone: (54) 11 4630 0100
 Fax: (54) 11 4918 1535
Total Employees of Company: 1,200
Total Employees at this Location: 150
Mill Locations:
Papelera del Plata, Zárate Mill, Camino de la Costa Brava Km.7, 2800 Zárate, Argentina, Capacity: 112,098 mt/y, (Paper mill)
 Phone: (54) 3487 428300/426615
 Fax: (54) 3487 428317
 Email: lpp-zarate@cmpc.com.ar

ⓜPapelera del Plata
Zárate Mill
Ownership: 100% by Empresas CMPC S.A.
Camino de la Costa Brava Km.7
2800 Zárate, Buenos Aires
Argentina
 Phone: (54) 3487 428300/426615
 Fax: (54) 3487 428317
 Email: lpp-zarate@cmpc.com.ar
 Web Address: www.papeleradelplata.com.ar
Personnel:
 Oper. Mgr.: Carlos Abella
 Phone: (54) 3487 428300/426615
 Fax: (54) 3487 428317
 Email: cabella@cmpc.com.ar
 Paper Mill Mgr.: Juan Caillabet
 Phone: (54) 3487 428300/426615
 Fax: (54) 3487 428317
 Email: jcaillabet@cmpc.com.ar
 Prod. Mgr.: Ernesto Rovitto
 Phone: (54) 3487 428300/426615
 Fax: (54) 3487 428317
 Email: erovitto@cmpc.com.ar

Convert. Tissue Mgr.: Fabián Montoya
 Phone: (54) 3487 428300/426615
 Fax: (54) 3487 428317
 Email: fmontoya@cmpc.com.ar
 Eng. Mgr.: Alejandro Pardo
 Phone: (54) 3487 428300/426615
 Fax: (54) 3487 428317
 Email: apardo@cmpc.com.ar
 Progr./ Purch. Mgr.: Jorge Gaite
 Phone: (54) 3487 428300/426615
 Fax: (54) 3487 428317
 Email: jgaite@cmpc.com.ar
 Mill Mgr. Sec: Ana Bellusci
 Phone: (54) 3487 428300/426615
 Fax: (54) 3487 428317
 Email: abellusci@cmpc.com.ar
Total Employees at this Location: 450
Type of Operation: Paper mill
Pulp Grades and Capacities:
 Total pulp capacity: 89,418 mt/y
 Recycled Pulping: 89,418 mt/y
Pulp Mill Data:
 Bleach Plant Systems: 1
 Recycled Pulping System, Type: DIP
 Recycled Fiber Treatment Lines:
 Flotation deinking lines: 1
Paper/Paperboard Grades and Capacities:
 Total paper and paperboard capacity: 112,098 mt/y
 Tissue: 112,098 mt/y
Paper and Paperboard Mill Data:
 Stock Preparation:
 Pulpers: 4
Paper Machines: 3
No. 1, crescent former, total capacity 34,986 mt/y, Trim width 2.7 m, Tissue, Uncoated woodfree/freesheet
No. 2, crescent former, total capacity 59,976 mt/y, Trim width 5.5 m, Tissue
No. 3, crescent former, total capacity 17,136 mt/y, Trim width 2.7 m, Tissue
Finishing Equipment:
 Rewinders: 1 at 20,000 mt/y
Energy Data:
Power boilers: 2
Electrical demand for mill: 388 MWh/D

ⓞPapel Prensa S.A.
Ownership: 49% by Clarín, 27.50% by Argentinian Government, 22.50% by La Nación newspaper
Bartolomé Mitre 739, Piso 2
1036 Buenos Aires, Buenos Aires
Argentina
 Phone: (54) 11 4328 1516
 Fax: (54) 11 4328 1586/4197
 Email: albertocuesta@ciudad.com.ar
 Web Address: www.papelprensa.com
Personnel:
 Pres.: Dr. Guillermo Gonzales Rosas
 Phone: (54) 11 4328 1516
 Fax: (54) 11 4328 1586/4197
 VP: Dr. Alberto G. Maquieira
 Phone: (54) 11 4328 1516
 Fax: (54) 11 4328 1586/4197
 Gen. Mgr.: Jorge J. Noseda
 Phone: (54) 11 4328 1587
 Fax: (54) 11 4328 1586
 Mktg. Mgr.: Alberto Cuesta
 Phone: (54) 11 4328 3811
 Email: albertocuesta@ciudad.com.ar
 Forestry Mgr: Ricardo Bratovich
 Phone: (54) 11 4328 1588
 Mill Mgr.: Herminio Liva
 Phone: (54) 3329 425 478
 Fax: (54) 3329 425 492
 Analysis Sen.: Eduardo Mario Ortiz
 Phone: (54) 11 4328 1516
 Fax: (54) 11 4328 1586/4197
 Asst. Mgr.: Diego Colabardini
 Phone: (54) 11 4328 1516
 Fax: (54) 11 4328 1586/4197
 Email: dcolabardini@papelprensa.com

Argentina

Total Employees of Company: 762
Total Employees at this Location: 100
Mill Locations:
Papel Prensa S.A., San Pedro Mill, Parque Industrial, 2930 San Pedro, Argentina, Capacity: 169,575 mt/y, (Pulp mill, Paper mill)
Phone: (54) 3329 426902
Fax: (54) 3329 425446
Email: plantasp@sanpedro.com.ar, plantasp@ictnet.com.ar

ⓂPapel Prensa S.A.
San Pedro Mill
Parque Industrial
2930 San Pedro, Buenos Aires
Argentina
Mailing Address: CC 157, 2930 San Pedro, Buenos Aires, Argentina
Phone: (54) 3329 426902
Fax: (54) 3329 425446
Email: plantasp@sanpedro.com.ar, plantasp@ictnet.com.ar
Web Address: www.papelprensa.com
Personnel:
Mill Mgr.: Ricardo H. Mariani
Phone: (54) 3329 425 478
Fax: (54) 3329 425 492
Email: rmariani@sanpedro.com.ar
HR Mgr.: Luis Guiricich
Phone: (54) 3329 426 902
Fax: (54) 3329 425 446
Process Eng.: Eduardo Alejandro Maglione
Phone: (54) 3329 426 902
Fax: (54) 3329 425 446
Email: eamaglione@ictnet.com.ar
Maint. Mgr.: Enrique Massaglia
Phone: (54) 3329 426 902
Fax: (54) 3329 425 446
Forestry Mgr: Manuel Climent
Phone: (54) 114 328 1588
Fax: (54) 114 328 1586
Mktg. Mgr.: Alberto Angel Cuesta
Phone: (54) 114 328 3811
Fax: (54) 114 328 1586
Total Employees at this Location: 350
Type of Operation: Pulp mill, Paper mill
Pulp Grades and Capacities:
Total pulp capacity: 160,638 mt/y
Mechanical Pulp: 149,301 mt/y
Recycled Pulping: 11,336 mt/y
Pulp Mill Data:
Mechanical Pulping Systems:
CTMP systems: 1
Pulp Lines: 1
Bleach Plant Systems: 2
Mechanical Pulping Process CMP, Type: Hardwood, Sequence: P
Recycled DIP Pulping System, Sequence: P
Recycled Fiber Treatment Lines:
Flotation deinking lines: 2 at 25,000 admt/y
Pulpers: 1 at 20,000 admt/y
Paper/Paperboard Grades and Capacities:
Total paper and paperboard capacity: 169,575 mt/y
Newsprint: 151,725 mt/y
Uncoated mechanical/groundwood: 17,850 mt/y
Paper and Paperboard Mill Data:
Stock Preparation:
Pulpers:
Paper Machines: 1
No. 1, (Suppliers: Valmet/Voith), DuoFormer D, total capacity 169,575 mt/y, Trim width 7.7 m, Newsprint, Uncoated mechanical/groundwood
Finishing Equipment:
Winders: 1 at 200,000 mt/y
Rewinders: 1 at 20,000 mt/y
Energy Data:
Power boilers: 2
Electrical demand for mill: 850 MWh/D

ⓄRainap S.A.
Av. García del Rio 2477 10° B
1429 Cdad. Buenos Aires
Argentina
Phone: (54) 11 4704 5900
Fax: (54) 11 4704 7333
Email: rainapsa@rainap.com.ar, emilioperez@rainap.com.ar
Web Address: www.rainap.com.ar
Personnel:
Pres.: Mr. Ricardo Rajnerman
Phone: (54) 11 4704 5900
Fax: (54) 11 4704 7333
Mill Locations:
Rainap S.A., Garín mill, Einstein esquina-Savio, 1619 Garín, Argentina, Capacity: 29,988 mt/y, (Paperboard mill)
Phone: (54) 11 4704-5900
Fax: (54) 3327 45 2105/ 3327 45 2105
Email: rainapsa@rainap.com.ar

ⓂRainap S.A.
Garín mill
Einstein esquina-Savio
1619 Garín, Buenos Aires
Argentina
Phone: (54) 11 4704-5900
Fax: (54) 3327 45 2105/ 3327 45 2105
Email: rainapsa@rainap.com.ar
Web Address: www.rainap.com.ar
Personnel:
Mill Mgr.: Eduardo Chimmel
Phone: (54) 11 153181 4743
Fax: (54) 3327 45 2105/ 3327 45 2105
Total Employees at this Location: 82
Type of Operation: Paperboard mill
Pulp Grades and Capacities:
Total pulp capacity: 30,456 mt/y
Recycled Pulping: 30,456 mt/y
Pulp Mill Data:
Recycled Fiber Treatment Lines:
Pulpers: 1 at 33,000
Paper/Paperboard Grades and Capacities:
Total paper and paperboard capacity: 29,988 mt/y
Corrugating medium/fluting: 29,988 mt/y
Paper and Paperboard Mill Data:
Paper Machines: 1
No. 1, fourdrinier, total capacity 29,988 mt/y, Trim width 2.5 m, Corrugating medium/fluting
Energy Data:
Power boilers
Electrical demand for mill: 53 MWh/D

ⓄPapelera Samseng S.A.
Ownership: 100% by Samtai Industrial Ltda
Chorroarin n° 1121
C 1427 Buenos Aires, Buenos Aires
Argentina
Phone: (54) 11 4553 9818/ 4551 9985
Fax: (54) 11 4552 9985 ext 123
Email: comex@papelera-samseng.com
Personnel:
Safety Mgr.: Macarena Luque
Phone: (54) 11 4553 9818/ 4551 9985
Fax: (54) 11 4552 9985
Mktg. Mgr.: Mariano R Mariano R
Phone: (54) 11 4553 9818/ 4551 9985
Fax: (54) 11 4552 9985
HR Mgr.: Eduardo M Eduardo M
Phone: (54) 11 4553 9818/ 4551 9985
Fax: (54) 11 4552 9985
Maint. Mgr.: Nicolás P Nicolás P
Phone: (54) 11 4553 9818/ 4551 9985
Fax: (54) 11 4552 9985
Mill Locations:
Papelera Samseng S.A., Pilar Mill, Parque Industrial Pilar, Ruta 61 y Calle 12, 1629 Pilar, Argentina, Capacity: 87,108 mt/y, (Paper mill)
Phone: (54) 23 2249 6050/58
Email: info@papelera-samseng.com, samseng@cuidad.com.ar

ⓂPapelera Samseng S.A.
Pilar Mill
Parque Industrial Pilar, Ruta 61 y Calle 12
1629 Pilar, Buenos Aires
Argentina
Phone: (54) 23 2249 6050/58
Email: info@papelera-samseng.com, samseng@cuidad.com.ar
Personnel:
Plant Mgr.: Carlos Gonzalez
Phone: (54) 23 2249 6050/58
Email: carlos.gonzalez@papelera-samseng.com
Total Employees at this Location: 350
Type of Operation: Paper mill
Pulp Grades and Capacities:
Total pulp capacity: 63,542 mt/y
Recycled Pulping: 63,542 mt/y
Pulp Mill Data:
Bleach Plant Systems: 1
Recycled Pulping System, Type: DIP
Recycled Fiber Treatment Lines:
Flotation deinking lines: 1
Paper/Paperboard Grades and Capacities:
Total paper and paperboard capacity: 87,108 mt/y
Tissue: 87,108 mt/y
Paper and Paperboard Mill Data:
Paper Machines: 3
No. 1, crescent former, total capacity 13,566 mt/y, Trim width 2 m, Tissue, Uncoated woodfree/freesheet
No. 2, twin-wire, total capacity 35,700 mt/y, Trim width 3.4 m, Tissue
No. 3, crescent former, total capacity 37,842 mt/y, Trim width 3.4 m, Tissue
Energy Data:
Power boilers
Electrical demand for mill: 344 MWh/D

ⓄⓂPapelera San Andrés de Giles S.A.
San Andrés de Giles Mill
Ruta 41, Km. 70
6720 San Andrés de Giles, Buenos Aires
Argentina
Phone: (54) 2325 440800, 11 4782 3787
Fax: (54) 2325 440120
Email: info@psag.com.ar
Web Address: www.psag.com.ar
Personnel:
CEO: Máximo V.G. Gagliardi
Phone: (54) 2325 440800
Fax: (54) 2325 440120
Email: mgagliardi@psag.com.ar
Converting Plt. Mgr.: Carlos Robutti
Phone: (54) 2325 442006
Fax: (54) 2325 440120
Email: crobutti@psag.com.ar
Purch. Agent: Daniel E. Santamaría
Phone: (54) 11 4702 0751
Fax: (54) 11 4704 9226
Email: dsantamaria@psag.com.ar
Sec.: Silvia Limonta
Phone: (54) 2325 442006 Ext. 101
Fax: (54) 2325 440120
Email: slimonta@psag.com.ar
Total Employees of Company: 126
Type of Operation: Paper mill
Paper/Paperboard Grades and Capacities:
Total paper and paperboard capacity: 18,000 mt/y
Tissue: 18,000 mt/y
Paper and Paperboard Mill Data:
Stock Preparation:
Pulpers: 1
Refiners: 1
Paper Machines: 1
PM 1, crescent former, total capacity 18,000 mt/y, Trim width 2.76 m, Tissue
Finishing Equipment:

Argentina

Rewinders: 3 at 10,000 mt/y
Energy Data:
Power boilers: 1

ⓘCelulosa San Pedro S.A.
Av. Bolivar 187, 3°C
1054 Buenos Aires, Buenos Aires
Argentina
Phone: (54) 11 4313 3277
Fax: (54) 11 4313 3744
Email: info@celulosasanpedro.com.ar
Personnel:
Pres.: Paulo Victor Planas
Phone: (54) 11 4313 3277
Mgr.: Miguel Planas
Phone: (54) 11 4313 3277
Email: miguel@celulosasanpedro.com.ar
Sls. Mgr.: Liliana Marzioni
Phone: (54) 11 4313 3277
Total Employees of Company: 80
Mill Locations:
Celulosa San Pedro S.A., Buenos Aires Mill, Calle Frers S/N°, Parque Industrial San Pedro, 2930 Buenos Aires, Argentina, Capacity: 7,000 mt/y, (Paper mill)
Phone: (54) 3329 425 943/633

ⓘCelulosa San Pedro S.A.
Buenos Aires Mill
Calle Frers S/N°, Parque Industrial San Pedro,
2930 Buenos Aires, Buenos Aires
Argentina
Phone: (54) 3329 425 943/633
Personnel:
Gen. Mgr.: Valentín
Phone: (54) 3329 425 943
Maint. Mgr.: Walter Morello
Phone: (54) 3329 425 943
Type of Operation: Paper mill
Paper/Paperboard Grades and Capacities:
Total paper and paperboard capacity: 7,000 mt/y
Corrugating medium/fluting: 7,000 mt/y
Paper and Paperboard Mill Data:
Paper Machines: 1
No. 1, total capacity 7,000 mt/y, Corrugating medium/fluting

ⓘⓜPapelera Santa Angela S.A.
General Pacheco Mill
Ruta 9 Km. 32.6
1617 General Pacheco, Tigre, Buenos Aires
Argentina
Phone: (54) 11 4736 0550/0660
Fax: (54) 11 4736 0880
Email: info@santaangela.com.ar
Personnel:
Dir.: Fernando Brozzoni
Phone: (54) 11 4736 0550/0660
Mill Mgr.: Helio Brozzoni
Phone: (54) 11 4736 0550/0660
Type of Operation: Paperboard mill
Paper/Paperboard Grades and Capacities:
Total paper and paperboard capacity: 20,000 mt/y
Linerboard: 20,000 mt/y
Paper and Paperboard Mill Data:
Paper Machines: 1
PM 1, total capacity 20,000 mt/y, Linerboard

ⓘSein y Cia. SA
Camino General Belgrano Km. 31
1886 Ranelagh, Buenos Aires
Argentina
Phone: (54) 11 4258 8604/8305/8738/4223 3754/0151
Fax: (54) 11 4258 8738
Email: info@seinycia.com.ar
Web Address: www.seinycia.com.ar
Personnel:
Pres.: Maria Sein de López Ramos
Phone: (54) 4258 8604

Fax: (54) 4258 8738
VP: Alberto Covatto
Phone: (54) 4258 8604
Fax: (54) 4258 8738
Dir.: Juan Ignacio Lopez Sein
Phone: (54) 4258 8604
Fax: (54) 4258 8738
Admin. Mgr.: Raúl Dieguez
Phone: (54) 4258 8604
Fax: (54) 4258 8738
Email: admin@seinycia.com.ar
Mill Locations:
Sein y Cia. SA, Ranelagh Mill, Camino General Belgrano Km. 31, 1886 Ranelagh, Argentina, Capacity: 10,000 mt/y, (Paper mill)
Phone: (54) 11 4258 8604/8305/8738/4223 3754/0151
Fax: (54) 11 4258 8738
Email: info@seinycia.com.ar

ⓘSein y Cia. SA
Ranelagh Mill
Camino General Belgrano Km. 31
1886 Ranelagh, Buenos Aires
Argentina
Phone: (54) 11 4258 8604/8305/8738/4223 3754/0151
Fax: (54) 11 4258 8738
Email: info@seinycia.com.ar
Web Address: www.seinycia.com.ar
Personnel:
Pres.: Maria Sein de López Ramos
Phone: (54) 11 4258 8604
Fax: (54) 11 4258 8738
VP: Alberto Covatto
Phone: (54) 11 4258 8604
Fax: (54) 11 4258 8738
Email: info@seinycia.com.ar
Dir.: Juan Ignacio Lopez Sein
Phone: (54) 11 4258 8604
Fax: (54) 11 4258 8738
Admin. Mgr.: Raúl Dieguez
Phone: (54) 11 4258 8604
Fax: (54) 11 4258 8738
Email: admin@seinycia.com.ar
Total Employees at this Location: 120
Type of Operation: Paper mill
Paper/Paperboard Grades and Capacities:
Total paper and paperboard capacity: 10,000 mt/y
Packaging papers
Specialty and industrial
Paper and Paperboard Mill Data:
Paper Machines: 2
PM 1, total capacity 3,500 mt/y, Trim width 2.2 m, Packaging papers, Specialty and industrial
PM 2, total capacity 6,500 mt/y

ⓘSmurfit Kappa de Argentina S.A.
Ownership: 80% by Smurfit Kappa Group
Roque Saenz Peña 308- 8° Piso
1642 San Isidro, Buenos Aires
Argentina
Phone: (54) 11 4732 6600/4743 2558
Fax: (54) 11 4742 1189/4743 2558
Web Address: www.smurfitkappa.com.ar
Personnel:
CEO Smurfit Argentina: Carlos Barrozzi
Phone: (54) 11 4732 6600/4743 2558
Fax: (54) 11 4742 1189/4743 2558
VP, Admin. & Finan.: Diego Carnevale
Phone: (54) 11 4732 6600/4743 2558
Fax: (54) 11 4742 1189/4743 2558
Pres. Sec.: Sandra Romar
Phone: Ext: 6639
Total Employees of Company: 770
Mill Locations:
Smurfit Kappa de Argentina S.A., Bernal Mill, Espora 200, 1876 Bernal, Argentina, Capacity: 62,832 mt/y, (Paper mill, Paperboard mill)
Phone: (54) 11 4259 6990/5253 7000

Fax: (54) 11 4259 9995/4259 3134
Smurfit Kappa de Argentina S.A., Coronel Suárez Mill, Av. M. Lloveras 531, 7540 Coronel Suárez, Argentina, Capacity: 49,980 mt/y, (Paperboard mill)
Phone: (54) 292 643 1700
Fax: (54) 292 642 4188

ⓜSmurfit Kappa de Argentina S.A.
Bernal Mill
Ownership: 80% by Smurfit Kappa Group
Espora 200
1876 Bernal, Buenos Aires
Argentina
Phone: (54) 11 4259 6990/5253 7000
Fax: (54) 11 4259 9995/4259 3134
Web Address: www.smurfitkappa.com.ar
Personnel:
VP (Paper Div.): Peter Osctoics
Phone: (54) 11 4259 6990/5253 7000
Fax: (54) 11 4259 9995/4259 3134
Email: posctoics@smurfit.com.ar
Gen. Mgr.: Gustavo Patat
Phone: (54) 11 4259 6990/5253 700
Fax: (54) 11 4259 9995/4259 3134
Email: gpatat@smurfit.com.ar
Prod. Mill Mgr.: Ing. Alejandro Roca
Phone: (54) 11 4259 6990/5253 7000 Ext. 7476
Fax: (54) 11 4259 9995/4259 3134
Email: aroca@smurfit.com.ar
Sls. Mgr. (Convert. Div.): German Gambini
Phone: (54) 11 4259 6990/5253 7000
Fax: (54) 11 4259 9995/4259 3134
Email: ggambini@smurfit.com.ar
Supt. Electrical.: Lucas Rotondo
Phone: (54) 11 4259 6990/5253 7000
Fax: (54) 11 4259 9995/4259 3134
Email: lrotondo@smurfit.com.ar
Sls. Mgr. (Paper Div.): Fernando Osinde
Phone: (54) 11 4259 6990/5253 7000
Fax: (54) 11 4259 9995/4259 3134
Email: fosinde@smurfit.com.ar
Total Employees at this Location: 100
Type of Operation: Paper mill, Paperboard mill
Pulp Grades and Capacities:
Total pulp capacity: 64,214 mt/y
Recycled Pulping: 64,214 mt/y
Pulp Mill Data:
Recycled Fiber Treatment Lines:
Recycled packaging pulping lines: 1
Paper/Paperboard Grades and Capacities:
Total paper and paperboard capacity: 62,832 mt/y
Linerboard: 37,842 mt/y
Corrugating medium/fluting: 24,990 mt/y
Paper and Paperboard Mill Data:
Stock Preparation:
Pulpers: 2
Refiners: 3
Paper Machines: 1
No. 11, fourdrinier, total capacity 62,832 mt/y, Trim width 3.6 m, Linerboard, Corrugating medium/fluting
Finishing Equipment:
Rewinders: 1
Energy Data:
Power boilers: 1
Electrical demand for mill: 70 MWh/D

ⓜSmurfit Kappa de Argentina S.A.
Coronel Suárez Mill
Ownership: 80% by Smurfit Kappa Group
Av. M. Lloveras 531
7540 Coronel Suárez, Buenos Aires
Argentina
Phone: (54) 292 643 1700
Fax: (54) 292 642 4188
Web Address: www.smurfitkappa.com.ar
Personnel:
Sls. Mgr. Sunchales corrugated plant: Cristian Marchisio
Phone: (54) 292 643 1700
Fax: (54) 292 642 4188

Argentina

Email: cristian.marchisio@smurfitkappa.com.ar
Plt Contr. Bag in Box: Diego De Pinto
Phone: (54) 292 643 1700
Fax: (54) 292 642 4188
Email: diego.depinto@smurfitkappa.com.ar
Total Employees at this Location: 80
Type of Operation: Paperboard mill
Pulp Grades and Capacities:
Total pulp capacity: 51,152 mt/y
Recycled Pulping: 51,152 mt/y
Pulp Mill Data:
Recycled Fiber Treatment Lines:
Pulpers: 2 at 55,500
Paper/Paperboard Grades and Capacities:
Total paper and paperboard capacity: 49,980 mt/y
Linerboard: 16,065 mt/y
Corrugating medium/fluting: 33,915 mt/y
Paper and Paperboard Mill Data:
Stock Preparation:
Pulpers: 2
Refiners: 2
Paper Machines: 1
No. 1, fourdrinier, total capacity 49,980 mt/y, Trim width 2.4 m, Linerboard, Corrugating medium/fluting
Finishing Equipment:
Rewinders: 1
Energy Data:
Power boilers: 2
Electrical demand for mill: 53 MWh/D

ⓘPapelera del Sur
Colonia y Perito Moreno
1754 San Justo, Buenos Aires
Argentina
Phone: (54) 11 4480 3400
Fax: (54) 11 4480 3443
Email: ventas@papeleradelsur.com.ar
Web Address: www.papeleradelsur.com.ar
Personnel:
Gen. Mgr.: Adrian Iglesias
Phone: (54) 11 4480 3421
Fax: (54) 11 4480 3402
Email: abarone@papeleradelsur.com.ar
Sls. Mgr.: Omar Espósito
Phone: (54) 11 4480 3400
Fax: (54) 11 4480 3443
Email: ventas@papeleadelsur.com.ar
Tech. Mgr.: Marcelo A. Soriano
Phone: (54) 11 4480 3421
Fax: (54) 11 4480 3402
Mgr. Asst.: Ana Gabriela Barone
Phone: (54) 11 44 803 421
Fax: (54) 11 44 803 402
Email: abarone@papeleradelsur.com.ar
Sales of Business International: Juan Martín Costa
Phone: (54) 11 4480 3400
Fax: (54) 11 4480 3443
Mill Locations:
Papelera del Sur, División Cartulinas de Interpack S.A., Tornquist Mill, Ruta 33 y 76, 8160 Tornquist, Argentina, Capacity: 89,964 mt/y, (Paperboard mill)
Phone: (54) 291 4940087/1119
Fax: (54) 291 4940087/1119
Email: rrhh@papeleradelsur.com.ar, compras@papeleradelsur.com.ar

ⓜPapelera del Sur, División Cartulinas de Interpack S.A.
Tornquist Mill
Ownership: Papelera del Sur
Ruta 33 y 76
8160 Tornquist, Buenos Aires
Argentina
Phone: (54) 291 4940087/1119
Fax: (54) 291 4940087/1119
Email: rrhh@papeleradelsur.com.ar, compras@papeleradelsur.com.ar
Web Address: www.papeleradelsur.com.ar
Personnel:
Mill Mgr.: Walter Dabós
Phone: (54) 291 4940087/1119
Total Employees at this Location: 219
Type of Operation: Paperboard mill
Pulp Grades and Capacities:
Total pulp capacity: 72,826 mt/y
Recycled Pulping: 72,826 mt/y
Pulp Mill Data:
Recycled Fiber Treatment Lines:
Recycled packaging pulping lines: 1
Paper/Paperboard Grades and Capacities:
Total paper and paperboard capacity: 89,964 mt/y
Boxboard/cartonboard: 89,964 mt/y
Paper and Paperboard Mill Data:
Stock Preparation:
Pulpers: 4
Refiners: 6
Paper Machines: 1
No. 1, fourdrinier (3), total capacity 89,964 mt/y, Trim width 2.3 m, Boxboard/cartonboard
Coating Machines: 4
No. 1, on machine
No. 2, on machine
No. 3, on machine
No. 4, on machine
Finishing Equipment:
Rewinders: 1
Sheeters: 2
Energy Data:
Power boilers: 2
Electrical demand for mill: 147 MWh/D

ⓘⓜSurpapel SA
Berazategui Mill
Ownership: 100% by Grupo Surpapel
Calle 14 y Camino Gral. Belgrano
1884 Berazategui, Buenos Aires
Argentina
Phone: (54) 11 4351 1281
Fax: (54) 11 4351 0622
Web Address: www.surpapel.com.ar
Personnel:
Contr.: Mariano Mucci
Phone: (54) 11 4351 1281
Fax: (54) 11 4351 0622
Admin. Mgr.: Mr. Guillermo Ravazzano
Phone: (54) 11 4351 1281
Fax: (54) 11 4351 0622
Qlty Contr. Mgr.: Luis Daniel Reyes Covena
Phone: (54) 11 4351 1281
Fax: (54) 11 4351 0622
Total Employees of Company: 148
Total Employees at this Location: 60
Type of Operation: Paper mill, Paperboard mill
Pulp Grades and Capacities:
Total pulp capacity: 23,566 mt/y
Recycled Pulping: 23,566 mt/y
Pulp Mill Data:
Recycled Fiber Treatment Lines:
Pulpers: 1 at 26,000
Paper/Paperboard Grades and Capacities:
Total paper and paperboard capacity: 23,205 mt/y
Linerboard: 14,280 mt/y
Corrugating medium/fluting: 8,925 mt/y
Paper and Paperboard Mill Data:
Stock Preparation:
Pulpers: 2
Refiners: 2
Paper Machines: 2
No. 1, multi-cylinder, total capacity 8,925 mt/y, Trim width 1.7 m, Corrugating medium/fluting
No. 2, multi-cylinder, total capacity 14,280 mt/y, Trim width 2.5 m, Linerboard
Finishing Equipment:
Rewinders: 2 at 21,000 mt/y
Energy Data:
Power boilers: 2
Electrical demand for mill: 33 MWh/D

ⓘⓜPapelera Don Torcuato S.A.
Don Torcuato Mill
Burgos 1380
B 1611 Don Torcuato, Buenos Aires
Argentina
Phone: (54) 11 4741 2292/2240
Email: info@papeleratorcuato.com
Web Address: www.papeleratorcuato.com
Personnel:
Pres.: Pedro Muiña
Phone: (54) 11 4741 2292/2240
Prod. Mgr.: Eduardo Marsoa
Phone: (54) 11 4741 2292/2240
Commer. Mgr.: Guillermo Echague
Phone: (54) 11 4741 2292/2240
Email: guillermoechague@papeleratorcuato.com
Total Employees at this Location: 95
Type of Operation: Paper mill
Pulp Grades and Capacities:
Total pulp capacity: 44,161 mt/y
Recycled Pulping: 44,161 mt/y
Pulp Mill Data:
Recycled Fiber Treatment Lines:
Recycled packaging pulping lines: 1
Paper/Paperboard Grades and Capacities:
Total paper and paperboard capacity: 43,197 mt/y
Packaging papers: 7,140 mt/y
Linerboard: 21,777 mt/y
Corrugating medium/fluting: 14,280 mt/y
Paper and Paperboard Mill Data:
Paper Machines: 2
No. 1, fourdrinier, total capacity 36,057 mt/y, Trim width 2.5 m, Corrugating medium/fluting, Linerboard
No. 2, fourdrinier, total capacity 7,140 mt/y, Trim width 1.5 m, Packaging papers
Energy Data:
Power boilers
Electrical demand for mill: 76 MWh/D

ⓘⓜPapelera Tucumán S.A.
San Justo, Tucuman II
Brig. General Juan Manuel de Rosas 2860
1754 San Justo, Buenos Aires
Argentina
Phone: (54) 11 4441 3400
Fax: (54) 11 4441 9560
Email: contacto@papeleratucuman.com.ar
Web Address: www.papeleratucuman.com.ar
Personnel:
Gen. Mgr.: Jorge Velasco
Phone: (54) 11 4441 3400
Fax: (54) 11 4441 9560
Email: pt@papeleratucuman.com.ar
Quality Mgr.: Carlos E. Peñalosa
Phone: (54) 11 4441 3400
Fax: (54) 11 4441 9560
Pers. Mgr.: Elida de Gonzalez Agüero
Phone: (54) 11 4441 3400
Fax: (54) 11 4441 9560
Commer. Dir.: Ing. Oscar Echevarría
Phone: (54) 11 4441 3400 Ext. 203
Fax: (54) 11 4441 9560
Email: oscech@papeleratucuman.com.ar
Asst Technical Dir.: Pablo Rospide
Phone: (54) 11 4441 3400
Fax: (54) 11 4441 9560
Total Employees at this Location: 120
Type of Operation: Paper mill
Mill Locations:
Papelera Tucumán S.A., General Pacheco, Tucuman III, Av. de los Constituyentes nº 2000 (ex. Ruta 9), 1617 General Pacheco, Argentina, Capacity: 12,000 mt/y, (Paper mill)
Phone: (54) 11 4736 4111
Fax: (54) 11 4736 4333
Papelera Tucumán S.A., Lules, Tucumán I Mill, Camino Potrero de las Tablas, Ruta 38, km 1526, Lules, Argentina, Capacity: 96,033 mt/y, (Pulp mill, Paper mill)
Phone: (54) 381 481 1155/1324/1690/1599

Argentina

Fax: (54) 381 481 2620
Email: info@papeleratucuman.com.ar
Paper/Paperboard Grades and Capacities:
Total paper and paperboard capacity: 18,000 mt/y
Packaging papers
Specialty and industrial
Paper and Paperboard Mill Data:
Stock Preparation:
Pulpers: 4
Refiners: 4
Paper Machines: 2
No. 1, Trim width 2.45 m
No. 2, Trim width 2.2 m
Finishing Equipment:
Rewinders: 4
Sheeters: 1

ⓂPapelera Tucumán S.A.
General Pacheco, Tucuman III
Av. de los Constituyentes n° 2000 (ex. Ruta 9)
1617 General Pacheco, Buenos Aires
Argentina
Phone: (54) 11 4736 4111
Fax: (54) 11 4736 4333
Web Address: www.papeleratucuman.com.ar
Personnel:
Dir.: Antonio Carlos de Sá
Phone: (54) 11 4736 4111
Fax: (54) 11 4736 4333
Pers. Mgr.: Luis Torrado
Phone: (54) 11 4736 4111
Fax: (54) 11 4736 4333
Email: luitor@papeleratucuman.com.ar
Prod. Mgr.: Juan Carlos Kise
Phone: (54) 11 4736 4111
Fax: (54) 11 4736 4333
Email: juakis@papeleratucuman.com.ar
Total Employees at this Location: 55
Type of Operation: Paper mill
Paper/Paperboard Grades and Capacities:
Total paper and paperboard capacity: 12,000 mt/y
Tissue: 12,000 mt/y
Paper and Paperboard Mill Data:
Stock Preparation:
Pulpers: 2
Refiners: 2
Paper Machines: 1
No. 1, Yankee dryer, Trim width 2.05 m, Tissue
Finishing Equipment:
Rewinders: 2
Sheeters: 2
Energy Data:
Power boilers: 1
Electrical demand for mill: 39 MWh/D

ⓂPapelera Tucumán S.A.
Lules, Tucumán I Mill
Camino Potrero de las Tablas, Ruta 38, km 1526
Lules, Tucumán
Argentina
Phone: (54) 381 481 1155/1324/1690/1599
Fax: (54) 381 481 2620
Email: info@papeleratucuman.com.ar
Web Address: www.papeleratucuman.com.ar
Personnel:
VP: Martín Chane
Phone: (54) 381 481 1155
Fax: (54) 381 481 2620
Email: marcha@papeleratucuman.com.ar
Qlty. Contr. Mgr.: Jefferson Ferreira
Phone: (54) 381 481 1155
Fax: (54) 381 481 2620
Email: jeffer@papeleratucuman.com.ar
Quality & Proc. Mgr.: Ing. Carlos Nunes
Phone: (54) 381 481 1155
Fax: (54) 381 481 2620
Email: carnun@papeleratucuman.com.ar
Process Mgr.: Ing. Miguel Zelarayan
Phone: (54) 381 481 1155
Fax: (54) 381 481 2620

Email: miguel.zelarayan@papeleratucuman.com.ar
VP. Asst. & Purch.: Patricia Sly
Phone: (54) 381 481 1155
Fax: (54) 381 481 2620
Email: patsly@papeleratucuman.com.ar
Total Employees at this Location: 250
Type of Operation: Pulp mill, Paper mill
Pulp Grades and Capacities:
Total pulp capacity: 76,038 mt/y
Recycled Pulping: 17,981 mt/y
Other Pulp: 58,057 mt/y
Pulp Mill Data:
Chemical Pulping Systems:
Batch digesters: 1
Bleach Plant Systems: 2
DIP
Nonwood pulp
Chemical Recovery Equipment:
Evaporator lines: 1
Recovery boilers: 1
Recycled Fiber Treatment Lines:
Flotation deinking lines: 1
Paper/Paperboard Grades and Capacities:
Total paper and paperboard capacity: 96,033 mt/y
Uncoated woodfree/freesheet: 96,033 mt/y
Paper and Paperboard Mill Data:
Stock Preparation:
Pulpers: 2
Refiners: 4
Paper Machines: 1
No. 1, fourdrinier, total capacity 96,033 mt/y, Trim width 7.6 m, Uncoated woodfree/freesheet
Finishing Equipment:
Rewinders: 2
Sheeters: 2
Energy Data:
Power boilers: 2
Steam turbines: 1 at 14.0 MW
Electrical demand for mill: 313 MWh/D

⒪ⓂUnión Papelera Platense
La Plata Mill
Camino Centenario y Calle 514 Ringuelet
1901 La Plata, Buenos Aires
Argentina
Phone: (54) 221 484 7099
Fax: (54) 221 484 7099
Email: unionpapeleraplatense@hotmail.com
Personnel:
Pres.: Fernando Godoy
Dir.: Castro Gustavo
Phone: (54) 221 484 7099
Total Employees at this Location: 60
Type of Operation: Paper mill, Paperboard mill
Pulp Grades and Capacities:
Paper/Paperboard Grades and Capacities:
Total paper and paperboard capacity: 17,800 mt/y
Uncoated woodfree/freesheet: 2,200 mt/y
Uncoated mechanical/groundwood: 3,000 mt/y
Coated woodfree/freesheet
Tissue: 2,400 mt/y
Packaging papers: 3,000 mt/y
Specialty and industrial
Linerboard: 7,200 mt/y
Corrugating medium/fluting
Paper and Paperboard Mill Data:
Stock Preparation:
Pulpers: 5
Refiners: 8
Paper Machines: 2
No. 1, fourdrinier, Trim width 2.5 m
No. 2, cylinder, twin-wire, Trim width 2.1 m
Coating Machines: 1
No. 1
Finishing Equipment:
Supercalenders: 1
Rewinders: 4
Energy Data:
Power boilers: 2

ⓄValot S.A.
Av. Belgrano 1250
C1093AAN Buenos Aires, Buenos Aires
Argentina
Phone: (54) 11 4381 3095/99
Fax: (54) 11 4381 2877
Email: info@valot.com.ar
Web Address: www.valot.com.ar
Personnel:
Dir. & Owner: Eduardo Valot
Phone: (54) 11 4381 3095/99
Fax: (54) 11 4381 2877
Email: eduardo.valot@valot.com.ar
Plant Mgr.: Fabian Danayo
Phone: (54) 11 4381 3095/99
Fax: (54) 11 4381 2877
Email: fabian.danayo@valot.com.ar
Export Mgr.: Jonathan Scher
Phone: (54) 11 4381 3095/99
Fax: (54) 11 4381 2877
Email: jonathan.scher@valot.com.ar
Sls. Mgr.: Miriam Mabel Ruquet
Phone: (54) 11 4381 3095/99
Fax: (54) 11 4381 2877
Email: miriam.ruquet@valot.com.ar
HR. Mgr.: Francisco Daniel Alfonso
Phone: (54) 11 4381 3095/99
Fax: (54) 11 4381 2877
Email: fransisco.alfonso@valot.com.ar
Mill Locations:
Valot S.A., Campana Mill, Ruta 12 Km 81,5, 2804
Campana, Argentina, Capacity: 13,000 mt/y, (Paper mill)
Phone: (54) 3489 424100/431113
Fax: (54) 3489 424100
Email: info@valot.com.ar

ⓂValot S.A.
Campana Mill
Ruta 12 Km 81,5
2804 Campana, Buenos Aires
Argentina
Phone: (54) 3489 424100/431113
Fax: (54) 3489 424100
Email: info@valot.com.ar
Web Address: www.valot.com.ar
Personnel:
Legal Affair: Alejandra Figueirido
Phone: (54) 3489 424100
Qlty. Mgr.: Mariano Andres Paladino
Phone: (54) 3489 424100
Sls. Mgr.: Gonzalo N. Martinez
Phone: (54) 3489 424100
Type of Operation: Paper mill
Pulp Mill Data:
Recycled Fiber Treatment Lines:
Pulpers: 2 at 30,000
Paper/Paperboard Grades and Capacities:
Total paper and paperboard capacity: 13,000 mt/y
Tissue: 7,000 mt/y
Specialty and industrial: 5,000 mt/y
Paper and Paperboard Mill Data:
Stock Preparation:
Pulpers: 1
Refiners: 2
Paper Machines: 1
No. 1, (second hand), fourdrinier, Yankee dryer, total capacity 13,000 mt/y, Trim width 3.7 m, Tissue, Specialty and industrial
Finishing Equipment:
Winders
Rewinders: 2
Energy Data:
Electrical demand for mill: 3 MWh/D

ⓄPapelera Vual S.A.
Lote 26 sector D, Parque Industrial Reconquista
3560 Reconquista, Santa Fé
Argentina

Bolivia

Phone: (54) 34 82428220
Web Address: www.papeleravual.com.ar
Mill Locations:
Papelera Vual S.A., Beccar Mill, José Ingenieros 1457, 1643 Beccar, Argentina, Capacity: 10,000 mt/y, (Paper mill)
Phone: (54) 4519 2684/85
Fax: (54) 11 4732 0832 0

ⓂPapelera Vual S.A.
Beccar Mill
José Ingenieros 1457
1643 Beccar, Buenos Aires
Argentina
Phone: (54) 4519 2684/85
Fax: (54) 11 4732 0832 0
Web Address: www.papeleravual.com.ar
Personnel:
Mill Mgr.: Carlos Quarin
Phone: (54) 15 5745 1324
Sec.: Mari Laura
Phone: (54) 11 4723 1688/4732 0832/4743 8012
Type of Operation: Paper mill
Paper/Paperboard Grades and Capacities:
Total paper and paperboard capacity: 10,000 mt/y
Tissue: 10,000 mt/y

ⒽⓂGrupo Zucamor
Ranelagh Mill
Av. Antártida Argentina y calle 258
B1886AMN Ranelagh, Buenos Aires
Argentina
Phone: (54) 11 4365 8100
Fax: (54) 11 4258 1212
Email: ventas@grupozucamor.com.ar
Web Address: www.grupozucamor.com
Personnel:
CEO: Eduardo Landín
Phone: (54) 11 4365 8100
Fax: (54) 11 4258 1212
Email: eduardo.landin@grupozucamor.com.ar
Pres.: Alberto Morra
Phone: (54) 11 4365 8100
Fax: (54) 11 4258 1212
Email: alberto.morra@grupozucamor.com.ar
VP: Marcelo Campo
Phone: (54) 11 4365 8100
Fax: (54) 11 4258 1212
Email: marcelo.campo@grupozucamor.com.ar
Indus. Dir.: Eduardo Andres Borges
Phone: (54) 11 4365 8100
Fax: (54) 11 4258 1212
Email: eduardo.borges@grupozucamor.com.ar
Logist. Mgr.: Esteban Boada
Phone: (54) 11 4365 8100
Fax: (54) 11 4258 1212
Email: esteban.boada@grupozucamor.com.ar
Sust. Environ. Mgr.: Oscar Panizza
Phone: (54) 11 4365 8100
Fax: (54) 11 4258 1212
Email: oscar.panizza@grupozucamor.com.ar
Total Employees of Company: 1,000
Total Employees at this Location: 93
Type of Operation: Paperboard mill
Mill Locations:
Papel Misionero S.A.I.F.C., Puerto Mineral Mill (96% owned), Puerto Mineral, Ruta 12 Km 1457, 3332 Capioví, Argentina, Capacity: 99,960 mt/y, (Pulp mill, Paper mill, Paperboard mill)
Phone: (54) 3743 493 700/444
Fax: (54) 3743 493 757/237
Email: info@grupozucamor.com.ar
Pulp Grades and Capacities:
Total pulp capacity: 81,428 mt/y
Recycled Pulping: 81,428 mt/y
Pulp Mill Data:
Recycled Fiber Treatment Lines:
Pulpers: 1 at 88,500 admt/y
Paper/Paperboard Grades and Capacities:
Total paper and paperboard capacity: 79,968 mt/y
Linerboard: 48,195 mt/y
Corrugating medium/fluting: 31,773 mt/y
Paper and Paperboard Mill Data:
Stock Preparation:
Pulpers:
Refiners: 3
Paper Machines: 1
No. 1, fourdrinier, total capacity 79,968 mt/y, Trim width 3.46 m, Corrugating medium/fluting, Linerboard
Finishing Equipment:
Rewinders: 1 at 80,000 mt/y
Energy Data:
Power boilers: 1
Steam turbines: 1
Electrical demand for mill: 127 MWh/D

BOLIVIA

ⒽⓂCompañía Papelera Mendoza S.A. (Copelme)
Cochabamba Mill
Av. Villazon Km. 4 1/2 carretera a Sacaba Zona Chacacollo
3503 Cochabamba
Bolivia
Phone: (591) 4 4720600/601/602/603/604
Fax: (591) 4 4720603
Email: info@copelme.com, produccion@copelme.com
Web Address: www.copelme.com
Personnel:
Owner & Pres.: Charbel Mendoza A.
Phone: (591) 4 4720600
Fax: (591) 4 4720603
Email: cmendoza@copelme.com
VP Admin.: Gonzalo Dorado
Phone: (591) 4 4720600
Fax: (591) 4 4720603
Email: gdorado@copelme.com
VP Accountant: Rocio Prado
Phone: (591) 4 4720600
Fax: (591) 4 4720603
Email: rprado@copelme.com
Prod. Mgr.: Bernardo Noya
Phone: (591) 4 4720600
Fax: (591) 4 4720603
Email: bnoya@copelme.com
Manuf. Mgr.: Jorge Saba
Phone: (591) 4 4720600
Fax: (591) 4 4720603
Email: jsaba@copelme.com
Assist. Maint. Mgr.: Omar Borda
Phone: (591) 4 4720600
Fax: (591) 4 4720603
Email: oborda@copelme.com
Total Employees of Company: 500
Total Employees at this Location: 100
Type of Operation: Paper mill
Pulp Grades and Capacities:
Total pulp capacity: 18,375 mt/y
Recycled Pulping: 18,375 mt/y
Pulp Mill Data:
Bleach Plant Systems: 1
Recycled Pulping System, Type: DIP
Recycled Fiber Treatment Lines:
Flotation deinking lines: 1
Paper/Paperboard Grades and Capacities:
Total paper and paperboard capacity: 22,134 mt/y
Tissue: 22,134 mt/y
Paper and Paperboard Mill Data:
Stock Preparation:
Pulpers: 3
Paper Machines: 1
No. 3, crescent former, total capacity 22,134 mt/y, Trim width 2.76 m, Tissue, Uncoated woodfree/freesheet
Finishing Equipment:
Sheeters: 5
Energy Data:
Power boilers: 1
Electrical demand for mill: 90 MWh/D

ⓂKimberly Bolivia S.A.
Santa Cruz Mill
Ownership: Kimberly-Clark Corp.
Parque Industrial M 5
6937 Santa Cruz de la Sierra
Bolivia
Phone: (591) 3 3465159
Fax: (591) 3 3470094
Web Address: www.kimberly-clark.com
Personnel:
Oper. Mgr.: Gilberto García
Phone: (591) 3 3465159
Fax: (591) 3 3470094
Email: ggarcia@kcc.com
Type of Operation: Paper mill
Paper/Paperboard Grades and Capacities:
Total paper and paperboard capacity: 17,000 mt/y
Tissue: 17,000 mt/y
Paper and Paperboard Mill Data:
Paper Machines: 1
No. 1, (second hand), total capacity 17,000 mt/y, Tissue

ⒽPapeles de Bolivia (Papelbol)
Av. Iturralde pasaje Chirinos 1067
La Paz
Bolivia
Phone: (591) 2 214 60 43/62
Fax: (591) 2 214 60 43
Email: produccion@papelesdebolivia.com
Web Address: www.produccion.gob.bo/content/papelbol
Personnel:
Gen. Dir.: Dr. Paulo Barragán Romano
Phone: (591) 2 214 60 43/62
Fax: (591) 2 214 60 43
Finan. Admin. Mgr.: Javier Campuzano
Phone: (591) 2 214 60 43/62
Fax: (591) 2 214 60 43
Acc. Mgr.: Freddy Ferrufino
Phone: (591) 2 214 60 43/62
Fax: (591) 2 214 60 43
Maint. Mgr.: Felipe Rodriguez Mendonca
Phone: (591) 2 214 60 43/62
Fax: (591) 2 214 60 43
Total Employees of Company: 60
Total Employees at this Location: 7
Mill Locations:
Papeles de Bolivia (Papelbol), Villa Tunari Mill, Villa Tunari, Cochabamba, Bolivia, Capacity: 15,000 mt/y, (Paper mill)
Phone: (591) 2 214 60 43/62
Fax: (591) 2 214 60 43
Email: produccion@papelesdebolivia.com

ⓂPapeles de Bolivia (Papelbol)
Villa Tunari Mill
Villa Tunari, Cochabamba
Bolivia
Phone: (591) 2 214 60 43/62
Fax: (591) 2 214 60 43
Email: produccion@papelesdebolivia.com
Web Address: papelbol.sedem.gob.bo/
Personnel:
Gen. Mgr.: Paulo Barragán Romano
Phone: (591) 2 214 60 43/62
Prod. Mgr.: Julio Quesada
Phone: (591) 72045440
Research & Dvlpmnt Mgr.: Ing. Ramiro V. Heredia Mendivil
Phone: (591) 22147001 - 76799967
Total Employees at this Location: 53
Type of Operation: Paper mill
Paper/Paperboard Grades and Capacities:
Total paper and paperboard capacity: 15,000 mt/y

Uncoated woodfree/freesheet: 15,000 mt/y
Paper and Paperboard Mill Data:
Stock Preparation:
Pulpers: 1
Refiners: 1
Paper Machines: 1
PM 1, (was originally due to start in September 2010, however was delayed until January 2014), fourdrinier, total capacity 15,000 mt/y, Newsprint, Uncoated woodfree/freesheet
Energy Data:
Power boilers: 1
Electrical demand for mill: 4 MWh/D

BRAZIL

ⓂAbbaspel Indústria e Comércio de Papéis Ltda.
Ownership: Private
Avenida Getúlio Vargas, 720, Bairro Cidade Nova
89400-000 Porto União, SC
Brazil
 Phone: (55) 42 3521 7300
 Fax: (55) 42 3523 3466
 Web Address: www.abbaspel.com.br
Personnel:
 Owner/Partner: Mohamad Abdul Abbas
 Phone: (55) 42 3521 7300
 Fax: (55) 42 3523 3466
 Owner/Partner: Ivone Wilhelms Abdul Abbas
 Phone: (55) 42 3521 7300
 Fax: (55) 42 3523 3466
 Owner/Partner: Omar Alexandre Abbas
 Phone: (55) 42 3521 7300
 Fax: (55) 42 3523 3466
 Owner/Partner: Jayle Cristine Abbas
 Phone: (1) 42 3521 7300
 Fax: (1) 42 3523 3466
 Owner/Partner: Abdo Marcelo Abbas
 Phone: (55) 42 3521 7300
 Fax: (55) 42 3523 3466
Mill Locations:
Abbaspel Indústria e Comércio de Papéis Ltda., Porto União Mill, Avenida Getúlio Vargas, 720, Bairro Cidade Nova, 89400-000 Porto União, SC, Brazil, Capacity: 3,500 mt/y, (Paper mill)
 Phone: (55) 42 3521 7300
 Fax: (55) 42 3523 3466
 Email: atendimento@abbaspel.com.br

ⓂAbbaspel Indústria e Comércio de Papéis Ltda.
Porto União Mill
Avenida Getúlio Vargas, 720, Bairro Cidade Nova
89400-000 Porto União, SC
Brazil
 Phone: (55) 42 3521 7300
 Fax: (55) 42 3523 3466
 Email: atendimento@abbaspel.com.br
 Web Address: www.abbaspel.com.br
Personnel:
 Owner/Partner: Mohamad Abdul Abbas
 Phone: (55) 42 3521 7300
 Fax: (55) 42 3523 3466
 Owner/Partner: Ivone Wilhelms Abdul Abbas
 Phone: (55) 42 3521 7300
 Fax: (55) 42 3523 3466
 Owner/Partner: Omar Alexandre Abbas
 Phone: (55) 42 3521 7300
 Fax: (55) 42 3523 3466
 Owner/Partner: Jayle Cristine Abbas
 Phone: (55) 42 3521 7300
 Fax: (55) 42 3523 3466
 Owner/Partner: Abdo Marcelo Abbas
 Phone: (55) 42 3521 7300
 Fax: (55) 42 3523 3466
Type of Operation: Paper mill
Paper/Paperboard Grades and Capacities:
Total paper and paperboard capacity: 3,500 mt/y
Tissue: 3,500 mt/y
Paper and Paperboard Mill Data:
Paper Machines: 2
PM 1, Trim width 1.69 m, Tissue
PM 2, Trim width 1.69 m, Tissue

ⓂAdami S.A. Madeiras
Rua Nereu Ramos, 196 - Centro
89500-000 Caçador, SC
Brazil
 Phone: (55) 49 3561 3200
 Fax: (55) 49 3561 3201
 Email: vendas@adami.com.br
 Web Address: www.adami.com.br
Personnel:
 Pres.: José Adami Neto
 Phone: (55) 49 3561 3200
 Fax: (55) 49 3561 3201
 Email: jose.adami@adami.com.br
 VP Dir.: Victor Batista Adami Filho
 Phone: (55) 49 3561 3200
 Fax: (55) 49 3561 3201
 Email: victor.adami@adami.com.br
 Corp. Commun. Supervisor: Adilson Padilha
 Phone: (55) 49 3561 3200
 Fax: (55) 49 3561 3201
 Email: adilson.padrilha@adami.com.br
 Dir. Sec.: Maria Eli Rocha
 Phone: (55) 49 3561 3032
 Fax: (55) 49 3561 3201
 Email: eli.rocha@adami.com.br
Total Employees of Company: 1,830
Mill Locations:
Adami S.A. Madeiras, Caçador Mill, Rod. SC 302, Km 6.5, Castelhano, 89500-000 Caçador, SC, Brazil, Capacity: 99,960 mt/y, (Paper mill, Paperboard mill)
 Phone: (55) 49 3561 3000
 Fax: (55) 49 3561 3065/62
 Email: fabrica@adami.com.br

ⓂAdami S.A. Madeiras
Caçador Mill
Rod. SC 302, Km 6.5, Castelhano
89500-000 Caçador, SC
Brazil
 Phone: (55) 49 3561 3000
 Fax: (55) 49 3561 3065/62
 Email: fabrica@adami.com.br
 Web Address: www.adami.com.br
Personnel:
 Paper Mill Mgr. (Prod. Mgr.): Francisco de Carvalho
 Phone: (55) 49 3561 3051
 Fax: (55) 49 3561 3065
 Email: francisco.carvalho@adami.com.br
 Sls. Mgr.: Alberto Domingues
 Phone: (55) 49 3561 3000
 Fax: (55) 49 3561 3065
 Email: alberto.domingues@adami.com.br
Total Employees at this Location: 225
Type of Operation: Paper mill, Paperboard mill
Pulp Grades and Capacities:
Total pulp capacity: 85,806 mt/y
Recycled Pulping: 85,806 mt/y
Pulp Mill Data:
Recycled Fiber Treatment Lines:
Recycled packaging pulping lines: 1 at 86,000
Paper/Paperboard Grades and Capacities:
Total paper and paperboard capacity: 99,960 mt/y
Linerboard: 59,976 mt/y
Corrugating medium/fluting: 39,984 mt/y
Paper and Paperboard Mill Data:
Stock Preparation:
Pulpers:
Paper Machines: 1
No. 1, (Former Type model: Fourdrinier Top/Bottom), fourdrinier (2), total capacity 99,960 mt/y, Trim width 2.2 m, Linerboard, Corrugating medium/fluting
Energy Data:
Power boilers: 1
Hydro turbines
Electrical demand for mill: 166 MWh/D

ⓂⓂÁguas Negras S.A. Ind. de Papel
Ituporanga Mill
Av. Brasil 1005, CP 67
88400-000 Ituporanga, SC
Brazil
 Phone: (55) 47 3533 8000
 Fax: (55) 47 3533 1202
 Email: contato@aguasnegras.ind.br
Personnel:
 CEO: Gerold Roland Purnhagen
 Phone: (55) 47 3533 1500
 Prod. Mgr.: Valdemar Machado
 Phone: (55) 47 3533 1500
 Finan. Mgr.: Adiomir Peters
 Phone: (55) 47 3533 1500
 Sls. Mgr.: Valdemir Bruering
 Phone: (55) 47 3533 1500
Total Employees of Company: 100
Type of Operation: Paper mill, Paperboard mill
Paper/Paperboard Grades and Capacities:
Total paper and paperboard capacity: 21,000 mt/y
Packaging papers: 13,000 mt/y
Linerboard: 4,000 mt/y
Corrugating medium/fluting: 4,000 mt/y
Paper and Paperboard Mill Data:
Paper Machines: 1
No. 1, total capacity 21,000 mt/y, Trim width 1.7 m, Packaging papers, Linerboard, Corrugating medium/fluting
Energy Data:
Hydro turbines: 1

ⓂAhlstrom Brasil Indústria e Comércio de Papéis Especiais Ltda.
Louveira Mill
Ownership: 100% by Ahlstrom Corporation Oy
Rua Armando Steck, 770
13290-000 Louveira, SP
Brazil
 Phone: (55) 19 3878 9200
 Fax: (55) 19 3878 9210
 Email: willy.bordignon@ahlstrom.com,
 investor@ahlstrom.com,
 corporate.communications@ahlstrom.com
 Web Address: www.ahlstrom.com
Personnel:
 VP Filtration & Prod. Man.: Willy Davis Bordignon
 Phone: (55) 19 3878 9200
 Fax: (55) 19 3878 9210
 Email: willy.bordignon@ahlstrom.com
 R&D and TCS Mgr.: Hermann Henrique Queiser
 Phone: (55) 19 3878 9200
 Fax: (55) 19 3878 9210
 HR Mgr.: José Laercio Pereira
 Phone: (55) 12 2127 9413
 Fax: (55) 19 3878 9210
 Email: laercio.pereira@ahlstrom.com
 Demand Mgr.: Uriel Barbosa Neto
 Phone: (55) 19 3878 9200
 Fax: (55) 19 3878 9210
Type of Operation: Paper mill
Pulp Grades and Capacities:
Paper/Paperboard Grades and Capacities:
Total paper and paperboard capacity: 9,000 mt/y
Specialty and industrial: 9,000 mt/y
Paper and Paperboard Mill Data:
Paper Machines: 1
No. 1, total capacity 9,000 mt/y, Specialty and industrial
Finishing Equipment:
Rewinders: 2

Brazil

ⒽⓂAlpes Celulose e Papéis Ltda.
São Luís Mill
Ownership: 100% by Grupo Auvepar
Porto do Tibiri, s/n, Bairro Tibiri
65055-072 São Luís, MA
Brazil
 Phone: (55) 98 3241 7142/2950
 Fax: (55) 98 3241 7057
 Email: diretoria@alpescelulose.com.br
 Web Address: www.alpescelulose.com.br
Personnel:
 Pres.: Carlos Thadeu Pinheiro Gaspar
 Phone: (55) 98 3241 2950
 Fax: (55) 98 3241 7057
 Supt. Dir.: Francisco de Assis Pinheiro Gaspar
 Phone: (55) 98 3241 2950
 Fax: (55) 98 3241 7057
 Mgr.: Antônio Silva
 Phone: (55) 98 3241 2950
 Fax: (55) 98 3241 7057
Total Employees of Company: 150
Total Employees at this Location: 150
Type of Operation: Paper mill
Paper/Paperboard Grades and Capacities:
 Total paper and paperboard capacity: 7,200 mt/y
 Tissue: 7,200 mt/y
Paper and Paperboard Mill Data:
Paper Machines: 1
 PM 1, total capacity 7,200 mt/y, Trim width 2.07 m, Tissue

ⒽAlta Papéis Ltda.
Rua Rio do Sul, 999, Cx. Postal 12, Bairro Alto Benedito
89124-000 Benedito Novo, SC
Brazil
Mailing Address: Benedito Novo, 12 Brazil
 Phone: (55) 47 3385 0708
 Fax: (55) 47 3385 0708
 Email: altapapeis@altapapeis.com.br
 Web Address: www.altapapeis.com.br
Personnel:
 Gen. Dir.: Geraldo Karam Westphalen Jr.
 Phone: (55) 47 3385 0708
 Fax: (55) 47 3385 0708
 Email: geraldo@altapapeis.com.br
 Commer. Dir.: Marli
 Phone: (55) 47 3385 0708
 Fax: (55) 47 3385 0708
 Email: marli@altapapeis.com.br
Mill Locations:
 Alta Papéis Ltda., Benedito Novo Mill, Rua Rio do Sul, 999, Cx. Postal 12, Bairro Alto Benedito, 89124-000 Benedito Novo, SC, Brazil, Capacity: 10,700 mt/y, (Paperboard mill)
 Phone: (55) 47 3385 0708
 Fax: (55) 47 3385 0708
 Email: altapapeis@altapapeis.com.br

ⓂAlta Papéis Ltda.
Benedito Novo Mill
Rua Rio do Sul, 999, Cx. Postal 12, Bairro Alto Benedito
89124-000 Benedito Novo, SC
Brazil
Mailing Address: Benedito Novo, 12 Brazil
 Phone: (55) 47 3385 0708
 Fax: (55) 47 3385 0708
 Email: altapapeis@altapapeis.com.br
 Web Address: www.altapapeis.com.br
Personnel:
 Gen. Dir.: Geraldo Karam Westphalen Jr.
 Phone: (55) 47 3385 0708
 Fax: (55) 47 3385 0708
 Email: geraldo@altapapeis.com.br
Type of Operation: Paperboard mill
Paper/Paperboard Grades and Capacities:
 Total paper and paperboard capacity: 10,700 mt/y
 Linerboard
 Corrugating medium/fluting: 10,700 mt/y

ⒽⓂIndústria Americana de Papel S.A.
São Paulo Mill
Rua Ulisses Cruz, 296 - Belenzinho
03077-000 São Paulo, SP
Brazil
 Phone: (55) 11 2291 2800
 Email: contato@americanapapel.com.br
 Web Address: www.americanapapel.com.br
Personnel:
 Gen. Dir.: Gladis Chade Cattini Maluf
 Phone: (55) 11 291 2800
 Finan. Dir.: Marina Chade Cattini Maluf
 Phone: (55) 11 291 2800
 Prod. Dir.: Afonso Martins
 Phone: (55) 11 2085 7070
 Email: afonso@saomiguel.ind.br
Type of Operation: Paper mill
Paper/Paperboard Grades and Capacities:
 Total paper and paperboard capacity: 7,000 mt/y
 Packaging papers

ⓂArjowiggins Ltda.
Salto Mill
Ownership: Arjowiggins SAS
Rodovia Salto-Itu 30
13324-195 Salto, SP
Brazil
 Phone: (55) 11 4028 9200
 Fax: (55) 11 4028 9309
 Email: lina.nonaka@arjowiggins.com
 Web Address: www.arjowiggins.com.br
Personnel:
 Gen. Dir.: Michel Jacques Giordani
 Phone: (55) 11 4028 9200
 Industrial Dir.: Valdeque Luis Roveri
 Phone: (55) 11 4028 9200
 Commer. & Mktg. Dir.: Ronald Carvalho Dutton
 Phone: (55) 11 4028 9200
Type of Operation: Paper mill
Pulp Grades and Capacities:
 Total pulp capacity: 3,500 mt/y
 Chemical Pulp: 3,500 mt/y
Pulp Mill Data:
 Chemical Pulping Systems:
 Batch digesters: 3
 Bleach Plant Systems: 1
 No. 1, Sequence: HDi, Capacity 1,500 admt/y
 Pulp Dryers:
 Air Float dryers 1
Paper/Paperboard Grades and Capacities:
 Total paper and paperboard capacity: 26,220 mt/y
 Coated woodfree/freesheet: 26,220 mt/y
Paper and Paperboard Mill Data:
 Stock Preparation:
 Pulpers: 4
 Refiners: 13
Paper Machines: 3
 No. 1, fourdrinier, Trim width 1.5 m
 No. 2, cylinder mould, Trim width 2.3 m
 No. 3, fourdrinier, Trim width 2.4 m
 Finishing Equipment:
 Supercalenders: 2
 Rewinders: 3
 Sheeters: 4

ⒽⓂIndústria e Comércio de Embalagens e Papéis Artivinco Ltda.
Santa Rosa do Viterbo Mill
Ownership: Rio Pardo - Indústrias de Papéis e Celulose
Fazenda Amália CP 85
14270-000 Santa Rosa do Viterbo, SP
Brazil
 Phone: (55) 16 3954 9100, 16 3954.9111
 Fax: (55) 16 3954 9127
 Email: admvendas@artivinco.com.br
 Web Address: www.artivinco.com.br
Personnel:
 Mill Mgr.: Douglas Rivas
 Phone: (55) 16 3954 9100
 Supervisor: Carlos Alexandre Pinto
 Phone: (55) 16 3954 9100
 Prod. Coord.: Marcos Alves
 Phone: (55) 16 3954 9100
Total Employees of Company: 400
Total Employees at this Location: 205
Type of Operation: Pulp mill, Paper mill, Paperboard mill
Pulp Grades and Capacities:
 Total pulp capacity: 161,636 mt/y
 Recycled Pulping: 136,349 mt/y
 Other Pulp: 25,287 mt/y
Pulp Mill Data:
 Chemical Pulping Systems:
 Batch digesters
 Pulp Lines: 1
 Recycled Fiber Treatment Lines:
 Pulpers: 1 at 63,470
Paper/Paperboard Grades and Capacities:
 Total paper and paperboard capacity: 162,078 mt/y
 Linerboard: 68,187 mt/y
 Corrugating medium/fluting: 93,891 mt/y
Paper and Paperboard Mill Data:
Paper Machines: 2
 No. 1, fourdrinier, total capacity 69,972 mt/y, Trim width 2.5 m, Linerboard, Corrugating medium/fluting
 No. 2, fourdrinier, total capacity 92,106 mt/y, Trim width 2.75 m, Linerboard, Corrugating medium/fluting
Energy Data:
 Power boilers
 Steam turbines: 1 at 4.5 MW
 Electrical demand for mill: 264 MWh/D

ⒽⓂAstória Papéis Ltda.
Gravataí Mill
Av. Antônio Gomes Corrêa, 1380, Parque dos Anjos
94190-300 Gravataí, RS
Brazil
 Phone: (55) 51 3484 8700
 Fax: (55) 51 3484 8727
 Email: vendas@astoriapapeis.com.br
 Web Address: www.astoriapapeis.com.br
Personnel:
 Gen. Dir.: Francisco José Justo
 Phone: (55) 51 3484 8700
 Ind. Dir.: Fernando José Ruschel Justo
 Phone: (55) 51 3484 8700
 Commer. Dir.: Paulo José Justo
 Phone: (55) 51 3484 8700
 Commer. Mgr.: Pércio Fernandez Jr.
 Phone: (55) 51 3484 8700
Total Employees of Company: 200
Total Employees at this Location: 200
Type of Operation: Paper mill
Paper/Paperboard Grades and Capacities:
 Total paper and paperboard capacity: 11,000 mt/y
 Tissue: 11,000 mt/y
Paper and Paperboard Mill Data:
Paper Machines: 1
 PM 3, total capacity 11,000 mt/y, Tissue

ⒽAvelino Bragagnolo S/A Indústria e Comércio
Distrito de Barra Grande
89696-000 Faxinal dos Guedes, SC
Brazil
 Phone: (55) 49 3436 7300
 Email: papel@bragagnolo.com.br, bragagnolo@bragagnolo.com.br
 Web Address: www.bragagnolo.com.br
Personnel:
 Pres. Owner: Avelino Bragagnolo
 Phone: (55) 49 3436 7300
 Email: bragagnolo@bragagnolo.com.br
Total Employees of Company: 800
Mill Locations:
 Avelino Bragagnolo S/A Indústria e Comércio, Faxinal

Brazil

dos Guedes Mill, Distrito de Barra Grande, 89696-000 Faxinal dos Guedes, SC, Brazil, Capacity: 72,000 mt/y, (Paperboard mill)
Phone: (55) 49 3436 7300
Email: bragagnolo@bragagnolo.com.br, papel@bragagnolo.com.br

ⓘⓜAvelino Bragagnolo S/A Indústria e Comércio
Faxinal dos Guedes Mill
Distrito de Barra Grande
89696-000 Faxinal dos Guedes, SC
Brazil
Phone: (55) 49 3436 7300
Email: bragagnolo@bragagnolo.com.br, papel@bragagnolo.com.br
Web Address: www.bragagnolo.com.br
Total Employees at this Location: 800
Type of Operation: Paperboard mill
Paper/Paperboard Grades and Capacities:
Total paper and paperboard capacity: 72,000 mt/y
Linerboard: 36,000 mt/y
Corrugating medium/fluting: 36,000 mt/y
Paper and Paperboard Mill Data:
Paper Machines: 2
PM 1, fourdrinier, total capacity 36,000 mt/y, Trim width 1.7 m, Linerboard, Corrugating medium/fluting
PM 2, total capacity 36,000 mt/y, Trim width 2.26 m, Corrugating medium/fluting, Linerboard
Energy Data:
Steam turbines: 1 at 4 MW

ⓘⓜBahia Specialty Cellulose S.A. ("BSC")
Camaçari Mill
Ownership: Sateri Holdings Limited
Rua Alfa 1033, AIN, COPEC
42810-290 Camaçari, BA
Brazil
Phone: (55) 71 3634 0401
Fax: (55) 71 3634 5462
Email: faleconosco@bahiaspeccell.com
Web Address: www.bahiaspeccell.com
Personnel:
Chmn Sateri International Ltd.: John Jeffrey Ying
Phone: (55) 71 3634 0401
Fax: (55) 71 3634 5462
CEO Sateri International Ltd.: Tey Wei Lin
Phone: (55) 71 3634 0401
Fax: (55) 71 3634 5462
CEO Sateri International Ltd.: Wil Hoon Wee Teng
Phone: (55) 71 3634 0401
Fax: (55) 71 3634 5462
Procurement Mgr.: Frederico Sa
Phone: (55) 71 3634 0401
Fax: (55) 71 3634 5462
Plann & Logist. Mgr.: Igor Noronha
Phone: (55) 71 3634 0401
Fax: (55) 71 3634 5462
Tech Service Mgr.: Alberto Lima
Phone: (55) 71 3634 0401
Fax: (55) 71 3634 5462
Finan. Dir.: Claudio Cotrim
Phone: (55) 71 3634 0401
Fax: (55) 71 3634 5462
Total Employees of Company: 650
Total Employees at this Location: 650
Type of Operation: Pulp mill
Pulp Grades and Capacities:
Total pulp capacity: 510,649 mt/y
Pulp available for market: 484,806 mt/y
Chemical Pulp: 510,649 mt/y
Pulp Mill Data:
Chemical Pulping Systems:
Batch digesters: 3
Pulp Lines: 2
Bleach Plant Systems: 2
Chemical Pulping System, Type: Hardwood - Ozone Process: MC, Sequence: O_2 AZP, Capacity 145,000 admt/y
Chemical Pulping System, Type: ECF - Hardwood Capacity 350,000 admt/y
Chemical Recovery Equipment:
Evaporator lines: 1
Recovery boilers: 2
Lime Kiln
Pulp Dryers:
Fourdriniers 1
Energy Data:
Power boilers: 1
Steam turbines: 2 at 14.0 MW
Electrical demand for mill: 1,240 MWh/D

ⓘⓜBignardi Indústria e Comércio de Papéis e Artefatos Ltda.
Jundiaí Mill / GB Millennium Mill
Ownership: 100% by Grupo Bignardi
Av. Antonio Pincinato, 7600, CP 32
13211-711 Jundiaí, SP
Brazil
Phone: (55) 11 4525 6000
Fax: (55) 11 4525 0170/6000
Email: sac@gbmillennium.com.br
Web Address: www.gbmillennium.com.br, www.bignardi.com.br
Personnel:
Pres.: José Bignardi Netto
Phone: (55) 11 4525 6000
Fax: (55) 11 4525 0170
Mill Mgr.: Kalil José Parizotto
Phone: (55) 11 4525 6044
Fax: (55) 11 4525 0020
Email: kalil.parizotto@bignardi.com.br
Tech. Mgr.: José Reinaldo Marquezini
Phone: (55) 11 4525 6087
Fax: (55) 11 4525 0020
Email: reinaldo@gbmillennium.com.br
Total Employees of Company: 418
Total Employees at this Location: 418
Type of Operation: Paper mill
Pulp Grades and Capacities:
Total pulp capacity: 9,344 mt/y
Recycled Pulping: 9,344 mt/y
Pulp Mill Data:
Recycled Fiber Treatment Lines:
Pulpers
Paper/Paperboard Grades and Capacities:
Total paper and paperboard capacity: 57,120 mt/y
Uncoated woodfree/freesheet: 57,120 mt/y
Paper and Paperboard Mill Data:
Stock Preparation:
Pulpers: 3
Refiners: 2
Paper Machines: 2
No. 1, fourdrinier, total capacity 14,280 mt/y, Trim width 2.04 m, Uncoated woodfree/freesheet
No. 2, fourdrinier, total capacity 46,410 mt/y, Trim width 2.2 m, Uncoated woodfree/freesheet
Coating Machines: 2
No. 1, total capacity 5,400 mt/y., off machine
No. 2, total capacity 5,400 mt/y., off machine
Finishing Equipment:
Calenders: 2
Rewinders: 4
Sheeters: 3
Energy Data:
Power boilers: 2
Electrical demand for mill: 125 MWh/D

ⓘⓜBenaion Indústria de Papel e Celulose S.A. - Bipacel
Manaus Mill
Ownership: 92% by Tocandira Benaion
Rua João Monte Fusco, 750, Santa Etelvina
69059-500 Manaus, AM
Brazil Phone: (55) 92 2121 1300
Fax: (55) 92 2121 1317
Email: bipacel@bipacel.com.br
Personnel:
Pres.: Tocandira Carreira Benaion
Phone: (55) 92 2121 1300
Fax: (55) 92 2121 1317
Email: tocandira@bipacel.com.br
Total Employees of Company: 200
Total Employees at this Location: 200
Type of Operation: Paper mill
Paper/Paperboard Grades and Capacities:
Total paper and paperboard capacity: 10,800 mt/y
Tissue: 10,800 mt/y
Paper and Paperboard Mill Data:
Paper Machines: 1
No. 1, total capacity 10,800 mt/y, Tissue

ⓘBL Bittar, Indústria de Papel
Rua Teixeira Marques, Vila Rosana
13485-127 Limeira, SP
Brazil
Phone: (55) 19 3446 8807, 19 3446-8800
Personnel:
Dir.: Rodrigo Bittar Lopes
Phone: (55) 19 3446 8800
Mill Dir.: Rogério Bittar
Phone: (55) 19 3446 8800
Partner Mgr.: Mara Rubia Bittar Lopes Ceres
Phone: (55) 19 3446 8800
Commer. Dir.: Eduardo Prado
Phone: (55) 19 3446 8800
Mill Locations:
BL Bittar, Indústria de Papel, Limeira Mill, Rua Teixeira Marques, Vila Rosana, 13485-127 Limeira, SP, Brazil, Capacity: 27,846 mt/y, (Paper mill)
Phone: (55) 19 3446 8807, 19 3446-8800

ⓘBL Bittar, Indústria de Papel
Limeira Mill
Rua Teixeira Marques, Vila Rosana
13485-127 Limeira, SP
Brazil
Phone: (55) 19 3446 8807, 19 3446-8800
Personnel:
Dir.: Rodrigo Bittar Lopes
Phone: (55) 19 3446 8807
Partner Mgr.: Mara Rubia Bittar Lopes Ceres
Phone: (55) 19 3446 8807
Total Employees at this Location: 150
Type of Operation: Paper mill
Pulp Grades and Capacities:
Total pulp capacity: 20,909 mt/y
Recycled Pulping: 20,909 mt/y
Pulp Mill Data:
Bleach Plant Systems: 1
Recycled Pulping System, Type: DIP
Recycled Fiber Treatment Lines:
Flotation deinking lines
Paper/Paperboard Grades and Capacities:
Total paper and paperboard capacity: 27,846 mt/y
Tissue: 27,846 mt/y
Paper and Paperboard Mill Data:
Paper Machines: 2
No. 1, fourdrinier, total capacity 13,566 mt/y, Trim width 2.5 m, Tissue
No. 2, crescent former, total capacity 14,280 mt/y, Trim width 2.5 m, Tissue
Energy Data:
Power boilers
Electrical demand for mill: 117 MWh/D

ⓘⓜBN - Papel Catarinense Ltda.
Benedito Novo Mill
Estrada BNV 447, Caixa Postal 47
89124-000 Benedito Novo, SC
Brazil
Phone: (55) 47 3385 2000/2002
Fax: (55) 47 3385 2025

Brazil

Email: administrativo@bnpapel.com.br
Web Address: www.bnpapel.com.br
Personnel:
Manuf. Mgr.: Gilberto Cristo Claro
Phone: (55) 47 3385 2000
Fax: (55) 47 3385 2025
Email: gilberto@bnpapel.com.br
Finan. Analyst.: Dirlei Giovani Filippi
Phone: (55) 47 3385 2000
Fax: (55) 47 3385 2025
Email: dirlei@bnpapel.com.br
Total Employees of Company: 99
Total Employees at this Location: 99
Type of Operation: Paper mill
Pulp Mill Data:
Recycled Fiber Treatment Lines:
Pulpers: 1 at 36,000 admt/y
Paper/Paperboard Grades and Capacities:
Total paper and paperboard capacity: 14,000 mt/y
Coated mechanical/groundwood: 14,000 mt/y
Packaging papers
Paper and Paperboard Mill Data:
Paper Machines: 1
No. 1, total capacity 14,000 mt/y, Trim width 2.5 m,
  Coated mechanical/groundwood, Packaging papers
Coating Machines: 1
No. 1, total capacity 3,600 mt/y., off machine
Finishing Equipment:
Winders: 1 at 3,600 mt/y
Calenders: 1
Rewinders: 1 at 3,600 mt/y
Energy Data:
Power boilers: 1
Electrical demand for mill: 40 MWh/D

ⓗⓜBom Pastor Indústria de Papel Ltda.
Divinópolis Mill
Rua Santa Rita de Cássia - Prolongamento Bairro Bom Pastor
35502-085 Divinópolis, MG
Brazil
Phone: (55) 37 3222 0700
Fax: (55) 37 3222 8049
Email: bompastorpapel@uol.com.br
Web Address: www.bompastorpapeis.com.br
Personnel:
Partner Mgr.: Ronaldo Fagunde
Phone: (55) 37 3222 0700
Fax: (55) 37 3222 8049
Partner Mgr.: Denis Soares Fagundes
Phone: (55) 37 3222 0700
Fax: (55) 37 3222 8049
Partner Mgr.: Maria Aparecida Fagundes
Phone: (55) 37 3222 0700
Fax: (55) 37 3222 8049
Partner Mgr.: José Lindolfo Fagundes
Phone: (55) 37 3222 0700
Fax: (55) 37 3222 8049
Total Employees of Company: 150
Total Employees at this Location: 150
Type of Operation: Paper mill
Paper/Paperboard Grades and Capacities:
Total paper and paperboard capacity: 10,350 mt/y
Tissue: 10,350 mt/y

ⓗⓜBonet Madeiras e Papéis Ltda.
Timbó Grande Mill
Rio Tamanduá, s/nº Vila Buriti
89545-000 Timbó Grande, SC
Brazil
Phone: (55) 49 3244 6190
Fax: (55) 49 3252 1101
Email: bonet@bonetsc.com.br
Web Address: www.bonetsc.com.br
Personnel:
Pres.: Hermes Antonio Bonet
Phone: (55) 49 3244 6190
Fax: (55) 49 3244 6184
Email: bonet@bonetsc.com.br
VP: Ary Adolfo Bonet
Phone: (55) 49 3244 6190
Fax: (55) 49 3244 6184
Supt.: Paulo Roberto Bonet
Phone: (55) 49 3244 6190
Fax: (55) 49 3244 6184
Ind. Mgr.: Paulo César Rufato
Phone: (55) 49 3244 6190
Fax: (55) 49 3244 6184
Email: rufato@bonetsc.com.br
Commer. Mgr.: Fernando Mauricio Signorini
Phone: (54) 49 3244 6190
Fax: (54) 49 3244 6184
Email: fernando@bonetsc.com.br
Total Employees of Company: 224
Total Employees at this Location: 96
Type of Operation: Paper mill, Paperboard mill
Pulp Grades and Capacities:
Total pulp capacity: 20,321 mt/y
Recycled Pulping: 20,321 mt/y
Pulp Mill Data:
Recycled Fiber Treatment Lines:
Pulpers: 1 at 22,610
Paper/Paperboard Grades and Capacities:
Total paper and paperboard capacity: 32,130 mt/y
Boxboard/cartonboard: 32,130 mt/y
Paper and Paperboard Mill Data:
Stock Preparation:
Pulpers: 4
Refiners: 3
Paper Machines: 1
No. 1, fourdrinier, total capacity 32,130 mt/y, Trim width 2.4 m, Boxboard/cartonboard
Coating Machines: 1
No. 1, total capacity 32,100 mt/y., on machine
Finishing Equipment:
Winders: 1 at 26,000 mt/y
Calenders: 3
Rewinders: 1 at 26,000 mt/y
Sheeters: 2 at 26,000 mt/y
Energy Data:
Power boilers: 1
Hydro turbines: 5 at 2.4 MW
Electrical demand for mill: 47 MWh/D

ⓗBrason Indústria de Papéis e Ondulados Ltda.
Av. Angelo Michielin 635
13601-010 Araras, SP
Brazil
  Phone: (55) 19 3542 8443 / 19 3544 5922
  Email: brason@terra.com.br,
  jaimebrason@terra.com.br
Personnel:
Pres.: Luiz Carlos Secundino
Phone: (55) 19 3544 5922
Email: luizsecundino@terra.com.br
Commer. Dir.: Jaime Brason
Phone: (55) 19 3544 5922
Email: jaimebrason@terra.com.br
Mill Locations:
Brason Indústria de Papéis e Ondulados Ltda.., Araras Mill, Av. Angelo Michielin 635, 13601-010 Araras, SP, Brazil, Capacity: 18,000 mt/y, (Paper mill)
Phone: (55) 19 3544 5922
Email: atendimento@brason.com.br

ⓜBrason Indústria de Papéis e Ondulados Ltda.
Araras Mill
Av. Angelo Michielin 635
13601-010 Araras, SP
Brazil
Phone: (55) 19 3544 5922
Email: atendimento@brason.com.br
Personnel:
Pres.: Luiz Carlos Secundino
Phone: (55) 19 3544 5922
Email: luizsecundino@terra.com.br
Commer. Dir.: Jaime Brason
Phone: (55) 19 3544 5922
Email: jaimebrason@terra.com.br
Type of Operation: Paper mill
Paper/Paperboard Grades and Capacities:
Total paper and paperboard capacity: 18,000 mt/y
Packaging papers
Linerboard
Corrugating medium/fluting
Paper and Paperboard Mill Data:
Paper Machines: 2
PM 1, total capacity 10,000 mt/y
PM 2, total capacity 8,000 mt/y

ⓗⓜCambará S.A. - Produtos Florestais
Cambará do Sul Mill
Ownership: 13.07% by Adrizo Adm e Participação Ldta, 5.32% by Antonio Pulchinelli, 23.95% by Dodreve Adm e Participação Ltda, 10.39% by Eduardo de Zorzi, 8.05% by Everton de Zorzi, 6% by Rumi Administracao e Participação Ltda
Rua Osvaldo Kroeff, s/n°, Bairro Ouro Verde
95480-000 Cambará do Sul, RS
Brazil
Phone: (55) 54 3251 8181
Fax: (55) 54 3251 8050
Email: cambara@cambarasa.com.br
Web Address: www.cambarasa.com.br
Personnel:
Prod. Mgr.: Alexandro Coelho
Phone: (55) 54 3251 8181
Fax: (55) 54 3251 8050
Email: alexandro.coelho@cambarasa.com.br
Total Employees of Company: 275
Total Employees at this Location: 275
Type of Operation: Pulp mill, Paper mill
Pulp Grades and Capacities:
Total pulp capacity: 30,000 mt/y
Pulp available for market: 30,000 mt/y
Pulp Mill Data:
Chemical Pulping Systems:
Batch digesters: 5
Pulp Lines: 1
Bleach Plant Systems: 1
No. 1, Sequence: O_2 EOP, Capacity 36,000 admt/y
Chemical Recovery Equipment:
Evaporator lines: 1
Pulp Dryers:
Fourdriniers 1
Paper/Paperboard Grades and Capacities:
Total paper and paperboard capacity: 10,000 mt/y
Tissue: 10,000 mt/y
Paper and Paperboard Mill Data:
Stock Preparation:
Pulpers: 1
Refiners: 1
Paper Machines: 1
No. 1, (second hand), fourdrinier, total capacity 10,000 mt/y, Trim width 2.4 m, Tissue
Energy Data:
Power boilers: 2
Steam turbines: 3 at 13 MW
Hydro turbines: 1 at 1.2 MW
Electrical demand for mill: 180 MWh/D

ⓗⓜCia. Canoinhas de Papel
Canoinhas Mill
Rod. BR 280 - S/N - Parque Industrial Nº 2, Campo d' Água Verde
89460-000 Canoinhas, SC
Brazil
Phone: (55) 47 3621 7000
Fax: (55) 47 3621 7090
Email: canoinhas@canoinhas.com.br
Web Address: www.canoinhas.com.br
Personnel:

Maint. Mgr.: Ricardo Motelewicz
Phone: (55) 47 3621 7000
Fax: (55) 47 3621 7090
Email: ricardo@canoinhas.com.br
HR Mgr.: Sergio Felipe De Souza
Phone: (55) 47 3621 7000
Fax: (55) 47 3621 7090
Email: sergiorh@canoinhas.com.br
Total Employees of Company: 510
Total Employees at this Location: 250
Type of Operation: Paper mill
Pulp Grades and Capacities:
Total pulp capacity: 46,094 mt/y
Recycled Pulping: 46,094 mt/y

Pulp Mill Data:
Bleach Plant Systems: 1
Recycled Pulping System, Type: DIP
Recycled Fiber Treatment Lines:
Flotation deinking lines: 1
Paper/Paperboard Grades and Capacities:
Total paper and paperboard capacity: 54,978 mt/y
Tissue: 54,978 mt/y
Paper and Paperboard Mill Data:
Paper Machines: 3
No. 1, crescent former, total capacity 12,852 mt/y, Trim width 2 m, Tissue, Uncoated woodfree/freesheet
No. 2, fourdrinier, total capacity 12,138 mt/y, Trim width 2.5 m, Tissue
No. 3, crescent former, total capacity 29,988 mt/y, Trim width 2.75 m, Tissue
Energy Data:
Power boilers
Electrical demand for mill: 187 MWh/D

ⒽCarta Fabril Ltda.
Ownership: 100% by Coutinho family
Rua Visconde de Sepetiba, 935 - 14th fl. - Centro
24020-206 Niterói, RJ
Brazil
 Phone: (55) 21 2159 9200, 2139-2929
 Email: sac@cartafabril.com.br, comercial@cartafabril.com.br
 Web Address: www.cartafabril.com.br
Personnel:
Dir.: Victor Leonardo Ferreira de Araujo Coutinho
Phone: (55) 21 2159-9200
Finan. Mgr.: Fabio Burgos
Phone: (55) 21 2159-9200
VP Finan.: Marcos Cattan
Phone: (55) 21 2159-9200
Admin. Mgr.: Fábio Rito Barbosa
Phone: (55) 21 2159 9200
Safety Mgr.: Steve Marcus Christensen
Phone: (55) 21 2159 9200
Email: cmarcus@cartafabril.com.br
Mill Locations:
Carta Fabril Ltda., Aracruz Mill, Rodovia Aracruz - Barra do Riacho, Aracruz, ES, Brazil, (Paper mill)
Email: cartafabril@cartafabril.com.br
Carta Fabril Ltda., Anápolis Mill, Distr. Agro Indl. Anápolis - Qd.09-Mód. 18/20, 75133-600 Anápolis, GO, Brazil, Capacity: 52,836 mt/y, (Paper mill)
Phone: (55) 62 4014 4601
Fax: (55) 62 4016 4601
Email: cartafabril@cartafabril.com.br, cartagoias@cartafabril.com.br
Carta Fabril Ltda., Carta Rio Mill, Av. Fued Moisés, 114, Tribobó, 24755-030 São Gonçalo, RJ, Brazil, Capacity: 27,132 mt/y, (Paper mill)
Phone: (55) 21 2159-9200 / 2139-2929
Email: comercial@cartafabril.com.br, sac@cartafabril.com.br

ⓂCarta Fabril Ltda.
Aracruz Mill
Mill is under construction (The first 2 PMs should kick off by 2015)
Ownership: 100% by Coutinho family
Rodovia Aracruz - Barra do Riacho
Aracruz, ES
Brazil
 Email: cartafabril@cartafabril.com.br
 Web Address: www.cartafabril.com.br
Type of Operation: Paper mill

ⓂCarta Fabril Ltda.
Anápolis Mill
Distr. Agro Indl. Anápolis - Qd.09-Mód. 18/20
75133-600 Anápolis, GO
Brazil
 Phone: (55) 62 4014 4601
 Fax: (55) 62 4016 4601
 Email: cartafabril@cartafabril.com.br, cartagoias@cartafabril.com.br
 Web Address: www.grupocartafabril.com.br, www.cartafabril.com.br
Personnel:
Proj. Mgr.: Luis Fernando Silva Rezende
Phone: (55) 62 4014 4601
Fax: (55) 62 4016 4601
Email: lrezende@cartafabril.com.br
Manuf. Mgr.: Marcione Bianchini Moraes
Phone: (55) 62 4014 4601
Email: 'mmoraes@cartafabril.com.br'
Total Employees at this Location: 120
Type of Operation: Paper mill
Pulp Grades and Capacities:
Total pulp capacity: 56,454 mt/y
Recycled Pulping: 56,454 mt/y

Pulp Mill Data:
Bleach Plant Systems: 1
Recycled Pulping System, Type: DIP
Recycled Fiber Treatment Lines:
Flotation deinking lines: 1
Paper/Paperboard Grades and Capacities:
Total paper and paperboard capacity: 52,836 mt/y
Tissue: 52,836 mt/y
Paper and Paperboard Mill Data:
Paper Machines: 3
No. 3, total capacity 10,710 mt/y, Trim width 2.2 m, Tissue, Uncoated woodfree/freesheet
No. 4, total capacity 12,138 mt/y, Trim width 2.4 m, Tissue, Uncoated woodfree/freesheet
No. 5, crescent former, total capacity 29,988 mt/y, Trim width 2.85 m, Tissue
Energy Data:
Power boilers

ⓂCarta Fabril Ltda.
Carta Rio Mill
Av. Fued Moisés, 114, Tribobó
24755-030 São Gonçalo, RJ
Brazil
 Phone: (55) 21 2159-9200 / 2139-2929
 Email: comercial@cartafabril.com.br, sac@cartafabril.com.br
 Web Address: www.cartafabril.com.br
Personnel:
Dir.: Victor Leonardo Ferreira de Araujo Coutinho
Phone: (55) 21 2159-9200 / 2139-2929
Dir. Plt.: José Carlos Pires Coutinho Jr.
Phone: (55) 21 2159-9200 / 2139-2929
Plann & Material Mgr.: Ricardo Fernandes
Phone: (55) 21 2159-9200 / 2139-2929
Plann & Logist. Mgr.: Jorge Medrado
Phone: (55) 21 2159-9200 / 2139-2929
Total Employees at this Location: 120
Type of Operation: Paper mill
Pulp Grades and Capacities:
Total pulp capacity: 29,022 mt/y
Recycled Pulping: 29,022 mt/y

Pulp Mill Data:
Bleach Plant Systems: 1
Recycled Pulping System, Type: DIP
Recycled Fiber Treatment Lines:
Flotation deinking lines: 1
Paper/Paperboard Grades and Capacities:
Total paper and paperboard capacity: 27,132 mt/y
Tissue: 27,132 mt/y
Paper and Paperboard Mill Data:
Paper Machines: 2
No. 1, crescent former, total capacity 12,852 mt/y, Trim width 2 m, Tissue, Uncoated woodfree/freesheet
No. 2, crescent former, total capacity 14,280 mt/y, Trim width 2.4 m, Tissue
Energy Data:
Power boilers
Electrical demand for mill: 132 MWh/D

ⒽⓂCataguazes Indústrias de Papel
Cataguases Mill
Rua Ondina Carvalheira Peixoto, 300, Chácara Palmeiras
36774-550 Cataguases, MG
Brazil
 Phone: (55) 32 3429 5000
 Fax: (55) 32 3429 5000
 Web Address: www.cataguazesdepapel.com.br
Personnel:
Pres.: João Gregório
Phone: (55) 32 3429 5000
Fax: (55) 32 3429 5000
Man. Dir.: Felix Santana
Phone: (55) 32 3429 5000
Fax: (55) 32 3429 5000
Industrial. Mgr.: José Wander Franzini
Phone: (55) 32 3429 5000
Fax: (55) 32 3429 5000
Tech. Mgr.: Charles Cipriano
Phone: (55) 32 3429 5000
Fax: (55) 32 3429 5000
Total Employees of Company: 200
Total Employees at this Location: 200
Type of Operation: Pulp mill, Paperboard mill
Pulp Grades and Capacities:
Total pulp capacity: 83,970 mt/y
Recycled Pulping: 83,970 mt/y

Pulp Mill Data:
Recycled Fiber Treatment Lines:
Recycled packaging pulping lines: 1 at 84,100
Paper/Paperboard Grades and Capacities:
Total paper and paperboard capacity: 82,824 mt/y
Linerboard: 40,698 mt/y
Corrugating medium/fluting: 42,126 mt/y
Paper and Paperboard Mill Data:
Paper Machines: 2
No. 1, fourdrinier, total capacity 42,126 mt/y, Trim width 2.5 m, Corrugating medium/fluting
No. 2, fourdrinier, total capacity 40,698 mt/y, Trim width 2.5 m, Linerboard
Energy Data:
Power boilers: 1
Electrical demand for mill: 148 MWh/D

ⒽCelulose Reciclada
Av. Dr. Rinaldo de Pinho Alves, 2680
53411-902 Paratibe, Paulista, PE
Brazil
 Phone: (55) 81 3542 1432, 11 7725 4154
 Email: contato@celulosereciclada.com.br
 Web Address: www.celulosereciclada.com.br
Personnel:
Bus. Dir.: Ailton Alves
Phone: (55) 81 3542 1432
Email: ailton@celulosereciclada.com.br
Commer. Mgr.: Bruno Peixoto
Phone: (55) 81 3542 1432
Email: bruno@celulosereciclada.com.br
Mill Locations:
Celulose Reciclada, Paulista Mill, Av. Dr. Rinaldo de Pinho Alves, 2680, 53411-902 Paratibe, Paulista, PE, Brazil, (Pulp mill)
Phone: (55) 81 3542 1432, 11 7725 4154
Email: contato@celulosereciclada.com.br

ⓂCelulose Reciclada
Paulista Mill
Av. Dr. Rinaldo de Pinho Alves, 2680

Brazil

53411-902 Paratibe, Paulista, PE
Brazil
 Phone: (55) 81 3542 1432, 11 7725 4154
 Email: contato@celuloseredclada.com.br
 Web Address: www.celuloseredclada.com.br
Personnel:
 Bus. Dir.: Ailton Alves
 Phone: (55) 81 3542 1432
 Email: ailton@celuloseredclada.com.br
 Commer. Mgr.: Bruno Peixoto
 Phone: (55) 81 3542 1432
 Email: bruno@celuloseredclada.com.br
 Asst. Bus. Dir.: Márcia Souza
 Phone: (55) 81 3542 1432
 Email: marcia@celuloseredclada.com.br
Type of Operation: Pulp mill
Pulp Grades and Capacities:
 Total pulp capacity: 12,000 mt/y
 Recycled Pulping: 12,000 mt/y

①⑩CELUPA - Industrial Celulose e Papel Guaíba Ltda.
Guaíba Mill
Ownership: 100% by Melitta Haushaltsprodukte GmbH & Co. KG
Estr. C. Ismael Chaves Barcellos ,150 - Bairro Engenho
92500-000 Guaíba, RS
Brazil
 Phone: (55) 51 3480 3336 / 2101 1100
 Fax: (55) 51 3480 2040 / 2101 1101
 Email: celupa@melitta.com.br
 Web Address: www.melitta.com.br
Personnel:
 Ind. Dir.: António Carlos da Silva
 Phone: (55) 51 2101 1100
 Fax: (55) 51 2101 1101
 Email: antonio.silva@melitta.com.br
 Asst. Ind. Dir.: Érica Batista do Nascimento
 Phone: (55) 51 2101 1136
 Fax: (55) 51 2101 1101
 Email: erica.nascimento@melitta.com.br
Type of Operation: Paper mill
Paper/Paperboard Grades and Capacities:
 Total paper and paperboard capacity: 30,900 mt/y
 Uncoated woodfree/freesheet: 17,000 mt/y
 Packaging papers: 2,500 mt/y
 Specialty and industrial: 11,400 mt/y
Paper and Paperboard Mill Data:
 Stock Preparation:
 Pulpers: 2
 Refiners: 9
Paper Machines: 1
 No. 2, fourdrinier, total capacity 30,900 mt/y, Trim width 2.4 m, Uncoated woodfree/freesheet, Specialty and industrial
Finishing Equipment:
 Supercalenders: 1 at 70,000 mt/y
 Rewinders: 2 at 38,500 mt/y
 Sheeters: 2
Energy Data:
 Power boilers: 3
 Combustion turbines: 1 at 1.2 MW

①CENIBRA - Celulose Nipo-Brasileira S.A.
Ownership: 100% by Japan Brazil Pulp & Paper Resources Development Co., Ltd.
Rua Bernardo Guimarães, 245 - 8° andar, Bairro Funcionários
30140-080 Belo Horizonte, MG
Brazil
Mailing Address: Caixa Postal 100, 35196-972 Distrito de Perpétuo Socorro, Belo Oriente, Brazil
 Phone: (55) 31 3235 4041
 Fax: (55) 31 3235 4002
 Email: leida.horst@cenibra.com.br
 Web Address: www.cenibra.com.br
Personnel:
 Pres.: Paulo Eduardo Rocha Brant
 Phone: (55) 31 3235 4041
 Fax: (55) 31 3235 4002
 Email: paulo.brant@cenibra.com.br
 Commer. Dir.: Satoshi Miyake
 Phone: (55) 31 3235 4041
 Fax: (55) 31 3235 4002
 Email: satoshi.miyake@cenibra.com.br
 Finan. Mgr.: Pauline Castillo
 Phone: (55) 31 3235 4041
 Fax: (55) 31 3235 4002
 Email: pauline.castillo@cenibra.com.br
 Tech. Dir.: Dierley Valadares
 Phone: (55) 31 3235 4041
 Fax: (55) 31 3235 4002
 Email: dierley.valadares@cenibra.com.br
 Exec. Assist.: Emiliani Ferreira
 Phone: (55) 31 3235 4015, 31 3235 4050
 Fax: (55) 31 3235 4002
 Email: emiliani.ferreira@cenibra.com.br
 Sls. Exec.: Fernando Costa Arantes
 Phone: (55) 31 3235 4038
 Fax: (55) 31 3235 4002
 Email: fernando.costa@cenibra.com.br
 Commer & Logist Mgr.: Alfredo Mavignier
 Phone: (55) 31 3235 4041
 Fax: (55) 31 3235 4002
 Email: alfredo.mavignier@cenibra.com.br
Mill Locations:
CENIBRA - Celulose Nipo-Brasileira S.A., Belo Oriente Mill, Rodovia BR 381, Km. 172, Distrito de Perpétuo Socorro, 35196-000 Belo Oriente, MG, Brazil, (Pulp mill)
 Phone: (55) 31 3829 5111/5010/5290
 Fax: (55) 31 3829 5260
 Email: comunicacacorporatival@cenibra.com.br

⑩CENIBRA - Celulose Nipo-Brasileira S.A.
Belo Oriente Mill
Rodovia BR 381, Km. 172, Distrito de Perpétuo Socorro
35196-000 Belo Oriente, MG
Brazil
Mailing Address: Caixa Postal 100, Belo Distrito de Perpétuo, 35196-972 Belo Oriente, MG, Brazil
 Phone: (55) 31 3829 5111/5010/5290
 Fax: (55) 31 3829 5260
 Email: comunicacacorporatival@cenibra.com.br
 Web Address: www.cenibra.com.br
Personnel:
 Mgr.: Edilson Vieira Dutra
 Phone: (55) 31 3829 5111
 Fax: (55) 31 3829 5260
 Email: edilson.vieira@cenibra.com.br
 Drying and Packaging Coordinator - Manuf. Dept.: Paulo Molinar Henrique
 Phone: (55) 31 3829 5541
 Fax: (55) 31 3829 5876
 Email: paulo.molinar@cenibra.com.br
Total Employees at this Location: 1,445
Type of Operation: Pulp mill
Pulp Grades and Capacities:
 Total pulp capacity: 1,353,818 mt/y
 Pulp available for market: 1,338,750 mt/y
 Chemical Pulp: 1,353,818 mt/y
Pulp Mill Data:
 Chemical Pulping Systems:
 Continuous digesters: 2
Pulp Lines: 2
 Bleach Plant Systems: 2
 Chemical Pulping System, Type: Hardwood, Sequence: O_2 DEopDP, Capacity 727,100 admt/y
 Chemical Pulping System - IsoThermail, Type: Hardwood Dith EopDP, Sequence: O_2 DEopD, Capacity 600,000 admt/y
 Chemical Recovery Equipment:
 Evaporator lines: 2
 Recovery boilers: 1
 Recovery boilers: 1
 Recovery boilers: 1
 Lime Kiln
 Pulp Dryers:
 Flakt dryer 1, Flakt dryer 1, Flakt dryer 1, Fourdriniers 1
Energy Data:
 Power boilers: 3
 Steam turbines: 2 at 44, 64 MW
 Electrical demand for mill: 2,323 MWh/D

①CEPASA - Celulose e Papel de Pernambuco S.A.
Ownership: Cia. Industrial Papelera Poblana S.A. de C.V.
Avenida Marquês de Olinda, n° 11, 8° andar
50030-000 Recife, PE
Brazil
 Phone: (55) 81 3419 9900
 Fax: (55) 81 3419 9960
Personnel:
 Dir. Pres.: José Bernardino Pereira dos Santos
 Phone: (55) 81 3419 9900
 Fax: (55) 81 3419 9960
 Dir. VP: Francisco de Jesus Penha
 Phone: (55) 81 3419 9900
 Fax: (55) 81 3419 9960
 Prod. Mgr.: Lázaro T Lázaro T
 Phone: (55) 81 3419 9900
 Fax: (55) 81 3419 9960
 Chief Eng, Eng. Mgr.: Juliana R Juliana R
 Phone: (55) 81 3419 9900
 Fax: (55) 81 3419 9960
Mill Locations:
CEPASA - Celulose e Papel de Pernambuco S.A., Jaboatão dos Guararapes Mill, Rua Vereador Sócrates Regueira Pinto de Souza, 183 – Padre Roma, 54110-000 Jaboatão dos Guararapes, PE, Brazil, Capacity: 69,972 mt/y, (Pulp mill, Paper mill, Paperboard mill)
 Phone: (55) 81 21198700
 Fax: (55) 81 34811298

⑩CEPASA - Celulose e Papel de Pernambuco S.A.
Jaboatão dos Guararapes Mill
Ownership: Cia. Industrial Papelera Poblana S.A. de C.V.
Rua Vereador Sócrates Regueira Pinto de Souza, 183 – Padre Roma
54110-000 Jaboatão dos Guararapes, PE
Brazil
 Phone: (55) 81 21198700
 Fax: (55) 81 34811298
Personnel:
 Plant. Mgr.: Adriano De Sa Pessoa
 Phone: (55) 81 21198700
 Fax: (55) 81 34811298
 Proj. Eng.: Fabricio Marques
 Phone: (55) 81 21198700
 Fax: (55) 81 34811298
Total Employees at this Location: 300
Type of Operation: Pulp mill, Paper mill, Paperboard mill
Pulp Grades and Capacities:
 Total pulp capacity: 72,660 mt/y
 Pulp available for market: 4,998 mt/y
 Other Pulp: 72,660 mt/y
Pulp Mill Data:
 Chemical Pulping Systems:
 Continuous digesters: 2
 Chemical Recovery Equipment:
 Evaporator lines: 1
 Recovery boilers: 1
 Lime Kiln
 Pulp Dryers:
 Flash dryers 3
Paper/Paperboard Grades and Capacities:
 Total paper and paperboard capacity: 69,972 mt/y
 Packaging papers: 39,984 mt/y
 Linerboard: 29,988 mt/y
Paper and Paperboard Mill Data:
 Stock Preparation:

Pulpers: 5
Refiners: 14
Paper Machines: 2
No. 2, fourdrinier, total capacity 29,988 mt/y, Trim width 1.4 m, Linerboard
No. 3, fourdrinier, total capacity 39,984 mt/y, Trim width 2.45 m, Packaging papers
Finishing Equipment:
Rewinders: 3
Energy Data:
Power boilers: 2
Steam turbines: 3 at 9 MW
Electrical demand for mill: 185 MWh/D

ⓂCibrapel S.A. Indústria de Papel e Embalagens
Ownership: 100% by private owners
Av. Brasil 22884, Guadalupe
21660-000 Rio de Janeiro, RJ
Brazil
Phone: (55) 21 3017 8787
Fax: (55) 21 3006 8900
Email: cibrapel@cibrapel.com.br
Web Address: www.cibrapel.com.br
Personnel:
Pres.: Rogério da Silva Oliveira
Phone: (55) 21 3017 8787
Fax: (55) 21 3006 8900
VP: Rosanne da Silva Oliveira
Phone: (55) 21 3017 8787
Fax: (55) 21 3006 8900
Finan. & Admin. Dir.: Ermelindo Bolfer Filho
Phone: (55) 21 3017 8787
Fax: (55) 21 3006 8900
Sls. Dir.: Eduardo Marcondes
Phone: (55) 21 3017 8787
Fax: (55) 21 3006 8900
Mill Locations:
Cibrapel S.A. Indústria de Papel e Embalagens, Guapimirim Mill, Estrada Comandante Bacellar 731, 25940-000 Guapimirim, RJ, Brazil, Capacity: 71,757 mt/y, (Paper mill, Paperboard mill)
Phone: (55) 21 2632 2313
Fax: (55) 21 2632 2040
Email: norma@cibrapel.com.br

ⓂCibrapel S.A. Indústria de Papel e Embalagens
Guapimirim Mill
Estrada Comandante Bacellar 731
25940-000 Guapimirim, RJ
Brazil
Phone: (55) 21 2632 2313
Fax: (55) 21 2632 2040
Email: norma@cibrapel.com.br
Web Address: www.cibrapel.com.br
Personnel:
Mill Mgr.: Milton Seixas
Phone: (55) 21 2632 2313
Fax: (55) 21 2632 2040
Email: milton@cibrapel.com.br
Controller: Vanilda Lopes da Motta
Phone: (55) 21 2632 2313
Fax: (55) 21 2632 2040
Email: vanilda@cibrapel.com.br
Total Employees at this Location: 250
Type of Operation: Paper mill, Paperboard mill
Pulp Grades and Capacities:
Total pulp capacity: 70,594 mt/y
Recycled Pulping: 70,594 mt/y

Pulp Mill Data:
Recycled Fiber Treatment Lines:
Recycled packaging pulping lines: 1
Paper/Paperboard Grades and Capacities:
Total paper and paperboard capacity: 71,757 mt/y
Corrugating medium/fluting: 42,840 mt/y
Boxboard/cartonboard: 28,917 mt/y
Paper and Paperboard Mill Data:
Stock Preparation:
Pulpers: 5
Refiners: 6
Paper Machines: 2
No. 1, fourdrinier, total capacity 28,917 mt/y, Trim width 2.46 m, Boxboard/cartonboard
No. 2, fourdrinier, total capacity 42,840 mt/y, Trim width 2.46 m, Corrugating medium/fluting
Coating Machines: 1
PM 1, total capacity 29,000 mt/y., on machine
Energy Data:
Power boilers: 1
Steam turbines: 1
Electrical demand for mill: 133 MWh/D

ⓂCICP Companhia Industrial de Celulose e Papel
Itaporanga d'Ajuda Mill
Ownership: 100% by Ondunorte, Cia. de Papéis e Papelão Ondulado do Norte
Rodovia BR 101, Km 114, Bairro Zona Rural
49120-000 Itaporanga d'Ajuda, SE
Brazil
Phone: (55) 79-3264-1324
Fax: (55) 79-3264-1071
Email: cicp@cicp.com.br
Web Address: www.ondunorte.com.br
Personnel:
Dir.: Pedro Américo Andrade
Phone: (55) 79-3264-1324
Fax: (55) 79-3264-1071
Email: pedroamerico@cicp.com.br
Type of Operation: Paper mill
Paper/Paperboard Grades and Capacities:
Total paper and paperboard capacity: 12,000 mt/y
Tissue: 12,000 mt/y
Paper and Paperboard Mill Data:
Paper Machines: 1
No. 1, total capacity 12,000 mt/y, Tissue

ⒽⓂCIPAC Indústria de Papéis Cantagalo Ltda.
Cantagalo Mill
Praça Miguel Santos, s/n, Bairro Centro
28500-000 Cantagalo, RJ
Brazil
Phone: (55) 22 2555 4069
Fax: (55) 22 2555 4001
Personnel:
Exec. Dir., Partner: Jorge Siqueira
Phone: (55) 22 2555 4069
Fax: (55) 22 2555 4001
Partner: Saulo Fonseca Padilha
Phone: (55) 22 2555 4069
Fax: (55) 22 2555 4001
Partner: José Renato Fonseca Padilha
Phone: (55) 22 2555 4069
Fax: (55) 22 2555 4001
Partner: Jussara Campanário Fonseca Padilha
Phone: (55) 22 2555 4069
Fax: (55) 22 2555 4001
Total Employees of Company: 170
Type of Operation: Paper mill
Paper/Paperboard Grades and Capacities:
Total paper and paperboard capacity: 12,800 mt/y
Tissue: 12,800 mt/y
Paper and Paperboard Mill Data:
Paper Machines: 2
PM 1, fourdrinier, total capacity 4,400 mt/y, Tissue
PM 2, fourdrinier, total capacity 8,400 mt/y, Tissue

ⒽⓂCITROPLAST- Ind. e Com. de Papéis e Plásticos Ltda.
Andradina Mill
Rodovia Euclides de Oliveira Figueiredo, km 188, Bairro Aparecida
16900-000 Andradina, SP
Brazil
Phone: (55) 18 3702 7000/7050
Fax: (55) 18 3702 7019/7010/7048
Email: citroplast@citroplast.com.br, vendas@citroplast.com.br
Web Address: www.citroplast.com.br
Personnel:
Commer. Representative: André Carreira
Phone: (55) 18 3702 7000
Fax: (55) 18 3702 7019
Email: alcandre@citroplast.com.br
Admin. Mgr.: Marco Antonio Nacfur
Phone: (55) 18 3702 7000
Fax: (55) 18 3702 7019
Email: marcoantonio@citroplast.com.br
Total Employees of Company: 100
Total Employees at this Location: 100
Type of Operation: Paper mill, Paperboard mill
Pulp Grades and Capacities:
Total pulp capacity: 83,850 mt/y
Recycled Pulping: 83,850 mt/y

Pulp Mill Data:
Recycled Fiber Treatment Lines:
Recycled packaging pulping lines: 1
Paper/Paperboard Grades and Capacities:
Total paper and paperboard capacity: 93,534 mt/y
Linerboard: 53,550 mt/y
Corrugating medium/fluting: 39,984 mt/y
Paper and Paperboard Mill Data:
Stock Preparation:
Pulpers:
Paper Machines: 2
No. 1, fourdrinier, total capacity 31,059 mt/y, Trim width 2.4 m, Corrugating medium/fluting, Linerboard
No. 2, (Former Type model: Fourdrinier Top/Bottom), fourdrinier, total capacity 62,475 mt/y, Trim width 2.5 m, Corrugating medium/fluting, Linerboard
Energy Data:
Power boilers: 1
Steam turbines: 1
Electrical demand for mill: 133 MWh/D

ⓂCMPC Celulose Riograndense
Guaíba Mill
Ownership: 100% by Empresas CMPC S.A.
Rua São Geraldo 1800, Bairro Ermo
92500-000 Guaíba, RS
Brazil
Phone: (55) 51 2139 7111/7211
Fax: (55) 51 2139 7186
Email: contato@cmpcrs.com.br
Web Address: www.celuloseriograndense.com.br
Personnel:
Pres. Dir.: Walter Lydian Nunes
Phone: (55) 51 2139 7111/7211
Fax: (55) 51 2139 7186
Mill. Mgr.: Jose Wilhelms Ventura
Phone: (55) 51 2139 7111/7211
Fax: (55) 51 2139 7186
Qlty. & Env. Mgr.: Clovis Zimmer
Phone: (55) 51 2139 7111/7211
Fax: (55) 51 2139 7186
IT Mgr.: Carlos Cesar Almeida
Phone: (55) 51 2139 7111/7211
Fax: (55) 51 2139 7186
Proj. Mgr.: Walter Martins
Phone: (55) 51 2139 7111/7211
Fax: (55) 51 2139 7186
Total Employees at this Location: 535
Type of Operation: Pulp mill, Paper mill
Pulp Grades and Capacities:
Total pulp capacity: 444,604 mt/y
Pulp available for market: 394,842 mt/y
Chemical Pulp: 444,604 mt/y

Pulp Mill Data:
Chemical Pulping Systems:
Continuous digesters: 1
Pulp Lines: 1
Bleach Plant Systems: 1
Chemical Pulping System, Type: Eucalyptus, Sequence: O_2 DEoDED, Capacity 430,000 admt/y
Chemical Recovery Equipment:

Brazil

Evaporator lines: 1
Recovery boilers: 1
Lime Kiln
Pulp Dryers:
Fourdriniers 1, Other dryers 1
Paper/Paperboard Grades and Capacities:
Total paper and paperboard capacity: 54,978 mt/y
Uncoated woodfree/freesheet: 54,978 mt/y
Paper and Paperboard Mill Data:
Stock Preparation:
Pulpers: 1
Refiners: 2
Paper Machines: 1
No. 1, fourdrinier, total capacity 54,978 mt/y, Trim width 2.79 m, Uncoated woodfree/freesheet
Finishing Equipment:
Winders: 1 at 58,500 mt/y
Calenders: 1
Sheeters: 1 at 22,000 mt/y
Energy Data:
Power boilers: 1
Steam turbines: 3 at 12.5, 12.5, 30 MW
Electrical demand for mill: 1,292 MWh/D

ⓘⓜ COCELPA - Companhia de Celulose e Papel do Paraná
Araucária Mill
Ownership: 100% by De Pauli family
Rdv. BR 476, Rdv. do Xisto, Km 14.5 CP 84
83707-440 Araucária, PR
Brazil
Phone: (55) 41 3641 3200
Fax: (55) 41 3643 3130
Email: cocelpa@cocelpa.com.br
Web Address: www.cocelpa.com.br
Personnel:
CEO: Sr. Rui Gerson Brandt
Phone: (55) 41 3641 3200
Fax: (55) 41 3643 3130
Commer. Dir.: Rinaldo Dalaqua
Phone: (55) 41 3641 3284, 41 3641 3285
Fax: (55) 41 3643 3130
Email: rinaldo.dalaqua@ecoverdi.com.br
Total Employees of Company: 550
Total Employees at this Location: 300
Type of Operation: Paper mill
Pulp Grades and Capacities:
Total pulp capacity: 50,000 mt/y
Chemical Pulp: 50,000 mt/y
Pulp Mill Data:
Chemical Pulping Systems:
Continuous digesters: 1
Pulp Lines: 1
Chemical Recovery Equipment:
Evaporator lines: 1
Recovery boilers: 1
Lime Kiln
Recycled Fiber Treatment Lines:
Flotation deinking lines: 1 at 550 admt/y
Recycled packaging pulping lines: 1 at 21,350 admt/y
Paper/Paperboard Grades and Capacities:
Total paper and paperboard capacity: 72,000 mt/y
Packaging papers: 36,000 mt/y
Linerboard: 36,000 mt/y
Paper and Paperboard Mill Data:
Stock Preparation:
Pulpers: 1
Refiners: 4
Paper Machines: 1
PM 2, (switch machine kraft paper - kraftliner), fourdrinier, total capacity 72,000 mt/y, Trim width 4.4 m, Packaging papers, Linerboard
Finishing Equipment:
Winders: 1 at 100,000 mt/y
Calenders: 1
Energy Data:
Power boilers: 2
Steam turbines: 3 at 2 x 6 MW
Electrical demand for mill: 279 MWh/D

ⓘⓜ Conpel - Cia Nordestina de Papel
Ownership: Ecoverdi
BR 101, Km 06, Vale do Gramame
58322-000 Conde
Brazil
Phone: (55) 83 3048-2300
Web Address: www.conpel.com.br
Personnel:
Pres.: Rui Brandt
Phone: (55) 83 3048-2300
Email: rui.brandt@cocelpa.com.br
Gen. Mgr.: Manoel Botelho
Phone: (55) 83 3048-2300
Email: manoelbotelho@conpel.com.br
Commer. Coord.: Vivianne Souza
Phone: (55) 41 3641 3287, 41 9698 0708
Email: vivianne.souza@cocelpa.com.br
Mill Locations:
Conpel - Cia Nordestina de Papel, Conde Mill, BR 101, Km 06, Vale do Gramame, 58322-000 Conde, PR, Brazil, Capacity: 63,600 mt/y, (Paperboard mill)
Phone: (55) 83 3048-2300

ⓘⓜ Conpel - Cia Nordestina de Papel
Conde Mill
Ownership: Ecoverdi
BR 101, Km 06, Vale do Gramame
58322-000 Conde, PR
Brazil
Phone: (55) 83 3048-2300
Web Address: www.conpel.com.br
Personnel:
Pres.: Rui Brandt
Phone: (55) 83 3048-2300
Email: rui.brandt@cocelpa.com.br
Gen. Mgr.: Manoel Botelho
Phone: (55) 83 3048-2300
Commer. Coord.: Vivianne Souza
Phone: (55) 41 3641 3287, 41 9698 0708
Email: vivianne.souza@cocelpa.com.br
Type of Operation: Paperboard mill
Paper/Paperboard Grades and Capacities:
Total paper and paperboard capacity: 63,600 mt/y
Packaging papers: 33,600 mt/y
Linerboard: 15,000 mt/y
Corrugating medium/fluting: 15,000 mt/y
Paper and Paperboard Mill Data:
Paper Machines: 1
PM 1, total capacity 63,600 mt/y, Linerboard, Corrugating medium/fluting, Packaging papers

ⓘⓜ COPAPA - Companhia Paduana de Papéis
Santo Antônio de Pádua Mill
Av. José Homem da Costa 635, CP 121710
28470-000 Santo Antônio de Pádua, RJ
Brazil
Phone: (55) 22 3854 9900
Fax: (55) 22 3854 9900
Email: copapa@copapa.com.br, contato@copapa.com.br
Web Address: www.copapa.com.br
Personnel:
Dir.: Mrs. Jussara Padilha
Phone: (55) 22 3854 9900
Fax: (55) 22 3854 9900
Email: jussara@copapa.com.br
Finan. Mgr.: Celso Ademir da Costa
Phone: (55) 22 3854 9900
Email: celso@copapa.com.br
Total Employees of Company: 450
Total Employees at this Location: 200
Type of Operation: Paper mill
Pulp Grades and Capacities:
Total pulp capacity: 30,026 mt/y
Recycled Pulping: 30,026 mt/y
Pulp Mill Data:
Bleach Plant Systems: 1
Recycled Pulping System, Type: DIP
Recycled Fiber Treatment Lines:
Flotation deinking lines: 1
Paper/Paperboard Grades and Capacities:
Total paper and paperboard capacity: 39,984 mt/y
Tissue: 39,984 mt/y
Paper and Paperboard Mill Data:
Paper Machines: 3
No. 1, fourdrinier, total capacity 4,641 mt/y, Trim width 1.68 m, Tissue
No. 2, fourdrinier, total capacity 7,497 mt/y, Trim width 2.45 m, Tissue
No. 4, crescent former, total capacity 27,846 mt/y, Trim width 2.5 m, Tissue
Energy Data:
Power boilers
Electrical demand for mill: 158 MWh/D

ⓘⓜ CVG - Cahdam Volta Grande
Rio Negrinho Mill
Rua Visconde de Mauá, 366 - Bairro Industrial do Norte
89295-000 Rio Negrinho, SC
Brazil
Phone: (55) 47 3646 1000
Fax: (55) 47 3646 1029
Email: cvg@cvg.ind.br
Web Address: www.cvg.ind.br
Personnel:
Industrial Dir.: Carlos Roberto Masutti
Phone: (55) 47 3646 1000
Fax: (55) 47 3646 1029
Email: carlosm@cvg.ind.br
Commer. Dir.: Paulo Cesar Forgati
Phone: (55) 47 3646 1000
Fax: (55) 47 3646 1029
Email: paulof@cvg.ind.br
Total Employees of Company: 230
Type of Operation: Pulp mill, Paper mill
Pulp Grades and Capacities:
Total pulp capacity: 40,123 mt/y
Recycled Pulping: 40,123 mt/y
Pulp Mill Data:
Bleach Plant Systems: 1
Recycled Pulping System, Type: DIP
Recycled Fiber Treatment Lines:
Flotation deinking lines: 1
Paper/Paperboard Grades and Capacities:
Total paper and paperboard capacity: 47,838 mt/y
Tissue: 47,838 mt/y
Paper and Paperboard Mill Data:
Stock Preparation:
Pulpers: 4
Refiners: 4
Paper Machines: 4
No. 1, fourdrinier, total capacity 6,069 mt/y, Trim width 1.8 m, Tissue
No. 2, crescent former, total capacity 16,779 mt/y, Trim width 2.3 m, Tissue
No. 3, crescent former, total capacity 13,209 mt/y, Trim width 2.3 m, Tissue
No. 4, crescent former, total capacity 11,781 mt/y, Trim width 2.7 m, Tissue
Finishing Equipment:
Rewinders: 1 at 10,000 mt/y
Energy Data:
Power boilers: 1
Electrical demand for mill: 170 MWh/D

ⓘⓜ Dall Pel Madeira e Papel
Grechinski Mill
Rua Ladislau Grechinski s/n, CP 171
84500-000 Irati, PR
Brazil
Phone: (55) 42 3423 1028
Fax: (55) 42 3423 1028
Email: dallpel@dallpel.com.br
Web Address: www.dallpel.com.br
Personnel:

Gen. Mgr.: Sylvio Bare Jr.
Phone: (55) 42 3423 1028
Fax: (55) 42 3423 1028
Email: sylvio@dallpel.com.br
Total Employees at this Location: 70
Type of Operation: Paperboard mill
Pulp Grades and Capacities:
Total pulp capacity: 40,207 mt/y
Recycled Pulping: 40,207 mt/y

Pulp Mill Data:
Recycled Fiber Treatment Lines:
Recycled packaging pulping lines: 1
Paper/Paperboard Grades and Capacities:
Total paper and paperboard capacity: 38,913 mt/y
Packaging papers: 25,347 mt/y
Linerboard: 6,783 mt/y
Corrugating medium/fluting: 6,783 mt/y
Paper and Paperboard Mill Data:
Paper Machines:
No. 1, fourdrinier, total capacity 38,913 mt/y, Trim width 2 m, Linerboard, Corrugating medium/fluting, Packaging papers
Energy Data:
Power boilers: 1
Electrical demand for mill: 69 MWh/D

①⑩DamaPel Comércio de Papéis Ltda
Guarulhos Mill
Av. Otávio Braga de Mesquita, 3748, CP 18 - Bairro Taboão
07140-230 Guarulhos, SP
Brazil
Phone: (55) 11 3809 8100/8001 22057
Fax: (55) 11 3809 8106/8129
Email: sac@damapel.com.br
Web Address: www.damapel.com.br
Personnel:
Pres.: Antonio Francisco Bonaccorso de Domenico
Phone: (55) 11 3809 8100
Fax: (55) 11 3809 8129
Mill Mgr.: Marcelo A. N. B. de Domenico
Phone: (55) 11 3809 8100
Fax: (55) 11 3809 8129
Email: marcelod@damapel.com.br
Commer. Mgr.: Carlos Ganancio
Phone: (55) 11 3809 8100
Fax: (55) 11 3809 8129
Email: carlosg@damapel.com.br
Maint. Mgr.: André Helderich
Phone: (55) 11 3809 8134
Fax: (55) 11 3809 8129
Email: andreh@damapel.com.br
Indus. Mgr.: César Moskewen
Phone: (55) 11 3809 8140
Fax: (55) 11 3809 8129
Email: cesarm@damapel.com.br
Total Employees of Company: 680
Total Employees at this Location: 272
Type of Operation: Pulp mill, Paper mill
Pulp Grades and Capacities:
Total pulp capacity: 25,017 mt/y
Recycled Pulping: 25,017 mt/y

Pulp Mill Data:
Mechanical Pulping Systems:
Conventional grinders: 3
Bleach Plant Systems: 1
Recycled Pulping System, Type: DIP
Recycled Fiber Treatment Lines:
Flotation deinking lines: 1
Pulpers: 2
Washing deinking lines: 1
Pulp Dryers:
Air Float dryers 1
Paper/Paperboard Grades and Capacities:
Total paper and paperboard capacity: 59,976 mt/y
Tissue: 59,976 mt/y
Paper and Paperboard Mill Data:
Stock Preparation:
Pulpers: 4
Refiners: 5
Paper Machines: 3
No. 1, crescent former, total capacity 11,067 mt/y, Trim width 2.5 m, Tissue
No. 2, crescent former, total capacity 18,921 mt/y, Trim width 2.9 m, Tissue
No. 3, crescent former, total capacity 29,988 mt/y, Trim width 2.7 m, Tissue
Finishing Equipment:
Rewinders: 6
Sheeters: 6
Energy Data:
Power boilers: 1
Electrical demand for mill: 203 MWh/D

①Eldorado Celulose e Papel
Ownership: 58.60% by J&F holding, 25% by MCL Empreendimentos, 8.20% by Funcef, 8.20% by Petros
Rua Alexandre Dumas, nº 2.100 - 6º andar
04717-913 Chácara Santo Antonio, São Pau, SP
Brazil
Phone: (55) 11 2505 0200
Fax: (55) 11 2505 0323
Web Address: www.eldoradobrasil.com.br
Personnel:
Pres. & CEO: José Carlos Grubisich Filho
Phone: (55) 11 2505 0200
Fax: (55) 11 2505 0323
Finan. Dir. and Relation with Investors: Hélio Baptista Novaes
Phone: (55) 11 2505 0200
Fax: (55) 11 2505 0323
Commer. Dir.: Giácoma Frasson Manhães
Phone: (55) 11 2505 0200
Fax: (55) 11 2505 0323
Email: giacoma.frasson@eldoradobrasil.com.br
Total Employees of Company: 2,800
Mill Locations:
Eldorado Celulose e Papel, Três Lagoas Mill, Rodovia BR 158 Km 231, 79641-300 Três Lagoas, MS, Brazil, (Pulp mill)
Phone: (55) 67 3509 0300

⑩Eldorado Celulose e Papel
Três Lagoas Mill
Rodovia BR 158 Km 231
79641-300 Três Lagoas, MS
Brazil
Phone: (55) 67 3509 0300
Web Address: www.eldoradobrasil.com.br
Personnel:
Gen. Mgr. (Eff. Feb. 2014): Fábio Nakano
Phone: (55) 67 3509 0300
Email: fabio.nakano@eldoradobrasil.com.br
Dir. Forest: Germano Vieira
Phone: (55) 67 3509 0167
Email: germano.vieira@eldoradobrasil.com.br
Tech. Dir.: Carlos Monteiro
Phone: (55) 67 3509 0300
Email: carlos.monteiro@eldoradobrasil.com.br
Maint. Mgr. (Eff. Feb 2014): Luiz Roberto Araújo
Phone: (55) 67 3509 0248
Email: luiz.araujo@eldoradobrasil.com.br
Total Employees at this Location: 800
Type of Operation: Pulp mill
Pulp Grades and Capacities:
Total pulp capacity: 1,515,573 mt/y
Pulp available for market: 1,500,114 mt/y
Chemical Pulp: 1,515,573 mt/y

Pulp Mill Data:
Chemical Pulping Systems:
Continuous digesters: 1
Pulp Lines: 1
Bleach Plant Systems: 1
No. 1, Type: ECF, Sequence: O_2 DEopDP, Capacity 1,695,750 admt/y
Chemical Recovery Equipment:
Evaporator lines: 7
Recovery boilers: 1
Lime Kiln
Pulp Dryers:
Air Float dryers 1, Air Float dryers 1, Twin Wire 1
Energy Data:
Power boilers: 1
Steam turbines: 2 at 182 MW
Electrical demand for mill: 2,482 MWh/D

①Estrela Indústria de Papel Ltda.
Ownership: 100% by Carraro family
Rua Gov. V. Parigot Souza, 1063, Bairro Lagoão
85555-000 Palmas, PR
Brazil
Phone: (55) 46 3263 1116
Fax: (55) 46 3262 3633
Web Address: www.estrelapapeis.com.br
Personnel:
Pres.: Dimovan Carraro
Phone: (55) 46 3263-1116
Fax: (55) 46 3262-3633
Purch. Mgr.: Jackson Carraro
Phone: (55) 46 3263-1116
Fax: (55) 46 3262-3633
Email: estrelacompras@proserv.com.br
Sls. Mgr.: Suew Cristina do Rio
Phone: (55) 46 3263-1116
Fax: (55) 46 3262-3633
Mill Locations:
Estrela Indústria de Papel Ltda., Palmas Mill, Rua Gov. V. Parigot Souza, 1063, Bairro Lagoão, 85555-000 Palmas, PR, Brazil, Capacity: 33,201 mt/y, (Paper mill, Paperboard mill)
Phone: (55) 46 3263 1116
Fax: (55) 46 3262 3633

⑩Estrela Indústria de Papel Ltda.
Palmas Mill
Rua Gov. V. Parigot Souza, 1063, Bairro Lagoão
85555-000 Palmas, PR
Brazil
Phone: (55) 46 3263 1116
Fax: (55) 46 3262 3633
Web Address: www.estrelapapeis.com.br
Personnel:
Pres.: Dimovan Carraro
Phone: (55) 46 3263 1116
Fax: (55) 46 3262-3633
Purch. Mgr.: Jackson Carraro
Phone: (55) 46 3263 1116
Fax: (55) 46 3262-3633
Email: estrelacompras@proserv.com.br
Sls. Mgr.: Suew Cristina do Rio
Phone: (55) 46 3263 1116
Fax: (55) 46 3262-3633
Total Employees at this Location: 100
Type of Operation: Paper mill, Paperboard mill
Pulp Grades and Capacities:
Total pulp capacity: 20,207 mt/y
Recycled Pulping: 20,207 mt/y

Pulp Mill Data:
Recycled Fiber Treatment Lines:
Recycled packaging pulping lines: 1
Paper/Paperboard Grades and Capacities:
Total paper and paperboard capacity: 33,201 mt/y
Tissue: 12,138 mt/y
Linerboard: 9,996 mt/y
Corrugating medium/fluting: 11,067 mt/y
Paper and Paperboard Mill Data:
Paper Machines: 2
No. 1, fourdrinier, total capacity 21,063 mt/y, Trim width 2 m, Linerboard, Corrugating medium/fluting
No. 2, fourdrinier, total capacity 12,138 mt/y, Trim width 2.76 m, Tissue, Uncoated woodfree/freesheet
Energy Data:
Power boilers: 1
Steam turbines: 1
Hydro turbines: 1
Electrical demand for mill: 72 MWh/D

Brazil

ⓘⓜFACEPA - Fábrica de Papel da Amazônia S.A.
Belém Mill
Passagem 3 de Outubro, 536, Sacramenta
66123-640 Belém, PA
Brazil
  Phone: (55) 91 4005 7300
  Fax: (55) 91 3233 0575
  Email: facepa@facepa.com.br
  Web Address: www.facepa.com.br
Personnel:
  Pres.: Antonio Georges Farah
  Phone: (55) 91 4005 7300
  VP: Cléa Chady Farah
  Phone: (55) 91 4005 7300
  Commer. Dir.: Carlos Georges Chady Farah
  Phone: (55) 91 4005 7300
  Finan. Dir.: Fernando Pessoa Diniz
  Phone: (55) 91 4005 7300
  Plan. Dir.: Edmar Acatauassu Freire
  Phone: (55) 91 4005 7300
Total Employees at this Location: 300
Type of Operation: Paper mill
Pulp Grades and Capacities:
  Total pulp capacity: 33,786 mt/y
  Recycled Pulping: 33,786 mt/y
Pulp Mill Data:
  Bleach Plant Systems: 1
  Recycled Pulping System, Type: DIP
  Recycled Fiber Treatment Lines:
  Flotation deinking lines: 1
Paper/Paperboard Grades and Capacities:
  Total paper and paperboard capacity: 64,974 mt/y
  Tissue: 64,974 mt/y
Paper and Paperboard Mill Data:
Paper Machines: 3
No. 2, fourdrinier, total capacity 12,138 mt/y, Trim width 2 m, Tissue, Uncoated woodfree/freesheet
No. 3, crescent former, total capacity 26,418 mt/y, Trim width 2.5 m, Tissue
No. 4, crescent former, total capacity 26,418 mt/y, Trim width 2.5 m, Tissue
Energy Data:
Power boilers
Electrical demand for mill: 214 MWh/D

ⓘⓜFernandez S.A. Indústria de Papel
Amparo Mill
Rod Amparo-Monte Alegre do Sul, Km. 2, CP 134
13900-000 Amparo, SP
Brazil
  Phone: (55) 19 3817 7100
  Fax: (55) 19 3817 7109
  Email: fernandez@fernandezpapel.com.br
  Web Address: www.fernandezpapel.com.br
Personnel:
  Pres & CEO: Benjamin Fernandez Rodriguez
  Phone: (55) 19 3817 7100
  Fax: (55) 19 3817 7109
  Asst. Accounting: Andréa Fernandez
  Phone: (55) 19 3817 7100
  Fax: (55) 19 3817 7109
  Prod. Engineer: Renato Antoun Izar
  Phone: (55) 19 3817 7100
  Fax: (55) 19 3817 7109
Total Employees at this Location: 165
Type of Operation: Paperboard mill
Pulp Grades and Capacities:
  Total pulp capacity: 180,502 mt/y
  Recycled Pulping: 180,502 mt/y
Pulp Mill Data:
  Recycled Fiber Treatment Lines:
  Recycled packaging pulping lines: 1 at 181,000
Paper/Paperboard Grades and Capacities:
  Total paper and paperboard capacity: 179,928 mt/y
  Linerboard: 34,986 mt/y
  Corrugating medium/fluting: 144,942 mt/y
Paper and Paperboard Mill Data:

Stock Preparation:
Pulpers:
Paper Machines: 3
No. 1, fourdrinier, total capacity 34,986 mt/y, Trim width 2 m, Linerboard
No. 2, fourdrinier, total capacity 57,834 mt/y, Trim width 2.5 m, Corrugating medium/fluting
No. 3, fourdrinier, total capacity 87,108 mt/y, Trim width 3 m, Corrugating medium/fluting
Energy Data:
Power boilers
Electrical demand for mill: 309 MWh/D

ⓘⓜIndústria e Comércio de Papel Fiberpap Ltda.
Limeira Mill
Avenida Campinas 2000, Bairro Vila Independência
13480-290 Limeira, SP
Brazil
Mailing Address: CP 113, 13480 Limeira, Brazil
  Phone: (55) 19 3451 3972
  Fax: (55) 19 3451 0984
  Email: fiberpap@terra.com.br
Personnel:
  Owner: Paulo Eneas Kuhl
  Phone: (55) 19 3451 3972
Type of Operation: Paper mill
Paper/Paperboard Grades and Capacities:
  Total paper and paperboard capacity: 4,000 mt/y
  Packaging papers: 4,000 mt/y

ⓘFibria Celulose SA
Ownership: 35.02% by shareholders, 29.42% by Votorantim Industrial - VID, 5.18% by Safra Bahamas Asset Management Ltd., 30.38% by BNDES
Alameda Santos 1357, 6° andar
01419-908 São Paulo, SP
Brazil
  Phone: (55) 11 2138 4000
  Fax: (55) 11 2138 4065
  Email: comunicacaofibria@fibria.com.br
  Web Address: www.fibria.com.br
Personnel:
  Chmn.: José Luciano Penido
  Phone: (55) 11 2138 4000
  Fax: (55) 11 2138 4065
  Email: jose.penido@fibria.com.br
  CEO: Marcelo Strufaldi Castelli
  Phone: (55) 11 2138 4000
  Fax: (55) 11 2138 4065
  Email: marcelo.castelli@fibria.com.br
  CFO & Investor Relations Director.: Guilherme Perboyre Cavalcanti
  Phone: (55) 11 2138 4000
  Fax: (55) 11 2138 4065
  Email: guilherme.cavalcanti@fibria.com.br
  Ind. Dir. : Paulo Silveira
  Phone: (55) 11 2138 4000
  Fax: (55) 11 2138 4065
  Email: paulo.silveira@fibria.com.br
  Commercial and International Logistics: Henri Philippe Van Keer
  Phone: (55) 11 2138 4000
  Fax: (55) 11 2138 4065
  Email: Henri.vankeer@fibria.com.br
  Human and Organizational Development: Luiz Fernando Torres Pinto
  Phone: (55) 11 2138 4000
  Fax: (55) 11 2138 4065
  Email: luiz.torres@fibria.com.br
  Forestry: Aires Galhardo
  Phone: (55) 11 2138 4000
  Fax: (55) 11 2138 4065
  Email: aires.galhardo@fibria.com.br
Total Employees of Company: 15,000
Total Employees at this Location: 234
Mill Locations:
Fibria Celulose SA, Aracruz Mill, Rodovia Aracruz - Barra do Riacho, s/n°, Km 25, 29197-900 Aracruz, ES, Brazil, (Pulp mill)
Phone: (55) 27 3270 2122
Fax: (55) 27 3270 2136
Fibria Celulose SA, Jacareí Mill, Rdv. Gen. Euryale J. Zerbini, km 84, 12340-010 Jacareí, SP, Brazil, (Pulp mill, Paper mill)
Phone: (55) 12 2128 1100
Fax: (55) 12 3957 1261
Fibria Celulose SA, Três Lagoas Mill, Rodovia MS 395 Km 20, CP 26, 79601-970 Três Lagoas, MS, Brazil, (Pulp mill, Paper mill)
Phone: (55) 67 3509 8041/1082
Fax: (55) 67 3509 1001
Veracel Celulose S.A., Veracel Pulp Mill (50% owned), Rodovia Fazenda Brazilândia BA 275, Km 24, Zona Rural, 45820-970 Eunápolis, BA, Brazil, (Pulp mill)
Phone: (55) 73 3166 8000
Fax: (55) 73 3166 8980
Email: veracel@veracel.com.br

ⓜFibria Celulose SA
Aracruz Mill
Rodovia Aracruz - Barra do Riacho, s/n°, Km 25
29197-900 Aracruz, ES
Brazil
  Phone: (55) 27 3270 2122
  Fax: (55) 27 3270 2136
  Web Address: www.fibria.com.br
Personnel:
  Mill Mgr.: Marcelo Oliveira
  Phone: (55) 27 3270 2122
  Fax: (55) 27 3270 2136
  Email: marcelo.oliveira@fibria.com.br
Total Employees at this Location: 1,750
Type of Operation: Pulp mill
Pulp Grades and Capacities:
  Total pulp capacity: 2,366,444 mt/y
  Pulp available for market: 2,340,135 mt/y
  Chemical Pulp: 2,366,444 mt/y
Pulp Mill Data:
  Chemical Pulping Systems:
  Continuous digesters: 3
  Pulp Lines: 3
  Bleach Plant Systems: 5
  Chemical Pulping System - line 5, Type: Hardwood, Sequence: O_2 A/DO EOP D D(P)
  Chemical Pulping System - lines 1, Type: Hardwood, Sequence: O_2 DoEopDPO
  Chemical Pulping System - lines 2, Type: Hardwood, Sequence: O_2 DoEopDPO
  Chemical Pulping System - lines 3, Type: Hardwood, Sequence: O_2 DEopDED
  Chemical Pulping System - lines 4, Type: Hardwood, Sequence: O_2 DEopDED
  Chemical Recovery Equipment:
  Evaporator lines: 5
  Recovery boilers: 3
  Lime Kiln
  Pulp Dryers:
  Air Float dryers 1, Air Float dryers 1, Air Float dryers 1, Air Float dryers 1, Air Float dryers 1
Energy Data:
Power boilers: 2
Steam turbines: 6 at 280 MW
Electrical demand for mill: 3,982 MWh/D

ⓜFibria Celulose SA
Jacareí Mill
Rdv. Gen. Euryale J. Zerbini, km 84
12340-010 Jacareí, SP
Brazil
  Phone: (55) 12 2128 1100
  Fax: (55) 12 3957 1261
  Web Address: www.fibria.com.br
Personnel:
  Mill. Mgr.: Paulo Gaia
  Phone: (55) 12 2128 1381
  Fax: (55) 12 3957 1261

Email: paulo.gaia@fibria.com.br
Eng & Proj Mgr.: Julio Cesar Rodrigues da Cunha
Phone: (55) 12 2128 1100
Fax: (55) 12 3957 1261
Email: julio.rodrigues@fibria.com.br
Tech Service Mgr.: Rosaria Mainieri
Phone: (55) 12 2128 1100
Fax: (55) 12 3957 1261
Email: rosaria.mainieri@fibria.com.br
Total Employees at this Location: 1,149
Type of Operation: Pulp mill, Paper mill
Pulp Grades and Capacities:
  Total pulp capacity: 1,109,510 mt/y
  Pulp available for market: 1,099,917 mt/y
  Chemical Pulp: 1,109,510 mt/y
Pulp Mill Data:
  Chemical Pulping Systems:
  Continuous digesters: 2
Pulp Lines: 2
  Bleach Plant Systems: 2
  Chemical Pulping system - B, Type: Hardwood (Eucalyptus) - Ozone process: MC, Sequence: O_2 OaZDP, Capacity 440,000 admt/y
  Chemical Pulping system - C, Type: Hardwood (Eucalyptus), Ozone process: HC, Sequence: O_2 Z/D(PO)D, Capacity 800,000 admt/y
  Chemical Recovery Equipment:
  Evaporator lines: 2
  Recovery boilers: 2
  Lime Kiln
  Pulp Dryers:
  Flakt dryer 1, Flakt dryer 1, Twin Wire 1, Twin Wire 1
Energy Data:
  Power boilers: 2
  Combustion turbines: 1 at 31 MW
  Steam turbines: 3 at 25, 38, 44 MW
  Electrical demand for mill: 1,953 MWh/D

ⓂFibria Celulose SA
Três Lagoas Mill
Rodovia MS 395 Km 20, CP 26
79601-970 Três Lagoas, MS
Brazil
  Phone: (55) 67 3509 8041/1082
  Fax: (55) 67 3509 1001
  Web Address: www.fibria.com.br
Personnel:
  Asst. Prod Mgr.: Andre Quatrini
  Phone: (55) 67 3509 8041/1082
  Fax: (55) 67 3509 1001
  Email: andre.quatrini@fibria.com.br
  Fiber Prod Specialist.: Vinicius Bassan Sierra
  Phone: (55) 67 3509 8041/1082
  Fax: (55) 67 3509 1001
  Email: vinicius.sierra@fibria.com.br
Total Employees at this Location: 897
Type of Operation: Pulp mill, Paper mill
Pulp Grades and Capacities:
  Total pulp capacity: 1,306,439 mt/y
  Pulp available for market: 1,299,837 mt/y
  Chemical Pulp: 1,306,439 mt/y
Pulp Mill Data:
  Chemical Pulping Systems:
  Continuous digesters: 1
Pulp Lines: 1
  Bleach Plant Systems: 1
  Chemical Pulping System, Type: ECF - Hardwood - A/DEoPDP
  Chemical Recovery Equipment:
  Evaporator lines: 1
  Recovery boilers: 1
  Lime Kiln
  Pulp Dryers:
  Air Float dryers 1, Twin Wire 1
Energy Data:
  Power boilers: 1
  Steam turbines: 2 at 170 MW
  Electrical demand for mill: 1,951 MWh/D

ⓂFibria Celulose SA
Eldorado
Rodovia MS 395 Km 20, CP 26
79601-970 Três Lagoas, MS
Brazil
  Phone: (55) 67 3509 8041/1082
  Fax: (55) 67 3509 1001
  Web Address: www.fibria.com.br
Total Employees at this Location: 536
Type of Operation: Pulp mill, Paper mill

ⓂFibria Celulose SA
Maranhão
Rodovia MS 395 Km 20, CP 26
79601-970 Três Lagoas, MS
Brazil
  Phone: (55) 67 3509 8041/1082
  Fax: (55) 67 3509 1001
  Web Address: www.fibria.com.br
Total Employees at this Location: 536
Type of Operation: Pulp mill, Paper mill

ⓂFibria Celulose SA
Maranhão
Rodovia MS 395 Km 20, CP 26
79601-970 Três Lagoas, MS
Brazil
  Phone: (55) 67 3509 8041/1082
  Fax: (55) 67 3509 1001
  Web Address: www.fibria.com.br
Total Employees at this Location: 536
Type of Operation: Pulp mill, Paper mill

ⓂFibria Celulose SA
Eldorado
Rodovia MS 395 Km 20, CP 26
79601-970 Três Lagoas, MS
Brazil
  Phone: (55) 67 3509 8041/1082
  Fax: (55) 67 3509 1001
  Web Address: www.fibria.com.br
Total Employees at this Location: 536
Type of Operation: Pulp mill, Paper mill

ⒽⓂFiliperson Papéis Especiais Ltda.
Rio de Janeiro Mill
Av. Canal do Rio Timbó 760, Inhaúma
21061-280 Rio de Janeiro, RJ
Brazil
  Phone: (55) 21 3265 3454
  Fax: (55) 21 3265 3454
  Email: sac@filiperson.com.br
  Web Address: www.filiperson.com.br
Personnel:
  Pres.: Ricardo Tannuri
  Phone: (55) 21 2560 8197/3265 3454
  Prod. Mgr.: Raivy Grifo
  Phone: (55) 21 2560 8197/3265 3454
Type of Operation: Paper mill
Paper/Paperboard Grades and Capacities:
  Total paper and paperboard capacity: 3,500 mt/y
  Uncoated woodfree/freesheet: 3,500 mt/y
Paper and Paperboard Mill Data:
Paper Machines: 1
  No. 1, total capacity 3,500 mt/y, Trim width 0.88 m, Uncoated woodfree/freesheet

ⒽⓂMadeireira Miguel Forte S.A.
União da Vitória Mill
Ownership: Domingos Forte Filho, José Forte, Vicente Forte
Avenida Marechal Deodoro, 2565, Rio d'Areia
84600-000 União da Vitória, PR
Brazil
  Phone: (55) 42 3522 3044, 3522-0300
  Fax: (55) 42 3522 3731
  Email: miforte@miforte.com.br, papel@miforte.com.br

Personnel:
  CEO : Cleyde Dalla Torre Forte
  Phone: (55) 42 3522 3044
  Fax: (55) 42 3522 3731
  Superintendent Dir.: Luiz Gustavo Forte
  Phone: (55) 11 3256 8863
  Email: lgforte@miforte.com.br
  Indus. Mgr. : Jose Miguel Forte
  Phone: (55) 42 3522 3044
  Fax: (55) 42 3522 3731
  Email: jmforte@miforte.com.br
  Mill Mgr.: Marco Antonio Caus
  Phone: (55) 42 3522 3044
  Fax: (55) 42 3522 3731
  Assist. Mgr.: Elinor Martinazzo
  Phone: (55) 42 3522 3044
  Fax: (55) 42 3522 3731
  Assist. Mgr.: Carlos Garcia
  Phone: (55) 42 3522 3044
  Fax: (55) 42 3522 3731
  Prod. Ass.: Valdomiro Voldiani
  Phone: (55) 42 3522 3044
  Fax: (55) 42 3522 3731
Total Employees of Company: 960
Total Employees at this Location: 300
Type of Operation: Pulp mill, Paper mill, Paperboard mill
Pulp Grades and Capacities:
  Total pulp capacity: 72,659 mt/y
  Mechanical Pulp: 5,696 mt/y
  Recycled Pulping: 66,963 mt/y
Pulp Mill Data:
  Mechanical Pulping Systems:
  Conventional grinders: 2
Pulp Lines: 2
  Recycled Fiber Treatment Lines:
  Recycled packaging pulping lines: 1
Paper/Paperboard Grades and Capacities:
  Total paper and paperboard capacity: 92,820 mt/y
  Linerboard: 42,840 mt/y
  Corrugating medium/fluting: 7,140 mt/y
  Boxboard/cartonboard: 42,840 mt/y
Paper and Paperboard Mill Data:
  Stock Preparation:
  Pulpers: 3
  Refiners: 5
Paper Machines: 2
  No. 1, fourdrinier, total capacity 42,840 mt/y, Trim width 2.4 m, Boxboard/cartonboard
  No. 2, fourdrinier, total capacity 49,980 mt/y, Trim width 2.4 m, Linerboard, Corrugating medium/fluting
Coating Machines: 1
  No. 1, on machine
Finishing Equipment:
  Winders: 1
  Calenders: 1
  Supercalenders
  Rewinders: 1
  Sheeters: 1 at 180 mt/y
Energy Data:
  Power boilers: 2
  Combustion turbines: 3 at 6 MW
  Steam turbines: 1 at 10 MW
  Electrical demand for mill: 113 MWh/D

ⒽⓂGênesis Papéis
Videira Mill
Rdv. SC 303, km 1
89560-000 Videira, SC
Brazil
  Phone: (55) 49 3533 2111
  Fax: (55) 49 3533 2111
  Email: genesis@genesispapeis.com.br
Personnel:
  Dir.: Mansur J. Zucchetti
  Phone: (55) 49 9116 4995
Total Employees of Company: 58
Type of Operation: Paper mill
Paper/Paperboard Grades and Capacities:

Brazil

Total paper and paperboard capacity: 7,200 mt/y
Tissue: 7,200 mt/y

⊕⊚Guaçu S.A. Papéis e Embalagens
Tambaú Mill
Estrada Tambaú - Mococa, km 5.2
13710-000 Tambaú, SP
Brazil
 Phone: (55) 19 3673 8166
 Fax: (55) 19 3673 1851
 Email: vendas@guacu.com.br
 Web Address: www.guacu.com.br
Personnel:
 Pres.: Fernando Ferrari
 Phone: (55) 19 3673 8166
 VP: Carlos Alberto Ferrari
 Phone: (55) 19 3673 1851
Total Employees of Company: 330
Total Employees at this Location: 150
Type of Operation: Paper mill, Paperboard mill
Pulp Grades and Capacities:
 Total pulp capacity: 62,275 mt/y
 Recycled Pulping: 62,275 mt/y
Pulp Mill Data:
 Recycled Fiber Treatment Lines:
 Recycled packaging pulping lines: 1
Paper/Paperboard Grades and Capacities:
 Total paper and paperboard capacity: 61,404 mt/y
 Linerboard: 30,702 mt/y
 Corrugating medium/fluting: 30,702 mt/y
Paper and Paperboard Mill Data:
Paper Machines: 2
 No. 1, fourdrinier, total capacity 30,702 mt/y, Trim width 2.5 m, Corrugating medium/fluting
 No. 2, fourdrinier, total capacity 30,702 mt/y, Trim width 2.5 m, Linerboard
Energy Data:
 Power boilers: 1
 Electrical demand for mill: 90 MWh/D

⊕⊚Indústria de Papel Guará Ltda.
Guaratinguetá Mill
Av. Rui Barbosa 1805
12500-000 Guaratinguetá, SP
Brazil
 Phone: (55) 12 3132 3599
 Fax: (55) 12 3132 3223
 Email: papelguara@yahoo.com.br
Personnel:
 Dir.: Plinio José César
 Phone: (55) 12 3132 3599
 Purch. Mgr.: Adauto Teixeira Santos
 Phone: (55) 12 3132 3599
 Sls. Mgr.: Isabel Cristina Faria Galvão Santos
 Phone: (55) 12 3132 3599
Type of Operation: Paper mill
Paper/Paperboard Grades and Capacities:
 Total paper and paperboard capacity: 14,000 mt/y
 Tissue: 14,000 mt/y
Paper and Paperboard Mill Data:
Paper Machines: 2
 PM 1, Trim width 1.5 m, Tissue
 PM 2, Trim width 1.5 m, Tissue

⊕⊚Hachmann S.A. Indústria e Comércio
Capinzal Mill
Ownership: 100% by Hachmann family
Rua Alexandre Thomazoni, 208
89665-000 Capinzal, SC
Brazil
Mailing Address: Localidade Barro Preto s/n° Cx. P. 01, 89665-000 Cidade Capinzal, Brazil
 Phone: (55) 49 3555 1099/1588
 Fax: (55) 49 3555 2203
 Email: hachmann@athila.com.br
Personnel:
 Pres.: Hellmuth Hachmann
 Phone: (55) 49 3555 1099/1588
 Dir.: Urbbano Hachmann
 Phone: (55) 49 3555 1099/1588
 Dir.: Henrique Hachmann
 Phone: (55) 49 3555 1099/1588
Type of Operation: Pulp mill
Pulp Grades and Capacities:
 Total pulp capacity: 8,000 mt/y
Pulp Mill Data:
 Mechanical Pulping Systems:
 Conventional grinders

⊚Heidrich Industrial Mercantil e Agricola S.A.
Taió Mill
Ownership: 100% by Heidrich family
Rua Coronel Feddersen 1044, Centro
89190-000 Taió, SC
Brazil
 Phone: (55) 47 3562 0111
 Fax: (55) 47 3562 0111
 Email: heidrich@heidrich.ind.br
 Web Address: www.heidrich.ind.br
Personnel:
 Dir Pres.: Bruno Heidrich Junior
 Phone: (55) 47 3562 0111
 Fax: (55) 47 3562 0111
 Finan. & Admin. Dir.: João Acácio Tomazoni
 Phone: (55) 47 3562 0111
 Fax: (55) 47 3562 0111
 Email: joaoacacio@heidrich.ind.br
 Sls. Mgr.: Ismael Block
 Phone: (55) 47 3562 0111
 Fax: (55) 47 3562 0111
 Email: ismael@heidrich.ind.br
Type of Operation: Paperboard mill
Paper/Paperboard Grades and Capacities:
 Total paper and paperboard capacity: 13,800 mt/y
 Boxboard/cartonboard: 13,800 mt/y

⊕⊚Ind. de Papelão Hörlle Ltda.
Campo Largo Mill
Ownership: Hörlle family
Rdv do Café, Km. 102.7
83607-000 Campo Largo, PR
Brazil
Mailing Address: 1143, 83601-980 Campo Largo, Brazil
 Phone: (55) 41 3649 8000
 Fax: (55) 41 3649 8001
 Email: horlle@horlle.com.br, dpcomex@horlle.com.br
 Web Address: www.horlle.com.br
Personnel:
 Man. Partner: Marcos Hörlle
 Phone: (55) 41 3649 8000
 Fax: (55) 41 3649 8001
 Email: marcos@horlle.com.br
 Indus. Dir: Milton Hörlle
 Phone: (55) 41 3649 8000
 Fax: (55) 41 3649 8001
 Email: milton@horlle.com.br
 Prod. Mgr.: Ildo Horlle Tschoke
 Phone: (55) 41 3649 8000
 Fax: (55) 41 3649 8001
 Email: ildo@horlle.com.br
Total Employees of Company: 170
Total Employees at this Location: 65
Type of Operation: Paper mill, Paperboard mill
Pulp Grades and Capacities:
 Total pulp capacity: 16,528 mt/y
 Recycled Pulping: 16,528 mt/y
Pulp Mill Data:
 Recycled Fiber Treatment Lines:
 Pulpers: 1 at 17,500
Paper/Paperboard Grades and Capacities:
 Total paper and paperboard capacity: 16,065 mt/y
 Boxboard/cartonboard: 16,065 mt/y
Paper and Paperboard Mill Data:
 Stock Preparation:
 Pulpers: 3
Paper Machines: 1
 No. 1, fourdrinier, total capacity 16,065 mt/y, Trim width 1.7 m, Boxboard/cartonboard
Finishing Equipment:
 Sheeters: 1
Energy Data:
 Power boilers: 1
 Electrical demand for mill: 21 MWh/D

⊕IBEMA - Cia. Brasileira de Papel
Ownership: 18% by Maia family, 60% by Ibema Participações, 22% by BNDESPar
Rua Padre Anchieta 2310 / 8° andar - Bigorrilho
80.730-000 Curitiba, PR
Brazil
 Phone: (55) 41 3240 7400
 Fax: (55) 41 3240 7442
 Email: administrativo@ibema.com.br, comercial@ibema.com.br
 Web Address: www.ibema.com.br
Personnel:
 CEO: Nei Senter Martins
 Phone: (55) 41 3240 7400
 Fax: (55) 41 3240 7442
 COO: Clecio Chiamulera
 Phone: (55) 41 3240 7400
 Fax: (55) 41 3240 7442
 Commer. Dir.: Jorge Luis Grandi
 Phone: (55) 41 3240 7400
 Fax: (55) 41 3240 7442
 Energy & Forest. Dir: Lourival Dos Santos E Souza
 Phone: (55) 41 3240 7400
 Fax: (55) 41 3240 7442
 Purch. Mgr.: Jomara Macedo Bahls
 Phone: (55) 41 3240 7400
 Fax: (55) 41 3240 7442
 Mktg. Mgr.: Juliana Neitdke
 Phone: (55) 41 3240 7427
Total Employees of Company: 770
Total Employees at this Location: 35
Mill Locations:
 IBEMA - Cia. Brasileira de Papel, Ibema Mill, Rodovia BR 277, Km. 545 - Distrito Industrial, 85150-000 Ibema, Cascavel, PR, Brazil, (Paper mill, Paperboard mill)
 Phone: (55) 45 3238 1281
 Fax: (55) 45 3238 1224
 Email: ibema-maq2@ibema.com.br
 IBEMA - Cia. Brasileira de Papel, Turvo Mill, Faxinal da Boa Vista, s/n°, 85150-000 Turvo, PR, Brazil, Capacity: 89,964 mt/y, (Pulp mill, Paperboard mill)
 Phone: (55) 42 3642 8000
 Fax: (55) 42 3642 8068
 Email: admturvo@ibema.com.br

⊚IBEMA - Cia. Brasileira de Papel
Ibema Mill
Rodovia BR 277, Km. 545 - Distrito Industrial
85150-000 Ibema, Cascavel, PR
Brazil
 Phone: (55) 45 3238 1281
 Fax: (55) 45 3238 1224
 Email: ibema-maq2@ibema.com.br
 Web Address: www.ibema.com.br
Personnel:
 Ind. Mgr.: Márcio Fontella
 Phone: (55) 45 3238 1281
 Fax: (55) 45 3238 1224
 Email: marcio@ibema.com.br
 Prod. Mgr: Roberto Binotto Júnior
 Phone: (55) 45 3238 1281
 Fax: (55) 45 3238 1224
 Maint. Mgr.: Cristiano Stefano Da Silva
 Phone: (55) 45 3238 1281
 Fax: (55) 45 3238 1224
Total Employees at this Location: 140
Type of Operation: Paper mill, Paperboard mill

Brazil

ⓜIBEMA - Cia. Brasileira de Papel
Turvo Mill
Faxinal da Boa Vista, s/n°
85150-000 Turvo, PR
Brazil
  Phone: (55) 42 3642 8000
  Fax: (55) 42 3642 8068
  Email: admturvo@ibema.com.br
  Web Address: www.ibema.com.br
Personnel:
  CEO: Nei Senter Martins
  Phone: (55) 41 3240 7400
  Fax: (55) 41 3240 7441
  COO: Clécio Chiamullera
  Phone: (55) 42 3642 8000
  Ind. Mgr.: Marcos Rodriguês Vaz
  Phone: (55) 42 3642 8005
  Email: vaz@ibema.com.br
  Maint. Mgr.: Georges Boabaid
  Phone: (55) 42 3642 8048
  Process Supervisor: Jufil Carneiro
  Phone: (55) 42 3642 8147
  Prod. Supervisor: João Matheus de Almeida
  Phone: (55) 42 3642 8129
  Janaine Silva
  Phone: (55) 42 3642 8005
  Manuf. Dir.: Sergio Hul
  Phone: (55) 42 3642 8000
  Fax: (55) 42 3642 8068
Total Employees at this Location: 351
Type of Operation: Pulp mill, Paperboard mill
Pulp Grades and Capacities:
  Total pulp capacity: 58,806 mt/y
  Mechanical Pulp: 20,909 mt/y
  Recycled Pulping: 37,897 mt/y
Pulp Mill Data:
  Mechanical Pulping Systems:
  Conventional grinders: 4
  Chemical Recovery Equipment:
  Evaporator lines: 1
  Recovery boilers: 1
  Recycled Fiber Treatment Lines:
  Pulpers: 3 at 45,000 admt/y
  Recycled packaging pulping lines: 1 at 40,000 admt/y
Paper/Paperboard Grades and Capacities:
  Total paper and paperboard capacity: 89,964 mt/y
  Boxboard/cartonboard: 89,964 mt/y
Paper and Paperboard Mill Data:
  Stock Preparation:
  Pulpers: 4
  Refiners: 5
Paper Machines: 1
No. 3, fourdrinier (3), total capacity 89,964 mt/y, Trim width 2.5 m, Boxboard/cartonboard
Coating Machines: 2
No. 1, total capacity 100 mt/y., on machine
No. 3, total capacity 330 mt/y., on machine
Finishing Equipment:
  Winders: 1 at 350 mt/y
  Calenders: 2
  Rewinders: 2 at 400 mt/y
  Sheeters: 3 at 260 mt/y
Energy Data:
  Power boilers: 3
  Hydro turbines: 5 at 12 MW
  Electrical demand for mill: 221 MWh/D

ⓜⓜIberkraft Indústria de Papel e Celulose Ltda.
Guarapuava Mill
Alto Xarquinho, Bairro Xarquinho, CP 446
85100-970 Guarapuava, PR
Brazil
  Phone: (55) 42 3629 8000
  Fax: (55) 42 3629 8000
  Email: iberkraft@iberkraft.com.br
Personnel:
  Gen. Dir.: Gonzalo Gallardo Diaz
  Phone: (55) 42 3629 8000
  Fax: (55) 42 3629 8000
  Gen. Mgr.: Benedito Maciel Arantes Junior
  Phone: (55) 42 3629 8000
  Fax: (55) 42 3629 8000
  Sls. Mgr.: Arimei Schascoski
  Phone: (55) 42 3629 8000
  Fax: (55) 42 3629 8000
  Prod. Mgr.: Pedro Siqueira
  Phone: (55) 42 3629 8000
  Fax: (55) 42 3629 8000
  Finan. Mgr.: Julio Sezar de L.
  Phone: (55) 42 3629 8000
  Fax: (55) 42 3629 8000
  Prod. Mgr.: Jose Carlos O.
  Phone: (55) 42 3629 8000
  Fax: (55) 42 3629 8000
Total Employees at this Location: 120
Type of Operation: Paper mill, Paperboard mill
Pulp Grades and Capacities:
  Total pulp capacity: 33,060 mt/y
  Recycled Pulping: 33,060 mt/y
Pulp Mill Data:
  Recycled Fiber Treatment Lines:
  Pulpers: 1 at 35,700
Paper/Paperboard Grades and Capacities:
  Total paper and paperboard capacity: 32,487 mt/y
  Linerboard: 32,487 mt/y
Paper and Paperboard Mill Data:
  Stock Preparation:
  Pulpers: 2
  Refiners: 2
Paper Machines: 1
No. 1, cylinder, total capacity 32,487 mt/y, Trim width 2.4 m, Linerboard
Energy Data:
  Power boilers: 1
  Electrical demand for mill: 35 MWh/D

ⓜIguaçu Celulose Papel S.A.
Ownership: 100% by Grupo Imaribo
Alameda Santa Mônica 1, São Domingos
83030-550 São José dos Pinhais, PR
Brazil
  Phone: (55) 41 2169 8080
  Fax: (55) 41 3283 5604
  Email: vendas@iguacucelulose.com.br,
  industrialsjp@iguacucelulose.com.br
  Web Address: www.iguacucelulose.com.br
Personnel:
  Pres. & Dir.: Paulo Roberto Pizani
  Phone: (55) 41 2169 8080
  Fax: (55) 41 3283 5604
  Email: roberto@iguacucelulose.com.br
  Exec. Sec.: Gelci Cardoso
  Phone: (55) 41 2169 8080
  Fax: (55) 41 3283 5604
  Email: gelci@iguacucelulose.com.br
  Commer. Mgr.: Oldair Jose Dominski
  Phone: (55) 41 2169 8009
  Fax: (55) 41 3283 5604
  Email: odominski@iguacucelulose.com.br
  Commer. Analyst: Kleyson Primo
  Phone: (55) 41 2169 8080
  Fax: (55) 41 3283 5604
  Email: primo@iguacucelulose.com.br
Total Employees of Company: 1,100
Mill Locations:
Iguaçu Celulose Papel S.A., Campos Novos/SC Mill, Rua Geral, s/n° - Ibicuí, 89620-000 Campos Novos, SC, Brazil, Capacity: 72,000 mt/y, (Paper mill)
Phone: (55) 49 3541 6100
Fax: (55) 49 3541 0423
Iguaçu Celulose Papel S.A., Frei Rogério Mill, R Geral, S/N°- Salto Correntes, 89530-000 Frei Rogério, SC, Brazil, Capacity: 5,400 mt/y, (Paperboard mill)
Phone: (55) 49 3292 2025/26
Fax: (55) 49 3292 2025/26
Email: industrialfr@iguacucelulose.com.br
Iguaçu Celulose Papel S.A., Piraí do Sul Mill, Rodovia PR 151, Km. 172, 640 CP 189, 84240-000 Piraí do Sul, PR, Brazil, Capacity: 79,968 mt/y, (Pulp mill)
Phone: (55) 42 3237 8300
Fax: (55) 42 3237 1130
Email: industrialps@iguacucelulose.com.br
Iguaçu Celulose Papel S.A., São José dos Pinhais Mill, Alameda Santa Mônica 1, São Domingo CP 73, 83030-550 São José dos Pinhais, PR, Brazil, Capacity: 16,065 mt/y, (Paper mill)
Phone: (55) 41 2169 8080
Fax: (55) 41 3283 5604
Email: industrialsjp@iguacucelulose.com.br

ⓜIguaçu Celulose Papel S.A.
Campos Novos/SC Mill
Rua Geral, s/n° - Ibicuí
89620-000 Campos Novos, SC
Brazil
  Phone: (55) 49 3541 6100
  Fax: (55) 49 3541 0423
  Web Address: www.iguacucelulose.com.br
Personnel:
  Adm. Coord.: Mauro Cezar
  Phone: (55) 49 3541 6100
  Fax: (55) 49 3541 0423
Total Employees at this Location: 460
Type of Operation: Paper mill
Paper/Paperboard Grades and Capacities:
  Total paper and paperboard capacity: 72,000 mt/y
  Packaging papers: 72,000 mt/y
Paper and Paperboard Mill Data:
Paper Machines: 2
PM 1, fourdrinier, total capacity 41,400 mt/y, Packaging papers
PM 2, fourdrinier, total capacity 29,000 mt/y, Packaging papers

ⓜIguaçu Celulose Papel S.A.
Frei Rogério Mill
R Geral, S/N°- Salto Correntes
89530-000 Frei Rogério, SC
Brazil
  Phone: (55) 49 3292 2025/26
  Fax: (55) 49 3292 2025/26
  Email: industrialfr@iguacucelulose.com.br
  Web Address: www.iguacucelulose.com.br
Personnel:
  Commer. Mgr.: Oldair Jose Dominski
  Phone: (55) 49 3292 2025/26
  Fax: (55) 41 3283 5604
  Email: odominski@iguacucelulose.com.br
  Maint. Coord.: Sergio Isley Liebel da Silva
  Phone: (55) 49 3292 2025/26
  Fax: (55) 41 3283 5604
Total Employees at this Location: 60
Type of Operation: Paperboard mill
Paper/Paperboard Grades and Capacities:
  Total paper and paperboard capacity: 5,400 mt/y
  Boxboard/cartonboard: 5,400 mt/y
Paper and Paperboard Mill Data:
Paper Machines: 1
PM 1, total capacity 5,400 mt/y, Boxboard/cartonboard

ⓜIguaçu Celulose Papel S.A.
Piraí do Sul Mill
Rodovia PR 151, Km. 172, 640 CP 189
84240-000 Piraí do Sul, PR
Brazil
  Phone: (55) 42 3237 8300
  Fax: (55) 42 3237 1130
  Email: industrialps@iguacucelulose.com.br
  Web Address: www.iguacucelulose.com.br
Personnel:
  Ind. Mgr.: Laércio Carlos Pereira
  Phone: (55) 42 3237 8300
  Fax: (55) 42 3237 1130
  Email: laercio@iguacucelulose.com.br
  Forest. Mgr.: Eder Fagundes Branco
  Phone: (55) 42 3237 8300
  Fax: (55) 42 3237 1130

Brazil

Admin. Asst. : Carlos Alberto Oelmuller Mainardes
Phone: (55) 42 3237 8300
Fax: (55) 42 3237 1130
Prod. Supervisor: Mauricio Pupo Ferreira
Phone: (55) 42 3237 8300
Fax: (55) 42 3237 1130
Plann Asst.: Erica Renata Piotrovski
Phone: (55) 42 3237 8300
Fax: (55) 42 3237 1130
HR Asst.: Lilian R. de Brito
Phone: (55) 42 3237 8300
Fax: (55) 42 3237 1130
Total Employees at this Location: 400
Type of Operation: Pulp mill
Pulp Grades and Capacities:
Total pulp capacity: 108,441 mt/y
Pulp available for market: 26,061 mt/y
Chemical Pulp: 108,441 mt/y
Pulp Mill Data:
Chemical Pulping Systems:
Batch digesters
Chemical Recovery Equipment:
Evaporator lines
Recovery boilers: 1
Lime Kiln
Pulp Dryers:
Fourdriniers 1, Pulp Dryers 1
Paper/Paperboard Grades and Capacities:
Total paper and paperboard capacity: 79,968 mt/y
Packaging papers: 79,968 mt/y
Paper and Paperboard Mill Data:
Paper Machines: 1
No. 1, fourdrinier, total capacity 79,968 mt/y, Trim width 3.4 m, Packaging papers
Energy Data:
Power boilers
Steam turbines
Electrical demand for mill: 244 MWh/D

ⓜIguaçu Celulose Papel S.A.
São José dos Pinhais Mill
Alameda Santa Mônica 1, São Domingo CP 73
83030-550 São José dos Pinhais, PR
Brazil
Phone: (55) 41 2169 8080
Fax: (55) 41 3283 5604
Email: industrialsjp@iguacucelulose.com.br
Web Address: www.iguacucelulose.com.br
Personnel:
Pres. & Dir.: Paulo Roberto Pizani
Phone: (55) 41 2169 8080
Fax: (55) 41 3283 5604
Exec. Sec. : Gelci Cardoso
Phone: (55) 41 2169 8080
Fax: (55) 41 3283 5604
Email: gelci@iguacucelulose.com.br
Comercial Mgr.: Oldair José Dominski
Phone: (55) 41 2169 8009, 41 2169 8080
Fax: (55) 41 3283 5604
Email: odominski@iguacucelulose.com.br
Commer. Analyst: Kleyson Primo
Phone: (55) 41 2169 8080
Fax: (55) 41 3283 5604
Email: primo@iguacucelulose.com.br
Ind. Mgr.: Elton Costantin
Phone: (55) 41 2169 8080
Fax: (55) 41 3283 5604
HR Analyst: Luciana Costa Ishibashi
Phone: (55) 41 2169 8080
Fax: (55) 41 3283 5604
Total Employees at this Location: 55
Type of Operation: Paper mill
Paper/Paperboard Grades and Capacities:
Total paper and paperboard capacity: 16,065 mt/y
Packaging papers: 4,641 mt/y
Specialty and industrial: 11,424 mt/y
Paper and Paperboard Mill Data:
Paper Machines: 1
No. 2, (Machine Glazed (MG)), fourdrinier, total capacity 16,065 mt/y, Trim width 2.75 m, Packaging papers, Specialty and industrial
Energy Data:
Power boilers
Electrical demand for mill: 42 MWh/D

ⓞⓜImporpel Ind. e Com. de Papéis Ltda.
Porto Ferreira Mill
Av. General Álvaro de Góes Valeriani 611, Serra d'Água
13660-000 Porto Ferreira, SP
Brazil
Phone: (55) 19 3581 4155
Fax: (55) 19 3581 2230
Email: importpel@imporpel.com.br, comercial@imporpel.com.br.
Web Address: www.imporpel.com.br
Personnel:
Pres.: Luis Felipe Figueiredo da Silva
Phone: (55) 19 3581 4155
Fax: (55) 19 3581 2230
Email: gerencia@imporpel.com.br
Admin. Mgr.: Luis Felipe Figueiredo da Silva Filho
Phone: (55) 19 3581 4155
Fax: (55) 19 3581 2230
Tech. Mgr.: Natal Nagasawa
Phone: (55) 19 3581 4155
Fax: (55) 19 3581 2230
Total Employees at this Location: 54
Type of Operation: Paperboard mill
Pulp Grades and Capacities:
Total pulp capacity: 18,841 mt/y
Recycled Pulping: 18,841 mt/y
Pulp Mill Data:
Recycled Fiber Treatment Lines:
Pulpers: 1 at 21,000
Paper/Paperboard Grades and Capacities:
Total paper and paperboard capacity: 18,564 mt/y
Corrugating medium/fluting: 18,564 mt/y
Paper and Paperboard Mill Data:
Paper Machines: 1
No. 1, fourdrinier, total capacity 18,564 mt/y, Trim width 2.5 m, Corrugating medium/fluting
Energy Data:
Power boilers: 1
Electrical demand for mill: 33 MWh/D

ⓞⓜIndústria de Papéis União
São Paulo Mill
Av. itaquera, 6785
08295-000 São Paulo, SP
Brazil
Fax: (55) 11 2749 5401
Email: miniflor@uol.com.br
Personnel:
Dir./Mgr.: Toshio Morita
Phone: (55) 11 2749 5401
Ind. Dir.: Clóvis Toshio Morita
Phone: (55) 11 2749 5401
HR: Fernando
Phone: (55) 11 2749 5401
Type of Operation: Paper mill
Paper/Paperboard Grades and Capacities:
Total paper and paperboard capacity: 2,800 mt/y
Tissue: 2,800 mt/y

ⓞⓜIndústria de Papel Dopel
Indaial Mill
Rua Dr. Blumenau, 5811
89130-000 Indaial, SC
Brazil
Phone: (55) 47 3333 2265
Fax: (55) 47 3333 2262
Email: papeldopel@terra.com.br
Personnel:
Dir.: Fabio Augusto Pires Dobuchak
Phone: (55) 47 3333 2265
Type of Operation: Paper mill
Paper/Paperboard Grades and Capacities:
Total paper and paperboard capacity: 2,200 mt/y
Tissue: 2,200 mt/y

ⓞIndústria e Comércio Papeis(INCOPA)
PEDRO GOMES DE NORÕES, 1353 – BAIRRO: MURITI
63132-150 Crato
Brazil
Mailing Address: P.O. Box 26
Phone: (55) 88 2101 7171
Web Address: www.incopa.com.br
Personnel:
Commer. Mgr. : Marcus Romyldo Pontes
Phone: (55) 88 2101 7171
Mill Locations:
Indústria e Comércio Papeis(INCOPA), Crato Mill, PEDRO GOMES DE NORÕES, 1353 – BAIRRO: MURITI, Crato, Brazil, Capacity: 8,000 mt/y, (Paper mill)
Phone: (55) 88 2101 7171

ⓜIndústria e Comércio Papeis(INCOPA)
Crato Mill
PEDRO GOMES DE NORÕES, 1353 – BAIRRO: MURITI
Crato
Brazil
Phone: (55) 88 2101 7171
Web Address: www.incopa.com.br
Personnel:
Commer. Mgr. : Marcus Romyldo Pontes
Phone: (55) 88 2101 7171
Type of Operation: Paper mill
Paper/Paperboard Grades and Capacities:
Total paper and paperboard capacity: 8,000 mt/y
Tissue: 8,000 mt/y

ⓞINPA - Indústria de Embalagens Santana S.A.
Av. das Américas 4200, Bloco II, Salas 112 a 116
22640-102 Bairro da Tijuca, RJ
Brazil
Phone: (55) 21 2136 9000
Fax: (55) 21 2136 9001
Web Address: www.inpa-embalagens.com.br
Personnel:
Pres.: Delvan Lima Telles
Phone: (55) 21 8119-0909
Fax: (55) 21 2136-9001
Email: delvan@inpa-embalagens.com.br
Total Employees of Company: 1,300
Mill Locations:
INPA - Indústria de Embalagens Santana S.A., Pirapetinga Mill, Rua Inpa, 186, 36730-000 Pirapetinga, MG, Brazil, Capacity: 144,942 mt/y, (Paperboard mill)
Phone: (55) 32 3465 3000
Fax: (55) 32 3465 3002
Email: inpa@inpa-embalagens.com.br
INPA - Indústria de Embalagens Santana S.A., Uberaba Mill, Rodovia BR 050, Km. 168, Distrito Industrial II, 38056-050 Uberaba, MG, Brazil, Capacity: 44,982 mt/y, (Paperboard mill)
Phone: (55) 34 2104 3100
Email: informatica@inpa-embalagens.com.br

ⓜINPA - Indústria de Embalagens Santana S.A.
Pirapetinga Mill
Rua Inpa, 186
36730-000 Pirapetinga, MG
Brazil
Phone: (55) 32 3465 3000
Fax: (55) 32 3465 3002
Email: inpa@inpa-embalagens.com.br
Web Address: www.inpa-embalagens.com.br
Personnel:

Industrial Dir.: Dirceu Martins
Phone: (55) 32 3465 3000
Fax: (55) 32 3465 3002
Email: dirceu@inpa-embalagens.com.br
Superintendent Dir.: Paulo Portugal
Phone: (55) 32 3465 3000
Fax: (55) 32 3465 3002
Email: paulo@inpa-embalagens.com.br
Environ. & Qlty. Contr. Mgr.: Ivan Antonio da Silva
Phone: (55) 32 3465 3046
Fax: (55) 32 3465 3002
Email: ivan@inpa-embalagens.com.br
Finan. Mgr.: Fernanda Lima Sobrinho
Phone: (55) 32 3465 3000
Fax: (55) 32 3465 3002
Email: fernanda@inpa-embalagens.com.br
Total Employees at this Location: 265
Type of Operation: Paperboard mill
Pulp Grades and Capacities:
Total pulp capacity: 140,542 mt/y
Recycled Pulping: 140,542 mt/y
Pulp Mill Data:
Recycled Fiber Treatment Lines:
Pulpers: 1 at 193,180
Paper/Paperboard Grades and Capacities:
Total paper and paperboard capacity: 144,942 mt/y
Linerboard: 79,968 mt/y
Corrugating medium/fluting: 64,974 mt/y
Paper and Paperboard Mill Data:
Stock Preparation:
Pulpers
Paper Machines: 2
No. 3, fourdrinier, total capacity 64,974 mt/y, Trim width 2.5 m, Corrugating medium/fluting
No. 4, fourdrinier (2), total capacity 79,968 mt/y, Trim width 2.5 m, Linerboard
Energy Data:
Power boilers: 6
Electrical demand for mill: 203 MWh/D

ⓜINPA - Indústria de Embalagens Santana S.A.
Uberaba Mill
Rodovia BR 050, Km. 168, Distrito Industrial II
38056-050 Uberaba, MG
Brazil
Phone: (55) 34 2104 3100
Email: informatica@inpa-embalagens.com.br
Web Address: www.inpa-embalagens.com.br
Personnel:
Mill Mgr.: Ricardo Baliviega
Phone: (55) 34 2104 3100
Total Employees at this Location: 150
Type of Operation: Paperboard mill
Pulp Grades and Capacities:
Total pulp capacity: 42,954 mt/y
Recycled Pulping: 42,954 mt/y
Pulp Mill Data:
Recycled Fiber Treatment Lines:
Pulpers
Paper/Paperboard Grades and Capacities:
Total paper and paperboard capacity: 44,982 mt/y
Linerboard: 27,132 mt/y
Corrugating medium/fluting: 17,850 mt/y
Paper and Paperboard Mill Data:
Stock Preparation:
Pulpers
Paper Machines: 1
No. 5, fourdrinier (2), total capacity 44,982 mt/y, Trim width 2.5 m, Linerboard, Corrugating medium/fluting
Energy Data:
Power boilers
Electrical demand for mill: 58 MWh/D

ⓞⓜINPOPEL - Indústrias Podolan de Papel Ltda.
Pitanga Mill
Rua Visconde de Guarapuava 320, CP 22
85200-000 Pitanga, PR
Brazil
Phone: (55) 42 3646 1406
Fax: (55) 42 3646 3142
Email: contato@inpopel.ind.br
Web Address: www.inpopel.ind.br
Personnel:
Mill Dir.: Wilson Podolan
Phone: (55) 42 3646 1406
Fax: (55) 42 3646 3142
Sls. Mgr.: Wagner Adriano Tizot
Phone: (55) 42 3646 1406
Fax: (55) 42 3646 3142
Finan. Mgr.: Fernando Podolan
Phone: (55) 42 3646 3142
Type of Operation: Paper mill
Paper/Paperboard Grades and Capacities:
Total paper and paperboard capacity: 5,000 mt/y
Tissue: 5,000 mt/y
Paper and Paperboard Mill Data:
Paper Machines: 1
PM 1, Tissue

ⓞⓜInternational Paper do Brasil Ltda.
Mogi Guaçu Mill
Ownership: International Paper Co.
Rodovia, SP-340, Km 171, CP 10
13840-970 Mogi Guaçu, SP
Brazil
Phone: (55) 19 3861 8593 / 8121
Fax: (55) 19 3861 8412 / 1098
Email: sac@ipaperbr.com
Web Address: www.internationalpaperdobrasil.com.br,
www.internationalpaper.com.br
Personnel:
Pres. IP Latin America, Snr. VP IP, (effective November 1, 2014): Glenn Landau
Phone: (55) 19 3861 8593
Fax: (55) 19 3861 8412
Email: glen.landau@ipaper.com
CIO Latin America: Pedro Oncken
Phone: (55) 19 3861 8593
Fax: (55) 19 3861 8412
Manuf. Dir.: Marcio Bertoldo
Phone: (55) 19 3861 8593
Fax: (55) 19 3861 8412
Email: marcio.bertoldo@ipaper.com
International Bus. Dir. : Raul Guaragna
Phone: (55) 19 3861 8593
Fax: (55) 19 3861 8412
Bus. Gen. Mgr. : Sergio Canela
Phone: (55) 19 3861 8593
Fax: (55) 19 3861 8412
Senior Supply Chain Mgr.: Rodrigo Giordano D'Arcadia
Phone: (55) 19 3861 8593
Fax: (55) 19 3861 8412
Senior Sls. Exec. Latin America: Luana Faria Cardozo
Phone: (55) 19 3861 8593
Fax: (55) 19 3861 8412
Email: luana.cardozo@ipaperbr.com
Senior Bus. Exec.: Monica Antoniazzi Araujo Machado
Phone: (55) 19 3861 8593
Fax: (55) 19 3861 8412
Email: monica.machado@ipaper.com
Sls. Oper. Mgr.: Angela Berti
Phone: (55) 19 3861 8593
Fax: (55) 19 3861 8412
Email: angela.berti@ipaperbr.com
HR Mgr.: Andreia Manera
Phone: (55) 19 3861 8593
Fax: (55) 19 3861 8412
Email: andreia.manera@ipaperbr.com
Tech. Asst. Cust. : Edson Eduardo Da Silva
Phone: (55) 19 3861 8593
Fax: (55) 19 3861 8412
Email: edson.eduardo@ipaperbr.com
Total Employees at this Location: 900
Type of Operation: Pulp mill, Paper mill
Mill Locations:
International Paper do Brasil Ltda., Luiz Antônio Mill, Rodovia SP 255, Km. 41, 240, 14210-000 Luiz Antonio, SP, Brazil, Capacity: 369,852 mt/y, (Pulp mill, Paper mill)
Phone: (55) 16 3986 9000
Fax: (55) 16 3986 1620
Email: sac@ipaperbr.com
International Paper do Brasil Ltda., Três Lagoas Mill, Rodovia MS 395 KM 21, 79601-970 Três Lagoas, MT, Brazil, Capacity: 204,918 mt/y, (Paper mill)
Phone: (55) 67 2105 6161
Fax: (55) 67 2105 6240
Email: sac@ipaperbr.com
Pulp Grades and Capacities:
Total pulp capacity: 418,714 mt/y
Pulp available for market: 39,984 mt/y
Chemical Pulp: 418,714 mt/y
Pulp Mill Data:
Chemical Pulping Systems:
Continuous digesters: 1
Pulp Lines: 1
Bleach Plant Systems: 1
Chemical Pulping System, Type: Hardwood (Eucalyptus), Sequence: O_2 D(EOP)D, Capacity 456,250 admt/y
Chemical Recovery Equipment:
Evaporator lines: 2
Recovery boilers: 2
Lime Kiln
Pulp Dryers:
Flakt dryer 1, Fourdriniers 1
Paper/Paperboard Grades and Capacities:
Total paper and paperboard capacity: 444,822 mt/y
Uncoated woodfree/freesheet: 444,822 mt/y
Paper and Paperboard Mill Data:
Stock Preparation:
Pulpers: 3
Refiners: 20
Paper Machines: 4
No. 3, fourdrinier, total capacity 62,832 mt/y, Trim width 3.36 m, Uncoated woodfree/freesheet
No. 4, fourdrinier, total capacity 93,177 mt/y, Trim width 4.2 m, Uncoated woodfree/freesheet
No. 5, fourdrinier, total capacity 134,946 mt/y, Trim width 4.2 m, Uncoated woodfree/freesheet
No. 6, fourdrinier, total capacity 153,867 mt/y, Trim width 4.2 m, Uncoated woodfree/freesheet
Finishing Equipment:
Winders: 4 at 440,000 mt/y
Rewinders: 2 at 15,000 mt/y
Sheeters: 4 at 210,000 mt/y
Energy Data:
Power boilers: 3
Steam turbines: 4 at 33 MW
Electrical demand for mill: 1,476 MWh/D

ⓜInternational Paper do Brasil Ltda.
Luiz Antônio Mill
Ownership: International Paper Co.
Rodovia SP 255, Km. 41, 240
14210-000 Luiz Antonio, SP
Brazil
Phone: (55) 16 3986 9000
Fax: (55) 16 3986 1620
Email: sac@ipaperbr.com
Web Address: www.internationalpaper.com.br
Personnel:
Gen. Mgr. : Luis Cesar Assin
Phone: (55) 16 3986 9000
Fax: (55) 16 3986 1620
Oper. Gen. Mgr. : Amaury Malia
Phone: (55) 16 3986 9000
Fax: (55) 16 3986 1620
Maint. Mgr.: Rogerio Zingra
Phone: (55) 16 3986 9000
Fax: (55) 16 3986 1620
HR Mgr.: Luciano Sgarbi
Phone: (55) 16 3986 9000
Fax: (55) 16 3986 1620

Brazil

Senior Sls. Exec. Latin America: Luana Faria Cardozo
Phone: (55) 19 3861 8593 / 8121
Fax: (55) 19 3861 8412 / 1098
Email: luana.cardozo@ipaperbr.com
Reliability Mgr.: Alberto Estevam Martinez
Phone: (55) 16 3986 9000
Fax: (55) 16 3986 1620
Total Employees at this Location: 649
Type of Operation: Pulp mill, Paper mill
Pulp Grades and Capacities:
Total pulp capacity: 426,245 mt/y
Pulp available for market: 119,952 mt/y
Chemical Pulp: 426,245 mt/y
Pulp Mill Data:
Chemical Pulping Systems:
Continuous digesters: 1
Pulp Lines: 1
Bleach Plant Systems: 1
Chemical Pulping System, Type: Hardwood, Ozone process: MC, Sequence: O_2 Z/DEopD, Capacity 420,000 admt/y
Chemical Recovery Equipment:
Evaporator lines: 1
Recovery boilers: 1
Lime Kiln
Pulp Dryers:
Wet Lap machine 1
Paper/Paperboard Grades and Capacities:
Total paper and paperboard capacity: 369,852 mt/y
Uncoated woodfree/freesheet: 369,852 mt/y
Paper and Paperboard Mill Data:
Stock Preparation:
Pulpers:
Refiners: 4
Paper Machines: 2
No. 1, DuoFormer D, total capacity 206,346 mt/y, Trim width 4.66 m, Uncoated woodfree/freesheet
No. 2, DuoFormer CF, total capacity 163,506 mt/y, Trim width 4.66 m, Uncoated woodfree/freesheet
Finishing Equipment:
Winders: 2
Rewinders: 1
Sheeters: 5 at 255,000 mt/y
Energy Data:
Power boilers: 3
Steam turbines: 2 at 34 MW
Electrical demand for mill: 1,447 MWh/D

ⓜInternational Paper do Brasil Ltda.
Três Lagoas Mill
Ownership: International Paper Co.
Rodovia MS 395 KM 21
79601-970 Três Lagoas, MT
Brazil
Phone: (55) 67 2105 6161
Fax: (55) 67 2105 6240
Email: sac@ipaperbr.com
Web Address: www.ipaper.com, www.internationalpaper.com/BRAZIL/EN/Company/Facilities/Tr%C3%AAs_Lagoas.html
Personnel:
Senior Sls. Exec. Latin America: Luana Faria Cardozo
Phone: (55) 19 3861 8593 / 8121
Fax: (55) 19 3861 8412 / 1098
Email: luana.cardozo@ipexbr.com
Asst. Admin.: Sabrina Carvalho
Phone: (55) 67 2105 6129, 67 2105 6161
Fax: (55) 67 2105 6240
Asst. Prod.: Mauro Pereira Borges
Phone: (55) 67 2105 6161
Fax: (55) 67 2105 6240
Total Employees at this Location: 125
Type of Operation: Paper mill
Pulp Mill Data:
Paper/Paperboard Grades and Capacities:
Total paper and paperboard capacity: 204,918 mt/y
Uncoated woodfree/freesheet: 204,918 mt/y
Paper and Paperboard Mill Data:
Paper Machines: 1
No. 1, DuoFormer, total capacity 204,918 mt/y, Trim width 5.2 m, Uncoated woodfree/freesheet
Energy Data:
Power boilers
Steam turbines: 2 at 162 MW
Electrical demand for mill: 387 MWh/D

ⓞⓜIpasa Indústria de Papel Apucarana S.A.
Apucarana Mill
Avenida Brasil, 714
86804-020 Apucarana, PR
Brazil
Phone: (55) 43 3427 7351/7424
Fax: (55) 43 3427 7500
Personnel:
Gen. Mgr.: Jurandil Depaola
Phone: (55) 43 3427 7351/7424
Fax: (55) 43 3427 7500
Mill Mgr.: Edivilson Volante
Phone: (55) 43 3427 7351/7424
Fax: (55) 43 3427 7500
Email: volante-ipasa@hotmail.com
Type of Operation: Paper mill
Paper/Paperboard Grades and Capacities:
Total paper and paperboard capacity: 5,000 mt/y
Tissue: 5,000 mt/y

ⓞⓜIPEL - Indaial Papel Embalagens Ltda.
Indaial Mill
Rua Dr. Blumenau 10.101, Passo Manso
89130-000 Indaial, SC
Brazil
Phone: (55) 47 3301 0191
Email: vendas@indaialpapel.com.br
Web Address: www.indaialpapel.com.br
Personnel:
Ind. Dir.: Júlio Dobuchak
Phone: (55) 47 3301 0191
Ind. Supt.: Roque Paulo Coelho
Phone: (55) 47 3301 0191
Email: industrial@indaialpapel.com.br
Commer. Superintendent: Luciana Dobuchak
Phone: (55) 47 3301 0191
Plant Supervisor: Juarez Zanluca
Phone: (55) 47 3301 0191
HR Analyst: Claudia Ipel
Phone: (55) 47 3301 0191
Total Employees at this Location: 315
Type of Operation: Paper mill
Pulp Grades and Capacities:
Total pulp capacity: 16,602 mt/y
Recycled Pulping: 16,602 mt/y
Pulp Mill Data:
Recycled Fiber Treatment Lines:
Pulpers: 1
Paper/Paperboard Grades and Capacities:
Total paper and paperboard capacity: 62,475 mt/y
Tissue: 62,475 mt/y
Paper and Paperboard Mill Data:
Paper Machines: 4
No. 1, fourdrinier, total capacity 3,927 mt/y, Trim width 2.4 m, Tissue
No. 2, crescent former, total capacity 12,138 mt/y, Trim width 2.8 m, Tissue
No. 3, crescent former, total capacity 19,992 mt/y, Trim width 2.8 m, Tissue
No. 4, crescent former, total capacity 26,418 mt/y, Trim width 2.8 m, Tissue
Energy Data:
Power boilers
Electrical demand for mill: 155 MWh/D

ⓞⓜIPELSA - Indústria de Celulose e Papel da Paraíba
Campina Grande Mill
Ownership: 100% by Renato R.C. Cruz e irmãos
Rua Antônio Vieira da Rocha, nº 100
58109-525 Campina Grande, PB
Brazil
Phone: (55) 83 2101 3000
Fax: (55) 83 2101 3020
Email: comercial@ipelsa.com.br
Personnel:
Accountant.: Neves Contadora
Phone: (55) 83 2101 3000
Fax: (55) 83 2101 3020
Total Employees of Company: 200
Total Employees at this Location: 200
Type of Operation: Paper mill
Pulp Mill Data:
Recycled Fiber Treatment Lines:
Pulpers: 2 at 15,000 admt/y
Paper/Paperboard Grades and Capacities:
Total paper and paperboard capacity: 9,600 mt/y
Tissue: 9,600 mt/y
Paper and Paperboard Mill Data:
Paper Machines: 1
No. 4, Yankee dryer, total capacity 9,600 mt/y, Trim width 1.8 m, Tissue
Energy Data:
Power boilers: 2
Electrical demand for mill: 21 MWh/D

ⓗCelulose Irani S.A.
Ownership: 100% by Habitasul Group
Rua General João Manoel, 157, 9th Fl. - Centro
90010-030 Porto Alegre, RS
Brazil
Phone: (55) 51 3220 3542
Fax: (55) 51 3220 3757
Email: superintendencia@irani.com.br
Web Address: www.irani.com.br
Personnel:
CEO: Péricles Pereira Druck
Phone: (55) 51 3220 3542
Fax: (55) 51 3220 3757
Email: periclesdruck@irani.com.br
CFO: Odivan Carlos Cargnin
Phone: (55) 51 3220 3542
Fax: (55) 51 3220 3757
Email: odivancargnin@irani.com.br
COO: Sérgio Ribas
Phone: (55) 51 3220 3542
Fax: (55) 51 3220 3757
Email: sergioribas@irani.com.br
Intelligence Mgr.: Gustavo Ferreira
Phone: (55) 51 3220 3542
Fax: (55) 51 3220 3757
Email: gustavoferreira@irani.com.br
Prod. Mgr.: Celio José Chiot
Phone: (55) 51 3220 3542
Fax: (55) 51 3220 3757
Asst. Exec.: Evelin Zarpelon
Phone: (55) 51 3220 3542
Fax: (55) 51 3220 3757
Dlvpmnt. Mgr.: Fábio Seminotti
Phone: (55) 51 3220 3542
Fax: (55) 51 3220 3757
Email: fabioseminotti@irani.com.br
Forest. Mgr.: Denis Baialuna
Phone: (55) 51 3220 3542
Fax: (55) 51 3220 3757
Total Employees of Company: 1,756
Total Employees at this Location: 15
Mill Locations:
Celulose Irani S.A., Vargem Bonita Mill, Rdv. BR 153, Km 47, Campina da Alegria, 89675-000 Vargem Bonita, SC, Brazil, Capacity: 202,419 mt/y, (Pulp mill, Paper mill, Paperboard mill)
Phone: (55) 49 3548 9000/69
Fax: (55) 49 3548 9255
Celulose Irani S.A., Santa Luzia Mill, Av. das Indústrias, 2445 Vila Olga, 33040-130 Santa Luzia, MG, Brazil, Capacity: 61,047 mt/y, (Paper mill, Paperboard mill)
Phone: (55) 31 2105 2850
Fax: (55) 31 2105 2862
Email: saoroberto@saoroberto.com.br

Brazil

ⓜCelulose Irani S.A.
Vargem Bonita Mill
Rdv. BR 153, Km 47, Campina da Alegria
89675-000 Vargem Bonita, SC
Brazil
 Phone: (55) 49 3548 9000/69
 Fax: (55) 49 3548 9255
 Web Address: www.irani.com.br
Personnel:
 Dir.: Sérgio Luiz Cotrim Ribas
 Phone: (55) 49 3548 9000/69
 Fax: (55) 49 3548 9255
 Email: sergioribas@irani.com.br
 Innovation Mgr.: Luiz Martins
 Phone: (55) 49 3548 9000/69
 Fax: (55) 49 3548 9255
 Email: luizmartins@irani.com.br
 Proj. Mgr.: Patric Schürhaus
 Phone: (55) 49 3548 9000/69
 Fax: (55) 49 3548 9255
 Email: Patricschurhaus@irani.com.br
Total Employees at this Location: 800
Type of Operation: Pulp mill, Paper mill, Paperboard mill
Pulp Grades and Capacities:
 Total pulp capacity: 203,926 mt/y
 Chemical Pulp: 83,431 mt/y
 Recycled Pulping: 120,495 mt/y
Pulp Mill Data:
 Chemical Pulping Systems:
 Batch digesters: 3
 Chemical Recovery Equipment:
 Evaporator lines: 1
 Recovery boilers: 1
 Lime Kiln
 Recycled Fiber Treatment Lines:
 Pulpers: 2 at 140,000 admt/y
 Recycled packaging pulping lines: 2 at 130,000 admt/y
Paper/Paperboard Grades and Capacities:
 Total paper and paperboard capacity: 202,419 mt/y
 Packaging papers: 71,043 mt/y
 Linerboard: 40,698 mt/y
 Corrugating medium/fluting: 90,678 mt/y
Paper and Paperboard Mill Data:
 Stock Preparation:
 Pulpers: 3
Paper Machines: 4
 No. 1, fourdrinier, total capacity 39,627 mt/y, Trim width 2.35 m, Linerboard, Packaging papers
 No. 2, fourdrinier, Yankee dryer, total capacity 21,777 mt/y, Trim width 2.05 m, Linerboard, Packaging papers
 No. 4, fourdrinier, Yankee dryer, total capacity 31,059 mt/y, Trim width 3 m, Packaging papers
 No. 5, (Former Type model: Fourdrinier Top/Bottom. Suppliers: Voith/Hergen.), fourdrinier, total capacity 109,956 mt/y, Trim width 2.45 m, Linerboard, Corrugating medium/fluting
Finishing Equipment:
 Rewinders: 4 at 202,500 mt/y
Energy Data:
 Power boilers: 1
 Steam turbines: 2 at 12 MW
 Hydro turbines: 6 at 9.5 MW
 Electrical demand for mill: 427 MWh/D

ⓜCelulose Irani S.A.
Santa Luzia Mill
Av. das Indústrias, 2445 Vila Olga
33040-130 Santa Luzia, MG
Brazil
 Phone: (55) 31 2105 2850
 Fax: (55) 31 2105 2862
 Email: saoroberto@saoroberto.com.br
 Web Address: www.saoroberto.com.br, www.irani.com.br
Personnel:
 Mill Mgr.: Mário Pinto de Oliveira
 Phone: (55) 11 2632 3000
 Indus. Mgr.: Wagner Rufino
 Phone: (55) 31 2105 2850
 Fax: (55) 31 2105 2862
 Forest. Mgr: Paulo de Tarso De Azambuja Ribeiro
 Phone: (55) 31 2105 2850
 Fax: (55) 31 2105 2862
 Logist. Mgr.: José Aristides da Fonseca
 Phone: (55) 31 2105 2850
 Fax: (55) 31 2105 2862
Total Employees at this Location: 162
Type of Operation: Paper mill, Paperboard mill
Pulp Grades and Capacities:
 Total pulp capacity: 62,059 mt/y
 Recycled Pulping: 62,059 mt/y
Pulp Mill Data:
 Recycled Fiber Treatment Lines:
 Recycled packaging pulping lines: 1
Paper/Paperboard Grades and Capacities:
 Total paper and paperboard capacity: 61,047 mt/y
 Linerboard: 48,909 mt/y
 Corrugating medium/fluting: 12,138 mt/y
Paper and Paperboard Mill Data:
 Stock Preparation:
 Pulpers: 3
 Refiners: 4
Paper Machines: 1
 No. 1, fourdrinier, total capacity 61,047 mt/y, Trim width 2.45 m, Corrugating medium/fluting, Linerboard
Finishing Equipment:
 Rewinders: 1 at 75,000 mt/y
Energy Data:
 Power boilers: 1
 Electrical demand for mill: 96 MWh/D

ⓜIndústria de Papel Irapuru Ltda.
Ribeirão Preto Mill
Rua Pernambuco, 2315
14085-570 Ribeirão Preto, SP
Brazil
 Phone: (55) 16 2101 2300
 Fax: (55) 16 3612 0770
 Email: irapuru@irapuru.ind.br
 Web Address: www.irapuru.ind.br
Personnel:
 CEO: Nazir José Nehemy Junior
 Phone: (55) 16 2101 2300
 Fax: (55) 16 3612 0770
 Dir.: Renato Neime
 Phone: (55) 16 2101 2300
 Fax: (55) 16 3612 0770
 Mill Mgr.: José Spinelli
 Phone: (55) 16 2101 2300
 Fax: (55) 16 3612 0770
Type of Operation: Paper mill
Paper/Paperboard Grades and Capacities:
 Total paper and paperboard capacity: 10,350 mt/y
 Tissue: 10,350 mt/y
Paper and Paperboard Mill Data:
Paper Machines: 3
 PM 2, fourdrinier, Trim width 1.35 m, Tissue
 PM 3, fourdrinier, Trim width 1.35 m, Tissue
 PM 4, fourdrinier, Trim width 1.75 m, Tissue

ⓜIndústria de Papéis para Embalagem Irmãos Siqueira Ltda.
Rua Soldado Aristides Gouveia, 326/25, Parque Novo Mundo
02188-090 São Paulo, SP
Brazil
 Phone: (55) 11 2207 6548
 Fax: (55) 11 2954 6248
 Email: vendas@ipapeis.com.br
 Web Address: www.ipapeis.com.br
Personnel:
 Sls. Mgr.: Alexandre Siqueira
 Phone: (55) 11 2954 6248
 Fax: (55) 11 2954 6248
Total Employees of Company: 294
Mill Locations:
Indústria de Papéis para Embalagem Irmãos Siqueira Ltda., Passa Quatro Mill, Av. Vereador Clementino J. Siqueira, 1061 - Bairro Pinheirinhos, 37460-000 Passa Quatro, MG, Brazil, Capacity: 29,988 mt/y, (Paper mill)
 Phone: (55) 35 3371 2133
 Fax: (55) 35 3371 2021
 Email: cartonagem@ipapeis.com.br

ⓜIndústria de Papéis para Embalagem Irmãos Siqueira Ltda.
Passa Quatro Mill
Av. Vereador Clementino J. Siqueira, 1061 - Bairro Pinheirinhos
37460-000 Passa Quatro, MG
Brazil
 Phone: (55) 35 3371 2133
 Fax: (55) 35 3371 2021
 Email: cartonagem@ipapeis.com.br
 Web Address: www.ipapeis.com.br
Personnel:
 Mill Mgr.: Edson Siqueira
 Phone: (55) 35 3371 2133
 Fax: (55) 35 3371 2021
 Email: edson@ipapeis.com.br
Total Employees at this Location: 86
Type of Operation: Paper mill
Pulp Grades and Capacities:
 Total pulp capacity: 30,746 mt/y
 Recycled Pulping: 30,746 mt/y
Pulp Mill Data:
 Recycled Fiber Treatment Lines:
 Pulpers: 1 at 33,700
Paper/Paperboard Grades and Capacities:
 Total paper and paperboard capacity: 29,988 mt/y
 Packaging papers: 7,854 mt/y
 Corrugating medium/fluting: 22,134 mt/y
Paper and Paperboard Mill Data:
Paper Machines: 1
 No. 1, fourdrinier, total capacity 29,988 mt/y, Trim width 2.5 m, Corrugating medium/fluting, Packaging papers
Energy Data:
 Power boilers
 Electrical demand for mill: 53 MWh/D

ⓜItararé Papéis Ltda.
R Gaudencio C Machado 3, VL Beca
18460 Itararé, SP
Brazil
 Phone: (55) 15 3532 6078
 Fax: (55) 15 3532 6078
 Email: itararepapeis@terra.com.br
Mill Locations:
Itararé Papéis Ltda., Itararé Mill, R Gaudencio C Machado 3, VL Beca, 18460 Itararé, SP, Brazil, Capacity: 5,000 mt/y, (Paper mill)
 Phone: (55) 15 3532 6078
 Fax: (55) 15 3532 6078
 Email: itararepapeis@terra.com.br

ⓜItararé Papéis Ltda.
Itararé Mill
R Gaudencio C Machado 3, VL Beca
18460 Itararé, SP
Brazil
 Phone: (55) 15 3532 6078
 Fax: (55) 15 3532 6078
 Email: itararepapeis@terra.com.br
Type of Operation: Paper mill
Paper/Paperboard Grades and Capacities:
 Total paper and paperboard capacity: 5,000 mt/y
 Tissue: 5,000 mt/y

ⓜⓜJaepel Papéis e Embalagens
Senador Canedo Mill
Rua Eixo Principal S/N - Quadra 02 - Módulo 01/20
75250-000 Senador Canedo, GO
Brazil
 Phone: (55) 62 3237-5200

Brazil

Fax: (55) 62 3237-5232
Email: jaepel@jaepel.com.br
Web Address: www.jaepel.com.br
Personnel:
Owner: José Roberto Garcia Amoroso
Phone: (55) 62 3237-5200
Fax: (55) 62 3237-5232
Owner: Adonis Jesus Garcia Amoroso
Phone: (55) 62 3237-5200
Fax: (55) 62 3237-5232
Owner: Edilza Terezinha Garcia Amoroso
Phone: (55) 62 3237-5200
Fax: (55) 62 3237-5232
Oper. Dir.: Ronaldo Thibes
Phone: (55) 62 3237-5200
Fax: (55) 62 3237-5232
Maint. Coord.: Elio Junior da Costa
Phone: (55) 62 3237-5200
Fax: (55) 62 3237-5232
Supply Mgr.: Dirceu Stern
Phone: (55) 62 3237-5200
Fax: (55) 62 3237-5232
Total Employees of Company: 350
Total Employees at this Location: 105
Type of Operation: Paperboard mill
Pulp Grades and Capacities:
Total pulp capacity: 69,690 mt/y
Recycled Pulping: 69,690 mt/y
Pulp Mill Data:
Recycled Fiber Treatment Lines:
Pulpers: 1 at 72,000
Paper/Paperboard Grades and Capacities:
Total paper and paperboard capacity: 71,757 mt/y
Linerboard: 47,838 mt/y
Corrugating medium/fluting: 23,919 mt/y
Paper and Paperboard Mill Data:
Stock Preparation:
Pulpers:
Paper Machines: 1
No. 1, (Former Type model: Fourdrinier Top/Bottom), fourdrinier, total capacity 71,757 mt/y, Trim width 2.5 m, Linerboard, Corrugating medium/fluting
Energy Data:
Power boilers
Electrical demand for mill: 111 MWh/D

⊕Jari Celulose, Papel e Embalagens S.A.

Ownership: 100% by Grupo Orsa
Alameda Mamoré 989, 23rd floor, Alphaville
06454-040 Barueri, SP
Brazil
Phone: (55) 11 2175 7500/4689 8700
Fax: (55) 11 4195 9506
Personnel:
Chmn.: Sergio Amoroso
Phone: (55) 11 2175 7500/4689 8700
Fax: (55) 11 4195 9506
Email: presidencia@grupoorsa.com.br
CEO: Jorge Henriques
Phone: (55) 11 2175 7500/4689 8700
Fax: (55) 11 4195 9506
Exec. Dir.: Luis Fernando Laranja Da Fonseca
Phone: (55) 11 2175 7500/4689 8700
Fax: (55) 11 4195 9506
Contr. Dir: Joao Eduardo Peres
Phone: (55) 11 2175 7500/4689 8700
Fax: (55) 11 4195 9506
Manuf. Dir.: Dino Ranzani
Phone: (55) 11 2175 7500/4689 8700
Fax: (55) 11 4195 9506
Indus. Dir.: Ricardo Galan
Phone: (55) 11 2175 7500/4689 8700
Fax: (55) 11 4195 9506
Plann. Mgr.: Daniel De Chiaro
Phone: (55) 11 2175 7500/4689 8700
Fax: (55) 11 4195 9506
Sls. Dir.: Patrick Nogueira
Phone: (55) 1 2175 7500/4689 8700
Fax: (55) 11 4195 9506
Email: kmsilva@grupoorsa.com.br
Bus. Dir.: Joao Prestes
Phone: (55) 11 2175 7500/4689 8700
Fax: (55) 11 4195 9506
Finan. Mgr.: Sandra Lima
Phone: (55) 11 2175 7500/4689 8700
Fax: (55) 11 4195 9506
IT Mgr.: Lari Papaleo
Phone: (55) 11 2175 7500/4689 8700
Fax: (55) 11 4195 9506
HR Mgr.: Luiz Bezerra
Phone: (55) 11 2175 7500/4689 8700
Fax: (55) 11 4195 9506
Total Employees of Company: 944
Total Employees at this Location: 111
Mill Locations:
Jari Celulose, Papel e Embalagens S.A., Monte Dourado Mill, Vila Munguba, s/n°, 68240-000 Monte Dourado, PA, Brazil, (Pulp mill)
Phone: (55) 93 3736 6201/6202
Fax: (55) 93 3736 1180

⊕Jari Celulose, Papel e Embalagens S.A.
Monte Dourado Mill

Mill is closed (stopped production January 15, 2013, being converted into a dissolving pulp producing site was expected to begin production in March 2014 however, this has been delayed until October 2014.)
Vila Munguba, s/n°
68240-000 Monte Dourado, PA
Brazil
Phone: (55) 93 3736 6201/6202
Fax: (55) 93 3736 1180
Personnel:
Ind. Dir.: Dino Angelo Ranzani
Phone: (55) 11 4689 8712
Email: dino.ranzani@grupojari.com.br
Plan. & Sls. Coord.: Leonardo Luz
Phone: (55) 11 2175 7538
Fax: (55) 11 4195 9506
Email: leonardo.luz@grupojari.com.br
Total Employees at this Location: 780
Type of Operation: Pulp mill
Pulp Mill Data:
Chemical Pulping Systems:
Batch digesters: 8
Pulp Lines: 1
Bleach Plant Systems: 1
Chemical Pulping System - 1, Type: ECF - Eucalyptus, Sequence: O_2 DoEoDD, Capacity 420,000 admt/y
Chemical Recovery Equipment:
Evaporator lines: 1
Recovery boilers: 1
Lime Kiln
Pulp Dryers:
Air Float dryers 1, Fourdriniers 1
Energy Data:
Power boilers: 2
Steam turbines: 1 at 55.0 MW

⊕Kimberly-Clark Brasil Ind. e Com. de Produtos de Higiene Ltda.

Ownership: Kimberly-Clark Corp.
Rua Olimpíadas, 205 - 6°/7° andar - Vila Olímpia
04551-000 São Paulo, SP
Brazil
Phone: (55) 11 4503 4500
Fax: (55) 11 4503 4715
Email: sacbrasil@kcc.com
Web Address: www.kimberly-clark.com.br, www.kcprofessional.com/br
Personnel:
Pres. Kimberly-Clark Brasil & VP Kimberly-Clark Latin America: João Luiz Damato
Phone: (55) 11 4503 4500
Fax: (55) 11 4503 4715
Dir.: Pedro Coletta
Phone: (55) 11 4503 4500
Fax: (55) 11 4503 4715
Finan. Dir.: Juan Lenis Bravo
Phone: (55) 11 4503 4500
Fax: (55) 11 4503 4715
HR Dir.: Ana Paula Bogus
Phone: (55) 11 4503 4500
Fax: (55) 11 4503 4715
Dir.: Douglas de Oliveira
Phone: (55) 11 4503 4500
Fax: (55) 11 4503 4715
Mill Locations:
Kimberly-Clark Brasil Ind. e Com. de Produtos de Higiene Ltda., Correia Pinto Mill, Rodovia BR 116, km 218 s/n°, 88535-000 Correia Pinto, SC, Brazil, Capacity: 57,834 mt/y, (Paper mill)
Phone: (55) 49 3243 6000
Fax: (55) 49 3243 6004
Email: sacprofessional@kcc.com
Kimberly-Clark Brasil Ind. e Com. de Produtos de Higiene Ltda., Mogi das Cruzes Mill, Estrada da Casa Grande, km 59 s/n°- Cocuera, 08710-971 Mogi das Cruzes, SP, Brazil, Capacity: 72,471 mt/y, (Paper mill)
Phone: (55) 11 4793 5000
Fax: (55) 11 4793 5000
Email: sacprofessional@kcc.com

⊕Kimberly-Clark Brasil Ind. e Com. de Produtos de Higiene Ltda.
Correia Pinto Mill

Ownership: Kimberly-Clark Corp.
Rodovia BR 116, km 218 s/n°
88535-000 Correia Pinto, SC
Brazil
Phone: (55) 49 3243 6000
Fax: (55) 49 3243 6004
Email: sacprofessional@kcc.com
Web Address: www.kcprofessional.com/br, www.kimberly-clark.com.br
Personnel:
Maint. Mgr.: Wagner M Paula
Phone: (55) 49 3243 6000
Fax: (55) 49 3243 6004
Email: wpaula@kcc.com
Total Employees at this Location: 200
Type of Operation: Paper mill
Pulp Grades and Capacities:
Total pulp capacity: 29,793 mt/y
Recycled Pulping: 29,793 mt/y
Pulp Mill Data:
Bleach Plant Systems: 1
Recycled Pulping System, Type: DIP
Recycled Fiber Treatment Lines:
Flotation deinking lines: 1
Paper/Paperboard Grades and Capacities:
Total paper and paperboard capacity: 57,834 mt/y
Tissue: 57,834 mt/y
Paper and Paperboard Mill Data:
Paper Machines: 1
No. 1, crescent former, total capacity 57,834 mt/y, Trim width 5.4 m, Tissue
Energy Data:
Power boilers: 1
Electrical demand for mill: 184 MWh/D

⊕Kimberly-Clark Brasil Ind. e Com. de Produtos de Higiene Ltda.
Mogi das Cruzes Mill

Ownership: Kimberly-Clark Corp.
Estrada da Casa Grande, km 59 s/n°- Cocuera
08710-971 Mogi das Cruzes, SP
Brazil
Phone: (55) 11 4793 5000
Fax: (55) 11 4793 5000
Email: sacprofessional@kcc.com
Web Address: www.kimberly-clark.com.br, www.kcprofessional.com/br
Personnel:

Brazil

Industrial Dir. (Family Care Division): Ricardo Casemiro Tobera
Phone: (55) 11 4793 5000
Fax: (55) 11 4793 5000
Email: rtobera@kcc.com
Methodology. Mgr: Claudio Heleno Rodrigues
Phone: (55) 11 4793 5000
Fax: (55) 11 4793 5000
Total Employees at this Location: 200
Type of Operation: Paper mill
Paper/Paperboard Grades and Capacities:
Total paper and paperboard capacity: 72,471 mt/y
Tissue: 72,471 mt/y
Paper and Paperboard Mill Data:
Paper Machines: 3
No. 4, crescent former, total capacity 21,420 mt/y, Trim width 2.65 m, Tissue
No. 7, crescent former, total capacity 28,917 mt/y, Trim width 2.65 m, Tissue, Uncoated woodfree/freesheet
No. 8, crescent former, total capacity 22,134 mt/y, Trim width 2.68 m, Tissue
Energy Data:
Power boilers: 1
Electrical demand for mill: 204 MWh/D

ⓜKlabin S.A.

Ownership: 59% by Klabin Irmãos & Cia., 20% by Monteiro Aranha S.A., 21% by others
Av. Brigadeiro Faria Lima, 3.600, 3°, 4° e 5° andares
04538-132 Itaim Bibi, São Paulo, SP
Brazil
Phone: (55) 11 3046 3438, 11 3046 5800
Fax: (55) 11 3046 5800
Email: klabin@klabin.com.br
Web Address: www.klabin.com.br
Personnel:
CEO: Fabio Schvartsman
Phone: (55) 11 3046 3438
Fax: (55) 11 3046 5800
Email: fschvartsman@klabin.com.br
CFO & Investor Rel. Dir.: Antonio Sergio Alfano
Phone: (55) 11 3046 3438
Fax: (55) 11 3046 5800
Email: asalfano@klabin.com.br
COO: Paulo Roberto Petterle
Phone: (55) 11 3046 3438
Fax: (55) 11 3046 5800
Email: prpetterle@klabin.com.br
Plan., Projects & Ind. Technology Officer: Francisco César Razzolini
Phone: (55) 11 3046 3438
Fax: (55) 11 3046 5800
Email: frazzolini@klabin.com.br
Commer. Dir. Coated Boards: Edgard Avezum Junior
Phone: (55) 11 3046 3438
Fax: (55) 11 3046 5800
Email: eavezum@klabin.com.br
Supply Chain Officer: Cristiano Cardoso Teixeira
Phone: (55) 11 3046 3438
Fax: (55) 11 3046 5800
Total Employees of Company: 14,430
Total Employees at this Location: 265
Mill Locations:
Klabin S.A., Angatuba Mill, Rodovia Raposo Tavases Km. 197, Bairro Palmital, 18240-000 Angatuba, SP, Brazil, Capacity: 99,960 mt/y, (Pulp mill, Paper mill, Paperboard mill)
Phone: (55) 15 3255 9000
Fax: (55) 15 3255 9011
Email: mhyamamoto@klabin.com.br
Klabin S.A., Correia Pinto Mill, Rodovia BR 116, Km. 218, 88535-000 Correia Pinto, SC, Brazil, Capacity: 209,916 mt/y, (Pulp mill, Paper mill)
Phone: (55) 49 3243 7000
Klabin S.A., Goiana Mill, Rod. PE 75, Km. 4.5, Engenho Pedregulho, 55900-000 Goiana, PE, Brazil, Capacity: 48,552 mt/y, (Paperboard mill)
Phone: (55) 81 3626 8200
Fax: (55) 81 3626 8287
Klabin S.A., Guapimirim Mill, Estrada Rio-Friburgo, 429 Km Zero, Parada Modelo, 25940-000 Guapimirim, RJ, Brazil, Capacity: 49,980 mt/y, (Paper mill, Paperboard mill)
Phone: (55) 21 2633 9700
Fax: (55) 21 2633 9734
Klabin S.A., Monte Alegre Mill, Fazenda Monte Alegre, Harmonia, 84275-000 Telêmaco Borba, PR, Brazil, Capacity: 1,066,002 mt/y, (Pulp mill, Paper mill, Paperboard mill)
Phone: (55) 42 3271 5000
Fax: (55) 42 3272 3246
Email: klabin@klabin.com.br
Klabin S.A., Otacílio Costa Mill, Av. Olinkraft, s/n, 6602, 88540-000 Otacílio Costa, SC, Brazil, Capacity: 349,860 mt/y, (Pulp mill, Paper mill, Paperboard mill)
Phone: (55) 49 3275 8200
Klabin S.A., Piracicaba Mill, Avenida Cristóvão Colombo 2307, 13412-224 Piracicaba, SP, Brazil, Capacity: 89,250 mt/y, (Paperboard mill)
Phone: (55) 19 3412 1300
Fax: (55) 19 3421 4132

ⓜKlabin S.A.
Angatuba Mill
Rodovia Raposo Tavases Km. 197, Bairro Palmital
18240-000 Angatuba, SP
Brazil
Phone: (55) 15 3255 9000
Fax: (55) 15 3255 9011
Email: mhyamamoto@klabin.com.br
Web Address: www.klabin.com.br
Personnel:
Ind. Mgr.: Ricardo Silva Franco Da Quinta
Phone: (55) 15 3255 9039
Fax: (55) 15 3255 9011
Email: rquinta@klabin.com.br
Qlty. Coord.: Vitor Barreto Cabral
Phone: (55) 15 3255 9012
Fax: (55) 15 3255 9011
Email: vbcabral@klabin.com.br
Total Employees at this Location: 195
Type of Operation: Pulp mill, Paper mill, Paperboard mill
Pulp Grades and Capacities:
Total pulp capacity: 51,250 mt/y
Chemical Pulp: 51,250 mt/y
Pulp Mill Data:
Chemical Pulping Systems:
Batch digesters: 3
Pulp Lines: 1
Chemical Recovery Equipment:
Evaporator lines: 1
Paper/Paperboard Grades and Capacities:
Total paper and paperboard capacity: 99,960 mt/y
Linerboard: 64,260 mt/y
Corrugating medium/fluting: 35,700 mt/y
Paper and Paperboard Mill Data:
Stock Preparation:
Pulpers: 3
Refiners: 6
Paper Machines: 1
No. 14, (Former Type model: Multi-Fourdrinier), four-drinier, total capacity 99,960 mt/y, Trim width 2.5 m, Linerboard, Corrugating medium/fluting
Finishing Equipment:
Winders: 1 at 135,000 mt/y
Calenders: 1 at 135,000 mt/y
Energy Data:
Power boilers: 3
Electrical demand for mill: 199 MWh/D

ⓜKlabin S.A.
Correia Pinto Mill
Rodovia BR 116, Km. 218
88535-000 Correia Pinto, SC
Brazil
Phone: (55) 49 3243 7000
Web Address: www.klabin.com.br
Personnel:
Industrial Dir.: Sadi Carlos de Oliveira
Phone: (55) 49 3275 8241
Fax: (55) 49 3243 1192
Email: saoliveira@klabin.com.br
Strat. & Market Specialist: Rogério Frediani
Phone: (55) 11 3046 3409
Email: rfrediani@klabin.com.br
Total Employees at this Location: 390
Type of Operation: Pulp mill, Paper mill
Pulp Grades and Capacities:
Total pulp capacity: 217,392 mt/y
Chemical Pulp: 170,653 mt/y
Recycled Pulping: 46,739 mt/y
Pulp Mill Data:
Chemical Pulping Systems:
Batch digesters: 8
Pulp Lines: 2
Chemical Recovery Equipment:
Evaporator lines: 1
Recovery boilers: 1
Lime Kiln
Recycled Fiber Treatment Lines:
Recycled packaging pulping lines: 1
Pulp Dryers:
Wet Lap machine 1
Paper/Paperboard Grades and Capacities:
Total paper and paperboard capacity: 209,916 mt/y
Packaging papers: 209,916 mt/y
Paper and Paperboard Mill Data:
Stock Preparation:
Refiners: 3
Paper Machines: 2
No. 16, fourdrinier, total capacity 129,948 mt/y, Trim width 4.4 m, Packaging papers
No. 17, fourdrinier, total capacity 79,968 mt/y, Trim width 3.4 m, Packaging papers
Finishing Equipment:
Winders: 1 at 130,000 mt/y
Calenders: 1
Rewinders: 1 at 300,000 mt/y
Energy Data:
Power boilers: 4
Steam turbines: 3 at 35 MW
Electrical demand for mill: 454 MWh/D

ⓜKlabin S.A.
Goiana Mill
Rod. PE 75, Km. 4.5, Engenho Pedregulho
55900-000 Goiana, PE
Brazil
Phone: (55) 81 3626 8200
Fax: (55) 81 3626 8287
Web Address: www.klabin.com.br
Personnel:
Prod & Tech Mgr.: Paulo Sergio Pereira da Silva
Phone: (55) 81 3626 8200
Fax: (55) 81 3626 8287
Indus. Mgr.: Angelo Brustolin
Phone: (55) 81 3626 8200
Fax: (55) 81 3626 8287
Maint. Mgr.: Netanias Lopes da Silva
Phone: (55) 81 3626 8200
Fax: (55) 81 3626 8287
Manuf. Dir.: Andre Possas
Phone: (55) 81 3626 8200
Fax: (55) 81 3626 8287
Total Employees at this Location: 97
Type of Operation: Paperboard mill
Pulp Grades and Capacities:
Total pulp capacity: 49,520 mt/y
Recycled Pulping: 49,520 mt/y
Pulp Mill Data:
Recycled Fiber Treatment Lines:
Pulpers: 2 at 59,000 admt/y
Paper/Paperboard Grades and Capacities:
Total paper and paperboard capacity: 48,552 mt/y
Linerboard: 9,996 mt/y
Corrugating medium/fluting: 38,556 mt/y
Paper and Paperboard Mill Data:

Brazil

Stock Preparation:
Pulpers: 2
Refiners: 3
Paper Machines: 1
No. 1, fourdrinier, total capacity 48,552 mt/y, Trim width 2.2 m, Corrugating medium/fluting, Linerboard
Finishing Equipment:
Winders: 1 at 47,000 mt/y
Rewinders: 1 at 47,000 mt/y
Energy Data:
Power boilers: 2
Electrical demand for mill: 90 MWh/D

Klabin S.A.
Guapimirim Mill
Estrada Rio-Friburgo, 429 Km Zero, Parada Modelo
25940-000 Guapimirim, RJ
Brazil
Phone: (55) 21 2633 9700
Fax: (55) 21 2633 9734
Web Address: www.klabin.com.br
Personnel:
Mill Mgr.: Mauro Haruo Yamamoto
Phone: (55) 15 3255 9001
Fax: (55) 15 3255 9011
Email: mhyamamoto@klabin.com.br
Total Employees at this Location: 95
Type of Operation: Paper mill, Paperboard mill
Pulp Grades and Capacities:
Total pulp capacity: 50,776 mt/y
Recycled Pulping: 50,776 mt/y

Pulp Mill Data:
Recycled Fiber Treatment Lines:
Pulpers: 1 at 88,457
Paper/Paperboard Grades and Capacities:
Total paper and paperboard capacity: 49,980 mt/y
Corrugating medium/fluting: 49,980 mt/y
Paper and Paperboard Mill Data:
Stock Preparation:
Pulpers: 2
Refiners: 5
Paper Machines: 1
No. 19, fourdrinier, total capacity 49,980 mt/y, Trim width 2.44 m, Corrugating medium/fluting
Finishing Equipment:
Winders: 3 at 28,350 mt/y, 28,350 mt/y, 49,000 mt/y
Energy Data:
Power boilers: 3
Electrical demand for mill: 64 MWh/D

Klabin S.A.
Monte Alegre Mill
Fazenda Monte Alegre, Harmonia
84275-000 Telêmaco Borba, PR
Brazil
Phone: (55) 42 3271 5000
Fax: (55) 42 3272 3246
Email: klabin@klabin.com.br
Web Address: www.klabin.com.br
Personnel:
Mill Mgr.: Arthur Canhisares
Phone: (55) 42 3271 5000
Fax: (55) 42 3272 3246
Gen. Mgr.: Flavio Deganutti
Phone: (55) 42 3271 5000
Fax: (55) 42 3272 3246
Email: fdeganutti@klabin.com.br
Assist. Tech.: Jorge Luiz Ferreira
Phone: (55) 42 3271 5000
Fax: (55) 42 3272 3246
Email: jferreira@klabin.com.br
Total Employees at this Location: 1,508
Type of Operation: Pulp mill, Paper mill, Paperboard mill
Pulp Grades and Capacities:
Total pulp capacity: 1,032,521 mt/y
Chemical Pulp: 884,229 mt/y
Mechanical Pulp: 148,291 mt/y
Pulp Mill Data:
Chemical Pulping Systems:
Continuous digesters: 2
Mechanical Pulping Systems:
CTMP systems: 1
Pulp Lines: 3
Bleach Plant Systems: 1
Chemical Pulping System, Type: ECF - Hardwood/Softwood, Sequence: O₂ DoEopD, Capacity 220,000 admt/y
Chemical Recovery Equipment:
Evaporator lines: 1
Recovery boilers: 2
Lime Kiln
Paper/Paperboard Grades and Capacities:
Total paper and paperboard capacity: 1,066,002 mt/y
Packaging papers: 19,992 mt/y
Linerboard: 359,142 mt/y
Boxboard/cartonboard: 686,868 mt/y
Paper and Paperboard Mill Data:
Stock Preparation:
Pulpers: 12
Refiners: 33
Paper Machines: 6
No. 1, (Former Type model: Fourdrinier/2nd HB), fourdrinier, total capacity 124,950 mt/y, Trim width 4.4 m, Linerboard
No. 3, fourdrinier, total capacity 28,917 mt/y, Trim width 2.6 m, Linerboard
No. 4, fourdrinier, total capacity 44,982 mt/y, Trim width 3.6 m, Linerboard, Packaging papers
No. 6, (Former Type model: Fourdrinier/D), fourdrinier, total capacity 180,285 mt/y, Trim width 6.6 m, Linerboard
No. 7, (Former Type model: Dourdrinier/BB/BL), fourdrinier, total capacity 329,868 mt/y, Trim width 6.1 m, Boxboard/cartonboard
No. 9, (Former Type model: Multi-Fourdrinier), fourdrinier, total capacity 357,000 mt/y, Trim width 6.6 m, Boxboard/cartonboard
Coating Machines: 3
No. 7, total capacity 330,000 mt/y., on machine
No. 9, total capacity 357,000 mt/y., on machine
MR2, total capacity 50,000 mt/y., off machine
Finishing Equipment:
Winders: 5
Calenders: 4
Rewinders: 2
Sheeters: 2
Energy Data:
Power boilers: 5
TMP Reboiler
Steam turbines: 4 at 6.25, 9.4, 23.5, 72 MW
Hydro turbines: 2 at 12.5, 11 MW
Electrical demand for mill: 3,633 MWh/D

Klabin S.A.
Otacílio Costa Mill
Av. Olinkraft, s/n, 6602
88540-000 Otacílio Costa, SC
Brazil
Phone: (55) 49 3275 8200
Web Address: www.klabin.com.br
Personnel:
Prod. Mgr.: Rubens Rovedo Scoz
Phone: (55) 49 3275 8241
Fax: (55) 49 3243 7201
Email: rscoz@klabin.com.br
Mill Mgr.: Arthur Canhisares
Total Employees at this Location: 563
Type of Operation: Pulp mill, Paper mill, Paperboard mill
Pulp Grades and Capacities:
Total pulp capacity: 362,654 mt/y
Chemical Pulp: 348,147 mt/y
Recycled Pulping: 14,506 mt/y
Pulp Mill Data:
Chemical Pulping Systems:
Batch digesters: 7
Pulp Lines: 2

Chemical Recovery Equipment:
Evaporator lines: 5
Recovery boilers: 2
Lime Kiln
Recycled Fiber Treatment Lines:
Pulpers: 2 at 35,500 admt/y
Paper/Paperboard Grades and Capacities:
Total paper and paperboard capacity: 349,860 mt/y
Linerboard: 349,860 mt/y
Paper and Paperboard Mill Data:
Stock Preparation:
Pulpers: 3
Refiners: 14
Paper Machines: 3
No. 11, fourdrinier, total capacity 44,982 mt/y, Trim width 2.4 m, Linerboard
No. 12, (Former Type model: Fourdrinier/2nd HB), fourdrinier, total capacity 79,968 mt/y, Trim width 2.4 m, Linerboard
No. 13, (Former Type model: Fourdrinier/2nd HB), fourdrinier, total capacity 224,910 mt/y, Trim width 4.4 m, Linerboard
Coating Machines: 1
No. 1, total capacity 30,000 mt/y., on machine
Finishing Equipment:
Rewinders: 3
Energy Data:
Power boilers: 3
Steam turbines: 3 at 16, 17 MW
Electrical demand for mill: 755 MWh/D

Klabin S.A.
Piracicaba Mill
Avenida Cristóvão Colombo 2307
13412-224 Piracicaba, SP
Brazil
Phone: (55) 19 3412 1300
Fax: (55) 19 3421 4132
Web Address: www.klabin.com.br
Personnel:
Prod. Mgr.: Fernando Inácio Torres
Phone: (55) 19 3412 1300
Fax: (55) 19 3421 4132
Maint. Mgr.: Renato Alexandre Pelegrino Boaratti
Phone: (55) 19 3412 1300
Fax: (55) 19 3421 4132
Eng. Mgr.: Cristiane Paiva
Phone: (55) 19 3412 1300
Fax: (55) 19 3421 4132
Total Employees at this Location: 104
Type of Operation: Paperboard mill
Pulp Grades and Capacities:
Total pulp capacity: 90,531 mt/y
Recycled Pulping: 90,531 mt/y

Pulp Mill Data:
Recycled Fiber Treatment Lines:
Recycled packaging pulping lines: 1
Paper/Paperboard Grades and Capacities:
Total paper and paperboard capacity: 89,250 mt/y
Linerboard: 35,700 mt/y
Corrugating medium/fluting: 53,550 mt/y
Paper and Paperboard Mill Data:
Stock Preparation:
Pulpers: 2
Refiners: 6
Paper Machines: 1
No. 21, (Former Type model: Fourdrinier Top/Bottom), fourdrinier, total capacity 89,250 mt/y, Trim width 2.5 m, Linerboard, Corrugating medium/fluting
Finishing Equipment:
Winders: 2 at 140,000 mt/y
Energy Data:
Power boilers: 4
Electrical demand for mill: 180 MWh/D

KM Papel
Ownership: 100% by Daniel Klabin Lorch Wurzmann
Av. Brig. Faria Lima, 2954, 5º andar, Cj. 53/54

Brazil

01451-000 São Paulo, SP
Brazil
 Phone: (55) 11 2010 1300
 Fax: (55) 11 2015-3280
 Email: contato@kmpapel.com.br
 Web Address: www.kmpapel.com.br
Personnel:
 Pres.: Daniel Klabin Wurzmann
 Phone: (55) 11 9981 8382
 Fax: (55) 11 2015 3280
 Finan. Dir.: Claucio Vergilio Leme Braga
 Phone: (55) 11 2010 1300
 Fax: (55) 11 2015 3280
 Sales Dir.: Fabricio Vanucci
 Phone: (55) 11 2010 1300
 Fax: (55) 11 2015 3280
 Ass. Pres.: Lilian Fernandes
 Phone: (55) 11 2010 1300
 Fax: (55) 11 2015 3280
Total Employees of Company: 300
Mill Locations:
 KM Papel, Bonsucesso Mill, Rua Prudente Arino Dos Reis Junqueira,199, 36720-000 Bonsucesso, Volta Grande, MG, Brazil, Capacity: 36,000 mt/y, (Paper mill)
 Phone: (55) 32 3463 1910
 Fax: (55) 32 3463 1250
 Email: contato@kmpapel.com.br

ⓜKM Papel
Bonsucesso Mill
Rua Prudente Arino Dos Reis Junqueira,199
36720-000 Bonsucesso, Volta Grande, MG
Brazil
 Phone: (55) 32 3463 1910
 Fax: (55) 32 3463 1250
 Email: contato@kmpapel.com.br
 Web Address: www.kmpapel.com.br
Personnel:
 Gen Mgr.: Ronaldo Oliveira
 Phone: (55) 32 3463 1910
 Fax: (55) 32 3463 1250
Total Employees at this Location: 180
Type of Operation: Paper mill
Paper/Paperboard Grades and Capacities:
 Total paper and paperboard capacity: 36,000 mt/y
 Uncoated woodfree/freesheet: 36,000 mt/y
Paper and Paperboard Mill Data:
Paper Machines: 1
 PM 1, total capacity 36,000 mt/y, Trim width 2.15 m, Uncoated woodfree/freesheet
Energy Data:
 Electrical demand for mill: 36 MWh/D

ⓟⓜLutepel Indústria e Com de Papel Ltda.
Lençóis Paulista Mill
Rua Ana Nery 365
18681-160 Lençóis Paulista, SP
Brazil
 Phone: (55) 14 3264 3900
 Fax: (55) 14 3264 3902
 Email: talithalima@lutepel.com.br
 Web Address: www.lutepel.com.br
Personnel:
 Dir.: Edenilson Grecca
 Phone: (55) 14 3264 3900
 Email: edenilson.grecca@lutepel.com.br
Total Employees of Company: 250
Total Employees at this Location: 75
Type of Operation: Paper mill
Paper/Paperboard Grades and Capacities:
 Total paper and paperboard capacity: 35,700 mt/y
 Packaging papers: 11,067 mt/y
 Specialty and industrial: 24,633 mt/y
Paper and Paperboard Mill Data:
Paper Machines: 2
 No. 1, Yankee dryer, total capacity 10,710 mt/y, Trim width 2.1 m, Packaging papers, Specialty and industrial
 No. 2, fourdrinier, total capacity 24,990 mt/y, Trim width 2.75 m, Specialty and industrial, Packaging papers
Finishing Equipment:
 Supercalenders: 2 at 8,000 mt/y
 Rewinders: 3 at 25,000 mt/y
Energy Data:
 Power boilers
 Electrical demand for mill: 82 MWh/D

ⓟⓜLwarcel Celulose Ltda.
Lençóis Paulista Mill
Ownership: 99.99% by The Lwart Group
Rodovia Marechal Rondon, Km. 303.5
18682-970 Lençóis Paulista, SP
Brazil
Mailing Address: 441, 18682-970 Lençóis Paulista, Brazil
 Phone: (55) 14 3269 5100
 Fax: (55) 14 3269 5101
 Email: grupolwart@lwart.com.br, comercial@lwarcel.com.br, corporativos@grupolwart.com.b
 Web Address: www.lwart.com.br
Personnel:
 Gen. Dir.: Luis Kunzel
 Phone: (55) 14 3269 5081
 Fax: (55) 14 3269 5005
 Email: lkunzel@lwarcel.com.br
 Mill Mgr.: Pedro Stefanini
 Phone: (55) 14 3269 5152
 Email: pstefanini@lwarcel.com.br
 Export Mgr.: Elio Moraes
 Phone: (55) 14 3269 5205
 Fax: (55) 14 3269 5101
 Email: emoraes@lwarcel.com.br
 Prod. Mgr.: Dalton Manzi
 Phone: (55) 14 3269 5211
 Fax: (55) 14 3269 5101
 Email: dmanzi@lwarcel.com.br
 Commer. Mgr.: José Wilson Petenazzi
 Phone: (55) 14 3269 5155
 Fax: (55) 14 3269 5101
 Email: jpettenazzi@lwarcel.com.br
 Recovery Mgr.: César Anfe
 Phone: (55) 14 3269 5190
 Fax: (55) 14 3269 5101
 Email: canfe@lwarcel.com.br
 Mktg. Mgr.: Eliane Oliveira da Silva
 Phone: (55) 14 3269 5051
 Email: esilva@lwarcel.com.br
 Maint. Mgr.: Joselio Rodriguez
 Phone: (55) 14 3269 5160
 Fax: (55) 14 3269 5101
 Prod. Eng.: Marcelino Freitas
 Phone: (55) 14 3269 5100
 Fax: (55) 14 3269 5101
 Maint. Eng.: Mauro Arrabal
 Phone: (55) 14 3269 5100
 Fax: (55) 14 3269 5101
 Maint. Coordinator: Luiz Fernando Attrot Vital
 Phone: (55) 14 3269 5100
 Fax: (55) 14 3269 5101
Total Employees of Company: 725
Total Employees at this Location: 462
Type of Operation: Pulp mill
Pulp Grades and Capacities:
 Total pulp capacity: 251,462 mt/y
 Pulp available for market: 249,900 mt/y
 Chemical Pulp: 251,462 mt/y
Pulp Mill Data:
 Chemical Pulping Systems:
 Continuous digesters: 1
Pulp Lines: 1
 Bleach Plant Systems: 1
 Chemical Pulping System, Type: Eucalyptus, Sequence: O_2 ADoEopD, Capacity 240,000 admt/y
 Chemical Recovery Equipment:
 Evaporator lines: 1
 Recovery boilers: 1
 Lime Kiln
 Pulp Dryers:
 Flakt dryer 1, Fourdriniers 1, Wet Lap machine 1
Energy Data:
 Power boilers: 2
 Steam turbines: 2 at 16.5, 21.7 MW
 Electrical demand for mill: 543 MWh/D

ⓜMadepar Papel e Celulose S.A.
Rua Oscar Gomes Cardim, 161
04580-040 São Paulo, SP
Brazil
 Phone: (55) 11 5033 4866
 Fax: (55) 11 5532 0411
 Email: sac@madepar.com.br
 Web Address: www.madeparpapel.com.br
Personnel:
 Pres.: Wilson Dissenha
 Phone: (55) 11 5033 4866
 Fax: (55) 11 5532 0411
 HR Asst.: Tatiana Ap. Silva de Camargo
 Phone: (55) 11 5033 4866
 Fax: (55) 11 5532 0411
Mill Locations:
 Madepar Papel e Celulose S.A., Aparecida Mill, Rua João Aprígio Costa 7, 125070-000 Aparecida, SP, Brazil, Capacity: 47,838 mt/y, (Paper mill, Paperboard mill)
 Phone: (55) 12 3104 2122
 Fax: (55) 12 3105 3129

ⓜMadepar Papel e Celulose S.A.
Aparecida Mill
Rua João Aprígio Costa 7
125070-000 Aparecida, SP
Brazil
 Phone: (55) 12 3104 2122
 Fax: (55) 12 3105 3129
 Web Address: www.madeparpapel.com.br
Personnel:
 Admin. Mgr.: Claudio Santi
 Phone: (55) 12 3104 2122
 Fax: (55) 12 3105 3129
 Email: claudio.santi@madeparpapel.com.br
Total Employees at this Location: 80
Type of Operation: Paper mill, Paperboard mill
Pulp Grades and Capacities:
 Total pulp capacity: 48,829 mt/y
 Recycled Pulping: 48,829 mt/y
Pulp Mill Data:
 Recycled Fiber Treatment Lines:
 Recycled packaging pulping lines: 1 at 49,000
Paper/Paperboard Grades and Capacities:
 Total paper and paperboard capacity: 47,838 mt/y
 Linerboard: 21,420 mt/y
 Corrugating medium/fluting: 26,418 mt/y
Paper and Paperboard Mill Data:
Paper Machines: 1
 No. 1, fourdrinier, total capacity 47,838 mt/y, Trim width 2.6 m, Corrugating medium/fluting, Linerboard
Finishing Equipment:
 Rewinders: 1
Energy Data:
 Power boilers: 1
 Electrical demand for mill: 81 MWh/D

ⓜManikraft Guaianazes Ind. de Celulose e Papel Ltda.
Rua Tupi 330/350 - Pacaembu
01233-902 São Paulo, SP
Brazil
 Phone: (55) 11 3825 7211
 Fax: (55) 11 3826 4744
 Email: manikraft@manikraft.com.br
 Web Address: www.manikraft.com.br
Personnel:
 Pres.: Francisco Caseiro
 Phone: (55) 11 3825 7211
 Fax: (55) 11 3826 4744
 Supt. Dir.: Olympio da Silva Caseiro
 Phone: (55) 11 3825 7211

Brazil

Fax: (55) 11 3826 4744
Comm. Dir./Admin. Dir.: Oswaldo da Silva Caseiro
Phone: (55) 11 3825 7211
Fax: (55) 11 3826 4744
Finan. Dir.: Luiz Gonçalves Caseiro
Phone: (55) 11 3825 7211
Fax: (55) 11 3826 4744
HR Mgr.: Rodrigo Pillat Caseiro
Phone: (55) 11 3825 7211
Fax: (55) 11 3826 4744
System Mgr.: Laerte Manikraft
Phone: (55) 11 3825 7211
Fax: (55) 11 3826 4744
IT Mgr.: Marcelo Carvalho
Phone: (55) 11 3825 7211
Fax: (55) 11 3826 4744
Mktg. Analyst: Fabio Cardi
Phone: (55) 11 3825 7211
Fax: (55) 11 3826 4744
Total Employees of Company: 700
Mill Locations:
Manikraft Guaianazes Ind. de Celulose e Papel Ltda., Guaianazes Mill, Rua S. Pascal, 269, 08430-820 Guaianazes, SP, Brazil, Capacity: 36,057 mt/y, (Paper mill)
Phone: (55) 11 2511 5888
Fax: (55) 11 6511 9747
Email: geraldo@manikraft.com.br

ⓜManikraft Guaianazes Ind. de Celulose e Papel Ltda.
Guaianazes Mill
Rua S. Pascal, 269
08430-820 Guaianazes, SP
Brazil
Phone: (55) 11 2511 5888
Fax: (55) 11 6511 9747
Email: geraldo@manikraft.com.br
Web Address: www.manikraft.com.br
Personnel:
Admin. Mgr.: José Geraldo
Phone: (55) 11 2511 5888
Fax: (55) 11 6511 9747
Tech. Dir.: Vicenzo Bove
Phone: (55) 11 2511 5888
Fax: (55) 11 6511 9747
Prod. Mgr.: João Torquato
Phone: (55) 11 2511 5888
Fax: (55) 11 6511 9747
Quality Mgr.: Silvana Pozzi
Phone: (55) 11 2511 5888
Fax: (55) 11 6511 9747
Asst. Sales: Daniel Ramos
Phone: (55) 11 2511 5888
Fax: (55) 11 6511 9747
Total Employees at this Location: 175
Type of Operation: Paper mill
Paper/Paperboard Grades and Capacities:
Total paper and paperboard capacity: 36,057 mt/y
Tissue: 36,057 mt/y
Paper and Paperboard Mill Data:
Paper Machines: 2
No. 1, fourdrinier, total capacity 16,422 mt/y, Trim width 1.85 m, Tissue, Uncoated woodfree/freesheet
No. 2, fourdrinier, total capacity 19,635 mt/y, Trim width 2.18 m, Tissue
Energy Data:
Power boilers
Electrical demand for mill: 103 MWh/D

ⓗⓜMarombas Indústria e Comércio de Madeiras e Papelão
Curitibanos Mill
Rua Valdir Ortigari, 220
89520-000 Curitibanos, SC
Brazil
Phone: (55) 49 3245 0871
Fax: (55) 49 3245 1876
Email: marombas@brturbo.com.br
Personnel:

Pres./Owner: Carlos Augusto Groene Bossardi
Phone: (55) 49 3245 0871
Admin. Dir./Owner: Mirian Ruth Groene Bossardi
Phone: (55) 49 3245 0871
Ind. Dir./Owner: Paulo Sérgio Groene Bossardi
Phone: (55) 49 3245 0871
Total Employees of Company: 95
Type of Operation: Paperboard mill
Paper/Paperboard Grades and Capacities:
Total paper and paperboard capacity: 12,000 mt/y
Boxboard/cartonboard: 12,000 mt/y
Paper and Paperboard Mill Data:
Paper Machines: 2
No. 1, total capacity 6,000 mt/y, Boxboard/cartonboard
No. 2, total capacity 6,000 mt/y, Boxboard/cartonboard

ⓗⓜMD Papéis Ltda.
Caieiras Mill
Ownership: Formitex Group
Rod. Pres. Tancredo de Almeida Neves, km 34, CP 21
07700-000 Caieiras, SP
Brazil
Phone: (55) 11 4441 7800
Fax: (55) 11 4605 2195
Email: sac@mdpapeis.com.br
Web Address: www.mdpapeis.com.br, www.formitex.com.br
Personnel:
Supt.: Carlos Barbosa
Phone: (55) 11 4441 7800
Fax: (55) 11 4605 2195
Email: cbarbosa@mdpapeis.com.br
Total Employees of Company: 1,032
Total Employees at this Location: 275
Type of Operation: Paper mill
Mill Locations:
MD Papéis Ltda., Limeira Mill, Rua Ferreira Bitencourt, 100, 13485-119 Limeira, SP, Brazil, Capacity: 55,000 mt/y, (Paperboard mill)
Phone: (55) 19 3446 7000
Fax: (55) 19 3451 1169
Paper/Paperboard Grades and Capacities:
Total paper and paperboard capacity: 61,047 mt/y
Packaging papers: 37,128 mt/y
Specialty and industrial: 23,919 mt/y
Paper and Paperboard Mill Data:
Stock Preparation:
Pulpers: 5
Refiners: 15
Paper Machines: 4
PM4, fourdrinier, total capacity 7,140 mt/y, Trim width 2.2 m, Packaging papers
PM5, fourdrinier, total capacity 9,996 mt/y, Trim width 2.2 m, Packaging papers
PM7, DuoFormer, total capacity 23,919 mt/y, Trim width 2.5 m, Specialty and industrial
PM8, fourdrinier, total capacity 19,992 mt/y, Trim width 2.6 m, Packaging papers
Finishing Equipment:
Supercalenders: 3
Rewinders: 4 at 80,000 mt/y
Sheeters: 1 at 10,000 mt/y
Energy Data:
Power boilers: 3
Electrical demand for mill: 73 MWh/D

ⓜMD Papéis Ltda.
Limeira Mill
Rua Ferreira Bitencourt, 100
13485-119 Limeira, SP
Brazil
Phone: (55) 19 3446 7000
Fax: (55) 19 3451 1169
Web Address: www.mdpapeis.com.br, www.formitex.com.br
Total Employees at this Location: 255
Type of Operation: Paperboard mill
Pulp Grades and Capacities:
Total pulp capacity: 60,000 mt/y

Paper/Paperboard Grades and Capacities:
Total paper and paperboard capacity: 55,000 mt/y
Boxboard/cartonboard: 55,000 mt/y
Paper and Paperboard Mill Data:
Paper Machines: 3
PM 1, (idle since 2009, due to restart for the second half of 2013.), total capacity 20,000 mt/y
PM 2, total capacity 31,000 mt/y, Boxboard/cartonboard
PM 3, total capacity 24,000 mt/y, Boxboard/cartonboard

ⓜMelhoramentos Florestal S.A.
Ownership: Empresas CMPC S.A.
Rua Tito 479
05051-000 São Paulo, SP
Brazil
Phone: (55) 11 3675-6463
Web Address: www.melhoramentos.com.br/v2/florestal/
Mill Locations:
Melhoramentos Florestal S.A., Carnanducaia Mill, Fazenda Levantina, s/n°, 37650-000 Camanducaia, MG, Brazil, (Pulp mill)
Phone: (55) 35 3433 8200
Fax: (55) 35 3433 8224
Email: jmoretti@melhoramentos.com.br

ⓜMelhoramentos Papéis Ltda.
Ownership: 100% by Empresas CMPC S.A.
Rua Tito 479
05051-000 São Paulo, SP
Brazil
Phone: (55) 11 3874 0600/0609
Fax: (55) 11 3874 0792
Web Address: www.melhoramentoscmpc.com.br
Personnel:
CEO: Sergio Sesiki
Phone: (55) 11 3874 0600/0609
Fax: (55) 11 3874 0792
Prod. Mgr.: Tatiana Schwanz
Phone: (55) 11 3874 0600/0609
Fax: (55) 11 3874 0792
Commer. Dir. (Institutional Div.): Eucário Cantanhede
Phone: (55) 11 3874 0600/0609
Fax: (55) 11 3874 0792
Email: ejcantan@cmpc.com.br
Logist. Mgr.: Paulo Andrade
Phone: (55) 11 3874 0600/0609
Fax: (55) 11 3874 0792
Mktg & Trade Mktg Mgr.: Thiago Garcia
Phone: (55) 11 3874 0600/0609
Fax: (55) 11 3874 0792
Indus. Mgr.: Marcio Matandos
Phone: (55) 11 3874 0600/0609
Fax: (55) 11 3874 0792
IT Mgr.: Julio Cezar Nicolosi Motta Junior
Phone: (55) 11 3874 0600/0609
Fax: (55) 11 3874 0792
Key Account Mgr.: Graziela Mól De Araújo Chaves
Phone: (55) 11 3874 0600/0609
Fax: (55) 11 3874 0792
Total Employees at this Location: 322
Mill Locations:
Melhoramentos Papéis Ltda., Caieiras Mill, Rodovia Pres. Tancredo de Almeida Neves, Km. 34, 07700-000 Caieiras, SP, Brazil, Capacity: 98,889 mt/y, (Pulp mill, Paper mill)
Phone: (55) 11 4441 7200
Fax: (55) 11 4441 7202
Email: comunica@cmpc.com.br
Melhoramentos Papéis Ltda., Mogi das Cruzes Mill, Av. Lourenço de Souza Franco, 2655, 08750-560 Mogi das Cruzes, SP, Brazil, Capacity: 33,915 mt/y, (Paper mill)
Phone: (55) 11 4795 9411
Fax: (55) 11 4727 2330

ⓜMelhoramentos Papéis Ltda.
Caieiras Mill
Ownership: 100% by Empresas CMPC S.A.

Brazil

Rodovia Pres. Tancredo de Almeida Neves, Km. 34
07700-000 Caieiras, SP
Brazil
 Phone: (55) 11 4441 7200
 Fax: (55) 11 4441 7202
 Email: comunica@cmpc.com.br
 Web Address: www.melhoramentos.com.br/papeis,
 www.cmpc.com.br
Personnel:
Industrial Dir.: Marcio David Carvalho
Phone: (55) 11 4441 7206
Fax: (55) 11 4441 7202
Email: mdcarvalho@cmpc.com.br
Mill Mgr.: Luciano Anastacio Nunes
Phone: (55) 11 4441 7340
Fax: (55) 11 4441 7202
Email: lanunes@cmpc.com.br
Proj. & Eng. Mgr.: Gilberto Emílio Genetti
Phone: (55) 11 4441 7919
Fax: (55) 11 4441 7202
Email: gegenetti@cmpc.com.br
Total Employees at this Location: 480
Type of Operation: Pulp mill, Paper mill
Pulp Grades and Capacities:
Total pulp capacity: 78,627 mt/y
Pulp available for market: 53,907 mt/y
Mechanical Pulp: 78,627 mt/y

Pulp Mill Data:
Mechanical Pulping Systems:
CTMP systems: 1
Bleach Plant Systems: 1
Mechanical Pulping System, Type: Hardwood,
Sequence: P
Chemical Recovery Equipment:
Evaporator lines: 1
Pulp Dryers:
Pulp Dryers 1
Paper/Paperboard Grades and Capacities:
Total paper and paperboard capacity: 98,889 mt/y
Tissue: 98,889 mt/y
Paper and Paperboard Mill Data:
Paper Machines: 3
No. 8, crescent former, total capacity 24,990 mt/y, Trim width 3.36 m, Tissue, Uncoated woodfree/freesheet
No. 9, crescent former, total capacity 53,907 mt/y, Trim width 3.5 m, Tissue, Uncoated woodfree/freesheet
No. 10, crescent former, total capacity 19,992 mt/y, Trim width 2.26 m, Tissue, Uncoated woodfree/freesheet
Energy Data:
Power boilers
TMP Reboiler
Steam turbines: 2
Electrical demand for mill: 781 MWh/D

ⓜMelhoramentos Florestal S.A.
Camanducaia Mill
Ownership: Empresas CMPC S.A.
Fazenda Levantina, s/nº
37650-000 Camanducaia, MG
Brazil
 Phone: (55) 35 3433 8200
 Fax: (55) 35 3433 8224
 Email: jmoretti@melhoramentos.com.br
 Web Address: www.melhoramentos.com.br/v2
Personnel:
Prod. Chief: Carlos Geraldo Mendes
Phone: (55) 35 3433 8250
Fax: (55) 35 3433 8224
Prod. Mgr.: Clovis Alcione P
Phone: (55) 35 3433 8200
Fax: (55) 35 3433 8224
Maint. Supervisor: Jose Volmir Pinto
Phone: (55) 35 3433 8200
Fax: (55) 35 3433 8224
Commer. Supervisor: Ilton Jose Rosolem
Phone: (55) 35 3433 8200
Fax: (55) 35 3433 8224
Supt.: Leandro B Leandro B
Phone: (55) 35 3433 8200
Fax: (55) 35 3433 8224

Total Employees at this Location: 137
Type of Operation: Pulp mill
Pulp Grades and Capacities:
Pulp available for market: 89,964 mt/y
Mechanical Pulp: 90,635 mt/y
Pulp Mill Data:
Mechanical Pulping Systems:
Not Given: 1
Bleach Plant Systems: 1
Mechanical Pulping System - TGW, Type: Hardwood/Softwood, Sequence: P
Pulp Dryers:
Fourdriniers 1
Energy Data:
Power boilers: 1
Steam turbines: 1 at 2 MW
Electrical demand for mill: 485 MWh/D

ⓜMelhoramentos Papéis Ltda.
Mogi das Cruzes Mill
Ownership: 100% by Empresas CMPC S.A.
Av. Lourenço de Souza Franco, 2655
08750-560 Mogi das Cruzes, SP
Brazil
 Phone: (55) 11 4795 9411
 Fax: (55) 11 4727 2330
 Web Address: www.cmpc.com.br
Personnel:
Chief Eng.: Nelson Nogueira Ignez
Phone: (55) 11 4795 9426
Fax: (55) 11 4727 2330
Email: nnignez@cmpc.com.br
Proj. & Eng. Mgr.: Gilberto Emílio Genetti
Phone: (55) 11 4441 7319
Fax: (55) 11 4441 7313
Email: gegenett@cmpc.com.br
Ind. Dir.: Alline Cunha
Phone: (55) 11 4795 9417
Fax: (55) 11 4727 6891
Email: amlcunha@cmpc.com.br
Total Employees at this Location: 350
Type of Operation: Paper mill
Paper/Paperboard Grades and Capacities:
Total paper and paperboard capacity: 33,915 mt/y
Tissue: 33,915 mt/y
Paper and Paperboard Mill Data:
Stock Preparation:
Pulpers: 1
Refiners: 2
Paper Machines: 1
No. 9, crescent former, total capacity 33,915 mt/y, Trim width 2.75 m, Tissue, Uncoated woodfree/freesheet
Finishing Equipment:
Rewinders: 1
Energy Data:
Power boilers: 3

ⓜMili S.A.
Ownership: Valdemar Lissoni, Vanderlei Micheletto
Rodovia BR 116, km 109, No. 21561, Pinheirinho
80690-500 Curitiba, PR
Brazil
 Phone: (55) 41 3227 8000
 Fax: (55) 41 3227 8008/9
 Web Address: www.mili.com.br
Personnel:
Pres.: Valdemar Lissoni
Phone: (55) 41 3227 8000
Fax: (55) 41 3227 8008/9
VP, Commer. Dir.: Vanderlei Micheletto
Phone: (55) 41 3227 8000
Fax: (55) 41 3227 8008/9
Tech. Dir.: Daniel Signori
Phone: (55) 41 3227 8000
Fax: (55) 41 3227 8008/9
Email: daniel@mili.com.br
Coord. Mktg.: Cinthia Micheletto
Phone: (55) 41 3227 8000
Fax: (55) 41 3227 8008/9

Email: cinthia@mili.com.br
IT Mgr.: Edvaldo P.
Phone: (55) 41 3227 8000
Fax: (55) 41 3227 8008/9
Chemical Eng.: Jefferson S.
Phone: (55) 41 3227 8000
Fax: (55) 41 3227 8008/9
Total Employees of Company: 1,100
Mill Locations:
Mili S.A., Tres Barras Mill, Rodovia SC 303, Km. 5.5, 89460-000 Tres Barras, SC, Brazil, Capacity: 137,445 mt/y, (Paper mill)
Phone: (55) 47 3621 4100
Fax: (55) 47 3621 4103
Email: falecom@mili.com.br

ⓜMili S.A.
Tres Barras Mill
Rodovia SC 303, Km. 5.5
89460-000 Tres Barras, SC
Brazil
 Phone: (55) 47 3621 4100
 Fax: (55) 47 3621 4103
 Email: falecom@mili.com.br
 Web Address: www.mili.com.br
Personnel:
Pres.: Valdemar Lissoni
Phone: (55) 47 3621 4100
Fax: (55) 47 3621 4103
VP, Commer. Dir.: Vanderlei Micheletto
Phone: (55) 47 3621 4100
Fax: (55) 47 3621 4103
Tech. Dir.: Daniel Signori
Phone: (55) 47 3621 4100
Fax: (55) 47 3621 4103
Email: daniel@mili.com.br
Coord. Mktg.: Cinthia Micheletto
Phone: (55) 47 3621 4100
Fax: (55) 47 3621 4103
Email: cinthia@mili.com.br
Total Employees at this Location: 426
Type of Operation: Paper mill
Pulp Grades and Capacities:
Total pulp capacity: 99,362 mt/y
Recycled Pulping: 99,362 mt/y
Pulp Mill Data:
Bleach Plant Systems: 1
Recycled Pulping System, Type: DIP
Recycled Fiber Treatment Lines:
Flotation deinking lines: 1
Paper/Paperboard Grades and Capacities:
Total paper and paperboard capacity: 137,445 mt/y
Tissue: 137,445 mt/y
Paper and Paperboard Mill Data:
Paper Machines: 6
No. 1, fourdrinier, total capacity 14,280 mt/y, Trim width 2.4 m, Tissue, Uncoated woodfree/freesheet
No. 2, fourdrinier, total capacity 7,140 mt/y, Trim width 1.2 m, Tissue, Uncoated woodfree/freesheet
No. 3, crescent former, total capacity 17,850 mt/y, Trim width 2.4 m, Tissue, Uncoated woodfree/freesheet
No. 4, crescent former, total capacity 30,345 mt/y, Trim width 2.8 m, Tissue, Uncoated woodfree/freesheet
No. 5, crescent former, total capacity 32,130 mt/y, Trim width 2.8 m, Tissue
No. 6, crescent former, total capacity 35,700 mt/y, Trim width 2.8 m, Tissue
Energy Data:
Power boilers
Steam turbines
Electrical demand for mill: 570 MWh/D

ⓜMimopel Papéis Higiénicos Ltda.
Estr. de Pau Grande 13
25935-000 MAGE, Rio de Janeiro, RJ
Brazil
 Phone: (55) 21 2659 4685
 Fax: (55) 21 2659 4685
Mill Locations:
Mimopel Papéis Higiénicos Ltda., Magé Mill, Estr. de

Brazil

Pau grande 13, Magé, RJ, Brazil, Capacity: 3,000 mt/y, (Paper mill)
Phone: (55) 212 659 4685
Fax: (55) 212 659 4685

ⓂMimopel Papéis Higiénicos Ltda.
Magé Mill
Estr. de Pau grande 13
Magé, RJ
Brazil
  Phone: (55) 212 659 4685
  Fax: (55) 212 659 4685
Type of Operation: Paper mill
Paper/Paperboard Grades and Capacities:
  Total paper and paperboard capacity: 3,000 mt/y
  Tissue: 3,000 mt/y

ⓄⓂMultiverde Papéis Especiais Ltda.
Mogi das Cruzes Mill
Ownership: 100% by Mogi Papers LLC (Delaware, USA)
Rua Presidente Campos Salles nº 6
08770-210 Mogi das Cruzes, SP
Brazil
Mailing Address: CP 90, 08770-210 Mogi das Cruzes, Brazil
  Phone: (55) 11 2159 1800/1884
  Fax: (55) 11 4791 3720
  Email: marketing@mvpapeis.com.br
  Web Address: www.multiverdepapeis.com, www.linhaimaginario.com.br
Personnel:
  CEO - Exec. Dir.: Marcus Vinicius Borba Melo
  Phone: (55) 11 2159 1800
  Fax: (55) 11 4791 3720
  Email: marcus.melo@mvpapeis.com.br
  Exec. Dir.: Fernando Carlos Pereira
  Phone: (55) 11 2159 1850
  Fax: (55) 11 4791 3720
  Email: fernando.pereira@mvpapeis.com.br
  Sls. & Mktg. Mgr.: Milton Rodrigues Alves
  Phone: (55) 11 2159 1800
  Fax: (55) 11 4791 3720
  Email: milton.alves@mvpapeis.com.br
  Qlty. Mgr.: Clovis Oliveira
  Phone: (55) 11 2159 1800
  Fax: (55) 11 4791 3720
  Email: clovis.oliveira@mvpapeis.com.br
Total Employees of Company: 219
Total Employees at this Location: 219
Type of Operation: Paper mill
Paper/Paperboard Grades and Capacities:
  Total paper and paperboard capacity: 25,000 mt/y
  Uncoated woodfree/freesheet: 8,000 mt/y
  Packaging papers
  Specialty and industrial: 17,000 mt/y
Paper and Paperboard Mill Data:
  Stock Preparation:
  Pulpers: 2
  Refiners: 4
Paper Machines: 2
  No. 1, fourdrinier, total capacity 15,000 mt/y, Trim width 2.04 m, Specialty and industrial
  No. 2, fourdrinier, Yankee dryer, total capacity 10,000 mt/y, Trim width 2.12 m, Specialty and industrial
Finishing Equipment:
  Winders: 2 at 25,000 mt/y
  Calenders: 2
  Rewinders: 3 at 25,000 mt/y
  Sheeters: 1 at 20,000 mt/y
Energy Data:
  Power boilers: 1
  Electrical demand for mill: 45 MWh/D

ⓂMunksjö Brasil Industria e Comercio de Comercio de papeis especiais Ltda.
Jacareí Paper Mill
Ownership: 100% by Munksjö Oyj
Rdv. Gen. Euryale de Jesus Zerbini, km 84
12340-010 Jacareí, SP
Brazil
  Phone: (55) 12 2127 9300
  Fax: (55) 12 2127 9330
  Email: info@munksjo.com
  Web Address: www.munksjo.com
Personnel:
  Mill Mgr.: Luis Coelho
  Phone: (55) 12 2127 9300
  Fax: (55) 12 2127 9330
  VP- Sales South America: Luciano Fernandes Neves
  Phone: (55) 12 2127 9300
  Fax: (55) 12 2127 9330
  HR Mgr.: José Laercio Pereira
  Phone: (55) 12 2127 9413
  Fax: (55) 12 2127 9330
  Maint. Mgr.: Luiz Eugênio Ribeiro Garcia
  Phone: (55) 12 2127 9300
  Fax: (55) 12 2127 9330
Total Employees at this Location: 233
Type of Operation: Paper mill
Paper/Paperboard Grades and Capacities:
  Total paper and paperboard capacity: 109,956 mt/y
  Specialty and industrial: 109,956 mt/y
Paper and Paperboard Mill Data:
  Stock Preparation:
  Pulpers: 1
  Refiners: 4
Paper Machines: 1
  No. 1, (Suppliers: Federal/Voith), fourdrinier, total capacity 109,956 mt/y, Trim width 4.2 m, Specialty and industrial
Coating Machines: 1
  No. 2, total capacity 79,500 mt/y., off machine
Finishing Equipment:
  Winders: 3 at 88,000 mt/y
  Sheeters: 3 at 61,600 mt/y
Energy Data:
  Electrical demand for mill: 285 MWh/D

ⓄⓂNittow Papel S.A.
Campinas Mill
Rua Coronel Alfredo Nascimento, 516 - Sousas
13106-000 Campinas, SP
Brazil
  Phone: (55) 19 3258 2125
  Fax: (55) 19 3258 2125
  Email: comercial@nittow.com.br
  Web Address: www.nittow.com.br
Personnel:
  Superintendent Dir.: Roberto Nakoto Nishiyama
  Phone: (55) 19 3258 2125
  Commer. Dir.: Marcelo Nishiyama
  Phone: (55) 19 3258 2125
Total Employees of Company: 55
Total Employees at this Location: 32
Type of Operation: Paper mill
Paper/Paperboard Grades and Capacities:
  Total paper and paperboard capacity: 14,000 mt/y
  Packaging papers: 10,000 mt/y
  Corrugating medium/fluting: 4,000 mt/y

ⓄⓂNobrecel S.A. Celulose e Papel
Pindamonhangaba Mill
Fazenda Coruputuba CP 01
12400-970 Pindamonhangaba, SP
Brazil
  Phone: (55) 12 3644 7000
  Fax: (55) 12 3643 2423
  Email: nobrecel@nobrecel.com.br
  Web Address: www.nobrecel.com.br
Personnel:
  Mill Dir.: Milva Monteiro Casagrande
  Phone: (55) 12 3644 7000
  Fax: (55) 12 3643 2423
  Finan. Dir.: Evandro Cesare Raimundo
  Phone: (55) 12 3644 7000
  Fax: (55) 12 3643 2423
  Tech. Dir.: Ivano Carvalho Simões
  Phone: (55) 12 3644 7000
  Fax: (55) 12 3643 2423
  Chief Eng. & Maint. Mgr.: Antonio Nelson de Campos
  Phone: (55) 12 3644 7000
  Fax: (55) 12 3643 2423
  Paper Admin. Accessory: Alfredo Ricardo da Palma Rodrigues
  Phone: (55) 12 3644 7000
  Fax: (55) 12 3643 2423
  Email: vendas@nobrecel.com.br
Total Employees of Company: 500
Total Employees at this Location: 180
Type of Operation: Pulp mill, Paper mill, Paperboard mill
Pulp Grades and Capacities:
  Total pulp capacity: 73,000 mt/y
  Pulp available for market: 20,000 mt/y
  Chemical Pulp: 73,000 mt/y
Pulp Mill Data:
  Chemical Pulping Systems:
  Batch digesters: 4
Pulp Lines: 1
  Bleach Plant Systems: 1
  No. 1, Sequence: CEoHH
  Chemical Recovery Equipment:
  Evaporator lines: 1
  Recovery boilers: 1
  Lime Kiln
  Pulp Dryers:
  Other dryers 1, Other dryers 1
Paper/Paperboard Grades and Capacities:
  Total paper and paperboard capacity: 42,000 mt/y
  Uncoated woodfree/freesheet: 24,000 mt/y
  Tissue: 18,000 mt/y
Paper and Paperboard Mill Data:
  Stock Preparation:
  Pulpers: 3
  Refiners: 7
Paper Machines: 4
  No. 1, Yankee dryer, total capacity 9,000 mt/y, Trim width 2.4 m, Tissue
  No. 2, cylinder, total capacity 10,000 mt/y, Trim width 2.4 m, Tissue
  No. 3, (idle, due to restart before July 2016), Yankee dryer, total capacity 11,000 mt/y, Trim width 2.3 m, Tissue
  No. 4, (idle, due to restart near end of 2014), fourdrinier, total capacity 25,000 mt/y, Trim width 2.8 m, Uncoated woodfree/freesheet
Coating Machines: 1
  No. 1, total capacity 7,200 mt/y., on machine
Finishing Equipment:
  Supercalenders: 1
  Rewinders: 4
  Sheeters: 3
Energy Data:
  Power boilers: 5
  Steam turbines: 1

ⓄⓂNorske Skog Pisa S.A.
Jaguariaíva Mill
Company is for sale
Ownership: 51% by Papeles Bío Bío, 49% by Norske Skogindustrier ASA
Rodovia PR 151, Km. 207.5
84200-000 Jaguariaíva, PR
Brazil
  Phone: (55) 43 3535 8000
  Fax: (55) 43 3535 2627
  Email: contato@norskeskog.com.br
  Web Address: www.norske-skog.com, www.norskeskog.com.br
Personnel:
  Gen. Mgr.: Alex Pornilio
  Phone: (55) 43 3535 8000
  Fax: (55) 43 3535 2627
  Bus. Develop. Mgr.: Stanley Melo
  Phone: (55) 43 3535 8000
  Fax: (55) 43 3535 2627

Tech. Dir.: Reinaldo Oliveira
Phone: (55) 43 3535 8000
Fax: (55) 43 3535 2627
Chief Eng., Eng. Mgr.: Lidiane A Lidiane A
Phone: (55) 43 3535 8000
Fax: (55) 43 3535 2627
Technol. Mgr.: Marcio P Marcio P
Phone: (55) 43 3535 8000
Fax: (55) 43 3535 2627
Purch. Mgr.: Leandro D Leandro D
Phone: (55) 43 3535 8000
Fax: (55) 43 3535 2627
Total Employees of Company: 317
Total Employees at this Location: 275
Type of Operation: Paper mill
Pulp Grades and Capacities:
Total pulp capacity: 161,378 mt/y
Mechanical Pulp: 161,378 mt/y
Pulp Mill Data:
Mechanical Pulping Systems:
Conventional grinders: 7
TMP systems: 1
Bleach Plant Systems: 1
Paper/Paperboard Grades and Capacities:
Total paper and paperboard capacity: 169,575 mt/y
Newsprint: 169,575 mt/y
Paper and Paperboard Mill Data:
Stock Preparation:
Pulpers: 3
Refiners: 5
Paper Machines: 1
No. 1, DuoFormer, total capacity 169,575 mt/y, Trim width 6.7 m, Newsprint
Finishing Equipment:
Winders: 1 at 185,000 mt/y
Calenders: 1
Rewinders: 1 at 4,000 mt/y
Energy Data:
Power boilers: 2
TMP Reboiler
Electrical demand for mill: 1,410 MWh/D

ⓂIndústrias Novacki S.A.
Ownership: 100% by Novacki family
Rua Júlia Amazonas, 30 - Centro
89400-000 Porto União, SC
Brazil
Phone: (55) 42 3521 7000
Fax: (55) 42 3521 7056
Email: novacki@novacki.com.br
Personnel:
Pres.: Mauro Novacki
Phone: (55) 42 3521 7000
Fax: (55) 42 3521 7056
Admin. & Finan. Dir.: Marcelo Novacki
Phone: (55) 42 3521 7000
Fax: (55) 42 3521 7056
Industrial Dir.: Mauro Novacki Jr.
Phone: (55) 42 3521 7000
Fax: (55) 42 3521 7056
Admin. Commer. Asst.: Marcos Bachmann
Phone: (55) 42 3521 7000
Fax: (55) 42 3521 7056
Email: marcosrb@novacki.com.br
Total Employees of Company: 723
Mill Locations:
Indústrias Novacki S.A., Porto União Mill, Rua Expedicionário Eugênio de Almeida, 30 - Santa Rosa, 89400-000 Porto União, SC, Brazil, Capacity: 25,500 mt/y, (Paper mill)
Phone: (55) 42 3522 1082
Fax: (55) 42 3522 1082
Email: novacki@novacki.com.br
Indústrias Novacki S.A., União da Vitória Mill, Avenida Porto Vitoria, s/no. - São Gabriel, União da Vitoria, PR, Brazil, Capacity: 89,964 mt/y, (Paperboard mill)
Phone: (55) 42 3521 3400
Fax: (55) 42 3523 3330
Email: novacki@novacki.com.br

ⓂIndústrias Novacki S.A.
Porto União Mill
Rua Expedicionário Eugênio de Almeida, 30 - Santa Rosa
89400-000 Porto União, SC
Brazil
Phone: (55) 42 3522 1082
Fax: (55) 42 3522 1082
Email: novacki@novacki.com.br
Personnel:
Ind. Dir.: José Roberto Mateus
Phone: (55) 42 3522 1082
Email: mateus@nvkpe.com.br
Supply Mgr.: Maruhan Antonio Abdalla
Phone: (55) 42 3522 1082
Email: maruhan@nvkpe.com.br
Type of Operation: Paper mill
Paper/Paperboard Grades and Capacities:
Total paper and paperboard capacity: 25,500 mt/y
Packaging papers: 25,500 mt/y
Paper and Paperboard Mill Data:
Paper Machines: 1
PM 1, fourdrinier, total capacity 24,000 mt/y, Trim width 2 m, Packaging papers

ⓂIndústrias Novacki S.A.
União da Vitória Mill
Avenida Porto Vitoria, s/no. - São Gabriel
União da Vitoria, PR
Brazil
Phone: (55) 42 3521 3400
Fax: (55) 42 3523 3330
Email: novacki@novacki.com.br
Personnel:
Mill Mgr.: Adoberto Gobato
Phone: (55) 42 3521 3400
Fax: (55) 42 3523 3330
HR Mgr.: Karina Novacki
Phone: (55) 42 3521 3400
Fax: (55) 42 3523 3330
Total Employees at this Location: 105
Type of Operation: Paperboard mill
Pulp Grades and Capacities:
Total pulp capacity: 85,791 mt/y
Recycled Pulping: 85,791 mt/y
Pulp Mill Data:
Recycled Fiber Treatment Lines:
Pulpers: 1 at 93,200
Paper/Paperboard Grades and Capacities:
Total paper and paperboard capacity: 89,964 mt/y
Linerboard: 69,972 mt/y
Corrugating medium/fluting: 19,992 mt/y
Paper and Paperboard Mill Data:
Stock Preparation:
Pulpers:
Paper Machines: 1
No. 1, fourdrinier, total capacity 89,964 mt/y, Trim width 2.5 m, Linerboard, Corrugating medium/fluting
Energy Data:
Power boilers
Electrical demand for mill: 146 MWh/D

ⓂOji Papéis Especiais Ltda
Piracicaba Mill
Ownership: 100% by Oji Holdings Corporation
Via Comendador Pedro Morganti, 3393 Bairro Monte Alegre
13415-900 Piracicaba, SP
Brazil
Phone: (55) 19 2106 9200, 19 2106 9609
Fax: (55) 19 2106 9619
Email: lucimara.didone@ojipapeis.com.br
Web Address: www.ojipapeis.com.br
Personnel:
CEO & Pres.: Gilberto 'Júlio' Piatto
Phone: (55) 19 2106 9602
Fax: (55) 19-2106-9619
Email: julio.piatto@ojipapeis.com.br
Production Exec. Officer: Marcelino Sacchi
Phone: (55) 19 2106 9601
Fax: (55) 19-2106-9619
Email: marcelino.sacchi@ojipapeis.com.br
Paper Prod. Mgr.: Fernando Antonio Elihimas Simione
Phone: (55) 19 2106 9689
Fax: (55) 19 2106 9610
Email: fernando.simione@ojipapeis.com.br
Eng. Maint. Utilities Mgr.: José Ernesto Rasera
Phone: (55) 19 2106 9618
Fax: (55) 19 2106 9632
Email: jose.rasera@ojipapeis.com.br
R&D Mgr.: Richardi Fernandes
Phone: (55) 19 2106 9651
Fax: (55) 19 2106 9653
Email: richardi.fernandes@ojipapeis.com.br
Commun. Assist.: Mayara F. Banow
Phone: (55) 11 2138 4195
Fax: (55) 19-2106-9619
Email: mayara.banow@ojipapeis.com.br
Commer. Dir.: Silney Szyszko
Phone: (55) 19 2106 9230
Fax: (55) 19-2106-9619
Email: silney.szyszko@ojipapeis.com.br
Finan. Dir.: Agostinho Monsserrocco Junior
Phone: (55) 19 2106 9686
Fax: (55) 19-2106-9619
Email: agostinho.momsserrocco@ojipapeis.com.br
HR Mgr.: Filipe Santarem Morassi
Phone: (55) 19-2106-9609
Fax: (55) 19-2106-9619
Email: filipe.morassi@ojipapeis.com.br
Total Employees at this Location: 573
Type of Operation: Paper mill
Paper/Paperboard Grades and Capacities:
Total paper and paperboard capacity: 114,988 mt/y
Uncoated woodfree/freesheet: 42,988 mt/y
Coated woodfree/freesheet: 72,000 mt/y
Paper and Paperboard Mill Data:
Stock Preparation:
Pulpers: 3
Refiners: 10
Paper Machines: 2
No. 1, (Major Rebuilds: drivers: hood, QCS. WFU (base paper for thermal & carbonless paper).), fourdrinier, total capacity 29,988 mt/y, Trim width 2.7 m, Uncoated woodfree/freesheet
No. 2, (Major Rebuilds: Duo former/Film Coating/Soft Calender. WFU (base paper for thermal & carbonless paper)), DuoFormer, total capacity 85,000 mt/y, Trim width 4.2 m, Coated woodfree/freesheet, Uncoated woodfree/freesheet
Coating Machines: 5
PC 1, total capacity 25,000 mt/y., off machine
PC 2, total capacity 18,000 mt/y., off machine
PC 3, total capacity 28,000 mt/y., off machine
PM 1, total capacity 25,000 mt/y., on machine
PM 2, total capacity 90,000 mt/y., on machine
Finishing Equipment:
Winders: 2 at 340,000 mt/y
Rewinders: 8 at 665,000 mt/y
Sheeters: 2 at 200,000 mt/y
Energy Data:
Power boilers: 2
Electrical demand for mill: 263 MWh/D

ⓂⓂOndunorte, Cia. de Papéis e Papelão Ondulado do Norte
Igarassu Mill
Rod. Br. 101, Km 29, s/n
53600-000 Igarassu, PE
Brazil
Phone: (55) 81 2121 6767
Fax: (55) 81 2121 6744
Email: ondunorte@ondunorte.com.br
Web Address: www.ondunorte.com
Personnel:
Pres.: Aluisio Pedrosa Pontes
Phone: (55) 81 2121 6767
Admn. & Finan. Dir.: Saulo Ribeiro Pontes

Brazil

Phone: (55) 81 2121 6767
Comer. Dir.: Sérgio Pontes
Phone: (55) 81 2121 6767
Control Dir.: Gilson Pontes
Phone: (55) 81 2121 6767
Ind. Mgr.: Luiz Frado
Phone: (55) 81 2121 6767
Total Employees at this Location: 160
Type of Operation: Paper mill, Paperboard mill
Mill Locations:
CICP Companhia Industrial de Celulose e Papel, Itaporanga d'Ajuda Mill, Rodovia BR 101, Km 114, Bairro Zona Rural, 49120-000 Itaporanga d'Ajuda, SE, Brazil, Capacity: 12,000 mt/y, (Paper mill)
Phone: (55) 79-3264-1324
Fax: (55) 79-3264-1071
Email: cicp@cicp.com.br
Pulp Grades and Capacities:
Total pulp capacity: 40,950 mt/y
Recycled Pulping: 40,950 mt/y
Pulp Mill Data:
Recycled Fiber Treatment Lines:
Pulpers: 1 at 44,430
Paper/Paperboard Grades and Capacities:
Total paper and paperboard capacity: 73,899 mt/y
Tissue: 33,915 mt/y
Linerboard: 27,489 mt/y
Corrugating medium/fluting: 12,495 mt/y
Paper and Paperboard Mill Data:
Stock Preparation:
Pulpers:
Paper Machines: 4
No. 1, crescent former, total capacity 12,138 mt/y, Trim width 2.5 m, Tissue, Uncoated woodfree/freesheet
No. 3, fourdrinier, total capacity 39,984 mt/y, Trim width 2.5 m, Linerboard, Corrugating medium/fluting
No. 4, crescent former, total capacity 5,712 mt/y, Trim width 2 m, Tissue
No. 5, crescent former, total capacity 16,065 mt/y, Trim width 2.8 m, Tissue, Uncoated woodfree/freesheet
Energy Data:
Power boilers
Combustion turbines
Electrical demand for mill: 156 MWh/D

ⓜ Orsa International Paper Embalagens S.A

Ownership: 100% by International Paper Co.
Alameda Mamoré, 989 - 25th Floor - Alphaville
06454-040 Barueri, SP
Brazil
 Phone: (55) 11 5054 7400
 Email: comercial.orsaip.com.br
 Web Address: www.orsaip.com.br
Personnel:
Chmn.: Sergio Amoroso
Phone: (55) 11 2175 7500/4689 8700
Fax: (55) 11 4195 9506
CEO: Jorge Henriques
Phone: (55) 11 2175 7500/4689 8700
Fax: (55) 11 4195 9506
Exec. Dir.: Luis Fernando Laranja Da Fonseca
Phone: (55) 11 2175 7500/4689 8700
Fax: (55) 11 4195 9506
Contr. Dir.: Joao Eduardo Peres
Phone: (55) 11 2175 7500/4689 8700
Fax: (55) 11 4195 9506
Manuf. Dir.: Dino Ranzani
Phone: (55) 11 2175 7500/4689 8700
Fax: (55) 11 4195 9506
Indus. Dir: Ricardo Galan
Phone: (55) 11 2175 7500/4689 8700
Fax: (55) 11 4195 9506
Plann. Mgr: Daniel De Chiaro
Phone: (55) 11 2175 7500/4689 8700
Fax: (55) 11 4195 9506
Bus. Dir.: Joao Prestes
Phone: (55) 11 2175 7500/4689 8700
Fax: (55) 11 4195 9506

Finan. Mgr.: Sandra Lima
Phone: (55) 11 2175 7500/4689 8700
Fax: (55) 11 4195 9506
IT Mgr.: Lari Papaleo
Phone: (55) 11 2175 7500/4689 8700
Fax: (55) 11 4195 9506
HR Mgr.: Luiz Bezerra
Phone: (55) 11 2175 7500/4689 8700
Fax: (55) 11 4195 9506
Total Employees of Company: 3,000
Mill Locations:
Orsa International Paper Embalagens S.A, Nova Campina Mill, Rodovia Luiz José Sguário, km 31 - Taquari Guassú, 18400-000 Nova Campina, SP, Brazil, Capacity: 183,141 mt/y, (Pulp mill, Paperboard mill)
Phone: (55) 15 3521 9600
Fax: (55) 15 3521 9718
Orsa International Paper Embalagens S.A, Franco da Rocha Mill, Av. Pacaembu 495 - Bairro dos Abreus, 07810 000 Franco da Rocha, SP, Brazil, Capacity: 49,980 mt/y, (Paperboard mill)
Phone: (55) 11 4811 8000
Email: comercial@orsaip.com.br
Orsa International Paper Embalagens S.A, Paulínia Mill, Rua Henedina R.O. Bresler, 150 - Bela Vista, 13140-000 Paulínia, SP, Brazil, Capacity: 132,090 mt/y, (Pulp mill, Paper mill, Paperboard mill)
Phone: (55) 19 3844 2600
Fax: (55) 19 3874 2279

ⓜ Orsa International Paper Embalagens S.A
Nova Campina Mill

Ownership: 100% by International Paper Co.
Rodovia Luiz José Sguário, km 31 - Taquari Guassú
18400-000 Nova Campina, SP
Brazil
Mailing Address: CP 82, 18400 Itapeva, SP, Brazil
 Phone: (55) 15 3521 9600
 Fax: (55) 15 3521 9718
 Web Address: www.orsaip.com.br
Personnel:
Mill Mgr.: Aparecido Cuba Tavares
Phone: (55) 15 3521 9600
Fax: (55) 15 3521 9718
Email: atavares@orsaip.com.br
Paper Mill Mgr.: Maximo Nogueira
Phone: (55) 15 3521 9600
Fax: (55) 15 3521 9718
Email: mnogueira@orsaip.com.br
Admin. Mgr.: Rene C. Silva
Phone: (55) 15 3521 9600
Fax: (55) 15 3521 9718
Email: rcsilva@orsaip.com.br
Tech. Mgr.: José Carlos Ferreira da Silva
Phone: (55) 15 3521 9600
Fax: (55) 15 3521 9645
Email: jcsilva@orsaip.com.br
Press Mgr.: Fernanda Ramos
Phone: (55) 15 3521 9600
Fax: (55) 15 3521 9718
Email: fernanda.ramos@orsaip.com.br
Commun. Mgr.: Marisa Coutinho
Phone: (55) 11 3797 5733
Email: marisa.coutinho@ipaper.com
Total Employees at this Location: 444
Type of Operation: Pulp mill, Paperboard mill
Pulp Grades and Capacities:
Total pulp capacity: 187,534 mt/y
Chemical Pulp: 166,074 mt/y
Recycled Pulping: 21,460 mt/y
Pulp Mill Data:
Chemical Pulping Systems:
Batch digesters: 6
Pulp Lines: 1
Chemical Recovery Equipment:
Evaporator lines: 1
Recovery boilers: 2
Lime Kiln
Recycled Fiber Treatment Lines:

Pulpers: 1 at 60,000 admt/y
Recycled packaging pulping lines: 1 at 60,000 admt/y
Paper/Paperboard Grades and Capacities:
Total paper and paperboard capacity: 183,141 mt/y
Linerboard: 183,141 mt/y
Paper and Paperboard Mill Data:
Stock Preparation:
Pulpers: 2
Refiners: 8
Paper Machines: 2
No. 1, fourdrinier, total capacity 68,187 mt/y, Trim width 2.5 m, Linerboard
No. 2, fourdrinier, total capacity 114,954 mt/y, Trim width 3.2 m, Linerboard
Finishing Equipment:
Winders: 2 at 177,500 mt/y
Calenders: 2
Rewinders: 2 at 177,500 mt/y
Energy Data:
Power boilers: 2
Steam turbines: 2 at 4.0, 10.0 MW
Hydro turbines: 2 at 2.0 MW
Electrical demand for mill: 351 MWh/D

ⓜ Orsa International Paper Embalagens S.A
Franco da Rocha Mill

Ownership: 100% by International Paper Co.
Av. Pacaembu 495 - Bairro dos Abreus
07810 000 Franco da Rocha, SP
Brazil
 Phone: (55) 11 4811 8000
 Email: comercial@orsaip.com.br
 Web Address: www.orsaip.com.br
Total Employees at this Location: 139
Type of Operation: Paperboard mill
Pulp Grades and Capacities:
Total pulp capacity: 50,430 mt/y
Recycled Pulping: 50,430 mt/y
Paper/Paperboard Grades and Capacities:
Total paper and paperboard capacity: 49,980 mt/y
Linerboard: 39,984 mt/y
Corrugating medium/fluting: 9,996 mt/y
Paper and Paperboard Mill Data:
Paper Machines: 1
No. 1, fourdrinier, total capacity 49,980 mt/y, Trim width 2.5 m, Linerboard, Corrugating medium/fluting
Energy Data:
Power boilers
Electrical demand for mill: 56 MWh/D

ⓜ Orsa International Paper Embalagens S.A
Paulínia Mill

Ownership: 100% by International Paper Co.
Rua Henedina R.O. Bresler, 150 - Bela Vista
13140-000 Paulínia, SP
Brazil
 Phone: (55) 19 3844 2600
 Fax: (55) 19 3874 2279
 Web Address: www.orsaip.com.br
Personnel:
Paper Mill Mgr.: Adroaldo José da Silva
Phone: (55) 19 3844 2654
Fax: (55) 19 3874 2279
Email: adasilva@orsaip.com.br
Total Employees at this Location: 236
Type of Operation: Pulp mill, Paper mill, Paperboard mill
Pulp Grades and Capacities:
Total pulp capacity: 133,908 mt/y
Recycled Pulping: 133,908 mt/y
Pulp Mill Data:
Recycled Fiber Treatment Lines:
Recycled packaging pulping lines: 1
Paper/Paperboard Grades and Capacities:
Total paper and paperboard capacity: 132,090 mt/y
Linerboard: 32,130 mt/y

Brazil

Corrugating medium/fluting: 99,960 mt/y
Paper and Paperboard Mill Data:
Stock Preparation:
Pulpers: 2
Refiners: 8
Paper Machines: 2
No. 1, fourdrinier, total capacity 39,984 mt/y, Trim width 2.2 m, Corrugating medium/fluting, Linerboard
No. 2, fourdrinier, total capacity 92,106 mt/y, Trim width 3.4 m, Corrugating medium/fluting, Linerboard
Finishing Equipment:
Rewinders: 2 at 40,000 mt/y, 92,000 mt/y
Energy Data:
Power boilers: 2
Electrical demand for mill: 173 MWh/D

ⓘOuro Verde Papéis e Embalagens Ltda.
Rodovia RS 211, s/n° - KM 14
99718-000 Paulo Bento, RS
Brazil
 Phone: (55) 54 3321 6133
 Fax: (55) 54 3520 2600
 Email: ouroverde@ouroverdepapeis.com.br
 Web Address: www.ouroverdepapeis.com.br
Personnel:
 Dir.: Grégori T Grégori T
 Phone: (55) 54 3321 6133
 Fax: (55) 54 3520 2600
 Admin. Mgr.: Luiz Carlos Pereira
 Phone: (55) 54 3321 6133
 Fax: (55) 54 3520 2600
 Chemist: Andreia Horszczaruk
 Phone: (55) 54 3321 6133
 Fax: (55) 54 3520 2600
Total Employees of Company: 99
Mill Locations:
Ouro Verde Papéis e Embalagens Ltda., Paulo Bento Mill, Rodovia RS 211, s/n° - KM 14, 99718-000 Paulo Bento, RS, Brazil, Capacity: 10,800 mt/y, (Paper mill)
 Phone: (55) 54 3321 6133
 Fax: (55) 54 3520 2600
 Email: ouroverde@ouroverdepapeis.com.br

ⓘOuro Verde Papéis e Embalagens Ltda.
Paulo Bento Mill
Rodovia RS 211, s/n° - KM 14
99718-000 Paulo Bento, RS
Brazil
 Phone: (55) 54 3321 6133
 Fax: (55) 54 3520 2600
 Email: ouroverde@ouroverdepapeis.com.br
 Web Address: www.ouroverdepapeis.com.br
Personnel:
 Dir.: Grégori T Grégori T
 Phone: (55) 54 3321 6133
 Fax: (55) 54 3520 2600
 Admin. Mgr.: Luiz Carlos Pereira
 Phone: (55) 54 3321 6133
 Fax: (55) 54 3520 2600
 Chemist: Andreia Horszczaruk
 Phone: (55) 54 3321 6133
 Fax: (55) 54 3520 2600
Total Employees at this Location: 99
Type of Operation: Paper mill
Paper/Paperboard Grades and Capacities:
Total paper and paperboard capacity: 10,800 mt/y
Tissue: 10,800 mt/y
Paper and Paperboard Mill Data:
Paper Machines: 1
PM 1, total capacity 10,800 mt/y, Trim width 2.1 m, Tissue
Energy Data:
Power boilers: 1

ⓘPaema Embalagens Ltda.
Estrada para Pinto Bandeira, s/n°, Barracão
95700-000 Bento Gonçalves, RS
Brazil
 Phone: (55) 2102 9500
 Fax: (55) 2102 9510
 Email: paema@paema.com.br
 Web Address: www.paema.com.br
Personnel:
 Dir.: Jucemar A. Buzin
 Phone: (55) 54 2102 9500
 Board Advisor: Paulo Henrique Cândido Fogaça
 Phone: (55) 54 2102 9500
 Indus. Mgr.: Cláudio Magalhães
 Phone: (55) 54 2102 9500
Mill Locations:
Paema Embalagens Ltda., Barracao Mill, Estrada para Pinto Bandeira, s/n°, Barracão, 95700-000 Bento Gonçalves, RS, Brazil, Capacity: 36,000 mt/y, (Paperboard mill)
 Phone: (55) 2102 9500
 Fax: (55) 2102 9510
 Email: paema@paema.com.br

ⓘⓘPaema Embalagens Ltda.
Barracao Mill
Estrada para Pinto Bandeira, s/n°, Barracão
95700-000 Bento Gonçalves, RS
Brazil
 Phone: (55) 2102 9500
 Fax: (55) 2102 9510
 Email: paema@paema.com.br
 Web Address: www.paema.com.br
Personnel:
 Ind. Mgr.: Cláudio Magalhães
 Phone: (55) 2102 9534
 Fax: (55) 2102 9510
 Email: claudio@paema.com.br
 Admin. Mgr.: Marcelo Rego
 Phone: (55) 2102 9500
 Fax: (55) 2102 9510
 Email: marcelorego@paema.com.br
Type of Operation: Paperboard mill
Paper/Paperboard Grades and Capacities:
Total paper and paperboard capacity: 36,000 mt/y
Linerboard: 18,000 mt/y
Corrugating medium/fluting: 18,000 mt/y
Paper and Paperboard Mill Data:
Paper Machines: 1
No. 1, fourdrinier, total capacity 36,000 mt/y, Trim width 2.47 m, Linerboard, Corrugating medium/fluting

ⓘPapel Tangará Ltda.
Pinheiro Preto
Brazil
Personnel:
 Owner: Sidney Melotti
Mill Locations:
Papel Tangará Ltda., Pinheiro Preto mill, Pinheiro Preto, SC, Brazil, Capacity: 18,000 mt/y, (Paper mill)

ⓘⓘPapel Tangará Ltda.
Pinheiro Preto mill
Pinheiro Preto, SC
Brazil
Personnel:
 Owner: Sidney Melotti
Type of Operation: Paper mill
Paper/Paperboard Grades and Capacities:
Total paper and paperboard capacity: 18,000 mt/y
Tissue: 18,000 mt/y
Paper and Paperboard Mill Data:
Paper Machines: 1
No. 1, (started up April 2011), total capacity 18,000 mt/y, Tissue

ⓘPapirus Indústria de Papel S.A.
Av. Santo Amaro, 3330 - 6th Floor
04556-300 São Paulo, SP
Brazil
 Phone: (55) 11 2125 3900
 Fax: (55) 11 2125 3927
 Email: vendas@papirus.com
 Web Address: www.papirus.com
Personnel:
 CEO & Pres.: Antonio Claudio Salce
 Phone: (55) 11 2125 3900
 Fax: (55) 11 2125 3927
 Commer. Dir.: Amando Varella
 Phone: (55) 11 2125 3900
 Fax: (55) 11 2125 3927
 Purch. & HR Dir.: Antonio Valdovino Pupin
 Phone: (55) 11 2125 3900
 Fax: (55) 11 2125 3927
 Commun. Analyst: Aline Teixeira
 Phone: (55) 19 2113 6200
Total Employees of Company: 366
Total Employees at this Location: 20
Mill Locations:
Papirus Indústria de Papel S.A., Limeira Mill, Via Anhanguera Km. 131, 13480-970 Limeira, SP, Brazil, Capacity: 89,964 mt/y, (Paperboard mill)
 Phone: (55) 19 2113 6100
 Fax: (55) 19 2113 6190
 Email: comunicacao@papirus.com

ⓘPapirus Indústria de Papel S.A.
Limeira Mill
Via Anhanguera Km. 131
13480-970 Limeira, SP
Brazil
 Phone: (55) 19 2113 6100
 Fax: (55) 19 2113 6190
 Email: comunicacao@papirus.com
 Web Address: www.papirus.com
Personnel:
 CEO & Pres.: Antonio Claudio Salce
 Phone: (55) 19 2113 6100
 Admin. & Finan. Dir.: Rubens Martins
 Phone: (55) 19 2113 6100
 Commer. Dir.: Amando Varella
 Phone: (55) 19 2113 6100
 Eng. Mgr.: José Claudio M
 Phone: (55) 19 2113 6200
 Oper. Mgr.: Maicom Margiotta Fonseca
 Phone: (55) 19 2113 6100
 Tech. Dir.: Thiago Roberto S
 Phone: (55) 19 2113 6200
Total Employees at this Location: 183
Type of Operation: Paperboard mill
Pulp Grades and Capacities:
Total pulp capacity: 39,568 mt/y
Recycled Pulping: 39,568 mt/y
Pulp Mill Data:
Recycled Fiber Treatment Lines:
Pulpers: 1 at 43,600
Paper/Paperboard Grades and Capacities:
Total paper and paperboard capacity: 89,964 mt/y
Boxboard/cartonboard: 89,964 mt/y
Paper and Paperboard Mill Data:
Paper Machines: 1
No. 1, (FormerType model: Multi-Fourdrinier), fourdrinier, total capacity 89,964 mt/y, Trim width 2.4 m, Boxboard/cartonboard
Coating Machines: 1
PM 1, total capacity 85,000 mt/y., on machine
Finishing Equipment:
Rewinders: 3
Sheeters: 4
Energy Data:
Power boilers: 4
Electrical demand for mill: 149 MWh/D

ⓘⓘParaibuna Embalagens Ltda.
Juiz de Fora Mill
Av. Antônio Simão Firjan 1205, Distrito Industrial
36092-000 Juiz de Fora, MG
Brazil
 Phone: (55) 32 2102 4000
 Fax: (55) 32 2102 4001
 Email: diretoria@paraibuna.com.br
 Web Address: www.paraibuna.com.br

Brazil

Personnel:
Pres.: Sergio Diaz
Phone: (55) 32 2102 4000
Fax: (55) 32 2102 4001
Man. Dir.: Mario Diaz Soto
Phone: (55) 32 2102 4000
Fax: (55) 32 2102 4001
Purch. Mgr.: Denim Peper
Phone: (55) 32 2102 4000
Fax: (55) 32 2102 4001
Finan. Dir.: Luis Barros
Phone: (55) 32 2102 4000
Fax: (55) 32 2102 4001
Total Employees of Company: 600
Total Employees at this Location: 110
Type of Operation: Paperboard mill
Pulp Grades and Capacities:
Total pulp capacity: 76,969 mt/y
Recycled Pulping: 76,969 mt/y
Pulp Mill Data:
Recycled Fiber Treatment Lines:
Recycled packaging pulping lines
Paper/Paperboard Grades and Capacities:
Total paper and paperboard capacity: 76,041 mt/y
Linerboard: 40,341 mt/y
Corrugating medium/fluting: 35,700 mt/y
Paper and Paperboard Mill Data:
Stock Preparation:
Pulpers:
Paper Machines: 1
No. 1, fourdrinier, total capacity 76,041 mt/y, Trim width 2.8 m, Linerboard, Corrugating medium/fluting
Energy Data:
Power boilers: 1
Electrical demand for mill: 129 MWh/D

ⓘPasa - Papelão Apucaraninha Ltda.
Rua Cândido Hartman, 570 27th floor cj 273
80730-440 Curitiba, PR
Brazil
Phone: (55) 41 3336 3893
Fax: (55) 41 3336 5615
Email: pasa@pasabr.com.br
Personnel:
Owner/Pres.: José Luis Dominges
Phone: (55) 41 3336 3893
Fax: (55) 41 3336 5615
Owner/Dir.: Leonardo Domingues
Phone: (55) 41 3336 3893
Fax: (55) 41 3336 5615
Total Employees of Company: 90
Total Employees at this Location: 2
Mill Locations:
Pasa - Papelão Apucaraninha Ltda., Londrina Mill, Fazenda Apucaraninha, 86125-000 Tamarana, PR, Brazil, Capacity: 13,000 mt/y, (Paperboard mill)
Phone: (55) 43 3399 2002
Email: pasa@pasabr.com.br

ⓂPasa - Papelão Apucaraninha Ltda.
Londrina Mill
Fazenda Apucaraninha
86125-000 Tamarana, PR
Brazil
Phone: (55) 43 3399 2002
Email: pasa@pasabr.com.br
Personnel:
Owner/Pres.: José Luiz Domingues
Phone: (55) 43 3399 2002
Mill Mgr.: Domingos Rampo
Phone: (55) 43 3399 2002
Type of Operation: Paperboard mill
Paper/Paperboard Grades and Capacities:
Total paper and paperboard capacity: 13,000 mt/y
Boxboard/cartonboard: 13,000 mt/y
Paper and Paperboard Mill Data:
Paper Machines: 1
No. 1, total capacity 13,000 mt/y, Boxboard/cartonboard

ⓂPaulispell, Indústria Paulista de Papéis e Chapas de Papelão
Aguaí Mill
Rodovia Aguaí - Pirassununga, km 3 - Itupeva
13860-970 Aguaí, SP
Brazil
Phone: (55) 19 3652 1516/9700
Fax: (55) 19 3652 1766
Email: paulispell@paulispell.com.br
Web Address: www.paulispell.com.br
Personnel:
Partner Mgr.: José Gallardo Diaz
Phone: (55) 19 3652 1516
Fax: (55) 19 3652 1766
Ind. Mgr.: Gilberto da Cunha
Phone: (55) 19 3652 1516
Fax: (55) 19 3652 1766
Email: ger.industrial@paulispell.com.br
Commer. Dir.: Ari Valverde
Phone: (55) 19 3652 1516
Fax: (55) 19 3652 1766
Email: arivalverde.comercial@paulispell.com.br
Total Employees at this Location: 103
Type of Operation: Paperboard mill
Pulp Grades and Capacities:
Total pulp capacity: 36,947 mt/y
Recycled Pulping: 36,947 mt/y
Pulp Mill Data:
Recycled Fiber Treatment Lines:
Recycled packaging pulping lines: 1
Paper/Paperboard Grades and Capacities:
Total paper and paperboard capacity: 36,057 mt/y
Linerboard: 19,992 mt/y
Corrugating medium/fluting: 16,065 mt/y
Paper and Paperboard Mill Data:
Paper Machines: 2
No. 1, fourdrinier, total capacity 16,422 mt/y, Trim width 2.25 m, Corrugating medium/fluting, Linerboard
No. 2, fourdrinier, total capacity 19,635 mt/y, Trim width 2.25 m, Corrugating medium/fluting, Linerboard
Energy Data:
Power boilers
Electrical demand for mill: 64 MWh/D

ⓘPaulispell, Indústria Paulista de Papéis e Chapas de Papelão
Rodovia Aguaí - Pirassununga, km 3 - Itupeva
13860-970 Aguaí, SP
Brazil
Phone: (55) 19 3652 1516/9700
Fax: (55) 19 3652 1766
Email: paulispell@paulispell.com.br
Web Address: www.paulispell.com.br
Personnel:
Partner Mgr.: José Gallardo Diaz
Phone: (55) 19 3652 1516/9700
Fax: (55) 19 3652 1766
Email: jgallardodiaz@paulispell.com.br
Ind. Mgr.: Gilberto da Cunha
Phone: (55) 19 3652 1516/9700
Fax: (55) 19 3652 1766
Email: gdacunha@paulispell.com.br
Commer. Dir.: Ari Valverde
Phone: (55) 19 3652 1516/9700
Fax: (55) 19 3652 1766
Email: arivalverde@paulispell.com.br
Contr.: Roberval Gondim
Phone: (55) 19 3652 1516/9700
Fax: (55) 19 3652 1766
Email: rgondim@paulispell.com.br
Mill Locations:
Paulispell, Indústria Paulista de Papéis e Chapas de Papelão, Aguaí Mill, Rodovia Aguaí - Pirassununga, km 3 - Itupeva, 13860-970 Aguaí, SP, Brazil, Capacity: 36,057 mt/y, (Paperboard mill)
Phone: (55) 19 3652 1516/9700
Fax: (55) 19 3652 1766
Email: paulispell@paulispell.com.br

ⓘPCE Embalagens
Ownership: 100% by Grupo CCE
Av. Grande Circular, 1000 - Pólo Industrial
60908-850 Manaus, AM
Brazil
Phone: (55) 92 2123 8800/8823
Fax: (55) 92 2123 8800
Email: vendas@pceembalagens.com.br
Web Address: www.pceembalagens.com.br
Personnel:
Gen. Mgr: Bruno di Crédico
Phone: (55) 92 8137 7273
Fax: (55) 92 2123 8800
Finan. Mgr: José Carlos Ferreira
Phone: (55) 92 2123 8800/8823
Fax: (55) 92 2123 8800
Email: jferreira@pceembalagens.com.br
Total Employees of Company: 370
Total Employees at this Location: 370
Mill Locations:
PCE Embalagens, Manaus Mill, Av. Grande Circular, 1000 - Pólo Industrial, 60908-850 Manaus, AM, Brazil, Capacity: 59,976 mt/y, (Paperboard mill)
Phone: (55) 92 2123 8800/8823
Fax: (55) 92 2123 8800
Email: vendas@pceembalagens.com.br

ⓂPCE Embalagens
Manaus Mill
Av. Grande Circular, 1000 - Pólo Industrial
60908-850 Manaus, AM
Brazil
Phone: (55) 92 2123 8800/8823
Fax: (55) 92 2123 8800
Email: vendas@pceembalagens.com.br
Web Address: www.pceembalagens.com.br
Personnel:
Gen. Mgr.: Bruno di Crédico
Phone: (55) 92 8137 7273
Finan. Mgr.: José Carlos Ferreira
Phone: (55) 92 2123 8800/8823
Email: jferreira@pceembalagens.com.br
Total Employees at this Location: 115
Type of Operation: Paperboard mill
Pulp Grades and Capacities:
Total pulp capacity: 58,936 mt/y
Recycled Pulping: 58,936 mt/y
Pulp Mill Data:
Recycled Fiber Treatment Lines:
Pulpers: 1 at 64,000
Paper/Paperboard Grades and Capacities:
Total paper and paperboard capacity: 59,976 mt/y
Packaging papers: 9,996 mt/y
Linerboard: 24,990 mt/y
Corrugating medium/fluting: 24,990 mt/y
Paper and Paperboard Mill Data:
Stock Preparation:
Pulpers:
Paper Machines: 1
No. 1, fourdrinier, total capacity 59,976 mt/y, Trim width 2.55 m, Linerboard, Corrugating medium/fluting, Packaging papers
Energy Data:
Power boilers: 1
Electrical demand for mill: 101 MWh/D

ⓘPenha Papéis e Embalagem Ltda.
Ownership: Fábrica de Papelão Nossa Senhora da Penha S/A
Av. Indianópolis, 1400 - Bairro Indianópolis
04062-001 São Paulo, SP
Brazil
Phone: (55) 11 5593 5800
Fax: (55) 11 5593 5808
Email: info@penha.com.br,
vendas@penha.com.br,
meioambiente@penha.com.br
Web Address: www.penha.com.br
Personnel:

Mill Mgr.: Maria Rafaela da Cruz
Phone: (55) 11 5593 5800
Fax: (55) 11 5593 5808
Email: rafaela@penha-ba.com.br
Admin. Mgr.: Marco Aurélio Rotoly
Phone: (55) 11 5593 5800
Fax: (55) 11 5593 5808
Email: rotoly@penha-ba.com.br
Indus. Mgr.: Maurício Ferreira de Andrade
Phone: (55) 11 5593 5800
Fax: (55) 11 5593 5808
Email: mauricio@penha.com.br
Prod. Mgr.: Cláudio Almeida da Silva
Phone: (55) 11 5593 5800
Fax: (55) 11 5593 5808
Email: claudioalmeida@penha-ba.com.br
Total Employees of Company: 2,050
Total Employees at this Location: 30
Mill Locations:
Penha Papéis e Embalagem Ltda., Santo Amaro Mill, Rod. BR 420, km 16 - Fazenda Pitinga, CP 48, 44200-000 Santo Amaro da Purificação, BA, Brazil, Capacity: 113,883 mt/y, (Paperboard mill)
Phone: (55) 75 3241 2000/8650
Fax: (55) 75 3241 2100
Email: penha@penha.com.br
Penha Papéis e Embalagem Ltda., Coronel Vivida Mill, Rodovia BR 158, km 495, 85550-000 Vivida, PR, Brazil, Capacity: 29,988 mt/y, (Paperboard mill)
Phone: (55) 46 3232 8100
Fax: (55) 46 3232 8119

ⓂPenha Papéis e Embalagem Ltda.
Santo Amaro Mill
Rod. BR 420, km 16 - Fazenda Pitinga, CP 48
44200-000 Santo Amaro da Purificação, BA
Brazil
Phone: (55) 75 3241 2000/8650
Fax: (55) 75 3241 2100
Email: penha@penha.com.br
Web Address: www.penha.com.br
Personnel:
Dir.: Maurício Ferreira de Andrade
Phone: (55) 41 8838 8741
Fax: (55) 75 3241 2100
Email: mauricio@penha.com.br
Comercial. Dir.: Carlos Edson Shiguematsu
Phone: (55) 75 3241 2000/8650
Fax: (55) 75 3241 2100
Tech Mgr.: Sergio Belli
Phone: (55) 41 8838 8741
Fax: (55) 75 3241 2100
Total Employees at this Location: 130
Type of Operation: Paperboard mill
Pulp Grades and Capacities:
Total pulp capacity: 115,766 mt/y
Recycled Pulping: 115,766 mt/y
Pulp Mill Data:
Chemical Pulping Systems:
Batch digesters: 5
Chemical Recovery Equipment:
Evaporator lines: 5
Recovery boilers: 1
Recycled Fiber Treatment Lines:
Pulpers: 2 at 108,000 admt/y
Paper/Paperboard Grades and Capacities:
Total paper and paperboard capacity: 113,883 mt/y
Linerboard: 12,495 mt/y
Corrugating medium/fluting: 101,388 mt/y
Paper and Paperboard Mill Data:
Stock Preparation:
Pulpers: 2
Refiners: 5
Paper Machines: 2
No. 1, fourdrinier, total capacity 63,903 mt/y, Trim width 2.45 m, Linerboard, Corrugating medium/fluting
No. 2, fourdrinier, total capacity 49,980 mt/y, Trim width 2.5 m, Linerboard, Corrugating medium/fluting
Finishing Equipment:
Rewinders: 2

Energy Data:
Power boilers: 2
Steam turbines: 1
Electrical demand for mill: 185 MWh/D

ⓂPenha Papéis e Embalagem Ltda.
Coronel Vivida Mill
Rodovia BR 158, km 495
85550-000 Vivida, PR
Brazil
Phone: (55) 46 3232 8100
Fax: (55) 46 3232 8119
Web Address: www.penha.com.br
Personnel:
Paper Mills Dir.: Maurício Ferreira de Andrade
Phone: (55) 41 8838 8741
Fax: (55) 46 3232 8119
Email: mauricio@penha.com.br
Total Employees at this Location: 82
Type of Operation: Paperboard mill
Pulp Grades and Capacities:
Total pulp capacity: 30,290 mt/y
Recycled Pulping: 30,290 mt/y
Pulp Mill Data:
Recycled Fiber Treatment Lines:
Recycled packaging pulping lines: 1
Paper/Paperboard Grades and Capacities:
Total paper and paperboard capacity: 29,988 mt/y
Linerboard: 8,925 mt/y
Corrugating medium/fluting: 21,063 mt/y
Paper and Paperboard Mill Data:
Paper Machines: 1
No. 1, (Suppliers: IPPEL/Voith), fourdrinier, total capacity 29,988 mt/y, Trim width 2.5 m, Corrugating medium/fluting, Linerboard
Energy Data:
Power boilers: 1
Electrical demand for mill: 52 MWh/D

ⓞⓂPinho Past Ltda.
Guarapuava Mill
Rio Coutinho-Saida p/ Pitanga, Km. 4, CP 7 - Rio Coutinho
85050-290 Guarapuava, PR
Brazil
Phone: (55) 42 3624 1200
Fax: (55) 42 3624 1200
Email: pinhopast@pinhopast.com.br
Web Address: www.pinhopast.com.br
Personnel:
Mill Mgr.: Sidney Ferreira
Phone: (55) 42 3624 1200
Admin. Dir.: Celso Luis Zagorski
Phone: (55) 42 3624 1200
Email: financeiro@pinhopast.com.br
Mkt. Mgr.: João Denck
Phone: (55) 42 3624 1200
Email: comercial@pinhopast.com.br
Type of Operation: Paperboard mill
Paper/Paperboard Grades and Capacities:
Total paper and paperboard capacity: 36,000 mt/y
Boxboard/cartonboard: 36,000 mt/y
Paper and Paperboard Mill Data:
Paper Machines: 1
PM 1, total capacity 36,000 mt/y, Boxboard/cartonboard
Energy Data:
Power boilers: 2

ⓞPiquiri Indústria e Comércio de Papéis Ltda.
Rua General João Carlos Lobo 395
Vila Maria, São Paulo, SP
Brazil
Phone: (55) 11 2954 4099
Email: piquiri@piquiri.com.br, piquiritr@piquiri.com.br
Web Address: www.piquiri.com.br
Personnel:

Supt. Dir.: Mozart Gaia Junior
Phone: (55) 11 2954 4099
Commer. Dir.: Cesar Magno
Phone: (55) 11 2954 4099
Prod. Supervisor: Jose Roberto Rosa
Phone: (55) 11 2954 4099
Mill Locations:
Piquiri Indústria e Comércio de Papéis Ltda., Guarapuava Mill, Principal s/n, Rio Piquiri, 85148-000 Campina do Simão, PR, Brazil, Capacity: 18,000 mt/y, (Paperboard mill)
Phone: (55) 42 3644 1135
Fax: (55) 42 3644 1135
Email: piquiri@piquiri.com.br

ⓂPiquiri Indústria e Comércio de Papéis Ltda.
Guarapuava Mill
Principal s/n, Rio Piquiri
85148-000 Campina do Simão, PR
Brazil
Mailing Address: CP 113, 85100-000 Guarapuava, Brazil
Phone: (55) 42 3644 1135
Fax: (55) 42 3644 1135
Email: piquiri@piquiri.com.br
Web Address: www.piquiri.com.br
Personnel:
Supt. Dir.: Mozart Gaia Jr.
Phone: (55) 42 3644 1135
Mill Mgr.: José Divozir
Phone: (55) 42 3644 1135
Total Employees at this Location: 107
Type of Operation: Paperboard mill
Paper/Paperboard Grades and Capacities:
Total paper and paperboard capacity: 18,000 mt/y
Corrugating medium/fluting: 18,000 mt/y
Paper and Paperboard Mill Data:
Paper Machines: 1
No. 1, total capacity 18,000 mt/y, Corrugating medium/fluting

ⓞPolpa de Madeiras Ltda.
Rua Frei Rogério, 415
88502-160 Lages, SC
Brazil
Phone: (55) 49 2101 8400
Email: polpa@polpademadeiras.com.br
Web Address: www.polpademadeiras.com.br
Personnel:
Eng. Mgr.: Lugindo Dall Asta Jr
Phone: (55) 49 2101 8400
Maint. Mgr.: Odair J Odair J
Phone: (55) 49 2101 8400
Contr.: Ritchaderson M Ritchaderson M
Phone: (55) 49 2101 8400
Mill Locations:
Polpa de Madeiras Ltda., Santa Cecília Mill, Vila Faxinal das Águas, s/n, 89540-000 Santa Cecília, SC, Brazil, Capacity: 23,000 mt/y, (Pulp mill, Paperboard mill)
Phone: (55) 49 3244 0823
Fax: (55) 49 3244 3280/2522
Email: polpa@polpademadeiras.com.br

ⓂPolpa de Madeiras Ltda.
Santa Cecília Mill
Vila Faxinal das Águas, s/n
89540-000 Santa Cecília, SC
Brazil
Phone: (55) 49 3244 0823
Fax: (55) 49 3244 3280/2522
Email: polpa@polpademadeiras.com.br
Personnel:
Gen. Mgr.: Valdir Nazário
Phone: (55) 49 3244 0823
Dir./Mktg. Mgr.: César Augusto Dall Asta
Phone: (55) 49 3244 0823
Finan. Dir./Economy Mgr.: Milton Mario Lando
Phone: (55) 49 3244 0823

Brazil

Pulp Mill Mgr.: Joao Pablo Felipe
Phone: (55) 49 3244 0823
Eng. Mgr: Lugindo Dall Asta Jr.
Phone: (55) 49 3244 0823
Total Employees at this Location: 95
Type of Operation: Pulp mill, Paperboard mill
Pulp Grades and Capacities:
Total pulp capacity: 2,000 mt/y
Mechanical Pulp: 2,000 mt/y
Pulp Mill Data:
Mechanical Pulping Systems:
Conventional grinders: 3
Pulp Dryers:
Flash dryers 13
Paper/Paperboard Grades and Capacities:
Total paper and paperboard capacity: 23,000 mt/y
Linerboard: 23,000 mt/y
Paper and Paperboard Mill Data:
Stock Preparation:
Pulpers: 3
Refiners: 3
Paper Machines: 1
No. 1, cylinder (3), total capacity 23,000 mt/y, Trim width 1.6 m, Linerboard
Finishing Equipment:
Supercalenders: 2
Energy Data:
Power boilers: 1
Combustion turbines: 3

ⓘⓜPorto Feliz S.A.
Porto Feliz Mill
Av. Atílio Fuser Jr, 21, Palmital
18540-000 Porto Feliz, SP
Brazil
Phone: (55) 15 3261 8000
Fax: (55) 15 3261 8016
Email: contato@portofelizsa.com.br
Web Address: www.portofelizsa.com.br
Personnel:
Ind. Mgr.: Rosivaldo Piazza
Phone: (55) 15 3261 8000
Fax: (55) 15 3261 8016
Pres.: Roberto Vetrano
Phone: (55) 15 3261 8000
Fax: (55) 15 3261 8016
Type of Operation: Paperboard mill
Paper/Paperboard Grades and Capacities:
Total paper and paperboard capacity: 30,000 mt/y
Linerboard: 17,000 mt/y
Corrugating medium/fluting: 13,000 mt/y
Paper and Paperboard Mill Data:
Stock Preparation:
Refiners: 2

ⓘⓜPrimo Tedesco S.A.
Caçador Mill
Ownership: 100% by Private
Rodovia Comendador Primo Tedesco, km 2,5. Bom Sucesso
89500-000 Caçador, SC
Brazil
Mailing Address: CP 481, 89500-000 Caçador, Brazil
Phone: (55) 49 3563 0600/3421 0600
Fax: (55) 49 3563 0537/3421 0604
Email: cacador@primotedesco.com.br
Web Address: www.primotedesco.com.br
Personnel:
Pres.: Julio André Ruas Tedesco
Phone: (55) 49 3563 0600
Fax: (55) 49 3563 0537
VP: Marco Antonio Tedesco
Phone: (55) 49 3563 0600
Fax: (55) 49 3563 0537
Superintendent Dir.: Elton Antonio Pigossi
Phone: (55) 49 3563 0600
Fax: (55) 49 3563 0537
ExecSec.: Cristine Machado
Phone: (55) 49 3563 0600
Fax: (55) 49 3563 0537
Commer. Mgr.: Vicente Luce Madeira
Phone: (55) 49 3563 0600
Fax: (55) 49 3563 0537
Indust. Mgr.: Valdomiro de Oliveira
Phone: (55) 49 3563 0600
Fax: (55) 49 3563 0537
Total Employees of Company: 440
Total Employees at this Location: 300
Type of Operation: Pulp mill, Paper mill, Paperboard mill
Pulp Grades and Capacities:
Total pulp capacity: 81,376 mt/y
Chemical Pulp: 62,704 mt/y
Recycled Pulping: 18,672 mt/y
Pulp Mill Data:
Chemical Pulping Systems:
Batch digesters: 3
Pulp Lines: 1
Chemical Recovery Equipment:
Evaporator lines: 5
Recovery boilers: 1
Lime Kiln
Recycled Fiber Treatment Lines:
Pulpers: 2 at 19,800 admt/y
Paper/Paperboard Grades and Capacities:
Total paper and paperboard capacity: 79,254 mt/y
Packaging papers: 11,067 mt/y
Linerboard: 68,187 mt/y
Paper and Paperboard Mill Data:
Stock Preparation:
Pulpers: 2
Refiners: 2
Paper Machines: 2
No. 1, fourdrinier, total capacity 23,562 mt/y, Trim width 1.6 m, Linerboard
No. 3, fourdrinier, total capacity 55,692 mt/y, Trim width 2.45 m, Packaging papers, Linerboard
Finishing Equipment:
Winders: 1 at 54,400 mt/y
Rewinders: 1 at 21,600 mt/y
Energy Data:
Power boilers: 2
Steam turbines: 1 at 1.4 MW
Hydro turbines: 3 at 1.1 MW
Electrical demand for mill: 141 MWh/D

ⓘPropaper
Ownership: Prolim
Rua Firo da Conceição, 500
Tremembé, SP
Brazil
Phone: (55) 12 3672 4430
Personnel:
Pres.: Edgard Almeida Pinto
Phone: (55) 3672 4430
Mill Mgr.: Neviton Santos
Phone: (55) 3672 4430
Qlty. Control Mgr.: Ana Paula
Phone: (55) 3672 4430
Commer. Dir.: Carlos Silva
Phone: (55) 3672 4430
Mill Locations:
Propaper, Tremembé Mill, Rua Firo da Conceição, 500, Tremembé, SP, Brazil, Capacity: 10,000 mt/y, (Paper mill)
Phone: (55) 12 3672 4430

ⓜPropaper
Tremembé Mill
Rua Firo da Conceição, 500
Tremembé, SP
Brazil
Phone: (55) 12 3672 4430
Web Address: www.propaper.com.br
Personnel:
Pres.: Edgard Almeida Pinto
Phone: (55) 12 3672 4430
Mill Mgr.: Neviton Santos
Phone: (55) 12 3672 4430
Qlty. Control Mgr.: Ana Paula
Phone: (55) 12 3672 4430
Commer. Dir.: Carlos Silva
Phone: (55) 12 3672 4430
Type of Operation: Paper mill
Paper/Paperboard Grades and Capacities:
Total paper and paperboard capacity: 10,000 mt/y
Tissue: 10,000 mt/y
Paper and Paperboard Mill Data:
Paper Machines: 1
PM 1, total capacity 10,000 mt/y, Trim width 2.8 m, Tissue

ⓘⓜPSA Indústria de Papel
São Leopoldo Mill
Rua Luiz Pedro Daudt 1200, CP 5
93025-730 São Leopoldo, RS
Brazil
Phone: (55) 51 3590 7800
Fax: (55) 51 3590 7839/7806
Email: vendas@sistemaflamingo.com.br
Web Address: www.sistemaflamingo.com.br
Personnel:
Pres.: Leo Moraes Poriuncula
Phone: (55) 51 3590 7800
Email: leo@sistemaflamingo.com.br
Silvia de Souza
Phone: (55) 51 3590 7810
Email: silvia@sistemaflamingo.com.br
Total Employees of Company: 100
Total Employees at this Location: 100
Type of Operation: Paper mill
Pulp Mill Data:
Recycled Fiber Treatment Lines:
Flotation deinking lines: 1 at 21,600 admt/y
Pulpers: 2 at 10,200 admt/y
Washing deinking lines: 1 at 21,600 admt/y
Paper/Paperboard Grades and Capacities:
Total paper and paperboard capacity: 10,200 mt/y
Tissue: 10,200 mt/y
Paper and Paperboard Mill Data:
Stock Preparation:
Pulpers: 2
Refiners: 3
Paper Machines: 1
PM 5, fourdrinier, total capacity 10,200 mt/y, Trim width 1.5 m, Tissue
Finishing Equipment:
Winders: 1 at 12,000 mt/y
Energy Data:
Power boilers: 2
Electrical demand for mill: 2 MWh/D

ⓘⓜIndústrias de Papel R. Ramenzoni S.A.
Cordeirópolis Mill
Rua Ary, 155, Vila Pereira, CP 09
13490-970 Cordeirópolis, SP
Brazil
Phone: (55) 19 3556 9020
Fax: (55) 19 3556 9024
Email: ramenzoni@ramenzoni.com.br, comercial@ramenzoni.com.br
Web Address: www.ramenzoni.com.br
Personnel:
Pres.: Roberto Antonio Augusto Ramenzoni
Phone: (55) 19 3556 9020
Fax: (55) 19 3556 9024
Email: roberto@ramenzoni.com.br
VP: Ricardo José Ramenzoni
Phone: (55) 19 3556 9020
Fax: (55) 19 3556 9024
Email: ricardo@ramenzoni.com.br
Prod. Mgr.: Jorge Miranda
Phone: (55) 19 3556 9020
Fax: (55) 19 3556 9024
Email: jorge@ramenzoni.com.br
RH Dir.: Lorival Batistela

Brazil

Phone: (55) 19 3556 9020
Fax: (55) 19 3556 9024
Email: lorival@ramenzoni.com.br
Total Employees at this Location: 200
Type of Operation: Paper mill, Paperboard mill
Pulp Grades and Capacities:
Total pulp capacity: 75,965 mt/y
Recycled Pulping: 75,965 mt/y
Pulp Mill Data:
Recycled Fiber Treatment Lines:
Pulpers: 1 at 73,000
Paper/Paperboard Grades and Capacities:
Total paper and paperboard capacity: 77,826 mt/y
Packaging papers: 13,923 mt/y
Corrugating medium/fluting: 13,923 mt/y
Boxboard/cartonboard: 49,980 mt/y
Paper and Paperboard Mill Data:
Stock Preparation:
Pulpers:
Paper Machines: 4
No. 1, fourdrinier, total capacity 4,998 mt/y, Trim width 2 m, Packaging papers
No. 2, fourdrinier, total capacity 8,925 mt/y, Trim width 2 m, Packaging papers
No. 3, fourdrinier, total capacity 13,923 mt/y, Trim width 2 m, Corrugating medium/fluting
No. 4, fourdrinier, total capacity 49,980 mt/y, Trim width 2 m, Boxboard/cartonboard
Coating Machines: 1
PM 4, total capacity 50,000 mt/y., on machine
Energy Data:
Power boilers: 1
Electrical demand for mill: 137 MWh/D

⊕⊚Indústrias Reunidas Cristo Rey Ltda.
Campo Mourão Mill
Estrada Barreiro das Frutas, km 8, C.P. 77 - Bairro Rio Ranchinho
87300-970 Campo Mourão, PR
Brazil
Phone: (55) 44 3525 1547
Fax: (55) 44 3525 1547
Personnel:
Admin. Dir.: Salvatore Milton
Phone: (55) 44 3525 1547
Total Employees at this Location: 56
Type of Operation: Paperboard mill
Pulp Grades and Capacities:
Total pulp capacity: 14,679 mt/y
Recycled Pulping: 14,679 mt/y
Pulp Mill Data:
Recycled Fiber Treatment Lines:
Recycled packaging pulping lines: 1 at 15,000
Paper/Paperboard Grades and Capacities:
Total paper and paperboard capacity: 14,280 mt/y
Corrugating medium/fluting: 14,280 mt/y
Paper and Paperboard Mill Data:
Paper Machines: 1
No. 1, fourdrinier, total capacity 14,280 mt/y, Trim width 2 m, Corrugating medium/fluting
Energy Data:
Power boilers: 1
Electrical demand for mill: 36 MWh/D

⊕⊚Indústrias de Papel Ribeirão Preto Ltda.
Ribeirão Preto Mill
Ownership: 100% by Marcelo Zucoloto
Rua Abílio Sampaio, 1331
14030-420 Ribeirão Preto, SP
Brazil
Phone: (55) 16 3456 3500
Fax: (55) 16 3456 3500
Email: papelribeirao@netsite.com.br
Personnel:
Mill Mgr. & Owner: Marcelo Zucoloto
Phone: (55) 16 3456 3500
Sls. Mgr.: Francis Rivia
Phone: (55) 16 3456 3500
Type of Operation: Paper mill
Paper/Paperboard Grades and Capacities:
Total paper and paperboard capacity: 13,000 mt/y
Corrugating medium/fluting: 4,000 mt/y

⊕Rigesa, Celulose, Papel e Embalagens Ltda.
Ownership: 100% by MeadWestvaco Corporation
Edifício Galleria Corporate, Av. Carlos Grimaldi, 1701, Fl. 5, Fazenda S. Quirino
13091-908 Campinas, SP
Brazil
Phone: (55) 19 3707 4000/4166
Fax: (55) 19 3707 4090
Web Address: www.rigesa.com.br, www.mwvrigesa.com.br
Personnel:
Pres.: Roberto Beckler
Phone: (55) 19 3707 4001
Fax: (55) 19 3707 4094
Finan. Dir.: Vanderlei Sakavicius
Phone: (55) 19 3707 4006
Fax: (55) 19 3707 4094
VP for Primary Products: Samuel Ice
Phone: (55) 19 3707 4004
Fax: (55) 19 3707 4094
Email: samuel.ice@rigesa.com.br
VP for Corr. Packg. Div.: Paulo Iserhard
Phone: (55) 19 3707 4009
Fax: (55) 19 3707 4094
Email: paulo.iserhard@rigesa.com.br
HR & Commun. Dir.: José Vegette
Phone: (55) 19 3707 4010
Fax: (55) 19 3707 4094
Strat. Plan. Mgr.: Luis Fernando Koutaka
Phone: (55) 19 3707 4045
Cons. Packag. Div. Dir.: Eduardo Scalese
Phone: (55) 19 3881 8839
Fax: (55) 19 3881 8839
Total Employees of Company: 2,300
Total Employees at this Location: 85
Mill Locations:
Rigesa, Celulose, Papel e Embalagens Ltda., Três Barras Mill, Av. Rigesa, 2.400, Bairro João Paulo II, 89490-000 Três Barras, SC, Brazil, Capacity: 434,826 mt/y, (Pulp mill, Paperboard mill)
Phone: (55) 47 3621 5400
Fax: (55) 47 3622 5324
Rigesa, Celulose, Papel e Embalagens Ltda., Valinhos Mill, Rua 13 de Maio 755 Centro, 13276 020 Valinhos, SP, Brazil, (Paperboard mill)
Phone: (55) 19 3869 9000/ 38699160
Fax: (55) 19 3869 9270
Email: antonio.puccinelli@mwv.com

⊚Rigesa, Celulose, Papel e Embalagens Ltda.
Três Barras Mill
Ownership: 100% by MeadWestvaco Corporation
Av. Rigesa, 2.400, Bairro João Paulo II
89490-000 Três Barras, SC
Brazil
Phone: (55) 47 3621 5400
Fax: (55) 47 3622 5324
Web Address: www.rigesa.com.br
Personnel:
Mill Mgr.: Aliomar Schmelzer
Phone: (55) 47 3621 5320
Email: aliomar.schmelzer@rigesa.com.br
Admin. Dir.: Haroldo Sussembach
Phone: (55) 47 3621 5329
Maint. Mgr.: Carlos E.R. Faria
Phone: (55) 47 3621 5223
Fax: (55) 47 3621 5249
Email: carlos.faria@rigesa.com.br
Purch. Agent: Fernando Krzesinki
Phone: (55) 47 3621 5390
Fax: (55) 47 3621 5399
Recov. Mgr.: Ferdinand Wessler
Phone: (55) 47 3621 5300
Fax: (55) 47 3621 5249
Sfty. & Effluent Treatment: Robson Carvalho
Phone: (55) 47 3621 5240
Eng. & Tech. Serv. Mgr.: Ali Abdul Ayoub
Phone: (55) 47 3621 5377
Fax: (55) 47 3621 5249
Email: ali.ayoub@rigesa.com.br
Pulp Mill & Wood Yard Mgr.: Narciso Zanatta
Phone: (55) 47 3621 5360
Fax: (55) 47 3621 5324
PM Mgr.: Anderson Frantz
Phone: (55) 47 3621 5353
Fax: (55) 47 3621 5324
Email: anderson.frantz@rigesa.com.br
Total Employees at this Location: 510
Type of Operation: Pulp mill, Paperboard mill
Pulp Grades and Capacities:
Total pulp capacity: 450,393 mt/y
Chemical Pulp: 346,421 mt/y
Recycled Pulping: 103,972 mt/y
Pulp Mill Data:
Chemical Pulping Systems:
Batch digesters: 5
Pulp Lines: 1
Chemical Recovery Equipment:
Evaporator lines: 1
Recovery boilers: 1
Lime Kiln
Recycled Fiber Treatment Lines:
Recycled packaging pulping lines: 1 at 125,000
Paper/Paperboard Grades and Capacities:
Total paper and paperboard capacity: 434,826 mt/y
Linerboard: 299,880 mt/y
Corrugating medium/fluting: 134,946 mt/y
Paper and Paperboard Mill Data:
Stock Preparation:
Refiners: 8
Paper Machines: 2
No. 3, fourdrinier, total capacity 134,946 mt/y, Trim width 4.4 m, Corrugating medium/fluting
No. 4, fourdrinier, total capacity 299,880 mt/y, Trim width 7.3 m, Linerboard
Finishing Equipment:
Winders: 1 at 240,000 mt/y
Calenders: 1
Rewinders: 1 at 260,000 mt/y
Energy Data:
Power boilers: 2
Steam turbines: 2 at 7.5, 25 MW
Electrical demand for mill: 866 MWh/D

⊚Rigesa, Celulose, Papel e Embalagens Ltda.
Valinhos Mill
Mill is closed (closed in late 2013)
Ownership: 100% by MeadWestvaco Corporation
Rua 13 de Maio 755 Centro
13276 020 Valinhos, SP
Brazil
Phone: (55) 19 3869 9000/ 38699160
Fax: (55) 19 3869 9270
Email: antonio.puccinelli@mwv.com
Web Address: www.rigesa.com.br
Personnel:
Paper Div. Dir.: Aliomar Schmelzer
Phone: (55) 19 3869 9194
Fax: (55) 19 3869 9270
Prod. Mgr.: Robson D. Souza
Phone: (55) 19 3869 9075
Fax: (55) 19 3869 9094
Paper Mill Mgr.: Antonio Carlos Puccinelli de Lima
Phone: (55) 19 3869 9194
Fax: (55) 19 3869 9270
Email: antonio.puccinelli@mwv.com
Convert. Dir.: Eduardo Brasil Gonçalves
Phone: (55) 38 69 9115

Brazil

Fax: (55) 19 3869 9295
Convert. Mgr.: Antonio Carlos Cardoso
Phone: (55) 19 3869 9157
Fax: (55) 19 3869 9295
Email: antonio.cardoso@mwv.com
Total Employees at this Location: 120
Type of Operation: Paperboard mill
Pulp Mill Data:
 Recycled Fiber Treatment Lines:
 Pulpers: 1 at 128,000 admt/y
Paper and Paperboard Mill Data:
 Stock Preparation:
 Pulpers: 1
 Refiners: 3
Paper Machines: 2
 No. 1, fourdrinier, total capacity 46,410 mt/y, Trim width 2.2 m
 No. 2, fourdrinier, total capacity 41,055 mt/y, Trim width 2.2 m
Finishing Equipment:
 Rewinders: 2 at 86,000 mt/y
Energy Data:
 Power boilers: 3

ⓘ Rio Jordão Papéis
Ownership: 100% by The Jaar Group
Rua Fernando Ferrari 1420 - Pav. III, CP 89
95680-000 Canela, RS
Brazil
 Phone: (55) (54) 3282.4111
 Email: rh@rjpapel.com.br.
 Web Address: rjpapel.com.br
Personnel:
 Prod. Mgr.: Leonardo Branco Pinto
 Materials Mgr.: Daisson Alencar Pilan Nunes
Mill Locations:
Rio Jordão Papéis, Canela Mill, Rua Fernando Ferrari 1420 - Pav. III, CP 89, 95680-000 Canela, RS, Brazil, Capacity: 57,120 mt/y, (Paper mill, Paperboard mill)
 Phone: (55) 54 3282 4111

ⓜ Rio Jordão Papéis
Canela Mill
Rua Fernando Ferrari 1420 - Pav. III, CP 89
95680-000 Canela, RS
Brazil
 Phone: (55) 54 3282 4111
 Web Address: rjpapel.com.br
Personnel:
 Prod. Mgr.: Clóvis Oliveira
 Phone: (55) 54 3282 4111
 HR Mgr.: Vanessa Lorenzoni Galle
 Phone: (55) 54 3282 4111
 Programmer: Jonas Baretta
 Phone: (55) 54 3282 4111
Total Employees at this Location: 140
Type of Operation: Paper mill, Paperboard mill
Pulp Grades and Capacities:
 Total pulp capacity: 58,215 mt/y
 Recycled Pulping: 58,215 mt/y
Pulp Mill Data:
 Recycled Fiber Treatment Lines:
 Recycled packaging pulping lines: 1 at 58,300
Paper/Paperboard Grades and Capacities:
 Total paper and paperboard capacity: 57,120 mt/y
 Corrugating medium/fluting: 57,120 mt/y
Paper and Paperboard Mill Data:
 Stock Preparation:
 Pulpers: 1
 Refiners: 3
Paper Machines: 1
 No. 2, fourdrinier, total capacity 57,120 mt/y, Trim width 2.23 m, Corrugating medium/fluting
Energy Data:
 Power boilers: 1
 Electrical demand for mill: 84 MWh/D

ⓘ Industrial e Agrícola Rio Verde Ltda.
Rua Coelho Neto, 3° Andar - Sala 34, CP 161
89160-000 Rio do Sul, SC
Brazil
 Phone: (55) 47 3521 0440/0682/2347
 Fax: (55) 47 3521 2108
 Email: rioverde@rioverde.ind.br
 Web Address: www.rioverde.ind.br
Personnel:
 Ind. Dir.: Frederico Faller
 Phone: (55) 47 3521 0440
 Fax: (55) 47 3521 2108
 Commer. Dept.: Vanderlei Deretti
 Phone: (55) 47 3521 0440
 Fax: (55) 47 3521 2108
Mill Locations:
Industrial e Agrícola Rio Verde Ltda., Rio do Campo Mill, Estrada Salto Rio d'Oeste Km. 4, s/n, 89198-000 Rio do Campo, SC, Brazil, Capacity: 21,000 mt/y, (Paperboard mill)
 Phone: (55) 47 3564 1300
 Fax: (55) 47 3564 1182
 Email: rioverde@rioverde.ind.br
Industrial e Agrícola Rio Verde Ltda., Taio Mill, Salto do Rio, Rahum, s/n, 89190-000 Taio, SC, Brazil, (Pulp mill)
 Email: rioverde@rioverde.ind.br

ⓜ Industrial e Agrícola Rio Verde Ltda.
Rio do Campo Mill
Estrada Salto Rio d'Oeste Km. 4, s/n
89198-000 Rio do Campo, SC
Brazil
 Phone: (55) 47 3564 1300
 Fax: (55) 47 3564 1182
 Email: rioverde@rioverde.ind.br
 Web Address: www.rioverde.ind.br
Personnel:
 Dir.: Valdir Erbs
 Phone: (55) 47 3564 1300
Type of Operation: Paperboard mill
Paper/Paperboard Grades and Capacities:
 Total paper and paperboard capacity: 21,000 mt/y Linerboard
 Corrugating medium/fluting
 Boxboard/cartonboard: 21,000 mt/y
Paper and Paperboard Mill Data:
Paper Machines: 1
 No. 1, total capacity 21,000 mt/y, Corrugating medium/fluting, Boxboard/cartonboard, Linerboard
Finishing Equipment:
 Calenders: 1
 Rewinders: 1
Energy Data:
 Power boilers: 2

ⓜ Industrial e Agrícola Rio Verde Ltda.
Taio Mill
Salto do Rio, Rahum, s/n
89190-000 Taio, SC
Brazil
 Email: rioverde@rioverde.ind.br
 Web Address: www.rioverde.ind.br
Personnel:
 Ind. Dir.: Frederico Faller
Type of Operation: Pulp mill
Pulp Grades and Capacities:
 Total pulp capacity: 10,000 mt/y
Pulp Mill Data:
 Mechanical Pulping Systems:
 Conventional grinders: 1
Pulp Lines: 1

ⓘⓜ RW Industria de Papel Ltda.
Palmeira Mill
Rod BR 277, s/n km 67
Palmeira
Brazil
 Phone: (55) 42 3252 3839
Type of Operation: Paper mill

Paper/Paperboard Grades and Capacities:
 Total paper and paperboard capacity: 10,000 mt/y
 Tissue: 10,000 mt/y

ⓘⓜ Samtai Industrial Ltda
Paulínia Mill
Paulínia city, SP
Brazil
 Phone: (55) 11 2671 1304
 Email: vendas@samtai.com.br
 Web Address: samtai.com
Type of Operation: Paper mill
Paper/Paperboard Grades and Capacities:
 Total paper and paperboard capacity: 35,000 mt/y
 Tissue: 35,000 mt/y
Paper and Paperboard Mill Data:
Paper Machines: 2
 PM 1, (started Q4, 2013), total capacity 17,500 mt/y, Trim width 3.7 m, Tissue
 PM 2, (due to start early 2014), total capacity 17,500 mt/y, Trim width 3.7 m, Tissue

ⓜ Santa Clara Indústria de Papéis Ltda.
Candoi Mill
Fazenda Rodeio Velho s/n
85140-000 Candoi, PR
Brazil
 Phone: (55) 42 3639 8000
 Fax: (55) 42 3639 8000
 Email: amauri@santaclarapapeis.com.br
 Web Address: www.santaclarapapeis.com.br
Personnel:
 Owner/Dir. Pres.: César Sguario Fadel
 Phone: (55) 42 3639 8000
 Fax: (55) 42 3639 8000
 Email: cesar@santaclarapapeis.com.br
 Mill Mgr.: Amauri de Paula
 Phone: (55) 42 3247 4000
 Fax: (55) 42 3639 8000
 Email: amauri@santaclarapapeis.com.br
Total Employees at this Location: 125
Type of Operation: Paperboard mill
Pulp Grades and Capacities:
 Total pulp capacity: 48,462 mt/y
 Recycled Pulping: 48,462 mt/y
Pulp Mill Data:
 Recycled Fiber Treatment Lines:
 Recycled packaging pulping lines: 1
Paper/Paperboard Grades and Capacities:
 Total paper and paperboard capacity: 47,838 mt/y
 Linerboard: 47,838 mt/y
Paper and Paperboard Mill Data:
Paper Machines: 1
 No. 1, fourdrinier, total capacity 47,838 mt/y, Trim width 1.7 m, Linerboard
Energy Data:
 Power boilers
 Electrical demand for mill: 81 MWh/D

ⓘⓜ Santa Clara Indústria de Papéis Ltda.
Ivaí Mill
Av. Principal, s/n - Palmital
84460-000 Ivaí, PR
Brazil
 Phone: (55) 42 3247 4000
 Fax: (55) 42 3247 4020
 Email: amauri@santaclarapapeis.com.br
 Web Address: www.santaclarapapeis.com.br
Personnel:
 Owner/Dir. Pres.: César Sguario Fadel
 Phone: (55) 42 3247 4000
 Fax: (55) 42 3247 4020
 Mill Mgr.: Amauri de Paula
 Phone: (55) 42 3247 4000
 Fax: (55) 42 3247 4020
 Email: amauri@santaclarapapeis.com.br
 Commer. Mgr.: Plínio Blanco

Phone: (55) 42 3247 4000
Fax: (55) 42 3247 4020
Total Employees at this Location: 100
Type of Operation: Paperboard mill
Mill Locations:
Santa Clara Indústria de Papéis Ltda., Candói Mill, Fazenda Rodeio Velho s/n, 85140-000 Candoi, PR, Brazil, Capacity: 47,838 mt/y, (Paperboard mill)
Phone: (55) 42 3639 8000
Fax: (55) 42 3639 8000
Email: amauri@santaclarapapeis.com.br
Pulp Grades and Capacities:
Total pulp capacity: 36,479 mt/y
Recycled Pulping: 36,479 mt/y
Pulp Mill Data:
Recycled Fiber Treatment Lines:
Pulpers: 1 at 40,500
Paper/Paperboard Grades and Capacities:
Total paper and paperboard capacity: 36,057 mt/y
Linerboard: 36,057 mt/y
Paper and Paperboard Mill Data:
Paper Machines: 1
No. 1, fourdrinier, total capacity 36,057 mt/y, Trim width 1.7 m, Linerboard
Energy Data:
Power boilers
Electrical demand for mill: 60 MWh/D

ⓘⓜSanta Maria Cia. de Papel e Celulose
Guarapuava Mill
BR 277 Km. 364, CP 3022, Rio Coutinho
85031-350 Guarapuava, PR
Brazil
Phone: (55) 42 3621 4000
Fax: (55) 42 3621 4059
Email: stamaria@santamaria.ind.br
Web Address: www.santamaria.ind.br
Personnel:
Pres.: Manuel Lacerda Cardoso Vieira
Phone: (55) 42 3621 4001
Finan. Dir.: Adriano Folador
Phone: (55) 42 3621 4001
Indus. Mgr.: Luiz Tadeu Perussolo
Phone: (55) 42 3621 4074
Fax: (55) 42 3621 4005
Logistics Mgr.: Saulo Bernardino
Phone: (55) 42 3621 4000
Fax: (55) 42 3621 4029
Email: saulo@santamaria.ind.br
Export Analyst: Bruna Barros
Phone: (55) 42 3621 4068
Fax: (55) 42 3621 4049
Commer. Mgr.: Mario Sterza
Phone: (55) 42 3621 4000
Process Coord.: Julio Cesar Ferrari
Phone: (55) 42 3621 4000
Total Employees at this Location: 200
Type of Operation: Paper mill
Paper/Paperboard Grades and Capacities:
Total paper and paperboard capacity: 99,960 mt/y
Uncoated woodfree/freesheet: 82,110 mt/y
Specialty and industrial: 17,850 mt/y
Paper and Paperboard Mill Data:
Stock Preparation:
Pulpers:
Paper Machines: 2
No. 1, fourdrinier, total capacity 35,700 mt/y, Trim width 2.5 m, Uncoated woodfree/freesheet, Specialty and industrial
No. 2, fourdrinier, total capacity 64,260 mt/y, Trim width 3.5 m, Uncoated woodfree/freesheet
Energy Data:
Power boilers: 1
Electrical demand for mill: 216 MWh/D

ⓘFábrica de Papel Santa Therezinha (SANTHER)
Av. Eusébio Matoso, 1375 - 9° andar
05423-180 São Paulo, SP
Brazil
Phone: (55) 11 3030 0200
Fax: (55) 11 3819 6132
Email: specialtypapers@santher.com.br
Web Address: www.santher.com.br
Personnel:
CEO: Ricardo Botelho
Phone: (55) 11 3030 0200
Fax: (55) 11 3819 6132
Email: Ricardo.botelho@santher.com.br
CFO: Marcelo Schmidt
Phone: (55) 11 3030 0200
Fax: (55) 11 3819 6132
Email: marcelo.schmidt@santher.com.br
Supply Chain Mgr.: Analucia Fonseca
Phone: (55) 11 3030 0200
Fax: (55) 11 3819 6132
Email: analucia.fonseca@santher.com.br
Domestic Market Mgr.: Paulo Segura
Phone: (55) 11 3819 6132
Fax: (55) 11 3819 6132
Email: paulo.segura@santher.com.br
Export Market Mgr.: Paula Borges
Phone: (55) 11 3819 6132
Fax: (55) 11 3819 6132
Email: paula.borges@santher.com.br
Total Employees at this Location: 46
Mill Locations:
Fábrica de Papel Santa Therezinha (SANTHER), Fadlo Haidar Mill, Rodovia Capitão, Barduíno Km. 98 CP 273, 12924-840 Bragança Paulista, SP, Brazil, Capacity: 121,023 mt/y, (Paper mill)
Phone: (55) 11 4481 8400
Fax: (55) 11 4031 1505
Email: san_ufh@santher.com.br
Fábrica de Papel Santa Therezinha (SANTHER), Governador Valadares Unit, Rodovia MG-04, Km. 05 CP 153, 35024-820 Capim, Governador Valadares, MG, Brazil, Capacity: 29,988 mt/y, (Paper mill)
Phone: (55) 33 2101 1212
Fax: (55) 33 3275 6910
Fábrica de Papel Santa Therezinha (SANTHER), Guaíba Mill, Vila Passo Fundo s/n°, CP 106, Bairro Passo Fundo, 92500-000 Guaíba, RS, Brazil, Capacity: 24,990 mt/y, (Paper mill)
Phone: (55) 51 3491 9400
Fax: (55) 51 3401 6090
Email: specialtypapers@santher.com.br
Fábrica de Papel Santa Therezinha (SANTHER), Penha Mill, Rua Aracati 275 - Penha, 03630-900 São Paulo, SP, Brazil, Capacity: 44,982 mt/y, (Paper mill)
Phone: (55) 11 2142 7876
Email: paula.borges@santher.com.br; irineu.palacio@santher.com.br

ⓘFábrica de Papel Santa Therezinha (SANTHER)
Fadlo Haidar Mill
Rodovia Capitão, Barduíno Km. 98 CP 273
12924-840 Bragança Paulista, SP
Brazil
Phone: (55) 11 4481 8400
Fax: (55) 11 4031 1505
Email: san_ufh@santher.com.br
Web Address: www.santher.com.br
Personnel:
Paper Prod. Mgr.: Mário Aguiar
Phone: (55) 11 4481 8417
Fax: (55) 11 4031 1505
Email: mario.aguiar@santher.com.br
Logist. Mgr.: José Aparecido Carvalho Silva
Phone: (55) 11 4481 8435
Fax: (55) 11 4031 1505
Email: jose@santher.com.br
Proj. Eng.: César Luis Canizela
Phone: (55) 11 4481 8489
Fax: (55) 11 4031 1505
Email: cesar.canizela@santher.com.br
Total Employees at this Location: 536
Type of Operation: Paper mill
Pulp Grades and Capacities:
Total pulp capacity: 54,636 mt/y
Recycled Pulping: 54,636 mt/y
Pulp Mill Data:
Bleach Plant Systems: 1
Recycled Pulping System, Type: DIP
Recycled Fiber Treatment Lines:
Flotation deinking lines: 1
Paper/Paperboard Grades and Capacities:
Total paper and paperboard capacity: 121,023 mt/y
Tissue: 121,023 mt/y
Paper and Paperboard Mill Data:
Stock Preparation:
Pulpers: 3
Refiners: 5
Paper Machines: 4
No. 3, fourdrinier, total capacity 27,846 mt/y, Trim width 2.76 m, Tissue, Uncoated woodfree/freesheet
No. 4, crescent former, total capacity 22,134 mt/y, Trim width 2.6 m, Tissue
No. 8, crescent former, total capacity 34,986 mt/y, Trim width 2.78 m, Tissue
No. 12, crescent former, total capacity 36,057 mt/y, Trim width 2.7 m, Tissue, Uncoated woodfree/freesheet
Energy Data:
Power boilers: 3
Electrical demand for mill: 430 MWh/D

ⓘFábrica de Papel Santa Therezinha (SANTHER)
Governador Valadares Unit
Rodovia MG-04, Km. 05 CP 153
35024-820 Capim, Governador Valadares, MG
Brazil
Phone: (55) 33 2101 1212
Fax: (55) 33 3275 6910
Web Address: www.santher.com.br
Personnel:
Indust. Mgr.: Alexandre Texeira
Phone: (55) 33 2101 1212
Fax: (55) 33 3275 6910
Prod. Mgr.: Jair Leite Da Silva
Phone: (55) 33 2101 1212
Fax: (55) 33 3275 6910
Total Employees at this Location: 172
Type of Operation: Paper mill
Pulp Grades and Capacities:
Total pulp capacity: 25,109 mt/y
Recycled Pulping: 25,109 mt/y
Pulp Mill Data:
Bleach Plant Systems: 1
Recycled Pulping System, Type: DIP
Recycled Fiber Treatment Lines:
Flotation deinking lines: 1
Pulpers: 3
Washing deinking lines: 1
Paper/Paperboard Grades and Capacities:
Total paper and paperboard capacity: 29,988 mt/y
Tissue: 29,988 mt/y
Paper and Paperboard Mill Data:
Stock Preparation:
Pulpers: 3
Refiners: 3
Paper Machines: 2
No. 6, fourdrinier, total capacity 14,994 mt/y, Trim width 2.38 m, Tissue, Uncoated woodfree/freesheet
No. 7, fourdrinier, total capacity 14,994 mt/y, Trim width 2.48 m, Tissue, Uncoated woodfree/freesheet
Finishing Equipment:
Rewinders: 3
Energy Data:
Power boilers: 3
Electrical demand for mill: 138 MWh/D

ⓘFábrica de Papel Santa Therezinha (SANTHER)
Guaíba Mill
Vila Passo Fundo s/n°, CP 106, Bairro Passo Fundo
92500-000 Guaíba, RS
Brazil

Brazil

Phone: (55) 51 3491 9400
Fax: (55) 51 3401 6090
Email: specialtypapers@santher.com.br
Web Address: www.santher.com.br
Total Employees at this Location: 130
Type of Operation: Paper mill
Paper/Paperboard Grades and Capacities:
Total paper and paperboard capacity: 24,990 mt/y
Tissue: 14,994 mt/y
Specialty and industrial: 9,996 mt/y
Paper and Paperboard Mill Data:
Stock Preparation:
Pulpers: 2
Refiners: 7
Paper Machines: 2
No. 9, fourdrinier, total capacity 9,996 mt/y, Trim width 2.8 m, Specialty and industrial
No. 11, fourdrinier, total capacity 14,994 mt/y, Trim width 2.8 m, Tissue, Uncoated woodfree/freesheet
Coating Machines: 1
PM9, total capacity 6,000 mt/y., off machine
Finishing Equipment:
Supercalenders: 1 at 3,600 mt/y
Rewinders: 2
Energy Data:
Power boilers: 1
Electrical demand for mill: 78 MWh/D

ⓂFábrica de Papel Santa Therezinha (SANTHER)
Penha Mill
Rua Aracati 275 - Penha
03630-900 São Paulo, SP
Brazil
Phone: (55) 11 2142 7876
Email: paula.borges@santher.com.br,
irineu.palacio@santher.com.br
Web Address: www.santher.com.br
Personnel:
HR Director.: Carolina Duque
Phone: (55) 11 2142 7876
Email: carolina.duque@santher.com.br
Total Employees at this Location: 200
Type of Operation: Paper mill
Paper/Paperboard Grades and Capacities:
Total paper and paperboard capacity: 44,982 mt/y
Tissue: 21,063 mt/y
Specialty and industrial: 23,919 mt/y
Paper and Paperboard Mill Data:
Stock Preparation:
Pulpers: 2
Refiners: 6
Paper Machines: 2
No. 1, Yankee dryer, total capacity 21,063 mt/y, Trim width 3 m, Tissue, Uncoated woodfree/freesheet
No. 2, Yankee dryer, total capacity 23,919 mt/y, Trim width 3.1 m, Specialty and industrial
Finishing Equipment:
Winders: 4 at 48,000 mt/y
Energy Data:
Power boilers: 2
Electrical demand for mill: 142 MWh/D

ⓄⓂSão Carlos SA Indústria de Papel e Embalagens
São Carlos Mill
Rodovia SP 318, Km. 236 CP 13 - Bairro Monjolinho
13560-970 São Carlos, SP
Brazil
Phone: (55) 16 3306 3900/09
Fax: (55) 16 3361 3900
Email: scarlosd@terra.com.br,
saocarlossa@linkway.com.br
Web Address: www.saocarlossa.com.br
Personnel:
Pres.: Mirella M. F. Zamparini
Phone: (55) 16 3306 3900
Fax: (55) 16 3361 3900
Dir. Supt.: Giorgio G. Foccorini

Phone: (55) 16 3306 3900
Fax: (55) 16 3361 3900
Ind. Dir.: Celso Luis Pedrino
Phone: (55) 16 3306 3900
Fax: (55) 16 3361 3900
Email: clpedrino@terra.com.br
Prod. Mgr.: Odalicio Bertolino Da Silva
Phone: (55) 16 3306 3900
Fax: (55) 16 3306 3900
Total Employees at this Location: 100
Type of Operation: Paper mill, Paperboard mill
Pulp Grades and Capacities:
Total pulp capacity: 72,866 mt/y
Recycled Pulping: 72,866 mt/y
Pulp Mill Data:
Recycled Fiber Treatment Lines:
Pulpers: 1 at 79,000
Paper/Paperboard Grades and Capacities:
Total paper and paperboard capacity: 71,400 mt/y
Linerboard: 28,560 mt/y
Corrugating medium/fluting: 42,840 mt/y
Paper and Paperboard Mill Data:
Paper Machines: 1
No. 1, fourdrinier, total capacity 71,400 mt/y, Trim width 3 m, Corrugating medium/fluting, Linerboard
Energy Data:
Power boilers: 1
Electrical demand for mill: 122 MWh/D

ⓂSão Gabriel Papéis Ltda.
União da Vitória Mill
Rua Autovia João Paulo Reolon, 3340 - São Gabriel
84600-000 União da Vitória, PR
Brazil
Phone: (55) 42 3523 9514
Fax: (55) 42 3523 9513/4
Email: comercial@sgabrielpapeis.com.br
Personnel:
Mill Mgr.: José Carlos Dissenha
Phone: (55) 42 3523 9514
Fax: (55) 42 3523 9513/4
Email: diretoria@sgabrielpapeis.com.br
Total Employees at this Location: 92
Type of Operation: Paperboard mill
Pulp Grades and Capacities:
Total pulp capacity: 43,292 mt/y
Recycled Pulping: 43,292 mt/y
Pulp Mill Data:
Recycled Fiber Treatment Lines:
Pulpers: 1 at 46,400
Paper/Paperboard Grades and Capacities:
Total paper and paperboard capacity: 42,840 mt/y
Linerboard: 20,706 mt/y
Corrugating medium/fluting: 22,134 mt/y
Paper and Paperboard Mill Data:
Paper Machines: 1
No. 1, fourdrinier, total capacity 42,840 mt/y, Trim width 2.5 m, Corrugating medium/fluting, Linerboard
Energy Data:
Power boilers: 1
Electrical demand for mill: 72 MWh/D

ⓄSão Gabriel Papéis Ltda.
Rua Autovia João Paulo Reolon, 3340 - São Gabriel
84600-000 União da Vitória
Brazil
Phone: (55) 42 3523 9514
Fax: (55) 42 3523 9513/4
Email: comercial@sgabrielpapeis.com.br
Personnel:
Mill Mgr.: José Carlos Dissenha
Phone: (55) 42 3523 9514
Fax: (55) 42 3523 9513/4
Email: diretoria@sgabrielpapeis.com.br
Total Employees at this Location: 140
Mill Locations:
São Gabriel Papéis Ltda., União da Vitória Mill, Rua Autovia João Paulo Reolon, 3340 - São Gabriel, 84600-000 União da Vitória, PR, Brazil, Capacity:

42,840 mt/y, (Paperboard mill)
Phone: (55) 42 3523 9514
Fax: (55) 42 3523 9513/4
Email: comercial@sgabrielpapeis.com.br

ⓄSAPELBA - Fábrica de Papel da Bahia S.A.
Rua Amazonas, 1020 CP 472, Pituba
41830-380 Salvador, BA
Brazil
Phone: (55) 71 3311 4877
Fax: (55) 71 3311 4879
Email: sapelba.ssa@sapelba.com.br
Personnel:
Pres.: Alexandre Visnevski
Phone: (55) 71 3311 4877
Fax: (55) 71 3311 4879
Dir.: Natalia Ferraz
Phone: (55) 71 3311 4877
Fax: (55) 71 3311 4879
Total Employees of Company: 220
Mill Locations:
SAPELBA - Fábrica de Papel da Bahia S.A., Feira de Santana Mill, Rodovia BR 101, Km 175, Humildes, CP 268, 44135-000 Feira de Santana, BA, Brazil, Capacity: 21,000 mt/y, (Paper mill)
Phone: (55) 75 3321 9700
Fax: (55) 75 3321 9737
Email: sapelba@sapelba.com.br

ⓂSAPELBA - Fábrica de Papel da Bahia S.A.
Feira de Santana Mill
Rodovia BR 101, Km 175, Humildes, CP 268
44135-000 Feira de Santana, BA
Brazil
Phone: (55) 75 3321 9700
Fax: (55) 75 3321 9737
Email: sapelba@sapelba.com.br
Personnel:
Pres.: Alexandre Visnevski
Phone: (55) 75 3321 9700
Fax: (55) 75 3321 9737
Ind. Dir.: Paulo Afonso Torres
Phone: (55) 75 3321 9700
Fax: (55) 75 3321 9737
Type of Operation: Paper mill
Paper/Paperboard Grades and Capacities:
Total paper and paperboard capacity: 21,000 mt/y
Linerboard
Corrugating medium/fluting
Paper and Paperboard Mill Data:
Paper Machines: 1
No. 1, Trim width 2.5 m, Containerboard

ⓄSchweitzer-Mauduit do Brasil
Ownership: 99% by Schweitzer-Mauduit International Inc.
Av. Nilo Peçanha, 50, cj 1509
20020-100 Rio de Janeiro, RJ
Brazil
Phone: (55) 21 2524 7824
Fax: (55) 21 2524 7853
Email: swmb@swmintl.com
Web Address: www.swmintl.com
Personnel:
Superintendent Dir.: Antonio Carlos Vilela
Phone: (55) 24 2447 5104
Fax: (55) 24 2447 5235
Email: dmonteiro@swmintl.com
Prod. Dlvpmnt Mgr.: Carlos Ragazzo
Phone: (55) 21 2524 7824
Fax: (55) 21 2524 7853
Total Employees of Company: 480
Total Employees at this Location: 6
Mill Locations:
Schweitzer-Mauduit do Brasil, Santanesia do Piraí Mill, Av. Darcy Vargas 325 5° Distrito de Piraí, 27195-000 Santanesia do Piraí, RJ, Brazil, Capacity: 37,000 mt/y, (Paper mill)

Brazil

Phone: (55) 24 2447 5000/5200
Fax: (55) 24 2443 5570

ⓂSchweitzer-Mauduit do Brasil
Santanesia do Piraí Mill
Ownership: 99% by Schweitzer-Mauduit International Inc.
Av. Darcy Vargas 325 5° Distrito de Piraí
27195-000 Santanesia do Piraí, RJ
Brazil
Phone: (55) 24 2447 5000/5200
Fax: (55) 24 2443 5570
Web Address: www.swmintl.com
Personnel:
Prod. Dir.: Julio Cesar Vasconcellos
Phone: (55) 24 2447 5000/5200
Tech. Mgr.: Marcos Aurélio Goldoni
Phone: (55) 24 2447 5000/5200
Logist. Mgr.: Milton Pedro Amorim
Phone: (55) 24 2447 5000/5200
Total Employees at this Location: 498
Type of Operation: Paper mill
Paper/Paperboard Grades and Capacities:
Total paper and paperboard capacity: 37,000 mt/y
Specialty and industrial: 37,000 mt/y
Paper and Paperboard Mill Data:
Stock Preparation:
Pulpers: 7
Refiners: 30
Paper Machines: 4
PM 1, Specialty and industrial
PM 3, total capacity 6,300 mt/y, Specialty and industrial
PM 4, total capacity 5,700 mt/y, Specialty and industrial
PM 6, total capacity 28,000 mt/y, Specialty and industrial
Energy Data:
Power boilers: 5

ⓂSengés Papel e Celulose Ltda.
Rua Gov. Manoel Ribas, 131
84220-000 Sengés, PR
Brazil
Phone: (55) 43 3567 8600
Fax: (55) 43 3567 8600
Email: sepace@uol.com.br
Web Address: www.sengespapel.com.br
Personnel:
Ind. Eng.: Ismair Miranda
Phone: (55) 43 3567 8600
Fax: (55) 43 3567 8600
Finan.&Commer. Dir.: Janey Rose Sguario
Phone: (55) 43 3567 8600
Fax: (55) 43 3567 8600
HR Mgr.: Marli Gregório
Phone: (55) 43 3567 8600
Fax: (55) 43 3567 8600
Purch.Mgr.: Carlos Eduardo Tobias Pedreira
Phone: (55) 43 3567 8600
Fax: (55) 43 3567 8600
Prod. Supervisor: Claudiomiro Camargo
Phone: (55) 43 3567 8600
Fax: (55) 43 3567 8600
Mill Locations:
Sengés Papel e Celulose Ltda., Senges Mill, Rua Luiz José Sguario s/n, 84220-000 Senges, PR, Brazil, Capacity: 3,187 mt/y, (Pulp mill, Paper mill)
Phone: (55) 43 3567 1335
Fax: (55) 43 3567 1335
Email: fabrica@sengespapel.com.br

ⓂSengés Papel e Celulose Ltda.
Senges Mill
Rua Luiz José Sguario s/n
84220-000 Senges, PR
Brazil
Phone: (55) 43 3567 1335
Fax: (55) 43 3567 1335
Email: fabrica@sengespapel.com.br
Web Address: www.sengespapel.com.br
Personnel:
Mill Mgr.: Shigueo
Phone: (55) 43 3567 1335
Fax: (55) 43 3567 1335
Email: shigueo@sengespapel.com.br
Type of Operation: Pulp mill, Paper mill
Pulp Grades and Capacities:
Total pulp capacity: 28,203 mt/y
Paper/Paperboard Grades and Capacities:
Total paper and paperboard capacity: 3,187 mt/y
Packaging papers: 3,187 mt/y

ⓄⓂSEPAC - Serrados e Pasta de Celulose Ltda.
Mallet Mill
Antiga Hidrelétrica
84570-000 Mallet, PR
Brazil
Phone: (55) 42 3542 1212/1286/41 3322 5606
Fax: (55) 42 3542 1216
Email: sepac@sepac.com.br
Web Address: www.sepac.com.br
Personnel:
Pres.: João Ferreira Dias
Phone: (55) 42 3542 1212/1286/41 3322 5606
Comm. Mgr.: Sonia Mabile
Phone: (55) 42 3542 1212/1286/41 3322 5606
Sales Admin. Mgr.: Tatiana Sescato
Phone: (55) 41 9932 3790
Email: tatiana@sepac.com.br
Total Employees at this Location: 350
Type of Operation: Paper mill
Paper/Paperboard Grades and Capacities:
Total paper and paperboard capacity: 130,662 mt/y
Tissue: 130,662 mt/y
Paper and Paperboard Mill Data:
Paper Machines: 5
No. 1, crescent former, total capacity 13,566 mt/y, Trim width 1.7 m, Tissue, Uncoated woodfree/freesheet
No. 2, crescent former, total capacity 13,566 mt/y, Trim width 1.7 m, Tissue, Uncoated woodfree/freesheet
No. 3, crescent former, total capacity 35,700 mt/y, Trim width 2.76 m, Tissue
No. 4, crescent former, total capacity 32,844 mt/y, Trim width 2.81 m, Tissue
No. 5, total capacity 34,986 mt/y, Trim width 4.8 m, Tissue
Energy Data:
Power boilers

ⓄⓂSerrana Papel e Celulose Ltda.
Serrana Mill
Ownership: 100% by Private
Rodovia SP 333 Km. 37.5, CP 29
14150-000 Serrana, SP
Brazil
Phone: (55) 16 3687-1011
Fax: (55) 16 3687-1017
Email: vendas@serranapapel.com.br
Personnel:
Pres.: Marcos Carreira
Prod. Mgr.: José Carlos Bispo
Sls. Mgr.: Edson Pereira
Total Employees at this Location: 125
Type of Operation: Paper mill
Paper/Paperboard Grades and Capacities:
Total paper and paperboard capacity: 23,919 mt/y
Tissue: 23,919 mt/y
Paper and Paperboard Mill Data:
Paper Machines: 2
No. 1, fourdrinier, total capacity 11,781 mt/y, Trim width 2.5 m, Tissue
No. 2, fourdrinier, total capacity 12,138 mt/y, Trim width 2.5 m, Tissue
Energy Data:
Power boilers
Electrical demand for mill: 73 MWh/D

ⓂSonoco do Brasil Ltda.
Londrina Mill
Ownership: Sonoco Products Co.
Rua Noitibó, 157, Vila Yara
86027-000 Londrina, PR
Brazil
Mailing Address: CP 2346, 86027-000 Londrina, Brazil
Phone: (55) 43 3377 7761
Fax: (55) 43 3377 7700
Email: antonio.silva@sonoco.com.br
Web Address: www.sonoco.com
Personnel:
Mill Mgr.: Otavio Baleoti
Phone: (55) 43 3377 7737
Paper Mill Mgr.: Carlos Amorin
Phone: (55) 43 3377 7761
Tech. Mgr.: Rafael Gauce
Phone: (55) 43 3377 7761
Purch. Agt./Acctg. Mgr.: Evaldo da Silva Lima
Phone: (55) 43 3377 7761
Supt. Prod.: Antônio César da Silva
Phone: (55) 43 3377 7761
Total Employees at this Location: 105
Type of Operation: Paper mill, Paperboard mill
Pulp Grades and Capacities:
Total pulp capacity: 41,905 mt/y
Recycled Pulping: 41,905 mt/y
Pulp Mill Data:
Recycled Fiber Treatment Lines:
Pulpers: 1 at 50,000 admt/y
Paper/Paperboard Grades and Capacities:
Total paper and paperboard capacity: 41,412 mt/y
Boxboard/cartonboard: 41,412 mt/y
Paper and Paperboard Mill Data:
Stock Preparation:
Pulpers: 1
Refiners: 2
Paper Machines: 1
No. 1, fourdrinier, total capacity 41,412 mt/y, Trim width 2.4 m, Boxboard/cartonboard
Finishing Equipment:
Rewinders: 1
Energy Data:
Power boilers: 1
Electrical demand for mill: 72 MWh/D

ⓄⓂSopasta S.A. Indústria e Comércio
Tangará Mill
Rua Rio Bonito 218 - Centro
89642-000 Tangará, SC
Brazil
Phone: (55) 49 3532 7000
Fax: (55) 49 3532 7020
Email: sopasta@sopasta.com.br
Web Address: www.sopasta.com.br
Personnel:
Owner: Milton Harasawa
Phone: (55) 49 3532 7000
Fax: (55) 49 3532 7020
Dir.: Renata Harasawa Paganini
Phone: (55) 49 3532 7000
Fax: (55) 49 3532 7020
Dir. Finan.: Dean M. B. Cendron
Phone: (55) 49 3532 7000
Fax: (55) 49 3532 7020
Finan. Mgr.: Gerson Luiz Santana
Phone: (55) 49 3532 7000
Fax: (55) 49 3532 7020
Admin. Mgr.: Andréa Thomazoni
Phone: (55) 49 3532 7000
Fax: (55) 49 3532 7020
Sls. Analyst: Rosiani Twardowski
Phone: (55) 49 3532 7000
Fax: (55) 49 3532 7020
Email: rct@sopasta.com.br
Sls. Supervisor: Gilson Balbinot
Phone: (55) 49 3532 7000
Fax: (55) 49 3532 7020

Brazil

Total Employees at this Location: 75
Type of Operation: Paperboard mill
Pulp Grades and Capacities:
  Total pulp capacity: 33,458 mt/y
  Recycled Pulping: 33,458 mt/y
Pulp Mill Data:
  Recycled Fiber Treatment Lines:
  Pulpers: 1 at 36,500
Paper/Paperboard Grades and Capacities:
  Total paper and paperboard capacity: 32,844 mt/y
  Linerboard: 32,844 mt/y
Paper and Paperboard Mill Data:
Paper Machines: 1
No. 1, fourdrinier, total capacity 32,844 mt/y, Trim width 2.5 m, Linerboard
Energy Data:
  Power boilers: 2
  Electrical demand for mill: 57 MWh/D

ⓗIndÚstria de Papel Sovel da Amazônia Ltda.

Ownership: 100% by Sovel Group
Rua Dr. João Paulo, 600 - Colônia Antônio Aleixo
69008-140 Manaus, AM
Brazil
  Phone: (55) 92 3616 2700 / 2736
  Fax: (55) 92 3616 2715
  Email: diretoria@sovel.com.br,
  comercial@sovel.com.br,
  secgerencia@sovel.com.br
  Web Address: www.sovel.com.br
Personnel:
  Dir. Pres.: Ali Yacub
  Phone: (55) 3616 2700
  Fax: (55) 92 3616 2715
  Prod. Mgr.: Gastão Justo
  Phone: (55) 3616 2700
  Fax: (55) 92 3616 2715
  Email: gastao.justo@sovel.com.br
  Prod. Coordinator: José Aparecido Batista
  Phone: (55) 3616 2700
  Fax: (55) 92 3616 2715
Mill Locations:
  Indústria de Papel Sovel da Amazônia Ltda., Manaus Mill, Rua Dr. João Paulo, 600 - Colônia Antônio Aleixo, 69008-140 Manaus, AM, Brazil, Capacity: 27,846 mt/y, (Paper mill, Paperboard mill)
  Phone: (55) 92 3616 2700
  Fax: (55) 92 3616 2715
  Email: diretoria@sovel.com.br

ⓜIndÚstria de Papel Sovel da Amazônia Ltda.
Manaus Mill

Rua Dr. João Paulo, 600 - Colônia Antônio Aleixo
69008-140 Manaus, AM
Brazil
  Phone: (55) 92 3616 2700
  Fax: (55) 92 3616 2715
  Email: diretoria@sovel.com.br
  Web Address: www.sovel.com.br
Personnel:
  Dir. Pres.: Ali Yacub
  Phone: (55) 92 3616 2700
  Fax: (55) 3616 2715
  Email: directoria@sovel.com.br
  Prod. Mgr.: Gastão Justo
  Phone: (55) 92 3616 2700
  Fax: (55) 3616 2715
  Email: gastao.justo@sovel.com.br
  Prod. Coordinator: José Aparecido Batista
  Phone: (55) 3616 2717, 8168 0621
  Fax: (55) 3616 2715
  Email: jose.batista@sovel.com.br
  Environ. Dir.: Fabiane S Fabiane S
  Phone: (55) 92 3616 2700
  Fax: (55) 3616 2715
Total Employees at this Location: 100
Type of Operation: Paper mill, Paperboard mill

Pulp Grades and Capacities:
  Total pulp capacity: 28,979 mt/y
  Recycled Pulping: 28,979 mt/y
Pulp Mill Data:
  Recycled Fiber Treatment Lines:
  Recycled packaging pulping lines: 1
Paper/Paperboard Grades and Capacities:
  Total paper and paperboard capacity: 27,846 mt/y
  Tissue: 4,998 mt/y
  Linerboard: 15,708 mt/y
  Corrugating medium/fluting: 7,140 mt/y
Paper and Paperboard Mill Data:
  Stock Preparation:
  Pulpers:
Paper Machines: 2
No. 2, Yankee dryer, total capacity 4,998 mt/y, Trim width 2.2 m, Tissue, Uncoated woodfree/freesheet
No. 3, Yankee dryer, total capacity 22,848 mt/y, Trim width 2.3 m, Linerboard, Corrugating medium/fluting
Energy Data:
  Power boilers: 1
  Steam turbines: 3
  Electrical demand for mill: 51 MWh/D

ⓗⓜStora Enso Arapoti Indústria de Papel Ltda.
Arapoti Mill

Ownership: 80% by Stora Enso Oyj, 20% by Celulosa Arauco y Constitucion S.A.
Rdv DR 01, Km 7 - Fazenda Barra Mansa, CP-11
84990-000 Arapoti, PR
Brazil
  Phone: (55) 43 3512 2100
  Fax: (55) 43 3512 2413
  Web Address: www.storaenso.com
Personnel:
  Head of Latin American Operations: Juan Carlos Bueno
  Phone: (55) 43 3512 2100
  Fax: (55) 43 3512 2413
  Email: juan.carlos@storaenso.com
  Mill Dir. & Group Safety Ambassador: Lucinei Damálio
  Phone: (55) 43 3512 2325
  Fax: (55) 43 3512 2411
  Email: lucinei.damalio@storaenso.com
  Fiber & Utilities Coord.: Rodrigo Biava
  Phone: (55) 43 3512 2100
  Fax: (55) 43 3512 2413
  Email: rodrigo.biava@storaenso.com
  Purch. Mgr.: Fernando Sanchez Laserna
  Phone: (55) 43 3512 2100
  Fax: (55) 43 3512 2413
  Email: fernando.laserna@storaenso.com
  Eng. Mgr.: Christiano Kluppel
  Phone: (55) 43 3512 2100
  Fax: (55) 43 3512 2413
  Email: christiano.kluppel@storaenso.com
Total Employees of Company: 336
Total Employees at this Location: 336
Type of Operation: Paper mill
Pulp Grades and Capacities:
  Total pulp capacity: 36,634 mt/y
  Mechanical Pulp: 36,634 mt/y
Pulp Mill Data:
  Mechanical Pulping Systems:
  TMP systems: 1
Pulp Lines: 1
  Bleach Plant Systems: 1
  Mechanical TMP Pulping System, Type: Eucalyptus/Softwood, Sequence: P, Capacity 100,000 admt/y
Paper/Paperboard Grades and Capacities:
  Total paper and paperboard capacity: 185,000 mt/y
  Coated mechanical/groundwood: 185,000 mt/y
Paper and Paperboard Mill Data:
  Stock Preparation:
  Pulpers: 2
  Refiners: 2
Paper Machines: 1
No. 1, DuoFormer CF, total capacity 185,000 mt/y, Trim width 5.24 m, Coated mechanical/groundwood
Coating Machines: 1
No. 1, total capacity 205,000 mt/y., off machine
Finishing Equipment:
  Winders: 1 at 205,000 mt/y
  Supercalenders: 2 at 205,000 mt/y
  Rewinders: 1 at 205,000 mt/y
Energy Data:
  Power boilers: 1
  TMP Reboiler: 1
  Electrical demand for mill: 873 MWh/D

ⓗⓜSulamericana Industrial Ltda.
Mogi Mirim Mill

Rua Nurollah Soltani 19 CP 108
13800-000 Mogi Mirim, SP
Brazil
  Phone: (55) 19 3805 8585
  Fax: (55) 19 3862 4596
  Email: sulamericanapapel@sulamericanapapel.com.br
  Web Address: www.silpapel.com.br
Personnel:
  Owner: Qodrat Ullah Soltani
  Phone: (55) 19 3805 8585
  Fax: (55) 19 3862 4596
  Pres.: Jorge H.M. Guerreiro
  Phone: (55) 19 3805 8585
  Fax: (55) 19 3862 4596
  Admin. Mgr. Finan.: Reinaldo G Reinaldo G
  Phone: (55) 19 3805 8585
  Fax: (55) 19 3862 4596
  Analyst.: Sergio G Sergio G
  Phone: (55) 19 3805 8585
  Fax: (55) 19 3862 4596
Total Employees at this Location: 52
Type of Operation: Paperboard mill
Pulp Grades and Capacities:
  Total pulp capacity: 30,479 mt/y
  Recycled Pulping: 30,479 mt/y
Pulp Mill Data:
  Recycled Fiber Treatment Lines:
  Recycled packaging pulping lines: 1
Paper/Paperboard Grades and Capacities:
  Total paper and paperboard capacity: 32,130 mt/y
  Linerboard: 32,130 mt/y
Paper and Paperboard Mill Data:
  Stock Preparation:
  Pulpers:
Paper Machines: 1
No. 1, fourdrinier, total capacity 32,130 mt/y, Trim width 2.6 m, Linerboard
Energy Data:
  Power boilers: 1
  Electrical demand for mill: 56 MWh/D

ⓗSuzanense Indústria e Comércio de Papéis Ltda.

Av. Vereador João Baptista Fittipaldi, 640
08685-000 Suzano, SP
Brazil
  Phone: (55) 11 4742 8875
  Fax: (55) 11 4742 8875
Personnel:
  Dir.: Aline Liao
  Phone: (55) 4742 8875
  Fax: (55) 4742 8875
  Dir.: Cheng Huliao
  Phone: (55) 4742 8875
  Fax: (55) 4742 8875
Mill Locations:
  Suzanense Indústria e Comércio de Papéis Ltda., Suzano Mill, Av. Vereador João Baptista Fittipaldi, 640, 08685-000 Suzano, SP, Brazil, Capacity: 7,200 mt/y, (Paper mill)
  Phone: (55) 11 4742 8875
  Fax: (55) 11 4742 8875
  Email: suzanensepapeis@terra.com.br

Brazil

ⓂSuzanense Indústria e Comércio de Papéis Ltda.
Suzano Mill
Av. Vereador João Baptista Fittipaldi, 640
08685-000 Suzano, SP
Brazil
 Phone: (55) 11 4742 8875
 Fax: (55) 11 4742 8875
 Email: suzanensepapeis@terra.com.br
Personnel:
Dir.: Aline Liao
 Phone: (55) 11 4742 8875
 Fax: (55) 4742 8875
Dir.: Cheng Huliao
 Phone: (55) 11 4742 8875
 Fax: (55) 4742 8875
Type of Operation: Paper mill
Paper/Paperboard Grades and Capacities:
Total paper and paperboard capacity: 7,200 mt/y
Uncoated woodfree/freesheet
Specialty and industrial: 7,200 mt/y
Paper and Paperboard Mill Data:
Paper Machines: 1
No. 1, total capacity 7,200 mt/y, Uncoated woodfree/freesheet, Specialty and industrial

ⓂSuzano Papel e Celulose S.A.
Ownership: 10% by Chemco International Inc., 90% by Nemo, Leon, and Max Feffer
Av. Brigadeiro Faria Lima 1355, 5°/10°
01452-919 São Paulo, SP
Brazil
 Phone: (55) 11 3503 9000/9326
 Fax: (55) 11 3815 7078
 Web Address: www.suzano.com.br
Personnel:
Chmn. of the Board: David Feffer
 Phone: (55) 11 3503 9000
 Fax: (55) 11 3815 7078
CEO: Walter Schalka
 Phone: (55) 11 3503 9000
 Fax: (55) 11 3815 7078
CFO (Eff. March 31, 2014): Marcelo Feriozzi Bacci
 Phone: (55) 11 3503 9000
 Fax: (55) 11 3815 7078
Head of Pulp Business Unit (Eff. February 2014): Carlos Aníbal De Almeida Jr.
 Phone: (55) 11 3503 9000
 Fax: (55) 11 3815 7078
COO: Ernesto Pousada Jr.
 Phone: (55) 11 3503 9000
 Fax: (55) 11 3815 7078
Total Employees of Company: 17,000
Mill Locations:
Suzano Papel e Celulose S.A., Limeira Mill, Estrada Limeira 391, s/n° - Bairro do Lageado, 13465-000 Limeira, SP, Brazil, Capacity: 379,848 mt/y, (Pulp mill, Paper mill)
 Phone: (55) 19 2108 3200/3311
 Fax: (55) 19 2108 3431
 Email: suzano@suzano.com.br
Suzano Papel e Celulose S.A., Maranhão Mill, Imperatriz city, MA, Brazil, (Pulp mill)
 Email: suzano@suzano.com.br
Suzano Papel e Celulose S.A., Mucuri Mill, Rod. BR 101 KM 945 - 4 + 7 Km à Esquerda S/N°, 45930-000 Mucuri, BA, Brazil, Capacity: 249,900 mt/y, (Pulp mill, Paper mill)
 Phone: (55) 73 3878 7500
 Fax: (55) 73 3292 3500
 Email: suzano@suzano.com.br
Suzano Papel e Celulose S.A., Rio Verde Unit, Av. Dr. Miguel Brada, Rio Baixo, 08613-010 Suzano, SP, Brazil, Capacity: 51,051 mt/y, (Paper mill)
 Phone: (55) 11 3636 7800
 Fax: (55) 11 4748 4388
 Email: faleconosco@suzano.com.br
Suzano Papel e Celulose S.A., Ripasa II Mill, Av. Elis Yazbek, 1502, 06803-902 Embu, SP, Brazil, Capacity: 49,980 mt/y, (Paper mill, Paperboard mill)
 Phone: (55) 11 2149 2800
 Fax: (55) 11 4704 2494
 Email: faleconosco@suzano.com.br
Suzano Papel e Celulose S.A., Suzano Mill, Av. Prudente de Moraes 3240/4006, 08613-900 Suzano, SP, Brazil, Capacity: 559,776 mt/y, (Pulp mill, Paper mill, Paperboard mill)
 Phone: (55) 11 3636 5000
 Fax: (55) 11 3636 5479

ⒽⓂSuzano Papel e Celulose S.A.
Limeira Mill
Ownership: 10% by Chemco International Inc., 90% by Nemo, Leon, and Max Feffer
Estrada Limeira 391, s/nº - Bairro do Lageado
13465-000 Limeira, SP
Brazil
Mailing Address: Caixa Postal 274, 13465-970 Americana, Brazil
 Phone: (55) 19 2108 3200/3311
 Fax: (55) 19 2108 3431
 Email: suzano@suzano.com.br
 Web Address: www.suzano.com.br
Personnel:
Paper Mill Mgr.: Edomar Raimundo
 Phone: (55) 19 2108 3200
 Fax: (55) 19 2108 3431
Purch. Mgr.: Francine Melo
 Phone: (55) 19 2108 3200
 Fax: (55) 19 2108 3431
Exec. Officer - Forest Bus. Unit: Paulo Celso Basseti
 Phone: (55) 19 2108 3200
 Fax: (55) 19 2108 3431
Prod. Mgr.: Rui Aureliano de Lima
 Phone: (55) 19 2108 3200
 Fax: (55) 19 2108 3431
Commun. Mgr.: Luciana Bueno
 Phone: (55) 19 2108 3200
 Fax: (55) 19 2108 3431
 Email: lucianabueno@conpacel.com.br
Total Employees at this Location: 1,300
Type of Operation: Pulp mill, Paper mill
Pulp Grades and Capacities:
Total pulp capacity: 642,654 mt/y
Pulp available for market: 339,864 mt/y
Chemical Pulp: 642,654 mt/y
Pulp Mill Data:
Chemical Pulping Systems:
Batch digesters: 9
Continuous digesters: 1
Pulp Lines: 2
Bleach Plant Systems: 2
Chemical Pulping System, Type: Hardwood - D(EOP) HP, Sequence: O_2 DEopD
Chemical Pulping System - STD/ECF, Type: Hardwood, Sequence: O_2 DEopD, Capacity 630,000 admt/y
Chemical Recovery Equipment:
Evaporator lines: 2
Recovery boilers: 3
Lime Kiln
Recycled Fiber Treatment Lines:
Pulpers: 2
Pulp Dryers:
Air Float dryers 1, Wet Lap machine 1
Paper/Paperboard Grades and Capacities:
Total paper and paperboard capacity: 379,848 mt/y
Uncoated woodfree/freesheet: 279,531 mt/y
Coated woodfree/freesheet: 100,317 mt/y
Paper and Paperboard Mill Data:
Stock Preparation:
Pulpers: 2
Paper Machines: 2
No. 1, DuoFormer D, total capacity 146,013 mt/y, Trim width 4.2 m, Coated woodfree/freesheet, Uncoated woodfree/freesheet
No. 2, GapFormer, total capacity 233,835 mt/y, Trim width 5.2 m, Coated woodfree/freesheet, Uncoated woodfree/freesheet
Coating Machines: 3
No. 3, total capacity 90,000 mt/y., off machine
PM 1's coater, total capacity 140,000 mt/y., on machine
PM 2's coater, off machine
Finishing Equipment:
Supercalenders: 2 at 40 mt/y, 25 mt/y
Rewinders: 2 at 300,000 mt/y
Sheeters: 4 at 238,000 mt/y
Energy Data:
Power boilers: 2
Steam turbines: 2 at 36 MW
Electrical demand for mill: 1,369 MWh/D

ⓂSuzano Papel e Celulose S.A.
Maranhão Mill
Imperatriz city, MA
Brazil
 Email: suzano@suzano.com.br
 Web Address: www.suzano.com.br
Total Employees at this Location: 780
Type of Operation: Pulp mill
Pulp Grades and Capacities:
Total pulp capacity: 1,111,388 mt/y
Pulp available for market: 1,100,274 mt/y
Chemical Pulp: 1,111,388 mt/y
Pulp Mill Data:
Chemical Pulping Systems:
Continuous digesters: 1
Pulp Lines: 1
Bleach Plant Systems: 1
Chemical Pulping System, Type: ECF, Sequence: O_2 DEpDP
Chemical Recovery Equipment:
Evaporator lines: 7
Recovery boilers: 1
Lime Kiln
Pulp Dryers:
Air Float dryers 1, Air Float dryers 1
Energy Data:
Power boilers
Steam turbines: 2 at 180 MW
Electrical demand for mill: 2,272 MWh/D

ⓂSuzano Papel e Celulose S.A.
Mucuri Mill
Rod. BR 101 KM 945 - 4 + 7 Km à Esquerda S/N°
45930-000 Mucuri, BA
Brazil
 Phone: (55) 73 3878 7500
 Fax: (55) 73 3292 3500
 Email: suzano@suzano.com.br
 Web Address: www.suzano.com.br
Personnel:
Industrial Mgr.: Sergio Adriani
 Phone: (55) 73 3878 7500
Pulp Mill Mgr.: Fabrício José da Silva
 Phone: (55) 73 3878 8253
Paper Mill Mgr.: Luis Claudio Zynger
 Phone: (55) 73 3878 7500
Supt.: Jean Carlos Da Silva Rego
 Phone: (55) 73 3878 7500
Total Employees at this Location: 1,506
Type of Operation: Pulp mill, Paper mill
Pulp Grades and Capacities:
Total pulp capacity: 2,009,188 mt/y
Pulp available for market: 1,785,000 mt/y
Chemical Pulp: 2,009,188 mt/y
Pulp Mill Data:
Chemical Pulping Systems:
Continuous digesters: 2
Pulp Lines: 2
Bleach Plant Systems: 2
Chemical Pulping System, Type: Hardwood (Eucalyptus) - D*DEopD(PO)
Chemical Pulping System - ECF, Type: Dual - Hardwood (Eucalyptus), Sequence: O_2 DEopDPo
Chemical Recovery Equipment:
Evaporator lines: 1
Recovery boilers: 1
Lime Kiln

Brazil

Pulp Dryers:
Air Float dryers 1, Air Float dryers 1, Fourdriniers 1
Paper/Paperboard Grades and Capacities:
Total paper and paperboard capacity: 249,900 mt/y
Uncoated woodfree/freesheet: 249,900 mt/y
Paper and Paperboard Mill Data:
Stock Preparation:
Pulpers:
Refiners: 4
Paper Machines: 1
No. 1, DuoFormer F, total capacity 249,900 mt/y, Trim width 7.78 m, Uncoated woodfree/freesheet
Finishing Equipment:
Winders: 1 at 250,000 mt/y
Calenders: 1
Rewinders: 1 at 5,000 mt/y
Sheeters: 2 at 90,000 mt/y
Energy Data:
Power boilers: 1
Steam turbines: 5 at 213.6 MW
Electrical demand for mill: 3,859 MWh/D

Ⓜ Suzano Papel e Celulose S.A.
Rio Verde Unit
Av. Dr. Miguel Brada, Rio Baixo
08613-010 Suzano, SP
Brazil
Phone: (55) 11 3636 7800
Fax: (55) 11 4748 4388
Email: faleconosco@suzano.com.br
Web Address: www.suzano.com.br
Total Employees at this Location: 186
Type of Operation: Paper mill
Pulp Grades and Capacities:
Total pulp capacity: 30,503 mt/y
Recycled Pulping: 30,503 mt/y
Pulp Mill Data:
Bleach Plant Systems: 1
Recycled Deinked Pulping System
Recycled Fiber Treatment Lines:
Flotation deinking lines: 1
Paper/Paperboard Grades and Capacities:
Total paper and paperboard capacity: 51,051 mt/y
Uncoated woodfree/freesheet: 51,051 mt/y
Paper and Paperboard Mill Data:
Stock Preparation:
Pulpers: 4
Refiners: 5
Paper Machines: 2
No. 1, fourdrinier, total capacity 30,702 mt/y, Trim width 2.15 m, Uncoated woodfree/freesheet
No. 2, fourdrinier, total capacity 20,349 mt/y, Trim width 2.15 m, Uncoated woodfree/freesheet
Finishing Equipment:
Supercalenders: 2
Rewinders: 2 at 60,000 mt/y
Sheeters: 2 at 40,000 mt/y
Energy Data:
Power boilers: 4
Electrical demand for mill: 148 MWh/D

Ⓜ Suzano Papel e Celulose S.A.
Ripasa II Mill
Av. Elis Yazbek, 1502
06803-902 Embu, SP
Brazil
Phone: (55) 11 2149 2800
Fax: (55) 11 4704 2494
Email: faleconosco@suzano.com.br
Web Address: www.suzano.com.br
Personnel:
Industrial Mgr.: Daniel Couto
Phone: (55) 11 2149 2800
Fax: (55) 11 4704 2494
Prod. Mgr.: Érico de Castro Ebeling
Phone: (55) 11 2149 2879
Fax: (55) 11 4704 2494
Maint. Mgr.: João Athayde de Oliveira Neto
Phone: (55) 11 2149 2831
Fax: (55) 11 4704 2494
Total Employees at this Location: 135
Type of Operation: Paper mill, Paperboard mill
Pulp Grades and Capacities:
Total pulp capacity: 10,162 mt/y
Recycled Pulping: 10,162 mt/y
Pulp Mill Data:
Recycled Fiber Treatment Lines:
Pulpers: 2
Paper/Paperboard Grades and Capacities:
Total paper and paperboard capacity: 49,980 mt/y
Boxboard/cartonboard: 49,980 mt/y
Paper and Paperboard Mill Data:
Stock Preparation:
Pulpers: 4
Refiners: 5
Paper Machines: 1
BM3, fourdrinier (3), total capacity 49,980 mt/y, Trim width 2.55 m, Boxboard/cartonboard
Coating Machines: 2
No. 1, total capacity 55,000 mt/y., on machine
No. 2, total capacity 55,000 mt/y., on machine
Finishing Equipment:
Winders: 1 at 70,000 mt/y
Calenders: 1
Sheeters: 2
Energy Data:
Power boilers: 3
Electrical demand for mill: 92 MWh/D

Ⓜ Suzano Papel e Celulose S.A.
Suzano Mill
Av. Prudente de Moraes 3240/4006
08613-900 Suzano, SP
Brazil
Phone: (55) 11 3636 5000
Fax: (55) 11 3636 5479
Web Address: www.suzano.com.br
Personnel:
Admin. Sec.: Célia Cristina Reis
Phone: (55) 11 3636 5000
Total Employees at this Location: 900
Type of Operation: Pulp mill, Paper mill, Paperboard mill
Pulp Grades and Capacities:
Total pulp capacity: 464,680 mt/y
Pulp available for market: 39,984 mt/y
Chemical Pulp: 464,680 mt/y
Pulp Mill Data:
Chemical Pulping Systems:
Batch digesters: 4
Continuous digesters: 1
Pulp Lines: 2
Bleach Plant Systems: 1
Chemical Pulping System - Line 3, Type: ECF - Hardwood, Sequence: O₂ DEopD, Capacity 494,000 admt/y
Chemical Recovery Equipment:
Evaporator lines: 2
Recovery boilers: 2
Lime Kiln
Pulp Dryers:
Flash dryers 1
Paper/Paperboard Grades and Capacities:
Total paper and paperboard capacity: 559,776 mt/y
Uncoated woodfree/freesheet: 269,892 mt/y
Coated woodfree/freesheet: 89,964 mt/y
Boxboard/cartonboard: 199,920 mt/y
Paper and Paperboard Mill Data:
Stock Preparation:
Pulpers: 22
Refiners: 19
Paper Machines: 4
No. 5, fourdrinier, total capacity 89,964 mt/y, Trim width 3.7 m, Coated woodfree/freesheet
No. 6, Fourdrinier (4), total capacity 199,920 mt/y, Trim width 4.6 m, Boxboard/cartonboard
No. 7, DuoFormer F, total capacity 109,956 mt/y, Trim width 4.7 m, Uncoated woodfree/freesheet
No. 8, twin-wire, total capacity 159,936 mt/y, Trim width 4.7 m, Uncoated woodfree/freesheet
Coating Machines: 2
MP2, total capacity 90,000 mt/y., off machine
PM 6, on machine
Finishing Equipment:
Supercalenders: 2
Rewinders: 8
Sheeters: 11
Energy Data:
Power boilers: 3
Combustion turbines: 1 at 25 MW
Steam turbines: 2 at 38.5 MW
Hydro turbines at 450 MW
Electrical demand for mill: 1,481 MWh/D

ⒽⓂ Três Portos S.A. Indústria de Papel
Esteio Mill
Rua Aurélio Porto 379 - Vila Três Portos
93250-090 Esteio, RS
Brazil
Phone: (55) 51 3473 0211
Fax: (55) 51 3473 0211
Personnel:
Pres.: José Carlos Chagas Feijó
Phone: (55) 51 3473 0211
Dir.: Manuel Francisco Chagas Feijó
Phone: (55) 51 3473 0211
Dir. Admin./Finan.: Atílio Garziera
Phone: (55) 51 3473 0211
Type of Operation: Paper mill
Paper/Paperboard Grades and Capacities:
Total paper and paperboard capacity: 14,100 mt/y
Tissue: 14,100 mt/y
Paper and Paperboard Mill Data:
Paper Machines: 4
No. 1, fourdrinier, Trim width 1.3 m, Tissue
No. 2, Yankee dryer, cylinder, total capacity 2,000 mt/y, Trim width 1.3 m, Tissue
No. 3, fourdrinier, Yankee dryer, total capacity 2,100 mt/y, Trim width 1.3 m, Tissue
No. 4, fourdrinier, Yankee dryer, total capacity 10,000 mt/y, Trim width 2.4 m, Tissue

ⒽⓂ Trombini Industrial S.A.
Curitiba Mill
Ownership: Trombini Embalagens Ltda.
Rua Olympio Trombini n° 619, Vista Alegre
82820-040 Curitiba, PR
Brazil
Phone: (55) 41 2169 1100
Fax: (55) 41 2169 1181
Email: mercado.papel@trombini.com.br
Web Address: www.trombini.com.br
Personnel:
Pres.: Renato Alcides Trombini
Phone: (55) 41 2169 1100
Fax: (55) 41 2169 1181
Email: rat@trombini.com.br
Mill Mgr.: Edelcio Baggio
Phone: (55) 41 2169 1175
Fax: (55) 41 2169 1181
Email: ebaggio@trombini.com.br
Div. Supt.: Wladimir Trombini
Phone: (55) 41 2169 1100
Fax: (55) 41 2169 1181
Email: wtrombini@trombini.com.br
Admin. Dir.: Luiz Sergio Trombini
Phone: (55) 41 2169 1100
Fax: (55) 41 2169 1181
Email: ltrombini@trombini.com.br
Comm. Dir.: Armando Machado Silva
Phone: (55) 41 2169 1100
Fax: (55) 41 2169 1181
Email: asilva@trombini.com.br
Corrugated Div. Dir.: Ricardo Lacombe Trombini
Phone: (55) 41 2169 1100
Fax: (55) 41 2169 1181
Email: rtrombini@trombini.com.br

Brazil

Prod. Mgr.: Sérgio Luis Toaldo
Phone: (55) 41 2169 1274
Fax: (55) 41 2169 1181
Email: stoaldo@trombini.com.br
Total Employees of Company: 1,100
Total Employees at this Location: 1,100
Type of Operation: Paper mill, Paperboard mill
Mill Locations:
Trombini Industrial S.A., Fraiburgo Mill, Av. René Frey 121- Centro, 89580-000 Fraiburgo, SC, Brazil, Capacity: 132,447 mt/y, (Pulp mill, Paper mill, Paperboard mill)
Phone: (55) 49 3256 2022
Fax: (55) 49 3256 2025
Email: trombini@fbo.trombini.com.br
Pulp Grades and Capacities:
Total pulp capacity: 71,133 mt/y
Recycled Pulping: 71,133 mt/y

Pulp Mill Data:
Recycled Fiber Treatment Lines:
Recycled packaging pulping lines: 1
Paper/Paperboard Grades and Capacities:
Total paper and paperboard capacity: 69,972 mt/y
Linerboard: 21,063 mt/y
Corrugating medium/fluting: 48,909 mt/y
Paper and Paperboard Mill Data:
Stock Preparation:
Pulpers: 3
Refiners: 4
Paper Machines: 1
No. 4, fourdrinier, total capacity 69,972 mt/y, Trim width 2.5 m, Corrugating medium/fluting, Linerboard
Energy Data:
Power boilers: 1
Steam turbines: 1
Electrical demand for mill: 113 MWh/D

ⓜTrombini Industrial S.A.
Fraiburgo Mill
Av. René Frey 121- Centro
89580-000 Fraiburgo, SC
Brazil
Phone: (55) 49 3256 2022
Fax: (55) 49 3256 2025
Email: trombini@fbo.trombini.com.br
Web Address: www.trombini.com.br
Personnel:
Mill Mgr.: Fernando A. Volpato
Phone: (55) 49 3256 2004
Fax: (55) 49 3256 2025
Email: fvolpato@fbo.trombini.com.br
Recovery & Utilities Mgr.: Alceu A. Scramocin
Phone: (55) 49 3256 2013
Fax: (55) 49 3256 2025
Email: ascramocin@fbo.trombini.com.br
Total Employees at this Location: 284
Type of Operation: Pulp mill, Paper mill, Paperboard mill
Pulp Grades and Capacities:
Total pulp capacity: 135,540 mt/y
Chemical Pulp: 86,598 mt/y
Recycled Pulping: 48,943 mt/y

Pulp Mill Data:
Chemical Pulping Systems:
Batch digesters: 4
Pulp Lines: 2
Chemical Recovery Equipment:
Evaporator lines: 1
Recovery boilers: 1
Lime Kiln
Recycled Fiber Treatment Lines:
Pulpers: 2 at 53,000 admt/y
Paper/Paperboard Grades and Capacities:
Total paper and paperboard capacity: 132,447 mt/y
Packaging papers: 44,982 mt/y
Linerboard: 87,465 mt/y
Paper and Paperboard Mill Data:
Stock Preparation:
Pulpers: 2
Refiners: 5
Paper Machines: 2
No. 3, fourdrinier, total capacity 44,982 mt/y, Trim width 2.4 m, Packaging papers
No. 4, (started up February 2011), fourdrinier, total capacity 87,465 mt/y, Trim width 2.5 m, Linerboard
Finishing Equipment:
Winders: 2 at 80,000 mt/y
Rewinders: 2 at 80,000 mt/y
Energy Data:
Power boilers: 2
Steam turbines: 2 at 18.4 MW
Electrical demand for mill: 301 MWh/D

ⓗⓜTrópicos Industrial e Comercial Ltda
Guarapuava Mill
Rodovia BR 227, Km. 330 Rio das Pedras
85100-000 Guarapuava, PR
Brazil
Phone: (55) 42 3622 4544
Fax: (55) 42 3622 1015
Email: comercial@tropicos.ind.br, tropicos@tropicos.ind.br
Web Address: www.tropicos.ind.br
Personnel:
Dir.: Luiz Aldemir Galvão
Phone: (55) 42 3622 4544
Fax: (55) 42 3622 1015
Email: aldemir@tropicos.ind.br
Commer. Dir.: Altamir Borges Camargo
Phone: (55) 42 3622 4544/42 8811 9181
Fax: (55) 42 3622 1015
Email: diretorcomercial@tropicos.ind.b
HR Mgr.: Jolinei
Phone: (55) 42 3622 4544
Fax: (55) 42 3622 1015
Email: Rh2@tropicos.ind.br
Total Employees at this Location: 100
Type of Operation: Paper mill
Paper/Paperboard Grades and Capacities:
Total paper and paperboard capacity: 21,063 mt/y
Tissue: 21,063 mt/y
Paper and Paperboard Mill Data:
Paper Machines: 1
No. 1, crescent former, total capacity 21,063 mt/y, Trim width 2.76 m, Tissue
Energy Data:
Power boilers
Electrical demand for mill: 59 MWh/D

ⓗⓜCartonifício Valinhos S.A.
Valinhos Mill
R. 12 de Outubro, 20 Vila Santana
13274-125 Valinhos, SP
Brazil
Phone: (55) 19 3871 9111
Fax: (55) 19 3871 9112/2754
Email: comercial.ondulado@cartonificiovalinhos.com.br
Web Address: www.cartonificiovalinhos.com.br
Personnel:
Dir. Pres.: Segismundo R.J. Celani
Phone: (55) 19 3871 9111
Dir. VP: Adelaida Cafarrena Acena Celani
Phone: (55) 19 3871 9111
Superintendent Dir.: Fernando Caffarena Celani
Phone: (55) 19 3871 9111
Email: diretoria@cartonificiovalinhos.com.br
Finan. Mgr.: Hélio Sebastião
Phone: (55) 19 3871 9111
Total Employees of Company: 150
Total Employees at this Location: 80
Type of Operation: Paperboard mill
Pulp Grades and Capacities:
Total pulp capacity: 65,814 mt/y
Recycled Pulping: 65,814 mt/y

Pulp Mill Data:
Recycled Fiber Treatment Lines:
Pulpers: 3 at 68,000 admt/y
Paper/Paperboard Grades and Capacities:
Total paper and paperboard capacity: 64,974 mt/y
Linerboard: 45,339 mt/y
Corrugating medium/fluting: 19,635 mt/y
Paper and Paperboard Mill Data:
Stock Preparation:
Pulpers: 3
Refiners: 5
Paper Machines: 1
No. 3, (Former Type model: Fourdrinier Top/bottom), fourdrinier, Yankee dryer, total capacity 64,974 mt/y, Trim width 2.4 m, Linerboard, Corrugating medium/fluting
Finishing Equipment:
Rewinders: 2
Energy Data:
Power boilers: 1
Electrical demand for mill: 106 MWh/D

ⓗⓜValpasa Indústria de Papel Ltda.
Tangará Mill
Linha Perotto, km 5, No 100, Cidade Industrial
89642-000 Tangará, SC
Brazil
Mailing Address: 64, Tangará, Brazil
Phone: (55) 49 3532 7900
Fax: (55) 49 3532 7927
Email: valpasa@valpasa.com.br
Web Address: www.valpasa.com.br
Personnel:
Dir./Pres.: Deoclides Cornachio
Phone: (55) 49 3532 7900
Fax: (55) 49 3532 7927
Contr.: Riquelmo Taiepti
Phone: (55) 49 3532 7900
Fax: (55) 49 3532 7927
Email: riquelmo@valpasa.com.br
Ind. Dir.: Claudimir Perotto
Phone: (55) 49 3532 7900
Fax: (55) 49 3532 7927
Total Employees at this Location: 88
Type of Operation: Paperboard mill
Pulp Grades and Capacities:
Total pulp capacity: 60,728 mt/y
Recycled Pulping: 60,728 mt/y

Pulp Mill Data:
Recycled Fiber Treatment Lines:
Pulpers: 1 at 65,850
Paper/Paperboard Grades and Capacities:
Total paper and paperboard capacity: 59,976 mt/y
Linerboard: 17,850 mt/y
Corrugating medium/fluting: 42,126 mt/y
Paper and Paperboard Mill Data:
Paper Machines: 1
No. 1, fourdrinier, total capacity 59,976 mt/y, Trim width 1.65 m, Corrugating medium/fluting, Linerboard
Energy Data:
Power boilers: 1
Electrical demand for mill: 98 MWh/D

ⓗⓜVeracel Celulose S.A.
Veracel Pulp Mill
Ownership: 50% by Stora Enso Oyj, 50% by Fibria Celulose SA
Rodovia Fazenda Brazilândia BA 275, Km 24, Zona Rural
45820-970 Eunápolis, BA
Brazil
Phone: (55) 73 3166 8000
Fax: (55) 73 3166 8980
Email: veracel@veracel.com.br
Web Address: www.veracel.com.br
Personnel:
Pres./Dir.: Antonio Sergio Alípio
Phone: (55) 73 3166 8000
Fax: (55) 73 3166 8980
Industrial Dir. Operations Dir.: Walter dos Santos Martins
Phone: (55) 73 3166 8965
Fax: (55) 73 3166 8980
Forestry Dir.: Sérgio da S. Borenstain

Cayman Islands

Phone: (55) 73 3166 8000
Fax: (55) 73 3166 8980
Email: sergio.borenstain@veracel.com.br
Sustainability Mgr.: Renato Carneiro
Phone: (55) 73 3166 8000
Fax: (55) 73 3166 8980
Finan. Mgr.: Anderson Angelo De Souza
Phone: (55) 73 3166 8000
Fax: (55) 73 3166 8980
Commun. Mgr: Debora Jorge
Phone: (55) 11 2138 4195
Fax: (55) 73 3166 8980
Email: debora.jorge@veracel.com.br
Forest. Mgr.: Jeronimo Christo
Phone: (55) 73 3166 8000
Fax: (55) 73 3166 8980
Eng. Mgr.: Ariovaldo Outa
Phone: (55) 73 3166 8000
Fax: (55) 73 3166 8980
Recovery & Utilities Mgr.: Amarildo Germiniani
Phone: (55) 73 3166 8000
Fax: (55) 73 3166 8980
Wood Supply Mgr.: Fabiano Stein
Phone: (55) 73 3166 8000
Fax: (55) 73 3166 8980
Total Employees of Company: 745
Type of Operation: Pulp mill
Pulp Grades and Capacities:
  Total pulp capacity: 1,157,537 mt/y
  Pulp available for market: 1,149,897 mt/y
  Chemical Pulp: 1,157,537 mt/y
Pulp Mill Data:
  Chemical Pulping Systems:
  Continuous digesters: 1
  Pulp Lines: 1
  Bleach Plant Systems: 1
  Chemical Pulping System, Type: Hardwood (Eucalyptus), Sequence: O_2 A/DO EOP D D(P)
  Chemical Recovery Equipment:
  Evaporator lines: 1
  Recovery boilers: 1
  Lime Kiln
  Pulp Dryers:
  Flakt dryer 1
Energy Data:
  Power boilers: 1
  Steam turbines: 1 at 126.6 MW
  Electrical demand for mill: 1,795 MWh/D

CAYMAN ISLANDS

ⓘYFY Cayman
Ownership: 79.65% by Yuen Foong Yu Inc., 20.35% by Nippon Paper Group
Marquee Place, Suite 300, 430 West Bay Road, PO Box 32052
KY1-1208 Grand Cayman
Cayman Islands
Mill Locations:
Jiangsu Yuen Foong Yu Paper (Yangzhou) Co., Ltd., Yangzhou Mill, No. 168, Chunjiang Road, Economy & Development Zone, Yangzhou 225000, China, Capacity: 914,500 mt/y, (Paper mill, Paperboard mill)
Phone: (86) 514 8752 9888
Fax: (86) 514 8752 9889
Yuen Foong Yu Packaging Inc., Chengkung Mill, No. 546, Sec. 3, Chung Shan Rd., Wu Jih District 41453, Taiwan, Capacity: 240,000 mt/y, (Paperboard mill)
Phone: (886) 4 23381126
Fax: (886) 4 23363154
Email: v0109@yfy.com, meg_wu@yfy.com
Yuen Foong Yu Packaging Inc., Hsin Wu Mill, 250, Hsia Chuangtsu, Tsu, Yuen An Tsun, Hsin Wu 32744, Taiwan, Capacity: 460,000 mt/y, (Paperboard mill)
Phone: (886) 3 4861701
Fax: (886) 3 4861078
Email: changjc@yfy.com

CHILE

ⓘCelulosa Arauco y Constitución S.A.
Ownership: 99.98% by Empresas COPEC S.A. (Public)
Av. El Golf 150, 14th floor
Las Condes, RM - Región Metro. de Santiago
Chile
Phone: (56) 2 461 7200
Fax: (56) 2 698 5967
Email: info@arauco.cl
Web Address: www.arauco.cl
Personnel:
Board Dir.: Jose Tomás Gusmán
Phone: (56) 2 461 7200
Fax: (56) 2 698 5967
Email: jose.gusman@arauco.cl
Vice Chmn: Roberto Angelini
Phone: (56) 2 461 7200
Fax: (56) 2 698 5967
Email: roberto.angelini@arauco.cl
Vice Chmn.: Manuel Enrique Bezanilla
Phone: (56) 2 461 7200
Fax: (56) 2 698 5967
Email: manuel.bezanilla@arauco.cl
CEO: Matias Domeyko
Phone: (56) 2 461 7200
Fax: (56) 2 698 5967
Email: matias.cassel@arauco.cl
Pres. & COO: Cristián Infante Bilbao
Phone: (56) 2 461 7200
Fax: (56) 2 698 5967
Email: cristian.bilbao@arauco.cl
CFO: Gianfranco Truffello
Phone: (56) 2 461 7200
Fax: (56) 2 698 5967
Email: gianfranco.truffello@arauco.cl
Snr. VP., Commercial & Corp. Affairs: Charles Kimber
Phone: (56) 2 461 7200
Fax: (56) 2 698 5967
Email: charles.kimber@arauco.cl
Snr. VP., Woodpulp: Franco Bozzalla
Phone: (56) 2 461 7200
Fax: (56) 2 698 5967
Email: franco.bozzalla@arauco.cl
Snr. VP., HR.: Camila Merino
Phone: (56) 2 461 7200
Fax: (56) 2 698 5967
Email: camila.merino@arauco.cl
Total Employees of Company: 9,034
Mill Locations:
Alto Paraná S.A., Misiones Mill, Ruta Nacional 12 Km 1589, N3378WCA Puerto Esperanza, Argentina, (Pulp mill)
Phone: (54) 3757 488000
Fax: (54) 3757 488099
Email: infocelulosa@altoparana.com
Celulosa Arauco y Constitución S.A., Arauco Pulp Mill, Los Horcones s/n, Casilla 8D, Arauco, Chile, (Pulp mill)
Phone: (56) 41 2509400
Fax: (56) 41 2509401
Celulosa Arauco y Constitución S.A., Constitución Mill, Av. Enrique MacIver 505, 3560132 Constitución, Chile, (Pulp mill)
Phone: (56) 71 200 800
Celulosa Arauco y Constitución S.A., Licancel Mill, Camino a Iloca km 3, Casilla 22, Licantén, Curico, Chile, (Pulp mill)
Phone: (56) 75 460 024/205 000
Fax: (56) 75 460 028/205 008
Celulosa Arauco y Constitución S.A., Nueva Aldea, Autopista del Itata, KM.21, Nueva Aldea, Ranquil, Chile, (Pulp mill)
Phone: (56) 41 286 2000
Fax: (56) 41 286 2006
Email: comunicaciones@arauco.cl
Celulosa Arauco y Constitución S.A., Valdivia Pulp Mill, Ruta 5 Sur, Km. 788, San José de la Mariquina, Valdivia, Chile, (Pulp mill)
Phone: (56) 63 631490
Fax: (56) 63 631412
Email: info@arauco.cl
Montes del Plata, Punta Pereira Mill (50% owned), Zona Franca, Punta Pereira, Uruguay, (Pulp mill)
Email: contacto@montesdelplata.com.uy

ⓜCelulosa Arauco y Constitución S.A.
Arauco Pulp Mill
Los Horcones s/n, Casilla 8D
Arauco, VIII - Región del Biobío
Chile
Phone: (56) 41 2509400
Fax: (56) 41 2509401
Web Address: www.plantaarauco.cl
Personnel:
Mill Mgr. & MAPA Project Manager: Edison Durán
Phone: (56) 41 2509 416
Fax: (56) 41 2509 402
Email: eduran@arauco.cl
Continuous Improvement Sub Mgr.: Andrés Mellado Rebolledo
Phone: (56) 41 2509 416
Fax: (56) 41 2509 402
Email: andres.mellado@arauco.cl
Maint. Mgr.: Mario Vergara
Phone: (56) 41 2509 416
Fax: (56) 41 2509 402
Email: mario.vergara@arauco.cl
Total Employees at this Location: 593
Type of Operation: Pulp mill
Pulp Grades and Capacities:
  Total pulp capacity: 798,952 mt/y
  Pulp available for market: 790,041 mt/y
  Chemical Pulp: 798,952 mt/y
Pulp Mill Data:
  Chemical Pulping Systems:
  Batch digesters: 7
  Continuous digesters: 1
  Pulp Lines: 2
  Bleach Plant Systems: 2
  Chemical Pulping System - Line 1 - Eucalyptus, Type: ECF, Sequence: O_2 DEopD, Capacity 290,000 admt/y
  Chemical Pulping System Line 2 - Pine, Type: ECF - Softwood, Sequence: O_2 DEopDED, Capacity 500,000 admt/y
  Chemical Recovery Equipment:
  Evaporator lines: 2
  Recovery boilers: 2
  Lime Kiln
  Pulp Dryers:
  Flakt dryer 1, Flash dryers 1, Fourdriniers 1, Fourdriniers 1
Energy Data:
  Power boilers: 4
  Combustion turbines: 1 at 24 MW
  Steam turbines: 5 at 96 (ST 2,3,4,5), 31 MW
  Electrical demand for mill: 1,948 MWh/D

ⓜCelulosa Arauco y Constitución S.A.
Constitución Mill
Av. Enrique MacIver 505
3560132 Constitución, VII - Región del Maule
Chile
Mailing Address: Casilla 93, 3560000 Constitución, VII - Región del Maule, Chile
Phone: (56) 71 200 800
Web Address: www.plantaconstitucion.cl
Personnel:
Mill Mgr.: Fernando Herrera Reyes
Phone: (56) 71 200 500
Fax: (56) 71 671 036
Email: fherrera@arauco.cl
Maint. Mgr.: Jaime Ojeda Greciet
Phone: (56) 71 200 600
Fax: (56) 71 671 036
Email: jojeda@arauco.cl
Prod. Mgr.: Juan Humberto Muñoz Gutierrez
Phone: (56) 71 200 700
Fax: (56) 71 671 036
Email: jhmunoz@arauco.cl

Tech. Contr. Mgr.: Jorge Mesa Mansilla
Phone: (56) 71 200 771
Fax: (56) 71 200 804
Email: jorge.mesa@arauco.cl
Environ. Mgr.: Juan Pablo Arroyo
Phone: (56) 71 200 790
Fax: (56) 71 671 036
Email: juanpablo.arroyo@arauco.cl
Plann. & Sls. Mgr.: Franco Mellafe
Phone: (56) 71 200 800
Fax: (56) 71 671 036
Email: franco.mellafe@arauco.cl
Total Employees at this Location: 324
Type of Operation: Pulp mill
Pulp Grades and Capacities:
Total pulp capacity: 360,116 mt/y
Pulp available for market: 354,858 mt/y
Chemical Pulp: 360,116 mt/y

Pulp Mill Data:
Chemical Pulping Systems:
Batch digesters: 10
Pulp Lines: 1
Chemical Recovery Equipment:
Evaporator lines: 1
Recovery boilers: 1
Lime Kiln
Pulp Dryers:
Air Float dryers 1, Fourdriniers 1
Energy Data:
Power boilers: 1
Steam turbines: 2 at 40 MW
Electrical demand for mill: 728 MWh/D

ⓜCelulosa Arauco y Constitución S.A.
Licancel Mill
Camino a Iloca km 3, Casilla 22
Licantén, Curico, VII - Región del Maule
Chile
Phone: (56) 75 460 024/205 000
Fax: (56) 75 460 028/205 008
Web Address: www.arauco.cl
Personnel:
Pulp Mill Mgr.: Alvaro Jimenez
Phone: (56) 75 205 004
Fax: (56) 75 205 008
Maint. Sub. Mgr.: René Arancet
Phone: (56) 75 460 024/205 000
Email: rarancet@arauco.cl
Mario Eckolt
Total Employees at this Location: 253
Type of Operation: Pulp mill
Pulp Grades and Capacities:
Total pulp capacity: 151,416 mt/y
Pulp available for market: 149,940 mt/y
Chemical Pulp: 151,416 mt/y

Pulp Mill Data:
Chemical Pulping Systems:
Batch digesters: 5
Pulp Lines: 2
Bleach Plant Systems: 1
Chemical Pulping System, Type: Hardwood/Softwood, Sequence: O_2 DEoDD, Capacity 140,000 admt/y
Chemical Recovery Equipment:
Evaporator lines: 1
Recovery boilers: 1
Lime Kiln
Pulp Dryers:
Air Float dryers 1
Energy Data:
Power boilers: 1
Steam turbines: 1 at 27 MW
Electrical demand for mill: 337 MWh/D

ⓜCelulosa Arauco y Constitución S.A.
Nueva Aldea
Autopista del Itata, KM.21, Nueva Aldea
Ranquil, VIII - Región del Biobío
Chile
Phone: (56) 41 286 2000
Fax: (56) 41 286 2006
Email: comunicaciones@arauco.cl
Web Address: www.complejonuevaaldea.cl, www.arauco.cl
Personnel:
Mill Mgr.: Felix Herneis
Phone: (56) 41 286 2000
Fax: (56) 41 286 2006
Email: fherneis@arauco.cl
Prod. Mgr.: Marco Vidal
Phone: (56) 41 286 2000
Fax: (56) 41 286 2006
Email: mvidal@arauco.cl
Adm. Mgr.: Hugo Castro
Phone: (56) 41 286 2000
Fax: (56) 41 286 2006
Email: hugo.castro@arauco.cl
Maint. Mgr.: Oscar Hidalgo
Phone: (56) 41 286 2000
Fax: (56) 41 286 2006
Email: oscar.hidalgo@arauco.cl
Env. Mgr.: Arturo Jiménez
Phone: (56) 41 286 2000
Fax: (56) 41 286 2006
Email: ajimene@arauco.cl
Plann. & Sls. Mgr.: Franco Mellafe Angelini
Phone: (56) 41 286 2011
Fax: (56) 41 286 2006
Email: franco.mellafe@arauco.cl
Mgr. Sec: Carmen Cartes
Phone: (56) 41 286 2011
Fax: (56) 41 286 2006
Email: carmen.cartes@arauco.cl
Total Employees at this Location: 463
Type of Operation: Pulp mill
Pulp Grades and Capacities:
Total pulp capacity: 1,035,430 mt/y
Pulp available for market: 1,026,732 mt/y
Chemical Pulp: 1,035,430 mt/y

Pulp Mill Data:
Chemical Pulping Systems:
Continuous digesters: 2
Pulp Lines: 2
Bleach Plant Systems: 2
Chemical Pulping System - Eucalyptus, Type: Hardwood (Eucalyptus), Sequence: O_2 DoEOPDD, Capacity 550,000 admt/y
Chemical Pulping System - Pine, Type: Softwood (P.Radiata), Sequence: O_2 DoEOPDD, Capacity 550,000 admt/y
Chemical Recovery Equipment:
Evaporator lines: 1
Recovery boilers: 1
Lime Kiln
Pulp Dryers:
Air Float dryers 1, Fourdriniers 1
Energy Data:
Power boilers: 4
Steam turbines: 2 at 140 MW
Electrical demand for mill: 2,447 MWh/D

ⓜCelulosa Arauco y Constitución S.A.
Valdivia Pulp Mill
Ruta 5 Sur, Km. 788, San José de la Mariquina
Valdivia, XIV - Región de Los Ríos
Chile
Phone: (56) 63 631490
Fax: (56) 63 631412
Email: info@arauco.cl
Web Address: www.arauco.cl
Personnel:
Mill Mgr.: Sergio H. Carreño
Phone: (56) 63 631400
Fax: (56) 63 631412
Email: scarreno@arauco.cl
Prod. Mgr.: Manuel A. González
Phone: (56) 63 631600
Fax: (56) 63 631412
Email: manuel.gonzalez@arauco.cl
Tech. Mgr.: Daniel Bustamante
Phone: (56) 63 631610
Fax: (56) 63 631531
Maint. Mgr.: Gastón R. Urrutia
Phone: (56) 63 631500
Fax: (56) 63 631412
Email: gurrutia@arauco.cl
Chief Eng.: Edmundo F. Alvarez
Phone: (56) 63 631580
Fax: (56) 63 631412
Email: ealvarez@arauco.cl
Environ. Mgr.: Miguel A. Osses
Phone: (56) 63 631497
Fax: (56) 63 631412
Email: mosses@arauco.cl
Process Eng.: Claudia Inzunza
Phone: (56) 63 631613
Fax: (56) 63 631413
Email: claudia.inzunza@arauco.cl
Total Employees at this Location: 348
Type of Operation: Pulp mill
Pulp Grades and Capacities:
Total pulp capacity: 554,773 mt/y
Pulp available for market: 549,780 mt/y
Chemical Pulp: 554,773 mt/y

Pulp Mill Data:
Chemical Pulping Systems:
Batch digesters: 10
Pulp Lines: 1
Bleach Plant Systems: 1
Chemical Pulping System, Type: Hardwood/Softwood, Sequence: O_2 DEopDD, Capacity 550,000 admt/y
Chemical Recovery Equipment:
Evaporator lines: 1
Recovery boilers: 1
Lime Kiln
Pulp Dryers:
Air Float dryers 1, Fourdriniers 1
Energy Data:
Power boilers: 1
Steam turbines: 2 at 70, 70 MW
Electrical demand for mill: 1,083 MWh/D

ⓜEmpresas CMPC S.A.
Ownership: 12.36% by Chilean pension funds, 0.30% by foreign investment funds, 31.50% by local shareholders, 55.84% by Matte family
Agustinas 1343
8340432 Santiago, RM - Región Metro. de Santiago
Chile
Mailing Address: PO Box 297, Correo Central, Santiago, Chile
Phone: (56) 2 441 2000
Fax: (56) 2 672 1115
Email: rlevy@gerencia.cmpc.cl
Web Address: www.cmpc.cl
Personnel:
Chmn.: Eliodoro Matte L.
Phone: (56) 2 441 2000
Fax: (56) 2 672 1115
Email: ematte@gerencia.cmpc.cl
CEO: Hernán Rodríguez wilson
Phone: (56) 2 441 2000
Fax: (56) 2 672 1115
Email: hernan.rodriguez@cmpc.cl
CFO: Luis Llanos Collado
Phone: (56) 2 441 2000
Fax: (56) 2 672 1115
Email: lllanos@gerencia.cmpc.cl
CEO CMPC Forestry & Wood Products: Francisco Ruiz-Tagle Edwards
Phone: (56) 2 441 2000
Fax: (56) 2 672 1115
Email: fruiztagle@cmpc.cl
Gen. Sec.: Gonzalo P. Garcia Balmaceda
Phone: (56) 2 441 2000
Fax: (56) 2 672 1115
Email: ggarcia@gerencia.cmpc.cl
Total Employees of Company: 16,000
Total Employees at this Location: 650
Mill Locations:

Chile

Absormex CMPC Tissue S.A. de CV, Altamira, Boulevard de los Ríos, Km 4.5, Puerto Industrial de Altamira, 89600 Altamira, Mexico, Capacity: 97,104 mt/y, (Paper mill)
Phone: (52) 833 260 0053/54/55/56/57
Email: korozco@gpoabs.com.mx

Cartulinas CMPC S.A., Maule Mill, Ruta L-25, Km. 28.5, Yerbas Buenas, Linares, Chile, Capacity: 359,856 mt/y, (Pulp mill, Paperboard mill)
Phone: (56) 71 52 3000
Fax: (56) 71 52 3004
Email: jconstabel@maule.cmpc.cl

Cartulinas CMPC S.A., Valdivia Mill, Avda. Balmaceda 8500, Valdivia, Chile, Capacity: 69,972 mt/y, (Pulp mill, Paperboard mill)
Phone: (56) 63 214 191
Fax: (56) 63 216 976
Email: nnavarro@valdivia.cmpc.cl

CMPC Celulosa S.A., Laja Mill, Balmaceda 30, Laja, Chile, Capacity: 76,398 mt/y, (Pulp mill, Paper mill)
Phone: (56) 43 334 000
Fax: (56) 43 334 015
Email: maceituno@celulosa.cmpc.cl

CMPC Celulosa S.A., Pacífico Mill, Avenida Jorge Alessandri 001, Mininco, Comuna Collipulli, Chile, (Pulp mill)
Phone: (56) 45 293300
Fax: (56) 45 293305

CMPC Celulosa S.A., Santa Fe Mill, Av. Julio Hammelmann 670, Nacimiento, Chile, (Pulp mill)
Phone: (56) 43 403 800
Fax: (56) 43 403 830
Email: fbackhouse@celulosa.cmpc.cl

CMPC Celulose Riograndense, Guaíba Mill, Rua São Geraldo 1800, Bairro Ermo, 92500-000 Guaíba, RS, Brazil, Capacity: 54,978 mt/y, (Pulp mill, Paper mill)
Phone: (55) 51 2139 7111/ 7211
Fax: (55) 51 2139 7186
Email: contato@cmpcrs.com.br

CMPC Papeles Cordillera S.A., Puente Alto Mill, Avda. Eyzaguirre, 01098 Puente Alto, Chile, Capacity: 314,874 mt/y, (Paper mill, Paperboard mill)
Phone: (56) 2 23675300, 23675700
Fax: (56) 2 28501118
Email: infocomercial@papeles.cmpc.cl

CMPC Tissue S.A., Puente Alto Mill, 01098 Eyzaguirre, Puente Alto, Chile, Capacity: 63,903 mt/y, (Paper mill)
Phone: (56) 2 366 6460/800 375 000
Fax: (56) 2 623 8539/366 6469

CMPC Tissue S.A., Talagante Mill, Camino Isla de Maipo, 0297 Talagante, Chile, Capacity: 108,528 mt/y, (Paper mill)
Fax: (56) 2 462 4511

IPUSA - Industria Papelera Uruguaya S.A., IPUSA Plant 3, Pando Mill (99.26% owned), Avenida España s/n PO Box 91000, Pando, Uruguay, (Paper mill)
Phone: (598) 2 292 2240 /2073
Fax: (598) 2 292 1358 /1362
Email: ipusa@ipusa.com.uy

Melhoramentos Papéis Ltda., Caieiras Mill, Rodovia Pres. Tancredo de Almeida Neves, Km. 34, 07700-000 Caieiras, SP, Brazil, Capacity: 98,889 mt/y, (Pulp mill, Paper mill)
Phone: (55) 11 4441 7200
Fax: (55) 11 4441 7202
Email: comunica@cmpc.com.br

Melhoramentos Florestal S.A., Camanducaia Mill, Fazenda Levantina, s/nº, 37650-000 Camanducaia, MG, Brazil, (Pulp mill)
Phone: (55) 35 3433 8200
Fax: (55) 35 3433 8224
Email: jmoretti@melhoramentos.com.br

Melhoramentos Papéis Ltda., Mogi das Cruzes Mill, Av. Lourenço de Souza Franco, 2655, 08750-560 Mogi das Cruzes, SP, Brazil, Capacity: 33,915 mt/y, (Paper mill)
Phone: (55) 11 4795 9411
Fax: (55) 11 4727 2330

Papeles Río Vergara S.A. , Nacimiento Mill, Av. Julio Hemmelman 330, Nacimiento, Chile, (Paper mill)
Phone: (56) 43 631300
Fax: (56) 43 511444

Papelera del Plata, Zárate Mill, Camino de la Costa Brava Km.7, 2800 Zárate, Argentina, Capacity: 112,098 mt/y, (Paper mill)
Phone: (54) 3487 428300/426615
Fax: (54) 3487 428317
Email: lpp-zarate@cmpc.com.ar

Protisa Colombia SA, Bogota Mill, Autopista Norte km 45, Bogotá Via Tunja, 15001000 Gachancipá, Colombia, Capacity: 28,560 mt/y, (Paper mill)
Phone: (57) 1 589 3333
Fax: (57) 1 589 3030

Protisa Peru S.A. - Productos Tissue del Peru, Santa Anita Mill, Av. Santa Rosa 550, Santa Anita, Peru, Capacity: 82,110 mt/y, (Paper mill)
Phone: (51) 1 362 0653
Fax: (51) 1 313 3031
Email: postmast@protisa.com.pe

Cartulinas CMPC S.A.
Maule Mill
Ownership: Empresas CMPC S.A.
Ruta L-25, Km. 28.5
Yerbas Buenas, Linares, VII - Región del Maule
Chile
Phone: (56) 71 52 3000
Fax: (56) 71 52 3004
Email: jconstabel@maule.cmpc.cl
Web Address: www.cartulinas-cmpc.com

Personnel:
Oper. Mgr.: Juan Constabel
Phone: (56) 2 440 3000
Fax: (56) 71 52 3004
Email: jconstabel@maule.cmpc.cl
Head of Production: Alfredo Lopez
Phone: (56) 2 440 3000
Fax: (56) 71 52 3004
Email: alopez@maule.cmpc.cl
Tech. Mgr.: Jorge Aldana
Phone: (56) 2 440 3000
Fax: (56) 71 52 3004
Email: jaldana@maule.cmpc.cl
Maint. Mgr.: Juan Cuevas
Phone: (56) 2 440 3000
Fax: (56) 71 52 3004
Email: jcuevas@maule.cmpc.cl
Admin. & Pers. Mgr.: Guillermo Rojas
Phone: (56) 71 52 3000
Fax: (56) 71 52 3004
Email: grojas@maule.cmpc.cl

Total Employees at this Location: 257
Type of Operation: Pulp mill, Paperboard mill
Pulp Grades and Capacities:
Total pulp capacity: 199,333 mt/y
Mechanical Pulp: 199,333 mt/y
Pulp Mill Data:
Mechanical Pulping Systems:
TMP systems: 2
Bleach Plant Systems: 1
Mechanical BCTMP Pulping System, Type: Softwood, Sequence: P
Paper/Paperboard Grades and Capacities:
Total paper and paperboard capacity: 359,856 mt/y
Boxboard/cartonboard: 359,856 mt/y
Paper and Paperboard Mill Data:
Stock Preparation:
Pulpers: 4
Refiners: 14
Paper Machines: 1
No. 19, (Suppliers: Voith/Metso.), fourdrinier, total capacity 359,856 mt/y, Trim width 4.8 m, Boxboard/cartonboard
Coating Machines: 1
No. 1 &3, total capacity 360,000 mt/y., on machine
Finishing Equipment:
Winders: 1
Rewinders: 1 at 36,000 mt/y
Sheeters: 6 at 195,000 mt/y
Energy Data:
Power boilers: 2

TMP Reboiler: 1
Electrical demand for mill: 1,514 MWh/D

Cartulinas CMPC S.A.
Valdivia Mill
Ownership: Empresas CMPC S.A.
Avda. Balmaceda 8500
Valdivia, X - Región de Los Lagos
Chile
Mailing Address: PO Box 5-D, Valdivia, X - Región de Los Lagos, Chile
Phone: (56) 63 214 191
Fax: (56) 63 216 976
Email: nnavarro@valdivia.cmpc.cl
Web Address: www.cartulinas-cmpc.com

Personnel:
Mill Mgr.: Nestor Navarro
Phone: (56) 63 216877
Email: nnavarro@valdivia.cmpc.cl
Prod. Mgr.: Romilio Bahamontes
Phone: (56) 63 21 4191 410
Oper. Mgr.: Juan Pablo Castro
Phone: (56) 63 21 4191 400
Email: jcastro@valdivia.cmpc.cl
Env. Mgr.: Carolina Escalona Muños
Phone: (56) 63 21 4191 520
Email: cescalona@valdivia.cmpc.cl
Maint. Mgr.: Patricio Rodriguez
Phone: (56) 63 21 4191 420
Email: prodriguezv@valdivia.cmpc.cl
Tech. Mgr.: Pablo Soto
Phone: (56) 63 21 4191 300
Email: psoto@valdivia.cmpc.cl

Total Employees at this Location: 121
Type of Operation: Pulp mill, Paperboard mill
Pulp Grades and Capacities:
Total pulp capacity: 40,079 mt/y
Mechanical Pulp: 26,719 mt/y
Recycled Pulping: 13,360 mt/y
Pulp Mill Data:
Mechanical Pulping Systems:
Conventional grinders: 3
Pulp Lines: 2
Recycled Fiber Treatment Lines:
Pulpers: 1 at 15,000 admt/y
Paper/Paperboard Grades and Capacities:
Total paper and paperboard capacity: 69,972 mt/y
Boxboard/cartonboard: 69,972 mt/y
Paper and Paperboard Mill Data:
Stock Preparation:
Pulpers: 3
Refiners: 3
Paper Machines: 1
No. 5, fourdrinier (3), total capacity 69,972 mt/y, Trim width 2.4 m, Boxboard/cartonboard
Coating Machines: 1
PM 5, total capacity 70,000 mt/y., on machine
Finishing Equipment:
Rewinders: 1
Sheeters: 1
Energy Data:
Power boilers: 2
Electrical demand for mill: 228 MWh/D

CMPC Celulosa S.A.
Ownership: Empresas CMPC S.A.
Agustinas 1343, 3rd floor
8340432 Santiago, RM - Región Metro. de Santiago
Chile
Mailing Address: Correo 21, 8340432 Santiago
Phone: (56) 2 441 2030/2000
Fax: (56) 2 698 2179
Email: sales@celulosa.cmpc.cl
Web Address: www.cmpccelulosa.cl

Personnel:
Pres.: Bernardo Matte
Phone: (56) 2 441 2030
Fax: (56) 2 698 2179
VP: Hernán Rodríguez

Chile

Phone: (56) 2 441 2030
Fax: (56) 2 698 2179
Mgr., Dir.: Sergio Colvin
Phone: (56) 2 441 2030
Fax: (56) 2 698 2179
CEO: Washington Williamon
Phone: (56) 2 441 2030
Fax: (56) 2 698 2179
Sal. Mgr.: Guillermo Mollins
Phone: (56) 2 441 2030
Fax: (56) 2 698 2179
Oper. Mgr.: Eckart Eitner
Phone: (56) 2 441 2030
Fax: (56) 2 698 2179
Tech. Dir.: Eugenio Grohnert
Phone: (56) 2 441 2030
Fax: (56) 2 698 2179
Total Employees of Company: 1,749
Mill Locations:
CMPC Celulosa S.A., Laja Mill, Balmaceda 30, Laja, Chile, Capacity: 76,398 mt/y, (Pulp mill, Paper mill)
Phone: (56) 43 334 000
Fax: (56) 43 334 015
Email: maceituno@celulosa.cmpc.cl
CMPC Celulosa S.A., Pacífico Mill, Avenida Jorge Alessandri 001, Mininco, Comuna Collipulli, Chile, (Pulp mill)
Phone: (56) 45 293300
Fax: (56) 45 293305
CMPC Celulosa S.A., Santa Fe Mill, Av. Julio Hammelmann 670, Nacimiento, Chile, (Pulp mill)
Phone: (56) 43 403 800
Fax: (56) 43 403 830
Email: fbackhouse@celulosa.cmpc.cl

ⓜCMPC Celulosa S.A.
Laja Mill
Ownership: Empresas CMPC S.A.
Balmaceda 30
Laja, VIII - Región del Biobío
Chile
Mailing Address: PO Box 108, Laja, Chile
Phone: (56) 43 334 000
Fax: (56) 43 334 015
Email: maceituno@celulosa.cmpc.cl
Web Address: www.cmpccelulosa.cl
Personnel:
Mill Mgr.: Marcelo Aceituno
Phone: (56) 43 334 000
Fax: (56) 43 334 015
Email: maceituno@celulosa.cmpc.cl
Mill Prod. Mgr.: Ramiro Peralta
Phone: (56) 43 334 000
Fax: (56) 43 334 015
Email: rperalta@celulosa.cmpc.cl
Pulp Mill Supt.: Marco Fernández
Phone: (56) 43 334 000
Fax: (56) 43 334 015
Email: mfernandez@celulosa.cmpc.cl
Fiber Supt.: Marco Rodríguez Tapia
Phone: (56) 43 334 000
Fax: (56) 43 334 015
Email: mrodriguez@celulosa.cmpc.cl
Recovery & Eng. Supt.: Leonel Vargas
Phone: (56) 43 334 374
Fax: (56) 43 334 015
Email: lvargas@celulosa.cmpc.cl
Cust. Serv. Mgr.: Jose Cuevas Le Bert
Phone: (56) 43 334 000
Fax: (56) 43 334 015
Email: jcuevaslb@celulosa.cmpc.cl
Environ. & Security Supt.: Juan Antonio López Díaz
Phone: (56) 43 334 000
Fax: (56) 43 334 015
Email: jdiaz@celulosa.cmpc.cl
Mech. Supt.: Mario Ormeño Muñoz
Phone: (56) 43 334 000
Fax: (56) 43 334 015
Email: mormeno@celulosa.cmpc.cl
Admin. Mgr.: Ana Gutierrez
Phone: (56) 43 334 374
Fax: (56) 43 334 015
Email: agutierrez@celulosa.cmpc.cl
Total Employees at this Location: 1,000
Type of Operation: Pulp mill, Paper mill
Pulp Grades and Capacities:
Total pulp capacity: 374,570 mt/y
Pulp available for market: 287,742 mt/y
Chemical Pulp: 374,570 mt/y
Pulp Mill Data:
Chemical Pulping Systems:
Batch digesters: 6
Continuous digesters: 1
Pulp Lines: 2
Bleach Plant Systems: 1
Chemical pulping System - BQ2, Type: Softwood, Sequence: O_2 DEopDED, Capacity 285,000 admt/y
Chemical Recovery Equipment:
Evaporator lines: 3
Recovery boilers: 2
Lime Kiln
Pulp Dryers:
Air Float dryers 1, Pulp Dryers 1
Paper/Paperboard Grades and Capacities:
Total paper and paperboard capacity: 76,398 mt/y
Packaging papers: 76,398 mt/y
Paper and Paperboard Mill Data:
Stock Preparation:
Pulpers: 1
Refiners: 9
Paper Machines: 2
No. 12, fourdrinier, total capacity 36,414 mt/y, Trim width 3.2 m, Packaging papers
No. 15, (20% of output is fluff pulp), fourdrinier, total capacity 39,984 mt/y, Trim width 3.2 m, Packaging papers
Finishing Equipment:
Winders: 2 at 80,000 mt/y
Rewinders: 1
Sheeters: 1 at 40,000 mt/y
Energy Data:
Power boilers: 2
Steam turbines: 2 at 19, 38 MW
Electrical demand for mill: 821 MWh/D

ⓜCMPC Celulosa S.A.
Pacífico Mill
Ownership: Empresas CMPC S.A.
Avenida Jorge Alessandri 001
Mininco, Comuna Collipulli, IX - Región de la Araucanía
Chile
Mailing Address: PO Box 11-D, Angol, IX - Región de la Araucanía, Chile
Phone: (56) 45 293300
Fax: (56) 45 293305
Web Address: www.cmpc.cl
Personnel:
Mill Mgr.: Gustavo Vera
Phone: (56) 45 293300
Fax: (56) 45 293305
Email: gvera@celulosa.cmpc.cl
Maint. & Eng. Mgr.: Claudio Barrios
Phone: (56) 45 293300
Fax: (56) 45 293305
Email: cbarrios@celulosa.cmpc.cl
Environ. & Safety Supt.: Victor Zambra
Phone: (56) 45 293300
Fax: (56) 45 293305
Email: vzambra@celulosa.cmpc.cl
Tech. Supt.: Raul Leung
Phone: (56) 45 293300
Fax: (56) 45 293305
Email: rleung@celulosa.cmpc.cl
Total Employees at this Location: 303
Type of Operation: Pulp mill
Pulp Grades and Capacities:
Total pulp capacity: 504,455 mt/y
Pulp available for market: 500,157 mt/y
Chemical Pulp: 504,455 mt/y
Pulp Mill Data:
Chemical Pulping Systems:
Continuous digesters: 1
Pulp Lines: 1
Bleach Plant Systems: 1
Chemical Pulping System, Type: Softwood, Sequence: DEopDD, Capacity 500,000 admt/y
Chemical Recovery Equipment:
Evaporator lines: 1
Recovery boilers: 1
Lime Kiln
Pulp Dryers:
Air Float dryers 1
Energy Data:
Power boilers: 3
Steam turbines: 2 at 38.8, 40 MW
Electrical demand for mill: 1,089 MWh/D

ⓜCMPC Celulosa S.A.
Santa Fe Mill
Ownership: Empresas CMPC S.A.
Av. Julio Hammelmann 670
Nacimiento, VIII - Región del Biobío
Chile
Phone: (56) 43 403 800
Fax: (56) 43 403 830
Email: fbackhouse@celulosa.cmpc.cl
Web Address: www.cmpccelulosa.cl
Personnel:
Mill Mgr.: Francis Backhouse
Phone: (56) 43 403701
Fax: (56) 43 403867
Email: fbackhouse@celulosa.cmpc.cl
Prod. Mgr.: Gerardo Vargas D.
Phone: (56) 43 403766
Fax: (56) 43 403867
Email: gvargas@celulosa.cmpc.cl
Maint. & Eng. Mgr.: Sergio Rebolledo
Phone: (56) 43 403815
Fax: (56) 43 403801
Email: srebolledo@celulosa.cmpc.cl
Tech. Supt.: José Soza
Phone: (56) 43 403772
Fax: (56) 43 403870
Email: jsoza@celulosa.cmpc.cl
Utilities Supt.: Hector Jara
Phone: (56) 43 635522
Fax: (56) 43 403830
Email: hjara@celulosa.cmpc.cl
Prod. Supt.: Victor Sepulveda C.
Phone: (56) 43 403716
Fax: (56) 43 403830
Email: vsepulveda@celulosa.cmpc.cl
Environ. & Safety Supt.: Juan Escalona G.
Phone: (56) 43 403918
Fax: (56) 43 403830
Email: jescalona@celulosa.cmpc.cl
Total Employees at this Location: 710
Type of Operation: Pulp mill
Pulp Grades and Capacities:
Total pulp capacity: 1,500,038 mt/y
Pulp available for market: 1,489,761 mt/y
Chemical Pulp: 1,500,038 mt/y
Pulp Mill Data:
Chemical Pulping Systems:
Continuous digesters: 2
Pulp Lines: 2
Bleach Plant Systems: 3
Chemical Pulping System - 1, Type: ECF - Hardwood, Sequence: DEopD
Chemical Pulping System - 2, Type: ECF - Hardwood, Sequence: DEopD
Chemical Pulping System - 3, Type: ECF - Hardwood, Sequence: O_2 DoEOPDD
Chemical Recovery Equipment:
Evaporator lines: 2
Recovery boilers: 2
Lime Kiln
Pulp Dryers:

Chile

Flakt dryer 1, Flakt dryer 1
Energy Data:
Power boilers: 1
Steam turbines: 3 at 120 MW
Electrical demand for mill: 2,152 MWh/D

ⓂCMPC Papeles Cordillera S.A.
Puente Alto Mill
Ownership: Empresas CMPC S.A.
Avda. Eyzaguirre
01098 Puente Alto, RM - Región Metro. de Santiago
Chile
Phone: (56) 2 23675300, 23675700
Fax: (56) 2 28501118
Email: infocomercial@papeles.cmpc.cl
Web Address: www.papelescordillera.cl
Personnel:
Mill Mgr.: Daniel Andres Rodriguez Navas
Phone: (56) 2 3675700
Fax: (56) 2 8501118
Email: drodriguez@papeles.cmpc.cl
Oper. Mgr.: Eduardo Alberto Huidobro
Phone: (56) 2 3675700
Fax: (56) 2 8501118
Email: ehuidobro@papeles.cmpc.cl
Eng. Mgr.: Luis Carrasco
Phone: (56) 2 3675700
Fax: (56) 2 8501118
Email: lcarrasco@papeles.cmpc.cl
Manuf. Dir.: Jorge Carrasco V.
Phone: (56) 2 3675700
Fax: (56) 2 8501118
Email: jcarrasco@papeles.cmpc.cl
Sls. Mgr.: Eduardo Gildemeister Meier
Phone: (56) 2 3675700
Fax: (56) 2 8501118
Email: egildeme@papeles.cmpc.cl
Total Employees at this Location: 322
Type of Operation: Paper mill, Paperboard mill
Pulp Grades and Capacities:
Total pulp capacity: 253,629 mt/y
Recycled Pulping: 253,629 mt/y
Pulp Mill Data:
Bleach Plant Systems: 1
DIP Capacity 18,000 admt/y
Recycled Fiber Treatment Lines:
Recycled packaging pulping lines: 1 at 254,000 admt/y
Paper/Paperboard Grades and Capacities:
Total paper and paperboard capacity: 314,874 mt/y
Uncoated woodfree/freesheet: 19,992 mt/y
Specialty and industrial: 9,996 mt/y
Linerboard: 134,946 mt/y
Corrugating medium/fluting: 149,940 mt/y
Paper and Paperboard Mill Data:
Stock Preparation:
Pulpers: 9
Refiners: 20
Paper Machines: 3
No. 8, fourdrinier, total capacity 19,992 mt/y, Trim width 3.2 m, Uncoated woodfree/freesheet
No. 10, Yankee dryer, total capacity 9,996 mt/y, Trim width 3.4 m, Specialty and industrial
No. 20, DuoFormer, total capacity 284,886 mt/y, Trim width 5.04 m, Linerboard, Corrugating medium/fluting
Coating Machines: 1
No. 1, total capacity 10,000 mt/y., off machine
Finishing Equipment:
Supercalenders: 2
Rewinders: 8 at 300,000 mt/y
Sheeters: 3 at 24,000 mt/y
Energy Data:
Power boilers: 3
Steam turbines: 2 at 6.0 MW
Electrical demand for mill: 388 MWh/D

ⓂCMPC Tissue S.A.
Puente Alto Mill
Ownership: Empresas CMPC S.A.
01098 Eyzaguirre, Puente Alto, RM - Región Metro. de Santiago
Chile
Phone: (56) 2 366 6460/800 375 000
Fax: (56) 2 623 8539/366 6469
Web Address: www.cmpctissue.cl
Personnel:
Pres.: Victor Infante Riveros
Phone: (56) 2 366 6460
Fax: (56) 2 623 8539
Email: vriveros@tisspte.cmpc.cl
Total Employees at this Location: 275
Type of Operation: Paper mill
Pulp Grades and Capacities:
Total pulp capacity: 60,644 mt/y
Recycled Pulping: 60,644 mt/y
Pulp Mill Data:
Bleach Plant Systems: 1
Recycled Pulping System, Type: DIP
Recycled Fiber Treatment Lines:
Pulpers: 3 at 72,000 admt/y
Paper/Paperboard Grades and Capacities:
Total paper and paperboard capacity: 63,903 mt/y
Tissue: 63,903 mt/y
Paper and Paperboard Mill Data:
Stock Preparation:
Pulpers: 6
Paper Machines: 3
No. 14, crescent former, total capacity 7,854 mt/y, Trim width 1.95 m, Tissue, Uncoated woodfree/freesheet
No. 16, twin-wire, total capacity 26,775 mt/y, Trim width 2.73 m, Tissue
No. 17, crescent former, total capacity 29,274 mt/y, Trim width 2.73 m, Tissue
Energy Data:
Power boilers
Electrical demand for mill: 281 MWh/D

ⓂCMPC Tissue S.A.
Talagante Mill
Ownership: Empresas CMPC S.A.
Camino Isla de Maipo
0297 Talagante, RM - Región Metro. de Santiago
Chile
Fax: (56) 2 462 4511
Web Address: www.cmpctissue.cl, www.cmpc.cl
Personnel:
Prod. Mgr.: Felipe Harding
Phone: (56) 2 462 4591
Total Employees at this Location: 500
Type of Operation: Paper mill
Pulp Grades and Capacities:
Total pulp capacity: 80,477 mt/y
Recycled Pulping: 80,477 mt/y
Pulp Mill Data:
Bleach Plant Systems: 1
Recycled Pulping System, Type: DIP
Recycled Fiber Treatment Lines:
Flotation deinking lines: 1
Paper/Paperboard Grades and Capacities:
Total paper and paperboard capacity: 108,528 mt/y
Tissue: 108,528 mt/y
Paper and Paperboard Mill Data:
Stock Preparation:
Pulpers: 2
Refiners: 2
Paper Machines: 3
No. 1, crescent former, total capacity 29,988 mt/y, Trim width 2.7 m, Tissue, Uncoated woodfree/freesheet
No. 2, ATMOS, total capacity 24,990 mt/y, Trim width 2.7 m, Tissue
No. 3, crescent former, total capacity 53,550 mt/y, Trim width 5.6 m, Tissue
Finishing Equipment:
Rewinders: 1
Energy Data:
Power boilers: 1
Electrical demand for mill: 409 MWh/D

ⓂForestal y Papelera Concepción S.A.
Ownership: 50% by Copapel Inversiones SA, 50% by Forestal e Industrial Curimaqui SA
Parque Ind. Escuadrón II, km 17.5
Coronel, VIII - Región del Biobío
Chile
Phone: (56) 41 2508 700, 41-2885000
Fax: (56) 41 2508 711
Email: fbebin@fpc.cl
Web Address: www.fpc.cl
Personnel:
Sls. Dir.: Gonzalo Pacheco
Phone: (56) 41 2508 700
Fax: (56) 41 2508 711
Email: gpacheco@fpc.cl
Total Employees of Company: 120
Mill Locations:
Forestal y Papelera Concepción S.A., Coronel Mill, Parque Ind. Escuadrón II, km 17.5, Coronel, Chile, Capacity: 104,958 mt/y, (Paper mill)
Phone: (56) 41 2885 000
Email: fbebin@fpc.cl

ⓂForestal y Papelera Concepción S.A.
Coronel Mill
Parque Ind. Escuadrón II, km 17.5
Coronel, VIII - Región del Biobío
Chile
Phone: (56) 41 2885 000
Email: fbebin@fpc.cl
Web Address: www.fpc.cl
Personnel:
Oper. Mgr.: Maurício Silva Martinez
Phone: (56) 41 2885 000
Fax: (56) 41 2508 711
Email: msilva@fpc.cl
Prod. Mgr.: Juan Fritz
Phone: (56) 41 2885 000
Fax: (56) 41 2508 711
Email: jfritz@fpc.cl
Comm. Dir.: Gonzalo Pacheco
Phone: (56) 41 2885 000
Fax: (56) 41 2508 711
Email: gpacheco@fpc.cl
Total Employees at this Location: 120
Type of Operation: Paper mill
Pulp Grades and Capacities:
Total pulp capacity: 104,965 mt/y
Recycled Pulping: 104,965 mt/y
Pulp Mill Data:
Recycled Fiber Treatment Lines:
Pulpers: 1 at 92,400
Paper/Paperboard Grades and Capacities:
Total paper and paperboard capacity: 104,958 mt/y
Linerboard: 34,986 mt/y
Corrugating medium/fluting: 69,972 mt/y
Paper and Paperboard Mill Data:
Paper Machines: 1
No. 1, twin-wire, total capacity 104,958 mt/y, Trim width 3.83 m, Corrugating medium/fluting, Linerboard
Energy Data:
Power boilers: 2
Steam turbines: 2 at 12, 2.8 MW
Electrical demand for mill: 162 MWh/D

ⓂⓂPapelera del Pacífico S.A.
San Francisco de Mostazal Mill
Ownership: 100% by Coipsa
Longitudinal Sur Km. 63
San Francisco de Mostazal, VI - Región Gen. O'Higgins
Chile
Phone: (56) 72 208 100
Fax: (56) 72 491 025
Email: info@cpp.cl
Web Address: www.cpp.cl
Personnel:
Indus. Mgr.: Cristian Jorquera
Phone: (56) 72 208 100

Fax: (56) 72 491 025
Email: cjorquera@cpp.cl
Commer. Mgr: Jaime Pavez
Phone: (56) 72 208 100
Fax: (56) 72 491 025
Email: jpavez@cpp.cl
Tech. Mgr.: Hipolito Lagos
Phone: (56) 72 208 100
Fax: (56) 72 491 025
Email: hlagos@cpp.cl
Export Mgr.: Eduardo Francke
Phone: (56) 72 208 100
Fax: (56) 72 491 025
Email: efrancke@cpp.cl
Sec. of Ind. Management: Carolina Zamorano
Phone: (56) 72 208 128
Fax: (56) 72 491 025
Email: czamorano@cpp.cl
Sec. Gen. Mgr.: Loreto Guerman
Phone: (56) 72 208 102
Fax: (56) 72 491 025
Email: lguerman@cpp.cl
Total Employees of Company: 160
Total Employees at this Location: 110
Type of Operation: Paper mill, Paperboard mill
Pulp Grades and Capacities:
Total pulp capacity: 90,985 mt/y
Recycled Pulping: 90,985 mt/y

Pulp Mill Data:
Recycled Fiber Treatment Lines:
Recycled packaging pulping lines: 1
Paper/Paperboard Grades and Capacities:
Total paper and paperboard capacity: 89,964 mt/y
Linerboard: 39,984 mt/y
Corrugating medium/fluting: 49,980 mt/y
Paper and Paperboard Mill Data:
Stock Preparation:
Pulpers: 3
Refiners: 8
Paper Machines: 1
No. 3, fourdrinier, total capacity 89,964 mt/y, Trim width 4.8 m, Corrugating medium/fluting, Linerboard
Coating Machines: 2
No. 1, off machine
No. 2, off machine
Energy Data:
Power boilers: 2
Electrical demand for mill: 133 MWh/D

ⓞⓜPapeles Bío Bío
Concepción Mill
Ownership: 30% by financing investors poll, 70% by Group BO/Pathfinder
Pedro Aguirre Cerda 1059, San Pedro de la Paz
Concepción, VIII - Región del Biobío
Chile
Mailing Address: Casilla 1097, 1054 Concepción, Chile
Phone: (56) 41 2500 000
Fax: (56) 41 2371 090
Web Address: www.papelesbiobio.cl
Personnel:
Gen. Mgr.: Glen Rybertt
Phone: (56) 41 2500 000
Fax: (56) 41 2371 090
Finan. Mgr.: Gerhard Baumgartner
Phone: (56) 41 2500 000
Fax: (56) 41 2371 090
Maint. Mgr.: Elias Valenzuela
Phone: (56) 41 2500 000
Fax: (56) 41 2371 090
Pulp Mill Mgr.: Ricardo D
Phone: (56) 41 2500 000
Fax: (56) 41 2371 090
Commer. Dir.: Enrique Guzmán
Phone: (56) 41 2500 000
Fax: (56) 41 2371 090
Email: enrique.guzman@pabio.cl
Commer. Mgr.: Gonzalo Hillerns
Phone: (56) 41 2500 000
Fax: (56) 41 2371 090
Email: gonzalo.hillerns@pabio.cl
Cust.Service Mgr.: Alvaro Olmos
Phone: (56) 41 2500 000
Fax: (56) 41 2371 090
Email: alvaro.olmos@pabio.cl
Total Employees of Company: 237
Total Employees at this Location: 237
Type of Operation: Pulp mill, Paper mill
Mill Locations:
Norske Skog Pisa S.A., Jaguariaíva Mill (51% owned), Rodovia PR 151, Km. 207.5, 84200-000 Jaguariaíva, PR, Brazil, Capacity: 169,575 mt/y, (Paper mill)
Phone: (55) 43 3535 8000
Fax: (55) 43 3535 2627
Email: contato@norskeskog.com.br
Pulp Grades and Capacities:
Total pulp capacity: 68,187 mt/y
Mechanical Pulp: 68,187 mt/y

Pulp Mill Data:
Mechanical Pulping Systems:
Pressurized grinders: 4
Bleach Plant Systems: 1
Mechanical PGW Pulping System, Type: Softwood
Paper/Paperboard Grades and Capacities:
Total paper and paperboard capacity: 116,739 mt/y
Newsprint: 37,485 mt/y
Uncoated mechanical/groundwood: 73,185 mt/y
Packaging papers: 6,069 mt/y
Paper and Paperboard Mill Data:
Stock Preparation:
Pulpers:
Paper Machines: 2
No. 1, (Former Type model: Twin-wire - DuoFormer HD), DuoFormer, total capacity 110,670 mt/y, Trim width 4.58 m, Newsprint, Uncoated mechanical/groundwood
No. 2, fourdrinier, total capacity 6,069 mt/y, Trim width 1.62 m, Packaging papers
Energy Data:
Power boilers: 1
Steam turbines: 1 at 7 MW
Electrical demand for mill: 685 MWh/D

ⓜPapeles Río Vergara S.A.
Nacimiento Mill
Mill is closed (closed early December, 2013.)
Ownership: 100% by Empresas CMPC S.A.
Av. Julio Hemmelman 330
Nacimiento, VIII - Región del Biobío
Chile
Mailing Address: Casilla 1791, Nacimiento, VIII - Región del Biobío, Chile
Phone: (56) 43 631300
Fax: (56) 43 511444
Web Address: www.cmpc.cl
Personnel:
Gen. Mgr.: Ing. Andrés Larraín Marchant
Phone: (56) 43 631300
Fax: (56) 43 511444
Paper Prod. Mgr.: Marcos Saavedra
Phone: (56) 43 631300
Fax: (56) 43 511444
Email: msaavedra@inforsa.cmpc.cl
Pulp Prod. Mgr.: Claudio Orellana L.
Phone: (56) 43 631300
Fax: (56) 43 511444
Email: corellana@inforsa.cmpc.cl
Eng. & Maint. Mgr.: Sergio Villagrán Valenzuela
Phone: (56) 43 631300
Fax: (56) 43 511444
Email: svillagran@inforsa.cmpc.cl
Total Employees at this Location: 300
Type of Operation: Paper mill

Pulp Mill Data:
Mechanical Pulping Systems:
TMP systems: 2
Pulp Lines: 2
Bleach Plant Systems: 1
Mechanical TMP Pulping System, Type: Softwood, Sequence: Di
Paper and Paperboard Mill Data:
Stock Preparation:
Refiners: 5
Paper Machines: 2
No. 1, GapFormer, total capacity 128,520 mt/y, Trim width 4.9 m
No. 1, twin-wire, total capacity 64,260 mt/y, Trim width 3.8 m, Newsprint
Finishing Equipment:
Rewinders: 1
Energy Data:
Power boilers: 2
TMP Reboiler: 1

ⓜPapeles Industriales S.A. (PISA)
Lampa Mill
Ownership: 100% by SCA - Svenska Cellulosa Aktiebolaget
Panamericana Norte
22550 Lampa, RM - Región Metro. de Santiago
Chile
Mailing Address: Casilla 50.990, Correo Central, 22550 Lampa, Chile
Phone: (56) 800 200 973, 2640 5200/5021/5270
Fax: (56) 2 733 1103/1031/1108
Email: contacto@pisa.cl, infochile@sca.com
Web Address: www.pisa.cl
Personnel:
Man. Dir.: Felipe Baraona
Phone: (56) 800 200 973
Fax: (56) 2 733 1031
Commer. Mgr.: Eduardo Hola
Phone: (56) 800 200 973
Fax: (56) 2 733 1031
Commer. Mgr. AFH SCA Chile: Francisco Salamé
Phone: (56) 800 200 973
Fax: (56) 2 733 1031
Sls. Mgr.: Cristian Ibañez
Phone: (56) 800 200 973
Fax: (56) 2 733 1031
Asst. Operations Mgr.: Nicolas Schilling
Phone: (56) 800 200 973
Fax: (56) 2 733 1031
Total Employees at this Location: 250
Type of Operation: Paper mill
Paper/Paperboard Grades and Capacities:
Total paper and paperboard capacity: 61,047 mt/y
Tissue: 61,047 mt/y
Paper and Paperboard Mill Data:
Paper Machines: 2
No. 2, crescent former, total capacity 29,988 mt/y, Trim width 2.76 m, Tissue, Uncoated woodfree/freesheet
No. 3, crescent former, total capacity 31,059 mt/y, Trim width 2.76 m, Tissue, Uncoated woodfree/freesheet
Energy Data:
Power boilers
Electrical demand for mill: 224 MWh/D

ⓞⓜSociedad Fábrica de Papel y Cartón Schorr y Concha S.A.
Talca Mill
Ownership: Familia Schorr y Concha
Av. Carlos Schorr 433, Casilla 185
Talca, VII - Región del Maule
Chile
Phone: (56) 71 510710
Fax: (56) 71 510715
Personnel:
Gen. Mgr.: Carlos Schorr Concha
Phone: (56) 71 510710
Prod. Mgr.: Jorge Schorr Concha
Phone: (56) 71 510710
Prod. Mgr.: Jimena Vivero
Phone: (56) 71 510710
Total Employees of Company: 135

Colombia

Total Employees at this Location: 135
Type of Operation: Paper mill, Paperboard mill
Paper/Paperboard Grades and Capacities:
Total paper and paperboard capacity: 6,000 mt/y
Packaging papers: 2,000 mt/y
Corrugating medium/fluting: 4,000 mt/y
Paper and Paperboard Mill Data:
Paper Machines: 1
PM 1, total capacity 6,000 mt/y, Packaging papers, Corrugating medium/fluting

COLOMBIA

ⓘCartones America SA - CAME
Ownership: 100% by CAME Group
Calle 70N No.2A-130 CAME
2393 Cali, Valle de Cauca
Colombia
Mailing Address: Aptdo. Aéreo 2393, Cali, Valle de Cauca, Colombia
  Phone: (57) 2 681 8888
  Fax: (57) 2 664 5282
  Email: info@cartonesamerica.com
  Web Address: www.cartonesamerica.com
Personnel:
  Pres.: Pierangelo Pacini Blanco
  Phone: (57) 2 681 8888
  Fax: (57) 2 664 5282
  CFO: Juan Negret
  Phone: (57) 2 681 8888
  Fax: (57) 2 664 5282
  Email: juanp.negret@cartonesamerica.com
  Mgr., VCC Venezuela Corrugating Div.: Mauricio Tapias
  Phone: (57) 2 681 8888
  Fax: (57) 2 664 5282
  Email: mauricio.tapias@cartonesamerica.com
  Proj. Mgr.: Juan Andújar Gabori
  Phone: (57) 2 681 8888
  Fax: (57) 2 664 5282
  Email: juan.andujar@cartonesamerica.com
Mill Locations:
Cartones America SA - CAME, Cali Mill, Calle 70N No.2A-130 CAME, 2393 Cali, Colombia, Capacity: 104,958 mt/y, (Paperboard mill)
  Phone: (57) 2 681 8888
  Fax: (57) 2 664 5282
  Email: info@cartonesamerica.com
Papelera del Sur S.A., Chincha Mill, Km. 202 Panamericana Sur Div. Chincha Baja, Chincha, Peru, Capacity: 61,761 mt/y, (Paperboard mill)
  Phone: (51) 56 2721 29

ⓜCartones America SA - CAME
Cali Mill
Calle 70N No.2A-130 CAME
2393 Cali, Valle de Cauca
Colombia
Mailing Address: Aptdo. Aéreo 2393, Cali, Colombia
  Phone: (57) 2 681 8888
  Fax: (57) 2 664 5282
  Email: info@cartonesamerica.com
  Web Address: www.cartonesamerica.com
Personnel:
  Pres.: Pierangelo Pacini Blanco
  Phone: (57) 2 681 8888
  Fax: (57) 2 664 5282
  Corp. Fin. Mgr.: Juan Pablo Negret
  Phone: (57) 2 681 8888
  Fax: (57) 2 664 5282
  Email: juanp.negret@cartonesamerica.com
  Mgr., VCC Venezuela Corrugating Div.: Mauricio Tapias
  Phone: (57) 2 681 8888
  Fax: (57) 2 664 5282
  Email: mauricio.tapias@cartonesamerica.com
  Proj. Mgr.: Juan Andújar Gabori
  Phone: (57) 2 681 8812
  Fax: (57) 2 664 5282
  Email: juan.andujar@cartonesamerica.com
Total Employees at this Location: 248
Type of Operation: Paperboard mill
Pulp Grades and Capacities:
Total pulp capacity: 100,734 mt/y
Recycled Pulping: 89,819 mt/y
Other Pulp: 10,915 mt/y
Pulp Mill Data:
  Chemical Pulping Systems:
  Batch digesters: 5
  Chemical Recovery Equipment:
  Recovery boilers: 1
  Recycled Fiber Treatment Lines:
  Pulpers: 4 at 97,000 admt/y
Paper/Paperboard Grades and Capacities:
Total paper and paperboard capacity: 104,958 mt/y
Linerboard: 44,982 mt/y
Corrugating medium/fluting: 24,990 mt/y
Boxboard/cartonboard: 34,986 mt/y
Paper and Paperboard Mill Data:
  Stock Preparation:
  Pulpers: 4
  Refiners: 8
Paper Machines: 2
No. 2, cylinder (3), total capacity 34,986 mt/y, Trim width 2.5 m, Boxboard/cartonboard
No. 3, fourdrinier, total capacity 69,972 mt/y, Trim width 2.5 m, Linerboard, Corrugating medium/fluting
Coating Machines: 1
PM 2, total capacity 28,600 mt/y., on machine
Finishing Equipment:
Rewinders: 2
Energy Data:
Power boilers: 1
Combustion turbines: 1 at 8 MW
Electrical demand for mill: 176 MWh/D

ⓘCartonal SAS
Ownership: 50% by Alberto Umaña, 50% by Jorge Ramon Mendoza
Carrera 16B 59-59 Sur
Santa Fe de Bogotá, Bogotá D.C.
Colombia
  Phone: (57) 1 568 5537
  Fax: (57) 1 568 5537-39
  Email: info@cartonalcolombia.com
  Web Address: www.cartonalcolombia.com
Personnel:
  Mgr.: Jorge Ramos
  Phone: (57) 57 1 568 5537
  Fax: (57) 57 1 568 5537
  Email: j.ramos@cartonalcolombia.com
  HR Mgr.: Fanny Pinzón
  Phone: (57) 57 1 568 5537
  Fax: (57) 57 1 568 5537
  Email: f.pinzon@cartonalcolombia.com
  Acct. Mgr.: Alexandra Párraga
  Phone: (57) 57 1 568 5537
  Fax: (57) 57 1 568 5537
  Email: a.parraga@cartonalcolombia.com
  Sls. Mgr: Riobueno Marisol
  Phone: (57) 57 1 568 5537
  Fax: (57) 57 1 568 5537
  Email: m.riobueno@cartonalcolombia.com
  Prod. Purch. Maint. Mgr: Alba Rojas
  Phone: (57) 57 1 568 5537
  Fax: (57) 57 1 568 5537
  Email: a.rojas@cartonalcolombia.com
Total Employees of Company: 40
Mill Locations:
Cartonal SAS, Santa Fe de Bogotá Mill, Carrera 16B 59-59 Sur, Santa Fe de Bogotá, Colombia, Capacity: 2,000 mt/y, (Paperboard mill)
  Phone: (57) 1 568 5537
  Fax: (57) 1 568 5537-39
  Email: info@cartonalcolombia.com

ⓜCartonal SAS
Santa Fe de Bogotá Mill
Carrera 16B 59-59 Sur
Santa Fe de Bogotá, Cundinamarca
Colombia
  Phone: (57) 1 568 5537
  Fax: (57) 1 568 5537-39
  Email: info@cartonalcolombia.com
  Web Address: www.cartonalcolombia.com
Personnel:
  Mill Mgr.: Jorge Ramos
  Phone: (57) 1 568 5537
  Fax: (57) 1 568 5537
  Email: j.ramos@cartonalcolombia.com
  HR Mgr.: Fanny Pinzón
  Phone: (57) 1 568 5537
  Fax: (57) 1 568 5537
  Email: f.pinzon@cartonalcolombia.com
  Sls. Mgr.: Marisol Riobueno
  Phone: (57) 1 568 5537
  Fax: (57) 1 568 5537
  Email: m.riobueno@cartonalcolombia.com
  Acct. Mgr: Alexandra Párraga
  Phone: (57) 1 568 5537
  Fax: (57) 1 568 5537
  Email: a.parraga@cartonalcolombia.com
  Prod. & Purch. & Maint. Mgr.: Alba Rojas
  Phone: (57) 1 568 5537
  Fax: (57) 1 568 5537
  Email: a.rojas@cartonalcolombia.com
Total Employees at this Location: 40
Type of Operation: Paperboard mill
Pulp Mill Data:
  Recycled Fiber Treatment Lines:
  Pulpers: 2 at 2,000 admt/y
Paper/Paperboard Grades and Capacities:
Total paper and paperboard capacity: 2,000 mt/y
Boxboard/cartonboard: 2,000 mt/y
Paper and Paperboard Mill Data:
Paper Machines: 2
PM 1, total capacity 1,000 mt/y, Trim width 0.5 m, Boxboard/cartonboard
PM 2, total capacity 1,000 mt/y, Trim width 0.5 m, Boxboard/cartonboard

ⓘⓜCarvajal Pulpa y Papel
Yumbo Mill, Plant 1
Ownership: Carvajal S.A. Group
Carretera Antigua Cali - Yumbo, Km 7
Yumbo, Valle de Cauca
Colombia
Mailing Address: Aptdo. Aéreo 4412, Cali, Valle del Cauca, Colombia
  Phone: (57) 2 651 2000
  Fax: (57) 2 651 2000 ext. 72205
  Email: servicio.cliente@propal.com.co, eugenio.castro@carvajal.com
  Web Address: www.propal.com.co, www.carvajal.com/
Personnel:
  Pres.: Henry Sanchez
  Phone: (57) (57 2) 6512000 Ext. 72210 or 72202
  Email: henry.sanchez@carvajal.com
  VP. Corp. Plan.: Eugenio Castro Carvajal
  Phone: (57) 2 6512202
  Fax: (57) 2 6512205
  Email: eugenio.castro@carvajal.com
  Bus. Mgr.: Otto Zufiga
  Phone: (57) 2 651 2000
  Oper. Mgr. (Plant No. 1): César Zuluaga
  Phone: (57) 2 6512214
  Oper. Mgr. (Plant No. 2): Oscar Holguín
  Phone: (57) 2 651 2000 Ext. 73400
  Fax: (57) 2 651 2000 Ext. 73415
  HR Mgr.: Jorge Mario Hurtado
  Phone: (57) 2 651 2000 Ext. 72412
  Fax: (57) 2 651 2000 Ext. 72415
  Innovation Mgr.: Juan Carlos Sadovnik
  Phone: (57) 2 651 2000
  Corporate Logistics Director: Alejandro Carvajal
  Phone: (57) (1) 410 0400 Ext.12144
  Fax: (57) (314) 771 2299
  Email: alejandro.carvajal@carvajal.com

Colombia

Logist. Mgr.: Guillermo Holguín
Phone: (57) 2 651 2000 Ext. 72600
Fax: (57) 2 651 2000 Ext. 72605
Qlty. Mgr.: Manuel Parra
Phone: (57) 2 651 2000 Ext. 72460
Fax: (57) 2 651 2000 Ext. 72415
Maint. Mgr.: Ricardo Hoyos
Phone: (57) 2 651 2000 Ext. 72830
Fax: (57) 2 651 2000 Ext. 72835
Asst. Exc.: Liliana Valencia Romero
Phone: (57) :(57) (2) 6512000 Ext.72202
Email: liliana.ValenciaRomero@carvajal.com
Total Employees of Company: 1,600
Total Employees at this Location: 578
Type of Operation: Pulp mill, Paper mill
Mill Locations:
Carvajal Pulpa y Papel, Guachené Mill, Plant 2, Km 3, Vía El Ingenio, La Cabaña - Parque Industrial, Guachené, Cauca, Colombia, Capacity: 126,021 mt/y, (Pulp mill, Paper mill)
Phone: (57) 2 651 2000
Fax: (57) 2 651 2658
Email: oscar.holguin@carvajal.com
Pulp Grades and Capacities:
Total pulp capacity: 86,457 mt/y
Other Pulp: 86,457 mt/y
Pulp Mill Data:
Chemical Pulping Systems:
Continuous digesters: 4
Pulp Lines: 1
Bleach Plant Systems: 1
Nonwood Pulping System, Type: Bagasse, Sequence: D(EOP)D, Capacity 100,000 admt/y
Chemical Recovery Equipment:
Evaporator lines: 1
Recovery boilers: 1
Lime Kiln
Paper/Paperboard Grades and Capacities:
Total paper and paperboard capacity: 118,167 mt/y
Uncoated woodfree/freesheet: 52,122 mt/y
Coated woodfree/freesheet: 32,487 mt/y
Packaging papers: 12,138 mt/y
Boxboard/cartonboard: 21,420 mt/y
Paper and Paperboard Mill Data:
Stock Preparation:
Pulpers: 3
Refiners: 5
Paper Machines: 3
No. 1, fourdrinier, total capacity 53,907 mt/y, Trim width 3.8 m, Boxboard/cartonboard, Coated woodfree/freesheet
No. 2, Yankee dryer, total capacity 12,138 mt/y, Trim width 3 m, Packaging papers
No. 3, fourdrinier, total capacity 52,122 mt/y, Trim width 3.8 m, Uncoated woodfree/freesheet
Coating Machines: 1
PM 3, total capacity 58,000 mt/y., off machine
Finishing Equipment:
Winders: 4
Supercalenders: 2
Rewinders: 1
Sheeters: 3
Energy Data:
Power boilers: 2
Steam turbines: 2 at 10, 15 MW
Electrical demand for mill: 339 MWh/D

ⓜCarvajal Pulpa y Papel
Guachené Mill, Plant 2
Km 3, Vía El Ingenio, La Cabaña - Parque Industrial
Guachené, Cauca, Valle de Cauca
Colombia
Phone: (57) 2 651 2000
Fax: (57) 2 651 2658
Email: oscar.holguin@carvajal.com
Web Address: www.carvajal.com/carvajal-pulpa-y-papel-2.html
Personnel:
Paper Mill Mgr.: Wilson Millan
Phone: (57) 2 651 2000 Ext. 73690
Fax: (57) 2 651 2658
Email: wilson.millan@carvajal.com
Pulp Mill Mgr.: Freddy Arroyo
Phone: (57) 2 651 2000 Ext. 73130
Fax: (57) 2 651 2658
Email: freddy.arroyo@carvajal.com
Scheduler: Hector Fabio Esquivel
Phone: (57) 2 651 2000 Ext. 73210
Fax: (57) 2 651 2658
Email: hector.esquivel@propal.com.co
Total Employees at this Location: 450
Type of Operation: Pulp mill, Paper mill
Pulp Grades and Capacities:
Total pulp capacity: 93,137 mt/y
Other Pulp: 93,137 mt/y
Pulp Mill Data:
Chemical Pulping Systems:
Continuous digesters: 1
Pulp Lines: 1
Bleach Plant Systems: 1
Chemical Pulping System, Type: Bagasse, Sequence: DEpD, Capacity 94,000 admt/y
Chemical Recovery Equipment:
Evaporator lines: 1
Recovery boilers: 1
Lime Kiln
Pulp Dryers:
Wet Lap machine 1
Paper/Paperboard Grades and Capacities:
Total paper and paperboard capacity: 126,021 mt/y
Uncoated woodfree/freesheet: 126,021 mt/y
Paper and Paperboard Mill Data:
Stock Preparation:
Pulpers: 2
Refiners: 4
Paper Machines: 1
No. 4, DuoFormer, total capacity 126,021 mt/y, Trim width 6 m, Uncoated woodfree/freesheet
Finishing Equipment:
Sheeters: 3 at 60,000 mt/y
Energy Data:
Power boilers: 1
Steam turbines: 1 at 17.0 MW
Electrical demand for mill: 380 MWh/D

ⓞⓜColombiana de Cartones Ltda.
Palmira, Cali Mill
Carrera 7, No. 34-120
696 Palmira, Cali, Valle de Cauca
Colombia
Phone: (57) 26669497
Personnel:
Asst. Mgr.: Luz Helena Valencia
Phone: (57) 26669497
Total Employees at this Location: 20
Type of Operation: Pulp mill, Paper mill, Paperboard mill
Paper/Paperboard Grades and Capacities:
Total paper and paperboard capacity: 20,000 mt/y
Boxboard/cartonboard: 20,000 mt/y
Paper and Paperboard Mill Data:
Paper Machines: 2
PM 1, Trim width 2.1 m, Boxboard/cartonboard
PM 2, Trim width 2.5 m, Boxboard/cartonboard

ⓞColombiana Kimberly Colpapel S.A.
Ownership: 100% by Kimberly-Clark Corp.
Carrera 11a # 94-45, piso 5
Bogotá
Colombia
Mailing Address: Apartado Aereo 90621, Bogotá D.C., Colombia
Phone: (57) 1 600 3300
Fax: (57) 1 600 3392
Email: KCPColombia.info@kcc.com
Web Address: www.kcc.com, www.kimberlypapelesfinos.com
Personnel:
Export Mgr. Colombia: Carlos Andres García Florez
Phone: (1) 631-311 7200 Ext. 2198
Fax: (1) 1 600 3392
Email: carlos.a.garcia@kcc.com
Corp. Affairs Mgr.: Elenita Mora Bendeck
Phone: (57) 1 600 3300 Ext. 1130
Fax: (57) 1 600 3392
Email: emorab@kcc.com
Mill Locations:
Colombiana Kimberly Colpapel S.A., Medellin Mill, Calle 12 # 1111 Vereda, Canaan Barbosa, Medellin, Colombia, Capacity: 22,848 mt/y, (Pulp mill, Paper mill)
Phone: (57) 4 3789200
Colombiana Kimberly Colpapel S.A., Puerto Tejada Mill, 201 mts después del Pte. El Hormiguero vía Cali - Pto Tejada, Puerto Tejada, Cauca, Colombia, Capacity: 64,974 mt/y, (Paper mill)
Phone: (57) 2 3187700 ext. 2084

ⓜColombiana Kimberly Colpapel S.A.
Medellin Mill
Ownership: 100% by Kimberly-Clark Corp.
Calle 12 # 1111 Vereda, Canaan Barbosa
Medellin, Antioquia
Colombia
Phone: (57) 4 3789200
Web Address: www.kcc.com, www.kimberlypapelesfinos.com
Personnel:
Mill. Mgr.: Nelson Morales
Phone: (57) 4 3789200
Email: nmorales@kcc.com
Maint. Mgr.: Jorge Andres P
Phone: (57) 4 3789200
Total Employees at this Location: 98
Type of Operation: Pulp mill, Paper mill
Paper/Paperboard Grades and Capacities:
Total paper and paperboard capacity: 22,848 mt/y
Tissue: 22,848 mt/y
Paper and Paperboard Mill Data:
Paper Machines: 1
No. 3, TAD, total capacity 22,848 mt/y, Trim width 2.6 m, Tissue
Energy Data:
Power boilers
Electrical demand for mill: 89 MWh/D

ⓜColombiana Kimberly Colpapel S.A.
Puerto Tejada Mill
Ownership: 100% by Kimberly-Clark Corp.
201 mts después del Pte. El Hormiguero vía Cali - Pto Tejada
Puerto Tejada, Cauca
Colombia
Phone: (57) 2 3187700 ext. 2084
Web Address: www.kcc.com, www.kimberlypapelesfinos.com
Personnel:
Mill Mgr. & Colombia Oper. Dir.: Carlos Morales
Phone: (57) 2 3187700 ext. 2084
Email: cmorales@kcc.com
Total Employees at this Location: 200
Type of Operation: Paper mill
Paper/Paperboard Grades and Capacities:
Total paper and paperboard capacity: 64,974 mt/y
Tissue: 64,974 mt/y
Paper and Paperboard Mill Data:
Paper Machines: 1
No. 1, twin-wire, total capacity 64,974 mt/y, Trim width 5.22 m, Tissue, Uncoated woodfree/freesheet
Energy Data:
Power boilers
Electrical demand for mill: 181 MWh/D

ⓞColombiana Tissue
Transversal 1 Cra 1 Parselación la Dolores
Palmira, Valle de Cauca
Colombia
Phone: (57) 2 666 9777
Web Address: www.colombianatissue.com

Colombia

Mill Locations:
Colombiana Tissue, Palmira Mill, Transversal 1 Cra 1 Parselación la Dolores, Palmira, Colombia, Capacity: 9,000 mt/y, (Paper mill)
Phone: (57) 2 666 9777

ⓜColombiana Tissue
Palmira Mill
Transversal 1 Cra 1 Parselación la Dolores
Palmira, Valle de Cauca
Colombia
Phone: (57) 2 666 9777
Web Address: www.colombianatissue.com
Type of Operation: Paper mill
Paper/Paperboard Grades and Capacities:
Total paper and paperboard capacity: 9,000 mt/y
Tissue: 9,000 mt/y

ⓗCorrugados de Colombia Ltda.
Cra. 113 N° 15C-81
Fontibón, Bogotá D.C.
Colombia
Mailing Address: Aptdo. Aéreo 80092, Bogotá D.C., Bogotá D.C., Colombia
Phone: (57) 1 415 4899
Fax: (57) 1 421 1163
Email: corrucol@etb.net.co, info.corrucol@etb.net.co
Web Address: www.corrucol.com.co
Personnel:
Pres. Junta Dir./Chmn.: Gabriele Garlatti Venturini
Phone: (57) 1 415 4899
Fax: (57) 1 421 1163
Admin. Dir.: Dony Ortiz
Phone: (57) 1 415 4899
Fax: (57) 1 421 1163
Email: diradm.corrucol@etb.net.co
HR Mgr.: Myriam Rozo
Phone: (57) 1 415 4899
Fax: (57) 1 421 1163
Email: rrhh.corrucol@etb.net.co
Total Employees of Company: 80
Mill Locations:
Corrugados de Colombia Ltda., Fontibón Mill, Cra. 113 N° 15C-81, Fontibón, Colombia, Capacity: 18,000 mt/y, (Paper mill, Paperboard mill)
Phone: (57) 1 415 4899
Fax: (57) 1 421 1163
Email: corrucol@etb.net.co, info.corrucol@etb.net.co

ⓜCorrugados de Colombia Ltda.
Fontibón Mill
Cra. 113 N° 15C-81
Fontibón, Bogotá D.C.
Colombia
Mailing Address: Aptdo. Aéreo 80092, Bogotá D.C., Colombia
Phone: (57) 1 415 4899
Fax: (57) 1 421 1163
Email: corrucol@etb.net.co, info.corrucol@etb.net.co
Web Address: www.corrucol.com.co
Personnel:
Pres. Junta Dir./Chmn.: Gabriele Garlatti Venturini
Phone: (57) 1 415 4899
Fax: (57) 1 421 1163
Gen. Mgr.: Dony Giovani Ortiz Vera
Phone: (57) 1 415 4899
Fax: (57) 1 421 1163
Email: diradm.corrucol@etb.net.co
Commercial Mgr.: Marisol Arias
Phone: (57) 1 415 4899
Fax: (57) 1 421 1163
Email: corrucol@etb.net.co
HR Mgr.: Marleny Rozo
Phone: (57) 1 415 4899
Fax: (57) 1 421 1163
Email: rrhh.corrucol@etb.net.co
Sls. Coord.: Gracie Avila
Phone: (57) 1 415 4899
Fax: (57) 1 421 1163
Email: ventas.corrucol@etb.net.co
Total Employees at this Location: 80
Type of Operation: Paper mill, Paperboard mill
Paper/Paperboard Grades and Capacities:
Total paper and paperboard capacity: 18,000 mt/y
Linerboard: 18,000 mt/y
Paper and Paperboard Mill Data:
Paper Machines: 4
No. 1, cylinder, total capacity 2,160 mt/y, Trim width 1.4 m, Linerboard
No. 2, total capacity 2,160 mt/y, Trim width 1.4 m, Linerboard
No. 3, total capacity 2,640 mt/y, Trim width 1.5 m, Linerboard
No. 4, fourdrinier, total capacity 4,800 mt/y, Trim width 1.7 m, Linerboard
Energy Data:
Power boilers: 2
TMP Reboiler: 1

ⓗEIC - Empaques Industriales Colombianos SA
Paso del Comercio, Variante Juanchito, Km 1
Caucaseco - Palmira, Valle de Cauca
Colombia
Mailing Address: Aptdo. Aéreo 4843, Cali, Valle de Cauca, Colombia
Phone: (57) 2 666 9471, 2 666 9460
Fax: (57) 2 666 9464
Email: guillermo.rodriguez@empicolsa.com
Web Address: www.empicolsa.com
Personnel:
Gen. Mgr.: Miguel Trefogli
Phone: (57) 5 334 8422
Fax: (57) 5 334 8467
Email: miguel.trefogli@empicolsa.com
Mill Mgr.: Guillermo Rodriguez
Phone: (57) 2 666 9460
Fax: (57) 2 666 9464
Email: guillermo.rodriguez@empicolsa.com
Total Employees of Company: 200
Total Employees at this Location: 200
Mill Locations:
EIC - Empaques Industriales Colombianos SA, Caucaseco - Palmira Mill, Paso del Comercio, Variante Junchito, Km 1, Caucaseco - Palmira, Colombia, Capacity: 39,984 mt/y, (Paper mill, Paperboard mill)
Phone: (57) 2 666 9471
Fax: (57) 2 666 9464
Email: guillermo.rodriguez@empicolsa.com

ⓜEIC - Empaques Industriales Colombianos SA
Caucaseco - Palmira Mill
Paso del Comercio, Variante Junchito, Km 1
Caucaseco - Palmira, Valle de Cauca
Colombia
Mailing Address: Aptdo. Aéreo 4843, Cali, Colombia
Phone: (57) 2 666 9471
Fax: (57) 2 666 9464
Email: guillermo.rodriguez@empicolsa.com
Personnel:
Gen. Mgr.: Miguel Trefogli
Phone: (57) 5 334 8422
Fax: (57) 5 334 8467
Email: miguel.trefogli@empicolsa.com
Mill Mgr.: Guillermo Rodriguez
Phone: (57) 2 666 9460
Fax: (57) 2 666 9464
Email: guillermo.rodriguez@empicolsa.com
Prod. Mgr.: Alberto Lopez
Phone: (57) 2 666 9460
Fax: (57) 2 666 9464
Email: alberto.lopez@empicolsa.com
Total Employees at this Location: 200
Type of Operation: Paper mill, Paperboard mill
Pulp Grades and Capacities:
Total pulp capacity: 40,594 mt/y
Recycled Pulping: 40,594 mt/y
Pulp Mill Data:
Recycled Fiber Treatment Lines:
Recycled packaging pulping lines: 1
Paper/Paperboard Grades and Capacities:
Total paper and paperboard capacity: 39,984 mt/y
Linerboard: 22,134 mt/y
Corrugating medium/fluting: 17,850 mt/y
Paper and Paperboard Mill Data:
Stock Preparation:
Pulpers: 3
Refiners: 6
Paper Machines: 2
No. 1, fourdrinier, total capacity 17,850 mt/y, Trim width 1.87 m, Corrugating medium/fluting
No. 2, fourdrinier, total capacity 22,134 mt/y, Trim width 1.8 m, Linerboard
Finishing Equipment:
Rewinders: 2 at 35,000 mt/y
Energy Data:
Power boilers: 2
Combustion turbines: 1 at 2.7 MW
Electrical demand for mill: 53 MWh/D

ⓜIndugevi S.A.
Sabaneta Mill
Calle 57 sur Nro 43A - 174
Sabaneta, Antioquia
Colombia
Phone: (57) 4 444 8296
Fax: (57) 4 288 6100
Email: servicioaldiente@indugevi.com.co
Web Address: www.indugevi.com.co
Personnel:
Mill Mgr.: Jorge Alonso Villegas
Phone: (57) 4 444 8296
Fax: (57) 4 2886100
Email: jvillegas@epm.net.co
Asst. Commer.: Sara Liliana Villegas Castrillon
Phone: (57) 4 444 8296
Fax: (57) 4 2886100
Total Employees at this Location: 55
Type of Operation: Paper mill, Paperboard mill
Pulp Grades and Capacities:
Total pulp capacity: 12,387 mt/y
Recycled Pulping: 12,387 mt/y
Pulp Mill Data:
Recycled Fiber Treatment Lines:
Recycled packaging pulping lines: 1
Paper/Paperboard Grades and Capacities:
Total paper and paperboard capacity: 12,138 mt/y
Linerboard: 7,140 mt/y
Corrugating medium/fluting: 4,998 mt/y
Paper and Paperboard Mill Data:
Paper Machines: 2
No. 1, fourdrinier, total capacity 4,998 mt/y, Trim width 1.2 m, Corrugating medium/fluting
No. 2, fourdrinier, total capacity 7,140 mt/y, Trim width 1.68 m, Linerboard
Energy Data:
Power boilers: 1
Electrical demand for mill: 21 MWh/D

ⓗIndugevi S.A.
Calle 57 sur Nro 43A - 174
Sabaneta, Antioquia
Colombia
Phone: (57) 4 444 8296
Fax: (57) 4 288 6100
Email: servicioaldiente@indugevi.com.co
Web Address: www.indugevi.com.co
Personnel:
Mill Mgr.: Jorge Alonso Villegas
Phone: (57) 4 444 8296
Fax: (57) 4 2886100
Email: jvillegas@epm.net.co
Asst. Commer.: Sara Liliana Villegas Castrillon
Phone: (57) 4 444 8296
Fax: (57) 4 2886100
Total Employees of Company: 200

Colombia

Total Employees at this Location: 200
Mill Locations:
Indugevi S.A., Sabaneta Mill, Calle 57 sur Nro 43A - 174, Sabaneta, Colombia, Capacity: 12,138 mt/y, (Paper mill, Paperboard mill)
Phone: (57) 4 444 8296
Fax: (57) 4 288 6100
Email: servicioalcliente@indugevi.com.co

ⓘⓜPapeles Nacionales S.A.
Pereira Mill
Ownership: 99.50% by Kruger Inc.
Paraje La Marina, Via Cartago
Puente Bolivar, Pereira, Risaralda
Colombia
Mailing Address: Apdto. Aéreo 483, Pereira, Colombia
Phone: (57) 2 2147500
Fax: (57) 2 2111014
Email: servicio.cliente@papelesnacionales.com
Web Address: www.papelesnacionales.com
Personnel:
Gen. Mgr.: Jose Miguel Carreira Lopez
Phone: (57) 2 2147500
Fax: (57) 2 2111014
CFO: Armando Hung
Phone: (57) 2 2147500
Fax: (57) 2 2111014
Email: armando.hung@papelesnacionales.com
HR & Pub. Rel.: Héctor Fabio Londoño
Phone: (57) 2 2147500
Fax: (57) 2 2111014
Email: hector.londono@papelesnacionales.com
Prod. Mgr.: Juan Andres Mesa
Phone: (57) 2 2147500
Fax: (57) 2 2111014
Email: juan.mesa@papelesnacionales.com
Converting Mgr.: Mauro De Andrade
Phone: (57) 2 2147500
Fax: (57) 2 2111014
Email: mauro.andrade@papelesnacionales.com
Total Employees of Company: 1,000
Total Employees at this Location: 380
Type of Operation: Paper mill
Pulp Grades and Capacities:
Total pulp capacity: 71,707 mt/y
Recycled Pulping: 71,707 mt/y
Pulp Mill Data:
Recycled Fiber Treatment Lines:
Flotation deinking lines: 3 at 62,000 admt/y
Pulpers: 3 at 80,000 admt/y
Washing deinking lines: 3 at 62,000 admt/y
Paper/Paperboard Grades and Capacities:
Total paper and paperboard capacity: 71,043 mt/y
Tissue: 71,043 mt/y
Paper and Paperboard Mill Data:
Stock Preparation:
Pulpers: 3
Refiners: 6
Paper Machines: 3
No. 1, fourdrinier, total capacity 9,282 mt/y, Trim width 3.48 m, Tissue, Uncoated woodfree/freesheet
No. 2, crescent former, total capacity 28,560 mt/y, Trim width 3.55 m, Tissue, Uncoated woodfree/freesheet
No. 3, crescent former, total capacity 33,201 mt/y, Trim width 3.55 m, Tissue
Finishing Equipment:
Rewinders: 2 at 24,000 mt/y
Energy Data:
Power boilers: 3
Electrical demand for mill: 290 MWh/D

ⓜPapeles Regionales S.A.
Dosquebradas Mill
Carrera 8 N° 35 -11 - Barrio Santa Isabel
Dosquebradas, Risaralda
Colombia
Phone: (57) 6 322 60 31
Fax: (57) 6 3222299
Email: info@papelesregionales.com
Web Address: www.papelesregionales.com
Personnel:
Mill Mgr.: Juan David Vanegas
Phone: (57) 6 322 4745
Email: papelesregionales@gmail.com
Finan. & Sls. Mgr.: Luis Felipe Vanegas
Phone: (57) 6 322 6031
Email: Papelesregionales2@gmail.com
Total Employees at this Location: 15
Type of Operation: Paper mill
Paper/Paperboard Grades and Capacities:
Total paper and paperboard capacity: 4,000 mt/y
Tissue: 4,000 mt/y
Paper and Paperboard Mill Data:
Paper Machines: 1
PM 1, fourdrinier, total capacity 5,400 mt/y, Tissue

ⓘPapeles Regionales S.A.
Cr8 35-11 Santa Isabel
Dosquebradas, Risaralda
Colombia
Phone: (57) 6 322 6031
Email: papelesregionales@gmail.com
Personnel:
Mill Mgr.: Juan David Vanegas
Phone: (57) 6 322 6031
Email: papelesregionales@gmail.com
Finan. & Sls. Mgr.: Luis Felipe Vanegas
Phone: (57) 6 322 6031
Email: Papelesregionales2@gmail.com
Mill Locations:
Papeles Regionales S.A., Dosquebradas Mill, Carrera 8 N° 35 -11 - Barrio Santa Isabel, Dosquebradas, Colombia, Capacity: 4,000 mt/y, (Paper mill)
Phone: (57) 6 322 60 31
Fax: (57) 6 3222299
Email: info@papelesregionales.com

ⓘⓜPAPELSA - Papeles y Cartones SA
Barbosa Mill
Ownership: Smurfit Kappa Group
Troncal del Nordeste km 1, Via Porce
Barbosa, Antioquia
Colombia
Phone: (57) 4 405 7000
Fax: (57) 4 406 2788
Email: alvaro.henao@papelsa.com
Web Address: www.papelsa.com, www.smurfitkappa.com
Personnel:
Gen. Man.: Alvaro José Henao Ramos
Phone: (57) 4 354 03 00
Fax: (57) 4 354 05 00
Email: alvaro.henao@papelsa.com
Controller: Ana Maria Zapata
Phone: (57) 4 405 70 00
Fax: (57) 4 354 05 00
Email: ana.zapata@papelsa.com
Sls. Mgr.: Juan Ramón Ospina
Phone: (57) 4 354 03 00
Fax: (57) 4 354 05 00
Email: juan.ospina@papelsa.com
Mgr.: Ricardo Sierra
Phone: (57) 4 354 03 00
Fax: (57) 4 354 05 00
Email: ricardo.sierra@papelsa.com
Total Employees of Company: 330
Total Employees at this Location: 98
Type of Operation: Paper mill, Paperboard mill
Pulp Grades and Capacities:
Total pulp capacity: 65,228 mt/y
Recycled Pulping: 65,228 mt/y
Pulp Mill Data:
Recycled Fiber Treatment Lines:
Pulpers: 1 at 125,000 admt/y
Paper/Paperboard Grades and Capacities:
Total paper and paperboard capacity: 64,260 mt/y
Linerboard: 46,410 mt/y
Corrugating medium/fluting: 17,850 mt/y
Paper and Paperboard Mill Data:
Stock Preparation:
Pulpers: 1
Refiners: 3
Paper Machines: 1
No. 1, fourdrinier, total capacity 64,260 mt/y, Trim width 3.2 m, Linerboard, Corrugating medium/fluting
Energy Data:
Power boilers: 3
Electrical demand for mill: 90 MWh/D

ⓘⓜProductos Familia SA
Medellin Mill
Ownership: 50% by SCA - Svenska Cellulosa Aktiebolaget
Calle 9 Sur
35160 Medellín, Antioquia
Colombia
Phone: (57) 4 360 9500 /9600 ,360 9522
Fax: (57) 4 361 3010, 4 360 9578
Email: servicioalclientemedellin@familia.com.co, margaritamm@familia.com.co
Web Address: www.familiasancela.com, www.grupofamilia.com.co, www.sca.com
Personnel:
Chmn. of Bd.: Alvaro Gomez Jaramillo
Phone: (57) 4 360 9500/ 9600
Fax: (57) 4 360 9578
Bd. Mbr.: Jan Schiavone
Phone: (57) 4 360 9500/ 9600
Fax: (57) 4 360 9578
Bd. Mbr.: Pablo Caicedo Gómez
Phone: (57) 4 360 9500/ 9600
Fax: (57) 4 360 9578
CEO: Dario Rey Mora
Phone: (57) 4 360 9500 /360 9522
Fax: (57) 4 360 9522
CFO: Juan Felipe Hoyos Botero
Phone: (57) 4 360 9500 /360 9522
Fax: (57) 4 361 3010
HR. Mgr.: Jesus Guillermo Caicedo Gerardino
Phone: (57) 4 360 9500 /360 9522
Fax: (57) 4 361 3010
Paper Mill/Div. Mgr.: Francisco Molina
Phone: (57) 4 360 9500 /360 9522
Fax: (57) 4 360 9577
Email: franciscoma@familia.com.co
Total Employees at this Location: 176
Type of Operation: Paper mill
Mill Locations:
Productos Familia Sancela del Ecuador S.A., Lasso Mill (50% owned), Panamericana Norte, Km. 20, Lasso, Ecuador, Capacity: 24,990 mt/y, (Paper mill)
Phone: (593) 3 271 8253/ 22484 352
Fax: (593) 22484 357/2484356-57
Productos Familia SA, Cajica Mill, Km 7.5 Via Cajicá Zipaquirá, Cajica, Colombia, Capacity: 74,970 mt/y, (Paper mill)
Phone: (57) 1593 84 84/43609500
Paper/Paperboard Grades and Capacities:
Total paper and paperboard capacity: 39,270 mt/y
Tissue: 39,270 mt/y
Paper and Paperboard Mill Data:
Paper Machines: 2
No. 3, crescent former, total capacity 13,566 mt/y, Trim width 2.16 m, Tissue, Uncoated woodfree/freesheet
No. 4, twin-wire, total capacity 25,704 mt/y, Trim width 3.3 m, Tissue, Uncoated woodfree/freesheet
Finishing Equipment:
Rewinders: 5
Sheeters: 5
Energy Data:
Power boilers
Electrical demand for mill: 150 MWh/D

ⓜProductos Familia SA
Cajica Mill
Ownership: 50% by SCA - Svenska Cellulosa Aktiebolaget

Colombia

Km 7.5 Via Cajicá Zipaquirá
Cajica, Cundinamarca
Colombia
 Phone: (57) 1593 84 84/43609500
 Web Address: www.familiasancela.com,
 www.grupofamilia.com.co,
 www.sca.com
Personnel:
 Prod. Mgr: Ivan Gonzales
 Phone: (57) 1593 84 84
 Email: ivango@familia.com.co
Total Employees at this Location: 292
Type of Operation: Paper mill
Pulp Grades and Capacities:
 Total pulp capacity: 49,076 mt/y
 Recycled Pulping: 49,076 mt/y
Pulp Mill Data:
 Bleach Plant Systems: 1
 Recycled Pulping System, Type: DIP
 Recycled Fiber Treatment Lines:
 Flotation deinking lines: 1 at 46,000
Paper/Paperboard Grades and Capacities:
 Total paper and paperboard capacity: 74,970 mt/y
 Tissue: 74,970 mt/y
Paper and Paperboard Mill Data:
Paper Machines: 2
 No. 6, crescent former, total capacity 34,986 mt/y, Trim
  width 3.46 m, Tissue, Uncoated woodfree/freesheet
 No. 7, crescent former, total capacity 39,984 mt/y, Trim
  width 3.46 m, Tissue, Uncoated woodfree/freesheet
Energy Data:
 Power boilers
 Electrical demand for mill: 343 MWh/D

ⓂProtisa Colombia SA
Bogota Mill
Ownership: Empresas CMPC S.A.
Autopista Norte km 45, Bogotá Via Tunja
15001000 Gachancipá, Cundinamarca
Colombia
 Phone: (57) 1 589 3333
 Fax: (57) 1 589 3030
Personnel:
 Mgr.: Ismael Ochoa
 Phone: (57) 1 589 3333
 Fax: (57) 1 589 3030
Total Employees at this Location: 210
Type of Operation: Paper mill
Paper/Paperboard Grades and Capacities:
 Total paper and paperboard capacity: 28,560 mt/y
 Tissue: 28,560 mt/y
Paper and Paperboard Mill Data:
Paper Machines: 1
 No. 1, crescent former, total capacity 28,560 mt/y, Trim
  width 2.85 m, Tissue, Uncoated woodfree/freesheet

ⒽⓂCartones y Papeles del Risaralda
Risaralda Mill
Cra 11 N°46-49 Barrio Los naranjos,
Dosquebradas
Dosquebradas, Pereira, Risaralda
Colombia
 Phone: (57) 6 322 8410
 Fax: (57) 6 322 8099
 Email: alicia@cyprisaralda.com
 Web Address: www.cyprisaralda.com
Personnel:
 Legal representative: Abraham Levy
 Phone: (57) 6 322 8410
 Fax: (57) 6 322 8099
 Mill Mgr.: Jimmy Levy
 Phone: (57) 6 322 8410
 Fax: (57) 6 322 8099
 Email: jimmy@cyprisaralda.com
 Mgr.: David Levy
 Phone: (57) 6 322 8410
 Fax: (57) 6 322 8099
 Prod./Tech. Mgr.: Luis Fernando Arias
 Phone: (57) 6 322 8410
 Fax: (57) 6 322 8099
 Mech. Eng.: Celio Bedoya
 Phone: (57) 6 322 8410
 Fax: (57) 6 322 8099
 Pres./Asst. Mill Mgr.: Alicia de Levy
 Phone: (57) 6 322 8410
 Fax: (57) 6 322 8099
Total Employees of Company: 100
Total Employees at this Location: 100
Type of Operation: Paper mill
Paper/Paperboard Grades and Capacities:
 Total paper and paperboard capacity: 24,990 mt/y
 Tissue: 24,990 mt/y
Paper and Paperboard Mill Data:
 Stock Preparation:
 Pulpers: 4
 Refiners: 2
Paper Machines: 1
 No. 4, Yankee dryer, total capacity 24,990 mt/y, Trim
  width 2.4 m, Tissue, Uncoated woodfree/freesheet
Finishing Equipment:
 Rewinders: 5
Energy Data:
 Power boilers: 2

ⓂSmurfit Kappa Cartón de Colombia SA
Ownership: 70% by Smurfit Kappa Group, 30% by Columbian investors
Calle 15 No. 18 - 109 Puerto Isaacs
Yumbo, Valle del Cauca, Valle de Cauca
Colombia
 Phone: (57) 2 651 6000
 Fax: (57) 2 651 6010
 Email: comunicaciones@smurfitkappa.com.co
 Web Address: www.smurfitkappa.com.co
Personnel:
 Pres. & CEO: Bernardo Guzmán Reyes
 Phone: (57) 2 691 4000
 Fax: (57) 2 691 4199
 Email: bernardo.guzman@smurfitkappa.com.co
 VP Pulp & Paper Mills: Julian Sánchez
 Phone: (57) 2 691 4000
 Fax: (57) 2 691 4199
 Email: julian.sanchez@smurfitkappa.com.co
 VP: Edgar Hernán Cortés
 Phone: (57) 2 281 8800
 Fax: (57) 2 281 8801
 Email: edgar.cortes@smurfitkappa.com.co
 VP Corrugated, Sls. & Mktg.: Jorge Alberto Angel
 Phone: (57) 2 691 4119
 Fax: (57) 2 691 4199
 Email: jorge.angel@smurfitkappa.com.co
 VP Corrugated, Sls. & Mktg.: Rudolf Rahn
 Phone: (57) 2 691 4000 Ex. 2119
 Fax: (57) 2 691 4173
 Email: rudolf.rahn@smurfitkappa.com.co
 Forest. Mgr.: Nicolas Pombo
 Phone: (57) 2 691 4000
 Fax: (57) 2 691 4199
 Email: nicolas.pombo@smurfitkappa.com.co
Total Employees of Company: 1,500
Mill Locations:
Smurfit Kappa Cartón de Colombia SA, Barranquilla Mill,
Vía 40 # 85 - 695 Las Flores, Barranquilla, Colombia,
Capacity: 58,905 mt/y, (Paperboard mill)
 Phone: (57) 5 373 4500/ 5373 4579
 Fax: (57) 5 373 4579
 Email: cesar.valencia@smurfitkappa.com.co
Smurfit Kappa Cartón de Colombia SA, Yumbo Mill,
Antigua Carretera a Yumbo Km. 15, Cali, Colombia,
Capacity: 251,685 mt/y, (Pulp mill, Paper mill,
Paperboard mill)
 Phone: (57) 2 691 4000
 Fax: (57) 2 691 4199
 Email: comunicaciones@smurfitkappa.com.co

ⓂSmurfit Kappa Cartón de Colombia SA
Barranquilla Mill
Ownership: 70% by Smurfit Kappa Group
Vía 40 # 85 - 695 Las Flores
Barranquilla, Atlántico
Colombia
 Phone: (57) 5 373 4500/ 5373 4579
 Fax: (57) 5 373 4579
 Email: cesar.valencia@smurfitkappa.com.co
 Web Address: www.smurfitkappa.com
Personnel:
 Gen. Mgr.: CesarValencia
 Phone: (57) 5 373 4521
 Fax: (57) 5 373 4579
 Email: cesar.valencia@smurfitkappa.com.co
 Mill Mgr.: Edgardo Vendries
 Phone: (57) 5 373 4551
 Fax: (57) 5 373 4579
 Email: edgardo.vendries@smurfitkappa.com.co
 Prod. Mgr.: Jose Rafael Salazar
 Phone: (57) 5 373 4500
 Fax: (57) 5 373 4579
 Email: jose.salazar@smurfitkappa.com.co
 Mktg. Mgr.: Enrique Gomez
 Phone: (57) 2 691 4186
 Fax: (57) 5 373 4579
 Email: enrique.gomez@smurfitkappa.com.co
Total Employees at this Location: 95
Type of Operation: Paperboard mill
Pulp Grades and Capacities:
 Total pulp capacity: 59,975 mt/y
 Recycled Pulping: 59,975 mt/y
Pulp Mill Data:
 Recycled Fiber Treatment Lines:
 Recycled packaging pulping lines: 1 at 60,000
Paper/Paperboard Grades and Capacities:
 Total paper and paperboard capacity: 58,905 mt/y
 Linerboard: 32,130 mt/y
 Corrugating medium/fluting: 26,775 mt/y
Paper and Paperboard Mill Data:
Paper Machines: 1
 No. 5, Ultraformer (5), total capacity 58,905 mt/y, Trim
  width 2.15 m, Linerboard, Corrugating medium/fluting
Coating Machines: 1
 CM1, off machine
Energy Data:
 Power boilers: 1
 Combustion turbines: 2 at 2.5, 2.5 MW
 Electrical demand for mill: 104 MWh/D

ⓂSmurfit Kappa Cartón de Colombia SA
Yumbo Mill
Ownership: 70% by Smurfit Kappa Group
Antigua Carretera a Yumbo Km. 15
Cali, Valle de Cauca
Colombia
Mailing Address: Aptdo. Aéreo 219, Cali, Colombia
 Phone: (57) 2 691 4000
 Fax: (57) 2 691 4199
 Email: comunicaciones@smurfitkappa.com.co
 Web Address: www.smurfitkappa.com.co
Personnel:
 VP Corrugated, Sls. & Mktg.: Jorge Alberto Angel
 Phone: (57) 2 691 4119
 Fax: (57) 2 691 4199
 Email: jorge.angel@smurfitkappa.com.co
 VP Mills Prod.: Jairo Cubillos
 Phone: (57) 2 691 4000
 Fax: (57) 2 691 4199
 Sls. Mgr. Mill Div.: Luis Carlos Vásquez
 Phone: (57) 2 691 4121
 Fax: (57) 2 691 4196
 Email: luis.vasquez@smurfitkappa.com.co
 Personnel Mgr.: Juan Carlos Gonzáles
 Phone: (57) 2 691 4002
 Fax: (57) 2 691 4110
 Mktg. Mgr.: Enrique Gomez
 Phone: (57) 2 691 4186
 Fax: (57) 2 691 4199
 Email: enrique.gomez@smurfitkappa.com.co
Total Employees at this Location: 957
Type of Operation: Pulp mill, Paper mill, Paperboard mill

Pulp Grades and Capacities:
Total pulp capacity: 249,623 mt/y
Pulp available for market: 7,140 mt/y
Chemical Pulp: 207,350 mt/y
Mechanical Pulp: 7,823 mt/y
Recycled Pulping: 34,450 mt/y
Pulp Mill Data:
Chemical Pulping Systems:
Batch digesters: 3
Mechanical Pulping Systems:
Conventional grinders: 1
Bleach Plant Systems: 1
No. 1
Chemical Recovery Equipment:
Evaporator lines: 1
Recovery boilers: 1
Lime Kiln
Recycled Fiber Treatment Lines:
Recycled packaging pulping lines: 1
Pulp Dryers:
Other dryers 1
Paper/Paperboard Grades and Capacities:
Total paper and paperboard capacity: 251,685 mt/y
Uncoated woodfree/freesheet: 91,749 mt/y
Packaging papers: 57,477 mt/y
Linerboard: 39,270 mt/y
Corrugating medium/fluting: 12,138 mt/y
Boxboard/cartonboard: 51,051 mt/y
Paper and Paperboard Mill Data:
Paper Machines: 4
No. 1, cylinder, total capacity 34,986 mt/y, Trim width 2.1 m, Boxboard/cartonboard
No. 3, cylinder, total capacity 36,771 mt/y, Trim width 2.1 m, Linerboard, Boxboard/cartonboard
No. 4, fourdrinier, total capacity 95,319 mt/y, Trim width 3.9 m, Linerboard, Corrugating medium/fluting, Packaging papers
No. 6, twin-wire, total capacity 91,749 mt/y, Trim width 3.9 m, Uncoated woodfree/freesheet
Coating Machines: 1
PM 1, total capacity 35,000 mt/y., on machine
Energy Data:
Power boilers: 1
Steam turbines: 1
Electrical demand for mill: 859 MWh/D

ⓘⓜSonoco de Colombia Ltda
Cali Mill
Ownership: Sonoco Products Co.
Carrera 7 No. 34-120
Cali, Valle de Cauca
Colombia
Mailing Address: Aptdo. Aéreo 6958, Cali, Colombia
Phone: (57) 2 681 8600
Fax: (57) 2 438 4736
Web Address: www.sonoco.com/sonoco/international/South+America/Colombia/
Personnel:
Gen. Mgr.: Juan Figallo
Phone: (57) 2 681 8600
Fax: (57) 2 438 4736
Main. Mgr: Edgar Salazar
Phone: (57) 2 681 8600
Fax: (57) 2 438 4736
Prod. Mgr.: Alexander Drada
Phone: (57) 2 681 8600
Fax: (57) 2 438 4736
Mktg. Mgr.: Francia Caicedo
Phone: (57) 2 681 8600
Fax: (57) 2 438 4736
Total Employees at this Location: 150
Type of Operation: Paperboard mill
Pulp Grades and Capacities:
Total pulp capacity: 32,536 mt/y
Recycled Pulping: 32,536 mt/y
Pulp Mill Data:
Recycled Fiber Treatment Lines:
Recycled packaging pulping lines
Paper/Paperboard Grades and Capacities:
Total paper and paperboard capacity: 33,558 mt/y
Linerboard: 8,211 mt/y
Boxboard/cartonboard: 25,347 mt/y
Paper and Paperboard Mill Data:
Paper Machines: 1
No. 1, cylinder, total capacity 33,558 mt/y, Trim width 2.5 m, Linerboard, Boxboard/cartonboard
Energy Data:
Power boilers: 1
Electrical demand for mill: 55 MWh/D

ⓘⓜFábrica de Bolsas de Papel UNIBOL SA
Soledad Mill
Autopista al Aeropuerto km. 7
Soledad, Atlántico
Colombia
Mailing Address: Aptdo. Aéro 350, Barranquilla, Atlántico, Colombia
Phone: (57) 575 336 6700
Fax: (57) 575 336 6797
Email: master@unibol.co, servidiente@unibol.com.co, expo@unibol.com.co
Web Address: www.unibol.co
Personnel:
Gen Mgr. & Converting Mgr.: George Zaher Jaar
Phone: (57) 575 336 6700
Fax: (57) 575 336 6797
Email: gzaher@unibol.com.co
Mill Mgr.: Iván Zaher Jaar
Phone: (57) 575 336 6700
Fax: (57) 575 336 6797
Email: izaher@unibol.com.co
Finan. Mgr.: Marta Gordillo
Phone: (57) 575 336 6700
Fax: (57) 575 336 6797
Email: mgordillo@unibol.com.co
Commer. Mgr.: Elias Zaher
Phone: (57) 575 336 6700
Fax: (57) 575 336 6797
Total Employees of Company: 400
Total Employees at this Location: 300
Type of Operation: Paper mill, Paper mill, Paper mill
Pulp Mill Data:
Recycled Fiber Treatment Lines:
Flotation deinking lines: 1 at 12,000 admt/y
Recycled packaging pulping lines: 1 at 8,000 admt/y
Paper/Paperboard Grades and Capacities:
Total paper and paperboard capacity: 20,000 mt/y
Tissue: 12,000 mt/y
Packaging papers: 8,000 mt/y
Paper and Paperboard Mill Data:
Stock Preparation:
Pulpers: 3
Refiners: 4
Paper Machines: 2
PM 1, crescent former, total capacity 12,000 mt/y, Trim width 3.06 m, Tissue
PM 2, fourdrinier, total capacity 9,000 mt/y, Trim width 3.2 m, Packaging papers
Finishing Equipment:
Rewinders: 4 at 12,500 mt/y
Energy Data:
Power boilers: 3
Combustion turbines: 2 at 2 MW
Electrical demand for mill: 50 MWh/D

COSTA RICA

ⓘⓜKimberly-Clark Costa Rica, SA
San José Mill
Ownership: 81% by Kimberly-Clark Corp.
San Antonio de Belen Aptdo. 10271
San José
Costa Rica
Mailing Address: PO Box 10271-1000, San José, Costa Rica
Phone: (506) 506 298 3100
Fax: (506) 506 239 0805
Web Address: www.kcc.com
Personnel:
Gen. Mgr.: Carlos Pasuelo
Phone: (506) 22983100
Email: cpasuelo@kcc.com
Prod. Mgr.: José M. Villalta
Phone: (506) 22983100
Email: jvillalta@kcc.com
Mktg. Dir.: Eduardo Rodriguez
Phone: (506) 22983100
Email: erodriguez@kcc.com
Purch. Dir.: Harold Phillips
Phone: (506) 22983100
Email: hphillips@kcc.com
Type of Operation: Pulp mill, Paper mill
Pulp Grades and Capacities:
Total pulp capacity: 21,508 mt/y
Recycled Pulping: 21,508 mt/y
Pulp Mill Data:
Bleach Plant Systems: 1
Recycled Pulping System, Type: DIP
Recycled Fiber Treatment Lines:
Flotation deinking lines: 1
Paper/Paperboard Grades and Capacities:
Total paper and paperboard capacity: 19,992 mt/y
Tissue: 19,992 mt/y
Paper and Paperboard Mill Data:
Paper Machines: 2
No. 1, fourdrinier, total capacity 9,282 mt/y, Trim width 2 m, Tissue, Uncoated woodfree/freesheet
No. 2, fourdrinier, total capacity 10,710 mt/y, Trim width 2 m, Tissue
Energy Data:
Power boilers
Electrical demand for mill: 85 MWh/D

CUBA

ⓘEmpresa Nacional del Papel - CUBAPEL
Ownership: 100% by Cuban State
Ave. 7ma. 2604 entre 26 y 28 Miramar
Playa
Cuba
Phone: (53) 7 2038944
Fax: (53) 7 2048127
Email: andres@pappyrus.minbas.cu
Web Address: www.cubapel.cubaindustria.cu/
Personnel:
Finan. Dir.: Pavel Ricardo Guerra
Phone: (53) 7 2051746
Fax: (53) 7 2048127
Email: pavel@pappyrus.minbas.cu
Tech. Dir.: Andrés Lopez Monterrey
Phone: (53) 7 2051748
Fax: (53) 7 2048127
Email: andres@pappyrus.minbas.cu
Oper. Dir.: Rafael Niebla Gonzalez
Phone: (53) 7 20 96997
Fax: (53) 7 2048127
Email: niebla@pappyrus.minbas.cu
Total Employees of Company: 1,156
Total Employees at this Location: 42
Mill Locations:
Papelera Damuji, Abreus Mill, CAI Guillermo Moncada, Abreus, Cuba, Capacity: 12,000 mt/y, (Pulp mill, Paperboard mill)
Phone: (53) 43 540140, 43 540590
Fax: (53) 43 286387- 286140
Email: pdamuji@enet.cu
Papelera Pulpa Cuba, Trinidad Mill, Carretera de Trinidad a Sancti Spiritus, KM 15 Iznaga, Trinidad, Cuba, Capacity: 29,988 mt/y, (Paper mill, Paperboard mill)

Dominican Republic

Phone: (53) 41 97212, 41 97216, 41 97390
Fax: (53) 41 97209
Email: pcubadir@enet.cu
Productos Sanitarios S.A. (PROSA), Matanzas Mill,
Carretera de Cárdenas a Sagua 7 1/2, Cárdenas,
Matanzas, Cuba, Capacity: 7,000 mt/y, (Paper mill)
Phone: (53) 45 613012
Fax: (53) 45 613010
Email: prosasec@psan.co.cu

Ⓜ Papelera Damují
Abreus Mill
Ownership: Empresa Nacional del Papel - CUBAPEL
CAI Guillermo Moncada
Abreus, Cienfuegos
Cuba
  Phone: (53) 43 540140, 43 540590
  Fax: (53) 43 286387- 286140
  Email: pdamuji@enet.cu
Personnel:
  Gen. Mgr., Dir.: Manuel Fernández Rogriguez
  Phone: (53) 43 540 140
  Fax: (53) 43 286 387
  Maint. Mgr.: Guillermo Rossell
  Phone: (53) 43 540 140
  Fax: (53) 43 286 387
  Tech. Mgr., Prod. Mgr.: Alexander Montalbo González
  Phone: (53) 43 540 140
  Fax: (53) 43 286 387
Total Employees at this Location: 214
Type of Operation: Pulp mill, Paperboard mill
Pulp Grades and Capacities:
  Total pulp capacity: 39,000 mt/y
  Recycled Pulping: 24,000 mt/y
Pulp Mill Data:
Pulp Lines: 2
  Recycled Fiber Treatment Lines:
  Pulpers: 1
  Recycled packaging pulping lines: 1 at 24,000 admt/y
Paper/Paperboard Grades and Capacities:
  Total paper and paperboard capacity: 12,000 mt/y
  Corrugating medium/fluting: 12,000 mt/y
Paper and Paperboard Mill Data:
  Stock Preparation:
  Pulpers: 1
  Refiners: 5
Paper Machines: 1
PM 1, fourdrinier, total capacity 12,000 mt/y, Trim width 3.25 m, Corrugating medium/fluting
Finishing Equipment:
  Winders: 1
  Calenders: 1
  Rewinders: 1
Energy Data:
  Power boilers: 1
  Electrical demand for mill: 48 MWh/D

Ⓜ Papelera Pulpa Cuba
Trinidad Mill
Ownership: Empresa Nacional del Papel - CUBAPEL
Carretera de Trinidad a Sancti Spiritus, KM 15 Iznaga
Trinidad, Sancti Spiritus
Cuba
  Phone: (53) 41 97212, 41 97216, 41 97390
  Fax: (53) 41 97209
  Email: pcubadir@enet.cu
Personnel:
  Gen. Dir.: Osvel Expósito
  Phone: (53) 41 97212, 41 97390
  Fax: (53) 41 97209
  Plant Mgr.: Israel Suarez
  Phone: (53) 41 97212, 41 97390
  Fax: (53) 41 97209
  Tech. Mgr.: Tomás Centeno
  Phone: (53) 41 97212, 41 97390
  Fax: (53) 41 97209
Total Employees at this Location: 90
Type of Operation: Paper mill, Paperboard mill
Pulp Grades and Capacities:
  Total pulp capacity: 30,756 mt/y
  Recycled Pulping: 30,756 mt/y
Pulp Mill Data:
  Recycled Fiber Treatment Lines:
  Pulpers: 1 at 33,300
Paper/Paperboard Grades and Capacities:
  Total paper and paperboard capacity: 29,988 mt/y
  Linerboard: 29,988 mt/y
Paper and Paperboard Mill Data:
  Stock Preparation:
  Pulpers: 1
  Refiners: 4
Paper Machines: 1
No. 1, fourdrinier, total capacity 29,988 mt/y, Trim width 2.6 m, Linerboard
Energy Data:
  Power boilers: 3
  Electrical demand for mill: 59 MWh/D

Ⓜ Ⓜ Productos Sanitarios S.A. (PROSA)
Matanzas Mill
Ownership: Empresa Nacional del Papel - CUBAPEL
Carretera de Cárdenas a Sagua 7 1/2, Cárdenas
Matanzas, Matanzas
Cuba
  Phone: (53) 45 613012
  Fax: (53) 45 613010
  Email: prosasec@psan.co.cu
Personnel:
  Board Dir. & Pres.: Juan Ramón Perez Armas
  Phone: (53) 45 613012 Ext. 222
  Fax: (53) 7 204 7595
  Email: gtegeneral@psan.co.cu
  Oper. Mgr.: Manuel Castellanos
  Phone: (53) 45 613012 Ext. 104
  Fax: (53) 45 613010
  Email: manuel@psan.co.cu
  Maint. Mgr.: Ignacio Concepción
  Phone: (53) 45 613012 Ext. 105
  Fax: (53) 45 613010
  Email: ignacio@psan.co.cu
  Exec. & Mgr. Asst.: Yamira Alvarez
  Phone: (53) 45 613012
  Fax: (53) 45 613010
  Email: yamira@psan.co.cu
Total Employees of Company: 186
Type of Operation: Paper mill
Pulp Mill Data:
  Recycled Fiber Treatment Lines:
  Pulpers: 3 at 10,000 admt/y
Paper/Paperboard Grades and Capacities:
  Total paper and paperboard capacity: 7,000 mt/y
  Tissue: 7,000 mt/y
Paper and Paperboard Mill Data:
  Stock Preparation:
  Pulpers: 3
  Refiners: 3
Paper Machines: 1
Tissue # 1, fourdrinier, total capacity 7,000 mt/y, Trim width 3.1 m, Tissue
Finishing Equipment:
  Rewinders: 1 at 10,000 mt/y
Energy Data:
  Power boilers: 1
  Electrical demand for mill: 34 MWh/D

Ⓜ Tejas Infinitas
Ownership: 100% by Empresa de Fibrocemento
Carretera a Siguaney Km 1, Siguaney Sancti Spiritu
Camaguey
Cuba
  Phone: (53) 141 681534/591, 322 91269
Personnel:
  Plt. Mgr.: Alexis Batan Bacallau
  Phone: (53) 322 91269
  Email: bacallau@pappyrus.minbas.cu
  Chief Eng.: Mario Alvarez
  Phone: (53) 322 91269
  Email: alvarez@pappyrus.minbas.cu
  Maint. Mgr.: Jaime Chavelli
  Phone: (53) 322 91269
  Email: chaveli@pappyrus.minbas.cu
  Prod. Mgr.: Carlos Hernandez Alonso
  Phone: (53) 322 91269
  Email: alonso@pappyrus.minbas.cu
Total Employees of Company: 176
Total Employees at this Location: 176
Mill Locations:
Tejas Infinitas, Camaguey Mill, Carretera de Cupey y línea de Ferrocaril Cama, Camaguey, Cuba, Capacity: 5,000 mt/y, (Paperboard mill)
Phone: (53) 322 91269

Ⓜ Tejas Infinitas
Camaguey Mill
Carretera de Cupey y línea de Ferrocaril Cama
Camaguey, Camaguey
Cuba
  Phone: (53) 322 91269
Personnel:
  Plt. Mgr.: Alexis Batan Bacallau
  Phone: (53) 322 91269
  Prod. Mgr.: Carlos Hernández Alonso
  Phone: (53) 322 91269
  Maint. Mgr.: Jaime Chaveli
  Phone: (53) 322 91269
  Chief Eng.: Mario Alvarez
  Phone: (53) 322 91269
Total Employees at this Location: 176
Type of Operation: Paperboard mill
Paper/Paperboard Grades and Capacities:
  Total paper and paperboard capacity: 5,000 mt/y
  Boxboard/cartonboard: 5,000 mt/y
Paper and Paperboard Mill Data:
Paper Machines: 1
PM 1, total capacity 5,000 mt/y, Trim width 1.83 m, Boxboard/cartonboard
Energy Data:
  Power boilers: 2

DOMINICAN REPUBLIC

Ⓜ Cesar Iglesias C. por A
San Pedro de Macorís Mill
Calle Cesar Iglesias No. 1
San Pedro de Macorís
Dominican Republic
  Phone: (809) 809 529 1461/ 809 529 2795
  Fax: (809) 529-1122
  Web Address: www.cesariglesias.com
Type of Operation: Paper mill
Paper/Paperboard Grades and Capacities:
  Total paper and paperboard capacity: 18,000 mt/y
  Tissue: 18,000 mt/y
Paper and Paperboard Mill Data:
Paper Machines: 1
No. 1, (started early in October 2010), crescent former, total capacity 18,000 mt/y, Tissue

ECUADOR

Ⓜ Absorpelsa Papeles Absorventes S.A.
Quito Mill
Ownership: Industrias Cartonera Asociada S.A. - INCASA
Panamericana Sur Km. 7 1/2, S26-183
1701-230 Quito, Pichincha
Ecuador

Pulp and Paper Mills - Latin America LOCKWOOD-POST DIRECTORY 2015-2016

Ecuador

Phone: (593) 267 7175 / 267 5774
Fax: (593) 267 5773
Email: ventas@absorpelsa.com.ec
Web Address: www.absorpelsa.com.ec
Personnel:
CEO: Carlos Alvarez Naranjo
Phone: (593) 2 267 3669, 267 1900
Fax: (593) 2 267 3672
Prod & Tech Mgr.: Patricio Jacome
Phone: (593) 2 267 1900
Fax: (593) 2 267 5776
Email: pjacome@incasa.com.ec
Type of Operation: Paper mill
Pulp Mill Data:
Recycled Fiber Treatment Lines:
Pulpers: 1
Paper/Paperboard Grades and Capacities:
Total paper and paperboard capacity: 3,000 mt/y
Tissue: 3,000 mt/y
Paper and Paperboard Mill Data:
Stock Preparation:
Refiners: 1
Paper Machines: 1
No. 1, fourdrinier, total capacity 3,000 mt/y, Trim width 1.92 m, Tissue
Finishing Equipment:
Rewinders: 1 at 10,000 mt/y
Energy Data:
Power boilers: 1
Electrical demand for mill: 12 MWh/D

ⓂCartopel S.A.
Cuenca Mill
Av. Cornelio Vintimilla y Carlos Tosi, Parque Industrial
Cuenca, Azuay
Ecuador
Phone: (593) 7 2860600
Fax: (593) 7 2862090
Email: ondutec1@cartopel.com,
webmaster@cartopel.com
Web Address: www.cartopel.com
Personnel:
Gen. Mgr.: Rafael Simon G.
Phone: (593) 7 2860600
Fax: (593) 7 2862090
Email: rafaelsg1@cartopel.com
Admin. Mgr.: Andres Roldan
Phone: (593) 7 2860600
Fax: (593) 7 2862090
Prod. Mgr.: Johnny Vega
Phone: (593) 7 2860600
Fax: (593) 7 2862090
Email: johnnyv1@cartopel.com
Purch. & Admin. Mgr.: Juan Andrade
Phone: (593) 7 2860600
Fax: (593) 7 2862090
Email: juana1@cartopel.com
Sec.: Gabriela Monteiro
Phone: (593) 7 2860600 Ext: 116
Fax: (593) 7 2862090
Email: gabrielam1@cartopel.com
Safety & Health Mgr.: Fausto Garzón
Phone: (593) 7 2860600
Fax: (593) 7 2862090
Total Employees at this Location: 115
Type of Operation: Paperboard mill
Pulp Grades and Capacities:
Total pulp capacity: 80,947 mt/y
Recycled Pulping: 80,947 mt/y
Pulp Mill Data:
Recycled Fiber Treatment Lines:
Recycled packaging pulping lines: 1 at 81,000
Paper/Paperboard Grades and Capacities:
Total paper and paperboard capacity: 79,968 mt/y
Linerboard: 29,988 mt/y
Corrugating medium/fluting: 49,980 mt/y
Paper and Paperboard Mill Data:
Stock Preparation:
Pulpers: 3
Refiners: 4
Paper Machines: 1
No. 1, fourdrinier, total capacity 79,968 mt/y, Trim width 2.85 m, Corrugating medium/fluting, Linerboard
Finishing Equipment:
Winders: 1 at 120,000 mt/y
Calenders: 1
Rewinders: 1
Energy Data:
Power boilers: 1
Electrical demand for mill: 111 MWh/D

ⓂProductos Familia Sancela del Ecuador S.A.
Ownership: 50% by SCA - Svenska Cellulosa Aktiebolaget, 50% by Productos Familia SA
Tadeo Benitez Oe 1-807 y Joaquín Mancheno
Quito, Pichincha
Ecuador
Phone: (593) 2 248 4359-60
Fax: (593) 2 248 4476, 248 4357
Web Address: www.familiasancela.com,
www.familiainstitucional.com
Personnel:
Mgr.: Gustavo Duque
Phone: (593) 2 2484 360
Fax: (593) 2 2484 476
Email: gustavodm@familia.com.co
Mill Locations:
Productos Familia Sancela del Ecuador S.A., Lasso Mill, Panamericana Norte, Km. 20, Lasso, Ecuador, Capacity: 24,990 mt/y, (Paper mill)
Phone: (593) 3 271 8253/ 22484 352
Fax: (593) 22484 357/2484356-57

ⓂProductos Familia Sancela del Ecuador S.A.
Lasso Mill
Ownership: 50% by SCA - Svenska Cellulosa Aktiebolaget, 50% by Productos Familia SA
Panamericana Norte, Km. 20
Lasso, Cotopaxi
Ecuador
Phone: (593) 3 271 8253/ 22484 352
Fax: (593) 22484 357/2484356-57
Web Address: www.sca.com,
www.familiasancela.com
Personnel:
Gen. Mgr.: Gustavo Duque
Phone: (593) 22484 352
Fax: (593) 22484 357
Email: gustavodm@familia.com.co
Plt. Mgr.: Juan Gabriel Ruiz
Phone: (593) 22484 352
Fax: (593) 22484 357
Proj. Mgr.: Benjamin Soto
Phone: (593) 22484 352
Fax: (593) 22484 357
Total Employees at this Location: 110
Type of Operation: Paper mill
Paper/Paperboard Grades and Capacities:
Total paper and paperboard capacity: 24,990 mt/y
Tissue: 24,990 mt/y
Paper and Paperboard Mill Data:
Paper Machines: 2
No. 3, fourdrinier, total capacity 11,067 mt/y, Trim width 2.45 m, Tissue, Uncoated woodfree/freesheet
No. 4, crescent former, total capacity 13,923 mt/y, Trim width 2.45 m, Tissue, Uncoated woodfree/freesheet
Energy Data:
Power boilers: 2
Electrical demand for mill: 92 MWh/D

ⒾⓂIndustrias Cartonera Asociada S.A. - INCASA
Quito Mill
Ownership: Industrias del Cartón S.A. - INCASA
Panamericana Sur Km. 7 1/2 N° S26-183
Quito, Pichincha
Ecuador
Mailing Address: Casilla de Correo, 17025208 Quito, Ecuador
Phone: (593) 2 267 1900
Fax: (593) 2 267 5776
Email: incasa@incasa.com.ec
Web Address: www.incasa.com.ec
Personnel:
CEO: Rodrigo Alvarez
Phone: (593) 2 267 400
Fax: (593) 2 267 5776
Email: ralvarez@incasa.com.ec
Gen. Mgr.: Angel Nunez
Phone: (593) 2 267 400
Fax: (593) 2 267 5776
Email: anunez@incasa.com.ec
Prod. & Tech. Mgr.: Patricio Jacome
Phone: (593) 2 267 400
Fax: (593) 2 267 5776
Email: pjacome@incasa.com.ec
Sls. Mgr.: Norberto Scholem
Phone: (593) 2 267 400
Fax: (593) 2 267 5776
Email: nscholem@incasa.com.ec
Total Employees at this Location: 150
Type of Operation: Paper mill, Paperboard mill
Mill Locations:
Absorpelsa Papeles Absorventes S.A., Quito Mill, Panamericana Sur Km. 7 1/2, S26-183, 1701-230 Quito, Ecuador, Capacity: 3,000 mt/y, (Paper mill)
Phone: (593) 267 7175 / 267 5774
Fax: (593) 267 5773
Email: ventas@absorpelsa.com.ec
Pulp Grades and Capacities:
Total pulp capacity: 29,956 mt/y
Recycled Pulping: 29,956 mt/y
Pulp Mill Data:
Recycled Fiber Treatment Lines:
Pulpers: 5 at 33,580 admt/y
Paper/Paperboard Grades and Capacities:
Total paper and paperboard capacity: 32,130 mt/y
Tissue: 2,856 mt/y
Linerboard: 25,704 mt/y
Corrugating medium/fluting: 3,570 mt/y
Paper and Paperboard Mill Data:
Stock Preparation:
Pulpers:
Refiners: 8
Paper Machines: 3
No. 1, total capacity 14,994 mt/y, Trim width 2.35 m, Linerboard
No. 2, fourdrinier, total capacity 14,280 mt/y, Trim width 2.05 m, Linerboard, Corrugating medium/fluting
No. 3, fourdrinier, total capacity 2,856 mt/y, Trim width 1.9 m, Tissue
Finishing Equipment:
Calenders: 1
Rewinders: 1 at 26,000 mt/y
Sheeters: 1 at 16,000 mt/y
Energy Data:
Power boilers: 2
Electrical demand for mill: 50 MWh/D

ⒾⓂIndustrial Papelera Ecuatoriana S.A (Inpaecsa)
Guayaquil Mill
Company is under construction
KM 10 1/2 Via Daule
Guayaquil
Ecuador
Type of Operation: Paper mill

ⒾⓂPapelera Nacional S.A.
Guayaquil Mill
Ownership: 100% by Inversancarlos s.a.
Box 09-01-7017, General Elizalde 114 entre Pichincha y Malecon
Guayaquil, Guayas
Ecuador

El Salvador

Phone: (593) 4 2729 027
Fax: (593) 4 2522 425
Email: ajimenez@panasa.com.ec,
rcrespo@panasa.es
Web Address: www.papeleranacional.com
Personnel:
Pres.: Mariano González P.
Phone: (593) 4 2321280
Fax: (593) 4 2326871
Email: mgonzalez@panasa.com.ec
Finan. Mgr.: Lino Antonio Rojas
Phone: (593) 4 2729002
Fax: (593) 4 2729002
Email: lrojas@panasa.com.ec
Chief of Sls.: Roger F. Crespo
Phone: (593) 4 2729007 ext 132
Fax: (593) 4 2729570
Email: rcrespo@panasa.com.ec
Tech. Mgr.: Carlos Arregui
Phone: (593) 4 2729 027
Fax: (593) 4 2722425
Email: carregui@panasa.com.ec
Sls. Mgr.: Andrés Jiménez
Phone: (593) 4 2729 027
Fax: (593) 4 2722425
Email: ajimenez@panasa.com.ec
Total Employees of Company: 397
Total Employees at this Location: 397
Type of Operation: Pulp mill, Paper mill, Paperboard mill
Pulp Grades and Capacities:
Total pulp capacity: 137,346 mt/y
Recycled Pulping: 126,201 mt/y
Other Pulp: 11,145 mt/y
Pulp Mill Data:
Chemical Pulping Systems:
Continuous digesters: 2
Recycled Fiber Treatment Lines:
Pulpers: 2
Paper/Paperboard Grades and Capacities:
Total paper and paperboard capacity: 141,015 mt/y
Packaging papers: 16,422 mt/y
Linerboard: 40,341 mt/y
Corrugating medium/fluting: 84,252 mt/y
Paper and Paperboard Mill Data:
Stock Preparation:
Pulpers: 2
Refiners: 9
Paper Machines: 2
No. 1, fourdrinier, total capacity 37,842 mt/y, Trim width 2.4 m, Linerboard, Corrugating medium/fluting, Packaging papers
No. 2, fourdrinier, total capacity 103,173 mt/y, Trim width 4.2 m, Linerboard, Corrugating medium/fluting
Finishing Equipment:
Rewinders: 2
Energy Data:
Power boilers: 3
Steam turbines: 1 at 4.0 MW
Electrical demand for mill: 219 MWh/D

ⓗⓜSurpapel Corp.
Guayas Mill
Ownership: 100% by Grupo Surpapel
Km 6.5 Vía Durán Tambo
Durán, Guayas
Ecuador
Phone: (593) 4 6011700
Fax: (593) 4 2800954
Web Address: www.gruposurpapel.com
Personnel:
Pres.: Pedro Huerta Barros
Phone: (593) 4 2599 112
Fax: (593) 4 2800 954
Email: pedro.huerta@spc.spg.ec
Proj. Mgr.: Hernan Pena
Phone: (593) 4 6011 700
Fax: (593) 4 2800 954
Total Employees at this Location: 145

Type of Operation: Paper mill
Pulp Grades and Capacities:
Total pulp capacity: 141,011 mt/y
Recycled Pulping: 141,011 mt/y
Pulp Mill Data:
Recycled Fiber Treatment Lines:
Pulpers: 1 at 131,000
Paper/Paperboard Grades and Capacities:
Total paper and paperboard capacity: 139,944 mt/y
Linerboard: 77,112 mt/y
Corrugating medium/fluting: 62,832 mt/y
Paper and Paperboard Mill Data:
Paper Machines: 1
No. 1, fourdrinier, total capacity 139,944 mt/y, Trim width 3.5 m, Corrugating medium/fluting, Linerboard
Energy Data:
Power boilers
Electrical demand for mill: 189 MWh/D

EL SALVADOR

ⓜAlas Doradas S.A. de C.V
San Juan Opico Mill
Km. 27 ½ Carretera a Santa Ana
San Juan Opico La Libertad
El Salvador
Phone: (503) 2304 2200
Fax: (503) 2304 2299/ 2261
Email: info@alas-doradas.com
Web Address: www.alas-doradas.com
Personnel:
Oper. Mgr. : Delia Avila
Phone: (503) 503 2304 2200
Fax: (503) 503 2304 2261
Email: davila@alas-doradas.com
Eng. Dir. :Jorge Alberto Zamora Castillejos
Phone: (503) 503 2304 2200
Fax: (503) 503 2304 2261
Email: jzamora@alas-doradas.com
Purch. Mgr.: Hazel Navas
Phone: (503) 503 2304 2200
Fax: (503) 503 2304 2261
Email: hnavas@alas-doradas.com
Total Employees at this Location: 200
Type of Operation: Paper mill
Pulp Grades and Capacities:
Total pulp capacity: 54,563 mt/y
Recycled Pulping: 54,563 mt/y
Pulp Mill Data:
Bleach Plant Systems: 1
Recycled Pulping System, Type: DIP
Recycled Fiber Treatment Lines:
Flotation deinking lines: 1
Paper/Paperboard Grades and Capacities:
Total paper and paperboard capacity: 51,051 mt/y
Tissue: 36,057 mt/y
Packaging papers: 14,994 mt/y
Paper and Paperboard Mill Data:
Paper Machines: 3
No. 2, fourdrinier, total capacity 14,994 mt/y, Trim width 2.6 m, Packaging papers
No. 3, fourdrinier, total capacity 12,138 mt/y, Trim width 2.4 m, Tissue, Uncoated woodfree/freesheet
No. 4, crescent former, total capacity 23,919 mt/y, Trim width 2.6 m, Tissue
Energy Data:
Power boilers: 3
Electrical demand for mill: 191 MWh/D

ⓗAlas Doradas S.A. de C.V
Km. 27 ½ Carretera a Santa Ana
San Juan Opico La Libertad, La Libertad
El Salvador
Phone: (503) 503 2304 2200
Fax: (503) 503 2304 2261
Email: info@alas-doradas.com

Web Address: www.alas-doradas.com
Personnel:
Oper. Mgr. : Delia Avila
Phone: (503) 503 2304 2200
Fax: (503) 503 2304 2261
Email: davila@alas-doradas.com
Eng. Mgr.: Jorge Zamora
Phone: (503) 503 2304 2200
Fax: (503) 503 2304 2261
Email: jzamora@alas-doradas.com
Purch. Mgr.: Hazel Navas
Phone: (503) 503 2304 2200
Fax: (503) 503 2304 2261
Email: hnavas@alas-doradas.com
Total Employees of Company: 250
Mill Locations:
Alas Doradas S.A. de C.V, San Juan Opico Mill, Km. 27 ½ Carretera a Santa Ana, San Juan Opico La Libertad, El Salvador, Capacity: 51,051 mt/y, (Paper mill)
Phone: (503) 2304 2200
Fax: (503) 2304 2299/ 2261
Email: info@alas-doradas.com

ⓗⓜKimberly-Clark de Centroamérica S.A.
Sitio Del Nino Mill
Ownership: 100% by Kimberly-Clark Corp.
Km. 32 Carretera a San Juan Opico
Sitio Del Nino, La Libertad
El Salvador
Phone: (503) 2319 4500
Web Address: www.kimberly-clarkcarreras.com
Personnel:
Mill Mgr.: Alamo Ramos
Phone: (503) 2319 4500
Email: alamo.ramos@kcc.com
Total Employees at this Location: 400
Type of Operation: Paper mill
Pulp Grades and Capacities:
Total pulp capacity: 69,915 mt/y
Recycled Pulping: 69,915 mt/y
Pulp Mill Data:
Bleach Plant Systems: 1
Recycled Pulping System, Type: DIP
Recycled Fiber Treatment Lines:
Flotation deinking lines: 1
Paper/Paperboard Grades and Capacities:
Total paper and paperboard capacity: 88,179 mt/y
Tissue: 88,179 mt/y
Paper and Paperboard Mill Data:
Paper Machines: 4
No. 1, fourdrinier, total capacity 11,781 mt/y, Trim width 1.7 m, Tissue, Uncoated woodfree/freesheet
No. 2, fourdrinier, total capacity 13,209 mt/y, Trim width 1.9 m, Tissue
No. 3, crescent former, total capacity 30,345 mt/y, Trim width 2.75 m, Tissue
No. 4, crescent former, total capacity 32,844 mt/y, Trim width 3.2 m, Tissue
Energy Data:
Power boilers
Electrical demand for mill: 380 MWh/D

GUATEMALA

ⓗPapelera del Pacífico S.A.
Ownership: Negocios Consolidados del Pacífico, S.A.
Av. 32-29 zona, 12 Colonia Santa Elisa Guatemala
01013 Pamplona, Guatemala
Guatemala
Phone: (502) 2 2446969, 2 24736241
Fax: (502) 2 2446970
Email: ppacific@intelnet.net.gt,
info@naturalecopapers.com
Web Address: www.papeleradelpacifico.com

Personnel:
Chmn./Pres./Man. Dir.: José R. Rolz
Phone: (502) 2 475 4119
Fax: (502) 2 475 2494
Mill Mgr.: Jose Alberto V
Phone: (502) 473 6241
Fax: (502) 475 2494
Indus. Dir.: Jorge G Jorge G
Phone: (502) 473 6241
Fax: (502) 475 2494
Finan. Mgr.: Romeo Toledo
Phone: (502) 473 6241
Purch. Dir.: Gina Rolz
Phone: (502) 473 6241
Fax: (502) 475 2494
Sls. Dir.: Michael Lacayo
Phone: (502) 473 6241
Tech. Dir.: Gustavo Solares
Phone: (502) 2 475 4119
Fax: (502) 2 475 2494
Total Employees of Company: 120
Total Employees at this Location: 60
Mill Locations:
Papelera del Pacífico S.A., Retalhuleu Mill, Carretera Litoral de Pacífico, Km 185 Ca-2, Recuerdo Ocosito, Retalhuleu, Guatemala, Capacity: 8,500 mt/y, (Paper mill)
Phone: (502) 2475 4119
Fax: (502) 2475 2494
Email: info@naturalecopapers.com

ⓜPapelera del Pacífico S.A.
Retalhuleu Mill
Carretera Litoral de Pacífico, Km 185 Ca-2, Recuerdo Ocosito
Retalhuleu
Guatemala
Phone: (502) 2475 4119
Fax: (502) 2475 2494
Email: info@naturalecopapers.com
Web Address: www.papeleradelpacifico.com
Personnel:
Tech. Mgr.: Eng. Julio Vasquez
Phone: (502) 2475 4119
Email: juliovasquez@papeleradelpacifico.com
Prod. Mgr.: Eddy Garcia
Phone: (502) 7771 1358/5608 8054
Email: eageyeye@gmail.com
Type of Operation: Paper mill
Pulp Grades and Capacities:
Total pulp capacity: 8,000 mt/y
Recycled Pulping: 8,000 mt/y
Pulp Mill Data:
Recycled Fiber Treatment Lines:
Recycled packaging pulping lines: 1
Paper/Paperboard Grades and Capacities:
Total paper and paperboard capacity: 8,500 mt/y
Packaging papers: 2,125 mt/y
Linerboard: 2,125 mt/y
Corrugating medium/fluting: 4,250 mt/y
Paper and Paperboard Mill Data:
Stock Preparation:
Refiners: 2
Paper Machines: 1
No. 1, fourdrinier, total capacity 8,500 mt/y, Packaging papers, Linerboard, Corrugating medium/fluting
Finishing Equipment:
Winders: 3
Calenders: 1
Rewinders: 1
Sheeters: 1 at 5,000 mt/y
Energy Data:
Power boilers: 2
Electrical demand for mill: 13 MWh/D

ⓜPapelera Internacional SA - PAINSA
Ownership: Corso family, Grand Bay International, A.V.V. (Kruger Inc.)
Km. 10 Ruta al Atlántico Zona 17
01017 Guatemala City
Guatemala
Phone: (502) 502 242 71300
Fax: (502) 502 242 71318
Email: sccorzo@painsak10.com.gt, informacion@papeleraintemacional.com.
Web Address: www.papeleraintemacional.com
Personnel:
Gen. Mgr.: Eduardo Font
Phone: (502) 502 242 71300
Fax: (502) 502 242 71318
Email: efont@painsak10.com.gt
Finan. Dir.: Israel Villarroel
Phone: (502) 502 242 71300
Fax: (502) 502 242 71318
Email: ivillarroel@painsak10.com.gt
Manuf. Dir.: Jose Ali Sanchez
Phone: (502) 502 242 71300
Fax: (502) 502 242 71318
Mill Mgr.: Jaime Cabrera
Phone: (502) 502 242 71300
Fax: (502) 502 242 71318
Email: jcabrera@painsak10.com.gt
Sls. Mgr. : Nestor Sanchez
Phone: (502) 502 242 71300
Fax: (502) 502 242 71318
Quality & Environ Mgr. : Mario Aguirre
Phone: (502) 502 242 71300
Fax: (502) 502 242 71318
Total Employees of Company: 250
Total Employees at this Location: 250
Mill Locations:
Papelera Internacional SA - PAINSA, Zacapa Mill, Km. 129 Teculután, 01017 Rio Hondo, Zacapa , Guatemala, Capacity: 37,128 mt/y, (Paper mill)
Phone: (502) 79291300
Fax: (502) 24271318
Email: sccorzo@painsak10.com.gt

ⓜPapelera Internacional SA - PAINSA
Zacapa Mill
Km. 129 Teculután
01017 Rio Hondo, Zacapa
Guatemala
Phone: (502) 79291300
Fax: (502) 24271318
Email: sccorzo@painsak10.com.gt
Web Address: www.papeleraintemacional.com
Personnel:
Gen. Mgr.: Eduardo Font
Phone: (502) 242 71300
Email: efont@painsak10.com.gt
Finan. Dir.: Israel Villarroel
Phone: (502) 242 71300
Email: ivillarroel@painsak10.com.gt
Manufacture Dir.: Jose Ali Sanchez
Phone: (502) 242 71300
Email: jsanchez@painsak10.com.gt
Mill Mgr.: Jaime Cabrera
Phone: (502) 242 71300
Email: jcabrera@painsak10.com.gt
Logist. Mgr.: Carlos Ramirez
Phone: (502) 242 71300
Email: cramirez@painsak10.com.gt
Maint. Mgr.: Ing. Augusio Castillo
Phone: (502) 242 71300
Email: augusto.castillo@painsak10.com.gt
Total Employees at this Location: 250
Type of Operation: Paper mill
Pulp Grades and Capacities:
Total pulp capacity: 39,803 mt/y
Recycled Pulping: 39,803 mt/y
Pulp Mill Data:
Bleach Plant Systems: 1
Recycled Pulping System, Type: DIP
Recycled Fiber Treatment Lines:
Recycled packaging pulping lines: 1
Paper/Paperboard Grades and Capacities:
Total paper and paperboard capacity: 37,128 mt/y
Tissue: 37,128 mt/y
Paper and Paperboard Mill Data:
Paper Machines: 4
No. 1, fourdrinier, total capacity 5,712 mt/y, Trim width 2.54 m, Tissue, Uncoated woodfree/freesheet
No. 2, crescent former, total capacity 7,497 mt/y, Trim width 2.54 m, Tissue, Uncoated woodfree/freesheet
No. 3, crescent former, total capacity 9,639 mt/y, Trim width 2.69 m, Tissue
No. 4, crescent former, total capacity 14,280 mt/y, Trim width 3.2 m, Tissue
Energy Data:
Power boilers
Electrical demand for mill: 147 MWh/D

MEXICO

ⓜAbsormex CMPC Tissue S.A. de CV
Ownership: 100% by Empresas CMPC S.A.
Avenida Fundadores 933 Colonia Valle Oriente
66000 San Pedro Garza García, Nuevo León
Mexico
Phone: (52) 81 8381 0034
Fax: (52) 81 8381 0035
Email: ventas@gpoabs.com.mx
Web Address: www.absormex.com.mx
Personnel:
Supply Chain Dir.: Cesar Leiva
Phone: (52) 81 8381 0034 Ext. 3600
Fax: (52) 81 8381 0035
Email: cesar.leyva@cmpc.com.mx
Sls. & Mktg. Dir. : Fernando Riquelme
Phone: (52) 81 8381 0034
Fax: (52) 81 8381 0035
Email: fernando.riquelme@cmpc.com.mx
Total Employees at this Location: 50
Mill Locations:
Absormex CMPC Tissue S.A. de CV, Altamira, Boulevard de los Ríos, Km 4.5, Puerto Industrial de Altamira, 89600 Altamira, Mexico, Capacity: 97,104 mt/y, (Paper mill)
Phone: (52) 833 260 0053/54/55/56/57
Email: korozco@gpoabs.com.mx

ⓜAbsormex CMPC Tissue S.A. de CV
Altamira
Ownership: 100% by Empresas CMPC S.A.
Boulevard de los Ríos, Km 4.5, Puerto Industrial de Altamira
89600 Altamira, Tamaulipas
Mexico
Phone: (52) 833 260 0053/54/55/56/57
Email: korozco@gpoabs.com.mx
Web Address: www.absormex.com.mx
Personnel:
Qlty. and R&D Mgr.: Oscar Fabian Cantu Guajardo
Phone: (52) 833 260 0053
Email: oscar.cantu@cmpc.com.mx
Purch. Mgr.: Luis Fuentes Alcantara
Phone: (52) 833 260 0053
Email: luis.fuentes@cmpc.com.mx
Asst Mill Mgr.: Carla Orozco
Phone: (52) 833 260 0053
Email: korozco@gpoabs.com.mx
Total Employees at this Location: 336
Type of Operation: Paper mill
Pulp Grades and Capacities:
Total pulp capacity: 42,839 mt/y
Recycled Pulping: 42,839 mt/y
Pulp Mill Data:
Bleach Plant Systems: 1
Recycled Pulping System, Type: DIP
Recycled Fiber Treatment Lines:
Flotation deinking lines: 1
Paper/Paperboard Grades and Capacities:
Total paper and paperboard capacity: 97,104 mt/y
Tissue: 97,104 mt/y

Mexico

Paper and Paperboard Mill Data:
Paper Machines: 3
No. 1, crescent former, total capacity 12,495 mt/y, Trim width 2.7 m, Tissue
No. 2, crescent former, total capacity 32,844 m/y, Trim width 2.75 m, Tissue, Uncoated woodfree/freesheet
No. 3, crescent former, total capacity 51,765 mt/y, Trim width 5.6 m, Tissue
Energy Data:
Power boilers: 2
Electrical demand for mill: 296 MWh/D

ⓗⓜBaja Paper Mills
Tijuana Mill
Ownership: 100% by Global Packaging solutions
Boulevard Pacifico 1069 Parque Industrial Pacifico
Tijuana, BCA
Mexico
  Phone: (52) 664 6260421
  Fax: (52) 664 6260553
  Email: sales@bajapapermill.com
  Web Address: www.bajapapermill.com
Type of Operation: Paperboard mill
Pulp Grades and Capacities:
  Total pulp capacity: 75,505 mt/y
  Recycled Pulping: 75,505 mt/y
Paper/Paperboard Grades and Capacities:
  Total paper and paperboard capacity: 74,970 mt/y
  Corrugating medium/fluting: 74,970 mt/y
Paper and Paperboard Mill Data:
Paper Machines: 1
No. 1, fourdrinier, total capacity 74,970 mt/y, Trim width 2.5 m, Corrugating medium/fluting
Energy Data:
Electrical demand for mill: 96 MWh/D

ⓗCelulosa y Papel del Bajío S.A.de C.V.
Ownership: 100% by Arcelus Group
Av. Quetzal 702, Col. Sta Rita
37450 León, Guanajuato
Mexico
  Phone: (52) 477 770 6051 / 6050 / 2525
  Fax: (52) 477 770 6052
  Email: materiaprima@ceypabasa.com.mx, ventas@ceypabasa.com.mx
  Web Address: www.ceypabasa.com.mx
Personnel:
  Gen. Mgr.: Ing. Ignacio Arcelus de Diego
  Phone: (52) 477 770 6051
  Fax: (52) 477 770 6052
  Email: direccion@ceypabasa.com.mx
  Prod. Mgr.: Basilio Salazar Ruvalcaba
  Phone: (52) 477 770 6051
  Fax: (52) 477 770 6052
  Email: produccion@ceypabasa.com.mx
Total Employees of Company: 165
Mill Locations:
Celulosa y Papel del Bajío S.A.de C.V., León Mill, Av. Quetzal 702, Col. Sta Rita, 37450 León, Mexico, Capacity: 32,130 mt/y, (Paperboard mill)
  Phone: (52) 477 770 6051
  Fax: (52) 477 770 6052
  Email: materiaprima@ceypabasa.com.mx

ⓜCelulosa y Papel del Bajío S.A.de C.V.
León Mill
Av. Quetzal 702, Col. Sta Rita
37450 León, Guanajuato
Mexico
  Phone: (52) 477 770 6051
  Fax: (52) 477 770 6052
  Email: materiaprima@ceypabasa.com.mx
  Web Address: www.ceypabasa.com.mx
Personnel:
  Gen. Mgr.: Ing. Ignacio Arcelus de Diego
  Phone: (52) 477 770 6051
  Fax: (52) 477 770 6052
  Tres.: Srita. Maria Isabel Arcelus de Diego
  Phone: (52) 477 770 6051
  Fax: (52) 477 770 6052
  Oper. Mgr.: Ing Basilio Salazar Ruvalcaba
  Phone: (52) 477 770 6050
  Fax: (52) 477 770 6052
  Email: produccion@ceypabasa.com.mx
  Finan. Mgr.: C.P. Jorge Mora Rios
  Phone: (52) 477 770 6051
  Fax: (52) 477 770 6052
  Maint. Mgr.: Joaquin Maldonado
  Phone: (52) 477 770 6051
  Fax: (52) 477 770 6052
  Email: mantenimiento@ceypabasa.com.mx
  Sls. Mgr.: Ing. Israel Solis
  Phone: (52) 477 770 6051
  Fax: (52) 477 770 6052
  Email: ventas@ceypabasa.com.mx
  Gen. Sec.: Erica Bregón
  Phone: (52) 477 770 6051
  Fax: (52) 477 770 6052
  Email: recepcion@ceypabasa.com.mx
Total Employees at this Location: 130
Type of Operation: Paperboard mill
Pulp Grades and Capacities:
  Total pulp capacity: 32,832 mt/y
  Recycled Pulping: 32,832 mt/y
Pulp Mill Data:
Recycled Fiber Treatment Lines:
  Pulpers: 1 at 35,300
Paper/Paperboard Grades and Capacities:
  Total paper and paperboard capacity: 32,130 mt/y
  Packaging papers: 3,213 mt/y
  Linerboard: 9,639 mt/y
  Corrugating medium/fluting: 19,278 mt/y
Paper and Paperboard Mill Data:
Paper Machines: 1
No. 1, fourdrinier, total capacity 32,130 mt/y, Trim width 4.17 m, Corrugating medium/fluting, Linerboard, Packaging papers
Energy Data:
Power boilers
Electrical demand for mill: 57 MWh/D

ⓗManufacturera de Papel Bidasoa S.A. de C.V.
Ownership: Manufacturas de Papel CA (MANPA) S.A.C.A.
Pasaje Interlomas N° 6-201
C.P. 52760 Col. Magno Centro, Huixquilucan
Mexico
  Phone: (52) 55 5290 6606/07
  Fax: (52) 55 5290 6592
  Email: slopez@prodigy.net.mx, mfrabidasoa@prodigy.net.mx
Personnel:
  Mill Mgr.: Ing. Esteban Larragain
  Phone: (52) 5 290 6606/07
  Fax: (52) 5 290 6592
  Tech. Mgr.: Ing. Octavio Ovalle
  Phone: (52) 5 290 6606/07
  Fax: (52) 5 290 6592
  Sls. Mgr.: Ing. Esteban larragain Gonzalez
  Phone: (52) 5 290 6606/07
  Fax: (52) 5 290 6592
  Admin. Mgr.: Ing. Victor Alejandro Márquez Ortiz Pinzón
  Phone: (52) 5 290 6606/07
  Fax: (52) 5 290 6592
Total Employees at this Location: 13
Mill Locations:
Manufacturera de Papel Bidasoa S.A. de C.V., Teotihuacan Mill, Antiguo Camino Real de Veracruz s/n Col. San Sebastian, 55800 Xolaltenco Teotihuacan, Mexico, Capacity: 32,000 mt/y, (Paper mill)
  Fax: (52) 594 9560 0300
  Email: bidasoam@abantel.net, mfradibasoa@prodigy.net.mx

ⓜManufacturera de Papel Bidasoa S.A. de C.V.
Teotihuacan Mill
Ownership: Manufacturas de Papel CA (MANPA) S.A.C.A.
Antiguo Camino Real de Veracruz s/n Col. San Sebastian
55800 Xolaltenco Teotihuacan, Edo. de México
Mexico
  Fax: (52) 594 9560 0300
  Email: bidasoam@abantel.net, mfradibasoa@prodigy.net.mx
Personnel:
  Pres. & Gen Mgr.: Ing. Esteban Larragain Gonzalez
  Plt. Mgr.: Cap. Jose Romero Hernández
  prod. Mgr.: Sr. Jose Octavio Ovalle nango
  Dir. Admin.: Ing. Victor Alejandro marquez Ortiz pinzon
Total Employees at this Location: 83
Type of Operation: Paper mill
Paper/Paperboard Grades and Capacities:
  Total paper and paperboard capacity: 32,000 mt/y
  Packaging papers: 32,000 mt/y
Paper and Paperboard Mill Data:
Paper Machines: 1
No. 1, fourdrinier, Trim width 2.2 m, Packaging papers

ⓗBio-PAPPEL, S.A.B. de C.V.
Edificio Torre Mayor, Avenida Paseo de la Reforma 505 piso 40
6500 Col. Cuauhtémoc
Mexico
  Phone: (52) 55-5729-7000
  Fax: (52) 55-5368-2413
  Web Address: www.biopappel.com
Personnel:
  Chmn. & CEO: Miguel Rincón Arredondo
  Phone: (52) 55-5729-7000
  Fax: (52) 55-5368-2413
  Email: mrincon@biopappel.com
  Chief Competitivity Officer: Martin Rincón Arredondo
  Phone: (52) 55-5729-7000
  Fax: (52) 55-5368-2413
  Email: martinrincon@biopappel.com
  CEO (BIO Pappel international): Ignacio Rincón Arredondo
  Phone: (52) 55-5729-7000
  Fax: (52) 55-5368-2413
  Email: irincon@biopappel.com
  CFO: Mayela De La Paz Rincon A Velasco
  Phone: (52) 55-5729-7000
  Fax: (52) 55-5368-2413
  CEO (BIO Pappel Printing & Kraft): Wilfrido Rincón Arredondo
  Phone: (52) 55-5729-7000
  Fax: (52) 55-5368-2413
  CEO (BIO Pappel Packaging): Miguel Rincon Barraza
  Phone: (52) 55-5729-7000
  Fax: (52) 55-5368-2413
  Gen. Counsel: Gabriel Villegas Salazar
  Phone: (52) 55-5729-7000
  Fax: (52) 55-5368-2413
Total Employees of Company: 7,977
Total Employees at this Location: 128
Mill Locations:
Bio-PAPPEL International, Prewitt Mill, County Rd 19, Prewitt, NM 87045, USA, Capacity: 226,709 mt/y, (Paperboard mill)
  Phone: (1) 505-876-2100
  Fax: (1) 505-876-2313
Bio-PAPPEL Kraft, Atenquique Mill, Km 160 Carretera libre Guadalajara Colima, 49820 Atenquique, Mexico, Capacity: 133,161 mt/y, (Pulp mill, Paper mill, Paperboard mill)
  Phone: (52) 371 415 0004
  Fax: (52) 371 415 0053
  Email: jfloresdelarocha@biopappel.com
Bio-PAPPEL Kraft, Cuesta El Registro mill, Km 26-Carretera Durango - Mexico, 34348 Cuesta El Registro, Mexico, Capacity: 269,892 mt/y, (Pulp mill, Paper mill, Paperboard mill)

Mexico

Phone: (52) 618 829 12 04/1202
Fax: (52) 618 829 12 69
Bio-PAPPEL Kraft, Monterrey Mill, Miguel Barragán 502 Pte Col Industrial, 66440 Monterrey, Mexico, Capacity: 129,948 mt/y, (Paper mill, Paperboard mill)
Phone: (52) 81 8375 7919
Fax: (52) 81 8372 6724
Email: dgarcia@biopappel.com
Bio-PAPPEL Kraft, Texcoco Mill, Km. 23.5, Carr. Mexico Texcoco, Col. La Magdalena, 56440 Los Reyes La Paz, Mexico, Capacity: 27,132 mt/y, (Paperboard mill)
Fax: (52) 26 138689
Bio-PAPPEL Kraft, Tizayuca Mill, Camino Tizayuca Tezóntepec No. 5, C.P. 43800 El Chopo, Tizayuca, Mexico, Capacity: 219,912 mt/y, (Paperboard mill)
Phone: (52) 779 796 9000
Fax: (52) 779 796 9017
Email: cpaulin@biopappel.com
Bio-PAPPEL Printing, Tres Valles Mill, Km. 66.5, Carretera La Tinaja - Ciudad Aleman, 95300 Tres Valles, Mexico, Capacity: 169,575 mt/y, (Paper mill)
Phone: (52) 288 88 690 00
Fax: (52) 288 88 690 60
Email: wgarperin@biopappel.com
Bio-PAPPEL Printing, Tuxtepec Mill, Ejido Benito Juarez S/N, Km. 9 Carr. , 68445 Tuxtepec, Mexico, Capacity: 184,926 mt/y, (Pulp mill, Paper mill)
Phone: (52) 287 875 9000
Fax: (52) 287 875 0090/17

ⓜBio-PAPPEL Kraft
Atenquique Mill

Ownership: 100% by Bio-PAPPEL, S.A.B. de C.V.
Km 160 Carretera libre Guadalajara Colima
49820 Atenquique, Jalisco
Mexico
 Phone: (52) 371 415 0004
 Fax: (52) 371 415 0053
 Email: jfloresdelarocha@biopappel.com
 Web Address: www.biopappel.com
Personnel:
 Mill Mgr.: Ing. Jaime Cortes
 Phone: (52) 371 415 0004
 Fax: (52) 371 415 0053
 Email: jcortes@biopappel.com
 Pulp Mgr.: Ing. Jorge Tapia Urzúa
 Phone: (52) 371 415 0004
 Fax: (52) 371 415 0053
 Email: jtapia@biopappel.com
 Finan. & Admin. Mgr.: Martin Cruz
 Phone: (52) 371 415 0004
 Fax: (52) 371 415 0053
 Email: mcruz@biopappel.com
 Dir.: Ing. Jaime Elizondo
 Phone: (52) 371 415 0004
 Fax: (52) 371 415 0053
 Email: jelizondo@biopappel.com
 Purch. Agt.: Felipe Rodriguez
 Phone: (52) 371 415 0004
 Fax: (52) 371 415 0053
 Email: frodriguez@biopappel.com
Total Employees at this Location: 300
Type of Operation: Pulp mill, Paper mill, Paperboard mill
Pulp Grades and Capacities:
 Total pulp capacity: 136,997 mt/y
 Chemical Pulp: 81,130 mt/y
 Recycled Pulping: 55,866 mt/y
Pulp Mill Data:
 Chemical Pulping Systems:
 Batch digesters: 1
 Chemical Recovery Equipment:
 Evaporator lines: 1
 Recovery boilers: 1
 Lime Kiln
 Recycled Fiber Treatment Lines:
 Pulpers: 2 at 61,000 admt/y
Paper/Paperboard Grades and Capacities:
 Total paper and paperboard capacity: 133,161 mt/y
 Linerboard: 87,465 mt/y
 Corrugating medium/fluting: 45,696 mt/y
Paper and Paperboard Mill Data:
 Stock Preparation:
 Pulpers: 2
 Refiners: 8
Paper Machines: 2
 No. 1, fourdrinier, total capacity 45,696 mt/y, Trim width 3.5 m, Corrugating medium/fluting
 No. 2, fourdrinier, total capacity 87,465 mt/y, Trim width 4.2 m, Linerboard
Finishing Equipment:
 Rewinders: 2
Energy Data:
 Power boilers: 3
 Steam turbines: 4 at 15.0 MW
 Electrical demand for mill: 303 MWh/D

ⓜBio-PAPPEL Kraft
Cuesta El Registro mill

Ownership: 100% by Bio-PAPPEL, S.A.B. de C.V.
Km 26-Carretera Durango - Mexico
34348 Cuesta El Registro, Durango
Mexico
 Phone: (52) 618 829 12 04/1202
 Fax: (52) 618 829 12 69
 Web Address: www.biopappel.com
Personnel:
 Gen. Dir.: Ing. Juan F. Montufar
 Phone: (52) 618 829 1902
 Fax: (52) 618 8291272
 Email: jmontufar@biopappel.com
 Mill Mgr.: Raul Castañeda R.
 Phone: (52) 618 829 1204
 Fax: (52) 618 829 12 69
 Email: rcastanedar@biopappel.com
 Maint. Mgr.: Ing. Daniel Sotelo
 Phone: (52) 618 8291240
 Fax: (52) 618 8291241
 Email: mantenimientoic@biopappel.com
Total Employees at this Location: 540
Type of Operation: Pulp mill, Paper mill, Paperboard mill
Pulp Grades and Capacities:
 Total pulp capacity: 273,796 mt/y
 Recycled Pulping: 273,796 mt/y
Pulp Mill Data:
 Recycled Fiber Treatment Lines:
 Recycled packaging pulping lines: 1 at 274,000
Paper/Paperboard Grades and Capacities:
 Total paper and paperboard capacity: 269,892 mt/y
 Linerboard: 180,999 mt/y
 Corrugating medium/fluting: 88,893 mt/y
Paper and Paperboard Mill Data:
 Stock Preparation:
 Pulpers: 2
 Refiners: 5
Paper Machines: 1
 No. 1, fourdrinier, total capacity 269,892 mt/y, Trim width 7 m, Linerboard, Corrugating medium/fluting
Finishing Equipment:
 Calenders: 1
 Rewinders: 1
Energy Data:
 Power boilers: 3
 Steam turbines: 2 at 12.5 MW
 Electrical demand for mill: 481 MWh/D

ⓗⓜBio-PAPPEL Kraft
Monterrey Mill

Ownership: 100% by Bio-PAPPEL, S.A.B. de C.V.
Miguel Barragán 502 Pte Col Industrial
66440 Monterrey, Nuevo León
Mexico
 Phone: (52) 81 8375 7919
 Fax: (52) 81 8372 6724
 Email: dgarcia@biopappel.com
 Web Address: www.biopappel.com
Personnel:
 Chmn & CEO: Miguel Rincon Arredondo
 Phone: (52) 81 8375 7919
 Fax: (52) 81 8372 6724
 Email: mrincon@biopappel.com
 Commer. Dir.: Edwin Mckey
 Phone: (52) 81 8375 7919
 Fax: (52) 81 8372 6724
 Email: emckey@biopappel.com
 Mgr. Corp. Accounts: Jose Ramirez Romero
 Phone: (52) 81 8156 0216
 Fax: (52) 81 8156 0260
 Email: jramirez@biopappel.com
Total Employees of Company: 320
Total Employees at this Location: 320
Type of Operation: Paper mill, Paperboard mill
Mill Locations:
Bio-PAPPEL Kraft, Atenquique Mill, Km 160 Carretera libre Guadalajara Colima, 49820 Atenquique, Mexico, Capacity: 133,161 mt/y, (Pulp mill, Paper mill, Paperboard mill)
 Phone: (52) 371 415 0004
 Fax: (52) 371 415 0053
 Email: jfloresdelarocha@biopappel.com
Bio-PAPPEL Kraft, Cuesta El Registro mill, Km 26-Carretera Durango - Mexico, 34348 Cuesta El Registro, Mexico, Capacity: 269,892 mt/y, (Pulp mill, Paper mill, Paperboard mill)
 Phone: (52) 618 829 12 04/1202
 Fax: (52) 618 829 12 69
Bio-PAPPEL Kraft, Texcoco Mill, Km. 23.5, Carr. Mexico Texcoco, Col. La Magdalena, 56440 Los Reyes La Paz, Mexico, Capacity: 27,132 mt/y, (Paperboard mill)
 Fax: (52) 26 138689
Bio-PAPPEL Kraft, Tizayuca Mill, Camino Tizayuca Tezóntepec No. 5, C.P. 43800 El Chopo, Tizayuca, Mexico, Capacity: 219,912 mt/y, (Paperboard mill)
 Phone: (52) 779 796 9000
 Fax: (52) 779 796 9017
 Email: cpaulin@biopappel.com
Pulp Grades and Capacities:
 Total pulp capacity: 132,731 mt/y
 Recycled Pulping: 132,731 mt/y
Pulp Mill Data:
 Recycled Fiber Treatment Lines:
 Recycled packaging pulping lines: 1
Paper/Paperboard Grades and Capacities:
 Total paper and paperboard capacity: 129,948 mt/y
 Linerboard: 45,339 mt/y
 Corrugating medium/fluting: 84,609 mt/y
Paper and Paperboard Mill Data:
 Stock Preparation:
 Pulpers: 4
 Refiners: 8
Paper Machines: 3
 No. 1, cylinder, total capacity 14,280 mt/y, Trim width 1.9 m, Linerboard, Corrugating medium/fluting
 No. 2, cylinder, total capacity 47,838 mt/y, Trim width 1.7 m, Linerboard, Corrugating medium/fluting
 No. 3, fourdrinier, total capacity 67,830 mt/y, Trim width 1.9 m, Linerboard, Corrugating medium/fluting
Energy Data:
 Power boilers: 1
 Steam turbines: 1
 Electrical demand for mill: 236 MWh/D

ⓜBio-PAPPEL Kraft
Texcoco Mill

Ownership: 100% by Bio-PAPPEL, S.A.B. de C.V.
Km. 23.5, Carr. Mexico Texcoco, Col. La Magdalena
56440 Los Reyes La Paz, Edo. de México
Mexico
 Fax: (52) 26 138689
 Web Address: www.biopappel.com
Personnel:
 Mill Mgr.: Ing. Hector Alcalde
 Phone: (52) 26 317711
 Prod. Mgr.: Ing. Angel Islas Rebollo
 Phone: (52) 26 317711
 Purch. Mgr.: Ing. Benito Valverde
 Phone: (52) 26 317711
 Mgr.: Ms. Sandra Galindo

Mexico

Phone: (52) 26 317711
Total Employees at this Location: 120
Type of Operation: Paperboard mill
Pulp Grades and Capacities:
Total pulp capacity: 27,535 mt/y
Recycled Pulping: 27,535 mt/y
Pulp Mill Data:
Recycled Fiber Treatment Lines:
Pulpers: 1 at 30,000
Paper/Paperboard Grades and Capacities:
Total paper and paperboard capacity: 27,132 mt/y
Corrugating medium/fluting: 27,132 mt/y
Paper and Paperboard Mill Data:
Stock Preparation:
Pulpers: 2
Refiners: 3
Paper Machines: 1
No. 1, fourdrinier, total capacity 27,132 mt/y, Trim width 2.2 m, Corrugating medium/fluting
Finishing Equipment:
Rewinders: 1
Energy Data:
Power boilers: 1
Electrical demand for mill: 44 MWh/D

ⓜBio-PAPPEL Kraft
Tizayuca Mill
Ownership: 100% by Bio-PAPPEL, S.A.B. de C.V.
Camino Tizayuca Tezóntepec No. 5
C.P. 43800 El Chopo, Tizayuca
Mexico
Phone: (52) 779 796 9000
Fax: (52) 779 796 9017
Email: cpaulin@biopappel.com
Web Address: www.biopappel.com
Personnel:
Plant Mgr.: Ing. Carlos Paulín
Phone: (52) 779 7969035/52
Email: cpaulin@biopappel.com
Oper. Dir.: Ing. Juan Montufar
Phone: (52) 779 796 9000
Email: jmontufar@biopappel.com
Prod. Mgr.: Ing. Aurelio Lopez
Phone: (52) 779 796 9000
Total Employees at this Location: 750
Type of Operation: Paperboard mill
Pulp Grades and Capacities:
Total pulp capacity: 222,705 mt/y
Recycled Pulping: 222,705 mt/y
Pulp Mill Data:
Recycled Fiber Treatment Lines:
Recycled packaging pulping lines: 1
Paper/Paperboard Grades and Capacities:
Total paper and paperboard capacity: 219,912 mt/y
Linerboard: 187,068 mt/y
Corrugating medium/fluting: 32,844 mt/y
Paper and Paperboard Mill Data:
Stock Preparation:
Pulpers: 2
Refiners: 13
Paper Machines: 1
No. 3, fourdrinier, total capacity 219,912 mt/y, Trim width 3.5 m, Linerboard, Corrugating medium/fluting
Coating Machines: 2
No. 1, on machine
No. 2, on machine
Finishing Equipment:
Rewinders: 2
Sheeters: 2
Energy Data:
Power boilers: 1
Steam turbines: 1 at 35 MW
Electrical demand for mill: 431 MWh/D

ⓜBio-PAPPEL Printing
Ownership: 100% by Bio-PAPPEL, S.A.B. de C.V.
Ejercito Nacional # 1130, Colonia Los Morales Polanco,
Delegacion Miguel Hidalgo
11510 Mexico, México, D.F.
Mexico
Phone: (52) 55 9126 6000
Web Address: www.biopappel.com
Personnel:
Chmn., Pres. & CEO: Miguel Rincon Arredondo
Gen. Dir.: Ing. Wilfrido Rincón
Phone: (52) 55 5729 7000/8111
Fax: (52) 55 5729 7067
Email: wrincon@biopappel.com
Oper. Dir.: Ing. Juan Montufar
Phone: (52) 55 5729 7000/8111
Fax: (52) 55 5729 7067
Gen. Attorney: Ing. Gabriel Villegas
Phone: (52) 55 5729 7000/8111
Fax: (52) 55 5729 7067
Sls. Mgr.: Horacio Acoltzin
Phone: (52) 55 5729 7000/8111
Fax: (52) 55 5729 7067
Email: horacioacoltzin@biopappel.com
Total Employees of Company: 1,720
Mill Locations:
Bio-PAPPEL Printing, Tres Valles Mill, Km. 66.5, Carretera La Tinaja - Ciudad Aleman, 95300 Tres Valles, Mexico, Capacity: 169,575 mt/y, (Paper mill)
Phone: (52) 288 88 690 00
Fax: (52) 288 88 690 60
Email: wgarperin@biopappel.com
Bio-PAPPEL Printing, Tuxtepec Mill, Ejido Benito Juarez S/N, Km. 9 Carr., 68445 Tuxtepec, Mexico, Capacity: 184,926 mt/y, (Pulp mill, Paper mill)
Phone: (52) 287 875 9000
Fax: (52) 287 875 0090/17

ⓜBio-PAPPEL Printing
Tres Valles Mill
Ownership: 100% by Bio-PAPPEL, S.A.B. de C.V.
Km. 66.5, Carretera La Tinaja - Ciudad Aleman
95300 Tres Valles, Veracruz
Mexico
Phone: (52) 288 88 690 00
Fax: (52) 288 88 690 60
Email: wgarperin@biopappel.com
Web Address: www.biopappel.com
Personnel:
Gen. Mgr.: Alejandro Peralta
Phone: (52) 288 88 690 00
Fax: (52) 288 88 690 60
Email: aperalta@biopappel.com
Paper Prod. Mgr.: Ing. J. Dante Marin R.
Phone: (52) 288 88 690 00
Fax: (52) 288 88 690 60
Email: dmarin@biopappel.com
Finan. & Admin. Mgr.: Carmelo Rangel T.
Phone: (52) 288 88 690 00
Fax: (52) 288 88 690 60
Email: crangel@biopappel.com
Maint. Mgr.: Ing. Miguel A. Feria
Phone: (52) 288 88 690 00
Fax: (52) 288 88 690 60
Email: mferia@biopappel.com
Total Employees at this Location: 690
Type of Operation: Paper mill
Pulp Grades and Capacities:
Total pulp capacity: 139,394 mt/y
Recycled Pulping: 139,394 mt/y
Pulp Mill Data:
Chemical Pulping Systems:
Batch digesters: 1
Bleach Plant Systems: 2
Nonwood Pulping System, Type: Bagasse
Recycled Deinked Pulping System, Type: DIP
Chemical Recovery Equipment:
Evaporator lines: 1
Recovery boilers: 1
Recycled Fiber Treatment Lines:
Flotation deinking lines: 1 at 90,000
Pulpers: 2
Paper/Paperboard Grades and Capacities:
Total paper and paperboard capacity: 169,575 mt/y
Uncoated woodfree/freesheet: 169,575 mt/y
Paper and Paperboard Mill Data:
Stock Preparation:
Pulpers: 3
Refiners: 3
Paper Machines: 1
No. 1, twin-wire, total capacity 169,575 mt/y, Trim width 6.39 m, Uncoated woodfree/freesheet
Finishing Equipment:
Rewinders: 1
Energy Data:
Power boilers: 3
Steam turbines: 2 at 18.2 MW
Electrical demand for mill: 443 MWh/D

ⓜBio-PAPPEL Printing
Tuxtepec Mill
Ownership: 100% by Bio-PAPPEL, S.A.B. de C.V.
Ejido Benito Juarez S/N, Km. 9 Carr.
68445 Tuxtepec, OAX
Mexico
Phone: (52) 287 875 9000
Fax: (52) 287 875 0090/17
Web Address: www.biopappel.com
Personnel:
Dir.: Ing. Walfred Casterin Gonzales
Phone: (52) 287 875 9000
Fax: (52) 287 875 0090/17
Prod. Mgr.: Ing. Francisco Javier Dominguez Fernandez
Phone: (52) 287 875 9000 Ext. 9080
Fax: (52) 287 875 0090/17
Email: fdominguez@biopappel.com
Finan. & Admin. Mgr.: CP Carmelo Rangel
Phone: (52) 287 875 9000
Fax: (52) 287 875 0090/17
Finishing Products Wharehouse Chief: Juan Pablo Sanchez
Phone: (52) 287 875 9000
Fax: (52) 287 875 0090/17
Total Employees at this Location: 350
Type of Operation: Pulp mill, Paper mill
Pulp Grades and Capacities:
Total pulp capacity: 191,111 mt/y
Recycled Pulping: 191,111 mt/y
Pulp Mill Data:
Bleach Plant Systems: 2
Mechanical TMP Pulping System, Type: Softwood
Recycled Deinked Pulping System
Recycled Fiber Treatment Lines:
Flotation deinking lines: 1
Paper/Paperboard Grades and Capacities:
Total paper and paperboard capacity: 184,926 mt/y
Newsprint: 99,960 mt/y
Uncoated mechanical/groundwood: 24,990 mt/y
Packaging papers: 35,700 mt/y
Corrugating medium/fluting: 24,276 mt/y
Paper and Paperboard Mill Data:
Paper Machines: 2
No. 1, fourdrinier, total capacity 59,976 mt/y, Trim width 4.4 m, Packaging papers, Corrugating medium/fluting
No. 2, Bel-Baie II, total capacity 124,950 mt/y, Trim width 6.7 m, Newsprint, Uncoated mechanical/groundwood
Energy Data:
Power boilers: 2
Electrical demand for mill: 446 MWh/D

ⓒCECSO - Celulosa y Corrugados de Sonora S.A. de C.V.
Pesqueira 90012 Sur
85870 Col. Juarez, Navojoa, Sonora
Mexico
Phone: (52) 642 422 4040
Fax: (52) 642 422 8116
Web Address: www.cecso.com.mx
Personnel:
Chmn.: German A. Tapia
Phone: (52) 642 422 4040
Fax: (52) 642 422 8116
CEO: Rafael Rodriguez Coronel

Phone: (52) 642 422 4040
Fax: (52) 642 422 8116
Mill Mgr.: Miguel F. Martinez
Phone: (52) 642 422 4040
Fax: (52) 642 422 8116
Purch. Dir.: Rafael Carmona Partida
Phone: (52) 642 422 4040
Fax: (52) 642 422 8116
Finan. Mgr.: Adrian Cerrano Camargo
Phone: (52) 642 422 4040
Fax: (52) 642 422 8116
Qlty. Mgr.: Teresa Lidia López
Phone: (52) 642 422 4040
Fax: (52) 642 422 8116
Mgr., Corrugating Bags: Mauricio Felix
Phone: (52) 642 422 4040
Fax: (52) 642 422 8116
Prod. Mgr.: Manuel Vargas
Phone: (52) 642 422 4040
Fax: (52) 642 422 8116

Total Employees of Company: 497
Total Employees at this Location: 97
Mill Locations:
CECSO - Celulosa y Corrugados de Sonora S.A. de C.V., Navojoa Mill, Carretera Int. Km 8.5 Navojoa Los Mochis Parque Industrial, 85800 Navojoa, Mexico, Capacity: 69,972 mt/y, (Paper mill, Paperboard mill)
Phone: (52) 642 425 8000-11
Fax: (52) 642 423 5246
Email: cecso@cecso.com.mx

Ⓜ CECSO - Celulosa y Corrugados de Sonora S.A. de C.V.
Navojoa Mill
Carretera Int. Km 8.5 Navojoa Los Mochis Parque Industrial
85800 Navojoa, Sonora
Mexico
Phone: (52) 642 425 8000-11
Fax: (52) 642 423 5246
Email: cecso@cecso.com.mx
Web Address: www.cecso.mx

Personnel:
CEO: Rafael Rodriguez Coronel
Phone: (52) 642 425 8000-11
Fax: (52) 642 423 5246
Email: rcoronel@cecso.com.mx
Mgr. Sec.: Teresita Felix
Phone: (52) 642 425 8000-11
Fax: (52) 642 423 5246
Email: tfelix@cecso.com.mx

Total Employees at this Location: 400
Type of Operation: Paper mill, Paperboard mill
Pulp Grades and Capacities:
Total pulp capacity: 71,205 mt/y
Recycled Pulping: 71,205 mt/y

Pulp Mill Data:
Recycled Fiber Treatment Lines:
Recycled packaging pulping lines: 1
Paper/Paperboard Grades and Capacities:
Total paper and paperboard capacity: 69,972 mt/y
Linerboard: 13,923 mt/y
Corrugating medium/fluting: 34,986 mt/y
Boxboard/cartonboard: 21,063 mt/y
Paper and Paperboard Mill Data:
Stock Preparation:
Pulpers: 4
Refiners: 4
Paper Machines: 2
No. 1, fourdrinier, total capacity 34,986 mt/y, Trim width 2.8 m, Corrugating medium/fluting
No. 2, cylinder, total capacity 34,986 mt/y, Trim width 2.5 m, Linerboard, Boxboard/cartonboard
Finishing Equipment:
Rewinders: 2
Energy Data:
Power boilers: 1
Steam turbines: 1
Electrical demand for mill: 86 MWh/D

Ⓜ Papelera de Chihuahua S.A. de C.V.
Chihuahua Mill
Ownership: 100% by Copamex, S.A. de C.V.
Plaza del Ferrocarril Kansas No. 1, Col. Popular
31350 Chihuahua, Chihuahua
Mexico
Phone: (52) 614 439 4200
Fax: (52) 614 439 9992
Email: pachisacorreo@copamex.com

Personnel:
Qlty. Contr. Mgr.: Hector Enriquez
Phone: (52) 614 439 4200
Fax: (52) 614 439 9992
Email: hector.enriquez@copamex.com
Area Mgr.: Isidro Burciaga
Phone: (52) 614 439 4200
Fax: (52) 614 439 9992
Email: isidro.burciaga@copamex.com

Total Employees at this Location: 169
Type of Operation: Paper mill
Pulp Grades and Capacities:
Total pulp capacity: 103,601 mt/y
Recycled Pulping: 103,601 mt/y

Pulp Mill Data:
Recycled Fiber Treatment Lines:
Pulpers: 1 at 47,200
Paper/Paperboard Grades and Capacities:
Total paper and paperboard capacity: 123,522 mt/y
Uncoated woodfree/freesheet: 18,564 mt/y
Packaging papers: 48,552 mt/y
Specialty and industrial: 4,998 mt/y
Linerboard: 29,988 mt/y
Corrugating medium/fluting: 21,420 mt/y
Paper and Paperboard Mill Data:
Stock Preparation:
Pulpers: 6
Refiners: 11
Paper Machines: 2
No. 1, fourdrinier, total capacity 26,061 mt/y, Trim width 2.1 m, Uncoated woodfree/freesheet, Specialty and industrial
No. 2, fourdrinier, total capacity 99,960 mt/y, Trim width 4 m, Linerboard, Packaging papers, Corrugating medium/fluting
Finishing Equipment:
Rewinders: 3
Sheeters: 1
Energy Data:
Power boilers: 3

Ⓗ Copamex, S.A. de C.V.
Av. Roble #300 2nd Floor Col. Valle del Campestre
66260 San Pedro Garza Garcia
Mexico
Phone: (52) 81 5000 6000
Fax: (52) 81 5000 6009/6119
Email: info@copamex.com
Web Address: www.copamex.com

Personnel:
Chmn. (From January 2014)): Ing. Antonio Rene Zarate Negrón
Phone: (52) 81 5000 6000
Fax: (52) 81 5000 6009
Email: antonio.negron@copamex.com
Pres & CEO (From January 2014): Alonso Gonzalez Ramirez
Phone: (52) 81 5000 6000
Fax: (52) 81 5000 6009
Procurement Mgr.: Jaime Gutierrez
Phone: (52) 81 5000 6000
Fax: (52) 81 5000 6009
Email: jaime.gutierrez@copamex.com
Innovation Dir.: Jose Peregrina
Phone: (52) 81 5000 6000
Fax: (52) 81 5000 6009
Email: jose.peregrina@copamex.com

Total Employees of Company: 3,100
Total Employees at this Location: 220
Mill Locations:
Papelera de Chihuahua S.A. de C.V., Chihuahua Mill, Plaza del Ferrocarril Kansas No. 1, Col. Popular, 31350 Chihuahua, Mexico, Capacity: 123,522 mt/y, (Paper mill)
Phone: (52) 614 439 4200
Fax: (52) 614 439 9992
Email: pachisacorreo@copamex.com
Copamex Industrias S.A. de C.V., Monterrey Mill, Av. de la Juventud 280, Col. Cuahutémoc, 66450 San Nicolas de los Garza, Mexico, Capacity: 160,650 mt/y, (Paper mill)
Phone: (52) 81 5000 7000
Fax: (52) 81 5000 7009
Pondercel, S.A. de C.V., Anahuac Mill, Domicilio Conocido Centro Agroindustrial Anahuac s/n, 31600 Anahuac, Mpio De Cuauhtemoc, Mexico, Capacity: 187,425 mt/y, (Pulp mill, Paper mill)
Phone: (52) 625 58 197 00
Fax: (52) 625 58 198 35
Email: luz.gonzalez@copamex.com

Ⓜ Copamex Industrias S.A. de C.V.
Monterrey Mill
Ownership: Copamex, S.A. de C.V.
Av. de la Juventud 280, Col. Cuahutérnoc
66450 San Nicolas de los Garza, Nuevo León
Mexico
Mailing Address: Aptdo. Postal 1428, 66450 Monterrey, Mexico
Phone: (52) 81 5000 7000
Fax: (52) 81 5000 7009
Web Address: www.copamex.com

Personnel:
Mill Mgr.: Jose Duron
Phone: (52) 81 5000 7060
Fax: (52) 81 5000 7009
Email: jose.duron@copamex.com
HR Dir.: Ing. Hector Jauregui
Phone: (52) 81 5000 7000 Ext. 7200
Fax: (52) 81 5000 7009
Email: hector.jauregui@copamex.com
Specialty Paper Sls.: Grethel Martinez
Phone: (52) 81 5000 7000
Fax: (52) 81 5000 7009
Email: grethel.martinez@copamex.com
R&D Mgr.: Ing. Sergio Garza
Phone: (52) 81 5000 7150
Fax: (52) 81 5000 7009
Email: sergio.garza@copamex.com

Total Employees at this Location: 450
Type of Operation: Paper mill
Pulp Grades and Capacities:
Total pulp capacity: 90,776 mt/y
Recycled Pulping: 90,776 mt/y

Pulp Mill Data:
Recycled Fiber Treatment Lines:
Recycled packaging pulping lines: 1
Paper/Paperboard Grades and Capacities:
Total paper and paperboard capacity: 160,650 mt/y
Packaging papers: 61,761 mt/y
Specialty and industrial: 34,986 mt/y
Linerboard: 46,053 mt/y
Corrugating medium/fluting: 17,850 mt/y
Paper and Paperboard Mill Data:
Stock Preparation:
Pulpers: 6
Refiners: 23
Paper Machines: 4
No. 1, fourdrinier, offset gravure, total capacity 41,769 mt/y, Trim width 2.5 m, Linerboard, Corrugating medium/fluting, Packaging papers
No. 2, fourdrinier, total capacity 9,639 mt/y, Trim width 2.2 m, Specialty and industrial
No. 3, fourdrinier, total capacity 83,895 mt/y, Trim width 3.1 m, Packaging papers, Linerboard
No. 4, (Machine Glazed (MG)), Yankee dryer, total capacity 25,347 mt/y, Trim width 3.5 m, Specialty and industrial
Finishing Equipment:
Supercalenders: 2

Mexico

Rewinders: 8
Sheeters: 3
Energy Data:
Power boilers: 4
Electrical demand for mill: 336 MWh/D

ⓂⓂCia. Papelera El Fenix S.A. de C.V.
Col. Arenal Mill
Av. Rio Consulado 375
02980 Col. Arenal, México, D.F.
Mexico
  Phone: (52) 55 5355 3211 / 2631 6672
  Fax: (52) 55 5355 3641
Personnel:
  CEO: Hector Fernandez Mancilla
  Phone: (52) 55 5355 3211 / 2631 6672
  Fax: (52) 55 5355 3641
Total Employees of Company: 256
Total Employees at this Location: 36
Type of Operation: Paper mill, Paperboard mill
Paper/Paperboard Grades and Capacities:
  Total paper and paperboard capacity: 25,600 mt/y
  Uncoated woodfree/freesheet: 19,600 mt/y
  Uncoated mechanical/groundwood
  Boxboard/cartonboard: 6,000 mt/y
Paper and Paperboard Mill Data:
  Stock Preparation:
  Pulpers: 3
  Refiners: 7
Paper Machines: 2
  No. 1, Trim width 1.8 m
  No. 2, Trim width 2 m
Coating Machines: 1
  No. 1
Finishing Equipment:
  Supercalenders: 1
  Rewinders: 2
  Sheeters: 1
Energy Data:
Power boilers: 2

ⓂCelulosa de Fibras Mexicanas S.A. de C.V.
Apizaco Mill
Ownership: Papelera Veracruzana S.A. de C.V.
Km. 1 Camino a Col. Morelos s/n
90308 Apizaco, Tlaxcala
Mexico
  Phone: (52) 241 417 0222 / 241 417 0241
  Fax: (52) 241 417 1777
  Email: celfimex@apizaco.podernet.com.mx,
  informacion@celfimex.com.mx
  Web Address: www.celfimex.com.mx
Personnel:
  Pres. & Paper Mill Mgr.: Ing. Enrique Morodo Santisteban
  Phone: (52) 241 417 0222
  Fax: (52) 241 417 1777
  Email: enrique.morodo@celfimex.com.mx
Total Employees at this Location: 170
Type of Operation: Paper mill
Paper/Paperboard Grades and Capacities:
  Total paper and paperboard capacity: 11,000 mt/y
  Packaging papers: 11,000 mt/y
  Specialty and industrial
  Boxboard/cartonboard
Paper and Paperboard Mill Data:
  Stock Preparation:
  Pulpers: 1
  Refiners: 3
Paper Machines: 2
  PM 3, Yankee dryer, total capacity 9,000 mt/y, Trim width 4 m
  PM 4, total capacity 2,000 mt/y
Finishing Equipment:
  Rewinders: 3
  Sheeters: 1
Energy Data:
Power boilers: 2

ⓂGrupo Gondi S.A. de C.V.
Calle de las Flores 42
51400 Los Reyes Acaquilpan, Edo. de México
Mexico
  Phone: (52) 55 52496000
  Fax: (52) 55 52496050
  Email: ventas.corporativas@grupogondi.com
  Web Address: www.grupogondi.com
Personnel:
  CEO: Eduardo Posada
  Phone: (52) 55 52496000
  Fax: (52) 55 52496050
  Email: eduardo.posada@grupogondi.com
  CFO: Francisco Rodriguez Tamayo
  Phone: (52) 55 52496000 Ext. 6013,6014,6018,6019
  Fax: (52) 55 5249600 Ext. 6613
  Email: francisco.rodriguez@grupogondi.com
  Gen. Dir.: Fernando Cimadevilla
  Phone: (52) 55 52496000
  Fax: (52) 55 52496050
  IT Manager: Carlos Guemez
  Phone: (52) 55 52496000
  Fax: (52) 55 52496050
  Strategic Mgr.: Adriana Chavez Medellin
  Phone: (52) 55 52496000
  Fax: (52) 55 52496050
  Man. Dir. (3 mills of Grupo Gondi): Jose Felix Rocha Echeverria
  Phone: (52) 55 52496000
  Fax: (52) 55 52496050
  Email: felix.rocha@grupogondi.com
Total Employees of Company: 5,000
Mill Locations:
Empaques Modernos de Guadalajara, S.A. de C.V., Guadalajara Mill, Km. 7.3 Carr. Guadalajara, 45680 El Salto, Mexico, Capacity: 199,920 mt/y, (Paper mill, Paperboard mill)
  Phone: (52) 33 32841300/08
  Fax: (52) 33 32841309
  Email: ventas.emg@grupogondi.com, info@grupogondi.com
Papelera Industrial Potosina S.A. de C.V., San Luis Potosi Mill, Zona Ind. Eje 114, No. 230 Col. Zona Industrial, 78090 San Luis Potosi, Mexico, Capacity: 57,120 mt/y, (Paper mill)
  Phone: (52) 444 8 248 484
  Fax: (52) 444 8 248 184
  Email: edernenegh@pipslp.com
Empaques Modernos San Pablo S.A. de C.V., Tlalnepantla Mill, Prol. Poniente N.150, Esq. Avenida de las Granjas S/N, Col. San Pablo Xalpa, 54090 Tlalnepantla, Mexico, Capacity: 179,928 mt/y, (Paper mill, Paperboard mill)
  Phone: (52) 55 5318 8800
  Fax: (52) 55 5382 1092
  Email: info@grupogondi.com

ⓂGrupo Corporativo Papelera S.A. de C.V. ("GCP")
Tepetlaoxtoc Mill
Prol. Xolaltenco No.1 Col. La Columna
56070 Tepetlaoxtoc
Mexico
Type of Operation: Paper mill
Paper/Paperboard Grades and Capacities:
  Total paper and paperboard capacity: 10,000 mt/y
  Tissue: 10,000 mt/y
Paper and Paperboard Mill Data:
Paper Machines: 1
  No. 1, total capacity 10,000 mt/y, Tissue

ⓂⓂHovomex S.A. de C.V.
Apizaco Mill
Ownership: Hollingsworth & Vose Co., Morodo Group
Km. 1.2, Camino a Col. Morelos
90308 Apizaco, Tlaxcala
Mexico
  Phone: (52) 241 41 72555/70773
  Fax: (52) 241 41 70708/80026
  Email: info@hovo.com.mx, bortiz@hovo.com.mx
  Web Address: www.hovo.com.mx
Personnel:
  Pres & CEO: Ing. Valentine Hollingsworth
  Phone: (52) 241 41 72555/70773
  Fax: (52) 241 41 70708/80026
  Email: val.hollingsworth@hovo.com
  VP & Chief Tech Officer: John Fitzgerald
  Phone: (52) 241 41 72555/70773
  Fax: (52) 241 41 70708/80026
  Email: john.fitzgerald@hovo.com
  VP Global Oper.: Don Bockoven
  Phone: (52) 241 41 72555/70773
  Fax: (52) 241 41 70708/80026
  Email: don.bockoven@hovo.com
  VP & Man Dir.: Josh Ayer
  Phone: (52) 241 41 72555/70773
  Fax: (52) 241 41 70708/80026
  Email: josh.ayer@hovo.com
  VP CFO: Jeff Sherer
  Phone: (52) 241 41 72555/70773
  Fax: (52) 241 41 70708/80026
  Email: jeff.sherer@hovo.com
  Mill Mgr.: Ing. Oscar Cano
  Phone: (52) 241 41 72555/70773
  Fax: (52) 241 41 70708/80026
  Email: oscar.cano@hovo.com
  VP HR: Ken Fausnacht
  Phone: (52) 241 41 72555/70773
  Fax: (52) 241 41 70708/80026
  Email: ken.fausnacht@hovo.com
  Sen Commun. Mgr.: Jodi Meltzer
  Phone: (52) 241 41 72555/70773
  Fax: (52) 241 41 70708/80026
  Email: jodi.meltzer@hovo.com
Total Employees of Company: 120
Type of Operation: Paper mill
Paper/Paperboard Grades and Capacities:
  Total paper and paperboard capacity: 9,000 mt/y
  Specialty and industrial: 9,000 mt/y
Paper and Paperboard Mill Data:
Paper Machines: 1
  No. 1, total capacity 9,000 mt/y, Trim width 2.2 m, Specialty and industrial
Finishing Equipment:
  Rewinders: 3

ⓂInternational Paper, Empaques Industriales de México S.A. de C.V.
Ownership: International Paper Co.
Avda. Uno No.1 Parque Industrial Iztaczoquitlan
94450 Iztaczoquitlan, Veracruz
Mexico
  Phone: (52) 272 72 820 00
  Fax: (52) 272 72 820 01
  Web Address: www.ipaper.com
Personnel:
  Chmn.: Ing. Enrique Prado
  Phone: (52) 272 72 820 00
  Fax: (52) 272 72 820 01
  Prod. Mgr.: Ing. Enrique Andrade Nadal
  Phone: (52) 272 72 820 00
  Fax: (52) 272 72 820 01
  Finan. Dir.: C.P. Romeo de Jesús Ramirez-Leal
  Phone: (52) 272 72 820 00
  Fax: (52) 272 72 820 01
  Sls. Mgr.: Ing. Luving Hernández
  Phone: (52) 272 72 820 00
  Fax: (52) 272 72 820 01
  Assist. Mgr.: Lic. Guillermo Hernández
  Phone: (52) 272 72 820 00
  Fax: (52) 272 72 820 01
Total Employees at this Location: 80
Mill Locations:
International Paper, Empaques Industriales de México S.A. de C.V., Xalapa Mill, Carretera Antigua Jalapa-Coatepec Km. 3.8 Predio La Yerbabuena, 91000 Xalapa, Mexico, Capacity: 24,276 mt/y, (Paper mill, Paperboard mill)

Phone: (52) 228 818 6777
Fax: (52) 228 818 3533

ⓜInternational Paper, Empaques Industriales de México S.A. de C.V.
Xalapa Mill
Ownership: International Paper Co.
Carretera Antigua Jalapa-Coatepec Km. 3.8 Predio La Yerbabuena
91000 Xalapa, Veracruz
Mexico
  Phone: (52) 228 818 6777
  Fax: (52) 228 818 3533
  Web Address: www.ipaper.com
Personnel:
Mill Mgr.: Ing. Enrique Prado Garza
  Phone: (52) 228 818 6777
  Fax: (52) 228 818 3533
  Email: enrique.prado@ipaper.com
Mgr. - Puebla Plt.: Lic. Romeo DeJesus Ramirez Leal
  Phone: (52) 222 210 6443 Ext. 112
  Fax: (52) 222 210 6354
  Email: romeo.ramirez@ipaper.com
Recycling Mgr.: Ing. Julio Cesar Dominguez
  Phone: (52) 228 841 8319
  Fax: (52) 228 818 3533
  Email: julio.dominguez@cbpr.ipaper.com
Oper. Mgr.: Ing. Jesús Raúl Perez
  Phone: (52) 228 818 6777
  Fax: (52) 228 818 3533
  Email: jesus.perez@ipaper.com
Total Employees at this Location: 110
Type of Operation: Paper mill, Paperboard mill
Pulp Grades and Capacities:
  Total pulp capacity: 24,804 mt/y
  Recycled Pulping: 24,804 mt/y

Pulp Mill Data:
  Recycled Fiber Treatment Lines:
  Recycled packaging pulping lines: 1 at 25,400
Paper/Paperboard Grades and Capacities:
  Total paper and paperboard capacity: 24,276 mt/y
  Linerboard: 12,138 mt/y
  Corrugating medium/fluting: 12,138 mt/y
Paper and Paperboard Mill Data:
  Stock Preparation:
  Pulpers: 2
  Refiners: 2
Paper Machines: 1
No. 1, fourdrinier, total capacity 24,276 mt/y, Trim width 2.05 m, Linerboard, Corrugating medium/fluting
Finishing Equipment:
  Supercalenders: 1
  Rewinders: 1
Energy Data:
Power boilers: 1
Electrical demand for mill: 36 MWh/D

ⓘⓜPapelera Iruña S.A. de C.V.
Iztapalapa Mill
Ownership: 100% by Arcelus Group
Av. Tlahuac 5921, Col. El Vergel
09880 Iztapalapa, México, D.F.
Mexico
  Phone: (52) 55 5804 3280
  Fax: (52) 55 5426 3589
  Email: info@iruna.com.mx, piruna@altavista.net
Personnel:
Prod. Control Mgr.: Víctor Águila
  Phone: (52) 5 426 5043 ext. 1257
  Fax: (52) 5 426 3589
  Email: juridico@denak.com.mx
Total Employees of Company: 360
Total Employees at this Location: 140
Type of Operation: Paper mill, Paperboard mill
Pulp Grades and Capacities:
  Total pulp capacity: 57,895 mt/y
  Recycled Pulping: 57,895 mt/y

Pulp Mill Data:
  Recycled Fiber Treatment Lines:
  Pulpers: 1 at 63,100
Paper/Paperboard Grades and Capacities:
  Total paper and paperboard capacity: 56,049 mt/y
  Packaging papers: 11,424 mt/y
  Linerboard: 16,422 mt/y
  Corrugating medium/fluting: 16,065 mt/y
  Boxboard/cartonboard: 12,138 mt/y
Paper and Paperboard Mill Data:
  Stock Preparation:
  Pulpers: 6
  Refiners: 8
Paper Machines: 5
No. 2, fourdrinier, total capacity 11,424 mt/y, Trim width 2 m, Linerboard
No. 3, fourdrinier, total capacity 11,424 mt/y, Trim width 2.25 m, Corrugating medium/fluting
No. 4, fourdrinier, total capacity 9,639 mt/y, Trim width 1.6 m, Linerboard, Corrugating medium/fluting
No. 5, cylinder, total capacity 12,138 mt/y, Trim width 1.65 m, Boxboard/cartonboard
No. 6, fourdrinier, total capacity 11,424 mt/y, Trim width 1.98 m, Packaging papers
Finishing Equipment:
  Rewinders: 6
  Sheeters: 3
Energy Data:
Power boilers: 4
Electrical demand for mill: 97 MWh/D

ⓜKimberly-Clark de México S.A. de C.V.
Ownership: Kimberly-Clark Corp.
Jaime Valmes 8, Piso 9 Col. los Morales Polanco
11510 Mexico, México, D.F.
Mexico
  Phone: (52) 555 282 7300
  Fax: (52) 555 282 7272
  Web Address: www.kimberly-clark.com.mx
Personnel:
Chmn. of the Board: Ing. Claudio X. Gonzalez Laporte
  Phone: (52) 555 282 7300
  Fax: (52) 555 282 7272
  Email: cgonzalez@kcc.com
CFO: C.P. Jorge A. Lara Flores
  Phone: (52) 555 282 7300
  Fax: (52) 555 282 7272
  Email: jlara@kcc.com
Man. Dir.: Pablo Roberto González Guajardo
  Phone: (52) 555 282 7300
  Fax: (52) 555 282 7272
  Email: pgonzalez@kcc.com
Sls. Dir.: Ing. Fernando Gonzalez Velazco
  Phone: (52) 555 282 7300
  Fax: (52) 555 282 7272
  Email: fgonzalez@kcc.com
HR Dir.: Ing. Alejandro Lascurain Curbelo
  Phone: (52) 555 282 7300
  Fax: (52) 555 282 7272
  Email: alascurain@kcc.com
Mktg. Dir.: Ing. Virgilio Isa
  Phone: (52) 555 282 7300
  Fax: (52) 555 282 7272
  Email: visa@kcc.com
Oper. Mgr.: Bernardo Aragon Paasch
  Phone: (52) 555 282 7300
  Fax: (52) 555 282 7272
  Email: bpaasch@kcc.com
Manuf. Dir.: Gabriel Lance brunet
  Phone: (52) 555 282 7300
  Fax: (52) 555 282 7272
  Email: gbrunet@kcc.com
Bus. Mgr.: Jorge Morales Rojas
  Phone: (52) 555 282 7300
  Fax: (52) 555 282 7272
  Email: jrojas@kcc.com
Finan. Mgr.: Xavier Cortes Lascurain
  Phone: (52) 555 282 7300
  Fax: (52) 555 282 7272
  Email: xlascurain@kcc.com

Proj. Mgr & Software Architect: Victor Alejandro Talavera Perez
  Phone: (52) 555 282 7300
  Fax: (52) 555 282 7272
  Email: valejandro@kcc.com
Total Employees of Company: 7,000
Mill Locations:
Kimberly-Clark de México S.A. de C.V., Bajio Mill, Av. Doctor Rafael Ayala, Echevarri Km. 0.5 Libramiento a Tequisquiapan, 76800 San Juan del Rio, Mexico, Capacity: 269,892 mt/y, (Paper mill)
  Phone: (52) 427 271 8500, 442 272 8282
  Fax: (52) 427 271 8504, 442 272 8030
Kimberly-Clark de México S.A. de C.V., Cepamisa, Domicilio Conocido, Ejido de Cointzio, Municipio de Morelia, 58341 Morelia, Mexico, Capacity: 44,982 mt/y, (Pulp mill, Paper mill)
  Phone: (52) 443 322 3700
  Fax: (52) 443 322 3709
Kimberly-Clark de México S.A. de C.V., Ecatepec Mill, Avenida de las Torres No. 87, Col. Jajalpa, San Cristobal, 55090 Ecatepec de Morelos, Mexico, Capacity: 142,086 mt/y, (Paper mill)
  Phone: (52) 55 5836 2400
  Fax: (52) 55 5836 2403 / 10
Kimberly-Clark de México S.A. de C.V., Orizaba Mill, Avenida San Juan 1, Escarnela Iztaczoquitlan, 94452 Orizaba, Mexico, Capacity: 94,962 mt/y, (Pulp mill, Paper mill)
  Phone: (52) 272 728 2800
  Fax: (52) 272 728 2844
  Email: salvador.ortegal@kcc.com
Kimberly-Clark de México S.A. de C.V., Ramos Arizpe Mill, Carretera Monterey Saltillo, Km. 21.4, 25900 Ramos Arizpe, Mexico, Capacity: 154,938 mt/y, (Paper mill)
  Phone: (52) 844 411 0100
  Fax: (52) 844 411 0137
Kimberly-Clark de México S.A. de C.V., San Martin Texmelucan Mill, Av. Revolucion No. 1, Santamaria, Moyotzingo, 74129 San Martin Texmelucan, Mexico, Capacity: 27,132 mt/y, (Paper mill)
  Phone: (52) 248 485 0477/0055
  Fax: (52) 248 485 0015

ⓜKimberly-Clark de México S.A. de C.V.
Bajio Mill
Ownership: Kimberly-Clark Corp.
Av. Doctor Rafael Ayala, Echevarri Km. 0.5 Libramiento a Tequisquiapan
76800 San Juan del Rio, Querétaro
Mexico
  Phone: (52) 427 271 8500, 442 272 8282
  Fax: (52) 427 271 8504, 442 272 8030
  Web Address: www.kimberly-clark.com.mx
Personnel:
HR. Dir. Kimberly-Clark de Mexico: Alejandro Lascurain Curbelo
  Phone: (52) 52 55 5282 7300
  Fax: (52) 52 55 5282 7282
Sls. Dir. Kimberly-Clark de Mexico: Fernando González Velasco
  Phone: (52) 52 55 5282 7300
  Fax: (52) 52 55 5282 7282
Mktg. Dir. Kimberly-Clark de Mexico: Virgilio Isa Cantillo
  Phone: (52) 52 55 5282 7300
  Fax: (52) 52 55 5282 7282
Plant Mgr. Querétaro Area: Laurentino Rodriguez
  Phone: (52) 427 271 8500, 442 272 8282
  Fax: (52) 427 271 8504, 442 272 8030
Purch. Mgr. Mexico City Area: Ricardo Quintana
  Phone: (52) 427 271 8500, 442 272 8282
  Fax: (52) 427 271 8504, 442 272 8030
Supt.: Ladislao Mendoza Zubieta
  Phone: (52) 427 271 8500, 442 272 8282
  Fax: (52) 427 271 8504, 442 272 8030
Total Employees at this Location: 970
Type of Operation: Paper mill
Pulp Grades and Capacities:
  Total pulp capacity: 83,420 mt/y

Mexico

Recycled Pulping: 83,420 mt/y
Pulp Mill Data:
Bleach Plant Systems: 1
Recycled Pulping System, Type: DIP
Recycled Fiber Treatment Lines:
Flotation deinking lines: 1
Paper/Paperboard Grades and Capacities:
Total paper and paperboard capacity: 269,892 mt/y
Tissue: 269,892 mt/y
Paper and Paperboard Mill Data:
Stock Preparation:
Pulpers: 6
Refiners: 6
Paper Machines: 4
No. 2, crescent former, total capacity 44,982 mt/y, Trim width 5.3 m, Tissue
No. 3, crescent former, total capacity 74,970 mt/y, Trim width 4.8 m, Tissue, Uncoated woodfree/freesheet
No. 4, TAD, total capacity 89,964 mt/y, Trim width 5.3 m, Tissue
No. 5, crescent former, total capacity 59,976 mt/y, Trim width 5.1 m, Tissue
Finishing Equipment:
Rewinders: 6
Sheeters: 2
Energy Data:
Power boilers: 3
Electrical demand for mill: 891 MWh/D

ⓜ Kimberly-Clark de México S.A. de C.V.
Cepamisa
Ownership: Kimberly-Clark Corp.
Domicilio Conocido, Ejido de Cointzio, Municipio de Morelia
58341 Morelia, Michoacán
Mexico
Phone: (52) 443 322 3700
Fax: (52) 443 322 3709
Web Address: www.kimberly-clark.com.mx
Personnel:
Corp. Treas.: Sergio Camacho Carmona
Phone: (52) 443 322 3700
Fax: (52) 443 322 3709
Email: scamacho@kcc.com
Total Employees at this Location: 375
Type of Operation: Pulp mill, Paper mill
Pulp Mill Data:
Chemical Pulping Systems:
Continuous digesters: 1
Bleach Plant Systems: 1
Chemical Recovery Equipment:
Evaporator lines: 1
Recovery boilers: 1
Pulp Dryers:
Air Float dryers 1
Paper/Paperboard Grades and Capacities:
Total paper and paperboard capacity: 44,982 mt/y
Tissue: 44,982 mt/y
Paper and Paperboard Mill Data:
Stock Preparation:
Pulpers: 3
Refiners: 4
Paper Machines: 1
No. 2, TAD, total capacity 44,982 mt/y, Trim width 3.56 m, Tissue
Finishing Equipment:
Supercalenders: 1
Rewinders: 2
Sheeters: 3
Energy Data:
Power boilers: 2
Steam turbines: 2 at 7.0 MW
Electrical demand for mill: 182 MWh/D

ⓜ Kimberly-Clark de México S.A. de C.V.
Ecatepec Mill
Ownership: Kimberly-Clark Corp.
Avenida de las Torres No. 87, Col. Jajalpa, San Cristobal
55090 Ecatepec de Morelos, Edo. de México
Mexico
Phone: (52) 55 5836 2400
Fax: (52) 55 5836 2403/10
Web Address: www.kimberly-clark.com.mx
Personnel:
Supt. Maint.: Epifanio Olivos
Phone: (52) 55 5836 2400
Fax: (52) 55 5836 2403
Total Employees at this Location: 428
Type of Operation: Paper mill
Pulp Grades and Capacities:
Total pulp capacity: 78,967 mt/y
Recycled Pulping: 78,967 mt/y
Pulp Mill Data:
Bleach Plant Systems: 1
Recycled Pulping System, Type: DIP
Recycled Fiber Treatment Lines:
Flotation deinking lines: 1
Paper/Paperboard Grades and Capacities:
Total paper and paperboard capacity: 142,086 mt/y
Tissue: 142,086 mt/y
Paper and Paperboard Mill Data:
Paper Machines: 4
No. 6, crescent former, total capacity 32,130 mt/y, Trim width 3.3 m, Tissue, Uncoated woodfree/freesheet
No. 7, crescent former, total capacity 49,980 mt/y, Trim width 5.4 m, Tissue
No. 8, crescent former, total capacity 29,988 mt/y, Trim width 3.5 m, Tissue
No. 9, crescent former, total capacity 29,988 mt/y, Trim width 3.5 m, Tissue
Energy Data:
Power boilers
Electrical demand for mill: 474 MWh/D

ⓜ Kimberly-Clark de México S.A. de C.V.
Orizaba Mill
Ownership: Kimberly-Clark Corp.
Avenida San Juan 1, Escamela Iztaczoquitlan
94452 Orizaba, Veracruz
Mexico
Phone: (52) 272 728 2800
Fax: (52) 272 728 2844
Email: salvador.ortegal@kcc.com
Web Address: www.kimberly-clark.com.mx
Personnel:
Chief Eng.: Salvador Ortega
Phone: (52) 272 728 2800
Fax: (52) 272 728 2844
Email: sortega@kcc.com
Admin. Mgr.: Rene Zarate
Phone: (52) 272 728 2800
Fax: (52) 272 728 2844
Email: rgzarate@kcc.com
Total Employees at this Location: 1,245
Type of Operation: Pulp mill, Paper mill
Pulp Mill Data:
Chemical Pulping Systems:
Continuous digesters: 2
Bleach Plant Systems: 2
No. 1, Sequence: CEH
No. 2, Sequence: CEopHS
Chemical Recovery Equipment:
Evaporator lines: 3
Recovery boilers: 2
Paper/Paperboard Grades and Capacities:
Total paper and paperboard capacity: 94,962 mt/y
Tissue: 94,962 mt/y
Paper and Paperboard Mill Data:
Stock Preparation:
Pulpers: 4
Refiners: 4
Paper Machines: 3
No. 5, crescent former, total capacity 24,990 mt/y, Trim width 4.2 m, Tissue
No. 6, crescent former, total capacity 29,988 mt/y, Trim width 4.2 m, Tissue, Uncoated woodfree/freesheet
No. 8, crescent former, total capacity 39,984 mt/y, Trim width 4.4 m, Tissue
Finishing Equipment:
Sheeters: 3
Energy Data:
Power boilers: 6
Electrical demand for mill: 291 MWh/D

ⓜ Kimberly-Clark de México S.A. de C.V.
Ramos Arizpe Mill
Ownership: Kimberly-Clark Corp.
Carretera Monterey Saltillo, Km. 21.4
25900 Ramos Arizpe, Coahuila
Mexico
Phone: (52) 844 411 0100
Fax: (52) 844 411 0137
Web Address: www.kimberly-clark.com.mx
Personnel:
Corp. Manuf. Systems & Process Mgr.: Ing. Gerardo Camacho Iberri
Phone: (52) 844 411 0120
Fax: (52) 844 411 0117
Email: gcamacho@kcc.com
Supt.: Arturo Baez
Phone: (52) 844 411 0100
Fax: (52) 844 411 0137
Email: abaez@kcc.com
Total Employees at this Location: 480
Type of Operation: Paper mill
Pulp Grades and Capacities:
Total pulp capacity: 99,100 mt/y
Recycled Pulping: 99,100 mt/y
Pulp Mill Data:
Recycled Fiber Treatment Lines:
Flotation deinking lines: 2
Pulpers: 2 at 60,000 admt/y
Washing deinking lines: 4
Paper/Paperboard Grades and Capacities:
Total paper and paperboard capacity: 154,938 mt/y
Tissue: 154,938 mt/y
Paper and Paperboard Mill Data:
Stock Preparation:
Pulpers: 2
Refiners: 2
Paper Machines: 3
No. 1, crescent former, total capacity 59,976 mt/y, Trim width 5.3 m, Tissue, Uncoated woodfree/freesheet
No. 2, crescent former, total capacity 59,976 mt/y, Trim width 5.3 m, Tissue, Uncoated woodfree/freesheet
No. 3, crescent former, total capacity 34,986 mt/y, Trim width 3.5 m, Tissue
Finishing Equipment:
Rewinders: 7
Energy Data:
Power boilers: 2
Electrical demand for mill: 503 MWh/D

ⓜ Kimberly-Clark de México S.A. de C.V.
San Martin Texmelucan Mill
Ownership: Kimberly-Clark Corp.
Av. Revolucion No. 1, Santamaria, Moyotzingo
74129 San Martin Texmelucan, Puebla
Mexico
Phone: (52) 248 485 0477/0055
Fax: (52) 248 485 0015
Web Address: www.kimberly-clark.com.mx
Personnel:
Mill Mgr.: Cruz Dominguez
Phone: (52) 248 485 0477/0055
Fax: (52) 248 485 0015
Oper. Mgr.: Gustavo Moreno Ayala
Phone: (52) 248 485 0477/0055
Fax: (52) 248 485 0015
Cost Acctg. Mgr.: Ing. Pedro Sanchez
Phone: (52) 248 485 0477/0055
Fax: (52) 248 485 0015
Total Employees at this Location: 220
Type of Operation: Paper mill
Pulp Grades and Capacities:

Total pulp capacity: 20,240 mt/y
Recycled Pulping: 20,240 mt/y
Pulp Mill Data:
Recycled Fiber Treatment Lines:
Flotation deinking lines: 1
Paper/Paperboard Grades and Capacities:
Total paper and paperboard capacity: 27,132 mt/y
Tissue: 27,132 mt/y
Paper and Paperboard Mill Data:
Stock Preparation:
Pulpers: 2
Refiners: 3
Paper Machines: 1
No. 51, crescent former, total capacity 27,132 mt/y, Trim width 3.1 m, Tissue
Finishing Equipment:
Rewinders: 1
Sheeters: 1
Energy Data:
Power boilers
Electrical demand for mill: 94 MWh/D

⓪ⓜPapeles Lozar S.A. de C.V.
Ixtapaluca Mill
Zaragoza 38, Col. La Venta
56530 Ixtapaluca, México, D.F.
Mexico
 Phone: (52) 55 5972 0022
 Fax: (52) 55 5972 0419
 Email: ventas@papeleslozar.com.mx,
 plozar@papeleslozar.com.mx
Personnel:
Board Mill Mgr.: Manuel Najera Rivera
 Phone: (52) 55 5972 0022
 Fax: (52) 55 5972 0419
Man. Dir.: Jesús Ramsol
 Phone: (52) 55 5972 0022
 Fax: (52) 55 5972 0419
Total Employees of Company: 100
Total Employees at this Location: 13
Type of Operation: Paper mill, Paperboard mill
Paper/Paperboard Grades and Capacities:
Total paper and paperboard capacity: 6,000 mt/y
Uncoated woodfree/freesheet: 4,800 mt/y
Boxboard/cartonboard
Paper and Paperboard Mill Data:
Stock Preparation:
Pulpers: 2
Refiners: 3
Paper Machines: 1
No. 1, fourdrinier, Trim width 2 m
Finishing Equipment:
Supercalenders: 1
Rewinders: 1
Sheeters: 1
Energy Data:
Power boilers: 1

ⓜEmpaques Modernos de Guadalajara, S.A. de C.V.
Guadalajara Mill
Ownership: 100% by Grupo Gondi S.A. de C.V.
Km. 7.3 Carr. Guadalajara
45680 El Salto, Jalisco
Mexico
 Phone: (52) 33 32841300/08
 Fax: (52) 33 32841309
 Email: ventas.emg@grupogondi.com,
 info@grupogondi.com
 Web Address: www.grupogondi.com
Personnel:
Gen. Mgr.: Ing. Juan Pablo González Cimadevilla
 Phone: (52) 33 32841300
 Fax: (52) 33 32841309
 Email: pablo.gonzalez@grupogondi.com
Mill Mgr.: Luis Alberto Baracaldo
 Phone: (52) 33 32841300
 Fax: (52) 33 32841309
Paper Mill Mgr.: José Refugio Rodriguez
 Phone: (52) 33 32841300
 Fax: (52) 33 32841309
 Email: refugio.rodriguez@grupogondi.com
Oper. Mgr. Corrugated Box Plant: Arturo Plaza
 Phone: (52) 33 32841300 Ext. 6550
 Fax: (52) 33 32841309
 Email: arturo.plaza@grupogondi.com
Total Employees at this Location: 180
Type of Operation: Paper mill, Paperboard mill
Pulp Grades and Capacities:
Total pulp capacity: 170,758 mt/y
Recycled Pulping: 170,758 mt/y
Pulp Mill Data:
Recycled Fiber Treatment Lines:
Recycled packaging pulping lines: 1
Paper/Paperboard Grades and Capacities:
Total paper and paperboard capacity: 199,920 mt/y
Corrugating medium/fluting: 79,968 mt/y
Boxboard/cartonboard: 119,952 mt/y
Paper and Paperboard Mill Data:
Stock Preparation:
Pulpers:
Paper Machines: 2
No. 1, cylinder, total capacity 79,968 mt/y, Trim width 3.2 m, Corrugating medium/fluting
No. 3, fourdrinier, total capacity 119,952 mt/y, Trim width 4.6 m, Boxboard/cartonboard
Coating Machines: 1
CM3, total capacity 120,000 mt/y., on machine
Energy Data:
Power boilers: 1
Electrical demand for mill: 314 MWh/D

⓪ⓜPapelera del Nevado S.A. de C.V.
Almoloyan Mill
Km. 16 Carretera Toluca Zitacuaro
50900 San Miguel Almoloyan, Almoloya de Juarez, México, D.F.
Mexico
 Phone: (52) 722 276 7120
 Fax: (52) 722 276 7123
 Email: info@nevado.com.mx
 Web Address: www.nevado.com.mx
Personnel:
Gen. Mgr.: Javier Manuel Arcelus Iroz
 Phone: (52) 722 276 7120
 Fax: (52) 722 276 7123
 Email: direccion@nevado.com.mx
Mgr.: Viridiana Hernández
 Phone: (52) 722 276 7120
 Fax: (52) 722 276 7123
 Email: rechum@nevado.com.mx
Total Employees of Company: 469
Total Employees at this Location: 322
Type of Operation: Paper mill, Paperboard mill
Pulp Grades and Capacities:
Total pulp capacity: 111,450 mt/y
Recycled Pulping: 111,450 mt/y
Pulp Mill Data:
Recycled Fiber Treatment Lines:
Recycled packaging pulping lines: 1
Paper/Paperboard Grades and Capacities:
Total paper and paperboard capacity: 108,528 mt/y
Packaging papers: 18,564 mt/y
Linerboard: 43,554 mt/y
Corrugating medium/fluting: 23,205 mt/y
Boxboard/cartonboard: 23,205 mt/y
Paper and Paperboard Mill Data:
Stock Preparation:
Pulpers: 4
Refiners: 8
Paper Machines: 3
No. 1, cylinder, total capacity 33,915 mt/y, Trim width 2.3 m, Boxboard/cartonboard, Linerboard
No. 2, Yankee dryer, total capacity 18,564 mt/y, Trim width 2 m, Packaging papers
No. 3, fourdrinier, total capacity 56,049 mt/y, Trim width 3.3 m, Linerboard, Corrugating medium/fluting
Finishing Equipment:
Rewinders: 3
Sheeters: 1
Energy Data:
Power boilers: 5
Electrical demand for mill: 158 MWh/D

ⓜPapelera del Pacífico S.A. de C.V.
Guadalajara Mill
Antiguo Camino Aviación No. 3177, Colonia La Nogalera
44460 Guadalajara, Jalisco
Mexico
Mailing Address: Aptdo. Postal 99-10, 44460 Guadalajara, Jalisco, Mexico
 Phone: (52) 33 3812 2975
 Fax: (52) 33 3812 2514
 Email: ppags13100@prodigy.net.mx
Personnel:
Gen. Mgr.: Ing. Brigido Rodriguez J.
 Phone: (52) 33 3812 2975
Mill Mgr.: Ing. Enrique Madrigal
 Phone: (52) 33 3812 2975
Total Employees at this Location: 50
Type of Operation: Paper mill

ⓜPapelera del Pacífico S.A. de C.V.
Antiguo Camino Aviación No. 3177, Colonia La Nogalera
44460 Guadalajara
Mexico
Mailing Address: Aptdo. Postal 99-10, 44460 Guadalajara
 Phone: (52) 33 3812 2975
 Fax: (52) 33 3812 2514
 Email: ppags13100@prodigy.net.mx
Personnel:
Gen. Mgr.: Brigido Rodriguez J.
 Phone: (52) 33 3812 2975
 Fax: (52) 33 3812 2514
Mill Mgr.: Enrique Madrigal
 Phone: (52) 33 3812 2975
 Fax: (52) 33 3812 2514
Total Employees at this Location: 50
Mill Locations:
Papelera del Pacífico S.A. de C.V., Guadalajara Mill, Antiguo Camino Aviación No. 3177, Colonia La Nogalera, 44460 Guadalajara, Mexico, (Paper mill)
 Phone: (52) 33 3812 2975
 Fax: (52) 33 3812 2514
 Email: ppags13100@prodigy.net.mx

⓪ⓜPCM-Papeles y Conversiones de México, S.A. de C.V.
Monterrey Mill
Cerro de La Silla 101, Las Huertas
67190 Monterrey, Guadalupe, Nuevo León
Mexico
 Phone: (52) 81 8127 7700
 Fax: (52) 52 81 8127 7701
 Web Address: www.pcm-net.com.mx
Personnel:
Dir.: Cesar Anaya
 Phone: (52) 81 8127 7700
 Fax: (52) 81 8127 7701
 Email: cesar@pcm-net.com.mx
HR. Mgr.: Francisco Javier Rendon Espinoza
 Phone: (52) 81 8127 7700
 Fax: (52) 81 8127 7701
Sls. Mktg.: Arturo Gonzalez
 Phone: (52) 81 8127 7700
 Email: jgonzalez@pcm-net.com.mx
Type of Operation: Paperboard mill
Pulp Grades and Capacities:
Total pulp capacity: 92,928 mt/y
Recycled Pulping: 92,928 mt/y
Paper/Paperboard Grades and Capacities:
Total paper and paperboard capacity: 92,106 mt/y
Linerboard: 50,694 mt/y
Corrugating medium/fluting: 41,412 mt/y

Mexico

Paper and Paperboard Mill Data:
Paper Machines: 1
No. 1, fourdrinier, total capacity 92,106 mt/y, Trim width 2.8 m, Linerboard, Corrugating medium/fluting
Energy Data:
Electrical demand for mill: 106 MWh/D

ⓘPCM-Papeles y Conversiones de México, S.A. de C.V.
Company is under construction
Cerro de La Silla 101, Las Huertas
67190 Guadalupe, Nuevo Leon, Nuevo León
Mexico
  Phone: (52) 52 81 8127 7700
  Fax: (52) 52 81 8127 7701
  Web Address: www.pcm-net.com.mx
Personnel:
Dir.: Cesar Anaya
Phone: (52) 81 8127 7700
Fax: (52) 81 8127 7701
Email: cesar@pcm-net.com.mx
Mill Locations:
PCM-Papeles y Conversiones de México, S.A. de C.V., Monterrey Mill, Cerro de La Silla 101, Las Huertas, 67190 Monterrey, Guadalupe, Mexico, Capacity: 92,106 mt/y, (Paperboard mill)
Phone: (52) 81 8127 7700
Fax: (52) 52 81 8127 7701

ⓘⓜCia. Industrial Papelera Poblana S.A. de C.V.
Chachapa Mill
Km. 136.5 Autopista México-Orizaba, San Diego Icatepec
72990 Chachapa, Puebla
Mexico
  Phone: (52) 222 286 0393-94
  Fax: (52) 222 286 0397
Personnel:
Chmn.: Ing. Gustavo T. Rugerio
Phone: (52) 555 872 2019
Fax: (52) 555 870 1533
Email: guscarton@gmail.com
Mill Mgr.: Ing. Alfonso Rugerio
Phone: (52) 222 286 1060
Fax: (52) 222 286 1060
Fin. Mgr.: Lic. Veronica Vasquez Roman
Phone: (52) 222 244 6300
Fax: (52) 222 286 0397
Total Employees of Company: 135
Total Employees at this Location: 105
Type of Operation: Paper mill, Paperboard mill
Mill Locations:
CEPASA - Celulose e Papel de Pernambuco S.A., Jaboatão dos Guararapes Mill, Rua Vereador Sócrates Regueira Pinto de Souza, 183— Padre Roma, 54110-000 Jaboatão dos Guararapes, PE, Brazil, Capacity: 69,972 mt/y, (Pulp mill, Paper mill, Paperboard mill)
Phone: (55) 81 21198700
Fax: (55) 81 34811298
Pulp Grades and Capacities:
Total pulp capacity: 45,935 mt/y
Recycled Pulping: 45,935 mt/y
Pulp Mill Data:
Recycled Fiber Treatment Lines:
Recycled packaging pulping lines: 1
Paper/Paperboard Grades and Capacities:
Total paper and paperboard capacity: 44,982 mt/y
Linerboard: 30,702 mt/y
Corrugating medium/fluting: 14,280 mt/y
Paper and Paperboard Mill Data:
Stock Preparation:
Pulpers: 2
Refiners: 2
Paper Machines: 2
No. 1, multi-cylinder, total capacity 14,280 mt/y, Trim width 2 m, Corrugating medium/fluting
No. 2, fourdrinier, total capacity 30,702 mt/y, Trim width 2 m, Linerboard

Finishing Equipment:
Rewinders: 2
Energy Data:
Power boilers: 1
Electrical demand for mill: 79 MWh/D

ⓜPondercel, S.A. de C.V.
Anahuac Mill
Ownership: Copamex, S.A. de C.V.
Domicilio Conocido Centro Agroindustrial Anahuac s/n
31600 Anahuac, Mpio De Cuauhtemoc, Chihuahua
Mexico
  Phone: (52) 625 58 197 00
  Fax: (52) 625 58 198 35
  Email: luz.gonzalez@copamex.com
  Web Address: www.copamex.com
Personnel:
Mill Mgr.: Ing. Carlos Najar Arreola
Phone: (52) 625 58 197 00
Fax: (52) 625 58 198 35
Email: carlos.arreola@copamex.com
Commodity Prod. Coord.: David Machuca
Phone: (52) 625 58 197 29 Ext: 9731
Fax: (52) 625 58 198 35
Email: david.machuca@copamex.com
Maint. Mgr. : Saul Armando Aguirre Aguirre
Phone: (52) 625 58 197 00
Fax: (52) 625 58 198 35
Email: saul.armando@copamex.com
Total Employees at this Location: 550
Type of Operation: Pulp mill, Paper mill
Pulp Mill Data:
Paper/Paperboard Grades and Capacities:
Total paper and paperboard capacity: 187,425 mt/y
Uncoated woodfree/freesheet: 187,425 mt/y
Paper and Paperboard Mill Data:
Stock Preparation:
Pulpers: 6
Refiners: 11
Paper Machines: 1
No. 1, fourdrinier, total capacity 187,425 mt/y, Trim width 5.5 m, Uncoated woodfree/freesheet
Finishing Equipment:
Rewinders: 3
Sheeters: 1
Energy Data:
Power boilers: 5
Electrical demand for mill: 430 MWh/D

ⓘCartones Ponderosa S.A. de C.V.
Ownership: 100% by Organización Editorial Mexicana
Libramiento a Tequisquiapan, Km. 4, Zona Industrial
76802 San Juan del Rio, Querétaro
Mexico
  Phone: (52) 427 271 9666/13/21
  Fax: (52) 427 271 9694
  Web Address: www.cartonesponderosa.com.mx
Personnel:
Pres. & Gen. Dir. : Don Mario Vásquez Raña
Phone: (52) 427 271 9600
Fax: (52) 427 271 9694
Pres. Paper Division: Antonio Rodriquez Demeneghi
Phone: (52) 427 271 9600
Fax: (52) 427 271 9694
Email: arodem@carpo.com.mx
Asst. Paper Div. Pres.: Gabriela Resendiz
Phone: (52) 427 271 9600
Fax: (52) 427 271 9694
Email: gresendiz@carpo.com.mx
Total Employees of Company: 594
Mill Locations:
Cartones Ponderosa S.A. de C.V., San Juan del Rio Mill, Libramiento a Tequisquiapan, Km. 4, Zona Industrial, 76802 San Juan del Rio, Mexico, Capacity: 239,904 mt/y, (Paperboard mill)
Phone: (52) 427 271 9600/13/21
Fax: (52) 427 271 9694

ⓜCartones Ponderosa S.A. de C.V.
San Juan del Rio Mill
Libramiento a Tequisquiapan, Km. 4, Zona Industrial
76802 San Juan del Rio, Querétaro
Mexico
  Phone: (52) 427 271 9600/13/21
  Fax: (52) 427 271 9694
  Web Address: www.cartonesponderosa.com.mx
Personnel:
Pres. & Gen. Dir.: Don Mario Vázquez Raña
Phone: (52) 427 271 9600
Fax: (52) 427 271 9694
Pres., Paper Division: Antonio Rodríguez Demeneghi
Phone: (52) 427 27 196 00
Fax: (52) 427 271 9694
Email: arodem@carpo.com.mx
General Mill Coordinator: Jose Saul Guzmán Espinosa
Phone: (52) 427 27 196 00
Fax: (52) 427 271 9694
Email: sguzman@carpo.com.mx
Manuf. Mgr.: Gustavo Guillén Bear
Phone: (52) 427 27 196 00
Fax: (52) 427 271 9694
Email: gguillen@carpo.com.mx
Sls. Dir.: Agustín Serrano
Phone: (52) 427 27 196 00
Fax: (52) 427 271 9694
Email: aserrano@carpo.com.mx
Ecofibers Coordinator: José Luis Michel
Phone: (52) 427 27 196 00
Fax: (52) 427 271 9694
Email: jlmichel@carpo.com.mx
Tech. Mgr.: Gustavo Maldonado Ramos
Phone: (52) 427 27 196 00
Fax: (52) 427 271 9694
Email: gmaldonado@carpo.com.mx
Total Employees at this Location: 409
Type of Operation: Paperboard mill
Pulp Grades and Capacities:
Total pulp capacity: 207,846 mt/y
Recycled Pulping: 207,846 mt/y
Pulp Mill Data:
Bleach Plant Systems: 1
Recycled Deinked Pulping System, Type: DIP
Recycled Fiber Treatment Lines:
Flotation deinking lines: 1
Recycled packaging pulping lines: 1
Paper/Paperboard Grades and Capacities:
Total paper and paperboard capacity: 239,904 mt/y
Boxboard/cartonboard: 239,904 mt/y
Paper and Paperboard Mill Data:
Stock Preparation:
Pulpers: 4
Refiners: 8
Paper Machines: 1
No. 1, fourdrinier (3), total capacity 239,904 mt/y, Trim width 3.3 m, Boxboard/cartonboard
Coating Machines: 1
PM 7, total capacity 228,500 mt/y., on machine
Finishing Equipment:
Rewinders: 3
Sheeters: 5
Energy Data:
Power boilers: 1
Combustion turbines: 3 at 19.5 MW
Steam turbines: 1 at 1.5 MW
Electrical demand for mill: 432 MWh/D

ⓘFábricas de Papel Potosí, S.A. de C.V.
Ownership: 50% by Gerardo Lopez, 50% by Isidro Lopez
Camino al Olivo, 15
05100 Lomas de Vistahermosa, México, D.F.
Mexico
  Phone: (52) 55 5246 3230
  Email: asistente_df@papelpotosi.com
  Web Address: www.papelpotosi.com
Personnel:
Pres. & CEO: Gerardo López Aramburu

Phone: (52) 55 5246 3230
Email: glopez@papelpotosi.com
Dir.: Esteban Lopez Ancona
Phone: (52) 55 5246 3230
Email: direccion2@papelpotosi.com
Account Executive: Sonia Arcos Guerrero
Phone: (52) 55 5246 3230
Head of Budget and Cost: Isaac Rodas
Phone: (52) 55 5246 3230
Prod. Mgr.: Carlos Barraza
Phone: (52) 55 5246 3230
Total Employees of Company: 580
Mill Locations:
Fábricas de Papel Potosí, S.A. de C.V., Potosí Mill, Eje 120 No. 315, Zona Industrial 1a. Sección, 78090 San Luis Potosí, Mexico, Capacity: 18,564 mt/y, (Paper mill)
Phone: (52) 444 824 5910
Fax: (52) 444 824 6224
Email: mcavazos@papelpotosi.com

⓪Fábricas de Papel Potosí, S.A. de C.V.
Potosí Mill
Eje 120 No. 315, Zona Industrial 1a. Sección
78090 San Luis Potosí, San Luis Potosi
Mexico
Phone: (52) 444 824 5910
Fax: (52) 444 824 6224
Email: mcavazos@papelpotosi.com
Web Address: www.papelpotosi.com
Personnel:
Pres. & CEO: Gerardo López Aramburu
Phone: (52) 5246 3230 231
Fax: (52) 5246 3230 260
Proj. Mgr.: Eduardo J. Cabal
Phone: (52) 444 824 5910 Ext. 580
Fax: (52) 444 824 6224
Email: ecabal@papelpotosi.com
Proj. & Maint. Mgr.: Sergio A. Lopez
Phone: (52) 444 824 5910 Ext. 550
Fax: (52) 444 824 6224
Email: slopez@papelpotosi.com
Sec.: Margarita Cavazos
Phone: (52) 444 824 5910 Ext. 512
Fax: (52) 444 824 6224
Email: mcavasos@papelpotosi.com
Maint. Eng. (Electric & Instriment): Eugenio Martínez
Phone: (52) 444 824 5910 Ext. 552
Fax: (52) 444 824 6224
Email: emartinez@papelpotosi.com
Prod. Mgr.: Alberto Rodríguez Sandoval
Phone: (52) 444 824 5910 Ext. 553
Fax: (52) 444 824 6224
Email: arodriguez@papelpotosi.com
Total Employees at this Location: 100
Type of Operation: Paper mill
Pulp Grades and Capacities:
Total pulp capacity: 20,003 mt/y
Recycled Pulping: 20,003 mt/y
Pulp Mill Data:
Bleach Plant Systems: 1
Recycled Pulping System, Type: DIP
Recycled Fiber Treatment Lines:
Flotation deinking lines: 1
Paper/Paperboard Grades and Capacities:
Total paper and paperboard capacity: 18,564 mt/y
Tissue: 18,564 mt/y
Paper and Paperboard Mill Data:
Stock Preparation:
Pulpers: 2
Refiners: 2
Paper Machines: 2
No. 1, fourdrinier, total capacity 9,996 mt/y, Trim width 3.4 m, Tissue, Uncoated woodfree/freesheet
No. 2, fourdrinier, total capacity 8,568 mt/y, Trim width 3 m, Tissue, Uncoated woodfree/freesheet
Finishing Equipment:
Winders: 4 at 35,000 mt/y
Energy Data:
Power boilers: 2
Electrical demand for mill: 79 MWh/D

⓪ⓜPapelera Industrial Potosina S.A. de C.V.
San Luis Potosi Mill
Ownership: 100% by Grupo Gondi S.A. de C.V.
Zona Ind. Eje 114, No. 230 Col. Zona Industrial
78090 San Luis Potosi, San Luis Potosi
Mexico
Phone: (52) 444 8 248 484
Fax: (52) 444 8 248 184
Email: edemenegh@pipslp.com
Web Address: www.papelera.educaredvirtual.com
Personnel:
Man. Dir.: Eugenio Lanz Ortiz
Phone: (52) 444 8 248 484
Fax: (52) 444 8 248 184
Controller: Martha Cruz
Phone: (52) 444 8 248 484
Fax: (52) 444 8 248 184
Ind. Rel. Dir.: Lourdes de la Rosa Castillo
Phone: (52) 444 8 248 484
Fax: (52) 444 8 248 184
Oper. Dir.: Eugenio de Meneghi
Phone: (52) 444 8 248 484
Fax: (52) 444 8 248 184
Tech. Mgr.: Guillermo González O.
Phone: (52) 444 8 248 484
Fax: (52) 444 8 248 184
Total Employees of Company: 170
Total Employees at this Location: 150
Type of Operation: Paper mill
Pulp Grades and Capacities:
Total pulp capacity: 58,011 mt/y
Recycled Pulping: 71,103 mt/y
Pulp Mill Data:
Recycled Fiber Treatment Lines:
Pulpers: 1 at 63,100
Paper/Paperboard Grades and Capacities:
Total paper and paperboard capacity: 57,120 mt/y
Corrugating medium/fluting: 57,120 mt/y
Paper and Paperboard Mill Data:
Paper Machines: 1
No. 1, fourdrinier, total capacity 57,120 mt/y, Trim width 2.65 m, Corrugating medium/fluting
Energy Data:
Power boilers
Electrical demand for mill: 99 MWh/D

⓪Procter & Gamble de Mexico S. de R.L. de C.V.
Ownership: 100% by Procter & Gamble Paper Products Co.
Loma Florida 32, Lomas de Vista Hermosa, Delegación Cuajimalpa
05100 Mexico, México, D.F.
Mexico
Phone: (52) 52 5724 2000/2075
Fax: (52) 52 5724 2024/2254
Email: oviedo.jl@pg.com
Web Address: www.pg.com.mx
Personnel:
Corporate Dir.: Claudia Herrera Moro
Phone: (52) 55 5724 2075/2000
Fax: (52) 55 5724 2254
Email: herreramoro.c@pg.com
Finan. & Purch. Dir.: Alexandro Diaz
Phone: (52) 55 5724 2075/2000
Fax: (52) 55 5724 2254
Sls./Mktg. Dir.: Isaac Figueroa
Phone: (52) 55 5724 2075/2000
Fax: (52) 55 5724 2254
Data Proc./Sys. Mgr.: Jorge Hernandez
Phone: (52) 55 5724 2075/2000
Fax: (52) 55 5724 2254
Corp. Dir. Sec.: Ms. Janet Skinfill
Phone: (52) ex: 2284
Email: skinfill.j@pg.com
Total Employees of Company: 660
Mill Locations:
Procter & Gamble de Mexico S. de R.L. de C.V., Apizaco Mill, Km. 115.5, Carretera Los Reyes Zacatepec, 90300 Apizaco, Mexico, Capacity: 74,970 mt/y, (Paper mill)
Phone: (52) 1 241 41 899 70
Email: tinajero@pg.com, reyes.mg.4@pg.com, lira.r.1@pg.com

ⓜProcter & Gamble de Mexico S. de R.L. de C.V.
Apizaco Mill
Ownership: 100% by Procter & Gamble Paper Products Co.
Km. 115.5, Carretera Los Reyes Zacatepec
90300 Apizaco, Tlaxacala
Mexico
Phone: (52) 1 241 41 899 70
Email: tinajero@pg.com,
reyes.mg.4@pg.com,
lira.r.1@pg.com
Web Address: www.pg.com.mx
Personnel:
Paper Mill Mgr.: Ing. Ricardo Peñafiel
Phone: (52) 1 241 41 899 70
Email: penafiel.r@pg.com
Converting Plt. Mgr.: Ing. Fernando del Río
Phone: (52) 1 241 41 899 70
Email: delrio.f@pg.com
Environ. Dir.: Ing. Carlos Segura
Phone: (52) 1 241 41 899 70
Email: segura.c@pg.com
Total Employees at this Location: 245
Type of Operation: Paper mill
Pulp Grades and Capacities:
Total pulp capacity: 80,576 mt/y
Recycled Pulping: 80,576 mt/y
Pulp Mill Data:
Bleach Plant Systems: 1
Recycled Pulping System, Type: DIP
Recycled Fiber Treatment Lines:
Flotation deinking lines: 1
Paper/Paperboard Grades and Capacities:
Total paper and paperboard capacity: 74,970 mt/y
Tissue: 74,970 mt/y
Paper and Paperboard Mill Data:
Paper Machines: 3
No. 1, Yankee dryer, total capacity 14,994 mt/y, Trim width 2.6 m, Tissue, Uncoated woodfree/freesheet
No. 2, Yankee dryer, total capacity 24,276 mt/y, Trim width 2.4 m, Tissue, Uncoated woodfree/freesheet
No. 3, Yankee dryer, total capacity 35,700 mt/y, Trim width 3.6 m, Tissue
Energy Data:
Power boilers
Combustion turbines: 1 at 45 MW
Electrical demand for mill: 361 MWh/D

⓪ⓜPronal, Productora Nacional de Papel, S.A. de C.V.
Pronal Mill
Ownership: 100% by Organización Editorial Mexicana
Km. 58 Carr. S. L. Potosi a San Felipe Guanajuato.
79500 Ejido San Miguel, Municipio Villa de Reyes, San Luis Potosi
Mexico
Phone: (52) 485 86 109 12/11
Fax: (52) 485 86 109 89
Email: ncervantes@pronal.com.mx
Personnel:
Pres.: Mario Vazquez Rana
Phone: (52) 485 861 0905
Mill Dir.: Edgar Ignacio Reyes
Phone: (52) 485 86 109 12/11
Finan. & Admin. Mgr.: Angel T. Oros Ovalle
Phone: (52) 485 86 109 12/11
Eng. Mgr.: René Guerrero
Phone: (52) 485 86 109 12/11
Total Employees of Company: 840

Mexico

Total Employees at this Location: 400
Type of Operation: Paper mill
Pulp Grades and Capacities:
  Total pulp capacity: 154,708 mt/y
  Recycled Pulping: 154,708 mt/y
Pulp Mill Data:
  Bleach Plant Systems: 2
  No. 1 Capacity 77,000 admt/y
  No. 2, Sequence: HS, Capacity 69,000 admt/y
  Recycled Fiber Treatment Lines:
  Flotation deinking lines: 1
Paper/Paperboard Grades and Capacities:
  Total paper and paperboard capacity: 149,940 mt/y
  Newsprint: 149,940 mt/y
Paper and Paperboard Mill Data:
  Stock Preparation:
  Pulpers: 3
Paper Machines: 2
  No. 1, Bel-Baie II, total capacity 80,325 mt/y, Trim width 5.4 m, Newsprint
  No. 2, Bel-Baie II, total capacity 69,615 mt/y, Trim width 6.1 m, Newsprint
Finishing Equipment:
  Rewinders: 2
Energy Data:
  HRSG boiler: 3
  Combustion turbines: 3 at 12.68 MW
  Electrical demand for mill: 397 MWh/D

ⓀⓂPROPASA - Productora de Papel S.A. de C.V.
San Nicolas de los Garza Mill
Ownership: 94% by Familia Garza Elizondo, 6% by Bio-PAPPEL Kraft
Via Matamoros, Km. 7, Estación Lagrange, Aptdo. Postal. 443
66490 San Nicolas de los Garza, Nuevo León
Mexico
  Phone: (52) 81 8158 90 00/05
  Fax: (52) 81 8158 90 81/84
  Email: atencionalpublico@productoradepapel.com, ventas@productoradepapel.com
  Web Address: www.productoradepapel.com/
Personnel:
  Gen. Dir.: Ing Juan Carlos Fuzy
  Phone: (52) 81 8158 90 00/05
  Fax: (52) 81 8158 90 81/84
  Email: jfuzy@productoradepapel.com
  Commer. Dir.: José Antonio Esquivel
  Phone: (52) 81 8158 90 00/05
  Fax: (52) 81 8158 90 81/84
  Logist. Mgr.: José Lira
  Phone: (52) 81 8158 90 00/05
  Fax: (52) 81 8158 90 81/84
  Proj. Mgr.: Guillermo Soto
  Phone: (52) 81 8158 90 00/05
  Fax: (52) 81 8158 90 81/84
  Email: gsoto@productoradepapel.com
  Purch. Mgr.: Juan Carlos Zaldo
  Phone: (52) 81 8158 90 00/05
  Fax: (52) 81 8158 90 81/84
  Sls. Mgr.: Teofilo Fernandez
  Phone: (52) 81 8158 90 00/05
  Fax: (52) 81 8158 90 81/84
  Email: tfernandez@productoradepapel.com
Total Employees of Company: 372
Total Employees at this Location: 225
Type of Operation: Pulp mill, Paper mill
Pulp Grades and Capacities:
  Total pulp capacity: 185,294 mt/y
  Recycled Pulping: 185,294 mt/y
Pulp Mill Data:
  Recycled Fiber Treatment Lines:
  Recycled packaging pulping lines: 1
Paper/Paperboard Grades and Capacities:
  Total paper and paperboard capacity: 189,210 mt/y
  Linerboard: 27,132 mt/y
  Corrugating medium/fluting: 29,988 mt/y
  Boxboard/cartonboard: 132,090 mt/y

Paper and Paperboard Mill Data:
  Stock Preparation:
  Pulpers: 4
  Refiners: 12
Paper Machines: 3
  No. 1, total capacity 27,132 mt/y, Trim width 2 m, Corrugating medium/fluting
  No. 2, total capacity 29,988 mt/y, Trim width 2 m, Linerboard, Corrugating medium/fluting
  No. 3, total capacity 132,090 mt/y, Trim width 3.3 m, Boxboard/cartonboard
Coating Machines: 3
  No. 1, off machine
  No. 2, off machine
  No. 3, off machine
Finishing Equipment:
  Rewinders: 3
Energy Data:
  Power boilers: 3
  Combustion turbines: 2 at 30.0 MW
  Electrical demand for mill: 231 MWh/D

ⓀⓂQF MEX, S.A. de C.V.
Iztapalapa Mill
Canal de Garay 485, Col. Cerro de la Estrella
09850 Iztapalapa, México, D.F.
Mexico
  Phone: (52) 55 5426 7562/ 7621/6164
  Fax: (52) 55 5426 6112
  Email: direccion@qfmex.com.mx, compras@qfmex.com.mx
  Web Address: qfmex.com
Personnel:
  Gen. Mgr.: Ing. Jesús Monroy
  Phone: (52) 55 5426 7621/7442
  Fax: (52) 55 5426 6112
  Finan. Mgr.: C.P. Pedro Fuente
  Phone: (52) 55 5426 7621/7442
  Fax: (52) 55 5426 6112
  Mill Mgr.: Ing. Jesus Olivares Vite
  Phone: (52) 55 5426 7621/7442
  Fax: (52) 55 5426 6112
  Tech. Mgr.: Ing. Guadalupe Rodriguez
  Phone: (52) 55 5426 7621/7442
  Fax: (52) 55 5426 6112
  Chief Eng.: Ing. Adolfo Anaya Villa
  Phone: (52) 55 5426 7621/7442
  Fax: (52) 55 5426 6112
  Purch. Mgr.: Ms. Margarita Lujan
  Phone: (52) 55 5426 7621/7442
  Fax: (52) 55 5426 6112
Total Employees of Company: 100
Total Employees at this Location: 18
Type of Operation: Paper mill
Pulp Mill Data:
  Recycled Fiber Treatment Lines:
  Pulpers: 3 at 400 admt/y
  Pulp Dryers:
  Flash dryers 19
Paper/Paperboard Grades and Capacities:
  Total paper and paperboard capacity: 13,000 mt/y
  Boxboard/cartonboard: 13,000 mt/y
Paper and Paperboard Mill Data:
  Stock Preparation:
  Pulpers: 3
  Refiners: 5
Paper Machines: 2
  No. 1, fourdrinier, Trim width 2 m
  No. 2, multi-former, Trim width 2.5 m
Finishing Equipment:
  Rewinders: 1
  Sheeters: 2

ⓀⓂFábrica de Papel San Francisco S.A. de C.V. (FAPSA)
Mexicali Mill
Ownership: 100% by Garcia Franco Group

Boulevard Lopez Mateos Km. 5.5, Centro Industrial Margar
21360 Mexicali, BCA
Mexico
  Phone: (52) 686 565 0127
  Email: fapsaweb@papelsanfrancisco.com
  Web Address: www.fapsa.com.mx
Personnel:
  Exec. Chmn.: Mario A. Garcia Franco
  Phone: (52) 68 6561 8341
  Fax: (52) 68 6561 7902
  Gen. Dir.: Abelardo Garcia
  Phone: (52) 68 6561 8341
  Fax: (52) 68 6561 7902
  Email: alberadog@fapsa.co.mx
  CIO: Sergio Colunga
  Phone: (52) 68 6561 8341
  Fax: (52) 68 6561 7902
  Sls. & Mktg. Dir.: Juan Jose Helu Villavicencio
  Phone: (52) 68 6561 8341
  Fax: (52) 68 6561 7902
  Prod. Mgr.: Julio César Rodríguez Lárraga
  Phone: (52) 68 6561 8341
  Fax: (52) 68 6561 7902
Total Employees of Company: 420
Total Employees at this Location: 394
Type of Operation: Pulp mill, Paper mill
Pulp Grades and Capacities:
  Total pulp capacity: 147,744 mt/y
  Recycled Pulping: 147,744 mt/y
Pulp Mill Data:
  Bleach Plant Systems: 1
  Recycled Pulping System, Type: DIP
  Recycled Fiber Treatment Lines:
  Flotation deinking lines: 1 at 130,000
Paper/Paperboard Grades and Capacities:
  Total paper and paperboard capacity: 137,802 mt/y
  Tissue: 137,802 mt/y
Paper and Paperboard Mill Data:
  Stock Preparation:
  Pulpers: 4
  Refiners: 3
Paper Machines: 5
  No. 1, crescent former, total capacity 17,850 mt/y, Trim width 2.4 m, Tissue, Uncoated woodfree/freesheet
  No. 3, crescent former, total capacity 29,988 mt/y, Trim width 2.7 m, Tissue, Uncoated woodfree/freesheet
  No. 4, crescent former, total capacity 29,988 mt/y, Trim width 2.6 m, Tissue
  No. 5, crescent former, total capacity 29,988 mt/y, Trim width 2.6 m, Tissue
  No. 6, OptiFormer, total capacity 29,988 mt/y, Trim width 2.7 m, Tissue
Energy Data:
  Power boilers: 1
  Steam turbines: 1
  Electrical demand for mill: 514 MWh/D

ⓀFábrica de Papel San José S.A. de C.V.
Km. 20.5 Carr. Mexico-Texcoco
56400 Los Reyes Acaquilpan, México, D.F.
Mexico
  Phone: (52) 5 58567647, 58550243, 58553766
  Fax: (52) 5 58553677
  Email: ventas@terra.com.mx
  Web Address: www.sajosa.com.mx
Personnel:
  Gen. Dir.: Juan Manuel Roja Gutiérrez
  Phone: (52) 58567647
  Fax: (52) 58553677
  Prod. Dir.: Pedro García Candás
  Phone: (52) 58567647
  Fax: (52) 58553677
  Sls. Mgr.: Tomas García Candás
  Phone: (52) 58567647
  Fax: (52) 58553677
  Admin. Mgr: Elvira U Elvira U
  Phone: (52) 58567647
  Fax: (52) 58553677

Mexico

Mill Locations:
Fábrica de Papel San José S.A. de C.V., Los Reyes Acaquilpan Mill, Km. 20.5 Carr. Mexico-Texcoco, 56400 Los Reyes Acaquilpan, Mexico, Capacity: 15,000 mt/y, (Paper mill)
Phone: (52) 5 58567647, 58550243, 58553766
Fax: (52) 5 58553677
Email: ventas@terra.com.mx

ⓜFábrica de Papel San José S.A. de C.V.
Los Reyes Acaquilpan Mill
Km. 20.5 Carr. Mexico-Texcoco
56400 Los Reyes Acaquilpan, México, D.F.
Mexico
  Phone: (52) 5 58567647, 58550243, 58553766
  Fax: (52) 5 58553677
  Email: ventas@terra.com.mx
  Web Address: www.sajosa.com.mx
Personnel:
  Gen. Dir.: Ing. Juan Manuel Roja Gutiérrez
  Phone: (52) 5 58567647, 58550243, 58553766
  Fax: (52) 58553677
  Prod. Dir.: Ing. Pedro García Candás
  Phone: (52) 5 58567647, 58550243, 58553766
  Fax: (52) 58553677
  Sls. Mgr.: Ing. Tomas García Candás
  Phone: (52) 5 58567647, 58550243, 58553766
  Fax: (52) 58553677
Total Employees at this Location: 120
Type of Operation: Paper mill
Pulp Grades and Capacities:
  Total pulp capacity: 51,100 mt/y
Paper/Paperboard Grades and Capacities:
  Total paper and paperboard capacity: 15,000 mt/y
  Uncoated woodfree/freesheet: 15,000 mt/y
Paper and Paperboard Mill Data:
Paper Machines: 2
  No. 1, fourdrinier, Trim width 1.9 m, Uncoated woodfree/freesheet
  No. 2, fourdrinier, Trim width 1.9 m, Uncoated woodfree/freesheet

ⓜEmpaques Modernos San Pablo S.A. de C.V.
Tlalnepantla Mill
Ownership: 100% by Grupo Gondi S.A. de C.V.
Prol. Poniente N.150, Esq. Avenida de las Granjas S/N,
Col. San Pablo Xalpa
54090 Tlalnepantla, Edo. de México
Mexico
  Phone: (52) 55 5318 8800
  Fax: (52) 55 5382 1092
  Email: info@grupogondi.com
  Web Address: www.grupogondi.com
Personnel:
  Prod. Mgr., Boxes: Ing. Enrique Ruiz
  Phone: (52) 55 5318 8800
  Fax: (52) 55 5382 1092
  Email: enrique.ruiz@grupogondi.com
  Prod. Mgr., Paper: Ing. Gabriel González
  Phone: (52) 55 5318 8800
  Fax: (52) 55 5382 1092
  Email: gabriel.gonzalez@grupogondi.com
  Sls & Mktg Mgr.: Alejandro Melendez
  Phone: (52) 55 5318 8800
  Fax: (52) 55 5382 1092
  Email: alejandro.melendez@grupogondi.com
  Gen. Dir. Sec.: Ms. Maria Isabel Aguilar Hernandez
  Phone: (52) 55 30035200
  Fax: (52) 55 30035205
  Email: isabel.aguilar@grupogondi.com
Total Employees at this Location: 200
Type of Operation: Paper mill, Paperboard mill
Pulp Grades and Capacities:
  Total pulp capacity: 182,950 mt/y
  Recycled Pulping: 182,950 mt/y
Pulp Mill Data:
Recycled Fiber Treatment Lines:
  Recycled packaging pulping lines: 1
Paper/Paperboard Grades and Capacities:
  Total paper and paperboard capacity: 179,928 mt/y
  Linerboard: 120,309 mt/y
  Corrugating medium/fluting: 59,619 mt/y
Paper and Paperboard Mill Data:
Paper Machines: 3
  No. 1, multi-cylinder, total capacity 19,992 mt/y, Trim width 2.14 m, Linerboard, Corrugating medium/fluting
  No. 2, fourdrinier, total capacity 59,976 mt/y, Trim width 4.16 m, Linerboard
  No. 3, fourdrinier, total capacity 99,960 mt/y, Trim width 4.65 m, Linerboard, Corrugating medium/fluting
Energy Data:
  Power boilers: 1
  Steam turbines: 3 at 15 MW
  Electrical demand for mill: 307 MWh/D

ⓜSCA Consumidor México y Centroamérica S.A. de C.V.
Sahagun Tissue Mill
Ownership: 100% by SCA - Svenska Cellulosa Aktiebolaget
Carretera Federal Ciudad Sahagún – Emiliano Zapata Km. 6.5, Comunidad Irolo, Municipio
43991 Tepeapulco, Hidalgo
Mexico
  Phone: (52) 79 1913 5456
  Email: comunicacion.scamexico@sca.com
  Web Address: www.sca.com
Personnel:
  Plt. Mgr.: Roberto Deleón
  Phone: (52) 79 1913 9144
  Email: roberto.deleon@sca.com
Type of Operation: Paper mill
Pulp Grades and Capacities:
  Total pulp capacity: 60,908 mt/y
  Recycled Pulping: 60,908 mt/y
Pulp Mill Data:
Bleach Plant Systems: 1
  Recycled Pulping System, Type: DIP
Recycled Fiber Treatment Lines:
  Flotation deinking lines: 1
Paper/Paperboard Grades and Capacities:
  Total paper and paperboard capacity: 57,120 mt/y
  Tissue: 57,120 mt/y
Paper and Paperboard Mill Data:
Paper Machines: 1
  No. 1, crescent former, total capacity 57,120 mt/y, Trim width 5.4 m, Tissue
Energy Data:
  Power boilers
  Electrical demand for mill: 247 MWh/D

ⓗSCA Consumidor México y Centroamérica S.A. de C.V.
Ownership: 100% by SCA - Svenska Cellulosa Aktiebolaget
Ave. Javier Barros Sierra No. 555, 5° Piso, Col. Santa Fe, Delegación Alvaro Obregón
01210 México, México, D.F.
Mexico
  Phone: (52) 52 55 5002 8600
  Fax: (52) 52 55 5002 8600
  Email: comunicacion.scamexico@sca.com
  Web Address: www.scamexico.com
Personnel:
  Pres. Unit: Don Lewis
  Phone: (52) 52 55 5002 8600
  Fax: (52) 52 55 5002 8600
  Dir. Gen.: Pablo Fuentes
  Phone: (52) 52 55 5002 8600
  Fax: (52) 52 55 5002 8600
  Email: comunicacion.scamexico@sca.com
Mill Locations:
SCA Consumidor México y Centroamérica S.A. de C.V., Sahagun Tissue Mill, Carretera Federal Ciudad Sahagún – Emiliano Zapata Km. 6.5, Comunidad Irolo, Municipio, 43991 Tepeapulco, Mexico, Capacity: 57,120 mt/y, (Paper mill)
Phone: (52) 79 1913 5456
Email: comunicacion.scamexico@sca.com
SCA Consumidor México y Centroamérica S.A. de C.V., Monterrey Tissue Mill, Avenida San Nicolás #300, Colonia Cuauthémoc, 66450 San Nicolas de los Garza, Mexico, Capacity: 59,976 mt/y, (Paper mill)
Phone: (52) 81 5000 7300
Fax: (52) 81 8 305 7317
Email: comunicacion.scamexico@sca.com
SCA Consumidor México y Centroamérica S.A. de C.V., Uruapan Tissue Mill, Boulevard Industrial No. 3201, Col. La Cofradía, 60221 Uruapan, Mexico, Capacity: 34,986 mt/y, (Pulp mill, Paper mill)
Phone: (52) 452 527 5200
Fax: (52) 452 527 5249
Email: comunicacion.scamexico@sca.com

ⓜSCA Consumidor México y Centroamérica S.A. de C.V.
Monterrey Tissue Mill
Ownership: 100% by SCA - Svenska Cellulosa Aktiebolaget
Avenida San Nicolás #300, Colonia Cuauthémoc
66450 San Nicolas de los Garza, Nuevo León
Mexico
  Phone: (52) 81 5000 7300
  Fax: (52) 81 8 305 7317
  Email: comunicacion.scamexico@sca.com
  Web Address: www.scamexico.com
Personnel:
  Mill Mgr.: Ing. Miguel A. Franco J.
  Phone: (52) 81 5000 7301
  Fax: (52) 81 5000 7303
  Email: miguel.franco@sca.com
  Converting Mgr.: Ing. Jorge A. Badillo
  Phone: (52) 81 5000 7304
  Fax: (52) 81 5000 7317
  Email: jorge.badillo@sca.com
  Snr. Sourcing Mgr.: Ing. José Carlos Rodriguez
  Phone: (52) 81 5000 7325
  Fax: (52) 81 5000 7317
  Email: jose.rodriguez@sca.com
  Admin. & Finan. Mgr.: C.P. Luis Enrique Rodriguez
  Phone: (52) 81 5000 7314
  Fax: (52) 81 5000 7317
  Email: luis.rodriguez@sca.com
  Safety, Health & Environ. Mgr.: Juan Muñoz
  Phone: (52) 81 5000 7345
  Fax: (52) 81 5000 7317
  Email: juan.munoz@sca.com
Total Employees at this Location: 200
Type of Operation: Paper mill
Pulp Grades and Capacities:
  Total pulp capacity: 64,076 mt/y
  Recycled Pulping: 64,076 mt/y
Pulp Mill Data:
Pulp Lines: 2
Bleach Plant Systems: 2
  Oxidative, Type: H_2O_2+NaOH
  Reductive, Type: Borol+Bisulfide
Recycled Fiber Treatment Lines:
  Flotation deinking lines: 2 at 60,995 admt/y
  Pulpers: 1 at 50,000 admt/y
  Pulpers: 1 at 85,410
  Recycled packaging pulping lines: 1 at 16,425 admt/y
  Washing deinking lines: 2 at 50,000 admt/y
Paper/Paperboard Grades and Capacities:
  Total paper and paperboard capacity: 59,976 mt/y
  Tissue: 59,976 mt/y
Paper and Paperboard Mill Data:
Stock Preparation:
  Pulpers: 2
  Refiners: 4
Paper Machines: 2
  No. 2, C-wrap, total capacity 24,276 mt/y, Trim width 3.3 m, Tissue, Uncoated woodfree/freesheet

Mexico

No. 3, crescent former, total capacity 35,700 mt/y, Trim width 3.5 m, Tissue
Finishing Equipment:
Rewinders: 1 at 5,000 mt/y
Energy Data:
Power boilers: 1
Electrical demand for mill: 205 MWh/D

ⓂSCA Consumidor México y Centroamérica S.A. de C.V.
Uruapan Tissue Mill
Ownership: 100% by SCA - Svenska Cellulosa Aktiebolaget
Boulevard Industrial No. 3201, Col. La Cofradía
60221 Uruapan, Michoacán
Mexico
Mailing Address: Aptdo. Postal 193, 60000 Uruapan, Mexico
Phone: (52) 452 527 5200
Fax: (52) 452 527 5249
Email: comunicacion.scamexico@sca.com
Web Address: www.sca.com
Personnel:
Mill Mgr.: Ing. Víctor Hernandez
Phone: (52) 452 527 5250
Fax: (52) 452 527 5252
Email: victor.hernandez@sca.com
Prod. Mgr.: Ing. Ramón Guajardo
Phone: (52) 452 527 5286
Fax: (52) 452 527 5249
Email: ramon.guajardo@sca.com
Tech. Mgr.: Ing. Alfredo Juárez
Phone: (52) 452 527 5280
Fax: (52) 452 527 5249
Email: alfredo.juarez@sca.com
Site Controller: CP Carlos Garibay
Phone: (52) 524 525 275 244
Email: carlos.garibay@sca.com
Tech. Mgr.: Ing. Alfredo Juarez
Phone: (52) 452 527 5280
Email: alfredo.juarez@sca.com
HR Mgr.: Lic. Jorge Fernandez
Phone: (52) 452 527 5260
Fax: (52) 452 527 5249
Total Employees at this Location: 125
Type of Operation: Pulp mill, Paper mill
Pulp Grades and Capacities:
Total pulp capacity: 37,488 mt/y
Recycled Pulping: 37,488 mt/y
Pulp Mill Data:
Bleach Plant Systems: 1
Recycled Pulping System, Type: DIP
Recycled Fiber Treatment Lines:
Flotation deinking lines: 1 at 54,000 admt/y
Pulpers: 1 at 77,143 admt/y
Washing deinking lines: 1 at 54,000 admt/y
Paper/Paperboard Grades and Capacities:
Total paper and paperboard capacity: 34,986 mt/y
Tissue: 34,986 mt/y
Paper and Paperboard Mill Data:
Stock Preparation:
Pulpers: 2
Refiners: 1
Paper Machines: 1
No. 1, crescent former, total capacity 34,986 mt/y, Trim width 3.5 m, Tissue
Energy Data:
Power boilers: 3
Combustion turbines at 10 MW
Electrical demand for mill: 176 MWh/D

ⒽGrupo Papelero Scribe, S.A. de C.V.
Company is for sale (Mexican paper and packaging producer Bio Pappel has signed an agreement to acquire 100% of the shares of Grupo Papelero Scribe. The transaction is subject to the approval of the Mexican antitrust authorities.)
Calle José Luis Lagrange 103, Piso 12, Col. Los Morales Polanco Del Miguel Hidalgo
11510 Mexico, México, D.F.
Mexico
Phone: (52) 55 5282 7400
Fax: (52) 55 5282 7490
Email: jibargue@scribe.com.mx
Web Address: www.grupopapeleroscribe.com, www.scribe.com.mx
Personnel:
CEO: Carlos Sacal
Phone: (52) 55 5282 7400
Fax: (52) 55 5282 7504
Email: carlos.sacal@cscribe.com.mx
VP Sls.: Juan Orozco
Phone: (52) 55 5282 7400
Fax: (52) 55 5282 7504
Email: juan.orozco@cscribe.com.mx
Sls Mgr.: Jorge Valdes
Phone: (52) 55 5282 7400
Fax: (52) 55 5282 7504
Email: jorge.valdes@cscribe.com.mx
Dir. Legal & HR: Arturo Luiz Perez Courtade
Phone: (52) 55 5282 7400
Fax: (52) 55 5282 7504
Email: arturo.perez@cscribe.com.mx
Corp. Purch. Mgr.: Javier Ibarguengoitia
Phone: (52) 55 5282 7400
Fax: (52) 55 5282 7504
Email: javier.ibarguengoitia@cscribe.com.mx
Finan. Dir.: Robert Payne
Phone: (52) 55 5282 7400
Fax: (52) 55 5282 7504
Email: robert.payne@cscribe.com.mx
National Mgr.: Alejandro Serina Carmona
Phone: (52) 55 5282 7400
Fax: (52) 55 5282 7504
Email: alejandro.carmona@cscribe.com.mx
Total Employees of Company: 1,500
Mill Locations:
Grupo Papelero Scribe, S.A. de C.V., Bajío Mill, Paseo central 2-A, Col. San Cayetano, 76800 San Juan del Rio, Mexico, Capacity: 142,800 mt/y, (Paper mill)
Phone: (52) 427 101 8300
Fax: (52) 427 101 8309
Grupo Papelero Scribe, S.A. de C.V., Morelia Mill, Domicilio Conocido, Ejido de Cointzio, Municipio de Morelia, 58341 Morelia, Mexico, Capacity: 60,690 mt/y, (Pulp mill, Paper mill)
Phone: (52) 443 322 3900
Fax: (52) 443 322 3903
Grupo Papelero Scribe, S.A. de C.V., Naucalpan Mill, Av. Uno # 9, Col. Alce Blanco, 53370 Naucalpan de Juarez, Mexico, Capacity: 35,700 mt/y, (Paper mill)
Phone: (52) 2629 9100
Fax: (52) 2629 9190
Grupo Papelero Scribe, S.A. de C.V., Orizaba Mill, Avenida San Juan 15, Escamela Iztaczoquitlan, 94450 Orizaba, Mexico, Capacity: 98,175 mt/y, (Paper mill)
Phone: (52) 272 728 3114/3100
Fax: (52) 272 728 3103

ⓂGrupo Papelero Scribe, S.A. de C.V.
Bajío Mill
Paseo central 2-A, Col. San Cayetano
76800 San Juan del Rio, Querétaro
Mexico
Phone: (52) 427 101 8300
Fax: (52) 427 101 8309
Web Address: www.grupopapeleroscribe.com, www.scribe.com.mx
Personnel:
Mill Mgr.: Enrique Barreto
Phone: (52) 427 101 8300
Fax: (52) 427 101 8309
Email: ebarreto@scribe.com.mx
Paper Mill Mgr.: Miguel Angel Villalobos
Phone: (52) 427 101 8300
Fax: (52) 427 101 8309
Email: mangelvillalobos@scribe.com.mx
Tech. Mgr.: Javier Corral
Phone: (52) 427 101 8300
Fax: (52) 427 101 8309
Email: jcorral@scribe.com.mx
Eng. Mgr.: Alejandro Blumenkron
Phone: (52) 427 101 8300
Fax: (52) 427 101 8309
Email: ablumenkron@scribe.com.mx
Assist. Mgr.: Nashieli Uribe Telez
Phone: (52) 427 101 8300
Fax: (52) 427 101 8309
Email: ntelez@scribe.com.mx
Total Employees at this Location: 989
Type of Operation: Paper mill
Paper/Paperboard Grades and Capacities:
Total paper and paperboard capacity: 142,800 mt/y
Uncoated woodfree/freesheet: 142,800 mt/y
Paper and Paperboard Mill Data:
Stock Preparation:
Pulpers:
Paper Machines: 1
No. 1, top former, total capacity 142,800 mt/y, Trim width 4.77 m, Uncoated woodfree/freesheet
Energy Data:
Power boilers: 3
Electrical demand for mill: 295 MWh/D

ⓂGrupo Papelero Scribe, S.A. de C.V.
Morelia Mill
Domicilio Conocido, Ejido de Cointzio, Municipio de Morelia
58341 Morelia, Michoacán
Mexico
Phone: (52) 443 322 3900
Fax: (52) 443 322 3903
Web Address: www.grupopapeleroscribe.com, www.scribe.com.mx
Personnel:
Mill Mgr.: German Castillo
Phone: (52) 443 322 3900
Paper Mill Mgr.: Fausto A. Cortes
Phone: (52) 443 322 3900
Pulp Mill Mgr.: Luis Estrada
Phone: (52) 443 322 3900
Tech. Mgr.: José Luis Mesa
Phone: (52) 443 322 3900
Maint. Mgr.: Eduardo Soltero
Phone: (52) 443 322 3900
Asst. Mill Mgr.: Maria del Socorro Ruiz Barajas
Phone: (52) 443 322 3900
Account Mgr.: Victor Hugo Tapia
Phone: (52) 443 322 3900
Forestry Mgr.: Ing. Rubén Abiña
Phone: (52) 443 322 3900
Total Employees at this Location: 229
Type of Operation: Pulp mill, Paper mill
Pulp Grades and Capacities:
Total pulp capacity: 50,719 mt/y
Chemical Pulp: 50,719 mt/y
Pulp Mill Data:
Chemical Pulping Systems:
Continuous digesters: 1
Pulp Lines: 1
Bleach Plant Systems: 1
Blanqueo, Type: Hardwood/Eucalyptus, Sequence: CEHH, Capacity 98,000 admt/y
Chemical Recovery Equipment:
Evaporator lines: 1
Recovery boilers: 1
Lime Kiln
Pulp Dryers:
Air Float dryers 1
Paper/Paperboard Grades and Capacities:
Total paper and paperboard capacity: 60,690 mt/y
Uncoated woodfree/freesheet: 60,690 mt/y
Paper and Paperboard Mill Data:
Stock Preparation:
Pulpers: 3
Refiners: 4
Paper Machines: 1
No. 21, twin-wire, total capacity 60,690 mt/y, Trim width 4.31 m, Uncoated woodfree/freesheet

Finishing Equipment:
Winders: 1 at 100,000 mt/y
Energy Data:
Power boilers: 1
Steam turbines: 2 at 3.5, 3.5 MW
Electrical demand for mill: 193 MWh/D

ⓂGrupo Papelero Scribe, S.A. de C.V.
Naucalpan Mill
Av. Uno # 9, Col. Alce Blanco
53370 Naucalpan de Juarez, Edo. de México
Mexico
 Phone: (52) 2629 9100
 Fax: (52) 2629 9190
 Web Address: www.grupopapeleroscribe.com, www.scribe.com.mx
Personnel:
CEO: Antonio Martinez Baez
 Phone: (52) 2629 9100
Plant Mgr.: René Aguilar Q.
 Phone: (52) 2629 9100
Purch. Mgr.: Javier Ibargüengoitia
 Phone: (52) 2629 9100
R&D Mgr.: Angela Lopez
 Phone: (52) 2629 9100
Tech. Mgr.: Israel Pacheco
 Phone: (52) 2629 9100
Ind. Rel. Mgr.: Alberto Modragón
 Phone: (52) 2629 9100
Total Employees at this Location: 225
Type of Operation: Paper mill
Paper/Paperboard Grades and Capacities:
Total paper and paperboard capacity: 35,700 mt/y
Uncoated woodfree/freesheet: 20,706 mt/y
Tissue: 14,994 mt/y
Paper and Paperboard Mill Data:
Stock Preparation:
Pulpers: 6
Paper Machines: 3
No. 1, fourdrinier, total capacity 15,351 mt/y, Trim width 2.4 m, Uncoated woodfree/freesheet
No. 2, Yankee dryer, total capacity 14,994 mt/y, Trim width 3 m, Tissue
No. 3, fourdrinier, total capacity 5,355 mt/y, Trim width 2.9 m, Uncoated woodfree/freesheet
Finishing Equipment:
Rewinders: 1
Energy Data:
Power boilers: 1
Electrical demand for mill: 37 MWh/D

ⓂGrupo Papelero Scribe, S.A. de C.V.
Orizaba Mill
Avenida San Juan 15, Escamela Iztaczoquitlan
94450 Orizaba, Veracruz
Mexico
 Phone: (52) 272 728 3114/3100
 Fax: (52) 272 728 3103
 Web Address: www.grupopapeleroscribe.com, www.scribe.com.mx
Personnel:
Mill Mgr.: Manuel Gamiño Mendez
 Phone: (52) 272 728 3114/3100
 Email: manuel.gamino@scribe.com.mx
Cost & Acct. Mgr.: Pedro Jacome Pintor
 Phone: (52) 272 728 3114/3100
Pulp Mill Mgr.: Ing. Carlos Mujíca
 Phone: (52) 272 728 3114/3100
Paper Mill Mgr.: José Rodriguez Lomeli
 Phone: (52) 272 728 3114/3100
Ind. Rel. Mgr.: Ing. Gonzalo Rosas
 Phone: (52) 272 728 3114/3100
Total Employees at this Location: 435
Type of Operation: Paper mill
Paper/Paperboard Grades and Capacities:
Total paper and paperboard capacity: 98,175 mt/y
Uncoated woodfree/freesheet: 98,175 mt/y
Paper and Paperboard Mill Data:
Stock Preparation:
Pulpers:
Paper Machines: 2
No. 4, fourdrinier, total capacity 43,554 mt/y, Trim width 3.1 m, Uncoated woodfree/freesheet
No. 7, fourdrinier, total capacity 54,621 mt/y, Trim width 3.8 m, Uncoated woodfree/freesheet
Coating Machines: 1
No. 1
Energy Data:
Power boilers: 6
Electrical demand for mill: 190 MWh/D

ⓂSmurfit Cartón y Papel de México S.A. de C.V.
Ownership: 100% by Smurfit Kappa Group
Jaime Balmes No.11 Torre D-7° Piso, Col. Los Morales Polanco
11510 Mexico, México, D.F.
Mexico
 Phone: (52) 55 57 29 23 00
 Fax: (52) 55 30 67 52 13
 Web Address: www.smurfitkappa.com.mx
Personnel:
CEO Paper and Board: Ing. Alain Baudant
 Phone: (52) 55 5729 2300
 Fax: (52) 55 3067 5233
CEO Corrugated & Converting: Roberto Villaquiran
 Phone: (52) 55 5729 2300
 Fax: (52) 55 3067 5233
COO: Tony Smurfit
 Phone: (52) 55 5729 2300
 Fax: (52) 55 3067 5233
VP Corrugated: Ing. Juan Michelsen
 Phone: (52) 55 5729 2300
 Fax: (52) 55 3067 5233
VP Finan.: CP. América Taracido
 Phone: (52) 55 5729 2300
 Fax: (52) 55 3067 5233
HR Dir.: Maria Teresa Zaldivar
 Phone: (52) 55 5729 2300
 Fax: (52) 55 3067 5233
Man. Dir.: Jose Luis Rivera Guerrero
 Phone: (52) 55 5729 2300
 Fax: (52) 55 3067 5233
HR Specialist: Myriam Mendoza
 Phone: (52) 55 5729 2300
 Fax: (52) 55 3067 5233
 Email: myriam.mendoza@smurfitkappa.com.mx
Total Employees of Company: 863
Total Employees at this Location: 63
Mill Locations:
Smurfit Cartón y Papel de México S.A. de C.V., Cerro Gordo Mill, Km. 15.5 Carr. Mexico-Laredo, 55540 Santa Clara Coatitla, Ecatepec de Morelos, Mexico, Capacity: 269,892 mt/y, (Pulp mill, Paperboard mill)
 Phone: (52) 55 5729 2300
 Fax: (52) 55 3067 5233
 Email: juancarlos.benavides@smurfitkappa.com.mx
Smurfit Cartón y Papel de México S.A. de C.V., Los Reyes Mill, Av. Presidente Juarez No 2030, 54090 Col. Los Reyes Iztacala, Tlalnepantla, Mexico, Capacity: 77,112 mt/y, (Paperboard mill)
 Phone: (52) 55 5729 2300
 Fax: (52) 55 3067 5204
 Email: josecarlos.nocetti@smurfitkappa.com.mx
Smurfit Cartón y Papel de México S.A. de C.V., Monterrey Mill, Carlos Salazar 1821 Oriente, 64010 Monterrey, BCA, Mexico, Capacity: 35,700 mt/y, (Paper mill, Paperboard mill)
 Phone: (52) 81 83545080
 Fax: (52) 81 83541990
 Email: ricardo.garcia@smurfitkappa.com.mx

ⓂSmurfit Cartón y Papel de México S.A. de C.V.
Cerro Gordo Mill
Ownership: 100% by Smurfit Kappa Group
Km. 15.5 Carr. Mexico-Laredo
55540 Santa Clara Coatitla, Ecatepec de Morelos, Edo. de México
Mexico
 Phone: (52) 55 5729 2300
 Fax: (52) 55 3067 5233
 Email: juancarlos.benavides@smurfitkappa.com.mx
 Web Address: www.smurfitkappa.com.mx
Personnel:
Prod Displays Division Mgr.: Juan Raul Martinez Nava
 Phone: (52) 55 5729 2300
 Fax: (52) 55 3067 5233
 Email: juan.martinez@smurfitkappa.com.mx
Sls. Mgr. Folding Cartons Div.: Gabriel Huerta
 Phone: (52) 55 5729 2300
 Fax: (52) 55 3067 5233
 Email: gabriel.huerta@smurfitkappa.com.mx
Total Employees at this Location: 360
Type of Operation: Pulp mill, Paperboard mill
Pulp Grades and Capacities:
Total pulp capacity: 254,904 mt/y
Recycled Pulping: 254,904 mt/y
Pulp Mill Data:
Recycled Fiber Treatment Lines:
Recycled packaging pulping lines: 1 at 255,000
Paper/Paperboard Grades and Capacities:
Total paper and paperboard capacity: 269,892 mt/y
Linerboard: 113,883 mt/y
Corrugating medium/fluting: 76,041 mt/y
Boxboard/cartonboard: 79,968 mt/y
Paper and Paperboard Mill Data:
Stock Preparation:
Pulpers:
Paper Machines: 2
No. 4, Ultraformer (5), total capacity 79,968 mt/y, Trim width 3.2 m, Boxboard/cartonboard
No. 5, fourdrinier, total capacity 189,924 mt/y, Trim width 5.5 m, Linerboard, Corrugating medium/fluting
Coating Machines: 1
PM 4, total capacity 80,000 mt/y., on machine
Energy Data:
Power boilers: 1
Electrical demand for mill: 384 MWh/D

ⓂSmurfit Cartón y Papel de México S.A. de C.V.
Los Reyes Mill
Ownership: 100% by Smurfit Kappa Group
Av. Presidente Juarez No 2030
54090 Col. Los Reyes Iztacala, Tlalnepantla, México, D.F.
Mexico
 Phone: (52) 55 5729 2300
 Fax: (52) 55 3067 5204
 Email: josecarlos.nocetti@smurfitkappa.com.mx
 Web Address: www.smurfitkappa.com.mx
Total Employees at this Location: 180
Type of Operation: Paperboard mill
Pulp Grades and Capacities:
Total pulp capacity: 68,425 mt/y
Recycled Pulping: 68,425 mt/y
Pulp Mill Data:
Recycled Fiber Treatment Lines:
Recycled packaging pulping lines: 1
Paper/Paperboard Grades and Capacities:
Total paper and paperboard capacity: 77,112 mt/y
Linerboard: 5,355 mt/y
Corrugating medium/fluting: 32,130 mt/y
Boxboard/cartonboard: 39,627 mt/y
Paper and Paperboard Mill Data:
Stock Preparation:
Pulpers: 8
Refiners: 7
Paper Machines: 2
No. 1, fourdrinier, total capacity 37,485 mt/y, Trim width 2.1 m, Linerboard, Corrugating medium/fluting
No. 3, cylinder (5), total capacity 39,627 mt/y, Trim width 2.1 m, Boxboard/cartonboard
Coating Machines: 1

Mexico

No. 3, total capacity 40,000 mt/y., on machine
Finishing Equipment:
  Rewinders: 2
  Sheeters: 2
Energy Data:
Power boilers: 3
Steam turbines: 1 at 1.8 MW
Electrical demand for mill: 141 MWh/D

ⓂSmurfit Cartón y Papel de México S.A. de C.V.
Monterrey Mill
Ownership: 100% by Smurfit Kappa Group
Carlos Salazar 1821 Oriente
64010 Monterrey, BCA
Mexico
  Phone: (52) 81 83545080
  Fax: (52) 81 83541990
  Email: ricardo.garcia@smurfitkappa.com.mx
  Web Address: www.smurfitkappa.com.mx
Personnel:
  Gen. Mgr.: Ing. Ricardo Garcia
  Phone: (52) 81 83545080
  Fax: (52) 81 83541990
  Email: ricardo.garcia@smurfitkappa.com.mx
  Plt. Mgr.: Ing. Julio Cesar Rodríguez
  Phone: (52) 81 83545080
  Fax: (52) 81 83541990
  Email: julio.rodriguez@smurfitkappa.com.mx
  Controller: Judith Alcala
  Phone: (52) 81 83545080
  Fax: (52) 81 83541990
  Email: judith.alcala@smurfitkappa.com.mx
  Sls. Mgr.: Guillermo Franco
  Phone: (52) 81 83545080
  Fax: (52) 81 83541990
  Email: guillermo.franco@smurfitkappa.com.mx
Total Employees at this Location: 82
Type of Operation: Paper mill, Paperboard mill
Pulp Grades and Capacities:
  Total pulp capacity: 36,369 mt/y
  Recycled Pulping: 36,369 mt/y
Pulp Mill Data:
  Recycled Fiber Treatment Lines:
  Pulpers: 1
Paper/Paperboard Grades and Capacities:
  Total paper and paperboard capacity: 35,700 mt/y
  Linerboard: 7,140 mt/y
  Corrugating medium/fluting: 28,560 mt/y
Paper and Paperboard Mill Data:
  Stock Preparation:
  Pulpers: 1
  Refiners: 2
Paper Machines: 1
No. 9, fourdrinier, total capacity 35,700 mt/y, Trim width 2 m, Linerboard, Corrugating medium/fluting
Energy Data:
Power boilers: 2
Electrical demand for mill: 56 MWh/D

ⓗⓂFábrica de Papel La Soledad S.A. de C.V.
Los Reyes Acaquilpan Mill
Km. 20.7 Carretera México-Texcoco
56400 Los Reyes Acaquilpan, México, D.F.
Mexico
Mailing Address: Aptdo. Postal 8938, 56400 Los Reyes Acaquilpan, La Paz, Mexico
  Phone: (52) 55 5855 0469/0075
  Fax: (52) 55 5855 0075/0186
Personnel:
  Dir. Gen.: Ing. Isidro Mier Fernández
  Phone: (52) 55 5855 0469
  Gen. Mgr.: Ing. Isidro Mier Hidalgo
  Phone: (52) 55 5855 0469
  Acct.: Ing. Francisco Espino Morquecho
  Phone: (52) 55 5855 0469
  Chief Eng.: Ing. Antonio Romero
  Phone: (52) 55 5855 0469
Total Employees of Company: 178
Total Employees at this Location: 20
Type of Operation: Paper mill
Paper/Paperboard Grades and Capacities:
  Total paper and paperboard capacity: 48,000 mt/y
  Packaging papers: 48,000 mt/y
  Specialty and industrial
Paper and Paperboard Mill Data:
Paper Machines: 3
No. 1, fourdrinier, total capacity 16,000 mt/y, Trim width 1.8 m
No. 2, fourdrinier, total capacity 16,000 mt/y, Trim width 2.5 m
No. 3, Yankee dryer, total capacity 16,000 mt/y, Trim width 2.4 m

ⓂSonoco de México, S.A. de C.V.
Ownership: 100% by Sonoco Products Co.
Ignacio Zaragoza No. 15, Col. Centro
52900 Atizapan de Zaragoza
Mexico
  Phone: (52) 5825 5648/49
  Fax: (52) 5825 5647
  Email: josefina.avalos@sonoco.com
  Web Address: www.sonoco.com, www.sonoco.com.mx
Personnel:
  Gen. Dir Mexico & South America: José Manuel Villafaña Nagel
  Phone: (52) 5825 5648/49
  Fax: (52) 5825 5647
  Mill. Mgr: Hector Rios Quintana
  Phone: (52) 5825 5648/49
  Fax: (52) 5825 5647
  Manuf. Dir. : Carlos Guillermo Ceniceros Matus
  Phone: (52) 5825 5648/49
  Fax: (52) 5825 5647
  Finan. Mgr.: Luis A Adame
  Phone: (52) 5825 5648/49
  Fax: (52) 5825 5647
Total Employees at this Location: 520
Mill Locations:
Sonoco de México, S.A. de C.V., Santa Clara Mill, Calle Hidalgo No. 175, 55540 Santa Clara Ecatepec, Mexico, Capacity: 59,976 mt/y, (Paperboard mill)
  Phone: (52) 55 9171 0100/101
  Fax: (52) 55 9171 0114/0110/0111
  Email: ofi.ventas@sonoco.com

ⓂSonoco de México, S.A. de C.V.
Santa Clara Mill
Ownership: 100% by Sonoco Products Co.
Calle Hidalgo No. 175
55540 Santa Clara Ecatepec, Edo. de México
Mexico
  Phone: (52) 55 9171 0100/101
  Fax: (52) 55 9171 0114/0110/0111
  Email: ofi.ventas@sonoco.com
  Web Address: www.sonoco.com
Personnel:
  Mill Mgr.: Ing. Alan Zetina
  Phone: (52) 55 9171 0100/101
  Email: alan.zetina@sonoco.com
  Manuf. Dir (Paper and Converting): Ing. Carlos Ceniceros
  Phone: (52) 55 9171 0100/101
  Email: carlos.ceniceros@sonoco.com
  Sls. Dir.: Ing. Rodrigo Vazquez Valle
  Phone: (52) 55 9171 0100/101
  Purch. Agt.: Lic. Manuel Maquiavelo Machado
  Phone: (52) 55 9171 0100/101
  HR. Dir.: Lic. Fernando Charles Nava
  Phone: (52) 55 9171 0100/101
Total Employees at this Location: 157
Type of Operation: Paperboard mill
Pulp Grades and Capacities:
  Total pulp capacity: 62,164 mt/y
  Recycled Pulping: 62,164 mt/y
Pulp Mill Data:
  Recycled Fiber Treatment Lines:
  Recycled packaging pulping lines: 1
Paper/Paperboard Grades and Capacities:
  Total paper and paperboard capacity: 59,976 mt/y
  Linerboard: 49,980 mt/y
  Boxboard/cartonboard: 9,996 mt/y
Paper and Paperboard Mill Data:
  Stock Preparation:
  Pulpers: 3
  Refiners: 4
Paper Machines: 2
No. 1, cylinder (4), total capacity 39,984 mt/y, Trim width 1.9 m, Linerboard
No. 2, cylinder (6), total capacity 19,992 mt/y, Trim width 2.3 m, Linerboard, Boxboard/cartonboard
Finishing Equipment:
  Rewinders: 4
  Sheeters: 1
Energy Data:
Power boilers: 2
Combustion turbines: 1
Electrical demand for mill: 92 MWh/D

ⓗⓂPapelera Tlaxcala S.A. de C.V.
Iztapaluca Mill
Km. 30.5 Carretera Federal México-Puebla
56530 Iztapaluca, Edo. de México
Mexico
  Phone: (52) 55 5972 0011
  Fax: (52) 55 5972 0014
  Email: adrimarin_68@yahoo.com.mx
Personnel:
  Pres.: Ing. Nicolas Resendiz
  Phone: (52) 55 5972 0011
  Fax: (52) 55 5972 0014
  Email: nresendiz@convertipap.com.mx
  Tech. Mgr.: Ing. Joel Martínez
  Phone: (52) 55 5972 0011
  Fax: (52) 55 5972 0014
  Email: jmartinez@convertipap.com.mx
  Acctg Mgr.: Ing. Jorge Maravilla Chávez
  Phone: (52) 55 5972 0011
  Fax: (52) 55 5972 0014
  Email: jchavez@convertipap.com.mx
Total Employees of Company: 377
Total Employees at this Location: 97
Type of Operation: Paper mill
Paper/Paperboard Grades and Capacities:
  Total paper and paperboard capacity: 17,500 mt/y
  Uncoated woodfree/freesheet: 17,500 mt/y
  Packaging papers
  Specialty and industrial
Paper and Paperboard Mill Data:
  Stock Preparation:
  Pulpers: 4
  Refiners: 10
Paper Machines: 2
No. 1, Yankee dryer, total capacity 8,800 mt/y, Trim width 3 m
No. 2, fourdrinier, total capacity 12,000 mt/y, Trim width 2 m
Coating Machines: 1
No. 1, total capacity 65,000 mt/y.
Finishing Equipment:
  Rewinders: 4
  Sheeters: 2
Energy Data:
Power boilers: 3

ⓗⓂTodo Papel S.A. de C.V.
Ixtapaluca Mill
Prolongación Municipio Libre S/N, Lote-11 Col. La Venta
56530 Ixtapaluca, México, D.F.
Mexico
  Phone: (52) 55 5972 3836
  Fax: (52) 55 5972 3836
Personnel:
  Pres.: Lic. Victor Ramos

Phone: (52) 55 5972 3836
Man. Dir.: Ing. José Luis Cruz Ramos
Phone: (52) 55 5972 3836
Finan. Mgr.: C.P. Eduardo Roque
Phone: (52) 55 5972 3836
Sls. Mgr.: Ms. Karla Lopéz
Phone: (52) 55 5972 3836
Purch. Agent: Ing. José Luis Fabían
Phone: (52) 55 5972 3836
Total Employees of Company: 74
Total Employees at this Location: 14
Type of Operation: Paper mill, Paperboard mill
Paper/Paperboard Grades and Capacities:
Total paper and paperboard capacity: 7,600 mt/y
Packaging papers: 1,600 mt/y
Linerboard: 3,000 mt/y
Corrugating medium/fluting: 3,000 mt/y
Paper and Paperboard Mill Data:
Paper Machines: 1
No. 1, fourdrinier, total capacity 7,600 mt/y, Trim width 2 m, Packaging papers, Containerboard

ⓜGrupo Unipak, S.A. de C.V. PT
Ownership: 100% by Grupo ECSA
Suderman 222, Col. Chapultepec Morales
11570 Mexico, México, D.F.
Mexico
 Phone: (52) 55 2581 0700
 Fax: (52) 55 2581 0701
 Email: unipak@grupak.com.mx, informacion@grupak.com.mx
 Web Address: www.grupak.com.mx
Personnel:
 Gen. Dir.: Ing. Santiago Durante
 Phone: (52) 55 2581 0700
 Fax: (52) 55 2581 0701
 Man. Dir.: Ing. Francisco Diaz
 Phone: (52) 55 2581 0700
 Fax: (52) 55 2581 0701
 Finan. Dir.: Ing. José Javier Lopéz
 Phone: (52) 55 2581 0700
 Fax: (52) 55 2581 0701
 Sls. Mgr.: Lic. Gerardo Sestier
 Phone: (52) 55 2581 0700
 Fax: (52) 55 2581 0701
 Planning Mgr.: Lic. Vicky Serrano
 Phone: (52) 55 2581 0700
 Fax: (52) 55 2581 0701
 Maint. Mgr.: Martin Espinoza
 Phone: (52) 55 2581 0700
 Fax: (52) 55 2581 0701
 Purch. Mgr.: Ana Maria Vazquez
 Phone: (52) 55 2581 0700
 Fax: (52) 55 2581 0701
 Prod. Mgr.: Juan Manuel Resendiz
 Phone: (52) 55 2581 0700
 Fax: (52) 55 2581 0701
Total Employees of Company: 435
Total Employees at this Location: 45
Mill Locations:
Grupo Unipak, S.A. de C.V. PT, Grupak Hidalgo, Emiliano Zapata, Mexico, Capacity: 220,000 mt/y, (Paperboard mill)
 Email: informacion@grupak.com.mx
Grupo Unipak, S.A. de C.V. PT, Cuernavaca Mill, Avenida Atlacomulco 117-A esq. Calle San Juan, Col. Chapultepec, 62450 Cuernavaca, Mexico, Capacity: 74,970 mt/y, (Paper mill, Paperboard mill)
 Phone: (52) 777 100 7200
 Fax: (52) 777 100 7201
 Email: unipakcv@grupak.com.mx

ⓞⓜGrupo Unipak, S.A. de C.V. PT
Grupak Hidalgo
Ownership: 100% by Grupo ECSA
Emiliano Zapata
Mexico
 Email: informacion@grupak.com.mx
 Web Address: www.grupak.com.mx

Total Employees of Company: 435
Type of Operation: Paperboard mill
Mill Locations:
Grupo Unipak, S.A. de C.V. PT, Cuernavaca Mill, Avenida Atlacomulco 117-A esq. Calle San Juan, Col. Chapultepec, 62450 Cuernavaca, Mexico, Capacity: 74,970 mt/y, (Paper mill, Paperboard mill)
 Phone: (52) 777 100 7200
 Fax: (52) 777 100 7201
 Email: unipakcv@grupak.com.mx
Paper/Paperboard Grades and Capacities:
Total paper and paperboard capacity: 220,000 mt/y
Linerboard: 110,000 mt/y
Corrugating medium/fluting: 110,000 mt/y
Paper and Paperboard Mill Data:
Paper Machines: 1
PM 1, (2nd hand, started September 2014), total capacity 220,000 mt/y, Trim width 5.6 m, Linerboard, Corrugating medium/fluting

ⓜGrupo Unipak, S.A. de C.V. PT
Cuernavaca Mill
Avenida Atlacomulco 117-A esq. Calle San Juan, Col. Chapultepec
62450 Cuernavaca, Morelos
Mexico
 Phone: (52) 777 100 7200
 Fax: (52) 777 100 7201
 Email: unipakcv@grupak.com.mx
 Web Address: www.grupak.com.mx
Personnel:
 Gen. Dir. & Oper. Mgr.: Ing. Francisco Diaz
 Phone: (52) 777 100 7200
 Fax: (52) 777 100 7201
 Paper Mill Mgr.: Ing. Jesús Salgado
 Phone: (52) 777 100 7200
 Fax: (52) 777 100 7201
 Prod. Mgr.: Ing. Juan Manuel Resendiz
 Phone: (52) 777 100 7200
 Fax: (52) 777 100 7201
 Maint. Mgr. (pulp): Martín Espinosa
 Phone: (52) 777 100 7200
 Fax: (52) 777 100 7201
 Corrugated Plant. Mgr.: Jose Gomez Moreno
 Phone: (52) 777 100 7200
 Fax: (52) 777 100 7201
 Process Ctrl Mgr.: Roque Diaz
 Phone: (52) 777 100 7200
 Fax: (52) 777 100 7201
Total Employees at this Location: 315
Type of Operation: Paper mill, Paperboard mill
Pulp Grades and Capacities:
Total pulp capacity: 76,175 mt/y
Recycled Pulping: 76,175 mt/y
Pulp Mill Data:
Recycled Fiber Treatment Lines:
Recycled packaging pulping lines: 1 at 77,000
Paper/Paperboard Grades and Capacities:
Total paper and paperboard capacity: 74,970 mt/y
Linerboard: 49,980 mt/y
Corrugating medium/fluting: 24,990 mt/y
Paper and Paperboard Mill Data:
Paper Machines: 2
No. 3, (Suppliers: Wolff/Sohne.), fourdrinier, total capacity 37,485 mt/y, Trim width 2.2 m, Linerboard, Corrugating medium/fluting
No. 4, fourdrinier, total capacity 37,485 mt/y, Trim width 2.2 m, Linerboard, Corrugating medium/fluting
Energy Data:
Power boilers: 1
Electrical demand for mill: 132 MWh/D

ⓞⓜPapelera Veracruzana S.A. de C.V.
Orizaba Mill
Ownership: 100% by Grupo Morodo
Poniente 15 Lotes del 2 al 8, Col. Urbana Librado Rivera
94380 Orizaba, Veracruz
Mexico
 Phone: (52) 272 725 2422/2504/3894
 Fax: (52) 272 725 2058
 Email: celftimex@prodigy.net.mx
Personnel:
 Pres.: Ing. Carlos Morodo S.
 Phone: (52) 272 725 2422/2504/3894
 Fax: (52) 272 725 2058
 VP: Ing. Enrique Morodo S.
 Phone: (52) 272 725 2422/2504/53894
 Fax: (52) 272 725 2058
 Mill Mgr.: Ing. Rogelio Hernandez
 Phone: (52) 272 725 2422/2504/3894
 Fax: (52) 272 725 2058
 Purch. Agent: Lic. Yadira Ortega
 Phone: (52) 272 725 2422/2504/3894
 Fax: (52) 272 725 2058
 Oper. Mgr.: Ing. Baudelio Candela
 Phone: (52) 272 725 2422/2504/3894
 Fax: (52) 272 725 2058
 Admin. Mgr.: C.P. Hector Hernández
 Phone: (52) 272 725 2422/2504/3894
 Fax: (52) 272 725 2058
Total Employees at this Location: 150
Type of Operation: Paper mill
Mill Locations:
Celulosa de Fibras Mexicanas S.A. de C.V., Apizaco Mill, Km. 1 Camino a Col. Morelos s/n, 90308 Apizaco, Mexico, Capacity: 11,000 mt/y, (Paper mill)
 Phone: (52) 241 417 0222 / 241 417 0241
 Fax: (52) 241 417 1777
 Email: celfimex@apizaco.podernet.com.mx, informacion@celfimex.com.mx
Paper/Paperboard Grades and Capacities:
Total paper and paperboard capacity: 240,000 mt/y
Packaging papers: 25,000 mt/y
Specialty and industrial
Boxboard/cartonboard: 215,000 mt/y
Paper and Paperboard Mill Data:
Stock Preparation:
Pulpers: 3
Refiners: 5
Paper Machines: 2
No. 2, Yankee dryer, fourdrinier, Trim width 2 m
No. 2, fourdrinier, Trim width 2 m
Finishing Equipment:
Rewinders: 2
Energy Data:
Combustion turbines: 1

PANAMA

ⓜPapelera Istmeña, S.A.
El Dorado Mill
Ownership: Kruger Inc.
Apdo. 0819-08589
El Dorado, Panama
Panama
 Phone: (507) 236 1611
 Fax: (507) 236 1479
 Email: lhoyos@papisa.com
 Web Address: www.papisa.com
Personnel:
 Gen. Mgr.: Javier Miro E.
 Phone: (507) 236 1611
 Fax: (507) 236 1479
 Email: javier.miro@papisa.com
 Commer. Dir.: Ana Lorena Palacios
 Phone: (507) 236 1811, 3005324
 Fax: (507) 236 1479
 Email: apalacios@papisa.com
Total Employees at this Location: 120
Type of Operation: Paper mill
Pulp Grades and Capacities:
Total pulp capacity: 22,662 mt/y
Recycled Pulping: 22,662 mt/y
Pulp Mill Data:
Bleach Plant Systems: 1

Paraguay

Recycled Pulping System, Type: DIP
Recycled Fiber Treatment Lines:
Flotation deinking lines: 1
Paper/Paperboard Grades and Capacities:
Total paper and paperboard capacity: 21,063 mt/y
Tissue: 21,063 mt/y
Paper and Paperboard Mill Data:
Paper Machines: 2
No. 1, fourdrinier, total capacity 10,353 mt/y, Trim width 2 m, Tissue, Uncoated woodfree/freesheet
No. 2, fourdrinier, total capacity 10,710 mt/y, Trim width 2 m, Tissue
Energy Data:
Power boilers
Electrical demand for mill: 90 MWh/D

Ⓟ Ⓜ Industria Panameña de Papel SA
Chilibre Mill
Ownership: 50% by Georgia-Pacific LLC, 50% by Grupo Galindo
Milla 15, Carretera Boyd Roosevelt
0816-02543 San Vicente, Zona Chilibre
Panama
Mailing Address: Apdo. 0816-02543, Milla 15 Agua buena, Chilibre, Panamá 5, Panama
Phone: (507) 216 6555/6031
Fax: (507) 16 6766
Email: vanipel@cw.panama.net
Web Address: www.e-galindo.com
Personnel:
Gen. Mgr.: Carlos Afre
Phone: (507) 216 6555
Fax: (507) 216 6766
Email: cafre@ipelpanama.com
Pub. Rel. Mgr.: Daniel Arias
Phone: (507) 216 6555
Fax: (507) 216 6766
Email: darias@e-galindo.com
Total Employees at this Location: 62
Type of Operation: Paper mill, Paperboard mill
Pulp Grades and Capacities:
Total pulp capacity: 30,730 mt/y
Recycled Pulping: 30,730 mt/y
Pulp Mill Data:
Recycled Fiber Treatment Lines:
Pulpers: 1 at 33,000
Paper/Paperboard Grades and Capacities:
Total paper and paperboard capacity: 29,988 mt/y
Packaging papers: 4,998 mt/y
Linerboard: 14,994 mt/y
Corrugating medium/fluting: 9,996 mt/y
Paper and Paperboard Mill Data:
Stock Preparation:
Pulpers: 1
Refiners: 1
Paper Machines: 1
No. 1, fourdrinier, total capacity 29,988 mt/y, Trim width 2.4 m, Corrugating medium/fluting, Linerboard, Packaging papers
Energy Data:
Power boilers: 1
Electrical demand for mill: 52 MWh/D

Ⓟ Papelera Istmeña, S.A.
Ownership: Kruger Inc.
Apdo. 0819-08589
El Dorado, Panama
Panama
Phone: (507) 236 1611
Fax: (507) 236 1479
Email: lhoyos@papisa.com
Web Address: www.papisa.com
Personnel:
Gen. Mgr.: Javier Miro E.
Phone: (507) 236 1611
Fax: (507) 236 1479
Email: jmiro@papisa.com
Gen. Commer.: Ana Lorena Palacios
Phone: (507) 236 1611
Fax: (507) 236 1479
Email: apalacios@papisa.com
Total Employees at this Location: 120
Mill Locations:
Papelera Istmeña, S.A., El Dorado Mill, Apdo. 0819-08589, El Dorado, Panama, Panama, Capacity: 21,063 mt/y, (Paper mill)
Phone: (507) 236 1611
Fax: (507) 236 1479
Email: lhoyos@papisa.com

PARAGUAY

Ⓟ Cartón Box del Paraguay S. A.
Ownership: 100% by Sr. Pablo Yoon
Cap. Pelayo Pratt Gill Nr. 423
Ñemby
Paraguay
Phone: (595) 595 21 960216, 960202, 960212, 960370
Fax: (595) 964200
Personnel:
Mill Mgr.: Ing. Enrique Fornells
Phone: (595) 992 248754
Email: enrique@cartonbox.com.py
Total Employees of Company: 275
Mill Locations:
Cartón Box del Paraguay S. A., Ñemby Mill, Capitan Pelayo Pratt Gill 423 Comp. Pa'i Nu, Ñemby, Paraguay, Capacity: 10,800 mt/y, (Paper mill)
Fax: (595) 595 21 964200
Email: info@cartonbox.com.py, enrique@cartonbox.com.py

Ⓜ Cartón Box del Paraguay S. A.
Ñemby Mill
Capitan Pelayo Pratt Gill 423 Comp. Pa'i Nu
Ñemby
Paraguay
Fax: (595) 595 21 964200
Email: info@cartonbox.com.py, enrique@cartonbox.com.py
Web Address: www.cartonbox.com.py
Personnel:
Mill Mgr.: Ing. Enrique Fornells
Phone: (595) 992 248754
Email: enrique@cartonbox.com.py
Total Employees at this Location: 275
Type of Operation: Paper mill
Paper/Paperboard Grades and Capacities:
Total paper and paperboard capacity: 10,800 mt/y
Tissue: 10,800 mt/y
Paper and Paperboard Mill Data:
Stock Preparation:
Pulpers: 6
Refiners: 3
Paper Machines: 4
No. 1, fourdrinier, total capacity 2,050 mt/y, Trim width 1.3 m, Tissue
No. 2, fourdrinier, total capacity 2,550 mt/y, Trim width 1.65 m, Tissue
No. 3, total capacity 2,600 mt/y, Trim width 1.9 m, Tissue
No. 4, fourdrinier, total capacity 3,600 mt/y, Tissue
Energy Data:
Power boilers: 2
Electrical demand for mill: 778 MWh/D

Ⓜ Corrugadora Paraguaya S.A.
Luque Mill
Ruta Generall Aquino Km. 12,5
Luque
Paraguay
Phone: (595) 21 642027/642399/647511
Email: cpsa@cpsa.com.py
Personnel:
Dir.: Andrés Losio
Phone: (595) 21 642027/642399/647511
Email: andreslosio@yahoo.com.ar
HR Mgr.: Zulma Gómez
Phone: (595) 21 642027/642399/647511
Type of Operation: Paperboard mill
Pulp Grades and Capacities:
Total pulp capacity: 10,000 mt/y
Pulp Mill Data:
Recycled Fiber Treatment Lines:
Flotation deinking lines: 1 at 10,000 admt/y
Paper/Paperboard Grades and Capacities:
Total paper and paperboard capacity: 9,600 mt/y
Linerboard: 9,600 mt/y
Paper and Paperboard Mill Data:
Paper Machines: 1
PM 1, total capacity 9,600 mt/y, Linerboard

Ⓟ Weig International
Ownership: Moritz J. Weig GmbH & Co. KG
Calle 6ta y Puerto Pinasco
Laurelty - Luque
Paraguay
Phone: (595) 21 640 048
Fax: (595) 21 643 565
Email: gerencia@cysa.com.py
Web Address: www.weig-karton.de
Personnel:
Pres. & Gen. Mgr.: Pablo Kalbermatten
Phone: (595) 21 659 9113
Fax: (595) 21 659 9105
Email: l.rabito@cysa.com.py
Ind. Dir. (CYSA): Omar Guzmán
Phone: (595) 21 659 9000
Fax: (595) 21 659 9143
Exec. Assit.: Leila Rabito
Phone: (595) 21 659 9113
Fax: (595) 21 659 9105
Email: l.rabito@cysa.com.py
Commer. Mgr.: Sergio Feliciangeli
Phone: (595) 21 659 9121
Fax: (595) 2651 / 84 - 329
Sls. Mgr.: Pedro Medina
Phone: (595) 21 659 9152
Fax: (595) 21 659 9105
Email: p.medina@cysa.com.py
Admin. Mgr.: Pablino Bogado
Phone: (595) 21 659 9103
Fax: (595) 21 659 9105
Mil Mgr. (East City): Horacio Almada
Phone: (595) 61 575 219
Fax: (595) 61 575 219
Prod. Mgr.: Stefan Hain
Phone: (595) 2651-84-171
Fax: (595) 2651 / 84 - 329
Email: stefan.hain@weig-karton.de
Materials & Purch. Mgr.: Torsten Asch
Phone: (595) 2651-84-233
Fax: (595) 2651 / 84 - 329
Email: torsten.asch@weig-karton.de
Total Employees of Company: 400
Total Employees at this Location: 150
Mill Locations:
Kartotec - Papeles Técnicos-, Villeta Mill, Calle Amambay 39, Zona Industrial Sur, Villeta, Paraguay, Capacity: 69,972 mt/y, (Paperboard mill)
Phone: (595) 225 952 680, 952 679
Fax: (595) 225 952 682
Email: ventas@kartotec.com.py

Ⓜ Envases Industriales S.A.
Villa Elisa Mill
Calle Paso Medin, Remanso
20090 Villa Elisa
Paraguay
Phone: (595) 21 940281
Fax: (595) 21 940281
Email: eisa1@tigo.com.py
Personnel:

Dir.: Ing. Alberto Osaky
Phone: (595) 21 940281
Mill Mgr.: Oscar Terraza
Phone: (595) 21 940281
Email: eisa1@tigo.com.py
Total Employees at this Location: 50
Type of Operation: Paperboard mill
Paper/Paperboard Grades and Capacities:
Total paper and paperboard capacity: 9,000 mt/y
Linerboard: 9,000 mt/y
Paper and Paperboard Mill Data:
Paper Machines: 1
PM 1, Trim width 1.7 m, Linerboard

ⓜKartotec - Papeles Técnicos-
Ownership: Weig International
Puerto Pinasco y Sexta Laurelty, Luque
1767 Asunción
Paraguay
Phone: (595) 21 659 9152
Fax: (595) 21 659 9105 / 9143
Email: ventas@kartotec.com.py
Web Address: www.kartotec.com.py
Personnel:
Quality & Sls Mgr.: Pedro Medina
Phone: (595) 21 659 9152
Fax: (595) 21 659 9143
Email: asesoria@kartotec.com.py
Export. Asst.: Marcelo Bon
Phone: (595) 21 659 9152
Fax: (595) 21 659 9143
Email: m.bon@kartotec.com.py
Head of Electricity & Instrumentation: Cesar Romero
Phone: (595) 21 659 9152
Fax: (595) 21 659 9143
Mill Locations:
Kartotec- Papeles Técnicos-, Villeta Mill, Calle Amambay 39, Zona Industrial Sur, Villeta, Paraguay, Capacity: 69,972 mt/y, (Paperboard mill)
Phone: (595) 225 952 680, 952 679
Fax: (595) 225 952 682
Email: ventas@kartotec.com.py

ⓜKartotec - Papeles Técnicos- Villeta Mill
Ownership: Weig International
Calle Amambay 39, Zona Industrial Sur
Villeta
Paraguay
Phone: (595) 225 952 680, 952 679
Fax: (595) 225 952 682
Email: ventas@kartotec.com.py
Web Address: www.kartotec.com.py
Personnel:
Tech. dir.: Dennis Salcedo
Phone: (595) 225 95 2680
Email: d.salcedo@kartotec.com.py
Maint. Mgr.: Herman Wagener
Phone: (595) 225 95 2680 Ext. 209
Email: h.wagener@kartotec.com.py
Proj. Mgr.: Marcelo Luzardi
Phone: (595) 225 95 2680 Ext. 210
Email: m.luzardi@kartotec.com.py
Eng. Mgr.: Nahi Lagraña
Phone: (595) 225 95 2680 Ext. 239
Email: n.lagrana@kartotec.com.py
Quality Mgr.: Pedro Medina
Phone: (595) 216 59 9152
Fax: (595) 216 59 9105
Total Employees at this Location: 150
Type of Operation: Paperboard mill
Pulp Grades and Capacities:
Total pulp capacity: 71,816 mt/y
Recycled Pulping: 71,816 mt/y
Pulp Mill Data:
Recycled Fiber Treatment Lines:
Pulpers: 1 at 78,000
Recycled packaging pulping lines: 1 at 72,000
Paper/Paperboard Grades and Capacities:
Total paper and paperboard capacity: 69,972 mt/y
Linerboard: 23,919 mt/y
Corrugating medium/fluting: 16,065 mt/y
Boxboard/cartonboard: 29,988 mt/y
Paper and Paperboard Mill Data:
Stock Preparation:
Pulpers: 1
Refiners: 4
Paper Machines: 1
KM7, (Supplier: PAMA Papiermaschinen.), fourdrinier, total capacity 69,972 mt/y, Trim width 2.6 m, Linerboard, Corrugating medium/fluting, Boxboard/cartonboard
Finishing Equipment:
Winders: 1 at 70,000 mt/y
Rewinders: 2 at 100,000 mt/y
Energy Data:
Power boilers: 2
Hydro turbines
Electrical demand for mill: 144 MWh/D

ⓜCelulosa Remanso S.A.
Mariano Roque Alonso Mill
Mill is operated by TransRiver International S.A. until 2018
Las Teresianas, calle 1 y calle 2
Mariano Roque Alonso
Paraguay
Phone: (595) 21 752665
Fax: (595) 21 752665
Email: ayz@conexion.com.py
Personnel:
Mill Mgr.: Ing. Carlos Avila
Phone: (595) 981 418605
Type of Operation: Paper mill
Paper/Paperboard Grades and Capacities:
Total paper and paperboard capacity: 7,000 mt/y
Tissue: 7,000 mt/y
Paper and Paperboard Mill Data:
Paper Machines: 1
PM 1, Yankee dryer, total capacity 6,000 mt/y, Trim width 2.3 m, Tissue
Finishing Equipment:
Rewinders: 1
Sheeters: 1
Energy Data:
Power boilers: 2

PERU

ⓞⓜIndustrial Papelera Atlas SA
Nana Mill
Ownership: 100% by Navarro Grau Group
Carretera Central Km. 19.5
100 Ñana, Lima, Lima
Peru
Phone: (51) 1 319 2777
Fax: (51) 1 359 3717
Email: inpasa@atlas.com.pe
Web Address: www.atlas.com.pe
Personnel:
Pres & Chmn.: Rolando Dávila Trinidad
Phone: (51) 1 319 2777
Fax: (51) 1 359 2303
Email: rdavila@atlas.com.pe
CEO: Joao Espinoza Aldana
Phone: (51) 1 319 2777
Fax: (51) 1 359 3717
Email: jespinoza@atlas.com.pe
Admin. Mgr.: Lilia Montoya
Phone: (51) 1 359 0092/0065
Fax: (51) 1 359 2303
Email: lmontoya@atlas.com.pe
Finan. Mgr.: Joao Espinoza
Phone: (51) 1 359 0092/0065
Fax: (51) 1 359 2303
Email: jespinoza@atlas.com.pe
Commer. Mgr.: Ricardo Temoche
Phone: (51) 1 359 0092/0065
Fax: (51) 1 359 2303
Email: rtemoche@atlas.com.pe
Prod. Mgr.: César Castillo
Phone: (51) 1 359 0092/0065
Fax: (51) 1 359 2303
Email: ccastillo@atlas.com.pe
Total Employees of Company: 400
Total Employees at this Location: 400
Type of Operation: Paper mill
Pulp Grades and Capacities:
Total pulp capacity: 6,000 mt/y
Recycled Pulping: 6,000 mt/y
Pulp Mill Data:
Recycled Fiber Treatment Lines:
Flotation deinking lines: 2 at 6,000 admt/y
Pulpers: 1 at 6,000 admt/y
Paper/Paperboard Grades and Capacities:
Total paper and paperboard capacity: 30,000 mt/y
Uncoated woodfree/freesheet: 30,000 mt/y
Paper and Paperboard Mill Data:
Stock Preparation:
Pulpers: 4
Refiners: 10
Paper Machines: 2
No. 1, fourdrinier, total capacity 15,000 mt/y, Trim width 2.2 m, Uncoated woodfree/freesheet
No. 2, fourdrinier, total capacity 15,000 mt/y, Trim width 2.3 m, Uncoated woodfree/freesheet
Finishing Equipment:
Supercalenders: 2
Rewinders: 3
Sheeters: 4
Energy Data:
Power boilers: 1
Electrical demand for mill: 72 MWh/D

ⓞPapelera del Sur S.A.
Ownership: 100% by Cartones America SA - CAME
Av. Industrial Km 36, Panamericana Sur
Lima
Peru
Phone: (51) 1 430 0660
Fax: (51) 1 430 2631
Web Address: www.cartonesamerica.com
Personnel:
Gen. Mgr.: Jose Luis Carreras Mariani
Phone: (51) 1 430 0660
Fax: (51) 1 430 2631
Email: josel.carreras@cartonesamerica.com
Prod. Mgr.: Giacomo De Col
Phone: (51) 1 430 0660
Fax: (51) 1 430 2631
Email: Giacomo.decold@cartonesamerica.com
Commer. Mgr.: Sergio Venero Vergani
Phone: (51) 1 430 0660
Fax: (51) 1 430 2631
Email: Sergio.venero@cartonesamerica.com
Mill Locations:
Papelera del Sur S.A., Chincha Mill, Km. 202 Panamericana Sur Div. Chincha Baja, Chincha, Peru, Capacity: 61,761 mt/y, (Paperboard mill)
Phone: (51) 56 2721 29

ⓜPapelera del Sur S.A.
Chincha Mill
Ownership: 100% by Cartones America SA - CAME
Km. 202 Panamericana Sur Div. Chincha Baja
Chincha, ICA
Peru
Mailing Address: Victor Mantilla 253 Surquillo, L-34
Lima, Peru
Phone: (51) 56 2721 29
Web Address: www.cartonesamerica.com
Personnel:
Gen. Mgr.: Santiago Reyna
Phone: (51) 1 430 0660

Peru

Fax: (51) 1 430 2631
Email: santiago.rayna@cartonesamerica.com
Purch. Mgr.: Claudia Tejeda
Phone: (51) 1 430 0660
Fax: (51) 1 430 2631
Email: claudia.tejeda@cartonesamerica.com
Paper Mill Mgr.: Ruben Avendaño
Phone: (51) 34 27219
Fax: (51) 34 272130
Email: ruben.avendano@cartonesamerica.com
Finan. Mgr.: Carlos Carrillo
Phone: (51) 1 430 0660
Fax: (51) 1 430 2631
Email: carlos.carrillo@cartonesamerica.com
Total Employees at this Location: 110
Type of Operation: Paperboard mill
Pulp Grades and Capacities:
Total pulp capacity: 62,278 mt/y
Recycled Pulping: 62,278 mt/y
Pulp Mill Data:
Recycled Fiber Treatment Lines:
Pulpers: 1 at 10,000 admt/y
Paper/Paperboard Grades and Capacities:
Total paper and paperboard capacity: 61,761 mt/y
Linerboard: 25,347 mt/y
Corrugating medium/fluting: 36,414 mt/y
Paper and Paperboard Mill Data:
Stock Preparation:
Refiners: 2
Paper Machines: 1
No. 5, fourdrinier, total capacity 61,761 mt/y, Trim width 2 m, Linerboard, Corrugating medium/fluting
Energy Data:
Power boilers: 1
Electrical demand for mill: 98 MWh/D

ⓘ CARVIMSA, Cartones Villa Marina S.A.
Ownership: Grupo COMECA
Autopista Panamericana Sur Km 19 Mz
Lima, Villa El Salvador
Peru
Phone: (51) 1 201 6600
Email: ventas@carvimsa.com
Web Address: www.carvimsa.com
Personnel:
HR Mgr.: Jimmy Montalvo A
Phone: (51) 1 201 6600
Email: rrhh@carvimsa.com
Mill Locations:
CARVIMSA, Cartones Villa Marina S.A., Nievería Mill, Lote B del 2° lote 2, Ex Fundo Nievería, Lurigancho-Chosica, Peru, Capacity: 43,000 mt/y, (Paper mill)
Phone: (51) 1 719 0552
Email: ventas@carvimsa.com

ⓜ CARVIMSA, Cartones Villa Marina S.A.
Nievería Mill
Lote B del 2° lote 2
Ex Fundo Nievería, Lurigancho-Chosica
Peru
Phone: (51) 1 719 0552
Email: ventas@carvimsa.com
Web Address: www.carvimsa.com
Personnel:
Plant Mgr.: Johony P Johony P
Phone: (51) 1 719 0552
Admin. Mgr.: Dick Calvo
Phone: (51) 1 719 0552
Type of Operation: Paper mill
Paper/Paperboard Grades and Capacities:
Total paper and paperboard capacity: 43,000 mt/y
Corrugating medium/fluting: 43,000 mt/y
Paper and Paperboard Mill Data:
Paper Machines: 1
No. 1, fourdrinier, total capacity 43,000 mt/y, Containerboard

ⓘ Gloria S.A.
Av. Republica de Panama 2461
13 Santa Catalina, Lima
Peru
Phone: (51) 1 470 7170
Fax: (51) 1 470 9837
Email: contactenos@gloria.com.pe
Web Address: www.grupogloria.com
Personnel:
Exec. Pres.: Jorge Rodríguez
Phone: (51) 1 470 7170
Fax: (51) 1 470 9837
COO: Jairo Molina
Phone: (51) 1 470 7170
Fax: (51) 1 470 9837
Email: jairomm@trupal.com.pe
Bus. International Dir.: Luis Alberto Tejada Diaz
Phone: (51) 1 470 7170
Fax: (51) 1 470 9837
HR. Dir.: Cesar Federico Palacios Reyes
Phone: (51) 1 470 7170
Fax: (51) 1 470 9837
Mill Locations:
Trupal S.A., Evitamiento Mill, Av. Evitamiento No. 3636, 100 El Agustino, Lima, Peru, Capacity: 44,982 mt/y, (Paper mill, Paperboard mill)
Phone: (51) 1 385 2043/42
Fax: (51) 1 385 2048
Email: serviciocliente@trupal.com.pe
Trupal S.A., Trujillo Mill, Santiago De Cao, Distrito de Malca, Trujillo, Peru, Capacity: 77,826 mt/y, (Pulp mill, Paper mill, Paperboard mill)
Phone: (51) 44 463043
Fax: (51) 44 463033/242962
Email: serviciocliente@trupal.com.pe

ⓘ Industrias del Cartón S.A. - INCASA
Ownership: 100% by Ciccia Group
Manuel Echeandía 303, Urb. El Pino
Lima
Peru
Email: incasa@incasa.com.pe
Web Address: www.incasa.com.pe
Personnel:
Pres.: Antonio Ciccia
Phone: (51) 1 326 3139, 326 5422
Fax: (51) 1 326 0372
Mgr.: Marco Antonio Ciccia Gabillo
Phone: (51) 1 326 3139, 326 5422
Fax: (51) 1 326 0372
Email: mciccia@incasa.com.pe
Mgr.: Uldarico Ossio
Phone: (51) 1 326 3139, 326 5422
Fax: (51) 1 326 0372
Commer. Dir.: Ricardo Carvajal Gonzales
Phone: (51) 1 326 3139, 326 5422
Fax: (51) 1 326 0372
Email: racg@incasa.com.pe
HR Mgr.: Pedro Bezada
Phone: (51) 1 326 3139, 326 5422
Fax: (51) 1 326 0372
Email: bezadape@incasa.com.pe
Mill Locations:
Absorpelsa Papeles Absorventes S.A., Quito Mill, Panamericana Sur Km. 7 1/2, S26-183, 1701-230 Quito, Ecuador, Capacity: 3,000 mt/y, (Paper mill)
Phone: (593) 267 7175 / 267 5774
Fax: (593) 267 5773
Email: ventas@absorpelsa.com.ec
Industrias Cartonera Asociada S.A. - INCASA, Quito Mill, Panamericana Sur Km. 7 1/2 N° S26-183, Quito, Ecuador, Capacity: 32,130 mt/y, (Paper mill, Paperboard mill)
Phone: (593) 2 267 1900
Fax: (593) 2 267 5776
Email: incasa@incasa.com.ec
Industrias del Cartón S.A. - INCASA, Cayalti Mill, Cayalti, Chiclayo, Peru, Capacity: 12,138 mt/y, (Paper mill, Paperboard mill)
Email: incasa@incasa.com.pt

ⓜ Industrias del Cartón S.A. - INCASA
Cayalti Mill
Cayalti, Chiclayo
Peru
Email: incasa@incasa.com.pt
Web Address: www.incasa.com.pe
Personnel:
Mgr.: Marco Antonio Ciccia Gabillo
Phone: (51) 1 326 3139
Fax: (51) 1 326 0372
Email: mciccia@incasa.com.pe
Total Employees at this Location: 74
Type of Operation: Paper mill, Paperboard mill
Pulp Grades and Capacities:
Total pulp capacity: 12,425 mt/y
Recycled Pulping: 12,425 mt/y
Pulp Mill Data:
Recycled Fiber Treatment Lines:
Recycled packaging pulping lines: 1
Paper/Paperboard Grades and Capacities:
Total paper and paperboard capacity: 12,138 mt/y
Packaging papers: 6,426 mt/y
Linerboard: 2,856 mt/y
Corrugating medium/fluting: 2,856 mt/y
Paper and Paperboard Mill Data:
Stock Preparation:
Pulpers: 1
Refiners: 2
Paper Machines: 1
No. 1, (second hand), fourdrinier, total capacity 12,138 mt/y, Trim width 2 m, Linerboard, Corrugating medium/fluting, Packaging papers
Finishing Equipment:
Rewinders: 1 at 10,800 mt/y
Energy Data:
Power boilers: 1
Electrical demand for mill: 21 MWh/D

ⓘⓜ Industrias del Papel S.A.
Chaclacayo Mill
Ownership: 100% by Lugon family
Km. 18.5, Carretera Central
Chaclacayo, Lima, Lima
Peru
Phone: (51) 1 359 0052
Fax: (51) 1 359 0402-115
Email: info@indupapel.com
Web Address: industriasdelpapel.com
Personnel:
Pres.: Julio Lugon Badaracco
Phone: (51) 1 359 0052
Fax: (51) 1 359 0402
Gen. Mgr.: José Arturo Lugon C.
Phone: (51) 1 359 0052
Fax: (51) 1 359 0402
Admin. & Finan. Mgr.: Juan Ugarte
Phone: (51) 1 359 0052
Fax: (51) 1 359 0402
Total Employees of Company: 150
Total Employees at this Location: 150
Type of Operation: Paper mill
Paper/Paperboard Grades and Capacities:
Total paper and paperboard capacity: 32,000 mt/y
Paper and Paperboard Mill Data:
Stock Preparation:
Pulpers: 2
Refiners: 4
Paper Machines: 2
PM 2, fourdrinier, total capacity 16,000 mt/y, Trim width 2.1 m
PM 3, total capacity 16,000 mt/y
Finishing Equipment:
Rewinders: 2
Sheeters: 1
Energy Data:
Power boilers: 2

Peru

①Papelera Inka S.A.
Ownership: 50% by Kruger Inc., 50% by Nicolini Hermanos
Av. El Sol 1033 La Campiña
Chorrillos, Lima
Peru
Phone: (51) 51 251 2840/1
Fax: (51) 51 251 3399
Email: geren@inkalim.com.pe
Web Address: www.papelerainka.com.pe
Mill Locations:
Papelera Inka S.A., Chincha Baja Mill, Predio San Roque N° 2, Chincha Baja, Chincha, Peru, Capacity: 8,000 mt/y, (Paper mill)
Phone: (51) 56 272178 /272179
Email: ettyr@incachin.com.pe, Raul.Villavicencio@papelerainka.com.pe

①Papelera Inka S.A.
Chincha Baja Mill
Ownership: 50% by Kruger Inc.
Predio San Roque N° 2
Chincha Baja, Chincha, ICA
Peru
Phone: (51) 56 272178 /272179
Email: ettyr@incachin.com.pe, Raul.Villavicencio@papelerainka.com.pe
Web Address: www.sanitisu.com
Personnel:
General Supt.: Martin Alonso Quezada Paredes
Phone: (51) 11 251 2840
Fax: (51) 11 251 3399
Mktg Mgr.: Raul Villavicencio
Phone: (51) 11 251 2840
Fax: (51) 11 251 3399
Email: raul.villavicencio@papelerainka.com.pe
Total Employees at this Location: 200
Type of Operation: Paper mill
Pulp Mill Data:
Bleach Plant Systems: 4
Recycled Fiber Treatment Lines:
Pulpers: 1 at 10,000 admt/y
Paper/Paperboard Grades and Capacities:
Total paper and paperboard capacity: 8,000 mt/y
Tissue: 8,000 mt/y
Paper and Paperboard Mill Data:
Stock Preparation:
Pulpers: 1
Refiners: 2
Paper Machines: 1
PM 1, fourdrinier, total capacity 8,000 mt/y, Trim width 2.5 m, Tissue

①⑩Kimberly-Clark Peru S.A.
Puente de Piedra Mill
Ownership: 100% by Kimberly-Clark Corp.
Av. del Pinar 180, Chacarilla del Estanque
Santiago de Surco, Lima
Peru
Mailing Address: Calle Bucare No. 598 Urbanizacion Camacho La Molina, Lima, Peru
Phone: (51) 1 618 1800
Fax: (51) 1 436 3189
Email: kcastellanos@kcc.com.pe, j.testino@kc.com
Web Address: www.kimberly-clark.com.pe
Personnel:
Dir.: Juan Carlos Belaúnde Cabieses
Phone: (51) 1 618 1800
Fax: (51) 1 436 3189
Gen. Mgr.: Blanca Quino
Phone: (51) 1 618 1800
Fax: (51) 1 436 3189
Finan. Mgr.: José Dagiau Roose
Phone: (51) 1 618 1800
Fax: (51) 1 436 3189
Mill Mgr.: Troy Delgadillo
Phone: (51) 1 618 1800
Fax: (51) 1 436 3189
Oper. Mgr.: Marcelo Hernández
Phone: (51) 1 618 1800
Fax: (51) 1 436 3189
Mktg. Mgr.: Mario Escudero Alay
Phone: (51) 1 618 1800
Fax: (51) 1 436 3189
HR Mgr.: Rafael Ravettino Cabieses
Phone: (51) 1 618 1800
Fax: (51) 1 436 3189
Prod. Mgr.: Miguel Navarrete
Phone: (51) 1 488 5020
Fax: (51) 1 488 5500
Email: mhernandez@kc.com.pe
Sls. Mgr.: Carlos Rupay
Phone: (51) 1 618 1800
Fax: (51) 1 436 3189
Purch. Agent Senior: Jorge Testino
Phone: (51) 1 488 5020
Fax: (51) 1 618 1800 Ext. 2296
Email: j.testino@kcc.com
Total Employees at this Location: 300
Type of Operation: Pulp mill, Paper mill
Pulp Grades and Capacities:
Total pulp capacity: 56,160 mt/y
Recycled Pulping: 56,160 mt/y
Pulp Mill Data:
Bleach Plant Systems: 1
Recycled Pulping System, Type: DIP
Recycled Fiber Treatment Lines:
Flotation deinking lines: 1 at 80,000 admt/y
Pulpers: 1 at 80,000 admt/y
Paper/Paperboard Grades and Capacities:
Total paper and paperboard capacity: 67,116 mt/y
Tissue: 67,116 mt/y
Paper and Paperboard Mill Data:
Stock Preparation:
Pulpers: 0
Paper Machines: 2
No. 1, twin-wire, total capacity 29,988 mt/y, Trim width 2.65 m, Tissue
No. 2, crescent former, total capacity 37,128 mt/y, Trim width 2.78 m, Tissue
Energy Data:
Power boilers: 2
Electrical demand for mill: 292 MWh/D

①Papelera Panamericana S.A.
Arequipa Mill
Eduardo Lopez de Romaña R-4, Pque. Industrial - Arequipa
Arequipa
Peru
Phone: (51) 54 214736/219326
Fax: (51) 236591
Web Address: www.panam.com.pe
Personnel:
Gen. Dir.: Alberto Muñoz-Najar
Phone: (51) 214736
Fax: (51) 236591
Type of Operation: Paper mill
Paper/Paperboard Grades and Capacities:
Total paper and paperboard capacity: 8,000 mt/y
Tissue: 8,000 mt/y
Paper and Paperboard Mill Data:
Paper Machines: 1
PM 1, fourdrinier, total capacity 8,000 mt/y, Trim width 2.4 m, Tissue

①Panasa, Papelera Nacional S.A.
Ownership: 100% by Fishman Group
Calle Luisa Bausejor 2450
1 Chacra Rios Norte Lima, Lima
Peru
Mailing Address: Casilla 2488, Lima, Peru
Phone: (51) 1 619 3131
Fax: (51) 1 336 5321
Email: quimpac@quimpac.com.pe
Web Address: www.panasa.com.pe
Personnel:
Chmn. of Bd.: Fishman Cotlear Marcos Shulim
Phone: (51) 1 619 3131
Fax: (51) 1 336 5321
Comm. Mgr.: Fernando Carranza
Phone: (51) 1 619 3131
Fax: (51) 1 336 5321
Email: fcarranza@quimpac.com.pe
Comm. Mgr. Paper: Aldo Casalino
Phone: (51) 1 619 3131
Fax: (51) 1 336 5321
Email: acasalino@panasa.com.pe
Admin. Asst.: Vanessa Oliva
Phone: (51) 1 619 3131
Fax: (51) 1 336 5321
HR Mgr.: Otto M.
Phone: (51) 1 619 3131
Fax: (51) 1 336 5321
Total Employees of Company: 500
Mill Locations:
Panasa, Papelera Nacional S.A., Paramonga Mill, Carretera Central Km. 18.5, Chaclacayo, Paramonga, Peru, Capacity: 94,962 mt/y, (Pulp mill, Paper mill, Paperboard mill)
Phone: (51) 1 2360351
Email: exportaciones@panasa.com.pe

①Panasa, Papelera Nacional S.A.
Paramonga Mill
Carretera Central Km. 18.5, Chaclacayo
Paramonga, Lima
Peru
Phone: (51) 1 2360351
Email: exportaciones@panasa.com.pe
Web Address: www.panasa.com.pe
Personnel:
Chmn. of Bd.: Fishman Cotlear Marcos Shulim
Phone: (51) 1 359 0052/0355
Gen. Mgr.: Luis Sobero
Phone: (51) 1 359 0052/0355
Email: lsobero@panasa.com.pe
Tech. Dir.: Serafin Serminario
Phone: (51) 1 359 0052/0355
Email: sserminario@panasa.com.pe
Mill Mgr.: Alberto Castillo
Phone: (51) 1 359 0052/0355
Pulp Mill Mgr.: Angel Minano
Phone: (51) 1 359 0052/0355
Conv. Plant Mgr.: Pedro Argote
Phone: (51) 1 359 0052/0355
Email: pargote@panasa.com.pe
Maint. Mgr.: Henry Chavez
Phone: (51) 44 360 351
Email: hchavez@panasa.com.pe
Total Employees at this Location: 500
Type of Operation: Pulp mill, Paper mill, Paperboard mill
Pulp Grades and Capacities:
Total pulp capacity: 79,885 mt/y
Recycled Pulping: 40,718 mt/y
Other Pulp: 39,167 mt/y
Pulp Mill Data:
Chemical Pulping Systems:
Continuous digesters: 4
Pulp Lines: 4
Bleach Plant Systems: 3
No. 1, Sequence: C, Capacity 30,000 admt/y
No. 2 Capacity 30,000 admt/y
No. 3, Sequence: DE, Capacity 30,000 admt/y
Chemical Recovery Equipment:
Evaporator lines: 1
Recovery boilers: 1
Lime Kiln
Recycled Fiber Treatment Lines:
Pulpers: 4 at 70,000 admt/y
Washing deinking lines: 2 at 6,000 admt/y
Paper/Paperboard Grades and Capacities:
Total paper and paperboard capacity: 94,962 mt/y
Uncoated woodfree/freesheet: 24,990 mt/y
Tissue: 14,994 mt/y

Peru

Packaging papers: 29,988 mt/y
Linerboard: 9,996 mt/y
Corrugating medium/fluting: 4,998 mt/y
Boxboard/cartonboard: 9,996 mt/y
Paper and Paperboard Mill Data:
Stock Preparation:
Pulpers:
Paper Machines: 4
No. 1, fourdrinier, total capacity 29,988 mt/y, Trim width 2.5 m, Packaging papers
No. 3, fourdrinier, total capacity 24,990 mt/y, Trim width 2.5 m, Linerboard, Corrugating medium/fluting, Boxboard/cartonboard
No. 5, fourdrinier, total capacity 24,990 mt/y, Trim width 2.9 m, Uncoated woodfree/freesheet
No. 6, fourdrinier, Yankee dryer, total capacity 14,994 mt/y, Trim width 4.2 m, Tissue, Uncoated woodfree/freesheet
Coating Machines: 1
PM 3, off machine
Energy Data:
Power boilers: 2
Steam turbines: 1 at 10 MW
Electrical demand for mill: 220 MWh/D

ⓘPapelera Panamericana S.A.
Eduardo Lopez de Romaña R-4, Pque. Industrial - Arequipa
Arequipa
Peru
Phone: (51) 214736/203973/213651
Fax: (51) 236591
Email: info@panam.com.pe
Web Address: www.panam.com.pe
Personnel:
Gen. Mgr.: Villena Penares Otto Alberto
Phone: (51) 214736/203973/213651
Fax: (51) 236591
Email: villena.o@panam.com.pe
Dir.: Mejia Panijo Arnaldo
Phone: (51) 214736/203973/213651
Fax: (51) 236591
Email: mejiapanizo.a@panam.com.pe
Mgr.: Laza Manrique Juan Salomon
Phone: (51) 214736/203973/213651
Fax: (51) 236591
Email: laza.m@panam.com.pe
Asst. Gen Mgr.: Marietta Pacheco
Phone: (51) 214736/203973/213651
Fax: (51) 236591
Email: pacheco.m@panam.com.pe
Sls. Mgr.: Marco Antonio Medrano Dominguez
Phone: (51) 214736/203973/213651
Fax: (51) 236591
Email: medranodominguez.m@panam.com.pe
Eng. Mgr.: Erick Lazo
Phone: (51) 214736/203973/213651
Fax: (51) 236591
Email: lazo.e@panam.com.pe
Mill Locations:
Papelera Panamericana S.A., Arequipa Mill, Eduardo Lopez de Romaña R-4, Pque. Industrial - Arequipa, Arequipa, Peru, Capacity: 8,000 mt/y, (Paper mill)
Phone: (51) 54 214736/219326
Fax: (51) 236591

ⓜProtisa Peru S.A. - Productos Tissue del Peru
Santa Anita Mill
Ownership: 100% by Empresas CMPC S.A.
Av. Santa Rosa 550
Santa Anita, Lima
Peru
Phone: (51) 1 362 0653
Fax: (51) 1 313 3031
Email: postmast@protisa.com.pe
Web Address: www.protisa.com.pe
Personnel:
Gen. Mgr.: Salvador-Calvo Perez
Phone: (51) 1 313 3030
Prod. Mgr.: Marcos Collantes
Phone: (51) 1 313 3030
Total Employees at this Location: 400
Type of Operation: Paper mill
Pulp Grades and Capacities:
Total pulp capacity: 53,154 mt/y
Recycled Pulping: 53,154 mt/y
Pulp Mill Data:
Bleach Plant Systems: 1
Recycled Pulping System, Type: DIP
Recycled Fiber Treatment Lines:
Flotation deinking lines: 1
Paper/Paperboard Grades and Capacities:
Total paper and paperboard capacity: 82,110 mt/y
Tissue: 82,110 mt/y
Paper and Paperboard Mill Data:
Stock Preparation:
Refiners: 2
Paper Machines: 3
No. 2, crescent former, total capacity 19,992 mt/y, Trim width 2.75 m, Tissue, Uncoated woodfree/freesheet
No. 3, crescent former, total capacity 29,988 mt/y, Trim width 2.75 m, Tissue
No. 4, crescent former, total capacity 32,130 mt/y, Trim width 2.75 m, Tissue
Energy Data:
Power boilers: 2
Electrical demand for mill: 326 MWh/D

ⓘⓜPapelera Reyes S.A.C.
Callao Mill
Av. Cml Nestor Gambeta Nro. 6693 Ind. la Chalaca
L-39 Callao, Lima
Peru
Phone: (51) 51 577 5024 /0505
Fax: (51) 51 577 1566
Web Address: www.papelerareyessac.com
Personnel:
Pres.: Renato Bayardo
Phone: (51) 1 577 0505/5024
Fax: (51) 1 577 1566
Gen. Mgr.: José Reyes
Phone: (51) 1 577 0505/5024
Fax: (51) 1 577 1566
Prod. Mill Mgr.: Jose Castello
Phone: (51) 1 577 0505/5024
Fax: (51) 1 577 1566
Finan. & Sls. Mgr.: Carlos Bocanegra
Phone: (51) 1 577 0505/5024
Fax: (51) 1 577 1566
Maint. Mgr.: Reinaldo Morales
Phone: (51) 1 577 0505/5024
Fax: (51) 1 577 1566
Total Employees of Company: 190
Total Employees at this Location: 190
Type of Operation: Paper mill
Pulp Grades and Capacities:
Total pulp capacity: 18,000 mt/y
Recycled Pulping: 18,000 mt/y
Pulp Mill Data:
Recycled Fiber Treatment Lines:
Flotation deinking lines: 1 at 10,000 admt/y
Pulpers: 3 at 18,000 admt/y
Paper/Paperboard Grades and Capacities:
Total paper and paperboard capacity: 18,000 mt/y
Tissue: 18,000 mt/y
Paper and Paperboard Mill Data:
Stock Preparation:
Refiners: 6
Paper Machines: 3
No. 1, fourdrinier, Yankee dryer, total capacity 5,000 mt/y, Trim width 2.2 m, Tissue
No. 2, fourdrinier, Yankee dryer, total capacity 5,000 mt/y, Trim width 2.2 m, Tissue
No. 3, fourdrinier, Yankee dryer, total capacity 7,280 mt/y, Trim width 2 m, Tissue
Energy Data:
Power boilers: 2

ⓜTrupal S.A.
Evitamiento Mill
Ownership: 100% by Gloria S.A.
Av. Evitamiento No. 3636
100 El Agustino, Lima, Lima
Peru
Phone: (51) 1 385 2043/42
Fax: (51) 1 385 2048
Email: servicioclente@trupal.com.pe
Web Address: www.grupogloria.com/trupal.html
Personnel:
Gen. Mgr.: Aldo Angobaldo
Phone: (51) 1 348 2342
Fax: (51) 1 385 2048
Email: aangoblado@trupal.com.pe
Prod. Superintendent: Jose Grijalba
Phone: (51) 1 385 1898
Fax: (51) 1 385 2048
Email: jgrijalba@gloria.com.pe
Total Employees at this Location: 690
Type of Operation: Paper mill, Paperboard mill
Pulp Grades and Capacities:
Total pulp capacity: 45,707 mt/y
Recycled Pulping: 45,707 mt/y
Pulp Mill Data:
Recycled Fiber Treatment Lines:
Pulpers: 2 at 46,800 admt/y
Paper/Paperboard Grades and Capacities:
Total paper and paperboard capacity: 44,982 mt/y
Packaging papers: 4,641 mt/y
Linerboard: 34,272 mt/y
Boxboard/cartonboard: 6,069 mt/y
Paper and Paperboard Mill Data:
Stock Preparation:
Pulpers: 2
Refiners: 4
Paper Machines: 2
No. 1, fourdrinier, total capacity 34,272 mt/y, Trim width 3.2 m, Linerboard
No. 2, fourdrinier, total capacity 10,710 mt/y, Trim width 1.5 m, Packaging papers, Boxboard/cartonboard
Energy Data:
Power boilers: 4
Electrical demand for mill: 74 MWh/D

ⓜTrupal S.A.
Trujillo Mill
Ownership: 100% by Gloria S.A.
Santiago De Cao, Distrito de Malca
Trujillo
Peru
Phone: (51) 44 463043
Fax: (51) 44 463033/242962
Email: servicioclente@trupal.com.pe
Web Address: www.grupogloria.com
Personnel:
Gen. Mgr.: Aldo Angobaldo
Phone: (51) 1 385 2042
Email: aangobaldo@trupal.com.pe
Logistics Mgr.: Luis Alvites Vasquez
Phone: (51) 44 463043
Email: lalvites@trupal.com.pe
Total Employees at this Location: 191
Type of Operation: Pulp mill, Paper mill, Paperboard mill
Pulp Grades and Capacities:
Total pulp capacity: 79,307 mt/y
Chemical Pulp: 51,337 mt/y
Recycled Pulping: 27,970 mt/y
Pulp Mill Data:
Chemical Pulping Systems:
Batch digesters: 4
Recycled Fiber Treatment Lines:
Pulpers: 4 at 220,000 admt/y
Paper/Paperboard Grades and Capacities:
Total paper and paperboard capacity: 77,826 mt/y
Linerboard: 7,854 mt/y
Corrugating medium/fluting: 69,972 mt/y

Paper and Paperboard Mill Data:
Stock Preparation:
Pulpers: 6
Refiners: 1
Paper Machines: 1
No. 7, fourdrinier, total capacity 77,826 mt/y, Trim width 5 m, Linerboard, Corrugating medium/fluting
Finishing Equipment:
Rewinders: 3
Sheeters: 2
Energy Data:
Power boilers: 1
Steam turbines: 1 at 15 MW
Electrical demand for mill: 188 MWh/D

①ⓜPapelera Zarate S.A.
Lima Mill
Mz- B Lote B Panamericana Norte Km. 24.5 Puente Piedra
Lima, Lima
Peru
Phone: (51) 1 551 1869
Fax: (51) 1 551 1858
Email: ventas@pzarate.com
Web Address: www.pzarate.com
Personnel:
Pres.: César Castrillón Rojas
Phone: (51) 1 551 1869
Fax: (51) 1 551 1858
Mill Mgr. & Tech. Mgr.: Rafael Castrillón R.
Phone: (51) 1 551 1869
Fax: (51) 1 551 1858
Email: pzarater@rednextel.com.pe
Total Employees of Company: 20
Type of Operation: Pulp mill, Paper mill
Pulp Grades and Capacities:
Total pulp capacity: 6,000 mt/y
Recycled Pulping: 6,000 mt/y

Pulp Mill Data:
Recycled Fiber Treatment Lines:
Flotation deinking lines: 1 at 5,400 admt/y
Pulpers: 4 at 6,000 admt/y
Paper/Paperboard Grades and Capacities:
Total paper and paperboard capacity: 4,000 mt/y
Tissue: 4,000 mt/y
Paper and Paperboard Mill Data:
Stock Preparation:
Refiners: 4
Finishing Equipment:
Rewinders: 5
Energy Data:
Power boilers

TRINIDAD AND TOBAGO

ⓜGrand Bay Paper Products Ltd
Arima Mill
Ownership: 100% by Trinidad Tissues Limited
Lot C Lennox Yearwood Expressway, O'Meara Industrial Estate
Arima
Trinidad and Tobago
Phone: (1) 868 6432519, 868 6432520
Fax: (1) 868 643 2522
Email: marketing@t-tissues.com
Web Address: www.t-tissues.com
Personnel:
VP Oper.: Alejandro Abes
Phone: (1) 868 6432520
Fax: (1) 868 643 2522
Dir.: Kevin Marcilliat
Phone: (1) 868 6432520
Fax: (1) 868 643 2522
Mechanical Eng.: Vashesh Sooknanan
Phone: (1) 868 6432520
Fax: (1) 868 643 2522
Plant Mgr.: Edmund Sorrillo
Phone: (1) 868 6432520
Fax: (1) 868 643 2522
Maint. Mgr.: Roopchand Persad
Phone: (1) 868 6432520
Fax: (1) 868 643 2522
Total Employees at this Location: 150
Type of Operation: Paper mill
Pulp Grades and Capacities:
Total pulp capacity: 29,538 mt/y
Recycled Pulping: 29,538 mt/y
Pulp Mill Data:
Pulp Lines: 2
Bleach Plant Systems: 1
Recycled Pulping System, Type: DIP
Recycled Fiber Treatment Lines:
Flotation deinking lines: 1
Paper/Paperboard Grades and Capacities:
Total paper and paperboard capacity: 32,130 mt/y
Tissue: 32,130 mt/y
Paper and Paperboard Mill Data:
Paper Machines: 1
No. 1, crescent former, total capacity 32,130 mt/y, Trim width 3.7 m, Tissue, Uncoated woodfree/freesheet
Energy Data:
Power boilers
Electrical demand for mill: 136 MWh/D

①Trinidad Tissues Limited
Ownership: Kruger Inc.
#40-41 Tissue Drive, New Industrial Estate
Trincity
Trinidad and Tobago
Mailing Address: Private Bag 174, Tunapuna, Trinidad and Tobago
Phone: (1) 640-4725, 640-6031
Fax: (1) 640 - 2811
Email: marketing@t-tissues.com
Web Address: www.t-tissues.com
Personnel:
Man. Dir.: Kevin Marcilliat
Phone: (1) 868 640 4725/640 6031
Fax: (1) 868 640 2811
Email: kevin.marcilliat@gbp.com.tt
Prod. Mgr.: Bernard Hoeger
Phone: (1) 868 640 4725/640 6031
Fax: (1) 868 640 2811
Email: bernard.hoeger@gbp.com.tt
Commun. Mgr.   : Farzan H Ali
Phone: (1) 643-2519/22 Ext. 4130 Direct:868 643 4130
Fax: (1) 868 643 522
Email: farzan.ali@gbp.com.tt
Total Employees of Company: 350
Mill Locations:
Grand Bay Paper Products Ltd, Arima Mill, Lot C Lennox Yearwood Expressway, O'Meara Industrial Estate, Arima, Trinidad and Tobago, Capacity: 32,130 mt/y, (Paper mill)
Phone: (1) 868 6432519, 868 6432520
Fax: (1) 868 643 2522
Email: marketing@t-tissues.com

URUGUAY

①FANAPEL - Fábrica Nacional de Papel S.A.
Ownership: 97.60% by Celulosa Argentina S.A.
Rincón 477, 6th Floor
11000 Montevideo
Uruguay
Phone: (598) 2 915 0917
Fax: (598) 2 916 3121
Email: fanapel@fanapel.com.uy
Web Address: www.fanapel.com.uy
Personnel:
Pres.: Dauglas Lee Albrecht
Phone: (598) 2 915 0917
Fax: (598) 2 916 3121
VP: Liberato Turinelli Ducassou
Phone: (598) 2 915 0917
Fax: (598) 2 916 3121
Email: lturinelli@fanapel.com.uy
Finan. Mgr.: Martin Echeguia Zusperreguy
Phone: (598) 2 915 0917
Fax: (598) 2 916 3121
Sls.Mgr.: Gonzalo Goni Altuna
Phone: (598) 2 915 0917
Fax: (598) 2 916 3121
Email: ggoni@fanapal.com.uy
Mill Mgr.: Horacio Faedo
Phone: (598) 2 915 0917
Fax: (598) 2 916 3121
Email: hfaedo@fanapel.com.uy
Project Mgr.: Carlos Giaudrone
Phone: (598) 2 915 0917
Fax: (598) 2 916 3121
Email: cgiaudrone@fanapel.com.uy
Total Employees of Company: 430
Mill Locations:
FANAPEL - Fábrica Nacional de Papel S.A., Juan Lacaze Mill, Av. Rep. Argentina s/n 102, 70001 Juan Lacaze, Uruguay, Capacity: 62,118 mt/y, (Pulp mill, Paper mill)
Phone: (598) 4586 2022
Fax: (598) 4586 2912
Email: planta.industrial@fanapel.com.uy

ⓜFANAPEL - Fábrica Nacional de Papel S.A.
Juan Lacaze Mill
Ownership: 97.60% by Celulosa Argentina S.A.
Av. Rep. Argentina s/n 102
70001 Juan Lacaze, Colonia
Uruguay
Mailing Address: Casilla 509, 11800 Montevidéo, Uruguay
Phone: (598) 4586 2022
Fax: (598) 4586 2912
Email: planta.industrial@fanapel.com.uy
Web Address: www.fanapel.com.uy
Personnel:
Mill Mgr.: Miguel Sica
Phone: (598) 4586 2022 Ext. 3213
Fax: (598) 4586 2912
Email: msica@fanapel.com.uy
Pulp Mill Mgr.: Gonzalo Gascue
Phone: (598) 4586 2022
Fax: (598) 4586 2912
Email: ggascue@fanapel.com.uy
Paper Production Mgr.: Gustavo Gorni
Phone: (598) 4586 2022
Fax: (598) 4586 2912
Email: ggorni@fanapel.com.uy
Maint. Mgr.: José Vázquez
Phone: (598) 4586 2022
Fax: (598) 4586 2912
Email: jvazquez@fanapel.com.uy
R&D Mgr.: Horacio Faedo
Phone: (598) 4586 2022
Fax: (598) 4586 2912
Email: hfaedo@fanapel.com.uy
Commer. Dep.: Ines Urrestarazu
Phone: (598) 2916 3858
Fax: (598) 2916 3121
Email: iurrestarazu@fanapel.com.uy
Total Employees at this Location: 350
Type of Operation: Pulp mill, Paper mill
Pulp Grades and Capacities:
Total pulp capacity: 36,097 mt/y
Chemical Pulp: 36,097 mt/y
Pulp Mill Data:
Chemical Pulping Systems:
Continuous digesters: 1

Uruguay

Bleach Plant Systems: 1
Chemical Pulping System, Type: Hardwood (planted Eucalyptus), Sequence: CEopH, Capacity 41,000 admt/y
Chemical Recovery Equipment:
Evaporator lines: 1
Recovery boilers: 1
Lime Kiln
Paper/Paperboard Grades and Capacities:
Total paper and paperboard capacity: 62,118 mt/y
Uncoated woodfree/freesheet: 14,994 mt/y
Coated woodfree/freesheet: 44,982 mt/y
Packaging papers: 2,142 mt/y
Paper and Paperboard Mill Data:
Stock Preparation:
Pulpers: 4
Refiners: 4
Paper Machines: 3
No. 1, (Former Type model: Foudrinier with Yankee), Yankee dryer, total capacity 2,142 mt/y, Trim width 2.2 m, Packaging papers
No. 2, fourdrinier, total capacity 14,994 mt/y, Trim width 2.2 m, Uncoated woodfree/freesheet
No. 3, fourdrinier, total capacity 44,982 mt/y, Trim width 2.8 m, Coated woodfree/freesheet
Coating Machines: 1
No. 1, total capacity 45,000 mt/y., off machine
Finishing Equipment:
Supercalenders: 1 at 40,000 mt/y
Rewinders: 2 at 60,000 mt/y
Sheeters: 3 at 35,000 mt/y
Energy Data:
Power boilers: 4
Steam turbines: 2 at 4 MW
Electrical demand for mill: 158 MWh/D

ⓂⒸIPUSA - Industria Papelera Uruguaya S.A.
IPUSA Plant 3, Pando Mill
Ownership: 99.26% by Empresas CMPC S.A.
Avenida España s/n PO Box 91000
Pando, Canelones
Uruguay
  Phone: (598) 2 292 2240 /2073
  Fax: (598) 2 292 1358 /1362
  Email: ipusa@ipusa.com.uy
  Web Address: www.ipusa.com.uy
Personnel:
  Paper Mill Mgr. & CEO: Ricardo Pereiras
  Phone: (598) 2 292 2073
  Fax: (598) 2 292 1358
  Email: rpereiras@ipusa.com.uy
  Mill Mgr.: Armando Zulian
  Phone: (598) 2 292 2073
  Fax: (598) 2 292 1358
  Email: azulian@ipusa.com.uy
  Chief Eng.: Pablo Bazzano
  Phone: (598) 2 292 2073
  Fax: (598) 2 292 1358
  Email: pbazzano@ipusa.com.uy
  Converting Plt. Mgr.: Carlos Silva
  Phone: (598) 2 292 2073
  Fax: (598) 2 292 1358
  Email: csilva@ipusa.com.uy
  Ind. Develop. Mgr.: Carlos Hirigoyen
  Phone: (598) 2 292 2073
  Fax: (598) 2 292 1358
  Email: chirigoyen@tissue.cmpc.cl
  Sls. Mgr.: Omar Manzo
  Phone: (598) 2 292 2073
  Fax: (598) 2 292 1358
  Email: omanzo@ipusa.com.uy
  Sec: Carina Behrens
  Phone: (598) 2 292 2073
  Fax: (598) 2 292 1358
  Email: cbehrens@ipusa.com.uy
Total Employees of Company: 14,382
Total Employees at this Location: 211
Type of Operation: Paper mill

Pulp Mill Data:
Bleach Plant Systems: 1
Recycled Pulping System, Type: DIP
Recycled Fiber Treatment Lines:
Flotation deinking lines: 1
Paper and Paperboard Mill Data:
Stock Preparation:
Pulpers: 4
Refiners: 4
Finishing Equipment:
Rewinders: 2 at 1,200 mt/y
Energy Data:
Power boilers: 3
Electrical demand for mill: 181 MWh/D

ⓂMontes del Plata
Ownership: 50% by Stora Enso Oyj, 50% by Celulosa Arauco y Constitución S.A.
Luis Alberto de Herrera 1248, Tower 3, Floor 9
11300 Montevideo
Uruguay
  Phone: (598) 2 623 6300
  Email: contacto@montesdelplata.com.uy
  Web Address: www.montesdelplata.com.uy
Personnel:
  CEO: Matías Domeyko
  Phone: (598) 2 623 6300
  Email: matias.cassel@arauco.cl
  Admin. & Finan. Mgr.: Diego Wollheim
  Phone: (598) 2 623 6300
  Sustainability & Corp. Aff's. Mgr.: Carolina Moreira Arenas
  Phone: (598) 2 623 6300
  Bd. Mbr.: Juan Carlos Bueno
  Phone: (598) 2 623 6300
  Forestry Mgr. MdP: Moacyr Fantini Jr.
  Phone: (598) 2 623 6300
Total Employees of Company: 5,000
Mill Locations:
Montes del Plata, Punta Pereira Mill, Zona Franca, Punta Pereira, Uruguay, (Pulp mill)
  Email: contacto@montesdelplata.com.uy

ⓂMontes del Plata
Punta Pereira Mill
Ownership: 50% by Stora Enso Oyj, 50% by Celulosa Arauco y Constitución S.A.
Zona Franca
Punta Pereira, Colonia
Uruguay
  Email: contacto@montesdelplata.com.uy
  Web Address: www.montesdelplata.com.uy
Personnel:
  Gen. Mgr.: Luis María Rodríguez
  Phone: (598) 4522 0658
  Mill Mgr.: Héctor Araneda
  Phone: (598) 4522 0658
  Prod. Mgr.: Andrés García González
  Phone: (598) 4522 0658
Type of Operation: Pulp mill
Pulp Grades and Capacities:
  Total pulp capacity: 1,050,806 mt/y
  Pulp available for market: 1,040,298 mt/y
  Chemical Pulp: 1,050,806 mt/y
Pulp Mill Data:
Pulp Lines: 1
Energy Data:
Electrical demand for mill: 1,734 MWh/D

ⓄPAMER - Papelera Mercedes S.A.
Luis A. de Herrera 3113
11800 Montevideo
Uruguay
  Phone: (598) 2 4804 242
  Fax: (598) 2 480 9630
  Email: info@pamer.com.uy
  Web Address: www.pamer.com.uy
Personnel:
  Man. Dir.: Andrés Caló
  Phone: (598) 2 4804 242
  Fax: (598) 2 480 9630
  Email: acalo@pamer.com.uy
  Sls. Mgr.: Joaquin Costas
  Phone: (598) 2 4804 242
  Fax: (598) 2 480 9630
  Email: jcostas@pamer.com.uy
  Finan. Admin. Dir.: Daniel Yanneo
  Phone: (598) 2 4804 242
  Fax: (598) 2 480 9630
  Email: dyanneo@pamer.com.uy
  Converting Mill Mgr.: Federico Algorta
  Phone: (598) 2 4804 242
  Fax: (598) 2 480 9630
  Email: falgorta@pamer.com.uy
  Paper Mill Mgr.: Luis Soria
  Phone: (598) 2 4804 242
  Fax: (598) 2 480 9630
  Email: lsoria@pamer.com.uy
  Sal. Exec.: Sebastián Ciliurczuk
  Phone: (598) 2 4804 242
  Fax: (598) 2 480 9630
Total Employees of Company: 340
Total Employees at this Location: 40
Mill Locations:
PAMER - Papelera Mercedes S.A., Mercedes, Soriano Mill, Ejido de Chacras, 75000 Mercedes, Soriano, Uruguay, Capacity: 34,986 mt/y, (Pulp mill, Paper mill, Paperboard mill)
  Phone: (598) 2 4532 3882
  Fax: (598) 2 4532 4355
  Email: info@pamer.com.uy

ⓄPAMER - Papelera Mercedes S.A.
Mercedes, Soriano Mill
Ejido de Chacras
75000 Mercedes, Soriano
Uruguay
  Phone: (598) 2 4532 3882
  Fax: (598) 2 4532 4355
  Email: info@pamer.com.uy
  Web Address: www.pamer.com.uy
Personnel:
  Man. Dir.: Andrés Caló
  Phone: (598) 2 4532 3882
  Fax: (598) 2 4532 4355
  Email: acalo@pamer.com.uy
  Plt. Mgr.: Luis Soria
  Phone: (598) 2 4532 3882 Ext: 247
  Fax: (598) 2 4532 4355
  Email: lsoria@pamer.com.uy
  Tech. Dir.: Carlos Moreira
  Phone: (598) 2 4804 242 Ext. 285
  Fax: (598) 2 4532 4355
  Email: cmoreira@pamer.com.uy
  Chief of Paper Prod.: Marianoel Gramajo
  Phone: (598) 2 4532 3882
  Fax: (598) 2 4532 4355
  Email: mgramajo@pamer.com.uy
  Corrugated Mgr.: Federico Algorta
  Phone: (598) 2 4532 3882 Ext: 267
  Fax: (598) 2 4532 4355
  Email: falgorta@pamer.com.uy
Total Employees at this Location: 105
Type of Operation: Pulp mill, Paper mill, Paperboard mill
Pulp Grades and Capacities:
  Total pulp capacity: 28,501 mt/y
  Recycled Pulping: 28,501 mt/y
Pulp Mill Data:
Recycled Fiber Treatment Lines:
Pulpers: 4 at 57,600
Paper/Paperboard Grades and Capacities:
  Total paper and paperboard capacity: 34,986 mt/y
  Tissue: 7,140 mt/y
  Linerboard: 18,921 mt/y
  Corrugating medium/fluting: 8,925 mt/y
Paper and Paperboard Mill Data:
Stock Preparation:

Pulpers:
Refiners: 6
Paper Machines: 2
No. 1, fourdrinier, total capacity 27,846 mt/y, Trim width 2.2 m, Linerboard, Corrugating medium/fluting
No. 3, fourdrinier, total capacity 7,140 mt/y, Trim width 2.1 m, Tissue
Finishing Equipment:
Rewinders: 3 at 30,000 mt/y
Sheeters: 1
Energy Data:
Power boilers: 2
Electrical demand for mill: 67 MWh/D

ⓂUPM Uruguay
Fray Bentos Pulp Mill
Ownership: UPM-Kymmene Corporation
Ruta Puente Puerto Km. 307
65000 Fray Bentos, Rio Negro
Uruguay
Phone: (598) 456 20100
Fax: (598) 456 26971
Web Address: www.upmuruguay.com.uy
Personnel:
Gen Mgr. (From February 2014): Juha Kääriäinen
Phone: (598) 456 25740
Fax: (598) 456 26971
Email: juha.kaariainen@upm.com
Commun. Mgr. UPM Uruguay operations: Matias Martinez
Phone: (598) 456 20100 Ext. 265, M: 993 71 339
Fax: (598) 456 26971
Email: matias.martinez@upm.com
Total Employees at this Location: 300
Type of Operation: Pulp mill
Pulp Grades and Capacities:
Total pulp capacity: 1,213,829 mt/y
Pulp available for market: 1,200,234 mt/y
Chemical Pulp: 1,213,829 mt/y
Pulp Mill Data:
Chemical Pulping Systems:
Continuous digesters: 1
Pulp Lines: 1
Bleach Plant Systems: 1
Chemical Pulping System, Type: Hardwood (Eucalyptus), Sequence: O₂ ADEOPDP
Chemical Recovery Equipment:
Evaporator lines: 7
Recovery boilers: 1
Lime Kiln
Pulp Dryers:
Air Float dryers 1, Air Float dryers 1
Energy Data:
Power boilers: 2
Steam turbines: 2 at 80, 80 MW
Electrical demand for mill: 1,620 MWh/D

VENEZUELA

ⓐA.B.C.D. Cartiere CA
Ownership: 100% by Giovanni Siciliano D.
Av. Francisco Solano, Edf. Yocoima, Piso 9 Of. 9-D Las Delicias, Sabana Grande
Caracas, Edo. Miranda
Venezuela
Phone: (58) 212 762 7036/763 3035
Fax: (58) 212 763 3035
Email: lecartiere@gmail.com
Web Address: www.lecartiere.com
Personnel:
Pres.: Giovanni Siciliano D.
Phone: (58) 212 762 7036/763 3035
Fax: (58) 212 763 3035
VP: Juan Carlos Siciliano Z.
Phone: (58) 212 762 7036/763 3035
Fax: (58) 212 763 3035
Tech. Dir.: Franco Conti
Phone: (58) 212 762 7036/763 3035
Fax: (58) 212 763 3035
Legal Dir.: Mauricio Siciliano Z.
Phone: (58) 212 762 7036/763 3035
Fax: (58) 212 763 3035
Admin. Dir.: Maria del Carmen Siciliano Z.
Phone: (58) 212 762 7036/763 3035
Fax: (58) 212 763 3035
Total Employees of Company: 27
Total Employees at this Location: 27
Mill Locations:
A.B.C.D. Cartiere CA, Charallave Mill, Urb. Ind. Cantarrana-Matalinda Av. 5, Esq. C/6, Charallave, Venezuela, Capacity: 1,200 mt/y, (Paper mill)
Phone: (58) 212 762 7036
Fax: (58) 212 763 3035
Email: lecartiere@gmail.com

ⓂA.B.C.D. Cartiere CA
Charallave Mill
Urb. Ind. Cantarrana-Matalinda Av. 5, Esq. C/6
Charallave, Edo. Miranda
Venezuela
Phone: (58) 212 762 7036
Fax: (58) 212 763 3035
Email: lecartiere@gmail.com
Web Address: www.lecartiere.com
Personnel:
Pres.: Giovanni Siciliano
Phone: (58) 212 762 7036
Tech. Dir.: Franco Conti
Phone: (58) 212 762 7036
Type of Operation: Paper mill
Paper/Paperboard Grades and Capacities:
Total paper and paperboard capacity: 1,200 mt/y
Uncoated woodfree/freesheet: 1,000 mt/y
Coated woodfree/freesheet: 200 mt/y
Paper and Paperboard Mill Data:
Paper Machines: 3
No. 1, Uncoated woodfree/freesheet
No. 2, Uncoated woodfree/freesheet
No. 3, Uncoated woodfree/freesheet
Finishing Equipment:
Sheeters: 2

ⓐCartonera del Caribe CA
Av. Urdaneta, Edf. Centro Financiero Latino, Piso 16, Of. 9
1010 Caracas, Edo. Miranda
Venezuela
Mailing Address: Aptdo. Postal 30056, 1010-A
Caracas, Venezuela
Phone: (58) 212 561 9411
Fax: (58) 212 563 8761
Email: ccaribe@cantv.net
Personnel:
Pres.: Saltiel Beracha
Phone: (58) 212 256 3339
Fax: (58) 212 563 8761
Email: bsaltiel@cantv.net
Plann. Mgr.: Elfas Fernando
Phone: (58) 212 561 9411
Fax: (58) 212 563 8761
Email: felias@cantv.net
Admin. Mgr.: Orlando Fragoso
Phone: (58) 212 561 9411
Fax: (58) 212 563 8761
Email: fragoso2@cantv.net
Total Employees of Company: 430
Total Employees at this Location: 60
Mill Locations:
Cartonera del Caribe CA, Maracay Mill, Zona Industrial San Vicente I, Maracay, Venezuela, Capacity: 26,400 mt/y, (Paperboard mill)
Phone: (58) 243 553 6522
Fax: (58) 243 553 6533
Email: cartoneracaribe@cantv.net

ⓂCartonera del Caribe CA
Maracay Mill
Zona Industrial San Vicente I
Maracay, Edo. Aragua
Venezuela
Phone: (58) 243 553 6522
Fax: (58) 243 553 6533
Email: cartoneracaribe@cantv.net
Web Address: www.cartoneracaribe.com.ve
Personnel:
Mill Mgr.: Ing. Elias Fernandez
Phone: (58) 243 553 6522
Fax: (58) 243 553 6533
Email: felias@cantv.net
Type of Operation: Paperboard mill
Paper/Paperboard Grades and Capacities:
Total paper and paperboard capacity: 26,400 mt/y
Linerboard
Corrugating medium/fluting
Boxboard/cartonboard: 26,400 mt/y
Paper and Paperboard Mill Data:
Paper Machines: 3
PM 1, Linerboard, Corrugating medium/fluting
PM 2
PM 3

ⓐⓂInvepal
Morón Mill
Ownership: 49% by Convinpa, 51% by state
Carr. Morón-Coro, Km. 10
2051 Morón, Edo. Carabobo
Venezuela
Phone: (58) 242 3607 019 / 125 / 062 / 048 / 166
Fax: (58) 242 3607 156
Web Address: www.invepal.com.ve
Personnel:
Pres.: Omar Romero Jose Marrero
Phone: (58) 242 3607 019
Fax: (58) 242 3607 156
Email: omarrero@invepal.com.ve
Prod. Mgr.: Carmen Pirona
Phone: (58) 242 3607 019
Fax: (58) 242 3607 156
Email: cpirona@invepal.com.ve
Admin & Finan. Mgr.: Enrique Melendez
Phone: (58) 242 3607 019
Fax: (58) 242 3607 156
Email: emelendez@invepal.com.ve
Maint. Mgr.: Alexis Hornebo
Phone: (58) 242 3607 019
Fax: (58) 242 3607 156
Email: ahornebo@invepal.com.ve
Total Employees at this Location: 300
Type of Operation: Pulp mill, Paper mill
Pulp Grades and Capacities:
Total pulp capacity: 132,629 mt/y
Recycled Pulping: 132,629 mt/y
Pulp Mill Data:
Chemical Pulping Systems:
Continuous digesters: 3
Bleach Plant Systems: 2
Chemical Pulping System, Type: bagasse (idle), Sequence: CEopH, Capacity 60,000 admt/y
Chemical Pulping System, Type: bagasse (idle), Sequence: CEopH, Capacity 60,000 admt/y
Chemical Recovery Equipment:
Evaporator lines: 1
Recovery boilers: 1
Recycled Fiber Treatment Lines:
Pulpers: 2 at 99,000 admt/y
Paper/Paperboard Grades and Capacities:
Total paper and paperboard capacity: 168,861 mt/y
Uncoated woodfree/freesheet: 39,984 mt/y
Packaging papers: 48,909 mt/y
Linerboard: 47,838 mt/y
Corrugating medium/fluting: 32,130 mt/y
Paper and Paperboard Mill Data:
Stock Preparation:

Venezuela

Pulpers: 11
Refiners: 45
Paper Machines: 4
No. 1, fourdrinier, total capacity 39,984 mt/y, Trim width 4.6 m, Uncoated woodfree/freesheet
No. 2, Yankee dryer, total capacity 17,850 mt/y, Trim width 4 m, Packaging papers
No. 4, fourdrinier, total capacity 79,968 mt/y, Trim width 4.3 m, Linerboard, Corrugating medium/fluting
No. 5, cylinder (8), total capacity 31,059 mt/y, Trim width 4 m, Packaging papers
Coating Machines: 2
No. 1, total capacity 38,500 mt/y., on machine
No. 2, on machine
Finishing Equipment:
Supercalenders: 4
Rewinders: 4
Sheeters: 6
Energy Data:
Power boilers: 4
Steam turbines: 4 at 40.5 MW
Electrical demand for mill: 284 MWh/D

ⓜKimberly-Clark Venezuela, C.A.
Ownership: Kimberly-Clark Corp.
Av. Francisco de Miranda and Av. del Parque, Centro Empresarial Dalipa, Torre C, Piso 11, El Rosal
Caracas
Venezuela
Phone: (58) 212 201 2500
Fax: (58) 212 201 2502
Web Address: www.kimberly-clark.com
Personnel:
Pres./Man. Dir.: Luis Padilla
Phone: (58) 212 201 2501
Email: luis.padilla@kcc.com
Sec.: Maria Megaro
Phone: (58) 212 201 2500
Fax: (58) 212 201 2502
Email: maria.s.megaro@kcc.com
Total Employees at this Location: 80
Mill Locations:
Kimberly-Clark Venezuela, C.A., Maracay Mill, Aptdo. 173, Zona Ind. La Hamaca 2da. transversal 160-4, Maracay, Venezuela, Capacity: 41,769 mt/y, (Paper mill)
Phone: (58) 243 550 1511
Fax: (58) 243 550 1502

ⓜKimberly-Clark Venezuela, C.A.
Maracay Mill
Ownership: Kimberly-Clark Corp.
Aptdo. 173, Zona Ind. La Hamaca 2da. transversal 160-4
Maracay, Edo. Aragua
Venezuela
Phone: (58) 243 550 1511
Fax: (58) 243 550 1502
Web Address: www.kcc.com
Personnel:
Pres.: Luiz Padilla
Phone: (58) 243 550 1511
Fax: (58) 243 550 1502
Manuf. Dir. Mill. Mgr.: Antonio D Antonio D
Phone: (58) 243 550 1511
Fax: (58) 243 550 1502
Total Employees at this Location: 154
Type of Operation: Paper mill
Paper/Paperboard Grades and Capacities:
Total paper and paperboard capacity: 41,769 mt/y
Tissue: 41,769 mt/y
Paper and Paperboard Mill Data:
Stock Preparation:
Pulpers: 4
Refiners: 5
Paper Machines: 2
No. 3, crescent former, total capacity 10,710 mt/y, Trim width 3.2 m, Tissue
No. 4, crescent former, total capacity 31,059 mt/y, Trim width 2.75 m, Tissue
Finishing Equipment:
Rewinders: 5
Energy Data:
Power boilers: 3
Electrical demand for mill: 120 MWh/D

ⓗManufacturas de Papel CA (MANPA) S.A.C.A.
Ownership: 100% by Larragain Family
Av. Francisco de Miranda, con Avenida Principal Edificio Torre Country Club
Chacaito, Caracas
Venezuela
Mailing Address: PO Box 2050, Chacaito, Caracas, Venezuela
Phone: (58) 212 901 2499
Fax: (58) 212 901 2310
Email: rrhh@manpa.com.ve
Web Address: www.manpa.com.ve/ingles/inghome1.html
Personnel:
Chmn. of Bd.: Carlos Delfino T.
Phone: (58) 212 901 2499
Fax: (58) 212 901 2310
Email: cdelfino@manpa.com.ve
Bd. Mbr.: Ricardo Delfino Monzon
Phone: (58) 212 901 2499
Fax: (58) 212 901 2310
Bd. Mbr.: Juan Carlos Carpio Delfino
Phone: (58) 212 901 2499
Fax: (58) 212 901 2310
Dir.: Arnaldo Anez D
Phone: (58) 212 901 2499
Fax: (58) 212 901 2310
VP Finan.: Juan Antonio Lovera V.
Phone: (58) 212 901 2499
Fax: (58) 212 901 2310
Email: jlovera@manpa.com.ve
COO: Egbert Dittmer
Phone: (58) 212 901 2434
Fax: (58) 212 901 2317
Email: edittmer@manpa.com.ve
Legal Counsel.: Nelly Gonzalez
Phone: (58) 212 901 2499
Fax: (58) 212 901 2310
Plann. Dir: Leticia Level
Phone: (58) 212 901 2499
Fax: (58) 212 901 2310
Email: llevel@manpa.com.ve
Asst. Exec. Pres.: Pedro Bosque
Phone: (58) 212 901 2306
Fax: (58) 212 901 2310
Email: pbosque@manpa.com.ve
Sls. Mgr.: Hector Rodriguez
Phone: (58) 212 901 2499
Fax: (58) 212 901 2310
Email: hrodriguez@manpa.com.ve
Total Employees of Company: 2,200
Mill Locations:
Manufacturera de Papel Bidasoa S.A. de C.V., Teotihuacan Mill, Antiguo Camino Real de Veracruz s/n Col. San Sebastian, 55800 Xolaltenco Teotihuacan, Mexico, Capacity: 32,000 mt/y, (Paper mill)
Fax: (52) 594 9560 0300
Email: bidasoam@abantel.net, mfradibasoa@prodigy.net.mx
Manufacturas de Papel CA (MANPA) S.A.C.A., Maracay Packaging Mill, Av. Aragua, cruce con Av. Mariño Sur Aptdo. 172, 2103 Maracay, Venezuela, Capacity: 119,595 mt/y, (Paper mill, Paperboard mill)
Phone: (58) 243 2401111
Fax: (58) 243 241045/340466
Email: ecarreño@manpa.com.ve
Manufacturas de Papel CA (MANPA) S.A.C.A., Maracay Tissue Mill, Calle Guayamure, Zona Industrial La Hamaca, 2103 Maracay, Venezuela, Capacity: 76,755 mt/y, (Pulp mill, Paper mill)
Phone: (58) 243 2407511
Fax: (58) 243 2723902
Email: atencionalconsumidor@manpa.com.ve

ⓜManufacturas de Papel CA (MANPA) S.A.C.A.
Maracay Packaging Mill
Av. Aragua, cruce con Av. Mariño Sur Aptdo. 172
2103 Maracay, Edo. Aragua
Venezuela
Phone: (58) 243 2401111
Fax: (58) 243 241045/340466
Email: ecarreño@manpa.com.ve
Web Address: www.manpa.com.ve/ingles/inghome1.html
Personnel:
Mill Mgr.: Ricardo Montilla
Phone: (58) 243 2401111
Fax: (58) 243 240 1086
Email: rmontilla@manpa.com.ve
Total Employees at this Location: 220
Type of Operation: Paper mill, Paperboard mill
Pulp Grades and Capacities:
Total pulp capacity: 86,194 mt/y
Recycled Pulping: 86,194 mt/y
Pulp Mill Data:
Bleach Plant Systems: 1
DIP
Recycled Fiber Treatment Lines:
Flotation deinking lines: 1
Recycled packaging pulping lines: 1
Paper/Paperboard Grades and Capacities:
Total paper and paperboard capacity: 119,595 mt/y
Uncoated woodfree/freesheet: 71,757 mt/y
Packaging papers: 32,844 mt/y
Linerboard: 9,282 mt/y
Corrugating medium/fluting: 5,712 mt/y
Paper and Paperboard Mill Data:
Stock Preparation:
Pulpers: 10
Refiners: 17
Paper Machines: 3
No. 1, fourdrinier, total capacity 14,280 mt/y, Trim width 2 m, Uncoated woodfree/freesheet
No. 2, fourdrinier, total capacity 47,838 mt/y, Trim width 3 m, Linerboard, Corrugating medium/fluting, Packaging papers
No. 3, fourdrinier, total capacity 57,477 mt/y, Trim width 4 m, Uncoated woodfree/freesheet
Finishing Equipment:
Rewinders: 6
Sheeters: 6
Energy Data:
Power boilers: 1
Steam turbines: 1
Electrical demand for mill: 267 MWh/D

ⓜManufacturas de Papel CA (MANPA) S.A.C.A.
Maracay Tissue Mill
Calle Guayamure, Zona Industrial La Hamaca
2103 Maracay, Edo. Aragua
Venezuela
Mailing Address: PO Box 72, 2104 Maracay, Edo. Aragua, Venezuela
Phone: (58) 243 2407511
Fax: (58) 243 2723902
Email: atencionalconsumidor@manpa.com.ve
Web Address: www.manpa.com.ve/ingles/inghome1.html
Personnel:
Chmn.: Carlos Delfino
Phone: (58) 212 901 2256
Fax: (58) 212 901 2130
Email: cdelfino@manpa.com.ve
Exec. Pres.: Alejandro Delfino
Phone: (58) 212 901 2313
Fax: (58) 212 901 2310
Email: adelfino@manpa.com.ve
COO: Egbert Dittmer

Venezuela

Phone: (58) 212 901 2434
Fax: (58) 212 901 2317
Email: edittmer@manpa.com.ve
Mill Mgr.: Gerardo Viloria
Phone: (58) 243 240 7529
Fax: (58) 243 240 4571
Email: gviloria@manpa.com.ve
Converting Plt. Mgr.: Alvaro Villamizar
Phone: (58) 243 240 7592
Fax: (58) 243 240 7239
Email: avillamizar@manpa.com.ve
Environ. Mgr.: Nilda Rosquete
Phone: (58) 243 240 1036
Fax: (58) 243 235 0812
Email: nrosquete@manpa.com.ve
Total Employees at this Location: 340
Type of Operation: Pulp mill, Paper mill
Pulp Grades and Capacities:
Total pulp capacity: 55,699 mt/y
Recycled Pulping: 55,699 mt/y

Pulp Mill Data:
Bleach Plant Systems: 1
Recycled Pulping System, Type: DIP
Recycled Fiber Treatment Lines:
Flotation deinking lines: 2 at 24,000 admt/y
Pulpers: 2 at 48,000 admt/y
Washing deinking lines: 2 at 24,000 admt/y
Pulp Dryers:
Air Float dryers 2
Paper/Paperboard Grades and Capacities:
Total paper and paperboard capacity: 76,755 mt/y
Tissue: 76,755 mt/y
Paper and Paperboard Mill Data:
Stock Preparation:
Pulpers: 5
Refiners: 12
Paper Machines: 4
No. 5, fourdrinier, total capacity 7,140 mt/y, Trim width 2 m, Tissue, Uncoated woodfree/freesheet
No. 6, fourdrinier, total capacity 16,779 mt/y, Trim width 2 m, Tissue, Uncoated woodfree/freesheet
No. 7, fourdrinier, total capacity 17,850 mt/y, Trim width 2 m, Tissue
No. 8, crescent former, total capacity 34,986 mt/y, Trim width 2.6 m, Tissue
Finishing Equipment:
Rewinders: 3
Energy Data:
Power boilers: 2
Combustion turbines: 2 at 40 MW
Electrical demand for mill: 328 MWh/D

ⓂSmurfit Kappa Cartón de Venezuela S.A.

Ownership: 78% by Smurfit Kappa Group
Av. Domingo Olavarría, Zona Ind. Sur
2003 Valencia, Edo. Carabobo
Venezuela
Mailing Address: P.O. Box 1382, 2003 Valencia, Edo. Carabobo, Venezuela
Phone: (58) 241 813 0966/70/00
Fax: (58) 241 813 0962/65
Web Address: www.smurfitkappa.com.ve
Personnel:
Pres & CEO: Edgar Londoño
Phone: (58) 241 813 0966/0970
Fax: (58) 241 813 0962/0965
Group CEO: Gary McGann
Phone: (58) 241 813 0966/0970
Fax: (58) 241 813 0962/0965
CEO Corrugated Division: Roberto Villaquiran
Phone: (58) 241 813 0966/0970
Fax: (58) 241 813 0962/0965
VP of Mills, Forestry & Eng. Projects: Alberto Ramirez
Phone: (58) 241 813 0966/0970
Fax: (58) 241 813 0962/0965
VPSec.: Joelle Falcon
Phone: (58) 241 813 0966/0970
Fax: (58) 241 813 0962/0965

Gen. Mgr.: Nang Cheng
Phone: (58) 241 813 0966/0970
Fax: (58) 241 813 0962/0965
Supt.: Amilcar Aponte Dubois
Phone: (58) 241 813 0966/0970
Fax: (58) 241 813 0962/0965
Mktg Analyst.: Juan Solórzano
Phone: (58) 0241 813 0630 Ex.0630
Fax: (58) 241 813 0962/0965
Email: Juan.Solorzano@smurfitkappa.com.ve
Mill Locations:
Smurfit Kappa Cartón de Venezuela S.A., Caracas Mill, Final Calle El Hatillo, 1070-A Petare, Caracas, Venezuela, Capacity: 23,919 mt/y, (Paperboard mill)
Phone: (58) 212 219 1100/01
Fax: (58) 212 219 1243
Smurfit Kappa Cartón de Venezuela S.A., San Felipe Mill, Carretera Morón-San Felipe, Zona Carbonero, 1010-A San Felipe, Venezuela, Capacity: 134,946 mt/y, (Pulp mill, Paperboard mill)
Phone: (58) 254 600 7215/6
Fax: (58) 254 600 7383
Smurfit Kappa Cartón de Venezuela S.A., Valencia Mill, Aptdo. Postal 448, Ave. Domingo Olavarria, Zona Industrial Sur, 2003 Valencia, Venezuela, Capacity: 80,682 mt/y, (Paperboard mill)
Phone: (58) 241 813 0401
Fax: (58) 241 813 0477

ⓂSmurfit Kappa Cartón de Venezuela S.A.
Caracas Mill
Ownership: 78% by Smurfit Kappa Group
Final Calle El Hatillo
1070-A Petare, Caracas, Edo. Miranda
Venezuela
Mailing Address: Aptdo. 609, 1010-A Petare, Caracas, Edo. Miranda, Venezuela
Phone: (58) 212 219 1100/01
Fax: (58) 212 219 1243
Web Address: www.smurfitkappa.com.ve
Personnel:
Gen & Mill Mgr.: Andres Acosta
Phone: (58) 212 219 1100/01
Fax: (58) 212 219 1243
Email: andres.acosta@smurfitkappa.com.ve
Prod. Mgr.: Alan Kment
Phone: (58) 212 219 1100/01
Fax: (58) 212 219 1243
Email: alan.kment@smurfitkappa.com.ve
Prod. Mgr.: Gerardo Yaremi
Phone: (58) 212 219 1100/01
Fax: (58) 212 219 1243
Email: gerardo.yaremi@smurfitkappa.com.ve
Mktg. Mgr.: Mauricio Pensa
Phone: (58) 212 219 1100/01
Fax: (58) 212 219 1243
Email: mauricio.pensa@smurfitkappa.com.ve
Total Employees at this Location: 83
Type of Operation: Paperboard mill
Pulp Grades and Capacities:
Total pulp capacity: 24,951 mt/y
Recycled Pulping: 24,951 mt/y
Pulp Mill Data:
Recycled Fiber Treatment Lines:
Recycled packaging pulping lines: 1 at 25,000
Paper/Paperboard Grades and Capacities:
Total paper and paperboard capacity: 23,919 mt/y
Boxboard/cartonboard: 23,919 mt/y
Paper and Paperboard Mill Data:
Stock Preparation:
Pulpers: 2
Refiners: 5
Paper Machines: 1
No. 1, fourdrinier, total capacity 23,919 mt/y, Trim width 1.7 m, Boxboard/cartonboard
Finishing Equipment:
Calenders: 1
Rewinders: 1 at 30,000 mt/y
Sheeters: 1

Energy Data:
Power boilers: 1
Electrical demand for mill: 46 MWh/D

ⓂSmurfit Kappa Cartón de Venezuela S.A.
San Felipe Mill
Ownership: 78% by Smurfit Kappa Group
Carretera Morón-San Felipe, Zona Carbonero
1010-A San Felipe, Yaracuy
Venezuela
Mailing Address: Aptdo. 111 Zona Carbonero, 1010-A San Felipe, Yaracuy, Venezuela
Phone: (58) 254 600 7215/6
Fax: (58) 254 600 7383
Web Address: www.smurfitkappa.com.ve
Personnel:
Gen & Mill Mgr.: Rafael Concepcion
Phone: (58) 254 600 7215
Fax: (58) 254 600 7383
Email: rafael.concepcion@smurfitkappa.com.ve
Prod. Mgr.: José De Abreu
Phone: (58) 254 600 7215
Fax: (58) 254 600 7383
Email: jose.deabreu@smurfitkappa.com.ve
Maint. Mgr.: Oswaldo Gomez
Phone: (58) 254 600 7215
Fax: (58) 254 600 7383
Email: oswaldo.gomez@smurfitkappa.com.ve
Total Employees at this Location: 340
Type of Operation: Pulp mill, Paperboard mill
Pulp Grades and Capacities:
Total pulp capacity: 138,157 mt/y
Chemical Pulp: 74,478 mt/y
Recycled Pulping: 63,679 mt/y
Pulp Mill Data:
Chemical Pulping Systems:
Batch digesters: 6
Continuous digesters: 1
Pulp Lines: 2
Chemical Recovery Equipment:
Evaporator lines: 1
Recovery boilers: 1
Lime Kiln
Recycled Fiber Treatment Lines:
Pulpers: 2 at 100,000 admt/y
Paper/Paperboard Grades and Capacities:
Total paper and paperboard capacity: 134,946 mt/y
Linerboard: 65,688 mt/y
Corrugating medium/fluting: 69,258 mt/y
Paper and Paperboard Mill Data:
Stock Preparation:
Pulpers: 2
Refiners: 5
Paper Machines: 1
No. 1, (Suppliers: Beloit/Carcano), fourdrinier, total capacity 134,946 mt/y, Trim width 4.25 m, Linerboard, Corrugating medium/fluting
Finishing Equipment:
Winders: 1 at 135,000 mt/y
Calenders: 1
Energy Data:
Power boilers: 4
Combustion turbines: 2 at 55.3, 55.3 MW
Steam turbines: 2 at 12.5, 12.5 MW
Electrical demand for mill: 325 MWh/D

ⓂSmurfit Kappa Cartón de Venezuela S.A.
Valencia Mill
Ownership: 78% by Smurfit Kappa Group
Aptdo. Postal 448, Ave. Domingo Olavarria, Zona Industrial Sur
2003 Valencia, Edo. Carabobo
Venezuela
Phone: (58) 241 813 0401
Fax: (58) 241 813 0477
Web Address: www.smurfitkappa.com.ve

Venezuela

Personnel:
Gen & Mill Mgr.: Juan Smola
Phone: (58) 241 813 0401
Fax: (58) 241 813 0477
Email: juan.smola@smurfitkappa.com.ve
Prod. Mgr.: Felix García
Phone: (58) 241 813 0401
Fax: (58) 241 813 0477
Email: felix.garcia@smurfitkappa.com.ve
Sls. Mgr.: Adolfo Marcano
Phone: (58) 241 813 0401
Fax: (58) 241 813 0477
Email: adolfo.marcano@smurfitkappa.com.ve
Total Employees at this Location: 130
Type of Operation: Paperboard mill
Pulp Grades and Capacities:
Total pulp capacity: 62,926 mt/y
Recycled Pulping: 62,926 mt/y
Pulp Mill Data:
Recycled Fiber Treatment Lines:
Recycled packaging pulping lines: 1
Paper/Paperboard Grades and Capacities:
Total paper and paperboard capacity: 80,682 mt/y
Boxboard/cartonboard: 80,682 mt/y
Paper and Paperboard Mill Data:
Stock Preparation:
Pulpers: 5
Refiners: 7
Paper Machines: 1
No. 7, Ultraformer (7), total capacity 80,682 mt/y, Trim width 2.8 m, Boxboard/cartonboard
Coating Machines: 2
No. 1, total capacity 80,000 mt/y., on machine
No. 2, total capacity 85,000 mt/y., on machine
Finishing Equipment:
Winders: 1
Rewinders: 1
Sheeters: 3
Energy Data:
Power boilers: 2
Combustion turbines: 2
Steam turbines: 2
Electrical demand for mill: 195 MWh/D

ⓂPapeles Venezolanos CA (PAVECA)

Ownership: 100% by Kruger Inc.
Carretera Nacional Guacara San Joaquín, Kilómetro 1, Aptdo. 003 (Principal de Los Ruices), Edif. PAVECA
2201 Guacara, Edo. Carabobo
Venezuela
Phone: (58) 245 400 3430/3280
Fax: (58) 245 400 3601/3643
Email: info@paveca.com.ve, paveca@paveca.com
Web Address: www.paveca.com.ve
Personnel:
Chmn.: Joseph Kruger
Phone: (58) 245 400 3430/3280
Fax: (58) 245 400 3601/3643
Email: bpatel@kruger.com
Gen. Mgr.: Torbjorn Lovas
Phone: (58) 245 400 3430/3280
Fax: (58) 245 400 3601/3643
Email: tlovas@paveca.com.ve
CFO: Gonzalo Alvarez
Phone: (58) 245 400 3430/3280
Fax: (58) 245 400 3601/3643
Email: galvarez@paveca.com.ve
Chief of Information: Igor Cegarra Noriega
Phone: (58) 245 400 3430/3280
Fax: (58) 245 400 3601/3643
Fin. Mgr.: Americo Valles
Phone: (58) 245 400 3430/3280
Fax: (58) 245 400 3601/3643
Email: avalles@paveca.com.ve
Eng. Mgr.: Alberto Matos Russe
Phone: (58) 245 400 3430/3280
Fax: (58) 245 400 3601/3643
Email: amatos@paveca.com.ve
VPSls.: Antonio Neri
Phone: (58) 245 400 3430/3280
Fax: (58) 245 400 3601/3643
Email: aneri@paveca.com.ve
Total Employees at this Location: 1,258
Mill Locations:
Papeles Venezolanos CA (PAVECA), Guacara Mill, Carretera Nacional Guacara San Joaquín, Kilómetro 1, Aptdo. 003, 2201 Guacara, Venezuela, Capacity: 102,816 mt/y, (Pulp mill, Paper mill)
Phone: (58) 245 400 3430/3280
Fax: (58) 245 400 3601/3643
Email: info@paveca.com, paveca@paveca.com

ⓂPapeles Venezolanos CA (PAVECA) Guacara Mill

Ownership: 100% by Kruger Inc.
Carretera Nacional Guacara San Joaquín, Kilómetro 1, Aptdo. 003
2201 Guacara, Edo. Carabobo
Venezuela
Phone: (58) 245 400 3430/3280
Fax: (58) 245 400 3601/3643
Email: info@paveca.com, paveca@paveca.com
Web Address: www.paveca.com.ve
Personnel:
Chmn.: Joseph Kruger
Phone: (58) 245 400 3430/3280
Email: bpatel@kruger.com
Gen. Mgr.: Torbjorn Lovas
Phone: (58) 245 400 3212
Fax: (58) 245 400 3602
Email: tlovas@paveca.com.ve
CFO: Gonzalo Alvarez
Phone: (58) 245 400 3214
Fax: (58) 245 400 3605
Email: galvarez@paveca.com.ve
Chief of Information: Igor Cegarra Noriega
Phone: (58) 245 400 3430/3280
Fax: (58) 245 400 3601/3643
Fin. Mgr.: Americo Valles
Phone: (58) 245 400 3430/3280
Email: avalles@paveca.com.ve
Eng. Mgr.: Alberto Matos Russe
Phone: (58) 245 400 3430
Fax: (58) 58 245 400 234
Email: amatos@paveca.com.ve
VPSls.: Antonio Neri
Phone: (58) 212 700 2238
Fax: (58) 212 700 2203
Email: aneri@paveca.com.ve
Total Employees at this Location: 500
Type of Operation: Pulp mill, Paper mill
Pulp Grades and Capacities:
Total pulp capacity: 79,637 mt/y
Mechanical Pulp: 33,160 mt/y
Recycled Pulping: 46,476 mt/y
Pulp Mill Data:
Mechanical Pulping Systems:
APMP Systems: 1
Bleach Plant Systems: 3
Mechanical Pulping System, Type: APMP
Recycled Pulping System, Type: DIP
Recycled Pulping System, Type: DIP
Recycled Fiber Treatment Lines:
Flotation deinking lines: 2
Paper/Paperboard Grades and Capacities:
Total paper and paperboard capacity: 102,816 mt/y
Tissue: 102,816 mt/y
Paper and Paperboard Mill Data:
Paper Machines: 6
No. 1, fourdrinier, total capacity 12,138 mt/y, Trim width 2.44 m, Tissue
No. 2, fourdrinier, total capacity 8,925 mt/y, Trim width 2.54 m, Tissue
No. 3, DuoFormer, total capacity 18,921 mt/y, Trim width 2.51 m, Tissue, Uncoated woodfree/freesheet
No. 4, inclined, total capacity 14,637 mt/y, Trim width 2.54 m, Tissue, Uncoated woodfree/freesheet
No. 5, crescent former, total capacity 34,986 mt/y, Trim width 4.83 m, Tissue
No. 6, crescent former, total capacity 13,209 mt/y, Trim width 2.75 m, Tissue
Energy Data:
Power boilers
Combustion turbines: 3 at 40 MW
Steam turbines: 1
Electrical demand for mill: 432 MWh/D

PULP and PAPER MILLS in Africa

ALGERIA

ⓘⓜAigle Paper Manufacturing Company - A.P.M.C.
Algiers Mill
Bir Mourad Raïs 13, Les Sources, Industrial Zone Rouïba
Algiers
Algeria
Phone: (213) 21 544041
Fax: (213) 21 544254
Email: djouider@yahoo.fr
Personnel:
Gen. Dir.: Boualem Djouider
Phone: (213) 21 544041
Total Employees at this Location: 40
Type of Operation: Paper mill
Paper/Paperboard Grades and Capacities:
Total paper and paperboard capacity: 5,000 mt/y
Tissue: 5,000 mt/y
Paper and Paperboard Mill Data:
Stock Preparation:
Pulpers: 1
Refiners: 2
Paper Machines: 1
No. 1-4, Tissue
Finishing Equipment:
Winders: 1 at 3,000 mt/y

ⓘFADERCO
Z.I. Les Eucalyptus, Lot n°22, route de Larbaâ
16057 Les Eucalyptus, Algiers, Wilaya d'Alger
Algeria
Phone: (213) 21 501 484 / 476
Fax: (213) 21 501 484 / 467
Email: contact@faderco.dz
Web Address: www.faderco.dz
Personnel:
Dir. Gen.: Amor Habes
Dir. Operations: Sid Ahmed Hasbellaoui
Dir. Exec: Riad Seddik Chikhaoui
Mill Locations:
FADERCO, Setif Mill, Zone Industriellle extension, Lot No. 21, Setif, Algeria, (Paper mill)
Email: contact@faderco.dz

ⓘFADERCO
Setif Mill
Mill is under construction (due to start for the second quarter of 2015)
Zone Industriellle extension, Lot No. 21
Setif
Algeria
Email: contact@faderco.dz
Web Address: www.faderco.dz
Type of Operation: Paper mill
Paper and Paperboard Mill Data:
Paper Machines: 1
PM 1, (due to start for the second quarter of 2015), Advantage DCT 100+, total capacity 30,000 mt/y, Tissue

ⓘGIPEC - Groupe Industriel des Papiers et de la Cellulose
Ownership: 100% by Algerian State
Route de la Gare
Baba Ali, Wilaya d'Alger
Algeria
Phone: (213) 21 309884/309291/308884
Fax: (213) 21 309194/309638
Email: info@gipec.dz.com, gipecdz@gipec.dz.com, info@gipec.com
Web Address: www.gipec.dz
Personnel:
Chmn. & CEO of GIPEC Group: Zaha Merssaud
Phone: (213) 21 309299
Fax: (213) 21 309174
Import & Mktg. Mgr.: Amal Tahourid
Phone: (213) 552 789022/21 309052
Fax: (213) 21 309052
Email: marketing-gipec@gipec.dz.com
Partnersh. Div. Mgr.: Amar Ferdja
Finan. & Account Div. Mgr.: A. Ferdjani
Phone: (213) 21 309884
Fax: (213) 21 309194
HR Mgr.: Ms. Nadia Chibout
Phone: (213) 21 309028
Fax: (213) 21 309194
Total Employees of Company: 1,528
Total Employees at this Location: 58
Mill Locations:
PAPCAS - Rebahia à Saïda, Saïda Mill, B.P. 92, 2000 Saïda, Algeria, Capacity: 31,500 mt/y, (Paperboard mill)
Phone: (213) 48 4623 32/22/27
Fax: (213) 48 4623 17
Email: gipecr@hotmail.com, gipec20@yahoo.fr

ⓜPapeterie de la Mitidja
La Chiffa Mill
Ownership: 100% by Bendriss Family
Route de Médéa
La Chiffa, Wilaya de Blida
Algeria
Phone: (213) 20 597956
Fax: (213) 20 597974
Personnel:
Gen. Mgr.: Mihoub Bendriss
Phone: (213) 772 896127
Commercial Mgr.: Badri Bendriss
Phone: (213) 20 597956
Prod. Foreman: Malki Boualem
Phone: (213) 20 597956
Total Employees at this Location: 45
Type of Operation: Paper mill
Pulp Grades and Capacities:
Total pulp capacity: 19,099 mt/y
Recycled Pulping: 19,099 mt/y
Pulp Mill Data:
Recycled Fiber Treatment Lines:
Pulpers: 2
Recycled packaging pulping lines: 1 at 20,000 admt/y
Paper/Paperboard Grades and Capacities:
Total paper and paperboard capacity: 19,000 mt/y
Linerboard: 10,000 mt/y
Corrugating medium/fluting: 9,000 mt/y
Paper and Paperboard Mill Data:
Stock Preparation:
Pulpers: 2
Refiners: 2
Paper Machines: 1
No. 1, fourdrinier, total capacity 19,000 mt/y, Trim width 2.4 m, Corrugating medium/fluting, Linerboard
Finishing Equipment:
Winders: 1
Rewinders: 1 at 15,000 mt/y
Energy Data:
Power boilers: 1
Electrical demand for mill: 28 MWh/D

ⓜPAPCAS - Rebahia à Saïda
Saïda Mill
Ownership: 100% by GIPEC - Groupe Industriel des Papiers et de la Cellulose
B.P. 92
2000 Saïda, Rebahia
Algeria
Phone: (213) 48 4623 32/22/27
Fax: (213) 48 4623 17
Email: gipecr@hotmail.com, gipec20@yahoo.fr
Personnel:
Gen. Mgr.: Hamoud El Habbas
Phone: (213) 4846 2347/770 861110
Man. Dir.: Boualem Souiyah
Phone: (213) 4846 2322
Finan. Mgr.: Moussa Chadli
Phone: (213) 4846 2327/773 810579
Total Employees at this Location: 255
Type of Operation: Paperboard mill
Pulp Grades and Capacities:
Total pulp capacity: 31,974 mt/y
Recycled Pulping: 31,974 mt/y
Pulp Mill Data:
Recycled Fiber Treatment Lines:
Pulpers: 1 at 31,500 admt/y
Paper/Paperboard Grades and Capacities:
Total paper and paperboard capacity: 31,500 mt/y
Linerboard: 20,000 mt/y
Corrugating medium/fluting: 11,500 mt/y
Paper and Paperboard Mill Data:
Stock Preparation:
Pulpers: 1
Refiners: 4
Paper Machines: 1
No. 1, fourdrinier, total capacity 31,500 mt/y, Trim width 4.2 m, Corrugating medium/fluting, Linerboard
Finishing Equipment:
Winders: 1 at 60,000 mt/y
Calenders: 1
Rewinders: 1
Energy Data:
Power boilers: 3
Electrical demand for mill: 47 MWh/D

ⓘTonic Industrie EPE
Ownership: 100% by Algerian State
Zone Industrielle Bou Ismail, No. 62, Route de Kolea
Bou Ismail, Wilaya d'Alger
Algeria
Phone: (213) 24 464140, 24 466143
Fax: (213) 24 461308
Email: info@tonic-industrie.com
Web Address: www.tonic-industrie.com
Personnel:
Pres., Gen. Dir.: Mourad Khobzi
Phone: (213) 24 464140
Fax: (213) 24 466143
Mill Mgr.: Tahar Fezari
Phone: (213) 24 464140
Fax: (213) 24 466143
Paper Recovery Mgr.: Amar Laouir
Phone: (213) 24 464140
Fax: (213) 24 466143
Paper Machine Mgr.: Sahri Belkacem
Phone: (213) 24 464140
Fax: (213) 24 466143
Tech. Asst.: Salah Saïdani
Phone: (213) 24 464140

Egypt

Fax: (213) 24 466143
Total Employees of Company: 2,500
Mill Locations:
Tonic Industrie EPE, Ouate Industrie Mill, Zone Industrielle Bou Ismail, No. 62, Route de Kolea, 42415 Bou Ismail, Algeria, Capacity: 168,000 mt/y, (Paper mill, Paperboard mill)
Phone: (213) 24 461722/464140/43
Fax: (213) 24 461308/468570
Email: info@tonic-industrie.com

ⓂTonic Industrie EPE
Ouate Industrie Mill
Zone Industrielle Bou Ismail, No. 62, Route de Kolea
42415 Bou Ismail, Wilaya d'Alger
Algeria
Phone: (213) 24 461722/464140/43
Fax: (213) 24 461308/468570
Email: info@tonic-industrie.com
Web Address: www.tonic-industrie.com
Personnel:
Pres., Gen. Dir.: Mourad Khobzi
Phone: (213) 24 461722/464140/43
Mill Mgr.: Tahar Fezari
Phone: (213) 24 468574
Fax: (213) 24 468574
Email: fezaritahar@yahoo.fr
Paper Recovery Mgr.: Amar Laouir
Phone: (213) 24 461722/464140/43
Paper Machine Mgr.: Sahri Belkacem
Phone: (213) 24 461722/464140/43
Tech. Asst.: Salah Saïdani
Phone: (213) 24 467355
Total Employees at this Location: 550
Type of Operation: Paper mill, Paperboard mill
Pulp Grades and Capacities:
Total pulp capacity: 148,382 mt/y
Recycled Pulping: 148,382 mt/y
Pulp Mill Data:
Bleach Plant Systems: 1
No. 1, Sequence: P
Recycled Fiber Treatment Lines:
Flotation deinking lines: 1 at 28,000 admt/y
Pulpers: 1 at 35,000 admt/y
Pulpers: 1
Recycled packaging pulping lines: 1 at 120,000 admt/y
Paper/Paperboard Grades and Capacities:
Total paper and paperboard capacity: 168,000 mt/y
Tissue: 25,000 mt/y
Packaging papers: 3,000 mt/y
Linerboard: 84,000 mt/y
Corrugating medium/fluting: 56,000 mt/y
Paper and Paperboard Mill Data:
Stock Preparation:
Pulpers: 2
Refiners: 3
Paper Machines: 2
No. 1, Advantage DCT 100, Yankee dryer, total capacity 28,000 mt/y, Trim width 2.75 m, Tissue, Uncoated woodfree/freesheet, Packaging papers
No. 2, fourdrinier (2), total capacity 140,000 mt/y, Trim width 2.6 m, Corrugating medium/fluting, Linerboard
Finishing Equipment:
Winders: 2
Calenders: 2
Rewinders: 2
Energy Data:
Power boilers: 3
Electrical demand for mill: 270 MWh/D

EGYPT

ⓄⓂAl Arouba Paper Co. M. Farghaly & Co.
Alexandria Mill
Nadi Elsied St, Moharem Bey
Alexandria, Iskanderiya
Egypt
Phone: (20) 1221 47242
Fax: (20) 3814 958
Email: khalaff_farghaly@hotmail.com
Personnel:
Owner & Mill Mgr.: Eng. Khalaff Farghaly
Phone: (20) 1221 47242
Email: khalaff_farghaly@hotmail.com
Mohamed Ibrahim
Total Employees of Company: 85
Total Employees at this Location: 85
Type of Operation: Paperboard mill
Paper/Paperboard Grades and Capacities:
Total paper and paperboard capacity: 7,500 mt/y
Linerboard
Corrugating medium/fluting: 7,500 mt/y
Paper and Paperboard Mill Data:
Paper Machines: 1
No. 1, total capacity 7,500 mt/y, Trim width 1.7 m, Corrugating medium/fluting, Linerboard

ⓄAl Bardi Paper Mill Co. (S.A.E.)
Ownership: 100% by Nuqul Group
90A Aamed Orabi St 6th floor
Mohandessen, Cairo
Egypt
Phone: (20) 23 833 0960/1922
Fax: (20) 23 833 0747
Email: bpm@albardifine.com
Personnel:
CEO: George Meghdi
Phone: (20) 23 833 0960/1922
Fax: (20) 23 833 0747
Total Employees of Company: 2,000
Mill Locations:
Al Bardi Paper Mill Co. (S.A.E.), 6 October City Mill, 4th Industrial zone, 6 October City, Egypt, Capacity: 20,000 mt/y, (Paper mill)
Phone: (20) 23 8330960/1922
Fax: (20) 23 8330747
Email: bpm@link.net, nt@nuqulgroup.com

ⓂAl Bardi Paper Mill Co. (S.A.E.)
6 October City Mill
Ownership: 100% by Nuqul Group
4th Industrial zone
6 October City, El Giza
Egypt
Phone: (20) 23 8330960/1922
Fax: (20) 23 8330747
Email: bpm@link.net, nt@nuqulgroup.com
Web Address: www.nuqulgroup.com
Personnel:
Purch. Dir.: Ms. Mary Samir
Phone: (20) 23 8330960
Fax: (20) 23 8330747
Email: msamir@nuqulgroup.com
Total Employees at this Location: 1,000
Type of Operation: Paper mill
Paper/Paperboard Grades and Capacities:
Total paper and paperboard capacity: 20,000 mt/y
Tissue: 20,000 mt/y
Paper and Paperboard Mill Data:
Paper Machines: 1
No. 1, twin-wire, Yankee dryer, total capacity 20,000 mt/y, Trim width 2.2 m, Uncoated woodfree/freesheet, Tissue
Finishing Equipment:
Winders: 1
Energy Data:
Power boilers
Combustion turbines at 13 MW
Electrical demand for mill: 52 MWh/D

ⓂAl Sindian Paper Mill Co. S.A.E.
6 October City Mill
Ownership: 100% by Nuqul Group
Plot 49-51, 4th Industrial Zone
6 October City, El Giza
Egypt
Mailing Address: PO Box 206, Cairo, Egypt
Phone: (20) 2 38330960/1922/1923
Fax: (20) 2 8330747
Email: shabib@albardifine.com, nt@nuqulgroup.com
Web Address: www.nuqulgroup.com
Personnel:
Gen. Mgr.: Magdi George
Phone: (20) 2 38330960
Fax: (20) 2 8330747
Email: mgeorge@nuqulgroup.com
Site Oper. Mgr.: Waheed Al Qannas
Phone: (20) 2 38330960
Fax: (20) 2 8330747
Email: wqannas@nuqulgroup.com
Total Employees at this Location: 1,000
Type of Operation: Paper mill
Paper/Paperboard Grades and Capacities:
Total paper and paperboard capacity: 54,000 mt/y
Tissue: 54,000 mt/y
Paper and Paperboard Mill Data:
Paper Machines: 1
No. 3, crescent former, Yankee dryer, total capacity 54,000 mt/y, Trim width 5.4 m, Tissue
Energy Data:
Power boilers
Combustion turbines at 13 MW
Electrical demand for mill: 142 MWh/D

ⓄⓂAl Zeina Tissue Mill
10th of Ramadan City Mill
Ownership: Eng. Abdul Karim Natout, Sultan Bin Mahfouz
Industrial Zone A-6
10th of Ramadan City, Sharkeya, East Province
Egypt
Phone: (20) 15 412816
Fax: (20) 15 412817 ex.255
Email: info@zeinatissue.com, info@alzeinamill.com
Web Address: www.alzeinamill.com/zeina_mill/index.aspx, www.zeinatissue.com/MILL/, www.zeinatissue.com
Personnel:
Chair. & CEO: Eng. Abdul Karim Natout
Phone: (20) 15 1412816
Fax: (20) 15 412817 ex.255
Man. Dir.: Mustafa El Naamani
Phone: (20) 18 2900039
Fax: (20) 15 412817 ex.255
Email: mnaamani@zeinagroup.com
Mill Mgr.: Eng. Ashraf Wagih
Phone: (20) 15 1412816
Fax: (20) 15 412817 ex.255
Email: awagih@zeinagroup.com
Commer. Dir.: Ahmed Natout
Phone: (20) 15 412816
Fax: (20) 15 412817 ex.255
Email: anatout@zeinagroup.com
Total Employees of Company: 250
Total Employees at this Location: 250
Type of Operation: Paper mill
Paper/Paperboard Grades and Capacities:
Total paper and paperboard capacity: 32,000 mt/y
Tissue: 32,000 mt/y
Paper and Paperboard Mill Data:
Paper Machines: 1
No. 1, crescent former, Yankee dryer, total capacity 32,000 mt/y, Trim width 2.75 m, Tissue, Uncoated woodfree/freesheet
Energy Data:
Power boilers
Electrical demand for mill: 82 MWh/D

Egypt

①⑩Alex Converta Co. SAE (Handy)
Alexandria Mill
Ownership: 100% by Private Sector
2nd. Zone 2, Block 13, New Borg El Arab, El-Gedeedah
Alexandria, Iskanderiya
Egypt
  Phone: (20) 3 4593605/1347/4378
  Fax: (20) 3 4592464
  Email: info@alexconverta.com,
  alexconverta@link.net,
  alexconverta_handy@hotmail.com
  Web Address: www.alexconverta.com
Personnel:
  Chmn.: Antoine Chaer
  Phone: (20) 3 4593605
  Fax: (20) 3 4592464
  Man. Dir.: Sabry Habib Awad
  Phone: (20) 3 4593605
  Fax: (20) 3 4592464
Type of Operation: Paper mill
Paper/Paperboard Grades and Capacities:
  Total paper and paperboard capacity: 10,000 mt/y
  Tissue: 10,000 mt/y
Paper and Paperboard Mill Data:
Paper Machines: 1
  No. 1, total capacity 10,000 mt/y, Trim width 1.85 m, Tissue

①⑩Carmen Tissue S.A.E.
6 October City Mill
Ownership: George Sarwat Bassily
1st Ind. Zone, Plot N° 192
6 October City, El Giza
Egypt
  Phone: (20) 23 8331612
  Fax: (20) 23 8331510
  Email: info@carmentissues.com,
  export@carmentissues.com
  Web Address: www.carmentissues.com
Personnel:
  Owner & Chmn.: Eng. George Sarwat Bassily
  Phone: (20) 23 8331612
  Prod. Mgr.: Eng. Joseph Anton Demetri
  Phone: (20) 12 2450000
Total Employees of Company: 200
Type of Operation: Paper mill
Paper/Paperboard Grades and Capacities:
  Total paper and paperboard capacity: 4,000 mt/y
  Tissue: 4,000 mt/y
Paper and Paperboard Mill Data:
Paper Machines: 1
  No. 1, (second hand), crescent former, total capacity 4,000 mt/y, Trim width 1.98 m, Tissue

①⑩Carta Misr
Maarouf, Cairo Mill
13 Abdel Hamid Said St.
Maarouf, Cairo
Egypt
  Phone: (20) 22 5786458
  Fax: (20) 22 5748385
  Email: info@cartamisr.com
  Web Address: www.cartamisr.com
Total Employees at this Location: 100
Type of Operation: Paperboard mill
Pulp Grades and Capacities:
  Total pulp capacity: 28,023 mt/y
  Recycled Pulping: 28,023 mt/y
Pulp Mill Data:
  Recycled Fiber Treatment Lines:
  Recycled packaging pulping lines: 1
Paper/Paperboard Grades and Capacities:
  Total paper and paperboard capacity: 40,000 mt/y
  Boxboard/cartonboard: 40,000 mt/y
Paper and Paperboard Mill Data:
Paper Machines: 1
  No. 2, cylinder, Yankee dryer, total capacity 40,000 mt/y, Trim width 2.9 m, Boxboard/cartonboard
Coating Machines: 1
  PM2, on machine
Energy Data:
  Power boilers
  Electrical demand for mill: 54 MWh/D

①⑩Delta Board Mills SAE
Cairo Mill
Ownership: Mr. Lucien Toutounzi (partly owned)
Ind. Zone, Plot 42-43
Badr City, Cairo
Egypt
  Phone: (20) 22 8640 926/314/327
  Fax: (20) 22 5290130
  Email: deltaboard@soficom.com
Personnel:
  Mill Mgr.: Serafeim Galaby
  Phone: (20) 22 8640 926/314/327
Total Employees of Company: 160
Total Employees at this Location: 160
Type of Operation: Paper mill
Pulp Grades and Capacities:
  Total pulp capacity: 14,990 mt/y
  Recycled Pulping: 14,990 mt/y
Pulp Mill Data:
  Recycled Fiber Treatment Lines:
  Recycled packaging pulping lines: 1
Paper/Paperboard Grades and Capacities:
  Total paper and paperboard capacity: 15,000 mt/y
  Linerboard: 9,000 mt/y
  Corrugating medium/fluting: 6,000 mt/y
Paper and Paperboard Mill Data:
Paper Machines: 1
  No. 1, fourdrinier, total capacity 15,000 mt/y, Trim width 2.3 m, Linerboard, Corrugating medium/fluting
Energy Data:
  Power boilers
  Electrical demand for mill: 21 MWh/D

①E.MAK Paper Manufacturing Co.
Ownership: Kharafy Group
71 Dr. Mohammed Hussein Hekel St.
Nasr City, 6th area, Cairo
Egypt
  Phone: (20) 2 2275 3893
  Fax: (20) 2 2670 8907
Personnel:
  Gen. Mgr.: Eng. Mohamed Ibrahim Saleh
  Phone: (20) 12 246 4559
Mill Locations:
  E.MAK Paper Manufacturing Co., Suez Mill, Ain el Sokhna Industrial Zone, Suez, Egypt, Capacity: 60,000 mt/y, (Paperboard mill)
  Phone: (20) 62 325 0420
  Fax: (20) 62 325 0427
  Email: emak_paper@emakacademy.com
  National Paper Co., Alexandria Mill, ElTabia, Rashid Rd., Alexandria, Egypt, Capacity: 82,000 mt/y, (Paper mill)
  Phone: (20) 3 5621712/810
  Fax: (20) 3 5621100

⑩E.MAK Paper Manufacturing Co.
Suez Mill
Ain el Sokhna Industrial Zone
Suez
Egypt
  Phone: (20) 62 325 0420
  Fax: (20) 62 325 0427
  Email: emak_paper@emakacademy.com
Personnel:
  Prod. Mgr.: Ghamel Ato
  Phone: (20) 10 667 1783
  Eng. Mgr.: Eng. Salah Nagia
  Phone: (20) 62 325 0420
Total Employees at this Location: 450
Type of Operation: Paperboard mill
Pulp Grades and Capacities:
  Total pulp capacity: 46,592 mt/y
  Recycled Pulping: 46,592 mt/y
Pulp Mill Data:
  Recycled Fiber Treatment Lines:
  Recycled packaging pulping lines: 1
Paper/Paperboard Grades and Capacities:
  Total paper and paperboard capacity: 60,000 mt/y
  Boxboard/cartonboard: 60,000 mt/y
Paper and Paperboard Mill Data:
  Stock Preparation:
  Pulpers: 6
  Refiners: 4
Paper Machines: 1
  No. 1, cylinder (8), Yankee dryer, total capacity 60,000 mt/y, Trim width 2.4 m, Boxboard/cartonboard
Coating Machines: 2
  No. 1
  No. 2
Finishing Equipment:
  Rewinders: 1 at 30,000 mt/y
  Sheeters: 1 at 60,000 mt/y
Energy Data:
  Power boilers: 2
  Electrical demand for mill: 82 MWh/D

①⑩El Dar El Beida
Alexandria Mill
New Borg El Arab, 3rd Area, Place 2,6, Block No. 15
Alexandria, Iskanderiya
Egypt
  Phone: (20) 3 4809764/5/4593702
  Fax: (20) 3 4592778
Personnel:
  Gen. Mgr.: Mahmoud Azab
  Phone: (20) 3 4592778
  Gen. Mgr.: Mohammed Radwan
  Phone: (20) 3 4809764/5/4593702
Total Employees at this Location: 200
Type of Operation: Paperboard mill
Paper/Paperboard Grades and Capacities:
  Total paper and paperboard capacity: 18,000 mt/y
  Boxboard/cartonboard: 18,000 mt/y
Paper and Paperboard Mill Data:
Paper Machines: 1
  No. 1, total capacity 18,000 mt/y, Trim width 2.35 m, Boxboard/cartonboard

①El Farouk Co. "Farco"
Ownership: Eng. Amr F. Osman
76 El Merghany St.
Heliopolis, Cairo
Egypt
  Phone: (20) 22 6903760/762
  Fax: (20) 22 6903736/2157565
  Email: amrosman@link.net
Personnel:
  Owner: Eng. Amr F. Osman
  Phone: (20) 12 210 9236
  Email: amrosman@link.net
Mill Locations:
  El Farouk Co. "Farco", El Obour Ind. City Mill, Block 12003/06 & /15 , Industrial zone, Obour, Egypt, Capacity: 75,000 mt/y, (Paperboard mill)
  Phone: (20) 2 61009 70/74 , 2 46650971
  Fax: (20) 2 61009 70
  Email: farco1@farcopaper.net , amrosman@link.net

⑩El Farouk Co. "Farco"
El Obour Ind. City Mill
Block 12003/06 & /15 , Industrial zone
Obour
Egypt
  Phone: (20) 2 61009 70/74 , 2 46650971
  Fax: (20) 2 61009 70
  Email: farco1@farcopaper.net,
  amrosman@link.net
Personnel:
  Chmn.: Eng. Amr F. Aly Osman
  Phone: (20) 12 210 9236
  Email: amrosman@link.net
Total Employees at this Location: 140

Egypt

Type of Operation: Paperboard mill
Pulp Grades and Capacities:
  Total pulp capacity: 68,114 mt/y
  Recycled Pulping: 68,114 mt/y
Pulp Mill Data:
  Recycled Fiber Treatment Lines:
  Recycled packaging pulping lines: 1
Paper/Paperboard Grades and Capacities:
  Total paper and paperboard capacity: 75,000 mt/y
  Packaging papers: 25,000 mt/y
  Linerboard: 50,000 mt/y
Paper and Paperboard Mill Data:
Paper Machines: 2
  No. 1, fourdrinier (2), total capacity 50,000 mt/y, Trim width 3.7 m, Linerboard
  No. 2, fourdrinier, total capacity 25,000 mt/y, Trim width 2.7 m, Packaging papers
Energy Data:
  Power boilers
  Electrical demand for mill: 114 MWh/D

El Nasr Carton Co.
Ownership: M. A. Bayoumi, Ms. Marwa & Eng. Ahmed Bayoumy
37 Abdel Khalik Tharwat St.
Cairo
Egypt
  Phone: (20) 2 23933667
  Fax: (20) 2 23933668
  Email: nasrgroup2002@yahoo.com, nasrgroup5@yahoo.com
  Web Address: nasrpack.webs.com
Total Employees of Company: 50
Mill Locations:
  El Nasr Carton Co., Borg El Arab El Gededah Mill, 3rd Zone, Block 20, Borg El Arab El - Gedeedah, Alexandria, Egypt, Capacity: 39,000 mt/y, (Paperboard mill)
  Phone: (20) 3 4592060/4592061/4592062/4591662
  Fax: (20) 3 5457080
  Email: nasrgroup2002@yahoo.com, nasrgroup5@yahoo.com

El Nasr Carton Co.
Borg El Arab El Gededah Mill
3rd Zone, Block 20
Borg El Arab El - Gedeedah, Alexandria
Egypt
Mailing Address: 15 Mina Street, Kafer Abdou, Alexandria, Egypt
  Phone: (20) 3 4592060/4592061/4592062/4591662
  Fax: (20) 3 5457080
  Email: nasrgroup2002@yahoo.com, nasrgroup5@yahoo.com
  Web Address: nasrpack.webs.com
Personnel:
  Chmn.: Mohamed Bayoumi
  Phone: (20) 3 4592060/4592061/4592062/4591662
  Mill Mgr.: Eng. Mohsen El-Shamy
  Phone: (20) 3 4300146/4592260/61
Total Employees at this Location: 50
Type of Operation: Paperboard mill
Pulp Grades and Capacities:
  Total pulp capacity: 39,370 mt/y
  Recycled Pulping: 39,370 mt/y
Pulp Mill Data:
  Recycled Fiber Treatment Lines:
  Pulpers: 1 at 43,000
Paper/Paperboard Grades and Capacities:
  Total paper and paperboard capacity: 39,000 mt/y
  Linerboard: 23,000 mt/y
  Corrugating medium/fluting: 16,000 mt/y
Paper and Paperboard Mill Data:
Paper Machines: 1
  No. 2, fourdrinier (2), total capacity 39,000 mt/y, Trim width 2.7 m, Corrugating medium/fluting, Linerboard
Energy Data:
  Power boilers
  Electrical demand for mill: 57 MWh/D

El Obour Co.
Heliopolis, Cairo Mill
Ownership: 100% by Sherif F. Osman
37 Ismail Ramzy St.
Heliopolis, Cairo
Egypt
  Phone: (20) 22 6440085/6397556
  Fax: (20) 22 6440086
  Email: sfosman@link.net
Personnel:
  Owner, Chmn & Mill Mgr.: Eng. Sherif F. Osman
  Phone: (20) 22 6440085/6397556
  Email: sfosman@link.net
Total Employees of Company: 350
Total Employees at this Location: 100
Type of Operation: Paper mill
Mill Locations:
  Superplast Co., El Obour Mill, 499 Port Said St., Bab El Shaaria, Cairo, Egypt, Capacity: 15,000 mt/y, (Paperboard mill)
  Phone: (20) 22 6440085/6
  Fax: (20) 22 6397556
  Email: sfosman@link.net
Pulp Grades and Capacities:
  Total pulp capacity: 52,854 mt/y
  Recycled Pulping: 52,854 mt/y
Pulp Mill Data:
  Recycled Fiber Treatment Lines:
  Recycled packaging pulping lines: 1
Paper/Paperboard Grades and Capacities:
  Total paper and paperboard capacity: 53,000 mt/y
  Linerboard: 28,000 mt/y
  Corrugating medium/fluting: 25,000 mt/y
Paper and Paperboard Mill Data:
Paper Machines: 1
  No. 3, fourdrinier, total capacity 53,000 mt/y, Trim width 3.8 m, Linerboard, Corrugating medium/fluting
Energy Data:
  Power boilers
  Electrical demand for mill: 74 MWh/D

El-Salam PaperMill
Alexandria Mill
Al Kabarey Road, Moharem Bey
Alexandria, Iskanderiya
Egypt
  Phone: (20) 3 3612794/3605801
  Fax: (20) 3 3608053
  Email: info@elsalampapermill.com
Personnel:
  Owner & Gen. Mgr.: Abdel Ali Khalifa
  Phone: (20) 3 3612794/3605801
  Owner: Khalifa Mohamed Khalifa
  Phone: (20) 3 3612794/3605801
  Prod. Mgr.: Sobhi Younes
  Phone: (20) 10 538 2492
Total Employees at this Location: 100
Type of Operation: Paperboard mill
Pulp Grades and Capacities:
  Total pulp capacity: 22,906 mt/y
  Recycled Pulping: 22,906 mt/y
Pulp Mill Data:
  Recycled Fiber Treatment Lines:
  Recycled packaging pulping lines: 1
Paper/Paperboard Grades and Capacities:
  Total paper and paperboard capacity: 26,500 mt/y
  Linerboard: 3,000 mt/y
  Corrugating medium/fluting: 2,000 mt/y
  Boxboard/cartonboard: 21,500 mt/y
Paper and Paperboard Mill Data:
Paper Machines: 1
  No. 1, cylinder (4), total capacity 26,500 mt/y, Trim width 1.8 m, Boxboard/cartonboard, Linerboard, Corrugating medium/fluting

Coating Machines: 1
  PM 1, total capacity 26,500 mt/y., on machine
Finishing Equipment:
  Sheeters
Energy Data:
  Power boilers: 1
  Electrical demand for mill: 40 MWh/D

El Shorouk (Motaheda)
Ownership: National Printing Company ("NPC"), Al Motaheda Paper & Board
8 Sibaweh El Masry St.
Nasr City, Cairo
Egypt
  Phone: (20) 24023399
  Fax: (20) 24037567
  Email: dar@shorouk.com
  Web Address: www.shorouk.com
Personnel:
  Exec. Mmbr of Board: Sharif Al Muallem
  Phone: (20) 24 023399
  Fax: (20) 24 037567
  Exec. Chrmn of Board: Eng. Ibrahim Al Muallem
  Phone: (20) 24 023399
  Fax: (20) 24 037567
  Man. Dir.: Eng. Ahmad Allam
  Phone: (20) 24 023399
  Fax: (20) 24 037567
Total Employees of Company: 800
Mill Locations:
  El Shorouk (Motaheda), El Obour Mill, 1st Industrial Zone El Obour City, El Obour, Cairo, Egypt, Capacity: 135,000 mt/y, (Paperboard mill)
  Phone: (20) 24 6100405
  Fax: (20) 24 6100485

El Shorouk (Motaheda)
El Obour Mill
1st Industrial Zone El Obour City
El Obour, Cairo
Egypt
  Phone: (20) 24 6100405
  Fax: (20) 24 6100485
Personnel:
  Tech. Mgr: Nabil Swailem
  Phone: (20) 24 6100405
  Fax: (20) 24 6100485
  Mgr.: Hany Abd El Hay
  Phone: (20) 24 6100405 225
  Fax: (20) 24 6100485
  Email: hahmed@shorouk.com
Total Employees at this Location: 200
Type of Operation: Paperboard mill
Pulp Grades and Capacities:
  Total pulp capacity: 109,424 mt/y
  Recycled Pulping: 109,424 mt/y
Pulp Mill Data:
  Recycled Fiber Treatment Lines:
  Recycled packaging pulping lines: 1
Paper/Paperboard Grades and Capacities:
  Total paper and paperboard capacity: 135,000 mt/y
  Boxboard/cartonboard: 135,000 mt/y
Paper and Paperboard Mill Data:
Paper Machines: 1
  No. 1, multi-wire, Yankee dryer, total capacity 135,000 mt/y, Trim width 2.6 m, Boxboard/cartonboard
Coating Machines: 1
  PM 1, on machine
Energy Data:
  Power boilers
  Electrical demand for mill: 220 MWh/D

ELF - Egyptian Co. for Manufacturing of Linerboard & Fluting
Ownership: Mohamed G. Mahmoud
21, El Obour Bldg., Salah Salam St.
11371 Cairo
Egypt

Egypt

Phone: (20) 22 4019131/32
Fax: (20) 22 4018045
Email: ddcmmg@gega.net,
info@ddc.com.eg
Web Address: www.mmgroup-egypt.com
Personnel:
Owner & Chmn.: Eng. Mohamed G. Mahmoud
Phone: (20) 22 4019131/32
Fax: (20) 22 4018045
Total Employees of Company: 350
Total Employees at this Location: 25
Mill Locations:
ELF - Egyptian Co. for Manufacturing of Linerboard & Fluting, 10th of Ramadan City Mill, Industrial Zone B2, 10th of Ramadan City, Cairo, Egypt, Capacity: 126,000 mt/y, (Paperboard mill)
Phone: (20) 15 361 386
Fax: (20) 15 361 542
Email: ddcmmg@gega.net

ⓜELF - Egyptian Co. for Manufacturing of Linerboard & Fluting
10th of Ramadan City Mill
Industrial Zone B2
10th of Ramadan City, Cairo, Sharkeya, East Province
Egypt
Phone: (20) 15 361 386
Fax: (20) 15 361 542
Email: ddcmmg@gega.net
Web Address: www.mmgroup-egypt.com
Personnel:
Mill Mgr.: Munir Hasan
Phone: (20) 16 400 3240
Total Employees at this Location: 325
Type of Operation: Paperboard mill
Pulp Grades and Capacities:
Total pulp capacity: 126,900 mt/y
Recycled Pulping: 126,900 mt/y
Pulp Mill Data:
Recycled Fiber Treatment Lines:
Recycled packaging pulping lines: 1
Paper/Paperboard Grades and Capacities:
Total paper and paperboard capacity: 126,000 mt/y
Linerboard: 81,000 mt/y
Corrugating medium/fluting: 45,000 mt/y
Paper and Paperboard Mill Data:
Paper Machines: 2
No. 1, fourdrinier (2), total capacity 40,000 mt/y, Trim width 2.65 m, Corrugating medium/fluting, Linerboard
No. 2, fourdrinier (2), total capacity 86,000 mt/y, Trim width 2.5 m, Corrugating medium/fluting, Linerboard
Energy Data:
Power boilers
Electrical demand for mill: 179 MWh/D

ⓜEtap Paper & Carton
Ownership: 100% by Moustafa Ashour Abdulla
201 Abdel El Salam Araf St.
Loran, Alexandria
Egypt
Phone: (20) 3 5833081/5850520
Fax: (20) 3 5821167
Personnel:
Chmn.: Eng. Hamdy Ashour Abdulla
Phone: (20) 10 1071384
Fax: (20) 3 5821167
Owner: Moustafa Ashour Abdulla
Phone: (20) 3 5833061/5850520
Fax: (20) 3 5821167
Total Employees of Company: 129
Total Employees at this Location: 6
Mill Locations:
Etap Paper & Carton, Borg El Arab El Gededah Mill, Ind. Zone 1, Block 35, Borg El Arab El Gededah, Egypt, Capacity: 72,000 mt/y, (Paperboard mill)
Phone: (20) 3 45921743
Fax: (20) 3 5821167

ⓜEtap Paper & Carton
Borg El Arab El Gededah Mill
Ind. Zone 1, Block 35
Borg El Arab El Gededah, Alexandria
Egypt
Phone: (20) 3 45921743
Fax: (20) 3 5821167
Personnel:
Owner & Mill Mgr.: Moustafa Ashour Abdulla
Phone: (20) 3 45921743
Total Employees at this Location: 220
Type of Operation: Paperboard mill
Pulp Grades and Capacities:
Total pulp capacity: 67,326 mt/y
Recycled Pulping: 67,326 mt/y
Pulp Mill Data:
Recycled Fiber Treatment Lines:
Recycled packaging pulping lines: 1
Paper/Paperboard Grades and Capacities:
Total paper and paperboard capacity: 72,000 mt/y
Linerboard: 34,000 mt/y
Corrugating medium/fluting: 23,000 mt/y
Boxboard/cartonboard: 15,000 mt/y
Paper and Paperboard Mill Data:
Paper Machines: 2
No. 1, cylinder, Yankee dryer, total capacity 15,000 mt/y, Trim width 1.95 m, Boxboard/cartonboard
No. 2, fourdrinier (2), total capacity 57,000 mt/y, Trim width 2.96 m, Corrugating medium/fluting, Linerboard
Coating Machines: 1
No. 1, total capacity 35,000 mt/y., off machine
Energy Data:
Power boilers: 1
Electrical demand for mill: 101 MWh/D

ⓞⓜFirst Co. For Industrial Development S.A.E
El Obour City Mill
1st Industrial Zone, Block 13003, Plot 10, Street 10
El Obour City
Egypt
Phone: (20) 2 46102370/71
Fax: (20) 2 46102373
Email: firstpaper@tedata.net.eg
Personnel:
Business Devlpt. Dir.: Eng. Mahmoud El Gazar
Phone: (20) 2 46102370/71
Mill Mgr. & Proj. Mgr.: Dr. Amr Darwish
Phone: (20) 2 46102370/71
Total Employees at this Location: 200
Type of Operation: Paperboard mill
Pulp Grades and Capacities:
Total pulp capacity: 99,927 mt/y
Recycled Pulping: 99,927 mt/y
Pulp Mill Data:
Recycled Fiber Treatment Lines:
Recycled packaging pulping lines: 1
Paper/Paperboard Grades and Capacities:
Total paper and paperboard capacity: 100,000 mt/y
Linerboard: 60,000 mt/y
Corrugating medium/fluting: 40,000 mt/y
Paper and Paperboard Mill Data:
Paper Machines: 2
No. 1, fourdrinier, total capacity 80,000 mt/y, Trim width 3.8 m, Linerboard, Corrugating medium/fluting
No. 2, fourdrinier, total capacity 20,000 mt/y, Trim width 2.5 m, Linerboard, Corrugating medium/fluting
Energy Data:
Power boilers: 2
Electrical demand for mill: 139 MWh/D

ⓞHorus Edfu
195 Gesr El Suez Str.
Heliopolis, Cairo
Egypt
Phone: (20) 02-26373919, 02-26373949, 02-26374209
Personnel:
Purch. Dir.: Alaa Kabil
Phone: (20) 22 6373919/6373949/6374209
Email: alaakabil@hotmail.com
Mill Locations:
Horus Edfu for Paper Industry, Beni Souef Mill, Beni Souef Industrial Zone, Beni Souef, Egypt, Capacity: 20,000 mt/y, (Paper mill)
Phone: (20) 82 9200924
Fax: (20) 82 9201050

ⓜHorus Edfu for Paper Industry
Beni Souef Mill
Ownership: Horus Edfu
Beni Souef Industrial Zone
Beni Souef
Egypt
Phone: (20) 82 9200924
Fax: (20) 82 9201050
Total Employees at this Location: 100
Type of Operation: Paper mill
Paper/Paperboard Grades and Capacities:
Total paper and paperboard capacity: 20,000 mt/y
Uncoated woodfree/freesheet: 20,000 mt/y
Paper and Paperboard Mill Data:
Paper Machines: 1
No. 1, fourdrinier, total capacity 20,000 mt/y, Trim width 2.75 m, Uncoated woodfree/freesheet
Energy Data:
Power boilers
Electrical demand for mill: 41 MWh/D

ⓜInterstate Paper Industries
Sadat City Mill
Ownership: Interstate Resources, Inc.
85 km North of Cairo Desert Road, P.O. Box 165
Sadat City, Menofeya
Egypt
Phone: (20) 4 8261 3080/77
Fax: (20) 4 8261 3076
Email: papermaking@indevcogroup.com,
pcd@indevcogroup.com,
info@ipitissue.com
Web Address: www.ipitissue.com,
www.indevcogroup.com
Personnel:
Regional Mgr., Tissue Oper.: George Mourad
Phone: (20) 4 8261 3080
Fax: (20) 4 8261 3076
Email: george.mourad@ipitissue.com
Project Mgr.: Eng. Samir Honeini
Phone: (20) 4 8261 3080
Fax: (20) 4 8261 3076
Email: samir.honeini@ipitissue.com
Qlty. & HSE Mgr.: Kamel J. Khalil
Phone: (20) 4 8261 3080 Ext. 2056
Fax: (20) 4 8261 3076
Email: kamel.khalil@ipitissue.com
Total Employees at this Location: 250
Type of Operation: Paper mill
Pulp Grades and Capacities:
Total pulp capacity: 26,671 mt/y
Recycled Pulping: 26,671 mt/y
Pulp Mill Data:
Recycled Fiber Treatment Lines:
Flotation deinking lines: 1
Paper/Paperboard Grades and Capacities:
Total paper and paperboard capacity: 75,000 mt/y
Tissue: 75,000 mt/y
Paper and Paperboard Mill Data:
Paper Machines: 3
No. 1, crescent former, Yankee dryer, total capacity 30,000 mt/y, Trim width 2.83 m, Tissue, Uncoated woodfree/freesheet
No. 2, crescent former, Yankee dryer, total capacity 30,000 mt/y, Trim width 2.83 m, Tissue, Uncoated woodfree/freesheet
No. 3, crescent former, Yankee dryer, total capacity 15,000 mt/y, Trim width 2.7 m, Tissue, Uncoated woodfree/freesheet

Egypt

Finishing Equipment:
Winders: 3 at 60,000 mt/y
Energy Data:
Power boilers
Combustion turbines
Electrical demand for mill: 216 MWh/D

ⓘIslamic Paper Manufacturing Co.
Ownership: Mr. Mostafa Saeed
Mubarak Ind. Zone, Kufur El-Raml
Quesna
Egypt
Phone: (20) 48 2590442/443
Fax: (20) 48 2590441
Email: itocomp@hotmail.com
Personnel:
Chmn.: Mostafa Saeed
Phone: (20) 48 2590442/443
Fax: (20) 48 2590441
Mill Mgr.: Mahmoud Soleyman
Phone: (20) 48 2590442/443
Fax: (20) 48 2590441
Total Employees at this Location: 600
Mill Locations:
Islamic Paper Manufacturing Co., Quesna Mill, Mubarak Ind. Zone, Kufur El-Raml, Quesna, Egypt, Capacity: 170,000 mt/y, (Paperboard mill)
Phone: (20) 48 2590442/443
Fax: (20) 48 2590441
Email: itocomp@hotmail.com

ⓜIslamic Paper Manufacturing Co.
Quesna Mill
Mubarak Ind. Zone, Kufur El-Raml
Quesna, Menofeya
Egypt
Phone: (20) 48 2590442/443
Fax: (20) 48 2590441
Email: itocomp@hotmail.com
Personnel:
Chmn.: Mostafa Saeed
Phone: (20) 48 2590442/443
Mill Mgr.: Eng. Mahmoud Soleyman
Phone: (20) 48 2590442/443
Total Employees at this Location: 600
Type of Operation: Paperboard mill
Pulp Grades and Capacities:
Total pulp capacity: 135,942 mt/y
Recycled Pulping: 135,942 mt/y
Pulp Mill Data:
Recycled Fiber Treatment Lines:
Recycled packaging pulping lines: 1
Paper/Paperboard Grades and Capacities:
Total paper and paperboard capacity: 170,000 mt/y
Packaging papers: 5,000 mt/y
Linerboard: 35,000 mt/y
Corrugating medium/fluting: 20,000 mt/y
Boxboard/cartonboard: 110,000 mt/y
Paper and Paperboard Mill Data:
Paper Machines: 2
No. 1, fourdrinier (2), total capacity 50,000 mt/y, Trim width 2.5 m, Packaging papers, Corrugating medium/fluting, Linerboard
No. 2, cylinder, Yankee dryer, total capacity 120,000 mt/y, Trim width 3.2 m, Boxboard/cartonboard, Linerboard
Coating Machines: 1
PM2, on machine
Energy Data:
Electrical demand for mill: 251 MWh/D

ⓘKishco Khodeir Paper Mill
Ownership: Mr. Kishu L. Vaswani
13 Abdel Hamid Said St.
Maarouf, Cairo
Egypt
Phone: (20) 23 8330890
Fax: (20) 23 8338704
Mill Locations:
Kishco Khodeir Paper Mill, 6 October City Mill, 3rd Industrial Zone, 6 October City, Egypt, Capacity: 15,000 mt/y, (Paperboard mill)
Phone: (20) 23 8330890
Fax: (20) 23 8338704

ⓜKishco Khodeir Paper Mill
6 October City Mill
3rd Industrial Zone
6 October City, El Giza
Egypt
Phone: (20) 23 8330890
Fax: (20) 23 8338704
Personnel:
Owner: Mr. K. L. Vaswani
Phone: (20) 23 8330890
Mill Mgr.: Eng. Maghdy Refaey
Phone: (20) 23 8330890
Total Employees at this Location: 40
Type of Operation: Paperboard mill
Pulp Grades and Capacities:
Total pulp capacity: 14,953 mt/y
Recycled Pulping: 14,953 mt/y
Pulp Mill Data:
Recycled Fiber Treatment Lines:
Recycled packaging pulping lines: 1
Paper/Paperboard Grades and Capacities:
Total paper and paperboard capacity: 15,000 mt/y
Corrugating medium/fluting: 15,000 mt/y
Paper and Paperboard Mill Data:
Paper Machines: 1
No. 1, fourdrinier, total capacity 15,000 mt/y, Trim width 2.25 m, Corrugating medium/fluting
Energy Data:
Power boilers
Electrical demand for mill: 21 MWh/D

ⓘⓜLotus for Paper Products
Sadat City Mill
Ind. Zone, Small Industries Complex, Plot 17418
Sadat City, Menofeya
Egypt
Phone: (20) 10 1566295
Personnel:
Mill Mgr. : Eng. Ehab Fatouh
Total Employees at this Location: 50
Type of Operation: Paperboard mill
Pulp Grades and Capacities:
Total pulp capacity: 19,986 mt/y
Recycled Pulping: 19,986 mt/y
Pulp Mill Data:
Recycled Fiber Treatment Lines:
Recycled packaging pulping lines: 1
Paper/Paperboard Grades and Capacities:
Total paper and paperboard capacity: 20,000 mt/y
Linerboard: 12,000 mt/y
Corrugating medium/fluting: 8,000 mt/y
Paper and Paperboard Mill Data:
Paper Machines: 1
No. 1, fourdrinier, total capacity 20,000 mt/y, Trim width 2.5 m, Linerboard, Corrugating medium/fluting
Energy Data:
Power boilers
Electrical demand for mill: 28 MWh/D

ⓘⓜMediterranean Tissue Company
Alexandria Mill
4th Ind. Zone, Block 33, Borg El Arab Industrial Area
Alexandria, Iskanderiya
Egypt
Phone: (20) 3 4599 146/7
Fax: (20) 3 4599144
Email: med_paper@yahoo.com
Web Address: www.medtissuemill.com
Personnel:
Owner: Ahmed Taha Chorbaji
Phone: (20) 1 1864 0005
Fax: (20) 3 4599 144
Email: ahmed@medtissuemill.com
Mill Mgr.: Samir El Fatth
Phone: (20) 3 4599 146/7
Fax: (20) 3 4599 144
Email: samir@medtissuemill.com
Prod. Mgr.: Hassan El Sayed
Phone: (20) 3 4599 146/7
Fax: (20) 3 4599 144
Email: hassan@medtissuemill.com
Logist. Mgr.: Sherif Belal
Phone: (20) 1 1900 7874
Fax: (20) 3 4599 144
Email: sherif@medtissuemill.com
Mktg. & Sls. Dir.: Hashem I. Al Batawy
Phone: (20) 2 2414 6995
Fax: (20) 2 2419 1427
Email: hashem@medtissuemill.com
Total Employees at this Location: 100
Type of Operation: Paper mill
Paper/Paperboard Grades and Capacities:
Total paper and paperboard capacity: 47,000 mt/y
Tissue: 47,000 mt/y
Paper and Paperboard Mill Data:
Paper Machines: 2
No. 1, twin-wire, Yankee dryer, total capacity 15,000 mt/y, Trim width 1.85 m, Tissue
No. 2, twin-wire, Yankee dryer, total capacity 32,000 mt/y, Trim width 2.75 m, Tissue
Energy Data:
Power boilers
Electrical demand for mill: 129 MWh/D

ⓘMenofeya for Paper & Cardboard
Ownership: Mahmoud Abu El Naser
1 Bank Misr Street
Cairo
Egypt
Phone: (20) 22 3927982
Fax: (20) 22 3933044
Personnel:
Owner: Mahmoud Abu El Naser
Phone: (20) 22 3927982
Fax: (20) 22 3933044
Gen. Mgr.: Sherin Saad Mahdy
Phone: (20) 22 3927982
Fax: (20) 22 3933044
Total Employees of Company: 500
Total Employees at this Location: 5
Mill Locations:
Menofeya for Paper & Cardboard - "Minobardy", Quissna Mill, Mubarak Industrial Area, Quissna, Egypt, Capacity: 24,000 mt/y, (Paper mill)
Phone: (20) 48 2590610/879

ⓜMenofeya for Paper & Cardboard - "Minobardy"
Quissna Mill
Ownership: Menofeya for Paper & Cardboard
Mubarak Industrial Area
Quissna, Menofeya
Egypt
Phone: (20) 48 2590610/879
Personnel:
Prod. Mgr.: Eng. Ahmed Wael
Phone: (20) 48 2590610/879
Total Employees at this Location: 200
Type of Operation: Paper mill
Pulp Grades and Capacities:
Total pulp capacity: 24,149 mt/y
Recycled Pulping: 24,149 mt/y
Pulp Mill Data:
Recycled Fiber Treatment Lines:
Recycled packaging pulping lines: 1
Paper/Paperboard Grades and Capacities:
Total paper and paperboard capacity: 24,000 mt/y
Linerboard: 12,000 mt/y
Corrugating medium/fluting: 12,000 mt/y
Paper and Paperboard Mill Data:

Egypt

Paper Machines: 2
No. 1, fourdrinier, total capacity 12,000 mt/y, Trim width 2.5 m, Linerboard, Corrugating medium/fluting
No. 2, fourdrinier, total capacity 12,000 mt/y, Trim width 2.5 m, Linerboard, Corrugating medium/fluting
Energy Data:
Power boilers: 2
Electrical demand for mill: 37 MWh/D

ⓜ Middle East Paper Co. (SIMO)
Ownership: government
37, Kasr El Nil St.
22819 Cairo
Egypt
 Phone: (20) 22 3934596
 Fax: (20) 22 3929362
 Email: atefyehya@hotmail.com
 Web Address: www.simo-eg.com
Personnel:
 Board Mmbr.: Wagdy Abdulnaby Allam
 Phone: (20) 22 3934596
 Fax: (20) 22 3929362
 Board Mmbr.: Farag Antar
 Phone: (20) 2 4824 3260
Total Employees of Company: 700
Total Employees at this Location: 10
Mill Locations:
Middle East Paper Co. (SIMO), Musturud Mill, 2 Bahtim Road, Musturud, Cairo, Egypt, Capacity: 21,000 mt/y, (Paperboard mill)
Phone: (20) 2 4220 4446, 4475 7314
Fax: (20) 2 4824 7942
Email: atefyehya@hotmail.com

ⓜ Middle East Paper Co. (SIMO)
Musturud Mill
2 Bahtim Road
Musturud, Cairo
Egypt
Mailing Address: P.O. Box 13753, Kalubia, Egypt
 Phone: (20) 2 4220 4446, 4475 7314
 Fax: (20) 2 4824 7942
 Email: atefyehya@hotmail.com
 Web Address: www.simo-eg.com
Personnel:
 Prod. Mgr.: Eid Wardani
 Phone: (20) 2 4824 5740
 Finan. Mgr.: Moustafa Ragab Mohammed
 Phone: (20) 2 4824 3260
 Admin. Mgr.: General El Sayed Abd El Aziz
 Phone: (20) 2 4824 5740
Total Employees at this Location: 610
Type of Operation: Paperboard mill
Pulp Grades and Capacities:
 Total pulp capacity: 20,309 mt/y
 Recycled Pulping: 20,309 mt/y
Pulp Mill Data:
 Chemical Pulping Systems:
 Batch digesters: 2
 Recycled Fiber Treatment Lines:
 Recycled packaging pulping lines: 1
Paper/Paperboard Grades and Capacities:
 Total paper and paperboard capacity: 21,000 mt/y
 Boxboard/cartonboard: 21,000 mt/y
Paper and Paperboard Mill Data:
 Stock Preparation:
 Pulpers: 3
 Refiners: 5
Paper Machines: 2
No. 1, cylinder (6), Yankee dryer, total capacity 14,000 mt/y, Trim width 2 m, Boxboard/cartonboard
No. 2, fourdrinier, total capacity 7,000 mt/y, Trim width 1 m, Boxboard/cartonboard
Finishing Equipment:
 Supercalenders: 1
 Rewinders: 1
 Sheeters: 1
Energy Data:
Power boilers
Electrical demand for mill: 28 MWh/D

ⓜ Misr Edfu for Pulp, Writing & Printing Paper Co. - MEPP-Co
Ownership: banks, National Sugar Co.
14 Gawad Hosny St.
Cairo
Egypt
 Phone: (20) 22 3952940/942
 Fax: (20) 22 3952941
 Email: Factoryhead@misredfu.com,
 edfumail@misredfu.com,
 meppco@link.net
 Web Address: www.misredfu.com
Personnel:
 Man. Dir.: Mr. M. M. Rashidy
 Phone: (20) 22 3952940/942
 Fax: (20) 22 3952941
Total Employees of Company: 1,000
Total Employees at this Location: 40
Mill Locations:
Misr Edfu for Pulp, Writing & Printing Paper Co. - MEPP-Co, Edfu Pulp Mill, Km. 7 from Edfu City, Koum El-Amir, Edfu, Aswan, Egypt, Capacity: 65,000 mt/y, (Pulp mill, Paper mill)
Phone: (20) 97 4790905/8
Fax: (20) 97 4790909
Email: factoryhead@misredfu.com

ⓜ Misr Edfu for Pulp, Writing & Printing Paper Co. - MEPP-Co
Edfu Pulp Mill
Km. 7 from Edfu City, Koum El-Amir
Edfu, Aswan
Egypt
 Phone: (20) 97 4790905/8
 Fax: (20) 97 4790909
 Email: factoryhead@misredfu.com
 Web Address: www.meppco.com
Personnel:
 Pres.: Eng. Abdel Rahman
 Phone: (20) 97 4790905/8
 Fax: (20) 23952941
 Email: chairman@misredfu.com
 Gen. Mgr.: Eng. Mohamed Abdella
 Phone: (20) 97 4790905/8
 Fax: (20) 97 4790909
 Email: mabdalla_meppco@yahoo.com
 Chem. Mgr.: Eng. Mohamed Shaker
 Phone: (20) 97 4790905/8
Total Employees at this Location: 750
Type of Operation: Pulp mill, Paper mill
Pulp Grades and Capacities:
 Total pulp capacity: 38,457 mt/y
 Other Pulp: 38,457 mt/y
Pulp Mill Data:
 Chemical Pulping Systems:
 Continuous digesters: 1
 Bleach Plant Systems: 1
 Hypo, Sequence: O_2 H, Capacity 250 admt/y
 Chemical Recovery Equipment:
 Evaporator lines: 3
 Pulp Dryers:
 Wet Lap machine 1
Paper/Paperboard Grades and Capacities:
 Total paper and paperboard capacity: 65,000 mt/y
 Uncoated woodfree/freesheet: 65,000 mt/y
Paper and Paperboard Mill Data:
Paper Machines: 1
No. 1, fourdrinier, total capacity 65,000 mt/y, Trim width 5.85 m, Uncoated woodfree/freesheet
Finishing Equipment:
 Winders: 1 at 75,000 mt/y
 Calenders: 1
 Sheeters: 5 at 30,000 mt/y
Energy Data:
Electrical demand for mill: 183 MWh/D

ⓜⓘ National Co. for Paper & Plastics
Ownership: Mr. Mohamed Hassan Madboli
Cairo-Alex Agricultural Road
Kaluib, Abo Sena
Egypt
 Phone: (20) 02 42155990
Personnel:
 Owner: Mohamed Hassan Madboli
 Phone: (20) 02 42155990, 12 2263714
Paper/Paperboard Grades and Capacities:
 Packaging papers
Paper and Paperboard Mill Data:
Paper Machines: 1
No. 1, Trim width 2.5 m, Packaging papers

ⓜ National Paper Co.
Alexandria Mill
Ownership: E.MAK Paper Manufacturing Co.
El Tabia, Rashid Rd.
Alexandria, Iskanderiya
Egypt
Mailing Address: P.O. Box 21916, El Tabia, Alexandria, Egypt
 Phone: (20) 3 5621712/810
 Fax: (20) 3 5621100
Personnel:
 Man. Dir.: Ibrahim Salah
 Phone: (20) 3 5621712/810
 Mill Mgr.: Eng. Taha Abd Rabouh
 Phone: (20) 10 668 8526
 Tech. Dir.: Eng. Ahmed El Magnme
 Phone: (20) 3 5621712/810
Total Employees at this Location: 900
Type of Operation: Paper mill
Pulp Grades and Capacities:
 Total pulp capacity: 85,705 mt/y
 Recycled Pulping: 24,520 mt/y
 Other Pulp: 61,185 mt/y
Pulp Mill Data:
 Chemical Pulping Systems:
 Continuous digesters: 1
 Chemical Recovery Equipment:
 Evaporator lines: 1
 Recovery boilers: 1
 Recycled Fiber Treatment Lines:
 Recycled packaging pulping lines: 1
Paper/Paperboard Grades and Capacities:
 Total paper and paperboard capacity: 82,000 mt/y
 Packaging papers: 35,000 mt/y
 Linerboard: 17,000 mt/y
 Corrugating medium/fluting: 30,000 mt/y
Paper and Paperboard Mill Data:
Paper Machines: 6
No. 1, fourdrinier, total capacity 9,000 mt/y, Trim width 2 m, Corrugating medium/fluting
No. 2, fourdrinier, total capacity 11,000 mt/y, Trim width 2 m, Linerboard
No. 3, fourdrinier, total capacity 6,000 mt/y, Trim width 2 m, Linerboard
No. 4, fourdrinier, total capacity 9,000 mt/y, Trim width 2 m, Packaging papers
No. 5, fourdrinier, total capacity 21,000 mt/y, Trim width 2.5 m, Corrugating medium/fluting
No. 6, fourdrinier, total capacity 26,000 mt/y, Trim width 3 m, Packaging papers
Energy Data:
Electrical demand for mill: 195 MWh/D

ⓜ Nefertiti Paper Co. Ltd
10th of Ramadan City Mill
Industrial Zone A2, Plot 1/5G
10th of Ramadan City, Sharkeya, East Province
Egypt
 Phone: (20) 10 5680125/ 15 411085
 Fax: (20) 15 413218
Personnel:
 Owner & Mill Mgr.: Samir Nashin Shahad
 Phone: (20) 12 319 5135
Total Employees at this Location: 130
Type of Operation: Paper mill
Paper/Paperboard Grades and Capacities:
 Total paper and paperboard capacity: 6,300 mt/y

Egypt

Tissue
Packaging papers
Paper and Paperboard Mill Data:
Paper Machines: 2
No. 1, total capacity 1,800 mt/y, Trim width 1.5 m, Tissue
No. 2, (second hand), Yankee dryer, total capacity 4,500 mt/y, Trim width 2.5 m, Tissue, Packaging papers

ⓗⓜPyramids Paper Mills S.A.E. - Flora
6th October City Mill
Ownership: 62.50% by Zeritis Group, 25% by MIRS Insurance Co.
Plot no. 194/195, 1st Industrial Zone
6th October City, El Giza
Egypt
Mailing Address: PO Box 17, 6th October City, Egypt
Phone: (20) 23 833 1400
Fax: (20) 23 833 1010/0500
Email: ppm@flora.com.eg
Web Address: www.flora.com.eg
Personnel:
Chmn. & Group Pres.: Panos Zeritis
Phone: (20) 23 833 1400
Man. Dir.: Eng. Christos Cavallis
Phone: (20) 23 833 1400
Mill Mgr.: Sobhy Ayad
Phone: (20) 23 833 1400
Dpty. Gen. Mgr. (Commerce): George Louis
Phone: (20) 23 833 1400
Dpty. Gen. Mgr. (Commerce): Medhat Ghoneim
Phone: (20) 23 833 1400
Costing & Planning Mgr.: Alexander Georgiadis
Phone: (20) 23 833 1400
Tech. Mgr.: Basem Aboul Wafa
Phone: (20) 23 833 1400
Purch. Mgr.: George Boulos
Phone: (20) 23 833 1400
Industrial Sls. Mgr.: Magdy Moussa
Phone: (20) 23 833 1400
Paper Prod. Mgr.: Eng. Samuel Saad
Phone: (20) 23 833 1400
Converting Prod. Mgr.: Wagdy Shafik
Phone: (20) 23 833 1400
Total Employees at this Location: 600
Type of Operation: Paper mill
Pulp Grades and Capacities:
Total pulp capacity: 24,010 mt/y
Recycled Pulping: 24,010 mt/y
Pulp Mill Data:
Recycled Fiber Treatment Lines:
Flotation deinking lines: 1
Paper/Paperboard Grades and Capacities:
Total paper and paperboard capacity: 55,000 mt/y
Tissue: 48,000 mt/y
Packaging papers: 7,000 mt/y
Paper and Paperboard Mill Data:
Stock Preparation:
Pulpers: 2
Refiners: 4
Paper Machines: 4
No. 1, fourdrinier, Yankee dryer, total capacity 10,000 mt/y, Trim width 2.54 m, Packaging papers, Tissue
No. 2, twin-wire, Yankee dryer, total capacity 25,000 mt/y, Trim width 2.74 m, Tissue, Uncoated woodfree/freesheet
No. 3, fourdrinier, Yankee dryer, total capacity 7,000 mt/y, Trim width 2.08 m, Tissue
No. 4, twin-wire, Yankee dryer, total capacity 13,000 mt/y, Trim width 2.54 m, Tissue
Finishing Equipment:
Rewinders: 2 at 20,000 mt/y
Sheeters: 1
Energy Data:
Power boilers: 2
Electrical demand for mill: 180 MWh/D

ⓗQuena Paper Industry Co. (QPIC)
3, Mamar Behler, Kasr-el-Nil Str.
Cairo
Egypt
Phone: (20) 22 3929268/4009
Fax: (20) 22 3921816
Email: info@qpicpaper.com
Web Address: www.qpicpaper.com
Personnel:
Chmn.: Eng. Daoud
Phone: (20) 22 3929268/4009
Fax: (20) 22 3921816
Commercial Dir.: Helmy Zayed
Phone: (20) 22 3929268/4009
Fax: (20) 22 3921816
Total Employees of Company: 1,000
Mill Locations:
Quena Paper Industry Co. (QPIC), Kous Mill, Kous, Quena, Egypt, Capacity: 120,000 mt/y, (Pulp mill, Paper mill)
Phone: (20) 96 6842775/6, 6843662/4
Fax: (20) 96 6843661/6843761
Email: info@qpicpaper.com

ⓜQuena Paper Industry Co. (QPIC)
Kous Mill
Kous, Quena
Egypt
Phone: (20) 96 6842775/6, 6843662/4
Fax: (20) 96 6843661/6843761
Email: info@qpicpaper.com
Web Address: www.qpicpaper.com
Personnel:
Prod. Mgr.: Ziad Mokhtar
Phone: (20) 96 6842775/6, 6843662/4
Email: ziad_mokhtar@hotmail.com
Commercial Dir.: Helmy Zayed
Phone: (20) 96 6842775/6, 6843662/4
Total Employees at this Location: 916
Type of Operation: Pulp mill, Paper mill
Pulp Grades and Capacities:
Total pulp capacity: 87,483 mt/y
Mechanical Pulp: 26,348 mt/y
Other Pulp: 61,135 mt/y
Pulp Mill Data:
Chemical Pulping Systems:
Continuous digesters: 1
Mechanical Pulping Systems:
CTMP systems: 1
Pulp Lines: 2
Bleach Plant Systems: 2
Chemical bagasse, Sequence: O_2 DEoD, Capacity 90,000 admt/y
Chemimechanical bagasse Capacity 60,000 admt/y
Chemical Recovery Equipment:
Recovery boilers: 1
Paper/Paperboard Grades and Capacities:
Total paper and paperboard capacity: 120,000 mt/y
Newsprint: 60,000 mt/y
Uncoated woodfree/freesheet: 60,000 mt/y
Paper and Paperboard Mill Data:
Paper Machines: 1
No. 1, DuoFormer CFD, total capacity 120,000 mt/y, Trim width 6.18 m, Newsprint, Uncoated woodfree/freesheet
Finishing Equipment:
Winders: 1
Rewinders: 1
Energy Data:
Turbines
Electrical demand for mill: 398 MWh/D

ⓗⓜRakta, General Co. for Paper Industry
Rakta Mill
Ownership: Ministry of Public Sector Enterprise
El-Tabia, Rashid Road
21916 Alexandria, Iskanderiya
Egypt
Phone: (20) 3 5615864/865/5601763/5615869
Fax: (20) 3 5615866/5601300
Email: rakta@alexcom.net
Web Address: www.rakta-eg.com
Personnel:
Chmn.: Eng. Mahmoud El Batuti
Phone: (20) 3 5615864/865/5601763/5615869
Chmn.: Eng. Abu Taleb
Phone: (20) 3 5615864/865/5601763/5615869
Mill Mgr.: Abdel Basset El Badry
Phone: (20) 123567517
Total Employees of Company: 1,200
Total Employees at this Location: 1,200
Type of Operation: Pulp mill, Paper mill, Paperboard mill
Pulp Grades and Capacities:
Total pulp capacity: 58,584 mt/y
Recycled Pulping: 43,061 mt/y
Other Pulp: 15,523 mt/y
Paper/Paperboard Grades and Capacities:
Total paper and paperboard capacity: 59,000 mt/y
Uncoated mechanical/groundwood: 15,000 mt/y
Packaging papers: 3,000 mt/y
Linerboard: 22,000 mt/y
Corrugating medium/fluting: 10,000 mt/y
Boxboard/cartonboard: 9,000 mt/y
Paper and Paperboard Mill Data:
Stock Preparation:
Pulpers: 7
Refiners: 42
Paper Machines: 4
No. 1, fourdrinier, total capacity 15,000 mt/y, Trim width 3.3 m, Corrugating medium/fluting, Linerboard
No. 2, fourdrinier, total capacity 15,000 mt/y, Trim width 3.3 m, Corrugating medium/fluting, Linerboard
No. 3, fourdrinier, total capacity 18,000 mt/y, Trim width 4.6 m, Uncoated mechanical/groundwood, Packaging papers
No. 4, cylinder (5), Yankee dryer, total capacity 11,000 mt/y, Trim width 2.2 m, Boxboard/cartonboard, Linerboard
Coating Machines: 1
No. 1, total capacity 11,000 mt/y., on machine
Finishing Equipment:
Rewinders: 4
Sheeters: 5
Energy Data:
Power boilers: 5
Steam turbines: 4 at 17.5 MW
Electrical demand for mill: 124 MWh/D

ⓗShotmed Paper Industries (SPI)
Ownership: 100% by Salama family
No. 156, 3rd Industrial Zone
12566 6th of October City, Giza, El Giza
Egypt
Phone: (20) 22 5783943/3 8342250
Fax: (20) 22 5755795/3 8303273
Email: info@spi-egypt.com, sales@spi-egypt.com
Web Address: www.spi-egypt.com
Personnel:
Owner & Man. Dir.: Karim Salama
Phone: (20) 578 9338
Fax: (20) 575 5795
Email: k_salama@shotmed.com
Purch. Dir.: Sami Sanad
Phone: (20) 22 5783943
Fax: (20) 22 5755795
Email: ssanad@spi-egypt.com
Total Employees of Company: 250
Mill Locations:
Shotmed Paper Industries (SPI), 6th of October City, Giza Mill, No. 156, 3rd Industrial Zone, 12566 6th of October City, Giza, Egypt, Capacity: 30,000 mt/y, (Paper mill)
Phone: (20) 23 834 2250
Fax: (20) 23 833 4744
Email: info@spi-egypt.com, sales@spi-egypt.com

ⓜShotmed Paper Industries (SPI)
6th of October City, Giza Mill
No. 156, 3rd Industrial Zone
12566 6th of October City, Giza, El Giza
Egypt

Phone: (20) 23 834 2250
Fax: (20) 23 833 4744
Email: info@spi-egypt.com,
sales@spi-egypt.com
Web Address: www.spi-egypt.com
Personnel:
Man. Dir.: Karim Salama
Phone: (20) 23 834 2250
Fax: (20) 23 833 4744
Email: k_salama@shotmed.com
Purch. Dir.: Sami Sanad
Phone: (20) 23 834 2250
Fax: (20) 23 833 4744
Email: ssanad@spi-egypt.com
Total Employees at this Location: 150
Type of Operation: Paper mill
Pulp Grades and Capacities:
Total pulp capacity: 1,121 mt/y
Recycled Pulping: 1,121 mt/y
Pulp Mill Data:
Recycled Fiber Treatment Lines:
Pulpers
Paper/Paperboard Grades and Capacities:
Total paper and paperboard capacity: 30,000 mt/y
Uncoated woodfree/freesheet: 30,000 mt/y
Paper and Paperboard Mill Data:
Paper Machines: 2
No. 1, fourdrinier, total capacity 15,000 mt/y, Trim width 2.4 m, Uncoated woodfree/freesheet
No. 2, fourdrinier, total capacity 15,000 mt/y, Trim width 2.4 m, Uncoated woodfree/freesheet
Energy Data:
Power boilers
Electrical demand for mill: 59 MWh/D

ⓜSuperplast Co.
El Obour Mill
Ownership: El Obour Co.
499 Port Said St.
Bab El Shaaria, Cairo
Egypt
Phone: (20) 22 6440085/6
Fax: (20) 22 6397556
Email: sfosman@link.net
Personnel:
Owner, Chmn & Mill Mgr.: Eng. Sherif F. Osman
Phone: (20) 22 6440085/6
Email: sfosman@link.net
Total Employees at this Location: 40
Type of Operation: Paperboard mill
Pulp Grades and Capacities:
Total pulp capacity: 15,196 mt/y
Recycled Pulping: 15,196 mt/y
Pulp Mill Data:
Recycled Fiber Treatment Lines:
Recycled packaging pulping lines: 1
Paper/Paperboard Grades and Capacities:
Total paper and paperboard capacity: 15,000 mt/y
Linerboard: 15,000 mt/y
Paper and Paperboard Mill Data:
Paper Machines: 1
No. 1, fourdrinier, total capacity 15,000 mt/y, Trim width 2.2 m, Linerboard
Energy Data:
Power boilers
Electrical demand for mill: 20 MWh/D

ETHIOPIA

ⓘⓜAnmol Products Ethiopia
Ginchi Mill
West Shoa Zone
Ginchi
Ethiopia
Phone: (251) 910047278
Fax: (251) 116621476

Email: anmol@ethionet.et
Personnel:
Man. Dir.: Arvind Sharma
Phone: (251) 910047278
Gen. Mgr.: Rajeev Sharma
Phone: (251) 910047278
Total Employees at this Location: 250
Type of Operation: Paper mill
Paper/Paperboard Grades and Capacities:
Total paper and paperboard capacity: 18,000 mt/y
Newsprint: 3,000 mt/y
Uncoated woodfree/freesheet: 15,000 mt/y
Paper and Paperboard Mill Data:
Paper Machines: 1
No. 1, (2nd hand), total capacity 18,000 mt/y, Newsprint, Uncoated woodfree/freesheet

ⓘEthiopian Pulp & Paper SC
Ownership: 70% by Govt. of Ethiopia, 30% by International Finance Corp.
Kef 15, Keb 30, H.No. 403/11
Addis Ababa
Ethiopia
Mailing Address: PO Box 790, Addis Ababa, Ethiopia
Phone: (251) 11 1 566122/566861
Fax: (251) 11 1566121
Email: eppsc.com@ethionet.et
Web Address: www.eppsc.com.et
Personnel:
Gen. Mgr.: Melaku Kebede
Phone: (251) 22 220 0800
Email: eth.pp@ethionet.et
Mktg. Mgr.: Addis Dessalegne
Phone: (251) 11 1566168
Email: eppsc.com@ethionet.et
Prod. Mgr.: Demelash Tebik
Phone: (251) 22 2200566
Tech. Mgr.: Abraham Teshome
Phone: (251) 22 2200567
Qlty. & Ass. Service Head: Wondosen Gizaw
Phone: (251) 22 2201242
MIS/A Head: Kasahun Debesay
Phone: (251) 22 2200693
Admin. & Manpower Mgr.: Testaye Yilma
Phone: (251) 22 2200568
Total Employees of Company: 555
Total Employees at this Location: 15
Mill Locations:
Ethiopian Pulp & Paper SC, Nazareth Mill, PO Box 70, Wonji, Nazareth, Ethiopia, Capacity: 12,000 mt/y, (Paper mill)
Phone: (251) 22 220 0075
Fax: (251) 22 220 0163
Email: eppsc.com@ethionet.et

ⓜEthiopian Pulp & Paper SC
Nazareth Mill
PO Box 70
Wonji, Nazareth
Ethiopia
Mailing Address: PO Box 790, Addis Ababa, Ethiopia
Phone: (251) 22 220 0075
Fax: (251) 22 220 0163
Email: eppsc.com@ethionet.et
Web Address: www.eppsc.com.et
Personnel:
Gen. Mgr.: Melaku Kebede
Phone: (251) 22 220 0800
Quality Mgr.: Mr. O. Wondwosen
Phone: (251) 22 220 0566
Total Employees at this Location: 540
Type of Operation: Paper mill
Paper/Paperboard Grades and Capacities:
Total paper and paperboard capacity: 12,000 mt/y
Uncoated woodfree/freesheet: 5,000 mt/y
Uncoated mechanical/groundwood: 2,000 mt/y
Packaging papers: 4,000 mt/y
Boxboard/cartonboard: 1,000 mt/y
Paper and Paperboard Mill Data:
Stock Preparation:

Pulpers: 1
Refiners: 2
Paper Machines: 1
No. 1, fourdrinier, total capacity 12,000 mt/y, Trim width 2.8 m, Uncoated woodfree/freesheet, Packaging papers, Boxboard/cartonboard, Uncoated mechanical/groundwood
Finishing Equipment:
Rewinders: 2
Sheeters: 3
Energy Data:
Power boilers: 5

GHANA

ⓘⓜSuper Paper Products Co. Ltd.
Tema Mill
PO Box 1133, 133 3rd Industrial Link, Heavy Industrial Area
Tema
Ghana
Phone: (233) 21 6650 16-5
Fax: (233) 21 663901-2
Email: sppcltd@yahoo.com
Web Address: www.sppcltd.com
Personnel:
Chmn.: Seth Anatsui
Phone: (233) 21 6650 16-5
Fax: (233) 21 663901-2
Exec. Vice Chmn.: Elkin Pianim
Phone: (233) 21 6650 16-5
Fax: (233) 21 663901-2
Man. Dir.: Jared Barnett
Phone: (233) 21 6650 16-5
Fax: (233) 21 663901-2
Dir.: Dr. Patrick Ata
Phone: (233) 21 6650 16-5
Fax: (233) 21 663901-2
Dir.: Ajomale Wole
Phone: (233) 21 6650 16-5
Fax: (233) 21 663901-2
Dir.: Ibrahim-Abu Samirah
Phone: (233) 21 6650 16-5
Fax: (233) 21 663901-2
Dir.: Yamoah Comfort
Phone: (233) 21 6650 16-5
Fax: (233) 21 663901-2
Prod. Mgr.: Mr. Kojo Omare
Phone: (233) 244 766 447
Fax: (233) 21 663901-2
Finan. Contr.: Moses Arthur
Phone: (233) 21 6650 16-5
Fax: (233) 21 663901-2
HR Mgr.: Enyo Akar
Phone: (233) 21 6650 16-5
Fax: (233) 21 663901-2
Head of Eng.: Edward Ackom
Phone: (233) 21 6650 16-5
Fax: (233) 21 663901-2
Total Employees at this Location: 270
Type of Operation: Paper mill
Paper/Paperboard Grades and Capacities:
Total paper and paperboard capacity: 3,650 mt/y
Tissue: 3,650 mt/y
Paper and Paperboard Mill Data:
Paper Machines: 2
PM 1, total capacity 1,650 mt/y, Trim width 1.73 m, Tissue
PM 2, total capacity 2,000 mt/y, Trim width 1.9 m, Tissue

KENYA

ⓘⓜChandaria Industries Ltd.
Chandaria Paper Mill
Ownership: Family-owned (Private)

Kenya

Baba Dogo Road, Ruaraka
Nairobi
Kenya
Mailing Address: PO Box 30621, Nairobi, Kenya
Phone: (254) 20 856 3252-5, 20 856 2124-6, 20 856 2740-2441
Fax: (254) 20 856 4271, 20 856 2130
Email: info@chandaria.com
Web Address: www.chandaria.com
Personnel:
Group Chmn.: M. M. Chandaria
Phone: (254) 20 856 3252-5/2124-6/2740-2441
Man. Dir.: H. Chandaria
Phone: (254) 20 856 3252-5/2124-6/2740-2441
Gen. Mgr.: A. K. Sharma
Phone: (254) 20 856 3252-5/2124-6/2740-2441
Sls. Mgr.: B. Tejani
Phone: (254) 20 856 3252-5/2124-6/2740-2441
Finan. Controller: R. Pradhu
Phone: (254) 20 856 3252-5/2124-6/2740-2441
Dir.: Mahesh Chandaria
Phone: (254) 20 856 3252-5/2124-6/2740-2441
Mill Mgr.: R. K. Acharya
Phone: (254) 20 856 3252-5/2124-6/2740-2441
Total Employees of Company: 600
Total Employees at this Location: 600
Type of Operation: Paper mill
Mill Locations:
Kenya Papermill Ltd., Thika Mill, PO Box 390, Thika, Kenya, Capacity: 30,000 mt/y, (Paper mill, Paperboard mill)
Phone: (254) 67 21299
Email: info@chandaria.com
Madhupaper Kenya Ltd., Madhupaper Mill, PO Box 78065, Nairobi, Kenya, Capacity: 12,000 mt/y, (Paper mill)
Phone: (254) 20 555366
Fax: (254) 20 540600
Email: info@chandaria.com
Tanpack Tissues Ltd., Dar-es-Salaam Mill, P.O.Box 21359, Dar-es-Salaam, Tanzania, Capacity: 3,000 mt/y, (Paper mill)
Phone: (255) 22 2700163/2773901-3
Fax: (255) 22 2700890
Email: info@tanpacktissue.com
Pulp Mill Data:
Recycled Fiber Treatment Lines:
Pulpers: 2
Paper/Paperboard Grades and Capacities:
Total paper and paperboard capacity: 8,400 mt/y
Tissue: 8,400 mt/y
Paper and Paperboard Mill Data:
Stock Preparation:
Pulpers: 2
Refiners: 5
Paper Machines: 2
No. 1, Yankee dryer, total capacity 4,200 mt/y, Trim width 1.8 m, Tissue
No. 2, Yankee dryer, total capacity 4,200 mt/y, Trim width 1.9 m, Tissue
Finishing Equipment:
Rewinders: 2
Sheeters: 1
Energy Data:
Power boilers: 3

ⓂHighland Paper Mills Ltd.
Eldoret Mill
Kambi Somali Road
10030 Eldoret, Western
Kenya
Mailing Address: PO Box 1425, 10030 Eldoret, Kenya
Phone: (254) 35 2030 262/612
Fax: (254) 5320 62269
Personnel:
Chmn.: N. P. Thakker
Phone: (254) 35 2030 262/612
Gen. Mgr.: Ramesh Chand Kapoor
Phone: (254) 721 267 634

Fax: (254) 53 32744
Email: rckhp@africaonline.co.ki
Mill Mgr./Prod. Mgr.: M. Nyongesa
Phone: (254) 722 90 9031
Fax: (254) 5320 62269
Factory Mgr. & Eng.: Joseph M. Linyerera
Phone: (254) 722 736301
Fax: (254) 53 62269
Accountant: David Taracha
Phone: (254) 722 909 064
Total Employees at this Location: 35
Type of Operation: Pulp mill, Paperboard mill
Pulp Grades and Capacities:
Total pulp capacity: 1,800 mt/y
Recycled Pulping
Pulp Mill Data:
Chemical Pulping Systems:
Batch digesters: 2
Paper/Paperboard Grades and Capacities:
Total paper and paperboard capacity: 11,500 mt/y
Specialty and industrial
Boxboard/cartonboard: 11,500 mt/y
Paper and Paperboard Mill Data:
Stock Preparation:
Pulpers: 3
Refiners: 2
Paper Machines: 1
No. 1, cylinder, total capacity 11,500 mt/y, Trim width 1.64 m, Boxboard/cartonboard
Energy Data:
Power boilers: 2

ⓂKenya Papermill Ltd.
Thika Mill
Ownership: Chandaria Industries Ltd.
PO Box 390
Thika, Central
Kenya
Phone: (254) 67 21299
Email: info@chandaria.com
Web Address: www.chandaria.com
Personnel:
Gen. Mgr.: A. K. Sharma
Phone: (254) 67 21299
Paper Mill Mgr.: R. Achar
Phone: (254) 67 21299
Prod. Mgr.: T. P. S. Saini
Phone: (254) 67 21299
Chief Eng.: F. Xavier
Phone: (254) 67 21299
Total Employees at this Location: 76
Type of Operation: Paper mill, Paperboard mill
Pulp Mill Data:
Recycled Fiber Treatment Lines:
Recycled packaging pulping lines: 1
Paper/Paperboard Grades and Capacities:
Total paper and paperboard capacity: 30,000 mt/y
Packaging papers
Specialty and industrial
Linerboard: 21,000 mt/y
Corrugating medium/fluting
Boxboard/cartonboard
Paper and Paperboard Mill Data:
Stock Preparation:
Pulpers: 1
Refiners: 2
Paper Machines: 2
No. 1, (idle), fourdrinier, Trim width 1.7 m
No. 2, (second hand), total capacity 21,000 mt/y, Containerboard, Linerboard, Corrugating medium/fluting, Packaging papers
Finishing Equipment:
Rewinders: 2
Sheeters: 2
Energy Data:
Power boilers: 2

ⓂMadhupaper Kenya Ltd.
Madhupaper Mill
Ownership: 100% by Chandaria Industries Ltd.
PO Box 78065
Nairobi
Kenya
Phone: (254) 20 555366
Fax: (254) 20 540600
Email: info@chandaria.com
Web Address: www.chandaria.com
Personnel:
Gen. Mgr.: A. K. Sharma
Phone: (254) 20 555366
Total Employees at this Location: 120
Type of Operation: Paper mill
Pulp Grades and Capacities:
Total pulp capacity: 10,000 mt/y
Recycled Pulping: 10,000 mt/y
Pulp Mill Data:
Recycled Fiber Treatment Lines:
Pulpers: 3
Paper/Paperboard Grades and Capacities:
Total paper and paperboard capacity: 12,000 mt/y
Tissue
Packaging papers
Paper and Paperboard Mill Data:
Stock Preparation:
Pulpers: 3
Refiners: 8
Paper Machines: 3
PM 1, Yankee dryer, total capacity 2,640 mt/y, Trim width 2 m, Tissue
PM 2, Yankee dryer, total capacity 3,300 mt/y, Trim width 2 m, Tissue, Packaging papers
PM 3, total capacity 6,000 mt/y, Packaging papers
Finishing Equipment:
Supercalenders: 1
Rewinders: 2
Sheeters: 1
Energy Data:
Power boilers: 4

ⓂPan Paper Mills
PO Box 535
Bungoma Di Webuye, Western
Kenya
Phone: (254) 55 30723
Mill Locations:
Pan Paper Mills, Webuye Mill, PO Box 535, 50205 Webuye, Bungoma District, Kenya, Capacity: 132,000 mt/y, (Pulp mill, Paper mill, Paperboard mill)
Fax: (254) 55 30723

ⓂPan Paper Mills
Webuye Mill
Mill is closed (closed since January 2012. The government plans to revive the mill but no dates given)
PO Box 535
50205 Webuye, Bungoma District, Western
Kenya
Fax: (254) 55 30723
Personnel:
Man. Dir.: Y. Pachiea
Gen. Mgr.: K. H. Kothari
Total Employees at this Location: 1,500
Type of Operation: Pulp mill, Paper mill, Paperboard mill
Pulp Grades and Capacities:
Total pulp capacity: 184,000 mt/y
Chemical Pulp: 100,000 mt/y
Mechanical Pulp: 22,500 mt/y
Recycled Pulping: 61,500 mt/y
Pulp Mill Data:
Chemical Pulping Systems:
Batch digesters: 5
Mechanical Pulping Systems:
Conventional grinders: 2

Pulp Lines: 3
Bleach Plant Systems: 2
No. 1, Sequence: CEpHH, Capacity 45,000 admt/y
No. 2, Sequence: P/HS, Capacity 15,000 admt/y
Chemical Recovery Equipment:
Evaporator lines: 1
Recovery boilers: 1
Lime Kiln
Recycled Fiber Treatment Lines:
Flotation deinking lines: 1 at 22,500 admt/y
Pulpers: 3 at 61,500 admt/y
Recycled packaging pulping lines: 1 at 39,000 admt/y
Washing deinking lines: 1 at 22,500 admt/y
Pulp Dryers:
Wet Lap machine 1
Paper/Paperboard Grades and Capacities:
Total paper and paperboard capacity: 132,000 mt/y
Newsprint: 12,000 mt/y
Packaging papers: 15,000 mt/y
Containerboard: 84,500 mt/y
Linerboard
Corrugating medium/fluting
Boxboard/cartonboard: 2,500 mt/y
Paper and Paperboard Mill Data:
Stock Preparation:
Pulpers: 7
Refiners: 18
Paper Machines: 4
No. 1, fourdrinier, total capacity 37,000 mt/y, Trim width 4.2 m, Packaging papers, Linerboard
No. 2, fourdrinier, total capacity 30,000 mt/y, Trim width 4.2 m, Newsprint, Uncoated woodfree/freesheet
No. 3, fourdrinier, total capacity 30,000 mt/y, Trim width 3.8 m, Linerboard, Corrugating medium/fluting
No. 4, total capacity 30,000 mt/y, Trim width 2.8 m, Linerboard, Corrugating medium/fluting, Boxboard/cartonboard
Coating Machines: 1
No. 4, total capacity 2,500 mt/y., on machine
Finishing Equipment:
Winders: 4 at 120,000 mt/y
Rewinders: 2 at 10,000 mt/y
Sheeters: 3 at 75,000 mt/y
Energy Data:
Power boilers: 3
Steam turbines: 2 at 12.5, 9.0 MW
Electrical demand for mill: 500 MWh/D

ⓗⓜPegant Ltd.
Nairobi Mill
Lunga Lunga Road
Nairobi
Kenya
Mailing Address: 42930, GPO, 00100 Nairobi, Kenya
Phone: (254) 20 651334/5
Fax: (254) 20 532911
Email: info@pegant.com
Personnel:
Man. Dir.: P. K. Shah
Phone: (254) 722 241111
Total Employees at this Location: 120
Type of Operation: Pulp mill, Paper mill
Pulp Grades and Capacities:
Total pulp capacity: 6,000 mt/y
Recycled Pulping: 6,000 mt/y
Pulp Mill Data:
Recycled Fiber Treatment Lines:
Flotation deinking lines: 1 at 6,000 admt/y
Pulpers: 2 at 5,000 admt/y
Paper/Paperboard Grades and Capacities:
Total paper and paperboard capacity: 6,000 mt/y
Tissue: 6,000 mt/y
Paper and Paperboard Mill Data:
Stock Preparation:
Pulpers: 2
Refiners: 2
Paper Machines: 1
No. 1, fourdrinier, total capacity 6,000 mt/y, Trim width 1.85 m, Tissue

Finishing Equipment:
Winders: 1
Rewinders: 2 at 4,000 mt/y
Energy Data:
Power boilers: 2
Electrical demand for mill: 1 MWh/D

MOROCCO

ⓞG.P.C. Mohammadia
Ownership: 100% by YNNA Holding - CHAABI Group
Route Cotière N° 111, Boîte postale 20800
Mohammadia
Morocco
Phone: (212) 523 327750/53
Fax: (212) 523 313445
Email: contact@gpccarton.com
Web Address: www.gpccarton.com, www.ynna.ma
Personnel:
Chmn.: Miloud Chaabi
Phone: (212) 523 327750/53
Fax: (212) 523 313445
Commercial Mgr.: Abdelali Alaoui
Phone: (212) 22 484737
Total Employees of Company: 100
Total Employees at this Location: 10
Mill Locations:
G.P.C. Mohammadia, Meknès Mill, Rte. D'Agourai, BP 296, Km 2.3, Meknès, Morocco, Capacity: 24,000 mt/y, (Paper mill, Paperboard mill)
Phone: (212) 535 537260/367215
Fax: (212) 535 538720
Email: contact@gpccarton.com

ⓜG.P.C. Mohammadia
Meknès Mill
Rte. D'Agourai, BP 296, Km 2.3
Meknès
Morocco
Phone: (212) 535 537260/367215
Fax: (212) 535 538720
Email: contact@gpccarton.com
Web Address: www.gpccarton.com, www.ynna.ma
Personnel:
Group Gen. Mgr.: Mounir Elbari
Phone: (212) 660 666855/ 661 156598
Fax: (212) 535 538720
Email: m.elbari@gpccarton.com
Prod. Mgr.: Hassan Harti
Phone: (212) 660 150351
Fax: (212) 535 538720
Email: h.harti@gpccarton.com
Maint. Mgr.: Badri Boutayeb
Phone: (212) 660 150350
Fax: (212) 535 538720
Email: b.boutayeb@gpccarton.com
Total Employees at this Location: 100
Type of Operation: Paper mill, Paperboard mill
Pulp Grades and Capacities:
Total pulp capacity: 23,987 mt/y
Recycled Pulping: 23,987 mt/y
Pulp Mill Data:
Recycled Fiber Treatment Lines:
Flotation deinking lines: 1
Pulpers: 2
Paper/Paperboard Grades and Capacities:
Total paper and paperboard capacity: 24,000 mt/y
Packaging papers: 10,000 mt/y
Linerboard: 9,000 mt/y
Corrugating medium/fluting: 5,000 mt/y
Paper and Paperboard Mill Data:
Stock Preparation:
Pulpers: 3

Paper Machines: 2
No. 1, fourdrinier, total capacity 14,000 mt/y, Trim width 2.4 m, Corrugating medium/fluting, Linerboard
No. 2, fourdrinier, Yankee dryer, total capacity 10,000 mt/y, Trim width 1.8 m, Packaging papers
Finishing Equipment:
Winders: 2 at 24,000 mt/y
Calenders: 1
Rewinders: 2
Sheeters: 2
Energy Data:
Power boilers: 3
Electrical demand for mill: 40 MWh/D

ⓞGroupe CMCP - La Compagnie Marocaine des Cartons et Papiers
Ownership: 100% by International Paper Co.
Quartier Industriel, Ain Sbaa, Boulevard A., B.P. 25, 95
Casablanca
Morocco
Phone: (212) 522 667878/350009
Fax: (212) 522 663 671/672/668
Email: contact@ipaper.com
Web Address: www.internationalpaper.com
Personnel:
Chmn/CEO: Bertrand Laplaud
Phone: (212) 522 667879
Commun. Mgr.: Mrs. Bouchra El Moufid
Phone: (212) 522 667878
Fax: (212) 522 663671/2
Email: bouchra.elmoufid@ipaper.com
Total Employees of Company: 1,300
Mill Locations:
Groupe CMCP - La Compagnie Marocaine des Cartons et Papiers, Kenitra Mill, Quartier Industriel, Boite Postale 94, MA 14000 Kenitra, Morocco, Capacity: 120,000 mt/y, (Paperboard mill)
Phone: (212) 537 399000
Fax: (212) 537 378557/8638
Email: contact@ipaper.com

ⓜGroupe CMCP - La Compagnie Marocaine des Cartons et Papiers
Kenitra Mill
Ownership: 100% by International Paper Co.
Quartier Industriel, Boite Postale 94
MA 14000 Kenitra
Morocco
Phone: (212) 537 399000
Fax: (212) 537 378557/8638
Email: contact@ipaper.com
Web Address: www.internationalpaper.com
Personnel:
Mill Mgr.: Philippe D'Adhemar
Phone: (212) 537 399000
Email: philippe.dadhemar@ipaper.com
Oper. Mgr.: Fabrice Jacqueroux
Phone: (212) 537 399009
Email: fabrice.jacqueroux@ipaper.com
Asst. Mill Mgr.: Mrs. Nazik Douiri
Phone: (212) 537 378558
Email: naziksalam.douiri@ipaper.com
HR Officer: Smail Latai
Phone: (212) 537 399000
Email: smail.latai@ipaper.com
Env. & Quality Officer, Risk Mgr.: Mohamed Dakkak
Phone: (212) 537 399000
Email: mohamed.dakkak@ipaper.com
Total Employees at this Location: 500
Type of Operation: Paperboard mill
Pulp Grades and Capacities:
Total pulp capacity: 108,889 mt/y
Recycled Pulping: 108,889 mt/y
Pulp Mill Data:
Recycled Fiber Treatment Lines:
Recycled packaging pulping lines: 1
Paper/Paperboard Grades and Capacities:
Total paper and paperboard capacity: 120,000 mt/y

Morocco

Linerboard: 40,000 mt/y
Corrugating medium/fluting: 35,000 mt/y
Boxboard/cartonboard: 45,000 mt/y
Paper and Paperboard Mill Data:
Stock Preparation:
Pulpers: 7
Refiners: 10
Paper Machines: 2
No. 1, cylinder (6), Yankee dryer, total capacity 40,000 mt/y, Trim width 3.65 m, Boxboard/cartonboard
No. 3, fourdrinier (2), total capacity 80,000 mt/y, Trim width 2.55 m, Corrugating medium/fluting, Linerboard, Boxboard/cartonboard
Coating Machines: 1
No. 1, on machine
Finishing Equipment:
Winders: 4
Supercalenders: 2
Rewinders: 1
Sheeters: 2 at 30,000 mt/y
Energy Data:
Power boilers: 5
Steam turbines: 2 at 6 MW
Electrical demand for mill: 175 MWh/D

ⓗⓜJeesr Industries Co.
Jeesr Industries Co.
Ownership: 100% by Novatis Group (Private)
76, Zone Industrielle
Berrechid
Morocco
Phone: (212) 5 22 32 72 00
Fax: (212) 5 22 32 72 05
Email: contact@novatis-group.com
Web Address: www.jeesr-industries.com
Total Employees of Company: 60
Total Employees at this Location: 60
Type of Operation: Paper mill
Paper/Paperboard Grades and Capacities:
Total paper and paperboard capacity: 30,000 mt/y
Tissue: 30,000 mt/y
Paper and Paperboard Mill Data:
Paper Machines: 1
No. 1, Advantage DCT 100+, Yankee dryer, total capacity 30,000 mt/y, Trim width 2.85 m, Tissue
Energy Data:
Power boilers
Electrical demand for mill: 75 MWh/D

ⓗLexpapier Sonacar S.A.
Ownership: 100% by Abdallah Jabri
Zone Industrielle El Jadida, Route de Safi
EL Jadida
Morocco
Phone: (212) 523 35 14 17/21
Fax: (212) 523 35 14 15
Email: sonacar@sonacar.ma
Web Address: sonacar.org
Personnel:
Pres. & CEO: Abdellah Jabri
Phone: (212) 523 35 14 17/21
Fax: (212) 523 35 14 15
Admin.: Aziz Jabri
Phone: (212) 523 35 14 17/21
Fax: (212) 523 35 14 15
Total Employees of Company: 54
Mill Locations:
Lexpapier Sonacar S.A., EL Jadida Mill, Zone Industrielle El Jadida, Route de Safi, EL Jadida, Morocco, Capacity: 36,000 mt/y, (Paper mill, Paperboard mill)
Phone: (212) 523 35 14 17/21
Fax: (212) 523 35 14 15
Email: lexpapier@sonacar.ma, sonacar@sonacar.ma

ⓗⓜLexpapier Sonacar S.A.
EL Jadida Mill
Zone Industrielle El Jadida, Route de Safi
EL Jadida
Morocco
Phone: (212) 523 35 14 17/21
Fax: (212) 523 35 14 15
Email: lexpapier@sonacar.ma, sonacar@sonacar.ma
Web Address: www.sonacar.com
Personnel:
Pres. & CEO: Abdellah Jabri
Phone: (212) 523 351417
Fax: (212) 523 351415
Email: sonacar@sonacar.ma
Gen. Mgr.: Mr. Michel Pliya
Phone: (212) 523 351417
Fax: (212) 523 351415
Tech. Mgr.: Mr. Mustapha Atif
Phone: (212) 663 797810
Fax: (212) 523 351415
Total Employees at this Location: 54
Type of Operation: Paper mill, Paperboard mill
Pulp Grades and Capacities:
Total pulp capacity: 36,055 mt/y
Recycled Pulping: 36,055 mt/y
Pulp Mill Data:
Recycled Fiber Treatment Lines:
Pulpers: 3
Paper/Paperboard Grades and Capacities:
Total paper and paperboard capacity: 36,000 mt/y
Linerboard: 17,000 mt/y
Corrugating medium/fluting: 17,000 mt/y
Boxboard/cartonboard: 2,000 mt/y
Paper and Paperboard Mill Data:
Stock Preparation:
Pulpers: 3
Refiners: 3
Paper Machines: 1
No. 1, fourdrinier, total capacity 36,000 mt/y, Trim width 2.4 m, Corrugating medium/fluting, Linerboard, Boxboard/cartonboard
Finishing Equipment:
Winders: 1 at 50,000 mt/y
Rewinders: 1 at 50,000 mt/y
Energy Data:
Power boilers: 2
Electrical demand for mill: 53 MWh/D

ⓗLa Cellulose du Maroc
Ownership: 62.70% by C.D.G. - Caisse de Dépôt et Gestion
12, Rue Tissa
Rabat
Morocco
Phone: (212) 537 708305
Fax: (212) 537 706135
Email: cellulose@menara.ma
Web Address: www.celluma.ma
Personnel:
Gen. Mgr.: Abderrahim Finjero
Phone: (212) 537 708305
Fax: (212) 537 706135
Email: a.finjero@celluma.ma
Commer. Mgr.: Mohamed Chaoui
Phone: (212) 537 737146
Email: m.chaoui@celluma.ma
Devlpt. Mgr.: Abdelaziz Rmili
Phone: (212) 537 708305
Fax: (212) 537 706135
Email: a.rmili@celluma.ma
HR Mgr.: Mr. Samir Fethi
Phone: (212) 537 708305
Fax: (212) 537 706135
Total Employees of Company: 255
Total Employees at this Location: 20
Mill Locations:
La Cellulose du Maroc, Sidi Yahia Pulp Mill, BP 68, Sidi Yahia Du Gharb, Morocco, (Pulp mill)
Phone: (212) 537 300053/54/708305/ 660106785/86
Fax: (212) 537 300014
Email: m.hassaouan@celluma.ma
MED Paper SA, Tangier Mill (23.72% owned), Zone Industrielle, Lot 19, Alleé 1, Bte postale 400, 9000 Tangier, Morocco, Capacity: 46,000 mt/y, (Paper mill)
Phone: (212) 539 36 2100
Fax: (212) 539 35 1144
Email: medpaper@medpaper.ma

ⓗLa Cellulose du Maroc
Sidi Yahia Pulp Mill
Mill is closed (Cellulose du Maroc suspended production of bleached eucalyptus kraft (BEK) pulp from late November 2013. Officially closed December 2013)
BP 68
Sidi Yahia Du Gharb, Kenitra
Morocco
Phone: (212) 537 300053/54/708305/ 660106785/86
Fax: (212) 537 300014
Email: m.hassaouan@celluma.ma
Web Address: www.celluma.ma
Personnel:
Mill Mgr.: Mahjoub Hassaouane
Phone: (212) 06 60106778
Email: m.hassaouan@celluma.ma
Prod. Officer: Boulahfa Seghir
Phone: (212) 537 300053/54/ 660106785/86
Mohamed Haoui
Total Employees at this Location: 215
Type of Operation: Pulp mill
Pulp Mill Data:
Chemical Pulping Systems:
Continuous digesters: 1
Pulp Lines: 1
Bleach Plant Systems: 1
No. 1, Sequence: O_2 C/DE/HDED, Capacity 151,000 admt/y
Chemical Recovery Equipment:
Evaporator lines: 1
Recovery boilers: 1
Lime Kiln
Pulp Dryers:
Air Float dryers 1
Energy Data:
Power boilers: 1
Steam turbines: 1 at 15 MW

ⓗⓜMED Paper SA
Tangier Mill
Ownership: 23.72% by La Cellulose du Maroc, 10.28% by C.D.G. - Caisse de Dépôt et Gestion, 60% by Sefrioui family
Zone Industrielle, Lot 19, Alleé 1, Bte postale 400
9000 Tangier
Morocco
Phone: (212) 539 36 2100
Fax: (212) 539 35 1144
Email: medpaper@medpaper.ma
Web Address: www.med-paper.ma
Personnel:
Gen. Dir.: Rachid Benchaaboun
Phone: (212) 539 362100
Fax: (212) 539 351144
Total Employees of Company: 280
Total Employees at this Location: 280
Type of Operation: Paper mill
Pulp Grades and Capacities:
Total pulp capacity: 6,285 mt/y
Recycled Pulping: 6,285 mt/y
Pulp Mill Data:
Recycled Fiber Treatment Lines:
Flotation deinking lines: 1 at 8,750 admt/y
Pulpers: 1
Paper/Paperboard Grades and Capacities:
Total paper and paperboard capacity: 46,000 mt/y
Uncoated woodfree/freesheet: 40,000 mt/y
Packaging papers: 6,000 mt/y
Paper and Paperboard Mill Data:
Stock Preparation:
Pulpers: 3

Nigeria

Refiners: 6
Paper Machines: 3
No. 1, fourdrinier, total capacity 6,000 mt/y, Trim width 2.45 m, Packaging papers
No. 2, fourdrinier, total capacity 15,000 mt/y, Trim width 2.46 m, Uncoated woodfree/freesheet
No. 3, fourdrinier, total capacity 25,000 mt/y, Trim width 2.7 m, Uncoated woodfree/freesheet
Finishing Equipment:
Winders: 3 at 51,000 mt/y
Calenders: 2
Rewinders: 4
Sheeters: 2
Energy Data:
Power boilers: 2
Electrical demand for mill: 88 MWh/D

ⓄⓂSocieté Industrielle Des Papiers "Tissues" (Sipat S.A.)
Meknès Mill
Ownership: 100% by private owners
Quartier Industriel Ain Slougui, BP 135
Meknès
Morocco
Phone: (212) 535 5005 26/27
Fax: (212) 535 500896
Email: sipatpap@yahoo.fr
Personnel:
Chmn. & CEO: Mohamed El Kendouci
Phone: (212) 535 5005 26/27
Man. Dir.: Moulay Driss El Kendouci
Phone: (212) 535 252406/07
Email: driss.elkendouci@gmail.com
Tech. Mgr.: Tayache Mohamed
Phone: (212) 664 564667
Finan. Dir.: Mohamed Hafidi
Phone: (212) 535 5005 26/27
Total Employees of Company: 145
Total Employees at this Location: 145
Type of Operation: Paper mill
Pulp Mill Data:
Recycled Fiber Treatment Lines:
Pulpers: 3 at 9,900 admt/y
Washing deinking lines: 1 at 9,000 admt/y
Paper/Paperboard Grades and Capacities:
Total paper and paperboard capacity: 17,000 mt/y
Tissue: 17,000 mt/y
Paper and Paperboard Mill Data:
Stock Preparation:
Pulpers: 3
Refiners: 2
Paper Machines: 2
PM 1, Yankee dryer, Trim width 1.92 m, Tissue
PM 2, crescent former, Yankee dryer, Trim width 2.75 m, Tissue
Finishing Equipment:
Winders: 2
Rewinders: 2 at 9,900 mt/y
Energy Data:
Power boilers: 2
Electrical demand for mill: 48 MWh/D

NIGERIA

ⓄBel Papyrus Ltd
Ownership: Boulos Group Ltd.
Plot 6, Kudirat, Abiola Way, Oregun Road Ikeja, Lagos, Lagos State, 241
Lagos State
Nigeria
Phone: (234) 1 7745232, 4960948
Fax: (234) 1 4968078
Web Address: www.groupboulos.com/companies.php#3
Mill Locations:
Bel Papyrus Ltd, Ogaba Mill, Plot 10, Block D Acme Road, Ogabas Industrial Scheme, 241 Ikeja, Lagos, Nigeria, Capacity: 38,000 mt/y, (Paper mill)
Phone: (234) 1 7745232/4960948/4964319/5557763
Fax: (234) 1 4968078
Bel Papyrus Ltd, Oregun Mill, Plot 6, Kudirat, Abiola Way, Oregun Road, 241 Ikeja, Lagos, Nigeria, Capacity: 5,000 mt/y, (Paper mill)
Phone: (234) 1 7745232/4960948/4964319/5557763
Fax: (234) 1 4968078

ⓂBel Papyrus Ltd
Ogaba Mill
Plot 10, Block D Acme Road, Ogabas Industrial Scheme
241 Ikeja, Lagos, Lagos State
Nigeria
Phone: (234) 1 7745232/4960948/4964319/5557763
Fax: (234) 1 4968078
Web Address: www.groupboulos.com/companies.php#3
Personnel:
Group Man. Dir.: Riad Joseph Baloukji
Phone: (234) 1 7745232
Fax: (234) 1 4968078
Email: r.baloukji@bpl.groupboulos.com
Total Employees at this Location: 120
Type of Operation: Paper mill
Pulp Mill Data:
Recycled Fiber Treatment Lines:
Flotation deinking lines: 1
Paper/Paperboard Grades and Capacities:
Total paper and paperboard capacity: 38,000 mt/y
Tissue: 38,000 mt/y
Paper and Paperboard Mill Data:
Paper Machines: 2
PM 2, crescent former, total capacity 15,000 mt/y, Trim width 2.75 m, Tissue
PM 3, (started up June 2013), crescent former, Yankee dryer, total capacity 23,000 mt/y, Trim width 2.85 m, Tissue
Energy Data:
Power boilers: 2
Steam turbines

ⓂBel Papyrus Ltd
Oregun Mill
Plot 6, Kudirat, Abiola Way, Oregun Road
241 Ikeja, Lagos, Lagos State
Nigeria
Phone: (234) 1 7745232/4960948/4964319/5557763
Fax: (234) 1 4968078
Web Address: www.groupboulos.com/companies.php#3
Type of Operation: Paper mill
Paper/Paperboard Grades and Capacities:
Total paper and paperboard capacity: 5,000 mt/y
Tissue: 5,000 mt/y
Paper and Paperboard Mill Data:
Paper Machines: 1
PM 1, fourdrinier, total capacity 5,000 mt/y, Trim width 1.85 m, Tissue

ⓄCrown Tissue
KM 36 Lagos-Abeokuta Express Way, Amje B/Stop, Alakuko Oshodi, Lagos, Lagos State,
Lagos State
Nigeria
Phone: (234) 1 817 2262
Fax: (234) 1 774 8235
Email: info@crowntissuegroup.com
Web Address: crowntissuegroup.com
Personnel:
Vice Chmn. & Group Man. Dir.: Bolaji Kuje
Phone: (234) 1 817 2262
Fax: (234) 1 774 8235
Commer. Dir.: Adedoyin Mebude
Phone: (234) 1 817 2262
Fax: (234) 1 774 8235
Email: ukashatadodomeb@yahoo.co.uk
Finan. Mgr.: Rasheed Haruna
Phone: (234) 1 817 2262
Fax: (234) 1 774 8235
Group Exec. Dir. Sls. & Mktg: Tola Bakare
Phone: (234) 1 817 2262
Fax: (234) 1 774 8235
Total Employees of Company: 100
Mill Locations:
Crown Tissue, Oshodi, Lagos Mill, KM 36 Lagos-Abeokuta Express Way, Amje B/Stop, Alakuko, Oshodi, Lagos, Nigeria, Capacity: 9,000 mt/y, (Paper mill)
Phone: (234) 1 817 2262
Fax: (234) 1 774 8235
Email: info@crowntissuegroup.com

ⓂCrown Tissue
Oshodi, Lagos Mill
KM 36 Lagos-Abeokuta Express Way, Amje B/Stop, Alakuko
Oshodi, Lagos, Lagos State
Nigeria
Phone: (234) 1 817 2262
Fax: (234) 1 774 8235
Email: info@crowntissuegroup.com
Web Address: crowntissuegroup.com
Personnel:
Vice Chmn.: Bolaji Kuje
Phone: (234) 1 817 2262
Fax: (234) 1 774 8235
Commer. Dir.: Adedoyin Mebude
Phone: (234) 1 817 2262
Fax: (234) 1 774 8235
Email: ukashatadodomeb@yahoo.co.uk
Finan. Mgr.: Rasheed Haruna
Phone: (234) 1 817 2262
Fax: (234) 1 774 8235
Total Employees at this Location: 100
Type of Operation: Paper mill
Paper/Paperboard Grades and Capacities:
Total paper and paperboard capacity: 9,000 mt/y
Tissue: 9,000 mt/y
Paper and Paperboard Mill Data:
Paper Machines: 1
PM 1, crescent former, total capacity 9,000 mt/y, Trim width 2.8 m, Tissue

ⓄEpesok Paper Mills Ltd.
Ownership: 100% by Onward Group of Companies
Obagun Avenue, Matori Industrial Estate
Oshodi, Lagos, Lagos State
Nigeria
Phone: (234) 1 - 7215299
Email: info@epesok.com
Web Address: epesok.com
Personnel:
Exec. Chmn.: M. O. Obagun
Phone: (234) 1 - 7215299
Man. Dir.: F.O. Obagun
Phone: (234) 1 - 2715295
Bus. Dev. Mgr.: Moruf Olaleye
Phone: (234) 1 - 2715295
Maint. Mgr.: Adekoya Stephen
Phone: (234) 1 - 2715295
Total Employees of Company: 320
Mill Locations:
Epesok Paper Mills Ltd., Oshodi, Lagos Mill, PMB 21356, Plot Y, Mobolaji Johnson Avenue, Alausa, Ikeja, Lagos, Nigeria, Capacity: 5,250 mt/y, (Paper mill)
Phone: (234) 1 - 2715295-6, 1 - 7740372
Email: info@epesok.com

ⓂEpesok Paper Mills Ltd.
Oshodi, Lagos Mill
PMB 21356, Plot Y, Mobolaji Johnson Avenue, Alausa

South Africa

Ikeja, Lagos, Lagos State
Nigeria
  Phone: (234) 1 - 2715295-6, 1 - 7740372
  Email: info@epesok.com
  Web Address: epesok.com
Personnel:
  Exec. Chmn: Chief M. O. Obagun
  Phone: (234) 1 - 7215299
  Man. Dir. : Mr. F. O. Obagun
  Phone: (234) 1 - 2715295
  Snr. Oper. Mgr.: Mr. Akinwande
  Phone: (234) 1 - 2715295
  Maint. Mgr.: Mr. Adekoya Stephen
  Phone: (234) 1 - 2715295
Total Employees at this Location: 320
Type of Operation: Paper mill
Paper/Paperboard Grades and Capacities:
  Total paper and paperboard capacity: 5,250 mt/y
  Tissue: 5,250 mt/y
Paper and Paperboard Mill Data:
Paper Machines: 1
  No. 1, total capacity 5,250 mt/y, Trim width 1.65 m, Tissue

ⓘⓜJebba Paper Mills Ltd.
Jebba Mill
Ownership: 100% by Manaksia Ltd.
21/23, Abimbola Street, Isolo Industrial Estate, P.O. Box 9024
Isolo, Lagos, Lagos State
Nigeria
  Phone: (234) 4529135 / 4529137 / 4528773
  Fax: (234) 4529136
  Email: minlisolo@multilinks.com, minl-ltd@multilink.com
  Web Address: www.manaksia.com
Personnel:
  Chmn, MINL: Mr. Suresh Kumar Agrawal
  Man. Dir., MINL: Mr. Koch Purkayasta
Total Employees of Company: 700
Type of Operation: Paper mill
Mill Locations:
  Jebba Paper Mills Ltd., Jebba Mill, Jebba, Nigeria, Capacity: 192,000 mt/y, (Pulp mill, Paperboard mill)
  Phone: (234) 4529135 / 4529137 / 4528773
  Fax: (234) 4529136
  Email: minlisolo@multilinks.com

ⓜJebba Paper Mills Ltd.
Jebba Mill
Jebba, Kwara State
Nigeria
Mailing Address: PO Box 581, Jebba, Kwara State, Nigeria
  Phone: (234) 4529135 / 4529137 / 4528773
  Fax: (234) 4529136
  Email: minlisolo@multilinks.com
Personnel:
  Gen. Mgr: Dinesh Kumar
  Phone: (234) 17756583
Type of Operation: Pulp mill, Paperboard mill
Paper/Paperboard Grades and Capacities:
  Total paper and paperboard capacity: 192,000 mt/y
  Linerboard
  Corrugating medium/fluting
Paper and Paperboard Mill Data:
  Stock Preparation:
  Pulpers: 6
  Refiners: 25
Paper Machines: 3
  No. 1, fourdrinier, cylinder, Trim width 2.1 m
  No. 2, fourdrinier, Trim width 4.29 m
  No. 3, fourdrinier, Trim width 4.29 m
Finishing Equipment:
  Rewinders: 4
  Sheeters: 2
Energy Data:
  Power boilers: 2
  Combustion turbines: 2 at 22.5 MW

ⓘⓜOku Iboku Pulp and Paper (OKIPP) Company Limited
Oku Iboku Mill
Company is closed (closed in the 1990's. In Feb. 2014, approval has been given for the rehabilitation and upgrade of the mill but no dates given.)
Ownership: 5.50% by Akwa Ibom State Govt. (AKSG), 4.50% by Cross River State Govt. (CRSG), 90% by Negris Holdings Limited
P.M.B. 1045, Itu Local Government Area
Ayadeghe, Oku Iboku, Akwa Ibom State
Nigeria
  Web Address: www.negrisgroup.com/okipp
Personnel:
  Bus. Devlpt. Mgr.: Sobo Sowemimo Jnr.
  Phone: (234) 82 3305 6226/5749 4491
  Email: sobo.sowemimo@negrisgroup.com
Type of Operation: Pulp mill, Paper mill
Pulp Grades and Capacities:
  Total pulp capacity: 100,000 mt/y
  Chemical Pulp: 100,000 mt/y
Paper/Paperboard Grades and Capacities:
  Total paper and paperboard capacity: 100,000 mt/y
  Newsprint
  Uncoated woodfree/freesheet
Paper and Paperboard Mill Data:
Paper Machines: 2
  No. 1, Trim width 4 m
  No. 2, Trim width 4 m

ⓘUna Ama Paper Mills Nigeria Ltd.
Ikot-Inyang Km 4, Ikot-Ekpene/Aba Road
Ikot-Ekpene
Nigeria
  Phone: (234) 803 6700532
Mill Locations:
  Una Ama Paper Mills Nigeria Ltd., Ikot-Ekpene Mill, Ikot-Inyang Km 4, Ikot-Ekpene/Aba Road, Ikot-Ekpene, Nigeria, Capacity: 700 mt/y, (Paper mill)
  Phone: (234) 8036700532

ⓜUna Ama Paper Mills Nigeria Ltd.
Ikot-Ekpene Mill
Ikot-Inyang Km 4, ikot-Ekpene/Aba Road
Ikot-Ekpene, Akwa Ibom State
Nigeria
  Phone: (234) 8036700532
Type of Operation: Paper mill
Paper/Paperboard Grades and Capacities:
  Total paper and paperboard capacity: 700 mt/y
  Tissue: 700 mt/y

SOUTH AFRICA

ⓘCape Waste Paper Pty. Ltd.
Ownership: 100% by Nick van Wyk
1 Beacon Way, Beaconville, Parow Vally
Cape Town, 7500
South Africa
Mailing Address: P.O. Box 1421, Parow Valley, Cape Town, 7499, South Africa
  Phone: (27) 21 931 7251
  Fax: (27) 21 933 4991
  Email: colin@capewaste.co.za
  Web Address: www.wykcogroup.com.za
Personnel:
  Owner: Nick van Wyk
  Phone: (27) 21 931 7251
  Fax: (27) 21 933 4991
  Email: nick@capewaste.co.za
  HR Mgr.: Johan Van Der Merwe
  Phone: (27) 21 931 7251
  Fax: (27) 21 933 4991
  Email: johan@capewaste.co.za
Total Employees at this Location: 140

Mill Locations:
K.Z.N. Tissue, Pietermaritzburg Mill, 21 Wiganthorpe, Willowton, Pietermaritzburg 3201, South Africa, Capacity: 5,000 mt/y, (Paper mill)
  Phone: (27) 33 345 1436
  Fax: (27) 33 394 7776
  Email: jay@kzntissue.co.za
Triwaste CC, Tongaat Mill, 21 Edmond Morewood Road, Truro Industries Estate, Tongaat 4400, South Africa, Capacity: 12,000 mt/y, (Paper mill)
  Phone: (27) 21931 17251
  Fax: (27) 32 944 1686
  Email: topco@iafrica.com

ⓘⓜConsolidated A One Trade and Invest 11 Pty. Ltd.
Chamdor, Krugersdorp Mill
Ownership: 50% by A. S. Jada, 50% by Mohammed S. Jada
22, Aschenberg Street
Chamdor, Krugersdorp, 1754, Gauteng
South Africa
Mailing Address: PO Box 60047, Langlaagte, 2102, South Africa
  Phone: (27) 11 762 6725/26
  Fax: (27) 11 762 6763
Personnel:
  Owner: Mohammed S. Jada
  Phone: (27) 11 762 6725/26
  Owner: A. S. Jada
  Phone: (27) 11 762 6725/26
  Finan. Dir.: Suliman Patel
  Phone: (27) 11 762 6725/26
  Email: spatel@yahoo.com
  Plant Mgr.: Riaz Aziz
  Phone: (27) 11 762 6725/26
Total Employees at this Location: 180
Type of Operation: Paper mill
Mill Locations:
  First A One Trade and Invest 11 Pty Ltd., Garankuwa Mill, 109 Main Str., Garankuwa, South Africa, Capacity: 6,000 mt/y, (Paper mill)
  Phone: (27) 12 703 6750/8769
  Fax: (27) 12 703 8758
Paper/Paperboard Grades and Capacities:
  Total paper and paperboard capacity: 6,500 mt/y
  Tissue: 6,500 mt/y
Paper and Paperboard Mill Data:
Paper Machines: 1
  PM 1, (second hand), fourdrinier, total capacity 6,500 mt/y, Tissue

ⓜCrescent Packaging Corporation, Pty. Ltd.
Heidelberg Mill
Ownership: Crystal Paper Group
15 Albert Street
Heidelberg, 1438, Gauteng
South Africa
Mailing Address: P.O. Box 1405, Heidelberg, 1438, Gauteng, South Africa
  Phone: (27) 16 341 6396/349 1330/349 2199/341 6805
  Fax: (27) 16 341 6386/341 3698
  Email: secretary@dosanigroup.co.za
  Web Address: www.tissuepaper.co.za
Personnel:
  Mill Mgr.: Mr. Buskar
  Phone: (27) 16 341 5920/73 092 9973
Total Employees at this Location: 38
Type of Operation: Paperboard mill
Paper/Paperboard Grades and Capacities:
  Total paper and paperboard capacity: 4,000 mt/y
  Boxboard/cartonboard: 4,000 mt/y
Paper and Paperboard Mill Data:
Paper Machines: 1
  No. 1, total capacity 4,000 mt/y, Trim width 1.8 m, Boxboard/cartonboard

South Africa

Energy Data:
Power boilers: 1

ⓂCrystal Paper Group
Ownership: 100% by Dosani family
15 Albert Street
Heidelberg, 1438, Gauteng
South Africa
Mailing Address: P.O. Box 1405, Heidelberg, Gauteng, South Africa
  Phone: (27) 16 341 6396, 16 341 6805
  Fax: (27) 16 341 6386, 16 341 3698
  Email: secretary@dosanigroup.co.za, expo@cybertrade.co.za
  Web Address: www.tissuepaper.co.za
Personnel:
  CEO: Rafik Dosani
  Phone: (27) 83 449 1188, 11 360 7183
  Fax: (27) 16 341 6386
Total Employees of Company: 180
Total Employees at this Location: 4
Mill Locations:
Crescent Packaging Corporation, Pty. Ltd., Heidelberg Mill, 15 Albert Street, Heidelberg 1438, South Africa, Capacity: 4,000 mt/y, (Paperboard mill)
  Phone: (27) 16 341 6396/349 1330/349 2199/341 6805
  Fax: (27) 16 341 6386/341 3698
  Email: secretary@dosanigroup.co.za
Egoli Tissue Mill (Pty) Ltd., Heidelberg Mill, 15 Albert Street, Heidelberg 1438, South Africa, Capacity: 6,700 mt/y, (Paper mill)
  Phone: (27) 16 341 6396/349 1330/349 2199/341 6805
  Fax: (27) 16 341 6386/341 3698
  Email: secretary@dosanigroup.co.za
Paper and Pulp Industries, Pty. Ltd., Heidelberg Mill, 15 Albert Street, Heidelberg 1438, South Africa, Capacity: 4,000 mt/y, (Paper mill)
  Phone: (27) 16 341 6396/349 1330/349 2199/341 6805
  Fax: (27) 16 341 6386/341 3698
  Email: secretary@dosanigroup.co.za, faruq@dosanigroup.co.za
South African Cartonboard Mills, Wadeville Mill, 10 Commercial Road, Wadeville 1422, South Africa, Capacity: 22,000 mt/y, (Paper mill, Paperboard mill)
  Phone: (27) 11 902 1096
  Fax: (27) 11 902 2044
  Email: secretary@dosanigroup.co.za

ⓂEgoli Tissue Mill (Pty) Ltd.
Heidelberg Mill
Ownership: Crystal Paper Group
15 Albert Street
Heidelberg, 1438, Gauteng
South Africa
Mailing Address: P.O. Box 1405, Heidelberg, 1438, South Africa
  Phone: (27) 16 341 6396/349 1330/349 2199/341 6805
  Fax: (27) 16 341 6386/341 3698
  Email: secretary@dosanigroup.co.za
  Web Address: www.tissuepaper.co.za
Personnel:
  Mill Mgr.: Ali Ahasan
  Phone: (27) 72 954 3299
Total Employees at this Location: 22
Type of Operation: Paper mill
Paper/Paperboard Grades and Capacities:
  Total paper and paperboard capacity: 6,700 mt/y
  Tissue: 6,700 mt/y
Paper and Paperboard Mill Data:
Paper Machines: 2
No. 1, total capacity 1,900 mt/y, Trim width 1.8 m, Tissue
No. 2, total capacity 4,800 mt/y, Trim width 2.5 m, Tissue

ⓂFirst A One Trade and Invest 11 Pty Ltd.
Garankuwa Mill
Ownership: Consolidated A One Trade and Invest 11 Pty. Ltd.
109 Main Str.
Garankuwa, Gauteng
South Africa
Mailing Address: P.O. Box 2676, Rosslyn, South Africa
  Phone: (27) 12 703 6750/8769
  Fax: (27) 12 703 8758
Personnel:
  Owner: Mohammed S. Jada
  Phone: (27) 11 762 6725/6
  Owner: A. S. Jada
  Phone: (27) 11 762 6725/6
  Man. Dir.: Suliman Patel
  Phone: (27) 11 762 6725/6
  Email: solly.patel@yahoo.com
  Mill Mgr.: Andre Gerder
  Phone: (27) 12 703 6750/8769
  Admin. Mgr. & Energy Eng.: Ms. C. A. Badenhorst
  Phone: (27) 12 703 6750/8769
  Clerk: Jonas Mabuso
  Phone: (27) 12 703 6750/8769
Total Employees at this Location: 60
Type of Operation: Paper mill
Pulp Mill Data:
  Recycled Fiber Treatment Lines:
  Pulpers: 2
Paper/Paperboard Grades and Capacities:
  Total paper and paperboard capacity: 6,000 mt/y
  Tissue: 6,000 mt/y
Paper and Paperboard Mill Data:
Paper Machines: 1
PM 1, total capacity 6,000 mt/y, Tissue
Energy Data:
Power boilers: 2

ⓄⓂGayatri Paper Mill
Germiston Mill
Ownership: Gayatri Paper Mills Pvt. Ltd.
1 Power Street Industries West
Germiston, 1400, Gauteng
South Africa
Mailing Address: P.O. Box 1116, Germiston, 1400, Gauteng, South Africa
  Phone: (27) 11 821 8600
  Fax: (27) 11 872 1884
  Email: sales@gayatripaper.co.za
Personnel:
  CEO: Kishor Chhita
  Phone: (27) 11 821 8600
  CEO: Raj Chhita
  Phone: (27) 11 821 8600
  CEO: Badresh Chhita
  Phone: (27) 11 821 8600
  Gen. Mgr.: Asha Chhita
  Phone: (27) 11 821 8600
  Email: asha@gayatripaper.co.za
  Mill Mgr.: Rao Varanasi
  Phone: (27) 11 821 8600
  Email: rao@gayatripaper.co.za
  Prod. Mgr.: Conrad Gykers
  Phone: (27) 11 821 8600
Total Employees of Company: 180
Total Employees at this Location: 100
Type of Operation: Paper mill, Paperboard mill
Pulp Grades and Capacities:
  Total pulp capacity: 91,200 mt/y
  Recycled Pulping: 91,200 mt/y
Pulp Mill Data:
  Recycled Fiber Treatment Lines:
  Recycled packaging pulping lines: 2
Paper/Paperboard Grades and Capacities:
  Total paper and paperboard capacity: 90,000 mt/y
  Linerboard: 50,000 mt/y
  Corrugating medium/fluting: 40,000 mt/y
Paper and Paperboard Mill Data:
Paper Machines: 2
No. 1, twin-wire, total capacity 50,000 mt/y, Trim width 2.44 m, Linerboard
No. 2, twin-wire, total capacity 40,000 mt/y, Trim width 2.44 m, Corrugating medium/fluting
Energy Data:
Power boilers: 2
Electrical demand for mill: 122 MWh/D

ⓄⓂGoodview Investments
Pietermaritzburg Mill
8 Roger De Klerk Road, M'Kondeni
Pietermaritzburg, KwaZulu-Natal
South Africa
  Phone: (27) 33 386 6710
  Fax: (27) 33 386 6708
Type of Operation: Paper mill
Paper/Paperboard Grades and Capacities:
  Total paper and paperboard capacity: 4,000 mt/y
  Tissue: 4,000 mt/y

ⓂHygienic Tissue Mills
Ownership: 100% by Jooma Family
19 Cardiff Rd., Willowton
Pietermaritzburg, 3201
South Africa
Mailing Address: P.O. Box 197, 3200 Pietermaritzburg
  Phone: (27) 33 397 9595
  Fax: (27) 86 531 4289
  Email: info@hygienictissuemill.com, htmill@iafrica.com
  Web Address: www.hygienictissuemills.com
Personnel:
  Mill Dir. & Mill Mgr.: Ashraf Jooma
  Phone: (27) 33 397 9595
  Fax: (27) 86 531 4289
  Email: htmill@iafrica.com
  Mill Dir.: Y. J. Effa
  Phone: (27) 33 397 9595
  Fax: (27) 86 531 4289
  Mill Dir.: Ismael Jooma
  Phone: (27) 33 397 9595
  Fax: (27) 86 531 4289
Total Employees at this Location: 150
Mill Locations:
Hygienic Tissue Mills, Pietermaritzburg Mill, 19 Cardiff Rd., Willowton, Pietermaritzburg 3201, South Africa, Capacity: 20,000 mt/y, (Paper mill)
  Phone: (27) 33 397 9595
  Fax: (27) 86 531 4289
  Email: htmill@iafrica.com

ⓂHygienic Tissue Mills
Pietermaritzburg Mill
19 Cardiff Rd., Willowton
Pietermaritzburg, 3201, Natal
South Africa
Mailing Address: P.O. Box 197, Pietermaritzburg, 3200, KwaZulu-Natal, South Africa
  Phone: (27) 33 397 9595
  Fax: (27) 86 531 4289
  Email: htmill@iafrica.com
  Web Address: www.hygienictissuemill.com
Personnel:
  Mill Dir. & Mill Mgr.: Ashraf Jooma
  Phone: (27) 83 554 7866
  Email: htmill@iafrica.com
  Mill Dir.: Y. J. Effa
  Phone: (27) 33 397 9595
  Mill Dir.: Ismael Jooma
Total Employees at this Location: 150
Type of Operation: Paper mill
Pulp Grades and Capacities:
  Total pulp capacity: 10,004 mt/y
  Recycled Pulping: 10,004 mt/y
Pulp Mill Data:
  Recycled Fiber Treatment Lines:

South Africa

Flotation deinking lines: 1 at 10,000 admt/y
Paper/Paperboard Grades and Capacities:
Total paper and paperboard capacity: 20,000 mt/y
Tissue: 20,000 mt/y
Paper and Paperboard Mill Data:
Paper Machines: 1
No. 1, twin-wire, Yankee dryer, total capacity 20,000 mt/y, Trim width 2.35 m, Tissue, Uncoated woodfree/freesheet
Energy Data:
Power boilers
Electrical demand for mill: 63 MWh/D

⑪Janjirker Paper Mill (Pty) Ltd
Ownership: 100% by Aziz Family
Sataar Business Park Unit 2, Sack Circle
Bellville, 7530
South Africa
Mailing Address: PO Box 1521, 7500 Parow
Phone: (27) 21 951 2270
Fax: (27) 21 951 2271
Email: green@mweb.co.za
Personnel:
Owner, Man. Dir. & Mill Mgr.: Majid Aziz
Phone: (27) 21 951 2270
Fax: (27) 21 951 2271
Owner & Finan. Mgr.: Zakir Aziz
Phone: (27) 21 951 2270
Fax: (27) 21 951 2271
Owner & Prod. Mgr.: Samad Aziz
Phone: (27) 21 951 2270
Fax: (27) 21 951 2271
Owner & Sls. Mgr.: Abdul Aziz
Phone: (27) 21 951 2270
Fax: (27) 21 951 2271
Mill Locations:
Janjirker Paper Mill (Pty) Ltd, Bellville Mill, Sataar Business Park Unit 2, Sack Circle, Bellville 7530, South Africa, Capacity: 14,000 mt/y, (Paper mill)
Phone: (27) 21 951 2270
Fax: (27) 21 951 2271
Email: green@mweb.co.za

⑪Janjirker Paper Mill (Pty) Ltd
Bellville Mill
Sataar Business Park Unit 2, Sack Circle
Bellville, 7530, Cape Town
South Africa
Mailing Address: PO Box 1521, Parow, 7500, Cape Town, South Africa
Phone: (27) 21 951 2270
Fax: (27) 21 951 2271
Email: green@mweb.co.za
Personnel:
Owner, Man. Dir. & Mill Mgr.: Majid Aziz
Phone: (27) 21 951 2270
Owner & Prod. Mgr.: Samad Aziz
Phone: (27) 21 951 2270
Owner & Sls. Mgr.: Abdul Aziz Aziz
Phone: (27) 21 951 2270
Owner & Finan. Mgr.: Zakir Aziz
Phone: (27) 21 951 2270
Type of Operation: Paper mill
Paper/Paperboard Grades and Capacities:
Total paper and paperboard capacity: 14,000 mt/y
Tissue: 14,000 mt/y
Paper and Paperboard Mill Data:
Paper Machines: 2
PM 1, total capacity 6,000 mt/y, Trim width 2.6 m, Tissue
PM 2, (started up December 2009), Jetformer, total capacity 8,000 mt/y, Trim width 2.6 m, Tissue

⑪Kimberly-Clark of SA (Pty) Ltd.
Ownership: Kimberly-Clark Corp.
Kimberly-Clark House, 8 Leicester Road
Bedfordview, 2008, Gauteng
South Africa
Phone: (27) 11 456 5700
Fax: (27) 11 456 5799

Email: connie.machitje@kcc.com
Web Address: www.kimberly-clark.com
Personnel:
Chmn.: Frank Berkeley
Phone: (27) 11 456 5700
Fax: (27) 11 456 5799
Man. Dir.: Garsh Towll
Phone: (27) 11 456 5823
Fax: (27) 11 456 5729
Gov. Dir.: V. H. Gaijar
Phone: (27) 11 456 5755
Fax: (27) 11 456 5874
Cust. Man. Dir.: W.J. Steenkamp
Phone: (27) 11 456 5824
Fax: (27) 11 456 5873
Dir. of Professional/Health Care: Ms. E. Abrie
Phone: (27) 11 456 5713
Fax: (27) 11 456 5919
Oper. Dir.: Mark Russell
Phone: (27) 11 456 5924
Fax: (27) 11 456 5797
Finan. Dir.: D. De Graaff
Phone: (27) 11 456 5835
Fax: (27) 11 456 5797
Consumer Mktg. Dir.: Ms. J. Siney
Phone: (27) 11 456 5803
Fax: (27) 11 456 5873
Supply Purch. Mgr.: G. S. Nell
Phone: (27) 11 456 5806
Fax: (27) 11 456 5797
Total Employees of Company: 58,000
Total Employees at this Location: 150
Mill Locations:
Kimberly-Clark of SA (Pty) Ltd., Enstra Mill, East Geduld Rd., Enstra, Springs 1560, South Africa, Capacity: 54,000 mt/y, (Paper mill)
Phone: (27) 11 360 7000
Fax: (27) 11 360 7001

⑪Kimberly-Clark of SA (Pty) Ltd.
Enstra Mill
Ownership: Kimberly-Clark Corp.
East Geduld Rd., Enstra
Springs, 1560, Gauteng
South Africa
Mailing Address: Private Bag X57, Springs, Gauteng, 1560, Gauteng, South Africa
Phone: (27) 11 360 7000
Fax: (27) 11 360 7001
Web Address: www.kimberly-clark.com
Personnel:
Mill Mgr.: Tony Hulme
Phone: (27) 11 360 7000
Fax: (27) 11 360 7001
Email: tony.hulme@kcc.com
Total Employees at this Location: 620
Type of Operation: Paper mill
Pulp Grades and Capacities:
Total pulp capacity: 31,504 mt/y
Recycled Pulping: 31,504 mt/y
Pulp Mill Data:
Recycled Fiber Treatment Lines:
Flotation deinking lines: 1
Paper/Paperboard Grades and Capacities:
Total paper and paperboard capacity: 54,000 mt/y
Tissue: 54,000 mt/y
Paper and Paperboard Mill Data:
Stock Preparation:
Pulpers: 3
Refiners: 4
Paper Machines: 2
No. 1, twin-wire, Yankee dryer, total capacity 19,000 mt/y, Trim width 3.3 m, Tissue
No. 2, twin-wire, Yankee dryer, total capacity 35,000 mt/y, Trim width 3.4 m, Tissue
Finishing Equipment:
Rewinders: 2
Energy Data:
Power boilers
Electrical demand for mill: 172 MWh/D

⑪K.Z.N. Tissue
Pietermaritzburg Mill
Ownership: Cape Waste Paper Pty. Ltd.
21 Wiganthorpe, Willowton
Pietermaritzburg, 3201, KwaZulu-Natal
South Africa
Mailing Address: P.O. Box 8595, Cumberwood, Pietermaritzburg, 3235, South Africa
Phone: (27) 33 345 1436
Fax: (27) 33 394 7776
Email: jay@kzntissue.co.za
Personnel:
Mill Mgr.: Jay Naidoo
Phone: (27) 82 697 5853
Total Employees at this Location: 50
Type of Operation: Paper mill
Paper/Paperboard Grades and Capacities:
Total paper and paperboard capacity: 5,000 mt/y
Tissue: 5,000 mt/y
Paper and Paperboard Mill Data:
Paper Machines: 2
No. 1, Tissue
No. 3, fourdrinier, Tissue

⑪Ligia Paper Industries
Ownership: 100% by private owners
83 ARRARAT ROAD, WELKOM, Free State 9459
Welkom, 9459
South Africa
Phone: (27) 573966818
Personnel:
Pres. & Owner: Yan Ren
Phone: (27) 573966818
Mill Locations:
Ligia Paper Industries, Welkom Mill, Welkom, South Africa, Capacity: 4,000 mt/y, (Pulp mill, Paper mill)

⑪Ligia Paper Industries
Welkom Mill
Welkom, Orange Free State
South Africa
Personnel:
Pres. & Owner: Ms. Yan Ren
Type of Operation: Pulp mill, Paper mill
Pulp Grades and Capacities:
Total pulp capacity: 4,000 mt/y
Recycled Pulping: 4,000 mt/y
Pulp Mill Data:
Pulp Lines: 2
Recycled Fiber Treatment Lines:
Washing deinking lines: 2 at 4,000 admt/y
Paper/Paperboard Grades and Capacities:
Total paper and paperboard capacity: 4,000 mt/y
Tissue: 4,000 mt/y
Paper and Paperboard Mill Data:
Paper Machines: 2
PM 1, cylinder, total capacity 2,000 mt/y, Trim width 1.58 m, Tissue
PM 2, cylinder, total capacity 2,000 mt/y, Trim width 1.58 m, Tissue

⑪⑪Lothlorien (Pty) Ltd
Lothlorien Pulp Mill
Ownership: 100% by V. Koekemoer
173 Immelman Rd.
Wadeville, 1407, Gauteng
South Africa
Mailing Address: PO Box 240, Alberton, 1450, Gauteng, South Africa
Phone: (27) 11 827 0512
Fax: (27) 11 827 6728
Email: info@lothpaper.co.za
Web Address: www.lothpaper.co.za, www.lothlorien.co.za
Personnel:
Man. Dir.: Eugene Koekemoer
Phone: (27) 11 827 0512

Pulp and Paper Mills - Africa

Fax: (27) 11 824 0748
Email: eugenek@lothpaper.co.za
Total Employees of Company: 160
Total Employees at this Location: 160
Type of Operation: Pulp mill, Paperboard mill
Pulp Grades and Capacities:
Total pulp capacity: 43,853 mt/y
Recycled Pulping: 43,853 mt/y

Pulp Mill Data:
Recycled Fiber Treatment Lines:
Pulpers: 3 at 40,000 admt/y

Paper/Paperboard Grades and Capacities:
Total paper and paperboard capacity: 43,000 mt/y
Packaging papers: 8,000 mt/y
Linerboard: 15,000 mt/y
Corrugating medium/fluting: 10,000 mt/y
Boxboard/cartonboard: 10,000 mt/y

Paper and Paperboard Mill Data:
Stock Preparation:
Pulpers: 3
Refiners: 2

Paper Machines: 2
No. 1, fourdrinier, total capacity 18,000 mt/y, Trim width 2.35 m, Corrugating medium/fluting, Packaging papers
No. 2, fourdrinier (2), total capacity 25,000 mt/y, Trim width 2.45 m, Boxboard/cartonboard, Linerboard

Finishing Equipment:
Rewinders: 3 at 60,000 mt/y

Energy Data:
Power boilers: 2
Electrical demand for mill: 52 MWh/D

ⓜMondi South Africa Division
Ownership: 100% by Mondi
44 Main Street
Johannesburg, 2001
South Africa
Mailing Address: 4th Floor, No. 3 Melrose Boulevard, Melrose Arch, 2196, Gauteng, South Africa
Phone: (27) 11 994 5400
Fax: (27) 11 994 5450
Web Address: www.mondigroup.com
Personnel:
CEO South Africa Div.: Ron Traill
Phone: (27) 11 994 5400
Fax: (27) 11 994 5450
Email: ron.traill@mondigroup.co.za
Total Employees of Company: 1,600
Total Employees at this Location: 15
Mill Locations:
Mondi Merebank, Merebank Mill, Travancore Dr., Merebank 4052, South Africa, Capacity: 265,000 mt/y, (Paper mill)
Phone: (27) 31 451 2111
Fax: (27) 31 451 2003
Email: service@mondigroup.com
Mondi Richards Bay, Richards Bay Mill, 7 Western Arterial, Alton, Richards Bay 3900, South Africa, Capacity: 280,000 mt/y, (Pulp mill, Paperboard mill)
Phone: (27) 35 902 2111
Fax: (27) 35 902 2537
Email: collette.vanstaden@mondigroup.com
Mondi Shanduka Newsprint, Merebank Mill (54% owned), Off Travancore Dr., Merebank 4052, South Africa, Capacity: 120,000 mt/y, (Pulp mill, Paper mill)
Phone: (27) 31 451 2111
Fax: (27) 31 461 1343

ⓜMondi
Ownership: 3% by Norges Bank, Public
4th Floor, No 3 Melrose Boulevard
Melrose Arch, Johannesburg, 2196
South Africa
Mailing Address: PostNet Suite # 444, Private Bag X1, Melrose Arch, 2076, South Africa
Phone: (27) 11 994 5400
Fax: (27) 86 520 4688
Email: info@mondigroup.com, zainfo@mondigroup.co.za
Web Address: www.mondigroup.com
Personnel:
Joint Chairman: Fred Phaswana
Phone: (27) 27 11 994 5400
Fax: (27) 27 86 520 4688
Joint Chairman: David Williams
Phone: (27) 27 11 994 5400
Fax: (27) 27 86 520 4688
CEO: David Hathorn
Phone: (27) 27 11 994 5418
Fax: (27) 27 86 520 4688
Email: david.hathorn@mondigroup.com
CFO: Andrew King
Phone: (27) 27 11 994 5415
Fax: (27) 27 86 520 4688
Email: andrew.king@mondigroup.com
CEO South Africa Division: Ron Trail
Phone: (27) 27 11 994 5400
Fax: (27) 27 86 520 4688
Group Tech. Dir.: John Lindahl
Phone: (27) 27 11 994 5400
Fax: (27) 27 86 520 4688
Email: john.lindahl@mondigroup.com
Group Commun. Mgr.: Kerry Crandon
Phone: (27) 27 11 994 5416
Fax: (27) 27 11 994 5506
Email: kerry.crandon@mondigroup.com
Comp. Sec.: Philip Laubscher
Phone: (27) 27 11 994 5400
Fax: (27) 27 86 520 4688
Email: philip.laubscher@mondigroup.com
Corporate Affairs Mgr. Group and South Africa Div.: Lora Rossler
Phone: (27) 27 31 451 2040
Fax: (27) 27 86 520 4688
Email: lora.rossler@mondigroup.co.za
Mktg. Mgr. South Africa Division: Gary Nossiter
Phone: (27) 27 31 451 2111
Fax: (27) 27 86 520 4688
Email: gary.nossiter@mondigroup.co.za
Forest Mgr. & Oper. Mgr.: Themba Vilane
Phone: (27) 27 11 994 5400
Fax: (27) 27 86 520 4688
Total Employees of Company: 24,578
Total Employees at this Location: 35
Mill Locations:
Mondi Dynäs AB, Väja Mill, SE-873 81 Väja, Sweden, Capacity: 250,000 mt/y, (Pulp mill, Paper mill)
Phone: (46) 612 83000
Fax: (46) 612 26511
Email: info.dynas@mondigroup.com
Mondi Frantschach GmbH, Frantschach Mill, Frantschach 5, A-9413 St. Gertraud, Austria, Capacity: 289,884 mt/y, (Pulp mill, Paper mill)
Phone: (43) 4352 530
Fax: (43) 4352 53073
Email: (firstname.lastname@mondigroup.com)
Mondi Neusiedler GmbH, Kematen mill, A-3331 Kematen, Austria, Capacity: 100,000 mt/y, (Pulp mill, Paper mill)
Phone: (43) 7475 500 0
Fax: (43) 7475 500 2259
Email: service@mondigroup.com
Mondi Lohja Oy, Lohja Mill, Kotkantie 5, FI-08100 Lohja, Finland, Capacity: 80,000 mt/y, (Paper mill)
Phone: (358) 2074 4611
Fax: (358) 2074 4610
Mondi Merebank, Merebank Mill, Travancore Dr., Merebank 4052, South Africa, Capacity: 265,000 mt/y, (Paper mill)
Phone: (27) 31 451 2111
Fax: (27) 31 451 2003
Email: service@mondigroup.com
Mondi, Pine Bluff Mill, 1701 Jefferson Parkway, Pine Bluff, AR 71601, USA, Capacity: 143,798 mt/y, (Paper mill)
Phone: (1) 870-541-5000
Fax: (1) 870-541-5060
Email: info@mondigroup.com
Mondi Raubling GmbH, Raubling Mill, Rosenheimer Str. 37, D-83064 Raubling, Germany, Capacity: 220,000 mt/y, (Paperboard mill)
Phone: (49) 8035 9090
Fax: (49) 8035 902 132
Email: (firstname.lastname@mondigroup.com)
Mondi Richards Bay, Richards Bay Mill, 7 Western Arterial, Alton, Richards Bay 3900, South Africa, Capacity: 280,000 mt/y, (Pulp mill, Paperboard mill)
Phone: (27) 35 902 2111
Fax: (27) 35 902 2537
Email: collette.vanstaden@mondigroup.com
Mondi SCP a.s., Ružomberok Mill, Tatranská cesta 3, SK-03417 Ružomberok, Slovakia, Capacity: 615,000 mt/y, (Pulp mill, Paper mill)
Phone: (421) 44 436 2222/2090
Fax: (421) 44 436 3824/2476
Email: mondiscp@mondigroup.com
Mondi Shanduka Newsprint, Merebank Mill, Off Travancore Dr., Merebank 4052, South Africa, Capacity: 120,000 mt/y, (Pulp mill, Paper mill)
Phone: (27) 31 451 2111
Fax: (27) 31 461 1343
Mondi Stambolijski EAD, Stambolijski Mill, 1, Zavodska Str., BG-4210 Stambolijski, Bulgaria, Capacity: 90,000 mt/y, (Pulp mill, Paper mill)
Phone: (359) 32 909 287
Fax: (359) 32 909 554
Mondi Štetí, Štetí Mill, Litoměrická 272, CZ-411 08 Štetí, Czech Republic, Capacity: 372,000 mt/y, (Pulp mill, Paper mill, Paperboard mill)
Phone: (420) 416 80 2184/1111/2603
Fax: (420) 416 80 2599 / 2233
Mondi Swiecie S.A., Swiecie Mill, Bydgoska Str. 1, PL-86100 Swiecie, Poland, Capacity: 1,399,000 mt/y, (Pulp mill, Paper mill, Paperboard mill)
Phone: (48) 52 332 1553
Fax: (48) 52 332 1931
Email: (firstname.surname@mondigroup.com), info.swiecie@mondigroup.com
Mondi Syktyvkar, Syktyvkar Mill, Bumazhnikov pr. 2, 167026 Syktyvkar, Russia, Capacity: 990,000 mt/y, (Pulp mill, Paper mill, Paperboard mill)
Phone: (7) 8212 699555
Fax: (7) 8212 620282
Email: olga.rimert@mondigroup.com
Mondi Neusiedler GmbH, Theresienthal Mill, A-3363 Ulmerfeld-Hausmening, Austria, Capacity: 287,000 mt/y, (Pulp mill, Paper mill)
Phone: (43) 7475 500 0
Fax: (43) 7475 500 2259
Email: service@mondigroup.com
Mondi Tire Kutsan Paper and Packaging Industry Inc., Tire Mill, Bekleme Mevkii, TR-35900 Tire, Turkey, Capacity: 135,000 mt/y, (Paper mill, Paperboard mill)
Phone: (90) 232 5121156/1943
Fax: (90) 232 5123871/1046
Email: info@tirekutsan.com.tr

ⓜMondi Merebank
Merebank Mill
Ownership: Mondi South Africa Division
Travancore Dr.
Merebank, 4052, KwaZulu-Natal
South Africa
Mailing Address: P.O. Box 31024, Merebank, 4059, KwaZulu-Natal, South Africa
Phone: (27) 31 451 2111
Fax: (27) 31 451 2003
Email: service@mondigroup.com
Web Address: www.mondigroup.com
Personnel:
Snr. Mech. Mgr.: James Gallagher
Phone: (27) 31 451 2111
Fax: (27) 31 451 2003
Email: james.gallagher@mondigroup.com
Oper. Mgr.: Wayne Simon
Phone: (27) 31 451 2111
Fax: (27) 31 451 2003
Email: wayne.simon@mondigroup.com
Head of Sls. & Mktg.: Gary Nossiter
Phone: (27) 31 451 2369

South Africa

Fax: (27) 31 451 2003
Email: gary.nossiter@mondigroup.co.za
Land & Forestry Dir.: Viv McMenamin
Phone: (27) 31 451 2401
Fax: (27) 31 451 2754
Email: viv.mcmenamin@mondibp.com
PR. & Commun. Officer: Deshni Govender
Phone: (27) 11 994 5416
Fax: (27) 86 575 2654
Email: deshni.govender@mondigroup.com
Total Employees at this Location: 350
Type of Operation: Paper mill
Paper/Paperboard Grades and Capacities:
Total paper and paperboard capacity: 265,000 mt/y
Uncoated woodfree/freesheet: 265,000 mt/y
Paper and Paperboard Mill Data:
Stock Preparation:
Pulpers: 9
Refiners: 15
Paper Machines: 1
No. 31, DuoFormerTQv, total capacity 265,000 mt/y, Trim width 6.4 m, Uncoated woodfree/freesheet
Finishing Equipment:
Winders: 1 at 265,000 mt/y
Calenders: 3
Rewinders: 1 at 15,000 mt/y
Sheeters: 7 at 265,000 mt/y
Energy Data:
Power boilers: 3
Steam turbines: 3 at 12.0, NA MW
Electrical demand for mill: 524 MWh/D

ⓜMondi Richards Bay
Richards Bay Mill
Ownership: Mondi South Africa Division
7 Western Arterial, Alton
Richards Bay, 3900, KwaZulu-Natal
South Africa
Mailing Address: PO Box 1551, Richards Bay, 3900, KwaZulu-Natal, South Africa
Phone: (27) 35 902 2111
Fax: (27) 35 902 2537
Email: collette.vanstaden@mondigroup.com
Web Address: www.mondigroup.com
Personnel:
Oper. Mgr.: Jay Oomadhram
Phone: (27) 35 902 2216
Fax: (27) 35 902 2263
Email: jay.oomadhram@mondigroup.co.za
Proj. Technologist Mgr.: Kevin Younghusband
Phone: (27) 35 902 2541
Fax: (27) 35 902 2537
Email: kevin.younghusband@mondigroup.co.za
Total Employees at this Location: 590
Type of Operation: Pulp mill, Paperboard mill
Pulp Grades and Capacities:
Total pulp capacity: 735,592 mt/y
Pulp available for market: 460,000 mt/y
Chemical Pulp: 735,592 mt/y
Pulp Mill Data:
Chemical Pulping Systems:
Batch digesters: 5
Continuous digesters: 1
Pulp Lines: 2
Bleach Plant Systems: 1
Kvaerner, Sequence: O_2 DEOpDEpD, Capacity 590,000 admt/y
Chemical Recovery Equipment:
Evaporator lines: 3
Recovery boilers: 2
Lime Kiln
Pulp Dryers:
Air Float dryers 1
Paper/Paperboard Grades and Capacities:
Total paper and paperboard capacity: 280,000 mt/y
Linerboard: 280,000 mt/y
Paper and Paperboard Mill Data:
Stock Preparation:
Pulpers: 2
Refiners: 8
Paper Machines: 1
No. 42, fourdrinier, total capacity 280,000 mt/y, Trim width 4.85 m, Linerboard
Finishing Equipment:
Supercalenders: 2
Rewinders: 1 at 30,000 mt/y
Sheeters: 7 at 134,000 mt/y
Energy Data:
Power boilers: 3
Combustion turbines: 1 at 27 MW
Steam turbines: 2 at 40 MW
Electrical demand for mill: 1,639 MWh/D

ⓞⓜMondi Shanduka Newsprint
Merebank Mill
Ownership: 54% by Mondi South Africa Division, 4% by Employee trust, 42% by Shanduka Resources
Off Travancore Dr.
Merebank, 4052, KwaZulu-Natal
South Africa
Mailing Address: P.O. Box X05, Merebank, 4059, KwaZulu-Natal, South Africa
Phone: (27) 31 451 2111
Fax: (27) 31 461 1343
Web Address: www.mondishanduka.co.za
Personnel:
Mgr.: David Laing
Phone: (27) 31 451 2111
Fax: (27) 31 461 1343
Email: david.laing@mondigroup.co.za
Total Employees of Company: 297
Total Employees at this Location: 167
Type of Operation: Pulp mill, Paper mill
Pulp Grades and Capacities:
Total pulp capacity: 122,196 mt/y
Mechanical Pulp: 67,208 mt/y
Recycled Pulping: 54,988 mt/y
Pulp Mill Data:
Mechanical Pulping Systems:
TMP systems: 4
Pulp Lines: 2
Bleach Plant Systems: 2
DIP, Sequence: P/Y
Mechanical Pulping System, Type: Softwood, Sequence: P
Recycled Fiber Treatment Lines:
Flotation deinking lines: 1 at 160,000 admt/y
Pulpers: 1 at 160,000 admt/y
Paper/Paperboard Grades and Capacities:
Total paper and paperboard capacity: 120,000 mt/y
Newsprint: 96,000 mt/y
Uncoated mechanical/groundwood: 24,000 mt/y
Paper and Paperboard Mill Data:
Stock Preparation:
Pulpers: 9
Refiners: 15
Paper Machines: 1
No. 5, DuoFormer F, total capacity 120,000 mt/y, Trim width 5.6 m, Newsprint, Uncoated mechanical/groundwood
Energy Data:
Electrical demand for mill: 673 MWh/D

ⓜMpact Limited
Ownership: 89.55% by Freefloat, 10.45% by Shanduka Packaging
4th Floor, No. 3 Melrose Boulevard
Melrose Arch, 2196, Gauteng
South Africa
Phone: (27) 11 994 5400
Fax: (27) 11 994 5506
Web Address: www.mpact.co.za
Personnel:
CEO: Bruce William Strong
Phone: (27) 11 994 5400
Fax: (27) 11 994 5506
CFO: Brett Clark
Phone: (27) 11 994 5400
Fax: (27) 11 994 5506
Man. Dir. Recycling: John William Hunt
Phone: (27) 11 994 5400
Fax: (27) 11 994 5506
CIO: Vuyokazi Menye
Phone: (27) 11 994 5400
Fax: (27) 11 994 5506
Man. Dir. Paper Manuf.: Hugh Michael Thompson
Phone: (27) 11 994 5400
Fax: (27) 11 994 5506
Man. Dir. Corrugated: Ralph Peter von Veh
Phone: (27) 11 994 5400
Fax: (27) 11 994 5506
Company Sec.: Noriah Sepuru
Phone: (27) 11 994 5400
Fax: (27) 11 994 5506
Total Employees of Company: 3,790
Total Employees at this Location: 30
Mill Locations:
Mpact Limited, Felixton Mill, Grantham Properties, Felixton, South Africa, Capacity: 150,000 mt/y, (Pulp mill, Paperboard mill)
Phone: (27) 35 791 6000
Fax: (27) 35 791 1029
Email: nhunt@mpact.co.za
Mpact Limited, Piet Retief Mill, Ermelo Rd., Vroegeveld Farm, Piet Retief, South Africa, Capacity: 134,000 mt/y, (Pulp mill, Paperboard mill)
Phone: (27) 17 826 9000
Fax: (27) 17 826 9136
Email: gbotes@mpact.co.za
Mpact Limited, Springs Mill, 82 - 84 Steel Street, New Era 1560, South Africa, Capacity: 137,000 mt/y, (Paperboard mill)
Phone: (27) 11 360 4100
Fax: (27) 11 813 4587

ⓜMpact Limited
Felixton Mill
Grantham Properties
Felixton, KwaZulu-Natal
South Africa
Phone: (27) 35 791 6000
Fax: (27) 35 791 1029
Email: nhunt@mpact.co.za
Web Address: www.mpact.co.za
Personnel:
Mill Mgr.: Brian Smith
Phone: (27) 35 791 6001
Fax: (27) 35 791 1029
Email: bsmith@mpact.co.za
Prod. Process Technician: Mike Button
Phone: (27) 35 791 6000
Fax: (27) 35 791 1029
Email: mbutton@mpact.co.za
Mill Chemist (Lab/Qlty. Mgr.): Annalie Sauer
Phone: (27) 35 791 6000
Fax: (27) 35 791 1029
Email: asauer@mpact.co.za
Mill Mgr. Secretary: Sandra Wright
Phone: (27) 35 791 6014
Fax: (27) 86 520 4471
Email: swright@mpact.co.za
Total Employees at this Location: 250
Type of Operation: Pulp mill, Paperboard mill
Pulp Grades and Capacities:
Total pulp capacity: 151,046 mt/y
Recycled Pulping: 81,049 mt/y
Other Pulp: 69,997 mt/y
Pulp Mill Data:
Chemical Pulping Systems:
Continuous digesters: 1
Chemical Recovery Equipment:
Recovery boilers: 1
Recycled Fiber Treatment Lines:
Recycled packaging pulping lines
Paper/Paperboard Grades and Capacities:
Total paper and paperboard capacity: 150,000 mt/y
Linerboard: 30,000 mt/y

South Africa

Corrugating medium/fluting: 120,000 mt/y
Paper and Paperboard Mill Data:
 Stock Preparation:
  Pulpers: 1
  Refiners: 6
Paper Machines: 1
 No. 3, fourdrinier, total capacity 150,000 mt/y, Trim width 4.5 m, Corrugating medium/fluting, Linerboard
Finishing Equipment:
 Rewinders: 2
Energy Data:
 Power boilers: 5
 Steam turbines: 1 at 0.5 MW
 Electrical demand for mill: 296 MWh/D

ⓜ Mpact Limited
Piet Retief Mill
Ermelo Rd., Vroegeveld Farm
Piet Retief, Mpumalanga
South Africa
Mailing Address: PO Box 290, Piet Retief, 2380, Mpumalanga, South Africa
 Phone: (27) 17 826 9000
 Fax: (27) 17 826 9136
 Email: gbotes@mpact.co.za
 Web Address: www.mpact.co.za
Personnel:
 Mill Mgr.: Richard Wass
 Phone: (27) 17 826 9002
 Fax: (27) 17 826 9136
 Email: rwass@mpact.co.za
 Tech. Serv. Mgr.: Johan Viviers
 Phone: (27) 17 826 9012
 Fax: (27) 17 826 9136
 Email: jviviers@mpact.co.za
 Head of Qlty. Contr.: Helene Vermaak
 Phone: (27) 17 826 9073
 Fax: (27) 17 826 9136
 Email: hvermaak@mpact.co.za
Total Employees at this Location: 274
Type of Operation: Pulp mill, Paperboard mill
Pulp Grades and Capacities:
 Total pulp capacity: 138,759 mt/y
 Chemical Pulp: 48,080 mt/y
 Recycled Pulping: 90,679 mt/y
Pulp Mill Data:
 Chemical Pulping Systems:
  Continuous digesters: 1
 Recycled Fiber Treatment Lines:
  Recycled packaging pulping lines
Paper/Paperboard Grades and Capacities:
 Total paper and paperboard capacity: 134,000 mt/y
 Linerboard: 134,000 mt/y
Paper and Paperboard Mill Data:
 Stock Preparation:
  Pulpers: 3
  Refiners: 7
Paper Machines: 1
 No. 4, fourdrinier (2), total capacity 134,000 mt/y, Trim width 4.5 m, Linerboard
Finishing Equipment:
 Winders: 1 at 132,000 mt/y
 Calenders: 1
 Rewinders: 1 at 3,000 mt/y
Energy Data:
 Power boilers: 4
 Steam turbines: 2 at 4.0, 4 MW
 Electrical demand for mill: 268 MWh/D

ⓜ Mpact Limited
Springs Mill
82 - 84 Steel Street
New Era, 1560, Gauteng
South Africa
Mailing Address: PO Box 608, Springs, 1560, Gauteng, South Africa
 Phone: (27) 11 360 4100
 Fax: (27) 11 813 4587
 Web Address: www.mpact.co.za
Personnel:
 Prod. Mgr. BM3 & VAP (Manuf. Mgr.): Andrew Reid
 Phone: (27) 11 360 4417
 Fax: (27) 86 520 2971
 Email: areid@mpact.co.za
 Eng. Mgr.: Geoff Botes
 Phone: (27) 11 360 4276
 Fax: (27) 86 520 3461
 Email: gbotes@mpact.co.za
Total Employees at this Location: 394
Type of Operation: Paperboard mill
Pulp Grades and Capacities:
 Total pulp capacity: 107,629 mt/y
 Recycled Pulping: 107,629 mt/y
Pulp Mill Data:
 Recycled Fiber Treatment Lines:
  Pulpers: 6 at 120,000 admt/y
Paper/Paperboard Grades and Capacities:
 Total paper and paperboard capacity: 137,000 mt/y
 Boxboard/cartonboard: 137,000 mt/y
Paper and Paperboard Mill Data:
 Stock Preparation:
  Pulpers: 6
  Refiners: 12
Paper Machines: 2
 No. 1, cylinder, total capacity 30,000 mt/y, Trim width 2.4 m, Boxboard/cartonboard
 No. 2, multi-fourdrinier, total capacity 107,000 mt/y, Trim width 3.9 m, Boxboard/cartonboard
Coating Machines: 1
 PM 2, total capacity 95,000 mt/y., on machine
Energy Data:
 Power boilers
 Electrical demand for mill: 242 MWh/D

ⓜ Nampak Ltd.
Ownership: Public
Nampak Centre, 114 Dennis Road, Atholl Gardens
Sandton, Johannesburg, 2146
South Africa
Mailing Address: P O Box 784 324, Sandton, 2146, South Africa
 Phone: (27) 11 719 6300
 Fax: (27) 11 444 4794
 Email: kirsten.tyler@za.nampak.com
 Web Address: www.nampak.co.za
Personnel:
 Chmn.: Tito Mboweni
 Phone: (27) 11 719 6300
 Fax: (27) 11 444 4794
 Email: tito.mboweni@za.nampak.com
 CEO: André de Ruyter
 Phone: (27) 11 719 6300
 Fax: (27) 11 444 4794
 CFO.: Gareth Griffiths
 Phone: (27) 11 719 6300
 Fax: (27) 11 444 4794
 Email: gareth.griffiths@za.nampak.com
 Mktg. Mgr.: Kirsten Tyler
 Phone: (27) 11 719 6423
 Fax: (27) 11 444 5761
 Email: kirsten.tyler@za.nampak.com
 Oper. Dir.: Peter Hartley
 Phone: (27) 11 719 6300
 Fax: (27) 11 444 4794
 Email: peter.hartley@za.nampak.com
 Group Mgr. Corp. Finan. & Treasury: Jacques Mol
 Phone: (27) 11 719 6300
 Fax: (27) 11 444 4794
 Email: jacques.mol@za.nampak.com
 Group Exec. Paper: Ephraim Msane
 Phone: (27) 11 719 6468
 Fax: (27) 11 444 5761
Total Employees of Company: 12,369
Total Employees at this Location: 250
Mill Locations:
Nampak Paper Ltd., Rosslyn Mill, 39E Hendrick van Eck St., Rosslyn 0200, South Africa, Capacity: 160,000 mt/y, (Paperboard mill)
 Phone: (27) 12 521 1700
 Fax: (27) 12 541 2988
Nampak Tissue (Pty) Ltd., Bellville Mill, Corner Mill & Marvello Streets, Bellville South 7530, South Africa, Capacity: 32,000 mt/y, (Pulp mill, Paper mill)
 Phone: (27) 21 959 5111
 Fax: (27) 21 959 522
 Email: info@nampak.co.za
Nampak Tissue (Pty) Ltd., Kliprivier Mill, Vereeniging Rd., Kliprivier 1871, South Africa, Capacity: 24,000 mt/y, (Pulp mill, Paper mill)
 Phone: (27) 11 617 1200
 Fax: (27) 11 903 8779
Nampak Tissue (Pty) Ltd., Durban Mill, Verulam, Riverview, South Africa, Capacity: 12,000 mt/y, (Paper mill)
 Phone: (27) 32 533 1122
 Fax: (27) 32 533 1548

ⓜ Nampak Paper Ltd.
Rosslyn Mill
Ownership: 100% by Nampak Ltd.
39E Hendrick van Eck St.
Rosslyn, 0200, Gauteng
South Africa
Mailing Address: PO Box 911-008, Rosslyn, Pretoria, 0200, Gauteng, South Africa
 Phone: (27) 12 521 1700
 Fax: (27) 12 541 2988
 Web Address: www.nampak.com
Personnel:
 Tech. Dir. Nampak Corrugated: Raymond Lund
 Phone: (27) 12 521 1702
 Fax: (27) 12 541 2988
 Email: raymond.lund@za.nampak.com
 Gen. Mgr.: Siva Gounden
 Phone: (27) 12 521 1700
 Fax: (27) 12 541 2988
 Email: siva.gounden@za.nampak.com
 Commer. Mgr.: Magda Bezuidenhout
 Phone: (27) 12 521 1700
 Fax: (27) 12 541 2988
 Email: magda.bezuidenhout@za.nampak.com
 Mgr.: Cindy Swart
 Phone: (27) 12 521 1700
 Fax: (27) 12 541 2988
 Email: cindy.swart@za.nampak.com
Total Employees at this Location: 151
Type of Operation: Paperboard mill
Pulp Grades and Capacities:
 Total pulp capacity: 161,150 mt/y
 Recycled Pulping: 161,150 mt/y
Pulp Mill Data:
 Recycled Fiber Treatment Lines:
  Pulpers: 2 at 108,000 admt/y
  Recycled packaging pulping lines: 1 at 161,000
Paper/Paperboard Grades and Capacities:
 Total paper and paperboard capacity: 160,000 mt/y
 Linerboard: 104,000 mt/y
 Corrugating medium/fluting: 56,000 mt/y
Paper and Paperboard Mill Data:
 Stock Preparation:
  Refiners: 1
Paper Machines: 2
 No. 1, fourdrinier, total capacity 50,000 mt/y, Trim width 2.4 m, Corrugating medium/fluting, Linerboard
 No. 2, DuoFormer, total capacity 110,000 mt/y, Trim width 2.45 m, Corrugating medium/fluting, Linerboard
Finishing Equipment:
 Rewinders: 12
Energy Data:
 Power boilers: 5
 Electrical demand for mill: 334 MWh/D

ⓜ Nampak Tissue (Pty) Ltd.
Ownership: 100% by Nampak Ltd.
Building 3, Bryanston Gate, 170 Curzon Rd
Bryanston, 2060, Gauteng
South Africa

South Africa

Mailing Address: Private Bag X85, Bryanston, 2021, Gauteng, South Africa
  Phone: (27) 11 799 7111
  Fax: (27) 11 799 7222
  Web Address: www.nampak.com
Personnel:
  Man. Dir. & Supply Chain Dir.: Mike Dennis
  Phone: (27) 82 800 8937
  Email: mike.dennis@za.nampak.com
  Sls. Dir.: John Duffy
  Phone: (27) 11 799 7111
  Fax: (27) 11 799 7222
  Mktg. Dir.: Farah Hukamdad
  Phone: (27) 11 799 7111
  Fax: (27) 11 799 7222
  Email: farah.hukamdad@za.nampak.com
  Finan. Dir.: Linday Olitzki
  Phone: (27) 11 799 7111
  Fax: (27) 11 799 7222
  Ops. Dir.: Mervyn Pillay
  Phone: (27) 11 799 7111
  Fax: (27) 11 799 7222
  HR Dir.: Charmaine Lernao
  Phone: (27) 11 799 7111
  Fax: (27) 11 799 7222
  Mktg. Mgr. (Away From Home): Claire Bowen
  Phone: (27) 11 799 7111
  Fax: (27) 11 799 7222
Total Employees of Company: 1,500
Total Employees at this Location: 110
Mill Locations:
  Nampak Tissue (Pty) Ltd., Bellville Mill, Corner Mill & Marvello Streets, Bellville South 7530, South Africa, Capacity: 32,000 mt/y, (Pulp mill, Paper mill)
  Phone: (27) 21 959 5111
  Fax: (27) 21 959 522
  Email: info@nampak.co.za
  Nampak Tissue (Pty) Ltd., Kliprivier Mill, Vereniging Rd., Kliprivier 1871, South Africa, Capacity: 24,000 mt/y, (Pulp mill, Paper mill)
  Phone: (27) 11 617 1200
  Fax: (27) 11 903 8779
  Nampak Tissue (Pty) Ltd., Durban Mill, Verulam, Riverview, South Africa, Capacity: 12,000 mt/y, (Paper mill)
  Phone: (27) 32 533 1122
  Fax: (27) 32 533 1548

Ⓜ Nampak Tissue (Pty) Ltd.
Bellville Mill
Ownership: 100% by Nampak Ltd.
Corner Mill & Marvello Streets
Bellville South, 7530, Cape Town
South Africa
Mailing Address: PO Box 153, Sanlamhof, 7532, South Africa
  Phone: (27) 21 959 5111
  Fax: (27) 21 959 522
  Email: info@nampak.co.za
  Web Address: www.nampak.com
Personnel:
  Mill Mgr.: Jason Naidoo
  Phone: (27) 21 959 5111
  Fax: (27) 21 959 522
  Email: jason.naidoo@za.nampak.com
  Oper. Dir.: Peter Hartley
  Phone: (27) 11 719 6300
  Fax: (27) 11 444 4794
  Email: peter.hartley@za.nampak.com
  Conv. Mgr.: Ronald Venecourt
  Phone: (27) 21 959 5111
  Fax: (27) 21 959 522
  Email: ronald.venecourt@za.nampak.com
  Sls. Mgr. of Wadding & Away From Home: Russell Davis
  Phone: (27) 21 959 5111
  Fax: (27) 21 959 522
  Email: russel.davis@za.nampak.com
Total Employees at this Location: 310
Type of Operation: Pulp mill, Paper mill
Pulp Grades and Capacities:
  Total pulp capacity: 34,266 mt/y
  Recycled Pulping: 34,266 mt/y
Pulp Mill Data:
  Recycled Fiber Treatment Lines:
  Flotation deinking lines: 2 at 40,000 admt/y
  Pulpers: 1 at 40,000 admt/y
Paper/Paperboard Grades and Capacities:
  Total paper and paperboard capacity: 32,000 mt/y
  Tissue: 29,000 mt/y
  Packaging papers: 3,000 mt/y
Paper and Paperboard Mill Data:
  Stock Preparation:
  Pulpers: 6
  Refiners: 11
Paper Machines: 2
  No. 2, fourdrinier, Yankee dryer, total capacity 8,000 mt/y, Trim width 1.8 m, Tissue, Packaging papers
  No. 4, twin-wire, Yankee dryer, total capacity 24,000 mt/y, Trim width 2.5 m, Tissue
Finishing Equipment:
  Rewinders: 4
  Sheeters: 1
Energy Data:
  Power boilers: 3
  Electrical demand for mill: 112 MWh/D

Ⓜ Nampak Tissue (Pty) Ltd.
Kliprivier Mill
Ownership: 100% by Nampak Ltd.
Vereniging Rd.
Kliprivier, 1871, Gauteng
South Africa
Mailing Address: PO Box 3, Kliprivier, 1871, Gauteng, South Africa
  Phone: (27) 11 617 1200
  Fax: (27) 11 903 8779
  Web Address: www.nampak.com
Personnel:
  Mill Mgr.: Craig Foster
  Phone: (27) 11 903 8649
  Fax: (27) 11 903 8779
  Email: craig.foster@za.nampak.com
  National Paper Manuf. Mgr.: Jack Steyn
  Phone: (27) 11 903 8649
  Fax: (27) 11 903 8779
  Email: jack.steyn@za.nampak.com
  Prod. Mgr.: Meshack Mnguni
  Phone: (27) 11 903 8649
  Fax: (27) 11 903 8779
  Email: meshack.mnguni@za.nampak.com
Total Employees at this Location: 85
Type of Operation: Pulp mill, Paper mill
Pulp Grades and Capacities:
  Total pulp capacity: 25,660 mt/y
  Recycled Pulping: 25,660 mt/y
Pulp Mill Data:
  Recycled Fiber Treatment Lines:
  Pulpers: 1 at 27,375 admt/y
Paper/Paperboard Grades and Capacities:
  Total paper and paperboard capacity: 24,000 mt/y
  Tissue: 24,000 mt/y
Paper and Paperboard Mill Data:
  Stock Preparation:
  Pulpers: 1
  Refiners: 1
Paper Machines: 1
  No. 3, twin-wire, Yankee dryer, total capacity 24,000 mt/y, Trim width 2.55 m, Tissue
Finishing Equipment:
  Rewinders: 1
Energy Data:
  Power boilers: 2
  Electrical demand for mill: 86 MWh/D

Ⓜ Nampak Tissue (Pty) Ltd.
Durban Mill
Ownership: 100% by Nampak Ltd.
Verulam, Riverview, KwaZulu-Natal
South Africa
  Phone: (27) 32 533 1122
  Fax: (27) 32 533 1548
  Web Address: www.nampak.co.za
Personnel:
  Mill Mgr.: Ramesh Gopalrethnam
  Phone: (27) 32 533 1122
  Fax: (27) 32 533 1548
  Email: ramesh.gopalrethnam@za.nampak.com
  Prod. Mgr.: Judy Dalais
  Phone: (27) 32 533 1122
  Fax: (27) 32 533 1548
  Email: judy.dalais@za.nampak.com
Total Employees at this Location: 50
Type of Operation: Paper mill
Pulp Grades and Capacities:
  Total pulp capacity: 12,807 mt/y
  Recycled Pulping: 12,807 mt/y
Pulp Mill Data:
  Recycled Fiber Treatment Lines:
  Flotation deinking lines: 1 at 22,000 admt/y
  Pulpers: 1 at 22,000 admt/y
Paper/Paperboard Grades and Capacities:
  Total paper and paperboard capacity: 12,000 mt/y
  Tissue: 12,000 mt/y
Paper and Paperboard Mill Data:
Paper Machines: 1
  No. 1, crescent former, Yankee dryer, total capacity 12,000 mt/y, Trim width 2.65 m, Tissue
Finishing Equipment:
  Rewinders: 1
Energy Data:
  Power boilers: 2
  Electrical demand for mill: 42 MWh/D

Ⓜ Paper and Pulp Industries, Pty. Ltd.
Heidelberg Mill
Ownership: Crystal Paper Group
15 Albert Street
Heidelberg, 1438, Gauteng
South Africa
Mailing Address: P.O. Box 1405, Heidelberg, 1438, Gauteng, South Africa
  Phone: (27) 16 341 6396/349 1330/349 2199/341 6805
  Fax: (27) 16 341 6386/341 3698
  Email: secretary@dosanigroup.co.za, faruq@dosanigroup.co.za
  Web Address: www.tissuepaper.co.za
Personnel:
  Mill Mgr.: Ali Ahasan
  Phone: (27) 16 341 6396/349 1330/349 2199/341 6805
Total Employees at this Location: 30
Type of Operation: Paper mill
Paper/Paperboard Grades and Capacities:
  Total paper and paperboard capacity: 4,000 mt/y
  Tissue: 4,000 mt/y
Paper and Paperboard Mill Data:
Paper Machines: 1
  PM 1, total capacity 4,000 mt/y, Trim width 2.36 m, Tissue

ⓄⓂ Rafalo Paper Mills
Phoenix, Durban Mill
154 Aberdare Dve, Phoenix Ind Park
Phoenix, Durban, 4051, KwaZulu-Natal
South Africa
  Phone: (27) 31 500 9466
  Fax: (27) 31 500 9480
  Email: edmon@correll.co.za
Personnel:
  Operations Dir.: Ravine Dukhi
  Phone: (27) 31 500 9466
  Tech. Mgr.: Willem Hendricks
  Phone: (27) 72 298 2210
  Finan. Mgr.: Eric Brown
  Phone: (27) 31 500 9466

Total Employees at this Location: 150
Type of Operation: Paper mill
Pulp Grades and Capacities:
 Recycled Pulping
Paper/Paperboard Grades and Capacities:
 Total paper and paperboard capacity: 11,000 mt/y
 Tissue: 11,000 mt/y
Paper and Paperboard Mill Data:
Paper Machines: 1
 No. 1, (second hand), total capacity 11,000 mt/y, Trim width 2.55 m, Tissue

⓪Sappi Limited

Ownership: 6.80% by Industrial Development Corporation (SA), 8.60% by Old Mutual Asset Managers (South Africa) (Pty) Ltd, 13.10% by Public Investment Commissioner (SA), 15.80% by Rand Merchant Bank (SA), 7.20% by Sanlam Investment Managers

48 Ameshoff St.
Johannesburg, 2001, Gauteng
South Africa
Mailing Address: PO Box 31560, Braamfontein, 2017, South Africa
 Phone: (27) 11 407 8111
 Fax: (27) 11 403 8236
 Email: celia.bayley@sappi.com
 Web Address: www.sappi.com
Personnel:
 CEO Sappi Limited (to step down on 30 June 2014): Roeloff (Ralph) Jacobus Boëttger
 Phone: (27) 11 407 8111
 Fax: (27) 11 403 8236
 Email: roeloff.boettger@sappi.com
 CFO (CEO starting July 1, 2014): Steve Robert Binnie
 Phone: (27) 11 407 8111
 Fax: (27) 11 403 8236
 Email: steve.binnie@sappi.com
 CFO (starting July 1, 2014): Glen Pearce
 Phone: (27) 11 407 8111
 Fax: (27) 11 403 8236
 CEO Sappi South Africa: Alexander van Coller Thiel
 Phone: (27) 11 407 8111
 Fax: (27) 11 403 8236
 Email: alexander.thiel@sappi.com
 Exec. VP, Specialized Cellulose: Gary Bowles
 Phone: (27) 11 407 8111
 Fax: (27) 11 403 8236
 Group Head Technology: Andrea Rossi
 Phone: (27) 11 407 8111
 Fax: (27) 11 403 8236
 Group CIO: Bradley Coward
 Phone: (27) 11 407 8111
 Fax: (27) 11 403 8236
 Email: bradley.coward@sappi.com
 Group Head HR: Lucia Adele Swartz
 Phone: (27) 11 407 8111
 Fax: (27) 11 403 8236
 Email: lucia.swartz@sappi.com
 Group Head Corp. Affairs: André Frederich Oberholzer
 Phone: (27) 11 407 8044
 Fax: (27) 86 673 1192
 Email: andre.oberholzer@sappi.com
 Commun. Mgr.: Celia Bayley
 Phone: (27) 11 407 8438
 Fax: (27) 86 673 1225
 Email: celia.bayley@sappi.com
Total Employees of Company: 13,700
Total Employees at this Location: 540
Mill Locations:
 Sappi Fine Paper Europe, Alfeld Mill, Mühlenmasch 1, D-31061 Alfeld (Leine), Germany, Capacity: 305,000 mt/y, (Pulp mill, Paper mill, Paperboard mill)
 Phone: (49) 5181 77-0
 Fax: (49) 5181 77208
 Email: infoalfeld@sappi.com
 Sappi Fine Paper Europe, Ehingen Mill, Biberacher Str. 73, D-89584 Ehingen, Germany, Capacity: 260,000 mt/y, (Pulp mill, Paper mill)
 Phone: (49) 7391 5010
 Fax: (49) 7391 501 315
 Email: renate.distelrath@sappi.com
 Sappi Fine Paper North America, Cloquet Mill, 2201 Avenue B, Cloquet, MN 55720, USA, Capacity: 330,348 mt/y, (Pulp mill, Paper mill)
 Phone: (1) 218-879-2300
 Fax: (1) 218-879-0648
 Sappi Fine Paper North America, Somerset Mill, 1329 Waterville Road, Skowhegan, ME 04976, USA, Capacity: 794,927 mt/y, (Pulp mill, Paper mill)
 Phone: (1) 207-238-3000
 Fax: (1) 207-453-4532
 Sappi Fine Paper North America, Westbrook Mill, 89 Cumberland St, Westbrook, ME 04092, USA, Capacity: 34,970 mt/y, (Paper mill)
 Phone: (1) 207-856-4000
 Fax: (1) 207-856-1346
 Email: info@sappi.com
 Sappi Paper and Paper Packaging South Africa (SA), Stanger Mill, Gledhow Mount, Stanger 4450, South Africa, Capacity: 111,000 mt/y, (Pulp mill, Paper mill)
 Phone: (27) 32 437 2222
 Fax: (27) 32 551 1622
 Sappi Fine Paper Europe, Gratkorn Mill, Brucker Str. 21, A-8101 Gratkorn, Austria, Capacity: 950,000 mt/y, (Pulp mill, Paper mill)
 Phone: (43) 3124 201 0
 Fax: (43) 3124 201 3038
 Email: gratkorn.mill@sappi.com
 Sappi Fine Paper Europe, Kirkniemi Mill, FI-08800 Kirkniemi, Finland, Capacity: 735,000 mt/y, (Pulp mill, Paper mill)
 Phone: (358) 1046 42999
 Fax: (358) 1046 42411
 Email: (firstname.lastname@sappi.com)
 Sappi Paper and Paper Packaging South Africa (SA), Cape Kraft Mill, 7 Esso Rd., Montague Gardens, Cape Town 7441, South Africa, Capacity: 60,000 mt/y, (Pulp mill, Paperboard mill)
 Phone: (27) 21 552 2127
 Fax: (27) 21 552 2152
 Sappi Paper and Paper Packaging South Africa (SA), Tugela Mill, Old Main Road, Mandini 4490, South Africa, Capacity: 200,000 mt/y, (Pulp mill, Paper mill, Paperboard mill)
 Phone: (27) 32 456 1111
 Fax: (27) 32 456 1484
 Sappi Fine Paper Europe, Lanaken Mill, Montaigneweg 2, B-3620 Lanaken, Belgium, Capacity: 500,000 mt/y, (Pulp mill, Paper mill)
 Phone: (32) 89 71 9719
 Fax: (32) 89 71 9222
 Email: lanaken.mill@sappi.com
 Sappi Fine Paper Europe, Maastricht Mill, Biesenweg 16, NL-6211 AA Maastricht, Netherlands, Capacity: 290,000 mt/y, (Paper mill)
 Phone: (31) 43 382 22 22
 Fax: (31) 43 382 27 31
 Email: maastricht.mill@sappi.com
 Sappi Paper and Paper Packaging South Africa (SA), Ngodwana Mill, N4 National Road, Ngodwana 1209, South Africa, Capacity: 370,000 mt/y, (Pulp mill, Paper mill, Paperboard mill)
 Phone: (27) 13 734 6111
 Fax: (27) 13 734 6535
 Sappi Paper and Paper Packaging South Africa (SA), Enstra Mill, East Geduld Rd., Enstra, Springs, South Africa, Capacity: 185,000 mt/y, (Pulp mill, Paper mill)
 Phone: (27) 11 360 0000
 Fax: (27) 11 360 0102
 Sappi Fine Paper Europe, Stockstadt Mill, Obernburger Strasse 1-9, D-63811 Stockstadt am Main, Germany, Capacity: 440,000 mt/y, (Pulp mill, Paper mill)
 Phone: (49) 6027 4200
 Fax: (49) 6027 420 245/823
 Email: stockstadt@sappi.com
 Sappi Chemical Cellulose, Saiccor Mill, Umkomanzi Drift, Umkomaas 4170, South Africa, (Pulp mill)
 Phone: (27) 39 973 8911
 Fax: (27) 866 862634

⓪Sappi Paper and Paper Packaging South Africa (SA)

Ownership: 100% by Sappi Limited

48 Ameshoff Street, Braamfontein
Johannesburg, 2001, Gauteng
South Africa
Mailing Address: PO Box 32706, Braamfontein, 2017, South Africa
 Phone: (27) 11 407 8111
 Fax: (27) 11 403 6929
 Web Address: www.sappi.com
Personnel:
 CEO: Jan Labuaschagne
 Phone: (27) 11 407 8111
 Fax: (27) 11 403 6929
 Man. Dir., Sappi Kraft: Albert Lubbe
 Phone: (27) 11 407 8077
 Man. Dir., Sappi Saiccor: Alan Tubb
 Phone: (27) 11 407 8111
 Fax: (27) 11 403 6929
 Gen. Mgr., Mktg.: Matt T. Spence
 Phone: (27) 11 407 8322
 Fax: (27) 11 339 6929
 Email: matt.spence@sappi.com
 Gen. Mgr., Finan.: John Anderssen
 Phone: (27) 11 407 8472
 Fax: (27) 11 339 4607
 Email: john.anderssen@sappi.com
Total Employees of Company: 2,310
Mill Locations:
 Sappi Paper and Paper Packaging South Africa (SA), Stanger Mill, Gledhow Mount, Stanger 4450, South Africa, Capacity: 111,000 mt/y, (Pulp mill, Paper mill)
 Phone: (27) 32 437 2222
 Fax: (27) 32 551 1622
 Sappi Paper and Paper Packaging South Africa (SA), Cape Kraft Mill, 7 Esso Rd., Montague Gardens, Cape Town 7441, South Africa, Capacity: 60,000 mt/y, (Pulp mill, Paperboard mill)
 Phone: (27) 21 552 2127
 Fax: (27) 21 552 2152
 Sappi Paper and Paper Packaging South Africa (SA), Tugela Mill, Old Main Road, Mandini 4490, South Africa, Capacity: 200,000 mt/y, (Pulp mill, Paper mill, Paperboard mill)
 Phone: (27) 32 456 1111
 Fax: (27) 32 456 1484
 Sappi Paper and Paper Packaging South Africa (SA), Ngodwana Mill, N4 National Road, Ngodwana 1209, South Africa, Capacity: 370,000 mt/y, (Pulp mill, Paper mill, Paperboard mill)
 Phone: (27) 13 734 6111
 Fax: (27) 13 734 6535
 Sappi Paper and Paper Packaging South Africa (SA), Enstra Mill, East Geduld Rd., Enstra, Springs, South Africa, Capacity: 185,000 mt/y, (Pulp mill, Paper mill)
 Phone: (27) 11 360 0000
 Fax: (27) 11 360 0102

ⓜSappi Paper and Paper Packaging South Africa (SA)
Stanger Mill

Ownership: 100% by Sappi Limited

Gledhow Mount
Stanger, 4450, KwaZulu-Natal
South Africa
Mailing Address: P.O. Box 725, Stanger, 4450, KwaZulu-Natal, South Africa
 Phone: (27) 32 437 2222
 Fax: (27) 32 551 1622
 Web Address: www.sappi.com
Personnel:
 Gen. Mgr.: Beverly Sukhdeo
 Phone: (27) 32 437 2101
 Fax: (27) 32 551 5384
 Email: beverly.sukhdeo@sappi.com
 Paper Prod. Mgr.: Derek Moonsamy
 Phone: (27) 32 437 2222
 Fax: (27) 32 551 1622

South Africa

Email: derek.moonsamy@sappi.com
Total Employees at this Location: 553
Type of Operation: Pulp mill, Paper mill
Pulp Grades and Capacities:
 Total pulp capacity: 60,006 mt/y
 Other Pulp: 60,006 mt/y
Pulp Mill Data:
 Chemical Pulping Systems:
 Continuous digesters: 1
 Bleach Plant Systems: 1
 No. 1, Sequence: CqEpH, Capacity 58,000 admt/y
 Chemical Recovery Equipment:
 Evaporator lines: 1
 Recovery boilers: 1
Paper/Paperboard Grades and Capacities:
 Total paper and paperboard capacity: 111,000 mt/y
 Coated woodfree/freesheet: 56,000 mt/y
 Tissue: 31,000 mt/y
 Specialty and industrial: 24,000 mt/y
Paper and Paperboard Mill Data:
 Stock Preparation:
 Pulpers: 5
 Refiners: 5
Paper Machines: 2
 No. 1, DuoFormer D, total capacity 80,000 mt/y, Trim width 3.2 m, Specialty and industrial, Coated woodfree/freesheet
 No. 2, Yankee dryer, total capacity 31,000 mt/y, Trim width 3.4 m, Tissue, Uncoated woodfree/freesheet
Coating Machines: 1
 PM 1, total capacity 81,000 mt/y., off machine
Finishing Equipment:
 Winders: 2 at 110,000 mt/y
 Calenders
 Supercalenders: 2 at 70,000 mt/y
 Rewinders: 2
 Sheeters: 2 at 35,000 mt/y
Energy Data:
 Power boilers: 4
 Electrical demand for mill: 322 MWh/D

ⓜSappi Paper and Paper Packaging South Africa (SA)
Cape Kraft Mill
Ownership: 100% by Sappi Limited
7 Esso Rd.
Montague Gardens, Cape Town, 7441, Cape Town
South Africa
Mailing Address: PO Box 185, Milnerton, Cape Town, 7435, South Africa
 Phone: (27) 21 552 2127
 Fax: (27) 21 552 2152
 Web Address: www.sappi.com
Personnel:
 Product Mgr.: Nazeem Philander
 Phone: (27) 21 552 2127
 Fax: (27) 21 552 2152
 Email: nazeem.philander@sappi.com
 SHEQ. Mgr.: Amanda Home
 Phone: (27) 21 552 2127
 Fax: (27) 21 552 2152
 Email: amanda.home@sappi.com
Total Employees at this Location: 130
Type of Operation: Pulp mill, Paperboard mill
Pulp Grades and Capacities:
 Total pulp capacity: 60,482 mt/y
 Recycled Pulping: 60,482 mt/y
Pulp Mill Data:
 Recycled Fiber Treatment Lines:
 Pulpers: 1 at 80,000 admt/y
Paper/Paperboard Grades and Capacities:
 Total paper and paperboard capacity: 60,000 mt/y
 Linerboard: 45,000 mt/y
 Corrugating medium/fluting: 15,000 mt/y
Paper and Paperboard Mill Data:
 Stock Preparation:
 Refiners: 2
Paper Machines: 1
 No. 1, fourdrinier, total capacity 60,000 mt/y, Trim width 2.4 m, Corrugating medium/fluting, Linerboard
Coating Machines: 1
 No. 1, total capacity 50,000 mt/y.
Finishing Equipment:
 Rewinders: 1 at 80,000 mt/y
Energy Data:
 Power boilers: 5
 Electrical demand for mill: 93 MWh/D

ⓜSappi Paper and Paper Packaging South Africa (SA)
Tugela Mill
Ownership: 100% by Sappi Limited
Old Main Road
Mandini, 4490, KwaZulu-Natal
South Africa
Mailing Address: Private Bag X6034, Mandeni, 4490, South Africa
 Phone: (27) 32 456 1111
 Fax: (27) 32 456 1484
 Web Address: www.sappi.com
Personnel:
 Gen. Mgr.: Louis Kruyshaar
 Phone: (27) 32 456 1111
 Fax: (27) 32 456 1484
 Email: louis.kruyshaar@sappi.com
 Services & Eng. Mgr.: Duncan Edwards
 Phone: (27) 32 456 1111
 Fax: (27) 32 456 1484
 Email: duncan.edwards@sappi.com
Total Employees at this Location: 429
Type of Operation: Pulp mill, Paper mill, Paperboard mill
Pulp Grades and Capacities:
 Total pulp capacity: 202,681 mt/y
 Chemical Pulp: 95,608 mt/y
 Recycled Pulping: 107,073 mt/y
Pulp Mill Data:
 Chemical Pulping Systems:
 Continuous digesters: 1
Pulp Lines: 2
 Chemical Recovery Equipment:
 Evaporator lines: 2
 Recovery boilers: 2
 Lime Kiln
 Recycled Fiber Treatment Lines:
 Recycled packaging pulping lines: 1 at 125,000
Paper/Paperboard Grades and Capacities:
 Total paper and paperboard capacity: 200,000 mt/y
 Linerboard: 100,000 mt/y
 Corrugating medium/fluting: 100,000 mt/y
Paper and Paperboard Mill Data:
 Stock Preparation:
 Pulpers: 7
 Refiners: 15
Paper Machines: 1
 No. 2, fourdrinier (2), total capacity 200,000 mt/y, Trim width 4.88 m, Linerboard, Corrugating medium/fluting
Finishing Equipment:
 Winders: 6
Energy Data:
 Power boilers: 10
 Steam turbines: 2 at 20.0 MW
 Electrical demand for mill: 452 MWh/D

ⓜSappi Paper and Paper Packaging South Africa (SA)
Ngodwana Mill
Ownership: 100% by Sappi Limited
N4 National Road
Ngodwana, 1209, Mpumalanga
South Africa
Mailing Address: Private Bag X1001, Ngodwana, 1209, Mpumalanga, South Africa
 Phone: (27) 13 734 6111
 Fax: (27) 13 734 6535
 Web Address: www.sappi.com
Personnel:
 Gen. Mgr.: SW Engelbrecht
 Phone: (27) 13 734 6367
 Fax: (27) 13 734 6325
 Email: sw.engelbrecht@sappi.com
 Tech. Mgr.: Nic Dreyer
 Phone: (27) 13 734 6210, (M): 82 876 7701
 Fax: (27) 13 734 6452
 Email: nick.dreyer@sappi.com
 Mill Mgr. Specialized Cellulose: Naresh Naidoo
 Phone: (27) 13 734 6166
 Fax: (27) 13 734 6044
 Email: naresh.naidoo@sappi.com
 Paper Mill Mgr.: John Bartleman
 Phone: (27) 13 734 6102
 Fax: (27) 13 734 6573
 Email: john.bartleman@sappi.com
 Eng. Mgr.: Piet Bisschoff
 Phone: (27) 13 734 6111
 Fax: (27) 13 734 6535
 Email: piet.bisschoff@sappi.com
Total Employees at this Location: 1,025
Type of Operation: Pulp mill, Paper mill, Paperboard mill
Pulp Grades and Capacities:
 Total pulp capacity: 579,837 mt/y
 Pulp available for market: 210,000 mt/y
 Chemical Pulp: 414,465 mt/y
 Mechanical Pulp: 122,967 mt/y
 Recycled Pulping: 42,405 mt/y
Pulp Mill Data:
 Chemical Pulping Systems:
 Batch digesters: 6
 Continuous digesters: 1
 Mechanical Pulping Systems:
 Conventional grinders: 8
 Pressurized grinders: 2
Pulp Lines: 2
 Bleach Plant Systems: 1
 No. 1, Sequence: O_2 ZDEDnD, Capacity 200,000 admt/y
 No. 2, Type: D-ZEop-D, HW, Sequence: Z/DEopD, Capacity 250,000 admt/y
 Chemical Recovery Equipment:
 Evaporator lines: 2
 Recovery boilers: 2
 Recycled Fiber Treatment Lines:
 Pulpers: 1 at 55,000 admt/y
 Pulp Dryers:
 Air Float dryers 1
Paper/Paperboard Grades and Capacities:
 Total paper and paperboard capacity: 370,000 mt/y
 Newsprint: 140,000 mt/y
 Linerboard: 230,000 mt/y
Paper and Paperboard Mill Data:
 Stock Preparation:
 Pulpers: 4
 Refiners: 9
Paper Machines: 2
 No. 1, fourdrinier (3), total capacity 230,000 mt/y, Trim width 6.8 m, Linerboard
 No. 2, Bel-Baie II, total capacity 140,000 mt/y, Trim width 6.58 m, Newsprint
Finishing Equipment:
 Winders: 2 at 240,000 mt/y, 140,000 mt/y
 Rewinders: 1 at 10,000 mt/y
Energy Data:
 Power boilers: 7
 Steam turbines: 2 at 117 MW
 Electrical demand for mill: 1,793 MWh/D

ⓜSappi Paper and Paper Packaging South Africa (SA)
Enstra Mill
Ownership: 100% by Sappi Limited
East Geduld Rd., Enstra
Springs, Gauteng
South Africa

Mailing Address: PO Box 3246, Springs, 1560, Gauteng, South Africa
  Phone: (27) 11 360 0000
  Fax: (27) 11 360 0102
  Web Address: www.sappi.co.za
Personnel:
  Gen. Mgr.: Matt Spence
  Phone: (27) 11 360 0110
  Fax: (27) 11 360 0102
  Email: matt.spence@sappi.com
  Paper Supply Mgr.: Gideon Oberholster
  Phone: (27) 11 360 0000
  Fax: (27) 11 360 0102
  Email: gideon.oberholster@sappi.com
  Procurement Mgr.: Lenet Smuts
  Phone: (27) 11 360 0000
  Fax: (27) 11 360 0102
  Email: lenet.smuts@sappi.com
  Pulp Prod. Mgr.: Piet Scheun
  Phone: (27) 11 360 0000
  Fax: (27) 11 360 0102
  Email: piet.scheun@sappi.com
Total Employees at this Location: 511
Type of Operation: Pulp mill, Paper mill
Pulp Mill Data:
  Chemical Pulping Systems:
  Batch digesters: 7
  Bleach Plant Systems: 2
  1, Sequence: O_2 DED, Capacity 70,000 admt/y
  2, Sequence: O_2 DED, Capacity 46,300 admt/y
  Chemical Recovery Equipment:
  Evaporator lines: 1
  Recovery boilers: 1
  Lime Kiln
Paper/Paperboard Grades and Capacities:
  Total paper and paperboard capacity: 185,000 mt/y
  Uncoated woodfree/freesheet: 185,000 mt/y
Paper and Paperboard Mill Data:
  Stock Preparation:
  Pulpers: 14
  Refiners: 19
Paper Machines: 3
No. 2, fourdrinier, total capacity 17,200 mt/y, Trim width 2.6 m, Uncoated woodfree/freesheet
No. 3, fourdrinier, total capacity 40,000 mt/y, Trim width 3 m, Uncoated woodfree/freesheet
No. 6, Bel-Bond, total capacity 127,800 mt/y, Trim width 4.7 m, Uncoated woodfree/freesheet
Finishing Equipment:
  Rewinders: 4
  Sheeters: 4
Energy Data:
  Power boilers: 6
  Steam turbines
  Electrical demand for mill: 388 MWh/D

ⓘⓜSappi Chemical Cellulose
Saiccor Mill
Ownership: 100% by Sappi Limited
Umkomanzi Drift
Umkomaas, 4170, KwaZulu-Natal
South Africa
Mailing Address: PO Box 62, Umkomaas, 4170, KwaZulu-Natal, South Africa
  Phone: (27) 39 973 8911
  Fax: (27) 866 862634
  Web Address: www.sappi.com
Personnel:
  Man. Dir.: Gary Bowles
  Phone: (27) 39 973 8001
  Fax: (27) 39 973 0668
  Email: gary.bowles@sappi.com
  Gen. Mgr.: Clive Oxley
  Phone: (27) 39 973 8050
  Fax: (27) 866 862634
  Email: clive.oxley@sappi.com
  Financial Mgr.: Pramy Moodley
  Phone: (27) 39 973 8007
  Fax: (27) 866 862634
  Email: pramy.moodley@sappi.com
  Mill. Mgr. Tech.: Wayne Weston
  Phone: (27) 39 9738626
  Fax: (27) 866 862634
  Email: wayne.weston@sappi.com
  Mill Mgr. Pulping & Recovery: Peter Morris
  Phone: (27) 39 9738332
  Fax: (27) 866 862634
  Email: peter.morris@sappi.com
  Mktg. Dir.: William Morrow
  Phone: (27) 39 973 8012
  Fax: (27) 39 973 0668
  Email: william.morrow@sappi.com
  Environmental Mgr.: Craig Daniel
  Phone: (27) 39 973 8152
  Fax: (27) 866 862634
  Email: craig.daniel@sappi.co.za
  Eng. Mgr.: Greg Taylor
  Phone: (27) 39 973 8143
  Fax: (27) 866 862634
  Email: greg.taylor@sappi.com
  SSC Gen.Mgr. - Tech. & COE: Tracy Wessels
  Phone: (27) 39 973 8420
  Fax: (27) 866 862634
  Email: tracy.wessels@sappi.com
Total Employees at this Location: 1,156
Type of Operation: Pulp mill
Pulp Grades and Capacities:
  Total pulp capacity: 840,703 mt/y
  Pulp available for market: 801,000 mt/y
  Chemical Pulp: 840,703 mt/y
Pulp Mill Data:
  Chemical Pulping Systems:
  Batch digesters: 35
Pulp Lines: 3
  Bleach Plant Systems: 3
  No. 3, Sequence: O_2 ODEDH(P)
  No. 4, Sequence: O_2 ODEDH(P)
  No. 5, Sequence: O_2 ODEDH(P)
  Chemical Recovery Equipment:
  Evaporator lines: 4
  Recovery boilers: 2
  Pulp Dryers:
  Air Float dryers 1, Air Float dryers 1, Air Float dryers 1, Fourdriniers 1
Finishing Equipment:
  Winders: 1 at 310,000 mt/y
  Rewinders: 1 at 310,000 mt/y
Energy Data:
  Power boilers: 6
  Steam turbines: 5 at 6, 6, 5, 28, 45 MW
  Electrical demand for mill: 1,691 MWh/D

ⓜSouth African Cartonboard Mills
Wadeville Mill
Ownership: Crystal Paper Group
10 Commercial Road
Wadeville, 1422, Gauteng
South Africa
Mailing Address: P.O. Box 15031, Wadeville, 1422, South Africa
  Phone: (27) 11 902 1096
  Fax: (27) 11 902 2044
  Email: secretary@dosanigroup.co.za
  Web Address: tissuepaper.co.za
Personnel:
  Mill Mgr.: Hanif Vosani
  Phone: (27) 11 902 1096
Total Employees at this Location: 40
Type of Operation: Paper mill, Paperboard mill
Pulp Grades and Capacities:
  Total pulp capacity: 16,355 mt/y
  Recycled Pulping: 16,355 mt/y
Pulp Mill Data:
  Recycled Fiber Treatment Lines:
  Recycled packaging pulping lines
Paper/Paperboard Grades and Capacities:
  Total paper and paperboard capacity: 22,000 mt/y
  Tissue: 6,000 mt/y
  Linerboard: 10,000 mt/y
  Corrugating medium/fluting: 6,000 mt/y
Paper and Paperboard Mill Data:
Paper Machines: 2
No. 1, fourdrinier, total capacity 16,000 mt/y, Trim width 2.35 m, Corrugating medium/fluting, Linerboard
No. 4, fourdrinier, total capacity 6,000 mt/y, Trim width 2.35 m, Tissue
Energy Data:
  Power boilers
  Electrical demand for mill: 40 MWh/D

ⓘSouth African Paper Mills (SAPM)
Ownership: Private
159 Bluff Road
Jacobs, Durban, 4026, KwaZulu-Natal
South Africa
  Phone: (27) 31 451 9600
  Fax: (27) 31 451 9629
  Email: info@sapaper.co.za
  Web Address: www.sapaper.co.za
Total Employees of Company: 120
Total Employees at this Location: 120
Mill Locations:
South African Paper Mills (SAPM), Durban Mill, 159 Bluff Road, Jacobs, Durban 4026, South Africa, Capacity: 26,000 mt/y, (Paper mill, Paperboard mill)
  Phone: (27) 31 451 9600
  Fax: (27) 31 451 9629
  Email: info@sapaper.co.za

ⓜSouth African Paper Mills (SAPM)
Durban Mill
159 Bluff Road
Jacobs, Durban, 4026, KwaZulu-Natal
South Africa
  Phone: (27) 31 451 9600
  Fax: (27) 31 451 9629
  Email: info@sapaper.co.za
  Web Address: www.sapaper.co.za
Personnel:
  Owner & Gen. Mgr.: Anesh Madaree
  Phone: (27) 82 552 3090
  Fax: (27) 31 451 9600
Total Employees at this Location: 120
Type of Operation: Paper mill, Paperboard mill
Pulp Grades and Capacities:
  Total pulp capacity: 26,779 mt/y
  Recycled Pulping: 26,779 mt/y
Pulp Mill Data:
  Recycled Fiber Treatment Lines:
  Recycled packaging pulping lines
Paper/Paperboard Grades and Capacities:
  Total paper and paperboard capacity: 26,000 mt/y
  Packaging papers: 11,000 mt/y
  Linerboard: 10,000 mt/y
  Corrugating medium/fluting: 5,000 mt/y
Paper and Paperboard Mill Data:
Paper Machines: 3
No. 1, fourdrinier, total capacity 5,000 mt/y, Trim width 1.7 m, Packaging papers
No. 2, fourdrinier, total capacity 6,000 mt/y, Trim width 2.2 m, Packaging papers
No. 4, fourdrinier, total capacity 15,000 mt/y, Trim width 3.05 m, Linerboard, Corrugating medium/fluting
Energy Data:
  Power boilers
  Electrical demand for mill: 42 MWh/D

ⓜTriwaste CC
Tongaat Mill
Ownership: Cape Waste Paper Pty. Ltd.
21 Edmond Morewood Road, Truro Industries Estate
Tongaat, 4400
South Africa
Mailing Address: P.O. Box 889, Tongaat, 4400, KwaZulu-Natal, South Africa
  Phone: (27) 21931 17251
  Fax: (27) 32 944 1686

Tanzania

Email: topco@iafrica.com
Personnel:
Mill Mgr.: Khaliq Nabeebuccas
Phone: (27) 32 944 4114
Total Employees at this Location: 180
Type of Operation: Paper mill
Paper/Paperboard Grades and Capacities:
Total paper and paperboard capacity: 12,000 mt/y
Tissue: 12,000 mt/y
Paper and Paperboard Mill Data:
Paper Machines: 2
PM 1, total capacity 4,800 mt/y, Trim width 2.5 m, Tissue
PM 2, total capacity 7,200 mt/y, Trim width 2.65 m, Tissue

TANZANIA

ⓜKibo Match Group Pulp and Paperboard Mill
Ownership: Chief Akundele, Kibo Match Group
P.O. Box 1819
Moshi
Tanzania
Phone: (255) 27 27 54425/6
Fax: (255) 27 27 50467
Personnel:
Owner: Chief Akundele
Phone: (255) 27 27 54425
Fax: (255) 27 27 50467
Man. Dir.: Marisa
Phone: (255) 27 27 54425
Fax: (255) 27 27 50467
Mill Mgr.: Mutisi
Phone: (255) 27 27 54425
Fax: (255) 27 27 50467
Total Employees of Company: 170
Mill Locations:
Kibo Match Group Pulp and Paperboard Mill, Moshi Mill, P.O. Box 1819, Moshi, Tanzania, Capacity: 10,000 mt/y, (Paper mill, Paperboard mill)
Phone: (255) 27 27 54425/6
Fax: (255) 27 27 50467

ⓜKibo Match Group Pulp and Paperboard Mill
Moshi Mill
Mill is closed (brought operations to a halt May 2014 after operating at a loss.)
P.O. Box 1819
Moshi
Tanzania
Phone: (255) 27 27 54425/6
Fax: (255) 27 27 50467
Personnel:
Owner: Chief Akundele
Phone: (255) 27 27 54425/6
Man. Dir.: Mr. Marisa
Phone: (255) 27 27 54425/6
Mill Mgr.: Mr. Mutisi
Phone: (255) 27 27 54425/6
Eng. Mgr.: Eng. Mosha
Phone: (255) 27 27 54425/6
Total Employees at this Location: 170
Type of Operation: Paper mill, Paperboard mill
Paper/Paperboard Grades and Capacities:
Total paper and paperboard capacity: 10,000 mt/y
Packaging papers
Linerboard: 10,000 mt/y
Paper and Paperboard Mill Data:
Paper Machines: 1
No. 1, total capacity 10,000 mt/y, Trim width 1.7 m, Packaging papers, Linerboard

ⓜMufindi Paper Mills (MPM)
Ownership: 99.99% by Angel Hurst Industries Limited
PO Box 1, Mufindi District
Mgololo, Iringa Region
Tanzania
Phone: (255) 78-3683125, 22-2863571
Fax: (255) 22-2863570
Email: svs@mufindipapermills.com
Web Address: mufindipaper.en.ecplaza.net
Personnel:
Mill Mgr.: Kishore Kumar Konakalla
Phone: (255) 22-2863571
Fax: (255) 22-2863570
Email: kumar@mufindipapermills.com
Total Employees of Company: 600
Mill Locations:
Mufindi Paper Mills (MPM), Mgololo Mill, PO Box 1, Mufindi District, Mgololo, Iringa Region, Tanzania, Capacity: 55,000 mt/y, (Pulp mill, Paper mill)
Phone: (255) 22-2863571
Fax: (255) 22-2863570
Email: svs@mufindipapermills.com

ⓜMufindi Paper Mills (MPM)
Mgololo Mill
PO Box 1, Mufindi District
Mgololo, Iringa Region
Tanzania
Phone: (255) 22-2863571
Fax: (255) 22-2863570
Email: svs@mufindipapermills.com
Personnel:
Man. Dir.: Mr. Jaswant Singh Rai
Phone: (255) 22-2863571
Fax: (255) 22-2863570
Email: jaswant@mufindipapermills.com
Mill Mgr.: Mr. Kishore Kumar Konakalla
Phone: (255) 22-2863571
Fax: (255) 22-2863570
Email: kumar@mufindipapermills.com
Total Employees at this Location: 600
Type of Operation: Pulp mill, Paper mill
Pulp Grades and Capacities:
Total pulp capacity: 50,000 mt/y
Chemical Pulp: 50,000 mt/y
Pulp Mill Data:
Chemical Pulping Systems:
Batch digesters: 3
Pulp Lines: 2
Bleach Plant Systems: 1
Chemical Recovery Equipment:
Evaporator lines: 1
Recovery boilers: 1
Paper/Paperboard Grades and Capacities:
Total paper and paperboard capacity: 55,000 mt/y
Packaging papers: 33,000 mt/y
Linerboard: 22,000 mt/y
Paper and Paperboard Mill Data:
Stock Preparation:
Pulpers: 3
Refiners: 6
Paper Machines: 2
No. 1, fourdrinier, total capacity 55,000 mt/y, Trim width 3.6 m, Packaging papers, Linerboard
No. 2, (idle, due to be rebuilt to produce extensible sack kraft), fourdrinier, total capacity 50,000 mt/y, Trim width 3.6 m
Finishing Equipment:
Rewinders: 1
Sheeters: 1
Energy Data:
Power boilers: 1
Steam turbines: 1 at 10.0 MW

ⓜTanpack Tissues Ltd.
Dar-es-Salaam Mill
Ownership: 100% by Chandaria Industries Ltd.
P.O. Box 21359
Dar-es-Salaam
Tanzania
Phone: (255) 22 2700163/2773901-3
Fax: (255) 22 2700890
Email: info@tanpacktissue.com
Web Address: www.chandaria.com
Personnel:
Chmn.: Manganlal M. Chandaria
Phone: (255) 22 2700163/2773901-3
Man. Dir.: Mahesh M. Chandaria
Phone: (255) 22 2700163/2773901-3
Gen. Mgr.: Rajesh Shah
Phone: (255) 744 327641
Mill Mgr.: John A. Philip
Phone: (255) 22 2700163/2773901-3
Operation Mgr.: Mehul Shah
Phone: (255) 765 630925
Maint. Mgr.: Pankaj Sharna
Total Employees at this Location: 120
Type of Operation: Paper mill
Paper/Paperboard Grades and Capacities:
Total paper and paperboard capacity: 3,000 mt/y
Tissue: 3,000 mt/y
Paper and Paperboard Mill Data:
Stock Preparation:
Pulpers: 1
Refiners: 2
Paper Machines: 1
No. 1, total capacity 3,000 mt/y, Trim width 1.65 m, Tissue
Finishing Equipment:
Rewinders: 2 at 4,000 mt/y
Energy Data:
Power boilers: 2

TUNISIA

ⓜAfri Paper
Ownership: 100% by SME-Société Méditérranéenne d'Emballages
GP1 - Route de M-Saken
4013 Messadine, Gouvernorat de Kairouan
Tunisia
Phone: (216) 73 323 025
Fax: (216) 73 323 033
Personnel:
Man. Dir.: Abdelfattah Mahjoub
Phone: (216) 73 284 025
Mill Locations:
Afri Paper, Chbika Mill, Avenue Abdelhamid Elkadhi, Chbika, Kairouan, Tunisia, Capacity: 50,000 mt/y, (Paperboard mill)
Phone: (216) 77 240 101
Fax: (216) 77 240 100
Email: afripaper@gnet.tn

ⓜAfri Paper
Chbika Mill
Avenue Abdelhamid Elkadhi
Chbika, Kairouan, Gouvernorat de Kairouan
Tunisia
Phone: (216) 77 240 101
Fax: (216) 77 240 100
Email: afripaper@gnet.tn
Personnel:
Owner: Abdelfattah Mahjoub
Phone: (216) 77 240 100
Gen. Mgr.: Mohamed Mahjoub
Phone: (216) 25 372348
Fax: (216) 77 240101
Total Employees at this Location: 45
Type of Operation: Paperboard mill
Pulp Grades and Capacities:
Total pulp capacity: 49,936 mt/y
Recycled Pulping: 49,936 mt/y
Pulp Mill Data:
Recycled Fiber Treatment Lines:
Pulpers: 1 at 55,140
Paper/Paperboard Grades and Capacities:

Tunisia

Total paper and paperboard capacity: 50,000 mt/y
Linerboard: 30,000 mt/y
Corrugating medium/fluting: 20,000 mt/y
Paper and Paperboard Mill Data:
Paper Machines: 1
No. 1, fourdrinier (2), total capacity 50,000 mt/y, Trim width 2.5 m, Corrugating medium/fluting, Linerboard
Finishing Equipment:
Winders: 1 at 50,000 mt/y
Rewinders: 1 at 80,000 mt/y
Energy Data:
Power boilers: 1
Steam turbines: 1 at 4.5 MW
Electrical demand for mill: 67 MWh/D

ⓜAZUR Papier
Zaghouan Mill
Mill is started in April 2013
Ownership: 100% by Société d'articles Hygiéniques (S.A.H)
9 Avenue de l'environnement
Hammam Zriba, Gouvernorat de Zaghouan
Tunisia
Type of Operation: Paper mill
Paper/Paperboard Grades and Capacities:
Total paper and paperboard capacity: 25,000 mt/y
Tissue: 25,000 mt/y
Paper and Paperboard Mill Data:
Paper Machines: 1
PM 1, (started in April 2013), total capacity 25,000 mt/y, Trim width 2.75 m, Tissue

ⓞⓜSAPB, Société Anonyme des Papeteries du Belvédére
Cité El Khadra, Tunis Mill
Ownership: 100% by private owners
108 Ave. Louis Braille
1003 Cité El Khadra, Tunis
Tunisia
Phone: (216) 71 770024
Fax: (216) 71 773931
Email: sapb@topnet.tn
Personnel:
Man. Dir. & Chmn.: Naceur Ben Ghorbal
Phone: (216) 71 770024
Tech. Mgr.: Adel Bencheikh
Phone: (216) 71 770024
Personnel Dir.: Rouis Habib
Phone: (216) 71 764 533
Fax: (216) 71 765 057
Commer. Officer: Adel Benmahmoud
Phone: (216) 770 024
Total Employees of Company: 115
Total Employees at this Location: 115
Type of Operation: Paper mill, Paperboard mill
Paper/Paperboard Grades and Capacities:
Total paper and paperboard capacity: 22,000 mt/y
Linerboard: 10,000 mt/y
Corrugating medium/fluting: 12,000 mt/y
Paper and Paperboard Mill Data:
Stock Preparation:
Pulpers: 3
Refiners: 2
Paper Machines: 3
No. 1, multi-cylinder, total capacity 10,000 mt/y, Trim width 2.8 m, Packaging papers
No. 3, multi-cylinder, total capacity 12,000 mt/y, Trim width 2.8 m, Corrugating medium/fluting
No. 4, (second hand, PM only operates as per demand), Yankee dryer, total capacity 2,000 mt/y, Trim width 2.2 m, Tissue
Finishing Equipment:
Winders: 2 at 20,000 mt/y
Rewinders: 2 at 20,000 mt/y
Energy Data:
Power boilers: 2
Electrical demand for mill: 36 MWh/D

ⓞⓜS.N.C.P.A. - Société Nationale de Cellulose et Papier Alfa
Kasserine Mill
Ownership: 100% by Tunisian State (Public)
6 Av. Habib Bourguiba
1200 Kasserine, Gouvernorat de Kasserine
Tunisia
Phone: (216) 71 349 633
Fax: (216) 71 342 985/77 474600
Email: sncpa@planet.tn
Web Address: www.sncpa.com.tn
Personnel:
Gen. Mgr. & Chmn.: Jlaïel Mongi
Phone: (216) 77 478358
Fax: (216) 71 342985
Commer. Mgr.: Mr. Hedi Mraihi
Phone: (216) 77 411 574
Fax: (216) 77 474 600
Email: sncpa.kasserine@planet.tn
Commercial Mgr. (Paper): Zohra Naili
Phone: (216) 71 349 633
Fax: (216) 71 342 988
Email: hammamizohra@planet.tn
Export Mgr.: Mohammed Ali Messaoud
Phone: (216) 71 349 633
Purch. Mgr.: Hamed Gassandi
Phone: (216) 71 348 168
Fax: (216) 71 42988
Mill Mgr.: Mr. Nourredine Salhi
Phone: (216) 77 475 560
Maint. Mgr.: Mr. Tidjani Chaabani
Phone: (216) 71 349 633
Total Employees of Company: 897
Total Employees at this Location: 600
Type of Operation: Pulp mill, Paper mill
Pulp Grades and Capacities:
Total pulp capacity: 4,526 mt/y
Chemical Pulp: 4,526 mt/y
Pulp Mill Data:
Chemical Pulping Systems:
Continuous digesters: 2
Pulp Lines: 1
Bleach Plant Systems: 1
No. 1, Sequence: CEH, Capacity 16,000 admt/y
Chemical Recovery Equipment:
Evaporator lines: 1
Recovery boilers: 1
Lime Kiln
Pulp Dryers:
Air Float dryers 1
Paper/Paperboard Grades and Capacities:
Total paper and paperboard capacity: 25,000 mt/y
Uncoated woodfree/freesheet: 25,000 mt/y
Paper and Paperboard Mill Data:
Stock Preparation:
Pulpers: 2
Refiners: 3
Paper Machines: 1
No. 1, fourdrinier, total capacity 25,000 mt/y, Trim width 3.6 m, Uncoated woodfree/freesheet
Finishing Equipment:
Rewinders: 1 at 1,400 mt/y
Sheeters: 1 at 3,570,000 mt/y
Energy Data:
Power boilers: 1
Steam turbines: 1 at 3.75 MW
Electrical demand for mill: 88 MWh/D

ⓞⓜSOPAFI, Société des Papiers Fins S.A.R.L.
Sbeitla Mill
Ownership: 100% by private company
Route de Sbiba, km 5
1250 Sbeitla, Gouvernorat de Kasserine
Tunisia
Phone: (216) 77 465 277/600
Fax: (216) 77 465 078
Email: adsopafi@topnet.tn
Personnel:
Gen. Mgr.: Ali Djellidi
Phone: (216) 77 465 600/277/601
Prod. Mgr.: Nasrali Khemaies
Phone: (216) 98 568 127 (gsm)
Email: adsopafi@topnet.tn
Commercial Mgr.: Ali Bahri
Phone: (216) 98 678 929 (gsm)
Procurement and Qlty. Officer: Fawzi Gueraoui
Phone: (216) 77 465 277/600
Maint. Mgr.: Missaoui Habib
Phone: (216) 77 465 277/600
Total Employees at this Location: 60
Type of Operation: Paper mill
Paper/Paperboard Grades and Capacities:
Total paper and paperboard capacity: 3,000 mt/y
Tissue: 3,000 mt/y
Paper and Paperboard Mill Data:
Stock Preparation:
Pulpers: 1
Refiners: 3
Paper Machines: 1
No. 1, Yankee dryer, fourdrinier, total capacity 3,000 mt/y, Trim width 2.2 m, Tissue
Finishing Equipment:
Winders: 1 at 5,250 mt/y
Rewinders: 1 at 3,000 mt/y
Sheeters: 1 at 1,400 mt/y
Energy Data:
Power boilers: 2
Electrical demand for mill: 13 MWh/D

ⓞSotipapier - Société Tunisienne Industrielle du Papier et du Carton - S.A.R.L.
Ownership: 28.99% by Hamrouni Group, 18.18% by Value Consulting, 18.18% by HAN TN, 1.01% by other Private, 33.64% by HAN LUX
Route de Sousse, Km. 6
8033 Megrine
Tunisia
Phone: (216) 71 434022
Fax: (216) 71 434793
Email: sotunol@planet.tn
Web Address: www.hamrouni.com
Personnel:
Chmn. & CEO: Abdelkader Hamrouni
Phone: (216) 71 732 928
Fax: (216) 71 434 793
Finan. Dir.: Lotfi Ayad
Phone: (216) 71 434022
Fax: (216) 71 434793
Total Employees of Company: 282
Mill Locations:
Sotipapier - Société Tunisienne Industrielle du Papier et du Carton - S.A.R.L., Belli Mill, Gouvernorat de Nabeul, 8022 Belli, Tunisia, Capacity: 55,000 mt/y, (Paperboard mill)
Phone: (216) 72 200 120/216
Fax: (216) 72 200 303
Email: messaoud.halleb@planet.tn

ⓜSotipapier - Société Tunisienne Industrielle du Papier et du Carton - S.A.R.L.
Belli Mill
Gouvernorat de Nabeul
8022 Belli
Tunisia
Phone: (216) 72 200 120/216
Fax: (216) 72 200 303
Email: messaoud.halleb@planet.tn
Web Address: www.hamrouni.com
Personnel:
Mill Mgr./Tech. Mgr.: Messaoud Halleb
Phone: (216) 98 342 389
Head of Mechanic Dept.: Jamel Mezghani
Phone: (216) 72 200 120/216
Maint. Mgr. (Electric Div.): Lotfi Ben Amara

Uganda

Phone: (216) 72 200 216
Email: lofti.benamara@planet.tn
Total Employees at this Location: 277
Type of Operation: Paperboard mill
Pulp Grades and Capacities:
  Total pulp capacity: 24,911 mt/y
  Recycled Pulping: 24,911 mt/y
Pulp Mill Data:
  Recycled Fiber Treatment Lines:
  Recycled packaging pulping lines
Paper/Paperboard Grades and Capacities:
  Total paper and paperboard capacity: 55,000 mt/y
  Packaging papers: 30,000 mt/y
  Linerboard: 10,000 mt/y
  Corrugating medium/fluting: 15,000 mt/y
Paper and Paperboard Mill Data:
  Stock Preparation:
  Pulpers: 5
  Refiners: 10
Paper Machines: 2
No. 2, fourdrinier, total capacity 30,000 mt/y, Trim width 3.2 m, Packaging papers
No. 3, fourdrinier, total capacity 25,000 mt/y, Trim width 2.65 m, Corrugating medium/fluting, Linerboard
Finishing Equipment:
  Winders: 3 at 90,000 mt/y
  Rewinders: 4
  Sheeters: 1 at 7,000 mt/y
Energy Data:
  Power boilers: 3
  Combustion turbines: 2 at 5.6, 5.6 MW
  Electrical demand for mill: 92 MWh/D

ⓘⓜ SPAC, Société Papier et Carton
Sbeitla Mill

Ownership: 100% by private company
Route de Sbiba, Km 5, BP 82
1250 Sbeitla, Gouvernorat de Kasserine
Tunisia
  Phone: (216) 77 466264
  Fax: (216) 77 466904
  Email: spac.tunisie@yahoo.fr
Personnel:
  Gen. Mgr.: Ahmed Aouni
  Phone: (216) 21 163693
  Commercial Department Head: Tlili Belgacem
  Phone: (216) 97 036035
  Admin. Officer: Siham Aouni
  Phone: (216) 77 466264
  Email: spac.tunisie@yahoo.fr
Total Employees of Company: 50
Total Employees at this Location: 50
Type of Operation: Paperboard mill
Pulp Mill Data:
  Recycled Fiber Treatment Lines:
  Pulpers at 3,000
Paper/Paperboard Grades and Capacities:
  Total paper and paperboard capacity: 3,000 mt/y
  Linerboard: 3,000 mt/y
Paper and Paperboard Mill Data:
  Stock Preparation:
  Pulpers: 2
  Refiners: 2
Paper Machines: 1
No. 1, multi-cylinder, total capacity 3,000 mt/y, Trim width 1.9 m, Linerboard
Finishing Equipment:
  Winders: 1 at 3,000 mt/y
  Rewinders: 1
  Sheeters: 1 at 3,000 mt/y
Energy Data:
  Power boilers: 1
  Electrical demand for mill: 7 MWh/D

ⓘⓜ Tunisie Ouate
Enfidha Mill

Ownership: 100% by private company
Industrial Zone
4030 Enfidha, Gouvernorat de Sousse
Tunisia
  Phone: (216) 73 250 480/307
  Fax: (216) 73 250 310
  Email: touate@gnet.tn
  Web Address: www.tunisieouate.com
Personnel:
  Man. Dir. & Chmn.: Abdelaziz Kooli
  Phone: (216) 98 404150
  Fax: (216) 73 250 955
  Depty. Man. Dir.: Aziz Ghassen Kooli
  Phone: (213) 73 250 480/307
  Tech. Mgr.: Mr. Smiri Belgacem
  Phone: (216) 97 596 637/98 402 789
  Commer. Mgr.: Mohamed Ali Kooli
  Phone: (216) 73 250 480
Total Employees of Company: 130
Total Employees at this Location: 130
Type of Operation: Paper mill
Pulp Grades and Capacities:
  Total pulp capacity: 4,926 mt/y
  Recycled Pulping: 4,926 mt/y
Pulp Mill Data:
  Recycled Fiber Treatment Lines:
  Flotation deinking lines: 1
Paper/Paperboard Grades and Capacities:
  Total paper and paperboard capacity: 21,000 mt/y
  Tissue: 21,000 mt/y
Paper and Paperboard Mill Data:
  Stock Preparation:
  Pulpers: 3
  Refiners: 4
Paper Machines: 2
No. 1, fourdrinier, Yankee dryer, total capacity 6,000 mt/y, Trim width 2.1 m, Uncoated woodfree/freesheet, Tissue
No. 2, crescent former, Yankee dryer, total capacity 15,000 mt/y, Trim width 2.7 m, Tissue
Finishing Equipment:
  Rewinders: 2 at 20,000 mt/y
Energy Data:
  Power boilers: 2
  Electrical demand for mill: 62 MWh/D

ⓘ Cartonnerie Tunisienne SA

Ownership: 100% by Utic group
Zone Industrielle d' Ariana B.P. 101
1080 Tunis Cedex
Tunisia
  Phone: (216) 70 837 780, 70 837 847
  Fax: (216) 70 838 611
  Email: cartonnerie@utic.com.tn,
  cartonnerie@utic.com.tn
  Web Address: www.cartonnerie.com.tn,
  www.utic.com.tn
Personnel:
  Chmn. & CEO: Mr. Omri Salah
  Phone: (216) 70 837780/817/441
  Fax: (216) 70 838611
  Email: salah.omri@utic.com.tn
  Purch. Dir.: Mr Nabli Hamad
  Phone: (216) 70 837780/817/441
  Fax: (216) 70 838611
Total Employees of Company: 107
Total Employees at this Location: 7
Mill Locations:
Cartonnerie Tunisienne SA, Enfidha Mill, Z.I. Enfidha BP 42, 4030 Enfidha, Tunisia, Capacity: 30,000 mt/y, (Paperboard mill)
  Phone: (216) 73 250 447
  Fax: (216) 73 250 476
  Email: cartonnerie@utic.com.tn

ⓜ Cartonnerie Tunisienne SA
Enfidha Mill

Z.I. Enfidha BP 42
4030 Enfidha, Gouvernorat de Sousse
Tunisia
  Phone: (216) 73 250 447
  Fax: (216) 73 250 476
  Email: cartonnerie@utic.com.tn
  Web Address: www.utic.com.tn
Personnel:
  Asst. to Gen. Dir.: Fethi Azzouz
  Phone: (216) 73 250293
  Email: fethi.azzouz@utic.com.tn
  Prod. Mgr.: Amor Mansar
  Phone: (216) 73 250293
  Email: amor.mansar@utic.com.tn
  Commer. Dir.: Zakaria Souayah
  Phone: (216) 97 642 466
  Email: zakaria.souayah@utic.com.tn
Total Employees at this Location: 100
Type of Operation: Paperboard mill
Pulp Grades and Capacities:
  Total pulp capacity: 25,107 mt/y
  Recycled Pulping: 25,107 mt/y
Pulp Mill Data:
  Recycled Fiber Treatment Lines:
  Recycled packaging pulping lines
Paper/Paperboard Grades and Capacities:
  Total paper and paperboard capacity: 30,000 mt/y
  Boxboard/cartonboard: 30,000 mt/y
Paper and Paperboard Mill Data:
  Stock Preparation:
  Pulpers: 6
  Refiners: 2
Paper Machines: 1
No. 1, cylinder, total capacity 30,000 mt/y, Trim width 2.3 m, Boxboard/cartonboard
Coating Machines: 1
No. 2, on machine
Finishing Equipment:
  Rewinders: 1 at 35,000 mt/y
  Sheeters: 3 at 40,000 mt/y
Energy Data:
  Power boilers: 2
  Electrical demand for mill: 48 MWh/D

UGANDA

ⓘⓜ Yueyang Paper International Uganda
Kampala Mill

Ownership: 100% by Mr. Xiaoming Lou
Nakawa Industrial Area
Kampala
Uganda
Type of Operation: Paper mill
Paper/Paperboard Grades and Capacities:
  Total paper and paperboard capacity: 2,000 mt/y
  Tissue: 2,000 mt/y
Paper and Paperboard Mill Data:
Paper Machines: 1
PM 1, total capacity 2,000 mt/y, Trim width 1.57 m, Tissue

ZAMBIA

ⓘⓜ Zambezi Paper Mills Ltd.
Ndola Mill

Ownership: 100% by The Sharma Group
Plot 4087/5/6/7, Mushili Rd., Heavy Industrial Area
Ndola
Zambia
Mailing Address: PO Box 71400, Ndola, Zambia
  Phone: (260) 212 650829/834/835
  Fax: (260) 212 650401/137
  Email: zpm@zamnet.zm,
  cdsharma@zambezipaper.net,
  inorgroup@zamnet.zm

Zimbabwe

Personnel:
Man. Dir.: Chantrakant D. Sharma
Phone: (260) 212 650829/834/835
Email: cdsharma@zambezipaper.net
Tech. Dir.: Raju D. Sharma
Phone: (260) 212 650829/834/835
Tech. Mgr.: Nigeefh Kumar
Total Employees at this Location: 295
Type of Operation: Paper mill
Pulp Grades and Capacities:
Total pulp capacity: 40,500 mt/y
Pulp available for market: 20,000 mt/y
Mechanical Pulp: 30,000 mt/y
Recycled Pulping: 10,500 mt/y

Pulp Mill Data:
Mechanical Pulping Systems:
CTMP systems: 1
TMP systems: 1
Recycled Fiber Treatment Lines:
Flotation deinking lines: 1 at 3,650 admt/y
Pulpers: 2 at 9,200 admt/y
Pulp Dryers:
Air Float dryers 1, Flash dryers 1
Paper/Paperboard Grades and Capacities:
Total paper and paperboard capacity: 12,000 mt/y
Tissue: 4,000 mt/y
Packaging papers
Containerboard
Paper and Paperboard Mill Data:
Stock Preparation:
Pulpers: 2
Refiners: 7
Paper Machines: 2
No. 1, fourdrinier, Yankee dryer, total capacity 4,000 mt/y, Trim width 2.1 m, Tissue
No. 2, fourdrinier, total capacity 8,000 mt/y, Trim width 2.5 m, Packaging papers, Containerboard
Finishing Equipment:
Supercalenders: 1
Rewinders: 3
Sheeters: 1
Energy Data:
Power boilers: 3

ZIMBABWE

ⓘ Art Corporation
Ownership: 100% by Amalgamated Regional Trading
202 Seke Road, Graniteside
Harare
Zimbabwe
Phone: (263) 4 770097
Fax: (263) 4 770137
Email: enquiries@artcorp.co.zw
Web Address: www.artcorp.co.zw
Personnel:
CEO: R. K. Zirobwa
Phone: (263) 4 770136
Fax: (263) 4 770137
Email: rzirobwa@artcorp.co.zw
CFO: Nomsa Dube
Phone: (263) 4 770129
Fax: (263) 4 770137
Email: ndube@artcorp.co.zw
COO: Tapiwa Makombe
Phone: (263) 4 770097
Fax: (263) 4 770137
Email: tmakombe@artcorp.co.zw
Group Tech. Dir.: Nesbert Marisa
Phone: (263) 4 770097
Fax: (263) 4 770135
Email: nmarisa@artcorp.co.zw
Total Employees of Company: 1,800
Total Employees at this Location: 49
Mill Locations:
KPM Kadoma Paper Mills, Kadoma Mill, Owl Mine Rd., Industrial Sites PO Box 250, Kadoma, Zimbabwe, Capacity: 19,000 mt/y, (Pulp mill, Paper mill)
Phone: (263) 68 22311/4/23605/24221
Fax: (263) 68 26608
Email: sales@kpm.artcorp.co.zw

ⓘ KPM Kadoma Paper Mills
Kadoma Mill
Ownership: 100% by Art Corporation
Owl Mine Rd., Industrial Sites PO Box 250
Kadoma
Zimbabwe
Phone: (263) 68 22311/4/23605/24221
Fax: (263) 68 26608
Email: sales@kpm.artcorp.co.zw
Web Address: www.artcorp.co.zw
Personnel:
Tech. Account Exec.: David Masina
Phone: (263) 68 22311
Fax: (263) 68 26608
Email: dmasina@artcorp.co.zw
Total Employees at this Location: 257
Type of Operation: Pulp mill, Paper mill
Pulp Grades and Capacities:
Total pulp capacity: 5,000 mt/y

Pulp Mill Data:
Chemical Pulping Systems:
Continuous digesters: 2
Paper/Paperboard Grades and Capacities:
Total paper and paperboard capacity: 19,000 mt/y
Uncoated woodfree/freesheet
Tissue: 5,000 mt/y
Linerboard: 9,000 mt/y
Corrugating medium/fluting: 5,000 mt/y
Paper and Paperboard Mill Data:
Stock Preparation:
Pulpers: 2
Refiners: 3
Paper Machines: 2
No. 1, Yankee dryer, total capacity 5,000 mt/y, Trim width 1.65 m, Tissue
No. 2, fourdrinier, total capacity 9,000 mt/y, Trim width 2 m, Uncoated woodfree/freesheet, Linerboard, Corrugating medium/fluting
Finishing Equipment:
Rewinders: 2
Energy Data:
Power boilers: 4

Pulp and Paper Grades Produced

Pulp Grades Produced

Chemical Pulp

Alberta-Pacific Forest Industries Inc. (Al-Pac)
Boyle Mill
Boyle, Alberta, Canada

Alto Paraná S.A.
Misiones Mill
Puerto Esperanza, Misiones, Argentina

An Hoa Paper and Pulp Factory
Vinh Loi Commune Mill
Vinh Loi Commune, Tuyen Quang, Vietnam

Anhui Huatai Forest Pulp & Paper Co., Ltd.
Anqing (Anhui Huatai) Mill
Anqing, Anhui, China

Appvion, Inc.
Roaring Spring Mill
Roaring Spring, Pennsylvania, United States

Arjowiggins Ltda.
Salto Mill
Salto, São Paulo, Brazil

Arkhangelsk Pulp & Paper Mill
Novodvinsk (Arkhangelsk - APPM) Mill
Novodvinsk, Arkhangelsk Region, Russia

Asia Symbol (Shandong) Pulp & Paper Co., Ltd.
Rizhao Mill
Rizhao, Shandong, China

Aurangabad Paper Mills Ltd.
Aurangabad Mill
Aurangabad, Maharashtra, India

Australian Paper
Maryvale Mill
Morwell, Victoria, Australia

AV Cell Inc.
Atholville Mill
Atholville, New Brunswick, Canada

AV Nackawic Inc.
Nackawic Mill
Nackawic, New Brunswick, Canada

AV Terrace Bay Pulp Inc.
Terrace Bay Mill
Terrace Bay, Ontario, Canada

Bahia Specialty Cellulose S.A. ("BSC")
Camaçari Mill
Camaçari, Bahia, Brazil

Baikalskiy Pulp and Paper Mill (Baikal)
Baikalsk Mill
Baikalsk, Irkutsk Region, Russia

Ballarpur Industries Ltd. (BILT)
Ballarshah (Unit Ballarpur)
Ballarshah, Maharashtra, India

Ballarpur Industries Ltd. (BILT)
Kamalapuram Mill
Mangapet, Warangal, Andhra Pradesh, India

Ballarpur Industries Ltd. (BILT)
Sewa Mill
Jeypore, Dist. Koratpur, Odisha, India

Ballarpur Industries Ltd. (BILT)
Shree Gopal Mill
Yamunanagar, Haryana, India

Bashundhara Paper Mills Ltd.
Unit 2
Sonargaon, New Town, Narayanganj, Bangladesh

BELIŠCE d.d.
Belišce Mill
Belišce, Salvonia, Croatia

BillerudKorsnäs AB
Frövi Mill
Frövi, Sweden

BillerudKorsnäs AB
Gävle Mill
Gävle, Sweden

BillerudKorsnäs AB
Gruvön Mill
Grums, Sweden

BillerudKorsnäs AB
Karlsborg Mill
Karlsborg, Sweden

BillerudKorsnäs AB
Skärblacka Mill
Skärblacka, Sweden

Bindal Papers Limited
Muzzaffarnagar Mill
Muzzaffarnagar, Uttar Pradesh, India

Bio-PAPPEL Kraft
Atenquique Mill
Atenquique, Jalisco, Mexico

Biocel Paskov a.s.
Paskov Mill
Paskov, Czech Republic

Boise Paper
International Falls Mill
International Falls, Minnesota, United States

Boise Paper
Jackson Mill
Jackson, Alabama, United States

Boise Paper
Wallula Mill
Wallula, Washington, United States

Borregaard ChemCell
Sarpsborg Mill
Sarpsborg, Norway

Bratsk Branch of Ilim Group
Bratsk Mill
Bratsk, Irkutsk Region, Russia

BUKOCEL, a.s.
Hencovce Mill
Hencovce, Slovakia

Caima-Indústria de Celulose S.A.
Constância Mill
Constância, Portugal

Canfor Pulp Ltd.
Intercontinental Mill
Prince George, British Columbia, Canada

Canfor Pulp Ltd.
Northwood Mill
Prince George, British Columbia, Canada

Canfor Pulp Ltd.
Prince George (Pulp & Paper) Mill
Prince George, British Columbia, Canada

Cariboo Pulp & Paper Co.
Cariboo Mill
Quesnel, British Columbia, Canada

Carter Holt Harvey Pulp & Paper
Kinleith Mill
Tokoroa, New Zealand

Carter Holt Harvey Pulp & Paper
Tasman Mill
Kawerau, Bay of Plenty, New Zealand

Cascade Pacific Pulp, LLC
Halsey Mill
Halsey, Oregon, United States

Catalyst Paper Corporation
Crofton Mill
Crofton, British Columbia, Canada

Celtejo - Empresa de Celulose do Tejo, S.A.
Celtejo Mill
Vila Velha de Rodão, Portugal

Celulosa Arauco y Constitución S.A.
Arauco Pulp Mill
Arauco, VIII - Región del Biobío, Chile

Celulosa Arauco y Constitución S.A.
Constitución Mill
Constitución, VII - Región del Maule, Chile

Celulosa Arauco y Constitución S.A.
Licancel Mill
Licantén, Curico, VII - Región del Maule, Chile

Celulosa Arauco y Constitución S.A.
Nueva Aldea
Ranquil, VIII - Región del Biobío, Chile

Chemical Pulp

Celulosa Arauco y Constitución S.A.
Valdivia Pulp Mill
Valdivia, XIV - Región de Los Ríos, Chile

Celulosa Argentina S.A.
Capitán Bermúdez Mill
Capitán Bermúdez, Santa Fé, Argentina

Celulosas de Asturias S.A. (CEASA)
Navia Mill
Navia, Asturias, Spain

Celulose Beira Industrial (Celbi) S.A.
Celbi Mill
Figueira da Foz, Portugal

Celulose Irani S.A.
Vargem Bonita Mill
Vargem Bonita, Santa Catarina, Brazil

CENIBRA - Celulose Nipo-Brasileira S.A.
Belo Oriente Mill
Belo Oriente, Minas Gerais, Brazil

Century Pulp & Paper
Lalkua Mill
Nainital, Uttarakhand, India

Chenming Paper Holdings Ltd.
Shouguang (Shouguang Chenming Specialty Paper No. 1) Mill
Shouguang, Shandong, China

Chongqing Lee & Man Paper Co., Ltd.
Chongqing Mill
Chongqing, Chongqing, China

Chouka Pulp & Paper Mill
Rezvanshahr Mill
Rezvanshahr, Iran

Chuetsu Pulp & Paper Co., Ltd.
Sendai Mill
Satsumasendai-shi, Kagoshima Pref., Japan

Chuetsu Pulp & Paper Co., Ltd.
Takaoka (Nohmachi) Mill
Takaoka-shi, Toyama Pref., Japan

Chung Hwa Pulp Corporation
Hualien Mill
Chi An, Hualien County, Taiwan

Clearwater Paper Corporation
Cypress Bend Mill, McGehee Mill
McGehee, Arkansas City, Arkansas, United States

Clearwater Paper Corporation
Lewiston Mill
Lewiston, Idaho, United States

CMPC Celulosa S.A.
Laja Mill
Laja, VIII - Región del Biobío, Chile

CMPC Celulosa S.A.
Pacífico Mill
Mininco, Comuna Collipulli, IX - Región de la Araucanía, Chile

CMPC Celulosa S.A.
Santa Fe Mill
Nacimiento, VIII - Región del Biobío, Chile

CMPC Celulose Riograndense
Guaíba Mill
Guaíba, Rio Grande do Sul, Brazil

COCELPA - Companhia de Celulose e Papel do Paraná
Araucária Mill
Araucária, Paraná, Brazil

Daio Paper Corp.
Kani Mill
Kani-shi, Gifu Pref., Japan

Daio Paper Corp.
Mishima Mill
Shikokuchuo-shi, Ehime Pref., Japan

Daishowa-Marubeni International Ltd.
Peace River Pulp Division
Peace River, Alberta, Canada

Delta Paper Mills Ltd.
Vendra Mill
Vendra, West Godavari Dist, Andhra Pradesh, India

Domsjö Fabriker
Örnsköldsvik Mill
Örnsköldsvik, Sweden

Domtar Corporation
Ashdown Mill
Ashdown, Arkansas, United States

Domtar Corporation
Dryden Mill
Dryden, Ontario, Canada

Domtar Corporation
Espanola Mill
Espanola, Ontario, Canada

Domtar Corporation
Hawesville Mill
Hawesville, Kentucky, United States

Domtar Corporation
Johnsonburg Mill
Johnsonburg, Pennsylvania, United States

Domtar Corporation
Kamloops Mill
Kamloops, British Columbia, Canada

Domtar Corporation
Kingsport Mill
Kingsport, Tennessee, United States

Domtar Corporation
Marlboro Mill
Bennettsville, South Carolina, United States

Domtar Corporation
Nekoosa Mill
Nekoosa, Wisconsin, United States

Domtar Corporation
Plymouth Mill
Plymouth, North Carolina, United States

Domtar Corporation
Rothschild Mill
Rothschild, Wisconsin, United States

Domtar Corporation
Windsor Mill
Windsor, Quebec, Canada

Dongyang Paper Mfg. Co., Ltd.
Asan Mill
Ansan-si, Chungcheongnam-do, South Korea

Double A (1991) Public Co., Ltd.
Prachinburi Mill
Amphur Sri Maha Phote, Prachinburi, Thailand

Eldorado Celulose e Papel
Três Lagoas Mill
Três Lagoas, Mato Grosso do Sul, Brazil

ENCE Energia y Celulosa SA
Huelva Mill
Huelva, Spain

ENCE Energia y Celulosa SA
Pontevedra Mill
Pontevedra, Spain

Europac Kraft Viana
Viana do Castelo Mill
Viana do Castelo, Portugal

Evergreen Packaging Inc.
Canton Mill
Canton, North Carolina, United States

Evergreen Packaging Inc.
Pine Bluff Mill
Pine Bluff, Arkansas, United States

Expera Specialty Solutions
Kaukauna Mill
Kaukauna, Wisconsin, United States

Expera Specialty Solutions
Mosinee Mill
Mosinee, Wisconsin, United States

FANAPEL - Fábrica Nacional de Papel S.A.
Juan Lacaze Mill
Juan Lacaze, Colonia, Uruguay

Faruki Pulp Mills Ltd.
Mangowal, Gujrat Mill
Mangowal, Gujrat, Punjab, Pakistan

Fibre Excellence Saint-Gaudens
St. Gaudens Mill
Saint Gaudens Cedex, France

Fibre Excellence Tarascon
Tarascon Mill
Tarascon Cedex, France

Fibria Celulose SA
Aracruz Mill
Aracruz, Espírito Santo, Brazil

Fibria Celulose SA
Jacareí Mill
Jacareí, São Paulo, Brazil

Fibria Celulose SA
Três Lagoas Mill
Três Lagoas, Mato Grosso do Sul, Brazil

Finch Paper, LLC
Glens Falls Mill
Glens Falls, New York, United States

Flambeau River Papers, LLC
Park Falls Mill
Park Falls, Wisconsin, United States

Fortress Specialty Cellulose Inc.
Thurso Mill
Thurso, Quebec, Canada

Chemical Pulp

Fujian Qingshan Paper Industry Co., Ltd.
Qingzhou Mill
Qingzhou, Fujian, China

Gascogne Paper
Mimizan Mill
Mimizan, Landes, France

Georgia-Pacific LLC
Big Island Mill
Big Island, Virginia, United States

Georgia-Pacific LLC
Brewton Mill
Brewton, Alabama, United States

Georgia-Pacific LLC
Camas Mill
Camas, Washington, United States

Georgia-Pacific LLC
Cedar Springs Mill
Cedar Springs, Georgia, United States

Georgia-Pacific LLC
Crossett Mill
Crossett, Arkansas, United States

Georgia-Pacific LLC
Monticello Mill
Monticello, Mississippi, United States

Georgia-Pacific LLC
Naheola Mill
Pennington, Alabama, United States

Georgia-Pacific LLC
Palatka Mill
Palatka, Florida, United States

Georgia-Pacific LLC
Port Hudson Mill
Zachary, Louisiana, United States

Georgia-Pacific LLC
Toledo Mill
Toledo, Oregon, United States

Georgia-Pacific LLC
Wauna Mill
Clatskanie, Oregon, United States

Glatfelter
Chillicothe Mill
Chillicothe, Ohio, United States

Glatfelter
Spring Grove Mill
Spring Grove, Pennsylvania, United States

Graphic Packaging International Inc.
Macon Mill
Macon, Georgia, United States

Graphic Packaging International Inc.
West Monroe Mill
West Monroe, Louisiana, United States

Grasim Industries Ltd
Harihar Polyfibers & Grasilene Division
Kumarpatanam, Karnataka, India

Green Bay Packaging Inc.
Morrilton Mill
Morrilton, Arkansas, United States

Greif Inc.
Riverville Mill
Amherst, Virginia, United States

Grupo Papelero Scribe, S.A. de C.V.
Morelia Mill
Morelia, Michoacán, Mexico

Grupo Portucel Soporcel
Fábrica de Cacia
Cacia, Aveiro, Portugal

Grupo Portucel Soporcel
Figueira da Foz Mill
Figueira da Foz, Coimbra, Portugal

Grupo Portucel Soporcel
Setúbal Mill
Setúbal, Portugal

Guangdong Dingfeng Paper Corporation
Zhaoqing Mill
Zhaoqing, Guangdong, China

Guangxi Fangchenggang Hongyuan Pulp & Paper Co., Ltd.
Fangchenggang Mill
Fangchenggang, Guangxi, China

Guangxi Forest Lipu Paper Co., Ltd.
Lipu Mill
Lipu, Guangxi, China

Guangxi Guitang (Group) Stock Co., Ltd
Guigang Mill
Guigang, Guangxi, China

Guangxi Guofa Forest & Paper Co. Ltd.
Liuzhou (Guangxi Guofa Forest & Paper) Mill
Liuzhou, Guangxi, China

Guangxi Heda Paper Co. Ltd.
Hezhou Mill
Hezhou, Guangxi, China

Guangxi Liangmianzhen Paper Co., Ltd.
Liuzhou Mill
Liuzhou, Guangxi, China

Guangxi Nanning Phoenix Pulp & Paper Co. Ltd.
Nanning Mill
Nanning, Guangxi, China

Hai Ha Pulp Mill
Bac Quang Dist. Mill
Bac Quang Dist., Ha Giang Province, Vietnam

Hainan Jinhai Pulp & Paper Industry Co., Ltd.
Yangpu (Hainan Jinhai Pulp & Paper Industry) Mill
Haikou, Hainan, China

Hartija Ko DOO
Kochani Mill
Kochani, Macedonia

Heilongjiang Fuyu Chenming Paper Co., Ltd.
Qiqihar (Heilongjiang Fuyu Chenming Paper) Mill
Qiqihar, Heilongjiang, China

Heilongjiang Yuejing Pulp & Paper Co., Ltd.
Harbin Mill
Harbin, Heilongjiang, China

Henan Yilin Paper Co., Ltd.
Xuchang Mill
Xuchang, Henan, China

Hindustan Newsprint Ltd.
Kottayam Dist. Mill
Kottayam Dist., Kerala, India

Hindustan Paper Corp. Ltd., CPM
Cachar Paper Mill
Cachar, Assam, India

Hindustan Paper Corp. Ltd., NPM
Nagaon Paper Mill
Morigaon, Assam, India

Hinton Pulp
Hinton Pulp
Hinton, Alberta, Canada

Hokuetsu Kishu Paper Co. Ltd.
Kishu Mill
Minamimuro-gun, Mie Pref., Japan

Hokuetsu Kishu Paper Co. Ltd.
Niigata Mill
Niigata-shi, Niigata Pref., Japan

Horizon Pulp & Paper Ltd.
Kehra Mill
Kehra, Estonia

Howe Sound Pulp and Paper Corporation
Port Mellon Mill
Port Mellon, British Columbia, Canada

Hubei Jianli Maxleaf Paper Co., Ltd.
Jingzhou Mill
Jingzhou, Hubei, China

Hunan Juntai Pulp & Paper Co., Ltd
Huaihua Mill
Huaihua, Hunan, China

Hunan Tiger Forest & Paper Group Co., Ltd
Yongzhou Mill
Yongzhou, Hunan, China

Hunan Tiger Forest & Paper Group Hongjiang Paper Co., Ltd
Hongjiang Mill
Huaihua, Hunan, China

Hunan Tiger Forest & Paper Group Yuanjiang Paper Co., Ltd.
Yuanjiang Mill
Yuanjiang, Hunan, China

Hunan Tiger Forest & Paper Group Yueyang Paper Co., Ltd.
Yueyang Mill
Yueyang, Hunan, China

Hunan Yueyang Fengli Pulp & Paper Co. Ltd.
Yueyang Mill
Yueyang, Hunan, China

Hyogo Pulp Industries, Ltd.
Tanigawa Mill
Tanba-shi, Hyogo Pref., Japan

Iggesund Paperboard AB
Iggesund Mill
Iggesund, Sweden

Chemical Pulp

Iguaçu Celulose Papel S.A.
Piraí do Sul Mill
Piraí do Sul, Paraná, Brazil

International Paper - Kwidzyn Sp. z o.o.
Kwidzyn Mill
Kwidzyn, Poland

International Paper APPM Ltd.
Rajahmundry Mill
Rajahmundry, East Godavari, Andhra Pradesh, India

International Paper Co.
Augusta Mill
Augusta, Georgia, United States

International Paper Co.
Bogalusa Mill
Bogalusa, Louisiana, United States

International Paper Co.
Courtland Mill
Courtland, Alabama, United States

International Paper Co.
Eastover Mill
Eastover, South Carolina, United States

International Paper Co.
Franklin Mill
Franklin, Virginia, United States

International Paper Co.
Georgetown Mill
Georgetown, South Carolina, United States

International Paper Co.
Mansfield Mill
Mansfield, Louisiana, United States

International Paper Co.
Orange Mill
Orange, Texas, United States

International Paper Co.
Pensacola Mill
Cantonment, Florida, United States

International Paper Co.
Pine Hill Mill
Pine Hill, Alabama, United States

International Paper Co.
Prattville Mill
Prattville, Alabama, United States

International Paper Co.
Red River Mill
Campti, Louisiana, United States

International Paper Co.
Riegelwood Mill
Riegelwood, North Carolina, United States

International Paper Co.
Riverdale Mill
Selma, Alabama, United States

International Paper Co.
Rome Mill
Rome, Georgia, United States

International Paper Co.
Savannah Mill
Savannah, Georgia, United States

International Paper Co.
Springfield Mill
Springfield, Oregon, United States

International Paper Co.
Texarkana Mill
Domino, Texas, United States

International Paper Co.
Ticonderoga Mill
Ticonderoga, New York, United States

International Paper Co.
Valliant Mill
Valliant, Oklahoma, United States

International Paper Co.
Vicksburg Mill
Vicksburg, Mississippi, United States

International Paper do Brasil Ltda.
Luiz Antônio Mill
Luiz Antonio, São Paulo, Brazil

International Paper do Brasil Ltda.
Mogi Guaçu Mill
Mogi Guaçu, São Paulo, Brazil

International Paper SA
Saillat Mill
Saint-Junien, France

Interstate Paper L.L.C.
Riceboro Mill
Riceboro, Georgia, United States

Irving Pulp & Paper, Ltd.
Saint John West Mill
Saint John, New Brunswick, Canada

IsraPaper Paper Industries Ltd.
Netanya Mill
Netanya, Israel

ITC Limited, Paperboards & Specialty Papers Division
Bhadrachalam Mill
Khammam, Bhadrachalam, Andhra Pradesh, India

Jiangsu Xinda Paper Co. Ltd.
Xinyi Mill
Xinyi, Jiangsu, China

Jilin Zhenlai Xinsheng Paper Co., Ltd.
Baicheng Mill
Baicheng, Jilin, China

JK Paper Ltd.
Central Pulp Mills-CPM, Songadh Mill
Fort Songadh, Dist. Tapi, Gujarat, India

JK Paper Ltd.
JK Paper Mills - JKPM
Jaykaypur, Rayagada Dist., Odisha, India

JSC Solikamskbumprom
Solikamsk Mill
Solikamsk, Perm Region, Russia

KapStone Kraft Paper Corporation
Longview Mill
Longview, Washington, United States

KapStone Kraft Paper Corporation
Roanoke Rapids Mill
Roanoke Rapids, North Carolina, United States

KapStone Paper Charleston Kraft LLC
North Charleston Mill
North Charleston, South Carolina, United States

Karnaphuli Paper Mills Ltd.
Chandraghona Mill
Chandraghona of Kaptai, Chittagong, Bangladesh

Kartontara, CJSC
Maykop Mill
Maykop, Adygheya Republic, Russia

Kitakami Hitec Paper Corp.
Kitakami-shi Mill
Kitakami-shi, Iwate Pref., Japan

Klabin S.A.
Angatuba Mill
Angatuba, São Paulo, Brazil

Klabin S.A.
Correia Pinto Mill
Correia Pinto, Santa Catarina, Brazil

Klabin S.A.
Monte Alegre Mill
Telêmaco Borba, Paraná, Brazil

Klabin S.A.
Otacílio Costa Mill
Otacílio Costa, Santa Catarina, Brazil

Kondopoga
Kondopoga Mill
Kondopoga, Karelia, Russia

Koryazhma Branch of Ilim Group
Kotlas Pulp and Paper Mill
Koryazhma, Arkhangelsk Region, Russia

Kotkamills Oy
Kotka Mill
Kotka, Finland

KPAQ Industries LLC
Saint Francisville Mill
Saint Francisville, Louisiana, United States

Kruger Wayagamack Inc.
Trois Rivières (Wayagamack) Mill
Trois-Rivières, Quebec, Canada

Kuantum Papers Ltd
Hoshiarpur Mill
Dist. Hoshiarpur, Punjab, India

La Cellulose du Maroc
Sidi Yahia Pulp Mill
Sidi Yahia Du Gharb, Kenitra, Morocco

Lake Utopia Paper
Saint George Mill
Utopia, New Brunswick, Canada

Lenzing AG
Lenzing Pulp Mill
Lenzing, Oberösterreich, Austria

Lwarcel Celulose Ltda.
Lençóis Paulista Mill
Lençóis Paulista, São Paulo, Brazil

Mackenzie Pulp Mill
Mackenzie Mill
Mackenzie, British Columbia, Canada

Marisky Pulp & Paper Mill
Volzhsk Mill
Volzhsk, Mari El Republic, Russia

Marusumi Paper Co., Ltd.
Kawanoe Mill
Shikokuchuo-shi, Ehime Pref., Japan

Chemical Pulp

Mazandaran Wood & Paper Industries Co.
Sari Mill
Sari, Mazandaran, Iran

MeadWestvaco Corporation
Covington Mill
Covington, Virginia, United States

MeadWestvaco Corporation
Evadale Mill
Evadale, Texas, United States

MeadWestvaco Corporation
Mahrt Mill
Cottonton, Alabama, United States

Metsä Board Husum
Husum Mill
Husum, Sweden

Metsä Fibre Oy
Äänekoski Mill
Äänekoski, Finland

Metsä Fibre Oy
Joutseno Mill
Joutseno, Finland

Metsä Fibre Oy
Kemi Mill
Kemi, Finland

Metsä Fibre Oy
Rauma Mill
Rauma, Finland

Mitsubishi Paper Mills Ltd.
Hachinohe Mill
Hachinohe-shi, Aomori, Japan

Mitsubishi Paper Mills Ltd.
Shirakawa Mill
Nishi-Shirakawa-gun, Fukushima Pref., Japan

Mondi
Pine Bluff Mill
Pine Bluff, Arkansas, United States

Mondi Dynäs AB
Väja Mill
Väja, Sweden

Mondi Frantschach GmbH
Frantschach Mill
St. Gertraud, Austria

Mondi Neusiedler GmbH
Kematen mill
Kematen, Niederösterreich, Austria

Mondi Richards Bay
Richards Bay Mill
Richards Bay, KwaZulu-Natal, South Africa

Mondi SCP a.s.
Ružomberok Mill
Ružomberok, Slovakia

Mondi Stambolijski EAD
Stambolijski Mill
Stambolijski, Bulgaria

Mondi Stetí
Štetí Mill
Štetí, Czech Republic

Mondi Swiecie S.A.
Swiecie Mill
Swiecie, Poland

Mondi Syktyvkar
Syktyvkar Mill
Syktyvkar, Komi Republic, Russia

Montes del Plata
Punta Pereira Mill
Punta Pereira, Colonia, Uruguay

Moorim P&P Co. Ltd.
Ulsan Mill
Ulsan-si, South Korea

Mopak Dalaman Pulp-Paper Cardboard Plant
Dalaman Mill
Mugla, Turkey

Mosaico Speciality Papers
Tolmezzo Mill
Tolmezzo, Udine, Italy

Mpact Limited
Piet Retief Mill
Piet Retief, Mpumalanga, South Africa

Mufindi Paper Mills (MPM)
Mgololo Mill
Mgololo, Iringa Region, Tanzania

Munksjö Aspa Bruk AB
Aspabruk Mill
Aspabruk, Sweden

Munksjö Paper AB
Billingsfors Mill
Billingsfors, Sweden

Munksjö Paper AB
Jönköping mill
Jönköping, Sweden

Myanma Paper and Chemical Industries (MPCI)
Sittuong No. 1 Paper Mill
Theinzayat, Mon State, Myanmar

Myanma Paper and Chemical Industries (MPCI)
Yeni Mill
Yedashe Township, Yeni, Bago Division, Myanmar

Mysore Paper Mills Ltd.
Shimoga Mill
Bhadravati, Shimoga, Karnataka, India

Nanaimo Forest Products Ltd
Harmac Mill
Nanaimo, British Columbia, Canada

Natron-Hayat d.o.o.
Maglaj Mill
Maglaj, Bosnia & Herzegovina

Neman Pulp & Paper Mill
Neman Mill
Neman, Kaliningrad Region, Russia

Neucel Specialty Cellulose Ltd.
Port Alice Mill
Port Alice, British Columbia, Canada

NewPage Corporation
Escanaba Mill
Escanaba, Michigan, United States

NewPage Corporation
Luke Mill
Luke, Maryland, United States

NewPage Corporation
Rumford Mill
Rumford, Maine, United States

NewPage Corporation
Wickliffe Mill
Wickliffe, Kentucky, United States

NewPage Corporation
Wisconsin Rapids Paper Mill
Wisconsin Rapids, Wisconsin, United States

Nine Dragons XingAn Paper Co., Ltd. (Inner Mongolia)
Zhalantun Mill
Zhalantun, Inner Mongolia, China

Nippon Paper Chemicals Co., Ltd.
Gotsu Mill
Gotsu-shi, Shimane Pref., Japan

Nippon Paper Industries Co., Ltd.
Akita Mill
Akita-shi, Akita Pref., Japan

Nippon Paper Industries Co., Ltd.
Fuji Mill
Fuji-shi, Shizuoka Pref., Japan

Nippon Paper Industries Co., Ltd.
Hokkaido Mill - Asahikawa
Asahikawa-shi, Hokkaido Pref., Japan

Nippon Paper Industries Co., Ltd.
Hokkaido Mill - Shiraoi
Shiraoi, Hokkaido Pref., Japan

Nippon Paper Industries Co., Ltd.
Hokkaido Mill - Yufutsu
Tomakomai-shi, Hokkaido Pref., Japan

Nippon Paper Industries Co., Ltd.
Ishinomaki Mill
Ishinomaki-shi, Miyagi Pref., Japan

Nippon Paper Industries Co., Ltd.
Iwakuni Mill
Iwakuni-shi, Yamaguchi Pref., Japan

Nippon Paper Industries Co., Ltd.
Iwanuma Mill
Iwanuma-shi, Miyagi Pref., Japan

Nippon Paper Industries Co., Ltd.
Kushiro Mill
Kushiro-shi, Hokkaido Pref., Japan

Nippon Paper Industries Co., Ltd.
Otake Mill
Otake-shi, Hiroshima Pref., Japan

Nippon Paper Industries Co., Ltd.
Yatsushiro Mill
Yatsushiro-shi, Kumamoto Pref., Japan

Nobrecel S.A. Celulose e Papel
Pindamonhangaba Mill
Pindamonhangaba, São Paulo, Brazil

Norampac
Cabano Mill
Cabano, Quebec, Canada

Chemical Pulp

Norampac
Trenton Mill
Trenton, Ontario, Canada

Nordic Paper Bäckhammar
Bäckhammars Bruk Mill
Kristinehamn, Sweden

Nordic Paper Seffle
Säffle Mill
Säffle, Sweden

Northern Pulp Nova Scotia Corporation
Pictou Mill
Abercrombie Point, Pictou County, Nova Scotia, Canada

OAO Pitkyaranta Pulp Mill
Pitkyaranta Mill
Pitkyaranta, Karelia, Russia

Oji F-Tex Co., Ltd.
Ebetsu Mill
Ebetsu-shi, Hokkaido Pref., Japan

Oji Materia Co., Ltd.
Kure Mill
Kure-shi, Hiroshima Pref., Japan

Oji Materia Co., Ltd.
Kushiro Mill
Kushiro-shi, Hokkaido Pref., Japan

Oji Materia Co., Ltd.
Nayoro Mill
Nayoro-shi, Hokkaido Pref., Japan

Oji Materia Co., Ltd.
Nikko Mill
Utsunomiya-shi, Tochigi Pref., Japan

Oku Iboku Pulp and Paper (OKIPP) Company Limited
Oku Iboku Mill
Ayadeghe, Oku Iboku, Akwa Ibom State, Nigeria

Old Town Fuel and Fiber
Maine Mill
Old Town, Maine, United States

Orient Paper Mills
Amlai mill
Shahdol, Madhya Pradesh, India

Orsa International Paper Embalagens S.A
Nova Campina Mill
Nova Campina, São Paulo, Brazil

OYKA Kagit Ve Ambalaj San Tic A.S.
Çaycuma Mill
Çaycuma, Zonguldak, Turkey

Packaging Corp. of America
Counce Mill
Counce, Tennessee, United States

Packaging Corp. of America
DeRidder Mill
DeRidder, Louisiana, United States

Packaging Corp. of America
Filer City Mill
Filer City, Michigan, United States

Packaging Corp. of America
Tomahawk Mill
Tomahawk, Wisconsin, United States

Packaging Corp. of America
Valdosta Mill
Valdosta, Georgia, United States

Pan Paper Mills
Webuye Mill
Webuye, Bungoma District, Western, Kenya

Panjapol Paper Industry Co. Ltd. and Panjapol Pulp Industry Public Co., Ltd.
Ayutthaya Mill
Bangsai District, Ayutthaya, Thailand

Papel Misionero S.A.I.F.C.
Puerto Mineral Mill
Capioví, Misiones, Argentina

Papelera del NOA S.A.
Rio Blanco Mill
Río Blanco, Jujuy, Jujuy, Argentina

Papelera Guipuzcoana de Zicuñaga S.A.
Hernani Mill
Hernani, Gipúzcoa, Spain

Paper Excellence Canada Holdings Corp
Skookumchuck Mill
Cranbrook, British Columbia, Canada

Papeteries de Saint-Girons
Saint-Girons Mill
Eycheil, Saint-Girons, France

Perm Pulp and Paper Mill
Perm Mill
Perm, Russia

Phoenix Pulp & Paper Public Company, Ltd.
Nam Phong Mill
Amphur Nampong, Khon Kaen, Thailand

Port Townsend Paper Corp.
Port Townsend Mill
Port Townsend, Washington, United States

Primo Tedesco S.A.
Caçador Mill
Caçador, Santa Catarina, Brazil

PT Indah Kiat Pulp & Paper Corp.
Perawang (PT Indah Kiat Pulp & Paper) Mill
Siak, Bengkalis, Riau, Sumatra, Indonesia

PT Lontar Papyrus Pulp & Paper Industry
Jambi (PT Lontar Papyrus Pulp & Paper) Mill
Jambi, South Sumatra, Indonesia

PT Riau Andalan Pulp & Paper (RAPP)
Riaupulp and Riaupaper Mill Kerinci
Pekanbaru - Riau, Riau, Sumatra, Indonesia

PT Tanjung Enim Lestari Pulp & Paper
Musi Pulp Mill
Kab. Muara Enim, South Sumatra, Indonesia

PT Toba Pulp Lestari Tbk. - TPL
Kec. Porsea, Kab. Toba Samosir Mill
Kec. Porsea, Kab. Toba Samosir, North Sumatra, Indonesia

PT Tri Daya Kreasi
Purwakarta Mill
Purwakarta, West Java, Indonesia

Rayonier Advanced Materials Inc.
Fernandina Beach Plant
Fernandina Beach, Florida, United States

Rayonier Advanced Materials Inc.
Jesup Plant
Jesup, Georgia, United States

Resolute Forest Products Canada Inc.
Fort Frances Mill
Fort Frances, Ontario, Canada

Resolute Forest Products Canada Inc.
Laurentide Mill
Grand-Mere, Quebec, Canada

Resolute Forest Products Canada Inc.
St Félicien Mill
Saint-Felicien, Quebec, Canada

Resolute Forest Products Canada Inc.
Thunder Bay Mill
Thunder Bay, Ontario, Canada

Rigesa, Celulose, Papel e Embalagens Ltda.
Três Barras Mill
Três Barras, Santa Catarina, Brazil

RockTenn Co.
Coshocton Mill
Coshocton, Ohio, United States

RockTenn Co.
Demopolis Mill
Demopolis, Alabama, United States

RockTenn Co.
Fernandina Beach Mill
Fernandina Beach, Florida, United States

RockTenn Co.
Florence Mill
Florence, South Carolina, United States

RockTenn Co.
Hodge Mill
Hodge, Louisiana, United States

RockTenn Co.
Hopewell Mill
Hopewell, Virginia, United States

RockTenn Co.
La Tuque Mill
La Tuque, Quebec, Canada

RockTenn Co.
Panama City Mill
Panama City, Florida, United States

RockTenn Co.
Stevenson Mill
Stevenson, Alabama, United States

RockTenn Co.
Tacoma Mill
Tacoma, Washington, United States

RockTenn Co.
West Point Mill
West Point, Virginia, United States

Rottneros, Vallviks Bruk AB
Vallvik Mill
Vallvik, Sweden

Chemical Pulp

S.N.C.P.A. - Société Nationale de Cellulose et Papier Alfa
Kasserine Mill
Kasserine, Gouvernorat de Kasserine, Tunisia

Sabah Forest Industries Sdn. Bhd.
Sipitang Mill
Sipitang, Sabah, Malaysia

Sanyo Paper Manufacturing Co., Ltd.
Tottori Mill
Tottori-shi, Tottori Pref., Japan

Sappi Chemical Cellulose
Saiccor Mill
Umkomaas, KwaZulu-Natal, South Africa

Sappi Fine Paper Europe
Alfeld Mill
Alfeld (Leine), Germany

Sappi Fine Paper Europe
Ehingen Mill
Ehingen, Germany

Sappi Fine Paper Europe
Gratkorn Mill
Gratkorn, Styria, Austria

Sappi Fine Paper Europe
Stockstadt Mill
Stockstadt am Main, Germany

Sappi Fine Paper North America
Cloquet Mill
Cloquet, Minnesota, United States

Sappi Fine Paper North America
Somerset Mill
Skowhegan, Maine, United States

Sappi Paper and Paper Packaging South Africa (SA)
Ngodwana Mill
Ngodwana, Mpumalanga, South Africa

Sappi Paper and Paper Packaging South Africa (SA)
Tugela Mill
Mandini, KwaZulu-Natal, South Africa

Satia Paper Mills Ltd.
Muktsar Mill
Dist. Muktsar, Punjab, India

Savon Sellu Oy
Savon Sellu
Kuopio, Finland

SCA Graphic Sundsvall AB
Östrand Pulp Mill
Timrå, Sweden

SCA Hygiene Products SE
Mannheim Mill
Mannheim, Germany

SCA Munksund AB
Piteå Mill
Piteå, Sweden

SCA Obbola AB
Obbola Mill
Obbola, Sweden

SCG Paper Public Co., Ltd.
BanPong Mill
BanPong, Ratchaburi, Thailand

Schweighofer Fiber GmbH
Hallein Mill
Hallein, Salzburg, Austria

Segezha Pulp & Paper Mill
Segezha Mill
Segezha, Karelia, Russia

Selenginsky Pulp & Board Mill
Selenginsk Mill
Selenginsk, Buryatia Republic, Russia

Seshasayee Paper & Boards Ltd.
Erode Mill
Erode, Tamil Nadu, India

Shandong Baron Paper Co., Ltd.
Laiwu Mill
Laiwu, Shandong, China

Shandong Bohui Paper Industry Co., Ltd.
Zibo Mill
Zibo, Shandong, China

Shandong Gaomi Silver Hawk Chemical Fibre Group Co., Ltd.
Gaomi Mill
Gaomi, Shandong, China

Shandong Huajin Paper Group
Jining Mill
Jining, Shandong, China

Shandong Jianghe Paper Co., Ltd.
Qihe Mill
Dezhou, Shandong, China

Shandong Rizhao Huatai Paper Co. Ltd.
Rizhao Mill
Rizhao, Shandong, China

Shandong Sun Paper Industry Joint Stock Co., Ltd.
Yanzhou Mill
Yanzhou, Shandong, China

Shandong Weifang Henglian Art Paper Co., Ltd.
Weifang Mill
Weifang, Shandong, China

Shandong Weifang Henglian Pulp & Paper Co., Ltd.
Weifang Mill
Weifang, Shandong, China

Siam Cellulose Co., Ltd.
Kanchanaburi Mill
Kanchanaburi, Kanchanaburi, Thailand

Sirpur Paper Mills Ltd.
Adilabad Mill
Sirpur-Kaghaznagar, Dist. Adilabad, Andhra Pradesh, India

Smurfit Kappa Cartón de Colombia SA
Yumbo Mill
Cali, Valle de Cauca, Colombia

Smurfit Kappa Cartón de Venezuela S.A.
San Felipe Mill
San Felipe, Yaracuy, Venezuela

Smurfit Kappa Cellulose du Pin
Facture mill
Biganos, France

Smurfit Kappa Kraftliner Piteå
Piteå Mill
Piteå, Sweden

Smurfit Kappa Nervión
Iurreta Mill
Iurreta, Vizcaya, Spain

Smurfit Kappa Nettingsdorfer, Nettingsdorfer Papierfabrik AG & Co. KG
Nettingsdorfer Mill
Haid bei Ansfelden, Oberösterreich, Austria

Smurfit Kappa Sangüesa Paper
Sanguesa Mill
Sangüesa, Navarra, Spain

Sniace S.A.
Torrelavega Mill
Torrelavega, Cantabria, Spain

Södra Cell AB
Mönsterås Mill
Mönsterås, Sweden

Södra Cell AB
Mörrum Mill
Mörrum, Sweden

Södra Cell AB
Värö Mill
Väröbacka, Sweden

Södra Cell Tofte
Tofte Mill
Tofte, Norway

Sokolsky Pulp & Paper Mill
Sokol Mill
Sokol, Vologodskaya obl., Russia

Solombalsky Pulp & Paper Mill
Arkhangelsk Mill
Arkhangelsk, Russia

Sonoco Products Co.
Hartsville Mill
Hartsville, South Carolina, United States

South India Paper Mills Ltd.
Nanjangud Mill
Nanjangud, Karnataka, India

Star Paper Mills Ltd.
Saharanpur Mill
Saharanpur, Uttar Pradesh, India

Stora Enso Biomaterials
Enocell Pulp Mill
Uimaharju, Finland

Stora Enso Biomaterials
Skutskär Pulp Mill
Skutskär, Sweden

Stora Enso Biomaterials
Sunila Mill
Kotka, Finland

Stora Enso Poland S.A.
Ostroleka Mill
Ostroleka, Poland

Stora Enso Printing and Reading
Nymölla Mill
Nymölla, Sweden

Chemical Pulp

Stora Enso Printing and Reading
Oulu Mill
Oulu, Finland

Stora Enso Printing and Reading
Varkaus Mill
Varkaus, Finland

Stora Enso Printing and Reading
Veitsiluoto Mill
Kemi, Finland

Stora Enso Renewable Packaging
Heinola Mill
Heinola, Finland

Stora Enso Renewable Packaging
Imatra Mills (Kaukopää & Tainionkoski)
Imatra, Finland

Stora Enso Renewable Packaging
Skoghall Mill
Skoghall, Sweden

Surya Chandra Paper Mills Ltd.
East Godavari Dist. Mill
East Godavari Dist., Andhra Pradesh, India

Suzano Papel e Celulose S.A.
Limeira Mill
Limeira, São Paulo, Brazil

Suzano Papel e Celulose S.A.
Maranhão Mill
Imperatriz city, Maranhão, Brazil

Suzano Papel e Celulose S.A.
Mucuri Mill
Mucuri, Bahia, Brazil

Suzano Papel e Celulose S.A.
Suzano Mill
Suzano, São Paulo, Brazil

Svetlogorskiy Pulp and Board Mill
Svetlogorsk Mill
Svetlogorsk, Gomel Region, Belarus

Svilosa AD
Svilocell EAD
Svishtov, Bulgaria

Syassky Pulp & Paper Mill
Syasstroy Mill
Syasstroy, Volkhovskiy rayon, Leningrad Region, Russia

Taiko Paper Mfg. Co., Ltd.
Fuji-shi Mill
Fuji-shi, Shizuoka Pref., Japan

Taiwan Pulp & Paper Corp.
Hsin Ying Mill
Hsinying District, Tainan City, Taiwan

Tamil Nadu Newsprint and Papers Limited (TNPL)
Kagithapuram Mill
Karur Dist., Kagithapuram, Tamil Nadu, India

Tan Hong Pulp Mill
Con Cuong Mill
Con Cuong, Vietnam

Tashkent Paper Mill of GPO Davlat Belgisi
Darkhan Mill
Vil. Darkhan, Tashkent Distr., Tashkentskaya obl., Uzbekistan

Tembec Inc.
Temiscaming Mill
Temiscaming, Quebec, Canada

Tembec Tartas
Tartas Mill
Tartas, France

The West Coast Paper Mills Ltd.
Dandeli Mill
Dandeli, Uttara Kannada, Karnataka, India

Tokushu Tokai Paper Co., Ltd.
Shimada Mill
Shimada-shi, Shizuoka Pref., Japan

Tolko Manitoba Kraft Papers
The Pas Mill
The Pas, Manitoba, Canada

Torraspapel S.A.
Zaragoza Mill
Zaragoza, Spain

Toyama Seishi KK
Toyama Mill
Toyama-shi, Toyama Pref., Japan

Trident Group
Barnala Mill
Dhaula, District Barnala, Punjab, India

Trombini Industrial S.A.
Fraiburgo Mill
Fraiburgo, Santa Catarina, Brazil

Trupal S.A.
Trujillo Mill
Trujillo, Peru

Turinsky Pulp & Paper Mill
Turinsk Mill
Turinsk, Sverdlovskaya obl., Russia

Twin Rivers Paper, LLC
Madawaska and Edmundston Mills (East Paper Operations)
Madawaska, Maine, United States

UPM Uruguay
Fray Bentos Pulp Mill
Fray Bentos, Rio Negro, Uruguay

UPM-Kymmene Corporation
Kaukas Mill
Lappeenranta, Finland

UPM-Kymmene Corporation
Kymi Mill
Kuusankoski, Kouvola, Finland

UPM-Kymmene Corporation
Pietarsaari Mill
Pietarsaari, Finland

Ust-Ilimsk Branch of Ilim Group
Ust-Ilimsk Mill
Ust-Ilimsk, Irkutsk Region, Russia

Vamsadhara Paper Mills Ltd.
Dist. Srikakulam Mill
Dist. Srikakulam, Andhra Pradesh, India

Veracel Celulose S.A.
Veracel Pulp Mill
Eunápolis, Bahia, Brazil

Verso Paper Corp.
Androscoggin Mill
Jay, Maine, United States

Verso Paper Corp.
Quinnesec Mill
Quinnesec, Michigan, United States

Viet Tri Paper Company
Viet Tri Mill
Viet Tri City, Phú Tho Province, Vietnam

Vietnam Paper Corporation (Vinapaco)-Bai Bang Paper
Bai Bang Paper
Phu Ninh District, Phú Tho Province, Vietnam

VISKOZA
Loznica Mill
Loznica, Serbia

Visy Pulp & Paper
Tumut, VPP9
Tumut, New South Wales, Australia

Vyborgskaya Cellulose, JSC
Sovetsky Mill
Vyborg, Sovetsky, Leningrad Region, Russia

Weyerhaeuser Co.
Columbus Mill
Columbus, Mississippi, United States

Weyerhaeuser Co.
Flint River Mill
Oglethorpe, Georgia, United States

Weyerhaeuser Co.
Longview Mill
Longview, Washington, United States

Weyerhaeuser Co.
New Bern Mill
Vanceboro, North Carolina, United States

Weyerhaeuser Co.
Port Wentworth Mill
Port Wentworth, Georgia, United States

Weyerhaeuser Company Ltd.
Grande Prairie Mill
Grande Prairie, Alberta, Canada

Yanbian Shixian Bailu Paper Co., Ltd.
Tumen Mill
Tumen, Jilin, China

Yanbian Shuanglu Chemical Fiber Co., Ltd.
Yanbian Mill
Longjing, Jilin, China

Yenisey Pulp and Paper Mill Inc.
Yenisey Pulp and Paper Mill
Krasnoyarsk, Russia

Yunnan Yun-Jing Forestry & Paper Mill Co., Ltd.
Jinggu Mill
Puer, Yunnan, China

ZAO International Paper
Svetogorsk Mill
Svetogorsk, Leningrad Region, Russia

Zellstoff Celgar Limited
Castlegar Mill
Castlegar, British Columbia, Canada

Mechanical Pulp

Zellstoff Pöls AG
Pöls Mill
Pöls, Styria, Austria

Zellstoff Stendal GmbH
Stendal Mill
Arneburg, Saxony-Anhalt, Germany

Zhanjiang Chenming Paper Pulp Co., Ltd.
Zhanjiang (Zhanjiang Chenming Pulp & Paper) Mill
Zhanjiang, Guangdong, China

ZPR, Zellstoff- und Papierfabrik Rosenthal GmbH
Rosenthal Mill
Blankenstein, Germany

Mechanical Pulp

Alberta Newsprint Co. Ltd.
Whitecourt Mill
Whitecourt, Alberta, Canada

Arctic Paper Mochenwangen GmbH
Mochenwangen Mill
Mochenwangen, Wolpertswende, Germany

AS Estonian Cell
Kunda Mill
Kunda, Lääne-Virumaa, Estonia

Aurangabad Paper Mills Ltd.
Aurangabad Mill
Aurangabad, Maharashtra, India

Baiersbronn Frischfaserkarton GmbH
Baiersbronn Mill
Baiersbronn, Germany

Balikesir Albayrak Kagit Fabrikasi
Balikesir Mill
Balikesir, Turkey

Bear Island Paper Co., LLC
Ashland Mill
Ashland, Virginia, United States

BillerudKorsnäs AB
Rockhammar Mill
Frövi, Sweden

Burgo Group SpA
Duino Mill
Duino, Trieste, Italy

Burgo Group SpA
Toscolano Mill
Toscolano Maderno, Brescia, Italy

Burgo Group SpA
Verzuolo Mill
Verzuolo, Cuneo, Italy

Canfor Corp.
Taylor Mill
Taylor, British Columbia, Canada

Cartiera Italiana Srl.
Serravalle Sesia Mill
Serravalle Sesia, Vercelli, Italy

Cartulinas CMPC S.A.
Maule Mill
Yerbas Buenas, Linares, VII - Región del Maule, Chile

Cartulinas CMPC S.A.
Valdivia Mill
Valdivia, X - Región de Los Lagos, Chile

Cascades Boxboard Group Inc.
Jonquière Mill
Jonquiere, Quebec, Canada

Cascades Djupafors AB
Kallinge Mill
Kallinge, Sweden

Cascades SAS
La Rochette Mill
La Rochette, France

Catalyst Paper Corporation
Crofton Mill
Crofton, British Columbia, Canada

Catalyst Paper Corporation
Port Alberni Mill
Port Alberni, British Columbia, Canada

Catalyst Paper Corporation
Powell River Mill
Powell River, British Columbia, Canada

Chenming Paper Holdings Ltd.
Shouguang (Shouguang Chenming No. 4) Mill
Shouguang, Shandong, China

Chuetsu Pulp & Paper Co., Ltd.
Takaoka (Futatsuka) Mill
Takaoka-shi, Toyama Pref., Japan

Daio Paper Corp.
Mishima Mill
Shikokuchuo-shi, Ehime Pref., Japan

Drvenjaca d.d.
Fuzine Mill
Fuzine, Gorski kotar, Croatia

Evergreen Packaging Inc.
Pine Bluff Mill
Pine Bluff, Arkansas, United States

F.F. Soucy SEC
Riviere du Loup Mill
Riviere du Loup, Quebec, Canada

Fabryka Papieru Myszków Sp. z o.o.
Myszkow Mill
Myszkow, Poland

Fujian Nanping Paper Co. Ltd.
Nanping Mill
Nanping, Fujian, China

Gold East Paper (Jiangsu) Co., Ltd.
Zhenjiang (Gold East Paper) Mill
Zhenjiang, Jiangsu, China

Great Northern Paper Co. LLC.
East Millinocket Mill
East Millinocket, Maine, United States

Guangxi Jingui Pulp & Paper Co., Ltd.
Qinzhou (Guangxi Jingui Pulp & Paper) Mill
Qinzhou, Guangxi, China

Hellefoss Paper
Hokksund Mill
Hokksund, Norway

Henan Jiaozuo Ruifeng Paper Co., Ltd.
Jiaozuo (Jiaozuo Ruifeng) Mill
Jiaozuo, Henan, China

Henan Puyang Longfeng Paper Co. Ltd
Puyang (Puyang Longfeng) Mill
Puyang, Henan, China

Henan Xinxiang Xinya Paper Group Co., Ltd.
Xinxiang (Cartonboard) Mill
Xinxiang, Henan, China

Hindustan Newsprint Ltd.
Kottayam Dist. Mill
Kottayam Dist., Kerala, India

Holmen AB
Braviken Paper Mill
Norrköping, Sweden

Holmen AB
Hallsta Mill
Hallstavik, Sweden

Howe Sound Pulp and Paper Corporation
Port Mellon Mill
Port Mellon, British Columbia, Canada

Hubei Chibi Chenli Paper Co., Ltd.
Chibi Mill
Chibi, Hubei, China

Hunan Tiger Forest & Paper Group Yueyang Paper Co., Ltd.
Yueyang Mill
Yueyang, Hunan, China

IBEMA - Cia. Brasileira de Papel
Turvo Mill
Turvo, Paraná, Brazil

Iggesund Paperboard (Workington) Ltd.
Workington Mill
Workington, Cumbria, United Kingdom

Inland Empire Paper Co.
Millwood Mill
Millwood, Spokane, Washington, United States

International Paper - Kwidzyn Sp. z o.o.
Kwidzyn Mill
Kwidzyn, Poland

Irving Paper
Saint John East Mill
Saint John, New Brunswick, Canada

Jeonju Paper Corporation, Ltd.
Jeonju Mill
Jeonju-si, Jeollabuk-do, South Korea

Jiangxi Chenming Paper Co., Ltd.
Nanchang (Jiangxi Chenming Paper) Mill
Nanchang, Jiangxi, China

JSC Solikamskbumprom
Solikamsk Mill
Solikamsk, Perm Region, Russia

Kama Pulp & Paper Mill
Krasnokamsk Mill
Krasnokamsk, Perm Region, Russia

Kartonfabrik Buchmann GmbH
Annweiler Mill
Annweiler, Germany

Katz GmbH & Co. KG
Weisenbach Mill
Weisenbach, Germany

Mechanical Pulp

Kimberly-Clark Australia Pty Ltd.
Millicent Mill
Millicent, South Australia, Australia

Klabin S.A.
Monte Alegre Mill
Telêmaco Borba, Paraná, Brazil

Kolicevo Karton d.o.o.
Kolicevo Mill
Domžale, Slovenia

Kondopoga
Kondopoga Mill
Kondopoga, Karelia, Russia

Kotkamills Oy
Kotka Mill
Kotka, Finland

Kruger Inc.
Bromptonville Mill
Sherbrooke, Quebec, Canada

Kruger Inc.
Corner Brook Mill
Corner Brook, Newfoundland and Labrador, Canada

Kruger Inc.
Trois-Rivières Mill
Trois-Rivières, Quebec, Canada

Kruger Wayagamack Inc.
Trois Rivierès (Wayagamack) Mill
Trois-Rivières, Quebec, Canada

Madeireira Miguel Forte S.A.
União da Vitória Mill
União da Vitória, Paraná, Brazil

Maragheh Paper Industries Company (M.P.I.C)
Maragheh Mill
Maragheh, East Azerbaijan, Iran

Marusumi Paper Co., Ltd.
Kawanoe Mill
Shikokuchuo-shi, Ehime Pref., Japan

Marusumi Paper Co., Ltd.
Ohe Mill
Shikokuchuo-shi, Ehime Pref., Japan

Mayr-Melnhof Eerbeek BV
Eerbeek Mill
Eerbeek, Netherlands

Mayr-Melnhof Karton GmbH
Frohnleiten Mill
Frohnleiten, Styria, Austria

Mazandaran Wood & Paper Industries Co.
Sari Mill
Sari, Mazandaran, Iran

MCC Paper Yinhe Co., Ltd.
Linqing Mill
Linqing, Shandong, China

Meadow Lake Mechanical Pulp
Meadow Lake Mill
Meadow Lake, Sasketchewan, Canada

Melhoramentos Florestal S.A.
Camanducaia Mill
Camanducaia, Minas Gerais, Brazil

Melhoramentos Papéis Ltda.
Caieiras Mill
Caieiras, São Paulo, Brazil

Metsä Board Joutseno
Joutseno Mill
Joutseno, Finland

Metsä Board Kaskinen
Kaskinen Mill
Kaskinen, Finland

Metsä Board Kyro
Kyro Mill
Kyröskoski, Finland

Metsä Board Simpele
Simpele Mill
Simpele, Finland

Millar Western Forest Products Ltd.
Whitecourt Pulp Mill
Whitecourt, Alberta, Canada

Mitsubishi Paper Mills Ltd.
Hachinohe Mill
Hachinohe-shi, Aomori, Japan

Mondi Shanduka Newsprint
Merebank Mill
Merebank, KwaZulu-Natal, South Africa

Mondi Syktyvkar
Syktyvkar Mill
Syktyvkar, Komi Republic, Russia

Mysore Paper Mills Ltd.
Shimoga Mill
Bhadravati, Shimoga, Karnataka, India

NewPage Corporation
Biron Mill
Wisconsin Rapids, Wisconsin, United States

NewPage Corporation
Duluth Paper Mill
Duluth, Minnesota, United States

NewPage Corporation
Escanaba Mill
Escanaba, Michigan, United States

NewPage Corporation
Rumford Mill
Rumford, Maine, United States

Nippon Paper Industries Co., Ltd.
Fuji Mill
Fuji-shi, Shizuoka Pref., Japan

Nippon Paper Industries Co., Ltd.
Hokkaido Mill - Asahikawa
Asahikawa-shi, Hokkaido Pref., Japan

Nippon Paper Industries Co., Ltd.
Hokkaido Mill - Yufutsu
Tomakomai-shi, Hokkaido Pref., Japan

Nippon Paper Industries Co., Ltd.
Ishinomaki Mill
Ishinomaki-shi, Miyagi Pref., Japan

Nippon Paper Industries Co., Ltd.
Iwanuma Mill
Iwanuma-shi, Miyagi Pref., Japan

Nippon Paper Industries Co., Ltd.
Kushiro Mill
Kushiro-shi, Hokkaido Pref., Japan

Nippon Paper Industries Co., Ltd.
Yatsushiro Mill
Yatsushiro-shi, Kumamoto Pref., Japan

Nippon Paper Industries USA Co., Ltd.
Port Angeles Mill
Port Angeles, Washington, United States

Norske Skog (Australia)
Albury Mill
Ettamogah via Albury, New South Wales, Australia

Norske Skog (Australia)
Boyer Mill
Boyer, Tasmania, Australia

Norske Skog ASA
Saugbrugs Mill
Halden, Norway

Norske Skog ASA
Skogn Mill
Skogn, Norway

Norske Skog Bruck GmbH
Bruck an der Mur Mill
Bruck an der Mur, Styria, Austria

Norske Skog Golbey SA
Golbey Mill
Golbey Cedex, France

Norske Skog Pisa S.A.
Jaguariaíva Mill
Jaguariaíva, Paraná, Brazil

Norske Skog Tasman
Tasman Mill
Kawerau, Bay of Plenty, New Zealand

Norske Skog Walsum GmbH
Walsum Mill
Duisburg, Germany

North Pacific Paper Corp. (Norpac)
Longview Mill
Longview, Washington, United States

Omniafiltra, LLC
Beaver Falls Mill
Beaver Falls, New York, United States

Pan Pac Forest Products Ltd.
Whirinaki Mill
Napier, Hawke's Bay, New Zealand

Pan Paper Mills
Webuye Mill
Webuye, Bungoma District, Western, Kenya

Pankaboard Oy
Pankakoski Mill
Pankakoski, Lieksa, Finland

Papel Prensa S.A.
San Pedro Mill
San Pedro, Buenos Aires, Argentina

Papeles Bío Bío
Concepción Mill
Concepción, VIII - Región del Biobío, Chile

Papeles Río Vergara S.A.
Nacimiento Mill
Nacimiento, VIII - Región del Biobío, Chile

Papeles Venezolanos CA (PAVECA)
Guacara Mill
Guacara, Edo. Carabobo, Venezuela

Mechanical Pulp

Papeteries de Vizille (Vicat)
Vizille Mill
Vizille, France

Papier Masson
Gatineau Mill
Gatineau, Quebec, Canada

Papierfabrik Utzenstorf AG
Utzenstorf Mill
Utzenstorf, Switzerland

Perlen Papier AG
Perlen Mill
Perlen, Switzerland

Polpa de Madeiras Ltda.
Santa Cecília Mill
Santa Cecília, Santa Catarina, Brazil

Ponderay Newsprint Co.
Usk Mill
Usk, Washington, United States

Portonogaro S.a.s. di Raffin Mario & C.
Casarsa della Delizia Mill
Casarsa della Delizia, Pordenone, Italy

Premium Board Finland Oy
Juankoski Board Mill
Juankoski, Finland

Quena Paper Industry Co. (QPIC)
Kous Mill
Kous, Quena, Egypt

Quesnel River Pulp Co.
Quesnel Mill
Quesnel, British Columbia, Canada

Resolute Forest Products Canada Inc.
Alma Mill
Alma, Quebec, Canada

Resolute Forest Products Canada Inc.
Amos Mill
Amos, Quebec, Canada

Resolute Forest Products Canada Inc.
Baie-Comeau Mill
Baie-Comeau, Quebec, Canada

Resolute Forest Products Canada Inc.
Clermont Mill
Clermont, Quebec, Canada

Resolute Forest Products Canada Inc.
Dolbeau Mill
Dolbeau, Quebec, Canada

Resolute Forest Products Canada Inc.
Fort Frances Mill
Fort Frances, Ontario, Canada

Resolute Forest Products Canada Inc.
Gatineau Mill
Gatineau, Quebec, Canada

Resolute Forest Products Canada Inc.
Iroquois Falls Mill
Iroquois Falls, Ontario, Canada

Resolute Forest Products Canada Inc.
Kenogami Mill
Jonquière, Quebec, Canada

Resolute Forest Products Canada Inc.
Laurentide Mill
Grand-Mere, Quebec, Canada

Resolute Forest Products Canada Inc.
Thunder Bay Mill
Thunder Bay, Ontario, Canada

Resolute FP Augusta LLC
Augusta Mill
Augusta, Georgia, United States

Rottneros Bruk AB
Rottneros Mill
Rottneros, Sweden

Rygene-Smith & Thommesen AS
Rykene Mill
Rykene, Norway

Sappi Fine Paper Europe
Kirkniemi Mill
Kirkniemi, Finland

Sappi Fine Paper Europe
Lanaken Mill
Lanaken, Belgium

Sappi Paper and Paper Packaging South Africa (SA)
Ngodwana Mill
Ngodwana, Mpumalanga, South Africa

SCA Graphic Sundsvall AB
Ortviken Mill
Sundsvall, Sweden

SCA Graphic Sundsvall AB
Östrand Pulp Mill
Timrå, Sweden

Shandong Bohui Paper Industry Co., Ltd.
Zibo Mill
Zibo, Shandong, China

Shandong Jianghe Paper Co., Ltd.
Qihe Mill
Dezhou, Shandong, China

Shandong Sun Paper Industry Joint Stock Co., Ltd.
Yanzhou Mill
Yanzhou, Shandong, China

Shandong Taiding Material Technology Co., Ltd.
Dezhou Mill
Dezhou, Shandong, China

Shandong Tianhe Paper Co., Ltd.
Taian Mill
Taian, Shandong, China

Shandong Zhongmao Shengyuan Pulp Co., Ltd.
Dezhou Mill
Dezhou, Shandong, China

Shklov Newsprint Mill (Zavod Gazetnoi Bumagi)
Shklov Newsprint Mill
Shklov, Mogilev region, Mogilev Region, Belarus

Shouguang Meilun Paper
Shouguang (Shouguang Meilun Paper) Mill
Shouguang, Shandong, China

Sicem-Saga SpA
Ciano di Canossa Mill
Ciano d'Enza, Reggio Emilia, Italy

Slave Lake Pulp Corp.
Slave Lake Pulp Mill
Slave Lake, Alberta, Canada

Smurfit Kappa Cartón de Colombia SA
Yumbo Mill
Cali, Valle de Cauca, Colombia

SP Fiber Technologies LLC (SPFT)
Newberg Mill
Newberg, Oregon, United States

Stadacona Inc.
Stadacona Mill
Quebec City, Quebec, Canada

Stora Enso Arapoti Indústria de Papel Ltda.
Arapoti Mill
Arapoti, Paraná, Brazil

Stora Enso Printing and Reading
Anjala Mill
Kouvola, Finland

Stora Enso Printing and Reading
Corbehem Mill
Corbehem, France

Stora Enso Printing and Reading
Hylte Mill
Hyltebruk, Sweden

Stora Enso Printing and Reading
Kabel Mill
Hagen, Germany

Stora Enso Printing and Reading
Kvarnsveden Mill
Borlänge, Sweden

Stora Enso Printing and Reading
Maxau Mill
Karlsruhe, Germany

Stora Enso Printing and Reading
Veitsiluoto Mill
Kemi, Finland

Stora Enso Renewable Packaging
Fors Mill
Fors, Sweden

Stora Enso Renewable Packaging
Imatra Mills (Kaukopää & Tainionkoski)
Imatra, Finland

Stora Enso Renewable Packaging
Ingerois Mill
Kouvola, Finland

Stora Enso Renewable Packaging
Skoghall Mill
Skoghall, Sweden

Syassky Pulp & Paper Mill
Syasstroy Mill
Syasstroy, Volkhovskiy rayon, Leningrad Region, Russia

Tan Mai Group Joint Stock Co.
Tan Mai Mill
Bien Hoa City, Dong Nai Province, Vietnam

Tembec Inc.
Matane Mill
Matane, Quebec, Canada

Other Pulp

Tembec Inc.
Spruce Falls Mill
Kapuskasing, Ontario, Canada

Tembec Inc.
Temiscaming Mill
Temiscaming, Quebec, Canada

Twin Rivers Paper, LLC
Madawaska and Edmundston Mills (East Paper Operations)
Madawaska, Maine, United States

UPM GmbH
Augsburg Mill
Augsburg, Germany

UPM GmbH
Ettringen Mill
Ettringen, Bavaria, Germany

UPM GmbH
Plattling Mill
Plattling, Germany

UPM GmbH
Schongau Mill
Schongau, Germany

UPM North America
Blandin Paper Mill
Grand Rapids, Minnesota, United States

UPM North America
Madison Paper Mill
Madison, Maine, United States

UPM-Kymmene (UK) Ltd.
Caledonian Paper Mill
Irvine, Scotland, United Kingdom

UPM-Kymmene Austria GmbH
Steyrermühl Mill
Steyrermühl, Oberösterreich, Austria

UPM-Kymmene Corporation
Jämsänkoski Mill
Jämsänkoski, Jämsä, Finland

UPM-Kymmene Corporation
Kaipola Mill
Kaipola, Jämsä, Finland

UPM-Kymmene Corporation
Kaukas Mill
Lappeenranta, Finland

UPM-Kymmene Corporation
Rauma Paper Mill
Rauma, Finland

Vafos Pulp
Kragerø Mill
Kragerø, Norway

Verso Paper Corp.
Androscoggin Mill
Jay, Maine, United States

Verso Paper Corp.
Bucksport Mill
Bucksport, Maine, United States

Vipap Videm Krško d.d.
Krško Mill
Krško, Ljubljana, Slovenia

Volga
Balakhna Mill
Balakhna, Nizhny Novgorod, Russia

Waggeryd Cell AB
Waggeryd Mill
Vaggeryd, Sweden

Winstone Pulp International Ltd.
Karioi Pulp Mill
Karioi, Ohakune, New Zealand

Zambezi Paper Mills Ltd.
Ndola Mill
Ndola, Zambia

ZAO International Paper
Svetogorsk Mill
Svetogorsk, Leningrad Region, Russia

Zubialde S.A.
Aizamazabal Mill
Aizamazabal, Gipúzcoa, Spain

Other Pulp

Bai Bang Paper Joint-stock Co., Ltd.
Ky Son Mill
Ky Son, Hoa Binh Province, Vietnam

Ballarpur Industries Ltd. (BILT)
Ballarshah (Unit Ballarpur)
Ballarshah, Maharashtra, India

Bulleh Shah Packaging (Private) Limited
Bulleh Shah Paper Mill
Kasur, Pakistan

Cartones America SA - CAME
Cali Mill
Cali, Valle de Cauca, Colombia

Carvajal Pulpa y Papel
Guachené Mill, Plant 2
Guachené, Cauca, Valle de Cauca, Colombia

Carvajal Pulpa y Papel
Yumbo Mill, Plant 1
Yumbo, Valle de Cauca, Colombia

Century Paper & Board Mills Ltd.
Kasur Mill
Bhai Pheru, Dist. Kasur, Pakistan

CEPASA - Celulose e Papel de Pernambuco S.A.
Jaboatão dos Guararapes Mill
Jaboatão dos Guararapes, Pernambuco, Brazil

Chongqing Lee & Man Paper Co., Ltd.
Chongqing Mill
Chongqing, Chongqing, China

Flying Board and Paper Products Ltd.
Sheikhupura Mill
Sheikhupura, Punjab, Pakistan

General Company for Paper Industry (GENCO)
Deir Ez-Zor Mill
Deir Ez-Zor, Syria

Guangdong Dingfeng Paper Corporation
Zhaoqing Mill
Zhaoqing, Guangdong, China

Guangdong Shaoneng Group
Nanxiong Mill
Nanxiong, Guangdong, China

Guangxi East Asia Paper Co., Ltd.
Chongzuo Mill
Chongzuo, Guangxi, China

Guangxi Fangchenggang Hongyuan Pulp & Paper Co., Ltd.
Fangchenggang Mill
Fangchenggang, Guangxi, China

Guangxi Heda Paper Co. Ltd.
Hezhou Mill
Hezhou, Guangxi, China

Guangxi Laibin Donta Paper Co., Ltd.
Laibin Mill
Laibin, Guangxi, China

Guangxi Liangmianzhen Paper Co., Ltd.
Liuzhou Mill
Liuzhou, Guangxi, China

Guangxi Yongkai Sugar and Paper Co., Ltd.
Nanning(liujing) Mill
Nanning, Guangxi, China

Guizhou Chitianhua Paper Industrial Co., Ltd
Chishui Mill
Chishui, Guizhou, China

Henan Neixiang Xianhe Special Paper & Pulp Co., Ltd.
Nanyang Mill
Nanyang, Henan, China

Henan Xinxiang Xinya Paper Group Co., Ltd.
Xinxiang No. 1 Mill
Xinxiang, Henan, China

Henan Xinxiang Xinya Paper Group Co., Ltd.
Xinxiang No. 2 Mill
Xinxiang, Henan, China

Henan Xinxiang Xinya Paper Group Co., Ltd.
Xinxiang No. 4 Mill
Xinxiang, Henan, China

Henan Xinxiang Xinya Paper Group Co., Ltd.
Xinxiang No. 6 Mill
Xinxiang, Henan, China

Henan Yilin Paper Co., Ltd.
Xuchang Mill
Xuchang, Henan, China

Henan Yinge Industrial Investment Co. Ltd.
Luohe (Yinge Industrial Investment) Mill
Luohe, Henan, China

Henan Zhumadian City Baiyun Paper Co., Ltd.
Zhumadian (Zhumadian Baiyun) Mill
Zhumadian, Henan, China

Hubei Chibi Chenli Paper Co., Ltd.
Chibi Mill
Chibi, Hubei, China

Other Pulp

Hunan Tiger Forest & Paper Group Yuanjiang Paper Co., Ltd.
Yuanjiang Mill
Yuanjiang, Hunan, China

Hunan Tiger Forest & Paper Group Yueyang Paper Co., Ltd.
Yueyang Mill
Yueyang, Hunan, China

Hunan Yueyang Fengli Pulp & Paper Co. Ltd.
Yueyang Mill
Yueyang, Hunan, China

Indústria e Comércio de Embalagens e Papéis Artivinco Ltda.
Santa Rosa do Viterbo Mill
Santa Rosa do Viterbo, São Paulo, Brazil

International Paper APPM Ltd.
Rajahmundry Mill
Rajahmundry, East Godavari, Andhra Pradesh, India

Jiangsu Xinda Paper Co. Ltd.
Xinyi Mill
Xinyi, Jiangsu, China

Jiangsu Yuen Foong Yu Paper (Yangzhou) Co., Ltd.
Yangzhou Mill
Yangzhou, Jiangsu, China

JK Paper Ltd.
Central Pulp Mills-CPM, Songadh Mill
Fort Songadh, Dist. Tapi, Gujarat, India

KR Pulp & Papers Ltd.
Shahjahanpur Mill
Shahjahanpur, Uttar Pradesh, India

Ledesma S.A.A.I.
Libertador General Mill
Libertador General San Martín, Jujuy, Argentina

Lepenka AD
Novi Knezevac Mill
Novi Knezevac, Vojvodina, Serbia

Liaoning Jincheng Paper Co., Ltd.
Linghai Mill
Linghai, Liaoning, China

Mandiali Paper Mill Ltd.
Sheikhupura Mill
Sheikhupura, Punjab, Pakistan

Marmara Kagit ve Ambalaj Sanayii ve Ticaret AS
Vezirhan Mill
Bilecik, Vezirhan, Bilecik, Turkey

MCC Meili Paper Industry Co., Ltd.
Zhongwei Mill
Zhongwei, Ningxia, China

MCC Paper Yinhe Co., Ltd.
Linqing Mill
Linqing, Shandong, China

Misr Edfu for Pulp, Writing & Printing Paper Co. - MEPP-Co
Edfu Pulp Mill
Edfu, Aswan, Egypt

Mopak Tasköprü Pulp and Cigarette Paper Plant
Kastamonu Mill
Kastamonu, Turkey

Mpact Limited
Felixton Mill
Felixton, KwaZulu-Natal, South Africa

Mysore Paper Mills Ltd.
Shimoga Mill
Bhadravati, Shimoga, Karnataka, India

Naini Papers Ltd.
Kashipur Mill
Kashipur, Uttarakhand, India

National Paper Co.
Alexandria Mill
Alexandria, Iskanderiya, Egypt

Ningxia Kejin Xiaguang Paper Co., Ltd.
Qingtongxia Mill
Qingtongxia, Ningxia, China

Ningxia Zijinghua Paper Industry Co. Ltd.
Yinchuan Mill
Yinchuan, Ningxia, China

Orient Paper Mills
Amlai mill
Shahdol, Madhya Pradesh, India

Panasa, Papelera Nacional S.A.
Paramonga Mill
Paramonga, Lima, Peru

Papelera Nacional S.A.
Guayaquil Mill
Guayaquil, Guayas, Ecuador

Papelera Tucumán S.A.
Lules, Tucumán I Mill
Lules, Tucumán, Argentina

Pars Paper Industrial Group
Ahwaz Mill
Ahwaz, Khuzestan, Iran

Quena Paper Industry Co. (QPIC)
Kous Mill
Kous, Quena, Egypt

Rakta, General Co. for Paper Industry
Rakta Mill
Alexandria, Iskanderiya, Egypt

Ruchira Papers Ltd.
Kala-Amb Mill
Kala-Amb, Himachal Pradesh, India

Sainsons Paper Industries Ltd.
Kurukshetra Mill
Dist. Kurukshetra, Haryana, India

Sappi Paper and Paper Packaging South Africa (SA)
Stanger Mill
Stanger, KwaZulu-Natal, South Africa

Seshasayee Paper & Boards Ltd.
Erode Mill
Erode, Tamil Nadu, India

Shandong Guihe Xianxing Paper Holding Pte. Ltd.
Zibo Mill
Zibo, Shandong, China

Shandong Huajin Paper Group
Jining Mill
Jining, Shandong, China

Shandong Tranlin Paper Co. Ltd.
Gaotang Mill
Liaocheng, Shandong, China

Shengda Group Jiangsu Shuangdeng Paper Co., Ltd.
Yancheng Mill
Yancheng, Jiangsu, China

Shree Bhageshwari Papers Ltd
Muzaffarnagar Mill
Muzaffarnagar, Uttar Pradesh, India

Shree Bhawani Paper Mills Ltd.
Rae Bareli Mill
Rae Bareli, Uttar Pradesh, India

Shree Rishabh Papers
Nawanshaher Mill
Banah, Dist. Nawanshahar, Punjab, India

Shreyans Papers
Ahmedgarh Mill
Ahmedgarh, Dist. Sangrur, Punjab, India

Sichuan Anxian Paper Co., Ltd.
Chengdu Mill
Chengdu, Sichuan, China

Sichuan Jianwei Fengsheng Paper Co. Ltd.
Leshan Mill
Leshan, Sichuan, China

Sichuan Meishan Fenghua Paper Co., Ltd.
Meishan Mill
Meishan, Sichuan, China

Sichuan Yinge Bamboo Pulp & Paper Co., Ltd.
Luzhou (Sichuan Yinge) Mill
Luzhou, Sichuan, China

Sichuan Yongfeng Paper-Making Joint-Stock Co., Ltd.
Leshan Mill
Leshan, Sichuan, China

Siddheshwari Paper Udhyog Ltd.
Kashipur Mill
Kashipur, Uttarakhand, India

Sidharth Papers Ltd.
Kashipur Mill
Kashipur, Uttarakhand, India

Tamil Nadu Newsprint and Papers Limited (TNPL)
Kagithapuram Mill
Karur Dist., Kagithapuram, Tamil Nadu, India

Vietnam Paper Corporation (Vinapaco)-Bai Bang Paper
Bai Bang Paper
Phu Ninh District, Phú Tho Province, Vietnam

Recycled Pulp

Xinjiang Bohu Reed Industry Stock Co., Ltd.
Kuerle (No.1) Mill
Kuerle, Xinjiang, China

Xinjiang Bohu Reed Industry Stock Co., Ltd.
Kuerle (No.2) Mill
Kuerle, Xinjiang, China

Yash Papers Ltd.
Faizabad Mill
Faizabad, Uttar Pradesh, India

Yibin Changyi Pulp Co., Ltd.
Yibin Mill
Yibin, Sichuan, China

Recycled Pulp

A & B Paper Ltd.
Dobrzejewice k/Torunia Mill
Dobrzejewice, k/Torunia, Poland

A. Merati - Cartiera di Laveno SpA
Laveno Mombello Mill
Laveno Mombello, Varese, Italy

A. Vl. Koliopoulos S.A. Pako
Pelasghia Mill
Pelasghia, Fthiotidos, Greece

Aarepapier AG
Niedergösgen Mill
Niedergösgen, Switzerland

Abelan Board and Packaging Solutions
Alcover Mill
Alcover, Tarragona, Spain

Abelan Board and Packaging Solutions
Viersen Mill
Viersen, Germany

Abelan Board and Packaging Solutions
Villava Mill
Villava, Navarra, Spain

Absormex CMPC Tissue S.A. de CV
Altamira
Altamira, Tamaulipas, Mexico

Abu Dhabi National Paper Mill
Abu Dhabi Mill
Abu Dhabi, Shaikhdom of Abu Dhabi, United Arab Emirates

Adami S.A. Madeiras
Caçador Mill
Caçador, Santa Catarina, Brazil

Adda Ondulati SpA
Annone di Brianza Mill
Annone di Brianza, Lecco, Italy

Adischevskaya Board Mill
Adischevo Mill
Adischevo, Ostrovsky District, Kostroma Region, Russia

Afri Paper
Chbika Mill
Chbika, Kairouan, Gouvernorat de Kairouan, Tunisia

Agustín Barral, S.A.
Barcelona Mill
La Pobla de Lillet (Barcelona), Spain

Ajin Paper Mfg. Co. Ltd.
Hyunpoong Mill
Dalseong-gun, Daegu-si, Daegu-si, South Korea

Akasan Adana Kagit San ve Tic. Ltd. Sti.
Adana Mill
Adana, Turkey

Alas Doradas S.A. de C.V
San Juan Opico Mill
San Juan Opico La Libertad, El Salvador

Alatyrskaya Paper Mill
Alatyr Mill
Alatyr, Chuvashkaya Republic, Russia

Albert Köhler GmbH & Co. KG
Gengenbach Mill
Gengenbach, Germany

Albertin Paperboard & Paper Mill
Slonim Mill
Slonim, Grodno Region, Belarus

Aleksinskaya Board & Paper Mill, CJSC
Aleksin Mill
Aleksin, Tula Region, Russia

Alier S.A.
Roselló Mill
Roselló, Lérida, Spain

Alkim Kagit Sanayi ve Ticaret A.S
Izmir Mill
Izmir, Izmir, Turkey

Allard Emballages
Varennes Mill
Aubigné-Racan, France

Amaravathi Sri Venkatesa Paper Mills Ltd.
Madathukulam Mill
Madathukulam, Coimbatore Dist., Tamil Nadu, India

Ambro SA Suceava
Suceava Mill
Suceava, Romania

American Eagle Paper Mills Inc.
Tyrone Mill
Tyrone, Pennsylvania, United States

Anand Duplex/Triplex Board Limited
Meerut Mill
Meerut District, Uttar Pradesh, India

Angren Pack
Bulbak Mill
Angren, pos. Bulbak, Tashkentskaya obl., Uzbekistan

Anhui Hefei Jinzhong Paper Co. Ltd.
Hefei Mill
Hefei, Anhui, China

Anhui Hefei Xingdong Paper Co., Ltd.
Hefei Mill
Hefei, Anhui, China

Anhui Huoshan County Chenfeng Paper Co., Ltd
LiuAn Mill
LiuAn, Anhui, China

Anhui Shanying Paper No. 1 Mill
Maanshan (No. 1) Mill
Maanshan, Anhui, China

Anhui Shanying Paper No. 2 Mill
Maanshan (No. 2) Mill
Maanshan, Anhui, China

Anhui Weilun Industry & Trade Co., Ltd.
Huainan Mill
Huainan, Anhui, China

Ansabo S.A.
Quilmes Mill
Quilmes, Buenos Aires, Argentina

APC Paper Company, Inc
Claremont Mill
Claremont, New Hampshire, United States

Appleton Coated LLC
Combined Locks Mill
Combined Locks, Wisconsin, United States

Arab Cardboard Mfg. Co.
Sahab Mill
Sahab, Jordan

Arab Company for Paper Product (Arapepco)
Aleppo Mill
Aleppo, Syria

Arab Paper Manufacturing Co. Ltd. (Waraq)
Dammam Mill
Dammam, Saudi Arabia

Argencraft S.A.
Andino Mill
Andino, Santa Fé, Argentina

Arjowiggins Le Bourray SAS
Le Bourray Mill
Saint-Mars-la-Brière, France

Aryan Paper Mills Pvt. Ltd.
Vapi Mill
Vapi, Gujarat, India

Asia Kraft Paper Co., Ltd.
Samut Sakhon Mill
Samut Sakhon, Thailand

Asia Paper Mfg. Co., Ltd.
Cheongwon Mill
Cheongwon-gun, Chungcheongbuk-do, South Korea

Asia Papertec Inc.
Shihwa Mill
Siheung-si, Gyeonggi-do, South Korea

ASL Paper Mills
Karachi Mill
Karachi, Sindh, Pakistan

Atas Paper (Pvt) Ltd.
Sheikhupura Mill
Sheikhupura, Punjab, Pakistan

Athena Paper Manufacturing Co., Ltd.
Okayama Mill
Okayama-shi, Okayama Pref., Japan

Atlantic Packaging Products Ltd.
Scarborough Mill
Scarborough, Ontario, Canada

Recycled Pulp

Atlantic Packaging Products Ltd.
Whitby Mill
Whitby, Ontario, Canada

Atlas Paper Mills LLC
Hialeah Mill
Hialeah, Florida, United States

Atrak Pulp & Paper Industry Company
Foulad Mill
Foulad Industrial City, Esfahan, Iran

Augusta Select Tissue, LLC
Augusta Mill
Augusta, Georgia, United States

Austell Boxboard
Austell Boxboard Mill # 2
Austell, Georgia, United States

Austell Boxboard
Austell Boxboard Mill #1
Austell, Georgia, United States

Australian Paper
Maryvale Mill
Morwell, Victoria, Australia

Aylesford Newsprint Ltd.
Aylesford Mill
Aylesford, Kent, United Kingdom

Bai Bang Paper Joint-stock Co., Ltd.
Ky Son Mill
Ky Son, Hoa Binh Province, Vietnam

Balkrishna Paper Mills Ltd.
Ambivli Mill
Taluka Kalyan, Dist. Thane, Maharashtra, India

Ballavpur Paper Mfg. Ltd.
Ballavpur Mill
Ballavpur, Raniganj, Dist. Bardhaman, West Bengal, India

Banglane Paper Mill Co., Ltd.
Nakhon Pathom Mill
Banglane District, Nakhon Pathom, Nakhon Pathom, Thailand

Bartoli F.lli SpA
Carraia Mill
Carraia, Lucca, Italy

Bashundhara Paper Mills Ltd.
Unit 2
Sonargaon, New Town, Narayanganj, Bangladesh

Bataan 2020
Baesa Mill
Baesa, Quezon City, Philippines

Bataan 2020
Samal Mill
Samal, Bataan, Philippines

Bazargaon Paper & Pulp Mills Pvt. Ltd.
Bazargaon Mill
Bazargaon, Nagpur, Maharashtra, India

Bear Island Paper Co., LLC
Ashland Mill
Ashland, Virginia, United States

Beijing Paper Mill No. 7 Co., Ltd.
Beijing Mill
Beijing, Beijing, China

BELIŠCE d.d.
Belišce Mill
Belišce, Salvonia, Croatia

Beloit Box Board Co
Beloit Mill
Beloit, Wisconsin, United States

Belovo Paper Mill S.A.
Belovo Mill
Belovo, Bulgaria

Berli Jucker Cellox Ltd.
Bangplee Mill
Bangchalong, Bangplee, Samut Prakarn, Thailand

Berli Jucker Cellox Ltd.
Prachinburi Mill
Srimahapoth, Prachinburi, Thailand

Best Paper Mills Pvt. Ltd.
Vapi Mill
Vapi, Gujarat, India

Bharat Papers Ltd.
Kathua Mill
Kathua, Jammu and Kashmir, India

Bignardi Indústria e Comércio de Papéis e Artefatos Ltda.
Jundiaí Mill / GB Millennium Mill
Jundiaí, São Paulo, Brazil

BillerudKorsnäs AB
Skärblacka Mill
Skärblacka, Sweden

BillerudKorsnäs Finland Oy
Tervasaari Mill
Valkeakoski, Finland

Bio-PAPPEL International
Prewitt Mill
Prewitt, New Mexico, United States

Bio-PAPPEL Kraft
Atenquique Mill
Atenquique, Jalisco, Mexico

Bio-PAPPEL Kraft
Cuesta El Registro mill
Cuesta El Registro, Durango, Mexico

Bio-PAPPEL Kraft
Monterrey Mill
Monterrey, Nuevo León, Mexico

Bio-PAPPEL Kraft
Texcoco Mill
Los Reyes La Paz, Edo. de México, Mexico

Bio-PAPPEL Kraft
Tizayuca Mill
El Chopo, Tizayuca, Mexico

Bio-PAPPEL Printing
Tres Valles Mill
Tres Valles, Veracruz, Mexico

Bio-PAPPEL Printing
Tuxtepec Mill
Tuxtepec, OAX, Mexico

Biodeal Laboratories Pvt. Ltd. (Paper Mill Div.)
Vapi Mill
Dist. Valsad, Gujarat, India

BL Bittar, Indústria de Papel
Limeira Mill
Limeira, São Paulo, Brazil

Boise Paper
Jackson Mill
Jackson, Alabama, United States

Boise Paper
Wallula Mill
Wallula, Washington, United States

Bonet Madeiras e Papéis Ltda.
Timbó Grande Mill
Timbó Grande, Santa Catarina, Brazil

Bormio SpA
Ponte Lambro Mill
Ponte Lambro, Como, Italy

Brianskaya Paper Mill
Belye Berega Mill
Pos. Belye Berega, Bryansk Region, Russia

Bulleh Shah Packaging (Private) Limited
Bulleh Shah Paper Mill
Kasur, Pakistan

Bulleh Shah Packaging (Private) Limited
Lahore Mill
Lahore, Punjab, Pakistan

Burgo Group SpA
Sarego Mill
Sarego, Vicenza, Italy

Burgo Group SpA
Sora Mill
Sora, Frosinone, Italy

Burgo Group SpA
Toscolano Mill
Toscolano Maderno, Brescia, Italy

C & C Srl
Broccostella Mill
Broccostella, Frosinone, Italy

C.C.R. - Cartiera Cooperativa Rivalta
Rivalta Veronese Mill
Brentino-Belluno, Verona, Italy

Calcarta S.R.L.
Chifenti Mill
Chifenti, Borgo a Mozzano, Lucca, Italy

California Paperboard Corp.
Santa Clara Mill
Santa Clara, California, United States

Carl Macher GmbH & Co. KG
Brunnenthal Mill
Brunnenthal, Germany

Carotell Paperboard
Taylors Mill
Taylors, South Carolina, United States

Carta Fabril Ltda.
Anápolis Mill
Anápolis, Goiás, Brazil

Carta Fabril Ltda.
Carta Rio Mill
São Gonçalo, Rio de Janeiro, Brazil

Recycled Pulp

Carta Misr
Maarouf, Cairo Mill
Maarouf, Cairo, Egypt

Cartaseta-Friedrich & Co.
Däniken Mill
Däniken, Switzerland

Carter Holt Harvey Pulp & Paper
Kinleith Mill
Tokoroa, New Zealand

Carter Holt Harvey Pulp & Paper
Penrose Mill
Penrose, Auckland, New Zealand

Cartesar SpA
Pellezano Mill
Pellezano, Salerno, Italy

Carthage Specialty Paperboard
Carthage Mill
Carthage, New York, United States

Cartiera Cama S.R.L.
Lallio Mill
Lallio, Bergamo, Italy

Cartiera Cerrone Francescantonio SpA
Cerrone Mill
Aquino, Frosinone, Italy

Cartiera Ciacci S.a.
San Marino Mill
Gualdicciolo, San Marino, San Marino

Cartiera del Chiese SpA
Montichiari Mill
Montichiari, Brescia, Italy

Cartiera dell' Adda SpA
Calolziocorte Mill
Calolziocorte, Lecco, Italy

Cartiera di Bosco Marengo SpA
Alessandria Mill
Bosco Marengo, Alessandria, Italy

Cartiera di Carbonera SpA
Camposampiero Mill
Camposampiero, Padua, Italy

Cartiera di Cologno SpA
Cologno Monzese Mill
Cologno Monzese, Milan, Italy

Cartiera di Ferrara SpA
Ferrara Mill
Ferrara, Ferrara, Italy

Cartiera di Momo SpA
Momo Mill
Momo, Novara, Italy

Cartiera di Nave SpA
Caino Mill
Caino, Brescia, Italy

Cartiera di Ponzano Srl
Ponzano Veneto Mill
Ponzano Veneto, Treviso, Italy

Cartiera di Porporano Srl
Porporano Mill
Porporano, Parma, Italy

Cartiera di Salerno di Mauro Benedetti
Salerno Mill
Salerno, Salerno, Italy

Cartiera Enrico Cassina SNC
Pinerolo Mill
Pinerolo, Turin, Italy

Cartiera Fornaci SpA
Fagnano Olona Mill
Fagnano Olona, Varese, Italy

Cartiera Francesco Imperato e Figli SNC
Palermo Mill
Palermo, Palermo, Italy

Cartiera Galliera srl
Galliera Veneta Mill
Galliera Veneta, Padua, Italy

Cartiera Giacosa SpA
Front Canavese Mill
Front Canavese, Turin, Italy

Cartiera Giorgione SpA
Castelfranco Veneto Mill
Castelfranco Veneto, Treviso, Italy

Cartiera Grillo sas di Giuseppe e Domenico Grillo
Genova-Voltri Mill
Genova-Voltri, Genova, Italy

Cartiera Mantovana S.R.L.
Maglio di Goito Mill
Maglio di Goito, Mantua, Italy

Cartiera Marchigiana Srl
Montelupone Mill
Montelupone, Macerata, Italy

Cartiera Nuova So.Car.Pi. S.r.l.
Piteglio Mill
Piteglio, Pistoia, Italy

Cartiera Olona Sas di Belvisi Dr. Davide & C.
Gorla Minore Mill
Gorla Minore, Varese, Italy

Cartiera Partenope S.r.l
Arzano Mill
Arzano, Naples, Italy

Cartiera Pasquini Srl
Bagni di Lucca Mill
Bagni di Lucca, Lucca, Italy

Cartiera Pieretti SpA
Marlia-Capannori Mill
Marlia-Capannori, Lucca, Italy

Cartiera Ponte A Villa s.r.l.
Villa Basilica Mill
Villa Basilica, Lucca, Italy

Cartiera Puglisi SRL
Castiglione di Sicilia Mill
Castiglione di Sicilia, Catania, Italy

Cartiera S.A.C.C.A. SpA
Calatabiano Mill
Calatabiano, Catania, Italy

Cartiera San Felice SpA
San Felice Mill
Piteccio, Pistoia, Italy

Cartiera San Giorgio S.r.l.
Genova-Voltri Mill
Genova-Voltri, Genova, Italy

Cartiera San Lorenzo S.R.L.
Gassano Mill
Gassano, Massa-Carrara, Italy

Cartiera San Martino SpA
Broccostella Mill
Broccostella, Frosinone, Italy

Cartiera San Rocco SpA
Villa Basilica Mill
Villa Basilica, Lucca, Italy

Cartiere del Garda SpA
Riva del Garda Mill
Riva del Garda, Trento, Italy

Cartiere del Polesine Spa
Adria Mill
Adria, Rovigo, Italy

Cartiere del Polesine Spa
Loreo Mill
Loreo, Rovigo, Italy

Cartiere di Trevi SpA
Trevi Mill
Trevi, Perugia, Italy

Cartiere Modesto Cardella SpA
San Pietro a Vico Mill
San Pietro a Vico, Lucca, Italy

Cartiere SACI SpA
Verona Mill
Cà di David, Verona, Italy

Cartiere Villa Lagarina Spa
Trento Mill
Trento, Trento, Italy

Cartitalia S.r.l.
Cartitalia Mill
Mesola, Ferrara, Italy

Cartocor S.A.
Arroyito Mill
Arroyito, Córdoba, Argentina

Cartones America SA - CAME
Cali Mill
Cali, Valle de Cauca, Colombia

Cartones Ponderosa S.A. de C.V.
San Juan del Rio Mill
San Juan del Rio, Querétaro, Mexico

Cartonificio Sandreschi S.R.L.
Villa Basilica Mill
Villa Basilica, Lucca, Italy

Cartonifício Valinhos S.A.
Valinhos Mill
Valinhos, São Paulo, Brazil

Cartonnerie Jean SA
Bonnat Mill
Bonnat, France

Cartonnerie Oudin
Truyes Mill
Truyes, France

Recycled Pulp

Cartonnerie Tunisienne SA
Enfidha Mill
Enfidha, Gouvernorat de Sousse, Tunisia

Cartonneries de Gondardennes SA
Wardrecques Mill
Wardrecques, Aire-Sur-La-Lys, France

Cartopel S.A.
Cuenca Mill
Cuenca, Azuay, Ecuador

Cartulinas CMPC S.A.
Valdivia Mill
Valdivia, X - Región de Los Lagos, Chile

Carval Cartiera Di Valletrompia Srl.
Concesio Mill
Concesio, Brescia, Italy

Casalino Carta S.r.l.
Mele Mill
Mele, Genova, Italy

Cascades Auburn Fiber, Inc.
Auburn Mill
Auburn, Maine, United States

Cascades Boxboard Group Inc.
East Angus Mill
East Angus, Quebec, Canada

Cascades Boxboard Group Inc.
Jonquière Mill
Jonquiere, Quebec, Canada

Cascades East Angus Inc.
East Angus Mill
East Angus, Quebec, Canada

Cascades Papier Kingsey Falls Inc.
Kingsey Falls Mill
Kingsey Falls, Quebec, Canada

Cascades Tissue Group
Candiac Mill
Candiac, Quebec, Canada

Cascades Tissue Group
Eau Claire Mill
Eau Claire, Wisconsin, United States

Cascades Tissue Group
Kingsey Falls Mill
Kingsey Falls, Quebec, Canada

Cascades Tissue Group
Lachute Mill
Lachute, Quebec, Canada

Cascades Tissue Group
Mechanicville Mill
Mechanicville, New York, United States

Cascades Tissue Group
Memphis Mill
Memphis, Tennessee, United States

Cascades Tissue Group
Ransom Mill
Ransom, Pennsylvania, United States

Cascades Tissue Group
Rockingham Mill
Rockingham, North Carolina, United States

Cascades Tissue Group
Saint Helens Mill
Saint Helens, Oregon, United States

Cascades Tissue Group
Scarborough Mill
Agincourt - Scarborough, Ontario, Canada

Cascades Tissue Group
Whitby Mill
Whitby, Ontario, Canada

Cataguazes Indústrias de Papel
Cataguases Mill
Cataguases, Minas Gerais, Brazil

CECSO - Celulosa y Corrugados de Sonora S.A. de C.V.
Navojoa Mill
Navojoa, Sonora, Mexico

Celu Paper S.A.
San Pedro Mill
San Pedro, Buenos Aires, Argentina

Celulosa Campana S.A.
Lima Mill
Lima, Buenos Aires, Argentina

Celulosa y Papel del Bajío S.A.de C.V.
León Mill
León, Guanajuato, Mexico

Celulose Irani S.A.
Santa Luzia Mill
Santa Luzia, Minas Gerais, Brazil

Celulose Irani S.A.
Vargem Bonita Mill
Vargem Bonita, Santa Catarina, Brazil

Celulose Reciclada
Paulista Mill
Paratibe, Paulista, Pernambuco, Brazil

Century Paper & Board Mills Ltd.
Kasur Mill
Bhai Pheru, Dist. Kasur, Pakistan

Century Pulp & Paper
Lalkua Mill
Nainital, Uttarakhand, India

CEREPA, a.s.
Cervená Recice Mill
Cervená Recice 107, Czech Republic

Chaltyr Paper Mill
Chaltyr Mill
Chaltyr, Russia

Charoen Aksorn Holding Group Co. Ltd. (CAS Group)
Singburi Mill
Amphur Muang, Singburi, Thailand

Cheema Paper Mills Pvt. Ltd.
Nainital Mill
Dist. Udham Singh Nagar, Uttarakhand, India

Cheng Fung Paper Co., Ltd.
Feng Yuan Mill
Feng Yuan District, Taichung City, Taiwan

Cheng Loong Corporation
Chu Pei Mill
Chu Pei, Hsinchu County, Taiwan

Cheng Loong Corporation
Hou Li Mill
Hou Li, Taichung City, Taiwan

Cheng Loong Corporation
Hsinchu Mill
Chung Pu Li, Hsinchu County, Taiwan

Cheng Loong Corporation Tayuan Mill
Ta Yuan Mill
Ta Yuan, Taoyuan County, Taiwan

Cheng Yang Paper Mill Co., Ltd.
Ben Cat Dist. (Cheng Yang Paper) Mill
Ben Cat Dist., Binh Duong Province, Vietnam

Chenming Paper Holdings Ltd.
Shouguang (Shouguang Chenming Newsprint No. 5) Mill
Shouguang, Shandong, China

China Sunshine Paper Holdings Company Limited
Weifang Mill
Weifang, Shandong, China

Chongqing Lee & Man Paper Co., Ltd.
Chongqing Mill
Chongqing, Chongqing, China

Chouka Pulp & Paper Mill
Rezvanshahr Mill
Rezvanshahr, Iran

Chuetsu Pulp & Paper Co., Ltd.
Sendai Mill
Satsumasendai-shi, Kagoshima Pref., Japan

Chuetsu Pulp & Paper Co., Ltd.
Takaoka (Futatsuka) Mill
Takaoka-shi, Toyama Pref., Japan

Cia. Canoinhas de Papel
Canoinhas Mill
Canoinhas, Santa Catarina, Brazil

Cia. Industrial Papelera Poblana S.A. de C.V.
Chachapa Mill
Chachapa, Puebla, Mexico

Cibrapel S.A. Indústria de Papel e Embalagens
Guapimirim Mill
Guapimirim, Rio de Janeiro, Brazil

Cincinnati Paperboard
Cincinnati Mill
Cincinnati, Ohio, United States

CITROPLAST- Ind. e Com. de Papéis e Plásticos Ltda.
Andradina Mill
Andradina, São Paulo, Brazil

Clearwater Paper Corporation
Ladysmith Mill
Ladysmith, Wisconsin, United States

CMPC Papeles Cordillera S.A.
Puente Alto Mill
Puente Alto, RM - Región Metro. de Santiago, Chile

CMPC Tissue S.A.
Puente Alto Mill
Eyzaguirre, Puente Alto, RM - Región Metro. de Santiago, Chile

CMPC Tissue S.A.
Talagante Mill
Talagante, RM - Región Metro. de Santiago, Chile

Recycled Pulp

Coldenhove Papier
Eerbeek Mill
Eerbeek, Netherlands

Compañía Papelera Mendoza S.A. (Copelme)
Cochabamba Mill
Cochabamba, Bolivia

Copamex Industrias S.A. de C.V.
Monterrey Mill
San Nicolas de los Garza, Nuevo León, Mexico

COPAPA - Companhia Paduana de Papéis
Santo Antônio de Pádua Mill
Santo Antônio de Pádua, Rio de Janeiro, Brazil

Copikas Kagit ve Oluklu Mukavva Kutu A.S.
Olmuksa Copikas Mill
Corum, Turkey

Corenso France
Soustre Mill
Saint-Seurin-Sur-L'Isle, France

Corenso North America
Wisconsin Rapids Mill
Wisconsin Rapids, Wisconsin, United States

Corenso United Oy Ltd.
Pori Coreboard Mill
Pori, Finland

Craft Corner Paper Mills Pvt. Ltd.
Vapi Dist., Valsad Mill
Dist. Valsad, Gujarat, India

Creative Paper Mills Ltd
Rupganj Mill
Rupganj, Narayanganj, Bangladesh

Crown Paper Mill Ltd.
Abu Dhabi Branch
Abu Dhabi, Shaikhdom of Abu Dhabi, United Arab Emirates

CVG - Cahdam Volta Grande
Rio Negrinho Mill
Rio Negrinho, Santa Catarina, Brazil

Dae Wang Paper Co., Ltd.
Gunsan Mill
Gunsan-si, Jeollabuk-do, South Korea

Daehan Paper Co., Ltd.
Cheongwon Mill
Cheongwon-gun, Chungcheongbuk-do, South Korea

Daehan Papertech Co., Ltd.
Danyang Mill
Daejeon-myeon, Damyang-gun, Jeollanam-do, South Korea

Daelim Paper Co. Ltd.
Daelim Paper
Osan-si, Gyeonggi-do, South Korea

Daewha Paper Board Mfg. Co., Ltd.
Gunpo Mill
Gunpo-si, Gyeonggi-do, South Korea

Daeyang Paper Mfg. Co. Ltd.
Ansan Mill
Ansan-si, Gyeonggi-do, South Korea

Daio Paper Corp.
Kani Mill
Kani-shi, Gifu Pref., Japan

Daio Paper Corp.
Mishima Mill
Shikokuchuo-shi, Ehime Pref., Japan

Daiwa Itagami Co., Ltd.
Daiwa Mill
Kashiwabara-shi, Osaka Pref., Japan

Dalkrovlya
Khabarovsk Mill
Khabarovsk, Russia

Dall Pel Madeira e Papel
Grechinski Mill
Irati, Paraná, Brazil

DamaPel Comércio de Papéis Ltda
Guarulhos Mill
Guarulhos, São Paulo, Brazil

Danalakshmi Paper Mills Pvt. Ltd.
Dindigul Mill
Nilakottai Taluk, Dindigul, Tamil Nadu, India

Decor Paper Mills Ltd.
Punjagutta, Hyderabad Mill
Punjagutta, Hyderabad, Andhra Pradesh, India

Delkeskamp Verpackungswerke GmbH
Nortrup Mill
Nortrup, Germany

Delta Board Mills SAE
Cairo Mill
Badr City, Cairo, Egypt

Delta Paper Mills Ltd.
Vendra Mill
Vendra, West Godavari Dist, Andhra Pradesh, India

Dentaş Ambalaj Ve Kagit San. A.S
Çorlu Mill
Çorlu, Tekirdag, Turkey

Dentaş Ambalaj Ve Kagit San. A.S
Denizli Mill
Denizli, Turkey

Dev Kiran Paper Mills (P) Ltd.
Bangalore Mill
Bangalore, Karnataka, India

Dev Priya Fibres Pvt. Ltd.
Meerut Mill
Meerut, Uttar Pradesh, India

Dev Priya Industries Limited
Meerut Mill
Meerut District, Uttar Pradesh, India

Dezhou Huisheng Pingyuan Paper Co., Ltd.
Dezhou Mill
Dezhou, Shandong, China

DICEPA Papelera de Enate S.L.
Enate Mill
Enate, Huesca, Spain

Dinatex Ltd. Co.
Adra Mill
Adra, Syria

Disley Tissue Ltd.
Disley Mill
Disley, North Stockport, Cheshire, United Kingdom

Dnepropetrovsk Paper Mill, Ltd.
Dnepropetrovsk Mill
Dnepropetrovsk, Ukraine

Dobrushskaya Paper Mill "Geroi Truda", OJSC
Dobrush Mill
Dobrush, Gomel Region, Belarus

Doh-Ei Paper Mfg. Co., Ltd.
Fuji Mill
Fuji-shi, Shizuoka Pref., Japan

Doh-Ei Paper Mfg. Co., Ltd.
Hokkaido Mill
Abuta-gun, Hokkaido Pref., Japan

Domtar Corporation
Nekoosa Mill
Nekoosa, Wisconsin, United States

Donetsk-Vtorma Ltd.
Donetsk Mill
Donetsk, Ukraine

Dongil Packaging
Jinju-si Mill
Jinju-si, Gyeongsangnam-do, South Korea

Dongil Paper Mfg. Co., Ltd.
Ansan Mill
Ansan-si, Gyeonggi-do, South Korea

Dongil Paper Mfg. Co., Ltd.
Uiryeong Mill
Uiryeong-gun, Gyeongsangnam-do, South Korea

Dongwon Paper Mfg. Co., Ltd.
Jeongup Mill
Jeongeup-si, Jeollabuk-do, South Korea

Donskaya Gofrotara
Rostov na Donu Mill
Rostov na Donu, Russia

Doruk Kagit San. T IC. A.S
Kayseri Mill
Kayseri, Turkey

Dresden Papier GmbH
Dresden Mill
Heidenau, Germany

DS Smith Chouanard
Coullons Mill
Coullons, Loiret, France

DS Smith Kaysersberg
Kaysersberg Mill
Kaysersberg, France

DS Smith Packaging Benelux B.V.
Eerbeek Mill
Eerbeek, Netherlands

DS Smith Packaging France
Contoire Hamel Mill
Contoire Hamel, France

Recycled Pulp

DS Smith Packaging France
Nantes Mill
Nantes Cedex 02, France

DS Smith Packaging Italia S.p.A.
Lucca Mill
Porcari, Lucca, Italy

DS Smith Paper
Kemsley Mill
Kemsley, Sittingbourne, Kent, United Kingdom

DS Smith Paper
Wansbrough Paper Mill
Watchet, Somerset, United Kingdom

DS Smith Paper Deutschland GmbH
Aschaffenburg Mill
Aschaffenburg, Germany

DS Smith Paper Deutschland GmbH
Witzenhausen Mill
Witzenhausen, Germany

Duropack GmbH
Trakia
Pazardzik, Glavinitza quarter, Bulgaria

E.MAK Paper Manufacturing Co.
Suez Mill
Suez, Egypt

Ecopaper JP Co. Ltd
Owariasahi Mill
Owariasahi-Shi, Aichi Pref., Japan

Edipack sh.p.k.
Durres Mill
Durres, Albania

EFW Tuscania Srl
Tuscania Mill
Tuscania, Viterbo, Italy

Ehime Paper Mfg. Co., Ltd.
Shikokuchuo-shi Mill
Shikokuchuo-shi, Ehime Pref., Japan

EIC - Empaques Industriales Colombianos SA
Caucaseco - Palmira Mill
Caucaseco - Palmira, Valle de Cauca, Colombia

EKA Industrial Paper Production Limited
Izmit Mill
Kosekoy, Izmit, Kocaeli, Turkey

El Farouk Co. "Farco"
El Obour Ind. City Mill
Obour, Egypt

El Nasr Carton Co.
Borg El Arab El Gededah Mill
Borg El Arab El - Gedeedah, Alexandria, Egypt

El Obour Co.
Heliopolis, Cairo Mill
Heliopolis, Cairo, Egypt

El-Salam PaperMill
Alexandria Mill
Alexandria, Iskanderiya, Egypt

ELF - Egyptian Co. for Manufacturing of Linerboard & Fluting
10th of Ramadan City Mill
10th of Ramadan City, Cairo, Sharkeya, East Province, Egypt

Elpap
Krakow Mill
Krakow, Poland

Emami Paper Mills Ltd.
Balasore Mill
Dist. Balasore, Odisha, India

EMBA spol. s. r.o.
Paseky nad Jizerou Mill
Paseky nad Jizerou, okr. Semily, Czech Republic

Emin Leydier
Champblain Mill
Saint-Vallier Cedex, France

Emin Leydier
Nogent-sur-Seine Mill
Nogent-sur-Seine, Aube, France

Empaques Modernos de Guadalajara, S.A. de C.V.
Guadalajara Mill
El Salto, Jalisco, Mexico

Empaques Modernos San Pablo S.A. de C.V.
Tlalnepantla Mill
Tlalnepantla, Edo. de México, Mexico

Encore Tissue
Laverton North Mill
Laverton North, Victoria, Australia

Erving Paper Mills Inc.
Erving Mill
Erving, Massachusetts, United States

Eska Graphic Board BV
Hoogezand Mill
Hoogezand, Netherlands

Eska Graphic Board BV
Sappemeer Mill
Sappemeer, Netherlands

Estrela Indústria de Papel Ltda.
Palmas Mill
Palmas, Paraná, Brazil

Etap Paper & Carton
Borg El Arab El Gededah Mill
Borg El Arab El Gededah, Alexandria, Egypt

Europac Alcolea de Cinca
Alcolea Mill
Alcolea de Cinca, Huesca, Spain

Europac Kraft Viana
Viana do Castelo Mill
Viana do Castelo, Portugal

Europac Papel Duenas
Dueñas Mill
Dueñas, Castilla y León, Spain

Europac Papeterie de Rouen
St. Etienne du Rouvray Mill
St. Etienne du Rouvray Cedex, France

Everbal
Evergnicourt Mill
Evergnicourt, France

Evergreen Packaging Inc.
Canton Mill
Canton, North Carolina, United States

Fábrica de Papel da Lapa Lda.
São Paio de Oleiros Mill
São Paio de Oleiros, Portugal

Fábrica de Papel de Torres Novas Lda.
Torres Novas Mill
Torres Novas, Portugal

Fábrica de Papel e Cartão da Zarrinha, S.A.
Rio Meão Mill
Rio Meão, Portugal

Fábrica de Papel San Francisco S.A. de C.V. (FAPSA)
Mexicali Mill
Mexicali, Baja California Norte, Mexico

Fábrica de Papel Santa Therezinha (SANTHER)
Fadlo Haidar Mill
Bragança Paulista, São Paulo, Brazil

Fábrica de Papel Santa Therezinha (SANTHER)
Governador Valadares Unit
Capim, Governador Valadares, Minas Gerais, Brazil

Fábricas de Papel Potosí, S.A. de C.V.
Potosí Mill
San Luis Potosí, San Luis Potosi, Mexico

Fabrika Hartije - PAP - DP
Beogradska Mill
Beograde, Serbia

Fabryka Papieru Czerwonak Sp. z o.o.
Czerwonak Mill
Czerwonak, Poland

Fabryka Papieru i Tektury "BESKIDY" S.A.
Wadowice Mill
Wadowice, Poland

Fabryka Papieru Kaczory Sp. z o.o.
Kaczory Mill
Kaczory, Poland

Fabryka Papieru Myszków Sp. z o.o.
Myszkow Mill
Myszkow, Poland

FACEPA - Fábrica de Papel da Amazônia S.A.
Belém Mill
Belem, Pará, Brazil

FAPAJAL - Fábrica de Papel de Tojal S.A.
São Julião do Tojal Mill
São Julião do Tojal, Portugal

Favini Spa
Rossano Veneto Mill
Rossano Veneto, Vicenza, Italy

Fedco Paper Corp.
Calamba City Mill
Calamba City, Laguna, Philippines

Fedrigoni S.P.A.
Arco Mill
Arco, Trento, Italy

Fedrigoni S.P.A.
Fabriano Mill
Fabriano, Ancona, Italy

Recycled Pulp

Fedrigoni S.P.A.
Varone Mill
Riva del Garda, Frazione Varone, Trento, Italy

Fedrigoni S.P.A.
Verona Mill
Verona, Verona, Italy

Feinpappenwerk Gebr. Schuster GmbH & Co. KG
Dachau Mill
Hebertshausen, Dachau, Germany

Fernandez S.A. Indústria de Papel
Amparo Mill
Amparo, São Paulo, Brazil

Fiber Marx Papers Ltd.
Kashipur Mill
Kashipur, Uttarakhand, India

Fibercorr Inc.
Massillon Mill
Massillon, Ohio, United States

Finch Paper, LLC
Glens Falls Mill
Glens Falls, New York, United States

Firma "W. Lewandowski" P.H.U.
Wloclawek Mill
Wloclawek, Poland

First Co. For Industrial Development S.A.E
El Obour City Mill
El Obour City, Egypt

Fiskeby Board AB
Norrköping Mill
Norrköping, Sweden

Flambeau River Papers, LLC
Park Falls Mill
Park Falls, Wisconsin, United States

Flying Kraft Paper Mills Ltd.
Charsadda Mill
Charsadda, Khyber Pakhtunkhwa, Pakistan

Forestal y Papelera Concepción S.A.
Coronel Mill
Coronel, VIII - Región del Bioblo, Chile

Foshan Gold Rich Union Paper Industry Co., Ltd.
Foshan Mill
Foshan, Guangdong, China

Fourstones Paper Mill Co. Ltd.
Sapphire Mills
Leslie, Scotland, United Kingdom

Fourstones Paper Mill Co. Ltd.
South Tyne Mill
Hexham, Northumberland, United Kingdom

Fox River Fiber Co., LLC
De Pere Mill
De Pere, Wisconsin, United States

FPHU "Filar" Sp. Jawna
Sadlno Mill
Sadlno, Gm Wierzbinek, Poland

French Paper Co.
Niles Mill
Niles, Michigan, United States

Fripa Papierfabrik Albert Friedrich KG
Miltenberg Mill
Miltenberg, Germany

FS-Karton GmbH
Neuss Mill
Neuss, Germany

Fthiotis Paper Mill SA
Damasta Mill
Damasta, Lamia, Greece

Fujian Dongxin (Zhangzhou) Paper Co., Ltd.
Zhangzhou Mill
Zhangzhou, Fujian, China

Fujian Dunxin Paper Co., Ltd.
Zhangzhou Mill
Zhangzhou, Fujian, China

Fujian Huafa (Fujian) Industrial Co., Ltd.
Longhai Mill
Longhai, Fujian, China

Fujian Jian'ou Taipingyang Paper Mill
Jian'ou Mill
Jian'ou, Fujian, China

Fujian Liansheng Paper (Longhai) Co., Ltd
Longhai Mill
Longhai City, Fujian, China

Fujian Liansheng Paper (Zhangzhou) Co., Ltd.
Zhangzhou Mill
Zhangzhou, Fujian, China

Fujian Lishu Pulp & Paper Co., Ltd.
Jianou Mill
Jianou, Fujian, China

Fujian Nanjing County Youlida Co., Ltd.
Zhangzhou Mill
Zhangzhou, Fujian, China

Fujian Nanping Paper Co. Ltd.
Nanping Mill
Nanping, Fujian, China

Fujian Qingshan Paper Industry Co., Ltd.
Qingzhou Mill
Qingzhou, Fujian, China

Fujian Quanzhou Guige Paper Co. Ltd.
Quanzhou Mill
Quanzhou, Fujian, China

Fujian Quanzhou Jingyu Paper Mill
Quanzhou Mill
Quanzhou, Fujian, China

Fujian Xinlida Paper Co., Ltd.
Zhangzhou Mill
Zhangzhou, Fujian, China

Fujieda Seishi Co. Ltd.
Fujieda-shi Mill
Fujieda-shi, Shizuoka Pref., Japan

Fukuda Paper Manufacturing Co., Ltd.
Iyomishima Mill
Shikokuchuo-shi, Ehime Pref., Japan

FutureMark Paper Group
Alsip Mill
Alsip, Illinois, United States

FutureMark Paper Group
Manistique Mill
Manistique, Michigan, United States

Fuyang Maohong Paper Co., Ltd.
Fuyang Mill
Fuyang, Zhejiang, China

G-P Gypsum LLC
San Leandro Mill
San Leandro, California, United States

G.F.F - Nikopol AD
Nikopol Mill
Cherkvitsa, Nikopol, Bulgaria

G.P.C. Mohammadia
Meknès Mill
Meknès, Morocco

Gain Hwang Paper Mfg. Co., Ltd.
Shan Hua Mill
Shan Hua, Tainan City, Taiwan

Gangotri Paper Mills Pvt Ltd.
Muzaffarnagar Mill
Muzaffarnagar, Uttar Pradesh, India

Gansu Hanfu Dongfang Paper Co., Ltd.
Tianshui Mill
Tianshui, Gansu, China

Gansu Tianshui Xuanyuan Paper Co., Ltd.
Tianshui Mill
Tianshui, Gansu, China

Gaya Baru Paper CV
Malang Mill
Malang, East Java, Indonesia

Gayatri Paper Mill
Germiston Mill
Germiston, Gauteng, South Africa

Gayatrishakti Paper & Boards Ltd.
Vapi Mill
Vapi, Gujarat, India

Gebr. Grünewald GmbH & Co. KG
Kirchhundem Mill
Kirchhundem-Hofolpe, Germany

Gemdoubs
Novillars Mill
Novillars, France

General Company for Paper Industry (GENCO)
Deir Ez-Zor Mill
Deir Ez-Zor, Syria

Genus Paper Products Limited
Moradabad Mill
Moradabad, Uttar Pradesh, India

Georgia-Pacific LLC
Big Island Mill
Big Island, Virginia, United States

Georgia-Pacific LLC
Broadway Street/West Mill
Green Bay, Wisconsin, United States

Georgia-Pacific LLC
Cedar Springs Mill
Cedar Springs, Georgia, United States

Recycled Pulp

Georgia-Pacific LLC
Halsey Mill
Halsey, Oregon, United States

Georgia-Pacific LLC
Monticello Mill
Monticello, Mississippi, United States

Georgia-Pacific LLC
Muskogee Mill
Muskogee, Oklahoma, United States

Georgia-Pacific LLC
Savannah River Mill
Rincon, Georgia, United States

Georgia-Pacific LLC
Toledo Mill
Toledo, Oregon, United States

Glatfelter
Chillicothe Mill
Chillicothe, Ohio, United States

Glucholaskie Zaklady Papiernicze Sp. z o.o.
Glucholazy Mill
Glucholazy, Poland

Godavari Pulp and Papers Mills (P) Ltd
Nasik Mill
Nasik, Maharashtra, India

Gomà-Camps S.A.U.
La Riba Mill
La Riba, Tarragona, Spain

Grand Bay Paper Products Ltd
Arima Mill
Arima, Trinidad and Tobago

Graphic Packaging International Inc.
Battle Creek Mill
Battle Creek, Michigan, United States

Graphic Packaging International Inc.
Kalamazoo Mill
Kalamazoo, Michigan, United States

Graphic Packaging International Inc.
Macon Mill
Macon, Georgia, United States

Graphic Packaging International Inc.
Middletown Mill
Middletown, Ohio, United States

Graphic Packaging International Inc.
Santa Clara Mill
Santa Clara, California, United States

Graphic Packaging International Inc.
West Monroe Mill
West Monroe, Louisiana, United States

Great Lakes Tissue Co.
Cheboygan Mill
Cheboygan, Michigan, United States

Green Bay Packaging Inc.
Green Bay Mill
Green Bay, Wisconsin, United States

Green Bay Packaging Inc.
Morrilton Mill
Morrilton, Arkansas, United States

Greenfield SAS
Château Thierry Pulp Mill
Château-Thierry, France

Greenpac Mill, LLC
Greenpac Mill
Niagara Falls, New York, United States

Greif Inc.
Massillon Mill
Massillon, Ohio, United States

Greif Inc.
Riverville Mill
Amherst, Virginia, United States

Groupe CMCP - La Compagnie Marocaine des Cartons et Papiers
Kenitra Mill
Kenitra, Morocco

Grupo Unipak, S.A. de C.V. PT
Cuernavaca Mill
Cuernavaca, Morelos, Mexico

Grupo Zucamor
Ranelagh Mill
Ranelagh, Buenos Aires, Argentina

Gruppo Cordenons SpA
Cordenons Mill
Cordenons, Pordenone, Italy

GS Paper & Packaging Group ("GSPP")
Banting Mill
Daerah Kuala Langat, Banting, Selangor Darul Ehsan, Malaysia

Guaçu S.A. Papéis e Embalagens
Tambaú Mill
Tambaú, São Paulo, Brazil

Guangdong City Baoli Paper Co., Ltd.
Dongguan Mill
Dongguan, Guangdong, China

Guangdong Dongguan Gaobu Qiangan Paper Mill
Dongguan Mill
Dongguan, Guangdong, China

Guangdong Dongguan Hongmei Lee & Man Paper Co., Ltd.
Dongguan (Hongmei) Milll
Dongguan, Guangdong, China

Guangdong Dongguan Huangyong Yinzhou Paper Industry Ltd.
Dongguan Mill
Dongguan, Guangdong, China

Guangdong Dongguan Jianhua Paper Co. Ltd.
Dongguan Mill
Dongguan, Guangdong, China

Guangdong Dongguan Jianhui Paper
Dongguan Mill
Dongguan, Guangdong, China

Guangdong Dongguan Jintian Paper Co., Ltd.
Dongguan Mill
Dongguan, Guangdong, China

Guangdong Dongguan Jinzhou Paper Co., Ltd.
Dongguan Mill
Dongguan, Guangdong, China

Guangdong Dongguan Lee & Man Paper Co., Ltd.
Dongguan (Huangyong) Mill
Dongguan, Guangdong, China

Guangdong Dongguan Nine Dragons Paper Industries Co., Ltd.
Dongguan Mill
Dongguan, Guangdong, China

Guangdong Dongguan Shenlian Paper Making Co., Ltd.
Dongguan Mill
Dongguan, Guangdong, China

Guangdong Dongguan Shuangzhou Paper Co., Ltd.
Dongguan Mill
Dongguan, Guangdong, China

Guangdong Dongguan Taichang Paper Co., Ltd.
Dongguan Mill
Dongguan, Guangdong, China

Guangdong Dongguan Zhonglian Paper Co., Ltd.
Dongguan Mill
Dongguan, Guangdong, China

Guangdong Donta Group Dongwen Paper Mill
Dongguan Mill
Dongguan, Guangdong, China

Guangdong Foshan Chengtong Paper Co., Ltd.
Foshan Mill
Foshan, Guangdong, China

Guangdong Green Forest (QingXin) Paper Industrial Limited
Qingyuan Mill
Qingyuan, Guangdong, China

Guangdong Guangzhou Panyu Lianhuashan Paper-Making Co., Ltd.
Guangzhou Mill
Guangzhou, Guangdong, China

Guangdong Heshan Paper Co., Ltd.
Heshan Mill
Heshan, Guangdong, China

Guangdong Huizhou Fook Woo Paper Co., Ltd.
Huizhou Mill
Huizhou, Guangdong, China

Guangdong Jiangmen City Qiaoyu Paper Co., Ltd.
Jiangmen Mill
Jiangmen, Guangdong, China

Guangdong Jiangmen Zhenlong Paper Mill Co., Ltd.
Jiangmen Mill
Jiangmen, Guangdong, China

Recycled Pulp

Guangdong Junye Paper Co., Ltd.
Dongguan Mill
Dongguan, Guangdong, China

Guangdong Mingxing Paper Co., Ltd.
Jiangmen Mill
Jiangmen, Guangdong, China

Guangdong Shantou Huashi Paper Industrial Co., Ltd.
Shantou Mill
Shantou, Guangdong, China

Guangdong Taiyuan Paper Co., Ltd.
Jiangmen Mill
Jiangmen, Guangdong, China

Guangdong Wanlida Paper
Guangzhou Mill
Guangzhou, Guangdong, China

Guangdong Zhongshan Rengo Hung Hing Paper Mfg. Co. Ltd.
Zhongshan Mill
Zhongshan, Guangdong, China

Guangdong Zhongshan Yongfa Paper Co., Ltd.
Zhongshan Mill
Zhongshan, Guangdong, China

Guangxi Forest Lipu Paper Co., Ltd.
Lipu Mill
Lipu, Guangxi, China

Guangxi Guigang Hongqi Paper Mill
Guigang mill
Guigang, Guangxi, China

Guangxi Jiayi Paper Co., Ltd.
Baise Mill
Baise, Guangxi, China

Guangxi Jindaxing Paper Group Co., Ltd.
Baise Mill
Baise, Guangxi, China

Guangzhou Paper Group Ltd. (Nansha)
Guangzhou Mill
Guangzhou, Guangdong, China

Guangzhou Victorgo Industry Co., Ltd.
Guangzhou (Guangzhou Victorgo) Mill
Guangzhou, Guangdong, China

Gugan Paper Mills Pvt Ltd
Gugan Paper Mills Pvt Ltd
Coimbatore, Tamil Nadu, India

Gulf Paper Industries Factory
Riyadh Mill
Riyadh, Saudi Arabia

Gulf Paper Manufacturing Free Zone Company
Dubai Mill
Jebel Ali Free Zone, Dubai, United Arab Emirates

Gulf Paper Mfg. Co. k.s.c.
Kuwait Mill
West Mina Abdulla, Ahmadi Governorate, Kuwait

GVG Paper Mills Ltd.
Palani Taluk Mill
Palani Taluk, Dist. Dindigul, Tamil Nadu, India

Hai Phong Paper Mill
Hai Phong City Mill
Hai Phong City, Hong Bang District, Vietnam

Halkali Kagit Karton San. ve Tic. A.S.
Istanbul Mill
Küçükçekmece, Istanbul, Turkey

Hamburger Hungaria Ltd
Dunaújváros Mill
Dunaújváros, Hungary

Hamburger Rieger GmbH & Co. KG
Spremberg-Schwarze Pumpe Mill
Spremberg-Schwarze Pumpe, Brandenburg, Germany

Hamburger Rieger GmbH & Co. KG
Trostberg Mill
Trostberg, Bavaria, Germany

Hanchang Paper Co., Ltd.
Yangsan-si Mill
Yangsan-si, Gyeongsangnam-do, South Korea

Hangzhou Huajin Specialty Paper Co., Ltd.
Hangzhou Mill
Hangzhou, Zhejiang, China

Hangzhou Jinjiang Paper Co., Ltd.
Linan Mill
Linan, Zhejiang, China

Hans Kolb Papierfabrik GmbH & Co. KG
Kaufbeuren Mill
Kaufbeuren, Germany

Hansol Paper Co. Ltd.
Daejeon Mill
Daejeon, Daejeon, South Korea

Harbor Paper LLC
Hoquiam Mill
Hoquiam, Washington, United States

Hariom Industries Limited
Kanpur Mill
Kanpur, Uttar Pradesh, India

Hartford City Paper, LLC
Hartford City Mill
Hartford City, Indiana, United States

Hayat Kagit ve Enerji A.S.
Corum Mill
Corum, Turkey

Hebei Baoding Mancheng Guanquan Paper Co., Ltd.
Baoding Mill
Baoding, Hebei, China

Hebei Baoding Orient Paper Co., Ltd.
Baoding Mill
Baoding, Hebei, China

Hebei Baoding Sanlian Paper Co., Ltd.
Baoding Mill
Baoding, Hebei, China

Hebei Chengda Paper Co., Ltd.
Tangshan Mill
Tangshan, Hebei, China

Hebei Dazhong Baolai Paper Co., Ltd.
Tangshan Mill
Tangshan, Hebei, China

Hebei Hongli Chenggong Paper Co., Ltd.
Tangshan Mill
Tangshan, Hebei, China

Hebei Huatai Paper Co., Ltd.
Shijiazhuang Mill
Shijiazhuang, Hebei, China

Hebei Huatong Paper Co., Ltd.
Langfang Mill
Langfang, Hebei, China

Hebei Lu Quan Shunfa Industrial Co., Ltd.
Luquan Mill
Luquan, Hebei, China

Hebei Luquan Yuanda Industrial Co., Ltd.
Luquan Mill
Luquan, Hebei, China

Hebei Qinhuangdao Fengman Paper Co., Ltd.
Qinghuangdao Mill
Qinghuangdao, Hebei, China

Hebei Qinhuangdao Haofeng Enterprise Group
Qinhuangdao Mill
Qinhuangdao, Hebei, China

Hebei Sanhe City Jingdong Shuhe Paper Mill
Sanhe Mill
Sanhe, Hebei, China

Hebei Sanhe City Youyi Paper Mill
Sanhe Mill
Sanhe, Hebei, China

Hebei Sanhe Xingwang Paper Mill
Sanhe Mill
Sanhe, Hebei, China

Hebei Sanhe Yangzhuang Dawotou Paper Mill
Sanhe Mill
Sanhe, Hebei, China

Hebei Sanhe Yanling Paper Mill
Sanhe Mill
Sanhe, Hebei, China

Hebei Sanhe Zhaotuzhuang Aimin Paper Mill
Sanhe Mill
Sanhe, Hebei, China

Hebei Tanghai Chenguang Paper Co., Ltd.
Tangshan Mill
Tangshan, Hebei, China

Hebei Tangshan Guotai Paper Co., Ltd.
Tangshan Mill
Tangshan, Hebei, China

Hebei Yongxin Paper Co., Ltd.
Tangshan (Hebei Yongxin) Mill
Tangshan, Hebei, China

Hebei Yuanshi County Jinpeng Paper Co., Ltd.
Shijiazhuang Mill
Shijiazhuang, Hebei, China

Recycled Pulp

Hebei Yutian Shunfa Paper Co., Ltd.
Tangshan Mill
Tangshan, Hebei, China

Henan Dongsheng Paper Co., Ltd.
Xinmi Mill
Xinmi, Henan, China

Henan Hongteng Paper Group Co., Ltd.
Xuchang Mill
Xuchang, Henan, China

Henan Longyuan Paper Co., Ltd.
Zhengzhou Mill
Zhengzhou, Henan, China

Henan Ningling County Longyuan Paper Co., Ltd.
Zhengzhou Mill
Zhengzhou, Henan, China

Henan No. 1 Sub-factory of Huixian City Paper Mill
Xinxiang Mill
Xinxiang, Henan, China

Henan Qinyang Haolin Paper Co., Ltd.
Qinyang Mill
Jiaozuo, Henan, China

Henan Xinxiang Hengli Paper Co., Ltd.
Huixian Mill
Huixian, Henan, China

Henan Xinxiang Hongda Paper Co., Ltd.
Xinxiang Mill
Xinxiang, Henan, China

Henan Xinxiang Hongtai Paper Co., Ltd.
Xinxiang Mill
Xinxiang, Henan, China

Henan Xinxiang Xinya Paper Group Co., Ltd.
Xinxiang No. 1 Mill
Xinxiang, Henan, China

Henan Xinxiang Xinya Paper Group Co., Ltd.
Xinxiang No. 4 Mill
Xinxiang, Henan, China

Henan Xuchang Feida Paper Co., Ltd.
Xuchang Mill
Xuchang, Henan, China

Henan Yingbo Paper Co., Ltd.
Mengzhou Mill
Mengzhou, Henan, China

Henan Yinge Packaging Paper Industry Co., Ltd.
Luohe (Yinge Packaging Paper) Mill
Luohe, Henan, China

Henan Zhengzhou Chunhui Paper Co., Ltd.
Xinmi Mill
Xinmi, Henan, China

Henan Zhengzhou Dongsheng Paper Co., Ltd.
Zhengzhou Mill
Zhengzhou, Henan, China

Hengshan Zhongkong International Paper Co., Ltd.
Hengyang Mill
Hengyang, Hunan, China

Hiang Seng Fibre Container Co., Ltd.
Samut Sakohn Mill
Amphur Muang, Samut Sakohn, Thailand

Highland Paper Mills Ltd.
Eldoret Mill
Eldoret, Western, Kenya

Hindustan Newsprint Ltd.
Kottayam Dist. Mill
Kottayam Dist., Kerala, India

Hogla-Kimberly Ltd.
Hadera Mill
Hadera, Israel

Hogla-Kimberly Ltd.
Naharya Mill
Naharya, Israel

Hokuetsu Kishu Paper Co. Ltd.
Kanto Ichikawa Mill
Ichikawa-shi, Chiba Pref., Japan

Hokuetsu Kishu Paper Co. Ltd.
Kanto Katsuta Mill
Hitachinaka-shi, Ibaraki Pref., Japan

Hokuetsu Kishu Paper Co. Ltd.
Kishu Mill
Minamimuro-gun, Mie Pref., Japan

Hokuetsu Kishu Paper Co. Ltd.
Niigata Mill
Niigata-shi, Niigata Pref., Japan

Holmen AB
Braviken Paper Mill
Norrköping, Sweden

Holmen Paper Madrid S.L.
Madrid Mill
Fuenlabrada, Madrid, Spain

HRA Papers Pvt Ltd
Kangra Mill
Village Tibbi, Kangra, Himachal Pradesh, India

Hsing Chung Paper Corp.
Wu Chieh Mill
Wu Chieh, Ilan County, Taiwan

Hubei Hongfa Renewable Resources Technology Development
Yichang Mill
Yichang, Hubei, China

Hubei Paima Paper Co., Ltd.
Jingzhou Mill
Jingzhou, Hubei, China

Hubei Wuhan Mulan Paper Co., Ltd.
Wuhan Mill
Wuhan, Hubei, China

Hubei Yadu Hengxing Paper Co., Ltd
Guangshui Mill
Guangshui, Hubei, China

Hubei Yichang Baota Paper Co., Ltd
Yichang Mill
Yichang, Hubei, China

Hunan Shuanghua Paper Co., Ltd.
Changsha Mill
Changsha, Hunan, China

Hunan Tiger Forest & Paper Group Yueyang Paper Co., Ltd.
Yueyang Mill
Yueyang, Hunan, China

Hygienic Tissue Mills
Pietermaritzburg Mill
Pietermaritzburg, Natal, South Africa

Hyogo Paper Mfg. Co., Ltd.
Himeji Mill
Himeji-shi, Hyogo Pref., Japan

IBEMA - Cia. Brasileira de Papel
Turvo Mill
Turvo, Paraná, Brazil

Iberkraft Indústria de Papel e Celulose Ltda.
Guarapuava Mill
Guarapuava, Paraná, Brazil

ICO-Industria Cartone Ondulato Srl
San Giovanni Teatino Mill
San Giovanni Teatino, Chieti, Italy

Imporpel Ind. e Com. de Papéis Ltda.
Porto Ferreira Mill
Porto Ferreira, São Paulo, Brazil

Ind. de Papelão Hörlle Ltda.
Campo Largo Mill
Campo Largo, Paraná, Brazil

Indugevi S.A.
Sabaneta Mill
Sabaneta, Antioquia, Colombia

Industria Cartaria Fenili S.p.A.
Coselli Capannori Mill
Coselli Capannori, Lucca, Italy

Industria Cartaria Pieretti SpA (ICP)
Marlia Mill
Marlia di Capannori, Lucca, Italy

Indústria de Papéis para Embalagem Irmãos Siqueira Ltda.
Passa Quatro Mill
Passa Quatro, Minas Gerais, Brazil

Indústria de Papel Sovel da Amazônia Ltda.
Manaus Mill
Manaus, Amazonas, Brazil

Indústria e Comércio de Embalagens e Papéis Artivinco Ltda.
Santa Rosa do Viterbo Mill
Santa Rosa do Viterbo, São Paulo, Brazil

Industria Panameña de Papel SA
Chilibre Mill
San Vicente, Zona Chilibre, Panama

Industrial Papelera Atlas SA
Nana Mill
Ñana, Lima, Lima, Peru

Industrias Cartonera Asociada S.A. - INCASA
Quito Mill
Quito, Pichincha, Ecuador

Recycled Pulp

Indústrias de Papel R. Ramenzoni S.A.
Cordeirópolis Mill
Cordeirópolis, São Paulo, Brazil

Industrias del Cartón S.A. - INCASA
Cayalti Mill
Cayalti, Chiclayo, Peru

Indústrias Novacki S.A.
União da Vitória Mill
União da Vitória, Paraná, Brazil

Indústrias Reunidas Cristo Rey Ltda.
Campo Mourão Mill
Campo Mourão, Paraná, Brazil

Inland Empire Paper Co.
Millwood Mill
Millwood, Spokane, Washington, United States

INPA - Indústria de Embalagens Santana S.A.
Pirapetinga Mill
Pirapetinga, Minas Gerais, Brazil

INPA - Indústria de Embalagens Santana S.A.
Uberaba Mill
Uberaba, Minas Gerais, Brazil

Inpol-Papier Sp. z o.o.
Bardo Mill
Bardo, Poland

Inter Pacific Paper Co., Ltd
Banpluang, Baansang Mill
Banpluang, Baansang, Prachinburi, Thailand

International Paper - Kwidzyn Sp. z o.o.
Kwidzyn Mill
Kwidzyn, Poland

International Paper APPM Ltd.
Kadiam Mill
Madhavarayudu Palem, East Godavari District, Andhra Pradesh, India

International Paper Co.
Bogalusa Mill
Bogalusa, Louisiana, United States

International Paper Co.
Cedar Rapids Mill
Cedar Rapids, Iowa, United States

International Paper Co.
Georgetown Mill
Georgetown, South Carolina, United States

International Paper Co.
Henderson Mill
Henderson, Kentucky, United States

International Paper Co.
Mansfield Mill
Mansfield, Louisiana, United States

International Paper Co.
Maysville Mill
Maysville, Kentucky, United States

International Paper Co.
Newport Mill
Cayuga, Indiana, United States

International Paper Co.
Orange Mill
Orange, Texas, United States

International Paper Co.
Pine Hill Mill
Pine Hill, Alabama, United States

International Paper Co.
Prattville Mill
Prattville, Alabama, United States

International Paper Co.
Red River Mill
Campti, Louisiana, United States

International Paper Co.
Riverdale Mill
Selma, Alabama, United States

International Paper Co.
Rome Mill
Rome, Georgia, United States

International Paper Co.
Savannah Mill
Savannah, Georgia, United States

International Paper Co.
Springfield Mill
Springfield, Oregon, United States

International Paper Co.
Valliant Mill
Valliant, Oklahoma, United States

International Paper Co.
Vicksburg Mill
Vicksburg, Mississippi, United States

International Paper, Empaques Industriales de México S.A. de C.V.
Xalapa Mill
Xalapa, Veracruz, Mexico

Interstate Paper Industries
Sadat City Mill
Sadat City, Menofeya, Egypt

Interstate Paper L.L.C.
Riceboro Mill
Riceboro, Georgia, United States

Invepal
Morón Mill
Morón, Edo. Carabobo, Venezuela

IPEL - Indaial Papel Embalagens Ltda.
Indaial Mill
Indaial, Santa Catarina, Brazil

IPUSA - Industria Papelera Uruguaya S.A.
IPUSA Plant 3, Pando Mill
Pando, Canelones, Uruguay

Iran Papyrus Co. Ltd.
Saveh Mill
Saveh, Markazi, Iran

Islamic Paper Manufacturing Co.
Quesna Mill
Quesna, Menofeya, Egypt

Isma 2000 (Ismaeco Group)
Marratxi Mill
Marratxi, Spain

Istituto Poligrafico e Zecca dello Stato
Foggia Mill
Foggia, Foggia, Italy

ITC Limited, Paperboards & Specialty Papers Division
Bhadrachalam Mill
Khammam, Bhadrachalam, Andhra Pradesh, India

ITC Limited, Paperboards & Specialty Papers Division
Kovai Mill
Coimbatore, Tamil Nadu, India

Itoman Co., Ltd.
Kawanoe Mill
Shikokuchuo-shi, Ehime Pref., Japan

Izmail Pulp & Paperboard Combine
Izmail Mill
Izmail, Odesskaya obl., Ukraine

J. Vilaseca S.A.
Capellades Mill
Capellades, Barcelona, Spain

Jack-Pol Sp. z o.o.
Olawa Mill
Olawa, Poland

Jackson Paper Manufacturing Co.
Sylva Mill
Sylva, North Carolina, United States

Jaepel Papéis e Embalagens
Senador Canedo Mill
Senador Canedo, Goiás, Brazil

Jeonju Paper Corporation, Ltd.
Cheongju mill
Cheongwon-gun, Chungcheongbuk-do, South Korea

Jeonju Paper Corporation, Ltd.
Jeonju Mill
Jeonju-si, Jeollabuk-do, South Korea

Jiangsu Chamfor Paper Industry Co. Ltd.
Danyang Mill
Danyang, Jiangsu, China

Jiangsu Fuxing Paper
Yancheng Mill
Yancheng, Jiangsu, China

Jiangsu Huaji Zhangjiagang Huaxing Papermaking Co. Ltd.
Zhangjiagang Mill
Zhangjiagang, Jiangsu, China

Jiangsu Huangli Paper Industry Co., Ltd.
Jiangyin Mill
Jiangyin, Jiangsu, China

Jiangsu Jiangyin Gushan Dongfang Paper Co., Ltd.
Jiangyin Mill
Jiangyin, Jiangsu, China

Jiangsu Lee & Man Paper Manufacturing Co. Ltd.
Changshu Mill
Changshu, Jiangsu, China

Jiangsu Longheng Paper Co. Ltd
Yancheng Mill
Yancheng, Jiangsu, China

Jiangsu Nine Dragons Paper Industries
Taicang Mill
Taicang, Jiangsu, China

Recycled Pulp

Jiangsu Taizhou Jinsong Paper Co., Ltd.
Taizhou Mill
Taizhou, Jiangsu, China

Jiangsu Wanda Paper Co., Ltd.
Changzhou Mill
Changzhou, Jiangsu, China

Jiangsu Wuxi Long Chen Paper Co., Ltd.
Wuxi Mill
Wuxi, Jiangsu, China

Jiangsu Xuzhou Xinyuan Paper Co.,Ltd
Xuzhou Mill
Xuzhou, Jiangsu, China

Jiangsu Yixing Zhangzhu Paper Mill
Yixing Mill
Yixing, Jiangsu, China

Jiangsu Yuen Foong Yu Paper (Yangzhou) Co., Ltd.
Yangzhou Mill
Yangzhou, Jiangsu, China

Jiangsu Zhangjiagang Mingxing Paper Co., Ltd.
Zhangjiagang Mill
Zhangjiagang, Jiangsu, China

Jiangxi Chenming Paper Co., Ltd.
Nanchang (Jiangxi Chenming Paper) Mill
Nanchang, Jiangxi, China

Jiangxi Dexing City Hengsheng Paper Co., Ltd.
Dexing Mill
Dexing, Jiangxi, China

Jiangxi Lee & Man Paper Co., Ltd.
Ruichang Mill
Ruichang, Jiangxi, China

Jiangyin Xinhao Recycling Paper Co., Ltd.
Jiangyin Mill
Jiangyin, Jiangsu, China

Jin Young Paper Co., Ltd.
Chilgok-gun Mill
Chilgok-gun, Gyeongsangbuk-do, South Korea

JIP - Papírny Vetrní,a.s.
Lukavice Mill
Zábreh, Czech Republic

JIP - Papírny Vetrní,a.s.
Vetrní Mill
Vetrni, Czech Republic

JK Paper Ltd.
Central Pulp Mills-CPM, Songadh Mill
Fort Songadh, Dist. Tapi, Gujarat, India

Jordan Paper & Cardboard Factories Co. Ltd.
Zarka Mill
Awajan, Zarka, Jordan

JSC 'Kondrovskaya Paper company'
Kondrovskaya Paper Company Mill
Kondrovo, Kaluga Region, Russia

JSC Grigiskes
Vilnius Mill
Vilnius, Lithuania

JSC Primsnabcontract Ussurijsk Paperboard Mill
Ussurijsk Mill
Ussurijsk, Russia

Julius Schulte Söhne GmbH & Co. KG
Düsseldorf Mill
Düsseldorf, Germany

Julius Schulte Trebsen GmbH & Co. KG
Trebsen Mill
Trebsen, Germany

Kaga Paper Mfg. Co., Ltd.
Kaga Paper Mill
Kanazawa-shi, Ishikawa Pref., Japan

Kahramanmaras Kagit San ve TIC A.S (KMK Paper)
Kahramanmaras Mill
Kahramanmaras, Turkey

Kahramanmaras Kagit San ve TIC A.S (KMK Paper)
Kütahya Mill
Kütahya, Turkey

Kahrizak Paper Mill
Tehran Mill
Tehran, Iran

Kamenskaya Board & Paper Mill, OJSC
Kuvshinovo Mill
Kuvshinovo, Tver Region, Russia

KapStone Kraft Paper Corporation
Cowpens Mill
Cowpens, South Carolina, United States

KapStone Kraft Paper Corporation
Longview Mill
Longview, Washington, United States

Karavaevo
Karavaevo Mill
Pos. Karavaevo, Moscow Region, Russia

Karl Kurz GmbH & Co. KG
Tullau Mill
Rosengarten-Tullau, Germany

Kartogroup España S.L.
Castellòn Mill
Burriana, Castellòn, Spain

Kartonfabrik Buchmann GmbH
Annweiler Mill
Annweiler, Germany

Kartonfabrik Kaierde GmbH & Co. Produktions KG
Delligsen Mill
Delligsen, Germany

Kartonfabrik Porstendorf GmbH
Porstendorf Mill
Porstendorf, Germany

Kartonsan - Karton Sanayi ve Ticaret AS
Kullar Koyu Mill
Izmit, Kocaeli, Turkey

Kartontara, CJSC
Maykop Mill
Maykop, Adygheya Republic, Russia

Kartontol
St. Petersburg Mill
St. Petersburg, Russia

Kartotec - Papeles Técnicos-
Villeta Mill
Villeta, Paraguay

Kasuga Seishi Kogyo Co., Ltd.
Fuji-shi Mill
Fuji-shi, Shizuoka Pref., Japan

Katz GmbH & Co. KG
Weisenbach Mill
Weisenbach, Germany

Kaveh Paper Industries Co.
Saveh Mill
Saveh, Markazi, Iran

KBK Ltd
Tuymazy Mill
Tuymazy, Respublika Bashkortostan, Russia

Khanna Paper Mills Pvt. Ltd.
Amritsar Mill
Amritsar, Punjab, India

Khatema Fibres Ltd.
Khatema Dist., Udham Singh Nagar Mill
Khatema Dist., Udham Singh Nagar, Uttar Pradesh, India

Kiev Cardboard and Paper Mill
Kiev Cardboard and Paper Mill
Obukhiv, Kyivska obl., Ukraine

Kimberly-Clark Brasil Ind. e Com. de Produtos de Higiene Ltda.
Correia Pinto Mill
Correia Pinto, Santa Catarina, Brazil

Kimberly-Clark Corp.
Loudon Mill
Loudon, Tennessee, United States

Kimberly-Clark Corp.
Mobile Mill
Mobile, Alabama, United States

Kimberly-Clark Corp.
Owensboro Mill
Owensboro, Kentucky, United States

Kimberly-Clark Costa Rica, SA
San José Mill
San José, Costa Rica

Kimberly-Clark de Centroamérica S.A.
Sitio Del Nino Mill
Sitio Del Nino, La Libertad, El Salvador

Kimberly-Clark de México S.A. de C.V.
Bajio Mill
San Juan del Rio, Querétaro, Mexico

Kimberly-Clark de México S.A. de C.V.
Ecatepec Mill
Ecatepec de Morelos, Edo. de México, Mexico

Kimberly-Clark de México S.A. de C.V.
Ramos Arizpe Mill
Ramos Arizpe, Coahuila, Mexico

Kimberly-Clark de México S.A. de C.V.
San Martin Texmelucan Mill
San Martin Texmelucan, Puebla, Mexico

Recycled Pulp

Kimberly-Clark GmbH
Koblenz Mill
Koblenz, Germany

Kimberly-Clark GmbH
Niederbipp Mill
Niederbipp, Switzerland

Kimberly-Clark Ltd.
Barrow-in-Furness Mill
Barrow-in-Furness, Cumbria, United Kingdom

Kimberly-Clark Ltd.
Coleshill Mill
Flint, United Kingdom

Kimberly-Clark Ltd.
Delyn Mill
Flint, United Kingdom

Kimberly-Clark of SA (Pty) Ltd.
Enstra Mill
Springs, Gauteng, South Africa

Kimberly-Clark Peru S.A.
Puente de Piedra Mill
Santiago de Surco, Lima, Peru

Kimberly-Clark Products (Malaysia) Sdn. Bhd.
Kluang Mill
Kluang, Johor Darul Takzim, Malaysia

Kimberly-Clark Thailand Ltd.
Pathumthani Mill
Amphur Muang, Pathumthani, Thailand

Kingston Paptech Pvt Ltd
Sabarkantha Mill
Sabarkantha district, Gujarat, India

Kishco Khodeir Paper Mill
6 October City Mill
6 October City, El Giza, Egypt

Kitakami Paper Co., Ltd.
Ichinoseki Mill
Ichinoseki-shi, Iwate Pref., Japan

Klabin S.A.
Correia Pinto Mill
Correia Pinto, Santa Catarina, Brazil

Klabin S.A.
Goiana Mill
Goiana, Pernambuco, Brazil

Klabin S.A.
Guapimirim Mill
Guapimirim, Rio de Janeiro, Brazil

Klabin S.A.
Otaclio Costa Mill
Otaclio Costa, Santa Catarina, Brazil

Klabin S.A.
Piracicaba Mill
Piracicaba, São Paulo, Brazil

Klaipedos Kartonas
Klaipeda Mill
Klaipeda, Lithuania

KleanNara Co., Ltd.
Chongju Mill
Cheongwon-gun, Chungcheongbuk-do, South Korea

Klingele Papierwerke GmbH & Co. KG
Weener Mill
Weener, Germany

Koa Kogyo Co., Ltd.
Fuji-shi Mill
Fuji-shi, Shizuoka Pref., Japan

Koehler Greiz GmbH & Co. KG
Greiz Mill
Greiz, Germany

Kohinoor Paper & Newsprint (P) Ltd
Parganas Mill
Parganas, West Bengal, India

Köknar Kagit Karton San ve Tic A.S.
Kirklareli Mill
Luleburgaz, Kirklareli, Turkey

Kolicevo Karton d.o.o.
Kolicevo Mill
Domžale, Slovenia

Kommunar Paper Mill
Kommunar Mill
Kommunar, Leningrad Region, Russia

Komotini Papermill SA - Elina
Elina Mill
Komotini, Greece

Korea Export Packing Ind. Co., Ltd.
Osan Mill
Osan-si, Gyeonggi-do, South Korea

Korea Paper Mfg. Co., Ltd.
Siheung-si Mill
Siheung-si, Gyeonggi-do, South Korea

KORONA Lochovice spol. s r.o.
Lochovice Mill
Lochovice, Czech Republic

Kostenez-HHI PLC
Kostenez Mill
Kostenez, Bulgaria

Kotkamills Oy
Kotka Mill
Kotka, Finland

Kotobuki Paper Co. Ltd.
Saga Mill
Ogi-shi, Saga Pref., Japan

Koyo Paper Mfg. Co., Ltd.
Honsha Mill
Fuji-shi, Shizuoka Pref., Japan

KPK St. Petersburg OOAO
Kommunar Mill
Kommunar, Leningrad Region, Russia

Krasnaya Zvezda
Krasnaya Zvezda Mill
Chashniki, Vitebsk region, Belarus

Krishna Mongkol Co., Ltd.
Nakhon Pathom Mill
Amphur Kampangsan, Nakhon Pathom, Nakhon Pathom, Thailand

Kruger Inc.
Bromptonville Mill
Sherbrooke, Quebec, Canada

Kruger Inc.
Corner Brook Mill
Corner Brook, Newfoundland and Labrador, Canada

Kruger Inc.
Place Turcot Mill
Montreal, Quebec, Canada

Kruger Products L.P.
Crabtree Mill
Crabtree, Quebec, Canada

Kuan Yuan Paper Mfg. Co. Ltd.
Taichung Mill
Dajia District, Taichung City, Taiwan

Kübler & Niethammer Papierfabrik Kriebstein AG
Kriebstein Mill
Kriebstein, Germany

Kuzbasskiy Skarabey
Kemerovo Mill
Kemerovo, Russia

Kyongsan Paper Co., Ltd.
Daegu-si Mill
Daegu-si, Daegu-si, South Korea

Ladhar Paper Mill
Jalandhar Mill
Dist. Jalandhar, Punjab, India

Lake Utopia Paper
Saint George Mill
Utopia, New Brunswick, Canada

Lamix
Witnica Mill
Witnica, Poland

Latif Paper Products Co.
Hashtgerd Mill
Hashtgerd, Markazi, Iran

LC Paper 1881, S.A.
Besalú Mill
Besalú, Girona, Spain

LEIPA Georg Leinfelder GmbH
Schrobenhausen Mill
Schrobenhausen, Germany

LEIPA Georg Leinfelder GmbH
Schwedt Mill
Schwedt, Germany

Lekok Paper Sdn Bhd
Melaka Mill
Melaka, Malaysia

Lenzing Papier GmbH
Lenzing Paper Mill
Lenzing, Oberösterreich, Austria

Lepenka
Trzic Mill
Trzic, Slovenia

Lepenka AD
Novi Knezevac Mill
Novi Knezevac, Vojvodina, Serbia

Levent Kağit San. ve TIC. A.S
Izmir Mill
Izmir, Izmir, Turkey

Recycled Pulp

Lexpapier Sonacar S.A.
ELJadida Mill
ELJadida, Morocco

Liaoning Hupo Paper
Fushun Mill
Fushun, Liaoning, China

Liberty Paper Inc.
Becker Mill
Becker, Minnesota, United States

Lien Tai Paper Co., Ltd.
Tsao Chiao mill
Tsao Chiao, Miaoli County, Taiwan

Ligia Paper Industries
Welkom Mill
Welkom, Orange Free State, South Africa

Long Chen Paper Co. Ltd.
Erh-Lin Mill
ErhLin, Changhua County, Taiwan

Lothlorien (Pty) Ltd
Lothlorien Pulp Mill
Wadeville, Gauteng, South Africa

Lucart SpA
Diecimo Mill
Diecimo, Lucca, Italy

Lucart SpA
Porcari Mill
Porcari, Lucca, Italy

Lutsky KRK
Lutsk Mill
Lutsk, Ukraine

Lvivkartonplast
Lviv Mill
Lviv, Ukraine

M.C.LIRI S.R.L.
Isola del Liri Mill
Frosinone, Frosinone, Italy

Madeireira Miguel Forte S.A.
União da Vitória Mill
União da Vitória, Paraná, Brazil

Madepar Papel e Celulose S.A.
Aparecida Mill
Aparecida, São Paulo, Brazil

Madhupaper Kenya Ltd.
Madhupaper Mill
Nairobi, Kenya

Magnum Ventures Ltd.
Ghaziabad Mill
Sahibabad, Dist. Ghaziabad, Uttar Pradesh, India

Mahachai Kraft Paper Co., Ltd.
Samut Sakohn Mill
Amphur Muang, Samut Sakohn, Thailand

Malaysian Newsprint Industries Sdn. Bhd.
Mentakab Mill
Mentakab, Pahang Darul Makmur, Malaysia

Malik Board and Paper Industries
Lahore Mill
Lahore, Punjab, Pakistan

Malu Paper Mills Ltd.
Nagpur 1 & 2 Mill
Dist. Nagpur, Maharashtra, India

Malu Paper Mills Ltd.
Nagpur 3 Mill
Dist. Nagpur, Maharashtra, India

Manufacturas de Papel CA (MANPA) S.A.C.A.
Maracay Packaging Mill
Maracay, Edo. Aragua, Venezuela

Manufacturas de Papel CA (MANPA) S.A.C.A.
Maracay Tissue Mill
Maracay, Edo. Aragua, Venezuela

Marisky Pulp & Paper Mill
Volzhsk Mill
Volzhsk, Mari El Republic, Russia

Marmara Kagit ve Ambalaj Sanayii ve Ticaret AS
Vezirhan Mill
Bilecik, Vezirhan, Bilecik, Turkey

Marui Paper Industry Co., Ltd.
Kuzawa
Fuji-shi, Shizuoka Pref., Japan

Marusan Paper Mfg. Co., Ltd.
Honsha Mill
Haramachi-ku, Minami-soma-shi, Fukushima Pref., Japan

Marusumi Paper Co., Ltd.
Kawanoe Mill
Shikokuchuo-shi, Ehime Pref., Japan

Marusumi Paper Co., Ltd.
Ohe Mill
Shikokuchuo-shi, Ehime Pref., Japan

Marutomi Paper Mfg. Co., Ltd.
Fujine Mill
Fuji-shi, Shizuoka Pref., Japan

Marutomi Paper Mfg. Co., Ltd.
Imaizumi Mill
Fuji-shi, Shizuoka Pref., Japan

Marutomi Paper Mfg. Co., Ltd.
Numazu Mill
Numazu-shi, Shizuoka Pref., Japan

Mashad Carton
Mashhad Mill
Mashhad, Khorsan, Iran

Matias Gomá Tomás S.A.
La Riba Mill
La Riba, Spain

Mayr-Melnhof Eerbeek BV
Eerbeek Mill
Eerbeek, Netherlands

Mayr-Melnhof Gernsbach GmbH
Gernsbach Mill
Gernsbach, Germany

Mayr-Melnhof Karton GmbH
Frohnleiten Mill
Frohnleiten, Styria, Austria

Mayr-Melnhof Karton GmbH
Hirschwang Mill
Reichenau an der Rax, Niederösterreich, Austria

Mazandaran Wood & Paper Industries Co.
Sari Mill
Sari, Mazandaran, Iran

MBD Group
Gagret town, Una district Mill
Gagret town, Una district, Himachal Pradesh, India

MCC Paper Yinhe Co., Ltd.
Linqing Mill
Linqing, Shandong, China

MeadWestvaco Corporation
Mahrt Mill
Cottonton, Alabama, United States

MED Paper SA
Tangier Mill
Tangier, Morocco

Mediterranean Paper Mills (MPM)
Lattakia Mill
Jableh, Lattakia, Syria

Meerssen Papier BV
Meerssen Mill
Meerssen, Netherlands

Meiji Seishi Co., Ltd.
Takaoka Mill
Fuji-shi, Shizuoka Pref., Japan

Mel Macedonian Paper Mills S.A.
Thessaloniki Mill
Thessaloniki, Greece

Melitta Haushaltsprodukte GmbH & Co. KG
Minden Mill
Minden, Germany

Menofeya for Paper & Cardboard - "Minobardy"
Quissna Mill
Quissna, Menofeya, Egypt

Merckens Karton- und Pappenfabrik GmbH
Schwertberg Mill
Schwertberg, Oberösterreich, Austria

Metro Paper Industries Tissue Group Ltd.
Portneuf Mill
Portneuf, Quebec, Canada

Metsä Tissue AB
Katrinefors Mill
Mariestad, Sweden

Metsä Tissue AB
Nyboholm Mill (Småland Mills)
Kvillsfors, Sweden

Metsä Tissue Corp.
Mänttä Mill
Mänttä, Finland

Metsä Tissue GmbH
Kreuzau Mill
Kreuzau, Germany

Recycled Pulp

Metsä Tissue GmbH
Raubach Mill
Raubach, Germany

Metsä Tissue S.A.
Krapkowice Mill
Krapkowice, Poland

Metsä Tissue Slovakia s.r.o.
Žilina (Tento) Mill
Žilina, Slovakia

Middle East Paper Co. (SIMO)
Musturud Mill
Musturud, Cairo, Egypt

Middle East Paper Company - (MEPCO)
Jeddah Mill
Jeddah, Saudi Arabia

Milano Papers Pvt. Ltd.
Rajkot Mill
Rajkot, Morbi, Gujarat, India

Mili S.A.
Tres Barras Mill
Tres Barras, Santa Catarina, Brazil

Millenium Papers Pvt. Ltd.
Morbi Mill
Morbi, Gujarat, India

Mimosa Sanitary Paper
Kaa El Rim. Bekaa Mill
Kaa El Rim. Bekaa, Lebanon

Mirae Paper Co., Ltd.
Jeonju Mill
Jeonju-si, Jeollabuk-do, South Korea

Mitsubishi Paper Mills Ltd.
Hachinohe Mill
Hachinohe-shi, Aomori, Japan

Mobile Paperboard Corp.
Mobile Mill
Mobile, Alabama, United States

Modern Karton Sanayi Ticaret AS
Çorlu Mill
Çorlu, Tekirdag, Turkey

Modinagar Paper Mills Ltd.
Modinagar Mill
Modinagar, Uttar Pradesh, India

Mohawk Fine Papers Inc.
Cohoes Mill
Cohoes, New York, United States

Mohawk Fine Papers Inc.
Waterford Mill
Waterford, New York, United States

Monalisa Co., Ltd.
Jeonju Mill
Jeonju-si, Jeollabuk-do, South Korea

Mondi
Pine Bluff Mill
Pine Bluff, Arkansas, United States

Mondi Raubling GmbH
Raubling Mill
Raubling, Germany

Mondi Shanduka Newsprint
Merebank Mill
Merebank, KwaZulu-Natal, South Africa

Mondi Stetí
Štetí Mill
Štetí, Czech Republic

Mondi Swiecie S.A.
Swiecie Mill
Swiecie, Poland

Mondi Tire Kutsan Paper and Packaging Industry Inc.
Tire Mill
Tire, Izmir, Turkey

Mondialcarta SpA
Diecimo Mill
Diecimo, Lucca, Italy

Mopak Dalaman Pulp-Paper Cardboard Plant
Dalaman Mill
Mugla, Turkey

Moritz J. Weig GmbH & Co. KG
Mayen Mill
Mayen, Germany

Mostafa Paper
Chittagong Mill
Chittagong, Chittagong, Bangladesh

Mpact Limited
Felixton Mill
Felixton, KwaZulu-Natal, South Africa

Mpact Limited
Piet Retief Mill
Piet Retief, Mpumalanga, South Africa

Mpact Limited
Springs Mill
New Era, Gauteng, South Africa

Muda Paper Mills Sdn. Bhd.
Kajang Mill
Kajang, Selangor Darul Ehsan, Malaysia

Muda Paper Mills Sdn. Bhd.
Tasek Mill
Seberang Prai Selatan, Penang, Malaysia

Multiwal Pulp & Board Mills Ltd.
Dist. Udham Singh Nagar Mill
Dist. Udham Singh Nagar, Uttarakhand, India

Munksjö Dettingen GmbH
Dettingen Mill
Dettingen an der Erms, Germany

Muratli Karton Fabrikasi
Tekirdag Mill
Tekirdag, Tekirdag, Turkey

Murli Industries Ltd.
Nagpur Mill
Nagpur, Maharashtra, India

Myagkaya Krovlya
Samara Mill
Samara, Russia

Naachiar Paper Boards Private Ltd.
Sivakasi Mill
Sivakasi, Tamil Nadu, India

Naberezhnye Chelny Paper & Board Mill
Naberezhnye Chelny Mill
Naberezhnye Chelny, Tatarstan Republic, Russia

Nakagawa Seishi KK
Mattsuto Mill
Hakusan-shi, Ishikawa Pref., Japan

Nampak Paper Ltd.
Rosslyn Mill
Rosslyn, Gauteng, South Africa

Nampak Tissue (Pty) Ltd.
Bellville Mill
Bellville South, Cape Town, South Africa

Nampak Tissue (Pty) Ltd.
Durban Mill
Verulam, Riverview, KwaZulu-Natal, South Africa

Nampak Tissue (Pty) Ltd.
Kliprivier Mill
Kliprivier, Gauteng, South Africa

National Gypsum Co.
Anniston Mill
Oxford, Alabama, United States

National Gypsum Co.
Milton Plant
New Columbia, Pennsylvania, United States

National Gypsum Co.
Pryor Mill
Pryor, Oklahoma, United States

National Paper Co.
Alexandria Mill
Alexandria, Iskanderiya, Egypt

Natron-Hayat d.o.o.
Maglaj Mill
Maglaj, Bosnia & Herzegovina

Neenah Paper, Inc.
Appleton Mill
Appleton, Wisconsin, United States

Neenah Paper, Inc.
Neenah Mill
Neenah, Wisconsin, United States

Neenah Paper, Inc.
Whiting Mill
Stevens Point, Wisconsin, United States

NEPA Ltd.
Nepanagar Mill
Nepanagar, Burhanpur District, Madhya Pradesh, India

New Forest Paper Mills LP
Scarborough Mill
Scarborough, Ontario, Canada

New Toyo Pulppy (Vietnam) Co., Ltd.
Thuan An District Mill
Thuan An District, Binh Duong Province, Vietnam

Newark America
Fitchburg Mill
Fitchburg, Massachusetts, United States

Newark Pacific Paperboard Corp.
Los Angeles Mill
Los Angeles, California, United States

Recycled Pulp

Newman & Company, Inc.
Philadelphia Mill
Philadelphia, Pennsylvania, United States

NewPage Corporation
Duluth Pulp Mill
Duluth, Minnesota, United States

Nibong Tebal Paper Mills Sdn. Bhd. (NTPM)
Seberang Prai Sel Mill
Nibong Tebal, Seberang Prai Sel, Penang, Malaysia

Nicol-Pack Corporation
Uchaly Mill
Uchaly, Respublika Bashkortostan, Russia

Nicol-Pack Imperial Co. Ltd.
Murom (Imperial) Mill
Murom, Vladimir oblast, Russia

Nine Dragons Paper (Tianjin) Co., Ltd.
Tianjin Mill
Tianjin, Tianjin, China

Nine Dragons Paper Industries (Chongqing) Co., Ltd.
Chongqing Mill
Chongqing, Chongqing, China

Nine Dragons Paper Industries (Quanzhou) Co., Ltd.
Quanzhou Mill
Quanzhou, Fujian, China

Nine Dragons Pulp & Paper (Leshan) Co., Ltd.
Leshan Mill
Leshan, Sichuan, China

Ningbo Muniu Paper Co. Ltd.
Ningbo Mill
Ningbo, Zhejiang, China

Ningxia Kejin Xiaguang Paper Co., Ltd.
Qingtongxia Mill
Qingtongxia, Ningxia, China

Nippon Paper Crecia Co., Ltd.
Tokyo Mill
Soka-shi, Saitama Pref., Japan

Nippon Paper Industries Co., Ltd.
Akita Mill
Akita-shi, Akita Pref., Japan

Nippon Paper Industries Co., Ltd.
Ashikaga Mill
Ashikaga-shi, Tochigi Pref., Japan

Nippon Paper Industries Co., Ltd.
Fuji Mill
Fuji-shi, Shizuoka Pref., Japan

Nippon Paper Industries Co., Ltd.
Hokkaido Mill - Asahikawa
Asahikawa-shi, Hokkaido Pref., Japan

Nippon Paper Industries Co., Ltd.
Hokkaido Mill - Yufutsu
Tomakomai-shi, Hokkaido Pref., Japan

Nippon Paper Industries Co., Ltd.
Ishinomaki Mill
Ishinomaki-shi, Miyagi Pref., Japan

Nippon Paper Industries Co., Ltd.
Iwanuma Mill
Iwanuma-shi, Miyagi Pref., Japan

Nippon Paper Industries Co., Ltd.
Kushiro Mill
Kushiro-shi, Hokkaido Pref., Japan

Nippon Paper Industries Co., Ltd.
Otake Mill
Otake-shi, Hiroshima Pref., Japan

Nippon Paper Industries Co., Ltd.
Soka Mill
Soka-shi, Saitama Pref., Japan

Nippon Paper Industries Co., Ltd.
Yatsushiro Mill
Yatsushiro-shi, Kumamoto Pref., Japan

Nippon Paper Industries USA Co., Ltd.
Port Angeles Mill
Port Angeles, Washington, United States

Nishinihon Eizai Co., Ltd.
Tatsuno-shi Mill
Tatsuno-shi, Hyogo Pref., Japan

Nisshinbo Paper Products, Inc.
Shimada Mill
Shimada-shi, Shizuoka Pref., Japan

Nisshinkogyo Co., Ltd.
Yamagata Mill
Yamagata-shi, Yamagata Pref., Japan

Nizhegorodsky Board & Asphalt Board Mill
Nizhegorodsky Mill
Nizhny Novgorod, Russia

Norampac
Cabano Mill
Cabano, Quebec, Canada

Norampac
Kingsey Falls Mill
Kingsey Falls, Quebec, Canada

Norampac
Mississauga Mill
Mississauga, Ontario, Canada

Norampac
Trenton Mill
Trenton, Ontario, Canada

Norampac Industries Inc.
Niagara Falls Mill
Niagara Falls, New York, United States

Norpaper Avot-Vallée SAS
Blendecques Mill
Blendecques, France

Norske Skog (Australia)
Albury Mill
Ettamogah via Albury, New South Wales, Australia

Norske Skog ASA
Skogn Mill
Skogn, Norway

Norske Skog Bruck GmbH
Bruck an der Mur Mill
Bruck an der Mur, Styria, Austria

Norske Skog Golbey SA
Golbey Mill
Golbey Cedex, France

North Pacific Paper Corp. (Norpac)
Longview Mill
Longview, Washington, United States

Novatissue SAS
Novatissue Mill
Laval-sur-Vologne, France

Nuove Cartiere di Tivoli S.R.L.
Villa Adriana Mill
Villa Adriana, Rome, Italy

OAO Mayak Technocell
Penza Mill
Penza, Russia

OAO Poligrafkarton
Balakhna Mill
Balakhna, Nizhny Novgorod, Russia

Obeikan Paper Industry
Riyadh Mill
Riyadh, Saudi Arabia

Ohio Paperboard Corp.
Baltimore Board Mill
Baltimore, Ohio, United States

Ohio Pulp Mills Inc.
Cincinnati Mill
Cincinnati, Ohio, United States

Oi Seishi Co., Ltd.
Ena Paper Mill
Ena-shi, Gifu Pref., Japan

Oita Seishi Corporation
Buzen Mill
Buzen-shi, Fukuoka Pref., Japan

Oita Seishi Corporation
Honsha Mill
Oita-shi, Oita Pref., Japan

Oji F-Tex Co., Ltd.
Fujinomiya Mill
Fujinomiya-shi, Shizuoka Pref., Japan

Oji F-Tex Co., Ltd.
Nakatsu Mill
Nakatsugawa-shi, Gifu Pref., Japan

Oji Materia Co., Ltd.
Edogawa Mill
Edogawa-ku, Tokyo, Japan

Oji Materia Co., Ltd.
Fuji Mill
Fuji-shi, Shizuoka Pref., Japan

Oji Materia Co., Ltd.
Gifu (Ena) Mill
Ena-shi, Gifu Pref., Japan

Oji Materia Co., Ltd.
Gifu (Nakatsugawa) Mill
Nakatsugawa-shi, Gifu Pref., Japan

Oji Materia Co., Ltd.
Kure Mill
Kure-shi, Hiroshima Pref., Japan

Oji Materia Co., Ltd.
Kushiro Mill
Kushiro-shi, Hokkaido Pref., Japan

Recycled Pulp

Oji Materia Co., Ltd.
Matsumoto Mill
Matsumoto-shi, Nagano Pref., Japan

Oji Materia Co., Ltd.
Nayoro Mill
Nayoro-shi, Hokkaido Pref., Japan

Oji Materia Co., Ltd.
Nikko Mill
Utsunomiya-shi, Tochigi Pref., Japan

Oji Materia Co., Ltd.
Oita Mill
Oita-shi, Oita Pref., Japan

Oji Materia Co., Ltd.
Osaka Mill
Osaka-shi, Osaka Pref., Japan

Oji Materia Co., Ltd.
Saga Mill
Saga-shi, Saga Pref., Japan

Oji Materia Co., Ltd.
Sobue Mill
Inazawa-shi, Aichi Pref., Japan

Oji Nepia Co., Ltd.
Tomakomai Mill
Tomakomai-shi, Hokkaido Pref., Japan

Okayama Paper Industries Co., Ltd.
Okayama-shi Mill
Okayama-shi, Okayama Pref., Japan

Okulovka P&P Mill Ltd.
Okulovka Mill
Okulovka, Novgorod Region, Russia

Oliveira Santos & Irmão, Lda.
Paços de Brandão Mill
Paços de Brandão, Santa Maria da Feira, Portugal

Olmuksa International Paper-Sabanci Ambalaj Sanayi ve Ticaret A.S.
Olmuksa Edirne Mill
Edirne, Turkey

Om Srinivasa Paper Boards Pvt. Ltd.
Sattur Mill
Sattur, Tamil Nadu, India

Omiya Seishi Co., Ltd.
Fuji Takaoka Mill
Fuji-shi, Shizuoka Pref., Japan

Omiya Seishi Co., Ltd.
Fujinomiya Mill
Fujinomiya-Shi, Shizuoka Pref., Japan

Ondunorte, Cia. de Papéis e Papelão Ondulado do Norte
Igarassu Mill
Igarassu, Pernambuco, Brazil

OOO Buprom-Pokrov
Pokrov, Petushinskiy rayon Mill
Pokrov, Petushinskiy rayon, Russia

OOO Nikmas
Chelyabinsk Mill
Chelyabinsk, Russia

OOO Triton-M
Tver Mill
Tver, Russia

Orchids Paper Products Co.
Pryor Mill
Pryor, Oklahoma, United States

Oriental Paper - Lanatex
Damascus Mill
Damascus, Syria

Orsa International Paper Embalagens S.A
Franco da Rocha Mill
Franco da Rocha, São Paulo, Brazil

Orsa International Paper Embalagens S.A
Nova Campina Mill
Nova Campina, São Paulo, Brazil

Orsa International Paper Embalagens S.A
Paulínia Mill
Paulínia, São Paulo, Brazil

Osaka Paper Co., Ltd.
Osaka-shi Mill
Osaka-shi, Osaka Pref., Japan

Otrokovické papírny a.s.
Otrokovice Mill
Otrokovice, Czech Republic

Otsego Paper Inc.
Otsego Mill
Otsego, Michigan, United States

Otsu-Paperboard Co., Ltd.
Otsu-shi Mill
Otsu-shi, Shiga Pref., Japan

Ox Paperboard LLC
Constantine Mill
Constantine, Michigan, United States

Ox Paperboard LLC
Halltown Mill
Halltown, West Virginia, United States

Ox Paperboard LLC
Pekin Mill
Pekin, Illinois, United States

OYKA Kagit Ve Ambalaj San Tic A.S.
Çaycuma Mill
Çaycuma, Zonguldak, Turkey

P.W. "APIS" S.J.
Chodecz Mill
Chodecz, Poland

P.W. "APIS" S.J.
Nowa Bystrzyca Mill
Stara Bystrzyca, Poland

PABCO Paper
Vernon Mill
Vernon, California, United States

Packaging Corp. of America
Counce Mill
Counce, Tennessee, United States

Packaging Corp. of America
DeRidder Mill
DeRidder, Louisiana, United States

Packaging Corp. of America
Filer City Mill
Filer City, Michigan, United States

Packaging Corp. of America
Tomahawk Mill
Tomahawk, Wisconsin, United States

Packprofil Sp. z o.o.
Kolonowskie Mill
Kolonowskie 1, Poland

PAKA Glashütter Pappen- und Kartonagenfabrik GmbH
Glashütte Mill
Glashütte, Germany

Palm Group
Eltmann Mill
Eltmann, Germany

Palm Group
Wörth Mill
Wörth am Rhein, Germany

Palm Paper Limited
King's Lynn Mill
King's Lynn, United Kingdom

Paloma-Sladkogorska Tovarna Papirja d.d. Sladki Vrh
Sladki Vrh Mill
Sladki Vrh, Slovenia

PAMER - Papelera Mercedes S.A.
Mercedes, Soriano Mill
Mercedes, Soriano, Uruguay

Pan Paper Mills
Webuye Mill
Webuye, Bungoma District, Western, Kenya

PAN Papirna Industrija d.o.o.
Zagreb Mill
Zagreb, Grad Zagreb, Croatia

Panasa, Papelera Nacional S.A.
Paramonga Mill
Paramonga, Lima, Peru

Panjapol Paper Industry Co. Ltd. and Panjapol Pulp Industry Public Co., Ltd.
Ayutthaya Mill
Bangsai District, Ayutthaya, Thailand

PAPCAS - Rebahia à Saïda
Saïda Mill
Saïda, Rebahia, Algeria

Papeco SA
Orval Mill
Orval, France

Papel Prensa S.A.
San Pedro Mill
San Pedro, Buenos Aires, Argentina

Papeleira Portuguesa S.A.
São Paio de Oleiros Mill
São Paio de Oleiros, Portugal

Papelera Andina S.A.
Papelera Andina
Godoy Cruz, Maipu, Mendoza, Argentina

Papelera Berazategui S.A.
Berazategui Mill
Berazategui, Buenos Aires, Argentina

Papelera Damují
Abreus Mill
Abreus, Cienfuegos, Cuba

Recycled Pulp

Papelera de Chihuahua S.A. de C.V.
Chihuahua Mill
Chihuahua, Chihuahua, Mexico

Papelera de la Alqueria S.L.
Alicante Mill
Alqueria de Aznar, Alicante, Spain

Papelera del Nevado S.A. de C.V.
Almoloyan Mill
San Miguel Almoloyan, Almoloya de Juarez, México, D.F., Mexico

Papelera del NOA S.A.
Rio Blanco Mill
Río Blanco, Jujuy, Jujuy, Argentina

Papelera del Pacífico S.A.
Retalhuleu Mill
Retalhuleu, Guatemala

Papelera del Pacífico S.A.
San Francisco de Mostazal Mill
San Francisco de Mostazal, VI - Región Gen. O'Higgins, Chile

Papelera del Plata
Zárate Mill
Zárate, Buenos Aires, Argentina

Papelera del Principado, S.A. (Paprinsa)
Mollerussa Mill
Mollerussa, Lérida, Spain

Papelera del Sur S.A.
Chincha Mill
Chincha, ICA, Peru

Papelera del Sur, División Cartulinas de Interpack S.A.
Tornquist Mill
Tornquist, Buenos Aires, Argentina

Papelera Don Torcuato S.A.
Don Torcuato Mill
Don Torcuato, Buenos Aires, Argentina

Papelera Entre Ríos S.A.
Paraná Mill
Paraná, Entre Ríos, Entre Ríos, Argentina

Papelera Industrial Potosina S.A. de C.V.
San Luis Potosi Mill
San Luis Potosi, San Luis Potosi, Mexico

Papelera Internacional SA - PAINSA
Zacapa Mill
Rio Hondo, Zacapa, Guatemala

Papelera Iruña S.A. de C.V.
Iztapalapa Mill
Iztapalapa, México, D.F., Mexico

Papelera Istmeña, S.A.
El Dorado Mill
El Dorado, Panama, Panama

Papelera Nacional S.A.
Guayaquil Mill
Guayaquil, Guayas, Ecuador

Papelera Pulpa Cuba
Trinidad Mill
Trinidad, Sancti Spiritus, Cuba

Papelera Reyes S.A.C.
Callao Mill
Callao, Lima, Peru

Papelera Samseng S.A.
Pilar Mill
Pilar, Buenos Aires, Argentina

Papelera Tucumán S.A.
Lules, Tucumán I Mill
Lules, Tucumán, Argentina

Papelera Zarate S.A.
Lima Mill
Lima, Lima, Peru

Papeles Nacionales S.A.
Pereira Mill
Puente Bolivar, Pereira, Risaralda, Colombia

Papeles Venezolanos CA (PAVECA)
Guacara Mill
Guacara, Edo. Carabobo, Venezuela

PAPELSA - Papeles y Cartones SA
Barbosa Mill
Barbosa, Antioquia, Colombia

Paper Corea Inc.
Gunsan Mill
Gunsan-si, Jeollabuk-do, South Korea

Paper Packaging Pvt. Ltd. Corp.
Mandli Mill
Mandli, Shimoga Dist., Karnataka, India

Papertech S.L.
Tudela Mill
Tudela, Navarra, Spain

PaperWorks Industries, Inc.
Philadelphia Mill
Philadelphia, Pennsylvania, United States

PaperWorks Industries, Inc.
Wabash Mill
Wabash, Indiana, United States

Papeterie de la Mitidja
La Chiffa Mill
La Chiffa, Wilaya de Blida, Algeria

Papeterie de Raon
Raon L'Etape Mill
Raon L'Etape, Vosges, France

Papeterie Saint Michel SAS Groupe Thiollet
St. Michel d'Entraygues Mill
St. Michel d'Entraygues, France

Papeteries de Bègles SAS
Bègles Mill
Bègles, France

Papeteries de Giroux SA
Giroux Mill
Olliergues, France

Papeteries des Chatelles SAS
Raon L'Etape Mill
Raon L'Etape, France

Papeteries du Rhin
Illzach Mill
Illzach, France

Papeteries et Cartonneries Lacaux Frères
Bosmie L'Aiguille Mill
Bosmie L'Aiguille, France

Papier- und Kartonfabrik Varel GmbH & Co. KG
Varel Mill
Varel, Niedersachsen, Germany

Papierfabriek Doetinchem BV
Doetinchem Mill
Doetinchem, Netherlands

Papierfabrik Adolf Jass GmbH & Co. KG
Fulda Mill
Fulda, Germany

Papierfabrik Adolf Jass GmbH & Co. KG
Rudolstadt-Schwarza Mill
Rudolstadt-Schwarza, Thüringen, Germany

Papierfabrik Fritz Peters GmbH & Co. KG
Gelsenkirchen Mill
Gelsenkirchen, Germany

Papierfabrik Hainsberg GmbH
Freital Mill
Freital-Hainsberg, Germany

Papierfabrik Niederauer Mühle GmbH
Kreuzau and Niederau Mills
Kreuzau, Germany

Papierfabrik Palm GmbH & Co KG
Aalen Mill
Aalen-Neukochen, Germany

Papierfabrik Schoellershammer
Düren Mill
Düren, Germany

Papierfabrik Tillmann
Zülpich-Sinzenich Mill
Zülpich-Sinzenich, Germany

Papierfabrik Utzenstorf AG
Utzenstorf Mill
Utzenstorf, Switzerland

Papierfabrik Vreden GmbH
Vreden Mill
Vreden, Germany

Papiernia Sieroslawice
Byczyna Mill
Byczyna, Poland

Papierwerk Sundern GmbH
Sundern Mill
Sundern, Germany

Papierwerke Lenk AG
Kappelrodeck Mill
Kappelrodeck, Germany

Papir-Mal
Malin Mill
Malin, Zhitomirskaya obl., Ukraine

Papirfabrika Ligatne Ltd.
Ligatne Mill
Ligatne, Latvia

Papiro Sarda S.R.L.
Assemini mill
Assemini, Como, Italy

Recycled Pulp

Papiro Sud Srl
Scafati Mill
Scafati, Salerno, Italy

Papirus Indústria de Papel S.A.
Limeira Mill
Limeira, São Paulo, Brazil

PAPOS v.o.s.
Ostrov Mill
Ostrov, Czech Republic

Pappenfabrik Nierfeld, J. Piront GmbH & Co. KG
Schleiden Mill
Schleiden, Germany

Pappenfabrik Trauchgau GmbH & Co. KG
Trauchgau Mill
Halblech, Germany

Papresa, S.L.
Rentería Mill
Rentería, Gipúzcoa, Spain

Paptol, Zaklad Produkcji Papieru Toaletowego
Kraków Mill
Kraków, Poland

Paraibuna Embalagens Ltda.
Juiz de Fora Mill
Juiz de Fora, Minas Gerais, Brazil

Paramount Paper Board Mills (Pvt) Ltd.
Haripur Mill
Haripur, Pakistan

Parenco B.V.
Renkum Mill
Renkum, Netherlands

Parteks Tekstil ve Kagit San Tic. Ltd. Sti.
Kayseri Mill
Kayseri, Turkey

Pascorp Paper Industries Bhd.
Bentong Mill
Bentong, Pahang Darul Makmur, Malaysia

Patoom Dhanee Paper Factory Ltd. Part
Pathumthani Mill
Amphur Muang, Pathumthani, Thailand

Paul Hartmann Ges.mbH
Grimmenstein Mill
Grimmenstein, Niederösterreich, Austria

Paulispell, Indústria Paulista de Papéis e Chapas de Papelão
Aguaí Mill
Aguaí, São Paulo, Brazil

PCE Embalagens
Manaus Mill
Manaus, Amazonas, Brazil

Pegant Ltd.
Nairobi Mill
Nairobi, Kenya

Pehart Tec SA Petresti
Petresti Mill
Petresti-Sebes, Romania

Pehlivanoglu Kagit, Kagit Mamülleri ve Ambalaj San.Tic. A.S.
Çerkezköy Mill
Çerkezköy, Tekirdag, Turkey

Penha Papéis e Embalagem Ltda.
Coronel Vivida Mill
Vivida, Paraná, Brazil

Penha Papéis e Embalagem Ltda.
Santo Amaro Mill
Santo Amaro da Purificação, Bahia, Brazil

Perlen Papier AG
Perlen Mill
Perlen, Switzerland

Perm Pulp and Paper Mill
Perm Mill
Perm, Russia

Peter Grant Papers Limited
Lancaster Mill
Lancaster, Lancashire, United Kingdom

Polotnyano-Zavodskaya Paper Mill
Polotnyany Zavod Mill
Polotnyany Zavod, Kaluga Region, Russia

Ponderay Newsprint Co.
Usk Mill
Usk, Washington, United States

Port Townsend Paper Corp.
Port Townsend Mill
Port Townsend, Washington, United States

Potsdam Specialty Paper Inc.
Cedar Mill
Potsdam, New York, United States

PPH Izopaper Sp. z o.o.
Chelmza Mill
Chelmza, Poland

PPHU 'KARAS'
Olawa Mill
Olawa, Poland

PPHU Rolls Sp. z o.o.
Wloclawek Mill
Wloclawek, Poland

Prado Karton S.A.
Tomar Mill
Tomar, Portugal

Prado-Cartolinas da Lousã S.A.
Lousã Mill
Lousã, Portugal

Pratt Industries (USA)
Conyers Mill
Conyers, Georgia, United States

Pratt Industries (USA)
Shreveport Mill
Shreveport, Louisiana, United States

Pratt Industries (USA)
Staten Island Mill
Staten Island, New York, United States

Primo Tedesco S.A.
Caçador Mill
Caçador, Santa Catarina, Brazil

Procter & Gamble de Mexico S. de R.L. de C.V.
Apizaco Mill
Apizaco, Tlaxacala, Mexico

Productos Familia SA
Cajica Mill
Cajica, Cundinamarca, Colombia

Proletariy, JSC
Surazh Mill
Surazh, Bryansk Region, Russia

Prolific Papers Pvt. Ltd.
Kashipur, Udham Singh Nagar Mill
Kashipur, Udham Singh Nagar, Uttarakhand, India

Pronal, Productora Nacional de Papel, S.A. de C.V.
Pronal Mill
Ejido San Miguel, Municipio Villa de Reyes, San Luis Potosi, Mexico

Propapier PM 1 GmbH
Burg Mill
Burg, Germany

Propapier PM 2 GmbH & Co. KG
Eisenhüttenstadt Mill
Eisenhüttenstadt, Brandenburg, Germany

PROPASA - Productora de Papel S.A. de C.V.
San Nicolas de los Garza Mill
San Nicolas de los Garza, Nuevo León, Mexico

Protisa Peru S.A. - Productos Tissue del Peru
Santa Anita Mill
Santa Anita, Lima, Peru

PROTISA, Productos Tinerfeños S.A.
Santa Cruz de Tenerife Mill
Santa Cruz de Tenerife, Spain

PT Adiprima Suraprinta
Gresik Mill
Gresik, East Java, Indonesia

PT Asia Paper Mills
Tangerang Mill
Tangerang, West Java, Indonesia

PT Aspex Kumbong
Bogor Mill
Bogor, West Java, Indonesia

PT Cipta Paperia
Serang, Banten Mill
Serang, Banten, West Java, Indonesia

PT Ekamas Fortuna
Malang (PT Ekamas Fortuna) Mill
Malang, Jawa Timur, Indonesia

PT Enggal Subur Kertas
Pati Mill
Pati, Central Java, Indonesia

PT Evergreen International Paper
Medan Mill
Deli Serdang, Medan, Sumatra, Indonesia

PT Fajar Surya Wisesa Tbk.
Bekasi Mill
Cikarang Barat, Bekasi, West Java, Indonesia

Recycled Pulp

PT Indah Kiat Pulp & Paper Corp.
Perawang (PT Indah Kiat Pulp & Paper) Mill
Siak, Bengkalis, Riau, Sumatra, Indonesia

PT Indah Kiat Pulp & Paper Corp.
Serang (PT Indah Kiat Pulp & Paper) Mill
Serang, West Java, Indonesia

PT Integra Lestari (Surabaya)
Kec. Ngoro Mill
Kec. Ngoro, Mojokerto, East Java, Indonesia

PT Kertas Blabak Megelang
Magelang Mill
Magelang, Central Java, Indonesia

PT Kertas Leces (Persero)
Probolinggo Mill
Probolinggo, East Java, Indonesia

PT Pabrik Kertas Indonesia (Pakerin)
Mojokerto Mill
Mojokerto, East Java, Indonesia

PT Pabrik Kertas Noree Indonesia
Bekasi Mill
Bekasi, West Java, Indonesia

PT Pabrik Kertas Tjiwi Kimia Tbk
Mojokerto (PT Pabrik Kertas Tjiwi Kimia) Mill
Mojokerto, East Java, Indonesia

PT Papertech Indonesia
Blabak Mill
Blabak, Mungkid, Central Java, Indonesia

PT Papertech Indonesia
Subang Mill
Subang, Jawa Barat, Indonesia

PT Papyrus Sakti
Bandung Mill
Banjaran, Bandung, West Java, Indonesia

PT Pelita Cengkareng Paper
Subang Mill
Subang, West Java, Indonesia

PT Pelita Cengkareng Paper
Tangerang Mill
Cengkareng, Tangerang, West Java, Indonesia

PT Pura Barutama
Kudus Mill
Kudus, Central Java, Indonesia

PT Pura Nusapersada
Terban, Kudus Mill
Terban, Kudus, Central Java, Indonesia

PT Setia Kawan
Tulungagung Mill
Tulungagung, East Java, Indonesia

PT Sinar Indah Kertas
Desa Pegandan Kecamatan Margorajo, Pati Mill
Desa Pegandan Kecamatan Margorejo, Pati, Central Java, Indonesia

PT Suparma, Tbk.
Surabaya Mill
Surabaya, East Java, Indonesia

PT Surabaya Agung Industri Pulp & Kertas
Driyorejo Mill
Gresik, East Java, Indonesia

PT Surabaya Mekabox
Driyorejo Mill
Surabaya, East Java, Indonesia

PT Tri Daya Kreasi
Purwakarta Mill
Purwakarta, West Java, Indonesia

PT Wirajaya Packindo
Tangerang Mill
Tangerang, West Java, Indonesia

Pudumjee Pulp & Paper Mills Ltd.
Pune Mill
Chinchwad, Pune, Maharashtra, India

Pulppy Corelex (Vietnam)
Hung Yen Mill
Hung Yen, Hung Yen Province, Vietnam

Pyramids Paper Mills S.A.E. - Flora
6th October City Mill
6th October City, El Giza, Egypt

Queenex Hygiene Paper Manufacturing L.L.C
Abu Dhabi Mill
Abu Dhabi, Shaikhdom of Abu Dhabi, United Arab Emirates

Queensland Tissue Products
Carole Park Mill
Brisbane, Queensland, Australia

Rafalo Paper Mills
Phoenix, Durban Mill
Phoenix, Durban, KwaZulu-Natal, South Africa

Rainap S.A.
Garín mill
Garín, Buenos Aires, Argentina

Rainbow Papers Ltd.
Mehsana Mill
Mehsana, Gujarat, India

Raipaper S.r.l.
Isola del Liri Mill
Isola del Liri, Frosinone, Italy

Rakta, General Co. for Paper Industry
Rakta Mill
Alexandria, Iskanderiya, Egypt

Rama Paper Mills Ltd.
Bijnor Mill
Kiratpur, Bijnor, Uttar Pradesh, India

Rand Whitney Containerboard
Montville Mill
Montville, Connecticut, United States

RDM Blendecques SAS
Blendecques Mill
Blendecques, Saint Omer Cedex, France

Reliable Paper (India) Pvt. Ltd.
Surat Mill
Bardoli, Taluka - Mahuva, Surat, Gujarat, India

Rengo Co., Ltd.
Amagasaki Mill
Kuise, Amagasaki-shi, Hyogo Pref., Japan

Rengo Co., Ltd.
Kanazu Mill
Awara-shi, Fukui Pref., Japan

Rengo Co., Ltd.
Tonegawa Mill
Bando-shi, Ibaraki Pref., Japan

Rengo Co., Ltd.
Yashio Mill
Yashio-shi, Saitama Pref., Japan

Rengo Co., Ltd.
Yodogawa Mill
Osaka-shi, Osaka Pref., Japan

Reno De Medici Arnsberg GmbH
Arnsberg Mill
Arnsberg, Germany

Reno De Medici SpA
Magenta Mill
Pontenuovo di Magenta, Milan, Italy

Reno De Medici SpA
Ovaro Mill
Ovaro, Udine, Italy

Reno De Medici SpA
Santa Giustina Mill
Santa Giustina Bellunese, Belluno, Italy

Reno De Medici SpA
Villa Santa Lucia Mill
Villa Santa Lucia, Frosinone, Italy

Reno De Medici, Iberica S.L.U.
Almazán Mill
Almazán, Soria, Spain

Renova - Fábrica de Papel do Almonda S.A.
Torres Novas Mill
Torres Novas, Portugal

Republic Paperboard Co. LLC
Lawton Mill
Lawton, Oklahoma, United States

Resolute Forest Products Canada Inc.
Alma Mill
Alma, Quebec, Canada

Resolute Forest Products Canada Inc.
Thorold Mill
Thorold, Ontario, Canada

Resolute Forest Products Canada Inc.
Thunder Bay Mill
Thunder Bay, Ontario, Canada

Resolute FP Augusta LLC
Augusta Mill
Augusta, Georgia, United States

Rigesa, Celulose, Papel e Embalagens Ltda.
Três Barras Mill
Três Barras, Santa Catarina, Brazil

Rigesa, Celulose, Papel e Embalagens Ltda.
Valinhos Mill
Valinhos, São Paulo, Brazil

RockTenn Co.
Battle Creek Mill
Battle Creek, Michigan, United States

RockTenn Co.
Chattanooga Mill
Chattanooga, Tennessee, United States

Recycled Pulp

RockTenn Co.
Cincinnati Mill
Cincinnati, Ohio, United States

RockTenn Co.
Coshocton Mill
Coshocton, Ohio, United States

RockTenn Co.
Dallas Mill
Dallas, Texas, United States

RockTenn Co.
Eaton Mill
Eaton, Indiana, United States

RockTenn Co.
Fernandina Beach Mill
Fernandina Beach, Florida, United States

RockTenn Co.
Florence Mill
Florence, South Carolina, United States

RockTenn Co.
Hodge Mill
Hodge, Louisiana, United States

RockTenn Co.
Hopewell Mill
Hopewell, Virginia, United States

RockTenn Co.
La Tuque Mill
La Tuque, Quebec, Canada

RockTenn Co.
Missisquoi Mill
Sheldon Springs, Vermont, United States

RockTenn Co.
Saint Paul Mill
Saint Paul, Minnesota, United States

RockTenn Co.
Seminole Mill
Jacksonville, Florida, United States

RockTenn Co.
Solvay Mill
Syracuse, New York, United States

RockTenn Co.
Stevenson Mill
Stevenson, Alabama, United States

RockTenn Co.
Stroudsburg Mill
Delaware Water Gap, Pennsylvania, United States

RockTenn Co.
Tacoma Mill
Tacoma, Washington, United States

RockTenn Co.
Uncasville Mill
Uncasville, Connecticut, United States

RockTenn Co.
West Point Mill
West Point, Virginia, United States

Romiley Board Mill
Stockport Mill
Stockport, Greater Manchester, Cheshire, United Kingdom

Rondo Ganahl AG
Frastanz Mill
Frastanz, Vorarlberg, Austria

Rossmann SAS
Ste. Croix aux Mines Mill
Ste. Croix aux Mines, France

Rubezhansky Cardboard and Packaging Mill
Rubezhnoye Mill
Rubezhnoye, Lugansk obl., Ukraine

Ruby Macons Ltd.
Morai Mill
Morai, Gujarat, India

Ruby Macons Ltd.
Vapi Mill
Vapi, Gujarat, India

Ruchira Papers Ltd.
Kala-Amb Mill
Kala-Amb, Himachal Pradesh, India

S.C. Comceh S. A.
Comceh Mill
Calarasi Judet, Romania

S.C. EcoPaper S.A.
Zarnesti Mill
Zarnesti, Romania

Sabarmati Papers Limited
Aglo Mill
Dist. Mehsana, Gujarat, India

Saffron Industries Ltd.
Nagpur Mill
Nagpur, Maharashtra, India

Sagheh Cellulose Iran Industrial Company (P.J.S.)
Takestan Mill
Takestan, Qazvin, Iran

SAICA - S.A. Industrias Celulosa Aragonesa
Fábrica I - Zaragoza Mill
Zaragoza, Spain

SAICA - S.A. Industrias Celulosa Aragonesa
Fábrica II, III & IV - El Burgo de Ebro Mill
El Burgo de Ebro, Zaragoza, Spain

SAICA Paper UK Ltd.
Partington Mill
Carrington, Manchester, Greater Manchester, United Kingdom

SAICA Vénizel
Vénizel Mill
Vénizel, France

Saigon Paper
My Xuan I Mill
Tan Thanh Dist., Ba Ria - Vung Tau, Dong Nam Bo, Vietnam

Saigon Paper
My Xuan II Mill
Tan Thanh Dist., Ba Ria - Vung Tau, Dong Nam Bo, Vietnam

Sainsons Paper Industries Ltd.
Kurukshetra Mill
Dist. Kurukshetra, Haryana, India

Samjung Pulp Ind. Co., Ltd.
Cheonan Mill
Cheonan-si, Dongnam-gu, Chungcheongnam-do, South Korea

Samjung Pulp Ind. Co., Ltd.
Haman Mill
Haman-gun, Gyeongsangnam-do, South Korea

Samjung Pulp Ind. Co., Ltd.
Pyeongtaek Mill
Godeok-myeon, Pyeongtaek-si, Gyeonggi-do, South Korea

San-Ei Regulator Co., Ltd.
Tokyo Mill
Kawasaki-shi, Kanagawa Pref., Japan

San-Paper Co., Ltd.
Nishiyatsushiro-gun Mill
Nishiyatsushiro-gun, Yamanashi Pref., Japan

Sanitex Paper Mill Ltd.
Kostinbrod Mill
Kostinbrod, Bulgaria

Santa Clara Indústria de Papéis Ltda.
Candoi Mill
Candoi, Paraná, Brazil

Santa Clara Indústria de Papéis Ltda.
Ivaí Mill
Ivaí, Paraná, Brazil

Sanyo Paper Manufacturing Co., Ltd.
Tottori Mill
Tottori-shi, Tottori Pref., Japan

São Carlos SA Indústria de Papel e Embalagens
São Carlos Mill
São Carlos, São Paulo, Brazil

São Gabriel Papéis Ltda.
União da Vitória Mill
União da Vitória, Paraná, Brazil

Sappi Fine Paper North America
Westbrook Mill
Westbrook, Maine, United States

Sappi Paper and Paper Packaging South Africa (SA)
Cape Kraft Mill
Montague Gardens, Cape Town, Cape Town, South Africa

Sappi Paper and Paper Packaging South Africa (SA)
Ngodwana Mill
Ngodwana, Mpumalanga, South Africa

Sappi Paper and Paper Packaging South Africa (SA)
Tugela Mill
Mandini, KwaZulu-Natal, South Africa

SAPSO Emballages Ondulés
Bazas Mill
Bazas, France

Saraswati Udyog India Ltd.
Namakkal Dist. Mill
Namakkal Dist., Tamil Nadu, India

Sastha Paper Mills
Kanchipuram Mill
Kanchipuram, Tamil Nadu, India

Recycled Pulp

Saudi Paper Manufacturing Co. (SPMC)
Dammam Mill
Dammam, Saudi Arabia

Savon Sellu Oy
Savon Sellu
Kuopio, Finland

Sayid Paper Mills
Lahore Mill
Lahore, Punjab, Pakistan

SCA Consumidor México y Centroamérica S.A. de C.V.
Monterrey Tissue Mill
San Nicolas de los Garza, Nuevo León, Mexico

SCA Consumidor México y Centroamérica S.A. de C.V.
Sahagun Tissue Mill
Tepeapulco, Hidalgo, Mexico

SCA Consumidor México y Centroamérica S.A. de C.V.
Uruapan Tissue Mill
Uruapan, Michoacán, Mexico

SCA France
Hondouville Mill
Louviers, France

SCA Hygiene Products AB
Edet Mill
Lilla Edet, Sweden

SCA Hygiene Products GmbH
Ortmann Mill
Ortmann, Pernitz, Niederösterreich, Austria

SCA Hygiene Products Russia LLC
Sovetsk Mill
Sovetsk, Shchekino Distr., Tula Region, Russia

SCA Hygiene Products Russia LLC
Svetogorsk Mill
Svetogorsk, Leningrad Region, Russia

SCA Hygiene Products SE
Goytside Mill
Chesterfield, Derbyshire, United Kingdom

SCA Hygiene Products SE
Mainz-Kostheim Mill
Mainz-Kostheim, Germany

SCA Hygiene Products SE
Prudhoe Mill
Prudhoe, Northumberland, United Kingdom

SCA Hygiene Products SE
Stubbins Mill
Ramsbottom, Bury, Lancashire, United Kingdom

SCA Munksund AB
Piteå Mill
Piteå, Sweden

SCA Nederlands BV
Cuijk Mill
Katwijk, Cuijk, Netherlands

SCA Obbola AB
Obbola Mill
Obbola, Sweden

SCA Tissue Finland Oy
Nokia Mill
Nokia, Finland

SCA Tissue North America, L.L.C.
Barton Mill
Cherokee, Alabama, United States

SCA Tissue North America, L.L.C.
Encore Paper
South Glens Falls, New York, United States

SCA Tissue North America, L.L.C.
Flagstaff Mill
Flagstaff, Arizona, United States

SCA Tissue North America, L.L.C.
Menasha Mill
Menasha, Wisconsin, United States

Schönfelder Papierfabrik GmbH
Annaberg-Buchholz Mill
Annaberg-Buchholz, Germany

Schumacher Packaging GmbH
Schwarzenberg Mill
Schwarzenberg, Germany

Schumacher Packaging Zaklad Grudziadz Sp.z o.o.
Grudziadz Mill
Grudziadz, Poland

Seaman Paper Company
Otter River Mill
Otter River, Massachusetts, United States

Seha Corporation
Hyunpoong Mill
Dalseong-gun, Daegu-si, Daegu-si, South Korea

Selenginsky Pulp & Board Mill
Selenginsk Mill
Selenginsk, Buryatia Republic, Russia

Selkasan Kagit ve Paketleme Malzemeleri Imalati San. ve Tic. AS
Manisa Mill
Manisa, Turkey

Servalakshmi Paper Ltd.
Servall Mill
Tirunelveli, Tamil Nadu, India

Seshasayee Paper & Boards Ltd.
Tirunelveli Mill
Mukkudal, Tirunelveli, Tamil Nadu, India

Seven Hills Paperboard, LLC
Lynchburg Mill
Lynchburg, Virginia, United States

Seyfert Paper S.A.S.
Descartes Mill
Descartes, France

Shaanxi Pucheng Wuyang Paper Co., Ltd.
Weinan Mill
Weinan, Shaanxi, China

Shaanxi Shenglong Paper Co., Ltd.
Baoji Mill
Baoji, Shaanxi, China

Shaanxi Xiongdi Paper Co., Ltd.
Xi-An Mill
Xi-An, Shaanxi, China

Shah Pulp & Paper Mills Ltd.
Valsad Mill
Vapi Pardi, Valsad, Gujarat, India

Shakumbhri Straw Products Ltd.
Moradabad Mill
Tehsil Bilari, Moradabad, Uttar Pradesh, India

Shandong Bohui Paper Industry Co., Ltd.
Zibo Mill
Zibo, Shandong, China

Shandong Chenlong Paper Co., Ltd.
Zibo Mill
Zibo, Shandong, China

Shandong Derong Paper Co., Ltd.
Zaozhuang Mill
Zaozhuang, Shandong, China

Shandong Dongming County Yongyue Paper Co., Ltd.
Heze Mill
Heze, Shandong, China

Shandong Dongyue Energy Co., Ltd.
Feicheng Mill
Feicheng, Shandong, China

Shandong Fengyuan Zhongke Biology Technology Co., Ltd.
Zaozhuang Mill
Zaozhuang, Shandong, China

Shandong Guanjun Paper Co., Ltd.
Dezhou Mill
Dezhou, Shandong, China

Shandong Guihe Xianxing Paper Holding Pte. Ltd.
Zibo Mill
Zibo, Shandong, China

Shandong Honghe Group Zoucheng Hengxiang Paper Co., Ltd.
Zoucheng Mill
Zoucheng, Shandong, China

Shandong Huajin Paper Group
Jining Mill
Jining, Shandong, China

Shandong Huapeng Paper Co. Ltd.
Zibo Mill
Zibo, Shandong, China

Shandong Huatai Group Co., Ltd.
Jiangmen Mill
Jiangmen, Guangdong, China

Shandong Jianghe Paper Co., Ltd.
Qihe Mill
Dezhou, Shandong, China

Shandong Qingdao Haiwang Paper Property Share Co., Ltd.
Qingdao Mill
Qingdao, Shandong, China

Shandong Rizhao Huatai Paper Co. Ltd.
Rizhao Mill
Rizhao, Shandong, China

Shandong Stora Enso Huatai Paper
Dawang Mill
Dongying, Shandong, China

Recycled Pulp

Shandong Taian Baichuan Paper Co., Ltd.
Taian Mill
Taian, Shandong, China

Shandong Taiding Material Technology Co., Ltd.
Dezhou Mill
Dezhou, Shandong, China

Shandong Texpack Paper Co., Ltd.
Dezhou Mill
Dezhou, Shandong, China

Shandong Tianhe Paper Co., Ltd.
Taian Mill
Taian, Shandong, China

Shandong Zaozhuang Huarun Paper Co., Ltd.
Zaozhuang Mill
Zaozhuang, Shandong, China

Shandong Zhucheng Xinxing Paper Co. Ltd.
Zhucheng Mill
Zhucheng, Shandong, China

Shandong Zibo Guotai Paper Co., Ltd.
Zibo Mill
Zibo, Shandong, China

Shandong Zibo Paperboard Co., Ltd.
Zibo Mill
Zibo, Shandong, China

Shanghai Chung Loong Paper Co., Ltd.
Shanghai Mill
Shanghai, Shanghai, China

Shanghai Fumin Paper Mill
Chongming Mill
Chongming, Shanghai, China

Shaniv Paper Industries Ltd.
Ofakim Paper Mill
Ofakim, Israel

Shanxi QiangWei Paper Co., Ltd.
Jinzhong Mill
Jinzhong, Shanxi, China

Shengda Group Jiangsu Shuangdeng Paper Co., Ltd.
Yancheng Mill
Yancheng, Jiangsu, China

Shenghua Group
Huzhou Mill
Huzhou, Zhejiang, China

Shihlin Paper Corp.
Yung An Mill
Hsin Wu, Taoyuan County, Taiwan

Shin-Ei Paper Mfg. Co., Ltd.
Fujinomiya-Shi Mill
Fujinomiya-Shi, Shizuoka Pref., Japan

Shinchang Paper
Asan Mill
Asan-si, Chungcheongnam-do, South Korea

Shindaeyang Paper Co., Ltd.
Ansan Mill
Ansan-si, Gyeonggi-do, South Korea

Shindaeyang Paper Co., Ltd.
Shihwa Mill
Ansan-si, Gyeonggi-do, South Korea

Shinpoong Paper Mfg. Co., Ltd.
Pyongtaek Mill
Pyeongtaek-si, Gyeonggi-do, South Korea

Shotmed Paper Industries (SPI)
6th of October City, Giza Mill
6th of October City, Giza, El Giza, Egypt

Shouguang Meilun Paper
Shouguang (Shouguang Meilun Paper) Mill
Shouguang, Shandong, China

SHP Harmanec, a.s.
Harmanec Mill
Harmanec, Slovakia

Shree Bhageshwari Papers Ltd
Muzaffarnagar Mill
Muzaffarnagar, Uttar Pradesh, India

Shree Bhawani Paper Mills Ltd.
Rae Bareli Mill
Rae Bareli, Uttar Pradesh, India

Shree Gopinath Paper Mills Pvt. Ltd
Surendranagar Mill
Surendranagar, Gujarat, India

Shree Krishna Paper Mills & Ind Ltd
Jaipur Mill
Jaipur, Rajasthan, India

Shree Rama Newsprint Ltd.
Barbhodan Mill
Barbhodan, Surat District, Gujarat, India

Siam Kraft Industry Co., Ltd.
BanPong Mill
BanPong, Ratchaburi, Thailand

SICAL
Lumbres Mill
Lumbres, France

Sichuan Chengdu Xiling Packaging Co., Ltd.
Chengdu Mill
Chengdu, Sichuan, China

Sichuan Guanghan City Shunfa Co., Ltd.
Deyang Mill
Deyang, Sichuan, China

Sichuan Yibin Lantian Paper
Yibin Mill
Yibin, Sichuan, China

Sicomo S.A.L.
Kab-Elias, Bekaa Mill
Kab-Elias, Bekaa, Lebanon

Siddheshwari Industries Ltd.
Muzaffarnagar Mill
Muzaffarnagar, Uttar Pradesh, India

Sidharth Papers Ltd.
Kashipur Mill
Kashipur, Uttarakhand, India

Sidharth Papers Ltd.
Kashipur Mill (Unit 2)
Kashipur, Uttarakhand, India

Simka Kagit San. Ve Tic A.S
Kayseri Mill
Kayseri, Turkey

SKG Pulp & Paper
New Alipore, Kolkata Mill
New Alipore, Kolkata, West Bengal, India

Skjern Papirfabrik A/S
Skjern Mill
Skjern, Denmark

Slavuta-Papir, JSC
Slavuta Mill
Slavuta, Ukraine

Smurfit Cartón y Papel de México S.A. de C.V.
Cerro Gordo Mill
Santa Clara Coatitla, Ecatepec de Morelos, Edo. de México, Mexico

Smurfit Cartón y Papel de México S.A. de C.V.
Los Reyes Mill
Col. Los Reyes Iztacala, Tlalnepantla, México, D.F., Mexico

Smurfit Cartón y Papel de México S.A. de C.V.
Monterrey Mill
Monterrey, Baja California Norte, Mexico

Smurfit Kappa Ania Paper
Ania Mill
Ponte all'Ania, Lucca, Italy

Smurfit Kappa Baden Karton GmbH
Gernsbach Mill
Gernsbach, Germany

Smurfit Kappa Cartón de Colombia SA
Barranquilla Mill
Barranquilla, Atlántico, Colombia

Smurfit Kappa Cartón de Colombia SA
Yumbo Mill
Cali, Valle de Cauca, Colombia

Smurfit Kappa Cartón de Venezuela S.A.
Caracas Mill
Petare, Caracas, Edo. Miranda, Venezuela

Smurfit Kappa Cartón de Venezuela S.A.
San Felipe Mill
San Felipe, Yaracuy, Venezuela

Smurfit Kappa Cartón de Venezuela S.A.
Valencia Mill
Valencia, Edo. Carabobo, Venezuela

Smurfit Kappa Cellulose du Pin
Facture mill
Biganos, France

Smurfit Kappa de Argentina S.A.
Bernal Mill
Bernal, Buenos Aires, Argentina

Smurfit Kappa de Argentina S.A.
Coronel Suárez Mill
Coronel Suárez, Buenos Aires, Argentina

Recycled Pulp

Smurfit Kappa GmbH Viersen Papier
Viersen Mill
Viersen, Germany

Smurfit Kappa Haupt Papier- und Pappenfabrik GmbH & Co. KG
Diemelstadt-Wrexen Mill
Diemelstadt-Wrexen, Germany

Smurfit Kappa Herzberger Papierfabrik GmbH
Herzberg Mill
Herzberg am Harz, Germany

Smurfit Kappa Kraftliner Piteå
Piteå Mill
Piteå, Sweden

Smurfit Kappa Mengíbar Paper
Mengíbar Mill
Mengíbar, Jaén, Spain

Smurfit Kappa Morava Paper
Žimrovice Mill
Žimrovice, Czech Republic

Smurfit Kappa Nettingsdorfer, Nettingsdorfer Papierfabrik AG & Co. KG
Nettingsdorfer Mill
Haid bei Ansfelden, Oberösterreich, Austria

Smurfit Kappa Orange County
Forney Mill
Forney, Texas, United States

Smurfit Kappa Papier & Kartonfabrik Hoya
Hoya Mill
Hoya/Weser, Germany

Smurfit Kappa Papier Recyclé France
Alfa d Avignon Mill
Le Pontet Cedex, France

Smurfit Kappa Papier Recyclé France
Papeteries de Saillat
Saint Junien Cedex, France

Smurfit Kappa Papier Recyclé France
Sault-les-Rethel mill
Sault-les-Rethel, France

Smurfit Kappa Roermond Papier BV
Roermond Mill
Roermond, Netherlands

Smurfit Kappa Sangüesa Paper
Sangüesa Mill
Sangüesa, Navarra, Spain

Smurfit Kappa Solid Board BV
Coevorden Mill
Coevorden, Netherlands

Smurfit Kappa Solid Board BV
Hoogkerk Mill
Groningen-Hoogkerk, Netherlands

Smurfit Kappa Solid Board BV
Nieuweschans Mill
Nieuweschans, Netherlands

Smurfit Kappa Solid Board BV
Oude Pekela Mill
Oude Pekela, Netherlands

Smurfit Kappa SSK
Birmingham Mill
Nechells, Birmingham, West Midlands, United Kingdom

Smurfit Kappa Townsend Hook
Snodland Mill
Snodland, Kent, United Kingdom

Smurfit Kappa Zülpich Papier GmbH
Zülpich Mill
Zülpich, Germany

Socarpi S.R.L.
Villa Basilica Mill
Villa Basilica, Lucca, Italy

Sofidel Group
Lancaster Mill
Lancaster, Lancashire, United Kingdom

SOLICAR-Société Libanaise de Carton
Beirut Mill
Beirut, Lebanon

Song Duong Tissue Paper Company
Long Bien District, Hanoi City Mill
Long Bien District, Hanoi City, Vietnam

Songhak Paper Co., Ltd.
Yangsan Mill
Yangsan-si, Gyeongsangnam-do, South Korea

Sonoco Alcore-Demolli srl
Ciriè Mill
Ciriè, Turin, Italy

Sonoco Board Mills Ltd.
Stainland Mill
Halifax, West Yorkshire, United Kingdom

Sonoco de Colombia Ltda
Cali Mill
Cali, Valle de Cauca, Colombia

Sonoco de México, S.A. de C.V.
Santa Clara Mill
Santa Clara Ecatepec, Edo. de México, Mexico

Sonoco do Brasil Ltda.
Londrina Mill
Londrina, Paraná, Brazil

Sonoco Hellas
Stavrohori Mill
Stavrohori, Kilkis, Greece

Sonoco Ltd.
Brantford Mill
Brantford, Ontario, Canada

Sonoco Ltd.
Trent Valley Mill
Glen Miller, Ontario, Canada

Sonoco Paper France SAS
Schweighouse Mill
Schweighouse sur Moder, France

Sonoco Products Co.
City of Industry Mill
City of Industry, California, United States

Sonoco Products Co.
Hartsville Mill
Hartsville, South Carolina, United States

Sonoco Products Co.
Holyoke Mill
Holyoke, Massachusetts, United States

Sonoco Products Co.
Hutchinson Mill
Hutchinson, Kansas, United States

Sonoco Products Co.
Menasha Mill
Menasha, Wisconsin, United States

Sonoco Products Co.
Newport Mill
Newport, Tennessee, United States

Sonoco Products Co.
Richmond Mill
Richmond, Virginia, United States

Sonoco Products Co.
Sumner Mill
Sumner, Washington, United States

Sonoco-Alcore Oy
Karhula Board Mill
Karhula, Finland

Sopasta S.A. Indústria e Comércio
Tangará Mill
Tangará, Santa Catarina, Brazil

Sotipapier - Société Tunisienne Industrielle du Papier et du Carton - S.A.R.L.
Belli Mill
Belli, Tunisia

Soundview Paper Co.
Elmwood Park Mill
Elmwood Park, New Jersey, United States

Soundview Paper Co.
Putney Mill
Putney, Vermont, United States

South African Cartonboard Mills
Wadeville Mill
Wadeville, Gauteng, South Africa

South African Paper Mills (SAPM)
Durban Mill
Jacobs, Durban, KwaZulu-Natal, South Africa

SP Fiber Technologies LLC (SPFT)
Dublin Mill
Dublin, Georgia, United States

SP Fiber Technologies LLC (SPFT)
Newberg Mill
Newberg, Oregon, United States

Spartak
Shklov Mill
Shklov, Mogilev Region, Belarus

Sprick GmbH & Co.
Mitte Mill
Diemelstadt, Germany

Sree Sakthi Paper Mills Ltd.
Chalakkudy Mill
Kanjirappilly, Chalakkudy, Kerala, India

Sree Sakthi Paper Mills Ltd.
Edayar Mill
Aluva, Kerala, India

Recycled Pulp

Sripathi Paper & Boards Pvt.Ltd
Sivakasi Mill
Sivakasi, Tamil Nadu, India

Ssangyong C&B
Chochiwon Mill
Jochiwon-eup, Yeongi-gun, Chungcheongnam-do, South Korea

Ssangyong Paper Co., Ltd.
Osan Mill
Osan-si, Gyeonggi-do, South Korea

ST Paper, LLC
Oconto Falls Mill
Oconto Falls, Wisconsin, United States

Stadfast Paper Mills Pvt. Ltd.
Valsad Mill
Dist. Bulsar, Gujarat, India

Steinbeis Papier Glückstadt GmbH & Co. KG
Glückstadt Mill
Glückstadt, Germany

Stora Enso Poland S.A.
Ostroleka Mill
Ostroleka, Poland

Stora Enso Printing and Reading
Hylte Mill
Hyltebruk, Sweden

Stora Enso Printing and Reading
Langerbrugge Mill
Gent, Belgium

Stora Enso Printing and Reading
Maxau Mill
Karlsruhe, Germany

Stora Enso Printing and Reading
Sachsen Mill
Eilenburg, Saxony, Germany

Stora Enso Renewable Packaging
Barcelona Mill
Castellbisbal, Catalonia, Spain

Stora Enso Renewable Packaging
Heinola Mill
Heinola, Finland

Stora Enso Renewable Packaging
Imatra Mills (Kaukopää & Tainionkoski)
Imatra, Finland

Strathcona Paper LP
Napanee Mill
Napanee, Ontario, Canada

Sukhonsky Pulp and Paper Mill
Sokol Mill
Sokol, Vologodskaya obl., Russia

Sulamericana Industrial Ltda.
Mogi Mirim Mill
Mogi Mirim, São Paulo, Brazil

Sunko Seishi Co., Ltd.
Shizuoka-shi Mill
Shimizu-ku, Shizuoka-shi, Shizuoka Pref., Japan

Superplast Co.
El Obour Mill
Bab El Shaaria, Cairo, Egypt

Supreme Coated Board Mills Pvt. Ltd.
Vembakottai Mill
Sivakasi, Tamil Nadu, India

Surpapel SA
Berazategui Mill
Berazategui, Buenos Aires, Argentina

Suyash Paper Mills
Basti district Mill
Basti district, Uttar Pradesh, Uttar Pradesh, India

Suzano Papel e Celulose S.A.
Rio Verde Unit
Suzano, São Paulo, Brazil

Suzano Papel e Celulose S.A.
Ripasa II Mill
Embu, São Paulo, Brazil

Svetlogorskiy Pulp and Board Mill
Svetlogorsk Mill
Svetlogorsk, Gomel Region, Belarus

Sweetwater Paperboard
Austell Mill
Austell, Georgia, United States

Syktyvkar Tissue Group, LLC
Syktyvkar Mill
Syktyvkar, Russia

Tacoma Paperboard
Tacoma Mill
Tacoma, Washington, United States

Taiho Paper Co., Ltd.
Kamo-gun Mill
Kamo-gun, Gifu Pref., Japan

Taisei Paper Industries Co., Ltd.
Tsuyama-shi Mill
Tsuyama-shi, Okayama Pref., Japan

Taishan Gypsum Co., Ltd.
Taian Mill
Taian, Shandong, China

Takano Paper Co., Ltd.
Fuji-shi Mill
Fuji-shi, Shizuoka Pref., Japan

Takasago Paper Co., Ltd.
Mitsukaido-shi Mill
Mitsukaido-shi, Ibaraki Pref., Japan

Tama Paperboard
Tama Mill
Tama, Iowa, United States

Tan Mai Group Joint Stock Co.
Tan Mai Mill
Bien Hoa City, Dong Nai Province, Vietnam

Tao Yuan Paper Mfg. Co., Ltd.
Lu Chu Mill
Lu Chu, Taoyuan County, Taiwan

Technocart SA
Tripolis Mill
Tripolis, Greece

Tenma Paper Mills (Thailand) Co., Ltd.
Pakkred Mill
Pakkred, Nonthaburi, Thailand

Tezol Tütün ve Kagit San ve Tic A.S.
Izmir Mill
Torbali, Izmir, Izmir, Turkey

Thai Cane Paper Public Co., Ltd.
Kanchanaburi Mill #1
Amphur Tha Muang, Kanchanaburi, Kanchanaburi, Thailand

Thai Cane Paper Public Co., Ltd.
Prachinburi Mill #2
Amphur Kabinburi, Prachinburi, Thailand

Thai Card Board Co Ltd.
Sampran Mill
Sampran, Nakhon Pathom, Thailand

Thai Development Paper Co., Ltd.
Samut Prakan Mill
Amphur Muang, Samut Prakan, Samut Prakarn, Thailand

Thai Kraft Paper Industry Co., Ltd.
Wangsala Mill
Tha Muang Distr., Kanchanaburi, Kanchanaburi, Thailand

Thai Paper Mill Co., Ltd.
Rayong Mill
Amphur Bankhai, Rayong, Thailand

Thai Union Paper Industry Co., Ltd.
Wangsala Mill
Tha Muang Distr., Kanchanaburi, Thailand

Thai Union Paper Public Co., Ltd.
Prapradaeng Mill
Prapradaeng, Samut Prakam, Thailand

The West Coast Paper Mills Ltd.
Dandeli Mill
Dandeli, Uttara Kannada, Karnataka, India

Thrace Paper Mill S.A.
Thrace (Diana) Mill
Xanthi, Greece

Three M Paper Mfg. Co. Pvt. Ltd.
Ratnagiri Mill
Ratnagiri, Maharashtra, India

Thurpapier, Model AG
Weinfelden Mill
Weinfelden, Switzerland

Tirthak Paper Mill Pvt. Ltd.
Morbi Mill
Morbi, Gujarat, India

Tokushu Tokai Paper Co., Ltd.
Shimada Mill
Shimada-shi, Shizuoka Pref., Japan

Tolentino S.r.l.
Tolentino Mill
Tolentino, Macerata, Italy

Tonic Industrie EPE
Ouate Industrie Mill
Bou Ismail, Wilaya d'Alger, Algeria

TOP S.A.
Katowice Mill
Katowice, Poland

TOP S.A.
Tychy Mill
Tychy, Poland

Toscopaper SpA
Ponte a Moriano Mill
Ponte a Moriano, Lucca, Italy

Recycled Pulp

TOV Poninki Cardboard and Paper Mill
Poninka Mill
Poninka, Polonsky rayon, Khmelnitska obl., Ukraine

Toyama Seishi KK
Toyama Mill
Toyama-shi, Toyama Pref., Japan

Toyo Paper Mfg. Co., Ltd.
Shikokuchuo-shi Mill
Shikokuchuo-shi, Ehime Pref., Japan

Trakya Kagit San ve TIC. A.S.
Tekirdag Mill
Tekirdag, Tekirdag, Turkey

Trio Paper Mills Sdn. Bhd.
Simpang Ampat Mill
Simpang Ampat, Pulau Pinang, Malaysia

Trombini Industrial S.A.
Curitiba Mill
Curitiba, Paraná, Brazil

Trombini Industrial S.A.
Fraiburgo Mill
Fraiburgo, Santa Catarina, Brazil

Trupal S.A.
Evitamiento Mill
El Agustino, Lima, Lima, Peru

Trupal S.A.
Trujillo Mill
Trujillo, Peru

Trust International Paper Corp. (TIPCO)
Mabalacat Mill
Mabalacat, Pampanga, Philippines

Tulsi Paper Mills Pvt. Ltd.
Bardoli Mill
Bardoli, Surat, Gujarat, India

Tung Chi Paper Corp.
Lung Ching Mill
Lung Ching District, Taichung City, Taiwan

Tunisie Ouate
Enfidha Mill
Enfidha, Gouvernorat de Sousse, Tunisia

Twin Rivers Paper, LLC
Madawaska and Edmundston Mills (East Paper Operations)
Madawaska, Maine, United States

U.S. Paper Mills Corp.
De Pere Mill
De Pere, Wisconsin, United States

UCAL Donusen Kagit San ve Tic A.S.
Sirapinar Mill
Sirapinar, Umraniye, Istanbul, Turkey

Umka AD, Fabrika Kartona
Umka Mill
Umka, Belgrade, Serbia

Unión Industrial Papelera S.A. (UIPSA)
La Pobla de Claramunt Mill
La Pobla de Claramunt, Barcelona, Spain

Union Paper Mills
Dubai Mill
Dubai, United Arab Emirates

Unipak Tissue Mill
Jbeil Mill
Jbeil, Jounieh, Lebanon

United Corrstack LLC
Reading Mill
Reading, Pennsylvania, United States

United Paper Public Co. Ltd.
Amphur Muang Mill
Amphur Muang, Prachinburi, Thailand

United Pulp & Paper Co., Inc.
Calumpit Mill
Calumpit, Bulacan, Philippines

United States Gypsum Co.
Galena Park Mill
Galena Park, Texas, United States

United States Gypsum Co.
North Kansas City Mill
North Kansas City, Missouri, United States

United States Gypsum Co.
Oakfield Mill
Oakfield, New York, United States

UPM GmbH
Augsburg Mill
Augsburg, Germany

UPM GmbH
Ettringen Mill
Ettringen, Bavaria, Germany

UPM GmbH
Hürth Mill
Hürth, Germany

UPM GmbH
Plattling Mill
Plattling, Germany

UPM GmbH
Schongau Mill
Schongau, Germany

UPM GmbH
Schwedt Mill
Schwedt/Oder, Germany

UPM-Kymmene (UK) Ltd.
Shotton Paper Mill
Shotton, Deeside, Wales, United Kingdom

UPM-Kymmene Austria GmbH
Steyrermühl Mill
Steyrermühl, Oberösterreich, Austria

UPM-Kymmene Corporation
Kaipola Mill
Kaipola, Jämsä, Finland

Urvashi Pulp & Paper Mills Pvt. Ltd.
Bharuch Mill
Ankleshwar, Dist. Bharuch, Gujarat, India

Valley Converting Co.
Toronto Mill
Toronto, Ohio, United States

Valpasa Indústria de Papel Ltda.
Tangará Mill
Tangará, Santa Catarina, Brazil

Van Houtum BV
Swalmen Mill
Swalmen, Netherlands

Venkraft Paper Mills Private Ltd.
Hosur Mill
Hosur, Tamil Nadu, India

Viet Tri Paper Company
Viet Tri Mill
Viet Tri City, Phú Tho Province, Vietnam

Viking Kagit ve Seluloz A.S.
Viking Paper Mill
Aliaga, Izmir, Turkey

Vina Kraft Paper
Ho Chi Minh City Mill
Ho Chi Minh City, Binh Duong Province, Vietnam

Viochartiki Paper Mill SA
Aspropirgos Mill
Aspropirgos, Attica, Greece

Vipap Videm Krško d.d.
Krško Mill
Krško, Ljubljana, Slovenia

VIS Containers Manufacturing SA
Volos Mill
Volos, Greece

Visy Pulp & Paper
Coolaroo Mill
Campbellfield, Victoria, Australia

Visy Pulp & Paper
Gibson Island, VPP8
Gibson Island, Queensland, Australia

Visy Pulp & Paper
Tumut, VPP9
Tumut, New South Wales, Australia

Visy Pulp & Paper
VPP2, Reservoir Mill
Reservoir, Victoria, Australia

Visy Pulp & Paper
VPP3/6, Smithfield Mill
Smithfield, New South Wales, Australia

Volga
Balakhna Mill
Balakhna, Nizhny Novgorod, Russia

Von Drehle Corp.
Cordova Mill
Cordova, North Carolina, United States

VPK Paper NV
Dendermonde Mill
Dendermonde, Belgium

Vrancart SA
Adjud Mill
Adjud, Vrancea, Romania

Vyborgskaya Cellulose, JSC
Sovetsky Mill
Vyborg, Sovetsky, Leningrad Region, Russia

W. Hamburger GmbH
Frohnleiten Mill
Frohnleiten, Styria, Austria

W. Hamburger GmbH
Pitten Mill
Pitten, Niederösterreich, Austria

WARTER - Fabryka Papieru i Tektury
Tarnowka Mill
Tarnowka, Poland

Recycled Pulp

Wausau Paper Towel & Tissue, LLC
Middletown Mill
Middletown, Ohio, United States

Weihai Longgang Paper Co., Ltd.
Weihai Mill
Weihai, Shandong, China

WELMAX Zaklad Produkcyjno-Handlowy Wieslaw Adamowicz
Wohyn Mill
Wohyń, Poland

WEPA Hygieneprodukte GmbH
Marsberg-Giershagen Mill
Marsberg-Giershagen, Germany

WEPA Hygieneprodukte GmbH
Arnsberg Mill
Arnsberg-Müschede, Germany

WEPA Hygieneprodukte GmbH
Mainz Mill
Mainz, Germany

WEPA Lille S.A.R.L.
Bousbecque Mill
Bousbecque, France

WEPA Professional Piechowice S.A.
Piechowice Mill
Piechowice, Poland

Werra Papier
Omega Mill
Wernshausen, Germany

West Linn Paper Co.
West Linn Mill
West Linn, Oregon, United States

White Pigeon Paper Co.
White Pigeon Mill
White Pigeon, Michigan, United States

Wisconsin Paperboard Corp.
Milwaukee Mill
Milwaukee, Wisconsin, United States

Wolsan Paper Mfg. Co., Ltd.
Haman Mill
Chilseo-myeon, Haman-gun, Gyeongsangnam-do, South Korea

WPT Eko-Klan Sp. z o.o.
Margonin Mill
Margonin, Poland

Xuan Duc Joint-Stock Paper Company
Ho Chi Minh City Mill
Ho Chi Minh City, Binh Duong Province, Vietnam

Yame Seishisho Co., Ltd.
Yame-shi Mill
Yame-shi, Fukuoka Pref., Japan

Yaroslavl Paper ZAO
Yaroslavl Mill
Yaroslavl, Yaroslavl obl., Russia

Yasar Ambalaj Kagit Bobin San. ve Tic. A.S.
Malatya Mill
Malatya, Turkey

Yeong Chaur Shing Paper Mill Sdn. Bhd.
Melaka Mill
Melaka, Malaysia

Youngpoong Paper Mfg. Co., Ltd.
Pyeongtaek-si Mill
Pyeongtaek-si, Gyeonggi-do, South Korea

Yuantong Paper (Shandong) Co., Ltd.
Zaozhuang Mill
Zaozhuang, Shandong, China

Yuen Foong Yu Packaging Inc.
Chengkung Mill
Wu Jih District, Taichung City, Taiwan

Yuen Foong Yu Packaging Inc.
Hsin Wu Mill
Hsin Wu, Taoyuan County, Taiwan

Yuhan-Kimberly Ltd.
Kimcheon Mill
Gimcheon-si, Gyeongsangbuk-do, South Korea

Yunnan Dali Huacheng Paper Co., Ltd.
Dali Mill
Dali, Yunnan, China

Yunnan Lujiang Paper Co., Ltd.
Kaiyuan Mill
Kaiyuan, Yunnan, China

Yunnan Yuxi Dongsheng Paper Co., Ltd.
Yuxi Mill
Yuxi, Yunnan, China

Zaman Paper and Board Mills Ltd.
Sheikhupura Mill
Sheikhupura, Punjab, Pakistan

Zambezi Paper Mills Ltd.
Ndola Mill
Ndola, Zambia

ZAO Altaykrovlya
Novoaltaysk Mill
Novoaltaysk, Altaisky Kray, Russia

ZAO MPK KRZ - Multibranch Production Company KRZ
Ryazan Mill
Ryazan, Russia

ZAO Suoyarvi Paperboard Mill
Suoyarvi Mill
Suoyarvi, Karelia, Russia

Zhejiang Cixi Longfeng Paper Co., Ltd.
Cixi Mill
Cixi, Zhejiang, China

Zhejiang Fuyang Chenggong Paper Co., Ltd.
Fuyang Mill
Fuyang, Zhejiang, China

Zhejiang Fuyang Chunsheng Paper Co., Ltd.
Fuyang Mill
Fuyang, Zhejiang, China

Zhejiang Fuyang City Huawei Paper Co., Ltd.
Fuyang Mill
Fuyang, Zhejiang, China

Zhejiang Fuyang City Huitai Paper Co., Ltd.
Fuyang Mill
Fuyang, Zhejiang, China

Zhejiang Fuyang City Huitai Paper Co., Ltd.
Fuyang Mill
Fuyang, Zhejiang, China

Zhejiang Fuyang Dingdian Paper Co., Ltd.
Fuyang Mill
Fuyang, Zhejiang, China

Zhejiang Fuyang Feima Paper Co., Ltd.
Fuyang Mill
Fuyang, Zhejiang, China

Zhejiang Fuyang Fuming Paper Co., Ltd.
Fuyang Mill
Fuyang, Zhejiang, China

Zhejiang Fuyang Futai Feifeng Paper Co., Ltd.
Fuyang Mill
Fuyang, Zhejiang, China

Zhejiang Fuyang Hualong Paper Co., Ltd.
Fuyang Mill
Fuyang, Zhejiang, China

Zhejiang Fuyang Huamao Paper Co., Ltd.
Fuyang Mill
Fuyang, Zhejiang, China

Zhejiang Fuyang Huatian Paper Co., Ltd.
Fuyang Mill
Fuyang, Zhejiang, China

Zhejiang Fuyang Jin Xin Paper Co., Ltd.
Fuyang Mill
Fuyang, Zhejiang, China

Zhejiang Fuyang Jinchang Paper Co., Ltd.
Fuyang Mill
Fuyang, Zhejiang, China

Zhejiang Fuyang Kangnan Paper Co., Ltd.
Fuyang Mill
Fuyang, Zhejiang, China

Zhejiang Fuyang Kraft Paper Mill
Fuyang Mill
Fuyang, Zhejiang, China

Zhejiang Fuyang Lingtai Paper Co., Ltd.
Fuyang Mill
Fuyang, Zhejiang, China

Zhejiang Fuyang Maoyuan Paper Co., Ltd.
Fuyang Mill
Fuyang, Zhejiang, China

Zhejiang Fuyang Nanfa Paper Co., Ltd.
Fuyang Mill
Fuyang, Zhejiang, China

Recycled Pulp

Zhejiang Fuyang Runtong Paper Co., Ltd.
Fuyang Mill
Fuyang, Zhejiang, China

Zhejiang Fuyang Shangyou Paper Industry Co., Ltd.
Fuyang Mill
Fuyang, Zhejiang, China

Zhejiang Fuyang Sunshi Paper Co., Ltd.
Fuyang Mill
Fuyang, Zhejiang, China

Zhejiang Fuyang Wansheng Paper Co., Ltd.
Fuyang Mill
Fuyang, Zhejiang, China

Zhejiang Fuyang Xinyuan Paper Co., Ltd.
Fuyang Mill
Fuyang, Zhejiang, China

Zhejiang Fuyang Zhenghua Paper Co., Ltd.
Fuyang Mill
Fuyang, Zhejiang, China

Zhejiang Gaoyang Paper Co., Ltd.
Fuyang Mill
Fuyang, Zhejiang, China

Zhejiang Haining Bangda Paper Co., Ltd.
Haining Mill
Haining, Zhejiang, China

Zhejiang Hangzhou Banqiao Paper Co., Ltd.
Fuyang Mill
Fuyang, Zhejiang, China

Zhejiang Hangzhou Dazhong Paper Co., Ltd.
Fuyang Mill
Fuyang, Zhejiang, China

Zhejiang Hangzhou Dongda Paper Co., Ltd.
Fuyang Mill
Fuyang, Zhejiang, China

Zhejiang Hangzhou Fuyang Jinying Industry Co., Ltd.
Fuyang Mill
Fuyang, Zhejiang, China

Zhejiang Hangzhou Guofeng Paper Co., Ltd.
Fuyang Mill
Fuyang, Zhejiang, China

Zhejiang Hangzhou Haichen Paper Co., Ltd.
Fuyang Mill
Fuyang, Zhejiang, China

Zhejiang Hangzhou Huasheng Paper Co., Ltd.
Fuyang Mill
Fuyang, Zhejiang, China

Zhejiang Hangzhou Jintai Paper Co., Ltd.
Fuyang Mill
Fuyang, Zhejiang, China

Zhejiang Hangzhou Ruixing Paper Co., Ltd.
Fuyang Mill
Fuyang, Zhejiang, China

Zhejiang Hangzhou Xushi Paper Co., Ltd.
Fuyang Mill
Fuyang, Zhejiang, China

Zhejiang Hangzhou Yinfa Paper Co., Ltd.
Fuyang Mill
Fuyang, Zhejiang, China

Zhejiang Hangzhou Yuanda Paper Co., Ltd.
Fuyang Mill
Fuyang, Zhejiang, China

Zhejiang Hangzhou Zhongyi Paper Co., Ltd.
Fuyang Mill
Fuyang, Zhejiang, China

Zhejiang Hongsheng Paper Co., Ltd.
Fuyang (Zhejiang Hongsheng Paper) Mill
Fuyang, Zhejiang, China

Zhejiang Huakang Paper Co., Ltd.
Ruian Mill
Ruian, Zhejiang, China

Zhejiang Huaxin Paper Co., Ltd.
Fuyang Mill
Fuyang, Zhejiang, China

Zhejiang Huayu Paper Co., Ltd.
Shaoxing Mill
Shaoxing, Zhejiang, China

Zhejiang Huayuan Paper Co., Ltd.
Fuyang Mill
Fuyang, Zhejiang, China

Zhejiang JiAn Paper Package Co., Ltd.
Jiaxing Mill
Jiaxing, Zhejiang, China

Zhejiang Jindong Paper Co., Ltd.
Fuyang Mill
Fuyang, Zhejiang, China

Zhejiang Jingxing Paper Joint Stock Co., Ltd.
Pinghu Mill
Pinghu, Zhejiang, China

Zhejiang Lanniao Paper Co., Ltd.
Fuyang Mill
Fuyang, Zhejiang, China

Zhejiang Linan Ma An Qianshi Paper Co., Ltd.
Linan Mill
Linan, Zhejiang, China

Zhejiang Long Chen Paper Co., Ltd.
Pinghu Mill
Pinghu, Zhejiang, China

Zhejiang Ningbo Asia Pulp and Paper Co., Ltd.
Beilun (Zhejiang Ningbo Asia Pulp and Paper) Mill
Xiaogang, Ningbo, Zhejiang, China

Zhejiang Ningbo Dongteng Paper Co., Ltd.
Ningbo Mill
Ningbo, Zhejiang, China

Zhejiang Ningbo Haishan Paper Co.
Ningbo Mill
Ningbo, Zhejiang, China

Zhejiang Ningbo Ningxing Paper Co., Ltd.
Ninghai Mill
Ninghai, Zhejiang, China

Zhejiang Ningbo Zhonghua Paper
Ningbo (Zhejiang Ningbo Zhonghua Paper) Mill
Ningbo, Zhejiang, China

Zhejiang Pinghu Fengli Paper Stock Co. Ltd.
Pinghu Mill
Pinghu, Zhejiang, China

Zhejiang Quzhou Shuangxiongmao Paper General Corp.
Quzhou Mill
Quzhou, Zhejiang, China

Zhejiang Rongsheng Paper Co., Ltd.
Pinghu Mill
Pinghu, Zhejiang, China

Zhejiang Sanxing Paper Co., Ltd.
Fuyang Mill
Fuyang, Zhejiang, China

Zhejiang Shengda Group
Hangzhou Mill
Hangzhou, Zhejiang, China

Zhejiang Tianting Paper Co., Ltd.
Jinhua Mill
Jinhua, Zhejiang, China

Zhejiang Wanxin Paper Co., Ltd.
Fuyang Mill
Fuyang, Zhejiang, China

Zhejiang Wenbo Paper Co., Ltd.
Fuyang (Zhejiang Wenbo Paper) Mill
Fuyang, Zhejiang, China

Zhejiang Wenfeng Paper Co., Ltd.
Fuyang Mill
Fuyang, Zhejiang, China

Zhejiang Xianglong Paper Co., Ltd.
Fuyang (Zhejiang Xianglong) Mill
Fuyang, Zhejiang, China

Zhejiang Yiwu City Huachuan Paper Co., Ltd.
Yiwu Mill
Yiwu, Zhejiang, China

Zhejiang Yiwu City YiNan Paper Co., Ltd.
Yiwu Mill
Yiwu, Zhejiang, China

Zhejiang Yongjin Paper Co., Ltd.
Fuyang Mill
Fuyang, Zhejiang, China

Newsprint

Zhejiang Yongtai Paper Group Co., Ltd.
Fuyang Mill
Fuyang, Zhejiang, China

Zhejiang Zhengda Holding Group Co., Ltd.
Fuyang Mill
Fuyang, Zhejiang, China

Zhydachiv Pulp & Paper Mill
Zhydachiv Mill
Zhydachiv, Lviv obl., Ukraine

Zhytomyr Paperboard Mill
Zhytomyr Mill
Zhytomyr, Ukraine

Paper and Paperboard Grades Produced

Newsprint

Ajanta Paper & General Products Ltd.
Jhagadia Mill
Jhagadia, Gujarat, India

Ajanta Paper & General Products Ltd.
Kalyan Mill
Dist. Thane, Maharashtra, India

Alberta Newsprint Co. Ltd.
Whitecourt Mill
Whitecourt, Alberta, Canada

Amaravathi Sri Venkatesa Paper Mills Ltd.
Madathukulam Mill
Madathukulam, Coimbatore Dist., Tamil Nadu, India

Anand Duplex/Triplex Board Limited
Meerut Mill
Meerut District, Uttar Pradesh, India

Anhui Shanying Paper No. 2 Mill
Maanshan (No. 2) Mill
Maanshan, Anhui, China

Anmol Products Ethiopia
Ginchi Mill
Ginchi, Ethiopia

Aurangabad Paper Mills Ltd.
Aurangabad Mill
Aurangabad, Maharashtra, India

Aylesford Newsprint Ltd.
Aylesford Mill
Aylesford, Kent, United Kingdom

Bai Bang Paper Joint-stock Co., Ltd.
Ky Son Mill
Ky Son, Hoa Binh Province, Vietnam

Balikesir Albayrak Kagit Fabrikasi
Balikesir Mill
Balikesir, Turkey

Bashundhara Paper Mills Ltd.
Unit 1
Sonargaon, Baranagar, Narayanganj, Bangladesh

Bashundhara Paper Mills Ltd.
Unit 2
Sonargaon, New Town, Narayanganj, Bangladesh

Bataan 2020
Samal Mill
Samal, Bataan, Philippines

Bear Island Paper Co., LLC
Ashland Mill
Ashland, Virginia, United States

Bio-PAPPEL Printing
Tuxtepec Mill
Tuxtepec, OAX, Mexico

Catalyst Paper Corporation
Crofton Mill
Crofton, British Columbia, Canada

Chandpur Enterprises Ltd.
Dist. Bijnor Mill
Dist. Bijnor, Uttar Pradesh, India

Charoen Aksorn Holding Group Co. Ltd. (CAS Group)
Singburi Mill
Amphur Muang, Singburi, Thailand

Chenming Paper Holdings Ltd.
Shouguang (Shouguang Chenming Newsprint No. 5) Mill
Shouguang, Shandong, China

Chuetsu Pulp & Paper Co., Ltd.
Takaoka (Futatsuka) Mill
Takaoka-shi, Toyama Pref., Japan

Coral Newsprints Limited
Jyotibaphulenagar Mill
Jia Phule Nagar, Uttar Pradesh, India

Cosboard Industries Ltd.
Jagatpur Mill
Dist. Cuttack, Odisha, India

Daehan Paper Co., Ltd.
Cheongwon Mill
Cheongwon-gun, Chungcheongbuk-do, South Korea

Daio Paper Corp.
Mishima Mill
Shikokuchuo-shi, Ehime Pref., Japan

Danalakshmi Paper Mills Pvt. Ltd.
Dindigul Mill
Nilakottai Taluk, Dindigul, Tamil Nadu, India

Ellora Paper Mills Ltd.
Tumsar, Dist. Bhandara Mill
Tumsar, Dist. Bhandara, Maharashtra, India

Emami Paper Mills Ltd.
Balasore Mill
Dist. Balasore, Odisha, India

Emami Paper Mills Ltd.
Kolkata Mill
Kolkata, West Bengal, India

F.F. Soucy SEC
Riviere du Loup Mill
Riviere du Loup, Quebec, Canada

Fabryka Papieru Myszków Sp. z o.o.
Myszkow Mill
Myszkow, Poland

Fujian Nanping Paper Co. Ltd.
Nanping Mill
Nanping, Fujian, China

Ganga Papers India
Pune Mill
Taluka Maval, Dist. Pune, Maharashtra, India

Gaurav Paper Mills
Chandrapur Mill
Chandrapur, Maharashtra, India

GRD Paper Industries PVT. Ltd
Howrah Mill
Howrah, West Bengal, India

Guangxi Jindaxing Paper Group Co., Ltd.
Baise Mill
Baise, Guangxi, China

Guangzhou Paper Group Ltd. (Nansha)
Guangzhou Mill
Guangzhou, Guangdong, China

GVG Paper Mills Ltd.
Palani Taluk Mill
Palani Taluk, Dist. Dindigul, Tamil Nadu, India

Hangzhou Huajin Specialty Paper Co., Ltd.
Hangzhou Mill
Hangzhou, Zhejiang, China

Hangzhou Jinjiang Paper Co., Ltd.
Linan Mill
Linan, Zhejiang, China

Hansson Paper Corp.
Pasig City Mill
Pasig City, Metro Manila, Philippines

Hebei Huatai Paper Co., Ltd.
Shijiazhuang Mill
Shijiazhuang, Hebei, China

Hebei Lu Quan Shunfa Industrial Co., Ltd.
Luquan Mill
Luquan, Hebei, China

Hebei Qinhuangdao Haofeng Enterprise Group
Qinhuangdao Mill
Qinhuangdao, Hebei, China

Henan Yingbo Paper Co., Ltd.
Mengzhou Mill
Mengzhou, Henan, China

Hindustan Newsprint Ltd.
Kottayam Dist. Mill
Kottayam Dist., Kerala, India

Holmen AB
Braviken Paper Mill
Norrköping, Sweden

Holmen Paper Madrid S.L.
Madrid Mill
Fuenlabrada, Madrid, Spain

Howe Sound Pulp and Paper Corporation
Port Mellon Mill
Port Mellon, British Columbia, Canada

HRA Papers Pvt Ltd
Kangra Mill
Village Tibbi, Kangra, Himachal Pradesh, India

Newsprint

Hubei Yichang Baota Paper Co., Ltd
Yichang Mill
Yichang, Hubei, China

Hyogo Paper Mfg. Co., Ltd.
Himeji Mill
Himeji-shi, Hyogo Pref., Japan

Indo Afrique Paper Mill
Pune Mill
Pune, Maharashtra, India

Inland Empire Paper Co.
Millwood Mill
Millwood, Spokane, Washington, United States

International Paper - Kwidzyn Sp. z o.o.
Kwidzyn Mill
Kwidzyn, Poland

Jeet Enterprises PVT. Ltd. (Sister Concern of Miglani Paper Mills)
Amritsar Mill
Amritsar, Punjab, India

Jeonju Paper Corporation, Ltd.
Cheongju mill
Cheongwon-gun, Chungcheongbuk-do, South Korea

Jeonju Paper Corporation, Ltd.
Jeonju Mill
Jeonju-si, Jeollabuk-do, South Korea

JSC Solikamskbumprom
Solikamsk Mill
Solikamsk, Perm Region, Russia

Kahramanmaras Kagit San ve TIC A.S (KMK Paper)
Kütahya Mill
Kütahya, Turkey

Kalptaru Papers Ltd.
Gandhinagar, Ahmadabad Mill
Gandhinagar, Ahmadabad, Gujarat, India

Kamakshi Papers Pvt. Ltd.
JP Nagar Mill
JP Nagar, Uttar Pradesh, India

Kaygaon Paper Mills Ltd.
Tq. Gangapur, Aurangabad Mill
Tq. Gangapur, Aurangabad, Maharashtra, India

Khanna Paper Mills Pvt. Ltd.
Amritsar Mill
Amritsar, Punjab, India

Kitakami Paper Co., Ltd.
Ichinoseki Mill
Ichinoseki-shi, Iwate Pref., Japan

Kondopoga
Kondopoga Mill
Kondopoga, Karelia, Russia

Kronex-Ukraina, Ltd.
Zmiev Mill
Zmiev, Kharkovskaya Obl., Ukraine

Kruger Inc.
Bromptonville Mill
Sherbrooke, Quebec, Canada

Kruger Inc.
Corner Brook Mill
Corner Brook, Newfoundland and Labrador, Canada

Kruger Inc.
Trois-Rivières Mill
Trois-Rivières, Quebec, Canada

Maa Chandi Papers Pvt. Ltd.
Burdwan Mill
Burdwan, West Bengal, India

Madhya Bharat Papers Ltd.
Dist. Janjgir-Champa Mill
Dist. Janjgir-Champa, Chattisgarh, India

Magnum Ventures Ltd.
Ghaziabad Mill
Sahibabad, Dist. Ghaziabad, Uttar Pradesh, India

Malaysian Newsprint Industries Sdn. Bhd.
Mentakab Mill
Mentakab, Pahang Darul Makmur, Malaysia

Malu Paper Mills Ltd.
Nagpur 3 Mill
Dist. Nagpur, Maharashtra, India

Marusumi Paper Co., Ltd.
Kawanoe Mill
Shikokuchuo-shi, Ehime Pref., Japan

Marusumi Paper Co., Ltd.
Ohe Mill
Shikokuchuo-shi, Ehime Pref., Japan

Mazandaran Wood & Paper Industries Co.
Sari Mill
Sari, Mazandaran, Iran

Mondi Shanduka Newsprint
Merebank Mill
Merebank, KwaZulu-Natal, South Africa

Mondi Syktyvkar
Syktyvkar Mill
Syktyvkar, Komi Republic, Russia

Mopak Dalaman Pulp-Paper Cardboard Plant
Dalaman Mill
Mugla, Turkey

Mostafa Paper
Chittagong Mill
Chittagong, Chittagong, Bangladesh

Murli Industries Ltd.
Nagpur Mill
Nagpur, Maharashtra, India

Mysore Paper Mills Ltd.
Shimoga Mill
Bhadravati, Shimoga, Karnataka, India

Nav Bharat Duplex Ltd.
Hapur Mill
Hapur, Uttar Pradesh, India

NEPA Ltd.
Nepanagar Mill
Nepanagar, Burhanpur District, Madhya Pradesh, India

Nippon Paper Industries Co., Ltd.
Fuji Mill
Fuji-shi, Shizuoka Pref., Japan

Nippon Paper Industries Co., Ltd.
Hokkaido Mill - Yufutsu
Tomakomai-shi, Hokkaido Pref., Japan

Nippon Paper Industries Co., Ltd.
Iwanuma Mill
Iwanuma-shi, Miyagi Pref., Japan

Nippon Paper Industries Co., Ltd.
Kushiro Mill
Kushiro-shi, Hokkaido Pref., Japan

Nippon Paper Industries Co., Ltd.
Yatsushiro Mill
Yatsushiro-shi, Kumamoto Pref., Japan

Norske Skog (Australia)
Albury Mill
Ettamogah via Albury, New South Wales, Australia

Norske Skog (Australia)
Boyer Mill
Boyer, Tasmania, Australia

Norske Skog ASA
Skogn Mill
Skogn, Norway

Norske Skog Bruck GmbH
Bruck an der Mur Mill
Bruck an der Mur, Styria, Austria

Norske Skog Golbey SA
Golbey Mill
Golbey Cedex, France

Norske Skog Pisa S.A.
Jaguariaíva Mill
Jaguariaíva, Paraná, Brazil

Norske Skog Tasman
Tasman Mill
Kawerau, Bay of Plenty, New Zealand

North Pacific Paper Corp. (Norpac)
Longview Mill
Longview, Washington, United States

NR Agarwal Industries Ltd.
Unit II
Vapi, Dist. Valsad, Gujarat, India

Oku Iboku Pulp and Paper (OKIPP) Company Limited
Oku Iboku Mill
Ayadeghe, Oku Iboku, Akwa Ibom State, Nigeria

Osaka Paper Co., Ltd.
Osaka-shi Mill
Osaka-shi, Osaka Pref., Japan

Palm Group
Eltmann Mill
Eltmann, Germany

Palm Paper Limited
King's Lynn Mill
King's Lynn, United Kingdom

Pan Paper Mills
Webuye Mill
Webuye, Bungoma District, Western, Kenya

Papel Prensa S.A.
San Pedro Mill
San Pedro, Buenos Aires, Argentina

Papeles Bío Bío
Concepción Mill
Concepción, VIII - Región del Biobío, Chile

Newsprint

Paper Corea Inc.
Gunsan Mill
Gunsan-si, Jeollabuk-do, South Korea

Papier Masson
Gatineau Mill
Gatineau, Quebec, Canada

Papierfabrik Palm GmbH & Co KG
Aalen Mill
Aalen-Neukochen, Germany

Papierfabrik Utzenstorf AG
Utzenstorf Mill
Utzenstorf, Switzerland

Papresa, S.L.
Rentería Mill
Rentería, Gipúzcoa, Spain

Perlen Papier AG
Perlen Mill
Perlen, Switzerland

Ponderay Newsprint Co.
Usk Mill
Usk, Washington, United States

Pragati Paper Industries Ltd.
Patiala Mill
Derabassi Dist., Patiala, Punjab, India

Pragati Paper Industries Ltd.
Sirmaur Mill
Dist. Sirmaur, Himachal Pradesh, India

Pronal, Productora Nacional de Papel, S.A. de C.V.
Pronal Mill
Ejido San Miguel, Municipio Villa de Reyes, San Luis Potosi, Mexico

PT Adiprima Suraprinta
Gresik Mill
Gresik, East Java, Indonesia

PT Aspex Kumbong
Bogor Mill
Bogor, West Java, Indonesia

PT Setia Kawan
Tulungagung Mill
Tulungagung, East Java, Indonesia

PT Surabaya Agung Industri Pulp & Kertas
Driyorejo Mill
Gresik, East Java, Indonesia

Purvi Bharat Paper & Power Ltd.
Cuttack Mill
Cuttack, Odisha, India

Quena Paper Industry Co. (QPIC)
Kous Mill
Kous, Quena, Egypt

Rainbow Papers Ltd.
Mehsana Mill
Mehsana, Gujarat, India

Rama Paper Mills Ltd.
Bijnor Mill
Kiratpur, Bijnor, Uttar Pradesh, India

Reliance Paper Mills
Bhairahawa Mill
Bhairahawa, Nepal

Resolute Forest Products Canada Inc.
Amos Mill
Amos, Quebec, Canada

Resolute Forest Products Canada Inc.
Baie-Comeau Mill
Baie-Comeau, Quebec, Canada

Resolute Forest Products Canada Inc.
Clermont Mill
Clermont, Quebec, Canada

Resolute Forest Products Canada Inc.
Gatineau Mill
Gatineau, Quebec, Canada

Resolute Forest Products Canada Inc.
Iroquois Falls Mill
Iroquois Falls, Ontario, Canada

Resolute Forest Products Canada Inc.
Thorold Mill
Thorold, Ontario, Canada

Resolute Forest Products Canada Inc.
Thunder Bay Mill
Thunder Bay, Ontario, Canada

Resolute FP Augusta LLC
Augusta Mill
Augusta, Georgia, United States

Rolex Paper Mills Ltd.
Vill. Chinta Parru Mill
Vill. Chinta Parru, Andhra Pradesh, India

Saffron Industries Ltd.
Nagpur Mill
Nagpur, Maharashtra, India

Sangal Papers Ltd.
Meerut Mill
Meerut, Uttar Pradesh, India

Sappi Paper and Paper Packaging South Africa (SA)
Ngodwana Mill
Ngodwana, Mpumalanga, South Africa

SCA Graphic Sundsvall AB
Ortviken Mill
Sundsvall, Sweden

Schönfelder Papierfabrik GmbH
Annaberg-Buchholz Mill
Annaberg-Buchholz, Germany

Servalakshmi Paper & Boards Ltd. (SLPB)
Nilakottai Talu Mill
Nilakottai Talu, Dindigul Dist., Tamil Nadu, India

Servalakshmi Paper Ltd.
Servall Mill
Tirunelveli, Tamil Nadu, India

Shah Pulp & Paper Mills Ltd.
Valsad Mill
Vapi Pardi, Valsad, Gujarat, India

Shakumbhri Straw Products Ltd.
Moradabad Mill
Tehsil Bilari, Moradabad, Uttar Pradesh, India

Shandong Chenlong Paper Co., Ltd.
Zibo Mill
Zibo, Shandong, China

Shandong Honghe Group Zoucheng Hengxiang Paper Co., Ltd.
Zoucheng Mill
Zoucheng, Shandong, China

Shandong Huatai Group Co., Ltd.
Jiangmen Mill
Jiangmen, Guangdong, China

Shandong Taiding Material Technology Co., Ltd.
Dezhou Mill
Dezhou, Shandong, China

Shandong Zhucheng Xinxing Paper Co. Ltd.
Zhucheng Mill
Zhucheng, Shandong, China

Shenghua Group
Huzhou Mill
Huzhou, Zhejiang, China

Shklov Newsprint Mill (Zavod Gazetnoi Bumagi)
Shklov Newsprint Mill
Shklov, Mogilev region, Mogilev Region, Belarus

Shree Bhawani Paper Mills Ltd.
Rae Bareli Mill
Rae Bareli, Uttar Pradesh, India

Shree Krishna Paper Mills & Ind Ltd
Jaipur Mill
Jaipur, Rajasthan, India

Shree Rajeshwaranand Paper Mills Ltd.
Dist. Bharuch Mill
Dist. Bharuch, Gujarat, India

Shree Rama Newsprint Ltd.
Barbhodan Mill
Barbhodan, Surat District, Gujarat, India

Shri Harikrishna Papers PVT. Ltd.
Palani Taluk Mill
Palani Taluk, Tamil Nadu, India

South India Paper Mills Ltd.
Nanjangud Mill
Nanjangud, Karnataka, India

SP Fiber Technologies LLC (SPFT)
Dublin Mill
Dublin, Georgia, United States

SP Fiber Technologies LLC (SPFT)
Newberg Mill
Newberg, Oregon, United States

Spaa Straw Board Ind. Pvt. Ltd.
Bolangir Mill
Bolangir, Odisha, India

Sri Luxmi Tulasi Agro Paper Pvt Ltd.
Rajahmundry Mill
Rajahmundry, Andhra Pradesh, India

Sri Ramalingeswara Paper Products (P) Ltd.
East Godavari Dist. Mill
East Godavari Dist., Andhra Pradesh, India

Stadacona Inc.
Stadacona Mill
Quebec City, Quebec, Canada

Uncoated woodfree/freesheet

Stora Enso Printing and Reading
Hylte Mill
Hyltebruk, Sweden

Stora Enso Printing and Reading
Langerbrugge Mill
Gent, Belgium

Stora Enso Printing and Reading
Sachsen Mill
Eilenburg, Saxony, Germany

Sumit Agro Products Ltd.
Meerut Mill
Meerut, Uttar Pradesh, India

Sun Paper Mills Co. Ltd.
Dist. Tirunelveli Mill
Dist. Trunelveli, Tamil Nadu, India

Surya Chandra Paper Mills Ltd.
East Godavari Dist. Mill
East Godavari Dist., Andhra Pradesh, India

Tan Mai Group Joint Stock Co.
Tan Mai Mill
Bien Hoa City, Dong Nai Province, Vietnam

Tembec Inc.
Spruce Falls Mill
Kapuskasing, Ontario, Canada

Three Star Paper Mills (P) Ltd.
Dist. Gautam Budh Nagar Mill
Dist. Gautam Budh Nagar, Uttar Pradesh, India

Trust International Paper Corp. (TIPCO)
Mabalacat Mill
Mabalacat, Pampanga, Philippines

UPM GmbH
Ettringen Mill
Ettringen, Bavaria, Germany

UPM GmbH
Hürth Mill
Hürth, Germany

UPM GmbH
Schongau Mill
Schongau, Germany

UPM GmbH
Schwedt Mill
Schwedt/Oder, Germany

UPM-Kymmene (UK) Ltd.
Shotton Paper Mill
Shotton, Deeside, Wales, United Kingdom

UPM-Kymmene Austria GmbH
Steyrermühl Mill
Steyrermühl, Oberösterreich, Austria

UPM-Kymmene Corporation
Kaipola Mill
Kaipola, Jämsä, Finland

V.G. Paper & Boards Ltd.
Unit 1 Swaminathapuram
Swaminathapuram, Tamil Nadu, India

Vedadri Paper Mill PVT. Ltd.
Kodad Mill
Chimiryala village, Kodad (M), Andhra Pradesh, India

Victory Paper & Boards (India) Ltd.
Pallakad Mill
Pallakad, Kerala, India

Vietnam Paper Corporation (Vinapaco)-Bai Bang Paper
Bai Bang Paper
Phu Ninh District, Phú Tho Province, Vietnam

Vipap Videm Krško d.d.
Krško Mill
Krško, Ljubljana, Slovenia

Vishnupriya Paper Mill Private Ltd.
Chennai Mill
Thiruvallur Dist., Chennai, Tamil Nadu, India

Volga
Balakhna Mill
Balakhna, Nizhny Novgorod, Russia

Yenisey Pulp and Paper Mill Inc.
Yenisey Pulp and Paper Mill
Krasnoyarsk, Russia

Zhejiang Linan Ma An Qianshi Paper Co., Ltd.
Linan Mill
Linan, Zhejiang, China

Uncoated woodfree/freesheet

A.B.C.D. Cartiere CA
Charallave Mill
Charallave, Edo. Miranda, Venezuela

A.P. Paper Mills Ltd
Patiala Mill
Dist. Mohali, Punjab, India

Ajanta Paper & General Products Ltd.
Kalyan Mill
Dist. Thane, Maharashtra, India

Alamigeon SA
Ruelle sur Touvre Mill
Ruelle sur Touvre, France

Alkim Kagit Sanayi ve Ticaret A.S
Izmir Mill
Izmir, Izmir, Turkey

Amaravathi Sri Venkatesa Paper Mills Ltd.
Madathukulam Mill
Madathukulam, Coimbatore Dist., Tamil Nadu, India

American Eagle Paper Mills Inc.
Tyrone Mill
Tyrone, Pennsylvania, United States

Anhui Chaohu Jinhe Paper Co. Ltd
Chaohu Mill
Chaohu, Anhui, China

Anhui Huatai Forest Pulp & Paper Co., Ltd.
Anqing (Anhui Huatai) Mill
Anqing, Anhui, China

Anhui Jing County Xuanzhi Mill
Jingxian Mill
Jingxian, Anhui, China

Anmol Products Ethiopia
Ginchi Mill
Ginchi, Ethiopia

Apex Paper Mills
Nagpur Mill
Nagpur, Maharashtra, India

Appleton Coated LLC
Combined Locks Mill
Combined Locks, Wisconsin, United States

Appvion, Inc.
Roaring Spring Mill
Roaring Spring, Pennsylvania, United States

Arctic Paper Kostrzyn S.A.
Kostrzyn Mill
Kostrzyn n/Odra, Poland

Arctic Paper Munkedals AB
Munkedal Mill
Munkedal, Sweden

Arjowiggins Chartham Ltd.
Chartham Paper Mill
Chartham, Canterbury, Kent, United Kingdom

Arjowiggins Fine Papers Pty. Ltd.
Stoneywood Mill
Aberdeen, Scotland, United Kingdom

Arjowiggins Fine Papers Pty. Ltd.
Stowford Mill
Ivybridge, Devon, United Kingdom

Arjowiggins Papiers Couchés S.A.
Aa Mill
Wizernes, Pas-de-Calais, France

Arjowiggins Rives SAS
Charavines Mill
Charavines, France

Arjowiggins Security B.V
Ugchelen Mill
Ugchelen, Netherlands

Arjowiggins Security SAS
Crèvecoeur Mill
Jouy-sur-Morin, France

Arkhangelsk Pulp & Paper Mill
Novodvinsk (Arkhangelsk - APPM) Mill
Novodvinsk, Arkhangelsk Region, Russia

Asia Paper Industrial Corp.
Valenzuela City Mill
East Canumay, Valenzuela City, Bulacan, Philippines

Asia Symbol (Guangdong) Paper Co., Ltd.
Jiangmen Mill
Jiangmen, Guangdong, China

ASL Paper Mills
Karachi Mill
Karachi, Sindh, Pakistan

Australian Paper
Maryvale Mill
Morwell, Victoria, Australia

Australian Paper
Shoalhaven Mill
Bomaderry, New South Wales, Australia

Bai Bang Paper Joint-stock Co., Ltd.
Ky Son Mill
Ky Son, Hoa Binh Province, Vietnam

Uncoated woodfree/freesheet

Balaji Paper Mills
Dist. Periyar Mill
Dist. Periyar, Tamil Nadu, India

Ballarpur Industries Ltd. (BILT)
Ashti Unit
Ashti, Maharashtra, India

Ballarpur Industries Ltd. (BILT)
Ballarshah (Unit Ballarpur)
Ballarshah, Maharashtra, India

Ballarpur Industries Ltd. (BILT)
Sewa Mill
Jeypore, Dist. Koratpur, Odisha, India

Ballarpur Industries Ltd. (BILT)
Shree Gopal Mill
Yamunanagar, Haryana, India

Bang Pa-In Paper Mill Industry Co., Ltd.
Ayutthaya Mill
Phra Nakhon Si Ayutthaya, Thailand

Banknote Paper Mill
Malin Mill
Malin, Zhitomirskaya obl., Ukraine

Banwari Paper Mills Ltd.
Kashipur Mill
Kashipur, Uttarakhand, India

Bashundhara Paper Mills Ltd.
Unit 1
Sonargaon, Baranagar, Narayanganj, Bangladesh

Bashundhara Paper Mills Ltd.
Unit 2
Sonargaon, New Town, Narayanganj, Bangladesh

Bataan 2020
Baesa Mill
Baesa, Quezon City, Philippines

Bataan 2020
Samal Mill
Samal, Bataan, Philippines

Bignardi Indústria e Comércio de Papéis e Artefatos Ltda.
Jundiaí Mill / GB Millennium Mill
Jundiaí, São Paulo, Brazil

Bindal Papers Limited
Muzzaffarnagar Mill
Muzzaffarnagar, Uttar Pradesh, India

Binh Minh Paper Company
Tien Du Mill
Tien Du, Bac Ninh Province, Vietnam

Bio-PAPPEL Printing
Tres Valles Mill
Tres Valles, Veracruz, Mexico

Boise Paper
International Falls Mill
International Falls, Minnesota, United States

Boise Paper
Jackson Mill
Jackson, Alabama, United States

Boise Paper
Wallula Mill
Wallula, Washington, United States

BPM, Inc.
Peshtigo Mill
Peshtigo, Wisconsin, United States

Bulleh Shah Packaging (Private) Limited
Bulleh Shah Paper Mill
Kasur, Pakistan

Büttenpapierfabrik Gmund GmbH & Co. KG
Gmund Mill
Gmund am Tegernsee, Germany

Canson SAS
Moulin du Roy Mill
St. Marcel les Annonay, France

Cartiera Ferdinando Amatruda di Amatruda Antonietta
Amalfi Mill
Amalfi, Salerno, Italy

Cartiera Sacchettificio Bonino
Borgaro Torinese Mill
Borgaro Torinese, Turin, Italy

Cartiere Ermolli S.p.a.
Moggio Udinese Mill
Moggio Udinese, Udine, Italy

Carvajal Pulpa y Papel
Guachené Mill, Plant 2
Guachené, Cauca, Valle de Cauca, Colombia

Carvajal Pulpa y Papel
Yumbo Mill, Plant 1
Yumbo, Valle de Cauca, Colombia

Celulosa Argentina S.A.
Capitán Bermúdez Mill
Capitán Bermúdez, Santa Fé, Argentina

Celulosa Argentina S.A.
Zárate Mill
Zárate, Buenos Aires, Argentina

CELUPA - Industrial Celulose e Papel Guaíba Ltda.
Guaíba Mill
Guaíba, Rio Grande do Sul, Brazil

Century Paper & Board Mills Ltd.
Kasur Mill
Bhai Pheru, Dist. Kasur, Pakistan

Century Pulp & Paper
Lalkua Mill
Nainital, Uttarakhand, India

Ceprohart SA
Braila Mill
Braila, Romania

Chen Ho Paper Mfg. Co., Ltd.
Pu Li Mill
Pu Li, Nantou County, Taiwan

Cheng Loong Corporation
Hou Li Mill
Hou Li, Taichung City, Taiwan

Chenming Paper Holdings Ltd.
Shouguang (Shouguang Chenming Art Paper No. 6) Mill
Shouguang, Shandong, China

Chenming Paper Holdings Ltd.
Shouguang (Shouguang Chenming Lightweight Coated Paper No. 2) Mill
Shouguang, Shandong, China

Chenming Paper Holdings Ltd.
Shouguang (Shouguang Chenming Specialty Paper No. 1) Mill
Shouguang, Shandong, China

Cholan Paper & Board Mills Ltd.
Kanchepuram Mill
Kanchepuram, Tamil Nadu, India

Chuetsu Pulp & Paper Co., Ltd.
Sendai Mill
Satsumasendai-shi, Kagoshima Pref., Japan

Chuetsu Pulp & Paper Co., Ltd.
Takaoka (Nohmachi) Mill
Takaoka-shi, Toyama Pref., Japan

Chung Hwa Pulp Corporation
Chiutang Mill
Ta Shu District, Kaohsiung City, Taiwan

Chung Hwa Pulp Corporation
Taitung Mill
Taitung, Taitung County, Taiwan

Chung Hwa Pulp Corporation
Hualien Mill
Chi An, Hualien County, Taiwan

Cia. Papelera El Fenix S.A. de C.V.
Col. Arenal Mill
Col. Arenal, México, D.F., Mexico

Circar Paper Mills Ltd.
Nellore Mill
Nellore, Andhra Pradesh, India

Clariana S.A.
Vila-Real Mill
Vila-Real, Castellón, Spain

CMPC Celulose Riograndense
Guaíba Mill
Guaíba, Rio Grande do Sul, Brazil

CMPC Papeles Cordillera S.A.
Puente Alto Mill
Puente Alto, RM - Región Metro. de Santiago, Chile

Coldenhove Papier
Eerbeek Mill
Eerbeek, Netherlands

Crane & Co., Inc.
Bay State Mill
Dalton, Massachusetts, United States

Crane & Co., Inc.
Byron Weston Mill
Dalton, Massachusetts, United States

Crane & Co., Inc.
Wahconah Mill
Dalton, Massachusetts, United States

Crane AB
Tumba Mill
Tumba, Sweden

Creative Paper Mills Ltd
Rupganj Mill
Rupganj, Narayanganj, Bangladesh

Uncoated woodfree/freesheet

Crocker Technical Papers
Fitchburg Mill
Fitchburg, Massachusetts, United States

Crown Van Gelder NV
Velsen-Noord Mill
Velsen-Noord, Netherlands

Daio Paper Corp.
Kani Mill
Kani-shi, Gifu Pref., Japan

Daio Paper Corp.
Mishima Mill
Shikokuchuo-shi, Ehime Pref., Japan

Danalakshmi Paper Mills Pvt. Ltd.
Dindigul Mill
Nilakottai Taluk, Dindigul, Tamil Nadu, India

De La Rue Currency
Overton Mill
Basingstoke, Hampshire, United Kingdom

De La Rue Security Papers
Bathford Paper Mill
Bath, Avon, Somerset, United Kingdom

Delta Paper Mills Ltd.
Vendra Mill
Vendra, West Godavari Dist, Andhra Pradesh, India

Diósgyőri Papírgyár Rt.
Miskolc Mill
Miskolc, Hungary

Dnepropetrovsk Paper Mill, Ltd.
Dnepropetrovsk Mill
Dnepropetrovsk, Ukraine

Dobrushskaya Paper Mill "Geroi Truda", OJSC
Dobrush Mill
Dobrush, Gomel Region, Belarus

Domtar Corporation
Ashdown Mill
Ashdown, Arkansas, United States

Domtar Corporation
Espanola Mill
Espanola, Ontario, Canada

Domtar Corporation
Hawesville Mill
Hawesville, Kentucky, United States

Domtar Corporation
Johnsonburg Mill
Johnsonburg, Pennsylvania, United States

Domtar Corporation
Kingsport Mill
Kingsport, Tennessee, United States

Domtar Corporation
Marlboro Mill
Bennettsville, South Carolina, United States

Domtar Corporation
Nekoosa Mill
Nekoosa, Wisconsin, United States

Domtar Corporation
Port Huron Mill
Port Huron, Michigan, United States

Domtar Corporation
Rothschild Mill
Rothschild, Wisconsin, United States

Domtar Corporation
Windsor Mill
Windsor, Quebec, Canada

Double A (1991) Public Co., Ltd.
Alizay Mill
Alizay, France

Double A (1991) Public Co., Ltd.
Prachinburi Mill
Amphur Sri Maha Phote, Prachinburi, Thailand

Dr. Franz Feurstein GmbH
Traun Mill
Traun, Oberösterreich, Austria

Drewsen Spezialpapiere GmbH & Co. KG
Lachendorf Mill
Lachendorf, Germany

Ecopaper JP Co. Ltd
Owariasahi Mill
Owariasahi-Shi, Aichi Pref., Japan

Ellora Paper Mills Ltd.
Tumsar, Dist. Bhandara Mill
Tumsar, Dist. Bhandara, Maharashtra, India

Emami Paper Mills Ltd.
Balasore Mill
Dist. Balasore, Odisha, India

Ethiopian Pulp & Paper SC
Nazareth Mill
Wonji, Nazareth, Ethiopia

Everbal
Evergnicourt Mill
Evergnicourt, France

Everest Paper Mills (P) Ltd.
Janakpurdham Mill
Mahendranagar, Janakpurdham, Dhausha District, Nepal

Evergreen Packaging Inc.
Canton Mill
Canton, North Carolina, United States

Fábrica de Papel de Fontes Lda.
Grijó Mill
Serzedo VNG Porto - Vila Nova de Gaia, Portugal

Fábrica de Papel San José S.A. de C.V.
Los Reyes Acaquilpan Mill
Los Reyes Acaquilpan, México, D.F., Mexico

Fábrica Nacional de Moneda y Timbre-FNMT
Burgos Mill
Burgos, Spain

FANAPEL - Fábrica Nacional de Papel S.A.
Juan Lacaze Mill
Juan Lacaze, Colonia, Uruguay

Favini Spa
Crusinallo Mill
Crusinallo di Omegna, Verbano-Cusio-Ossola, Italy

Favini Spa
Rossano Veneto Mill
Rossano Veneto, Vicenza, Italy

Fedco Paper Corp.
Calamba City Mill
Calamba City, Laguna, Philippines

Fedrigoni S.P.A.
Fabriano Mill
Fabriano, Ancona, Italy

Fedrigoni S.P.A.
Pioraco Mill
Pioraco, Macerata, Italy

Fedrigoni S.P.A.
Varone Mill
Riva del Garda, Frazione Varone, Trento, Italy

Fedrigoni S.P.A.
Verona Mill
Verona, Verona, Italy

Felix Schoeller Jr. Foto & Spezialpapiere GmbH
Weissenborn Mill
Weissenborn, Germany

Fiber Marx Papers Ltd.
Kashipur Mill
Kashipur, Uttarakhand, India

Filiperson Papéis Especiais Ltda.
Rio de Janeiro Mill
Rio de Janeiro, Rio de Janeiro, Brazil

Finch Paper, LLC
Glens Falls Mill
Glens Falls, New York, United States

Flambeau River Papers, LLC
Park Falls Mill
Park Falls, Wisconsin, United States

Flying Board and Paper Products Ltd.
Sheikhupura Mill
Sheikhupura, Punjab, Pakistan

French Paper Co.
Niles Mill
Niles, Michigan, United States

Fuji Paper Mill Cooperatives
Awagami Mill
Oe-gun, Tokushima Pref., Japan

Fujian Nanping Paper Co. Ltd.
Nanping Mill
Nanping, Fujian, China

Fujian Youlanfa Group
Jinjiang Mill
Jinjiang, Fujian, China

Fujifilm Corp.
Fujinomiya Mill
Fujinomiya-Shi, Shizuoka Pref., Japan

Gahir Paper Mills Ltd.
Sangrur Mill
Sangrur, Punjab, India

Ganga Papers India
Pune Mill
Taluka Maval, Dist. Pune, Maharashtra, India

Uncoated woodfree/freesheet

Georgia-Pacific LLC
Camas Mill
Camas, Washington, United States

Georgia-Pacific LLC
Port Hudson Mill
Zachary, Louisiana, United States

Gharb Paper Ind. Co.
Tehran Mill
Tehran, Iran

Glatfelter
Chillicothe Mill
Chillicothe, Ohio, United States

Glatfelter
Spring Grove Mill
Spring Grove, Pennsylvania, United States

Globe Paper Mills
Keng Hua Mill
Malabon, Metro Manila, Philippines

Gold Huasheng Paper (Suzhou Industrial Park) Co., Ltd.
Suzhou (Gold Huasheng Paper) Mill
Suzhou, Jiangsu, China

Goricane, tovarna papirja Medvode, d.d.
Medvode Mill
Medvode, Slovenia

GRD Paper Industries PVT. Ltd
Howrah Mill
Howrah, West Bengal, India

Grupo Papelero Scribe, S.A. de C.V.
Bajío Mill
San Juan del Río, Querétaro, Mexico

Grupo Papelero Scribe, S.A. de C.V.
Morelia Mill
Morelia, Michoacán, Mexico

Grupo Papelero Scribe, S.A. de C.V.
Naucalpan Mill
Naucalpan de Juarez, Edo. de México, Mexico

Grupo Papelero Scribe, S.A. de C.V.
Orizaba Mill
Orizaba, Veracruz, Mexico

Grupo Portucel Soporcel
Figueira da Foz Mill
Figueira da Foz, Coimbra, Portugal

Grupo Portucel Soporcel
Setúbal Mill
Setúbal, Portugal

Gruppo Cordenons SpA
Cordenons Mill
Cordenons, Pordenone, Italy

Gruppo Cordenons SpA
Scurelle Mill
Scurelle, Trento, Italy

Guangdong Dongguan Nine Dragons Paper Industries Co., Ltd.
Dongguan Mill
Dongguan, Guangdong, China

Guangdong Foshan City Gaoming Hongyuan Paper Co., Ltd.
Foshan Mill
Foshan, Guangdong, China

Guangdong Jiangnan Paper Co. Ltd.
Zhaoqing Mill
Zhaoqing, Guangdong, China

Guangdong Shaoneng Group
Nanxiong Mill
Nanxiong, Guangdong, China

Guangdong Zhanjiang Guanlong Paper Co., Ltd.
Zhanjiang Mill
Zhanjiang, Guangdong, China

Guangdong Zhongsheng Paper Co., Ltd
Zhaoqing Mill
Zhaoqing, Guangdong, China

Guangdong Zhuhai Jiangqiao Special Paper Co. Ltd.
Zhuhai Mill
Zhuhai, Guangdong, China

Guangxi Binyang Daqiao Paper Co., Ltd.
Nanning (Binyang Daqiao) Mill
Nanning, Guangxi, China

Guangxi Guitang (Group) Stock Co., Ltd
Guigang Mill
Guigang, Guangxi, China

Guangxi Guofa Forest & Paper Co. Ltd.
Liuzhou (Guangxi Guofa Forest & Paper) Mill
Liuzhou, Guangxi, China

Guangxi Huaken Paper
Laibin Mill
Laibin, Guangxi, China

Guangxi Hwagain Group
Nanning Mill
Nanning, Guangxi, China

Guangxi Jiayi Paper Co., Ltd.
Baise Mill
Baise, Guangxi, China

Guangxi Nanning Jindaxing Pulp & Paper Co., Ltd.
Nanning Mill
Nanning, Guangxi, China

Guarro Casas S.A.
Gelida Mill
Gelida, Spain

GVG Paper Mills Ltd.
Palani Taluk Mill
Palani Taluk, Dist. Dindigul, Tamil Nadu, India

Hadera Paper-Printing & Writing Paper Ltd
Hadera Mill
Hadera, Israel

Hahnemühle FineArt GmbH
Dassel Mill
Dassel, Germany

Hankuk Paper Mfg. Co., Ltd.
Onsan Mill
Ulsan-si, Gyeongsangnam-do, South Korea

Hansol Artone Paper Co., Ltd.
Sintanjin Mill
Daedeok-gu, Daejeon, South Korea

Hansol Paper Co., Ltd.
Changhang Mill
Seocheun-gun, Chungcheongnam-do, South Korea

Hansol Paper Co., Ltd.
Chonan Mill
Cheonan-si, Chungcheongnam-do, South Korea

Hansson Paper Corp.
Pasig City Mill
Pasig City, Metro Manila, Philippines

Hanuman Agro Industries Ltd.
Raipur Mill
Raipur, Chattisgarh, India

Hartija Ko DOO
Kochani Mill
Kochani, Macedonia

Hebei Baoding Banknote Paper Mill
Baoding Mill
Baoding, Hebei, China

Hebei Baoding Orient Paper Co., Ltd.
Baoding Mill
Baoding, Hebei, China

Hebei Chengda Paper Co., Ltd.
Tangshan Mill
Tangshan, Hebei, China

Henan Jianghe Paper Co., Ltd.
Jiaozuo Mill
Jiaozuo, Henan, China

Henan Longquan Group Yubei Co., Ltd.
Xinxiang Mill
Xinxiang, Henan, China

Henan Luohe Yinge Specialty Paper Co., Ltd.
Luohe (Yinge Specialty) Mill
Luohe, Henan, China

Henan Neixiang Xianhe Special Paper & Pulp Co., Ltd.
Nanyang Mill
Nanyang, Henan, China

Henan Puyang Longfeng Paper Co. Ltd
Puyang (Puyang Longfeng) Mill
Puyang, Henan, China

Henan Tianbang Group Paper Co., Ltd.
Xinxiang Mill
Xinxiang, Henan, China

Henan Wuzhi Guangyuan Paper Mill
Jiaozuo Mill
Jiaozuo, Henan, China

Henan Xinxiang Hongtai Paper Co., Ltd.
Xinxiang Mill
Xinxiang, Henan, China

Uncoated woodfree/freesheet

Henan Xinxiang Xinya Paper Group Co., Ltd.
Xinxiang No. 2 Mill
Xinxiang, Henan, China

Henan Xinxiang Xinya Paper Group Co., Ltd.
Xinxiang No. 3 Mill
Xinxiang, Henan, China

Henan Xinxiang Xinya Paper Group Co., Ltd.
Xinxiang No. 5 Mill
Xinxiang, Henan, China

Henan Xinxiang Xinya Paper Group Co., Ltd.
Xinxiang No. 6 Mill
Xinxiang, Henan, China

Henan Yilin Paper Co., Ltd.
Xuchang Mill
Xuchang, Henan, China

Henan Yinge Industrial Investment Co. Ltd.
Luohe (Yinge Industrial Investment) Mill
Luohe, Henan, China

Henan Zhumadian City Baiyun Paper Co., Ltd.
Zhumadian (Zhumadian Baiyun) Mill
Zhumadian, Henan, China

Hindustan Paper Corp. Ltd., CPM
Cachar Paper Mill
Cachar, Assam, India

Hindustan Paper Corp. Ltd., NPM
Nagaon Paper Mill
Morigaon, Assam, India

Hokuetsu Kishu Paper Co. Ltd.
Kishu Mill
Minamimuro-gun, Mie Pref., Japan

Hokuetsu Kishu Paper Co. Ltd.
Niigata Mill
Niigata-shi, Niigata Pref., Japan

Hongwon Paper Mfg. Co., Ltd.
Jinwi Mill
Pyeongtaek-si, Gyeonggi-do, South Korea

Horus Edfu for Paper Industry
Beni Souef Mill
Beni Souef, Egypt

HRA Papers Pvt Ltd
Kangra Mill
Village Tibbi, Kangra, Himachal Pradesh, India

Hsing Chung Paper Corp.
Wu Chieh Mill
Wu Chieh, Ilan County, Taiwan

Hubei Chibi Chenli Paper Co., Ltd.
Chibi Mill
Chibi, Hubei, China

Hubei Wuhan Chenming Paper Co. Ltd.
Wuhan (Wuhan Chenming Hanyang Paper No. 2 Mill) Mill
Wuhan, Hubei, China

Hubei Yichang Baota Paper Co., Ltd
Yichang Mill
Yichang, Hubei, China

Hunan Tiger Forest & Paper Group Yuanjiang Paper Co., Ltd.
Yuanjiang Mill
Yuanjiang, Hunan, China

Hunan Tiger Forest & Paper Group Yueyang Paper Co., Ltd.
Yueyang Mill
Yueyang, Hunan, China

IdemPapers SA
Virginal Mill
Virginal-Samme, Belgium

Illig'sche Papierfabrik
Mühltal Mill
Mühltal, Germany

Indo Afrique Paper Mill
Pune Mill
Pune, Maharashtra, India

Industrial Papelera Atlas SA
Nana Mill
Ñana, Lima, Lima, Peru

International Paper - Kwidzyn Sp. z o.o.
Kwidzyn Mill
Kwidzyn, Poland

International Paper APPM Ltd.
Kadiam Mill
Madhavarayudu Palem, East Godavari District, Andhra Pradesh, India

International Paper APPM Ltd.
Rajahmundry Mill
Rajahmundry, East Godavari, Andhra Pradesh, India

International Paper Co.
Eastover Mill
Eastover, South Carolina, United States

International Paper Co.
Georgetown Mill
Georgetown, South Carolina, United States

International Paper Co.
Riverdale Mill
Selma, Alabama, United States

International Paper Co.
Ticonderoga Mill
Ticonderoga, New York, United States

International Paper do Brasil Ltda.
Luiz Antônio Mill
Luiz Antonio, São Paulo, Brazil

International Paper do Brasil Ltda.
Mogi Guaçu Mill
Mogi Guaçu, São Paulo, Brazil

International Paper do Brasil Ltda.
Três Lagoas Mill
Três Lagoas, Mato Grosso, Brazil

International Paper SA
Saillat Mill
Saint-Junien, France

Invepal
Morón Mill
Morón, Edo. Carabobo, Venezuela

ITC Limited, Paperboards & Specialty Papers Division
Bhadrachalam Mill
Khammam, Bhadrachalam, Andhra Pradesh, India

ITC Limited, Paperboards & Specialty Papers Division
Tribeni Mill
Chandrahati, Hooghly, West Bengal, India

J&K Pulp & Paper Pvt. Ltd.
Jammu Mill
Bari Brahmana, Dist. Jammu, Jammu and Kashmir, India

J. Tönnesmann & Vogel, Papierfabrik Hönnetal GmbH
Menden Mill
Menden, Germany

J. Vilaseca S.A.
Capellades Mill
Capellades, Barcelona, Spain

James Cropper
Kendal Mill
Kendal, Cumbria, United Kingdom

Jeet Enterprises PVT. Ltd. (Sister Concern of Miglani Paper Mills)
Amritsar Mill
Amritsar, Punjab, India

Jejani Pulp and Paper Mills Pvt. Ltd.
Gadchiroli Mill
Gadchiroli, Madras State, India

Jiangsu Nine Dragons Paper Industries
Taicang Mill
Taicang, Jiangsu, China

Jiangsu Oji Paper Nantong Co., Ltd.
Nantong Mill
Nantong, Jiangsu, China

Jiangsu UPM, Changshu Paper Industry Co., Ltd.
Changshu Mill
Changshu, Jiangsu, China

Jiangxi Dexing City Hengsheng Paper Co., Ltd.
Dexing Mill
Dexing, Jiangxi, China

Jiangxi Ganzhou Hwagain Paper Co., Ltd
Ganzhou Mill
Ganzhou, Jiangxi, China

Jih Sun Paper Ind. Co., Ltd.
Kuanyin Hsiang Mill
Kuanyin Hsiang, Taoyuan County, Taiwan

Jilin Chenming Paper Co. Ltd.
Jilin (Jilin Chenming Paper) Mill
Jilin, Jilin, China

JK Paper Ltd.
Central Pulp Mills-CPM, Songadh Mill
Fort Songadh, Dist. Tapi, Gujarat, India

Uncoated woodfree/freesheet

JK Paper Ltd.
JK Paper Mills - JKPM
Jaykaypur, Rayagada Dist., Odisha, India

Joung Yin Enterprise Co., Ltd.
Hsin Kang Mill
Hsin Kang, Chia-I County, Taiwan

Jujo Thermal Ltd.
Kauttua Mill
Kauttua, Finland

Kanzan Spezialpapiere GmbH
Neumühl Mill
Düren, Germany

Karnaphuli Paper Mills Ltd.
Chandraghona Mill
Chandraghona of Kaptai, Chittagong, Bangladesh

Karthikeya Paper & Board Ltd.
Erode District Mill
Erode District, Tamil Nadu, India

Kasuga Seishi Kogyo Co., Ltd.
Fuji-shi Mill
Fuji-shi, Shizuoka Pref., Japan

Khanna Paper Mills Pvt. Ltd.
Amritsar Mill
Amritsar, Punjab, India

Kitakami Hitec Paper Corp.
Kitakami-shi Mill
Kitakami-shi, Iwate Pref., Japan

KM Papel
Bonsucesso Mill
Bonsucesso, Volta Grande, Minas Gerais, Brazil

Koehler Greiz GmbH & Co. KG
Greiz Mill
Greiz, Germany

Koehler Kehl GmbH
Kehl Mill
Kehl, Germany

Kohinoor Paper & Newsprint (P) Ltd
Parganas Mill
Parganas, West Bengal, India

Kombassan San. ve Tic. AS
Konya Mill
Selcuklu, Konya, Turkey

Koryazhma Branch of Ilim Group
Kotlas Pulp and Paper Mill
Koryazhma, Arkhangelsk Region, Russia

KPM Kadoma Paper Mills
Kadoma Mill
Kadoma, Zimbabwe

KR Pulp & Papers Ltd.
Shahjahanpur Mill
Shahjahanpur, Uttar Pradesh, India

Krasnokamskaya Paper Mill Goznak
Krasnokamsk Mill
Krasnokamsk, Perm Region, Russia

Kronex-Ukraina, Ltd.
Zmiev Mill
Zmiev, Kharkovskaya Obl., Ukraine

KRPA Paper, a.s.
Krpa Papir Mill
Hostinné, Czech Republic

Kuantum Papers Ltd
Hoshiarpur Mill
Dist. Hoshiarpur, Punjab, India

Kyrgyz-Chinese Paper Mill
Chuj-Tokmok Mill
Chuj-Tokmok, Chujskaya Obl., Kyrgyzstan

Ladhar Paper Mill
Jalandhar Mill
Dist. Jalandhar, Punjab, India

Lana Papiers Speciaux
Strasbourg Mill
Strasbourg, France

Landqart AG
Landqart Mill
Landquart, Switzerland

Ledesma S.A.A.I.
Libertador General Mill
Libertador General San Martín, Jujuy, Argentina

Lenzing Papier GmbH
Lenzing Paper Mill
Lenzing, Oberösterreich, Austria

Lessebo Paper
Lessebo Paper Mill
Lessebo, Sweden

Liaoning Jincheng Paper Co., Ltd.
Linghai Mill
Linghai, Liaoning, China

Liaoning Yingkou Paper Mill
Yingkou Mill
Yingkou, Liaoning, China

Maa Chandi Papers Pvt. Ltd.
Burdwan Mill
Burdwan, West Bengal, India

Madhya Bharat Papers Ltd.
Dist. Janjgir-Champa Mill
Dist. Janjgir-Champa, Chattisgarh, India

Magnani Srl
Pescia Mill
Pescia, Pistoia, Italy

Malik Board Mills
Sheikhupura Mill
Sheikhupura, Punjab, Pakistan

Manaylux Papers & Boards (P) Ltd. Yediyur
Taluk Tumkur Mill
Taluk Tumkur, Karnataka, India

Mandiali Paper Mill Ltd.
Sheikhupura Mill
Sheikhupura, Punjab, Pakistan

Mandya National Paper Mills Ltd.
Belagola Mill
Belagola, Karnataka, India

Manufacturas de Papel CA (MANPA) S.A.C.A.
Maracay Packaging Mill
Maracay, Edo. Aragua, Venezuela

MBD Group
Gagret town, Una district Mill
Gagret town, Una district, Himachal Pradesh, India

MCC Meili Paper Industry Co., Ltd.
Zhongwei Mill
Zhongwei, Ningxia, China

MCC Paper Yinhe Co., Ltd.
Linqing Mill
Linqing, Shandong, China

MED Paper SA
Tangier Mill
Tangier, Morocco

Meerssen Papier BV
Meerssen Mill
Meerssen, Netherlands

MELECKY a.s. závod Papírna Aloisov
Aloisov Mill
Ruda nad Moravou, Czech Republic

Metsä Board Husum
Husum Mill
Husum, Sweden

Metsä Board Zanders GmbH
Zanders Gohrsmühle Mill
Bergisch Gladbach, Germany

Miquel y Costas & Miquel S.A.
Mislata mill
Mislata, Valencia, Spain

Misr Edfu for Pulp, Writing & Printing Paper Co. - MEPP-Co
Edfu Pulp Mill
Edfu, Aswan, Egypt

Mitsubishi HiTec Paper Europe GmbH
Bielefeld Mill
Bielefeld, Germany

Mitsubishi HiTec Paper Europe GmbH
Flensburg Mill
Flensburg, Germany

Mitsubishi Paper Mills Ltd.
Hachinohe Mill
Hachinohe-shi, Aomori, Japan

Mitsubishi Paper Mills Ltd.
Kyoto Mill
Nagaokakyo-shi, Kyoto Pref., Japan

Mitsubishi Paper Mills Ltd.
Takasago Mill
Takasago-shi, Hyogo Pref., Japan

Mohammadi Paper & Board Industries (Pvt.) Ltd.
Sheikhupura Lahore Unit 1
Sheikhupura Lahore, Punjab, Pakistan

Mohawk Fine Papers Inc.
Cohoes Mill
Cohoes, New York, United States

Mohawk Fine Papers Inc.
Waterford Mill
Waterford, New York, United States

Mohit Paper Mills Ltd.
Bijnor Mill
Bijnor, Uttar Pradesh, India

Molza Corp.
Muge Mill
Seki-shi, Gifu Pref., Japan

Uncoated woodfree/freesheet

Monadnock Paper Mills, Inc.
Bennington Mill
Bennington, New Hampshire, United States

Mondi Merebank
Merebank Mill
Merebank, KwaZulu-Natal, South Africa

Mondi Neusiedler GmbH
Kematen mill
Kematen, Niederösterreich, Austria

Mondi Neusiedler GmbH
Theresienthal Mill
Ulmerfeld-Hausmening, Niederösterreich, Austria

Mondi SCP a.s.
Ružomberok Mill
Ružomberok, Slovakia

Mondi Syktyvkar
Syktyvkar Mill
Syktyvkar, Komi Republic, Russia

Moorim P&P Co. Ltd.
Ulsan Mill
Ulsan-si, South Korea

Moorim Paper Co., Ltd.
Jinju Mill
Jinju-si, Gyeongsangnam-do, South Korea

Moorim SP Co., Ltd.
Daegu Mill
Buk-gu, Daegu-si, South Korea

Mopak Dalaman Pulp-Paper Cardboard Plant
Dalaman Mill
Mugla, Turkey

Mopak Kagit Karton San. ve Tic. A.S.
Kemalpasa Mill
Kemalpasa, Izmir, Turkey

Mopak Tasköprü Pulp and Cigarette Paper Plant
Kastamonu Mill
Kastamonu, Turkey

Mosaico Speciality Papers
Tolmezzo Mill
Tolmezzo, Udine, Italy

Mostafa Paper
Chittagong Mill
Chittagong, Chittagong, Bangladesh

Multiverde Papéis Especiais Ltda.
Mogi das Cruzes Mill
Mogi das Cruzes, São Paulo, Brazil

Multiwal Pulp & Board Mills Ltd.
Dist. Udham Singh Nagar Mill
Dist. Udham Singh Nagar, Uttarakhand, India

Munksjö Arches SAS
Arches Mill
Arches, France

Munksjö Dettingen GmbH
Dettingen Mill
Dettingen an der Erms, Germany

Murli Industries Ltd.
Nagpur Mill
Nagpur, Maharashtra, India

Myanma Paper and Chemical Industries (MPCI)
Sittuong No. 1 Paper Mill
Theinzayat, Mon State, Myanmar

Myanma Paper and Chemical Industries (MPCI)
Thabaung Pulp & Paper Mill
Thabaung, Pathein, Ayeyewaddy, Myanmar

Myanmar Jute Enterprise
Pantaput village, Maubin town Mill
Pantaput village, Maubin town, Myanmar

Mysore Paper Mills Ltd.
Shimoga Mill
Bhadravati, Shimoga, Karnataka, India

Nachiketa Papers Ltd.
Dist. Patiala Mill
Dist. Mohali, Punjab, India

Naini Papers Ltd.
Kashipur Mill
Kashipur, Uttarakhand, India

Nav Bharat Duplex Ltd.
Hapur Mill
Hapur, Uttar Pradesh, India

Neenah Paper, Inc.
Appleton Mill
Appleton, Wisconsin, United States

Neenah Paper, Inc.
Neenah Mill
Neenah, Wisconsin, United States

Neenah Paper, Inc.
Whiting Mill
Stevens Point, Wisconsin, United States

Neman Pulp & Paper Mill
Neman Mill
Neman, Kaliningrad Region, Russia

Neo-Print
Tbilisi Mill
Tbilisi, Georgia

NewPage Corporation
Escanaba Mill
Escanaba, Michigan, United States

NewPage Corporation
Rumford Mill
Rumford, Maine, United States

NewPage Corporation
Wickliffe Mill
Wickliffe, Kentucky, United States

Ningxia Kejin Xiaguang Paper Co., Ltd.
Qingtongxia Mill
Qingtongxia, Ningxia, China

Nippon Paper Industries Co., Ltd.
Akita Mill
Akita-shi, Akita Pref., Japan

Nippon Paper Industries Co., Ltd.
Fuji Mill
Fuji-shi, Shizuoka Pref., Japan

Nippon Paper Industries Co., Ltd.
Hokkaido Mill - Asahikawa
Asahikawa-shi, Hokkaido Pref., Japan

Nippon Paper Industries Co., Ltd.
Hokkaido Mill - Shiraoi
Shiraoi, Hokkaido Pref., Japan

Nippon Paper Industries Co., Ltd.
Hokkaido Mill - Yufutsu
Tomakomai-shi, Hokkaido Pref., Japan

Nippon Paper Industries Co., Ltd.
Ishinomaki Mill
Ishinomaki-shi, Miyagi Pref., Japan

Nippon Paper Industries Co., Ltd.
Iwakuni Mill
Iwakuni-shi, Yamaguchi Pref., Japan

Nippon Paper Industries Co., Ltd.
Ohtake Mill
Ohtake-shi, Hiroshima Pref., Japan

Nippon Paper Industries Co., Ltd.
Yatsushiro Mill
Yatsushiro-shi, Kumamoto Pref., Japan

Nippon Paper Papylia Co., Ltd.
Harada Mill
Fuji-shi, Shizuoka Pref., Japan

Nisshinbo Paper Products, Inc.
Tokushima Mill
Tokushima-shi, Tokushima Pref., Japan

Nobrecel S.A. Celulose e Papel
Pindamonhangaba Mill
Pindamonhangaba, São Paulo, Brazil

NR Agarwal Industries Ltd.
Unit-V (Sarigam)
Sarigam, Valsad, Gujarat, India

OAO Toshkent Qogoze
Tashkent Mill
Tashkent, Tashkentskaya obl., Uzbekistan

Oji F-Tex Co., Ltd.
Ebetsu Mill
Ebetsu-shi, Hokkaido Pref., Japan

Oji Papéis Especiais Ltda
Piracicaba Mill
Piracicaba, São Paulo, Brazil

Oku Iboku Pulp and Paper (OKIPP) Company Limited
Oku Iboku Mill
Ayadeghe, Oku Iboku, Akwa Ibom State, Nigeria

OOO ASS-Korostyshiv Paper Mill
Korostyshiv Mill
Korostyshiv, Ukraine

OP Papírna s.r.o.
Olšany Mill
Olšany, Czech Republic

Orient Paper Mills
Amlai mill
Shahdol, Madhya Pradesh, India

Panasa, Papelera Nacional S.A.
Paramonga Mill
Paramonga, Lima, Peru

Papelera de Chihuahua S.A. de C.V.
Chihuahua Mill
Chihuahua, Chihuahua, Mexico

Uncoated woodfree/freesheet

Papelera del Oria, S.A.
Zizurkil Mill
Zizurkil, Gipúzcoa, Spain

Papelera Guipuzcoana de Zicuñaga S.A.
Hernani Mill
Hernani, Gipúzcoa, Spain

Papelera Paysandú S.A.I.C.
Wilde Mill
Wilde, Buenos Aires, Argentina

Papelera Tlaxcala S.A. de C.V.
Iztapaluca Mill
Iztapaluca, Edo. de México, Mexico

Papelera Tucumán S.A.
Lules, Tucumán I Mill
Lules, Tucumán, Argentina

Papeles de Bolivia (Papelbol)
Villa Tunari Mill
Villa Tunari, Cochabamba, Bolivia

Papeles Lozar S.A. de C.V.
Ixtapaluca Mill
Ixtapaluca, México, D.F., Mexico

Paperlogic
Turners Falls Mill
Turners, Falls, Massachusetts, United States

Papeterie de Mandeure SA
Mandeure Mill
Mandeure, Doubs, France

Papeterie Zuber Rieder
Boussières Mill
Boussières, France

Papeteries de Clairefontaine
Etival-Clairefontaine Mill
Etival-Clairefontaine, France

Papeteries de Vizille (Vicat)
Vizille Mill
Vizille, France

Papeteries des Chatelles SAS
Raon L'Etape Mill
Raon L'Etape, France

Papeteries des Vosges (PDV)
Laval-sur-Vologne Mill
Laval-sur-Vologne, France

Papeteries du Leman (PDL)
Thonon-les-Bains Mill
Thonon-les-Bains Cédex, France

Papierfabrik August Koehler AG
Oberkirch Mill
Oberkirch (Baden), Germany

Papierfabrik Hainsberg GmbH
Freital Mill
Freital-Hainsberg, Germany

Papierfabrik Louisenthal GmbH
Gmund am Tegernsee Mill
Gmund am Tegernsee, Germany

Papierfabrik Louisenthal GmbH
Königstein Mill
Königstein, Saxony, Germany

Papierfabrik Schleipen
Bad Dürkheim Mill
Bad Dürkheim, Germany

Papierfabrik Schoellershammer
Düren Mill
Düren, Germany

Papierfabrik Zerkall Renker & Söhne GmbH & Co. KG
Hürtgenwald-Zerkall Mill
Hürtgenwald-Zerkall, Germany

Paramount Paper Mills
Panchkula Mill
Panchkula, Haryana, India

Pars Paper Industrial Group
Ahwaz Mill
Ahwaz, Khuzestan, Iran

Pearl Paper & Board Mills Ltd.
Dhamrai Mill
Dhamrai, Dhaka, Bangladesh

Phoenix Pulp & Paper Public Company, Ltd.
Nam Phong Mill
Amphur Nampong, Khon Kaen, Thailand

Pitambar Coated Papers Ltd.
Bhiwadi Mill
Bhiwadi, Rajasthan, India

Polska Wytwornia Papierow Wartosciowych S.A.
Warsaw Mill
Warsaw, Poland

Pondercel, S.A. de C.V.
Anahuac Mill
Anahuac, Mpio De Cuauhtemoc, Chihuahua, Mexico

Poneder Halbstoff-Fabrik GmbH
Ulmerfeld-Hausmening Mill
Ulmerfeld-Hausmening, Niederösterreich, Austria

Pragati Paper Industries Ltd.
Patiala Mill
Derabassi Dist., Patiala, Punjab, India

Pragati Paper Industries Ltd.
Sirmaur Mill
Dist. Sirmaur, Himachal Pradesh, India

Pragati Paper Mills Ltd.
Dist. Ghaziabad Mill
Dist. Ghaziabad, Uttar Pradesh, India

Prolific Papers Pvt. Ltd.
Kashipur, Udham Singh Nagar Mill
Kashipur, Udham Singh Nagar, Uttarakhand, India

PT Aspex Kumbong
Bogor Mill
Bogor, West Java, Indonesia

PT Esa Kertas Nusantara
Karawang Mill
Karawang, West Java, Indonesia

PT Gunung Jaya Agung
Karawaci Mill
Karawaci, Tangerang, Jawa Barat, Indonesia

PT Indah Kiat Pulp & Paper Corp.
Perawang (PT Indah Kiat Pulp & Paper) Mill
Siak, Bengkalis, Riau, Sumatra, Indonesia

PT Indah Kiat Pulp & Paper Corp.
Tangerang (PT Indah Kiat Pulp & Paper) Mill
Serpong, Tangerang, West Java, Indonesia

PT Jaya Kertas
Nganjuk Mill
Nganjuk, East Java, Indonesia

PT Kertas Basuki Rachmat
Banyuwangi Mill
Banyuwangi, East Java, Indonesia

PT Kertas Leces (Persero)
Probolinggo Mill
Probolinggo, East Java, Indonesia

PT Kertas Padalarang
Padalarang Mill
Padalarang, Bandung, West Java, Indonesia

PT Pabrik Kertas Tjiwi Kimia Tbk
Mojokerto (PT Pabrik Kertas Tjiwi Kimia) Mill
Mojokerto, East Java, Indonesia

PT Papyrus Sakti
Bandung Mill
Banjaran, Bandung, West Java, Indonesia

PT Parisindo Pratama
Bogor Mill
Bogor, West Java, Indonesia

PT Pindo Deli Pulp & Paper Mills
Karawang No. 1 (PT Pindo Deli Pulp & Paper Mills) Mill
Karawang, West Java, Indonesia

PT Pindo Deli Pulp & Paper Mills
Karawang No. 2 (PT Pindo Deli Pulp & Paper Mills) Mill
Karawang, West Java, Indonesia

PT Pura Barutama
Kudus Mill
Kudus, Central Java, Indonesia

PT Riau Andalan Pulp & Paper (RAPP)
Riaupulp and Riaupaper Mill Kerinci
Pekanbaru - Riau, Riau, Sumatra, Indonesia

PT Surabaya Agung Industri Pulp & Kertas
Driyorejo Mill
Gresik, East Java, Indonesia

PT Unipa Daya
Tangerang Mill
Karawaci, Tangerang, Jawa Barat, Indonesia

Pudumjee Pulp & Paper Mills Ltd.
Pune Mill
Chinchwad, Pune, Maharashtra, India

Purvi Bharat Paper & Power Ltd.
Cuttack Mill
Cuttack, Odisha, India

Quena Paper Industry Co. (QPIC)
Kous Mill
Kous, Quena, Egypt

Radece Papir Nova
Radece Mill
Radece Zidani most, Slovenia

Rainbow Papers Ltd.
Mehsana Mill
Mehsana, Gujarat, India

Uncoated woodfree/freesheet

Rama Paper Mills Ltd.
Bijnor Mill
Kiratpur, Bijnor, Uttar Pradesh, India

Rama Pulp & Papers Ltd.
Vapi, Dist. Valsad Mill
Vapi, Dist. Valsad, Gujarat, India

Rana Mohendra Paper Ltd.
Dist. Ropar Mill
Dist. Ropar, Punjab, India

Rehman Classic Pvt. Ltd
Gujranwala Mill
Gujranwala, Punjab, Pakistan

Reliance Paper Mills
Bhairahawa Mill
Bhairahawa, Nepal

Renova - Fábrica de Papel do Almonda S.A.
Torres Novas Mill
Torres Novas, Portugal

Rolex Paper Mills Ltd.
Vill. Chinta Parru Mill
Vill. Chinta Parru, Andhra Pradesh, India

Ruchira Papers Ltd.
Kala-Amb Mill
Kala-Amb, Himachal Pradesh, India

S.N.C.P.A. - Société Nationale de Cellulose et Papier Alfa
Kasserine Mill
Kasserine, Gouvernorat de Kasserine, Tunisia

Sabah Forest Industries Sdn. Bhd.
Sipitang Mill
Sipitang, Sabah, Malaysia

Sai Rayalaseema Paper Mills Ltd. (SRPML)
Kurnool Mill
Kurnool, Andhra Pradesh, India

Salzer Papier GmbH
Stattersdorf Mill
St. Pölten, Niederösterreich, Austria

Samil Paper Co., Ltd.
Hanam Mill
Hanam-si, Gyeonggi-do, South Korea

Samwha Paper Co., Ltd.
Chongwon Mill
Cheongwon-gun, Chungcheongbuk-do, South Korea

Santa Maria Cia. de Papel e Celulose
Guarapuava Mill
Guarapuava, Paraná, Brazil

Sappi Fine Paper Europe
Stockstadt Mill
Stockstadt am Main, Germany

Sappi Paper and Paper Packaging South Africa (SA)
Enstra Mill
Springs, Gauteng, South Africa

Satia Paper Mills Ltd.
Muktsar Mill
Dist. Muktsar, Punjab, India

Saurashtra Paper & Board Mills Ltd.
Shapar Mill
Rajkot, Gujarat, India

Sayid Paper Mills
Lahore Mill
Lahore, Punjab, Pakistan

Schönfelder Papierfabrik GmbH
Annaberg-Buchholz Mill
Annaberg-Buchholz, Germany

Schut Papier
Heelsum Mill
Heelsum, Netherlands

Security Papers Ltd.
Karachi Mill
Karachi, Sindh, Pakistan

Security Printing and Minting Corporation Of India Limited (SPMCIL)
Hoshangabad Mill
Hoshangabad, Madhya Pradesh, India

Serpukhovskaya Paper Mill
Serpukhov Mill
Serpukhov, Moscow Region, Russia

Servalakshmi Paper & Boards Ltd. (SLPB)
Nilakottai Talu Mill
Nilakottai Talu, Dindigul Dist., Tamil Nadu, India

Servalakshmi Paper Ltd.
Servall Mill
Tirunelveli, Tamil Nadu, India

Seshasayee Paper & Boards Ltd.
Erode Mill
Erode, Tamil Nadu, India

Seshasayee Paper & Boards Ltd.
Tirunelveli Mill
Mukkudal, Tirunelveli, Tamil Nadu, India

Shaheen Paper & Board Industries (pvt) Ltd
Raiwind Lahore Mill
Raiwind Lahore, Pakistan

Shakumbhri Straw Products Ltd.
Moradabad Mill
Tehsil Bilari, Moradabad, Uttar Pradesh, India

Shandong Baron Paper Co., Ltd.
Laiwu Mill
Laiwu, Shandong, China

Shandong Bohui Paper Industry Co., Ltd.
Zibo Mill
Zibo, Shandong, China

Shandong Dezhou Huabei Paper (Group) Co., Ltd.
Dezhou Mill
Dezhou, Shandong, China

Shandong Dezhou Huadong Paper Group
Dezhou Mill
Dezhou, Shandong, China

Shandong Feicheng Dongsheng Paper Co., Ltd.
Feicheng Mill
Feicheng, Shandong, China

Shandong Gaoqing Qingyuan Paper Co. Ltd.
Zibo Mill
Zibo, Shandong, China

Shandong Gaotang No. 2 Paper Mill
Liaocheng Mill
Liaocheng, Shandong, China

Shandong Gold Shankou Paper Co., Ltd.
Taian Mill
Taian, Shandong, China

Shandong Guanjun Paper Co., Ltd.
Dezhou Mill
Dezhou, Shandong, China

Shandong Heze City Hongtai Paper Co., Ltd.
Heze Mill
Heze, Shandong, China

Shandong Huajin Paper Group
Jining Mill
Jining, Shandong, China

Shandong Jianghe Paper Co., Ltd.
Qihe Mill
Dezhou, Shandong, China

Shandong Jining Jinsheng Paper Co., Ltd.
Jining Mill
Jining, Shandong, China

Shandong Linqu Yulong Paper Co., Ltd.
Weifang Mill
Weifang, Shandong, China

Shandong Lu An Paper Co., Ltd.
Anqiu Mill
Anqiu, Shandong, China

Shandong Qingdao Haiwang Paper Property Share Co., Ltd.
Qingdao Mill
Qingdao, Shandong, China

Shandong Qunxing Paper Holdings Co., Ltd.
Binzhou Mill
Binzhou, Shandong, China

Shandong Shouguang Liben Papermaking
Shouguang (Shandong Shouguang Liben Papermaking) Mill
Shouguang, Shandong, China

Shandong Sun Paper Industry Joint Stock Co., Ltd.
Yanzhou Mill
Yanzhou, Shandong, China

Shandong Tianhe Paper Co., Ltd.
Taian Mill
Taian, Shandong, China

Shandong Tranlin Paper Chiping Co., Ltd.
Liaocheng Mill
Liaocheng, Shandong, China

Shandong Tranlin Paper Co. Ltd.
Gaotang Mill
Liaocheng, Shandong, China

Grades Produced

Uncoated woodfree/freesheet

Shandong Tranlin Paper Xiajin Co., Ltd.
Xiajin Mill
Dezhou, Shandong, China

Shandong Weifang Henglian Art Paper Co., Ltd.
Weifang Mill
Weifang, Shandong, China

Shandong Yantai Jinhong Paper Co. Ltd.
Yantai Mill
Yantai, Shandong, China

Shandong Zibo Guotai Paper Co., Ltd.
Zibo Mill
Zibo, Shandong, China

Shandong Zibo Paperboard Co., Ltd.
Zibo Mill
Zibo, Shandong, China

Shotmed Paper Industries (SPI)
6th of October City, Giza Mill
6th of October City, Giza, El Giza, Egypt

Shree Bhawani Paper Mills Ltd.
Rae Bareli Mill
Rae Bareli, Uttar Pradesh, India

Shree Karthik Papers Ltd.
Dist. Coimbatore Mill
Dist. Coimbatore, Tamil Nadu, India

Shree Rajeshwaranand Paper Mills Ltd.
Dist. Bharuch Mill
Dist. Bharuch, Gujarat, India

Shree Rama Newsprint Ltd.
Barbhodan Mill
Barbhodan, Surat District, Gujarat, India

Shree Rishabh Papers
Nawanshaher Mill
Banah, Dist. Nawanshahar, Punjab, India

Shree Satpura Tapi Parisar Sahkari Sakhar Karkhanal Ltd.
Dist. Nandurban Mill
Dist. Nandurban, Maharashtra, India

Shree Shyam Pulp & Board Mills Ltd.
Kashipur Mill
Udham Singh Nagar, Uttakhand, Uttarakhand, India

Shree Sitaram Paper Mills Ltd.
Dist. Kohlapur Mill
Dist. Kohlapur, Maharashtra, India

Shree Sudarshan Paper Mills Ltd.
Mettupalamam Mill
Mettupalamam, Tamil Nadu, India

Shree Vindhya Paper Mills Ltd.
Jalgaon Mill
Bhusaval, Jalgaon, Maharashtra, India

Shreyans Papers
Ahmedgarh Mill
Ahmedgarh, Dist. Sangrur, Punjab, India

Shri Harikrishna Papers PVT. Ltd.
Palani Taluk Mill
Palani Taluk, Tamil Nadu, India

Sichuan Anxian Paper Co., Ltd.
Chengdu Mill
Chengdu, Sichuan, China

Sichuan Meishan Fenghua Paper Co., Ltd.
Meishan Mill
Meishan, Sichuan, China

Sichuan Mingshan County Yunxiang Paper Co., Ltd.
Yaan Mill
Yaan, Sichuan, China

Sichuan Yinge Bamboo Pulp & Paper Co., Ltd.
Luzhou (Sichuan Yinge) Mill
Luzhou, Sichuan, China

Sichuan Yongfeng Paper-Making Joint-Stock Co., Ltd.
Leshan Mill
Leshan, Sichuan, China

Sirisak Paper Industries Co., Ltd.
Kanchanaburi Mill
Amphur Muang, Kanchanaburi, Kanchanaburi, Thailand

Sirpur Paper Mills Ltd.
Adilabad Mill
Sirpur-Kaghaznagar, Dist. Adilabad, Andhra Pradesh, India

Smurfit Kappa Cartón de Colombia SA
Yumbo Mill
Cali, Valle de Cauca, Colombia

Sonali Paper & Board Mills Ltd.
Dhaka Mill
Dhaka, Dhaka, Bangladesh

South India Paper Mills Ltd.
Nanjangud Mill
Nanjangud, Karnataka, India

Spaa Straw Board Ind. Pvt. Ltd.
Bolangir Mill
Bolangir, Odisha, India

Speciality Papers Ltd.
Valsad Mill
Vapi, Dist. Valsad, Gujarat, India

SPM - Security Paper Mill a.s.
Štetí Mill
Štetí, Czech Republic

Sri Luxmi Tulasi Agro Paper Pvt Ltd.
Rajahmundry Mill
Rajahmundry, Andhra Pradesh, India

Sri Ramalingeswara Paper Products (P) Ltd.
East Godavari Dist. Mill
East Godavari Dist., Andhra Pradesh, India

St. Petersburg Paper Mill Goznak
St. Petersburg Mill
St. Petersburg, Russia

Star Paper Mills Ltd.
Saharanpur Mill
Saharanpur, Uttar Pradesh, India

Steinbeis Papier Glückstadt GmbH & Co. KG
Glückstadt Mill
Glückstadt, Germany

Stora Enso Printing and Reading
Nymölla Mill
Nymölla, Sweden

Stora Enso Printing and Reading
Varkaus Mill
Varkaus, Finland

Stora Enso Printing and Reading
Veitsiluoto Mill
Kemi, Finland

Sumit Agro Products Ltd.
Meerut Mill
Meerut, Uttar Pradesh, India

Sun Paper Mills Co. Ltd.
Dist. Tirunelveli Mill
Dist. Trunelveli, Tamil Nadu, India

Sunglim Paper
Yongin Mill
Yongin-si, Gyeonggi-do, South Korea

Supreme Paper Mills Ltd.
Chakdaha Mill
Nadia, West Bengal, India

Surya Chandra Paper Mills Ltd.
East Godavari Dist. Mill
East Godavari Dist., Andhra Pradesh, India

Suzanense Indústria e Comércio de Papéis Ltda.
Suzano Mill
Suzano, São Paulo, Brazil

Suzano Papel e Celulose S.A.
Limeira Mill
Limeira, São Paulo, Brazil

Suzano Papel e Celulose S.A.
Mucuri Mill
Mucuri, Bahia, Brazil

Suzano Papel e Celulose S.A.
Rio Verde Unit
Suzano, São Paulo, Brazil

Suzano Papel e Celulose S.A.
Suzano Mill
Suzano, São Paulo, Brazil

Taiwan Chi Suen Enterprise Co., Ltd.
Pu Li Mill
Pu Li, Nantou County, Taiwan

Taiwan Pulp & Paper Corp.
Hsin Ying Mill
Hsinying District, Tainan City, Taiwan

Tamil Nadu Newsprint and Papers Limited (TNPL)
Kagithapuram Mill
Karur Dist., Kagithapuram, Tamil Nadu, India

Tan Mai Group Joint Stock Co.
Binh An Mill
Binh An Ward, Di An District, Binh Duong Province, Vietnam

Tan Mai Group Joint Stock Co.
Dong Nai Mill
Bien Hoa City, Dong Nai Province, Vietnam

Tan Mai Group Joint Stock Co.
Tan Mai Mill
Bien Hoa City, Dong Nai Province, Vietnam

Technocell Dekor GmbH & Co. KG
Osnabrück Mill
Osnabrück, Germany

Uncoated mechanical/groundwood

Teppatana Paper Mill Co., Ltd.
Amphur Muan Mill
Amphur Muang, Phathum Thani, Thailand

Tervakoski Oy
Tervakoski Mill
Tervakoski, Finland

Thai Paper Co., Ltd.
BanPong Mill
BanPong, Ratchaburi, Thailand

The Eastern Industrial Co., Ltd.
Pathumthani Mill
Amphur Muang, Pathumthani, Thailand

The Industrial Krungthai Co., Ltd.
Pathumthani Mill
Amphur Muang, Pathumthani, Thailand

The West Coast Paper Mills Ltd.
Dandeli Mill
Dandeli, Uttara Kannada, Karnataka, India

Three Star Paper Mills (P) Ltd.
Dist. Gautam Budh Nagar Mill
Dist. Gautam Budh Nagar, Uttar Pradesh, India

Tokushu Tokai Paper Co., Ltd.
Gifu Mill
Gifu-Shi, Gifu Pref., Japan

Tokushu Tokai Paper Co., Ltd.
Mishima Mill
Sunto-Gun, Shizuoka Pref., Japan

Toprak Temizlik Kagidi San. Tic. A.S.
Bozuyuk Mill
Bozuyuk, Bilecik, Turkey

Torraspapel S.A.
Sarriá de Ter Mill
Sarriá de Ter, Girona, Spain

Torraspapel S.A.
Zaragoza Mill
Zaragoza, Spain

Transnational Paper Corp.
Cavite Mill
Calvite City, Calabarzon, Laguna, Philippines

Trident Group
Bamala Mill
Dhaula, District Barnala, Punjab, India

Tullis Russell Papermakers Ltd.
Markinch Mill
Markinch, Glenrothes, Scotland, United Kingdom

Turinsky Pulp & Paper Mill
Turinsk Mill
Turinsk, Sverdlovskaya obl., Russia

Twin Rivers Paper, LLC
Madawaska and Edmundston Mills (East Paper Operations)
Madawaska, Maine, United States

Unión Papelera Platense
La Plata Mill
La Plata, Buenos Aires, Argentina

Unitary Enterprise (UE) "Paper Mill of Goznak"
Borisov Mill
Borisov, Minskaya obl., Belarus

United Paper Boards Limited
Patna Mill
Patna, Bihar, India

UPM GmbH
Nordland Mill
Dörpen, Germany

UPM-Kymmene Corporation
Kymi Mill
Kuusankoski, Kouvola, Finland

V.G. Paper & Boards Ltd.
Unit 1 Swaminathapuram
Swaminathapuram, Tamil Nadu, India

Van Diem Paper Joint-Stock Co.
Phu Xuyen Mill
Phu Xuyen District, Ha Tay Province, Vietnam

Ve-Ge Hassas Kagit ve Yapistirici Bant San. ve Tic. A.S.
Kemalpasa Mill
Kemalpasa, Izmir, Turkey

Vedadri Paper Mill PVT. Ltd.
Kodad Mill
Chimiryala village, Kodad (M), Andhra Pradesh, India

Verso Paper Corp.
Androscoggin Mill
Jay, Maine, United States

Verso Paper Corp.
Bucksport Mill
Bucksport, Maine, United States

Viet Thang Paper & Packing Co., Ltd.
Thuong Tin Dist. Mill
Thuong Tin Dist., Ha Tay Province, Vietnam

Viet Tri Paper Company
Viet Tri Mill
Viet Tri City, Phú Tho Province, Vietnam

Vietnam Paper Corporation (Vinapaco)-Bai Bang Paper
Bai Bang Paper
Phu Ninh District, Phú Tho Province, Vietnam

Vishal Coaters Ltd.
Patiala Mill
Patiala, Punjab, India

Whatman International Ltd.
Springfield Mill
Maidstone, Kent, United Kingdom

Whiting Paper Co.
Menasha Mill
Menasha, Wisconsin, United States

Xinjiang Bohu Reed Industry Stock Co., Ltd.
Kuerle (No.1) Mill
Kuerle, Xinjiang, China

Xinjiang Tianhong Paper Co., Ltd.
Shihezi Mill
Shihezi, Xinjiang, China

Xuan Duc Joint-Stock Paper Company
Ho Chi Minh City Mill
Ho Chi Minh City, Binh Duong Province, Vietnam

Yantai Longxiang Paper Co., Ltd.
Yantai Mill
Yantai, Shandong, China

Yashlyk Pulp & Paper Mill
Yashlyk, Akbuldai etrat Mill
Yashlyk, Akbuldai etrat, Gyaurs district, Akhal velat, Turkmenistan

Yunnan Changning Jianxing Paper Co., Ltd.
Baoshan Mill
Baoshan, Yunnan, China

ZAO International Paper
Svetogorsk Mill
Svetogorsk, Leningrad Region, Russia

Zhanjiang Chenming Paper Pulp Co., Ltd.
Zhanjiang (Zhanjiang Chenming Pulp & Paper) Mill
Zhanjiang, Guangdong, China

Zhejiang Halberd Paper Co., Ltd.
Quzhou Mill
Quzhou, Zhejiang, China

Zhejiang Hangzhou Banqiao Paper Co., Ltd.
Fuyang Mill
Fuyang, Zhejiang, China

Zhejiang Tiantianhong Paper Co., Ltd.
Quzhou Mill
Quzhou, Zhejiang, China

Zhejiang Winbon Special Paper Co. Ltd.
Quzhou Mill
Quzhou, Zhejiang, China

Zhejiang Yiwu City YiNan Paper Co., Ltd.
Yiwu Mill
Yiwu, Zhejiang, China

Zhenjiang Dadong Pulp & Paper Co. Ltd.
Zhenjiang Mill
Zhenjiang, Jiangsu, China

Ziegler Papier AG
Grellingen Mill
Grellingen, Switzerland

Uncoated mechanical/groundwood

Arctic Paper Mochenwangen GmbH
Mochenwangen Mill
Mochenwangen, Wolpertswende, Germany

Arctic Paper Munkedals AB
Munkedal Mill
Munkedal, Sweden

Arjowiggins Le Bourray SAS
Le Bourray Mill
Saint-Mars-la-Brière, France

Arjowiggins Security SAS
Crèvecoeur Mill
Jouy-sur-Morin, France

Bio-PAPPEL Printing
Tuxtepec Mill
Tuxtepec, OAX, Mexico

Catalyst Paper Corporation
Port Alberni Mill
Port Alberni, British Columbia, Canada

Uncoated mechanical/groundwood

Catalyst Paper Corporation
Powell River Mill
Powell River, British Columbia, Canada

Cia. Papelera El Fenix S.A. de C.V.
Col. Arenal Mill
Col. Arenal, México, D.F., Mexico

Daehan Paper Co., Ltd.
Cheongwon Mill
Cheongwon-gun, Chungcheongbuk-do, South Korea

Daini Seishi Co., Ltd.
Fuji-shi Mill
Fuji-shi, Shizuoka Pref., Japan

Daio Paper Corp.
Mishima Mill
Shikokuchuo-shi, Ehime Pref., Japan

Ellora Paper Mills Ltd.
Tumsar, Dist. Bhandara Mill
Tumsar, Dist. Bhandara, Maharashtra, India

Ethiopian Pulp & Paper SC
Nazareth Mill
Wonji, Nazareth, Ethiopia

Evergreen Packaging Inc.
Pine Bluff Mill
Pine Bluff, Arkansas, United States

F.F. Soucy SEC
Riviere du Loup Mill
Riviere du Loup, Quebec, Canada

Fábrica Nacional de Moneda y Timbre-FNMT
Burgos Mill
Burgos, Spain

Fabryka Papieru Myszków Sp. z o.o.
Myszkow Mill
Myszkow, Poland

FutureMark Paper Group
Manistique Mill
Manistique, Michigan, United States

Hellefoss Paper
Hokksund Mill
Hokksund, Norway

Henan Longquan Group Yubei Co., Ltd.
Xinxiang Mill
Xinxiang, Henan, China

Henan Puyang City Tongyu Paper Co., Ltd.
Puyang Mill
Puyang, Henan, China

Henan Xinxiang Hongtai Paper Co., Ltd.
Xinxiang Mill
Xinxiang, Henan, China

Holmen AB
Braviken Paper Mill
Norrköping, Sweden

Holmen AB
Hallsta Mill
Hallstavik, Sweden

Holmen Paper Madrid S.L.
Madrid Mill
Fuenlabrada, Madrid, Spain

Hubei Chibi Chenli Paper Co., Ltd.
Chibi Mill
Chibi, Hubei, China

Hunan Tiger Forest & Paper Group Yueyang Paper Co., Ltd.
Yueyang Mill
Yueyang, Hunan, China

Inland Empire Paper Co.
Millwood Mill
Millwood, Spokane, Washington, United States

Irving Paper
Saint John East Mill
Saint John, New Brunswick, Canada

Istituto Poligrafico e Zecca dello Stato
Foggia Mill
Foggia, Foggia, Italy

Jeonju Paper Corporation, Ltd.
Jeonju Mill
Jeonju-si, Jeollabuk-do, South Korea

Jiangxi Chenming Paper Co., Ltd.
Nanchang (Jiangxi Chenming Paper) Mill
Nanchang, Jiangxi, China

Julius Glatz GmbH Papierfabriken
Neidenfels Mill
Neidenfels, Germany

Kahramanmaras Kagit San ve TIC A.S (KMK Paper)
Kütahya Mill
Kütahya, Turkey

Kasuga Seishi Kogyo Co., Ltd.
Fuji-shi Mill
Fuji-shi, Shizuoka Pref., Japan

Koa Kogyo Co., Ltd.
Fuji-shi Mill
Fuji-shi, Shizuoka Pref., Japan

Maragheh Paper Industries Company (M.P.I.C)
Maragheh Mill
Maragheh, East Azerbaijan, Iran

Marusumi Paper Co., Ltd.
Kawanoe Mill
Shikokuchuo-shi, Ehime Pref., Japan

Mazandaran Wood & Paper Industries Co.
Sari Mill
Sari, Mazandaran, Iran

MCC Paper Yinhe Co., Ltd.
Linqing Mill
Linqing, Shandong, China

MELECKY a.s. závod Papírna Aloisov
Aloisov Mill
Ruda nad Moravou, Czech Republic

Mondi Shanduka Newsprint
Merebank Mill
Merebank, KwaZulu-Natal, South Africa

NewPage Corporation
Duluth Paper Mill
Duluth, Minnesota, United States

Nippon Paper Industries Co., Ltd.
Fuji Mill
Fuji-shi, Shizuoka Pref., Japan

Nippon Paper Industries Co., Ltd.
Yatsushiro Mill
Yatsushiro-shi, Kumamoto Pref., Japan

Nippon Paper Industries USA Co., Ltd.
Port Angeles Mill
Port Angeles, Washington, United States

Norske Skog (Australia)
Boyer Mill
Boyer, Tasmania, Australia

Norske Skog ASA
Saugbrugs Mill
Halden, Norway

Norske Skog ASA
Skogn Mill
Skogn, Norway

Norske Skog Bruck GmbH
Bruck an der Mur Mill
Bruck an der Mur, Styria, Austria

Norske Skog Golbey SA
Golbey Mill
Golbey Cedex, France

Norske Skog Tasman
Tasman Mill
Kawerau, Bay of Plenty, New Zealand

North Pacific Paper Corp. (Norpac)
Longview Mill
Longview, Washington, United States

Palm Paper Limited
King's Lynn Mill
King's Lynn, United Kingdom

Papel Prensa S.A.
San Pedro Mill
San Pedro, Buenos Aires, Argentina

Papelera Paysandú S.A.I.C.
Wilde Mill
Wilde, Buenos Aires, Argentina

Papeles Bío Bío
Concepción Mill
Concepción, VIII - Región del Biobío, Chile

Papierfabrik Hainsberg GmbH
Freital Mill
Freital-Hainsberg, Germany

Papierfabrik Schleipen
Bad Dürkheim Mill
Bad Dürkheim, Germany

Papierfabrik Utzenstorf AG
Utzenstorf Mill
Utzenstorf, Switzerland

Papierfabrik Zerkall Renker & Söhne GmbH & Co. KG
Hürtgenwald-Zerkall Mill
Hürtgenwald-Zerkall, Germany

Coated woodfree/freesheet

Papresa, S.L.
Rentería Mill
Rentería, Gipúzcoa, Spain

Parenco B.V.
Renkum Mill
Renkum, Netherlands

Perlen Papier AG
Perlen Mill
Perlen, Switzerland

Rakta, General Co. for Paper Industry
Rakta Mill
Alexandria, Iskanderiya, Egypt

Resolute Forest Products Canada Inc.
Alma Mill
Alma, Quebec, Canada

Resolute Forest Products Canada Inc.
Dolbeau Mill
Dolbeau, Quebec, Canada

Resolute Forest Products Canada Inc.
Kenogami Mill
Jonquière, Quebec, Canada

Sangal Papers Ltd.
Meerut Mill
Meerut, Uttar Pradesh, India

Sanko Seishi Kogyo KK
Fuji-shi Mill
Fuji-shi, Shizuoka Pref., Japan

Sanzen Paper Mfg. Co., Ltd.
Kanazawa Mill
Kanazawa-shi, Ishikawa Pref., Japan

SCA Graphic Sundsvall AB
Ortviken Mill
Sundsvall, Sweden

Schönfelder Papierfabrik GmbH
Annaberg-Buchholz Mill
Annaberg-Buchholz, Germany

Shandong Baron Paper Co., Ltd.
Laiwu Mill
Laiwu, Shandong, China

Shandong Bohui Paper Industry Co., Ltd.
Zibo Mill
Zibo, Shandong, China

Shandong Dezhou Huabei Paper (Group) Co., Ltd.
Dezhou Mill
Dezhou, Shandong, China

Shandong Dezhou Huadong Paper Group
Dezhou Mill
Dezhou, Shandong, China

Shandong Golden Cailun Paper Co., Ltd.
Liaocheng Mill
Liaocheng, Shandong, China

Shandong Guanjun Paper Co., Ltd.
Dezhou Mill
Dezhou, Shandong, China

Shandong Lianxi Paper Co. Ltd.
Rizhao Mill
Rizhao, Shandong, China

Shandong Stora Enso Huatai Paper
Dawang Mill
Dongying, Shandong, China

Shandong Taian Baichuan Paper Co., Ltd.
Taian Mill
Taian, Shandong, China

Shandong Taiding Material Technology Co., Ltd.
Dezhou Mill
Dezhou, Shandong, China

Shandong Tranlin Paper Co. Ltd.
Gaotang Mill
Liaocheng, Shandong, China

Stadacona Inc.
Stadacona Mill
Quebec City, Quebec, Canada

Stora Enso Printing and Reading
Anjala Mill
Kouvola, Finland

Stora Enso Printing and Reading
Kvarnsveden Mill
Borlänge, Sweden

Stora Enso Printing and Reading
Langerbrugge Mill
Gent, Belgium

Stora Enso Printing and Reading
Maxau Mill
Karlsruhe, Germany

Stora Enso Printing and Reading
Sachsen Mill
Eilenburg, Saxony, Germany

Tembec Inc.
Spruce Falls Mill
Kapuskasing, Ontario, Canada

Twin Rivers Paper, LLC
Madawaska and Edmundston Mills (East Paper Operations)
Madawaska, Maine, United States

Unión Papelera Platense
La Plata Mill
La Plata, Buenos Aires, Argentina

UPM GmbH
Augsburg Mill
Augsburg, Germany

UPM GmbH
Ettringen Mill
Ettringen, Bavaria, Germany

UPM GmbH
Plattling Mill
Plattling, Germany

UPM GmbH
Schongau Mill
Schongau, Germany

UPM North America
Madison Paper Mill
Madison, Maine, United States

UPM-Kymmene Austria GmbH
Steyrermühl Mill
Steyrermühl, Oberösterreich, Austria

UPM-Kymmene Corporation
Jämsänkoski Mill
Jämsänkoski, Jämsä, Finland

UPM-Kymmene Corporation
Kaipola Mill
Kaipola, Jämsä, Finland

UPM-Kymmene Corporation
Rauma Paper Mill
Rauma, Finland

Verso Paper Corp.
Bucksport Mill
Bucksport, Maine, United States

Vipap Videm Krško d.d.
Krško Mill
Krško, Ljubljana, Slovenia

Yunnan Changning Jianxing Paper Co., Ltd.
Baoshan Mill
Baoshan, Yunnan, China

Coated woodfree/freesheet

A.B.C.D. Cartiere CA
Charallave Mill
Charallave, Edo. Miranda, Venezuela

Ahlstrom Osnabrück GmbH
Osnabrück Mill
Osnabrück, Germany

Alkim Kagit Sanayi ve Ticaret A.S
Izmir Mill
Izmir, Izmir, Turkey

Appleton Coated LLC
Combined Locks Mill
Combined Locks, Wisconsin, United States

Arctic Paper Grycksbo AB
Grycksbo Mill
Grycksbo, Sweden

Arjowiggins Ltda.
Salto Mill
Salto, São Paulo, Brazil

Arjowiggins Papiers Couchés S.A.
Aa Mill
Wizernes, Pas-de-Calais, France

Arjowiggins Papiers Couchés SAS
Bessé-sur-Braye Mill
Bessé-sur-Braye, France

Ballarpur Industries Ltd. (BILT)
Pune Mill
Bhigwan, Dist. Pune, Maharashtra, India

Burgo Group SpA
Sarego Mill
Sarego, Vicenza, Italy

Burgo Group SpA
Sora Mill
Sora, Frosinone, Italy

Burgo Group SpA
Toscolano Mill
Toscolano Maderno, Brescia, Italy

Coated woodfree/freesheet

Cartiere del Garda SpA
Riva del Garda Mill
Riva del Garda, Trento, Italy

Carvajal Pulpa y Papel
Yumbo Mill, Plant 1
Yumbo, Valle de Cauca, Colombia

Cheng Loong Corporation
Hou Li Mill
Hou Li, Taichung City, Taiwan

Chenming Paper Holdings Ltd.
Shouguang (Shouguang Chenming Coated Woodfree Paper No. 3) Mill
Shouguang, Shandong, China

Chuetsu Pulp & Paper Co., Ltd.
Takaoka (Nohmachi) Mill
Takaoka-shi, Toyama Pref., Japan

Chung Hwa Pulp Corporation
Chiutang Mill
Ta Shu District, Kaohsiung City, Taiwan

Chung Hwa Pulp Corporation
Hualien Mill
Chi An, Hualien County, Taiwan

Crocker Technical Papers
Fitchburg Mill
Fitchburg, Massachusetts, United States

Daio Paper Corp.
Mishima Mill
Shikokuchuo-shi, Ehime Pref., Japan

Fábrica Nacional de Moneda y Timbre-FNMT
Burgos Mill
Burgos, Spain

FANAPEL - Fábrica Nacional de Papel S.A.
Juan Lacaze Mill
Juan Lacaze, Colonia, Uruguay

Fedrigoni S.P.A.
Arco Mill
Arco, Trento, Italy

Fujian Qingshan Youxi Paper Co., Ltd.
Sanming Mill
Sanming, Fujian, China

Fujifilm Corp.
Fujinomiya Mill
Fujinomiya-Shi, Shizuoka Pref., Japan

Gold East Paper (Jiangsu) Co., Ltd.
Zhenjiang (Gold East Paper) Mill
Zhenjiang, Jiangsu, China

Gold Huasheng Paper (Suzhou Industrial Park) Co., Ltd.
Suzhou (Gold Huasheng Paper) Mill
Suzhou, Jiangsu, China

Goricane, tovarna papirja Medvode, d.d.
Medvode Mill
Medvode, Slovenia

Guangdong Jiangnan Paper Co. Ltd.
Zhaoqing Mill
Zhaoqing, Guangdong, China

Hahnemühle FineArt GmbH
Dassel Mill
Dassel, Germany

Hainan Jinhai Pulp & Paper Industry Co., Ltd.
Yangpu (Hainan Jinhai Pulp & Paper Industry) Mill
Haikou, Hainan, China

Hankuk Paper Mfg. Co., Ltd.
Onsan Mill
Ulsan-si, Gyeongsangnam-do, South Korea

Hansol Artone Paper Co., Ltd.
Osan Mill
Ohsan-si, Gyeonggi-do, South Korea

Hansol Artone Paper Co., Ltd.
Sintanjin Mill
Daedeok-gu, Daejeon, South Korea

Hansol Paper Co., Ltd.
Changhang Mill
Seocheun-gun, Chungcheongnam-do, South Korea

Heilongjiang Mudanjiang Daewoo Paper Mfg. Co. Ltd.
Mudanjiang Mill
Yangming District, Mudanjiang, Heilongjiang, China

Henan Puyang Longfeng Paper Co. Ltd
Puyang (Puyang Longfeng) Mill
Puyang, Henan, China

Hokuetsu Kishu Paper Co. Ltd.
Niigata Mill
Niigata-shi, Niigata Pref., Japan

Hollingsworth & Vose Co.
East Walpole Mill
East Walpole, Massachusetts, United States

Hongwon Paper Mfg. Co., Ltd.
Jinwi Mill
Pyeongtaek-si, Gyeonggi-do, South Korea

Hunan Tiger Forest & Paper Group Yueyang Paper Co., Ltd.
Yueyang Mill
Yueyang, Hunan, China

IdemPapers SA
Virginal Mill
Virginal-Samme, Belgium

Illig'sche Papierfabrik
Mühltal Mill
Mühltal, Germany

ITC Limited, Paperboards & Specialty Papers Division
Bhadrachalam Mill
Khammam, Bhadrachalam, Andhra Pradesh, India

Jiangsu Oji Paper Nantong Co., Ltd.
Nantong Mill
Nantong, Jiangsu, China

Jiangsu Stora Enso Suzhou Paper Co. Ltd.
Suzhou Mill
Suzhou, Jiangsu, China

Jiangsu UPM, Changshu Paper Industry Co., Ltd.
Changshu Mill
Changshu, Jiangsu, China

JK Paper Ltd.
JK Paper Mills - JKPM
Jaykaypur, Rayagada Dist., Odisha, India

Koryazhma Branch of Ilim Group
Kotlas Pulp and Paper Mill
Koryazhma, Arkhangelsk Region, Russia

Lalji Board Industries (P) Ltd.
Firozabad Mill
Firozabad, Uttar Pradesh, India

Ledesma S.A.A.I.
Libertador General Mill
Libertador General San Martín, Jujuy, Argentina

Lenzing Papier GmbH
Lenzing Paper Mill
Lenzing, Oberösterreich, Austria

Marusumi Paper Co., Ltd.
Ohe Mill
Shikokuchuo-shi, Ehime Pref., Japan

MCC Meili Paper Industry Co., Ltd.
Zhongwei Mill
Zhongwei, Ningxia, China

Metsä Board Husum
Husum Mill
Husum, Sweden

Mitsubishi Paper Mills Ltd.
Hachinohe Mill
Hachinohe-shi, Aomori, Japan

Monadnock Paper Mills, Inc.
Bennington Mill
Bennington, New Hampshire, United States

Moorim P&P Co. Ltd.
Ulsan Mill
Ulsan-si, South Korea

Moorim Paper Co., Ltd.
Jinju Mill
Jinju-si, Gyeongsangnam-do, South Korea

Moorim SP Co., Ltd.
Daegu Mill
Buk-gu, Daegu-si, South Korea

Mopak Dalaman Pulp-Paper Cardboard Plant
Dalaman Mill
Mugla, Turkey

Mosaico Speciality Papers
Lugo di Vicenza Mill
Lugo di Vicenza, Vicenza, Italy

Nath Pulp & Paper Mills Ltd.
Aurangabad Mill
Aurangabad, Maharashtra, India

Neo-Print
Tbilisi Mill
Tbilisi, Georgia

NewPage Corporation
Escanaba Mill
Escanaba, Michigan, United States

NewPage Corporation
Luke Mill
Luke, Maryland, United States

Coated woodfree/freesheet

NewPage Corporation
Rumford Mill
Rumford, Maine, United States

NewPage Corporation
Wickliffe Mill
Wickliffe, Kentucky, United States

NewPage Corporation
Wisconsin Rapids Paper Mill
Wisconsin Rapids, Wisconsin, United States

Nippon Paper Industries Co., Ltd.
Akita Mill
Akita-shi, Akita Pref., Japan

Nippon Paper Industries Co., Ltd.
Fuji Mill
Fuji-shi, Shizuoka Pref., Japan

Nippon Paper Industries Co., Ltd.
Hokkaido Mill - Shiraoi
Shiraoi, Hokkaido Pref., Japan

Nippon Paper Industries Co., Ltd.
Ishinomaki Mill
Ishinomaki-shi, Miyagi Pref., Japan

Nippon Paper Industries Co., Ltd.
Iwakuni Mill
Iwakuni-shi, Yamaguchi Pref., Japan

Nippon Paper Industries Co., Ltd.
Iwanuma Mill
Iwanuma-shi, Miyagi Pref., Japan

Nippon Paper Papylia Co., Ltd.
Harada Mill
Fuji-shi, Shizuoka Pref., Japan

Oji Papéis Especiais Ltda
Piracicaba Mill
Piracicaba, São Paulo, Brazil

Opel Paper Mill Ltd.
Vapi Mill
Vapi, Gujarat, India

Papel Aralar S.A.
Amezqueta Mill
Amezqueta, Gipúzcoa, Spain

Papeterie de la Banque de France
Vic-le-Comte Mill
Vic-le-Comte, France

Papeteries de Condat
Condat le Lardin Mill
Le Lardin St. Lazare, France

Papierfabrik Scheufelen GmbH & Co. KG
Lenningen Mill
Lenningen, Baden-Württemberg, Germany

Papierfabrik Zerkall Renker & Söhne GmbH & Co. KG
Hürtgenwald-Zerkall Mill
Hürtgenwald-Zerkall, Germany

Papirnica Vevce d.o.o.
Vevce Mill
Ljubljana-Dobrunje, Slovenia

Pitambar Coated Papers Ltd.
Bhiwadi Mill
Bhiwadi, Rajasthan, India

PT Esa Kertas Nusantara
Karawang Mill
Karawang, West Java, Indonesia

PT Jaya Kertas
Nganjuk Mill
Nganjuk, East Java, Indonesia

PT Pabrik Kertas Tjiwi Kimia Tbk
Mojokerto (PT Pabrik Kertas Tjiwi Kimia) Mill
Mojokerto, East Java, Indonesia

PT Pindo Deli Pulp & Paper Mills
Karawang No. 1 (PT Pindo Deli Pulp & Paper Mills) Mill
Karawang, West Java, Indonesia

Renova - Fábrica de Papel do Almonda S.A.
Torres Novas Mill
Torres Novas, Portugal

Sappi Fine Paper Europe
Ehingen Mill
Ehingen, Germany

Sappi Fine Paper Europe
Gratkorn Mill
Gratkorn, Styria, Austria

Sappi Fine Paper Europe
Lanaken Mill
Lanaken, Belgium

Sappi Fine Paper Europe
Maastricht Mill
Maastricht, Netherlands

Sappi Fine Paper Europe
Stockstadt Mill
Stockstadt am Main, Germany

Sappi Fine Paper North America
Cloquet Mill
Cloquet, Minnesota, United States

Sappi Fine Paper North America
Somerset Mill
Skowhegan, Maine, United States

Sappi Paper and Paper Packaging South Africa (SA)
Stanger Mill
Stanger, KwaZulu-Natal, South Africa

Schut Papier
Heelsum Mill
Heelsum, Netherlands

Serpukhovskaya Paper Mill
Serpukhov Mill
Serpukhov, Moscow Region, Russia

Shandong Baron Paper Co., Ltd.
Laiwu Mill
Laiwu, Shandong, China

Shandong Linqu Yulong Paper Co., Ltd.
Weifang Mill
Weifang, Shandong, China

Shandong Lu An Paper Co., Ltd.
Anqiu Mill
Anqiu, Shandong, China

Shandong Sun Paper Industry Joint Stock Co., Ltd.
Yanzhou Mill
Yanzhou, Shandong, China

Shandong Tranlin Paper Co. Ltd.
Gaotang Mill
Liaocheng, Shandong, China

Shandong Weifang Henglian Art Paper Co., Ltd.
Weifang Mill
Weifang, Shandong, China

Shouguang Meilun Paper
Shouguang (Shouguang Meilun Paper) Mill
Shouguang, Shandong, China

Shree Krishna Paper Mills & Ind Ltd
Haryana Coating Division
Bahadurgarh, Haryana, India

SPM - Security Paper Mill a.s.
Štetí Mill
Štetí, Czech Republic

St. Petersburg Paper Mill Goznak
St. Petersburg Mill
St. Petersburg, Russia

Stora Enso Printing and Reading
Oulu Mill
Oulu, Finland

Stora Enso Printing and Reading
Uetersen Mill
Uetersen, Germany

Sudhir Papers Ltd.
Bangalore Mill
Bangalore, Karnataka, India

Sukhraj Agro Papers Ltd.
Dist. Sangrur Mill
Dist. Sangrur, Punjab, India

Suzano Papel e Celulose S.A.
Limeira Mill
Limeira, São Paulo, Brazil

Suzano Papel e Celulose S.A.
Suzano Mill
Suzano, São Paulo, Brazil

T.T.K. Pharma Ltd. (Paper division)
Dist. Erode Mill
Dist. Erode, Tamil Nadu, India

Tamil Nadu Newsprint and Papers Limited (TNPL)
Kagithapuram Mill
Karur Dist., Kagithapuram, Tamil Nadu, India

Tervakoski Oy
Tervakoski Mill
Tervakoski, Finland

Thai Paper Co., Ltd.
BanPong Mill
BanPong, Ratchaburi, Thailand

Thai Union Paper Public Co., Ltd.
Prapradaeng Mill
Prapradaeng, Samut Prakarn, Thailand

Torraspapel S.A.
Motril Mill
Motril, Granada, Spain

Torraspapel S.A.
Sant Joan les Fonts Mill
Sant Joan les Fonts, Girona, Spain

Coated mechanical/groundwood

Torraspapel S.A.
Zaragoza Mill
Zaragoza, Spain

Twin Rivers Paper, LLC
Madawaska and Edmundston Mills (East Paper Operations)
Madawaska, Maine, United States

Unión Papelera Platense
La Plata Mill
La Plata, Buenos Aires, Argentina

UPM GmbH
Nordland Mill
Dörpen, Germany

UPM-Kymmene Corporation
Kymi Mill
Kuusankoski, Kouvola, Finland

Verso Paper Corp.
Androscoggin Mill
Jay, Maine, United States

Verso Paper Corp.
Quinnesec Mill
Quinnesec, Michigan, United States

Viet Thang Paper & Packing Co., Ltd.
Thuong Tin Dist. Mill
Thuong Tin Dist., Ha Tay Province, Vietnam

West Linn Paper Co.
West Linn Mill
West Linn, Oregon, United States

Whatman International Ltd.
Springfield Mill
Maidstone, Kent, United Kingdom

Coated mechanical/groundwood

Appleton Coated LLC
Combined Locks Mill
Combined Locks, Wisconsin, United States

Arjowiggins Le Bourray SAS
Le Bourray Mill
Saint-Mars-la-Brière, France

BN - Papel Catarinense Ltda.
Benedito Novo Mill
Benedito Novo, Santa Catarina, Brazil

Burgo Group SpA
Duino Mill
Duino, Trieste, Italy

Burgo Group SpA
Toscolano Mill
Toscolano Maderno, Brescia, Italy

Burgo Group SpA
Verzuolo Mill
Verzuolo, Cuneo, Italy

Burgo Group SpA
Villorba Mill
Villorba, Treviso, Italy

Catalyst Paper Corporation
Port Alberni Mill
Port Alberni, British Columbia, Canada

Chenming Paper Holdings Ltd.
Shouguang (Shouguang Chenming Lightweight Coated Paper No. 2) Mill
Shouguang, Shandong, China

Chuetsu Pulp & Paper Co., Ltd.
Sendai Mill
Satsumasendai-shi, Kagoshima Pref., Japan

Daio Paper Corp.
Mishima Mill
Shikokuchuo-shi, Ehime Pref., Japan

Evergreen Packaging Inc.
Pine Bluff Mill
Pine Bluff, Arkansas, United States

Hokuetsu Kishu Paper Co. Ltd.
Niigata Mill
Niigata-shi, Niigata Pref., Japan

Hunan Tiger Forest & Paper Group Yueyang Paper Co., Ltd.
Yueyang Mill
Yueyang, Hunan, China

Jiangxi Chenming Paper Co., Ltd.
Nanchang (Jiangxi Chenming Paper) Mill
Nanchang, Jiangxi, China

Kama Pulp & Paper Mill
Krasnokamsk Mill
Krasnokamsk, Perm Region, Russia

Kotkamills Oy
Kotka Mill
Kotka, Finland

Kruger Wayagamack Inc.
Trois Rivierès (Wayagamack) Mill
Trois-Rivières, Quebec, Canada

Kübler & Niethammer Papierfabrik Kriebstein AG
Kriebstein Mill
Kriebstein, Germany

LEIPA Georg Leinfelder GmbH
Schwedt Mill
Schwedt, Germany

Maragheh Paper Industries Company (M.P.I.C)
Maragheh Mill
Maragheh, East Azerbaijan, Iran

Marusumi Paper Co., Ltd.
Ohe Mill
Shikokuchuo-shi, Ehime Pref., Japan

Mazandaran Wood & Paper Industries Co.
Sari Mill
Sari, Mazandaran, Iran

NewPage Corporation
Biron Mill
Wisconsin Rapids, Wisconsin, United States

NewPage Corporation
Escanaba Mill
Escanaba, Michigan, United States

NewPage Corporation
Rumford Mill
Rumford, Maine, United States

Nippon Paper Industries Co., Ltd.
Fuji Mill
Fuji-shi, Shizuoka Pref., Japan

Nippon Paper Industries Co., Ltd.
Hokkaido Mill - Asahikawa
Asahikawa-shi, Hokkaido Pref., Japan

Nippon Paper Industries Co., Ltd.
Ishinomaki Mill
Ishinomaki-shi, Miyagi Pref., Japan

Nippon Paper Industries Co., Ltd.
Iwanuma Mill
Iwanuma-shi, Miyagi Pref., Japan

Norske Skog (Australia)
Boyer Mill
Boyer, Tasmania, Australia

Norske Skog Bruck GmbH
Bruck an der Mur Mill
Bruck an der Mur, Styria, Austria

Norske Skog Walsum GmbH
Walsum Mill
Duisburg, Germany

Perlen Papier AG
Perlen Mill
Perlen, Switzerland

Sappi Fine Paper Europe
Kirkniemi Mill
Kirkniemi, Finland

Sappi Fine Paper Europe
Lanaken Mill
Lanaken, Belgium

SCA Graphic Sundsvall AB
Ortviken Mill
Sundsvall, Sweden

Steinbeis Papier Glückstadt GmbH & Co. KG
Glückstadt Mill
Glückstadt, Germany

Stora Enso Arapoti Indústria de Papel Ltda.
Arapoti Mill
Arapoti, Paraná, Brazil

Stora Enso Printing and Reading
Anjala Mill
Kouvola, Finland

Stora Enso Printing and Reading
Kabel Mill
Hagen, Germany

Stora Enso Printing and Reading
Veitsiluoto Mill
Kemi, Finland

UPM GmbH
Augsburg Mill
Augsburg, Germany

UPM GmbH
Plattling Mill
Plattling, Germany

UPM North America
Blandin Paper Mill
Grand Rapids, Minnesota, United States

Tissue

UPM-Kymmene (UK) Ltd.
Caledonian Paper Mill
Irvine, Scotland, United Kingdom

UPM-Kymmene Corporation
Kaipola Mill
Kaipola, Jämsä, Finland

UPM-Kymmene Corporation
Kaukas Mill
Lappeenranta, Finland

UPM-Kymmene Corporation
Rauma Paper Mill
Rauma, Finland

Verso Paper Corp.
Androscoggin Mill
Jay, Maine, United States

Verso Paper Corp.
Bucksport Mill
Bucksport, Maine, United States

Vipap Videm Krško d.d.
Krško Mill
Krško, Ljubljana, Slovenia

Tissue

A & B Paper Ltd.
Dobrzejewice k/Torunia Mill
Dobrzejewice, k/Torunia, Poland

Abbaspel Indústria e Comércio de Papéis Ltda.
Porto União Mill
Porto União, Santa Catarina, Brazil

ABC Tissue Products Pty. Ltd.
Wetherill Park Mill
Fairfield, Sydney, New South Wales, Australia

Absormex CMPC Tissue S.A. de CV
Altamira
Altamira, Tamaulipas, Mexico

Absorpelsa Papeles Absorventes S.A.
Quito Mill
Quito, Pichincha, Ecuador

Abu Dhabi National Paper Mill
Abu Dhabi Mill
Abu Dhabi, Shaikhdom of Abu Dhabi, United Arab Emirates

Adischevskaya Board Mill
Adischevo Mill
Adischevo, Ostrovsky District, Kostroma Region, Russia

Aigle Paper Manufacturing Company - A.P.M.C.
Algiers Mill
Algiers, Algeria

Ak Gida San. ve Tic. A.Ş
Pamukova Mill
Pamukova, Turkey

Al Alamiyya Paper Mill
Amman Mill
Amman, Jordan

Al Bardi Paper Mill Co. (S.A.E.)
6 October City Mill
6 October City, El Giza, Egypt

Al Keena Hygienic Paper Mill Co. Ltd.
Amman Mill
Al-Jiza, Amman, Jordan

Al Sindian Paper Mill Co. S.A.E.
6 October City Mill
6 October City, El Giza, Egypt

Al Snobar Hygienic Paper Mill
Amman Mill
Al-Jiza, Amman, Jordan

Al Zeina Tissue Mill
10th of Ramadan City Mill
10th of Ramadan City, Sharkeya, East Province, Egypt

Alas Doradas S.A. de C.V
San Juan Opico Mill
San Juan Opico La Libertad, El Salvador

Albatros Paper Mill
Dnepropetrovsk Mill
Dnepropetrovsk, Ukraine

Albertin Paperboard & Paper Mill
Slonim Mill
Slonim, Grodno Region, Belarus

Alex Converta Co. SAE (Handy)
Alexandria Mill
Alexandria, Iskanderiya, Egypt

Almaty Maolin Paper
Almaty Mill
Karasai District, Almaty Obl., Kazakhstan

Alpes Celulose e Papéis Ltda.
São Luís Mill
São Luís, Maranhão, Brazil

Amal
Bishkek Mill
Bishkek, Kyrgyzstan

AMS - Gomà Camps S.A.
Vila Velha de Ródão Mill
Vila Velha de Ródão, Portugal

Angren Pack
Bulbak Mill
Angren, pos. Bulbak, Tashkentskaya obl., Uzbekistan

Anhui Bilun Tissue Paper Co. Ltd.
Maanshan Mill
Maanshan, Anhui, China

Anhui HengAn Wuhu Paper Co., Ltd
Wuhu Mill
Wuhu, Anhui, China

Anhui Weilun Industry & Trade Co., Ltd.
Huainan Mill
Huainan, Anhui, China

Ariete Srl
Cava Dè Tirreni Mill
Cava Dè Tirreni, Salerno, Italy

Arjowiggins Le Bourray SAS
Le Bourray Mill
Saint-Mars-la-Brière, France

Astória Papéis Ltda.
Gravataí Mill
Gravataí, Rio Grande do Sul, Brazil

Athens Paper Mill SA
Athens Mill
Athens, Greece

Atlas Paper Mills LLC
Hialeah Mill
Hialeah, Florida, United States

Augusta Select Tissue, LLC
Augusta Mill
Augusta, Georgia, United States

Baoda Paper
Jiangmen Mill
Jiangmen, Guangdong, China

Bashundhara Paper Mills Ltd.
Unit 3
Gazaria, Munshigonj, Bangladesh

Bataan 2020
Samal Mill
Samal, Bataan, Philippines

Beijing Vinda Paper (Beijing) Co., Ltd.
Beijing Mill
Beijing, Beijing, China

Bel Papyrus Ltd
Ogaba Mill
Ikeja, Lagos, Lagos State, Nigeria

Bel Papyrus Ltd
Oregun Mill
Ikeja, Lagos, Lagos State, Nigeria

Belovo Paper Mill S.A.
Belovo Mill
Belovo, Bulgaria

Benaion Indústria de Papel e Celulose S.A. - Bipacel
Manaus Mill
Manaus, Amazonas, Brazil

Berli Jucker Cellox Ltd.
Bangplee Mill
Bangchalong, Bangplee, Samut Prakarn, Thailand

Berli Jucker Cellox Ltd.
Prachinburi Mill
Srimahapoth, Prachinburi, Thailand

BL Bittar, Indústria de Papel
Limeira Mill
Limeira, São Paulo, Brazil

Bom Pastor Indústria de Papel Ltda.
Divinópolis Mill
Divinópolis, Minas Gerais, Brazil

Bulleh Shah Packaging (Private) Limited
Lahore Mill
Lahore, Punjab, Pakistan

C&S Paper Co., Ltd.
Jiangmen Mill
Jiangmen, Guangdong, China

C&S Paper Co., Ltd.
Jiaxing Mill
Jiaxing, Zhejiang, China

C&S Paper Co., Ltd.
Tangshan Mill
Tangshan, Hebei, China

Tissue

C&S Paper Co., Ltd.
Xiaogan Mill
Xiaogan, Hubei, China

C&S Paper Co., Ltd.
Yunfu Mill
Yunfu, Guangdong, China

C&S Paper Co., Ltd.
Zhongshan Mill
Zhongshan, Guangdong, China

Calcarta S.R.L.
Chifenti Mill
Chifenti, Borgo a Mozzano, Lucca, Italy

Cambará S.A. - Produtos Florestais
Cambará do Sul Mill
Cambará do Sul, Rio Grande do Sul, Brazil

Carmen Tissue S.A.E.
6 October City Mill
6 October City, El Giza, Egypt

Carta Fabril Ltda.
Anápolis Mill
Anápolis, Goiás, Brazil

Carta Fabril Ltda.
Carta Rio Mill
São Gonçalo, Rio de Janeiro, Brazil

Cartaseta-Friedrich & Co.
Däniken Mill
Däniken, Switzerland

Cartiera Capostrada SpA
Tullio Carrara Mill
Capostrada, Pistoia, Italy

Cartiera Carma Srl
Pistoia Mill
Pescia-Pietrabuona, Pistoia, Italy

Cartiera Carma Srl
Pratovecchio Mill
Pratovecchio, Arezzo, Italy

Cartiera Confalone S.R.L.
Salerno Mill
Maiori, Salerno, Italy

Cartiera del Vignaletto Srl
Santa Maria di Zevio Mill
Santa Maria di Zevio, Verona, Italy

Cartiera Della Basilica SRL
Bagni di Lucca Mill
Bagni di Lucca, Lucca, Italy

Cartiera Della Basilica SRL
Villa Basilica Mill
Botticino, Lucca, Italy

Cartiera di Cagliari Srl
Assemini (Sardinia) Mill
Assemini, Cagliari, Italy

Cartiera di Carbonera SpA
Camposampiero Mill
Camposampiero, Padua, Italy

Cartiera di Ponzano Srl
Ponzano Veneto Mill
Ponzano Veneto, Treviso, Italy

Cartiera Europaper SpA
Monzone-Fivizzano Mill
Monzone-Fivizzano, Massa-Carrara, Italy

Cartiera Francesco Imperato e Figli SNC
Palermo Mill
Palermo, Palermo, Italy

Cartiera Giusta Srl
Pracando Mill
Pracando-Villa Basilica, Lucca, Italy

Cartiera Nuova So.Car.Pi. S.r.l.
Piteglio Mill
Piteglio, Pistoia, Italy

Cartiera Partenope S.r.l
Arzano Mill
Arzano, Naples, Italy

Cartiera Pasquini Srl
Bagni di Lucca Mill
Bagni di Lucca, Lucca, Italy

Cartiera Ponte A Villa s.r.l.
Villa Basilica Mill
Villa Basilica, Lucca, Italy

Cartiera Ponte d'Oro Ansalcarta Srl
Pracando Mill
Pracando Villa Basilica, Lucca, Italy

Cartiera San Giorgio S.r.l.
Genova-Voltri Mill
Genova-Voltri, Genova, Italy

Cartiera San Lorenzo S.R.L.
Gassano Mill
Gassano, Massa-Carrara, Italy

Cartiera San Rocco SpA
Villa Basilica Mill
Villa Basilica, Lucca, Italy

Cartiera Val di Lima S.R.L.
Bagni di Lucca Mill
Bagni di Lucca, Lucca, Italy

Cartiere Villa Lagarina Spa
Trento Mill
Trento, Trento, Italy

Cartón Box del Paraguay S. A.
Ñemby Mill
Ñemby, Paraguay

Cartones y Papeles del Risaralda
Risaralda Mill
Dosquebradas, Pereira, Risaralda, Colombia

Casalino Carta S.r.l.
Mele Mill
Mele, Genova, Italy

Cascades Tissue Group
Candiac Mill
Candiac, Quebec, Canada

Cascades Tissue Group
Eau Claire Mill
Eau Claire, Wisconsin, United States

Cascades Tissue Group
Kingsey Falls Mill
Kingsey Falls, Quebec, Canada

Cascades Tissue Group
Lachute Mill
Lachute, Quebec, Canada

Cascades Tissue Group
Mechanicville Mill
Mechanicville, New York, United States

Cascades Tissue Group
Memphis Mill
Memphis, Tennessee, United States

Cascades Tissue Group
Ransom Mill
Ransom, Pennsylvania, United States

Cascades Tissue Group
Rockingham Mill
Rockingham, North Carolina, United States

Cascades Tissue Group
Saint Helens Mill
Saint Helens, Oregon, United States

Cascades Tissue Group
Scarborough Mill
Agincourt - Scarborough, Ontario, Canada

Cascades Tissue Group
Whitby Mill
Whitby, Ontario, Canada

Celu Paper S.A.
San Pedro Mill
San Pedro, Buenos Aires, Argentina

Celulosa Baradero S.A.
Baradero Mill
Baradero, Buenos Aires, Argentina

Celulosa Campana S.A.
Lima Mill
Lima, Buenos Aires, Argentina

Celulosa Remanso S.A.
Mariano Roque Alonso Mill
Mariano Roque Alonso, Paraguay

Century Pulp & Paper
Lalkua Mill
Nainital, Uttarakhand, India

CEREPA, a.s.
Cervená Recice Mill
Cervená Recice 107, Czech Republic

Cesar Iglesias C. por A
San Pedro de Macorís Mill
San Pedro de Macorís, Dominican Republic

Chaltyr Paper Mill
Chaltyr Mill
Chaltyr, Russia

Chandaria Industries Ltd.
Chandaria Paper Mill
Nairobi, Kenya

Chang Tang Industrial Co., Ltd.
Yuanlin Mill
Yuanlin, Changhua County, Taiwan

Cheng Dah Paper Co., Ltd
Pu Shin Mill
Pu Shin, Changhua County, Taiwan

Cheng Loong Corporation
Chu Pei Mill
Chu Pei, Hsinchu County, Taiwan

Chi Sheng Paper Product Co., Ltd.
Hua Tan Mill
Pu Hsin, Changhua County, Taiwan

Chiao Feng Paper Co., Ltd.
Yuanlin Mill
Yuanlin, Changhua County, Taiwan

Tissue

Chongqing HengAn Paper Co., Ltd.
Chongqing Mill
Chongqing, Chongqing, China

Chongqing Longjing Paper
Chongqing Mill
Chongqing, Chongqing, China

Chongqing Wei Er Mei Paper
Chongqing Mill
Chongqing, Chongqing, China

Cia. Canoinhas de Papel
Canoinhas Mill
Canoinhas, Santa Catarina, Brazil

CICP Companhia Industrial de Celulose e Papel
Itaporanga d'Ajuda Mill
Itaporanga d'Ajuda, Sergipe, Brazil

CIPAC Indústria de Papéis Cantagalo Ltda.
Cantagalo Mill
Cantagalo, Rio de Janeiro, Brazil

CJSC ESEIRA
Panevezys Mill
Panevezys, Lithuania

Clearwater Paper Corporation
East Hartford Mill
East Hartford, Connecticut, United States

Clearwater Paper Corporation
Ladysmith Mill
Ladysmith, Wisconsin, United States

Clearwater Paper Corporation
Lakeview Mill
Neenah, Wisconsin, United States

Clearwater Paper Corporation
Las Vegas Mill
North Las Vegas, Nevada, United States

Clearwater Paper Corporation
Lewiston Mill
Lewiston, Idaho, United States

Clearwater Paper Corporation
Natural Dam Mill
Gouverneur, New York, United States

Clearwater Paper Corporation
Saint Catharines Mill
Saint Catharines, Ontario, Canada

Clearwater Paper Corporation
Shelby Mill
Shelby, North Carolina, United States

Clearwater Paper Corporation
Wiggins Mill
Wiggins, Mississippi, United States

CMPC Tissue S.A.
Puente Alto Mill
Eyzaguirre, Puente Alto, RM - Región Metro. de Santiago, Chile

CMPC Tissue S.A.
Talagante Mill
Talagante, RM - Región Metro. de Santiago, Chile

Colombiana Kimberly Colpapel S.A.
Medellin Mill
Medellin, Antioquia, Colombia

Colombiana Kimberly Colpapel S.A.
Puerto Tejada Mill
Puerto Tejada, Cauca, Colombia

Compañía Papelera Mendoza S.A. (Copelme)
Cochabamba Mill
Cochabamba, Bolivia

Consolidated A One Trade and Invest 11 Pty. Ltd.
Chamdor, Krugersdorp Mill
Chamdor, Krugersdorp, Gauteng, South Africa

COPAPA - Companhia Paduana de Papéis
Santo Antônio de Pádua Mill
Santo Antônio de Pádua, Rio de Janeiro, Brazil

Crown Paper Mill Ltd.
Abu Dhabi Branch
Abu Dhabi, Shaikhdom of Abu Dhabi, United Arab Emirates

Crown Tissue
Oshodi, Lagos Mill
Oshodi, Lagos, Lagos State, Nigeria

CVG - Cahdam Volta Grande
Rio Negrinho Mill
Rio Negrinho, Santa Catarina, Brazil

Dae Wang Paper Co., Ltd.
Gunsan Mill
Gunsan-si, Jeollabuk-do, South Korea

Daejin Paper Mfg. Co., Ltd.
Daegu Mill
Buk-gu, Daegu-si, Daegu-si, South Korea

Daewang Paper Co. Ltd.
Gunpo Mill
Gunpo-si, Gyeonggi-do, South Korea

Daio Paper Corp.
Kani Mill
Kani-shi, Gifu Pref., Japan

Daio Paper Corp.
Mishima Mill
Shikokuchuo-shi, Ehime Pref., Japan

DamaPel Comércio de Papéis Ltda
Guarulhos Mill
Guarulhos, São Paulo, Brazil

Deerfield Tissue, LLC
Augusta Mill
Augusta, Georgia, United States

Delicarta SpA
Monfalcone Mill
Monfalcone, Gorizia, Italy

Delicarta SpA
Porcari Mill
Porcari, Lucca, Italy

Delicarta SpA
Valdottavo Mill
Valdottavo di Borgo a Mozzano, Lucca, Italy

Delipapier GmbH
Arneburg Mill
Arneburg, Saxony-Anhalt, Germany

Delipapier S.A.S.
Frouard Mill
Frouard, France

Delipapier S.A.S.
Roanne Mill
Roanne Cédex, France

Delitissue Sp. z.o.o.
Ciechanow Mill
Ciechanow, Poland

Diana Paper
Tien Du Mill
Tien Du, Bac Ninh Province, Vietnam

DICEPA Papelera de Enate S.L.
Enate Mill
Enate, Huesca, Spain

Dinatex Ltd. Co.
Adra Mill
Adra, Syria

Disley Tissue Ltd.
Disley Mill
Disley, North Stockport, Cheshire, United Kingdom

Dnepropetrovsk Paper Mill, Ltd.
Dnepropetrovsk Mill
Dnepropetrovsk, Ukraine

Doh-Ei Paper Mfg. Co., Ltd.
Fuji Mill
Fuji-shi, Shizuoka Pref., Japan

Doh-Ei Paper Mfg. Co., Ltd.
Hokkaido Mill
Abuta-gun, Hokkaido Pref., Japan

Drenik A.D.
Belgrade Mill
Belgrade, Serbia

Durga Paper Mills
Kathua Mill
Kathua, Jammu and Kashmir, India

E-papertech Co. Ltd.
Yesan-gun Mill
Yesan-gun, Chungcheongnam-do, South Korea

Egoli Tissue Mill (Pty) Ltd.
Heidelberg Mill
Heidelberg, Gauteng, South Africa

Ehime Paper Mfg. Co., Ltd.
Shikokuchuo-shi Mill
Shikokuchuo-shi, Ehime Pref., Japan

EKA Industrial Paper Production Limited
Izmit Mill
Kosekoy, Izmit, Kocaeli, Turkey

Elikon
Murygino Mill
Murygino, Kirovskaya Obl., Russia

Elpap
Krakow Mill
Krakow, Poland

Encore Tissue
Laverton North Mill
Laverton North, Victoria, Australia

Tissue

Eng Fong Paper Co., Ltd.
Yuanlin Mill
Yuanlin, Changhua County, Taiwan

Epesok Paper Mills Ltd.
Oshodi, Lagos Mill
Ikeja, Lagos, Lagos State, Nigeria

Erving Paper Mills Inc.
Erving Mill
Erving, Massachusetts, United States

Estrela Indústria de Papel Ltda.
Palmas Mill
Palmas, Paraná, Brazil

Eurocartiera
Pietramelara Mill
Pietramelara, Caserta, Italy

Fábrica de Bolsas de Papel UNIBOL SA
Soledad Mill
Soledad, Atlántico, Colombia

Fábrica de Papel San Francisco S.A. de C.V. (FAPSA)
Mexicali Mill
Mexicali, Baja California Norte, Mexico

Fábrica de Papel Santa Therezinha (SANTHER)
Fadlo Haidar Mill
Bragança Paulista, São Paulo, Brazil

Fábrica de Papel Santa Therezinha (SANTHER)
Governador Valadares Unit
Capim, Governador Valadares, Minas Gerais, Brazil

Fábrica de Papel Santa Therezinha (SANTHER)
Guaíba Mill
Guaíba, Rio Grande do Sul, Brazil

Fábrica de Papel Santa Therezinha (SANTHER)
Penha Mill
São Paulo, São Paulo, Brazil

Fábricas de Papel Potosí, S.A. de C.V.
Potosí Mill
San Luis Potosí, San Luis Potosí, Mexico

Fabryka Papieru Czerwonak Sp. z o.o.
Czerwonak Mill
Czerwonak, Poland

Fabryka Papieru i Tektury "BESKIDY" S.A.
Wadowice Mill
Wadowice, Poland

Fabryka Papieru Kaczory Sp. z o.o.
Kaczory Mill
Kaczory, Poland

Fabryka Papieru Kaczory Sp. z o.o.
Margonin Mill
Margonin, Poland

FACEPA - Fábrica de Papel da Amazônia S.A.
Belém Mill
Belem, Pará, Brazil

FAPAJAL - Fábrica de Papel de Tojal S.A.
São Julião do Tojal Mill
São Julião do Tojal, Portugal

FE "Myuniks" LLC
Minsk Mill
Smolevichi, Minsk region, Minskaya obl., Belarus

Fibrocellulosa S.p.A
Bagni di Lucca Mill
Bagni di Lucca, Lucca, Italy

Firma "W. Lewandowski" P.H.U.
Wloclawek Mill
Wloclawek, Poland

First A One Trade and Invest 11 Pty Ltd.
Garankuwa Mill
Garankuwa, Gauteng, South Africa

First Quality Tissue LLC
Anderson Mill
Anderson, South Carolina, United States

First Quality Tissue LLC
Lock Haven Mill
Lock Haven, Pennsylvania, United States

Flower City Tissue Mills Co.
Rochester Mill
Rochester, New York, United States

Fourstones Paper Mill Co. Ltd.
Sapphire Mills
Leslie, Scotland, United Kingdom

Fourstones Paper Mill Co. Ltd.
South Tyne Mill
Hexham, Northumberland, United Kingdom

FPHU "Filar" Sp. Jawna
Sadlno Mill
Sadlno, Gm Wierzbinek, Poland

Fripa Papierfabrik Albert Friedrich KG
Miltenberg Mill
Miltenberg, Germany

Fujian Annuo Paper (Fujian) Co., Ltd.
Fuding Mill
Fuding, Fujian, China

Fujian HengAn (China) Paper Co., Ltd.
Jinjiang Mill
Jinjiang, Fujian, China

Fujian Jian'ou Hengfeng Paper Co., Ltd.
Jian'ou Mill
Jian'ou, Fujian, China

Fujian Nan'an Hengli Paper Products Co., Ltd.
Nanan Mill
Nanan, Fujian, China

Fujian Nanyang Paper Co., Ltd.
Fuding Mill
Fuding, Fujian, China

Fujian Youlanfa Group
Jinjiang Mill
Jinjiang, Fujian, China

Fujieda Seishi Co. Ltd.
Fujieda-shi Mill
Fujieda-shi, Shizuoka Pref., Japan

Fukuda Paper Manufacturing Co., Ltd.
Iyomishima Mill
Shikokuchuo-shi, Ehime Pref., Japan

G.F.F - Nikopol AD
Nikopol Mill
Cherkvitsa, Nikopol, Bulgaria

Gênesis Papéis
Videira Mill
Videira, Santa Catarina, Brazil

Georgia-Pacific LLC
Broadway Street/West Mill
Green Bay, Wisconsin, United States

Georgia-Pacific LLC
Camas Mill
Camas, Washington, United States

Georgia-Pacific LLC
Crossett Mill
Crossett, Arkansas, United States

Georgia-Pacific LLC
Day Street/East Mill
Green Bay, Wisconsin, United States

Georgia-Pacific LLC
Halsey Mill
Halsey, Oregon, United States

Georgia-Pacific LLC
Muskogee Mill
Muskogee, Oklahoma, United States

Georgia-Pacific LLC
Naheola Mill
Pennington, Alabama, United States

Georgia-Pacific LLC
Palatka Mill
Palatka, Florida, United States

Georgia-Pacific LLC
Plattsburgh Mill
Plattsburgh, New York, United States

Georgia-Pacific LLC
Port Hudson Mill
Zachary, Louisiana, United States

Georgia-Pacific LLC
Savannah River Mill
Rincon, Georgia, United States

Georgia-Pacific LLC
Wauna Mill
Clatskanie, Oregon, United States

Globe Paper Mills
Keng Hua Mill
Malabon, Metro Manila, Philippines

Glucholaskie Zaklady Papiernicze Sp. z o.o.
Glucholazy Mill
Glucholazy, Poland

Glucholaskie Zaklady Papiernicze Sp. z o.o.
Niedomice Mill
Niedomice, Poland

Gold Hongye Paper (Hubei)
Xiaogan (Gold Hongye Paper) Mill
Xiaogan, Hubei, China

Gold Hongye Paper (Suzhou Industrial Park) Co., Ltd.
Suzhou (Gold Hongye Paper) Mill
Suzhou, Jiangsu, China

Tissue

Gomà-Camps S.A.U.
La Riba Mill
La Riba, Tarragona, Spain

Gorlovskaya Paper Mill 000
Gorlovka Mill
Gorlovka, Ukraine

Grand Bay Paper Products Ltd
Arima Mill
Arima, Trinidad and Tobago

Great Lakes Tissue Co.
Cheboygan Mill
Cheboygan, Michigan, United States

Green Papertech
Daejeon Mill
Daejeon-si, Daejeon, South Korea

Grupo Papelero Scribe, S.A. de C.V.
Naucalpan Mill
Naucalpan de Juarez, Edo. de México, Mexico

Guangdong Dongguan Baojian Paper Co., Ltd.
Dongguan Mill
Dongguan, Guangdong, China

Guangdong Dongguan White Swan Paper Co., Ltd.
Dongguan Mill
Dongguan, Guangdong, China

Guangdong Dongguan Yongchang Paper Co., Ltd.
Dongguan Mill
Dongguan, Guangdong, China

Guangdong Foshan Gaoming Super Trans Paper Co., Ltd.
Foshan Mill
Foshan, Guangdong, China

Guangdong Guangzhou Panyu Lianhuashan Paper-Making Co., Ltd.
Guangzhou Mill
Guangzhou, Guangdong, China

Guangdong Guangzhou Smile Daily Necessities Co., Ltd.
Guangzhou Mill
Guangzhou, Guangdong, China

Guangdong Huizhou Fook Woo Paper Co., Ltd.
Huizhou Mill
Huizhou, Guangdong, China

Guangdong Jiangmen City Xinlong Paper Co., Ltd.
Jiangmen Mill
Jiangmen, Guangdong, China

Guangdong Jiangmen Renke Lvzhou Paper Industry Co., Ltd.
Jiangmen Mill
Jiangmen, Guangdong, China

Guangdong Jieyang City Xinda Paper Co., Ltd.
Jieyang Mill
Jieyang, Guangdong, China

Guangdong Vinda Paper (Guangdong) Co., Ltd.
Xinhui Mill
Xinhui, Guangdong, China

Guangdong Vinda Paper (Jiangmen) Co., Ltd.
Jiangmen Mill
Jiangmen, Guangdong, China

Guangdong Vinda Paper Co., Ltd.
Sanjiang Mill
Jiangmen, Guangdong, China

Guangdong Zhongshan Polly Paper Manufacture Co., Ltd.
Zhongshan Mill
Zhongshan, Guangdong, China

Guangdong Zhongshan Sanjiao Paper Manufacture Co., Ltd.
Zhongshan Mill
Zhongshan, Guangdong, China

Guangdong Zhuhai Doumen Baijiao Yuanyuan Paper Manufacturing Co., Ltd.
Zhuhai Mill
Zhuhai, Guangdong, China

Guangxi Guitang (Group) Stock Co., Ltd
Guigang Mill
Guigang, Guangxi, China

Guangxi Huayi Paper Co., Ltd.
Guigang Mill
Guigang, Guangxi, China

Guangxi Hwagain Group
Nanning Mill
Nanning, Guangxi, China

Guangxi Jeanper Paper Co., Ltd. (Jiebao Paper)
Guiping Mill
Guigang, Guangxi, China

Guangxi Laibin Donta Paper Co., Ltd.
Laibin Mill
Laibin, Guangxi, China

Guangxi Nanning Jiada Paper
Nanning Mill
Nanning, Guangxi, China

Guangxi Nanning Lianli Paper Co., Ltd
Nanning Mill
Nanning, Guangxi, China

Guangxi Nanning Phoenix Pulp & Paper Co. Ltd.
Nanning Mill
Nanning, Guangxi, China

Guangxi Nanning Tianran Paper Co., Ltd.
Nanning Mill
Nanning, Guangxi, China

Guangxi Tianlin County Lisen Paper Co., Ltd.
Baise Mill
Baise, Guangxi, China

Guangxi Tianyang Huamei Paper Co., Lt.d
Tianyang Mill
Baise, Guangxi, China

Guangxi Xiangzhou Liangui Paper Co., Ltd.
Laibin Mill
Laibin, Guangxi, China

Gulf Paper Industries Factory
Riyadh Mill
Riyadh, Saudi Arabia

Gulf Paper Mfg. Co. k.s.c.
Kuwait Mill
West Mina Abdulla, Ahmadi Governorate, Kuwait

Hai Ming Paper Mills Sdn Bhd
Kota Samarahan Mill
Kota Samarahan, Sarawak, Borneo, Malaysia

Hai Phong Paper Joint-Stock Co. (Hapaco)
Hai Phong City Mill
Hai Phong City, Vietnam

Hainan Gold Hongye Paper Co., Ltd.
Yangpu (Gold Hongye Paper) Mill
Haikou, Hainan, China

Hainan Gold Shengpu Paper Co., Ltd.
Haikou (Gold Shengpu Paper) Mill
Haikou, Hainan, China

Hanke Tissue Spólka z o.o.
Kostrzyn Mill
Kostrzyn, Poland

Harir Khuzestan Tissue Co.
Haft-Tappeh, Shoosh Mill
Haft-Tappeh, Shoosh, Khuzestan, Iran

Hayat Kimya A.S.
Mersin Mill
Mersin, Turkey

Hayat Kimya A.S.
Yeniköy (Kocaeli) Mill
Yeniköy, Izmit, Kocaeli, Turkey

Hayat Kimya A.S.
Zencan Mill
Zencan, Iran

Hebei Baoding Chenguang Paper Co., Ltd.
Baoding Mill
Baoding, Hebei, China

Hebei Baoding Dongsheng Hygiene Products Co., Ltd.
Baoding Mill
Baoding, Hebei, China

Hebei Baoding Gangxing Paper Co., Ltd.
Baoding Mill
Baoding, Hebei, China

Hebei Baoding Hengfa Paper Co., Ltd.
Baoding Mill
Baoding, Hebei, China

Hebei Baoding Hengtai Paper Co., Ltd.
Baoding Mill
Baoding, Hebei, China

Tissue

Hebei Baoding Mancheng Donggou Paper Mill
Baoding Mill
Baoding, Hebei, China

Hebei Baoding Mancheng Fukang Paper Co., Ltd.
Baoding Mill
Baoding, Hebei, China

Hebei Baoding Mancheng Guanquan Paper Co., Ltd.
Baoding Mill
Baoding, Hebei, China

Hebei Baoding Mancheng Huifeng Paper Co., Ltd.
Baoding Mill
Baoding, Hebei, China

Hebei Baoding Mancheng Jifa Paper Co., Ltd.
Baoding Mill
Baoding, Hebei, China

Hebei Baoding Mancheng Lida Paper Mill
Baoding Mill
Baoding, Hebei, China

Hebei Baoding Mancheng Yikang Paper Co., Ltd.
Baoding Mill
Baoding, Hebei, China

Hebei Baoding Mancheng Yongxing Paper Mill
Baoding Mill
Baoding, Hebei, China

Hebei Baoding Mancheng Yuexing Paper Mill
Baoding Mill
Baoding, Hebei, China

Hebei Baoding No. 5 Paper Mill
Baoding Mill
Baoding, Hebei, China

Hebei Baoding Ruifeng Paper Co., Ltd.
Baoding Mill
Baoding, Hebei, China

Hebei Baoding Xinghua Paper Mill
Baoding Mill
Baoding, Hebei, China

Hebei Daiyu Paper Co., Ltd.
Xingtai Mill
Xingtai, Hebei, China

Hebei Linhai Paper Co., Ltd.
Baoding Mill
Baoding, Hebei, China

Hebei Mancheng Changfa Paper Co., Ltd.
Baoding Mill
Baoding, Hebei, China

Hebei Mancheng Chenggong Paper Co., Ltd.
Baoding Mill
Baoding, Hebei, China

Hebei Mancheng Chengxin Paper Co., Ltd.
Baoding Mill
Baoding, Hebei, China

Hebei Mancheng Hongda Paper Co., Ltd.
Baoding Mill
Baoding, Hebei, China

Hebei Mancheng Hongsheng Paper Co., Ltd.
Baoding Mill
Baoding, Hebei, China

Hebei Mancheng Jinguang Paper Co., Ltd.
Baoding Mill
Baoding, Hebei, China

Hebei Mancheng Shunli Paper Co., Ltd.
Baoding Mill
Baoding, Hebei, China

Hebei Mancheng Yiyuan Paper Mill
Baoding Mill
Baoding, Hebei, China

Hebei Mancheng Yongfa Paper Co., Ltd.
Baoding Mill
Baoding, Hebei, China

Hebei Sanhe City Jingdong Shuhe Paper Mill
Sanhe Mill
Sanhe, Hebei, China

Hebei Sanhe City Youyi Paper Mill
Sanhe Mill
Sanhe, Hebei, China

Hebei Sanhe Xingwang Paper Mill
Sanhe Mill
Sanhe, Hebei, China

Hebei Sanhe Yangzhuang Dawotou Paper Mill
Sanhe Mill
Sanhe, Hebei, China

Hebei Sanhe Yanling Paper Mill
Sanhe Mill
Sanhe, Hebei, China

Hebei Sanhe Zhaotuzhuang Aimin Paper Mill
Sanhe Mill
Sanhe, Hebei, China

Hebei Tangshan Boda Paper Mill Co., Ltd.
Thangshan Mill
Thangshan, Hebei, China

Hebei Xiaorenguo Paper Co., Ltd.
Baoding Mill
Baoding, Hebei, China

Hebei Xuesong Paper Co., Ltd.
Baoding Mill
Baoding, Hebei, China

Hebei Yaguang Paper Co., Ltd.
Baoding Mill
Baoding, Hebei, China

Hebei Zhongxin Paper Co., Ltd.
Baoding Mill
Baoding, Hebei, China

Heilongjiang Kaifeng Paper Produce Co., Ltd.
Daqing Mill
Daqing, Heilongjiang, China

Heilongjiang Xinhua Hygiene & Specialty Paper Co., Ltd.
Acheng Mill
Acheng, Heilongjiang, China

Henan Hulijia Industry Co. Ltd.
Zhoukou Mill
Zhoukou, Henan, China

Henan Luohe Yinge Tissue Paper Industry Co., Ltd.
Luohe (Yinge Tissue) Mill
Luohe, Henan, China

Henan Puyang City Tongyu Paper Co., Ltd.
Puyang Mill
Puyang, Henan, China

Henan Xinxiang Xinya Paper Group Co., Ltd.
Xinxiang No. 3 Mill
Xinxiang, Henan, China

Henan Xinxiang Xinya Paper Group Co., Ltd.
Xinxiang No. 4 Mill
Xinxiang, Henan, China

Henan Xinxiang Xinya Paper Group Co., Ltd.
Xinxiang No. 5 Mill
Xinxiang, Henan, China

Henan Xinxiang Xinya Paper Group Co., Ltd.
Xinxiang No. 6 Mill
Xinxiang, Henan, China

Henan Yuzhou Shengxuan Paper Co., Ltd.
Yuzhou Mill
Yuzhou, Henan, China

Henan Zhengzhou Dongsheng Paper Co., Ltd.
Zhengzhou Mill
Zhengzhou, Henan, China

Higi Papersoft Co. Ltd.
Szolnok Mill
Szolnok, Hungary

Hogla-Kimberly Ltd.
Hadera Mill
Hadera, Israel

Hogla-Kimberly Ltd.
Naharya Mill
Naharya, Israel

Hubei Enshi Jinhua Group
Enshi Mill
Enshi, Hubei, China

Hubei Jingzhou Zhiyin Paper
Jingzhou Mill
Jingzhou, Hubei, China

Tissue

Hubei Vinda Paper (Hubei) Co., Ltd.
Xiaogan Mill
Xiaogan, Hubei, China

Hubei Wuhan Chenming Paper Co. Ltd.
Wuhan (Wuhan Chenming Hanyang Paper No. 2 Mill) Mill
Wuhan, Hubei, China

Hunan Changde HengAn Paper Co., Ltd.
Changde Mill
Changde, Hunan, China

Hunan Jingtianren Paper Co., Ltd.
Yueyang Mill
Yueyang, Hunan, China

Hygienic Tissue Mills
Pietermaritzburg Mill
Pietermaritzburg, Natal, South Africa

Ibertissue S.L.U.
Buñuel Mill
Buñuel, Navarra, Spain

ICT France SAS
Montargis Mill
Pannes, Montargis, Loiret, France

ICT Ibérica, S.L.U
El Burgo de Ebro Mill
El Burgo de Ebro, Zaragoza, Spain

ICT Italy
Piano della Rocca Mill
Borgo a Mozzano, Lucca, Italy

ICT Italy
Piano di Coreglia Mill
Piano di Coreglia, Lucca, Italy

ICT Poland Sp. z o.o.
Kostrzyn Mill
Kostrzyn, Poland

Ideal Cart SpA
Sermoneta Mill
Sermoneta, Latina, Italy

Industria Cartaria Fenili S.p.A.
Coselli Capannori Mill
Coselli Capannori, Lucca, Italy

Indústria de Papéis União
São Paulo Mill
São Paulo, São Paulo, Brazil

Indústria de Papel Dopel
Indaial Mill
Indaial, Santa Catarina, Brazil

Indústria de Papel Guará Ltda.
Guaratinguetá Mill
Guaratinguetá, São Paulo, Brazil

Indústria de Papel Irapuru Ltda.
Ribeirão Preto Mill
Ribeirão Preto, São Paulo, Brazil

Indústria de Papel Sovel da Amazônia Ltda.
Manaus Mill
Manaus, Amazonas, Brazil

Industrias Cartonera Asociada S.A. - INCASA
Quito Mill
Quito, Pichincha, Ecuador

INPOPEL - Indústrias Podolan de Papel Ltda.
Pitanga Mill
Pitanga, Paraná, Brazil

Interstate Paper Industries
Sadat City Mill
Sadat City, Menofeya, Egypt

Intertissue Ltd.
Port Talbot Mill
Briton Ferry, Neath, Wales, United Kingdom

Ipasa Indústria de Papel Apucarana S.A.
Apucarana Mill
Apucarana, Paraná, Brazil

Ipek Kagit San. ve Tic. A.S.
Karamürsel Mill
Yalova, Turkey

IPEL - Indaial Papel Embalagens Ltda.
Indaial Mill
Indaial, Santa Catarina, Brazil

IPELSA - Indústria de Celulose e Papel da Paraíba
Campina Grande Mill
Campina Grande, Paraíba, Brazil

Irving Tissue Inc.
Fort Edward Mill
Fort Edward, New York, United States

Irving Tissue Inc.
Saint John Mill
Saint John, New Brunswick, Canada

Irving Tissue Inc.
Toronto Mill
Toronto, Ontario, Canada

Isma 2000 (Ismaeco Group)
Marratxi Mill
Marratxi, Spain

IsraPaper Paper Industries Ltd.
Netanya Mill
Netanya, Israel

ITC Limited, Paperboards & Specialty Papers Division
Tribeni Mill
Chandrahati, Hooghly, West Bengal, India

Itoman Co., Ltd.
Kawanoe Mill
Shikokuchuo-shi, Ehime Pref., Japan

Jack-Pol Sp. z o.o.
Olawa Mill
Olawa, Poland

Janjirker Paper Mill (Pty) Ltd
Bellville Mill
Bellville, Cape Town, South Africa

Jerusalem White Paper & Neeman (2000) Ltd
Kiryat Gat Mill
Kiryat Gat, Israel

Jiangsu Jinlian Paper Co.
HuaiAn Mill
HuaiAn, Jiangsu, China

Jiangsu Oji Paper Nepia (Suzhou) Co., Ltd.
Suzhou Mill
Suzhou, Jiangsu, China

Jiangsu Yuen Foong Yu Paper (Kunshan) Co. Ltd.
Kunshan Mill
Kunshan, Jiangsu, China

Jiangsu Yuen Foong Yu Paper (Yangzhou) Co., Ltd.
Yangzhou Mill
Yangzhou, Jiangsu, China

Jiangxi Ganzhou Hwagain Paper Co., Ltd
Ganzhou Mill
Ganzhou, Jiangxi, China

Jilin Zhenlai Xinsheng Paper Co., Ltd.
Baicheng Mill
Baicheng, Jilin, China

Jin Diing Co Ltd.
Hsin Ying Mill
Hsinying District, Tainan City, Taiwan

JSC 'Kondrovskaya Paper company'
Kondrovskaya Paper Company Mill
Kondrovo, Kaluga Region, Russia

JSC Grigiskes
Vilnius Mill
Vilnius, Lithuania

Juei Fong Paper Co., Ltd.
Pi Tou Mill
Be Tou, Changhua County, Taiwan

Juei Fong Paper Co., Ltd.
Pu Shin Mill
Pu Hsin, Changhua County, Taiwan

K.T.G. (USA) L.P.
Memphis Mill
Memphis, Tennessee, United States

K.Z.N. Tissue
Pietermaritzburg Mill
Pietermaritzburg, KwaZulu-Natal, South Africa

Karina Trading PLC
Almaty Mill
Almaty, Almaty Obl., Kazakhstan

Kartogroup España S.L.
Castellòn Mill
Burriana, Castellòn, Spain

Kasuga Seishi Kogyo Co., Ltd.
Fuji-shi Mill
Fuji-shi, Shizuoka Pref., Japan

KBK Ltd
Tuymazy Mill
Tuymazy, Respublika Bashkortostan, Russia

Kiev Cardboard and Paper Mill
Kiev Cardboard and Paper Mill
Obukhiv, Kyivska obl., Ukraine

Tissue

Kimberly Bolivia S.A.
Santa Cruz Mill
Santa Cruz de la Sierra, Bolivia

Kimberly-Clark Australia Pty Ltd.
Millicent Mill
Millicent, South Australia, Australia

Kimberly-Clark Brasil Ind. e Com. de Produtos de Higiene Ltda.
Correia Pinto Mill
Correia Pinto, Santa Catarina, Brazil

Kimberly-Clark Brasil Ind. e Com. de Produtos de Higiene Ltda.
Mogi das Cruzes Mill
Mogi das Cruzes, São Paulo, Brazil

Kimberly-Clark Corp.
Beech Island Mill
Beech Island, South Carolina, United States

Kimberly-Clark Corp.
Chester Mill
Chester, Pennsylvania, United States

Kimberly-Clark Corp.
Fullerton Mill
Fullerton, California, United States

Kimberly-Clark Corp.
Jenks Mill
Jenks, Oklahoma, United States

Kimberly-Clark Corp.
Loudon Mill
Loudon, Tennessee, United States

Kimberly-Clark Corp.
Marinette Mill
Marinette, Wisconsin, United States

Kimberly-Clark Corp.
Mobile Mill
Mobile, Alabama, United States

Kimberly-Clark Corp.
New Milford Mill
New Milford, Connecticut, United States

Kimberly-Clark Corp.
Owensboro Mill
Owensboro, Kentucky, United States

Kimberly-Clark Costa Rica, SA
San José Mill
San José, Costa Rica

Kimberly-Clark de Centroamérica S.A.
Sitio Del Nino Mill
Sitio Del Nino, La Libertad, El Salvador

Kimberly-Clark de México S.A. de C.V.
Bajio Mill
San Juan del Rio, Querétaro, Mexico

Kimberly-Clark de México S.A. de C.V.
Cepamisa
Morelia, Michoacán, Mexico

Kimberly-Clark de México S.A. de C.V.
Ecatepec Mill
Ecatepec de Morelos, Edo. de México, Mexico

Kimberly-Clark de México S.A. de C.V.
Orizaba Mill
Orizaba, Veracruz, Mexico

Kimberly-Clark de México S.A. de C.V.
Ramos Arizpe Mill
Ramos Arizpe, Coahuila, Mexico

Kimberly-Clark de México S.A. de C.V.
San Martin Texmelucan Mill
San Martin Texmelucan, Puebla, Mexico

Kimberly-Clark GmbH
Koblenz Mill
Koblenz, Germany

Kimberly-Clark GmbH
Niederbipp Mill
Niederbipp, Switzerland

Kimberly-Clark Ltd.
Barrow-in-Furness Mill
Barrow-in-Furness, Cumbria, United Kingdom

Kimberly-Clark Ltd.
Coleshill Mill
Flint, United Kingdom

Kimberly-Clark Ltd.
Delyn Mill
Flint, United Kingdom

Kimberly-Clark Ltd.
Northfleet Mill
Northfleet, Gravesend, Kent, United Kingdom

Kimberly-Clark of Canada
Huntsville Mill
Huntsville, Ontario, Canada

Kimberly-Clark of SA (Pty) Ltd.
Enstra Mill
Springs, Gauteng, South Africa

Kimberly-Clark Peru S.A.
Puente de Piedra Mill
Santiago de Surco, Lima, Peru

Kimberly-Clark Products (Malaysia) Sdn. Bhd.
Kluang Mill
Kluang, Johor Darul Takzim, Malaysia

Kimberly-Clark S.A.
Bernal Mill
Bernal, Buenos Aires, Argentina

Kimberly-Clark S.A.
Salamanca Mill
Doñinos, Salamanca, Spain

Kimberly-Clark SAS
Sotteville-les-Rouen Mill
Sotteville-les-Rouen, France

Kimberly-Clark SNC
Toul Mill
Toul, France

Kimberly-Clark Srl
Alanno Scalo Mill
Alanno Scalo, Pescara, Italy

Kimberly-Clark Srl
Romagnano Sesia Mill
Romagnano Sesia, Novara, Italy

Kimberly-Clark Taiwan
Chungli Mill
Hsin Wu, Taoyuan County, Taiwan

Kimberly-Clark Taiwan
Hsinying Mill
Hsinying, Tainan City, Taiwan

Kimberly-Clark Taiwan
Tayuan Mill
Tayuan, Taoyuan County, Taiwan

Kimberly-Clark Thailand Ltd.
Pathumthani Mill
Amphur Muang, Pathumthani, Thailand

Kimberly-Clark Thailand Ltd.
Samut Prakan Mill
Amphur Phrapradaeng, Samut Prakarn, Thailand

Kimberly-Clark Venezuela, C.A.
Maracay Mill
Maracay, Edo. Aragua, Venezuela

Kitakami Hitec Paper Corp.
Kitakami-shi Mill
Kitakami-shi, Iwate Pref., Japan

KleanNara Co., Ltd.
Chongju Mill
Cheongwon-gun, Chungcheongbuk-do, South Korea

Komotini Papermill SA - Elina
Elina Mill
Komotini, Greece

Kostenez-HHI PLC
Kostenez Mill
Kostenez, Bulgaria

Kotobuki Paper Co. Ltd.
Saga Mill
Ogi-shi, Saga Pref., Japan

Koyo Paper Mfg. Co., Ltd.
Honsha Mill
Fuji-shi, Shizuoka Pref., Japan

KPM Kadoma Paper Mills
Kadoma Mill
Kadoma, Zimbabwe

Kruger Products L.P.
Crabtree Mill
Crabtree, Quebec, Canada

Kruger Products L.P.
Gatineau Mill
Gatineau, Quebec, Canada

Kruger Products L.P.
Lennoxville Mill
Sherbrooke, Quebec, Canada

Kruger Products L.P.
New Westminster Mill
New Westminster, British Columbia, Canada

Krymbumaga
Simferopol Mill
Simferopol, Ukraine

Kyrgyz-Chinese Paper Mill
Chuj-Tokmok Mill
Chuj-Tokmok, Chujskaya Obl., Kyrgyzstan

Lalskaya Paper Mill
Lalsk Mill
Lalsk, Kirovskaya Obl., Russia

Lamix
Witnica Mill
Witnica, Poland

Tissue

Latif Paper Products Co.
Hashtgerd Mill
Hashtgerd, Markazi, Iran

LC Paper 1881, S.A.
Besalú Mill
Besalú, Girona, Spain

Lepenka
Trzic Mill
Trzic, Slovenia

Levent Kağit San. ve TIC. A.S
Izmir Mill
Izmir, Izmir, Turkey

Liaoning Dandong Fengcheng Dongfeng Paper Co., Ltd.
Fengcheng Mill
Fengcheng, Liaoning, China

Liaoning Dandong Hengyao Paper Co., Ltd.
Fengcheng Mill
Fengcheng, Liaoning, China

Liaoning Hupo Paper
Fushun Mill
Fushun, Liaoning, China

Liaoning Jincheng Paper Jinbao Paper Co., Ltd.
Linghai Mill
Linghai, Liaoning, China

Liaoning Jinzhou Jinri Paper Co., Ltd.
Linhai Mill
Linhai, Liaoning, China

Liaoning Jinzhou Nuerhe Paper Co., Ltd.
Jinzhou Mill
Jinzhou, Liaoning, China

Liaoning Shangyang Paper Co., Ltd.
Tieling Mill
Tieling, Liaoning, China

Liaoning Tieling Qinghe Gangxing Paper Co., Ltd.
Tieling Mill
Tieling, Liaoning, China

Liaoning Xingqi Paper Co., Ltd.
Liaoyang Mill
Liaoyang, Liaoning, China

Liberty Paper Mill, Inc.
Malinta Mill
Valenzuela, Bulacan, Philippines

Ligia Paper Industries
Welkom Mill
Welkom, Orange Free State, South Africa

Lila Kagit San. ve Tic. A.S.
Çorlu-Takrdad Mill
Çorlu-Takrdad, Tekirdag, Turkey

Lincoln Paper and Tissue, LLC
Lincoln Mill
Lincoln, Maine, United States

Linh Xuan Paper Joint-Stock Co.
Ho Chi Minh City Mill
Thu Duc District, Ho Chi Minh City, Binh Duong Province, Vietnam

LLC Pulp Invest
Kazan Mill
Kazan, Tatarstan Republic, Russia

Lua Viet Paper Joint-Stock Co.
Ha Hoa District Mill
Ha Hoa District, Phú Tho Province, Vietnam

Lucart France SAS
Troyes Mill
La Rivière de Corps, France

Lucart SpA
Castelnuovo Mill
Castelnuovo di Garfagnana, Lucca, Italy

Lucart SpA
Diecimo Mill
Diecimo, Lucca, Italy

Lucart SpA
Porcari Mill
Porcari, Lucca, Italy

Lvivkartonplast
Lviv Mill
Lviv, Ukraine

Madhupaper Kenya Ltd.
Madhupaper Mill
Nairobi, Kenya

Mai Lan Paper Joint-Stock Company
Tan Binh Mill
Tan Binh, Ho Chi Minh City, Vietnam

Manikraft Guaianazes Ind. de Celulose e Papel Ltda.
Guaianazes Mill
Guaianazes, São Paulo, Brazil

Manufacturas de Papel CA (MANPA) S.A.C.A.
Maracay Tissue Mill
Maracay, Edo. Aragua, Venezuela

Marlboro Paper Inc.
Drummondville Mill
Drummondville, Quebec, Canada

Marusan Paper Corparation
Shikokuchuo-shi Mill
Shikokuchuo-shi, Ehime Pref., Japan

Marutomi Paper Mfg. Co., Ltd.
Fujine Mill
Fuji-shi, Shizuoka Pref., Japan

Marutomi Paper Mfg. Co., Ltd.
Imaizumi Mill
Fuji-shi, Shizuoka Pref., Japan

Marutomi Paper Mfg. Co., Ltd.
Numazu Mill
Numazu-shi, Shizuoka Pref., Japan

Max Fortune (FZ) Paper Products
Fuzhou Mill
Fuzhou, Fujian, China

MC Tissue SpA
Tassignano Mill
Tassignano/Capannori, Lucca, Italy

Mediterranean Paper Mills (MPM)
Lattakia Mill
Jableh, Lattakia, Syria

Mediterranean Tissue Company
Alexandria Mill
Alexandria, Iskanderiya, Egypt

Mei Ho Paper Mfg. Co., Ltd.
Ho Mei Mill
Ho Mei, Changhua County, Taiwan

Meiji Seishi Co., Ltd.
Takaoka Mill
Fuji-shi, Shizuoka Pref., Japan

Melhoramentos Papéis Ltda.
Caieiras Mill
Caieiras, São Paulo, Brazil

Melhoramentos Papéis Ltda.
Mogi das Cruzes Mill
Mogi das Cruzes, São Paulo, Brazil

Metro Paper Industries Tissue Group Ltd.
Portneuf Mill
Portneuf, Quebec, Canada

Metsä Tissue AB
Katrinefors Mill
Mariestad, Sweden

Metsä Tissue AB
Nyboholm Mill (Småland Mills)
Kvillsfors, Sweden

Metsä Tissue AB
Paulistr̈om Mill (Småland Mills)
Paulistr̈om, Sweden

Metsä Tissue Corp.
Mänttä Mill
Mänttä, Finland

Metsä Tissue GmbH
Kreuzau Mill
Kreuzau, Germany

Metsä Tissue GmbH
Raubach Mill
Raubach, Germany

Metsä Tissue GmbH
Stotzheim Mill
Euskirchen-Stotzheim, Germany

Metsä Tissue S.A.
Krapkowice Mill
Krapkowice, Poland

Metsä Tissue Slovakia s.r.o.
Žilina (Tento) Mill
Žilina, Slovakia

Mili S.A.
Tres Barras Mill
Tres Barras, Santa Catarina, Brazil

Millenium Paper Mill
Sokhna, Zarqa Mill
Sokhna, Zarqa, Jordan

Mimosa Sanitary Paper
Kaa El Rim. Bekaa Mill
Kaa El Rim. Bekaa, Lebanon

Mirae Paper Co., Ltd.
Jeonju Mill
Jeonju-si, Jeollabuk-do, South Korea

Tissue

Mokvynska Paper Mill, Ltd.
Mokvyn Mill
Mokvyn, Ukraine

Monalisa Co., Ltd.
Jeonju Mill
Jeonju-si, Jeollabuk-do, South Korea

Naberezhnye Chelny Paper & Board Mill
Naberezhnye Chelny Mill
Naberezhnye Chelny, Tatarstan Republic, Russia

Nampak Tissue (Pty) Ltd.
Bellville Mill
Bellville South, Cape Town, South Africa

Nampak Tissue (Pty) Ltd.
Durban Mill
Verulam, Riverview, KwaZulu-Natal, South Africa

Nampak Tissue (Pty) Ltd.
Kliprivier Mill
Kliprivier, Gauteng, South Africa

Natural - Indústria de Papel, Lda.
Povolide (Viseu) Mill
Povolide, Viseu, Portugal

Nefertiti Paper Co. Ltd
10th of Ramadan City Mill
10th of Ramadan City, Sharkeya, East Province, Egypt

New Toyo Pulppy (Vietnam) Co., Ltd.
Thuan An District Mill
Thuan An District, Binh Duong Province, Vietnam

Nibong Tebal Paper Mills Sdn. Bhd. (NTPM)
Seberang Prai Sel Mill
Nibong Tebal, Seberang Prai Sel, Penang, Malaysia

Niko Seishi Co., Ltd.
Honsha Mill
Ihara-gun, Shizuoka Pref., Japan

Ninex Paper
Beirut Mill
Beirut, Lebanon

Ningxia Kejin Xiaguang Paper Co., Ltd.
Qingtongxia Mill
Qingtongxia, Ningxia, China

Ningxia Zijinghua Paper Industry Co. Ltd.
Yinchuan Mill
Yinchuan, Ningxia, China

Nippon Paper Crecia Co., Ltd.
Kaisei Mill
Ashigarakami-gun, Kanagawa Pref., Japan

Nippon Paper Crecia Co., Ltd.
Kyoto Mill
Fukuchiyama-shi, Kyoto Pref., Japan

Nippon Paper Crecia Co., Ltd.
Tokyo Mill
Soka-shi, Saitama Pref., Japan

Nishinihon Eizai Co., Ltd.
Tatsuno-shi Mill
Tatsuno-shi, Hyogo Pref., Japan

Nisshinbo Paper Products, Inc.
Shimada Mill
Shimada-shi, Shizuoka Pref., Japan

Nittoku Co., Ltd.
Fuji-shi Mill
Fuji-shi, Shizuoka Pref., Japan

Nobrecel S.A. Celulose e Papel
Pindamonhangaba Mill
Pindamonhangaba, São Paulo, Brazil

Northwood & Wepa Limited
Llangynwyd (Bridgend) Mill
Bridgend, Wales, United Kingdom

Novatissue SAS
Novatissue Mill
Laval-sur-Vologne, France

Novzohour Co. Ltd.
Tehran Mill
Tehran, Iran

Nuova Cartiera della Toscana SpA
Villa Basilica Mill
Villa Basilica, Lucca, Italy

Nuove Cartiere di Tivoli S.R.L.
Villa Adriana Mill
Villa Adriana, Rome, Italy

OAO Kohavinska Paper Mill
Gnizdychiv Mill
Gnizdychiv, Zhydachivsky rayon, Ukraine

OAO Toshkent Qogoze
Tashkent Mill
Tashkent, Tashkentskaya obl., Uzbekistan

Oita Seishi Corporation
Buzen Mill
Buzen-shi, Fukuoka Pref., Japan

Oita Seishi Corporation
Honsha Mill
Oita-shi, Oita Pref., Japan

Oji Nepia Co., Ltd.
Nagoya Mill
Kasugai-shi, Aichi Pref., Japan

Oji Nepia Co., Ltd.
Tokushima Mill
Anan-shi, Tokushima Pref., Japan

Oji Nepia Co., Ltd.
Tomakomai Mill
Tomakomai-shi, Hokkaido Pref., Japan

Olayan Kimberly-Clark (Bahrain) W.L.L.
Isa Town Mill
Isa Town, Bahrain, Bahrain

Omer Tissue Mills (Pvt) Ltd
Lahore Mill
Lahore, Punjab, Pakistan

Omiya Seishi Co., Ltd.
Fuji Takaoka Mill
Fuji-shi, Shizuoka Pref., Japan

Omiya Seishi Co., Ltd.
Fujinomiya Mill
Fujinomiya-Shi, Shizuoka Pref., Japan

Omsk Paper Mill
Klyuchi Mill
Klyuchi, Russia

Ondunorte, Cia. de Papéis e Papelão Ondulado do Norte
Igarassu Mill
Igarassu, Pernambuco, Brazil

OOO Ametist
Chernigov Mill
Chernigov, Ukraine

OOO Bely Kamen Paper Mill
Bely Kamen Mill
Bely Kamen, Ukraine

OOO Bumy
Lyskovo Mill
Lyskovo, Nizhny Novgorod, Russia

OOO Buprom-Pokrov
Pokrov, Petushinskiy rayon Mill
Pokrov, Petushinskiy rayon, Russia

OOO First Donetsk Paper Mill
Donetsk Mill
Donetsk, Ukraine

OOO Interecoline
Kharkiv Mill
Kharkiv, Ukraine

OOO KubanPapir
Krasnodar Mill
Krasnodar, Russia

OOO Nikmas
Chelyabinsk Mill
Chelyabinsk, Russia

OOO Tissue-Bumaga
Krasnodar Mill
Krasnodar, Russia

OOO Triton-M
Tver Mill
Tver, Russia

OOO Yarovoy
Cherkassy Mill
Cherkassy, Ukraine

Orchids Paper Products Co.
Pryor Mill
Pryor, Oklahoma, United States

Orient Paper Mills
Amlai mill
Shahdol, Madhya Pradesh, India

Oriental Paper - Lanatex
Damascus Mill
Damascus, Syria

Ouro Verde Papéis e Embalagens Ltda.
Paulo Bento Mill
Paulo Bento, Rio Grande do Sul, Brazil

P.W. "APIS" S.J.
Chodecz Mill
Chodecz, Poland

Paloma-Sladkogorska Tovarna Papirja d.d. Sladki Vrh
Sladki Vrh Mill
Sladki Vrh, Slovenia

PAMER - Papelera Mercedes S.A.
Mercedes, Soriano Mill
Mercedes, Soriano, Uruguay

Tissue

Panasa, Papelera Nacional S.A.
Paramonga Mill
Paramonga, Lima, Peru

Papeco SA
Orval Mill
Orval, France

Papelera del Plata
Zárate Mill
Zárate, Buenos Aires, Argentina

Papelera Inka S.A.
Chincha Baja Mill
Chincha Baja, Chincha, ICA, Peru

Papelera Internacional SA - PAINSA
Zacapa Mill
Rio Hondo, Zacapa, Guatemala

Papelera Istmeña, S.A.
El Dorado Mill
El Dorado, Panama, Panama

Papelera Panamericana S.A.
Arequipa Mill
Arequipa, Peru

Papelera Reyes S.A.C.
Callao Mill
Callao, Lima, Peru

Papelera Samseng S.A.
Pilar Mill
Pilar, Buenos Aires, Argentina

Papelera San Andrés de Giles S.A.
San Andrés de Giles Mill
San Andrés de Giles, Buenos Aires, Argentina

Papelera Tucumán S.A.
General Pacheco, Tucuman III
General Pacheco, Buenos Aires, Argentina

Papelera Vual S.A.
Beccar Mill
Beccar, Buenos Aires, Argentina

Papelera Zarate S.A.
Lima Mill
Lima, Lima, Peru

Papeles Industriales S.A. (PISA)
Lampa Mill
Lampa, RM - Región Metro. de Santiago, Chile

Papeles Nacionales S.A.
Pereira Mill
Puente Bolívar, Pereira, Risaralda, Colombia

Papeles Regionales S.A.
Dosquebradas Mill
Dosquebradas, Risaralda, Colombia

Papeles Venezolanos CA (PAVECA)
Guacara Mill
Guacara, Edo. Carabobo, Venezuela

Paper and Pulp Industries, Pty. Ltd.
Heidelberg Mill
Heidelberg, Gauteng, South Africa

Paper Pak Industries
La Verne Mill
La Verne, California, United States

Paper Pak Industries
Washington Mill
Washington, Georgia, United States

papergroup® SpA
San Gennaro Mill
Capannori, Lucca, Italy

Papierfabriek Doetinchem BV
Doetinchem Mill
Doetinchem, Netherlands

Papierfabrik Netstal AG
Netstal Mill
Netstal, Glarus, Switzerland

Papierfabrik Nettemühle GmbH & Co. KG
Mayen Mill
Mayen, Germany

Papiernia Sieroslawice
Byczyna Mill
Byczyna, Poland

Papierwerk Sundern GmbH
Sundern Mill
Sundern, Germany

Papir-Mal
Malin Mill
Malin, Zhitomirskaya obl., Ukraine

Papirpak D. O. O. Preduzece za proizvodnju i promet papirne konfekcije
Cacak-Preljina Mill
Cacak-Preljina, Serbia

Paptol, Zaklad Produkcji Papieru Toaletowego
Kraków Mill
Kraków, Poland

Papyros Paper Mill S.A.
Papyros Mill
Katerini, Greece

Parteks Tekstil ve Kagit San Tic. Ltd. Sti.
Kayseri Mill
Kayseri, Turkey

Patras Paper Mills SA
Patras Mill
Patras, Achaia, Greece

Paul Hartmann Ges.mbH
Grimmenstein Mill
Grimmenstein, Niederösterreich, Austria

Pegant Ltd.
Nairobi Mill
Nairobi, Kenya

Pehart Tec SA Petresti
Petresti Mill
Petresti-Sebes, Romania

Peter Grant Papers Limited
Lancaster Mill
Lancaster, Lancashire, United Kingdom

Petrocart SA
Piatra Neamt Mill
Piatra Neamt, Romania

Poly Paper & Board Mills (Pvt.) Ltd.
Sheikhupura Mill
Sheikhupura, Punjab, Pakistan

PPH Izopaper Sp. z o.o.
Chelmza Mill
Chelmza, Poland

PPHU 'KARAS'
Olawa Mill
Olawa, Poland

PPHU Rolls Sp. z o.o.
Wloclawek Mill
Wloclawek, Poland

Premier Tissues India Ltd.
Mysore Mill
Bannur, Mysore, Karnataka, India

Procter & Gamble de Mexico S. de R.L. de C.V.
Apizaco Mill
Apizaco, Tlaxcala, Mexico

Procter & Gamble Paper Products Co.
Albany Mill
Albany, Georgia, United States

Procter & Gamble Paper Products Co.
Box Elder Mill
Brigham City, Utah, United States

Procter & Gamble Paper Products Co.
Cape Girardeau Mill
Cape Girardeau, Jackson, Missouri, United States

Procter & Gamble Paper Products Co.
Fox River Plant
Green Bay, Wisconsin, United States

Procter & Gamble Paper Products Co.
Mehoopany Mill
Mehoopany, Pennsylvania, United States

Procter & Gamble Paper Products Co.
Oxnard Mill
Oxnard, California, United States

Productos Celulosicos S.A. - Procesa
Azuqueca de Henares Mill
Azuqueca de Henares, Spain

Productos Familia SA
Cajica Mill
Cajica, Cundinamarca, Colombia

Productos Familia SA
Medellin Mill
Medellín, Antioquia, Colombia

Productos Familia Sancela del Ecuador S.A.
Lasso Mill
Lasso, Cotopaxi, Ecuador

Productos Sanitarios S.A. (PROSA)
Matanzas Mill
Matanzas, Matanzas, Cuba

Propaper
Tremembé Mill
Tremembé, São Paulo, Brazil

Protisa Colombia SA
Bogota Mill
Gachancipá, Cundinamarca, Colombia

Protisa Peru S.A. - Productos Tissue del Peru
Santa Anita Mill
Santa Anita, Lima, Peru

Tissue

PROTISA, Productos Tinerfeños S.A.
Santa Cruz de Tenerife Mill
Santa Cruz de Tenerife, Spain

PSA Indústria de Papel
São Leopoldo Mill
São Leopoldo, Rio Grande do Sul, Brazil

PT Graha Cemerlang Paper Utama (Grace Paper)
Cikampek, Karawang Mill
Cikampek, Karawang, Jawa Barat, Indonesia

PT Gunung Jaya Agung
Karawaci Mill
Karawaci, Tangerang, Jawa Barat, Indonesia

PT Indo Paper Primajaya
Tangerang Mill
Tangerang, Jawa Barat, Indonesia

PT Java Paperindo Utama Industries
Mojokerto Mill
Mojokerto, East Java, Indonesia

PT Jaya Kertas
Nganjuk Mill
Nganjuk, East Java, Indonesia

PT Kertas Leces (Persero)
Probolinggo Mill
Probolinggo, East Java, Indonesia

PT Lispap Rayasentosa
Tangerang, Banten Mill
Tangerang, Banten, Jawa Barat, Indonesia

PT Lontar Papyrus Pulp & Paper Industry
Jambi (PT Lontar Papyrus Pulp & Paper) Mill
Jambi, South Sumatra, Indonesia

PT Panca Usaha Paramita
Banten Mill
Tangerang, Banten, Jawa Barat, Indonesia

PT Pindo Deli Pulp & Paper Mills
Karawang No. 1 (PT Pindo Deli Pulp & Paper Mills) Mill
Karawang, West Java, Indonesia

PT Pindo Deli Pulp & Paper Mills
Karawang No. 2 (PT Pindo Deli Pulp & Paper Mills) Mill
Karawang, West Java, Indonesia

PT Pindo Deli Pulp & Paper Mills Hive
Perawang (Pindo Deli Pulp & Paper Mills Hive) Mill
Siak, Bengkalis, Riau, Sumatra, Indonesia

PT Sopanusa Tissue
Mojokerto Mill
Mojokerto, East Java, Indonesia

PT Suparma, Tbk.
Surabaya Mill
Surabaya, East Java, Indonesia

PT The Univenus Co. Ltd.
Perawang (PT The Univenus) Mill
Perawang, Riau, Sumatra, Indonesia

Pudumjee Industries Ltd. (PIL)
Pune Mill
Pune, Maharashtra, India

Pulppy Corelex (Vietnam)
Hung Yen Mill
Hung Yen, Hung Yen Province, Vietnam

Pyramids Paper Mills S.A.E. - Flora
6th October City Mill
6th October City, El Giza, Egypt

Qafqaz Kagit Sanaye, Caucasus Paper Industry
Baku Mill
Baku, Binagadi District, Azerbaijan

Queenex Hygiene Paper Manufacturing L.L.C
Abu Dhabi Mill
Abu Dhabi, Shaikhdom of Abu Dhabi, United Arab Emirates

Queensland Tissue Products
Carole Park Mill
Brisbane, Queensland, Australia

Rafalo Paper Mills
Phoenix, Durban Mill
Phoenix, Durban, KwaZulu-Natal, South Africa

Rama Paper Mills Ltd.
Bijnor Mill
Kiratpur, Bijnor, Uttar Pradesh, India

Rama Pulp & Papers Ltd.
Vapi, Dist. Valsad Mill
Vapi, Dist. Valsad, Gujarat, India

Rang Dong Paper Joint-stock Co.
Dien Khanh District Mill
Dien Khanh District, Khanh Hoa Province, Vietnam

Reliable Paper (India) Pvt. Ltd.
Surat Mill
Bardoli, Taluka - Mahuva, Surat, Gujarat, India

Renova - Fábrica de Papel do Almonda S.A.
Torres Novas Mill
Torres Novas, Portugal

Rexcell Tissue & Airlaid AB
Skåpafors Mill
Bengtsfors, Sweden

Riverpro Pulp & Paper Co., Ltd.
Saraburi Mill
Saraburi, Thailand

Roses Southeast Papers, LLC
Sanford Mill
Sanford, Florida, United States

Royal Paper
Gila Bend
Phoenix, Arizona, United States

S.C. Comceh S. A.
Comceh Mill
Calarasi Judet, Romania

Saber Swiss Quality Paper AG
Balsthal Mill
Balsthal, Switzerland

Saffouri Company for Tissue Manufacturing
Damascus Mill
Damascus, Syria

Saigon Paper
My Xuan I Mill
Tan Thanh Dist., Ba Ria - Vung Tau, Dong Nam Bo, Vietnam

Saigon Paper
My Xuan II Mill
Tan Thanh Dist., Ba Ria - Vung Tau, Dong Nam Bo, Vietnam

Samjung Pulp Ind. Co., Ltd.
Cheonan Mill
Cheonan-si, Dongnam-gu, Chungcheongnam-do, South Korea

Samjung Pulp Ind. Co., Ltd.
Haman Mill
Haman-gun, Gyeongsangnam-do, South Korea

Samjung Pulp Ind. Co., Ltd.
Pyeongtaek Mill
Godeok-myeon, Pyeongtaek-si, Gyeonggi-do, South Korea

Samtai Industrial Ltda
Paulínia Mill
Paulínia city, São Paulo, Brazil

San-Ei Regulator Co., Ltd.
Fujinomiya Mill
Fujinomiya-Shi, Shizuoka Pref., Japan

San-Ei Regulator Co., Ltd.
Tokyo Mill
Kawasaki-shi, Kanagawa Pref., Japan

San-Paper Co., Ltd.
Nishiyatsushiro-gun Mill
Nishiyatsushiro-gun, Yamanashi Pref., Japan

Sanitex Paper Mill Ltd.
Kostinbrod Mill
Kostinbrod, Bulgaria

Sappi Paper and Paper Packaging South Africa (SA)
Stanger Mill
Stanger, KwaZulu-Natal, South Africa

Saudi Paper Manufacturing Co. (SPMC)
Dammam Mill
Dammam, Saudi Arabia

SC Monte Bianco SA
Targoviste Mill
Targoviste, Romania

SCA Consumidor México y Centroamérica S.A. de C.V.
Monterrey Tissue Mill
San Nicolas de los Garza, Nuevo León, Mexico

SCA Consumidor México y Centroamérica S.A. de C.V.
Sahagun Tissue Mill
Tepeapulco, Hidalgo, Mexico

SCA Consumidor México y Centroamérica S.A. de C.V.
Uruapan Tissue Mill
Uruapan, Michoacán, Mexico

SCA France
Gien Mill
Gien Cedex, France

SCA France
Hondouville Mill
Louviers, France

Tissue

SCA France
Kunheim Mill
Muntzenheim, France

SCA Hygiene Products
Collodi Mill
Collodi, Pistoia, Italy

SCA Hygiene Products AB
Edet Mill
Lilla Edet, Sweden

SCA Hygiene Products Australasia
Box Hill Mill
Box Hill, Victoria, Australia

SCA Hygiene Products Australasia
Kawerau Mill
Kawerau, Bay of Plenty, New Zealand

SCA Hygiene Products GmbH
Ortmann Mill
Ortmann, Pernitz, Niederösterreich, Austria

SCA Hygiene Products GmbH
Witzenhausen Tissue Mill
Witzenhausen, Germany

SCA Hygiene Products Manchester Ltd.
Manchester (Trafford Park) Mill
Manchester, United Kingdom

SCA Hygiene Products Operations SNC
Orléans Mill
Saint Cyr en Val, Orléans, France

SCA Hygiene Products Russia LLC
Sovetsk Mill
Sovetsk, Shchekino Distr., Tula Region, Russia

SCA Hygiene Products Russia LLC
Svetogorsk Mill
Svetogorsk, Leningrad Region, Russia

SCA Hygiene Products S.A./N.V.
Stembert Mill
Stembert, Belgium

SCA Hygiene Products S.L.
La Riba Mill
La Riba, Tarragona, Spain

SCA Hygiene Products S.L.
Mediona Mill
Mediona, Barcelona, Spain

SCA Hygiene Products S.L.
Puigpelat (Valls) Mill
Puigpelat, Tarragona, Spain

SCA Hygiene Products SE
Goytside Mill
Chesterfield, Derbyshire, United Kingdom

SCA Hygiene Products SE
Mainz-Kostheim Mill
Mainz-Kostheim, Germany

SCA Hygiene Products SE
Mannheim Mill
Mannheim, Germany

SCA Hygiene Products SE
Neuss Mill
Neuss, Germany

SCA Hygiene Products SE
Oakenholt Mill
Oakenholt, Flint, Wales, United Kingdom

SCA Hygiene Products SE
Prudhoe Mill
Prudhoe, Northumberland, United Kingdom

SCA Hygiene Products SE
Stubbins Mill
Ramsbottom, Bury, Lancashire, United Kingdom

SCA Hygiene Products SpA
Altopascio Mill
Altopascio, Loc. Badia Pozzeveri, Lucca, Italy

SCA Hygiene Products SpA
Lucca 1 Tissue Mill
Porcari, Lucca, Italy

SCA Hygiene Products Supply SAS
Le Theil Mill
Le Theil sur Huisne, France

SCA Nederlands BV
Cuijk Mill
Katwijk, Cuijk, Netherlands

SCA Patras
Patras Mill
Ag. Stefanos - Patras, Achaia, Greece

SCA Spain
Allo Mill
Allo, Navarra, Spain

SCA Tissue Finland Oy
Nokia Mill
Nokia, Finland

SCA Tissue North America, L.L.C.
Barton Mill
Cherokee, Alabama, United States

SCA Tissue North America, L.L.C.
Encore Paper
South Glens Falls, New York, United States

SCA Tissue North America, L.L.C.
Flagstaff Mill
Flagstaff, Arizona, United States

SCA Tissue North America, L.L.C.
Menasha Mill
Menasha, Wisconsin, United States

Seaman Paper Company
Otter River Mill
Otter River, Massachusetts, United States

SEPAC - Serrados e Pasta de Celulose Ltda.
Mallet Mill
Mallet, Paraná, Brazil

Serrana Papel e Celulose Ltda.
Serrana Mill
Serrana, São Paulo, Brazil

Shaanxi Xi-An Lintong District Hanxing Co., Ltd.
Xi-An Mill
Xi-An, Shaanxi, China

Shandong Baron Paper Co., Ltd.
Laiwu Mill
Laiwu, Shandong, China

Shandong Dongyue Energy Co., Ltd.
Feicheng Mill
Feicheng, Shandong, China

Shandong Gaotang Quanjie Paper Co., Ltd.
Liaocheng Mill
Liaocheng, Shandong, China

Shandong Haiyang Yongping Paper Co., Ltd.
Haiyang Mill
Haiyang, Shandong, China

Shandong Lianxi Paper Co. Ltd.
Rizhao Mill
Rizhao, Shandong, China

Shandong Linyi Sensen Paper Co., Ltd.
Linyi Mill
Linyi, Shandong, China

Shandong Rizhao Huatai Paper Co. Ltd.
Rizhao Mill
Rizhao, Shandong, China

Shandong Sun Paper Industry Joint Stock Co., Ltd.
Yanzhou Mill
Yanzhou, Shandong, China

Shandong Tianhe Paper Co., Ltd.
Taian Mill
Taian, Shandong, China

Shandong Tranlin Paper Co. Ltd.
Gaotang Mill
Liaocheng, Shandong, China

Shandong Weifang HengAn Paper Co. Ltd.
Weifang Mill
Weifang, Shandong, China

Shandong Weifang Henglian Meilin Life-Uses Paper Limited Co.
Weifang Mill
Weifang, Shandong, China

Shandong Yantai Jinhong Paper Co. Ltd.
Yantai Mill
Yantai, Shandong, China

Shandong Zhucheng City Qixianzi Products Co., Ltd.
Weifang Mill
Weifang, Shandong, China

Shanghai Kimberly-Clark (China) Paper Co. Ltd.
Shanghai Mill
Shanghai, Shanghai, China

Shanghai Orient Champion Huajie Paper Co., Ltd.
Jinshan Mill
Shanghai, Shanghai, China

Shaniv Paper Industries Ltd.
Ofakim Paper Mill
Ofakim, Israel

Shanxi Linyi Lida Paper Co., Ltd.
Yuncheng Mill
Yuncheng, Shanxi, China

Tissue

Shawano Specialty Papers
Shawano Mill
Shawano, Wisconsin, United States

Shengda Group Jiangsu Shuangdeng Paper Co., Ltd.
Yancheng Mill
Yancheng, Jiangsu, China

Shenyang Jinxin Pulp & Paper Co., Ltd
Xinmin (Shenyang Jinxin Pulp & Paper) Mill
Xinmin, Liaoning, China

Shin-Ei Paper Mfg. Co., Ltd.
Fujinomiya-Shi Mill
Fujinomiya-Shi, Shizuoka Pref., Japan

Shinchang Paper
Asan Mill
Asan-si, Chungcheongnam-do, South Korea

Shine Yan Paper Co., Ltd.
Fengyuan Mill
Fengyuan District, Taichung City, Taiwan

Shouguang Meilun Paper
Shouguang (Shouguang Meilun Paper) Mill
Shouguang, Shandong, China

SHP CELEX AD
Banja Luka Mill
Banja Luka, Bosnia & Herzegovina

SHP Harmanec, a.s.
Harmanec Mill
Harmanec, Slovakia

SHP Slavošovce, a.s.
Slavošovce Mill
Slavošovce, Slovakia

Shree Bhageshwari Papers Ltd
Muzaffarnagar Mill
Muzaffarnagar, Uttar Pradesh, India

Sichuan Anxian Paper Co., Ltd.
Chengdu Mill
Chengdu, Sichuan, China

Sichuan Chengdu Jiexin Paper Co., Ltd.
Chengdu Mill
Chengdu, Sichuan, China

Sichuan Chengdu Jinghua Paper Co., Ltd.
Chengdu Mill
Chengdu, Sichuan, China

Sichuan Chengdu Yuanzhou Industrial Co., Ltd.
Shifang Mill
Shifang, Sichuan, China

Sichuan Meishan City Hongyuan Paper Co., Ltd.
Meishan Mill
Meishan, Sichuan, China

Sichuan Mingshan County Yunxiang Paper Co., Ltd.
Yaan Mill
Yaan, Sichuan, China

Sichuan Pengzhou Daliang Paper
Pengzhou Mill
Pengzhou, Sichuan, China

Sichuan Santai Sanjiao Living Paper Manufacture Co., Ltd.
Mianyang Mill
Mianyang, Sichuan, China

Sichuan WanAn Paper Co., Ltd.
Leshan Mill
Leshan, Sichuan, China

Sichuan Xilong Paper Co., Ltd.
Meishan Mill
Meishan, Sichuan, China

Sichuan Zhongshun Tiantian Paper Co., Ltd.
Chengdu Mill
Pengzhou, Chengdu, Sichuan, China

Sichuan Zigong Tissue Paper Mill
Zigong Mill
Zigong, Sichuan, China

Socarpi S.R.L.
Villa Basilica Mill
Villa Basilica, Lucca, Italy

Societé Industrielle Des Papiers "Tissues" (Sipat S.A.)
Meknès Mill
Meknès, Morocco

Soffass S.p.A.
Soffass Mill
Porcari, Lucca, Italy

Sofidel America Corporation
Haines City Mill
Haines City, Florida, United States

Sofidel Benelux
Duffel Mill
Duffel, Antwerp, Belgium

Sofidel Group
Kamns Mill
Leicester, United Kingdom

Sofidel Group
Lancaster Mill
Lancaster, Lancashire, United Kingdom

Song Duong Tissue Paper Company
Long Bien District, Hanoi City Mill
Long Bien District, Hanoi City, Vietnam

SOPAFI, Société des Papiers Fins S.A.R.L.
Sbeitla Mill
Sbeitla, Gouvernorat de Kasserine, Tunisia

Soundview Paper Co.
Elmwood Park Mill
Elmwood Park, New Jersey, United States

Soundview Paper Co.
Putney Mill
Putney, Vermont, United States

South African Cartonboard Mills
Wadeville Mill
Wadeville, Gauteng, South Africa

SP Exclusive
Grodno Mill
Grodno, Grodno Region, Belarus

Spartak
Shklov Mill
Shklov, Mogilev Region, Belarus

Speciality Papers Ltd.
Valsad Mill
Vapi, Dist. Valsad, Gujarat, India

Ssangyong C&B
Chochiwon Mill
Jochiwon-eup, Yeongi-gun, Chungcheongnam-do, South Korea

ST Paper, LLC
Oconto Falls Mill
Oconto Falls, Wisconsin, United States

Sunglim Paper
Yongin Mill
Yongin-si, Gyeonggi-do, South Korea

Sunshine Paper India Ltd
Kakinada Mill
Kakinada, Andhra Pradesh, India

Super Paper Products Co. Ltd.
Tema Mill
Tema, Ghana

Suyash Paper Mills
Basti district Mill
Basti district, Uttar Pradesh, Uttar Pradesh, India

Svenska Pappersbruket
Klippan Mill
Klippan, Sweden

Swedish Tissue AB
Kisa Mill
Kisa, Sweden

Syassky Pulp & Paper Mill
Syasstroy Mill
Syasstroy, Volkhovskiy rayon, Leningrad Region, Russia

Syktyvkar Tissue Group, LLC
Semibratovo Mill
Semibratovo, Yaroslavl obl., Russia

Syktyvkar Tissue Group, LLC
Syktyvkar Mill
Syktyvkar, Russia

Taiping Paper Mills Sdn. Bhd.
Taiping Mill
Taiping, Perak, Malaysia

Takano Paper Co., Ltd.
Fuji-shi Mill
Fuji-shi, Shizuoka Pref., Japan

Tanpack Tissues Ltd.
Dar-es-Salaam Mill
Dar-es-Salaam, Tanzania

Tezol Tütün ve Kagit San ve Tic A.S.
Izmir Mill
Torbali, Izmir, Izmir, Turkey

Thai Victory Paper Co., Ltd.
Bangkok Mill
Samaedam, Bangkhuntian, Bangkok, Bangkok, Thailand

Thanatarn Paper Co., Ltd.
Taparak Mill
Taparak, Samut Prakam, Thailand

Tissue

Thrace Paper Mill S.A.
Thrace (Diana) Mill
Xanthi, Greece

Thüringer Hygiene Papier GmbH
Thüringer Mill
Schmalkalden, Germany

Tianjin Golden Camel Group
Tianjin Mill
Tianjin, Tianjin, China

Tianjin Zhongchao Paper Co. Ltd.
Tianjin Mill
Tianjin, Tianjin, China

Tonic Industrie EPE
Ouate Industrie Mill
Bou Ismail, Wilaya d'Alger, Algeria

Toprak Temizlik Kagidi San. Tic. A.S.
Bozuyuk Mill
Bozuyuk, Bilecik, Turkey

TOV Novy Kyiv (New Kiev) Paper Mill
Raketnaya Mill
Raketnaya, Ukraine

Toyo Paper Mfg. Co., Ltd.
Shikokuchuo-shi Mill
Shikokuchuo-shi, Ehime Pref., Japan

Trakya Kagit San ve TIC. A.S.
Tekirdag Mill
Tekirdag, Tekirdag, Turkey

Três Portos S.A. Indústria de Papel
Esteio Mill
Esteio, Rio Grande do Sul, Brazil

Triwaste CC
Tongaat Mill
Tongaat, South Africa

Trópicos Industrial e Comercial Ltda
Guarapuava Mill
Guarapuava, Paraná, Brazil

Truc Bach Paper Joint-Stock Co.
Hanoi City Mill
Thanh Tri District, Hanoi City, Vietnam

Tung I Paper Corp.
Feng Yuan Mill
Feng Yuan District, Taichung City, Taiwan

Tunisie Ouate
Enfidha Mill
Enfidha, Gouvernorat de Sousse, Tunisia

Una Ama Paper Mills Nigeria Ltd.
Ikot-Ekpene Mill
Ikot-Ekpene, Akwa Ibom State, Nigeria

Unión Papelera Platense
La Plata Mill
La Plata, Buenos Aires, Argentina

Union Paper Industries Sdn. Bhd.
Bentung Mill
Bentung, Pahang Darul Makmur, Malaysia

Unipak Tissue Mill
Jbeil Mill
Jbeil, Jounieh, Lebanon

Valot S.A.
Campana Mill
Campana, Buenos Aires, Argentina

Van Houtum BV
Swalmen Mill
Swalmen, Netherlands

Velgiiskaya Paper Mill
Borovichi Mill
Borovichi, Novgorod Region, Russia

Velvet CARE sp. z o.o.
Klucze Mill
Klucze, Poland

Vien Dong Paper Joint-Stock Company
Ho Chi Minh City Mill
Ho Chi Minh City, Binh Duong Province, Vietnam

Viet Tri Paper Company
Viet Tri Mill
Viet Tri City, Phú Tho Province, Vietnam

Viking Kagit ve Seluloz A.S.
Viking Paper Mill
Aliaga, Izmir, Turkey

Vinda Paper (Liaoning) Co., Ltd.
Anshan Mill
Anshan, Liaoning, China

Vinda Paper (Sichuan) Co. Ltd.
Deyang Mill
Deyang, Sichuan, China

Vinda Paper (Zhejiang) Co., Ltd.
Quzhou Mill
Quzhou, Zhejiang, China

Vinh Hue Paper Joint-Stock Co. (Vihimex)
Ho Chi Minh City Mill
Thu Duc District, Ho Chi Minh City, Binh Duong Province, Vietnam

Viochartiki Paper Mill SA
Aspropirgos Mill
Aspropirgos, Attica, Greece

Virtisú S.L.
Capellades Mill
La Torre de Claramunt, Barcelona, Spain

Von Drehle Corp.
Cordova Mill
Cordova, North Carolina, United States

Vrancart SA
Adjud Mill
Adjud, Vrancea, Romania

Wang N.T. Paper Co., Ltd.
Lopburi Mill
Thaluang Distr., Lopburi, Thailand

Wausau Paper Towel & Tissue, LLC
Harrodsburg Mill
Harrodsburg, Kentucky, United States

Wausau Paper Towel & Tissue, LLC
Middletown Mill
Middletown, Ohio, United States

WELMAX Zaklad Produkcyjno-Handlowy Wieslaw Adamowicz
Wohyn Mill
Wohyń, Poland

WEPA Hygieneprodukte GmbH
Marsberg-Giershagen Mill
Marsberg-Giershagen, Germany

WEPA Hygieneprodukte GmbH
Arnsberg Mill
Arnsberg-Müschede, Germany

WEPA Hygieneprodukte GmbH
Mainz Mill
Mainz, Germany

WEPA Leuna GmbH
Leuna Mill
Leuna, Spergau, Germany

WEPA Lille S.A.R.L.
Bousbecque Mill
Bousbecque, France

WEPA Lucca Srl
Cassino Mill
Cassino, Frosinone, Italy

WEPA Lucca Srl
Fosso Raletta Mill
Porcari, Lucca, Italy

WEPA Papierfabrik Sachsen GmbH
Kriebethal Mill
Kriebethal, Germany

WEPA Professional Piechowice S.A.
Piechowice Mill
Piechowice, Poland

Werra Papier
Omega Mill
Wernshausen, Germany

WPT Eko-Klan Sp. z o.o.
Margonin Mill
Margonin, Poland

Xiamen Xinyang Paper
Xiamen Mill
Xiamen, Fujian, China

Xinjiang Tianhong Paper Co., Ltd.
Shihezi Mill
Shihezi, Xinjiang, China

Yame Seishisho Co., Ltd.
Yame-shi Mill
Yame-shi, Fukuoka Pref., Japan

Yeong Chaur Shing Paper Mill Sdn. Bhd.
Melaka Mill
Melaka, Malaysia

Yuen Foong Yu Inc.
Beijing Mill
Beijing, Beijing, China

Yuen Foong Yu Consumer Products Co., Ltd
Ching Shui Mill
Ching Shui District, Taichung City, Taiwan

Yuen Foong Yu Consumer Products Co., Ltd.
Yang-Mei Mill
Yang Mei, Taoyuan County, Taiwan

Yueyang Paper International Uganda
Kampala Mill
Kampala, Uganda

Yuhan-Kimberly Ltd.
Daejeon Mill

Packaging papers

Daejeon-si, Daejeon, South Korea

Yuhan-Kimberly Ltd.
Kimcheon Mill
Gimcheon-si, Gyeongsangbuk-do, South Korea

Yuhan-Kimberly Ltd.
Kunpo Mill
Gunpo-si, Gyeonggi-do, South Korea

Yung Fang Paper Mfg. Co
Hsi Chou Mill
Hsi Chou, Changhua County, Taiwan

Yunnan Hanguang Paper Co., Ltd.
Yuxi Mill
Yuxi, Yunnan, China

Yunnan Jiangchuan Cuifeng Paper Co., Ltd.
Yuxi Mill
Yuxi, Yunnan, China

Yunnan Kunming Zhenlong Paper Mill
Kunming Mill
Kunming, Yunnan, China

Yunnan Lujiang Paper Co., Ltd.
Kaiyuan Mill
Kaiyuan, Yunnan, China

Yunnan Wenshan Yunhe Paper Industry Co., Ltd.
Wenshan Mill
Wenshan, Yunnan, China

Zambezi Paper Mills Ltd.
Ndola Mill
Ndola, Zambia

ZAO Altaykrovlya
Novoaltaysk Mill
Novoaltaysk, Altaisky Kraý, Russia

ZAO ATMSS
Kazan Mill
Kazan, Tatarstan Republic, Russia

ZAO MPK KRZ - Multibranch Production Company KRZ
Ryazan Mill
Ryazan, Russia

ZAO Uralskaya Bumaga
Sukhoy Log Mill
Sukhoy Log, Sverdlovskaya obl., Russia

Zhejiang Fuyang City Huawei Paper Co., Ltd.
Fuyang Mill
Fuyang, Zhejiang, China

Zhejiang Fuyang Dingdian Paper Co., Ltd.
Fuyang Mill
Fuyang, Zhejiang, China

Zhejiang Haining Bangda Paper Co., Ltd.
Haining Mill
Haining, Zhejiang, China

Zhejiang Jintong Paper Co., Ltd.
Jinhua Mill
Jinhua, Zhejiang, China

Zhejiang Quzhou Shuangxiongmao Paper General Corp.
Quzhou Mill
Quzhou, Zhejiang, China

Zhejiang Welfare Paper Co., Ltd.
Shaoxing Mill
Shaoxing, Zhejiang, China

Zywieckie Zaklady Papiernicze "SOLALI" S.A.
Zywiec Mill
Zywiec, Poland

Packaging papers

A.P. Paper Mills Ltd
Patiala Mill
Dist. Mohali, Punjab, India

Afsons Industrial Corporation Ltd.
Raigad Mill
Raigad, Maharashtra, India

Águas Negras S.A. Ind. de Papel
Ituporanga Mill
Ituporanga, Santa Catarina, Brazil

Akshat Papers Ltd.
Surat Mill
Surat, Gujarat, India

Alas Doradas S.A. de C.V
San Juan Opico Mill
San Juan Opico La Libertad, El Salvador

Alatyrskaya Paper Mill
Alatyr Mill
Alatyr, Chuvashkaya Republic, Russia

Albertin Paperboard & Paper Mill
Slonim Mill
Slonim, Grodno Region, Belarus

Alier S.A.
Roselló Mill
Roselló, Lérida, Spain

Amaravathi Sri Venkatesa Paper Mills Ltd.
Madathukulam Mill
Madathukulam, Coimbatore Dist., Tamil Nadu, India

Amol Paper Mills (P) Ltd
Raigad Mill
Raigad, Maharashtra, India

Amritsar Pulp & Board Mills (P) Ltd.
Amritsar Mill
Amritsar, Punjab, India

Anand Tissues Ltd.
Meerut Mill
Meerut, Uttar Pradesh, India

Anhui Huoshan County Chenfeng Paper Co., Ltd
LiuAn Mill
LiuAn, Anhui, China

APC Paper Company, Inc
Claremont Mill
Claremont, New Hampshire, United States

Arkhangelsk Pulp & Paper Mill
Novodvinsk (Arkhangelsk - APPM) Mill
Novodvinsk, Arkhangelsk Region, Russia

Ashi Dipi Paper Mills Pvt. Ltd.
Ujjain Mill
Ujjain, Madhya Pradesh, India

Asia Paper Mfg. Co., Ltd.
Cheongwon Mill
Cheongwon-gun, Chungcheongbuk-do, South Korea

Atas Paper (Pvt) Ltd.
Sheikhupura Mill
Sheikhupura, Punjab, Pakistan

Aurangabad Paper Mills Ltd.
Aurangabad Mill
Aurangabad, Maharashtra, India

Australian Paper
Maryvale Mill
Morwell, Victoria, Australia

Awade Pulp and Paper Mills Pvt. Ltd.
Abdul-Lat Mill
Sahakari Soot Girani, Abdul-Lat, Maharashtra, India

Ballarpur Industries Ltd. (BILT)
Ballarshah (Unit Ballarpur)
Ballarshah, Maharashtra, India

Bansi Pulp & Paper Mills Pvt. Ltd.
Miraj, Sangli District Mill
Dist. Sangli, Maharashtra, India

Bashundhara Paper Mills Ltd.
Unit 2
Sonargaon, New Town, Narayanganj, Bangladesh

Bashundhara Paper Mills Ltd.
Unit 3
Gazaria, Munshigonj, Bangladesh

Bedse Pulp Conversion Industries (P) Ltd.
Aurangabad Mill
Aurangabad, Maharashtra, India

Belovo Paper Mill S.A.
Belovo Mill
Belovo, Bulgaria

Best Paper Mills Pvt. Ltd.
Vapi Mill
Vapi, Gujarat, India

Bhandari Deepak Industries Ltd
Solan Mill
Solan, Himachal Pradesh, India

Bhikusa Papers Pvt. Ltd.
Nasik Mill
Panchwati, Maharashtra, India

BillerudKorsnäs AB
Gruvön Mill
Grums, Sweden

BillerudKorsnäs AB
Karlsborg Mill
Karlsborg, Sweden

BillerudKorsnäs AB
Skärblacka Mill
Skärblacka, Sweden

BillerudKorsnäs Finland Oy
Pietarsaari Mill
Pietarsaari, Finland

Packaging papers

BillerudKorsnäs Finland Oy
Tervasaari Mill
Valkeakoski, Finland

Bindals Duplex Ltd.
Muzaffarnagar Mill
Muzaffarnagar, Uttar Pradesh, India

Binh Minh Paper Company
Tien Du Mill
Tien Du, Bac Ninh Province, Vietnam

Bio-PAPPEL International
Prewitt Mill
Prewitt, New Mexico, United States

Bio-PAPPEL Printing
Tuxtepec Mill
Tuxtepec, OAX, Mexico

BN - Papel Catarinense Ltda.
Benedito Novo Mill
Benedito Novo, Santa Catarina, Brazil

Brahmaputra Paper Pvt. Ltd.
Tezpur Mill
Tezpur, Assam, India

Brason Indústria de Papéis e Ondulados Ltda.
Araras Mill
Araras, São Paulo, Brazil

Brianskaya Paper Mill
Belye Berega Mill
Pos. Belye Berega, Bryansk Region, Russia

Canfor Pulp Ltd.
Prince George (Pulp & Paper) Mill
Prince George, British Columbia, Canada

Cartiera Bocci Ponte di Gemolano Srl
Pescia Mill
Pescia, Pistoia, Italy

Cartiera del Chiese SpA
Montichiari Mill
Montichiari, Brescia, Italy

Cartiera di Nebbiuno S.R.L.
Nebbiuno Mill
Nebbiuno, Novara, Italy

Cartiera G.I.C. S.r.l.
Francavilla di Sicilia Mill
Francavilla di Sicilia, Messina, Italy

Cartiera Galliera srl
Galliera Veneta Mill
Galliera Veneta, Padua, Italy

Cartiera Giacosa SpA
Front Canavese Mill
Front Canavese, Turin, Italy

Cartiera Grillo sas di Giuseppe e Domenico Grillo
Genova-Voltri Mill
Genova-Voltri, Genova, Italy

Cartiera Mantovana S.R.L.
Maglio di Goito Mill
Maglio di Goito, Mantua, Italy

Cartiera Partenope S.r.l
Arzano Mill
Arzano, Naples, Italy

Cartiera Pasquini Srl
Bagni di Lucca Mill
Bagni di Lucca, Lucca, Italy

Cartiera Puglisi SRL
Castiglione di Sicilia Mill
Castiglione di Sicilia, Catania, Italy

Cartiera Sacchettificio Bonino
Borgaro Torinese Mill
Borgaro Torinese, Turin, Italy

Cartiere SACI SpA
Verona Mill
Cà di David, Verona, Italy

Carvajal Pulpa y Papel
Yumbo Mill, Plant 1
Yumbo, Valle de Cauca, Colombia

Celulosa Argentina S.A.
Capitán Bermúdez Mill
Capitán Bermúdez, Santa Fé, Argentina

Celulosa de Fibras Mexicanas S.A. de C.V.
Apizaco Mill
Apizaco, Tlaxacala, Mexico

Celulosa y Papel del Bajío S.A.de C.V.
León Mill
León, Guanajuato, Mexico

Celulose Irani S.A.
Vargem Bonita Mill
Vargem Bonita, Santa Catarina, Brazil

CELUPA - Industrial Celulose e Papel Guaíba Ltda.
Guaíba Mill
Guaíba, Rio Grande do Sul, Brazil

CEPASA - Celulose e Papel de Pernambuco S.A.
Jaboatão dos Guararapes Mill
Jaboatão dos Guararapes, Pernambuco, Brazil

Chadha Papers Ltd
Bilaspur, Dist. Rampur Mill
Dist. Rampur, Uttar Pradesh, India

Chandpur Enterprises Ltd.
Dist. Bijnor Mill
Dist. Bijnor, Uttar Pradesh, India

Chouka Pulp & Paper Mill
Rezvanshahr Mill
Rezvanshahr, Iran

Chuetsu Pulp & Paper Co., Ltd.
Sendai Mill
Satsumasendai-shi, Kagoshima Pref., Japan

Chuetsu Pulp & Paper Co., Ltd.
Takaoka (Nohmachi) Mill
Takaoka-shi, Toyama Pref., Japan

Circar Paper Mills Ltd.
Nellore Mill
Nellore, Andhra Pradesh, India

Cita Peuchoon Paper Mills Sdn. Bhd.
Sungai Petani Mill
Sungai Petani, Kedah, Malaysia

CMPC Celulosa S.A.
Laja Mill
Laja, VIII - Región del Biobío, Chile

Coastal Agro Industries Ltd
West Godavari Mill
West Godavari, Tanuku, Andhra Pradesh, India

COCELPA - Companhia de Celulose e Papel do Paraná
Araucária Mill
Araucária, Paraná, Brazil

Cochin Kagaz Ltd.
Ernakulam Mill
Ernakulam, Kerala, India

Coldenhove Papier
Eerbeek Mill
Eerbeek, Netherlands

Copamex Industrias S.A. de C.V.
Monterrey Mill
San Nicolas de los Garza, Nuevo León, Mexico

COPSI Compañía Papelera Sinsacate S.R.L.
Sinsacate Mill
Sinsacate, Córdoba, Argentina

Coral Newsprints Limited
Jyotibaphulenagar Mill
Jia Phule Nagar, Uttar Pradesh, India

Cosboard Industries Ltd.
Jagatpur Mill
Dist. Cuttack, Odisha, India

Cottrell Paper Co., Inc.
Rock City Falls Mill
Rock City Falls, New York, United States

Crocker Technical Papers
Fitchburg Mill
Fitchburg, Massachusetts, United States

Daini Seishi Co., Ltd.
Fuji-shi Mill
Fuji-shi, Shizuoka Pref., Japan

Daio Paper Corp.
Kani Mill
Kani-shi, Gifu Pref., Japan

Daio Paper Corp.
Mishima Mill
Shikokuchuo-shi, Ehime Pref., Japan

Dalkrovlya
Khabarovsk Mill
Khabarovsk, Russia

Dall Pel Madeira e Papel
Grechinski Mill
Irati, Paraná, Brazil

Decor Paper Mills Ltd.
Punjagutta, Hyderabad Mill
Punjagutta, Hyderabad, Andhra Pradesh, India

Delux Kraft Board Ltd.
Vapi Mill
Vapi, Gujarat, India

DICEPA Papelera de Enate S.L.
Enate Mill
Enate, Huesca, Spain

Dnepropetrovsk Paper Mill, Ltd.
Dnepropetrovsk Mill
Dnepropetrovsk, Ukraine

Packaging papers

Dobrushskaya Paper Mill "Geroi Truda", OJSC
Dobrush Mill
Dobrush, Gomel Region, Belarus

Dong Fa Paper Mfg. Co., Ltd.
Puyen Mill
Pu Yien, Changhua County, Taiwan

Dongguan Landsing (Lianxing) Packaging Co., Ltd.
Dongguan Mill
Dongguan, Guangdong, China

Doruk Kagit San. T IC. A.S
Kayseri Mill
Kayseri, Turkey

DS Smith Paper
Wansbrough Paper Mill
Watchet, Somerset, United Kingdom

EKA Industrial Paper Production Limited
Izmit Mill
Kosekoy, Izmit, Kocaeli, Turkey

El Farouk Co. "Farco"
El Obour Ind. City Mill
Obour, Egypt

Elikon
Murygino Mill
Murygino, Kirovskaya Obl., Russia

Ethiopian Pulp & Paper SC
Nazareth Mill
Wonji, Nazareth, Ethiopia

Expera Specialty Solutions
Rhinelander Mill
Rhinelander, Wisconsin, United States

Fábrica de Bolsas de Papel UNIBOL SA
Soledad Mill
Soledad, Atlántico, Colombia

Fábrica de Papel da Lapa Lda.
São Paio de Oleiros Mill
São Paio de Oleiros, Portugal

Fábrica de Papel de Ponte Redonda S.A.
Silvalde, Espinho Mill
Silvalde, Espinho, Portugal

Fábrica de Papel de Torres Novas Lda.
Torres Novas Mill
Torres Novas, Portugal

Fábrica de Papel La Soledad S.A. de C.V.
Los Reyes Acaquilpan Mill
Los Reyes Acaquilpan, México, D.F., Mexico

Fabryka Papieru Sp. z.o.o. w Dabrowicy
Jelenia Gora Mill
Jelenia Gora, Poland

FANAPEL - Fábrica Nacional de Papel S.A.
Juan Lacaze Mill
Juan Lacaze, Colonia, Uruguay

FAPAJAL - Fábrica de Papel de Tojal S.A.
São Julião do Tojal Mill
São Julião do Tojal, Portugal

Fedco Paper Corp.
Calamba City Mill
Calamba City, Laguna, Philippines

Flying Kraft Paper Mills Ltd.
Charsadda Mill
Charsadda, Khyber Pakhtunkhwa, Pakistan

Fujian Qingshan Paper Industry Co., Ltd.
Qingzhou Mill
Qingzhou, Fujian, China

FutureMark Paper Group
Manistique Mill
Manistique, Michigan, United States

G.P.C. Mohammadia
Meknès Mill
Meknès, Morocco

Gain Hwang Paper Mfg. Co., Ltd.
Shan Hua Mill
Shan Hua, Tainan City, Taiwan

Gajanan Paper Mill (P) Ltd
Buldana Mill
Buldana, Maharashtra, India

Ganga Papers India
Pune Mill
Taluka Maval, Dist. Pune, Maharashtra, India

Garg Duplex & Paper Mills Pvt. Ltd.
Muzaffarnagar Mill
Muzaffarnagar, Uttar Pradesh, India

Gascogne Paper
Mimizan Mill
Mimizan, Landes, France

Gayatri Paper Mills Pvt. Ltd.
Raigarh Mill
Raigarh, Maharashtra, India

General Company for Paper Industry (GENCO)
Deir Ez-Zor Mill
Deir Ez-Zor, Syria

Georgia-Pacific LLC
Palatka Mill
Palatka, Florida, United States

Git-Vijay Paper Mills (P) Ltd.
Mehsana Mill
Mehsana, Gujarat, India

Glucholaskie Zaklady Papiernicze Sp. z o.o.
Glucholazy Mill
Glucholazy, Poland

Glucholaskie Zaklady Papiernicze Sp. z o.o.
Niedomice Mill
Niedomice, Poland

Goodwill Team Papers Ltd
Usilampatti Mill
Usilampatti, Madurai, Tamil Nadu, India

Goraya Straw Board Mills (P) Ltd
Udham Singh Nagar Mill
Kashipur, Uttarakhand, India

Graphic Packaging International Inc.
West Monroe Mill
West Monroe, Louisiana, United States

Greenland Paper Mill Ltd
Kollam Mill
Kollam, Kerala, India

Guangxi East Asia Paper Co., Ltd.
Chongzuo Mill
Chongzuo, Guangxi, China

Guangxi Forest Lipu Paper Co., Ltd.
Lipu Mill
Lipu, Guangxi, China

Hardoli Paper Mills Ltd.
Nagpur Mill
Nagpur, Maharashtra, India

Hari Ohm Paper Mills (P) Ltd.
Surat Mill
Surat, Gujarat, India

Harisar Papers Ltd
Ludhiana Mill
Ludhiana, Punjab, India

Hartford City Paper, LLC
Hartford City Mill
Hartford City, Indiana, United States

Hebei Qinhuangdao Haofeng Enterprise Group
Qinhuangdao Mill
Qinhuangdao, Hebei, China

Heilongjiang Fuyu Chenming Paper Co., Ltd.
Qiqihar (Heilongjiang Fuyu Chenming Paper) Mill
Qiqihar, Heilongjiang, China

Heilongjiang Longjiangfu Pulp & Paper Co., Ltd.
Jiamusi Mill
Jiamusi, Heilongjiang, China

Hemkunt Paper Mills Ltd
Ludhiana Mill
Ludhiana, Punjab, India

Hiang Seng Fibre Container Co., Ltd.
Samut Sakohn Mill
Amphur Muang, Samut Sakohn, Thailand

Hoang Van Thu Paper Joint Stock Company
Thai Nguyen City Mill
Thai Nguyen City, Thai Nguyen Province, Vietnam

Hollingsworth & Vose Co.
East Walpole Mill
East Walpole, Massachusetts, United States

Hollingsworth & Vose Co.
Easton Mill
Greenwich, New York, United States

Hollingsworth & Vose Co.
West Groton Mill
West Groton, Massachusetts, United States

Packaging papers

Horizon Pulp & Paper Ltd.
Kehra Mill
Kehra, Estonia

Hsing Chung Paper Corp.
Wu Chieh Mill
Wu Chieh, Ilan County, Taiwan

Hunan Tiger Forest & Paper Group Co., Ltd
Yongzhou Mill
Yongzhou, Hunan, China

Hunan Tiger Forest & Paper Group Hongjiang Paper Co., Ltd
Hongjiang Mill
Huaihua, Hunan, China

Hunan Tiger Forest & Paper Group Yuanjiang Paper Co., Ltd.
Yuanjiang Mill
Yuanjiang, Hunan, China

Iguaçu Celulose Papel S.A.
Campos Novos/SC Mill
Campos Novos, Santa Catarina, Brazil

Iguaçu Celulose Papel S.A.
Piraí do Sul Mill
Piraí do Sul, Paraná, Brazil

Iguaçu Celulose Papel S.A.
São José dos Pinhais Mill
São José dos Pinhais, Paraná, Brazil

Indústria Americana de Papel S.A.
São Paulo Mill
São Paulo, São Paulo, Brazil

Indústria de Papéis para Embalagem Irmãos Siqueira Ltda.
Passa Quatro Mill
Passa Quatro, Minas Gerais, Brazil

Indústria e Comércio de Papel Fiberpap Ltda.
Limeira Mill
Limeira, São Paulo, Brazil

Industria Panameña de Papel SA
Chilibre Mill
San Vicente, Zona Chilibre, Panama

Indústrias de Papel R. Ramenzoni S.A.
Cordeirópolis Mill
Cordeirópolis, São Paulo, Brazil

Industrias del Cartón S.A. - INCASA
Cayalti Mill
Cayalti, Chiclayo, Peru

Indústrias Novacki S.A.
Porto União Mill
Porto União, Santa Catarina, Brazil

International Paper Co.
Savannah Mill
Savannah, Georgia, United States

Invepal
Morón Mill
Morón, Edo. Carabobo, Venezuela

Islamic Paper Manufacturing Co.
Quesna Mill
Quesna, Menofeya, Egypt

Ivex Specialty Paper, LLC
Peoria Mill
Peoria, Illinois, United States

J B Daruka Paper Ltd
Sitapur Mill
Sitapur, Uttar Pradesh, India

J. Tönnesmann & Vogel, Papierfabrik Hönnetal GmbH
Menden Mill
Menden, Germany

JIP - Papírny Vetrní,a.s.
Lukavice Mill
Zábreh, Czech Republic

JIP - Papírny Vetrní,a.s.
Vetrní Mill
Vetrní, Czech Republic

Julius Schulte Söhne GmbH & Co. KG
Düsseldorf Mill
Düsseldorf, Germany

Kahramanmaras Kagit San ve TIC A.S (KMK Paper)
Kütahya Mill
Kütahya, Turkey

Kalptaru Papers Ltd.
Gandhinagar, Ahmadabad Mill
Gandhinagar, Ahmadabad, Gujarat, India

Kao Nan Pulp & Paper Mfg. Co., Ltd.
Nan Tzyy Dist Mill
Nan Tzyy District, Kaohsiung City, Taiwan

KapStone Kraft Paper Corporation
Longview Mill
Longview, Washington, United States

KapStone Kraft Paper Corporation
Roanoke Rapids Mill
Roanoke Rapids, North Carolina, United States

KapStone Paper Charleston Kraft LLC
North Charleston Mill
North Charleston, South Carolina, United States

Karanja Industries (P) Ltd., Paper Division
Bidar Mill
Bidar, Karnataka, India

Karavaevo
Karavaevo Mill
Pos. Karavaevo, Moscow Region, Russia

Karnaphuli Paper Mills Ltd.
Chandraghona Mill
Chandraghona of Kaptai, Chittagong, Bangladesh

Kartontol
St. Petersburg Mill
St. Petersburg, Russia

Karur KCP Packagings Ltd.
Pondicherry Mill
Pondicherry, Pondicherry, India

Kasuga Seishi Kogyo Co., Ltd.
Fuji-shi Mill
Fuji-shi, Shizuoka Pref., Japan

Kay Power & Paper Limited
Satara Mill
Satara, Maharashtra, India

Kaygaon Paper Mills Ltd.
Tq. Gangapur, Aurangabad Mill
Tq. Gangapur, Aurangabad, Maharashtra, India

Kenya Papermill Ltd.
Thika Mill
Thika, Central, Kenya

Kibo Match Group Pulp and Paperboard Mill
Moshi Mill
Moshi, Tanzania

Klabin S.A.
Correia Pinto Mill
Correia Pinto, Santa Catarina, Brazil

Klabin S.A.
Monte Alegre Mill
Telêmaco Borba, Paraná, Brazil

Komal Straw Board & Mill Board Industries
Gurdaspur Mill
Gurdaspur, Punjab, India

Kommunar Paper Mill
Kommunar Mill
Kommunar, Leningrad Region, Russia

Kondopoga
Kondopoga Mill
Kondopoga, Karelia, Russia

Korea Green Paper Mfg., Co. Ltd. - KGP
Asan Mill
Asan-si, Chungcheongnam-do, South Korea

Koryazhma Branch of Ilim Group
Kotlas Pulp and Paper Mill
Koryazhma, Arkhangelsk Region, Russia

Kostenez-HHI PLC
Kostenez Mill
Kostenez, Bulgaria

Kotkamills Oy
Kotka Mill
Kotka, Finland

Kovai Maruthi Papers & Boards (P) Ltd.
Salem Mill
Salem, Tamil Nadu, India

KPAQ Industries LLC
Saint Francisville Mill
Saint Francisville, Louisiana, United States

KR Pulp & Papers Ltd.
Shahjahanpur Mill
Shahjahanpur, Uttar Pradesh, India

Krasnaya Zvezda
Krasnaya Zvezda Mill
Chashniki, Vitebsk region, Belarus

Kronex-Ukraina, Ltd.
Zmiev Mill
Zmiev, Kharkovskaya Obl., Ukraine

Kulik Paper Industries (P) Ltd.
Raiganj Mill
Uttar Dinajpur, West Bengal, India

Kwality Pulp & Paper Mills
Valsad Mill
Valsad, Gujarat, India

Packaging papers

Lalji Board Industries (P) Ltd.
Firozabad Mill
Firozabad, Uttar Pradesh, India

Lalskaya Paper Mill
Lalsk Mill
Lalsk, Kirovskaya Obl., Russia

Laxmi Paper Mills
Thane Mill
Dist. Ahmednagar, Maharashtra, India

LC Paper 1881, S.A.
Besalú Mill
Besalú, Girona, Spain

LEIPA Georg Leinfelder GmbH
Schrobenhausen Mill
Schrobenhausen, Germany

Lih Tai Industrial Corp.
Chu Tien Mill
Chu Tien, Pingtung County, Taiwan

Lintec Corp.
Kumagaya Mill
Kumagaya-shi, Saitama Pref., Japan

Lintec Corp.
Mishima Mill
Shikokuchuo-shi, Ehime Pref., Japan

Lothlorien (Pty) Ltd
Lothlorien Pulp Mill
Wadeville, Gauteng, South Africa

Lua Viet Paper Joint-Stock Co.
Ha Hoa District Mill
Ha Hoa District, Phú Tho Province, Vietnam

Lucart SpA
Porcari Mill
Porcari, Lucca, Italy

Lutepel Indústria e Com de Papel Ltda.
Lençóis Paulista Mill
Lençóis Paulista, São Paulo, Brazil

Lutsky KRK
Lutsk Mill
Lutsk, Ukraine

Lydall, Inc.
Rochester Mill
Rochester, New Hampshire, United States

M.P. Boards & Paper Mills (P) Ltd.
Dist. Vidisha Mill
Dist. Vidisha, Madhya Pradesh, India

Madhupaper Kenya Ltd.
Madhupaper Mill
Nairobi, Kenya

Madhya Bharat Papers Ltd.
Dist. Janjgir-Champa Mill
Dist. Janjgir-Champa, Chattisgarh, India

Magura Paper Mills Ltd.
Narayanganj Mill
Narayanganj, Narayanganj, Bangladesh

Maheshwari Paper Limited
Tal Palanpur Mill
Tal Palanpur, Gujarat, India

Manaylux Papers & Boards (P) Ltd. Yediyur
Taluk Tumkur Mill
Taluk Tumkur, Karnataka, India

Mandya National Paper Mills Ltd.
Belagola Mill
Belagola, Karnataka, India

Manufacturas de Papel CA (MANPA) S.A.C.A.
Maracay Packaging Mill
Maracay, Edo. Aragua, Venezuela

Manufacturera de Papel Bidasoa S.A. de C.V.
Teotihuacan Mill
Xolaltenco Teotihuacan, Edo. de México, Mexico

Marisky Pulp & Paper Mill
Volzhsk Mill
Volzhsk, Mari El Republic, Russia

Marusan Paper Corparation
Shikokuchuo-shi Mill
Shikokuchuo-shi, Ehime Pref., Japan

Marusumi Paper Co., Ltd.
Kawanoe Mill
Shikokuchuo-shi, Ehime Pref., Japan

MD Papéis Ltda.
Caieiras Mill
Caieiras, São Paulo, Brazil

MED Paper SA
Tangier Mill
Tangier, Morocco

Meenu Paper Mills (P) Ltd.
Muzaffarnagar Mill
Muzaffarnagar, Uttar Pradesh, India

Middle East Paper Company - (MEPCO)
Jeddah Mill
Jeddah, Saudi Arabia

Mien Tay Packing Co. Ltd.
Can Tho City Mill
Can Tho City, Vietnam

Mier
Lviv Mill
Lviv, Ukraine

Mohammadi Paper & Board Industries (Pvt.) Ltd.
Sheikhupura Lahore Unit 2
Sheikhupura Lahore, Punjab, Pakistan

Mokvynska Paper Mill, Ltd.
Mokvyn Mill
Mokvyn, Ukraine

Mondi
Pine Bluff Mill
Pine Bluff, Arkansas, United States

Mondi Dynäs AB
Väja Mill
Väja, Sweden

Mondi Frantschach GmbH
Frantschach Mill
St. Gertraud, Austria

Mondi SCP a.s.
Ružomberok Mill
Ružomberok, Slovakia

Mondi Stambolijski EAD
Stambolijski Mill
Stambolijski, Bulgaria

Mondi Stetí
Štetí Mill
Štetí, Czech Republic

Mondi Swiecie S.A.
Swiecie Mill
Swiecie, Poland

Mosaico Speciality Papers
Tolmezzo Mill
Tolmezzo, Udine, Italy

Mostafa Paper
Chittagong Mill
Chittagong, Chittagong, Bangladesh

Mufindi Paper Mills (MPM)
Mgololo Mill
Mgololo, Iringa Region, Tanzania

Multiverde Papéis Especiais Ltda.
Mogi das Cruzes Mill
Mogi das Cruzes, São Paulo, Brazil

Multiwal Pulp & Board Mills Ltd.
Dist. Udham Singh Nagar Mill
Dist. Udham Singh Nagar, Uttarakhand, India

Myanma Paper and Chemical Industries (MPCI)
Yeni Mill
Yedashe Township, Yeni, Bago Division, Myanmar

Nakagawa Seishi KK
Mattsuto Mill
Hakusan-shi, Ishikawa Pref., Japan

Namgang Paper Co., Ltd.
Chinju Mill
Jinju-si, Gyeongsangnam-do, South Korea

Nampak Tissue (Pty) Ltd.
Bellville Mill
Bellville South, Cape Town, South Africa

Nath Pulp & Paper Mills Ltd.
Aurangabad Mill
Aurangabad, Maharashtra, India

National Co. for Paper & Plastics
Kaluib, Abo Sena Mill
Kaluib, Abo Sena, Egypt

National Paper Co.
Alexandria Mill
Alexandria, Iskanderiya, Egypt

Natron-Hayat d.o.o.
Maglaj Mill
Maglaj, Bosnia & Herzegovina

Nefertiti Paper Co. Ltd
10th of Ramadan City Mill
10th of Ramadan City, Sharkeya, East Province, Egypt

Nelsun Paper Mills Ltd.
Chennai Mill
Thanjavur, Tamil Nadu, India

Packaging papers

New Bombay Paper Mills Pvt Ltd.
Bombay Mill
Dist. Raigarh, Maharashtra, India

Nice Papers Ltd.
Kamleshwar, Dist. Nagpur Mill
Dist. Nagpur, Maharashtra, India

Nikita Paper (P) Ltd.
Shamli Mill
Dist. Muzzaffarnagar, Uttar Pradesh, India

Nine Dragons Pulp & Paper (Leshan) Co., Ltd.
Leshan Mill
Leshan, Sichuan, China

Nine Dragons XingAn Paper Co., Ltd. (Inner Mongolia)
Zhalantun Mill
Zhalantun, Inner Mongolia, China

Nippon Paper Industries Co., Ltd.
Hokkaido Mill - Asahikawa
Asahikawa-shi, Hokkaido Pref., Japan

Nittow Papel S.A.
Campinas Mill
Campinas, São Paulo, Brazil

Nordic Paper Bäckhammar
Bäckhammars Bruk Mill
Kristinehamn, Sweden

Norpapel S.A.I.C.
Villa Ocampo Mill
Villa Ocampo, Santa Fé, Argentina

Nuove Cartiere di Tivoli S.R.L.
Villa Adriana Mill
Villa Adriana, Rome, Italy

OAO Technicheskaya Bumaga
Rybinskiy rayon Mill
Rybinskiy rayon, Yaroslavl obl., Russia

Oji Materia Co., Ltd.
Kure Mill
Kure-shi, Hiroshima Pref., Japan

Omer Tissue Mills (Pvt) Ltd
Lahore Mill
Lahore, Punjab, Pakistan

Omniafiltra, LLC
Beaver Falls Mill
Beaver Falls, New York, United States

OYKA Kagit Ve Ambalaj San Tic A.S.
Çaycuma Mill
Çaycuma, Zonguldak, Turkey

Paalson Paper & Board
Puddukottai Mill
Puddukottai, Tamil Nadu, India

Palode Paper Mills Ltd.
Thiruvananthapuram Dist. Mill
Trivendrum, Kerala, India

Pan Paper Mills
Webuye Mill
Webuye, Bungoma District, Western, Kenya

Panasa, Papelera Nacional S.A.
Paramonga Mill
Paramonga, Lima, Peru

Papel Misionero S.A.I.F.C.
Puerto Mineral Mill
Capioví, Misiones, Argentina

Papelera de Brandia S.A.
La Coruña Mill
Santiago de Compostela, La Coruña, Spain

Papelera de Chihuahua S.A. de C.V.
Chihuahua Mill
Chihuahua, Chihuahua, Mexico

Papelera del Nevado S.A. de C.V.
Almoloyan Mill
San Miguel Almoloyan, Almoloya de Juarez, México, D.F., Mexico

Papelera del Pacífico S.A.
Retalhuleu Mill
Retalhuleu, Guatemala

Papelera Don Torcuato S.A.
Don Torcuato Mill
Don Torcuato, Buenos Aires, Argentina

Papelera Guipuzcoana de Zicuñaga S.A.
Hernani Mill
Hernani, Gipúzcoa, Spain

Papelera Iruña S.A. de C.V.
Iztapalapa Mill
Iztapalapa, México, D.F., Mexico

Papelera Nacional S.A.
Guayaquil Mill
Guayaquil, Guayas, Ecuador

Papelera Paysandú S.A.I.C.
Wilde Mill
Wilde, Buenos Aires, Argentina

Papelera Tlaxcala S.A. de C.V.
Iztapaluca Mill
Iztapaluca, Edo. de México, Mexico

Papelera Tucumán S.A.
San Justo, Tucuman II
San Justo, Buenos Aires, Argentina

Papelera Veracruzana S.A. de C.V.
Orizaba Mill
Orizaba, Veracruz, Mexico

Papeles Bío Bío
Concepción Mill
Concepción, VIII - Región del Biobío, Chile

Paper Corea Inc.
Gunsan Mill
Gunsan-si, Jeollabuk-do, South Korea

Paperland, Inc.
Quezon City Mill
Quezon City, Philippines

Papeterie de Raon
Raon L'Etape Mill
Raon L'Etape, Vosges, France

Papeteries de Fures
Tullins Mill
Fures, Tullins, France

Papeteries de Montségur
Montségur-sur-Lauzon Mill
Montségur-sur-Lauzon, France

Papierfabriek Doetinchem BV
Doetinchem Mill
Doetinchem, Netherlands

Papierwerke Lenk AG
Kappelrodeck Mill
Kappelrodeck, Germany

Papir-Mal
Malin Mill
Malin, Zhitomirskaya obl., Ukraine

Parijat Paper Mills Ltd.
Muzaffarnagar Mill
Muzaffarnagar, Uttar Pradesh, India

Paswara Paper Mill Limited
Meerut Mill
Meerut, Uttar Pradesh, India

PCE Embalagens
Manaus Mill
Manaus, Amazonas, Brazil

Port Townsend Paper Corp.
Port Townsend Mill
Port Townsend, Washington, United States

Premium Paper & Boards Ind. Ltd.
Surat Mill
Surat, Gujarat, India

Primo Tedesco S.A.
Caçador Mill
Caçador, Santa Catarina, Brazil

Progressive Paper Mills (P) Ltd.
Kolkata Mill
Kolkata, West Bengal, India

Proletariy, JSC
Surazh Mill
Surazh, Bryansk Region, Russia

Prolific Papers Pvt. Ltd.
Kashipur, Udham Singh Nagar Mill
Kashipur, Udham Singh Nagar, Uttarakhand, India

PT Gunung Jaya Agung
Karawaci Mill
Karawaci, Tangerang, Jawa Barat, Indonesia

PT Jaya Kertas
Nganjuk Mill
Nganjuk, East Java, Indonesia

PT Karya Tulada
Karawaci Mill
Tangerang, Banten, West Java, Indonesia

PT Kertas Blabak Megelang
Magelang Mill
Magelang, Central Java, Indonesia

PT Pabrik Kertas Tjiwi Kimia Tbk
Mojokerto (PT Pabrik Kertas Tjiwi Kimia) Mill
Mojokerto, East Java, Indonesia

PT Parisindo Pratama
Bogor Mill
Bogor, West Java, Indonesia

PT Pura Barutama
Kudus Mill
Kudus, Central Java, Indonesia

PT Pura Nusapersada
Terban, Kudus Mill
Terban, Kudus, Central Java, Indonesia

Packaging papers

PT Sinar Hoperindo
Bogor Mill
Bogor, West Java, Indonesia

PT Suparma, Tbk.
Surabaya Mill
Surabaya, East Java, Indonesia

PT Unipa Daya
Tangerang Mill
Karawaci, Tangerang, Jawa Barat, Indonesia

Pyramids Paper Mills S.A.E. - Flora
6th October City Mill
6th October City, El Giza, Egypt

R A Shaikh Paper Mills Pvt. Ltd.
Valsad Mill
Vapi, Gujarat, India

Raipaper S.r.l.
Isola del Liri Mill
Isola del Liri, Frosinone, Italy

Rajesh Paper Mills Ltd.
Shikohabad Mill
Shikohabad, Uttar Pradesh, India

Rakta, General Co. for Paper Industry
Rakta Mill
Alexandria, Iskanderiya, Egypt

Rama Shyma Papers Ltd.
Bareilly Mill
Bareilly, Uttar Pradesh, India

Raman Boards Ltd.
Mysore Mill
Mysore, Karnataka, India

Rana Mohendra Paper Ltd.
Dist. Ropar Mill
Dist. Ropar, Punjab, India

Rana Papers Ltd.
Muzaffarnagar Mill
Muzaffarnagar, Uttar Pradesh, India

Ravindra Paper Mills (P) Ltd.
Karnal Mill
Karnal, Haryana, India

Rayana Paper & Board Industries Ltd.
Basti Mill
Basti, Uttar Pradesh, India

Reliance Paper Mills
Bhairahawa Mill
Bhairahawa, Nepal

Remco Paper & Board Industries Pvt. Ltd.
Valsad Mill
Valsad, Gujarat, India

Renova - Fábrica de Papel do Almonda S.A.
Torres Novas Mill
Torres Novas, Portugal

Rolex Paper Mills Ltd.
Vill. Chinta Parru Mill
Vill. Chinta Parru, Andhra Pradesh, India

Roshan Lal Paper Mills Pvt Ltd
Bhatinda Mill
Bhatinda, Punjab, India

S.N. Paper Mills (P) Ltd.
Dist. Ludhiana Mill
Dist. Ludhiana, Punjab, India

Sainath Paper Mills
Dist. Valsad Mill
Dist. Valsad, Gujarat, India

Saiyed Paper Mills Ltd.
Vapi Mill
Vapi, Gujarat, India

Sangal Papers Ltd.
Meerut Mill
Meerut, Uttar Pradesh, India

Sanyo Paper Co., Ltd.
Sennan-shi Mill
Sennan-shi, Osaka Pref., Japan

Saraogi Paper Mills (P) Ltd.
Kishanganj Mill
Kishanganj, Bihar, India

Sardhana Papers (P) Ltd.
Sardhana Mill
Sardhana, Uttar Pradesh, India

Satyam Industries Private Ltd.
Panipat Mill
Panipat, Haryana, India

Saurashtra Paper & Board Mills Ltd.
Navagam Mill
Rajkot, Gujarat, India

SCA Hygiene Products SE
Mannheim Mill
Mannheim, Germany

Segezha Pulp & Paper Mill
Segezha Mill
Segezha, Karelia, Russia

Sein y Cia. SA
Ranelagh Mill
Ranelagh, Buenos Aires, Argentina

Selenginsky Pulp & Board Mill
Selenginsk Mill
Selenginsk, Buryatia Republic, Russia

Sengés Papel e Celulose Ltda.
Senges Mill
Senges, Paraná, Brazil

Shah Paper Mills Ltd.
Valsad Mill
Valsad, Gujarat, India

Shakumbhri Pulp & Paper Mills Ltd.
Muzaffarnagar Mill
Muzaffarnagar, Uttar Pradesh, India

Shalimar Krafts and Tissue (P) Ltd.
Muzaffarnagar Mill
Muzaffarnagar, Uttar Pradesh, India

Shalimar Paper Mills (P) Ltd.
Muzaffarnagar Mill
Muzaffarnagar, Uttar Pradesh, India

Shamli Paper Mills Ltd.
Vill. Sikka Shamli Mill
Vill. Sikka Shamli, Uttar Pradesh, India

Shandong Lianxi Paper Co. Ltd.
Rizhao Mill
Rizhao, Shandong, China

Shandong Qingdao Haiwang Paper Property Share Co., Ltd.
Qingdao Mill
Qingdao, Shandong, China

Shandong Rizhao Huatai Paper Co. Ltd.
Rizhao Mill
Rizhao, Shandong, China

Shandong Taiding Material Technology Co., Ltd.
Dezhou Mill
Dezhou, Shandong, China

Shayona Pulp Conversion Mills Pvt. Ltd.
Aurangabad Mill
Aurangabad, Maharashtra, India

Shelavi Pulp & Paper Mills (P) Ltd.
Mehsana Mill
Chhatral, Dist. Mehsana, Gujarat, India

Shiroyama Paper Mfg. Co., Ltd.
Shikokuchuo-shi Mill
Shikokuchuo-shi, Ehime Pref., Japan

Shiv Shakti Kraft Board Mills (P) Ltd.
Dist. Aurangabad Mill
Dist. Aurangabad, Maharashtra, India

Shiva Shakti Paper Mills Ltd.
Vidisha Mill
Vidisha, Madhya Pradesh, India

Shree Ajit Pulp and Paper Ltd.
Dist. Valsad Mill
Dist. Valsad, Gujarat, India

Shree Ambeshwar Paper Mills Ltd.
Ankleshwar Mill
Ankleshwar, Gujarat, India

Shree Badri Kedar Papers (P) Ltd.
Najibabad Mill
Najibabad, Uttar Pradesh, India

Shree Bhageshwari Papers Ltd
Muzaffarnagar Mill
Muzaffarnagar, Uttar Pradesh, India

Shree Gajanan Papers & Boards (P) Ltd.
Vapi, Dist. Valsad Mill
Vapi, Dist. Valsad, Gujarat, India

Shree Ganesh Agroils (Paper Division)
Ludhiana Mill
Ludhiana, Punjab, India

Shree Jagdambe Paper Mills Ltd.
Sirsa Mill
Sirsa, Haryana, India

Shree Kaiwal Paper Mill
Dist. Panchmahal Mill
Dist. Panchmahal, Gujarat, India

Shree Marathawada Paper Mills (P) Ltd.
Dist. Beed Mill
Dist. Beed, Maharashtra, India

Shree Raj- Rajeshwari Pap-Chem Industries (P) Ltd.
Nasik Mill
Dist. Nasik, Maharashtra, India

Packaging papers

Shree Sitaram Paper Mills Ltd.
Bharuch Mill
Dist. Bharuch, Gujarat, India

Shri Bankey Bihari Lal Board Mills
Ghaziabad Mill
Ghaziabad, Uttar Pradesh, India

Shri Krishna Paper & Board Mills
Dombivli Mill
Dombivli, Maharashtra, India

Shri Ramchander Straw Products Ltd.
Dist. Moradabad Mill
Dist. Moradabad, Uttar Pradesh, India

Siam Paper J.N.K. Industrial Co., Ltd.
Bangkok Mill
Bangkok, Bangkok, Thailand

Sichuan Yinge Bamboo Pulp & Paper Co., Ltd.
Luzhou (Sichuan Yinge) Mill
Luzhou, Sichuan, China

Sichuan Yongfeng Paper-Making Joint-Stock Co., Ltd.
Leshan Mill
Leshan, Sichuan, China

Slavuta-Papir, JSC
Slavuta Mill
Slavuta, Ukraine

Smurfit Kappa Cartón de Colombia SA
Yumbo Mill
Cali, Valle de Cauca, Colombia

Smurfit Kappa Nervión
Iurreta Mill
Iurreta, Vizcaya, Spain

Smurfit Kappa Sangüesa Paper
Sanguesa Mill
Sangüesa, Navarra, Spain

Sociedad Fábrica de Papel y Cartón Schorr y Concha S.A.
Talca Mill
Talca, VII - Región del Maule, Chile

Sokolsky Pulp & Paper Mill
Sokol Mill
Sokol, Vologodskaya obl., Russia

Solid Containers Ltd.
Thane Mill
Thane, Maharashtra, India

Solombalsky Pulp & Paper Mill
Arkhangelsk Mill
Arkhangelsk, Russia

Somes SA Dej
Dej Mill
Dej, Judet Cluj, Romania

Sona Paper & Boards Ltd.
Patiala Mill
Dist. Mohali, Punjab, India

Songhak Paper Co., Ltd.
Yangsan Mill
Yangsan-si, Gyeongsangnam-do, South Korea

Sotipapier - Société Tunisienne Industrielle du Papier et du Carton - S.A.R.L.
Belli Mill
Belli, Tunisia

South African Paper Mills (SAPM)
Durban Mill
Jacobs, Durban, KwaZulu-Natal, South Africa

South India Paper Mills Ltd.
Nanjangud Mill
Nanjangud, Karnataka, India

SP Fiber Technologies LLC (SPFT)
Dublin Mill
Dublin, Georgia, United States

Spaa Straw Board Ind. Pvt. Ltd.
Bolangir Mill
Bolangir, Odisha, India

Spartak
Shklov Mill
Shklov, Mogilev Region, Belarus

Speciality Papers Ltd.
Valsad Mill
Vapi, Dist. Valsad, Gujarat, India

Sprick GmbH & Co.
Mitte Mill
Diemelstadt, Germany

Sri Luxmi Tulasi Agro Paper Pvt Ltd.
Rajahmundry Mill
Rajahmundry, Andhra Pradesh, India

Sri Vinayaka Paper Boards (P) Ltd.
Rajanagaram Mandal Mill
Rajanagaram Mandal, Andhra Pradesh, India

Ssangyong Paper Co., Ltd.
Osan Mill
Osan-si, Gyeonggi-do, South Korea

Stadfast Paper Mills Pvt. Ltd.
Valsad Mill
Dist. Bulsar, Gujarat, India

Stora Enso Poland S.A.
Ostroleka Mill
Ostroleka, Poland

Stora Enso Renewable Packaging
Imatra Mills (Kaukopää & Tainionkoski)
Imatra, Finland

Suchak Paper Manufacturing Co. (P) Ltd.
Dist. Thane Mill
Dist. Thane, Maharashtra, India

Sukhraj Agro Papers Ltd.
Dist. Sangrur Mill
Dist. Sangrur, Punjab, India

Sundaram Multi Pap Ltd.
Nagpur Mill
Kanhan, Dist. Nagpur, Maharashtra, India

Super Deluxe Paper Mills Pvt. Ltd.
Vapi, Dist. Valsad Mill
Dist. Valsad, Gujarat, India

Surya Paper Mills
Raipur Mill
Raipur, Chattisgarh, India

Svetlogorskiy Pulp and Board Mill
Svetlogorsk Mill
Svetlogorsk, Gomel Region, Belarus

T.T.K. Pharma Ltd. (Paper division)
Dist. Erode Mill
Dist. Erode, Tamil Nadu, India

Taiko Paper Mfg. Co., Ltd.
Fuji-shi Mill
Fuji-shi, Shizuoka Pref., Japan

Tan Mai Group Joint Stock Co.
Dong Nai Mill
Bien Hoa City, Dong Nai Province, Vietnam

Technocart SA
Tripolis Mill
Tripolis, Greece

Tehri Pulp & Paper Ltd.
Muzaffarnagar Mill
Muzaffarnagar, Uttar Pradesh, India

Tej Card Board & Paper Industries (P) Ltd.
Dist. Amritsar Mill
Dist. Amritsar, Punjab, India

Tejal Paper Mills Pvt. Ltd.
Mehsana Mill
Mehsana, Gujarat, India

Thai Kraft Paper Industry Co., Ltd.
Wangsala Mill
Tha Muang Distr., Kanchanaburi, Kanchanaburi, Thailand

The Rahuri Pulp & Paper Mills
Ahmednagar Mill
Ahmednagar, Maharashtra, India

Theen Seng Paper Manufacturing Sdn. Bhd.
Rasa Mill
Rasa, Hulu Selangor, Selangor Darul Ehsan, Malaysia

Three Star Paper Mills (P) Ltd.
Dist. Gautam Budh Nagar Mill
Dist. Gautam Budh Nagar, Uttar Pradesh, India

Todo Papel S.A. de C.V.
Ixtapaluca Mill
Ixtapaluca, México, D.F., Mexico

Tolko Manitoba Kraft Papers
The Pas Mill
The Pas, Manitoba, Canada

Tonic Industrie EPE
Ouate Industrie Mill
Bou Ismail, Wilaya d'Alger, Algeria

Trakya Kagit San ve TIC. A.S.
Tekirdag Mill
Tekirdag, Tekirdag, Turkey

Travancore Paper Mills (P) Ltd.
Alappuzha Dist. Mill
Alappuzha Dist., Karnataka, India

Trombini Industrial S.A.
Fraiburgo Mill
Fraiburgo, Santa Catarina, Brazil

Trupal S.A.
Evitamiento Mill
El Agustino, Lima, Lima, Peru

Specialty and industrial

UCAL Donusen Kagit San ve Tic A.S.
Sirapinar Mill
Sirapinar, Umraniye, Istanbul, Turkey

Umesh Board & Paper Mills (P) Ltd.
Tq. & Dist. Aurangabad Mill
Tq. & Dist. Aurangabad, Maharashtra, India

Unión Papelera Platense
La Plata Mill
La Plata, Buenos Aires, Argentina

Unitech Paper & Board Industries (P) Ltd.
Dist. West Midnapore Mill
Dist. West Midnapore, West Bengal, India

Unitech Paper Mills (P) Ltd.
Midnapore Mill
Midnapore, West Bengal, India

United Paper Boards Limited
Patna Mill
Patna, Bihar, India

UPP Pulp & Paper (M) Sdn Bhd
Batang Berjuntai Mill
Ijok, Batang Berjuntai, Selangor Darul Ehsan, Malaysia

Vaibhav Paper Boards (P)Ltd.
Vapi, Dist. Valsad Mill
Vapi, Dist. Valsad, Gujarat, India

Vaishnav Fibers Ltd.
Rajgarh Mill
Rajgarh, Madhya Pradesh, India

Valaichenai Paper Mills
Valaichenai Mill
Valaichenai, Sri Lanka

Vamsadhara Paper Mills Ltd.
Dist. Srikakulam Mill
Dist. Srikakulam, Andhra Pradesh, India

Vapi Paper Mills Ltd.
Vapi, Dist. Valsad Mill
Vapi, Dist. Valsad, Gujarat, India

Ved Cellulose Limited
Ghaziabad Mill
Ghaziabad, Uttar Pradesh, India

Velgiiskaya Paper Mill
Borovichi Mill
Borovichi, Novgorod Region, Russia

Vijayalakshmi Paper Mills
Dindigul Mill
Dindigul, Tamil Nadu, India

Vinh Hue Paper Joint-Stock Co. (Vihimex)
Ho Chi Minh City Mill
Thu Duc District, Ho Chi Minh City, Binh Duong Province, Vietnam

Viochartiki Paper Mill SA
Aspropirgos Mill
Aspropirgos, Attica, Greece

Vishal Paper Mills Ltd.
Malerkotla Mill
Malerkotla, Punjab, India

Vishnupriya Paper Mill Private Ltd.
Chennai Mill
Thiruvallur Dist., Chennai, Tamil Nadu, India

Vishwa Paper Mills
Aurangabad Mill
Dist. Aurangabad, Maharashtra, India

Volga
Balakhna Mill
Balakhna, Nizhny Novgorod, Russia

Vrancart SA
Adjud Mill
Adjud, Vrancea, Romania

Well Pack Papers & Containers Ltd.
Mehsana Mill
Varnaj, Kadi, Mehsana, Gujarat, India

Windsor-Stevens Inc.
Poquonock Mill
Windsor, Connecticut, United States

Wood Papers Ltd.
Bilimora Mill
Bilimora, Gujarat, India

Yaroslavl Paper ZAO
Yaroslavl Mill
Yaroslavl, Yaroslavl obl., Russia

Yash Papers Ltd.
Faizabad Mill
Faizabad, Uttar Pradesh, India

Yung Chi Paper Co., Ltd.
Chu Pei Mill
Chu Pei, Hsinchu County, Taiwan

Yung-Seng Development Enterprise Co., Ltd.
Taoyuan Mill
Taoyuan, Taoyuan County, Taiwan

Zambezi Paper Mills Ltd.
Ndola Mill
Ndola, Zambia

ZAO MPK KRZ - Multibranch Production Company KRZ
Ryazan Mill
Ryazan, Russia

Zaveri Paper & Board Mills
Dist. Dohad Mill
Dist. Dohad, Gujarat, India

Zellstoff Pöls AG
Pöls Mill
Pöls, Styria, Austria

Zhejiang Fuyang Kraft Paper Mill
Fuyang Mill
Fuyang, Zhejiang, China

Zhejiang Fuyang Wanfang Paper Co., Ltd.
Fuyang Mill
Fuyang, Zhejiang, China

Zhejiang Hangzhou Fulun Paper Co., Ltd.
Fuyang Mill
Fuyang, Zhejiang, China

Zhejiang Winbon Special Paper Co. Ltd.
Quzhou Mill
Quzhou, Zhejiang, China

Zhydachiv Pulp & Paper Mill
Zhydachiv Mill
Zhydachiv, Lviv obl., Ukraine

Specialty and industrial

3M Tilton
Tilton Mill
Tilton, New Hampshire, United States

Agarwal Duplex Board Mills Ltd.
Muzzaffarnagar Mill
Muzzaffarnagar, Uttar Pradesh, India

Ahlstrom Binzhou
Binzhou Mill
Binzhou, Shandong, China

Ahlstrom Brasil Indústria e Comércio de Papéis Especiais Ltda.
Louveira Mill
Louveira, São Paulo, Brazil

Ahlstrom Engine Filtration, L.L.C.
Taylorville Mill
Taylorville, Illinois, United States

Ahlstrom Filtration LLC
Madisonville Plant
Madisonville, Kentucky, United States

Ahlstrom Filtration LLC
Mount Holly Springs Mill
Mount Holly Springs, Pennsylvania, United States

Ahlstrom Korea Co., Ltd.
Hyunpoong Mill
Daegu-si, Daegu-si, South Korea

Ahlstrom Osnabrück GmbH
Osnabrück Mill
Osnabrück, Germany

Ahlstrom Packaging SA
St. Séverin Mill
Saint Séverin, France

Ahlstrom Specialties SA
Bousbecque Mill
Bousbecque, France

Ahlstrom Specialties SA
Pont-Audemer Mill
Pont Audemer, France

Ahlstrom Tampere Oy
Kauttua Mill
Kauttua, Finland

Ahlstrom Yulong Specialty Paper Company Ltd.
Longkou Mill
Longkou, Shandong, China

Alabama Paper Products, LLC
Tuscaloosa Mill
Tuscaloosa, Alabama, United States

Alamigeon SA
Ruelle sur Touvre Mill
Ruelle sur Touvre, France

Albertin Paperboard & Paper Mill
Slonim Mill
Slonim, Grodno Region, Belarus

Specialty and industrial

Anhui Huabon Specialty Paper Co. Ltd.
Huangshan Mill
Huangshan, Anhui, China

Anhui Jingfeng Paper Co., Ltd.
Huainan Mill
Huainan, Anhui, China

Anhui Mikitoku Paper Co., Ltd
Anqing Mill
Anqing, Anhui, China

Anhui Winbon Gaosen Paper Manufacture Co., Ltd.
Anqing Mill
Anqing, Anhui, China

Appleton Coated LLC
Combined Locks Mill
Combined Locks, Wisconsin, United States

Arctic Paper Grycksbo AB
Grycksbo Mill
Grycksbo, Sweden

Arjowiggins Fine Papers Pty. Ltd.
Stowford Mill
Ivybridge, Devon, United Kingdom

Arjowiggins Papiers Couchés S.A.
Aa Mill
Wizernes, Pas-de-Calais, France

Arjowiggins SAS
Palalda Mill
Amélie-les-Bains, France

Arjowiggins Security SAS
Crèvecoeur Mill
Jouy-sur-Morin, France

Arkhangelsk Pulp & Paper Mill
Novodvinsk (Arkhangelsk - APPM) Mill
Novodvinsk, Arkhangelsk Region, Russia

Atas Paper (Pvt) Ltd.
Sheikhupura Mill
Sheikhupura, Punjab, Pakistan

Awa Paper Manufacturing Co., Ltd.
Anan Mill
Anan-shi, Tokushima Pref., Japan

Awa Paper Manufacturing Co., Ltd.
Tokushima Mill
Tokushima, Tokushima Pref., Japan

Azumi Filter Paper Co., Ltd.
Honsha Mill
Osaka-shi, Osaka Pref., Japan

Bashundhara Paper Mills Ltd.
Unit 1
Sonargaon, Baranagar, Narayanganj, Bangladesh

Bashundhara Paper Mills Ltd.
Unit 3
Gazaria, Munshigonj, Bangladesh

Bernard Dumas SAS
Creysse Mill
Creysse, France

BillerudKorsnäs AB
Beetham Mill
Milnthorpe, Cumbria, United Kingdom

BillerudKorsnäs AB
Gruvön Mill
Grums, Sweden

BillerudKorsnäs AB
Karlsborg Mill
Karlsborg, Sweden

BillerudKorsnäs AB
Skärblacka Mill
Skärblacka, Sweden

BillerudKorsnäs Finland Oy
Pietarsaari Mill
Pietarsaari, Finland

BillerudKorsnäs Finland Oy
Tervasaari Mill
Valkeakoski, Finland

Boise Paper
International Falls Mill
International Falls, Minnesota, United States

Boise Paper
Wallula Mill
Wallula, Washington, United States

BPM, Inc.
Peshtigo Mill
Peshtigo, Wisconsin, United States

Brigl & Bergmeister GmbH
Niklasdorf Mill
Niklasdorf, Styria, Austria

Burrows Paper
Lyonsdale Mill
Lyons Falls, New York, United States

Burrows Paper
Mill Street Facility
Little Falls, New York, United States

Burrows Paper
Mohawk Valley Facility
Little Falls, New York, United States

Burrows Paper
Pickens Mill
Pickens, Mississippi, United States

Camose Srl
del Serra Mill
Buti, Pisa, Italy

Cartiera di Guarcino S.p.A.
Guarcino Mill
Guarcino, Frosinone, Italy

Cartiera Galliera srl
Galliera Veneta Mill
Galliera Veneta, Padua, Italy

Cartiera Giacosa SpA
Front Canavese Mill
Front Canavese, Turin, Italy

Cartiera Ponte d'Oro Ansalcarta Srl
Pracando Mill
Pracando Villa Basilica, Lucca, Italy

Cartiera S. Giovanni di Figli di Checchi G. S.R.L.
Pietrabuona di Pescia Mill
Pietrabuona di Pescia, Pistoia, Italy

Cartiera Sicars S.R.L.
Aci Bonaccorsi Mill
Aci Bonaccorsi, Catania, Italy

Cartiere Ermolli S.p.a.
Moggio Udinese Mill
Moggio Udinese, Udine, Italy

Cartiere Panigada S.R.L.
Piteglio Mill
Piteglio, Pistoia, Italy

Cascades Lupel Inc.
Trois-Rivières Mill
Trois-Rivières, Quebec, Canada

Celulosa de Fibras Mexicanas S.A. de C.V.
Apizaco Mill
Apizaco, Tlaxacala, Mexico

CELUPA - Industrial Celulose e Papel Guaíba Ltda.
Guaíba Mill
Guaíba, Rio Grande do Sul, Brazil

Century Paper & Board Mills Ltd.
Kasur Mill
Bhai Pheru, Dist. Kasur, Pakistan

Cham Paper Group Italia S.p.A.
Carmignano Mill
Carmignano di Brenta, Padua, Italy

Cham Paper Group Italia S.p.A.
Condino Mill
Condino, Trento, Italy

Chang Chun Plastics Co., Ltd.
Ta Liao Mill
Ta Liao District, Kaohsiung City, Taiwan

Chenming Paper Holdings Ltd.
Shouguang (Shouguang Chenming Art Paper No. 6) Mill
Shouguang, Shandong, China

Chi Hsiang Paper Co., Ltd.
Tou Liu Mill
Tou Liu, Yunlin County, Taiwan

China Tobacco Mauduit (Jiangmen) Paper Industry Company Ltd.
Jiangmen Mill
Jiangmen, Guangdong, China

Chuetsu Pulp & Paper Co., Ltd.
Takaoka (Nohmachi) Mill
Takaoka-shi, Toyama Pref., Japan

Chung Rhy Special Paper Mfg. Co., Ltd.
Pu Li Mill
Pu Li, Nantou County, Taiwan

Cita Peuchoon Paper Mills Sdn. Bhd.
Sungai Petani Mill
Sungai Petani, Kedah, Malaysia

Clearwater Paper Corporation
Menominee Mill
Menominee, Michigan, United States

Clearwater Paper Corporation
Saint Catharines Mill
Saint Catharines, Ontario, Canada

Specialty and industrial

Clearwater Paper Corporation
Wiggins Mill
Wiggins, Mississippi, United States

CMPC Papeles Cordillera S.A.
Puente Alto Mill
Puente Alto, RM - Región Metro. de Santiago, Chile

Copamex Industrias S.A. de C.V.
Monterrey Mill
San Nicolas de los Garza, Nuevo León, Mexico

Cottrell Paper Co., Inc.
Rock City Falls Mill
Rock City Falls, New York, United States

Crane & Co., Inc.
Byron Weston Mill
Dalton, Massachusetts, United States

Crocker Technical Papers
Fitchburg Mill
Fitchburg, Massachusetts, United States

Daio Paper Corp.
Kani Mill
Kani-shi, Gifu Pref., Japan

Der Lih Paper Co., Ltd.
Tou Liu Mill
Tou Liu, Yunlin County, Taiwan

Dev Kiran Paper Mills (P) Ltd.
Bangalore Mill
Bangalore, Karnataka, India

Devon Valley Ltd.
Devon Valley Mill
Hele, Exeter, Devon, United Kingdom

Diósgyöri Papírgyár Rt.
Miskolc Mill
Miskolc, Hungary

Dobrushskaya Paper Mill "Geroi Truda", OJSC
Dobrush Mill
Dobrush, Gomel Region, Belarus

Domtar Corporation
Espanola Mill
Espanola, Ontario, Canada

Domtar Corporation
Marlboro Mill
Bennettsville, South Carolina, United States

Domtar Corporation
Port Huron Mill
Port Huron, Michigan, United States

Dong Da Paper Mfg. Co., Ltd.
Ming Chien Mill
Ming Chien, Nantou County, Taiwan

Dongyang Paper Mfg. Co., Ltd.
Asan Mill
Ansan-si, Chungcheongnam-do, South Korea

Dr. Franz Feurstein GmbH
Traun Mill
Traun, Oberösterreich, Austria

Dresden Papier GmbH
Dresden Mill
Heidenau, Germany

Drewsen Spezialpapiere GmbH & Co. KG
Lachendorf Mill
Lachendorf, Germany

Dunafin Kft.
Dunaujvaros Mill
Dunaujvaros, Hungary

Dunn Paper
Port Huron Mill
Port Huron, Michigan, United States

Dynic Corporation
Fuji Mill
Fuji-shi, Shizuoka Pref., Japan

Ecologicheskie Tekhnologii Ltd
Balakhna Mill
Balakhna, Nizhny Novgorod, Russia

Elikon
Murygino Mill
Murygino, Kirovskaya Obl., Russia

Erfurt & Sohn KG
Wuppertal Mill
Wuppertal, Germany

Evergreen Packaging Inc.
Canton Mill
Canton, North Carolina, United States

Expera Specialty Solutions
Kaukauna Mill
Kaukauna, Wisconsin, United States

Expera Specialty Solutions
Mosinee Mill
Mosinee, Wisconsin, United States

Expera Specialty Solutions
Nicolet Mill
De Pere, Wisconsin, United States

Expera Specialty Solutions
Rhinelander Mill
Rhinelander, Wisconsin, United States

Fábrica de Papel de Medros, Lda.
Barcelinhos Mill
Barcelinhos, Barcelos, Portugal

Fábrica de Papel La Soledad S.A. de C.V.
Los Reyes Acaquilpan Mill
Los Reyes Acaquilpan, México, D.F., Mexico

Fábrica de Papel Santa Therezinha (SANTHER)
Guaíba Mill
Guaíba, Rio Grande do Sul, Brazil

Fábrica de Papel Santa Therezinha (SANTHER)
Penha Mill
São Paulo, São Paulo, Brazil

Fábrica Nacional de Moneda y Timbre-FNMT
Burgos Mill
Burgos, Spain

Fabryka Papieru Malta Decor S.A.
Poznan Mill
Poznan, Poland

Fabryka Papieru Malta Decor S.A.
Rudawa Mill
Nowy Swietów, Poland

Fedrigoni S.P.A.
Fabriano Mill
Fabriano, Ancona, Italy

FiberMark North America, Inc.
Brattleboro Mill
Brattleboro, Vermont, United States

Filtros Anoia, S.A.
Sant Pere de Riudebitlles Mill
Sant Pere de Riudebitlles, Barcelona, Spain

Fujian Naoshan Paper Group Co. Ltd
Sanming Mill
Sanming, Fujian, China

Fujian Youlanfa Group
Jinjiang Mill
Jinjiang, Fujian, China

Fujikyowa Paper Mfg. Co., Ltd.
Fuji Mill
Fuji-Shi, Shizuoka Pref., Japan

Gai Chin Paper Co, Ltd.
Hou Lung Mill
Hou Lung, Miaoli County, Taiwan

Gascogne Paper
Mimizan Mill
Mimizan, Landes, France

Gebr. Grünewald GmbH & Co. KG
Kirchhundem Mill
Kirchhundem-Hofolpe, Germany

Gebr. Hoffsümmer Spezialpapier GmbH & Co. KG
Düren Mill
Düren, Germany

Georgia-Pacific LLC
Palatka Mill
Palatka, Florida, United States

Glassine Canada Inc.
Quebec City Mill
Quebec City, Quebec, Canada

Glatfelter
Scaër Mill
Scaër, France

Glatfelter
Spring Grove Mill
Spring Grove, Pennsylvania, United States

Glatfelter Gernsbach GmbH & Co. KG
Gernsbach Mill
Gernsbach, Germany

Glatfelter UK Ltd.
Lydney Paper Mill
Lydney, Gloucestershire, United Kingdom

Glatz Finepaper Vietnam Co. Ltd.
Ho Chi Minh City Mill
Thu Dau Mot, Binh Duong Province, Vietnam

Gold East Paper (Jiangsu) Co., Ltd.
Zhenjiang (Gold East Paper) Mill
Zhenjiang, Jiangsu, China

Specialty and industrial

Goricane, tovarna papirja Medvode, d.d.
Medvode Mill
Medvode, Slovenia

GrünPerga Papier GmbH
Grünhainichen Mill
Grünhainichen, Germany

Gruppo Cordenons SpA
Cordenons Mill
Cordenons, Pordenone, Italy

Guangxi Forest Lipu Paper Co., Ltd.
Lipu Mill
Lipu, Guangxi, China

Guangxi Guilin No. 2 Paper Mill
Guilin Mill
Guilin, Guangxi, China

Guangxi Guilin Qifeng Paper Co., Ltd.
Guilin Mill
Guilin, Guangxi, China

Guangzhou Zhujiang Specialty Paper Co., Ltd.
Guangzhou Mill
Guangzhou, Guangdong, China

Gusmer Enterprises Inc.
Waupaca Mill
Waupaca, Wisconsin, United States

GusmerCellulo
Fresno Mill
Fresno, California, United States

Halong Trading Company
Tien Yen District Mill
Tien Yen District, Quang Ninh Province, Vietnam

Hangzhou Huatian Paper Co., Ltd.
Linan Mill
Linan, Zhejiang, China

Hangzhou Huawang New Material Co., Ltd.
Hangzhou Mill
Hangzhou, Zhejiang, China

Hanuman Chromocoates Ltd.
Chhindwara Mill
Chhindwara, Madhya Pradesh, India

Hapaco Joss Paper Mill
Tran Yen District Mill
Tran Yen District, Yen Bai Province, Vietnam

Hapaco Paper Mill
Van Ban District Mill
Van Ban District, Lao Cai Province, Vietnam

Hapaco Pulp Mill
Mai Chau District Mill
Mai Chau District, Hoa Binh Province, Vietnam

Hartford City Paper, LLC
Hartford City Mill
Hartford City, Indiana, United States

Hebei Baoding Xingji Specialty Paper Mill
Baoding Mill
Baoding, Hebei, China

Hebei Huixing Paper Co., Ltd.
Baoding Mill
Baoding, Hebei, China

Heilongjiang Mudanjiang Hengfeng Paper Group Co., Ltd.
Mudanjiang Mill
Mudanjiang, Heilongjiang, China

Henan Huifeng Paper Co., Ltd.
Zhoukou Mill
Zhoukou, Henan, China

Henan Neixiang Xianhe Special Paper & Pulp Co., Ltd.
Nanyang Mill
Nanyang, Henan, China

Highland Paper Mills Ltd.
Eldoret Mill
Eldoret, Western, Kenya

Hokuetsu Kishu Paper Co. Ltd.
Kishu Mill
Minamimuro-gun, Mie Pref., Japan

Hokuetsu Kishu Paper Co. Ltd.
Nagaoka Mill
Nagaoka-shi, Niigata Pref., Japan

Hollingsworth & Vose Co.
East Walpole Mill
East Walpole, Massachusetts, United States

Hollingsworth & Vose Co.
Easton Mill
Greenwich, New York, United States

Hollingsworth & Vose Co.
Greenwich Mill
Greenwich, New York, United States

Hollingsworth & Vose Co.
Hawkinsville Mill
Hawkinsville, Georgia, United States

Hollingsworth & Vose Co.
West Groton Mill
West Groton, Massachusetts, United States

Hollingsworth & Vose Co. Ltd.
Postlip Mills
Cheltenham, Gloucestershire, United Kingdom

Hollingsworth & Vose GmbH
Hatzfeld Mill
Hatzfeld, Germany

Hovomex S.A. de C.V.
Apizaco Mill
Apizaco, Tlaxacala, Mexico

Hubei Enshi Jinhua Group
Enshi Mill
Enshi, Hubei, China

Hunan Tiger Forest & Paper Group Yuanjiang Paper Co., Ltd.
Yuanjiang Mill
Yuanjiang, Hunan, China

Hunan Tiger Forest & Paper Group Yueyang Paper Co., Ltd.
Yueyang Mill
Yueyang, Hunan, China

Hunan Xiangfeng Specialty Paper Co., Ltd. No. 2 Branch Mill
Shaoyang Mill
Shaoyang, Hunan, China

Hunan Xiangfeng Specialty Paper Co., Ltd., No. 1 Branch Mill
Shaoyang Mill
Shaoyang, Hunan, China

Hussain Pulp, Paper & Board Mills Ltd.
Dhaka Mill
Dhaka, Dhaka, Bangladesh

IdemPapers SA
Virginal Mill
Virginal-Samme, Belgium

Iguaçu Celulose Papel S.A.
São José dos Pinhais Mill
São José dos Pinhais, Paraná, Brazil

Illig'sche Papierfabrik
Mühltal Mill
Mühltal, Germany

Interface Solutions Altenkirchen GmbH
Altenkirchen Mill
Altenkirchen, Germany

International Paper APPM Ltd.
Rajahmundry Mill
Rajahmundry, East Godavari, Andhra Pradesh, India

ITC Limited, Paperboards & Specialty Papers Division
Bhadrachalam Mill
Khammam, Bhadrachalam, Andhra Pradesh, India

ITC Limited, Paperboards & Specialty Papers Division
Tribeni Mill
Chandrahati, Hooghly, West Bengal, India

J. Tönnesmann & Vogel, Papierfabrik Hönnetal GmbH
Menden Mill
Menden, Germany

J. Vilaseca S.A.
Capellades Mill
Capellades, Barcelona, Spain

James Cropper
Kendal Mill
Kendal, Cumbria, United Kingdom

Jeng Chia Paper Product Co., Ltd.
Tai Pao Mill
Tai Pao, Chia-I County, Taiwan

Jiangsu Taizhou Jinsong Paper Co., Ltd.
Taizhou Mill
Taizhou, Jiangsu, China

Jiangxi Jinggangshan Paper Co., Ltd.
Jinggangshan Mill
Jinggangshan, Jiangxi, China

JIP - Papírny Vetrní, a.s.
Vetrní Mill
Vetrni, Czech Republic

Jujo Thermal Ltd.
Kauttua Mill
Kauttua, Finland

Specialty and industrial

Julius Glatz GmbH Papierfabriken
Frankeneck Mill
Frankeneck, Germany

Julius Glatz GmbH Papierfabriken
Neidenfels Mill
Neidenfels, Germany

Kao Nan Pulp & Paper Mfg. Co., Ltd.
Nan Tzyy Dist Mill
Nan Tzyy District, Kaohsiung City, Taiwan

KapStone Kraft Paper Corporation
Longview Mill
Longview, Washington, United States

Keio Paper Mfg. Co., Ltd.
Fuji-shi Mill
Fuji-shi, Shizuoka Pref., Japan

Kenya Papermill Ltd.
Thika Mill
Thika, Central, Kenya

Khatema Fibres Ltd.
Khatema Dist., Udham Singh Nagar Mill
Khatema Dist., Udham Singh Nagar, Uttar Pradesh, India

Kingdecor (Zhejiang) Co., Ltd.
Quzhou Mill
Quzhou, Zhejiang, China

KJ Specialty Paper Co., Ltd.
Fuji Mill
Fuji-shi, Shizuoka Pref., Japan

Koehler Kehl GmbH
Kehl Mill
Kehl, Germany

Kommunar Paper Mill
Kommunar Mill
Kommunar, Leningrad Region, Russia

Korea Green Paper Mfg., Co. Ltd. - KGP
Asan Mill
Asan-si, Chungcheongnam-do, South Korea

Korea Green Paper Mfg., Co. Ltd. - KGP
Pyoengtaek Mill
Pyeongtaek-si, Gyeonggi-do, South Korea

Koryazhma Branch of Ilim Group
Kotlas Pulp and Paper Mill
Koryazhma, Arkhangelsk Region, Russia

Kosino Paper Mill
Kosino Mill
Kosino, Zuevskiy rayon, Kirovskaya Obl., Russia

Krasnokamskaya Paper Mill Goznak
Krasnokamsk Mill
Krasnokamsk, Perm Region, Russia

Krempel-Group
Thalheim Mill
Thalheim, Germany

KRPA Paper, a.s.
Krpa Papir Mill
Hostinné, Czech Republic

Kukil Paper Mfg. Co., Ltd.
Idong-myeon, Yongin-si Mill
Idong-myeon, Yongin-si, Gyeonggi-do, South Korea

Kuo Zong Paper Mfg. Co., Ltd.
Kuan Tien Mill
Kuan Tien District, Tainan City, Taiwan

Kyoku-Ei Paper Mfg. Co., Ltd.
Fuji-shi Mill
Fuji-shi, Shizuoka Pref., Japan

Lalskaya Paper Mill
Lalsk Mill
Lalsk, Kirovskaya Obl., Russia

Lana Papiers Speciaux
Strasbourg Mill
Strasbourg, France

Lenzing Papier GmbH
Lenzing Paper Mill
Lenzing, Oberösterreich, Austria

Lintec Corp.
Kumagaya Mill
Kumagaya-shi, Saitama Pref., Japan

Lintec Corp.
Mishima Mill
Shikokuchuo-shi, Ehime Pref., Japan

Lucart SpA
Porcari Mill
Porcari, Lucca, Italy

Lutepel Indústria e Com de Papel Ltda.
Lençóis Paulista Mill
Lençóis Paulista, São Paulo, Brazil

Lydall Filtration Separation SAS
Melrand Mill
Melrand, France

Lydall, Inc.
Green Island Mill
Green Island, New York, United States

Lydall, Inc.
Rochester Mill
Rochester, New Hampshire, United States

M.P. Boards & Paper Mills (P) Ltd.
Dist. Vidisha Mill
Dist. Vidisha, Madhya Pradesh, India

Mahachai Kraft Paper Co., Ltd.
Samut Sakohn Mill
Amphur Muang, Samut Sakohn, Thailand

Malyn - Weidmann Paper Mill VAT
Malyn Mill
Malyn, Zhitomirskaya obl., Ukraine

Marisky Pulp & Paper Mill
Volzhsk Mill
Volzhsk, Mari El Republic, Russia

Marusan Paper Corparation
Shikokuchuo-shi Mill
Shikokuchuo-shi, Ehime Pref., Japan

Marusan Paper Mfg. Co., Ltd.
Honsha Mill
Haramachi-ku, Minami-soma-shi, Fukushima Pref., Japan

Maryland Paper
Williamsport Mill
Williamsport, Maryland, United States

MB Papeles Especiales
La Pobla de Claramunt Mill
La Pobla de Claramunt, Barcelona, Spain

MD Papéis Ltda.
Caieiras Mill
Caieiras, São Paulo, Brazil

Melitta Haushaltsprodukte GmbH & Co. KG
Minden Mill
Minden, Germany

Metsä Board Kyro
Kyro Mill
Kyröskoski, Finland

Metsä Tissue Corp.
Mänttä Mill
Mänttä, Finland

Metsä Tissue GmbH
Düren Mill
Düren, Germany

Miki Tokushu Paper Mfg. Co., Ltd.
Kawanoe Mill
Shikokuchuo-shi, Ehime Pref., Japan

Miquel y Costas & Miquel S.A.
de Besos mill
Barcelona, Spain

Miquel y Costas & Miquel S.A.
Mislata mill
Mislata, Valencia, Spain

Mitsubishi Paper Mills Ltd.
Shirakawa Mill
Nishi-Shirakawa-gun, Fukushima Pref., Japan

Mitsubishi Paper Mills Ltd.
Takasago Mill
Takasago-shi, Hyogo Pref., Japan

Molza Corp.
Muge Mill
Seki-shi, Gifu Pref., Japan

Mondi Frantschach GmbH
Frantschach Mill
St. Gertraud, Austria

Mondi Lohja Oy
Lohja Mill
Lohja, Finland

Mondi Stetí
Štetí Mill
Štetí, Czech Republic

Moorim SP Co., Ltd.
Daegu Mill
Buk-gu, Daegu-si, South Korea

Mopak Taşköprü Pulp and Cigarette Paper Plant
Kastamonu Mill
Kastamonu, Turkey

Mosaico Speciality Papers
Chiampo Mill
Chiampo, Vicenza, Italy

Mosaico Speciality Papers
Lugo di Vicenza Mill
Lugo di Vicenza, Vicenza, Italy

Specialty and industrial

Mosaico Speciality Papers
Tolmezzo Mill
Tolmezzo, Udine, Italy

Mosaico Speciality Papers
Treviso Mill
Carbonera, Treviso, Italy

Multiverde Papéis Especiais Ltda.
Mogi das Cruzes Mill
Mogi das Cruzes, São Paulo, Brazil

Munksjö Arches SAS
Arches Mill
Arches, France

Munksjö Dettingen GmbH
Dettingen Mill
Dettingen an der Erms, Germany

Munksjö Italia S.p.A.
Turin Mill
Mathi Canavese, Turin, Italy

Munksjö LabelPack
La Gère Mill
Pont Evêque, France

Munksjö LabelPack
Rottersac Mill
Lalinde, France

Munksjö LabelPack
Stenay Mill
Stenay, France

Munksjö Paper AB
Billingsfors Mill
Billingsfors, Sweden

Munksjö Paper AB
Jönköping mill
Jönköping, Sweden

Munksjö Paper GmbH
Unterkochen Mill
Aalen-Unterkochen, Germany

Munksjö Paper S.A.
Tolosa Mill
Berástegui, Gipúzcoa, Spain

Munktell & Filtrak GmbH
Bärenstein Mill
Bärenstein, Germany

Mysore Paper Mills Ltd.
Shimoga Mill
Bhadravati, Shimoga, Karnataka, India

Nakagawa Seishi KK
Mattsuto Mill
Hakusan-shi, Ishikawa Pref., Japan

Nath Pulp & Paper Mills Ltd.
Aurangabad Mill
Aurangabad, Maharashtra, India

Neenah Gessner GmbH
Bruckmühl Mill
Bruckmühl, Germany

Neenah Gessner GmbH
Feldkirchen-Westerham Mill
Feldkirchen-Westerham, Germany

Neenah Lahnstein
Lahnstein Mill
Lahnstein, Germany

Neenah Paper, Inc.
Munising Mill
Munising, Michigan, United States

Neo-Print
Tbilisi Mill
Tbilisi, Georgia

Neu Kaliss Spezialpapier GmbH
Neu Kaliss Mill
Neu Kaliss, Germany

Neukölln Spezialpapier NK GmbH & Co. KG
Berlin Mill
Berlin, Germany

NewPage Corporation
Escanaba Mill
Escanaba, Michigan, United States

NewPage Corporation
Luke Mill
Luke, Maryland, United States

NewPage Corporation
Rumford Mill
Rumford, Maine, United States

NewPage Corporation
Stevens Point Mill
Stevens Point, Wisconsin, United States

Nine Dragons Pulp & Paper (Leshan) Co., Ltd.
Leshan Mill
Leshan, Sichuan, China

Nippon Paper Industries Co., Ltd.
Akita Mill
Akita-shi, Akita Pref., Japan

Nippon Paper Industries Co., Ltd.
Fuji Mill
Fuji-shi, Shizuoka Pref., Japan

Nippon Paper Industries Co., Ltd.
Hokkaido Mill - Asahikawa
Asahikawa-shi, Hokkaido Pref., Japan

Nippon Paper Industries Co., Ltd.
Otake Mill
Otake-shi, Hiroshima Pref., Japan

Nippon Paper Papylia Co., Ltd.
Harada Mill
Fuji-shi, Shizuoka Pref., Japan

Nippon Paper Papylia Co., Ltd.
Harada Mill (Yodahashi)
Fuji-shi, Shizuoka Pref., Japan

Nippon Paper Papylia Co., Ltd.
Kochi Mill
Agawa-Gun, Kochi Pref., Japan

Nippon Paper Papylia Co., Ltd.
Suita Mill
Suita-shi, Osaka Pref., Japan

Nisshinbo Paper Products, Inc.
Fuji Mill
Fuji-shi, Shizuoka Pref., Japan

Nisshinkogyo Co., Ltd.
Yamagata Mill
Yamagata-shi, Yamagata Pref., Japan

Nordic Paper Åmotfors
Åmotfors Bruk Mill
Åmotfors, Sweden

Nordic Paper Bäckhammar
Bäckhammars Bruk Mill
Kristinehamn, Sweden

Nordic Paper Greåker AS
Greåker Mill
Greåker, Norway

Nordic Paper Seffle
Säffle Mill
Säffle, Sweden

OAO Mayak Technocell
Penza Mill
Penza, Russia

OAO Toshkent Qogoze
Tashkent Mill
Tashkent, Tashkentskaya obl., Uzbekistan

Oji F-Tex Co., Ltd.
Dai-ichi Mill
Fuji-shi, Shizuoka Pref., Japan

Oji F-Tex Co., Ltd.
Ebetsu Mill
Ebetsu-shi, Hokkaido Pref., Japan

Oji F-Tex Co., Ltd.
Fuji Mill
Fuji-shi, Shizuoka Pref., Japan

Oji F-Tex Co., Ltd.
Iwabuchi Mill
Fujikawa-cho, Ihara-gun, Shizuoka Pref., Japan

Oji F-Tex Co., Ltd.
Nakatsu Mill
Nakatsugawa-shi, Gifu Pref., Japan

Ojsc 'Troitskaya Paper Mill'
Troitskaya Mill
Kondrovo, Kaluga Region, Russia

Omniafibre srl
Alife Mill
Alife, Caserta, Italy

Omniafiltra, LLC
Beaver Falls Mill
Beaver Falls, New York, United States

Onyx Specialty Papers, Inc
South Lee Mill
South Lee, Massachusetts, United States

OP Papírna s.r.o.
Olšany Mill
Olšany, Czech Republic

Opel Paper Mill Ltd.
Vapi Mill
Vapi, Gujarat, India

Palode Paper Mills Ltd.
Thiruvananthapuram Dist. Mill
Trivendrum, Kerala, India

Papel Aralar S.A.
Amezqueta Mill
Amezqueta, Gipúzcoa, Spain

Papelera de Brandia S.A.
La Coruña Mill
Santiago de Compostela, La Coruña, Spain

Specialty and industrial

Papelera de Chihuahua S.A. de C.V.
Chihuahua Mill
Chihuahua, Chihuahua, Mexico

Papelera Guipuzcoana de Zicuñaga S.A.
Hernani Mill
Hernani, Gipúzcoa, Spain

Papelera La Helice S.A.I.C.
San Fernando Mill
San Fernando, Buenos Aires, Argentina

Papelera Munné S.A.
Capellades Mill
Capellades, Barcelona, Spain

Papelera Paysandú S.A.I.C.
Wilde Mill
Wilde, Buenos Aires, Argentina

Papelera Tlaxcala S.A. de C.V.
Iztapaluca Mill
Iztapaluca, Edo. de México, Mexico

Papelera Tucumán S.A.
San Justo, Tucuman II
San Justo, Buenos Aires, Argentina

Papelera Veracruzana S.A. de C.V.
Orizaba Mill
Orizaba, Veracruz, Mexico

Papeles PM S.A.I.C.
San Martín Mill
San Martín, Buenos Aires, Argentina

Papeterie de Raon
Raon L'Etape Mill
Raon L'Etape, Vosges, France

Papeteries de Mauduit SA
Mauduit Mill
Quimperlé, France

Papeteries de Saint-Girons
Saint-Girons Mill
Eycheil, Saint-Girons, France

Papeteries de Vizille (Vicat)
Vizille Mill
Vizille, France

Papeteries Léon Martin SA
Engomer Mill
Engomer, France

Papierfabrik August Koehler AG
Oberkirch Mill
Oberkirch (Baden), Germany

Papierfabrik Cordier
Bad Dürkheim Mill
Bad Dürkheim, Germany

Papierfabrik Netstal AG
Netstal Mill
Netstal, Glarus, Switzerland

Papierfabrik Poerringer GmbH & Co. KG
Annweiler Mill
Annweiler am Trifels, Germany

Papierfabrik Wattens GmbH & Co KG
Wattens Mill
Wattens, Tyrol, Austria

Papírna Perštejn s.r.o., Keseg & Rathouský
Perštejn nad Ohří Mill
Perštejn nad Ohří, Czech Republic

Papirnica Vevce d.o.o.
Vevce Mill
Ljubljana-Dobrunje, Slovenia

Pfleiderer Spezialpapiere
Teisnach Mill
Teisnach, Germany

Pitambar Coated Papers Ltd.
Bhiwadi Mill
Bhiwadi, Rajasthan, India

Polska Wytwornia Papierow Wartosciowych S.A.
Warsaw Mill
Warsaw, Poland

Potsdam Specialty Paper Inc.
Cedar Mill
Potsdam, New York, United States

Prat Dumas & Cie.
Lalinde Mill
Lalinde, France

PT Bukit Muria Jaya
Karawang Mill
Karawang, West Java, Indonesia

PT Chiral Filindo Utama
Jakarta, Sukabumi Mill
Jakarta, Sukabumi, West Java, Indonesia

PT Eureka Aba
Mojosari Mill
Mojokerto, East Java, Indonesia

PT Java Paperindo Utama Industries
Mojokerto Mill
Mojokerto, East Java, Indonesia

PT Juara Prayasa Jawa
Genteng, Surabaya Mill
Genteng, Surabaya, East Java, Indonesia

PT Kertas Padalarang
Padalarang Mill
Padalarang, Bandung, West Java, Indonesia

PT Klambir Jaya
Deli Serdang Mill
Deli Serdang, North Sumatera, Indonesia

PT Niki Tunggal
Lumajang Mill
Lumajang, East Java, Indonesia

PT Pabrik Kertas Tjiwi Kimia Tbk
Mojokerto (PT Pabrik Kertas Tjiwi Kimia) Mill
Mojokerto, East Java, Indonesia

PT Pindo Deli Pulp & Paper Mills Hive
Perawang (Pindo Deli Pulp & Paper Mills Hive) Mill
Siak, Bengkalis, Riau, Sumatra, Indonesia

PT Pura Barutama
Kudus Mill
Kudus, Central Java, Indonesia

PT Sekarindo Inti Serasi
Bogor Mill
Bogor, West Java, Indonesia

PT Simanda
Serdang, Medan Mill
Serdang, Medan, North Sumatera, Indonesia

PT Sopanusa Tissue
Mojokerto Mill
Mojokerto, East Java, Indonesia

PT Surabaya Agung Industri Pulp & Kertas
Driyorejo Mill
Gresik, East Java, Indonesia

PT Surya Mas Aditama
Banten Mill
Banten, West Java, Indonesia

PT Surya Zig Zag
Kediri Mill
Kediri, East Java, Indonesia

PT Triguna Pratama
Karawang Mill
Karawang, West Java, Indonesia

PT Uninga Bima Sakti
Sukabumi Mill
Sukabumi, West Java, Indonesia

Pu Li Paper Mfg. Co., Ltd.
Pu Li Mill
Pu Li, Nantou County, Taiwan

Pucaro Elektro-Isolierstoffe GmbH
Roigheim Mill
Roigheim, Germany

Pudumjee Industries Ltd. (PIL)
Pune Mill
Pune, Maharashtra, India

Pudumjee Pulp & Paper Mills Ltd.
Pune Mill
Chinchwad, Pune, Maharashtra, India

Radece Papir Nova
Radece Mill
Radece Zidani most, Slovenia

Rampal Paper Mills
Dist. Malda Mill
Dist. Malda, West Bengal, India

Reliable Paper (India) Pvt. Ltd.
Surat Mill
Bardoli, Taluka - Mahuva, Surat, Gujarat, India

Remco Paper & Board Industries Pvt. Ltd.
Valsad Mill
Valsad, Gujarat, India

Saber Swiss Quality Paper AG
Balsthal Mill
Balsthal, Switzerland

Sam Bard Co., Ltd.
Min Hsiung Mill
Min Hsiung, Chia-I County, Taiwan

Samil Paper Co., Ltd.
Hanam Mill
Hanam-si, Gyeonggi-do, South Korea

San Yang Paper Making Co., Ltd.
Pai Ho Mill
Pai Ho District, Tainan City, Taiwan

Specialty and industrial

San Yi Paper Industry Co., Ltd.
Chung Pu Mill
Chung Pu, Chia-I County, Taiwan

Santa Maria Cia. de Papel e Celulose
Guarapuava Mill
Guarapuava, Paraná, Brazil

Sanzen Paper Mfg. Co., Ltd.
Kanazawa Mill
Kanazawa-shi, Ishikawa Pref., Japan

Sappi Fine Paper Europe
Alfeld Mill
Alfeld (Leine), Germany

Sappi Fine Paper North America
Somerset Mill
Skowhegan, Maine, United States

Sappi Fine Paper North America
Westbrook Mill
Westbrook, Maine, United States

Sappi Paper and Paper Packaging South Africa (SA)
Stanger Mill
Stanger, KwaZulu-Natal, South Africa

SCA Graphic Sundsvall AB
Ortviken Mill
Sundsvall, Sweden

SCA Hygiene Products SE
Mannheim Mill
Mannheim, Germany

Schut Papier
Heelsum Mill
Heelsum, Netherlands

Schweitzer-Mauduit do Brasil
Santanesia do Piraí Mill
Santanesia do Piraí, Rio de Janeiro, Brazil

Schweitzer-Mauduit International Inc.
Ancram Mill
Ancram, New York, United States

Schweitzer-Mauduit International Inc.
Medan Mill
Medan, Sumatra, Indonesia

Schweitzer-Mauduit International Inc.
Spotswood Mill
Spotswood, New Jersey, United States

Sealed Air Corp.
Lenoir Mill
Lenoir, North Carolina, United States

Sealed Air Corp.
Modena Mill
Modena, Pennsylvania, United States

Sealed Air Corp.
Reading Mill
Reading, Pennsylvania, United States

Seaman Paper Company
Otter River Mill
Otter River, Massachusetts, United States

Sein y Cia. SA
Ranelagh Mill
Ranelagh, Buenos Aires, Argentina

Senapathy-Whiteley (P) Ltd.
Ramangram Mill
Ramangram, Karnataka, India

SER.PA.M S.A.
Serres Mill
Serres, Greece

Serpukhovskaya Paper Mill
Serpukhov Mill
Serpukhov, Moscow Region, Russia

Seshasayee Paper & Boards Ltd.
Erode Mill
Erode, Tamil Nadu, India

Shandong Dezhou Huabei Paper (Group) Co., Ltd.
Dezhou Mill
Dezhou, Shandong, China

Shandong Guihe Xianxing Paper Holding Pte. Ltd.
Zibo Mill
Zibo, Shandong, China

Shandong Heze City Hongtai Paper Co., Ltd.
Heze Mill
Heze, Shandong, China

Shandong Kaili Paper Co. Ltd.
Rongcheng Mill
Rongcheng, Shandong, China

Shandong Laizhou Lutong Speciality Paper Co., Ltd.
Laizhou Mill
Laizhou, Shandong, China

Shandong Laizhou Yintong Paper Co., Ltd.
Laiyang Mill
Laiyang, Shandong, China

Shandong Lunan Paper Industry Group
Linyi Mill
Linyi, Shandong, China

Shandong Qifeng New Material Co., Ltd.
Zibo Mill
Zibo, Shandong, China

Shandong Qingdao Haiwang Paper Property Share Co., Ltd.
Qingdao Mill
Qingdao, Shandong, China

Shandong Qingdao Paper Mill
Qingdao Mill
Qingdao, Shandong, China

Shandong Qingzhou Dongxin Paper Co., Ltd.
Qingzhou Mill
Qingzhou, Shandong, China

Shandong Qinshi Group Co., Ltd.
Zaozhuang Mill
Zaozhuang, Shandong, China

Shandong Qunxing Paper Holdings Co., Ltd.
Binzhou Mill
Binzhou, Shandong, China

Shandong Taian Baichuan Paper Co., Ltd.
Taian Mill
Taian, Shandong, China

Shandong Taiding Material Technology Co., Ltd.
Dezhou Mill
Dezhou, Shandong, China

Shandong Tianhe Paper Co., Ltd.
Taian Mill
Taian, Shandong, China

Shandong Weifang Henglian Art Paper Co., Ltd.
Weifang Mill
Weifang, Shandong, China

Shandong Weifang Henglian Cellophane Co., Ltd.
Weifang Mill
Weifang, Shandong, China

Shandong Weifang Huisheng Group
Weifang Mill
Weifang, Shandong, China

Shandong Weifang Yongxin Paper Co., Ltd.
Changle Mill
Changle, Shandong, China

Shandong Xincheng Paper Co., Ltd.
Liaocheng Mill
Liaocheng, Shandong, China

Shawano Specialty Papers
Shawano Mill
Shawano, Wisconsin, United States

Shelavi Pulp & Paper Mills (P) Ltd.
Mehsana Mill
Chhatral, Dist. Mehsana, Gujarat, India

Shihlin Paper Corp.
Yung An Mill
Hsin Wu, Taoyuan County, Taiwan

Shin Kwang Hwa Paper Mfg. Co., Ltd.
Pu Li Mill
Pu Li, Nantou County, Taiwan

Shree Karthik Papers Ltd.
Dist. Coimbatore Mill
Dist. Coimbatore, Tamil Nadu, India

Shree Sudarshan Paper Mills Ltd.
Mettupalamam Mill
Mettupalamam, Tamil Nadu, India

Shri Harikrishna Papers PVT. Ltd.
Palani Taluk Mill
Palani Taluk, Tamil Nadu, India

Shri Krishna Fire Works
Sivakasi Mill
Sivakasi, Tamil Nadu, India

Sichuan Anxian Paper Co., Ltd.
Chengdu Mill
Chengdu, Sichuan, China

Sichuan Jinfeng Paper Holdings Co. Ltd.
Chengdu Mill
Chengdu, Sichuan, China

Specialty and industrial

Sichuan Xicheng Paper Co., Ltd.
Leshan
Leshan, Sichuan, China

Smurfit Kappa Sangüesa Paper
Sanguesa Mill
Sangüesa, Navarra, Spain

Sonoco Paper France SAS
Schweighouse Mill
Schweighouse sur Moder, France

Speciality Papers Ltd.
Valsad Mill
Vapi, Dist. Valsad, Gujarat, India

Spezialpapierfabrik Oberschmitten GmbH
Nidda/Ober-Schmitten Mill
Nidda/Ober-Schmitten, Germany

Ssangyong Paper Co., Ltd.
Osan Mill
Osan-si, Gyeonggi-do, South Korea

St. Petersburg Paper Mill Goznak
St. Petersburg Mill
St. Petersburg, Russia

Star Paper Mills Pvt. Ltd.
Kotri Mill
Kotri, Sindh, Pakistan

Stora Enso Poland S.A.
Ostroleka Mill
Ostroleka, Poland

Stora Enso Printing and Reading
Uetersen Mill
Uetersen, Germany

Stora Enso Renewable Packaging
Imatra Mills (Kaukopää & Tainionkoski)
Imatra, Finland

Sudhir Papers Ltd.
Bangalore Mill
Bangalore, Karnataka, India

Sun Thing Co., Ltd.
Houbi Mill
Houbi District, Tainan City, Taiwan

Sunshine Oji (Shouguang) Specialty Paper Ltd.
Shouguang Mill
Weifang, Shandong, China

Suzanense Indústria e Comércio de Papéis Ltda.
Suzano Mill
Suzano, São Paulo, Brazil

Taiko Paper Mfg. Co., Ltd.
Fuji-shi Mill
Fuji-shi, Shizuoka Pref., Japan

Tashkent Paper Mill of GPO Davlat Belgisi
Darkhan Mill
Vil. Darkhan, Tashkent Distr., Tashkentskaya obl., Uzbekistan

Technocell Canada Inc.
Drummondville Mill
Drummondville, Quebec, Canada

Technocell Dekor GmbH & Co. KG
Günzach Mill
Günzach, Germany

Technocell Dekor GmbH & Co. KG
Neustadt Mill
Titisee-Neustadt, Germany

Technocell Dekor GmbH & Co. KG
Osnabrück Mill
Osnabrück, Germany

Technocell Dekor GmbH & Co. KG
Penig Mill
Penig, Germany

Tentok Paper Co., Ltd.
Fuji-shi Mill
Fuji-shi, Shizuoka Pref., Japan

Terranova Papers
La Pobla de Claramunt Mill
La Pobla de Claramunt, Barcelona, Spain

Tervakoski Oy
Tervakoski Mill
Tervakoski, Finland

Texon Möckmühl GmbH
Möckmühl Mill
Möckmühl, Germany

Thai Union Paper Public Co., Ltd.
Prapradaeng Mill
Prapradaeng, Samut Prakarn, Thailand

The West Coast Paper Mills Ltd.
Dandeli Mill
Dandeli, Uttara Kannada, Karnataka, India

Theen Seng Paper Manufacturing Sdn. Bhd.
Rasa Mill
Rasa, Hulu Selangor, Selangor Darul Ehsan, Malaysia

Tianjin Zhongchao Paper Co. Ltd.
Tianjin Mill
Tianjin, Tianjin, China

Tokushu Tokai Paper Co., Ltd.
Mishima Mill
Sunto-Gun, Shizuoka Pref., Japan

Tokushu Tokai Paper Co., Ltd.
Shimada Mill
Shimada-shi, Shizuoka Pref., Japan

Tokushu Tokai Paper Co., Ltd.
Yokoi mill
Shimada-shi, Shizuoka Pref., Japan

Tokyo Paper Mfg. Co., Ltd.
Fujinomiya-Shi Mill
Fujinomiya-Shi, Shizuoka Pref., Japan

Tomoegawa Paper Co., Ltd.
Shizuoka Mill
Shizuoka-Shi, Shizuoka Pref., Japan

Torraspapel S.A.
Motril Mill
Motril, Granada, Spain

Toyo Paper Mfg. Co., Ltd.
Shikokuchuo-shi Mill
Shikokuchuo-shi, Ehime Pref., Japan

Trio Paper Mills Sdn. Bhd.
Simpang Ampat Mill
Simpang Ampat, Pulau Pinang, Malaysia

Tsyurupinsk Paper Company
Tsyurupinsk Mill
Tsyurupinsk, Kherson obl., Ukraine

Tullis Russell Papermakers Ltd.
Markinch Mill
Markinch, Glenrothes, Scotland, United Kingdom

Tung Chi Paper Corp.
Lung Ching Mill
Lung Ching District, Taichung City, Taiwan

Twin Rivers Paper, LLC
Madawaska and Edmundston Mills (East Paper Operations)
Madawaska, Maine, United States

Unión Papelera Platense
La Plata Mill
La Plata, Buenos Aires, Argentina

Union Paper Corp.
Lin Nei Mill
Lin Nei, Yunlin County, Taiwan

Union Papertech
Simpson Clough Paper Mill
Heywood, Lancashire, United Kingdom

Unitary Enterprise (UE) "Paper Mill of Goznak"
Borisov Mill
Borisov, Minskaya obl., Belarus

UPM-Kymmene Corporation
Jämsänkoski Mill
Jämsänkoski, Jämsä, Finland

UPM-Kymmene Corporation
Tervasaari Mill
Valkeakoski, Finland

UPP Pulp & Paper (M) Sdn Bhd
Batang Berjuntai Mill
Ijok, Batang Berjuntai, Selangor Darul Ehsan, Malaysia

Valaichenai Paper Mills
Valaichenai Mill
Valaichenai, Sri Lanka

Valot S.A.
Campana Mill
Campana, Buenos Aires, Argentina

Ved Cellulose Limited
Ghaziabad Mill
Ghaziabad, Uttar Pradesh, India

Verso Paper Corp.
Androscoggin Mill
Jay, Maine, United States

Verso Paper Corp.
Bucksport Mill
Bucksport, Maine, United States

Vezirköprü Orman Ürünleri ve Gida Ticaret As.
Samsun Mill
Samsun, Turkey

Vinh Hue Paper Joint-Stock Co. (Vihimex)
Ho Chi Minh City Mill
Thu Duc District, Ho Chi Minh City, Binh Duong Province, Vietnam

Vyborgskaya Cellulose, JSC
Sovetsky Mill
Vyborg, Sovetsky, Leningrad Region, Russia

Weifang Huagang Packing Material Co. Ltd
Weifang Mill
Weifang, Shandong, China

Whatman International Ltd.
Springfield Mill
Maidstone, Kent, United Kingdom

Windsor-Stevens Inc.
Poquonock Mill
Windsor, Connecticut, United States

Wolsan Paper Mfg. Co., Ltd.
Haman Mill
Chilseo-myeon, Haman-gun, Gyeongsangnam-do, South Korea

Yash Papers Ltd.
Faizabad Mill
Faizabad, Uttar Pradesh, India

Yen Son Joint-Stock Co.
Yen Bai Town Mill
Yen Bai Town, Yen Bai Province, Vietnam

YenBai Joint-Stock Forest Agricultural and Foodstuff Company
Yen Bai City Mill
Yen Bai City, Yen Bai Province, Vietnam

Yenisey Pulp and Paper Mill Inc.
Yenisey Pulp and Paper Mill
Krasnoyarsk, Russia

Yuen Min Paper Product Co., Ltd.
Chu Nan Mill
Chu Nan, Miaoli County, Taiwan

Yunnan Hongta Blue Eagle Paper Co., Ltd.
Honghe Mill
Honghe District, Yunnan, China

ZAO NPP Filter Materials
Otradnoye Mill
Otradnoye, Russia

Zellstoff Pöls AG
Pöls Mill
Pöls, Styria, Austria

Zhejiang Fuyang Fuchunwan Paper Co., Ltd.
Fuyang Mill
Fuyang, Zhejiang, China

Zhejiang Fuyang Senyuan Paper Co., Ltd.
Fuyang Mill
Fuyang, Zhejiang, China

Zhejiang Halberd Paper Co., Ltd.
Quzhou Mill
Quzhou, Zhejiang, China

Zhejiang Hangzhou Huafeng Paper Co., Ltd.
Hangzhou Mill
Hangzhou, Zhejiang, China

Zhejiang Hangzhou Xinfeng Paper Co., Ltd.
Hangzhou Mill
Hangzhou, Zhejiang, China

Zhejiang Hangzhou Xinhua Paper Industry Co., Ltd.
Hangzhou Mill
Hangzhou, Zhejiang, China

Zhejiang Kaifeng Paper Co., Ltd.
Quzhou Mill
Quzhou, Zhejiang, China

Zhejiang Kan Specialty Material Co., Ltd.
Lishui Mill
Lishui, Zhejiang, China

Zhejiang Linan Ma An Qianshi Paper Co., Ltd.
Linan Mill
Linan, Zhejiang, China

Zhejiang Linglong Paper Group Co. Ltd.
Linan Mill
Linan, Zhejiang, China

Zhejiang Minfeng Benkete Paper Co., Ltd.
Jiaxing Mill
Jiaxing, Zhejiang, China

Zhejiang Minfeng Robert Special Paper Co., Ltd.
Jiaxing Mill
Jiaxing, Zhejiang, China

Zhejiang Minfeng Special Paper Co., Ltd.
Jiaxing Mill
Jiaxing, Zhejiang, China

Zhejiang Minfeng Zanders Special Paper Co., Ltd
Jiaxing Mill
Jiaxing, Zhejiang, China

Zhejiang Purico Speciality Paper Company Limited
Jiaxing Mill
Jiaxing, Zhejiang, China

Zhejiang Rongchang Paper Co., Ltd.
Quzhou Mill
Quzhou, Zhejiang, China

Zhejiang Rongfeng Paper
Jiaxing Mill
Jiaxing, Zhejiang, China

Zhejiang Tann Longyou Paper Industry Co., Ltd.
Longyou Mill
Longyou, Zhejiang, China

Zhejiang Tianting Yalun Paper Group Co., Ltd.
Quzhou Mill
Quzhou, Zhejiang, China

Containerboard

Zhejiang Winbon Special Paper Co. Ltd.
Quzhou Mill
Quzhou, Zhejiang, China

Zhejiang Xianhe Specialty Paper
Quzhou Mill
Quzhou, Zhejiang, China

Zhejiang Yiwu City Huachuan Paper Co., Ltd.
Yiwu Mill
Yiwu, Zhejiang, China

Zhejiang Yongtai Paper Group Co., Ltd.
Fuyang Mill
Fuyang, Zhejiang, China

Zhenjiang Dadong Pulp & Paper Co. Ltd.
Zhenjiang Mill
Zhenjiang, Jiangsu, China

Zywieckie Zaklady Papiernicze "SOLALI" S.A.
Zywiec Mill
Zywiec, Poland

Containerboard

Brücher GmbH, Pappen- und Papierfabrik
Bensheim Mill
Bensheim, Germany

Elikon
Murygino Mill
Murygino, Kirovskaya Obl., Russia

Henan Luohe Paperboard Mill
Luohe Mill
Luohe, Henan, China

Henan Zhengzhou Chunhui Paper Co., Ltd.
Xinmi Mill
Xinmi, Henan, China

Hubei Shuailun Paper Co. Ltd.
Wuhan Mill
Wuhan, Hubei, China

My Huong Paper Joint-stock Co.
Hai Phong Mill
Hai Phong City, Vietnam

OAO Toshkent Qogoze
Tashkent Mill
Tashkent, Tashkentskaya obl., Uzbekistan

Pan Paper Mills
Webuye Mill
Webuye, Bungoma District, Western, Kenya

Papeterie de Gromelle
Saint-Saturnin Mill
Saint-Saturnin-les-Avignon, France

PT Buana Megah
Pasuruan Mill
Pasuruan, East Java, Indonesia

PT Eureka Aba
Mojosari Mill
Mojokerto, East Java, Indonesia

Linerboard

PT Jaya Kertas
Nganjuk Mill
Nganjuk, East Java, Indonesia

Quang Phat Co., Ltd.
Ho Chi Minh City Mill
Ho Chi Minh City, Binh Duong Province, Vietnam

Shree Ram Krupa Paper Mill
Surendranagar Mill
Surendranagar, Gujarat, India

Sichuan Longchang Yuhong Paper Co., Ltd.
Neijiang Mill
Neijiang, Sichuan, China

SIPCO-Soc. Ind. de Papier et de Carton Ondule SAL
Beirut Mill
Kfarchima, Beirut, Lebanon

Tektura Sp. z o.o.
Mikolow Mill
Mikolow, Poland

Thanakorn Paper Industry Co., Ltd.
Amphur Muang, Pathumthani Mill
Amphur Muang, Pathumthani, Thailand

Zambezi Paper Mills Ltd.
Ndola Mill
Ndola, Zambia

Linerboard

A. Vl. Koliopoulos S.A. Pako
Korinthias Mill
Velo, Korinthias, Greece

A. Vl. Koliopoulos S.A. Pako
Pelasghia Mill
Pelasghia, Fthiotidos, Greece

Aarepapier AG
Niedergösgen Mill
Niedergösgen, Switzerland

Adami S.A. Madeiras
Caçador Mill
Caçador, Santa Catarina, Brazil

Afri Paper
Chbika Mill
Chbika, Kairouan, Gouvernorat de Kairouan, Tunisia

Águas Negras S.A. Ind. de Papel
Ituporanga Mill
Ituporanga, Santa Catarina, Brazil

Agustín Barral, S.A.
Barcelona Mill
La Pobla de Lillet (Barcelona), Spain

Ajin Paper Mfg. Co. Ltd.
Hyunpoong Mill
Dalseong-gun, Daegu-si, Daegu-si, South Korea

Akasan Adana Kagit San ve Tic. Ltd. Sti.
Adana Mill
Adana, Turkey

Al Arouba Paper Co. M. Farghaly & Co.
Alexandria Mill
Alexandria, Iskanderiya, Egypt

Alatyrskaya Paper Mill
Alatyr Mill
Alatyr, Chuvashkaya Republic, Russia

Albertin Paperboard & Paper Mill
Slonim Mill
Slonim, Grodno Region, Belarus

Allard Emballages
Varennes Mill
Aubigné-Racan, France

Alta Papéis Ltda.
Benedito Novo Mill
Benedito Novo, Santa Catarina, Brazil

Ambro SA Suceava
Suceava Mill
Suceava, Romania

An Binh Paper Corporation-ABPAPER
Di An District Mill
Di An District, Binh Duong Province, Vietnam

Angren Pack
Bulbak Mill
Angren, pos. Bulbak, Tashkentskaya obl., Uzbekistan

Anhui Huoshan County Chenfeng Paper Co., Ltd
LiuAn Mill
LiuAn, Anhui, China

Anhui Shanying Paper No. 1 Mill
Maanshan (No. 1) Mill
Maanshan, Anhui, China

Anhui Shanying Paper No. 2 Mill
Maanshan (No. 2) Mill
Maanshan, Anhui, China

Ansabo S.A.
Quilmes Mill
Quilmes, Buenos Aires, Argentina

Arab Company for Paper Product (Arapepco)
Aleppo Mill
Aleppo, Syria

Arab Paper Manufacturing Co. Ltd. (Waraq)
Dammam Mill
Dammam, Saudi Arabia

Arbumprom-Kartontara, LLC
Yerevan Mill
Yerevan, Gorod Yerevan, Armenia

Arctic Paper Grycksbo AB
Grycksbo Mill
Grycksbo, Sweden

Argencraft S.A.
Andino Mill
Andino, Santa Fé, Argentina

Arkhangelsk Pulp & Paper Mill
Novodvinsk (Arkhangelsk - APPM) Mill
Novodvinsk, Arkhangelsk Region, Russia

Aryan Paper Mills Pvt. Ltd.
Vapi Mill
Vapi, Gujarat, India

Asia Kraft Paper Co., Ltd.
Samut Sakhon Mill
Samut Sakhon, Thailand

Asia Paper Mfg. Co., Ltd.
Cheongwon Mill
Cheongwon-gun, Chungcheongbuk-do, South Korea

Asia Papertec Inc.
Shihwa Mill
Siheung-si, Gyeonggi-do, South Korea

Atlantic Packaging Products Ltd.
Scarborough Mill
Scarborough, Ontario, Canada

Atlantic Packaging Products Ltd.
Whitby Mill
Whitby, Ontario, Canada

Australian Paper
Maryvale Mill
Morwell, Victoria, Australia

Balkrishna Paper Mills Ltd.
Ambivli Mill
Taluka Kalyan, Dist. Thane, Maharashtra, India

Ballavpur Paper Mfg. Ltd.
Ballavpur Mill
Ballavpur, Raniganj, Dist. Bardhaman, West Bengal, India

Bashundhara Paper Mills Ltd.
Unit 2
Sonargaon, New Town, Narayanganj, Bangladesh

BELIŠĆE d.d.
Belišće Mill
Belišće, Salvonia, Croatia

Bharat Papers Ltd.
Kathua Mill
Kathua, Jammu and Kashmir, India

BillerudKorsnäs AB
Gävle Mill
Gävle, Sweden

BillerudKorsnäs AB
Gruvön Mill
Grums, Sweden

Bio-PAPPEL International
Prewitt Mill
Prewitt, New Mexico, United States

Bio-PAPPEL Kraft
Atenquique Mill
Atenquique, Jalisco, Mexico

Bio-PAPPEL Kraft
Cuesta El Registro mill
Cuesta El Registro, Durango, Mexico

Bio-PAPPEL Kraft
Monterrey Mill
Monterrey, Nuevo León, Mexico

Bio-PAPPEL Kraft
Tizayuca Mill
El Chopo, Tizayuca, Mexico

Biodeal Laboratories Pvt. Ltd. (Paper Mill Div.)
Vapi Mill
Dist. Valsad, Gujarat, India

Bormio SpA
Ponte Lambro Mill
Ponte Lambro, Como, Italy

Linerboard

Brason Indústria de Papéis e Ondulados Ltda.
Araras Mill
Araras, São Paulo, Brazil

Bratsk Branch of Ilim Group
Bratsk Mill
Bratsk, Irkutsk Region, Russia

Brianskaya Paper Mill
Belye Berega Mill
Pos. Belye Berega, Bryansk Region, Russia

Bulleh Shah Packaging (Private) Limited
Bulleh Shah Paper Mill
Kasur, Pakistan

C & C Srl
Broccostella Mill
Broccostella, Frosinone, Italy

California Paperboard Corp.
Santa Clara Mill
Santa Clara, California, United States

Carter Holt Harvey Pulp & Paper
Kinleith Mill
Tokoroa, New Zealand

Cartesar SpA
Pellezano Mill
Pellezano, Salerno, Italy

Cartiera di Carbonera SpA
Camposampiero Mill
Camposampiero, Padua, Italy

Cartiera di Porporano Srl
Porporano Mill
Porporano, Parma, Italy

Cartiera di Salerno di Mauro Benedetti
Salerno Mill
Salerno, Salerno, Italy

Cartiera Galliera srl
Galliera Veneta Mill
Galliera Veneta, Padua, Italy

Cartiera Giacosa SpA
Front Canavese Mill
Front Canavese, Turin, Italy

Cartiera Giorgione SpA
Castelfranco Veneto Mill
Castelfranco Veneto, Treviso, Italy

Cartiera Pieretti SpA
Marlia-Capannori Mill
Marlia-Capannori, Lucca, Italy

Cartiere del Polesine Spa
Adria Mill
Adria, Rovigo, Italy

Cartiere Villa Lagarina Spa
Trento Mill
Trento, Trento, Italy

Cartitalia S.r.l.
Cartitalia Mill
Mesola, Ferrara, Italy

Cartocor S.A.
Arroyito Mill
Arroyito, Córdoba, Argentina

Cartonera del Caribe CA
Maracay Mill
Maracay, Edo. Aragua, Venezuela

Cartones America SA - CAME
Cali Mill
Cali, Valle de Cauca, Colombia

Cartonifício Valinhos S.A.
Valinhos Mill
Valinhos, São Paulo, Brazil

Cartonneries de Gondardennes SA
Wardrecques Mill
Wardrecques, Aire-Sur-La-Lys, France

Cartopel S.A.
Cuenca Mill
Cuenca, Azuay, Ecuador

Cataguazes Indústrias de Papel
Cataguases Mill
Cataguases, Minas Gerais, Brazil

CECSO - Celulosa y Corrugados de Sonora S.A. de C.V.
Navojoa Mill
Navojoa, Sonora, Mexico

Celulosa y Papel del Bajío S.A.de C.V.
León Mill
León, Guanajuato, Mexico

Celulose Irani S.A.
Santa Luzia Mill
Santa Luzia, Minas Gerais, Brazil

Celulose Irani S.A.
Vargem Bonita Mill
Vargem Bonita, Santa Catarina, Brazil

CEPASA - Celulose e Papel de Pernambuco S.A.
Jaboatão dos Guararapes Mill
Jaboatão dos Guararapes, Pernambuco, Brazil

Chang Shin Paper Mfg. Co., Ltd.
Dah Yuan Mill
Dah Yuan, Taoyuan County, Taiwan

Charoen Chai Co., Ltd.
Bangkok Mill
Bangkok, Bangkok, Thailand

Cheema Paper Mills Pvt. Ltd.
Nainital Mill
Dist. Udham Singh Nagar, Uttarakhand, India

Cheng Fung Paper Co., Ltd.
Feng Yuan Mill
Feng Yuan District, Taichung City, Taiwan

Cheng Loong Corporation
Hou Li Mill
Hou Li, Taichung City, Taiwan

Cheng Loong Corporation
Hsinchu Mill
Chung Pu Li, Hsinchu County, Taiwan

Cheng Loong Corporation Tayuan Mill
Ta Yuan Mill
Ta Yuan, Taoyuan County, Taiwan

Cheng Yang Paper Mill Co., Ltd.
Ben Cat Dist. (Cheng Yang Paper) Mill
Ben Cat Dist., Binh Duong Province, Vietnam

China Sunshine Paper Holdings Company Limited
Weifang Mill
Weifang, Shandong, China

Chizhovskaya Paper Mill
Novograd-Volynskiy Mill
Chizhovka, Novograd-Volynskiy rayon, Zhitomirskaya obl., Ukraine

Chongqing Lee & Man Paper Co., Ltd.
Chongqing Mill
Chongqing, Chongqing, China

Chouka Pulp & Paper Mill
Rezvanshahr Mill
Rezvanshahr, Iran

Cia. Industrial Papelera Poblana S.A. de C.V.
Chachapa Mill
Chachapa, Puebla, Mexico

Cita Peuchoon Paper Mills Sdn. Bhd.
Sungai Petani Mill
Sungai Petani, Kedah, Malaysia

CITROPLAST- Ind. e Com. de Papéis e Plásticos Ltda.
Andradina Mill
Andradina, São Paulo, Brazil

CMPC Papeles Cordillera S.A.
Puente Alto Mill
Puente Alto, RM - Región Metro. de Santiago, Chile

COCELPA - Companhia de Celulose e Papel do Paraná
Araucária Mill
Araucária, Paraná, Brazil

Container Corp. of the Philippines
Quezon City Mill
Quezon City, Philippines

Copamex Industrias S.A. de C.V.
Monterrey Mill
San Nicolas de los Garza, Nuevo León, Mexico

Coromandel Papers
Dindigul Mill
Dindigul, Tamil Nadu, India

Corrugadora Paraguaya S.A.
Luque Mill
Luque, Paraguay

Corrugados de Colombia Ltda.
Fontibón Mill
Fontibón, Bogotá D.C., Colombia

Creative Paper Mills Ltd
Rupganj Mill
Rupganj, Narayanganj, Bangladesh

Daehan Papertech Co., Ltd.
Danyang Mill
Daejeon-myeon, Damyang-gun, Jeollanam-do, South Korea

Daeyang Paper Mfg. Co. Ltd.
Ansan Mill
Ansan-si, Gyeonggi-do, South Korea

Daio Paper Corp.
Mishima Mill
Shikokuchuo-shi, Ehime Pref., Japan

Linerboard

Dall Pel Madeira e Papel
Grechinski Mill
Irati, Paraná, Brazil

Decor Paper Mills Ltd.
Punjagutta, Hyderabad Mill
Punjagutta, Hyderabad, Andhra Pradesh, India

Delkeskamp Verpackungswerke GmbH
Nortrup Mill
Nortrup, Germany

Delta Board Mills SAE
Cairo Mill
Badr City, Cairo, Egypt

Dentaş Ambalaj Ve Kagit San. A.S
Çorlu Mill
Çorlu, Tekirdag, Turkey

Dentaş Ambalaj Ve Kagit San. A.S
Denizli Mill
Denizli, Turkey

Dev Kiran Paper Mills (P) Ltd.
Bangalore Mill
Bangalore, Karnataka, India

Dev Priya Fibres Pvt. Ltd.
Meerut Mill
Meerut, Uttar Pradesh, India

Dev Priya Industries Limited
Meerut Mill
Meerut District, Uttar Pradesh, India

Dezhou Huisheng Pingyuan Paper Co., Ltd.
Dezhou Mill
Dezhou, Shandong, China

Dhanlaxmi Paper Mills Pvt Ltd
Coimbatore Mill
Coimbatore, Tamil Nadu, India

Dnepropetrovsk Paper Mill, Ltd.
Dnepropetrovsk Mill
Dnepropetrovsk, Ukraine

Dobrushskaya Paper Mill "Geroi Truda", OJSC
Dobrush Mill
Dobrush, Gomel Region, Belarus

Donetsk-Vtorma Ltd.
Donetsk Mill
Donetsk, Ukraine

Dongil Packaging
Jinju-si Mill
Jinju-si, Gyeongsangnam-do, South Korea

Dongil Paper Mfg. Co., Ltd.
Ansan Mill
Ansan-si, Gyeonggi-do, South Korea

Dongwon Paper Mfg. Co., Ltd.
Jeongup Mill
Jeongeup-si, Jeollabuk-do, South Korea

Donskaya Gofrotara
Rostov na Donu Mill
Rostov na Donu, Russia

DS Smith Kaysersberg
Kaysersberg Mill
Kaysersberg, France

DS Smith Packaging Benelux B.V.
Eerbeek Mill
Eerbeek, Netherlands

DS Smith Packaging France
Contoire Hamel Mill
Contoire Hamel, France

DS Smith Packaging France
Nantes Mill
Nantes Cedex 02, France

DS Smith Packaging Italia S.p.A.
Lucca Mill
Porcari, Lucca, Italy

DS Smith Paper
Kemsley Mill
Kemsley, Sittingbourne, Kent, United Kingdom

DS Smith Paper
Wansbrough Paper Mill
Watchet, Somerset, United Kingdom

DS Smith Paper Deutschland GmbH
Aschaffenburg Mill
Aschaffenburg, Germany

DS Smith Paper Deutschland GmbH
Witzenhausen Mill
Witzenhausen, Germany

Duropack GmbH
Trakia
Pazardzik, Glavinitza quarter, Bulgaria

East India Paper & Board Mills
Howeah Mill
Howeah, West Bengal, India

Ecologicheskie Tekhnologii Ltd
Balakhna Mill
Balakhna, Nizhny Novgorod, Russia

Edipack sh.p.k.
Durres Mill
Durres, Albania

Ehime Paper Mfg. Co., Ltd.
Shikokuchuo-shi Mill
Shikokuchuo-shi, Ehime Pref., Japan

EIC - Empaques Industriales Colombianos SA
Caucaseco - Palmira Mill
Caucaseco - Palmira, Valle de Cauca, Colombia

El Farouk Co. "Farco"
El Obour Ind. City Mill
Obour, Egypt

El Nasr Carton Co.
Borg El Arab El Gededah Mill
Borg El Arab El - Gedeedah, Alexandria, Egypt

El Obour Co.
Heliopolis, Cairo Mill
Heliopolis, Cairo, Egypt

El-Salam PaperMill
Alexandria Mill
Alexandria, Iskanderiya, Egypt

ELF - Egyptian Co. for Manufacturing of Linerboard & Fluting
10th of Ramadan City Mill
10th of Ramadan City, Cairo, Sharkeya, East Province, Egypt

Emin Leydier
Champblain Mill
Saint-Vallier Cedex, France

Emin Leydier
Nogent-sur-Seine Mill
Nogent-sur-Seine, Aube, France

Empaques Modernos San Pablo S.A. de C.V.
Tlalnepantla Mill
Tlalnepantla, Edo. de México, Mexico

Envases Industriales S.A.
Villa Elisa Mill
Villa Elisa, Paraguay

Estrela Indústria de Papel Ltda.
Palmas Mill
Palmas, Paraná, Brazil

Etap Paper & Carton
Borg El Arab El Gededah Mill
Borg El Arab El Gededah, Alexandria, Egypt

Europac Kraft Viana
Viana do Castelo Mill
Viana do Castelo, Portugal

Europac Papel Duenas
Dueñas Mill
Dueñas, Castilla y León, Spain

Fábrica de Papel da Lapa Lda.
São Paio de Oleiros Mill
São Paio de Oleiros, Portugal

Fábrica de Papel de Ponte Redonda S.A.
Silvalde, Espinho Mill
Silvalde, Espinho, Portugal

Fábrica de Papel de Torres Novas Lda.
Torres Novas Mill
Torres Novas, Portugal

Fabrika Hartije - PAP - DP
Beogradska Mill
Beograde, Serbia

Fernandez S.A. Indústria de Papel
Amparo Mill
Amparo, São Paulo, Brazil

Fibre Foils Ltd.
Khalapur Mill
Khalapur, Raigad, Maharashtra, India

First Co. For Industrial Development S.A.E
El Obour City Mill
El Obour City, Egypt

Forestal y Papelera Concepción S.A.
Coronel Mill
Coronel, VIII - Región del Biobío, Chile

FS-Karton GmbH
Neuss Mill
Neuss, Germany

Linerboard

Fthiotis Paper Mill SA
Damasta Mill
Damasta, Lamia, Greece

Fujian Dunxin Paper Co., Ltd.
Zhangzhou Mill
Zhangzhou, Fujian, China

Fujian Liansheng Paper (Longhai) Co., Ltd
Longhai Mill
Longhai City, Fujian, China

Fujian Liansheng Paper (Zhangzhou) Co., Ltd.
Zhangzhou Mill
Zhangzhou, Fujian, China

Fujian Quanzhou Guige Paper Co. Ltd.
Quanzhou Mill
Quanzhou, Fujian, China

Fujian Quanzhou Jingyu Paper Mill
Quanzhou Mill
Quanzhou, Fujian, China

Fujian Xinlida Paper Co., Ltd.
Zhangzhou Mill
Zhangzhou, Fujian, China

Fujian Zhangzhou Gangxing Group Gangxing Paper Co., Ltd
Zhangzhou Mill
Zhangzhou, Fujian, China

Fuyang Maohong Paper Co., Ltd.
Fuyang Mill
Fuyang, Zhejiang, China

G.P.C. Mohammadia
Meknès Mill
Meknès, Morocco

Gangotri Paper Mills Pvt Ltd.
Muzaffarnagar Mill
Muzaffarnagar, Uttar Pradesh, India

Gayatri Paper Mill
Germiston Mill
Germiston, Gauteng, South Africa

Gemdoubs
Novillars Mill
Novillars, France

Genus Paper Products Limited
Moradabad Mill
Moradabad, Uttar Pradesh, India

Georgia-Pacific LLC
Big Island Mill
Big Island, Virginia, United States

Georgia-Pacific LLC
Brewton Mill
Brewton, Alabama, United States

Georgia-Pacific LLC
Cedar Springs Mill
Cedar Springs, Georgia, United States

Georgia-Pacific LLC
Monticello Mill
Monticello, Mississippi, United States

Georgia-Pacific LLC
Palatka Mill
Palatka, Florida, United States

Georgia-Pacific LLC
Toledo Mill
Toledo, Oregon, United States

Globe Paper Mills
Keng Hua Mill
Malabon, Metro Manila, Philippines

Grand Holding Mill
Yerevan Mill
Yerevan, Gorod Yerevan, Armenia

Green Bay Packaging Inc.
Green Bay Mill
Green Bay, Wisconsin, United States

Green Bay Packaging Inc.
Morrilton Mill
Morrilton, Arkansas, United States

Greenpac Mill, LLC
Greenpac Mill
Niagara Falls, New York, United States

Greif Inc.
Riverville Mill
Amherst, Virginia, United States

Groupe CMCP - La Compagnie Marocaine des Cartons et Papiers
Kenitra Mill
Kenitra, Morocco

Grupo Unipak, S.A. de C.V. PT
Cuernavaca Mill
Cuernavaca, Morelos, Mexico

Grupo Unipak, S.A. de C.V. PT
Grupak Hidalgo
Emiliano Zapata, Mexico

Grupo Zucamor
Ranelagh Mill
Ranelagh, Buenos Aires, Argentina

GS Paper & Packaging Group ("GSPP")
Banting Mill
Daerah Kuala Langat, Banting, Selangor Darul Ehsan, Malaysia

Guaçu S.A. Papéis e Embalagens
Tambaú Mill
Tambaú, São Paulo, Brazil

Guangdong Dongguan Gaobu Qiangan Paper Mill
Dongguan Mill
Dongguan, Guangdong, China

Guangdong Dongguan Hongmei Lee & Man Paper Co., Ltd.
Dongguan (Hongmei) Milll
Dongguan, Guangdong, China

Guangdong Dongguan Huangyong Yinzhou Paper Industry Ltd.
Dongguan Mill
Dongguan, Guangdong, China

Guangdong Dongguan Jianhua Paper Co. Ltd.
Dongguan Mill
Dongguan, Guangdong, China

Guangdong Dongguan Jianhui Paper
Dongguan Mill
Dongguan, Guangdong, China

Guangdong Dongguan Jinzhou Paper Co., Ltd.
Dongguan Mill
Dongguan, Guangdong, China

Guangdong Dongguan Lee & Man Paper Co., Ltd.
Dongguan (Huangyong) Mill
Dongguan, Guangdong, China

Guangdong Dongguan Nine Dragons Paper Industries Co., Ltd.
Dongguan Mill
Dongguan, Guangdong, China

Guangdong Dongguan Taichang Paper Co., Ltd.
Dongguan Mill
Dongguan, Guangdong, China

Guangdong Dongguan Zhonglian Paper Co., Ltd.
Dongguan Mill
Dongguan, Guangdong, China

Guangdong Green Forest (QingXin) Paper Industrial Limited
Qingyuan Mill
Qingyuan, Guangdong, China

Guangdong Heshan Paper Co., Ltd.
Heshan Mill
Heshan, Guangdong, China

Guangdong Jiangmen Zhenlong Paper Mill Co., Ltd.
Jiangmen Mill
Jiangmen, Guangdong, China

Guangdong Junye Paper Co., Ltd.
Dongguan Mill
Dongguan, Guangdong, China

Guangdong Mingxing Paper Co., Ltd.
Jiangmen Mill
Jiangmen, Guangdong, China

Guangdong Shunde Sugar Co., Ltd.
Foshan Mill
Foshan, Guangdong, China

Guangdong Wanlida Paper
Guangzhou Mill
Guangzhou, Guangdong, China

Guangdong Zhongshan Rengo Hung Hing Paper Mfg. Co. Ltd.
Zhongshan Mill
Zhongshan, Guangdong, China

Guangxi Forest Lipu Paper Co., Ltd.
Lipu Mill
Lipu, Guangxi, China

Guangxi Guofa Forest & Paper Co. Ltd.
Liuzhou (Guangxi Guofa Forest & Paper) Mill
Liuzhou, Guangxi, China

Gugan Paper Mills Pvt Ltd
Gugan Paper Mills Pvt Ltd
Coimbatore, Tamil Nadu, India

Gulf Paper Industries Factory
Riyadh Mill
Riyadh, Saudi Arabia

Linerboard

Gulf Paper Manufacturing Free Zone Company
Dubai Mill
Jebel Ali Free Zone, Dubai, United Arab Emirates

Gulf Paper Mfg. Co. k.s.c.
Kuwait Mill
West Mina Abdulla, Ahmadi Governorate, Kuwait

Halkali Kagit Karton San. ve Tic. A.S.
Istanbul Mill
Küçükçekmece, Istanbul, Turkey

Hamburger Hungaria Ltd
Dunaújváros Mill
Dunaújváros, Hungary

Hamburger Rieger GmbH & Co. KG
Spremberg-Schwarze Pumpe Mill
Spremberg-Schwarze Pumpe, Brandenburg, Germany

Hamburger Rieger GmbH & Co. KG
Trostberg Mill
Trostberg, Bavaria, Germany

Hans Kolb Papierfabrik GmbH & Co. KG
Kaufbeuren Mill
Kaufbeuren, Germany

Hayat Kagit ve Enerji A.S.
Corum Mill
Corum, Turkey

Hebei Baoding Sanlian Paper Co., Ltd.
Baoding Mill
Baoding, Hebei, China

Hebei Dazhong Baolai Paper Co., Ltd.
Tangshan Mill
Tangshan, Hebei, China

Hebei Hongli Chenggong Paper Co., Ltd.
Tangshan Mill
Tangshan, Hebei, China

Hebei Lu Quan Shunfa Industrial Co., Ltd.
Luquan Mill
Luquan, Hebei, China

Hebei Qinhuangdao Fengman Paper Co., Ltd.
Qinghuangdao Mill
Qinghuangdao, Hebei, China

Hebei Tanghai Chenguang Paper Co., Ltd.
Tangshan Mill
Tangshan, Hebei, China

Hebei Yongxin Paper Co., Ltd.
Tangshan (Hebei Yongxin) Mill
Tangshan, Hebei, China

Hebei Yutian Shunfa Paper Co., Ltd.
Tangshan Mill
Tangshan, Hebei, China

Hemkunt Paper Mills Ltd
Ludhiana Mill
Ludhiana, Punjab, India

Henan Chenyang Paper Co., Ltd.
Xuchang Mill
Xuchang, Henan, China

Henan Hongteng Paper Group Co., Ltd.
Xuchang Mill
Xuchang, Henan, China

Henan Luoyang City Longxiang Paper Co., Ltd.
Luoyang Mill
Luoyang, Henan, China

Henan Ningling County Longyuan Paper Co., Ltd.
Zhengzhou Mill
Zhengzhou, Henan, China

Henan Xuchang Feida Paper Co., Ltd.
Xuchang Mill
Xuchang, Henan, China

Henan Yinge Packaging Paper Industry Co., Ltd.
Luohe (Yinge Packaging Paper) Mill
Luohe, Henan, China

Henan Zhengzhou Chunhui Paper Co., Ltd.
Xinmi Mill
Xinmi, Henan, China

Hiang Seng Fibre Container Co., Ltd.
Samut Sakohn Mill
Amphur Muang, Samut Sakohn, Thailand

Hoang Van Thu Paper Joint Stock Company
Thai Nguyen City Mill
Thai Nguyen City, Thai Nguyen Province, Vietnam

Hubei Hongfa Renewable Resources Technology Development
Yichang Mill
Yichang, Hubei, China

Hubei Shuailun Paper Co. Ltd.
Wuhan Mill
Wuhan, Hubei, China

Hyogo Paper Mfg. Co., Ltd.
Himeji Mill
Himeji-shi, Hyogo Pref., Japan

Iberkraft Indústria de Papel e Celulose Ltda.
Guarapuava Mill
Guarapuava, Paraná, Brazil

ICO-Industria Cartone Ondulato Srl
San Giovanni Teatino Mill
San Giovanni Teatino, Chieti, Italy

Indugevi S.A.
Sabaneta Mill
Sabaneta, Antioquia, Colombia

Industria Cartaria Pieretti SpA (ICP)
Marlia Mill
Marlia di Capannori, Lucca, Italy

Indústria de Papel Sovel da Amazônia Ltda.
Manaus Mill
Manaus, Amazonas, Brazil

Indústria e Comércio de Embalagens e Papéis Artivinco Ltda.
Santa Rosa do Viterbo Mill
Santa Rosa do Viterbo, São Paulo, Brazil

Industria Panameña de Papel SA
Chilibre Mill
San Vicente, Zona Chilibre, Panama

Industrial e Agrícola Rio Verde Ltda.
Rio do Campo Mill
Rio do Campo, Santa Catarina, Brazil

Industrias Cartonera Asociada S.A. - INCASA
Quito Mill
Quito, Pichincha, Ecuador

Industrias del Cartón S.A. - INCASA
Cayalti Mill
Cayalti, Chiclayo, Peru

Indústrias Novacki S.A.
União da Vitória Mill
União da Vitoria, Paraná, Brazil

INPA - Indústria de Embalagens Santana S.A.
Pirapetinga Mill
Pirapetinga, Minas Gerais, Brazil

INPA - Indústria de Embalagens Santana S.A.
Uberaba Mill
Uberaba, Minas Gerais, Brazil

Inpol-Papier Sp. z o.o.
Bardo Mill
Bardo, Poland

Inter Pacific Paper Co., Ltd
Banpluang, Baansang Mill
Banpluang, Baansang, Prachinburi, Thailand

International Paper Co.
Bogalusa Mill
Bogalusa, Louisiana, United States

International Paper Co.
Cedar Rapids Mill
Cedar Rapids, Iowa, United States

International Paper Co.
Henderson Mill
Henderson, Kentucky, United States

International Paper Co.
Mansfield Mill
Mansfield, Louisiana, United States

International Paper Co.
Maysville Mill
Maysville, Kentucky, United States

International Paper Co.
Newport Mill
Cayuga, Indiana, United States

International Paper Co.
Orange Mill
Orange, Texas, United States

International Paper Co.
Pensacola Mill
Cantonment, Florida, United States

International Paper Co.
Pine Hill Mill
Pine Hill, Alabama, United States

International Paper Co.
Prattville Mill
Prattville, Alabama, United States

Linerboard

International Paper Co.
Red River Mill
Campti, Louisiana, United States

International Paper Co.
Rome Mill
Rome, Georgia, United States

International Paper Co.
Savannah Mill
Savannah, Georgia, United States

International Paper Co.
Springfield Mill
Springfield, Oregon, United States

International Paper Co.
Valliant Mill
Valliant, Oklahoma, United States

International Paper Co.
Vicksburg Mill
Vicksburg, Mississippi, United States

International Paper, Empaques Industriales de México S.A. de C.V.
Xalapa Mill
Xalapa, Veracruz, Mexico

Interstate Paper L.L.C.
Riceboro Mill
Riceboro, Georgia, United States

Invepal
Morón Mill
Morón, Edo. Carabobo, Venezuela

Iran Papyrus Co. Ltd.
Saveh Mill
Saveh, Markazi, Iran

Islamic Paper Manufacturing Co.
Quesna Mill
Quesna, Menofeya, Egypt

Izmail Pulp & Paperboard Combine
Izmail Mill
Izmail, Odesskaya obl., Ukraine

Jaepel Papéis e Embalagens
Senador Canedo Mill
Senador Canedo, Goiás, Brazil

Jebba Paper Mills Ltd.
Jebba Mill
Jebba, Kwara State, Nigeria

Jiangsu Chamfor Paper Industry Co. Ltd.
Danyang Mill
Danyang, Jiangsu, China

Jiangsu Huangli Paper Industry Co., Ltd.
Jiangyin Mill
Jiangyin, Jiangsu, China

Jiangsu Jiangyin Gushan Dongfang Paper Co., Ltd.
Jiangyin Mill
Jiangyin, Jiangsu, China

Jiangsu Lee & Man Paper Manufacturing Co. Ltd.
Changshu Mill
Changshu, Jiangsu, China

Jiangsu Nine Dragons Paper Industries
Taicang Mill
Taicang, Jiangsu, China

Jiangsu Wanda Paper Co., Ltd.
Changzhou Mill
Changzhou, Jiangsu, China

Jiangsu Wuxi Long Chen Paper Co., Ltd.
Wuxi Mill
Wuxi, Jiangsu, China

Jiangsu Yuen Foong Yu Paper (Yangzhou) Co., Ltd.
Yangzhou Mill
Yangzhou, Jiangsu, China

Jiangxi Lee & Man Paper Co., Ltd.
Ruichang Mill
Ruichang, Jiangxi, China

Jin Young Paper Co., Ltd.
Chilgok-gun Mill
Chilgok-gun, Gyeongsangbuk-do, South Korea

Johmewah Maju Paper Mill Sdn. Bhd.
Yong Peng Mill
Yong Peng, Johor Darul Takzim, Malaysia

John Hargreaves (C&S) Ltd.
Stalybridge Mill
Stalybridge, Cheshire, Greater Manchester, United Kingdom

Jordan Paper & Cardboard Factories Co. Ltd.
Zarka Mill
Awajan, Zarka, Jordan

JSC 'Kondrovskaya Paper company'
Kondrovskaya Paper Company Mill
Kondrovo, Kaluga Region, Russia

JSC Primsnabcontract Ussurijsk Paperboard Mill
Ussurijsk Mill
Ussurijsk, Russia

Julius Schulte Trebsen GmbH & Co. KG
Trebsen Mill
Trebsen, Germany

Kagazy Recycling LLP
Almaty Mill
Karasai district, Almaty, Almaty Obl., Kazakhstan

Kahramanmaras Kagit San ve TIC A.S (KMK Paper)
Kahramanmaras Mill
Kahramanmaras, Turkey

Kahramanmaras Kagit San ve TIC A.S (KMK Paper)
Kütahya Mill
Kütahya, Turkey

Kahrizak Paper Mill
Tehran Mill
Tehran, Iran

Kamenskaya Board & Paper Mill, OJSC
Kuvshinovo Mill
Kuvshinovo, Tver Region, Russia

KapStone Kraft Paper Corporation
Cowpens Mill
Cowpens, South Carolina, United States

KapStone Kraft Paper Corporation
Longview Mill
Longview, Washington, United States

KapStone Kraft Paper Corporation
Roanoke Rapids Mill
Roanoke Rapids, North Carolina, United States

KapStone Paper Charleston Kraft LLC
North Charleston Mill
North Charleston, South Carolina, United States

Karavaevo
Karavaevo Mill
Pos. Karavaevo, Moscow Region, Russia

Karnal Card Board Industries
Karnal Mill
Karnal, Haryana, India

Kartontara, CJSC
Maykop Mill
Maykop, Adygheya Republic, Russia

Kartotec - Papeles Técnicos-
Villeta Mill
Villeta, Paraguay

Kaveh Paper Industries Co.
Saveh Mill
Saveh, Markazi, Iran

KBK Ltd
Tuymazy Mill
Tuymazy, Respublika Bashkortostan, Russia

Kenya Papermill Ltd.
Thika Mill
Thika, Central, Kenya

Khatema Fibres Ltd.
Khatema Dist., Udham Singh Nagar Mill
Khatema Dist., Udham Singh Nagar, Uttar Pradesh, India

Kibo Match Group Pulp and Paperboard Mill
Moshi Mill
Moshi, Tanzania

Kiev Cardboard and Paper Mill
Kiev Cardboard and Paper Mill
Obukhiv, Kyivska obl., Ukraine

Kingston Paptech Pvt Ltd
Sabarkantha Mill
Sabarkantha district, Gujarat, India

Kitakami Paper Co., Ltd.
Ichinoseki Mill
Ichinoseki-shi, Iwate Pref., Japan

Klabin S.A.
Angatuba Mill
Angatuba, São Paulo, Brazil

Klabin S.A.
Goiana Mill
Goiana, Pernambuco, Brazil

Klabin S.A.
Monte Alegre Mill
Telêmaco Borba, Paraná, Brazil

Klabin S.A.
Otacílio Costa Mill
Otacílio Costa, Santa Catarina, Brazil

Linerboard

Klabin S.A.
Piracicaba Mill
Piracicaba, São Paulo, Brazil

Klaipedos Kartonas
Klaipeda Mill
Klaipeda, Lithuania

Klingele Papierwerke GmbH & Co. KG
Weener Mill
Weener, Germany

Koa Kogyo Co., Ltd.
Fuji-shi Mill
Fuji-shi, Shizuoka Pref., Japan

Kolicevo Karton d.o.o.
Kolicevo Mill
Domžale, Slovenia

Kommunar Paper Mill
Kommunar Mill
Kommunar, Leningrad Region, Russia

Korea Export Packing Ind. Co., Ltd.
Osan Mill
Osan-si, Gyeonggi-do, South Korea

Korea Paper Mfg. Co., Ltd.
Siheung-si Mill
Siheung-si, Gyeonggi-do, South Korea

Koryazhma Branch of Ilim Group
Kotlas Pulp and Paper Mill
Koryazhma, Arkhangelsk Region, Russia

KPAQ Industries LLC
Saint Francisville Mill
Saint Francisville, Louisiana, United States

KPK St. Petersburg OOAO
Kommunar Mill
Kommunar, Leningrad Region, Russia

KPM Kadoma Paper Mills
Kadoma Mill
Kadoma, Zimbabwe

Krasnaya Zvezda
Krasnaya Zvezda Mill
Chashniki, Vitebsk region, Belarus

Kruger Inc.
Place Turcot Mill
Montreal, Quebec, Canada

Kübler & Niethammer Papierfabrik Kriebstein AG
Kriebstein Mill
Kriebstein, Germany

Kuzbasskiy Skarabey
Kemerovo Mill
Kemerovo, Russia

Lam Son Paper Joint-Stock Company
Nong Cong Mill
Nong Cong District, Thanh Hoa Province, Vietnam

LEIPA Georg Leinfelder GmbH
Schwedt Mill
Schwedt, Germany

Lepenka AD
Novi Knezevac Mill
Novi Knezevac, Vojvodina, Serbia

Lexpapier Sonacar S.A.
El Jadida Mill
El Jadida, Morocco

Liaoning Hupo Paper
Fushun Mill
Fushun, Liaoning, China

Liaoning Nine Dragons Paper Industries
Shenyang Mill
Xinmin, Shenyang, Liaoning, China

Liberty Paper Inc.
Becker Mill
Becker, Minnesota, United States

Linh Xuan Paper Joint-Stock Co.
Ho Chi Minh City Mill
Thu Duc District, Ho Chi Minh City, Binh Duong Province, Vietnam

Long Chen Paper Co. Ltd.
Erh-Lin Mill
ErhLin, Changhua County, Taiwan

Lothlorien (Pty) Ltd
Lothlorien Pulp Mill
Wadeville, Gauteng, South Africa

Lutsky KRK
Lutsk Mill
Lutsk, Ukraine

Madeireira Miguel Forte S.A.
União da Vitória Mill
União da Vitória, Paraná, Brazil

Madepar Papel e Celulose S.A.
Aparecida Mill
Aparecida, São Paulo, Brazil

Magura Paper Mills Ltd.
Narayanganj Mill
Narayanganj, Narayanganj, Bangladesh

Mahachai Kraft Paper Co., Ltd.
Samut Sakohn Mill
Amphur Muang, Samut Sakohn, Thailand

Malu Paper Mills Ltd.
Nagpur 1 & 2 Mill
Dist. Nagpur, Maharashtra, India

Mamta Papers Pvt Ltd
Jagatpur Mill
Jagatpur, Odisha, India

Mandya National Paper Mills Ltd.
Belagola Mill
Belagola, Karnataka, India

Manufacturas de Papel CA (MANPA) S.A.C.A.
Maracay Packaging Mill
Maracay, Edo. Aragua, Venezuela

Marisky Pulp & Paper Mill
Volzhsk Mill
Volzhsk, Mari El Republic, Russia

Marmara Kagit ve Ambalaj Sanayii ve Ticaret AS
Vezirhan Mill
Bilecik, Vezirhan, Bilecik, Turkey

Marusan Paper Mfg. Co., Ltd.
Honsha Mill
Haramachi-ku, Minami-soma-shi, Fukushima Pref., Japan

Mashad Carton
Mashhad Mill
Mashhad, Khorsan, Iran

Matias Gomá Tomás S.A.
La Riba Mill
La Riba, Spain

Mazandaran Wood & Paper Industries Co.
Sari Mill
Sari, Mazandaran, Iran

MCC Meili Paper Industry Co., Ltd.
Zhongwei Mill
Zhongwei, Ningxia, China

MELECKY a.s. závod Papírna Aloisov
Aloisov Mill
Ruda nad Moravou, Czech Republic

Menofeya for Paper & Cardboard - "Minobardy"
Quissna Mill
Quissna, Menofeya, Egypt

Metsä Board Husum
Husum Mill
Husum, Sweden

Metsä Board Kemiart Liners
Kemi Mill
Kemi, Finland

Middle East Paper Company - (MEPCO)
Jeddah Mill
Jeddah, Saudi Arabia

Mier
Lviv Mill
Lviv, Ukraine

Mimosa Sanitary Paper
Kaa El Rim. Bekaa Mill
Kaa El Rim. Bekaa, Lebanon

Modern Karton Sanayi Ticaret AS
Çorlu Mill
Çorlu, Tekirdag, Turkey

Mohammadi Paper & Board Industries (Pvt.) Ltd.
Sheikhupura Lahore Unit 2
Sheikhupura Lahore, Punjab, Pakistan

Mondi Raubling GmbH
Raubling Mill
Raubling, Germany

Mondi Richards Bay
Richards Bay Mill
Richards Bay, KwaZulu-Natal, South Africa

Mondi Stetí
Štetí Mill
Štetí, Czech Republic

Mondi Swiecie S.A.
Swiecie Mill
Swiecie, Poland

Linerboard

Mondi Syktyvkar
Syktyvkar Mill
Syktyvkar, Komi Republic, Russia

Mondi Tire Kutsan Paper and Packaging Industry Inc.
Tire Mill
Tire, Izmir, Turkey

Mondialcarta SpA
Diecimo Mill
Diecimo, Lucca, Italy

Mopak Dalaman Pulp-Paper Cardboard Plant
Dalaman Mill
Mugla, Turkey

Moritz J. Weig GmbH & Co. KG
Mayen Mill
Mayen, Germany

Mpact Limited
Felixton Mill
Felixton, KwaZulu-Natal, South Africa

Mpact Limited
Piet Retief Mill
Piet Retief, Mpumalanga, South Africa

Muc Son Paper Paper Joint-Stock Co.
Tho Xuan Mill
Tho Xuan District, Thanh Hoa Province, Vietnam

Muda Paper Mills Sdn. Bhd.
Kajang Mill
Kajang, Selangor Darul Ehsan, Malaysia

Muda Paper Mills Sdn. Bhd.
Tasek Mill
Seberang Prai Selatan, Penang, Malaysia

Mufindi Paper Mills (MPM)
Mgololo Mill
Mgololo, Iringa Region, Tanzania

My Huong Paper Joint-stock Co.
Hai Phong Mill
Hai Phong City, Vietnam

Naberezhnye Chelny Paper & Board Mill
Naberezhnye Chelny Mill
Naberezhnye Chelny, Tatarstan Republic, Russia

Nakagawa Seishi KK
Mattsuto Mill
Hakusan-shi, Ishikawa Pref., Japan

Nampak Paper Ltd.
Rosslyn Mill
Rosslyn, Gauteng, South Africa

Nath Pulp & Paper Mills Ltd.
Aurangabad Mill
Aurangabad, Maharashtra, India

National Paper Co.
Alexandria Mill
Alexandria, Iskanderiya, Egypt

Natron-Hayat d.o.o.
Maglaj Mill
Maglaj, Bosnia & Herzegovina

New Forest Paper Mills LP
Scarborough Mill
Scarborough, Ontario, Canada

Newark America
Fitchburg Mill
Fitchburg, Massachusetts, United States

Nicol-Pack Corporation
Uchaly Mill
Uchaly, Respublika Bashkortostan, Russia

Nikita Paper (P) Ltd.
Shamli Mill
Dist. Muzzaffarnagar, Uttar Pradesh, India

Nine Dragons Paper (Tianjin) Co., Ltd.
Tianjin Mill
Tianjin, Tianjin, China

Nine Dragons Paper Industries (Chongqing) Co., Ltd.
Chongqing Mill
Chongqing, Chongqing, China

Nine Dragons Paper Industries (Quanzhou) Co., Ltd.
Quanzhou Mill
Quanzhou, Fujian, China

Ningxia Kejin Xiaguang Paper Co., Ltd.
Qingtongxia Mill
Qingtongxia, Ningxia, China

Nippon Paper Industries Co., Ltd.
Akita Mill
Akita-shi, Akita Pref., Japan

Nippon Paper Industries Co., Ltd.
Otake Mill
Otake-shi, Hiroshima Pref., Japan

Nippon Paper Industries Co., Ltd.
Soka Mill
Soka-shi, Saitama Pref., Japan

Nippon Paper Industries Co., Ltd.
Yoshinaga Mill
Fuji-shi, Shizuoka Pref., Japan

Norampac
Kingsey Falls Mill
Kingsey Falls, Quebec, Canada

Norampac
Mississauga Mill
Mississauga, Ontario, Canada

Norpapel S.A.I.C.
Villa Ocampo Mill
Villa Ocampo, Santa Fé, Argentina

Norpaper Avot-Vallée SAS
Blendecques Mill
Blendecques, France

Nuove Cartiere di Tivoli S.R.L.
Villa Adriana Mill
Villa Adriana, Rome, Italy

OAO Mayak Technocell
Penza Mill
Penza, Russia

OAO Technicheskaya Bumaga
Rybinskiy rayon Mill
Rybinskiy rayon, Yaroslavl obl., Russia

Oi Seishi Co., Ltd.
Ena Paper Mill
Ena-shi, Gifu Pref., Japan

Oji Materia Co., Ltd.
Gifu (Ena) Mill
Ena-shi, Gifu Pref., Japan

Oji Materia Co., Ltd.
Kushiro Mill
Kushiro-shi, Hokkaido Pref., Japan

Oji Materia Co., Ltd.
Matsumoto Mill
Matsumoto-shi, Nagano Pref., Japan

Oji Materia Co., Ltd.
Nayoro Mill
Nayoro-shi, Hokkaido Pref., Japan

Oji Materia Co., Ltd.
Nikko Mill
Utsunomiya-shi, Tochigi Pref., Japan

Oji Materia Co., Ltd.
Oita Mill
Oita-shi, Oita Pref., Japan

Oji Materia Co., Ltd.
Osaka Mill
Osaka-shi, Osaka Pref., Japan

Oji Materia Co., Ltd.
Saga Mill
Saga-shi, Saga Pref., Japan

Oji Materia Co., Ltd.
Sobue Mill
Inazawa-shi, Aichi Pref., Japan

Okulovka P&P Mill Ltd.
Okulovka Mill
Okulovka, Novgorod Region, Russia

Oliveira Santos & Irmão, Lda.
Paços de Brandão Mill
Paços de Brandão, Santa Maria da Feira, Portugal

Olkhovka Board Mill, JSC
Olkhovka Mill
Olkhovka, Grodno Region, Belarus

Olmuksa International Paper-Sabanci Ambalaj Sanayi ve Ticaret A.S.
Olmuksa Edirne Mill
Edirne, Turkey

Ondunorte, Cia. de Papéis e Papelão Ondulado do Norte
Igarassu Mill
Igarassu, Pernambuco, Brazil

OOO Astrakhanskaya Paperboard Mill
Solyanka Mill
Solyanka, Russia

Orsa International Paper Embalagens S.A
Franco da Rocha Mill
Franco da Rocha, São Paulo, Brazil

Orsa International Paper Embalagens S.A
Nova Campina Mill
Nova Campina, São Paulo, Brazil

Orsa International Paper Embalagens S.A
Paulínia Mill
Paulínia, São Paulo, Brazil

Linerboard

Otsu-Paperboard Co., Ltd.
Otsu-shi Mill
Otsu-shi, Shiga Pref., Japan

OYKA Kagit Ve Ambalaj San Tic A.S.
Çaycuma Mill
Çaycuma, Zonguldak, Turkey

PABCO Paper
Vernon Mill
Vernon, California, United States

Packaging Corp. of America
Counce Mill
Counce, Tennessee, United States

Packaging Corp. of America
DeRidder Mill
DeRidder, Louisiana, United States

Packaging Corp. of America
Valdosta Mill
Valdosta, Georgia, United States

Palm Group
Wörth Mill
Wörth am Rhein, Germany

PAMER - Papelera Mercedes S.A.
Mercedes, Soriano Mill
Mercedes, Soriano, Uruguay

Pan Paper Mills
Webuye Mill
Webuye, Bungoma District, Western, Kenya

PAN Papirna Industrija d.o.o.
Zagreb Mill
Zagreb, Grad Zagreb, Croatia

Panasa, Papelera Nacional S.A.
Paramonga Mill
Paramonga, Lima, Peru

Panjapol Paper Industry Co. Ltd. and Panjapol Pulp Industry Public Co., Ltd.
Ayutthaya Mill
Bangsai District, Ayutthaya, Thailand

PAPCAS - Rebahia à Saïda
Saïda Mill
Saïda, Rebahia, Algeria

Papel Misionero S.A.I.F.C.
Puerto Mineral Mill
Capioví, Misiones, Argentina

Papeleira Portuguesa S.A.
São Paio de Oleiros Mill
São Paio de Oleiros, Portugal

Papelera Berazategui S.A.
Berazategui Mill
Berazategui, Buenos Aires, Argentina

Papelera de Chihuahua S.A. de C.V.
Chihuahua Mill
Chihuahua, Chihuahua, Mexico

Papelera de la Alqueria S.L.
Alicante Mill
Alqueria de Aznar, Alicante, Spain

Papelera del Nevado S.A. de C.V.
Almoloyan Mill
San Miguel Almoloyan, Almoloya de Juarez, México, D.F., Mexico

Papelera del Pacífico S.A.
Retalhuleu Mill
Retalhuleu, Guatemala

Papelera del Pacífico S.A.
San Francisco de Mostazal Mill
San Francisco de Mostazal, VI - Región Gen. O'Higgins, Chile

Papelera del Sur S.A.
Chincha Mill
Chincha, ICA, Peru

Papelera Don Torcuato S.A.
Don Torcuato Mill
Don Torcuato, Buenos Aires, Argentina

Papelera Entre Ríos S.A.
Paraná Mill
Paraná, Entre Ríos, Entre Ríos, Argentina

Papelera Iruña S.A. de C.V.
Iztapalapa Mill
Iztapalapa, México, D.F., Mexico

Papelera Mediterránea S.A.
Córdoba Mill
Córdoba, Córdoba, Argentina

Papelera Nacional S.A.
Guayaquil Mill
Guayaquil, Guayas, Ecuador

Papelera Paysandú S.A.I.C.
Wilde Mill
Wilde, Buenos Aires, Argentina

Papelera Pulpa Cuba
Trinidad Mill
Trinidad, Sancti Spiritus, Cuba

Papelera Santa Angela S.A.
General Pacheco Mill
General Pacheco, Tigre, Buenos Aires, Argentina

PAPELSA - Papeles y Cartones SA
Barbosa Mill
Barbosa, Antioquia, Colombia

Paper Packaging Pvt. Ltd. Corp.
Mandli Mill
Mandli, Shimoga Dist., Karnataka, India

Papeterie de la Mitidja
La Chiffa Mill
La Chiffa, Wilaya de Blida, Algeria

Papeterie Saint Michel SAS Groupe Thiollet
St. Michel d'Entraygues Mill
St. Michel d'Entraygues, France

Papeteries de Giroux SA
Giroux Mill
Olliergues, France

Papeteries et Cartonneries Lacaux Frères
Bosmie L'Aiguille Mill
Bosmie L'Aiguille, France

Papier- und Kartonfabrik Varel GmbH & Co. KG
Varel Mill
Varel, Niedersachsen, Germany

Papierfabrik Adolf Jass GmbH & Co. KG
Fulda Mill
Fulda, Germany

Papierfabrik Adolf Jass GmbH & Co. KG
Rudolstadt-Schwarza Mill
Rudolstadt-Schwarza, Thüringen, Germany

Papierfabrik Fritz Peters GmbH & Co. KG
Gelsenkirchen Mill
Gelsenkirchen, Germany

Papierfabrik Niederauer Mühle GmbH
Kreuzau and Niederau Mills
Kreuzau, Germany

Papierfabrik Palm GmbH & Co KG
Aalen Mill
Aalen-Neukochen, Germany

Papierfabrik Schoellershammer
Düren Mill
Düren, Germany

Papierfabrik Tillmann
Zülpich-Sinzenich Mill
Zülpich-Sinzenich, Germany

Papierfabrik Vreden GmbH
Vreden Mill
Vreden, Germany

Papir-Mal
Malin Mill
Malin, Zhitomirskaya obl., Ukraine

Papirfabrika Ligatne Ltd.
Ligatne Mill
Ligatne, Latvia

Paraibuna Embalagens Ltda.
Juiz de Fora Mill
Juiz de Fora, Minas Gerais, Brazil

Paramount Paper Board Mills (Pvt) Ltd.
Haripur Mill
Haripur, Pakistan

Parteks Tekstil ve Kagit San Tic. Ltd. Sti.
Kayseri Mill
Kayseri, Turkey

Pascorp Paper Industries Bhd.
Bentong Mill
Bentong, Pahang Darul Makmur, Malaysia

Patoom Dhanee Paper Factory Ltd. Part
Pathumthani Mill
Amphur Muang, Pathumthani, Thailand

Paulispell, Indústria Paulista de Papéis e Chapas de Papelão
Aguaí Mill
Aguaí, São Paulo, Brazil

PCE Embalagens
Manaus Mill
Manaus, Amazonas, Brazil

Pehlivanoglu Kagit, Kagit Mamülleri ve Ambalaj San.Tic. A.S.
Çerkezköy Mill
Çerkezköy, Tekirdag, Turkey

Penha Papéis e Embalagem Ltda.
Coronel Vivida Mill
Vivida, Paraná, Brazil

Linerboard

Penha Papéis e Embalagem Ltda.
Santo Amaro Mill
Santo Amaro da Purificação, Bahia, Brazil

Perm Pulp and Paper Mill
Perm Mill
Perm, Russia

Pham Thu Processing and Trading Co., Ltd
Ho Chi Minh City Mill
Ho Chi Minh City, Binh Duong Province, Vietnam

Phu Giang Paper and Packaging Co., Ltd.
Tien Du Mill
Tien Du, Bac Ninh Province, Vietnam

Pioneer Board Products (Pvt) Ltd.
Lahore Mill
Lahore, Punjab, Pakistan

Polotnyano-Zavodskaya Paper Mill
Polotnyany Zavod Mill
Polotnyany Zavod, Kaluga Region, Russia

Polpa de Madeiras Ltda.
Santa Cecília Mill
Santa Cecília, Santa Catarina, Brazil

Port Townsend Paper Corp.
Port Townsend Mill
Port Townsend, Washington, United States

Porto Feliz S.A.
Porto Feliz Mill
Porto Feliz, São Paulo, Brazil

Pratt Industries (USA)
Conyers Mill
Conyers, Georgia, United States

Pratt Industries (USA)
Shreveport Mill
Shreveport, Louisiana, United States

Pratt Industries (USA)
Staten Island Mill
Staten Island, New York, United States

Premium Paper & Boards Ind. Ltd.
Surat Mill
Surat, Gujarat, India

Primo Tedesco S.A.
Caçador Mill
Caçador, Santa Catarina, Brazil

Proletariy, JSC
Surazh Mill
Surazh, Bryansk Region, Russia

Propapier PM 1 GmbH
Burg Mill
Burg, Germany

Propapier PM 2 GmbH & Co. KG
Eisenhüttenstadt Mill
Eisenhüttenstadt, Brandenburg, Germany

PROPASA - Productora de Papel S.A. de C.V.
San Nicolas de los Garza Mill
San Nicolas de los Garza, Nuevo León, Mexico

PT Asia Paper Mills
Tangerang Mill
Tangerang, West Java, Indonesia

PT Ekamas Fortuna
Malang (PT Ekamas Fortuna) Mill
Malang, Jawa Timur, Indonesia

PT Enggal Subur Kertas
Pati Mill
Pati, Central Java, Indonesia

PT Eureka Aba
Mojosari Mill
Mojokerto, East Java, Indonesia

PT Evergreen International Paper
Medan Mill
Deli Serdang, Medan, Sumatra, Indonesia

PT Fajar Surya Wisesa Tbk.
Bekasi Mill
Cikarang Barat, Bekasi, West Java, Indonesia

PT Gunung Jaya Agung
Karawaci Mill
Karawaci, Tangerang, Jawa Barat, Indonesia

PT Indah Kiat Pulp & Paper Corp.
Perawang (PT Indah Kiat Pulp & Paper) Mill
Siak, Bengkalis, Riau, Sumatra, Indonesia

PT Indah Kiat Pulp & Paper Corp.
Serang (PT Indah Kiat Pulp & Paper) Mill
Serang, West Java, Indonesia

PT Integra Lestari (Surabaya)
Kec. Ngoro Mill
Kec. Ngoro, Mojokerto, East Java, Indonesia

PT Jaya Kertas
Nganjuk Mill
Nganjuk, East Java, Indonesia

PT Pabrik Kertas Indonesia (Pakerin)
Mojokerto Mill
Mojokerto, East Java, Indonesia

PT Pelita Cengkareng Paper
Subang Mill
Subang, West Java, Indonesia

PT Pelita Cengkareng Paper
Tangerang Mill
Cengkareng, Tangerang, West Java, Indonesia

PT Pura Barutama
Kudus Mill
Kudus, Central Java, Indonesia

PT Pura Nusapersada
Terban, Kudus Mill
Terban, Kudus, Central Java, Indonesia

PT Sinar Indah Kertas
Desa Pegandan Kecamatan Margorajo, Pati Mill
Desa Pegandan Kecamatan Margorejo, Pati, Central Java, Indonesia

PT Surabaya Mekabox
Driyorejo Mill
Surabaya, East Java, Indonesia

PT Tri Daya Kreasi
Purwakarta Mill
Purwakarta, West Java, Indonesia

PT Wirajaya Packindo
Tangerang Mill
Tangerang, West Java, Indonesia

Rakta, General Co. for Paper Industry
Rakta Mill
Alexandria, Iskanderiya, Egypt

Rampal Paper Mills
Dist. Malda Mill
Dist. Malda, West Bengal, India

Rana Mohendra Paper Ltd.
Dist. Ropar Mill
Dist. Ropar, Punjab, India

Rana Papers Ltd.
Muzaffarnagar Mill
Muzaffarnagar, Uttar Pradesh, India

Rand Whitney Containerboard
Montville Mill
Montville, Connecticut, United States

Rang Dong Paper Joint-stock Co.
Dien Khanh District Mill
Dien Khanh District, Khanh Hoa Province, Vietnam

Rayevka
Rayevka Mill
Rayevka, Minskaya obl., Belarus

Rengo Co., Ltd.
Amagasaki Mill
Kuise, Amagasaki-shi, Hyogo Pref., Japan

Rengo Co., Ltd.
Tonegawa Mill
Bando-shi, Ibaraki Pref., Japan

Rengo Co., Ltd.
Yashio Mill
Yashio-shi, Saitama Pref., Japan

Rengo Co., Ltd.
Yodogawa Mill
Osaka-shi, Osaka Pref., Japan

Republic Paperboard Co. LLC
Lawton Mill
Lawton, Oklahoma, United States

Rigesa, Celulose, Papel e Embalagens Ltda.
Três Barras Mill
Três Barras, Santa Catarina, Brazil

RockTenn Co.
Fernandina Beach Mill
Fernandina Beach, Florida, United States

RockTenn Co.
Florence Mill
Florence, South Carolina, United States

RockTenn Co.
Hodge Mill
Hodge, Louisiana, United States

RockTenn Co.
Hopewell Mill
Hopewell, Virginia, United States

RockTenn Co.
La Tuque Mill
La Tuque, Quebec, Canada

RockTenn Co.
Panama City Mill
Panama City, Florida, United States

Linerboard

RockTenn Co.
Seminole Mill
Jacksonville, Florida, United States

RockTenn Co.
Solvay Mill
Syracuse, New York, United States

RockTenn Co.
Tacoma Mill
Tacoma, Washington, United States

RockTenn Co.
West Point Mill
West Point, Virginia, United States

Rondo Ganahl AG
Frastanz Mill
Frastanz, Vorarlberg, Austria

Rossmann SAS
Ste. Croix aux Mines Mill
Ste. Croix aux Mines, France

Rubezhansky Cardboard and Packaging Mill
Rubezhnoye Mill
Rubezhnoye, Lugansk obl., Ukraine

Ruby Macons Ltd.
Morai Mill
Morai, Gujarat, India

Ruby Macons Ltd.
Vapi Mill
Vapi, Gujarat, India

Ruchira Papers Ltd.
Kala-Amb Mill
Kala-Amb, Himachal Pradesh, India

Ruloni
Tbilisi Mill
Tbilisi, Georgia

S.C. EcoPaper S.A.
Zarnesti Mill
Zarnesti, Romania

S.N. Paper Mills (P) Ltd.
Dist. Ludhiana Mill
Dist. Ludhiana, Punjab, India

Sadeque Paper & Board Mills Ltd.
Kaliakoir, Gazipur Mill
Kaliakoir, Gazipur, Gazipur, Bangladesh

SAICA - S.A. Industrias Celulosa Aragonesa
Fábrica I - Zaragoza Mill
Zaragoza, Spain

SAICA - S.A. Industrias Celulosa Aragonesa
Fábrica II, III & IV - El Burgo de Ebro Mill
El Burgo de Ebro, Zaragoza, Spain

SAICA Paper UK Ltd.
Partington Mill
Carrington, Manchester, Greater Manchester, United Kingdom

SAICA Vénizel
Vénizel Mill
Vénizel, France

Saigon Paper
My Xuan I Mill
Tan Thanh Dist., Ba Ria - Vung Tau, Dong Nam Bo, Vietnam

Saigon Paper
My Xuan II Mill
Tan Thanh Dist., Ba Ria - Vung Tau, Dong Nam Bo, Vietnam

Sainath Paper Mills
Dist. Valsad Mill
Dist. Valsad, Gujarat, India

Sainsons Paper Industries Ltd.
Kurukshetra Mill
Dist. Kurukshetra, Haryana, India

Saiyed Paper Mills Ltd.
Vapi Mill
Vapi, Gujarat, India

Santa Clara Indústria de Papéis Ltda.
Candoi Mill
Candoi, Paraná, Brazil

Santa Clara Indústria de Papéis Ltda.
Ivaí Mill
Ivaí, Paraná, Brazil

São Carlos SA Indústria de Papel e Embalagens
São Carlos Mill
São Carlos, São Paulo, Brazil

São Gabriel Papéis Ltda.
União da Vitória Mill
União da Vitória, Paraná, Brazil

SAPB, Société Anonyme des Papeteries du Belvédére
Cité El Khadra, Tunis Mill
Cité El Khadra, Tunis, Tunisia

SAPELBA - Fábrica de Papel da Bahia S.A.
Feira de Santana Mill
Feira de Santana, Bahia, Brazil

Sappi Fine Paper Europe
Alfeld Mill
Alfeld (Leine), Germany

Sappi Paper and Paper Packaging South Africa (SA)
Cape Kraft Mill
Montague Gardens, Cape Town, Cape Town, South Africa

Sappi Paper and Paper Packaging South Africa (SA)
Ngodwana Mill
Ngodwana, Mpumalanga, South Africa

Sappi Paper and Paper Packaging South Africa (SA)
Tugela Mill
Mandini, KwaZulu-Natal, South Africa

Sastha Paper Mills
Kanchipuram Mill
Kanchipuram, Tamil Nadu, India

SCA Graphic Sundsvall AB
Ortviken Mill
Sundsvall, Sweden

SCA Munksund AB
Piteå Mill
Piteå, Sweden

SCA Obbola AB
Obbola Mill
Obbola, Sweden

Schumacher Packaging Zaklad Grudziadz Sp.z o.o.
Grudziadz Mill
Grudziadz, Poland

Selenginsky Pulp & Board Mill
Selenginsk Mill
Selenginsk, Buryatia Republic, Russia

Selkasan Kagit ve Paketleme Malzemeleri Imalati San. ve Tic. AS
Manisa Mill
Manisa, Turkey

Seyfert Paper S.A.S.
Descartes Mill
Descartes, France

Shaanxi Xi-An Weiyangqu Efang Paperboard Co., Ltd.
Xi-An Mill
Xi-An, Shaanxi, China

Shakumbhri Straw Products Ltd.
Moradabad Mill
Tehsil Bilari, Moradabad, Uttar Pradesh, India

Shalimar Paper Mills (P) Ltd.
Muzaffarnagar Mill
Muzaffarnagar, Uttar Pradesh, India

Shamli Paper Mills Ltd.
Vill. Sikka Shamli Mill
Vill. Sikka Shamli, Uttar Pradesh, India

Shandong Bohui Paper Industry Co., Ltd.
Zibo Mill
Zibo, Shandong, China

Shandong Derong Paper Co., Ltd.
Zaozhuang Mill
Zaozhuang, Shandong, China

Shandong Gaoqing Qingyuan Paper Co. Ltd.
Zibo Mill
Zibo, Shandong, China

Shandong Guihe Xianxing Paper Holding Pte. Ltd.
Zibo Mill
Zibo, Shandong, China

Shandong Huapeng Paper Co. Ltd.
Zibo Mill
Zibo, Shandong, China

Shandong Jianghe Paper Co., Ltd.
Qihe Mill
Dezhou, Shandong, China

Shandong Qingdao Haiwang Paper Property Share Co., Ltd.
Qingdao Mill
Qingdao, Shandong, China

Linerboard

Shandong Taian Baichuan Paper Co., Ltd.
Taian Mill
Taian, Shandong, China

Shanghai Chung Loong Paper Co., Ltd.
Shanghai Mill
Shanghai, Shanghai, China

Shindaeyang Paper Co., Ltd.
Shihwa Mill
Ansan-si, Gyeonggi-do, South Korea

Shiv Shakti Kraft Board Mills (P) Ltd.
Dist. Aurangabad Mill
Dist. Aurangabad, Maharashtra, India

Shouguang Meilun Paper
Shouguang (Shouguang Meilun Paper) Mill
Shouguang, Shandong, China

Shree Papers Ltd.
East Godavari Mill
East Godavari, Andhra Pradesh, India

Siam Kraft Industry Co., Ltd.
BanPong Mill
BanPong, Ratchaburi, Thailand

SICAL
Lumbres Mill
Lumbres, France

Sichuan Guanghan City Shunfa Co., Ltd.
Deyang Mill
Deyang, Sichuan, China

Sichuan Longchang Yuhong Paper Co., Ltd.
Neijiang Mill
Neijiang, Sichuan, China

Siddheshwari Industries Ltd.
Muzaffarnagar Mill
Muzaffarnagar, Uttar Pradesh, India

Sidharth Papers Ltd.
Kashipur Mill
Kashipur, Uttarakhand, India

Silvertoan Papers Ltd.
Muzaffarnagar Mill
Muzaffarnagar, Uttar Pradesh, India

SIPCO-Soc. Ind. de Papier et de Carton Ondule SAL
Beirut Mill
Kfarchima, Beirut, Lebanon

SKG Pulp & Paper
New Alipore, Kolkata Mill
New Alipore, Kolkata, West Bengal, India

Slavuta-Papir, JSC
Slavuta Mill
Slavuta, Ukraine

Smurfit Cartón y Papel de México S.A. de C.V.
Cerro Gordo Mill
Santa Clara Coatitla, Ecatepec de Morelos, Edo. de México, Mexico

Smurfit Cartón y Papel de México S.A. de C.V.
Los Reyes Mill
Col. Los Reyes Iztacala, Tlalnepantla, México, D.F., Mexico

Smurfit Cartón y Papel de México S.A. de C.V.
Monterrey Mill
Monterrey, Baja California Norte, Mexico

Smurfit Kappa Ania Paper
Ania Mill
Ponte all'Ania, Lucca, Italy

Smurfit Kappa Cartón de Colombia SA
Barranquilla Mill
Barranquilla, Atlántico, Colombia

Smurfit Kappa Cartón de Colombia SA
Yumbo Mill
Cali, Valle de Cauca, Colombia

Smurfit Kappa Cartón de Venezuela S.A.
San Felipe Mill
San Felipe, Yaracuy, Venezuela

Smurfit Kappa Cellulose du Pin
Facture mill
Biganos, France

Smurfit Kappa de Argentina S.A.
Bernal Mill
Bernal, Buenos Aires, Argentina

Smurfit Kappa de Argentina S.A.
Coronel Suárez Mill
Coronel Suárez, Buenos Aires, Argentina

Smurfit Kappa GmbH Viersen Papier
Viersen Mill
Viersen, Germany

Smurfit Kappa Haupt Papier- und Pappenfabrik GmbH & Co. KG
Diemelstadt-Wrexen Mill
Diemelstadt-Wrexen, Germany

Smurfit Kappa Kraftliner Piteå
Piteå Mill
Piteå, Sweden

Smurfit Kappa Mengibar Paper
Mengibar Mill
Mengibar, Jaén, Spain

Smurfit Kappa Morava Paper
Žimrovice Mill
Žimrovice, Czech Republic

Smurfit Kappa Nettingsdorfer, Nettingsdorfer Papierfabrik AG & Co. KG
Nettingsdorfer Mill
Haid bei Ansfelden, Oberösterreich, Austria

Smurfit Kappa Orange County
Forney Mill
Forney, Texas, United States

Smurfit Kappa Papier & Kartonfabrik Hoya
Hoya Mill
Hoya/Weser, Germany

Smurfit Kappa Papier Recyclé France
Alfa d Avignon Mill
Le Pontet Cedex, France

Smurfit Kappa Papier Recyclé France
Papeteries de Saillat
Saint Junien Cedex, France

Smurfit Kappa Papier Recyclé France
Sault-les-Rethel mill
Sault-les-Rethel, France

Smurfit Kappa Roermond Papier BV
Roermond Mill
Roermond, Netherlands

Smurfit Kappa Sangüesa Paper
Sangüesa Mill
Sangüesa, Navarra, Spain

Smurfit Kappa SSK
Birmingham Mill
Nechells, Birmingham, West Midlands, United Kingdom

Smurfit Kappa Zülpich Papier GmbH
Zülpich Mill
Zülpich, Germany

SOLICAR-Société Libanaise de Carton
Beirut Mill
Beirut, Lebanon

Sona Paper & Boards Ltd.
Patiala Mill
Dist. Mohali, Punjab, India

Song Lam Paper Joint-Stock Co.
Hung Nguyen Dist. Mill
Hung Nguyen Dist., Vietnam

Sonoco de Colombia Ltda
Cali Mill
Cali, Valle de Cauca, Colombia

Sonoco de México, S.A. de C.V.
Santa Clara Mill
Santa Clara Ecatepec, Edo. de México, Mexico

Sonoco Ltd.
Trent Valley Mill
Glen Miller, Ontario, Canada

Sopasta S.A. Indústria e Comércio
Tangará Mill
Tangará, Santa Catarina, Brazil

Sotipapier - Société Tunisienne Industrielle du Papier et du Carton - S.A.R.L.
Belli Mill
Belli, Tunisia

South African Cartonboard Mills
Wadeville Mill
Wadeville, Gauteng, South Africa

South African Paper Mills (SAPM)
Durban Mill
Jacobs, Durban, KwaZulu-Natal, South Africa

SP Fiber Technologies LLC (SPFT)
Dublin Mill
Dublin, Georgia, United States

SPAC, Société Papier et Carton
Sbeitla Mill
Sbeitla, Gouvernorat de Kasserine, Tunisia

Spartak
Shklov Mill
Shklov, Mogilev Region, Belarus

Sprick GmbH & Co.
Mitte Mill
Diemelstadt, Germany

Linerboard

Sree Sakthi Paper Mills Ltd.
Edayar Mill
Aluva, Kerala, India

Sripathi Paper & Boards Pvt.Ltd
Sivakasi Mill
Sivakasi, Tamil Nadu, India

Stallion Duplex (P) Ltd.
Karnal Mill
Karnal, Haryana, India

Stora Enso Poland S.A.
Ostroleka Mill
Ostroleka, Poland

Stora Enso Printing and Reading
Uetersen Mill
Uetersen, Germany

Stora Enso Renewable Packaging
Skoghall Mill
Skoghall, Sweden

Suhar Paper Mill
Suhar Mill
Suhar, Oman

Sukhonsky Pulp and Paper Mill
Sokol Mill
Sokol, Vologodskaya obl., Russia

Sulamericana Industrial Ltda.
Mogi Mirim Mill
Mogi Mirim, São Paulo, Brazil

Sunko Seishi Co., Ltd.
Shizuoka-shi Mill
Shimizu-ku, Shizuoka-shi, Shizuoka Pref., Japan

Superplast Co.
El Obour Mill
Bab El Shaaria, Cairo, Egypt

Surpapel SA
Berazategui Mill
Berazategui, Buenos Aires, Argentina

Suyash Paper Mills
Basti district Mill
Basti district, Uttar Pradesh, Uttar Pradesh, India

Svetlogorskiy Pulp and Board Mill
Svetlogorsk Mill
Svetlogorsk, Gomel Region, Belarus

T.T.K. Pharma Ltd. (Paper division)
Dist. Erode Mill
Dist. Erode, Tamil Nadu, India

Ta Chang Paper Mfg. Co., Ltd.
Lungchin Mill
Long Ching District, Taichung City, Taiwan

Taiho Paper Co., Ltd.
Kamo-gun Mill
Kamo-gun, Gifu Pref., Japan

Taisei Paper Industries Co., Ltd.
Tsuyama-shi Mill
Tsuyama-shi, Okayama Pref., Japan

Tao Yuan Paper Mfg. Co., Ltd.
Lu Chu Mill
Lu Chu, Taoyuan County, Taiwan

Technocart SA
Tripolis Mill
Tripolis, Greece

Thai Cane Paper Public Co., Ltd.
Prachinburi Mill #2
Amphur Kabinburi, Prachinburi, Thailand

Thai Kraft Paper Industry Co., Ltd.
Wangsala Mill
Tha Muang Distr., Kanchanaburi, Kanchanaburi, Thailand

Thai Paper Mill Co., Ltd.
Rayong Mill
Amphur Bankhai, Rayong, Thailand

Thanakorn Paper Industry Co., Ltd.
Amphur Muang, Pathumthani Mill
Amphur Muang, Pathumthani, Thailand

Thurpapier, Model AG
Weinfelden Mill
Weinfelden, Switzerland

Todo Papel S.A. de C.V.
Ixtapaluca Mill
Ixtapaluca, México, D.F., Mexico

Tokushu Tokai Paper Co., Ltd.
Shimada Mill
Shimada-shi, Shizuoka Pref., Japan

Tolentino S.r.l.
Tolentino Mill
Tolentino, Macerata, Italy

Tong Long Paper Co., Ltd.
Ta Liao Mill
Ta Liao District, Kaohsiung City, Taiwan

Tonic Industrie EPE
Ouate Industrie Mill
Bou Ismail, Wilaya d'Alger, Algeria

TOP S.A.
Tychy Mill
Tychy, Poland

Top-Comment Technology Enterprise Co. Ltd.
Chiayi Mill
Ming Hsiung, Chia-I County, Taiwan

TOV Poninki Cardboard and Paper Mill
Poninka Mill
Poninka, Polonsky rayon, Khmelnitska obl., Ukraine

Transnational Paper Corp.
Cavite Mill
Calvite City, Calabarzon, Laguna, Philippines

Tri-Asia Paper Mill, Inc.
Cabuyao Mill
Cabuyao City, Laguna, Philippines

Trombini Industrial S.A.
Curitiba Mill
Curitiba, Paraná, Brazil

Trombini Industrial S.A.
Fraiburgo Mill
Fraiburgo, Santa Catarina, Brazil

Trupal S.A.
Evitamiento Mill
El Agustino, Lima, Lima, Peru

Trupal S.A.
Trujillo Mill
Trujillo, Peru

Tung Yuan Paper Mfg. Co., Ltd.
Chiao Tou Mill
Chiao Tou District, Kaohsiung City, Taiwan

Umesh Board & Paper Mills (P) Ltd.
Tq. & Dist. Aurangabad Mill
Tq. & Dist. Aurangabad, Maharashtra, India

Unión Industrial Papelera S.A. (UIPSA)
La Pobla de Claramunt Mill
La Pobla de Claramunt, Barcelona, Spain

Unión Papelera Platense
La Plata Mill
La Plata, Buenos Aires, Argentina

Union Paper Mills
Dubai Mill
Dubai, United Arab Emirates

United Paper Public Co. Ltd.
Amphur Muang Mill
Amphur Muang, Prachinburi, Thailand

United Pulp & Paper Co., Inc.
Calumpit Mill
Calumpit, Bulacan, Philippines

UPP Pulp & Paper (M) Sdn Bhd
Batang Berjuntai Mill
Ijok, Batang Berjuntai, Selangor Darul Ehsan, Malaysia

Valaichenai Paper Mills
Valaichenai Mill
Valaichenai, Sri Lanka

Valpasa Indústria de Papel Ltda.
Tangará Mill
Tangará, Santa Catarina, Brazil

Van Diem Paper Joint-Stock Co.
Phu Xuyen Mill
Phu Xuyen District, Ha Tay Province, Vietnam

Veerachola Papers
Veerachola Papers
Tirupur, Tamil Nadu, India

Venkraft Paper Mills Private Ltd.
Hosur Mill
Hosur, Tamil Nadu, India

Vietnam Lee & Man Paper Manufacturing Ltd
Hau Giang Mill
Chau Thanh district, Ha Giang Province, Vietnam

Vina Kraft Paper
Ho Chi Minh City Mill
Ho Chi Minh City, Binh Duong Province, Vietnam

VIS Containers Manufacturing SA
Volos Mill
Volos, Greece

Visy Pulp & Paper
Coolaroo Mill
Campbellfield, Victoria, Australia

Visy Pulp & Paper
Gibson Island, VPP8
Gibson Island, Queensland, Australia

Visy Pulp & Paper
Tumut, VPP9
Tumut, New South Wales, Australia

Visy Pulp & Paper
VPP2, Reservoir Mill
Reservoir, Victoria, Australia

Visy Pulp & Paper
VPP3/6, Smithfield Mill
Smithfield, New South Wales, Australia

VPK Paper NV
Dendermonde Mill
Dendermonde, Belgium

Vrancart SA
Adjud Mill
Adjud, Vrancea, Romania

Vyborgskaya Cellulose, JSC
Sovetsky Mill
Vyborg, Sovetsky, Leningrad Region, Russia

W. Hamburger GmbH
Pitten Mill
Pitten, Niederösterreich, Austria

Weihai Longgang Paper Co., Ltd.
Weihai Mill
Weihai, Shandong, China

Wolsan Paper Mfg. Co., Ltd.
Haman Mill
Chilseo-myeon, Haman-gun, Gyeongsangnam-do, South Korea

Xuan Duc Joint-Stock Paper Company
Ho Chi Minh City Mill
Ho Chi Minh City, Binh Duong Province, Vietnam

Yaroslavl Paper ZAO
Yaroslavl Mill
Yaroslavl, Yaroslavl obl., Russia

Youngpoong Paper Mfg. Co., Ltd.
Pyeongtaek-si Mill
Pyeongtaek-si, Gyeonggi-do, South Korea

Yuantong Paper (Shandong) Co., Ltd.
Zaozhuang Mill
Zaozhuang, Shandong, China

Yuen Foong Yu Packaging Inc.
Hsin Wu Mill
Hsin Wu, Taoyuan County, Taiwan

Yung-Seng Development Enterprise Co., Ltd.
Taoyuan Mill
Taoyuan, Taoyuan County, Taiwan

ZAO Altaykrovlya
Novoaltaysk Mill
Novoaltaysk, Altaisky Kray, Russia

ZAO MPK KRZ - Multibranch Production Company KRZ
Ryazan Mill
Ryazan, Russia

Zhejiang Fuyang Jinchang Paper Co., Ltd.
Fuyang Mill
Fuyang, Zhejiang, China

Zhejiang Fuyang Wansheng Paper Co., Ltd.
Fuyang Mill
Fuyang, Zhejiang, China

Zhejiang Huakang Paper Co., Ltd.
Ruian Mill
Ruian, Zhejiang, China

Zhejiang Huayu Paper Co., Ltd.
Shaoxing Mill
Shaoxing, Zhejiang, China

Zhejiang JiAn Paper Package Co., Ltd.
Jiaxing Mill
Jiaxing, Zhejiang, China

Zhejiang Jingxing Paper Joint Stock Co., Ltd.
Pinghu Mill
Pinghu, Zhejiang, China

Zhejiang Long Chen Paper Co., Ltd.
Pinghu Mill
Pinghu, Zhejiang, China

Zhejiang Rongsheng Paper Co., Ltd.
Pinghu Mill
Pinghu, Zhejiang, China

Zhejiang Shengda Group
Hangzhou Mill
Hangzhou, Zhejiang, China

Zhejiang Yiwu City YiNan Paper Co., Ltd.
Yiwu Mill
Yiwu, Zhejiang, China

Zhydachiv Pulp & Paper Mill
Zhydachiv Mill
Zhydachiv, Lviv obl., Ukraine

Zhytomyr Paperboard Mill
Zhytomyr Mill
Zhytomyr, Ukraine

Corrugating medium/fluting

A. Vl. Koliopoulos S.A. Pako
Pelasghia Mill
Pelasghia, Fthiotidos, Greece

Aarepapier AG
Niedergösgen Mill
Niedergösgen, Switzerland

Adami S.A. Madeiras
Caçador Mill
Caçador, Santa Catarina, Brazil

Adda Ondulati SpA
Annone di Brianza Mill
Annone di Brianza, Lecco, Italy

Afri Paper
Chbika Mill
Chbika, Kairouan, Gouvernorat de Kairouan, Tunisia

Águas Negras S.A. Ind. de Papel
Ituporanga Mill
Ituporanga, Santa Catarina, Brazil

Agustín Barral, S.A.
Barcelona Mill
La Pobla de Lillet (Barcelona), Spain

Ajin Paper Mfg. Co. Ltd.
Hyunpoong Mill
Dalseong-gun, Daegu-si, Daegu-si, South Korea

Akasan Adana Kagit San ve Tic. Ltd. Sti.
Adana Mill
Adana, Turkey

Al Arouba Paper Co. M. Farghaly & Co.
Alexandria Mill
Alexandria, Iskanderiya, Egypt

Alatyrskaya Paper Mill
Alatyr Mill
Alatyr, Chuvashkaya Republic, Russia

Albertin Paperboard & Paper Mill
Slonim Mill
Slonim, Grodno Region, Belarus

Allard Emballages
Varennes Mill
Aubigné-Racan, France

Alta Papéis Ltda.
Benedito Novo Mill
Benedito Novo, Santa Catarina, Brazil

Ambro SA Suceava
Suceava Mill
Suceava, Romania

An Binh Paper Corporation-ABPAPER
Di An District Mill
Di An District, Binh Duong Province, Vietnam

Angren Pack
Bulbak Mill
Angren, pos. Bulbak, Tashkentskaya obl., Uzbekistan

Anhui Hefei Jinzhong Paper Co. Ltd.
Hefei Mill
Hefei, Anhui, China

Anhui Hefei Xingdong Paper Co., Ltd.
Hefei Mill
Hefei, Anhui, China

Ansabo S.A.
Quilmes Mill
Quilmes, Buenos Aires, Argentina

Arab Cardboard Mfg. Co.
Sahab Mill
Sahab, Jordan

Arab Company for Paper Product (Arapepco)
Aleppo Mill
Aleppo, Syria

Arab Paper Manufacturing Co. Ltd. (Waraq)
Dammam Mill
Dammam, Saudi Arabia

Argencraft S.A.
Andino Mill
Andino, Santa Fé, Argentina

Arkhangelsk Pulp & Paper Mill
Novodvinsk (Arkhangelsk - APPM) Mill
Novodvinsk, Arkhangelsk Region, Russia

Aryan Paper Mills Pvt. Ltd.
Vapi Mill
Vapi, Gujarat, India

Asia Kraft Paper Co., Ltd.
Samut Sakhon Mill
Samut Sakhon, Thailand

Corrugating medium/fluting

Atlantic Packaging Products Ltd.
Scarborough Mill
Scarborough, Ontario, Canada

Atlantic Packaging Products Ltd.
Whitby Mill
Whitby, Ontario, Canada

Baron-Well GmbH
Goslar Mill
Goslar, Germany

Bataan 2020
Baesa Mill
Baesa, Quezon City, Philippines

Bazargaon Paper & Pulp Mills Pvt. Ltd.
Bazargaon Mill
Bazargaon, Nagpur, Maharashtra, India

BELIŠCE d.d.
Belišce Mill
Belišce, Salvonia, Croatia

Bharat Papers Ltd.
Kathua Mill
Kathua, Jammu and Kashmir, India

BillerudKorsnäs AB
Gruvön Mill
Grums, Sweden

BillerudKorsnäs AB
Skärblacka Mill
Skärblacka, Sweden

Bio-PAPPEL International
Prewitt Mill
Prewitt, New Mexico, United States

Bio-PAPPEL Kraft
Atenquique Mill
Atenquique, Jalisco, Mexico

Bio-PAPPEL Kraft
Cuesta El Registro mill
Cuesta El Registro, Durango, Mexico

Bio-PAPPEL Kraft
Monterrey Mill
Monterrey, Nuevo León, Mexico

Bio-PAPPEL Kraft
Texcoco Mill
Los Reyes La Paz, Edo. de México, Mexico

Bio-PAPPEL Kraft
Tizayuca Mill
El Chopo, Tizayuca, Mexico

Bio-PAPPEL Printing
Tuxtepec Mill
Tuxtepec, OAX, Mexico

Boise Paper
Wallula Mill
Wallula, Washington, United States

Bormio SpA
Ponte Lambro Mill
Ponte Lambro, Como, Italy

Brason Indústria de Papéis e Ondulados Ltda.
Araras Mill
Araras, São Paulo, Brazil

Brianskaya Paper Mill
Belye Berega Mill
Pos. Belye Berega, Bryansk Region, Russia

Bulleh Shah Packaging (Private) Limited
Bulleh Shah Paper Mill
Kasur, Pakistan

C & C Srl
Broccostella Mill
Broccostella, Frosinone, Italy

C.C.R. - Cartiera Cooperativa Rivalta
Rivalta Veronese Mill
Brentino-Belluno, Verona, Italy

California Paperboard Corp.
Santa Clara Mill
Santa Clara, California, United States

Carter Holt Harvey Pulp & Paper
Kinleith Mill
Tokoroa, New Zealand

Carter Holt Harvey Pulp & Paper
Penrose Mill
Penrose, Auckland, New Zealand

Cartesar SpA
Pellezano Mill
Pellezano, Salerno, Italy

Cartiera Ciacci S.a.
San Marino Mill
Gualdicciolo, San Marino, San Marino

Cartiera di Cologno SpA
Cologno Monzese Mill
Cologno Monzese, Milan, Italy

Cartiera di Porporano Srl
Porporano Mill
Porporano, Parma, Italy

Cartiera di Salerno di Mauro Benedetti
Salerno Mill
Salerno, Salerno, Italy

Cartiera Enrico Cassina SNC
Pinerolo Mill
Pinerolo, Turin, Italy

Cartiera S.A.C.C.A. SpA
Calatabiano Mill
Calatabiano, Catania, Italy

Cartiere del Polesine Spa
Adria Mill
Adria, Rovigo, Italy

Cartiere del Polesine Spa
Loreo Mill
Loreo, Rovigo, Italy

Cartiere di Trevi SpA
Trevi Mill
Trevi, Perugia, Italy

Cartiere Modesto Cardella SpA
San Pietro a Vico Mill
San Pietro a Vico, Lucca, Italy

Cartiere SACI SpA
Verona Mill
Cà di David, Verona, Italy

Cartiere Villa Lagarina Spa
Trento Mill
Trento, Trento, Italy

Cartitalia S.r.l.
Cartitalia Mill
Mesola, Ferrara, Italy

Cartocor S.A.
Arroyito Mill
Arroyito, Córdoba, Argentina

Cartonera del Caribe CA
Maracay Mill
Maracay, Edo. Aragua, Venezuela

Cartones America SA - CAME
Cali Mill
Cali, Valle de Cauca, Colombia

Cartonifício Valinhos S.A.
Valinhos Mill
Valinhos, São Paulo, Brazil

Cartonneries de Gondardennes SA
Wardrecques Mill
Wardrecques, Aire-Sur-La-Lys, France

Cartopel S.A.
Cuenca Mill
Cuenca, Azuay, Ecuador

CARVIMSA, Cartones Villa Marina S.A.
Niveria Mill
Ex Fundo Nieveria, Lurigancho-Chosica, Peru

Cataguazes Indústrias de Papel
Cataguases Mill
Cataguases, Minas Gerais, Brazil

CECSO - Celulosa y Corrugados de Sonora S.A. de C.V.
Navojoa Mill
Navojoa, Sonora, Mexico

Celulosa San Pedro S.A.
Buenos Aires Mill
Buenos Aires, Buenos Aires, Argentina

Celulosa y Papel del Bajío S.A.de C.V.
León Mill
León, Guanajuato, Mexico

Celulose Irani S.A.
Santa Luzia Mill
Santa Luzia, Minas Gerais, Brazil

Celulose Irani S.A.
Vargem Bonita Mill
Vargem Bonita, Santa Catarina, Brazil

Charoen Chai Co., Ltd.
Bangkok Mill
Bangkok, Bangkok, Thailand

Cheeyee Enterprise Corp.
Ping Tung Mill
Pingtung, Pingtung County, Taiwan

Chen Tjun Paper Mill Industrial Co., Ltd.
Chu Nan Mill
Chu Nan, Miaoli County, Taiwan

Cheng Loong Corporation
Hou Li Mill
Hou Li, Taichung City, Taiwan

Corrugating medium/fluting

Cheng Loong Corporation Tayuan Mill
Ta Yuan Mill
Ta Yuan, Taoyuan County, Taiwan

Cheng Yang Paper Mill Co., Ltd.
Ben Cat Dist. (Cheng Yang Paper) Mill
Ben Cat Dist., Binh Duong Province, Vietnam

Chilya Corrugated Board Mills Ltd
Karachi Mill
Karachi, Sindh, Pakistan

China Sunshine Paper Holdings Company Limited
Weifang Mill
Weifang, Shandong, China

Chizhovskaya Paper Mill
Novograd-Volynskiy Mill
Chizhovka, Novograd-Volynskiy rayon, Zhitomirskaya obl., Ukraine

Chouka Pulp & Paper Mill
Rezvanshahr Mill
Rezvanshahr, Iran

Cia. Industrial Papelera Poblana S.A. de C.V.
Chachapa Mill
Chachapa, Puebla, Mexico

Cibrapel S.A. Indústria de Papel e Embalagens
Guapimirim Mill
Guapimirim, Rio de Janeiro, Brazil

CITROPLAST- Ind. e Com. de Papéis e Plásticos Ltda.
Andradina Mill
Andradina, São Paulo, Brazil

CMPC Papeles Cordillera S.A.
Puente Alto Mill
Puente Alto, RM - Región Metro. de Santiago, Chile

Container Corp. of the Philippines
Quezon City Mill
Quezon City, Philippines

Copamex Industrias S.A. de C.V.
Monterrey Mill
San Nicolas de los Garza, Nuevo León, Mexico

Copikas Kagit ve Oluklu Mukavva Kutu A.S.
Olmuksa Copikas Mill
Corum, Turkey

Craft Corner Paper Mills Pvt. Ltd.
Vapi Dist., Valsad Mill
Dist. Valsad, Gujarat, India

Daehan Papertech Co., Ltd.
Danyang Mill
Daejeon-myeon, Damyang-gun, Jeollanam-do, South Korea

Daelim Paper Co. Ltd.
Daelim Paper
Osan-si, Gyeonggi-do, South Korea

Dall Pel Madeira e Papel
Grechinski Mill
Irati, Paraná, Brazil

Delkeskamp Verpackungswerke GmbH
Nortrup Mill
Nortrup, Germany

Delta Board Mills SAE
Cairo Mill
Badr City, Cairo, Egypt

Dentaş Ambalaj Ve Kagit San. A.S
Çorlu Mill
Çorlu, Tekirdag, Turkey

Dentaş Ambalaj Ve Kagit San. A.S
Denizli Mill
Denizli, Turkey

Dev Kiran Paper Mills (P) Ltd.
Bangalore Mill
Bangalore, Karnataka, India

Dev Priya Industries Limited
Meerut Mill
Meerut District, Uttar Pradesh, India

Dnepropetrovsk Paper Mill, Ltd.
Dnepropetrovsk Mill
Dnepropetrovsk, Ukraine

Dobrushskaya Paper Mill "Geroi Truda", OJSC
Dobrush Mill
Dobrush, Gomel Region, Belarus

Donetsk-Vtorma Ltd.
Donetsk Mill
Donetsk, Ukraine

Dongil Paper Mfg. Co., Ltd.
Ansan Mill
Ansan-si, Gyeonggi-do, South Korea

Dongil Paper Mfg. Co., Ltd.
Uiryeong Mill
Uiryeong-gun, Gyeongsangnam-do, South Korea

Donskaya Gofrotara
Rostov na Donu Mill
Rostov na Donu, Russia

Doruk Kagit San. TIC. A.S
Kayseri Mill
Kayseri, Turkey

DS Smith Packaging Benelux B.V.
Eerbeek Mill
Eerbeek, Netherlands

DS Smith Packaging France
Contoire Hamel Mill
Contoire Hamel, France

DS Smith Packaging Italia S.p.A.
Lucca Mill
Porcari, Lucca, Italy

DS Smith Paper
Kemsley Mill
Kemsley, Sittingbourne, Kent, United Kingdom

DS Smith Paper Deutschland GmbH
Aschaffenburg Mill
Aschaffenburg, Germany

DS Smith Paper Deutschland GmbH
Witzenhausen Mill
Witzenhausen, Germany

Duropack GmbH
Trakia
Pazardzik, Glavinitza quarter, Bulgaria

Ecologicheskie Tekhnologii Ltd
Balakhna Mill
Balakhna, Nizhny Novgorod, Russia

Ecopaper JP Co. Ltd
Owariasahi Mill
Owariasahi-Shi, Aichi Pref., Japan

Edipack sh.p.k.
Durres Mill
Durres, Albania

EFW Tuscania Srl
Tuscania Mill
Tuscania, Viterbo, Italy

Ehime Paper Mfg. Co., Ltd.
Shikokuchuo-shi Mill
Shikokuchuo-shi, Ehime Pref., Japan

EIC - Empaques Industriales Colombianos SA
Caucaseco - Palmira Mill
Caucaseco - Palmira, Valle de Cauca, Colombia

El Nasr Carton Co.
Borg El Arab El Gededah Mill
Borg El Arab El - Gedeedah, Alexandria, Egypt

El Obour Co.
Heliopolis, Cairo Mill
Heliopolis, Cairo, Egypt

El-Salam PaperMill
Alexandria Mill
Alexandria, Iskanderiya, Egypt

ELF - Egyptian Co. for Manufacturing of Linerboard & Fluting
10th of Ramadan City Mill
10th of Ramadan City, Cairo, Sharkeya, East Province, Egypt

Emin Leydier
Champblain Mill
Saint-Vallier Cedex, France

Emin Leydier
Nogent-sur-Seine Mill
Nogent-sur-Seine, Aube, France

Empaques Modernos de Guadalajara, S.A. de C.V.
Guadalajara Mill
El Salto, Jalisco, Mexico

Empaques Modernos San Pablo S.A. de C.V.
Tlalnepantla Mill
Tlalnepantla, Edo. de México, Mexico

Estrela Indústria de Papel Ltda.
Palmas Mill
Palmas, Paraná, Brazil

Etap Paper & Carton
Borg El Arab El Gededah Mill
Borg El Arab El Gededah, Alexandria, Egypt

Corrugating medium/fluting

Europac Alcolea de Cinca
Alcolea Mill
Alcolea de Cinca, Huesca, Spain

Europac Papeterie de Rouen
St. Etienne du Rouvray Mill
St. Etienne du Rouvray Cedex, France

Fábrica de Papel da Lapa Lda.
São Paio de Oleiros Mill
São Paio de Oleiros, Portugal

Fábrica de Papel de Ponte Redonda S.A.
Silvalde, Espinho Mill
Silvalde, Espinho, Portugal

Fábrica de Papel de Torres Novas Lda.
Torres Novas Mill
Torres Novas, Portugal

Fábrica de Papel e Cartão da Zarrinha, S.A.
Rio Meão Mill
Rio Meão, Portugal

Fabrika Hartije - PAP - DP
Beogradska Mill
Beograde, Serbia

Fernandez S.A. Indústria de Papel
Amparo Mill
Amparo, São Paulo, Brazil

Fibercorr Inc.
Massillon Mill
Massillon, Ohio, United States

First Co. For Industrial Development S.A.E
El Obour City Mill
El Obour City, Egypt

Forestal y Papelera Concepción S.A.
Coronel Mill
Coronel, VIII - Región del Biobío, Chile

Foshan Gold Rich Union Paper Industry Co., Ltd.
Foshan Mill
Foshan, Guangdong, China

Fthiotis Paper Mill SA
Damasta Mill
Damasta, Lamia, Greece

Fujian Dongxin (Zhangzhou) Paper Co., Ltd.
Zhangzhou Mill
Zhangzhou, Fujian, China

Fujian Huafa (Fujian) Industrial Co., Ltd.
Longhai Mill
Longhai, Fujian, China

Fujian Liansheng Paper (Longhai) Co., Ltd
Longhai Mill
Longhai City, Fujian, China

Fujian Liansheng Paper (Zhangzhou) Co., Ltd.
Zhangzhou Mill
Zhangzhou, Fujian, China

Fujian Lishu Pulp & Paper Co., Ltd.
Jianou Mill
Jianou, Fujian, China

Fujian Nanjing County Youlida Co., Ltd.
Zhangzhou Mill
Zhangzhou, Fujian, China

Fujian Quanzhou Jingyu Paper Mill
Quanzhou Mill
Quanzhou, Fujian, China

Fukuyama Paper Co., Ltd.
Osaka Mill
Osaka, Osaka Pref., Japan

G.P.C. Mohammadia
Meknès Mill
Meknès, Morocco

Gansu Hanfu Dongfang Paper Co., Ltd.
Tianshui Mill
Tianshui, Gansu, China

Gansu Tianshui Xuanyuan Paper Co., Ltd.
Tianshui Mill
Tianshui, Gansu, China

Gayatri Paper Mill
Germiston Mill
Germiston, Gauteng, South Africa

Gemdoubs
Novillars Mill
Novillars, France

General Company for Paper Industry (GENCO)
Deir Ez-Zor Mill
Deir Ez-Zor, Syria

Georgia-Pacific LLC
Big Island Mill
Big Island, Virginia, United States

Georgia-Pacific LLC
Cedar Springs Mill
Cedar Springs, Georgia, United States

Georgia-Pacific LLC
Toledo Mill
Toledo, Oregon, United States

Glucholaskie Zaklady Papiernicze Sp. z o.o.
Glucholazy Mill
Glucholazy, Poland

Godavari Pulp and Papers Mills (P) Ltd
Nasik Mill
Nasik, Maharashtra, India

Grand Holding Mill
Yerevan Mill
Yerevan, Gorod Yerevan, Armenia

Graphic Packaging International Inc.
West Monroe Mill
West Monroe, Louisiana, United States

Green Bay Packaging Inc.
Green Bay Mill
Green Bay, Wisconsin, United States

Green Bay Packaging Inc.
Morrilton Mill
Morrilton, Arkansas, United States

Greif Inc.
Massillon Mill
Massillon, Ohio, United States

Greif Inc.
Riverville Mill
Amherst, Virginia, United States

Groupe CMCP - La Compagnie Marocaine des Cartons et Papiers
Kenitra Mill
Kenitra, Morocco

Grupo Unipak, S.A. de C.V. PT
Cuernavaca Mill
Cuernavaca, Morelos, Mexico

Grupo Unipak, S.A. de C.V. PT
Grupak Hidalgo
Emiliano Zapata, Mexico

Grupo Zucamor
Ranelagh Mill
Ranelagh, Buenos Aires, Argentina

GS Paper & Packaging Group ("GSPP")
Banting Mill
Daerah Kuala Langat, Banting, Selangor Darul Ehsan, Malaysia

Guaçu S.A. Papéis e Embalagens
Tambaú Mill
Tambaú, São Paulo, Brazil

Guangdong Dongguan Hongmei Lee & Man Paper Co., Ltd.
Dongguan (Hongmei) Milll
Dongguan, Guangdong, China

Guangdong Dongguan Huangyong Yinzhou Paper Industry Ltd.
Dongguan Mill
Dongguan, Guangdong, China

Guangdong Dongguan Jianhua Paper Co. Ltd.
Dongguan Mill
Dongguan, Guangdong, China

Guangdong Dongguan Jinzhou Paper Co., Ltd.
Dongguan Mill
Dongguan, Guangdong, China

Guangdong Dongguan Lee & Man Paper Co., Ltd.
Dongguan (Huangyong) Mill
Dongguan, Guangdong, China

Guangdong Dongguan Nine Dragons Paper Industries Co., Ltd.
Dongguan Mill
Dongguan, Guangdong, China

Guangdong Dongguan Shenlian Paper Making Co., Ltd.
Dongguan Mill
Dongguan, Guangdong, China

Guangdong Dongguan Shuangzhou Paper Co., Ltd.
Dongguan Mill
Dongguan, Guangdong, China

Corrugating medium/fluting

Guangdong Dongguan Zhonglian Paper Co., Ltd.
Dongguan Mill
Dongguan, Guangdong, China

Guangdong Donta Group Dongwen Paper Mill
Dongguan Mill
Dongguan, Guangdong, China

Guangdong Green Forest (QingXin) Paper Industrial Limited
Qingyuan Mill
Qingyuan, Guangdong, China

Guangdong Jiangmen City Qiaoyu Paper Co., Ltd.
Jiangmen Mill
Jiangmen, Guangdong, China

Guangdong Junye Paper Co., Ltd.
Dongguan Mill
Dongguan, Guangdong, China

Guangdong Mingxing Paper Co., Ltd.
Jiangmen Mill
Jiangmen, Guangdong, China

Guangdong Shantou Huashi Paper Industrial Co., Ltd.
Shantou Mill
Shantou, Guangdong, China

Guangdong Shunde Sugar Co., Ltd.
Foshan Mill
Foshan, Guangdong, China

Guangdong Taiyuan Paper Co., Ltd.
Jiangmen Mill
Jiangmen, Guangdong, China

Guangdong Wanlida Paper
Guangzhou Mill
Guangzhou, Guangdong, China

Guangdong Zhongshan Rengo Hung Hing Paper Mfg. Co. Ltd.
Zhongshan Mill
Zhongshan, Guangdong, China

Guangdong Zhongshan Yongfa Paper Co., Ltd.
Zhongshan Mill
Zhongshan, Guangdong, China

Guangxi Guigang Hongqi Paper Mill
Guigang mill
Guigang, Guangxi, China

Guangxi Guitang (Group) Stock Co., Ltd
Guigang Mill
Guigang, Guangxi, China

Guangxi Jiayi Paper Co., Ltd.
Baise Mill
Baise, Guangxi, China

Gugan Paper Mills Pvt Ltd
Gugan Paper Mills Pvt Ltd
Coimbatore, Tamil Nadu, India

Gulf Paper Industries Factory
Riyadh Mill
Riyadh, Saudi Arabia

Gulf Paper Manufacturing Free Zone Company
Dubai Mill
Jebel Ali Free Zone, Dubai, United Arab Emirates

Gulf Paper Mfg. Co. k.s.c.
Kuwait Mill
West Mina Abdulla, Ahmadi Governorate, Kuwait

GVG Paper Mills Ltd.
Palani Taluk Mill
Palani Taluk, Dist. Dindigul, Tamil Nadu, India

Halkali Kagit Karton San. ve Tic. A.S.
Istanbul Mill
Küçükçekmece, Istanbul, Turkey

Hamburger Hungaria Ltd
Dunaújváros Mill
Dunaújváros, Hungary

Hans Kolb Papierfabrik GmbH & Co. KG
Kaufbeuren Mill
Kaufbeuren, Germany

Hariom Industries Limited
Kanpur Mill
Kanpur, Uttar Pradesh, India

Hartford City Paper, LLC
Hartford City Mill
Hartford City, Indiana, United States

Hayat Kagit ve Enerji A.S.
Corum Mill
Corum, Turkey

Hebei Baoding Orient Paper Co., Ltd.
Baoding Mill
Baoding, Hebei, China

Hebei Huatong Paper Co., Ltd.
Langfang Mill
Langfang, Hebei, China

Hebei Qinhuangdao Fengman Paper Co., Ltd.
Qinghuangdao Mill
Qinghuangdao, Hebei, China

Hebei Tanghai Chenguang Paper Co., Ltd.
Tangshan Mill
Tangshan, Hebei, China

Hebei Tangshan Guotai Paper Co., Ltd.
Tangshan Mill
Tangshan, Hebei, China

Hebei Yuanshi County Jinpeng Paper Co., Ltd.
Shijiazhuang Mill
Shijiazhuang, Hebei, China

Hellbut & Co. GmbH
Ilfeld Mill
Ilfeld, Germany

Henan Dongsheng Paper Co.,Ltd.
Xinmi Mill
Xinmi, Henan, China

Henan Hongteng Paper Group Co., Ltd.
Xuchang Mill
Xuchang, Henan, China

Henan Longyuan Paper Co., Ltd.
Zhengzhou Mill
Zhengzhou, Henan, China

Henan No. 1 Sub-factory of Huixian City Paper Mill
Xinxiang Mill
Xinxiang, Henan, China

Henan Qinyang Haolin Paper Co., Ltd.
Qinyang Mill
Jiaozuo, Henan, China

Henan Xinxiang Hengli Paper Co., Ltd.
Huixian Mill
Huixian, Henan, China

Henan Xinxiang Hongda Paper Co., Ltd.
Xinxiang Mill
Xinxiang, Henan, China

Henan Xinxiang Xinya Paper Group Co., Ltd.
Xinxiang No. 1 Mill
Xinxiang, Henan, China

Henan Xinxiang Xinya Paper Group Co., Ltd.
Xinxiang No. 4 Mill
Xinxiang, Henan, China

Henan Xuchang Feida Paper Co., Ltd.
Xuchang Mill
Xuchang, Henan, China

Henan Zhengzhou Chunhui Paper Co., Ltd.
Xinmi Mill
Xinmi, Henan, China

Hengshan Zhongkong International Paper Co., Ltd.
Hengyang Mill
Hengyang, Hunan, China

Hiang Seng Fibre Container Co., Ltd.
Samut Sakohn Mill
Amphur Muang, Samut Sakohn, Thailand

Hoang Van Thu Paper Joint Stock Company
Thai Nguyen City Mill
Thai Nguyen City, Thai Nguyen Province, Vietnam

Horng Ming Paper Co., Ltd.
Chu Nan Mill
Chu Nan, Miaoli County, Taiwan

Hubei Shuailun Paper Co. Ltd.
Wuhan Mill
Wuhan, Hubei, China

Hubei Wuhan Mulan Paper Co., Ltd.
Wuhan Mill
Wuhan, Hubei, China

Hubei Yadu Hengxing Paper Co., Ltd
Guangshui Mill
Guangshui, Hubei, China

Hunan Shuanghua Paper Co., Ltd.
Changsha Mill
Changsha, Hunan, China

Corrugating medium/fluting

Hunan Tiger Forest & Paper Group Yueyang Paper Co., Ltd.
Yueyang Mill
Yueyang, Hunan, China

ICO-Industria Cartone Ondulato Srl
San Giovanni Teatino Mill
San Giovanni Teatino, Chieti, Italy

Imporpel Ind. e Com. de Papéis Ltda.
Porto Ferreira Mill
Porto Ferreira, São Paulo, Brazil

Indugevi S.A.
Sabaneta Mill
Sabaneta, Antioquia, Colombia

Industria Cartaria Pieretti SpA (ICP)
Marlia Mill
Marlia di Capannori, Lucca, Italy

Indústria de Papéis para Embalagem Irmãos Siqueira Ltda.
Passa Quatro Mill
Passa Quatro, Minas Gerais, Brazil

Indústria de Papel Sovel da Amazônia Ltda.
Manaus Mill
Manaus, Amazonas, Brazil

Indústria e Comércio de Embalagens e Papéis Artivinco Ltda.
Santa Rosa do Viterbo Mill
Santa Rosa do Viterbo, São Paulo, Brazil

Industria Panameña de Papel SA
Chilibre Mill
San Vicente, Zona Chilibre, Panama

Industrial e Agricola Rio Verde Ltda.
Rio do Campo Mill
Rio do Campo, Santa Catarina, Brazil

Industrias Cartonera Asociada S.A. - INCASA
Quito Mill
Quito, Pichincha, Ecuador

Indústrias de Papel R. Ramenzoni S.A.
Cordeirópolis Mill
Cordeirópolis, São Paulo, Brazil

Indústrias de Papel Ribeirão Preto Ltda.
Ribeirão Preto Mill
Ribeirão Preto, São Paulo, Brazil

Industrias del Cartón S.A. - INCASA
Cayalti Mill
Cayalti, Chiclayo, Peru

Indústrias Novacki S.A.
União da Vitória Mill
União da Vitória, Paraná, Brazil

Indústrias Reunidas Cristo Rey Ltda.
Campo Mourão Mill
Campo Mourão, Paraná, Brazil

INPA - Indústria de Embalagens Santana S.A.
Pirapetinga Mill
Pirapetinga, Minas Gerais, Brazil

INPA - Indústria de Embalagens Santana S.A.
Uberaba Mill
Uberaba, Minas Gerais, Brazil

Inpol-Papier Sp. z o.o.
Bardo Mill
Bardo, Poland

Inter Pacific Paper Co., Ltd
Banpluang, Baansang Mill
Banpluang, Baansang, Prachinburi, Thailand

International Paper Co.
Cedar Rapids Mill
Cedar Rapids, Iowa, United States

International Paper Co.
Henderson Mill
Henderson, Kentucky, United States

International Paper Co.
Mansfield Mill
Mansfield, Louisiana, United States

International Paper Co.
Maysville Mill
Maysville, Kentucky, United States

International Paper Co.
Newport Mill
Cayuga, Indiana, United States

International Paper Co.
Pine Hill Mill
Pine Hill, Alabama, United States

International Paper Co.
Valliant Mill
Valliant, Oklahoma, United States

International Paper Co.
Vicksburg Mill
Vicksburg, Mississippi, United States

International Paper, Empaques Industriales de México S.A. de C.V.
Xalapa Mill
Xalapa, Veracruz, Mexico

Invepal
Morón Mill
Morón, Edo. Carabobo, Venezuela

Islamic Paper Manufacturing Co.
Quesna Mill
Quesna, Menofeya, Egypt

Izmail Pulp & Paperboard Combine
Izmail Mill
Izmail, Odesskaya obl., Ukraine

Jackson Paper Manufacturing Co.
Sylva Mill
Sylva, North Carolina, United States

Jaepel Papéis e Embalagens
Senador Canedo Mill
Senador Canedo, Goiás, Brazil

Jebba Paper Mills Ltd.
Jebba Mill
Jebba, Kwara State, Nigeria

Jiangsu Chamfor Paper Industry Co. Ltd.
Danyang Mill
Danyang, Jiangsu, China

Jiangsu Huaji Zhangjiagang Huaxing Papermaking Co. Ltd.
Zhangjiagang Mill
Zhangjiagang, Jiangsu, China

Jiangsu Lee & Man Paper Manufacturing Co. Ltd.
Changshu Mill
Changshu, Jiangsu, China

Jiangsu Nine Dragons Paper Industries
Taicang Mill
Taicang, Jiangsu, China

Jiangsu Wuxi Long Chen Paper Co., Ltd.
Wuxi Mill
Wuxi, Jiangsu, China

Jiangsu Xuzhou Xinyuan Paper Co.,Ltd
Xuzhou Mill
Xuzhou, Jiangsu, China

Jiangsu Yixing Zhangzhu Paper Mill
Yixing Mill
Yixing, Jiangsu, China

Jiangsu Yuen Foong Yu Paper (Yangzhou) Co., Ltd.
Yangzhou Mill
Yangzhou, Jiangsu, China

Jin Young Paper Co., Ltd.
Chilgok-gun Mill
Chilgok-gun, Gyeongsangbuk-do, South Korea

Johmewah Maju Paper Mill Sdn. Bhd.
Yong Peng Mill
Yong Peng, Johor Darul Takzim, Malaysia

Jordan Paper & Cardboard Factories Co. Ltd.
Zarka Mill
Awajan, Zarka, Jordan

JSC 'Kondrovskaya Paper company'
Kondrovskaya Paper Company Mill
Kondrovo, Kaluga Region, Russia

JSC Primsnabcontract Ussurijsk Paperboard Mill
Ussurijsk Mill
Ussurijsk, Russia

Julius Schulte Trebsen GmbH & Co. KG
Trebsen Mill
Trebsen, Germany

Kagazy Recycling LLP
Almaty Mill
Karasai district, Almaty, Almaty Obl., Kazakhstan

Kahramanmaras Kagit San ve TIC A.S (KMK Paper)
Kahramanmaras Mill
Kahramanmaras, Turkey

Kahramanmaras Kagit San ve TIC A.S (KMK Paper)
Kütahya Mill
Kütahya, Turkey

Kahrizak Paper Mill
Tehran Mill
Tehran, Iran

Kamenskaya Board & Paper Mill, OJSC
Kuvshinovo Mill
Kuvshinovo, Tver Region, Russia

KapStone Kraft Paper Corporation
Cowpens Mill
Cowpens, South Carolina, United States

Corrugating medium/fluting

KapStone Kraft Paper Corporation
Longview Mill
Longview, Washington, United States

KapStone Paper Charleston Kraft LLC
North Charleston Mill
North Charleston, South Carolina, United States

Karavaevo
Karavaevo Mill
Pos. Karavaevo, Moscow Region, Russia

Karnaphuli Paper Mills Ltd.
Chandraghona Mill
Chandraghona of Kaptai, Chittagong, Bangladesh

Kartontara, CJSC
Maykop Mill
Maykop, Adygheya Republic, Russia

Kartontol
St. Petersburg Mill
St. Petersburg, Russia

Kartotec - Papeles Técnicos-
Villeta Mill
Villeta, Paraguay

KBK Ltd
Tuymazy Mill
Tuymazy, Respublika Bashkortostan, Russia

Kenya Papermill Ltd.
Thika Mill
Thika, Central, Kenya

Kiev Cardboard and Paper Mill
Kiev Cardboard and Paper Mill
Obukhiv, Kyivska obl., Ukraine

Kishco Khodeir Paper Mill
6 October City Mill
6 October City, El Giza, Egypt

Klabin S.A.
Angatuba Mill
Angatuba, São Paulo, Brazil

Klabin S.A.
Goiana Mill
Goiana, Pernambuco, Brazil

Klabin S.A.
Guapimirim Mill
Guapimirim, Rio de Janeiro, Brazil

Klabin S.A.
Piracicaba Mill
Piracicaba, São Paulo, Brazil

Klaipedos Kartonas
Klaipeda Mill
Klaipeda, Lithuania

Klingele Papierwerke GmbH & Co. KG
Weener Mill
Weener, Germany

Knijna Fabrika "Iskar" JSC
Paper Factory Iskar AD
Sofia, Bulgaria

Koa Kogyo Co., Ltd.
Fuji-shi Mill
Fuji-shi, Shizuoka Pref., Japan

Kommunar Paper Mill
Kommunar Mill
Kommunar, Leningrad Region, Russia

Koryazhma Branch of Ilim Group
Kotlas Pulp and Paper Mill
Koryazhma, Arkhangelsk Region, Russia

Kostenez-HHI PLC
Kostenez Mill
Kostenez, Bulgaria

KPM Kadoma Paper Mills
Kadoma Mill
Kadoma, Zimbabwe

Krasnaya Zvezda
Krasnaya Zvezda Mill
Chashniki, Vitebsk region, Belarus

Krishna Mongkol Co., Ltd.
Nakhon Pathom Mill
Amphur Kampangsan, Nakhon Pathom, Nakhon Pathom, Thailand

Kuzbasskiy Skarabey
Kemerovo Mill
Kemerovo, Russia

Kyongsan Paper Co., Ltd.
Daegu-si Mill
Daegu-si, Daegu-si, South Korea

Lake Utopia Paper
Saint George Mill
Utopia, New Brunswick, Canada

Lam Son Paper Joint-Stock Company
Nong Cong Mill
Nong Cong District, Thanh Hoa Province, Vietnam

Lekok Paper Sdn Bhd
Melaka Mill
Melaka, Malaysia

Lepenka AD
Novi Knezevac Mill
Novi Knezevac, Vojvodina, Serbia

Lexpapier Sonacar S.A.
El Jadida Mill
El Jadida, Morocco

Liaoning Nine Dragons Paper Industries
Shenyang Mill
Xinmin, Shenyang, Liaoning, China

Long Chen Paper Co. Ltd.
Erh-Lin Mill
ErhLin, Changhua County, Taiwan

Lothlorien (Pty) Ltd
Lothlorien Pulp Mill
Wadeville, Gauteng, South Africa

Lutsky KRK
Lutsk Mill
Lutsk, Ukraine

Madeireira Miguel Forte S.A.
União da Vitória Mill
União da Vitória, Paraná, Brazil

Madepar Papel e Celulose S.A.
Aparecida Mill
Aparecida, São Paulo, Brazil

Magura Paper Mills Ltd.
Narayanganj Mill
Narayanganj, Narayanganj, Bangladesh

Mahachai Kraft Paper Co., Ltd.
Samut Sakohn Mill
Amphur Muang, Samut Sakohn, Thailand

Malu Paper Mills Ltd.
Nagpur 1 & 2 Mill
Dist. Nagpur, Maharashtra, India

Manufacturas de Papel CA (MANPA) S.A.C.A.
Maracay Packaging Mill
Maracay, Edo. Aragua, Venezuela

Marisky Pulp & Paper Mill
Volzhsk Mill
Volzhsk, Mari El Republic, Russia

Marmara Kagit ve Ambalaj Sanayii ve Ticaret AS
Vezirhan Mill
Bilecik, Vezirhan, Bilecik, Turkey

Marusan Paper Mfg. Co., Ltd.
Honsha Mill
Haramachi-ku, Minami-soma-shi, Fukushima Pref., Japan

Master Papers (Pvt) Ltd
Karachi Mill
Karachi, Sindh, Pakistan

Matias Gomá Tomás S.A.
La Riba Mill
La Riba, Spain

Mazandaran Wood & Paper Industries Co.
Sari Mill
Sari, Mazandaran, Iran

MCC Paper Yinhe Co., Ltd.
Linqing Mill
Linqing, Shandong, China

Menofeya for Paper & Cardboard - "Minobardy"
Quissna Mill
Quissna, Menofeya, Egypt

Middle East Paper Company - (MEPCO)
Jeddah Mill
Jeddah, Saudi Arabia

Mier
Lviv Mill
Lviv, Ukraine

Modern Karton Sanayi Ticaret AS
Corlu Mill
Corlu, Tekirdag, Turkey

Modinagar Paper Mills Ltd.
Modinagar Mill
Modinagar, Uttar Pradesh, India

Mohammadi Paper & Board Industries (Pvt.) Ltd.
Sheikhupura Lahore Unit 2
Sheikhupura Lahore, Punjab, Pakistan

Mondi Raubling GmbH
Raubling Mill
Raubling, Germany

Mondi Swiecie S.A.
Swiecie Mill
Swiecie, Poland

Corrugating medium/fluting

Mondi Tire Kutsan Paper and Packaging Industry Inc.
Tire Mill
Tire, Izmir, Turkey

Mpact Limited
Felixton Mill
Felixton, KwaZulu-Natal, South Africa

Muda Paper Mills Sdn. Bhd.
Kajang Mill
Kajang, Selangor Darul Ehsan, Malaysia

Muda Paper Mills Sdn. Bhd.
Tasek Mill
Seberang Prai Selatan, Penang, Malaysia

My Huong Paper Joint-stock Co.
Hai Phong Mill
Hai Phong City, Vietnam

Naberezhnye Chelny Paper & Board Mill
Naberezhnye Chelny Mill
Naberezhnye Chelny, Tatarstan Republic, Russia

Nampak Paper Ltd.
Rosslyn Mill
Rosslyn, Gauteng, South Africa

National Paper Co.
Alexandria Mill
Alexandria, Iskanderiya, Egypt

Natron-Hayat d.o.o.
Maglaj Mill
Maglaj, Bosnia & Herzegovina

New Forest Paper Mills LP
Scarborough Mill
Scarborough, Ontario, Canada

Nicol-Pack Corporation
Uchaly Mill
Uchaly, Respublika Bashkortostan, Russia

Nine Dragons Paper (Tianjin) Co., Ltd.
Tianjin Mill
Tianjin, Tianjin, China

Nine Dragons Paper Industries (Chongqing) Co., Ltd.
Chongqing Mill
Chongqing, Chongqing, China

Nine Dragons Pulp & Paper (Leshan) Co., Ltd.
Leshan Mill
Leshan, Sichuan, China

Ningbo Muniu Paper Co. Ltd.
Ningbo Mill
Ningbo, Zhejiang, China

Nippon Paper Industries Co., Ltd.
Ashikaga Mill
Ashikaga-shi, Tochigi Pref., Japan

Nippon Paper Industries Co., Ltd.
Soka Mill
Soka-shi, Saitama Pref., Japan

Nittow Papel S.A.
Campinas Mill
Campinas, São Paulo, Brazil

Norampac
Cabano Mill
Cabano, Quebec, Canada

Norampac
Kingsey Falls Mill
Kingsey Falls, Quebec, Canada

Norampac
Trenton Mill
Trenton, Ontario, Canada

Norampac Industries Inc.
Niagara Falls Mill
Niagara Falls, New York, United States

Norpapel S.A.I.C.
Villa Ocampo Mill
Villa Ocampo, Santa Fé, Argentina

Nuove Cartiere di Tivoli S.R.L.
Villa Adriana Mill
Villa Adriana, Rome, Italy

OAO Mayak Technocell
Penza Mill
Penza, Russia

OAO Miropol Paper Mill
Miropol Mill
Miropol, Romanovskiy rayon, Zhitomirskaya obl., Ukraine

OAO Poligrafkarton
Balakhna Mill
Balakhna, Nizhny Novgorod, Russia

OAO Technicheskaya Bumaga
Rybinskiy rayon Mill
Rybinskiy rayon, Yaroslavl obl., Russia

Ohio Paperboard Corp.
Baltimore Board Mill
Baltimore, Ohio, United States

Oji Materia Co., Ltd.
Fuji Mill
Fuji-shi, Shizuoka Pref., Japan

Oji Materia Co., Ltd.
Gifu (Ena) Mill
Ena-shi, Gifu Pref., Japan

Oji Materia Co., Ltd.
Gifu (Nakatsugawa) Mill
Nakatsugawa-shi, Gifu Pref., Japan

Oji Materia Co., Ltd.
Nayoro Mill
Nayoro-shi, Hokkaido Pref., Japan

Oji Materia Co., Ltd.
Nikko Mill
Utsunomiya-shi, Tochigi Pref., Japan

Oji Materia Co., Ltd.
Saga Mill
Saga-shi, Saga Pref., Japan

Okayama Paper Industries Co., Ltd.
Okayama-shi Mill
Okayama-shi, Okayama Pref., Japan

Okulovka P&P Mill Ltd.
Okulovka Mill
Okulovka, Novgorod Region, Russia

Olmuksa International Paper-Sabanci Ambalaj Sanayi ve Ticaret A.S.
Olmuksa Edirne Mill
Edirne, Turkey

Ondunorte, Cia. de Papéis e Papelão Ondulado do Norte
Igarassu Mill
Igarassu, Pernambuco, Brazil

OOO Altyn Ajydaar
Bishkek Mill
Bishkek, Kyrgyzstan

OOO Astrakhanskaya Paperboard Mill
Solyanka Mill
Solyanka, Russia

Orsa International Paper Embalagens S.A
Franco da Rocha Mill
Franco da Rocha, São Paulo, Brazil

Orsa International Paper Embalagens S.A
Paulínia Mill
Paulínia, São Paulo, Brazil

P.W. "APIS" S.J.
Nowa Bystrzyca Mill
Stara Bystrzyca, Poland

Packaging Corp. of America
DeRidder Mill
DeRidder, Louisiana, United States

Packaging Corp. of America
Filer City Mill
Filer City, Michigan, United States

Packaging Corp. of America
Tomahawk Mill
Tomahawk, Wisconsin, United States

Palm Group
Wörth Mill
Wörth am Rhein, Germany

PAMER - Papelera Mercedes S.A.
Mercedes, Soriano Mill
Mercedes, Soriano, Uruguay

Pan Paper Mills
Webuye Mill
Webuye, Bungoma District, Western, Kenya

PAN Papirna Industrija d.o.o.
Zagreb Mill
Zagreb, Grad Zagreb, Croatia

Panasa, Papelera Nacional S.A.
Paramonga Mill
Paramonga, Lima, Peru

Panjapol Paper Industry Co. Ltd. and Panjapol Pulp Industry Public Co., Ltd.
Ayutthaya Mill
Bangsai District, Ayutthaya, Thailand

PAPCAS - Rebahia à Saïda
Saïda Mill
Saïda, Rebahia, Algeria

Papeleira Portuguesa S.A.
São Paio de Oleiros Mill
São Paio de Oleiros, Portugal

Papelera Andina S.A.
Papelera Andina
Godoy Cruz, Maipu, Mendoza, Argentina

Corrugating medium/fluting

Papelera Berazategui S.A.
Berazategui Mill
Berazategui, Buenos Aires, Argentina

Papelera Damují
Abreus Mill
Abreus, Cienfuegos, Cuba

Papelera de Chihuahua S.A. de C.V.
Chihuahua Mill
Chihuahua, Chihuahua, Mexico

Papelera de la Alqueria S.L.
Alicante Mill
Alqueria de Aznar, Alicante, Spain

Papelera del Nevado S.A. de C.V.
Almoloyan Mill
San Miguel Almoloyan, Almoloya de Juarez, México, D.F., Mexico

Papelera del NOA S.A.
Rio Blanco Mill
Río Blanco, Jujuy, Jujuy, Argentina

Papelera del Pacífico S.A.
Retalhuleu Mill
Retalhuleu, Guatemala

Papelera del Pacífico S.A.
San Francisco de Mostazal Mill
San Francisco de Mostazal, VI - Región Gen. O'Higgins, Chile

Papelera del Sur S.A.
Chincha Mill
Chincha, ICA, Peru

Papelera Don Torcuato S.A.
Don Torcuato Mill
Don Torcuato, Buenos Aires, Argentina

Papelera Entre Ríos S.A.
Paraná Mill
Paraná, Entre Ríos, Entre Ríos, Argentina

Papelera Industrial Potosina S.A. de C.V.
San Luis Potosi Mill
San Luis Potosi, San Luis Potosi, Mexico

Papelera Iruña S.A. de C.V.
Iztapalapa Mill
Iztapalapa, México, D.F., Mexico

Papelera La Helice S.A.I.C.
San Fernando Mill
San Fernando, Buenos Aires, Argentina

Papelera Mediterránea S.A.
Córdoba Mill
Córdoba, Córdoba, Argentina

Papelera Nacional S.A.
Guayaquil Mill
Guayaquil, Guayas, Ecuador

Papelera Paysandú S.A.I.C.
Wilde Mill
Wilde, Buenos Aires, Argentina

PAPELSA - Papeles y Cartones SA
Barbosa Mill
Barbosa, Antioquia, Colombia

Papeltex Argentina S.A.I.C.
Lanus Oeste Mill
Lanus Oeste, Buenos Aires, Argentina

Paper Packaging Pvt. Ltd. Corp.
Mandli Mill
Mandli, Shimoga Dist., Karnataka, India

Paperland, Inc.
Quezon City Mill
Quezon City, Philippines

Papeterie de la Mitidja
La Chiffa Mill
La Chiffa, Wilaya de Blida, Algeria

Papeterie Saint Michel SAS Groupe Thiollet
St. Michel d'Entraygues Mill
St. Michel d'Entraygues, France

Papeteries et Cartonneries Lacaux Frères
Bosmie L'Aiguille Mill
Bosmie L'Aiguille, France

Papier- und Kartonfabrik Varel GmbH & Co. KG
Varel Mill
Varel, Niedersachsen, Germany

Papierfabrik Adolf Jass GmbH & Co. KG
Fulda Mill
Fulda, Germany

Papierfabrik Adolf Jass GmbH & Co. KG
Rudolstadt-Schwarza Mill
Rudolstadt-Schwarza, Thüringen, Germany

Papierfabrik Fritz Peters GmbH & Co. KG
Gelsenkirchen Mill
Gelsenkirchen, Germany

Papierfabrik Niederauer Mühle GmbH
Kreuzau and Niederau Mills
Kreuzau, Germany

Papierfabrik Palm GmbH & Co KG
Aalen Mill
Aalen-Neukochen, Germany

Papierfabrik Schoellershammer
Düren Mill
Düren, Germany

Papierfabrik Tillmann
Zülpich-Sinzenich Mill
Zülpich-Sinzenich, Germany

Papierfabrik Vreden GmbH
Vreden Mill
Vreden, Germany

Papir-Mal
Malin Mill
Malin, Zhitomirskaya obl., Ukraine

Papirfabrika Ligatne Ltd.
Ligatne Mill
Ligatne, Latvia

Papiro Sarda S.R.L.
Assemini mill
Assemini, Como, Italy

Papiro Sud Srl
Scafati Mill
Scafati, Salerno, Italy

Paraibuna Embalagens Ltda.
Juiz de Fora Mill
Juiz de Fora, Minas Gerais, Brazil

Parteks Tekstil ve Kagit San Tic. Ltd. Sti.
Kayseri Mill
Kayseri, Turkey

Pascorp Paper Industries Bhd.
Bentong Mill
Bentong, Pahang Darul Makmur, Malaysia

Patoom Dhanee Paper Factory Ltd. Part
Pathumthani Mill
Amphur Muang, Pathumthani, Thailand

Paulispell, Indústria Paulista de Papéis e Chapas de Papelão
Aguaí Mill
Aguaí, São Paulo, Brazil

PCE Embalagens
Manaus Mill
Manaus, Amazonas, Brazil

Pehlivanoglu Kagit, Kagit Mamülleri ve Ambalaj San.Tic. A.S.
Çerkezköy Mill
Çerkezköy, Tekirdag, Turkey

Penha Papéis e Embalagem Ltda.
Coronel Vivida Mill
Vivida, Paraná, Brazil

Penha Papéis e Embalagem Ltda.
Santo Amaro Mill
Santo Amaro da Purificação, Bahia, Brazil

Perm Pulp and Paper Mill
Perm Mill
Perm, Russia

Pham Thu Processing and Trading Co., Ltd
Ho Chi Minh City Mill
Ho Chi Minh City, Binh Duong Province, Vietnam

Phu Giang Paper and Packaging Co., Ltd.
Tien Du Mill
Tien Du, Bac Ninh Province, Vietnam

Phu Thinh Paper Co., Ltd.
Ho Chi Minh City Mill
Ho Chi Minh City, Binh Duong Province, Vietnam

Piquiri Indústria e Comércio de Papéis Ltda.
Guarapuava Mill
Campina do Simão, Paraná, Brazil

Polotnyano-Zavodskaya Paper Mill
Polotnyany Zavod Mill
Polotnyany Zavod, Kaluga Region, Russia

Port Townsend Paper Corp.
Port Townsend Mill
Port Townsend, Washington, United States

Porto Feliz S.A.
Porto Feliz Mill
Porto Feliz, São Paulo, Brazil

Pratt Industries (USA)
Conyers Mill
Conyers, Georgia, United States

Corrugating medium/fluting

Pratt Industries (USA)
Shreveport Mill
Shreveport, Louisiana, United States

Pratt Industries (USA)
Staten Island Mill
Staten Island, New York, United States

Proletariy, JSC
Surazh Mill
Surazh, Bryansk Region, Russia

Propapier PM 1 GmbH
Burg Mill
Burg, Germany

Propapier PM 2 GmbH & Co. KG
Eisenhüttenstadt Mill
Eisenhüttenstadt, Brandenburg, Germany

PROPASA - Productora de Papel S.A. de C.V.
San Nicolas de los Garza Mill
San Nicolas de los Garza, Nuevo León, Mexico

PT Asia Paper Mills
Tangerang Mill
Tangerang, West Java, Indonesia

PT Cipta Paperia
Serang, Banten Mill
Serang, Banten, West Java, Indonesia

PT Ekamas Fortuna
Malang (PT Ekamas Fortuna) Mill
Malang, Jawa Timur, Indonesia

PT Enggal Subur Kertas
Pati Mill
Pati, Central Java, Indonesia

PT Eureka Aba
Mojosari Mill
Mojokerto, East Java, Indonesia

PT Evergreen International Paper
Medan Mill
Deli Serdang, Medan, Sumatra, Indonesia

PT Fajar Surya Wisesa Tbk.
Bekasi Mill
Cikarang Barat, Bekasi, West Java, Indonesia

PT Indah Kiat Pulp & Paper Corp.
Serang (PT Indah Kiat Pulp & Paper) Mill
Serang, West Java, Indonesia

PT Integra Lestari (Surabaya)
Kec. Ngoro Mill
Kec. Ngoro, Mojokerto, East Java, Indonesia

PT Jaya Kertas
Nganjuk Mill
Nganjuk, East Java, Indonesia

PT Kertas Blabak Megelang
Magelang Mill
Magelang, Central Java, Indonesia

PT Kertas Leces (Persero)
Probolinggo Mill
Probolinggo, East Java, Indonesia

PT Pabrik Kertas Indonesia (Pakerin)
Mojokerto Mill
Mojokerto, East Java, Indonesia

PT Pelita Cengkareng Paper
Subang Mill
Subang, West Java, Indonesia

PT Pelita Cengkareng Paper
Tangerang Mill
Cengkareng, Tangerang, West Java, Indonesia

PT Pola Pulpindo Mantap
Lampung Mill
Lampung, Sumatra, Indonesia

PT Pura Barutama
Kudus Mill
Kudus, Central Java, Indonesia

PT Pura Nusapersada
Terban, Kudus Mill
Terban, Kudus, Central Java, Indonesia

PT Setia Kawan
Tulungagung Mill
Tulungagung, East Java, Indonesia

PT Sinar Indah Kertas
Desa Pegandan Kecamatan Margorajo, Pati Mill
Desa Pegandan Kecamatan Margorejo, Pati, Central Java, Indonesia

PT Surabaya Mekabox
Driyorejo Mill
Surabaya, East Java, Indonesia

PT Tri Daya Kreasi
Purwakarta Mill
Purwakarta, West Java, Indonesia

PT Wirajaya Packindo
Tangerang Mill
Tangerang, West Java, Indonesia

Rainap S.A.
Garín mill
Garín, Buenos Aires, Argentina

Rakta, General Co. for Paper Industry
Rakta Mill
Alexandria, Iskanderiya, Egypt

Rang Dong Paper Joint-stock Co.
Dien Khanh District Mill
Dien Khanh District, Khanh Hoa Province, Vietnam

Rengo Co., Ltd.
Amagasaki Mill
Kuise, Amagasaki-shi, Hyogo Pref., Japan

Rengo Co., Ltd.
Kanazu Mill
Awara-shi, Fukui Pref., Japan

Rengo Co., Ltd.
Yashio Mill
Yashio-shi, Saitama Pref., Japan

Republic Paperboard Co. LLC
Lawton Mill
Lawton, Oklahoma, United States

Rigesa, Celulose, Papel e Embalagens Ltda.
Três Barras Mill
Três Barras, Santa Catarina, Brazil

RockTenn Co.
Coshocton Mill
Coshocton, Ohio, United States

RockTenn Co.
Saint Paul Mill
Saint Paul, Minnesota, United States

RockTenn Co.
Seminole Mill
Jacksonville, Florida, United States

RockTenn Co.
Solvay Mill
Syracuse, New York, United States

RockTenn Co.
Stevenson Mill
Stevenson, Alabama, United States

RockTenn Co.
Uncasville Mill
Uncasville, Connecticut, United States

RockTenn Co.
West Point Mill
West Point, Virginia, United States

Rossmann SAS
Ste. Croix aux Mines Mill
Ste. Croix aux Mines, France

Rubezhansky Cardboard and Packaging Mill
Rubezhnoye Mill
Rubezhnoye, Lugansk obl., Ukraine

Ruby Macons Ltd.
Morai Mill
Morai, Gujarat, India

Ruby Macons Ltd.
Vapi Mill
Vapi, Gujarat, India

Ruloni
Tbilisi Mill
Tbilisi, Georgia

S.C. EcoPaper S.A.
Zarnesti Mill
Zarnesti, Romania

Sagheh Cellulose Iran Industrial Company (P.J.S.)
Takestan Mill
Takestan, Qazvin, Iran

SAICA - S.A. Industrias Celulosa Aragonesa
Fábrica I - Zaragoza Mill
Zaragoza, Spain

SAICA - S.A. Industrias Celulosa Aragonesa
Fábrica II, III & IV - El Burgo de Ebro Mill
El Burgo de Ebro, Zaragoza, Spain

SAICA Paper UK Ltd.
Partington Mill
Carrington, Manchester, Greater Manchester, United Kingdom

SAICA Vénizel
Vénizel Mill
Vénizel, France

Saigon Paper
My Xuan I Mill
Tan Thanh Dist., Ba Ria - Vung Tau, Dong Nam Bo, Vietnam

Corrugating medium/fluting

Saigon Paper
My Xuan II Mill
Tan Thanh Dist., Ba Ria - Vung Tau, Dong Nam Bo, Vietnam

Sainsons Paper Industries Ltd.
Kurukshetra Mill
Dist. Kurukshetra, Haryana, India

Sanyo Paper Manufacturing Co., Ltd.
Tottori Mill
Tottori-shi, Tottori Pref., Japan

São Carlos SA Indústria de Papel e Embalagens
São Carlos Mill
São Carlos, São Paulo, Brazil

São Gabriel Papéis Ltda.
União da Vitória Mill
União da Vitória, Paraná, Brazil

SAPB, Société Anonyme des Papeteries du Belvédére
Cité El Khadra, Tunis Mill
Cité El Khadra, Tunis, Tunisia

SAPELBA - Fábrica de Papel da Bahia S.A.
Feira de Santana Mill
Feira de Santana, Bahia, Brazil

Sappi Paper and Paper Packaging South Africa (SA)
Cape Kraft Mill
Montague Gardens, Cape Town, Cape Town, South Africa

Sappi Paper and Paper Packaging South Africa (SA)
Tugela Mill
Mandini, KwaZulu-Natal, South Africa

SAPSO Emballages Ondulés
Bazas Mill
Bazas, France

Sastha Paper Mills
Kanchipuram Mill
Kanchipuram, Tamil Nadu, India

Savon Sellu Oy
Savon Sellu
Kuopio, Finland

Schumacher Packaging Zaklad Grudziadz Sp.z o.o.
Grudziadz Mill
Grudziadz, Poland

Selkasan Kagit ve Paketleme Malzemeleri Imalati San. ve Tic. AS
Manisa Mill
Manisa, Turkey

Seyfert Paper S.A.S.
Descartes Mill
Descartes, France

Shaanxi Pucheng Wuyang Paper Co., Ltd.
Weinan Mill
Weinan, Shaanxi, China

Shaanxi Shenglong Paper Co., Ltd.
Baoji Mill
Baoji, Shaanxi, China

Shaanxi Xiongdi Paper Co., Ltd.
Xi-An Mill
Xi-An, Shaanxi, China

Shakumbhri Straw Products Ltd.
Moradabad Mill
Tehsil Bilari, Moradabad, Uttar Pradesh, India

Shandong Dongming County Yongyue Paper Co., Ltd.
Heze Mill
Heze, Shandong, China

Shandong Fengyuan Zhongke Biology Technology Co., Ltd.
Zaozhuang Mill
Zaozhuang, Shandong, China

Shandong Guihe Xianxing Paper Holding Pte. Ltd.
Zibo Mill
Zibo, Shandong, China

Shandong Jianghe Paper Co., Ltd.
Qihe Mill
Dezhou, Shandong, China

Shanghai Fumin Paper Mill
Chongming Mill
Chongming, Shanghai, China

Shindaeyang Paper Co., Ltd.
Ansan Mill
Ansan-si, Gyeonggi-do, South Korea

Shree Bhageshwari Papers Ltd
Muzaffarnagar Mill
Muzaffarnagar, Uttar Pradesh, India

Shree Gopinath Paper Mills Pvt. Ltd
Surendranagar Mill
Surendranagar, Gujarat, India

Siam Kraft Industry Co., Ltd.
BanPong Mill
BanPong, Ratchaburi, Thailand

SICAL
Lumbres Mill
Lumbres, France

Sichuan Chengdu Xiling Packaging Co., Ltd.
Chengdu Mill
Chengdu, Sichuan, China

Sichuan Guanghan City Shunfa Co., Ltd.
Deyang Mill
Deyang, Sichuan, China

Sichuan Longchang Yuhong Paper Co., Ltd.
Neijiang Mill
Neijiang, Sichuan, China

Siddheshwari Paper Udhyog Ltd.
Kashipur Mill
Kashipur, Uttarakhand, India

Simka Kagit San. Ve Tic A.S
Kayseri Mill
Kayseri, Turkey

SIPCO-Soc. Ind. de Papier et de Carton Ondule SAL
Beirut Mill
Kfarchima, Beirut, Lebanon

SKG Pulp & Paper
New Alipore, Kolkata Mill
New Alipore, Kolkata, West Bengal, India

Slavuta-Papir, JSC
Slavuta Mill
Slavuta, Ukraine

Smurfit Cartón y Papel de México S.A. de C.V.
Cerro Gordo Mill
Santa Clara Coatitla, Ecatepec de Morelos, Edo. de México, Mexico

Smurfit Cartón y Papel de México S.A. de C.V.
Los Reyes Mill
Col. Los Reyes Iztacala, Tlalnepantla, México, D.F., Mexico

Smurfit Cartón y Papel de México S.A. de C.V.
Monterrey Mill
Monterrey, Baja California Norte, Mexico

Smurfit Kappa Ania Paper
Ania Mill
Ponte all'Ania, Lucca, Italy

Smurfit Kappa Cartón de Colombia SA
Barranquilla Mill
Barranquilla, Atlántico, Colombia

Smurfit Kappa Cartón de Colombia SA
Yumbo Mill
Cali, Valle de Cauca, Colombia

Smurfit Kappa Cartón de Venezuela S.A.
San Felipe Mill
San Felipe, Yaracuy, Venezuela

Smurfit Kappa de Argentina S.A.
Bernal Mill
Bernal, Buenos Aires, Argentina

Smurfit Kappa de Argentina S.A.
Coronel Suárez Mill
Coronel Suárez, Buenos Aires, Argentina

Smurfit Kappa GmbH Viersen Papier
Viersen Mill
Viersen, Germany

Smurfit Kappa Haupt Papier- und Pappenfabrik GmbH & Co. KG
Diemelstadt-Wrexen Mill
Diemelstadt-Wrexen, Germany

Smurfit Kappa Mengibar Paper
Mengibar Mill
Mengibar, Jaén, Spain

Smurfit Kappa Morava Paper
Žimrovice Mill
Žimrovice, Czech Republic

Smurfit Kappa Orange County
Forney Mill
Forney, Texas, United States

Smurfit Kappa Papier & Kartonfabrik Hoya
Hoya Mill
Hoya/Weser, Germany

Corrugating medium/fluting

Smurfit Kappa Papier Recyclé France
Papeteries de Saillat
Saint Junien Cedex, France

Smurfit Kappa Roermond Papier BV
Roermond Mill
Roermond, Netherlands

Smurfit Kappa SSK
Birmingham Mill
Nechells, Birmingham, West Midlands, United Kingdom

Smurfit Kappa Zülpich Papier GmbH
Zülpich Mill
Zülpich, Germany

Sociedad Fábrica de Papel y Cartón Schorr y Concha S.A.
Talca Mill
Talca, VII - Región del Maule, Chile

Song Lam Paper Joint-Stock Co.
Hung Nguyen Dist. Mill
Hung Nguyen Dist., Vietnam

Sonoco Products Co.
Hartsville Mill
Hartsville, South Carolina, United States

Sonoco Products Co.
Menasha Mill
Menasha, Wisconsin, United States

Sotipapier - Société Tunisienne Industrielle du Papier et du Carton - S.A.R.L.
Belli Mill
Belli, Tunisia

South African Cartonboard Mills
Wadeville Mill
Wadeville, Gauteng, South Africa

South African Paper Mills (SAPM)
Durban Mill
Jacobs, Durban, KwaZulu-Natal, South Africa

SP Fiber Technologies LLC (SPFT)
Dublin Mill
Dublin, Georgia, United States

Spartak
Shklov Mill
Shklov, Mogilev Region, Belarus

Specialty Paper Mills Inc.
Santa Fe Springs Mill
Santa Fe Springs, California, United States

Sprick GmbH & Co.
Mitte Mill
Diemelstadt, Germany

Sree Sakthi Paper Mills Ltd.
Edayar Mill
Aluva, Kerala, India

Sripathi Paper & Boards Pvt.Ltd
Sivakasi Mill
Sivakasi, Tamil Nadu, India

Stora Enso Poland S.A.
Ostroleka Mill
Ostroleka, Poland

Stora Enso Renewable Packaging
Heinola Mill
Heinola, Finland

Stragarit
Stragari Mill
Stragari, Serbia

Suhar Paper Mill
Suhar Mill
Suhar, Oman

Sukhonsky Pulp and Paper Mill
Sokol Mill
Sokol, Vologodskaya obl., Russia

Surpapel SA
Berazategui Mill
Berazategui, Buenos Aires, Argentina

Svetlogorskiy Pulp and Board Mill
Svetlogorsk Mill
Svetlogorsk, Gomel Region, Belarus

Ta Chang Paper Mfg. Co., Ltd.
Lungchin Mill
Long Ching District, Taichung City, Taiwan

Taiho Paper Co., Ltd.
Kamo-gun Mill
Kamo-gun, Gifu Pref., Japan

Technocart SA
Tripolis Mill
Tripolis, Greece

Thai Cane Paper Public Co., Ltd.
Kanchanaburi Mill #1
Amphur Tha Muang, Kanchanaburi, Kanchanaburi, Thailand

Thai Kraft Paper Industry Co., Ltd.
Wangsala Mill
Tha Muang Distr., Kanchanaburi, Kanchanaburi, Thailand

Thai Paper Mill Co., Ltd.
Rayong Mill
Amphur Bankhai, Rayong, Thailand

Thanakorn Paper Industry Co., Ltd.
Amphur Muang, Pathumthani Mill
Amphur Muang, Pathumthani, Thailand

Thurpapier, Model AG
Weinfelden Mill
Weinfelden, Switzerland

Todo Papel S.A. de C.V.
Ixtapaluca Mill
Ixtapaluca, México, D.F., Mexico

Tokushu Tokai Paper Co., Ltd.
Shimada Mill
Shimada-shi, Shizuoka Pref., Japan

Tolentino S.r.l.
Tolentino Mill
Tolentino, Macerata, Italy

Tonic Industrie EPE
Ouate Industrie Mill
Bou Ismail, Wilaya d'Alger, Algeria

TOP S.A.
Tychy Mill
Tychy, Poland

Toscopaper SpA
Ponte a Moriano Mill
Ponte a Moriano, Lucca, Italy

TOV Poninki Cardboard and Paper Mill
Poninka Mill
Poninka, Polonsky rayon, Khmelnitska obl., Ukraine

Toyama Seishi KK
Toyama Mill
Toyama-shi, Toyama Pref., Japan

Transnational Paper Corp.
Cavite Mill
Calvite City, Calabarzon, Laguna, Philippines

Tri-Asia Paper Mill, Inc.
Cabuyao Mill
Cabuyao City, Laguna, Philippines

Trio Paper Mills Sdn. Bhd.
Simpang Ampat Mill
Simpang Ampat, Pulau Pinang, Malaysia

Trombini Industrial S.A.
Curitiba Mill
Curitiba, Paraná, Brazil

Trupal S.A.
Trujillo Mill
Trujillo, Peru

Tung Yuan Paper Mfg. Co., Ltd.
Chiao Tou Mill
Chiao Tou District, Kaohsiung City, Taiwan

UCAL Donusen Kagit San ve Tic A.S.
Sirapinar Mill
Sirapinar, Umraniye, Istanbul, Turkey

Unión Industrial Papelera S.A. (UIPSA)
La Pobla de Claramunt Mill
La Pobla de Claramunt, Barcelona, Spain

Unión Papelera Platense
La Plata Mill
La Plata, Buenos Aires, Argentina

Union Paper Mills
Dubai Mill
Dubai, United Arab Emirates

United Corrstack LLC
Reading Mill
Reading, Pennsylvania, United States

United Paper Public Co. Ltd.
Amphur Muang Mill
Amphur Muang, Prachinburi, Thailand

United Pulp & Paper Co., Inc.
Calumpit Mill
Calumpit, Bulacan, Philippines

UPP Pulp & Paper (M) Sdn Bhd
Batang Berjuntai Mill
Ijok, Batang Berjuntai, Selangor Darul Ehsan, Malaysia

Urvashi Pulp & Paper Mills Pvt. Ltd.
Bharuch Mill
Ankleshwar, Dist. Bharuch, Gujarat, India

Valaichenai Paper Mills
Valaichenai Mill
Valaichenai, Sri Lanka

Valpasa Indústria de Papel Ltda.
Tangará Mill
Tangará, Santa Catarina, Brazil

Boxboard/cartonboard

Veerachola Papers
Veerachola Papers
Tirupur, Tamil Nadu, India

Venkraft Paper Mills Private Ltd.
Hosur Mill
Hosur, Tamil Nadu, India

Vietnam Lee & Man Paper Manufacturing Ltd
Hau Giang Mill
Chau Thanh district, Ha Giang Province, Vietnam

Vina Kraft Paper
Ho Chi Minh City Mill
Ho Chi Minh City, Binh Duong Province, Vietnam

Visy Pulp & Paper
Coolaroo Mill
Campbellfield, Victoria, Australia

Visy Pulp & Paper
Gibson Island, VPP8
Gibson Island, Queensland, Australia

Visy Pulp & Paper
VPP2, Reservoir Mill
Reservoir, Victoria, Australia

Visy Pulp & Paper
VPP3/6, Smithfield Mill
Smithfield, New South Wales, Australia

VPK Paper NV
Dendermonde Mill
Dendermonde, Belgium

Vrancart SA
Adjud Mill
Adjud, Vrancea, Romania

W. Hamburger GmbH
Pitten Mill
Pitten, Niederösterreich, Austria

Weihai Longgang Paper Co., Ltd.
Weihai Mill
Weihai, Shandong, China

Wolsan Paper Mfg. Co., Ltd.
Hanan Mill
Chilseo-myeon, Haman-gun, Gyeongsangnam-do, South Korea

Yaroslavl Paper ZAO
Yaroslavl Mill
Yaroslavl, Yaroslavl obl., Russia

Yenisey Pulp and Paper Mill Inc.
Yenisey Pulp and Paper Mill
Krasnoyarsk, Russia

Yuen Foong Yu Packaging Inc.
Chengkung Mill
Wu Jih District, Taichung City, Taiwan

Yung-Seng Development Enterprise Co., Ltd.
Taoyuan Mill
Taoyuan, Taoyuan County, Taiwan

Yunnan Dali Huacheng Paper Co., Ltd.
Dali Mill
Dali, Yunnan, China

Yunnan Yuxi Dongsheng Paper Co., Ltd.
Yuxi Mill
Yuxi, Yunnan, China

ZAO Altaykrovlya
Novoaltaysk Mill
Novoaltaysk, Altaisky Kraý, Russia

ZAO MPK KRZ - Multibranch Production Company KRZ
Ryazan Mill
Ryazan, Russia

Zhejiang Cixi Longfeng Paper Co., Ltd.
Cixi Mill
Cixi, Zhejiang, China

Zhejiang Fuyang Chenggong Paper Co., Ltd.
Fuyang Mill
Fuyang, Zhejiang, China

Zhejiang Fuyang Fuming Paper Co., Ltd.
Fuyang Mill
Fuyang, Zhejiang, China

Zhejiang Fuyang Huamao Paper Co., Ltd.
Fuyang Mill
Fuyang, Zhejiang, China

Zhejiang Fuyang Shangyou Paper Industry Co., Ltd.
Fuyang Mill
Fuyang, Zhejiang, China

Zhejiang Fuyang Zhenghua Paper Co., Ltd.
Fuyang Mill
Fuyang, Zhejiang, China

Zhejiang Huakang Paper Co., Ltd.
Ruian Mill
Ruian, Zhejiang, China

Zhejiang Huayu Paper Co., Ltd.
Shaoxing Mill
Shaoxing, Zhejiang, China

Zhejiang JiAn Paper Package Co., Ltd.
Jiaxing Mill
Jiaxing, Zhejiang, China

Zhejiang Long Chen Paper Co., Ltd.
Pinghu Mill
Pinghu, Zhejiang, China

Zhejiang Ningbo Dongteng Paper Co., Ltd.
Ningbo Mill
Ningbo, Zhejiang, China

Zhejiang Ningbo Haishan Paper Co.
Ningbo Mill
Ningbo, Zhejiang, China

Zhejiang Ningbo Ningxing Paper Co., Ltd.
Ninghai Mill
Ninghai, Zhejiang, China

Zhejiang Pinghu Fengli Paper Stock Co. Ltd.
Pinghu Mill
Pinghu, Zhejiang, China

Zhejiang Rongsheng Paper Co., Ltd.
Pinghu Mill
Pinghu, Zhejiang, China

Zhejiang Shengda Group
Hangzhou Mill
Hangzhou, Zhejiang, China

Zhejiang Yiwu City Huachuan Paper Co., Ltd.
Yiwu Mill
Yiwu, Zhejiang, China

Zhejiang Yiwu City YiNan Paper Co., Ltd.
Yiwu Mill
Yiwu, Zhejiang, China

Zhejiang Zhengda Holding Group Co., Ltd.
Fuyang Mill
Fuyang, Zhejiang, China

Zhydachiv Pulp & Paper Mill
Zhydachiv Mill
Zhydachiv, Lviv obl., Ukraine

Zhytomyr Paperboard Mill
Zhytomyr Mill
Zhytomyr, Ukraine

Boxboard/cartonboard

3M Tilton
Tilton Mill
Tilton, New Hampshire, United States

A. Merati - Cartiera di Laveno SpA
Laveno Mombello Mill
Laveno Mombello, Varese, Italy

Abelan Board and Packaging Solutions
Alcover Mill
Alcover, Tarragona, Spain

Abelan Board and Packaging Solutions
Viersen Mill
Viersen, Germany

Abelan Board and Packaging Solutions
Villava Mill
Villava, Navarra, Spain

Afsons Industrial Corporation Ltd.
Raigad Mill
Raigad, Maharashtra, India

Agarwal Duplex Board Mills Ltd.
Muzzaffarnagar Mill
Muzzaffarnagar, Uttar Pradesh, India

Agustín Barral, S.A.
Barcelona Mill
La Pobla de Lillet (Barcelona), Spain

Albert Köhler GmbH & Co. KG
Gengenbach Mill
Gengenbach, Germany

Albertin Paperboard & Paper Mill
Slonim Mill
Slonim, Grodno Region, Belarus

Aleksinskaya Board & Paper Mill, CJSC
Aleksin Mill
Aleksin, Tula Region, Russia

Alier S.A.
Roselló Mill
Roselló, Lérida, Spain

Boxboard/cartonboard

Amaravathi Sri Venkatesa Paper Mills Ltd.
Madathukulam Mill
Madathukulam, Coimbatore Dist., Tamil Nadu, India

Anand Duplex/Triplex Board Limited
Meerut Mill
Meerut District, Uttar Pradesh, India

Anhui Chaohu Jinhe Paper Co. Ltd
Chaohu Mill
Chaohu, Anhui, China

Anhui Hefei Jinzhong Paper Co. Ltd.
Hefei Mill
Hefei, Anhui, China

Anhui Hefei Xingdong Paper Co., Ltd.
Hefei Mill
Hefei, Anhui, China

Anhui Huoshan County Chenfeng Paper Co., Ltd
LiuAn Mill
LiuAn, Anhui, China

Anhui Shanying Paper No. 1 Mill
Maanshan (No. 1) Mill
Maanshan, Anhui, China

APO Pappenfabrik Apostelmühle GmbH
Rodalben Mill
Rodalben, Germany

Arab Company for Paper Product (Arapepco)
Aleppo Mill
Aleppo, Syria

Arab Paper Manufacturing Co. Ltd. (Waraq)
Dammam Mill
Dammam, Saudi Arabia

Arctic Paper Grycksbo AB
Grycksbo Mill
Grycksbo, Sweden

Arjowiggins Papiers Couchés SAS
Bessé-sur-Braye Mill
Bessé-sur-Braye, France

Asia Paper Mfg. Co., Ltd.
Cheongwon Mill
Cheongwon-gun, Chungcheongbuk-do, South Korea

Asia Symbol (Shandong) Pulp & Paper Co., Ltd.
Rizhao Mill
Rizhao, Shandong, China

Athena Paper Manufacturing Co., Ltd.
Okayama Mill
Okayama-shi, Okayama Pref., Japan

Atrak Pulp & Paper Industry Company
Foulad Mill
Foulad Industrial City, Esfahan, Iran

Austell Boxboard
Austell Boxboard Mill # 2
Austell, Georgia, United States

Austell Boxboard
Austell Boxboard Mill # 1
Austell, Georgia, United States

Baiersbronn Frischfaserkarton GmbH
Baiersbronn Mill
Baiersbronn, Germany

Balaji Cellulose Products Ltd.
Muzaffarnagar Mill
Muzaffarnagar, Uttar Pradesh, India

Balkrishna Paper Mills Ltd.
Ambivli Mill
Taluka Kalyan, Dist. Thane, Maharashtra, India

Ballarpur Industries Ltd. (BILT)
Shree Gopal Mill
Yamunanagar, Haryana, India

Banglane Paper Mill Co., Ltd.
Nakhon Pathom Mill
Banglane District, Nakhon Pathom, Nakhon Pathom, Thailand

Bartoli F.lli SpA
Carraia Mill
Carraia, Lucca, Italy

Bashundhara Paper Mills Ltd.
Unit 2
Sonargaon, New Town, Narayanganj, Bangladesh

Beijing Paper Mill No. 7 Co., Ltd.
Beijing Mill
Beijing, Beijing, China

Beloit Box Board Co
Beloit Mill
Beloit, Wisconsin, United States

Belovo Paper Mill S.A.
Belovo Mill
Belovo, Bulgaria

Bharat Papers Ltd.
Kathua Mill
Kathua, Jammu and Kashmir, India

BillerudKorsnäs AB
Frövi Mill
Frövi, Sweden

BillerudKorsnäs AB
Gävle Mill
Gävle, Sweden

BillerudKorsnäs AB
Gruvön Mill
Grums, Sweden

Biltube Europe Ltd.
St. Didier-en-Velay Mill
St. Didier-en-Velay, France

Bindals Duplex Ltd.
Muzaffarnagar Mill
Muzaffarnagar, Uttar Pradesh, India

Biwa Paper Mfg. Co., Ltd.
Nagahama-shi Mill
Nagahama-shi, Shiga Pref., Japan

Bonet Madeiras e Papéis Ltda.
Timbó Grande Mill
Timbó Grande, Santa Catarina, Brazil

Brücher GmbH, Pappen- und Papierfabrik
Bensheim Mill
Bensheim, Germany

Bulleh Shah Packaging (Private) Limited
Bulleh Shah Paper Mill
Kasur, Pakistan

Carl Macher GmbH & Co. KG
Brunnenthal Mill
Brunnenthal, Germany

Carotell Paperboard
Taylors Mill
Taylors, South Carolina, United States

Carta Misr
Maarouf, Cairo Mill
Maarouf, Cairo, Egypt

Carta Riedenburg GmbH
Riedenburg Mill
Riedenburg, Germany

Carthage Specialty Paperboard
Carthage Mill
Carthage, New York, United States

Cartiera Cama S.R.L.
Lallio Mill
Lallio, Bergamo, Italy

Cartiera Cerrone Francescantonio SpA
Cerrone Mill
Aquino, Frosinone, Italy

Cartiera dell' Adda SpA
Calolziocorte Mill
Calolziocorte, Lecco, Italy

Cartiera di Bosco Marengo SpA
Alessandria Mill
Bosco Marengo, Alessandria, Italy

Cartiera di Ferrara SpA
Ferrara Mill
Ferrara, Ferrara, Italy

Cartiera di Momo SpA
Momo Mill
Momo, Novara, Italy

Cartiera di Nave SpA
Caino Mill
Caino, Brescia, Italy

Cartiera di Rivignano SpA
Rivignano Mill
Rivignano, Udine, Italy

Cartiera Fornaci SpA
Fagnano Olona Mill
Fagnano Olona, Varese, Italy

Cartiera Marchigiana Srl
Montelupone Mill
Montelupone, Macerata, Italy

Cartiera Olona Sas di Belvisi Dr. Davide & C.
Gorla Minore Mill
Gorla Minore, Varese, Italy

Cartiera Pieretti SpA
Marlia-Capannori Mill
Marlia-Capannori, Lucca, Italy

Cartiera S. Giovanni di Figli di Checchi G. S.R.L.
Pietrabuona di Pescia Mill
Pietrabuona di Pescia, Pistoia, Italy

Boxboard/cartonboard

Cartiera San Felice SpA
San Felice Mill
Piteccio, Pistoia, Italy

Cartiera San Martino SpA
Broccostella Mill
Broccostella, Frosinone, Italy

Cartiere di Trevi SpA
Trevi Mill
Trevi, Perugia, Italy

Cartonal SAS
Santa Fe de Bogotá Mill
Santa Fe de Bogotá, Cundinamarca, Colombia

Cartonera del Caribe CA
Maracay Mill
Maracay, Edo. Aragua, Venezuela

Cartones America SA - CAME
Cali Mill
Cali, Valle de Cauca, Colombia

Cartones Compactos S.L.
Barberá del Vallés Mill
Barberá del Vallés, Barcelona, Spain

Cartones Ponderosa S.A. de C.V.
San Juan del Rio Mill
San Juan del Rio, Querétaro, Mexico

Cartonificio Sandreschi S.R.L.
Villa Basilica Mill
Villa Basilica, Lucca, Italy

Cartonnerie Jean SA
Bonnat Mill
Bonnat, France

Cartonnerie Oudin
Truyes Mill
Truyes, France

Cartonnerie Tunisienne SA
Enfidha Mill
Enfidha, Gouvernorat de Sousse, Tunisia

Cartulinas CMPC S.A.
Maule Mill
Yerbas Buenas, Linares, VII - Región del Maule, Chile

Cartulinas CMPC S.A.
Valdivia Mill
Valdivia, X - Región de Los Lagos, Chile

Carvajal Pulpa y Papel
Yumbo Mill, Plant 1
Yumbo, Valle de Cauca, Colombia

Carval Cartiera Di Valletrompia Srl.
Concesio Mill
Concesio, Brescia, Italy

Cascades Boxboard Group Inc.
East Angus Mill
East Angus, Quebec, Canada

Cascades Boxboard Group Inc.
Jonquière Mill
Jonquiere, Quebec, Canada

Cascades Djupafors AB
Kallinge Mill
Kallinge, Sweden

Cascades Papier Kingsey Falls Inc.
Kingsey Falls Mill
Kingsey Falls, Quebec, Canada

Cascades SAS
La Rochette Mill
La Rochette, France

CECSO - Celulosa y Corrugados de Sonora S.A. de C.V.
Navojoa Mill
Navojoa, Sonora, Mexico

Celulosa de Fibras Mexicanas S.A. de C.V.
Apizaco Mill
Apizaco, Tlaxacala, Mexico

Century Paper & Board Mills Ltd.
Kasur Mill
Bhai Pheru, Dist. Kasur, Pakistan

Century Pulp & Paper
Lalkua Mill
Nainital, Uttarakhand, India

Ceprohart SA
Braila Mill
Braila, Romania

Chao Yang Paper Mfg. Co., Ltd.
Tsao Chiao Mill
Tsao Chiao, Miaoli County, Taiwan

Cheema Paper Mills Pvt. Ltd.
Nainital Mill
Dist. Udham Singh Nagar, Uttarakhand, India

Cheng Loong Corporation
Chu Pei Mill
Chu Pei, Hsinchu County, Taiwan

Cheng Loong Corporation
Hou Li Mill
Hou Li, Taichung City, Taiwan

Chenming Paper Holdings Ltd.
Shouguang (Shouguang Chenming No. 4) Mill
Shouguang, Shandong, China

China Sunshine Paper Holdings Company Limited
Weifang Mill
Weifang, Shandong, China

Ching Mei Paper Co., Ltd.
Kuan Yin Mill
Kuan Yin, Taoyuan County, Taiwan

Chuetsu Pulp & Paper Co., Ltd.
Takaoka (Nohmachi) Mill
Takaoka-shi, Toyama Pref., Japan

Chung Hwa Pulp Corporation
Taitung Mill
Taitung, Taitung County, Taiwan

Cia. Papelera El Fenix S.A. de C.V.
Col. Arenal Mill
Col. Arenal, México, D.F., Mexico

Cibrapel S.A. Indústria de Papel e Embalagens
Guapimirim Mill
Guapimirim, Rio de Janeiro, Brazil

CIFIVE S.A.I.C.
Recreo Sur Mill
Recreo Sur, Santa Fé, Argentina

Cincinnati Paperboard
Cincinnati Mill
Cincinnati, Ohio, United States

Circar Paper Mills Ltd.
Nellore Mill
Nellore, Andhra Pradesh, India

Cita Peuchoon Paper Mills Sdn. Bhd.
Sungai Petani Mill
Sungai Petani, Kedah, Malaysia

Clearwater Paper Corporation
Cypress Bend Mill, McGehee Mill
McGehee, Arkansas City, Arkansas, United States

Clearwater Paper Corporation
Lewiston Mill
Lewiston, Idaho, United States

Coastal Agro Industries Ltd
West Godavari Mill
West Godavari, Tanuku, Andhra Pradesh, India

Coldenhove Papier
Eerbeek Mill
Eerbeek, Netherlands

Colombiana de Cartones Ltda.
Palmira, Cali Mill
Palmira, Cali, Valle de Cauca, Colombia

Container Corp. of the Philippines
Quezon City Mill
Quezon City, Philippines

COPSI Compañía Papelera Sinsacate S.R.L.
Sinsacate Mill
Sinsacate, Córdoba, Argentina

Corenso France
Soustre Mill
Saint-Seurin-Sur-L'Isle, France

Corenso North America
Wisconsin Rapids Mill
Wisconsin Rapids, Wisconsin, United States

Corenso United Oy Ltd.
Pori Coreboard Mill
Pori, Finland

Cosboard Industries Ltd.
Jagatpur Mill
Dist. Cuttack, Odisha, India

Cottrell Paper Co., Inc.
Rock City Falls Mill
Rock City Falls, New York, United States

Crescent Packaging Corporation, Pty. Ltd.
Heidelberg Mill
Heidelberg, Gauteng, South Africa

Crocker Technical Papers
Fitchburg Mill
Fitchburg, Massachusetts, United States

Daewha Paper Board Mfg. Co., Ltd.
Gunpo Mill
Gunpo-si, Gyeonggi-do, South Korea

Daiwa Itagami Co., Ltd.
Daiwa Mill
Kashiwabara-shi, Osaka Pref., Japan

Boxboard/cartonboard

Dalkrovlya
Khabarovsk Mill
Khabarovsk, Russia

Daman Ganga Papers Mills (P) Ltd.
Vapi Mill
Vapi, Dist. Valsad, Gujarat, India

Dev Priya Papers Pvt. Ltd.
Meerut Mill
Meerut, Uttar Pradesh, India

Dezhou Huisheng Pingyuan Paper Co., Ltd.
Dezhou Mill
Dezhou, Shandong, China

DS Smith Chouanard
Coullons Mill
Coullons, Loiret, France

DS Smith Kaysersberg
Kaysersberg Mill
Kaysersberg, France

DS Smith Paper
Kemsley Mill
Kemsley, Sittingbourne, Kent, United Kingdom

DS Smith Paper
Wansbrough Paper Mill
Watchet, Somerset, United Kingdom

Durga Duplex Mill Private Limited
Malerkotla Mill
Malerkotla, Punjab, India

E.MAK Paper Manufacturing Co.
Suez Mill
Suez, Egypt

East India Paper & Board Mills
Howeah Mill
Howeah, West Bengal, India

El Dar El Beida
Alexandria Mill
Alexandria, Iskanderiya, Egypt

El-Salam PaperMill
Alexandria Mill
Alexandria, Iskanderiya, Egypt

EMBA spol. s. r.o.
Paseky nad Jizerou Mill
Paseky nad Jizerou, okr. Semily, Czech Republic

Empaques Modernos de Guadalajara, S.A. de C.V.
Guadalajara Mill
El Salto, Jalisco, Mexico

Eska Graphic Board BV
Hoogezand Mill
Hoogezand, Netherlands

Eska Graphic Board BV
Sappemeer Mill
Sappemeer, Netherlands

Etap Paper & Carton
Borg El Arab El Gededah Mill
Borg El Arab El Gededah, Alexandria, Egypt

Ethiopian Pulp & Paper SC
Nazareth Mill
Wonji, Nazareth, Ethiopia

Everest Paper Mills (P) Ltd.
Ganganagar Mill
Kolkata, West Bengal, India

Evergreen Packaging Inc.
Canton Mill
Canton, North Carolina, United States

Evergreen Packaging Inc.
Pine Bluff Mill
Pine Bluff, Arkansas, United States

Fábrica de Papel de Ponte Redonda S.A.
Silvalde, Espinho Mill
Silvalde, Espinho, Portugal

Fábrica de Papel de Torres Novas Lda.
Torres Novas Mill
Torres Novas, Portugal

Fabryka Papieru i Tektury "BESKIDY" S.A.
Wadowice Mill
Wadowice, Poland

Feinpappenwerk Gebr. Schuster GmbH & Co. KG
Dachau Mill
Hebertshausen, Dachau, Germany

Fibre Foils Ltd.
Khalapur Mill
Khalapur, Raigad, Maharashtra, India

Fiskeby Board AB
Norrköping Mill
Norrköping, Sweden

Flexipack International Wunderlich GmbH + Co KG
Baar-Ebenhausen Mill
Baar-Ebenhausen, Germany

Flexipack International Wunderlich GmbH + Co KG
Gerlingen Mill
Wenden, Germany

FS-Karton GmbH
Neuss Mill
Neuss, Germany

Fthiotis Paper Mill SA
Damasta Mill
Damasta, Lamia, Greece

Fujian Jian'ou Taipingyang Paper Mill
Jian'ou Mill
Jian'ou, Fujian, China

Fujian Liansheng Paper (Longhai) Co., Ltd
Longhai Mill
Longhai City, Fujian, China

Fujian Quanzhou Guige Paper Co. Ltd.
Quanzhou Mill
Quanzhou, Fujian, China

Fukuyama Paper Co., Ltd.
Osaka Mill
Osaka, Osaka Pref., Japan

G-P Gypsum LLC
San Leandro Mill
San Leandro, California, United States

Gahir Paper Mills Ltd.
Sangrur Mill
Sangrur, Punjab, India

Gaya Baru Paper CV
Malang Mill
Malang, East Java, Indonesia

Gayatrishakti Paper & Boards Ltd.
Vapi Mill
Vapi, Gujarat, India

Georgia-Pacific LLC
Brewton Mill
Brewton, Alabama, United States

Georgia-Pacific LLC
Crossett Mill
Crossett, Arkansas, United States

Georgia-Pacific LLC
Naheola Mill
Pennington, Alabama, United States

Georgia-Pacific LLC
Thorold Mill
Thorold, Ontario, Canada

Gojo Paper Mfg. Co., Ltd.
Fuji Mill
Fuji-shi, Shizuoka Pref., Japan

Goraya Straw Board Mills (P) Ltd
Udham Singh Nagar Mill
Kashipur, Uttarakhand, India

Gramox Paper & Boards Ltd.
Ernakulam Mill
Ernakulam, Kerala, India

Graphic Packaging International Inc.
Battle Creek Mill
Battle Creek, Michigan, United States

Graphic Packaging International Inc.
Kalamazoo Mill
Kalamazoo, Michigan, United States

Graphic Packaging International Inc.
Macon Mill
Macon, Georgia, United States

Graphic Packaging International Inc.
Middletown Mill
Middletown, Ohio, United States

Graphic Packaging International Inc.
Santa Clara Mill
Santa Clara, California, United States

Graphic Packaging International Inc.
West Monroe Mill
West Monroe, Louisiana, United States

Groupe CMCP - La Compagnie Marocaine des Cartons et Papiers
Kenitra Mill
Kenitra, Morocco

Guangdong City Baoli Paper Co., Ltd.
Dongguan Mill
Dongguan, Guangdong, China

Guangdong Dongguan Dongfa Paper Industry Co., Ltd.
Dongguan Mill
Dongguan, Guangdong, China

Boxboard/cartonboard

Guangdong Dongguan Hongmei Lee & Man Paper Co., Ltd.
Dongguan (Hongmei) Mill
Dongguan, Guangdong, China

Guangdong Dongguan Jianhui Paper
Dongguan Mill
Dongguan, Guangdong, China

Guangdong Dongguan Jintian Paper Co., Ltd.
Dongguan Mill
Dongguan, Guangdong, China

Guangdong Dongguan Nine Dragons Paper Industries Co., Ltd.
Dongguan Mill
Dongguan, Guangdong, China

Guangdong Zhuhai S.E.Z. Hongta Renheng Paper Co. Ltd.
Zhuhai (Gaolangang) Mill
Zhuhai, Guangdong, China

Guangdong Zhuhai S.E.Z. Hongta Renheng Paper Co. Ltd.
Zhuhai (Qianshan) Mill
Zhuhai, Guangdong, China

Guangxi East Asia Paper Co., Ltd.
Chongzuo Mill
Chongzuo, Guangxi, China

Guangxi Guofa Forest & Paper Co. Ltd.
Liuzhou (Guangxi Guofa Forest & Paper) Mill
Liuzhou, Guangxi, China

Guangxi Jingui Pulp & Paper Co., Ltd.
Qinzhou (Guangxi Jingui Pulp & Paper) Mill
Qinzhou, Guangxi, China

Guangzhou Victorgo Industry Co., Ltd.
Guangzhou (Guangzhou Victorgo) Mill
Guangzhou, Guangdong, China

Gulf Paper Industries Factory
Riyadh Mill
Riyadh, Saudi Arabia

Gulf Paper Manufacturing Free Zone Company
Dubai Mill
Jebel Ali Free Zone, Dubai, United Arab Emirates

Gulf Paper Mfg. Co. k.s.c.
Kuwait Mill
West Mina Abdulla, Ahmadi Governorate, Kuwait

Gusmer Enterprises Inc.
Waupaca Mill
Waupaca, Wisconsin, United States

GVG Paper Mills Ltd.
Palani Taluk Mill
Palani Taluk, Dist. Dindigul, Tamil Nadu, India

Hai Phong Paper Mill
Hai Phong City Mill
Hai Phong City, Hong Bang District, Vietnam

Halkali Kagit Karton San. ve Tic. A.S.
Istanbul Mill
Küçükçekmece, Istanbul, Turkey

Hamburger Rieger GmbH & Co. KG
Spremberg-Schwarze Pumpe Mill
Spremberg-Schwarze Pumpe, Brandenburg, Germany

Hamburger Rieger GmbH & Co. KG
Trostberg Mill
Trostberg, Bavaria, Germany

Hanchang Paper Co., Ltd.
Yangsan-si Mill
Yangsan-si, Gyeongsangnam-do, South Korea

Hansol Paper Co. Ltd.
Daejeon Mill
Daejeon, Daejeon, South Korea

Hebei Baoding Xinghua Paper Mill
Baoding Mill
Baoding, Hebei, China

Hebei Dazhong Baolai Paper Co., Ltd.
Tangshan Mill
Tangshan, Hebei, China

Hebei Luquan Yuanda Industrial Co., Ltd.
Luquan Mill
Luquan, Hebei, China

Hebei Tanghai Chenguang Paper Co., Ltd.
Tangshan Mill
Tangshan, Hebei, China

Hebei Tangshan Guotai Paper Co., Ltd.
Tangshan Mill
Tangshan, Hebei, China

Hebei Yongxin Paper Co., Ltd.
Tangshan (Hebei Yongxin) Mill
Tangshan, Hebei, China

Heidrich Industrial Mercantil e Agricola S.A.
Taió Mill
Taió, Santa Catarina, Brazil

Hemkunt Paper Mills Ltd
Ludhiana Mill
Ludhiana, Punjab, India

Henan Dongsheng Paper Co.,Ltd.
Xinmi Mill
Xinmi, Henan, China

Henan Shangqiu Xinhao Paper Co., Ltd.
Shangqiu Mill
Shangqiu, Henan, China

Henan Xinxiang Xinya Paper Group Co., Ltd.
Xinxiang (Cartonboard) Mill
Xinxiang, Henan, China

Henan Xinxiang Xinya Paper Group Co., Ltd.
Xinxiang No. 2 Mill
Xinxiang, Henan, China

Henan Zhengzhou Chunhui Paper Co., Ltd.
Xinmi Mill
Xinmi, Henan, China

Highland Paper Mills Ltd.
Eldoret Mill
Eldoret, Western, Kenya

Hokuetsu Kishu Paper Co. Ltd.
Kanto Ichikawa Mill
Ichikawa-shi, Chiba Pref., Japan

Hokuetsu Kishu Paper Co. Ltd.
Kanto Katsuta Mill
Hitachinaka-shi, Ibaraki Pref., Japan

Hokuetsu Kishu Paper Co. Ltd.
Niigata Mill
Niigata-shi, Niigata Pref., Japan

Hollingsworth & Vose Co.
East Walpole Mill
East Walpole, Massachusetts, United States

Hua Te Mei Paper Co., Ltd.
Pu Hsing mill
Pu Hsing, Changhua County, Taiwan

Hubei Junma Paper Co. Ltd
Jingzhou Mill
Jingzhou, Hubei, China

Hubei Paima Paper Co., Ltd.
Jingzhou Mill
Jingzhou, Hubei, China

Hunan No. 1 Paperboard Co., Ltd.
Shaoyang Mill
Shaoyang, Hunan, China

IBEMA - Cia. Brasileira de Papel
Turvo Mill
Turvo, Paraná, Brazil

Iggesund Paperboard (Workington) Ltd.
Workington Mill
Workington, Cumbria, United Kingdom

Iggesund Paperboard AB
Iggesund Mill
Iggesund, Sweden

Iguaçu Celulose Papel S.A.
Frei Rogério Mill
Frei Rogério, Santa Catarina, Brazil

Ind. de Papelão Hörlle Ltda.
Campo Largo Mill
Campo Largo, Paraná, Brazil

Industria Cartaria Pieretti SpA (ICP)
Marlia Mill
Marlia di Capannori, Lucca, Italy

Industrial e Agrícola Rio Verde Ltda.
Rio do Campo Mill
Rio do Campo, Santa Catarina, Brazil

Indústrias de Papel R. Ramenzoni S.A.
Cordeirópolis Mill
Cordeirópolis, São Paulo, Brazil

International Paper & Sun Paper Cartonboard Co., Ltd.
Yanzhou Mill
Yanzhou, Shandong, China

International Paper - Kwidzyn Sp. z o.o.
Kwidzyn Mill
Kwidzyn, Poland

International Paper Co.
Augusta Mill
Augusta, Georgia, United States

International Paper Co.
Newport Mill
Cayuga, Indiana, United States

Boxboard/cartonboard

International Paper Co.
Riegelwood Mill
Riegelwood, North Carolina, United States

International Paper Co.
Texarkana Mill
Domino, Texas, United States

Iran Papyrus Co. Ltd.
Saveh Mill
Saveh, Markazi, Iran

Islamic Paper Manufacturing Co.
Quesna Mill
Quesna, Menofeya, Egypt

ITC Limited, Paperboards & Specialty Papers Division
Bhadrachalam Mill
Khammam, Bhadrachalam, Andhra Pradesh, India

ITC Limited, Paperboards & Specialty Papers Division
Kovai Mill
Coimbatore, Tamil Nadu, India

Jammu Paper (P) Ltd.
Jammu Tawi Mill
Jammu, Jammu and Kashmir, India

Jiangsu Fuxing Paper
Yancheng Mill
Yancheng, Jiangsu, China

Jiangsu Huangli Paper Industry Co., Ltd.
Jiangyin Mill
Jiangyin, Jiangsu, China

Jiangsu Jiangyin BESTO Special Paper Board Co., Ltd.
Jiangyin Mill
Jiangyin, Jiangsu, China

Jiangsu Jiangyin Gushan Dongfang Paper Co., Ltd.
Jiangyin Mill
Jiangyin, Jiangsu, China

Jiangsu Jiuxing Paper Co., Ltd.
Yancheng Mill
Yancheng, Jiangsu, China

Jiangsu Longheng Paper Co. Ltd
Yancheng Mill
Yancheng, Jiangsu, China

Jiangsu Nine Dragons Paper Industries
Taicang Mill
Taicang, Jiangsu, China

Jiangsu Taizhou Weidmann High Voltage Insulation Co. Ltd
Taizhou Mill
Taizhou, Jiangsu, China

Jiangsu Zhangjiagang Mingxing Paper Co., Ltd.
Zhangjiagang Mill
Zhangjiagang, Jiangsu, China

Jiangyin Xinhao Recycling Paper Co., Ltd.
Jiangyin Mill
Jiangyin, Jiangsu, China

Jilin Meihekou City Chuangda Paper Co., Ltd.
Meihekou Mill
Meihekou, Jilin, China

Jilin Meihekou Haishan Paper Mill
Meihekou Mill
Meihekou, Jilin, China

JK Paper Ltd.
Central Pulp Mills-CPM, Songadh Mill
Fort Songadh, Dist. Tapi, Gujarat, India

Jollyboard Limited
Mumbai Mill
Mumbai, Maharashtra, India

Jordan Paper & Cardboard Factories Co. Ltd.
Zarka Mill
Awajan, Zarka, Jordan

Julius Schulte Söhne GmbH & Co. KG
Düsseldorf Mill
Düsseldorf, Germany

Kaga Paper Mfg. Co., Ltd.
Kaga Paper Mill
Kanazawa-shi, Ishikawa Pref., Japan

Kahramanmaras Kagit San ve TIC A.S (KMK Paper)
Kahramanmaras Mill
Kahramanmaras, Turkey

KapStone Paper Charleston Kraft LLC
North Charleston Mill
North Charleston, South Carolina, United States

Karanja Industries (P) Ltd., Paper Division
Bidar Mill
Bidar, Karnataka, India

Karavaevo
Karavaevo Mill
Pos. Karavaevo, Moscow Region, Russia

Karl Kurz GmbH & Co. KG
Tullau Mill
Rosengarten-Tullau, Germany

Karnal Card Board Industries
Karnal Mill
Karnal, Haryana, India

Kartonfabriek Henri Goossens
Huizingen Mill
Huizingen, Belgium

Kartonfabrik Buchmann GmbH
Annweiler Mill
Annweiler, Germany

Kartonfabrik Kaierde GmbH & Co. Produktions KG
Delligsen Mill
Delligsen, Germany

Kartonfabrik Porstendorf GmbH
Porstendorf Mill
Porstendorf, Germany

Kartonsan - Karton Sanayi ve Ticaret AS
Kullar Koyu Mill
Izmit, Kocaeli, Turkey

Kartontara
Velikie Luki Mill
Velikie Luki, Pskov obl., Russia

Kartontol
St. Petersburg Mill
St. Petersburg, Russia

Kartotec - Papeles Técnicos-
Villeta Mill
Villeta, Paraguay

Katz GmbH & Co. KG
Weisenbach Mill
Weisenbach, Germany

Kaveh Paper Industries Co.
Saveh Mill
Saveh, Markazi, Iran

Kenya Papermill Ltd.
Thika Mill
Thika, Central, Kenya

Khanna Paper Mills Pvt. Ltd.
Amritsar Mill
Amritsar, Punjab, India

Kherani Paper Mills Ltd.
Valsad Mill
Dist. Valsad, Gujarat, India

Kiev Cardboard and Paper Mill
Kiev Cardboard and Paper Mill
Obukhiv, Kyivska obl., Ukraine

Klabin S.A.
Monte Alegre Mill
Telêmaco Borba, Paraná, Brazil

KleanNara Co., Ltd.
Chongju Mill
Cheongwon-gun, Chungcheongbuk-do, South Korea

Köknar Kagit Karton San ve Tic A.S.
Kirklareli Mill
Luleburgaz, Kirklareli, Turkey

Kolicevo Karton d.o.o.
Kolicevo Mill
Domžale, Slovenia

KORONA Lochovice spol. s r.o.
Lochovice Mill
Lochovice, Czech Republic

Kosino Paper Mill
Kosino Mill
Kosino, Zuevskiy rayon, Kirovskaya Obl., Russia

Koyo Paper Mfg. Co., Ltd.
Honsha Mill
Fuji-shi, Shizuoka Pref., Japan

KPK St. Petersburg OOAO
Kommunar Mill
Kommunar, Leningrad Region, Russia

Krempel-Group
Kuppenheim Mill
Kuppenheim, Germany

Krempel-Group
Zwönitz Mill
Zwönitz, Germany

Kuan Yuan Paper Mfg. Co. Ltd.
Taichung Mill
Dajia District, Taichung City, Taiwan

Boxboard/cartonboard

Kuan Yuan Paper Mfg. Co., Ltd.
Chunan Mill
Chu Nan, Miaoli County, Taiwan

Kuzbasskiy Skarabey
Kemerovo Mill
Kemerovo, Russia

LEIPA Georg Leinfelder GmbH
Schrobenhausen Mill
Schrobenhausen, Germany

Lepenka
Trzic Mill
Trzic, Slovenia

Lepenka AD
Novi Knezevac Mill
Novi Knezevac, Vojvodina, Serbia

Lexpapier Sonacar S.A.
El Jadida Mill
El Jadida, Morocco

Lothlorien (Pty) Ltd
Lothlorien Pulp Mill
Wadeville, Gauteng, South Africa

Lutsky KRK
Lutsk Mill
Lutsk, Ukraine

Lvivkartonplast
Lviv Mill
Lviv, Ukraine

M.C.LIRI S.R.L.
Isola del Liri Mill
Frosinone, Frosinone, Italy

Madeireira Miguel Forte S.A.
União da Vitória Mill
União da Vitória, Paraná, Brazil

Maghan Paper Mills (P) Ltd.
Sangrur Mill
Sangrur, Punjab, India

Magnum Ventures Ltd.
Ghaziabad Mill
Sahibabad, Dist. Ghaziabad, Uttar Pradesh, India

Malik Board and Paper Industries
Lahore Mill
Lahore, Punjab, Pakistan

Malik Board Mills
Sheikhupura Mill
Sheikhupura, Punjab, Pakistan

Malyn - Weidmann Paper Mill VAT
Malyn Mill
Malyn, Zhitomirskaya obl., Ukraine

Marombas Indústria e Comércio de Madeiras e Papelão
Curitibanos Mill
Curitibanos, Santa Catarina, Brazil

Marui Paper Industry Co., Ltd.
Kuzawa
Fuji-shi, Shizuoka Pref., Japan

Mayr-Melnhof Eerbeek BV
Eerbeek Mill
Eerbeek, Netherlands

Mayr-Melnhof Gernsbach GmbH
Gernsbach Mill
Gernsbach, Germany

Mayr-Melnhof Karton GmbH
Frohnleiten Mill
Frohnleiten, Styria, Austria

Mayr-Melnhof Karton GmbH
Hirschwang Mill
Reichenau an der Rax, Niederösterreich, Austria

MD Papéis Ltda.
Limeira Mill
Limeira, São Paulo, Brazil

MeadWestvaco Corporation
Covington Mill
Covington, Virginia, United States

MeadWestvaco Corporation
Evadale Mill
Evadale, Texas, United States

MeadWestvaco Corporation
Mahrt Mill
Cottonton, Alabama, United States

Mel Macedonian Paper Mills S.A.
Thessaloniki Mill
Thessaloniki, Greece

Merckens Karton- und Pappenfabrik GmbH
Schwertberg Mill
Schwertberg, Oberösterreich, Austria

Metsä Board Äänekoski
Äänekoski Board Mill
Äänekoski, Finland

Metsä Board Kyro
Kyro Mill
Kyröskoski, Finland

Metsä Board Simpele
Simpele Mill
Simpele, Finland

Metsä Board Tako
Tako Mill
Tampere, Finland

Middle East Paper Co. (SIMO)
Musturud Mill
Musturud, Cairo, Egypt

Middle East Paper Company - (MEPCO)
Jeddah Mill
Jeddah, Saudi Arabia

Milano Papers Pvt. Ltd.
Rajkot Mill
Rajkot, Morbi, Gujarat, India

Millenium Papers Pvt. Ltd.
Morbi Mill
Morbi, Gujarat, India

Mimosa Sanitary Paper
Kaa El Rim, Bekaa Mill
Kaa El Rim, Bekaa, Lebanon

Mitsubishi Paper Mills Ltd.
Hachinohe Mill
Hachinohe-shi, Aomori, Japan

Mladost Cuprija A.D.G.D.
Cuprija Mill
Cuprija, Serbia

Mobile Paperboard Corp.
Mobile Mill
Mobile, Alabama, United States

Mohammadi Paper & Board Industries (Pvt.) Ltd.
Sheikhupura Lahore Unit 2
Sheikhupura Lahore, Punjab, Pakistan

Mondi Syktyvkar
Syktyvkar Mill
Syktyvkar, Komi Republic, Russia

Mopak Dalaman Pulp-Paper Cardboard Plant
Dalaman Mill
Mugla, Turkey

Moritz J. Weig GmbH & Co. KG
Mayen Mill
Mayen, Germany

Mosaico Speciality Papers
Lugo di Vicenza Mill
Lugo di Vicenza, Vicenza, Italy

Mpact Limited
Springs Mill
New Era, Gauteng, South Africa

Muda Paper Mills Sdn. Bhd.
Tasek Mill
Seberang Prai Selatan, Penang, Malaysia

Multiwal Pulp & Board Mills Ltd.
Dist. Udham Singh Nagar Mill
Dist. Udham Singh Nagar, Uttarakhand, India

Muratli Karton Fabrikasi
Tekirdag Mill
Tekirdag, Tekirdag, Turkey

Murli Industries Ltd.
Nagpur Mill
Nagpur, Maharashtra, India

Myagkaya Krovlya
Samara Mill
Samara, Russia

Naachiar Paper Boards Private Ltd.
Sivakasi Mill
Sivakasi, Tamil Nadu, India

Nabha Paper Mills Ltd.
Malerkotla Mill
Malerkotla, Punjab, India

Nabha Paper Mills Ltd.
Nabha Mill
Dist. Patiala, Punjab, India

Nath Pulp & Paper Mills Ltd.
Aurangabad Mill
Aurangabad, Maharashtra, India

National Gypsum Co.
Anniston Mill
Oxford, Alabama, United States

National Gypsum Co.
Milton Plant
New Columbia, Pennsylvania, United States

Boxboard/cartonboard

National Gypsum Co.
Pryor Mill
Pryor, Oklahoma, United States

Newark America
Fitchburg Mill
Fitchburg, Massachusetts, United States

Newark Pacific Paperboard Corp.
Los Angeles Mill
Los Angeles, California, United States

Newman & Company, Inc.
Philadelphia Mill
Philadelphia, Pennsylvania, United States

Nicol-Pack Corporation
Uchaly Mill
Uchaly, Respublika Bashkortostan, Russia

Nicol-Pack Imperial Co. Ltd.
Murom (Imperial) Mill
Murom, Vladimir oblast, Russia

Nine Dragons Paper (Tianjin) Co., Ltd.
Tianjin Mill
Tianjin, Tianjin, China

Nine Dragons Paper Industries (Chongqing) Co., Ltd.
Chongqing Mill
Chongqing, Chongqing, China

Ningbo Muniu Paper Co. Ltd.
Ningbo Mill
Ningbo, Zhejiang, China

Nippon Paper Industries Co., Ltd.
Ashikaga Mill
Ashikaga-shi, Tochigi Pref., Japan

Nippon Paper Industries Co., Ltd.
Hokkaido Mill - Asahikawa
Asahikawa-shi, Hokkaido Pref., Japan

Nippon Paper Industries Co., Ltd.
Soka Mill
Soka-shi, Saitama Pref., Japan

Nippon Paper Industries Co., Ltd.
Yoshinaga Mill
Fuji-shi, Shizuoka Pref., Japan

Nizhegorodsky Board & Asphalt Board Mill
Nizhegorodsky Mill
Nizhny Novgorod, Russia

NR Agarwal Industries Ltd.
Unit III and Unit IV
Vapi, Dist. Valsad, Gujarat, India

NR Agarwal Industries Ltd.
Vapi, Valsad (Unit I) Mill
Vapi, Valsad, Gujarat, India

Nuova Cartiera Sordini S.R.L.
Foligno Mill
Foligno, Perugia, Italy

Nuova F.lli Alimonti srl
Castelmadama Mill
Castelmadama, Rome, Italy

OAO Aleksandrovbumprom (ABP)
Krasnopolyanskij Paperboard Mill
Pos. Krasnaya Polyana, Ostrovskiy rayon, Kostroma Region, Russia

OAO Poligrafkarton
Balakhna Mill
Balakhna, Nizhny Novgorod, Russia

OAO Technicheskaya Bumaga
Rybinskiy rayon Mill
Rybinskiy rayon, Yaroslavl obl., Russia

Obeikan Paper Industry
Riyadh Mill
Riyadh, Saudi Arabia

Ohio Paperboard Corp.
Baltimore Board Mill
Baltimore, Ohio, United States

Oji F-Tex Co., Ltd.
Fujinomiya Mill
Fujinomiya-shi, Shizuoka Pref., Japan

Oji F-Tex Co., Ltd.
Shibakawa Mill
Fuji-gun, Shizuoka Pref., Japan

Oji Materia Co., Ltd.
Edogawa Mill
Edogawa-ku, Tokyo, Japan

Oji Materia Co., Ltd.
Nayoro Mill
Nayoro-shi, Hokkaido Pref., Japan

Oji Materia Co., Ltd.
Nikko Mill
Utsunomiya-shi, Tochigi Pref., Japan

Oji Materia Co., Ltd.
Oita Mill
Oita-shi, Oita Pref., Japan

Oji Materia Co., Ltd.
Saga Mill
Saga-shi, Saga Pref., Japan

Oji Materia Co., Ltd.
Sobue Mill
Inazawa-shi, Aichi Pref., Japan

Okayama Paper Industries Co., Ltd.
Okayama-shi Mill
Okayama-shi, Okayama Pref., Japan

Okitsugawa Seishi Co., Ltd.
Shizuoka-shi Mill
Shizuoka-shi, Shizuoka Pref., Japan

Olympia Paper & Board Mills (Pvt) Ltd
Peshawar Mill
Peshawar, Khyber Pakhtunkhwa, Pakistan

Om Srinivasa Paper Boards Pvt. Ltd.
Sattur Mill
Sattur, Tamil Nadu, India

Omniafiltra, LLC
Beaver Falls Mill
Beaver Falls, New York, United States

Omskkrovlya
Omsk Mill
Omsk, Russia

Osaka Paper Co., Ltd.
Osaka-shi Mill
Osaka-shi, Osaka Pref., Japan

Otrokovické papírny a.s.
Otrokovice Mill
Otrokovice, Czech Republic

Otsego Paper Inc.
Otsego Mill
Otsego, Michigan, United States

Ox Paperboard LLC
Constantine Mill
Constantine, Michigan, United States

Ox Paperboard LLC
Halltown Mill
Halltown, West Virginia, United States

Ox Paperboard LLC
Pekin Mill
Pekin, Illinois, United States

PABCO Paper
Vernon Mill
Vernon, California, United States

Packprofil Sp. z o.o.
Kolonowskie Mill
Kolonowskie 1, Poland

PAKA Glashütter Pappen- und Kartonagenfabrik GmbH
Glashütte Mill
Glashütte, Germany

Pan Paper Mills
Webuye Mill
Webuye, Bungoma District, Western, Kenya

PAN Papirna Industrija d.o.o.
Zagreb Mill
Zagreb, Grad Zagreb, Croatia

Panasa, Papelera Nacional S.A.
Paramonga Mill
Paramonga, Lima, Peru

Pankaboard Oy
Pankakoski Mill
Pankakoski, Lieksa, Finland

Papeleira Portuguesa S.A.
São Paio de Oleiros Mill
São Paio de Oleiros, Portugal

Papelera del Nevado S.A. de C.V.
Almoloyan Mill
San Miguel Almoloyan, Almoloya de Juarez, México, D.F., Mexico

Papelera del Principado, S.A. (Paprinsa)
Mollerussa Mill
Mollerussa, Lérida, Spain

Papelera del Sur, División Cartulinas de Interpack S.A.
Tornquist Mill
Tornquist, Buenos Aires, Argentina

Papelera Iruña S.A. de C.V.
Iztapalapa Mill
Iztapalapa, México, D.F., Mexico

Papelera Munné S.A.
Capellades Mill
Capellades, Barcelona, Spain

Papelera Veracruzana S.A. de C.V.
Orizaba Mill
Orizaba, Veracruz, Mexico

Boxboard/cartonboard

Papeles Lozar S.A. de C.V.
Ixtapaluca Mill
Ixtapaluca, México, D.F., Mexico

Papeltex Argentina S.A.I.C.
Lanus Oeste Mill
Lanus Oeste, Buenos Aires, Argentina

Papertech S.L.
Tudela Mill
Tudela, Navarra, Spain

PaperWorks Industries, Inc.
Philadelphia Mill
Philadelphia, Pennsylvania, United States

PaperWorks Industries, Inc.
Wabash Mill
Wabash, Indiana, United States

Papeterie de Gromelle
Saint-Saturnin Mill
Saint-Saturnin-les-Avignon, France

Papeteries de Bègles SAS
Bègles Mill
Bègles, France

Papeteries du Rhin
Illzach Mill
Illzach, France

Papier- und Kartonfabrik Varel GmbH & Co. KG
Varel Mill
Varel, Niedersachsen, Germany

Papierfabrik Carl Lenz GmbH & Co.
Wehr Mill
Wehr, Germany

Papierfabrik Fritz Peters GmbH & Co. KG
Gelsenkirchen Mill
Gelsenkirchen, Germany

Papierfabrik Poerringer GmbH & Co. KG
Annweiler Mill
Annweiler am Trifels, Germany

Papirfabrika Ligatne Ltd.
Ligatne Mill
Ligatne, Latvia

Papírna APIS, s.r.o.
Ceská Kamenice Mill
Ceská Kamenice, Czech Republic

Papirus Indústria de Papel S.A.
Limeira Mill
Limeira, São Paulo, Brazil

PAPOS v.o.s.
Ostrov Mill
Ostrov, Czech Republic

Pappenfabrik A. Obenauf GmbH & Co. KG
Bad Harzburg Mill
Bad Harzburg, Germany

Pappenfabrik Nierfeld, J. Piront GmbH & Co. KG
Schleiden Mill
Schleiden, Germany

Pappenfabrik Trauchgau GmbH & Co. KG
Trauchgau Mill
Halblech, Germany

Paramount Paper Board Mills (Pvt) Ltd.
Haripur Mill
Haripur, Pakistan

Pasa - Papelão Apucaraninha Ltda.
Londrina Mill
Tamarana, Paraná, Brazil

Petrocart SA
Piatra Neamt Mill
Piatra Neamt, Romania

Pinho Past Ltda.
Guarapuava Mill
Guarapuava, Paraná, Brazil

Pioneer Board Products (Pvt) Ltd.
Lahore Mill
Lahore, Punjab, Pakistan

Prado Karton S.A.
Tomar Mill
Tomar, Portugal

Prado-Cartolinas da Lousã S.A.
Lousã Mill
Lousã, Portugal

Pragati Paper Mills Ltd.
Dist. Ghaziabad Mill
Dist. Ghaziabad, Uttar Pradesh, India

Pranavraj Paper Mills Pvt. Ltd.
Vapi, Dist. Valsad Mill
Vapi, Dist. Valsad, Gujarat, India

Prayas Papers (P) Ltd.
Parganas Mill
North 24-Parganas, West Bengal, India

Premium Board Finland Oy
Juankoski Board Mill
Juankoski, Finland

Premium Paper & Boards Ind. Ltd.
Surat Mill
Surat, Gujarat, India

Proletariy, JSC
Surazh Mill
Surazh, Bryansk Region, Russia

PROPASA - Productora de Papel S.A. de C.V.
San Nicolas de los Garza Mill
San Nicolas de los Garza, Nuevo León, Mexico

PT Ekamas Fortuna
Malang (PT Ekamas Fortuna) Mill
Malang, Jawa Timur, Indonesia

PT Fajar Surya Wisesa Tbk.
Bekasi Mill
Cikarang Barat, Bekasi, West Java, Indonesia

PT Indah Kiat Pulp & Paper Corp.
Serang (PT Indah Kiat Pulp & Paper) Mill
Serang, West Java, Indonesia

PT Jaya Kertas
Nganjuk Mill
Nganjuk, East Java, Indonesia

PT Karya Tulada
Karawaci Mill
Tangerang, Banten, West Java, Indonesia

PT Kertas Blabak Megelang
Magelang Mill
Magelang, Central Java, Indonesia

PT Pabrik Kertas Indonesia (Pakerin)
Mojokerto Mill
Mojokerto, East Java, Indonesia

PT Pabrik Kertas Noree Indonesia
Bekasi Mill
Bekasi, West Java, Indonesia

PT Pabrik Kertas Tjiwi Kimia Tbk
Mojokerto (PT Pabrik Kertas Tjiwi Kimia) Mill
Mojokerto, East Java, Indonesia

PT Papertech Indonesia
Blabak Mill
Blabak, Mungkid, Central Java, Indonesia

PT Papertech Indonesia
Subang Mill
Subang, Jawa Barat, Indonesia

PT Papertech Indonesia
Unit II, Kabupaten Magelang
Kecamatan Mungkid, Kabupaten Magelang, Jawa Tengah, Indonesia

PT Papyrus Sakti
Bandung Mill
Banjaran, Bandung, West Java, Indonesia

PT Pelita Cengkareng Paper
Tangerang Mill
Cengkareng, Tangerang, West Java, Indonesia

PT Pindo Deli Pulp & Paper Mills
Karawang No. 1 (PT Pindo Deli Pulp & Paper Mills) Mill
Karawang, West Java, Indonesia

PT Pola Pulpindo Mantap
Lampung Mill
Lampung, Sumatra, Indonesia

PT Pura Nusapersada
Terban, Kudus Mill
Terban, Kudus, Central Java, Indonesia

PT Suparma, Tbk.
Surabaya Mill
Surabaya, East Java, Indonesia

PT Surabaya Agung Industri Pulp & Kertas
Driyorejo Mill
Gresik, East Java, Indonesia

PT Surya Pamenang
Kediri Mill
Kediri, East Java, Indonesia

PT Tri Daya Kreasi
Purwakarta Mill
Purwakarta, West Java, Indonesia

PT Wirajaya Packindo
Tangerang Mill
Tangerang, West Java, Indonesia

Pucaro Elektro-Isolierstoffe GmbH
Roigheim Mill
Roigheim, Germany

Boxboard/cartonboard

Pukhovichskaya Paperboard Mill
Pukhovichskaya Paperboard Mill
Svetly Bor, Pukhovichskiy rayon, Minskaya obl., Belarus

QF MEX, S.A. de C.V.
Iztapalapa Mill
Iztapalapa, México, D.F., Mexico

Rainbow Papers Ltd.
Mehsana Mill
Mehsana, Gujarat, India

Rakta, General Co. for Paper Industry
Rakta Mill
Alexandria, Iskanderiya, Egypt

Rama Paper Mills Ltd.
Bijnor Mill
Kiratpur, Bijnor, Uttar Pradesh, India

Raman Boards Ltd.
Mysore Mill
Mysore, Karnataka, India

Rampal Paper Mills
Dist. Malda Mill
Dist. Malda, West Bengal, India

Räpina Paberivabrik AS
Räpina Mill
Räpina, Estonia

Rayevka
Rayevka Mill
Rayevka, Minskaya obl., Belarus

RDM Blendecques SAS
Blendecques Mill
Blendecques, Saint Omer Cedex, France

Reliable Paper (India) Pvt. Ltd.
Surat Mill
Bardoli, Taluka - Mahuva, Surat, Gujarat, India

Remco Paper & Board Industries Pvt. Ltd.
Valsad Mill
Valsad, Gujarat, India

Rengo Co., Ltd.
Amagasaki Mill
Kuise, Amagasaki-shi, Hyogo Pref., Japan

Rengo Co., Ltd.
Tonegawa Mill
Bando-shi, Ibaraki Pref., Japan

Rengo Co., Ltd.
Yashio Mill
Yashio-shi, Saitama Pref., Japan

Reno De Medici Arnsberg GmbH
Arnsberg Mill
Arnsberg, Germany

Reno De Medici SpA
Ovaro Mill
Ovaro, Udine, Italy

Reno De Medici SpA
Santa Giustina Mill
Santa Giustina Bellunese, Belluno, Italy

Reno De Medici SpA
Villa Santa Lucia Mill
Villa Santa Lucia, Frosinone, Italy

Reno De Medici, Iberica S.L.U.
Almazán Mill
Almazán, Soria, Spain

Republic Paperboard Co. LLC
Lawton Mill
Lawton, Oklahoma, United States

RockTenn Co.
Battle Creek Mill
Battle Creek, Michigan, United States

RockTenn Co.
Chattanooga Mill
Chattanooga, Tennessee, United States

RockTenn Co.
Cincinnati Mill
Cincinnati, Ohio, United States

RockTenn Co.
Dallas Mill
Dallas, Texas, United States

RockTenn Co.
Demopolis Mill
Demopolis, Alabama, United States

RockTenn Co.
Eaton Mill
Eaton, Indiana, United States

RockTenn Co.
La Tuque Mill
La Tuque, Quebec, Canada

RockTenn Co.
Saint Paul Mill
Saint Paul, Minnesota, United States

RockTenn Co.
Stroudsburg Mill
Delaware Water Gap, Pennsylvania, United States

Rogan Paperboard Mill
Rogan Mill
Rogan, Kharkovskaya Obl., Ukraine

Romiley Board Mill
Stockport Mill
Stockport, Greater Manchester, Cheshire, United Kingdom

Ruby Macons Ltd.
Vapi Mill
Vapi, Gujarat, India

Ruchira Papers Ltd.
Kala-Amb Mill
Kala-Amb, Himachal Pradesh, India

S.N. Paper Mills (P) Ltd.
Dist. Ludhiana Mill
Dist. Ludhiana, Punjab, India

Sabarmati Papers Limited
Aglo Mill
Dist. Mehsana, Gujarat, India

Sadeque Paper & Board Mills Ltd.
Kaliakoir, Gazipur Mill
Kaliakoir, Gazipur, Gazipur, Bangladesh

Saigon Paper
My Xuan II Mill
Tan Thanh Dist., Ba Ria - Vung Tau, Dong Nam Bo, Vietnam

Sanyo Itagami Kogyo KK
Okayama-shi Mill
Okayama-shi, Okayama Pref., Japan

Sappi Fine Paper Europe
Alfeld Mill
Alfeld (Leine), Germany

Saraswati Udyog India Ltd.
Namakkal Dist. Mill
Namakkal Dist., Tamil Nadu, India

Schumacher Packaging GmbH
Schwarzenberg Mill
Schwarzenberg, Germany

Seha Corporation
Hyunpoong Mill
Dalseong-gun, Daegu-si, Daegu-si, South Korea

Senapathy-Whiteley (P) Ltd.
Ramangram Mill
Ramangram, Karnataka, India

Seshasayee Paper & Boards Ltd.
Erode Mill
Erode, Tamil Nadu, India

Seven Hills Paperboard, LLC
Lynchburg Mill
Lynchburg, Virginia, United States

Sevenhills Papers (P) Ltd.
East Godavari Dist. Mill
East Godavari Dist., Andhra Pradesh, India

Severny Kommunar
Sivinskiy Mill
Severny Kommunar, Sivinskiy rayon, Perm Region, Russia

Severoceská papírna s.r.o.
Novosedlice Mill
Novosedlice, Czech Republic

Shaanxi Shenglong Paper Co., Ltd.
Baoji Mill
Baoji, Shaanxi, China

Shaanxi Xi-An Weiyangqu Efang Paperboard Co., Ltd.
Xi-An Mill
Xi-An, Shaanxi, China

Shandong Bohui Paper Industry Co., Ltd.
Zibo Mill
Zibo, Shandong, China

Shandong Dadi Paper Co., Ltd.
Taian Mill
Taian, Shandong, China

Shandong Huajin Paper Group
Jining Mill
Jining, Shandong, China

Shandong Jianghe Paper Co., Ltd.
Qihe Mill
Dezhou, Shandong, China

Shandong Qingdao Haiwang Paper Property Share Co., Ltd.
Qingdao Mill
Qingdao, Shandong, China

Boxboard/cartonboard

Shandong Sun Paper Industry Joint Stock Co., Ltd.
Yanzhou Mill
Yanzhou, Shandong, China

Shandong Taian Baichuan Paper Co., Ltd.
Taian Mill
Taian, Shandong, China

Shandong Texpack Paper Co., Ltd.
Dezhou Mill
Dezhou, Shandong, China

Shandong Weifang Huisheng Group
Weifang Mill
Weifang, Shandong, China

Shandong Zaozhuang Huarun Paper Co., Ltd.
Zaozhuang Mill
Zaozhuang, Shandong, China

Shanghai Jinfengyuan Paper (Shanghai) Co., Ltd.
Shanghai (Shanghai Jinfengyuan Paper) Mill
Shanghai, Shanghai, China

Shanxi QiangWei Paper Co., Ltd.
Jinzhong Mill
Jinzhong, Shanxi, China

Shihlin Paper Corp.
Yung An Mill
Hsin Wu, Taoyuan County, Taiwan

Shinpoong Paper Mfg. Co., Ltd.
Pyongtaek Mill
Pyeongtaek-si, Gyeonggi-do, South Korea

Shree Jee Paper Industries
Nagda Mill
Nagda, Madhya Pradesh, India

Shree Papers Ltd.
East Godavari Mill
East Godavari, Andhra Pradesh, India

Shree Saptashringi Board & Paper Mill (P) Ltd.
Dist. Aurangabad Mill
Dist. Aurangabad, Maharashtra, India

Shree Swami Harigiri Paper Mills Ltd.
Bharuch Mill
Dist. Bharuch, Gujarat, India

Shreyas Papers Pvt. Ltd.
Dandeli Mill
Dandeli, Karnataka, India

Sichuan Longchang Yuhong Paper Co., Ltd.
Neijiang Mill
Neijiang, Sichuan, China

Sichuan Yibin Lantian Paper
Yibin Mill
Yibin, Sichuan, China

Sicomo S.A.L.
Kab-Elias, Bekaa Mill
Kab-Elias, Bekaa, Lebanon

Sidharth Papers Ltd.
Kashipur Mill (Unit 2)
Kashipur, Uttarakhand, India

SIPCO-Soc. Ind. de Papier et de Carton Ondule SAL
Beirut Mill
Kfarchima, Beirut, Lebanon

Sirpur Paper Mills Ltd.
Adilabad Mill
Sirpur-Kaghaznagar, Dist. Adilabad, Andhra Pradesh, India

Skjern Papirfabrik A/S
Skjern Mill
Skjern, Denmark

Smurfit Cartón y Papel de México S.A. de C.V.
Cerro Gordo Mill
Santa Clara Coatitla, Ecatepec de Morelos, Edo. de México, Mexico

Smurfit Cartón y Papel de México S.A. de C.V.
Los Reyes Mill
Col. Los Reyes Iztacala, Tlalnepantla, México, D.F., Mexico

Smurfit Kappa Baden Karton GmbH
Gernsbach Mill
Gernsbach, Germany

Smurfit Kappa Cartón de Colombia SA
Yumbo Mill
Cali, Valle de Cauca, Colombia

Smurfit Kappa Cartón de Venezuela S.A.
Caracas Mill
Petare, Caracas, Edo. Miranda, Venezuela

Smurfit Kappa Cartón de Venezuela S.A.
Valencia Mill
Valencia, Edo. Carabobo, Venezuela

Smurfit Kappa Haupt Papier- und Pappenfabrik GmbH & Co. KG
Diemelstadt-Wrexen Mill
Diemelstadt-Wrexen, Germany

Smurfit Kappa Herzberger Papierfabrik GmbH
Herzberg Mill
Herzberg am Harz, Germany

Smurfit Kappa Papier & Kartonfabrik Hoya
Hoya Mill
Hoya/Weser, Germany

Smurfit Kappa Solid Board BV
Coevorden Mill
Coevorden, Netherlands

Smurfit Kappa Solid Board BV
Hoogkerk Mill
Groningen-Hoogkerk, Netherlands

Smurfit Kappa Solid Board BV
Nieuweschans Mill
Nieuweschans, Netherlands

Smurfit Kappa Solid Board BV
Oude Pekela Mill
Oude Pekela, Netherlands

SOLICAR-Société Libanaise de Carton
Beirut Mill
Beirut, Lebanon

Solid Containers Ltd.
Thane Mill
Thane, Maharashtra, India

Song Lam Paper Joint-Stock Co.
Hung Nguyen Dist. Mill
Hung Nguyen Dist., Vietnam

Sonoco Alcore-Demolli srl
Ciriè Mill
Ciriè, Turin, Italy

Sonoco Board Mills Ltd.
Stainland Mill
Halifax, West Yorkshire, United Kingdom

Sonoco de Colombia Ltda
Cali Mill
Cali, Valle de Cauca, Colombia

Sonoco de México, S.A. de C.V.
Santa Clara Mill
Santa Clara Ecatepec, Edo. de México, Mexico

Sonoco do Brasil Ltda.
Londrina Mill
Londrina, Paraná, Brazil

Sonoco Hellas
Stavrohori Mill
Stavrohori, Kilkis, Greece

Sonoco Ltd.
Brantford Mill
Brantford, Ontario, Canada

Sonoco Ltd.
Trent Valley Mill
Glen Miller, Ontario, Canada

Sonoco Paper France SAS
Schweighouse Mill
Schweighouse sur Moder, France

Sonoco Products Co.
City of Industry Mill
City of Industry, California, United States

Sonoco Products Co.
Hartsville Mill
Hartsville, South Carolina, United States

Sonoco Products Co.
Holyoke Mill
Holyoke, Massachusetts, United States

Sonoco Products Co.
Hutchinson Mill
Hutchinson, Kansas, United States

Sonoco Products Co.
Menasha Mill
Menasha, Wisconsin, United States

Sonoco Products Co.
Newport Mill
Newport, Tennessee, United States

Sonoco Products Co.
Richmond Mill
Richmond, Virginia, United States

Sonoco Products Co.
Sumner Mill
Sumner, Washington, United States

Sonoco-Alcore Oy
Karhula Board Mill
Karhula, Finland

Boxboard/cartonboard

South East Asia Paper Ltd.
Bankae Mill
Bangkae Nua, Bankae, Bangkok, Thailand

Spartak
Shklov Mill
Shklov, Mogilev Region, Belarus

Sree Raja Rajeswari Paper Mills Ltd
Bapulapadu Branch
Krishna, Andhra Pradesh, India

Sree Sakthi Paper Mills Ltd.
Chalakkudy Mill
Kanjirappilly, Chalakkudy, Kerala, India

Sripathi Paper & Boards Pvt.Ltd
Sivakasi Mill
Sivakasi, Tamil Nadu, India

St. Petersburg Paper Mill Goznak
St. Petersburg Mill
St. Petersburg, Russia

Stallion Duplex (P) Ltd.
Karnal Mill
Karnal, Haryana, India

Stora Enso Printing and Reading
Uetersen Mill
Uetersen, Germany

Stora Enso Renewable Packaging
Barcelona Mill
Castellbisbal, Catalonia, Spain

Stora Enso Renewable Packaging
Fors Mill
Fors, Sweden

Stora Enso Renewable Packaging
Imatra Mills (Kaukopää & Tainionkoski)
Imatra, Finland

Stora Enso Renewable Packaging
Ingerois Mill
Kouvola, Finland

Stora Enso Renewable Packaging
Skoghall Mill
Skoghall, Sweden

Strathcona Paper LP
Napanee Mill
Napanee, Ontario, Canada

Sun-Ka Kagit ve Karton San. ve Tic. Ltd. sti
Çorum Mill
Çorum, Turkey

Supatrtanagorn Paper Mill Co., Ltd.
Angtong Mill
Posa District, Ang Thong Province, Thailand

Supreme Coated Board Mills Pvt. Ltd.
Vembakottai Mill
Sivakasi, Tamil Nadu, India

Surat Board & Paper Mills Pvt. Ltd.
Surat Mill
Surat, Gujarat, India

Suzano Papel e Celulose S.A.
Ripasa II Mill
Embu, São Paulo, Brazil

Suzano Papel e Celulose S.A.
Suzano Mill
Suzano, São Paulo, Brazil

Svetlogorskiy Pulp and Board Mill
Svetlogorsk Mill
Svetlogorsk, Gomel Region, Belarus

Sweetwater Paperboard
Austell Mill
Austell, Georgia, United States

Tacoma Paperboard
Tacoma Mill
Tacoma, Washington, United States

Taishan Gypsum Co., Ltd.
Taian Mill
Taian, Shandong, China

Takasago Paper Co., Ltd.
Mitsukaido-shi Mill
Mitsukaido-shi, Ibaraki Pref., Japan

Tama Paperboard
Tama Mill
Tama, Iowa, United States

Tejas Infinitas
Camaguey Mill
Camaguey, Camaguey, Cuba

Tektura Sp. z o.o.
Mikolow Mill
Mikolow, Poland

Tembec Inc.
Temiscaming Mill
Temiscaming, Quebec, Canada

Tenma Paper Mills (Thailand) Co., Ltd.
Pakkred Mill
Pakkred, Nonthaburi, Thailand

Teppatana Paper Mill Co., Ltd.
Amphur Muan Mill
Amphur Muang, Phathum Thani, Thailand

Thai Card Board Co Ltd.
Sampran Mill
Sampran, Nakhon Pathom, Thailand

Thai Development Paper Co., Ltd.
Samut Prakan Mill
Amphur Muang, Samut Prakan, Samut Prakarn, Thailand

Thai Product Paper Mill Co., Ltd.
Chachoengsao Mill
Amphur Muang, Chachoengsao, Thailand

Thai Union Paper Industry Co., Ltd.
Wangsala Mill
Tha Muang Distr., Kanchanaburi, Thailand

Thai Union Paper Public Co., Ltd.
Prapradaeng Mill
Prapradaeng, Samut Prakarn, Thailand

The Eastern Industrial Co., Ltd.
Pathumthani Mill
Amphur Muang, Pathumthani, Thailand

The West Coast Paper Mills Ltd.
Dandeli Mill
Dandeli, Uttara Kannada, Karnataka, India

Three M Paper Mfg. Co. Pvt. Ltd.
Ratnagiri Mill
Ratnagiri, Maharashtra, India

Tirthak Paper Mill Pvt. Ltd.
Morbi Mill
Morbi, Gujarat, India

Titagarh Paper Mills Co. Ltd.
No. 1 Mill
Titagarh, West Bengal, India

Tokushu Tokai Paper Co., Ltd.
Shimada Mill
Shimada-shi, Shizuoka Pref., Japan

TOP S.A.
Katowice Mill
Katowice, Poland

Trakya Kagit San ve TIC. A.S.
Tekirdag Mill
Tekirdag, Tekirdag, Turkey

Trio Paper Mills Sdn. Bhd.
Simpang Ampat Mill
Simpang Ampat, Pulau Pinang, Malaysia

Trupal S.A.
Evitamiento Mill
El Agustino, Lima, Lima, Peru

Tullis Russell Papermakers Ltd.
Markinch Mill
Markinch, Glenrothes, Scotland, United Kingdom

Tulsi Paper Mills Pvt. Ltd.
Bardoli Mill
Bardoli, Surat, Gujarat, India

Tung Chi Paper Corp.
Lung Ching Mill
Lung Ching District, Taichung City, Taiwan

U.S. Paper Mills Corp.
De Pere Mill
De Pere, Wisconsin, United States

UCAL Donusen Kagit San ve Tic A.S.
Sirapinar Mill
Sirapinar, Umraniye, Istanbul, Turkey

Umka AD, Fabrika Kartona
Umka Mill
Umka, Belgrade, Serbia

Union Paper Mills
Dubai Mill
Dubai, United Arab Emirates

United Paper Boards Limited
Patna Mill
Patna, Bihar, India

United States Gypsum Co.
Galena Park Mill
Galena Park, Texas, United States

United States Gypsum Co.
North Kansas City Mill
North Kansas City, Missouri, United States

United States Gypsum Co.
Oakfield Mill
Oakfield, New York, United States

UPP Pulp & Paper (M) Sdn Bhd
Batang Berjuntai Mill
Ijok, Batang Berjuntai, Selangor Darul Ehsan, Malaysia

Boxboard/cartonboard

Vadbhag Paper & Board Mills (P) Ltd.
Hooghly Mill
Hooghly, West Bengal, India

Valaichenai Paper Mills
Valaichenai Mill
Valaichenai, Sri Lanka

Valley Converting Co.
Toronto Mill
Toronto, Ohio, United States

Vanson Paper Industrial Corp.
Valenzuela Mill
Marulas, Valenzuela, Metro Manila, Philippines

Venkraft Paper Mills Private Ltd.
Hosur Mill
Hosur, Tamil Nadu, India

Viet Tri Paper Company
Viet Tri Mill
Viet Tri City, Phú Tho Province, Vietnam

Vishal Paper Mills Ltd.
Malerkotla Mill
Malerkotla, Punjab, India

Visy Pulp & Paper
Coolaroo Mill
Campbellfield, Victoria, Australia

Visy Pulp & Paper
VPP2, Reservoir Mill
Reservoir, Victoria, Australia

VPK Paper NV
Dendermonde Mill
Dendermonde, Belgium

Vrancart SA
Adjud Mill
Adjud, Vrancea, Romania

W & M Pappen GmbH & Co. KG
Elbrinxen Mill
Lügde / Elbrinxen, Germany

WARTER - Fabryka Papieru i Tektury
Tarnowka Mill
Tarnowka, Poland

Weidmann Electrical Technology AG
Rapperswil Mill
Rapperswil, Switzerland

Weidmann Electrical Technology Inc.
Saint Johnsbury Mill
Saint Johnsbury, Vermont, United States

Weidmann Whiteley Ltd.
Otley Mill
Otley, West Yorkshire, United Kingdom

Weyerhaeuser Co.
Longview Mill
Longview, Washington, United States

White Pigeon Paper Co.
White Pigeon Mill
White Pigeon, Michigan, United States

Wisconsin Paperboard Corp.
Milwaukee Mill
Milwaukee, Wisconsin, United States

Yasar Ambalaj Kagit Bobin San. ve Tic. A.S.
Malatya Mill
Malatya, Turkey

Yenisey Pulp and Paper Mill Inc.
Yenisey Pulp and Paper Mill
Krasnoyarsk, Russia

Youngpoong Paper Mfg. Co., Ltd.
Pyeongtaek-si Mill
Pyeongtaek-si, Gyeonggi-do, South Korea

Yuantong Paper (Shandong) Co., Ltd.
Zaozhuang Mill
Zaozhuang, Shandong, China

Yuen Foong Yu Packaging Inc.
Hsin Wu Mill
Hsin Wu, Taoyuan County, Taiwan

Zaman Paper and Board Mills Ltd.
Sheikhupura Mill
Sheikhupura, Punjab, Pakistan

Zamindara Paper & Board Mill Ltd.
Sheikhupura Mill
Sheikhupura, Punjab, Pakistan

ZAO Altaykrovlya
Novoaltaysk Mill
Novoaltaysk, Altaisky Kraý, Russia

ZAO International Paper
Svetogorsk Mill
Svetogorsk, Leningrad Region, Russia

ZAO MPK KRZ - Multibranch Production Company KRZ
Ryazan Mill
Ryazan, Russia

ZAO Suoyarvi Paperboard Mill
Suoyarvi Mill
Suoyarvi, Karelia, Russia

Zhejiang Fuyang Chunsheng Paper Co., Ltd.
Fuyang Mill
Fuyang, Zhejiang, China

Zhejiang Fuyang City Huitai Paper Co., Ltd.
Fuyang Mill
Fuyang, Zhejiang, China

Zhejiang Fuyang City Huitai Paper Co., Ltd.
Fuyang Mill
Fuyang, Zhejiang, China

Zhejiang Fuyang Dongcheng Paper Co., Ltd.
Fuyang Mill
Fuyang, Zhejiang, China

Zhejiang Fuyang Feima Paper Co., Ltd.
Fuyang Mill
Fuyang, Zhejiang, China

Zhejiang Fuyang Futai Feifeng Paper Co., Ltd.
Fuyang Mill
Fuyang, Zhejiang, China

Zhejiang Fuyang Gaoyang Paper Co., Ltd.
Fuyang Mill
Fuyang, Zhejiang, China

Zhejiang Fuyang Huali Paper Co., Ltd.
Fuyang Mill
Fuyang, Zhejiang, China

Zhejiang Fuyang Hualong Paper Co., Ltd.
Fuyang Mill
Fuyang, Zhejiang, China

Zhejiang Fuyang Huatian Paper Co., Ltd.
Fuyang Mill
Fuyang, Zhejiang, China

Zhejiang Fuyang Jin Xin Paper Co., Ltd.
Fuyang Mill
Fuyang, Zhejiang, China

Zhejiang Fuyang Kangnan Paper Co., Ltd.
Fuyang Mill
Fuyang, Zhejiang, China

Zhejiang Fuyang Lingtai Paper Co., Ltd.
Fuyang Mill
Fuyang, Zhejiang, China

Zhejiang Fuyang Maoyuan Paper Co., Ltd.
Fuyang Mill
Fuyang, Zhejiang, China

Zhejiang Fuyang Nanfa Paper Co., Ltd.
Fuyang Mill
Fuyang, Zhejiang, China

Zhejiang Fuyang Runtong Paper Co., Ltd.
Fuyang Mill
Fuyang, Zhejiang, China

Zhejiang Fuyang Shangyou Paper Industry Co., Ltd.
Fuyang Mill
Fuyang, Zhejiang, China

Zhejiang Fuyang Sunshi Paper Co., Ltd.
Fuyang Mill
Fuyang, Zhejiang, China

Zhejiang Fuyang Xinyuan Paper Co., Ltd.
Fuyang Mill
Fuyang, Zhejiang, China

Zhejiang Gaoyang Paper Co., Ltd.
Fuyang Mill
Fuyang, Zhejiang, China

Zhejiang Hangzhou Banqiao Paper Co., Ltd.
Fuyang Mill
Fuyang, Zhejiang, China

Zhejiang Hangzhou Dazhong Paper Co., Ltd.
Fuyang Mill
Fuyang, Zhejiang, China

Boxboard/cartonboard

Zhejiang Hangzhou Dongda Paper Co., Ltd.
Fuyang Mill
Fuyang, Zhejiang, China

Zhejiang Hangzhou Fuyang Jinying Industry Co., Ltd.
Fuyang Mill
Fuyang, Zhejiang, China

Zhejiang Hangzhou Guofeng Paper Co., Ltd.
Fuyang Mill
Fuyang, Zhejiang, China

Zhejiang Hangzhou Haichen Paper Co., Ltd.
Fuyang Mill
Fuyang, Zhejiang, China

Zhejiang Hangzhou Huasheng Paper Co., Ltd.
Fuyang Mill
Fuyang, Zhejiang, China

Zhejiang Hangzhou Jintai Paper Co., Ltd.
Fuyang Mill
Fuyang, Zhejiang, China

Zhejiang Hangzhou Ruixing Paper Co., Ltd.
Fuyang Mill
Fuyang, Zhejiang, China

Zhejiang Hangzhou Xushi Paper Co., Ltd.
Fuyang Mill
Fuyang, Zhejiang, China

Zhejiang Hangzhou Yinfa Paper Co., Ltd.
Fuyang Mill
Fuyang, Zhejiang, China

Zhejiang Hangzhou Yuanda Paper Co., Ltd.
Fuyang Mill
Fuyang, Zhejiang, China

Zhejiang Hangzhou Zhongyi Paper Co., Ltd.
Fuyang Mill
Fuyang, Zhejiang, China

Zhejiang Hongsheng Paper Co., Ltd.
Fuyang (Zhejiang Hongsheng Paper) Mill
Fuyang, Zhejiang, China

Zhejiang Huaxin Paper Co., Ltd.
Fuyang Mill
Fuyang, Zhejiang, China

Zhejiang Huayuan Paper Co., Ltd.
Fuyang Mill
Fuyang, Zhejiang, China

Zhejiang Jindong Paper Co., Ltd.
Fuyang Mill
Fuyang, Zhejiang, China

Zhejiang Jingxing Paper Joint Stock Co., Ltd.
Pinghu Mill
Pinghu, Zhejiang, China

Zhejiang Lanniao Paper Co., Ltd.
Fuyang Mill
Fuyang, Zhejiang, China

Zhejiang Ningbo Asia Pulp and Paper Co., Ltd.
Beilun (Zhejiang Ningbo Asia Pulp and Paper) Mill
Xiaogang, Ningbo, Zhejiang, China

Zhejiang Ningbo Zhonghua Paper
Ningbo (Zhejiang Ningbo Zhonghua Paper) Mill
Ningbo, Zhejiang, China

Zhejiang Sanxing Paper Co., Ltd.
Fuyang Mill
Fuyang, Zhejiang, China

Zhejiang Tianting Paper Co., Ltd.
Jinhua Mill
Jinhua, Zhejiang, China

Zhejiang Wanxin Paper Co., Ltd.
Fuyang Mill
Fuyang, Zhejiang, China

Zhejiang Wenbo Paper Co., Ltd.
Fuyang (Zhejiang Wenbo Paper) Mill
Fuyang, Zhejiang, China

Zhejiang Wenfeng Paper Co., Ltd.
Fuyang Mill
Fuyang, Zhejiang, China

Zhejiang Wuxing Paper Co., Ltd
Quzhou Mill
Quzhou, Zhejiang, China

Zhejiang Xianglong Paper Co., Ltd.
Fuyang (Zhejiang Xianglong) Mill
Fuyang, Zhejiang, China

Zhejiang Yiwu City Huachuan Paper Co., Ltd.
Yiwu Mill
Yiwu, Zhejiang, China

Zhejiang Yiwu City YiNan Paper Co., Ltd.
Yiwu Mill
Yiwu, Zhejiang, China

Zhejiang Yongjin Paper Co., Ltd.
Fuyang Mill
Fuyang, Zhejiang, China

Zhejiang Yongtai Paper Group Co., Ltd.
Fuyang Mill
Fuyang, Zhejiang, China

Zhejiang Zhengda Holding Group Co., Ltd.
Fuyang Mill
Fuyang, Zhejiang, China

Zhenjiang Dadong Pulp & Paper Co. Ltd.
Zhenjiang Mill
Zhenjiang, Jiangsu, China

Zhydachiv Pulp & Paper Mill
Zhydachiv Mill
Zhydachiv, Lviv obl., Ukraine

Lockwood-Post
Directory of Pulp & Paper Mills

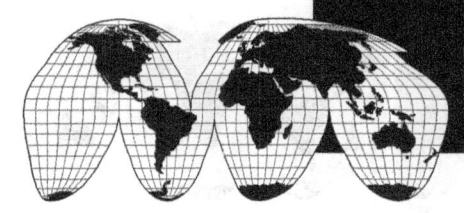

Measurements

Imperial units of measurement are used in the U.S. mill entries in this directory. Metric units of measurement are used in mill entries of all other countries.

Abbreviations:

Ⓗ preceding company denotes the company's headquarters location.
Ⓜ preceding company denotes a mill location.
mt/y = metric tonnes per year
st/y = short tons per year
admt/y = air dried metric tonnes per year
adst/y = air dried short tons per year
in = inches
MWh/d = Megawatt hours per day

C = chlorination
E = caustic extraction
H = hypochlorite
D = chlorine dioxide
O = oxygen
P = peroxide
R = reductive agent
Z = ozone

Grade list

PAPER
GRAPHIC PAPER
 Newsprint
 Uncoated woodfree/freesheet (WFU/UCFS)
 Uncoated mechanical/groundwood
 Coated woodfree/freesheet
 Coated mechanical/groundwood
TISSUE
PACKAGING PAPERS
 Kraft Papers
 Bag/Wrapping Papers
 Recycled Packaging Papers
SPECIALTY AND INDUSTRIAL
 Release Liner
 Filter Paper
 Other Specialty and Industrial

PAPERBOARD
CONTAINERBOARD
 Linerboard
  Kraftliner
  Recycled Linerboard
 Corrugating medium/fluting
  Semichemical medium
  Recycled medium
BOXBOARD/CARTONBOARD
OTHER PAPERBOARD

PULP
CHEMICAL PULP
 Bleached Softwood Kraft Pulp
 Bleached Hardwood Kraft Pulp
 Unbleached Kraft Pulp
 Bleached Fluff Pulp
 Sulfite Pulp

MECHANICAL PULP
 Stone Groundwood Pulp
 Pressurized Groundwood Pulp
 Refiner Mechanical Pulp
 Thermomechanical Pulp
 Chemithermomechanical Pulp (CTMP)
 Alkaline peroxide mechanical pulp (APMP)
OTHER PULP
 Semichemical pulp
 Dissolving pulp
 Nonwood pulp
RECYCLED PULPING

For a full list of terms commonly used in the industry, please use the Paper Toolkit at http://www.risiinfo.com/toolcontent?toolkit=paperhelp Please also refer to the help sections from Asset Data base: http://www.risiinfo.com/millassets/help.html

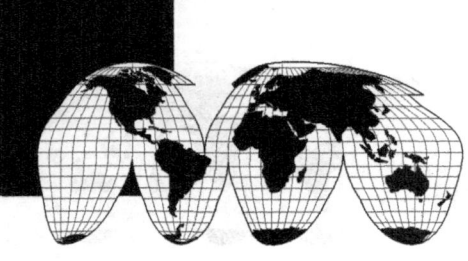

Country Index

Country/State/Province .... Index

NORTH AMERICA
United States
- Alabama 1
- Arizona 5
- Arkansas 6
- California 7
- Connecticut 10
- Florida 13
- Georgia 16
- Idaho 24
- Illinois 25
- Indiana 27
- Iowa 28
- Kansas 28
- Kentucky 28
- Louisiana 30
- Maine 32
- Maryland 36
- Massachusetts 37
- Michigan 41
- Minnesota 45
- Mississippi 47
- Missouri 49
- Nevada 49
- New Hampshire 49
- New Jersey 51
- New Mexico 52
- New York 52
- North Carolina 59
- Ohio 62
- Oklahoma 66
- Oregon 67
- Pennsylvania 69
- South Carolina 74
- Tennessee 77
- Texas 81
- Utah 85
- Vermont 85
- Virginia 85
- Washington 88
- Wisconsin 95

Canada
- Alberta 105
- British Columbia 107
- Manitoba 113
- New Brunswick 113
- Newfoundland and Labrador 115
- Nova Scotia 115
- Ontario 116
- Quebec 122
- Sasketchewan 135

EUROPE
- Albania 137
- Austria 137
- Belarus 146
- Belgium 149
- Bosnia & Herzegovina 152
- Bulgaria 153
- Croatia 155
- Czech Republic 156
- Denmark 160
- Estonia 160
- Finland 161
- France 176
- Germany 199
- Greece 237
- Hungary 241
- Ireland 242
- Italy 243
- Latvia 275
- Lithuania 275
- Macedonia 276
- Netherlands 276
- Norway 281
- Poland 284
- Portugal 295
- Romania 300
- Russia 303
- San Marino 324
- Serbia 325
- Slovakia 326
- Slovenia 328
- Spain 329
- Sweden 347
- Switzerland 363
- Ukraine 366
- United Kingdom 372

ASIA AND OCEANIA
- Armenia 385
- Australia 385
- Azerbaijan 389
- Bahrain 389
- Bangladesh 389
- China 393
  - Anhui 393
  - Beijing 397
  - Chongqing 398
  - Fujian 399
  - Gansu 405
  - Guangdong 406
  - Guangxi 425
  - Guizhou 435
  - Hainan 435
  - Hebei 436
  - Heilongjiang 452
  - Henan 454
  - Hubei 465
  - Hunan 468
  - Inner Mongolia 472
  - Jiangsu 472
  - Jiangxi 481
  - Jilin 482
  - Liaoning 483
  - Ningxia 486
  - Shaanxi 487
  - Shandong 488
  - Shanghai 511
  - Shanxi 512
  - Sichuan 513
  - Tianjin 520
  - Xinjiang 521
  - Yunnan 523
  - Zhejiang 525
- Fiji 550
- Georgia 550
- Hong Kong 550
- India 552
- Indonesia 625
- Iran 644
- Israel 648
- Japan 650
- Jordan 690
- Kazakhstan 691
- Kuwait 692
- Kyrgyzstan 692
- Laos 693
- Lebanon 693
- Malaysia 694
- Myanmar 699
- Nepal 700
- New Zealand 700
- Oman 702
- Pakistan 702
- Philippines 709
- Saudi Arabia 712
- Singapore 714
- South Korea 714
- Sri Lanka 729
- Syria 729
- Taiwan 731
- Thailand 743
- Turkey 755
- Turkmenistan 767
- United Arab Emirates 767
- Uzbekistan 768
- Vietnam 769

LATIN AMERICA
- Argentina 781
- Bolivia 792
- Brazil 793
- Cayman Islands 832
- Chile 832
- Colombia 838
- Costa Rica 843
- Cuba 843
- Dominican Republic 844
- Ecuador 844
- El Salvador 846
- Guatemala 846
- Mexico 847
- Panama 863
- Paraguay 864
- Peru 865
- Trinidad and Tobago 869
- Uruguay 869
- Venezuela 871

AFRICA
- Algeria 875
- Egypt 876
- Ethiopia 883
- Ghana 883
- Kenya 883
- Morocco 885
- Nigeria 887
- South Africa 888
- Tanzania 898
- Tunisia 898
- Uganda 900
- Zambia 900
- Zimbabwe 901

General Index

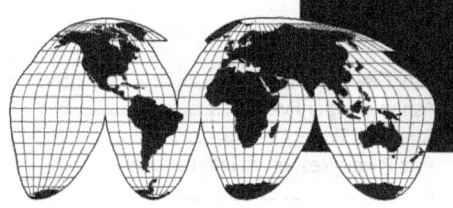

Alphabetical listing of pulp and paper company executive offices, headquarters, pulp and paper mills.

3M Tilton..49

A

Aarepapier AG..363
Abbaspel Indústria e Comércio de Papéis Ltda.......................................793
A.B.C.D. Cartiere CA..............................871
ABC Tissue Products Pty. Ltd................385
Abelan Board and Packaging Solutions................................217, 329, 330
Abhishek Industries Ltd........................552
A & B Paper Ltd.....................................284
Absormex CMPC Tissue S.A. de CV........847
Absorpelsa Papeles Absorventes S.A....844
Abu Dhabi National Paper Mill..............767
Adami S.A. Madeiras..............................793
Adda Ondulati SpA................................243
Adischevskaya Board Mill......................303
Aditya Birla Group..................................553
Afri Paper...898
Afsons Industrial Corporation Ltd........553
Agarwal Duplex Board Mills Ltd............553
Águas Negras S.A. Ind. de Papel...........793
Agustín Barral, S.A.................................331
Ahlstrom Binzhou..................................488
Ahlstrom Brasil Indústria e Comércio de Papéis Especiais Ltda..........................793
Ahlstrom Chirnside Ltd..................372, 373
Ahlstrom Corporation Oy......................161
Ahlstrom Engine Filtration, L.L.C............25
Ahlstrom Filtration LLC.....................28, 69
Ahlstrom Korea Co., Ltd.........................714
Ahlstrom Osnabrück GmbH..................199
Ahlstrom Packaging SA..........................176
Ahlstrom Specialties SA.........................177
Ahlstrom Tampere Oy...........................162
Ahlstrom Turin SpA...............................243
Ahlstrom Yulong Specialty Paper Company Ltd...488
Aigle Paper Manufacturing Company - A.P.M.C..875
Ajanta Paper & General Products Ltd...553
Ajin Paper Mfg. Co. Ltd..........................714
Akabira Paper Corporation K.K.............652
Akasan Adana Kagit San ve Tic. Ltd. Sti....755
Ak Gida San. ve Tic. A.S.........................755
Akshat Papers Ltd..................................554

Alabama Paper Products, LLC...................1
Al Alamiyya Paper Mill...........................690
Alamigeon SA...177
Al Arouba Paper Co. M. Farghaly & Co...876
Alas Doradas S.A. de C.V........................846
Alatyrskaya Paper Mill...........................304
Al Bardi Paper Mill Co. (S.A.E.)...............876
Albatros Paper Mill................................366
Albay Agro Industrial Development Corp. (Alindeco)...709
Albayrak Sirketler Grubu.......................755
Alberta Newsprint Co. Ltd.....................105
Alberta-Pacific Forest Industries Inc. (Al-Pac)...105
Albertin Paperboard & Paper Mill.........146
Albert Köhler GmbH & Co. KG...............210
Aleksinskaya Board & Paper Mill, CJSC....304
Alex Converta Co. SAE (Handy).............877
Alier S.A..330
Al Keena Hygienic Paper Mill Co. Ltd....690
Alkim Kagit Sanayi ve Ticaret A.S..........755
Allard Emballages..................................177
Almaty Maolin Paper.............................691
Alpes Celulose e Papéis Ltda.................794
Al Sindian Paper Mill Co. S.A.E..............876
Al Snobar Hygienic Paper Mill...............690
Alta Papéis Ltda.....................................794
Alto Paraná S.A......................................781
Al Zeina Tissue Mill................................876
Amal..692, 693
Amaravathi Sri Venkatesa Paper Mills Ltd....554
Ambro SA Suceava.................................300
A. Merati - Cartiera di Laveno SpA........261
American Eagle Paper Mills Inc...............69
Amol Paper Mills (P) Ltd........................554
Amritsar Pulp & Board Mills (P) Ltd......554
AMS - Gomà Camps S.A........................295
Anand Duplex/Triplex Board Limited....554, 555
Anand Tissues Ltd.................................555
Ananta Paper Mills Pvt. Ltd...................389
An Binh Paper Corporation-ABPAPER...769
Angren Pack...768
An Hoa Paper and Pulp Factory............769
Anhui Bilun Tissue Paper Co. Ltd..........393
Anhui Chaohu Jinhe Paper Co. Ltd........393
Anhui Hefei Jinzhong Paper Co. Ltd......393
Anhui Hefei Xingdong Paper Co., Ltd....393, 394
Anhui HengAn Wuhu Paper Co., Ltd.....394
Anhui Huabon Specialty Paper Co. Ltd....396
Anhui Huatai Forest Pulp & Paper Co., Ltd..394
Anhui Huoshan County Chenfeng Paper Co., Ltd..394

Anhui Jing County Xuanzhi Mill............394
Anhui Jingfeng Paper Co., Ltd...............394
Anhui Kailai Paper Co., Ltd....................395
Anhui Linping Paper Co., Ltd.................395
Anhui Mikitoku Paper Co., Ltd..............395
Anhui Ningguo Zhaofeng Paper Co., Ltd....395
Anhui Shanying Paper Industry Co., Ltd....395
Anhui Shanying Paper No. 1 Mill..........395
Anhui Shanying Paper No. 2 Mill..........395
Anhui Snow Dragon Fiber Technology Co., Ltd................................396
Anhui Weilun Industry & Trade Co., Ltd....396
Anhui Winbon Gaosen Paper Manufacture Co., Ltd.............................396
Anji Huayingtai Paper Co., Ltd..............525
Anmol Products Ethiopia.......................883
Ansabo S.A...781
APC Paper Company, Inc........................50
APC Paper Company of New York, Inc....52
Apex Paper Mills....................................555
APO Pappenfabrik Apostelmühle GmbH....199
A.P. Paper Mills Ltd................................555
Appleton Coated LLC..............................95
Appvion, Inc.....................................70, 95
Arab Cardboard Mfg. Co........................690
Arab Company for Paper Product (Arapepco)...729
Arab Paper Manufacturing Co. Ltd. (Waraq)..712
Arbumprom-Kartontara, LLC................385
Arctic Paper Grycksbo AB.....................347
Arctic Paper Kostrzyn S.A......................285
Arctic Paper Mochenwangen GmbH....199
Arctic Paper Munkedals AB..................347
Arctic Paper S.A.....................................285
Argencraft S.A..781
Ariete Srl..244
Arjowiggins Chartham Ltd....................373
Arjowiggins Fine Papers Pty. Ltd..........373
Arjowiggins Le Bourray SAS..................178
Arjowiggins Ltda....................................794
Arjowiggins Papiers Couchés S.A.........178
Arjowiggins Rives SAS...........................179
Arjowiggins SAS............................178, 179
Arjowiggins Security B.V.......................276
Arjowiggins Security SAS......................179
Arjun Pulp And Paper (india) Private Limited..............................555, 556
Arkhangelsk Pulp & Paper Mill.............304
Arkhbum Tissue Group.........................305
Art Corporation.....................................901
Aryan Paper Mills Pvt. Ltd.....................556
AS Estonian Cell....................................160

Index

Ashi Dipi Paper Mills Pvt. Ltd. 556
Ashmita Paper Pvt. Ltd. 556
Asia Kraft Paper Co., Ltd. 743
Asia Pacific Resources International -
APRIL 714
Asia Paper Industrial Corp. 709
Asia Paper Mfg. Co., Ltd. 714, 715
Asia Papertec Inc. 715
Asia Pulp & Paper (APP) 625
Asia Symbol (Guangdong) Paper Co., Ltd. 409
Asia Symbol (Shandong) Pulp &
Paper Co., Ltd. 490
ASL Paper Mills 702
Astória Papéis Ltda. 794
Astron Paper & Board Ltd 556
Atas Paper (Pvt) Ltd. 703
Athena Paper Manufacturing Co., Ltd. ... 650
Athens Paper Mill SA 237
Atlantic Packaging Products Ltd. 116
Atlas Paper Mills LLC 13
Atrak Pulp & Paper Industry Company ... 644
Augusta Select Tissue, LLC 16
Aurangabad Paper Mills Ltd. 556, 557
Austell Boxboard 16
Australian Paper 385, 386
AV Cell Inc. 113
Avelino Bragagnolo S/A Indústria
e Comércio 794, 795
Aviretta GmbH 200
A. Vl. Koliopoulos S.A. Pako 238
AV Nackawic Inc. 113
AV Terrace Bay Pulp Inc. 116
Awade Pulp and Paper Mills Pvt. Ltd. 557
Awa Paper Manufacturing Co., Ltd. 650
Aylesford Newsprint Ltd. 373
Azumi Filter Paper Co., Ltd. 650
AZUR Papier 899

B

Bahia Specialty Cellulose S.A. ("BSC") 795
Bai Bang Paper Joint-stock Co., Ltd. 770
Baiersbronn Frischfaserkarton GmbH 200
Baikalskiy Pulp and Paper Mill (Baikal) ... 305
Baja Paper Mills 848
Balaji Cellulose Products Ltd. 557
Balaji Paper Mills 557
Balikesir Albayrak Kagit Fabrikasi 756
Balkrishna Industries Ltd. 557
Balkrishna Paper Mills Ltd. 557
Ballarpur Industries Ltd. (BILT) .557, 558, 559
Bangladesh Chemical Industries Corp. ... 389
Bangladesh Monospool Paper
Mfg. Co. Ltd. (MPMC) 390
Banglane Paper Mill Co., Ltd. 743
Bang Pa-In Paper Mill Industry Co., Ltd. .. 743
Banknote Paper Mill 367
Bank Note Paper Mill India
Private Limited 559
Bansi Pulp & Paper Mills Pvt. Ltd. 559

Banwari Paper Mills Ltd. 560
Baoda Paper 406
Baoding Aisen Paper Co., Ltd. 436
Baoding City Jinneng Sanitary
Products Co., Ltd. 436
Baoding Jinboshi Paper Co., Ltd. 436
Baoding Yazi Paper Co., Ltd. 436
Baoding Yusen Hygiene Products Co., Ltd 436
Baron-Well GmbH 200
Bartoli F.lli SpA 244
Bashundhara Paper Mills Ltd. 390
Bataan 2020 709
Bazargaon Paper & Pulp Mills Pvt. Ltd. ... 560
Bear Island Paper Co., LLC 85
Bedse Pulp Conversion
Industries (P) Ltd. 560
Beijing Paper Mill No. 7 Co., Ltd. 397
Beijing Vinda Paper (Beijing) Co., Ltd. 397
Beijing Xinghe Paper Co., Ltd. 397
BELIŠCE d.d. 155
Bellesbumprom 146
Belnatsionalservis 146
Beloit Box Board Co. 95
Belovo Paper Mill S.A. 153
Bel Papyrus Ltd 887
Benaion Indústria de Papel e
Celulose S.A. - Bipacel 795
Berli Jucker Cellox Ltd. 744
Bernard Dumas SAS 183
Best Paper Mills Pvt. Ltd. 560
Bhandari Deepak Industries Ltd 560
Bharat Papers Ltd. 560
Bhikusa Papers Pvt. Ltd. 561
Bignardi Indústria e Comércio
de Papéis e Artefatos Ltda. 795
BillerudKorsnäs AB ...347, 348, 349, 351, 374
BillerudKorsnäs Finland Oy 161, 162
Biltube Europe Ltd. 180
Bindal Papers Limited 561
Bindals Duplex Ltd. 561
Binh Minh Paper Company 770
Biocel Paskov a.s. 156
Biodeal Laboratories Pvt. Ltd.
(Paper Mill Div.) 561
Bio-PAPPEL International 52, 81
Bio-PAPPEL Kraft 849, 850
Bio-PAPPEL Printing 850
Bio-PAPPEL, S.A.B. de C.V. 848
Biwa Paper Mfg. Co., Ltd. 651
BL Bittar, Indústria de Papel 795
Blue Paper SAS 180
BN - Papel Catarinense Ltda. 795
Boise Paper 1, 24, 45, 88, 89
Bolloré Thin Papers 180
Bolton Hellas 237
Bom Pastor Indústria de Papel Ltda. 796
Bonet Madeiras e Papéis Ltda. 796
Bormio SpA 245
Borregaard ChemCell 281
Botou Longda Paper Co., Ltd. 436

BPM, Inc. 96
Brahmaputra Paper Pvt. Ltd. 561
Brason Indústria de Papéis
e Ondulados Ltda. 796
Bratsk Branch of Ilim Group 308
Brianskaya Paper Mill 305
Brigl & Bergmeister GmbH 137
Brücher GmbH, Pappen-
und Papierfabrik 200
BUKOCEL, a.s. 326
Bulleh Shah Packaging (Private)
Limited 703, 706
Burgo Ardennes 149
Burgo Group SpA 245, 246, 247, 248
Burrows Paper 47, 52, 53
Büttenpapierfabrik Gmund
GmbH & Co. KG 201

C

Caima-Indústria de Celulose S.A. 295
Calcarta S.R.L. 248
California Paperboard Corp. 7
Cambará S.A. - Produtos Florestais 796
Camose Srl 248, 249
Canfor Corp. 107
Canfor Pulp Ltd. 107, 108
Canlubang Pulp Mfg. Corp. 710
Canson SAS 180
Cape Waste Paper Pty. Ltd. 888
Capital Paper & Pulp Industries Ltd. 391
Caraustar Industries, Inc. 16
Cariboo Pulp & Paper Co. 108
Carl Macher GmbH & Co. KG 213
Carmen Tissue S.A.E. 877
Carotell Paperboard 74
Carta Fabril Ltda. 797
Carta Misr. 877
Carta Riedenburg GmbH 222
Cartaseta-Friedrich & Co. 363
Carter Holt Harvey Pulp & Paper 700, 701
Cartesar SpA 250
Carthage Specialty Paperboard 53, 54
Cartiera Bocci Ponte di Gemolano Srl 245
Cartiera Cama S.R.L. 248
Cartiera Capostrada SpA 249
Cartiera Carma Srl 249
Cartiera Carmenta 249
Cartiera Cerrone Francescantonio SpA .. 251
Cartiera Ciacci S.a. 324
Cartiera Confalone S.R.L. 252
Cartiera del Chiese SpA 251
Cartiera Della Basilica SRL 244
Cartiera dell' Adda SpA 243
Cartiera Delle Alpi S.r.l. 253
Cartiera del Vignaletto Srl 274
Cartiera di Bosco Marengo SpA 245
Cartiera di Cagliari Srl. 248
Cartiera di Carbonera SpA 249
Cartiera di Cologno SpA 252

Cartiera di Ferrara SpA ... 256
Cartiera di Guarcino S.p.A. ... 258
Cartiera di Momo SpA ... 262
Cartiera di Nave SpA ... 263
Cartiera di Nebbiuno S.R.L. ... 263
Cartiera di Ponzano Srl ... 266
Cartiera di Porporano Srl ... 266
Cartiera di Rivignano SpA ... 268
Cartiera di Salerno di Mauro Benedetti ... 245
Cartiera Enrico Cassina SNC ... 250
Cartiera Europaper SpA ... 254
Cartiera Eurotec srl ... 254
Cartiera Ferdinando Amatruda di Amatruda Antonietta ... 244
Cartiera Fornaci SpA ... 256
Cartiera Francesco Imperato e Figli SNC .. 259
Cartiera Galliera srl ... 256
Cartiera Giacosa SpA ... 257
Cartiera G.I.C. S.r.l. ... 257
Cartiera Giorgione SpA ... 257
Cartiera Giusta Srl ... 257
Cartiera Grillo sas di Giuseppe e Domenico Grillo ... 258
Cartiera Italiana Srl. ... 259
Cartiera Logudoro S.r.l. ... 250
Cartiera Mantovana S.R.L. ... 261
Cartiera Marchigiana Srl ... 261
Cartiera Nuova So.Car.Pi. S.r.l. ... 263
Cartiera Olona Sas di Belvisi Dr. Davide & C. ... 263
Cartiera Partenope S.r.l. ... 264
Cartiera Pasquini Srl ... 264
Cartiera Pieretti SpA ... 265
Cartiera Ponte A Villa s.r.l. ... 266
Cartiera Ponte d'Oro Ansalcarta Srl ... 266
Cartiera Puglisi SRL ... 266, 267
Cartiera S.A.C.C.A. SpA ... 268
Cartiera Sacchettificio Bonino ... 269
Cartiera San Felice SpA ... 269
Cartiera San Giorgio S.r.l. ... 269
Cartiera San Lorenzo S.R.L. ... 269
Cartiera San Martino SpA ... 269
Cartiera San Rocco SpA ... 270
Cartiera S. Giovanni di Figli di Checchi G. S.R.L. ... 269
Cartiera Sicars S.R.L. ... 271
Cartiera S. Stefano Di Sodini Davide & C. SAS ... 272
Cartiera Torre Mondovi ... 273
Cartiera Val di Lima S.R.L. ... 274
Cartiere del Garda SpA ... 257
Cartiere del Polesine Spa ... 265
Cartiere di Trevi SpA ... 273
Cartiere Ermolli S.p.a. ... 254
Cartiere Modesto Cardella SpA ... 262
Cartiere Panigada S.R.L. ... 264
Cartiere Rodolfo Reguzzoni SRL ... 267
Cartiere SACI SpA ... 269
Cartiere Villa Lagarina Spa ... 274
Cartitalia S.r.l. ... 250

Cartocor S.A. ... 782, 783
Cartonal SAS ... 838
Cartón Box del Paraguay S. A. ... 864
Cartonera del Caribe CA ... 871
Cartones America SA - CAME ... 838
Cartones Compactos S.L. ... 332
Cartones Ponderosa S.A. de C.V. ... 856
Cartones y Papeles del Risaralda ... 842
Cartonificio Sandreschi S.R.L. ... 270
Cartonifício Valinhos S.A. ... 831
Cartonnerie de la Boème ... 180
Cartonnerie Jean SA ... 187
Cartonnerie Oudin ... 191
Cartonneries de Gondardennes SA ... 186
Cartonnerie Tunisienne SA ... 900
Cartopel S.A. ... 845
Cartulinas CMPC S.A. ... 834
Carvajal Pulpa y Papel ... 838
Carval Cartiera Di Valletrompia Srl ... 250
CARVIMSA, Cartones Villa Marina S.A. ... 866
Casalino Carta S.r.l. ... 250
Cascade Pacific Pulp, LLC ... 67
Cascades Auburn Fiber, Inc. ... 32
Cascades Boxboard Group Inc. ... 123
Cascades Djupafors AB ... 349
Cascades East Angus Inc. ... 123
Cascades Inc. ... 122
Cascades Lupel Inc. ... 124
Cascades Papier Kingsey Falls Inc. ... 124
Cascades SAS ... 180
Cascades Tissue Group ... 53, 59, 68, 70 77, 96, 117, 124, 125
Cataguazes Indústrias de Papel ... 797
Catalyst Paper Corporation ... 108, 109
C.C.R. - Cartiera Cooperativa Rivalta ... 251
C & C Srl ... 248
CECSO - Celulosa y Corrugados de Sonora S.A. de C.V. ... 850, 851
CEL Technologies & Systems, S.L. ... 331, 332
Celtejo - Empresa de Celulose do Tejo, S.A. ... 295
Celtex S.p.a ... 251
Celulosa Arauco y Constitución S.A. 832, 833
Celulosa Argentina S.A. ... 782
Celulosa Baradero S.A. ... 782
Celulosa Campana S.A. ... 783
Celulosa de Fibras Mexicanas S.A. de C.V. 852
Celulosa de Levante S.A. (CELESA) ... 338
Celulosa Remanso S.A. ... 865
Celulosa San Pedro S.A. ... 789
Celulosas de Asturias S.A. (CEASA) ... 332
Celulosa y Papel del Bajío S.A.de C.V. ... 848
Celulose Beira Industrial (Celbi) S.A. ... 295
Celulose Irani S.A. ... 808, 809
Celulose Reciclada ... 797
CELUPA - Industrial Celulose e Papel Guaíba Ltda. ... 798
Celu Paper S.A. ... 783
CENIBRA - Celulose Nipo-Brasileira S.A. ... 798
Century Paper & Board Mills Ltd. ... 703

Century Pulp & Paper ... 562
CEPASA - Celulose e Papel de Pernambuco S.A. ... 798
Ceprohart SA ... 300
CEREPA, a.s. ... 156
Cesar Iglesias C. por A ... 844
Chadha Papers Ltd ... 562
Chaltyr Paper Mill ... 306
Cham Paper Group Italia S.p.A. ... 251
Chandaria Industries Ltd. ... 883
Chandpur Enterprises Ltd. ... 562
Chang Chun Plastics Co., Ltd. ... 731
Chang Shin Paper Mfg. Co., Ltd. ... 731
Chang Tang Industrial Co., Ltd. ... 731
Chao Yang Paper Mfg. Co., Ltd. ... 731
Charoen Aksorn Holding Group Co. Ltd. (CAS Group) ... 744
Charoen Chai Co., Ltd. ... 744
Cheema Paper Mills Pvt. Ltd. ... 562
Cheeyee Enterprise Corp. ... 731
Cheney Pulp & Paper Co. ... 62
Cheng Dah Paper Co., Ltd ... 732
Chengdu Jujia Family Life Paper Making Co., Ltd. ... 513
Chengdu R Paper Co., Ltd. ... 513
Chengdu Yatai Paper Industry Co., Ltd. ... 513
Chengdu Zhihao Paper Co., Ltd. ... 514
Cheng Fung Paper Co., Ltd. ... 732
Cheng Loong Corporation ... 732, 733
Cheng Loong Corporation Tayuan Mill ... 733
Cheng Yang Paper Mill Co., Ltd. ... 770
Chen Ho Paper Mfg. Co., Ltd. ... 731
Chenming Paper Holdings Ltd. 491, 492, 493
Chen Tjun Paper Mill Industrial Co., Ltd. ... 732
Chenzhou Yunong Paper Co. Ltd ... 468
Chhattisgarh Industries Ltd. ... 563
CHH Pacific Paper Sdn Bhd (CHHPP) ... 694
Chiao Feng Paper Co., Ltd. ... 733
Chi Hsiang Paper Co., Ltd. ... 733
Chilya Corrugated Board Mills Ltd ... 703
China Chengtong Holding Group Ltd. ... 397
China Sunshine Paper Holdings Company Limited ... 488, 489
China Tobacco Mauduit (Jiangmen) Paper Industry Company Ltd. ... 407
Ching Mei Paper Co., Ltd ... 733
Chi Sheng Paper Product Co., Ltd. ... 733
Chizhovskaya Paper Mill ... 367
Cholan Paper & Board Mills Ltd. ... 563
Chongqing HengAn Paper Co., Ltd ... 398
Chongqing Lee & Man Paper Co., Ltd. ... 398
Chongqing Lee & Man Tissue Manufacturing Ltd. ... 398
Chongqing Longjing Paper ... 398
Chongqing Longzhang Paper Co., Ltd. ... 398
Chongqing Qianzheng Paper Co., Ltd. ... 399
Chongqing Wei Er Mei Paper ... 399
Chouka Pulp & Paper Mill ... 645
Chuetsu Pulp & Paper Co., Ltd. ... 651
Chung Hwa Pulp Corporation ... 733

Index

Chung Rhy Special Paper Mfg. Co. Ltd. 734
Cia. Canoinhas de Papel 796
Cia. Industrial Papelera Poblana
S.A. de C.V. 856
Cia. Papelera El Fenix S.A. de C.V. 852
Cibrapel S.A. Indústria de Papel
e Embalagens 799
CICP Companhia Industrial de
Celulose e Papel 799
CIFIVE S.A.I.C. 783
Cincinnati Paperboard 62
CIPAC Indústria de Papéis Cantagalo Ltda. 799
Circar Paper Mills Ltd. 563
Cita Peuchoon Paper Mills Sdn. Bhd. 695
CITROPLAST- Ind. e Com. de Papéis
e Plásticos Ltda. 799
CJSC ESEIRA 275
Clariana S.A. 332
Clearwater Paper Corporation 6, 10, 24, 41
    47, 49, 54, 59, 89, 96, 117
CMPC Celulosa S.A. 834, 835
CMPC Celulose Riograndense 799
CMPC Papeles Cordillera S.A. 836
CMPC Tissue S.A. 836
Coastal Agro Industries Ltd. 563
COCELPA - Companhia de Celulose
e Papel do Paraná 800
Cochin Kagaz Ltd. 563
Coldenhove Papier 276
Colombiana de Cartones Ltda. 839
Colombiana Kimberly Colpapel S.A. 839
Colombiana Tissue 839, 840
Compañía Papelera Mendoza S.A.
(Copelme) 792
Conpel - Cia Nordestina de Papel 800
Consolidated A One Trade and
Invest 11 Pty. Ltd. 888
Consolidated Paper Mills PLC 306
Container Corp. of the Philippines 710
Continental Management Plc 306
Cooperativa Pachi Lara 784
Copamex Industrias S.A. de C.V. 851
Copamex, S.A. de C.V. 851
COPAPA - Companhia Paduana
de Papéis 800
Copikas Kagit ve Oluklu Mukavva
Kutu A.S. 756
COPSI Compañía Papelera
Sinsacate S.R.L. 784
Coral Newsprints Limited 563
Cordier Spezialpapier GmbH 201
Corelex Co., Ltd. 652
Corenso France 181
Corenso North America 97
Corenso United Oy Ltd. 162, 163
Coromandel Papers 564
Corrugadora Paraguaya S.A. 864
Corrugados de Colombia Ltda. 840
Cosboard Industries Ltd. 564
Cosmo Specialty Fibers, Inc. 89, 90

Cotton South S.L. (CELSUR) 332
Cottrell Paper Co., Inc. 54
Craft Corner Paper Mills Pvt. Ltd. 564
Crane AB 349
Crane & Co., Inc. 37
Creative Paper Mills Ltd. 391
Crescent Packaging Corporation,
Pty. Ltd. 888
Crocker Technical Papers 38
Crown Paper Mill Ltd. 767
Crown Tissue 887
Crown Van Gelder NV 276
Crystal Paper Group 889
C&S Paper Co., Ltd. 407, 436, 465, 525
CVG - Cahdam Volta Grande 800

D

Daehan Paper Co., Ltd. 715
Daehan Papertech Co., Ltd. 716
Daejin Paper Mfg. Co., Ltd. 716
Daelim Paper Co. Ltd. 716
Daewang Paper Co. Ltd. 716
Dae Wang Paper Co., Ltd. 715
Daewha Paper Board Mfg. Co., Ltd. 716
Daeyang Paper Mfg. Co. Ltd. 716
Daini Seishi Co., Ltd. 652
Daio Paper Corp. 652, 653
Daishowa-Marubeni
International Ltd. 105, 109
Daiwa Itagami Co., Ltd. 653
Dalkrovlya 306
Dall Pel Madeira e Papel 800
Daman Ganga Papers Mills (P) Ltd. 564
DamaPel Comércio de Papéis Ltda. 801
Danalakshmi Paper Mills Pvt. Ltd. 564
Decor Paper Mills Ltd. 565
Deerfield Tissue, LLC 17
De La Rue Currency 374
De La Rue plc. 374
De La Rue Security Papers 374
delfortgroup AG 137
Delicarta SpA 253
Delipapier GmbH 201
Delipapier S.A.S. 182
Delitissue Sp. z.o.o. 286
Delkeskamp Verpackungswerke
GmbH 201
Delta Board Mills SAE 877
Delta Paper Mills Ltd. 565
Delux Kraft Board Ltd. 565
Dentas Ambalaj Ve Kagit San. A.S. 756
Deoria Paper Mills Ltd. 565
Der Lih Paper Co., Ltd. 735
Dev Kiran Paper Mills (P) Ltd. 565
Devon Valley Ltd. 375
Dev Priya Fibres Pvt. Ltd. 566
Dev Priya Industries Limited 566
Dev Priya Papers Pvt. Ltd. 566
Dev Priya Product Ltd. 566

Dezhou Huisheng Pingyuan
Paper Co., Ltd. 489
Dhanlaxmi Paper Mills Pvt Ltd 566
Dhruv Craft Mill Private Limited (DCMPL) 566
Diana Paper 770
DICEPA Papelera de Enate S.L. 333
Dinatex Ltd. Co. 729
Diósgyöri Papírgyár Rt. 241
Disley Tissue Ltd. 375
Dnepropetrovsk Paper Mill, Ltd. 367
Dobrushskaya Paper Mill
"Geroi Truda", OJSC 146
Doh-Ei Paper Mfg. Co., Ltd. 653, 654
Domsjö Fabriker 349
Domtar Corporation 6, 28, 41, 59, 70, 74
    77, 97, 109, 117, 125
Donetsk-Vtorma Ltd. 367, 368
Dong Da Paper Mfg. Co., Ltd. 735
Dong Fa Paper Mfg. Co., Ltd. 735
Dongguan Dalin Paper 407
Dongguan Enxing Paper Co., Ltd. 408
Dongguan Huaixing Paper Co., Ltd. 408
Dongguan Landsing (Lianxing)
Packaging Co., Ltd. 411
Dongguan Weihong Paper Co., Ltd. 408
Dongguan Xuantong Paper 408
Dongguan Youngsun Paper Co., Ltd 408
Dongguan Zhongqiao Paper Co., Ltd. 408
Dongil Packaging 717
Dongil Paper Mfg. Co., Ltd. 717
Dongwon Paper Mfg. Co., Ltd. 717
Dongyang Paper Mfg. Co., Ltd. 717
Donskaya Gofrotara 306
Doruk Kagit San. T IC. A.S. 756, 757
Double A (1991) Public
Co., Ltd. 182, 744, 745
Drenik A.D. 325
Dresden Papier GmbH 202
Drewsen Spezialpapiere
GmbH & Co. KG 201
Dr. Franz Feurstein GmbH 138
Drvenjaca d.d. 155
DS Smith Chouanard 183
DS Smith Kaysersberg 182, 183
DS Smith Packaging Benelux B.V. 277
DS Smith Packaging France 182, 183
DS Smith Packaging Italia S.p.A. 253
DS Smith Paper 375, 376
DS Smith Paper Deutschland GmbH 202
DS Smith Plc. 375
Duerbote Mongolian Autonomous
County Haida Paper Co., Ltd. 452
Dunafin Kft. 241
Duni AB 350
Dunn Paper 41
Durga Duplex Mill Private Limited ... 566, 567
Durga Paper Mills 567
Duropack GmbH 138, 153
Dynic Corporation 654

Index

E

East India Paper & Board Mills 567
Ecologicheskie Tekhnologii Ltd 307
Ecopaper JP Co. Ltd. 654
Edipack sh.p.k. 137
EFW Tuscania Srl 254
Egoli Tissue Mill (Pty) Ltd. 889
Ehime Paper Mfg. Co., Ltd. 654
EIC - Empaques Industriales
Colombianos SA 840
EKA Industrial Paper Production Limited .. 757
Eko Pulp & Paper Sdn. Bhd. 695
El Dar El Beida 877
Eldorado Celulose e Papel 801
El Farouk Co. "Farco" 877
ELF - Egyptian Co. for Manufacturing
of Linerboard & Fluting 878, 879
Elikon 307
Ellora Paper Mills Ltd. 567
El Nasr Carton Co. 878
El Obour Co. 878
Elpap 286
El-Salam PaperMill 878
El Shorouk (Motaheda) 878
E.MAK Paper Manufacturing Co. 877
Emami Paper Mills Ltd. 567, 568
EMBA spol. s. r.o. 156
Emin Leydier 183, 184
Empaques Modernos
de Guadalajara, S.A. de C.V. 855
Empaques Modernos
San Pablo S.A. de C.V. 859
Empresa Nacional del Papel -
CUBAPEL 843
Empresas CMPC S.A. 833
ENCE Energia y Celulosa SA 333
Encore Tissue 386
Eng Fong Paper Co., Ltd. 735
Envases Industriales S.A. 864
Environment Pulp and Paper Co., Ltd. ... 745
E-papertech Co. Ltd. 718
Epesok Paper Mills Ltd. 887
Erfurt & Sohn KG 202
Ertok Oluklu Mukavva San.ve tic.ltd. Sti. .. 757
Erving Industries Inc. 38
Erving Paper Mills Inc. 38
Eska Graphic Board BV 277
Essel Selüloz ve Kagıt Sanayi Ticaret A.S . 757
Estrela Indústria de Papel Ltda. 801
Etap Paper & Carton 879
Ethiopian Pulp & Paper SC 883
Eurocartiera 254
Europac Alcolea de Cinca 334
Europac Kraft Viana 296
Europac Papel Duenas 334
Europac - Papeles y Cartones
de Europa S.A. 334
Europac Papeterie de Rouen 184
Europac Portugal 296

Everbal 184
Everest Paper Mills (P) Ltd. 568, 700
Evergreen Packaging Inc. 6, 60, 78
Exacompta Clairefontaine 184
Expera Specialty Solutions 97, 98

F

Fábrica de Bolsas de Papel UNIBOL SA 843
Fábrica de Papel Aveirense Lda. 295
Fábrica de Papel da Lapa Lda. 296, 297
Fábrica de Papel de Fontes Lda. 296
Fábrica de Papel de Medros, Lda. .. 296, 297
Fábrica de Papel de Ponte Redonda S.A. . 297
Fábrica de Papel de Torres Novas Lda. ... 300
Fábrica de Papel e Cartão
da Zarrinha, S.A. 300
Fábrica de Papel La Soledad S.A. de C.V. . 862
Fábrica de Papel San Francisco
S.A. de C.V. (FAPSA) 858
Fábrica de Papel San José S.A. de C.V. 858, 859
Fábrica de Papel Santa Therezinha
(SANTHER) 825, 826
Fábrica Nacional de Moneda y
Timbre-FNMT 334
Fábricas de Papel Potosí,
S.A. de C.V. 856, 857
Fabrika Hartije - PAP - DP 325
Fabryka Papieru Czerwonak Sp. z o.o. ... 286
Fabryka Papieru i Tektury "BESKIDY" S.A. .. 285
Fabryka Papieru Kaczory
Sp. z o.o. 286, 287, 289
Fabryka Papieru Malta Decor S.A. 290
Fabryka Papieru Myszków Sp. z o.o. 291
Fabryka Papieru Sp. z.o.o. w Dabrowicy . 286
FACEPA - Fábrica de Papel
da Amazônia S.A. 802
FADERCO 875
Fa. Katharina Tillmann Papier- und
Wellpappenfabrik e.K. 232
FANAPEL - Fábrica Nacional de Papel S.A. 869
FAPAJAL - Fábrica de Papel de Tojal S.A. .. 296
Faruki Pulp Mills Ltd. 703, 704
Favini Spa 254, 255
Fedco Paper Corp. 710
Fedrigoni S.P.A. 255, 256
Feinpappenwerk Gebr. Schuster
GmbH & Co. KG 227
Felix Schoeller Jr. Foto &
Spezialpapiere GmbH 225
FE "Myuniks" LLC 147
Fengyuan (Xingtai) Specialty
Paper Co., Ltd. 436
Fernandez S.A. Indústria de Papel 802
F.F. Soucy SEC 126
Fibercorr Inc. 62
FiberMark North America, Inc. 38, 85
Fiber Marx Papers Ltd. 568
Fiber Pattana Co., Ltd. 745
Fibre Excellence Saint-Gaudens 185

Fibre Excellence Tarascon 185
Fibre Foils Ltd. 568
Fibria Celulose SA 802, 803
Fibrocellulosa S.p.A 256
Filiperson Papéis Especiais Ltda. 803
Filtros Anoia, S.A. 334
Finch Paper, LLC 54
Firma "W. Lewandowski" P.H.U. 289, 290
First A One Trade and Invest 11 Pty Ltd. .. 889
First Co. For Industrial Development S.A. E879
First Quality Tissue LLC 55, 71, 74
Fiskeby Board AB 350
Flambeau River Papers, LLC 99
Flexipack International
Wunderlich GmbH + Co KG 202, 203
Florelle Tissue Corporation 55
Flower City Tissue Mills Co. 55
Flying Board and Paper Products Ltd. ... 704
Flying Group of Industries Ltd. 704
Flying Kraft Paper Mills Ltd. 704
Fook Woo Group 550
Forestal y Papelera Concepción S.A. 836
Fortress Global Cellulose Ltd 126
Fortress Paper Ltd. 110
Fortress Specialty Cellulose Inc. 126
Fortune Paper Mills 568
Foshan Gold Rich Union Paper
Industry Co., Ltd. 408
Fourstones Paper Mill Co. Ltd. 376
Fox River Fiber Co., LLC 99
FPHU "Filar" Sp. Jawna 287
French Paper Co. 42
Fripa Papierfabrik Albert Friedrich KG .. 203
Froeb-Verpackungen GmbH 203
FS-Karton GmbH 203
Fthiotis Paper Mill SA 237
Fujian Annuo Group 399
Fujian Annuo Paper (Fujian) Co., Ltd. ... 399
Fujian Dongxin (Zhangzhou)
Paper Co., Ltd. 399
Fujian Dunxin Group 399
Fujian Dunxin Paper Co., Ltd. 400
Fujian HengAn (China) Paper Co., Ltd. .. 400
Fujian Hengan International Group 400
Fujian Huafa (Fujian) Industrial Co., Ltd. .. 400
Fujian Huamin Paper Co., Ltd. 401
Fujian Jian'ou Hengfeng Paper Co., Ltd. .. 401
Fujian Jian'ou Taipingyang Paper Mill ... 401
Fujian Liansheng Paper (Longhai) Co., Ltd 401
Fujian Liansheng Paper (Zhangzhou)
Co., Ltd. 401
Fujian Lishu Pulp & Paper Co., Ltd. 401, 402
Fujian Luoyuan Xiongfeng Paper Mill ... 402
Fujian Lvjin Huamei Paper Co., Ltd. 405
Fujian Nan'an Hengli Paper
Products Co., Ltd. 400
Fujian Nanjing County Youlida Co., Ltd. . 402
Fujian Nanping Paper Co. Ltd. 402
Fujian Nanyang Paper Co., Ltd. 402
Fujian Naoshan Paper Group Co. Ltd ... 403

Index

Fujian Qingshan Paper Industry Co., Ltd... 403
Fujian Qingshan Youxi Paper Co., Ltd........ 403
Fujian Quanzhou Guige Paper Co. Ltd....... 403
Fujian Quanzhou Jingyu Paper Co., Ltd..... 403
Fujian Quanzhou Jingyu Paper Mill............ 403
Fujian Tengrongda Pulp Co., Ltd 404
Fujian Xinlida Paper Co., Ltd..................... 404
Fujian Xiyuan Paper Co., Ltd..................... 404
Fujian Youlanfa Group 404
Fujian Zhangzhou Gangxing Group
Gangxing Paper Co., Ltd........................... 404
Fujieda Seishi Co. Ltd. 655
Fujifilm Corp.. 655
Fujikyowa Paper Mfg. Co., Ltd.................. 655
Fuji Paper Mill Cooperatives..................... 655
Fuji Satowa Paper Co., LTD...................... 655
Fukuda Paper Manufacturing Co., Ltd...... 655
Fukuyama Paper Co., Ltd......................... 655
Fulida Group Holding Co., Ltd 525
Fushun Huasheng Paper Products
Co., Ltd. 483
Fusion Paperboard.................................... 11
FutureMark Paper Group 11, 25, 42
Fuyang Jinfeng Paper Co., Ltd.................. 525
Fuyang Maohong Paper Co., Ltd.............. 525

G

Gahir Paper Mills Ltd................................ 569
Gai Chin Paper Co, Ltd............................ 735
Gain Hwang Paper Mfg. Co., Ltd.............. 735
Gajanan Paper Mill (P) Ltd 569
Ganga Papers India 569
Gangotri Paper Mills Pvt Ltd..................... 569
Gansu Hanfu Dongfang Paper Co., Ltd..... 405
Gansu Jingning HengDa Paper Co., Ltd.... 406
Gansu Tianshui Xuanyuan Paper Co., Ltd. 406
Gansu Xinglong Paper Co., Ltd 406
Gansu Zhangye City Mingyang
Paper Mill 406
Garg Duplex & Paper Mills Pvt. Ltd........... 569
Gascogne Paper....................................... 185
Gascogne SA 185
Gaurav Paper Mills......................... 569, 570
Gaya Baru Paper CV................................ 629
Gayatri Paper Mill 889
Gayatri Paper Mills Pvt. Ltd...................... 570
Gayatrishakti Paper & Boards Ltd............. 570
Gebr. Grünewald GmbH & Co. KG........... 204
Gebr. Hoffsümmer Spezialpapier
GmbH & Co. KG..................................... 206
Gemdoubs... 186
General Company for Paper Industry
(GENCO).. 730
Gênesis Papéis 803
Genus Paper Products Limited 570
Georgia-Pacific LLC. 1, 2, 7, 13, 17, 18, 30, 48
            55, 66, 68, 86, 90, 99, 118
G.F.F - Nikopol AD 154
Gharb Paper Ind. Co. 645

GIPEC - Groupe Industriel
des Papiers et de la Cellulose................. 875
Git-Vijay Paper Mills (P) Ltd..................... 570
Glassine Canada Inc. 126
Glatfelter............................... 63, 71, 186
Glatfelter Gernsbach GmbH & Co. KG..... 203
Glatfelter UK Ltd. 376
Glatz Finepaper Vietnam Co. Ltd. 770
Globe Paper Mills.................................... 710
Gloria S.A. 866
Glucholaskie Zaklady
Papiernicze Sp. z o.o. 287
Godavari Pulp and Papers Mills (P) Ltd.... 571
Gofrotara OOO 307
Gojo Paper Mfg. Co., Ltd......................... 656
Gold East Paper (Jiangsu) Co., Ltd. 472
Gold Hongye Paper (Hubei) 465
Gold Hongye Paper
(Suzhou Industrial Park) Co., Ltd............ 473
Gold Huasheng Paper
(Suzhou Industrial Park) Co., Ltd............ 473
Golzern Holding GmbH............................ 204
Gomà-Camps S.A.U. 335
Goodview Investments............................ 889
Goodwill Team Papers Ltd 571
Goraya Straw Board Mills (P) Ltd 571
Gorham Paper and Tissue, LLC................. 50
Goricane, tovarna papirja Medvode, d.d. . 328
Gorlovskaya Paper Mill OOO 368
Goshika Seishi Co. Ltd............................ 656
GP Cellulose, LLC.................. 2, 13, 18, 48
G.P.C. Mohammadia................................ 885
G-P Gypsum LLC.. 8
Gramox Paper & Boards Ltd.................... 571
Grand Bay Paper Products Ltd 869
Grand Holding Mill 385
Graphic Packaging International Inc. 8, 18, 19
                                            30, 42, 63
Grasim Industries Ltd.............................. 571
GRD Paper Industries PVT. Ltd................. 571
Great Lakes Tissue Co. 43
Great Northern Paper Co. LLC............ 32, 33
Green Bay Packaging Inc................... 7, 100
Greenfield SAS 186
Greenland Paper Mill Ltd................ 571, 572
Greenpac Mill, LLC............................. 55, 57
Green Papertech 718
Greif Inc... 63, 86
Groupe CMCP - La Compagnie
Marocaine des Cartons et Papiers........... 885
GrünPerga Papier GmbH......................... 204
Grupo Corporativo Papelera
S.A. de C.V. ("GCP")................................ 852
Grupo Gondi S.A. de C.V......................... 852
Grupo Papelero Scribe, S.A. de C.V. .860, 861
Grupo Portucel Soporcel 298
Grupo Unipak, S.A. de C.V. PT................. 863
Grupo Zucamor....................................... 792
Gruppo Cordenons SpA 252
GS Paper & Packaging Group ("GSPP").... 695

Guaçu S.A. Papéis e Embalagens 804
Guangan Anqi Paper Co., Ltd................... 514
Guangdong Baoli Paper Co., Ltd.............. 409
Guangdong Dingfeng Paper Corporation. 409
Guangdong Dongguan Baojian
Paper Co., Ltd. 409
Guangdong Dongguan Dongfa
Paper Industry Co., Ltd................... 409, 410
Guangdong Dongguan Duorong
Paper Co., Ltd 410
Guangdong Dongguan Gaobu
Qiangan Paper Mill................................ 410
Guangdong Dongguan Hongmei
Lee & Man Paper Co., Ltd. 410
Guangdong Dongguan Huangyong
Yinzhou Paper Industry Ltd. 414
Guangdong Dongguan Jianhua
Paper Co. Ltd. 410
Guangdong Dongguan Jianhui Paper 410, 411
Guangdong Dongguan Jintian
Paper Co., Ltd. 411
Guangdong Dongguan Jinzhou
Paper Co., Ltd. 411
Guangdong Dongguan Lee & Man
Paper Co., Ltd. 412
Guangdong Dongguan Nine Dragons
Paper Industries Co., Ltd. 412
Guangdong Dongguan Shenlian
Paper Making Co., Ltd. 412
Guangdong Dongguan Shuangzhou
Paper Co., Ltd. 413
Guangdong Dongguan Shunyu
Paper Co., Ltd. 413
Guangdong Dongguan Taichang Paper Co.,
Ltd. 413
Guangdong Dongguan White Swan
Paper Co, Ltd. 413
Guangdong Dongguan Yongan
Paper Co., Ltd. 414
Guangdong Dongguan Zhonglian
Paper Co., Ltd. 414
Guangdong Donta Group Co., Ltd........... 415
Guangdong Donta Group
Dongwen Paper Mill 415
Guangdong Foshan Chengtong
Paper Co., Ltd. 415
Guangdong Foshan City Gaoming
Hongyuan Paper Co., Ltd. 415
Guangdong Foshan Gaoming Super
Trans Paper Co., Ltd. 415
Guangdong Foshan Shanshui Kelun
Paper Co., Ltd 416
Guangdong Green Forest (QingXin)
Paper Industrial Limited 416
Guangdong Guangzhou Panyu
Lianhuashan Paper-Making Co., Ltd. 416
Guangdong Guangzhou Smile
Daily Necessities Co., Ltd. 416
Guangdong Guanhao
High-Tech Co., LTD. 416, 417

Guangdong Heshan Paper Co., Ltd............417
Guangdong Huizhou Fook Woo
Paper Co., Ltd. 417
Guangdong Jiangmen City Qiaoyu
Paper Co., Ltd. 417
Guangdong Jiangmen City Xinlong
Paper Co., Ltd. 417
Guangdong Jiangmen Jingang
Paper Co., Ltd. 418
Guangdong Jiangmen Renke Lvzhou
Paper Industry Co., Ltd. 418
Guangdong Jiangmen Zhenlong
Paper Mill Co., Ltd. 418
Guangdong Jiangnan Paper Co. Ltd. 418
Guangdong Jieyang City Xinda
Paper Co., Ltd. 418
Guangdong Junye Paper Co., Ltd. 418
Guangdong Mingxing Paper Co., Ltd. 419
Guangdong Regall Group Co., Ltd. 419
Guangdong Shantou City WanAn
Paper Co., Ltd. 419
Guangdong Shantou Huashi Paper
Industrial Co., Ltd. 419
Guangdong Shaoneng Group 419, 420
Guangdong Shunde Sugar Co., Ltd. 420
Guangdong Taiyuan Paper Co., Ltd. 420
Guangdong Vinda Paper Co., Ltd. 420
Guangdong Vinda Paper
(Guangdong) Co., Ltd. 420
Guangdong Vinda Paper
(Jiangmen) Co., Ltd. 420
Guangdong Wanlida Paper 421
Guangdong Zhanjiang Guanlong
Paper Co., Ltd. 421
Guangdong Zhaoqing Kelun Paper Co., Ltd 421
Guangdong Zhongshan Polly
Paper Manufacture Co., Ltd. 421
Guangdong Zhongshan Rengo Hung
Hing Paper Mfg. Co. Ltd. 422
Guangdong Zhongshan Sanjiao
Paper Manufacture Co., Ltd. 421
Guangdong Zhongshan Yajieli
Paper Co., Ltd. 422
Guangdong Zhongshan Yongfa
Paper Co., Ltd. 422
Guangdong Zhongsheng Paper Co., Ltd. 422
Guangdong Zhuhai Jiangqiao
Special Paper Co. Ltd. 423
Guangdong Zhuhai S.E.Z. Hongta
Renheng Paper Co. Ltd. 422, 423
Guangxi Baise Hezhong Paper Co., Ltd. 425
Guangxi Binyang Daqiao Paper Co., Ltd. ...425
Guangxi Binyang Jiangnan Paper Co., Ltd.425
Guangxi Boguan Paper Co., Ltd. 425
Guangxi Chongzuo Daming
Paper Co., Ltd. 425
Guangxi Chongzuo Daming
Paper Co., Ltd. 425
Guangxi Chongzuo Huamei
Paper Co., Ltd. 425

Guangxi East Asia Paper Co., Ltd. 426
Guangxi Fangchenggang Hongyuan
Pulp & Paper Co., Ltd. 426
uangxi Fengtang Luzhai Paper Co., Ltd. 426
Guangxi Forest Lipu Paper Co., Ltd. 427
Guangxi Gold Zhuyuan Paper Co., Ltd. 426
Guangxi Guangui Sugar Co., Ltd. 426
Guangxi Guigang Hongqi Paper Mill 427
Guangxi Guilin No. 2 Paper Mill.....................427
Guangxi Guilin Paper Inc. 427
Guangxi Guilin Qifeng Paper Co., Ltd. 427
Guangxi Guitang (Group) Stock Co., Ltd .. 428
Guangxi Guitang Paper Group Co., Ltd. 428
Guangxi Guofa Forest & Paper Co. Ltd. 428
Guangxi Haolin Paper Co., Ltd. 428
Guangxi Heda Paper Co. Ltd. 428
Guangxi Heng County Jiabao
Paper Co., Ltd. 429
Guangxi Heng County Jiangnan
Paper Co., Ltd. 429
Guangxi Huaken Paper 429
Guangxi Huayi Paper Co., Ltd. 429
Guangxi Hwagain Group 429, 430
Guangxi Jeanper Paper Co., Ltd.
(Jiebao Paper) 430
Guangxi Jiayi Paper Co., Ltd. 430
Guangxi Jindaxing Paper Group Co., Ltd...430
Guangxi Jingui Pulp & Paper Co., Ltd. 431
Guangxi Jinrong Paper Co., Ltd. 431
Guangxi Laibin Donta Paper Co., Ltd. 431
Guangxi Laibin Huamei Paper Co., Ltd 431
Guangxi Liangmianzhen Paper Co., Ltd. 431
Guangxi Liuzhou Guizhong Paper Co., Ltd.432
Guangxi Liuzhou Liulin Paper Co., Ltd. 432
Guangxi Liuzhou Zhongdi Paper Co., Ltd...432
Guangxi Longzhou Nanhua
Paper Co., Ltd. 432
Guangxi Nanning Huaze Pulp &
Paper Co., Ltd. 432
Guangxi Nanning Jiabao Paper Co., Ltd. 432
Guangxi Nanning Jiada Paper 432
Guangxi Nanning Jindaxing
Pulp & Paper Co., Ltd. 432
Guangxi Nanning Lianli Paper Co., Ltd 433
Guangxi Nanning Phoenix
Pulp & Paper Co. Ltd. 433
Guangxi Nanning Tianran Paper Co., Ltd. . 433
Guangxi Paiji Paper Co., Ltd. 433
Guangxi Pumiao Paper Co., Ltd. 433
Guangxi Sky Power Natural
Material Co., Ltd. 434
Guangxi Tianlin County Lisen
Paper Co., Ltd. 434
Guangxi Tianyang Huamei Paper Co., Ltd.434
Guangxi Tianyang Nanhua Paper Co., Ltd 434
Guangxi Xiangzhou Liangui Paper Co., Ltd.434
Guangxi Xinrui Paper Co., Ltd. 434, 435
Guangxi Yongkai Sugar and Paper Co., Ltd.435
Guangxi Yongxin Huatang Group
Laibin Paper Co., Ltd. 435

Guangzhou Hongjieda Paper Co., Ltd. 423
Guangzhou Paper Group Ltd. (Nansha)... 423
Guangzhou Qiming Paper Co., Ltd. 423
Guangzhou Ronglong Paper Co., Ltd. 419
Guangzhou Victorgo Industry Co., Ltd. 423
Guangzhou Zhujiang Specialty
Paper Co. ,Ltd. 424
Guarro Casas S.A. 335
Gugan Paper Mills Pvt Ltd 572
Guizhou Chitianhua Paper
Industrial Co., Ltd 435
Gulf Paper Industries Factory 712
Gulf Paper Manufacturing
Free Zone Company 768
Gulf Paper Mfg. Co. k.s.c. 692
GusmerCellulo 8
Gusmer Enterprises Inc. 100
GVG Paper Mills Ltd. 572

H

Hachmann S.A. Indústria e Comércio 804
Hadera Paper Industries Ltd. 648
Hadera Paper-Printing & Writing Paper Ltd649
Hahnemühle FineArt GmbH 205
Hai Ha Pulp Mill 770
Hai Ming Holdings Bhd. 695
Hai Ming Paper Mills Sdn Bhd......................695
Hainan Gold Hongye Paper Co., Ltd. 435
Hainan Gold Shengpu Paper Co., Ltd. 435
Hainan Jinhai Pulp & Paper
Industry Co., Ltd. 435
Hai Phong Paper Joint-Stock Co.
(Hapaco) 771
Hai Phong Paper Mill 771
Hakle GmbH 205
Halkali Kagit Karton San. ve Tic. A.S. 757
Halong Trading Company 771
Hamburger Hungaria Ltd 241
Hamburger Rieger GmbH & Co. KG 205, 206
Hana Paper Co., Ltd. 718
Hanchang Paper Co., Ltd. 718
Hangzhou Dahua Paper Co., Ltd. 525, 526
Hangzhou Fulton Industry Co.,Ltd. 526
Hangzhou Huajin Specialty Paper Co., Ltd.526
Hangzhou Huatian Paper Co., Ltd. 526
Hangzhou Huawang Group 526
Hangzhou Huawang New Material
Co., Ltd. 526
Hangzhou Jinjiang Paper Co., Ltd. 526
Hanke Tissue Spólka z o.o. 287
Hankuk Paper Mfg. Co., Ltd. 718
Hans Kolb Papierfabrik GmbH & Co. KG...210
Hansol Artone Paper Co., Ltd. 719
Hansol Paper Co. Ltd. 719, 720
Hansson Paper Corp. 710
Hanuman Agro Industries Ltd. 572
Hanuman Chromocoates Ltd. 572
Hapaco Joss Paper Mill 771
Hapaco Paper Mill..771

Index

Hapaco Pulp Mill 771
Harbor Paper LLC 90
Hardoli Paper Mills Ltd. 572
Hari Ohm Paper Mills (P) Ltd. 573
Hariom Industries Limited 573
Harir Khuzestan Tissue Co. 645
Harisar Papers Ltd 573
Hartford City Paper, LLC 27
Hartija Ko DOO 276
Hattori Seishi K.K. 656
Havix Corporation Ltd. 656
Hayat Kagit ve Enerji A.S. 758
Hayat Kimya A.S. 645, 758
Hebei Baoding Banknote Paper Mill 436, 437
Hebei Baoding Baojie Paper Co., Ltd. 437
Hebei Baoding Chenguang
Paper Co., Ltd. 437
Hebei Baoding Dayi Paper Co., Ltd. 437
Hebei Baoding Dongsheng Hygiene
Products Co., Ltd. 437
Hebei Baoding Gangxing Paper Co., Ltd. ... 437
Hebei Baoding Haofeng Paper Co., Ltd. 438
Hebei Baoding Hengfa Paper Co., Ltd. 438
Hebei Baoding Hengtai Paper Co., Ltd. 438
Hebei Baoding Mancheng Donggou
Paper Mill 438
Hebei Baoding Mancheng Fukang
Paper Co., Ltd. 438, 439
Hebei Baoding Mancheng Guanquan
Paper Co., Ltd. 439
Hebei Baoding Mancheng Huifeng
Paper Co., Ltd. 439
Hebei Baoding Mancheng Jifa
Paper Co., Ltd. 439
Hebei Baoding Mancheng Lida Paper Mill 439
Hebei Baoding Mancheng Yikang
Paper Co., Ltd. 440
Hebei Baoding Mancheng Yongxing
Paper Mill 440
Hebei Baoding Mancheng Yuexing
Paper Mill 440
Hebei Baoding No. 5 Paper Mill 440
Hebei Baoding Orient Paper Co., Ltd. 440
Hebei Baoding Orient Paper
Milling Co., Ltd. 441
Hebei Baoding Ruifeng Paper Co., Ltd. 441
Hebei Baoding Sanlian Paper Co., Ltd. 441
Hebei Baoding Xiangyu Paper Co., Ltd. 441
Hebei Baoding Xinghua Paper Mill 441
Hebei Baoding Xingji Specialty Paper Mill 441
Hebei Baoding Zhengda Paper Co., Ltd. ... 442
Hebei Birou Paper Co., Ltd. 442
Hebei Changtai Paper 442
Hebei Chengda Paper Co., Ltd. 442
Hebei Dafa Paper Co., Ltd. 442
Hebei Daiyu Paper Co., Ltd. 442
Hebei Dazhong Baolai Paper Co., Ltd. 443
Hebei Haotong Paper Co., Ltd. 443
Hebei Hengwei Paper Co., Ltd. 443
Hebei Hongli Chenggong Paper Co., Ltd. . 443

Hebei Hualin Textile Raw
Materials Co., Ltd. 443
Hebei Huashuo Paper Co., Ltd. 443
Hebei Huatai Paper Co., Ltd. 444
Hebei Huatong Paper Co., Ltd. 443
Hebei Huixing Paper Co., Ltd. 444
Hebei Jigao Chemical Fiber Co., Ltd. 444
Hebei Jurun Paper Co., Ltd. 444
Hebei Kaishide Specialty Paper Co., Ltd. .. 444
Hebei Kangda Paper Group 444
Hebei Linhai Paper Co., Ltd. 444, 445
Hebei Longyuan Paper Co., Ltd. 445
Hebei Lu Quan Shunfa Industrial Co., Ltd. 445
Hebei Luquan Yuanda Industrial Co., Ltd. 445
Hebei Mancheng Anxin Paper Co., Ltd. 445
Hebei Mancheng Changfa Paper Co., Ltd. 445
Hebei Mancheng Chenggong
Paper Co., Ltd. 445
Hebei Mancheng Chengxin
Paper Co., Ltd. 446
Hebei Mancheng Chenyu Paper Co., Ltd. 446
Hebei Mancheng Hongda Paper Co., Ltd. 446
Hebei Mancheng Hongsheng
Paper Co., Ltd. 446
Hebei Mancheng Jinguang Paper Co., Ltd. 446
Hebei Mancheng Jinli Paper Co., Ltd. 447
Hebei Mancheng Shunli Paper Co., Ltd. ... 447
Hebei Mancheng Shuntong
Paper Co., Ltd. 447
Hebei Mancheng Xinyu
Paper Co., Ltd. 447
Hebei Mancheng Yiyuan Paper Mill 447
Hebei Mancheng Yongfa
Paper Co., Ltd. 447, 448
Hebei Qinhuangdao Fengman
Paper Co., Ltd. 448
Hebei Qinhuangdao Haofeng
Enterprise Group 448
Hebei Qu Zhai Group 448
Hebei Sanhe City Jingdong Shuhe
Paper Mill 448
Hebei Sanhe City Youyi Paper Mill 448, 449
Hebei Sanhe Xingwang Paper Mill 449
Hebei Sanhe Yangzhuang Dawotou
Paper Mill 449
Hebei Sanhe Yanling Paper Mill 449
Hebei Sanhe Zhaotuzhuang Aimin
Paper Mill 449
Hebei Tanghai Chenguang Paper Co., Ltd. 450
Hebei Tangshan Boda Paper Mill Co., Ltd. 450
Hebei Tangshan Guotai Paper Co., Ltd. 449
Hebei Xiaorenguo Paper Co., Ltd. 450
Hebei Xierman Nengwei Paper Co., Ltd. .. 450
Hebei Xingchang Paper Co., Ltd. 450
Hebei Xuesong Paper Co., Ltd. 451
Hebei Yaguang Paper Co., Ltd. 451
Hebei Yihoucheng Commodity Co. Ltd .. 451
Hebei Yongxin Paper Co., Ltd. 451
Hebei Yuanshi County Jinpeng
Paper Co., Ltd. 451

Hebei Yutian Shunfa Paper Co., Ltd. 451
Hebei Zhongxin Paper Co., Ltd. 452
Hefei Jiadong Paper Co., Ltd. 396
Heidrich Industrial Mercantil
e Agricola S.A. 804
Heilongjiang Dongshun Paper Co., Ltd 454
Heilongjiang Fuyu Chenming
Paper Co., Ltd. 452
Heilongjiang Kaifeng Paper
Produce Co., Ltd. 452, 453
Heilongjiang Longjiangfu Pulp &
Paper Co., Ltd. 453
Heilongjiang Mudanjiang Daewoo
Paper Mfg. Co. Ltd. 453
Heilongjiang Mudanjiang Hengfeng
Paper Group Co., Ltd. 453
Heilongjiang Xinhua Hygiene &
Specialty Paper Co., Ltd. 454
Heilongjiang Yuejing Pulp &
Paper Co., Ltd. 454
Heinzel Holding GmbH 139
Hellbut & Co. GmbH 206
Hellefoss Paper 281
Hemkunt Paper Mills Ltd 573
Henan Anyang Huaxian Paper 454
Henan Anyang Senyuan Paper Co., Ltd. .. 454
Henan Aobo Paper Co., Ltd. 454
Henan Chenyang Paper Co., Ltd. 455
Henan Dahe Paper Co., Ltd. 455
Henan Dongsheng Paper Co., Ltd. 455
Henan Fangzheng Paper Co., Ltd. 455
Henan Feida Group 455
Henan Fengyuan Paper Co., Ltd. 455
Henan Haiyang Chemical
Fiber Group Co., Ltd. 455
Henan Hebi Ruizhou Paper Co., Ltd. 455
Henan Hongteng Paper Group Co., Ltd. . 456
Henan Hongwei Paper Co., Ltd 456
Henan Huifeng Paper Co., Ltd. 456
Henan Hulijia Industry Co. Ltd. 456
Henan Jianghe Paper Co., Ltd. 456
Henan Jiaozuo Ruifeng Paper Co., Ltd. 456
Henan Jiyuan Tengsheng Paper Co., Ltd. 457
Henan Longquan Group Co., Ltd. 457
Henan Longquan Group Qilong Co., Ltd. 457
Henan Longquan Group Yubei Co., Ltd. .. 457
Henan Longyuan Paper Co., Ltd. 457
Henan Luohe Paperboard Mill 458
Henan Luohe Yinge Specialty
Paper Co., Ltd. 458
Henan Luohe Yinge Tissue
Paper Industry Co., Ltd. 458
Henan Luoshan Hengyuan Paper Co., Ltd 458
Henan Luoyang City Longxiang
Paper Co., Ltd. 458
Henan Mintong Huarui Paper Co., Ltd. 458
Henan Neixiang Xianhe Special
Paper & Pulp Co., Ltd. 458
Henan Ningling County Longyuan
Paper Co., Ltd. 459

Index

Henan No. 1 Sub-factory of Huixian City Paper Mill 460
Henan No. 1 Sub-factory of Huixian City Paper Mill 460
Henan Puyang City Tongyu Paper Co., Ltd. 459
Henan Puyang Longfeng Paper Co. Ltd 459
Henan Qinyang Haolin Paper Co., Ltd. 459
Henan Shangqiu Xinhao Paper Co., Ltd. ... 459
Henan Shangqiu Xinrong Paper Co., Ltd. .. 460
Henan Shengyuan Paper Co., Ltd. 460
Henan Tengfei Paper Co., Ltd. 460
Henan Tianbang Group Paper Co., Ltd. 460
Henan Weierte Chemical Fiber Co., Ltd. ... 460
Henan Wugang Qunwang Paper Co., Ltd. 460
Henan Wuzhi Guangyuan Paper Mill 460
Henan Xinxiang Hengli Paper Co., Ltd. 461
Henan Xinxiang Hongda Paper Co., Ltd. ... 461
Henan Xinxiang Hongtai Paper Co., Ltd. .. 461
Henan Xinxiang Runyang Chemical Fiber Co., Ltd. 461
Henan Xinxiang Xinya Paper Group Co., Ltd. 461, 462, 463
Henan Xuchang Feida Paper Co., Ltd. 463
Henan Yilin Paper Co., Ltd. 463
Henan Yingbo Paper Co., Ltd. 463
Henan Yinge Industrial Investment Co. Ltd. 463
Henan Yinge Packaging Paper Industry Co., Ltd. 464
Henan Yuzhou Shengxuan Paper Co., Ltd. 464
Henan Zhengzhou Dongsheng Paper Co., Ltd. 464
Henan Zhumadian City Baiyun Paper Co., Ltd. 465
Hengshan Zhongkong International Paper Co., Ltd. 472
Hiang Seng Fibre Container Co., Ltd. 746
Higher Kings Mill Ltd 377
Highland Paper Mills Ltd 884
Higi Papersoft Co. Ltd. 242
Hindustan Newsprint Ltd. 574
Hindustan Paper Corp. Ltd. 573
Hindustan Paper Corp. Ltd., CPM 573
Hinton Pulp 106
Hoa Binh Pulp Mill 771
Hoang Van Thu Paper Joint Stock Company 771
Hogla-Kimberly Ltd. 649
Hokuetsu Kishu Paper Co. Ltd. 656, 657
Hollingsworth & Vose Co. .. 19, 38, 39, 55, 56
Hollingsworth & Vose Co. Ltd. 377
Hollingsworth & Vose GmbH 206
Holmen AB 350, 351
Holmen Paper Madrid S.L. 335
Honen Seishi K.K. 682
Hongwon Paper Mfg. Co., Ltd. 720
Hood Container Corporation 78
Hop Fung Group Holdings Limited 551

Horizon Pulp & Paper Ltd. 161
Horng Ming Paper Co., Ltd. 735
Horus Edfu 879
Horus Edfu for Paper Industry 879
Hovomex S.A. de C.V. 852
Howe Sound Pulp and Paper Corporation 110
HRA Papers Pvt Ltd 574
Hsing Chung Paper Corp. 735
Hua Te Mei Paper Co., Ltd. 736
Hubei Baoli Paper Co., Ltd. 465
Hubei Chibi Chenli Paper Co., Ltd. 465
Hubei Enshi Jinhua Group 465
Hubei Hengfeng Paper Co., Ltd. 466
Hubei Hongfa Renewable Resources Technology Development 466
Hubei Jianli Maxleaf Paper Co., Ltd. 466
Hubei Jingzhou Zhiyin Paper 466
Hubei Junma Paper Co. Ltd. 466
Hubei Maxleaf Paper Co., Ltd. 466
Hubei Paima Paper Co., Ltd. 466
Hubei Shuailun Paper Co. Ltd. 467
Hubei Shulin Paper Co., Ltd. 467
Hubei Shuyun Paper Co., Ltd. 467
Hubei Vinda Paper (Hubei) Co., Ltd. 467
Hubei Wuhan Chenming Paper Co. Ltd. .. 467
Hubei Wuhan Mulan Paper Co., Ltd. 467
Hubei Yadu Hengxing Paper Co., Ltd 468
Hubei Yichang Baota Paper Co., Ltd. 468
Hubei Yingqiang Paper Co., Ltd. 468
Hubei Zhencheng Paper Co., Ltd. 468
Hunan Baoqing Group Union Paper Co., Ltd 468
Hunan Changde HengAn Paper Co., Ltd. . 469
Hunan Dongshun Paper Co., Ltd 469
Hunan Huayao Pulp & Paper Co., Ltd. 469
Hunan Jianhongda Group 469
Hunan Jingtianren Paper Co., Ltd. 469
Hunan Jintaiyang Paper Co., Ltd. 469
Hunan Juntai Pulp & Paper Co., Ltd 471
Hunan Linyuan Paper Co., Ltd 469
Hunan No. 1 Paperboard Co., Ltd. 470
Hunan Shuanghua Paper Co., Ltd. 470
Hunan Tiger Forest & Paper Group Co., Ltd 470, 472
Hunan Tiger Forest & Paper Group Hongjiang Paper Co., Ltd 471
Hunan Tiger Forest & Paper Group Yuanjiang Paper Co., Ltd 471
Hunan Tiger Forest & Paper Group Yueyang Paper Co., Ltd. 470
Hunan Tuopu Bamboo and Flax Industry Development Co., Ltd. 471
Hunan Xiangfeng Specialty Paper Co., Ltd., No. 1 Branch Mill 471
Hunan Xiangfeng Specialty Paper Co., Ltd. No. 2 Branch Mill 472
Hunan Yueyang Fengli Pulp & Paper Co. Ltd. 472
Hussain Pulp, Paper & Board Mills Ltd. ... 391
Hygienic Tissue Mills 889

Hyogo Paper Mfg. Co., Ltd. 657
Hyogo Pulp Industries, Ltd. 658

I

IBEMA - Cia. Brasileira de Papel 804, 805
Iberkraft Indústria de Papel e Celulose Ltda. 805
Iberpapel 336
Ibertissue S.L.U. 336
Ichikawa Seishi K.K. 658
ICO-Industria Cartone Ondulato Srl 258
ICT France SAS 187
ICT Ibérica, S.L.U 336
ICT Italy 258, 259
ICT Poland Sp. z o.o. 288
Ideal Cart SpA 259
IdemPapers SA 150
Ide Shigyo K.K. 658
Iexon Enterprises Co., Ltd. 736
Iggesund Paperboard AB 351
Iggesund Paperboard (Workington) Ltd. .. 377
Iguaçu Celulose Papel S.A. 805, 806
Ilim Group 307
Illig'sche Papierfabrik 207
Imporpel Ind. e Com. de Papéis Ltda. 806
Ind. de Papelão Hörlle Ltda. 804
INDEVCO - Industrial Development Company sal 693
Indo Afrique Paper Mill 574
Indugevi S.A. 840
Indústria Americana de Papel S.A. 794
Industria Cartaria Fenili S.p.A. 256
Industria Cartaria Pieretti SpA (ICP) 265
Indústria de Papéis para Embalagem Irmãos Siqueira Ltda. 809
Indústria de Papéis União 806
Indústria de Papel Dopel 806
Indústria de Papel Guará Ltda. 804
Indústria de Papel Irapuru Ltda. 809
Indústria de Papel Sovel da Amazônia Ltda. 828
Indústria e Comércio de Embalagens e Papéis Artivinco Ltda. 794
Indústria e Comércio de Papel Fiberpap Ltda. 802
Indústria e Comércio Papeis(INCOPA) 806
Industrial e Agrícola Rio Verde Ltda. 824
Industrial Papelera Atlas SA 865
Industrial Papelera Ecuatoriana S.A (Inpaecsa) 845
Industria Panameña de Papel SA 864
Industrias Cartonera Asociada S.A. - INCASA 845
Industrias del Cartón S.A. - INCASA 866
Industrias del Papel S.A. 866
Indústrias de Papel Ribeirão Preto Ltda. .. 823
Indústrias de Papel R. Ramenzoni S.A. 822
Indústrias Novacki S.A. 817
Indústrias Reunidas Cristo Rey Ltda. 823

Index

Inland Empire Paper Co. 90
Innovio Papers 278
INPA - Indústria de Embalagens
Santana S.A. 806, 807
Inpol-Papier Sp. z o.o. 288
INPOPEL - Indústrias Podolan
de Papel Ltda. 807
Interface Solutions Altenkirchen GmbH 207
International Paper APPM Ltd. 574, 575
International Paper Co. 2, 3, 14, 19, 20, 27
                              28, 29, 31, 48, 56, 60, 66,
                              68, 74, 75, 78, 82, 86
International Paper do Brasil Ltda. 807, 808
International Paper, Empaques
Industriales de México S.A. de C.V. ..852, 853
International Paper (Europe) SA 150
International Paper - Kwidzyn Sp. z o.o. 288
International Paper SA 187
International Paper &
Sun Paper Cartonboard Co., Ltd. 489
Inter Pacific Paper Co., Ltd. 746
Interstate Paper Industries 879
Interstate Paper L.L.C. 20
Interstate Resources, Inc. 86
Intertissue Ltd. 378
Invepal 871
Investlesprom 309
Ipasa Indústria de Papel
Apucarana S.A. 808
Ipek Kagit San. ve Tic. A.S. 758, 759
IPEL - Indaial Papel Embalagens Ltda. 808
IPELSA - Indústria de Celulose
e Papel da Paraíba 808
IPUSA - Industria Papelera Uruguaya S.A. 870
Iran Papyrus Co. Ltd. 645
Iran Wood-Paper Industries 646
Irving Paper 114
Irving Pulp & Paper, Ltd. 114
Irving Tissue Inc. 56, 114, 118
Islamic Paper Manufacturing Co. 880
Isma 2000 (Ismaeco Group) 336
IsraPaper Paper Industries Ltd. 649
Istituto Poligrafico e Zecca dello Stato 259
Itararé Papéis Ltda. 809
ITC Limited 575
ITC Limited, Paperboards &
Specialty Papers Division 575, 576
Itoman Co., Ltd. 658
IVEX Protective Packaging 25
Ivex Specialty Paper, LLC 25
Iwaki Daio Paper Corp. 659
Izmail Pulp & Paperboard Combine 368
Izumi Seishi K.K. 658

J

Jack-Pol Sp. z o.o. 288
Jackson Paper Manufacturing Co. 60
Jaepel Papéis e Embalagens 809
James Cropper 374

Jammu Paper (P) Ltd. 576
Janjirker Paper Mill (Pty) Ltd. 890
Jari Celulose, Papel e Embalagens S.A. 810
Jayanti Board Mills Ltd. 577
J B Daruka Paper Ltd. 576
J.D. Irving, Ltd. 113
Jebba Paper Mills Ltd. 888
Jeesr Industries Co. 886
Jeet Enterprises PVT. Ltd.
(Sister Concern of Miglani Paper Mills).....577
Jejani Pulp and Paper Mills Pvt. Ltd. 577
Jeng Chia Paper Product Co., Ltd. 736
Jeonju Paper Corporation, Ltd. 720
Jerusalem White Paper &
Neeman (2000) Ltd. 649
Jiangmen Hongxiang
Paper Co. Ltd (YY Group) 424
Jiangmen Rijia Paper Co., Ltd. 424
Jiangmen Xinghui Paper Mill Co., Ltd. 424
Jiangsu Bohui Paper Industry Co., Ltd. 473
Jiangsu Chamfor Paper Industry Co. Ltd. .. 473
Jiangsu Changshun Paper Co., Ltd. 474
Jiangsu Feixiang Paper Co., Ltd 474
Jiangsu Fuxing Paper 474
Jiangsu Huaji Zhangjiagang
Huaxing Papermaking Co. Ltd. 474
Jiangsu Huangli Paper Industry Co., Ltd. ...474
Jiangsu Jiangyin BESTO Special
Paper Board Co., Ltd. 474
Jiangsu Jiangyin Gushan Dongfang
Paper Co., Ltd. 475
Jiangsu Jiangyin YFY Mfg. Co, Ltd. 475
Jiangsu Jinhuang Paper Co., Ltd. 475
iangsu Jinlian Paper Co. 475
Jiangsu Jiuxing Paper Co., Ltd. 475
Jiangsu Lee & Man Paper
Manufacturing Co. Ltd. 475
Jiangsu Longheng Paper Co. Ltd 476
Jiangsu Nantong Xianglong Paper Co., Ltd 476
Jiangsu Nine Dragons Paper Industries 476
Jiangsu Oji Paper Nantong Co., Ltd. 476
Jiangsu Oji Paper Nepia
(Suzhou) Co., Ltd. 476
Jiangsu Peibo Paper Co., Ltd. 476
Jiangsu Shuangsheng Paper
Technology Development Co. Ltd. 480
Jiangsu Stora Enso Suzhou Paper Co. Ltd.477
Jiangsu Suqian Tiancheng Paper Co., Ltd. 477
Jiangsu Taizhou Jinsong Paper Co., Ltd. 477
Jiangsu Taizhou Weidmann
High Voltage Insulation Co. Ltd 477
Jiangsu UPM, Changshu
Paper Industry Co., Ltd. 477
Jiangsu Wanda Paper Co., Ltd. 477, 478
Jiangsu Wanxing Paper Co., Ltd. 478
Jiangsu Wuxi Long Chen Paper Co., Ltd.... 478
Jiangsu Xinda Paper Co. Ltd. 478
Jiangsu Xuzhou Xinyuan Paper Co.,Ltd 478
Jiangsu Yixing Zhangzhu Paper Mill 478
Jiangsu Yuen Foong Yu Paper

(Kunshan) Co. Ltd. 479
Jiangsu Yuen Foong Yu Paper
(Yangzhou) Co., Ltd. 479
Jiangsu Yujie Paper Co., Ltd. 479
Jiangsu Zhangjiagang Mingxing
Paper Co., Ltd. 479
Jiangsu Zhangjiagang Mingxing
Paper Co., Ltd. 479
Jiangxi Chenming Paper Co., Ltd. 481
Jiangxi Dexing City Hengsheng
Paper Co., Ltd. 481
Jiangxi Fuzhou Sihai Paper Co., Ltd. 481
Jiangxi Ganzhou Hwagain Paper Co., Ltd ..481
Jiangxi Jinggangshan Paper Co., Ltd. 481
Jiangxi Lee & Man Paper Co., Ltd. 482
Jiangyin Xinhao Recycling Paper Co., Ltd.. 479
Jih Sun Paper Ind. Co., Ltd. 736
Jilin Baishan Qixiang Paper Co., Ltd. 482
Jilin Chenming Paper Co. Ltd. 482
Jilin Meihekou City Chuangda
Paper Co., Ltd. 482
Jilin Meihekou Haishan Paper Mill 482
Jilin Zhenlai Xinsheng Paper Co., Ltd. 482
Jinan Haoyuan Paper Co., Ltd. 489
Jin Diing Co Ltd 736
Jin Young Paper Co., Ltd. 721
JIP - Papírny Vetrní,a.s. 157
Jiujiang Hengsheng Chemical
Fiber Co., Ltd. 482
JK Paper Ltd. 577
J&K Pulp & Paper Pvt. Ltd. 578
Jofel Industrial S.A. 336
Johmewah Maju Paper Mill Sdn. Bhd. 695
John Hargreaves (C&S) Ltd. 377
Jollyboard Limited 578
Jordan Paper & Cardboard
Factories Co. Ltd. 691
Joung Yin Enterprise Co., Ltd. 736
JR Group... 578
JSC Grigiskes 275
JSC 'Kondrovskaya Paper company' 311
JSC Primsnabcontract Ussurijsk
Paperboard Mill 318
JSC Solikamskbumprom 320
J. Tönnesmann & Vogel,
Papierfabrik Hönnetal GmbH 232
Juei Fong Paper Co., Ltd. 736
Jujo Thermal Ltd. 163
Julius Glatz GmbH Papierfabriken 204
Julius Schulte Söhne GmbH & Co. KG 226
Julius Schulte Trebsen GmbH & Co. KG ... 226
J. Vilaseca S.A. 346

K

Kabool(Lianyungang) Rayon Co., Ltd. 480
Kaga Paper Mfg. Co., Ltd. 659
Kagazy Recycling LLP 691
Kahramanmaras Kagit San
ve TIC A.S (KMK Paper) 759

Index

Kahrizak Paper Mill 646
Kalptaru Papers Ltd. 578
Kamakshi Papers Pvt. Ltd. 578
Karna Pulp & Paper Mill 309
Kamenskaya Board & Paper Mill, OJSC 309
Kämmerer GmbH 208
Kanzan Spezialpapiere GmbH 208
Kao Nan Pulp & Paper Mfg. Co., Ltd. 736
KapStone Kraft Paper Corporation. 60, 75, 91
KapStone Paper and Packaging Corp 26
KapStone Paper Charleston Kraft LLC 75
Karanja Industries (P) Ltd., Paper Division 578
Karavaevo 310
Karina Trading PLC 692
Karl Kurz GmbH & Co. KG 211
Karnal Card Board Industries 579
Karnaphuli Paper Mills Ltd. 391
Karthikeya Paper & Board Ltd. 579
Kartogroup España S.L. 337
Kartonfabriek Henri Goossens 149
Kartonfabriek St. Leonard NV 150
Kartonfabrik Buchmann GmbH 200
Kartonfabrik Kaierde GmbH & Co.
Produktions KG 208
Kartonfabrik Porstendorf GmbH 221
Kartonsan - Karton Sanayi ve Ticaret AS ... 759
Kartontara 310
Kartontara, CJSC 313
Kartontol 310
Kartotec - Papeles Técnicos- 865
Karur KCP Packagings Ltd. 579
Kasuga Seishi Kogyo Co., Ltd. 659
Katz GmbH & Co. KG 208
Kaveh Paper Industries Co. 646
Kawamura Seishi K.K. 659
Kawano Seishi K.K. 659
Kaygaon Paper Mills Ltd. 579
Kay Power & Paper Limited 579
Kazakhstan Kagazy 691
KBK Ltd 310
Keio Paper Mfg. Co., Ltd. 659
Kenya Papermill Ltd. 884
Khanna Paper Mills Pvt. Ltd. 579
Khatema Fibres Ltd. 580
Kherani Paper Mills Ltd. 580
Kibo Match Group Pulp and
Paperboard Mill 898
Kiev Cardboard and Paper Mill 368
Kimberly Bolivia S.A. 792
Kimberly-Clark Australia Pty Ltd. 386
Kimberly-Clark Brasil Ind. e Com.
de Produtos de Higiene Ltda. 810
Kimberly-Clark Corp. 3, 8, 11, 29, 66, 71
                                         75, 79, 82, 100
Kimberly-Clark Costa Rica, SA. 843
Kimberly-Clark de Centroamérica S.A. 846
Kimberly-Clark de México S.A. de C.V. 853, 854
Kimberly-Clark GmbH 208, 363
Kimberly-Clark Ltd. 378, 379
Kimberly-Clark of Canada 119

Kimberly-Clark of SA (Pty) Ltd. 890
Kimberly-Clark Peru S.A. 867
Kimberly-Clark Products
(Malaysia) Sdn. Bhd. 696
Kimberly-Clark S.A. 337, 784
Kimberly-Clark SAS 187
Kimberly-Clark SNC 187
Kimberly-Clark Srl 259, 260
Kimberly-Clark Taiwan 736, 737
Kimberly-Clark Thailand Ltd. 746, 747
Kimberly-Clark Venezuela, C.A. 872
Kingdecor (Zhejiang) Co., Ltd. 526
King Paper(Xiamen) Co., Ltd. 405
Kingston Paptech Pvt Ltd 580
Kinsei Seishi Co. Ltd. 660
Kipas Kagit Sanayi Isletmeleri A.S 760
Kishco Khodeir Paper Mill 880
Kitakami Hitec Paper Corp. 660
KJ Specialty Paper Co., Ltd. 660
Klabin S.A. 811, 812
Klaipedos Kartonas 275
KleanNara Co., Ltd. 721
Klingele Papierwerke GmbH & Co. KG 209
KM Papel 812, 813
Knijna Fabrika "Iskar" JSC 154
Koa Kogyo Co., Ltd. 660
Koehler Greiz GmbH & Co. KG 209
Koehler Kehl GmbH 209
Kohinoor Paper & Newsprint (P) Ltd 580
Kohinoor Pulp & Paper Pvt. Ltd 580
Köknar Kagit Karton San ve Tic A.S. 760
Kolicevo Karton d.o.o. 328
Komal Straw Board & Mill
Board Industries 581
Kombassan Holding 760
Kombassan San. ve Tic. AS 761
Kommunar Paper Mill 311
Komotini Papermill SA - Elina 238
Kondopoga 311
Kookil Paper (Zhangjiagang) Mfg. Co., Ltd. 480
Korea Export Packaging Ind. Co., Ltd. 721
Korea Export Packing Ind. Co., Ltd. 721
Korea Green Paper Mfg., Co. Ltd. - KGP ... 722
Korea Paper Mfg. Co., Ltd. 722
Korindo Group 632
KORONA Lochovice spol. s r.o. 157
Koryazhma Branch of Ilim Group 308
Koryo Seishi K.K. 650
Kosino Paper Mill 311
Kostenez-HHI PLC 154
Kotkamills Oy 163
Kotobuki Paper Co. Ltd. 661
Kovai Maruthi Papers & Boards (P) Ltd 581
Koyo Paper Mfg. Co., Ltd. 661
KPAQ Industries LLC 31, 32
KPK St. Petersburg OOAO 312, 319
KPM Kadoma Paper Mills 901
Krasnaya Zvezda 147
Krasnokamskaya Paper Mill Goznak 312
Krempel-Group 210, 211

Krishna Mongkol Co., Ltd. 747
Kronex-Ukraina, Ltd. 369
KRPA Paper, a.s. 158
KR Pulp & Papers Ltd. 581
Kruger Inc. 115, 127, 128
Kruger Products L.P. 111, 119, 128
Kruger Wayagamack Inc. 128
Krymbumaga 369
K.T.G. (USA) L.P. 80
Kuantum Papers Ltd 581
Kuan Yuan Paper Mfg. Co. Ltd. 737
Kübler & Niethammer
Papierfabrik Kriebstein AG 211
Kukil Paper Mfg. Co., Ltd. 722
Kulik Paper Industries (P) Ltd. 581
Kunert Gruppe, Paul &
Co GmbH & Co. KG 211
Kuo Zong Paper Mfg. Co., Ltd. 738
Kuzbasskiy Skarabey 312
Kwality Pulp & Paper Mills 581
Kyoku-Ei Paper Mfg. Co. 661
Kyoku-Ei Paper Mfg. Co., Ltd. 661
Kyongsan Paper Co., Ltd. 723
Kyrgyz-Chinese Paper Mill 693
K.Z.N. Tissue 890

L

Laakirchen Papier AG 139
La Cellulose du Maroc 886
Ladhar Paper Mill 582
Lake Utopia Paper 114, 115
Lalji Board Industries (P) Ltd. 582
Lalskaya Paper Mill 312
Lamix 289
Lam Son Paper Joint-Stock Company 772
Lana Papiers Speciaux 188
Landqart AG 364
Latif Paper Co. 646
Latif Paper Products Co. 646
Laxmi Board & Paper Mills Ltd. 582
Laxmi Paper Mills 582
LC Paper 1881, S.A. 337
Lecta S.A. 337
Ledesma S.A.A.I. 784, 785
Lee & Man Paper Manufacturing Ltd. 551
LEIPA Georg Leinfelder GmbH 212
Lekok Paper Sdn Bhd 696
Lenzing AG 139
Lenzing Papier GmbH 140
Lepenka 328
Lepenka AD 325
Lessebo Paper 352
Lessebo Pulp 352
Levent Kagit San. ve TIC. A.S. 761
Lexpapier Sonacar S.A. 886
Liaoning Dandong Fengcheng
Dongfeng Paper Co., Ltd. 483
Liaoning Dandong Hengyao
Paper Co., Ltd. 483

Index

Liaoning Hupo Paper ... 484
Liaoning Jincheng Paper Co., Ltd. ... 484
Liaoning Jincheng Paper Jinbao Paper Co., Ltd. ... 484
Liaoning Jinzhou Jinri Paper Co., Ltd. ... 484
Liaoning Jinzhou Nuerhe Paper Co., Ltd. ... 484
Liaoning Nine Dragons Paper Industries ... 484
Liaoning Panjin Dongsheng Paper Co., Ltd. ... 484
Liaoning Panjin Zhenxing Ecology Paper Co., Ltd ... 485
Liaoning Shangyang Paper Co., Ltd. ... 485
Liaoning Tieling Qinghe Gangxing Paper Co., Ltd. ... 485
Liaoning Tongsheng Paper Co., Ltd. ... 485
Liaoning Xingqi Paper Co., Ltd. ... 485
Liaoning Yingkou Paper Mill ... 485
Liberty Diversified Industries ... 46
Liberty Paper Inc. ... 46
Liberty Paper Mill, Inc. ... 710
Lien Tai Paper Co., Ltd. ... 738
Ligia Paper Industries ... 890
Lih Tai Industrial Corp. ... 738
Lila Kagit San. ve Tic. A.S. ... 761
Lincoln Paper and Tissue, LLC ... 33
Lindian Haida Paper Co., Ltd. ... 454
Linh Xuan Paper Joint-Stock Co. ... 772
Lintec Corp. ... 661, 662
Little Rapids Corp. ... 101
Liuan Zihao Paper Co., Ltd. ... 397
LLC Pulp Invest ... 312
Long Chen Paper Co. Ltd. ... 738
Long Van ... 693
Lothlorien (Pty) Ltd ... 890
Lotus for Paper Products ... 880
Lua Viet Paper Joint-Stock Co. ... 772
Lucart France SAS ... 188
Lucart SpA ... 260
Lunzenauer Papier- und Pappenfabrik GmbH & Co. KG ... 213
Lutepel Indústria e Com de Papel Ltda. ... 813
Lutsky KRK ... 369
Luzhou Shengfeng Paper Co., Ltd. ... 514
Lvivkartonplast ... 370
Lwarcel Celulose Ltda. ... 813
Lydall Filtration Separation SAS ... 188
Lydall, Inc. ... 11, 50, 56

M

Maa Chandi Papers Pvt. Ltd. ... 582
Mackenzie Pulp Mill ... 111
Madeireira Miguel Forte S.A. ... 803
Madepar Papel e Celulose S.A. ... 813
Madhupaper Kenya Ltd. ... 884
Madhya Bharat Papers Ltd. ... 582, 583
MAF Newsprint Mills Ltd (MAF NFL) ... 391
Maghan Paper Mills (P) Ltd. ... 583
Magnani Srl ... 261
Magnum Ventures Ltd. ... 583

Magura Group ... 392
Magura Paper Mills Ltd. ... 392
Mahachai Kraft Paper Co., Ltd. ... 747
Maheshwari Paper Limited ... 583
Mai Lan Paper Joint-Stock Company ... 772
Maki Seishi K.K. ... 662
Malaysian Newsprint Industries Sdn. Bhd. 696
Malik Board and Paper Industries ... 704, 705
Malik Board Mills ... 705
Malu Paper Mills Ltd. ... 583, 584
Malyn - Weidmann Paper Mill VAT ... 370
Mamta Papers Pvt Ltd ... 584
Manaylux Papers & Boards (P) Ltd. Yediyur ... 584
Mandiali Paper Mill Ltd. ... 705
Mandya National Paper Mills Ltd. ... 584
Manikraft Guaianazes Ind. de Celulose e Papel Ltda. ... 813, 814
Manufacturas de Papel CA (MANPA) S.A.C.A. ... 872
Manufacturera de Papel Bidasoa S.A. de C.V. ... 848
Maragheh Paper Industries Company (M.P.I.C) ... 646, 647
Marisky Pulp & Paper Mill ... 313
Marlboro Paper Inc. ... 129
Marmara Kagit ve Ambalaj Sanayii ve Ticaret AS ... 761
Marombas Indústria e Comércio de Madeiras e Papelão ... 814
Marubeni Corporation ... 662
Marui Paper Industry Co., Ltd. ... 662
Marukin Seishi K.K. ... 662
Marusan Paper Corparation ... 663
Marusan Paper Mfg. Co., Ltd. ... 662
Marusumi Paper Co., Ltd. ... 663
Marutomi Paper Mfg. Co., Ltd. ... 663, 664
Maryland Paper ... 36
Mashad Carton ... 647
Master Papers (Pvt) Ltd ... 705
Masuko Seishi K.K. ... 664
Matias Gomá Tomás S.A. ... 338
Matsuoka Seishi K.K. ... 664
Mauro Benedetti S.p.A. ... 244
Max Fortune (FZ) Paper Products ... 405
MAXI S.A. ... 238
Mayr-Melnhof Eerbeek BV ... 278
Mayr-Melnhof Gernsbach GmbH ... 213
Mayr-Melnhof Karton AG ... 140
Mayr-Melnhof Karton GmbH ... 140, 141
Mazandaran Wood & Industries (MWPI) ... 647
Mazandaran Wood & Paper Industries Co. 647
MBD Group ... 584
MB Papeles Especiales ... 338
MCC Meili Paper Industry Co., Ltd. ... 486
MCC Meili Paper (Laishan) Co., Ltd. ... 514
MCC Paper Group Co., Ltd. ... 397
MCC Paper Yinhe Co., Ltd. ... 489
M.C.LIRI S.R.L ... 261
MC Tissue SpA ... 261

MD Papéis Ltda. ... 814
Meadow Lake Mechanical Pulp ... 135
MeadWestvaco Corporation ... 3, 84, 87
Mediterranean Paper Mills (MPM) ... 730
Mediterranean Tissue Company ... 880
MED Paper SA ... 886
Meenu Paper Mills (P) Ltd. ... 584
Meerssen Papier BV ... 278
Mei Ho Paper Mfg. Co., Ltd. ... 738
Meiji Seishi Co., Ltd. ... 664
MELECKY a.s. závod Papírna Aloisov ... 158
Melhoramentos Florestal S.A. ... 814, 815
Melhoramentos Papéis Ltda. ... 814, 815
Melitta Haushaltsprodukte GmbH & Co. KG ... 214
Mel Macedonian Paper Mills S.A. ... 238
Menofeya for Paper & Cardboard ... 880
Menofeya for Paper & Cardboard - "Minobardy" ... 880
Merckens Karton- und Pappenfabrik GmbH ... 141
Metro Knight (M) Sdn. Bhd. ... 696
Metro Paper Industries Tissue Group Ltd. ... 119
Metsä Board ... 166
Metsä Board Äänekoski ... 167
Metsä Board Husum ... 352
Metsä Board Joutseno ... 167
Metsä Board Kaskinen ... 167
Metsä Board Kemiart Liners ... 163
Metsä Board Kyro ... 168
Metsä Board Simpele ... 168
Metsä Board Tako ... 164
Metsä Board Zanders GmbH ... 214
Metsä Fibre Oy ... 164, 165
Metsä Group ... 165
Metsä Tissue AB ... 353
Metsä Tissue Corp. ... 166
Metsä Tissue GmbH ... 214, 215
Metsä Tissue S.A. ... 290
Metsä Tissue Slovakia s.r.o. ... 327
Middle East Paper Company - (MEPCO) ... 713
Middle East Paper Co. (SIMO) ... 881
Mien Tay Packing Co. Ltd. ... 772
Mier ... 370
Mifuji Seishi K.K. ... 664
Miki Tokushu Paper Mfg. Co., Ltd. ... 665
Milano Papers Pvt. Ltd. ... 584
Mili S.A. ... 815
Millar Western Forest Products Ltd. ... 106
Millenium Paper Mill ... 691
Millenium Papers Pvt. Ltd. ... 585
Mimopel Papéis Higiénicos Ltda. ... 815, 816
Mimosa Sanitary Paper ... 693
Miquel y Costas & Miquel S.A. ... 338, 339
Mirae Paper Co., Ltd. ... 723
Misr Edfu for Pulp, Writing & Printing Paper Co. - MEPP-Co ... 881
Mississippi River Corp. ... 48
Mitsubishi HiTec Paper Europe GmbH ... 215
Mitsubishi Paper Holding

Index

(Europe) GmbH......................................215
Mitsubishi Paper Mills Ltd...............665, 666
Mladost Cuprija A.D.G.D.........................325
MMK FollaCell A.S....................................282
Mobile Paperboard Corp............................4
Modern Karton Sanayi Ticaret AS............762
Modinagar Paper Mills Ltd......................585
Mohammadi Paper & Board
Industries (Pvt.) Ltd................................705
Mohawk Fine Papers Inc....................56, 57
Mohit Paper Mills Ltd.............................585
Mokvynska Paper Mill, Ltd......................370
Molza Corp..666
Monadnock Paper Mills, Inc................50, 51
Monalisa Co., Ltd....................................723
Mondi..7, 891
Mondialcarta SpA...................................262
Mondi Dynäs AB.....................................353
Mondi Europe & International Division...141
Mondi Frantschach GmbH.....................142
Mondi Lohja Oy......................................166
Mondi Merebank.....................................891
Mondi Neusiedler GmbH........................142
Mondi Raubling GmbH..........................216
Mondi Richards Bay................................892
Mondi SCP a.s..327
Mondi Shanduka Newsprint..................892
Mondi South Africa Division..................891
Mondi Stambolijski EAD........................154
Mondi Stetí..158
Mondi Swiecie S.A..................................290
Mondi Syktyvkar....................................313
Mondi Tire Kutsan Paper and
Packaging Industry Inc..........................762
Montes del Plata....................................870
Moorim Paper Co., Ltd..........................723
Moorim P&P Co. Ltd..............................724
Moorim SP Co., Ltd................................724
Mopak Dalaman Pulp-Paper
Cardboard Plant....................................762
Mopak Kagit Karton San. ve Tic. A.S......763
Mopak Tasköprü Pulp and
Cigarette Paper Plant............................763
Moritz J. Weig GmbH & Co. KG.............235
Mosaico Speciality Papers.............246, 247
Mostafa Paper..392
Most China International Ltd................551
Mpact Limited................................892, 893
M.P. Boards & Paper Mills (P) Ltd..........582
M.P. Hygiene, S.A.S................................189
Muc Son Paper Paper Joint-Stock Co......773
Muda Holdings Berhad..........................697
Mudanjiang Sandu Specialty
Paper Co., Ltd..454
Muda Paper Mills Sdn. Bhd...................697
Mufindi Paper Mills (MPM)...................898
Multiverde Papéis Especiais Ltda..........816
Multiwal Pulp & Board Mills Ltd............585
Munksjö Arches SAS..............................189
Munksjö Aspa Bruk AB..........................354
Munksjö Brasil Industria e Comercio
de Comercio de papeis especiais Ltda...816
Munksjö Dettingen GmbH.....................216
Munksjö Italia S.p.A...............................262
Munksjö LabelPack................................190
Munksjö Oyj...353
Munksjö Paper AB..........................354, 355
Munksjö Paper GmbH............................216
Munksjö Paper S.A.................................339
Munktell & Filtrak GmbH......................216
Muratli Karton Fabrikasi........................763
Murli Industries Ltd...............................585
Myagkaya Krovlya..................................314
Myanma Paper and Chemical
Industries (MPCI)...........................699, 670
Myanmar Jute Enterprise......................700
My Huong Paper Joint-stock Co............773
Mysore Paper Mills Ltd..........................586

N

Naachiar Paper Boards Private Ltd........586
Naberezhnye Chelny Paper &
Board Mill..314
Nabha Paper Mills Ltd...........................586
Nachiketa Papers Ltd.............................587
Naini Papers Ltd....................................587
Nakagawa Seishi KK..............................666
Namgang Paper Co., Ltd.......................724
Nampak Ltd...893
Nampak Paper Ltd.................................893
Nampak Tissue (Pty) Ltd................893, 894
Nanaimo Forest Products Ltd................110
Nath Pulp & Paper Mills Ltd..................587
National Co. for Paper & Plastics...........881
National Gypsum Co...................4, 61, 66, 72
National Paper Co..................................881
National Paper Co. Ltd. (NPCL).............729
Natron-Hayat d.o.o................................152
Natural - Indústria de Papel, Lda..........297
Nav Bharat Duplex Ltd..........................587
Neenah Gessner GmbH.........................216
Neenah Lahnstein..................................217
Neenah Paper, Inc....................20, 43, 101
Nefertiti Paper Co. Ltd..........................881
Nelsun Paper Mills Ltd....................587, 588
Neman Pulp & Paper Mill...............314, 315
Neo-Print...550
NEPA Ltd...588
Neucel Specialty Cellulose Ltd................111
Neu Kaliss Spezialpapier GmbH............217
Neukölln Spezialpapier NK
GmbH & Co. KG....................................217
Newark America......................................39
Newark Pacific Paperboard Corp..............9
Newark Recycled Paperboard Solutions...51
New Bombay Paper Mills Pvt Ltd...........588
New Forest Paper Mills LP.....................119
New-Indy Containerboard LLC.............8, 9
Newman & Company, Inc.......................72
NewPage Corporation.........29, 33, 37, 43, 46
                                   64, 101, 102
Newtech Pulp Inc....................................710
Newton Falls Fine Papers Company, LLC....57
New Toyo Pulppy (Hong Kong) Limited....551
New Toyo Pulppy (Vietnam) Co., Ltd.......773
Nibong Tebal Paper Mills Sdn.
Bhd. (NTPM)..697
Nice Papers Ltd......................................588
Nicol-Pack Corporation..........................315
Nicol-Pack Imperial Co. Ltd...................308
Nikita Paper (P) Ltd...............................588
Niko Seishi Co., Ltd................................666
Nine Dragons Paper (Holdings) Ltd.......551
Nine Dragons Paper Industries
(Chongqing) Co., Ltd.............................399
Nine Dragons Paper Industries
(Quanzhou) Co., Ltd..............................405
Nine Dragons Paper (Tianjin) Co., Ltd...520
Nine Dragons Pulp & Paper
(Leshan) Co., Ltd...................................514
Nine Dragons XingAn Paper Co., Ltd.
(Inner Mongolia)....................................472
Ninex Paper..693
Ningbo Muniu Paper Co. Ltd.................527
Ningbo Stainless Paper Industry Co., Ltd...527
Ningxia Kejin Xiaguang Paper Co., Ltd...486
Ningxia Zijinghua Paper Industry Co. Ltd...486
Nippon Paper Chemicals Co., Ltd.........668
Nippon Paper Crecia Co., Ltd................668
Nippon Paper Industries Co., Ltd...666, 667
                                   668, 669, 670, 671, 672
Nippon Paper Industries USA Co., Ltd....91
Nippon Paper Papylia Co., Ltd.......672, 673
Nishinihon Eizai Co., Ltd.......................673
Nisshinbo Paper Products, Inc........673, 674
Nisshinkogyo Co., Ltd............................674
Nittoku Co., Ltd.....................................674
Nittow Papel S.A....................................816
Nizhegorodsky Board & Asphalt Board Mill...315
Noah's Paper Mills, Inc..................710, 711
Nobrecel S.A. Celulose e Papel..............816
Norampac...........................119, 120, 129, 130
Norampac Industries Inc.........................57
Nordic Paper Åmotfors..........................355
Nordic Paper Bäckhammar....................355
Nordic Paper Greåker AS......................282
Nordic Paper Holding AB......................355
Nordic Paper Seffle................................355
Norpapel S.A.I.C....................................786
Norpaper Avot-Vallée SAS.....................190
Norske Skog ASA............................282, 283
Norske Skog (Australia)...................386, 387
Norske Skog Bruck GmbH.....................143
Norske Skog Golbey SA.........................190
Norske Skog PanAsia.............................714
Norske Skog Pisa S.A.............................816
Norske Skog Tasman.............................701
Norske Skog Walsum GmbH.................218
Northern Pulp Nova Scotia Corporation....115

Index

North Pacific Paper Corp. (Norpac) 92
Northwood Group 379
Northwood & Wepa Limited 379
Novatissue SAS 191
Novzohour Co. Ltd. 647
NR Agarwal Industries Ltd. 588, 589
Nuova Cartiera della Toscana SpA 273
Nuova Cartiera Sordini S.R.L. 273
Nuova F.lli Alimonti srl 243
Nuove Cartiere di Tivoli S.R.L. 273
Nuqul Group 691

O

OAO Aleksandrovbumprom (ABP) ... 304, 316
OAO Kohavinska Paper Mill 369
OAO Mayak Technocell 313
OAO Miropol Paper Mill 370
OAO Pitkyaranta Pulp Mill 317
OAO Poligrafkarton 318
OAO Technicheskaya Bumaga 322
OAO Toshkent Qogoze 769
Obeikan Paper Industry 713
Ohio Paperboard Corp. 64
Ohio Pulp Mills Inc. 64
Ohtaka Seishi K.K. 674
Oi Seishi Co., Ltd. 674
Oita Seishi Corporation 674, 675
Oji F-Tex Co., Ltd. 675, 676
Oji Holdings Corporation 679
Oji Materia Co., Ltd. 676, 677, 678, 680, 682
Oji Nepia Co., Ltd. 678
Oji Papéis Especiais Ltda. 817
Oji Paper Co., Ltd. 680, 681
Ojsc 'Troitskaya Paper Mill' 323
Okayama Paper Industries Co., Ltd. 682
Okitsugawa Seishi Co., Ltd. 682
Oku Iboku Pulp and Paper (OKIPP)
Company Limited 888
Okulovka P&P Mill Ltd. 316
Olayan Kimberly-Clark (Bahrain) W.L.L. 389
Old Town Fuel and Fiber 34
Oliveira Santos & Irmão, Lda. 297
Olkhovka Board Mill, JSC 147
Olmuksa International Paper-Sabanci
Ambalaj Sanayi ve Ticaret A.S. 763
Olympia Paper & Board Mills (Pvt) Ltd 706
Omer Tissue Mills (Pvt) Ltd. 706
Omiya Seishi Co., Ltd. 683
Omniafibre srl 263
Omniafiltra, LLC 57
Omskkrovlya 316
Omsk Paper Mill 316
Om Srinivasa Paper Boards Pvt. Ltd. 589
Ondunorte, Cia. de Papéis e
Papelão Ondulado do Norte 817
Ono Seishi K.K. 683
Onyx Specialty Papers, Inc. 39
OOO Altyn Ajydaar 692, 693
OOO Ametist 366

OOO ASS-Korostyshiv Paper Mill 366
OOO Astrakhanskaya
Paperboard Mill 305, 317
OOO Bely Kamen Paper Mill 367
OOO Bumy 305, 317
OOO Buprom-Pokrov 305, 317
OOO First Donetsk Paper Mill 368
OOO Interecoline 368
OOO KubanPapir 312, 317
OOO Nikmas 315
OOO Tissue-Bumaga 317, 323
OOO Triton-M 317, 323
OOO Yarovoy 372
Opel Paper Mill Ltd. 589
OP Papírna s.r.o. 159
Orchids Paper Products Co. 66
Oriental Paper - Lanatex 730
Orient Paper & Industries Ltd. 589
Orient Paper Mills 589
Orora Ltd 387
Orsa International Paper Embalagens S.A 818
Osaka Paper Co., Ltd. 683
Otrokovické papírny a.s. 159
Otsego Paper Inc. 43
Otsu-Paperboard Co., Ltd. 683
Ouro Verde Papéis e Embalagens Ltda 819
Ox Paperboard LLC 25, 44, 94
OYKA Kagit Ve Ambalaj San Tic A.S. 764

P

Paalson Paper & Board 590
PABCO Paper 9
Pabianicka Fabryka Papieru Sp. z.o.o. 291
Packaging Corp. of America 20, 26, 30
                                            44, 80, 102
Packprofil Sp. z o.o. 291
Paema Embalagens Ltda. 819
PAKA Glashütter Pappen-
und Kartonagenfabrik GmbH 219
Palm Group 219, 220
Palm Paper Limited 379
Palode Paper Mills Ltd. 590
Paloma-Sladkogorska Tovarna
Papirja d.d. Sladki Vrh 328
PAMER - Papelera Mercedes S.A. 870
Panasa, Papelera Nacional S.A. 867
Panjapol Paper Industry Co. Ltd.
and Panjapol Pulp Industry
Public Co., Ltd. 747
Pankaboard Oy 168
Pan Pac Forest Products Ltd. 701
Pan Paper Mills 884
PAN Papirna Industrija d.o.o. 155
PAPCAS - Rebahia à Saïda 875
Papeco SA 191
Papel Aralar S.A. 331
Papeleira Portuguesa S.A. 299
Papelera Andina S.A. 781
Papelera Berazategui S.A. 782

Papelera Damují 844
Papelera de Brandia S.A. 331
Papelera de Chihuahua S.A. de C.V. 851
Papelera de la Alqueria S.L. 330, 331
Papelera del Nevado S.A. de C.V. 855
Papelera del NOA S.A. 785, 786
Papelera del Oria, S.A. 339
Papelera del Pacífico S.A. 836
Papelera del Pacífico S.A. 846, 847
Papelera del Pacífico S.A. de C.V. 855
apelera del Plata 787
Papelera del Principado, S.A. (Paprinsa) .. 340
Papelera del Sur 790
Papelera del Sur, División Cartulinas
de Interpack S.A. 790
Papelera del Sur S.A. 865
Papelera Don Torcuato S.A. 790
Papelera Ecker S.A. 333
Papelera Entre Ríos S.A. 784
Papelera Guipuzcoana de Zicuñaga S.A. ... 335
Papelera Industrial Potosina S.A. de C.V. .. 857
Papelera Inka S.A. 867
Papelera Internacional SA - PAINSA 847
Papelera Iruña S.A. de C.V. 853
Papelera Istmeña, S.A. 863, 864
Papelera La Helice S.A.I.C. 784
Papelera Mediterránea S.A. 785
Papelera Munné S.A. 339
Papelera Nacional S.A. 845
Papelera Panamericana S.A. 867, 868
Papelera Paysandú S.A.I.C. 787
Papelera Pulpa Cuba 844
Papelera Reyes S.A.C. 868
Papelera Rio Quequén 786
Papelera Samseng S.A. 788
Papelera San Andrés de Giles S.A. 788
Papelera Santa Angela S.A. 789
Papeleras del Arlanzón, S.A. 331
Papelera Tlaxcala S.A. de C.V. 862
Papelera Tucumán S.A. 790, 791
Papelera Veracruzana S.A. de C.V. 863
Papelera Vual S.A. 791, 792
Papelera Zarate S.A. 869
Papeles Bío Bío 837
Papeles de Bolivia (Papelbol) 792
Papeles Industriales S.A. (PISA) 837
Papeles Lozar S.A. de C.V. 855
Papeles Nacionales S.A. 841
Papeles PM S.A.I.C. 786
Papeles Regionales S.A. 841
Papeles Río Vergara S.A. 837
Papeles Venezolanos CA (PAVECA) 874
Papel Misionero S.A.I.F.C. 785
Papel Pampa. NOA 786
Papel Prensa S.A. 787, 788
PAPELSA - Papeles y Cartones SA 841
Papel Tangará Ltda. 819
Papeltex Argentina S.A.I.C. 787
Paper and Pulp Industries, Pty. Ltd. 894
Paper Corea Inc. 724

Paper Excellence Canada Holdings Corp 111, 112	Papierwerke Lenk AG 212	Phu Thinh Paper Co., Ltd............................... 774
Paper Excellence Group................................... 110	Papierwerk Sundern GmbH..........................231	Pingliang Xiamen Paper Co., Ltd.................406
papergroup® SpA.. 264	Papirfabrika Ligatne Ltd................................. 275	Pinho Past Ltda...821
Paperland, Inc... 711	Papir-Mal..371	Pioneer Board Products (Pvt) Ltd. 707
Paperlogic 40	Papírna APIS, s.r.o. 156, 159	Piquiri Indústria e Comércio de Papéis Ltda...821
Paper Packaging Pvt. Ltd. Corp......................590	Papírna Perštejn s.r.o., Keseg & Rathouský 159	Pitambar Coated Papers Ltd........................591
Paper Pak Industries.............................. 9, 10, 21	Papirnica Vevce d.o.o..................................... 329	Polotnyano-Zavodskaya Paper Mill 318
Papertech S.L... 339	Papiro Sarda S.R.L... 264	Polpa de Madeiras Ltda.................................821
PaperWorks Industries, Inc......................27, 72	Papiro Sud Srl 264	olska Wytwornia Papierow Wartosciowych S.A. 292
Papeterie de Gromelle.................................... 187	Papirpak D. O. O. Preduzece za proizvodnju i promet papirne konfekcije .. 326	
Papeterie de la Banque de France 179	apirus Indústria de Papel S.A. 819	Polymerkrovlya..318
Papeterie de la Mitidja.................................. 875	PAPOS v.o.s. 159	Poly Paper & Board Mills (Pvt.) Ltd............707
Papeterie de Mandeure SA............................ 189	Pappenfabrik A. Obenauf GmbH & Co. KG...218	Ponderay Newsprint Co.................................92
Papeterie de Raon..192		Pondercel, S.A. de C.V....................................856
Papeterie Saint Michel SAS Groupe Thiollet.. 191	Pappenfabrik Nierfeld, J. Piront GmbH & Co. KG..218	Poneder Halbstoff-Fabrik GmbH 143
		Port Hawkesbury Paper................................. 116
Papeteries de Bègles SAS 179	Pappenfabrik Trauchgau GmbH & Co. KG 232	Porto Feliz S.A.. 822
Papeteries de Clairefontaine 181	Papresa, S.L..340	Portonogaro S.a.s. di Raffin Mario & C...... 266
Papeteries de Condat..................................... 181	Paptol, Zaklad Produkcji Papieru Toaletowego... 292	Port Townsend Paper Corp............................92
Papeteries de Fures... 185		Potsdam Specialty Paper Inc.........................58
Papeteries de Giroux SA 186	Papyros Paper Mill S.A....................................239	Powerflute Oyj... 168
Papeteries de Mauduit SA............................. 189	Paraibuna Embalagens Ltda........................819	PPH Izopaper Sp. z o.o. 288
Papeteries de Montségur.............................. 189	Paramount Paper Board Mills (Pvt) Ltd. ... 706	PPHU 'KARAS' 289
Papeteries de Saint-Girons............................193	Paramount Paper Mills 590	PPHU Rolls Sp. z o.o. 292
Papeteries des Chatelles SAS 181	Parenco B.V. 278, 279	Prado-Cartolinas da Lousã S.A. 299
Papeteries des Vosges (PDV)....................... 199	Parijat Paper Mills Ltd...................................590	Prado Karton S.A..299
Papeteries de Vizille (Vicat)......................... 198	Pars Paper Industrial Group.........................648	Pragati Paper Industries Ltd. 591
Papeteries du Leman (PDL) 188	Parteks Tekstil ve Kagit San Tic. Ltd. Sti...... 764	Pranavraj Paper Mills Pvt. Ltd......................591
Papeteries du Rhin..192	Pasa - Papelão Apucaraninha Ltda............. 820	Prat Dumas & Cie. 191
Papeteries et Cartonneries Lacaux Frères. 188	Pascorp Paper Industries Bhd......................698	Pratt Industries (USA)...........................21, 32, 58
Papeteries Léon Martin SA............................ 189	Paswara Paper Mill Limited................590, 591	Prayas Papers (P) Ltd.....................................591
Papeterie Zuber Rieder.................................. 199	Patoom Dhanee Paper Factory Ltd. Part... 748	Premier Paper Mills Ltd. 591, 707
Papierfabriek Doetinchem BV 277	Patras Paper Mills SA.....................................239	Premier Tissues India Ltd. 592
Papierfabrik Adolf Jass GmbH & Co. KG... 207	Paul Hartmann Ges.mbH 139	Premium Board Finland Oy........................ 169
Papierfabrik August Koehler AG..................209	Paulispell, Indústria Paulista de Papéis e Chapas de Papelão........................ 820	Premium Paper & Boards Ind. Ltd............. 592
Papierfabrik Carl Lenz GmbH & Co. 212		Preston Board and Packaging Ltd.............379
Papierfabrik Cordier.. 201	PCE Embalagens...820	Prietopapel..340
Papierfabrik Fritz Peters GmbH & Co. KG .220	PCM-Papeles y Conversiones de México, S.A. de C.V. 855, 856	Primo Tedesco S.A. 822
Papierfabrik Hainsberg GmbH....................205		Procter & Gamble de Mexico S. de R.L. de C.V. 857
Papierfabrik Louisenthal GmbH.................. 213	Pearl Paper & Board Mills Ltd..................... 392	
Papierfabrik Meldorf GmbH & Co. KG....... 213	Pegant Ltd.. 885	Procter & Gamble Paper Products Co. .. 10, 21 49, 64, 73, 85, 102
Papierfabrik Netstal AG.................................364	Pehart Tec SA Petresti 301, 302	
Papierfabrik Nettemühle GmbH & Co. KG 217	Pehlivanoglu Kagit, Kagit Mamülleri ve Ambalaj San.Tic. A.S......................................764	Productos Celulosicos S.A. - Procesa.........340
Papierfabrik Niederauer Mühle GmbH 217		Productos Familia SA 841
Papierfabrik Palm GmbH & Co KG.............. 219	Penha Papéis e Embalagem Ltda......820, 821	Productos Familia Sancela del Ecuador S.A..845
Papierfabrik Poerringer GmbH & Co. KG..220	Pere Valls S.A. 340	
Papierfabrik Scheufelen GmbH & Co. KG 225	Perlen Papier AG 365	Productos Sanitarios S.A. (PROSA) 844
Papierfabrik Schleipen 225	Perm Pulp and Paper Mill.............................317	Pro-Gest S.p.A.. 266
Papierfabrik Schoellershammer.................. 226	Peter Grant Papers Limited.......................... 377	Progressive Paper Mills (P) Ltd. 592
Papierfabrik Tillmann.................................... 232	Peterson Packaging AS 283	Progroup AG..221
Papierfabrik Utzenstorf AG...........................364	Petrocart SA... 302	Proletariy, JSC...318
Papierfabrik Vreden GmbH.......................... 234	Pfleiderer Spezialpapiere 220	Prolific Papers Pvt. Ltd. 592
Papierfabrik Wattens GmbH & Co KG 145	Pham Thu Processing and Trading Co., Ltd 773	Pronal, Productora Nacional de Papel, S.A. de C.V. 857
Papierfabrik Zerkall Renker & Söhne GmbH & Co. KG................................ 236		
	Phoenix Pulp & Paper Public Company, Ltd. 748	Propaper... 822
Papier Masson... 130		Propapier PM 1 GmbH 221
Papiernia Sieroslawice 291	Phu Giang Paper and Packaging Co., Ltd. 773	Propapier PM 2 GmbH & Co. KG 221
Papier- und Kartonfabrik Varel GmbH & Co. KG.. 234	Phuong Nam Kenaf Pulp Mill and Paper Company.. 774	PROPASA - Productora de Papel S.A. de C.V. 858

Index

Protisa Colombia SA. 842
Protisa Peru S.A. - Productos Tissue
del Peru 868
PROTISA, Productos Tinerfeños S.A. 341
PSA Indústria de Papel 822
PT Adiprima Suraprinta 625
PT Asia Paper Mills 625
PT Aspex Kumbong 626
PT Buana Megah 627, 638
PT Bukit Muria Jaya 627
PT Chiral Filindo Utama 627
PT Cipta Paperia 627
PT Ekamas Fortuna 627
T Enggal Subur Kertas 628
PT Esa Kertas Nusantara 628
PT Eureka Aba 628
PT Evergreen International Paper 628, 637
PT Fajar Surya Wisesa Tbk. 628
T Graha Cemerlang Paper Utama (
Grace Paper) 629
PT Gunung Jaya Agung 629
PT Indah Kiat Pulp & Paper Corp. 629, 630
PT Indo Paper Primajaya 630, 631
PT Integra Lestari (Surabaya) 631, 637
PT Java Paperindo Utama Industries 631
PT Jaya Kertas 631
PT Juara Prayasa Jawa 631
PT Karya Tulada 631
PT Kertas Basuki Rachmat 626
PT Kertas Blabak Megelang 627
PT Kertas Leces (Persero) 632
PT Kertas Nusantara 632
PT Kertas Padalarang 634
PT Klambir Jaya 632
PT Lispap Rayasentosa 632
PT Lontar Papyrus Pulp & Paper Industry . 633
PT Mount Dreams 638
PT Niki Tunggal 633
PT Pabrik Kertas Indonesia (Pakerin) 633
PT Pabrik Kertas Noree Indonesia 633
PT Pabrik Kertas Tjiwi Kimia Tbk. 643
PT Panca Usaha Paramita 634
PT Papertech Indonesia 634, 635
PT Papyrus Sakti 635
PT Parisindo Pratama 635
PT Pelita Cengkareng Paper 636
PT Pindo Deli Pulp & Paper Mills 636, 637
PT Pindo Deli Pulp & Paper Mills Hive 637
PT Pola Pulpindo Mantap 637
PT Pura Barutama 638
PT Pura Nusapersada 639
PT Riau Andalan Pulp & Paper (RAPP) 639
PT Sekarindo Inti Serasi 640
PT Setia Kawan 640
PT Simanda 638, 640
PT Sinar Hoperindo 640
PT Sinar Indah Kertas 638, 640
PT Sopanusa Tissue 640
PT Sun Paper Source 641
PT Suparma, Tbk. 641

PT Surabaya Agung Industri
Pulp & Kertas 641
PT Surabaya Mekabox 642
PT Surya Mas Aditama 642
PT Surya Pamenang 642
PT Surya Zig Zag 638
PT Tanjung Enim Lestari Pulp & Paper 642
PT The Univenus Co. Ltd. 644
PT Toba Pulp Lestari Tbk. 643
PT Toba Pulp Lestari Tbk. - TPL 643
PT Tri Daya Kreasi 638
PT Triguna Pratama 643
PT Uninga Bima Sakti 644
PT Unipa Daya 644
PT Wirajaya Packindo 638, 644
Pucaro Elektro-Isolierstoffe GmbH 221
Pudumjee Industries Ltd. (PIL) 592
Pudumjee Pulp & Paper Mills Ltd. 593
Pukhovichskaya Paperboard Mill 147
Pu Li Paper Mfg. Co., Ltd. 738
Pulp Mill Holding GesmbH 143
Pulppy Corelex (Vietnam) 774
Pulp Specialties Philippines, Inc. (PSPI) ... 711
Pura Group 639
Purico Group (China) 527
Purico Group Ltd. 380
Purvi Bharat Paper & Power Ltd. 593
P.W. "APIS" S.J. 284, 285
Pyramids Paper Mills S.A.E. - Flora 882

Q

Qadria Board Mills 707
Qafqaz Kagit Sanaye, Caucasus
Paper Industry 389
QF MEX, S.A. de C.V. 858
Quang Phat Co., Ltd. 774
Quanta Paper Corporation 711
Quanzhou Huaxiang Paper Co., Ltd. 405
Queenex Hygiene Paper
Manufacturing L.L.C. 768
Queensland Tissue Products 387
Quena Paper Industry Co. (QPIC) 882
Quesnel River Pulp Co. 112

R

Radece Papir Nova 328
Rafalo Paper Mills 894
Rainap S.A. 788
Rainbow Papers Ltd. 593, 594
Raipaper S.r.l. 267
Rajesh Paper Mills Ltd. 594
Rakta, General Co. for Paper Industry 882
Raman Boards Ltd. 595
Rama Paper Mills Ltd. 594
Rama Pulp & Papers Ltd. 594
Rama Shyma Papers Ltd. 595
Rampal Paper Mills 595
Rana Papers Ltd. 595

Rand Whitney Containerboard 12
Rang Dong Paper Joint-stock Co. 774
Räpina Paberivabrik AS 161
R A Shaikh Paper Mills Pvt. Ltd. 593
Ravindra Paper Mills (P) Ltd. 595
Rayana Paper & Board Industries Ltd 595
Rayevka 148
Rayonier Advanced Materials Inc. 14, 21
RDM Blendecques SAS 192
Reflex Premium Papier AG 222
Rehman Classic Pvt. Ltd. 707
Reinsberger Spezialpapier GmbH 222
Reliable Paper (India) Pvt. Ltd. 595
Reliance Paper Mills 700
Remco Paper & Board
Industries Pvt. Ltd. 596
Rengo Co., Ltd. 683, 684
Reno De Medici Arnsberg GmbH 222
Reno De Medici, Iberica S.L.U. 341
Reno De Medici SpA 267, 268
Renova - Fábrica de Papel do
Almonda S.A. 299
Republic Group 192
Republic Paperboard Co. LLC 67
Resolute Forest Products Canada Inc. 120, 21
130, 131, 132, 133
Resolute FP Augusta LLC 22
Resolute FP US Inc. 4, 44, 48, 76, 80, 94
Resolute Paper Korea Ltd. 715
Rexcell Tissue & Airlaid AB 356
Ricoh Co., Ltd. 685
Rigesa, Celulose, Papel e
Embalagens Ltda. 823
Rio Jordão Papéis 824
Riverpro Group 748
Riverpro Pulp & Paper Co., Ltd. 748
RockTenn Co. 4, 5, 12, 14, 15, 22, 28, 32
44, 46, 58, 65, 73, 76, 81,
84, 85, 87, 88, 93; 133
Rogan Paperboard Mill 371
Rolex Paper Mills Ltd. 596
Rolland Enterprises Inc. 133
Romiley Board Mill 380
Rondo Ganahl AG 144
Roses Southeast Papers, LLC 15, 52
Roshan Lal Paper Mills Pvt Ltd 596
Rossmann SAS 193
Roto-cart SpA 268
Rottneros AB 356
Rottneros Bruk AB 356
Rottneros, Vallviks Bruk AB 356
Royal Paper 5
Rubezhansky Cardboard and
Packaging Mill 371
Ruby Macons Ltd. 596
Ruchira Papers Ltd. 597
Ruloni 550
RW Industria de Papel Ltda. 824
Rygene-Smith & Thommesen AS 283

Index

S

Sabah Forest Industries Sdn. Bhd. 698
Sabarmati Papers Limited 597
Sabarmati Papers Pvt Limited 597
Saber Group 597
Saber Swiss Quality Paper AG 365
Sadeque Paper & Board Mills Ltd. 392
Saffouri Company for Tissue
Manufacturing 730
Saffron Industries Ltd. 597
Sagheh Cellulose Iran Industrial
Company (P.J.S.) 648
SAICA Paper UK Ltd. 380
SAICA - S.A. Industrias Celulosa
Aragonesa 341, 342
SAICA Vénizel 193
Saigon Paper 775
Saigon Paper Joint Stock Company 774
Sainath Paper Mills 598
Sainsons Paper Industries Ltd. 598
Sai Rayalaseema Paper Mills Ltd.
(SRPML) 597, 598
Saiyed Paper Mills Ltd. 598
Salzer Papier GmbH 144
Sam Bard Co., Ltd. 739
Samil Paper Co., Ltd. 725
Samjung Pulp Ind. Co., Ltd. 725
Samson Paper Holdings Limited 552
Samtai Industrial Ltda 824
Samwha Paper Co. Ltd. 725, 726
Sandeep Paper Mills Pvt. Ltd. 598
San-Ei Regulator Co., Ltd. 685
Sangal Papers Ltd. 598, 599
Sanitex Paper Mill Ltd. 154
Sanko Seishi K.K. 658
Sanko Seishi Kogyo KK 685
San-Paper Co., Ltd. 685
Santa Clara Indústria de Papéis Ltda. 824
Santa Maria Cia. de Papel e Celulose 825
Sant'Andrea Spa 270
Sanwa Seishi K.K. 685
San Yang Paper Making Co., Ltd. 739
San Yi Paper Industry Co., Ltd. 739
Sanyo Itagami Kogyo KK 685
Sanyo Paper Co., Ltd. 685
Sanyo Paper Manufacturing Co., Ltd. 685
Sanzen Paper Mfg. Co., Ltd. 686
São Carlos SA Indústria de Papel
e Embalagens 826
São Gabriel Papéis Ltda. 826
SAPB, Société Anonyme des
Papeteries du Belvédére 899
SAPELBA - Fábrica de Papel
da Bahia S.A. 826
Sappi Chemical Cellulose 897
Sappi Fine Paper Europe .. 144, 150, 151, 169
222, 223, 279
Sappi Fine Paper North America 34, 40, 47
Sappi Limited 895

Sappi Paper and Paper Packaging
South Africa (SA) 895, 896
SAPSO Emballages Ondulés 193
Saraburi Paper Co., Ltd 748, 749
Saraogi Paper Mills (P) Ltd. 599
Saraswati Udyog India Ltd. 599
Sardhana Papers (P) Ltd. 599
Sastha Paper Mills 599
Sateri Holdings Limited 552
Satia Paper Mills Ltd. 600
Satyam Industries Private Ltd. 600
Saudi Paper Manufacturing Co. (SPMC) ... 713
Saurashtra Paper & Board Mills Ltd. 600
Savon Sellu Oy 169
Sayid Paper Mills 707
SCA Consumidor México y
Centroamérica S.A. de C.V. 859, 860
SCA France 194
SCA Graphic Sundsvall AB 358
SCA Hygiene Products 270
SCA Hygiene Products AB 359
SCA Hygiene Products Australasia 387, 701
SCA Hygiene Products GmbH . 144, 145, 224
SCA Hygiene Products Manchester Ltd. 380
SCA Hygiene Products Operations SNC ... 194
SCA Hygiene Products Russia LLC 319
SCA Hygiene Products S.A./N.V. 151
SCA Hygiene Products SE. 223, 224, 380, 381
SCA Hygiene Products S.L. 342, 343
SCA Hygiene Products SpA 270, 271
SCA Hygiene Products Supply SAS 194
SCA Munksund AB 359
SCA Nederlands BV 279
SCA Obbola AB 359
SCA Patras 239
SCA Spain 342
SCA - Svenska Cellulosa Aktiebolaget 356
SCA Tissue Finland Oy 170
SCA Tissue North America, L.L.C. 5, 58, 73, 103
S.C. Comceh S. A. 301
S.C. EcoPaper S.A. 301
SCG Paper Public Co., Ltd. 749
Schönfelder Papierfabrik GmbH 226
Schumacher Packaging GmbH 227
Schumacher Packaging Zaklad
Grudziadz Sp.z o.o. 292
Schut Papier 279
Schwarzwald Papierwerke AG 227
Schweighofer Fiber GmbH 142
Schweitzer-Mauduit do Brasil 826, 827
Schweitzer-Mauduit International Inc. ... 23, 51
59, 636
SC Metalicplas Impex SRL 301
SC Monte Bianco SA 302
Sealed Air Corp. 51, 61, 73
Seaman Paper Company 40, 41
Security Papers Ltd. 708
Security Printing and Minting Corporation
Of India Limited (SPMCIL) 600
Segezha Pulp & Paper Mill 319

Seha Corporation 726
Sein y Cia. SA 789
Selenginsky Pulp & Board Mill 319
Selkasan Kagit ve Paketleme
Malzemeleri Imalati San. ve Tic. AS 764
Senapathy-Whiteley (P) Ltd. 600, 601
Sengés Papel e Celulose Ltda. 827
SEPAC - Serrados e Pasta de
Celulose Ltda. 827
SER.PA.M S.A. 239
Serpukhovskaya Paper Mill 320
Serrana Papel e Celulose Ltda. 827
Servalakshmi Paper &
Boards Ltd. (SLPB) 601
Servalakshmi Paper Ltd. 601
Seshasayee Paper & Boards Ltd. 601, 602
Seven Hills Paperboard, LLC 88
Sevenhills Papers (P) Ltd. 602
Severny Kommunar 320
Severoceská papírna s.r.o. 160
Seyfert Paper S.A.S. 194
SFT Group 320
Shaanxi Pucheng Wuyang Paper Co., Ltd. 487
Shaanxi Shenglong Paper Co., Ltd. 487
Shaanxi Xi-An Lintong District
Hanxing Co., Ltd. 487
Shaanxi Xi-An Weiyangqu Efang
Paperboard Co., Ltd. 487
Shaanxi Xingbao Group Co., Ltd 488
Shaanxi Xiongdi Paper Co., Ltd. 488
Shaheen Paper & Board
Industries (pvt) Ltd. 708
Shah Paper Mills Ltd. 602
Shah Pulp & Paper Mills Ltd. 602
Shakumbhri Pulp & Paper
Mills Ltd. 602, 603
Shakumbhri Straw Products Ltd. 603
Shalimar Krafts and Tissue (P) Ltd. 603
Shalimar Paper Mills (P) Ltd. 603
Shamli Paper Mills Ltd. 603
Shandong Baron Paper Co., Ltd. 490
Shandong Bohui Paper Industry
Co., Ltd. 490, 491
Shandong Bowen Paper Co., Ltd 491
Shandong Chenlong Paper Co., Ltd. 491
Shandong Dadi Paper Co., Ltd. 493
Shandong Deguang Gongmao Co., Ltd. ... 493
Shandong Derong Paper Co., Ltd. 493
Shandong Dezhou Huabei Paper
(Group) Co., Ltd. 494
Shandong Dezhou Huadong
Paper Group 494
Shandong Dongming County Yongyue
Paper Co., Ltd. 494
Shandong Dongshun Paper Group 494
Shandong Dongyue Energy Co., Ltd. 495
Shandong Feicheng Dongsheng
Paper Co., Ltd. 495
Shandong Fengyuan Zhongke
Biology Technology Co., Ltd. 495

Index

Shandong Gaomi Silver Hawk Chemical Fibre Group Co., Ltd. 495
Shandong Gaoqing Qingyuan Paper Co. Ltd. 495
Shandong Gaotang No. 2 Paper Mill 495
Shandong Gaotang Quanjie Paper Co., Ltd. 496
Shandong Golden Cailun Paper Co., Ltd. 496
Shandong Gold Shankou Paper Co., Ltd. 496
Shandong Guanghua Paper Group 496
Shandong Guanjun Paper Co., Ltd. 496
Shandong Guihe Paper Group Co., Ltd. 496
Shandong Guihe Xianxing Paper Holding Pte. Ltd. 497
Shandong Haiyang Yongping Paper Co., Ltd. 497
Shandong Helon Co., Ltd. 497
Shandong Henglian Paper Group C., Ltd. 497
Shandong Heze City Hongtai Paper Co., Ltd. 509
Shandong Heze Luchen Paper Co., Ltd. 497
Shandong Heze Mudan Paper Co., Ltd. 497
Shandong Honghe Group Zoucheng Hengxiang Paper Co., Ltd. 497
Shandong Huajin Paper Group 498
Shandong Huapeng Paper Co. Ltd. 498
Shandong Huatai Group Co., Ltd. 424
Shandong Huatai Paper Co., Ltd. 498
Shandong Huatai Qinghe Industrial Co., Ltd 499
Shandong Jianghe Paper Co., Ltd. 493
Shandong Jining Jinsheng Paper Co., Ltd. 499
Shandong Jining Lianhe Paper Co., Ltd. 499
Shandong Kaili Paper Co. Ltd. 499
Shandong Laiwu Hengli Paper Co., Ltd. 499
Shandong Laiwu Ronghe Paper Co., Ltd. 499
Shandong Laizhou Lutong Speciality Paper Co., Ltd. 500
Shandong Laizhou Yintong Paper Co., Ltd. 500
Shandong Lianxi Paper Co. Ltd. 500
Shandong Linqu Yulong Paper Co., Ltd. 500
Shandong Linyi Sensen Paper Co., Ltd. 500
Shandong Liying Paper Co., Ltd. 500
Shandong Longkou Yulong Paper Co., Ltd. 500
Shandong Lu An Paper Co., Ltd. 500
Shandong Lunan Paper Industry Group 501
Shandong Qifeng New Material Co., Ltd. 501
Shandong Qingdao Haiwang Paper Property Share Co., Ltd. 501
Shandong Qingdao Paper Mill 501
Shandong Qingzhou Dongxin Paper Co., Ltd. 502
Shandong Qingzhou Dongyang Paper Co., Ltd. 502
Shandong Qinshi Group 502
Shandong Qinshi Group Co., Ltd. 502
Shandong Qunxing Paper Holdings Co., Ltd. 502
Shandong Renfeng Special Materials Co., Ltd. 502
Shandong Rizhao Huatai Paper Co. Ltd. 502
Shandong Rongcheng Haisheng Paper Co., Ltd. 503
Shandong Ronghua Paper Co., Ltd. 503
Shandong Shengquan Paper Co., Ltd. 503
Shandong Shouguang Liben Papermaking 503
Shandong Stora Enso Huatai Paper 503
Shandong Sun Paper Industry Joint Stock Co., Ltd. 503
Shandong Taian Baichuan Paper Co., Ltd. 504
Shandong Taiding Material Technology Co., Ltd. 504
Shandong Texpack Paper Co., Ltd. 504
Shandong Tiandiyuan Industry Co., Ltd. 504, 505
Shandong Tianhe Paper Co., Ltd. 505
Shandong Tianjian Paper Co., Ltd. 505
Shandong Tranlin Paper Chiping Co., Ltd. 506
Shandong Tranlin Paper Co. Ltd. 505
Shandong Tranlin Paper Xiajin Co., Ltd. 506
Shandong Wanhao Paper Group Co., Ltd. 506
Shandong Weifang HengAn Paper Co. Ltd. 506
Shandong Weifang Henglian Art Paper Co., Ltd. 506
Shandong Weifang Henglian Cellophane Co., Ltd. 506
Shandong Weifang Henglian Meilin Life-Uses Paper Limited Co. 506
Shandong Weifang Henglian Pulp & Paper Co., Ltd. 507
Shandong Weifang Huisheng Group 507
Shandong Weifang Yongxin Paper Co., Ltd. 507
Shandong Xincheng Paper Co., Ltd. 507
Shandong Xinma Paper Co., Ltd. 507
Shandong Yantai Jinhong Paper Co. Ltd. 507
Shandong Yiren Paper Co., Ltd. 508
Shandong Yongtai Paper Co., Ltd 508
Shandong Zaozhuang Huarun Paper Co., Ltd. 508
Shandong Zhangqiu Huashi Paper Co., Ltd 508
Shandong Zhongmao Shengyuan Pulp Co., Ltd. 508
Shandong Zhucheng City Qixianzi Products Co., Ltd. 509
Shandong Zhucheng Haoyang Paper Co., Ltd. 509
Shandong Zhucheng Xinxing Paper Co. Ltd. 509
Shandong Zibo Guotai Paper Co., Ltd. 509
Shandong Zibo Paperboard Co., Ltd. 509
Shanghai Chung Loong Paper Co., Ltd. 511
Shanghai Fumin Paper Mill 511
Shanghai Jinfengyuan Paper (Shanghai) Co., Ltd. 511
Shanghai Kimberly-Clark (China) Paper Co. Ltd. 512
Shanghai Orient Champion Huajie Paper Co., Ltd. 512
Shanghai Prosperous Paper Co., Ltd. 512
Shanghai Stora Enso Asia Pacific 512
Shanghai Welfare Group Co., Ltd. 512
Shaniv Paper Industries Ltd. 649
Shantou Piaohe Paper Co., Ltd. 424
Shanxi Linyi Lida Paper Co., Ltd. 512
Shanxi QiangWei Paper Co., Ltd. 513
Shanxi Taiyuan Jiasheng Paper Co., Ltd. 513
Shawano Specialty Papers 103
Shayona Pulp Conversion Mills Pvt. Ltd. 603
Shelavi Pulp & Paper Mills (P) Ltd. 603
Shengda Group Jiangsu Shuangdeng Paper Co., Ltd. 480
Shenghua Group 527
Shenyang Jinxin Pulp & Paper Co., Ltd 485
Shenyang Stainless Paper Industry Co., Ltd. 485
Shihlin Paper Corp. 739
Shinbashi Seishi K.K. 686
Shinchang Paper 726
Shindaeyang Paper Co., Ltd. 726, 727
Shin-Ei Paper Mfg. Co., Ltd. 686
Shine Yan Paper Co., Ltd. 739
Shin Kwang Hwa Paper Mfg. Co., Ltd. 739
Shinpoong Paper Mfg. Co., Ltd. 727
Shiroyama Paper Mfg. Co., Ltd. 686
Shiva Shakti Paper Mills Ltd. 604
Shiv Shakti Kraft Board Mills (P) Ltd 604
Shklov Newsprint Mill (Zavod Gazetnoi Bumagi) 148
Shotmed Paper Industries (SPI) 882
Shouguang Meilun Paper 509
Showa Seishi K.K. 686
SHP CELEX AD 153
SHP Harmanec, a.s. 327
SHP Slavošovce, a.s. 327
Shree Ajit Pulp and Paper Ltd. 604
Shree Ambeshwar Paper Mills Ltd. 604
Shree Badri Kedar Papers (P) Ltd. 604
Shree Bhageshwari Papers Ltd. 604
Shree Bhawani Paper Mills Ltd. 605
Shree Gajanan Papers & Boards (P) Ltd. 605
Shree Ganesh Agroils (Paper Division) 605
Shree Gopinath Paper Mills Pvt. Ltd. 605
Shree Jagdambe Paper Mills Ltd. 606
Shree Jee Paper Industries 606
Shree Kaiwal Paper Mill 606
Shree Karthik Papers Ltd. 606
Shree Krishna Paper Mills & Ind Ltd 606
Shree Marathawada Paper Mills (P) Ltd. 607
Shree Papers Ltd. 607
Shree Rajeshwaranand Paper Mills Ltd. 607
Shree Raj- Rajeshwari Pap-Chem Industries (P) Ltd. 607
Shree Rama Newsprint Ltd 594, 607
Shree Ram Krupa Paper Mill 607
Shree Rishabh Papers 608

Index

Shree Saptashringi Board &
Paper Mill (P) Ltd. 608
Shree Satpura Tapi Parisar Sahkari
Sakhar Karkhanal Ltd. 608
Shree Shyam Pulp & Board Mills Ltd. 608
Shree Sitaram Paper Mills Ltd. 608
Shree Sudarshan Paper Mills Ltd. 608, 609
Shree Swami Harigiri Paper Mills Ltd. 609
Shree Vindhya Paper Mills Ltd. 609
Shreyans Industries Ltd. 609
Shreyans Papers. 609
Shreyas Papers Pvt. Ltd. 609
Shri Bankey Bihari Lal Board Mills..............609
Shri Harikrishna Papers PVT. Ltd................609
Shri Krishna Fire Works 610
Shri Krishna Paper & Board Mills 610
Shri Ramchander Straw Products Ltd. 610
Siam Cellulose Co., Ltd. 749
Siam Kraft Industry Co., Ltd. 750
Siam Nippon Industrial Paper Co. 750
Siam Paper J.N.K. Industrial Co., Ltd. 750
SICAL 195
Sicem-Saga SpA 271
Sichuan Anxian Paper Co., Ltd. 514
Sichuan Beiaijia Paper Co., Ltd. 514
Sichuan Changning Zhuhai Paper Co., Ltd.514
Sichuan Chaolan Paper Co., Ltd. 515
Sichuan Chengdu Jiexin Paper Co., Ltd. 515
Sichuan Chengdu Lianda Paper Co., Ltd ...515
Sichuan Chengdu Xiling
Packaging Co., Ltd. 515
Sichuan Chengdu Yuanzhou
Industrial Co., Ltd. 515
Sichuan Eupon(youbang)
Paper Co., Ltd. 515, 516
Sichuan F. Source Paper 516
Sichuan Gold Hongye Paper Co., Ltd. 516
Sichuan Guanghan City Shunfa Co., Ltd..516
Sichuan Haiteng Paper Co., Ltd. 516
Sichuan Hefeng Paper Co., Ltd. 516
Sichuan Huaqiao Fenghuang
Paper Co., Ltd. 516
Sichuan Jiajiang Huarun Paper Co., Ltd......516
Sichuan Jiajiang Huifeng Paper Co., Ltd. 516
Sichuan Jiajiang Ruijie Paper Co., Ltd. 517
Sichuan Jianwei Fengsheng
Paper Co. Ltd. 517
Sichuan Jiayi Paper Co., Ltd. 517
Sichuan Jin'an Pulp Co. Ltd. 517
Sichuan Jinfeng Paper Holdings Co. Ltd. ...517
Sichuan Longchang Yuhong
Paper Co., Ltd. 517
Sichuan Meishan City Hongyuan
Paper Co., Ltd. 517
Sichuan Meishan Fenghua Paper Co., Ltd.518
Sichuan Meishan Jieai Paper Co., Ltd. 518
Sichuan Mingshan County Yunxiang
Paper Co., Ltd. 518
Sichuan Pengzhou Daliang Paper 518
Sichuan Ruilong Group Co., Ltd. 518

Sichuan Santai Sanjiao Living
Paper Manufacture Co., Ltd. 518
Sichuan Tianzhu Development
of Bamboo Resource Co., Ltd. 518
Sichuan WanAn Paper Co., Ltd. 518
Sichuan Xicheng Paper Co., Ltd. 518
Sichuan Xilong Paper Co., Ltd. 519
Sichuan Xinjihong Paper Co., Ltd. 519
Sichuan Xinjin Chenlong Paper Co., Ltd.....519
Sichuan Yajie Paper Co., Ltd. 519
Sichuan Yibin Lantian Paper 520
Sichuan Yibin Paper Industry Co., Ltd. 519
Sichuan Yinge Bamboo Pulp &
Paper Co., Ltd. 519
Sichuan Yongfeng Paper-Making
Joint-Stock Co., Ltd. 520
Sichuan Zhongshun Tiantian
Paper Co., Ltd. 513
Sichuan Zigong Tissue Paper Mill 520
Sicomo S.A.L. 694
Siddheshwari Industries Ltd. 610
Siddheshwari Paper Udhyog Ltd 610
Sidharth Papers Ltd. 610, 611
Silvertoan Papers Ltd. 611
Simka Kagit San. Ve Tic A.S. 765
Simkins Industries Inc. 12
Simpson Paper Co. 93
SIPCO-Soc. Ind. de Papier et de
Carton Ondule SAL 694
Sirisak Paper Industries Co., Ltd. 750
Sirpur Paper Mills Ltd. 611
SKG Pulp & Paper 611, 612
Skjern Papirfabrik A/S 160
Slave Lake Pulp Corp. 106
Slavuta-Papir, JSC 371
Smurfit Cartón y Papel de México
S.A. de C.V. 861, 862
Smurfit Kappa Ania Paper 271
Smurfit Kappa Baden Karton GmbH 227
Smurfit Kappa Cartón de Colombia SA 842
Smurfit Kappa Cartón de Venezuela S.A...873
Smurfit Kappa Cellulose du Pin 196
Smurfit Kappa de Argentina S.A. 789
Smurfit Kappa Europe 195
Smurfit Kappa GmbH Viersen Papier 228
Smurfit Kappa Group 242
Smurfit Kappa Haupt Papier- und
Pappenfabrik GmbH & Co. KG 228
Smurfit Kappa Herzberger
Papierfabrik GmbH...............................228
Smurfit Kappa Kraftliner Piteå 359
Smurfit Kappa Mengibar Paper 343
Smurfit Kappa Morava Paper 160
Smurfit Kappa Nervión 343
Smurfit Kappa Nettingsdorfer,
Nettingsdorfer Papierfabrik AG & Co. KG..145
Smurfit Kappa Orange County 10, 84
Smurfit Kappa Papier & Kartonfabrik Hoya228
Smurfit Kappa Papier Recyclé France196, 197
Smurfit Kappa Roermond Papier BV 279

Smurfit Kappa Sangüesa Paper 343
Smurfit Kappa Solid Board BV 280
Smurfit Kappa SSK 381
Smurfit Kappa Townsend Hook 381
Smurfit Kappa Zülpich Papier GmbH........228
S.N.C.P.A. - Société Nationale de Cellulose et
Papier Alfa 899
Sniace S.A. 343, 344
S.N. Paper Mills (P) Ltd. 597
Socarpi S.R.L. 271
Sociedad Fábrica de Papel y Cartón
Schorr y Concha S.A. 837
Societé Industrielle Des Papiers
"Tissues" (Sipat S.A.) 887
Södra Cell AB 360
Södra Cell Tofte 283
Soffass S.p.A. 271
Sofidel America Corporation 15
Sofidel Benelux 151
Sofidel Group 271, 381, 382
Sokolsky Pulp & Paper Mill 320
SOLICAR-Société Libanaise de Carton 694
Solid Containers Ltd. 612
Solidpack B.V. 280
Solombalales Managing Company 321
Somes SA Dej 302
Sonali Paper & Board Mills Ltd. 392
Sona Paper & Boards Ltd. 612
Song Duong Tissue Paper Company 775
Songhak Paper Co., Ltd. 727
Song Lam Paper Joint-Stock Co. 775
Sonoco Alcore-Demolli srl 272
Sonoco Alcore NV 151
Sonoco-Alcore Oy 170
Sonoco Board Mills Ltd. 382
Sonoco de Colombia Ltda 843
Sonoco de México, S.A. de C.V. 862
Sonoco do Brasil Ltda. 827
Sonoco Hellas 239
Sonoco Ltd. 121
Sonoco Paper France SAS 197
Sonoco Products Co. 10, 28, 41, 76, 81,
                                                    88, 93, 103
SOPAFI, Société des Papiers Fins S.A.R.L..899
Sopasta S.A. Indústria e Comércio 827
Sotipapier - Société Tunisienne Industrielle
du Papier et du Carton - S.A.R.L. 899
Soundview Paper Co. 52, 85
South African Cartonboard Mills 897
South African Paper Mills (SAPM) 897
South East Asia Paper Ltd. 750
Southern Cellulose Products Inc. 81
South India Paper Mills Ltd. 612
South Pacific Waste Recyclers 550
Spaa Straw Board Ind. Pvt. Ltd. 612
SPAC, Société Papier et Carton 900
Spartak 148
Speciality Papers Ltd. 613
Specialty Paper Mills Inc. 10
SP Exclusive 148

Index

Spezialpapierfabrik Oberschmitten GmbH 218
SP Fiber Technologies LLC (SPFT) 23, 69
SPM - Security Paper Mill a.s. 160
Sprick GmbH Bielefelder Papier-
und Wellpappenwerke & Co. 229
Sprick GmbH & Co. 229
Sree Raja Rajeswari Paper Mills Ltd 613
Sree Sakthi Paper Mills Ltd. 613
Sri Luxmi Tulasi Agro Paper Pvt Ltd. 613
Sripathi Paper & Boards Pvt.Ltd 614
Sri Ramalingeswara Paper
Products (P) Ltd. 614
Sri Vinayaka Paper Boards (P) Ltd 614
Ssangyong C&B 727
Ssangyong Paper Co., Ltd. 727
SSYMB BM12 307
Stadacona Inc. 133
Stadfast Paper Mills Pvt. Ltd. 614
Stallion Duplex (P) Ltd. 615
Star Kraft Co., Ltd. 750, 751
Star Paper Mills Ltd. 615
Star Paper Mills Pvt. Ltd. 708
St Cuthberts Mill Limited 382
Steinbeis Papier Glückstadt
GmbH & Co. KG 229
Stora Enso Arapoti Indústria
de Papel Ltda. 828
Stora Enso Biomaterials 172, 173, 361
Stora Enso Oyj. 170
Stora Enso Poland S.A. 292
Stora Enso Printing and Reading 152, 171,
172, 173, 197, 230, 231, 361, 362
Stora Enso Renewable Packaging 172, 173
344, 361, 362
ST Paper, LLC 103
St. Petersburg Paper Mill Goznak 321
Stragarit 326
Strathcona Paper LP 121
ST Tissue, LLC 88
Suchak Paper Manufacturing Co. (P) Ltd. .. 615
Sudhir Papers Ltd. 615
Sudirman Paper Private Ltd. 615
Suhar Paper Mill 702
Sukhonsky Pulp and Paper Mill 321
Sukhraj Agro Papers Ltd. 615
Sulamericana Industrial Ltda. 828
Sultan Paper Board Mills Ltd. 708
Sumit Agro Products Ltd. 615
Sundaram Multi Pap Ltd. 616
Sunglim Paper 728
Sun-Ka Kagit ve Karton San. ve Tic. Ltd. stl 765
Sunko Seishi Co., Ltd. 686
Sun Paper Mills Co. Ltd. 616
Sunshine Oji (Shouguang) Specialty
Paper Ltd. 510
Sunshine Paper India Ltd 616
Sun Thing Co., Ltd. 739
Supatrtanagorn Paper Mill Co., Ltd. 751
Super Deluxe Paper Mills Pvt. Ltd. 616
Super Paper Products Co. Ltd. 883

Superplast Co. 883
Supreme Coated Board Mills Pvt. Ltd. 616
Dupreme Paper Mills Ltd. 616
Surat Board & Paper Mills Pvt. Ltd. 617
Surpapel Corp. 846
Surpapel SA. 790
Surya Chandra Paper Mills Ltd. 617
Surya Paper Mills 617
Sushila Pulp & Paper Limited 617
Suyash Paper Mills 617
Suzanense Indústria e Comércio
de Papéis Ltda. 828, 829
Suzano Papel e Celulose S.A. 829, 830
Svanskog Bruk AB 362
Svenska Pappersbruket 362
Svetlogorskiy Pulp and Board Mill 149
Svilosa AD. 155
Swedish Tissue AB 362
SwedPaper AB 363
Sweetwater Paperboard 24
Syassky Pulp & Paper Mill 322
Syktyvkar Tissue Group, LLC 322
Syropaper 729, 730

T

Ta Chang Paper Mfg. Co., Ltd. 739
Tacoma Paperboard 93
Tagonoura Pulp K.K. 686
Taiho Paper Co., Ltd. 686
Taiko Paper Mfg. Co., Ltd. 687
Tai Kuang Paper Co., Ltd. 740
Taiping Paper Mills Sdn. Bhd. 698
Taisei Paper Industries Co., Ltd. 687
Taishan Gypsum Co., Ltd. 510
Taiwan Chi Suen Enterprise Co., Ltd. 740
Taiwan Pulp & Paper Corp. 740
Takano Paper Co., Ltd. 687
Takasago Paper Co., Ltd. 687
Takizawa Seishi K.K. 687
Tama Paperboard 28
Tamil Nadu Newsprint and Papers
Limited (TNPL) 618
Tangshan Sanyou Group 452
Tan Hong Export-Import Joint-stock Co. .. 775
Tan Hong Pulp Mill 776
Tan Mai Group Joint Stock Co. 776
Tanpack Tissues Ltd. 898
Tao Yuan Paper Mfg. Co., Ltd. 740
Tashkent Paper Mill of GPO Davlat Belgisi 769
Tateyama Paper Mill Co., Ltd. 687
Technocart SA 239
Technocell Canada Inc. 134
Technocell Dekor GmbH & Co. KG .. 225, 231
Tehri Pulp & Paper Ltd. 618
Tejal Paper Mills Pvt. Ltd. 618
Tejas Infinitas 844
Tej Card Board & Paper Industries (P) Ltd. 618
Tektura Sp. z o.o. 293
Telangana Paper Mills Ltd. 619

Tembec Inc. 122, 134
Tembec Tartas 197
Tenma Paper Mills & Co. 687
Tenma Paper Mills (Thailand) Co., Ltd. 751
Tentok Paper Co., Ltd. 688
Teppatana Paper Mill Co., Ltd. 751
Terranova Papers 339
Tervakoski Oy 173
Texon Möckmühl GmbH 231
Tezol Tütün ve Kagit San ve Tic A.S. 765
Thai Cane Paper Public Co., Ltd. 751, 752
Thai Card Board Co Ltd. 752
Thai Development Paper Co., Ltd. 752
Thai Gorilla Pulp Ltd. (TGP) 752
Thai Kraft Paper Industry Co., Ltd. 752
Thai Paper Co., Ltd. 753
Thai Paper Mill Co., Ltd. 753
Thai Product Paper Mill Co Ltd. 753
Thai Union Paper Industry Co., Ltd. 754
Thai Union Paper Public Co., Ltd. 753
Thai Victory Paper Co., Ltd. 754
Thanakom Paper Industry Co., Ltd. 754
Thanatarn Paper Co., Ltd. 754
The Eastern Industrial Co., Ltd. 745
Theen Seng Paper Manufacturing
Sdn. Bhd. 698
The Industrial Krungthai Co., Ltd. 746
The Rahuri Pulp & Paper Mills 593
The Sirpur Paper Mills Ltd. 611
The West Coast Paper Mills Ltd. 624
Thrace Paper Mill S.A. 240
Three M Paper Mfg. Co. Pvt. Ltd. 619
Three Star Paper Mills (P) Ltd. 619
Thüringer Hygiene Papier GmbH 231
Thurpapier, Model AG 365
Tianjin Golden Camel Group 521
Tianjin Guangjuyuan Paper Co., Ltd 521
Tianjin Wanli Natural Fiber Co., Ltd. 521
Tianjin Zhongchao Paper Co. Ltd. 521
Tirthak Paper Mill Pvt. Ltd. 619
Titagarh Paper Mills Co. Ltd. 619, 620
T. K. Paper Products Ltd. 393
Todo Papel S.A. de C.V. 862
Toho Tokushu Pulp Co., Ltd. 688
Tokai Seishi Kougyou Co., Ltd. 688
Tokushu Tokai Paper Co., Ltd. 688, 689
Tokyo Paper Mfg. Co., Ltd. 689
Tolentino S.r.l. 273
Tolko Industries Ltd. 112
Tolko Manitoba Kraft Papers 113
Tolyatti Paper Mill (TPM) 323
Tomoegawa Paper Co., Ltd. 689
Tong Long Paper Co., Ltd. 740
Tonic Industrie EPE 875, 876
Top-Comment Technology
Enterprise Co. Ltd. 740
Toprak Temizlik Kagidi San. Tic. A.S. 765
TOP S.A. 293
Torraspapel S.A. 344, 345
Toscopaper SpA 273

Index

TOV Novy Kyiv (New Kiev) Paper Mill 370
TOV Poninki Cardboard and Paper Mill 371
Toyama Seishi KK 689
Toyo Paper Mfg. Co., Ltd. 689
Toyo Tokushi Seishi K.K. 690
Trakya Kagit San ve TIC. A.S. 766
Transnational Paper Corp. 711
Travancore Paper Mills (P) Ltd. 620
Três Portos S.A. Indústria de Papel 830
Tri-Asia Paper Mill, Inc. 711
Trinidad Tissues Limited 869
Trio Paper Mills Sdn. Bhd. 698
Triwaste CC 897
Trombini Industrial S.A. 830, 831
Trópicos Industrial e Comercial Ltda 831
Truc Bach Paper Joint-Stock Co. 776
Trupal S.A. 868
Trust International Paper Corp. (TIPCO) .. 711
Tsyurupinsk Paper Company 372
T.T.K. Pharma Ltd. (Paper division) ... 617, 620
Tullis Russell Papermakers Ltd. 382
Tulsi Paper Mills Pvt. Ltd. 620
Tung Chi Paper Corp. 741
Tung I Paper Corp. 741
Tung Yuan Paper Mfg. Co., Ltd. 741
Tunisie Ouate 900
Turanlar Group 766
Turinsky Pulp & Paper Mill 323
Twin Rivers Paper, LLC 34, 35

U

UCAL Donusen Kagit San ve Tic A.S. 766
Umesh Board & Paper Mills (P) Ltd. 620
Umiya Board & Paper Mills 620
Umka AD, Fabrika Kartona 326
Una Ama Paper Mills Nigeria Ltd. 888
Unión Industrial Papelera S.A. (UIPSA) 346
Unión Papelera Platense 791
Union Paper Corp. 741
Union Paper Industries Sdn. Bhd. 699
Union Paper Mills 768
Union Papertech 382
Unipak Tissue Mill 694
Unitary Enterprise (UE)
"Paper Mill of Goznak" 147
Unitech Paper & Board Industries (P) Ltd. 620
Unitech Paper Mills (P) Ltd. 620
United Corrstack LLC 74
United for Paper Industries (UNI PAPER) .. 731
United Paper Boards Limited 620
United Paper Industries 692
United Paper Public Co. Ltd. 754
United Pulp & Paper Co., Inc. 712
United States Gypsum Co. 26, 49, 59, 84
UPM 198
UPM GmbH 232, 233, 234
UPM-Kymmene Austria GmbH 145
UPM-Kymmene Corporation 174, 175, 176
UPM-Kymmene (UK) Ltd. 383

UPM North America 26, 35, 47
UPM Uruguay 871
UPP Holdings Limited 714
UPP Pulp & Paper (M) Sdn Bhd 699
Urvashi Pulp & Paper Mills Pvt. Ltd. 620
U.S. Paper Mills Corp. 104
Ust-Ilimsk Branch of Ilim Group 308

V

Vadbhag Paper & Board Mills (P) Ltd. 621
Vafos Pulp 284
Vaibhav Paper Boards (P)Ltd. 621
Vaishnav Fibers Ltd. 621
Vajda-Papir Scandinavia AS 284
Valaichenai Paper Mills 729
Valley Converting Co. 65
Valot S.A. 791
Valpasa Indústria de Papel Ltda. 831
Vamsadhara Paper Mills Ltd. 621
Van Diem Paper Joint-Stock Co. 777
Van Houtum BV 281
Vanson Paper Industrial Corp. 712
Vapi Paper Mills Ltd. 621
Vedadri Paper Mill PVT. Ltd. 622
Ved Cellulose Limited 622
Veerachola Papers 622
Veer Industries Limited 622
Ve-Ge Hassas Kagit ve Yapistirici
Bant San. ve Tic. A.S. 766
Velgiiskaya Paper Mill 323
Velvet CARE sp. z o.o. 293
Venkraft Paper Mills Private Ltd. 622
Veracel Celulose S.A. 831
Verso Paper Corp. 35, 36, 45, 81
Vertaris/Delion France SA 198
Vezirköprü Orman Ürünleri ve
Gida Ticaret As. 766
V.G. Paper & Boards Ltd. 622
Victory Paper & Boards (India) Ltd. 622
Vien Dong Paper Joint-Stock Company .. 777
Vietnam Lee & Man Paper
Manufacturing Ltd. 778
Vietnam Paper Corporation
(Vinapaco) 778
Vietnam Paper Corporation
(Vinapaco)-Bai Bang Paper 770
Viet Thang Paper & Packing Co., Ltd. 777
Viet Tri Paper Company 777
Vijayalakshmi Paper Mills 622
Viking Kagit ve Seluloz A.S. 766
Vina Kraft Paper 778
Vinda International Holdings Limited 552
Vinda Paper (Liaoning) Co., Ltd. 486
Vinda Paper (Shandong) Co., Ltd. 510
Vinda Paper (Sichuan) Co. Ltd. 520
Vinda Paper (Zhejiang) Co., Ltd. 527
Vinh Hue Paper Joint-Stock Co.
(Vihimex) 778
Viochartiki Paper Mill SA 240

Vipap Videm Krško d.d. 329
Virtisú S.L. 346
VIS Containers Manufacturing SA 240
Vishal Coaters Ltd. 623
Vishal Paper Mills Ltd. 623
Vishnupriya Paper Mill Private Ltd. 623
Vishwa Paper Mills 623
VISKOZA 326
Visy Pulp & Paper 388, 389
Volga 324
Von Drehle Corp. 49, 61
VPK Packaging Group 152
VPK Paper NV 152
Vrancart SA 303
Vyborgskaya Cellulose, JSC 324

W

Waggeryd Cell AB 363
Wang N.T. Paper Co., Ltd. 755
WARTER - Fabryka Papieru i Tektury 293, 294
Wausau Paper Corp. 104
Wausau Paper Towel & Tissue, LLC 30, 65
Weidmann Electrical Technology AG 365
Weidmann Electrical Technology Inc. .. 66, 85
Weidmann Whiteley Ltd. 383
Weifang Huagang Packing
Material Co. Ltd. 510
Weig International 864
Weihai Longgang Paper Co., Ltd. 510
Wellkistenfabrik Fritz Peters
GmbH & Co. KG 220
Well Pack Papers & Containers Ltd. 623
WELMAX Zaklad Produkcyjno-Handlowy
Wieslaw Adamowicz 294
WEPA Hygieneprodukte GmbH 235, 236
WEPA Leuna GmbH 236
WEPA Lille S.A.R.L. 199
WEPA Lucca Srl 274
WEPA Papierfabrik Sachsen GmbH 236
WEPA Professional Piechowice S.A. 294
Werra Papier 236
West Linn Paper Co. 69
Weyerhaeuser Co. 24, 49, 61, 93, 94
Weyerhaeuser Company Ltd. 106, 112
Whakatane Mill Ltd. 701, 702
W. Hamburger GmbH 138, 138
Whatman International Ltd. 383
White Birch Paper Company 12
White Pigeon Paper Co. 45
Whiting Paper Co. 104
Wicor Group 365
Windsor-Stevens Inc. 13
Winstone Pulp International Ltd. 702
Wisconsin Paperboard Corp. 104
W & M Pappen GmbH & Co. KG 236
Wolsan Paper Mfg. Co., Ltd. 728
Woodland Pulp LLC 36
Wood Papers Ltd. 624
WPT Eko-Klan Sp. z o.o. 286, 294

Index

Wuhan Golden Phoenix Paper Co., Ltd. 468
Wuhan Shenlong Paper Co., Ltd.................468

X

Xiamen Xinyang Paper.................................405
Xian Dubang Paper Co., Ltd........................488
Xingping Jinlong Chemical Fiber Co., Ltd..488
Xingtai Jinbai Pulp Co., Ltd........................452
Xinjiang Bazhou Mingxing Paper Co., Ltd..521
Xinjiang Bohu Reed Industry
Stock Co., Ltd...............................521, 522
Xinjiang Helon Co., Ltd..............................522
Xinjiang Manasi Aoyang
Technology Co., Ltd..................................522
Xinjiang Silver Hawk Gongmao
Co., Ltd..522
Xinjiang Taichang Industry Co., Ltd...........522
Xinjiang Tianhong Paper Co., Ltd...............522
Xinjiang Tianli Paper Co., Ltd.....................523
Xuan Duc Joint-Stock Paper Company......778

Y

Yamakyo Paper Mills Ltd............................690
Yame Seishisho Co., Ltd.............................690
Yanbian Hanji Paper Co., Ltd......................483
Yanbian Shixian Bailu Paper Co., Ltd.........483
Yanbian Shuanglu Chemical
Fiber Co., Ltd..482
Yantai Longxiang Paper Co., Ltd................511
Yaroslavl Paper ZAO..................................324
Yasar Ambalaj Kagit Bobin
San. ve Tic. A.S...767
Yashlyk Pulp & Paper Mill..........................767
Yash Papers Ltd..624
Yawatahama Shigyo K.K............................690
YenBai Joint-Stock Forest Agricultural and
Foodstuff Company..................................779
Yenisey Pulp and Paper Mill Inc.................324
en Son Joint-Stock Co...............................779
Yeong Chaur Shing Paper Mill Sdn. Bhd...699
YFY Cayman..832
Yibin Changyi Pulp Co., Ltd.......................520
Youngpoong Paper Mfg. Co., Ltd...............728
Younus Paper Mills Ltd..............................393
Yuantong Paper (Shandong) Co., Ltd.........511
Yuen Foong Yu Consumer
Products Co., Ltd.....................................742
Yuen Foong Yu Inc............................398, 741
Yuen Foong Yu Packaging Inc...................742
Yuen Min Paper Product Co., Ltd..............743
Yueyang Paper International Uganda.......900
Yuhan-Kimberly Ltd...........................728, 729
Yung Fang Paper Mfg.,Co..........................743
Yung-Seng Development
Enterprise Co., Ltd..................................743
Yunnan Changning Jianxing
Paper Co., Ltd..523
Yunnan Dali Huacheng Paper Co., Ltd......523

Yunnan Hanguang Paper Co., Ltd..............523
Yunnan Hongta Blue Eagle Paper Co., Ltd.523
Yunnan Jiangchuan Cuifeng
Paper Co., Ltd..524
Yunnan Kunming Zhenlong Paper Mill......524
Yunnan Lincang Nanhua Paper Co., Ltd...524
Yunnan Lujiang Paper Co., Ltd..................524
Yunnan Luliang Yinhe Paper Co., Ltd.......523
Yunnan Wenshan Yunhe
Paper Industry Co., Ltd............................524
Yunnan Xinping Nanen Sugar
and Paper Co., Ltd..................................524
Yunnan Yun-Jing Forestry &
Paper Mill Co., Ltd..................................524
Yunnan Yuxi Dongsheng Paper Co., Ltd....525

Z

Zaman Paper and Board Mills Ltd.............708
Zambezi Paper Mills Ltd............................900
Zamindara Paper & Board Mill Ltd............709
ZAO Altaykrovlya......................................304
ZAO ATMSS..305
ZAO International Paper...........................309
ZAO MPK KRZ - Multibranch
Production Company KRZ......................314
ZAO NPP Filter Materials.........................303
ZAO Suoyarvi Paperboard Mill..................321
ZAO Uralskaya Bumaga...........................303
Zaveri Paper & Board Mills......................625
Zellstoff Celgar Limited.............................112
Zellstoff Pöls AG.......................................143
Zellstoff Stendal GmbH............................229
Zeritis Group..241
Zhangzhou Xinyan Environmental
Protection Products Co. Ltd...................405
Zhanjiang Chenming Paper Pulp Co., Ltd.424
Zhejiang Anji Yatong Paper Co., Ltd.........527
Zhejiang Cixi Longfeng Paper Co., Ltd.527, 528
Zhejiang Dingxing Paper Co., Ltd.............528
Zhejiang Fuyang Chenggong
Paper Co., Ltd..528
Zhejiang Fuyang Chunsheng
Paper Co., Ltd..528
Zhejiang Fuyang City Huawei
Paper Co., Ltd..528
Zhejiang Fuyang City Huitai
Paper Co., Ltd..528
Zhejiang Fuyang Dingdian Paper Co., Ltd.529
Zhejiang Fuyang Dongcheng
Paper Co., Ltd..529
Zhejiang Fuyang Feima Paper Co., Ltd....529
Zhejiang Fuyang Fuchunwan
Paper Co., Ltd..529
Zhejiang Fuyang Fulong Paper Co., Ltd...530
Zhejiang Fuyang Fuming Paper Co., Ltd..530
Zhejiang Fuyang Futai Feifeng
Paper Co., Ltd..530
Zhejiang Fuyang Gaoyang Paper Co., Ltd.530
Zhejiang Fuyang Huali Paper Co., Ltd.....530

Zhejiang Fuyang Hualong Paper Co., Ltd..530
Zhejiang Fuyang Huamao Paper Co., Ltd.530
Zhejiang Fuyang Huatian Paper Co., Ltd..531
Zhejiang Fuyang Jinchang Paper Co., Ltd.531
Zhejiang Fuyang Jin Xin Paper Co., Ltd...531
Zhejiang Fuyang Kangnan Paper Co., Ltd.531
Zhejiang Fuyang Kraft Paper Mill.............532
Zhejiang Fuyang Lingtai Paper Co., Ltd...532
Zhejiang Fuyang Maoyuan Paper Co., Ltd.532
Zhejiang Fuyang Nanfa Paper Co., Ltd....532
Zhejiang Fuyang Runtong Paper Co., Ltd.532
Zhejiang Fuyang Senyuan Paper Co., Ltd.533
Zhejiang Fuyang Shangyou Paper Industry
Co., Ltd..533
Zhejiang Fuyang Sunshi Paper Co., Ltd...533
Zhejiang Fuyang Wanfang Paper Co., Ltd.533
Zhejiang Fuyang Wansheng
Paper Co., Ltd..533
Zhejiang Fuyang Xinyuan Paper Co., Ltd..534
Zhejiang Fuyang Zhenghua Paper Co., Ltd.534
Zhejiang Gaoyang Paper Co., Ltd............534
Zhejiang Haijing Paper Co., Ltd...............534
Zhejiang Haining Bangda Paper Co., Ltd..534
Zhejiang Halberd Paper Co., Ltd..............534
Zhejiang Hangzhou Banqiao
Paper Co., Ltd..534
Zhejiang Hangzhou Dazhong
Paper Co., Ltd..535
Zhejiang Hangzhou Dongda
Paper Co., Ltd..535
Zhejiang Hangzhou Fulun Paper Co., Ltd.535
Zhejiang Hangzhou Fuyang
Jinying Industry Co., Ltd........................535
Zhejiang Hangzhou Guofeng
Paper Co., Ltd..536
Zhejiang Hangzhou Haichen
Paper Co., Ltd..536
Zhejiang Hangzhou Huafeng
Paper Co., Ltd..536
Zhejiang Hangzhou Huasheng
Paper Co., Ltd..536
Zhejiang Hangzhou Jintai Paper Co., Ltd.536
Zhejiang Hangzhou Ruixing
Paper Co., Ltd..537
Zhejiang Hangzhou Tongda Paper Co., Ltd 537
Zhejiang Hangzhou Xinfeng
Paper Co., Ltd..537
Zhejiang Hangzhou Xinhua
Paper Industry Co., Ltd...........................537
Zhejiang Hangzhou Xushi
Paper Co., Ltd..537
Zhejiang Hangzhou Yinfa
Paper Co., Ltd..538
Zhejiang Hangzhou Yuanda
Paper Co., Ltd..538
Zhejiang Hangzhou Zhongyi
Paper Co., Ltd..538
Zhejiang Hengda Paper Co., Ltd..............538
Zhejiang Hongan Paper Co., Ltd..............538
Zhejiang Hongsheng Paper Co., Ltd........539

Index

Zhejiang Huachuan Industrial Group......... 539
Zhejiang Huakang Paper Co., Ltd................ 539
Zhejiang Huaxin Paper Co., Ltd.................. 539
Zhejiang Huayuan Paper Co., Ltd................ 539
Zhejiang Huayu Paper Co., Ltd.................... 539
Zhejiang JiAn Paper Package Co., Ltd......... 540
Zhejiang Jiashan Yongquan
Paper Co., Ltd.. 540
Zhejiang Jindong Paper Co., Ltd.................. 540
Zhejiang Jindong Paper Co., Ltd.................. 540
Zhejiang Jingxing Paper Joint
Stock Co., Ltd.. 540
Zhejiang Jintong Paper Co., Ltd................... 541
Zhejiang Kaifeng Paper Co., Ltd.................. 541
Zhejiang Kan Specialty Material Co., Ltd.... 541
Zhejiang Lanniao Paper Co., Ltd................. 541
Zhejiang Linan Ma An Qianshi
Paper Co., Ltd.. 541
Zhejiang Linglong Paper Group Co., Ltd. ... 542
Zhejiang Long Chen Paper Co., Ltd. 542
Zhejiang Minfeng Benkete
Paper Co., Ltd.. 542
Zhejiang Minfeng Robert Special
Paper Co., Ltd.. 542
 Zhejiang Minfeng Special Paper Co., Ltd. 542
Zhejiang Minfeng Zanders Special
Paper Co., Ltd 542
Zhejiang Ningbo Asia Pulp and
Paper Co., Ltd. 543

Zhejiang Ningbo Dongteng
Paper Co., Ltd. 543
Zhejiang Ningbo Haishan Paper Co. 543
Zhejiang Ningbo Ningxing Paper Co., Ltd. 543
Zhejiang Ningbo Zhonghua Paper 543
Zhejiang Pinghu Fengli Paper
Stock Co. Ltd... 544
Zhejiang Purico Speciality Paper
Company Limited 544
Zhejiang Quzhou Shuangxiongmao
Paper General Corp................................... 544
Zhejiang Rongchang Paper Co., Ltd.......... 544
Zhejiang Rongfeng Paper.......................... 544
Zhejiang Rongsheng Paper Co., Ltd.......... 545
Zhejiang Sanxing Paper Co., Ltd................ 545
Zhejiang Shangyu Blue Star Paper Co., Ltd 545
Zhejiang Shengda Group 545
Zhejiang Shunpu Paper Co., Ltd. 545
Zhejiang Tann Longyou Paper
Industry Co., Ltd. 545, 546
Zhejiang Tiantianhong Paper Co., Ltd. 546
Zhejiang Tianting Paper Co., Ltd............... 546
Zhejiang Tianting Yalun Paper
Group Co., Ltd.. 546
Zhejiang Tongxiang Fuli Paper Co., Ltd 546
Zhejiang Wanxin Paper Co., Ltd........546, 547
Zhejiang Wanzhong Paper Co., Ltd. 547
Zhejiang Welbon Pulp & Paper Group 547
Zhejiang Welfare Paper Co., Ltd................ 547

Zhejiang Wenbo Paper Co., Ltd................... 547
Zhejiang Wenfeng Paper Co., Ltd. 547
Zhejiang Winbon Special Paper Co. Ltd. ... 547
Zhejiang Wuxing Paper Co., Ltd 548
Zhejiang Wuzhou Specialty
Paper Co., Ltd. 548
Zhejiang Xianglong Paper Co., Ltd.............. 548
Zhejiang Xianhe Specialty Paper................. 548
Zhejiang Yiwu City Huachuan
Paper Co., Ltd. 548
 Zhejiang Yiwu City YiNan Paper Co., Ltd. 549
Zhejiang Yongjin Paper Co., Ltd.................. 549
Zhejiang Yongtai Paper Group Co., Ltd..... 549
Zhejiang Zhengda Holding
Group Co., Ltd.. 549
Zhejiang Zhenghua Paper Co., Ltd. 550
Zhenjiang Dadong Pulp & Paper Co. Ltd..480
Zhenjiang Wanfa Chemical Fiber Co., Ltd. 481
Zhucheng East-Honor Industry
& Trade Co., Ltd.. 511
Zhydachiv Pulp & Paper Mill....................... 372
Zhytomyr Paperboard Mill......................... 372
Ziegler Papier AG... 366
ZPR, Zellstoff- und Papierfabrik
Rosenthal GmbH 237
Zubialde S.A. 346
Zywieckie Zaklady Papiernicze
"SOLALI" S.A. 294

RISI

RISI helps Suppliers to the forest products industry strategically grow their business.

RISI's mill and machine data and supply and demand analysis will empower your sales, marketing, business intelligence, and corporate strategy teams. It will enable them to stay ahead of market developments and drive smarter decisions related to:

Business Growth — Get data on new market investments. Forecast growth in the market to build a business development plan focused on retention and new opportunities.

Market Investments — Leverage RISI supply and demand analysis to invest in the right geographies and industries to help you prosper.

Competitive Analysis — Understand which assets are at risk of closure, and which ones have a sustainable competitive position

Risk Assessment — Weigh supply and demand developments to support your customers. Plan geographic and grade investments based on global forest product growth trends.

Identifying the right customer for your product is important, but finding the right customer at the time he needs you most is invaluable. With detailed mill and industry trend data, as well as unbeatable news teams to track market investments, RISI helps identify the best prospects to present your solution at the most critical time.

Supplier's sales, marketing, and corporate strategy executives use RISI:

News Products to track new market investments, follow customers and pinpoint new opportunities on which to bid.

Mill Asset Data to target specific geographies, paper grades or pulping sequences. Understand what new projects and new investments are coming up in specific regions around the world to make sure you can identify new potential opportunities to bid on.

Cost Benchmarking to understand the cost curve for specific mills so you can identify how your product can have an efficiency impact. Finding the "cost pain points" and mapping your product's impact gives your sales team a key insight for success.